PENGUIN BOOKS

The Penguin Guide to Jazz on CD

Praise for the previous editions

'It must be one of the most elegantly written and useful books ever to have appeared about jazz'
Adam Lively, *Mail on Sunday*

'Suitably monumental ... admirably thorough ... an impressive achievement – any serious collector of jazz recordings ought to have it on his or her shelf'
James Maxfield, *Cadence*

'A volume whose scholarship is matched by its sassy wit ... you find something new on every read'
Christopher Hawtree, *The Times*

'Discerning and conscientious ... a splendid source of information at a bargain price' *Jazz Times*

'Highly recommended ... the book is a valuable reference tool, a thorough catalogue, and a credible guide through the ocean of discs that flood the stores' *Fanfare*

'Comprehensive, endlessly fascinating and informative ... I was lost in admiration' *Literary Review*

'This masterpiece of compilation ... provides the newcomer with an easy to use and accessible introduction ... for the regular jazz collector it is the first truly comprehensive and critical reference source (of its kind)'
Sinan Carter Savaskan, *The Times Educational Supplement*

ABOUT THE AUTHORS

Richard Cook was born in Kew and still lives in a leafy enclave of west London. An early passion for record collecting helped push him towards jazz and both interests have endured, although the records have caused some space problems over the years. He got paid for a piece of music writing in 1979 and was so impressed that he kept going. He edited the *Wire* for seven years and is currently in the same role at *Jazz Review*; meanwhile, he turns up from time to time in other publications, and has once or twice been heard on the wireless. He still likes selling hurdles but can't make up his mind about banded racing. If anyone pours him a glass of a fine old Islay malt, they've made a friend for life.

Brian Morton was born in Paisley and, spookily, fifty years later his son was born there too, quite by accident. He has been listening to jazz for most of that time and writing about it for the last thirty years. He is married to photographer Sarah MacDonald, who came along just in time. They have (so far) one child, who might have been Thelonious Sphere Morton or even Miles Dewey Morton, but is plain John Robert. They all live on a small farm on the west coast of Scotland with Zen the border collie and, from time to time, Brian's older daughters Fiona and Alice. The CDs are stored in a converted cowshed; the saxophones look as plaintive as abandoned agricultural equipment.

The Penguin Guide to **Jazz** on CD

Richard Cook and Brian Morton

Seventh edition

PENGUIN BOOKS

PENGUIN BOOKS

Published by the Penguin Group
Penguin Books Ltd, 80 Strand, London WC2R 0RL, England
Penguin Group (USA) Inc., 375 Hudson Street, New York, New York 10014, USA
Penguin Books Australia Ltd, 250 Camberwell Road, Camberwell, Victoria 3124, Australia
Penguin Books Canada Ltd, 10 Alcorn Avenue, Toronto, Ontario, Canada M4V 3B2
Penguin Books India (P) Ltd, 11, Community Centre, Panchsheel Park, New Delhi – 110 017, India
Penguin Group (NZ), cnr Airborne and Rosedale Roads, Albany, Auckland 1310, New Zealand
Penguin Books (South Africa) (Pty) Ltd, 24 Sturdee Avenue, Rosebank 2196, South Africa

Penguin Books Ltd, Registered Offices: 80 Strand, London WC2R 0RL, England

www.penguin.con

First published 1992
Second edition 1994
Third edition 1996
Fourth edition 1998
Fifth edition 2000
Sixth edition 2002
Seventh edition 2004
1

This book was produced using Librios® authoring and content management technology
Typeset by Letterpart
Designed by Richard Marston
Printed in Finland by WS Bookwell

Contents

Introduction

Jelly Roll Morton always said he started it; so did Nick LaRocca. Perhaps it was born in New Orleans; maybe it just sort of drifted that way and bloomed there. Either way, jazz has been around since the beginning of the last century, even if it didn't start being recorded until about 1917, when the Original Dixieland Jazz Band first went into a studio. We shall never know what Buddy Bolden, the first 'king' of New Orleans cornet-playing, sounded like, since he never recorded; and many other opportunities were also missed by the American industry. King Oliver and Jelly Roll Morton, both prominent figures before 1917, didn't arrive in the studios until the 1920s; Freddie Keppard, whose band was a sensation in the 1910s, allegedly refused to make records lest anyone steal his sound. In fact, very little significant recording was done in New Orleans, the supposed birthplace of jazz, until the 1940s. So a white band in New York made 'Darktown Strutters' Ball' in January 1917: at that time, they were described on the record labels as the 'Original Dixieland Jass Band'.

Jazz (or jass) has become as widely documented on record as any music. It has rushed through its history – from traditional jazz to swing to bebop to free jazz and back again – in less than a century, and the gramophone has enjoyed the unique position of being able to document it at almost every step along the way. Although many will always hold that jazz is primarily a live music, at its best created in the immediacy of a concert setting of some kind, it has long been disseminated, listened to and argued about via the medium of records. Jazz was, indeed, the first music to be dramatically affected *by* records. As the 78-rpm medium gave way to the LP format, the confining bonds of the three-minute disc were abandoned and jazz performance became longer, less contained, more multifarious.

It is one of the paradoxes of the jazz life that, although the musicians who play the music are seldom as financially rewarded as their counterparts in rock and classical music, they often get to make many more records. Jazz recordings are relatively economical to produce compared with the studio time which rock and classical records seem to demand. Starting your own label has often been the way by which musicians themselves disseminate their work, and there are many, many entrepreneurial spirits whose eagerness to record and distribute the music has helped to keep the jazz record scene a burgeoning phenomenon. Today, more jazz records than ever are recorded and released, despite jazz's allegedly marginal status.

There is also the matter of some eight decades of 'catalogue' to be reissued. The advent of the compact disc brought new life to many a neglected jazz archive. Most of the major catalogues of the past – RCA's Bluebird, Warner Bros' Atlantic, the great modern archives of Blue Note, Verve and Prestige – have been restored to circulation via CD. As many of the earlier recordings have fallen out of copyright, independent enterprises such as Classics, Frog and Retrieval have embarked on extensive CD reissues of the jazz of the 1920s, '30s and '40s. This has extended to the 1950s: the LP era itself is now (to the consternation of many in the industry) becoming 'available'.

Our aim in this book has been to try to provide as comprehensive an overview as possible of this vast and bewilderingly diverse area of recorded music. Newcomers to jazz are always hard-pressed to know both where to start and where to proceed from there. Most will have heard of Miles Davis's *Kind Of Blue* or John Coltrane's *Giant Steps*, two of the most famous jazz albums ever released. But both those musicians have enormous discographies, and this presents a formidable problem to collectors on a limited budget or to those who wish to acquire just a few examples of Davis or Coltrane on record. At the same time, more experienced fans and collectors deserve a detailed summary and evaluation of what exactly is available by both major and minor figures in the jazz field. That is what we've tried to do here.

As in the areas routinely defined by the terms 'rock' or 'classical', the diversity of music covered by the term 'jazz' is extraordinary. Our aim is to list and discuss as many records currently available in the field as possible – but, since jazz itself remains a difficult area to define, this has inevitably led to problems over what to include and what to leave out. Although jazz and blues are inextricably bound up in each other, we have omitted such musicians as Bessie Smith and Joe Turner, even though their records are listened to and enjoyed by countless numbers of 'jazz fans': the blues demands a volume to itself, which should be documented by safer hands than ours (we hope that the long-awaited *Penguin Guide to Blues* is going to be completed soon!). Singers, too, are difficult to make clear judgement-calls on: the old argument as to what is a jazz singer has never been resolved, and it could be contended that, if we have included Mel Torme (as we have), then why not Peggy Lee, or Bing Crosby, or Frank Sinatra, all of whom made records of a jazz inclination? Often we have been guided by the nature of the accompaniments, and in some cases we have chosen to include only the jazz-directed output of a particular artist. In the case of Nat Cole, for instance, we've omitted the bulk of his vocal recordings, while his instrumental ones have remained; much the same applies to George Benson. We don't wish to discriminate against an artist seeking pop status, but we try to stick to discussing jazz records.

The advent of 'free music' placed a further strain on jazz classification: the work of such musicians as Derek Bailey may, often at their own insistence, have little to do with any jazz tradition. But the connections between jazz and improvised music are indisputable, and there is no feasible reason to discriminate against free music by excluding it from this book.

It hardly needs saying that it's impossible to include every jazz record from every part of the globe. The sixth edition of the *Guide* reached a physical limit in terms of size, and for this one we have had to be ever more selective in terms of what's been included. Even so, literally thousands of new discs have been considered for inclusion. The flow of new material is as prodigious as ever. To those who missed out this time around, our apologies: but the *Guide* can only get so big. In addition, the increasing bulk of the jazz back-catalogue is another issue. While many records have disappeared from circulation since last time, it is increasingly the practice of major jazz labels such as ECM and Black Saint/Soul Note to keep their entire catalogues in print. But we still try to cover as much of significance as we can out of what was available at the time of our cut-off point (spring 2004). More on this further on.

In situations where there is a big overlap in the reissues of early material, as is now the case with some major artists, we've simply tried to choose the best records to list. Compilations, either of a single artist or of some style of jazz genre, have been flooding out in recent years, as major labels seek to put a bit of fresh life (as they see it) into comparatively quiescent areas of their catalogue. We've omitted many of these, unless they're a really effective piece of cherrypicking.

As usual, we rarely list those records which amount to little more than easy-listening instrumental or vocal music with only the vaguest of jazz connotations. The radio format in America known as 'smooth jazz' includes a great deal of this kind of thing. Many such records have little to do with what we (and most of our readers) understand as jazz – and if that seems an élitist view, we prefer to see it as a pragmatic one. There's a substantial grey area between jazz and contemporary composition: some musicians, such as Fred Rzewski, move freely between these genres, and there are many records – particularly from such companies as Bvhaast – which count jazz as an element (though not perhaps the defining one) in their make-up. On this issue, we've used our discretion here as best we can.

How do we get the records we review? Many companies and indeed the artists themselves are kind enough to send us review copies – although they can all vouch for the fact that this has no bearing on what we think of the music we listen to! Some may be astonished to hear that many, many records were also purchased, across the counter, by ourselves – just as most of our readers do. We like to think that we haven't entirely lost touch with how collectors and fans approach building their personal library of music. But if nobody has sent us a disc, and we haven't been able to lay our hands on a copy, it won't be listed here. If a disc is literally impossible to find, even if theoretically available, it does no kind of service to collectors to give it coverage.

Other discs may have arrived too late for inclusion. Some we have deemed too poor to be even worth listing. Some we may have simply missed altogether. A few of our correspondents take obvious delight in pointing out discs which we've omitted, to which we can only say ... excuse us, but no one's perfect.

One trend of late has been for some of the major labels to issue limited-edition releases – Blue Note with their Connoisseur series, Verve with their Elite Editions. Here and there we have listed a few of these titles, where we think the release is of particular significance and the reader stands a good chance of finding a copy: some 'limited editions' seem to last a long time.

This is designed to be a practical book, to assist our readership in putting together a collection of jazz music which they can enjoy and be proud of. None of the judgements herein is set in stone: further listening and pondering on the music may yield different opinions in the fullness of time, and – as always – here and there assiduous readers may again spot a slight change of opinion from our previous editions. In that respect, we share a characteristic that is surely common to all jazz-listeners: that of living and developing with this music as it continues to evolve and grow. We have tried not to be sentimental about our evaluations: it is all too tempting to overrate some records on the basis that the jazz musician's lot is trying enough without having to endure negative criticism. But the first responsibility of a guide such as this is to the listeners and record-buyers. Building even a modestly representative library of jazz CDs is an expensive business, and even the keenest fan will be able to invest in only a fraction of what is available to them in the current record marketplace. Our primary aim has been to assist in deciding how best to make that choice and to suggest areas of the music which may yield hitherto unrealized pleasures.

Evaluation

While some may consider it iniquitous to define the merits of a record using a star-system, we feel that it's simply the most useful shorthand as a starting point for discussing the disc in question. But we cannot stress too strongly that the reader should consult the text in addition to the star rating for our overall evaluation of the record. We have chosen to make use of between one and four stars: parentheses round a single star indicate that some small reservation prevents our placing it in the higher category. Brackets around all of the stars denote a basic reservation which usually has something to do with the presentation.

**** Very fine: an outstanding record that yields consistent pleasure and is a notable example of the artist's work.

***(*) An excellent record, with some exceptional music. Only kept out of the front rank by some minor reservations.

*** A good, middleweight set; one that lacks the stature or consistency of the finest records, but which will reward the listener tuned to its merits.

**(*) Worthwhile things here, but some significant flaws in either performance or presentation tell against it. Maybe for completists of the artist in question only.

** Not good. There are many better records to listen to.

*(*) Awful. A waste of their time and your money.

* Confiscate their instruments.

A few further words on grading. Inevitably, a great many records end up with a three-star rating, which is basically an average mark. By its very nature, this is going to be a populous category. Such records may well provide a lot of pleasure, but they're never going to be part of an 'essential' library. Such a rating might also be considered in the context of the artist in question: a three-star record by one of the giants of the music is likely to be an inferior example of that musician at work, but for many lesser figures, it could be their signature session. As ever, interpret these gradings in tandem with the text.

When push comes to shove, though, we would admit that anyone looking to build an 'essential' collection can pass up anything under three-and-a-half stars without loss of sleep. Life's too short, and CDs are too costly. There aren't all that many discs of two stars or less which we even list, and even then it's more in the nature of a warning than anything else: our space (and listening time) is at enough of a premium to oblige us to dismiss most dross out of hand.

In a *very* few cases we have chosen to award a special token of merit; in our *Guide*, it takes the form of a crown. This is to denote records we feel a special admiration or affection for: a purely personal choice, which we hope our readers will deem as such. We hope our readers will indulge this whim!.

Core Collection

This book rates thousands of CDs but, modern life being what it is, very few readers can hope to make time for even a significant percentage of the total. With that in mind, for our seventh edition we have selected some 200 discs which are suggested as a 'Core Collection': a basic library of jazz records which readers on a budget or those who wish for only a small holding of jazz CDs might consider as their first-priority purchases. These are highlighted as such in the text. It is meant as a balanced selection covering every strain in the music; but we anticipate that debate will inevitably rage over what has and hasn't been included in this list!

Recording Quality

Our first concern is with the music itself, and most contemporary jazz records are engineered to the customary high standards which are the norm for the industry; they therefore require little further comment – although, whenever there is some particular felicity or problem with the production, we have noted it as such. Far more important, however, is the question of the remastering of older material for CD reissue. Remastering from 78s continues to be an area which excites controversy, just as it was in the LP era, and numerous issues have caused us disappointment in this regard. Set against this is the magnificent work which has been done by, in particular, John R. T. Davies, the doyen of the field. We have attempted to be as scrupulous as possible in our evaluation of this issue. We might also mention that we have frequently discovered many instances when the CD version of even a relatively modern record offers no noticeable improvement over the LP issue: LP-loving audiophiles are a small but vocal minority, and they are unlikely ever to be satisfied with the now-standard format. Overall, however, we are glad to note that, as the CD era has matured, standards of remastering have become much more consistent, and more often than not there is evidence of real craftsmanship in a typical CD reissue.

A good deal of fuss has been made (by the industry) over such new standards as 24-bit remastering. In reality, the 'noticeable improvements' in such editions are a marketing deception. Since domestic CD players are at present still no more than 16-bit, the 'superior' sound is currently converted down in any case.

Pricing

The jazz record business is a global one and, with the rise in internet commerce and international retailing, CD pricing is a far from static issue: the price of a disc in one territory may conflict with its cost as an import in another. As usual, we do not denote whether an issue is full- or mid-price, or indeed at budget. The latter bracket is still a rarity among jazz CDs but, with labels such as Naxos and Proper launching their own series and with many of the major companies releasing compilation series which are at least close to the budget point, it's an increasingly populated area.

Layout of Text

Musician-entries are listed alphabetically.

Here is a typical record-entry:

***(*) **The Return of Tal Farlow**
Original Jazz Classics OJC 356 *Farlow; John Scully (p); Jack Six (b); Alan Dawson (d).* 9/69.

The star-rating is followed by the title of the record; its label and catalogue number follow. Next we list the musicians who are playing on the disc, together with their instrumental credits, and – where available – the date of the recording (month/year). All personnel are listed collectively – that is, it shouldn't be implied that every musician listed for a record is featured on every track. A full list of instrument abbreviations follows this introduction. Where there are multiple records in an entry, each change in personnel is duly noted – although, rather than listing the same musicians over again, subsequent details may begin with 'As above, except ...'. Sometimes, where there may be some minor changes between complex lists of personnel, we have chosen to say 'similar to above' or suchlike. Where the recording dates span a number of different sessions, as is the case for many compilations, they are listed as, for example, 5/74–10/80. While we've tried to present the clearest possible picture of who recorded what and when, this is a guide, not a discography, and we've attempted to be sensible over the listing of minutiae. We hope our readers will indulge any slight discrepancies of style which may result.

We have tried to be as accurate as possible over listing catalogue numbers, but neither we nor our publishers can be held responsible for mistakes which may have eluded our checking. By and large, we have attempted to simplify the situation as far as possible by concentrating on the 'core' number which most records are assigned. Many CDs now show a seemingly baffling array of digits, but often these refer to bar-code configurations as well as the core number. It has become an industry standard to use the suffix -2 to denote a CD issue. Independent companies often use very simple systems of cataloguing – which we wish the major companies would avail themselves of! Most record companies are seeking to standardize their catalogue-number system to ensure that a worldwide release uses the same central number. Columbia seems to be one of the few which doesn't, necessarily.

We always advise that, when ordering records, readers state in full the title and artist and desired format, as well as the catalogue numbers. Experienced dealers will be able to spot any possible confusion over the number when furnished with these extra details.

Biography

We have again chosen to preface each artist's entry with a few lines – in some cases, no more than a few words – which offer some biographical information, or frequently a simple pointer to the kind of player he or she is. We've no wish to charge into the sort of territory inhabited by the several excellent biographical A–Z jazz works which are already out there; this is more of a 'sighter' on the artist in question.

Formats: Can the CD Survive, Again?

Last time we suggested that 'the compact disc continues to be king in the music marketplace, but the throne is wobbling'. It still is. The huge revenues lost to the industry from free downloads and piracy of various kinds have been almost devastating. However, there were signs in 2004 that the tide was turning. Downloading music via the World Wide Web has itself become institutionalized and a recognized revenue source for the major companies. CDs, though, continue to hang around. The jazz audience find them a useful and manageable medium and even with the rise of computers and iPods as a hip alternative to hi-fi systems, these new technologies haven't displaced the compact disc's capacity to present clear, clean and hi-fi sound (if anything's driving these new media, it's convenience, not sound quality). The new format of SACD is, though, a remarkable one, judged on the relatively few examples currently available in the jazz field, and at the audiophile end of the market nay have a substantial impact soon enough.

As ever, though, most of us, whether musicians or listeners, still tend to think in terms of jazz albums. Watch this space.

Deletions

A book like this can never be as up to date as we would wish. Many records will have appeared since our manuscript went to press, and a number of those listed here may have fallen victim to the deletions axe. Records often stay in circulation even after they have been officially 'deleted': dealers and independent distributors may hold stocks, and a diligent search can often locate a supposedly extinct item. All this will be familiar to experienced collectors, who know how difficult it can be to locate a particular record; but we counsel that a patient reader should try more than one source if confronted with an initial response that a record is deleted and therefore impossible to obtain. For that purpose we have included a list of distributors at the end of this introduction.

What's In, What's Out?

As mentioned earlier, we have been under intense pressure this time as regards our available space. In consequence, some hard decisions have had to be taken over what to include and what to leave out. The glut of editions of pre-1950 material has led to competing collections of major artists such as Louis Armstrong, Duke Ellington, Billie Holiday and Django Reinhardt – sometimes to an absurd degree of duplication. Certain European labels of sometimes doubtful provenance have also started issuing sets with titles such as *The Complete Blue Note Recordings of ...*, which have not been welcomed in America. We've tried to list what we feel is the most effective and appropriate issue of the music in question, wherever possible, without taking up excessive space in discussing what may be minute points of difference.

As far as newer music is concerned, our aim has been to offer a fair spread of coverage to different schools and different territories, in an attempt to reflect jazz's pluralism and global outreach. So there is music from Australia and Portugal, and music by revivalists, avant-gardists, hard boppers and dixielanders. We only wish we could include everything we've heard!

Limited-edition releases and semi-professional issues on CD-Rs are also out there in abundance. We've included some, but tried to be sensible and realistic about it. As for Mosaic, the distinguished company which handles high-quality, limited-edition reissues, a couple of reviewers have as usual taken us to task for ignoring them, although in one case an example cited had actually sold out by the time the point was made. We can only suggest you visit www.mosaicrecords.com.

Overview 2004–2005

Once again it is vocalists who have dominated the business end of jazz – even if the performers in question have, at best, a tangential relationship with the music (and hasn't it always been thus?). The enormous sales enjoyed by Norah Jones for her two albums have brought a lot of revenue into Blue Note's coffers, and if we have decided not to list her work in our book, no slight is intended: as with the UK phenom Jamie Cullum, the jazz content of music which has been marketed primarily to pop audiences is at best modest. To Jones's credit (and unlike Cullum) she hardly talks about jazz anyway.

What this has tended to do is accelerate the major labels' move away from investing in jazz instrumentalists. Wynton Marsalis was signed by Blue Note, which began to look like the last label with a 'major' affiliation that was prepared to pursue a consistent programme of new, straightahead releases. That said, there were some fresh signings elsewhere: The Bad Plus and James Carter at Columbia, for two. Brad Mehldau (Warners) and Dave Douglas (RCA) hung on. But this has been the most difficult period for the major labels for many years, and the dramatic consequences of downloading and plunging CD sales has impacted across every area of the business. Small labels have had hard times, too, with high-street retailers putting an increasing squeeze on independent distributors and in many cases driving indie-label releases out of their stores altogether.

Even so, recording activity has scarcely abated. Major-minors such as Criss Cross and Steeplechase continue to record and release albums as regularly as ever. Musician-owned labels still proliferate, and some artists who enjoyed brief major-label status have gone back to their own resources (Branford Marsalis, founder of Marsalis Music, is one high-profile example). And reissues are more abundant than ever. Now that the LP era is entering the out-of-copyright arena, the archives of Blue Note and Prestige, amongst others, are starting to be plundered by independent labels in Europe. More legitimate acts of licensing have allowed independents to reissue much material which the majors simply aren't bothered with. In a curious example of retrogression, there is probably more jazz recorded in the 1950s and '60s currently available than ever before; in contrast, the music of the '80s is comparatively neglected, much of it now waiting its turn to be reissued.

As a recognizable idiom, jazz is under continuous, if friendly, fire. World jazz, Nu jazz, fusions of one sort or another: it's fair game for everybody with a festival to programme, a radio series to fill up or an institutional grant to apply for. 'Jazz' can, it seems, mean anything some people want it to, these days. But the music discussed in this book is, as far as we can hear, all part of a distinct idiom which has its own defining characteristics. As the pianist Jason Moran recently said: 'I don't understand people who say there's nothing new in jazz. I mean, I'm not just making fries here.' Amen to that.

Acknowledgements

Our burden in compiling the seventh edition of this overweight tome has, as always, been greatly lightened by the kindness and affable co-operation of many friends involved in the jazz business, both in the UK and abroad. Our special thanks in this regard go to (alphabetically!) Hiroshi Aono, Debbie Ballard, Derek Day, Wendy Day, Tim Dunn, Polly Eldridge, Carl Ericson, David Fraser, Mark Gillinson, Florence Halfon, George Haslam, Terri Hinte, John Jack, Sian Matthews, Ian Moody, Leonard Newman, Bill Trythall, Oliver Weindling. We should also thank the many readers who have written to us with suggestions or corrections: always gratefully received, even if not always acknowledged. Our peerless editor Nigel Wilcockson ('When exactly do you think you'll be finished by?') has been a marvel, even if he still can't tell King Oliver from Grover Washington. Alas, Rachael Arthur decided to depart for pastures new towards the end of our production schedule (nothing to do with us, we hope) but Daisy Jackson carried on in her shoes and did a great job. This time we are also finally giving a mention to our indefatigable agent Anthony Goff. Thanks, Anthony!

As usual, two people who've shared our listening time – not always to their own satisfaction – get the biggest thanks: love always to Lee Ellen and Sarah.

Richard Cook
Brian Morton

Distributors

The following UK distributors may be able to help in obtaining records. We have appended the names of some of the labels they deal with, where appropriate.

New Note Distribution, Electron House, Cray Avenue, Orpington, Kent BR5 3RJ
(Tel. : 01689 877884; Fax: 01689 877891)
Concord, ECM, Hep, Label Bleu, N2K, Nagel Heyer, Stretch, TCB, Timeless, Tutu, Zephyr

Harmonia Mundi Ltd, 19–21 Nile St, London N1 7LR
(Tel.: 020 7253 0863; Fax: 020 7253 3237)
Black Saint, Emanem, Flapper, hatOLOGY, Soul Note, Winter & Winter

Cadillac Distribution, 15 King's Exchange, Tileyard Road, London N7 9AH
(Tel.: 020 7619 9111; Fax: 020 7619 0901;
email john@cadillacjazz.co.uk).
Arbors, Baldwin Street, Bvhaast, Cadillac, Calligraph, Dragon, 504, FMP, Frog, Geestgronden, Gemini, ICP, Jazz Focus, Jazz Hour, Jazz Oracle, Leo, Matchless, Ogun, PEK Sound, Phono Suecia, Reservoir, Wave

Spotlite, 103 London Road, Sawbridgeworth, Herts CM21 9JJ
(Tel.: 01279 724572)
Sackville, Spotlite

Discovery Records, Nursteed Road, Devizes, Wilts SN10 3DY
(Tel.: 01380 728000).
Classics, Cool N Blue, Definitive, Fresh Sound, Steeplechase, Stunt, Sunnyside

Proper Distribution, The Powerhouse, Cricket Lane, Beckenham, Kent BR3 1LW
(Tel.: 020 8676 5131)
A, Black Lion, Candid, Challenge, Chesky, Criss Cross, Delmark, High Note, Lake, Proper, Retrieval, Savant

Support your local record shop! However, since mail order is often the only available option for many, we recommend: Crazy Jazz, 1 Hearn Road, Romford RM1 2DP
(Tel.: 08707 469210; Fax: 01708 726796;
or visit www.crazyjazz.co.uk).

Artists or companies who have records which they feel should be heard by the authors for the next edition are invited to contact Richard Cook via email at: RDCookJazz@aol.com.

Abbreviations

acc	accordion
acl	alto clarinet
af	alto flute
ahn	alto horn
arr	arranger
as	alto saxophone
b	bass
bal	balalaika
ban	bandoneon
bb	brass bass
bcl	bass clarinet
bf	bass flute
bhn	baritone horn
bj	banjo
bs	baritone saxophone
bsn	bassoon
bsx	bass saxophone
b-t	bass trumpet
btb	bass trombone
c	cornet
cbcl	contrabass clarinet
cbsx	contrabass saxophone
cbsrspn	contrabass sarrusophone
cel	celeste
cl	clarinet
clo	cello
Cmel	C-melody saxophone
comp	composer
cond	conductor
cor	cor anglais
d	drums
elec	electronics
eng hn	english horn
euph	euphonium
f	flute
flhn	flugelhorn
frhn	french horn
g	guitar
gfs	goofus
g-syn	guitar synthesizer
hca	harmonica
hn	horn
hp	harp
hpd	harpsichord
ky	keyboards
kz	kazoo
mand	mandolin
mar	marimba
mel	mellophone
ob	oboe
org	organ
p	piano
perc	percussion
picc	piccolo
picc t	piccolo trumpet
pkt-t	pocket-trumpet
sax	saxophone
sno	sopranino saxophone
sop-cl	soprano-clarinet
sou	sousaphone
srspn	sarrusophone
ss	soprano saxophone
syn	synthesizer
t	trumpet
tb	trombone
tba	tuba
thn	tenor horn
ts	tenor saxophone
uke	ukulele
v	vocal
vib	vibraphone
vla	viola
vn	violin
vtb	valve trombone
wbd	washboard
xy	xylophone

Juhani Aaltonen (born 1935)

TENOR AND ALTO SAXOPHONES, FLUTE, ALTO FLUTE, PICCOLO

Born in Kuovala, Aaltonen worked in various musical situations before arriving in Helsinki in 1961 and working in numerous big-band and studio settings. In the '70s he came to wider prominence, with Edward Vesala and Heikki Sarmanto, and an association with Arild Andersen; but in the '90s he worked largely away from jazz and has only recently made a return on record.

★★★★ **Etiquette**
Love LRCD 119 *Aaltonen; Sakari Kukko (ts); Hasse Walli (g); Jouhani Poutanen (vla); Pekka Sarmanto, Teppo Hauta-aho (b); Edward Vesala (d, syn, v).* 3–9/74.

★★★(★) **Strings**
Love LRCD 160 *Aaltonen; Seppo Peltola (tb); Esko Linnavalli (p); Rune Gustafsson (g); Ilkka Willman (b); Esko Rosnell (d); Sabu Martinez, Tapani Ikonen (perc); strings.* 1/76.

Aaltonen figured as a great voice in the European jazz of the '70s and his retreat from prominence in the '80s and '90s must be accounted a major disappointment. These albums for the Finnish Love label were long overdue for CD reissue and their appearance is greatly welcomed. Both suffer a little from dated touches in matters such as the sound of electric keyboards, but the playing remains compelling. *Etiquette* is basically a collaboration with Edward Vesala, who contributes several themes, and it opens on an almost brutal dissection of 'But Not For Me', which is executed with Rollins-like authority. As if to remind us that Aaltonen is one of the few saxophonists who can play flute with the same intensity as his other horn, the succceeding 'Fountain' is a stinging solo for overdubbed flutes. 'Bhanki' explores some of the territory Garbarek and Rypdal had been staking out, but if anything even more fiercely, while the title-piece is an almost ritualistic frenzy for alto saxophone. 'Perhaps' is a mystifying coda. Both Aaltonen and Vesala give their all throughout.

Strings is co-credited with composer Otto Donner (who doesn't play on the record) and is a fascinating showcase for Aaltonen's craggy lyricism. Against dark, looming string charts, the saxophonist plays with enormous power and energy. 'Och Det Gar, Det Gar' is a stunning tour de force for his flute-playing and the closing 'My Next And Only Love' turns the jazzman-with-strings ballad on its head, the playing seemingly hewn out of rock, even when the closing measures hint at the American ballad which the title paraphrases. Both discs have been excellently remastered.

★★★★ **Mother Tongue**
TUM CD 002 *Aaltonen; Uffe Krokfors (b); Tom Nekljudow (d).* 10/02.

★★★(★) **Strings Revisited**
TM CD 03 *Aaltonen; Reggie Workman (b); Andrew Cyrille (d); Avanti! Chamber Orchestra; Henrik Otto Donner (cond).* 11/03.

★★★(★) **Reflections**
TUM CD 007 *Aaltonen; Reggie Workman (b); Andrew Cyrille (d).* 11/03.

These arrived right on our deadline and have received only the briefest of scrutinies, but it's clearly a marvellous return for Aaltonen. The concert recording with his new trio is beautifully pitched, bass and drums moving in shadowy formation behind the saxophone and flute, and the leader's playing has lost nothing in the way of power and expressiveness. The group is so simpatico that even the later set with Workman and Cyrille is a shade less involving, although there's still some tremendous music here, including Aaltonen's current musings on Coltrane in 'Selflessness'. This one was recorded the day after the sessions for *Strings Revisited*, which takes a fresh look at some of Donner's themes from the classic *Strings* date plus some new works. The new version of 'My Next And Only Love' is hauntingly beautiful. Welcome back, master.

AALY Trio

GROUP

Swedish improv power trio, on each occasion abetted by guest, Ken Vandermark.

★★★ **Stumble**
Wobbly Rail 002 *Mats Gustafsson (ts, f, fluteophone); Ken Vandermark (ts, cl, bcl); Peter Janson (b); Kjell Nordeson (d).* 1/98.

★★★(★) **Live At The Glenn Miller Café**
Wobbly Rail 008 *As above.* 3/99.

Gustafsson, Janson and Nordeson are a formidable team in their own right, starting off from loose but palpable structures and charging into black, unlit space. But this is not all blood and iron. There is a rather beautiful and affecting version of Charlie Haden's 'Song For Che' on the earlier disc, with a long and superbly accomplished bass improvisation by Nordeson. Nevertheless, it's the cathartic sequences on both discs that make the most impact. Both sets were cut live, and the somewhat remote sound on *Stumble*, set down at a Chicago concert on an American tour, detracts from the group's viscerality. Vandermark and Gustafsson are formidably like-minded, at least in the way they want the band to make its impression, and the sound of the quartet in full flight has a harsh, narcotic edge to it. The Glenn Miller Café in Stockholm hosted the second event, and this one is a twist more immediate and – in its way – sensual. There is an absolutely overwhelming treatment of Albert Ayler's 'Ghosts' and a vibrant version of Joe Harriott's 'Idioms', which sounds better than anything on Vandermark's own Joe Harriott Project record.

★★★(★) **I Wonder If Was Screaming**
Crazy Wisdom 013111-2 *As above.* 3/00.

Recorded this time under studio conditions in Stockholm (the city is still standing), the trio plus one strike again. Surprisingly, there's no dramatic increase in sonic fidelity, and Janson and Nordeson could have used a more powerful mix. But there's still plenty of power to spare in episodes such as the opening assault on Fred Anderson's '3 On 2', after which the soothing introduction to 'There Is A Balm In Gilead' (eventually obliterated by Gustafsson) might be blessed relief. They've thought through what they can do to get further into – and further away from – the power-trio situation. The result is a rounded, more rational record than its predecessors, which some who prefer the heat of battle may enjoy less. Vandermark tends to dominate operations – three of the six themes are his, and only Janson's 'Würzburg' emanates from the trio itself. All that said, a record brimming with intensity.

***** Double Or Nothing**

Okkadisk OD 12035 *Mats Gustafsson (as, ts); Ken Vandermark (ts, cl, bcl); Kent Kessler, Ingebrigt Håker Flaten (b); Kjell Nordeson, Hamid Drake (d).* 9/99.

This one double-billed the AALY Trio with Vandermark's DKV Trio (and brought in Flaten for Janson). Thirty years earlier, this would likely have emerged as an undifferentiated blowout, but informed by all that's happened since – although still wishing to partake of some ecstatic beating of wings – the music and the musicians manage to find some coherence and resolution even in the tumult of the three long pieces on display here: one Vandermark original (in dedication to Henry Grimes), Ayler's 'Ghosts' and Don Cherry's 'Awake Nu'. While the two horn players delight in the duel, the bassists and drummers find it harder to work either cooperatively or in productive combat – or maybe that's just our ears failing to get to grips with a soundmix which is naturalistic but consequentially inadequate.

Eivind Aarset

GUITAR, COMPUTERS

The talented young Norwegian has previously collaborated with trumpeter Nils Petter Molvaer and the multi-talented Bugge Wesseltoft, between them the advance guard of a vital new Scandinavian movement to unite jazz and contemporary popular forms.

***** Electronique Noir**

Jazzland 558 128-2 *Aarset; Nils Petter Molvaer (t); Vidar Johannesen (bcl); Ketil Bjerkestrand, Kjetil Saunes, Bugge Wesseltoft (ky); Bjørn Kjellemyr, Jonny Sjo (b); Kim Ofstad (d).* 97.

Rarely has the guitar gone through quite so many transformations: flanged, reverbed, echoed, tweaked, distorted. Rarely, too, has jazz danced so promiscuously with other styles and genres. Aarset has assembled a technically ingenious, technologically astute montage of techno, ambient, drum'n'bass with blues-based jazz.

How far it is effective rather depends on attitudes to the source material. American attempts to work similar syntheses – the legacy of M-Base and like-minded musicians – have rarely sounded as innocent or as whole-hearted. Aarset is perhaps too enamoured of his gadgets and widgets to be entirely engaging. There is a hint of muso self-indulgence, and yet the very enthusiasm carries the day and *Electronique Noir* is wonderfully infectious and enjoyable. A subsequent record for Jazzland does, however, appear to have sent Aarset into an entirely ambient field, which is rather outside our remit.

Abbs, Tom

BASS, TUBA

Bassist and occasional tuba-player, busy on the New York scene since arriving there in 1991.

****(*) Conscription**

CIMP 288 *Abbs; Brian Settles (ts, f); Okkyung Lee (clo); Chad Taylor (d, vib).* 4/03.

Abbs has done string work with the likes of Ori Kaplan and Steve Swell, but this is the first of his own groups (named Frequency Response) to record. While there's some strong playing, particularly from Lee, the music feels rather dissolute and under-prepared. A free bop piece such as 'Conscription' needs a lot more in the way of both flair and discipline to make it work, and the contrast between that and the merely rambling 'Turbulence', which immediately follows, suggests that this is a group which simply isn't all that sure of itself and where it's going. At least Abbs picks unclichéd titles: two of them are 'Redundant Triangulation' and 'Anti-torpidity'.

Ahmed Abdul-Malik (1927–93)

DOUBLE BASS, OUD

Abdul-Malik worked with Randy Weston and Thelonious Monk as a bassist, but he turned to his education in African music and made the lute-like oud a viable jazz instrument. His rare excursions as leader are interesting but by no means essential.

***** Jazz Sounds Of Africa**

Prestige 24279 *Abdul-Malik; Tommy Turrentine, Richard Williams (t); Taft Chandler, Eric Dixon (ts); Bilal Abdurrahman (cl, reeds, perc); Calo Scott (vn, clo); Rudy Collins, Andrew Cyrille (d); Chief Bey, Montego Joe (perc).* 57–58.

****(*) Jazz Sahara**

Original Jazz Classics OJCCD 1820 *Abdul-Malik; Johnny Griffin (ts); Naim Karacand (vn); Jack Ghanaim (kanon); Al Harewood (d); Bilal Abdurrahman, Mike Hamway (perc).* 10/58.

***** East Meets West: Musique of Ahmed Abdul-Malik**

RCA 74321 25723 *As above, except add Lee Morgan (t); Curtis Fuller (tb); Benny Golson (ts); Jerome Richardson (f); replace Ghanaim with Ahmed Yetman (kanon).* 3/59.

Abdul-Malik was briefly touted at the end of the '50s as the cutting edge of East–West crossover music. As a bass-player, he saw service in some of the most innovative jazz groups of the time, including Thelonious Monk's, and the presence of Griffin, Golson and Fuller on these albums attests to his mainstream acceptance. However, he tended to gravitate towards leaders who were similarly interested in investigating some sort of rapprochement between Asian or African musics and American jazz; hence his engagements with Randy Weston and, more briefly, John Coltrane. As with so many such experiments, one sometimes feels that Eastern and Western elements are juxtaposed rather than properly synthesized. That is certainly true of the opening tracks on the latter pair of records. On the long 'Ya Annas (Oh, People)' which launches *Jazz Sahara*, he begins on the lute-like *oud*, before switching to bass to set up a rhythmic pattern for Griffin's first entrance. Much the same happens on 'E-Lail (The Night)' on the later album, 80 seconds of 'ethnic' ostinati with an unfamiliar scalar feel, except that Lee Morgan doesn't seem to need a 'jazz' context, playing comfortably and often inspirationally even without conventional changes and showing some understanding in his slides and growls of the microtonal basis of Abdul-Malik's music. Even without a settled tonality, the music has a minor-key feel which affords the jazz players – and particularly the brass-players – room for manoeuvre, though Griffin (a partner in the 1958 Monk quartet) and Golson both respond positively. The only straightforward jazz writing on either disc is 'Searchin'' on *East Meets West*, a relatively conventional blowing theme that highlights Abdul-Malik's slightly fruity bass sound (something of a cross between Wilbur Ware and a camp Paul Chambers) and his interesting approach to textures. Arranged for trombone, flute, tenor and rhythm, and stripped of the shimmering 72-stringed *kanon* and the Middle Eastern percussion, it manages to sound both familiar and alien.

Recently reissued, *Jazz Sounds Of Africa* brings together two early LPs, *The Music Of Ahmed Abdul-Malik* and *Sounds Of Africa*. Of most interest to watchers of the avant-garde may be the appearance of Cyrille in the personnel, already exploring new rhythmic patterns to get out of jazz's relentless oscillation between 4/4 and 6/8. It's hard to match these tracks for sheer atmosphere and for a synthesis of musics that is as advanced in its way as what John Coltrane would be doing on his Afro–Asian pilgrimage. Abdul-Malik plays bass mostly, but with oud overdubbed on a number of tracks. Abdurrahman adds an exotic tinge with his ethnic instruments. 'Nights On Saturn' may sound like a Sun Ra piece, but it's just one of many fine Abdul-Malik originals. Though he was perhaps something of a singleton, an isolated experimenter who happened to chime with aspects of a wider musical environment, Abdul-Malik still repays attention.

Ahmed Abdullah (born 1947)

TRUMPET, FLUGELHORN, VOCAL

Began almost as a swing stylist, but subsequently followed paths to freedom from the '70s onwards.

***** Dedication**

CIMP 152 *Abdullah; Carlos Ward (as, f); Masujaa (g); Alex Blake (b); Cody Moffett (d).* 6/97.

***** Actual Proof**

CIMP 192 *Abdullah; Alex Harding (bs, bcl); Masa Kamaguchi (b); Jimmy Weinstein (d).* 1/99.

Abdullah's original inspiration was Louis Armstrong, but his main areas of activity have more to do with the free playing of the '70s and '80s.

Dedication is his first record in a while. The music tends to be dominated by Cody Moffett (playing his father's kit), and he creates a fine, swinging drive for the big pieces, 'Amanpondo' and 'Song Of The Holy Warrior'. Ward seems a little sidelined and Abdullah again lacks authority as a player; but the music has a cheerful, celebratory feel, old-fashioned like a free-bop date of 25 years before, and it's quite a warming experience, though Abdullah's singing on 'La Vie En Rose' is one track that many will prefer to skip.

The spirit of Charles Moffett hangs over *Actual Proof* as well. Drummer Jimmy Weinstein met the veteran in a Brooklyn store, and then heard Abdullah at Moffett's funeral service. Through a sequence of circumstances, NAM was formed and this record, whose title refers to the Buddhist belief in something like synchronicity, is the result. Abdullah is in stronger voice than on previous records and the group is altogether better balanced than on *Dedication*. A long 'Naima' and Gunter Hampel's 'Serenade For Marion Brown' occupy the heart of the set, though once again Abdullah's interest in the nexus of New Orleans and Africa is a dominant concern. The final 'Song Of Time/Shaka Zulu' is dedicated to the late Fred Hopkins, but the most straightforwardly moving cut is Abdullah's own 'Song Of Tenderness', on which his muted solo floats over a bass line that old Fred would have loved.

John Abercrombie (born 1944)

GUITAR, GUITAR SYNTHESIZER, ELECTRIC MANDOLIN, GUITAR MANDOLIN, PIANO

Like several gifted young guitarists, Abercrombie got a professional start – after four years at Berklee – with Chico Hamilton's group, before going on to record with drummer Billy Cobham. His characteristic style, which some would regard as definitive of the ECM label, is limpid and evocative and makes imaginative use of electronic sweetening and extensions. It's hard to pin down obvious influences; Abercrombie is very much his own man.

****** Timeless**

ECM 829114-2 *Abercrombie; Jan Hammer (p, ky); Jack DeJohnette (d).* 6/74.

***** Sargasso Sea**

ECM 835015-2 *Abercrombie; Ralph Towner (g, p).* 5/76.

*****(*) Characters**

ECM 829372-2 *Abercrombie (g solo).* 11/77.

All credit to ECM for spotting and signing up the often understated Abercrombie. There's more filigree than flash on the early *Timeless*, and it's left to DeJohnette (the first of several tough-minded drummers Abercrombie has used as foils) and the underrated Hammer to give the set the propulsion it calls for. It would be unfair, though, to suggest that the guitarist doesn't punch his weight. There is always more to his playing than hits the ear first time around, and this is a session that has grown in stature with familiarity, an altogether tougher and more resilient label debut than anyone remembers. (And if anyone is wondering where *Gateway* and its successors have gone, may we recommend a quick flip to the G-spot, where this properly collaborative group is now listed separately.)

Sargasso Sea is a very different pile of weed, a winsome, diffident affair on which only the timbral variation of Towner's 12-string and piano figures sustains interest. This is the sort of thing that gave ECM its (mostly) undeserved reputation for unfunky pastel-jazz and, though the album still has its advocates, it's less than representative of Abercrombie's real strengths. If American popular music can be seen as a long struggle between 3/4 and 4/4, then Abercrombie is squarely on the side of the waltzers; 6/8 and 12/8 are actually his most effective settings, but he rations both.

Though an eponymous album was still, for some unexplained reason, some years off, *Characters* was Abercrombie's most overt manifesto and calling-card, a demonstration of styles and moods and, even at this point in his career, influences too. If they weren't obvious before, Jim Hall and Tal Farlow are evident in the mix, and there's a touch of Wes Montgomery that was to come out again in the '90s trio with Dan Wall and Adam Nussbaum.

***** Night**

ECM 823212-2 *Abercrombie; Michael Brecker (ts); Jan Hammer (p, ky); Jack DeJohnette (d).* 4/84.

★★★(★) Current Event
ECM 827770-2 *Abercrombie; Marc Johnson (b); Peter Erskine (d).* 9/85.

★★★ Getting There
ECM 833494-2 *As above, except add Michael Brecker (ts).* 4/87.

★★★ John Abercrombie
ECM 837756-2 *As above, except omit Brecker.* 4/88.

★★★★ Animato
ECM 841779-2 *Abercrombie; Vince Mendoza (syn); Peter Erskine (d).* 10/89.

By the later '80s, Abercrombie had something of an image problem. In terms of sheer bankability, he had been overtaken by John Scofield, and Bill Frisell's bag of tricks was significantly more capacious. Mercifully, whatever was discussed across the table at ECM (or, more realistically, whatever went on in Manfred Eicher's or Abercrombie's own head), there were to be no career-boosting gimmicks. These albums mark a period of consolidation during which Abercrombie simply dug in and got on with what he was good at. The self-titled record says nothing other than 'Here I am; this is what I do; hope you like it', and if it doesn't quite come up to the strength of *Current Event*, which introduces two of the guitarist's most sympathetic and responsive partners, it is still a very strong statement. The decision to include standard material – in particular a truly beautiful 'Stella By Starlight' and an unexpected reading of 'Haunted Heart' – was a good one at this point.

Night demonstrated two things: first, that Abercrombie had outgrown the association with Hammer in particular, probably because increasingly he could give those evocative keyboard figures his own spin, using pedals and, later, guitar synth; and secondly, that he never sounds entirely easy in the company of a horn player whose main strength is rapid-fire changes work. Brecker comes on like the hired gun who takes over the whole show, as he always does, and there's perhaps too generous an allocation of space to both Johnson and Erskine on *John Abercrombie*, a further hint that the guitarist isn't quite selfish enough to stamp himself on the music (though, to be fair, these albums are among the first to feature ECM's later habit of giving individual group members an opportunity to develop their own thing; it sometimes works, sometimes not).

Animato is interesting in this regard. Though it seems to contradict the point about not needing an effects man any more, it includes in Mendoza a synthesizer player very like Hammer in general conception and it gives considerable (and justified) prominence to the drummer. However, longer retrospect reveals this as one of Abercrombie's most cohesive and swinging sets. He sounds completely in control of the music, and it is almost axiomatic, given the label concerned, that the production is flawless. This probably wouldn't be most people's desert island choice, but time and the sea-change that followed have given it a new gloss and urgency.

★★★(★) Now It Can Be Played
Steeplechase SCCD 31314 *Abercrombie; Andy LaVerne (p); Steve LaSpina (b); Jeff Hirshfield (d).* 4/92.

During the '90s Abercrombie flirted with a couple of other labels. The knee-jerk was to turn Jewish mother and declare that he wouldn't get the Eicher and Kongshaug treatment from anyone else, but in fact the rather more homecooked sound on the Steeplechase serves him very well indeed. 'Cat Nap' and 'Waltz King' are both exceptional performances, with LaVerne strongly featured as co-leader.

★★★★ November
ECM 519073-2 *Abercrombie; John Surman (ss, bs, bcl); Marc Johnson (b); Peter Erskine (d).* 11/92.

Reconvening the trio with Johnson and Erskine was a masterstroke. Teaming them with stablemate Surman was little short of genius. In keeping with ECM's later policy, this isn't so much an Abercrombie record as a collaborative set that allows all four players to develop ideas. The title-track, though, is for the trio and it is one of the very best things Abercrombie has ever done: moody, faintly bleak but undeniably hard-edged and without sentiment. Johnson's 'Right Brain Patrol', which on his own projects has always seemed slightly winsome and out-of-focus, emerges here as a compelling addition to the modern repertory, while Surman's contribution to the freely improvised opening number, 'The Cat's Back', suggests strongly that he had familiarized himself with at least some of Abercrombie's back-catalogue before turning up to play. The retread of 'John's Waltz' suggests it's a theme we will be hearing again and, unexpectedly in this context, there is an arrangement of a standard, 'Come Rain Or Come Shine'. Superb, evocative modern jazz. One day, we'll get the out-takes as well.

★★★(★) While We're Young
ECM 517352-2 *Abercrombie; Dan Wall (org); Adam Nussbaum (d).* 6/92.

★★★ Speak Of The Devil
ECM 849648-2 *As above.* 7/93.

★★★(★) Tactics
ECM 533680-2 *As above.* 7/96.

No one expected this to last. It was widely assumed in 1992 that Abercrombie's organ trio – poised somewhere between Wes Montgomery and Lifetime – was a one-off idea, a forgivable self-indulgence that actually worked better than anyone had any right to expect. In fact, its great success has largely defined Abercrombie's recent career and has very significantly kick-started his playing. The most recent of the trio was recorded live at Visiones in New York and it represents a working band who have come to understand each other's needs very well. Nussbaum, like Christensen and Erskine before him, doesn't so much drive the thing along as provide injections of fuel when they are needed. There are signs that much of the material on the second album was written especially for the trio, but perhaps with some pragmatic haste. It must have been fun to play, but there is too little for the listener to get a purchase on. The live album, *Tactics*, is much stronger: churning but still delicate Hammond shapes, a rock-steady bass, and some of Abercrombie's lightest and most dancing jazz-playing.

★★★(★) Open Land
ECM 557652-2 *As above, except add Kenny Wheeler (t, flhn), Joe Lovano (ts), Mark Feldman (vn).* 9/98.

There was no particular need to augment or spice up the existing trio, which still had lots of mileage, but this was an intriguing collaboration. The revelation of the set is Feldman, who is as fiery and antagonistic in places as Leroy Jenkins or Billy Bang, and he blends brilliantly with both organ and guitar. Wheeler, as ever, has more sinew in his playing than at first appears, and his attack is notably sharper and more plosive here than in his usual guest-musician mode. The slight disappointment is Lovano who very much sounds as though he's around for a casual sit-in; Joe never plays badly or with less than imagination, but there's no fire to his work. Both the title-track and 'Free Piece Suite' are quite free in conception, and Wall's open-ended dissonances leave any amount of room for imaginative improvisation. Like most current ECM sets, this feels very much like a collaborative project rather than leader-plus-group; but Abercrombie does seem firmly, quietly in charge here, steering the performances in his distinctive, hard to define way.

*****(*) The Hudson Project**

Stretch 9024 *Abercrombie; John Patitucci (b); Peter Erskine (d).* 99.

Classic trio jazz from three masters, sensitively produced by Paul Siegel and label boss Chick Corea. Our only reservation is that the record somewhat lacks light and shade. Abercrombie's two compositions are the most upbeat and buoyant on the set, bracketed by Bob Mintzer's 'Runferyerlife' and 'Modern Day Tuba'. John's 'Little Swing' shows how comfortably he remains in possession of a classic jazz guitar idiom, while his solos on 'Cats & Kittens' and 'Well', composed by Erskine and Patitucci respectively, suggest once again how much wit and humour there is in his playing.

****** Cat'n'Mouse**

ECM 014001-2 *Abercrombie; Mark Feldman (vn); Marc Johnson (b); Joe Baron (d).* 12/00.

A quietly beautiful record. 'A Nice Idea' opens the record with softly brushed figures from Baron, ensembles and exchanges between Abercrombie and Feldman (who sound like two wisely passionate old philosophers) and some notably earthbound and focused playing from Johnson. 'Convolution' moves the music some way towards abstraction, as do the collectively improvised 'Third Stream Samba' and 'Show of Hands', but it's that second track's edgy detail that shows how sympathetic and responsive a group this is, and when Abercrombie rocks out the final two minutes they're with him every inch.

John sounds in great form, but it's very often the fiddle that cuts through the mix to make the most emphatic statements. The more obviously processed lines work better than the cleaner, acoustic-sounding passages, but the production is in no way at fault. Manfred Eicher and engineer James Farber have found a sound-balance ideally suited to this extraordinary group and a thoroughly satisfying performance.

****** Class Trip**

ECM 038118-2 *As above.* 2/03.

Another disc which arrived right on our deadline, but even a brief examination suggests that John and Manfred Eicher were right to give this quartet another turn in the studio. As with the previous date, it's quiet, thoughtful, and about as remote from the current axis of American jazz guitar (Scofield–Metheny) as the one non-original, Bela Bartók's 'Soldier's Song'. But it's still four American guys in a New York studio, and the playing is informed by many traditions. As gentle as many of the pieces are, the session feels like it works at a steady lilt, and Abercrombie's fascination with waltz time seems to run through most of it, even when they're playing in a different metre. 'Dansir' is a lovely start, and the closing improvisation is a surprisingly tart finale.

Rabih Abou-Khalil (born 1958)

OUD, FLUTE

Abou-Khalil is a young Lebanese master forced into German exile in 1978 by the increasingly chaotic civil war. After a period studying flute, he returned to the traditional oud. A follower of the great Wadih Al-Safi, he has maintained a passionate commitment to the 'new music' while taking account of the singing and playing traditions of Western jazz. His playing is as fleet and rhythmic as that of any jazz guitarist.

***** Between Dusk And Dawn**

MMP 170886 *Abou-Khalil; Charlie Mariano (as, ss); Christian Burchard (mar); Michael Armann (p); Glen Moore (b); Glen Velez (frame d, bodhran, darabukka, perc); Ramesh Shotham (tavil, ghatam, mouth hp, dholak, kanjira, perc).* 86.

*****(*) Nafas**

ECM 835781-2 *Abou-Khalil; Selim Kusur (nay, v); Glen Velez (frame d); Setrak Sarkissian (darabukka).* 2/88.

****** Bukra**

MMP 170889 *Abou-Khalil; Sonny Fortune (as); Glen Moore (b); Glen Velez (frame d, perc, v); Ramesh Shotham (South Indian d, perc).* 3/88.

*****(*) Al-Jadida**

Enja 6090 *Abou-Khalil; Sonny Fortune (as); Glen Moore (b); Ramesh Shotham (South Indian d, perc); Nabil Khaiat (frame d, perc).* 10/90.

***** Roots And Sprouts**

MMP 170890 *Abou-Khalil; Selim Kusur (nay); Yassin El-Achek (v); Glen Moore (b); Glen Velez (frame d); Mohammad Al-Sous (darabukka).* 11/90.

*****(*) Tarab**

Enja 7083 *Abou-Khalil; Selim Kusur (nay); Glen Moore (b); Nabil Khaiat (frame d, perc); Ramesh Shotham (Indian d, perc).* 2–3/92.

****** Blue Camel**

Enja 7053 *Abou-Khalil; Charlie Mariano (as); Kenny Wheeler (t, flhn); Steve Swallow (b); Milton Cardona (perc); Nabil Khaiat (frame d); Ramesh Shotham (Indian d, perc).* 5/92.

***** The Sultan's Picnic**

Enja 8078 *Abou-Khalil; Kenny Wheeler (t, flhn); Charlie Mariano (as); Howard Levy (hca); Michel Godard (tba, serpent); Steve Swallow (b); Mark Nauseef (d); Milton Cardona, Nabil Khaiat (perc).* 3/94.

***** Odd Times**

Enja ENJ 9330 *Similar to above.* 96.

Jazz is only one of the world's great improvising traditions. Within Arab music, there has always been a substantial area of freedom for the virtuoso performer, and the 11-string *oud* has occupied a role in classical and more popular forms roughly analogous to that of the piano and guitar in the West. The 'new music' of which Abou-Khalil is an exponent – *al-Jadida* – is new not just in the sense of modern, but also in the sense that Western homophony was once dubbed 'new'. A composition like 'Ornette Never Sleeps' (*Al-Jadida*) gives off no obvious irony; like much of Abou-Khalil's work, it is intended as sincere hommage. Those well disposed towards Oregon's proto-'world music' will feel most comfortable with the magnificent *Between Dusk And Dawn*, but *Bukra* is in some regards more challenging. Like early jazz, much of the emphasis is on ensemble improvisation rather than more obviously virtuosic soloing. Apart from the leader's cleanly picked multi-directional lines, it's also worth mentioning Moore's marvellously sonorous bass and Mariano's familiarly 'Eastern' mode. Fortune is more of a revelation. Staying mainly with the alto saxophone, which is perhaps a more promising choice in this harmonic context, he sounds absolutely familiar with the idiom, and it's the saxophonist who gives *Bukra* much of its compelling power. His unaccompanied introduction to 'Kibbe' is breathtaking, matched for sheer surprise only by Glen Velez's perfectly controlled overtone singing on 'Remember ... The Desert'.

Restored to the catalogue just as the early *Bitter Harvest* on MMP was disappearing, *Nafas* is notable for a brilliant performance by Selim Kusur, a leading performer on the bamboo *nay* flute. Recent sets have also leant heavily on guest players, as Abou-Khalil's own playing increasingly takes a back seat to a more ensemble approach with occasional vivid highlighting. *Blue Camel*, with Wheeler, Swallow and Mariano all guesting, might on the surface appear to be his 'jazz' album, but the mix is very much as usual. *Tarab* returns unequivocally to a highly traditional style, as if to refute any suspicion of commercial sell-out, but again the slightly disappointing *Sultan's Picnic* looks to be aimed at a crossover audience, as is the more recent *Odd Times*. Even so, because it is so uncompromised, it is hard to see this music ever reaching a mass audience. But it is highly attractive none the less, and the laminated digipacks Enja have now seemingly reserved for Abou-Khalil are among the most attractive around.

*** Yara

Enja 9360 *Abou-Khalil; Dominique Pifarély (vn); Vincent Courtois (clo); Nabil Khaiat (frame d).* 99.

This is a film project, the soundtrack to a film by Yilmaz Arslan, but the album stands up very well as a pure listening experience. As with previous records, there is a strong multi-cultural feel. 'Imminent Journey' sounds almost Karnatic in idiom while 'On A Bus (To Beirut)' is much closer to jazz, albeit in a weirdly off-kilter metre. The set is generally low key, but the ending – 'The Knowledge Of A Child' – is decidedly sombre, perhaps reflecting the dynamic of a film we have not seen, but which is contextualized in Harry Lachner's extensive liner-essay. An attractive and successful album, but not for every taste.

**** The Cactus Of Knowledge

Enja 9401 *Abou-Khalil; Eddie E. J. Allen, Dave Ballou (t); Tom Varner (frhn); Dave Bargeron (euph); Michel Godard (tba); Ellery Eskelin (ts); Gabriele Mirabassi (cl); Vincent Courtois (clo); Jarrod Cagwin (d); Nabil Khaiat (frame d).* 7/00.

This is Abou-Khalil's most ambitious disc to date, a fulsomely arranged and densely textured work that ironically downplays the *oud*, even though the leader remains the main featured soloist. Where the previous album was introspective and generally low-key, *The Cactus Of Knowledge* has a more upbeat and, yes, spiky quality that is very engaging. Hart and Allen bring a strong jazz sensibility to the project, but they are not in any way inclined to turn Abou-Khalil's Mediterranean aesthetic into NY bebop. 'Fraise Et Crème Fraîche' is as delightful and toothsome as the dish that gives it its name, and 'Oum Said' and 'Maltese Chicken Farm' are both pungently beautiful. There is also a brisk wit about this session that hasn't been in evidence before. Very strongly recommended.

*** Il Sospiro

Enja ENJ 9401 *Abou-Khalil (oud solo). n.d.*

No sooner had Abou-Khalil delivered his most developed and highly structured performance than he released this radically stripped-down and neo-traditional set. Though his compositions are still strikingly original, it is clear that for this debut solo disc he has returned to his roots. The intimacy of his playing is somewhat marred by a recording that leaves some of the attacks raw and distorted, but there is no mistaking the intensity of these performances, which are darker and more inward than usual. Of the 11 compositions, 'Le Jardin De Chine' and 'La Ladra Di Cuori' are most compelling, utilizing multiple lines and a range of overtones that is almost lost in group settings. This might be a very good place to start exploring Abou-Khalil's work, though most listeners will, we suspect, prefer the more upbeat recordings.

*** Morton's Foot

Enja 9462 *Abou-Khalil; Michel Godard (tba); Gabriele Mirabassi (cl); Luciano Bondini (acc); Jarrod Chagwin (d) Gavina Murgia (v).* 1–3/03.

Morton's foot is a condition in which the second toe is longer than the big toe. Its relevance here is uncertain but however easily stubbed such crossover projects are, this one comes off triumphantly, as the oud player explores all sorts of Mediterranean influences, and track titles range from English to German to Italian and French, with references to Malta and North Africa thrown in. The band, Mirabassi in particular, play with commitment and passion. Murgia is a remarkable singer and the leader's oud-playing is ever more confidently inscribed.

Muhal Richard Abrams (born 1930)

PIANO, SYNTHESIZER, CLARINET, COMPOSER

Abrams's contribution to the new music goes back all the way to 1961 when he formed the Experimental Band. Unlike the scorched-earth philosophers who followed him, Abrams was deeply versed in jazz history and regarded the work of the legendary Association for the Advancement of Creative Musicians as a combination of lab work and archive. His enormous influence outweighs his recorded output.

*** Levels And Degrees Of Light

Delmark CD 413 *Abrams; Anthony Braxton (as); Maurice McIntyre (ts); Leroy Jenkins (vn); Gordon Emmanuel (vib); Charles Clark, Leonard Jones (b); Thurman Barker (d); David Moore, Penelope Taylor (v).* 1–7/67.

***(*) Young At Heart / Wise In Time

Delmark CD 423 *Abrams; Wadada Leo Smith (t, flhn); Henry Threadgill (as); Lester Lashley (b); Thurman Barker (d).* 7-8/69.

There is no absolute or reliable means of measuring artistic influence. If there were, Muhal Richard Abrams would surely stand higher in the canon of recent American jazz than he does (or seems to) in the hearts of jazz fans. Like any physical catalyst, he seems curiously unchanged by the forces he has set in motion, as composer, performer and educator. In a curious way, he has no 'style' of his own; that is his strength. In its place, a free array of Black and European idioms, everything from stride to serialism, deployed within an intensely rhythmic, but often quite complex framework.

Levels And Degrees Of Light would be a slightly difficult record to place in a blindfold test. It is certainly not untypical of the Chicago experimentalism of the period, except in that it seems much less chaotic, much more responsive to European models. It opens in almost prayerful mood, with Penelope Taylor's wavering vocalize giving way to Abrams's unvirtuosic but strangely effective clarinet (which bears much the same relation to his keyboard work as Keith Jarrett's occasional soprano outbreaks do to his piano playing). The lyrical content of the very long 'Bird Song' is much less effective, though the inclusion of Jenkins and Jones gives the music an almost orchestral depth of focus, and Barker too contributes enormously, as he does on both records; one of the most musical drummers of his generation.

Young/Wise combines the definitive Abrams solo performance of the period with a group of tracks of burning intensity. 'Wise In Time', the piano piece, is both a good representation of Abrams's strengths and the clearest indication of his limits as a solo performer. It's packed with powerful striding metres and wonderful left-hand geometries that recall the greats of the piano, Tatum, James P. Johnson and Bud, but overlaid with ideas that come from a very different tradition altogether.

*****(*) Things To Come From Those Now Gone**

Delmark CD 430 *Abrams (p solo).* 10/72.

The title says it all. *Things To Come* is a ringing assertion of Abrams's lifelong belief that musical advancement can only be achieved by observing the lessons of tradition. In what's best heard as an extended autobiographical/historical suite, he investigates every conceivable angle and dimension of the jazz and popular tradition, synthesizing ragtime, stride, boogie and swing styles with a complex free idiom. It is rare to hear Abrams unaccompanied and the pianism is not immediately identifiable, only its kinship with earlier masters James P. Johnson and even Willie 'The Lion' Smith. An enormously valuable reissue, released in 2000, *Things To Come ...* now sounds like a complex musical manifesto, a template for the next 30 years of dogged effort and exploration.

***** 1-OQA+19**

Black Saint 120017-2 *Abrams; Anthony Braxton (as, sno, f, cl, v); Henry Threadgill (as, ts, f, v); Leonard Jones (b, v); Steve McCall (d, perc, v).* 11–12/77.

***** Spihumonesty**

Black Saint 120032-2 *Abrams; George E. Lewis (tb, sou, syn); Roscoe Mitchell (as, f); Amina Claudine Myers (p, electric p, org); Youssef Yancey (theremin); Leonard Jones (b); Jay Clayton (v).* 7/79.

Like other American radicals (Bill Dixon and George Lewis are other good examples) Abrams has had to rely on European labels – and in particular on the Italian-based Black Saint – to make his music heard. These two discs underline how early Giovanni Bonandrini's adventurous imprints actually were. This is music that still retains the experimental edge of earlier years, but with a much more settled approach and a highly sophisticated group sound.

Myers's contribution to *Spihumonesty* (a typically punning title that recalls the gnomic titles of bebop, like 'Klactoveeseedstene') is much more focused than on the duo set. This drummerless band moves through the charts like information through a printed circuit, and there is an impressive simultaneity to some of the cues which suggests that at least some of this music was predetermined and meticulously rehearsed. Abrams still isn't a great soloist in any conventional sense, but like Ellington he has a rare gift for taking and retaining strong personalities and yet making them part of an overall sound which is very much greater than the parts.

The earlier record has on the face of it a more impressive starting line-up, though also a far more conventionally jazz-based sound. Though Threadgill is a much less demanding player than Roscoe Mitchell, Anthony Braxton is one of the certain masters of modern jazz and perhaps Abrams's most gifted pupil. The music they make together is complex, scurryingly allusive and seldom directly appealing. Braxton's title-composition is handled with great intelligence and reserve and so is 'Charlie In The Parker', but there are question marks elsewhere.

***** Mama And Daddy**

Black Saint 120041-2 *Abrams; Baikida Carroll (t, flhn); George E. Lewis (tb); Bob Stewart (tba); Vincent Chancey (hn); Wallace McMillan (as, bs, ts, f, perc); Leroy Jenkins (vn); Brian Smith (b); Andrew Cyrille (d, perc).* 12/79.

***** Rejoicing With The Light**

Black Saint 120071-2 *Abrams; Baikida Carroll (t, flhn); Vincent Chancey (hn); Wallace McMillan (as, bs, ts, f, perc); Marty Ehrlich (as, f, cl); Patience Higgins (cl, acl, bs); Jean-Paul Bourelly (g); Abdul Wadud (clo); Rick Rosie (b); Warren Smith (vib, timp, perc).* 1/83.

If there is a 'transitional' period in the career of a musician as doggedly exploratory as Abrams, then this has to be it. These albums seem more compelling now than they did when they first came out, because it is clear where the leader's ideas are going, even if it wasn't (yet) to some of even his most devoted followers. The addition of the powerful Carroll (who sounds like Leo Smith cross-matched with Fats Navarro), the estimable Lewis and, to be an Abrams regular after *Rejoicing*, Patience Higgins gives these records a sonic authority which isn't yet matched by either writing or playing.

****(*) Duet**

Black Saint 120051-2 *Abrams; Amina Claudine Myers (p).* 5/81.

*****(*) Duets And Solos**

Black Saint 120133-2 *Abrams; Roscoe Mitchell (reeds, f).* 3/90.

Unfortunately still missing is the 1975 *Sightsong*, a duo album with Malachi Favors, a richly textured meditation on the bass tradition of Wilbur Ware, another great Chicagoan. The encounters with Mitchell and Myers are both somewhat later, dating from a time when Abrams's interests seem to be settling down to composition rather than improvised structures. Retrospect hasn't changed our view that the two pianists simply get in each other's way on the earlier record. Mitchell, though, is a consummate duo performer, a listening musician who delivers a telling statement every time he allows himself to step forward. His flute playing is perhaps less well documented than his other reeds, and it is that frail but hard-edged sound which is most to be treasured here.

***** View From Within**

Black Saint 120081-2 *Abrams; Stanton Davis (t, flhn); John Purcell (as, ss, f, ts, bcl); Marty Ehrlich (picc, f, as, ts, cl, bcl); Warren Smith (vib, mar, perc); Rick Rosie (b); Thurman Barker (d, perc); Ray Mantilla (perc).* 9/84.

★★★ Colors In Thirty-Third

Black Saint 120091-2 *Abrams; John Purcell (ts, ss, bcl); John Blake (vn); Dave Holland (b, clo); Fred Hopkins (b); Andrew Cyrille (d).* 12/86.

Like the slightly later *Colors In Thirty-Third, View* sounds like a thoroughly personal statement. The multi-instrumental approach lends it a fluid, unsettled quality, but with a huge timbral and textural range. Again much of the energy transfers between Abrams, articulating patiently and without overt drama, and the estimable Barker.

The later record continues the experiment with texture and harmonic depth by building in string lines, Holland on cello an obvious asset on a set like this. This might be thought to be Purcell's finest hour, but everyone contributes. The basic personnel divides into trio, quartet, quintet and, for the title-piece and the significantly named 'Introspection', full sextet. Cyrille matches Thurman Barker for sheer strength and personality, and richly deserves the dedication of 'Drumman'.

★★★(★) The Hearinga Suite

Black Saint 120103-2 *Abrams; Cecil Bridgewater, Frank Gordon, Ron Tooley, Jack Walrath (t); Clifton Anderson, Dick Griffin (tb); Jack Jeffers, Bill Lowe (btb); John Purcell (ts, f, cl); Marty Ehrlich (as, picc, f, cl); Patience Higgins (ts, bcl); Courtney Wynter (bsn, bcl, ts); Charles Davis (bs, ss); Dierdre Murray (clo); Fred Hopkins (b); Andrew Cyrille (d).* 1/89.

This marks something of a quantum shift, a move towards something larger and more cohesive. The spirit of Ellington isn't far away here. Pieces like 'Hearinga' itself, 'Seesall' and 'Bermix' are self-contained and robustly structured, though one finds oneself wishing now and again for a more relaxed and open-ended performance. Ehrlich, Higgins, Wynter and Davis might have been given a bit more room to expand, though this time out the rhythm section could hardly be bettered. Hopkins is still underrated, though this is one of Cyrille's very best recorded performances.

★★★★ Blu Blu Blu

Black Saint 120117-2 *Abrams; Joel Brandon (whistle); Jack Walrath (t); Alfred Patterson (tb); Mark Taylor (frhn); Joe Daley (tba); John Purcell (as, f, bcl); Robert DeBellis (as, cl, bcl); Eugene Ghee (ts, cl, bcl); David Fiuczynski (g); Lindsey Horne, Brad Jones (b); Warren Smith (vib, tim); Thurman Barker (d).* 11/90.

Abrams's best album for some time is almost hijacked by the extraordinary Brandon, who has also worked with David Murray. His high, bird-like tones could almost be produced by a synth, were they not so rapidly and naturally articulated. 'One For The Whistler' is a *tour de force*, and elsewhere on the record Brandon demonstrates his own and his overlooked instrument's viability as an improvising voice; he should be picking up 'miscellaneous instrument' citations like litter.

Abrams really gets going as a pianist only on the final 'Stretch Time', leaving most of the foreground to a tonally varied and adventurous band. The title-track is a dedication to McKinley Morganfield (better known as Muddy Waters). Fiuczynski's howling guitar initially sounds out of place, but it settles back into a sophisticated chart in which Abrams brings together much of the continuum of recent black music. Of the brasses, Walrath is the unchallenged star: punchy, accurate and full of droll wit. As ever, Barker takes control of the engine room. To be set alongside Sun Ra's later work and the better of Butch Morris's 'Conduction' experiments, this is among the most important contemporary big-band records.

★★★(★) Family Talk

Black Saint 120132-2 *Abrams; Jack Walrath (t); Patience Higgins (ts, bcl, eng hn); Warren Smith (vib, timp, mar, gongs); Brad Jones (b); Reggie Nicholson (d, mar, bells).* 3/93.

A fine record which transcends individual contributions. Higgins is a somewhat limited soloist, probably best deployed as a colourist on a session like this. His tenor solo on 'Illuso' is so forcedly naïve, we begin to wonder if he is putting us on. By contrast, Walrath this time out sounds too knowing and technically assured, as if trying to distance himself from his confrères. On the long 'DizBirdMonkBudMax' he sounds poised and at ease, but he's the wrong man for the moodier and more complex tracks like 'Drumbutu', where he simply reworks the cod-Gothick effects he has patented on his own records.

As on a couple of occasions before, *Family Talk* really belongs to the rhythm section. Abrams is securely anchored and the addition of tuned percussion allows him to play quite abstractly when he feels the need. His synthesizer work, which goes in and out of focus, is mainly reserved here for introductory sketches and background washes, but it adds an important element to the overall sound. Smith is excellent on vibes and marimba. The woodier tones mix well with Jones's bass, and overall the album has a lovely rich sound.

★★★(★) Think All, Focus One

Black Saint 120141-2 *Abrams; Eddie E. J. Allen (t); Alfred Patterson (tb); Eugene Ghee (ts, bcl); David Gilmore (g); Brad Jones (b); Reggie Nicholson (d).* 7/94.

Henry Threadgill's liner-notes come in the form of a poem, a free-form rhapsody that invokes hunger, fear, delight, pursuit and the sheer playful exuberance of language. The music doesn't quite come up to the level of Threadgill's emotive response, but it's fine, toughly thought jazz all the same.

Abrams's own playing is still relatively unemphatic but, by this stage in the game, his 'instrument' is the whole band, and these musicians understand exactly what he is about. 'The Harmonic Veil' and 'Scaledance' are relatively technical opuses, and Abrams has interspersed these with more associative pieces like 'Crossbeams' and 'The Junction', both of which seem to strike specific chords in Threadgill. The title-track, which comes right at the end, is a small-scale classic, a piece of jazz writing which manages to collapse a whole lifetime of experience into just five and a half minutes.

That said, there is something almost routine about the playing, almost as if this repertoire had been rehearsed and workshopped to the point where all spontaneity ceased.

★★★(★) Song For All

Black Saint 120161-2 *Abrams; Eddie E. J. Allen (t); Craig Harris (tb); Aaron Stewart (ts, ss); Bryan Carrott (vib, perc); Brad Jones (b); Reggie Nicholson (d).* 95.

Again, the presence of a vibist makes a significant difference to Abrams's own approach. He sounds more concerned with colours and shapes than with the forward momentum of a piece, and this is all to the good. The group has a somewhat unfamiliar aspect. Allen is a bouncy, often provocative player, sounding almost as if he comes from an earlier generation. Harris is a star, of course, and cannot keep his light under even a row of bushels, beaming out of the ensembles like the boy who habitually sticks out his tongue in the school photo. Stewart is not so much anonymous as easily overlooked, but he makes an attractive noise.

The two long tracks, 'GMBR' and 'Over The Same Over', are richly constructed and intelligently paced. The opening 'Song For All' and 'Dabba Dabba Doo' which follows it are probably the best on the record, though. One of those sets which palls a little over the full length and which is probably better sampled a track at a time.

****** One Line, Two Views**
New World 80469 *Abrams; Eddie E. J. Allen (t, perc, v); Marty Ehrlich (as, bcl, perc, v); Patience Higgins (ts, bcl, perc, v); Mark Feldman (vn, perc, v); Tony Cedras (acc, perc, v); Anne LeBaron (hp, perc, v); Bryan Carrott (vib, perc, v); Lindsey Horner (b, perc, v); Reggie Nicholson (d, perc, v).* 6/95.

This is the record Abrams has been promising for years, and it is perhaps ironic that it should appear other than on Black Saint, who have kept faith with the man for a decade and a half. As expected, it's characterized by tight, intelligent charts, an imaginative approach to timbre, and a headlong freedom that remains intact from early days. Higgins still isn't an impressive soloist – neither Hodges nor Gonsalves – but he does fit this music very well. Ehrlich's reappearance brings in a whole range of sounds, and Abrams finds key roles for harpist LeBaron (herself an important composer) and accordionist Cedras. At the heart of the set, a brief, heartfelt threnody to Julius Hemphill and Don Pullen, fellow-composers who left in a hurry with much undone. The longer pieces never drag, though there are moments in the closing 'Ensemble Song' which border on self-indulgence. A triumph, and an essential purchase for Abrams enthusiasts.

*****(*) The Open Air Meeting**
New World 80512 *Abrams; Marty Ehrlich (as, cl).* 8/96.

Recorded at the Brooklyn Museum, outdoors and in high summer, this is a fresh, mostly sunlit performance from two old friends whose association isn't always easy to unpick from a larger group performance. Two Ehrlich compositions – 'Dark Sestina' and 'Bright Canto' – set the expressive parameters of the set, the latter a glorious example of duo playing at the very highest level. Ehrlich's clarinet stands out strongly: vigorous, reedy and oddly traditional in articulation. Abrams deals with a less than wonderful piano with his usual lack of fuss, dodging round what sound like a couple of slightly dead keys. Good stuff, and a welcome return to the duet experiments of the early '80s.

***** The Visibility Of Thought**
Mutable Music 725052 2 *Abrams; Joseph Kubera (p); Todd Reynolds, Mary Rowell (vn); Ralph Ferris (vla); Dorothy Lawson (clo); Thomas Buckner (v).* 3/01.

This is a curious record, not because it 'isn't jazz' but because it seems to touch too many stylistic dimensions at once. The stately title-piece is a carefully crafted and strongly felt computer composition. It leaves one wishing to hear more of Abrams's work in this area, which clearly relates closely to both his ensemble and solo piano work. The long closing piano improvisation is a worthwhile companion piece, but one wonders about the role and provenance of the remaining works, a duet for double bass and piano (very understated), for violin and piano (Feldman at least expending some energy) and for label owner Buckner with the Ethel String Quartet. There is also a duet with Kubera which is mystifyingly lacking in content, purpose or energy.

Abrams has rarely been more enigmatic. If he wishes to reinvent himself as a composer, he may find his admirers were for once well in advance of him.

Bruce Adams (born 1951)

TRUMPET, FLUGELHORN

Grew up in Glasgow and began working the local scene in his teens, before moving south and staking a corner of the British mainstream as a forthright, ebullient stylist, rather in the Roy Eldridge tradition.

***** Good Bait**
Jazz House JHCD 063 *Adams; Dave Cliff (g); Leon Clayton (b); Martin Drew (d).* 5–6/00.

***** All The Way!**
Mainstem MCD 0016 *Adams; Brian Dee (p).* 11/00.

***** Always And Forever**
Woodville WVCD 104 *Adams; Dave Cliff (g); Leon Clayton (b); Ralph Salmins (d).* 12/03.

Adams is a socking player whose big range and armoury of licks will appeal to anyone who's a fan of the grandstanding end of the trumpet tradition. At the same time, he likes to mumble away in the middle register at more cooling moments, which gives his playing a certain unpredictability in the dynamics. It also makes him sound like a cross between Clark Terry and Roy Eldridge with a degree of bebop stirred in – impressive, if not especially individual. *Good Bait* is a typical live blow by Adams and his quartet, blustering along, although the ballads have their share of sugar. It was a good idea to enlist the unflappable Cliff for the group: putting an excitable pianist in would have overcooked everything. Dee is not prone to excitability either, and his duet session with Bruce is an amiable dialogue – nothing like as memorable as the encounter between Warren Vaché and Bill Charlap, but pleasing enough.

The latest quartet session, for Alan Barnes's new label, works best when the tempos are down – Pat Metheny's title track is beautifully handled. Adams isn't always precise enough to come away from some of his phrases without a stagger and there are times when it doesn't seem to make any difference which of the fast pieces he's playing on. But there's plenty to enjoy – and Cliff, Clayton and the cheerfully swinging Salmins are excellent value.

George Adams (1940–92)

TENOR SAXOPHONE, FLUTE, BASS CLARINET, VOCAL

The much-missed Georgian worked with Charles Mingus, Gil Evans and McCoy Tyner but had his first and major starring role in a collaborative group with Don Pullen. His saxophone style was deep and earthy, with many modernist elements but also a deep awareness of the blues.

****(*) Sound Suggestions**
ECM 517755-2 *Adams; Kenny Wheeler (t, flhn); Heinz Sauer (ts); Richie Beirach (p); Dave Holland (b); Jack DeJohnette (d).* 5/79.

***** Don't Loose Control**

Soul Note 121104-2 *Adams; Don Pullen (p); Cameron Brown (b); Dannie Richmond (d).* 11/79.

***** Hand To Hand**

Soul Note 121107-2 *Adams; Jimmy Knepper (tb); Hugh Lawson (p); Mike Richmond (b); Dannie Richmond (d).* 2/80.

What an irony that George Adams should have inspired one of the most heartfelt personal memorials of recent times, a tune almost on a par with 'Goodbye Pork Pie Hat', from a friend and partner who was fated to survive him for no more than three short years. Don Pullen's 'George, We Hardly Knew Ya' celebrated a working relationship that was close and instinctive and produced some of the fieriest small-group jazz of the '80s. Pullen was perhaps the dominant partner in terms of compositional ideas, but it was big George's hot, fruity tone that dominated the groups. An essentially melodic player in the tradition of Sonny Rollins, Adams had listened to enough of the avant-garde to bring in aspects of Coltrane's harmonic revolution and of Albert Ayler's unfettered testifying. If the elements weren't always comfortably blended – and the reissued *Sound Suggestions* conveys a man in search of his creative identity – the results were always exciting. Listening to the solitary ECM (an association which doesn't seem to have satisfied either side) alongside the first of the Soul Notes, recorded six months later, boldly underlines Pullen's role in Adams's emergence. He thrives on the big, vamped chords and gospelly runs and the basic vocabulary is all in place. The strengths of the ECM lie in Adams's interplay with Holland and DeJohnette. Beirach and Wheeler are scarcely sympathetic partners and there is no need for a second saxophonist, especially when the horns are panned hard right and left. Only two compositions are credited to the leader, the remainder to Wheeler and, inexplicably, to the anonymous Sauer, reinforcing the sense that this was an uneasy collaboration, not really Adams's own session. Only on his own 'Imani's Dance' and 'Got Somethin' Good For You' does he feel confident enough to let rip.

Hand To Hand was another co-led session, cementing what was to be another important association, with Mingus's favourite drummer, Dannie Richmond. The trombonist is much more like the thing than Wheeler, a raw, regressive player who sounds as if he has completely missed out on J. J. Johnson's revisionist teachings.

***** Gentlemen's Agreement**

Soul Note 121057-2 *Adams; Jimmy Knepper (tb); Hugh Lawson (p); Mike Richmond (b); Dannie Richmond (d).* 2/83.

An interesting reunion of the Adams/Richmond unit which suggests that both men might have been looking for alternative directions and a much broader tonal and timbral range. 'Prayer For A Jitterbug' and 'Symphony For Five' are redolent of Eric Dolphy's work on *Iron Man*, and Lawson (who registers more strongly with each return visit) combines lyricism with a blunt strength, almost like a selected hybrid of Beirach and Pullen. Less sheerly exciting than the quartets, but not to be overlooked.

***** Live At The Village Vanguard**

Soul Note 121094-2 *Adams; Don Pullen (p); Cameron Brown (b); Dannie Richmond (d).* 8/83.

***** Live At The Village Vanguard: Volume 2**

Soul Note 121144-2 *As above.* 8/83.

The working band *in excelsis*, rounding off a half-decade of concentrated activity with a couple of heated – sometimes overheated – sets. Perhaps oddly, given the chemistry, this is a band that always sounded better in the studio. The Village Vanguard sets are slightly ramshackle (compare the live version of 'Thank You Very Much, Mr Monk' with the one on the deleted *City Gates*), and much of the interest now lies in hearing how much Adams anticipates what David Murray was going to be doing (sambas, spirituals) at the end of the decade. With various sets for Timeless and Blue Note now deleted, there isn't much great Adams available at present.

Pepper Adams (1930–86)

BARITONE SAXOPHONE

Park Adams III was touring with Lionel Hampton in his teens and, after army duty, he worked in Detroit during the early '50s. From 1958 he based himself in New York, and among his principal associations were spells with Charles Mingus, a co-led quintet with Donald Byrd, and the Thad Jones–Mel Lewis Orchestra, as well as many dates under his own leadership.

***** 10 To 4 At The 5-Spot**

Original Jazz Classics OJC 031 *Adams; Donald Byrd (t); Bobby Timmons (p); Doug Watkins (b); Elvin Jones (d).* 4/58.

The baritone sax was as unpopular with hard-bop musicians as it was with the original boppers and, come to that, with the swing-era saxophonists. Pepper Adams, more than anyone, came close to making it a congenial instrument in the hot-house environment of hard bop. He had a dry, unsentimental tone – very different from either Serge Chaloff or Gerry Mulligan – and a penchant for full-tilt solos that gave no shred of concession to the horn's 'cumbersome' reputation. The live session, made with a frequent partner at the time, Donald Byrd, is typical of Adams's kind of date, with muscular blow-outs of the order of 'Hastings Street Bounce' sitting next to a clear-headed ballad reading of 'You're My Thrill'. That said, it's sometimes only the novelty value of hearing a baritone in the ensembles that lifts the music out of a professional hard-bop routine.

***** Out Of This World**

Fresh Sound FSR-CD 137 *Adams; Donald Byrd (t); Herbie Hancock (p); Teddy Charles (vib); Laymon Jackson (b); Jimmy Cobb (d).* 61.

Though sometimes listed under either Byrd's name or Adams's, we have elected to include this album under the saxophonist's entry. One might expect a bluff, no-nonsense kind of hard bop, but this session tends to spotlight the gentler side of the two leaders. The Fresh Sound date, originally released on Warwick and produced by Teddy Charles, has some genuinely lyrical touches: Adams's solo turn on 'Day Dream', for instance, with a pleasing early solo by Hancock.

***** Pepper Adams Plays Charlie Mingus**

Fresh Sound FSR-CD 177 *Adams; Thad Jones (t); Bennie Powell (tb); Charles McPherson (as); Zoot Sims (ts); Hank Jones (p); Paul Chambers, Bob Cranshaw (b); Dannie Richmond (d).* 9/63.

Adams led this date with his usual unfussy authority. There are nine Mingus tunes and a mixture of Mingusians and – in the case of Zoot Sims – at least one musician about as far removed from being a Mingus sideman as one could imagine, though Zoot deals with the situation as imperturbably as always. The results, split between a quintet and an octet, are akin to a pocket-size edition of a typical Mingus band: 'Haitian Fight Song' and 'Fables Of Faubus' are as swinging as any Mingus version (Chambers is at the top of his game), but 'Better Git In Your Soul' (*sic*) is comparatively watery, and Jones is a lot more dapper than a Mingus pianist might have been.

*****(*) Encounter!**
Original Jazz Classics OJC 892 *Adams; Zoot Sims (ts); Tommy Flanagan (p); Ron Carter (b); Elvin Jones (d).* 12/68.

A very good one. The band is absolutely stellar, full of Detroit homeboys, and Sims was a fail-safe choice for the front-line partner. If anything, Jones overdoes the bashing, and the up-tempo pieces are a battle, but the saxophonists don't falter at any point. There is a fine Adams ballad in 'I've Just Seen Her', as well as a choice arrangement of 'Star-Crossed Lovers'.

*****(*) Conjuration: Fat Tuesday's Session**
Reservoir RSR 113 *Adams; Kenny Wheeler (t, flhn); Hank Jones (p); Clint Houston (b); Louis Hayes (d).* 8/83.

This live set emphasizes Pepper's virtues – the muscularity of sound, oversized tone and plangent phrasing – so decisively that one overlooks any scent of routine in the playing. Kenny Wheeler, an unlikely partner, adds sparkle and some good material, and Hank Jones is sublimely buoyant, as are Houston and Hayes.

Julian 'Cannonball' Adderley (1928–75)

ALTO SAXOPHONE

Born in Tampa, Florida, he taught music and led groups only part-time but was persuaded to try his luck in New York in 1955. Joined Miles Davis, 1957–9, then re-formed band with brother Nat, touring and recording more or less continuously thereafter until his death from a stroke. A great popularizer, and a leader in the soul-jazz style of the '60s, Cannon was a much-loved figure who helped keep jazz before an audience at a time when it was losing listeners.

***** Julian 'Cannonball' Adderley**
Verve 830381-2 *Adderley; Nat Adderley (c); J J Johnson, Jimmy Cleveland (tb); Jerome Richardson (ts, f); Cecil Payne (bs); John Williams (p); Paul Chambers (b); Kenny Clarke, Max Roach (d).* 7–8/55.

***** Jump For Joy**
Verve 528699-2 *Adderley; Emmett Berry (t); Bill Evans (p); Barry Galbraith (g); Milt Hinton (b); Jimmy Cobb (d).* 10/55–8/58.

*****(*) Sophisticated Swing**
Verve 528408-2 2CD *Adderley; Nat Adderley (c); Junior Mance (p); Sam Jones, Al McKibbon (b); Specs Wright, Jimmy Cobb (d).* 7/56–3/58.

***** Portrait Of Cannonball**
Original Jazz Classics OJC 361 *Adderley; Blue Mitchell (t); Bill Evans (p); Sam Jones (b); Philly Joe Jones (d).* 7/58.

*****(*) Things Are Getting Better**
Original Jazz Classics OJC 032 *Adderley; Wynton Kelly (p); Milt Jackson (vib); Percy Heath (b); Art Blakey (d).* 10/58.

***** Quintet In Chicago**
Verve 559770-2 *Adderley; John Coltrane (ts); Wynton Kelly (p); Paul Chambers (b); Jimmy Cobb (d).* 2/59.

***** Ultimate Cannonball Adderley**
Verve 559710-2 *As Verve albums listed above.* 58–62.

Long a critically undervalued figure, Cannonball Adderley's status as a master communicator in jazz has increased since his sadly early death. The blues-soaked tone and hard, swinging delivery of his alto lines are as recognizable a sound as anything in the aftermath of bebop and, while many have been quick to criticize his essentially derivative manner – Cannonball frequently fell back on clichés, because he just liked the sound of them – there's a lean, hard-won quality about his best playing that says a lot about one man's dedication to his craft.

Julian 'Cannonball' Adderley was his first date for Emarcy and his third appearance in a recording studio, yet the confidence and brio is already in place and seemingly unstoppable. The session's organized as a kind of routine around the leading soloist and offers little in the way of creative succour, but even a formulaic setting like the one for 'The Song Is You' gets Cannonball burning.

When he joined Miles Davis, Adderley's cameo appearances on *Milestones* and *Kind Of Blue* were somewhat outclassed by the leader's returning-the-favour guest spot on *Somethin' Else*. But something else distinguishes the Adderley sessions of this period: the superb line-up of supporting players. There is marvellous sparring with Milt Jackson on *Things Are Getting Better* and with Kelly, Heath and Blakey also in great form; and 'The Sidewalks Of New York' is an inspired revision which only Ellington's incomparable 1940 version can surpass. *Portrait Of Cannonball* (which includes three alternative takes on the CD issue) finds Blue Mitchell taking some welcome limelight – though he sounds no more facile than the oft-maligned Nat – and an early glimpse of Bill Evans feeling his way through 'Nardis'. The session with Coltrane is really the Miles Davis band without Miles, and it's a bit of good fun, both hornmen flexing their muscles on the blues and a ballad feature apiece. There really isn't a dud record in this batch.

Verve have filled in the picture of this period by putting together Cannonball's Emarcy sessions. *Sophisticated Swing* pulls together all the LPs *Sophisticated Swing, Cannonball En Route* and *Cannonball's Sharpshooters*, plus Nat's date, *To The Ivy League From Nat*, in a double-disc reissue. The clipped, punchy format of most of the tracks suits the playing, and there is some of the altoist's freshest music hidden in some otherwise unpromising songs. *Jump For Joy* puts Cannonball with Richard Hayman's strings for the first half, and it's not the happiest of combinations, though the sheer alacrity of Adderley's sound energizes some otherwise tepid writing. The second half, arranged by Bill Russo to accommodate a string quartet beside a familiar rhythm section, works better, and there is some felicitous work by all hands. Excellent remastering of both discs.

It was a gracious touch to have Joe Zawinul select favourites by his old boss for the *Ultimate* compilation. No surprises here, although since there's nothing from the period when Joe himself was in the band (because none of that music belongs to Verve) there's a degree of pointlessness about it too.

CORE COLLECTION

★★★★ Somethin' Else

Blue Note 95392-2 *Adderley; Miles Davis (t); Hank Jones (p); Sam Jones (b); Art Blakey (d).* 3/58.

A classic Blue Note, and while the record has been somewhat unfairly credited to Miles Davis as the distinguishing spirit, it is at least as much Cannonball's achievement. The long, sublimely relaxed lope through 'Autumn Leaves' is the track every listener remembers, but there isn't a rote moment on the record, and the rhythm section – Sam Jones making a rare appearance in the Blue Note studios – take much credit too. The contrast between Adderley's vitally energized playing and the narrow-eyed lyricism of Davis is a treat, yet each man makes his own kind of impression, very deep.

★★★ In San Francisco

Original Jazz Classics OJC 035 *Adderley; Nat Adderley (c); Bobby Timmons (p); Sam Jones (b); Louis Hayes (d).* 10/59.

★★★ What Is This Thing Called Soul

Original Jazz Classics OJC 801 *Adderley; Nat Adderley (c); Victor Feldman (p); Sam Jones (b); Louis Hayes (d).* 11/60.

★★★ Paris 1960

Pablo PACD-5303-2 *As above.* 11/60.

Adderley's regular quintet has often been damned with such faint praise as 'unpretentious' and 'soulful'. This was a hard-hitting, rocking band which invested blues and blowing formulae with an intensity that helped to keep one part of jazz's communication channels open at the time of Ornette Coleman, Eric Dolphy and other seekers after new forms. The earlier live album is a memorably rowdy and exciting session. *In San Francisco* is a little overstretched, with four tracks nudging the 12-minute mark and some of the solos running out of steam too soon. *What Is This Thing Called Soul* is taken from European concerts: the band is on cracking form on Jimmy Heath's 'Big P', and the rest of the set is up to scratch. *Paris 1960* is a recent discovery with six favourites from the band's book: scarcely essential, given the several versions of titles like 'Dis Here' in the discography, but no disappointments about the form of the band.

★★★ African Waltz

Original Jazz Classics OJC 258 *Adderley; Clark Terry, Ernie Royal, Joe Newman, Nick Travis (t); Nat Adderley (c); Bob Brookmeyer (vtb); Melba Liston, Arnette Sparrow, George Matthews, Jimmy Cleveland, Paul Faulise (tb); George Dorsey (as, f); Jerome Richardson, Oliver Jackson (ts, f); Arthur Clarke (bs); Wynton Kelly (p); Sam Jones (b); Don Butterfield (tba); Louis Hayes, Charli Persip (d); Ray Barretto, Olatunji (perc).* 2–5/61.

A departure from and an extension of what the Adderleys were doing in their small groups. Ernie Wilkins arranges a set of fulsome, top-heavy charts which Adderley has to jostle with to create their own space, and the music's worth hearing for its sheer brashness and impact. But the simple clarity of the Adderley small groups is a casualty of the setting, and the altoman isn't as convincingly at home here as he is in the *Great Jazz Standards* album with Gil Evans, one of his finest hours.

★★★ Know What I Mean?

Original Jazz Classics OJC 105 *Adderley; Bill Evans (p); Percy Heath (b); Connie Kay (d).* 1–3/61.

★★★ Cannonball Adderley Quintet Plus

Original Jazz Classics OJC 306 *Adderley; Nat Adderley (c); Victor Feldman (p, vib); Wynton Kelly (p); Sam Jones (b); Louis Hayes (d).* 5/61.

★★(★) In New York

Original Jazz Classics OJC 142 *Adderley; Nat Adderley (c); Yusef Lateef (ts, ob); Joe Zawinul (p); Sam Jones (b); Louis Hayes (d).* 1/62.

★★★ Jazz Workshop Revisited

Capitol 29441-2 *As above.* 9/62.

★★★ Cannonball's Bossa Nova

Capitol 22667-2 *Adderley; Pedro Paulo (t); Paulo Moura (as); Sergio Mendes (p); Durval Ferreria (g); Octavio Bailly Jr (b); Dom Um Romao (d).* 12/62.

★★★ Nippon Soul

Original Jazz Classics OJC 435 *Adderley; Nat Adderley (c); Yusef Lateef (ts, ob, f); Joe Zawinul (p); Sam Jones (b); Louis Hayes (d).* 7/63.

★★★ Dizzy's Business

Milestone MCD-47069-2 *As above.* 9/62–7/63.

★★★ Lugano 1963

TCB TDE 02032 *As above.* 3/63.

Cannonball continued to turn out records for Riverside at a cracking pace and, while there are no classics here, his own big-hearted playing seldom falters. At this point, though, the regimen of tours and records begins to fossilize some aspects of his own playing. Having stratified bop licks and set the pace for so-called 'soul jazz', Adderley found there wasn't much left to do but play them over again. If he plays with undiminished verve, the power of his improvising declines. The quartet date with Bill Evans was one of the last chances to hear him as sole horn, and he sounds fine; *Plus* brings in Wynton Kelly on a few tracks, enabling Feldman to play some more vibes, but it's otherwise a routine Adderley band date. Bringing in Joe Zawinul and Yusef Lateef energized the band anew, but the records are all vaguely disappointing. Zawinul is still no more than a good bandsman, and Lateef's touches of exotica – such as the oboe solo on 'Brother John' (*Nippon Soul*) or his furry, Roland Kirk-like flute improvisations – are an awkward match for the sunnier disposition of the customary material. Nevertheless *Nippon Soul* is perhaps the best of this bunch, although the new edition of *Jazz Workshop Revisited* runs it close: on favourite turf in San Francisco, the band are in good fettle. *Dizzy's Business* patches together some out-takes from the sessions for *Jazz Workshop Revisited* and *Nippon Soul*: not bad, with the title-track a solidly turned cooker. The Lugano date is another characteristic concert from one of the hardest-working bands of their era: familiar songs, though done as well as anywhere, and one nice note with 'Jessica's Birthday'. Recorded by Swiss Radio and in good fidelity. The men who earn exemption from criticism on all these records are Sam Jones and Louis Hayes: seldom remembered as a major rhythm section, their unflagging tempos and generosity of spirit centre the music at all times.

Cannonball's Bossa Nova finds Adderley on a Brazilian vacation, with some of the local talent. Little more than a sweet-natured excursion into some of the indigenous music, it's a pleasing diversion.

***** Live Session**

Capitol 97934-2 *Adderley; Nat Adderley (c); Joe Zawinul (p); Sam Jones (b); Louis Hayes (d); Ernie Andrews(v).* 9/62, 10/64.

***** Mercy, Mercy, Mercy**

Capitol 29915-2 *Adderley; Nat Adderley (c); Joe Zawinul (p); Victor Gaskin (b); Roy McCurdy (d).* 10/66.

***** Inside Straight**

Original Jazz Classics OJC 750 *Adderley; Nat Adderley (c); Hal Galper (p); Walter Booker (b); Roy McCurdy (d); King Errisson (perc).* 6/73.

****(*) Pyramid**

Original Jazz Classics OJC 952 *As above, except add George Duke (ky), Jimmy Jones (p), Phil Upchurch (g); omit Errisson.* 74.

Adderley kept on recording regularly until his death, but many of his later albums are currently in limbo so far as the catalogues are concerned. Close to 20 Capitol albums have been boiled down to what's on offer here. Given that many of the later records were misfire attempts at fusion of one sort or another, maybe it's not such a bad thing. The *Live Session* actually comes from gigs two years apart, and were meant to launch the singing voice of Andrews as much as Adderley. He sounds fine, but the band take a back seat to the singer, and for Cannonball fans this one's secondary. *Mercy, Mercy, Mercy* is a hard-swinging live album with one of Cannon's hottest outings in 'Sticks'.

Inside Straight is a welcome addition to latter-day Cannon on CD. This was one of his live-in-the-studio sessions with a late edition of the band: Galper plays smart, probing electric piano, and Booker and McCurdy generate considerable heat. The tunes are a little more severe than before: only the title-track can be called a typical Adderley slice of soul-jazz. 'Inner Journey', 'Snakin' The Grass' and 'Second Son' are more sidelong looks at the band's playing methods, and more interesting for it. No masterpiece, but a hint of other paths the group might have explored. Less valuable is *Pyramid*, which imports Duke and Upchurch for some modish touches and gets righteous mostly with a more traditionally inclined 'Bess, Oh Where's My Bess'.

Nat Adderley (1931–2000)

CORNET, TRUMPET

One of the few modern brass players to have specialized on cornet, Nat had a sharp, staccato tone in melody statements which could give way to the most unctuous and syrupy of deliveries when he played ballads. He worked with J. J. Johnson and Woody Herman and, most famously, with his older brother, Cannonball, to whom he was an ideal foil.

***** Introducing Nat Adderley**

Verve 543 828 *Adderley; Julian 'Cannonball' Adderley (as); Horace Silver (p); Paul Chambers (b); Roy Haynes (d).* 9/55.

The Adderley brothers helped keep a light burning for jazz when rock'n'roll was dominating the industry 'demographics'. Neither was ever particularly revolutionary or adventurous in style, but saxophonist Cannonball's enormous personality and untimely death, together with his participation in such legendary dates as Miles's *Kind Of Blue*, have sanctified his memory with young fans who would have found his live performances rather predictable.

Nat was always the more incisive soloist, with a bright, ringing tone that most obviously drew on the example of Dizzy Gillespie but in which could be heard a whole raft of influences from Clark Terry to Henry 'Red' Allen to the pre-post-modern Miles of the '50s.

Interestingly, the brothers' recording debut was made under Nat's leadership. *Introducing* is a buoyant, exuberant set created by a band who sound as if they have absolutely nothing to prove. All the tunes are by Nat and Cannonball and some of them – most obviously the opening triptych of 'Watermelon', 'Two Brothers' and 'Little Joanie Walks' – would be standard fare for the Adderleys, together and apart, for years to come.

Though Charlie Parker had been dead for some time and the search was already on for his successor, an accolade that would later settle on Cannonball, he doesn't sound unduly affected by Bird and his phrasing is much more reminiscent of Willie Smith and Benny Carter. Nat was then and remained a musical descendant of the Eldridge/Shavers era and his punchy, precise attack on 'New Arrival' and 'Blues For Bohemia' is a delight. Hard to imagine that when this record was made, the Adderleys were still pretty much unknown. The fact that they managed to assemble such a stellar rhythm section suggests that fellow-musicians knew where the action was going to be in future.

***** Branching Out**

Original Jazz Classics OJC 255 *Adderley; Johnny Griffin (ts); The Three Sounds (Gene Harris (p); Andy Simpkins (b); Bill Dowdy (d)).* 9/58.

****** Work Song**

Original Jazz Classics OJC 363 *Adderley; Bobby Timmons (p); Wes Montgomery (g); Keter Betts, Sam Jones (b); Louis Hayes, Percy Heath (d).* 1/60.

In the late '50s the cornetist was playing at his peak, and these sessions do genuinely merit the 'classic' tag, though 'original' is probably stretching things a bit. *Branching Out* is an attractive enough set, but Griff doesn't seem to be the right saxophone player for the gig, too noisy and rapid-fire on things like 'I Got Plenty of Nuthin''. *Work Song* is the real classic, of course, laced with a funky blues feel but marked by some unexpectedly lyrical playing (on 'Violets For Your Furs' and 'My Heart Stood Still') from the leader. Montgomery manages to produce something more enterprising than his trademark octave-runs and hits a tense, almost threatening groove. Timmons is more predictable, but just right for this sort of set; compare *In San Francisco* (OJC 035), which was made under Cannonball's name.

***** Much Brass**

Original Jazz Classics OJCCD 848 *Adderley; Slide Hampton (tb); Wynton Kelly (p); Laymon Jackson, Sam Jones (b); Albert 'Tootie' Heath (d).* 3/59.

Some interesting arrangements here, presumably largely the work of Hampton, and some delicately interwoven playing which largely belies the bluster implied in the title. 'Israel' is gorgeous, as is the closing 'Sometimes I Feel Like A Motherless Child'. Not immediately identifiable as a 'typical' Nat Adderley record, but a beautiful statement all the same.

★★★(★) That's Right

Original Jazz Classics OJC 791 *Adderley; Julian 'Cannonball' Adderley (as); Yusef Lateef (ts, f, ob); Jimmy Heath, Charlie Rouse (ts); Tate Houston (bs); Wynton Kelly (p); Jim Hall, Les Spann (g); Sam Jones (b); Jimmy Cobb (d).* 9/60.

★★★ In The Bag

Original Jazz Classics OJC 648 *Adderley; Julian 'Cannonball' Adderley (as); Nat Perrilliat (ts); Ellis Marsalis (p); Sam Jones (b); James Black (d).* 6/62.

That's Right is a bit of an oddity, with Nat's cornet placed in front of what was billed, quite accurately, as the Big Sax Section. Lateef's multi-instrumentalism is kept to a minimum. He leads the ensemble on flute for 'My Old Country' but switches back to tenor for a rich, folksy solo. His oboe doesn't quite work out on 'Night After Night'; back in 1960 there weren't that many soprano specialists around to take a part made for one of them. Heath and Rouse are well featured, taking fine solos either side of Nat and the pianist on Heath's own 'Chordnation'. One of the high points of a thoroughly enjoyable record.

In The Bag is welcome for a further glimpse of the brothers playing together but isn't specially exciting. Watch out for the little-known Perrilliat, who plays a firm-toned and steady tenor, with some interesting quirks. The CD has added a couple of rather inconsequential bonus tracks.

★★★★ Little Big Horn!

Original Jazz Classics OJC 1001 *Adderley; Junior Mance (p); Kenny Burrell, Jim Hall (g); Bob Cranshaw (b); Mickey Roker (d).* 9–10/63.

Nat was still working with his brother's group when this was recorded, and it disappeared from sight surprisingly quickly after first release. Restored, it suggests again what a fine writer the wee man was. There's nothing as powerful as 'Work Song', but 'Loneliness' is an almost archetypal Nat tune and solo, and the penultimate track, 'Roses For Your Pillow', one of eight composed by the leader, is beautifully pitched and harmonized, a ballad worthy of frequent revival. Listening to this after a gap of – in our case – 15 years, it's hard to understand why such a quiet gem has slipped through the net.

★★★ Sayin' Somethin'

Atlantic 81222 72393 2 *Adderley; Joe Henderson (ts); Herbie Hancock (p); Bob Cranshaw (b); Mickey Roker (d).* 2/66.

Hearing Nat in the presence of both Joe Henderson and Herbie Hancock provides ample reminder that his approach to hard bop and soul-jazz was one that very much stayed up with the times. His solo on Herbie's 'Canteloupe Island' is simplicity itself, but none the less effective for avoiding over-elaboration. 'Hippodelphia' and 'Manchild' are funky treatments and even the pop tune, 'Call Me', seems to fit the setting comfortably enough. Very dated sound, which remastering hasn't smoothed out. Also now available in digipack accompanied by a liner interview with Nat. Example: *Q.* What are you saying with the album title, Nat? *A.* I'm saying nothing. It was Nesuhi Ertegun who picked it ... Hmm.

★★(★) The Soul Of The Bible

Blue Note 53217 *Adderley; Julian 'Cannonball' Adderley (as); George Duke (p, ky); Walter Booker (b); Roy McCurdy (d); Francisco Centeno, Mayuto Octavio, King Errison, Airto Moreira (perc); Rick Holmes (v).* 72.

Not quite as dismal as '70s concept album *Love, Sex and the Zodiac*, but coming close. Framed by gospel readings from Holmes, this seems to lack a solid enough rationale and limps along in a self-consciously soulful way. Given how comfortably Motown and Stax musicians of the time were synthesizing sacred and profane in popular music, the Adderleys' approach is lame in the extreme. Some strong playing from the horns but percussion-heavy and drably produced. By no means an essential buy.

★★★ Don't Look Back

Steeplechase SCCD 31059 *Adderley; Ken McIntyre (as, bcl, ob, f); John Stubblefield (ts, ss); Onaje Allan Gumbs (p, ky); Fernando Gumbs (b); Ira Buddy Williams (d); Victor See Yuen (perc).* 8/76.

Adderley's reputation as a mainstream traditionalist takes a knock with sets like these. Unfortunately, the results aren't by any means commensurate with the daring of the line-up. McIntyre is an important catalyst in the re-voicing of jazz horns but, like a true catalyst, he remains largely untouched by what is going on round him and he solos as if alone. Stubblefield is fierier and provokes some of the leader's best returns of fire. Whatever Onaje Allen Gumbs's qualities, he's patently wrong for this gig, and the rest of the group circle round him somewhat uneasily. A bold effort, but not quite there.

★★★ A Little New York Midtown Music

Original Jazz Classics OJCCD 1008 *Adderley; Johnny Griffin (ts); Victor Feldman (p); Ron Carter (b); Roy McCurdy (d).* 9/78.

A resilient and tough-minded hard-bop session, this late-'70s set is distinguished by some expert accompaniment from Victor Feldman and by superb solos from Nat and Johnny Griffin. Vic chips in with an original theme, 'Whipitup', but the bulk of the material, as ever, comes from Nat himself, and of his four compositions the title-track and 'Fortune's Child' are the best. Which means it's an album that peaks too soon, waning in interest after the first few cuts. Very much of its day, it has a brittle register which pervades the playing as well as the recording. Carter is poorly recorded, suggesting that even producer Orrin Keepnews could have an off-day.

★★★ Good Company

Challenge 70009 *Adderley; Antonio Hart (as); Rob Bargad (p); Walter Booker (b); Jimmy Cobb (d).* 6/94.

★★★ Live At The Floating Jazz Festival 1994

Chiaroscuro 334 2CD *As above, except omit Hart; add Vincent Herring (as).* 10/94.

By the mid-'90s, Nat had become something of an elder statesman of the music and one of its living historians. As the chops faltered, the monologues between numbers tended to get longer, and on the double festival CD the chat outweighs solo playing from the leader at least. His account of the origins of Sam Jones's 'Unit Seven' (heard to good effect on *Good Company*) has already entered jazz mythology, a hilarious performance, even if after a first hearing one starts to wish for a little more jazz. Most of the serious solo honours now fall to young Herring and to Bargad, both of whom sound poised and confident in such senior company.

Opening with Hank Mobley's 'This I Dig Of You' and Walter Booker's 'Soudade', the Floating Jazz set soon moves in more familiar directions, with fine versions of 'Work Song' and, rather briefly, 'Mercy, Mercy, Mercy'. Nat's most effective feature is his solo on 'Once I Had A Secret Love', on which the tone of the old days comes back ripe and fat and buttery. Bargad is excellent on the Chiaroscuro disc and he is rewarded with inclusion of two new compositions, 'War Zone' and 'Rob's New Tune'.

Hart is a more intuitive soloist than Herring, and his ensemble work is tighter and more obviously integrated with the leader's idiom, and yet he lacks his fellow-altoist's simplicity of tone. Producer Hein Van De Geyn goes for a plain but resonant sound and he seems to have boosted Nat in places, which is no more than his due.

Christopher Adler

PIANO

Gifted young pianist and musicologist on the San Diego scene.

***** Transcontinental**
9 Winds NWCD0262 *Adler; Alan Lechusza (woodwinds); Vikas Srivastava (d).* 1/01.

Adler has explored the musics and musical instruments of Thailand, specializing in the *khaen* (on which he has recorded) and the xylophone-like *ranaat ek*. His main musical language, though, appears to be a flowing, improvisatory idiom. His main statement on the opening 'Aloft' is reminiscent of Borah Bergman, though quieter and less percussive. Elsewhere on this rewarding album, which was originally released as a CD-R on Black Phone Records, he comps and vamps with an easy intensity, occupying an improbable territory between Jay McShann and Cecil Taylor. Lechusza is rather dominant in the recording and Srivastava's cymbal work is disconcertingly sibilant. A vivid and compelling slice of free improvisation, however.

Ron Affif (born 1965)

GUITAR

Post-bop guitarist, tougher than the average while working from a fundamentally conventional jazz viewpoint.

***** Ron Affif**
Pablo 2310-949-2 *Affif; Brian O'Rourke (p); Andy Simpkins (b); Colin Bailey (d).* 10/92.

*****(*) Vierd Blues**
Pablo 2310-954-2 *As above, except add Ron Anthony (g), Brian Kilgore (d).* 12/93–2/94.

****** 52nd Street**
Pablo 2310-958-2 *Affif; Essiet Essiet (b); Jeff Tain Watts (d).* 10/95.

*****(*) Ringside**
Pablo 2310-962-2 *Affif; Essiet Essiet (b); Colin Bailey (d).* 2/97.

***** Solotude**
Pablo 2310-965-2 *Affif (g solo).* 99.

It's a little surprising at first to read that Afiff was never a rock player, since his hard tone is at odds with the sweeter, warmer jazz feel of Montgomery, Pass or Hall, three clear role-models to judge from the interesting debut set, *Ron Affif*. There's something of a pull between the guitarist's obvious chopsmanship and his reluctance to take all the limelight: O'Rourke is just as readily featured, and nothing Affif does takes up too much space. Nevertheless this is still a fundamentally traditional-modern guitar programme, with standards the main bill of fare. *Vierd Blues* is a surprising advance. The programme is all Miles Davis tunes or dedications, and Affif goes at it with a startling blend of irreverence and homage. 'Solar' is turned into a helter-skelter samba tune; 'So What' is genuinely hard-bitten, a striking antidote to the many softer versions of the past 30 years. Affif puts some fresh light on most of the tunes, and his gutsy playing is capable enough to silence any talk of mere disrespect.

52nd Street is mostly bebop, but done with such skill and intensity that one never thinks of revivalism. On pure bop tunes such as 'Bohemia After Dark' Affif goes at it like a terrier, reeling off lines without relinquishing a finesse which is clearly his trademark. Yet there are subtle performances here too, especially the remarkable treatment of 'You Don't Know What Love Is', which starts out as a straightforward ballad and gets tougher and darker as it proceeds. There is superb support from Essiet and Watts, and they're all granted a wonderful sound in the studio. That pristine focus softens a little on *Ringside*, which has a frisson of excitement provided by a live-in-the-studio audience. If this one seems a shade more prosaic than before, there's no dimming of Affif's intensity or his capacity to build big-scale solos.

Perhaps the solo album was inevitable but, for a player who seems to thrive on interaction, this is a predictably quiescent and so-so situation. The music offers all the virtues of the earlier records, minus the intensity, and to that extent it's a disappointing continuation.

Oskar Aichinger

PIANO

Austrian sound-poet who swings in his own unorthodox way.

***** Elements Of Poetry**
Between the Lines btl 5 *Aichinger; Achim Tang (b); Paul Skrepek (b).* 00.

***** To Touch A Distant Soul**
Between the Lines btl 14 *Aichinger; Peter Raab (t); Max Nagl (ss, as); Martin Siewert (g); Achim Tang (b); Paul Skrepek (d).* 11/00.

***** Synapsis**
Between the Lines btl 29 *As for Elements of Poetry; add Stefan Nemeth (syn).* 12/02.

The personnel on the first disc suggests a relatively orthodox piano trio format. The reality, as listeners to Aichinger's earlier *Poemia* will understand, is very different. The pianist is interested in complex sonority rather than line, and rarely plays on the changes. *Elements Of Poetry* touches on various jazz styles, anything from a slowed-down bebop to the abstract-Latin tinge of 'Loose Calypso', but by and large concentrates on Aichinger's own evocative sound-world. There is less overt classicism than one might initially assume, though Debussy, Ravel and Webern are all part of the mix. The trio partners are completely sympathetic to the working philosophy and contribute substantially to the record's success, especially on the freely improvised tracks 'Perdendosi', 'Air', 'Ridicolosamente' and that strange 'Calypso'.

To Touch A Distant Soul expands the same concept in interesting directions. Again, what looks like a conventional jazz grouping is put to uses that are closer in parts to Webern's *Klangfarben* approach, using different instruments for different elements of the composition. That is evident on the long 'Nucleus', the lovely 'Initials To A Ballad' (which presumably uses the old classical trick of deriving a line from musicians' initials) and the improvised 'Attraction And Sudden Solitude'. Aichinger is very much the centre of attention, but Nagl's soprano and Raab's trumpet (somewhat reminiscent of label boss Franz Koglmann) play their part as well.

The addition of Nemeth on the third record pushes the sonorities still further out and allows Aichinger (who doubles on synthesizer himself this time out) to explore sliding tonalities and areas of colour not available on the piano. It's another lovely disc and one that presents a more accessible face to the uninitiated but without compromising on Aichinger's essential vision. We're hard pressed to recommend one of these ahead of the others. At a push, though, we'd say go for them in chronological order and hear the development of a very distinctive European voice.

Air / New Air

GROUP

Almost definitive of the experimental Chicago sound of the '70s, Air and New Air combined radical free improvisation with the democratic levelling of so-called 'little instruments'.

CORE COLLECTION

**** Air Time

Nessa NCD 12 *Henry Threadgill (as, ts, f, bf, hubkaphone); Fred Hopkins (b); Steve McCall (d, perc). 11/77.*

Air were capable of riveting live performance, but one suspects that the intimate, almost hermetic atmosphere of the studio usually brought out their most characteristic work. *Air Time* is a particularly valuable entry in a catalogue which currently still has very little available by this important group, and we've no hesitation in giving it the nod ahead of the others. Listening in detail to its five tracks – two of them very short indeed and one, Threadgill's 'Keep Right On Playing Through The Mirror Over The Water', developing so seamlessly out of 'Subtraction' as to appear to be the same piece – helps illuminate much of the group's language, its vivid exploitation of splintered tempi, deliberately awkward and raucous phrasing, devices from other musical traditions (like the Burundi music which lies behind Hopkins's 'G.v.E.'), and most particularly the use of percussion as another voiced and pitched instrument.

*** Live Air

Black Saint 120034-2 *As above. 10/77.*

*** Air Mail

Black Saint 120049-2

As above. 12/80.

*** New Air: Live At The Montreal International Jazz Festival

Black Saint 120084-2 *As above, except add Pheeroan akLaff (d, perc). 7/83.*

Air's first ever gig was a theatre performance of Scott Joplin themes, played as rags and as a basis for jazz improvisation. It remained a key source. The group always placed great emphasis on tightly coordinated ensemble work while at the same time exploring the kind of sonic *terra incognita* represented by Threadgill's hubkaphone, which is exactly what it says: an array of automobile accessories yielding a sound that is neither urban nor 'ethnic', but profoundly strange. It figures in the improvised conclusion to Threadgill's long 'Subtraction' (*Air Time*), almost the only non-scored element of the piece, except for some of Hopkins's bass embellishments behind the flute, and it's put to good effect on the first of the Black Saints.

Listening to *Air Time* clarifies some unresolved aspects to the other albums listed in which the improvisational component became dominant over fixed forms. *Live Air*, recorded a month earlier, almost sounds like a dry run and it benefits enormously from a hearing in tandem. McCall is immense, probably the only player of his generation (and that includes Sunny Murray, Andrew Cyrille and Milford Graves) who can sound this far out and at the same time so firmly anchored in tradition. Such a rating inevitably damns the born-again New Air. Pheeroan akLaff acquits himself well but rather conventionally. He works closer to the motoric drive Cyrille and Murray brought to Cecil Taylor's music and lacks McCall's ability to work melodically around the saxophonist, subtilizing his powerful, shouting lines. Hopkins is uneasily placed in the live recordings and asserts himself only on *Air Mail* which, along with the Morton and Joplin arrangements on the deleted RCA *Air Lore*, is the most instantly approachable of the group's records. Much of their music remains unissued on CD and they have been marginalized as a result.

Noël Akchoté (born 1968)

GUITAR

The young Parisian studied with Chet Baker and Barney Wilen, as well as with fellow guitarists John Abercrombie and Philip Catherine. He has emerged as the European Bill Frisell, a player with a gift for atmosphere and an iron-clad musical understanding.

***(*) Lust Corner

Winter & Winter 910 019-2 *Akchoté; Eugene Chadbourne (g, bjo, v); Marc Ribot (g). 6/96–7/97.*

It's no great surprise to find this debut album from the young Frenchman dominated by Ornette Coleman compositions. Ornette's liberation of the guitar must have figured prominently in Akchoté's musical education, and he takes to 'New York' (with Ribot), 'Street Woman', 'Peace Warriors' and that magnificent dirge, 'Broken Shadows' (with the more abrasive Chadbourne), as if they had been written for him.

The impressive thing about Akchoté is how comfortably he has synthesized the clean-picked single lines of classic jazz with a more contemporary, noise-based approach. A piece like 'Chadology' recalls Frisell's duets with Living Color frontman Vernon Reid on *Smash And Scatteration*, but with a more graceful and laid-back quality.

Akchoté has greatly impressed as a member of drummer Steve Arguëlles's Recyclers group and with Tim Berne's touring band. Striking out on his own, he suggests he's not going to be a sideman for long. *Lust Corner* is an impressive and confidently understated coming-out.

***** J'en doute encore**

Stupeur & Trompette 1015 *Akchoté; Jo Thirion (org, v); Pakito Bolino, Maki, Yves Miara (g, v); Didier Roth (g, perc, v); Gilles Gampaux (d, v).* 99.

We're still not sure either. Akchoté is clearly a gifted and clever man, anxious to spread his wings creatively, but this set of experimental, guitar-led songs isn't half as groovy as the players seem to think. Indulgent is the word, and our indulgence would have been stretched past breaking point if it hadn't been for some genuinely lovely moments along the way, not least in the lovely closing 'Appendice'.

**** Noël Akchoté & Bruno Meillier**

SMI 209 *Akchoté; Bruno Meillier (as, cl, f, bendir).* 99.

Dismally recorded and musically shapeless, this sounds as if someone ran a tape during a day's un-urgent jamming and put out the result. Meillier isn't much of a multi-instrumentalist, and he manages to sound derivative whatever he happens to be playing. The guitarist makes some interesting noises, but they need much more work before we should be expected to put down dollars and pounds – or even euros – for them.

****(*) Rien**

Winter & Winter 910057-2 *Akchoté; Erik Minkkinen (computer); Andrew Sharpley (turntables, sampler).* 10/99.

With the exception of the title-track, the pieces on this low-key set are given terse verbs as titles – in English, 'Spit', 'Cry', 'Shout', 'Speak', and so on. It's an odd decision, since the music is so blandly adjectival. Few of the pieces have much structure; the main exception is the closing 'Pousse', which is the best thing on the record and the only occasion when Akchoté seems to be playing straight guitar. Minkkinen and Sharpley (the latter a member of Stock, Hausen and Walkman) contribute interesting sounds and effects, but if anything detract from any sense of purpose and direction. If your taste is for easy-going ambient, this may be your cup of tea. We'd prefer coffee.

***** Alike Joseph**

Rectangle AM1 *Akchoté (g solo).* 00.

***** Simple Joseph**

Rectangle AM2 *As above.* 01.

These are curious records. Very little happens, rather slowly and mostly quietly. Tracks are identified by numbers – '3', '00', '101', '202', etc. – and there is no obvious or likely programmatic content. And yet they are subtly involving performances. Even when it sounds as though the guitarist is merely working through some of the technical resources of his instrument and his amplifier, there is a sense of not-quite-definable structure. Some effects suggest a kinship with avant-garde rock and pop, and listeners coming from that direction may well find much to enjoy. We're slightly mystified, but intrigued.

Toshiko Akiyoshi (born 1929)

PIANO, COMPOSER

Akiyoshi was born in Manchuria and managed to study classical piano before the militaristic ethos of pre-war Japan imposed restrictions on what musicians might listen to and play. Already a formidable presence in her native Japan, Akiyoshi went to the United States in 1956 under the tutelage of Oscar Peterson. She met Charlie Mariano while a student at Berklee and the couple married in 1959. Her second husband is the saxophonist Lew Tabackin. Her style combines a historically aware jazz feel, an unfailing swing, and a still unexpected admixture of non-Western harmonies.

***** Live At Birdland**

Fresh Sound FSRCD 1021 *Akiyoshi; Charlie Mariano (as); Gene Cherico (b); Eddie Marshall (d).* 4/60–10/61.

*****(*) Toshiko–Mariano Quartet**

Candid 79012 *As above.* 12/60.

Akiyoshi's playing was based closely but not slavishly on Bud Powell's, an influence that was to surface from time to time over the years. The Candid session, made with new husband Mariano, is forceful and intelligent, and the only sign of 'orientalism' in the small-group playing (there have always been engaging oddities of scoring in the big-band arrangements) is a willingness to mix modes, as on the Mariano-composed 'Little T', dedicated to her, and on the closing 'Long Yellow Road'.

Recorded with an established band (the excellent Eddie Marshall had signed up a few months before), the set has a coherence of tone and enthusiasm which provides Mariano with the impetus for some of his best recorded playing. Supervised by Nat Hentoff, the balances and registrations are ahead of their time.

The Birdland sets, one before and one after the studio recording, are worthwhile in themselves, but they also offer a useful way of judging how much the band developed in its short life. A later version of 'Blues For Father' (introduced by stand-in compère Maynard Ferguson on the April 1960 date as a new composition) is taken rather slower and Mariano's solo opens on a sequence of held notes that feed directly off Akiyoshi's accompaniment, rather than varying the melody. Unfortunately, the sound is much poorer on the later session, roughening his tone and significantly muting the piano and bass.

*****(*) Toshiko Mariano And Her Big Band: Recorded In Tokyo**

Vee Jay VJ 023 *Akiyoshi; Tetsuo Fushimini, Terumaso Hino, Hisao Mori, Shigeru Takemura (t); Taleshi Aoki, Teruhiko Kataoka, Mitsuhiko Matsumoto, Hiroshi Suzuki (tb); Hiroshi Ozazaki, Shigeo Suzuki (as); Sleepy Matsumoto, Akira Mayazawa (ts); Tadayuki Harada (bs); Paul Chambers (b); Jimmy Cobb (d).* 65.

The war was only 20 years over when this remarkable record was cut in Tokyo. Never before had a basically Japanese unit – albeit driven by two powerful American rhythm-players – come together to create such music. Even so, the arrangements are definitely home-grown. The opening 'Kisrazu Jink' is traditional, a theme cast in 5/4 and dominated by the pianist. It's followed by J. J. Johnson's 'Lament', done by the trio and a theme which sits very comfortably for Akiyoshi's approach; after that, there is a version of Mariano's 'The Shout', John Carisi's 'Israel' and, arranged for tenors and trio, the blues 'Walkin'', a Miles Davis staple. Sleepy Matsumoto, who seems to have stayed awake for whatever was going on in the States, switches to soprano and manages to sound both like Trane and like no one you ever heard before, all in one track.

The other tracks are Mariano's 'Santa Barbara' and, placed just after Mariano's arrangement of 'Israel', a version of 'Land

Of Peace' by Leonard Feather, who supervised the original recording. There may come a moment when Akiyoshi's music is fully assimilated. For the moment, though, it's the underlying hint of strangeness that makes her so compelling. These are marvellous cuts; a valuable reissue.

****** Hiroshima: Rising From The Abyss**
True Life 10008 *Akiyoshi; John Eckert, Jim O'Connor, Mike Ponella, Jim Rotondi (t); Steve Armour, Scott Whitfield (tb); Tim Newman (btb); Dave Pietro, Jim Snidero (as, f); Tom Christensen, Lew Tabackin (ts, f); Paul Gill (b); George Kawaguchi, Andy Watson (d); Valtinho (perc).* 7/02.

After a relatively fallow period, Akiyoshi and Tabackin have started producing big band records of real quality again, although most have only been released in Japan. The most effective of these is the Hiroshima album, not just because the world was again facing the prospect of war around the time of its release, but because it is a genuinely effective musical statement. Divided into movements – 'Futility', 'Survivor', 'Hope', 'Wishing Peace' – it does not so much suggest a single continuous work as a loose amalgam of roughly similar ideas, united by strong emotion.

Joe Albany (1924–88)

PIANO, VOCAL

Somewhat of a bebop legend, Albany was Charlie Parker's room-mate and worked with him and in the Boyd Raeburn orchestra, also recording with Lester Young. But his career was constantly interrupted by drug addiction and spells in prison. He was hardly recorded until his rediscovery in the '70s.

*****(*) The Right Combination**
Original Jazz Classics OJC 1749 *Albany; Warne Marsh (ts); Bob Whitlock (b).* 57.

Albany remains a frustrating enigma. Legendary in his time, as the sleeve to this album proclaims, he was allegedly one of Parker's favourite accompanists but never made a studio recording with him. In fact he didn't make any kind of studio sessions until the '70s. This reissue was spliced together from an impromptu session at engineer Ralph Garretson's home which caught Albany and Marsh jamming together on seven standards (the last of which, 'The Nearness Of You', is only a fragment). While the sound is very plain and the piano in particular is recessed, the music is intermittently remarkable. Albany's style is a peculiar amalgam of Parker and Art Tatum: the complexity of his lines suggests something of the older pianist, while the horn-like figures in the right hand might suggest a bop soloist. Yet Albany's jumbled, idiosyncratic sense of time is almost all his own, and his solos are cliff-hanger explorations. Marsh is at his most fragmentary, his tone a foggy squeal at some points, yet between them they create some compelling improvisations: 'Body And Soul', done at fast and slow tempos, is as personal as any version, and a dreamy, troubled 'Angel Eyes' shows off Albany's best work. No wonder, with the next 25 years spoiled by narcotic and personal problems, that Albany seemed like a wasted talent.

**** Birdtown Birds**
Steeplechase SCCD 1003 *Albany; Hugo Rasmussen (b); Hans Nymand (d).* 4/73.

****(*) Two's Company**
Steeplechase SCCD 1019 *Albany; Niels-Henning Orsted Pedersen (b).* 2/74.

Once rediscovered, first through a home-made tape which forms the basis of *Joe Albany At Home*, a now-deleted comeback album on Spotlite, and then on subsequent European sojourns and New York appearances, Albany made a dozen or so albums during the '70s. While much talked-up at the time, none of them has worn at all well. The best music comes on *Two's Company*, where the duets with bassist NHOP are elaborately conceived and confidently dispatched. But many of Albany's ideas are beset by misfingerings, and the famously off-kilter conception of time can sometimes sound more like clumsiness than anything else.

Albion Jazz Band

GROUP

Veteran British tradsters, on their holidays.

**** One For The Guv'nor**
Stomp Off 1206 *Tony Pringle (c, v); Jim Klippert (tb, v); Gerry Green (cl); Bob Pelland (p); Mike Cox (bj, v); Mike Fay (b); Mike McCombe (d).* 3/90.

****(*) They're All Nice Tunes**
Stomp Off 1249 *As above.* 3/92.

A couple of waggish trad sessions by a troupe of cheerful British Luddites, transported to Vancouver for the occasion (both times!). The first album is a tribute to Ken Colyer and is pretty effortful stuff, with Colyer's dogged primitivism overshadowing their more sprightly moments. The subsequent *They're All Nice Tunes* is a smidgeon more lively and gets an extra notch for the sheer cheek of turning the Beatles' 'I'll Follow The Sun' into a George Lewis-like dirge. Some of the horn playing is stunningly ham-fisted, but the band have a knack of sticking an extra chorus on to the end of most of the tunes, which always seem to pick up a ragged second wind as a result.

Alvin Alcorn (born 1912)

TRUMPET

Alcorn was leading groups in his native New Orleans when still a teenager. He toured with Don Albert in the '30s, based himself in his home town in the '40s, and had a very successful stint with the Kid Ory band of the '50s. Thereafter he performed back at home and on European tours, one with the Chris Barber band.

***** Sounds Of New Orleans Vol. 6**
Storyville STCD 6012 *Alcorn; Jack Delaney, Bill Matthews (tb); Raymond Burke (cl); Stanley Mendelson (p); Lawrence Marrero (bj); Chink Martin, Sherwood Mangiapane, Alcide 'Slow Drag' Pavageau (b); Abbie Brunies (d).* 12/52–11/53.

****(*) Live At Earthquake McGoon's Vol. 1**
GHB BCD-238 *Alcorn; Big Bill Bissonnette (tb); Paul 'Polo' Barnes (cl, as); James 'Sing' Miller (p); Jim Tutunjian (b); Alex Bigard (d).* 7/69.

****(*) Live At Earthquake McGoon's Vol. 2**
GHB BCD-239 *As above.* 7/69.

Alcorn was lightly recorded as a leader, and he might almost be termed a cool hornman in comparison with some of his New Orleans peers. His contribution to Storyville's archive series of sessions consists of two live dates from Joe Mares's Place and an informal studio session by the Alcorn Jazz Babies, all using largely the same personnel. As so often, the group plays with more spirit than finesse, but Alcorn's controlled lead (he is never much of a soloist) settles a certain steady-rolling fluency on much of the playing.

In 1969, at Turk Murphy's club, four New Orleanians sat down with Bissonnette and played through a stack of old numbers. The music has its ragged edges, but what compensates is a gentlemanly camaraderie that is rather different from the fierceness of much authentic New Orleans playing. Alcorn still sounds better as ensemble man than as improviser, and Bissonnette's barking trombone can sound overly heated; it's Barnes's charmingly old-fashioned alto playing which is the most distinctive thing. History may be glad that there are two volumes, but most will settle for the first. Bissonnette has cleaned up the original tapes quite respectably.

Howard Alden (born 1958)

GUITAR

A classic example of the jazz 'young fogey', Alden is a Californian who began playing banjo in pizza parlours before working in numerous swing-to-mainstream outfits. His Concord records began in a conservative vein and have since diversified into a sophisticated and personal take on jazz history. He remains much in demand for session work in several styles.

****(*) Hand-Crafted Swing**

Concord CCD 4513 *Alden; George Van Eps (g); Dave Stone (b); Jake Hanna (d).* 6/91.

**** Seven & Seven**

Concord CCD 4584 *As above, except omit Stone and Hanna.* 12/92.

Alden's earlier Concords have been deleted, so these guitar-duo records are where his listing starts off at present. It's interesting to hear Alden playing alongside a man who himself played alongside Eddie Lang more than 60 years before. Van Eps prefers stately chord-based playing and, while it might not inhibit the younger man, Alden certainly scales down his approach to accommodate his senior. (He also had a seven-string guitar made in the fashion of Van Eps's instrument.) The first record is pleasant, but the second is dull. Without any rhythm players to egg them on, they're too slow and quiet, and the sluggish tempos tend to push the music into the background.

****** Take Your Pick**

Concord CCD 4743 *Alden; Lew Tabackin (ts, f); Renee Rosnes (p); Michael Moore (b); Bill Goodwin (d).* 5/96.

Is anyone making better mainstream-to-modern records than Alden? Another impeccable choice of tunes sets Ellington and Herbie Nichols alongside Berlin and Porter, and Alden's masterstroke is to treat them all on the same terms. When he does Nichols's 'The Gig' and follows it with a gorgeous (yet unsentimental) 'My Funny Valentine', it's clear how thoroughly and effectively he's developed his own idiom out of jazz's compositional history. The band could hardly be better; Tabackin's gruff, swinging intensity (he gets the flute out only for 'U.M.M.G.') sits perfectly next to Rosnes's crackling solos and accompaniments and, with Moore and Goodwin both flawless, this is music that thrills with its own calm intensity.

*****(*) Full Circle**

Concord CCD2-4788-2 2CD *Alden; Jimmy Bruno (g); Michael Moore (b); Alan Dawson (d).* 3/95.

Recorded before *Take Your Pick* but not released until 1998, this mellifluous but steely series of duets with fellow stringsman Bruno will appeal most to guitar followers. Compared to the albums that came before, this seems like lightweight stuff, but the beautifully measured touch of both men is a pleasure in itself on the likes of 'Polka Dots And Moonbeams'. Played softly, it makes for very hip easy-listening. There is a bonus CD of the *Jazz/Concord* album cut in 1973 by a quartet with Herb Ellis and Joe Pass, making this a particularly attractive package.

***** In A Mellow Tone**

Concord CCD-2207-2 *Alden; Bucky Pizzarelli (g).* 12/00.

Concord seem to have a particular penchant for multiple-guitar records. This one's nice enough, but two seven-stringers playing acoustic across an entire CD of otherwise unaccompanied duets is always going to have a hard time escaping monotony, particularly when the tunes are as familiar as these.

*****(*) My Shining Hour**

Concord CCD –4841-2 *Alden (g solo).* 01.

Alden's such a consummate group player that the notion of a solo set has less appeal than it otherwise might, and this has some almost inescapable moments of dryness. However, even familiars such as 'My Shining Hour', 'Girl From Ipanema' and 'Gone With The Wind' are revitalized by the guitarist's mastery. He seems to think about the nuance of every plucked string, without making the interpretations seem merely academic, and with the superb recording the physicality of the instrument is felt as it rarely is on a jazz-guitar record. Jelly Roll Morton's 'Sweet Substitute', performed on acoustic, is a lovely transformation. Two Dick Hyman melodies – written for, but not used in Woody Allen's *Sweet And Lowdown* – are a nice bonus.

Terrie Richards Alden

VOCAL

Debut appearance for American singer, wife of guitarist Howard Alden.

***** Voice With Heart**

Nagel-Heyer 048 *Alden; Warren Vaché (c, flhn, v); Howard Alden (g); Michael Moore (b); Jackie Williams (d).* 8/96.

****(*) Love**

Nagel-Heyer 071 *Alden; Howard Alden (g).* 12/00.

A sexy voice, and the heart's certainly in the right place. She covers some tunes that are probably a shade too familiar, but she does get a sting or a twist out of several of them that isn't so obvious: try the bluesy tang in 'Comes Love' or the *a cappella* intro to 'Dindi'. That isn't an especially successful treatment of the Jobim tune, though, and she sounds happier on old-fashioned standards with a jazz legacy, such as 'Gee Baby Ain't I Good To You' or the delicious stroll through 'Please Don't Talk About Me When I'm Gone', which opens the record. The backings are surprisingly sparse, and a courageous thing for a singer to try on her debut. Vaché and Mr Alden play some ear-tickling cameos throughout.

The duo record is a bit disappointing. This time Terrie makes only a mild impression on the material, and she doesn't get 'Miss Otis Regrets' at all. Howard plays with his usual polish, but it's not quite enough.

Eric Alexander (born 1968)

TENOR SAXOPHONE

He grew up in Washington State and studied in Indiana, moving to Chicago and playing on the club scene there. He moved to New York in 1992 and has since freelanced.

***** Straight Up**
Delmark 461 *Alexander; Jim Rotondi (t); Harold Mabern (p); John Webber (b); George Fludas (d).* 8/92.

***** New York Calling**
Criss Cross 1077 *Alexander; John Swana (t, flhn); Richard Wyands (p); Peter Washington (b); Kenny Washington (d).* 12/92.

***** Up, Over And Out**
Delmark 476 *Alexander; Harold Mabern (p); John Ore (b); Joe Farnsworth (d).* 8/93.

***** Full Range**
Criss Cross 1098 *Alexander; John Swana (t); Kenny Barron (p); Peter Bernstein (g); Peter Washington (b); Carl Allen (d).* 1/94.

***** Stablemates**
Delmark DE-488 *Alexander; Lin Halliday (ts); Jodie Christian (p); Dan Shapera (b); Wilbur Campbell (d).* 95.

In his early records, Alexander stands four-square in the tradition of big Chicago tenors. The first disc was made on local turf, the second in the city of the title, and in either milieu he sounds completely assured. This is old-fashioned tenor playing: fat, bruising, wide-bodied, but limber enough to handle bebop tempos and inner complexities, even if Alexander prefers a more seasoned tradition. His laggardly way with the beat makes one think of Dexter Gordon. Still, neither of these records is a world-beater, and the next two – again, one from Chicago, one from New York – show no specific advance. Each of the Delmark albums includes some professorial work from Mabern, even while the other players are unexceptional. *Up, Over And Out* is arguably the best of the three for its tough, uncompromising take on Monk's 'Eronel' and – the other side of Alexander's persona – the tender trap of 'The Nearness Of You'. Both the Criss Cross dates are good value yet neither really lifts itself out of the blowing-session convention that is wearing after a few tracks. Alexander's writing shows only modest promise, and he sounds more like an executant than a leader; but it will be interesting to hear him marshal a properly prepared record. *Stablemates* is more an off-the-cuff interlude than anything. Alexander shares front-and-centre with veteran tenorman Halliday in a specific attempt to revitalize the two-tenor fisticuffs of yore. They certainly strike sparks on the up-tempo pieces, and there is a fetching ballad medley of 'Polka Dots And Moonbeams' and 'Old Folks', but otherwise this goes down as little more than a good potboiler.

***** Eric Alexander In Europe**
Criss Cross 1114 *Alexander; Melvin Rhyne (org); Bobby Broom (g); Joe Farnsworth (d).* 4/95.

*****(*) 2 Soon 2 Tell**
Sharp Nine 1006 *Alexander; Jim Rotondi (t, flhn); Steve Davis (tb); David Hazeltine (p); Peter Washington (b); Joe Farnsworth (d).* 2/97.

Cut in The Netherlands following a tour, *In Europe* features a format of which Alexander already has plenty of experience, and he sounds very comfortable. The date still falls prey to its essentially conservative programme – blues, ballads and a couple of mildly engaging originals – but Alexander and Broom in particular settle themselves into long solos which they can carry off with aplomb. Broom's 'The Edge' is a particularly well-cast original.

The Sharp Nine album was made live at a New York club where the band had already been working for a while, and here Alexander comes into his own in a band of strong spirits. The Messengers format is adapted and surpassed. There are several impressive originals, Rotondi and Davis are executants who want to go their own way too, and Alexander sounds transfigured by the situation. He's probably never played a better solo than the one on 'Visionary'.

****** Man With A Horn**
Milestone 9293-2 *Alexander; Jim Rotondi (t); Steve Davis (tb); Cedar Walton (p); Dwayne Burno (b); Joe Farnsworth (d).* 1/97.

***** Mode For Mabes**
Delmark 500 *Alexander; Jim Rotondi (t); Steve Davis (tb); Harold Mabern (p); John Webber (b); George Fludas (d).* 5/97.

***** Alexander The Great**
High Note HCD 7013 *Alexander; Jim Rotondi (t); Charles Earland (org); Peter Bernstein (g); Joe Farnsworth (d).* 5/97.

*****(*) Solid!**
Milestone 9283-2 *Alexander; Jim Rotondi (t); John Hicks (p); Joe Locke (vib); George Mraz (b); Idris Muhammad (d).* 4–5/98.

Alexander's patient but inexorable progress is enjoyable to watch. In the course of a few years, he's bloomed into a tenorman of formidable authority and adaptability. The only danger now is that, via sideman and leadership work, he might be over-recorded. The High Note and Delmark albums are sound, foot-perfect hard-bop dates, *Alexander The Great* (ahem!) nudges just ahead for the splendid work by Earland on one of his last sessions. But the Milestone albums suggest something of the eminence which Alexander is working towards. Beautifuly recorded, *Man With A Horn* is a quartet date (Rotondi and Davis play on three tracks) where the saxophonist luxuriates in the rhythm section (Walton on top form) and peels off some of his most expansive and full-blooded improvising. Years of working on his sound have developed a magisterial voice on the tenor, massive in the mid-register and smoothly convincing when he goes towards the top. *Solid!* is in some ways more ambitious, since the programme features hard-bop nuggets like 'Solid' (Rollins), 'Little Melonae' (McLean), 'My Conception' (Sonny Clark) and 'Straight Street' (Coltrane), the leader apparently out to settle his credentials in the heaviest company. This is a slightly less convincing rhythm section – Muhammad plays well but never as capably as Farnsworth on the other date – and to that degree it's a less imposing record, but Alexander's sound is again tremendous; some of his most precocious solos, vaulting into double-time, are enough to have one reaching for the repeat button.

*****(*) The First Milestone**
Milestone 9302-2 *Alexander; Harold Mabern (p); Pat Martino (g); Peter Washington (b); Joe Farnsworth (d).* 11/99.
*****(*) The Second Milestone**
Milestone 9315-2 *As above, except Jim Rotondi (t) replaces Martino.* 12/00.

They're generic records, which might disappoint some in search of breakthrough reports, but the steady-state progress suggested by the titles is manifest enough in the music. While Alexander is working with distinguished veterans such as Mabern and Martino, the line-ups aren't exactly fashionable, and he's gone for unflashy situations over chopsmanship. In each case, the choice of material is idiosyncratic, sometimes suggesting an Eddie Harris take on looking for tunes: the theme from *The Towering Inferno* on the first, 'Matchmaker, Matchmaker' and Henry Mancini's 'Moment To Moment' on the second. Nor does Alexander rattle through his uptempo solos with the abandon of his early discs. There's a feel of much power held in gracious reserve, rather than being unwillingly checked. And the focus is very much on the saxophone. Other solos seem like interludes, and Rotondi, kept to three appearances, is there mainly as an ensemble foil. Eric's ballad playing has taken a stride or two, too – 'Estate' is beautifully modulated and unsentimental on the second set. Keep watching.

*****(*) Summit Meeting**
Milestone 9322-2 *Alexander; Nicholas Payton (); Harold Mabern (p); John Webber (b); Joe Farnsworth (d).* 12/01.
*****(*) Nightlife In Tokyo**
Milestone 9330-2 *Alexander; Harold Mabern (p); Ron Carter (b); Joe Farnsworth (d).* 12/02.

Summit Meeting signs Payton on for four tunes, and the sparks never stop flying. Mabern sounds like he's enjoying every second of the date and gets both horns to give of their best. It's not all good news – 'Something's Gotta Give' is taken at a tempo which really is too fast, and we're not fond of 'A House Is Not A Home' as a jazz piece – but most of it is terrific. *Nightlife In Tokyo* asks Alexander to act as sole horn again, but Mabern's still pushing hard, and if there are too many blues pieces, the small miracle is that Alexander keeps it all so fresh as far as the chief improviser's role is concerned. Diminishing returns seem inevitable soon enough, but not quite yet.

Monty Alexander (born 1944)

PIANO

There have been many attempts to hybridize jazz and Afro-Cuban music, but relatively few to bring the rhythms of reggae, ska and mento into a jazz context. Jamaican-born Alexander remains the prime exponent, using steel pans in his Ivory and Steel group and exploiting Caribbean backbeats to a jazz idiom influenced by Nat Cole and Oscar Peterson.

*****(*) Jamento**
Original Jazz Classics OJCCD 904 *Alexander; Ernest Ranglin (g); Andy Simpkins (b); Roger Bethelny, Duffy Jackson (d); Vince Charles (steel d); Larry McDonell (perc).* 6/78.

Only Tommy Smith has a more variable accent. Kingston-born, Alexander has never quite decided whether he is a Jamaican homeboy, an enthusiastic *norteamericano*, or indeed a European. He has fronted a style of jazz in which swing is recast in Caribbean rhythms, signalled by the steel pans, but also marked out by great formal control. Alexander now has an impressive back-catalogue of (mostly trio) recordings which reveal an exuberant sensibility schooled – sometimes a little too doctrinairely – in the School of Oscar Peterson. Typical of that tendency, he has a tone which is both percussive and lyrical, heavy on the triplets and arpeggiated chords, melodically inspired in the main (i.e. no long, chordal ramblings), maximal but controlled.

Recorded in Hollywood, this is one of the best of Alexander's synoptic essays in jazz-plus-reggae/merengue/mento. The presence of the irrepressible Ranglin is some sort of guarantee and the groove the guitarist lays down on 'Sugar Loaf At Twilight' and the closing 'Mango Rengue' is deep and wide enough to ride a bus down. Alexander produced the session himself, and if we have quibbles they have to do with the balance of sound, which is less than faithful to the component parts. Much of the percussion sounds off-stage, and the piano is oddly located in the mixing, seeming to phase across its range. Good stuff of its kind, though.

***** Triple Scoop**
Concord 2122 2CD *Alexander; Herb Ellis (g); John Frigo (vn); Ray Brown (b).* 3/82–6/87.

Alexander worked with both Ray Brown and Milt Jackson before breaking through as a solo artist. The vibes were close enough to the steel drums to be familiar, but his approach to the lower end is interesting and untypical and Alexander bassists are often found playing *arco*, favouring big-toned pedals against which he can punch out sometimes surprisingly complex augmented chords.

There are wonderful things on the original *Triple Treat* ('Body And Soul' and, ahem, the 'Flintstones' theme). In the drummerless *Triple Treat II*, recorded live like its successor, he used the violinist, John Frigo, alongside Brown and Herb Ellis, to similar effect. Though they were recorded at the same time, *III* is a more interesting record, and the quartet interpretation of 'My One And Only Love' stands out. The rather lowly rating largely stems from a very poor sound, with everything jumbled together towards the middle. Concord, having lost Monty's services, have been repackaging early albums; *Triple Scoop* usefully brings together all three albums on a double disc. Kicking off with '(Meet The) Flintstones', followed by a now legendary version of 'Body and Soul', was a masterstroke. Few could resist.

***** Ivory And Steel**
Concord CCD 4124 *Alexander; Othello Molineaux (steel d); Gerald Wiggins (b); Frank Gant (d); Robert Thomas Jr (perc).* 3/80.

***** Jamboree**
Concord CCD 4359 *Alexander; Othello Molineaux, Len 'Boogsie' Sharpe (steel d); Marshall Wood, Bernard Montgomery (b); Robert Thomas Jr (perc); Marvin 'Smitty' Smith (d).* 2–3/88.

***** Island Grooves**
Concord CCD2-4940-2 2CD *As above.* 3/80–3/88.

One of the most interesting aspects of Alexander's career has been his attempt to assimilate the steel-drum sound of his native Jamaica to the conventional jazz rhythm section. In the earlier disc, the new sound is still a little tacked-on and Gant in particular seems slightly uneasy, but the balance of instrumentation is good and Alexander finds sufficient space on *Ivory And Steel* to rattle off some of his most joyous solos.

Jamboree is a marvellous record, partly because the playing is so good, but also because of the imaginative selection of covers. Bob Marley's 'No Woman, No Cry' and Joni Mitchell's 'Big Yellow Taxi' have not previously figured too prominently in the average fake book; indeed, with the very considerable exception of avant-garde trumpeter Leo Smith, reggae has made remarkably little impact on contemporary jazz. 'Smitty' Smith was an inspired addition on the later date, and he lifts the energy level a further notch. Both are highly recommended, but go for *Jamboree*. One love.

Island Grooves puts both albums together in an attractive box set, though again the original releases may still be offered for sale.

***** Threesome**

Soul Note 121152 *Alexander; Niels-Henning Orsted Pedersen (b); Grady Tate (d, v).* 11–12/85.

Well used to top-drawer rhythm sections, Alexander makes the most of this one, turning in a sparkling set with sufficient variety to suggest his responsiveness to others. The version of 'All Blues' is interesting, but the material is otherwise a little lack-lustre.

***** Caribbean Circle**

Chesky JD 80 *Alexander; Jon Faddis, E Dankworth (t); Slide Hampton (tb); Frank Foster (ts); Dave Glasser (as); Ira Coleman, Anthony Jackson (b); Othello Molineaux (steel d); Herlin Riley, Steve Ferrone (d); Robert Thompson Jr, Marjorie Whylie (perc).* 6/92.

An extension of his work with Ivory and Steel and the nearest thing to a big band Alexander has mustered so far, this is a jolly, romping session that slightly overplays the Jamaican accent that Alexander jokingly phoneticizes in his sleeve-notes. Credit for the arrangements goes to Hampton. They're characteristically bright and uncluttered, and features like Dankworth's solo on a bluebeat version of 'When The Saints' or Marjorie Whylie's one-woman-band percussion-breaks fit neatly into them. What don't are Alexander's own solos, which tend to go off in odd directions, a bit like his jivey monologues, which you'll find either charming or plain irritating, like the 'Cowboy Ska Melody'. A tribute to Miles called 'Oh Why?' shows the pianist still capable of writing and playing feelingly, but it's exceptional.

***** Yard Movement**

Island 524 232 *Alexander; Dwight Dawes (ky); Ernest Ranglin (g); Robert Thomas Jr, Roland Wilson (d).* 7/95.

During the '90s, Alexander started to explore a rootsier and less sun-kissed aspect of Jamaican music. *Yard Movement* is a flawed but powerful record with a punchy, electric sound that suits Monty surprisingly well, especially when he is mixed forward and gated quite sharply on the recording. The legendary Ernest Ranglin is part of the group, chuffing out shuffle rhythms and reggae chords with no apparent effort, and every now and then punctuating a line with what seems to be pure sound, harmonically unrelated to what he's playing. It would be fascinating to hear the rehearsal tapes and alternatives from these sessions; our assumption is that they must be much rougher (in an entirely positive sense) and more exploratory than the rather polished final product. *Yard Movement* is a more compelling and authentic record than the later tribute to the music of Bob Marley, but it does rely on uneasy stylistic compromise.

*****(*) Echos Of Jilly's**

Concord CCD 4769 *Alexander; John Patitucci (b); Troy Davis (d).* 97.

Thirty years after he first moved to New York from his first exile in Miami, Alexander meditates on the legacy of Jilly's most famous habitué. By the start of the last year of his life, jazz tributes to Frank Sinatra were becoming more frequent. Having played at the club himself, Alexander could claim a closeness of connection few others had and there is something about this session which recalls those years with exceptional vividness. It's partly the nicotine blue of the piano lines, partly the choice of Sinatra-connected material; but more importantly it's an attitude that hovers between aggression and devil-may-care relaxation. 'Strangers In The Night' comes from later in Frank's career, but it's full of that dry, threatening spirit. An exceptional record, from a musician whose shifts of identity and changeable solidarities have done him no favours. This is his most effective turf.

*****(*) Concord Jazz Heritage Series: Monty Alexander**

Concord CCD 4812 *As above.* 79–97.

***** Ballad Essentials**

Concord CCD 4903 *As above.* 80–96.

The end of Monty's Concord years, left the label with an enormous back catalogue of marketable jazz. Some earlier albums have been reissued as twofer, as mentioned above, but these two compilations are worthy of notice if you haven't yet caught up with Monty, or need a back-up copy of favourite tracks for the car. The Heritage Series disc puts the emphasis on mid-paced swingers and familiar themes, while the ballad selection is inevitably a bit more laid back and meditative, on reflection not the kind of thing you might want to be listening to on the freeway. A superb 'Body And Soul', with Ray Brown and Herb Ellis, and a solo reading of 'Estate' are among the stand-out tracks.

***** Stir It Up: The Music Of Bob Marley**

Telarc 83469 *Alexander; Steve Turre (tb); Dwight Dawes (ky); Robert Angus, Daniel Dicenzo (g); Glen Browne, Tony MacKenzie, J. J. Wiggins (b); Troy Davis, Sly Dunbar, Rolando Wilson (d).* 99.

***** Monty Meets Sly and Robbie**

Telarc 83494 *Alexander; Steve Jankowski (t); Jay Davidson (saxes); Handel Tucker (ky); Robbie Shakespeare (b); Desmond Jones, Sly Dunbar (d).* 01.

Stir It Up was one of those rare jazz albums that simply flew off the shelves, thanks largely to the composer. It's not, to be frank, particularly strong, though there are some excellent set-pieces, like Steve Turre's solos on 'I Shot The Sheriff', which is taken at real high-speed pursuit pace and 'Running Away' (ditto). The title-track is very good, and more than one critic has rightly pointed out the debt to Ahmad Jamal. Indeed, the whole set smacks of the pop covers of an earlier day. Pointless to be snobbish about it, but Alexander has created a rod for his own back by combining a jazz trio with the Jamaican members of the Gumption Band, who know this stuff like the back of their hands and aren't going to let some bunch of jazzers steal it away from them.

The acid test was always going to be 'No Woman, No Cry' and it is a very strong performance, with Monty turning in some of his most compelling playing on an otherwise rather anonymous set. Mostly, though, the two rhythm sections cancel one another out and Monty is left to pick over rather unadorned melody lines. The album also includes a reworking of 'Could You Be Loved' by the legendary Sly Dunbar who, to his credit, puts heart and soul into his cameo.

The legendary duo return on the follow-up record, which frankly is better because it seems so much less self-conscious. Glen Browne produces as if he were making a straight reggae record. Alexander may have managed to get the piano moved a bit forward, but what one hears is the group sound, not an individual solo voice with accompaniment. 'Moanin'', 'Monty's Groove' and the melodica-led tribute to reggae organist Jackie Mittoo (why not on organ?) are beautifully done, and there is a vivid version of '(Do The) Kool Step'. A clever, effective crossover record, with big market appeal, though not perhaps the surprise value of its predecessor.

**(*) Goin' Yard

Telarc 83527 *Alexander; Dwight Dawes (ky); Wayne Armond, Robert Browne (g); Glen Browne (b); Desmond Jones (d); Robert Thorns Jr (perc).* 10/00.

After the success of *Stir It Up*, Monty was always going to extend the reggae concept. A couple of Marley tunes – 'Could You Be Loved', 'Exodus' – are included here, but the meat of the set is original material, including 'Grub', 'Trust', 'Hurricane' and 'Hype'. It sounds almost like Alexander-by-numbers, drifting between vivid rockers and strangely dry and sour ballad forms. A disappointing follow-up to what was presumably his most successful disc to date.

*** My America

Telarc 83552 *Alexander; Leroy Barbie Romans (ky); Dalton Browne, Derek Dicenzo (g); Glen Browne, Leon Duncan (b); Desi Jones (d); Bobby Thomas Jr (perc); Cat, Freddy Cole, Kevin Mahogany, John Pizzarelli (v).* 3-4/02.

Perhaps aware that his recent career has been somewhat overdetermined by the reggae influence, Alexander sets out in this one to show what other musical influences fed into his imagination. A reggaefied version of Duke and Harry Carney's 'Rocking In Rhythm' – or 'Riddim' here – underlines that Caribbean influences aren't too far away, while 'Mack The Knife' is probably part of every jazz guy's armoury. The more surprising cuts are things like James Brown's 'Sex Machine' and Marvin Gaye's 'Sexual Healing', not tunes that necessarily lend themselves to jazz improvisation. Alexander gives 'The Battle Hymn Of The Republic' a certain sentimental grandeur (similar in impact to the singing of 'La Marseillaise' in *Casablanca*) but for the most part this album feels like a self-conscious playing with styles, saved from cynicism by the sheer verve of the performances, though marred by some ill-judged vocal performances from Freddy Cole, Kevin Mahogany, John Pizzarelli and Cat.

Rashied Ali (born 1935)

DRUMS

The former Robert Patterson played R&B in his native Philadelphia before moving to New York, where he became involved in the avant-garde and came within the orbit of John Coltrane, in whose group he succeeded his own greatest influence, Elvin Jones. After Trane's death, Ali continued to work in the master's shadow, developing his little-understood rhythmic ideas. Ali founded his own record label and started his own jazz club.

*** Live At Tonic

DIW 940 *Ali; Louis Belogenis (ts); Wilber Morris (b).* 00.

No musician has greater title to the legacy of Coltrane and yet one instinctively feels that this is perhaps one tribute too many. Opening on Belogenis's 'Invocation: Trane Is In The House', the set meanders through a sequence of collective improvisations before concluding – with admitted poignancy – on 'Brazilia' and a briefly stated 'Spiritual'. Ali is boilingly intense throughout and Belogenis gives his usual convincing performance, making a virtue of his very different tonality. Morris drifts in and out of the mix, perhaps deliberately because the real action remains that drum/saxophone axis that is so much part of this story. If you get the chance to sample the record, try the fifth track: 'Heavenly Start' is another Belogenis composition, and one of his very best, delivered crisply and feelingly. Impressive, but not representative of a rather shapeless set.

*** Deals, Ideas & Ideals

Hopscotch HOP 6 *Ali; Assif Tsahar (ts, bcl); Peter Kowald (b).* 5/00.

This is a powerful unit, but it's the late bassist who gives it its coherence and much of its vigour. Much of the music is in Albert Ayler mode, but with some strong contemporary references, as on 'The Rap', which isn't quite the trendy, streetwise thing it maybe sounds. The other long track is the title piece, which again leans heavily on Kowald's supple lines. Tsahar knows his instruments inside out, but occasionally lapses into technique for its own sake. Ali himself has sounded stronger, and there are places where his energy seems to flag. However, anyone who appreciates free jazz of this vintage will enjoy the record

Jan Allan (born 1934)

TRUMPET

Began as a pianist but switched to trumpet as his main instrument in the '50s. Worked in the Carl-Henrik Norin orchestra, then in numerous small groups with his contemporaries. Also holds a doctorate in particle physics.

♛ **** Jan Allan – 70

Phono Suecia PSCD 130 *Allan; Lennart Axelsson, Weine Renliden, Bertil Lövgren, Rolf Ericson (t); Olle Holmqvist, George Vernon, Jörgen Johansson (tb); Olle Lind (btb); Sven-Ake Landström, Bengt Belfrage (frhn); Arne Domnérus (as); Lennart Aberg (ts, ss, f); Claes Rosendahl (ts, f); Bernt Rosengren (ts); Bengt Christianson, Jerker Halldén (f, picc); Nils Lindberg, Bobo Stenson (p); Rune Gustafsson (g); Palle Danielsson, Roman Dylag (b); Egil Hohansen, Jon Christensen (d); Rupert Clemendore (perc).* 12/68–9/69.

*****(*) Sweet And Lovely**

Dragon DRCD 254 *Allan; Rune Gustafsson (g); Georg Riedel (b).* 3/92.

Allan's small number of records as a leader is an inadequate showing for one of the most eminent Swedish modernists: poised between a cool lyricism and a bashful affection for the long melodic line, the trumpeter's unfussy and effortless playing refuses to draw attention to itself.

His finest hour stretches back more than 30 years, to the marvellous *Jan Allan – 70*, released at last on CD. There are two small-group scores by Carl-Axel Dominique and one piece by Palle Danielsson, but the main focus of the record is on the three superlative scores by Nils Lindberg, 'Polska With Trumpet', 'Ballad For Trumpet' and 'Rolf Billberg In Memoriam'. Lindberg's writing is full of almost Byzantine detail at times, yet the music flows along without any difficulty and the sonorities of brass and woodwind are richly compelling. 'Polska With Trumpet' sparkles with rhythmic and harmonic invention and the 'Ballad' is serenely beautiful, but it's the deeply felt and profoundly moving dedication to Rolf Billberg that brings out the best in composer, soloist and orchestra. In what might almost be an answer record to the likes of *Miles Ahead*, Allan refuses to preen or overplay: his solos are part of a genuine dialogue with the orchestra, and he never loses his way or seems unsettled by such a demanding opportunity. A record that should be in every collection.

A long jump from there to *Sweet And Lovely*. Here, with two very old friends, he sketches a sequence of wonderful miniatures. Since Lars Gullin, Reinhold Svensson and Jan Johansson – three major contemporaries of Allan's – are all represented as composers, the record also stands as a meditation on the achievements (still sorely undervalued) of one of the great schools of modern jazz in Europe. Some may be reminded of many of Chet Baker's later sessions; but Allan, Gustafsson and Riedel, all in prime, easy-going form, sustain the flow of these 14 tunes with few difficulties.

*****(*) Software**

Imogena IGCD 068 *Allan; Erik Norstrom (ts); Rune Gustafsson (g); Yasuhito Mori (b).* 11/98.

Some old friends at work here. Aside from Mori, who's been on the Swedish scene long enough to earn honorary-member status anyway, these are veterans of an old-time Swedish modernity, when Getz, Mulligan and the more sinewy kind of West Coast cool held sway. The music is in that vein, wrinkled a little by experience, but yielding nothing to more 'contemporary' styles. Allan's soft delivery has, as ever, an undisclosed streak of iron in it, and Norstrom (who co-leads and writes most of the originals) is an able partner.

Geri Allen (born 1957)

PIANO, SYNTHESIZER

Studied piano as a child, then later taught in Washington, DC, before moving to New York in 1980. Associated with the M-Base Collective early on, but came to work in a broad variety of contexts and has recorded for Blue Note and Verve as a leader.

*****(*) Etudes**

Soul Note 121162 *Allen; Charlie Haden (b); Paul Motian (d).* 9/87.

***** In The Year Of The Dragon**

Winter & Winter *As above.* 3/89.

To suggest that Geri Allen is something of an enigma is not to withdraw our enthusiasm for her work. She is a formidable technician, drawing elements from all over the modern piano tradition – Bud Powell, Monk, tinges of Cecil Taylor, less celebrated figures like Herbie Nichols and Mary Lou Williams – and from non-pianists like Eric Dolphy, whose spiky, restless ideas are also reflected in her writing. And yet, for all this creative weaponry, there is something unaccountably soft-centred, almost whimsical about much of Allen's work under her own name. Therein lies the puzzle, for Allen has often seemed a more confident and accomplished performer on other leaders' dates than on her own. These records seem to confirm, both positively and negatively, our feeling that Allen fares better when relieved of leadership. She was officially guest soloist with the veteran Haden/Motian team, but hogged the praise for *Etudes* so completely that she was officially inducted into the freemasonry, immediately losing the freshness and the spontaneity that had made the 1987 record so striking.

In The Year Of The Dragon was restored to catalogue in 2002, when Winter & Winter began reissuing the JMT catalogue. It's one of the best of the trio sets, kicking off with Bud Powell's 'Oblivion' and moving from there into new compositions that were at the time the benchmark for piano-trio jazz. What followed is slightly mysterious in that Allen seemed poised to sweep all before her. Motherhood and a certain resistance – at best inertia – in the business did her no favours.

***** Some Aspects Of Water**

Storyville STCD 4212 *Allen; Johnny Coles (flhn); Henrik Bolberg Pedersen (t, flhn); Kjeld Ipsen (tb); Axel Windfeld (tba); Michael Hove (as, f, cl); Uffe Markussen (ts, ss, bcl, f); Palle Danielsson (b); Lenny White (d).* 3/96.

The Danish Jazz Centre gave Allen the 1996 Jazzpar Prize, a striking acknowledgement of her growing international reputation. The payback was a pair of concerts which were to include a commissioned work – the long title-piece here – and to involve a contingent of Scandinavian players.

The Copenhagen performance included long trio versions of Allen compositions, 'Skin' and 'Feed The Fire', with a flowing rendition of the Jules Styne and Sammy Cahn classic, 'A Beautiful Friendship', once again underlining how insecure Allen can still be on standards; she plays as if she understands the chords but has only recently heard the melody for the first time. Danielsson and White are both excellent. Wallace Roney was supposed to have guested with the trio but was detained on his own tour. Taking his place, the veteran Johnny Coles hijacks 'Old Folks' with his warm, buttery tone and unhurryable approach. To her credit, Allen enjoys the moment for what it is and shows no signs of wanting to recapture the spotlight.

The commissioned piece is a multi-part suite that sounds as if it had been assembled out of a good many sketchy ideas in Allen's workbasket. It certainly isn't incoherent (Allen is now far too consistent a stylist for that) but the title gives away the essentially episodic character. Coles is again the star and there is an excellent bass clarinet passage from Uffe Markussen, who is also a featured soloist on 'Smooth Attitudes', a piece commissioned for the nonet from Jens Winther, an earlier Jazzpar artist.

Allen's own contributions are gracefully Ellingtonian, but not quite arresting enough to secure ownership in a competent group performance, not quite note-perfect but accomplished enough, given limited rehearsal time and unfamiliar charts.

Harry Allen (born 1966)

TENOR SAXOPHONE

Born in Washington, DC, Allen studied at Rutgers in New Jersey and was soon hanging out in jazz clubs. He has been lionized as a young mainstreamer and plays in the manner of the swing masters rather than in the post-Coltrane idiom of his contemporaries.

****(*) How Long Has This Been Going On?**
Progressive 7082 *Allen; Keith Ingham (p); Major Holley (b); Oliver Jackson (d).* 6/88.

***** Someone To Light Up My Life**
Mastermix CHECD 00100 *Allen; John Horler (p); Peter Morgan (b); Oliver Jackson (d).* n.d.

***** I Know That You Know**
Mastermix CHECD 00104 *Allen; John Colianni (p); Michael Moore (b).* 1/92.

***** I'll Never Be The Same**
Mastermix CHECD 00106 *Allen; Howard Alden (g); Simon Woolf (b).* 11/92.

*****(*) Jazz Im Amerika Haus Vol. 1**
Nagel-Heyer 011 *Allen; John Bunch (p); Dennis Irwin (b); Duffy Jackson (d).* 5/94.

Allen has been acclaimed by an audience waiting for the Four Brothers to come back, if not the big bands. His full-blooded tenor sound offers countless tugs of the forelock to Zoot, Lester, Hawkins and whichever other standard-issue swing tenor one can think of; and it's hardly surprising that these enjoyable records have been given the kind of approbation that was heaped on the early Scott Hamilton albums. Allen plays nothing but standards, delivers them with a confidence and luxuriance that belie his then twenty-something age, and generally acts as if Coltrane and Coleman had never appeared at all. On their own terms, there is much to enjoy in all these records. The two earlier discs are a little too stratified by tenor-and-rhythm clichés but, by cannily removing any sign of a drummer on the later records, Allen frees himself up just enough to suggest that he might eventually do more than act the young fogey. Certainly the interplay with Alden, who has also found a way of investing more of himself into mainstream vocabulary, offers some piquant moments.

Allen has been doing some solid sideman duty all the way through, but his entry in the *Jazz Im Amerika Haus* series suggests that he's getting more authoritative all the time. His improvisation on 'Deed I Do' has a steamrollering sense of swing, and he's sewing phrases and licks together with the kind of assurance once associated with Zoot Sims. Since the rhythm section goes along with the same ineluctable purpose, this has to go down as Allen's best to this point.

***** A Night At Birdland Vol. 1**
Nagel-Heyer 5002 *Allen; Randy Sandke (t); Brian Dee (p); Len Skeat (b); Oliver Jackson (d).* 11/93.

***** A Night At Birdland Vol. 2**
Nagel-Heyer 010 *As above.* 11/93.

***** Live At Renouf's**
Mastermix CHECD 00117 *Allen; John Colianni (p); Phil Flanigan (b); Duffy Jackson (d).* 8/96.

***** The Music Of The Trumpet Kings**
Nagel-Heyer 037 *Allen; Randy Sandke, Greg Bowen, Dieter Bilsheim, Till Bronner, Christian Grabandt (t); Thomas Loup, John Marshall, Soren Fischer, Andy Grossman (tb); Norbert Nagel, Klaus Marmulla (as); Walter Gauchel, Gregoire Peters (ts); Helmut Wenzel (bs); Ingo Cramer (g); Kai Rautenberg (p); Hajo Lange (b); Holger Nell (d).* 11/96.

*****(*) A Little Touch Of Harry**
Mastermix CHECD 00118 *Allen; Kenny Barron (p); George Mraz (b); Al Foster (d).* 97.

***** Love Songs Live!**
Nagel-Heyer 1014 *As Nagel-Heyer sessions above.* 93–96.

Allen is clearly a favourite of the Nagel-Heyer set-up, and the two Birdland (Hamburg, not New York) sessions will be snapped up by the label's genre devotees. The rhythm section is perhaps no more than adequate, though Jackson, on some of his final recordings, seems enlivened by the situation, and interest centres on two principals: Allen doesn't quite have Sandke's catholic taste, but they strike some pleasing sparks. The second shades out the first (now reissued in a new mastering), though one disc from two might have been a better bet anyway. The *Trumpet Kings* session is really more Sandke's than Allen's, even though the tenorman's name comes first on the sleeve. Sandke arranged nearly all the charts for the RIAS Big Band of Berlin, and he and Allen are the featured soloists. It's intriguing to hear a discovery attributed to Beiderbecke, 'Cloudy', on which Allen rather than Sandke solos; and 'The Moontrane' and 'All Blues' are more modern pieces that go well enough, though the band sounds over-bright and over-eager in its delivery.

The quartet format is where Allen's destiny lies. *Live At Renouf's* is blemished by a thin and clinky-sounding piano, and there's too much space for bass solos. But Allen himself, though he takes some of his ballad statements far too slowly, sounds imperious. The way he flies through 'The Man I Love' is almost boppish in its fleet intensity. He likes to stretch out, and he can make it work for him. *A Little Touch Of Harry* is more contained in that respect. It also has far and away the best rhythm section he's ever worked with, and a thoughtful blend of familiar and more elusive standards. One point away from the masterpiece he may have in him. *Love Songs Live!* pulls together a sequence of ballads from various of the Nagel-Heyer outings featuring Allen, with four 'new' tracks as a bonus. It's very good, though since it skips the more swinging side of the saxophonist, one for more particular tastes.

*****(*) Harry Allen Meets The John Pizzarelli Trio**
BMG Novus 74321 37397-2 *Allen; Ray Kennedy (p); John Pizzarelli (g); Martin Pizzarelli (b).* 12/95.

*****(*) Tenors Anyone?**
BMG Novus 74321 50684-2 *As above.* 11/96.

Recorded by Ikuyoshi Hirakawa, initially for Japanese release, these meetings with the Pizzarelli trio are so affably swinging that they play through without a murmur of dissent from us. The impression they offer is of smart young professionals, absolutely in love with this music but unafraid to stamp themselves on what's often deemed to be a conservative idiom. To pick one instance, listen to the joyful romp through 'I Want To Be Happy' on the first disc. Allen's tone isn't always as conventionally lovely as you'd expect – he isn't really a breathy Webster type, and his ballads are leaner and a little quirkier than is at first noticeable. Pizzarelli is temperamentally akin, and his trio is a great team to have comping behind you. Soundwise, the second date is that bit fuller and livelier.

*** Night Birds

Gemini GMCD 95 *Allen; George Masso (tb); Totti Bergh (ss, ts); Per Husby (p); Bjørn Alterhaug (b); Per Hulten (d).* 8/97.

Recorded on a stopover in Oslo, Allen guests with some distinguished locals, as well as fellow visitor George Masso. Light and polite, but pleasantly done. There are some nice features, notably, Bergh's treatment of 'Don't Explain', with a superb introduction from Husby.

***(*) Eu Não Quero Dança – I Won't Dance

RCA Victor 74321 58126-2 *Allen; Larry Goldings (p); Dori Caymmi (g, v); Joe Cohn (g); Dennis Irwin (b); Duduka Fonseca (d); Maúcha Adnét (v).* 12/97.

**** Day Dream

RCA Victor 74321 67152-2 *Allen; Tommy Flanagan (p); Peter Washington (b); Lewis Nash (d).* 9/98.

For a change of pace, Allen did a sort of bossa nova album in *I Won't Dance* – sort of, because he swings it a lot harder than Getz chose to. Instead of the melodies billowing off balmy breezes, there's the odd tropical storm along the way, and it's an agreeable variation on what might have been expected. 'Desafinado', for instance, is given the office by Fonseca, and Adnét's vocal is darker than Astrud Gilberto ever sounded. A good record, but *Day Dream* looks like the one set up to be a definitive statement, and it's hard to argue with the results. Flanagan is still one of the best people to have in this situation, and the unfussy elegance of his style is a handsome fit with Allen's own demeanour. Bass and drums sit out on every other selection through the programme, and the five duets are beautifully handled by both men, measured and unsentimental. Washington and Nash lend a snap and immediacy that has been missing from some of Allen's other rhythm sections, and the sheer classy ebullience of 'I'm Checking Out, Goombye' hits a peak that Harry's often even-tempered records rarely find. In other words, four stars. These albums were again sponsored by the Japanese wing of RCA, and it's a shame that Allen hasn't found further support on American labels since.

Henry 'Red' Allen (1908–67)

TRUMPET, VOCAL

Born in New Orleans, Allen's father ran a renowned brass band and he became a trumpeter himself. Joined King Oliver in 1927, then (in New York) Luis Russell in 1929 and Fletcher Henderson in 1933. He recorded extensively as a small-group leader in the '30s and '40s, and managed to work through the '50s and early '60s in the same format, despite the depressed state of traditional jazz. He remained an idiosyncratic, unique stylist and was fêted as an avant-garde player by the young trumpeter, Don Ellis. He died from cancer in 1967, following a final European tour.

CORE COLLECTION

**** Henry 'Red' Allen & His Orchestra 1929–1933

Classics 540 *Allen; Otis Johnson (t); J. C. Higginbotham, Jimmy Archey, Dicky Wells, Benny Morton (tb); Charlie Holmes (cl, ss, as); Russell Procope, Edward Inge, Albert Nicholas, William Blue (cl, as); Hilton Jefferson (as); Teddy Hill (cl, ts); Coleman Hawkins, Greely Walton (ts); Luis Russell (p, cel); Don Kirkpatrick, Horace Henderson (p); Will Johnson (bj, g, v); Bernard Addison (g); Bob Ysaguirre, George 'Pops' Foster (bb, b); Ernest 'Bass' Hill (bb); Walter Johnson, Manzie Johnson, Paul Barbarin (d); Victoria Spivey, The Four Wanderers (v).* 7/29–11/33.

Henry Allen was once described as 'the last great trumpet soloist to come out of New Orleans', but that was before Wynton Marsalis and his followers. He was, though, the last to make a mark on the '20s, recording his astonishing debut sessions as a leader for Victor in the summer of 1929 and immediately causing a stir. The four tracks are 'It Should Be You', 'Biff'ly Blues', 'Feeling Drowsy' and 'Swing Out', magnificently conceived and executed jazz, with the whole band – actually the nucleus of the Luis Russell Orchestra, where Allen had already set down some superb solos – playing with outstanding power and finesse, while Allen's own improvisations outplay any trumpeter of the day aside from Louis Armstrong. While his playing is sometimes a little unfocused, Allen's ideas usually run together with few seams showing, and the controlled strength of his solo on 'Feeling Drowsy' is as impressive as the more daring flights of 'Swing Out'. The beautifully sustained solo on 'Make A Country Bird Fly Wild' sees him through a tricky stop-time passage and shows how he was both like and unlike Armstrong: there's the same rhythmic chance-taking and nobility of tone, but Allen is often less predictable than Armstrong and can shy away from the signalled high notes which Louis always aimed at. He can even suggest a faintly wistful quality in an otherwise heated passage. The tracks for Victor, though, are abetted by his choice of companions: Higginbotham is wonderfully characterful on trombone, agile but snarlingly expressive, and the vastly underrated Charlie Holmes matches the young Johnny Hodges for a hard-hitting yet fundamentally lyrical alto style. Foster and Barbarin, too, are exceptionally swinging. This was an outstanding band which should have made many more records than it did.

***(*) Henry Allen Collection Vol. 1

Collector's Classics COCD 1 *Allen; Jimmy Lord (cl); Pee Wee Russell (cl, ts); Joe Sullivan, Fats Waller (p); Eddie Condon (bj); Jack Bland (g); Al Morgan, George 'Pops' Foster (b); Zutty Singleton (d); Billy Banks (v).* 4–10/32.

*** Henry 'Red' Allen–Coleman Hawkins 1933

Hep 1028 *As above, except add Russell Smith, Bobby Stark (t), Claude Jones (tb), John Kirby (b); omit Blue, Johnson, Higginbotham, Archey, Russell, Holmes, Walton, Johnson, Foster, Barbarin, Spivey.* 3–10/33.

The Classics CD omits the alternative takes which filled up the earlier edition on JSP (still deleted) and carries on through the first sessions by the Allen–Coleman Hawkins Orchestra. Both men were then working with Fletcher Henderson, and this could have been an explosive combination, but their records are comparatively tame, with pop-tune material and Allen's admittedly engaging vocals taking up a lot of space. The Hep CD includes all the Allen–Hawkins tracks (the final three are on the next Classics disc) and adds the 1933 session under Horace Henderson's leadership, which includes what might be the most swinging 'Ol' Man River' on record and a splendid feature for Hawkins in 'I've Got To Sing A Torch Song'. Excellent remastering here: the Classics CD is patchy in comparison but most will find it very listenable. The first volume of the Collector's Classics edition brings together all the tracks released under the nominal leadership of Billy Banks and Jack Bland; if you can stomach Banks's singing, there's some very hot playing from what is basically an Eddie Condon group. Superb transfers.

***** Henry 'Red' Allen 1933–1935**
Classics 551 *Allen; Pee Wee Irwin (t); J. C. Higginbotham, Dicky Wells, Benny Morton, Keg Johnson, George Washington (tb); Buster Bailey, Cecil Scott, Albert Nicholas (cl); Edward Inge (cl, as); Hilton Jefferson (as); Coleman Hawkins, Chu Berry (ts); Horace Henderson (p); Bernard Addison (bj, g); Lawrence Lucie (g); Bob Ysaguirre (bb); John Kirby (b, bb); Elmer James, George 'Pops' Foster (b); Manzie Johnson, Kaiser Marshall, Walter Johnson, Paul Barbarin, George Stafford (d).* 11/33–7/35.

***** Henry Allen Collection Vol. 2**
Collector's Classics COCD 2 *Similar to above.* 10/32–7/35.

***** Henry 'Red' Allen 1935–1936**
Classics 575 *Allen; J. C. Higginbotham (tb); Albert Nicholas (cl); Rudy Powell, Hildred Humphries (cl, as); Cecil Scott (cl, ts); Pete Clark, Tab Smith (as); Happy Caldwell, Joe Garland, Ted McRae (ts); Edgar Hayes, Norman Lester, Jimmy Reynolds, Clyde Hart (p); Lawrence Lucie (g); Elmer James, John Kirby (b); O'Neil Spencer, Cozy Cole, Walter Johnson (d).* 11/35–8/36.

***** Henry Allen Collection Vol. 3**
Collector's Classics COCD 10 *Similar to above.* 35–36.

***** Henry 'Red' Allen 1936–1937**
Classics 590 *Allen; Gene Mikell, Buster Bailey, Glyn Paque (cl); Tab Smith (as); Ted McRae, Sonny Fredericks, Harold Arnold (ts); Clyde Hart, Billy Kyle, Luis Russell (p); Danny Barker (g); John Kirby, John Williams (b); Cozy Cole, Alphonse Steele, Paul Barbarin (d).* 10/36–4/37.

***** Henry Allen Collection Vol. 4**
Collector's Classics COCD 15 *Similar to above.* 10/36–6/37.

*****(*) Henry 'Red' Allen 1937–1941**
Classics 628 *Allen; Benny Morton, J. C. Higginbotham (tb); Glyn Paque, Edmond Hall (cl); Tab Smith (as); Harold Arnold, Sammy Davis (ts); Luis Russell, Billy Kyle, Lil Hardin Armstrong, Kenny Kersey (p); Danny Barker, Bernard Addison (g); John Williams, George 'Pops' Foster, Billy Taylor (b); Paul Barbarin, Alphonse Steele, Zutty Singleton, Jimmy Hoskins (d).* 6/37–7/41.

*****(*) Henry Allen Collection Vol. 5**
Collector's Classics COCD 23 *As above.* 9/37–7/41.

***** Henry Allen Collection Vol. 6**
Collector's Classics COCD 24 *Allen; J. C. Higginbotham (tb); Edmond Hall (cl); Don Stovall (as); Kenny Kersey, Al Williams, Bill Thompson (p); Billy Taylor, Clarence Moten (b); Jimmy Hoskins, Alvin Burroughs, Eddie Bourne (d).* 4/41–7/46.

***** Henry 'Red' Allen 1944–1947**
Classics 1067 *As above, except add Buster Bailey (cl), Johnny Guarnieri (p), Roy Ross (acc).* 5/44–3/47.

***** The Alternative Takes 1929–1941**
Neatwork RP 2031 *As various discs above.* 7/29–4/41.

Maybe Allen was a man out of his time: he arrived just too late to make a significant impact on the first jazz decade, and he had to work through the Depression – and the early part of the swing era – recording what were really novelty small-group sessions, most of which are little-known today. Like Armstrong and Waller, he had to record at least as many bad songs as good ones and, though he was an entertaining singer, he couldn't match either Fats or Louis as master of whatever material came his way. Still, the chronological Classics and Collector's Classics sequences are a valuable and pretty consistent documentation. The groups tend to be rough-and-ready but, whenever he's partnered by the superb Higginbotham, Allen comes up with marvellously exuberant jazz. And sometimes unpromising material releases a classic performance: hear, for instance, the completely wild version of 'Roll Along, Prairie Moon' on Classics 551/COCD 2, in which the trombonist blows such a fine solo that Allen insists on handing over his own solo space. The CDs in the middle of the sequence have too many duff tunes on them, but the 1937–41 set is stronger, since Allen switched labels (to Decca) in 1940 and started recording uncompromised jazz again. Sessions with Ed Hall, Zutty Singleton and Benny Morton are a little too brash, perhaps, but Allen's own playing is stirring throughout.

The sound on all five Classics CDs is mostly very good, with just a few transfers suffering from noticeable blemishes, but they are outdone by the excellent Collector's Classics edition, which gets our first choice. This has now been extended to six discs. Volume Six is a very erratic set: there's some dispiritingly bad music, such as 'Get The Mop' and 'Drink Hearty', and in general Allen seems a little lost for direction, but a few excellent pieces salvage everything: 'The Crawl', two takes of 'Indiana' and the blues 'Let Me Miss You Baby' which Allen turned into a great set-piece on his 1957 Victor date. Classics 1067 covers much the same ground but adds three tracks from a Saturday Night Swing Session and a sextet date for Apollo from 1947. 'Dark Eyes' and 'Sweet Lorraine' are almost extended trumpet solos by themselves and Bailey gets to do his extravagant thing on 'Indiana'. The Apollo tracks are restrained jump-band music with a lot of mugging on 'Old Fool Do You Know Me?'

The Neatwork compilation is mostly from the 1929–32 period and, given that these are alternates of some of Red's finest work, it's well worth having. There are also sides with Billy Banks, Jack Bland and a single alternate from a Buster Bailey date.

****(*) The Hot Trumpets Of Joe Newman And Henry 'Red' Allen**
Prestige 24232 *Allen; Lannie Scott (p); Franklin Skeete (b); Jerry Potter (d).* 6/62.

*****(*) Live, 1965**
Storyville STCD 8290 *Allen; Sam Price, Lannie Scott (p); Clarence Moten (b); George Reed (d).* 6/65.

*****(*) Henry 'Red' Allen With Alex Welsh**
Jazzology JCD-318 *Allen; Alex Welsh (t); Roy Wiliams (tb); Al Gay (cl, ts); Fred Hunt (p); Jim Douglas (g); Ronnie Rae (b); Lennie Hastings (d).* 67.

Allen's best latter-day recordings are out of print, and unless they are restored to CD he will soon be a very distant player. His share of the Prestige reissue (rather oddly coupled with a Joe Newman session) is frankly disappointing. Originally issued as the Prestige LP, *Mr Allen*, the great, generous tone seems thin and under-recorded and the accompanists are undistinguished. Even so, there are still some characteristic moments of Allen extravagance – as on the growling cadences of 'There's A House In Harlem For Sale' – and completists will want it.

The Storyville set dates from an engagement at a Long Island lounge and finds him in good enough late form, but the recording is pretty awful, dropping in and out all the way through, and the group isn't exactly performing with distinction.

The session with Alex Welsh dates from his final tour and he was already very ill, but the astonishing spirit of the man makes the record both a poignant and delightful farewell. If some of his phrases fall down, others show the old Allen bravado still alive, and he enthusiastically MCs the band, who clearly loved playing with him.

J. D. Allen (born 1974)

TENOR SAXOPHONE

Allen served a fairly rugged apprenticeship with the likes of Betty Carter, Wallace Roney and drummers Winard Harper and Cindy Blackman before setting out on his own. He favours a varied rhythmic approach and seems comfortable at all metres.

***** In Search Of ...**

Red 123283 *Allen; Fabio Morgera (t); Sheldrick Mitchell (p); Eric Revis (b); Rodney Green (d).* 99.

***** Pharoah's Children**

Criss Cross 1221 *Allen; Jeremy Pelt (t); Orrin Evans (p); Eric Revis (b); Gene Jackson (d).* 12/01.

The presence of Ornette Coleman's 'Lonely Woman' at the end of the debut album might have been a quiet reminder that Allen was not one of those Coltrane-obsessed tenors who dominated the '80s and early '90s. His interest is above all in melody and rhythm and his ability to weave solos on those grounds is the most impressive aspect of both records. *In Search Of ...* might have benefited from a couple more standard or repertory tunes, but the youngster is obviously anxious to set out his stall and his colleagues are well versed in the original charts. Trumpeter Morgera is a superb foil and Green is a revelation at the kit.

Gene Jackson does the business on *Pharoah's Children* as well and may well be the dedicatee of 'House Of Eugene'. Pelt has made his own record for Criss Cross and is very much in the same boldly retro mould. 'Mademoiselle Blackman' also repays a debt, but it's the more thoughtful tracks, 'The Annex' and 'Queen Elisabeth' (Betty Carter?), that will intrigue. Clearly a talent to watch, Allen has made the most convincing of starts.

Ben Allison (born 1966)

DOUBLE BASS

Allison is the talented and tireless artistic director of the Jazz Composers' Collective in New York City and a leading light in the research, performance and recording group the Herbie Nicols Project. Mingus-inspired as a bassist and composer, he combines power and subtlety.

***** Seven Arrows**

Koch Jazz 3-7832-2 *Allison; Ron Horton (t); Ted Nash (ts, cl, f); Frank Kimbrough (p); Tim Horner (d).* 6/95–4/96.

***** Medicine Wheel**

Palmetto PM 2038 *As above, except omit Horner; add Michael Blake (sax); Thomas Ulrich (clo).* 98.

*****(*) Third Eye**

Palmetto PM 2054 *As above, except add Ara Dinkjian (oud, cumbus).* 99.

****** Riding The Nuclear Tiger**

Palmetto PM 2067 *As above.* 5/00.

Even in an industry prone to hype and oversell, Allison always looked likely to make a major impact. His sophistication was evident from the very first record, in compositions as buoyantly various as 'Dragzilla', 'King Of A One Man Planet' and the Monkish 'Delirioso'.

All these records bespeak a settled understanding among the players and many, many hours spent developing ideas. There is not a slackly run-down idea on any of them. Allison's is seldom the dominant voice, though the pairing of bass and cello in the group that became known as Medicine Wheel offers an intriguing counterbalance to the horns and piano. The structures are very solid and patiently worked out.

The gentleness of the debut album largely evaporates on *Medicine Wheel*; Allison may have been listening to or hanging out with the Knitting Factory crowd. It's a more assertively downtown album, marked by some notably pungent conceptions. 'Blabbermouth' and 'Apostles Of The Ugly' stand out, while 'Spy' has touches of John Zorn. There's the beginnings of a synthesis and a consolidation on *Third Eye*, but it's the bold sweep of *Riding The Nuclear Tiger*, all the way from its exhilarating opening on the title-track to its reworking of Charles Mingus in 'Love Chant Remix', that grabs and holds the attention. The group now has a thoroughly seasoned feel and a desire to explore yet more new textures. The addition of oud hadn't made much impact on *Third Eye* but here pianist Kimbrough plays direct on open strings and prepares his piano on 'Swiss Cheese D', while on 'Weazy' saxophonist Blake plays two horns simultaneously (and without sounding like Roland Kirk!). Horton has more than one bag to dip into: some of his statements are smokingly pungent, reminiscent of Booker Little, but he can also play with a melting simplicity. Kimbrough is a seasoned leader in his own right and it is worth tracking his contributions through these records: a model of control.

*****(*) Peace Pipe**

Palmetto PM 2086 *Allison; Michael Blake (ss, ts, bcl); Peter Apfelbaum (ts); Frank Kimbrough (ky); Tomas Ulrich (clo); Mamadou Diabate (kora); Michel Sarin (d).* 3/02.

Allison continues to progress and to surprise. Though there are obvious precedents on earlier recordings, the new element here is kora player Diabate, who features strongly on the opening 'Third Rail'. It's inspired by Duke Ellington and marked by an Allison solo plucked with a subway ticket and some astonishing prepared piano from Kimbrough. Diabate also makes a superb entrance on 'Slap Happy' and figures in an amazing duet with the leader – 'Music Is Music' – which was taped at rehearsal. He can also be heard in duet with drummer Sarin on the brilliant 'Disposable Genius'.

Interestingly, Allison is now sufficiently aware of his own playing history to include a new version of 'Mantra' from *Third Eye*, an entirely reconceived interpretation which takes the tune's secondary subject and lifts it into new prominence. The album breaks new ground with an intriguing cover of Neil Young's 'Goin' Back', a showcase for the melodious Blake, but it also shows Allison attempting to underline his jazz dues with the straightahead 'Realization', which uses relatively orthodox changes.

Mose Allison (born 1927)

PIANO, VOCAL, TRUMPET

The quintessential Mississippi jazzman, Allison learned both piano and trumpet as a child, and soaked up the local black music as well as bebop. He played countless southern gigs before moving to New York in 1956. Though he is a good band pianist and played with Getz, Mulligan and Sims, his principal setting is the piano trio, where he sings the most knowingly world-weary songs over idiosyncratic, bumpy rhythms. A huge influence on many singers, players and songwriters alike, and a special favourite in England.

*****(*) Back Country Suite**
Original Jazz Classics OJC 075 *Allison; Taylor LaFargue (b); Frank Isola (d).* 3/57.

***** Local Color**
Original Jazz Classics OJC 457 *Allison; Addison Farmer (b); Nick Stabulas (d).* 11/57.

*****(*) Autumn Song**
Original Jazz Classics OJC 894 *Allison; Addison Farmer (b); Ronnie Free (d).* 58.

***** Down Home Piano**
Original Jazz Classics OJC 922 *Allison; Addison Farmer (b); Nick Stabulas, Ronnie Free (d).* 58.

*****(*) Creek Bank**
Prestige PRCD-24055-2 *As above.* 1–8/58.

***** Greatest Hits**
Original Jazz Classics OJC 6004 *As above five records.* 3/57–2/59.

****** Sings And Plays**
Prestige CDJZD 007 *As above.* 3/57–2/59.

By the time Mose Allison came to listen to bebop, a little of which creeps into his playing, he was already hooked on the light and steady kind of swing playing that Nat Cole's trio exemplified. Mose has always been a modernist: his hip fatalism and mastery of the wry put-down ('When you're walking your last mile / Baby, don't forget to smile') have always been paired with a vocal style that is reluctantly knowing, as though he tells truths which he has to force out. Coupled with a rhythmically juddering, blues-directed piano manner, he's made sure that there's been no one else quite like him, as influential as he's been.

Back Country Suite, his debut, remains arguably his best record as an instrumentalist and composer: the deft little miniatures which make up the 'suite' are winsome and rocking by turns, and LaFargue and Isola read the leader's moves beautifully. *Local Color* is nearly as good, with a rare glimpse of Allison's muted trumpet on 'Trouble In Mind', an unusual Ellington revival in 'Don't Ever Say Goodbye' and his first and best treatment of Percy Mayfield's 'Lost Mind'. *Autumn Song* is nicely balanced between his vocal set-pieces ('Eyesight To The Blind', one of his classic one-liners) and his 'serious' stuff, with a rare piece of straight bebop in 'Groovin' High'. *Down Home Piano* returns to the countrified feel of *Back Country Suite*, with 'Crepuscular Air', 'Devil In The Cane Field' and 'Mojo Woman' collating another suite's worth of impressionism. *Creek Bank* couples the album of that name with the slightly earlier *Young Man Mose* and is an excellent package: more standards, blues and Allison vignettes in generous playing time. *Greatest Hits* concentrates on Allison the singer/recitalist rather than the pianist/composer: a well-planned selection, but it bows to John Crosby's excellent compilation, *Sings And Plays*, which brings together all his vocal cuts for Prestige as well as ten instrumentals on an excellent-value 23-track CD. It's hard to go wrong with Allison in this period: any of these records will give much pleasure.

*****(*) High Jinks**
Columbia/Epic/Legacy J3K 64275 3CD *Allison; Addison Farmer, Henry Grimes, Aaron Bell, Bill Crow (b); Paul Motian, Jerry Segal, Osie Johnson, Gus Johnson (d).* 12/59–9/60.

Recorded across four different sessions, this three-disc set collects three original LPs – *I Love The Life I Live, V-8 Ford Blues* and *The Transfiguration Of Hiram Brown* – and adds a smattering of unreleased extras to each disc. The 'Hiram Brown' suite which takes up half of one of the discs is Allison's best instrumental work outside of the 'Back Country Suite', another tough, charming evocation of country-meets-the-city, while each of the other discs has its share of gems: 'A Pretty Girl Is Like A Melody', 'Life Is Suicide', 'Make Yourself Comfortable'. Nice remastering, a reminiscent note by Mose on each one, and some neat packaging.

****** I Don't Worry About A Thing**
Rhino/Atlantic R2 71417 *Allison; Addison Farmer (b); Osie Johnson (d).* 3/62.

No real change or advance, but this is for some the classic Allison album. Here are the first versions of two of his sharpest pieces, 'Your Mind Is On Vacation' and the title-song; one of his best Nat Cole treatments, 'Meet Me At No Special Place'; and three of his own oblique pieces of Americana for piano, bass and drums. Short shrift on playing time, but extra tracks would have spoiled the balance of a marvellous record.

CORE COLLECTION

****** The Word From Mose**
Atlantic 8122-72394-2 *Allison; Ben Tucker (b); Don Lundberg (d).* 3/64.

The absolute favourite of one of us, despite what is noted above. 'Don't Forget To Smile', 'I'm Not Talking', 'Look Here' and 'Days Like This' should go on anybody's list of the best songs ever written. Don't have it? Get it.

***** Ever Since The World Ended**
Blue Note 48015 *Allison; Bob Malach (as, ts); Arthur Blythe (as); Bennie Wallace (ts); Kenny Burrell (g); Dennis Irwin (b); Tom Whaley (d).* 5–6/87.

***** My Backyard**
Blue Note 93840 *Allison; Tony Dagradi (ts); Steve Masakowski (g); Bill Huntington (b); John Vidacovich (d).* 12/89.

***** The Earth Wants You**
Blue Note 827640-2 *Allison; Randy Brecker (t); Joe Lovano (as); Bob Malach (ts); Hugh McCracken (hca); John Scofield (g); Ratzo Harris (b); Paul Motian (d); Ray Mantilla (perc).* 94.

After 30-plus years in the studios, some of Mose's world-view has become institutionalized, and his slip-on brand of fatalism might seem old hat to some. These are good, solid Allison albums, nevertheless. Blue Note's efforts to update him a little aren't especially successful: the guest-star turns on *Ever Since The World Ended* add weight but no special substance to the music, and the New Orleans team that supports him on *My Backyard* has its own agenda as well as following the leader. Allison's distinctive touch still comes through on 'The Gettin' Paid Waltz' and 'I Looked In The Mirror'.

After a further break came *The Earth Wants You*. Another cast of Blue Note heavies make themselves useful, none more so than the unerringly versatile Scofield, whose blues fills on 'You Can't Push People Around' and 'Natural Born Malcontent' make solid sense. Motian's return to the Allison fold after 30-odd years is another pleasure, and 'Certified Senior Citizen' is as canny a lyric as Mose has ever come up with. Excellent fun.

*****(*) Gimcracks And Gewgaws**
Blue Note 823211-2 *Allison; Mark Shim (ts); Russell Malone (g); Ratzo Harris (b); Paul Motian (d).* 5/97.

It seems boring to say it, but here's another great one from Mose. Some of his targets are a mite too easy, such as folks who live by their faxes and cellular phones ('The More You Get'), but Ben Sidran's production has sharpened up the music: new guy on the label Mark Shim is keen to please, and he does; Malone is right on it; Motian loves this gig; Ratzo's right there; and if the old guy's voice is shakier than it used to be, he's holding on tight.

*****(*) The Mose Chronicles – Live In London Volume 1**
Blue Note 29747-2 *Allison; Roy Babbington (b); Mark Taylor (d).* 1/00.

*****(*) The Mose Chronicles – Live In London Volume 2**
Blue Note 29748-2 *As above except add Jim Mullen (g).* 1/00.

A nice stroll round the block for the great man, at 'the only gig left in the world where you can play three weeks in a row, six nights a week, twice a year'. To the shame of the United States, the venue is London's Pizza Express in Dean Street. This isn't a bought-in British rhythm section, either – Mose says he's played over a thousand gigs with them. From a rip-roaring 'Excursion And Interlude' onwards, it's classic Allison. On the second volume, Jim Mullen arrives to join in the fun, and fun they have, over the course of seventeen Allison chestnuts. Is there a more consistently enjoyable record-maker in the music?

John Allred

TROMBONE

The son of trombonist Bill Allred, John is very much a chip off the same block. He has a bright and attractive tone and is an adept soloist in a swing setting.

***** In the Beginning ...**
Arbors ARCD 19115 *Allred; Betty O'Hara (euph); Johnny Varo (p); David Stone (b); Ed Metz Jr (d).* 92.

***** Head To Head**
Arbors ARCD 19261 *Allred; Wycliffe Gordon (tb, v); John Sheridan (p); Charlie Silva (b); Ed Metz Jr (d).* 12/01.

It must be rather reassuring for Allred senior to see the lad growing up right. John's approach is very straight down the line, with only the occasional modernist touch, like the multi-tracked 'bone 'section' on the second album's most adventurous track, 'The Curse Of An Aching Heart', which also features an unexpected Gordon scat vocal.

The debut disc is bright and breezy and sticks very much to familiar material, though John confidently kicks off with an original tune, 'I Got Your Letter', which showcases his full tone and dextrous delivery very nicely. 'Autumn Leaves' is mellow and fruitful and there are some intriguing sidebars to his reading of 'Jitterbug Waltz'. The real highlight of the set, though, is a guest slot on double bell euphonium by Betty O'Hara, on a rollicking 'Stomping At The Savoy'. Worth it for that alone.

The line-up on *Head To Head* inevitably recalls those Jay & Kai sessions of old. On that logic, Gordon takes the J. J. Johnson role, while John is happier with the more linear Winding approach. They pay explicit tribute to J.J. on John Lewis's 'Afternoon In Paris', one of the weaker things on the set. The Ellington/Strayhorn material is nicely handled and 'America The Beautiful' is done with the merest hint of irony. 'Walkin' My Baby Back Home' is a feature for the rhythm section, a generous touch not fully recompensed. Expect no fireworks or extended technique from this trombonist; but be assured of some solid playing.

Karrin Allyson

VOCAL, PIANO

Born in Kansas, Allyson studied piano at Nebraska University and worked around the Mid-West. She is again based in Kansas.

*****(*) I Didn't Know About You**
Concord CCD 4543 *Allyson; Gary Sivils (c); Mike Metheny (flhn); Joe Cartwright, Russ Long, Paul Smith (p); Rod Fleeman, Danny Embrey (g); Bob Bowman, Gerald Sparts (b); Todd Strait (d); Doug Auwarter (perc); Bryan Hicks (v).* 92.

***** Sweet Home Cookin'**
Concord CCD 4593 *Allyson; Randy Sandke (t); Bob Cooper (ts); Alan Broadbent, Paul Smith (p); Rod Fleeman (g); Putter Smith, Bob Bowman (b); Sherman Ferguson, Todd Strait (d).* 6–9/93.

***** Azure-Te**
Concord CCD 4641 *Allyson; Stan Kessler (t, flhn); Mike Metheny (flhn); Kim Park (as, ts); Randy Weinstein (hca);*

Paul Smith, Laura Caviani (p); Claude Williams (vn); Rod Fleeman, Danny Embrey (g); Bob Bowman, Gerald Sparts (b); Todd Strait (d). 11/94.

The debut album established Allyson's sexy, fresh-faced delivery as something different in the (then) small group of new jazz singers. With a background rather vaguely rooted in rock, she doesn't feel uptight about including material from writers like Randy Newman or Janis Ian, although her zestful rhythmic sense and solid scat capabilities let her walk in the tradition when she wants. A small-hours blues such as Newman's 'Guilty' sounds terrific here, and all the standards she tackles come off well, her large cast of supporting players creating a wide variety of settings. If *Sweet Home Cookin'* was a slight disappointment as a follow-up, it's because it's that much more homogeneous, with Alan Broadbent's arrangements and horn charts fashioning a more familiar West Coast feel. Allyson herself still sounds fine. The same with *Azure-Te*, though again the material seems less catholic and more classic, with standards and bop tunes making up the programme. Heartbreaker: the slowly sighing 'Some Other Time'.

***** Collage**

Concord CCD 4709 *Allyson; Mike Metheny (flhn); Kim Park (as); Claude Williams (vn); Randy Weinstein (hca); Laura Caviani, Paul Smith (p); Rod Fleeman, Danny Embrey (g); Bob Bowman (b); Todd Strait (d).* 1/96.

***** Daydream**

Concord CCD4773 *As above, except add Randy Brecker (flhn), Gary Burton (vib); omit Metheny, Williams.* 1/96–3/97.

Allyson is edging away from jazz and further into a kind of adult pop, which given her broad sympathies doesn't hurt. Neither of these discs will convert any sceptics, but they're coolly effective, the lilt in her voice and its slight crack on a wistful line both working in her favour. *Collage* puts Billy Joel next to Clifford Brown next to Monk next to 'Cherokee' next to the Beatles, and her lack of pretension somehow carries it off. *Daydream* has more Monk and 'Donna Lee', which suggests that she isn't leaving jazz at all, although the show tune 'Show Me' and a lovely 'Everything Must Change' come from somewhere else.

****(*) From Paris To Rio**

Concord CCD 4865-2 *Allyson; Kim Park (as, f); Paul Smith (ky); Gil Goldstein (acc); Rod Fleeman, Danny Embrey (g); Bob Bowman (b); Todd Strait, Doug Auwarter (d); strings.* 98.

This feels like a disappointing misfire, which is a surprise given that Allyson has been performing a lot of this kind of material in live situations. She doesn't seem to characterize such widely different composers as Caetano Veloso, Ivan Lins, Ennio Morricone and Jacques Brel with enough distinctiveness to make the songs stand out from each other; Brel's 'Ne Me Quitte Pas' is entirely wrong. It's an amenable record, but for once in her discography she sounds little more than bland.

*****(*) Ballads – Remembering John Coltrane**

Concord CCD4950-2 *Allyson; Steve Wilson (ss); James Carter, Bob Berg (ts); James Williams (p); John Patitucci (b); Lewis Nash (d).* 11/00.

Back to jazz. Saying that your favourite Coltrane album is *Ballads* is a bit like admitting that you're the class wimp, but you'd hardly expect Karrin to pick out *Live In Japan*. Her set follows the programme of the original exactly, then adds 'Naima', 'Why Was I Born?' and 'Everytime We Say Goodbye'. If she's been listening to Krall, or at least looking at her chart positions, then at least she has a direct, top-drawer band behind her, unsweetened by strings or other needless candy. The three saxophonists go toe-to-toe (without appearing on any of each other's tracks), and the singer herself sustains eleven mostly slow tracks ('All Or Nothing At All' is given a good groove) with aplomb. It's focused and serious.

*****(*) In Blue**

Concord CCD-2106-2 *Allyson; Steve Wilson (ss, as); Mulgrew Miller (p); Danny Embrey (g); Peter Washington (b); Lewis Nash (d).* 2/02.

The Coltrane album was a hit record, and Karrin has found herself as Concord's leading female vocalist in consequence. The follow-up is all blues – although genuine twelve-bars are mixed in with 'Long As You're Living', 'Angel Eyes' and 'Blue Motel Room', so it's blue in feel rather than form. Minus sax stars and plus Miller and Embrey, the music's relaxed without being laid-back, and some of it ('Love Me Like A Man', also recently covered by Krall) really smoulders. Allyson's on fine form, and since she's visited this kind of thing often enough before, there's no sense of tacked-together concept.

Mikhail Alperin

PIANO, MELODICA, VOICE

Ukranian pianist-bandleader with a sorrowful European aesthetic.

****(*) Waves Of Sorrow**

ECM 839621-2 *Alperin; Arkady Shilkloper (frhn, flhn, v).* 7/89.

***** Folk Dreams**

Jaro 4187 *As above, except add Sergey Starostin (v, reeds); Russkaja Pesnja Folk Choir.* 92.

***** North Story**

ECM 531022-2 *As above, except add Tore Brunborg (ts); Terje Gewelt (b); Jon Christensen (d).* 9/95.

*****(*) First Impression**

ECM 557650-2 *Alperin; Arkady Shilkloper (frhn, flhn); John Surman (ss, bs); Terje Gewelt (b); Jon Christensen (d); Hans-Kristian Kjos Sørenson (mar, perc).* 12/97.

***** Night**

ECM 014431-2 *Alperin; Anja Lechner (clo); Hans-Kristian Kjos Sørensen (perc, mar, v).* 4/98.

'I saw a group of Moldavian square-dance musicians at a countryside wedding, performing a Beethoven sonata, dressed in studded leather jackets.' Misha Alperin's musical vision is attractively unconstrained but it only rarely breaks out of its own charmed and charming circle. Along with Shilkloper, who is wedded to melancholy by his choice of instrument, he has carved out a corner of world jazz and made it his own, a gentle, folksy idiom which never quite sounds so much improvised as tentatively remembered from long ago.

Reverie is the abiding characteristic of *North Story*. It's a sequence of eight impressionistic compositions filled out by the late Norwegian composer Harald Saeverud's chorale 'Kristi-Blodsdraper'. Why 'Ironical Evening' should come between

'Morning' and the long, slow 'Afternoon' isn't clear, but there is a coherent logic to the sequence, which deserves to be heard entire. Brunborg and the redoubtable Christensen provide an attractive range of variations on the rather limited range of sound offered by French horn and piano, as do the voices on *Folk Dreams*, an album which seems pretty remote from any jazz sensibility but for Alperin's occasional – and perhaps unconscious – echoes of Bill Evans.

First Impression is readily mistakable as a John Surman record, perhaps some anachronistic hybrid of his solo *Westering Home* experiment and some of the more recent group recordings. Alperin's hand takes a moment or two to detect, but once one starts to hear his delicately folksy/classical approach, it is clear who is in charge. The title-track, which follows a deceptively naïve 'Overture', has the limpid inconsequence of one of Satie's 'Gnossiennes'. Later 'Impressions' and other tracks involve Surman and the group and are more grabbing and alert. Alperin is most convincingly an improviser in his responsiveness to nuance. 'Twilight Hour', 'City Dance' and 'Movement' represent a suite-within-a-suite, a quietly dancing interlude dropped into the quiet spaces Alperin likes to leave between notes and ideas. One of the quietest and most contemplative records you could ever hope to encounter.

Looked at more closely, the line-up on *Night* is not so dissimilar from that of a conventional jazz piano trio. Alperin doubles on claviola and Sørensen (who like the others has a classical background) uses marimba as well as percussion; otherwise, no real difference. What really does set this apart, though, is that there is considerable room for improvisation, and a wise use of silence and stillness, but almost no identifiably jazz language at all. That isn't to belittle or exclude a powerful set, recorded live at the Vossa Jazz festival on the group's first public appearance; but be warned that they won't be doing 'In Walked Bud', 'Gloria's Step' or 'Misty', though the last of these would probably suit Misha's temperament.

Myriam Alter

COMPOSER

Composer working in a post-bop idiom, though not actually playing on her own records.

***(*) **Alter Ego**
Intuition 3258-2 *Ron Miles (t); Billy Drewes (ts, cl); Kenny Werner (p); Marc Johnson (b); Joey Baron (d).* 12/97.

*** **If**
Enja 9451-2 *John Ruocco (cl); Kenny Werner (p); Dino Saluzzi (band); Greg Cohen (b); Joey Baron (d).* 6/01.

Alter avers in her sleeve-note to the first record that 'When you write music, the most important thing is not necessarily to play it yourself'. Instead, a crack New York team was assembled for this graceful look through her book – ten compositions given an eloquent reading indeed. Cool stylists such as Miles and Drewes were well-chosen for the front line, and the rhythm section is about as apposite as it could get. Which puts a lot of expectation on the music, given that it has to function as expressively as the players. There are some unexpected quirks along the way: the dreamlike 'Funny Story' shifts between a vaguely disquieting cycle and sections where there's a satiric tango lick to offset the horns. More characteristic, perhaps, are interludes such as 'Stay Close To Me', gentle manipulations of ballad form which draw strength from the improvising. One could complain that it's all a little pat (almost every track runs out to the same length), although an advocate would prefer to suggest that the programme is finished and finely tailored. Either way it merits an attentive listen.

The Enja album enlists Werner and Baron again but otherwise switches towards the kind of folkish strain which is running through a lot of Italian jazz at present, with clarinet and bandoneon evoking a nostalgic feel of some faintly familiar parlour music. It's sweetly done and warmly enjoyable as such, but the tougher elements of the earlier record have ebbed away.

Barry Altschul (born 1943)

DRUMS, PERCUSSION

A sophisticated and subtle stylist who studied with Charli Persip, Altschul combines accurate, orthodox timekeeping with free-form ideas. His recording career as leader faltered in the mid-'80s.

*** **For Stu**
Soul Note 121015 *Altschul; Ray Anderson (tb); Anthony Davis (p); Rick Rozie (b).* 2/79.

*** **Brahma**
Sackville 3023 *Ray Anderson (tb, perc); Mark Helias (b, clo, perc).* 1/80.

*** **Irina**
Soul Note 121065 *Altschul; Enrico Rava (t); John Surman (ss, bs); Mark Helias (b).* 2/83.

Contrasting records from a fertile period in Altschul's career. Anderson was a very sympathetic collaborator and the two records which feature him are marked by some fine interplay that mixes free form improvisation with other, often older styles of jazz. The two-horn front line and more sombre 'European' sound-world of *Irina* probably suits the drummer better, but he is a formidable time keeper as well. *For Stu* – dedicated to a fellow drummer, the late Stu Martin – is an engagingly varied session, probably the best introduction to Altschul's work, though less musically adventurous. The title-track is a long, multi-dimensional exploration of rhythmic and tonal ideas, contrasting with Davis's typically thoughtful and oddly engaging 'Sleepwalker'. Altschul takes a solo spot on 'Drum Role', more interesting than these things usually are, but the highlight is a rousing interpretation of Mingus's 'Orange Was The Colour Of Her Dress, Then Silk Blues'.

Brahma was missed in previous editions and it's nice to be reminded of it and of how arresting a player Altschul could be in this company. There is a lovely version of the ballad 'Irina', which was a staple part of Barry's repertoire, and there are a few moments which point back to classic jazz, whether as a result of the trombonist's influence or Altschul's own explorations isn't clear.

On *Irina*, the leader suffers again from a rather patchy mix. This doesn't feel like fully three-dimensional Altschul. In the absence of a piano, he takes on an accompanist's role and does it very successfully, often leaving Helias to keep the count, though his own metre is rock steady. Rava and Surman don't quite gel early on and the album really comes alight only towards the end with a jolly tango and a rousing, almost ten-minute version of Waller's 'Jitterbug Waltz'.

****(*) That's Nice**

Soul Note 121115 *Altschul; Glenn Ferris (tb); Sean Bergin (as, ts); Mike Melillo (p); Andy McKee (b).* 11/85.

This is where the story peters out. Since the mid-80s there have been, to our knowledge, no more records under Altschul's leadership. The reasons can only be guessed at but, despite some engaging playing from all concerned and a lively dedication to three great predecessors, 'For Papa Jo, Klook And Philly Too', the drummer's heart doesn't seem to be in it.

The quartet tracks with just horns are more arrestingly original than the two with pianist Melillo, who shifts the direction back towards the mainstream. Bergin has some incendiary moments and Ferris and McKee bring in some interesting compositional material – 'Afra Love' and 'Blues Interrogation' – which maybe hints at declining confidence on the leader's part. Not a memorable set and a disappointing (if temporary) end to Altschul's solo career.

Amalgam

GROUP

Powerful British improvising unit which along with free bop and open form improvisation explored aspects of folk melody as well.

♛ ** Prayer For Peace**

FMR 109 *Trevor Watts (as); Jeff Clyne, Barry Guy (b); John Stevens (d).* 5/69.

Amalgam – and the associated Splinters – created some of the most vivid and powerful improvised music to be heard in Britain at the cusp of the '70s. This classic album remained on the deleted list for thirty years, but it comes across as freshly and powerfully as ever. The opening 'Tales Of Sadness' is an Ornettish dirge (somewhat in the manner of Coleman's 'Broken Shadows') that starts in open-ended C minor before breaking out into total freedom. Watts's wailing alto figure sounds like a Celtic folk theme. Sounded across a heavy bass pedal, its repetitive power slowly triggers some of the closest and most empathetic improvisation the group ever played in public. The remaining tracks would be anti-climactic if they were not so good. The three parts of 'Judy's Smile' build into a suite of majesty and real power, with Stevens generating much of the musical information on his tiny kit. Clyne only appears on the title-track and it's Guy who provides those richly resonant chords and fast-fingered ghost melodies that run through the whole astonishing set. Great music by a classic band.

*****(*) Innovation**

FMR 119 *Trevor Watts (as); Keith Tippett (p); Kent Carter, Lindsay Cooper (b); John Stevens (d); Terri Quaye (perc).* 12/74.

Strongly marked by Watts's growing interest in rhythmic repetition and shift, *Innovation* is very different to its predecessor. The addition of Tippett and a second bass changes the nature of things considerably. Keith drives along the harmony and plays some astonishingly beautiful things behind Watts. Stevens is somewhat lost in all this, particularly given the presence of a percussionist, but when he plays out of time his contribution is most interesting. The whole set ends with one of the breeziest knees-up you'll ever hear, a slow fade and segue out of 'Suzie Jay' into a piece called 'Austrian Roll' that should have, and may have, started a whole dance craze on its own. It lacks the dark power of *Prayer for Peace* but *Innovation* has its own fulsome delights.

***** Another Time**

FMR 116 *Trevor Watts (as); Steve Hayton (g); Pete Cowling (b); Liam Genockey (d).* 6/76.

The Watts/Stevens partnership foundered and Trevor went on to form an equally strong and in the event longer lasting relationship with drummer Liam Genockey. The other new members were a reflection of Watts's developing new direction, which would lead him to the Moire Music experiments of the following decade. There is enough continuity with the old group, however, to justify keeping the name. 'Suzie Jay' is still there from the old set list, but delivered now with a much funkier beat. A 'Tribute To Trane' points to one of the saxophonist's off-and-on influences while the long title-track and 'Chips' show that Watts could still improvise within this newer, more song-based outfit.

Ari Ambrose (born 1973)

TENOR SAXOPHONE

Studied sax in Washington, DC, and played in the local scene, then studied at Manhattan School from 1991. Played and recorded in sundry sideman situations before these leadership dates.

***** Introducing Ari Ambrose**

Steeplechase SCCD 31450 *Ambrose; Dennis Irwin (b); Billy Hart (d).* 4/98.

*****(*) Cyclic Episode**

Steeplechase SCCD 31472 *Ambrose; George Colligan (p); Joe Martin (b); Billy Drummond (d).* 12/98.

The gruff, almost barking sound suggests a lineage back through Rollins to Jacquet and early Webster, even if Ambrose does start the debut CD with a Coltrane tune. He says he wanted to make a three-man date that sounded more like a piano trio than a sax burn-out session, and the splendid playing of Irwin and Hart certainly helps in that direction. The awkwardness of Monk's 'Ugly Beauty' is smoothed away without sacrificing any grittiness of tone. But Ambrose is not quite imaginative enough to carry the slow tempo convincingly, and the playing ends up as a string of bits and pieces. That sense of disjunction afflicts all of these tracks to some degree. While it's a relief to find a tenorman not bent on flying past each harmonic hurdle, it's still only intermittently effective.

The quartet session benefits from Colligan's astuteness, which immediately cools off the excessive heat: this time Ambrose seems determined to tear 'Gingerbread Boy' limb from limb, but actually the opener is the only piece to divert from what's essentially a rather inscrutable set of interpretations. Although themes like Sam Rivers's title-track or Bobby Hutcherson's 'Roses Poses' are turned over and over by the quartet, they're made to seem like excerpts from even longer pieces. Ambrose never quite presents conclusive evidence that he knows where his improvising's going, but there are surprising and often fascinating passages in all his solos here. Ambitious and worth following.

*****(*) Chainsaw**
Steeplechase SCCD 31481 *Ambriose; Luis Perdomo (p); Carlo De Rosa (b); Ari Hoenig (d).* 5/99.

*****(*) Early Song**
Steeplechase SCCD 31496 *Ambrose; George Colligan (p); Joe Martin (b); Rick Montalbano (d).* 99.

Hoenig is a terrific partner for Ambrose on *Chainsaw*. He crisply centres the music, even as the saxophonist is careering all over the place, and his rhythm part for 'Think Of One' is a one-man show by itself. Sometimes the leader is almost needlessly grotesque on standards such as 'Ghost Of A Chance', although at least he avoids any accusations of being a sound-alike tenor. Perdomo is a little more facile than Colligan, but the music is full of real excitement.

And there's more on *Early Song*. Colligan returns, and continues an absorbing dialogue with Ambrose. The 24-bar blues of 'Waiting' is appetizing food for thought, and there's a particularly engaging reading of a Jobim tune which normally escapes jazz attention, 'Useless Landscape'. There's not much distance in time between all these records, but it's not too fanciful to hear Ambrose growing more confident and effective, even as he's surrendering nothing in terms of energy.

*****(*) United**
Steeplechase SCCD 31518 *Ambrose; Jay Anderson (b); Jeff Williams (d).* 12/02.

***** Jazmin**
Steeplechase SCCD 31535 *Ambrose; Michael Leonhardt (p); Joe Martin (b); Rick Monalbano (d).* 3/01.

These two seem to have been released out of sequence, and with seven albums in barely four years, Ambrose is certainly being given his head at Steeplechase. The strong trio set underlines that Ambrose prefers enough open country that he can get fast and loose with the structures; on the quartet record, he isn't becalmed, just a bit more hemmed in. Both are satisfying, although no more so than the earlier dates, and maybe he now needs a more interventionist producer or label.

AMM

IMPROVISING ENSEMBLE

AMM's 35-year history is one of the most extraordinary and disciplined in improvised music. It is also completely sui generis. The group's membership has changed over the years, with only Eddie Prévost and Keith Rowe remaining from the original configuration; what has remained consistent is the members' devotion to engaged music-making that is neither abstract nor conventionally expressive but always intensely beautiful.

*****(*) AMMusic 1966**
Matchless/rer no number *Cornelius Cardew (p, transistor radio); Lou Gare (ts, vn); Eddie Prévost (d); Keith Rowe (g, transistor radio); Lawrence Sheaff (cl, acc, transistor radio).* 6/66.

****** The Crypt – 12 June 1968**
Matchless MRCD 05 2CD *Cornelius Cardew (p, clo); Lou Gare (ts, vn); Christopher Hobbs, Eddie Prévost (perc); Keith Rowe (g, elec).* 6/68.

****** Laminal**
Matchless MRCD 31 3CD *As above, except add John Tilbury (p).* 12/69–5/94.

In a rather dense and difficult book called *Noise* (*Bruits*), the French cultural theorist Jacques Attali identifies four main stages in the political economy of music. It is a process that culminates in a final utopian phase which Attali calls composition. This is a music 'beyond exchange ... performed for the musician's own enjoyment, as self-communication, fundamentally outside all other communication, as self-transcendence, a solitary, egotistical, noncommercial act'. It's an argument and a model that applies very cogently, though not always entirely accurately, to the music of AMM, who for three decades have stood outside every commercial and critical nexus and continued to make rich, astonishing music. One would have to quibble with 'egotistical', for it is almost axiomatic of 'AMMusic' (no other category exists) that ego is effectively suspended. AMM's origin lies in the British free-jazz movement, but the political and philosophical instincts of the founding members quickly dictated its transformation into an improvising collective in which process rather than gesture was important and which redefined the growing division in new music between performers and audience. Early AMM performances were conducted in the dark – *The Crypt* seems an entirely appropriate setting – and often deliberately blurred starting and finishing times.

Though 'beyond exchange' and defined entirely by the context and the collective understanding of the changing membership, the music has begun to enjoy a second life on record. The advent of CD meant that for the first time whole performances could be issued without breaks or editing, and founder member Eddie Prévost has used his own Matchless imprint to document the group's early and ongoing history. *The Crypt* was previously available in a two-LP boxed set, but the improvement in sound-quality, a richness of texture and of detail in quieter passages, is revelatory, here and throughout the older catalogue. In a superb liner-note to the earliest performance, Prévost points out that the *Jazz Journal* once identified the group as the 'Cornelius Cardew Quartet', a nonsensical and ironic attribution on all sorts of counts.

This is a music which rejects instrumentalism. It matters very little after a few minutes who is playing what, particularly when conventional technique is almost entirely overthrown. In later years, as can be heard in the later performances on *Laminal*, Prévost was to return to something that demonstrated at least a kinship with jazz drumming, and Tilbury's piano playing is more conventionally expressive than Cardew's. Rowe is perhaps the key to the sound-world. He is credited as 'guitarist', but only in the most deconstructionist sense, laying the instrument flat on a table and manipulating feedback, overtones, percussive effects and accidentals, using the instrument as a sound source without a playing history. Veterans will insist that the 1966 record and *The Crypt* are essential texts, but the newcomer should certainly settle on *Laminal*, which documents an early overseas performance (in Aarhus, Denmark) with much later work from what was to become the '90s version of the group. There is much more (and perhaps better) from them below, but the juxtaposition of their intent, uneffusive music with the turbulent swirl of the late-'60s group is instructive.

***** At The Roundhouse**
Anomalous ICES 01 *Lou Gare (ts); Eddie Prévost (d).* 8/72.

***** To Hear And Back Again**
Matchless MRCD 03 *As above* 6/73–4/75.

Like the similarly convened Spontaneous Music Ensemble, AMM functioned for a time as a duo. What's odd about these early-to-mid-'70s tracks and what distinguishes them most clearly from the Trevor Watts/John Stevens version of SME is the extent to which Gare and Prévost seem to have reverted to the free-jazz idiom they were presumed to have left behind more than a decade before. The two long studio tracks which occupied sides one and two of the original LP, 'To Hear' and 'Back Again', are very much more abstract than the half-hour's worth of live performances from London and Berlin that fill out the CD reissue. It's the additional material, and particularly the opening item, 'Unity First', which reminds the listener that Gare and Prévost started out as Sonny Rollins and Max Roach acolytes and retained a good measure of that basic sound feel, that sense of musical organization in even their most 'out' performances. Three stars may seem diffident, or even damning. It's simply that this disc is far from representative of AMM and, while Prévost could doubtless point up some quite obvious continuities, this is probably better grouped with the recordings made under his own name.

Issued for the first time in 2004, *At The Roundhouse* is a surprisingly good quality recording of AMM's appearance at Harvey Matusow's International Carnival of Experimental Sound event. The single continuous performance, titled 'The Sound Of Indifference' here (though what is meant by 'indifference' should be looked at carefully), is punctuated by silences and occasional drone passages, where Prévost plays underneath sustained tones from the saxophonist. Some of the duo's later work, including purely drone-based gigs, is anticipated here. A most valuable document of a remarkable period in British free jazz.

***** Generative Themes**
Matchless MRCD 06 *John Tilbury (p); Keith Rowe (g, elec); Eddie Prévost (d).* 12/82.

***** Combine + Laminates + Treatise '84**
Matchless MRCD 26 *As above.* 84.

*****(*) The Inexhaustible Document**
Matchless MRCD 13 *As above, except add Rohan De Saram (clo).* 87.

****** The Nameless Uncarved Block**
Matchless MRCD 20 *As above, except replace De Saram with Lou Gare (ts).* 4/90.

The trio represented on *Generative Themes* and *Combine + Laminates* was to be the basic AMM line-up thereafter. Interestingly, the early '80s saw the group rethinking and in some respects greatly simplifying the approach of the Cardew years. Tilbury is a more conventionally expressive, but by no means a conventional, player. His use of space, light and shade is extraordinary, constantly suggesting (as does Prévost) the *possibility* of linear development without ever allowing it to emerge. That is particularly clear on *Generative Themes*, which can be heard as a sequence of five potential compositions in which the transformational rules and functions are laid out but given no straightforwardly meaningful substance. On reflection, this is perhaps the most abstract record AMM has issued. That is an attempt at description, not criticism. The third item on the 1984 album (originally a Pogus LP of a performance at the Arts Club in Chicago) introduced material which drew on Cardew's theoretical/conceptual work, suggesting that, just a year or two after his untimely death, his partners were working through ideas and procedures which it had not been possible hitherto to accommodate in AMM terms. The addition of cellist Rohan De Saram, who appears on *The Inexhaustible Document*, was a reminder of Cardew's other instrumental voice, except that de Saram, a member of the blue-chip new music group, the Arditti Quartet, is probably closer in instinct to a philosophical tradition in which suspension of the self is a premiss rather than a problematic goal. He certainly fits into the music seamlessly.

Gare, who reappears on the 1990 album, is a more problematic presence. Critics gleefully queued up to nominate *The Nameless Uncarved Block* as AMM's 'rock' record – ironically enough, given Prévost's very fruitful association with high-octane outfit God and other groups later in the decade when AMM began to receive paternity suits as progenitors of the new ambient and process-driven music. Again, the saxophonist doesn't sound quite in context. There are moments in the huge 'Igneous' (there are many longer AMM tracks, but this one feels burstingly oversized) when the whole thing seems poised on the brink of a catastrophic finale, much as John Coltrane's long-form improvisations with Pharoah Sanders did. There the similarities end, of course. This is music which is not exhausted by repetition, and even seasoned AMM admirers (ourselves included), who might once have rejected the very idea of 'mechanical reproduction', have begun to accept the importance of documentation. This is music which transcends its moment. It does make sense to listen to it many times. It is never the same, always fresh, always developing, or developing new pathways in the listener.

****** Newfoundland**
Matchless MRCD 23 *Keith Rowe (g, elec); John Tilbury (p); Eddie Prévost (d).* 7/92.

****** Live In Allentown USA**
Matchless MRCD 30 *As above.* 4/94.

*****(*) From A Strange Place**
Modern Music PSFD 80 *As above.* 10/95.

*****(*) Before Driving To The Chapel We Took Coffee With Rick And Jennifer Reed**
Matchless MRCD 35 *As above.* 4/96.

Composer Howard Skempton's sleeve-note for the marvellous *Newfoundland* makes salutary reading. 'It is surely easy to resort to adjectives' – we have tried to resist – 'this music is so stunningly immediate, so palpable, that it makes a nonsense of such musings.' Emphatically, yes, but it still demands some kind of response, and reactions to AMM are notoriously difficult to verbalize. Comparison is perhaps the safest resort. In purely timbral, textural terms, recent performances have been gentler, less confrontational than of yore. Some of this may be explained by passing years, some by changing expectations. In the '90s AMM have been hailed as the progenitors of a whole slew of post-rock idioms, and there may be some subconscious attempt to build bridges to a younger generation. The dynamics of a trio are always intriguing. Prévost continues to suggest and imply a pulse even when it cannot be securely quantified. Tilbury is delicacy itself, somewhere between Satie and Bill Evans, but filtered through gauze. It's Rowe who is the anarchist, the deconstructor, splashing colours across the Allentown set and providing the most significant estrangements on *From A Strange Place*, a rare AMM appearance on another label. It is extraordinarily hard to separate these sessions. Different as they are, each has its beauties, and all three have their longueurs. The most recent of the bunch – and if there's a longer or worse album-title in the book you should probably claim discount – is curiously formulaic, cast in a language that often seems to be striving after effect rather than going straight for the unfettered *jouissance* that makes this music so absolute and so exceptional.

***** Tunes Without Measure Or End**
Matchless MRCD 44 *As above.* 5/00.

*****(*) Fine**
Matchless MRCD 46 *As above.* 5/01.

We were present when the first of these was recorded, as part of the Free RadiCCAls event in Glasgow's McLellan Galleries, the temporary home of CCA. As a recorded experience, it is even more subtly detailed and inflected than the original performance, and eminently listenable. Taken as a pair, these records strongly reflect Matchless's marketing tag-line about AMM records being as like and unalike as trees. The sound-world is now instantly identifiable, but in constant variation and flux. We marginally prefer *Fine*, which was recorded at a festival in France and in the company of Fine Kwiatkowski. It's not for us to comment on the relationship between music and physical movement, but there is a wonderful grace and centredness to the almost hour-long set, and one can almost envisage using it as a meditation or Tai Chi device.

***** AMM/Formanex**
Fibrr 005 *As above, except add John White, Laurent Dailleau (elec).* 7/02.

An unusual festival collaboration with French electro-acoustic ensemble Formanex, who had previously recorded parts of Cornelius Cardew's *Treatise*. Recorded in Nancy, it blends found sound (including some intriguing pastoral noises) with white and pink noise, but as ever it's Tilbury and Prévost who command attention with their almost telepathic understanding. The addition of other instrumental voices, notably Dailleau's theremin, is interesting, but the language of AMM music is by now so completely *sui generis* and familiar/unfamiliar that any outside influence is faintly corrosive. This will be hard to find, in any case.

Albert Ammons (1907–49)

PIANO

Played in Chicago from the mid-'20s but didn't start recording until 1936. Made much success during the boogie-woogie craze of the late '30s and persisted through the '40s, but a final illness ended his career.

*****(*) Albert Ammons 1936–1939**
Classics 715 *Ammons; Guy Kelly (t); Dalbert Bright (cl, as); Ike Perkins (g); Israel Crosby (b); Jimmy Hoskins (d).* 2/36–10/39.

*****(*) The Boogie Woogie Man**
ASV AJA 5305 *As above, except add Harry James, Frankie Newton, Hot Lips Page (t), J. C. Higginbotham, Vic Dickenson (tb), Meade Lux Lewis, Pete Johnson (p), Teddy Bunn (g), Johnny Williams (b), Eddie Dougherty, Big Sid Catlett, James F. Hoskins (d).* 2/36–2/44.

One-third of the great boogie-woogie triumvirate (with Pete Johnson and Meade Lux Lewis), Albert Ammons was arguably the least individual of the three, though he lacked nothing in power and swinging. The Classics CD usefully rounds up all his tracks from the '30s: there are two Decca sessions by his Rhythm Kings, but the meat is in the 18 piano solos, cut for Vocalion, Solo Art and Blue Note, with a session of airshots from Chicago making up the balance. 'Shout For Joy' and 'Boogie Woogie Stomp' are classics of boogie-woogie exuberance, but his 1939 Solo Art session proved he was also a considerable blues piano man: 'Chicago In Mind' contemplates the form with genuine insight. The CD offers mixed reproduction, mostly not bad.

ASV go for a broader cross-section, with material from various band sessions for Blue Note and Commodore, although it does duplicate some of the Classics material.

Gene Ammons (1925–74)

TENOR SAXOPHONE

Son of pianist Albert, Gene Ammons, also known as Jug, worked with Billy Eckstine and Woody Herman before leading his own bands through the '50s and '60s, although prison terms for drug offences blighted his career. Despite that, he recorded a huge number of albums and continued to work until his death from pneumonia. A swing-to-bop stylist, his playing was one of the models for the soul-jazz movement of the '60s.

****(*) Gene Ammons 1947–1949**
Classics 1251 *Ammons; Gail Brockman, Jesse Miller (t); Ernest Macdonald (as); Leo Parker, John Dungee (as, bs); James Craig, Junior Mance, Christine Chatman (p); Leo Blevins (g); Gene Wright, Leroy Jackson, Lowell Pointer (b); Chuck Williams, Ellis Bartee, Wesley Landers, Ike Day (d); Mary F. Graham, Earl Coleman, Marcel Daniels (v).* 6/47–2/49.

****(*) Gene Ammons 1949–1950**
Classics 1329 *Ammons; Jesse Miller, Bill Massey (t); Matthew Gee, Eph Greenlea, Bennie Green (tb); Ernest Macdonald (as, bs); Christine Chatman (p, v); Junior Mance, Duke Jordan, Charlie Bateman (p); Leo Blevins (g); Lowell Pointer, Leroy Jackson, Tommy Potter, Gene Wright (b); Ike Day, Wesley Landers, Jo Jones, Art Blakey (d); Teddy Williams (v).* 2/49–5/50.

*****(*) The Gene Ammons Story: The 78 Era**
Prestige PRCD-24058-2 *Ammons; Bill Massey, Nat Woodyard (t); Matthew Gee, Eli Dabney, Bennie Green, Henderson Chambers (tb); Sonny Stitt, Rudy Williams, McKinley Easton (bs); Duke Jordan, Charlie Bateman, Junior Mance, Clarence 'Sleepy' Anderson, John Houston (p); Gene Wright, Earl May, Ernie Shepard, Ben Stuberville, Tommy Potter (b); Art Blakey, Wesley Landers, Teddy Stewart, George Brown (d); Earl Coleman (v).* 4/50–2/55.

*****(*) All Star Sessions**
Original Jazz Classics OJC 014 *Ammons; Art Farmer, Bill Massey (t); Alfred 'Chippie' Outcalt (tb); Lou Donaldson (as); Sonny Stitt (ts, bs); Duke Jordan, Junior Mance, Charlie Bateman, Freddie Redd (p); Tommy Potter, Gene Wright, Addison Farmer (b); Jo Jones, Wesley Landers, Teddy Stewart, Kenny Clarke (d).* 3/50–6/55.

***** The Happy Blues**
Original Jazz Classics OJC 013 *Ammons; Art Farmer, Jackie McLean (as); Duke Jordan (p); Addison Farmer (b); Art Taylor (d); Candido Camero (perc).* 4/56.

★★(★) Jammin' With Gene
Original Jazz Classics OJC 211 *Ammons; Donald Byrd (t); Jackie McLean (as); Mal Waldron (b); Doug Watkins (b); Art Taylor (d).* 7/56.

★★★ Funky
Original Jazz Classics OJC 244 *As above, except Art Farmer (t) replaces Byrd; add Kenny Burrell (g).* 1/57.

★★ Jammin' In Hi Fi
Original Jazz Classics OJC 129 *Ammons; Idrees Sulieman (t); Jackie McLean (as); Mal Waldron (p); Kenny Burrell (g); Paul Chambers (b); Art Taylor (d).* 4/57.

★★★ The Big Sound
Original Jazz Classics OJC 651 *Ammons; John Coltrane (as); Paul Quinichette (ts); Pepper Adams (bs); Jerome Richardson (f); Mal Waldron (p); George Joyner (b); Art Taylor (d).* 1/58.

★★★ Groove Blues
Original Jazz Classics OJC 723 *As above.* 1/58.

★★★(★) Blue Gene
Original Jazz Classics OJC 192 *Ammons; Idrees Sulieman (t); Pepper Adams (bs); Mal Waldron (p); Doug Watkins (b); Art Taylor (d); Ray Barretto (perc).* 5/58.

Gene Ammons made a lot of records, and a surprising number are now in print on CD, thanks mainly to the extensive OJC/Prestige reissue programme. Classics have started to deal with what is effectively Jug's pre-history, the small-combo sessions he set down for Mercury, Aladdin, Chess and Aristocrat at the very end of the '40s. Classics 1251 starts with two very bleary-sounding sessions where the energy level seems negligible, but subsequent dates for Mercury are livelier, even though there's very little here beyond boppin'-the-blues clichés, and the final date with singer-pianist Chatman is in very low-fi sound. More sessions for Aristocrat and Mercury open Classics 1329 before they pick up the start of Jug's dates for Prestige (duplicated on *The 78 Era*). There's really very little here to return to once heard. The leader's own style had been forged as a first-generation bopper, first with Billy Eckstine, then under his own name, but his early records find him walking a line between bop and R&B honking. *The 78 Era* is rough-and-ready music, and listening to it is like thumbing coins into a jukebox of the day. Jug liked to enjoy his music, and perhaps the darker passions of a Parker were beyond him. The earliest tracks on *All Star Sessions* are also typical of the kind of stuff he recorded prior to the LP era, roistering through two-tenor battles with Sonny Stitt, a close kindred spirit. A later date with Farmer and Donaldson is more restrained until the collective whoop of 'Madhouse'.

The next six records all follow similar patterns: long, expansive tracks – at most four to a record – and variations on the blues and some standards for the material. Ammons himself takes the leading solos, but he so often resorts to quotes and familiar phrases that one is left wishing for a less open-ended environment; of the other players involved, McLean and Waldron are the most reliably inventive. *Jammin' In Hi Fi* is the weakest of the six, the whole session sounding like a warm-up, while *Jammin' With Gene* has a very long and overcooked 'Not Really The Blues' balancing two superior slow pieces. *Funky* and *Blue Gene* are decent if unremarkable, but the session that makes up both *The Big Sound* and *Groove Blues* has a couple of interesting points in featuring one of John Coltrane's few appearances on alto (undistinguished though it is) and some unexpectedly piquant flute solos by Richardson to vary the palette a little. These all count as playable but unexceptional discs.

★★★ The Gene Ammons Story: Organ Combos
Prestige PRCD-24071-2 *Ammons; Joe Newman (t); Frank Wess (ts, f); Jack McDuff, Johnny 'Hammond' Smith (org); Wendell Marshall, Doug Watkins (b); Art Taylor, Walter Perkins (d); Ray Barretto (perc).* 6/60–11/61.

★★★ Boss Tenor
Prestige 7180 *Ammons; Tommy Flanagan (p); Doug Watkins (b); Art Taylor (d); Ray Barretto (perc).* 6/60.

★★★ Jug
Original Jazz Classics OJC 701 *Ammons; Richard Wyands (p); Clarence 'Sleepy' Anderson (org); Doug Watkins (b); J. C. Heard (d).* 1/61.

★★★(★) The Gene Ammons Story: Gentle Jug
Prestige PRCD-24079-2 *Ammons; Richard Wyands, Patti Bown (p); George Duvivier, Doug Watkins (b); J. C. Heard, Ed Shaughnessy (d).* 1/61–4/62.

★★(★) Live! In Chicago
Original Jazz Classics OJC 395 *Ammons; Eddie Buster (org); Gerald Donovan (d).* 8/61.

★★★ Up Tight!
Prestige PRCD-24140-2 *Ammons; Walter Bishop Jr, Patti Bown (p); Arthur Davis, George Duvivier (b); Art Taylor (d); Ray Barretto (perc).* 10/61.

★★ Preachin'
Original Jazz Classics OJC 792 *Ammons; Clarence 'Sleepy' Anderson (org); Sylvester Hickman (b); Dorral Anderson (d).* 5/62.

★★★ Jug And Dodo
Prestige PRCD-24021-2 *Ammons; Michael 'Dodo' Marmarosa (p); Sam Jones (b); Marshall Thompson (d).* 5/62.

★★(★) Bad! Bossa Nova
Original Jazz Classics OJC 351 *Ammons; Hank Jones (p); Bucky Pizzarelli, Kenny Burrell (g); Norman Edge (b); Oliver Jackson (d); Al Hayes (perc).* 9/62.

★★(★) We'll Be Together Again
Original Jazz Classics OJC 708 *Ammons; Sonny Stitt (as, ts); John Houston (p); Buster Williams (b); George Brown (d).* 68.

★★(★) The Boss Is Back!
Prestige PRCD-24129-2 *Ammons; Prince James, Houston Person (ts); Junior Mance (p); Sonny Phillips (org); Billy Butler (g); Buster Williams, Bob Bushnell (b); Frankie Jones, Bernard Purdie (d); Candido Camero (perc).* 11/69.

There is a lot of Gene Ammons available again. It's sad that the albums are so spotty and inconsistent, but that seemed to be his way. Great performances can follow weary ones, even on the same record, and there doesn't seem to be a particular setting that turns him on to his best form. The clinkers here are *Preachin'*, a set of gospel tunes that he can barely be bothered to blow through, and *The Boss Is Back!*, which combines the original *Boss Is Back* (not bad) and *Brother Jug* (rotten). *We'll Be Together Again* should have been an incendiary meeting with Sonny Stitt, but it leaves a trail of smoke rather than any fire – the tracks are cut off short before they can really work up steam. *Bad! Bossa Nova* sounds like a duff corporate idea, setting him to work on bossa nova rhythms, but he blows hard enough to make it worthwhile. *Boss Tenor*, *Jug* and especially *Organ Combos* (which combines the original albums, *Twisting*

The Jug and the fine *Angel Eyes*) are solid and worth the shelf-space. The best records, though, are probably *Jug And Dodo*, an unlikely, sometimes compelling meeting with Dodo Marmarosa in one of the pianist's rare recordings, and the splendid *Gentle Jug*. This at last puts on CD one of his best Prestige dates, *The Soulful Moods Of Gene Ammons*, where he plays with Hawkins-like authority, and adds the similarly inclined *Nice An' Cool* session from a year earlier. *Up Tight!* is the most recent addition to the sequence, collecting the contents of two 1961 LPs, *Up Tight* and *Boss Soul*. A couple of good ones, too, though if anyone feels confused by the similarity of all these titles, much the same can be said about a lot of the music.

***** The Chase!**
Prestige 24166 *Ammons; Dexter Gordon (ts); John Young, Jodie Christian (p); Cleveland Eaton, Rufus Reid (b); Steve McCall, Wilbur Campbell (d); Vi Redd (v).* 7/70.

Not exactly a rekindling of the old two-tenor team, since either Ammons or Gordon sits out a lot of the time. But there are a few entertaining sparks struck off some old (and much-saddled) bebop warhorses and, with two down-home Chicagoan rhythm sections in attendance, there's plenty of fun.

***** Legends Of Acid Jazz**
Prestige 24188 *Ammons; Sonny Stitt (ts); Leon Spencer, Don Patterson (org); Harold Mabern (p); George Freeman, Paul Weeden (g); Ron Carter (b); Idris Muhammad, Bill James (d); strings.* 62–68.

This is a useful sampling of Jug's music, since it combines the albums *The Black Cat* and *You Talk That Talk* and adds two tracks from a 1962 date with Don Patterson. The later disc offers some typical fisticuffs with Sonny Stitt while the *Black Cat* tracks include a couple of pieces with strings, some blues and a 'Piece To Keep Away Evil Spirits'. Ammons blows on regardless.

****(*) Greatest Hits, Vol. 1: The Sixties**
Original Jazz Classics OJC 6005 *Ammons; Joe Newman (t); Frank Wess (ts); Jack McDuff, Johnny Hammond Smith (org); Richard Wyands, Hank Jones, Tommy Flanagan (p); Kenny Burrell, Bucky Pizzarelli (g); Doug Watkins, Norman Edge, Wendell Marshall (b); Art Taylor, Oliver Jackson, Walter Perkins (d); Ray Barretto, Al Hayes (perc).* 61–69.

***** Soul Summit**
Prestige PRCD-24118-2 *Ammons; various others.* 6/61–4/62.

Two useful if sometimes frustrating compilations. The *Hits* collection isn't a bad trawl through some of his '60s sessions, though any of the better albums listed above would do just as well as a sampling of Ammons in this decade. *Soul Summit* is shared with Sonny Stitt and Jack McDuff, and Jug turns up on a couple of tracks with a big band as well as sparring with Stitt.

***** Fine And Mellow**
Prestige 24281-2 *Ammons; Sonny Phillips (org, p); Ernie Hayes (org); Hank Jones (p); Joe Beck, Maynard Parker (g); Ron Carter (b); Idris Muhammed, Mickey Roker, Billy Cobham (d).* 10–11/72.

***** God Bless Jug And Sonny**
Prestige 11019-2 *Ammons; Sonny Stitt (as, ts); Cedar Walton (p); Sam Jones (b); Billy Higgins (d).* 6/73.

***** Left Bank Encores**
Prestige 11022-2 *As above.* 6/73.

****(*) Gene Ammons And Friends At Montreux**
Original Jazz Classics OJC 1023 *Ammons; Nat Adderley (c); Julian 'Cannonball' Adderley (as); Dexter Gordon (ts); Hampton Hawes (p); Bob Cranshaw (b); Kenny Clarke (d); Kenneth Nash (perc).* 7/73.

Almost the end of the line for Jug (although he actually made another five albums after these!). *Fine And Mellow* doubles up *Got My Own* and *Big Bad Jug*, where he lumbers through pop material, some standards and three oversweetened string charts, still sounding like Jug: if the backings don't exactly suit him, they don't trouble him – and they remind that, in an age when smooth-jazz saxophonists are as polite as they can be, players of Ammons's individuality are a rare breed indeed. The meeting with Stitt comes from a Baltimore club date, and it's abrim with atmosphere, even if the playing has its faltering moments. Stitt sounds the stronger, perhaps inevitably, but there's still much fun to be had in the two of them playing tag at the moments where the horns are asked to properly joust with each other. It might have been pushing it a bit to have released a second session from the same date, but in the event there isn't much to choose between this one and *Left Bank Encores*: no masterpiece in this set either, but nothing disgraceful from two veterans of thousands of blowing gigs.

The Montreux affair isn't as good. Gene plays 'Yardbird Suite' and 'Sophisticated Lady' as if nothing had changed, but his era was virtually over and what looks on paper like a classic live session feels tired. Nat, Dexter and Cannonball join in only on the final 'Treux Blues'. It's sad to think that they're all now gone, as are Hawes and Clarke.

Franck Amsallem (born 1961)

PIANO

Algerian-born, Amsallem went to the USA two decades ago after graduating from Nice Conservatory. His list of credits since then includes gigs with A-list names like Gerry Mulligan, Charles Lloyd and Bobby Watson. He has also been MD at the Grand Casino in Monte Carlo.

****** Another Time**
Challenge A 73117 *Amsallem; Gary Peacock (b); Bill Stewart (d).* 7/90.

*****(*) Is That So**
Sunnyside SSC 1071 *Amsallem; Tim Ries (ts); Leon Parker (d, perc).* 97.

***** Years Gone By**
Challenge A 73129 *Amsallem; Tim Ries (ts); Riccardo Del Frà (b); Daniel Humair (d).* 98.

***** On Second Thought**
Naïve 226105 *Amsallem; Tim Ries (ss, as); Johannes Weidenmuller (b); Marc Miralta (d).* 2/01.

Amsallem comes from Oran, the city that was home to Albert Camus, and, though no outsider and lacking all the usual symptoms of alienation and estrangement, he has certainly cut his own distinctive furrow. Periods of study in Nice, at Berklee, and at the Manhattan School of Music refined what was already an obvious talent, and Amsallem quickly became a first-call player. His debut recording was originally released on OMD as *Out A Day*. The writing is exquisite. '... And Keep This Place In Mind For A Better One Is Heart [*sic*] To Find' and the following two tracks, 'Running After Eternity' and 'Dee', are among the best things we have heard for piano trio in a long time. Peacock's huge sound and Bill Stewart's now widely recognized delicacy and grace contribute substantially.

The next record introduces a partnership with Tim Ries that has remained in place ever since. It's obviously a *simpatico* relationship, but we remain unpersuaded by the saxophonist, who always seems to be trying too hard to impress. The trio with Parker is more effective and there are very good things on *Years Gone By*, where Ries sounds brisker and less cluttered.

Until the release of *On Second Thought* it was hard to go past the debut record but 2001 saw a new facet to Amsallem's small-group writing. Both 'Chanson Triste' and 'Thirty Two More Bars To Go' are vividly expressive ideas and the group (still anchored by the improving Ries) makes fascinating play with them both. 'Affreusement Votre' – which translates as something like 'Horribly Yours' – is more of a *jeu d'esprit*, but like everything Franck writes, it has a solid backbone of harmonic intelligence. The sound is very live and very present, with nice separation between the component instruments. As a soloist, Amsallem is impressive rather than totally engaging; too many notes, sometimes not enough reflection, and yet the outline of something grander is always evident.

Amsterdam String Trio

ENSEMBLE

Challenging chamber jazz from three gifted Dutch improvisers.

***** Winter Theme**

Winter & Winter New Edition 910 060 2 *Maurice Horsthuis (vla); Ernst Reijseger (clo); Ernst Glerum (b).* 11/99.

This uncategorizable group has previously veered between free-form improvisation and what sounds like formal new music, as the line-up might have suggested. Previous records, like *Dodekakania*, failed to make much impact but this one deserves to be heard, if only for Stefan Winter's impeccable production. Horsthuis is the only composer credited (which raises a question about how much of the music is improvised) but it is the producer who merits – and judging by the winter-dominated titles gets – all the credit. Intriguing and challenging.

Curtis Amy (born 1927)

TENOR AND SOPRANO SAXOPHONES

A Texas tenorman, Amy learned saxophone in an army band and based himself in Los Angeles from 1955, playing in many hard-bop and soul-jazz groups in the area.

*****(*) Katanga**

Pacific Jazz 94850-2 *Amy; Dupree Bolton, Marcus Belgrave (t); Roy Brewster (vtb); John Houston, Jack Wilson (p); Ray Ayers (vib); Ray Crawford (g); Victor Gaskin, George Morrow (b); Doug Sides, Tony Bazley (d).* 62–63.

***** Peace For Love**

Fresh Sound FSR 5004 *Amy; Steve Huffsteter (t, flhn); Bob McChesney (b); Frank Strazzeri (p); Donn Wyatt (ky); John B Williams (b); Leon Ndugu Chancler (d); Merry Clayton, Jessie Williams (v).* 6/94.

The reissue of *Katanga* will be welcomed by collectors not so much for Amy's work as for the glimpse of a semi-legendary figure, Dupree Bolton, who made hardly any other records yet was a fascinating stylist: his solos have a headlong momentum that is buoyed up by a poise which keeps the logic of the playing intact. The rest of the playing and the tunes are more ordinary, but these surviving fragments of a lost talent (Bolton served a prison sentence not long afterwards) are fascinating. Amy's own big-bodied Texas tenor is reliable and likeable, but none of his early records ever really stands out from each other, and there are several more Pacific Jazz albums yet to reappear. The CD has a bonus of three tracks from the earlier *Way Down*.

The Fresh Sound set is a rare latter-day record from the old pro. This easy-going date, while never striking more than a few sparks, is the jazz equivalent of comfort food. Amy's thick, soft tenor lines and insinuating tone are fine, but the best features are the astute writing for the three-horn front line and the slowly unfolding groove which the splendid rhythm section put together for most of the tunes. Mrs Amy, Merry Clayton, adds wordless vocals to track one.

Arild Andersen (born 1945)

DOUBLE BASS

Like many players of his generation in Scandinavia, Andersen was much influenced by exiled guru George Russell's Lydian Chromatic approach to harmony. The bassist has worked in a wide range of contexts and was leader of Masqualero. His characteristic manner is resonant and fleet, with much of the harmonic complexity Russell's influence imbued.

*****(*) Molde Concert**

ECM 159497-2 *Andersen; John Taylor (p); Bill Frisell (g); Alphonse Mouzon (d).* 8/81.

This is that rarity, an ECM reissue with extra material. The original concert album has been expanded to some 78 minutes of music with four extra tracks. It's an untypical Andersen group: Mouzon is a combative and over-aggressive drummer, but for once the Norwegian bassist seems to enjoy working alongside such naked power, and Frisell treats it almost as a power-trio situation. Taylor has to find his own way into this, but he's adept enough to do so, and we still consider 'The Sword Under His Wings' especially to be a memorable group performance. The extra tracks add weight, which the intense performance is able to carry.

*****(*) Sagn**

ECM 849647-2 *Andersen; Bendik Hofseth (ts, ss); Bugge Wesseltoft (ky); Frode Alnaes (g); Nana Vasconcelos (perc, v); Kirsten Braten Berg (v).* 8/90.

***** If You Look Far Enough**

ECM 513902-2 *Andersen; Ralph Towner (g); Audun Kleive (d); Nana Vasconcelos (perc).* 88, 7/91, 2/92.

****** Hyperborean**

ECM 537342-2 *Andersen; Bendik Hofseth (ts); Tore Brunborg (ts, ss); Kenneth Knudsen (ky); Paolo Vinaccia (d, perc); Cikada String Quartet.* 12/96.

*****(*) Achirana**

ECM 1728 *Andersen; Vassilis Tsabropoulos (p); John Marshall (d).* 10/99.

***** The Triangle**

ECM 038121-2 *As above.* 1/03.

Andersen's music is an intriguingly unstable amalgam of Miles Davis (an influence evident in the bassist's group, Masqualero) and Norwegian folk forms. *Sagn* is weighted towards the latter, an early shot in ECM's effort to integrate the Nordic tradition and American jazz and one of the most successful, though Berg is not as compelling a presence as her countrywomen, Agnes Buen Gårnas or Mari Boine. She is the weak link in an otherwise splendid record.

If You Look Far Enough is constrained by its origins – recorded over nearly four years – and by the original purpose of much of the material. Written as a soundtrack for the film *Blucher*, it limps along for lack of supporting images, and some of the playing is notably limp, too. It does, however, feature Andersen prominently as soloist, sometimes unadorned, sometimes making use of real-time delay and a cathedral-proportioned reverb. The lines positively sing.

Hyperborean is a reference to the cool, ageless land the Greeks believed lay beyond the northern mountains. The music is disciplined, unromantic and timeless. Andersen dispenses with effects pedals, combining his increasingly elaborate improvisations in real time with keyboards and string quartet, lending the whole – ironically enough – a jazzier feel than anything he has done since Masqualero. Hofseth and Brunborg are reduced to supporting cast and it's the Cikada Quartet that dominates the first half. Things loosen up later, albeit leaving an uneasy sense that Andersen has delivered his main ideas upfront and is then struggling to fill the slot. Though structurally less elaborate than *Sagn*, which is organized as a three-part suite, *Hyperborean* has a unity of tone and an overall sense of direction lacking on the earlier discs. Andersen dominates completely. His sound is immense and his soloing involved and compelling, once again prompting the question why he hasn't yet recorded unaccompanied.

Achirana resembles nothing more than Paul Bley's trios of the early '70s with Kent Carter and Barry Altschul. Tsabropoulos favours tiny, disengaged phrases strung together into long, long lines. Marshall has long been an unsung hero – why *is* he heard so little of on record? – and Andersen is in top form on 'The Spell' and 'She's Gone'. Lovely, delicately cadenced jazz.

The follow-up record is almost a retread of the first, which is not to say that it lacks interest. Some of the pieces are almost explicitly classical in conception; 'Choral' ('Chorale', surely?) is Tsabropoulos's composition and 'Pavane' is the pianist's arrangement of Ravel's lovely piece 'for a princess of a bygone age'. See Larry Coryell's version for comparison. The only improvised track is the relatively brief 'European Triangle'. Andersen's own tunes, led off by the fine 'Saturday', are mostly in the same modal, lyrical style he deployed with Masqualero. This bids fair to be his most durable group since then.

Ernestine Anderson (born 1928)

VOCAL

Sang with the Johnny Otis road show in the late '40s and early '50s, then in clubs, and made five albums for Mercury during 1958–60, most of which have never been reissued on CD. In the '80s she made many albums for Concord, moving between torch-song and R&B styles.

***** My Kinda Swing**

Verve 842409-2 *Anderson; Ernie Wilkins Orchestra.* 60.

***** Never Make Your Move Too Soon**

Concord CCD 4147 *Anderson; Monty Alexander (p); Ray Brown (b); Frank Gant (d).* 8/80.

****(*) When The Sun Goes Down**

Concord CCD 4263 *Anderson; Red Holloway (ts); Gene Harris (p); Ray Brown (b); Gerryck King (d).* 8/84.

Ernestine Anderson isn't the kind of singer one expected to find on Concord: she was originally more of a rhythm-and-blues shouter, and her 1958 debut for Mercury (now back in limbo) was a typical girl-singer date in which she sounded fine on the belters and less sure with the ballads. Verve have recently issued her 1960 set *My Kinda Swing*, originally on Mercury, in their LPR series, and already she's starting to sound like the more urbane performer of later years, even though the setlist includes 'See See Rider' alongside the likes of 'All Of My Life' and 'Black Moonlight'. Ernie Wilkins's charts are on the tepid side, which doesn't assist the ballads, but band and singer each have their moments.

The typically classy situations she was placed in at Concord may on the face of it seem to be inappropriate. Yet the least satisfying session here is the most 'bluesy', *When The Sun Goes Down*, which wastes the subtleties in Anderson's voice on lesser material, with Holloway and Harris also sounding stuck in routine. *Never Make Your Move Too Soon* also has too many familiar tunes on it, but Alexander's knowing vivacity is a tonic. Since leaving Concord, there's been little to add to the discography.

Fred Anderson (born 1929)

TENOR SAXOPHONE

Anderson wasn't the first and won't be the last musician to give up active playing to run a joint of his own. Fortunately the Chicagoan has resurfaced in the '90s to re-establish a recording career that was late enough in starting but which even then seemed to stall prematurely.

***** Dark Day: Live in Verona 1979**

Atavistic 218 *Anderson; Billy Brimfield (t); Steven Palmore (b); Hamid Drake (d).* 5/79.

***** The Milwaukee Tapes: Volume 1**

Atavistic 62204 *As above, except omit Palmore; add Larry Hayrod (b).* 80.

The first of these is an important release, coming on an imprint devoted to recovering music that has previously only had limited availability. The title is slightly misleading in that the set includes material recorded back home in Chicago as well as in Italy less than a week later.

The real delight of this – apart from a glimpse of Anderson in what should have been his pomp but was a time of relative obscurity, enjoying the patronage of the small Message Records – is a first hearing of the young Hamid Drake. He resembles nothing more than Tony Williams at similar age, though there is a touch of the even more precocious Denardo Coleman as well. Trumpeter Billy Brimfield has never been widely acknowledged, though he was a respected member of the AACM collective, and bassist Steven Palmore is another fine musician. 'Dark Day' is the definitive Anderson performance, sombre and cutting by turns, packed with muscular phrases but also strangely tender and vulnerable.

The Milwaukee sessions are pretty much of a piece with the slightly earlier set, but there is a tendency to meander through solos in what sounds like a second-gear version of late Coltrane. Fred's blues sensibility surfaces more frequently than we've heard elsewhere, especially on the opening 'Ballad For Rita'. Not the cleanest or most faithful of recordings, but more than reasonable for the vintage and provenance.

*****(*) The Missing Link**
Nessa NCD 23 *Anderson; Larry Hayrod (b); Hamid Drake (d); Adam Rudolph (perc).* 9/79.

***** Vintage Duets: 1.11.1980**
Okkadisk OD 12001 *Anderson; Steve McCall (d).* 1/80.

***** Birdhouse**
Okkadisk OD 12007 *Anderson; Jim Baker (p); Harrison Bankhead (b); Hamid Drake (d).* 4/94, 2/95.

It's irritating to hear people talk about having *seen* a musician when they really mean they've *heard* him. With Fred Anderson, as with a few others, the two are more than usually connected. Not for him the upright stance and relaxed shoulders the manuals suggest. The veteran Chicagoan dips, stoops and crouches and, what's more, you can hear him do it. Anderson always sounds in pursuit of what he has to say, in struggle with the sheer intransigence of the music. If he is a missing link, as the title of the very welcome Nessa reissue suggests, what he's bridging is the gap between the spare, blues-soaked sound of early Ornette and the clean-sweep radicalism of AACM.

Anderson first made his presence felt three decades ago on fellow-saxophonist Joseph Jarman's ground-breaking Delmark record, *Song For*. Thereafter he disappeared for a decade and more, so far as a wider record-buying public was concerned, concentrating on running his South Side jazz joint, the Velvet Lounge. It was only in the '80s, and then again more securely in the '90s that he became a presence on the scene. He shares with Von Freeman a knack for sounding absolutely contemporary and completely steeped in the tradition. There is an excellent Okkadisk release under Marilyn Crispell's nominal leadership, called *Destiny* with Hamid Drake, which underlines the point perfectly.

If there is a single reference-point for his playing, it has to be Gene Ammons; it's in the phrasing and in the shape of almost every solo. Anderson is raw and spare, feeding directly off the percussion rather than the chords, which is why he never sounds quite as focused working with a piano player. Like Jug, he doesn't rush to make his point. The duets with McCall (the only other percussionist on the planet who really taps into what he's about) are as laid back and unhurried as could ever be, sometimes to the point where the listener feels excluded. It isn't so much a dialogue as two overlapping soliloquies, with McCall relying on the sheer suppleness of his deceptively straightforward count to keep Fred on his toes.

The Missing Link catches him early enough for all the components – Jug, Ornette, the AACM experiment – to be severally audible. It now reappears with a long extra track, Hamid Drake's composition 'Tabla Peace', and is certainly the disc of choice. *Birdhouse* never quite fires, perhaps because the pianist is so restrictive, though 'Like Sonny', a tribute to Sonny Stitt with no hint of pastiche, is worth the wait. The duets suffer from a poor transfer which leaves the splendid McCall sounding as if he's in another place.

***** Chicago Chamber Music**
Okka Disk 12010 *Anderson; Tatsu Aoki (b); Afif Phillard (d).* 96.

***** Fred Anderson & DKV Trio**
Okka Disk 12014 *Anderson; Ken Vandermark (reeds); Kent Kessler (b); Hamid Drake (d).* 12/96.

The DKV Trio collaboration was an important turning point in perceptions of Fred Anderson's music, since these younger players were leading something of a charge in contemporary Chicagoan jazz. 'Planet E' had been part of Fred's bag for some time (it figures on *The Milwaukee Tapes*), and it is an absolutely steaming opener. We've noted a slight tendency for Fred's performances to start gamely and then fizzle out, though whether this is the result of listener fatigue is hard to judge.

The other album has a potentially misleading title, since this is nothing to do with any neo-Third Stream project. In fact the record is very similar to Fred's recordings of the period, marked by the same qualities and occasional qualifications. Fred sometimes overplays to cover for the absence of a chordal instrument, and this is one occasion where he lapses into that fault, though he doesn't always seem entirely secure with his drummer, a relative unknown, and tries to pack the metre.

*****(*) Live At The Velvet Lounge**
Okkadisk OD 12023 *Anderson; Peter Kowald (b); Hamid Drake (d).* 6/98.

The live session comes from Anderson's own club, and it has the self-indulgent relaxation of focus that comes with a home gig. Kowald is a master, but even he seems to be taking a night off and, apart from the emotionally driven 'To Those Who Know', barely registers as anything more than an accompanist. Drake is more forceful, but he drifts into an over-emphatic grandstanding which doesn't suit the occasion. The opening track, 'Straight, But Not Straight', may well be a homage to Monk, but it lacks the master's wry refusal of self-importance. Anderson is more of a stalwart than an innovator. His impact on the Chicago scene has been considerable, and he's spoken of affectionately by two generations of players there. Not quite a players' player, but not quite defined enough for stardom.

***** Fred Anderson Quartet: Volume 1**
Asian Improv 00049 *Anderson; Billy Brimfield (t); Tatsu Aoki (b); Chad Taylor (d).* 98.

Around this time, many of Fred's admirers were pointing out his similarity to the older-school tenormen. Comparisons ranged from Gene Ammons to Hank Mobley. We were also struck by how much he seems to have drawn from the neglected John Gilmore, though how much of this is simple coincidence of vision and how much an actual influence, it is difficult to tell. The group sounds tight and well organized, and these discs rarely drift off into the slightly noodling, hectoring sound that mars some items in the Anderson discography.

*****(*) Duets 2001: Live at the Empty Bottle**
Thrill Jockey 101 *Anderson; Robert Barry (d).* 5/99.

A cracking set of mostly fairly short live duets with the former Arkestra percussionist. Fred sounds in buoyant form on the opening 'Bouncing', but tightens up his tone and phrasing somewhat as the set continues. Barry is a powerful drummer, well used to marshalling the most chaotic and anarchic of ensembles, but here he can be quite delicate, and only a recording of this quality would have captured all of his quieter figures. Anderson's reputation grows apace and sets like this can only enhance it further.

**** On the Run: Live at the Velvet Lounge**
Delmark 534 *Anderson; Tatsu Aoki (b); Hamid Drake (d).* 3/00.

Compared to the duo album with Robert Barry, this is a rather slackly conceived and executed album, overfull of saxophone posturing and rambling solo construction. In other words, not at all the kind of tight, muscular set we've come to expect from Fred. Sometimes, working your own gaff isn't the easiest gig, and it may be that Fred has his mind on other things. Either way, we suspect that he's had many a better night in the place, and it's a pity that this one should have been picked for release.

Ray Anderson (born 1952)

TROMBONE, ALTO TROMBONE, OTHER BRASS AND PERCUSSION, VOCALS

Anderson came to New York in 1972 and five years later joined Anthony Braxton's quartet, replacing his teacher, George Lewis. His work encompasses the avant-garde, jazz and funk, all of it handled in an old-fashioned tailgating style that is usually irresistible.

***** Right Down Your Alley**
Soul Note 121087-2 *Anderson; Mark Helias (b); Gerry Hemingway (d).* 2/84.

Ray Anderson always gives the impression that he goes to work with a smile. Whether playing in a – more or less – straight jazz context, or with the relative freedom of the BassDrumBone group with Mark Helias and Gerry Hemingway, or most obviously with his R&B unit, Slickaphonics, there is an exuberance and verve about his playing which is impossible to resist.

The trio with Helias and Hemingway is much freer and more open-ended, with a greater emphasis on blurts, smears and huge portamento effects. Like George Lewis, Anderson favours a horn with an F-key, a thumb-operated valve which allows him to drop the sound a fourth as required, and there's a depth to the sound that here and there almost suggests a bass instrument. Timbrally, it's engaging enough, but *Right Down Your Alley* is a drier and more demanding listen than the Enja record.

***** It Just So Happens**
Enja 5037 *Anderson; Stanton Davis (t); Perry Robinson (cl); Bob Stewart (tba); Mark Desser (b); Ronnie Burrage (d).* 1–2/87.

Reissued in Enja's Vintage Series, this isn't one of Anderson's classics, but it does explore some of the jazz matters which particularly tickle him – Dixieland, brass bands, and the way they can be intermingled with the jollier side of the avant-garde. The band isn't really focused, as if their leader's instructions mystified them a bit, but they all play gamely enough.

*****(*) Funkorific**
Enja ENJ 9340-2 *Anderson; Amina Claudine Myers (p, org, v); Jerome Harris (g); Lonnie Plaxico (b); Tommy Campbell (d).* 1/98.

****** Where Home Is**
Enja ENJ 9366-2 *Anderson; Lew Soloff (t); Matt Perine (sou); Bobby Previte (d).* 11/98.

The disappearance of Anderson's hat ART albums, *Azurety*, *Cheer Up* and *Slide Ride*, leave a hole in the catalogue; who knows when and whether any of these will reappear? These more recent sessions don't quite plug the gap, but they do go some way towards it.

What colour is lapis lazuli? Blue, blue, blue. *Funkorific* is blue to its core, a blues album of the fastest and most evocative dye. Signing up Amina Claudine Myers was a brilliant notion. She is the key element in the new Lapis Lazuli band, creating funky but edgy accompaniments for Anderson's latest extension of the Slickaphonics concept, a roots band with a toe dipped in the avant-garde. 'Hammond Eggs' and 'Willie & Muddy' are as down-home as it gets, while the opening 'Pheromonical' shows how much Anderson and Myers have drawn from stylistically more experimental settings.

The Pocket Brass Band featured on *Where Home Is* consciously closes the distance between the early days of jazz and the contemporary, saxophone-haunted scene. Moving on from the all-trombone front line which made *Slideride* for hat ART, this line-up calls on the fierce, stabbing attack of Lew Soloff and the eclectic bass lines of Matt Perrine, who has worked in every genre from straight brass to reggae. 'The Alligatory Abagua' recalls previous bands, a strutting, confident performance that is deeply rooted in brass-band idiom. There are absences to regret in Anderson's discography but, as long as he turns out albums as strong as these, there is going to be little time to mourn them.

Reid Anderson

BASS

Contemporary bassist at work on the current New York scene. He is now renowned as one of the three members of The Bad Plus.

*****(*) Dirty Show Tunes**
Fresh Sound FSNT 030 *Anderson; Mark Turner (ts); Ethan Iverson (p); Jorge Rossy (d).* 5/97.

****** Abolish Bad Architecture**
Fresh Sound FSNT 062 *As above, except Jeff Ballard (d) replaces Rossy.* 5/99.

Despite the title of the first disc (also Anderson's publishing name), no show tunes, dirty or otherwise, and not a lot to bed these down among the conventions of tenor-and-rhythm either. Anderson writes material that continually changes its shape as it goes forward. The harmonic structure of each piece is elusive: it never seems to be made particularly manifest, and there's a feeling of clear freedom even as each component seems to lead inevitably to the next. Tempos evolve out of the collective playing, slowing or accelerating as the internal dynamics demand. The music is more melodious than tied to set lines of melody. It's at least fascinating, often utterly compelling: listen to the absolutely extraordinary 'Mystery Girl' on *Abolish Bad Architecture*, which is not a ballad in feel but is as serenely contemplative as any conventional bit of post-bop lyricism, yet from another, oblique world. It helps Anderson that he has two magnificent contributors in Turner and Iverson, players who are themselves very out of the ordinary, as their own discs suggest. The second disc is the superior one because the empathy seems even more attuned, and Ballard is a less conventionally swinging drummer than Rossy, and he suits this unconventional music better (Ballard even uses relatively simple rock patterns at times, as on 'Hommage; Mahler'). This is one place jazz is going next.

****** The Vastness Of Space**
Fresh Sound FSNT 096 *Anderson; Andrew D'Angelo (as); Bill McHenry (ts); Ben Monder (g); Marlon Browden (d).* 3/00.

Why is Anderson's record and group different from so many other, seemingly similar records and groups? Is it his book of tunes, all morning-fresh yet naggingly familiar in many of their turnings? His mix of inscrutability and open, free sounds? His band of contrary personalities who manage to play as a seamless ensemble? The way drummer Browden plays simple propulsion without once being simplistic? The way 'Reclusive' has no improvising, yet feels entirely spontaneous? The way the pale timbres of McHenry and D'Angelo conceal an often terrific ferocity? The way Monder shifts in and out of focus, playing guitar, or piano on guitar, or saxophone on guitar, and making it all work? The way the leader himself roves around the rest of the music, the melodic heart as well as the rhythmical one? Sustained across almost 65 minutes and recorded with an unglossy immediacy, the impression is of a kind of workshop-music, maybe a bit like some of the earliest and most ingenious George Russell small-group records – but something that could only have been played just moments ago.

Ulf Andersson (born 1940)

TENOR SAXOPHONE

Veteran Swedish modernist, a sideman with Eje Thelin in the '60s and a journeyman leader since, often seen with Monica Zetterlund.

***** Flying Carpet**
Four Leaf Clover FLC CD 1673 *Andersson; Marten Lundgren (t); Ewan Svensson (g); Hans Backenroth (b); Rune Carlsson (d).* 4/98.

Andersson leads this strong sounding band through 11 originals, and along with lots of meaty blowing the composing has a neat lyrical turn which softens the lines in the music. Two other key virtues are Svensson's guitar – used as harmonic filler in the ensemble but with uncommon deftness – and the beautiful drumming of Carlsson; whom the leader says has the 'capacity of being able to create a feeling of weightlessness, a "flying carpet" feeling'. A very satisfying 65 minutes of music.

Luke Annesley

ALTO SAXOPHONE

Young British hopeful.

***** Beginning**
FMR CD93 *Annesley; Dave Cliff (g); Simon Thorpe (b); Matt Skelton (d).* 02.

There's no pretension about the title. This is very much a first shot for the young but already seasoned professional who favours a Cool School approach and a highly melodic way of playing standards. Cliff is the secret weapon, not just on the originals 'Waiting' and 'Dishevelled', but also on the standards – two Cole Porter tunes and a wonderfully unexpected revision of 'Daisy, Daisy'. There's bound to be better to come, but this is a fine start.

The Antique Six

GROUP

British trad, well weathered.

****(*) Roadshow**
PEK Sound PKCD-132 *Alan Bateman (t, cl, as, v); Keith Hockin (tb); Dick Chapman (cl, ts, v); Peter Long (bj); Jackie Chapman (b); Richard Rose (d); Ted Higham (v).* 6/99.

This sextet of senior tradsters make a fair go at putting together what is presumably a souvenir of their live shows. In their favour is a programme of mostly unhackneyed material, Jackie Chapman's usefully sprightly electric bass lines, and some spirited ensemble playing. Against: solos are a very mixed bag (Bateman, who looks like the baby of the group, completely loses his way on 'King Of The Mardi Gras'), and their very name is asking for trouble. Higham shows up only to sing on 'Miss Jenny's Ball', but he needn't have bothered. Recorded in Swindon.

****(*) New Orleans To Chicago**
A6CD05 *Tony Billingsley (t, v); Keith Hockin (tb); Dick Chapman (cl, saxes, v); Clinton Sedgley (bj, g); Jackie Chapman (b); Graham Smith (d).* 12/01.

**** Six Of One Half A Dozen Of Another**
A6CD06 *As above, except Chris Mercer (c) replaces Billingsley; add Richard Leach (tb).* n.d.

The Antiques continue on their merry way. They're on to their third trumpet/cornet man in three years with the third CD, but the horns continue to be their weak link: Jackie Chapman is still the star of the band! This time there are too many hackneyed tunes on both discs – they really can't compete with the Stomp Off division of traditional outfits at this level – and the brass playing simply isn't good enough.

Jimmy Archey (1902–67)

TROMBONE

In New York from 1927 and played in many of the major big bands in the '30s. Later, he was more familiarly seen in revivalist bands but could always move easily between trad, swing and mainstream styles.

***** Dr Jazz Vol. 4**
Storyville STCD 6044 *Archey; Henry Goodwin (t); Benny Waters (cl, ss, as); Dick Wellstood (p); George 'Pops' Foster (b); Tommy Benford (d).* 1–4/52.

**** Reunion**
GHB BCD-310 *Archey; Punch Miller (t); Albert Burbank (cl); Dick Griffith (bj); Dick McCarthy (b); Sammy Penn (d).* 2/67.

Rare examples of this redoubtable 'bone man as leader. The Storyville disc is from the *Dr Jazz* series of radio broadcasts, and though as usual the band was encouraged to play overheated Dixieland, some excellent moments survive. Waters, not often in the limelight at this stage of his career, is in top form, and the rarely heard Goodwin stands comfortably beside the leader.

Archey was from Virginia, but the *Reunion* with a group of New Orleans players actually took place in Connecticut. The material is bedraggled – and so, alas, is much of the playing: Burbank's agile phrasing is flawed by his terribly squeaky tone, and Punch Miller was having an indifferent day. Archey's spirited, melodic solos are much more encouraging, though, and the rhythm players make sure that the music clatters along.

Julian Arguëlles (born 1966)

TENOR SAXOPHONE

Emerged from the Loose Tubes collective as a singular musician in his own right. Has often worked with brother Steve but is asserting himself as a group leader and recording artist.

***** Home Truths**

Babel BDV 9503 *Arguëlles; Mike Walker (g); Steve Swallow (b); Martin France (d).* 5/95.

The Arguëlles brothers – Julian and Steve – are, along with the Mondesirs, the Traceys and the Bancrofts in Scotland, the closest thing to a significant family dynasty in British jazz. Both are richly talented; both have created music of considerable individuality. *Home Truths* is an encouragingly personal sax-and-rhythm date for the British saxophonist. Abjuring obvious role-models has apparently led him in the direction of such players as Warne Marsh and some of the modern European masters. If Arguëlles is a Good Thing, then so, too, is Oliver Weindling's Babel label, which has dedicated itself to some of the most creative music around. It is a measure of the reputation of young Brits like Arguëlles and guitarist Mike Walker that Steve Swallow should find time in a busy schedule to come and record a session like this. To be frank, he makes it. Weaving in and around both Walker and Arguëlles, he creates a skein of sound that is almost too beguiling, and the listener may end up pulled away from the main action.

*****(*) Scapes**

Babel BDV 9674 *Arguëlles; Steve Arguëlles (d, perc).* 95.

The duos on *Scapes* are brief, clever, funny and thoroughly musical. Julian's multi-instrumentalism has never been a pose, and increasingly he has developed a definite character on all his instruments. Steve's contributions are more than functional. He inhabits the music and propels it at the same time, turning the shortest tracks into mini-odysseys that go in unexpected directions. A fine, comradely album.

***** Skull View**

Babel BDV 9719 *Arguëlles; Mark Bassey (tb); Django Bates (thn); Iain Dixon (ts, bcl, cl); Mario Laginha (p); Mike Walker (g); Steve Watts (b); Martin France (d).* 96.

Skull View is ambitiously conceived and contoured, an album that suggests Arguëlles will develop into a fine composer for larger units. His command of small detail is matched by a generous musical sweep, and there is a mature exuberance even to pieces which seem to flirt with the macabre humour that one thought was left behind in Loose Tubes days.

****** Escapade**

Provocateur PVC 1019 *Arguëlles; Django Bates (thn); Iain Dixon (ts, cl, bcl); Mario Laginha (p); Mike Walker (g); Steve Watts (b); Martin France (d).* 6/99.

This is one of the best British jazz albums of recent memory, a subtle, compelling record which repays the closest attention or one that can be put on simply for the groove. 'The Pow Wow' is reminiscent of things John Surman and John McLaughlin were doing at the time of *Extrapolation*, and the whole album has all the serious, insouciant perversity of those days, locked into a compelling groove but also brimming over with ideas.

Guitarist Walker has a hefty reputation on the scene but one which, until now, has not seemed to transfer easily to record. The delicacy of his understated chordal introduction to the brief '9 Grammes Of Lead' is a measure of how subtle he can be. Mark Bassey's mournful brass-band trombone and Django's now familiar peckhorn lines are singularly adapted to Arguëlles's slower compositions, but even when the tempo is frenetic, as on the scratch 'Coffee And Diesel' (which might almost be a Tim Berne out-take), the band is ideally attuned to the material. Pianist Laginha is a revelation, though occasionally he and Walker seem to have each other's charts.

***** As Above So Below**

Provocateur PVC 1033 *Arguëlles; Henry Lowther (t, flhn); Jim Rattigan (fr hn); Stan Sulzmann (f, af); Iain Dixon (cl, bcl); Mike Walker (g); Steve Watts (b); Martin France (d); strings.* 5/03.

Arguëlles has been in outstanding form, live and on record, since a recent move to Scotland, but this new record for Provocateur seems discouragingly tame and even unambitious after the excellent *Escapade*. The string parts are nicely done, the ensembles are sleekly tailored, but while the saxophonist plays well, the impression is of a curiously introverted assemblage of notions: the players seem engaged, but there's little enough to do the same for the listener. Longer acquaintance may help.

Steve Arguëlles (born 1963)

DRUMS

British drummer/percussionist, brother of saxophonist Julian, who emerged as part of the Loose Tubes collective in the '80s and has latterly based himself in Paris; numerous projects include The Recyclers.

***** Blue Moon In A Function Room**

Babel BDV 9402 *Arguëlles; Stuart Hall (g, v); Billy Jenkins (g); Steve Watts (b).* 90.

***** Busy Listening**

Babel BDV 9406 *Arguëlles; Julian Arguëlles (as); Stuart Hall (g, v); Huw Warren (acc); Mick Hutton (b).* 9/93.

So richly and sympathetically has Britain nourished and nurtured talent like Arguëlles's that he has had to move to France to find an acceptable amount of paid work. A familiar story, and a very galling one. It has taken Steve somewhat out of the recording picture at home. The earliest of these goes back some way and is still a little self-conscious, bearing the stamp of Jenkins's maverick genius. Items like 'Vision On', theme music to a British television programme for deaf children, seem unlikely in a jazz context, alongside 'Tiger Rag', 'Lady Be Good' (which is segued with 'Johnny B. Goode') and 'Ruby (Don't Take Your Love To Town)'. Hugely entertaining, but not by any means as interesting as what Arguëlles has done more recently with The Recyclers (who are reviewed separately) and on *Busy Listening*, both of which are splendidly mature but not solemn, and packed with ideas without becoming po-faced. Arguëlles lays down a crackling groove for his colleagues on both sets. Some of the laddishness has worn off, and the music is all the better for it. We could do with a new record from Steve at this point.

Lil Hardin Armstrong (1898–1971)

PIANO, VOCAL

Born in Memphis, Lillian Hardin demonstrated pianos at a Chicago store before working with some of the best bands in the city, eventually joining King Oliver and meeting her future husband, Louis Armstrong. She helped drive his career early on, but they eventually divorced in 1938. She led groups of her own and was house pianist at Decca for a spell. From the '40s onwards she was a familiar presence once again on the Chicago club scene.

***** Lil Hardin Armstrong And Her Swing Orchestra 1936–1940**

Classics 564 *Armstrong; Joe Thomas, Shirley Clay, Ralph Muzillo, Johnny McGee, Reunald Jones, Jonah Jones (t); Al Philburn, J. C. Higginbotham (tb); Buster Bailey, Tony Zimmers (cl); Don Stovall (as); Russell Johns, Prince Robinson, Robert Carroll, Chu Berry (ts); Frank Froeba, James Sherman, Teddy Cole (p); Arnold Adams, Huey Long, Dave Barbour (g); John Frazier, Wellman Braud, Haig Stephens (b); O'Neil Spencer, Sam Weiss, George 'Pops' Foster, Manzie Johnson (d); Midge Williams, Hilda Rogers (v).* 10/36–3/40.

Although she was a real modernist in her youth, the former Mrs Armstrong never advanced very much as a piano player, which may be why keyboard duties were entrusted to others on most of these sessions. But her vocal talents are still likeable, and on these now largely forgotten sides she comes on like a precursor of Nellie Lutcher and other, vaguely racy, post-war singers. The accompaniments offer a rough distillation of small-band swing and rather older styles, suggested by the presence of such veterans of the '20s as Robinson and Clay, alongside the more modernistic Thomas and Berry. Titles such as '(I'm On A) Sit-down Strike For Rhythm' have a self-explanatory charm, and there's a more distinctive jazz content in the typically hot and fluent playing of Bailey. On the final, 1940 date, Mrs Armstrong returns to the piano and leaves the singing to others. A mixed bag as far as reproduction goes, but mostly dubbed from decent originals.

***** Lil Hardin Armstrong – Chicago: The Living Legends**

Original Jazz Classics OJC 1823 *Armstrong; Bill Martin, Roi Nabors, Eddie Smith (t); Preston Jackson, Al Wynn (tb); Darnell Howard, Franz Jackson (cl); George 'Pops' Foster (b); Booker Washington (d).* 9/61.

This group of old-timers plays with astonishing vitality, even mania, on some of these tracks. 'Royal Garden Blues' has seldom had such a shaking-down as it gets here: Howard's clarinet goes from a woody moan to a near-shriek, and the trumpeters all take their turn to rattle the roof. There is also some solid blues, an enjoyable feature for Lil's singing on 'Clip Joint', and 'Boogie Me', where she duets with Washington and makes one wonder why she didn't play piano like that with the Hot Five. Hardly subtle, but much merriment.

Louis Armstrong (1901–71)

TRUMPET, CORNET, VOCAL

Born in New Orleans, Armstrong learned the cornet after being sent to a waifs' home in 1913. By 1919 he was already a formidable player, and he began recording with King Oliver in 1923, as second cornet. He went to New York a year later and joined the Fletcher Henderson orchestra, then he began recording under his own name in 1925 with the Hot Five and Hot Seven for Okeh Records in Chicago. By the end of the '20s he was a great star as a soloist, and his playing had influenced everybody in jazz, shifting the emphasis from group playing to solo improvising. He also created a vocal style for all jazz singers. In the '30s he worked in a big-band context and began touring with what had been the Luis Russell Orchestra in 1935. In 1947, his career at a comparatively low ebb despite Hollywood appearances and an invincible personality, he switched to small groups and began leading his All Stars, a sextet format he remained with for the rest of his touring career. In the '60s he had worldwide pop hits with the likes of 'Hello Dolly' and 'What A Wonderful World'. Though illness left him faltering at times in his later years, he was always the greatest ambassador in jazz and he remains its best-loved individual figure.

♕ ** Hot Fives & Sevens**

JSP LOUISBOX 100 *As JSP discs, listed individually below.* 25–30.

Armstrong's music is one of the cornerstones of jazz and, while his most famous records – principally, the small-group sides made under the names The Hot Five and The Hot Seven – are now antiquarian in terms of their place in the jazz chronology, his playing remains a marvel. While we are envious of any who are discovering the likes of 'Wild Man Blues' or 'Tight Like This' for the first time, we acknowledge that the sound of the records – particularly the earliest, acoustic dates by The Hot Five from 1925 – can seem as 'difficult' to ears raised on digital sound as anything from the pre-LP era. Considering he was playing with his peers – Kid Ory and Johnny Dodds were two of the most respected performers in their field – the group's basic sound seems unexpectedly rough and unsophisticated, at least on the earlier sessions. Yet when one focuses on Armstrong himself, shortcomings seem to fall away in the face of his youthful mastery. Not yet 25 and still playing cornet when the sessions for OKeh started, he is still trying out for greatness, even if his spell with Fletcher Henderson a year earlier had already alerted the growing jazz community to his incipient brilliance. Earlier pieces like 'Jazz Lips' or 'Cornet Chop Suey' have a rough-and-ready quality which Armstrong's blossoming power either barges past or transcends, and although there is a degree of vaudeville in his music already – exemplified by pieces like 'Heebie Jeebies' and 'Muskrat Ramble', with their comic studio routines – a lot of the time he elevates his surroundings through sheer charisma. By the time of the Hot Seven dates, beginning in 1927, with Dodds assuming a second-voice role that has even Armstrong compelled to play at his best, the music seems mystical in its poetry and majesty. 'Potato Head

Blues', with its incredible stop-time solo, the astounding improvisation on 'Wild Man Blues' and the glittering blues playing on 'Willie The Weeper' are but three examples of the artistry that at that moment was reducing everyone else in jazz to a bit-player. By the time of the 'second' series of Hot Fives, with Earl Hines arriving on piano, Armstrong was already approaching the stature of a concerto soloist, a role he would play more or less throughout the next decade, which makes these final small-group sessions something like a reluctant farewell to jazz's first golden age. Since Hines is also magnificent on these discs (and their insouciant exuberance is a marvel on the duet showstopper, 'Weather Bird'), the results seem like eavesdropping on great men speaking almost quietly among themselves. There is nothing in jazz finer or more moving than the playing on 'West End Blues', 'Tight Like This', 'Beau Koo Jack' and 'Muggles'.

It should go almost without saying that we consider these tracks indispensable in any jazz collection. They have been reissued many times over the years, and OKeh's excellent studio sound has been faithfully transferred to a number of LP editions from the '60s onwards. We are delighted to acknowledge the superlative four-disc edition remastered by John R. T. Davies for JSP which should be generally available. Besides the basic Hot Five and Seven library, they also include such pieces as a Butterbeans and Susie duet which the group play behind, two tracks with Carroll Dickerson's Savoyagers, the classic 'Knockin' A Jug' date with Jack Teagarden and Eddie Lang, and the first 1929–30 sessions where Armstrong plays in front of the Luis Russell band. The four discs are available separately, but they can be bought in a four-disc slipcase to which we must inevitably accord a crown rating.

CORE COLLECTION

♛ ** The Complete Hot Five And Hot Seven Recordings**
Columbia C4K 63527 4CD *As listed below.* 25–30.

Columbia were for a long time mystifyingly neglectful of these great recordings, but in 2000 they finally released their own 'definitive' edition. There has been some controversy among Armstrong scholars as to whether this or the JSP is the superior edition, a matter which we will not take sides on: to our ears, while there are numerous differences along the way, both sets do a remarkable job on the material, and it's hard to see anyone being disappointed with either. Columbia certainly score heavily with the magnificently produced book which comes with the CDs. In addition, they include a few rare takes and offer 'Cornet Chop Suey' at two different speeds (and hence in two different keys). Delightful to find all this music so comprehensively available at last.

****** Hot Fives And Hot Sevens Vol. 1**
JSP CD 312 *Armstrong; Kid Ory (tb); Johnny Dodds (cl, as); Lil Hardin Armstrong (p); Johnny St Cyr (bj); Butterbeans & Susie, May Alix (v).* 11/25–11/26.

****** Louis Armstrong 1925–1926**
Classics 600 *As above.* 11/25–11/26.

****** Hot Fives And Hot Sevens Vol. 2**
JSP CD 313 *As above, except add Bill Wilson (c), Honore Dutrey, John Thomas (tb), Boyd Atkins (cl, ss, as), Albert Washington (ts), Earl Hines (p), Lonnie Johnson (g), Rip Bassett (bj, g), Pete Briggs (bb), Baby Dodds, Tubby Hall (d).* 5–12/27.

****** Hot Fives And Hot Sevens Vol. 3**
JSP CD 314 *Armstrong; Homer Hobson (t); Fred Robinson, Jack Teagarden (tb); Jimmy Strong (cl, ts); Don Redman (cl, as); Bert Curry, Crawford Wetherington (as); Happy Caldwell (ts); Earl Hines, Joe Sullivan (p); Carroll Dickerson (vn); Eddie Lang (g); Mancy Cara (bj, v); Dave Wilborn (bj, g); Pete Briggs (tba); Zutty Singleton, Kaiser Marshall (d).* 5–12/27.

****** Louis Armstrong 1926–1927**
Classics 585 *As above.* 11/26–12/27.

****** Hot Fives and Hot Sevens Vol. 4**
JSP CD 315 *Armstrong; Homer Hobson, Henry 'Red' Allen, Otis Johnson (t); J. C. Higginbotham, Fred Robinson (tb); Jimmy Strong (cl, ts); Charlie Holmes, Albert Nicholas, William Blue (cl, as); Bert Curry, Crawford Wetherington (as); Teddy Hill (ts); Carroll Dickerson (vn); Gene Anderson (p, cel); Luis Russell, Buck Washington (p); Lonnie Johnson, Will Johnson (g); Eddie Condon, Mancy Cara (bj); Pete Briggs (tba); George 'Pops' Foster (b); Zutty Singleton, Paul Barbarin (d); Hoagy Carmichael (v).* 3/29–4/30.

****** The 25 Greatest Hot Fives And Hot Sevens**
ASV AJA 5171 *Basically as above.* 25–29.

***** Fireworks**
Dreyfus FDM 36710-2 *As various discs above.* 28.

***** Heebie Jeebies**
Naxos Jazz Legends 8.120541 *As discs above.* 25–30.

****** The Complete Hot Five And Hot Seven Recordings Vol. 1**
Columbia CK 86999 *As discs above.* 11/25-11/26

****** The Complete Hot Five And Hot Seven Recordings Vol. 2**
Columbia CK 87010 *As discs above.* 11/26-12/27.

****** The Complete Hot Five And Hot Seven Recordings Vol. 3**
Columbia CK 87011 *As discs above.* 12/27-12/28.

Inevitably, this great music has become available in numerous other editions. These are among the ones you're most likely to encounter. Classics have done their usual job, but their editions pale next to the other sets. The ASV disc isn't far behind the best in terms of sound and, as a single-disc representation of some of the best in the series, this works pretty well.

Fireworks takes the interesting tack of including only sides which Armstrong cut in 1928, 'his richest vintage in masterpieces'. Unfortunately we are less happy with the sound than we are with many of the reissues in this usually strong Dreyfus series: too much echo. Naxos chip in with their own selection of 18 tracks from 1925–30, and it's a nice budget release, if no more than a pendant to the full editions. Columbia have pared their four-disc set back to three individual items, minus the various alternates and rarities. It plays very well.

****** Louis Armstrong & His Orchestra 1928–1929**
Classics 570 *Personnel as listed under appropriate dates above.* 6/28–3/29.

****** Louis Armstrong & His Orchestra 1929–1930**
Classics 557 *Armstrong; Homer Hobson (t); Fred Robinson, Jack Teagarden, J. C. Higginbotham (tb); Jimmy Strong (cl, ts); Albert Nicholas, Charlie Holmes, Bert Curry, William Blue, Crawford Wethington (as); Happy Cauldwell (ts); Joe*

Sullivan, Luis Russell, Buck Washington (p); Eddie Lang, Lonnie Johnson (g); Eddie Condon (bj); George 'Pops' Foster (b); Paul Barbarin, Kaiser Marshall (d); Hoagy Carmichael (v). 3/29–5/30.

****** Louis Armstrong & His Orchestra 1930–1931**
Classics 547 *Armstrong; Leon Elkins, George Orendorff, Harold Scott (t); Lawrence Brown, Luther Graven (tb); Leon Herriford, Willie Stark, Marvin Johnson (as); Les Hite (as, bs); Charlie Jones (cl, ts); Wiliam Franz (ts); Harvey Brooks, Henry Prince (p); Bill Perkins, Ceele Burke (bj, g); Reggie Jones (tba); Joe Bailey (b); Lionel Hampton (d, vib).* 7/30–4/31.

****** Louis Armstrong & His Orchestra 1931–1932**
Classics 536 *Armstrong; Zilmer Randolph (t); Preston Jackson (tb); George James (cl, ss, as); Lester Boone (cl, as); Albert Washington (cl, ts); Charlie Alexander (p); Mike McKendrick (g, bj); John Lindsay (b); Tubby Hall (d).* 4/31–3/32.

Following the final Hot Five records, Armstrong recorded almost exclusively as a soloist in front of big bands, at least until the formation of the All Stars in the '40s. Although the records became much more formal in shape – most of them are recordings of contemporary pop tunes, opened by an Armstrong vocal and climaxing in a stratospheric solo – the finest of them showcase Louis as grandly as anything he'd already recorded, and they certainly provide him with his best opportunities to sing. Since his vocal stylings were becoming at least as influential as his trumpet playing, it was critical that he get some of the best tunes of the day – and at this stage in his career, he did. Classics 557 covers the period when Armstrong was fronting the Luis Russell band. 'Black And Blue', 'Dallas Blues' and 'After You've Gone' offer superb improvisations against bland but functional backdrops and, while some of the sheer daring has gone out of Armstrong's playing, he's become more poised, more serenely powerful than before. Finer still, though, are the records made in Los Angeles in 1930 with, among others, the young Lionel Hampton. There are few Armstrong performances superior to 'Body And Soul', 'I'm A Ding Dong Daddy From Dumas' and 'Memories Of You', where his singing is as integral and inventive as his trumpet-playing, and the sequence culminates in the moving and transcendent performance of 'Sweethearts On Parade'. The 1931–2 sessions find him in front of another anonymous orchestra and, although arrangements and performances are again merely competent, they serve to throw the leader's own contributions into sharper relief, with 'Star Dust', 'Lawd, You Made The Night Too Long' and 'Chinatown, My Chinatown' among the outstanding tracks. These were his final recordings for OKeh before a move to Victor in 1933.

The Classics sequence has the merit of uninterrupted chronological presentation at an attractive price and, while their transfers aren't always of the finest, there are no serious problems with the overall sound. As noted above, some of the earlier tracks are on the fourth disc in the JSP edition.

****** Louis Armstrong & His Orchestra 1932–1933**
Classics 529 *Armstrong; Louis Bacon, Louis Hunt, Billy Hicks, Charlie Gaines, Elmer Whitlock, Zilmer Randolph (t); Charlie Green, Keg Johnson (tb); Pete Clark, Scoville Brown, George Oldham (cl, as); Edgar Sampson (as, vn); Louis Jordan, Arthur Davey (as); Budd Johnson (cl, ts); Elmer Williams, Ellsworth Blake (ts); Don Kirkpatrick, Wesley Robinson, Teddy Wilson (p); Mike McKendrick (bj, g); John Trueheart (g); Edgar Hayes, Bill Oldham (bb, b); Elmer James (b); Chick Webb, Benny Hill, Yank Porter (d).* 12/32–4/33.

Armstrong's Victor records of 1932–3 are among his most majestic statements. If he had simplified his style, the breadth of his tone and seeming inevitability of timing and attack have been fashioned into an invincible creation: the way he handles 'I Gotta Right To Sing The Blues' or 'Basin Street Blues' makes them seem like conclusive offerings from jazz's greatest virtuoso. Even so, weaker material was already starting to creep into his repertoire, and it planted the seeds for the often unfortunate choices of tune that would beset his years at Decca. The Classics series continues apace and gathers in most of the Victor material on to one CD.

****** Louis Armstrong & His Orchestra 1934–1936**
Classics 509 *Armstrong; Jack Hamilton, Leslie Thompson, Leonard Davis, Gus Aiken, Louis Bacon, Bunny Berigan, Bob Mayhew (t); Lionel Guimaraes, Harry White, Jimmy Archey, Al Philburn (tb); Pete Duconge (cl, as); Sid Trucker (cl, bs); Henry Tyre, Henry Jones, Charlie Holmes, Phil Waltzer (as); Alfred Pratt, Bingie Madison, Greely Walton, Paul Ricci (ts); Herman Chittison, Luis Russell, Fulton McGrath (p); Maceo Jefferson, Lee Blair, Dave Barbour (g); German Artango, George 'Pops' Foster, Pete Peterson (b); Oliver Tynes, Paul Barbarin, Stan King (d).* 10/34–2/36.

*****(*) Rhythm Saved The World**
GRP 051602-2 *Largely as above.* 10/35–2/36.

*****(*) Louis Armstrong & His Orchestra 1936–1937**
Classics 512 *As above, except add Snub Mosley, Bobby Byrne, Joe Yukl, Don Mattison (tb), Jimmy Dorsey, Jack Stacey (cl, as), Fud Livingston, Skeets Herfurt (cl, ts), Bobby Van Eps (p), George Archer, Harry Baty (g, v), Roscoe Hillman (g), Sam Koki (stg), Andy Iona (uke, v), Jim Taft, Joe Nawahi (b), Ray McKinley, Lionel Hampton (d), Bing Crosby, Frances Langford, The Mills Brothers (v).* 2/36–4/37.

****** Louis Armstrong & His Orchestra 1937–1938**
Classics 515 *Armstrong; Shelton Hemphill, Louis Bacon, Henry 'Red' Allen (t); George Matthews, George Washington, J. C. Higginbotham, Wilbur De Paris (tb); Pete Clark, Charlie Holmes, Rupert Cole (as); Albert Nicholas, Bingie Madison (cl, ts); Luis Russell (p); Lee Blair (g); George 'Pops' Foster, Red Callender (b); Paul Barbarin (d); The Mills Brothers (v).* 6/37–5/38.

*****(*) Louis Armstrong & His Orchestra 1938–1939**
Classics 523 *As above, except add Bob Cusumano, Johnny McGee, Otis Johnson, Frank Zullo, Grady Watts, Sonny Dunham (t); Al Philburn, Murray McEachern, Russell Rauch, Pee Wee Hunt (tb); Sid Stoneburn (cl); Art Ralston, Clarence Hutchenrider (as); Pat Davis, Dan D'Andrea, Joe Garland (ts); Kenny Sargent (bs); Nat Jaffe, Howard Hall (p); Jack Blanchette, Dave Barbour (g); Haig Stephens, Stan Dennis (b); Sam Weiss, Big Sid Catlett, Tony Briglia (d).* 5/38–4/39.

***** Heart Full Of Rhythm Vol. 2**
GRP 051620-2 *As above discs.* 4/36–12/38.

***** Louis Armstrong 1939–1940**
Classics 615 *Armstrong; Shelton Hemphill, Otis Johnson, Henry 'Red' Allen, Bernard Flood (t); Wilbur De Paris, George Washington, J. C. Higginbotham (tb); Charlie Holmes, Rupert Cole (cl, as); Joe Garland, Bingie Madison (ts); Luis Russell (p); Lee Blair (g); George 'Pops' Foster (b); Big Sid Catlett (d); The Mills Brothers (v).* 4/39–4/40.

*****(*) Louis Armstrong 1940–1942**

Classics 685 *As above, except add Gene Prince, Frank Galbreath (t), Claude Jones, Norman Greene, Henderson Chambers, James Whitney (tb), Sidney Bechet (cl, ss), Carl Frye (as), Prince Robinson (cl, ts), Bernard Addison, Lawrence Lucie (g), John Simmons, Hayes Alvis, Wellman Braud (b), Zutty Singleton (d).* 5/40–4/42.

Armstrong's Decca recordings in the '30s have been a maligned group of records, always the least favoured part of his career. This is both a right and a wrong view. While there are many throwaway songs and plain bad ideas – even Louis couldn't do much with 'She's The Daughter Of A Planter From Havana' and its sorry ilk – he does rise above the circumstances much as Fats Waller and Billie Holiday do in the same period: the sheer *sound* of Armstrong, whether singing or playing trumpet, is exhilarating, and there are merits in these sessions which have often been overlooked. Decca's studio sound is often very handsome and they caught a silvery quality in Armstrong's tone which is not often apparent on his other records. He was playing with a particularly steely finesse at this point, far from the bubbling genius of a decade earlier but not yet the benign maestro of a decade hence. There is also his singing: whatever the lyric, Pops gives it his full measure.

The sequential Classics issues have to compete with the GRP reissues, which collectors will want for some rare alternative takes. The 1934–5 Classics disc includes a memorable session made in Paris with a local band including the very fine pianist, Herman Chittison, with a terrific 'St Louis Blues'; from there, Armstrong is backed mostly by a Luis Russell band, and it performs very creditably, with some members stepping forward for occasional solos. (This seems a good point to mention *Louis Armstrong And Friends*, a compilation in Emarcy's excellent 'Jazz In Paris' series of reissues, 013979-2. It includes the seven titles from this date and adds other '30s sessions by Freddy Johnson, Arthur Briggs, Danny Polo, Greta Keller and even a title by Marlene Dietrich – a good choice for anyone collecting Armstrong material from sources other than the Classics issues.) 1936–7 includes two tremendous pieces in 'Swing That Music' and 'Mahogany Hall Stomp' as well as a peculiar meeting with a Hawaiian group and two dates with the Mills Brothers. The fine session from January 1938 is on the next disc, with Albert Nicholas almost stealing the occasion on 'Struttin' With Some Barbecue' until Louis's own solo. The 1938–9 record has a session with the Casa Loma Orchestra, another with a rather white-toned gospel group, the lovely 'My Walking Stick' with the Mills Brothers and a concluding date which remakes 'West End Blues' and Don Redman's 'Save It, Pretty Mama'. Classics 615 has some miserable stuff of the order of 'Me And Brother Bill' but peaks on a new 'Confessin'', a fine 'Wolverine Blues' and a stunning new 'Sweethearts On Parade'. The final disc in the sequence, Classics 685, is again rather dated, although it includes the complete reunion date with Bechet from May 1940 and has a majestic 'When It's Sleepy Time Down South' – not the last track, but a suitable climax. We must award all these high marks, if only for the occasions when the material, music and Armstrong himself are all strong. The transfers are consistent enough.

The first GRP compilation takes a look at one of the most enjoyable of this run of sessions, from 1935–6, with 'I've Got My Fingers Crossed', 'Solitude' and 'I'm Putting All My Eggs In One Basket' among the standouts. Having creamed off the best of those, the second disc, *Heart Full Of Rhythm*, is a little less consistent, though there are still half a dozen tracks that any Armstrong collector should have; together, these two make a good sampler of the period. Some may prefer the highly cleaned-up sound of these transfers using the NoNoise system.

*****(*) The Alternative Takes Vol. 1**

Neatwork RP 2020 *As various discs above, plus Harry Hoffman (vn), Seger Ellis, Jimmie Rodgers (v).* 5/26–12/35.

***** The Alternative Takes Vol. 2**

Neatwork RP 2029 *As various discs above.* 10/35–12/44.

The first disc includes the three titles where Louis played behind the awful vocalist Seger Ellis, little-known sideman features which were certainly worth saving, and the famous 'Blue Yodel No. 9', where Pops and Lil backed none other than the Singing Brakeman, Jimmie Rodgers (once issued in the UK on a Regal Zonophone 78!). The second disc isn't quite so interesting, though there are alternates of two titles from the V-Disc Jam Session.

****** Louis Armstrong 1944–1946**

Classics 928 *Armstrong; Roy Eldridge, Billy Butterfield, Jesse Brown, Fats Ford, Sleepy Grider, Lester Currant, Charlie Shavers, Moons Mullens, Neal Hefti, Chieftie Scott (t); Bobby Hackett (c); Jack Teagarden (tb, v); Russell Moore, Adam Martin, Norman Powe, Al Cobbs, Taswell Baird, Larry Anderson, Lou McGarity (tb); Barney Bigard, Ernie Caceres, Jimmy Hamilton (cl); Bill Stegmeyer (as, ts, cl); John Brown, Willard Brown, Johnny Hodges, Sid Stoneburn, Jules Rubin, George Koenig, Donald Hill, Amos Gordon (as); Don Byas, Jack Greenberg, Art Drelinger, Coleman Hawkins, Joe Garland, Johnny Sparrow, Ted McRae, Dexter Gordon, Nick Caiazza, Arthur Rollini (ts); Ernest Thompson, Paul Ricci, Milton Shatz (bs); Duke Ellington, Billy Strayhorn, Ed Swanston, Joe Bushkin, Art Tatum, Dave Bowman, Johnny Guarnieri (p); Al Casey, Emmitt Slay, Herb Ellis, Carl Kress, Remo Palmieri, Danny Perri, Elmer Warner (g); Trigger Alpert, Chubby Jackson, Arvell Shaw, Oscar Pettiford, Alfred Moore, Al Hall, Bob Haggart (b); Big Sid Catlett, James Harris, Cozy Cole, Johnny Blowers, Sonny Greer, Butch Ballard (d); Ella Fitzgerald, Velma Middleton, Dorothy Dandridge (v).* 1/44–4/46.

A very fine cross-section of Armstrong as guest star and bandleader during this period. The five tracks from the Esquire Metropolitan Opera House Jam Session are by a peerless supergroup – Pops, Teagarden, Tatum, Eldridge, Hawkins, Bigard and more – and despite scrappy ensembles the music lives up to the billing. Two sessions for Decca bookend two V-Discs, including a superb 'Jack-Armstrong' Blues, where for once Tea duets with Lou McGarity and Armstrong solos by himself. Another Esquire date has Louis with Ellington and others on a lovely 'Long Long Journey', before two sweet duets with Ella and a Bob Haggart band; then a final big-band session for Decca with Armstrong playing excellently on five titles. A delightful pot-pourri in mostly excellent sound.

*****(*) Louis Armstrong 1946–1947**

Classics 992 *Armstrong; Bob Butler, Sleepy Grider, Ed Mullens, William Scott, Louis Gray, Fats Ford (t); Vic Dickenson, Alton Moore, Russell Moore, Waddet Williams, Nathaniel Allen, James Whitney, Jack Teagarden (tb); Edmond Hall, Barney Bigard (cl); Don Hill, Amos Garden, Arthur Dennis (as); Joe Garland, Johnny Sparrow, Lucky Thompson, Flip Phillips (ts); Ernest Thompson (bs); Charlie Beal, Leonard*

Feather, Earl Mason, Charlie Bateman (p); Allen Reuss, Bud Scott, Elmer Warner (g); Red Callender, Johnny Williams, Arvell Shaw (b); Big Sid Catlett, Zutty Singleton, Minor Hall, Jimmy Crawford, James Harris (d); Billie Holiday (v). 9/46–4/47.

****** Louis Armstrong 1947**

Classics 1072 *Armstrong; Bobby Hackett (c); Jack Teagarden, Tommy Dorsey (tb); Benny Goodman, Peanuts Hucko, Barney Bigard (cl); Ernie Caceres (cl, bs); Charlie Barnet (as); Lionel Hampton (vib); Dick Cary, Mel Powell (p); Al Casey, Al Hendrickson (g); Bob Haggart, Harry Babasin, Arvell Shaw, Al Hall (b); Big Sid Catlett, George Wettling, Cozy Cole, Louie Bellson (d); Jeri Sullivan, Golden Gate Quartet (v).* 5–11/47.

After some years of comparative neglect, Armstrong bounced back via the film *New Orleans*, which was made during the period covered by the earliest tracks here, and the formation of the All Stars, a move initiated by the celebrated 1947 New York Town Hall concert. Classics 992 starts with four little-known tracks cut for the French Swng label, excellent sides, and has three final big-band sessions for RCA, including the fine 'The Blues Are Brewin'', and some stray V-Disc material, including 'Do You Know What It Means To Miss New Orleans' alongside Holiday and an interview with Louis. Mixed stuff, but entertaining.

Classics have their own six tracks from the Town Hall event, all of the four-title session for Victor cut a month later, two jam-session tracks with an all-star band for Capitol and the first ten tracks by the 'original' All Stars. Throughout all this material Armstrong sounds like a maestro ready to resume his eminence: his playing here on 'Back O'Town Blues' and 'Jack-Armstrong Blues' has riveting intensity. Teagarden matches him with his own playing. Indispensable.

CORE COLLECTION

****** The Complete RCA Victor Recordings**

Bluebird 09026-63846-2 4CD *As various discs above.* 32–56.

Rather hard to place this edition in its correct place, since it covers not only all the 1932-3 sessions, but also the complete All Stars, Town Hall and Esquire Award Winners dates of 1946–7 and a stray pair of tracks with a Hal Mooney studio band of 1956. In a well-groomed package of four discs with a typically excellent Dan Morgenstern sleeve-note, this must be first choice if this is the Armstrong material you want. Dennis Farrante's transfers are beautifully clean and clear, with great presence, one of the best examples of the CEDAR restoration process we've heard, although here and there the music seems to have a vaguely metallic edge to it.

***** C'est Si Bon**

Proper Properbox 24 4CD *As various discs above, plus Billie Holiday (v), Louis Jordan's Tympany Five, Sy Oliver Orchestra.* 4/40–8/50.

***** C'est Si Bon**

Dreyfus FDM 36730-2 *As above.* 41–50.

Beginning with the date with Sidney Bechet and closing on sessions where Pops featured alongside Billie Holiday, Louis Jordan and the Sy Oliver band, the Proper package skims through most of Louis' studio dates of the decade. Nothing that can't be heard elsewhere, and the mastering (from uncredited sources) is no better or worse than in other editions. Dreyfus's set (with the same title!) is a sometimes curious assemblage from the same period, and at least it sounds better than their earlier Armstrong set.

*****(*) Satchmo At Symphony Hall**

GRP 051661-2 *Armstrong; Jack Teagarden (tb, v); Barney Bigard (cl); Dick Cary (p); Arvell Shaw (b); Big Sid Catlett (d); Velma Middleton (v).* 11/47.

Live from Boston with some 70 minutes of music, this is a re-run of the Town Hall situation with some bonus points. One is hearing Sid Catlett at some length on two titles, a rarity in that this master drummer seldom has more than ensemble work to show in his recorded career. Another is the interplay between Armstrong and Teagarden, if anything even more affectionate than it was in New York. Valuable.

***** Live At Winter Garden New York And Blue Note Chicago**

Storyville STCD 8242 *Armstrong; Bobby Hackett (c); Jack Teagarden (tb, v); Barney Bigard, Peanuts Hucko (cl); Ernie Caceres (bs); Dick Cary, Earl Hines (p); Jack Lesberg, Arvell Shaw (b); George Wettling, Big Sid Catlett (d).* 6/47–12/48.

Two brief broadcasts by two editions of the All Stars – though the group wasn't formally in existence at the time of the first (June 1947). This is comparatively scrappy material, and even Pops and Hines sound in less than their best form, but as a survival it's worthwhile.

***** Louis Armstrong 1950-1951**

Classics 1233 *Armstrong; Aaron Izenhall (t); Jack Teagarden (tb, v); Barney Bigard (cl); Louis Jordan (as, v); Josh Jackson (ts); Bill Doggett, Billy Kyle, Earl Hines (p); Bill Jennings, Everett Barksdale (g); Bob Bushnell, Arvell Shaw, Joe Benjamin (b); Chris Columbus, Cozy Cole, Johnny Blowers (d); Ella Fitzgerald, Velma Middleton (v); Sy Oliver Orchestra.* 6/50-1/51.

***** Louis Armstrong 1951-1952**

Classics 1283 *Similar to above, with orchestras led by Gordon Jenkins, Sy Oliver, John Scott Trotter, Dave Barbour; add Bing Crosby (v).* 2/51-8/52.

*****(*) Satchmo Serenades**

Verve 543792-2 *Armstrong; orchestras led by Sy Oliver, Toots Camarata.* 9/49–10/53.

***** Satchmo In Style**

Verve 549594-2 *Armstrong; orchestras led by Gordon Jenkins.* 9/49–4/54.

Armstrong's early '50s sides for Decca have been only spottily available for some time, and these two sets impose some sort of order on the situation. Produced by Milt Gabler, at least they had a jazzman at the helm, and Oliver's sessions, for instance, used the likes of Charlie Holmes, Budd Johnson, Horace Henderson and even Buck Clayton in the personnels. Jenkins, though no jazz arranger, adored Armstrong, and gave him as much free rein as possible – which wasn't all that much, given that these were records aimed at the new charts, then in the strange netherworld between swing and before rock. As jazz records, these are both nothing much, but as Armstrong showcases they're consistently delightful, and in some ways more exciting and characterful than the numerous 'recreation' sessions he would embark on for Columbia. There are a few feeble songs, but not many, and even then Pops makes something amusing out of them – listen to what he does to 'Chloe' and 'Trees' on *In Style*. The latter set is less successful, if only because of the welter of strings and choirs, but that extraordinary voice – and trumpet – keep taking over. The remastering of both sets is excellent, the sound having a presence to match the voice, which is saying something!

Classics continue their journey with two discs which cover much the same material. Classics 1233 includes all of the Pasadena 1951 concert by the All Stars, a good enough example of the group on a typical one-nighter; the rest is studio material, which also takes up Classics 1283. This does include quite a few singles missed off the Verve albums, such as the immortal 'Gone Fishin'' with Bing, although the plain packaging doesn't exactly honour the material.

*****(*) Plays W. C. Handy**
Columbia CK 64925 *Armstrong; Trummy Young (tb); Barney Bigard (cl); Billy Kyle (p); Arvell Shaw (b); Barrett Deems (d); Velma Middleton (v).* 6/54.

***** Satch Plays Fats**
Columbia CK 64927 *As above (plus personnel from sessions of 6/28–3/32).* 4–5/55.

The new edition of *Plays W. C. Handy* includes a brief, rather touching interview with Handy himself and a sequence of rehearsal tracks by the group who show how seriously they were taking this project. It still sounds like one of the very best of Armstrong's latter-day records. If he is most himself on the slower tunes, there's still a geniality about 'The Memphis Blues' and even in 'Loveless Love' which is comparatively rare. The Waller collection is nearly as good, although here the showbiz characteristics which stick to many of the tunes renege on their jazz content. The All Stars were playing well enough, but Young is scarcely a strong replacement for Teagarden, no matter how lax the latter might become. The latest edition of this album has been padded out with seven tracks from various Okeh sessions of 1928–32, where Armstrong was covering Waller tunes for the first time – a nice, if somewhat peculiar touch.

****** The California Concerts**
GRP 050613-2 4CD *Armstrong; Jack Teagarden, Trummy Young (tb, v); Barney Bigard (cl, v); Earl Hines, Billy Kyle (p); Arvell Shaw (b); Barrett Deems, Cozy Cole (d); Velma Middleton (v).* 1/51–1/55.

*****(*) The Great Chicago Concert 1956**
Columbia C2K 65119 2CD *As above, except add Edmond Hall (cl), Dale Jones (b); omit Teagarden, Bigard, Hines, Shaw, Cole and Middleton.* 6/56.

Armstrong's period with the All Stars has often been treated unfairly over the years. While there have been many indifferent and low-fi concert recordings floating around on dubious labels, these well-packaged and handsomely remastered collections call for a new appraisal of the group. The superb MCA set, spread across four CDs, covers two dates four years apart: the original All Stars with Teagarden and Hines, and the more familiar later group with Young and Kyle. Pops is in good form throughout and, though the vaudevillian aspects of the group often take precedence, there is always some piece of magic from the leader that transforms routine; his singing, as nearly always, is beyond reproof. There are many previously unreleased tracks and a good deal of straight-ahead jazz. The *Chicago Concert* date is slighter stuff, but there are still memorable takes of 'Black And Blue', 'Tenderly' and 'Struttin' With Some Barbecue' – not exactly revisionist, more the master shedding new light on old favourites via a few inflexions.

***** Satchmo – A Musical Autobiography**
Verve 543822-2 *Armstrong; Yank Lawson (t); Jack Teagarden, Trummy Young (tb); Edmond Hall, Barney Bigard (cl); George Dorsey (as, f); Lucky Thompson (ts); Dave McRae (bs, bsx, bcl); Dick Cary, Earl Hines, Billy Kyle (p); Everett Barksdale, George Barnes (g); Squire Gersh, Arvell Shaw (b); Cozy Cole, Big Sid Catlett, Barrett Deems (d); Kenny John, Velma Middleton (v).* 11/47–1/57.

Armstrong tells something of his life and career in the spoken intros to most of the tracks on these three CDs. This should have been some of the most worthwhile Armstrong of the period, with the material including plenty of tunes he hadn't returned to for many years, but the arrangements by Bob Haggart or Sy Oliver are a bit tight and Dixielandish, with the tempos a shade too taut to suit him. That said, it's still a pleasure to hear him go back to the likes of 'Knockin' A Jug'. Previously included as a European edition, we are now listing the new Verve set, which offers a great improvement in sound and a de-luxe package.

***** Satchmo The Great**
Columbia CK 62170 *Armstrong; Trummy Young (tb); Edmond Hall (cl); Billy Kyle (p); Dale Jones (b); Barrett Deems (d); Edward Murrow (narration); orchestra conducted by Leonard Bernstein.* 1–7/56.

***** Ambassador Satch**
Columbia CK 64926 *As above, except omit Jones, Murrow and orchestra, add Arvell Shaw (b).* 12/55–3/56.

The soundtrack to a film biography of Armstrong, with amusingly effulgent narration by Ed Murrow. Doesn't make much sense as a listening experience, though the performances are from a decent All Stars vintage. Leonard Bernstein conducts the Lewisohn Stadium Symphony for a mighty 'St Louis Blues'. *Ambassador Satch* strings together a number of European concert shows (and one from Hollywood), and they caught some likeable performances: 'Tin Roof Blues', a majestic reprise of 'West End Blues', a neat 'Someday You'll Be Sorry'. Some of the tracks are studio masquerades.

***** Louis And The Angels / Louis And The Good Book**
Universal MLCD 19379 *Armstrong; Trummy Young (tb); Hank D'Amico, Edmond Hall (cl); George Dorsey, Phil D'Urso (as, f); Lucky Thompson (ts); Dave Macrae (bs); Billy Kyle (p); Nick Tragg (org); Everett Barksdale, George Barnes (g); Mort Herbert, Joe Benjamin, Sid Block (b); Rudy Taylor, Barrett Deems (d); strings, choir.* 1/57–2/58.

Armstrong's two 'sacred' albums for Decca are about as secular as one can imagine. *Louis And The Angels* is more arranged and dependent on the strings, with chestnuts like 'A Sinner Kissed An Angel' alongside 'Angela Mia'; *Louis And The Good Book* is more fun, Armstrong swapping notes with his very white-sounding choir, although there's a surprisingly feelingful 'Nobody Knows The Trouble I've Seen' along the way. If this is all a bit light and obvious, it's still hugely enjoyable, and Louis himself is in great singing voice. *Louis And The Good Book* is now separately available as a Verve Master Edition (549593-2), with a few other tracks from different Armstrong eras rather annoyingly used as padding. *Louis And The Angels* has received a similar treatment (549592-2), but with no extra tracks this time!

****(*) Louis Armstrong: The Silver Collection**
Verve 823446-2 *Armstrong; Russell Garcia Orchestra.* 8/57.

***** Louis Armstrong Meets Oscar Peterson**

Verve 539060-2 *Armstrong; Oscar Peterson (p); Herb Ellis (g); Ray Brown (b); Louie Bellson (d).* 7–10/57.

***** Verve Jazz Masters: Louis Armstrong**

Verve 519818-2 *Armstrong; Trummy Young (tb); Edmond Hall (cl); Billy Kyle, Oscar Peterson (p); Herb Ellis (g); Ray Brown, Dale Jones (b); Louie Bellson, Barrett Deems (d); Ella Fitzgerald (v); Russell Garcia Orchestra.* 8/56–10/57.

***** Jazz Around Midnight: Louis Armstrong**

Verve 843422-2 *As above, except add Tyree Glenn (tb), Buster Bailey (cl), Marty Napoleon (p), Alfred Di Lernia (bj), Buddy Catlett (b), Danny Barcelona (d).* 7/57–5/66.

*****(*) Let's Do It**

Verve 529017-2 2CD *As above discs, except add Big Chief Russell Moore (tb), Joe Darensbourg (cl), Everett Barksdale (g), Arvell Shaw (b).* 8/57–9/64.

Verve recorded Armstrong with a little more initiative as regards concepts, but it didn't always work out. *The Silver Collection* finds Armstrong fronting Russell Garcia's hearty though not graceless orchestra with his usual aplomb; comparing, say, 'I Gotta Right To Sing The Blues' with his version of some 25 years earlier isolates the maturity of Armstrong's later art: he hasn't the chops for grandstand improvisations any more, but his sense of timing and his treatment of pure melody are almost as gratifying. Yet some of the songs end up as merely dull.

The meeting with Oscar Peterson's trio, now reissued in one of Verve's Master Edition series, is perhaps a mixed success but nevertheless an intriguing disc. Peterson can't altogether avoid his besetting pushiness, yet he's just as often *sotto voce* in accompaniment, and on the slower tunes especially – 'Sweet Lorraine' and 'Let's Fall In Love' – the chemistry works, and Louis is certainly never intimidated. It's good to hear him on material more obviously 'modern' than he normally tackled and, although he sometimes gets the feel of a song wrong, he finds a surprising spin for several of the lyrics. Both of the two compilations are quite thoughtfully chosen and, with the spotlight primarily on Louis's singing, the VJM disc is a good sampler of the period.

Dan Morgenstern's selection and notes for *Let's Do It*, a comprehensive overview of Louis with Verve, make a good case for reconsidering this period. If one wants a single selection here, this is certainly the one to go for, with some of his very best moments with Ella, Russ Garcia and Peterson carefully sequenced.

*****(*) I've Got The World On A String / Louis Under The Stars**

Verve 559831-2 2CD *Armstrong; Paul Smith (p); Russell Garcia Orchestra.* 8/57.

In this very fine remastering it's the sheer grandeur of Pops the vocalist and interpreter that comes off this double-disc set. His voice sounds huge. Some of the songs, such as 'Little Girl Blue', don't really suit him, and there is very little trumpet to offset Russell Garcia's swooning strings, but the magnetism of the man is sometimes awe-inspiring. There are a lot of alternative takes to pad out the two discs, but most of them offer little but extra weight.

***** Mack The Knife**

Pablo 2310941 *Armstrong; Trummy Young (tb, v); Edmond Hall (cl); Billy Kyle (p); Squire Gersh (b); Barrett Deems (d).* 7/57.

There seem to be many, many All Stars concerts which have survived on tape, and this is no better or worse than any for the period, though it includes a slightly more concentrated amount of jazz material.

*****(*) Porgy And Bess**

Verve 827475-2 *Armstrong; Ella Fitzgerald (v); Russell Garcia Orchestra.* 8/57.

*****(*) Ella And Louis**

Verve 543304-2 *Armstrong; Oscar Peterson (p); Herb Ellis (g); Ray Brown (b); Louie Bellson (d); Ella Fitzgerald (v).* 57.

*****(*) Ella And Louis Again**

Verve 825374-2 *As above.* 57.

***** Verve Jazz Masters 24: Ella Fitzgerald & Louis Armstrong**

Verve 521851-2 *As above discs.* 56–57.

*****(*) The Complete Ella Fitzgerald & Louis Armstrong On Verve**

Verve 537284-2 3CD *As above.* 56–57.

We have been dismissive of these sessions in the past and perhaps they *are* disappointing: the two greatest voices in jazz ought to have been a dream pairing, but with Pops used to trading innuendo with Velma Middleton and Ella always going her own queenly way, maybe it was never a match made in jazz heaven. But there are compensations which make a lot of the music hard to resist. *Porgy And Bess* has never been highly regarded among the numerous jazz versions of Gershwin's opera, yet though Russell Garcia's orchestra tends to loom over the music, there are a handful of sublime moments which make up for the stiffness: 'Summertime', in particular, is turned into a profoundly moving meditation, and the closing bars of this version are as transcendent as anything in the work of Ella and Louis. The two small-group dates have material that suits Fitzgerald rather than her partner, and some of the tunes end up either bland or merely workmanlike; yet others are a delight, especially 'I Won't Dance' and 'Isn't This A Lovely Day', and there is the deftest support from Peterson and his team. The *Jazz Masters* compilation isn't bad, but we would quarrel with some of the tune choices. *The Complete* puts the whole lot in one place, though the concertina packaging is somewhat eccentric.

***** I Love Jazz!**

Verve 543747-2 *Armstrong; Taft Jordan, William Scott, Charlie Shavers (t); Jack Teagarden, Trummy Young, Al Cobbs, Elmer Crumbley, Paul Seiden (tb); Peanuts Hucko, Barney Bigard, Edmond Hall (cl); Omer Simeon (ss); Eddie Miller (ts); Billy Kyle, Earl Hines (p); Al Hendrickson, Danny Barker, George Barnes (g); Mort Herbert, Arvell Shaw, Squire Gersh (b); Danny Barcelona, Cozy Cole, Barrett Deems (d); choir.* 4/50–10/58.

'The cats was really boppin' that time, wasn't they, folks?' Thus Pops at the end of a comic version of 'Twelfth Street Rag', from this curious set of All Stars tracks covering most of the '50s (one track features a bigger band). It's a hotchpotch of material, but it's interesting to hear Armstrong tackle 'Frog-I-More Rag', which dates back to his time with Oliver. Excellent sound.

****** Louis Armstrong & Duke Ellington: The Complete Sessions**
Roulette 793844-2 2 CD *Armstrong; Trummy Young (tb); Barney Bigard (cl); Duke Ellington (p); Mort Herbert (b); Danny Barcelona (d).* 4/61.

****** The Great Summit – The Master Takes**
Roulette 24547-2 *As above.* 4/61.

These sessions have never been highly regarded: Ellington is more or less slumming it with the All Stars, and some of his piano parts do sound eccentrically isolated. Yet this is Armstrong's date, not his, even with all the material composed by Duke: Louis stamps his imprimatur on it from the first vocal on 'Duke's Place'. His occasional frailties and the sometimes tired tempos only personalize further his single opportunity to interpret his greatest contemporary at length. On the extraordinarily affecting 'I Got It Bad And That Ain't Good' or the superbly paced 'It Don't Mean A Thing', Louis reflects on a parallel heritage of tunes which his traditional proclivities perhaps denied him; and the results are both moving and quietly eloquent. The complete edition has lots of warm-ups and chatter; if you want just the music pure and simple, go to *The Master Takes*.

****(*) In Chicago August 1 1962**
Storyville 101 8327 *Armstrong; Trummy Young (tb); Joe Darensbourg (cl); Billy Kyle (p); Billy Cronk (b); Danny Barcelona (d).* 8/62.

Made before Armstrong's health began to impair his performing, this is a game enough All Stars date. Not a priority unless you want everything the man did, but not as poor as many of the later survivals either.

**** The Legendary Berlin Concert**
Jazzpoint 1062 *Armstrong; Tyree Glenn (tb); Eddie Shu (cl); Billy Kyle (p); Arvell Shaw (b); Danny Barcelona (d); Jewel Brown (v).* 3/65.

**** The Legendary Berlin Concert Part II**
Jazzpoint 1063 *As above.* 3/65.

**** The Best Live Concert Vol. 1**
Emarcy 013030-2 *As above.* 6/65.

**** The Best Live Concert Vol. 2**
Emarcy 013031-2 *As above.* 6/65.

By the mid-'60s, Armstrong's powers as a trumpeter were finally in serious decline, and there are sad moments among the glimmers of greatness which remain. Numerous All Stars shows seem to have survived, and most of them get called 'Legendary' or 'The Greatest'. Neither of these holds a candle to vintage Armstrong, and not only because his own playing was in decline – the rest of the band indulge in so much showboating, instead of offering sensitive support to the boss, that the music palls very quickly. The Berlin show at least has a fine 'Black And Blue', and Pops' singing lives on.

****(*) What A Wonderful World**
MCA 811876-2 *Armstrong; strings.* 68.

The spirit abides in this late set, but the showbiz material hurts, and only his great heart gets him through it to any effectiveness.

**** Louis Armstrong And His Friends**
RCA Victor Gold 74321 747942 *Armstrong; orchestra led by Oliver Nelson.* 5/70.

His farewell. He doesn't play, and for a lot of the way he talks more than he sings. But the old humour abides: in Pharoah Sanders's awful 'The Creator Has A Master Plan', he can spot a load of baloney when he hears it.

Kenneth Arnström (born 1946)

ALTO, TENOR AND BARITONE SAXOPHONES, CLARINET, BASS CLARINET

Having made a name for himself in Sweden as a prodigious saxophonist in a trad-to-mainstream style, the enigmatic Arnström disappeared from the scene for 15 years and worked as a carpenter. In the '90s he returned to more active duty, picking up where he left off. He also founded the Kenneth jazz label.

***** Saxcess**
Phontastic NCD 8836 *Arnström; Jan Stolpe (t); Pelle Larsson (p); Dan Berglund (b); Hasse Linskog (d); Sabina Have (v).* 1–7/95.

***** Rhythm King**
Opus 3 19502 *Arnström; Bent Persson (c, t); Tomas Ornberg (cl, ss); Keith Durston (p); Olle Nyman (g, bj); Goran Eriksson (bj); Bo Juhlin (sou); Tomas Ekstrom (b).* 4–5/95.

****(*) Hittin' The Roots**
Phontastic PHONTCD 8849 *Arnström; Peter Kjellin (t); Fredrik John (tb); Per Notini (p); Rune Gustafsson (g); Christian Franck (b); Sven Stahlberg, Peter Ostlund (d).* 3/95–2/96.

Arnström originally impressed as a big-toned tenorman in the classic manner. *Saxcess* seems to be the first album under his own name, after he was tempted back to playing following a long sabbatical, and only the cursory support and off-the-cuff tune-choices withhold a higher commendation: his own playing is in the top class. He musters a fluent delivery, but it's edged by a black tone that intensifies when his phrases turn vehement – scarcely a solo goes by without some seemingly angry turn of expression. Partnered by Stolpe, who comes on as if Louis Armstrong was still everybody's main influence on the horn, this gives the front line a rare virility.

Rhythm King is quite different, a set of mostly very old tunes (one surprise: Paul Gonsalves's 'Solitariness') given a rather steely recitation by a small group. Minus any drums, the sparse setting grants an odd, almost metallic feel to the sound and, when they handle pieces like 'Funny Feathers' or 'Forty And Tight' (or 'Somebody Stole My Gal', done as a duet for banjo and bass clarinet!), it seems more like an essay on traditional forms than anything. A charismatic but rather rarefied date. *Hittin' The Roots* seems much more prosaic and rather less successful, the rhythm section tying down the horns and the result a playable if unremarkable session. Arnström himself remains an enigma.

*****(*) Jazz Feeling Vol 1: Baby Face**
Phontastic NCD8855 *Arnström; Uf Johansson (p, tb); Olle Brostedt (b); Bert Dale (Nils-Bertil Dahlander) (d).* 10/97.

Recorded in the dancehall ambience of Swedish Radio Studio 3, this informal swing session is unpretentious joy. Johansson's knowing stylings – he picks up the trombone on only one track – suit Arnström's idiosyncratic way with his material beautifully, and the two veterans in the rhythm section sound like they're having a good time (the four participants were each born in different decades). The leader's fractious tendencies work very much to the music's advantage, and there is character in everything from 'Winin' Boy Blues' to a Latin-flavoured original, 'Karin'.

Lynne Arriale

PIANO

A piano-competition winner, Arriale is from Wisconsin and is a late starter: classical music took up her time until she was 24. She works out of New York, mostly with her regular trio.

*****(*) A Long Road Home**
TCB 97952 *Arriale; John Patitucci (b); Steve Davis (d).* 4/97.

***** Melody**
TCB 99552 *Arriale; Scott Colley (b); Steve Davis (d).* 12/98.

*****(*) Live At Montreux**
TCB 20252 *Arriale; Jay Anderson (b); Steve Davis (d).* 7/99.

****** Inspiration**
TCB 22102 *As above.* 8/00.

Arriale's dedication to melody and her concentration on improvising with logic and relevance to the material sets her somewhat apart from the plethora of contemporary piano-players, and each of these sets has piano jazz of an exceptionally high order. She gets a lovely tone out of the instrument, possibly a result of her classical training, and she rarely gets far away from her thematic starting point: everything is designed with sometimes extravagant care. That can take a little of the juice out of the music, and you don't listen to Arriale for surprise, but her recitalist's way with the melodies is mainly ravishing, as well as refreshingly uncluttered.

A Long Road Home was her first for TCB and, while some may feel that her take on Monk ('Bye-Ya') is too cultivated, at least she avoids the obvious imitative touches that most pianists throw in. The slow version of 'Wouldn't It Be Loverly' is marvellous, and 'A Night In Tunisia' is serenely modelled and delivered. *Melody* doesn't seem quite so good: one or two tracks seem, for once, a shade over-extended, and the set could use another faster piece, though she is very good with 'Touch Her Soft Lips And Part'. The Montreux set is focused and intense. On jazz themes such as 'Evidence' and 'Seven Steps To Heaven', she makes it new, without debasing the material. Best so far is *Inspiration*: a perfect balance of material ('America', 'Blackbird', 'A House Is Not A Home', 'The Nearness Of You'), a trio that sounds as one, and personalizations of each piece which are fully individual without resorting to radicalism.

*****(*) Arise**
Motema MTM 71372 *As above.* 8/02.

Perhaps this isn't quite as close to perfect as the previous set: on a couple of the fastest pieces Arriale sounds less sure of herself, and the executive virtuosity which seems de rigueur among contemporary pianists may not fall under her fingers quite as easily as some. But at the medium tempo of 'American Woman' or the Latin lilt of 'Esperanza', where she feels completely comfortable with her fellow players, she's peerless. This is eloquent and notably individual piano-trio music, as good in its way as the recent best of Mehldau, Moran and Hersch, and Arriale should be commanding the attention of piano fans everywhere.

Art Ensemble Of Chicago

GROUP

Born out of Chicago's Association for the Advancement of Creative Musicians, this co-operative grew out of a Roscoe Mitchell small group. Phillip Wilson drummed for them early on, but it was the quartet of Mitchell, Lester Bowie, Joseph Jarman and Malachi Favors which went to live and play in Europe in 1969. They returned to the US to work in 1972 and were joined by drummer Famoudou Don Moye. They became a leading concert attraction during the late '70s, '80s and '90s, but as a group they recorded only occasionally, each member often busy with other projects. Nevertheless, they symbolize the creative spirit of Chicago's black avant-gardists of the '60s.

CORE COLLECTION

****** Art Ensemble 1967–68**
Nessa NCD-2500 5CD *Lester Bowie (t, flhn, perc); Roscoe Mitchell (saxes, perc); Joseph Jarman (saxes, bsn, cl); Malachi Favors (b, zith, perc); Charles Clark (b); Phillip Wilson, Thurman Barker, Robert Crowder (d).* 67–68.

Those who know the Art Ensemble of Chicago only by their considerable reputation may be disappointed by their work as it's been documented on record. Bowie, Jarman, Favors and Mitchell, later joined by percussionist Famoudou Don Moye, have been celebrated as among the most radical and innovative musicians in the intensely creative environment which was centred on Chicago's AACM movement in the '60s. Not surprisingly, they had to uproot and head for Europe in order to find work and recording opportunities at the time, and most of their music remains on European labels. As a mix of personalities, the Ensemble has always been in a crisis of temperament, with Bowie's arsenal of sardonic inflexions pitched against Mitchell's schematic constructions, Jarman's fierce and elegant improvising and Favors's other-worldly commentaries from the bass. Satire, both musical and literal, has sustained much of their music; long- and short-form pieces have broken jazz structure down into areas of sound and silence. At their best, they are as uncompromisingly abstract as the most severe European players, yet their materials are cut from the heart of the traditions of black music in Chicago and St Louis.

The Nessa five-disc set (which is a limited though very expensive edition) compiles three previously issued LPs – Mitchell's *Congliptious* and *Old/Quartet*, and Bowie's *Numbers 1 & 2* – along with some two and a half hours of previously unreleased workshop tapes, alternative takes and some demos. Historically, with relatively little of the Chicago free masters having been documented at the time, this is of great importance and, while the best music is probably that heard on those original albums, there are some fascinating things in the sometimes messy alternative tracks and rehearsals, with the legendary Clark and drummers Crowder and Barker making rare appearances. For specialists, arguably, but there is much here that deserves wider circulation.

Their French recordings of 1969 are an important group, but the music has been packaged in all sorts of editions over the past 30 years and we do not feel comfortable about listing any of it as currently available. It's time it was given a respectful complete edition.

***** Live**

Delmark DE-432 *As above, except add Famoudou Don Moye (d).* 1/72.

*****(*) Bap-Tizum**

Atlantic 7567-80757-2 *As above.* 9/72.

*****(*) Fanfare For The Warriors**

Koch 8501/Atlantic 8122-7235-2 *As above, except add Muhal Richard Abrams (p).* 9/73.

***** Nice Guys**

ECM 827876-2 *As above, except omit Abrams.* 5/78.

***** Full Force**

ECM 829197-2 *As above.* 1/80.

*****(*) Urban Bushmen**

ECM 829394-2 2CD *As above.* 5/80.

The Ensemble made only a handful of discs in the '70s, and most are now back in circulation. The live session, recorded at Chicago's Mandel Hall in 1972, has been remastered by Delmark. This was something of a homecoming affair and there is much jubilation in the playing, but the recording remains imperfect, the detail skimped, and in a continuous 76-minute performance there are inevitable dead spots which the Ensemble have never truly found a way of avoiding. *Bap-Tizum* is another concert set, from the 1972 Ann Arbor Festival, and is better – more coherent, more purposeful. The studio *Fanfare For The Warriors* is one of their most finished efforts, with Mitchell's 'Nonaah' and 'Tnoona' among their most challenging original structures and Jarman's fierce title-piece delivered with real, concentrated force. As guest, Abrams thickens the stew and acts as something of a binding force: no theatre, just hard music. Even here, though, the production isn't really up to evoking a true picture of the Ensemble's sound.

It wasn't until they secured a deal with ECM that they were finally given the opportunity to record in the sonic detail which their work always demanded. Even so, the two studio albums were good yet unexceptional instances of the group at work. *Nice Guys* has two absorbing Jarman pieces in '597-59' and 'Dreaming Of The Master', but the attempt at a ska beat in 'JA' is unconvincing and much of the music seems almost formulaic, the improvisation limited. *Full Force* is a little more outgoing without cutting loose, and the lengthy 'Magg Zelma' seems long-winded rather than epic in its movement. The Ensemble's concert appearances could still generate music of blistering power, which made their apparently desultory records all the more frustrating. So the live *Urban Bushmen*, while still somewhat muted and inevitably deprived of the theatrical impact of the Ensemble's in-person charisma, proved to be their most worthwhile record for many years. Spread over 90 minutes, the group displayed their virtuosity on a vast panoply of devices (Jarman alone is credited with playing 14 different wind instruments, along with sundry items of percussion) and the patchwork of musics adds up to a tying together of their many endeavours in form and content. Revisiting the music, it does not seem to have worn as well as we remembered, but it remains a useful introduction to their work.

****(*) The Third Decade**

ECM 823213-2 *As above.* 6/84.

A dispiriting continuation after another longish absence from the studios. Embarking on their third decade together suggested nothing so much as the atrophy of a once-radical band. The horn players are as spikily creative as ever in those moments when the Ensemble parts to reveal them, but the crucial decline is in the quality of interaction: several of these pieces dispel the collective identity of the group rather than binding it together.

***** Live In Japan**

DIW 8005 *As above.* 4/84.

***** The Complete Live In Japan**

DIW 8021/2 2CD *As above.* 4/84.

The AEOC commenced a new contract with the Japanese DIW company with this worthwhile though hardly enthralling live set (the first record is a distillation of the concert, which appears in its totality on the subsequent double-CD). Some of the earlier ECM material reappears in concert form: the differences in emphasis are interesting, if little more. Acceptable rather than outstanding sound.

***** Naked**

DIW 8011 *As above.* 11/85–7/86.

****(*) Ancient To The Future: Dreaming Of The Masters Vol. 1**

DIW 8014 *As above, except add Bahnamous Lee Bowie (ky).* 3/87.

The group's recording for DIW continued with records which, because of their limited distribution, caused little excitement. But the music continued to be a revisiting of old haunts rather than anything strikingly new; Mitchell and Bowie were, in any case, more active elsewhere. A taste for fanciful, zigzagging hard bop lightens some of *Naked*, and the impeccable recording affords some pleasure in just listening to the sound of Jarman, Mitchell and Favors in particular. But the attempts at rounding up 'the tradition' on DIW 8014 include poorly conceived stabs at 'Purple Haze' and 'No Woman No Cry' which mock their mastery.

****** The Alternate Express**

DIW 8033 *As above.* 1/89.

A remarkable record from a period when it seemed that the Ensemble's powers were all but spent. The huge, blustering 'Kush' rekindles the wildness of their best improvising; 'Imaginary Situations' is a ghostly collective sketch; 'Whatever Happens' catches Bowie at his melancholy best, while Mitchell's title-piece is a fine tribute to the group's survivalist spirit. A valuable and welcome document that might be called a comeback.

****(*) Art Ensemble Of Soweto**

DIW 837 *As above, except add Elliot Ngubane (v, ky, perc); Joe Leguabe (v, perc); Zacheuus Nyoni, Welcome Max Bhe Bhe, Kay Ngwazene (v).* 12/89–1/90.

This might have seemed like a logical collaboration, between the Ensemble and the African male chorus Amabutho, but the results tend to declare the differences between the two groups rather than their allegiances. The harmonic dignity of Amabutho stands alone on the three tracks they're featured on, while the best instrumental music comes on Mitchell's 'Fresh Start', an invigorating blast of free bop. Worth hearing, but not the grand encounter which must have been intended.

***** Live At The Eighth Tokyo Music Joy 1990**

DIW 842 *Lester Bowie, Stanton Davis, Eddie E. J. Allen, Gerald Brazel (t); Vincent Chancey (frhn); Steve Turre, Clifton*

Anderson (tb); Roscoe Mitchell, Joseph Jarman (reeds); Bob Stewart (tba); Malachi Favors (b); Famoudou Don Moye, Vinnie Johnson (d). 2/90.

A meeting between two great ensembles, the AEOC and Bowie's Brass Fantasy. Each has three tracks of its own and there are four collective pieces, of which Steve Turre's arrangement of 'The Emperor' seems to prove the idea that he is the real leader of Brass Fantasy – or, at least, the one who knows how to make it work for the best. A celebratory meeting but not an altogether successful one.

***** Thelonious Sphere Monk: Dreaming Of The Masters Vol. 2**

DIW 846 *Lester Bowie (t); Roscoe Mitchell, Joseph Jarman (reeds); Cecil Taylor (p, v); Malachi Favors (b); Famoudou Don Moye (d).* 1–3/90.

***** Dreaming Of The Masters Suite**

DIW 854 *As above, except omit Taylor.* 1–3/90.

It seemed a curiously neo-classic device for the Ensemble to be so specifically paying tribute to senior spirits, which was on the face of it the kind of laborious dues-paying which Bowie in particular was critical of in many of today's younger players. Their approach is, of course, different: the colouristic interchanges between Mitchell and Jarman, Bowie's inimitable irreverence and the patient, other-worldly bass of Favors all ensure that. But neither of these records is anything much more than a reminder of the AEOC's existence; certainly no specific new ground is broken, and in that sense the encounter with Cecil Taylor is a disappointment, although Taylor's singing is actually a fascinating embellishment of the Ensemble's own tradition. When he plays piano, the two sides – perhaps inevitably – don't really meet. Oddly, neither record is much about its respective dedicatees: there are only two Monk tunes and three by Coltrane here, though 'Impressions' is a fine repertory performance. The Ensemble still exists as a performing unit but its status as an ongoing contributor is in doubt: it now seems to belong to the past.

***** Coming Home Jamaica**

Birdology FDM 37003-2 *As above, except omit Jarman; add Bahnamous Bowie (ky).* 12/95–1/96.

With Jarman retiring from active duty and Bowie now gone, this was seemingly the final AEOC album. From the R&B shuffle of 'Grape Escape' to the portly ska of 'Strawberry Mango', it's a good-natured farewell. All the real electricity went out of the group some time ago, but as a kind of repertory exercise this has its share of moments: Bowie plays well and, if Jarman's elegance is sadly missed, Mitchell's deadpan aggression still has its say. The new edition has three previously unheard tracks: a brief Bowie lament, 'Villa Tiamo'; a dense Mitchell essay, 'C Monster'; and a 'classic' AEOC freakout, 'Blue Hole/Mr Freddy', which shows that the group's spirit endured even if its routines had become familiar.

***** Tribute To Lester**

ECM 017066-2 *As above, except omit Bowie.* 9/01

***** The Meeting**

PI 07 *As above, except Jarman returns.* n.d.

Tribute To Lester isn't exactly subdued, but with the Ensemble down to three and with neither Bowie nor Jarman there, much of the music seems beset by absences – Mitchell, Favors and Moye play with serene heart, yet the differing energies of the two missing spirits do seem irreplaceable. 'Suite For Lester' itself finds Mitchell working through soprano, flute and bass sax, and the final 'He Speaks To Me Often In Dreams' is a thoughtful ensemble improv which offers some resolution, even if it also suggests unfinished business.

In the end, Jarman decided to return to the Ensemble's ranks, but with Favors now gone too, this is surely the real finale to the group's work. There is something poignant in seeing these great crusaders as the four old men, wrapped up against what may have been a Chicago winter, on the cover of the CD. As ritualistic as they ever were, from the solemn gaiety of Jarman's 'Hail We Now Sing Joy' inwards, this is a necessarily autumnal record, reflective, and though it occasionally bursts into stiffly volatile life – as on Mitchell's 'Tech Ritter And The Megabytes' – it's mostly a musing creation which the less sympathetic might feel is merely rambling. Fittingly, perhaps, Favors' piece 'It's The Sign Of The Times', which commences with a solo turn by each man, is the AEOC at its most delicately effective – and there's an eerie moment towards the end where somebody plays something which sounds uncannily like a Lester Bowie break.

Art Studio

GROUP

Formed in Turin in 1974, Art Studio brought together four young avant-gardists from the local scene. They worked together as a group until the mid-'80s, and reunited for the 1997 Splasc(h) session.

****(*) The Complete C.M.C. Sessions**

Splasc(h) CDH 503/4.2 2CD *Carlo Actis Dato (ts, bs, bcl); Irene Robbins (p, v); Claudio Lodati (g); Enrico Fazio (b); Fiorenzo Sordini (d, vib).* 7/78–11/85.

***** Off Limits**

Splasc(h) CDH 656.2 *As above, except omit Robbins.* 12/97.

The four young men (average age, 20) who formed Art Studio in 1974 have become distinguished members of Italy's contemporary jazz movement. Their early adventures were captured on four albums for C.M.C., re-issued on the Splasc(h) double set; the first album actually dates from 1978. Though the sleeve-notes make much of a link with the Ornette Coleman quartet, the music sounds more like offcuts from the jazz-rock workbench which was being set up in many parts of Europe at the time, even if Art Studio was directed more towards jazz than rock. The earliest session *Diagnosi* is comparatively unfocused and at times tedious. *Paralisi*, the second, added Robbins to the line-up; her wordless vocals are unimpressive, but her piano was a productive fifth element. The long blast of 'Acquario', featuring Dato at his most extreme, begins strongly before petering out; smaller pieces such as 'Ariete' are more effective. The five-piece line-up continues for *Presagio* and *Pensieri*. There is more exploration of space, sound, form and dynamics – suggesting an influence from the Chicagoans of that period – than of improvising within conventionally swinging forms. Inevitably it is hit and miss. 'Pensieri' moves from a dull guitar prelude to a dark and surprising collective. 'Sud Suite' is fast freebop. The mixes have plenty of inappropriate studio echo, and although the playing tries hard, it is finally not all that interesting.

The 1997 reunion came after all four had worked productively elsewhere. Lodati has added to his technical arsenal (he uses a mostly unglamorous open tone on the old records), Robbins has disappeared, and the playing has a lot more muscle, purpose and humour. The group still has a tendency to grind an idea to powder rather than genuinely develop it, though Dato's spry demeanour now makes a more effective contrast with Lodati's gloomier prognoses.

Joe Ascione (born 1961)

DRUMS

An Italian-American from Long Island, Ascione started by worshipping Krupa and Rich. His CV has since stretched from Cab Calloway to Donald Fagen, and he seems at home in any style from swing onwards.

***** My Buddy**
Nagel-Heyer 036 *Ascione; Randy Sandke (t); Dan Barrett (tb); Brian Ogilvie (cl, as, ts); Billy Mitchell (ts); Mark Shane (p); James Chirillo (g); Bob Haggart (b).* 11/96.

***** Post No Bills**
Arbors ARCD 19174 *Ascione; Jerry Weldon (ts); Dave LaLama (p); Ron Affif (g); Tim Givens (b).* 12/96.

Ascione idolized Buddy Rich; *My Buddy* is a set of tunes associated with the man and is a worthy homage. The band is drawn from what is now the Nagel-Heyer repertory crew and is none the worse for that, though it's nice to welcome the gruff, booting tenor of Billy Mitchell – frayed round the edges, but more distinctive than many a saxophonist of today – back to the studios. The trumpet–drums duet of 'Nica's Dream' and the floating tempo on 'Soft Winds', deliciously set up by Barrett, are useful changes of pace, even if much of the music is the kind of thing we've heard many times before. The closing blues is a bit of a marathon.

Post No Bills takes some similar cues, but it is generally much more boppishly inclined and is built round the trio of Ascione, LaLama and Givens. The pianist's neat touch finds some soft light on 'Chelsea Bridge', played at a very quiescent pace, and, with Weldon adding muscular tenor to the likes of 'Moment's Notice', this is a slight step outside Nagel-Heyer's mainstream methods.

Dorothy Ashby (1932–86)

HARP

The first jazz harpist? Not quite – Casper Reardon got there first.

*****(*) In A Minor Groove**
Prestige PCD 24120 *Ashby; Frank Wess (f); Eugene Wright, Herman Wright (b); Roy Haynes, Art Taylor (d).* 3–12/58.

***** Afro-Harping**
Verve B00008 *Ashby; arrangements by Richard Evans.* 68.

The New Grove Dictionary of Jazz describes Ashby as 'the only important bop harpist', which might seem a rather empty accolade, given a somewhat scant subscription to the instrument in this music. On balance, though, it's fair comment. Ashby came to notice in her early 20s, playing with no less a man than Louis Armstrong. Remarkably, she saw a place for herself in the new idiom and managed to fit her seemingly unwieldy instrument to the contours of an essentially horn-dominated style. There are affinities between her harp-playing and some contemporary guitar stylings, notably Wes Montgomery's, but she also learned something from bebop pianists like Bud Powell, bringing an unusually dark tonality and timbre to a notoriously soft-voiced instrument. Ashby's determination to lead her own groups allowed her to develop a personal language and style. Although she recruited such fine players as Roy Haynes and Jimmy Cobb, her most fruitful association was with Frank Wess, whose flute-playing (still much undervalued) was perfect for her. The best of their partnership can be sampled on the Prestige. This found her working with two equally good rhythm-sections, Haynes and Gene Wright, and Art Taylor and Herman Wright, the absence of a more familiar piano or guitar left some of the harmonies quite open, and there are unexpected chromatic sweeps in some of these tracks – 'It's A Minor Thing' and 'Alone Together' – which seem ahead of their time.

Afro-Harping is a plusher affair, but Ashby's lead lines are still as strong and unfussy as ever, and her soloing has real power, right from the opening 'Soul Vibrations'. The title-piece is a terse, folksy original with a sophisticated arrangement; there are also fine versions of 'The Look Of Love' (which might have been drowned in celestial harp plus strings, but isn't) and André Previn's theme from *The Valley Of The Dolls*, which has an authentic whiff of danger.

Harold Ashby (born 1925)

TENOR SAXOPHONE

Ashby was born in Kansas and worked in relative obscurity in the Mid-West until moving to New York in the late '50s. He worked with Duke Ellington on and off before joining permanently in 1968. His records represent an Indian summer in the recording studios.

***** Scufflin'**
Black & Blue BB932.2 *Ashby; Booty Wood (tb); Raymond Fol (p); Aaron Bell (b); Sam Woodyard (d).* 5/78.

***** The Viking**
Gemini GM 60 *Ashby; Norman Simmons (p); Paul West (b); Gerryck King (d).* 8/88.

***** What Am I Here For?**
Criss Cross 1054 *Ashby; Mulgrew Miller (p); Rufus Reid (b); Ben Riley (d).* 11/90.

A late arrival in the Duke Ellington Orchestra, Harold Ashby was really Ben Webster's replacement; he kept the Webster huff on ballads and the grouchy, just-woke-up timbre on faster tunes. Quicker tempos don't bother him as much as they did Webster, but he liked to take his time, and he fashions storytelling solos which can freshen up the material. It's all done consistently enough to ensure that there's little to choose between these four recordings for four labels. Recently arrived is the reissued Black & Blue album, which is about as kosher as an Ellington small-group can be without the master at the piano. It was, in fact, Raymond Fol's last date, and he plays with a lovely touch that suggests he was delighted to be in this company. Themes such as 'Salty Mama' and 'Earma Jean' are nothing much compositionally, but they're a prop for some generous, happy blowing.

What Am I Here For? is an ideal programme of Ellingtonia and, though it is a little too long to sustain interest, the playing is jauntily assured from track to track. The Gemini set sounds perkier, perhaps because the rhythm section is less of a signed-up star group and because Ashby sounds expansive and happy with the four original lines he came up with for the date.

Mickey Ashman (born 1927)

BASS

A veteran mainstay of British trad rhythm sections, Ashman has worked with Barber, Colyer, Lyttelton, Lightfoot and Sunshine, among others.

***** Through Darkest Ashman**

Lake LACD86 *Ashman; Stan Sowden, Sonny Morris (t); Peter Jamieson, Brian Cotton (tb); Gerry Turnham (cl); Dickie Bishop, Martin Boorman (bj); Trevor Glenroy, Billy Loch (d).* 8/58–1/61.

Mickey Ashman is still playing the kind of absolute bass heard on these tracks – turn to the Neville Dickie entry for details. This is a reissue of a fondly remembered Pye LP by a good trad outfit: Turnham's woodsy clarinet and Morris's brisk trumpet stand out on a set of tunes all with some kind of jungle connection, the standout arguably a surprisingly fine treatment of Ellington's 'Jungle Nights In Harlem'. As a bonus, there are four tracks from a rare 1958 EP of old-time tunes, which goes out on an astonishingly full-tilt 'If Those Lips Could Only Speak'. Those were remastered off vinyl and sound a bit rough, but the Pye tracks are beautifully clear and Mickey's bass comes through mightily.

Svend Asmussen (born 1916)

VIOLIN, VIBRAPHONE, VOCAL

Asmussen has been working professionally since the '30s, although much of his post-war output was closer to salon music than to jazz. His celebrated LP with John Lewis, European Encounter, has yet to appear on CD.

***** Musical Miracle 1935–1940**

Phontastic PHONTCD 9306 *Asmussen; Svend Hauberg (t, cl, g); Olaf Carlson (t); Kai Ewans (cl); Aage Voss, Kai Moller, Johnny Campbell (as); Henry Hagemann, Banner Jansen, Valdemar Nielsen (ts); Kjeld Bonfils (p, vib); Kjeld Norregaard (p); Hans Ulrik Neumann, Helge Jacobsen, Jimmy Campbell, Borge Ring, Oscar Aleman (g); Niels Foss, Christian Jensen, Alfred Rasmussen (b); Bibi Miranda, Erik Frederiksen, Rik Kragh (d).* 11/35–12/40.

Asmussen should be celebrated as one of the major jazz violinists, yet he remains relatively little-known outside his native Denmark. Like, say, Bengt Hallberg, his musical tastes stretch to areas of music remote from jazz and have led him into light-music byways that have perhaps not done his reputation much good. Nevertheless he remains preposterously neglected by CD reissues, and a listen to some of the tracks on this early collection will make one wonder why. He is at least as fluent as Grappelli or South, with little of the sweetness or strictness that sometimes mars their work. Try, for example, the rigorous variation on the theme of 'Limehouse Blues' (1938) or the flawless impetus of 'After You've Gone' (1940). The earliest tracks feature him as a sideman, but the majority are by small groups designed to feature him as a violinist, an occasional vibesman and an agreeable if Armstrong-derived vocalist. Aside from Aleman, present on only two tracks, none of the guitarists really challenges him the way Reinhardt did Grappelli, and there's a hint of café society kitsch here and there; otherwise, this is an excellent programme. Remastering is a little tubby in the bass, and 'Jazz Potpourri 2' is from a swishy original 78, but the sound is fine in most respects.

**** Prize Winners**

Music Mecca 2060-2 *Asmussen; Kenny Drew (p); Niels-Henning Orsted Pedersen (b); Ed Thigpen (d).* 2/78–11/80.

Originally recorded for Drew's own (and short-lived) Matrix label, this is a disappointment, especially considering that the quartet had worked together to some acclaim on the concert stage. The material is very mixed, and often given bizarrely inappropriate treatment: 'You Are The Sunshine Of My Life' is turned into a funereal ballad, and Asmussen makes 'A Pretty Girl is Like A Melody' into an inebriated stagger. Six routine tracks by the trio minus Asmussen are a dubious bonus.

***** Fiddling Around**

Imogena IGCD 039 *Asmussen; Jacob Fischer (g); Jesper Lundgaard (b); Aage Tanggaard (d).* 3/93.

Interesting, but Asmussen's originals here are insubstantial, and the arrangements of the more familiar material are inconsistent – a slow, thoughtful 'Cherokee' is set beside a merely silly 'Alabama Barbecue'. Still, the rest of the group are in fine fettle and, the violinist has lost none of his panache.

*****(*) Still Fiddling**

Storyville 101 4252 *As above.* 6–11/99.

At 83 Asmussen still sounds like a powerful force. The material is a typically unpredictable bag – Grieg, 'My Yiddishe Momme', 'Down South Camp Meeting' and an original tribute to Stuff Smith are among the highlights – and the group has improved from the Imogena album. But the intriguing thing is, inevitably, comparing Asmussen and Grappelli in their respective old ages. Where Steff grew ever sweeter, ever more in thrall to his kind of rhapsodizing, Svend is more suspicious of old-fashioned romance. They both share a love of kitsch, but the Dane's version is more arcane – Jewish music, blues as European folklore. Moreover, Asmussen still seems to be thinking about the future, rather than the past. The music's lean and sinewy, and there's no kiss-kiss sentiment.

Peter Asplund (born 1969)

TRUMPET, FLUGELHORN

Studied in Stockholm's Royal College of Music, then played big-band gigs and led his own group.

***** Open Mind**

Dragon DRCD281 *Asplund; Johan Hörlén (ss, as); Ion Baciu (p); Christian Spering (b); Johan Löfcrantz (d).* 95.

***** Melos**

Sittel SITCD 9260 *Asplund; Johan Hörlen (ss, as, f); Anders Holtz (ky); Jacob Karlzon (p); Dan Berglund (b); Johan Löfcrantz (d); Rigmor Gustafsson (v).* 1/99.

Asplund is a post-bop trumpeter who likes to push hard – there's nothing laid-back or very impressionistic about his view of the modern mainstream. He's focused on a result in every track. Löfcrantz is a drummer who picks up and carries the rest of the band if he feels they're lagging behind, and that sense of urgency carries over into all but the most sedate pieces. *Open Mind* benefits from the decisiveness, since in and of itself it's not an especially individual programme of material. Some attractively resolved melodies, and the horns have sufficient to chew on, but nothing leaves an indelible mark. Asplund saves some of his best for a very long and detailed look at 'Stardust'.

Melos is a shade different, though perhaps not quite as removed from orthodoxy as the leader's notes imply. He claims that the use of a female voice and occasional synths introduce a romantic element which he's been moving towards in his writing. Gustafsson is used both in a wordless role and as a lyric interpreter and, if anything, this brings the record closer to the cool lyricism that is a Swedish strain which followers of that music will readily identify. Oddly enough, Asplund himself seems to take a less forthright role as soloist here, leaving Karlzon in particular to make the most distinctive impression.

Gilad Atzmon (born 1963)

SOPRANO AND ALTO SAXOPHONES, CLARINET, SOL

An Israeli who came to Britain in the early '90s, Atzmon plays his own styling of post-bop with suitably self-confident chutzpah.

***** Take It Or Leave It ...**

Face Jazz (no number) *Atzmon; Val Manix (b); Sam Anstice Brown (d).* n.d.

***** Gilad Atzmon & The Orient House Ensemble**

Tiptoe 888839-2 *Atzmon; Frank Harrion (p, melod); Oli Hayhurst (b); Asaf Sirkis (d, bandir).* n.d.

***** Nostalgico**

Tiptoe 888841-2 *As above, except add Joe de Jesus (t, tb), Brian Neil (g).* n.d.

Anyone expecting some sort of fusion of bop and klezmer jollity may be pulled up short by the attacking sound of *Take It Or Leave It ...*, recorded in Somerset and made up mostly of standards and jazz tunes given a sharp-witted, crisp despatch by the energetic trio. Atzmon isn't a relentless note-merchant, though, and some of his phrasing is actually quite spare when you expect volleys of sound. He approaches 'My Funny Valentine', done on clarinet, in a very sideways manner, and this is an unexpectedly musing performance, as is the mid-tempo 'These Foolish Things' which follows. The record has a bit of a home-brewed quality and the originals are nothing special, but it's a refreshing turn.

For the first of the Tiptoe albums, Atzmon seems to have consciously decided to 'mature': he puts down the alto, sets the jazz and standard material aside (aside from Davis and Shorter derivations), picks up the sol and introduces Turkish and Ladino tunes. The results are much tamer, and there's a sense that the fire which Atzmon customarily injects into his live performances has been smoothed away in the studio; but there's some beautiful playing nevertheless: 'Miserlu', the Turkish piece, is quite lovely.

Nostalgico follows similar paths but more intensely. We are not sure that the pastiche of '20th Century', which juggles 'It Ain't Necessarily So' and 'Caravan', actually counts for much, and if Atzmon has a difficulty here it's that he's trying to cover too many bases. To play 'Petit Fleur' as sweetly as this and line it up next to a fuming 'Love For Sale' is almost vaudevillian. No classic yet, but across the three discs there's much to enjoy.

Georgie Auld (1919–90)

SOPRANO, ALTO AND TENOR SAXOPHONES

Born John Altweger in Toronto, Auld was already bandleading in New York before he was out of his teens. After sideman work with Bunny Berigan and Artie Shaw, he led his own big band, then worked through the '40s and '50s as a freelance, sometimes in sweet settings. He can also be seen in Martin Scorsese's New York, New York.

***** Georgie Auld 1940–1945**

Classics 1322 *Auld; Chuck Peterson, Nelson Shellady, Bernie Privin, John Best, Harry Geller, Charlie Shavers, Sonny Berman, Manny Fox, Howard McGhee, George Schwartz, Billy Butterfield, Dizzy Gillespie, Al Killian, Jimmy Roma, Freddy Webster (t); George Arus, Les Jenkins, Harry Rodgers, Rude De Luca, Jerry Dorn, Bobby Lord, John D'Agostino, Eli Robinson, Trummy Young, Bob Ascher, Roger Smith (tb); Les Robinson, Harry Freeman, Musky Ruffo, Gene Zanoni (as); Ben Webster, Ronnie Perry, Coleman Hawkins, Tony Pastor, Al Cohn, Irv Roth, Al Epstein, Joe Megro, Jack Schwartz (ts); Manny Albam, Irv Greenberg, Larry Molinelli (bs); Bob Kitsis, Bill Rowland, Harry Biss, Erroll Garner, Tony Aless (p); Dave Barbour, Hy White, Mike Bryan, Turk Van Lake, Al Avola (g); Dick Horvath, Israel Crosby, Morris Rayman, Chubby Jackson, Doc Goldberg (b); Ralph Hawkins, Henry Adler, Specs Powell, Lou Fromm, Shadow Wilson, Irv Kluger (d); Patti Powers, Kay Foster, Kay Little, Gordon Drake (v).* 1/4–3/45.

This is a curious string of sessions. The first two are by a band which was really Artie Shaw's, with Auld at the helm after the leader had disappeared on one of his famous sabbaticals. Then comes a session by a sextet where the saxophonist shares the front line with Ben Webster and Coleman Hawkins (and stands his ground, surprisingly well). Finally, three 1944–45 dates where the 'genuine' Auld big band holds forth, with the likes of Dizzy Gillespie and Erroll Garner in the orchestra as well as Sonny Berman, Billy Butterfield and Trummy Young. Auld was a swing man much in the Hawkins mould, and his featured solos on the likes of 'Taps Miller' and 'I Can't Get Started' are accomplished variations on the theme: hardly individual, but managed with some style. The 1945 tracks hint at bebop without the meat of it, and Gillespie and Garner get in a few exciting bursts. A bit of a hotchpotch, but plenty to listen to.

Lovie Austin (1887–1972)

PIANO

Born in Chattanooga, Austin was an educated musician who ran her own vaudeville show, before settling in Chicago and leading pit bands and record dates as a Paramount house-pianist. She later worked in munitions and, after the war, played in dance instruction classes, recording again in the early '60s.

***** Lovie Austin 1924–1926**

Classics 756 *Austin; Tommy Ladnier, Bob Shoffner, Natty Dominique (c); Kid Ory (tb); Jimmy O'Bryant, Johnny Dodds (cl); Eustern Woodfork (bj); W. E. Burton (d); Ford & Ford, Edmonia Henderson, Viola Bartlette, Henry Williams (v).* 9/24–8/26.

A remarkable woman, and one of the first female musicians to make a significant contribution to jazz, the Tennessee-born Austin became house-pianist at Paramount in the early '20s. She settled in Chicago, but after the end of the decade she scarcely recorded again until the early '60s. There are 17 surviving sides by her Blues Serenaders, plus various accompaniments to blues and vaudeville singers, and they're all on this valuable CD. Austin's music was a tight, sophisticated variation on the barrelhouse style that was prevalent in Chicago at the time. The two sides by the trio of Austin, Ladnier and O'Bryant create a densely plaited counterpoint which seems amazingly advanced for its time. The quartet and quintet sides are harsher, with Burton's clumping drumming on what sounds like a military side-drum taking unfortunate precedence, but the simple breaks and stop-time passages have a rough poetry about them that transcends the very grimy recording. This CD adds to the old Fountain LP by including nine tracks in which Austin and some of her colleagues accompany various blues singers. The transfers are a very mixed bag, as usual with Classics: two tracks by Edmonia Henderson are terribly noisy, and none of the original Paramount recordings are better than average; but practised ears will listen through the noise to some classic Chicago jazz of its day. It really is time these sides were given a fresh remastering, though.

In 1961, when in her seventies, Austin was persuaded to record again, as accompanist to Alberta Hunter. The results are available on Original Blues Classics OBC-510.

AustraLYSIS

GROUP

Band of Australian improvisers, led by expatriate bassist-keyboardist Roger Dean and growing out of his earlier London-based group LYSIS.

***** Moving The Landscape**
Tall Poppies TP007 *Sandy Evans (ss, ts); Roger Dean (ky); Tony Buck (perc, elec).* 91.

****(*) The Next Room**
Tall Poppies TP050 2CD *As above.* 1/92.

****(*) Present Tense**
Tall Poppies TP109 *As above, except Greg White (elec, etc) replaces Buck.* 9/95–11/96.

AustraLYSIS might best be seen as a vehicle for the gently experimental musings and sonic-sketchpads of Roger Dean, a familiar figure in British improvising and fusion before his move to Sydney in the '80s. The problem with all these discs is that they've dated quickly: relatively slow technology which, under Dean's jurisdiction, has a certain theoretical weight dissipated by the furiously fast pace of progress in music involving electronics over recent years. Both *Moving The Landscape* and *The Next Room* take their energy from the work of Evans and Buck rather than Dean's ponderous structures and fussy procedures. Evans in particular contributes some engrossing arguments to what are often discouragingly undernourished and unhelpful settings. The first record is based around briefer episodes, but *The Next Room* is two big pieces accommodated on two CDs. Both sets have their rewards, but it's hard to see listeners bothering to return to them more than once or twice.

Present Tense, with White's sound manipulations and programming replacing the more conventional rhythmic contributions of Buck, is more specifically computer-orientated, although again it's Evans's acoustic playing which makes the most interesting sounds. A piece such as 'Nordic Humes' sounds like one of Klaus Schulze's tone poems and here and there it feels like a journey through a New Age retailer. A further record from the same source, *Acouslytic*, is seemingly dedicated entirely to electroacoustic composition and doesn't belong here.

Available Jelly

GROUP

A Netherlands-based group under the direction of Eric Boeren and Michael Moore, performing free-bop jazz of its own making.

***** Available Jelly**
Ramboy 014 *Jimmy Serensky (t); Michael Moore (as, cl, p); Barry Block, Stuart Curtis (ss, ts); Gregg Moore (b); Michael Vatcher (d, perc).* 84.

Michael Moore and later Eric Boeren masterminded most of the material for this band, which grew out of a group that worked as accompanists to a mime troupe in the '70s. These early records, originally on Square, were once hard to find but had a reputation well beyond their actual availability, and it's wonderful to have them on CD and find out that the fuss was entirely justified.

The eponymous first disc, which might actually be called *Le Jelly* judging by the chopped off front cover, features a wonderfully eclectic range of material, from Dizzy Gillespie's classic bebopper 'Salt Peanuts' to Mingus's 'Fables Of Faubus' to material by Sean Bergin and Abdullah Ibrahim. Moore is certainly the lead voice but only in that he seems to tie together much of the thematic material. Otherwise, it's very much a collaborative effort.

***** Monuments**
Ramboy 07 *Eric Boeren (t, c); Jimmy Sernesky (t); Gregg Moore (tb, tba, b); Michael Moore (cl, bcl, as, p, hmca); Tobias Delius (ts, hca); Alexei Levin (p, org, acc); Eric Calmes (b); Michael Vatcher (d).* 8–10/93.

***** Happy Camp**
Ramboy 10 *Eric Boeren (c, melodica); Wolter Wierbos (tb); Michael Moore (as, cl, bcl); Tobias Delius (ts); Ernst Glerum (b); Michael Vatcher (d).* 6/96.

Monuments wasn't one of their best: the band's then-new members added extra weight but they sometimes seem like excess baggage. The firecracker playing that Boeren contributed to the earlier sets seems to have been swamped by the arrangements, some of which are merely lugubrious, and the concert-hall ambience of the sound-mix doesn't suit them. But there are still some moments to savour, such as Moore's doleful 'Shotgun Wedding', a classic sad-sack dirge, and a couple of Boeren's neatest miniatures. *Happy Camp* is the loosest and liveliest of their records, recorded live at the BIM-Huis. Here the band seem ready to go back to jazz, what with two Ellington tunes (a lovely version of 'The Feeling Of Jazz') and the extra weight lost as the instrumentation goes back to six. Glerum makes the band swing more, and he fits well with Vatcher. Moore does most of the writing and he savours the counterpoint as it proceeds.

Franck Avitabile

PIANO

Sponsored by two of the giants of French jazz piano, Martial Solal and the late Michel Petrucciani, Avitabile is a brilliantly gifted youngster with a deep background in musical theory gained at the Ecole Normale Supérieure in his home town of Lyon. His work is marked by a deft touch and an effortless swing at all tempos.

***** Lumières**

Dreyfus FDM 3545 2 *Avitabile; Louis Petrucciani (b); Thomas Grimmonprez (d).* 98.

***** In Tradition**

Dreyfus FDM 3569 2 *Avitabile; Riccardo Del Fra (b); Luigi Bonafede (d).* 99.

***** Right Time**

Dreyfus FDM 36608 2 *Avitabile; Niels-Henning Orsted Pedersen, Louis Petrucciani (b); Roberto Gatto (d).* 2/00.

*****(*) Bemsha Swing**

Dreyfus FDM 36639 2 *Avitabile; Rémi Vignolo (b); Dré Pallmaerts (d).* 5/02.

Bud Powell is the main jazz influence on the young Frenchman, who seems to have been inspired by Francis Paudras's touching account of life with the troubled Bud. Where the American could be dark and brooding, there is nothing but sunshine and optimism in Avitabile's playing, added to which is an obvious interest in the farther shores of harmony. The first album, produced by Michel Petrucciani, is in some ways the most direct, but it is perhaps too engagingly simple. Avitabile has more to offer than this and succeeding records have delivered steadily more food for thought.

The pianist's understanding of bebop doesn't merely extend to reworking standard material. His own composition 'Right Time!' is a brilliantly idiomatic piece, strongly abetted by NHOP. Franck continues to show his breadth of rhythmic understanding with a Latin-tinged original, 'Facin' Up', and a delightful waltz, 'Miss Laurence', also on the third album.

With *Bemsha Swing* he seems to have gained full confidence in his skills. There are nods here and there to both Petrucciani and Solal, but the Monk tune that gives the record its title, a stunningly good 'Body And Soul' and an unaccompanied version of Duke's 'Prelude To A Kiss' all suggest that Avitabile is a pianist to watch very carefully. He may have recorded too much and too quickly and one would like to have heard each of these groups recorded during a long residency somewhere; however, there is nothing pat or studio-conscious about them and lovers of piano trios will enjoy the experience every time.

Omer Avital (born 1971)

BASS, VOCAL

Israeli-born bassist now part of the ever-burgeoning 'new jazz' community at work in New York.

***** Think With Your Heart**

Fresh Sound New Talent FSNT 104 *Avital; Myron Walden (as); Gregory Tardy (ts, bcl); Jay Collins (ts, ss, f); Jimmy Greene (ss, ts); Joel Frahm (ts); Joshua Levitt (nay f, v); Daniel Freedman (d, v).* 9/00.

***** Third World Love Songs**

Fresh Sound New Talent FSNT 114 *Avital; Avishai Cohen (t); Yonatan Avishai (p); Daniel Freedman (d).* 02.

Avital's music has a strongly vocalized quality, even if the only actual singing is done by Freedman, Avital and Levitt on 'Marrakesh'. Having no fewer than six woodwind players (and there are never fewer than four in attendance on any one track) in the band, with only bass and drums as the other contributors, makes for a diverse gathering of voices, to be sure, although none of these players is exactly a tonal extremist. It's more about a sometimes fierce but usually harmonious blending of timbres.

That said, the record has a strange, almost untutored feel, for all the virtuosity in the group. Avital shoulders all writing responsibilities bar Bob Marley's 'Redemption Song', done as a bass solo, which opens the disc, and 'Stella By Starlight', which is a melody that tends to show up the leader's own attempts. The juxtaposition of 'Andaluz' and 'Marrakesh' offers a Middle East dropped down into a New York pulse. Solos are shared out among the saxophonists, and these improvisations centre the jazz feel of music which might otherwise drift off into worldly modal jamming. For all its rough-and-ready-ness and its sometimes messy execution, the set has a vitality and vividness which many more expensive sessions struggle to touch on.

Third World Love Songs extends the promise and also introduces young Yonatan (Jonathan) Avishai, who has worked with Tzadik artist Danny Zamir and who brings a fresh and idiosyncratic vision to the session, mixing in Hebrew melodies, stray folk-tunes from unidentifiable trading cultures and a touch that can be as soft as Bill Evans and as percussive as Abdullah Ibrahim. It's a fine follow-up from the bassist, even if his thunder is stolen by the piano-player.

Bent Axen (born 1925)

PIANO

Studied Charlie Parker's music as it appeared in Denmark, and began playing regularly at Copenhagen's Vingaarden club in the late '50s. Backed many visiting Americans during this period, but eventually moved into theatre and TV work and left jazz behind.

****(*) Axen**

Steeplechase SCCD 36003 *Axen; Allan Botschinsky (t); Bent Jaedig, Frank Jensen (ts); Niels-Henning Orsted Pedersen, Ole Laumann, Erik Molbach (b); Finn Frederiksen, Jorn Elniff (d).* 12/59–10/60.

The back pages of Danish jazz history. Axen subsequently left the music, but he helped pioneer modern jazz on record in Denmark and this documents some early steps. The CD gathers in three sessions, two quintets and a trio, for what are rough-and-ready approximations of the American bebop model, refracted through the Scandinavian affection for Getzian cool. NHOP was still only fourteen when he made the trio tracks and Botschinsky was barely out of his teens. Nothing startling here, really: Axen's tunes follow familiar models and his own playing is decent if unexceptional. The most interesting player is probably Jaedig, who was as close to a genuine hard-bopper in delivery as anyone in that scene at the time. The sound is rather rough and tends to distort on volume peaks.

Albert Ayler (1936–70)

TENOR, ALTO AND SOPRANO SAXOPHONES

Born in Cleveland, Ayler played R&B on alto as a teenager, then switched to tenor during army service. Left for Sweden in 1962, recorded in Europe, and returned to the USA in 1963, recording for ESP and later Impulse! through the rest of the decade. The most intense of avant-gardists, his recordings map out much of what happened to jazz in the '60s, including its decline into attempted populism. Found dead in New York's East River in 1970.

***(*) The First Recordings: Volume 2

DIW 349 *Ayler; Torbjørn Hultcrantz (b); Sune Spångberg (d).* 10/62.

Ayler's style has been subjected to just as many conspiracy theories as his life and death. It is now generally considered to be a highly personal amalgam of New Orleans brass, rhythm and blues (to which Ayler unapologetically returned in his last two years) and some of the more extreme timbral innovations of the '60s New Thing.

The first recordings, made in Denmark, are astonishingly sparse. With no harmony instrument and a concentration on stark melodic variations in and out of tempo, they sound influenced by early Ornette Coleman; but what is immediately distinctive about Ayler is the almost hypnotic depth of his concentration on a single motif, which he repeats, worries, splinters into constituent harmonics, until even familiar standards are virtually unrecognizable. Ayler's impatience with bebop is evident throughout and, for all their unrelieved starkness, these rather solitary experiments are still remarkably refreshing. Not called on to keep time, Hultcrantz and Spangberg occasionally resort to marking it, but they seem unfazed by Ayler's primitivism. Why a regular working band should be so lackadaisical about music as unexpected as this remains mysterious. There is some evidence that Ayler didn't want these sessions to be released, or at the very least that he was sceptical about their merits. The second batch of material from October 1962 consists of four disjointed repertory pieces – 'Moanin'', 'Good Bait', 'I Didn't Know What Time It Was' and a take of 'Softly, As In A Morning Sunrise' – which see Albert effectively ignore the harmonic structure of the song and simply follow the logic of his own invention. Not once, though, does the rhythm section follow him 'out', and it is already clear that the saxophonist needs not only sympathetic interpreters but also a new body of material. John Coltrane's dismantling and reconfiguration of the popular song was not to be Ayler's recourse, though the impact of his radicalized hymns and marches had a similar, arguably even greater emotional impact.

***(*) Witches and Devils

1201 Music 9006 *Ayler; Norman Howard (t); Henry Grimes, Earle Henderson (b); Sunny Murray (d).* 64.

Like much of the discography, this is cobbled together from two sessions. Arguably, this is the first recorded glimpse of Ayler in full flow. He reaches peaks of intensity here that are among the most arresting and evocative in his brief career. The title-piece has an eldritch, haunted quality, but it is 'Holy, Holy', on which Grimes (with his bow) plays a central role, that is the real high-spot, a lowing, pungent wail that hovers between anguish and ecstatic celebration. Indeed, were there no titles to direct the listener, it would be difficult to gauge the emotional temperature of many of these performances. Howard was a friend from home in Cleveland; like Don Ayler, he is not a virtuosic or even technically secure player, but unlike Don lacks a saving expressiveness as a soloist. The real action, much as in Coltrane's work with both Elvin Jones and critically with Rashied Ali, is between saxophone and drums and Murray is a towering presence throughout.

***(*) Prophecy

Get Back 1046 *Ayler; Gary Peacock (b); Sunny Murray (d).* 6/64.

*** Bells

Calibre 1010 *As above; add Donald Ayler (t); Charles Tyler (as); Lewis Worrell (b).* 5/65.

***(*) Bells / Prophecy

ESP 1010 *As above.* 6/64, 5/65.

Prophecy was Ayler's first session for the ESP label, though it was not released until after *Spiritual Unity*. It was an important session in laying down some of the basic language of the saxophonist's career and also the problematic issue of titles and themes. Few artists have been so consistently misattributed on sleeves and in discographies, and we are happy to shoulder our share of blame for this. Two versions of 'Ghosts' represent the central action of the record. The difference is less in Ayler's playing, which is definitive, but in the role of Murray and Peacock. In the first to be taped, the bassist provides a drone figure which underpins the saxophone's wilder utterances; in the second, his playing is more obviously rhythmic. These recordings have had a chequered history and this disc may also be found under the Calibre imprint.

Bells was the notorious one-sided LP, a token that here was music so powerful you'd probably only manage 20 minutes of it before switching off the hi-fi and taking deep gulps of air. As a single, hectic performance, it still retains its power, but it's short shrift for a CD, which is why it has now also appeared paired with *Prophecy*, giving a decent duration and a hefty wallop of Ayler at his most unfettered.

CORE COLLECTION

♛ **** Spiritual Unity

ESP Disk 1002 *Ayler; Gary Peacock (b); Sunny Murray (d).* 7/64.

The poet Ted Joans likened the impact of this trio to hearing someone scream the word 'fuck' in St Patrick's Cathedral. Subjectively, there may be some validity in this, but it makes a nonsense of what was actually going on in this group. The intensity of interaction among the three individuals, their attentiveness to what the others were doing, ruled out any such gesture. Even amid the noise, the 1964 Ayler trio was

quintessentially a listening band, locked in a personal struggle which it is possible only to observe, awe-struck, from the side-lines.

We noted in our previous edition that the Ayler catalogue was in a rather shambolic state. As will be seen below, much of it has been restored, though the ESP catalogue has passed through several hands.

**(*) New York Eye and Ear Control

Calibre 1012 *Ayler; Don Cherry (t); Roswell Rudd (tb); John Tchicai (as); Gary Peacock (b); Sunny Murray (d).* 7/64.

Recorded as soundtrack music to a now-forgotten short film, this is an overrated and needlessly chaotic session that sounds like little more than an unrehearsed jam. The music comes in two undigested blocks, and though glimpses of Rudd and Tchicai are valuable at this juncture, neither has anything of great moment to impart. Ayler himself was not in any sense an abstract player and he sounds ill at ease on the session. Though he always used dynamics structurally, here power takes the place of musical thought.

*** The Copenhagen Tapes

Ayler 33 *As above; add Don Cherry (t).* 9/64.

This is a compilation of a live club performance at the Jazzhus Montmartre in Copenhagen with a studio session recorded a week later. Listeners will be used to the relatively narrow thematic repertoire of Ayler recordings and this is an extreme example, with the same melodies repeated throughout. Given the technical differences between the studio session and the Montmartre material, this is perhaps more off-putting than on other releases, but it does help understanding of Ayler's thematic and dynamic variation of a theme. Cherry's playing on the club session helps underline some of Ayler's debt to Ornette Coleman. Like his namesake, Albert's brother Don plays with a fieriness that overturns concerns about his pitching. Peacock as usual veers between a harmonic and a rhythmic role, freeing up Murray for some astonishingly powerful free playing.

*** Spirits Rejoice

Calibre 1020 *Ayler; Donald Ayler (t); Charles Tyler (as); Call Cobbs (hpd); Henry Grimes, Gary Peacock (b); Sunny Murray.* 9/65.

Anyone who argues that Ayler turned to R&B at the end of his life has missed an important detail: that black popular music was an essential component of what he had done from the very beginning. Here, at what might be thought a transitional period, it is clearly evident as both source and destination. 'Holy, Holy' might almost be some brash bar-walking theme instead of a profound spiritual statement. The addition of Call Cobbs on harpsichord gives the music some of its alien quality; rarely can the older keyboard have had such an important role in a modern jazz recording. The session was taped in concert at Judson Hall, then an important venue for new music in New York City. The intensity is extreme and the addition of a second saxophonist alongside the Ayler brothers adds to the stew. Tyler has never enjoyed great critical recognition, but he adds his voice to 'Angels' and the other tunes and finds a place to work. Interesting to compare the dynamics and the harmonic language of this session to Ornette Coleman's problematic *Crisis* with Don Cherry and Dewey Redman in the parallel roles and similar problems with the track listings.

***(*) At Slug's

Get Back 1018 *Ayler; Donald Ayler (t); Michael Sampson (vn); Lewis Worrell (b); Ronald Shannon Jackson (d).* 5/66.

Recorded on May Day 1966, this is a session of incendiary power and ranks with some of the very best Ayler performances. 'Bells' is a magnificently powerful thing, beginning with a mournful violin figure and then bringing in trumpet – Donald in characteristically raw and expressive form – then bass and saxophone with a significant harmonic shift. 'Truth Is Marching In' has never sounded so close to its origins in 'Battle Hymn of the Republic' and its anguished intensity marks as significant a subversion of familiar and homely material as Coltrane's 'My Favorite Things'. The other interesting aspect of this set is an early glimpse of Ronald Shannon Jackson, who was to have such an impact during Ornette Coleman's harmolodic experiments and as an incendiary leader. For a live recording, the sound quality is pretty good, though there are moments of unevenness.

***(*) Lörrach, Paris 1966

hatOLOGY 3500 *Ayler; Donald Ayler (t); Michael Sampson (vn); Bill Folwell (b); Beaver Harris (d).* 11/66.

Back in catalogue again, thank goodness, and still a shock and delight to listen to. More than ever, Ayler sounds like a radical preacher, taking energy from the murmured 'Amen's and 'Praise God's of his fellow-players, but basically ignoring them as he creates ever more intense harmonic rainbows across these deceptively childlike themes. This is perhaps a preacher speaking to children or to those with no grasp of abstract theology/harmony, who need everything told by example. 'Bells' and 'Ghosts' (two versions and occasional allusions elsewhere) are both part of the sermon; there is a huge version of 'Truth Is Marching In' and a long medley of 'Spiritual Rebirth'/'Light In Darkness', which freezes the blood before it warms the heart. Sampson's violin is integral to it all, though it's to be doubted whether he understood what this group was about any better than troubled brother Don did. They came and played their parts, leaving it to Albert out front to bring the congregation in. Magnificent.

**** Live In Greenwich Village: The Complete Impulse Recordings

Impulse! IMP 12732 2 CD *Ayler; Donald Ayler (t); George Steele (tb); Michel Sampson (vn); Joel Freedman (clo); William Folwell, Henry Grimes, Alan Silva (b); Beaver Harris, Sunny Murray (d).* 3/65–2/67.

Whatever technical and aesthetic shortcomings the Lörrach and Paris live sessions may have had (there is a nihilistic, fragmentary quality to the latter), the Village Theater and Village Vanguard sessions are hugely affirmative and satisfyingly complete without losing a jot of Ayler's angry and premonitory force. These are some of the essential post-war jazz recordings, and they include some of Ayler's best playing on both alto ('For John Coltrane', ironically or self-protectively) and tenor (the apocalyptic 'Truth Is Marching In'). The second bass, in addition to either violin or cello, actually sharpens the sound considerably, producing a rock-solid foundation for Ayler's raw witness.

This splendid reissue continues the progress towards a new sound. It supersedes *In Greenwich Village* and *The Village Concerts* without adding very much of significance towards what was already a remarkable record. There is a single track

('Holy Ghost') from March 1965, originally issued on the Impulse! compilation, *The New Wave In Jazz.* One other track, 'Universal Thoughts', is incomplete, presumably because the tape ran out. However, having these performances together on one set is of value. John Coltrane was present, ailing and tired, when 'Truth Is Marching In' and 'Our Prayer' were recorded at the Village Vanguard. John was to die in the summer of the following year, but his spirit is everywhere here, even though Ayler was firmly in command of his own style and approach. These are Don Ayler's finest moments. Always an approximate technician, but driven by loyalty to his brother, he produces a stream of pure sound which is unique in jazz. Not even Ornette Coleman on brass sounds so alien. A remarkable record, to be prized by anyone who shares Ayler's lonely vigil on the planet.

*** Love Cry

Impulse! GRD 108 *Ayler; Donald Ayler (t); Call Cobbs (hpd); Alan Silva (b); Milford Graves (d).* 8/67.

By the summer of 1967, Donald's mental health was increasingly unsteady and this was his last appearance on a record with his brother. Not long after this strange and strangely beautiful session, he was hospitalized. If it was difficult to characterize the philosophy of Ayler's great trio, the group that made *Spiritual Unity*, it is near impossible to define with any precision what this group was about. The unsettling jangle of Call Cobbs's harpsichord and the ferocious desynchronization of Milford Graves's drumming are by this stage the first things you hear. Ayler's wail is almost familiar and insofar as it cleaves to a melodic logic, almost comforting. Albert's forays into the false upper register are increasingly controlled, though.

Love Cry has rarely featured on anyone's list of his best or more controversial works. It is certainly one of the best recorded. The tunes are mostly very short and pungent, though 'Love Cry II' extends over seven minutes. The CD reissue includes two takes each of 'Universal Indians' and 'Zion Hill', but these only tend to emphasize how tight a rein Albert was keeping on songs and his fellow players.

*** Music Is The Healing Force Of The Universe

Impulse! 9191 *Ayler; Bobby Few (p); Henry Vestine (g); James Folwell, Stafford James (b); Muhammad Ali (d); Mary Maria (v).* 8/69.

Endlessly controversial, frequently guyed, but equally frequently used to suggest a radical new direction in Albert's music. Radical, that is, in the sense of going back to roots. This is not quite the R&B album that some readers and listeners may have been led to expect. It certainly has some of that quality and the addition of Canned Heat guitarist Henry Vestine on 'Drudgery' underlines the connection. But *Music Is The Healing Force ...* also includes some wonderful playing from Albert and some of his most innovative use of sound; the addition of bagpipes and ocarina to 'Masonic Inborn' perhaps pointed the way to a new approach. Impulse! records were, by the standards of their time in jazz strong on production values and producer Ed Michel gives the sound new layers and a new richness of tone that is much more interesting than questions of commercial 'sell-out'.

Even if the album is not demonized, one of the band has been. Mary Parks (here Mary Maria) was Albert's business manager and girlfriend and as such might seem to be a questionable presence on record. But repeated hearings and recent revelations about the last months of Albert's life suggest that she had a natural musicality ('Island Harvest' is hers) and a genuine commitment to the saxophonist's vision; pointless to dismiss her as if she was Linda McCartney.

Music ... is not the best Albert Ayler album, but it is not the laughable monstrosity it has sometimes been painted. Albert's singing on 'Oh Love Is Life' is initially risible but uses that fact to deliver a real emotional punch, and that is a lesson to be drawn from his music as a whole. This final studio statement touches on all the major themes of Ayler's life: sorrow, loss, guilt and, above all, redemption.

**(*) Nuits De La Fondation

Maeght Water 103 *Ayler; Call Cobbs (p); Steve Tintweiss (b); Allan Blairman (d); Mary Parks (v, ss).* 7/70.

Recorded in the south of France a matter of months before his disappearance and death, this now stands as a final manifestation of one of jazz's most complex and most readily misunderstood geniuses. Given the line-up and the sensibilities of players like Blairman and Tintweiss, this has less of an R&B stamp than *Music Is The Healing Force ...* The title-tune of that album is included as a curtain-piece here and there is a further version of 'Truth Is Marching In', but without Donald's bugling lines or a mournful violin, the latter lacks bite and real intensity. On piano, Cobbs is a competent but rather ordinary player and he coasts through much of this session. It may be that further live tapes of Ayler at this or earlier periods will surface for release. It's important not to fetishize final statements since they are only that by unhappy accident, not design. Albert's message to the planet was in awkward, alien speech that we have not yet deciphered. We are still unsure of its emotional temper. Listening to these unsatisfactory cuts again, cold and without prejudice, it is hard to reconcile them with some of the great statements of previous years, but it is also hard to miss the precarious balance of anger, pain and sheer, uncomplicated joy.

Azimuth

GROUP

The trio of Taylor, Wheeler and Winstone, subsequently built on but as basic an improvising chamber-jazz group as can be thought of.

***(*) Azimuth / The Touchstone / Départ

ECM 523010-2 3CD *Kenny Wheeler (t, flhn); John Taylor (ky); Norma Winstone (v); Ralph Towner (g on Départ only).* 3/77–12/79.

**(*) Azimuth '85

ECM 827520-2 *As above, except omit Towner.* 3/85.

*** 'How It Was Then ... Never Again'

ECM 523820-2 *As above.* 4/94.

The repackaging of Azimuth's first three records, and the appearance of a new disc after a break of some years, offered a chance to reassess the work of a notably understated trio whose live appearances (at least one gig every year since 1977; no mean achievement in this branch of music) are often far more rugged and sharply inflected than the recorded product would suggest. Initially, the group was a duo format for the then-married Taylor and Winstone. On the debut album, her voice floats with a characteristic balance between freedom and control over Taylor's minimalistic piano figures. Any doubts that these are jazz-trained and jazz-centred performers are immediately dispelled, and the second track, called simply 'O', is not much more than a blowing shape, over which Winstone and Wheeler (whose inclusion was suggested by ECM producer and demi-urge, Manfred Eicher, with a characteristic instinct for the appropriate touch) improvise freely. The very next track, significantly the title-cut, is the first to use the studio as a compositional device, building up layers of keyboard, voice and trumpets into a grand acoustic edifice that constantly reveals new areas of interest.

The most obvious difference between the first and third albums and the middle one of the original group is that on *Touchstone* there is no lyric component as such. Here Winstone vocalizes, turning her voice into a third and equal part in the mix. Taylor abandons the synthesizer swirls of *Azimuth* in favour of the organ's richly *breathing* sound. The result is perhaps the group's masterpiece, combining jazz, classical and contemporary composition, and sheer sound in a mix that is as invigorating as it is thought-provoking. The outstanding track is without a doubt the glorious 'See'.

Azimuth and Ralph Towner met at ECM's Oslo studios, where the guitarist was finishing an album of his own. The end of the '70s probably marked the high-water mark of the label's more experimental ethos, with Eicher encouraging previously untried permutations. Much as he does on Weather Report's *I Sing The Body Electric*, Towner sounds as if he comes from outside the basic conception of the group, but with a genuine understanding and appreciation of what it's all about. His contribution is perhaps most emphatic on 'Arrivée', which is a companion-piece to the title-track, linking the whole disc into a continuous suite. As such, it's perhaps slightly too mannered and deliberate, but none the less effective for that.

Succeeding years presented fewer opportunities to record as a unit, presumably to some extent because Wheeler in particular was busy on projects of his own. Azimuth's return to the studio was the pretty disappointing '85. With '85, Azimuth fell into the trap Towner's Oregon has always avoided: that of making style an end in itself. There is no fixed requirement that musicians or bands 'develop' stylistically, but, for all the quality of writing and performance, *Azimuth '85* did seem to be an unconfident step back.

It was then nearly a decade before the group recorded again, an awkward gap of time in critical and commercial terms. The signs are, though, that the energies of the first record have been significantly re-channelled and re-directed. '*How It Was Then ... Never Again*' suggests a backward-looking and even nostalgic subtext; the music within is as progressive and empirical as anything the group had done in 20 years. Taylor restricts himself to piano and to a compositional style that has acquired a new, though entirely non-linear, logic. Titles like 'Whirlpool' and 'Full Circle' very accurately convey his ability to infuse harmonic and melodic stasis with hints of tremendous energy. Winstone's voice is as pure and reed-like as ever, and the only question marks relate to Wheeler, who increasingly seemed to be speaking in a different musical language.

Jay Azzolina

GUITAR

Former Spyro Gyra man, but all is forgiven.

***** Past Tense**

Double Time 162 *Azzolina; Chris Potter (ss, ts); Charles Blenzig (p); John Patitucci (b); Adam Nussbaum (d).* 1/00.

***** Live At One Station Plaza**

Azziz 01 *Azzolina; Gary Versace (org); Adam Nussbaum (d).* 12/01.

The guitarist's first record, *Never Too Late*, was a dozen years old when *Past Tense* was released, prompting some surprise at Azzolina's slow delivery. The other surprise, of course, is that this is a straight jazz album, mostly of sharply written originals, and far removed from the smooth fusion of Spyro Gyra. You might be forgiven for mistaking parts of this with early Scofield, except that it's Azzolina who sounds the more committed jazz guy. He hasn't quite got Sco's chops, but on his own 'Inside Pie Eyes', the Gershwin-rooted 'Rhythms Change' and the one standard, Weill's 'My Ship', he plays terse lead lines that roll and weave round Potter's exuberant saxophone-playing. Blenzig is pretty much unknown, but knows his way round the keyboard. Patitucci is masterful and rich-toned; Nussbaum keeps it all together. A delightful surprise all round.

The live record is released on Azzolina's own label and may be difficult to get. It's worth the persistence, though. Working with an organ trio might seem a cue to let loose with his rock thang, but Jay sticks to his jazz guns with a vengeance, even throwing in his own variation on Coltrane's most famous composition, 'So Steps The Giant'. The opening number, 'It's All About You', is deceptively mild-mannered compared to the rest. Surprise on surprise; it's a thoroughly intelligent and adventurous gig that threatens to rival John Abercrombie's experiments in this direction.

Ab Baars

CLARINET, SOPRANO, TENOR AND BARITONE SAXOPHONES

Dutch improviser specializing in the reed family, a sideman with Maarten Altena, and a notably individual voice in the overpopulated family of reed players.

**** Krang**

Geestgronden 2 *Baars (solo).* 12/87–6/89.

****(*) 3900 Carol Court**

Geestgronden 12 *Baars; Wilbert De Joode (b); Martin Van Duynhoven (d).* 3–6/92.

***** Sprok**

Geestgronden 14 *As above.* 2–5/94.

****(*) Verderame**

Geestgronden 17 *Baars (solo).* 1/95.

***** Hef**

Terp 02 *Baars; Terrie Ex (g).* 00.

Baars makes very heavy weather of *Krang*. Rather than improvising in any specific direction, his solos tend to circle in on themselves or to reach a spurious climax of increasingly harsh repetitions. This makes the soprano solo 'Geel en Rood' barely listenable, a different application of Steve Lacy's methods to sometimes grisly ends. But the blustering weight of the baritone on 'Spaat' or the false pathos of the tenor on the title-track are more interesting.

There's another version of 'Krang' on the first trio album. After the abstractions of the solo record, it comes as a mild shock to hear him with an almost conventionally swinging rhythm section on John Lewis's 'Plastic Dreams'. But the other pieces, revolving round remote kinds of interplay among the three players, are more typical of what Baars is after. The leader's solos still tend to grind through curtly defined areas of timbre and phrasing, but at least they're leavened by the inquiring bass and drum parts.

Sprok seems like a loosening-up and a further clarifying at the same time. Baars makes his clarinet and tenor sound more dry and stone-faced than ever, but bass and drums shift smoothly between free playing and courtly, strict time. Not bad at all.

His second solo disc, though, isn't much less drear and mirthless than the first one. Various dedications – to Han Bennink, Misha Mengelberg, Pee Wee Russell, John Carter – are writ intimidatingly large, as if he wants to express only the starkest and most harsh aspects of his influences. He sticks to clarinet and tenor, and several of the pieces have a morse-code brevity of layout. Taken one or two at a time it is quite powerful, but a whole disc (even at only 40 minutes) is pretty hard going.

The duos with guitarist Ex pursue an ever more radical (if that word counts for anything any longer in free playing) fragmentation of form, technique and expectation. With 14 tracks despatched inside three-quarters of an hour, it's hard to suggest that anything outstays its welcome, and in these compact, rigorous displays there's little sense of anything which could be called 'development': every piece seems to aspire to a life entirely independent of every other piece. Difficult to know how to rate such music, given that it seems entirely *sui generis* but if these words have done enough to intrigue the prospective listener, perhaps Baars will have achieved his aim.

*****(*) Party At The Bimhuis**

Wig 09 *Baars; Mariëtte Roupe Van Der Voort (as, f, bf, picc); Guus Janssen, Misha Mengelberg (p); Ig Henneman (vla); Wilbert De Joude (b); Martin Van Duynhoven (d).* 1/03.

Baars throws a party to celebrate ten years of his trio (they start with a revisit to '3900 Carol Court') and invites some guests along to join in the fun. And great fun it is, with the pianists joining in at different points and all seven players getting together for three tracks where the ensemble has a real particularity – makes you wish that Baars convened a septet more often. Baars takes a terrific tenor solo on Monk's 'Reflections' and there are dedications to Von Freeman and Roswell Rudd, as well as a John Carter tune. Well worth attending.

Alice Babs (born 1924)

VOCAL, PIANO

Born in Kalmar, Babs was more of a pop-MOR singer in her native Sweden, but her affiliations with jazz were recognized by Duke Ellington, who featured her with the band on several occasions from 1963.

***** Swing It!**

Phontastic PHONTCD 9302 *Babs; Thore Ehrling, Gosta Redlig, Gosta Torner, Rolf Ericson, Rune Ander, Olle Jacobson, Nisse Skoog, Anders Sward (t); George Vernon, Bertil Jacobson, Sven Bohman, Karl-Erik Lennholm, Sverre Oredsson (tb); Sven Gustafsson, Ove Lind, Putte Wickman, Charlie Redland (cl); Casper Hjukstrom (cl, as); John Bjorling, Ove Ronn, Arne Domnérus, O Thalen (as); Carl-Henrik Norin, Gunnar Lunden-Velden, Gosta Theselius, Curt Blomqvist (ts); Lars Schonning (bs); Stig Holm, Allan Johansson, Rolf Larsson, Charles Norman, Rolf Svensson (p); Bosse Callstrom (vib); Erik Frank, Nisse Lind (acc); Rolf Berg, B. Larsson, Folke Eriksberg, Sven Stiberg, Jonny Bossman, Nils-Erik Sandell, Sten Carlberg, Kalle Lohr (g); Thore Jederby, Henry Lundin, Gunnar Almstedt, Romeo Sjoberg, Simon Brehm, Rolf Bengtsson (b); Ake Brandes, Andrew Burman, Henry Wallin, Gosta Heden, Thord Waerner, Gosta Oddner (d).* 5/39–4/53.

*****(*) Metronome-Aren 1951–1958**

Metronome 4509-93189-2 2CD *Babs; orchestras of Charlie Norman, Harry Arnold, Gunnar Lunden-Velden, Anders Burman, Ernie Englund.* 51–58.

***** Far Away Star**

Bluebell ABCD 005 *Babs; Money Johnson, Johnny Coles, Barry Lee Hall, Willie Cook, Mercer Ellington, Americo Bellotto, Bertil Lövgren, Jan Allan, Håkan Nyqvist (t); Vince Prudente, Chuck Connors, Art Baron, Torgny Nilsson, Lars Olofsson, Bertil Strandberg, Sven Larsson (tb); Harry Carney, Russell Procope, Harold Minerve, Harold Ashby, Parcy Marion, Arne Domnérus, Claes Rosendahl, Lennart Aberg, Ulf Andersson, Erik Nilsson (reeds); Duke Ellington, Nils Lindberg (p); Rune Gustafsson (g); Joe Benjamin, Red Mitchell (b); Quentin White Jr, Nils-Erik Slorner (d).* 6/73–5/76.

***** There's Something About Me ...**

Bluebell ABCD 052 *As above, except omit Ellington personnel; add Jan Allan (t), Anders Lindskog (ts), Erik Nilsson (bs), Davor Kajfes (ky), Rune Carlsson (d).* 5/73–9/78.

Along with the very different stylist, Monica Zetterlund, Alice 'Babs' Nilsson is Sweden's most renowned vocalist in the jazz world – although, like Zetterlund, she has often touched only peripherally on jazz surroundings. Her early tracks feature on the useful compilation, *Swing It!*, which is in many ways the most jazz-orientated of all four discs. She tackles everything from 'Some Of These Days' and 'Darktown Strutters Ball' to 'Yodel In Swing' and 'Opus In Scat', in settings that range from accordion trios to impressive big bands. Three airchecks with a small group including Rolf Ericson (terrific on 'Truckin'') offer some of the best music, but the entire disc has much to enjoy, not least Babs's light but amazingly confident handling of the English lyrics. The earliest track dates from before her sixteenth birthday, yet she seems fearless in all this music. The Metronome two-disc set is of much more limited appeal. Sung mainly in Swedish, this includes a lot of pop material which has marginal jazz content and, though Babs is unfailingly charming, in parts it can be a struggle.

She first worked with Ellington in 1963, and she remained a favourite with Duke: the four 1973 tracks with the band on *Far Away Star* are a souvenir of one of their final collaborations, though the tracks from an Ellington memorial concert the following year with a Swedish group are actually rather better. So is *There's Something About Me ...*, which has some more Ellington material – 'Checkered Hat', 'Me And You' and the title-piece – but which is most interesting for five songs co-written by John Lewis. Babs, whose cool, slightly impassive but fundamentally emotional delivery seems well suited to this material, produces some of her best work here. There is much more still awaiting reissue.

Back Bay Ramblers

GROUP

An 'occasional' American repertory group playing the hot dance music of the '20s.

***** 'Leven Thirty Saturday Night**

Stomp Off CD 1262 *Peter Ecklund (c); Bob Connors (tb); Steve Wright (cl, as, ts, bs, bsx); Bill Novick (cl, as); Butch Thompson (p); Peter Bullis (g, bj); Stu Gunn (tba, b); Bill Reynolds (d); Karen Cameron (v).* 1/93

***** My Mamma's In Town!**

Stomp Off CD 1279 *As above, except omit Thompson and Gunn; add Mark Shane, Bob Pilsbury (p), Vince Giordano (tba, bsx, b) ; Andy Stein (vn), Jimmy Mazzy (v).* 1/94.

Of the many repertory bands recording for Stomp Off, the Ramblers pay some of the most dutiful homage to their inspirations – usually the hot dance music of the '20s rather than the out-and-out jazz of the period. So the first CD includes arrangements drawn from the books of Bob Haring, Jack Pettis and Spike Hughes, while the second relies heavily on the work of Jean Goldkette, Annette Hanshaw and Ted Lewis. None of the players makes a special impression by himself – they're playing for the band, and the lilt and deferential swing of this music is its reason to exist. Ecklund has some agreeable 16-bar interludes, Connors is splendidly versatile, and Novick and Wright are skilled interpreters of the old-time reedsman's role. That said, the music can seem almost airlessly polite at times. Cameron sings sweetly, Mazzy with a bit more gusto on the second disc. Little to choose between the two discs, and it's a churl who would deny that it's pleasant to find a group ready to perform something like Phil Napoleon's 'You Can't Cheat A Cheater' in the godless '90s.

*****(*) Cuttin' Up**

Stomp Off CD 1355 *Jon-Erik Kellso (c); Bob Connors (tb); Billy Novick (cl, as); John Clark (cl, as, ts, bs); Ross Petot (p); Scott Philbrick (g); Peter Bullis (bj); Vince Giordano (bsx, b, tba); Bill Reynolds (d); Karen Cameron (v).* 10/99.

Zestier than ever, this hot dance outfit is getting hotter. Bob Connors did all the work on the arrangements, faithful to such sources as Andy Kirk, Bennie Moten, Bill Brown and His Brownies and even Dunk Rendelman and His Alabamians, and the latest line-up works hard at getting them right without sacrificing any of the good-humoured enjoyment they seem to get out of what should be fun music to play. Karen Cameron returns for some more sweet-toned vocals. Twenty-four titles is a lot to get through, but that's just the Stomp Off philosophy of value for money!

Back Door

GROUP

Bass-led British fusioneers. Ancestors of Morphine and Jaco Pastorius.

***** Back Door**

Warners 2716 *Ron Aspery (as, f, ky); Colin Hodgkinson (b); Tony Hicks (d).* 72.

***** 8th Street Nites**

Warners 2753 *As above.* 73.

*****(*) The Human Bed**

Hux 31 *As above; add Dave McRae (p).* 73–74.

British males of a certain age wilt in nostalgia when the name is mentioned. Back Door were loud, rough and in their way surprisingly sophisticated. In the time-honoured spirit of what goes around comes around, they have become mildly fashionable again. Hodgkinson's rolling bass is the key element, a lo-fi throb that still beguiles even when it seems as passé as Morgan sports cars and Spangles. 'Slivadiv' is the fondest memory of the first album, while old Leadbelly and Robert Johnson blues are the highlight of the Felix Pappalardi-produced *8th Street Nites.* The BBC sessions on *The Human Bed* are probably the best representation of the band, despite the inexplicable horror of 'The Dashing White Sergeant'. Permit us our moment of nostalgia ... and embarrassment.

Gerard Badini (born 1931)

TENOR SAXOPHONE

Sometimes known as 'Mr Swing', this Parisian tenorman has a big bruising sound in the Lockjaw Davis mould. Originally a trad man on the local scene, he subsequently played regularly with Claude Bolling, and led small groups and big bands under the name (Super) Swing Machine. Health problems have latterly obliged him to lead from the piano and give up the tenor.

***** A Night At The Popcorn**

Black & Blue BB 966-2 *Badini; Milt Buckner (p); Jimmy Woode (b); Sam Woodyard, Panama Francis (d).* 3/75.

A boisterous night in Geneva, where Badini led this multinational crew through a suitably rowdy couple of sets. Sam Woodyard and Milt Buckner seem endlessly pleased to be in each other's company, joshing their way through the music, and Badini hollers and roars his way through the tunes, mostly blues of one sort or another. Panama Francis sits in on one tune, possibly while Sam was refreshing himself at the bar. High-spirited fun, although best heard a few tracks at a time.

Bad Plus, The

GROUP

A project which grew out of various collaborations between the three protagonists, and now a high-profile matter in new American jazz.

****** The Bad Plus**

Fresh Sound FSNT 107 *Ethan Iverson (p); Reid Anderson (b); David King (d).* 12/00.

*****(*) These Are The Vistas**

Columbia 510666-2 *As above.* 10/02.

****** Give**

Columbia 515307-2 *As above.* 10/03.

We previously listed the first album under Iverson's name, but The Bad Plus have quickly evolved into a singular entity and a hot property, signing to Columbia in 2002 and releasing two albums which carry on the work of the first disc. You don't expect the stately trinity of piano–bass–drums to qualify as any kind of power trio, but that's what happens with this unit. On the debut, Iverson, Anderson and the 'certifiable mid-western drum star' David King go at a group of their own originals, one standard ('Blue Moon') and two pop tunes. The treatment of Abba's 'Knowing Me Knowing You' is a textbook example of the jazz transformation of an uneventful melody, and Nirvana's 'Smells Like Teen Spirit' (which the others had to force Iverson into even learning!) is turned into a glorious, helter-skelter set-piece, the tune stirred and thickened by the pianist's voicings while King's drums swing them off the stand. The five originals are fascinating: 'Labyrinth' severely beautiful, '1972 Bronze Medalist' peculiarly funky.

For sheer freshness the debut probably remains our favourite, but as produced by Tchad Blake, the trio have gained presence in the studio and the Columbia albums are exhilarating, funny, surprising. There are some remakes of tunes from the debut on *These Are The Vistas*. The Aphex Twin's 'Film' is a beautiful set-piece and Blondie's 'Heart Of Glass' is destruction. Blake manages to get a mix which gives each man equal prominence, and while some have complained that King's drums are too loud and too rock, careful listening – and this band asks for just that – reveals both charges as misguided. Anderson is, in his way, just as loud.

Although they do a semi-apocalyptic 'Iron Man' (from Black Sabbath's songbook) to close *Give*, the originals are getting more prominence, and they're played with fierce conviction. In America, the group have excited an almost absurd degree of controversy, with complaints coming that they're being pushed forward because they're white and likely to appeal to neanderthal rock audiences. What we hear is three talented musicians going in a very individual direction. Either way, at least some of this music is required listening.

Benny Bailey (born 1925)

TRUMPET, FLUGELHORN

Bailey won his spurs in three of the most important big bands of his day, Jay McShann's, Dizzy Gillespie's and Lionel Hampton's, staying with the last for almost five years. His bright, hard-edged tone softens markedly in small-group settings, but without losing its burnish. Bailey spent a considerable time in Europe, where he worked with Eric Dolphy and where he has sustained a regular recording schedule.

*** Big Brass

Candid CCD 79011 *Bailey; Julius Watkins (hn); Phil Woods (as, bcl); Les Spann (f, g); Tommy Flanagan (p); Buddy Catlett (b); Art Taylor (d).* 11/60.

Bailey is probably best known as first trumpet in the Kenny Clarke/Francy Boland big bands of the '60s. He is also an impressive and entertaining soloist, with a number of distinguishing marks on his musical passport, noticeably his much-commented-upon octave plummets and his enigmatic lines that seem to have neither melodic nor harmonic significance, just a strangely specific logic all their own. His bebop background is still evident on *Big Brass*, certainly his finest available record (though the deleted *Serenade To The Planet* is considered essential documentation). The themes have begun to stretch out, though, into long, quasi-modal strings that contain any number of potential resolutions. Flanagan is a sympathetic accompanist. Woods and Rouse could hardly be more different, but Bailey responds magnanimously to the challenge posed by each.

***(*) Grand Slam

Storyville 8271 *Bailey; Charlie Rouse (ts); Richard Wyands (p); Sam Jones (b); Billy Hart (d).* 10/78.

Originally released on Jazzcraft, this pungent set is one of Bailey's best. The inclusion of three tunes by arranger Fritz Pauer is a bit over the top, but there are also fine originals by Benny – 'Theloniousassault' and 'Who's Bossa Now?' – which cover a good bit of his range, from fiery bebop to a more gently swinging sound. An alternative take of Pepper Adams's 'Reflectory' is less emphatic than the issued version, but Rouse's two solos and Wyands's generous accompaniment make the track a welcome addition. Bailey sounded capable of anything in these years. He has always quoted classic recordings – almost unconsciously, one suspects – and it's interesting here to see how often he seems to make reference to Dizzy, Fats and Howard McGhee in the course of his solos, even when the material is far removed from orthodox bebop or Afro-Cuban. A fine album, recommended to Bailey newcomers and established fans alike.

*** The Satchmo Legacy

Enja 9407 *Bailey; John Bunch (p); Bucky Pizzarelli (g); Jay Leonhart (b); Grady Tate (d).* 99.

A welcome addition to the Bailey catalogue, albeit a relatively low-key affair. Benny's tone doesn't have the bite and snap of past years and he very wisely makes no attempt to pastiche Pops on this tribute record. Kicking off with a bright but also thoughtful 'Some Day You'll Be Sorry', Benny mostly avoids predictable material. Only 'Do You Know What It Means To Miss New Orleans' sounds like it comes from a self-conscious Satchmo project. The other tracks very much bear Benny's individual stamp and are all the better for it. In Bunch and Pizzarelli, he has sidemen who know and respect this material, but who are able to bring something individual to it. Grady Tate knows all the words and most of these performances offer a reminder that astonishing as Armstrong was on the trumpet, he was also one of the most important singers in jazz.

Buster Bailey (1902–67)

CLARINET

Bailey learned from a noted classical teacher in college in Chicago and was already a virtuoso by the time he joined Fletcher Henderson in 1924, staying until 1937. In the '50s he often played with Henry Allen, then freelanced until ending his career back with his Henderson colleague, Louis Armstrong, in the All Stars.

**(*) Buster Bailey 1925–1940

Classics 904 *Bailey; Henry 'Red' Allen, Charlie Shavers, Frankie Newton (t); J. C. Higginbotham (tb); Pete Brown, Benny Carter, Russell Procope (as); Clarence Todd, Charlie Beal, Don Frye, Billy Kyle (p); Danny Barker, James McLin (g); Buddy Christian (bj); Elmer James, Johnny Williams, John Kirby (b); Walter Johnson, O'Neil Spencer, Zutty Singleton (d); Jerry Kruger, Judy Ellington (v).* 5/25–6/40.

Bailey's many records with Fletcher Henderson are probably his best legacy. Certainly these sessions under his own name are a disappointing lot. His single coupling for Banner in 1925, with Clarence Todd and the vigorous Buddy Christian, is rather good, but it's dubbed from a very rough 78 and 'Squeeze Me' has some outrageous artificial echo. A 1934 session with Allen,

Higginbotham and Carter is good if restrained, but most of the remaining dates – many with variations of the John Kirby line-up in which Bailey was a regular – are drearily bouncy light music, with the ludicrous tea-dance version of 'Pine Top's Boogie Woogie' a low point and the endearing if ridiculous 'Man With A Horn Goes Berserk' making one wonder what kind of musician Bailey saw himself as. The transfers, after the disastrous start, are just about acceptable.

Derek Bailey (born 1930)

GUITAR

A figure of immeasurable importance in contemporary music, Bailey has remained true to a radical philosophy of improvisation which dispenses with all the conventional parameters of music: line, rhythm, vertical harmony. The Yorkshireman was a key figure in the development of free jazz and in groups like Josef Holbrooke, Iskra 1903 and the Spontaneous Music Ensemble; other key associations were with drummer Tony Oxley and saxophonist Evan Parker, with whom he founded Incus records. Bailey was also for many years ringmaster of the annual Company week of free improvisation.

***** Fairly Early With Postscripts**
Emanem 4027 *Bailey; Anthony Braxton (reeds, f); Kent Carter (b); John Stevens (d).* 7/71–10/98.

***** Solo Guitar: Volume 1**
Incus CD10 *Bailey (g, syn solo).* 2/71.

***** Outcome**
Potlatch P299 *Bailey; Steve Lacy (ss).* 73.

*****(*) Dynamics Of The Impromptu**
Entrophy ESR004 *Bailey; Trevor Watts (ss); John Stevens (d, bugle).* 12/73-1/74.

****** Incus Taps: Solo Guitar 101-104**
Organ of Corti 10 *Bailey (g solo).* 73.

***** Improvisation**
Ampersand ampere 2 *Bailey (g solo).* 75.

****** Domestic & Public Pieces**
Emanem 4001 *As above.* 75–77.

Bailey's sometimes forbidding but always challenging music illuminates certain important differences between European and American improvisers. Whereas American free jazz and improvisation have tended to remain individualistic – the most convenient image is the soloist stepping forward from the ensemble – European improvisers have tended to follow a broadly collectivist philosophy which downplays personal expression in favour of a highly objectified or process-dominated music. Perhaps the best concrete illustration of the difference can be found in Bailey's duo performances with the multi-instrumentalist Anthony Braxton. Despite considerable mutual admiration, these confirm the old saw about Britons and Americans being divided by a common language. Braxton's formulations are still conditioned by the deep structures of jazz, Bailey's according to a mysterious metalanguage by which a performance offers few guidelines as to its presumed origins and underlying processes. (The guitarist did once record a splendidly ironic version of 'The Lost Chord'.)

Like a good many European improvisers, Bailey underwent an accelerated and virtually seamless transition from jazz to free jazz to free music. He has performed with such innovative groups as Josef Holbrooke and Iskra 1903, but since 1976 his activities have centred on solo and duo work (where he is most influential as a performer) and on his loosely affiliated collective, Company, locus of some of the most challenging musical and para-musical performance of recent years. Company has been sufficiently unlimited to draw in musicians from a straight jazz background (most strikingly Lee Konitz), avant-garde composer–performers such as trombonist Vinko Globokar, and even dancer Katie Duck, as well as long-standing associates Evan Parker, Jamie Muir, Barre Phillips, Han Bennink and Tristan Honsinger, with all of whom Bailey has made significant duo recordings.

Bailey's music resists exact description and evaluation. Eschewing special effects (apart from a swell pedal on his amplified performances and a one-off use of VCS3 synthesizer on *Solo Guitar: Volume 1*), he plays intensely and abstractly. The early solo records are still the best place to start with Bailey, though the release of *Fairly Early* offers a glimpse of Derek playing solo and with other musicians who share his philosophy. It also offers a rare insight into his political view, as he discusses current affairs to a free-form accompaniment in a series of 'cassette letters' to label-owner Martin Davidson. The CD has the additional advantage of offering material from a nearly 30-year span, valuable if you want a quick introduction.

But a word of warning. If you don't open yourself without prejudice to what is happening on these tight, intense and dynamic numbers and on the three solo guitar records, it seems improbable to unlikely that you will respond to anything else that Bailey has recorded. The playing is, as even classical players have admitted, entirely idiomatic. It owes nothing to any existing style, though Bailey did make one BBC interviewer's jaw drop when (though famously resistant to any discussion of influence) he mentioned Teddy Bunn of the Spirits of Rhythm as a major source. In the most curious way, *Solo Guitar* now sounds quite old-fashioned – not anachronistic, but redolent of an earlier, more innocent phase in the free movement when the moment was everything.

This is still the spirit that governs *Domestic & Public Pieces* which, as the title suggests, brings performance material together with what can't be described as 'rehearsal' in this context but is closer to a process of private musing, diary-keeping, monologue. Some of these acoustic guitar pieces have spoken commentaries, which are, as ever, wry if mostly unenlightening. The amplified concert-pieces are more familiar in nature but no less appealing to the Bailey enthusiast. As ever, Martin Davidson has done a meticulous job.

The 1973 duos with Lacy aren't quite the dialogue of the deaf his original encounter with Braxton sometimes seems but there are similar problems. Lacy is still very wedded to melody, albeit of the most heterodox sort, and Bailey at this stage is so averse to any hint of structure that they don't really meet in the middle. The work with another soprano saxophonist, Trevor Watts, and with drummer John Stevens was recorded at the legendary Little Theatre Club in London. This material is at the root of much of what happened in British improvisation, so it has a historical importance beyond its slightly ramshackle aesthetic. Even Bailey doesn't sound as if he's quite doing it for real in places. One of Bailey's first attempts to sell his music commercially was in boxes of quarter-inch tape on three-inch reels. Some of these pieces are now reissued as *Incus Taps (sic)*, documenting four fantastically aggressive and committed episodes of improvisation that still represent the most unfettered work he was ever prepared to release. They make for tough listening, but they're an essential part of the Derek Bailey story.

***** Tristan (Duo)**

Incus CD 53 *Bailey; Tristan Honsinger (clo, v).* 10/75, 2/76.

Bailey met the cellist at Massy near Paris in 1975 and immediately asked him to join in on the concert. The first half-dozen tracks are taken from that occasion. Honsinger's yelps and shouts are a form of deranged scat singing; the crowd seem uneasy how to respond, but they get used to it and as the dynamics gradually build they respond more warmly to the astonishing interplay of two very different stringed instruments. The remainder were originally released on Incus as *Duo* and are included here without sweetening or post-production of any sort. Derek uses his regular electric and his 19 (approximately) string guitar, as well as a gizmo called the Waiswich crackle box on 'The Shadow'.

***** New Sights, Old Sounds**

Incus 48/49 *Bailey (g solo).* 78.

This reissue usefully torpedoes any notion that before the '90s Bailey was not interested in playing anything that had identifiable form or a rhythmic groove. On the very long 'Live In Kavalinka', he plays what sounds like flamenco and elsewhere there are outbreaks of blues and Spirits of Rhythm-era swing. For the most part, though, what one hears is a Westerner modifying his language to reach out to his Japanese hosts and in the process influencing a whole generation of Japanese guitarists and free players, who tend to regard Bailey as a demigod. A valuable double set of solo work, long unavailable.

***** Cyro**

Incus CD01 *Bailey; Cyro Baptista (perc).* 86.

***** 1972**

Cortical CD14 *Bailey; Han Bennink (perc).* 72.

*****(*) Han**

Incus CD02 *As above.* 3/86.

Bailey has generally preferred to work in the company of percussionists, and a quick comparison of his recordings with the elegant Baptista and the forceful and witty Bennink demonstrates how thoughtfully contextualized all his work is. The best point of comparison between these sets is illustrated on a later album, *Village Life*, with the African percussionists Louis Moholo and the younger Thebe Lipere. Like Thebe, Baptista seems content to gloss and embellish Derek's ideas rather than take a proactive stance. Bennink is more like Moholo, driving the music along not in a rhythmic groove but by the sheer force and intensity of his sound. He can sound like one of the great swing drummers of the '30s, or like a Jean Tinguely sculpture, deconstructing itself. It is a relationship that has lasted many years and, apart from Tony Oxley, no other musician has ever shown a closer appreciation of what Bailey is about.

***** Drops**

Ictus/New Tone rdc 5037 *Bailey; Andrea Centazzo (perc).* 4/76.

Presumably misdated on the sleeve (which suggests 1967), this was originally released on Centazzo's own vinyl label, Ictus, which is now being reissued in some bulk. As often when working with percussionists, Bailey is in exceptional form, negotiating nine relatively short pieces on both acoustic and electric, spinning out his dry, unemphatic lines with characteristic authority and esprit. Centazzo might almost be confused with Paul Lovens on this showing, playing abstractly but with an undercurrent of melody never far from breaking surface. 'How Long Has This Been Going On?' bears no discernible relation to the standard, lest anyone picks it up in the hope that Bailey has been caught out doing some swing; there are better reasons for buying this unusual, original record.

***** Dynamics Of The Impromptu**

Entropy 4 *Bailey; Trevor Watts (ss, as); John Stevens (d, c).* n.d.

Though the Spontaneous Music Ensemble was co-led by John Stevens and Trevor Watts, Bailey was a core member and the perfect embodiment of the group's stance on radical abstraction. These self-title improvisations are cast in a language which will be immediately familiar to anyone who came up with the British improvised scene in the early '70s. Once heard, Watts's plangent alto and Stevens's rushing, almost swing-inspired percussion are unforgettable, and Bailey seems to hold the balance of forces here. More than 70 minutes of music, played with absolute concentration and balance.

*****(*) Aida**

Incus 40 *Bailey (g solo).* 8/80.

Miles Davis was much drawn to *Aida* as a source of rich funkable tunes. Bailey, almost needless to say, isn't thinking along those lines at all on this remarkable set, with its three broad slabs of guitar sound. As ever, Bailey keeps the effects and articulation devices pared to the bone, and his fretting and fingering have an unexpected softness and precision which occasionally suggest something graspable amid the abstraction. Even without reference points, this is intensely involving music.

*****(*) Arch Duo**

Rastascan 45 *Bailey; Evan Parker (ss, ts).* 82.

A recent 'archive' release from old associates who have been making this kind of music for decades, and yet they still find new means of communication each time they meet. Parker utilizes ever-higher harmonics and extremes of tone; Bailey's characteristic idiom is still a furious hardscrabble. Together, they create a unique language, not so much unintelligible to others as beyond simple decipherment.

****** Figuring**

Incus CD05 *Bailey; Barre Phillips (b).* 5/87–9/88.

Dialogue in the conventional musical sense rarely occurs (with Braxton it sounds like a dialogue of the deaf), and there have been charges that Bailey is not an unsympathetic player, is unwilling to compromise his driven and focused approach by having to respond to what anyone else is doing. With Phillips, interestingly, he seems to be doing just that, throwing back jagged and sometimes almost hostile reshapings of the bassist's typically complex and volatile ideas. This is perhaps the most accessible of the duo records and is certainly of the highest musical standard.

****** Drop Me Off At 96th**

Scatter 02 *Bailey (g solo).* 5/86.

*****(*) Lace**

Emanem 4013 *As above.* 12/89.

*****(*) Solo Guitar: Volume 2**

Incus CD11 *As above.* 6/91.

It's still Bailey's solo performances that afford the clearest impression of his pitchless, metreless playing, and these examples are among the best of their kind. Twenty years on from the first *Solo Guitar*, the basic premisses seem not to have changed one iota, though by this time in his career Bailey was opening up to all sorts of unexpected influences and associations. The sound is less dry, but that may simply be because recording technology has moved on a step.

Drop Me Off, issued by the Glasgow-based Scatter label, is a strong statement, and one of the toughest sets Bailey had released for many years, unexpectedly so in some respects. Though it isn't a particularly sophisticated recording, it picks up a lot of low-level detail and sounds true to the dynamics of live performance. *Lace* was recorded in Los Angeles (hence the acrostic title) and consists of just two long pieces and a short encore, 'Which Bit Would You Like Again?' – a characteristic Bailey comment to the audience. Bailey had worked in LA a few times before and is regarded there as something of a visiting celebrity. Certainly, this concert seems to have been a prodigal homecoming, and the playing is as warm and committed as ever, with Bailey's pre-war Epiphone Triumph sounding full-voiced and hugely atmospheric.

*****(*) Village Life**

Incus CD09 *Bailey; Thebe Lipere (perc, v); Louis Moholo (d, perc, v).* 9/91.

As ever, Bailey is inspired and inspirational in the company of inventive percussionists, here two African modernists with very different musical styles. The young Lipere is more obviously decorative and takes what is basically an associate's role, leaving the main dialogue between Bailey, who rips and tugs at his strings with delightful abandon, and the astonishing Moholo. The latter is much closer to Bailey's aesthetic than initially appears. An Afro-modernist, he moves freely between the most joyously groove-driven of township sounds to the most outside evasion of pulse. An exhilarating album.

*****(*) Playing**

Incus CD14 *Bailey; John Stevens (d, mini-t).* 8/92.

Despite Bailey's long association with Stevens, there was almost no duo material featuring the two together until *Playing* was recorded. Concentrated and flowing, it offers an ideal opportunity, as Steve Beresford points out in his liner-note, to examine at close quarters how this music works. Beresford's analogy to the 'butterfly effect', in which tiny events have disproportionately significant outcomes at considerable physical or temporal distances, is completely apt.

***** Wireforks**

Shanachie 5011 *Bailey; Henry Kaiser (g).* 95.

*****(*) Banter**

O0 Discs 20 *Bailey; Gregg Bendian (perc).* 95

*****(*) Harras**

Avant AVAN 056 *Bailey; John Zorn (as); William Parker (b).* 95.

****** The Last Wave**

DIW 903 *Bailey; Bill Laswell (b); Tony Williams (d).* 4/95

Typically, Bailey celebrated his 65th birthday with a fresh challenge rather than a comfortable downshift. The last few years have been extremely productive ones in Bailey's life, though a spell of bad health did seem to throw additional emphasis on the CD output. The duets with Kaiser and Bendian are interesting in the context of our earlier comments about the difficulties he has sometimes had squaring his radical conception with the more groove-based work of Americans. With neither of these players does he have any problem, nor with the self-aware but cartoonish post-bop of Zorn on the apparently big-selling *Harras* CD, which is a recommended place for newcomers to approach the later work. Of the others, Bendian is a fantastically open-minded musician whose interests embrace straight composition, folk forms, free jazz and more straightahead, pulse-driven things, while Kaiser is an eccentric (in the strict sense) who is always able to put his instincts out on the line and take chances. On all three of these discs it is the absolute *concentration* of Bailey's playing that compels attention.

The real shocker is *The Last Wave*, which can be described as a post-modern revenant of Williams's notorious Lifetime by a group officially known as Arcana. One simply isn't used to hearing Derek Bailey in a context like this. It is both exhilarating and rather unsettling, like seeing a favourite uncle give up chitting seed potatoes and debudding chrysanthemums in order to take up ju-jitsu.

****** Soho Suites**

Incus CD CD 26/27 2CD *Bailey; Tony Oxley (d, perc).* 2/77–9/95.

Bailey's contribution to Tony Oxley's '60s work was definitive: clangorous guitar chords which echoed the amplified strings and metal percussion the drummer added to his kit in those days. Latter-day Oxley is still utterly unmistakable, and these extraordinary sides roll back the years like nobody's business. Bailey always sounds relaxed, almost conversational in the company of his old friend, and these two discs seem to pass by in moments, when in fact they are among the most substantial performances from either man in recent years. The sound could be better, but the quality of playing and the sense of mutual involvement are beguiling enough to overcome that.

*****(*) Takes Fakes And Dead She Dances**

Incus 31 *Bailey (g, v solo).* 9/95–5/97.

A mixture of studio improvisations and a quite extraordinary concert performance of Bailey accompanying his own recitation of Peter Riley's poem 'Dead She Dances', a bleak work of verse that might have come from one of the neglected corners of a Paul Haines opera. Derek manipulates what might become melodic figures into dark, mutant shapes, spattering atonal sound all over the room.

***** Saisoro**

Tzadik 7205 *Bailey; Masuda Ryuishi (b); Yoshida Tatsuya (d).* 95.

****(*) Tohjinbo**

Paratactile PLE 1101 *As above, except omit Ryuishi; add Sasaki Hisashi (b).* 4/97.

After Derek and the Dominoes, this is Derek and the Ruins, further evidence of Bailey's fruitful association with Japanese performers. The surprise is how much of the music recalls the free jazz of the '60s, and again how completely at ease Bailey sounds, without having to alter his usual attack and trajectory one whit. Tatsuya is the key element, a bright, lateral-thinking percussionist whose stop–start playing and use of vocals irresistibly recall the Scottish-born but Asian-influenced Ken Hyder. The earlier album, which apparently represented the

Ruins' first attempt at live improvisation in the studio, has a freshness and candour that doesn't carry over into the second, which seems by contrast rather deliberate and mannered. Item by item, it's difficult to be greatly enthused by *Tohjinbo* but, like most of Bailey's projects with young Japanese rockers, it has a certain cumulative impact.

***(*) Guitar, Drums 'N' Bass

Avant AVAN 060 *Bailey; DJ Ninj (d prog).* 96.

Guitar, Drums 'N' Bass became one of the most talked-about records of recent years, and further proof of Bailey's extraordinary adaptability and willingness to experiment with new genres. As so often before, though, what one hears isn't a synthesis so much as an intriguing conjunction of almost entirely unconnected elements. Bailey certainly doesn't accommodate himself to drum'n'bass but simply carries on doing his own thing against a sequence of backgrounds which become ever less relevant to his spasmodic and abrasive discourse as the record proceeds. By the end, the exercise seems almost entirely played out, and many listeners have reported rapidly diminishing returns. We're inclined to think better of it than that, but lengthening retrospect suggests this may soon seem like an amusing sidebar rather than the revelatory change of direction that was hailed on first release. Bailey's own comments on the project tend to reinforce that impression.

*** Close to the Kitchen: London Guitar Duos August 96

Blue Chopsticks 6 *Bailey; Noël Akchoté (g).* 8/96.

A studio recording, this was originally issued on a French label before being taken up by the small Chicago imprint. Whatever the provenance, it is a fine performance by Bailey and Akchoté, though in terms of existing track record it must count as a more significant addition to Akchoté's discography than to Bailey's which is – as you are seeing – enormous. Both men play electric, Bailey in his usual manner, the Frenchman in a fiery hardscrabble that occasionally calls for some preparation of the guitar strings. On one number, 'Toi Et Moi', the guitars are heard unamplified.

**** The Sign Of Four

Knitting Factory KFW 197 3CD *Bailey; Pat Metheny (g); Gregg Bendian, Paul Wertico (perc).* 12/96.

Dear old Pat Metheny continues to throw himself into the roughest, toughest playing situations, like the boy at school who gets cheerfully creamed game after game just so no one will think he's wimping out. This specially priced three-CD set was recorded live and in studio during Bailey's pre-Christmas '96 visit to New York. Apart from the short studio track, 'The Rule Of Three', on which Wertico bows out, all the material is for twinned guitars and percussion, with Bailey and Wertico sharing the right channel, Metheny and Bendian the left. Most of the material is for amplified instruments, though both guitarists play acoustically on 'The Rule Of Three', which features Pat's sitar-guitar. The whole of the first disc is taken up with the live 'A Study In Scarlet', which sounds like an edited live performance. The Sherlock Holmes titling doesn't seem to have any particular significance, for the music is as resolutely abstract as ever. Bendian plays wonderfully, conjuring a huge range of sound from his arco disc and other percussion, often vying with the guitarists for the foreground.

**** No Waiting

Potlatch P 198 *Bailey; Joelle Léandre (b).* 5/97.

In anthropology, a potlatch is an extreme form of conspicuous consumption, a gift-giving splurge intended to show how generously funded the giver is. That's almost the opposite of what is going on in these quiet, grave interchanges. Léandre has, of course, worked with Bailey before, most obviously under the aegis of his Company project. Like Barre Phillips, she is one of the few players with whom he seems prepared to exchange ideas and challenges, rather than galloping along on his own course. There are moments on the second and third improvisations (all of which were recorded at Les Instants Chavires), when *he* almost seems to be accompanying *her*. Léandre's low, sonorous line is reminiscent of the jazz bass of people like Scott LaFaro, Eddie Gomez and Marc Johnson, and here and there Bailey willy-nilly strays into quasi-harmonic territory that wouldn't have startled Bill Evans had he still been around. More than ever, we are convinced that the guitarist absorbs historical influences without even being aware of it. On this occasion, the results are absolutely fascinating.

**** Trio Playing

Incus CD 28 *Bailey; John Butcher (ts, ss); Oren Marshall (tba).* 97.

With the exception of 'I'd Love A Key', which is almost a quarter of an hour in length, these are all relatively short pieces, seven expansive and almost jazz-like trios that recall nothing more than Jimmy Giuffre's early groups with Paul Bley and Steve Swallow; though the idiom is very different, there is the same lightness of touch and something of Giuffre's folksy abstraction. Marshall has established himself as a considerable improviser on an improbable instrument, and Butcher is now one of the most effective free players in Europe: exact, unfussy and full of ideas. The studio sound is good, but one can't help wanting to see this group in a live setting as well.

*** Play Backs

Bingo 4 *Bailey; Henry Kaiser, Jim O'Rourke (g); Bundy K. Brown, John French, Sasha Frere-Jones, John Herndon, Darryl Moore, John Oswald, Casey Rice, Ko Thein, Tied and Tickled Trio (various).* 98.

**(*) Viper

Avant AVAN 50 *Bailey; Min Xiao-Fen (pipa).* 98.

*** Flying Dragons

Incus 51 *As above.* 99.

More explorations of sound, in the company of more recent collaborators. The guitar/pipa duets on *Viper* are as close as it will ever get to Derek Bailey Lite, an oddly unsatisfying experience and somewhat grating over the span of a whole CD. The live cuts from New York on *Flying Dragons* are better but still not essential Bailey material. The associations on *Play Backs* are more various, but hard to pin down verbally. We've found it to be one of his oddest records of recent years, without being able to describe its elusive essence.

*** Departures

Volatile VCD002 *Bailey; Vadim Budman (g, c, reed c); Ron de Jong (d, perc).* 5/98.

Bailey in London in company with the Canadian duo Vertrek Ensemble, whose previous release, *Another Idea of North*, was one of the freshest free-improvising records of the late '90s. Most of the titles here come from American poet Wallace

Stevens, who is an ideal inspiration for improvisers, given his belief that the imagination can transform everything. De Jong is a wonderfully playful percussionist who resembles Han Bennink more than any other familiar name, but still has his own approach and idiom. Budman is obviously influenced by Bailey's free-form approach, but is more given to electronic manipulation of his sound. The opening 'A Moving Part Of A Motion, A Discovery' is a guitar/percussion duet. The following piece, 'More Nights, More Days, More Clouds, More Worlds' is for guitar and cornet, a choice of horn that will inevitably conjure up memories of the late SME founder John Stevens's bugle passages. Derek's acoustic guitar almost plays chordal accompaniment to Budman's muted 'solo', further sign of Bailey's willingness to work closer to a jazz aesthetic in recent years. The trio 'Waving Adieu, Adieu, Adieu' is perhaps the least effective thing on the set, but there are wonderful things on the solo-driven 'Stockwell Suite'. A remarkable record all round, beautifully recorded by Tony (Hrycek-)Robinson, who seems to be the guitarist's engineer of choice.

***** Unanswered Questions – Intermission**

BvHaast 9906 *Bailey; Klaas Hekman (bsx); Chris Burn (p); Wilbert de Joode, William Parker, Hideji Taninaka (b); Gilius van Bergeijk (elec).* 2/98.

Intermission is an extraordinary group consisting of one bass saxophonist and three double bassists. The association with Bailey was an important one in terms of public profile and of this CD, which also features contributions from Burn and from sound artist van Bergeijk. The low-frequency sound, mixed with high harmonics and overtones, is immensely powerful and provides a setting for Bailey's playing which is both hugely suggestive and also interestingly restrictive. He plays differently in this context is all we're able to say, without being too specific. This is an unusual item in the discography and thus not perhaps to everyone's taste. Best sampled once you've got used to the major items in the Bailey canon.

****** LOCationAL**

Incus CD37 *Bailey; Alex Ward (cl).* 10/98, 1/99.

Ward's vocalized lines have a plaintive immediacy that comes across with great power on the opening studio cut. It finds him improvising freely over sustained drones and feedback-like tones from Bailey, who seems increasingly interested in exploring static, almost monumental shapes in contrast to his usual skittering hyperactivity. Ward's control in overblowing is as impressive as Bailey's command of electronic signals. At the start of 'Studio 2', he moves to a softer chalumeau register while Derek examines a koto-like voice interspersed with jagged single notes. There is one more studio track, two 'domestic' pieces recorded in 'rehearsal' and a long live piece which despite a very shaky recording, distant and echoey, confirms what a close working relationship exists between these players. Recommended.

***** Mirakle**

Tzadik 7603 *Bailey; Jamaaladeen Tacuma (b); Calvin Weston (d).* 99.

Derek's involvement with the kind of hard-edged noise-funk one associates with John Zorn and the Tzadik label has been one of his most fruitful directions over the last few years. As ever, he refuses to hook his usual claim on radical freedom on to fixed energy lines. The guitarist skates ahead of his companions, often playing with flashing speed, but equally often delivering sounds that have no reference to context. Not quite as startling as *Guitar, Drums 'N' Bass* seemed on first appearance, five years ago, but a wallopingly unexpected album nevertheless.

***** Post Improvisation, Volume 2: Air Mail Special**

Incus 35 *Bailey; Han Bennink (d).* 99.

Needless to say, they don't do a swinging cover of 'Air Mail Special' (though a standards set was unexpectedly on the way from Derek). The idea was ridiculously simple. In default of a face to face encounter, the two old friends would post one another taped performances, over which the relevant improvisation would then be dubbed. This is the closest to 'post'-production that a Bailey project has got. Only seasoned listeners will notice anything different and even then they won't be sure. Whether the overdubs were made 'live' (i.e. at first hearing) or whether there was a sneak audition beforehand we'll never know, but there is certainly no sign of second-guessing anywhere here. Derek is brisk and to the point on most of the tracks, and it's Han who seems the more expansive and ebullient, much as you might expect. More than a gimmick, this one-off seems a perfectly logical extension of Bailey's lifelong improvisational networking. Volume 1 has been credited to the drummer, since he starts it off

***** Daedal**

Incus CD 36 *Bailey; Susie Ibarra (d).* 99.

***** Bids**

Incus CD 52 *As above.* 99.

Ibarra comes out of the free-jazz tradition of Murray, Graves and Cyrille, but brings to it her own highly developed lyricism, a tough and thoroughly engaged idiom that is still taking shape. She is more than up to the challenge of working opposite Bailey, who loves guitar and percussion duos perhaps more than any other working context. Ibarra gives him few hints of a metre or even a trajectory but, unlike some other younger partners, she does not always defer, tending to match gesture with gesture. Confronted by Derek's characteristic surges of volume she does not batter or declaim but simply puts her own emphatic signature on the moment. Impressive stuff, though these days such duo releases are perhaps more important to the junior partner than to the great man himself.

There's some strong stuff on *Bids*, which was recorded at the Kongsberg Jazz Festival in Norway. Bailey seems ever more interested in exploring feedback as a creative resource and here he loops great wailing sheets of it round Ibarra's strangely rockish drumming. At moments we might almost be hearing onstage mayhem from some lost heavy metal bootleg. Impressive and physical.

****** Ore**

Arrival 01 *Bailey; Eddie Prévost (d).* 3/00.

Two of the Desert Fathers of British improvisation, heard together in a rare but never rarefied collaboration. All of the tracks are named after metallic elements, and there is an elemental condensation of language on the shorter pieces. The opening 'Bismuth' is there to facilitate an X-ray of the duo's language. It's slightly too long and almost discursive, but it fires Derek and Eddie into some of the most remarkable playing of both their careers. The drummer is a master of implied rhythm;

he is also capable of playing with extraordinary delicacy, and in this department at least he can on his day make Max Roach sound like Ringo Starr. Derek is almost filigreed in places, leaving more space between his notes than usual and allowing the decays to do more work than the attacks. On 'Ruthenium' he plays acoustic, and one wouldn't have been astonished to hear him break into song, some raspy old tale of northern mills and canals. A great record, released in Canada, but as with so much of this discography well worth the search.

** And

Rectangle S2 *Bailey; Pat Thomas (elec); Steve Noble (perc).* 8/97.

A disappointing performance that finds Bailey sounding almost formulaic and hasty. Noble is as ever a compelling player, but the trio doesn't sound as if it's communicating or working any kind of convincing parallelism. Not a priority item, by any means.

** String Theory

Paratactile 11092 *Bailey; Vanessa Mackness (v); Alex Ward (phone).* 00.

Jimi Hendrix wasn't the first guitarist to explore the creative potential of feedback, but he certainly raised accident to the level of art and made those squally overtones an integral component of his improvising style. Bailey has always done the same, but this is the first time that he has created a whole album of feedback effects. No sign here of his distinctive dry picking or those big, pedal-swelled dissonances. Some of the tracks are dull, and it is hard to say how often anyone will want to listen to this album. Mackness's contribution is interesting. She matches her voices to the harmonics, thereby creating beats and pulses which are intriguingly reminiscent of Derek's recent experiments with rhythm. It might have been interesting to have involved other musicians; Evan Parker, for instance, understands this territory better than anyone on the planet. Young Alex Ward isn't strictly a performer at all. He merely phones Derek, interrupting the final number.

*** Llaer

Sofa 503 *Bailey; Ingar Zach (d, perc).* 10/00.

*** Seven

Incus CD 54 *As above.* 01

Recorded in Norway in the autumn of 2000, *Llaer* catches Bailey in one of his favourite settings, working opposite a percussionist. Zach is virtually unknown outside his local scene, but he more than stands his own here. There are a few occasions where he manages to upstage Bailey, though by the same token he does occasionally defer to the guitarist, who plays amplified throughout. There are a couple of solo spots, and again the percussionist confirms his talent and his ability (reminiscent of another recent Bailey partner, Englishman Eddie Prévost) to suggest timekeeping while remaining unfettered by metre or bar lines.

Seven is equally interesting. This time Bailey plays acoustically and Zach rises to the challenge with a freer and edgier sound that is so closely wired to the guitarist's thinking that at moments it might almost be a single musician. The tracks are named after stages in a card game: 'Shuffle', 'Cut', 'Deal', etc., but with no sense that there is a definitive show at the end. Both players play their discards with as much care as their raises. They're in it together. It's us who're being taken along.

*** Duos London 2001

Incus CD 51 *Bailey; Alan Wilkinson (bs, v); Julian Kytaasy (f, bandura); Roger Turner (perc).* 3 & 10/01.

These were recorded at different times and locations, which explains a variation in acoustic as well as improvising dynamic. Bailey knows both Wilkinson (perpetually underrated) and Turner very well indeed and there is a kind of elided understanding to some of the playing with both of them. The passages with the saxophonist are heavy and almost aggressive in places but also suprisingly delicate. Bailey loves working with percussionists and his duos with Turner are brilliant, clever and ironic but never arch. The work with the flautist is too similar to his duets with pipa player Min Xiao-fen, which has always been one of our least favourite Derek Bailey projects.

**(*) Barcelona

Hopscotch HOP 10 *Bailey; Agusti Fern.ndez (p).* 11/01.

We're not convinced by this one. Fern.ndez (so spelt) favours the water-drop and trill style of improvised piano-playing and rarely sounds as if he's listening to his partner. In the same spirit, Bailey clanks and scratches away on his own. There are odd outbreaks of inside work on the piano and some temporary 'preparation' of the strings, but it's all too keyboard-centred and self-consciously haphazard to be really interesting.

**** Ballads

Tzadik 7007 *Bailey (g solo).* 02.

The idea of Derek Bailey playing standards would once have seemed absurd. Indeed, we've often mentioned it in an ironic context. Bailey's language doesn't come off a blank page but exists in the presence of a vast reservoir of blues, swing, bop, free and, yes, ballads. This project was seemingly suggested by Tzadik executive producer John Zorn, and it is quite wonderful. Bailey approaches these 12 themes (two versions each of 'Gone With The Wind' and 'Rockin' Chair') with an awkward tenderness, hinting at the melody rather than stating it and certainly not troubling himself over much with the changes, though it's clear from 'Body And Soul' that he knows them inside out. The delicacy of his playing is astonishing, and there is something profoundly moving about the whole set, almost like hearing Samuel Beckett sit down in a bar snug to sing old Irish songs. We never thought we'd see the day. Really.

**** Limescale

Incus CD 56 *Bailey; Alex Ward (cl); Tony Bevan (bsx); T. H. F. Drenching (Dictaphone); Sonic Pleasure (amp bricks).* 02.

It's no longer any surprise, after *Ballads* and the drum'n'bass projects, to hear Derek Bailey playing something like conventional jazz guitar, and there are a couple of moments here, notably on the short closing track, 'Titles By Drenching', when he might again be the bastard son of Teddy Bunn and the Spirits of Rhythm. Halfway into the track, he lays down a row of big chunky chords, utterly different from his usual triple-light acoustic work. For the most part, though, his playing is as unfettered and unconstrained as we've come to expect of him, though it's interesting that at some point in all six improvisations someone picks up what sounds momentarily like a rhythm line. It's usually brief, but it does act as a point of focus for the piece, particularly on subsequent hearings.

As often as not, it's Tony Bevan's bass saxophone that provides it, sounding not unlike a brass bass in a New Orleans band. Then, within a breath's length, he's lowing like a steer again. It's a wonderful sound, resolutely old-fashioned and a perfect foil to Alex Ward's wheedling clarinet, sometimes a bit lost in the recording, but packed with musical intelligence. His work on 'Charity Singles Ball' and 'French Archive' is stunning.

The two remaining participants are T. H. F. Drenching and Sonic Pleasure, credited with Dictaphone and 'bricks' respectively. Because there is no clear aural expectation for either of these, their contributions are harder to assess. Which is probably how it should be, because this is a genuine collective. Bailey is the senior figure and works in an idiom now so familiarly strange that most of us can recognize him from a couple of notes. One of the most stimulating records in the recent catalogue.

*** Poetry & Playing

Paratactile PLE 1116-2 *Bailey (g, v solo).* 02.

'Sometimes beauty turns my attention by endeavour…' It presumably isn't intended so, but the line from Lyn Hejinian's *Writing Is An Aid To Memory* might almost serve as a motto for Derek Bailey's career. After the drum'n'bass, the avant-rock and the ballads, here's the poetry album. As a totalizing artist, with a generous philosophy of improvisation, it makes perfect sense. Though most often cast as a leader, or maybe oracle, Bailey is also a deep listener.

His long endeavour has almost always been in the presence of other artists, sometimes audible, sometimes in the deep background, everyone from Teddy Bunn to nameless northern entertainers. The latter loom somewhat here, in these guitar improvisations and recitations from three very different poets. The lineage is most obvious in the tracks derived from Peter Riley's *Lines On The Liver*, purportedly the words of an old tramp called John Dooley speaking in a disconnected callbox on the North Staffordshire moors. Their addled intelligence and alternate vividity and flatness are a perfect foil to Bailey's guitar-playing. The opening piece by Lyn Hejinian is more overtly philosophical. She is a lyricist at heart and a very good one. There isn't a regular foot or metre in the whole thing but their musicality is evident even without the accompaniment. Bailey is not providing a musical background to the three poets' work, but an extension of it into dimensions not catered for in language. Steve Dalachinsky's *A Superintendent's Eyes* is described by the author as a 'cyclopean almost myopian ala odyssean journey' into the heart of New York. It's the least immediately engaging of the record's three elements, but it's also the one on which Bailey's contribution is most integral.

*** Scale Points On The Fever Curve

Emanem 4099 *Bailey; Milo Fine (cl, ky, d).* 3/03.

Minneapolis-based Fine has worked closely with guitarist Steve Gnitka in his own Free Jazz Ensemble. He first corresponded with Bailey twenty years before this British visit. Recorded in a pub basement, the set was their first playing encounter. No one can doubt the empathy they established and it has to be said that these four pieces are a good deal more interesting than anything Fine has done with Gnitka or the augmented FJE. Even so, he is prone to repetition and one wonders what prompted Martin Davidson to edit the two middle performances when CD length clearly wasn't the only issue. Fine's use of keyboard and clarinet was relatively restricted here, and as ever Bailey sounds most engaged when working with a percussionist.

Mildred Bailey (1904–51)

VOCAL

Mildred Rinker sent a demo record to Paul Whiteman, who hired her in 1929. After four years (and a signature hit, 'Rockin' Chair') she went solo on record and sang with husband Red Norvo's group. She was a star for the rest of the '30s, but a tempestuous personality and health problems saw her decline in the '40s, and she was hospitalized in 1949, dying after a brief comeback in 1951.

*** Mildred Bailey 1929–1932

Classics 1061 *Bailey; Andy Secrest, Charlie Margulis, Harry Goldfield, Nat Natoli,Joe Hostetter, Bo Ashford, Bobby Jones (t); Bill Rank, Jack Fulton, Fritz Hummel, Pee Wee Hunt, Billy Ruach (tb); Bernard Dalky, Charles Strickfadden, Izzy Friedman, Min Leibrook, Chester Hazlett, Frankie Trumbauer, Ray McDermott, Glen Gray, Clarence Hutchenrider, Kenny Sargent, Pat Davis (reeds); Mel Jenssen, Henry Whiteman, Joe Venuti, Matt Malneck, Mischa Russell, Kurt Dieterle, John Bowman (vn); Hoagy Carmichael, Roy Bargy, Joe Hall (p); Eddie Lang, Fritz Ciccone, Gene Gifford (g); Mike Trafficante, Pierre Olker, Art Miller, Stanley Dennis (b); George Marsh, Tony Briglia (d).* 10/29–8/32.

***(*) Mildred Bailey 1932–1936

Classics 1080 *Bailey; Bunny Berigan, Sonny Dunham, Grady Watts, Bobby Jones, Gordon Griffin, Ziggy Elman, Manny Klein (t); Tommy Dorsey, Pee Wee Hunt, Billy Rauch (tb); Artie Shaw (cl); Jimmy Dorsey, Clarence Hutchenrider (cl, as); Johnny Hodges, Kenny Sargent (as); Larry Binyon, Pat Davis, Chu Berry, Francis Lowe (ts); Luton McGrath, Joe Hall, Teddy Wilson (p); Red Norvo (xy); Mel Jenssen, Matt Malneck (vn); Dick McDonough, Gene Gifford, Dave Barbour (g); Artie Bernstein, Stanley Dennis, John Kirby (b); Stan King, Tony Briglia, Eddie Dougherty, Cozy Cole (d).* 8/32–11/36.

Mildred Bailey has now secured some comprehensive representation on CD. She had claims to be fêted on a par with Holiday and Fitzgerald – and she started recording well before either of them, with her first version of her signature, 'Rockin' Chair', dating back to 1931 – yet she was more of a transitional figure than either of those giants. Her early records suggest a singer struggling, gently, with the old style of Broadway belting (difficult enough for someone with a small voice), while some of the later ones are almost too placid and formal; yet she never lost the vaudevillian tang of the classic blues singers of the '20s, which helped her put over risqué numbers like 'Jenny' or the wartime novelty, 'Scrap Your Fat'. Lacking either Holiday's modern pathos or Fitzgerald's monumental swing, her art is modest, stylized and innately graceful.

Classics 1061 starts with Bailey as the unlisted vocalist on sides by Eddie Lang, Frankie Trumbauer and Paul Whiteman, plus a featured date with the Casa Loma Orchestra. Thereafter she gets top billing, mostly with rather schmaltzy and often unidentified bands. Most of her material seems to be songs of longing or regret, and the disc has a rather weepy feel to it. Classics 1080 sees her hitting her stride in earnest. Sessions with Berigan and the Dorsey brothers are assured, fun on 'Is That Religion?', sweet on 'Harlem Lullaby', hot on 'Doin' The Uptown Lowdown'. Sessions for Vocalion and Decca include four tracks with Berigan, Hodges and Wilson, and throughout

Bailey's voice keeps its appeal while swinging the material: she was selling plenty of records. Transfers generally seem good enough.

***** Mildred Bailey 1937–1938**

Classics 1114 *Bailey; Roy Eldridge, Bill Hyland, Stew Pletcher, Eddie Sauter, Buck Clayton, George Wendt, Louis Mucci, Jimmy Blake, Zeke Zarchy, Barney Zudecoff (t); Alex Mastren, Wes Hein (tb); Edmond Hall (cl); Hank D'Amico (cl, as); Scoops Carey, Len Goldstein, Charles Lamphere, Frank Simeone (as); Herbie Haymer, Herschel Evans, Chu Berry, Jerry Jerome (ts); Teddy Cole, Joe Liss, James Sherman, Bill Miller, Teddy Wilson (p); Red Norvo (xy); John Collins, Dave Barbour, Freddy Green, Red McGarvey, Allan Reuss, Allen Hanlon (g); Walter Page, Truck Parham, Pete Peterson (b); Zutty Singleton, Maurice Purtill, Jo Jones, Dave Tough, George Wettling (d).* 1/37–3/38.

***** Mildred Bailey 1938**

Classics 1160 *Bailey; Jimmy Blake, Zeke Zarchy, Barney Zudecoff, John Owens, Jack Palmer, Charlie Shavers (t); Wes Hein, Andy Russo, Al George (tb); Buster Bailey, Hank D'Amico (cl); Len Goldstein, Russell Procope (as); Charles Lamphere, Jerry Jerome, George Berg, Maurice Kogan (ts); Bill Miller, Billy Kyle (p); Red Norvo (xy); Allen Hanlon (g); Pete Peterson, John Kirby (b); George Wettling, O'Neil Spencer (d).* 4–12/38.

***** Mildred Bailey 1939**

Classics 1187 *Bailey; Charlie Shavers (t); Buster Bailey (cl); Russell Procope (as); Billy Kyle, Mary Lou Williams (p); Red Norvo (xy); Floyd Smith (g); John Kirby, John Williams (b); O'Neil Spencer, Eddie Dougherty, Cozy Cole (d).* 1–6/39.

***** Mildred Bailey 1940–1942**

Classics 1279 *Bailey; Roy Eldridge, Billy Butterfield (t); Jack Jenney (tb); Jimmy Lytell (cl); Robert Burns, Jimmy Carroll (cl, as); Carl Prager, Sal Franzella (bcl); Eddie Powell (f); Mitch Miller (ob, cor); Teddy Wilson, Billy Kyle, Herman Chittison (p); John Collins, Dave Barbour, Carmen Mastren (g); Pete Peterson, Frenchy Covetti, Charlie Barber (b); O'Neil Spencer, Bill Beason, Kenny Clarke, Jimmy Hoskins (d); Delta Rhythm Boys (v).* 4/40–2/42.

*****(*) Mildred Bailey 1943–1945**

Classics 1316 *Bailey; Louis Armstrong, Roy Eldridge, Charlie Shavers, Dick Vance (t); Jack Teagarden, Henderson Chambers (tb); Barney Bigard, Hank D'Amico (cl); Aaron Sachs (cl, as); Coleman Hawkins, Emmett Carls (ts); Teddy Wilson, Vernon Duke, Ellis Larkins, Danny Negri (p); Red Norvo (vib); Al Casey, Tommy Kay, Chuck Wayne, Remo Palmieri (g); Oscar Pettiford, Clyde Lombardi, Billy Taylor, Al Hall (b); Sid Catlett, Eddie Dell, Specs Powell, J. C. Heard (d); Paul Baron Orchestra.* 11/43–12/45.

*****(*) Mildred Bailey 1945–1947**

Classics 1337 *Bailey; Dick Vance, Irving Randolph (t); Henderson Chambers (tb); Hank D'Amico (cl); Emmett Carls (ts); Ellis Larkins (p); Red Norvo (vib); Chuck Wayne, Art Ryerson, Barry Galbraith, Gene Fields (g); Billy Taylor, Beverley Peer (b); J. C. Heard, Specs Powell, Jimmy Crawford (d); Julian Work Orchestra.* 12/45–3/47.

Classics have quickly completed their Bailey survey (the only missing titles are two Decca sides dating from 1950). It's an impressive run, but as with so many prolific recording artists of the period, material is often the problem: the singer has to mix quality songs with topical novelties and weaker tunes. Her accompanists – up to 1940 or so most of her backings were directed by Red Norvo – often included good soloists, but they rarely get much of a chance to step out, and a lot will depend on how much Bailey's voice and straightforward manner appeal. There are also backings by the embryonic John Kirby group. Track for track, though, Mildred rarely gives less than a sympathetic and often a great performance. Classics 1316 is nearly all made up of V-Disc recordings and it starts with four superb titles with Teddy Wilson as sole accompanist (and her delightful fluff on the intro to 'Rockin' Chair' was luckily preserved). It must have hurt her to have to sing 'Scrap Your Fat' but she still turns in a sterling effort. This is one of the best discs in the sequence. But Classics 1337 isn't far behind, and shows how Bailey's art deepened over the years: grown-up songs such as 'These Foolish Things' and 'I'll Close My Eyes' are given thoughtful, tender or quietly passionate readings. Hank D'Amico's clarinet is often her answering voice in the ensemble, and he's very good, as is the discreet Ellis Larkins.

***** The Blue Angel Years**

Baldwin Street Music BJH-306 *Bailey; Dick Vance, Max Kaminsky (t); Henderson Chambers, Miff Mole (tb); Hank D'Amico, Pee Wee Russell (cl); Emmett Carls (ts); Red Norvo (vib); Ellis Larkins, Cliff Jackson, Vernon Duke (p); Chuck Wayne, Eugene Fields (g); Eddie Safranski, Billy Taylor, George 'Pops' Foster (b); J. C. Heard, George Wettling (d).* 44–49.

Late-period Bailey with many felicitous moments. Despite very lengthy sleeve-notes, the exact provenance of all this material isn't clear, although much of it comes from her final studio dates for Majestic and Victor, and there are two closing tracks from a VOA broadcast with a Dixieland group. Though she'd been suffering health problems, the voice shows very little damage or strain on most of these pieces, and many of the trio tracks with Ellis Larkins are a delight, with a few rarer songs such as 'I Don't Want To Miss Mississippi' and 'Gone On That Guy'. The sound is mostly pretty flat, though admirers shouldn't be deterred.

*****(*) Mrs Swing**

Proper Properbox 57 4CD *As various discs above.* 29–42.

Proper's survey takes in early sessions with the Dorsey Brothers and goes up as far as her 1942 studio dates. They might have made room for some of her often more affecting later work, but it's a decent selection, packaged with their usual attractive documentation.

Victor Bailey

BASS GUITAR, VOCALS

Inventive fusion player inspired by Stanley Clarke and by Jaco Pastorius, his predecessor in Weather Report.

***** Low Blow**

ESC 4904 *Bailey; Kenny Garrett (ss, as); Michael Bearden (p, ky); Henry Hey (ky); Jim Beard (ky, v); Wayne Krantz (g); Dennis Chambers, Omar Hakim (d).* 3/99.

***** That's Right**

ESC 03676 *Bailey; Bill Evans (ss, ts, bs); Bennie Maupin (ts, bcl); Jim Beard (p, ky); Dean Brown (g); Lenny White (d).* 4/01.

Bailey's first record, *Bottom's Up*, was made a decade earlier and the gap seems on the face of it surprising. He is a bright, melodic player, with an ability to turn unexpected material into thoughtful jazz fusion. *Low Blow* pays fulsome tribute to Pastorius with a version of Jaco's 'Continuum' and a slightly dodgy vocal on 'Do You Know Who', as well as to Sly Stone's bassist Larry Graham with 'Graham Cracker'. It also includes lots of material that might have come from a Stanley Clarke album of an earlier decade. Memories of Bailey's stint with Weather Report are reinforced by the presence of Omar Hakim. The longer tracks, like the closing 'Brain Teaser', tend to drag a bit, but Bailey proves himself to be a master of crisp jazz funk and his playing, while not in the Clarke/Pastorius league, is more than workmanlike.

The follow-up album pins its colours to the mast with a tight medley of 'Knee Deep' and 'One Nation Under A Groove' from the legendary Funkadelic songbook. Benny Maupin's 'Steamy' is an interesting inclusion and there is a moving original in 'Joey', apparently dedicated to a cousin of Bailey's killed during a robbery. There are fine spots over both records from the likes of Maupin, Garrett and Evans and the production is distinctly of the moment, even given that Bailey's thing is very much '70s fusion. All credit to him for sticking to his last all these years, doing gigs for everyone from Aztec Camera to Mary J. Blige until he found a label willing to put out his kind of music.

Chet Baker (1929–88)

TRUMPET, FLUGELHORN, VOCAL

Baker was the archetypal, some would say stereotypical, 'young man with the horn', brilliant, inward, self-destructive. He grew up in Oklahoma but was in New York to witness the birth of bebop. He played briefly with Charlie Parker and developed a sound that was similar to Miles Davis's: quiet, restricted in range, and melodic rather than harmonically virtuosic. The famous pianoless quartet with Gerry Mulligan and Chet's keynote performance of 'My Funny Valentine' were important moments in the development of cool jazz. Chet's heroin habit led not so very indirectly to the loss of his teeth; the film star looks gave way to a sunken and haunted image that was all too easily projected on to the music. However low he sank – and, in later years, Chet was playing only to cover his drug bill – his technique was precise and his range of expression, whether playing trumpet or singing, remained unaffected.

**** Live At The Trade Winds 1952**

Fresh Sound FSCD-1001 *Baker; Ted Ottison (t); Sonny Criss (as); Wardell Gray, Jack Montrose, Dave Pell (ts); Les Thompson (hca); Jerry Mandell, Al Haig (p); Harry Babasin (clo); Bob Whitlock, Dave Bryant (b); Larance Marable, Larry Bunker (d).* 3–8/52.

***** LA Get Together**

Fresh Sound FSRCD 1022 *Baker; Stan Getz (ts); Russ Freeman (p); Joe Mondragon, Carson Smith (b); Larry Bunker, Shelly Manne (d).* 6 & 12/53.

***** Witch Doctor**

Original Jazz Classics OJC 609 *Baker; Rolf Ericson (t); Bud Shank (as, bs); Jimmy Giuffre, Bob Cooper (ts); Russ Freeman, Claude Williamson (p); Howard Rumsey (b); Max Roach, Shelly Manne (d).* 9/53.

***** Ensemble And Sextet**

Fresh Sound FSRCD 175 *Baker; Bob Brookmeyer (tb); Jack Montrose, Phil Urso (ts); Herb Geller (as, ts); Bobby Gordon, Bud Shank (bs); Russ Freeman, Bobby Timmons (p); Jimmy Bond, Joe Mondragon, Carson Smith (b); Peter Littman, Shelly Manne (d).* 12/53, 9/54, 7/56.

***** Big Band**

Pacific Jazz 81201 *Baker; Norman Raye, Conte Candoli (t); Bob Burgess, Frank Rosolino (tb); Bob Brookmeyer (vtb); Art Pepper, Fred Waters (as); Bud Shank (as, bs); Phil Urso (ts, bs, as); Bob Graf, Bill Perkins (ts); Bill Hood (bs); Russ Freeman, Bobby Timmons (p); Jimmy Bond, Carson Smith (b); Peter Littman, James McLean, Shelly Manne, Larance Marable (d).* 9/54, 10/56.

***** Young Chet**

Pacific Jazz 36194 *Baker; Bob Brookmeyer (vtb); Bud Shank (f); Herb Geller (as, ts); Jack Montrose (ts); Bobby Gordon (bs); Russ Freeman, Pete Jolly (p); Corky Hale (hp); Jimmy Bond, Red Mitchell, Joe Mondragon, Carson Smith, Leroy Vinnegar, Bob Whitlock (b); Larry Bunker, Stan Levey, Peter Littman, Shelly Manne, Larance Marable, Bob Neel, Bobby White (d).* 7/53–7/56.

Baker's crucial years came right at the beginning of his career, 1952–3, when he played with Charlie Parker (undocumented in the studios) and in Gerry Mulligan's pianoless quartet; Stan Getz joined Chet in a similar group at the Haig in LA in June 1953 (recorded on *LA Get Together*), returning that Christmas for a more conventional, piano-driven quintet. Some of the Monday-night jam sessions at the Trade Winds Club in Inglewood, California, produced the music collected on the first Fresh Sound CD: scrappily recorded, it doesn't make much of an album, but Baker already sounds like himself – cool, restrained, diffidently lyrical – and Criss is very much himself, a fire-engine next to Baker's roadster. Gray, Montrose and the mysterious Les Thompson garner other features, but it's nothing special. *Witch Doctor* was recorded at the Lighthouse and sounds superior, though again the diffuseness of the jam-session atmosphere tends to militate against it standing up as a record in its own right.

Ensemble And Sextet cobbles a bunch of Jack Montrose and Bill Holman arrangements, recorded in Hollywood in 1953 and 1954 (and originally released on a 10-inch LP), with a single track from a later Forum Theater engagement which is reviewed below. The September 1954 material also appears on the Pacific *Big Band* CD, which pairs it with the ensemble tracks from an October 1956 band recording. It's unfortunate that the material falls the way it does, because collectors will certainly want to have all these sessions, irrespective of the overlap. Both are mono sets, but the Pacific probably has a shade more oomph.

Young Chet is one of a proliferating sub-genre of (mainly) vocal compilations. Individual sessions can probably be identified by reference to dates, but this is unlikely to be of interest to serious collectors. Insomniac romantics may well find it pleasing.

***** Chet Baker & Charlie Parker: Complete Jam Sessions**

Definitive DRCD 11231 *Baker; Charlie Parker, Sonny Criss (as); Russ Freeman, Al Haig, Jimmy Rowles (p); Harry Babasin, Carson Smith (b); Shelly Manne, Larance Marable (d).* 6/52, 11/53.

When Charlie Parker auditioned for a new trumpeter on the West Coast in 1952, it seems that Chet's name was at the head of his list. There was an immediate rapport between the two, not apparently cemented by drugs, as cynics think, but by a genuine musical chemistry. That's evident on these fascinating sessions. The first was taped at the Inglewood Club in June with Harry Babasin's All Stars. The 22-year-old Baker was no more uncomfortable a bebopper than Miles turns out to be, but on this occasion the playlist didn't include any of the Parker originals and contrefacts recorded the following year at the University of Oregon, but less recondite material like 'Indiana', 'Liza', 'They Didn't Believe Me' and Tadd Dameron's 'The Squirrel', which turns into a nutty chase. Sonny Criss comes across like Bird's more sober self. His articulation is nothing like as assured as Parker's and on a couple of occasions, Chet seems to mimic his faint stutter on the attack of a phrase. Baker keeps his best and most open-shouldered work for 'The Chase' and takes his choruses with ease and grace. He's on less certain ground in the November 1953 session with Jimmy Rowles, Carson Smith and Shelly Manne. The tempo seems to trouble him on 'Ornithology' and he doesn't have much to offer on 'Barbados' either, beyond a reworking of tried and tested licks. A fascinating document. Bird went back east and told Miles there was a boy in California who could 'eat him up'. The reaction is not recorded.

***** Chet Baker With Strings**

Columbia Legacy 65662 *Baker; Mario Pezzotta (tb); Bud Shank (as, f); Jack Montrose, Zoot Sims (ts); Gianni Basso, Fausto Papetti (reeds); Russ Freeman (p); Giulio Libano (p, cel); Franco Cerri, Joe Mondragon (b); Shelly Manne (d); strings.* 53–54.

Being asked to record with strings was at this period a sign that you had arrived. Chet takes to it with languid ease, floating through and over a set of arrangements by Marty Paich, Shorty Rogers and Johnny Mandel, and turning in some lovely, well-crafted solos. The mainly Italian orchestra is well drilled and nicely nuanced. He still wasn't entirely confident as a singer and so there are no vocal spots on a session that would have been ideally suited to a couple of torchy numbers.

Given the quality of the band, and Chet's relative youth, it was inevitable that one or two of the other players would be asked to take solos. Zoot and Bud are nicely featured and Russ Freeman takes the spotlight on his own composition, 'The Wind', which is one of the high-points of the date. Three extra tracks – alternative versions of 'You Don't Know What Love Is', 'You Better Go Now' and Jack Montrose's 'A Little Duet For Zoot And Chet' – were included on the reissue.

*****(*) This Time The Dream's On Me: Chet Baker Quartet Live, Volume 1**

Blue Note 25248 *Baker; Russ Freeman (p); Carson Smith (b); Larry Bunker (d).* 53, 54.

*****(*) Out Of Nowhere: Quartet Live, Volume 2**

Blue Note 25263 *As above, except omit Bunker; add Bob Neel (d).* 7–8/54.

*****(*) My Old Flame: Quartet Live, Volume 3**

Blue Note 31573 *As above.* 7–8/54.

***** West Coast Live**

Blue Note 35634 *Baker; Stan Getz (ts); Russ Freeman (p); Joe Mondragon, Carson Smith (b); Shelly Manne, Bobby White (d).* 6/53–8/54.

***** Boston, 1954**

Uptown 2735 *Baker; Russ Freeman (p); Carson Smith (b); Bob Neel (d).* 54.

The first of these was Chet's first recorded performance as a leader, and it finds him in fine, relaxed form. The disc combines material from Los Angeles with a later gig recorded at a Masonic Temple in Michigan. There are a few problems with the source material which distorts some of Chet's sustained notes; it seems surprising that these couldn't be corrected during the remastering process, given that the background isn't too busy or intrusive. 'My Funny Valentine', always a signature piece, gets off to a slightly weird start with Bunker sounding as though he's introducing a high-wire artist.

That might have been more appropriate to 'Carson City Stage' on *Out Of Nowhere*, the second release from this early period. Written by the bassist, it's a wild shoot-em-up of a piece, not at all the kind of thing that would be associated with Chet in later years. Smith is also dominant on 'No Ties'. The later material on this disc was recorded at the Tiffany Club in LA (the rest is from the Civic Auditorium in Santa Cruz) and it carries over into Volume 3, *My Old Flame*. The Tiffany had a certain reputation, and that may explain the rather edgy and even abrasive character of the music. These are important discs in the Baker oeuvre, a clear sign that in early days at least he was much closer, certainly in a live context, to the bop idiom that he seemed to be leaving behind. Hearing him with a piano-player also reminds how he could play when the chords were securely laid out under him. Even given the enormous and sprawling nature of the discography, these are records that even more casual Chet fans should make space for. If you didn't feel you could stump up for the Mosaic box set, here's your chance.

The other Blue Note makes officially available material that most ardent Chetophiles will have either bought or righteously spurned in bootleg form. These are scrupulously mastered and historically important, not least since Chet and Getz apparently loathed one another on sight. Gerry Mulligan was in the slammer at the time, which was why the stand-in was necessary. The earlier set was at the Haig in LA, the latter at the notorious Tiffany again, though here the sparky energy of the quartet sessions has been lost. Trumpet and sax seem to chase one another round the houses without getting down to any real musical interaction. It's a slightly dispiriting performance, though again historically very significant, and to that degree worthy of its place on the shelf.

The Uptown airshots from the Storyville club in Boston are also worth having. Chet sings on 'Time After Time' but for the most part plays bright, up-tempo jazz with a bop tinge. 'Maid In Mexico' and 'A Line For Lyons' were both regularly programmed at this period and these are good performances of both. Some tracks are very short, presumably in response to a red light from the broadcast guys, but the set has some coherence.

*****(*) The Best Of Chet Baker Plays**

Pacific Jazz 97161 *Baker; Conte Candoli, Norman Faye (t); Frank Rosolino (tb); Bob Brookmeyer (vtb); Bud Shank (as, bs); Herb Geller, Art Pepper (as); Richie Kamuca, Jack Montrose, Phil Urso, Bill Perkins (ts); Russ Freeman, Bobby Timmons, Pete Jolly, Carl Perkins (p); Carson Smith, Joe Mondragon, Curtis Counce, Leroy Vinnegar, Jimmy Bond (b); Larry Bunker, Larance Marable, Shelly Manne, Stan Levey, Peter Littman (d); Bill Loughborough (perc).* 7/53–10/56.

****** Let's Get Lost: The Best Of Chet Baker Sings**

Pacific Jazz 92932 *Baker; Russ Freeman (p); Carson Smith, Jimmy Bond, Joe Mondragon (b); Shelly Manne, Bob Neel, Larance Marable, Peter Littman (d).* 2/53–10/56.

***(*) Chet Baker Sings

Pacific Jazz 1222 *Baker; Jimmy Bond (p); Russ Freeman (p, cel); James E. Bond, Carson Smith (b); Larance Marable, Bob Neel (d).* 2/54, 7/56.

*** The Route

Pacific Jazz 92931 *Baker; Art Pepper (as); Richie Kamuca (ts); Pete Jolly (p); Leroy Vinnegar (b); Stan Levey (d).* 7/56.

*** At The Forum Theater

Fresh Sound FSRCD-168 *Baker; Phil Urso (ts); Bobby Timmons (p); Jimmy Bond (b); Peter Littman (d).* 7/56.

***(*) Chet Baker And Crew

Pacific Jazz 82671 *As above.* 7/56.

*** Chet Baker Cools Out

Boplicity CDBOP 013 *As above, except add Art Pepper (as), Richie Kamuca (ts), Pete Jolly (p), Leroy Vinnegar (b), Stan Levey (d).* 7/56.

Richard Bock began recording Baker as a leader when the quartet with Mulligan began attracting rave notices and even a popular audience, and the records the trumpeter made for Pacific Jazz remain among his freshest and most appealing work. The material is currently a little scattered across the seven releases listed above, two of which are best-ofs, and one – *The Route* – which was subsequently put together from tracks strewn across various compilations over the years. *The Route* is effective: Kamuca is strong enough to match the other horns, and the rhythm section does a surprisingly better job on what are mostly standards. On *Forum Theater* and *Cools Out*, Urso's almost mentholated tenor is an apposite foil, but the music is rather underachieved and all too similar to many of the sessions being cut in the city in this period. A couple of tracks duplicate each other on these two CDs (not all the tracks were made for Pacific), and the Boplicity disc includes a single item from the *Route* band. The appearance in 1993 of *And Crew*, with two previously unissued tracks and material formerly issued on Jazz West Coast and Crown, offers pretty definitive coverage of this material, and there's no earthly reason to plump for the Fresh Sound instead.

To hear the best of Baker himself, one must turn to the other records. Controversy has simmered over the extent of Baker's powers: a poor reader, a restrained technician, he sticks to the horn's middle range and picks at bebop lines as if they were something that might do him harm; yet he can play with sometimes amazing accomplishment. The blues 'Bea's Flat' (on *The Best Of Chet Baker Plays*), a scintillating line by Russ Freeman, provokes a solo of agility enough to dismiss charges of Baker's incompetence as ludicrous. It was on the various quartet sessions with Freeman that Baker did most of his best work for Pacific. The five tracks on *Plays* cover some of them. The rest of the compilation makes an intelligent choice from the trumpeter's other sessions, and – as the title suggests – it's all trumpet and no vocals.

The other disc contains what are still Baker's most popular recordings, his first vocal sessions for Pacific. The 20 tracks include all of the original *Chet Baker Sings* LP ... and purists have been loudly wishing ever since that he didn't, except that Chet's voice has a quiet, almost creepy beauty that became steadily more sepulchral as the years went by. Even this early, he sounds as if he's crooning quietly to himself. He certainly doesn't *project*. The new edition of the original album is also in catalogue: it's programmed out of chronological sequence so that the 1956 material, by far the most accomplished, is heard first, and only then do we get the February 1954 session that began his career as a vocalist. It's fair to remember that Louis Armstrong was almost as revolutionary a vocalist as he was a trumpet-player. It's difficult to make that claim for Chet, but listening to 'Like Someone In Love' or (inevitably) 'Valentine' from the '54 date, it's evident how different he must have seemed from just about anyone else on the scene at the time.

***(*) Chet Baker In Paris

Emarcy 543547-2 *Baker; Benny Vasseur (tb); Jean Aldegon, Teddy Hameline (as); Armand Migiani, Jean-Louis Chautemps (ts); William Boucaya (bs); Francy Boland, Raymond Fol, Richard Twardzik, Gérard Gustin (p); Jimmy Bond, Benoît Quersin, Eddie De Haas (b); Jean-Louis Viale, Nils-Bertil Dahlander, Pierre Lemarchand, Peter Littman (d).* 55–56.

***(*) Verve Jazz Masters 32

Verve 840632-2 *Baker; Benny Vasseur (tb); Jean Aldegon (as); Frank Strozier (as, f); Stan Getz, Armand Migiani, Jean-Louis Chautemps, Phil Urso (ts); William Boucaya (bs); Leon Cohen, Wilford Holcombe, Henry Freeman, Seldon Powell, Alan Ross (reeds); Francy Boland, Jodie Christian, Richard Twardzik, Hank Jones, Hal Galper, Gerard Goustin, Bob James, René Urtreger (p); Everett Barksdale (g); Caterina Valente (g, v); Jimmy Bond, Eddie De Haas, Richard Davis, Michael Fleming, Victor Sproles (b); Nils-Bertil Dahlander, Connie Kay, Charlie Rice, Charles Saudrais, Marshall Thompson (d).* 10/55–6/65.

Baker's Parisian sessions are among his finest and most considered work. Unfortunately, the fine four-disc survey of this music, previously on Emarcy, has now been boiled down to a single disc, with several important pieces missing, and for that reason we dock it at least one notch from our rating. What's here is still excellent: spare and introspective quartet music, more swinging larger groups, and it's by no means all pale and melancholic: what's striking is the firmness of Baker's lines and his almost Tristano-like logic on occasion. For non-specialists, though, the *Jazz Masters* compilation is good value. It includes a track from the October '55 sessions, with later European material and a group of tracks recorded back in America in 1964 and 1965; the best of these are probably the four songs recorded with Urso and Strozier in New York, November 1964, a highlight for that period.

*** Chet Baker Introduces Johnny Pace

Original Jazz Classics OJCCD 433 2 *Baker; Herbie Mann (ts, f); Joe Berle (p); Jimmie Burke (b); Philly Joe Jones, Ed Thigpen (d); Johnny Pace (v).* 58.

By rights this should have been the baritone's album, and there is something very attractive about Pace's Sinatra-influenced delivery, but it's Chet's relaxed fills and solos which really command attention. On 'All Or Nothing At All', he strays outside the bar-lines to deliver a passionate declaration, while on 'We Could Make Such Beautiful Music', 'It Might As Well Be Spring' and 'Yesterdays' horn and voice combine in three seductive duets.

*** The Art Of The Ballad

Prestige 11011 *Baker; George Coleman, Zoot Sims (ts); Pepper Adams (bs); Herbie Mann (f); Bob Corwin, Kenny Drew, Bill Evans, Al Haig, Kirk Lightsey, Renato Sellani (p); Kenny Burrell (g); Paul Chambers, Earl May, George Morrow,*

Franco Serri, Herman Wright (b); Roy Brooks, Clifford Jarvis, Philly Joe Jones, Connie Kay, Gene Victory (d). 8/58–8/65.

This is one of the first of a veritable rash of themed collections, mostly late-night smokers and romantic torch songs. Many of them we have overlooked. This isn't vintage Chet either, but it has some fine things on it and creams some of his best slower-tempo recordings for Prestige. There are only a couple of vocals, which will appeal to those unconvinced by Chet's papery whisper. 'Polka Dots And Moonbeams' is fantastic and 'Almost Like Being In Love' is fleet enough to get the pulse racing, robust for a ballads album.

***** It Could Happen To You**

Original Jazz Classics OJC 303 *Baker; Kenny Drew (p); George Morrow, Sam Jones (b); Dannie Richmond, Philly Joe Jones (d).* 8/58.

***** Chet Baker In New York**

Original Jazz Classics OJC 207 *Baker; Johnny Griffin (ts); Al Haig (p); Paul Chambers (b); Philly Joe Jones (d).* 9/58.

***** Chet**

Original Jazz Classics OJC 087 *Baker; Herbie Mann (ts, f); Pepper Adams (bs); Bill Evans (p); Kenny Burrell (g); Paul Chambers (b); Connie Kay, Philly Joe Jones (d).* 3/59.

***** Plays The Best Of Lerner & Loewe**

Original Jazz Classics OJC 137 *Baker; Herbie Mann (ts, f); Zoot Sims (ts, as); Pepper Adams (bs); Bill Evans, Bob Corwin (p); Earl May (b); Clifford Jarvis (d).* 7/59.

Perhaps Baker wanted nothing more than to be a part of the modern-jazz mainstream; certainly, after his earlier adventures, his records were taking on the appearance of another bebop trumpeter wandering from session to session. These are all worthwhile records, but without any regular cast of players Chet sounds like a man trying to be one of the boys. He has no problem with the assertiveness of the group on *In New York*, which shows how far he'd come from the supposed early fumblings (never very apparent from the actual records). But this set, and the Lerner & Loewe collection and the similarly directed *Chet*, aren't very different from the standard bop outings of the time: good, but working off a solid routine. *It Could Happen To You* is more of a singing record, and it includes a couple of his most charming efforts on 'Do It The Hard Way' and 'I'm Old Fashioned'.

***** With Fifty Italian Strings**

Original Jazz Classics OJC 492 *Baker; Mario Pezzotta (tb); Glauco Masetti (as); Gianni Basso (ts); Fausto Papetti (bs); Giulio Libano (p, cel); Franco Cerri (b); Gene Victory (d); strings.* 9/59.

****(*) In Milan**

Original Jazz Classics OJC 370 *As above, except add Renato Sellani (p); omit Pezzotta, Papetti, Libano.* 9–10/59.

Back in Europe, Baker lived in Italy, where he eventually ended up in jail. The strings album is a rather good one of its kind: it was inevitable that Baker would go with this treatment eventually, and by now he was assured enough not to let the horn solos blow away on the orchestral breeze. 'Violets For Your Furs', for instance, makes the most of both the melody and the changes. *In Milan* features a good band – Basso was one of the leading Italians of the day – but it's an uneventful session.

***** Picture Of Heath**

EMI 9332 *Baker; Art Pepper (as); Phil Urso (ts); Carl Perkins (p); Curtis Counce (b); Larance Marable (d).* 61.

This is probably better known as *Playboys* and for a notorious album cover showing a topless blonde covering her assets with two glove puppets. This version is more PC, just a monochrome shot of the guys in studio. The music is pretty good, though it was the prospect of two of the most celebrated junkies on the West Coast actually working together that gave the album its spurious cachet. In fact, it's Urso who consistently impresses, particularly when he digs in behind the unusual chords Perkins favours and blows hard. Baker is less prominent than on some sessions, but plays with an interesting economy and often trades ideas with Pepper. The title isn't a misprint; most of the selections were written by Jimmy Heath and the best of them – 'CTA', 'For Minors Only' and 'For Miles And Miles' – might have been written for the trumpeter, so comfortably do they sit in his register and tempo.

***** The Italian Sessions**

RCA 68590 *Baker; Bobby Jaspar (ts, f); Amadeo Tommasi (p); René Thomas (g); Benoît Quersin (b); Daniel Humair (d).* 62.

***** Somewhere Over The Rainbow**

RCA Bluebird 61060 *As above.* 62.

A fine group – it was mostly Bobby Jaspar's, with local man Tommasi sitting in – and Baker has to work hard to get some room. Quersin and Humair are a grooving rhythm section, Thomas gets in some voluble solos, and Jaspar is his usual mix of detachment and intensity; Baker, though, seems undecided whether to play hot or cool. *Somewhere Over The Rainbow* offers a budget-price version of the same music, minus two tracks.

***** Chet Is Back**

BMG International 79619 *Baker; Bobby Jaspar (ts, f); Benoît Quersin (b); Daniel Humair (d).* 1/62.

Hearing Chet with Bobby Jaspar is the closest you'll get to a Chet/Pres summit, and it works very well indeed on this 'comeback' record. The material is very varied and quite adventurous, kicking off with Monk's 'Well, You Needn't' and including Rollins's 'Pent-Up House' and a blues ballad by Tommasi. In fact, Chet has rarely concentrated so doggedly on blues tonalities as he does here, as if he were working through the basic idiom all over again.

***** Baby Breeze**

Verve 538328 *Baker; Phil Urso (ts); Frank Strozier (as, f); Hal Galper, Hilary James, Bobby Scott (p); Kenny Burrell (g); Michael Fleming (b); Charlie Rice (d).* 1/64, 2/65.

***** The Most Important Jazz Album Of 1964/65**

Roulette Jazz 81829 *As above.* 64-65.

Chet came back from Europe trying to get his act back together but also finding that the scene had changed quite considerably since his departure. The new group was an effort to toughen up his sound, in line with the new vogue for hard bop and a certain suspicion of West Coast cool. There is a nice little story behind this session on which Chet has to play with a borrowed flugelhorn, having lost his own trumpet to an opportunistic thief. The sound is obviously still his but there is something slightly different about it, and every now and then Chet seems to hesitate fractionally on a phrase as if the action is unfamiliar under the fingers. And yet he is very good indeed on the Hal Galper tunes and on familiar stuff like 'Everything Depends On You' and 'Born To Be Blue'. The pianist is in fine, expressive form, as is Bobby Scott, who comes in for some of the later tracks, though he overcooks some of his own material. A couple of alternative takes fill out a welcome reissue. Sorry to obsess, but if you were recording on 14 February 1965, isn't there a song you might think of playing, or at least alluding to?

The second disc, with that hopeful title, is dominated by Tadd Dameron tunes, not an area of repertoire that you'd normally associate with Chet but obviously a source of inspiration to him as he glides through 'Soultrane', 'Mating Call' and 'Tadd's Delight', a clever way of aligning Baker with such nascent stars as John Coltrane.

*** Baker's Holiday

Emarcy 838204-2 *Baker; Alan Ross, Henry Freeman, Seldon Powell, Leon Cohen, Wilford Holcombe (reeds); Everett Barksdale (g); Hank Jones (p); Richard Davis (b); Connie Kay (d).* 65.

Chet on flugelhorn and as a vocalist obeying what he thought was the most impressive aspect of Billie Holiday's singing, that she never raised her voice. It's a warm, swinging session that is kept quite deliberately low-key. On the bigger horn, Chet actually doesn't sound so very different, a little broader, a little less clipped in faster passages, but essentially the same. Richard Davis emerges much more clearly than on the LP, and he and Jones provide the springboard for graceful solos on 'Travelin' Light' and 'That Ole Devil Called Love', our personal favourites from an album with a box-of-chocolates flavour.

*** Groovin' With The Chet Baker Quintet

Prestige PR20 7460-2 *Baker; George Coleman (ts); Kirk Lightsey (p); Herman Wright (b); Roy Brooks (d).* 8/65.

*** Comin' On With The Chet Baker Quintet

Prestige PR20 7478-2 *As above.* 8/65.

*** Cool Burnin' With The Chet Baker Quintet

Prestige PR20 7496-2 *As above.* 8/65.

*** Boppin' With The Chet Baker Quintet

Prestige PR20 7512-2 *As above.* 8/65

The pairing with Coleman might at first seem like *la belle et la bête*, except that Big George has always had a more sophisticated harmonic awareness than seems obvious at first hearing and an ability to enunciate a soft and unemphatic melody line with absolute directness of purpose. Factor in the magnificent Lightsey, and these sessions begin to make sense. There is certainly too much material spread too thinly, and it might have been just about possible to make one very strong or two very decent records out of the tracks available. As things stand, the quality is spread rather thin.

These records have previously been available under other names, but this restores the sequence to its original set of titles and to completion. The parallel with the classic Miles Davis discs, *Relaxin'*, *Cookin'*, and so on, was conscious and deliberate, designed to enhance Chet's reputation as the 'white Miles'. The main audible difference was that Baker played on flugelhorn throughout, getting a broad, 'fat' tone that worked superbly on ballads. There is scarcely a dud track in the sequence, but one or two inevitably stand out. 'On A Misty Night' (*Boppin'*) is wonderful, there is an unexpected reading of Tadd Dameron's 'The 490' on *Cool Burnin'* and that record also closes with a delicious interpretation of Jimmy Mundy's 'Sleeping Susan'. If you really can afford only one of the discs, it's the one to go for, but these have been reissued at an attractive budget price and Chetophiles can indulge their completism without breaking the bank.

*** You Can't Go Home Again

Verve 543516-2 2CD *Baker; Paul Desmond (as); Michael Brecker (ts); Hubert Laws (f, bf, picc); John Scofield (g); Richie Beirach (p, ky); Kenny Barron, Don Sebesky (ky); Ron Carter (b); Alphonso Johnson, Tony Williams (d); Ralph McDonald (perc); strings.* 5/72.

*** She Was Too Good To Me

Columbia 40804 *Baker; Paul Desmond (as); Hubert Laws (f); Romeo Penque, George Marge (woodwinds); Bob James (p); Dave Friedman (vib); Ron Carter (b); Jack DeJohnette (d); strings.* 7 & 11/74.

In 1968, having moved to San Francisco, Baker was attacked and severely beaten, suffering the kind of injuries to his mouth that horn-players dread. The incident has been explained as a random mugging, and as a 'reminder' of defaulted drug payments by a local supplier. Whatever the explanation, the loss of several teeth and a nearly unbreakable narcotics habit gave his face that caved-in, despairing look that it wears on a score of album covers from the '80s. If Chet began as a golden youth, he ended his days as a death's-head.

F. Scott Fitzgerald wrote that there were no second acts in American lives. To an extent, Chet bore that out. The years between 1970 and his rather mysterious death in 1988 were a prolonged curtain. What they did confirm was the truth of another literary tag, Thomas Wolfe's 'You can't go home again', which was used for a wonderful quartet piece, recorded by the slowly rehabilitating trumpeter in 1972 with Paul Desmond, by far the best thing on the A&M album, though by no means representative of its rather slick, fusion-tinged product. America really didn't know what to do with him, other than wrap him up in no-substance parcels like this, but for *She Was Too Good To Me* he was cushioned as carefully as possible. Creed Taylor lined up some very safe playing partners, including the peerless Paul Desmond, and sweetened some of the arrangements with strings. The opening 'Autumn Leaves' is confident enough to leave you wondering why Chet had been away and whether he really had. His chops sound in good shape and his phrasing is effortlessly melodic.

The group pretty much envelops him on occasion, and some will find that his quieter passages are swamped in detail; but it was the '70s and if a record didn't make you feel you were being drenched in 'production' from head to toe, you'd probably have asked for your money back. He might have included 'Valentine', just to underline that he was back in business and relatively intact. As it is, 'Tangerine' is the big show-stopper, a genuinely beautiful performance.

*** In Concert

India Navigation IN 1052 *Baker; Lee Konitz (as); Michael Moore (b); Beaver Harris (d).* 74.

Not a label on which one would expect to find either of the two front-men, concentrating as it did largely on avant-garde music. This set, apparently Baker's first in America for some time, was recorded at Ornette Coleman's New York City loft. It's standard bop fare, freeze-dried and then set to the quite demanding rhythm set up by Moore and Harris. Sonny Rollins's 'Airegin' gets things moving, followed by a long 'Au Privave'. Later tracks are more representative of Chet's style, and he shapes some lovely solos on 'Body And Soul' (demonstrating that it's not just a tenor saxophonist's number), 'Willow Weep For Me' and 'Walkin''. The sound is rather poor but the music is interesting enough and fills in an awkward gap in the current discography.

*****(*) Once Upon A Summertime**

Original Jazz Classics OJC 405 *Baker; Greg Herbert (ts); Harold Danko (p); Ron Carter (b); Mel Lewis (d).* 2/77.

For the remainder of his life, Chet lived out of a suitcase. He enjoyed cult status in Europe and followed an exhausting and seemingly futile itinerary, 'going single' with local musicians. Having moved over to flugelhorn after his beating, he gradually restored his lip. The late sound is frail, airy, almost ethereal. Usually assumed to be a development of Miles Davis's style (and Chet followed a similar repertoire of standards), it was actually more reminiscent of Fats Navarro at his most delicate and attenuated. Unlike Miles, Chet did not favour mutes but developed a quiet, breathy delivery that made such accessories irrelevant.

Originally released on Galaxy, this is a fine, straightforward jazz session. Herbert isn't particularly well known, but he acquits himself with honour in a no-frills ballad style, with occasional glimpses of a tougher, hard-bop diction peeking through. Chet plays very cleanly and sounds in better lip than at any time in the previous ten years. The rhythm section can't be faulted. Good versions of 'E.S.P.' and 'The Song Is You', with Danko well to the fore on the latter.

***** Sings/Plays Live At The Keystone Korner**

High Note 7112 *Baker; Roger Rosenberg (ss, bs); unknown (ts); Phil Markowitz (p); Jon Burr (b); Jeff Brillinger (d).* 2/78.

The piano apart, this sounds like an attempt to recapture the sound of the old Baker–Mulligan quartet. It no more than half succeeds. The story is that Chet broke his dentures shortly before going onstage, which is probably why the singing takes precedence. Baker's problems are only evident on 'Secret Love', the longest of four tunes, when he muffs part of his first entrance. For the most part, his playing is as effective as ever, as is the singing, if you are partial to it. Rosenberg has a delightful time, switching to soprano on the Richie Beirach tune 'Broken Wing' and wuffling through some nice choruses on baritone on 'But Not For Me'. The mystery of the set is the identity of the tenor player who sits in on 'Secret Love' and a rather staccato 'Blue'n'Boogie'. Suggestions would be welcome. Markowitz and Brillinger were part of the regular line-up at this time but it's Burr who wins plaudits for his firm melodic lines.

****** Live At Nick's**

Criss Cross Jazz 1027 *Baker; Phil Markowitz (p); Scott Lee (b); Jeff Brillinger (d).* 11/78.

***** Oh You Crazy Moon**

Enja 9453 *As above.* 12/78.

****(*) Two A Day**

Dreyfus Jazz Line FDM 365092 *As above, except Jean-Louis Rassinfosse (b) replaces Lee.* 12/78.

Distinguished by a notably fresh choice of material, the Criss Cross is another fine jazz set. Richie Beirach's 'Broken Wing' was written specially for Chet, but the long version of Wayne Shorter's 'Beautiful Black Eyes' (it can also be heard on the later France's Concert session) is the product of an unexpected enthusiasm that fed the trumpeter with new and relatively untried material. Markowitz is an admirably responsive accompanist and fully merits 'featured' billing on the sleeve. The Shorter track is by far the longest thing on the session, though two CD bonuses, the relatively predictable standards, 'I Remember You' and 'Love For Sale', are both over ten minutes. Gerry Teekens is too sophisticated and demanding a producer to have settled for just another ballad album and, with the exception of the last two tracks, this is extremely well modulated, one of a mere handful of records from the last two decades of Chet's career that have to be considered essential.

Oh, You Crazy Moon is another part of Enja's *Legacy* sequence. Whatever Chet's condition at the time (and this heavily documented year finds him in reasonable shape, despite embouchure problems), his ability to pick out effective songs and make them his own was unparalleled. A 14-minute version of 'Beautiful Black Eyes' is one of his best performances of this final decade. By contrast, 'Love For Sale' is done as jazz-lite, though Lee turns in a perceptive solo.

By contrast, the live session from Hérouville, France, is pretty nondescript, though recorded only a month later and with essentially the same band. Those who saw Baker on this trip will confirm that 'two a day' wasn't the reality of the situation at all, and it shows in the playing. Where *Live At Nick's* finds him crisp and pointed (albeit according to his own laid-back standard), the later session is merely messy and not helped by a cack-handed recording.

****** Broken Wing**

Emarcy 013043 *Baker; Phil Markowitz (p); Jean-François Jenny-Clark (b); Jeff Brillinger (d).* 12/78.

Stunningly good, and a fine opportunity to hear Chet tackle challenging contemporary fare (two takes of Wayne Shorter's 'Black Eyes', as well as the Richie Beirach-composed title-tune). The trumpeter is in great form, as laid back as ever, but still with an occasional crackle of unexpected energy in his mid-tempo solos. Brillinger is a decent enough accompanist, but it is Jenny-Clark who really shines, a complete star. Oddly, Chet's vocal on 'Oh, You Crazy Moon' is well off the money, one of his poorest on record, but it's easily made up for by the long, mostly jammed 'Blue Gilles' which completes the 'official session' and leaves the listener whetted for those extra takes.

*****(*) The Touch Of Your Lips**

Steeplechase SCCD 31122 *Baker; Doug Raney (g); Niels-Henning Orsted Pedersen (b).* 6/79.

***** Daybreak**

Steeplechase SCCD 31142 *As above.* 10/79.

***** This Is Always**

Steeplechase SCCD 31168 *As above.* 10/79.

***** Someday My Prince Will Come**

Steeplechase SCCD 31180 *As above.* 10/79.

Chet greatly relished this format (and returned to it to even greater effect with Philip Catherine and Jean-Louis Rassinfosse in the mid-'80s). The absence of a drummer allowed him to develop long, out-of-tempo lines that were reminiscent of Miles Davis's ballad experiments in the '50s in which bar-lines were largely ignored and phrases were overlapped or elided. This broke down the conventional development of a solo, replacing it with a relatively unstructured sequence of musical incidents, all of them directly or more obliquely related to the main theme. This was easier to do on ballads, and Chet's dynamics became increasingly restrictive in the last few years. *Chet's Choice*, below, is more varied in pace, but in 1979 Baker was still suffering some intonation problems, presumably as a result of losing teeth, and he fluffs some of the faster transitions. On slower material he sounds masterful and is ably accompanied by Raney's soft-bop guitar and NHOP's towering bass (a studio duo album with the great Dane would have been something to hear). Steeplechase are often guilty of issuing poorly recorded *audio vérité* sessions with little adjustment of balance or volume. *The Touch Of Your Lips*, though, is admirably done, though there's more than an element of overkill in the other three sessions, apparently from later that same year, in which there really isn't enough good material for more than one carefully edited CD, a double at most.

*** No Problem

Steeplechase SCCD 31131 *Baker; Duke Jordan (p); Niels-Henning Orsted Pedersen (b); Norman Fearrington (d).* 10/79.

A more-than-usually boppish set for this vintage. Though none of the material is orthodox bebop, there is something about Chet's phrasing and Jordan's tight, unelaborate comping that looks back to a much earlier period. That may recommend the session to those who find the later material too far removed from the blues. Others may feel that Baker had moved too far beyond this kind of approach to be able to return to it comfortably.

***(*) Burnin' At Backstreet

Fresh Sound FSR CD 128 *Baker; Drew Salperto (p); Michael Formanek (b); Art Frank (d).* 2/80.

Unconsciously or no, this turns into a tribute by the white Miles Davis to the original and only Miles Davis. Three Davis compositions – 'Tune Up', 'Milestones' and 'Four' – and a version of 'Stella By Starlight' that twice quotes from the classic version. Baker often did these tunes, but seldom with this concentration. He had behind him a very good young band, including the excellent Formanek, and he had at the time (so it is said) a belief that every date could be his last. There was to be nearly a decade more of last dates and missed deadlines, but there were few better nights than this. The sound is our only problem with it. Recorded in the Backstreet Club in New Haven, it is no better than it might be, and there are a few off-mike moments that disturb the flow of solos. Strongly recommended, all the same.

***(*) Live At Fat Tuesday's

Fresh Sound FSR CD 131 *Baker; Bud Shank (as); Hal Galper, Phil Markowitz (p); Ron Carter (b); Ben Riley (d).* 4/81.

A great shame that Shank wasn't able to sit in on 'You Can't Go Home Again', thus wakening memories of the superb Baker–Desmond version; but there's no doubt that the altoist gives Chet a shot in the arm on their two tracks together. 'In Your Own Sweet Way' is handled with more fire than normal. Shank's tone (well captured on CD) is clear and bright, and Chet sounds more pungent and full-bodied than usual. Warmly recommended.

**** Blues For A Reason

Criss Cross Jazz 1010 *Baker; Warne Marsh (ts); Hod O'Brien (p); Cecil McBee (b); Eddie Gladden (d).* 9/84.

It has always been a matter of considerable debate whether or not Chet belongs in the 'Cool School', is a Tristano disciple, or has the authentic 'West Coast sound'. Just as it's now recognized in most quarters that Tristano was a much more forceful and swinging player than the conventional image allows, so it's clear that the near-abstraction and extreme chromaticism of Chet's last years were a perfectly logical outgrowth of bebop. Warne Marsh's style has been seen as equally problematic, 'cold', 'dry', 'academic', the apparent antithesis of Chet's romantic expressionism. When the two are put together, as on this remarkable session, it's clear that unsubstantiated generalizations and categorizations quickly fall flat. While Baker is quite clearly no longer an orthodox changes player, having followed Miles's course out of bop, he's still able to live with Marsh's complex harmonic developments. *Blues For A Reason* stands out from much of the work of the period in including relatively unfamiliar original charts, including three by Chet himself. The best of these, 'Looking Good Tonight', is heard in two versions, demonstrating how the trumpeter doesn't so much rethink his whole strategy on a solo as allow very small textural changes to dictate a different development. Marsh, by contrast, sounds much more of a *thinking* player and, to that extent, just a little less spontaneous. The saxophonist's 'Well Spoken', with which the set begins, is perhaps the most challenging single item Baker tackled in his final decade, and he sounds as confident with it as with the well-worn 'If You Could See Me Now' and 'Imagination'. This is an important and quietly salutary album that confounds the more casual dismissals of the trumpeter's latter-day work.

***(*) Diane

Steeplechase 1207 *Baker; Paul Bley (p).* 2/85.

Considerably undervalued as a standards player, Bley is exactly the right duo partner for Chet. His accompaniments frequently dispense with the chords altogether, holding on to the theme with the lightest of touches and allowing the basic rhythm to stretch out and dismantle itself. Typically of this period, the material is quite straightforward, but the treatments are far from orthodox and *Diane* would certainly merit an unqualified fourth star were it not for rather murky sound.

**** Chet's Choice

Criss Cross 1016 *Baker; Philip Catherine (g); Jean-Louis Rassinfosse, Hein Van De Geyn (b).* 6/85.

This was the most productive year of Baker's last decade, and in the association with Catherine he hit a purple patch. It was a format he liked and had used to great effect in the 1979 sessions with Doug Raney and NHOP. The Criss Cross session is the most completely satisfying studio record of the period. Playing a basic standards set, he sounds refocused and clear-voiced, with a strength and fullness of tone that is undoubtedly helped by Gerry Teeken's typically professional production job. All three players are recorded in tight close-up, but with excellent separation.

*** Round Midnight

Challenge 70052 *Baker; Jean-Paul Florens (g); Henri Florens (p); Jim Richardson (b); Tony Mann (d); Rachel Gould (v).* 85.

Not another Paris date, as the personnel might suggest, but a London session on which Chet turns out to have been in exceptionally good form. Jean-Paul is particularly impressive, and often he and Baker are caught in duet and in some very effective interplay. 'Phil's Bossa' is the guitarist's composition, and though it sounds run down on the spot, it's extremely good. Rachel Gould adds a dimension, and doubtless she'll remember the day for ever.

**** Symphonically**
Soul Note 121134-2 *Baker; Mike Melillo (p); Massimo Moriconi (b); Giampaola Ascolese (d); Orchestra Filarmonica Marchigiana.* 7/85.

Baker often performed well in front of big orchestras, but this was an over-produced and rather heavy-handed session and contains little of interest. The sound is very slushy and Chet is made to sound rather cavernous.

*****(*) When Sunny Gets Blue**
Steeplechase SCCD 31121 *Baker; Butch Lacy (p); Jesper Lundgaard (b); Jukkis Uotila (d).* 2/86.

A rather melancholic session, but one of the better ones from the period. Lacy is a much-underrated piano player. He gives Baker a great deal of room, leaving chords suspended in unexpected places and rarely resorting to predetermined structures even on very familiar tunes. Indeed, he sets up conventional expectations on 'Here's That Rainy Day' and 'You'd Be So Nice To Come Home To' and then confounds them utterly with altered tonalities and out-of-tempo figures. Lundgaard and Uotila are both thoroughly professional and contribute to a fine, unpredictable set.

***** Mister B / As Time Goes By / Cool Cat**
Timeless TTD 251/3 3CD *Baker; Harold Danko, Michel Grallier (p); Jon Burr, Riccardo Del Fra (b); Ben Riley (d).* 5/83–85.

***** Live In Rosenheim / Sings Again / Heartbreak**
Timeless TTD 280 3CD *Baker; Harold Danko, Luca Alex Flores (p); Nicola Stilo (g, f); Marc Abrams (b); Ben Riley (d); strings; other personnel.* 6/83–4/88.

As with Eric Dolphy, who also died in Europe, there has been an unseemly rush to claim Baker's 'last' recording. The date released as *Live In Rosenheim* is billed as his 'last as quartet', which opens the field for anyone with trio and duo material to jump on the same bandwagon. These three-CD reissues usefully mop up some interesting but inessential material from Chet's last years. These have never been his most interesting records, but for the prurient fascination of watching him and listening to him get through another gig and make it to the airport for the next stage of the journey. They also begin the process of posthumous tinkering with Baker sessions; *Heartbreak* was arranged for strings after Chet was gone, with very mixed results. *Mister B* has been remixed to iron out the dull spots and fluffs. Chet's status as Melmoth the Wanderer was established in these years. There are great musical moments – 'If I Should Lose You' from Rosenheim, 'Round Midnight' from *Cool Cat*, indeed almost any version of 'Round Midnight' from this period, when he clearly recognized that it was. Danko, Burr and Riley provided sterling support and Harold's own lyrical gift is often to the fore, on his own material and the standards. On nights when he is obviously covering for Chet, the session becomes effectively his own, though this is rarer than you might expect.

Ginger Baker (born 1940)

DRUMS

Began as a trad drummer, moved to R&B, attained superstar status with rock trio, Cream, dissipated his success in the '70s, re-emerged in the '80s as a ginger-greybeard master-drummer/bandleader and now firmly ensconsed as a paterfamilias.

***** Horses & Trees**
Terrascape TRS 4123 *Baker; Robert Musso, Bernie Worrell (org); Nicky Skopelitis (g); Shankar (vn); Foday Musa Suso (douss'n gouni); Nana Vasconcelos (berimbau, perc); Bill Laswell (b); Aiyb Dieng, Daniel Ponce (perc).* 86.

***** Unseen Rain**
Day Eight DEMCD 028 *Baker; Jens Johansson (p); Jonas Hellborg (b).* 92.

*****(*) Going Back Home**
Atlantic 7567 82652 *Baker; Bill Frisell (g); Charlie Haden (b).* 3/94.

*****(*) Falling Off The Roof**
Atlantic 7567 82900 *As above, except add Bela Fleck (bj); Jerry Hahn (g).* 12/95, 3/96.

****** Coward Of The County**
Atlantic 7567 83168-2 *Baker; Ron Miles (t); Fred Hess (ts); James Carter (bs, bcl); Eric Gunnison (p); Shamie Royston (org); Todd Ayers (g); Glenn Taylor (pedal steel g); Artie Moore (b).* 9/98.

Ginger Baker made his professional debut playing in Dixieland groups. Even with rock supergroup Cream, even – dare we say it? – amid the confused eclecticism and sheer overload of later projects like Airforce and the ill-fated Baker–Gurvitz Army, he has remained loyal to his jazz roots. Perhaps the main model was Phil Seamen, who was briefly recruited to Airforce towards the end of his playing life, but Baker has a sound very much his own, superficially reminiscent of Paul Motian, but with heavier emphases and with a less delicate cadence.

Horses & Trees sounds like the work of a man who has still to unload a lot of baggage from years gone by. It's a clotted, overwrought album which affords tiny glimpses of something extraordinary but never manages to rise above a drab, rock-inflected production. One might almost be listening to a less-than-compelling jazz-rock record from a decade earlier, basically an augmented organ/guitar trio with overmixed drums.

Unseen Rain is the closest to a straight jazz set we're likely to get from Ginger, a set of eight themes of pretty much equal length, delivered with panache and a subtly experimental edge. It's not quite clear on 'Worlds Within Worlds' or 'The Great Festival Of Destruction' when or whether the music is going to undergo some sort of explosive fission and fly off in every direction. That it doesn't is entirely down to Ginger's skill as a bandleader.

Anyone sharp-eared enough to recognize either Frisell or Haden on the excellent Atlantics might guess that Motian is the drummer, but Motian has never done anything as direct and resolute as the 'Straight, No Chaser' on *Goin' Back Home*, nor has he ever matched the sheer ferocity of Ginger's own anti-colonialist 'East Timor' on the same record. If anything, the follow-up is better. 'Bemsha Swing' is absolutely on the money and there is a totally unexpected version of 'Au Privave' with Bela Fleck guesting on banjo. Startling there, more obviously idiomatic on something like Haden's country-tinged 'Taney County' and Frisell's softly swinging 'Amarillo Barbados'. Jerry

Hahn doubles up on just one track, Haden's 'Sunday At The Hillcrest', an appearance brief enough to wonder why Frisell wasn't simply double-tracked.

Unlike the Stones' Charlie Watts, who can afford to indulge his own bebop passions from time to time, Ginger is rooted in this music with the kind of imperative commitment that guarantees it keeps changing. *Coward Of The County* is a cracking record. The band is credited as the DJQ2O – the Denver Jazz Quintet-To-Octet – but the key relationship is that between Ginger and the album's main composer. Baker seems to have got involved with trumpeter, composer and educator Ron Miles and put on some polo and jazz evenings. Shoulder surgery and a set of cracked ribs (courtesy of a ballsy gelding called Clyde) put him out of action for a while, but he and Miles struck up an instantly sympathetic relationship and the trumpeter wrote some strong material with Ginger in mind. 'Daylight' is a storming idea, bleak and intense and full of scope for improvisation. 'Ginger Spice' was apparently written by Miles in complete ignorance of Ms Geri Halliwell, though we beg leave to doubt this, citing an unmistakable though momentary quote from the Girls' 'Spice Up Your Life'. One thing is sure. The Spices were never asked to sing and dance to a hybrid of 9/8 and 12/8.

The other key presence on the album is saxophonist Carter, who restricts himself to the lower end of his range, on baritone and bass clarinet. He honks righteously through 'Cyril Davies', a dedication to the harmonica player in Alexis Korner's Blues Incorporated and weaves a prayerful bass clarinet sound on 'Jesus Loves Me' and 'Jesus, I Just Want To Go To Sleep'. The first of these is a mazy rhythmic exercise; the latter – which has also featured on a Ron Miles record – a moody and graceful farewell on which bassist Artie Moore also features. The title-track has nothing to do with the Johnny Cash song of that name, though it shares something of its down-home stoicism. With this beautiful collaborative album, Baker's reinvention seems complete.

Kenny Baker (1921–99)

TRUMPET

A Yorkshireman who learned to play in brass bands, Baker played lead in the Ted Heath band of the '40s and helped cement its reputation for precision. Led his Baker's Dozen band in the '50s and recorded much sweet as well as hot music. Countless (anonymous) studio dates from the '60s onwards, abetted by frequent club appearances, and finally a starring role in both the posthumous Ted Heath Orchestra and the London Big Band. A musician's musician, regarded with much affection by his community.

***** Birth Of A Legend '41–'46**

Hep CD 58 *Baker; David Wilkins, Tommy McQuater, Stan Roderick, Alfie Noakes, Harry Letham, Alan Franks (t); Lad Busby, George Chisholm, Don McCaffer, Harry Roche, Jock Bain, Eric Breeze, Bruce Campbell, George Flynn, Jack Bentley, Jimmy Coombes, Woolf Phillips (tb); Harry Parry, Carl Barriteau (cl); Harry Hayes, Duggie Robinson, Reg Owen, Les Gilbert (as); Buddy Featherstonehaugh (cl, ts); George Evans, Reggie Dare, Aubrey Franks, Andy McDevitt, Jimmy Skidmore, Johnny Gray, Frank Reidy (ts); Bill Lewington, Charles Granville, Phil Goody, Jimmy Durant (bs); George Shearing, Dick Katz, Harry Rayner, Billy Munn, Ralph Sharon, Norman Stenfalt (p); Frank Deniz, Joe Deniz, Vic Lewis, Ivor Mairants, Archie Slavin, Dave Goldberg (g); Tommy Bromley, Charlie Short, Jack Collier (b); George Fierstone, Jock Cummings, Jack Parnell, Carlo Krahmer, Bobby Midgley (d).* 11/41–1/46.

***** The Half Dozen / After Hours**

Lake LACD88 *Baker; George Chisholm (tb); Bruce Turner (cl, as); Derek Collins (cl, ts); Harry Smith, Dill Jones (p); Jack Fallon, Frank Clarke (b); Lennie Hastings, Derek Price (d).* 5/55–4/57.

***** Ain't Misbehavin'**

Zephyr ZECD 17 *Baker; Warren Vaché (c); Brian Lemon (p); Howard Alden (g); Dave Green (b); Allan Ganley (d).* 9/96–7/97.

****(*) Size 10**

Raymer Sound RSCD677 *Baker; Ceri Williams (t); Terry Wiliams (tb); Zoe Lambeth (reeds); Henry Davies (p); Martyn Mills (b); Brian Price (d).* 5/98.

Baker has left a vast legacy on record but little under his own name. Hep's fascinating compilation rounds up tracks by the likes of the Melody Maker Competition Band and First English Public Jam Session, as well as sessions under the leadership of Chisholm, Featherstonehaugh and Shearing, and early Ted Heath tracks. It's clear that from the start Baker was a tough nut and a pro's pro, his solos needle-fine in their precision and standing out among bands that were dance orchestras rather than jazz outfits. Harking back to a time when saxophone players had names like Aubrey Franks and Reggie Dare, the few enlightened souls – Baker, Shearing, Chisholm and Featherstonehaugh – sound like radicals. None of this is deathless music but it steps out of history well enough.

Baker's Dozen were more renowned for their regular broadcasts than for any records, and the legacy is disappointingly slight. Lake's CD gathers together tracks from one Pye and one Polygon LP. A mix of swing, jump-band music and a more relaxed mainstream, the music has a faceless feel which the solos at least put some colour into, and Baker remains impeccable.

John Bune should take credit for organizing the sessions for *Ain't Misbehavin'*, since this will probably turn out to be Baker's last featured recording. In his seventies, he was still turning in generous and enthusiastic playing, and it is hard to envisage that there is a 30-year difference in age between him and Vaché, who is enjoying himself just as much: the bubbling treatment of 'Who's Sorry Now' is marvellous. Alden slips in a few typically astute remarks along the way.

Kenny sat in as a guest with The Beachcombers, a trad–swing band that works around the Bristol area, in 1998. Once past the idiotic opening of 'Fanfare For The Common Man', it settles down nicely into an agreeable blow for those involved, with Baker raising everyone's game; but docked a notch for a few lamentable lapses of judgement, such as the (uncredited) singing.

Jon Balke (born 1955)

PIANO, KEYBOARDS

Brilliant Norwegian with rock and other influences whose atmospheric albums help define the much-disputed 'ECM sound'.

***** Nonsentration**

ECM 1445 *Balke; Nils Petter Molvaer (t); Dag Einar Eilertsen, Torbjørn Sunde (tb); Erick Balke (as, bs); Tore*

Brunborg (ss, ts); Arne Frang (ts, bsx); Olave Dale (bs); Carl Morten Iversen (b); Jon Christensen, Audun Kleive (d); Miki N'Doye (perc). 91.

★★★(★) Further

ECM 1517 *Balke; Jens Petter Antonsen (t); Per Jørgenson (t, v); Morten Halle (as); Tore Brunborg (ss, ts); Anders Jormin (b); Audun Kleive (d); Marilyn Mazur (perc); string quartet.* 6/93.

★★★★ Kyanos

ECM 1822 *Balke; Arve Henrikson, Per Jørgenson (t); Morten Halle (sax, f); Svante Henryson (clo); Anders Jormin (b); Audun Kleive (d).* 11/01.

Like Jan Garbarek and Edward Vesala, Balke favours slow developments, dense textures and a very open-ended harmonic approach. The first album, which followed a promising LP *One to One*, features Oslo 13 and sounds as quintessentially Norwegian as the schuss of skis or the wintry whistle of ptarmigans. Balke is an effective writer and leader, though here the suspicion is that this is a keyboard album writ large rather than idiomatic writing for large ensemble.

There are New Age longueurs on the second album but, given that most of the tracks are brief and to the point, these rarely get in the way for long. Apart from the leader, soloing is relatively sparse. Brunborg, Halle and Jørgenson are featured in the central section of what is effectively a continuous suite; otherwise the emphasis is on ensemble-playing. The entrance of the strings, played pizzicato, on 'Horizontal Song' shows how crafty Balke can be. Many of these pieces function as wry musical puzzles, deceptively straightforward at first hearing, but constantly opening up layers of interest.

The third album, credited to Balke and the Magnetic North Orchestra, is a meditation on blue – '*kyanos*' in Greek – and therefore tinged with the blues. His first record for ECM for almost a decade, it's by far the best, making full use of some now very experienced soloists and much more confident in its language; there is a simplicity and straightforwardness about the arrangements which wasn't there before. Paring back the string-writing to a single cello was a brilliant stroke. Balke still solos prominently, but again the emphasis is on ensemble-writing and the album seems to work best as a suite of related ideas rather than as single tracks.

Kenny Ball (born 1930)

TRUMPET, VOCAL

Born in Ilford, Ball worked in dance-band small groups before leading his own trad-to-Dixie outfit from 1958. His band introduced a new professionalism to the genre, and their records for Pye were commercial enough to score several hits in the early '60s. Lip trouble interrupted his career later that decade, but since then Ball has been unstoppable as a touring attraction.

★★★(★) Back At The Start

Lake LACD114 *Ball; John Bennett (tb); Dave Jones (cl); Colin Bates, Ron Weatherburn (p); Dickie Bishop, Diz Disley, Paddy Lightfoot (bj); Vic Pitt (b); Tony Budd, Ron Bowden (d).* 6/59–3/62.

★★★ Great British Jazz Bands Vol. 8: Kenny Ball & His Jazzmen 1960–1961

Lake LACD76 *As above, except add Lonnie Donegan (bj); omit Bishop, Budd.* 5/60–5/61.

★★★(★) The Pye Jazz Albums

Castle CMKBX 794 6CD *Ball (t, v); John Bennett (tb); Dave Jones (cl); Ron Weatherburn, Colin Bates (p); Paddy Lightfoot (bj, v); Diz Disley (bj, g, v); Bill Dixon, Lonnie Donegan (bj) Vic Pitt (b); Ron Bowden (d).* 5/60 – 11/64.

★★★(★) The Pye Jazz Anthology

Castle CMDDD 138 2CD *As above discs.* 60–74.

★★ The Very Best Of Kenny Ball

Timeless TTD 598 *As above, except Hugh Ledigo (p) replaces Swift.* 91–5.

★★(★) That's A Plenty

Timeless TTD 629 *As above, except Nick Millward (d) replaces Bowden; omit Fenner.* 3–4/99.

Ball's early records may surprise any who only know his subsequent cabaret-styled jazz. He led a tough, hard-hitting outfit which his own powerful lead directed with great skill. John Bennett, one of the longest-serving sidemen in jazz, played urbane but gutsy trombone, and the rhythm section had a tautness that evaded many lesser trad outfits. Ball's signing to Pye, engineered by Lonnie Donegan, was the commercial making of the band, and Ball was almost ruthless in pursuing a style of Dixieland that was disciplined enough to attract a popular audience (unthinkable today, but plausible in the chart environment of 1960). The two Lake discs bring together all of his early recordings, and they're an impressive lot, particularly *Back At The Start*, which opens with three obscure 1959 tracks made for the Collector label and proceeds through the early Pye material. Ball's own playing is what stands out – unfussy, but surprisingly risk-taking at points. If his chops later bothered him, there's no evidence of it here. The second disc, while nearly as good, sows the seeds of Ball's move towards trad as pop. 'Teddy Bear's Picnic' and 'I Got Plenty Of Nuthin'' are the kind of things that would later be the staple ingredients of his chicken-in-a-basket set. These are the discs to get if you want Kenny's early years in detail, but as a single source the Castle *Pye Jazz Anthology* makes an attractive collection. All the hits are here, taking the story up to the '70s, and a well-chosen sampling of their hardcore material; 'Cornet Chop Suey' and Bechet's 'The Pay Off' may surprise any who regard the Jazzmen as mere showbiz players. Fine notes with an absorbing interview with Kenny.

Even more comprehensive is Castle's six-disc marathon, which takes in all of the Pye albums and adds the bonus of *Kenny Ball In Japan*, cut in Tokyo in 1964 and previously only available to Japanese fans (they included a couple of Japanese army songs – Ball always knew his audience better than anyone else). Pretty strange concept, since the whole programme is made up of marches, with the even more bizarre exception of The Singing Nun's 'Dominique'! At a bargain price, this makes a very appealing buy all told.

There's a big jump from there to the latter-day output of the Jazzmen. The compilation of Ball's '90s recordings is less appealing since the front line sounds increasingly prone to either fluffs or fatigue, even as the rhythms sound more chipper than ever. *That's A Plenty* has an ounce more bounce thanks to new boy Nick Millward and, though they might have thought of one or two less obvious tunes to play, it's not bad. Sadly, Kenny has lately been obliged to give up on the trumpet, but he's still leading and singing with the band.

Iain Ballamy (born 1964)

TENOR AND SOPRANO SAXOPHONES

Born in Guildford, Ballamy was a significant player in the new London jazz of the '80s. Since then he has worked steadily as a leader, and collected a lot of saxophones.

★★★★ Food

Feral Records ASFA 101 *Ballamy; Arve Henriksen (t, v, elec); Mats Eilertsen (b); Thomas Strönen (d, perc).* 7/98.

Though he had been leading bands since his late teens, it was only with the formation of Loose Tubes that Iain Ballamy came to wider notice. This shambolic collective – originally started by Graham Collier as a rehearsal band – became the talent pool for white British jazz in the '80s, but it also became something of a jail for those of its members who weren't prepared to sit their finals and move on. Ballamy always sounded like a man who wanted to learn as well as blow. He gravitated towards the Greenwich-based Voice of God Collective run by guitarist Billy Jenkins, and he became a member (with Django Bates, who'd been in his teenage group) of Bill Bruford's group, Earthworks. The end result, coupled with some personal misfortune, meant that his own career seemed to go on the back-burner for quite extended periods of time.

Food was a complete surprise, and this time the credit has to be shared evenly. Ballamy's Norwegian colleagues create an entirely new environment for him: rich, tense and unfamiliarly abstract. This allows him to place his notes not with more care but with a more relaxed cadence. At moments, particularly on a track like 'Strange Burn', the music harks back to the British free jazz of the late '60s, which is another of Ballamy's sources. Recorded live to two-track at the Molde Jazz Festival, the sound is very raw and immediate, with Eilertsen's bass foregrounded and plenty of roomy ambience. The tracks are attractively spare and unindulgent, with a stark quality to the horns (Henriksen occasionally plays more than one trumpet simultaneously) that implies a much bigger sound-world than is actually present. Food for thought and, at its best, nourishment to the spirit as well.

★★★ Pepper Street Interludes

Feral ASFA 102 *Ballamy; Stan Carstensen (acc); Matthew Sharp (clo); Martin France (d); Norma Winstone (v).* 1/00.

Carstensen and Ballamy make for quite a team, tenor sax and button accordion a rare combination even now. But the album passes by insubstantially, with 14 tracks finished in 40 minutes. Winstone sings a beautiful 'Midnight Sun' and the theme to *White Horses* is an odd way to bring proceedings to a climax.

★★★(★) Food Organic & GM

Feral ASFA 104 *Ballamy; Arve Henriksen (t, v, elec); Mats Eilertsen (b, elec); Thomas Strönen (d, elec).* 5–6/00.

★★★(★) Veggie

Rune Grammofon RCD 2027 *As above.* 02.

Completely different. Recorded after a tour with the (Norwegian) group, the music is a deft and often exceptionally sensitive blend of folkish tunes, sparingly used electronics and grooving group performances. Since no one timbre gains the upper hand, there's neither Nordic brooding nor mere whimsy to deter the unconvinced. When they get to the final 'Technojoshi', Ballamy really digs in, which suggests that this combination of muscle and mood-painting suits him very nicely.

Veggie sees samplers and other electronic manipulations taking over even more, to the extent that the two horns are rarely heard in their own voices. The first track is almost all processed, spookily atmospheric. Henriksen opens 'Eat' in Miles Davis (or maybe Leo Smith) mode over scraped bass and random percussion and electronic effects. Trumpet and saxophone join in delicate canon here and there, but over rumbly electric bass line or mock-orchestral effects. 'Chickpea' uses beats as a background to some highly processed horn lines, which sound as if they're being emailed in from a space station.

Dave Ballou (born 1963)

TRUMPET, FLUGELHORN

Ballou took his place in the New York scene at the beginning of the '90s and has been regularly seen as a sideman, with these dates for Steeplechase his leadership work to date.

★★(★) Amongst Ourselves

Steeplechase SCCD 31436 *Ballou; Tony Malaby (ts); Michael Formanek (b); Jeff Williams (d).* 9/97.

★★★ Volition

Steeplechase SCCD 31460 *Ballou; Cameron Brown (b); Jeff Williams (d).* 4/98.

★★★(★) The Floating World

Steeplechase SCCD *Ballou; George Colligan (p); Doug Weiss (b); Darren Beckett (d).* 12/99.

★★★ On This Day

Steeplechase SCCD 31504 *Ballou; Billy Drewes (ss, as); Tony Malaby (ts); Michael Formanek (b); Tom Rainey (d).* 12/00.

Ballou's clear, cool tone and deft abilities on the horn are an undoubted plus for a band in need of a capable trumpet, but these entries for Steeplechase are decidedly mixed. *Amongst Ourselves* gets off to a strong start in 'All About Joey' and the stately 'Blake's Vision', but there is too much reliance on Ballou's own writing, which seems stiff and scholarly at times, as if he were working out ideas in public. The quartet plays well enough, but a preponderance of slow tempos don't really help; some of this is just dreary. It was a brave move to go to a bare-bones trio setting for *Volition*, and there are some excellent moments here. However, the presence of Monk's 'Light Blue' and Booker Little's beautiful 'Opening Statement' again shows up the weaknesses in Ballou's own writing, and his originals make little impact on the memory.

The Floating World is easily his best set. The only session with a piano is abetted by the splendid Colligan, and the greater emphasis on familiar material (five covers of differing sources) is surely an assist. 'Pannonica' brings in Monk again, and Ballou gets a nicely personal sound out of the flugelhorn, while the trumpet and piano of 'Memories Of You' provide a real, challenging partnership.

On This Day is another all-original programme and, without carping too much about the writing, it simply isn't as good. Ballou exposes one or two technical weaknesses here, and what sounds like an essay on certain aspects of free-ish playing has a kind of intellectual intrigue to it. But others may find the whole thing simply introverted. What Ballou may simply need is an interventionist producer.

Tom Bancroft

DRUMS

Brother of saxman Phil and a prominent force in the new Scottish jazz of the '90s and beyond, Bancroft also co-runs the 'local' jazz label, Caber.

*** Pieology

Caber 001 *Bancroft; Claude Deppa, Eddie Severn, Colin Steele (t); Paul Jayasinha (t, clo); Rick Taylor (tb); Lindsay Cooper, Oren Marshall (tba); Phil Bancroft (ts); Jorrit Dykstra (as, cl); Dick Lee (as, cl, bcl); John Burgess (as); Karen Wimhurst (cl, bcl); John Telfer (bs); Brian Kellock, Chick Lyall (p, ky); Kevin MacKenzie (g); Kenny Ellis (b); John Rae (d).* 2/93–2/97.

The first issue on the Bancrofts' own cottage – or should that be crofting? – label is a fairly random selection of live and broadcast cuts, but enough to show that Tom's desire to be the Scottish Basie and Ellington isn't so far off the pace. London's legendary Loose Tubes collective are the other obvious and more recent point of comparison, except that Bancroft's charts lack the wilful perversity that crept into the Tubes' act.

The opening 'Cat And Mouse' is a clever call-and-response theme, with a vocal line originally written for Fionna Duncan. It tees up the first of several superb solos from trumpeter Claude Deppa and Phil Bancroft. The tenor saxophonist is the dedicatee of the title-piece, 'Pieology', which was an early big-band effort by his brother, showing the joins here and there but still a generously proportioned blowing tune. 'Scottish Heart' was a bold synthesis of jazz and traditional Scottish ideas, dominated by Brian Kellock's Ellingtonian statement. 'The Piano Is A Dark Horse' features a fine duo between Phil Bancroft and Scotland's other ranking jazz pianist, Chick Lyall. 'Sleep Head' is an exquisite ballad with little or no solo play. The only non-Bancroft composition on the disc is Ennio Morricone's 'The Ballad Of Algiers', intended as a tribute to John Zorn and elevated by more wonderful playing from guitarist Kevin MacKenzie and tubist Oren Marshall. For much of the album, Bancroft cedes the drum stool to John Rae, head of another of Scotland's inventive musical families. Although Tom has lately been busier with actually running the label, he can also be found under Trio AAB.

Billy Bang (born 1947)

VIOLIN

Bang was born in Alabama and served with the military in Vietnam, a combination of experiences which perhaps helps explain his passionate resistance to racial inequality. He began playing seriously relatively late, drawing inspiration from Ramsay Ameen and Leroy Jenkins, but also from the classic exponent of swing violin, Stuff Smith. His characteristic sound is combative, sometimes harsh, but always melodic.

**** Rainbow Gladiator

Soul Note 121016-2 *Bang; Charles Tyler (as, bs); Michele Rosewoman (p); Wilber Morris (b); Dennis Charles (d).* 6/81.

*** Invitation

Soul Note 121036-2 *As above, except Curtis Clark (p) replaces Rosewoman.* 4/82.

Rainbow Gladiator is a terrific record, bright, percussive and packed with ideas. The group has a unique and immediately identifiable sound, especially when Tyler is playing baritone, and this has to count as one of Rosewoman's best early recordings, reminiscent in places of Marilyn Crispell, with whom Bang recorded *Spirit Music*. The violinist's articulation is as precise as ever and ranges between a huge, raw vibrato and a lighter, dry, almost bleached effect. The title-track opens the album on a high; almost a quarter of an hour in length, it doesn't let up for a moment. Everything else is a good deal shorter. 'Ebony Minstrel Man', 'Broken Strings' and 'Bang's Bounce' are less than five minutes each, but they show how comfortable Bang is with song forms: a dedication to Laurel Van Horn, 'Yaa – Woman Born On Thursday', is extraordinary.

It's not clear why the second record is so disappointing. Certainly one misses the distinctiveness of Rosewoman's attack, but Clark is an excellent player and idiosyncratic enough not to leave a hole. It is simply that there is nothing very distinctive about any of the music, and Bang's own playing seems lacklustre and formulaic. The sound too is rather disappointing, though both these records gained immeasurably from transfer to CD.

***(*) The Fire From Within

Soul Note 121086-2 *Bang; Ahmed Abdullah (t); Oscar Sanders (g); William Parker (b); Thurman Barker (mar, perc); John Betsch (d); Charles Bobo Shaw (perc).*

*** Live At Carlos I

Soul Note 121136-2 *As above, except omit Abdullah, Betsch, Shaw; add Roy Campbell (t); Zen Matsuura (d); Eddie Conde (congas).* 11/86.

The combination of trumpet, guitar and percussion makes an effective foil for Bang's grainy lines, especially when the splendid Barker turns to his marimba. The sheer woodiness of the sound – with Parker also making a strong contribution – is beguiling, and the melodic and rhythmic language rich. The live record underlines the distinctiveness of this group – by default, unfortunately. Campbell is a much less individual player than Abdullah, whose debt to Louis Armstrong is always evident, even when playing outside. Betsch understands Bang's music as well as anyone and, Barker apart, seems the ideal sideman. The club date (Carlos I is an establishment in Greenwich Village) has a slightly plodding quality that even the mercurial William Parker can't quite mitigate.

**** Valve No. 10

Soul Note 121186-2 *Bang; Frank Lowe (ts); Sirone (b); Dennis Charles (d).* 2/88.

A definite high-point and Bang's most convincing performance since *Rainbow Gladiator*. The album was recorded on the eve of a long European tour which saw the violinist and his group cement a truly creative artistic relationship; some of the performances were uncanny and it would be fascinating to have a recording of these same tracks made a month later. Bang has always been drawn to bassists who think of their instruments as bass fiddles (William Parker frequently describes his in precisely those terms) and who try to accentuate the singing harmonies of violin and cello; scandalously under-recorded Sirone (formerly Norris Jones) is just such a player. In Frank Lowe, Bang has a saxophonist who has managed to combine the freedoms and intensity of the avant-garde with a huge respect for tradition. Lowe himself cites Coleman Hawkins, Ben

Webster and Lucky Thompson and dismisses his own sound as 'basic'; it is certainly unadorned, but it calls to mind nothing more than a latter-day Chu Berry.

The album opens strongly with 'P.M.', an attention-grabber with its odd structure and tendency to begin solos mid-chorus and allow them to leak over into the next. Charles is the featured soloist here and establishes a strong presence on the rest of the record as well. 'Bien Hoa Blues' is a reminiscence of Bang's Vietnam posting, and there are two tributes to John Coltrane, to mark the 20th anniversary of his death; the disc closes with a searingly mournful 'Lonnie's Lament' on which Lowe's determination *not* to sound like Trane pays unexpected dividends. 'September 23rd' is less successful, a poem to Coltrane which draws on familiar album titles *and* the 'Love Supreme' chant.

*** A Tribute To Stuff Smith

Soul Note 121216-2 *Bang; Sun Ra (p); John Ore (b); Andrew Cyrille (d).* 9/92.

Bang worked with Sun Ra's Intergalactic Arkestra for a time at the start of the '80s. It was his first regular contact with standard material, and his first full exposure to large-ensemble playing. Sun Ra's presence on this record, a rare appearance as a sideman, is the most remarkable thing about a set that never quite adds up to its promise or to more than the sum of its personnel. Cyrille is the key element, constantly suggesting new routes, changing the pace, lying back almost out of the picture, and then erupting in with another flurry of ideas. He and Sun Ra seem to be engaged in a constant dialogue, leaving the two strings to pick their way through some surprisingly conventional material. The opening track is Stuff Smith's 'Only Time Will Tell', and there is one other tune by the great fiddler, 'Bugle Blues'. For the rest, slightly uneven, neither entirely authentic nor ironic readings of 'Satin Doll', 'Deep Purple', 'Foggy Day In London Town', 'April In Paris', a rather good 'Lover Man' and a weak 'Yesterdays'. A fascinating item in the Bang discography but, make no mistake, not a classic.

*** Spirits Gathering

CIMP 109 *Bang; Brett Allen (g); Akira Ando (b); Dennis Charles (d).* 2/96.

This was a session beset with technical problems from the start, and they rebound on the music more than a little. CIMP pride themselves on a straight, unadorned recording technique; what is played is what you get. Bang seems to have had difficulties with his pickup from the start and, after various efforts to resolve them, was obliged to press ahead regardless. He sounds less open than usual, and there are a few occasions when extraneous noise is evident, most obviously on the opening 'Tanko-bushi' and the following title-track. This is a strong group. As so often before, Bang doesn't seem to need or want a straightforward harmony instrument, using the guitar colouristically and for additional punctuation to the melody. The two standards – 'Softly, As In A Morning Sunrise' and 'My Funny Valentine' – are both excellent, idiomatic and original, but elsewhere there is little that startles, and the limitations of the sound become more and more evident as time passes. A fascinating session that doesn't quite transcend its circumstances.

**** Bang On!

Justin Time JUST 105 *Bang; D. D. Jackson (p); Akira Ando (b); Ronnie Burrage (d).* 4/97.

A complete surprise. This is by far the straightest and most mainstream sound Bang has ever committed to record, on the opening tracks at least. 'Sweet Georgia Brown' and then later 'Willow Weep For Me' and 'Yesterdays' are given light, sweet readings that concentrate heavily on the melody. 'Spirits Entering' is moodier and almost threatening, with Bang using drawn-out wails and glissandi to underpin a strong central idea. Jackson is superb, almost hijacking the session with his rapid-fire delivery and invention. Burrage deserves to be better known and is particularly effective on the slower tunes, using his cymbals to great effect and constantly referring to the tune. An excellent record from a master craftsman who, at 50, has learnt the virtues of a quieter approach.

***(*) Commandment (For The Sculpture Of Alain Kirili)

No More Records NO 5 *Bang (vn solo).* n.d.

The sheer physicality of this – recorded without sweetening in sculptor Kirili's loft – is astonishing. Bang sighs, stomps, taps his feet, *moves* to the music. The material is as eclectic as ever: Butch Morris's 'Music For The Love Of It', Sun Ra's 'They Plan To Leave', a gently busked 'Swing Low, Sweet Chariot', sounded pizzicato, and a performance of Bang's own quasi-classical 'Daydreams'. If you were never to hear another Billy Bang record, this would almost be enough. What's missing is his extraordinary ear, his ability to interact with other musicians and, to a large extent, his jazz sense. This should have the widest possible circulation; but to get a true measure of the man it will be necessary to look elsewhere.

***(*) Vietnam: The Aftermath

Justin Time JUST 165 *Bang; Ted Daniel (t); Frank Lowe (ts); Sonny Fortune (f); John Hicks (p); Curtis Lundy (b); Michael Carvin (d); Ron Brown (perc); Butch Morris (cond).* 4/01.

It seems a long time after the event to be attempting an exorcism, but this remarkable suite of pieces inspired by Bang's scarifying tour of duty in Southeast Asia is far from the doom-laden horrorfest one might have expected. Instead of attempting to convey just the horrors of the Vietnam war – experiences which drove the violinist to the brink of insanity – Bang has created a sound-picture of a wider world. He uses what sound like authentically Asian themes and scales to build up a surprisingly gentle collage into which the few eruptions of real violence – 'Tunnel Rat' and 'Tet Offensive' – arrive with even greater dramatic force. Billy's patented range of sonics, percussive stops, scratched dissonances and eldritch wails, have never been more dramatically appropriate.

At least one other member of the group shared the Vietnam experience and Ted Daniel brings his own emotional agenda to the set, playing strong and proud but with an aching vulnerability as well. We are not sure if Frank Lowe or Sonny Fortune saw similar service, but they certainly understand the emotional dictates of Bang's music, and the band sounds as if it has been together for years, a musical platoon united by comradeship and mutual need.

There seems to be some doubt whether the track details on the sleeve are correct. Some inconsistencies suggest that the order is not as given, but either way the pieces identified as 'Ho Chi Minh' and 'KIAMIA' ('killed/missing in action') are among the best Billy has recorded for years. A fine record and a brave personal testimony.

Billy Banks (1908–67)

VOCAL

Heard in a Cleveland club by Irving Mills, Banks arrived in New York in 1932 and worked at Connie's Inn, then with Noble Sissle. He was in residence at the Diamond Horseshoe club all through the '40s before working in Europe, the Far East and Australia. He died in Tokyo.

*** Billy Banks 1932

Classics 969 *Banks; Henry 'Red' Allen (t, v); Tommy Dorsey (tb); Jimmy Lord (cl); Pee Wee Russell (cl, ts); Happy Caldwell (ts); Fats Waller (p, v); Joe Sullivan (p); Jack Bland (g); Eddie Condon (bj); George 'Pops' Foster, Al Morgan (b); Gene Krupa, Zutty Singleton (d); Chick Bullock (v); plus two unknown bands.* 4–10/32.

Banks himself is a minor personality in New York jazz of the '30s, and he hardly makes for an imposing presence on these sessions. Nevertheless, they're remembered with affection by 78 collectors as slightly eccentric examples of small-group hot music of that time. Banks seldom appears on the first session, which includes an instrumental 'Bugle Call Rag' and features Henry Allen, not Banks, taking the vocal on 'Oh Peter'. When Billy finally gets some space, on 'Margie', it's a shock to hear his light, sweet tenor (which is immediately followed by a Pee Wee Russell tenor solo). But he wasn't a bad scat singer, and he gets more space on the two Victor dates, which feature otherwise unknown personnel. Waller arrives for the July 1932 session and is in top form. The disc is filled out by a session under Jack Bland's nominal leadership; Banks is absent, and Chick Bullock does the singing, though Allen takes over on 'Someone Stole Gabriel's Horn'. An entertaining if second-division survival.

Denys Baptiste

TENOR AND SOPRANO SAXOPHONES

London tenorman turned on to jazz by his father's record collection. Studied at Guildhall and joined Gary Crosby's Nu Troop.

*** Be Where You Are

Dune CD03 *Baptiste; Andrew McCormack (p); Larry Bartley (b); Daniel Crosby, Tom Skinner (d); Juliet Roberts, Sian Lord, Kevin Leo (v).* 99.

*** Alternating Currents

Dune CD05 *Baptiste; Kevin Robinson (t, flhn); Winston Rollins, Harry Brown (tb); Andrew McCormack (p); Martin Taylor (g); Larry Bartley (b); Tom Skinner (d); Juliet Roberts, Cleveland Watkiss, Nedia Baptiste (v).* 01.

A skilful player with a big sound, Baptiste seems much in thrall to the obvious tenor forebears, and his original 'Rollinstone' and a blushing treatment of 'Naima' make that debt even more specific. His own writing seems rather green, but it's the playing that counts. A sound, serious date which is enjoyable for its lack of pretension. There's a rousing version of Stevie Wonder's 'Have A Talk With God' voiced by Juliet Roberts, but it's hard to see why it's there, beyond a sense that it's trying to snare listeners who wouldn't care about a regular tenor-and-rhythm date.

Alternating Currents is a confident and often striking successor. Baptiste's composing has taken a stride or two, 'The Kraken', easily his most interesting piece so far, toys with funk and ska rhythms while rooting itself in recurring changes which Baptiste and Martin Taylor eat up as they go. 'Mind The Gap' updates the New Orleans march, and 'City Of Clouds' and 'Namesake' prettily voice an ECM kind of ballad sound. 'Stop And Look Around' and 'Inner City Blues' provide further features for Juliet Roberts. An absorbing blend, but the record is badly let down by its muted sound, which takes so much of the punch out of the music that even Baptiste sounds remote a lot of the time.

***(*) Let Freedom Ring!

Dune CD010 *Baptiste; Abram Wilson (t); Trevor Mires (tb); Nathaniel Facey (as); Andrew McCormack (p); Robin Bannerjee, Adam Goldsmith (g); Omar Puente (vn); Jenny Adejayan (clo); Gary Crosby (b); Rod Youngs (d); Satin Singh (perc); Ben Okri (v).* 7/03.

A vivid piece of political art, as Baptiste turns a festival commission into a powerful recording – using Martin Luther King's famous 1963 speech as a springboard for a four-part suite, he then draws on Ben Okri's poetry to reflect on King's original message. With something to focus his composing on, Baptiste sounds much more confident, and if the written materials do seem derivative of sources such as Charles Mingus and Carla Bley, the music is played fiercely enough to convince by itself (and Jason Yarde's production is distinctly superior to the earlier discs). The biggish band really hits its stride on the title-section, where Baptiste is as righteous and inflamed as any of his free-playing antecedents, and the music hangs in for the controlled intensity of the finale. Not quite the masterpiece it was greeted as in some quarters, but a fine piece of work.

Paul Barbarin (1899–1969)

DRUMS

Barbarin played in the New Orleans Young Olympian Brass Band as a teenager, and thereafter also worked in New York and Chicago with Oliver, Keppard and Henry Allen. From the '30s he based himself in New Orleans but played frequent guest gigs in the northern cities. He died after leading his band in the hitherto segregated Proteus procession in 1969.

*** Streets Of The City

504 CD 9 *Barbarin; Ernest Cagnolotti, John Brunious (t); Eddie Pierson, Worthia Thomas (tb); Albert Burbank, Willie Humphrey (cl); Lester Santiago (p); Edmond Souchon (bj, v); Richard McLean, Ricard Alexis (b).* 9/50–4/56.

*** Paul Barbarin And His Band

Storyville STCD 6008 *As above, except add Johnny St Cyr (bj); omit Brunious, Thomas, Burbank, Souchon, Alexis.* 51.

*** In Concert 1951–1959

504 CD 48 *Barbarin; Jack Willis (t); Ernie Cagnolotti (t, v); Waldron Joseph, Bob Thomas (tb); Albert Burbank, Louis Cottrell (cl); Lester Santiago (p); Emanuel Sayles (g, bjo); Gerald Adams, Richard McLean (b).* 51–59.

*** Paul Barbarin And His New Orleans Band

Atlantic 90977-2 *Barbarin; John Brunious (t); Bob Thomas (tb); Willie Humphrey (cl); Lester Santiago (p); Danny Barker (bj); Milt Hinton (b).* 55.

***** Oxford Series Vol. 15**

American Music AMCD-35 *As above, except Ricard Alexis (b) replaces Hinton.* 3/56.

One of the major New Orleans drummers, Paul Barbarin was most visibly active in the '30s, when he played and toured with such leaders as Louis Armstrong and Luis Russell; but it was the revival of interest in New Orleans jazz which let him record as a leader. He had a hard yet restless manner of playing the beat, and his bands swing with a kind of relentlessness that can be very exciting. The Storyville disc catches his group at a peak: the horns are all excellent soloists as well as vivid ensemble players, with Pierson a shouting trombonist, Burbank terrifically agile and Cagnolotti making light work of sounding tough and imaginative at the same time. There's an uproarious version of 'Clarinet Marmalade' and, though all the material is staple Dixieland repertoire, they play it with seasoned rather than hackneyed dedication. The sound is a little flat but perfectly acceptable. *Streets Of The City* collects three sessions by two bands: with Cagnolotti and Burbank the music is more deeply traditional, with Brunious and the versatile Humphrey a blend of looking back and glancing forward. Barbarin himself, a four-square traditionalist even though he worked on some very modern sessions two decades earlier, adds gravitas to every passage.

The live material on the recently issued 504 CD offers more of the same. The recordings are somewhat rough and ready in places but there is enough musical substance throughout a mixed bag of material to satisfy Barbarin admirers. 'Gettysburg March' and a long version of 'Tiger Rag' stand out, not least for the leader's proud and accurate playing. Barbarin sounds almost gracious on some of these cuts, a long way from the thumping crudity of many fellow-traditionalists.

The 1955 edition of the group – which includes some major New Orleanians – is perhaps less exciting than the one which made the 1951 sessions. The music is otherwise much as before, though Hinton's flexible bass gives the underlying rhythms a more varied sense of swing, and this is certainly the clearest sound of Barbarin's available music. The Oxford session, by basically the same band, suffers from a wobbly balance, but the dominant musician here is certainly Humphrey, whose graceful lines are paradigmatic of New Orleans clarinet. All five discs are worth hearing and keeping.

Chris Barber (born 1930)

TROMBONE, BASS TRUMPET, VOCALS

Chris Barber has been playing jazz for half a century, which is also half the lifetime of the music itself. He was born in Welwyn Garden City and studied at the Guildhall in London. In the early '50s, he took over leadership of the Ken Colyer band and has been a leader ever since. The Barber band adapted its strategy to take account of the growing boom in blues, but otherwise has remained consistent in its approach to traditional jazz. Other soloists and vocalists have perhaps been more important to the band's sound and success, but Chris Barber's consistent presence has been the key to the band's longevity and high standard.

CORE COLLECTION

****** The Complete Decca Sessions 1954/55**

Lake LACDD 141/2 *Barber; Pat Halcox (c); Monty Sunshine (cl); Bertie King (as); Lonnie Donegan (bj); Jim Bray (b, bb); Ron Bowden (d); Beryl Bryden (wbd); Ottilie Patterson (v).* 7/54, 1/55.

Barber had been leading bands while still in his teens, but his first serious attempt was a co-operative group pulled together in 1953 during bandleader Ken Colyer's extended 'vacation' in New Orleans. Although Barber and Colyer subsequently worked together, the band split over their ultimate direction, and while Colyer (who felt the Armstrong Hot Fives were too modern) went back to elemental New Orleans playing, Barber assumed not only leadership but the mantle of the entire trad movement, with Humphrey Lyttelton already moving towards swing mainstream. The crucial early documents are these sessions for Decca, here beautifully remastered in an indispensable two-disc set. While the ensemble's the thing – as it was with Colyer – Barber thinks much more creatively about arrangements, the place of solos, counterpoint and rhythm, and it's surprising to hear how strongly this music survives the years. It sounds youthful and energetic, and it reminds that it was still being played by men in their early 20s. The very first track, the highly improbable 'Bobby Shaftoe', works up a terrific head of steam, yet it's clearly all under control. Some of the shibboleths of the trad movement – such as the plunk of the banjo – are there to be sure, but Barber's men were too good to let it seem like anything but a necessary part of the music. Halcox is still a bit green, but Sunshine is already masterful, and the leader's own playing has a terrific bark to it. Donegan contributes his 'Skiffle Group' session, which spawned the hit 'Rock Island Line', and paved the way not only for the skiffle boom but British beat music itself. The live tracks on disc two are just as impressive, and are greeted with applause the like of which hasn't been heard again at a jazz concert in Britain (at least, prior to the Jamie Cullum era). And with guest spots for Bertie King and material as diverse as 'Skokiaan' and 'Salutation March', Barber was already serving notice that as far as he was concerned, his musical remit was going to be as wide as he wanted.

***** The Original Copenhagen Concert**

Storyville STCD 5527 *As above, except omit Bryden and King.* 10/54.

*****(*) Ottilie Patterson With Chris Barber's Jazzband, 1955–1958**

Lake LACD 30 *As above, except add Eddie Smith (bj), Dickie Bishop (b).* 3/55–1/58.

****** The Chris Barber Concerts**

Lake LACD 55/56 2CD *As above, except omit Bishop, Donegan; add Graham Burbidge (d), Dick Smith (b).* 12/56, 1 & 3/58.

***** Chris Barber At The BBC**

Upbeat URCD 158 *Barber; Pat Halcox (t); Ian Wheeler (cl, as); Joe Harriott (as); Ian Armit (p); Eddie Smith (g, bj); Dick Smith (b); Graham Burbidge (d); Bobby Breen, Ottilie Patterson (v).* 12/63.

*****(*) Chris Barber At The BBC Vol. 2**

Upbeat URCD 177 *As above, except Tony Coe (as), Fred Hunt (p) replace Harriott, Armit and Breen.* 61–63.

Barber's live recordings probably outnumber his studio dates, as many of those as there are. Lake LACD 30 and 55/56 document what was, 50 years ago, the biggest musical draw in Britain, filling the Royal Festival Hall ten days before Christmas 1956 and packing venues elsewhere round the country with that full-hearted sound. Ottilie Patterson's occasional spots are uneven but tend to confirm her blues credentials. Barber's groups were at their peak in the late '50s. At the end of the decade they became the first British group to play the blue-riband Ed Sullivan Show, and they also built a huge following in Germany. It's important to recognize with what respect and seriousness Barber's brand of jazz was regarded in the Eastern bloc. In the communist countries, traditional jazz was the spontaneous music of an oppressed proletariat, uncomplicated by formalism or individualism, created collectively. All of this collective spirit is handsomely caught on the Lake issues.

The Upbeat records are drawn from BBC Jazz Club broadcasts at the beginning of the following decade, and already there are shifts – some subtle, some not remotely – in Barber's approach. On the first one, he lets Bobby Breen sing 'Route 66' and brings on guest Joe Harriott for four tunes, including his own 'Revival'. Humphrey Lyttelton is the MC. The sound is unfortunately rather dusty. Volume two comes in better fidelity and although there's a feature each for guests Coe and Hunt, this one – drawn from various broadcasts over a two-year period – feels more like 'traditional' Barber.

****** The Pye Jazz Anthology**

Castle CMDDD 139 2CD *As various discs above.* 56–59.

This can sit happily beside the Lake *Complete Decca Sessions* as all that the less than fanatical need to know about Barber in the '50s. Two discs' worth of live and studio material from Chris's sequence of albums for Pye/Nixa, excellently mastered, in a smart package that includes an entertaining interview with him.

*****(*) In Barber's Chair**

Lake LACD 185 *Barber; Pat Halcox (t); Ian Wheeler (cl, as); Monty Sunshine (cl, ss); Eddie Smith (g, bj); Dick Smith (b); Graham Burbidge (d); Ottilie Patterson (v).* 4/60–7/62.

This is one of the first issues in Lake's new series, releasing material from Denis Preston's Lansdowne recording operation. It gathers in the contents of four scarce EPs (*In Barber's Chair, Monty, Pat* and *Introducing Ian*), and adds on four other pieces which didn't turn up on the LPs of the period. The various features for Halcox, Wheeler and Sunshine are graciously handled by each of the soloists – it's a measure of Barber's confidence in his sidemen in that the leader doesn't even play on ten of these 20 tracks! There's a very fine 'Mood Indigo', a couple of good vocals for Ottilie, and a notably swinging attack on 'Till We Meet Again' (which Bunk Johnson did at his final session).

***** American Jazz Band**

Black & Blue 965.2 *Barber; Sidney De Paris (t, v); Edmond Hall (cl); Hank Duncan (p); Hayes Alvis (b); Joe Marshall (d).* 11/61.

Considering that many of these men were close to twice Barber's age when he made this record on an American visit, the leader acquits himself without a trace of nerves. The material's all too familiar but the playing has real verve.

***** Collaboration**

Jazzology BCD 40 *Barber; Pat Halcox (t); Ian Wheeler (cl, as); Graham Paterson (p); Stu Morrison (bj); Brian Turnock (b); Barry Martyn (d).* 9/66.

***** The Grand Reunion Concert**

Timeless TTD 553 *Barber; Pat Halcox (t, flhn, v); Monty Sunshine (cl); John Crocker (cl, as, v); Lonnie Donegan (bj, g, v); Johnny McCallum (bj, g); John Slaughter (g); Jim Bray (b); Ron Bowden, Graham Burbidge (d).* 6/75.

***** Echoes Of Ellington: Volume 1**

Timeless TTD 555 *Barber; Pat Halcox (t, flhn); John Crocker (cl, as, ts); Russell Procope (cl, as); Wild Bill Davis (p); John Slaughter (g); Johnny McCallum (g, bj); Jackie Flavelle (b); Pete York (d).* 6/76.

***** Echoes Of Ellington: Volume 2**

Timeless TTD 556 *As above.* 6/76.

Just because he was successful, Barber never forgot the origins of the music he loved. He has become an important practical historian of early 'hot' music in Britain and has constantly purified his own style, though not to the extent of shunning contact with other styles (witness the 1976 Ducal sessions, recorded in St Ives, with Ellingtonian Russell Procope), and he keeps a weather eye on shifts in public taste. In important essentials, though, Barber's approach has not changed in four decades; adaptability has never meant compromise. The later material, notably *Reunion*, betrays some signs of rote playing from some of the band, but Sunshine (who went off to make a career of his own on the back of 'Petite Fleur', a 1959 clarinet feature on which Barber did not solo but which became a major band hit) is an elegant and often moving performer, and Halcox has grown in stature with the years. The *Collaboration* with drummer Martyn is an interesting by-blow (taped by the late Doug Dobell, who was something of a legend on the British jazz scene).

***** Panama!**

Timeless CD TTD 568 *Barber; Wendell Brunious (t, v); Pat Halcox (t); Ian Wheeler (cl, as); John Crocker (cl, ts); Johnny McCallum (bj, g); John Slaughter (g); Vic Pitt (b); Russell Gilbrook (d).* 1/91.

***** Chris Barber And His New Orleans Friends**

Timeless TTD 573 *Barber; Percy Humphrey (t); Willie Humphrey (cl); Jeanette Kimball (p); Frank Fields (b); Barry Martyn (d).* 8/91.

The August 1991 meeting with members of the legendary Preservation Hall Band is as much of a disappointment as most of their activities. These may be the senior practitioners of the New Orleans style, but they make it sound a lot more pedestrian in the charmed air of New Orleans (albeit in a campus auditorium at Tulane University) than Barber's regular band can do in a small-town arts centre in the Home Counties. It's relatively unusual to hear him backed by a piano, but Jeanette Kimball isn't a particularly unusual player; indeed, she seems content to stay within reach of half a dozen trademark chords and runs at all times.

Panama! is really a showcase for the young New Orleanian trumpeter, who supplants the long-serving Halcox on most of the solo slots. Brunious builds a lovely solo on the extended 'Georgia On My Mind' and sings in a mournful, wavery mid-tenor. 'Careless Love' features clarinet before the vocal and then continues with a soft, cry-baby wah-wah chorus on trumpet (presumably from Brunious) that drops behind a delicate banjo and bass accompaniment; McCallum doubles the time on his own intriguingly jittery solo-line. Typically well crafted and intelligent, Barber's arrangements of 'Oh! Lady Be Good' and William Tyers's title-tune reflect traditional jazz at its best. Barber fans shouldn't miss it and trad enthusiasts should jump at the opportunity to hear Brunious in sympathetic company.

***** Forty Years Jubilee At The Opera House, Nürnberg**
Timeless TTD 590 *Barber; Pat Halcox (t); Monty Sunshine (cl); Ian Wheeler, John Crocker (cl, as); John Slaughter (g); Lonnie Donegan, Johnny McCallum (bj); Jim Bray, Vic Pitt (b); Ron Bowden, Russell Gilbrook (d).* 5/94.

The old gang's back in town. Two resurrected bands revisit one of their old stamping-grounds (and this corner of Europe is very much a hotbed of Barber loyalism), sounding in pretty good form. The chops, inevitably, aren't quite what they were, but the inclusion of Sunshine and a fit-sounding Donegan (who'd had cardiac problems) pushes the energy level well up. Delightful stuff from start to finish, though a better bet for collectors and nostalgia freaks than for newcomers, who might find it all a bit old-pals-ish.

***** Live In Munich**
Timeless CD TTD 600 *Barber; Pat Halcox (t, c, flhn); John Crocker (as, ts, cl); Ian Wheeler (as, cl); John Slaughter (g); Paul Sealey (bj, g); Vic Pitt (b); Alan 'Sticky' Wickett (d).* 2/95.

As so often, the Barber band goes down a storm in Germany, though this time in Bavaria where for a time there was a certain resistance to jazz. The line-up is familiar enough, and so is the programme. 'Tin Roof Blues' is stretched out long to give everybody a moment up in the sun. There's a fine if brief Duke Ellington medley which gives the saxophonists a nice lyrical feature, and the inclusion of 'Big Noise From Winnetka/Pitt's Extract' and 'Magnolia's Wedding Day' allows Barber to indulge some more ambitious material right in the middle of the set. A must for collectors and a good buy too for anyone who simply wants to sample later Barber work.

***** That's It Then!**
Timeless CD TTD619 *Barber; Pat Halcox (t); Acker Bilk (cl); John Crocker, Ian Wheeler (cl, sax, f); Paul Sealey (bj, g); John Slaughter (g); Vic Pett (b); Alan 'Sticky' Wickett (d).* 12/96.

Recorded in Manchester and Harrogate, these live dates are co-credited to Acker Bilk, whose 'Stranger On The Shore' dominates the first half of the CD, still haunting after all these years. The standard material ('Just A Closer Walk With Thee', 'Bugle Boy March', 'Wabash Blues', 'On The Sunny Side Of The Street' and 'High Society') is also high-calibre, with Barber in particular sounding very strong and convincing in his features. The evergreen Pat Halcox completes the horn line-up and shows no sign of ever changing his breezy, off-the-cuff approach. It may sound like an old act whose time has gone, but it is hard to argue with the musicianship all round.

***** Live 1998 – Cornbread, Peas And Black Molasses**
Timeless TTD 628 *Barber; Pat Halcox (t, v); John Crocker (cl, as, ts); John Defferary (cl, ts); John Slaughter (g); Paul Sealey (g, bj); Vic Pitt (b); Colin Miller (d).* 12/98.

*****(*) Misty Morning**
Timeless TTD 641 *As above, except add Mike Henry (t), Bob Hunt (tb), Nick Payton (as, cl, bs).* 12/00.

*****(*) The First Eleven**
Timeless TTD 650 *As above.* 12/01.

New recruits Defferary and Miller come in for the 1998 session, but this is basically business as usual on an enjoyable if unexceptional live record. More significant are the two subsequent discs, which debut the Big Chris Barber Band – Hunt, Payton and Henry coming in on an occasional basis with the specific brief of assisting in the creation of an Ellingtonian sound. Most of *Misty Morning* is indeed Ellington material, although there's a wider diversity on the later disc. This makes a nice fillip to a discography which was in danger of becoming atrophied in routine, and while the discs are in and of themselves nothing extraordinary, there's some very satisfying ensemble playing which underlines what an exceptional bandmaster Barber has been over the years. As we went to press, this amazing man was preparing to celebrate the 50th anniversary of his group.

Patricia Barber

PIANO, ORGAN, VOCAL

Studied psychology and classical piano in college and began piano and vocal work in clubs in the '80s. Recent work for Blue Note has brought her to prominence.

****(*) A Distortion Of Love**
Antilles 512235-2 *Barber; Wolfgang Muthspiel (g); Marc Johnson (b); Adam Nussbaum (d).* 11/91.

***** Café Blue**
Blue Note/Premonition 521810-2 *Barber; John McLean (g); Michael Arnopol (b); Mark Walker (d).* 6–7/94.

*****(*) Modern Cool**
Blue Note/Premonition 521811-2 *As above, except add Dave Douglas (t), Jeff Stitely (udu).* 1–2/98.

*****(*) Companion**
Blue Note/Premonition 522963-2 *As above, except add Eric Montzka (d), Jason Narducy (v); omit Douglas and Walker.* 7/99.

Barber made an album for Antilles in the early '90s which had disappeared without trace, but in the light of her recent success Universal have reissued it. Starting on a sparse, self-conscious trawl through 'Summertime', the record rather awkwardly mixes five originals (including the first two tries at 'Yellow Car') and four standards she never sounds comfortable with, although the impromptu stab at 'My Girl' isn't bad. The originals step towards the more dramatic persona of her later albums and admirers will want to hear them, but the record sounds like a label wondering what to do with a talented artist.

Her two Premonition records, subsequently licensed by Blue Note, had the feel of a cult sensation in the making. She uses pop material in a tough, unsparing way, and her songwriting has a metropolitan wit that sits well beside the few standards that she tackles. *Café Blue* has some weaknesses: her piano playing is interesting, but she doesn't really sustain the very long 'Nardis' or 'Yellow Car III', and 'Too Rich For My Blood' is needlessly extended. However, there are alternately sexy and troubling versions of 'A Taste Of Honey' and 'Ode To Billie Joe' and some smart originals. *Modern Cool* is the breakthrough record, with a string of the cleverest lyrics this side of Dave Frishberg and a delivery to match. Barber sounds best when she's using her contralto in its huskiest and most stand-offish tone, and that puts a proper erotic spin on 'Light My Fire', anti-coquette and all. Her band plays slinky, cool-cat combo music, with McLean outstanding and guest Douglas playing a little blues.

The quickie live album *Companion* is a fill-in release, but it has two of her most telling performances in covers of Sonny and Cher's 'The Beat Goes On' and Bill Withers's 'Use Me'. This could all get hung up in pure artifice, but Barber's been around, she keeps her distance in a very effective way and her method resists mere posturing.

*****(*) Nightclub**

Blue Note 27290-2 *Barber; Charlie Hunter (g); Michael Arnopol, Marc Johnson (b); Adam Cruz (d).* 5/00.

Barber's implicit aim here was to evoke the last-set feel at a club, where only the dedicated few have held on, and musicians and audience are thinking and feeling more or less as one. Tough to do in the studio, but this excellent continuation of the previous sequence makes a good shot at it. Hard to imagine at this point that Barber will be seeking dramatic departures in her work. It's already a process of refinement, and reduction to essences, but her piano solo in the opening 'Bye Bye Blackbird' suggests a method not much less distinctive than her singing, and in these two settings – two trios, with Hunter sitting in for three tracks – she makes an impressive stab at putting her own mark on such run-down staples as 'Yesterdays', 'Autumn Leaves' and 'All Or Nothing At All'. She refuses to muddle the sense of a lyric, hangs on to the melody as gospel, and manages to turn songs around without undue mannerism, unless you think her whole style is mannerism. Arguable, but we prefer to hear a remarkable performer in her prime.

***** Verse**

Blue Note/Premonition 39856-2 *Barber; Dave Douglas (t); Neal Alger (g); Michael Arnopol (b); Joey Baron, Eric Montzka (d); strings.* 2/02.

Taking a surprisingly baroque turn, *Verse* is – well, the title's a clue! – more a poetry record than a song collection, with the likes of 'The Moon' and 'Pieces' emerging as half-spoken half-sung recitations, while Douglas and Alger fiddle and decorate. 'Dansons La Gigue' is even an adaptation from Verlaine. It could be termed a natural progression from the beat-culture feel of some of the earlier records, and there's an abundance of striking lines. But many who loved the more groovesome situations of the earlier sets will find this march into capital-A art disappointingly unyielding – even selfish. 'You Gotta Go Home' and 'If I Were Blue' make up a fetching finale, and the faithful will need to hang in there.

Leandro 'Gato' Barbieri (born 1934)

TENOR SAXOPHONE, FLUTE, PERCUSSION, VOICE

Barbieri's intense, vocalized sound and upper-register screams can easily tip over into self-parody, but he remains a greatly underrated figure whose more radical and innovative work has been eclipsed by pop and film projects. Born in Rosario, Argentina, Barbieri moved to Buenos Aires in his teens and began his professional career in Lalo Schifrin's orchestra as an altoist and clarinettist. He then switched to tenor and began to create his own distinctive hybrid of jazz and South American folk forms.

***** In Search Of The Mystery**

ESP Disk 1049 *Barbieri; Calo Scott (clo); Sirone (b); Bobby Kapp (d).* 68.

***** Hamba Khale**

Fuel 2000 061187 *Barbieri; Dollar Brand (p).* 69.

As we have noted before, Barbieri is also a classic victim of what is known as Rodin's Syndrome: being best known for your least representative work. Two decades before making it big with the *Last Tango* soundtrack, he had been one of the most innovative young horn players working in Europe, where he cut a classic set with Don Cherry, *Complete Communion*, and the intermittently available *In Search Of The Mystery* under his own name, before establishing himself in the Jazz Composers' Orchestra.

To anyone who only knows the Latin Barbieri, or even more jarringly the disco-friendly Barbieri of the later '70s, this early disc and the duets with Dollar Brand will come as a complete shock. In keeping with ESP's philosophy and reflecting Barbieri's often overlooked similarity to Albert Ayler, the group album is howlingly intense and unremitting. 'Obsession' (a name chosen for at least one reissue) is the key theme, insistent, nagging and delivered at full pitch. 'Cinematheque' is prescient in suggesting that this musican's work was always likely to find its way onto a film soundtrack.

The duets with Brand (later Abdullah Ibrahim) are in a similar vein, though here in place of the roiling string figures created by cellist Scott and bassist Sirone (aka Norris Jones) he has the South African's percussive ostinato figures pounding away below him. It's an unexpectedly successful encounter, though Barbieri sounds more constrained than usual.

****** El Pampero**

RCA Victor 6369 418 *Barbieri; Lonnie Liston Smith (p); Chuck Rainey (b); Bernard Purdie (d); Sonny Morgan, NaNa (perc, berimbau).* 6/71.

Over the past few years Barbieri's '70s work has been reissued on RCA, though it may be that some items are difficult to find outside continental Europe, where the Argentinian has always had a loyal following and a critically serious reputation.

El Pampero was recorded at the Montreux Jazz Festival, where Barbieri also guested with Oliver Nelson and Eddie 'Cleanhead' Vinson as sax battlers in front of a United Nations big band. The small-group set with his regular band of the time is no less incendiary, with that extraordinary upper-register shriek kicking in less than a chorus into the title-track. 'Brasil' and 'Buenos Aires Querido' are both equally strong-voiced and Smith's electric piano, which had yet to slide into its egregious disco wobble, provides a strong harmonic base.

***** Fenix**

RCA Victor 37506 *Barbieri; Lonnie Liston Smith (p); Joe Beck (g); Ron Carter (b); Lenny White (d); Nana Vasconcelos (berimbau, perc); Gene Golden (perc).* 4/71.

*****(*) Under Fire**

RCA Victor 37507 *Barbieri; Lonnie Liston Smith (p); John Abercrombie (g); Stanley Clarke (b); Roy Haynes (d); Airto Moreira, Mtume (perc); Moulay Ali Hafid (dumbeq).* 71.

***** Bolivia**

RCA Victor 22105 *As above, except add Jean-François Jenny-Clark (b).* 73.

Fenix is one of the fieriest of the sessions Barbieri did for the Flying Dutchman label. It was one of a group of albums by the saxophonist which help deliver an audience previously largely uninterested even in the crossover style of Charles Lloyd and Miles Davis. The emphasis is laid pretty heavily on the saxophone throughout, and Barbieri's solos (still showing some of the influence of his avant-garde days) are raw and intense. His entry on 'Bahia' suggests an artist who is never going to surrender contentedly to mere prettiness.

Under Fire is, by contrast, the least incendiary of the Flying Dutchman albums. Abercrombie contributes significantly to a measured and lyrical approach, but the star player is Clarke. The material is heavily tinged with folk themes, and big Stanley's counter-melodies on 'Parana' and 'Maria Domingas' show how effortlessly he had assimilated similar material under Chick Corea's tutelage. Barbieri overdubs a second saxophone part on 'Antonico', a scaled-down version of the orchestrations he got from Nelson. A strong record from a vintage period.

The live *Bolivia* (like *El Pampero* before it) is a useful reminder of just how strong an improviser Barbieri was in a live context as well as in the studio. The traditional 'Eclypse' and 'Vidala Triste' stand out, with the saxophone ranging restlessly over single-chord vamps from Smith on the Rhodes.

**** Last Tango In Paris

Rykodisc 10724 *Barbieri; Franco D'Andrea (p); Wolmer Beltrani, Franco Goldani (acc); Oliver Nelson (cond); strings.* 11/72.

We are in some doubt as to whether this astonishing soundtrack strictly belongs in a jazz guide, but it is the record which made and hijacked Barbieri's reputation, and it is still an invigorating listen. Bernardo Bertolucci's film worked some pretty far-fetched variations on Rodin's 'The Kiss', but it was also accompanied by music of sensual grace, which always hinted at the darkness of passion and an almost nihilistic despair and self-concealment underlying the eroticism. The title-piece is intended to suggest thwarted climax, a steadily rising howl of desire and loss.

The focus is almost always on either the saxophonist or the accordions, but Oliver Nelson's lush arrangements are very much part of the mood of the film, velvety and intoxicated. This new issue is attractive for the inclusion of a 'Last Tango In Paris Suite', assembled by Barbieri from almost 30 cues from the original score. A plus for Barbieri fans and for collectors of film music.

**** Latino America

Impulse! 052236-2 2CD *Barbieri; Helio Delmiro, Ricardo Lew, Quela Palacios, Lee Ritenour (g); Osvaldo Bellingieri (p); Dino Saluzzi (bandoneon); Isoca Fumero (charango); Daudeth De Azevado, Raul Mercado (quena); Amadeo Monges (hp); Adalberto Cevasco, Novelli (b); Pocho Lapuble, Paulinho (d); Domingo Cura (Indian d); Antonio Pantoja (various instruments); Jorge Padin, El Zurdo Roizner (perc); percussion section of Escola do Samba do Niteroi* 73–74.

Having boosted his way to fame on the back of an (albeit controversial) film, and the quality of Barbieri's soundtrack was the one thing nobody disagreed about, it is no surprise that he, wife Michelle and producer Ed Michel should have been inclined to view the progress of his career cinematically. The two first albums for Impulse!, fulfilling the former Lalo Schifrin sideman's dream of recording for Coltrane's label, were called *Chapter One* and *Chapter Two* respectively, a practice that continued with their successors. This CD reissue puts them together, along with some previously unreleased material: a long version of 'Nunca Mas', a shorter 'single' version of the splendidly titled 'La China Leoncia Arreo La Correntinada Trajo Entre La Muchachada La Flore De La Juventud', and a single, 'Gato Gato', recorded with Lee Ritenour and an LA rhythm section. The pattern of almost all the music on both sets is a slow accretion of complex rhythm lines and very slowly shifting major–minor chord-patterns, over which Barbieri lifts steadily into the altissimo stratosphere. It is undeniably exciting stuff, even when it does lapse into histrionics. *Chapter One* ended, just to underline the filmic analogy, with 'To Be Continued', a two-minute curtain-call, in which Barbieri calls in the instruments one by one, like Vivian Stanshall on *Tubular Bells* or with the Bonzos.

Chapter Two also has additional tracks, the best of them being the alternative of 'Latino America' itself, and complete versions of 'Para Nostros' and 'Marissea', the latter minus the overdubbed flute part Gato added after the sessions, just one of several signs that these performances were both problematic and also an opportunity to experiment with collage effects. There is also an unreleased 'Mate', which is almost as stimulating as that beverage and which brings the set to a promising end. It seems clear that, between them, Michelle, Michel and engineer Baker Bigsby were Barbieri's Teo Macero, editing down sometimes cumbersomely long live performances to meet the exigencies of LP dimensions. Hearing these familiar tracks at full length isn't always as revelatory as one might have expected. There is, though, a trance-like quality to a Barbieri performance which comes across well and, for those who love his sound, more is very definitely better.

*** Yesterdays

BMG International 7432 147797 2 *Barbieri; George Dalto (p); Paul Metzke (g); Ron Carter (b); Pretty Purdie (d); Babafemi, Raymond Mantilla (perc).* 74.

The hugely underrated Metzke was to be an important part of the Barbieri set up over the next period, a player of elegance and occasional fire who never really emerged from the shadows. Though itself overshadowed by the brilliant *Chapter Four: Alive In New York*, this album rewards attention, not least because it sees Barbieri closing with the spirits of both Coleman Hawkins (on the opening 'Yesterdays') and with John Coltrane, on a drastic reworking of 'Village Blues'. Barbieri also reveals his filmic obsessions with a reworking of Bernard Herrmann's main theme from Hitchcock's *Marnie*. Ron Carter sounds as capable on electric bass as he always does on the upright version and it's him who hold things together here, leaving pianist Dalto to fill in the backgrounds and Metzke to open up the textures.

**(*) Caliente!

A & M 394 597 *Barbieri; Marvin Stamm, Bernie Glow, Randy Brecker, Irvin Marvovitz (t); Wayne Andre, David Taylor, Paul Faulise (tb); Don Grolnick, Eddie Martinez (ky); Joe Beck, Eric Gale, David Spinozza (g); Gary King (b); Lenny White (d); Ralph MacDonald, Cachete Maldonado, Mtume (perc); strings.* 76.

Caliente! catches Barbieri halfway into his disco-god mode. There is some excellent playing, as usual, though oddly the upper-register stuff sounds far more overheated in this context than it ever did in the more way-out sessions, and the orchestrations (by Jay Chattaway) are as tight and crisp as anything that came out of the fusion movement. Whatever else, Herb Alpert knows how to produce this sort of thing, and there can be few quibbles on technical grounds. However, apart from the opening 'Fireflies' and the evocative 'Behind The Rain', which contains a tiny, almost subliminal reference to a similarly titled Coltrane piece, there is not much of any great substance here.

*** Que Pasa

Columbia CK 67855 *Barbieri; Jim Hynes (t); Michael Davis (tb); Andy Snitzer (as); Philippe Saisse (ky, prog); Jeff Golub (g); Ron Jenkins, Mario Rodriguez (b); Dennis Chambers, Poogie Bell, Robbie Gonzalez (d); Cyro Baptista (perc); Vanessa Falabella (v).* 97.

It means 'what's happening'. This is Barbieri's *What's Going On?*, a meditation on life, violence, prejudice and the environment which manages to remain commercially astute. The key moment in Barbieri's recent life was the death of his wife, partner and helpmeet, Michelle. She is the dedicatee of 'The Woman I Remember', the strongest track on an album that is somewhat overpowered with something called 'sound design'. Barbieri has always been interested in the studio as a musical instrument in its own right, and he has always been able to find the appropriate techniques to match his conception. Here, though, he seems overwhelmed by the technology.

Interesting to hear him working with other horns on a couple of tracks. Barbieri has usually preferred to be sole front man, albeit in front of a huge range of percussion, but on 'Mystica' (dedicated to Jacques Tati) and 'Granada' (a poem to the bullfight) he brings in some solo brass and woodwind. Otherwise, producer Saisse is the main component of the sound on keyboards, and the range of percussion has been cut back dramatically. Not a classic record, but an intriguing one at this juncture. Almost 25 years after *Last Tango*, Barbieri is able to give his erotic soundtracking of the planet a very definite political spin.

** Gato Barbieri's Finest Hour

Verve 490671 *Personnel as for early items above.*

The 'finest hour' concept implies that you're being presented with a key or epochal moment in an artist's career. In point of fact, what you get in this series is a rather conventional career survey/best-of compilation. We'd question this collection even on that premise. Apart from 'Nunca Mas' and 'Bahia', most of these ten tracks seem somewhat peripheral to the main story. The inclusion of 'To Be Continued' from Chapter One seems perverse, given its nature (basically a count-in of instruments) and its position as a statement of intent. Disappointing.

*** The Shadow Of The Cat

Peak PKD 8509 2 *Barbieri; Herb Alpert, Barry Daniellian (t); Ozzie Melendez (tb); Oscar Hernandez (p); Jason Miles (ky, d, prog); Dean Brown, Russ Freeman, Dal Lowe, Romero Lubambo, Jeff Mironov, Peter White (g); Mark Egan, James Genus (b); Vinnie Colaiuta, Richie Morales (d); Steven Wolf (d prog); Cyro Baptista, Sheila E, Marc Quinones (perc); Lisa Fischer, Cassandra Reed (v).* 02.

The Cat may be less lithe than before, but he still caterwauls impressively. This is the most open and emotionally naked record from Barbieri for some time and arranger/programmer Jason Miles has combined old and new beautifully. As a saxophonist, he is still hugely underrated. Only the perceptive Dave Liebman has attested to the influence of Barbieri's trademark vocalized tone. The opening cut here is a tribute to the late Chico O'Farrill and features the delightful trumpet playing of Herb Alpert, the man sometimes damned for having led Barbieri away from free jazz and into disco. Herb also turns up on the title tune and the magnificent 'Para Todos'. Barbieri's liking for guitar players surfaces here as well with Jeff Mironov, Peter White and notably Russ Freeman engaging in some inventive exchanges. The leader is often seen and heard as a cat who prefers to walk by himself, but even a casual listen to 'Beautiful Walk' reveals how careful a listener he is as well. Barbieri's singing is more usually a recitation, but tracks like 'Ai Ai Ai Ai' suggest how close the horn and the voice sit in his imagination. He also finds space on 'Si Tu Me Quisieras' for Cassandra Reed, who has some of her namesake's jazz chops.The pay-off track is a latter-day reworking of the *Last Tango* theme, still broodingly erotic but these days much lighter and less fraught. Tonally brighter and more straightforward in articulation, the old gaucho can still cut it.

Sam Bardfeld (born 1968)

VIOLIN

Violin still has a rather peripheral role in improvised music, but Bardfeld has devised a language which takes in classical models, jazz harmony and pure sound.

*** Taxidermy

CIMP 195 *Bardfeld; Ken Wessel (g); Drew Gress (b); Mike Sarin (d).* 2/99.

CIMP had already experimented with improv violin in the shape of Billy Bang. Perhaps oddly, *until* you hear Bardfeld, he's not the first name in the young New Yorker's list of influences. These include Jean-Luc Ponty and Zbigniew Seifert – and we'd want to add the ill-fated Seifert's fellow-countryman, Michal Urbaniak, as well.

This line-up, which goes out as Cabal Fatale, had been around for some years before making a recording and there is obvious rapport between the players. The three string guys all have very different approaches and functions. Bardfeld favours a middle register and quite elaborate lines, however staccato the phrasing seems. Gress is reminiscent of the late David Izenzon and there are occasions when this might almost be an Ornette project.

'El Judio Demonstro Calidad' – 'the Jew demonstrated quality' – was a line about Bardfeld in a Colombian newspaper. 'One For Bill' is a tribute to the leader's teacher, saxophonist Bill Barron, while 'Curve' is a kind of abstract narrative, designed to feature the drummer over what is effectively a string ensemble. The title-piece, a protest against stuffed music, develops quite slowly, but actually has a rather sophisticated structure, revealing Bardfeld's interest in classical form.

Rob Bargad

PIANO

Played in rock and blues bands before more serious jazz work, with Nat Adderley and others.

*** Better Times

Criss Cross 1086 *Bargad; Eddie Henderson (t, flhn); Tom Williams (t); Steve Wilson (as, ss); Donald Harrison (as); Peter Washington (b); Billy Drummond (d); Daniel Sadownick (perc).* 12/92, 12/93.

There's something refreshingly simple but studied in Bargad's approach, and it's testimony to his powers as a writer of themes that the seven originals on *Better Times* all sound like things other bandleaders should pick up on. A duo performance of one of them, 'Is It Love?', on which he is partnered by Eddie Henderson, has the *déjà-écouté* quality of something that sounds as though it must have been around for years. Bargad has been singularly fortunate in his fellow-musicians on this debut recording. Henderson is a fierce and swinging trumpeter who manages to maintain beauty of tone even at full stretch. Wilson is an excellent partner. The two tracks from a December 1992 session – both standards, interestingly enough – feature Williams and Harrison instead and, while the former is in cracking form on 'When I Fall In Love', the partnership wouldn't be quite right for Bargad's own material. Of it, 'The Snake', 'Little J.J.' and 'Tears' are the most memorable themes, the last of them perfectly illustrating what the composer has learnt from rock. Still Bargad's only record as leader.

Guy Barker (born 1957)

TRUMPET

The London-born trumpeter studied and worked in NYJO before making his mark as a sideman in local bands and taking countless sessionman credits. In the '90s he emerged as a forthright group leader and increasingly powerful composer, leading an international band and making a sequence of high-calibre studio dates.

*****(*) Isn't It?**

Spotlite SPJ-CD 545 *Barker; Jamie Talbot (ss); Nigel Hitchcock (as, ts); Peter King (as); Julian Joseph, Stan Tracey (p); Jim Mullen (g); Alec Dankworth (b); Clark Tracey (d).* 7–8/91.

Barker's standing as the doyen of Britain's younger trumpeters has scarcely resulted in a flood of recordings under his own name, but this belated effort as leader bristles with fine music. His own three originals suggest a witty composer as well as a polished musical mind, with the title-track a particularly lucid and clever line, while the trumpet-and-rhythm setting of 'Amandanita' strikes a measured balance between poise and tenderness. Some of his solos err on the side of self-consciousness, such as that on 'Sheldon The Cat', where both he and the garrulous saxman Hitchcock are outdone by Jim Mullen's flowing improvisation; but there is trumpet playing of sometimes awesome finesse scattered through the session. No complaints about anyone else's contribution, either.

****** What Love Is**

Emarcy 558331-2 *Barker; Perico Sambeat (as); Dave Hartley, Bernardo Sassetti (p); Geoff Gascoyne (b); Gene Calderazzo (d); Sting (v); London Metropolitan Orchestra.* 11/97.

Superbly orchestrated by Colin Towns, the third of the trumpeter's Universal releases has him in his most characteristic mood: romantic, thoughtful and exquisitely poised. Working without another horn casts him more clearly in focus than ever before; Sambeat appears only once, and he shakes up the pace, for the record isn't all relaxed and smoochy by any means. The saxophonist has his moment on an Ornette Coleman medley that's there to startle, coming just after a boisterous 'Monk's Mood' and just before 'The Things We Did Last Summer' and 'Angel Eyes'. What's also startling is that there are no originals this time out. Barker is perfectly capable of holding his own in company like this, though it may have been a good market decision to issue more familiar material at this point in his progress. Opening with a richly textured version of Jimmy Rowles's 'The Peacocks' was a masterstroke and, unlike *Timeswing*, the modulations of mood and harmonic profile are well observed throughout. Ellington's 'Star-Crossed Lovers' is perhaps the most sheerly perfect solo Barker has yet to record, a statement of touching simplicity and great emotional maturity. The strings and additional winds, courtesy of the London Metropolitan Orchestra, are tastefully balanced with the band, and Sting's vocal has a throaty intensity despite its bar-stool relaxation. (It's even more of a pleasure than a relief to one of the authors to be able to register so positive a response, since his colleague is credited as joint producer of both records.)

****** Soundtrack**

Provocateur PVC 1030 *Barker; Barnaby Dickinson (tb); Rosario Giuliani (as); Denys Baptiste (ts); Jim Watson (p, org); Bernardo Sassetti (b); Orlando Le Fleming, Geoff Gascoyne (b); Sebastiaan De Krom (d).* 11/01.

This is a remarkable album, very clean-limbed and straightforward in conception but packed with unexpected strengths. Barker programmes in a couple of imaginary cinematic pieces (hence the title) that don't really require any programme, especially the more abstract 'Sounds In Black And White', and it isn't entirely clear why he feels he needs this extraneous matter adhering to what are already brilliant charts. The opening 'Underdogs' sounds unimpeachably authentic and very American. Barker plays big, ringing tones against an organ-fuelled background; Giuliani is raw and bluesy. On 'Waiting For The Delay' – one of those tunes that seem terribly familiar even when you know you haven't heard it before – Barker sits out for much of the track and only really kicks in right before the end, like a *deus ex machina*. 'Queen Of The Night' has nothing to do with Mozart, except there is an almost masonic simplicity and mystery to the backing from just bass and drums. 'Purr' is miscast here, but there is a beautiful version of 'Nature Boy' that (partly, one suspects, because of memories of *Moulin Rouge*) is far more filmic than the supposed soundtrack pieces. Great stuff from Guy.

Dale Barlow (born 1959)

SAXOPHONES, FLUTE

A Sydneysider, Barlow's no-nonsense hard-bop derived style has found various homes around the world, but he still spends much of his time in Australia, building on playing experience with the likes of Art Blakey and Guy Barker. Recent albums have seen him trying more open-ended areas to work in.

***** Windmills On Mars**

Hipnotation 003 *Barlow; Walter Lampe (p).* 9/99.

****(*) Where We Live**

Hipnotation 002 *Barlow; Alan Dargin, Matt Doyle (didg); Guy Strazzullo, Guy LeClaire (g); Steve Hunter (b); Nick McBride, Toby Hall (d).* 2–3/00.

*****(*) Live**

Jazzhead 028 *Barlow; Mark Fitzgibbon (p); Matt Clohesy (b); Dave Beck (d).* 3–4/01.

Barlow's most familiar persona has been hard-bop tough guy, and these more questing releases may surprise those familiar with his earlier playing. The duo record with Lampe – a former Sydney room-mate – was an impromptu studio meeting with the two musicians setting about a few standards and what seem to be a couple of improvisations. Recorded in acute close-up, Barlow's tone has an intriguingly feathery and almost wounded sound, which makes 'Over The Rainbow' and 'Like Someone In Love' unusually affecting. But the more open pieces have both men falling back on pattern-playing and don't work so well.

Where We Live is by two different editions of Barlow's Nomads group, which puts him alongside guitar, didgeridoo and percussion, as well as the occasional 'sonic device' of Australian origin. Whether this can been portrayed as a particularly Australian fusion may be a moot point, and hitherto the didgeridoo has frankly struggled to quantify its jazz credentials, but *Where We Live* at least stands as a lively setting for the leader's musical thinking. The problem is that there's nothing for him to kick against in the group. The didgeridoo players work as background drones and the guitarists stitch in a thin harmonic framework, and Dale is all too often reduced to polite decorative work. Some nice atmospheres are worked up along the way, but little really lingers in the mind.

It's almost a relief to find him back in the meat-and-potatoes blowing situation of the live date, recorded in two Melbourne locations with another longtime confrere in Mark Fitzgibbon. 'Jazz Couch' is lavishly furnished across 17 minutes and it could easily have gone on much longer; a wonderfully sustained blow that springs off an agreeably lyrical base. Here and in the following 'Bunyip' one can follow how Barlow's appropriated the spearing wail of some of his American mentors and applied it to a vocabulary which mixes swift jabs with more complicated bouts of phrasing that play deftly with the underlying time. Fitzgibbon is no slouch and Clohesy and Beck swing hard. A very enjoyable place to make Barlow's acquaintance.

Bob Barnard (born 1933)

CORNET, VOCAL

Born in Melbourne, he played in various Australian trad–mainstream outfits, including the Graeme Bell group. He led his own groups to much acclaim in the '70s and '80s, but occasional trips abroad have left him less widely known than he might be.

****(*) Stardust**

La Brava LB9711 *Barnard; Kenny Powell (ky); George Golla, Jim Kelly (g); Chris Qua, Darcy Wright (b); Len Barnard, Laurie Bennett (d).* 5-7/79.

***** Cornet Chop Suey**

Opus 3 19503 *Barnard; Lars-Erik Eriksson, Tomas Ornberg (cl); Kalle Nygren, Johan Bijkerk (p); Olle Nyman (g, bj); Bjorn Hagerman (b).* 6–7/95.

***** New York Notes**

Sackville SKCD2-3061 *Barnard; Keith Ingham (p); Cal Collins (g); Earl May (b); Jackie Williams (d).* 12/95.

***** The Man From The South**

La Brava LB9701 *Barnard; Tom Baker (c, tb, cl, ts, v); Kevin Hunt (p); David Seidel (b); Len Barnard (d, wbd).* 10/96–2/97.

***** Presents Oz Originals**

La Brava LB9811 *Barnard; Ed Wilson (tb, bt); Don Burrrows (cl, ts); Paul Furniss (cl, ss); Chris Tapperell, Dave Macrae, Graeme Bell (p); Ian Date (g); Ed Gaston, Deiter Vogt (b); Len Barnard, Lawrie Thompson (d).* 4/97.

***** The Joint Is Jumpin'**

La Brava LB0012 *Barnard; Don Burrows, John McCarthy (cl); Ralph Sutton (p); Ed Gaston (b); Len Barnard (d).* 4/99.

Barnard is an Australian whose occasional sojourns abroad have sometimes resulted in a record or two, as here. He admits to copying everything Armstrong did early on in his career, and that primary colour has since been assimilated into a modest style, marked by careful choices of notes, shaded dynamics and a clean melody-line. *Cornet Chop Suey* was done in Stockholm and is the more avowedly traditional record, with Barnard taking a notably reflective look at Armstrong staples such as 'West End Blues'. If there's such a thing as chamber-trad, this may be it, and the Swedes give him graceful support. *New York Notes* betrays the scholarly hand of Ingham at work, with many of the tracks resurrecting tunes unheard for decades. Barnard takes it in his stride and plays some of his most wistful horn. Comparatively uneventful but pleasing music. Bob has since recorded highlights from his 1999 Jazz Party at home in Australia, available on the homegrown Nif Nuf label (Nif Nuf 43/001), and he is listed on a companion release in the Marty Grosz entry. But the Australian La Brava label has some of his releases too. The 1979 strings session isn't much more than a pleasant light-music date, with the string charts entirely perfunctory. The recent stuff is much more like it. Barnard shares the front line with the multi-instrumentalist Tom Baker on *The Man From The South* and the music – mostly '20s and '30s material, with three originals tossed in – goes with a good-humoured bounce. *Oz Originals* presents a programme of material all from Australian composers – including John Sangster, Dave Dallwitz and Sandie Williams, as well as some of the players on the record – and runs the gamut from Graeme Bell's ragtime to Dallwitz's Ellingtonian 'Dawn Over Euroa'. If anything the music's presented a little too modestly, and while everything passes agreeably, little really jumps out. Much jumping on the final disc, which is a Waller programme with the assistance of the then-visiting Ralph Sutton. They had the sense to keep away from some of the more hackneyed Waller tunes. Probably the pick of these three, although even here the music lacks something that would take it a step away from merely decent swing mainstream.

Alan Barnes (born 1959)

CLARINET, ALTO AND BARITONE SAXOPHONES

Born in Altrincham, Barnes made waves as the saxophonist in the Tommy Chase band of the early '80s. Besides hard-bop gigs, he has also worked in the Humphrey Lyttelton band and the Pizza Express Modern Jazz Sextet. He can handle any swing-to-bop style, and virtually any member of the saxophone family, with the same facility.

***** Like Minds**

Fret FJCD 105 *Barnes; David Newton (p).* 7/93.

***** A Sleepin' Bee**

Zephyr ZECD7 *Barnes; Brian Lemon (p).* 12/95.

*****(*) Here Comes Trouble**

Fret FJCD 110 *Barnes; Steve Hamilton (p); Mick Hutton (b); Bryan Spring (d).* 1/96.

*****(*) Yesterdays**

Zephyr ZECD11 *Barnes; Brian Lemon (p); Dave Green (b).* 2/96.

***** Young Minds – Old Hands**

Zephyr ZECD13 *Barnes; Gerard Presencer (t); Iain Dixon (reeds); Andy Panayi (reeds, f); Brian Lemon (p); Anthony Kerr (vib); Dave Green, Alec Dankworth (b); Clark Tracey (d).* 3/96.

***** A Dotty Blues**

Zephyr ZECD26 *Barnes; Gerard Presencer (t, flhn); Mark Nightingale (tb); Andy Panayi (ts, f, picc); Iain Dixon (cl, ts); Brian Lemon (p); Anthony Kerr (vib); Dave Green (b); Steve Brown (d).* 1–6/97.

Barnes has been a stalwart saxophonist in all kinds of British jazz situations since the early '80s. His rush of recording in the '90s, thanks to the independent labels Fret and Zephyr, is a welcome testament by an unassuming yet significantly talented musician. Given the relative isolation of British musicians from the world jazz stage, it's sometimes difficult to get a handle on how good they really are. Barnes won't decimate any opposition, but he won't let anybody cut him either. He seems like a bopper by inclination – Phil Woods comes to mind as a possible model – who often ends up in mainstream situations, as happens on most of these records.

We have singled out two discs as the best examples of what he can do. *Here Comes Trouble* is a quartet date brimming with energy and chops. Barnes sticks to alto and baritone and handles what's almost an old Blue Note set-list (standards, Mobley, a Charlie Parker line) with ferocious aplomb. His principal activist in the group is the mercurial Spring, too rarely heard from these days, and it's a retro-hard-bop date of great character. The other one is the Zephyr set *Yesterdays*, with house pianist Lemon offering staunch support and bassist Green walking in here and there. It gets the nod over the similar *A Sleepin' Bee* if only for the quite sublime treatment of 'The Folks Who Live On The Hill'. Barnes and Lemon take few liberties with tunes and structure, and on a difficult one like 'Last Night When We Were Young' the embellishments are at the service of the song. *Like Minds* matches Barnes with the more introspective Newton: very good, if on a comparatively low flame.

The one disappointment, arguably, is the octet date, *Young Minds – Old Hands*, which brings a splendid group rather deliberately to heel on nine tunes. Barnes himself plays with notable finesse and there are plenty of good solos to enjoy, but the music could use a jolt of something here and there, produced with too benign a hand to strike many sparks.

A Dotty Blues is his latest from the Zephyr stable. Panayi, Presencer and Lemon all take a turn, but it's mainly Alan's own arrangements that power the nine-strong band, of everything from 'Birdland' to Kid Ory's 'Savoy Blues'. All done with a nice sleight-of-hand, but the even-tempered nature of it all bespeaks a British reserve that to some may suggest indifference. There are, inevitably, some warming solos: Presencer, beautifully athletic on 'All The Things You Are', and the inextinguishable Lemon on 'It Had To Be You'.

*****(*) The Pollwinners Playing Girl Talk**

Zephyr ZECD 28 *Barnes; Warren Vaché (t); Roy Williams (tb); Tony Coe (ts); Brian Lemon (p); Dave Cliff (g); Dave Green (b); Clark Tracey (d).* 7/99.

John Bune's Zephyr has quickly established itself as one of the shrewdest and most effective mainstream labels in the music, and his patronage of Barnes is an enlightened policy indeed. Besides genre favourites such as 'Girl Talk' and 'Tangerine', here's Clifford Brown's 'LaRue' and 'Once In Love With Amy'; besides making sure that everyone feels relaxed and comfortable, Barnes puts sufficient prickle in his charts to make sure that nobody's asleep. The results are a fine mix of masterclass, homage and new spirit. And the studio sound is beautifully sympathetic.

*****(*) Summertime**

Concord CCD 4905-2 *Barnes; David Newton (p).* 1/00.

*****(*) Manhattan**

Concord CCD 4847-2 *As above, except add Conte Candoli (t); Matt Miles (b); Steve Brown (d).* 4/00.

The duo record has its eccentricities – 'Tico Tico' for one – but some of this is quite sublime duo playing. The material is a connoisseur's cross-section of jazz history, from Ellington's 'Black And Tan Fantasy', superbly realized for soprano and piano, to a haunting alto treatment of 'Street Of Dreams' and an unexpected bass clarinet sortie on Don Weller's 'Di's Waltz'. Recorded in close-up, a memorable one-two. The quintet isn't far behind. Candoli, in one of his last appearances on record, is right at home in Alan's charts, fresh and alert in '2 Degrees East, 3 Degrees West' and briskly boppish on 'Jigsaw'. They skirt with repertory exercise here and there, but mostly it's a loving and gracefully tempered record.

***** Cannonball**

ASC CD 36 *Barnes; Steve Fishwick (t); Don Weller (ts); John Donaldson (p); Alec Dankworth (b); Steve Brown (d).* 5/00.

Live in Wakefield, this was the only way to record this tribute band – but, fine as the playing is, it takes second place to pretty much any in-person Adderley album.

*****(*) Swingin' The Samba**

Woodville WVCD 102 *Barnes; Art Themen (ss, ts); John Donaldson (p); Simon Thorpe (b); Dave Barry (d).* 6/02.

***** The Sherlock Holmes Suite**

Woodville WVCD 103 2CD *Barnes; Bruce Adams (t, flhn); Mark Nightingale (tb); Robert Fowler (ts, cl); Stan Sulzmann (as, ts, f); David Newton (p); Simon Thorpe (b); Clark Tracey (d); Alan Mitchell (narration).* 1/03.

Barnes has set up his own label and it's already delivered these first records. The *Samba* record addresses Latin-flavoured material with a superbly zesty aplomb, from Alan's own 'La-Teen-O' inwards, taking in Ellington, Silver, Burrell and Rollins tunes along the way. Themen's wrangling tenor proves a great foil and the whole session has a feel poised between knockabout and high-street spicy – not remotely authentic, and all the better for it.

The Sherlock Holmes Suite indulges in the British penchant for suites, and doing a jazz version of Conan Doyle is surely something that would come out of no other jazz territory. There's fruity dialogue by Alan Mitchell to go with programmatic music that sometimes stretches the credulity a bit – Mark Nightingale, that most urbane of trombonists, hardly personifies the Hound of the Baskervilles – and two CDs of all this is perhaps a bit much. But approached with a bit of tongue in cheek, there's some great fun too.

Emil Barnes (1892–1970)

CLARINET

A minor New Orleans legend who was taught by George Baquet, Barnes rarely recorded in the early days but figures in a number of location recordings from later in his life.

** Emil Barnes' Harmony Four The Very First Recordings 1946

American Music AMCD-102 *Barnes; De De Pierce, Charlie Love, Lawrence Tocca (t); Joe Avery, Harrison Brazlee (tb); Israel Gorman (cl); Billie Pierce, Sweet Emma Barrett (p); Albert Jiles, George Henderson, Willie Wilson (d).* 7/46–8/54.

These are rare recordings, the first four tracks from the dawn of New Orleans revivalism, with Barnes, Billie and De De Pierce and Willie Wilson in 1946. There's a 1954 session by Israel Gorman's band and two final tracks by a De De Pierce group. Rather peculiar that Barnes, under whose name this CD appears, is on only 4 of the 17 tracks, but that's American Music for you! While the performances have a certain dance-hall charm, this is ramshackle music that in all likelihood will appeal to diehard New Orleans campaigners only.

*** The Louisiana Joymakers Introducing De De & Billie Pierce

American Music AMCD-13 *Barnes; De De Pierce (t, v); Lawrence Tocca (t); Harrison Brazley (tb); Billie Pierce (p, v); Albert Glenny (b); Cie Frazier (d).* 8/51.

Alden Ashforth helped organize this date and his sleeve-notes bring the occasion back to vivid life. A lot of it may seem shambolic to those unacquainted with New Orleans practice (and we might be held up as apologists on that basis), but there's tremendous spirit at work. Billie Pierce's vocals have a serene majesty akin to the classic blues women, and De De's rambunctious delivery of 'Eh! La Bas' is jubilant. When the band is really smoking along, as in 'Hindustan', it's electric. Barnes plays his part, but once again he's hardly the mainstay of the CD!

** Opening Night At Preservation Hall

American Music AMCD-86 *Barnes; George 'Kid Sheik' Cola (t); Eddie Summers (tb); Emanuel Sayles (bj); Alcide 'Slow Drag' Pavageau (b); Alex Bigard (d).* 6/61.

A little bit of history. These are rediscovered tapes of the first night at the most famous shrine of the revival in New Orleans, Preservation Hall. Barnes was the nominal leader of a group of the old guys, and they sound in good spirits, even if from time to time the music is sloppy to the point of a shambles. Soloists come across with gusto, including the vigorous Sayles, but the ensembles really are all over the place, and the sound is pretty dire. Still, scholars will welcome a valuable document of its kind, and the notes – by the Hall's real founder, Ken Mills – show how fiscal politics intruded even here.

John Barnes (born 1932)

CLARINET, ALTO, BARITONE, TENOR AND SOPRANO SAXOPHONES

Barnes was recording in British trad circles in the middle '50s and entered into long-term associations with Alan Elsdon and Alex Welsh in the '60s, specializing on baritone. He was with Humphrey Lyttelton all through the '80s and has since tried his hand in various mainstream situations.

*** Like We Do

Lake LACD 69 *Barnes; Digby Fairweather (t); Roy Williams (tb); Fred Hunt (p); Jim Douglas (g, bj); Pete Skivington (b); Roger Nobes (d, vib).* 1/75.

*** The Talk Of The Town

Raymer Sound RSCD 722 *Barnes; Roy Williams (tb); Craig Milverton (p); Tony Marshall (g); Mike Thorn (b).* 9/00.

A dependably rousing voice on many a mainstream stage, Barnes has shown few inclinations to lead on record, although maybe he's never been offered the opportunity. This date for the Rediffusion label from 1975 found him sharing name honours with Roy Williams, but the band is basically the Alex Welsh line-up of the day with a young Digby Fairweather sitting in for Alex, who was contractually unable to appear. It's good British mainstream, very cleanly recorded, although the most interesting piece is 'Fascinating Rhythm', where trombone and baritone work with just bass and drums and the result is a startling copy of the Mulligan-Brookmeyer sound. Williams also has the temerity to essay 'Struttin' With Some Barbecue' as a bossa nova.

Barnes and Williams got together to guest with Milverton's trio at a gig at the Ordulph Arms in Tavistock, and the microphones caught a good one. Barnes seems to have left his baritone at home, since it's all alto and clarinet here, but the playing from both horns is delightful, and Milverton's men play copybook mainstream which gives them all they need. One might have hoped for one warhorse or two less, just to spice up the session.

Charlie Barnet (1913–91)

TENOR, ALTO AND SOPRANO SAXOPHONES

Born into a wealthy New York family, Barnet took up playing sax and was at work in Harlem – where he broke the colour bar – and everywhere in the city by the mid-'30s. But his band struggled until 1939, when he began making records for Bluebird, and broke big. He kept on through the '40s but disliked the way big-band music was going and quit bandleading in 1949, going into hotel management and leading groups only when he pleased, in the '50s, '60s and '70s. As an alto and soprano player, he idolized Johnny Hodges. He was married more times than even Dinah Washington.

*** Charlie Barnet 1933–1936

Classics 1133 *Barnet; Toots Camarata, Gordon Griffin, Eddie Myers; Eddie Sauter, Frank Amaral, Kermit Simmons, Joe Hostetter (t); Russ Jenner, Bill McVeigh, Buzz Smith, John Doyle (tb); George Bone, Les Cooper, Don Morres, Jack Henderson, George Vaughan (cl, as); Willard Brady, Bob Parks (ts); Billy Miller, Red Norvo, Horace Diaz (p); Buford Turner, Frank Klinger (g); Pete Peterson, Sid Weiss (b); Rudy de Julius, Bill Gussak, Julie Mendelson (d); Helen Heath, Harry Von Zell, Jackie Martin, Marion Nichols, Laura Deane (v).* 10/33–6/36.

Although a handful of Barnet's records – especially his big hits, 'Cherokee' and 'Skyliner' – stand as staples of the big-band era, he's generally been less than well served critically and by jazz collectors: there is still relatively little available on CD at present. His own playing – which always points to Johnny Hodges as a first influence, and splendidly so – is usually restricted to a few telling bars, but he was an enthusiastic advocate of other, greater players, and he remains one of the few bandleaders to have virtually ignored racial distinctions. It may have cost him dear in career terms, too, though Barnet never seems to have cared very much.

Classics have now made a start on his output. The first four sessions, cut for Banner in 1933–4, are extremely routine Manhattan dance music with jazz barely getting a look in. The debut session for Bluebird, six titles from January 1935, fields an uncertain personnel but a much more lively and exciting outfit. They may not have the finesse of many of their contemporaries, but the Benny Carter charts for 'Nagasaki' and 'On A Holiday' are played with terrific gusto (interesting to hear how the prescient Barnet was offering solo space to his guitarist, too). There are some mannered but oddly likeable vocals from Marion Nichols, which are an awful lot better than the terrible ones by a certain Harry von Zell on the early sessions. Next come four pretty ordinary titles for ARC before a return to Bluebird for the final two tracks. 'I'm An Old Cowhand' is taken at a surprisingly brisk clip and has some fine Beriganish trumpet (Amaral?) and 'But Definitely' is a forgotten but agreeable tune given a spirited delivery.

****(*) Charlie Barnet 1936–1937**

Classics 1159 *Barnet; Joe Hostetter (t, v); Frank Amaral, Kermit Simmons, Irving Goodman, George Kennedy, Art Lombardi, Frank Borati, Al Stuart (t); Buzz Smith, John Doyle, Sonny Lee, Bob Fishel, James Curry (tb); George Vaughan, Don Morres, Henry Galtman (cl, as); Dave Gotwalls, Joe Estren (as); Bob Parks (ts, v); Willard Brady, Murray Williams, Kurt Bloom (ts); Horace Diaz, John Nicolino (p); Frank Klinger, Tom Morgan, Buford Turner, Scoop Thomson (g); Sid Weiss, Bob Elden (b); Julius Mendelson, Billy Flanagan, Buddy Schutz (d); Kathleen Long, The Barnet Modernaires (v).* 6/36–5/37.

***** Charlie Barnet 1937–1939**

Classics 1194 *Barnet; Irving Goodman, Frank Amaral, Al Stuart, Frankie Newton, Jack Koven, Jimmy Milazzo, Bob Burnet, Johnny Mendell, Charles Huffine (t); Bob Fishel, James Curry, John D'Agostino, Ben Hall, Don Ruppersberg, Bill Robertson (tb); Henry Galtman (cl, as); Joe Estren, Dave Gotwalls, Gene Kinsey, Harry Carrel, Ernie Diven (as); Kurt Bloom (ts, v); Don McCook, James Lamare (ts); John Nicolini, Ludwig Flato, Joe Myrow, Nat Jaffe (p); Tom Morgan, George Cuomo, Bus Etri (g); Bob Elden, John Kirby, Harry Sulkin, Phil Stevens (b); Buddy Schutz, Joe Dale, Weesley Dean (d); Kathleen Long, The Four Stars, Judy Ellington (v).* 5/37–3/39.

Barnet's progress wasn't especially quick: much of the second volume in the Classics sequence is still little more than so-so dance music, with some dreary material such as 'The Milkman's Matinee'. A stray date for Varsity – under the old California Ramblers name! – has a bit more go in it. But Barnet could boast no outstanding soloists at this point.

The next is definitely up a notch. A couple of 1937 dates for Variety feature guest trumpeter Frankie Newton and include a spirited cover of Ellington's 'Emperor Jones' (alias 'Jubilesta'), which anticipates Barnet's regular borrowings from both Ellington and Basie. 'Surrealism' and 'Overheard In A Cocktail Lounge' are (to say the least) unexpected after some of the previous material. But with his return to Bluebird in 1939, and a new residency at the Famous Door club (celebrated in 'Knockin' At The Famous Door') Barnet's music hits its stride. If he was already deliberately derivative of the black swing orchestras rather than seeking a style of his own, as a consequence the music stands up all the better at this distance. Certainly the likes of 'I'm Prayin' Humble', 'Jump Session' and 'Swing Street Strut' go over as well as anything Dorsey, say, was doing at the same period. Judy Ellington, his new singer, was also an appealing addition. Remastering of the Bluebird material is good enough, but be warned that some of the Variety sides are poor.

***** Charlie Barnet 1939–1940**

Classics 1266 *Barnet; Bob Burnet, John Owens, Lyman Vunk, Billy May (t); Ben Hall, Don Ruppersberg, Bill Robertson, Spud Murphy (tb); Kurt Bloom, Gene Kinsey, Skippy Martin, Noni Bernardi (as); Don McCook, James Lamare (ts); Bill Miller, Phil Moore (p); Bus Etri (g); Phil Stevens (b); Ray Michaels, Cliff Leeman (d); Judy Ellington, Del Casino, Mary Ann McCall (v).* 9/39–3/40.

***** Charlie Barnet 1940**

Classics 1318 *As above, except omit Hall, Bernardi, McCook, Moore, Michaels, Casino, Ellington; add Larry Taylor (v).* 2–5/40.

Classics 1266 starts with the excellent 'The Duke's Idea' and its sessionmate 'The Count's Idea', but thereafter the tracks are the usual assortment of dance-band ballads and the occasional swinger. Mary Ann McCall arrives as new regular vocalist, here sounding very young indeed. 'Clap Hands, Here Comes Charlie' is a frantic instrumental. A mixed bag. McCall also sings on no fewer than 18 tracks on Classics 1318, but the band do get their chances: 'Leapin' At The Lincoln' is a cracking showcase, and the closing 'Flying Home', if hardly abandoned in the Hampton manner, is crisply done.

***** The Transcription Performances 1941**

Hep CD 53 *Barnet; Bernie Privin, Bob Burnet, George Esposito, Lyman Vunk (t); Spud Murphy, Don Ruppersberg, Bill Robertson, Ford Leary (tb); Leo White, James Lamare, Conn Humphries (as); Kurt Bloom (ts); Bill Miller (p); Bus Etri (g); Phil Stevens (b); Cliff Leeman (d); Lena Horne, Bob Carroll (v).* 1/41.

***** Swingsation**

GRP 059952-2 *Barnet; Peanuts Holland, Lyman Vunk, Johnny Martel, Jack Mootz, Irving Berger, Chuck Zimmerman, Joe Ferrante, Ernie Figueroa, Roy Eldridge, Art House, Jimmy Pupa, Paul Webster, Al Killian, Everett Macdonald, Art Robey, Ed Stress (t); Russ Brown, Kahn Keene, Bill Robertson, Dave Hallett, Ed Fromm, Porky Cohen, Tommy Pederson, Walt Baron, Ben Pickering, Charles Coolidge, Gerald Foster, Dave Hallett, Burt Johnson (tb); Buddy DeFranco (cl); Harold Herzon, Joe Meisner, George Bohn, Murray Williams, Conn Humphries, Ray De Geer, Gene Kinsey (as); Kurt Bloom, Ed Pripps, James Lamare, Andy Pinot, Kenny Dehlin, Dave Matthews (ts); Bob Poland, Danny Bank, Bob Dawes (bs); Michael 'Dodo' Marmarosa, Bill Miller, Marty Napoleon, Sheldon Smith (p); Barney Kessel, Tommy Moore, Turk Van Lake, Dennis Sandole (g); Howard Rumsey, Bob Elden, John Chance, Andy Riccardi, Irv Lang (b); Harold Hahn, Cliff Leeman, Mickey Scrima (d).* 8/44–3/46.

A Lang–Worth transcription date fills the Hep CD, featuring a strong edition of Barnet's band, even if it lacks a little in star soloists. It's the gutsy ensemble playing that endured, even when the programme is biased towards the sweeter end of Barnet's repertoire, as it often is here. Carroll is a lugubrious crooner on his features but the young Lena Horne makes an impact in her two songs, and there are some useful Billy May arrangements, as well as several originals by 'Dale Bennett' (a Barnet *nom de plume* that he used to help him out with his alimony problems). Excellent remastering.

Barnet's allotment in the GRP *Swingsation* series is a miserly eight tracks on a CD shared with Jimmy Dorsey. 'Skyliner' and some other fine stuff is here, in very bright transfers, but this is short measure on a bandleader whose records are already suffering neglect.

*****(*) The Capitol Big Band Sessions**

Capitol 21258-2 *Barnet; Jack Hansen, Irv Lewis, Dave Nichols, Lamar Wright Jr, Dave Burns, Tony DiNardi, John Howell, Doc Severinsen, Rolf Ericson, Ray Wetzel, Maynard Ferguson, John Coppola, Carlton McBeath, Al Del Simone, Marvin Rosen (t); Karle De Karske, Herbie Harper, Phil Washburne, Dick Kenney, Obie Massingill, Kenny Martlock, Bob Burgess, Harry Betts, Dave Wells (tb); Frank Pappalardo, Walt Weidler, Vinnie Dean, Art Raboy, Ruben Leon, Dick Meldonian (as); Al Curtis, Bud Shank, Kurt Bloom, Dave Matthews, Dick Hafer, Bill Holman, Jack Laird (ts); Bob Dawes, Danny Bank, Manny Albam (bs); Claude Williamson, Don Trenner (p); Iggy Shevak, Eddie Safranski, Ed Mihelich (b); Dick Shanahan, Cliff Leeman, Tiny Kahn, John Markham (d); Carlos Vidal (perc, v); Francisco Alvarez, Diego Ibarra, Ivar Jaminez (perc); Trudy Richards (v); strings.* 8/48–12/50.

This was Barnet's 'bebop' band. He knew he couldn't play the new jazz and that he didn't really want that kind of band, but he was shrewd enough to hire players who were adept enough to handle a really tough score such as 'Cu-ba', the sort of thing that was coming out of Dizzy Gillespie's book. Arrangers such as Manny Albam and Pete Rugolo posed plenty of challenges for the band, and here and there are pieces which pointed the Barnet men in the direction of Stan Kenton, which was the last thing their leader wanted. After he famously broke the band up in 1949, there came a new version, which cut the last four 1950 tracks here, with strings added. This is little-known jazz and it's a welcome addition to Barnet's CD showing, even if much of it is atypical of his best work.

Joey Baron (born 1955)

DRUMS, ELECTRONICS

One of the house-drummers for the New York downtown scene in the '80s and '90s, Baron also leads his own bands and now moves in wider, post-bop repertory circles.

***** Down Home**

Intuition INT 3503 2 *Baron; Arthur Blythe (as); Bill Frisell (g); Ron Carter (b).* 97.

*****(*) We'll Soon Find Out**

Intuition INT 3515 2 *As above.* 00.

Baron's discography as a sideman hasn't yet been matched by his output as leader or co-leader, but he has produced a number of highly effective albums. Earlier editions covered work like the fine *RAIsedpleasuredot* and *Crackshot*, both of which may still be found. The association with Blythe, Frisell and Carter was a fruitful one for the drummer. *Down Home* is aptly titled, an earthy, blues-soaked journey back into the tradition in the company of four master musicians. Blythe's resurgent alto has rarely been heard in a more effective setting and Frisell thrives in contexts like these. The tempo is rarely faster than a mule on a hot day, and even when a 'Wide Load' has to be delivered, the urgency is kept pretty well damped down. Here and elsewhere, Frisell plays straight, unadorned accompaniment but still manages, as does Baron himself, to make a straightforward count of four sound much more complicated. Once or twice it sounds as though Carter may have gone back to Fender bass, though his articulation on the upright instrument is so powerful and resonant, it may be that we're hearing. His walking intro to 'The Crock Pot' gives little hint of what is to come from Frisell and Blythe, who take a simple idea and turn it into something much more expansive without once departing from the basic changes.

Reconvened a couple of years later, the personnel is much more coherent and intuitive. Frisell plays much as he might on one of his own records and Blythe gets into some intriguing territory. The blues feel is precisely that, an atmosphere rather than a strict appropriation. Baron is the sole composer, which is confident and brave. 'M' and 'Closer Than You Think' are outstanding ideas, pitched in the same rhythmic free-bop idiom that dominates another strong and entertaining session.

Dan Barrett (born 1955)

TROMBONE, CORNET

Born in Pasadena, Barrett played in California revivalist groups before moving to New York in 1983 and working with Benny Goodman and Buck Clayton. He is a mainstream sideman par excellence.

***** Jubilesta!**

Arbors ARCD 19107 *Barrett; Ray Sherman (p); David Stone (b); Jake Hanna (d).* 12/91–2/92.

***** Reunion With Al**

Arbors ARCD 19124 *As above, except add Al Jenkins (tb, v), Rick Fay (cl, ss, ts).* 3/93.

Barrett doesn't sound much like Teagarden, but his manner makes one think of the great man: he plays a melody with a singer's grace and vibrancy. This session is beautifully done, horn and rhythm section in simple, effective empathy; but the drowsy material takes the edge off, and even when he picks up the plunger mute Barrett doesn't really push himself. Or so one thinks. *Reunion With Al* seems meant primarily as a comeback showcase for octogenarian trombonist Jenkins. Despite the lavish praise in the sleeve-notes, Jenkins sounds unsurprisingly slow and careful in his playing, but the music still goes off at an agreeable lilt and, with Barrett sticking to cornet this time, the front line has a pleasing balance.

***** Two Sleepy People**

Arbors ARCD 19116 *Barrett; John Sheridan (p).* 2/94.

***** In Australia**

Arbors ARCD 19143 *Barrett; Bob Barnard (c); Tom Baker (ts, as, c); Chris Tapperell (p); Ian Date (g); Don Heap (b); Lynn Wallis (d).* 10/94.

*****(*) Moon Song**

Arbors ARCD 19158 *Barrett; Bryan Shaw (t, c); Scott Robinson (cl, as, ts, bsx); Brian Ogilvie (cl, ts); Dave Frishberg (p, cel); Bucky Pizzarelli (g); Joel Forbes (b); Jeff Hamilton (d); Rebecca Kilgore (v, g).* 12/95.

Two Sleepy People strolls good-naturedly through 13 standards and a Billie Holiday medley, Barrett dividing his time between trumpet and cornet, Sheridan a gentleman accompanist. They don't fail to please. It's just that the record could use a few peaks, and it's so even-tempered. Barrett and Baker were on a trip down under when they made *In Australia* with a local crew. Nothing amiss here either: Barnard sits in on only three tracks, which is a pity, though Baker's tenor gets nicely tough at quicker tempos. The rhythm section is fine, but they aren't blessed with a very friendly sound. Best of this batch is certainly *Moon Song*, lovingly crafted out of a programme of a fine and unhackneyed list of songs and lifted up an extra notch by the presence of Becky Kilgore, who takes six excellent vocals. She isn't on the old Billie Holiday chestnut 'Miss Brown To You', but the band make a beautiful job of it.

*****(*) Melody In Swing**

Arbors ARCD 19191 *Barrett; Ray Sherman (p); Eddie Erickson (g, bj); Dave Stone (b); Jeff Hamilton (d); Ed Slauson (perc).* 7–10/97.

A top-notch performance, from a starting position that is hardly at the height of fashion: trombone player, with only rhythm section support, tackles mainstream obscurities. Not all that obscure, to be sure, but 'I'm Nobody's Baby' and 'My Mother's Eyes' are hardly hit-parade material today. Barrett uses plunger, mel-o-wah and old-felt-hat mutes on different tunes, plays 'What Is This Thing Called Love?' as a yawning lament, but gets almost boppishly freaky on 'Besame Mucho'. The band is attentive and admirable.

****(*) Being A Bear**

Arbors ARCD 19228 *Barrett; Spanky Davis (t, v); Jim Galloway (ss, bs); Scott Robinson (cl, bs, bsx, bcl, as); John Sheridan (p); Paul Keller (b); Jeff Hamilton (d); Rebecca Kilgore (v).* 9/99.

*****(*) Blue Swing**

Arbors ARCD 19232 *Barrett; Jon-Erik Kelso (t); Brian Ogilvie (c, ts); John Smith (ss, as); Ray Sherman (p); Eddie Erickson (g, bj, v); Joel Forbes (b); Jeff Hamilton (d); Rebecca Kilgore (v).* 9/99.

***** International Swing Party**

Nagel-Heyer 9067 *As above, except add Tom Baker (t, tb, as, ts), Scott Robinson (cl, as, ts, normaphone), Chris Hopkins (p); omit Kelso, Ogilvie, Smith, Sherman, Kilgore.* 10/00.

An animated soundtrack, *Being A Bear* outplays most cartoon film music but by itself is nothing special, and the likes of 'At The Jazz Bears Jamboree' may appeal only to those who are trying to get an offspring started in the right stuff. Better is *Blue Swing*, another immaculate show of small-group swing, just enough players to give it the feel of something bigger than average and with the chops and knowledge to transcend the most obvious clichés of the idiom. There's a sense that Barrett and his cohorts may already have taken this kind of thing as far as it can go, but even as a repertory exercise this has enough class to stroll past the obvious pitfalls.

The Nagel-Heyer set is another live show that dusts off pieces such as 'Early Session Hop' and 'Hindustan' – the sort of thing that might qualify as 'neglected', if the entire genre itself hadn't lain all but untouched for so long. Live sound is a bit rough, but it musses things up in a useful way.

Bill Barron (1927–89)

TENOR SAXOPHONE

Elder brother of pianist Kenny, Bill was already in his 30s when he made his debut on Cecil Taylor's Love For Sale. He made only a few recordings as a leader when in his prime and spent much of his last two decades in education. There are a few later sessions for Muse which we listed in our first edition.

*****(*) Modern Windows Suite**

Savoy 92878-2 *Baron; Ted Curson (t); Jay Cameron (bs); Kenny Barron (p); Eddie Khan, Jimmy Garrison (b); Pete LaRoca, Frankie Dunlop (d).* 2–6/61.

***** Now, Hear This!**

Fresh Sound FSR 323 *Barron; Ted Curson (t); Kenny Barron (p); Ronnie Boykins (b); Dick Berk (d).* 64.

****(*) Compilation**

Cadence CJR 1119 *Barron; Bill Lowe (tb, tba); Fred Simmons (p); Jay Hoggard (vib); Wes Brown (b); Ed Blackwell (d).* 10/84–3/85.

The Savoy reissue is a welcome coupling of the original LPs *Modern Windows Suite* and *The Tenor Stylings Of Bill Barron*, although only the title-piece of the former is included. Both sessions are a striking departure from hard-bop convention. Barron's writing, involving modal forms, blues and – in the 'Suite' especially – some queer Mingus-like tonalities, sounds like little else that was going on at the time. Both he and Curson register strongly as improvisers; listen to their contrasting approaches to the ostinato section of the eerie 'Ode To An Earth Girl'. Cameron, absent on *Tenor Stylings*, is rather less impressive. Both were recorded poorly by Savoy, and Kenny's piano is so far back in the mix, particularly in the 'Suite', that at times it almost sounds as if it is a pianoless group. But for Bill's playing alone this is a valuable and vivid document of a strong and rather wilful tenor voice at its peak.

Now, Hear This! is a date which has drifted around in various editions on vinyl; this may be its CD debut. The originals are a provocative lot. 'Big Bill' is a sort of boogie march, 'The Leopard' wrings everything out of a single central chord, 'Dwackdi Mun Fudalick' is a Messengers-like shuffle. Some of the tracks feel a bit foreshortened, and 'In A Monastery Garden' is a queer choice of cover, but for in-your-face intensity the horn solos are hard to beat, even if Curson sounds wayward at times.

The Cadence collection offers tracks sifted from the collection of tapes kept by Bill's widow Anna and recorded, during his long tenure at Wesleyan University. The sound is mostly rough but serviceable, the tracks from gigs made during 1984–5. It's an eccentric choice combining the virtually free 'Waiting For You', a marathon blues, a solo-piano treatment of 'My Funny Valentine' and a final march through 'Giant Steps'. Hoggard appears only on the first piece and Lowe's tuba solos are a bit of a trial, but over Ed Blackwell's thumping beats the leader plays with undiminished energy, and there is a lot of fine saxophone oratory in his mature post-Trane style.

Kenny Barron (born 1943)

PIANO, CLARINET

The younger brother of saxophonist Bill Barron, Kenny was a phenomenally talented youngster who developed into a soloist of graceful and gracious presence, the perfect sideman, but also a leader of genuine presence and authority.

★★★(★) At The Piano

Prevue CD PR 3 *Barron (p solo).* 2/81.

This fulfilled producer Don Schlitten's long-standing desire to create an album of Barron playing solo; to realize it, he booked the same room, RCA Studio C, and the same nine-foot Steinway on which the likes of Artur Rubinstein and Van Cliburn had recorded. This is certainly classic jazz, if not classical music. The opening bars of 'Bud-Like' are already too warped and subversive to sustain that categorization. It's the first of four Barron originals on the set. 'Calypso' sketches in an enthusiasm which has come out ever stronger in later years, while 'Enchanted Flower' builds on an idea first encountered on *Sunset To Dawn*, and an extra track, 'Wazuri Blues', suggests how much Barron had been influenced at this stage by the African rhythmic investigations of Tootie Heath, whose creative presence can readily be discerned here.

Monk and Ellington are the other tutelary presences, with versions of 'Misterioso', 'Rhythm-A-Ning' and 'The Star-Crossed Lovers', but it's the lyrical style of Billy Strayhorn that most profoundly influences the melody lines and improvisations. The sound, as one might expect, is very full and lush, and perhaps a little too curtained and veneered for some of the funkier material. An ideal place to follow Barron's procedures and take a measure on his expressive character.

★★★★ Green Chimneys

Criss Cross 1008 *Barron; Buster Williams (b); Ben Riley (d).* 7/83.

★★★(★) Rhythm-A-Ning

Candid CCD 79044 *Barron; John Hicks (p); Walter Booker (b); Jimmy Cobb (d).* 9/89.

Barron's group work is always characterized by a sensitive balance of resources, and these records range from the stretching and unconventional piano-trio format of *Green Chimneys* to outwardly more mainstream sets.

Hicks's presence on *Rhythm-A-Ning* is puzzling since he and Barron share so many strengths. Their collaboration doesn't quite strike sparks, largely because shared loyalties are less interesting than a degree of contention. Of the bunch, though, *Green Chimneys* is a neglected masterpiece with great character and a lovely balanced sound.

★★★ The Only One

Reservoir RSR CD 115 *Barron; Ray Drummond (b); Ben Riley (d).* 90.

★★★(★) The Artistry Of Kenny Barron

Wave CD 34. *Barron; Peter Ind (b); Mark Taylor (d).* 3/90.

★★★ Invitation

Criss Cross 1044 *Barron; Ralph Moore (ts); David Williams (b); Lewis Nash (d).* 12/90.

★★★(★) Lemuria–Seascape

Candid CCD 79508 *Barron; Ray Drummond (b); Ben Riley (d).* 1/91.

Some of the '80s work is disappointing but, like many musicians of his generation, Barron had a sudden boost at the start of the new decade. *Invitation* is well worth having. A highlight is Barron's own 'And Then Again' (that's the way he plays, setting out an idea, stating its converse, trying it out on the band if he has one, and then, as often as not, replacing it with the second subject or counter-melody rather than merely recapitulating). It's a brisk blues with the strong bebop overtones Barron brings to most of his work. There is much the same mix of inputs on the Wave CD, which was recorded on a memorable night at the Bass Clef club in London. Barron was in storming form and the long readings of 'Like Someone In Love', 'Body And Soul' and 'Lover Man' stand out in the work of recent years, suggesting that the only way to capture the quicksilver genius of this artist is to catch him in concert and unawares.

The trio on *Lemuria–Seascape* also features some good original material. The two title-tunes, at top and bottom of the programme, are more impressionistic than usual, though the rhythm section keeps the music driving forward. Riley's brushwork is prominently featured on 'Have You Met Miss Jones?'. The same 'and then again ...' effect transforms Monk's 'Ask Me Now' into an altogether less spiky number. *Lemuria–Seascape* is one of Barron's most attractively romantic sessions, a lighter and less rooted conception. Though none of them scales the heights, there are of course good things on almost all of these records, and Barron, who has suffered the kind of critical invisibility that comes with ubiquity, shouldn't be overlooked.

★★★★ But Beautiful

Steeplechase SCCD 31295 *Barron; Joe Locke (vib).*

The Steeplechase website refers to one of the tracks as 'Single *Pedal* Of A Rose', which makes a perverse kind of sense, for Barron's use of dynamics, damped notes and sustains is never more evident than on this lovely duo with vibist Locke. A set of romantic standards, played with authority and relaxed conviction. 'You Don't Know What Love Is' and the title-piece are almost symphonic in conception, with Locke's arpeggiated chords sounding like a whole string section. We've always had some doubts about piano/vibes combinations, but this one is exquisite.

★★(★) Freefall

Uptown/Universal 549706 *Barron; Regina Carter (vn).* 00.

Carter and Barron had gigged a couple of times in New York before this disc was cut, which explains the easy rapport between them, evident right from the opening 'Softly, As In A Morning Sunrise'. It also gets them through some tricky moments on Hodges's 'Squatty Roo', Shorter's 'Footprints' and Monk's 'Misterioso'. The title-piece is a free improvisation, quite boldly executed; but, perhaps with an eye to a more commercial audience, there is a cover of Sting's Green anthem, 'Fragile'. So far, so good; but why our relatively lowly rating? Simply because repeated listens to *Freefall* have left us largely unmoved and unstirred. It's effortlessly competent and thoroughly musical, but it lacks a certain saving passion.

Bruce Barth (born 1958)

PIANO

Unassuming post-bop pianist seeking to make his mark with a set of dates under his own name.

*** Don't Blame Me

Double-Time DTRCD-129 *Barth; Ed Howard (b); Billy Drummond (d). 6/97.*

*** Somehow It's Time

Double-Time DTRCD-168 *Barth; Terell Stafford (t); Adam Kolker (ts); Ugonna Okegwo (b); Billy Hart (d); Duduka Fonseca (perc). 2/00.*

Barth balances an earnest pianism with a fine touch. He doesn't exactly caress the keys, but he dislikes banging the piano, and each disc has a mellifluous quality that seems to emanate from the piano. The trio record suffers slightly from Barth's touch of circumspection. When he plays Monk's 'Evidence', even though that composer is clearly an influence on his own writing, it comes out rather bland and forceless and one can only conclude that Barth is not a natural Monkian. The two ballads at the heart of the record, 'Song For Alex' and 'For Clara', are the best examples of his virtues as both composer and performer, and they're handled impeccably. *Somehow It's Time* returns to a horns and rhythm setting and feels crowded some of the way. 'Tom Tom Thing' is a herculean group performance which sounds like a Coltrane ensemble and makes the following piano–rhythm treatment of 'Estate' seem like a drink of water. A couple of Monk covers pursue Barth's interest in the bop master, although the most interesting note is struck by three separate solo versions of 'Criss Cross', the first two no more than a chorus each, the third a more detailed take. A bag of bits and pieces.

*** Live at the Village Vanguard

Max Jazz MXJ 205 *Barth; Ugonna Okegwo (b); Al Foster (d). 8/02.*

*** East And West

Max Jazz MXJ 201 *As above, except add Terell Stafford (t, flhn), Steve Wilson (ss, as, cl), Adam Kolker (ts, bcl), Sam Newsome (ss). 12/00.*

The ensemble set is a more carefully thought-out and considered record than its predecessors, but still not yet the breakthrough album that Barth seems capable of delivering. The horns are used more sparingly than the personnel listing perhaps suggests, and the basic anchor of the group is the trio with Okegwo and Foster, which is featured without winds on a couple of tracks. But Bruce seems anxious to show himself off in very different contexts and with a self-conscious change of pace. 'The Lexter' is a hard-driving original which strongly features both Stafford and Steve Wilson. 'Sundown Time' is arranged for clarinets, and has more of a midnight feel, with Kolker groaning away mournfully at the back.

The trio record is much more consistent in tone and delivery, as might be expected of a live project. Foster is a model of attention, providing a structure to Barth's curiously unrhythmic approach and Okegwo delivers a strong but flexible harmonic basis for the pianist. Barth's odd devotion to Monk (odd, given his playing personality) is evident again: 'Evidence' again, but this time free-ish versions of 'San Francisco Holiday' and 'Let's Call This'. Nice, unfussy sound-mix from Max Jazz.

Gary Bartz (born 1940)

ALTO AND SOPRANO SAXOPHONES, SOPRANINO SAXOPHONE, CLARINET, FLUTE, WOOD FLUTE, PERCUSSION

Born in Baltimore, he studied at Juilliard and Peabody and played with hard-bop bands in the '60s before a stint with Miles Davis in 1970. Tried an increasingly dissipated fusion, but moved back to acoustic hard-bop in the '80s. Has lately taken to acting and production, and freelances as he pleases.

*** Libra / Another Earth

Milestone MCD 47077 2 *Bartz; Jimmy Owens, Charles Tolliver (t, flhn); Pharoah Sanders (ts); Albert Dailey, Stanley Cowell (p); Richard Davis, Reggie Workman (b); Billy Higgins, Freddie Waits (d). 5/67–6/68.*

A slightly lumpy pairing of Bartz recording for Milestone, mismatched not just because the two groups are so different but because the saxophonist's interest in mystical science-fiction never quite seems to blend with his raw blues phrasing. The second album, with its roster of avant-gardists, is a more satisfactory blend, and Tolliver turns in some wonderful throaty horn. The version of 'Lost In The Stars' is well worth having, but also worth comparing with 'Cabin In The Sky' on the earlier half of the disc, where Bartz really doesn't seem to know quite what he's trying to do with this new hybrid sound.

*** Harlem Bush Music – Taifa / Uhuru

BGP CD 108 *Bartz; Juni Booth (b); Harold White (d); Nat Bettis (perc); Chief Bey (v). 11/70–1/71.*

**(*) JuJu Street Songs

Prestige PRCD 24181 *Bartz; Chief Bey (p, perc, v); Herbert Eaves (p); Herbert Centeno (g); Stafford James (b, perc, v); Howard King (d, perc, v). 10/72–6/73.*

Bartz's raw, intense sound reversed the usual tendency for other instrumentalists to be influenced by the dominant saxophone sound of the day. He was more obviously affected by brass players, mainly Lee Morgan and Grachan Moncur III, with whom he studied. His precocious talents won him a place in the Jazz Messengers, though by this time Bartz had already formed his Ntu Troop, a group which changed rapidly in style over succeeding years.

At the start of the '70s he was recruited to Miles Davis's electric band, a prominent gig which did much to harden up what was already a strong interest in Afro-funk. Specializing, as he had from his early years, in soprano, he developed an affecting if unadorned delivery which on the earlier disc (pairing two albums, *Taifa* and *Uhuru* under the *Harlem Bush Music* title) sounds unaffectedly original. *JuJu Street Songs* is much less clearly defined, a disappointing follow-up.

The years that followed were to be somewhat eclipsed. Bartz made a fairytale album for kids, called *Singerella*, and was active in politics and education. There was no sign that he had much appetite for jazz, and it was widely thought that his early promise (which had also included stints with Woody Shaw and Max Roach) would go no further.

** Music Is My Sanctuary

Blue Note 80733 *Bartz; Ray Brown, Eddie Henderson (t); George Cables (p); Larry Mizell (ky, v); Juewet Bostick, David T. Walker, John Rowin, Wah Wah Watson (g); Welton Gite,*

Curtis A. Robertson; (b) James Gadson, Howard King, Nate Neblett (d); Mtume, Bill Summers (perc); Syreeta Wright (v). 77.

It would be churlish to waste too much invective on music of such charm and energy, and it's worth saying that Bartz was something of a pioneer in trying to make jazz work alongside disco. However, this isn't an album that has worn well and despite its club cachet, it's unlikely to spend a lot of time on your machine. Larry Mizell's arrangements are big, over the top and endlessly danceable, but even with some fine soloists in the roster, there's little room for creative improvisation of any sort here. We're secretly fond but publicly have to be stern and dismissive.

★★(★) Monsoon

Steeplechase SCCD 31234 *Bartz; Butch Lacy (p); Clint Houston (b); Billy Hart (d).* 4/88.

★★(★) Reflections Of Monk

Steeplechase SCCD 31248 *Bartz; Eddie Henderson (t); Bob Butta (p); Geoff Harper (b); Billy Hart (d); Jenelle Fisher, Mekea Keith (v).* 11/88.

In the early '70s Bartz was collecting poll wins like beer mats. By the end of the decade he was playing drab pop, a shift of idiom legitimized to a degree by the sponsorship of Miles Davis, but lacking the boss's innate musicality.

Bartz had been picked out as a possible successor to Jackie McLean; while any such comparison went out of the window in the '70s, it was to return when, at near 50, Bartz began to record jazz again. Both of these albums are a good deal more tentative than the run of live gigs at the time. There is a fine 'Soul Eyes' on *Monsoon*, but the Monk covers are slightly robotic despite strong contributions from Henderson. The superadded vocals on 'Monk's Mood' and 'Reflections' were a mistake – Jenelle Fisher is certainly no Abbey Lincoln. However, enough of the *Wunderkind* survives to guarantee Bartz listenability, if not much more than that.

★★★(★) West 42nd Street

Candid CCD 79049 *Bartz; Claudio Roditi (t, flhn); John Hicks (p); Ray Drummond (b); Al Foster (d).* 3/90.

Just occasionally, when a saxophone player climbs the stand at Birdland, a portly ghost in a pale suit wobbles out from the shadows and whispers in his ear. Bartz learned to be like Bird through Jackie McLean, but on this record he seems inclined to dig back deeper into the source material, and he plays like a man inspired. 'It's Easy To Remember' becomes a huge romantic edifice, from which he soars into 'Cousins' and a surprisingly Coltrane-ish 'The Night Has A Thousand Eyes'. Hicks is the best piano-player Bartz has come across in years, and Al Foster sends little whiplash figures along the line of the metre, coaxing the three main soloists on to even better things. Slightly exhausting, in the way a hot club set teeters between euphoria and growing weariness, but a more than welcome confirmation of Bartz's long-latent qualities. Strongly recommended.

★★★★ There Goes The Neighbourhood!

Candid CCD 79506 *Bartz; Kenny Barron (p); Ray Drummond (b); Ben Riley (d).* 11/90.

His finest hour. The opening 'Racism' is a boiling blues, an original played with an increasingly noticeable Coltrane inflexion. The first of two Tadd Dameron compositions, 'On A Misty Night' was originally recorded in the mid-'50s in a band that included Coltrane; the mid-point of the set is a severe interpretation of 'Impressions'. Bartz's homage isn't limited to a growing repertoire of anguished cries and dissonant transpositions. He has also paid attention to how the younger Coltrane framed a solo; working against the trajectory of Dameron's theme, but sitting comfortably inside the beat, he constructs an ascending line that culminates each time in a beautifully placed false note. The result is as lovely as it is unsettling.

Johnny Mercer's 'Laura' receives a serene and stately reading, with Drummond featured. Bartz's coda restatement is masterful. He tackles 'Impressions' in the most boiled-down way, with only minimal rhythmic support, concentrating on the basics. Barron returns to the foreground for 'I've Never Been In Love' and the closing 'Flight Path', his own composition. Throughout, his touch is light but definite, freeing his accompaniments of any excess baggage.

Though Charles McPherson and Bobby Watson have previously laid claim to Parker's alto crown, Bartz appears to have come into his kingdom at last. A superb album that will grace and enliven any collection; recorded live at Birdland, it's well balanced and free from extraneous noise.

★★★ Children Of Harlem

Challenge CHR 70001 *Bartz; Larry Willis (p); Buster Williams (b); Ben Riley (d).* 1/94.

There's nothing on *Children Of Harlem* in terms of emotional urgency or social polemic that Bartz hadn't already done on *There Goes* … The 1994 session is dedicated to Paul Laurence Dunbar, tagged with lines by Countee Cullen, another poet of the Harlem Renaissance, and kicked off with a version of the Amos'n'Andy theme. An unlikely parallel, maybe, but where Charlie Haden's Quartet West project works precisely because it is so determinedly unapologetic in its sentimentality, Bartz seems determined to throw in ironic nods and winks, quotes and antagonistic outbursts that don't really fit the mood of the thing. That said, the playing is generally good (if recorded a bit crudely by Rudy Van Gelder's usual standard), and the long 'If This Isn't Love' stands up with anything Bartz has done in recent years.

★★★ Live @ The Jazz Standard: Volume 1

OYO 021 *Bartz; Barney McAll (p); Kenny Davis (b); Greg Bandy (d).* 99.

Given the vagaries of his recording career, it's not surprising to find Gary setting up his own label. This debut release keeps it basic (and inexpensive) with a club gig that's clearly intended to show off the leader's chops in an emphatic statement of intent. The material is harder and more boppish than has been the case in recent years. 'But Not For Me' has become a Bartz favourite and the reading here is again long and highly developed, while keeping the energy level high. Walter Davis Jr's 'Uranus' is a strong opener, and there are two originals 'Soulstice' and 'Eastern Blues'. The former is an aggressive showstopper, the latter a more mysterious scalar conception that sees Gary execute curious shifts on his horn, almost as if he loses sight of the original line and has to do some intricate stepwork to get by.

Though Barney McAll isn't the most exciting of piano-players, the group is solid and palpably aware that its role is to keep the boss topped up with cues. Run your own label and you even get to do your own cover art. For the first issue on his own imprint, this one is modestly conceived. Nothing inside is quite as startling as Gary's liner-painting.

*****(*) The Montreal Concert**
DSM 3037 *Bartz; Peter Leitch (g).* 10/99.

An unusual duo but an extremely effective partnership in the event. Leitch is a superb harmonist with a profound affection for the great standards. He feeds Gary an endless flow of ideas on three long medleys, of which 'The Touch of Your Lips' and 'But Not For Me' are the most impressive, a seemingly staunchless flow of ideas that will delight the casual listener but which will supply players with a pool of ideas. Neither of these men ever falls back on a conventional lick when they can attempt something a little more inventive, and whether on alto or soprano Gary always sounds as if he's looking for something more. Given the instrumentation, the record might sound rather mild at a distance. Heard attentively, though, it's as tough-minded as could be.

Count Basie (1904–84)

PIANO, ORGAN

Born in Red Bank, New Jersey, William Basie settled in Kansas City after experience in clubs and vaudeville. He joined the Bennie Moten band there in 1929, and eventually took over its leadership in 1935. His band moved to New York in 1936 and became one of the most eminent of its day, with many important soloists and with a uniquely swinging rhythm section characterized by Basie's own minimalist piano style. He also ran small groups within the big band, and cut back to an octet for a while (1950–51) when the big band proved too expensive to run. European tours in the '50s and '60s restored the band's popularity; Basie's final period of recording, with the Pablo label, was the most prolific of his career, despite some spells of illness and finally having to lead the band from a motorized wheelchair. The band is still a working unit, now under the leadership of long-time Basieite, Grover Mitchell.

CORE COLLECTION

♛ ** The Original American Decca Recordings**
MCA GRP 36112 3CD *Basie; Buck Clayton, Joe Keyes, Carl Smith, Ed Lewis, Bobby Moore, Karl George, Harry 'Sweets' Edison, Shad Collins (t); Eddie Durham (tb, g); George Hunt, Dan Minor, Benny Morton, Dicky Wells (tb); Jack Washington (as, bs); Caughey Roberts, Earl Warren (as); Lester Young, Herschel Evans (cl, ts); Chu Berry (ts); Claude Williams, Freddie Green (g); Walter Page (b); Jo Jones (d); Jimmy Rushing, Helen Humes (v).* 1/37–2/39.

The arrival of the Count Basie band – on an East Coast scene dominated by Ellington, Lunceford and Henderson – set up a new force in the swing era, and hearing their records from the late '30s is still a marvellous, enthralling experience. Basie's Kansas City band was a rough-and-ready outfit compared with Lunceford's immaculate drive or Ellington's urbane mastery. But rhythmically it might have been the most swinging band of its time, based not only around the perfectly interlocking team of Basie, Green, Page and Jones, but also in the freedom of soloists such as Lester Young, Buck Clayton and Herschel Evans, in the intuitive momentum created within the sections (famously, Basie had relatively few arrangements written out and would instead evolve head-arrangements on the stand) and in the best singing team of all the big bands, Helen Humes and the incomparable Jimmy Rushing. There are paradoxical elements – the minimalism of the leader's piano solos that is nevertheless as invigorating as any chunk of fast stride piano, Green's invisible yet indispensable chording, the power of the band which still seems to drift rather than punch its way off the record. They all go to make up an orchestra unique in jazz.

This is desert-island music and this three-disc set is, as a single representation of Basie, a priority for collectors. Universal should really go back and remaster it again at this point, but even in this comparatively early CD edition the music still sounds very strong.

****** Listen ... You Shall Hear**
Hep CD 1025 *As above.* 1–10/37.

****** Do You Wanna Jump ...?**
Hep CD 1027 *As above.* 1–11/38.

****** Basie Rhythm**
Hep CD 1032 *As above, except add Harry James (t), Jess Stacy (p).* 10/36–2/39.

***** Jive At Five**
ASV AJA 5089 *As above.* 12/32–2/39.

****** Count Basie 1936–1938**
Classics 503 *As MCA disc, except omit Collins, Edison, Wells, Berry and Humes.* 10/36–1/38.

****** Count Basie 1938–39**
Classics 504 *As above, except omit Keyes, Smith, Hunt, Roberts and Williams; add Harry 'Sweets' Edison, Shad Collins (t), Dicky Wells (tb), Helen Humes (v).* 1/38–1/39.

(***) Lester–Amadeus
Phontastic CD 7639 *As above discs.* 10/36–9/38.

(***) Rock-A-Bye-Basie
Vintage Jazz Classics VJC-1033 *As above discs.* 38–9.

*****(*) Swingsation**
GRP 059920-2 *As above discs.* 37–9.

There are too many great individual records to cite here, and instead we shall note only that there are two significant early periods covered by reissues, the Decca tracks (1937–9) and the subsequent recordings for Vocalion, OKeh and Columbia (1939–42). A contractual oddity is that Basie's first session – credited to Jones–Smith Inc., and marking the astonishing debut of Lester Young on record – was made for Columbia rather than Decca. Two of them are on the hotchpotch *Jive At Five*, but the first Classics CD has them all together. For a definitive study of the Decca sides, one must look to either the Hep or the MCA CDs listed above. The Hep discs have been completed with *Basie Rhythm* and, besides having the four Jones–Smith Inc. tracks, the valuable thing here is the addition of eight tracks under the nominal leadership of Harry James but with Basie personnel dominating the line-up (also available under James's name on Classics). James himself sounds better than he does on most of his own records, but otherwise the outstanding figure is saxophonist Herschel Evans, always at least as interesting as Lester Young. There is actually very little to choose between the transfers: the Hep remastering is sometimes a little more full-bodied, but the MCA is mostly smoother and often a little brighter.

The Classics CDs, as usual, ignore any label boundaries and simply go through all the music chronologically, although no alternative takes are included. The transfers here are unpredictable. Some seem to have a lot of reverberation, which suggests second-hand tape transfers, and while all the discs sound good enough, they can't compete with the Hep or MCA sets.

The Phontastic CD, though named for Lester Young, is nearly all Basie airshots and concert material. There are some rarities, such as two allegedly unreleased tracks from a 1938 Carnegie Hall concert, but sound-quality is often poor; for fanatics only.

Rock-A-Bye-Basie, which is all airshots, also comes in very rough fidelity, but the standard of performances is high enough to warrant giving it an audition. If you can stand sound that seems to be crackling out of a pre-war receiver, this will be an exciting, surprising disc. There are some fine treatments and individual spots by the usual stars, as well as undervalued performers such as Jack Washington. Edison especially gets a better shot in than on many of the studio sides: hear his chorus of trumpet on 'Moten Swing'.

Released to cash in on the fad for swing music in the '90s, the *Swingsation* compilation is nevertheless an excellent choice of tracks from this vintage period.

*****(*) Count Basie 1939**

Classics 513 *Basie; Buck Clayton, Ed Lewis, Harry 'Sweets' Edison, Shad Collins (t); Dicky Wells, Benny Morton, Dan Minor (tb); Earl Warren (as); Jack Washington (as, bs); Chu Berry, Buddy Tate, Lester Young (cl, ts); Freddie Green (g); Walter Page (b); Jo Jones (d); Jimmy Rushing, Helen Humes (v).* 1–4/39.

*****(*) Count Basie 1939 Vol. 2**

Classics 533 *As above, except omit Berry.* 5–11/39.

***** Count Basie 1939–1940**

Classics 563 *As above, except add Al Killian (t), Tab Smith (ss, as); omit Collins.* 11/39–10/40.

***** Count Basie 1940–1941**

Classics 623 *As above, except add Ed Cuffee (tb), Paul Bascomb, Coleman Hawkins (ts).* 11/40–4/41.

***** Count Basie 1941**

Classics 652 *As above, except add Robert Scott, Eli Robinson (tb), Kenny Clarke (d), Paul Robeson, Lynne Sherman (v); omit Hawkins.* 5–11/41.

***** Count Basie 1942**

Classics 684 *As above, except add Jerry Blake (cl, as), Caughey Roberts (as), Henry Nemo (v); omit Minor, Cuffee, Robeson.* 5/41–7/42.

The great change which began this Basie era was the sad death of Herschel Evans, 'the greatest jazz musician I ever played with in my life', as Jo Jones remembered him. In many ways the band was never the same again. Evans's partnership with Lester Young had given the reed section its idiosyncratic fluency, and perhaps his death marked the end of the original Basie era, when the band relied on its individual players to combine and create the instinctive Basie sound. That said, Chu Berry was a more than capable replacement for Evans, and the orchestra was still approaching a technical peak. Other arrivals – Shad Collins, Tab Smith (who also wrote some strong arrangements) and, later, Buddy Tate (when Berry departed) – also had an impact on the band, and emerging arrangers (Andy Gibson, Buck Clayton) had a beneficial effect. But Basie was already steeped in a routine of riffs, conventional harmonies and familiar patterns which even the soloists (including the finally disenfranchised Young) couldn't really transcend, let alone transform. Taken a few at a time, these tracks are fine, but all together they can sometimes be dull as full-length records.

Highlights to listen for are 'Evil Blues', a memorable band performance, Lester Young's solo on 'Taxi War Dance' (both Classics 513), 'Clap Hands, Here Comes Charlie' and the Kansas City Seven date of September 1939 (all Classics 533), 'Blow Top' (Classics 563), Clayton's 'Love Jumped Out' and Helen Humes's delightful vocal on 'My Wanderin' Man' (both Classics 623). There are plenty of other interludes and solos to savour – this was too good a band to lack interest. Coleman Hawkins also makes a guest appearance on two tracks on Classics 623. But the paucity of genuinely memorable compositions and Basie's own leaning towards ensemble punch and exactness over personal flair sow the seeds of the band's decline.

There are also Basie's own piano 'solos' (actually with the rhythm section), ten of which were recorded in 1938–9 (they are split among Classics 503, 504 and 513). Basie had long since started to pare away the more florid and excitable elements of his early stride style and by now was cutting down to the bone. It works best on the elegance of 'How Long' and the almost playful feel accorded to 'Fare Thee Well, Honey, Fare Thee Well'. They also let the great rhythm section display itself away from the confines of the band, and one can hear how perfectly the team interlocks. But they also expose something of the repetitiousness and sometimes false economies of Basie's playing, even at the curtailed 78-rpm length.

The next two Classics compilations take the story up to 1942. Classics 652 shows the band playing with unimpaired vitality, but the material is often grim. Saving graces include 'Diggin' For Dex' and 'Platterbrains', and there is Paul Robeson's one jazz appearance on 'King Joe'. Classics 684 is considerably better: some excellent Rushing blues performances, eight titles by the Basie All-American Rhythm Section (all traditional blues), with Clayton and Byas featured on four of them, and a final date that produced a minor classic in Clayton's arrangement of 'It's Sand, Man!'.

*****(*) The Jubilee Alternatives**

Hep CD 38 *Basie; Harry 'Sweets' Edison, Al Killian, Ed Lewis, Snooky Young (t); Eli Robinson, Robert Scott, Louis Taylor, Dicky Wells (tb); Jimmy Powell, Earl Warren (as); Buddy Tate, Lester Young, Illinois Jacquet (ts); Rudy Rutherford (bs, cl); Freddie Green (g); Rodney Richardson (b); Jo Jones, Buddy Rich (d); Thelma Carpenter, Jimmy Rushing (v).* 12/43–10/44.

***** Count Basie 1943–1945**

Classics 801 *Similar to above, except add Buck Clayton, Al Stearns, Joe Newman (t), Lucky Thompson (ts), Jack Washington (bs), Shadow Wilson (d).* 7/43–1/45.

Splendidly remastered in crisp sound, these studio 'alternatives' to AFRS Jubilee show broadcasts give a useful impression of a transitional Basie band. Buddy Rich and Illinois Jacquet replace Jones and Young on some tracks, and the brass section is largely different from the previous commercial studio tracks. There are some good charts here – Andy Gibson's freshly paced 'Andy's Blues', Clayton's excellent 'Avenue C' and Tab Smith's 'Harvard Blues', one of the best of the later Columbias, with a repeat performance of the *tour de force* vocal by Jimmy Rushing – and many of the soloists sound in unusually lively form.

Classics picks up the story again with a group of V-Discs and one Columbia session. This covers some of the VJC material (below) and, as usual, no sources are listed for the transfers.

*** Count Basie And His Orchestra – 1944

Circle CCD-60 *Similar to above.* 1/44.

Cut in a single three-hour session, these are 16 transcriptions from the Lang–Worth service. Another solid Basie session with staples from his then current book, three rather gooey ballads sung by Earl Warren and only two features for Rushing. Hardly essential, but the sound of the transcriptions is exceptionally clear and fresh.

**(*) Count Basie And His Orchestra 1944 & 1945

Circle CCD-130 *Similar to above.* 1/44–2/45.

Another 17 transcriptions, remastered in very good sound. Too many vocals, perhaps, even though two of them are by Rushing, and jazz survives only in a couple of unremarkable Dicky Wells tunes, Earl Warren's predictable 'Rockin' The Blues' and Al Killian's boisterous 'Let's Jump'.

**(*) Count Basie 1945–1946

Classics 934 *Basie; Harry 'Sweets' Edison, Al Killian, Joe Newman, Ed Lewis, Karl George, Emmett Berry, Snooky Young (t); Dicky Wells, Ed Donnelly, Eli Robinson, Louis Taylor, J. J. Johnson (tb); Jimmy Powell, Earl Warren, Preston Love, George Dorsey (as); Buddy Tate, Illinois Jacquet, Lucky Thompson (ts); Rudy Rutherford (bs, cl); Freddie Green (g); Rodney Richardson (b); Shadow Wilson (d); Jimmy Rushing, Lynne Sherman, Taps Miller (v); strings.* 2/45–2/46.

Rather a thin bunch of Basie – one scratchy-sounding session for V-Disc, a misguided date for strings and three others for Columbia with some particularly undistinguished titles among them. The studio version of Clayton's 'Avenue C' is the main point of interest.

*** Brand New Wagon

RCA Bluebird ND 82292 *Basie; Harry 'Sweets' Edison, Ed Lewis, Emmett Berry, Snooky Young (t); Bill Johnson, Ted Donnelly, George Matthews, Dicky Wells, George Simon, George Washington, Eli Robinson (tb); Preston Love, Rudy Rutherford, C. Q. Price (as); Paul Gonsalves, Buddy Tate (ts); Jack Washington (bs); Freddie Green (g); Walter Page (b); Jo Jones (d); Jimmy Rushing (v).* 1–12/47.

*** Count Basie 1947

Classics 1018 *As above, except add Bob Bailey (v).* 5–12/47.

Basie signed a three-year contract with Victor in 1947, and the results have usually been regarded as something of a low point in his discography. But this set of 21 tracks from that initial year presents some good Basie performances, even if they show little sign of any marked change from the formula that had been enveloping the orchestra over the previous seven years. Gonsalves, seldom remembered as a Basieite, turns in some strong solos, 'Swingin' The Blues' and 'Basie's Basement' trim the band down to a small group without losing any impact, and there is the usual ration of features for Jimmy Rushing, always worth hearing. The sound hasn't been best served by the NoNoise process of remastering but will suffice.

The Classics disc covers the same ground but includes some tracks which the Bluebird set skips – not always to the listener's advantage, since they include fluff like Bob Bailey's feature on 'Blue And Sentimental'. But Basie collectors will welcome the complete approach, and the transfers seem respectable.

**(*) Blues By Basie

Columbia 501651-2 *As various discs above.* 5/39–11/50.

***(*) Swinging The Blues

Dreyfus FDM 36711-2 *As varous discs above.* 6/38–4/39.

These compilations show how it should and shouldn't be done. Columbia's release offers a mere 12 tracks of various blues numbers from a 12-year span. It's a straight reissue of an old '60s LP and sounds like it's scarcely been updated at all. The music's good, but this is poor value. Dreyfus has chosen 20 tracks from a similar period, with full documentation, handsome packaging (if you go for their 'modern art' look) and good transfers. One or two maverick choices jostle with what's otherwise a greatest hits of this Basie era .

***(*) America's #1 Band!

Columbia 512892-2 4CD *As various discs above.* 11/36–11/50.

Basie fans will hardly know whether to be enraged or elated by this release. Columbia's archive of Basie material is superb, but instead of doing a genuinely comprehensive overview – which would have been quite feasible – they've cherrypicked tracks from every era up to the Octet sessions of 1950, missing out many fine numbers in favour of adding an entire CD of airshots. These are interesting enough, especially for Basie scholars, but most of them have been out before (admittedly on semi-authorized editions) and most hard core Basie followers will likely have them already. What *is* here is admirably packaged and remastered, but it's a pity that many fine Columbia tracks have been left off.

*** Shoutin' Blues

RCA Bluebird 07863 66158 2 *Basie; Harry 'Sweets' Edison, Emmett Berry, Clark Terry, Gerald Wilson, Jimmy Nottingham (t); Ted Donnelly, Dicky Wells, George Matthews, Melba Liston (tb); C. Q. Price, Earl Warren (as); Paul Gonsalves, Weasel Parker, Georgie Auld (ts); Gene Ammons (ts, bs); Jack Washington (bs); Freddie Green (g); Singleton Palmer, Al McKibbon (b); Butch Ballard, Gus Johnson (d); Jimmy Rushing, Billy Valentine, Taps Miller, Google Eyes (v).* 4/49–2/50.

The final sessions before Basie disbanded the orchestra in 1950. Bop sidles into some of the arrangements here, notably 'Slider' and 'Normania', and it gives Basie's men no trouble – after all, this was one of the most accomplished of bands. There is some dreadful stuff as far as material is concerned, and it's only on the various permutations of the blues that the music settles down and grooves. Good moments for Wells, Edison and Rushing, as ever, and mostly fine remastering.

***(*) The Count Basie Story

Proper Properbox 19 4CD *As various discs above.* 11/36–11/50.

Basie's entry in the budget-box series initiated by the British label Proper offers a detailed overview of his vintage years: 99 tracks across four CDs, with full documentation. Besides the more obvious studio material, there are several V-Disc tracks and one or two more idiosyncratic picks. A solid introduction to an important figure, even if the material (from unlisted sources) may count as an opportunistic gathering.

*** Count Basie 1952

Classics 1281 *Basie; Paul Campbell, Joe Newman, Wendell Culley, Charlie Shavers, Reunald Jones (t); Henry Coker, Benny Powell, Jimmy Wilkins (tb); Marshal Royal (cl, as); Ernie Wilkins (as, ts); Eddie 'Lockjaw' Davis, Paul Quinichette (ts); Charlie Fowlkes (bs); Freddie Green (g); Jimmy Lewis (b); Gus Johnson (d); Bixie Crawford (v).* 1–7/52.

★★★ **King Of Swing**

Verve 837433-2 *As above, except add Joe Wilder, Thad Jones (t), Henderson Chambers, Bill Hughes (tb), Johnny Mandel (btb), Frank Foster, Frank Wess (ts), Eddie Jones (b); omit Shavers, Wilkins, Davis, Quinichette, Lewis, Crawford.* 12/53–8/54.

Basie reformed the big band and signed up to Norman Granz's Clef operation in 1952. The band sound happy, relaxed and confident, new charts by Neal Hefti help out, and there's fresh blood arriving in the solo ranks too. Classics 1281 covers the first sessions for Granz and there are good moments for Newman and Quinichette especially. *King Of Swing* is at present the earliest 'original' album available from Verve and it sports the first appearances of Franks Foster and Wess. Neither disc is really classic Basie but both show him settling into the failsafe guide of his 'mature' band after some years in a comparative wilderness.

★★★ **April In Paris**

Verve 521402-2 *Basie; Reunald Jones, Thad Jones, Joe Newman, Wendell Culley (t); Benny Powell, Henry Coker, Matthew Gee (tb); Marshal Royal (cl, as); Bill Graham (as); Frank Wess (ts, f); Frank Foster (ts); Charlie Fowlkes (bs); Freddie Green (g); Eddie Jones (b); Sonny Payne (d); Joe Williams (v).* 1/56.

★★★ **Basie In London**

Verve 833805-2 *As above.* 9/56.

★★★★ **Count Basie Swings, Joe Williams Sings**

Verve 519852-2 *As above, except Bill Hughes (tb) replaces Gee.* 7/55–6/56.

★★★(★) **The Greatest!!**

Verve 833774-2 *As above.* 57.

★★★(★) **Count Basie At Newport**

Verve 0602498617618 *As above, except add Roy Eldridge (t), Illinois Jacquet, Lester Young (ts), Jo Jones (d), Jimmy Rushing (v).* 7/57.

Basie had been obliged to work with an octet rather than a full band in 1950–51, but he put a new orchestra together the following year, and from then on he always remained in charge of a big band. It was the start of the 'modern' Basie era. By taking arrangements from a new team, of whom the most important was Neal Hefti, Basie made the most of a formidable new reed section, trumpets that streamlined the old Basie fire with absolute precision, and the first of a line of effusive drummers, Gus Johnson. Basie's belief in the primacy of the riff now led inexorably to arrangements that had screaming brass piled on top of crooning reeds on top of thunderous drums: it was a fearsome and, in its way, exciting effect. At the moment, though, the beginning of this period is not properly represented on CD. Facsimile editions of some of the most significant of Basie's Verve albums from the '50s – *Dance Session No. 1* and *No. 2*, and *The Band Of Distinction* – have yet to appear. Of the three originals now on CD, *April In Paris* and *Basie In London* are typical Basie fare of the period: bustling charts, leathery solos and pinpoint timing. The new Master Edition of *April In Paris* has been quite handsomely restored in sonic terms and is lengthened by seven alternative takes, none of them especially revealing. *At Newport* is a fun reunion with some of Basie's old sidemen (though Young sounds as wayward as he usually then was) and features Eldridge going several miles over the top on 'One O'Clock Jump'. The outstanding albums are probably the two featuring Joe Williams. The debut appearance on 519852-2 is a classic of big-band singing. The original versions of 'Alright, OK, You Win', 'Every Day I Have The Blues' and 'In The Evening', material on which Williams made his name, still have terrific zip and élan, and the remastered sound has real clout. *The Greatest!!* concentrates on standards but is another faultless performance. Rich-toned, as oleaginous as Billy Eckstine could be, yet with a feeling for the blues which came some way near the irreplaceable Rushing, Williams's smoothness and debonair manner fitted the new Basie band almost perfectly.

CORE COLLECTION

★★★★ **The Complete Atomic Mr Basie**

Roulette 793273-2 *Basie; Joe Newman, Thad Jones, Wendell Culley, Snooky Young (t); Benny Powell, Henry Coker, Al Grey (tb); Marshal Royal, Frank Wess (as); Eddie 'Lockjaw' Davis, Frank Foster (ts); Charlie Fowlkes (bs); Freddie Green (g); Eddie Jones (b); Sonny Payne (d).* 10/57.

Basie opened his contract for Roulette with the great show-stopping album that this band had in it, *The Atomic Mr Basie* (complete with mushroom cloud on the cover, a Cold War classic). It might be the last great Basie album. He had Neal Hefti (who already had scored most of the hottest numbers in the band's recent book) do the whole record, and Hefti's zesty, machine-tooled scoring reached its apogee in 'The Kid From Red Bank', 'Flight Of The Foo Birds', 'Splanky' and the rest. But it also had a guest soloist in the great Lockjaw Davis, whose splenetic outbursts gave just the right fillip to what might otherwise have been a too cut-and-dried effort. The record has been reissued in its full form, properly remastered (early pressings were flawed), with all the available extra tracks.

★★★ **Basie Swings, Bennett Sings**

Roulette 93899-2 *As above, except add Ralph Sharon (p), Tony Bennett (v); George Duvivier (b) replaces Jones.* 1/59.

★★★ **The Best Of Count Basie – The Roulette Years**

Roulette 97969 *Similar to above.* 57–62.

★★★ **Atomic Swing**

Roulette 97871 *Similar to above.* 57–62.

These Roulette albums are as prosaic and sensible as the rest of Basie's latter-day output. The meeting with Tony Bennett will please Bennett fans more than Basie admirers, but it's an enjoyable record. The rest of the Roulette catalogue seems to have disappeared for now, but there are two different best-ofs available. *Atomic Swing* has 13 tracks, *The Best Of Count Basie* a more generous 20, though the former has the slightly superior sound. The original *Atomic* album, though, ought to suffice as a representative sample.

★★★(★) **Count On The Coast Vol. 1**

Phontastic PHONT CD 7574 *Basie; Snooky Young, Thad Jones, Wendell Culley, Joe Newman (t); Benny Powell, Henry Coker, Al Grey (tb); Frank Wess (as, f); Billy Mitchell, Frank Foster (ts); Charlie Fowlkes (bs); Freddie Green (g); Eddie Jones (b); Sonny Payne (d); Joe Williams (v).* 6–7/58.

★★★(★) **Count On The Coast Vol. 2**

Phontastic PHONT CD 7575 *As above.* 6–7/58.

*** Basie's Golden '58
Phontastic PHONT NCD 8839 *As above.* 6–7/58.

*** Fresno, California
Jazz Unlimited JUCD 2039 *As above.* 4/59.

***(*) Live 1958–59
Status STCD 110 *As above, except add John Anderson (t), Marshal Royal (as, cl).* 6/58–11/59.

These are exceptionally strong live recordings. The three Phontastic CDs and the Status disc are all in such clear and powerful sound that the recordings belie their age. Basie's men sound in particularly muscular and good-humoured form, especially on the Status set, which includes a few uncommon parts of the Basie repertoire and some dry runs for the Roulette sessions that were coming up. Foster is a titan among the soloists, but Powell, Wess and Newman also have their moments, and Williams is very good on the Phontastic discs; *Basie's Golden '58* carries on the tradition of the two earlier discs. The date in Fresno caught another good one by the band, though the way the applause has been trimmed out you'd hardly know there was any encouragement for them. Sound is a little harsh, as if brightened from a dull master-tape, but listenable.

***(*) Breakfast Dance And Barbecue
Roulette 31791-2 *Basie; Thad Jones, Joe Newman, Wendell Culley, Snooky Young, Harry 'Sweets' Edison (t); Al Grey, Henry Coker, Benny Powell (tb); Marshal Royal (as); Frank Wess (ts, as, f); Frank Foster, Billy Mitchell (ts); Charlie Fowlkes (bs); Freddie Green (g); Eddie Jones (b); Sonny Payne (d); Joe Williams (v).* 5/59.

A rare glimpse of a complete Basie show: flown in from a Birdland residency to play a one-night dance at a Miami record convention, the band sounds like it's having a good time. The original album has been extended to include a full 18 tracks, and there are expected highlights such as 'Splanky' and the Joe Williams features. Harry Edison gets up at the end to guest on 'One O'Clock Jump'. The music's probably neither better nor worse than most such Basie survivals, but it's loaded with atmosphere.

*** Count Basie And The Kansas City Seven
Impulse! 051202-2 *Basie; Thad Jones (t); Eric Dixon (ts, cl, f); Frank Foster (ts, cl); Frank Wess (f); Eddie Jones (b); Sonny Payne (d).* 3/62.

A small-group one-off for Impulse!, this had the ingredients for a classic – Basie returning to a combo setting, the material ('Shoe Shine Boy', 'Lady Be Good') recalling the earliest recordings with Lester Young, and a congenial gathering of Basieites ready to give of their best. But Bob Thiele's overly cute production seems to have smothered all the spontaneity out of the date, there's too much flute and not enough saxophone, and apart from 'Lady Be Good' the music actually sounds formulaic. Still some nice moments, but a missed opportunity.

** This Time By Basie
Reprise 45162 *Basie; Don Rader, Sonny Cohn, Fip Ricard, Al Aarons, Edward Preston, Wallace Davenport, Sam Noto (t); Benny Powell, Henderson Chambers, Al Grey, Bill Hughes, Gordon Thomas, Grover Mitchell, Henry Coker, Urbie Green (tb); Marshal Royal, Frank Wess, Eddie 'Lockjaw' Davis, Bobby Plater, Frank Foster, Eric Dixon, Charlie Fowlkes (reeds); Freddie Green (g); Wyatt Ruther, Buddy Catlett (b); Louie Bellson, Sonny Payne (d); Leon Thomas (v).* 4/63.

** Basie's Beatle Bag
Verve 557455-2 *Similar to above.* 66.

Basie was at a low ebb in the mid-'60s, and record producers were probably asking themselves what to do with such a venerable and prolific recording artist. *This Time By Basie* is one of the misguided attempts to make the Count go pop. Competent, but any decent radio orchestra could have done just as good a job. We think that the less said about *Basie's Beatle Bag*, the better.

*** Verve Jazz Masters: Count Basie
Verve 519819-2 *As appropriate discs above.* 8/54–10/65.

Old favourites and the obvious choices from Basie's Verve tenure – 'April In Paris', 'Shiny Stockings', 'Sent For You Yesterday' and 13 more.

*** Straight Ahead
GRP Chessmates 051822-2 *Basie; Al Aarons, Oscar Brashear, Gene Coe, Sonny Cohn (t); Dick Boone, Steve Galloway, Bill Hughes, Grover Mitchell (tb); Bobby Plater (as, f); Marshal Royal (as); Eddie 'Lockjaw' Davis (ts); Eric Dixon (ts, f); Charlie Fowlkes (bs); Freddie Green (g); Norman Kennan (b); Harold Jones (d).* 10/68.

Originally released on Dot, this is a stray entry from the late '60s, entirely written and arranged by Sammy Nestico. 'Everything he does fits the band so well,' says Basie in the sleeve-notes, and it's too true: in other words, Nestico comes out as just another faceless Basie hack. That said, the band seems to like the situation, and there are some spirited solos along with the usual machine-like playing.

*** The Board Of Directors & Annual Report
MCA MCLD 19366 *Basie; Al Aarons (t, flhn); Gene Coe, Nat Pavone, Ernie Royal, Oscar Brashear, Sonny Cohn (t); Richard Boone, Harlan Floyd, Grover Mitchell, Steve Galloway (tb); Bill Hughes (btb); Marshal Royal (cl, as); Bobby Player (as, f); Eric Dixon (ts, f); Frank Foster, Eddie 'Lockjaw' Davis (ts); Charlie Fowlkes (bs); Freddie Green (g); Norman Keenan (b); Sol Gubin, Harold Jones (d); Mills Brothers (v).* 11/67–7/68.

Given the number of silly ideas that seemed to be flying across Basie's desk in the '60s, this collaboration is less absurd than many: the band with the Mills Brothers for two sets of decidedly old-fashioned tunes (exception: 'I Dig Rock And Roll Music', which is sheer idiocy). At its best, a swinging encounter. Notably fine studio sound.

*** Basie On The Beatles
Ocium OCM 0022 *Basie; Gene Goe, Sonny Cohn, Luis Gasca, Waymon Reed (t); Grover Mitchell, Mel Wanzo, Frank Hooks (tb); Bill Hughes (btb); Marshal Royal (cl, as); Bobby Plater (as, f); Eric Dixon, Eddie 'Lockjaw' Davis (ts); Charlie Fowlkes (bs); Freddie Green (g); Norman Kennan (b); Harold Jones (d).* 12/69.

Basie's second stab at a Beatles album is comparatively little-known, yet is a lot better than *Basie's Beatle Bag*. The arrangements by Bob Florence are surprisingly witty and inventive, and the band sound in very good shape, even managing to make something palatable out of the dreary 'Something'.

**(*) Afrique
RCA Victor Gold 74321 796182 *Basie; Paul Cohen, Sonny Cohn, Pete Minger, Waymon Reed (t, flhn); Steve Galloway, Bill Hughes, Mel Wanzo, John Watson (tb); Bill Adkins, Eddie*

'Lockjaw' Davis, Eric Dixon, Oliver Nelson, Bob Ashton (reeds); Hubert Laws (f); Buddy Lucas (hca); Warren Smith (mar); Freddie Green (g); Norman Keenan, John B. Williams (b); Harold Jones (d); Richard Landrum, Sonny Morgan (perc). 12/70.

Oliver Nelson's turn in the arranger's chair. Five tunes of his own, plus the spectacle of the Basie band tackling an Albert Ayler tune. As was par for the course in this period, there are foolhardy attempts to 'update' Basie. Norman Keenan's only allowed to work on the opening flagwaver, and Williams plays electric bass thereafter; Buddy Lucas wails on harmonica on 'Hobo Flats'; Hubert Laws comes tootling in; and there's a lot of noisy percussion on several tracks. Overall, not great.

***** Basie Jam**

Pablo 2310-718 *Basie; Harry 'Sweets' Edison (t); J. J. Johnson (tb); Eddie 'Lockjaw' Davis (ts); Zoot Sims (ts); Irving Ashby (g); Ray Brown (b); Louie Bellson (d).* 12/73.

***** The Bosses**

Original Jazz Classics OJC 821 *As above, except add Joe Turner (v).* 12/73.

***** For The First Time**

Pablo 2310-712 *Basie; Ray Brown (b); Louie Bellson (d).* 5/74.

***** For The Second Time**

Original Jazz Classics OJC 600 *As above.* 8/75.

***** Satch And Josh**

Original Jazz Classics OJC 959 *Basie; Oscar Peterson (p); Freddie Green (g); Ray Brown (b); Louie Bellson (d).* 12/74.

*****(*) Basie & Zoot**

Original Jazz Classics OJC 822 *Basie; Zoot Sims (ts); John Heard (b); Louie Bellson (d).* 4/75.

**** Jam Session At Montreux 1975**

Original Jazz Classics OJC 933 *Basie; Roy Eldridge (t); Johnny Griffin (ts); Milt Jackson (vib); Niels-Henning Orsted Pedersen (b); Louie Bellson (d).* 7/75.

***** Basie Big Band**

Pablo 2310-756 *Basie; Pete Minger, Frank Szabo, Dave Stahl, Bob Mitchell, Sonny Cohn (t); Al Grey, Curtis Fuller, Bill Hughes, Mel Wanzo (tb); Bobby Plater (as, f); Danny Turner (as); Eric Dixon, Jimmy Forrest (ts); Charlie Fowlkes (bs); Freddie Green (g); John Duke (b); Butch Miles (d).* 8/75.

****(*) Basie And Friends**

Pablo 2310-925 *Basie; Oscar Peterson (p); Freddie Green (g); Ray Brown, John Heard, Niels-Henning Orsted Pedersen (b); Louie Bellson (d).* 12/74–11/81.

Norman Granz signed Basie to his new Pablo label and began taking down albums more prolifically than ever before, some three dozen in the last ten years of the bandleader's life. The old wizard was effectively reborn as a recording artist. Eight new albums were set down in the first 18 months. *The Bosses* was a fine beginning, setting Basie alongside Joe Turner, who is in mellow but not reticent mood. There are too many remakes of his old hits here, but Turner and Basie make a magisterial combination, and the horns aren't too intrusive. *Basie Jam* was the first and perhaps the best of a series of studio jam sessions. The formula is, let it be said, predictable: fast blues, slow blues, fast blues, slow blues ... sort-of-fast blues. Basie plays as minimally as he ever has, but he presides grandly from the rear, and there are entertaining cameos from Johnson, Sims and Davis. The *Montreux Jam* is a bore, with Eldridge past his best and the others simply going on too long, while *Basie Big Band* was his first set for Pablo with the regular orchestra. This was a more than encouraging start. Sam Nestico, who wrote all nine charts, offered no radical departures from the Basie method, but at least he had had time to settle in since the *Straight Ahead* session and was starting to look for more interesting harmonies and section colours. There were some fine players in the band again: Jimmy Forrest, Bobby Mitchell, Curtis Fuller. Butch Miles, the least self-effacing of Basie's drummers, had also arrived, but was so far behaving, and Granz's dry studio sound suited the clean and direct lines rather well.

As far as Basie the pianist went, he made his first trio album in *For The First Time* (a formula repeated on *For The Second Time*) and traded licks with Oscar Peterson, his stylistic opposite, in the amusing *Satch And Josh*. Neither record was exactly a revelation, since Basie basically carried on in the style he'd played in for the last 40 years, but as fresh areas of work after 25 years of making the same kind of record, it must have been invigorating; and he plays as if it was. *Basie And Friends* is a collection of out-takes from various sessions, mainly made in this period, though a couple date from later on.

One of the best of all of Basie's Pablos is the meeting with Zoot Sims on *Basie & Zoot*. It's almost worth having just for the snorting blues choruses they put down on 'Hardav'. Basie gets a bit too ripe when he turns to the organ for a wallow through 'I Surrender Dear' but Sims always has a swinging line to put down, and this was a well-made match.

***** I Told You So**

Original Jazz Classics OJC 824 *As above, except John Thomas, Jack Feierman (t) replace Szabo and Stahl.* 1/76.

***** Basie Jam No. 2**

Original Jazz Classics OJC 631 *Basie; Clark Terry (t); Al Grey (tb); Benny Carter (as); Eddie 'Lockjaw' Davis (ts); Joe Pass (g); John Heard (b); Louie Bellson (d).* 5/76.

****(*) Basie Jam No. 3**

Original Jazz Classics OJC 687 *As above.* 5/76.

****(*) Prime Time**

Pablo 2310-797 *Basie; Pete Minger, Lyn Biviano, Bob Mitchell, Sonny Cohn (t); Al Grey, Curtis Fuller, Bill Hughes, Mel Wanzo (tb); Danny Turner, Bobby Plater (as); Jimmy Forrest, Eric Dixon (ts); Charlie Fowlkes (bs); Nat Pierce (p); Freddie Green (g); John Duke (b); Butch Miles (d).* 1/77.

**** Montreux '77**

Original Jazz Classics OJC 377 *As above, except Waymon Reed (t), Dennis Wilson (tb) replace Minger and Fuller.* 7/77.

***** Jam Montreux '77**

Original Jazz Classics OJC 379 *Basie; Roy Eldridge (t); Vic Dickenson, Al Grey (tb); Benny Carter (as); Zoot Sims (ts); Ray Brown (b); Jimmie Smith (d).* 7/77.

***** Kansas City Five**

Original Jazz Classics OJC 888 *Basie; Milt Jackson (vib); Joe Pass (g); John Heard (b); Louie Bellson (d).* 1/77.

***** Satch And Josh ... Again**

Original Jazz Classics OJC 960 *Basie; Oscar Peterson (p); John Heard (b); Louie Bellson (d).* 9/77.

Basie continued his Pablo run with a steady stream of solid, good or at least credible albums. The two further *Basie Jam* albums are lesser editions of the previous set, though, like all such records, they have a moment or two when things start happening. Carter and Davis are the most reliable soloists on hand. *I Told You So* and *Prime Time* were the second and third full-orchestra albums for Pablo and, while the first one is solid, the second misfires a few times. 'Bundle O'Funk' was exactly the kind of modishness that Basie's return to traditionalism should have eschewed, and some of the soloists sound tired. But it's better than the desperately routine live set from Montreux which wanders joylessly through a stale Basie set.

The small-band jam from the same year is much better. Carter's gorgeous solo on 'These Foolish Things', Sims wherever he plays, and even the by-now-unreliable Eldridge all make something good out of it. The second *Satch And Josh* album follows the same sort of pattern as the first and takes much of its energy from the grooving beat laid down by Heard and Bellson. 'Home Run', for instance, is deliciously spry and merry. *Kansas City Five* sets the unpretentious pairing of Basie and Jackson on their inevitable programme of blues and jazz chestnuts so old they ought to be roasted to a crisp by now. The veteran campaigners still find a wrinkle or two. Especially warm: 'Frog's Blues'.

***** Live In Japan '78**

Pablo 2308-246 *Basie; Pete Minger, Sonny Cohn, Nolan Smith, Waymon Reed (t); Mel Wanzo, Bill Hughes, Dennis Wilson, Alonzo Wesley (tb); Bobby Plater, Danny Turner (as); Eric Dixon (ts, f); Kenny Hing (ts); Charlie Fowlkes (bs); Freddie Green (g); John Clayton (b); Butch Miles (d).* 5/78.

***** Night Rider**

Original Jazz Classics OJC 688 *Basie; Oscar Peterson (p); John Heard (bb); Louie Bellson (d).* 2/78.

***** The Timekeepers**

Original Jazz Classics OJC 790 *As above.* 2/78.

***** Yessir, That's My Baby**

Pablo 2310-923 *As above.* 2/78.

***** On the Road**

Original Jazz Classics OJC 854 *Basie; Pete Minger, Sonny Cohn, Paul Cohen, Raymond Brown (t); Booty Wood, Bill Hughes, Mel Wanzo, Dennis Wilson (tb); Charlie Fowlkes, Eric Dixon, Bobby Plater, Danny Turner, Kenny Hing (reeds); Freddie Green (g); Keter Betts (b); Mickey Roker (d).* 7/79.

***** Get Together**

Pablo 2310-924 *Basie; Clark Terry (t, flhn); Harry 'Sweets' Edison (t); Budd Johnson (ts, bs); Eddie 'Lockjaw' Davis (ts); Freddie Green (g); John Clayton (b); Gus Johnson (d).* 9/79.

The Japanese concert must have been a happy experience for the band, since they sound in excellent spirits and familiar charts take on a springier life. The sound is unfortunately slightly constricted and certainly isn't as wide-bodied as the punchy crescendos secured on *On The Road*, which is another of the better live albums from this stage of Basie's career. The sheer wallop of 'Wind Machine' and 'Splanky' sums up the kind of unhindered and creaseless power that Basie's orchestra worked to secure and, while it says little of any personal nature, taken a few tracks at a time it certainly knocks the listener over. The three albums with Peterson are good enough on their own terms, but anyone who has either of the earlier discs won't find anything different here. Peterson carries most of the weight, and Basie answers with his patented right-hand fills and occasional brow-furrowing left-hand chords. If anything makes the music happen, though, it's again the exemplary swing of Heard and Bellson. *Get Together* is yet another small-group jam on a few old favourites, but the presence of the great Budd Johnson adds a few more felicitous moments than usual.

***** Kansas City Seven**

Original Jazz Classics OJC 690 *Basie; Freddie Hubbard (t); J. J. Johnson (tb); Eddie 'Lockjaw' Davis (ts); Joe Pass (g); John Heard (b); Jake Hanna (d).* 4/80.

****(*) Kansas City Shout**

Pablo 2310-859 *Basie; Pete Minger, Sonny Cohn, Dale Carley, Dave Stahl (t); Booty Wood, Bill Hughes, Dennis Wilson, Grover Mitchell, Dennis Rowland (tb); Eddie 'Cleanhead' Vinson (as, v); Eric Dixon, Bobby Plater (as); Danny Turner, Kenny Hing (ts); John Williams (bs); Freddie Green (g); Cleveland Eaton (b); Duffy Jackson (d); Joe Turner (v).* 4/80.

***** Warm Breeze**

Original Jazz Classics OJC 994 *As above, except add Bob Summers, Willie Cook, Harry 'Sweets' Edison, Frank Szabo (t), Harold Jones, Gregg Field (d); omit Rowland, Stahl, Minger.* 9/81.

***** Farmers Market Barbecue**

Original Jazz Classics OJC 732 *As above, except Chris Albert (t), James Leary (b) replace Eaton, Jackson, Vinson, Jones and Turner.* 5/82.

***** Me And You**

Original Jazz Classics OJC 906 *As above, except Steve Furtado, Frank Szabo (t), Eric Schneider (ts), Chris Woods (as), Dennis Mackrel (d) replace Albert, Hing, Dixon, Plater, Field.* 2/83.

****(*) 88 Basie Street**

Pablo 2310-901 *As above.* 5/83.

****(*) Fancy Pants**

Original Jazz Classics OJC 1038 *As above, except Jim Crawford (t) replaces Furtado.* 12/83.

***** Kansas City Six**

Original Jazz Classics OJC 449 *Basie; Willie Cook (t); Eddie 'Cleanhead' Vinson (as, v); Joe Pass (g); Niels-Henning Orsted Pedersen (b); Louie Bellson (d).* 11/81.

***** Mostly Blues ... And Some Others**

Pablo 2310-919 *Basie; Snooky Young (t); Eddie 'Lockjaw' Davis (ts); Joe Pass, Freddie Green (g); John Heard (b); Roy McCurdy (d).* 6/83.

Basie carried on, regardless of encroaching arthritis, eventually working the stage from a wheelchair. The big-band records from this patch are some of his best Pablos, for the simple reason that Granz was recording the band to more telling effect: studio mixes had improved, the weight and balance of the orchestra came through more smoothly and arrived with a bigger punch and, since those virtues counted for more with Basie than did individual solos or any other idiosyncrasy, the band just sounded bigger and better. The arrangements on the final albums are shared among a number of hands. Sam Nestico was again responsible for most of *Warm Breeze* and *Fancy Pants*, while other band-members contributed to the remaining three discs, which also featured numbers by Ernie Wilkins and Basie himself. *Warm Breeze* is a particularly shapely album, with Willie Cook featured on a couple of tunes, Harry 'Sweets' Edison guesting on 'How Sweet It Is' and the themes standing among Nestico's more melodic efforts. *Me And You* and *Farmers Market Barbecue* are both split between a full band and a smaller edition of the orchestra. The latter has a splendid 'Blues For The Barbecue' and fine tenor by Kenny Hing on 'St Louis Blues', while the former includes an overripe Booty Wood solo on a dead slow 'She's Funny That Way' as well as a look all the way back to 'Moten Swing'. *88 Basie Street* and *Fancy Pants* are a little more routine, even by Basie standards, but the slickness and precision are unfaltering. *Kansas City Shout* and *Six* are fun albums with Vinson and Turner vying for attention and Basie refereeing with stately calm at the piano. But the two best records from this closing period are probably *Kansas City Seven* and *Mostly Blues ... And Some Others*. The former features a cracking line-up, and though Hubbard sometimes goes too far and Hanna's cymbals are annoyingly overbusy, it makes for some steaming music. The latter is as slow, full-flavoured and hefty as Basie seemed to want his blues to be. Pass and the imperturbable Green make a memorable combination, and Young and Davis blow things that turn out just fine. The pianist, of course, does his usual.

***** Fun Time**

Pablo 2310-945 *Basie; Sonny Cohn, Frank Szabo, Pete Minger, Dave Stahl, Bob Mitchell (t); Al Grey, Curtis Fuller, Mel Wanzo, Bill Hughes (tb); Eric Dixon, Danny Turner, Bobby Plater, Jimmy Forrest, Charlie Fowlkes (reeds); Freddie Green (g); John Duke (b); Butch Miles (d); Bill Caffey (v).* 7/75.

The first of what could have been many more Basie records yet, although if Pablo has any kind of stockpile, it currently seems to be keeping quiet about it. This is the orchestra at Montreux in 1975, a grand edition of the band, and delivering on all cylinders. Big and clear concert sound.

***** The Best Of Count Basie**

Pablo 2405-408 73–83

***** The Best Of The Count Basie Big Band**

Pablo 2405-422 73–83

Two solid compilations from a vast trove of recordings. The first concentrates on the small groups, the second on the orchestra, and either will serve as a sampler of the later Basie.

****** The Golden Years**

Pablo 4419-2 4CD *As Pablo and OJC albums listed above.* 73–83.

His last decade on record did little to challenge the memories of his (real) golden age, and none of the original albums really stands out as a classic. So this intelligent and smilingly prepared four-disc compilation is a welcome retrieval of many of the best moments from a prolific Indian summer in the studios and on stage. Two discs of big bands, one of small groups and one where he assists various singers. Little to argue about in the choosing, either.

***** Live At El Morocco**

Telarc CD-83312 *Mike Williams, Melton Mustafa, Derrick Gardner, Bob Ojeda (t); Mel Wanzo, Clarence Banks, Robert Trowers, Bill Hughes (tb); Danny Turner (as, picc); Manny Boyd (as, f); Kenny Hing, Doug Miller (ts, f); Frank Foster (ts); John Williams (bs, bcl); George Caldwell (p); Charlie Johnson (g); Cleveland Eaton (b); David Gibson (d).* 2/92.

***** Basie's Bag**

Telarc CD-83358 *As above.* 11/92.

Given that the big band as it stood under Basie in the final years was as sleek and hard as polished steel, the idea of a ghost band seems more plausible than an Ellington, Goodman or Herman survival group. Frank Foster worked hard to maintain the standards of the group, and these records are convincing reminders of Basie's legacy, even if they don't shake the earth. The live disc is warm enough to stir the blood a little. *Basie's Bag* has a grand set-piece in the 'Count Basie Remembrance Suite' and a few solid reshuffles from the band book. Foster, by now an eminence of Basie-esque stature himself, presides with fine authority. The band is now looked after by Grover Mitchell, and its anniversary concerts at Ronnie Scott's in 1999 were warmly received. A great institution lives on.

The Basin Street Six

GROUP

Formed in New Orleans in the mid-'40s by a gang of young men, partly as a way to get into football games for nothing. They began taking the music more seriously and started recording in 1950, though the group fell apart a few years later when trumpeter Girard began leading his own bands.

***** The Complete Circle Recordings**

GHB BCD–103 *George Girard (t); Joe Rotis (tb); Pete Fountain (cl, ts); Roy Zimmerman (p); Bunny Franks (b); Charlie Duke (d).* 8–11/50.

Tom Stagg's notes detail the history of the Basin Street Six, which was important for setting up the careers of two particular figures, Girard and Fountain. Girard already sounds head and shoulders above the others on this set of 11 Dixieland staples, and his elegantly hot playing is what makes the music endure. An exceptional musician, his early death denied him recognition in the music's history. Fountain, who went on to become a pop–Dixieland major, is merely competent in comparison. Circle weren't noted for their hi-fi recordings, and these are no exception, though it won't trouble those used to vintage New Orleans survivals.

Piero Bassini (born 1952)

PIANO, KEYBOARDS

Italian pianist working in the post-bop mainstream of the local music.

****(*) Into The Blue**

Red 123218-2 *Bassini; Flavio Boltro (t); Michele Bozza (ts); Riccardo Fioravanti (b); Giampiero Prina (b).* 11/87.

****(*) Lush Life**

Splasc(h) H 341-2 *Bassini (p solo); with Erminio Cella (ky).* 6/90.

Bassini's earlier records for Red are out of print, but he plays a useful role in the quintet session, which is otherwise under no single leader. All six tunes are based round the blues and, given the plain speaking of the group, the results are inevitably sound but unexceptional, with Boltro and Bozza sounding facile rather than involving. *Lush Life* is an energetic solo album that's let down somewhat by the hard piano-sound which accentuates Bassini's already percussive, almost belligerent manner – not much of his underlying romanticism comes through, though 'Night Moon' is a composition worth saving.

***** Intensity**

Red 123266-2 *Bassini; Luca Garlaschelli (b); Ettore Fioravanti, Massimo Pintori (d).* 2/95.

***** Portrait With In**

Splasc(h) 615 *As above, except omit Pintori.* 2/97.

These trio records are a stronger statement by Bassini, though they have a schematic flavour which sometimes gets in the way of the music making a deeper impact. The Red album has titles like 'Segment', 'Interval', 'Two Chords' and so on, while the Splasc(h) date relies on a similar distancing of emotion while attempting to plumb less obvious depths. The results are impressive in a somewhat detached way. The trio play with earnest concentration, and the music feels worked-through, thought-out, while missing a degree of spontaneity that might otherwise take these discs into the top bracket. The most exceptional moment comes in Bassini's solo 'Looking At The Hills' on the Splasc(h) album, a beautiful and less deliberate meditation.

Django Bates (born 1960)

PIANO, KEYBOARDS, TENOR HORN

After stints with London bands Borderline and Zila, Bates worked with his own Human Chain and was a central player in the big band, Loose Tubes. Became an international property in the '90s, with orchestral commissions, prizes and association with the Tim Berne circle of players.

*****(*) Like Life**

Storyville STCD 4221 *Bates; Palle Bolvig, Jan Kohlin, Henrik Bolberg Pederssen, Benny Rosenfeld, Jens Winther (t, flhn); Vincent Nilsson (tb, bhn); Steen Hansen, Kjeld Ipsen (tb); Klaus Lohrer (btb); Axel Windfeld (btb, tba); Terje Aadne (frhn); Nikolaj Schultz (f, bf); Iain Ballamy, Christina Von Bülow, Tomas Franck, Michael Hove, Flemming Madsen, Uffe Markussen, Jan Zum Vorde (reeds); Nikolaj Bentzon (ky); Anders Chico Lindvall (g); Michael Mondesir, Thomas Ovesen (b); Martin France, Jonas Johansen (d); Ethan Weisgard (perc).* 3/97.

Bates was the second Briton in three years to scoop the Jazzpar Prize. Coming as he did between Geri Allen and 1998 winner Jim Hall only reinforced the honour. As always, the prize provides for a recording with the winner's own group and with the Danish Radio Jazz Orchestra. It's the orchestra that tackles the three key compositions on the disc, a central section that must represent the most concentrated and effective music of Django's career to date.

The longest single item is 'The Strange Voyage Of Donald Crowhurst', a haunting, haunted evocation of the round-the-world yachtsman who pretended to be making potentially winning progress when in fact he was doing nothing more than sailing in circles and radioing in false bearings. It may be that Crowhurst took his own life rather than be exposed. Bates turns the story into a bitter-sweet epic, a feature for his own peck-horn and for Uffe Markussen's tenor. Bracketing it are two shorter pieces, 'Misplaced Swans', which sounds like scaled-up Loose Tubes, and the anarchic 'The Importance Of Boiling Water', another horn feature and a good example of Bates's fascination with the musicality, as he expatiates on the correct procedure for making tea.

The recording also featured a special Jazzpar version of Bates's band, Delightful Precipice, bringing in the estimable Ballamy, who solos beautifully on 'Tightrope' (on alto), 'The Loneliness Of Being Right' and the more skittish 'Armchair March' (both on soprano). Other Britons who made the trip were bassist Mondesir and drummer France. One suspects the DRJO may have found Bates's charts a little wayward; some of the playing is stiff and 'correct', and there is an immediate loosening of tension on the Delightful Precipice tracks. The writing is as extraordinary as ever, though, and it is that, and the Crowhurst piece in particular, which makes this such a special album.

*****(*) Quiet Nights**

Screwgun screwu 70007 *Bates; Iain Ballamy (sax, bass hca, lipo-sax); Michael Mondesir (b); Martin France (d, perc); Josefine Crønholm (v).* 98.

A standards album seemed a good bet at some point in the near future, but it was a racing certainty that a Django Bates solo album wasn't going to be a run-of-the-mill affair. 'Hi Lilli Hi Lo' segues into an abstract 'Solitude', with Ellington's opening chords played on a 'prepared' piano, accompanied by Martin France's wooden percussion and what we take to be Ballamy's lipo-sax. Two originals, 'And The Mermaid Laughed' and 'Is There Anyone Up There?', are idiosyncratic Batesian sound-scapes. The opening 'Speak Low' reveals Crønholm's skills as a standards singer. Later, on Jobim's 'Quiet Nights Of Quiet Night Stars' and 'Solitude', she is required to sing in a deadened monotone. 'Like Someone In Love' begins with electronic squawks, settles into a version Jimmy Van Heusen might just have recognized, before exploding into a punkish thrash and then vanishing in a sad repetition of the hook down a phone line. Django is even further off-mike on 'Over The Rainbow', a faraway, offstage vocal amid the birdsong and Sibelius chords.

Weighing in light at less than 45 minutes, *Quiet Nights* is nevertheless near perfectly pitched: a clever, wry album full of unexpected twists and turns and some full-on beauty as well.

Stefano Battaglia (born 1966)

PIANO

Born in Milan, Battaglia studied the classical piano literature before turning to jazz, moving between free playing and post-bop structure.

***** Auryn**

Splasc(h) H 161-2 *Battaglia; Paolino Dalla Porta (b); Manhu Roche (d).* 5/88.

*****(*) Explore**

Splasc(h) H 304-2 *Battaglia; Tony Oxley (d).* 2/90.

*****(*) Confession**

Splasc(h) H 344-2 *Battaglia; Paolino Dalla Porta (b); Roberto Gatto (d).* 3/91.

Battaglia is a formidable young player from Italy's impressive contemporary movement. His first album for Splasc(h), *Things Ain't What They Used To Be*, has yet to appear on CD, but the programme of original material on *Auryn* is a reasonable place to start: the rubato structure of 'The Real Meaning (Of The Blues)' and the Jarrett-like melodies elsewhere are vehicles for full-blooded and essentially romantic improvisations, though sometimes one feels they aren't really going anywhere much. The two later discs suggest a wider range of interests, starting with the unexpected meeting with Oxley. Most of the duo pieces on *Explore* are quite brief and contained, and structurally there's little sense of anything but careful preparation; yet spontaneity runs all through the music, whether in full-tilt, crashing interplay with the drummer or in small-voiced dialogue which shows great sensitivity. *Confession* is a much more closely developed trio music than that of his earlier releases, all three men taking virtually equal roles in a triologue that they sustain with few problems over the course of several very long tracks. These are distinctive and worth seeking out.

***** Bill Evans Compositions Vol. One**

Splasc(h) H 400-2 *Battaglia; Paolino Dalla Porta (b); Aldo Romano (d).* 12/92.

***** Bill Evans Compositions Vol. Two**

Splasc(h) 410-2 *As above.* 12/92.

The relatively small number of direct homages to Evans – as compared with the countless ones to Monk or Ellington – hints at the difficulty of getting inside the skin of his music, as opposed to decorating its surface. Battaglia looks to celebrate rather than scrutinize, and he sounds fully at ease on the likes of 'Five', 'Loose Bloose' and 'Nardis'. But when it comes to 'Time Remembered' or 'My Bells', the luminosity of the originals is what one thinks of, as charmingly as Battaglia plays.

***** Life Of A Petal**

Splasc(h) 422 *Battaglia (p solo).* 5/93.

*****(*) Baptism**

Splasc(h) 417 *Battaglia (p solo).* 12/93.

*****(*) Sulphur**

Splasc(h) 430 *Battaglia; Paolino Dalla Porta (b); Tony Oxley (d).* 10/93.

*****(*) Unknown Flames**

Splasc(h) 471/2 2CD *As above, except Roberto Gatto (d) replaces Oxley.* 7/95.

The solo records are interesting if rarefied. Battaglia doesn't amble unduly – a dozen pieces are dispatched inside an hour on the first set – but these miniatures often seem to be seeking an individual point that never arrives. There are some clever touches in 'Etude', 'Recitative' and 'Blowed' which would stand expansion within a trio format; but the title-piece is a particularly lyrical solo that stands on its own. *Baptism* pursues a similar path, and some of it offers a discrete viewpoint of the piano tradition, in pieces such as 'Tristano'. But the pyrotechnic cycles of 'Observe' and the stark spaces of 'Requiem Pour Renée Daumal' are the work of a very singular imagination altogether.

Sulphur is a rematch with Tony Oxley, this time with Dalla Porta also on hand. Battaglia meets Oxley on his own terms, and damping the strings or otherwise subverting his natural romanticism doesn't seem to trouble him, even if the blossoming 'Science Of The Heart' sounds more his sort of thing. Just as important here, though, is Dalla Porta, whose five compositions – particularly the dedications to Duchamp, Picasso and Klee – are the most striking and adventurous music on the record, with Oxley conspiring with characteristic unorthodoxy.

Unknown Flames offers an extravagant two hours of music from a Siena concert. Gatto is a much more conventional drummer and isn't favoured with ideal sound, but the trio work with an enthusiasm that overcomes most doubts. A second version of 'Lifebeat' and the Evans recollections of 'Orbit' and 'I've Grown Accustomed To Her Face' align the two faces of Battaglia's music, and the pianist continues to work on a blend of Bley, Jarrett and Evans which he can make into something entirely his own. Not there yet, but it's an absorbing journey.

***** Gesti**

Splasc(h) 901 *Battaglia; Michael Gassmann (t); Mirco Mariottini (cl); Stefano Fanceschini, Dmitri Grechi Espinoza, Filiberto Palermini, Mirko Guerrini, Daniele Malvisi (reeds); Milko Ambrogini, Nino Pellegrini, Gianluca Renzi (b); Paolo Corsi, Riccardo Ienna, Alessio Riccio (d).* 6/97.

Two long pieces featuring players taught by Battaglia in his classes. These workshop pieces suggest the pianist's deftness in creating frameworks free enough for some uproar but ready to fall back into recognizable form. More experienced musicians might have given the music a bigger impact, but the enthusiasm of these musicians has merit in itself. A plausible interlude in his discography.

*****(*) When We Were**

Splasc(h) 690 *Battaglia; Michael Gassman (t); Pierre Favre (d).* 12/97.

*****(*) Omen**

Splasc(h) 691 *As above, except omit Gassman.* 12/97.

Two sessions recorded in Zurich for Swiss Radio. Battaglia responds to Favre's mixture of kit-based rhythms and freely spaced percussive commentary in diverse ways: sometimes darkly lyrical, or playful, or turning to prepared-piano sound in the opening 'Landing'. Gassman joins in for *When We Were*, and while a piece such as 'Code And Disorder' is jittery and living on its nerves, there is some cool, even limpid playing which serves up some beautiful stuff in the likes of 'Like Tears In The Rain'.

Conrad Bauer (born 1943)

TROMBONE, ELECTRONICS

Born in Halle, one of two trombonist brothers, Connie Bauer was a key player in the small group of East German improvisers at work from the end of the '60s. Although only infrequently sighted on record, he is one of those who helped form the improvising vocabulary for free-jazz trombonists.

***** Toronto Tone**

Victo CD017 *Bauer (tb, elec solo).* 10/91.

***** Three Wheels – Four Directions**

Victo CD023 *Bauer; Peter Kowald (b); Gunter Sommer (d etc.).* 10/92.

*****(*) Bauer Bauer**

Intakt CD 040 *Bauer; Johannes Bauer (tb).*

****** Plie**

Intakt CD 037 *Bauer; Ernst-Ludwig Petrowsky (as, cl, f); Ulrich Gumpert (p); Gunter Sommer (d).* 2/94.

Working out of the former East Germany for many years, Bauer is perhaps the least known of the great European trombone impressionists. Heard in successive years at Canada's Victoriaville Festival, he makes a good if less than outstanding account on these souvenirs of the occasions. The solo engagement finds him colouring his improvisations with a variety of electronics: chorus effects, loops, echo. Sometimes one feels that the FX are used for impressionistic rather than musical effect, although – as with similar projects by Bill Frisell or Eberhard Weber – the results can be entertaining enough to overcome doubts. As a plain soloist, Bauer can't match Paul Rutherford or Gunter Christmann for sheer inventiveness, but his folksy blares and long, sung tones have their own impact.

With Kowald and Sommer he uses the unadorned slide trombone. There are four group improvs and a solo apiece: Sommer's soliloquy is merely silly, and his lumpy kind of momentum can hold the group back, but there is some excellent stuff on 'Trio Goes East' and 'Trio Goes North'. Kowald, as usual, is beyond reproach, and his *arco* solo is intense enough to blister paint.

Bauer Bauer is a duo concert with his brother Johannes, recorded in the room inside Leipzig's Monument to the Battle of Nations, where there's a natural 20-second echo. The results are almost predictably beautiful, given the sonorities involved, and it must have been a temptation to remain with the long-held notes and counterpoint of 'Dialog 1' and 'Dialog 4' for the whole set; but there is some taut, snickering interplay elsewhere, and the senior Bauer uses some electronics to spare and judicious effect on his solo (there are six duets and a solo apiece).

Plie should properly be credited to the Zentralquartett, since this band of old cronies go under that name when working together. In the aftermath of free jazz (not to mention the DDR), the four players work through a bad-tempered kind of free bop that seems to blossom reluctantly into lyricism at the most unexpected moments. Fragments of blues piano, hard bop, hot solos and harsh ensemble-work permeate what turns out to be an absolutely engrossing record. Cantankerous and highly entertaining sleeve-notes by Christian Broecking fit the record perfectly.

*****(*) Reflections**
FMP CD 74 *Bauer; Johannes Bauer (tb); Uwe Kropinski, Joe Sachse (g).* 10/86.

*****(*) Aventure Québécoise**
Victo 065 *As above.* 5/98.

Strictly speaking, these are by the group Doppelmoppel. Although on the shelf for ten years before release, *Reflections* sounds fresh, and the interplay – at once skeletal and dense, with the spidery lines of the guitarists scuttling around the blurting, blaring horns – hasn't lost its wit and brightness. The tone sometimes comes down to the monochromatic, but these are imaginative players and they have a lot to say. Reconvening after a dozen years, the quartet seem invigorated by the occasion (a Victoriaville Festival set) and play with a matching intensity and cleverness.

****** Between Heaven And Earth**
Intakt CD 079 *Bauer; Peter Kowald (b); Gunter Sommer (d).* 12/01.

Recorded just a few months before Peter Kowald's premature death, this captures the bassist with two of his most sympathetic collaborators, perhaps united by years spent on the 'wrong' side of the Iron Curtain. The 11 improvisations are so titled and organized as to suggest a progress through life from birth to rebirth. Bauer is the dominant voice, but both Kowald and Sommer are so attuned to this idiom that one hears a group rather than individuals. Right in the middle of the set, 'Travelling' and 'Loving' represent its emotional core, intense and quietly fiery improvisations that would be hard to improve upon. Another first-rate release from Intakt and a further poignant footnote to the magnificent career of Europe's most influential free-jazz bassist.

Johannes Bauer (born 1954)

TROMBONE

Perhaps the slightly lesser-known of the Bauer brothers, Johannes is nevertheless a powerful trombone voice in European free playing.

*****(*) Organo Pleno**
FMP CD 56 *Bauer; Fred Van Hove (p, acc); Annick Nozati (v).* 7/92.

Johannes is a blunter and less discursive player than brother Connie, these days wholly dedicated to free improvised music. The present trio is relatively long-standing by the usual measure of such things, and *Organo Pleno* bespeaks considerable understanding between the members. Van Hove is an enormously underrated player whose continued involvement in other areas of musical enterprise may be reflected in his patiently normative role, roping in the group's wilder excesses. As is the way of such things, the trio swing between spiky, open-form blasts that ruthlessly avoid anything resembling a groove and gentler, almost song-like patterns, such as 'Pars IV', on which piano gives way to organ, starbursts and broken-glass runs to soft, wheezy washes. In general the mood is fairly laid-back. There are plenty of sub-two-minute miniatures, and one mammoth work-out which approaches half an hour in length. Nozati tires and runs low on ideas here, and it is left to Bauer's post-Mangelsdorff phrase-making to give the thing a sense of direction. He is a wonderfully clean articulator with a very distinctive attack and a real dramatic presence.

Agneta Baumann

VOCAL

Swedish vocalist with much experience in theatre and cabaret music, here moving into a mainstream jazz idiom.

***** A Time For Love**
Touché TMCCD 006 *Baumann; Anders Lindskog (ts); Staffan Hallgren (f); Carl Fredrik Orrje (p); Per-Ola Gadd (b); Bengt Stark (d).* 8/96.

*****(*) Comes Love**
Touché TMCCD 011 *Baumann; Bosse Broberg (t); Gösta Rundqvist (p); Hans Backenroth (b); Johan Löfcrantz (d).* 6/99.

Baumann's career in Sweden has been a mix of pop, jazz and cabaret singing, but she is at her slow-burning best on *A Time For Love*, a set of 15 standards, most of them delivered at a stately pace. She has a steady and soft-spoken way with a lyric that induces a sort of motionless drama into a song such as 'More Than You Know' (done with the verse complete) and, although this makes the album a bit tiring over 70 minutes, it's impressive taken a few tracks at a time. Playing honours mainly go to the rhythm section: Hallgren is pretty, and Lindskog comes on as a comatose Lester Young.

Comes Love repeats the trick, but just that bit better: familiar but very suitable tunes, the rhythm section scintillates, and Broberg keeps popping up to take brief, surprising solos, a bright, sharp light in an otherwise nocturnal sound. Baumann does what she did last time, but she's getting better, too.

Jim Beard (born 1960)

KEYBOARDS, PERCUSSION

Keyboard player and composer-arranger, Beard has also done extensive work as a producer on various jazz- and fusion-related projects.

***** Lost At The Carnival**

Lipstick LIP 89027 *Beard; Bill Evans (ts, ss); Stan Harrison (cl, bcl, f, af); Jon Herington (g, hca, perc); Ron Jenkins, Steve Rodby (b); Scooter Warner, Mike Mecham, Billy Ward (d).* 94.

Beard has worked extensively with the Breckers, Sco and John McLaughlin, and a prejudiced eye wonders why he didn't try to get one or more of them in on his first solo project. The results are actually more interesting than they promise to be. The album has a rough concept, held together by fairground organ; the device allows Beard to wander, slightly distractedly, through the 'carnivalized' world of contemporary jazz, rock and funk, touching on styles and approaches, committing to none, discarding none. It's quite exhilarating in a headachey sort of way; the voicings on 'Chunks And Chairknobs' are interesting enough to hear again, and 'Poke' has an insistent harmonic oddity that quickly overcomes its initial cheesy impression.

***** Truly ...**

ESC 03652-2 *As above, except add Aaron Heick (f, picc, cl, cor, ob), Todd Reynolds (vn), Erik Friedlander (clo), John Patitucci (b), Billy Ward (d), Mark Ledford (v, picc-t), David Blamires (v), Marc Quinones (perc); omit Jenkins, Rodby, Warner, Mecham.* 97.

Beard has, in the interim, become a rather ubiquitous figure in the world of electric, somewhat jazzed instrumental music. He's probably able to make a decent living at pop if he wants it, but his heart seems to be in these engagingly oddball projects which fashion a sophisticate's take on current trends in jazz-funk and its various offspring. Hiring Ledford and Blamires to sing their doo-doo-wop vocals on some tracks and directing a good if faceless team of studio players throughout, Beard (who dresses the part on the sleeve) seems like some court-composer to us gentrified patrons. Who else is going to buy this understated virtuosity, based around handsomely orchestrated keyboards, soufflé-light funk rhythms and a pasticheur's wittiest remarks on his chosen milieu? A lot of it passes uneventfully enough, but try the beautifully handled 'Gone Was, Gone Will Be'. If his next is that good all through, Beard will have more than won his spurs.

***** Ad.Vo.Cate**

ESC 03663-2 *Beard; Bob Malach (ts, f, cl, bcl, basset); Pete Davenport (f, v); Jon Herington (g, bj); Matthew Garrison, Tim Lefebvre (b); Gene Lake, Zach Danziger (d); Arto Tuncboyaciyan (perc, v).* 2–6/99.

No, not quite as good as all that, and partly because the silliness sometimes gets the better of the music-making. Beard hams it up in the sleeve photos and that trait gets the better of him in too many of these tracks. Several pieces sound like the Weather Report of the early '80s, with the edges buffed to a pop shine. He has the cheek to call one tune 'Jazz'. But when he leans back, thins out the textures and lets the melody speak – as on 'Hope', 'Relief', 'Jambolay' – he's good company.

Sidney Bechet (1897–1959)

SOPRANO SAXOPHONE, CLARINET; ALSO TENOR AND BASS SAXOPHONES, PIANO, BASS, DRUM

Bechet is the first great soloist in jazz. Even before Louis Armstrong came along, he was playing vertical improvisations on the chords of a tune, rather than simple melodic breaks. Like Pops, Bechet grew up in New Orleans, transported his style north and then became the American star in Europe. A pioneer of the soprano saxophone, Sidney managed to combine its intense, sometimes treacherous tonality with the warm, woody sound of the clarinet.

***** Sidney Bechet, 1923–1936**

Classics 583 *Bechet; Clarence Brereton, Wendell Culley, Demas Dean, Tommy Ladnier (t); Billy Burns, Chester Burrill, Teddy Nixon (tb); Chauncey Haughton (cl, as); Ralph Duquesne, Rudy Jackson (cl, as, ss); Ramon Usera (cl, ts); Jerome Pasquall, Gil White (ts); Harry Brooks, Henry Duncan, Lloyd Pinckney, Clarence Williams (p); Oscar Madera (vn); Buddy Christian, Frank Ethridge (bj); Jimmy Miller (g); Wilson Myers (b, v); Edward Coles (bb); Jimmy Jones (b); Jack Carter, Wilbert Kirk, Morris Morland (d); Billy Banks, Lena Horne, Billy Maxey, Noble Sissle (v).* 10/23–3/36.

***** Young Sidney Bechet**

Timeless CBC 1-028 *Similar to above.* 23–25.

*****(*) Sidney Bechet, 1937–1938**

Classics 593 *Bechet; Clarence Brereton, Wendell Culley, Demas Dean, Charlie Shavers (t); Chester Burrill (tb); Chauncey Haughton (cl, as); Jerome Pasquall, Gil White (ts); Ernie Caceres (bs); Oscar Madera (vn); Dave Bowman, Harry Brooks, Erskine Butterfield, Sam Price (p); Teddy Bunn, Jimmy Miller, Leonard Ware (g); Richard Fulbright, Jimmy Jones, Henry Turner (b); Wilbert Kirk, Zutty Singleton (d); O'Neil Spencer (d, v); Billy Banks, The Two Fishmongers, Trixie Smith (v).* 4/37–11/38.

Bechet himself contributed to the heav'n-taught image surrounding his early days. His autobiography, *Treat It Gentle*, is a masterpiece of contrived ingenuousness – the opposite, one might say, of Charles Mingus's ruthlessly disingenuous rants in *Beneath the Underdog*. The fact is that Bechet was an exceptionally gifted and formally aware musician whose compositional skills greatly outshine those of Louis Armstrong, his rival for canonization as the first great jazz improviser. Armstrong's enormous popularity – abetted by his sky-writing top Cs and vocal performance – tended to eclipse Bechet everywhere except in France. Yet the musical evidence is that Bechet was an artist of equal and parallel standing. His melodic sense and ability to structure a solo round the harmonic sequence of the original theme (or with no theme whatsoever) have been of immense significance in the development of modern jazz. Bechet made a pioneering switch to the soprano saxophone (a stronger-voiced and more projective instrument than the clarinet) in the same year as Ansermet's essay, having found a second-hand horn in a London shop. Within a few years, his biting tone and dramatic tremolo were among the most distinctive sounds in jazz.

Bechet made a relatively slow start to his recording career. His first cuts as 'leader' are as accompanist on two tracks made in New York in October and credited to Rosetta Crawford & the King Bechet Trio. The early sessions with Clarence Williams and a variety of modestly talented singers include carefully annotated breaks and solos from Bechet, largely on soprano saxophone; but these sessions are of specialist interest in the main. His clarinet style (on tracks with Eva Taylor) is still strongly coloured by that of Alphonse Picou and Lorenzo Tio, who gave the precocious Bechet lessons, and is markedly less individual than his saxophone playing. The Timeless compilation is very attractive, and John R. T. Davies's remastering is pitch perfect, an appropriately flattering context for these marvellous early performances.

The Classics compilation is less detailed, but it includes material with Noble Sissle's orchestra not included on either of the other available options; in fact, only the two Rosetta Crawford tracks are in common. The sound is rather abrasive and these early sessions are essential only for a brief, brilliant soprano solo on 'Loveless Love'. According to John Chilton, Bechet is also responsible, on this and two other tracks (he solos only on the initially rejected 'In A Café On The Road To Calais'), for the bass saxophone parts, which are not credited in the Classics notes. The session of 15 September 1932 is one of Bechet's best yet, with superb solos on 'I Want You Tonight' and 'Maple Leaf Rag'. The later disc is generally more professional and every bit as compelling musically. Bechet reached a new high with two quintet tracks credited to Noble Sissle's Swingsters, an offshoot of the main band. His solos on 'Okey-Doke' and 'Characteristic Blues' are classic performances, full of extravagantly bent notes, trills and time-changes. Using both clarinet and soprano saxophone, Bechet creates an atmosphere of considerable tension that is discharged only during a phenomenal solo on 'Characteristic Blues'. Later, in 1938, there was controversy over the exact authorship of 'Hold Me Tight', which Bechet claimed was based on his earlier 'I Want Some Seafood, Mama', but which was declared obscene and withdrawn from radio stations. The real controversy, however, was directed towards what seemed to be a new way of playing jazz, and in that context the session of April 1937 is absolutely critical, not just to Bechet's development but to that of jazz itself.

***(*) Sidney Bechet, 1938–1940

Classics 608 *Bechet; Tommy Ladnier, Frankie Newton, Kenneth Roane (t); J. C. Higginbotham (tb); Mezz Mezzrow (cl, ts); Meade Lux Lewis, Willie 'The Lion' Smith, Sonny White (p); Teddy Bunn, Charlie Howard (g); Elmer James, Olin Aderhold, Wilson Myers, John Williams (b); Big Sid Catlett, Kenny Clarke, Manzie Johnson, Leo Warney (d).* 11/38–40.

*** Sidney Bechet, 1940

Classics 619 *Bechet; Sidney De Paris (t); Muggsy Spanier (c); Sandy Williams (tb); Cliff Jackson (p); Bernard Addison, Teddy Bunn, Carmen Mastren (g); Josh White (g, v); Wellman Braud, George 'Pops' Foster, Wilson Myers (b); Big Sid Catlett (d).* 3–6/40.

***(*) Sidney Bechet, 1940–1941

Classics 638 *Bechet; Gus Aiken, Henry 'Red' Allen, Henry Goodwin, Henry Levine, Charlie Shavers (t); Rex Stewart (c); Jack Epstein, Vic Dickenson, J. C. Higginbotham, Sandy Williams (tb); Alfie Evans (cl); Rudolph Adler, Lem Johnson (ts); Don Donaldson, Earl Hines, Cliff Jackson, Mario Janarro, Willie 'The Lion' Smith, James Toliver (p); Everett Barksdale, Tony Colucci (g); Wellman Braud, John Lindsay, Wilson Myers, Harry Patent, Ernest Williamson (b); Baby Dodds, J. C. Heard, Arthur Herbert, Manzie Johnson, Nat Levine (d); Herb Jeffries (v).* 9/40–10/41.

In April 1941 Bechet fulfilled the logic of his increasingly self-reliant musical conception (Hines suggested that his quietly 'evil' mood on the day of the 1940 sessions was characteristic of New Orleans players at the time when dealing with Northerners) by recording two unprecedented 'one-man-band' tracks, overdubbing up to six instruments. 'Sheik Of Araby' is for the full 'band' of soprano and tenor saxophones, clarinet, piano, bass and drums; so time-consuming was the process that a second item, 'Blues For Bechet', had to be completed without bass or drums, leaving a fascinating fragment for RCA to release.

In September of the same year, Bechet made another classic trio recording, this time with Willie 'The Lion' Smith and the relative unknown, Everett Barksdale, on electric guitar. Though the two sidemen provide no more than incidental distractions, the trio sessions were more compelling than the full band assembled on that day (Charlie Shavers plays monster lines on 'I'm Coming Virginia', as on the October 'Mood Indigo', but is otherwise ill-suited); 'Strange Fruit' is one of Bechet's most calmly magisterial performances, and the two takes of 'You're The Limit' seem too good to have been dumped in the 'unreleased' bin, though perhaps the absence on either of a commanding solo from Bechet (who may not have liked Smith's uncomplicated tune) put the label off. But what did they know? A month later, in the same session that realized 'Mood Indigo', Bechet cut the utterly awful 'Laughin' In Rhythm', a New Orleans version of 'The Laughing Policeman' that, despite a taut soprano solo, hardly merits revival. Dickenson, whose humour was usually reliable, also plays beautifully on 'Blue In The Air', one of the finest of Bechet's recorded solos and one that merits the closest attention.

A lot of this material is available elsewhere. However, it's always good to have the simply and exactly documented Classics discs, and there are some useful inclusions and corrections, like the correct attribution of 'Ti Ralph' and 'Meringue D'Amour' from the Willie 'The Lion' Smith date of November 1939; these have been inverted on most reissues in recent times. The 'Original Haitian Music' with Smith is an oddity from a decidedly odd band, and one has a strong sense that Bechet was finding it harder over this period following his brief sabbatical in 1938 to set up completely sympathetic sessions. More and more often one finds him in bands where piano, not guitar, dominates the rhythm section, and he is paired with other saxophone players. It was always characteristic of Bechet's VSOP sound that it didn't marry well with sharper vintages, however potent they were in isolation. One would still want to recommend these discs, but with the proviso that they have their downs as well as ups.

Blues In Thirds is dominated by Sidney's somewhat hostile relationship with piano players. Earl Hines has spoken of the saxophonist's 'evil' mood on the day of their September 1940 encounter, when he refused to nominate which Hines tune was next on the programme. It turned out to be 'Blues In Thirds', and the trio with the pianist and Baby Dodds is a classic. So confused is the Bechet discography that it is becoming virtually impossible to offer reasoned preferences. Technically, these are sub-standard transfers, flat and unresonant.

*** Sidney Bechet, 1941–1944

Classics 860 *Bechet; Sidney De Paris, Charlie Shavers (t); Henry Goodwin (t, v); Vic Dickenson, Wilbur De Paris (tb); Gene Cedric (ts, cl); Don Donaldson, Art Hodes, Cliff Jackson,*

Willie 'The Lion' Smith (p); Everett Barksdale (g); Wellman Braud, George 'Pops' Foster, Wilson Myers, Ernest Williamson (b); Big Sid Catlett, Eddie Dougherty, Wilbert Kirk, Manzie Johnson (d). 10/41–44.

This picks up where Classics 638 left off. Better things were to follow later in October, but two other tracks from that session, 'Blues In The Air' and 'The Mooche', test the quality of this fine band. Duke was obviously on his mind at this time (unless it was Vic Dickenson who was pressing Ellington's suit), because he also includes 'Mood Indigo' on the 24 October session, and plays it quite beautifully. Willie The Lion is on top form and lets rip on 'Oh! Lady Be Good' and '12th Street Rag'. It was to be some time before Bechet recorded again; there were three V-Discs in December 1943, reworkings of jazz and blues classics, and then nothing for a further year, until the second of the saxophonist's contacts with Blue Note. This was the session that yielded 'Blue Horizon', a solo of structural perfection and exquisite grace, not very well transferred here but very welcome for all that. 'St Louis Blues' and 'Muskrat Ramble' aren't quite up to that quality, but the combination of Bechet, Sidney De Paris, Dickenson, Art Hodes, Pops Foster and Manzie Johnson was a potent one, and these sides are widely and rightly admired. The very next day, Bechet made a session as sideman with pianist Cliff Jackson's Village Cats, an artist whose work is shortly to be covered by Classics. Released on Black & White, these are agreeable enough sides, and Bechet is featured often enough to please his fans, but even 'Jeepers Creepers' and 'Quiet Please' don't do much more than fill out an otherwise thin disc.

*** Up A Lazy River

Good Time Jazz 12064 *Bechet; Muggsy Spanier (c); Henry Goodwin, Albert Snaer (t); Jimmy Archey, George Brunies, Wilbur De Paris, George Wettling (tb); Buster Bailey, Albert Nicholas, Bob Wilber (cl); James P. Johnson, Dick Wellstood (p); Danny Barker, Carmen Mastren (g); Wellman Braud, George 'Pops' Foster, Walter Page (b); Tommy Benford (d).* 40–44.

*** Weary Blues

Jazz Hour 73553 *Bechet; Louis Armstrong, Clarence Brereton, Tommy Ladnier, Sidney De Paris (t); Claude Jones (tb); Albert Nicholas (cl); Mezz Mezzrow (cl, ts); Happy Caldwell, Gil White (ts); Ernie Caceres (bs); Dave Bowman, Harry Brooks, Cliff Jackson, Meade Lux Lewis, Jelly Roll Morton, Luis Russell (p); Bernard Addison, Teddy Bunn, Charlie Howard, Lawrence Lucie, Jimmy Miller, Leonard Ware (g); Wellman Braud, George 'Pops' Foster, Elmer James, Henry Turner (b); Big Sid Catlett, Kenny Clarke, Manzie Johnson, Zutty Singleton (d).*

Two attractive enough compilations of mostly familiar material, but with nothing to recommend them to anyone who wants more than a random sampling of Bechet material. There are enough chronological discs around which – even allowing for the technical shortcomings of the Classics format – tell the story in a reasonably logical fashion for the proliferation of career compilations to become simply confusing. Experienced Bechet listeners will be able to do their own chronologies based on personnel; more casual purchasers may not be concerned.

Weary Blues is very inconsistent in sound, with no attempt (laudably or laughably, depending on your point of view) to smooth out differences in source masters. On the other disc, the transfers are clean and unexceptionable and the only quibble might be a slightly artificial bass roll-off which isn't obvious elsewhere. The cover shows Sidney with a fishing rod rather than a saxophone.

*** Runnin' Wild

Blue Note 21259 *Bechet; Wild Bill Davison (c); Jimmy Archey, Bob Diehl (tb); Art Hodes, Joe Sullivan (p); George 'Pops' Foster, Walter Page (b); Slick Jones, Freddie Moore (d).* 49–50.

Bechet was Blue Note's token traditionalist in the '40s, a figure substantial enough to stand alongside the fierce hard-boppers. The partnership with Davison works well throughout the set, with Bill's punchy and ringing tone blending superbly with Bechet on 'Basin Street Blues' and 'Runnin' Wild' itself. There are alternative takes of it and of 'Ain't Gonna Give Nobody None Of My Jelly Roll', which is raunchy enough to merit a reprise.

***(*) Jazz Classics: Volume 1

Blue Note 789384 *Bechet; Bunk Johnson, Max Kaminsky, Frankie Newton, Sidney De Paris (t); Jimmy Archey, Vic Dickenson, J. C. Higginbotham, George Lugg, Sandy Williams (tb); Albert Nicholas (cl); Art Hodes, Cliff Jackson, Meade Lux Lewis (p); Teddy Bunn (g); George 'Pops' Foster, John Williams (b); Big Sid Catlett, Manzie Johnson (d); Fred Moore (d, v).* 6/39–11/51.

*** Jazz Classics: Volume 2

Blue Note 789385 *As above.* 6/39–11/51.

Bechet and Blue Note make an irresistible combination, but not an immediately obvious one. Though the label had its roots in earlier R&B and jazz, having recorded both Albert Ammons and Meade Lux Lewis, its stock-in-trade was to be hard bop and the more accommodating aspects of the avant-garde. Bechet had approached Alfred Lion, wanting to record a long version of 'Summertime' (*Volume 1*, also available on Classics, above), something he had not been able to do for another label. The session of June 1939, the earliest of the dates represented on these compilations, isn't vintage Bechet by any stretch of the imagination, but there are some striking moments. With Lewis all over the place, Bunn lays down a wonderfully simple accompaniment and, with no other horn to hand, Bechet plays a vivid solo that was to boost the original 78 into hit sales. The 1939 session came shortly after the death of Tommy Ladnier, and the full band recorded a less than morose 'Blues For Tommy' (*Volume 2*) on which only Bechet sounds as if he might honestly miss his old partner.

The association with Blue Note continued intermittently over the next few years. In March 1940, with the excellent Bunn again on hand, Bechet recorded 'Dear Old Southland' (*Volume 1*). The 1944 cuts with Sidney de Paris, Vic Dickenson and Art Hodes are less than wholly compelling; but the saxophonist's encounter with the enigmatic Bunk Johnson in March 1945 is a different matter. Bechet sounds cautiously respectful; Bunk sounds like a man whose mind is elsewhere. Nevertheless 'Milenberg Blues' and 'Days Beyond Recall' have a historic significance that goes well beyond their intrinsic value as performances.

The final Blue Note session was recorded a dozen years after the first, and it's a mellowing Bechet who plays the appropriately titled 'Changes Made' with de Paris again, and trombonist Jimmy Archey. Looked at objectively, these sides have taken on a certain sheen purely because of the label that recorded them.

Technically, they're first class; historically, they're full of interest; but musically, they're second-order Bechet.

★★★★ King Jazz: Volume 1

GHB BCD 501/502 2CD *Bechet; Hot Lips Page (t); Mezz Mezzrow (cl); Sammy Price, Fritz Weston (p); Danny Barker (g); George 'Pops' Foster (b); Big Sid Catlett, Kaiser Marshall (d); Douglas Daniels, Pleasant Joseph (v).* 3–8/45.

★★★(★) King Jazz: Volume 2

GHB BCD 503/504/505 3CD *As above, except omit Page, Joseph, Daniels, Barker; add Sox Wilson (p), Coot Grant (v).* 9/46, 12/47.

The Bechet centenary came and went in 1997 with little more than a mild flurry of interest. Perhaps because there is no 'problematic' about Bechet, no need to rescue him from obscurity or debunk his undentable popularity, there was no real leverage for a reassessment. The one big event of the year, record-wise, was the appearance of the legendary King Jazz catalogue on CD. By rights, the label was the brainchild of Mezz Mezzrow, an extraordinary booster and self-promoter who managed to raise enough cash from a man who had made his pile in the war selling radar equipment to get the label under way. But Mezzrow was no better as a businessman than he was as a clarinettist, and he quickly got distracted into writing his (fictionalized) autobiography, *Really the Blues*, with the help of journalist Bernard Wolfe. However, the label's policy of recording much more than could be issued pays dividends now. The first sessions on the disc are of pianist Sammy Price with and without vocalist Pleasant Joseph. There follow, though, sessions from July and August with the Bechet–Mezzrow group. Some of these tracks – 'Revolutionary Blues', 'Perdido Street Stomp', 'The Sheik Of Araby' and 'Minor Swoon' – are classics of post-war Dixieland and, though Mezzrow's technical insufficiencies are in no way glossed over in the transfer, the brightness and unselfconscious ease of these performances warm the heart. For once Pops Foster and Danny Barker can be heard clearly, and the balance of the sound is as good as it is likely to get. Sammy Price plays on all the *Volume 1* sides except those from the August sessions. He's a decent player, slightly florid and overcooked as a soloist, but he comes into his own as a group accompanist, bettered only by Art Hodes. Fritz Weston comes in for the later dates and isn't remotely as idiomatic or as good.

Volume 2 doesn't reach the same heights but it does contain a generous amount of music and the chance to hear the basic band working at some length. 'Chicago Function' exists in alternative takes, as do several other tracks, and it's clear from these that, while Mezzrow has to plough pretty much the same furrow each time, Sidney throws off ideas like a meteor shower. The King Jazz story was a short one and, in the final analysis, no different from a thousand other small labels optimistically begun and naïvely mismanaged. Along the way, though, it threw up some wonderful music.

★★★ Bunk & Bechet In Boston

Jazz Crusade 3040 *Bechet; Bunk Johnson (t); Hank Duncan, Ray Parker (p); George 'Pops' Foster (b); Freddie Moore, George Thompson (d).* 4/45.

Like Louis Armstrong, Bunk Johnson did not like to share leadership with anyone. In 1945 he was something of a living legend, but he was also profoundly erratic and subject to drinking jags. On these radio sessions, Sidney backs him manfully and leaps in whenever the trumpeter loses the plot. Even allowing for such lapses and the rather shaky source material, the sessions are fascinating for the variation in personal styles. Johnson sounds like a man out on his back porch, while Bechet climbs all over the melody and, when things are not going disastrously wrong, merely proceeding at a pedestrian pace, he simply ignores what Bunk is doing and skyrockets off on his own. This material is also available on the Classics compilation below, but these transfers are very good indeed.

★★★ Sidney Bechet, 1945–1946

Classics 954 *Bechet; Bunk Johnson, Max Kaminsky, Frankie Newton (t); George Brunies, George Lugg, Sandy Williams (tb); Albert Nicholas (cl); Art Hodes, Cliff Jackson, Joe Sullivan (p); George 'Pops' Foster, Jack Lesberg (b); Danny Alvin, Manzie Johnson, George Wettling (d); Freddie Moore (d, v).* 45–46.

As inclusive and as muddy as ever, this further Classics volume takes the Bechet story on another step of the way, concentrating on sessions under his own name at the end of the war. The transfers seem uglier than ever here, but having this material, including such classic performances as the 1945 'Salty Dog' and 'Weary Blues', on just one CD is most welcome.

★★★ Ken Burns Jazz: Sidney Bechet

Columbia Legacy 61441 *Bechet; Clarence Brereton, Arthur Briggs, Demas Dean, Sidney De Paris, Tommy Ladnier (t); Louis Armstrong, Muggsy Spanier, Thomas Morris (c); Chester Burrill, Billy Burns, Vic Dickenson, J. C. Higginbotham, Charles Irvis, John Mayfield, Teddy Nixon, Sandy Williams (tb); Ralph Duquesne, Rudy Jackson (ss, as, cl); Chauncey Haughton, Harvey Boone (as, cl); Jim Tolliver, Gil White (ts); Ernie Caceres (bs); Dave Bowman, Harry Brooks, Erskine Butterfield, Henry Duncan, Art Hodes, Cliff Jackson, Lloyd Pinckney, Clarence Williams (p); Bernard Addison, Teddy Bunn, Howard Hill, Carmen Mastren, Jimmy Miller, Leonard Ware (g); Buddy Christian (bj); Wellman Braud, George 'Pops' Foster, Jimmy Jones, Henry Turner, John Williams (b); Wilson Myers (b, v); Jack Carter, Big Sid Catlett, J. C. Heard, Arthur Herbert, Manzie Johnson, Wilbert Kirk, Morris Morland, Zutty Singleton, O'Neill Spencer (d); Noble Sissle, Eva Taylor (v).* 23–47.

Burns's approaching-legendary television series did little to shake a consensus about the history of America's most significant vernacular musics, but it did bring many new listeners to jazz, and to that degree we have to acknowledge his achievement, even while dissenting from some of his premises and many of his conclusions.

The associated series of 22 compilations by major innovators offers a decent grounding to the absolute newcomer. The Bechet volume covers early work with Clarence Williams (a decision which might elevate it over other collections which start later), through to Noble Sissle and to Bechet's own groups. Of course, it overlaps considerably with other anthologies but it does include most of the obvious things and at a decent price.

CORE COLLECTION

★★★★ Shake 'Em Up

Avid 694 2CD *Bechet; Wild Bill Davison, Muggsy Spanier (c); Clarence Brereton, Johnny Glasel, Frankie Newton (t); Vic Dickenson, J. C. Higginbotham, Bob Mielke (tb); Bob Wilber (cl); Ernie Caceres (ts, bs); Gil White (ts, cl, v); Dave Bowman, Harry Brooks, Don Donaldson, Art Hodes, Meade Lux Lewis, Lloyd Phillips, Joe Sullivan, Dick Wellstood (p); Teddy Bunn, Jimmy Miller, Leonard Ware (g); Josh White (g, v); Wellman Braud, George 'Pops' Foster, Jimmy Jones, Wilson Myers, Henry Turner, John Williams (b); Big Sid Catlett, Arthur Herbert, Wilbert Kirk, Freddie Moore, Zutty Singleton, Danny Strong, George Wettling (d); O'Neill Spencer (v).* 38–47.

This is a very good career survey, covering the decade from 1938 to 1947 and squeezing 45 tracks on to two CDs. Most of the material is available elsewhere and the one-man-band 'Sheikh Of Araby' is a near inevitable inclusion on a Bechet compilation; but one big bonus is the complete Big Four date with Muggsy Spanier. The sound transfers are pretty good, though once or twice there is a curious variance from one track to the next, which is momentarily distracting. A very attractive introduction to Bechet's classic period.

***** Sidney Bechet 1949**

Classics 1141 *Bechet; Buster Bailey, Wild Bill Davison (c); Albert Snaer (t); Wilbur De Paris, Benny Vasseur, Munn Ware (tb); Bill Reinhart (cl); Art Hodes, Don Ewell, James P. Johnson (p); Jean-Pierre Sasson (g); Guy Defatto, Walter Page, Sid Thall (b); Wally Gordon, Wilmore Slick Jones, Freddie Moore, George Wettling (d).* 1–5/49.

***** Sidney Bechet 1949, Volume 2**

Classics 1186 *Bechet; Bill Coleman, Pierre Dervaux, Henry Goodwin (t); Claude Phillippe (t, bj); Jimmy Archey, Mowgli Jospin, Benny Vasseur (tb); Claude Luter, Bob Wilber (cl); Christian Azzi, Roland Bianchini, Charlie Lewis, Dick Wellstood (p); Duke Of Iron (vn); Jean-Pierre Sasson (g); George 'Pops' Foster, Pierre Michelot (b); Tommy Benford, Kenny Clarke, André Jourdan (d).* 5–10/49.

At the start of the final decade of his life, Bechet was already coasting. His tone sounds drier and more pungent than of yore, though the broad vibrato is still there and the solos are still constructed with the same arrogant authority. We cannot say that there are any classic sessions documented here, but Bechet fans will find their man playing with absolute reliability. As for much of his career, Bechet was flitting back and forth between France and the United States, hence the international line-ups.

***** Spreadin' Joy: 1940–1950**

Naxos 8120531 *Bechet; Henry 'Red' Allen, Humphrey Lyttelton (t); Muggsy Spanier (co); Keith Christie, J. C. Higginbotham, Bob Mielke (tb); Bob Wilber (cl); Art Hodes, Ralph Sutton, Jim Tolliver, Dick Wellstood (p); Everett Barksdale, Carmen Mastren (g); Wellman Braud, Jack Lesbert, Walter Page, Charles Traeger (b); J. C. Heard, Manzie Johnson, Wilmore Slick Jones, Danny Strong, George Wettling (d).* 40–50.

***** From New York To Paris**

EPM Musique 159962 *Bechet; Bill Coleman, Sidney De Paris, Pierre Dervaux, Henry Goodwin, Hot Lips Page (t); Claude Phillippe (t, bj); Vic Dickenson, Mowgli Jospin, Sandy Williams, Bernard Zacharias (tb); Claude Luter, Mezz Mezzrow, Albert Nicholas (cl); Christian Azzi, Don Donaldson, Earl Hines, Art Hodes, Charlie Lewis, Sammy Price, Sox Wilson (p); Bernard Addison, Danny Barker (g); Roland Bianchini, George 'Pops' Foster, Pierre Michelot, Ernest Williamson (b); Danny Alvin, Big Sid Catlett, Baby Dodds, Manzie Johnson (d).* 40–49.

Kicking off with the overdubbed 'Sheikh Of Araby', the Naxos set is bent on presenting Bechet as a virtually godlike soloist, capable of doing almost anything on his own. It's not a strictly representative collection, with more gaps than continuities, but the sound transfers are, we find, very good indeed and, given Naxos's budget profile, this is a very attractive introduction to Sidney's work during his last really creative period.

The other set covers similar ground, but includes cuts with Hot Lips Page and Mezz Mezzrow that are sure to be of interest. It is also well transferred, though there is a slight deadness of sound here and there which we didn't find attractive.

***** In New York, 1950–1951**

Storyville 6039 *Bechet; Vic Dickenson, Big Chief Russell Moore (tb); Ken Kersey, Red Richards (p); Herb Ward (b); Cliff Leeman, Art Trappier (d).* 50–51.

The live New York material contains some great moments, including a number of tracks, originally on Pumpkin, which modestly feature Russell Moore, a hugely affable player whose contribution to the music of the time is still not wholly valued. Bechet himself is in good form, with a harder than usual tone and some decidedly spikey moments.

Gordon Beck (born 1938)

PIANO, ELECTRIC PIANO, ELECTRONICS

A veteran British modernist, Beck drew attention in the Tubby Hayes group of the '60s, as Ronnie Scott's house-pianist and with Phil Woods, 1969–72. Since then has freelanced, worked as an educator and helmed occasional albums.

****** Experiments With Pops**

Art of Life 1001-2 *Beck; John McLaughlin (g); Jeff Clyne (b); Tony Oxley (d).* 8/67.

****** Gyroscope**

Art of Life 1003 *As above, except omit McLaughlin.* 68.

It may be no comfort to the astonishingly gifted Beck, whose later work was critically praised and then neglected, but now two of his early albums are available on CD. *Experiments* introduces the nascent talent of 'Johnny' McLaughlin, apparently a late inclusion on what otherwise was meant to be a trio date. Given the pop provenance of the material, it was a brilliant wheeze bringing him aboard. John transforms the set, adding a gear and providing the kind of forceful attack he would later demonstrate on *Extrapolation* and with the Mahavishnu Orchestra.

The songs themselves are standard fodder: 'Norwegian Wood' and 'Michelle' from the Fabs, 'These Boots Were Made For Walking', Jimmy Webb's 'Up, Up And Away' and a solo reading from Beck of 'Sunny'. It would be another 20 years before creative jazz players seriously explored the improvisational reaches of chart pop. With Clyne and Oxley also on the strength, this is a major find. All credit to producer Ray Horricks for suggesting the repertoire, and to Art of Life for bringing it out again.

Gyroscope is a very different project, freer and more intense in scope. The title piece, which also provided the name of a later Beck group, is one of his most enduring conceptions, a whirling, beautifully balanced trio performance that gives each player equal weight and significance. 'Suite No. 1' is collectively improvised and sounds very slightly dated now but the long closing medley of 'And Still She is With Me/Oxus' is as good a piece as any to emerge from the British free-jazz scene. Another hugely welcome recovery from the vaults.

***** Once Is Never Enough**
FMR CD 28 *Beck; Stan Sulzmann (ts, f); Chris Laurence (b); Paul Clarvis (d, perc).* 2/96.

At long last, a British label recognizes Beck's brilliance. Unfortunately, the chemistry never quite fires, and this remains a better record in potential than in fact. Sulzmann and Beck divide writing duties, and big Stan's three pieces, including the title-track, are impressive for their deceptive familiarity, almost as if each is drawn from a standard.

The piano at Gateway Studios sounds in excellent shape, and Beck dwells more often than usual on richly sustained chords, allowing phrases to blend together, a change from his usual rather clean-edged delivery. Laurence provides a steady reference point, and the only serious quibble (beyond the rather tentative sound) is Clarvis, who always sounds disengaged from whichever band he's nominally in, pattering away in an undertone.

Mick Beck

TENOR SAXOPHONE, BASSOON, RECORDER

Based in Yorkshire, Beck has been a regular in British improvising circles since the middle '80s.

***** Picture August**
Bruce's Fingers BF 34 *Beck; Stephen Grew (p).* 8/99.

***** The Three B's**
Fencing Flatworm 019 *Beck; Pat Thomas (ky, elec); Paul Hession (d).* 11/00.

While it has plenty of violence, the opening duet of 'Upflucht' on *Picture August* has a quality of composed chamber music: refined in its steady dynamic variation, moving quickly between harmonic composure and rattled, furious duelling, it covers a lot of ground in 12 minutes. It's so good, actually, that the rest of the disc is something of an anti-climax. Grew sounds like a reformed classicist and on 'Is There A Race Against Time' he seems to be picking out a sonata against Beck's huffs and puffs. The other pieces are briefer and sometimes wryly amusing, especially when Beck picks up his bassoon, but it's finally a bit stentorian and could use a dram less intensity.

The trio set was recorded at one of Leeds's Termite Club Festivals and has a bracing 45 minutes of trio interchange. As loud as he can be, Beck is occasionally buried beneath the sonic onslaught of what's coming off Thomas's keyboards and electronics, while Hession is as full on as usual. Recorded in a tight, gritty close-up, it's a typical gig-CDR presentation, but it doesn't half make a good racket.

Harry Beckett (born 1935)

TRUMPET, FLUGELHORN

A Barbadian, he came to London in 1954, began playing in clubs and eventually rose to be a major presence on the British contemporary scene, working with all its major protagonists over decades. More recently lionized by Europe, with recordings in Germany and association with the French National Jazz Orchestra.

*****(*) Flare Up**
Jazzprint JPVP 124 *Beckett; John Surman (ss, bs); Mike Osborne (as); Alan Skidmore (ts); Frank Ricotti (vib, perc); John Taylor (ky); Chris Laurence (b); John Webb (d).* 7/70.

***** All Four One**
Spotlite SPJ CD 547 *Beckett; Chris Batchelor, Jon Corbett, Claude Deppa (flhn); Alistair Gavin (p); Fred Thelonious Baker (b); Tony Marsh (d); Jan Ponsford (v).* 91.

*****(*) Images Of Clarity**
Evidence EVCD 315 *Beckett; Didier Levallet (b); Tony Marsh (d).* 12/92.

Too vital a presence to be merely a father-figure, Beckett lent a rugged, avuncular blessing to the reintegration of young black musicians into post-free British jazz. Like many of the African- and Caribbean-born musicians who fell within the circle of Chris McGregor's Brotherhood of Breath, Beckett moves without strain between free and mainstream improvisation. His essential qualities are an untroubled romanticism and a brightly lyrical tone (to which he adds gruff asides and occasionally startling rhythmic punctuations). His 1970 session (originally for Philips) is a welcome new reissue. Beckett and Graham Collier wrote most of the tunes and they're a bustling, creative lot, with the horns obliged to push for their own space, and a fondness for some clarion ensemble voicings which (the limited soundmix aside) makes for some exciting jazz. Osborne is superb on 'Flow Stream Flow' and Beckett himself referees with a fine sense of what will and won't work within the parameters of the tunes.

Though some of the best of Beckett's work is on sessions for other leaders, his re-emergence as a recording artist (no more than his deserts, albeit on small labels) finds him consolidating his strengths as an improviser. A pity he hasn't recorded more frequently in the sparse but richly contoured setting of *Images Of Clarity*. Levallet has a gorgeous touch (and chips in with two lovely themes it would be nice to hear again). Marsh is among the most musical of European drummers, embellishing softly without ever losing track of an already delicate pulse. Beckett sounds pensive and slightly wry, and he keeps a thread of humour running through the set, as he has throughout his career.

Beckett's All Four One project is based on a four-flugelhorn front line, an instrumentation capable of great richness but also, one fears and quickly hears confirmed, too little variety. There are some excellent moments. Mingus's 'Better Git It In Your Soul' is just right for this group and 'The Outstanding Light', a very Beckettian original, sits perfectly for the group, but it might have been better to have made an album on which this personnel appeared once or twice; they don't, alas, sustain the full distance. A partially successful idea, then, that neverthless confirms this much-loved musician's continuing desire to experiment. Harry's other albums for RCA, as well as the sets by his Joy Unlimited group, are all overdue for CD release.

Tom Beckham

VIBRAPHONE

Raised in Washington DC, Beckham studied marimba and classical percussion as a teenager but settled for vibes. He arrived in New York in the '90s.

***(*) Suspicions

Fresh Sound NT 075 *Beckham; Chris Cheek (ss, ts); Reid Anderson (b); George Schuller (d).* 6/99.

Another groundbreaking discovery from Fresh Sound's New Talent imprint. This is no perfumed, chamberish quartet. Beckham plays and writes tough music, with Schuller surely the brashest ever drummer in a vibes-led band, and Cheek's saxophones a piquant ingredient. The music is a compilation of Beckham's writing to date, and its considered strands – bop, blues, modal playing – suggest the best bits from a stockpile. A piece such as 'Ascent' suggests emotional complexity as well as thoughtful lines and squares, and the concentrated delivery by all four makes this a real band record, even if Beckham is responsible for all the directions. A pretty impressive start. Pity there's no follow-up yet!

Allen Beechey

CORNET

One of the principals in a new wave of British trad, Beechey leads his Bright Stars Of Jazz, a gang of improbably youthful Londoners tackling the Chicago jazz idiom with aplomb.

***(*) Bridging The Gap

Lake LACD 169 *Beechey; Graham Hughes (tb); Jason Downes (cl, as); George Fagg (p); Andrew Ruiz-Palma (g); Heather Birt (b); Dominic Coles (d); Tamsin West (v).* 3/02.

Even the idea of a band of twentysomethings playing jazz in this style rather than the ubiquitous post-bop idiom is enough to tickle jaded palates, and Beechey's group don't disappoint on their maiden outing. Excellent work by the horns, a nod to the trad tradition of taking on unlikely material ('Skater's Waltz'!) and a lively if sometimes too-polite rhythm section (possibly a little let down by the underdone production) make this an enormously enjoyable outing. Tamsin West guests on 'Jazz Me Blues' and is irresistible.

Bix Beiderbecke (1903–31)

CORNET

The quintessence of jazz legend, Leon 'Bix' Beiderbecke was born in Davenport, Iowa, and was mostly self-taught on both piano and cornet. He joined the Wolverine Orchestra and made his first records in 1923, but it was his periods with Jean Goldkette (St Louis, 1926–7) and Paul Whiteman (New York, 1928–30) which brought him to a wider attention, as well as his record dates with Frankie Trumbauer and under his own name. Alcoholism ruined his health and he died of pneumonia. Though comparatively little known in his lifetime, he became idolized after his death as a unique figure – a cool stylist with a bell-like tone, the flip-side to Louis Armstrong's forthright playing.

*** Bix Beiderbecke And The Wolverines

Timeless CBC 1-013 *Beiderbecke; Jimmy McPartland (c); Miff Mole, Tommy Dorsey, George Brunies, Al Gandee (tb); Don Murray (cl); Jimmy Hartwell (cl, as); Frankie Trumbauer (Cmel); George Johnson (ts); Dick Voynow, Rube Bloom, Paul Mertz (p); Bob Gillett, Howdy Quicksell (bj); Min Leibrook (tba); Vic Moore, Tom Gargano (d).* 2–12/24.

*** Bix Beiderbecke And The Chicago Cornets

Milestone MCD-47019-2 *As above, except add Muggsy Spanier (c), Guy Carey (tb), Volly DeFaut (cl), Mel Stitzel (p), Marvin Saxbe (bj, g), Vic Berton (d).* 2–12/24.

Bix Beiderbecke, the cornetist from Davenport, Iowa, remains among the most lionized and romanticized of jazz figures, nearly 70 years after his death. Beiderbecke's understated mastery, his cool eloquence and precise improvising were long cherished as the major alternative to Louis Armstrong's clarion leadership in the original jazz age, and his records have endured remarkably well, even though comparatively few of them were in the uncompromised jazz vein of Armstrong's studio work. These CDs collect virtually everything he made in his first year in the studios, with the Wolverine Orchestra, the Sioux City Six and Bix's Rhythm Jugglers. With no vocalists to hinder them, these young white bands were following in the footsteps of the Original Dixieland Jazz Band, and although they sometimes seem rather stiff and unswinging, the ensembles are as daring as almost anything that was being recorded at the time. Despite the presence of such players as Mole, Dorsey and Murray, only Beiderbecke's solos have retained much independent life; the beautiful little contribution to 'Royal Garden Blues', for instance, shines through the dull recording and staid surroundings. The record also includes two tracks made after McPartland had replaced Bix in the Wolverines. Some of the original Gennett masters will never sound better than dusty and muffled, but John R. T. Davies has done his usual peerless job on the remastering for Timeless, and there is a fine essay by Beiderbecke scholar, Richard Sudhalter. Milestone's *Chicago Cornets* disc includes all this material but also adds five tracks by Chicago's Bucktown Five, fronted by the teenaged Muggsy Spanier – a not inconsiderable bonus, though overall the remastering isn't quite as good as that on the Timeless CD.

**** Bix Beiderbecke Vol. 1 Singin' The Blues

Columbia CK 45450 *Beiderbecke; Hymie Farberman (t); Bill Rank (tb); Don Murray (cl, bs); Jimmy Dorsey (cl, as); Frankie Trumbauer (Cmel); Red Ingle, Bobby Davis (as); Adrian Rollini (bsx); Paul Mertz, Itzy Riskin, Frank Signorelli (p); Joe Venuti (vn); Eddie Lang (g); John Cali (bj); Joe Tarto (tba); Chauncey Morehouse, Vic Berton (d); Sam Lanin (perc); Irving Kaufman, Seger Ellis (v).* 2–9/27.

This follows Beiderbecke chronologically through 1927, arguably his greatest year in the studios, and it also includes his curious piano solo, 'In A Mist'. Most of the tracks are under Frankie Trumbauer's leadership, and his own slippery, imaginative solos are often as inventive as Bix's, demonstrating why Lester Young named him as a primary influence. But most listeners will be waiting for the shining, affecting cornet improvisations on 'Singin' The Blues', 'Clarinet Marmalade',

'For No Reason At All In C' and the rest. The contributions of Lang and Dorsey are a further bonus. The Columbia sound seems quite light and clear.

****** Bix Beiderbecke Vol. 2 At The Jazz Band Ball**

Columbia CK 46175 *Beiderbecke; Charlie Margulis (t); Bill Rank (tb); Pee Wee Russell (cl); Jimmy Dorsey, Issy Friedman, Charles Strickfadden (cl, as); Don Murray (cl, bs); Frankie Trumbauer (Cmel); Adrian Rollini, Min Leibrook (bsx); Frank Signorelli, Arthur Schutt (p); Tom Satterfield (p, cel); Joe Venuti, Matty Malneck (vn); Carl Kress, Eddie Lang (g); Chauncey Morehouse, Harold MacDonald (d); Bing Crosby, Jimmy Miller, Charlie Farrell (v).* 10/27–4/28.

***** The Bix Beiderbecke Story**

Columbia 501645-2 2CD *As Columbia discs above.* 2/27–4/28.

The survey of Beiderbecke's OKeh recordings has the advantage of eliminating the Whiteman material and concentrating on his most jazz-directed music; this disc includes some of the best of the Bix And His Gang sides, including the title-piece, 'Jazz Me Blues' and 'Sorry', plus further dates with Trumbauer. As a leader, Beiderbecke wasn't exactly a progressive – some of the material harks back to the arrangements used by the Original Dixieland Jazz Band – but his own playing is always remarkable: lean, bruised, a romantic's sound, but one that feels quite at home in what were still rough and elementary days for jazz.

Columbia's two single-disc compilations are now augmented by what's effectively a reissue of an old compilation from the vinyl era with extras. It simply duplicates the contents of the other two sets, and our ears detect no difference in the mastering. A cheap effort by the company. Inside is the legend 'Neo-Vintage Jazz', whatever that means.

***** Bix Beiderbecke With Paul Whiteman 1927–1928**

Classics 1208 *Beiderbecke; Henry Busse, Charlie Margulis, Henry Busse, Eddie Pinder (t); Jack Fulton (tb, v); Tommy Dorsey, Boyce Cullen, Wilbur Hall, Bill Rank (tb); Jimmy Dorsey, Chester Hazlett, Charlie Strickfaden, Hal Mclean, Frankie Trumbauer, Jack Mayhew, Nye Mayhew, Rube Crozier, Izzy Friedman, Red Mayer (reeds); Hoagy Carmichael (p, v); Harry Perrella, Tom Satterfield, Roy Bargy, Ferdie Grofe (p); Kurt Dieterle, Mischa Russell, Marlo Perry, Matt Malneck, Charles Gaylord, John Bowman (strings); Wilbur Hall, Carl Kress (g); Mike Pingitore (bj); Min Leibrook (tba, bsx); Mike Trafficante, Steve Brown (b); Harold McDonald (d); Bing Crosby, Al Rinker, Harry Barris, Austin Young, Charles Gaylord, Olive Kline, Lambert Murphy (v); Paul Whiteman (cond).* 11/27–4/28.

Beiderbecke's tenure with the Whiteman orchestra is a mix of triumph and frustration. Though often buried in the massed ranks of the ensemble, he's still audible in the brass section-work, and when his solos come up, a light comes on. As usual with all dance music of the period, the soloists are mostly rationed to eight, 16 or (sometimes) 32 bars, yet even within this framework Beiderbecke shines in 'Lonely Melody' and 'Dardanella'. There are occasional sidebars such as the small-group treatment of 'San', as well as the bonus of the young Bing Crosby on many of the 24 tracks. Transfers seem solid enough.

CORE COLLECTION

****** Bix And Tram**

JSP CD913 4CD *As appropriate discs above.* 26-29.

A fully comprehensive Beiderbecke collection, properly remastered and from a reputable source, is still not widely available. This JSP set at least covers all of the Gang titles and every session with Trumbauer, and given the fine transfers and bargain price, this is easily first choice among what is now a crowded field of compilations and the like. Mosaic has issued one of its exceptional sets which covers Beiderbecke, Trumbauer and some associated Jack Teagarden sessions in a seven-disc edition (MD7-211), superbly transferred by Doug Pomeroy. The American Sunbeam label has also created three three-disc sets, *Bix Restored Vols. 1-3*, which covers most of the Beiderbecke canon; but this edition is also hard to obtain and we have not been able to audition it. With Bix slipping further back into history one wonders how this young man's reputation is going to hold up over the next period of jazz appreciation.

***** Bix Beiderbecke 1924–1927**

Classics 778 *As appropriate discs above.* 2/24–10/27.

***** Bix Beiderbecke 1927–1930**

Classics 788 *As appropriate discs above.* 10/27–9/30.

Classics enters the fray with these two discs that start with the Wolverines' titles, go on through all of the Bix and his Gang tracks, and finish with the 1930 sessions for Hoagy Carmichael and Irving Mills, together with the final three Victors under his own name. As so often with this series, reproduction is rather up-and-down.

***** The Alternative Takes 1924-1930**

Neatwork RP 2060 *As various discs above.* 5/24–9/30.

Bix with the Wolverines, Jean Goldkette, Trumbauer (three takes from the Chicago Loopers session), Irving Mills and Hoagy Carmichael. Unless you have one of the Sunbeam or Mosaic editions, this is an attractive gap-filler. Nothing remarkable about the alternates, but it's a decent sampler of Bix's various working environments.

Richie Beirach (born 1947)

PIANO, KEYBOARDS

Studied at Berklee and in Manhattan before making a mark with Dave Liebman in the '70s, a continuing association. Only rarely leads his own groups on record, but he has many credits in his book and is much admired as a harmonic theoretician in particular.

***** Too Grand**

Steeplechase SCCD 31333 *Beirach; Andy LaVerne (p).* 11/92.

***** Universal Mind**

Steeplechase SCCD 31325 *As above.* 11/93.

This New Yorker's pianism is entirely unmistakable. Throughout his career, Beirach has attempted to blend jazz harmony with elements of European classical music: Chopin, Debussy's impressionism most obviously, and also the densely chromatic language of the Second Viennese School. He is most successful as a solo performer, but much of the early catalogue is currently out of circulation and it's quite difficult to get a fix on his development. Some of his best work has been with saxophonist Dave Liebman and in the context of groups like Quest and Lookout Farm, but these are also in need of revival.

Two fine duet albums, the second of which is unusual in jazz terms for being a four-hands project, using just one piano. The culminating part is 'The Town Hall Suite', four Bill Evans compositions, played with great freedom and inventiveness. For the rest, the dominating presence is Miles Davis, whose 'Solar' and 'Blue In Green' are both included. There is also a fresh outing for Beirach's 'Elm'. The earlier record also includes two Miles tunes, 'Milestones' and 'So What', as well as material by Monk, Brubeck, Tyner, Shorter and a lovely version of 'Nature Boy'. Andy and Richie swap treble and bass duties throughout the four-hands record, but they seem to do the same instinctively, even when there are two pianos. The performance of Brubeck's 'In Your Own Sweet Way' is particularly forceful in this regard, a huge spread of sound that might be from a much bigger ensemble were it not for the rich piano chording and the percussive off-accents.

***** The Snow Leopard**
Evidence ECD 22193 *Beirach; Gregor Huebner (vn); George Mraz (b); Billy Hart (d).* 6/96, 6/97.

*****(*) Round About Bartók**
ACT 9276 2 *As above, except omit Hart.* 12/99.

The Snow Leopard is a wonderfully varied trio set – Huebner appears on just three tracks – that covers material by Coltrane ('Expression' and 'Naima'), Bill Evans ('Peace Piece'), Billy Hart's wonderful 'Redemption' and classical themes by Mompou and Bartók. There is also a moving and profoundly effective 'In The Wee Small Hours Of The Morning', on which Mraz references Frank Sinatra's famous recording of the song. Beirach's own compositions are typically eclectic. 'The Snow Leopard' is as rarefied and elusive as the creature itself, and as beautiful. 'Citizen Code' and 'Elm' are more generic, but none the less effective.

The more recent, drummerless set is a further extension of Beirach's desire to synthesize jazz and the language of modern classical music. He draws on themes by Scriabin and Kodály as well as Bartók, and juxtaposes folk themes from Eastern Europe with his own 'Zal'. Working without percussion emphasizes the classical feel of the trio, and Mraz works much of the time down in cello range. The recording is flawless, warm and intimate, and impeccably balanced.

***** Round About Monteverdi**
ACT 9412 2 *Beirach; Gregor Huebner (vn); George Mraz (b).* 10/02.

All that is wrong with this delightful set is – perversely, by our usual standard – there is too much jazz in it. Monteverdi's music, like Bach's, is one of the wellsprings of the Western classical tradition, so primal and unmuddied that it seems almost vandalism to overwork it as Beirach does on occasion here. The material is drawn from all over the master's canon, with themes stated relatively straight before being subjected to variation and 'fantasy'. The key player is Mraz, who provides some wonderful tonalities and seems anxious not to over-egg. Listeners who've never encountered Monteverdi may well be captivated and may well find themselves hunting down more orthodox performances. Those familiar with the canon may well find they don't return to this in a hurry. On its own perfectly respectable terms, though, a fine contribution to Beirach's thoughtful series.

Bob Belden (born 1956)

TENOR AND SOPRANO SAXOPHONES, KEYBOARDS

Belden grew up in South Carolina and studied in Texas, before working with Woody Herman and Donald Byrd. His own large ensemble played and recorded in 1989–90 and secured a reputation which allowed him subsequently to work with high-profile names such as Sting and Herbie Hancock. He is now in demand as an arranger, with a versatile CV.

****(*) Treasure Island**
Sunnyside SSC 1041D *Belden; Jim Powell, Tim Hagans (t, flhn); John Fedchock (tb); George Moran (btb); Peter Reit (frhn); Tim Ries, Craig Handy (ss, ts); Chuck Wilson (cl, f); Mike Migliore (as, f, picc); Ron Kozak (bcl, f); Glenn Wilson (bs); Marc Cohen (ky); Carl Kleinsteuber (tba); Jay Anderson (b); Jeff Hirshfield (d).* 8/89.

***** La Cigale**
Sunnyside SSC 1097D *As above, except Larry Farrell (tb), Marc Copland (p) replace Fedchock and Cohen.* 10/90.

Belden's first record as a leader was belated, but it's not terribly exciting. His own 'Treasure Island Suite' is a cumbersome piece of scoring with nothing compelling in it, and the rest of this well-recorded CD (which runs for nearly 80 minutes) offers an eclectic bunch of modern big-band workouts. Migliore and Wilson, at least, add purposeful improvising.

La Cigale was recorded live at the 1990 Paris Jazz Festival. The programme has a similar feel to the studio date, but it's looser knit, and the soloists in the band get to show their paces with some aplomb. 'Psalm No. 1 (For The Heavens)' emerges as a rather attractive piece of mood music.

***** Black Dahlia**
Blue Note 523883-2 *Belden; Lew Soloff, Alan Rubin, Tony Kadleck, Tim Hagans (t); John Fedchock, Conrad Herwig (tb); George Flynn (btb); John Clark, Ann Ellsworth, Jeff Lange, Bob Carlisle (frhn); Lawrence Feldman (as); Joe Lovano (ts); Scott Robinson (cbsx); Tim Ries (af); Lou Marini, Mike Migliore (bf); Charles Pillow (cor); Marc Copland, Kevin Hays (p); Scott Kinsey (ky); Ira Coleman, David Dyson (b); Billy Kilson (d); Bobby Previte, Zach Danziger, Bruce Hall (perc); strings.* 5/00.

This is Belden's symphony *noir*. Where Charlie Haden's Los Angeles records are all misty memorials to a sweeter age, Belden is looking for 'the seamier side of Hollywood', drawing ideas from James Ellroy and Jerry Goldsmith's *Chinatown* score; 'City Of Angels', a setting for Tim Hagans, sounds like Goldsmith's main theme. A 65-piece orchestra frames 13 different soloists. Fitted up with concert-hall echo, the music sounds luscious and is put together and performed with the finest of diligence. Whether it adds up to much more than brainy easy-listening is a matter for debate. It's hard to discern any new ground, and it does suggest that Belden's talents are as a capable pasticheur.

Roberto Bellatalla

DOUBLE BASS

Brilliant freestyle player and now an effective leader, Bellatalla has previously worked with Elton Dean, John Law and Louis Moholo.

***** Borrowed Time**
Slam CD 239 *Bellatalla; Claude Deppa (t, flhn); Jason Yarde (ss, as); Brian Abrahams (d).* 12/98.

Bellatalla's involvement in the South African diaspora in Britain gives his work a comfortable foothold in both melodic, almost folksy playing and powerful free-form improvisation. Some of the tracks here start in relatively simple, certainly discernible melodies and then explode. 'A Blessing In The Eyes' will recall the great days of Dudu Pukwana and Mongezi Feza. Bellatalla is not Harry Miller but he has some of Harry's melodic power. 'On The Eastern Side Of The Lake Of The Flowers' might threaten something drably impressionistic, but it is a tour de force for bowed bass and soprano saxophone. Abrahams is an important presence throughout, not so commanding as Louis Moholo, but endlessly authoritative and thoroughly listenable.

Louie Bellson (born 1924)

DRUMS

Born Luigi Paolino Balassoni, the drummer was working with Goodman, Dorsey and James in the '40s, but his most famous early association was with Duke Ellington, whom he joined in 1951. He continued to work in big bands until the mid-'60s, whereupon he led his own groups of varying size, although his most authoritative work remains in the orchestral situation.

***** Live At Flamingo Hotel 1959**
Jazz Hour JH-1026 *Bellson; Guido Basso, Johnny Frock, Ralph Clark, Wally Buttogello, Fred Thompson (t); Juan Tizol, Earl Swope, Nick Di Maio (tb); Joe Di Angelis (frhn); Frank Albright, Herb Geller (as); Aaron Sachs, Nick Nicholas (ts); George Perry (bs); Ed Diamond (p); Lawrence Lucy (g); Truck Parham (b); Jack Arnold (vib, perc).* 6/59.

***** Louie In London**
DRG 8471 *Bellson; Stan Reynolds, Stan Roderick, Greg Bowen, Kenny Wheeler, Eddie Blair, Pete Winslow, Freddy Staff, Harry Rochie, Wally Smith, Don Lusher, Bobby Lamb, Bill Geldard, Ken Goldie (tb); Roy Willox, Peter Hughes, Dennis Walton, Bob Efford, Brian Ashe, Bernie George, Keith Bird, George Hunter (reeds); Frank Horrox (p); Ernie Shear (g); Frank Donnison, Arthur Watts (b); Derek Warne (perc).* 5/70.

****(*) Jam With Blue Mitchell**
Original Jazz Classics OJC 802 *Bellson; Blue Mitchell (t, flhn); Pete Christlieb (ts); Ross Tompkins (p); Bob Bain (g); Gary Pratt (b); Emil Richards (vib, perc).* 9/78.

**** Cool, Cool Blue**
Original Jazz Classics OJC 825 *Bellson; Ted Nash (ss, ts); Matt Catingub (ss, as); Frank Strazzeri (p); George Duvivier (b).* 11/82.

****(*) The Best Of Louie Bellson**
Pablo 2405-407 *Bellson; Blue Mitchell, Snooky Young, Bobby Shew, Dick Mitchell, Dick Cooper, Cat Anderson, Conte Candoli, Walter Johnson, Ron King (t); Nick Di Maio, Gil Falco, Ernie Tack, Mayo Tiana, Bob Payne, Alan Kaplan, Dana Hughes (tb); Don Menza, Pete Christlieb, Dick Spencer, Larry Covelli, Bill Byrne, Ted Nash, Andy Mackintosh (reeds); Nat Pierce, Ross Tompkins (p); Emil Richards (vib, perc); Mitch Holder, Grant Geissman, Bob Bain (g); John Williams, Joe DiBartolo, Gary Pratt (b); Paulo Magalhaes, Dave Levine, John Arnold, Gene Estes (perc).* 5/75–9/78.

**** The Louie Bellson Explosion**
Original Jazz Classics OJC 728 *Similar to above.* 5/75.

***** Matterhorn Original**
Jazz Classics 1096 *Bellson; Conte Candoli, Walter Johnson, Ron King, Bobby Shew, Snooky Young (t); William C. Both, Gil Falco, Dana Hughes, Alan Kaplan, Bob Payne (tb); Pete Christlieb, Andy Mackintosh, Don Menza, Joe Romano, Richard Spencer (saxes); Ross Tompkins (p); Grant Geissman (g); Joel DiBartolo (b); John E. Arnold, Robert Zimmitti (perc).* 12/78.

Louie Bellson is one of the last survivors of a breed of tough and tirelessly energetic men who powered big bands and small groups alike with the same mix of showmanship and sheer muscle. His comprehensive work with the big-band élite – including Goodman, Basie, James and especially Ellington – gave him a nearly unrivalled experience, and his own groups are marked out by an authority which is often masked by Bellson's comparatively restrained style: virtuoso player that he is, he always plays for the band.

The Jazz Hour CD resurrects a typical hotel engagement by his band as it stood at the end of the '50s. Location sound is excellent and the authentic whomp of the Bellson kit fires up the band, though soloists are left precious little space to shine: Basso and Geller get some time to themselves in 'Blast Off', but there isn't much more than that. *Louie In London* uncovers three days of recording with a British big band from 1970. Mostly co-written by Bellson and Jack Hayes, the titles are a tourist's notebook ('London Suite', 'Proud Thames' and so forth) and the playing is spick-and-span in the worthy way of British big bands, but Bellson sounds as if he must have enjoyed it.

Many of Bellson's records from the '70s and '80s are blemished by a shallow attempt at crossover and unhappy eclecticism. Several have now returned on CD. The *Jam* date with Mitchell is decent, even though Blue isn't his old self, and Christlieb supplies the most reliable solos. *Cool, Cool Blue* has very little going on. The *Best Of* is no great shakes, but it distils some of the superior moments from what were otherwise dispensable records. The 1975 *Explosion* has its moments, but the best of them are on the compilation. *Matterhorn* is the latest to return and, though we didn't have happy memories of it, it does stand up rather well. Conceived as a whopping 'Suite For Drums', there's a whiff of '70s excess which Bellson manages to transmute through sheer skill and bravado – somehow he manages this sort of thing without resorting to the bombast of Buddy Rich. It's a crack team of studio pros and there is the odd solo which livens things further.

*****(*) Inferno!**
Concord CCD2-2158-2 *Bellson; Bobby Shew, Stuart Blumberg, Frank Szabo. Conte Candoli, Blue Mitchell, Harry Edison, Nelson Hatt, Walt Johnson, Ron King, John Thomas (t, flhn); Charlie Loper, Frank Rosolino, Gil Falco, Dana Hughes, Nick Di Maio, Mayo Taina, Bob Payne, Alan Kaplan (tb); Dick Spencer, Larry Covelli, Don Menza, Pete Christlieb, Bill*

Byrne, Matt Catingub, Andy Mackintosh, Gordon Goodwin (saxes); Nat Pierce, Ross Tompkins, Frank Collett (p); Mundell Lowe, John Chiodini, Timothy May (g); John Williams (b); Jack Arnold, Joe Porcaro (perc). 5/74–8/79.

Of Bellson's eight earlier albums for Concord, a much more consistent sequence than his Pablo records, this two-disc repackage of *150 MPH* and *Dynamite!* makes an attractive buy. There are a few nice cameos from the likes of Edison, Candoli and Rosolino on *150 MPH*, and a fine Bill Holman chart for 'Hello Young Lovers': minus any of the modish fluff which spoiled the Pablo albums, this is one of Louie's best. The later set was cut live at the 1979 Concord Festival and for sheer big-band exuberance the likes of 'Sambandrea Swing' hit the bullseye dead centre.

****(*) Their Time Was The Greatest!**
Concord CCD 4683 *Bellson; Conte Candoli, Pete Candoli, Walt Johnson, Frank Szabo, Snooky Young (t); Thurman Green, Andy Martin, Jimmy Zito (tb); Mike Wimberley (btb); Sal Lozano, Ray Reed (as); Pete Christlieb, Tommy Newsom (ts); Bill Green (bs); Frank Strazzeri (p); Dave Carpenter (b); Jack Arnold (perc).* 8/95.

Paying homage to 12 'super-drummers', from Chick Webb to Steve Gadd, this feels too worked-over. Bellson himself sounds anything but tired and his various nods to his peer group have impeccable élan. The band, though, seem unable to bring any special fizz to the occasion and one waits in vain for the kind of over-the-top attack which gives the Buddy Rich tribute albums their punch.

Gregg Bendian

PERCUSSION

An improvising drummer–percussionist, Bendian first played in art-rock situations but moved into free music and has been associated with many leading improvisers.

***** Definite Pitch**
Aggregate CD 001 *Bendian (perc solo).* 94.

*****(*) Counterparts**
CIMP 105 *Bendian; Paul Smoker (t, flhn); Vinny Golia (sno, cl, bcl); Mark Dresser (b).* 1/96.

*****(*) Interzone**
Eremite MTE 03 *Bendian; Nels Cline (g); Mark Dresser (b); Alex Cline (d, perc).* 8/96.

Like Gerry Hemingway, whom he in many ways resembles, Bendian was originally excited by rock music, before discovering the richness of percussion-aware composers like Edgard Varèse. He has pointed out that the main influences on his development of a solo improvisational approach were not other percussionists but free players like Cecil Taylor (who has recorded some Bendian compositions) and Derek Bailey (with whom he has since recorded). With one exception, the pieces on *Definite Pitch* are all written for tuned instruments, hence the title; Bendian uses chimes, timps, chromatic boobams, electronic keyboard percussion, vibes, but only on one track does he attempt to create an ensemble effect by moving among different instruments. This is a work-in-progress recording with an emphasis on repaying debts. There are tributes to Bailey associate Jamie Muir, one of the most extravagant contemporary percussion improvisers, to Captain Beefheart/Don Van Vliet, to film-maker Stan Brakhage, physicist Richard Feynmann and others.

Brakhage and Beefheart are interesting figures to acknowledge because much of Bendian's work is surreal and associative, and this is very much the mood of his first group-recording, in which he takes a more conventional drummer's part but reinterprets it in that same, rather maverick way. Smoker, Golia and Dresser are kindred spirits in this. The pieces (rather dimly recorded, it should be said, on *Caden* magazine's own label) are for the most part long and open-formed, and they integrate arranged themes with what sound like totally free passages. Precisely where one begins and the other ends remains unclear, and there is a constant sense, as in Braxton's works, of multiple subjects being engaged, sometimes sequentially, sometimes overlapping slightly, sometimes simultaneous as in a palimpsest. CIMP's dedication to this music is admirable, but its as-it-happens approach to the sound is a little troubling and might be addressed in future issues. These are, after all, expensive items and not everyone wants the warts and all.

Interzone seems to be and sounds like a settled performing unit. Bendian concentrates on vibes and glockenspiel, leaving more conventional time-keeping to Alex Cline, and relying on the two string players for much of the texture and colour in the set, and there is no shortage of either. Most of the tracks are long and detailed and are structured round quite complex rhythmic ideas. 'I-Zones' is unembarrassedly abstract and uncompromisingly lateral in approach. 'Sunblade Strafe The Continent' is more obviously evocative (though it certainly doesn't have an identifiable programme) and the enigmatic 'Blood: Sassoon zi tavit' might almost be an offcut from some unreleased project of John Zorn's. This is a strong set, faithfully recorded and well engineered by Michael Ehlers and Jon Rosenberg. A tip of the hat to them, as well.

*****(*) Espiritu**
Truemedia D 98715 *Bendian; Alex Cline (perc).* 2/97.

*****(*) Trio Pianissimo**
Truemedia D 99205 *Bendian; Steve Hunt (p); John Lockwood (b).* 98.

Two beautifully inflected discs by a musician who grows more musical with every record. The piano trio is, of course, not a conventional piano trio at all, though Bendian does kick back here and there and settle into an accompanist's groove that suggests nothing more – however unlikely this sounds – than Paul Motian's work with Bill Evans. This is probably the closest the percussionist will ever come to a straight jazz setting, albeit a fractured and asymmetrical bebop.

The opening 'Doshi' is a bustling, urgent thing that shifts between two subtly differentiated time-counts. 'Silvia' is more of a pianist's feature, with drum and cymbal accents flawlessly placed. There is something of a sameness about later tracks, though it is Lockwood who sounds one-dimensional; properly, most of the interest rests with Bendian himself. The closing 'Hysteresis' redeems any shortcomings; opening with fruity bass chords, it develops into a free-flowing improvisation built round an idea that might have come straight from Bud Powell's notebooks. A strong, beautifully executed album that might have been improved only by the inclusion of more varied material.

The duets with Alex Cline are heart-liftingly good, percussion playing of the highest order and unfailingly musical. All the tracks were recorded over one convivial evening and, though seemingly not sequenced on the record as performed, they have the flow and logic of an actual performance. Bendian's rippling vibraphone has all the expressive character one would expect of masters like Milt Jackson and Bobby Hutcherson, and yet it probably comes from somewhere closer to the music of John Cage and Lou Harrison. The opening 'Breakthrough' is breathtaking, and the pace scarcely lags thereafter. A lovely record.

★★★★ Interstellar Space: The Music Of John Coltrane
Atavistic ALP 102 *Bendian; Nels Cline (g).* 2-4/98.

One of the most interesting of a whole shelfload of Coltrane anniversary records, this one appeared long after the due date and was largely overlooked. Basically, it is a retread of Trane and Rashied Ali's experimental duets on *Interstellar Space.* Interestingly, Nels Cline, brother of Interzone's Alex, does not push his powerfully amped guitar up into the multiphonic and harmonically complex atmospheres which the great saxophonist claimed for jazz in the '60s, relying instead on much simpler lines and an almost delicate phrasing.

Bendian is so wholly besotted by free-jazz drumming that he adopts the mannerisms with absolute authenticity. As pastiche, this would be wonderful. As a tribute to the permanent revolution in modern music, it is nearly grand, a superbly modulated performance from both players. The zodiacal themes from *Interstellar Space* would have been easy to overcook, but there is a plainness and humility to these *hommages* which refreshes the original more than we would have thought possible. Hard to listen to this contemporary pairing without returning to the source material. Hard to revisit that without wanting to hear Bendian and Cline again. The bonus live performance of 'Lonnie's Lament' is as good as anything Bill Frisell and Joey Baron have committed to record: atmospheric, moving, not a whit self-indulgent.

★★★ Myriad
Atavistic 119 *Bendian; Nels Cline (g); Steuart Liebig (b); Alex Cline (d, perc).* 99.

★★★ Requiem For Jack Kirby
Atavistic 125 *As above, except omit Liebig; add Joel Hamilton (d).* 00.

Unlike fellow-percussionist Alex Cline, who appears again on the first of this pair, Bendian has evolved toward an edgy surrealism that remains rhythmically based. The second of the pair is a tribute to the great era of comic book art and one can see how and what Bendian draws from that aesthetic.

Gregg concentrates largely on vibraphone and glockenspiel on these Atavistic dates, leaving Cline to fill in his trademark textures. Nels Cline reinforces the similarities with the kind of art-rock that figured at the beginning of the leader's career, and though some of his hotter solos veer towards pastiche, they're executed with enough strength and intelligence to avoid parody. Hard to single out tracks on either album, except to say that 'Diaspora' (*Myriad*) and 'Teaneck In the Marvel Age' (*Requiem*) outstay their welcome somewhat. Bendian now seems more convincing when he restricts himself to a shorter duration. Even so, these are fine, intelligent records which point to a new kind of jazz fusion. Along with the Cline brothers' work they may seem of growing significance as the years go by.

Roni Ben-Hur

GUITAR

Born in Israel, Ben-Hur arrived in the US in 1985, and studied improvisation with Barry Harris. He plays in a brisk bop style.

★★★ Backyard
TCB 95902 *Ben-Hur; Barry Harris (p); Lisle Atkinson (b); Leroy Williams (d); Amy London (v).* 94.

★★★(★) Sofia's Butterfly
TCB 98802 *As above; omit Harris.* 97.

★★★(★) Anna's Dance
Reservoir RSR 127 *Ben-Hur; Charles Davis (ts); Barry Harris (p); Walter Booker (b); Leroy Williams (d).* 11/00.

For his debut, Ben-Hur shrewdly recruited one of the genuine surviving bop giants. The still effervescent Barry Harris coasts through these relatively unfamiliar tunes with a smile you can almost hear. 'The Thrill Is Gone' opens the album on what is possibly its high point, but the following 'Dance Of The Infidels' which the man from the Holy Land invests with scope and drama and with a certain pre-modern quality that suggests the theme might have originated on a Crusader march. Sonny Rollins's 'Audubon' is rarely covered but reveals another brightly plumaged bopper. 'Backyard' is Harris's clever contrafact on 'Embraceable You'. Singer Amy London – Mrs Ben-Hur – turns in a solitary vocal on 'Something To Live For'.

Ben-Hur has been likened to Kenny Burrell and Jimmy Raney. If anything, he sounds more like Jimmy's son Doug, with the same quiet urgency and willingness to hang back on the beat before pressing down on the gas and scurrying through ten phrases in the space left for eight. The second album is a better showcase of his guitar playing than the debut, which inevitably relied heavily on Harris. Roni keeps Atkinson and Williams on board, and gives the missis a vocal spot, but in the trio format he's pushed out into the spotlight. Two Harris tunes, 'Like This' and 'Choices', sound as if they might have formed the basis for past lessons, so briskly does the guitarist despatch them. The Bud Powell tune this time is 'The Fruit' and there is a fresh Latin tinge to 'Tin Tin Deo'.

On the third record, Ben-Hur closes with another bop master whose work he has studied closely. As a member of Bertha Hope's Elmolennium Project, Roni came across Elmo Hope's 'So Nice' which kicks off *Anna's Dance* again with its strongest component. Sadly, there are no other Hope themes on the set, a pity given the return of Harris who understands this material like no one else now living. The other ambitious reading is of Charlie Parker's seldom-played blues 'Visa', which puts guitar and piano into an interesting new relation. Booker is another Ben-Hur employer and his firm, chunky bass is a great asset, spurring on some of the quieter and less emphatic numbers.

Han Bennink (born 1942)

DRUMS, PERCUSSION, TROMBONE, TENOR AND SOPRANO SAXOPHONES, CLARINET, HARMONICA, ANYTHING/EVERYTHING

Born in Zaandam, Bennink went the classic route of working on liners to have the chance of hearing American jazz, and he played drums for US visitors to Amsterdam all through the '60s. At the same time, he began working with Misha Mengelberg as

a duo and soon evolved into a key figure in European free music, an eminence he has maintained ever since, although he still enjoys more boppish playing situations too.

***** Nerve Beats**
Atavistic Unheard Music UMS/ALP 206 *Bennink (d etc solo).* 9/73.

*****(*) Jazz Bunker**
Leo Golden Years GY 7/8 2CD *Bennink; Toshinori Kondo (t, euph, perc, v); Eugene Chadbourne (g, p, v).* 2/80.

***** Serpentine**
Songlines SGL 1510 *Bennink; Dave Douglas (t).* 1/96.

*****(*) When We're Smilin'**
Incus CD 34 *Bennink; Derek Bailey (g).* n.d.

***** In Edamo**
ICP 037 *Bennink; Steve Beresford (p, elec).* 2/00.

There's no substitute for seeing Bennink in performance, and the 1973 survival *Nerve Beats* is a tour de force which seems entirely one-dimensional, given that we can only experience the aural element. Starting with a drum fusillade which sounds like the work of ten men at least, then proceeding through a further 40 minutes of percussion, trombone, clarinet, primitive drum machines, tabla playing, noise and music off radios and more, it transcends the clichés about period charm and feels vividly alive, although one can only guess what this extraordinary man is doing some of the way.

The 1980 session with Kondo and Chadbourne is a meeting of three masters of cracked extravagance and features everything from trombone–euphonium dialogues to a war of attrition over respective volume levels. In a curious way, it is much more traditional in flavour than most European improvised music; importing bluegrass, brass-band music and pre-bop swing into its delivery, for much of the way it hardly feels avant garde at all, for all the chaos. The quality of the recording isn't outstanding, but as a constantly surprising, intense and funny piece of documentation, it ranks highly in this area.

The duo with Douglas offers 13 mostly short tracks, interspersing extemporized originals, a couple of tunes that sound as if they've had some preparatory work done on them, and a couple of standards, most startlingly 'Cherokee', which is a vividly comic but also deeply felt performance. 'Too Close For Comfort' is prefaced by 'Two Clogs For Comfort', but mostly the tone is quite sober. Both 'Serpentine' and 'Delft', the two most substantial pieces, are written by Douglas, but he seems to defer to the drummer in performance.

Bennink and Bailey is another partnership that goes back a long way. According to its brief sleevenote, each man posted the other some music, and each played along with the received result, creating a set of virtual duets. Bennink refuses to do anything except swing, even when he's not playing a countable time, and he always lifts Bailey's abstractions into something which at least approaches jazz (perhaps to the guitarist's exasperation). A brief and delightful record.

The English pianist Beresford is no match for Misha Mengelberg in duet with the ferocious Dutchman, and his resorting to toy electronics soon becomes a bit tiresome, but the drummer's unstinting enthusiasms bridge any weak spots and a modern recording highlights Han's superb stickwork.

****(*) Tempo Comodo**
Data 823 *Bennink (perc solo).* n.d.

Another solo set from the Dutchman. We don't have a date for this, but if it is very recent it rather suggests that Bennink has settled into a 'style' that is increasingly predictable. Dates like this always make demanding listening, but behind the generic titles – 'Sticktrick', 'Traps 1/Rims', and the brief, hilarious 'Dropsticks' – there is some far from generic playing going on. The problem with an artist from whom one always expects the unexpected is that the degree of unexpectedness perhaps stretches too far. A glorious technician, Bennink has by now learned enough technical tricks to keep the most avid percussion junkie going for months; for most listeners, though, a fairly tough listen.

***** Train Kept A Rollin' (21 Years Later)**
Leo 324 *Bennink; Eugene Chadbourne (g, bjo, p).* 01.

Han and the good Doctor in a series of hilariously unexpected duets. Most of the tracks are freely improvised and bear a version of the subtitle ('One Year Later', 'Five Years Later' and so on) but there is also a version of Jobim's 'Corcovado' and, in honour of Han's association with Eric Dolphy, a lovely and completely unexpected take on the saxophonist's best known composition 'Miss Ann'. As ever, Chadbourne has his selection of stringed tricks at the ready and somewhat dominates the set.

***** The Laughing Owl**
Atavistic 10 *Bennink; Terrie Ex (g).* 01.

Just as Derek Bailey had been experimenting with drum'n'bass groups and with DJs, so Bennink chipped in with this set with the guitarist of Dutch punk group The Ex. The songs are mostly short, intense, and fairly haphazard in tone, but the whole project is saved by Bennink's manic humour and Ex's delightful hardscrabble approach. Any comparison with the Chadbourne set will reveal how different a sensibility is at work.

***** Grass Is Greener**
Psi 02.02 *Bennink; Evan Parker (ts).* 01.

Released on Parker's own label, this is a strangely disappointing set in the sense that the two long opening tracks, 'Traps of Appetite', 'Traps of Instinct', have no obvious logic, no real shape and only a rather obscure registration on the recording, which was made under professional circumstances. The shorter pieces are much more effective and 'The Empty Hook' is a small masterpiece. Parker is a wonderful tenor player, a detail often eclipsed by his virtuosic soprano performances, and his strong, gritty tone is heard to maximum effect here. Bennink has a wealth of musical ideas and the intricacy of his playing is breathtaking in places. A shame about those opening pieces, though. Some listeners might not get past the first half hour and one wonders if Parker's judgement was sound in including them.

George Benson (born 1943)

GUITAR, VOCAL

Sang from an early age and made R&B records as a teenager. Then focused on guitar, touring with Jack McDuff from 1962, his own albums from 1965, and sideman appearances with Miles Davis and others. Broke through to major crossover success in the '70s, first as a guitarist, then with a return to singing and upmarket soft-soul hits. Occasional forays back towards some kind of straight-ahead playing as his pop audience has waned.

***** The New Boss Guitar**

Original Jazz Classics OJC 460 *Benson; Red Holloway (ts); Jack McDuff (org); Ronnie Boykins (b); Montego Joe (d).* 5/64.

The huge success Benson earned in the '70s and '80s as a light-soul vocalist has obscured some of the impact of his guitar playing. He is a brilliant musician. His first records were made when Wes Montgomery was alive and the acknowledged master of the style which Benson developed for his own ends: a rich, liquid tone, chunky chording which evolved from Montgomery's octave technique, and a careful sense of construction which makes each chorus tell its own story. At his best Benson can fire off beautiful lines and ride on a 4/4 rhythm with almost insolent ease; strain is never a part of his playing. Almost any record that he plays guitar on has its share of great moments, although this early date with his then-boss McDuff is comparatively routine. Its short tracks and meagre playing-time are very much in the organ-combo genre that churned out scores of records in the early and middle '60s. But it's still very good.

***** Giblet Gravy**

Verve 543754-2 *Benson; Ernie Royal, Snooky Young (t); Jimmy Owens (t, flhn); Alan Raph (btb); Pepper Adams (bs); Herbie Hancock (p); Eric Gale, Carl Lynch (g); Ron Carter, Bob Cranshaw (b); Billy Cobham (d); Johnny Pacheco (perc); Eileen Gilbert, Albertine Robinson, Los Winter (v).* 68.

***** The Silver Collection**

Verve 823450-2 *Benson; Jimmy Owens (t, flhn); Clark Terry, Ernie Royal, Snooky Young (t); Garnett Brown (tb); Alan Raph (btb); Arthur Clarke, George Marge (ts, f); Pepper Adams (bs); Buddy Lucas (hca); Herbie Hancock, Paul Griffin (p); Jimmy Smith (org); Eric Gale (g); Jack Jennings (vib, perc); Bob Cranshaw, Ron Carter, Chuck Rainey (b); Billy Cobham, Jimmy Johnson Jr, Idris Muhammad, Donald Bailey (d); Johnny Pacheco (perc); strings.* 1/67–11/68.

***** Talkin' Verve**

Verve 553780-2 *Similar to above.* 2–11/68.

***** George Benson: Verve Jazz Masters 21**

Verve 521861-2 *Similar to above discs.* 2/68–11/69.

After leaving McDuff, Benson cast around for success without really breaking through. His clean, funky but restrained style was hardly the thing in Hendrix's era, and the easy-listening option, to which Montgomery fell prey, had yet to envelop him while at Columbia and Verve. The *Silver Collection* and *Jazz Masters* sets are very similar, each an intelligent cross-section of Benson's small number of recordings in the period. A hot quintet with Hancock, Carter and Cobham glide through 'Billie's Bounce' and 'Thunder Walk', while 'I Remember Wes' is a sensitive tribute to the recently deceased Montgomery. The tracks with a larger band are ordinary, but hint at Benson's growing versatility and suggest that he was already seen as Montgomery's natural successor. *Talkin' Verve* concentrates on tracks from two original LPs, *Giblet Gravy* and *Goodies*, and to that extent is slightly more restricted in range. The original of *Giblet Gravy* has returned as a Verve Master Edition, and though George wouldn't be caught dead eating in the kind of place in the cover photo these days, the album makes a case for itself; the compilations are at least as good. None of this is deathless music but it's begun to gather a period appeal to go with the virtues of Benson's playing.

***** Beyond The Blue Horizon**

CTI ZK 65130 *Benson; Clarence Palmer (org); Ron Carter (b); Jack DeJohnette (d); Michael Cameron, Albert Nicholson (perc).* 2/71.

****(*) Body Talk**

CTI/Epic 5051692 *Benson; Jon Faddis, John Gatchell, Waymon Reed (t); Gerald Chamberlain, Dick Griffin (tb); Frank Foster (ts); Harold Mabern (p); Earl Klugh (g); Ron Carter, Gary Kind (g); Jack DeJohnette (d); Mobutu (perc).* 7/73.

**** Bad Benson**

CTI/Epic 505285-2 *Benson; Kenny Barron (p); Phil Upchurch (g); Ron Carter (b); Steve Gadd (d); orchestra.* 5–6/74.

Creed Taylor's CTI label set the standard for easy-listening jazz in its early-70s heyday, and while some of this music has worn rather better than we expected (which may be more a comment on how lamentable the current smooth-jazz fad has become), it's scarcely provocative. Given Taylor's proclivities for stupefying charts and tick-tock rhythms, it's surprising that there's as much decent music as there is here. The latest edition of *Beyond The Blue Horizon* still has claims on being one of Benson's best records. 'So What' and 'The Gentle Rain' are among the high points of Benson's CTI work, lyrical but quite hard-bitten in their handling, and with the excellent rhythm section behind him the guitarist finds plenty of room to stretch out. 'Somewhere In The East' is a curious bit of early world-jazz. Aside from Benson himself, DeJohnette does very well.

Body Talk sees formula taking over. DeJohnette sticks closer to a rock-funk pulse, Klugh plays dreary counterpoint, and Benson's originals are disappointingly thin. The title-piece (there is an alternative take in the new edition) opens the doors to the disco. Yet even here the guitarist salvages some good licks for himself. *Bad Benson* has Steve Gadd at the kit and is often plain boring; an interesting extra is a long Don Sebesky piece, 'Serbian Blue', which at least allows George to play the blues at length, even if he sounds emasculated by the mix.

***** Breezin'**

Warner Archive/Rhino 76713-2 *Benson; Ronnie Foster, Jorge Dalto (ky); Phil Upchurch (g); Stanley Banks (b); Harvey Mason (d); Ralph McDonald (perc); strings.* 1/76.

**** In Flight**

Warner Bros 256327 *As above.* 8–11/76.

***** Weekend In L.A.**

Warner Bros 3139-2 2CD *As above, except omit strings.* 2/77.

Breezin' was the first jazz album to go platinum and sell a million copies, but more important for the listener was its reconciliation of Taylor's pop-jazz approach with a small-group backing in which Benson could feel genuinely at home. Claus Ogerman's arrangements are still fluffy, and the tunes are thin if not quite anodyne, but Benson and his tightly effective band get the most out of them. The new edition adds two extra tracks, one of which, 'Shark Bite', is rather tougher and less polite than the rest of the record. *In Flight* re-introduces Benson as a vocalist (he actually began as a singer in the '50s) and 'Nature Boy' blueprints the direction he would take next, but the record is too patently a retread of the previous one. *Weekend In L.A.* is a live set that shows how the band can hit a groove outside the studio. Benson's treatment of 'On Broadway' is an infectious classic because he lives out the song; the session as a whole is a bit deodorized, but smoothness is the guitarist's trademark, and his solos are full of singing melodies, tied to their own imperturbable groove.

**** Tenderly**

Warner Bros 25907 *Benson; McCoy Tyner (p); Ron Carter (b); Louis Hayes, Al Foster (d).* 89.

**** Big Boss Band**

Warner Bros 26295 *Benson; Bob Ojeda, Byron Stripling, Randy Brecker, Jon Faddis, Lew Soloff, Larry Farrell (t); Paul Faulise, Earl Gardner, Keith O'Quinn, James Pugh (tb); David Glasser (as); Frank Foster (ts); Barry Eastmond, Richard Tee, Terry Burrus, David Witham (ky); Ron Carter (b); Carmen Bradford (v); Count Basie Orchestra; Robert Farnon Orchestra.* 90.

***** Best Of George Benson: The Instrumentals**

Warners 946660-2 *As Warner albums above.*

Most of Benson's records after *Weekend In L.A.* fall outside the scope of this book, although many rate as high-calibre light soul. But of late he's been investigating a return to more jazz-orientated material, possibly as a result of a somewhat waning general popularity. Guest appearances as a sideman with such friends as Earl Klugh and Jimmy Smith haven't yielded much, though, and these two sets must be counted as great disappointments. *Tenderly* is far too relaxed: Benson's singing sounds tired, and his playing is as uneventful as that of the others involved, although such seasoned pros always deliver a few worthwhile touches. Weaker still is *Big Boss Band*, a collaboration with Frank Foster's Count Basie band that runs aground on fussy arrangements, material Basie himself wouldn't have touched (the soporific 'How Do You Keep The Music Playing'); the track with Robert Farnon's band ('Portrait Of Jennie') suggests that a shot at Nat Cole's repertoire might have been the next thing on George's agenda (it wasn't, as it turned out). His guitar playing takes an entirely minor role. The new instrumental *Best Of* makes a game effort at distilling the jazz ingredients in Benson's pop albums of 1976–93; it's agreeable enough even though several pieces sound like a master musician reduced to the sappiest of instrumental pop.

Benson has since signed to GRP for records that try to make his pop-jazz contemporary again. He has gone steadily back towards the hard stuff with the albums *That's Right* and *Standing Together*, and the 2000 release *Absolute Benson* comes close to his old form. Players like Joe Sample, Christian McBride and even Cindy Blackman are on hand to up the ante. But there is a distant veil of synthesizers on most tracks so as not to upset smooth-jazz radio, and by the end it's clear that George is long past the point of risking losing what remains of his easy-listening audience. In the last few years he seems to have called time on any straight-ahead activity, as star sideman or leader alike, and he surely belongs to the jazz past now.

Bob Berg (1951–2002)

TENOR SAXOPHONE, SOPRANO SAXOPHONE

The New Yorker's career began early with Brother Jack McDuff, in whose group he played as a teenager. Technically less astute than Michael Brecker, whom he somewhat resembles, Berg always overcame technical limitations by his sheer power and conviction, and his records never quite had the authority of his live appearances. A complex man who had his share of problems, Berg always has a story to tell, however haltingly. The story ended with his death in a car accident at the end of 2002.

*****(*) Steppin'**

Red RR123178-2 *Berg; Danilo Rea (p); Enzo Pietropaoli (b); Roberto Gatto (d).* 82.

A stint with Miles Davis, far from pushing Berg into the limelight, set his always-promising solo career back a good album or two. Miles, for reasons obvious from his earlier CV, was less than generous to his latter-day reedmen, obviously looking on the sax as a regressive instrument *vis-à-vis* happening things like 'lead' bass guitars, synths and drum machines.

Berg was a hugely talented mainstream player with a well-assimilated Coltrane influence who could never realistically have been expected to fit into Miles's avant-disco conception. What he was expected to put in is now history, but what did he take away with him? Listening to him on *Steppin'*, which was recorded live in Europe with a decent but uninspiring band, the answer to that is as ambiguous as the question. In later years, Miles moved ever closer to the blues, and it's possible to hear Berg attempt the same simplification of idiom in almost every track on the Italian date, even when the material is reasonably complex. Tom Harrell's 'Terrestris' was an interesting composition to include; it isn't a tune that sits easily for the saxophone, but Bob turns it into a taut harmonic essay. His own 'Arja' is as lovely a thing as he ever did but it is marred by a very distant recording. Another original, 'Luce di Fulvia', and an imaginative version of Stevie Wonder's 'Secret Life Of Plants' round out the record.

****** Another Standard**

Stretch SCD 9013 *Berg; Randy Brecker (t); David Kikoski (p); Mike Stern (g); Ed Howard (b); Gary Novak (d).* 96.

Another Standard was the record some observers felt Berg should have made some years earlier, as a way of demonstrating that he could work someone else's turf convincingly and not just hide behind his own material. Not surprisingly, what transpires is an album that has Bob Berg written all over it: wry, witty, anarchic and sternly disciplined in one carefully assembled package. The outstanding performance is on 'It Was a Very Good Year', which Berg deconstructs from the bottom up, weaving a soprano line round Kikoski's piano. Adding Randy Brecker on two tracks ('My Man's Gone Now' and 'I Could Write A Book') suggests that Berg has absorbed himself in the work of Miles's quintet with Coltrane, while Mike Stern's walk-on part on 'No Trouble' is extremely effective, another Miles alumnus who has learnt to do things his way. Berg's desire to keep close to the original tunes is admirable, though more often honoured in the breach, for these are highly intelligent reinventions, packed with ideas and unflaggingly interesting. He subsequently did other sideman records, but this proved to be Berg's swansong as a leader.

Anders Bergcrantz (born 1961)

TRUMPET, CORNET, FLUGELHORN

Danish post-bop trumpeter with an increasing international reputation.

***** Live At Sweet Basil**

Dragon DRCD 225 *Bergcrantz; Rick Margitza (ts); Richie Beirach (p); Ron McClure (b); Adam Nussbaum (d).* 2/92.

*****(*) In This Together**

Dragon DRCD 261 *As above, except omit Margitza.* 8/94.

Bergcrantz is a gifted hard-bop trumpeter whose fiery early days are settling into a more considered but still attacking manner. Some earlier records for Dragon have yet to make it to CD, and the enjoyable *Live At Sweet Basil* is unfortunately something of a pot-boiler. Bergcrantz is among peers for this New York visit, and he takes a firm lead with two interesting originals of his own and a striking recasting of 'Body And Soul' among other themes, but the sound of the group lacks the clear weave of his Swedish bands and the music isn't as tautly sustained as his earlier records. Margitza makes a useful partner – there's a nice touch of European bleakness about his tone – and Beirach, McClure and Nussbaum are this time dependable and classy rather than inspired. The sound is a little fuzzy when it ought to bite.

In This Together is very, very good. In the studio, the quartet comes together perfectly: Beirach plays in his most concentrated style, and McClure and Nussbaum swing mightily. Bergcrantz takes a more measured course than usual, pacing himself through his solos and finding a mellow, woodsmoked sound on flugelhorn. He comes up with tones and phrasings which no American trumpeter would play and, set against the strong yet thoughtful pulse of the others, the result is a rare kind of post-bop. Even so, it's difficult to sustain a trumpet quartet date for an hour, and just here and there one wishes for another horn for some piquancy, or to propel Bergcrantz in a fresh direction. Exemplary recording, done in New York.

****** C**

Dragon DRCD 293 *As above.* 10/96.

It's a wonderful group, and this on-tour CD caught them at a playing peak. The 'C' is for Coltrane, and the four men give a pretty amazing impression of the great quartet on the title-track without resorting to mere copycat tricks. Beirach sounds bigger and stronger than he ever has, McClure is the epitome of the invisible, soulful bassman, and Nussbaum simply ransacks the kit for every bit of Elvin he can find. They do similar things on 'Footprints' and the rather more mysterious 'Renfield', but there's a lovely flugelhorn ballad on 'I Won Her Heart' and a quite thoughtful look at 'Stella By Starlight'. Interestingly, Bergcrantz chooses to play cornet more often than not, and it seems to put a bit of extra jab into his quicker phrases. His long solos have fire, ingenuity and elegance in as close to equality as one can hope. A great live one.

*****(*) Twenty-Four Hours**

Dragon DRCD 312 *Bergcrantz; Roy Wall, Anders Gustafsson (t); Vincent Nilsson (tb); Helge Albin (as); Fredrik Carlquist, Inge Petersson (cl, ts); Cennet Jönsson (ss, ts, bcl); Terje Thiwang (f); Jacob Christoffersen (ky); Sven Bergcrantz (p); Hans Andersson (b); Lennart Gruvstedt (d).* 98.

A spiritedly ambitious programme from Bergcrantz this time. The title piece is a six-part suite which takes the listener through a single day – hardly a daring concept, but realized with flair and a lack of fuss which makes the music very appealing. Scored for four brass and rhythm section, the music has a plangent bite and the soloists rise to their featured moments with a good deal of bravado. There are two tracks where Anders' father Sven plays piano on his own compositions – poignantly, not long before his death – although the funk beat chosen for 'Den Lille Malcolm' is less appealing. The final 'Thank You And Farewell' is another commissioned piece that works through some attractive harmonic writing very much in an old Scandinavian tradition. Not every step works, but still a very attractive set.

Karl Berger (born 1935)

VIBRAPHONE, PIANO

Born in Heidelberg, Berger learned to play jazz piano in the company of visiting Americans. After musical study at home and in Berlin, he switched his interest to free jazz and moved first to Paris (with Don Cherry) and then to the USA, where he and Ornette Coleman founded the Creative Music Studio at Woodstock, NY. In recent years, Berger has arranged for musicians as diverse as Jeff Buckley and the Cardigans. These and educational activities have limited his recorded output.

***** Just Play**

Emanem 4037 *Berger; Ed Blackwell (d, perc).* 3/76.

****(*) All Kinds Of Time**

Sackville SKCD2-3010 *Berger; Dave Holland (b).* 4/76.

Berger and Blackwell had worked together in Don Cherry's group and it was to be an important association for the vibist. This session was recorded in Albany, New York, by the estimable Martin Davidson. The 1979 Quark LP has long been out of circulation. Five of the tracks are for vibes (without fans) and drum kit, but the longest and most adventurous compositions are for African balafon and osi – or slit – drum. The two pieces, 'Balafon Samba' and 'Wood And Skin Works', occupy almost half the record between them. The shorter tracks are more dynamic but don't recapture the same, almost hypnotic, quality. Blackwell is in great form, perfectly in balance with Berger's own delicate touch.

The duos with Holland have a faintly academic bent – some impeccable interplay and finely judged nuancing of the very bare textures involved – but even over what is no more than a vinyl LP's length, the record sometimes struggles to hold the interest.

*****(*) Transit**

Black Saint 100922-2 *Berger; Dave Holland (b); Ed Blackwell (d).* 8/86.

The best of Berger's recorded output lies in the trio with Holland and Blackwell. 'Dakar Dance' and 'Ornette' on *Transit* are both open-hearted and expressive. Holland is a completely sympathetic collaborator; this is very much his territory. One wonders about the choice of Blackwell rather than a European drummer better adapted to these abstractions. There's a sense that he's having to work harder than the others, giving the quieter tracks a rather tense quality that presumably isn't intentional.

***** Around**
Black Saint 120112 *Berger; Koji Paul Shigihara (g); Santi Debriano (b); Leroy Williams (d).* n.d.

In recent years, Berger has shown an interest in working with guitarists, and has struck up an impressive rapport with Shigihara. An album of duets is in the works, but their collaboration here is self-explanatory on 'Guitar Vibes'. Berger's free-music roots are less and less in evidence, but 'Travel South' has interesting elements of freedom. Debriano and Williams are more than bit players, but one wonders if they are surplus to requirements.

***** Conversations**
In + Out 7027 *Berger; Ray Anderson (tb); Carlos Ward (as, f); James Blood Ulmer (g); Mark Feldman (vn); Dave Holland (b); Ingrid Sertso (v).* 01.

Given the dearth of recent albums bearing Berger's name, this is especially welcome, though it rather tellingly features him in scattered contexts with a variety of old friends and sparring partners. Musically, some of these encounters are more surprising than effective. The guitar/piano duet with Blood Ulmer on 'North' is a bold idea that doesn't really come off. Rather better conceived is a pair of pieces with Dave Holland, 'Presently' and 'Still', which at least sound as if they come from the same sound-world. Mark Feldman also seems to enjoy the challenge and old partner Ingrid Sertso is there once more, but the surprise package of the set is a romping piano and trombone version of Monk's 'Bemsha Swing', which immediately makes you wish for an entire set of Berger and Anderson duos. The only other artist who prompts that response is the still-underrated Carlos Ward, who contributes beautiful alto and flute to 'Out There Alone' and 'At Last'.

***** No Man Is An Island**
Knitting Factory 3004 *Berger; Enrico Rava (t); Arkady Shilkloper (frhn); Bernd Konrad (sax, cl); Jean-Louis Matinier (acc); Barbara Krummer (vn); Ernst Reijseger (clo); Marc Abraham (b); Bill Elgart (d, perc); Ingrid Sertso (v).* 01.

An intriguing multi-movement work that underlines Berger's interest in orchestral scoring. Some aspects of this sound very much like off-shoots of recent commercial work, but the overall structure is very open and free, with some room for improvisation and a nice variation of instrumental colour. The piece's programme is familiar enough to seem almost hackneyed, but at a time when isolationism and international responsibility are again competing philosophies in America's corridors of power, the piece has a wider currency than one might suspect. Nicely recorded, with a lot of individual detail, though the strings are forwarded somewhat relative to the horns.

Totti Bergh (born 1935)

TENOR AND SOPRANO SAXOPHONES

Began on clarinet and later switched to tenor. Worked on cruise ships during the '60s and since then has worked on a semi-pro basis. An exemplar of Norway's jazz mainstream.

*****(*) I Hear A Rhapsody**
Gemini GMCD 48 *Bergh; Per Husby, Egil Kapstad (p); Terje Venaas (b); Egil Johansen, Ole Jacob Hansen (d).* 8/85.

***** Tenor Gladness**
Gemini GMCD 53 *As above, except add Al Cohn (ts); omit Husby and Johansen.* 8/86.

***** On The Trail!**
Gemini GMCD 78 *As above, except Plas Johnson (ts) replaces Cohn.* 8/91.

*****(*) Remember**
Gemini GMCD 88 *Bergh; Joe Cohn (g); Erik Amundsen (b); Tom Olstad (d); Laila Dalseth (v).* 3/95.

***** Warm Valley**
Gemini GMCD 91 *Bergh; Einar Iversen (p); Kare Garnes (b); Eyvind Olsen (d).* 10/96.

Totti Bergh is a master saxophonist whose home-base of Norway has never managed to release him on to a wider audience. That shouldn't deter listeners from seeking out at least one of these handsome records. Bergh plays with the timeless authority of the mainstream saxman and there's scarcely a step out of place on any of these five sessions. *I Hear A Rhapsody* is a luscious set of ballads, the tenor curling round the melodies and huffing through solos that barely bother to move; lovely stuff, though, and the rhythm sections are good enough never to let the music bog down in treacle. Bergh's meeting with Al Cohn calls to mind the many Zoot-and-Al partnerships, perhaps slightly to Bergh's disadvantage, though Cohn (near the end of his life) was also taking things steady that day. The meeting with Plas Johnson is a bit livelier and there is some enjoyable banter on the likes of 'Smooth Sailing' and 'Tickle Toe'.

Bergh has never had a better sound in the studio than he has on the two most recent records. *Remember* is perhaps the best record the tenorman has made: Joe Cohn is a deft and encouraging partner who persuades the leader into his most beguiling form on 'Two Funky People' and 'Foolin' Myself'. Laila Dalseth (alias Mrs Bergh) sings five of her Merrillesque vocals and a long record never outstays its welcome. *Warm Valley* is another set of ballads which this time is just a shade too quiescent to hold the interest throughout, although any five minutes from the record will surely delight a casual listener. Bergh's grand tone and patient phrasing remain a steadfast pleasure.

Borah Bergman (born 1933)

PIANO

For a time, Borah Bergman concentrated exclusively on playing with his left hand in order to build up strength, suppleness and the kind of right-brain co-ordination that now underpin his formidable technique. Though most obviously of the Cecil Taylor school, his astonishing solo performances also recall the 'two pianists' illusion associated with Art Tatum, though in a fragmentary and disorderly sound-world far removed from Tatum's or that of the stride and ragtime pianists who are also part of Bergman's background.

****** A New Frontier**
Soul Note 121030 *Bergman (p solo).* 1/83.

***** The Fire Tale**
Soul Note 121252 *Bergman; Evan Parker (ss).*

*****(*) The Human Factor**
Soul Note 121212 *Bergman; Andrew Cyrille (d).* 6/92.

**** First Meeting

Knitting Factory Works KFW 175 *Bergman; Roscoe Mitchell (as, ss); Thomas Buckner (v).* 12/94.

Record companies insist that no overdubs, multi-tracking or tape-speeding have been used on their records only when something rather special is going on inside. That is certainly the case with Borah Bergman, whose initial impact as a player can be likened – however lame a cliché this has become – only to that of Cecil Taylor. Bergman is both a composer and an improviser, and it is often difficult to draw lines between the two. What he has done is to break down any residual distinction between left- and right-hand functions in piano playing. On the two large-scale pieces which make up *A New Frontier* he sets up huge whirling shapes with each hand, which then engage in dialogue – often confrontational dialogue, at that. There is something slightly mechanistic about the playing on 'Night Circus' that makes one think of the player-piano pieces of Conlon Nancarrow, but this is eliminated on the remarkable 'Time For Intensity', a more richly coloured pair of contrasting pieces, the second of which, 'Webs And Whirlpools', must be one of the most purely astonishing piano performances of all time.

In contrast to these, the duos with Evan Parker are almost conventional, conforming to the basic idiomatic conventions of improvised music. Nevertheless there is a scope to 'The Fire Tale', a piece about the survival and extinction of creativity, and to 'Red Desert', which Bergman has recorded before, for which only classical parallels effectively apply. If some of the solo pieces are symphonic, the duos have to be heard as bizarre concertos in which the element of contention has once again taken over from simple concord.

The disc with Cyrille is both exhilarating and exhausting. Framed by two approaches to the title-theme and, more surprisingly, two takes of 'Chasin' The Trane' (why didn't he record that with Parker?), it is both visceral and intellectually challenging. 'Red Shadows' reappears from the earlier record, and Bergman enthusiasts must already be aware how doggedly and self-critically he pursues certain ideas. Even with Cyrille in harness, Ayler might perhaps be a more accurate analogy than Taylor, though for sheer thump there's not much in it.

Even given the variety of the foregoing, what a complete surprise *First Meeting* is. Coming to it with expectations based on the earlier records, on some knowledge of Mitchell's fierce saxophone poetry, or simply on reputation, one is astonished by the delicacy and precision, the sheer *quietness* of these pieces. 'Clear Blue' particularly has a limpid quality, as if every note had been gently diluted in water before being exposed to the air. Mitchell's breath-sounds are often louder than the actual reed-notes. Thomas Buckner was there as producer only, but it was decided that he should take part, and he did so, unrehearsed, on the suite, 'One Mind', bringing a further dimension to a riveting, gentle and perfectly centred hour of creative music.

*** Reflections On Ornette Coleman And The Stone House

Soul Note 121280 *Bergman; Hamid Drake (d).* 95.

Ornette bid farewell to the piano early in his career, not finally, but to all intents and purposes. So Bergman's appropriation of these Coleman themes is both challenging and wilfully perverse. Drake is the natural successor to Ed Blackwell and so is completely at ease on long explorations of 'Focus On Sanity' and 'Lonely Woman', the two pieces that open the album and are its most successful reworkings. Bergman's tendency to envelop themes in vast curtains of sound is less evident here than on some projects and Drake has the ability to keep the texture open and flowing.

**** Eight By Three

Mixtery M00001 *Bergman; Anthony Braxton, Peter Brötzmann (reeds).* 4/96.

*** Exhilaration

Soul Note 121330 *Bergman; Peter Brötzmann (as); Andrew Cyrille (d).* 9/96, 1/97.

*** Ride Into The Blue

Konnex 5069 *Bergman; Peter Brötzmann (as, tarogato); Thomas Borgmann (ts).* 96.

*** Blue Zoo

Konnex 5074 *As above.* 96.

Exhilaration consists of four stunning trio tracks and a further duo session with Bergman and Brötzmann, all recorded at the Knitting Factory. If the prevailing mood is exhilaration as in the first item, then it's of a particularly hectic and troubled sort. Bergman goes off like an express train, leaving nothing but sparks and cinders in his wake, and more or less abandoning Cyrille and even the normally sanguine Brötzmann standing in their tracks. Later tracks are quieter and more reserved, and with much more attention to structure. For the most part, though, this is a headlong set that demands much of the listener.

The set with Braxton is measured, cool and almost alien in its absence of expressionist dramas. The balance of two horns and piano is a hard one to sustain at length, but Bergman is a caustic enough player not to be troubled by it. They try the same formula, one that obviously appeals to Bergman, on *Ride Into The Blue* and *Blue Zoo.* What's increasingly evident about the pianist is that he is not just a powerhouse with a radically expanded technique but also a delicate player who uses silence effectively and knows when to drop either hand from the mix. Brötzmann has a similar PR problem, which is why critics still register surprise whenever he plays something softly or with warmth; check the discography and it's always been there. Borgmann is probably the weak link, but only because one constantly strains to hear what is going on between Brötzmann and Bergman.

*** Toronto 1997

Boxholder BXH 033 *Bergman; Thomas Chapin (sax, f).* 97.

There was something in the air at this remarkable meeting of two very different musicians whose careers have gone radically different ways. Bergman has only become a star later in life; Chapin's star was snuffed out less than a year after this recording, a victim of leukaemia. Unusually – though a more meditative strain runs through all of Bergman's work, even the most turbulent – the pianist almost acts as accompanist here, leaving the louder and edgier playing to Chapin, who was rarely heard in this free context with his own groups. Chapin's multiphonics anticipate the extreme chromaticism of Bergman's playing, where almost any note seems the basis for some new vertical alignment. This isn't the most comfortable listen, but as a record of two important musicians, one now gone, one only slowly being assimilated, it is of immense value.

***** A New Organization**

Soul Note 121322 2 *Bergman; Oliver Lake (as).* 99.

Recorded live at the Knitting Factory, this is a fascinating encounter between two very different avant-gardists who have drawn on different and opposite aspects of twentieth-century music. Whether their work does represent a further step towards a new organization of musical language is more questionable, because much of this sounds like basic improv, stripped of its more schematic and abstract qualities. The intensity of 'I Kiss Your Eyes' and 'Forever Fervent' is not just a function of their titles, but something genuinely residing in the music, which toys with major–minor oppositions and slithers in and out of polytonality but which ultimately depends on melody, and melody alone, for its impact.

****** The River Of Sounds**

Boxholder 024 *Bergman; Conrad Bauer (tb); Mat Maneri (vn).* 5/00.

There is a strange, poetic programme behind this astonishing record though, by this stage in his career, the words 'Bergman' and 'astonishing' are securely welded. The main characters, 'Spindell Kresge', 'Jim' and 'The Blond Woman', are presented in long passages dominated by microtones, free-form passages and sudden incursions of what sound like composed material. 'The Blond Woman' is more or less a duet for fiddle and piano and has a kind of cracked romanticism.

The instrumentation is fabulously rich, with Maneri's six-string electric violin providing a whole range of tone-colours and harmonic variations. While the piano is firmly locked into the Western scale, the presence of two inherently microtonal instruments allows Bergman to develop his musical language in the most sympathetic of surroundings. A very fine record from an increasingly important figure.

***** The Italian Concert**

Soul Note 121342 *Bergman; Roscoe Mitchell (ss, as).*

Obviously the major points of comparison are the duos with Lake and Chapin. Mitchell's output is so small relative to his enormous importance that any appearance places the attention squarely on his sharp reed sound. Except here, where Bergman all but overwhelms him with huge, rolling figures, dense chords and Cowell-like clusters. The two long opening pieces almost exhaust Mitchell's input and one gets the feeling that on some of the later, shorter tracks, he is unwilling to follow Bergman or unable to penetrate his densely layered sound.

*****(*) Meditations For Piano**

Tzadik TZ7180 *Bergman (p solo).* 01.

***** Double Idea**

Boxholder 024 *As above.* 02.

Bergman's solo work remains the key to his art. He is such a massively dominant player that he threatens to overwhelm playing partners and sometimes his own ideas with sheer volume of sound. That is why the Tzadik set, consisting of quieter and more reflective pieces, is such a revelation. Bergman still gets the same richness and intensity of sound, a mixture of solid attack and clever use of pedals, but he also brings in a keening, almost elegiac quality that is immensely attractive. Indeed, as the album progresses toward the tiny final 'Meditation', his approach to the keyboard becomes ever sparer, with no gratuitous embellishment. Suddenly, the Ornette Coleman record of some years back starts to make more sense.

Jerry Bergonzi (born 1947)

TENOR AND SOPRANO SAXOPHONES

A Bostonian, Bergonzi studied at Berklee and went to New York in the early '70s, spending a period in the Dave Brubeck group, before returning home in 1981 to teach and play.

****(*) Jerry On Red**

Red 123224 *Bergonzi; Salvatore Bonafede (p); Dodo Goya (b); Salvatore Tranchini (d).* 5/88.

***** Inside Out**

Red 123230-2 *As above, except Bruce Gertz (b) replaces Goya.*

****(*) Lineage**

Red 123237 *Bergonzi; Mulgrew Miller (p); Dave Santoro (b); Adam Nussbaum (d).* 10/89.

***** Tilt**

Red 123245-2 *Bergonzi; Andy LaVerne, Salvatore Bonafede (p); Bruce Gertz (b); Salvatore Tranchini (d).* 5/90.

Bergonzi already had many years in jazz behind him before he made these dates; a quartet from 1983 on the Plug label is worth seeking out as a vinyl rarity. The Red albums may disappoint those who've heard him in more excellent sideman situations, but the studio sound doesn't flatter him and we still find these to be unrepresentative of his talents. From moment to moment the records impress, but there isn't enough to make one much want to return. None of these is truly outstanding, and Bergonzi's harshness and false-register cries are often more ugly than powerful. *Lineage* keeps up a high level of energy and inventiveness on its own terms. The best records, though, are *Inside Out* and *Tilt*. Gertz and Tranchini create a solid foundation with few distractions, and Bergonzi's rather spare writing works best in this context. 'Jones', from *Tilt*, makes the most of its simple bass motif, and the other tunes provide just enough material to keep the long, dissonant tenor solos on a particular track.

***** Etc Plus One**

Red 123249-2 *Bergonzi; Fred Hersch (p); Steve LaSpina (b); Jeff Hirshfield (d).* 3/91.

***** Peek A Boo**

Evidence 22119 *Bergonzi; Tiger Okoshi (t, flhn); Joachim Kühn (p); Dave Santoro (b); Daniel Humair (d).* 10/92.

Bergonzi's records have been growing in stature. *Etc Plus One* documents his meeting with Fred Hersch's trio, the pianist's elegance of line a shrewd counter to the saxophonist's spilling energy and hard sound. The result is a record that tends to drift between sensibilities, interesting if never quite compelling, and there are probably a few tracks where an extra take could have secured a higher result.

Peek A Boo is more conventional. Bergonzi's command of the horn is one of the striking qualities here, and the expertise of this quintet can be enjoyed by itself, though again nothing in the set really stands out as unmissable.

***** Just Within**

Double-Time DTRCD 127 *Bergonzi; Dan Wall (org); Adam Nussbaum (d).* 12/96.

*****(*) Lost In The Shuffle**

Double-Time DTRCD-142 *As above.* 1/98.

The Double-Time discs document a fruitful partnership with Wall – whose second-banana status to many a frontman can make one miss how good he is – and the skilful Nussbaum. Nothing like an old-time bluesologist on the Hammond, Wall plays with no shortage of guts but the harmonic shading and soft melodic fills are a necessary counterweight to a musician like Bergonzi. Nussbaum is big and brawny at the kit, and the music has a quality of inexorable forward motion to go with the thoughtful aspects. Both of these dates are meritorious, and the second is that bit more expansive and substantial.

***(*) Wiggy

Double-Time DTRCD-173 *As above.* 8/99.

***(*) A Different Look

Double-Time DTRCD-184 *As above.* 8/99.

In a world of soundalike tenors, Jerry Bergonzi expresses himself. The curious paraphrase of the 'Just In Time' melody lets the unwary know from the start that this isn't a typical tenor–organ date. The third in this trio's sequence is a very, very good set. Bergonzi has sometimes been a problem to catch right in the studios, but the full range of his tone and execution are truthfully exposed here, and his admiration for Rollins features strongly (and to his advantage) in every track. 'Channeling', which ends unexpectedly on a fade, is a superb workout, while the following ballad 'Committed' manages to be both hushed and intense. Wall and Nussbaum follow the leader with complete understanding.

A Different Look is basically leftovers from the same session, but there's nothing second-rate, just more excellent playing on fertile material. A cooker like 'Con Brio' is exciting, but perhaps it's on the more restrained pieces such as the 3/4 'You Can Tell' that the trio's musicality really impresses.

*** Live Gonz!

Double-Time DTRCD-190 *Bergonzi; Renato Chicco (p); Dave Santoro (b); Andrea Michelutti (d).* n.d.

A recent (though undated) set from a French club gig, this finds Gonz in spirited form. He blazes through a scarcely recognizable 'Have You Met Miss Jones' and plays a thoughtfully intricate solo on his own 'Different Places Together'. Next to the studio trio dates, though, this is more routine, with unexceptional support from the rhythm section and the curious difficulty of catching his sound just right left unsolved.

***(*) Dreaming Out Loud

Whaling City Sound WCS 020 *Bergonzi; Bruce Gertz (b); Bob Kaufman (d).* n.d.

Bergonzi seems ideally suited by the trio format, and this grouping settles him into music which is coming to personify a style more personal than one would have guessed from the records of a decade and more ago: oblique, melodious but many-noted, hookless – Bergonzi's writing is based around intervallic techniques – and with the dynamics very spaciously spread, the music sounds muscular but soft, or pliable. No phrases are barked out, and even when he goes into something like a false register, it feels like a fluent transition. It's akin to a Tristanoite approach, though at the same time nothing much like it. Gertz and Kaufman play with splendid accord. A kind of jazz which is unlikely to appeal to many tastes, but he's certainly asserting an individual approach.

Gunnar Bergsten

BARITONE SAXOPHONE

Swedish baritone saxophonist, a Mulligan man from a younger generation.

***(*) The Good Life

Arietta ADCD 5 *Bergsten; Peter Nordahl (p); Patrik Boman (b); Rune Carlsson (d).* 6/95.

***(*) Somewhere

Arietta ADCD 17 *As above, except Leif Wennerstrom (d) replaces Carlsson.* 1/98.

Gullin, Mulligan, Chaloff, Carney: Bergsten belongs in the highest company that this low instrument has kept. His light-bodied sound allows him a mobility which the big horn needs to get around a ballad without making it seem overweight and, while he prefers a steady mid-tempo, a quicker pace here and there gives him no difficulties. Listen to what he does with the old Gene Ammons chestnut, 'Ca Purange', on *Somewhere*: every idea is extracted from the theme, still kept in sight, but by the end Bergsten has been on a long and masterfully navigated voyage. 'Ask Me Now' on *The Good Life* is that rarity, a Monk interpretation which has little of Monk about it and a great deal of its interpreter. This is unambitious music in the way of its delivery – Bergsten pretends to nothing revolutionary, any more than the excellent Nordahl does – but in terms of poise and generosity these are wonderfully playable records.

**** Play Lars Gullin

Proprius PRCD 2001-06-29 *Bergsten; Peter Nordahl (p).* 1/00.

Paying homage to Lars Gullin's music is, perhaps, almost a matter of duty for Swedish jazz players, but it's surely never been approached with as much tenderness and insight as here. Bergsten is both like and unlike the master: while he seldom goes for the power-in-reserve drive which fuelled Gullin's improvising, he has the same failsafe fluency in his melodic thinking. Elaborating on these lovely themes comes as easily to him as reciting them. Not that this is one of those occasions where the material is merely a prop for the solos. Both men take the texts as a matter of profound importance, with only the sparest and most tactful embellishment allowed.

The result is a record that has one musing quietly on the achievements of Gullin the composer. While some of these pieces were inflated into much grander situations for bigger ensembles, two pairs of hands distil them with no sense of diminution. 'Primavera', which we know better as 'Manchester Fog', is a slice of loneliness which is as bittersweet as anything in the jazz book. Conversely, the sly 'Mazurka' is a vehicle for humorous banter which the two men handle impeccably. 'I've Seen' is as close to perfection as any duet can get, every gesture aptly answered, every direction beautifully resolved. Nordahl refuses to overplay, but he's a full partner in these pieces, and in the roving cadences of 'Fine Together' he's magnificent.

Bunny Berigan (1908–42)

TRUMPET

He had college-band experience behind him when he joined Fred Rich in 1931, then Paul Whiteman, though he disliked the music and took every chance at a hot solo on a studio session.

He was a big hit with Benny Goodman – and, later, Tommy Dorsey – but his own big bands were commercial disasters and he had to fight off bankruptcy. His greatest playing – with its huge sound, fascination with the low register and swinging poise – could cut most other players of his time, but chronic alcoholism and depression destroyed him, and he died in 1942.

***** Portrait Of Bunny Berigan**

ASV Living Era AJACD 5060 *Berigan; Nate Kazebier, Joe Aguanno, John Fallstitch, Irving Goodman, George Johnston, Steve Lipkins, Ralph Muzillo, Jerry Neary, Charlie Spivak, Jimmy Welch, Carl Warwick, Joe Bauer, Bob Cusumano, Johnny Napton (t); Glenn Miller, Morey Samuel, Red Ballard, Jack Lacy, Marc Pasco, Al Jennings, Ray Conniff, Bob Jenny, Tommy Dorsey, Red Bone, Al George, Sonny Lee, Les Jenkins (tb); Johnny Mintz, Matty Matlock, Benny Goodman (cl); Fred Stulce, Clyde Rounds, Henry Saltman, Toots Mondello, Hymie Schertzer, Charlie DiMaggio, Jack Goldie (as); Gus Bivona, Murray Williams, Sid Pearlmutter, Joe Dixon (cl, as); Eddie Miller (cl, ts); Bud Freeman, Georgie Auld, Dick Jones, Don Lodice, Harry Walsh, Arthur Rollini, Dick Clark, Stewart Anderson (ts); Frank Froeba, Joe Lippman, Claude Thornhill, Fats Waller, Edwin Ross, Joe Bushkin (p); Eddie Condon, Larry Hall, Dick McDonough, Carmen Mastren, Tommy Moore, Tom Morgan, George Van Eps, Dick Wharton, Allan Reuss (g); Harry Goodman, Arnold Fishkind, Delmar Kaplan, Grachan Moncur, Pete Peterson, Mort Stuhlmaker, Gene Traxler, Hank Wayland (b); Ray Bauduc, Cozy Cole, Paul Collins, Eddie Jenkins, Gene Krupa, Dave Tough, George Wettling (d); Wingy Manone, Jack Leonard (v); Paul Hamilton and His Orchestra; Frankie Trumbauer and His Orchestra* 32–37.

*****(*) Bunny Berigan 1935–1936**

Classics 734 *Berigan; Jack Lacey (tb); Joe Marsala, Slats Long, Artie Shaw, Paul Ricci (cl); Edgar Sampson (cl, as); Eddie Miller (cl, ts); Forrest Crawford, Art Drelinger, Bud Freeman, Herbie Haymer (ts); Joe Bushkin, Frank Froeba, Cliff Jackson (p); Dave Barbour, Bobby Bennett, Eddie Condon, Clayton Duerr (g); Artie Bernstein, Artie Shapiro, Mort Stuhlmaker, Grachan Moncur (b); Ray Bauduc, Maurice Purtill, Cozy Cole, Dave Tough (d); Chick Bullock, Tempo King, Midge Williams (v).* 12/35–8/36.

*****(*) Bunny Berigan 1936–1937**

Classics 749 *Berigan; Irving Goodman, Harry Greenwald, L. Brown, Cliff Natalie, Steve Lipkins (t); Morey Samuel, Sonny Lee, Frank D'Annolfo, Ford Leary, Red Jessup (tb); Matty Matlock (cl); Sid Pearlmutter, Joe Dixon, Slats Long, Henry Freling (cl, as); Toots Mondello, Hymie Schertzer (as); Artie Drelinger, Babe Russin, Clyde Rounds, Georgie Auld (ts); Joe Bushkin, Les Burness, Joe Lippman (p); Eddie Condon, Tom Morgan (g); Arnold Fishkind, Mort Stuhlmaker (b); Manny Berger, George Wettling (d); Art Gentry, Ruth Bradley, Johnny Hauser, Carol McKay, Sue Mitchell (v).* 11/36–6/37.

****** Bunny Berigan 1937**

Classics 766 *Berigan; Irving Goodman, Steve Lipkins (t); Morey Samuel, Sonny Lee, Al George (tb); Mike Doty, Sid Pearlmutter, Joe Dixon (cl, as); Clyde Rounds, Georgie Auld (ts); Joe Lippman (p); Tom Morgan (g); Arnold Fishkind, Hank Wayland (b); George Wettling (d); Ruth Bradley, Gail Reese (v).* 6–12/37.

****** Bunny Berigan 1937–1938**

Classics 785 *As above, except add Ray Conniff, Nat Lobovsky (tb), Graham Forbes, Fulton McGrath (p), Dick Wharton (g), Dave Tough (d), Ruth Gaylor (v).* 12/37–5/38.

*****(*) Bunny Berigan 1938**

Classics 815 *As above, except add John Napton (t), George Bohn, Gus Bivona, Milton Schatz, Murray Williams (cl, as), Buddy Rich (d), Jayne Dover, Kitty Lane, Bernie Mackey (v).* 6–11/38.

***** Gangbusters**

Hep CD 1036 *Berigan; Steve Lipkins, Irving Goodman, George Johnston, Jack Koven, Johnny Napton (t); Nat Lobovsky, Ray Conniff, Bob Jenney, Andy Russo (tb); Gigi Bohn, Milton Schatz, Hank Saltman, Murray Williams (as); Gus Bivona (cl, as); Georgie Auld, Don Lodice (ts); Clyde Rounds, Larry Walsh (ts, bs); Joe Bushkin (p); Dick Wharton, Allan Reuss (g); Hank Wayland (b); Eddie Jenkins, Buddy Rich (d); Jayne Dover, Kitty Lane, Bernie Mackey (v).* 9/38–3/39.

***** Bunny Berigan 1938–1942**

Classics 844 *Berigan; Joe Aguanno, John Fallstitch, Irving Goodman, Bobby Mansell, Arthur Mellor, Johnny Napton, Freddy Norton, Jack Koven, George Johnston, Carl Warwick (t); Ray Conniff, Max Smith, Charlie Stewart, Mark Pasco, Al Jennings, Bob Jenny (tb); Gus Bivona, Charlie DiMaggio, Jack Goldie, Henry Saltman, Walt Mellor, George Quinty, Murray Williams (cl, as); Georgie Auld, Stewart Anderson, Don Lodice, Neil Smith, Red Lang, Larry Walsh (ts); Joe Bushkin, Eugene Kutch, Edwin Ross (p); Tommy Moore, Allan Reuss (g); Mort Stuhlmaker, Tony Estren, Hank Wayland (b); Paul Collins, Eddie Jenkins, Buddy Rich, Jack Sperling (d); Kathleen Long, Danny Richards, Nita Sharon (v).* 1/38–1/42.

Bunny Berigan's only flaw, in Louis Armstrong's opinion, was that he didn't live long enough. At the height of his career as an independent bandleader he was making impossible demands on an uncertain constitution. As a leader, he could be wildly exciting or beautifully lyrical, cutting solos like those on the concerto-like signature-piece, 'I Can't Get Started' (there are two versions, but the 1937 one is the classic); he was always one of the boys in the band but was utterly inept as an organizer. Stints with disciplinarians like Goodman and Tommy Dorsey (who valued his genius too much to pitch him out) didn't change his ways.

Though he died prematurely burnt out, Berigan left a legacy of wonderful music. The ASV Living Era package is good, but converts will certainly want the Classics documentation in full. Berigan's tone was huge and 'fat', a far cry from the tinny squawk with which he started out. Typical devices are his use of 'ghost' notes and rapid chromatic runs that inject a degree of tension into music that, on his most commercial dates, often sounds ready to fall asleep.

By contrast, the small groups anthologized on the first Classics volume are sparky, tight and wholly inventive. Chick Bullock's vocals are no great asset, except on those occasions when they give Berigan the chance to mimic his singer's phrasing. The disc also includes six tracks under Frank Froeba's leadership and featuring Midge Williams, who later went on to make her own records. Pretty obscure stuff, this, but worth having for Berigan's buoyant fills.

That Berigan's time-sense and ability to play instant counter-melodies were God-given there is no doubt, but it's also clear that he studied Armstrong closely and learned a great deal from him. That's evident from the solos on 'Sing! Sing! Sing!' and 'On Your Toes'. The second volume continues with the June 1938 sessions and kicks off with the best track yet, a rousing 'Shanghai Shuffle' with Auld and Dixon bracketing Berigan himself; Dixon returns for another couple of choruses on alto at the end. Ray Conniff is featured on 'I Never Knew (I Could Love Anybody)', but it's not so much the solos that stand out as the section playing which often sounds like a much bigger band, yet is also marvellously detailed.

The Hep set is also an excellent buy. It offers a detailed documentation of autumn 1938, which must be considered a final peak before Berigan's financial and alcoholic slide of the following year. There is a substantial mythology attached to Berigan's drinking. Looking at the 1938 recording schedule suggests he may have been as much a workaholic as an alcoholic. The falling away, perfectly evident on the final Classics volume, was doubtless tragic, but it came after a period of sustained excellence, a body of work attained by few who lived twice as long. The high point, undoubtedly, came in 1937 and 1938, and serious enthusiasts should make the relevant Classics volumes their priority. Long for its time at four minutes and forty seconds, 'I Can't Get Started' is exemplary jazz playing, with that mix of sheer bravura and pathos that was Berigan's signature. His solo on 'The Wearin' Of The Green' on the 1937–8 volume is a nod to Irish ancestry, blustering and demonstrative, but also touchingly guileless. Berigan's ability to sustain power throughout his impressive range was one of his most durable characteristics, and he retains the ability to say more in fewer notes than any of his rivals. His development is logical, and impressively simple; he tackles 'Russian Lullaby' without the onion-y emotion most players of the time brought to Irving Berlin's tune, and his deep-toned solo on 'A Serenade To The Stars' is as moving as trumpet gets before Miles Davis came along. These days, certainly among younger listeners and recent jazz converts, Berigan is little known. He should, rather, be remembered and heard as one of the great hornmen in the music. Almost any of the above discs will provide the evidence.

David Berkman

PIANO

Pianist and composer at work in today's New York jazz community, though originally from Cleveland.

****** Communication Theory**
Palmetto PM 2059 *Berkman; Sam Newsome (ss); Steve Wilson (as, ss); Chris Cheek (ts, ss); Ugonna Okegwo (b); Brian Blade (d).* 1/00.

*****(*) Leaving Home**
Palmetto PM 2078 *As above, except Dick Oatts (as) replaces Wilson.* 9/01.

The brilliant *Communication Theory* immediately establishes Berkman as a composer of substance. 'Every original tune of mine is supposed to put the band into some space, some zone,' he's said, and rather than working from standards and their prefigured areas of expectation, he's fashioned interesting settings which give the players something new to work with. The miracle is that little or nothing here is obtuse, obscurantist or drearily unmelodic, in the unfortunate modern way. Without going into a track-by-track account, unmissable are the blues regeneration of 'Blutocracy', the unexpected harmonizing of the horns in 'Colby' and the nouveau nostalgia of 'Back In The 90's', which manages the impossible by turning Branford Marsalis into an influence. It helps that he gets terrific performances out of a great team, but his own playing is no composer-on-the-bench fill-in.

The follow-up misses some of the lightness of the earlier set, though one reason may be the circumstances of the recording (it took place on the two days following certain events in New York in September 2001). Still, there's a greater ratio of slower pieces. Where Berkman scores again is his sense of economy; solos are contained within supportive, evolving structures and existentialism is discouraged. At the end, he gives himself the luxury of 'Embraceable You', though it's played at a pace somewhere below slow motion.

***** Start Here, Finish There**
Palmetto PM 2098 *Berkman; Dick Oatts (ss, as); Ugonna Okegwo (b); Nasheet Waits (d).* 9/03.

This is now Berkman's regular quartet, of two years' standing, and live performances of this material early in 2004 sounded terrific. The CD emerges at a lower voltage, although that's partly through a curious choice of track order, which places the more downcast material in such a way as to give it undue prominence. Pick out the more vital-sounding tracks, such as 'Penultimatum', and the group persist at Berkman's high standard. Pared back to a quartet, the group misses some of the richness of the earlier sets, and perhaps sounds more conventional too – but it's still quite a band. Oatts, formerly considered mostly as a cut-and-dried bebop man, is pushed into areas which – as on 'Old Forks' – he delights in exploring.

Berlin Contemporary Jazz Orchestra

GROUP

The name tells the story, although this is only a very 'occasional' ensemble, with its participants usually busy with other matters.

****** Berlin Contemporary Jazz Orchestra**
ECM 841777-2 *Benny Bailey, Thomas Heberer, Henry Lowther (t); Kenny Wheeler (t, flhn); Henning Berg, Hermann Breuer, Hubert Katzenbeier (tb); Ute Zimmermann (btb); Paul Van Kamenade, Felix Wahnschaffe (as); Gerd Dudek (ts, ss, cl, f); Walter Gauchel (ts); Ernst Ludwig Petrowsky (bs); Willem Breuker (bs, bcl); Misha Mengelberg, Aki Takase (p); Günter Lenz (b); Ed Thigpen (d); Alexander von Schlippenbach (cond).* 5/89.

Much as Barry Guy's London Jazz Composers Orchestra has turned in recent years to large-scale composition, the Berlin Contemporary Jazz Orchestra presented its conductor/organizer with a more formal and structured resource for presentation of large-scale scored pieces with marked tempi for improvising orchestra. One outwardly surprising inclusion in the line-up is drummer Ed Thigpen, normally associated with conventional mainstream jazz. This superb set features one long piece by Canadian trumpeter Kenny Wheeler and two rather less melancholy pieces by Misha Mengelberg. Wheeler's 'Ana' is a long, almost hymnic piece whose mournful aspect nevertheless doesn't soften some powerful soloing; Thomas Heberer, Aki Takase and Gerd Dudek are just the most notable contributors, and the piece is held together as much by Thigpen's robust swing as by Wheeler's detailed score. Mengelberg's

'Reef Und Kneebus' and 'Salz' are very much in the line of a post-war Dutch style in which jazz is almost as dominant an element as serial procedures. Mengelberg's music is frequently satirical, then unexpectedly melancholy. Benny Bailey's bursting solo on 'Salz' prepares the way for some determined overblowing on the second piece, which fits jazz themes into a 'Minuet', 'Rigaudon', 'Bourrée' matrix. (If the middle element is less familiar, it relates to another seventeenth-century danceform with a sharp rhythmic hop at the opening and a central bridge passage which sharply changes the direction of both music and dancers. Of such turns are both of Mengelberg's compositions made.) Outstanding solos from Dudek again and van Kamenade, while, on 'Salz', Breuker almost matches Bailey for sheer brass – or, in this case, woodwind. Thoroughly enjoyable and thought-provoking music.

Tim Berne (born 1954)

ALTO AND BARITONE SAXOPHONES, VOICE

Berne is never going to be considered one of the great instrumentalists of modern jazz, but his dogged self-determination and application to a starkly challenging idiom commend him as an experimenter who would surely have found a willing berth in the loft scene of the '60s. He is devoted to the music and the earthly philosophy of Julius Hemphill, a challenging guru for any musician.

*** Empire Box

Screwgun no number 5 CD *Berne; Olu Dara (c); Glenn Ferris, James Harvey, John Rapson (tb); John Carter (cl); Vinny Golia (bs, picc, f, afl, bsn, khene); Mark Goldsbury (ss, ts); Nels Cline (g); John Lindberg, Roberto Miranda, Ed Schuller (b); Alex Cline (d).* 79–82.

Tim Berne called his first album *The Five Year Plan*. He released it himself, apparently unwilling to wait around for the bigger labels to get their heads together and totally unwilling to spend five or ten years hacking it as a sideman. *Empire Box* is a release on Berne's own label and it brings together the records he released as an unsigned independent between 1979 and 1982. This was a raw and in some respects unfocused period in Berne's development, and listening to these records after a gap of some years suggests a stash of rehearsal and workshop tapes that wouldn't otherwise have seen the light of day. This is not to decry them, because by 1979 genuine experimentation was at an appallingly low ebb in jazz. Berne's first release begins with a piece dedicated to Hemphill on his intense, squalling alto; it's a sound that was not to change significantly over the next couple of years. The Cline brothers were to be responsive partners, and Vinny Golia, a deft and clever instrumentalist, fills in a lot of ground that Berne himself is unable to cover technically. The material on *7X* was smoother and more harmonically centred, with trombone and guitar combining to give Berne's sour-toned forays a more settled foundation. The last of the bunch, *Songs And Rituals In Real Time*, was stripped down – just two saxophones, bass and drums – but our favourite remains the 1981 *Spectres*, with its three-horn front line and stunningly inventive rhythm section of Alex Cline and either Ed Schuller or John Lindberg on bass.

Heard in bulk and after a lapse of more than 20 (!) years, some of this sounds unbearably callow, and it might have been better to have filleted out a double CD of the strongest material – say 'The Glasco Cowboy' (that Hemphill posy from the debut disc), '7X' and 'Flies' from the second record, 'Grendel' and 'Stroll' from *Spectres*, and maybe the hugely ambitious 'The Ancient Ones' from *Songs And Rituals*. These, though, are subjective preferences and could change by tomorrow morning. Whatever, this reissue is too exhaustive to be entirely compelling.

*** The Ancestors

Soul Note 121061 *Berne; Herb Robertson (t, pkt-t, c, flhn); Ray Anderson (tb, tba); Mack Goldsbury (ts, ss); Ed Schuller (b); Paul Motian (d, perc).* 2/83.

*** Mutant Variations

Soul Note 121091 *As above, except omit Anderson, Goldsbury.* 3/83.

*** Fulton Street Maul

Koch Jazz 7826 *Berne; Bill Frisell (g); Hank Roberts (clo, v); Alex Cline (perc, v).* 86.

*** Sanctified Dreams

Koch 7825 *Berne; Herb Robertson (t, pkt-t, flhn, c); Hank Roberts (clo, v); Mark Dresser (b); Joey Baron (d).* 10/87.

The Ancestors was a first sign that Berne was willing to slow down, look about him and take stock. Recorded live, it's a measured, authoritative set, rhythmically more coherent than previous and later sessions, with passages of almost Asiatic beauty from Berne and some classic trombone from the developing Anderson. Berne's charts are increasingly adventurous, and ensemble passages are well played and registered in a typically professional Soul Note production. The set's coherence might be credited to the veteran Motian – he takes a fine solo on one piece and holds together the excellent *Mutant Variations*, with its leaner, punchier line-up – who makes an effective rhythmic anchor with Schuller, a veteran of Berne albums.

Bizarrely, Berne was signed to Columbia in the mid-'80s – which was either a stroke of creative generosity on the corporation's part or a wooden horse operation, or a simple mistake. Certainly, the saxophonist does not appear to bow to major-label pressure, and he delivers a tough, antagonistic set that even after 15 years has a sandbagging power and thuggish authority. Like the leader, Frisell doesn't know his own strength. A bold reissue for Koch, which has rescued some valuable recordings over the last couple of years, though none as uncompromising as this.

Sanctified Dreams was originally released on Columbia in 1988, but as at various stages in his career Berne has regained control of the material and seen it reissued. After a decade it still sounds fresh, if a touch crude and over-eager, though that must be accounted a description rather than a criticism of what Berne does. The key players here are Robertson and Baron, always forthright when they appear, but relishing this setting and turning in career-best performances which make up for an occasionally lacklustre showing by the leader, who is also maddeningly, even perversely, inconsistent.

*** Fractured Fairy Tales

Winter & Winter 919030 *Berne; Herb Robertson (t, laryngeal crowbar); Hank Roberts (clo, elec); Mark Dresser (b, diffus, bungy); Joey Baron (d, elec).* 6/89.

*** Pace Yourself

Winter & Winter 919040 *Berne; Herb Robertson (t); Steve Swell (tb); Marc Ducret (g); Mark Dresser (b); Bobby Previte (d).* 11/90.

Originally released on the now-vanished JMT, the first of these reads and listens like a spoof on the 'little instruments' aesthetic of early AACM dates. It's an impression cemented by Berne's fleeting resemblance on alto to Anthony Braxton: the same sourish tone and fractured bop. Robertson's trumpet is the other key element, but it's his 'laryngeal crowbar' which leads off an impressive armoury of unusual 'instruments'. Others are Baron's low-budget 'Shacktronics' and Dresser's 'diffus' and 'bungy'. As he was to do later, Berne segues together compositions into longer and longer forms and again the obvious parallel is Braxton's palimpsests where he blends different compositions into a single piece. The difference is that Berne does it consecutively rather than simultaneously. Here, 'Hong Kong Sad Song' and 'More Coffee' are yoked together, dominating an album that starts relatively quietly and becomes more anarchic and surreal as it progresses.

The Caos Totale group was one of many Berne outfits of the period, a habit of named bands which has continued to the present. The trumpeter is a joy again, sounding like some big band player of the '40s just out of Bellevue. Robertson's use of mute is as far from Miles's soft rasp as you'll hear; instead, big, blaring figures that are almost comic in effect until you unpack their virtuosic components. Dresser is also fundamental to the group, but this time round it's Ducret who takes over Roberts' role and ties together the different elements, leaving the bass to go its own way. The opening 'Bass Voodoo', one of six relatively short pieces on the set, is a sign that the lower registers are important here. Berne's later use of baritone, not yet part of his bag, is anticipated throughout these tracks. Two fine, exhausting records; welcome back.

*** Unwound

Screwgun SCREW U 70001 3CD *Berne; Chris Speed (ts, cl); Michael Formanek (b); Jim Black (d).* 3–4/96.

With the demise of JMT, Berne was once again thrown back on his own resources. He formed Screwgun and with this unvarnished live recording kicked off his own imprint. The performances, from Berlin and Ann Arbor, are raw, immediate and proudly unproduced, long versions of things like 'Blood Count' and 'What Are The Odds?', which on its own would have occupied the whole of an old-fashioned LP. Berne seems determined to go for the jugular with every tune, blazing away with an indiscriminate ferocity that alienates and attracts in equal proportion. Black is astonishingly good, clattering and riffing in a manner that suggests Joey Baron crossed with some fallen angel of percussion. Speed keeps his end up … just, but really isn't either passionate or charismatic enough for the material. Most of the attention is focused on the leader; never a virtuosic player, never a man who can move with a beautiful tone or a graceful phrase, he relies on a hectoring, abrasive sound that is less lovely than it is forceful.

*** Please Advise

Screwgun SCREW U 70001 *Berne; Drew Gress (b); Tom Rainey (d).* 96.

***(*) Visitation Rites

Screwgun SCREW U 70002 *As above.* 96.

Sample five large, raw slabs of music, one composition by each of the three players, packaged with ugly artwork and unreadable texts, and still find yourself drawn in by Berne's other group of the moment. This is the group he calls Paraphrase. Whether that's the approach to written material he encourages isn't clear, but certainly there is nothing literal or one-dimensional about the attacks. *Please Advise* is just two long tracks, recorded live and furiously focused from start to finish. Rainey plays almost like a rock drummer in places, sounding as if he might – duh! – be feigning a brainless thud through the chart but actually keeping it very tightly and demandingly on the brink of breakdown. Gress is the anchor man, hinting at harmonies, solidifying the beat but never succumbing to regular metre. 'Piano Justice' is the longest piece on *Visitation Rites*, a peculiar, almost perverse agglomeration of ideas. Rainey and Gress are heroic, making the best of what sounds like an unpromising acoustic and an unyielding crowd. Berne remains oblivious to everything except his own soapbox rant. It isn't pretty, but isn't it compulsive?

*** Big Satan

Winter & Winter 910 005 *Berne; Marc Ducret (g); Tom Rainey (d).* 5/96.

Much less rough and raw than the live sets on Screwgun – this was also recorded in concert, at *Instants chavires* in Montreuil – but music of relentless violence all the same. The closing 'Description Du Tunnel' is one of the most unrelieved pieces Berne has ever recorded. 'Dialectes' and 'Yes, Dear' are more subtle, the latter perhaps intended as some sort of nod in the direction of Thelonious Monk. Ducret emerges as the hero of the session, playing with a rare intensity, but subtilizing some of Berne's harsher passages and introducing small areas of calm here and there. Tim's baritone is becoming increasingly dominant, a broad, bludgeoning tone, but with a touch of warmth as well.

*** Saturation Point

Screwgun SCREW U 70004 *Berne; Chris Speed (ts, cl); Django Bates (ky); Marc Ducret (g); Drew Gress, Mike Formanek, Mike Mondesir (b); Jim Black, Tom Rainey, Martin France (d).* 96–98.

Originally a limited release obtainable only direct from the label, this seems to be in general circulation now. It's not the most accessible of Berne records, which might explain its clubby exclusivity, but it has all the familiar elements: hectic improvisation over deceptively crude ostinati and rhythms, a strong resemblance to the frenetic ensembles of early jazz and a notional foundation in the blues that usually submerges before the minute, but is rarely lost for good. Culled from live performances over a period of time, it isn't as coherent as some of the records surprisingly are. Berne himself is pretty dominant, but the groups all perform brilliantly and it's worth tracking down, even if you do have to write away for it.

*** Ornery People

Little Brother 013 *Berne; Michael Formanek (b).* 98.

Recorded in the dry air of Arizona, these duo compositions and improvisations strip away some of the extraneous detail and highlight Berne's approach to melody. 'Emerger' was written by the bass player, but it's Berne who leads, with a blunt saxophone solo. The compliment is reversed on 'Byram's World', a Berne tune that provides Formanek with his most individual feature. The duo come together on the closing 'Brincident' which seems to be improvised and has Berne switch to baritone for a bruising and hostile encounter that will leave most listeners feeling a bit shell-shocked.

***** Cause & Reflect**

Level 22004 *Berne; Hank Roberts (clo).* 98.

This is duo improvisation of a very high order. It's also completely bonkers in places. 'Invasion Of The Freudian Shrimp' might almost be something by Mingus, arranged by Raymond Scott. Berne and old friend Roberts know each other's moves intimately and are capable of producing a riotous sound – as on 'More Than Once Dance' – as well as the almost folksy 'Showdown!' The two players check each other out, throw in ideas, withdraw them and then when the other chap agrees to go off in a new direction, return to the original idea as if nothing had happened. It must have been an astonishing vibe in the studio. It comes across on record, but be warned, this isn't an easy or a comfortable listen.

*****(*) The Shell Game**

Thirsty Ear 57099 *Berne; Craig Taborn (ky); Tom Rainey (d).* 01.

****** Science Friction**

Screwgun 013 *As above, except add Marc Ducret (g).* 12/01.

All the familiar signatures are there: dense, jagged themes, dizzy humour, and a weird tightrope between structure and anarchy. Berne and Rainey have built up an astonishing understanding over the years and these records are payoff. The trio disc depends heavily on Taborn's electronic soundscapes, but it is alto and drums which carry the bulk of the action. 'Twisted/Straight Jacket' is a riveting performance, with so much drama that its 20-minutes-plus duration passes like five. 'Heavy Metal' is dedicated to Wayne Krantz, and 'Thin Ice', well, it skates on that treacherous surface for most of its 30 minutes and still leaves the listener exhilarated.

The earlier addition of Ducret was a masterstroke and he's vital to this set as well. This is one of the most effective groups that Berne has ever convened. The guitarist gives Berne an enormous range of options, as he demonstrates on the co-composed 'Sigh Fry'. Though the partnership with Rainey is still the defining energy, Taborn's electronic keyboards define the textural landscape of most of the pieces. They range in length from a dozen minutes – 'Manatee Woman' and 'Clown Finger' – down to just 64 seconds on the enigmatic 'The Mallomar Manoeuvre'. David Torn produces and gives the set a big, boisterous sound that puts the saxophone right in there with the other instruments creating blocks of sound rather than discernible lines. Great stuff, but as challenging as ever.

*****(*) Open, Coma**

Screwgun 012 2CD *Berne; Herb Robertson; Lars Vissing (t); Kasper Tranberg (c); Mads Hyhne (tb); Lotte Anker (ss); Peter Fuglsang (cl); Thomas Agergaard (ts, f); Thomas Clausen (p); Marc Ducret (g); Nils Davisen (b); Anders Mogensen (d); Copenhagen Arts Ensemble.* 9/00.

Spread over two CDs, these are huge and somewhat sprawling interpretations of Berne compositions. This is reminiscent, in spirit if not in sonority, of Miles Davis's *Aura*, an attempt to give a great improviser a genuinely monumental context for his music. The material is drawn from *Bloodcount* and *Caos Totale* days, but the title-track is new and more obviously fitted to the 'sinfonietta' format. Three are concert recordings, but the title-piece was taped in the studio which helps to reinforce the impression of coherence. The Danish soloists are more than adequate, and Clausen's far from old-fashioned sounding Fender Rhodes brings an idiosyncratic richness to the ensembles. However, it's the breezy trumpet of Herb Robertson and Berne's own distinctively pitched alto which cut through. Purely as a listening experience, *Open, Coma* is a compelling experience. Its real importance, though, is in clinching Berne's emergence as a major composer.

***** The Sevens**

New World 80586 *Berne; Beat Hofstetter (ss); Sascha Armbruster (as); Andrea Formenti (ts); Bent Kappeler (bs); Marc Ducret, David Torn (g).* 01.

Further sign of Berne's desire to spread his wings and demonstrate his range beyond post-bop jazz. The members of the Arte Quartet try manfully not to come on like a conservatory saxophone ensemble and for the most part generate a tense, funky sound that complements the leader's still raw delivery. The really interesting collaborators here, though, are the two guitarists. Long tracks like 'Repulsion' and 'Quicksand' – both epic ventures – are broadly familiar in contour from Berne's previous albums, but it's on the shorter pieces that Ducret and particularly Torn shine. 'Tonguefarmer' is a remarkable piece, as difficult to categorize as it is to forget. A very unusual and intriguing disc.

****** The Sublime And**

Thirsty Ear 57139 *Berne; Craig Taborn (p, ky, elec); Marc Ducret (g); Tom Rainey (d).* 4/03.

The Sublime And finds the band doing very much the business onstage in Switzerland. There is probably more straight (i.e. unprocessed) playing but Taborn's laptop electronics make a huge difference and Ducret's guitar is critical. He lays down big gestural washes on the opening 'Van Gundy's Retreat', building on the melody and the underlying rhythmic code until the music sounds distantly abstracted from the original theme. At the beginning of the second set, 'Smallfry' is almost ambient, as far removed from the Coleman and Hemphill influenced linearity of earlier years as you could imagine. 'Jalapeno Diplomacy' rocks like nobody's business, hotter than chilli. Taborn's laptop effects and 'virtual organ' haven't completely overtaken his piano playing but increasingly diffuse it; it has less to do with line now and more with texture. Rainey has a hard job picking his way through it, but on tracks like 'Mrs Subliminal/Clownfinger' and the closing 'Stuckon U', he is absolutely central. Through it all, Berne cuts a solitary furrow, a proud outsider with a wonky understanding of harmonic basics who, like Ornette before him, refuses to surrender to orthodoxy. Wonderful stuff and a pointer to the way ahead.

Marc Bernstein

SOPRANO, ALTO AND TENOR SAXOPHONES

Supple and inventive reedman with a small but effective body of recording.

***** Blue Walls**

Storyville STCD 4223 *Bernstein; Olivier Antunes (p); Mads Vinding (b); Billy Hart (d).* 99.

★★★(★) **Dear Tom Harrell**

Storyville STCD 4251 *Bernstein; Tom Harrell (flhn); Chris Rogers (t); Hans Ulrik (bcl); Henrik Sorensen (p); Michel Camilo (vla); Tom Bramer (b); Morten Lund (d) Alfonso Correa Leite (perc).* 01.

The debut album is very much a vehicle for Bernstein and Hart. The drummer is featured quite prominently and his bustling presence sometimes overshadows the saxophone player. The later record is more successful, but the same thing happens: any record that features a guesting Tom Harrell is likely to sound like a Tom Harrell record. Here he is the dedicatee and the star. The trumpeter brings in his own 'Madrid' and 'Recitation' and these are far and away the best pieces on the set.

Peter Bernstein (born 1967)

GUITAR

A New Yorker who learned from several teachers in the city, Bernstein has been an increasingly ubiquitous presence during the '90s as sideman and, more recently, as leader.

★★(★) **Somethin's Burnin'**

Criss Cross 1079 *Bernstein; Brad Mehldau (p); John Webber (b); Jimmy Cobb (d).* 12/92.

★★★ **Signs Of Life**

Criss Cross 1095 *Bernstein; Brad Mehldau (p); Christian McBride (b); Gregory Hutchinson (d).* 12/94.

Bernstein's anonymous tone and easy fluency send the blameless *Somethin's Burnin'* on the way to mediocrity. Precious little here really burns – Mehldau's jabbing solos are a good deal more interesting than the leader's, who tends to come off the Grant Green axis without much to call his own. The follow-up is an improvement, though Bernstein has to lean very heavily on Mehldau and McBride to keep up the level of interest. Some promising signs of life, though.

★★★ **Brain Dance**

Criss Cross 1130 *Bernstein; Steve Davis (tb); Eric Alexander (ts); Larry Goldings (org); Billy Drummond (d).* 12/96.

★★★ **Earth Tones**

Criss Cross 1151 *Bernstein; Larry Goldings (org); Bill Stewart (d).* 12/97.

Bernstein has been racking up some impressive sideman credits recently and now there's little denying his fluency and wit in that role. As a leader, though, he tends to make agreeable records that frequently lose out in the battle for priority-plays. Nothing wrong with either *Brain Dance* or, especially, *Earth Tones*, the latter featuring a trio that has played together regularly (if on-and-off) since 1989. The sustained elegance of his improvising on 'The Acrobat' will delight guitar-followers. But the blowing formats of these discs don't find enough in them to transcend the occasion, so they end up in a bracket of nothing to disappoint but little to remember.

★★★★ **Heart's Content**

Criss Cross 1233 *Bernstein; Brad Mehldau (p); Larry Grenadier (b); Bill Stewart (d).* 02.

Ten years on, Bernstein is back with Mehldau, Grenadier and Stewart are also on hand, and the music is little short of sublime – unfussy, skilful, complex in tone even as it's directly communicative as a straight-ahead hard bop record. Perhaps so much has already been essayed in this medium that even a great record is hard to spot, but the playing here works at both macro- and micro-level: line by line it's beautifully pitched and sensitive, but it lacks little in excitement and larger impact. Bernstein's tunes have utilitarian blowing value, and finesse too. Mehldau, away from the spotlight of his leadership records, simply plays one telling solo after another.

Chu Berry (1910–41)

TENOR SAXOPHONE

Leon Berry played with several New York bands before a spell with Fletcher Henderson, from 1935, then with Cab Calloway, from 1937. He also cut small-group sessions with Roy Eldridge and Lionel Hampton. A Hawkins follower, but with a character of his own, he was a popular man who was much mourned when he died after injuries received in a car crash.

★★★(★) **Chu Berry, 1937–1941**

Classics 784 *Berry; Roy Eldridge, Hot Lips Page, Irving Randolph (t); Keg Johnson, George Mathews (tb); Buster Bailey (cl); Charlie Ventura (ts); Horace Henderson, Clyde Hart, Benny Payne (p); Danny Barker, Al Casey (g); Israel Crosby, Milt Hinton, Al Morgan, Artie Shapiro (b); Big Sid Catlett, Cozy Cole, Leroy Maxey, Harry Yeager (d).* 3/37–9/41.

Sixty years after his premature death, Berry's reputation is still in eclipse. He died just a little too soon for the extraordinary revolution in saxophone playing that followed the end of the war. He had a big sound, not unlike that of Coleman Hawkins – who considered him an equal – with a curiously fey inflexion that was entirely his own and which appealed strongly to Young Turks like Frank Lowe, who began to listen to Berry again in the '70s.

For someone who recorded a good deal, the catalogue has always been sparse. A self-effacing sort of character, Berry often found himself in the shadow of more celebrated figures such as Herschel Evans, Basie's right-hand man until his premature death. Berry was only ever a dep in the Basie orchestra, but he turned in one classic, 'Lady Be Good'. He had more prominence in the Calloway outfit, with whom he was employed at the time of his death. Too often under other leaders he was restricted to brief excursions from the woodwind bench, and Berry was a player who needed time and space to have his say.

The partnership with Roy Eldridge was a matey, happy affair, and the 'Little Jazz' Ensembles of November 1938 are among Chu's best small-group performances. The version of 'Body And Soul' sits very well alongside the great ones. The opening number, 'Sittin' In', is introduced conversationally by the two principals. Talking or playing, they're both in rumbustious form, and the warmth of the partnership was equalled only by the late sessions with Hot Lips Page, made within weeks of the road accident which ended Chu's short life. 'On The Sunny Side Of The Street' had Page laying out, and it's an interesting place to study Berry as an improviser. The existing release doesn't include any alternative takes, but these do exist, and here and elsewhere they expose a rather thin sense of structure; solos always seemed to follow much the same trajectory. Chu was a wonderfully complete player in every other regard, and with a strong band behind him he was up with the very best. When he died, they left his chair in the Cab Calloway band sitting empty.

Tony Bevan

TENOR, SOPRANO AND BASS SAXOPHONES

Less well known than some of his saxophone-playing contemporaries in Britain, Bevan has carved his own quiet – or, rather, quietly abrasive – course. His use of overblowing and seemingly unmusical sound is very subtle and strangely elegant, in the way that primitive folksong has an unexpected elegance.

***** Original Gravity**
Incus CD 03 *Bevan; Greg Kingston (g, rec, tapes, toys); Matt Lewis (perc, bird calls).* 9/88.

****** Bigshots**
Incus CD 08 *Bevan; Paul Rogers (b); Steve Noble (perc).* 7/91.

****** Twisters**
Scatter 06CD *Bevan; Alexander Frangenheim (b); Steve Noble (perc).* 4 & 5/95.

***** Three Oranges**
Foghorn FOGCD001 *Bevan (bsx).* 7/98.

Bevan is a gritty British improviser who's managed to spell out an idiom sufficiently different from the dominant but hard-to-emulate Evan Parker style. The earliest of these sessions is engagingly spiny and good-humoured, with a few nods (Lewis's duck-calls most obviously) in the direction of John Zorn's freestyle. The beery track-titles – '1044°–1050°', 'Original Gravity', 'Best Before End' – are a bit of a giveaway, for there's a boys'-night-out feel to the proceedings which makes you wonder if it wasn't a lot more fun for the participants than it could ever be for CD listeners.

That certainly isn't true of *Bigshots*, which is wonderfully controlled and dramatic, three absolutely compatible players working at full stretch, listening carefully to one another without surrendering a shred of autonomy. Rogers, as so often in these settings, is the dominant voice, and it's sometimes difficult not to home in exclusively on his rumbling lines. Bevan himself has started to play more smoothly, even lyrically in passages, and it suits him. Only on the long closing 'The Last Shot' does he appear to run out of ideas – though, listening to the track again, one almost wonders whether it wasn't actually an initial try-out rather than a curtain-call, so tentative are some of its components. The title-track is much more compelling. Noble comes into his own with a vengeance and Bevan truffles up ideas of real originality.

Noble is excellent again on *Twisters*: alternating long and short tracks, dense outbursts of sound with quieter and more spacious ideas. Closer to orthodox freebop – if there is such a thing as freebop orthodoxy – than on previous records, Bevan's own contribution is more linear and orderly, and 'Belly Of The Whale' might even be some mid-'60s group like Amalgam or Splinters. It, though, is an exception. This is fresh, undogmatic music, without a hint of retro styling or nostalgia.

Solo bass saxophone is a fairly recherché area of musical practice, and Bevan hasn't the depth of understanding which Roscoe Mitchell and Anthony Braxton have brought to such projects. The comfort is that the album is very short, more of an EP than an LP, and is played very expressively, with a nice modulation of mood. Even so, very much an acquired taste, and don't expect the echo of Prokofiev in the title to be reflected in the music.

***** The Sale Of Tickets For Money Was Abolished**
Balance Point Acoustics 002 *Bevan; Scott R. Looney (p, elec); Damon Smith (b).* 4/00.

*****(*) Nothing Is Permanent But Woe**
Foghorn FOGCD 002 *Bevan; John Edwards (b); Mark Sanders (d).* 9–10/00.

Bevan at work in Oakland and London. The American disc offers a lot of dark, scuffling, mysterious sound, heavy on the bass frequencies (Bevan uses only bass sax on both these sets). Moments such as the piano–sax duet of 'To Accept Errors Is Not To Contradict Fate' bring a welcome ray or two of light. Smith's job is, apparently, queuing for rock concert tickets – this set was set down after he'd been waiting in line for a Lou Reed show.

The British trio follows much the same course, though it has a better studio sound and Sanders, a very fine drummer in this music, makes an important difference: Bevan likes to stay almost obsessively earthbound on the big horn, digging the heftiest sonorities he can out of it, and the percussionist's momentum raises what might otherwise be overly sluggish playing. Edwards, who seems incapable of playing at less than the highest level, finds an intriguing middle path between solo and ensemble playing – a classic improviser's doctrine.

***** Under Tracey's Bed**
Foghorn FOGCD-R02 *Bevan; Derek Bailey (g).* 11/02.

A rough-and-ready gig souvenir, recorded in Oxford. Bevan's dedication to the bass sax is paying bigger dividends the more he goes on with it, and with paterfamilias Bailey doing his usual, the tonal palette is surprisingly rich. A pity that the recording isn't more professional.

Faruq Z. Bey

ALTO AND TENOR SAXOPHONES

Detroit-based player and former leader of the obscure but influential Griot Galaxy. Bey returned to playing after serious injury in a motorcycle accident.

****(*) 19 Moons**
Entropy Stereo ESR 011 *Bey; Leonard Bukowski (contra acl); Mike Carey (ts, f); Mike Gilmore (vib, baritone g); Mike Johnston (b); Nick Ashton (d).* 02.

***** Ashirai Pattern**
Entropy Stereo ESR 013 *As above.* 6–11/02.

In Griot Galaxy days, Bey had no great love of the studio and it is no surprise that both these albums, made in collaboration with Michigan-based Northwoods Improvisers, should be concert performances. The recipe is the same in both cases: dense rhythm patterns that hover between funk and free jazz, extreme sonority (best represented by Bukowski's contra-alto clarinet and Gilmore's baritone guitar), coupled to a brooding expressiveness.

The long 'After Death' on *19 Moons* is a retread of a Griot Galaxy composition; 'Moors' is longer and more developed; but while Bey's compositions dominate these recordings, he sounds more like a guest artist with a talented ensemble who work in a slightly different idiom, a situation Anthony Braxton has found himself in on more than one occasion. The second set is the more compelling of the two: 'Mathanawi' is a rousing opener, and while nothing else quite matches up to its energy, the music is rich, varied and hugely enjoyable.

Barney Bigard (1906–80)

CLARINET, TENOR SAXOPHONE

Born Albany Leon Bigard in New Orleans, his first major job was with King Oliver in Chicago, but he joined Duke Ellington at the start of his Cotton Club residency in 1927 and stayed till 1942. There followed five years with the Louis Armstrong All Stars, with a second brief stay in 1960, and general work as a freelance. He retired from full-time playing in 1965 but was a frequent guest and visitor to festivals.

***** Barney Bigard 1944**

Classics 896 *Bigard; Shorty Sherock, Norman Bowden, Joe Thomas (t); John 'Shorty' Haughton (tb); Les Robinson (as); Eddie Miller, Georgie Auld (ts); Stan Wrightsmann (p, cel); Pete Johnson, Leonard Feather, Fred Washington (p); Nappy Lamare, Bud Scott, Remo Palmieri, Chuck Wayne (g); Hank Wayland, Al Hall, Billy Taylor (b); Nick Fatool, Shelly Manne, Zutty Singleton, Stan Levey (d); Peggy Lee, Etta Jones (v); strings.* 1–12/44.

***** Barney Bigard 1944–1945**

Classics 930 *Bigard; Joe Thomas, Ray Linn (t); Vic Dickenson (tb); Willie Smith (as); Joe Thomas (ts, v); Georgie Auld (ts); Cyril Haynes, Leonard Feather, Calvin Jackson, Eddie Beal, Art Tatum, Johnny Guarnieri (p); Allan Reuss, Chuck Wayne (g); Billy Taylor, Red Callender (b); Zutty Singleton, Stan Levey, Cozy Cole (d); Wini Beatty, Claude Trenier, Monette Moore (v).* 12/44–12/45.

The conventional wisdom is that Bigard did all his best work with Ellington, and the rest isn't up to anything much. While some of the jazz on these two interesting compilations of his freelance work is less than immortal, his own playing is seldom less than fine. Classics 896 starts with four excellent titles by The Capitol International Jazzmen, including good work from Robinson and Miller as well as Bigard, and two charming vocals by Peggy Lee. A trio session for Signature is fluent and swinging and, though two dates with Zutty Singleton are less impressive and four titles with strings are unremarkable, the final four titles with Etta Jones and Joe Thomas include some excellent blues playing by Barney. Classics 930 brings together a string of largely less-than-classic dates, four of them accompanying singers, and some of these tracks are very obscure indeed: but there is an excellent quintet date for Keynote which offers Bigard at his best on 'Rose Room' and 'Bojangles', and a pair of titles for the Lamplighter label have some entertaining jousting with Vic Dickenson. Transfers are decent, especially considering that some of these tracks weren't exactly finessed by the microphones in the first place.

***** Bucket's Got A Hole In It**

Delmark DE-211 *Bigard; Nap Trottier (t); George Brunis (tb); Art Hodes (p); Rail Wilson (b); Barrett Deems (d).* 1/68.

A delightful reunion of old-timers, with the sextet ambling through this alternately rousing and bluesy date with evident enjoyment. The timing is rather off here and there, despite the reliable Deems, and Trottier and the engaging Brunis (who goes back almost to pre-history as far as jazz recording is concerned) aren't players of the stature of Bigard and Hodes, but the feeling is so warm and cheerful that the occasional frailties don't matter.

**** Barney Bigard And The Pelican Trio**

Jazzology JCD-228 *Bigard; Duke Burrell (p); Barry Martyn (d).* 76.

This one, though, should be left on the shelf. Bigard sounds well past his best and, though Burrell and Martyn play with great spirit, they tend to overpower the old man.

Acker Bilk (born 1929)

CLARINET

Best known, after nearly 40 years, for his 'Stranger On The Shore' hit, Bilk was the chart-topping star of British trad whose credentials – going as far back as the early Ken Colyer band – were actually impeccable. He has continued to perform, with strings, choirs and his own Paramount Jazzband, ever since.

****** Mr Acker Bilk And His Paramount Jazzband**

Lake LACD 48 *Bilk; Ken Sims (t); John Mortimer (tb); Jay Hawkins, Roy James (bj); Ernest Price (b); Ron McKay (d).* 3/58–1/59.

***** Acker**

Lake LACD 186 *Bilk; Ken Sims, Colin Smith (t); John Mortimer (tb); Stan Greig, Dave Collett (p); Roy James (bj); Ernie Price (b); Ron McKay (d, v).* 10/59–8/60.

*****(*) Stranger On The Shore / A Taste Of Honey**

Redial 546458-2 *Bilk; strings, choir, directed by Leon Young.* 61–65.

Barber, Ball and Bilk – the 'Three Bs' – were the heirs of Ken Colyer's trad revolution. If Barber 'prettified' Colyer's rough-edged approach, Bilk brought an element of showmanship and humour, speaking in a disconcerting Zummerzet accent, dressing his Paramount Jazzband in Edwardian waistcoats and bowlers, notching two enormous hits with 'Summer Set' (a further punning reference to the county of his birth) and 'Stranger On The Shore', a tune still much requested at autumnal wedding receptions. The idea had come from producer Dennis Preston, who wanted Bilk to record with strings. The clarinettist reworked a theme that was originally dedicated to his daughter, recorded it with the Leon Young String Chorale, saw it picked up as the signature-tune to a similarly titled television serial, and started counting the royalties. Bilk's success – 'Stranger' sold more than two million copies – and photogenic presentation attracted an inevitable mixture of envy and disdain, and it's often forgotten how accomplished and 'authentic' a musician he actually is. Working with Colyer in the mid-'50s, he played in a raw-edged George Lewis style very different from the silky, evocative vibrato he cultivated in later years.

The choice of a single Bilk album for a sample collection of British trad is made easier by the appearance on Lake of sessions from the Nixa 'Jazz Today' collection. These dates from 1958 and 1959 capture the Paramount Jazzband at its best, doing blues and rags with a raw, unembellished quality. 'Willie The Weeper' is pretty authentic, and things like 'Blaze Away' and 'Higher Ground' give the band plenty of scope for raucous to-and-froing. *Acker* also features the Paramount Jazz Band in its toughest, most unprettified form: there are nods to variety with the likes of 'White Cliffs Of Dover', but at this point this was more to do with the New Orleans tradition of covering pop tunes of every generation rather than playing for the chicken-in-a-basket crowd that Acker courted in later years. The front line tends to go for punch rather than finesse, and Ken Sims wouldn't be anybody's choice for a firm lead trumpet, but the tracks don't half go off at an argumentative lick. Stan Greig comes in on piano on the later tracks. 'Snake Rag' and 'Milenberg Joys' blaze along, and an original such as 'Fancy Pants' shows Bilk's good ear for a pop hook, even if here he's playing it straight and hot. Paul Adams has cleaned off some of the reverb on the original LP, which makes it all sound leaner and even more in your face.

The Redial reissue of the original *Stranger On The Shore* and *A Taste Of Honey* on a two-on-one CD will be greatly welcomed by admirers of the 'popular' Bilk. Whatever reservations one has about the setting, his own clarinet remains markedly individual and there are a few delightful surprises along the way, such as his own original 'Evening Shadows'.

Bilk is an impressive middle-register player who seldom uses the coloratura range for spurious effect, preferring to work melodic variations on a given theme. Though he repeats certain formulae, he tends to do so with variations that stop them going stale. A major figure in British jazz, Bilk has to be separated from a carefully nurtured image. On record, he's consistently impressive and continued to produce the goods right into the '90s. Illness has slowed him down of late, but it was good to find him enjoying himself in the company of some other British veterans on the 2002 release, *British Jazz Legends Together* (Decca 470271-2).

David Bindman

TENOR SAXOPHONE

East Coast American based in Brooklyn who works extensively around the New York–Connecticut axis.

***** Imaginings**

CIMP 151 *Bindman; Joe Fonda (b); Kevin Norton (d).* 7/97.

Bindman's style is energy-based but fundamentally conservative. He sometimes goes in for tonal distortions, but the more he pushes them, the less convincing he sounds. His full, brawny sound comes out best in the middle-lower register and many of his improvisations stick to that area and wring it out for inspiration. Some of these simple melodic themes suit him fine, and his bleak revamping of 'Jitterbug Waltz' is interesting, but ten shots of this music are a little wearing over CD length. Fonda and Norton, familiar partners, are noisily propulsive, and this is one occasion where CIMP's 'natural' sound detracts: the drums need extra width to accommodate Norton's brusque attack.

Binney, David (born 1961)

SOPRANO AND ALTO SAXOPHONES

Firm-toned saxophonist with strong improvising ideas.

*****(*) Luxury Of Guessing**

Audioquest 1030 *Binney; Donny McCaslin (ts); Uri Caine (p); Ben Monder (g); Scott Colley (b); Jeff Hirshfield (d); Daniel Sadownick (perc).* 2/95.

***** Afinidad**

Red RR 12134 *Binney; Edward Simon (p); Adam Rogers (g); Scott Colley (b); Brian Blade, Adam Cruz (d); Lucia Pulida (v).* 4/00.

*****(*) South**

ACT 9279 *Binney; Uri Caine (p); Chris Potter (ts); Scott Colley (b); Brian Blade (d).* 6/00.

***** Balance**

ACT 9411 *Binney; Donny McCaslin (sax); Uri Caine (p); Wayne Krantz (g); Tim Lefebvre (b); Jim Black (d).* 7–8/01.

Binney's brand of vigorous post-bop is touched here and there with free-form playing. On all these records, he sounds adventurous but also self-possessed. The writing is clear, authoritative and always seems to lead from A to B. It's actually very difficult to make discriminatory judgements between the discs, so consistently good are they, but we very much like his interplay with Potter on *South* and the whole rhythmic conception of the middle albums, where some strong recruitments have yielded highly creative results. The one question mark hangs over the Red disc; it's actually co-led by pianist Simon, who has ideas of his own; the main objection, though, is that the sound is flat and uninviting.

Binney seems on the brink of genuinely remarkable things. His ability to sustain a regular band is laudable, but what he needs now is to push off into deeper water and follow through on the promise of these fine discs; a more detailed examination next time.

The Birdlanders

GROUP

Pick-up dates from the New York session scene of the early '50s.

****(*) The Birdlanders Volume 1**

Original Jazz Classics OJC 1930-2 *J. J. Johnson, Kai Winding (tb); Al Cohn (ts); Milt Jackson (p, vib); Duke Jordan, Henri Renaud (p); Percy Heath, Gene Ramey (b); Charlie Smith, Lee Abrams (d).* 1–3/54.

***** The Birdlanders Volume 2**

Original Jazz Classics OJC 1931-2 *As above, except add Tal Farlow (g); Oscar Pettiford (b, clo); Max Roach, Denzil Best (d); omit Johnson, Jackson, Heath, Smith and Abrams.* 3/54.

These sessions might almost be listed under Henri Renaud's name, since he organized and produced them for the Period label, as well as playing piano on all but five titles. Originally scattered across three LPs, the four separate sessions have been re-sequenced in order. Much of the music is amiable jamming on the blues and standards, but there are a few tickles of interest in the material: a sketch by Gerry Mulligan, 'East Lag', and early appearances of Duke Jordan originals such as 'Jordu' (here as 'Minor Escamp'). The first disc, despite the presence of Jackson, is pretty ordinary, with Jordan's five trio tracks sounding very flat. The second has rather more interest, with Farlow and the reliable Cohn taking solo honours. Still, these are very much bebop's backwaters. The original sound is on the dusty side.

Walter Bishop Jr (1927–98)

PIANO

Swing-to-bop pianist who followed in the footsteps of a renowned swing-era musician.

*****(*) Trio, 1965**
Original Jazz Classics OJC 1896 *Bishop; Butch Warren (b); Jimmy Cobb, Granville T. Hogan (d).* 62, 10/63.

***** Summertime**
Fresh Sound FSCD 11 *As above, except omit Hogan.* 64.

If there was an obvious influence on Bish's solo style, it was Erroll Garner, but despite being widely regarded it was some time before he either felt confident enough or was deemed to be marketable enough to make a record of his own. We're slightly confused about the titling of the OJC set. The cover clearly reads 1965, which may have been the year of issue, but there are references to sessions in spring 1962 and, with Cobb as drummer, autumn 1963, and this seems to be correct. Whatever the date, the playing is fine. Hogan plays on the four earlier selections only, and Cobb is certainly much more polished. A good deal of the material is co-credited to Bishop and supervisor Addison Amor, which suggests that it was run down in the studio. Fortunately, Bishop's improvisational skills are sufficient to sustain the quality. *Summertime* is marred only by poor sound. The playing is well up to scratch, and it's a beautifully constructed set, evidence of Bishop's taste as a leader. Butch Warren is poorly served in the mastering, and there is a fog over much of the music, though this is not serious enough to put off enthusiasts.

Michael Bisio

BASS

West Coast improviser and free-bop bassist, here given the opportunity to lead his own dates.

****(*) Covert Choreography**
Cadence CJR 1063 *Bisio; Rob Blakeslee (t); Eyvind Kang (vn); Bob Nell (p); Ed Pias (d).* 96.

***** Finger Wigglers**
CIMP 127 *Bisio; Joe McPhee (ts).* 9/96.

The quintet album offers some vigorous playing by a worthwhile group, but it comes across as a rather messily recorded document of a studio jam for much of its length. The title-piece runs for 40 minutes and fades from free to bop and back again with all too many desultory passages. The three remaining pieces are better focused, and Blakeslee is always worth hearing, but it's nothing special.

Bisio's duets with McPhee are harsh, even gruelling stuff. Two takes of 'Lonely Woman' leave the tune almost unrecognizable, as is 'Blue Monk'. Although 'Here's That Rainy Day' emerges into the light after a long bass introduction, McPhee is at his most intractable for much of this and everything else. Not without its rewards, and it has the merit of the saxophonist sticking to tenor for the whole date, which lets one examine his peculiarly cruel lyricism at length.

*****(*) Undulations**
Omnitone 15001 *Bisio; Rob Blakeslee (c, t, flhn); Bob Nell (p); Jim Nolet (vla); Ed Pias (d).* 6/96.

On the shelf for four years prior to release, this enticing quintet record is Bisio's most effective one. An unusual line-up and a slightly more conventional approach – 'Injury Or Malpractice?' is basic freebop, and the helter-skelter finale of 'Legends' is much the same – centre Bisio's interests as an organizer and player. A dedication to Henry Grimes particularizes the bassist's dedication to his instrument in its traditional–modern role, and in using players like Blakeslee and Nell he's opting for two worlds in sync. The result is seven creative themes and an inventive ensemble.

***** Zebulon**
CIMP 179 *Bisio; Joe McPhee (as, ts).* 7/98.

****(*) MBEK**
Meniscus 005 *Bisio; Eyvind Kang (vn).* 11/98.

****(*) Concerted**
Cadence CJR 1121 *Bisio; Dan Blunck (ss, ts).* 4/00.

Looks like Bisio's making a speciality out of the duo record. The return match with McPhee goes much the way of the first, though this time the saxophonist also has an alto to hand, and the grudging lyricism of 'Kind Of A Ballad', at least, is some kind of concession. Should suit severe tastes. Playing *MBEK* straight afterwards is a bit of a shock, given the difference between Meniscus's rich, resonant sound and the crabby naturalism of CIMP (whichever is the more truthful is up to the listener). The music, though, is no less demanding. Bisio and Kang bow and scrape their way through a long recital – 'Cardinal Waters', at over 20 minutes, is a real endurance test, partly because Kang's exaggerated vibrato and distortions become tiresome uncomfortably quickly. It might be unfair to criticize this setting as dry, but a bass–violin duo is a test for listeners as well as performers.

With Blunck, the music goes through wild mood-swings. The further out the saxophonist gets, the less convincing he sounds, ending up entirely lost at the end of 'Dragonfly Suite' for one. He does better with something to work from, such as 'Harlem Nocturne' or his own 'Big Al'. But for much of the time this feels unfortunately close to a repertory exercise, of musicians playing at, rather than in, free music.

Ketil Bjørnstad (born 1952)

PIANO

Classically trained, but more interested in bringing that aesthetic into an area touched by jazz.

***** Water Stories**
ECM 519076-2 *Bjørnstad; Terje Rypdal (g); Bjorn Kjellemyr (b); Jon Christensen, Per Hillestad (d).* 1/93.

***** The Sea**
ECM 521718-2 *Bjørnstad; David Darling (clo); Terje Rypdal (g); Jon Christensen (d).* 9/94.

*****(*) The Sea II**
ECM 537341-2 *As above.* 12/96.

***** Epigraphs**
ECM 543159-2 *Bjørnstad; David Darling (clo).* 9/98.

All those expensive lessons – wasted! Bjørnstad is a classically trained pianist who was turned on to jazz by *In A Silent Way* and hasn't looked back since. The debut album is a linked sequence of pieces inspired by the land and seascape of Rosendal in western Norway. The first few sections evoke a glacier cutting its path through the mountains. Here at least it makes sense that the music is held in check, though one can almost hear Rypdal pumping the brakes. As things progress, the pace gradually increases, and Hillestad, who's played with underrated rockers A-Ha, replaces Christensen, bringing a more headlong sound.

Frankly, we find it difficult to distinguish between the two *Sea* records. Had they been recorded at the same time, and *Sea II* a set of offcuts, it would all make more sense, but to reconvene the same band 27 months on in order to record what sounds like the same material seems perverse in the extreme. To be fair to Bjørnstad, there has been some attempt to roughen up the textures a bit and to give the follow-up record a semblance of grit and fibre. Too late, though. Immaculate sound, thrown away on spindrift.

Epigraphs brings together two of the most pacific spirits on a label roster which isn't exactly brimming with warmongers. The settings of Dufay, Byrd, Gibbons and Aichinger are as gentle and sweetly voiced as the originals, all of it at a pace which rarely moves above slow motion. Beautiful – and goodbye to jazz.

***** Grace**

Emarcy 013622-2 *Bjørnstad; Bendik Hofseth (ts, v); Eivind Aarset (g); Arild Andersen (b); Trilok Gurtu (perc); Jan Bang (sampling); Anneli Drecker (v).* 4/00.

Settings of John Donne, written by Bjørnstad and performed by a Norwegian supergroup of sorts, all working around the serene but tough vocals of Drecker and, oddly, the more vulnerable-sounding Hofseth. In other words, art song. Recorded at the 2000 Voss Festival, the sound is spacious, resonant with Bang's sampling and treatments, and Bjørnstad finds some lovely chords. As we were saying – goodbye to jazz.

***** The Nest**

Emarcy 067 153 2 *Bjørnstad; Ketil Bjerkestrand (ky, elec, perc); Eivind Aarset (g); Nora Takdal (vla); Anneli Drecker (v).* 8–12/02.

This is another intensely beautiful album, only peripherally related to jazz, but driven by a complex spectrum of inspirations. The title comes from Eva-Maria Riegler's photograph of the same name, while some of the songs are inspired by Norwegian novelist Sigrid Undset and by American poet Hart Crane's difficult epic *The Bridge*. Bjørnstad's piano playing is part of a process he calls 'reconstruction', which seems to fall somewhere between orthodox song-setting (though Anneli Drecker is here as guest vocalist) and the use of lyrics rather than melody as the basis for improvisation. The dominant instrumental voice is Takdal's viola, though it does little more than soar gracefully over the piano voicings. At its best, *The Nest* achieves profound insight – Crane's 'Old Song' is stunning – but there is an inescapably vacuous quality to some of the arrangements. However, it's a hugely enjoyable set and if it turns listeners on to the beauties of Crane (and Undset) it will have fulfilled an extra purpose.

The Blackbottom Stompers

GROUP

Many bands have used this monicker over the years. This one hails from the British home counties, led by trombonist Goddard.

***** Friends**

PEK Sound PKCD-213 *Dennis Field (c, t, flhn); John Goddard (tb, v); George Dawson (ss, cl); Keith Nichols (p, tb, v); Andy Ford (bj); Terry Lewis (b); Norman Davey (d).* 1/03.

Live at the Charles Cryer Studio Theatre, Carshalton, the Stompers here meet a guest star in the shape of Keith Nichols, who's perfectly at home with the likes of 'Davenport Blues' and gets a few features to himself. Mercifully little time is wasted on vocals and the group has a pleasing feel to the ensembles, although some of the solos could use a degree more aptitude. A souvenir of a good night out.

Black Eagle Jazz Band

GROUP

Veteran traditionalists from Boston who first played together in 1971 and have been going ever since.

***** New Black Eagle Jazz Band**

GHB BCD-59 *Tony Pringle (c, v); Stan Vincent (tb); Stan McDonald (cl, ss); Bob Pilsbury (p); Eli Newberger (tba); Peter Bullis (bj); Pam Pameijer (d).* 4–9/72.

***** Some Sweet Day**

Lake LACD065 *As above, except add Rudy Balliеu (cl), Hugh Clackwell (cl, as), Butch Thompson (p); omit McDonald.* 7/81–2/84.

***** Don't Monkey With It**

Stomp Off CD1147 *As above, except add Billy Novick (cl, ss, as); omit Ballieu, Blackwell and Thompson.* 6/87.

*****(*) Jersey Lightning**

Stomp Off CD1224 *As above.* 6/90.

***** Hear Me Talkin' To Ya**

Stomp Off CD1356 *As above.* 6/90.

****(*) On Tour In England**

Stomp Off CD1257 *As above, except Ray Foxley (p) replaces Pilsbury.* 8/92.

***** When Your Hair Has Turned To Silver**

Stomp Off CD1303 *As above, except Bob Pilsbury (p, v) replaces Foxley.* 6/95.

*****(*) Skeletons In The Closet**

BE(CD) 2004 *As above.* 6/95.

*****(*) The Black Eagles At Naworth Castle**

Lake LACD95 *As above.* 8/96.

There's now plenty available by this Bostonian institution, who've been playing the traditional repertoire for decades. The GHB issue documents some of their earliest sessions: at this point still in thrall to traditional conventions, with a sometimes rickety-tick quality to the quicker tempos, and when they tackle an unimprovable such as 'Potato Head Blues' the comparison makes them suffer. Yet the playing is skilful in an honest and pleasurable way, the best tracks genuinely hot and adept.

Most of the Stomp Off sessions are live, and so is much of *Some Sweet Day*, which was recorded at a Dutch festival in 1981 with guests Ballieu and Thompson. Five studio tracks come from some time later. A bit of a scratch issue, but the Dutch music is very much in the Black Eagles mould, even with the guest players. The Stomp Off discs portray a mature band that knows exactly how it wants to deal with the vast legacy of old jazz: programmes which mix staples with rarities, a very occasional original, an emphasis on ensemble-work over solos but space enough for gentle improvisation, and a particularly fine judgement of tempo. They can play incredibly slowly at times and never make it sound like a crawl, as in the stately version of 'Wild Man Blues' on *Don't Monkey With It*, in which Pilsbury's piano solo is some kind of miracle of trad minimalism.

Jersey Lightning has perhaps their most engaging programme of material and some of the best playing, although *Don't Monkey With It* is really only a notch behind. *Hear Me Talkin' To Ya* is a belated release of the rest of the material from the *Jersey Lightning* concerts, and if they used the best on the other disc, this one still has lots to enjoy, though Pringle's vocals are less than delightful. *On Tour In England* isn't so good – the recording's only average and here and there the redoubtable Pringle seems shakier than usual (although, since he modelled himself on that renowned note-cracker Kid Cola, it's often hard to tell when he's putting it on). *Skeletons In The Closet* is the only one of several CDs on their label which we've heard: a gig in Connecticut, and another set with a particularly strong run of tunes, from 'Mabel's Dream' to 'Saturday Night Function'. *When Your Hair Has Turned To Silver* returns them to the Mount Gretna Playhouse (scene of the *Jersey Lightning* sessions): good, but not one of our favourites. However, British fans caught a fine set when the Eagles played at Naworth Castle. It was a bit of a cheek for Pringle to take on Ken Colyer's 'Goin' Home' (and his voice is really starting to give out), but the band are in excellent fettle.

Cindy Blackman (born 1959)

DRUMS, PERCUSSION

A third-generation musician, Blackman is a formidable player. Her jazz recording career has been interrupted by forays into rock, not least with the talented Lenny Kravitz. She suits both idioms, playing her jazz with an unembellished simplicity that has often attracted 'masculine' labels, except that it is so tunefully and tastefully nuanced.

***** In The Now**
High Note 7024 *Blackman; Ravi Coltrane (ss, ts); Jacky Terrasson (p); Ron Carter (b).* 98.

*****(*) Works On Canvas**
High Note 7038 *Blackman; J. D. Allen III (ts); Carlton Holmes (p, ky); George Mitchell (b).* 4/99.

***** Someday**
High Note 7063 *As above.* 4/00.

Cindy's jazz career break as Lenny Kravitz's drummer is acknowledged at the end of *In The Now* with a brisk and well-shaped version of Lennie's 'Let Love Rule'. For the rest, though, she is very much back to normal business. An interpretation of Ornette's 'Happy House' sticks out a little uncomfortably but her originals are very strong and the long 'A King Among Men' is classic Blackman.

Works On Canvas is very impressive indeed. It starts with a very unusual re-interpretation of 'On Green Dolphin Street' and a pair of compositions by Blackman's colleagues on the set: Allen's 'Mudee Ya' and Holmes's 'My Isha', before introducing a sequence of pieces inspired by Van Gogh. The tonality throughout is dark, vibrant and, on 'Sword Of The Painter', almost threatening. Saxophonist and pianist are in superb form (why have we not heard more from them?) and are destined for great things. The interplay on Holmes's 'Beautiful World' is exquisite, and the set includes half a dozen items which might well make it into the repertoire.

The third of the group is not quite so impressive, but Blackman is playing with a new confidence, and here she constructs a thoughtful, sometimes provocative set, built round three 'Calls To The Ancestors'. As often before, she establishes her credentials at the start of the set with a reworking of a familiar standard, this time 'My Funny Valentine'. What follows is clever, sharp-witted modern jazz.

Ed Blackwell (1929–92)

DRUMS

Born in New Orleans, he began playing in local R&B groups in the '40s and later moved to Los Angeles, working with Ornette Coleman, then, in the '60s, with Don Cherry, Coltrane, Dolphy and Coleman again. His playing was curtailed to some extent by his dependence on a dialysis machine, but he carried on through the '80s, always a dynamic member of a group.

*****(*) Walls-Bridges**
Black Saint 120153 *Blackwell; Dewey Redman (ts); Cameron Brown (b).* 2/92.

Like a lot of drummers, Blackwell appeared on a huge number of records, but very rarely indeed as leader. The Black Saint, taped at the beginning of the last year of his life, finds him a little swamped by Redman's over-the-top improvising, in which he consistently seems to ignore Blackwell's pulse and floats free of any restraint. Even on tunes like 'Take The "A" Train', there's not much respect accorded the material. Best to concentrate on what Ed is doing with the underrated Cameron Brown at the back of the stand. Their empathy on Miles's 'Half Nelson' and the long following 'Everything Happens To Me' is worth the slog through this rather noisy and one-dimensional disc.

Brian Blade

DRUMS, PERCUSSION

The talented drummer was part of Kenny Garrett's trio and had amassed an impressive array of credits before making his debut as lead.

****(*) Brian Blade Fellowship**
Blue Note 59417-2 *Blade; Myron Walden (as); Melvin Butler (ts, ss); Jon Cowherd (p, org); Daniel Lanois, Jeff Parker (g); Dave Easley (pedal steel g); Christopher Thomas (b).* 97.

***** Perceptual**
Blue Note 23571-2 *As above, except add Kurt Rosenwinkel (g), Joni Mitchell (v); omit Parker.* 99.

Blade's debut recording as leader is strikingly similar to early projects by fellow-percussionist Jack DeJohnette, and it shares some of their limitations. *Fellowship* is more impressionistic than dynamic, and the textures on the opening 'Red River

Revel', an evocation of the annual festival in his home town of Shriveport, Louisiana, are surpassingly gentle, thanks largely to producer Lanois's mando-guitar and Dave Easley's pedal steel. The most obvious link with DeJohnette is 'Folklore', a collage of voices (apparently the Babenzele pygmies) and instrumental sounds. Whereas DeJohnette's world-music excursions almost always have a solid core, this has nothing but surface. The two saxophones pick up the pace here and there, and the basic group, with soul-brother Cowherd supplying 'Lifeline' and Thomas commanding the engine-room with old-fashioned string bass, has a coherence that suggests they probably sound great live. On this showing, though, not very forceful.

Blue Note's confidence in his talent is better borne out by the second record, which builds on the strengths of the debut and turns them in a more positive direction. Blade is rarely more than a subtle background presence, taking no solo spotlight and acting as a quiet dynamo to the guitar and saxophone front line, which is nicely balanced. The use of pedal steel has become a signature, enhanced this time by a further cameo from Daniel Lanois and a rather frail and plangent vocal from Joni Mitchell on 'Steadfast'. The most effective tracks are 'Evinrude Fifty (Trembling)' and the long, suite-like 'Variations Of A Bloodline', which might be influenced by the maverick Terry Allen of the Panhandle Mystery Band.

Eubie Blake (1883–1983)

PIANO

Born in Baltimore, he wrote 'The Charleston Rag' while still a teenager. Later teamed up with Noble Sissle to write the first all-black revue and a string of hit songs. The swing era left him behind, but Eubie enjoyed an Indian summer towards the end of his life performing his songs and rags, an example of living musical history.

***** Memories Of You**

Shout! Factory 30146 *Blake (p rolls); Steve 'Syco Steve' Williams (p); Gertrude Baum (p rolls); Noble Sissle (v).* 15–73.

(***) Tricky Fingers

Quicksilver 9003 *Blake (p solo).* n.d.

If he'd known he was going to live so long, Eubie Blake famously stated, he'd have taken better care of himself. As it was, Blake was a part of American music from the very birth of jazz till his death in 1983, just days after his hundredth birthday. For all his longevity, there is very little remaining in print. Some concerts and recitals on which he tells the story of his life and career are available in LP form on the Eubie Blake imprint, and there is a good sample of his piano playing on a compilation of *Jazz Piano Masters* (Chiaroscuro 170), but the above are the only readily available discs.

Memories Of You is probably the only Blake album anyone really needs. Using original piano rolls, but also a 1973 performance of the hit 'I'm Just Wild About Harry', it takes the story from 'The Charleston Rag' onwards and includes some wonderful fleet performances and some good guest spots, from Noble Sissle and Gertrude Baum (on 'Fizz Water'). The two best cuts, though, are probably the evergreen 'Boll Weevil Blues' and the closing Blake/Razaf charmer 'Memories Of You'. Great stuff.

Some of the same tunes appear on *Tricky Fingers*, an undated and unprovenanced set of material that is identifiably Blake but hardly an ideal introduction. A little basic scholarship would probably track down the recording dates and details, but frankly we haven't the time. Stick to *Memories Of You*.

Michael Blake (born 1964)

TENOR AND SOPRANO SAXOPHONES

A charter member of the Lounge Lizards, the gifted Canadian has managed to combine world music influences with avant-garde freedoms to create some powerfully original music.

***** Kingdom Of Champa**

Intuition 3189 *Blake; Steven Bernstein (t); Marcus Rojas (tba); Thomas Chapin (picc, f, bf, bs); Bryan Carrott (vib); David Tronzo (slide g); Tony Scherr (b, lute); Scott Neumann (d); Billy Martin (d).* 97.

***** Drift**

Intuition 3213 *Blake; Steven Bernstein (t); Ron Horton (t, flhn); Peck Allmond (t, ts, peck horn); Marcus Roja (tba); Briggan Krauss (as, bs); Frank Kimbrough (p); Tony Scherr (g); Ben Allison (b); Matt Wilson (d); Mauro Refosco (perc).* 9/98–1/99.

Blake's debut record as a solo artist was produced by none other than Teo Macero and is every bit as elegantly eclectic as you'd expect from that, mixing jazz, rock and Vietnamese influences with impressive surety. There is a folksong arrangement among the originals, of which 'Purple City' is the most substantial and impressive.

There is a workshopped feel to the second album, which is reminiscent in many ways of bassist Ben Allison's own projects. The writing is tinged with Mingus devices, not least a preference for a mid-to-low register for the main voicings, but no one will confuse Blake with any other writer. He is a genuine original, capable of delivering strong, feeling solos while negotiating a demanding chord structure. 'Duty Free Suite' and 'The Creep' are both outstanding.

Ran Blake (born 1935)

PIANO, KEYBOARDS

Born in Springfield, Massachusetts, Blake studied at Bard and Lenox and was working as an accompanist–partner to Jeanne Lee from the late '50s. More renowned as an academic, at New England Conservatory, Blake's records arrive like unexpected lightning and are a mostly fascinating blend of his musical studies and what he's drawn from jazz tradition.

***** Duke Dreams**

Soul Note 121027 *Blake (p solo).* 5 & 6/81.

A set of intelligently reimagined Duke Ellington compositions, handled as only Blake can. His ability to switch inside to outside on a composition as seemingly one-dimensional as 'Drop Me Off In Harlem' is evidence of his own ability as both performer and composer. The only other compositions included are Blake's overture to the set, which is the title-track, Dave Brubeck's 'Duke' and a totally unexpected version of 'Animal Crackers', which seems to have strayed in from another session, though it fits like a glove musically.

*** Improvisations

Soul Note 121022 *Blake; Jaki Byard (p).* 6/81.

Piano duos can be messily unsatisfactory affairs; one thinks of the Cecil Taylor/Mary Lou Williams imbroglio in particular. This, though, is an exception. Blake and Byard don't so much share a common conception as an ecumenical willingness to meet each other half-way, a characteristic noted on Byard's remarkable Festival Hall, London, encounter with the British improviser Howard Riley. The formalism of 'Sonata For Two Pianos' is mostly in the title; it's a limber, well-spaced piece with considerable harmonic interest. Almost inevitably, there is a taut, academic undercurrent to 'Tea For Two' and 'On Green Dolphin Street'. The pianos don't register quite as well as they might in some of the more exuberant passages but the sound is generally good, given the difficulties of recording this kind of music. A little more crispness in the bass might have helped, but the music is good enough to merit a sprinkle of stars.

*** Suffield Gothic

Soul Note 121077 *Blake; Houston Person (ts).* 9/83.

A most unlikely pairing, but a completely successful one, and cleverly weighted to solo performance with Person wheeled on for just four cuts. The best part of the album is a tribute to Mahalia Jackson, evidence of Blake's passion for female singers. Person sounds completely at ease on some difficult themes, at odds with Clifford Jordan's occasional discomfort on the later Mapeshade date *Masters of Different Worlds.*

**** Painted Rhythms: Volume 1

GM 3007 *Blake (p solo).* 12/85.

**** Painted Rhythms: Volume 2

GM 3008 *As above.* 12/85.

Like trumpeter Franz Koglmann, Blake takes a highly personal stance on the jazz tradition, reinterpreting classic material with a curious mixture of respectful precision and free-floating innovation. The most striking instances of that are the *four* versions of 'Maple Leaf Rag' that straddle these two remarkable discs. The third of them, bringing Volume 1 to a close, is dislocated, rediscovering Joplin's tune from a whirlpool of atonality and fractured rhythms. The second, by contrast, is played with a kind of sweet abandon that's the other side to Blake's sometimes rather severe approach. Volume 1 is largely concerned with jazz repertoire, originals like Duke's 'Azure' and 'Skrontch', Mary Lou Williams's 'What's Your Story, Morning Glory?', more recent things like George Russell's 'Ezzthetic' and the Stan Kenton tune that gives the set its name. Volume 2 casts the net a lot wider, searching for that 'Spanish tinge' which Jelly Roll Morton thought was a constant in jazz. Blake has long been interested in Sephardic music, and its distinctive harmonies (parallel to those familiar from the blues and jazz) provide this volume with new colours. Volume 2 also features Blake the composer. 'Shoah!' and 'Storm Warning' both seem to hint at historical urgency, an impression heightened by the quotes from Shostakovich in the second, and by Blake's adaptation of Olshanetsky and Wolfson's *klezmer*-based 'Vilna', a mourning tune memorializing the victims of a Nazi massacre. 'Babbitt', presumably dedicated to the composer, is a more abstract exploration of sound and silence, each pushed to the limit in its power to communicate with the immediacy of images.

CORE COLLECTION

**** The Short Life Of Barbara Monk

Soul Note 121127 *Blake; Ricky Ford (ts); Ed Felson (b); Jon Hazilla (d).* 8/86.

This is a truly marvellous album, and it makes Blake's apparent unwillingness to work in ensemble settings all the more galling. The first part ends with the title-piece, dedicated to Thelonious Monk's daughter, Barbara, who died of cancer in 1984. It's a complex and moving composition that shifts effortlessly between a bright lyricism and an edgy premonition; Blake plays quite beautifully, and his interplay with the young but supremely confident rhythm section is a revelation. A death also lies behind the closing track on part two. 'Pourquoi Laurent?' expresses both a hurt need to understand and a calm desire to heal, written in the face of French jazz critic Laurent Goddet's suicide. 'Impresario Of Death' is equally disturbing but so intelligently constructed as to resolve its inner contradiction perfectly. 'Vradiazi', by the Greek composer Theodorakis is a favourite of Blake's, as is the Sephardic melody 'Una Matica De Ruda' (two eye-blink takes), which also features on *Painted Rhythms 2* (above). To lighten the mix a little, there are astonishing versions of Stan Kenton's theme, 'Artistry In Rhythm', and, as an entirely unexpected opener, 'I've Got You Under My Skin'. Blake's Falcone Concert Grand sounds in perfect shape and the session – a single day of concentrated music-making – is superbly recorded and pressed.

***(*) Epistrophy

Soul Note 121177 *Blake (p solo).* 4/91.

Epistrophy is probably the most representative of Blake's records currently available. He touches base with the title-tune no fewer than three times on the record and adopts characteristically acute angles on the others. Where Blake departs from Monk is in the regularity and precision of the pulse. There is not a trace of the original begetter's anarchic time-shifts and slippages. In their place an exactness which is admirable in its consistency, even if it seems alien to those who have spent most of their time in different cloisters.

*** Memory Of Vienna

hatOLOGY CD 6134 *Blake; Anthony Braxton (reeds).*

A pairing which is both predictable and full of surprises. Blake's moments of wildness are tempered by Braxton's cool precision and emphasis on control. The sound of the duo is very clear, very sharp, with the suffocating clarity one would find at two or three atmospheres, and this is where the set goes wrong. There is no spontaneity, just a clash of intellects communicating at a level above that of ordinary mortals. Slightly mandarin, and just a touch pointless.

***(*) Unmarked Van

Soul Note 121227 *Blake; Tiziano Tononi (d).* 12/94.

Blake's passion for singers has been well attested over the years, but no one was quite prepared for this astonishing tribute to the genius of Sarah Vaughan. Sassie's huge range and ability to texture and retexture a single tone made her one of the great instrumentalists of the music, and Blake has settled on that aspect of her singing, rather than its emotional components (arguable as these remain) in constructing his homage. The opening piece is an original composition which conjures up some of her most characteristic phrasing devices, including that famous deep roll up off the bottom of a chord. Sassie recorded Debussy's 'Reverie' more than once and Blake has attempted to capture the less obviously classical interpretation. That oscillation between more and less formal interpretations runs through the whole album, not least on four separate takes of 'Tenderly', the last of which closes the disc on a moment of romantic uncertainty, less definitive than the title-tune, a Blake original which quotes Vaughan's version of the Lord's Prayer. This is a record which demands and repays a little effort, not one which communicates immediately and straightforwardly. Nothing in Blake's previous output quite prepares the listener for it, and yet everything is absolutely characteristic.

***(*) Something To Live For

hatOLOGY 527 *Blake; Guillermo Gregorio (cl); David Fabris (g).* 3/98.

Unpredictable as ever in his choice of material and settings, Blake nevertheless delivers a characteristic record in this filigree recital. Nineteen tracks are dispatched in a little over 50 minutes, ten of them duets with either Gregorio or Fabris: many pieces are so cut back to the bone that they're little more than epigrams, and even when he indulges himself over five or six minutes, as in 'Memphis', each chord seems meticulously selected. Not that this is effete or even very introspective as a programme: Blake may be sparing, but he doesn't spare the keyboard, and every piece is defined and crisply delineated, however oblique the structures may seem. Gregorio and Fabris do their best to enter into the spirit, though at times they might be wondering where they are. If you're not a Blake believer, this set won't do anything to convert you, but its astringency will delight any of the already-hooked.

*** Horace Is Blue: A Silver Noir

hatOLOGY 570 *Blake; James Merenda (as); James Knife Fabris (g).* 00.

Blake's ability to personalize almost any compositional style has never been more clearly evidenced than on this fascinating set of Horace Silver tunes. There are two versions each of 'Ecaroh' and the peerless 'Song For My Father', which further show how thoroughly Blake is prepared to reinvent a melody on each performance. These are probably the heart of a slightly unwieldy set, on which the other players are surplus to requirements and probably only recruited as a favour to former students. The sound is nicely enclosed, reflecting Blake's thoughtful and introspective approach.

**** Sonic Temples

GM 3046 2CD *Blake; Nicole Kampgen-Schuller (as); Ed Schuller (b); George Schuller (d, perc).* 01.

Unusual to hear Blake in a relatively conventional piano-trio setting, but the Schullers are so well versed in the pianist's brand of classically aware jazz that they fit in with the concept seamlessly. Hearing 'The Short Life Of Barbara Monk' in this context is absolutely fascinating, but the real delight of this two-CD set is the extraordinary 'Stormy Weather' which opens the second half of the set with heart-stopping grace.

We take the title to suggest the extent to which Blake has paid his respects, made his obeisances and sung his praises within these mainly familiar themes. The material is mostly standards-based – 'Nature Boy', 'Tangerine', 'Skylark', 'How High The Moon' – but leavened with some typically elegant Blake originals. Ed Schuller is represented by a couple of tracks – including 'Dra-Kumba', which features his wife Nicole on alto – and a couple of numbers sound as if they have been collectively improvised. Good as the rhythm section and guest are, it's Ran's record. How much he now resembles his namesake, William: immense experience tempered by a gentle innocence of purpose, apocalyptic vividness matched by delicacy of touch, radical and traditional in equal measure.

Ron Blake

TENOR AND SOPRANO SAXOPHONES

Cut his teeth in bassist Christian McBride's group and shows considerable promise as a leader.

*** Lest We Forget

Mack Avenue MAC 1012 *Blake; Rashwan Ross (t); Joey DeFrancesco (org); David Gilmore (g); Christian McBride (b); Greg Hutchinson (d).* 03.

Blake's self-released debut is unapologetically old-fashioned in cast, a homage to the soul-jazz of the '50s and '60s. With Joey DeFrancesco aboard, the Hammond sound of Charles Earland and Groove Holmes is very much to the fore, but Blake has the ability and the confidence to steer the project his way. 'Mister Magic' is a heartfelt tribute to the late Grover Washington Jr, played not as pastiche but tackled as a standard. 'Minor Chant' is a cool but vaguely threatening groove that makes the most of the fine rhythm section, which includes a returning-the-favour bassist called McBride. Top marks to him, as always, but all praise to drummer Greg Hutchinson, a veteran of another great bassist's band, and here showing all the supple time-feel he learned from Ray Brown.

Blake's tough, sardonic delivery is evident from the opening 'Sara's Dance' but really comes into its own on the second track 'More Today Than Yesterday', which is the high point of the set and might have been better placed later on. 'You Must Believe In Spring' gives Ron a chance to pace himself against the masters and he comes out very respectably indeed with a typically well-crafted and intelligent solo.

The basic organ-trio format has been imaginatively augmented. McBride is more than a time-keeper and guitarist Gilmore does intriguing things behind the two horns. Ross is perhaps the weak point, but since he's the least familiar name here, it may be that he deserves a longer and more detailed listen. A fine debut from a guy whose conservative stance doesn't mask a lack of ambition.

Seamus Blake (born 1969)

TENOR AND SOPRANO SAXOPHONES

Canadian-born, Blake made a mark as one of the crop of young saxophonists to enter the New York scene in the '90s.

*** The Call

Criss Cross 1088 *Blake; Kurt Rosenwinkel (g); Kevin Hays (p); Larry Grenadier (b); Bill Stewart (d).* 12/93.

*****(*) Four Track Mind**
Criss Cross 1126 *Blake; Tim Hagans (t); Mark Turner (ts); Kevin Hays (p, ky); Larry Grenadier (b); Billy Drummond (d).* 12/94.

***** The Bloomdaddies**
Criss Cross 1110 *Blake; Chris Cheek (ts); Jesse Murphy (b); Jorge Rossy, Dan Reiser (d).* 12/95.

Blake has paid due respect to his masters – fellow-saxophonist Joe Lovano, fellow-Canadian Kenny Wheeler – without in any way standing in thrall to them. He has very quickly mapped out his own path, and the appearance of subsequent Criss Cross releases amply justifies label boss Gerry Teekens's confidence in giving the then 24-year-old a date as leader. For some reason, Blake's sessions for the label have been issued out of chronological sequence, as the issue numbers suggest. Perhaps Teekens wanted to highlight the 'other' side of his young signing, in the company of his electric band, The Bloomdaddies. Perhaps he had some doubts about the quality of *Four Track Mind.* If the latter, it's a surprising conclusion. The 1994 album is self-consciously a showcase, intended to demonstrate Blake's range and diversity. If there is a criticism, it is that the set has very little consistency. It opens with the funky title-track, and an off-the-peg blues, 'Dittee', before Blake shows any real originality either of conception or of execution. That comes with 'Jali', a tribute to former boss Victor Lewis, featuring Blake on soprano and Tim Hagans coming to the fore. The most striking piece on the album is 'In A Warring Absence', a jagged, almost serial piece written by Blake's violinist girlfriend, Farran, the same 'Miss James' who inspires the set's one romantic ballad and who probably bought young Seamus the Debussy discs he'd obviously been listening to.

Though there is an inevitable overlap of styles, *The Bloomdaddies* is a very different animal: loud, sometimes overemphatic and heavily processed, it's marked by rock and hip-hop sensibilities. Bass guitar, twinned drummers and, again, closely interwoven saxophone parts contribute to a dense, slightly programmed sound. Blake cedes some of the writing duties to partner Chris Cheek, specifically the last two tunes and the ballad feature, but by the time they come along the album has started to lose its way a little. A clangorous medley restores a forceful, upbeat feel after Cheek's 'Shelter', which is a lovely conception, and it might have been preferable to close proceedings at that point. Signs that Berklee-trained Blake hasn't yet got a comfortable range of material under his belt. He dabbles briefly with harmolodics on 'To Be Ornette To Be' and seems to decide he's a traditionalist – albeit a noisy one – after all, following up with Louis Prima's 'Sing, Sing, Sing'. Throughout, the emphasis is on tight ensemble playing, unlike the more open, blowing feel of *The Call.* It's often difficult to say which of the two saxophonists is to the fore, and how much is played as live and how much is a studio artefact.

***** Stranger Things Have Happened**
Fresh Sound FSNT 063 *Blake; Kurt Rosenwinkel, Jesse Harris (g); Larry Grenadier (b); Jorge Rossy (d).* 3/99.

An interesting continuation, but the music feels rather shapeless, even melancholy: an uncredited vocalist (presumably Blake himself) sings on the doleful 'Northern Light' and, while Rosenwinkel's effects and free gestures leave the harmonic picture wide open, Blake tends to amble through it, focusing himself here and there, and just as often sounding unsure of quite where he is.

***** Sunsol**
Fresh Sound New Talent 087 *Blake; Avishai Cohen (b); Marc Miralta (d).* 00.

*****(*) Echonomics**
Criss Cross 1197 *Blake; David Kikoski (p); Ed Howard (b); Victor Lewis (d).* 00.

Blake and Miralta are old roomies and they sound good together on this free-flowing and pretty open-ended set. By this stage in his career, Cohen is able to take on just about any challenge, and he contributes some of the strongest material, notably the opening 'Go', which works interesting variations on a blues pattern. 'Boston In 3/4' is also strong and the title-piece rounds out a cracking set.

Echonomics is in a 'new standards' vein, taking tunes like Brian Wilson's 'God Only Knows' and Stevie Wonder's 'Rain Your Love Down' and using them as a basis for relatively orthodox, though by no means formulaic, jazz improvisation. Blake's daring is still in evidence but he's also trying to consolidate a style, and this is the album that does it for us. Lewis and Howard anchor the sound effectively.

***** Mosh For Lovers**
Fresh Sound New Talent FSNT 178 *Blake; Chris Cheek (ts); Jesse Murphy (b); Tony Mason (d).* 01.

A fairly routine return for The Bloomdaddies band. Blake's soloing sounds perfunctory in places, but the group as a whole now coheres like the working unit it is and past fans will not be too disappointed. Not his best, though.

Rob Blakeslee

TRUMPET, CORNET, FLUGELHORN

Free-bop brassman, working in the community of improvisers and players associated with Vinny Golia's Nine Winds label in California.

****(*) Lifeline**
Nine Winds NWCD 0147 *Blakeslee; Vinny Golia (ss, bs, f, bcl); Tad Weed (p); Ken Filiano (b); Billy Mintz (d).* 3/92.

***** Long Narrows**
Nine Winds NWCD 0167 *As above, except Michael Bisio (b), Bob Meyer (d) replace Filiano and Mintz.* 7/94.

Blakeslee is the unassuming leader for two records that are effectively free-bop exercises by the repertory cast of Nine Winds. Both feature much food for thought, yet neither makes a very distinctive impact, sometimes through circumstances outside the playing. The sound on *Lifeline* is terribly thin and unfocused, and it tends to take all the sting out of the music, which suffers further from tracks which simply go on too long ('Absence Of Mallets' runs past 21 minutes). *Long Narrows* is better, more lucid and more decisive all round, without offering the rewards which these players have each managed to proffer up in other circumstances.

*****(*) Spirit Of The Times**
Nine Winds NWCD 0208 *Blakeslee; Vinny Golia (cl, bcl); Ken Filiano (b); Billy Mintz (d).* 5/97.

While there's still a suspicion that these performances sometimes outstay their welcome, this is otherwise a poised and inventive set of themes, and Blakeslee has never sounded better in a studio. 'Just Off The Avenue' is a worthy dedication to

Bobby Bradford, the leader's playing finding the clarion pure tone which Bradford uses, and with Golia restricting himself to two members of the clarinet family, there's a clear echo of the old Bradford–Carter quartet records for Revelation. A fine piece of work.

*****(*) Last Minute Gifts**

Louie 019 *Blakeslee; Michael Vlatkovich (tb); Clyde Reed (b); Dave Storrs (d).* 8/00.

The beautiful dialogues between Blakeslee and Vlatkovich form the body of this set. Both are conservative radicals in terms of their individual playing, able to turn on a brass player's full range of expressionist effects but reluctant to do so very often. It helps that Reed and Storrs have a graceful way with the rhythms, keeping out of the way most of the time in order to let the front-line blow. The tunes imitate folk melody or copy Ornette – often the same thing anyway – but they're an individual lot, and there are some light touches of humour along the way too.

Art Blakey (1919–90)

DRUMS

Pittsburgh-born and self-taught as a pianist, Blakey was leading his own big band at 15, though he switched to drums when Erroll Garner came in. In New York he joined the powerhouse Billy Eckstine band and stayed for three years until it broke up in 1947. Freelancing and occasional bandleading followed until the 1954 Blue Note sessions which led to the formation of the Jazz Messengers (the name Blakey used for all his subsequent groups), the most famous academy in jazz, through which passed countless young and up-and-coming players. A master percussionist who investigated African and other styles along with his own swing-to-bop beginnings, he was peerless in support of soloists. He also loved to speak up on behalf of jazz, and he kept the standard unswervingly until his death in 1990.

CORE COLLECTION

****** A Night At Birdland Vol. 1**

Blue Note 32146-2 *Blakey; Clifford Brown (t); Lou Donaldson (as); Horace Silver (p); Curley Russell (b).* 2/54.

****** A Night At Birdland Vol. 2**

Blue Note 32147-2 *As above.* 2/54.

It was still called the Art Blakey Quintet, but this was the nexus of the band that became the Jazz Messengers, one of the most durable bywords in jazz, even if the name was first used on a Horace Silver album-cover. Blakey wasn't as widely acknowledged as Max Roach or Kenny Clarke as one of the leaders in establishing bop drumming, and in the end he was credited with working out the rhythms for what came after original bebop, first heard to significant effect on these records. Much of it is based on sheer muscle. Blakey played very loud and very hard, accenting the off-beat with a hi-hat snap that had a thunderous abruptness and developing a snare roll that possessed a high drama all its own. As much as he dominates the music, though, he always plays for the band, and inspirational leadership is as apparent on these early records as it is on his final ones. Both horn players benefit: Donaldson makes his Parkerisms sound pointed and vivacious, while Brown is marvellously mercurial, as well as sensitive on his ballad feature 'Once In A While' from Volume 1 (Donaldson's comes on 'If I Had You' on the second record). Silver, too, lays down some of the tenets of hard bop, with his poundingly funky solos and hints of gospel melody. The latest RVG editions of the albums restore the original ten-inch cover art, and for once a new mastering has really bounced the sound up an extra level.

*****(*) At The Café Bohemia Vol. 1**

Blue Note 32148-2 *Blakey; Kenny Dorham (t); Hank Mobley (ts); Horace Silver (p); Doug Watkins (b).* 11/55.

*****(*) At The Café Bohemia Vol. 2**

Blue Note 32149-2 *As above.* 11/55.

A different band but results of equal interest to the Birdland session (the second volume of the Bohemia date was made 12 days after Volume 1). Hank Mobley is a somewhat unfocused stylist, and nothing quite matches the intensity which the quintet secured at Birdland, yet the playing is finally just as absorbing. Dorham's elusive brilliance was seldom so extensively captured, his 'Yesterdays' ballad feature displaying a rare tenderness which faces off against the contentious dynamism of his fast solos that seem to forge a link between Dizzy Gillespie and Miles Davis. Long, mid-tempo pieces such as 'Soft Winds' and 'Like Someone In Love' find Silver and Blakey in reflective competition, but the drummer never slackens his grip; listen to what he does behind Dorham on 'Minor's Holiday'. There's some added charm in the announcements by Mobley and Dorham before their features. Once again, the RVG remastering in these new editions of this great music brings the sound up to a fresh height and even if you think you know these dates well, they're worth returning to.

*****(*) The Jazz Messengers**

Columbia CK 65265 *Blakey; Donald Byrd (t); Hank Mobley (ts); Horace Silver (p); Doug Watkins (b).* 4–5/56.

An expanded and revised version of the original Columbia date, with five extra tracks. Byrd and Mobley weren't the greatest front line Blakey had, and when McLean arrived shortly afterwards the group had a flash more fire about it; but these are still elegant and powerful tracks, and about as authentic as hard bop could be – tough, unfussy, swinging. It's a handsome new package with splendid photos and notes.

***** Hard Bop / Paris Concert Collectables**

COL-5675 *Blakey; Bill Hardman, Lee Morgan (t); Jackie Mclean (as); Benny Golson (ts); Sam Dockery (p), Bobby Timmons; Spanky DeBrest, Jymie Merritt (b).* 12/56–12/58.

Combining sessions two years apart by two entirely different editions of the Messengers, this offers the Hardman–McLean frontline on a studio date followed by Morgan–Golson live in Paris. The latter tend to take the honours, since the studio date seems unsympathetically produced and lacks much in the way of real fire (the ballad feature 'My Heart Stood Still' has been dropped to fit both albums on to one CD). That said, the concert set, with marathon treatments of 'Moanin' (which follows a rote solo course after a beautiful statement of the theme) and 'Justice', does suffer from some long-windedness. Morgan's handsome 'I Remember Clifford' and the steaming finale of 'Just By Myself' are worth waiting for.

♛ **** Art Blakey's Jazz Messengers With Thelonious Monk

Atlantic/Rhino R2 75598 *Blakey; Bill Hardman (t); Johnny Griffin (ts); Thelonious Monk (p); Spanky DeBrest (b).* 3/57.

Blakey appeared on several of Monk's seminal Blue Note sessions, and he had a seemingly intuitive knowledge of what the pianist wanted from a drummer. Griffin, volatile but serene in his mastery of the horn, was an almost ideal yet very different interpreter of Monk's music. This set of five Monk tunes and one by Griffin is a masterpiece. If Hardman wasn't on the same exalted level as the other three, he does nothing to disgrace himself, and DeBrest keeps calm, unobtrusive time. The continuous dialogue between Blakey and Monk comes out most clearly in passages such as Monk's solo on 'In Walked Bud', but almost any moment on the session illustrates their unique empathy. Both use simple materials, which makes the music unusually clear in its layout, yet the inner complexities are astonishing, and as a result the music retains an uncanny freshness more than 40 years later; no passage is like another, and some of the tempos, such as those chosen for 'Evidence' and 'I Mean You', are almost unique in the annals of Monk interpretations. In its new Atlantic/Rhino edition, the music comes with three alternative takes, frankly inessential, but we welcome the superior sound of this remastering. Absolutely indispensable jazz.

*** Orgy In Rhythm

Blue Note 56586 *Blakey; Herbie Mann (f); Ray Bryant (p); Wendell Marshall (b); Jo Jones, Art Taylor, Specs Wright (d); Sabu Martinez (perc, v); Carlos Patato Valdes, Jose Valiente, Ubal Nieto, Evilio Quintero (perc).* 3/57.

A good bash. The drummers get 'Split Skins' to themselves, and the rest is an entertaining if somewhat exhausting barrage of Latinesque licks provided by the massed percussionists, pepped up by Sabu's singing and Herbie's tootling flute. If the idea was to make a record that would fit in with the craze for exotic lounge music, Blakey was probably having little of that. The two original LPs have fitted on to a single CD.

*** A Night In Tunisia

Bluebird 09026-63896-2 *Blakey; Bill Hardman (t); Jackie McLean (as); Johnny Griffin (ts); Sam Dockery (p); Spanky DeBrest (b).* 4/57.

*** A Night In Tunisia / Play Lerner And Loewe

Collectables COL-CD-2811 2CD *As above.* 3–4/57.

Compared to the session which goes under the same title for Blue Note this is rather more routine, but it's still the kind of band which would have crowds cheering in any jazz club today. The star among the horns is the superfast Griffin: his solos on both versions of 'Theory Of Art' are boisterous blowouts which still stack up as thoughtful designs. Three alternative takes provide almost 30 minutes of extra music and in the smart digipaks, which this series comes in, an attractive buy.

Collectables set a poser for collectors by doubling up the same session (minus the alternative takes) with the lesser-known *Play Lerner And Loewe* on a somewhat ungenerous twofer (both discs only just top the 80-minute mark in total). The latter was clearly a record-company man's idea and judging from the sleeve-notes it was very hard work (Hardman recalled that 'I can't remember when I felt so beat after it was all over'). McLean is absent but Griffin is again operating at tornado velocity, and though the ensembles seem stiff and unsure, the solos have no shortage of fireworks.

***(*) Moanin'

Blue Note 95324-2 *Blakey; Lee Morgan (t); Benny Golson (ts); Bobby Timmons (p); Jymie Merritt (b).* 10/58.

*** 1958 Paris Olympia

Emarcy 832659-2 *As above.* 11–12/58.

*** Des Femmes Disparaissent / Les Tricheurs

Fontana 834752-2 *As above.* 12/58.

*** Les Liaisons Dangereuses 1960

Fontana 812017-2 *Blakey; Lee Morgan (t); Barney Wilen (ss, ts); Duke Jordan, Bobby Timmons (p); Jymie Merritt (b); John Rodriguez, Willie Rodriguez, Tommy Lopez (perc).* 7/59.

Benny Golson wasn't a Jazz Messenger for long – *Moanin'* was his only American album with the band – but he still contributed three of the most enduring themes to its book, all of them on *Moanin'*: the title-track, 'Blues March' and 'Along Came Betty'. These versions might seem almost prosaic next to some of the grandstand readings which other Blakey bands would later create, but Golson's own playing shows great toughness, and the ebullient Morgan, also making his Messengers debut, is a splendid foil. Another release in the Rudy Van Gelder Edition which is Blue Note's latest polishing of their catalogue. The set played at the Paris Olympia follows a similar pattern. Golson plays with riveting urgency (if imperfect control), and only the more distant sound keeps this one on the B-list of Messengers albums. The soundtrack for Eduardo Molinaro's *Des Femmes Disparaissent* is one of the least known of Blakey's albums, directed mainly by Golson. Made up of fragments of Messengers tunes, motifs, drum-rolls and blues, it scarcely hangs together as a Messengers session, but the components are impeccably conceived and finished, and the superb studio sound allows a close-up hearing of how this band worked.

Another soundtrack, *Les Liaisons Dangereuses*, offers a brief look at Barney Wilen in the band. The music is less than abundant in terms of material (most of it gets played twice for the purposes of the film) but Wilen acquits himself courageously, his tenor on 'Valmontana' and soprano on 'Prelude In Blue' both impressive.

***(*) At The Jazz Corner Of The World

Blue Note 28888-2 2CD *Blakey; Lee Morgan (t); Hank Mobley (ts); Bobby Timmons (p); Jymie Merritt (b).* 4/59.

A brief interlude with Hank Mobley returning to the tenor chair. He sounds comfortable enough – and gets to contribute three tunes of his own, even if they're hardly in the class set by the next tenorman to step in. Any live event with the Messengers in this period was worth saving, and this one sounds terrifically loud, up-front and spirited, with the master of the traps in imperious form. Originally on two separate LPs, now on a double-CD set.

*** The Big Beat

Blue Note 46400-2 *Blakey; Lee Morgan (t); Wayne Shorter (ts); Bobby Timmons (p); Jymie Merritt (b).* 3/60.

**** A Night In Tunisia

Blue Note 84049-2 *As above.* 8/60.

**** Roots And Herbs

Blue Note 21956-2 *As above, except add Walter Davis Jr (p).* 2–5/61.

*****(*) The Freedom Rider**

Blue Note 21287-2 *As above, except omit Davis.* 2–5/61.

*****(*) The Witch Doctor**

Blue Note 21957-2 *As above.* 3/61.

After Golson came Shorter, the most individual of composers and an invaluable source for the Messengers. *A Night In Tunisia* is a long-standing favourite among Messengers followers. Besides the wildly over-the-top version of the title-tune, there's Shorter's lovely 'Sincerely Diana' and two charming Lee Morgan themes. Shorter's playing had a dark, corrosive edge to it that turned softly beseeching when he played ballads, but some of his solos don't come off; that on 'The Chess Players' from the patchy *The Big Beat* never gets started. *The Freedom Rider* is beefed up with three extra tracks, including the Morgan themes 'Pisces' and 'Uptight'; this is a lesser-known Blakey album, but it still has Blakey's title-track drum solo (a celebration of the Freedom Ride anti-segregationists), Shorter's magnificent 'El Toro' (with a superb tenor improvisation) and the usual share of intensities. *The Witch Doctor* is a new arrival and a welcome one: Morgan's 'Afrique' and the title-tune are more New York than dark continent, but Shorter's mysterious 'Those Who Sit And Wait' was worth waiting for. Even more bountiful, though, is *Roots And Herbs*, which is arguably the great forgotten Blakey album. All six themes are by Shorter (and there are three alternative takes as a bonus), and from the ferocious 'Ping Pong' onwards the music hits a rare intensity, allied with the composer's enigmatic elegance. Davis sits in for Timmons on two titles.

***** Live In Stockholm 1959**

DIW 313 *Blakey; Lee Morgan (t); Wayne Shorter (ts); Walter Bishop Jr (p); Jymie Merritt (b).* 11/59.

***** Live In Stockholm 1959**

Dragon DRCD 182 *As above.* 11/59.

***** Live In Stockholm 1960**

DIW 344 *As above, except Bobby Timmons (p) replaces Bishop.* 12/60.

***** Lausanne 1960 First Set**

TCB 02058 *As above.* 12/60

***** Lausanne 1960 Second Set**

TCB 02062 *As above.* 12/60.

***** Unforgettable Lee!**

Fresh Sound FSCD-1020 *As above.* 4–6/60.

***** More Birdland Sessions**

Fresh Sound FSCD-1029 *As above, except add Walter Davis Jr (p).* 6–11/60.

Though one might imagine live Messengers recordings to be hotter than their studio counterparts, the band was able to generate the same intensity in both locations. Still, these live sessions from a couple of European visits are useful supplements to the Blue Note albums. There is little variation between the three Stockholm sets, although the 1959 Dragon issue includes some more interesting themes, recorded on the same day as the DIW disc but apparently using some different material. With the recordings probably emanating from radio tapes, the sound is consistently clear, if not as full-bodied as the studio sessions; in any event, Morgan and Shorter are always worth hearing as a youthful partnership, creating the kind of idiosyncratic front-line that seems lost among today's more faceless technicians. The two *Lausanne* discs are from Swiss Radio archives and find the band on another European stopover – same tour, same calibre of playing, and probably for completists only.

The Fresh Sound disc sorts together nine tracks from various Birdland sessions in the spring of 1960 (it is nominally credited to Morgan and has his picture on the CD sleeve), and although anyone who has the other discs listed here will have the material in other versions, this catches the Messengers on a very hot streak. A brief 'Justice' finds Morgan in explosive form on his solo, and he sounds particularly exciting on most of the tracks on a generously packed CD. The sound, though, is rather grainy and suffers from some drop-outs. *More Birdland Sessions* sweeps together some more offcuts from the same year. Shorter is at his most eccentric in the 'Lester Left Town' solo, but there is interesting stuff from both him and Morgan throughout. Indifferent sound, though.

*****(*) Jazz Messengers**

Impulse! 051175-2 *Blakey; Freddie Hubbard (t); Curtis Fuller (tb); Wayne Shorter (ts); Cedar Walton (p); Jymie Merritt (b).* 6/61.

****** Mosaic**

Blue Note 46523-2 *As above.* 10/61.

****** Buhaina's Delight**

Blue Note 84104-2 *As above.* 11–12/61.

*****(*) Three Blind Mice Vol. 1**

Blue Note 84451 *As above.* 3/62.

*****(*) Three Blind Mice Vol. 2**

Blue Note 84452 *As above.* 3/62.

***** Caravan**

Original Jazz Classics OJC 038 *As above, except Reggie Workman (b) replaces Merritt.* 10/62.

*****(*) Ugetsu**

Original Jazz Classics OJC 090 *As above.* 6/63.

****** Free For All**

Blue Note 84170 *As above.* 2/64.

***** Kyoto**

Original Jazz Classics OJC 145 *As above.* 2/64.

Exit Morgan, enter Hubbard and Fuller. By now it was clear that Blakey's Jazz Messengers were becoming a dynasty unto themselves, with the drummer driving everything from his kit. As musical director, Shorter was still providing some startling material which Hubbard and Fuller, outstanding players but undercharacterized personalities, could use to fashion directions of their own. Cedar Walton was another significant new man; after the lightweight work of Bobby Timmons, Walton's deeper but no less buoyant themes added extra weight to the band's impact.

In some ways this was the most adventurous of all Messengers line-ups. The three masterpieces are the amazingly intense *Free For All*, which reasserts Blakey's polyrhythmic firepower as never before and finds Shorter at his most ferocious on the title-tune and 'Hammer Head'; *Mosaic*, where the complex title-piece (by Walton) shows how the expanded voicings of the band added orchestral sonority to rhythmic power; and *Buhaina's Delight*, which opens on the swaggering 'Backstage Sally' and leads to Shorter's stone-faced 'Contemplation' and vivid arrangement of 'Moon River'. Hubbard's feisty brightness and Fuller's sober, quickfire solos are a memorable counterweight to Shorter's private, dark improvisations. The tenorman is less evident on *Kyoto*, a breezier session dominated by Fuller and

Hubbard, and although the live-at-Birdland *Ugetsu* is fine, it doesn't catch fire in quite the way the band might have been expected to in concert, though Shorter's feature on 'I Didn't Know What Time It Was' is ponderously impressive. More exciting are the two *Three Blind Mice* sets, mostly made at an engagement at the Renaissance in Los Angeles. Less finished than the studio recordings, but it's a thrill to hear Shorter and Hubbard tear into the likes of 'It's Only A Paper Moon' as well as the originals in the book. Walton is often rather remote in the mix.

Caravan is another solid though slightly less imposing set. The earliest date for Impulse! seems to have been organized more by the producer than by the musicians since it consists almost entirely of standards; though capably done, it's not what this edition of the band was about.

*** The African Beat

Blue Note 22666-2 *Blakey; Yusef Lateef (ts, f, ob, cow horn, perc); Ahmed Abdul-Malik (b); Solomon G. Ilori (v, whistle, perc); Chief Bey, Montego Joe, Garvin Masseaux, James Ola Folami, Robert Crowder, Curtis Fuller (perc).* 1/62.

A little more serious than *Orgy In Rhythm*, though the end result isn't all that different. No doubt Blakey was fascinated by the possibilities of African and American percussionists working together, and the recording is a starburst of energy, the master's kit-patterns surrounded by congas, telegraph drums, *chekeres, maracas, bambara* drums and more. Lateef is right at home in this setting, and there is the unique presence of Curtis Fuller as a tympanist. In the end, though, the music feels packaged for its surroundings, the hard bop of the Blue Note catalogue, with the various pieces either foreshortened or otherwise shaped to fit to an LP's needs.

**** The Best Of Art Blakey And The Jazz Messengers

Blue Note 93205-2

*** The Best Of Art Blakey

Emarcy 848245-2 *Blakey; Lee Morgan, Chuck Mangione, Valery Ponomarev (t); Bobby Watson (as); Benny Golson, Barney Wilen, Wayne Shorter, Frank Mitchell, David Schnitter (ts); Bobby Timmons, Walter Davis Jr, Keith Jarrett, James Williams (p); Jymie Merritt, Reggie Johnson, Dennis Irwin (b).* 12/58–2/79.

The Blue Note compilation is well chosen, with 'Moanin'', 'Blues March' and 'Dat Dere' covering the most popular Messengers tunes and 'Mosaic', 'Free For All' and 'Lester Left Town' their most challenging. 'A Night In Tunisia' is also here. Emarcy's collection includes four tracks with Barney Wilen opposite Morgan in the 1958–9 band, a 1966 reading of 'My Romance' which is included mainly for the presence of Keith Jarrett, and a somewhat desultory 1979 version of 'Blues March' by a less than distinguished line-up; a patchwork but worthwhile disc.

***(*) A Jazz Message

Impulse! 547964-2 *Blakey; Sonny Stitt (ts, as); McCoy Tyner (p); Art Davis (b).* 7/63.

Loose-limbed, flying, four great musicians having a high old time of it one day in the Van Gelder studios (though this wasn't a Blue Note date). It's just some blues and three standards, and it's no immortal statement, but Blakey sounds like he's enjoying himself hugely, and though Stitt rarely let himself go in the studios, he plays some of his most shining licks here. Tyner and the super-solid Davis go along for the ride.

**(*) Child's Dance

Prestige 24130-2 *Blakey; Woody Shaw (t); Buddy Terry (ss); Ramon Morris (ts, f); Carter Jefferson (ts); Manny Boyd (f); George Cables, Cedar Walton, John Hicks, Walter Davis Jr (p); Essien Nkrumah (g); Stanley Clarke, Mickey Bass (b); Nathaniel Bettis, Sonny Morgan, Pablo Landrums, Emmanuel Rahid, Ray Mantilla, Tony Waters (perc).* 3/73.

*** Mission Eternal

Prestige 24159-2 *Blakey; Woody Shaw (t); Steve Turre (tb); Carter Jefferson (ss, ts); Cedar Walton (p); Michael Howell (g); Mickey Bass (b); Tony Waters (perc); Jon Hendricks (v).* 3/73.

This Messengers period is scarcely represented in the catalogues at all at present. They cut three albums for Prestige at this time; the balance of two of them is presented on *Child's Dance*, with a long-unreleased track as a bonus. Musically, it's pretty poor stuff. The ramshackle percussion tracks, modish electric pianos, preponderance of flutes and generally rambling solos give little focus to a band that was stuck between past and future. The one figure of substance (aside from Blakey himself) is Shaw, who cuts out a few hard-edged solos and gives a slightly overcooked but mainly convincing reading of 'I Can't Get Started' as the anachronistic but solid centre of the disc.

Mission Eternal mops up the rest of the material and is a much better bet. Shaw again takes the honours, his solos full of snap but with a thoughtful, almost musing quality at times which militates against the volatility of the typical Messengers approach. Turre appears on three tracks and Hendricks guest-stars on a jolly treatment of 'Along Came Betty'. There is a worthwile bonus in the previously unheard 'Siempre Mi Amor'.

*** Blakey's Beat

Concord CCD2-2234-2 2CD *Blakey; Valery Ponomarev, Wynton Marsalis (t); Bobby Watson (as); David Schnitter, Bill Pierce (ts); James Wiliams (p); Dennis Irwin, Charles Fambrough (b).* 5/78–8/81.

The relatively quiet time Blakey had of it in the studios in the '70s says something about how his kind of jazz had slipped out of fashion, and his albums for Concord seemed to consign this perpetual standard-bearer to a mere repertory role. The first disc in this twofer reissue, originally *In This Korner*, suggests that the Messengers had become so much hot air, solos padded out to the point of obesity and the newer items in the band's book lacking the kind of instant-classic qualities which had gone before. On disc two (originally *Straight Ahead*) Wynton Marsalis takes up the cudgels and everything starts to change. Read on.

***(*) Keystone 3

Concord CCD 4196 *Blakey; Wynton Marsalis(t); Branford Marsalis (as); Billy Pierce (ts);Donald Brown (p); Charles Fambrough (b).* 1/82.

Wynton Marsalis's arrival was a turning point for both Blakey and jazz in the '80s. His peculiar assurance and whipcrack precision, at the age of 19, heralded a new school of Messengers graduates of rare confidence and ability. Once Marsalis took over as MD, the ensembles took on a fresh bite and the soloists sound leaner, more pointed. *Keystone 3* was recorded live at San Francisco's Keystone Korner and finds a renewed involvement from Blakey himself, who's well served by the crisp recording. Watson's departure was a shade disappointing, given the tickle of creative confrontation between himself and Marsalis, but brother Branford's arrival, though he sounds as yet unformed, lends another edge of anxiety-to-please to the ensembles.

*****(*) Coast To Coast**
Concord CCD2-4926-2 2CD *Blakey; Terence Blanchard (t); Donald Harrison (as); Jean Toussaint (ts); Mulgrew Miller (p); Lonnie Plaxico (b).* 4/84.

Even after Wynton Marsalis departed the band, the Messengers continued their winning streak. Blanchard, whom one might call the first post-Marsalis trumpeter, proved another inspiring MD, and his partnership with Harrison made the front-line sizzle. Two trumpet solos, on 'Oh By The Way' and 'Tenderly', show off intelligence, fire and perfectly calculated risk in some abundance. Miller and Plaxico renewed the rhythm section with superlative technique, and the old man sounds as aggressive as ever. Toussaint's brawny solos are closely in the Messengers tradition and Harrison was a lucid foil to Blanchard in particular (they made a few albums together for Columbia after this). This twofer doubles up the single albums *New York Scene* and *Live At Kimball's.*

****(*) Not Yet**
Soul Note 121105-2 *Blakey; Philip Harper (t); Robin Eubanks (tb); Javon Jackson (ts); Benny Green (p); Peter Washington (b).* 3/88.

****(*) I Get A Kick Out Of Bu**
Soul Note 121550-2 *As above, except Leon Dorsey (b) replaces Washington.* 11/88.

Blakey's status as a bandmaster for all seasons was now as widely celebrated as anything in jazz, and taking a place in the Messengers was one of the most widespread ambitions among young players. Of those in this edition, only Jackson seems less than outstanding, with Eubanks splendidly peppery, Harper another Marsalis type with a silvery tone, and Green one of the funkiest pianists since the band's earlier days. Yet they never made a truly outstanding Messengers record together. By this time, much of the excitement about neo-classic jazz had subsided, and the players had a hard time escaping the scent of technique-over-feeling which was beginning to invade a lot of precision-orientated young bands. Blakey's own playing remains thunderously powerful, and he makes a lot of things happen which might otherwise have slipped away, yet the Soul Note records seem made by rote, and there's an overall feeling of transition and that Blakey himself was too late in his career to move forward.

Terence Blanchard (born 1962)

TRUMPET, PIANO

Came to prominence as a late-period Jazz Messenger and has since recorded as a leader and become heavily involved in film music, initially scoring several Spike Lee movies.

***** The Billie Holiday Songbook**
Columbia CK 57793 *Blanchard; Bruce Barth (p); Chris Thomas (b); Troy Davis (d); Jeanie Bryson (v); orchestra.* 10/93.

****** Romantic Defiance**
Columbia 480489 *Blanchard; Kenny Garrett (ts); Edward Simon (p); Chris Thomas (b); Troy Davis (d).* 12/94.

*****(*) The Heart Speaks**
Columbia 483638-2 *Blanchard; Ivan Lins (p, v); Edward Simon (p); Oscar Castro-Nueves (g); David Pulphus (b); Paulinho Da Costa (perc); Fred Zlotkin, David Bohanovich (v).* 95.

****** Jazz In Film**
Columbia SK 60671 *Blanchard; Steve Turre (tb); Donald Harrison (as); Joe Henderson (ts); Kenny Kirkland (p); Reginald Veal (b); Carl Allen (d).* 3–4/98.

Blanchard plays with a minimum of fuss and with admirable directness, simple and declarative: name, rank and number – though, if you're looking for a fancier way to describe what he does and how he sounds 'romantic defiance' serves well. If he looks more and more like Dizzy as the years go by, his sound seems to come from an earlier generation, 'Sweets' Edison and Buck Clayton foremost. An intriguing segue from the original 'Glass J' to 'Mo' Better Blues' and thence to Ornette's 'Lonely Woman' (on an earlier Columbia album, *Simply Stated*) serves as a brief but effective history lesson.

Blanchard took over Wynton Marsalis's chair in the Jazz Messengers (that was where he met sidekick, Donald Harrison, who'd stepped into Branford Marsalis's shoes) but though there are superficial similarities of approach he's a more open-hearted player, less hung up on self-defeating standards of authenticity. Earlier albums for Columbia are currently in the dead-letter office, but these more recent entries remain available. One wonders how exactly the Billie Holiday project was A&R'd. 'Songbook' albums are popular again, and though Lady was no composer, she gave the material she sang such a personal cast that a whole raft of songs – not just 'Strange Fruit' – seem eternally associated with her. At what point, though, was Jeanie Bryson brought in as soloist? Whatever, it's the key to this extremely patchy session. Blanchard finds interesting things to do with 'Good Morning Heartache', a tune that sits comfortably for a brass player, and solos with some emotion on 'I Cover The Waterfront'. But the band trudges through the rest, and it's only on Bryson's five songs that things get seriously interesting. 'Strange Fruit' is always a bit of a gamble for other singers. Only Nina Simone has ever got a hold of its sheer weirdness, but Bryson takes it simply and unaffectedly, unlike her dizzy reading of 'What A Little Moonlight Can Do'. Encouragingly, it's an album that gets better as it goes along. The closing 'Lady Sings The Blues' instrumental gets at the elements of Herbie Nichols's tune that are often overlooked, and Blanchard provides a nice coda.

Romantic Defiance remains his best to date. It sounds as though it was recorded by a seasoned working band. Garrett, who has been growing on his own account in recent years, plays with tremendous poise and conviction, and the rhythm section is subtly different in emphasis from the Marsalis-orbit players who had been round Blanchard until this point. A smashing record by any standard.

The Heart Speaks is very pleasing, if something of an interlude in the work of a musician who has progressed some way beyond mere gigging; his filmscore work for Spike Lee (*Malcolm X, Mo' Better Blues* and *Clockers*) he may count among his most important work. This is nevertheless a charming and particularly warm set of interpretations of songs by Ivan Lins, the sometimes sappy melodiousness of Brazilian song firmed up by the trumpeter's gently assertive lines.

Jazz In Film continued the interest in soundtrack music and confirms Blanchard's now substantial reputation. The material covered is as recent and close at hand as Blanchard's own score for *Clockers*, and as classic as Alex North's *A Streetcar Named Desire* and Elmer Bernstein's *The Man With The Golden Arm*. North's music for the Tennessee Williams play loses its *Suthuhn* feyness and comes out brisk and streetwise. Turre's solo is less shop-soiled than Blanche Dubois, but no less beguiling – the quote from 'It Don't Mean A Thing' is expertly timed. Blanchard's own intervention has none of the brutishness the theme might suggest. It's one of the most elegant he has committed to record.

The other material covered includes Jerry Goldsmith's theme for *Chinatown* (exquisitely introduced by the late lamented Kirkland), Duke's *Anatomy Of A Murder* and *Degas' Racing World*, Previn's *The Subterraneans* and Bernard Herrmann's chilling last work, the theme for *Taxi Driver*. Throughout, Blanchard is impeccably voiced, pitched just in front of an excellent band. Joe Henderson raises the ante whenever he plays, not content to let this lapse into easy filmic impressionism. His betting stubs are all on the table for the second of the Ellington pieces, a minor miracle of jazz impressionism.

**** Wandering Moon

Sony Classics SK 89111 *Blanchard; Aaron Fletcher (as); Branford Marsalis, Brice Winston (ts); Edward Simon (p); Dave Holland (b); Eric Harland (d).* 6/99.

Under benign exile to Sony Classics, Blanchard goes for a long (over 75 minutes), ballad-orientated record which seems full of near-darkness. Originals such as 'Luna Viajera' and 'If I Could, I Would' distil a sense of melancholy which is mitigated by the serenity of the playing. Even though there are one or two tear-ups, from Marsalis in particular, what one remembers about the record is its poise, its cool dedication to instrumental mastery. None is more masterful than the leader himself. The closing version of 'I Thought About You', taken at the slowest of tempos, is a definitive treatment which silences criticism and in its final moments leaves the listener dumbfounded.

***(*) Let's Get Lost

Sony Classics SK 89607 *Blanchard; Brice Winston (ts); Edward Simon (p); Derek Nievergelt (b); Eric Harland (d); Diana Krall, Jane Monheit, Dianne Reeves, Cassandra Wilson (v).* 00.

One of the few small-group instrumentalists who's working on a big budget at present, Blanchard must be spending handsomely to get this quartet of singers involved in this homage to songwriter Jimmy McHugh. The singers handle seven of 11 tracks, with appropriate concentration (even Wilson seems less mannered than usual), but the voice to hear remains Blanchard's trumpet – dignified, sonorous, implacably balanced. Once again, he settles on a tempo so slow ('Lost In A Fog') that it seems the group is barely moving – and still makes it work.

***(*) Bounce

Blue Note 90953-2 *Blanchard; Brice Winston (ss, ts); Aaron Parks (p); Robert Glasper (ky); Lionel Loueke (g, v); Brandon Owens (b); Eric Harland (d).* 2/03.

Blanchard moved over to Blue Note at about the same time as another trumpet-playing son of New Orleans, and although the electric keyboards and guitar made this debut look ominously like a fusion sidestep, the hip-hop elements are used sparingly enough to keep what is a very strong run of records on the right track. Wayne Shorter's 'Footprints' unexpectedly benefits from this treatment, rather than another plain old hard-bop reading. Terence himself sounds completely in command of both horn and setting and he continues to make a case for considering him jazz's leading ballad player on the slower pieces. Where he goes next is certainly an intriguing poser.

Walter Blanding (born 1972)

TENOR SAXOPHONE

Made his name with the Tough Young Tenors, but has also worked with Wynton Marsalis and the Lincoln Center Jazz Orchestra.

*** The Olive Tree

Criss Cross 1186 *Blanding; Ryan Kisor (t); Farid Barron (p); Rodney Whitaker (b); Rodney Green (d).* 00.

Blanding's track record speaks for itself and this debut album is everything one would have hoped. He has a clean, biting attack and is best on faster themes where his ability to swing a relatively complex line is shown to greatest advantage. Including tunes by Wayne Shorter and Thelonious Monk alongside 'Jitterbug Waltz' and some original material suggests a desire to establish a persona responsive to tradition as well as the lessons of the avant-garde. The group is very strong as well, with Kisor shining on almost every track. Whitaker has established himself as a valued section player and both Barron and Green keep the energy level high.

Carla Bley (born 1938)

PIANO, ORGAN, SYNTHESIZERS, COMPOSER

Noted first as a composer and co-led Jazz Composers Orchestra in New York from 1964, some form of which is still her basic performing ensemble. Her label JCOA transformed into Watt, which releases most of her music. Also performs in small-group situations, mostly with Steve Swallow; her piano and organ playing, somewhat minimalist, seems to be progressing to a lead instrument of late.

***(*) Escalator Over The Hill

JCOA/ECM 839 310 2 2CD *Bley; Michael Mantler (t, vtb, p); Enrico Rava, Michael Snow (t); Don Cherry (t, f, perc, v); Sam Burtis, Jimmy Knepper, Roswell Rudd (tb); Jack Jeffers (btb); Bob Carlisle, Sharon Freeman (frhn); John Buckingham, Howard Johnson (tba); Peggy Imig, Perry Robinson (cl); Souren Baronian (cl, dumbec); Jimmy Lyons, Dewey Redman (as); Gato Barbieri (ts); Chris Woods (bs); Sam Brown, John McLaughlin (g); Karl Berger (vib); Don Preston (syn, v); Jack Bruce (b, v solo); Charlie Haden, Ron McClure, Richard Youngstein (b); Leroy Jenkins (vn); Nancy Newton (vla); Calo Scott (clo); Bill Morimando (bells); Paul Motian (d); Roger Dawson (perc); Jane Blackstone, Paul Jones, Sheila Jordan, Jeanne Lee, Timothy Marquand, Tod Papageorge, Linda Ronstadt, Bob Stewart, Viva (v solo); Jonathan Cott, Steve Gebhardt, Tyrus Gerlach, Eileen Hale, Rosalind Hupp (v).* 11/68–6/71.

Though initially influenced by the likes of Monk and Miles, with all that that implies, Carla Bley was profoundly influenced by European classical music and by the darker reaches of *chanson*. She quickly became disenchanted with free-form improvisation and, from the late '60s onwards, began experimenting with large-scale composition. No jazz composition is as large and ungainly as the massive 'chronotransduction', *Escalator Over The Hill*. We fall in and out of love with this strange, perverse work. Like all genuinely original artistic experiments, it is an uneasy hybrid of genius – vivid and uplifting – and unbelievable tosh. Written to an impenetrable libretto by Paul Haines, it is more closely related to the non-linear, associative cinema of avant-garde film-makers Kenneth Anger, Stan Brakhage, Maya Deren and Jonas Mekas (at whose Cinemathèque some of the sessions were recorded) than to any musical parallel. The repetitious dialogue – 'again' is repeated *ad infinitum* – is largely derived from Gertrude Stein and it's perhaps best to take Stein's Alice-in-Wonderland advice and treat everything as meaning precisely what one chooses it to mean. Musically, it's a patchwork of raucous big-band themes like the opening 'Hotel Overture' (many of the events take place in Cecil Clark's Hotel with its pastiche Palm Court band) which has fine solos from Barbieri, Robinson, Haden and Rudd, heavy rock numbers like the apocalyptic 'Rawalpindi Blues' (McLaughlin, Bruce, Motian), ethnic themes from Don Cherry's Desert Band, and mysterious, ring-modulated 'dream sequences'. There is an element of recitative that, as with most opera recordings, most listeners will prefer to skip, since it doesn't advance understanding of the 'plot' one millimetre, and it's probably best to treat *Escalator* as a compilation of individual pieces with dispensable continuity. The slightly earlier *A Genuine Tong Funeral* is a genuine masterpiece on a slightly less ambitious scale and it, rather than *Escalator* (which was as much Paul Haines's work as Bley's), established her musical idiom of the '70s.

Perhaps it's time now to re-record an edited version of *Escalator*, with a new cast. Or would that simply dispel the maddeningly chaotic magic of a flawed masterpiece?

***(*) Tropic Appetites

Watt/1 *Bley; Michael Mantler (t, vtb); Gato Barbieri (ts, perc); Howard Johnson (ss, bs, bsx, cl, bcl, tba, v); Dave Holland (b, clo) Toni Marcus (vn, vla); Paul Motian (d, perc); Julie Tippetts (v).* 9/73–2/74.

Tropic Appetites is the work that *Escalator* might have been with a little judicious editing. Its sheer strangeness is endlessly beguiling and the fact that this, unlike its bulky predecessor, has been out of circulation for some time lends the reissue a fizzy freshness. Haines's words are much more effective when not squeezed into a larger, quasi-narrative template and Julie Tippetts' voice is completely compelling; she is one of those rare creatures who would be worth hearing even if she were singing the phone book.

The instrumentation is gloriously cadenced. Howard Johnson is a complete horn section in himself, Barbieri was at his most freakishly expressionistic and Bley herself ranges over a whole spectrum of keyboards, doing her 'composer's piano' thing with a wry recognition of her own lack of virtuosity. The backgrounds she creates for 'What Will Be Left Between Us And The Moon Tonight?' and 'Song Of The Jungle Stream' are definitive of the Bley approach, correct but wacky, linear and perverse in the same breath. The latter track, dedicated to Tadd Dameron, reveals how much Bley owes to her predecessors and to the jazz tradition.

Motian's drumming and Dave Holland's bass lines cement the astonishing architecture, while the horns create an illusion of scale that still surprises 30 years on.

*** Dinner Music

Watt/6 *Bley; Michael Mantler (t); Roswell Rudd (tb); Bob Stewart (tba); Carlos Ward (as, ts); Richard Tee (p); Eric Gale, Cornell Dupree (g); Gordon Edwards (b); Steve Gadd (d).* 7–9/76.

*** European Tour 1977

Watt/8 *Bley; Michael Mantler (t); Roswell Rudd (tb); John Clark (frhn); Elton Dean (as); Gary Windo (bs); Terry Adams (p); Hugh Hopper (b); Andrew Cyrille (d, perc).* 77.

*** Musique Mécanique

Watt/9 *Bley; Michael Mantler (t); Roswell Rudd (tb); John Clark (frhn); Bob Stewart (tba); Alan Braufman (f, cl, as); Gary Windo (bcl, ts); Terry Adams (p, org); Eugene Chadbourne (g, radio); Steve Swallow (b); D. Sharpe (d); Karen Mantler (glockenspiel).* 8–11/78.

This is an awkward period in Bley's and Watt's development, largely because there is no development. There was an understandable retreat from ambitious experimentation, and yet these records document a highly individual approach that draws on no obvious precedents. Something of a muchness, they are harmonically quirky, sometimes plain eccentric, song shapes delivered with a maximum of spin. The Brits on the European tour seemed to get the point straight away, paving a course for Carla's European bands of the '80s and after. Earlier editions give a more detailed breakdown of these records; time makes it harder to choose among them.

*** Social Studies

Watt/11 *Bley; Michael Mantler (t); Gary Valente (tb); Joe Daley (euph); Earl McIntyre (tba); Carlos Ward (as, ss); Tony Dagradi (cl, ts); Steve Swallow (b); D. Sharpe (d).* 12/80.

***(*) Live!

Watt/12 *Bley; Michael Mantler (t); Gary Valente (tb); Vincent Chancey (frhn); Earl McIntyre (tba, btb); Steve Slagle (as); Tony Dagradi (ts); Arturo O'Farrill (p, org); Steve Swallow (b); D. Sharpe (d).* 8/81.

It's at this point that Bley's imagination makes a sharp left away from the European art-music models that haunted her throughout the '70s and towards a more recognizable jazz idiom which may be less authentically individual but which gains immeasurably in sheer energy. *Live!* is a treat, representing one of the finest performances by her and Mantler on record. *Social Studies* shouldn't be missed; a bookish cover masks some wonderfully wry music.

** I Hate To Sing

Watt/12 *Bley; Michael Mantler (t); Gary Valente (tb); Vincent Chancey (frhn); Earl McIntyre (tba, btb, v); Steve Slagle (as); Tony Dagradi (ts); Arturo O'Farrill (p, org, v); Steve Swallow (b, d); D. Sharpe (d, v).* 8/81–1/83.

** Heavy Heart

Watt/14 *Bley; Michael Mantler (t); Gary Valente (tb); Earl McIntyre (tba); Steve Slagle (f, as, bs); Hiram Bullock (g); Kenny Kirkland (p); Steve Swallow (b); Victor Lewis (d); Manolo Badrena (perc).* 9–10/83.

****(*) Night-Glo**
Watt/16 *Bley; Randy Brecker (t, flhn); Tom Malone (tb); Dave Taylor (btb); John Clark (frhn); Paul McCandless (ob, eng hn, ss, ts, bcl); Hiram Bullock (g); Larry Willis (p); Steve Swallow (b); Victor Lewis (d); Manolo Badrena (perc).* 6–8/85.

This is a disappointing vintage in Bley's music. Despite the undoubted popularity of *I Hate To Sing*, it is one of her least imaginative small-group albums, heavily reliant on a limited range of ideas that are far more heavily embellished than usual, with camouflaging percussion and timbral effects. *Heavy Heart* is similarly disappointing, though the arrangements and voicings transfer well to CD. *Night-Glo* is by far the best of the trio; Oregon's Paul McCandless produces some striking woodwind effects and Hiram Bullock's guitar, not yet promoted beyond 'other ranks' status, is used more sensibly than on the first item below. Completists – and there must be lots – will be happy enough. New listeners would do better elsewhere.

****(*) Sextet**
Watt/17 *Bley; Hiram Bullock (g); Larry Willis (p); Steve Swallow (b); Victor Lewis (d); Don Alias (perc).* 12/86–1/87.

***** Duets**
Watt/20 *Bley; Steve Swallow (b).* 7–8/88.

Towards the end of the '80s, Bley's emphasis shifted towards smaller and more intimate units. Though never a virtuosic soloist, she grew in stature as a performer. *Sextet* was unusual in having no horns, but Bley's chords are so voiced as to suggest whole areas of harmonic interest that here and in the *Duets* with Swallow remain implicit rather than fully worked out. Bullock is perhaps too insistent a spokesman, though he takes his more promising cues from the veteran bass man. By this time there is an almost telepathic understanding between Bley and Swallow; the duets make an ironic but uncynical commentary on the cocktail-lounge conventions of piano-and-bass duos. It's an entertaining album and an ideal primer on Bley's compositional and improvising techniques.

*****(*) Fleur Carnivore**
Watt/21 839 662 *Bley; Lew Soloff, Jens Winther (t); Frank Lacy (frhn, flhn); Gary Valente (tb); Bob Stewart (tba); Daniel Beaussier (ob, f); Wolfgang Puschnig (as, f); Andy Sheppard (ts, cl); Christof Lauer (ts, ss); Roberto Ottini (bs, ss); Karen Mantler (hca, org, vib, chimes); Steve Swallow (b); Buddy Williams (d); Don Alias (perc).* 11/88.

This is something like a masterpiece. Having concentrated pretty much on small bands during the '80s, Bley returned wholeheartedly to large-scale scoring and arranging, touring with a Big Band and a Very Big Band, working in an idiom that was not only unmistakably jazz but also plain unmistakable. The relation of parts to whole is far more confident than in times gone by and the solos are uniformly imaginative, with Lauer, Soloff and Mantler, K., deserving special commendation. The writing is acute and the concert recording manages to balance 'live' energy with studio precision and fullness of sound.

***** The Very Big Carla Bley Band**
Watt/23 *Bley; Guy Barker, Steven Bernstein, Claude Deppa, Lew Soloff (t); Richard Edwards, Gary Valente, Fayyaz Virji (tb); Ashley Slater (btb); Roger Jannotta (ob, f, cl, ss); Wolfgang Puschnig (as, f); Andy Sheppard (ts, ss); Pete Hurt (ts, cl); Pablo Calogero (bs); Karen Mantler (org); Steve Swallow (b); Victor Lewis (d); Don Alias (perc).* 10/90.

A stirring live outfit, the Very Big Band translates well to record, with plenty of emphasis on straightforward blowing from featured soloists Soloff, Valente, Puschnig and Sheppard. 'United States' opens with splashy percussion, low, threatening brass figures, with the theme only really hinted at in Lew Soloff's sensuous growl solo. The riff and horn voicings that follow are unmistakably Bley's, as is the sudden, swinging interpolation of an entirely new theme. 'Strange Arrangement' opens with an almost childish piano figure, which gives way to huge, shimmering harmonics that instantly explain its logic. 'Who Will Rescue You?' grows out of an almost gospelly vamp, but by this time the album has lost at least some of its initial impetus, and 'Lo Ultimo' is a rather limping curtain-piece.

***** Go Together**
Watt/24 *Bley; Steve Swallow (b).* 92.

An intriguingly relaxed and unhurried survey of (mostly) older material, this includes beautifully judged performances of 'Sing Me Softly Of The Blues', 'Mother Of The Dead Man' and 'Fleur Carnivore'. Students of Bley – and there are growing numbers, even in academia – will find much of interest in these slender, relatively unadorned arrangements. Everyone else can simply enjoy them.

***** Big Band Theory**
Watt/25 *Bley; Lew Soloff, Guy Barker, Claude Deppa, Steve Waterman (t); Gary Valente, Richard Edwards, Annie Whitehead (tb); Ashley Slater (btb); Roger Jannotta (ss, f); Wolfgang Puschnig (as, f); Andy Sheppard (ts, ss); Pete Hurt (ts); Julian Arguëlles (bs); Karen Mantler (org); Alex Balanescu (vn); Steve Swallow (b); Dennis Mackrel (d).* 7/93.

This never quite fulfils the promise of some exciting arrangements (notably of Mingus's 'Goodbye Pork Pie Hat') and a rash of hot soloists, including regulars Sheppard, Soloff, Puschnig and Swallow, and guest Alex Balanescu, who gets down to it with a will. 'Birds Of Paradise' was a commission for the Glasgow Jazz Festival and was a serious disappointment there. Typically, though, it has been reworked and sharpened up considerably, and it comes across much more forcefully on record.

The main reservation about *Big Band Theory* stems from the overall balance of the recording. Though in a warm, expansive analogue, it muffles and blurs some of the horn passages and exaggerates the rhythm tracks, often to the detriment of subtle voicings.

***** Songs With Legs**
Watt/26 *Bley; Andy Sheppard (ts, ss); Steve Swallow (b).* 5/94.

A matey trawl round Europe by three chums with a bag of songs. It isn't much more complicated than that, and just sometimes it conveys precisely that had-to-be-there feel that can be off-putting if you weren't. Carla's compositions have become modern classics and it is fascinating to hear 'Real Life Hits' and 'Wrong Key Donkey' given this stripped-down treatment. She doesn't put a foot wrong throughout, but then these performances were hand-picked from six different locations, so the selection process obviously played a part.

*****(*) The Carla Bley Big Band Goes To Church**

Watt/27 *Bley; Lew Soloff, Guy Barker, Claude Deppa, Steve Waterman (t); Gary Valente, Pete Beachill, Chris Dean (tb); Richard Henry (btb); Roger Jannotta (ss, as, f); Wolfgang Puschnig (as); Andy Sheppard, Jerry Underwood (ts); Julian Arguëlles (bs); Karen Mantler (org, hca); Steve Swallow (b); Dennis Mackrel (d).* 7/96.

Another episode from the road, so titled not just because of the gospelly, preaching tone that predominates but more immediately because these six cracking tracks were recorded in concert at the beautiful Chiesa San Francesco Al Prato, an important venue for the Umbria Jazz Festival. The acoustic is surprisingly dry and, but for occasional ripples of applause, *Goes To Church* might almost be a live studio recording.

The long (almost 25 minutes) opening piece, 'Setting Calvin's Waltz', was written on commission for the Berlin Jazz Festival. Opening on a soft, confessional dialogue between Bley and Swallow, it opens up into an episodic curtain-raiser featuring most of the major soloists: Sheppard, Soloff, Valente, Karen Mantler and Puschnig, who emerges as the favoured pupil this time with no fewer than five feature spots on the disc. The best of them come on the two closing tracks, 'Permanent Wave' and 'Who Will Rescue You?', on which his slightly dry tone and plangent delivery work to perfection.

As ever, Swallow's cleanly picked bass guitar lines are well to the fore, but Bley herself seems increasingly content on Big Band dates to disappear into the background, reserving herself for the occasional intro and, perhaps, for the small groups. Here and there, though, she provides some instinctive colours, and her quirky scales and chords are the thread on which Sheppard, Soloff and the highly accomplished Mackrel string their 'Beads'. The best Bley album since *Fleur Carnivore*?

***** Fancy Chamber Music**

Watt/28 *Bley; Alison Hayhurst (f); Sarah Lee (cl, glock); Steve Morris (vn); Andrew Byrt (vla); Emma Black (clo); Steve Swallow (b); Chris Wells (perc).* 12/97.

Bley is one of a small group of jazz composers who have attracted the admiring attention of conservatory and academic musicians. For a time, there was a Bley Band at Leicester Polytechnic (now de Montfort University) in England, dedicated to 'classical' performance of her repertoire. The material here, though, had its origins back in 1985 when Carla was asked to write some pieces for the Lincoln Center Chamber Music Society. A commission followed from avant-garde pianist Ursula Oppens and the Hamburg group, L'Art Pour L'Art. The first of these pieces, 'Copertone', for the LCCMS, seems to be lost to history, but 'Romantic Notions' and 'Tigers In Training', written for the latter pair, are included here.

The key work, though, is 'End Of Vienna' – and what a raft of associations is buried in that title! It was composed for the 300th jazz workshop conducted by North German Radio. The momentum continued with further work for the Guildhall in London, and the sequence ends with a moving piece called 'Jon Benet', the name of a little girl reported kidnapped by her family – involving the infamous '*War And Peace* of ransom notes' – and subsequently found murdered in the family cellar.

Bley's attraction to 'Fancy Chamber Music', ties and tails rather than jeans and trainers, was obvious from the first. What is immediately clear from these immaculately performed tracks is that there is very little in essence separating the fancy from the funky, except that well-brought-up music fans know not to applaud in the wrong places. It's a pity that this material wasn't recorded live and on the road. All it lacks is that fear of the mistimed cough or dropped programme. Otherwise, vintage Bley.

***** Are We There Yet?**

Watt/29 *Bley; Steve Swallow (b).* 10/98.

Just now and again, one wonders if having a 'home' recording label has done Carla Bley any real favours. While it's been an admirably disciplined imprint, without a hint of self-indulgence, there are moments like this when the output seems to require a level of editorial oversight which neither Carla nor Steve Swallow seems ready to bring.

The worst that can be said about *Are We There Yet?* is that it represents 80 minutes of self-indulgent noodling, recorded live on tour in Europe. The best that can be said of it is that Carla and Steve's public pillow-talk is infinitely more interesting than anyone else's. Like *Duets* and *Go Together*, it plays on certain expectations and confounds them at the same time. A duo re-run of 'Musique Mécanique' apart, the bulk of the music here is written by Swallow, with a rather lovely version of 'Lost In The Stars' thrown in for good measure. Steve's cleanly articulated bass lines represent not just a second but in some respects the main lead instrument. He is awesome on 'A Dog's Life' and 'Satie For Two', two clever, witty compositions that (like Bley's recent chamber pieces) flout any distinction between 'jazz' and 'classical' forms.

*****(*) 4 × 4**

Watt 159457 *Bley; Lew Soloff (t); Gary Valente (tb); Wolfgang Puschnig (as); Andy Sheppard (ts); Larry Goldings (org); Steve Swallow (b); Victor Lewis (d).* 7/99.

Strictly speaking, it ought to be 4 + 4 to reflect the neatly paired double-quartet formation of the new band, but with music as impressive and as ambitious as this, who's complaining? The album gets off to a rollicking start with 'Blues In 12 Bars/Blues In 12 Other Bars', a long, rolling piece with plenty of solo space and a lot of substance under the jolly surface. The pairings aren't the obvious (instrumental) familial ones: Carla and Steve have, of course, their own special interaction and telepathy, but Soloff and Goldings seem twinned, especially on that first track, and Andy Sheppard seems to have excellent rhythmic rapport with the formidable Lewis, leaving Puschnig and Valente to conduct an oddly effective dialogue of the deaf – and deaf is how you end up, working too close to Gary, one of the loudest players on the scene.

'Sidewinders In Paradise' is intriguing. Is it really an attempt to cast Lee Morgan in *Kismet*? Sounds that way. Bley has rarely been as open-hearted and puckish as this; for all the brooding quality of the closing 'Utviklingssang', it's a very happy record. Like the players, the tracks seem to come in twos. Just before that closing piece, 'Baseball' is a danceable Latin theme. However, the most important piece comes in three parts. 'Les Trois Lagons' is inspired by a Matisse work and falls into a conventional jazz opening, a song-like second section and then a very unexpected finale that combines rag and stride effects with what sounds like a complex tone-row. The best quarter-hour we've heard from Carla Bley in many years.

*****(*) Looking For America**

Watt/31 *Bley; Giampaolo Casati, Earl Gardner, Lew Soloff, Byron Stripling (t); Dave Bargeron, Jim Pugh, David Taylor, Gary Valente (tb); Robert Routch (frhn); Lawrence Feldman (ss, as, f); Wolfgang Puschnig (as, f); Craig Handy, Andy Sheppard (ts); Gary Smulyan (bs); Karen Mantler (org, glock); Steve Swallow (b); Billy Drummond (b); Don Alias (perc).* 10/02.

There's a curious disclaimer on the back of the liner booklet to the effect that 'the views expressed do not necessarily reflect those of the musicians in the band or the record company'. The question is: expressed *where*? Carla's loving deconstruction of 'The Star Spangled Banner' (and parts of 'O Canada') is as ironically loving or lovingly ironic as Jimi Hendrix's and surely couldn't cause any possible offence. So presumably it's ironic. We're a long way from *Skies Of America* on 'OG Can UC' and Patrick Hinely's photographic juxtaposition of Carla with John Wayne and a haulage truck shouldn't be read as a profound political comment.

As an exploration of Americana, this is a fine and fun set. Any jazz album that ends with a big band version of 'Old MacDonald Had A Farm' is all right with us; with Gary Smulyan's outrageous intro and Lew Soloff well to the fore, it swings like a monkey. In probably the most mixed set she's produced for a while Carla builds in a group of tracks dedicated to Miss Liberty or to the eternal feminine: 'Grand Mother', 'Step Mother', 'God Mother'. 'Tijuana Traffic' is a south of the border knees up with just a reminder of Charles Mingus. 'Fast Lane' is a hard, outside lane bopper.

Paul Bley (born 1932)

PIANO

The Canadian pianist is astonishingly prolific, having recorded over 100 discs down the years, by our reckoning. He is also extremely eclectic, ranging from free bop and ballads to electronic settings and larger groups. Consistently, though, he has produced vivid, vital jazz couched in an advanced and challenging idiom. Born in Montreal, he moved to New York, played in hard-bop groups and then crossed coasts to California, where he was nominal leader on one of Ornette Coleman's most important documented live dates. Bley then began to develop his own distinctive style, built on unexpected harmonic shifts, a steady but subtly varied pulse and powerful melodic statements.

*****(*) Introducing Paul Bley**
Original Jazz Classics OJC 201 *Bley; Charles Mingus (b); Art Blakey (p).* 11/53.

***** Paul Bley**
Emarcy 9107 *Bley; Percy Heath, Peter Ind (b); Al Levitt (d).* 2 & 8/54.

*****(*) The Fabulous Paul Bley Quintet**
Musidisc MU 500542 *Bley; Don Cherry (t); Ornette Coleman (as); Charlie Haden (b); Billy Higgins (d).* 7/58.

****** Touching**
Black Lion BLCD 760195 *Bley; Kent Carter, Mark Levinson (b); Barry Altschul (d).* 11/65, 11/66.

****** Open, To Love**
ECM 827751-2 *Bley (p solo).* 9/72.

***** Tango Palace**
Soul Note 121090 *As above.* 5/83.

*****(*) Solo**
Justin Time Just 28 *As above.* 87.

***** Solo Piano**
Steeplechase SCCD 31236 *As above.* 4/88.

***** Blues For Red**
Red Records RR 123238 *As above.* 5/89.

*****(*) Changing Hands**
Justin Time Just 40 *As above.* 2/91.

*****(*) Caravan Suite**
Steeplechase SCCD 31316 *As above.* 4/92.

***** Paul Bley At Copenhagen Jazz House**
Steeplechase SCCD 31348 *As above.* 11/92.

There is probably no other pianist currently active with a stylistic signature as distinctively inscribed as Paul Bley's – which is ironic, for he is a restless experimenter with an inbuilt resistance to stopping long in any one place. It is difficult to formulate exactly what unifies his remarkable body of work, beyond a vague sense that Bley's enunciation and accent are different from other people's, almost as if he strikes the keyboard differently. He favours curiously ambiguous diminuendo effects, tightly pedalled chords and sparse right-hand figures, often in challengingly different metre; working solo, he creates variety and dramatic interest by gradually changing note-lengths within a steady pulse (a device introduced to keyboard literature by a minor German improviser called Ludwig van Something) and generates considerable dramatic tension by unexpectedly augmenting chords, shifting the harmonic centre constantly.

The early Emarcy date has recently returned to catalogue and it's useful to hear where Bley was coming from. At this stage in his career, he's a very orthodox bopper, aware of the blues but certainly not restricted to them, possibly exploring aspects of Tristano's evolution as well, and certainly listening to classical pianists for technique and harmonic ideas. These are not classic cuts and most casual listeners would be hard pressed to identify the pianist, but they are fascinating as a record of his earlier development and they help to fill in a rather sketchy picture.

Though he has played in a number of classic groups – notably with Jimmy Giuffre and Steve Swallow, that astonishing debut with Mingus and Blakey, on which he sounds edgy and a little cautious on the standards but absolutely secure in his technique, and, more recently, with John Surman and Bill Frisell – Bley is still perhaps best heard as a solo performer. The 1958 Hillcrest Club session has an almost legendary status, by no means hindered by the shaky recording. Though it is often discussed as if it were an Ornette Coleman record (and indeed the saxophonist dominates it), it was Bley's date. Having sacked vibraphonist Dave Pike to recruit Ornette and Cherry, Bley then had to absorb their radical new music at high speed; *Something Else* had been released a short time before and, though he was winning a critical following, Ornette was still considered a radical outsider. The first track was a version of 'Klactoveesedstene', which proceeds in a predictable bebop manner until the saxophonist takes off into his solo, at which point it is immediately obvious that something revolutionary is taking place. Bley audibly does his best to stick with it but, of course, even at this stage Ornette had very little use for an orthodox accompanist. The piano solo is a little spindly, but CD transfer has put a certain amount of meat on it. Bley's contributions to the two Ornette compositions, 'The Blessing' and 'Free', are much less assured. This is clearly an important record and, technical deficiencies aside, it should be in all modern collections. However, it isn't central to Bley's recorded output.

The earlier solo set neatly oversteps the most uncomfortably eclectic phase of Bley's career, when he turned to electronics in a largely unsuccessful bid to increase his tonal vocabulary. Bley claims that he only listens to his own records nowadays. Tongue in cheek or not, there are certainly enough of them on the backlist to occupy the bulk of his non-playing time (if bulk is the right word for a musician so promiscuously active). There are also signs that Bley listens to his past records in a quite constructive sense, constantly revising and modifying his thematic development (as in these intense reveries), constantly alluding to other melodies and performances. There is, perhaps, inevitably a hint of *déjà vu* here and there, but the terrain is always much too interesting for that to become a problem.

The 1965 sessions on Black Lion were once available on an Arista Freedom double-LP which featured one of the most unpleasant covers in the history of recorded music. The playing was superb, though, and it's a great shame that the whole disc hasn't been reproduced. Long tracks like 'Mister Joy' are missing, though other Annette Peacock and Carla Bley tracks are strongly in evidence, and Paul Bley's own 'Mazatalan' suggests that he's no slouch as a writer when he so chooses. Carter and Altschul offer solid support, but the focus is all on the piano.

Solo and *Changing Hands* are uniquely thoughtful piano solos, recorded back home in Montreal on a beautifully tempered instrument (and producer Jim West has to be congratulated for the immediacy and precision of the sound). Any suspicion that Bley may have become one-dimensionally meditative is allayed by the vigorous 'Boogie' on *Solo* and *Changing Hands*' remarkable interpretation of 'Summertime'. If it came down to a hard choice, the earlier album is marginally to be preferred; don't be seduced by the prettier cover.

Much of his recorded output has been on small-scale European labels, many of them in Italy, like the *Blues* set on Red. (See also *Lyrics*, below, on Splasc(h), which mixes vocal tracks by Tizia Ghiglioni with solo pieces.) *Blues For Red* is typical in all but content. Bley doesn't normally play as much in a blues mode as this, and it's pretty effective, though by no means orthodox. There are fine things on the Soul Note session (also recorded in Italy), but it is a mellow, after-dinner affair compared to the iced-vodka shocks of *Open, To Love*, one of Bley's finest-ever performances and the beginning of a productive relationship with ECM that really flowered only much later. Stand-out track is a fresh reading of ex-wife Carla Bley's uneasy 'Ida Lupino'. The 1988 Steeplechase has excellent sound and features the pianist in meditative mood; his reading of 'You Go To My Head' is so oblique as to suggest another tune entirely. Nevertheless there is little of the vapid meandering that afflicts so much piano improvisation; Bley is a tremendously disciplined improviser and this is one of his most intellectually rigorous albums.

Caravan Suite is an extended examination on Ellington. There's a long version of 'In My Solitude', notably sombre accounts of 'I Got It Bad And That Ain't Good' and 'I'm Beginning To See The Light', and an extended, four-part meditation on 'Caravan'. The Steeplechase piano is very crisp and exact, suiting the material admirably. It's certainly a better instrument than the one at the Jazz House, which has a couple of unpleasant idiosyncrasies, not helped by the close-up recording of the top end. Good playing, though.

*** Paul Bley With Gary Peacock

ECM 843162-2 *Bley; Gary Peacock (b); Paul Motian, Billy Elgart (d).* 4/63.

In November 1953, Bley had recorded a disc for Charles Mingus's Debut label, now available on a 12-CD compilation of all the Debut performances. A trio consisting of Charles Mingus and Art Blakey was a pretty decent coming-of-age present for a 21-year-old from Montreal, and it gave Bley a taste he was never to lose for strongly individual, not just blandly supportive sidemen. There are good things, too, from what was to be Bley's established trio. Up until that point, most of the trio's best work seems to have gone unrecorded. The ECM label's third release – following a superb Mal Waldron session and a thoroughly forgettable band led by the enigmatic Alfred Harth – highlighted 'When Will The Blues Leave'.

***(*) Barrage

ESP/Calibre 1008 *Bley; Dewey Johnson (t); Marshall Allen (as); Eddie Gomez (b); Milford Graves (d).* 10/64.

**** Closer

ESP/Calibre 1021 *Bley; Steve Swallow (b); Barry Altschul (d).* 12/65.

Bley's brief association with the forward-thinking ESP yielded one classic trio and one now largely-forgotten quintet date. The earlier date saw Bley recruiting two horn men from the Sun Ra Arkestra and much of the interest of the album, which like its successor consists entirely of Carla Bley tunes, is in hearing Johnson and Allen in a small group context. The music is fairly hard-edged and the presence of two such confrontational players (the trumpeter was to appear on Coltrane's *Ascension*) gives the set an uncomfortably fiery complexion that tends to singe away its more subtle moments. The interplay with Gomez is really the key to the set, and on 'Ictus' and 'Walking Woman' – the two best tracks – a trio performance would have been preferred.

Closer is still a delight nearly 40 years after first release. The key track here is Carla's classic 'Ida Lupino', which her former husband turns into a rolling, almost filmic narrative with layers of detail that belie the simple materials. Some have noted a continuing cross-fertilization of ideas with Ornette Coleman on these tracks. That's harder to hear if you aren't aware of the association, but certainly the staccato rhythms and bitten-off melodic ideas do point in that direction.

***(*) Paul Bley In Haarlem

TJC TKCB 71620 *Bley; Barry Levinson (b); Barry Altschul (d).* 66.

And that's Haarlem in the Netherlands rather than Harlem in New Amsterdam. This is a legendary Bley session, issued many times in different formats, but one for which we have a particular affection, despite its technical shortcomings and the slightly shambolic nature of the long performances of 'Blood' and 'Mister Joy', both of which are wrongly attributed to Carla Bley instead of Annette Peacock.

Altschul is fiery and uncompromising, though he loses paces during 'Mr Joy', but Levinson is a very average player, and certainly not in the creative league of Gary Peacock, Steve Swallow and Kent Carter, all of whom have seen similar duty in Bley trios. Warts and all, though, this is a thoroughly entertaining album, even when Bley appears to lose interest and start tinkering with the inside of his piano instead of the keyboard.

***** Quiet Song**

Improvising Artists 123839 *Bley; Jimmy Giuffre (cl); Bill Connors (g).* 12/74.

This in many respects anticipates the trio with Giuffre and bass guitarist Steve Swallow a decade and a half later. Most of the pieces are improvised and most are thoughtful and introspective rather than dramatic. Giuffre's slightly dry chalumeau is very nicely captured, though there are touches of distortion here and there when the full trio is playing, suggesting that microphone positions were too close or not sufficiently baffled. It's a minor point, but it mars some lovely group playing where subtle interactions of harmony are vital to the success of a piece.

***** Japan Suite**

Improvising Artists 123849 2 *Bley; Gary Peacock (b); Barry Altschul (d).* 7/76.

It seems that technical problems delayed the start of this concert and annoyed the crowd who were about to turn nasty when the trio came on and proceeded to blow them away with a set of remarkable intensity, even by the standards of these fiery players. Altschul is a particular revelation here, hammering his kit as if to outdo Bley's own percussive attack, but still managing to sound tuneful and focused. Peacock isn't well served in the mix, though it does seem to improve as the rather short set progresses.

***** Axis**

Improvising Artists 123853 *Bley (p solo).* 7/77.

Axis might seem to belong with the solo recordings listed unchronologically above, but it stands somewhat apart in Bley's output. It's a meditative and in some ways rather melancholy set that draws on both familiar material, Carla's 'El Cordobes' and the much less familiar 'Music Matador', a theme by Prince Lasha, a school friend of Ornette Coleman's and Dolphyist saxophonist. It's an intriguing blend of styles and ideas and the album would have been better still if the piano had been more robust or better tuned. There are edgy overtones on some of the softer passages and a bass buzz that is irritating when Bley is playing one of his romantic chorales.

****(*) The Paul Bley Group**

Soul Note 121140 *Bley; John Scofield (g); Steve Swallow (b); Barry Altschul (d).* 3/85.

***** Fragments**

ECM 829280-2 *Bley; John Surman (ss, bcl, bs); Bill Frisell (g); Paul Motian (d).* 1/86.

***** The Paul Bley Quartet**

ECM 835250-2 *As above.*

Fragments is denied a further star only by the width of the band-book. As on the Soul Note session, recorded a year before, the writing and arranging are surprisingly below par and the recording isn't quite as clean as it might be. The Soul Note features a fine reading of Bley's staple 'Mazatalan', but little else of really compelling interest; Scofield and Swallow blend almost seamlessly, and Altschul has always been the perfect conduit for Bley's more advanced rhythmic cues. By contrast, the ECM band seems all texture, and much less structure; Frisell's almost apologetically discordant lines and reverberations blend unexpectedly well with Surman's almost equally introspective lines, and Motian – with whom Bley has duo'd to great effect – varies his emphases almost by the bar to accommodate whoever is in the forefront. The long 'Interplay' on the later, eponymous set, is disappointing enough to ease that album back a stellar notch. All three, though, are fine examples of a remarkable musician at work without preconceptions, doctrinaire stylistic theories or ego.

***** Questions**

Steeplechase SCCD 1205 *Bley; Jesper Lundgaard (b); Aage Tanggaard (d).* 2/85.

***** My Standard**

Steeplechase SCCD 1214 *As above, except replace Tanggaard with Billy Hart (d).* 12/85.

****(*) Live**

Steeplechase SCCD 1223 *As above, except omit Hart.* 3/86.

***** Live Again**

Steeplechase SCCD 1230 *As above.* 3/86.

***** Montmartre Live**

Steeplechase SCCD 31243 *As for Live/Live Again.* 3/86.

****** Indian Summer**

Steeplechase SCCD 31286 *Bley; Ron McClure (b); Barry Altschul (d).* 5/87.

The mid-'80s trios for Steeplechase mark a consistent high point in Bley's now capacious output. The Danish rhythm section isn't all that special on *Questions* but it functions more than adequately. The duos with Lundgaard are pretty dry; oddly, the best performances have been held over for the follow-up *Live Again.* Bley needs a bassist with a little more poke (step forward Swallow, Peacock and the better-known Dane, NHOP – see below) or a drummer who doesn't get swamped by the sheer profusion of Bley's notes. Hart tends to drive things along quite hard, and it's only really on *Indian Summer* that one feels the chemistry is just right. This is one of the pianist's periodic blues-based programmes. Engineered by Kazunori Sigiyama, who's responsible for DIW's output, it registers brightly, essential for music which is as softly pitched as much of this is. The high points are Bley's own 'Blue Waltz' and an ironic 'The More I See You', in which he works through variations in much the same way as he had on *Caravan Suite* for the same label, reconstructing the melodies rather than simply going through the changes. It's a fine record by any standards, but it stands out prominently among the later trios.

***** Paul Bley/NHOP**

Steeplechase SCCD 31005 *Bley; Niels-Henning Orsted Pedersen (b).* 6–7/73.

***** Notes**

Soul Note 121190 *Bley; Paul Motian (d).* 7/87.

Years of standing behind Oscar Peterson did nothing to blunt NHOP's appetite for the job. He complements Bley's haunting chords perfectly, and on the inaugural 'Meeting' constructs an *arco* solo of great beauty over huge, ringing piano pedals (played on the electric instrument which reappears to good effect on the closing 'Gesture Without Plot' by Annette Peacock). 'Later' is perhaps the best-balanced duo performance; followed by the lively and intriguingly oblique 'Summer', it underlines once again Bley's sensitivity to his fellow-players and the emotional range of his playing. He is, nevertheless, absolutely distinctive. The opening notes of 'Meeting' could not be by anyone else, and a random sampling of any track uncovers his signature within half a dozen bars. The piano is appropriately well recorded and the bass is well forward with no flattening of the bottom notes (which is where NHOP works best) and no teeth-jangling distortion of his bridgework.

Motian is always wonderful, seeming to work in a time-scale all his own, conjuring tissues of sound from the kit that seem to have nothing to do with metal or skin. Their interplay in the most demanding of all improvisational settings is intuitive and perfectly weighted.

***** The Nearness Of You**

Steeplechase SCCD 31246 *Bley; Ron McClure (b); Billy Hart (d).* 11/88.

For those who find Bley a shade too dry, 'Take The "A" Train' rousts along like it was trying to make up time between stops. By sharp contrast, the title-track is a long reverie punctuated by angry interpolations, almost as if a whole relationship is replaying on some inner screen. Compelling music as always, with an uncharacteristically laid-back rhythm section that on a couple of cuts might just as well have sat out and left the pianist to do his own remarkable thing. Good, well-rounded sound.

*****(*) Rejoicing**

Steeplechase SCCD 31274 *Bley; Michal Urbaniak (vn); Ron McClure (b); Barry Altschul (d).* 5/89.

The vibrant amplified sound of the Polish-born violinist works very effectively in the context of Bley's music. Add a rhythm section as sympathetic as McClure and Altschul, and you have a formula for something rather different and unpredictable. The Monk opening is certainly unexpected and leaves Urbaniak standing, but he recovers well enough to steal a couple of well-trodden standards – 'I Can't Get Started' and 'All The Things You Are' – and to make a dramatic contribution to 'Ictus', a tune that Bley had recorded with Jimmy Giuffre and Steve Swallow back in 1961, and again on the ESP Disk. A slightly unusual item in Bley's list, this is nevertheless well worth sampling. Recorded live at Sweet Basil, it has a convincing live feel without too much dirt in the sound.

****** BeBopBeBopBeBopBeBop**

Steeplechase SCCD 31259 *Bley; Bob Cranshaw (b); Keith Copeland (d).* 12/89.

There's a certain irony in the fact that the man who headed the palace coup that overthrew bebop at the Hillcrest Club in 1958 (the date is often credited to Ornette Coleman, but Bley was the nominal leader) should be the one to produce such an exacting and forward-looking variation on bop language in the '80s. Far from a nostalgia album, or an easy ride for soloist and sidemen, *BeBop* is a taxingly inventive and constantly surprising run through a dozen kenspeckle bop tunes, including (a circular tribute to the label) 'Steeplechase'. Bley's chording and lower-keyboard runs on 'My Little Suede Shoes' pull that rather banal theme apart; Cranshaw's solo is superb. 'Ornithology' and 'The Theme' receive equally extended attention; the closing '52nd Street Theme' is a suitably elliptical commentary on the whole era.

****** The Life Of A Trio: Saturday**

Owl 014.731 2 *Bley; Jimmy Giuffre (ss, cl); Steve Swallow (b).* 12/89.

*****(*) The Life Of A Trio: Sunday**

Owl 014.735 2 *As above.* 12/89.

***** Partners**

Owl 014 730 *As above, except omit Giuffre.* 12/89.

This was a wonderful group and the reissue is doubly welcome. Bley has always enjoyed contexts where individual members play solos and duos as well as ensemble tracks. Here, all three members contribute substantially to the success of the album, not just as trio players, but very largely as soloists. Bley's own performances include 'Foreplay' and 'Even Steven' (*Saturday*) and the wonderful 'Mephisto' (*Sunday*), but this time out, he is substantially outclassed by Jimmy Giuffre in his pomp. The clarinettist's opening piece on the first disc is a reminder of what a wonderful, controlled voice he has on the black stick. His soprano playing, heard later, is wilder and more frenetic, in some respects untypical of what we expect from Giuffre, whose 'Sensing', done as a trio piece, opens the second disc. Swallow is as solid and harmonically imaginative as ever. He also keeps a clear pulse running through every track he's involved with, even keeping the occasionally uncertain Giuffre on line on the duo 'We Agree'. Anyone who heard this group live will recognize that these brief pieces are only tasters for what the trio could do in a live setting and with no restriction on time.

Valuable documents nonetheless and well worth renewing acquaintance even if you've heard them before. Bley's harmonic resource is astonishing and all the more remarkable when you consider that these three records were recorded over just three days. It isn't clear whether the duo set was always planned or whether Giuffre dropped out of the December 18 session (he did suffer some ill health around this time). Whatever the reason, the alternation of bass and piano solos with duo pieces works wonderfully and one has a strong impression of both players listening to each other's ideas and incorporating them into their own solos, often on completely different tracks. Consider for instance the trade-off between Bley's solo 'Majestique' and Peacock's 'Gently Gently', or between the opening duo 'Again Anew' and the stunning, brief version of Ornette Coleman's 'Latin Genetics'.

****** Memoirs**

Soul Note 121240 *Bley; Charlie Haden (b); Paul Motian (d).* 7/90.

A dream line-up that promises much and delivers royally. If anything pricks the bubble of the concurrent trio featuring Geri Allen, it is this fine set. Bley's finely spun chromatic developments are now so well judged as to give an impression of being quite conventionally resolved. Given the title and the strategically placed 'Monk's Dream' and Ornette's 'Latin Genetics', it's tempting to read the set as an attempt to summarize Bley's career over the past three decades. Haden's 'Dark Victory' and 'New Flame' and Bley's own 'Insanity' suggest how far Bley, Haden and Motian have pushed the conventional piano trio. Tremendous stuff.

***** Lyrics**

Splasc(h) H 348-2 *Bley; Tiziana Ghiglioni (v).* 3/91.

Ghiglioni's rather strained delivery does little more than point out the melody on the vocal tracks. These are interspersed by instrumental originals, which are a commentary (though recorded prior to the vocal track) on five otherwise uneventful standards. It's these re-readings which lift this rather low-key set. They're further testimony to Bley's remarkable harmonic imagination, and it may be that Ghiglioni felt constrained rather than inspired by them. The idea is an intriguing one, but one would like to hear him try it with a more sophisticated vocal artist, like Sheila Jordan.

★★★(★) In The Evenings Out There

ECM 517469-2 *Bley; John Surman (bs, bcl); Gary Peacock (b); Tony Oxley (d). 9/91.*

It's not clear quite how to attribute this one, since material from the same session has been released under Surman's name as *Adventure Playground.* The music is entirely collaborative and there are solo tracks, duos and trios, with only one substantial group track, so the emphasis is on intimate communications across small but significant musical distances. Oxley might not at first seem to be the ideal drummer for Bley, having played regularly with Cecil Taylor and in an almost antagonistic branch of the music. They play face to face only briefly, but it is enough to suggest that Bley's style is at least capable of re-incorporating some aspects of the free jazz he appeared to have left behind.

★★★(★) Paul Plays Carla

Steeplechase SCCD 31303 *Bley; Marc Johnson (b); Jeff Williams (d). 12/91.*

This contains a number of tunes by ex-wife Carla Bley that have criss-crossed Bley's playing career from the beginning. They still fall comfortably under his fingers. It's possible to trace through some of the tunes, 'Vashkar' and 'Ictus' particularly, how and where Bley's playing has changed over the years. His left-hand accents are now stronger and more insistently rhythmic, and he has largely stripped away the grace notes and embellishments that once would have surrounded the solo line. It's all much cleaner and more exact, without in any way losing its romantic lilt. Compare the versions recorded in New York a year later and released as *Homage to Carla*, below.

★★★(★) Annette

hatOLOGY 564 *Bley; Franz Koglmann (t, flhn); Gary Peacock (b). 4/92.*

★★★★ Homage To Carla

Owl 013 427 2 *Bley (p solo). 4/92.*

Anyone who remembers Bley's live sets from Copenhagen and Haarlem will remember the sheer sensuous delight of tunes like 'Touching', 'Blood' and 'Mr Joy', Annette Peacock compositions which both receive fresh and freshly delightful readings here on the reissue of *Annette.* The only non-Peacock item on the set is the improvised title track, which somehow manages to capture her essence. On take one of 'Touching' (a second closes the album), Bley can be heard singing along to his solo reading, which is as spare and unembellished as any he has done of the piece. 'El Cordobes' and the peerless 'Cartoon' follow, bringing in Peacock and Koglmann, and on the latter track the level of abstraction and timbral complexity increases a good deal.

One has the strong impression throughout the disc that these are songs without words, which is much as they were written. Annette's intention was to provide Bley with challenging environments for improvisation. As such, they are more open-ended and ambiguous than the wry, pungent themes he received from Carla Bley. The albums were recorded a fortnight apart, *Annette* in Switzerland, *Homage to Carla* in New York City, solo and on a magnificent Bosendorfer that seems to chime and resonate with the slightest touch. Though Bley's music uses the same dark, minor tonalities and untroubled dissonance, the two composers are very different and on the Carla album it is not so much melody and harmonic development one notices as the overall structure and colour of pieces like 'Ictus', 'Closer' and 'Vashkar', which have admittedly gained a certain familiarity from long use. Bley's use of special techniques, like the softly dampened open strings on 'Closer', is sparing but stunningly good.

Two rather different sets, then, but devoted to the two most important musical associations of Bley's life. As an inspiration and interpreter, he is without peer and these sets underline his conviction that whether playing solo or in a group, improvisation is always a collaborative act.

★★★★ Mindset

Soul Note 121213 *Bley; Gary Peacock (b). 10/92.*

Peacock's place in the history of modern jazz is less immediately obvious than Bley's but ironically is more secure because much of his career has been in the service of other visions. Increasingly in recent years, he has come out as a performer of absolute individuality, and the solo components of this remarkable record provide a primer to two men whose musical language – shared and several – is as rich and complex as any on the planet. They have worked together before, of course, not least in an early ECM session, and have always demonstrated a closeness of understanding that goes beyond basic stylistic similarities. The pattern is very straightforward: a solo from each and then a duet, repeated four times, with just a tiny coda of Ornette's 'Circle With The Hole In The Middle' to complete the engagement. As often as not, Bley is accompanying the bassist, as on 'Duality' and on parts of the long 'Mindset', and here he drifts easily into a flat-handed chording style that rolls back the years and demonstrates again how much he remains in touch with his own younger selves. On 'Duality' the pair explore just about every aspect of their stylistic changes from the '50s to now, swing, bebop, cool, abstraction and resolute freedom. It's a hugely compelling performance. A shame that it lay around for five years before release – though, given the number of Bley records out there, one can hardly be surprised.

★★★(★) If We May

Steeplechase SCCD 31344 *Bley; Jay Anderson (b); Adam Nussbaum (d). 4/93.*

Not perhaps as successful as the slightly earlier Steeplechase trios (for which, see above) but a sterling performance all the same, and further testimony to Bley's willingness to reinvent himself and his repertoire. Nussbaum gives him a spacious rhythm, allowing him to stretch out on 'All The Things You Are' and 'Confirmation', two of his best-crafted solos of recent years. Once again the Steeplechase studio delivers the goods triumphantly, digital recording of marked sensitivity and warmth.

★★★ Know Time

Justin Time JUST 57 *Bley; Herbie Spanier (t, flhn); Geordie McDonald (d, perc). 8/93.*

A free session by three Canadians whose paths have crossed in different permutations over the years but who have never been able to preserve this type of gig on tape. McDonald is the wild card, a composer–improviser with a huge range of sounds at his disposal. Though the stated aim is the old one of finding a basis for improvisation that goes far beyond conventional song form, there is a persistent sense that this is exactly what lies behind these 13 shortish pieces. However, items like 'Seascape', 'Cave Painting' and 'Matrix' do suggest that the prevailing analogy is not musical at all but the visual arts, and that these are not so much songs as images. They are less static than this suggests, and it is possible to hear Bley in particular hesitate between linear logic (never something he has been wedded to) and a more impressionistic, flat-plane sound that generates very different patterns of sound. Though in some respects it sounds unresolved and even uncertain, in years to come this may be seen as one of Bley's most important later recordings, signalling yet another change of direction.

*** Speechless

Steeplechase SCCD 31363 *Bley; Jay Anderson (b); Victor Lewis (d).* 93.

Bley was to record again, and more convincingly, with this trio somewhat later. For some reason, it fails to fire on this occasion. Anderson is exactly the kind of bass he likes and needs, Haden-influenced, deep-toned and a reliable purveyor of root notes when the harmonics become complex, while Victor Lewis is one of the most musical drummers around. Whatever the reason, things failed to fire on the day. The later *Reality Check* is much better.

CORE COLLECTION

**** Time Will Tell

ECM 523819-2 *Bley; Evan Parker (ts, ss); Barre Phillips (b).* 1/94.

Superb. This is the kind of group that makes you wish you ran a festival or owned a club. The material is divided into seven trios, two duets pairing Bley with Phillips or Parker, and two excellent Parker/Phillips encounters. These are not apprentice players in a hurry but mature artists who can afford the time to let their music unfold organically. Every piece gives off a sense of having evolved spontaneously. The original intention was to create a setting very similar to the then recently reconvened Giuffre/Bley/Swallow trio (whose first two records had been reissued on ECM), but the strong personalities of three players who had not worked as a trio before very quickly asserted themselves. 'Poetic Justice' has a more restless quality than the rest, but the title-track is a near-perfect illustration of the way three senior players with yard-long CVs and utterly distinctive voices are still able to touch base with their own musical upbringing. Parker's Coltrane inflexions are only the most obvious example; Bley and Phillips dig deep into their own memories as well. A superb album, recommendable to anyone.

*** Chaos

Soul Note 121285 2 *Bley; Furio Di Castri (b); Tony Oxley (d, perc).* 3/94.

Not strictly a Bley album since it involves solos by all three participants and just five trio tracks. The pieces mostly evolve slowly and rather quietly, with an emphasis on clearly articulated detail and small shifts of timbre and tonality rather than anything more dramatic. The piano/drums duet 'Soft Touch' is the signature track, coming in after each player has played alone. After it, 'Poetic Justice' is the first trio improvisation: highly focused, crisply articulated and thoroughly logical from start to finish. Bley's piano sounds as if it might have gone out of tune during the recording, or only been tuned half way through, but it doesn't mar the angular beauty of these sessions. Oxley's genius is equally evident and the less familiar Di Castri acquits himself magnificently.

*** Outside In

Justin Time JUST 69 *Bley; Sonny Greenwich (g).* 7/94.

A very spontaneous and – apparently – unrehearsed studio session following one of the guitarist's relatively rare concert appearances at the Festival International de Jazz de Montréal in 1994. The aim was to explore a batch of songs from without and within, working in both directions simultaneously. The process is easier to follow on the standard and repertoire material, a very oblique interpretation of 'These Foolish Things' and versions of Eldridge's 'I Remember Harlem', Rollins's 'Pent Up House' and Charlie Parker's 'Steeplechase', a nod in the direction of Bley's other sponsoring label. Some of the material is clearly improvised on the spot or is based on material run down at the concert earlier. The playing is calm, detailed and resolutely un-intense. If improvising players now try to resist the 'conversational' analogy for what they do, this record seems to restore it. It's full of the elisions, repetitions, non-sequiturs and sheer playfulness found in any dialogue between friends, old or new.

**** Reality Check

Steeplechase SCCD 31379 *Bley; Jay Anderson (b); Victor Lewis (d).* 10/94.

Bley still jokes that he only listens to his own records these days. Such is the flow of material, it's all too possible, but the joke also contains a serious pointer, because he sounds like a man who inhabits his own musical world. It is now a very long time since it has been possible to say of him that he sounds like Monk, or Taylorish, or in the spirit of Bud Powell. Oddly, then, this is an album that seems to want to re-establish precisely some of those connections. Perhaps that is what he means by 'Reality Check', a stark, spare, stripped-down piece that builds up into a glorious abstract improvisation with a strictly limited palette and an unlimited range of ideas. Mark Gardner suggests that 'For George', exquisitely introduced on brushes by Victor Lewis, is dedicated to George Wallington, one of the lesser-known figures on the New York scene in the '50s. Or it may simply be that memories of a friend have conjured up an older style of playing. There is certainly more than a whiff of Bill Evans throughout the record. In what would have been Bill's 75th year, perhaps his spirit was abroad again. Even Bley's approach to 'I Surrender, Dear' has an element of a more delicate and lyrical style in it, a softness of focus that balances the blunt, blocky chords and fierce stabs of colour. The trio is working as a unit, but with ample space for individual expression. Anderson's solo on 'Do Something' is good enough to cue back and play again, and Lewis doesn't put a foot wrong, often taking a forward role while Bley chords restlessly round an idea. A superb album, and one which stands out in a now crowded catalogue.

*** Not Two, Not One

ECM 1860 *Bley; Gary Peacock (b); Paul Motian (d).* 95.

One of the more disappointing Bley albums of recent years and an unconscious omission from our last edition, because we don't entirely know what to make of it. No one can possibly mistake the level of understanding and sympathy that exists between these three senior players. And yet the impression given here is of musicians anticipating one another to such an extent that the conversation becomes private and solipsistic. There are lovely passages and Peacock is in absolutely magisterial form, Motian less so. It's not so much that the parts don't cohere as that a highly coherent sound refuses to yield up the drama of its making.

***** Sweet Time**
Justin Time 56 *Bley (p solo).* 95.
***** Hands On**
Evidence ECD 22184 *As above.* 96.

Sweet Time is a fascinating set that underlines how deeply Bley is immersed in the blues, gospel, ragtime and a host of other piano idioms. The title piece is a clotted blues rag, densely structured but rhythmically pungent. 'Contrary' draws on a host of classical references, some explicit, most of them very carefully absorbed into the structure. 'Never Again' is one of his seemingly spontaneous compositions, a minimal line packed with information and with emotion. 'Turnham Bay' seems to relate to something deeply personal and is as lovely as anything he's produced in years, while 'Pointillist' is a return to a more abstractionist approach.

The Evidence disc is more discursive and in some respects more demanding of the listener, but the quality of sound is stunning, with Bley conjuring layers of sound out of the Bosendorfer Imperial, an instrument big enough to contain his increasingly philosophical vision. Two of the best Bley solo records of recent years.

****** Sankt Gerold**
ECM 157899 *Bley; Evan Parker (ss, ts); Barre Phillips (b).* 4/96.

This trio is now a fairly long-standing association and the three principals play with astonishing sympathy and understanding. This time the recording was made in the Sankt Gerold monastery in Austria, a setting that must have made an impact on three individuals with their own spiritual and philosophical understandings.

The concert is presented as a set of 12 'variations', though on what is never made entirely clear (an omission that didn't hold Elgar back, to be fair). Some are solo pieces, and Bley's two features, 'Variations 6/9', are vintage performances: free, rhythmic and intense, but with a floating lyricism that is borrowed in part from the graceful Phillips, who really holds this session together. Barre's solo is a model of its kind, idiomatic but also intensely musical.

Whether the Austrian setting prompted thoughts of Webern, Berg and Schoenberg can't be guessed at, but there is certainly a hint of that drily romantic idiom floating through these astonishing tracks. Another lovely record from ECM in a collaborative format that has paid enormous creative dividends in recent years.

*****(*) Notes On Ornette**
Steeplechase SCCD 31437 *Bley; Jay Anderson (b); Jeff Hirshfield (d).* 9/97.

'Turnaround' has always been the Ornette theme that appeals to piano players. Hampton Hawes memorably recorded it with Charlie Haden, and now Bley, who worked with Ornette at the Hillcrest Club in California all those years ago, makes it his own in a long and deeply thoughtful reading. There are a couple of surprises on the set, the inclusion of 'Lorraine' and 'Crossroads', but the key inclusion, all too short, is 'When Will The Blues Leave', the composer's most rawly evocative work. Though only half the length of the other Ornette pieces (there is also a closing original 'AARP'), it's the defining cut on a heartfelt and very effective album.

*****(*) Basics**
Justin Time JUST 154 *Bley (p solo).* 7/00.

'Monk's Mood' is the only non-original on this solo set of mostly new and unfamiliar material, almost all of it couched in Bley's signature post-bop style, but tempered by unexpected nods in the direction of Dave Brubeck *and* Ray Charles ('Told You So') and the pianoless Baker/Mulligan groups ('Chet'). The piano sounds lovely and full-voiced and the engineering gives it lots of presence and warmth.

Oddbjørn Blindheim

PIANO

Norwegian mainstreamer with vivid approach.

***** Horace Hello**
Gemini GMCD 102 *Blindheim; Svein Olav Blindheim (b); Hakon Mjaset Johansen, Eyvind Olsen (d).* 6/99.

A tribute to Horace Silver by his Nordic admirer. Blindheim knows how to swing and his fleet delivery never fails to please. 'Ecaroh' and 'Horace-scope' are both absolutely in the groove, and the reading of 'Lady From Johannesburg' is lovely as well. Olsen is in for one track only, and it's a pity he couldn't have stayed for longer: a subtler and more propulsive drummer than Johansen. Otherwise, the trio is excellent and this is an attractive package.

Jane Ira Bloom (born 1954)

SOPRANO SAXOPHONE

Bloom went to Berklee and then Yale, before settling in New York and choosing to focus on soprano sax. She began recording on her own Outline label in 1979 and had a brief spell at Columbia before going her own way.

***** Mighty Lights**
Enja 4044-2 *Bloom; Fred Hersch (p); Charlie Haden (b); Ed Blackwell (d).* 11/82.

***** As One**
Winter & Winter 919003-2 *Bloom; Fred Hersch (p).* 9/84.

*****(*) Art And Aviation**
Arabesque AJ0107 *Bloom; Kenny Wheeler (t, flhn); Ron Horton (t); Kenny Werner (p); Rufus Reid, Michael Formanek (b); Jerry Granelli (d).* 7/92.

Bloom remains among the few musicians who play exclusively on the soprano sax. Recordings from the '80s – a pair of quickly deleted albums for Columbia, which found her dabbling with electronics – suggested she was becoming disenchanted with the possibilities of the instrument in a straight-ahead jazz format; but the earlier disc is a distinctive acoustic setting. She has a sparse, considered delivery, eschewing vibrato and sentimentality: Leroy Anderson's 'Lost In The Stars' is awarded an attractively tart reading. Particularly impressive are two tracks in which Hersch sits out and Bloom, Haden and Blackwell hit a propulsive groove.

The Winter & Winter record is a reissue of a duo album for JMT. We dismissed it rather peremptorily in our first edition, but returning to it has been a modest pleasure. Bloom's partnership with Hersch has gone on to more profound levels since, but they find attractive common ground straight away in the opening 'Waiting For Daylight', and the mild tension between Hersch's romanticism and Bloom's starker delivery brings some interesting bounty.

After a quiet period Bloom returned with the fine *Art And Aviation*. The seven originals are titled to suggest a concept of flying through dark, outer-space skies, and with the peripatetic Wheeler in wonderful form and spare, sharply attuned playing by the rhythm players, the music does indeed soar and glide when it wants to. The plangency of Wheeler's brass and Bloom's acerbic delivery grant a pleasingly frosty feel to much of the playing, as if they really were performing in a still, cold atmosphere. 'Hawkins' Parallel Universe' dovetails the two horns so acutely that they might be figure-skating the melodies. In context, the cover of Monk's 'Straight No Chaser' and the farewell of 'Lost In The Stars' work perfectly; and the occasional flicker of live electronics is much better adapted than on Bloom's earlier records.

**** The Nearness

Arabesque AJ0120 *Bloom; Kenny Wheeler (t, flhn); Julian Priester (tb); Fred Hersch (p); Rufus Reid (b); Bobby Previte (d).* 95.

The surprise card is Priester and, with no electronics and several standards in the programme, this might have been an orthodox blowing record. Instead, Bloom recasts every melody and form in refreshing ways. Incredibly, she manages to find something new in 'Round Midnight', here done as a sober dance for the horns, and the ballads 'The Nearness Of You' and 'In The Wee Small Hours Of The Morning' are played – spoken, almost – with cadences of melody soft enough to suggest music drifting down from the stars. Wheeler is his usual irresistible self, the rhythm section are marvellous, and an original such as 'It's A Corrugated World' stops the music becoming too navel-gazing. Very fine.

**** The Red Quartets

Arabesque AJO144 *Bloom; Fred Hersch (p); Mark Dresser (b); Bobby Previte (d).* 5/97–1/99.

Another session with Hersch, and another marvellous record from Bloom. Though in other ways she is quite unlike him, she shares something of Steve Lacy's anti-virtuosity on the fish horn, often going aggravatingly against the grain of an otherwise busy dynamic in which the rest of the group are involved. She has stuck with her austere tone, which can at times seem baleful but at other moments – as in the extraordinary bittersweetness of 'Time After Time' – be uncommonly affecting. Without other horns to converse with, she forges an even closer alliance with Hersch. For all the excellent work put in by Dresser and Previte, it's their dialogue which is the heartbeat of the record, with Hersch's flowing lyricism filling out all the possibilities inherent in Bloom's themes.

***(*) Sometimes The Magic

Arabesque AJO 155 *Bloom; Vincent Bourgeyx (p); Mark Dresser (b); Bobby Previte (d).* 6–7/00.

Divided between solos, trio and quartet tracks, this isn't the best of Bloom, though it's a worthy addition to her Arabesque sequence. Bourgeyx is no match for Hersch, although the rhythm section plays with authority on the five quartet tunes; 'Truth In Timbre' is especially effective. In soliloquy, on 'Bewitched' and 'How Are Things In Glocca Morra?', Bloom seems to be thinking to herself, and the performances aren't very outgoing. But she continues to work her particular combination of standards, post-bop playing and atmospheric abstraction to remarkable ends.

Blue Goat Quartet

GROUP

Formed in 1996, this Swiss quartet sort through the contemporary vocabulary in seach of something individual.

*** Talking Idly

Altrisuoni LC 0504 *Costi Topalidis (ss, ts); Jodok Hess (p); Markus Fischer (b); Tobias Friedli (d).* 11/01.

With some years of work behind them before they made their debut CD, the BGQ sound confident and in full command of their music on this impressively well-turned and vibrant set of pieces (all credited to pianist Hess). The music has a near pop-tune feel, but lacks little in the way of musical muscle: the rhythm players are likely to settle into a rockish beat here and there, yet the interplay between the group is smart and sensitive. Hess uses the Fender Rhodes on some tracks, which tends to underline the notion of a fusion leaning, and Topalidis likes the soprano at least as much as the tenor. The improvising makes no deep impression: the record's about a quick, grooving band, and is very enjoyable on those terms.

Blue Notes

GROUP

A rare recording by the legendary South African group with their original line-up.

*** Live In South Africa, 1964

Ogun OGCD 007 *Chris McGregor (p); Mongezi Feza (t); Dudu Pukwana (as); Nick Moyake (ts); Johnny Mbizo Dyani (b); Louis Moholo (d).* 64.

The dateline tells you much of what you need to know. Two years after Sharpeville, a mixed-race group (Chris McGregor was white) playing jazz in Durban. Not long after this recording was made, the Blue Notes went to Europe to perform at the St Juan-les-Pins Jazz Festival and never returned. The early Blue Notes were more mixed stylistically than hindsight might have suggested. This is essentially a swing band, playing mostly in common time and with very few bebop accents. Moholo, later to be a fantastically lateral drummer, mainly keeps it straight, and the solos are delivered straight with none of the boiling dissonance that was to be a feature of later groups like Pukwana's Spear and Zila. They, of course, were founded amidst the agonies of exile and it would be idle to speculate how these six musicians (of whom only Moholo is still playing) might have developed – or not – had they lived untroubled in a liberal climate. As the set progresses, a mixture of McGregor and Pukwana tunes, with 'I Cover The Waterfront' featuring a Gonsalves-like Moyake, it becomes possible to hear some intimations of the later style. Pukwana's 'B My Dear' has a tender plangency that was to be reasserted when the piece was re-arranged for the Dedication Orchestra in 1993 (see below). Feza is less assertive than one expects, and the bulk of the solo space is devoted to alto and piano. Acoustically, the quality is no worse than one might expect, given the circumstances. Dyani is quite audible relative to McGregor, and the Kid's trumpet seems to be pointing away in another direction, which might offer some insight into the position of the mike. These are secondary issues, though. This is an important historical release for anyone interested in the development of the South African strain in British and European jazz. It conveys, particularly on the closing 'Dorkay House', something of the raw excitement of those extraordinary years.

Hamiet Bluiett (born 1940)

BARITONE SAXOPHONE, ALTO CLARINET

Settled in with the St Louis Black Artists Group in 1969, and in the '70s sparsely recorded before his association with World Saxophone Quartet. In the '90s he has been very active in the studios and is asserting his own career. Though the sound's been mollified by time, he can still make an elegant avant-garde roar on the big horn.

**** Birthright

India Navigation IN 1030 *Bluiett (bs solo). 77.*

The baritone saxophone enjoyed a brief but historically unspecific boom in the '50s. Why then? Harry Carney had turned it into a viable solo instrument; there were probably more good ensemble players around, conscious equally of the run-down on paying gigs with big bands and of the attractions of a little solo spotlight; lastly, the prevailing role-models on alto and tenor were, perhaps, a little too dominant. By contrast, no established baritone style developed; Gerry Mulligan was as different from Serge Chaloff as Chaloff was from Pepper Adams; and round the fringes there were players like Sahib Shihab and Nick Brignola doing very different things indeed.

Currently, the situation is much the same. The three most interesting baritonists all play in markedly different styles. The young Amerasian Fred Houn is very much a Carney disciple; Britain's John Surman blows baritone as if it were a scaled-up alto (which by and large it is); Hamiet Bluiett, on the other hand, gives the big horn and his 'double', alto clarinet, a dark, Mephistophelian inflexion, concentrating on their lower registers, but also capable of pushing both horns up into extraordinary ranges more reminiscent of the soprano. A fine section-player – and his work with the World Saxophone Quartet is an extension of that – he is a highly distinctive soloist.

Heard unaccompanied on this set from The Kitchen, he is dark, rootsy and at moments almost unbearably intense. 'In Tribute To Harry Carney' is a deeply personal testimonial, redolent of the blues as the whole album is. The saxophonist's wife Ebu is the dedicatee of a short and heartful song which compresses much of his music to date. Other family members, including Hamiet Sr, are invoked in 'My Father's House', the longest single piece on the record. Recorded without overdubbing or effects, but with multiple microphones to capture a sense of movement and of spatial relationships, the sound is very authentic and hauntingly present. As ever, it remains in the lower register for much of the duration of the concert, a vocalized sound that never becomes discursive but harks back to the most primitive of music-making and the most sophisticated gestures of the avant-garde.

***(*) Saying Something For All

Just A Memory JAM 9134-2 *Bluiett; Muhal Richard Abrams (p). 7/77, 79.*

Justin Time has been very generous to Bluiett in recent years. These remarkable recordings are issued on the Canadian label's archive imprint. Abrams has always been a formidable duo player, endlessly challenging and responsive, hugely generous as well. His contribution, as writer and performer, to the two opening tracks – 'Night Dreams For Daytime Viewing' – calls for a separate credit. He is less in evidence later on when Bluiett compositions take over. The title-piece sounds like a spontaneous improvisation, but one which draws on both men's catalogues of work.

'Suite Pretty Tune' is a flute feature, light-toned and agreeably slight. 'Solo Flight' foregrounds the horn still more, but the real pay-off comes not from the duo's Environ gig – recorded in New York in 1977 – but from two years later when Bluiett was touring with the Sam Rivers band. 'Requiem For Kent State' was apparently recorded at the Ohio college where four anti-Vietnam protesters were shot dead by the National Guard. Emotionally it's a compelling piece, but it is also perhaps the best available sampling of Bluiett's technical resources on the big horn. Honks, slaps, vocalized overtones, toneless keying: all play their part in what is probably the definitive Bluiett performance. You can almost sense the silent band behind him watching in awe.

***(*) Resolution

Black Saint 120014 *Bluiett; Don Pullen (p); Fred Hopkins (b); Famoudou Don Moye (perc). 11/77.*

**** Im/possible To Keep

India Navigation IN 1072 2CD *As above. 77.*

*** EBU

Soul Note 121088 *Bluiett; John Hicks (p); Fred Hopkins (b); Marvin 'Smitty' Smith (d). 2/84.*

Compared to the clutter (or exuberance – tastes vary) of the later, Africanized albums, the earlier recordings are stripped down (or downright sparse – ditto), muscular and sometimes chillingly abrasive. The *Resolution* quartet is perhaps heard to better effect on the deleted *SOS* (India Navigation IN 1039), a live New York set of near-identical vintage, but the studio cuts are still absolutely compelling. Bluiett, on baritone only, is in sterling form, relaxed in perhaps the most conducive company he has assembled on record. Pullen and Hopkins are masters of this idiom, and Moye curbs his occasionally foolish excesses. Production values aren't as hot as on the Soul Note sessions, but the music is way out in front.

The reappearance of the material on *Im/possible To Keep* is a huge bonus to this rather truncated discography. There is more than two and a quarter hours of concentrated music here, including a massive version of 'Sobre Una Nube' and a splendid reading of Miles's 'Tune Up'. The band sound is very authentic and unadorned, with a live ambience and no undue sweetening. Hopkins is in great shape throughout, sounding big and fast and unfailingly musical. Bluiett shifts from baritone to clarinet and flutes, playing fluently and with unmistakable passion. Strongly recommended.

A generous mix and better-than-average registration of the lead horn (the CD is first class) redeems *EBU*'s rather slack execution and raises it to the front rank. Hicks is a much lighter player than Pullen and is perhaps too much of an instinctive lyricist to combine well with Bluiett's increasingly declamatory responses. The rhythm section sometimes lacks incisiveness, fatally so on a rather odd 'Night In Tunisia'.

*** Dangerously Suite

Soul Note 121018 *Bluiett; Bob Neloms (p); Buster Williams (b); Billy Hart (d); Chief Bey (African perc); Irene Datcher (v).* 4/81.

*** Nali Kola

Soul Note 121188 *Bluiett; Hugh Masekela (t, flhn); James Plunky Branch (ss); Billy Spaceman Patterson (g); Donald Smith (b); Okyerema Asante, Chief Bey, Titos Sompa, Seku Tonge (perc); Quincy Troupe (poet).* 7/87.

Bluiett's pan-Africanism of the early '80s opened up for him a whole book of new rhythmic codes that helped ease him out of the still impressive but palpably finite resources of his original post-bop orientation. *Dangerously* is a transitional exercise in that it merely grafts African percussion and voice on to the basic horn/piano/rhythm quartet. It is a fine album none the less, neither tentative nor blandly 'experimental'. *Nali Kola* is certainly not tentative, but it lacks the clearly methodological premisses someone like Marion Brown brings to projects of this type. The awkward instrumentation is intriguingly handled and well recorded – though the channel separation is a little crude – and Bluiett seems comfortable in his interplay with the still-adventurous Masekela and the little-known Branch and Smith, who are casual additions to the long title-track. It also features the 'verse' of Quincy Troupe, now better known for his ghosting of Miles's autobiography. As a whole, it is somewhat reminiscent of Archie Shepp's remarkable 1969 collaboration with Philly Joe Jones. And none the worse for that!

**(*) The Clarinet Family

Black Saint 120097 *Bluiett; Dwight Andrews (sno cl, s cl); Don Byron, Gene Ghee, John Purcell (s cl, bcl); Buddy Collette (s cl, acl); J. D. Parran (sno cl, s cl, acl, contralto cl); Sir Kidd Jordan (cbcl); Fred Hopkins (b); Ronnie Burrage (d).* 11/84.

Utterly remarkable. The ten-minute egg of hard-boiled clarinet revivalism. Bluiett's inspired project may initially sound like a discursive guide to the woodwinds; in practice, it's a deeply celebratory, almost pentecostal rediscovery of the clarinet – once the jazz voice *par excellence* – and its preterite cousins and second cousins. Kidd Jordan's hefty contrabass instrument, hitherto associated only with Anthony Braxton, must count as a second cousin, twice removed; pitched at double B flat, it has an extraordinary tonality, as on 'River Niger', a Jordan composition that conjures up oddly disconnected echoes of Paul Robeson in *Sanders of the River*.

There's a strong sense of tradition through this fine live set, recorded in Berlin: two long tributes to Machito – a very different 'Macho' from the one credited to Steve Turre on the Brass Fantasy's ECM *Avant Pop* – and Duke Ellington, well-shared-out compositional credits, a startling bass solo from Hopkins, and, following it, a beautifully judged climax. After *Resolution* and the better of the WSQ albums, this is the essential Bluiett album, albeit one in which he plays a collective and slightly understated role.

***(*) Libation For The Baritone Saxophone Nation

Justin Time JTR 8470-2 *Bluiett; James Carter, Alex Harding, Patience Higgins (bs); Ronnie Burrage (d).* 97.

This is what in certain circles is called turning up mob-handed. Bluiett first experimented with these forces in 1972 with the Baritone Saxophone Retinue, co-led with Pat Patrick and Charles Davis, and featuring Cecil Payne. Twenty years later, he revived the idea with the more anonymous International Baritone Conspiracy. The latest incarnation is the most convincingly idiomatic yet. Introducing the band at the 1997 Montreal Jazz Festival on *Libation*, Bluiett calls in his three baritone-wielding colleagues and the up-for-it Burrage as if he was warming up for James Brown on a funk revival tour. Bluiett is a master of upper-register playing, and some of his top lines are light and fleet enough to sound like rootsy alto. On 'Discussion Among Friends' – otherwise the most prosaic performance on the record – he further extends the big horn's range with vocalized chord effects; but for the most part he sticks to the instrument's middle register, leaving the foundation work to Higgins and Harding.

Carter has, of course, carved his own path through this kind of repertoire; his composition, 'J.B. Groove', is a tribute to the master, but one cast in a version of Bluiett's own groovy hybrid of r'n'b and the avant-garde. The other material is splendidly varied, with a reading of Sam Rivers's 'Revival', a brassy version of trombonist Frank Lacy's 'Settegast Strut' and with E. J. Allen's 'Discussion Amongst Friends' used as a set exercise for the ensemble.

*** Makin' Whoopee: Tribute To The King Cole Trio

Mapleshade 040932 *Bluiett; Ed Cherry (g); Keter Betts (b).* 97.

Weird as this sometimes is, it's a model demonstration of how to record a small acoustic group in which one member – the saxophonist, natch – is always likely to overpower the rest of the group. Bluiett's devotion to Nat Cole seems improbable only until one thinks of his devotion to vocal jazz, soul and the vivid, harmonic swing that Nat bequeathed to American music. These cuts are not going to be to everyone's taste and there is an occasional mismatch of material and performance, but the overall effect is gorgeous and 'Route 66' is just about the boldest remake of an American classic that you'll ever hear.

***(*) Same Space

Justin Time JUST 109-2 *Bluiett; D. D. Jackson (p, ky); Mor Thiam (v, djembe).* 97.

***(*) Join Us

Justin Time 124-2 *As above.* 10/98.

A rainbow coalition band, and a distinctive new sound for Bluiett. Initially, the emphasis seems to be firmly placed on vocal chants and dark, swampy rhythms, but there is a freedom as well which recalls nothing more strongly than legendary British group, The Trio, with baritonist John Surman, Barre Phillips and Stu Martin. For a change, Bluiett's baritone is at something of a discount, though his opening on 'Ayse' (*Join Us*) over djembe and piano is exquisitely thoughtful. Both records apportion writing credits very evenly; indeed Bluiett contributes only three atypical tunes to *Same Space*. African-born Mor Thiam and the rapidly developing Jackson, who won his spurs on the burgeoning Canadian scene, are unmistakably co-leaders. Serious Bluiett collectors should be aware that these are not headlining albums for the big man.

Jackson's funky organ might seem to pitch the music in the direction of jukebox r'n'b, but even here the initial impression is deceptive for, once the percussion kicks in, the count goes seriously wild. 'A Little Calypso' tips its hat to Sonny Rollins, but goes its own distinctive way. Both are studio recordings, although spoken introductions and vocal interjections, raps and poems give a strong impression of live immediacy. Apart from 'Mon Dieu' on the earlier record and D. D. Jackson's 'One Night' on *Join Us*, the tracks are mostly short and relaxedly conversational.

***** With Eyes Wide Open**

Justin Time 138 *Bluiett; Ed Cherry (g); Jaribu Shahid (b); Nasheet Waits (d).* 11/99.

Credited simply to 'Bluiett' – he seems to have abandoned the first name, à la 'don't call me James' Moody – *With Eyes Wide Open* combines original compositions with two pieces by the late Don Pullen. The first of these, 'Sing Me A Song Everlasting', is perhaps the most effective piece on a perhaps too varied and eclectic set which seems to be heading in several directions at once. The new group is securely anchored on a funky, accurate rhythm-section, and one scarcely ever feels the need for a second horn. Bluiett's playing has rarely been more soulful and melodic, but there are confrontational moments with Cherry which raise the temperature and see the saxophonist head up into his very controlled false upper register. This is an aspect of his playing which is now so finely attuned that on songs like 'Enum' and 'Mystery Tune' it is genuinely difficult in some measures to determine which member of the saxophone family is involved. That's a minor issue. The more important point is that Bluiett is playing as well and as adventurously as ever. Not the most coherent of albums, but every track suggests a project.

***** The Calling**

Justin Time 162 *Bluiett; D. D. Jackson (p, org, ky); Kahil El'Zabar (d, perc, v).* 10/00.

A most unusual and effective record, *The Calling* showcases compositions by Jackson and El'Zabar organized round a central improvisation, 'Ask And You Shall Find'. It is disconcertingly brief, but this is intended very much as an album of songs rather than long-form improvisations. El'Zabar contributes four numbers, including the very powerful 'Open My Eyes' which sets the tone for the disc. At the other extreme, 'Blues Grind' is a raw and dirty showcase for Bluiett's characteristically muscular baritone and for Jackson's organ grooves. Hamiet switches to bamboo flute for 'Ask And You Shall Find' but sticks mainly to his big horn, which more than ever is presented as a singing voice and here as a foil to El'Zabar's plaintive, folky vocals.

***** Blueblack**

Justin Time 158 *Bluiett; James Carter (bs, cbcl); Patience Higgins, Alex Harding (bs, bcl); Lee Person, Kahil el'Zabar (d, perc).* 1/01.

If you still use an ink pen, peer into a bottle of Quink blue/black for a sense of this album's basic tonality. The lower registers are well catered for, and it takes a player of Bluiett's extraordinary range to make such a project interesting. The most effective use of the massed baritones and bass clarinets comes on 'Humpback' by the intriguing black composer Coleridge Taylor Perkinson, the first of a number of his compositions covered on a record which kicks off with a Motown cover and then disappears in precisely the opposite direction. Bluiett is still a genuine experimenter, prepared to let a very restrictive format drive him forwards. Some listeners will find this a difficult album to like, but patience and a certain aural recalibration do pay dividends and we recommend it.

Larry Bluth

PIANO

A pianist, bassist and drummer working together in the Lennie Tristano idiom, the trio's records are all drawn from concerts played during the '90s.

***** Live At Orfeo**

Zinnia 105 *Bluth; Don Messina (b); Bill Chattin (d).* 11/91–1/92.

***** Five Concerts And A Landscape**

Zinnia 109 *As above.*

***** Formations**

Zinnia 114 *As above.* 10/96–2/98.

We are listing these records under Bluth's name purely for alphabetical convenience, since this is clearly a co-operative effort among three like-minded and accomplished thinkers in the Tristano tradition. Recorded in front of various small audiences at concerts in and around New York, the music consists of somewhat old-fashioned and deferential improvisations on some notable chord-sequences. The music will sound comfily familiar to those attuned to the Warne Marsh/Peter Ind sessions of the late '50s or to anything by Sal Mosca (there is a dedication to Mosca on the third record). There's little to choose between the three discs, although the audiences were noisier in the early days of the trio, and the recording quality, which is hit and miss on the first two albums, has improved considerably by the time of *Formations*. There's a documentary feel, which results in, say, the music suddenly disappearing at the end of 'Shoals', on *Formations*, the kind of stroke which no major record label would allow. Bluth hints at melodies without quite realizing them, Messina plays a roving, modestly virtuosic line, and Chattin sets up the quietest of swinging grooves. There is always the fun of playing spot-the-standard, hidden under titles like 'Sundays At Elke's', although the later records own up to which tunes they're playing. Although the music spans seven years of work, there's no 'development' as such, more a sense that they're patiently working out directions that it will take them the rest of their performing lives to investigate. These are men playing for the music rather than for themselves, and the rarity of this kind of jazz makes these enjoyable sessions all the more satisfying.

Arthur Blythe (born 1940)

ALTO SAXOPHONE

Also known as Black Arthur, Blythe originally divided his career between relatively orthodox bebop and an innovative style of jazz that united the passionate immediacy of the early pioneers with non-Western harmonies and rhythms. Brilliant but erratic, he is still not well represented on record.

*****(*) In Concert**

India Navigation IN 1029 *Blythe; Ahmed Abdullah (t); Bob Stewart (tba); Abdul Wadud (clo); Steve Reid (d); Muhammad Abdullah (perc).* 2/77.

Arthur Blythe is a marvellous musician whose path has often seemed luckless. His India Navigation sets of the late '70s were breathtakingly original, and his form-sheet included demanding and chops-quickening stints with Gil Evans and Horace

Tapscott, with whom he was a founding member of two radical co-operatives, Artists Ascension and Union of God's Musicians.

In Concert covers two major pieces, 'Metamorphosis' and 'The Grip'. The band has the sort of dark, experimental feel of Tapscott's West Coast collectives. The use of Stewart is brilliant and the absence of a string bassist irrelevant in face of his robust *legato* playing. Ahmed Abdullah is sharp and forceful, combining elements of Pops with Roy Eldridge and Charlie Shavers (and, frankly, nothing more contemporary than that). Blythe's solo formation isn't always entirely secure, but he is brimming over with ideas, and he attempts to string them together at least logically.

CORE COLLECTION

♛ **** Lenox Avenue Breakdown

Koch KOC CD 7871 *Blythe; Bob Stewart (tba); James Newton (f); James Blood Ulmer (g); Cecil McBee (b); Jack DeJohnette (d); Guilherme Franco (perc).* 79.

In 1979 Blythe signed with Columbia and produced what became one of the lost masterpieces of modern jazz, reissued on CD only 20 years after its first appearance. *Lenox Avenue Breakdown* is a superlative piece of imaginative instrumentation, similar to the India Navigation set, but with the lighter and more complex sound of James Newton's flute backing the leader's extraordinary blues wail. There is scarcely a flat moment on the album, despite all four pieces being built round relatively static and repetitive ideas.

Stewart's long solo on the title-piece is one of the few genuinely important tuba statements in jazz, a nimble sermon that promises storms and sunshine. McBee has his moment on 'Slidin' Through', and Blythe himself saves his main contribution for the final track, the Eastern-sounding 'Odessa', on which he cries like a *muezzin*, a *cantor* and a storefront Salvationist, all in one impeccably structured arc. DeJohnette came of age with this record, playing with fire and authority, and with the sophisticated understanding of how rhythm and melody can combine which was to characterize his own later projects; *Special Edition*, which included Blythe, was recorded in the same year as this. His work behind Blythe on that final track deserves the closest attention. The other key element to the sound is Ulmer, who in those days was (like Blythe himself) moving comfortably between 'inside' and 'outside' projects.

There were more fine albums to come, but then Blythe's wind went, and he seemed lost. Much of his work in intervening years was in a pop vein, a watered-down version of the deep, urban groove he found on *Lenox Avenue Breakdown*. In recording terms, there is a long gap at this point. Worth dwelling just a moment longer with this extraordinary disc.

*** Hipmotism

Enja ENJ 6088-2 *Blythe; Hamiet Bluiett (bs); Kelvyn Bell (g); Gust William Tsilis (vib, mar); Bob Stewart (tba); Arto Tuncboyacyan (perc, v); Famoudou Don Moye (d).* 3/91.

*** Retroflection

Enja ENJ 8046-2 *Blythe; John Hicks (p); Cecil McBee (b); Bobby Battle (d).* 6/93.

***(*) Calling Card

Enja ENJ 9051-2 *As above.* 6/93.

Blythe returned to jazz proper in the mid-'80s, seemingly unblunted by his dalliance with commercial music. For all the personal references and dedications, he still betrays a lack of essential spirit on *Hipmotism*. There are also signs, most seriously on the opening trio and the concluding, unaccompanied 'My Son Ra', that a certain laziness of articulation had become second nature. The Village Vanguard session that makes up *Retroflection* finds him in better voice, technically speaking, but decidedly short of ideas. A more or less routine re-run of 'Lenox Avenue Breakdown' is relieved by crisp, sensitive playing from the group. Hicks is a total professional, and McBee is absolutely on the spot, both harmonically and rhythmically. No complaints whatever there, but still an unsatisfyingly hollow centre.

The blend of instrumental voices on *Hipmotism* is intriguing enough to carry the day. There are only three all-in tracks, 'Matter Of Fact' and 'Bush Baby', both of them notably abstract, and the title-piece, which is simple and roistering. Blythe sounds good on them all, feeding off the deeper, darker sounds of Stewart's tuba and guest Bluiett's brassy baritone. The sparser settings expose him mercilessly and 'Miss Eugie', for alto saxophone, tuba and Tuncboyacyan's percussion and voice, requires a more forceful performance.

Oddly enough, the second issue of material from the June 1993 Village Vanguard sessions is a good deal more satisfying than the first. There is the same stiltedness of delivery, but the material on *Calling Card* is looser and more expressive. Once again, Hicks's 'Naima's Love Song' is the crowning moment of a modern-jazz set, played feelingly and with lovely shifts of time and register throughout. 'Jitterbug Waltz' might almost be read as a nod to the example of Eric Dolphy. It isn't played on Eric's first choice of horn for this tune, but it has the same intriguing mix of familiarity and alienation. Battle is exceptionally good on these cuts, though here and there problems of registration surface on the two-track recording, which may have persuaded Enja to hold back these performances for later release. For our money, though, this is the better record.

***(*) Today's Blues

CIMP 158 *Blythe; David Eyges (clo).* 8/97.

One of those out-of-nowhere records that sends a thrill of excitement through the unprepared listener. The meeting with Eyges, who plays amplified cello, rekindles memories of Blythe with Abdul Wadud, many years earlier, and the saxophonist's beautifully responsive and articulate lines are wonderful to hear. The lovely, ripe vibrato he puts on the end of some of his phrases, the rich, singing tone and speech-like reflexes all sound like Arthur at his best – and it's good to have him back on record sounding so strong. Eyges is no match for Wadud – much less Blythe – but he plays second fiddle to the alto master with a fine good humour.

**** Night Song

Clarity 1016 *Blythe; Chico Freeman (bcl, perc); Gust William Tsilis (vib, mar); Bob Stewart (tba); David Frazier, Josh Jones, Arto Tuncboyaciyan (perc).* 97.

This finds Arthur in top form: raw, stylish, inventive and mixing tradition and experiment with great confidence. He varies an already enterprising personnel from track to track, calling on producer Freeman for some effective bass clarinet here and there. He combines brilliantly with Stewart's parping tuba. The use of three-hand drummers gives parts of the set an almost ceremonial parade feel, something that has surfaced in Arthur's work here and there over the years. The title-piece –

strictly 'Cancion De La Noche' – is a collaboration with vibist Tsilis and was set to become one of Arthur's signature pieces over the next few years, gently swinging, but also pointing at depths of harmony and of historical awareness. There is a nod to the modern-jazz tradition in a middle section that follows Monk's 'We See' (Monk is clearly an important source) with Strayhorn's mournful 'Blood Count'. A thoroughly enjoyable and thought-provoking album.

***** Spirits In The Field**
Savant 2024 *Blythe; Bob Stewart (tba); Cecil Brooks III (d).* 99.

Recorded live at the BIM Huis in Amsterdam, this catches Blythe on a good night, playing with an intensity and focus which is not fairly represented in the recording. Stewart sounds muffled and the drums are overloud but compositions as varied as the classic 'Lenox Avenue Breakdown' and Don Pullen's threnody for George Adams 'Ah, George, We Hardly Knew Ya' are delightful performances and show that Arthur is still enjoying his purple streak.

***** Blythe Bite**
Savant 2036 *Blythe; John Hicks (p); Dwayne Dolphin (b); Cecil Brooks III (d).* 3/01.

Largely dominated by Monk themes – 'Blue Monk', 'Ruby My Dear', 'Light Blue' – and graced by a fine interpretation of Trane's 'Naima', this is an appealing if slightly anonymous set. Relative to recent form, Arthur is a little low-key and leaves an unexpectedly large amount of space for Hicks and Dolphin. And yet it is the drummer who frequently captures the spotlight, a crisp and capable accompanist, with musical ideas of his own. The closing rendition of 'What A Friend We Have In Jesus' is Blythe at his best – emotive, forceful and intense.

*****(*) Focus**
Savant 2044 *Blythe; Gust William Tsilis (b mar); Bob Stewart (tba); Cecil Brooks (d).* 4/02.

This is essentially the same group Arthur has worked with for a number of years. The instrumentation is a near perfect illustration of his desire to balance early jazz with 'avant-garde' philosophies and his fellow-players seem consistently alert to the concept. Both Stewart and Tsilis contribute bass lines and harmonic accompaniment. Their readings of two relatively unknown Monk tunes, 'Children's Song' and 'Stuffy Turkey', are a mixture of simplicity and sophistication, as is a rugged romp through 'C. C. Rider'. Blythe and Tsilis reprise the excellent 'Night Song', but the best of the writing is Arthur's. 'My Son Ra' is a moving and clearly very personal theme while 'Hip Toe' suggests a range of listening that includes Ellington as well as Monk; sure enough, Duke's 'In A Sentimental Mood' is the album closer, but for the title track, which is not much more than a solo coda.

Arthur's tone is stronger and more stringent than ever. He has a preacher's intensity and an increasingly vocalized attack that gives these tracks the immediacy and the power of song. Another excellent record.

Jimmy Blythe (1901–31)

PIANO

He arrived in Chicago around 1918 and over the next dozen years worked extensively in the South Side music business, recording from 1924 until shortly before his death. He recorded prolifically as soloist, accompanist and small-group leader, in a style that bridged the blues and the more rough-and-ready jazz of the area.

***** Jimmy Blythe 1924–1931**
RST JPCD-1510-2 *Blythe; Alfred Bell, Punch Miller (c); Darnell Howard (cl); Leroy Pickett (vn); Charlie Clark (p); William Lyle (b); W. E. Burton (d, kz); Jimmy Bertrand (wbd); Viola Bartlette, Alexander Robinson, Frankie Jaxon (v).* 4/24–3/31.

***** State Street Ramblers 1927–1928**
RST JPCD-1512 *Blythe; Natty Dominique (c); Johnny Dodds, Baldy McDonald (cl); Bill Johnson (b); W. E. Burton (wbd, kz, v); Baby Dodds (wbd); Marcus H. Norman (d).* 8/27–7/28.

***** State Street Ramblers 1928–1931**
RST JPCD-1513 *As above, except add Alfred Bell (c, kz, v), Roy Palmer (tb), Darnell Howard (cl), Ed Hudson (bj, v), Cliff Jones (d); omit Dominique, Dodds, Norman.* 7/28–3/31.

***** State Street Ramblers 1928–1931**
Cygnet CYG 1003 *As above, except add Charlie Clark (p), James 'Bat' Robinson, Ed 'Fats' Hudson (v).* 7/28–3/31.

Blythe was originally from Kentucky: Michael Moore's exemplary research has filled in many of the gaps in an elusive life, detailed in the notes to the first CD, but we still know little enough about him. The pianist should be remembered as an integral part of Chicago's South Side jazz in the '20s, and his extensive work for Paramount, Gennett and Vocalion mixes a strong blues-piano approach with flakes of stride and boogie-woogie that show a determined and creative thinker. Many of the band sides collected on the State Street Ramblers CDs are relatively knockabout stuff: Blythe's driving piano parts have kept alive what are often jazz relics. Dodds appears on the earliest tracks and plays well enough, if not quite up to his best. The music shows no 'advance' by the later sessions, but the playing is more confident. For a good one-disc portrait of Blythe, though, either the first RST item or the Cygnet release will do. On the former, there are some doleful blues accompaniments and one or two items where Blythe's presence is dubious, but it includes all his piano solos, with 'Mr Freddie Blues' and 'Alley Rat' outstanding, a terrific coupling by Jimmy Bertrand's Washboard Wizards and two nimble duets with his cousin, Charlie Clark. The Cygnet release is generally in considerably better sound than the RST records and offers 15 tracks by the Ramblers, five with Fats Hudson and Bat Robinson singing, and the two Clark duets. Meningitis killed Jimmy only weeks after this final session.

Peter Bocage (1887–1967)

TRUMPET, VIOLIN

He started as a violinist but was taught cornet by Bunk Johnson. Worked with Fate Marable in New Orleans but left and recommended young Louis Armsrong as his replacement. Spent ten years with A.J. Piron's orchestra and was still playing in New Orleans at the end of a long life.

**** Peter Bocage With His Creole Serenaders And The Love–Jiles Ragtime Orchestra**
Original Jazz Classics OJC 1835-2 *Bocage; Charlie Love (t); Homer Eugene, Albert Warner (tb); Louis Cottrell, Paul 'Polo'*

Barnes (cl); Benjamin Turner (p); Sidney Pflueger (g); Emanuel Sayles (bj); McNeal Breaux, Auguste Lanoix (b); Alfred Williams, Albert Jiles (d). 6/60–1/61.

One of the weakest entries in Riverside's *New Orleans: The Living Legends* series, and it does no justice to a brassman who first recorded with A. J. Piron in the early '20s. Bocage sounds faltering and shaky on the tracks where he leads his Creole Serenaders and, though Cottrell provides some bright moments, this is pretty lame stuff. Bocage plays violin as a sideman in the Love–Jiles group, which handles five rags without a great deal of panache – Warner in particular plays some atrocious trombone. Definitely one for hardcore specialists only.

Eric Boeren (born 1959)

CORNET

Dutch brassman of the generation of improvisers that came after Mengelberg, Bennink and Breuker.

*****(*) Cross Breeding**

Bimhuis 005 *Boeren; Michael Moore (as, bcl); Jan Willem Van der Ham, Paul Termos (as); Ab Baars (cl, ts); Tobias Delius, Sean Bergin (ts); Wilbert De Joode, Ernst Glerum (b); Wim Janssen, Michael Vatcher (d).* 8/95.

***** Joy Of A Toy**

Bvhaast CD 9907 *Boeren; Michael Moore (cl, alto-cl, as); Wilbert De Joode (b); Han Bennink (d).* 6/97–3/99.

Boeren's sleeve-note to *Joy Of A Toy* confesses that he has often had his compositions described as sounding like those of Ornette Coleman (he took it as a compliment), so he has grasped the nettle by mixing his own originals with Coleman themes for both of these this tribute-cum-repertory exercises. The playing is strong and sensitively shaped, but, as with attempts to play the Hot Five or the Red Hot Peppers, the originals tend to cast an unflattering shadow on the new versions. Still, it's often very joyfully done. We prefer the earlier disc, cut over two nights at the BIM Huis. Boeren had been listening hard to each of Coleman's Atlantic sessions and had been presenting material from each album at individual concerts. 'Mapa' features Baars on tenor; the next four tracks include Moore on alto; then, most audaciously of all, Boeren revises Coleman's 'Free Jazz' as a double-quintet plus one (himself), mixing the theme of 'Free Jazz' itself and 'Happy House' alongside six of his own pieces. This is a striking adaptation of Coleman's music to Boeren's own. It's a pity that the sound is rather flat and lacking in detail.

On *Joy Of A Toy*, which was much more widely noticed on its appearance than the earlier disc, Boeren doesn't attempt to stray too far from the form of his models and, with Bennink his usual over-powerful self, too many of these pieces seem a fraction too fast; 'Joy Of A Toy' itself, for instance, has a clockwork feel to it. They do better on the gentler themes like 'Peace'. The opening track, 'A Fuzzphony', strays in from an earlier date, but the rest was recorded at a single 1999 concert, in slightly clattery sound.

Paul Bollenback (born 1959)

GUITAR

Born in Hinsdale, Illinois, Bollenback listened to rock, fusion and jazz, apparently in that order, and studied jazz at Miami University. He spent several years in the Joey DeFrancesco group.

*****(*) Original Visions**

Challenge CHR 70022 *Bollenback; Gary Thomas (ts, f); Joey DeFrancesco (org); Ed Howard (b); Terri Lyne Carrington (d).* 2/95.

***** Double Gemini**

Challenge CHR 70046 *Bollenback; Joey DeFrancesco (org); Jeff Tain Watts (d).* 3/97.

****(*) Soul Grooves**

Challenge CHR 70064 *Bollenback; Jim Rotondi (t); Steve Davis (tb); Steve Wilson (as); Eric Alexander (ts); Joey DeFrancesco (org); Jeff Tain Watts (d); Broto Roy (perc).* 12/98.

Bollenback has progressed from able sideman to leader comfortably enough, even if these records seldom stand out from the crowd. He seems divided, on *Original Visions*, between a harder, rockier route to catharsis and a more rigorous jazz achievement. He isn't helped by the bottom-heavy sound and an indifferent choice of material: his originals don't do much, and the standards are obvious. Thomas, who seldom does this kind of gig these days, does little of interest. Yet when guitar, organ and drums lock together and the groove toughens and intensifies, the music sometimes takes off.

Bollenback has worked often with DeFrancesco and they are clearly very *simpatico*. 'Breaking The Girl', which opens *Double Gemini*, is about as swinging and hard-hitting a guitar–organ blowout as one can imagine. The set this time blends four originals with six pop tunes (and we mean Hootie and the Blowfish, not Cole Porter) and Bollenback seems more at home here than he did on the earlier disc. Some of it sounds like merely engaging mood-music, even if Sting's 'Fields Of Gold' comes out pretty as a picture, but the burners are genuinely exciting. If Bollenback himself rarely impresses as a singular voice, he has some good moves.

Soul Grooves takes the route of drawing on old-fashioned soul for its source material: Stevie Wonder, Marvin Gaye and The Temptations. So Bollenback has actually regressed, after the programme of *Double Gemini*. The crack horn section are on hand mostly to play charts (Wilson gets some agreeable space on 'Papa Was A Rolling Stone'). Three originals add some variation, but the pop tunes aren't so dramatically revised as to startle: it's nice, easy-going, and forgettable. The record could use one real jolt, musicianly though it is.

***** Dreams**

Challenge 70082 *Bollenback; Joe Locke (vib); Ray Drummond (b); Jeff 'Tain' Watts (d).* 01.

The presence of the Rolling Stones' 'Wild Horses' in the set-list raised a few hackles but Bollenback pulls it off with typical aplomb, turning the Jagger wail into a soft, almost Latin swinger. It's typical of his approach on this, his most immediately approachable album. The trio format sounds very settled and communicative and the addition of Joe Locke on the opening 'Estate' is a plus but by no means a prop. Paul's appropriately romantic on 'I Fall In Love Too Easily', but he adds a barb as well. His interpretation of Michel Legrand's 'Summer of '42 (The Summer Knows)' is a stroke of genius, altering the big, swelling theme with a tight rhythmic conception in which Watts (dedicatee of 'Taining In' – one of just three originals) plays his usual emphatic part. There's a Kenny Kirkland song as well, 'Chance', which is a welcome airing for the late pianist's too rarely explored theme. A fine record all round and a delight for anyone who's disillusioned with recent Sco discs.

Claude Bolling (born 1930)

PIANO, BANDLEADER

Bolling has been at the heart of French swing for decades. He was bandleading in his teens and has led big bands on and off since the '50s, with much success in film scoring too. Not many days go by in France without a Bolling record being heard on radio or television.

***** Tribute To The Piano Greats**
Fremeaux FA 458 *Bolling; Paul Piguillem (g); Max Hedigeur (b); Marcel Sabiani (d).* 75.

(***) Inspirations
Magnum CDSB 1013 *As above.* 75.

*****(*) Rolling With Bolling**
Fremeaux FA 5029 3CD *Bolling; Maurice Thomas, Pierre Sellin, J. Claude Naude, Fernand Verstraete, Louis Vezan, Patrick Artero (t); Bill Tamper, Francois Guin, Benny Vasseur, Charles Verstraete, Michel Camicas, Emile Vilain, Jean Orieux (tb); Jacques Nourredine, Jean Aldegon, Marcel Canillar, Denis Fournier (as); André Villégér, Gérard Badini (ts); Jean-Louis Chautemps (ts); Pierre Gossez (bs); Francis Lemarguer, Pierre Cullaz, Barthy Raffo (g); Max Hediguer, Guy Pedersen, Marc Michel (b); Pierre-Alkain Dahan, Michael Silva, Marcel Sabiani, Maurice Bouchon, André Arpino (d).* 73–83.

***** Black Brown And Beige / A Drum Is A Woman**
Milan 35877-2 2CD *Bolling; Philippe Corcuff, Guy Bodet, Michel Delakian, Fernand Verstraete, Christian Martinez, Michel Bonnet (t); Benny Vasseur, Damien Verherve, Jean-Christophe Vilain, Emile Vilain, Michel Camicas, André Paquinet (tb); Jean Aldegon, Jean Eteve, Claude Tissendier, Pierre Schirrer, Philippe Portejoie, Francis Cournet, Romain Mayoral (saxes); Patrice Fontanarosa (vn); Christine Icart (hp); Jean-Paul Charlap (g); Pierre-Yves Sorin, Pierre Maingourd (b); Vincent Cordelette, (d); Pierre-Michel Balthazar (perc); Jeffery Smith, Laika, Guylenn (v).* 1/89–96.

***** Paris Swing**
Milan 80484-2 *Bolling; Christian Martinez, Guy Bodet, Michel Delakian, Philippe Slominski (t); André Paquinet, Benny Vasseur, Jean-Christophe Vilain, Emile Vilain (tb); Philippe Portejoie (ss, as); Claude Tissendier (as, cl); Pierre Schirrer (ts, f); Romain Mayoral (trs); André Villégér (bs, cl); Jean Eteve (cl); Jean-Paul Charlap (g); Pierre Maingourd (b); Vincent Cordelette (d); Maud, Marc Thomas (v).* 6/00.

Bolling is a hugely popular figure in France, but though his name is well-enough known elsewhere, few of his records have made much international impact, and even we have been neglectful of him! The ideal place to catch up is with the very enjoyable three-disc *Rolling With Bolling*, which covers a decade of big-band sessions. Although all 43 tunes are Bolling originals, many of them sound like ingenious Ellington steals, and Claude's obvious affection for the Ducal manner comes across as humorously respectful rather than the work of a hack pasticheur. There are plenty of juicy and hot solos to enjoy and he gets the band to swing at all times.

The double of *Black Brown And Beige* and *A Drum Is A Woman* is his most direct Ellington tribute, and in its way a pretty remarkable one: to replay the latter in its entirety (it's a concert recording) was impressive, even if it seems strange to hear the narration done in French! The band couldn't be mistaken as genuinely Ellingtonian and sections of *BB&B* are on the perfunctory side, but a nice document to have. *Paris Swing* celebrates his 70th in fine style, with a swing through some great Parisian hits, from 'La Mer' and 'C'est Si Bon' to 'Un Homme Et Une Femme', with a prelude of his own Basiesque 'Suivez Le Chef'. Basie does, indeed, sound to have supplanted Ellington as the Bolling band blueprint, and they do a good take on that well-oiled machine.

Tribute To The Piano Greats is a useful place to sample his own piano-playing. From a start in ragtime and stride, he progressed to a sort of Basie-Peterson synthesis which is fun to hear, even if he rarely touches any great depths. Each of the dozen compositions is a little *hommage* to a piano great, and he does his usual sly job of catching each personality about right. Beware the Magnum set listed as *Inspirations*: it's actually the same session, even though the notes misleadingly suggest that this is a live big-band date from 1979!

Flavio Boltro

TRUMPET, BUGLE

Italian trumpeter working with a Franco-Italian alliance.

***** Road Runner**
Blue Note 233422-2 *Boltro; Stefano Di Battista (ss); Daniele Scannapieco (ts); Eric Legnini (ky); Marcello Giuliani (g, b); Louis Winsberg (g); Pippo Matino (b); Stéphane Huchard, Paco Sery (d); Nantha Kumar (perc).* 99.

Boltro has been spotted in several sideman situations, but this Blue Note debut – a daring move for the label to go with such a musician, even if distribution is limited – is a confident and surprisingly effective nugget of modern fusion – even if much of it harks back to various phases of Miles Davis's electric music. Most of the mainly brief tracks pivot on an old-school groove of some sort, but the clarity of the sound, the individuality of each musician's contribution and the carefully judged shape of each piece is something rather more contemporary and skilful. Boltro gets good support from di Batista and Legnini in particular. We've heard it all before, but perhaps not quite in this way and this order.

Sharkey Bonano (1904–72)

TRUMPET, CORNET, VOCAL

Joseph Bonano was born in New Orleans and is associated mainly with NO revivalism. In the '20s, though, he drifted around several musical jobs across America, and he was a hit with his own band in New York in the later '30s. He had a second career with the revivalists of the '40s and '50s and continued to work and play, although poor health wound down his career from the '60s onwards.

*** Sharkey Bonano 1928–1937

Timeless CBC 1-001 *Bonano; Shorty Sherock (t); Santo Pecora, Moe Zudecoff, Julian Lane, George Brunies (tb); Meyer Weinberg (cl, as); Sidney Arodin (cl, tin whistle); Joe Marsala, Irving Fazola (cl); Hal Jordy (as, bs); Dave Winstein (ts); Johnnie Miller, Clyde Hart, Joe Bushkin, Stan Wrightman, Freddy Newman, Armand Hug (p); Joe Cupero, Frank Federico, Eddie Condon (g); Bill Bourjois (bj, g); Steve Brou (bj); Luther Lamar (tba, b); Chink Martin, Ray Bonitas, Thurman Teague, Artie Shapiro, Hank Wayland (b); Monk Hazel (d, mel, v); Leo Adde, Augie Schellange, Ben Pollack, George Wettling, Al Sidell, Riley Scott (d).* 4/28–4/37.

Bonano is conventionally placed as a New Orleans man, but though he was a native of the town his early career points elsewhere – he tried out as replacement for Beiderbecke with both The Wolverines and Jean Goldkette, for instance. The first two (little-known) sessions here, though, are among the very few home-grown New Orleans sessions of the '20s – both showing an ironic New York influence, but with fine clarinet by Sidney Arodin and Bonano proving that he had a light but curiously engaging lead as a cornetist. A jump forward to 1936 brings a more Dixieland-orientated sound, and three further sessions from 1936–7 find him in New York with a band largely made up of Condonites. Four tracks by a Santo Pecora group with Shorty Sherock on trumpet round off the disc. Bonano's vaudevillian vocals dominate several tracks, but when his trumpet emerges he sounds in good fettle, and there are useful glimpses of the New Orleans clarinet of Fazola. A mixed but entertaining bag, and the remastering is fine.

*** Sharkey Bonano At Lenfant's Lounge

Storyville STCD 6015 *Bonano; Jack Delaney (tb); Bujie Centobie (cl); Stanley Mendelson (p); Arnold 'Deacon' Loyacano (b); Abbie Brunies, Monk Hazel (d); Lizzie Miles (v).* 8–9/52.

*** Sharkey Bonano And His Band

Storyville STCD 6011 *As above, except omit Hazel and Miles.* 12/52.

Bonano almost inevitably returned to New Orleans and spent most of the rest of his life there, working and recording frequently in the aftermath of the New Orleans revival of the '40s and '50s. Location recordings catch his able band in lively form. The leader's own playing suggests that he was more convincing as a front man than as a soloist: if he tries to push too hard, his tone thins out and his phrases buckle. But Delaney and Centobie are both perfectly assured soloists, and Bonano sensibly gives them the lion's share of the attention. Lizzie Miles sings a couple of vocals on the first record and shouts encouragement too. The recordings are clear enough, though they don't have much sparkle, but the swing of the band stands up well: another valuable document of a genuine New Orleans outfit, playing to orders – the material is very familiar – but making the most of it.

Joe Bonner (born 1948)

PIANO

Easy at first hearing to dismiss Bonner as a watery disciple of McCoy Tyner. The truth is more individual and more challenging. Born in Thelonious Monk's home town of Rocky Mount, North Carolina, Bonner's piano style embraces some elements of Monk's quirky individuality, but also some of the milder elements of Cecil Taylor's unique atonality.

***(*) Parade

Steeplechase SCCD 31116 *Bonner; Johnny Mbizo Dyani (b); Billy Higgins (d).* 2/79.

*** Devotion

Steeplechase SCCD 31182 *Bonner (p solo).* 2/83.

*** Suburban Fantasies

Steeplechase SCCD 31176 *Bonner; Johnny Mbizo Dyani (b).* 2/83.

*** Two & One

Steeplechase SCCD 37033/34 2CD *As above.*

Bonner is an impressive modernist whose occasional resemblance to Thelonious Monk probably stems from the fact that he has listened and paid attention to the same swing-era players that Monk did. He has a surprisingly light touch (too light on some of the Steeplechases, where the miking sounds a bit remote) and he can seem a little diffident. He is, though, a fine solo performer, with a rolling, gospelly delivery, and an adventurous group leader. Much of his most distinctive work has been with the late Johnny Dyani, who has the same combination of dark strength and lyrical delicacy; over several albums they developed a rapport that seems to cement ever more strongly as they moved outwards from settled bop progressions and into freer territory.

Suburban Fantasies is a lovely record, but oddly substanceless, as if worked up from scratch and on the spur of the moment. *Two & One* is a valuable mid-price compilation of Bonner's relationship with Dyani. It has the same rather slack-paced fascination of the single album but, over time, the sheer conversational magic of the relationship begins to work its spell.

***(*) Suite For Chocolate

Steeplechase SCCD 31215 *Bonner; Khan Jamal (vib); Jesper Lundgaard (b); Leroy Lowe (d).* 11/85.

*** New Life

Steeplechase SCCD 31239 *Bonner; Hugo Rasmussen (b); Aage Tanggaard (d).* 8/86.

*** The Lost Melody

Steeplechase SCCD 31227 *Bonner; Bob Rockwell (ts); Jesper Lundgaard (b); Jukkis Uotila (d).* 3/87.

*** Impressions Of Copenhagen

Evidence ECD 22024 *Bonner; Eddie Shu (t); Gary Olson (tb); Holly Hoffman (f); Paul Warburton (b); J. Thomas Tilton (d); Carol Michalowski (vn); Carol Garrett (vla); Beverley Woolery (clo).*

The African elements also emerge in the lovely *Suite For Chocolate*. Working with the under-recorded Khan Jamal, who has had his own records issued on Steeplechase, gives Bonner a detailed stipple of sound over which to lay his discontinuous melody lines. A surprising record in many ways, it veers between experiment and conservatism, eventually coming down on the side of easy, unstressed swing.

The Lost Melody is a good group-session, marked by strong charts and just the right element of freedom for Rockwell, a fine soloist within his own square of turf, but apt to flounder beyond it. *Impressions Of Copenhagen* (formerly on Theresa) has been available for some time now on Evidence, with a bonus version of 'Lush Life'. There are some effectively impressionistic moments, and the use of strings is quite original and uncluttered, but it's a bit of a by-blow and not really consistent in either tone or quality with Bonner's impressive jazz output. To the best of our knowledge, another Theresa LP, *New Beginnings*, with singer Laurie Antonioli, has not yet emerged on CD, leaving that aspect of the pianist's career, his gifts as an accompanist, still obscure.

***** Monkisms**

Capri 74030 *Bonner (p solo).* 7/91.

We didn't much like the sound of Monk*ism*, let alone its plural form. Such ventures almost invariably turn into mannerisms all too quickly. Bonner avoids that by a whisker, though it does seem a touch perverse to take some of Monk's most idiosyncratic compositions – and all the usual suspects are included here – only to render them down into rather conventional jazz tunes, with little of the spikiness and intensity of attack associated with the begetter. Most of the tunes are very short indeed, with no extended development. 'Monk's Dream', already an ambiguous structure, is pushed out to over six minutes, but it is the longest track by some way; 'Straight, No Chaser' has become such a hackneyed blowing theme that it is quite attractive hearing it played so directly, though again it lacks a degree of abrasion and impatience. An accomplished and, in some small regards, challenging record from a still marginal figure.

Thomas Borgmann (born 1955)

SOPRANINO, SOPRANO AND TENOR SAXOPHONES, WHISTLES

Born in Münster, Borgmann is a free improviser in the grand tradition of European free playing, although so far his exposure on record has been comparatively limited.

*****(*) Orkestra Kith 'N Kin**

Cadence CJR 1081 *Borgmann; Martin Mayes (frhn); Lol Coxhill (ss); Erik Balke (as, sno); Dietmar Diesner (as, ss); Jonas Akerblom (bsx); Pat Thomas (p, elec); Hans Reichel (g, daxophon); Christoph Winckel (b); Mark Sanders (d).* 5/95.

*****(*) Boom Swing**

Konnex KCD 5082 *Borgmann; Wilber Morris (b); Dennis Charles (d).* 97.

***** Stalker Songs**

CIMP 160 *As above, except add Peter Brötzmann (ts, cl, tarogato).* 9/97.

***** BMN Trio ... You See What We're Sayin'?**

CIMP 188 *As above, except add Reggie Nicholson (d); omit Brötzmann and Charles.* 10/98.

Borgmann is no spring chicken as a free player, although he's made only a few records as a leader. The 1995 ensemble recording has a spirited hour-long piece (and a foolish ten-minute encore, which could profitably have been omitted). There are few 'solos' as such, more disparate lines drawn by different groupings, with the rousingly arranged finale raising the spirits. But the amateurish recording spoils much of the interest in what's going on.

Borgmann's trio with Morris and Charles was a regular working outfit in Europe and America. The Konnex album seems to be live (the documentation is a bit mysterious) and, though intense enough, it also suffers from a cloudy mix which obscures too much detail. *Stalker Songs* is much better. Brötzmann seems to be scaling himself down a bit for the occasion, and CIMP's 'truthful' sound isn't entirely adequate, but these two half-hour improvisations are good and gripping. Charles died a few months later, and a new trio convened to make the later *You See What We're Sayin'?*, which starts with a sombre dedication to the departed drummer before thundering forward through three more intense blows. Borgmann doesn't really impress as an individual voice: he synthesizes a lot of the familiar uproar of his forebears to ends which are intermittently dramatic. He puts his trust in an old-fashioned energy music. Not misplaced, though: such raw playing is always a welcome counter to the conventional language.

***** The Cooler Suite**

Grob 539 *Borgmann; Peter Brötzmann (as, ts, cl); William Parker (b); Rashied Bakr (d)* 1/97.

Although recorded almost by chance (on a spare tape Borgmann had in his pocket), this gig from the now-defunct Cooler club in New York has plenty of presence. Parker is often relegated to the background on many of his sessions but he comes through here with surprising clarity. That said, at moments of extreme stress (of which there are plenty), the recording is clearly inadequate, especially for Bakr. What survives is the unmitigated punch of the playing. Borgmann is once again in grand company here and he holds his own, but perhaps this is, for all its extremism, still just a gig souvenir at bottom.

Michiel Borstlap

PIANO, KEYBOARDS

A keyboardist looking for new combinations of post-bop playing and electric situations.

****** The Sextet Live!**

Challenge CHR 70030 2CD *Borstlap; Eric Vloeimans (t); Benjamin Herman (as, Cmel); Yuri Honing (ss, ts); Anton Drukker (b); Joost Lijbaart (d).* 4/95.

***** Body Acoustic**

Emarcy 538976-2 *Borstlap; Eric Vloeimans (t); Tom Beek (ts, bcl); Jesse Van Ruller (g); Anton Drukker, Ernst Glerum (b); Hans Eijkenaar, Han Bennink (d); Jeroen de Rijk (perc).* 2/99.

****(*) Liveline**

Emarcy 159111-2 *Borstlap; Eric Vloeimans (t); Jimmy Haslip (b); Hans Eijkenaar (d); Jeroen de Rijk (perc).* 2/00.

***** Gramercy Park**

Emarcy 014326-2 3CD *Borstlap; Jeroen Rietbergen (ky); Essiet Okun Essiet, Stefan Lievenstro, Boudewijn Lucas, Michel Van Schie (b); Jeff Tain Watts, Roy Dackus, Sebastiaan Kaptein (d); Ronald Molendijk (turntables); Hans Teeuwen (v).* n.d.

The Challenge record documents a remarkable concert at Amsterdam's BIM Huis. For once a record feels too short – the two sets only muster 85 minutes across the two CDs, and the level of invention is so high that you're left wanting more. Borstlap's originals use all the resources of the sextet. The horns are asked to employ all kinds of dynamic variation in charts which are full of sweet-sour tonalities and surprising uses of space – often everything stops for a long, *a capella* horn passage. It helps that Borstlap has a terrific band: Vloiemans is brilliant on 'Curve' and 'Just In Town', and Honing and Herman are only a beat behind. 'Day Off' is a rush hour of chords overlaid with quicksilver improvising. It ends with 'Basin Street Blues', gorgeously delivered as a pristine lament. Using a typical Jazz Messengers line-up, Borstlap came up with something disarmingly fresh.

His Emarcy records have been, in comparison, curiously disappointing. *Body Acoustic* was an audacious start, arranging Weather Report material for an acoustic band (van Ruller excepted). There are some interesting transformations and one splendid bit of virtuosity – Borstlap's duet with guest Bennink on 'Three Views Of A Secret'. But the chosen pieces are an odd lot, and deprived of Zawinul's signature electronics some of the material is exposed as charmless and not very nourishing for improvisers.

Still, Borstlap clearly wants to make his own kind of fusion, and *Liveline* introduces synthesizer and Fender Rhodes. In a band which is co-led with Haslip, grooves have replaced jazz rhythms for much of the way, and instead of space there's density. Borstlap still plays lots of Yamaha grand, and his regular front-liner Vloiemans is again excellent, but it's another live recording, and there are too many boring bass and percussion interludes.

Gramercy Park is too much of a good thing, Borstlap showing us what he can do across three CDs (admittedly, the third is only 20 minutes of music). One disc of solos sets out to impress, with long versions of 'Dolphin Dance' and 'Body And Soul', as well as Chopin's Opus 20 Scherzo; a second disc of trios, American and Dutch, runs through a bag of standards, but one misses the spacious elegance of the sextet music. Phans of Phuture Jazz may respond most readily to the two tracks on disc three, where Borstlap collaborates with the electric group Soulvation. It sounds more interesting than anything the re-incarnated Headhunters did.

Ralph Bowen

TENOR SAXOPHONE

Experienced post-bopper made a considered leadership debut for Criss Cross and now offered a belated follow-up.

***(*) Movin' On

Criss Cross Criss 1066 *Bowen; Jim Beard (p); Jon Herington (g); Anthony Jackson (b); Ben Perowsky (d).* 12/92.

An able and in-demand sideman, Bowen took his time before recording a debut solo album. It was worth the wait. Bowen has been writing and putting by original themes since he was in his teens, and it's a symptom of his remarkable self-possession that he should have picked seven of them for *Movin' On* rather than opting for more familiar repertoire material. The title-piece is entirely characteristic, a lean but lyrical tune that propels him into the first of what is to be a batch of fine solos. Apprenticeship with Horace Silver has left an unmistakable mark on Bowen's writing, but it is Silver the melodist who predominates. Bowen rarely forces the pace, allowing each theme to dictate its own momentum. 'A Little Silver In My Pocket' is the most direct homage, and Jim Beard turns in a completely idiomatic solo with a brisk, bouncy left-hand part. Only on the longish 'Just Reconnoitering' does Bowen start to repeat himself. To some extent the piece draws on Coltrane's 'sheets of sound' approach, but this isn't a comfortable route, and the piece resolves itself much more conventionally. Mixed well up, the two guitars bring a soulful groove to 'Thru Traffic'; Herington draws heavily on Pat LaBarbera licks, but it's Jackson who impresses with a fluid legato.

***(*) Soul Proprietor

Criss Cross 1216 *Bowen; John Swana (t); Sam Yahel (org); Peter Bernstein (g); Brian Blade (d).* 5/01.

Bowen's belated follow-up is a burnished beauty. Outwardly, it's organ, guitar, rhythm and two horns, a formula as prone to routine as any in post-bop jazz. And the material's mostly familiar, the structures never untoward. What sets it up is the absolute confidence and sophistication of the playing. Bowen's big tone is all over 'My Ideal', as indolent with the beat as Dexter Gordon, yet on the pushier pieces he thinks nothing of over-blowing a note, or stepping on some toes. Swana – a fellow regular on Philadelphia bandstands – is a good second banana on this occasion, while Bernstein and Yahel know their vocabularies for the situation and aren't afraid to introduce subtleties and discretions which the organ combo text rarely permits. Finally, there's Blade, one of the best American drummers of today. Perhaps it's *too* admirable a record – a little 'insiderish' – to really demand classic status, but anyone who thinks this kind of jazz setting is played out should lend a receptive ear. Bowen can also be heard in excellent fettle on records by the Criss Cross pianist Orrin Evans.

*** Keep The Change

Criss Cross 1243 *Bowen; Ryan Kisor (t); Orrin Evans (p); Reuben Rogers (b); Gregory Hutchinson (d).* 10/03.

A decent continuation, but frankly a little disappointing after the last two. For once Bowen doesn't seem able to really do a transformation act on the material, and the hit-and-miss Kisor, who can often fall back on failsafe licks when the spirit deserts him, wasn't the ideal pick as front-line partner. Still some powerful moments, and there's always that rhythm section to listen to even when things aren't happening out front.

Lester Bowie (1940–99)

TRUMPET, FLUGELHORN

Born in Maryland, Bowie grew up in St Louis and based himself in Chicago from the mid-'60s, becoming a major force in both the AACM and the Art Ensemble Of Chicago, with which he performed until the end of his life. He lived and worked in Jamaica and Africa for some spells, and finally found his most popular niche with his nearly-all-brass band, Brass Fantasy. His 60-strong Sho' Nuff Orchestra was unfortunately never recorded. A pioneer of expressionist playing in a modern vernacular, Bowie was a great renegade spirit in the music and fiercely critical of what he saw as the jazz conservatism of the '80s and '90s. He died from liver cancer in 1999.

***** The Fifth Power**

Black Saint 120020-2 *Bowie; Arthur Blythe (as); Amina Claudine Myers (p, v); Malachi Favors (b); Phillip Wilson (d).* 4/78.

Bowie's '70s band provides a more straightforward kind of post-Chicago jazz, but this quintet is loaded with expressive talent. Blythe and Myers are the outsiders here, yet their different kinds of playing – Blythe is swaggeringly verbose, Myers a gospelish spirit – add new flavours to Bowie's sardonic music. The 18 minutes of 'God Has Smiled On Me' are several too many, although the ferocious free-for-all in the middle is excitingly done, while '3 In 1' finds a beautiful balance between freedom and form.

***** The Great Pretender**

ECM 829369-2 *Bowie; Hamiet Bluiett (bs); Donald Smith (ky); Fred Wilson (b); Phillip Wilson (d); Fontella Bass, David Peaston (v).* 6/81.

****(*) All The Magic!**

ECM 810625-2 2CD *As above, except Ari Brown (ss, ts), Art Matthews (p) replace Bluiett and Smith.* 6/82.

This was a disappointing band, at least on record. In concert David Peaston's rendition of 'Everything Must Change' was astonishingly uplifting, but the version on *All The Magic!* is disarmingly tame. *The Great Pretender* began Bowie's exploration of pop standards as vehicles for extended free-jazz satire, but it tends to go on for too long. Perhaps the typically resplendent ECM recording didn't suit the group, although 'Rios Negroes' is a fine feature for the leader. The second half of *All The Magic!*, though, multitracks Bowie's trumpet into a gallery of grotesques; his style has matured into a lexicon of smears, growls, chirrups and other effects, and here he uses it as an expressionist cartoon.

****(*) I Only Have Eyes For You**

ECM 825902-2 *Bowie; Stanton Davis, Malachi Thompson, Bruce Purse (t); Steve Turre, Craig Harris (tb); Vincent Chancey (frhn); Bob Stewart (tba); Phillip Wilson (d).* 2/85.

****(*) Avant Pop**

ECM 829563-2 *As above, except Rasul Siddik (t), Frank Lacy (tb) replace Purse and Harris.* 3/86.

***** Serious Fun**

DIW 834/8035 *Bowie; Stanton Davis, Eddie E. J. Allen, Gerald Brezel (t); Steve Turre, Frank Lacy (tb); Vincent Chancey (frhn); Bob Stewart (tba); Vinnie Johnson, Ken Crutchfield (d); Famoudou Don Moye (perc).* 4/89.

These records are by Bowie's group, Brass Fantasy, a band with an unprecedented instrumentation, at least in modern jazz. But the brass-heavy line-up has obvious echoes of marching bands and the oldest kinds of jazz, and one expects a provocative kind of neo-traditionalism with Bowie at the helm. But Brass Fantasy seldom delivers much more than a lightweight irreverence on record. The first two albums have some surprising choices of covers, including Whitney Houston's 'Saving All My Love For You' and Lloyd Price's 'Personality', but the studio seems to stifle some of the freewheeling bravado of the ensemble, and Bowie himself resorts to a disappointing self-parody. Just as one thinks it can go no further the DIW disc displayed a fresh maturity; the brass voicing acquires a broader resonance, the section-work sounds funkier, and although the improvising is still too predictable, it suggests altogether that the group still has plenty left to play.

***** Works**

ECM 837274-2 *Bowie; various groups.* 81–86.

A respectable compilation from Bowie's four ECM records, plus one track ('Charlie M') from the AEOC's *Full Force.*

*****(*) My Way**

DIW 835 *Bowie; Stanton Davis, Eddie E. J. Allen, Gerald Brazel, Earl Garner (t); Steve Turre (tb, conch); Frank Lacy (tb, v); Gregory Williams (frhn); Bob Stewart (tba); Vinnie Johnson, Ken Crutchfield (d); Famoudou Don Moye (perc).* 1/90.

In the past this project seemed like an amusing, if not especially productive, vehicle for Bowie to mess around with. This album brought a new focus to bear. The three originals which lead off *My Way* explore the sonorities of the band as never before; the playing glitters with a new finesse, and the improvising has real gravitas. 'My Way' itself should have been too cornball and obvious, but the superb central solo by Turre denies all that. 'I Got You' really is too obvious, but the closing 'Honky Tonk' is a good one.

*****(*) The Odyssey Of Funk And Popular Music Vol. 1**

BirdologyFDM 37004-2 *Bowie; Joseph 'Mac' Gollehon, Ravi Best, Gerald Brazel (t); Joseph Bowie (tb, v); Luis Bonilla, Josh Roseman, Gary Valente (tb); Vincent Chancey (frhn); Bob Stewart (tba); Victor See Yuen (d); Dean Bowman (v).* 9–10/97.

****(*) When The Spirit Returns**

Birdology 83471-2 *As above, except omit Joseph Bowie.* 9–11/99.

Bowie kept working until his illness overtook him. By this time, the Brass Fantasy had become a regular showbiz gig, and there is no longer any shock value in hearing them tackle 'Don't Cry For Me Argentina' or 'Nessun Dorma', let alone Marilyn Manson's 'Beautiful People' or the Spice Girls' 'Two Become One'. But it still sounds very good. The later record, finished shortly before the leader's death, is much less appealing: Lester's work was pretty much done.

JoAnne Brackeen (born 1938)

PIANO

JoAnne Grogan grew up in California and moved to New York after divorcing the saxophonist Charles Brackeen. She worked with Art Blakey, Joe Henderson and Stan Getz, developing a muscular but harmonically limpid solo style.

*****(*) Turnaround**

Evidence 22123 *Brackeen; Donald Harrison (as); Cecil McBee (b); Marvin 'Smitty' Smith (d).* 2/92.

Always useful as a jazz trivia stumper: which white woman played piano for the Jazz Messengers? JoAnne Brackeen hung on to the piano chair with Blakey between 1969 and 1971. It was a poorly recorded spell, and with earlier albums for Choice, Freedom, Timeless, MPS, Columbia, Antilles, Palo Alto and Concord all now languishing as either rare vinyl or deleted

CDs, it's difficult to follow what was a very interesting progress through the '70s and '80s. On *Turnaround*, taped at Sweet Basil in New York, Brackeen's group kicks into top gear straight away with a finely judged version of 'There Is No Greater Love'. The set is dominated, though, by the original 'Picasso' (no discernible relation to the famous Coleman Hawkins solo) and by Ornette Coleman's title-tune, which is played very straight and confounds any notion that Brackeen avoids playing in orthodox blues formats. Harrison is hesitant here and there, forming his solos with unusual care, perhaps thrown off slightly by the pianist's use of unconventional supplementary harmonies. Smith and McBee are a dream combination, and the whole set is very well recorded, if a little toppy in places.

★★★(★) Power Talk

Turnipseed Music TMCD 08 *Brackeen; Ira Coleman (b); Tony Reedus (d). 4/94.*

The concert documented on *Power Talk* takes the wheel on an extra turn. Opening with a magnificent stop-action reading of 'There Is No Greater Love', Brackeen powers through a mostly standards trio, repeating 'Picasso' and 'Cosmic Ties And Mud Pies' from *Where Legends Dwell* and giving both the big treatment. Her young colleagues don't show her undue deference, forging ahead a couple of times as she pauses to elaborate points and then defiantly accelerating again as she changes pace to catch up. It must have been an exhilarating night. Incidentally, Turnipseed Music operates out of Metairie, Louisiana.

★★★★ Pink Elephant Magic

Arkadia 70371 *Brackeen; Nicholas Payton (t); David Liebman (ss); Chris Potter (ss, ts); John Patitucci (b); Horacio El Negro Hernanadez (d); Jamey Haddad (perc); Kurt Elling (v). 3/99.*

This sounds like a template for about five different albums and a proving ground for as many unpredictable and creative bands. As a soloist Brackeen is not as prominent as on her trio recordings, but she is emphatically in charge of the music, and the set showcases half a dozen wildly original new numbers. 'Beethoven Meets The Millennium In Spain' is a clever meeting of musical languages, the title-piece is sheer playfulness and wit, and 'What's Your Choice, Rolls Royce?' (which seems to contain references to Mary Lou Williams) provides Kurt Elling with a wacky feature. His is not the only guest voice on the album. The ever-inventive Liebman is supreme on two numbers. Perhaps the centrepiece of the album is an unaccompanied variation on Dave Brubeck's 'Strange Meadowlark', a meditative but by no means sombre excursion that transforms the old ballad into something quite mysterious and fugitive.

★★★(★) Popsicle Illusion

Arkadia 70372 *Brackeen (p solo). 7/99.*

Her second solo record has the feel of a fire hydrant being turned on, at least in the number of bases it touches. Though we rate it highly, it's more for its individual, track-by-track achievements. As a record, it can be either tiring or even bewildering to listen to all the way through, given the sweeping changes which Brackeen brings. Boogie and blues variations jostle with what sound like homages to modern composers and a version of 'From This Moment On' that feels like the tune's being turned inside out. Strong and accomplished work from a very individual figure, but sample a track or two at a time.

Don Braden (born 1964)

TENOR SAXOPHONE

Braden is a swinging mainstream player with a sophisticated harmonic sense and a good deal of taste. He proved his worth as an accompanist on Betty Carter's Grammy winner Look What I Got and won another with Jeanie Bryson. He often plays with a light, slightly feminine tone, contrasting with powerful pedal notes in a much lower register.

★★★ The Time Is Now

Criss Cross Criss 1051 *Braden; Tom Harrell (t, flhn); Benny Green (p); Christian McBride (b); Carl Allen (d). 1/91.*

★★★(★) Wish List

Criss Cross 1069 *As above, except add Steve Turre (tb). 12/91.*

Braden's debut album, *The Time Is Now*, was widely praised, but it wasn't a patch on *Wish List*, an elegant set of standards and refreshingly straightforward originals. Instead of overloading themes with harmonic changes, Braden builds in bridge sections which shift the tempo from fours to threes. He's an intelligent arranger, too. Turre and Harrell wouldn't on the face of it be everyone's notion of a *simpatico* brass-line, but Braden has them working in easy tandem without diluting what each does best. Harrell is unwontedly fiery on 'Just The Facts', a schematic minor blues with a gentle twist in its tail. It's the title-track, appropriately closing the record, that confirms Braden's enormous potential, a dreamy, almost wistful song that steadily uncovers its hidden riches. Braden has already played with the best – Carter, Tony Williams, Wynton Marsalis – so this record isn't a wish-list date in that sense. Braden palpably doesn't need the support of star names, just the company of like-minded and equally dedicated players.

★★★★ After Dark

Criss Cross 1081 *Braden; Scott Wendholt (t, flhn); Noah Bless (tb); Steve Wilson (as); Darrell Grant (p); Christian McBride (b); Carl Allen (d). 5/93.*

Braden's third Criss Cross record marks a sudden and dramatic maturing of his style. Not only is he playing as well as before; suddenly his writing and arranging skills seem to have made a quantum step forward. There is a nocturnal programme to the record which gives it a darker and more sombre emphasis. Originals like the uneasy 'R.E.M.' and the gently upbeat 'Dawn' are interspersed with 'You And The Night And The Music', 'Monk's Dream' and Stevie Wonder's 'Creepin''. The group plays well, and trombonist Bless must have staked a claim with producer Gerry Teekens for a solo outing of his own.

★★★(★) The Open Road

Double Time DTRCD 114 *Braden; Tim Hagans (t); Kenny Werner (p); Larry Grenadier (b); Billy Hart (d). 7/96.*

It is remarkable how quickly Braden has developed an identifiable creative personality. From the opening moments of the title-track, which begins the album, there can be no doubt who is playing. Yes, there are influences on view – and there is no point rehearsing them here – but the voice is assured, individual and one of a kind. Even when he tackles well-signposted themes like 'Maiden Voyage' or 'Someday My Prince Will Come', which has Miles's pawprint all over it, he manages to find things of his own to say. The group contributes more than its share to the success of the session. Werner is still an unsung hero of the current scene, an adaptable player who never submerges his own ideas in the ensemble but keeps the interests of the two afloat and side by side. Grenadier and Hart work in easy combination. The closing 'Lush Life' is the most mature work we've heard from Braden yet, and if the album as a whole lacks a touch of focus, it's still moving in interesting directions.

***** Contemporary Standards Ensemble**

Double Time 177 *Braden; Terell Stafford (t); Vincent Herring (as); George Colligan (p); Richie Goods (b); Ralph Peterson (d).* 00.

Miles Davis, and later Herbie Hancock, led the way in showing young players that the concept of standards should be stretched to meet more recent pop material. Here, Braden covers material by Donny Hathaway ('The Closer I Get To You'), Roberta Flack ('Feel Like Making Love'), Stevie Wonder ('Overjoyed') and Walter Becker and Donald Fagen of Steely Dan ('Kid Charlemagne'), as well as original compositions. 'Dance Of The One' is outstanding, raunchy and thoughtful by turns, and 'The Vail Jumpers' is terse and pungent.

Colligan emerges as an able accompanist and an excellent solo performer, happy to lie back but equally willing to take the spotlight when occasion demands. Herring's Cannonball influence is much in evidence but by no means obtrusive. Impressive stuff from a leader whose career progresses quietly.

****** Brighter Days**

High Note 7076 *Braden; Xavier Davis (p); Dwayne Burno (b); Cecil Brooks III (d).* 01.

This is as straightforward and swinging as it gets, a top-notch hard-bop set with no pretensions and more swing than the biggest kids' playground you ever saw. Don pays tribute to Stanley Turrentine on 'Sweet T', nods to Coltrane on 'My Favorite Things', while still making the song his own, and even manages to banish memories of Duke's great soloists on his interpretation of 'Prelude To A Kiss'. Don's never made a more coherent or a more relaxed album, and one wonders whether he hasn't previously been hampered by concepts, label demands or a simple lack of confidence that he has the chops to deliver a set as good as this. His reading of 'I Hear A Rhapsody' is packed with ideas that allude to, rather than quote, previous performances, and the album saves a big pay-off till last in the superb title-track. Full marks to the band but … The Don – he's really got there this time.

*****(*) The New Hang**

High Note HCD 7117 *Braden; Conrad Herwig (tb); Kyle Koehler (org); Cecil Brooks III (d).* 11/03.

The 'new hang' is what the guys christened drummer and producer Cecil Brooks's New Jersey night club. Cecil and Don have been friends and associates since the early '90s. The other two players were less obvious as first calls. Herwig is a drier and more inward player than Steve Turre, but one can immediately hear on the tight-head ensemble of 'Through The Fire' why Braden wanted him for the gig. Tonally and timbrally, they're amazingly close and when they reprise 'Wish List' itself, the harmonics blossom. The young Philadelphian Koehler isn't from the wheeze and grind school of Hammond playing. He has a softer and more shimmering approach, less exuberantly Leslied, and his solo lines are spacious and expansive. He comes into his own on a delightful duo version of 'When I Fall In Love', dedicated to the saxophonist's wife. 'Mother's Wish' is an equally heartfelt tribute to the first Mrs Braden, one of three tracks without trombone.

Braden's writing has never sounded crisper or more assured, and the confirmation of that is how confidently he reinvents 'Wish List' for this group. However fine Herwig is as second horn and however thoughtful and expressive the organist, it's Brooks who really makes the record. As producer, he's entitled to ease himself forward in the mix, but what's impressive is how cleanly he separates his cymbals from the Hammond sound, with no tizz or hash, and how cleanly his toms articulate the metre behind the horns. This is Braden's most polished disc to date, not necessarily his best, but certainly the most accomplished.

Bobby Bradford (born 1934)

TRUMPET, CORNET

Played with Ornette Coleman in Los Angeles in the '50s, and eventually replaced Don Cherry in the quartet in 1961; then closely associated with John Carter, as both a duo and in group contexts. Now mostly teaches in LA.

**** Lost In LA**

Soul Note 121068 *Bradford; James Kousakis (as); Roberto Miguel Miranda, Mark Dresser (b); Sherman Ferguson (d).* 6/83.

**** One Night Stand**

Soul Note 121168 *Bradford; Frank Sullivan (p); Scott Walton (b); Billy Bowker (d).* 11/86.

Bradford's best work with Ornette is supposed to have gone the way of desert flowers, and the recordings made under his own name are curiously unsatisfactory, full of good things (like his superbly constructed solos) but ultimately underachieved. There isn't much in the catalogue at present, anyway. *Lost In LA* has precious few striking moments and the single-horn format of *One Night Stand* prompts some more of his bravura and his most thoughtful solos; but these are largely indifferent works. An important and adventurous player, Bradford has yet to recapture the brilliance of the 1973 *Secrets* with Carter; even the live sets seem to lose something of their burnish at the mixing desk. Bradford's been badly neglected in the CD era and some important appearances are overdue for reissue.

***** Purple Gums**

Asian Improv AIR 0064 *Bradford; Francis Wong (ts, f); William Roper (tba, perc).* 10/02.

Nice to welcome a new Bradford record to the listings, even if this feels somewhat atypical. The nine pieces are all co-credited – 'No notes, no discussions, just horn to the lips, blow some air'. Which makes the rounded, harmonious results some tribute to a very simpatico threesome. Cornet, tenor and tuba would once have been a very scarce instrumentation and Bradford's place in the development of chamber-jazz is likeably honoured by such a set. Everyone does, though, play carefully and deferentially and across 71 minutes one might wish for the occasional eruption. Roper contributes a shaggy dog story or two as a spoken-word component and they fit in rather well. Bradford's elegance and choice of notes are unimpaired, though he wobbles a little here and there.

Ruby Braff (1927–2003)

CORNET, TRUMPET

Reuben – hence Ruby – Braff left his native Boston at the start of the '50s and began to record in New York with the likes of Vic Dickenson and Urbie Green. His powerful, melodic cornet is one of the most distinctive sounds in mainstream jazz, backed by a seemingly limitless flow of ideas. After a brief eclipse in his career – which some would put down to a volatile temperament – Braff continued to make fine records into his seventh and eighth decade, before his death in 2003.

*** Linger Awhile

Vanguard 79608 *Braff; Buck Clayton (t); Vic Dickenson, Benny Morton (tb); Samuel Margolis (ts, cl); Buddy Tate (ts); Edmond Hall (cl); Jimmy Jones, Nat Pierce, Sir Charles Thompson (p); Steve Jordan (g); Aaron Bell, Walter Page (b); Jo Jones (d).* 52, 53, 54.

Early material that has only recently come back into circulation. Some of the tracks are under Dickenson's leadership, but it's Ruby who's the main solo voice throughout, in a variety of partnerships. A long 'Sweet Sue, It's You' finds him in company with saxophonist Samuel Margolis, over whom posterity has drawn a veil. It bookends the disc with a wonderful 'I Can't Get Started', where Ruby is partnered by the effervescent Clayton, an interesting exercise in contrasting trumpet styles. Lots of good things in between, including 'Ghost Of A Chance' and 'I Cover The Waterfront', all played at length. Nice moments, too, from Morton, Hall, Tate and Thompson; all-star cast and a great find for Braff fans.

**** 2 × 2: Ruby Braff And Ellis Larkins Play Rodgers And Hart

Vanguard 8507 *Braff; Ellis Larkins (p).* 10/55.

A dream ticket. Larkins is the consummate accompanist and he knew more about these songs than almost anyone currently working. Ruby is in full voice, both pungent and lyrical on 'My Funny Valentine', 'I Could Write A Book' (compare with Miles Davis's floating filigree) and the less well-known 'Where Or When' and 'I Married An Angel'. The sound is up close and very faithful to both instruments.

*** Hi-Fi Salute To Bunny

RCA 2118250 *Braff; Benny Morton (tb); Pee Wee Russell (cl); Dick Hafer (ts); Nat Pierce (p); Steve Jordan (g); Walter Page (b); Buzzy Drootin (d).* 3–4/57.

***(*) Easy Now

RCA 211852 *Braff; Emmett Berry, Roy Eldridge (t); Bob Wilber (cl, ts); Hank Jones (p); Mundell Lowe (g); Leonard Gaskin (b); Don Lamond (d).* 8/58.

Not the most personable or accommodating figure to do business with (the 'Mr Hyde and Mr Hyde' joke has been heard in his vicinity more than once), Braff is a hugely entertaining performer whose cornet style seems to have arrived a generation too late. It has an almost vocal agility that balances delicacy of detail with a strong underlying pulse and harmonic richness. Like Roy Eldridge, who joins him on some of the *Easy Now* tracks, he is a player who bridges the gap between early jazz and swing, and then between swing and (hard as it may be to square this with his conservative/mainstream niching) bebop. Listen, though, to the phrasing on the tribute to Bunny Berigan, and it is possible to hear strong intimations of Fats Navarro and even that other style-switcher Charlie Shavers.

The two RCAs see him develop into a different player, and in embryo the protean stylist he was to remain until the '90s. Comparing these lushly mastered sessions with a recent Concord does the RCA technical department no favours, but it also confirms that Braff's mature style was in place almost from the beginning rather than coming along later in a bid to keep pace with the youngsters. One further indication of his bridge-building capacity is that old-school players like Morton and Russell manage to sound comfortable alongside the bustly Hafer.

*** Grand Reunion

Chiaroscuro 117 *Braff; Ellis Larkins (p).* 72.

This was the first reunion of a duo that had got together in 1955 and was to repeat the experiment 20 years later. The pace is mostly gentle, partly to suit Larkins, who is a fine ballad player, but also to highlight a more reflective side to Braff. Ruby invests even his most languid solos with a hint of fires beneath, and when occasion demands he simply doubles up the tempo and raises the ante that way. There are a couple of extra tracks not on the original LP, but the best of the session is still to be found in 'Love Walked In' and a lively but philosophical version of 'Ain't Misbehavin''.

***(*) Live At The New School

Chiaroscuro CRD 126 *Braff; George Barnes, Wayne Wright (g); Michael Moore (b).* 4/74.

In the end, despite the amiably waspish chat on the first of these, they couldn't get along together, but while they were playing rather than squabbling Braff and Barnes produced some of the best small-group jazz of the day. Needless to say, the critics were looking in the other direction at the time. The Chiaroscuro documents an entire concert at the prestigious New School for Social Research, a recording made by the audio engineering class. It was actually the last gig in an influential series known as Jazz Ramble, and it seems appropriate that it should have been a group touching so many stylistic bases that rang down the curtain. Braff's sponsorship of the young wasn't limited to having students in the booth. The inclusion of young Michael Moore in the quartet was a master-stroke, bringing forward one of the best mainstream–modern bassists of his generation and taxing him to the limit. You can almost *hear* Moore learning on some of the less familiar material, things like 'With Time For Love' and Don Redman's 'Nobody Else But You', just two of ten tracks that were not included on the original release. A doubly valuable document, then, of a short-lived group that continued for only a few months more.

*** Ruby And Woody: It Had To Be Us

Chiaroscuro 204 *Braff; Woody Herman (cl, v); John Bunch (p); Wayne Wright (g); Michael Moore (b); Jake Hanna (d).* 75.

Augmented by three alternates and an interview with George Avakian, this is a welcome part of the current Braff discography and will, of course, appeal to Herman collectors as well. The partnership is outstanding on 'I Hadn't Anyone Till You' and 'There Is No Greater Love', with both men blending tradition with a thoroughly modern approach. The group sounds as if it is having a fine time.

*** R & R

Chiaroscuro 211 *Braff; Ralph Sutton (p); Jack Lesberg (b); Gus Johnson (d).* 10/79.

Back in 1980, Ralph Sutton released a batch of duo performances on the Chaz label. This is one of the most valuable, brought back from obscurity in 2002 by Chiaroscuro. Braff is in fine form and relishes the partnership from start to finish. There are lots of Armstrong references in Ruby's solos; 'Royal Garden Blues', 'Big Butter and Egg Man' and the closing 'Dinah', always a favourite, are pungently authentic. The recording quality is a bit shaky, with some distortion here and there, but given the quality of the music more than acceptable.

*** America, The Beautiful

Arbors 19269 *Braff; Dick Hyman (org).* 4/82.

Brass and organ has been a winning combination for 400 years, and this is no exception. The slightly emphysemic organ pretends to be older and poorer-winded than it is, and Hyman turns in lovely, flowing lines. Braff is responsive and alert, but also deeply evocative. This was originally issued as part of the George Wein Collection under the off-putting title *Pipe Organ Recital Plus One*, but in the wake of the World Trade Center attacks, interest in sentimental Americana increased exponentially and this reissue has probably started tears coursing many times since. Few of the tunes are overtly nationalistic: 'When It's Sleepy Time Down South', 'Muskrat Ramble' and a rumbustious 'Dinah' are probably the best cuts.

*** The Canadian Sessions

Sackville 5005 2CD *Braff; Gene DiNovi (p); Ed Bickert (g); Don Thompson (b); Terry Clarke (d).* 79–84.

Themed much as big Dave McKenna likes to programme a set, with songs about love and the heart, the first half of this is clever, allusive and entirely convincing. The doubts creep in a bit later, when Ruby is playing with Thompson and Clarke and the pace somehow drops, not so much rhythmically as emotionally. The Gershwin and Berlin material is expertly played, but without much excitement. DiNovi has spent too many years in the shadows, but sounds convincing here, bringing his own agenda to the material without crowding the boss.

*** As Time Goes By

Candid 79741 *Braff; Howard Alden (g); Frank Tate (b).* 5/91.

Recorded live in London, with a thoroughly sympathetic group and an intriguing programme of songs. Braff is in excellent form, trying out variants on familiar harmonies and sometimes wholly recasting old songs. Mary Lou Williams's wonderful 'Lonely Moments' is too rarely covered and following 'Shoe Shine Boy' as it does, gets the album off to a stunning start which isn't quite sustained. Not a bad track in the bunch, though.

***(*) Live At The Regattabar

Arbors ARCD 9131 *Braff; Gray Sargent (p); Jon Wheatley (g); Marshall Wood (b).* 11/93.

*** Controlled Nonchalance

Arbors ARCD 9134 *As above, except add Scott Hamilton (ts), Dave McKenna (p), Chuck Riggs (d); omit Wheatley.* 11/93.

The earlier of these – by just a few days – was recorded on the 30th anniversary of President John F. Kennedy's assassination and in the heart of Kennedy country – the Regattabar is in the Charles Hotel, Cambridge, Massachusetts. Though there is no mention of the date's significance on the record, can it be that it contributed something to the quiet centredness of the session, which conveys a mood closer to melancholy than to nonchalance? Control, though, definitely. Braff's activities had been curtailed somewhat in the previous couple of years by attacks of the wind player's curse, emphysema; but he was fit enough to take charge of both these groups, leading them through two superbly crafted programmes of standard material. 'No One Else But You' is revived and gives Jon Wheatley his most effective feature, and here Braff's increasingly obvious interest in playing saxophone lines on cornet (Ben Webster is his avowed model) is given full rein. Gray Sargent has a more plangent, blues-influenced style, which is effectively deployed on 'Give My Regards To Broadway' and on the brand-new 'Orange' – a departure in the Braff canon in that the composer introduces it on piano. That warms the instrument up nicely for big Dave McKenna, four nights later with the augmented group. Qualitatively there really isn't much to choose between these groups, but one misses the stillness and precision of the drummerless quartet and the slight sense that, except for 'Struttin' With Some Barbecue' (played with a Latin spin) and 'Sunday', both of which are triumphant, Braff is slightly eclipsed by the others.

**(*) Ruby Braff And Dick Hyman Play Nice Tunes

Arbors ARCD 19141 *Braff; Dick Hyman (p).* 94.

Indeed they do – but, for some reason, perhaps because Braff sounds short-winded and weary, they don't get much firmer than that. This is a curiously drab album, with a flat and uninvolving sound, and while both men play with great competence, there is nothing that lifts it up out of the ordinary.

CORE COLLECTION

**** Calling Berlin: Volume 1

Arbors ARCD 19139 *Braff; Ellis Larkins (p); Bucky Pizzarelli (g).* 6–7/94.

The cover has them huddled round a kitchen table, with a shortwave receiver, cans and a mic, except that the Berlin they're calling on isn't the German capital but the great composer. This is the kind of intimate setting and this is the sort of material that suits Braff to a 't', and he plays superbly. 'Blue Skies' and 'Alexander's Ragtime Band' on the first volume are impossible to fault, and 'How Deep Is The Ocean?' has a wise and almost philosophical quality that is utterly engaging. Working with Ella Fitzgerald turned Larkins into a front-row accompanist. He is never less than interesting; even when he and Braff seem to start in different keys, the pianist makes something of a virtue of their displacement.

*** Calling Berlin: Volume 2

Arbors ARCD 19140 *As above, except omit Pizzarelli.* 6–7/94.

Pizzarelli doesn't appear on the second volume at all, a pity because he adds light and shade to 'It's A Lovely Day Today' and 'Russian Lullaby', and it would have been good to get more of him.

*** Concord Jazz Heritage Series

Concord Jazz 4833 *As for various Concord releases.* 74–95.

As with so many of these estimable records, the real value will be for those who either don't know Ruby's work or can't afford to amass the original discs. All the things you'd expect to find are here, along with a couple of wild cards like the original

'Here's Carl', a dedication to the label's president. Inevitably, it lacks the logic and shading of an official release but, track for track, it's a jewel.

★★★(★) Being With You: Ruby Braff Remembers Louis Armstrong

Arbors ARCD 19163 *Braff; Joe Wilder (flhn); Jon-Erik Kellso (c); Dan Barrett (tb); Scott Robinson (bs, cl); Jerry Jerome (ts); Bucky Pizzarelli (g); Johnny Varro (p); Bob Haggart (b); Jim Gwin (d).* 4/96.

Pops was always the single greatest influence on Braff's playing, and this nicely crafted tribute shows some of the ways. The group is a mixture of the great-and-good (Wilder, Barrett, Pizzarelli) and relative unknowns, but the playing is of the highest quality; though fellow-cornetist Joe is around for only a single track, the long 'Royal Garden Blues', he brings such colour and vibrancy to it as to colour the whole album. The opening take on 'I Never Knew (Where Roses Grew)' sets the tone for a richly varied session that ends on the theme tune ('When It's Sleepy Time Down South') and on a point of rest. There isn't anyone else around who could have invested this material with such conviction and grace.

★★★★ Braff Plays Wimbledon: First Set

Zephyr ZECD 15 *Braff; Warren Vaché (flhn); Roy Williams (tb); Brian Lemon (p); Howard Alden (g); Dave Green (b); Allan Ganley (d).* 9/96.

★★★(★) Braff Plays Wimbledon: The Second Set

ZECD 16 *As above.* 9/96.

Not, as it probably sounds, a live album but an exquisitely crafted studio session that sees Braff tackling a batch of unusual and rarely visited standards and bringing to them all a now familiar but no less startling creative verve. His ability to climb inside the harmonic structure of the tune and to reinvent it wholesale is endlessly satisfying, and on this occasion he is joined by three players – Vaché, the estimable Williams and Zephyr's leading light, Lemon – to create two hours of vibrant and intelligent jazz. The first set includes a long version of 'Take The "A" Train' and 'The Very Thought Of You', while the second majors on an extended reading of the Sweets and Basie jumper, 'Jive At Five'. Williams is supreme, poised and unflustered by the fastest and sometimes not the most secure change of pace and key; and the rhythm section, which has been tested almost to destruction over the years, delivers a rich, elastic beat that is the perfect platform for Braff. Two excellent records that should gladden the hearts of every mainstream fan on the planet.

★★★ You Can Depend On Me

Arbors 19165 *Braff; Johnny Varro (p); Bucky Pizzarelli (g); Bob Haggart (b); Jim Gwin (d).* 9/98.

Rising 70, Ruby is sly and subtle, turning familiar material like 'The Man I Love' into rich exercises in harmony and melody. The group is supportive but slightly anonymous, with the exception of the wonderful Pizzarelli, who bounces from tune to tune, agile and unflappable. Ruby's solos on 'S'posin" and 'Big Butter And Egg Man' are among his best in recent years.

★★★(★) Born To Play

Arbors 19203 *Braff; Kenny Davern (cl); Howard Alden, Bucky Pizzarelli, Jon Wheatley (g); Michael Moore, Marshall Wood (b); Jim Gwin (d).* 4/99.

This is not a collective personnel but the actual line-up for a most unusual band, Braff as ever experimenting and trying out new combinations of sound. The combination of three guitars is excellent, filling out a rich harmonic backdrop for the two horns. Davern is in quiet and thoughtful form, but Ruby goes for broke with big solos on Charlie Chaplin's 'Smile' and on the opening 'Avalon'. He decides to sing on the final number, 'Born To Lose', but the performance is so weighted with irony that one is inclined to grant him the small self-indulgence in return for so imaginative and unexpected a set.

★★★ Ruby Braff And Strings

Arbors 19219 *Braff; John Bunch, Brian Lemon (p); Bucky Pizzarelli (g); Lennie Bush, Michael Moore (b); Terry Jenkins, Kenny Washington (d); strings.* 11/78–3/99.

The former of these is an elegant and mostly very good strings session, marked by solid and unspectacular solos. Lemon is masterly and Bucky Pizzarelli lopes along with amiable inattention, often sounding as if he's listening to some other set on headphones. The passage of time confirms its quiet authority.

The other set offers more recent material from the Big Apple. The emphasis was on tunes associated with Bing Crosby and Frank Sinatra, but there's nothing either gently crooning or unduly blue-eyed about Braff's playing, which is as pugnacious and forthright as ever. Some of the ballad playing does sound as if it is past everyone's bedtime, but Ruby keeps the interest up, throwing in some unexpected items like the Irish song 'Too-Ra-Loo-Ra-Loo-Rai' from the New York sessions and a brilliant rendition of 'Go Fly A Kite'. The NY band is fantastic, with Pizzarelli and Bunch providing the kind of accompaniment that allows Ruby to take flight.

★★★(★) The Cape Codfather

Arbors 19222 *Braff; Kenny Davern (cl); Tommy Newsom (ts); John Bunch (p); Howard Alden (g); Michael Moore (b); Kenny Washington (d).* 3/99.

★★★ Music For The Still Of The Night

Arbors 19221 *As above; omit Davern, Newsom.* 00.

Arbors have done him proud over the last few years, and Ruby turns in another cracking set on *The Cape Codfather.* Nothing to set the heather on fire, innovation-wise, but solid standards jazz and a rare Braff original in 'Orange' which is just about the shortest thing on the set but certainly one of the most compelling. Davern is his grouchy, curmudgeonly best (let's hope they didn't have to share a dressing room), and the now familiar line-up does its stuff with impressive ease and assurance.

Music For The Still Of The Night carries on the theme. Lest anyone think this is a mild, late-nite set of slow jazz ballads, it actually comes across much more pungently than that, a set of mid-tempo swingers that allows Ruby to do his stuff with uncomplicated authority. 'When It's Sleepy Time Down South' and 'Willow Weep For Me' are astonishingly good, and completely unsurprising. The miracle is that Ruby continues to turn in quality jazz performances well past his 70th birthday when he could easily kick back and watch the racing on the tube.

★★★(★) I Hear Music

Arbors 19244 *Braff; Tommy Newsom (ts); Bill Charlap (p); Bucky Pizzarelli (g); John Beal (b); Tony DeNicola (d); Daryl Sherman (d).* 7/00.

A new band this time out, but not much significant difference in the sound. Ruby is in great form on 'Wouldn't It Be Loverly?' and a brisk and breezy 'Chicago Medley'. His tone and attack sound as supple and responsive as ever, and he deliberately softens his approach around Newsom. All the way from the opening title-track to the last bars of the original 'We're All Through', this exudes delight.

***** Watch What Happens ...**
Arbors 19259 *Braff; Dick Hyman (p); Howard Alden (g); Jake Hanna (d).* 9/01.

You wouldn't know it from the music, but this was recorded in Manhattan just one day after the World Trade Center attacks. Ruby is in spanking form and if the trauma of the day before hit him at all, it wasn't until after this beautifully crafted set was put to bed. There was no bass player, possibly because of disruption in the city and Alden had to be called in to sub for Bucky Pizzarelli, but you wouldn't think that was anything other than the planned session. 'The Blue Room' is a tour de force, and it's only topped by a lovely reading of 'Over The Rainbow' and by a version of 'Shadowland', which counts as one of Ruby's best solos of recent years. He and Hyman have a telepathic partnership and Hanna is in the groove from start to finish. Accomplished and beautiful and thank god Ruby and Dick didn't re-record 'America, The Beautiful'.

***** Variety Is The Spice Of Braff**
Arbors 19194 *Braff; Joe Wilder (t); Randy Reinhart (co); George Masso (tb); Kenny Davern (cl); Jack Stuckey (as); Chuck Wilson (as, cl); Tommy Newsom (ts); Scott Robinson (bs); Bill Charlap, Skitch Henderson (p); Howard Alden, Bucky Pizzarelli (g); John Beal (b); Joe Ascione, Sherrie Maricle (d).* 02.

No single group on this, which blunts the impact slightly. Tommy Newsom's arrangements are slick and unfussy, and give Braff lots of room for extended soloing, which he does with ease and with no sign of declining health, but the overall impact of the album is less than on slightly earlier work. Despite a good showing on 'Jumpin' At The Woodside' and 'Somebody Stole My Gal', both hefty performances, Ruby doesn't seem to be overstretched and is if anything rather dismissive of his accompanists, jumping the beat a couple of times, foreshortening ensembles with solo entries at others.

George Braith (born 1939)

SOPRANO, ALTO AND TENOR SAXOPHONES, STRITCH

A New Yorker, Braith followed Roland Kirk's idea of playing two horns at once. A brief spell with Blue Note took him nowhere in particular, and he spent much of the '70s and '80s as a street musician, though he has lately been working with John Patton.

***** The Complete Blue Note Sessions**
Blue Note 24558-2 2CD *Braith; Billy Gardner (org); Grant Green (g); Donald Bailey, Hugh Walker, Clarence Johnston (d).* 9/63–3/64.

Braith's three Blue Note albums, *Two Souls In One, Soul Stream* and *Extension*, are obscurities which this double-disc edition rescues, though the curious may be disappointed. Braith's two-horn sound, usually stritch and soprano in tandem, is less pyrotechnic than Roland Kirk's and touched by an interesting hollowed-out timbre. It makes material like the calypso 'Mary Ann' suit him rather well, although 'Mary Had A Little Lamb' – improbably turned into a fast burner – suggests that they were stuck for ideas at times. Vocalizing on blues licks and taking his sweet time on the marathon 'Braith-A-Way', the saxophonist departs from what might have been merely capable soul-jazz dates. Gardner and Green are present on all three dates; only the drummers change. The imaginative treatments of 'The Man I Love' and 'Ev'ry Time We Say Goodbye' are encouraging, although some of the originals are less so, and on a straightforward blow like 'Boop Bop Bing Bash' Braith sounds less secure than the reliable Green. An engaging footnote in Blue Note history.

Anthony Braxton (born 1945)

ALTO SAXOPHONE, ALL OTHER SAXOPHONES AND CLARINETS, FLUTE, ELECTRONICS, PERCUSSION

Few modern musicians, in any genre, can have been so extensively documented as the Chicago-born multi-instrumentalist, and yet the very density of the documentation serves only to heighten the enigma that is Anthony Braxton. His cultural background is very much the experimental ethos of the AACM and its devotion to new sound-sources and an abandonment of old hierarchies. But Braxton is a rather special kind of radical. He claims the close harmony of Frankie Lymon and the Teenagers as an influence; having worked, somewhat improbably, in one of Dave Brubeck's groups, he adduces the cool, white sound of Paul Desmond and Warne Marsh as being important to his development as a saxophonist. Braxton's enormous composition list combines relatively straightforward pulse-driven themes, akin to jazz composition, with quasi-conceptual work for unconventional instrumentation (including amplified shovels) and with grand music-theatre projects with a strong ritual component. He has also projected future work for performance on orbiting space stations, which makes Stockhausen's 'Helicopter Quartet' seem rather tame. It will obviously be many years before such projects are realizable, which is perhaps the point. A line of André Gide's applies admirably to Braxton: 'Please do not understand me too quickly.'

***** Three Compositions Of New Jazz**
Delmark DS 423 *Braxton; Wadada Leo Smith (t, perc); Leroy Jenkins (vn, vla, perc); Muhal Richard Abrams (p, clo, cl).* 4–5/68.

***** Anthony Braxton/B-X/N-0-147A**
Sunspot 524 *As above; omit Abrams; add Steve McCall (perc).* 9/69.

***** This Time ...**
Sunspot 525 *As above.* 1/70.

It would be a brave man indeed who would now claim a more than passing familiarity with the whole of the Anthony Braxton discography. The simple statistic is that there is now more material bearing Braxton's name in the public domain than there is by John Coltrane and Ornette Coleman *put together.* Whether or not this reflects his real importance to the American music of today is scarcely the point. It is a fact, and it means that assessing his body of recorded work is enormously and increasingly difficult. The number of imprints featuring his work increases by the month, and the appearance of his own imprint, Braxton House, in the '90s almost seals the issue. In what follows, we have attempted to do little more than register the main recordings and their relative merits. There will, inevitably, be omissions, but we hope they occur only in the more ephemeral and elusive corners of the picture. The question of what Braxton's music *is*, generically speaking, is one that should no longer worry anyone. Whatever the prevailing definition of jazz, Braxton's music conforms majestically: rhythmic, virtuosic, powerfully emotive, constantly reinventing itself. He has been able to translate his solo concept (in the late '60s he pioneered unaccompanied saxophone performance) to the largest orchestral scale.

The dateline on *Three Compositions Of New Jazz* is significant. Braxton's first major statement – indeed, his recording debut as leader – came in the year of revolutions (or at least of revolutionary thinking throughout America and Europe) and openly declares itself as standing at the end of a played-out cultural tradition. Though he can expect to rake over the ashes of that tradition for some time, this is the critical historical moment which Braxton's music addresses. The disc contains three compositions of decreasing length, two by Braxton, one by Smith. As John Litweiler suggests in a useful biographical liner-note, the middle piece is the one in which the new language that Braxton, Smith and Abrams are articulating can most readily be accessed. The saxophonist still sounds hot and fierce, the disciple of Parker and Dolphy rather than of the cooler, whiter voices (Desmond, Marsh) he turned to in the '80s. All the same, these graduation exercises by the 1968 AACM show class. The loose, drummerless concept works well for all three, and the music, though still slightly raw, stands up well after 30-plus years.

The recently reissued quartets with Jenkins, Smith and McCall, originally on BYG/Actuel, are a welcome reappearance of two sets that illustrate the AACM aesthetic with equal clarity. The addition of a percussionist gives the music a superficial impression of regular metres, but it's a fleeting impression. The two non-Braxton compositions are Smith's 'The Light On The Dalta' (sic) and Jenkins's 'Simple Like', the former a brooding processional that anticipates much of his later work, Jenkins's piece a howling atavistic 'blues'. Braxton's own structures were at this time closer to free improvisation than they became later and any understanding of the music is hampered by the shaky sound-quality, which blurs most of the detail. The other set suffers similar problems, and the multi-instrumentalism often seems wilful rather than purposeful, but these fill in important parts of the Braxton story.

♛ ★★★★ For Alto

Delmark 420 *Braxton (as solo).* 10/68.

Three Compositions Of New Jazz was, for all its radicalism, still recognizably within a group-jazz tradition. Not so its successor. *For Alto* challenged every parameter of the music, tonal, textural, rhythmic and structural. Now reissued on CD, it offers eloquent testimony not just of Braxton's unfolding vision, but of the boldness of a cash-strapped record label in releasing two LPs of unaccompanied saxophone improvisations with scarcely a bebop lick in evidence to calm less adventurous listeners.

One thinks at once of Charlie Parker's headlong saxophone breaks, some of them taped after the rest of the band has stopped, and sometimes of Eric Dolphy's wild, angular solos. But with the well-named *For Alto* Braxton virtually deconstructs his instrument. The piece dedicated to John Cage moves into areas where the saxophone is no longer played idiomatically or even identifiably but creates it own instant sound-world, a philosophy very much in keeping with Cage's own. Bent notes, smears, trills and tongue-slaps are by no means new in jazz, indeed they have always been part of the jazz musician's dialect, but what Braxton does here is to make them the basis of an entirely new language.

There are moments when he appears to invoke and to subvert the structure of the blues, and it is possible to hear the whole of *For Alto* as a radical gloss on the blues, a jazz parallel to *Die Kunst der Fuge*. And yet this is to reduce a work of profound feeling and genuine spirituality to a set of exercises. Just as Bach always transcends the merely technical dimensions of the quiddity he has set himself, so too Braxton creates a highly personal drama and one that was to provide the template for much of what he was to do over the next 30 years. Some pieces anticipate the speech-based works he attempted in the late '90s. Still others point forward to his abstract or theatrical compositions. All, however, seem technically assured and entirely achieved; in other words, this lacks the open-ended tentativeness of 'experimental' music. *For Alto* is one of the genuinely important American recordings. While some landmark performances retain only a mystical aura of their original significance, it remains powerfully listenable and endlessly fascinating. (There are still problems with the track listing; readers should refer to Graham Lock's painstaking editorial work on Braxton's oeuvre.)

★★★★ News From The 70s

Felmay 7005 *Braxton; Kenny Wheeler (flhn); George E. Lewis (tb); Dave Holland (b); Barry Altschul (d).* 5/72–11/76.

Braxton's second creative high-water mark came through his membership of Circle and his association with Chick Corea, Kenny Wheeler, Dave Holland and Barry Altschul. The latter trio provide the anchor to this valuable set, which is edited by the musicologist Francesco Martinelli, using tapes long hidden away in Braxton's home. Long-standing fans who these days are used to very high opus numbers indeed will be excited by the inclusion of 'Composition 8c/g', two striking solo horn performances) and even more enticingly 'Compositions -1 & -2'. The first of these is a Town Hall recording of Braxton on clarinet with Dave Holland on cello, and it has been heard before. 'Four Winds' is also familiar (though not this version) from Holland's classic *Conference Of The Birds* disc on ECM. Braxton is immensely engaging on his high-end instruments (including piccolo) and Lewis is in powerful, almost tailgating form. Wheeler's flugelhorn work is as intense and thoughtful as ever on the other quartet piece. Rounding out the set, a very effective clarinet/bass duo with Dave Holland.

Braxton's articulation is still boppish and phrase-based, but one can also hear him break his line down into constituent parts, experiment with drones and almost toneless passages, and delve into rhythmic complexities which draw something from late Coltrane (or, rather, Coltrane-plus-Ali). Even on material not intended or considered inadequate for release, he sounds assured and authoritative.

It seems puzzling that this material has not been made available till now but, given the pace and proactive nature of Braxton's career, it is perhaps not surprising that he should have overlooked these recordings. We can all be grateful to Signor Martinelli for making them available; they help fill in a now somewhat neglected corner of the Braxton story.

★★(★) What's New In The Tradition

Steeplechase 37003 2CD *Braxton; Tete Montoliu (p); Niels-Henning Orsted Pedersen (b); Albert 'Tootie' Heath (d).* 5/74.

The two-volume *In The Tradition* was Braxton's first sustained essay in revisionism, his first attempt to show that underneath the hard edge there was a jazz spirit. It's an awkward and in some respects unappealing session, largely because the piano player, the blind Catalan, Tete Montoliu, was so patently at odds with his intentions. Braxton's lyrical lines on shibboleths like 'Ornithology' are so clearly drawn as to render the chords and Montoliu's embellishments almost redundant. The bass and drums by contrast are almost ideally adapted to Braxton's needs, a particular tribute to NHOP's resilience and catholicity of taste. The bassist's finest moment is a sombre contrabass/contrabass clarinet duet on 'Goodbye Pork Pie Hat', the most funereal of funeral music. Over a quarter of a century on, these records sound almost antiquated and grievously lacking in subtlety. However adaptable Braxton's chops at the time, he was to prove himself in later years a much finer and more responsive performer of jazz material. Never a player of powerful emotion, more of ideas, he doesn't quite have the rhetoric yet to convince.

Even a further audition of the reissued set – in line with Steeplechase's admirable policy of doubling up vintage sets – doesn't persuade us to a more generous view. Nor does it make us think that a single strong or themed CD might make a more coherent write-up of this experiment.

***** First Duo Concert**

Emanem 4006 *Braxton; Derek Bailey (g).* 6/74.

We were present at this much-heralded and thoroughly extraordinary encounter, and what a revelation it turned out to be. Braxton and Bailey, representing (as became increasingly clear) two very different approaches to improvisation, met and rehearsed the day before the concert and swapped notes. It was made clear that Braxton did not want to improvise freely, while Bailey, who came from precisely that idiom, did not want to play predetermined structures. The ensuing concert represented a compromise in which each piece – or 'area' – was about certain types and categories of sound: staccato, sustained, and so on. Two pieces were set aside as solos. Braxton's 'Area 9' is one of his unaccompanied alto solos, very much in line with what he had been doing in that direction for some time: quite straightforward, jazz-based and emotionally unemphatic. By contrast, Bailey seems much more anarchic and ironic, and the conclusion, now as then, is that this was a mismatch of creative personalities which nevertheless managed to yield some fascinating music.

***** Quartet (Dortmund) 1976**

hatOLOGY 548 *Braxton; George Lewis (tb); Dave Holland (b); Barry Altschul (d).* 76.

A vintage line-up and a very powerful set that finds Braxton brokering turf between post-bop, free improvisation (which is very much Lewis's bag) and a more structured approach to jazz composition. The sound quality is good and all four players clearly defined, though Holland is a bit muffled and rumbly in some passages.

***** Quintet (Basel) 1977**

hatOLOGY 545 *Braxton; George E. Lewis (tb); Muhal Richard Abrams (p); Mark Helias (b); Charles Bobo Shaw (d).* 7/77.

Concentrating very largely on Braxton's 'Composition No. 69' and its derivatives, this finds him once again in the company of the catalytic Muhal Richard Abrams. At some distance, the music seems simpler, more discursive and unexpectedly open-textured, perhaps because the pianist hints constantly at generic source material. Shaw is a touch uncomfortable in the percussion role, a little inclined to treat the material as if it were merely expanded bebop, which it had ceased being some few years previously. Lewis, on the other hand, revels in his role and manages once again to cement the association between Braxton's radicalism and his deep awareness of the jazz and swing traditions. The recording quality is more than decent and each of the players is sufficiently registered to allow an assessment of their contributions. Braxton on this occasion limits himself to alto, sopranino and clarinet.

*****(*) Solo (Köln) 1978**

Golden Years of New Jazz 17 *Braxton (as solo).* 78.

****** Solo (Milano) 1979: Volume 1**

Golden Years of New Jazz 20 *As above.* 79.

These rare tapes have only been issued a quarter-century after Braxton made them in Germany and Italy, on tours that must have carried some echo of Eric Dolphy's lonely sojourn in Europe fifteen years previously. There is more of Dolphy's outside-inside tonality, timbral inventiveness and wilfulness about these recordings than one might expect. Braxton seemed to jump from Parker to a language all of his own, but the influence is certainly there. As usual, he mixes original compositions and heterodox standards interpretations. The first date has a wonderful 'Impressions', which was something of a signature piece for Braxton in those years, but even that is topped by the brilliant 'I Remember Clifford' and 'Out Of Nowhere' on the Milano date. These are stunning performances, as are 'Compositions 8g/I' and 'Composition 77b', both again on the Italian session, which is the one we recommend, especially with the promise of a second volume to follow.

***** Composition No. 94 For Three Instrumentalists (1980)**

Leo/Golden Years of New Jazz GY 3 *Braxton; Ray Anderson (tb); James Emery (g, elec).* 4/80.

Braxton's association with Ray Anderson was one of the happiest and most fruitful of his career, albeit brief. It offered him a range of singing tonalities not available from other instruments, and whenever the two worked together Braxton's own playing seemed to open out with ever greater generosity of spirit. Recorded live in Bologna, just a few months before that city was tragically changed for ever, the three sections of 'Composition No. 94' are played forwards and then, risible as it may sound, played backwards. This is apparently the only recording of the trio, which mitigates its poor quality somewhat, though only somewhat. Graham Lock points out in his informed and illuminating liner-note that Braxton was increasingly thinking in terms of visual parallels at this time, and much of the piece seems to be concerned with the movement of water or cloud, or with the shifting patterns of fabric. It's a good analogy for a composer who is often, unfairly, thought to be abstract and drily cerebral.

*****(*) Composition No. 96**

Leo CD LR 169 *Braxton (cond); Dave Scott, James Knapp (t); Julian Priester, Scott Reeves (tb); Richard Reed (frhn); Rick Byrnes (tba); Nancy Hargerud, Rebecca Morgan, Denise Pool (f); Aileen Munger, Laurri Uhlig (ob); Bob Davis (eng hn); Marlene Weaver (bsn); Paul Pearse, Bill Smith (cl); Ray*

Downey (bcl); Denny Goodhew (as); Julian Smedley, Mathew Pederson, Jeannine Davis, Libby Poole, Jeroen Van Tyn, Sandra Guy, Becky Liverzey, Mary Jacobson (vn); Betty Agent, Jean Word, Sam Williams, Beatrice Dolf (vla); Page Smith-Weaver, Scott Threlkold, Marjorie Parbington (clo); Scott Weaver, Deborah De Loria (b); Motter Dean (hp); Ed Hartman, Matt Kocmieroski (perc). 5/81.

Dating from the end of the '70s, *Composition No. 96* is a large-scale composition dedicated to Karlheinz Stockhausen and reflecting Braxton's interest in the relationship between 'dynamic symbolism' (the Jungian archetypes, close enough) and planetary change. The symbols are realized as photographic slides of actual physical phenomena, which are then projected as part of a strict parallelism between perceptual systems. Braxton's earlier experiments with large-scale orchestral 'composition' – difficult to hear any of it as uniformly scored – were not particularly happy. It's ironic that while one of the routine criticisms levelled at his small-group work is that it is too rigidly formalized, his orchestral works can sound unproductively chaotic. *Composition No. 96*, which comes from a particularly fruitful phase in Braxton's career, is a huge, apocalyptic thing that might serve as a soundtrack for some post-creationist epic of the Next Frontier.

Graham Lock's immensely detailed liner-note explains the genesis and structure of the music, but essentially *Composition No. 96* consists of 16 separate elements and their numerological product, seven distinct parts, which move from the vibrant collisions of the opening through slower and faster sections, punctuated by *fermata* or pauses like those that signal the beginning of cadenzas in classical concertos. Braxton's large-scale works were a logical extension of what he had been doing throughout the 1970s, but they were also part of his effort to raise Afro-American music out of the 'jazz' ghetto. Even at the level of pure sound, with no reference to its complex structural synchronization, *Composition No. 96* is an impressive achievement. The Composers and Improvisers Orchestra has a rather *ad hoc* feel, and some of the transitions sound fudged and incomplete. The only recognizable jazz name in the ensemble is trombonist Julian Priester, and one wonders how sympathetic some of the players actually were to Braxton's conception. There are places when the playing is more exact and 'legitimate' than the context seems to demand; but such perceptions may be the result of residual expectations of what jazz musicians are 'supposed' to sound like, and for that reason alone should be resisted.

***** Four Compositions (Quartet) 1984**
Black Saint 120086 *Braxton; Marilyn Crispell (p); John Lindberg (b); Gerry Hemingway (d).* 9/84.

*****(*) Quartet (London) 1985**
Leo CD LR 200/201 2CD *As above, except Mark Dresser (b) replaces Lindberg.* 11/85.

*****(*) Quartet (Birmingham) 1985**
Leo CD LR 202/3 2CD *As above.* 11/85.

****** Quartet (Coventry) 1985**
Leo CD LR 204/205 2CD *As above.* 11/85.

*****(*) Five Compositions (Quartet) 1986**
Black Saint 120106 *As above, except David Rosenboom (p) replaces Crispell.* 7/86.

For all his compositions for amplified shovels, 100 tubas and galactically dispersed orchestras, the core of Braxton's conception remains the recognizably four-square jazz quartet. This is where he was heard to best advantage in the '80s. The minimally varied album-titles are increasingly confusing; for instance, *Four Compositions (Quartet) 1983* with George Lewis has now disappeared, leaving the near-identical-sounding set above. Fortunately, there is a straightforward rule of thumb: if Marilyn Crispell is on it, buy it. The Braxton Quartet of 1984–5 was of remarkable vintage and Crispell's Cecil Taylor-inspired but increasingly individual piano-playing was one of its outstanding features. There are unauthorized recordings of this band in circulation, but the Leo sets are absolutely legitimate, and pretty nearly exhaustive; the CDs offer good-quality transfers of the original boxed set, six sides of quite remarkable music that, in conjunction with the other quartet sessions, confirm Braxton's often stated but outwardly improbable interest in the Lennie Tristano school, and in particular the superb harmonic improvisation of Warne Marsh. Those who followed the 1985 British tour may argue about the respective merits of different nights and locations, but there really isn't much to separate the London, Coventry and Birmingham sets for the non-specialist. For reference, the material performed on each pair of discs is as follows: London – Compositions 122 (+ 108A), 40(O), 52, 86 (+ 32 + 96), 115, 105A, piano solo from 96, 40F, 121, 116; Birmingham – 110A (+ 96 + 108B), 69M (+ 10 + 33 + 96), 60 (+ 96 + 108C), 85 (+ 30 + 108D), 105B (+ 5 + 32 + 96), 87 (+ 108C), 23J, 69H (+ 31 + 96), 40(O); Coventry – 124 (+ 30 + 96), 88 (+ 108C + 30 + 96), piano solo from 30, 23G (+ 30 + 96), 40N, 69C (+ 32 + 96), percussion solo from 96, 69F, 69B, bass solo from 96, 6A. It will be noted how often compositions in the above list are 'collaged' with 'Composition No. 96', the 'multiple-line' orchestral piece listed above. It serves as a reference point, most obviously in the Coventry concert. This also includes an intriguing conversation interview with Braxton, conducted by Graham Lock and covering such subjects as Frankie Lymon, John Coltrane, Warne Marsh, chess, the blues, and the nature of music itself.

Though the Birmingham set reaches a hectic climax with an encore performance of 'Kelvin 40(O)' that does further damage to Braxton's undeserved reputation as a po-faced number-cruncher, the extra half-star has to go to Coventry, first for the interview material, but also for the most sheerly beautiful performance in Braxton's entire recorded output, the peaceful clarinet music on 'Composition No. 40(N)' that ends the first set. Nothing else on the remaining five discs quite reaches that peak of perfection. Rosenboom is a poor substitute for Crispell on the 1986 set, but the rhythm section of Dresser or Lindberg and Hemingway was beginning to sound custom-made by this stage, perfectly attuned to the music.

The music from this tour has now been rationalized and issued with fascinating interview material which goes some way to setting out Braxton's complex heritage and musical philosophy.

***** Victoriaville 1988**
Victo 7 *Braxton; Paul Smoker (t); George Lewis (tb); Evan Parker (ts); Bobby Naughton (vib); Joelle Leandre (b); Gerry Hemingway (d).* 10/88.

This has an indefinable 'supergroup' feel to it, an awkward sense that the participants are playing to the audience and not listening to one another with the usual intensity. Consisting of two long Braxton compositions – 141 and 142, the latter only a fifth the length of the titanic opener – it's familiar enough territory, but marked out by some extraordinary showmanship from Braxton, Smoker and Lewis, all of whom seem to be having great fun. Parker is more reserved, but also seems to be most conscious of what is happening elsewhere in the group, notably bass and vibraphone, where the harmonic decryption is going on. We can't quite pin down our reservations. A genuinely enjoyable set, notwithstanding.

**** Six Monk's Compositions (1987)

Black Saint 120 116 *Braxton; Mal Waldron (p); Buell Neidlinger (b); Bill Osborne (d).* 7/87.

Braxton more than most had eventually to prove himself as a performer of standards. Even before *In The Tradition* it was clear that he was deeply rooted and by no means the scorched-earth revolutionary sceptics liked to think him. The Monk sessions are a triumph. Far from the usual pastiche, these are reinvented versions of a half-dozen obscurer items from the monastic œuvre. Pianist Mal Waldron is there to confirm the apostolic succession, but Braxton's readings are thoroughly apostate, furiously paced and unapologetically maximal.

***(*) 2 Compositions (Järvenpää) 1988

Leo CD LR 233 *Braxton; Mircea Stan (tb); Seppo Paakkunainen (ts, bs, f); Pentti Lahti (as, ss, f); Pepa Päivinen (ts, ss, bcl, f); Mikko-Ville Luolajan-Mikkola (vn); Teppo Hauta-aho (b, clo); Jukka Wasama (d).* 11/88.

In the autumn of 1988, Braxton toured Finland with an *ad hoc* group called Ensemble Braxtonia. It is to their credit – considerable collective experience notwithstanding – that they coped so well with numbers 144 and 145, and the ease with which these were communicated to a highly enthusiastic audience at the Tampere Jazz Happening (Järvenpää is Sibelius's home and a point of pilgrimage for Finnish musicians) gives some sense of the movement of Braxton's work from the far periphery to something near the hub of contemporary creative music. There is nothing here that would frighten the horses, just intense, very focused music of a high order. Only the recording lets it down.

CORE COLLECTION

**** Eugene (1989)

Black Saint 120137 *Braxton; Rob Blakeslee, Ernie Carbajal, Jorn Jensen (t); Mike Heffley, Tom Hill, Ed Kammerer (tb); Thom Bergeron, Jeff Homan, Carl Woideck (reeds); Mike Vannice (reeds, p); Toddy Barton (syn); Joe Robinson (g); Forrest Moyer (b); Charles Dowd (vib, perc); Tom Kelly (perc).* 1/89.

Eugene is one of Braxton's finest discs, and certainly the most accessible of the larger-group recordings; this features eight compositions dating from 1975 to 1989, and was recorded in Eugene, Oregon, during a 'creative orchestra' tour of the Pacific North-West. Much of the credit for the project has to go to trombonist Mike Heffley, who originally proposed and subsequently organized the tour. The earliest of the pieces, 'Composition No. 45', was written for a free-jazz festival in Baden-Baden and is defined by Braxton in his _Composition Notes C_ as 'an extended platform for the challenge of post-Coltrane/Ayler functionalism'. A march, it anticipates the more complex 'Composition No. 58' (not included here) but demonstrates how creatively Braxton has been able to use the large-scale 'outdoor' structures he draws from Henry Brant, Sun Ra and traditional marching music, to open up unsuspected areas of improvisatory freedom; the link with Ayler's apocalyptic 'Truth Is Marching In' is immediately obvious. 'Composition No. 91' is a delicately pointillistic piece with a much more abstract configuration. Less propulsive than 'No. 45' or the more conventional ensemble-and-soloists outline of 'No. 71', it underlines the composer's brilliant grasp of instrumental colour; synthesizer and electric guitar provide some unfamiliar tonalities in the context of Braxton's work and, perhaps in reaction, he limits his own playing to alto saxophone. Braxton's work has taken on an increasingly ritualistic quality, as in the processional opening and steady two-beat pulse of the most recent piece, 'Composition No. 134'. As such, it stands beside the work of Stockhausen and the composers mentioned above. If its underlying philosophy is millennial, its significance is commensurate with that.

*** Duo (Amsterdam) 1991

Okkadisk OD 12018 *Braxton; Georg Graewe (p).* 10/91.

To the best of our understanding, these two long, one short pieces were spontaneously improvised, with no predetermined logic or direction for the music. Even so, there are continual hints and reminders of Braxton's current compositional interests, palindromic shapes and stretching pulses, which suggest the extent to which he used public performance of this sort as a laboratory for ideas which would take on a more detailed form later. Braxton's flute and clarinet playing is extremely impressive, the former especially.

**** Four (Ensemble) Compositions

Black Saint 120124 *Braxton; Robert Rumboltz (t); Roland Dahinden, John Rapson (tb); Don Byron (cl, bcl); Marty Ehrlich (f, picc, cl, as, ts); J. D. Parran (f, cl, bcl, acl, bamboo f); Randy McKean (cl, as, bcl); Ted Reichman, Guy Klucevesek (acc); Amina Claudine Myers (org, v); Jay Hoggard (vib, mar); Lyndon Achee, Warren Smith (perc).* 92.

***(*) Composition No. 165

New Albion NA 050 *Braxton; University of Illinois Creative Music Orchestra: Thomas Tait, Jeff Helgesen, Judd G. Danby (t); Erik Lund, Douglas Farwell, Keith Moore (tb); Jesse Seifert-Gram (tba); Paul Martin Zonn (as, cl, slide sax); Graham Kessler (as, cl); Andrew Mitroff (ts, f); Kevin Engel (ts, bsn, cl); Mark Barone (bs, bcl); Tom Paynter (p); Mark Zanter (g); Drew Krause (syn); Adam Davis (b); Justin Kramer, Tom Sherwood (perc).* 2/92.

The material on *Four (Ensemble) Compositions* is a combination of brand-new compositions – numbers 163 and 164 – with a fascinating performance of the pivotal 'Composition No. 96'. This time, the orchestra includes time-served jazz players and improvisers, and the piece takes on a limber, relaxed charm that it can't altogether claim on the Leo recording. 'Composition No. 165', on the New Albion, is surprisingly direct and unfussy, but it lacks the element of sheer shock that Braxton used to bring, and there are moments when it is drifts perilously close to cosy classicism. Once again, one wonders to what extent these players understand where Braxton is coming from. The wonderful thing about the ensemble on the Black Saint is that they've all been there too. These sessions, like some of their predecessors, pose one intriguing question about Braxton's future work. Will he come to see himself more and more as a composer/conductor, less and less as an improvising instrumentalist; or does he believe that he can sustain both strands? For the sake of improvised music, one hopes so.

***** (Victoriaville) 1992**
Victo 21 *Braxton; Marilyn Crispell (p); Mark Dresser (b); Gerry Hemingway (d).* 8/92.

It's more than tempting to refer to this as the 'classic Anthony Braxton Quartet'. The analogy with John Coltrane is reinforced by a stirring encore rendition of Trane's blues-based 'Impressions', which had become something of a signature piece for Braxton. The group is in wonderful form, perhaps less engaged and certainly less well recorded than on their closely documented British tour in 1985, but still in powerful form. 'Composition 147' serves as the multiple line anchor piece in most of these improvisations, much as 'Composition 96' did in earlier days, and it's worth spending some time listening in detail to the structures and practices Braxton deploys here. Any sense that such analysis is inimical to enjoyment means you're not yet attuned to Braxton's challenging aesthetic.

*****(*) 9 Standards (Quartet) 1993**
Leo CD LR 237/238 2CD *Braxton; Fred Simmons (p); Paul Brown (b); Leroy Williams (d).* 2/93.

An intriguing view of Braxton working, not with a regular ensemble, but with what is effectively a pick-up group, albeit a highly experienced one. Simmons is known to have worked with Dewey Redman, while Brown and Williams were a useful hard-bop partnership in the '70s. As a working unit, they sound seamless and instinctive. With the exception of Simmons's opening 'In Motion', all the tunes are standards or blowing themes. The set includes Braxton's first documented version of 'On Green Dolphin Street', though we must correct Art Lange's suggestion that Braxton hasn't tackled Coltrane's 'Impressions' more than once before. There are two or three versions currently available, none more straightforwardly in the tradition of the classic quartet than this, though.

Performing 'What's New' on flute is an interesting oddity. This is now one of Braxton's least-used instruments, and it's fascinating to hear him negotiate the changes at some speed (in vertical terms, if not in actual enunciation). 'Cherokee' is not much more than a settler, to follow the Simmons tune and give the band some familiar material to stretch out on. Heard unannounced, Braxton sounds resolutely mainstream, suggesting one of the white saxophonists of the '50s, curbing any hint of whoop or holler. A fascinating double set, but two more CDs for the Braxtonophile to negotiate.

****** Duo (London) 1993**
Leo CD LR 193 *Braxton; Evan Parker (ts).* 5/93.

****** Trio (London) 1993**
Leo CD LR 197 *As above, except add Paul Rutherford (tb).* 5/93.

Braxton has been quoted as saying that these recordings gave him more solace in times of doubt and uncertainty than anything he had played for many years. Contrary to expectation, both men sound cool and thoughtful. The understanding with Parker is almost telepathic as intricate, bleached lines spiral upwards at ever higher levels of organization. Parker in particular sounds as though he has awakened ancestral ghosts, at a couple of points sounding disconcertingly like one of Braxton's masters, Warne Marsh, and hovering on the verge of harmonic improvisation throughout the set. In strict harmonic terms, he may even be ahead of his partner in this sort of project. He seems to be able to hear harmonics two places above the ostensible playing position and to bring them into play quite seamlessly and unforcedly.

He is doing the same thing on the trio set, recorded at the same London festival. Rutherford's contribution is to make the music more abstract. Any intention on Braxton's part to restore elements of jazz language is confounded and, as so often in a European environment, he is pushed out into unfamiliar and very challenging territory, where he is obliged to examine his procedures note by note. These are exhilarating performances, among his most radical small-group works.

*****(*) The Braxton Quartet Plays Twelve Braxton Compositions**
Music & Arts CD 835 2CD *Braxton; Marilyn Crispell (p); Mark Dresser (b); Gerry Hemingway (d, mar).* 7/93.

How wonderful to hear the 'classic quartet' recorded again. Everyone who heard the group during their residencies in Santa Cruz and at Yoshi's nightclub in Oakland (near his old stamping ground of Mills College) concedes that it was playing at its peak, while these recordings are probably the best and most generously balanced this line-up had enjoyed to date, which undoubtedly helps the complex, richly textured music to make its maximum impact. Braxton dips back into his composition books to revive some early ideas like '23C' and '40(O)', one of the early Kelvin series, but he also includes some of the more recent, theatre-based works, such as 'Composition 173', later documented with a full orchestral ensemble and released on Black Saint. The choice of material is slightly less varied on the Yoshi's discs which were released on hat ART and are currently deleted, and the playing is rather compressed in places. However, Crispell (who is the only other member of the group photographed on the cover) is in exceptional form and plays with unqualified brilliance from start to finish, demonstrating how far she has travelled since. In this version it sounds inevitably much closer to jazz roots, and the two performances make for a fascinating comparison. For most listeners, though, the best route here is simply to allow these long performances to impinge slowly over time. Whether one recognizes compositional strategies, let alone numbers, is ultimately irrelevant.

(***) Composition No. 174
Leo CD LR 217 *Arizona State University Percussion Ensemble.* 2/94.

Though we stand by our assertion that Braxton's music is readily accommodatable on CD, one wonders about this piece, which is written for percussion ensemble and constructed environment and which seems to concern a party of mountaineers and an expedition that is a cross between *The Ascent Of F6* and a virtual reality primer to Braxton's compositional method. There are oddities in the registration of the instruments – a broad-ranging percussion ensemble – which demand an answer to the question as to whether the music is played accurately or whether hitches and uncertainties have persisted in this première performance. Unless you are Anthony Braxton, impossible to judge.

***** Knitting Factory (Piano/Quartet): Volume 1**
Leo CD LR 222/223 2CD *Braxton; Marty Ehrlich (as, ss, cl); Joe Fonda (b); Pheeroan akLaff (d).* 94.

***** Piano Quartet, Yoshi's, 1994**
Music & Arts CD 849 4CD *As above, except omit akLaff; add Arthur Fuller (d, perc).* 6/94.

*** Knitting Factory (Piano/Quartet) 1994: Volume 2

Leo CDLR 297/298 *As above.* 6/94.

It was no surprise to anyone who has heard him play keyboard that Braxton should want to release something of this sort; he is also an accomplished drummer, and we can't rule out a future percussion project. What is astonishing is that he should have permitted the release of *six* CDs, with the explicit promise of more – volumes three, four? more? – on Leo. These are exclusively jazz repertoire sessions, a detailed and highly respectful examination of composers who have affected Braxton and his music. The range of material is astonishing: Mingus, Brubeck, Monk, Golson, Noble, Miles, Dolphy, Gryce and (on the Leo) Shorter, Mingus and Monk again, Ellington, Tristano. It is difficult to gauge how we might assess these performances if the pianist were anyone but Braxton. In a sense, he does not sound 'like himself'. The switch of register, the harmonic resource, the relative unfamiliarity, all make a profound difference, and yet it is clear that he is directing operations in a quite interventionist way. Ehrlich is a strong player but not a particularly passionate structuralist, and he seems to follow where Braxton leads, allowing his pitching and coloration to be determined quite explicitly by the chords and by a deep-level 'pulse' in the music.

**(*) Duo (Wesleyan) 1994

Leo CDLR 228/229 2CD *Braxton; Abraham Adzinyah (perc).* 94.

The percussionist's name is listed first on the cover, seemingly at Braxton's insistence. From a less generous and open-spirited man, one might almost suspect that this selflessness camouflages a recognition that this is less than a central Braxton recording. Overlong at 100 minutes of continuous music spread over two CDs, verbose in the extreme and curiously difficult to relate to Braxton's current projects.

***(*) Small Ensemble Music (Wesleyan) 1994

Splasc(h) 2034 *Braxton; Roland Dahinden (tb); Jeanne Choe (p); other personnel.* 94.

An unexpected artist to launch the usually bop-orientated Italian label's international series, but a chance to revisit one of Braxton's classic compositions. 'Composition No. 107' was originally performed by Garret List and Marianne Schroeder, and it returns here with a pleasurable shock of familiarity. Braxton's duo and trio appearances are also attractively accessible and only the mostly new sextet work packs any kind of alien punch. An unexpected release, but a very welcome one.

(***) Composition No. 173

Black Saint 120166 *Braxton; Melinda Newman (ob); Brandon Evans (sno, bcl); Jennifer Hill (cl); Bo Bell (bsn); Nickie Braxton, Danielle Langston (vn); Brett W. Larner (koto); Kevin O'Neil (g); Sandra Miller, Jacob Rosen (clo); Dirck Westervelt, Joe Fonda (b); Josh Rosenblatt (perc); actors.* 12/94.

'"I hear an influence coming in from the CKA areas," cried Miss Tishingham' is about the most illuminating commentary on this one. Another of Braxton's multi-media pieces, it transfers to disc no more incompletely and insecurely than its successor (which was recorded first). Like 'No. 174', it has moments of real musical beauty, especially here when the woodwinds are soloing; but to what extent the 'score' can be separated from the *mise en scène* and the stage apparatus is beyond our competence. It may still be jazz music, but not as we know it, Jim.

**** 11 Compositions (Duo) 1995

Leo CDLR 244 *Braxton; Brett Larner (koto).* 3/95.

Braxton acknowledges the prior example of Tony Scott, Joe Harriott and Don Cherry in introducing the multi-stringed *koto* to this kind of improvisational environment. His own intentions are no less supra-national, even cosmic, and with Larner he creates a web of sounds of great complexity and gentleness, hard to locate culturally but equally and typically hard to tie to 'story-lines' other than those which determine areas of sound and time. 'Composition 72H' is said to be 'solemn and grave and without forgiveness' and, later, like a 'slow freight train', one of those Mid-West monsters which despite its movement gives an impression of eternity. In 'Composition 72F', another of the series, the voices murmur up and down, one slowly ceding to the other, one quietly dominating. A near-perfect album of duo improvisation, unexpected in sonority, rich in association, played magnificently.

*** 10 Compositions (Duet) 1995

Konnex 5071 *Braxton; Joe Fonda (b).* 8/95.

**** Four Compositions (Quartet) 1995

Braxton House 5 *Braxton; Ted Reichman (acc); Joe Fonda (b); Kevin Norton (d, vib, perc).* 8/95.

Braxton has never been short of sympathetic collaborators, and Fonda is just the latest in a line. That is not to dismiss his contribution here. The duets album includes three of his compositions, of which the well-named 'Restlessness' is the most substantial. The set is bracketed by a couple of standards, most notably a majestic reading of 'Autumn In New York'.

The second disc includes finely detailed and refreshingly clear-sighted performances of four closely related compositions – numbers 181 to 184 – which very clearly establish the lineage of the recent Ghost Trance Musics back to the improvisational structures of past years. If there is an obvious point of comparison for this record, it is early recordings with Chick Corea, Dave Holland and Barry Altschul. The dynamics and the relaxed, almost meditative drive are the same. The soundscape is very different, of course, but identifying the similarities once again focuses attention on how consistent Braxton's course has been. Brightly recorded in performance at Wesleyan University, the music communicates well on CD.

**** Sextet (Istanbul) 1995

Braxton House 1 2CD *Braxton; Roland Dahinden (tb); Jason Hwang (vn); Ted Reichman (acc); Joe Fonda (b); Kevin Norton (d, vib, mar, perc).* 10/95.

This is perhaps the clearest and most coherent invocation of Braxton's newest line of development, what he refers to as the Ghost Trance Musics. These long, powerful improvisations, recorded at a jazz festival in Turkey, attempt to put players and listeners close to the heightened consciousness experienced in Native-American and Eastern ritual, prolonged improvisation of an unmannered, ego-less sort that for the first time seems closer to the long-form, process-dominated music of AMM and other British ensembles than to the jazz tradition (though, of course, Braxton continues to espouse this line as well, in both musical language and instrumentation). 'Composition No. 186' is titanic, almost exactly an hour in length and reminiscent in its focus and intensity of some of the late Coltrane sessions when standard material was shredded, reconstituted and finally re-created as something new and transcendent. Though not based on any recognizable melodic material, Braxton's usual dependency on simple motifs and cells is less evident here because in sheer durational terms the development is much further from the statement. It would be a mistake, though, to suggest that this is dramatically different or apart from the continuum of his work. Like Miles Davis, Braxton seems consumed with a need to change, but in change he always remains consistent with his own ongoing concerns.

**** Ensemble (New York) 1995

Braxton House 7 *Braxton; J. D. Parran (cl, bsx); Lily White (as); Aaron Stewart (ts); Libby Van Cleeve (eng hn); Melinda Newman (ob); Jacquie Carrasco, Gwen Laster (vn); Nioka Workman (clo); Joe Fonda (b); Kevin Norton (d, vib, perc).* 11/95.

**** Octet (New York) 1995

Braxton House 6 *Braxton; Roland Dahinden (tb); Brandon Evans (f, wood f, bcl, ss, ts); Andre Vida (f, ss, as, ts, bs); Jason Hwang (vn); Ted Reichman (acc); Joe Fonda (b); Kevin Norton (d, vib, perc).* 11/95.

The group of the moment caught live at a special Braxton event held at the Knitting Factory in New York City. Having surrounded himself with like-minded multi-reed persons, Braxton himself carries less of the sheer weight of the music than he once did. Now that there are second-generation players around who understand his premisses as well as his intentions, he has been able to devolve at least some of the responsibilities of leadership. The period of Ghost Trance Musics is pretty well established by now. If some of this and other records are reminiscent of Minimalism, that is not accidental. Braxton has not been entirely forthcoming about stylistic antecedents for this phase of his career, perhaps because in the past he has been able to espouse unfashionable sources. Here he runs the risk of *appearing* to jump on a bandwagon that has already begun to lose momentum. There were, of course, Minimalist elements in his work before now – less Glass and Reich than Young and Riley – and these have been more or less widely acknowledged. It is surprising to find them occupying the foreground at this juncture, but there is no mistaking the vitality and the rigour with which Braxton has invested them.

Both records contain just one long composition. *Ensemble*, with its expanded sound-palette (and some striking compositional echoes of Ornette Coleman's early experiments with legitimate formations), is devoted to 'Composition No. 187'. This is one of the best representations of his 'Tri-Centric' philosophy, the three-in-one of structure, ideas and ritual; architecture, philosophy and ritual; symbolic function, structured space and mutable logic. The balance of voices is clearly still very important, but more so is the need to read off very different parameters in the music, functioning all at once. 'Composition No. 188', which occupies the second of the two records from the event, is a more straightforward piece in some respects, but also more abrasively rhythmic and propulsive. Both are absolutely compelling and should be sought out by anyone interested in the future direction of American music.

*** Solo Piano (Standards) 1995

No More Records No. 2 2CD *Braxton (p solo).* 12/95.

Stories abound of Braxton playing piano and even drums behind young musicians in informal settings and at masterclasses. It was presumably only a matter of time before a solo piano album came along – and it would have been worth taking odds that it would be a double set. Strictly speaking, this isn't a standards set at all, but a collection of jazz compositions. Coltrane's 'Central Park West', one of the few tunes on which he didn't solo, is an interesting choice, with McCoy Tyner's flowing solo replicated in more angular and abrasive form; 'Straight Street' is less familiar and less satisfactory. A couple of takes of 'Pannonica' and one of 'Skippy' establish Braxton's relationship to Monk. There are a couple of Mingus compositions and material by Wayne Shorter, Mal Waldron (two versions of 'Dee's Dilemma') and Benny Golson. The first of the two discs is perhaps the stronger, and there is every reason to think that an edited single would have been quite adequate in this case. Braxton's debt to Dave Brubeck, with whom he once recorded, is pretty clear, but he is as much his own man on piano as on reeds. An accomplished, thoroughly enjoyable record.

*** Composition No. 102

Braxton House 3 *Braxton; Sam Hoyt, Steve Laronga, Zach See (t); Taylor Bynum (flhn); Daniel Young (c); John Speck (tb); Stewart Gillmor (euph); Niko Higgins, David Kasher, Matthew Lee, Allen Livermore (as); Jackson Moore (as, cl); April Monroe, Christine Whitledge (f); Rafael Cohen (ob); Sung Kim (hca); Michael Buescher, Ronaldo Garces, Eric Ronick, Michael Thompson, Kevin Uehinger (p); Edmond Cho, Nathaniel Delafield, Thom Loubet, Kevin O'Neil (g); Nickie Braxton (vn); Vivian Lee, Anil Seth (clo); Brett Larner (koto); Dave Gilbert (g); Michael Lenore (b); Rene Muslin, Josh Rosenblatt (perc).* 96.

Originally written in 1982 and premièred in Houston, Texas, 'Composition No. 102' is scored for orchestra and puppet theatre and cuts across European, American and African folklores to create an environment of calm mystery. Like much of Braxton's work, so forbiddingly complex on the surface, it is made up of relatively simple materials, rising and falling figures, shifts of dynamics and attack, and rhythmic variation right across the field of the orchestra. Like many of the composer's recent works, it probably makes less than complete sense as a purely aural experience and it would be wonderful to see a video version of a complete performance. This – or some more sophisticated audio-visual technology – seems an inevitable next step for Braxton. Much as we admire the music here, it is difficult to be excited about it. The Wesleyan orchestra is well-drilled and seemingly very precise, though how much of its occasional stiffness is intended (perhaps to suggest or reflect puppet movements) again remains hard to assess.

*** 14 Compositions (Traditional) 1996

Leo CDLR 259 *Braxton; Stewart Gillmor (t, frhn, p).* 3/96.

It's not clear what Braxton means by 'traditional' here, since the material covered takes in songs by Hoagy Carmichael ('Skylark'), Duke Ellington ('In A Sentimental Mood'), W. C. Handy ('Memphis Blues') and the Wesleyan University football fight song, Wesleyan being Braxton's academic base of operations. Gillmor is a responsive collaborator, but not much more than that, and the record is another opportunity to sample Anthony's astonishing multi-instrumentalism, with starring roles for the extreme sonority of bass saxophone and contrabass clarinet. The tracks weigh in at a fairly standard length and there is something slightly 'by rote' about the playing but, longueurs aside, there is plenty to enjoy.

*** Composition 192

Leo Records CDLR 251 *Braxton; Lauren Newton (v).* 6/96.

This piece for two musicians in a constructed environment consisting of a fairground Wheel of Fortune and a video projection of the environs of New York City through a car windshield is said to be the first of Braxton's new cycle of Ghost Trance Music. This is what Braxton has described as a 'new image logic', seemingly a way of converting ordinary, even domestic environments into cosmic spaces by endless, weaving melodies, here played on saxophones and clarinets, while Lauren Newton recites the letters of the alphabet. This was the first encounter between Braxton and Newton, curiously enough. Whatever she thought and however much she understood of the music's premisses, she enters into it with great enthusiasm and with a wry humour.

***(*) Tentet (New York) 1996

Braxton House 4 *Braxton; Roland Dahinden (tb); J. D. Parran (acl, picc); Brandon Evans (ss, as, ts, bcl, f); Andre Vida (ss, as, ts, bs); Jacquie Carrasco, Gwen Laster (vn); Ted Reichman (acc); Joe Fonda (b); Kevin Norton (d, vib, perc).* 6/96.

A large, saxophone-dominated ensemble for 'Composition No. 193' and a very fine performance from all concerned. Reichman is profoundly clued in to Braxton's music, and the two fiddlers both contribute substantially to the very textured and modulated sound Braxton has tried to achieve with this recent work. Generically, it seems to sit somewhere between his pulse-driven and jazz-derived works and his more obviously theatrical output. The interweaving of the horns suggests some of Stan Kenton's more spacious endeavours, and there are phrases here and there towards the end which recall Bob Graettinger arrangements, so perhaps Braxton has added yet another arrow to his quiver of stylistic derivations.

** Trillium R: Shala Fears For The Poor – Composition No. 162

Braxton House BH 008 *Braxton; Steve Swell (tb); Libby Van Cleeve (frhn); Mark Whitecage (ss); David Bindman (ts); Aaron Stewart (bs); Rob Brown (f); Perry Robinson (cl); Brandon Evans (bcl); Joseph Celli (ob); Lisa Bielawa, Mellissa Fathman, Elizabeth Henreckenson-Farnum, Heather Dea Jennings, Matthew Pass, Benjamin Sosland, Melton Sawyer, Gregory Purnhagen, Peter Stewart (v); Tri-Centric Orchestra.* 10/96.

Catholic and inclusive though we like to be, the music in this curious music-theatre project (dedicated to Nelson Mandela) falls very largely outside the scope of this book. We found the proceedings sparse and unengaging. However, the *Trillium* cycle is as central to Braxton's oeuvre as *Skies Of America* was to Ornette Coleman's, and on that analogy we beg leave to wonder if this dry performance genuinely reflects the wishes and intentions of the composer.

The line-up is extraordinary, but there is very little scope for instrumentalists of the quality of Robinson and Swell to make much impact. The voices are indifferently recorded and the whole package seems remote and abstract.

**** Ninetet (Yoshi's) 1997: Volume 1

Leo CDLR 343/344 2CD *Braxton; Brandon Evans (sno, C-ss, ts, bcl, f); James Fei (ss, as, bcl); Jackson Moore (as, bb cl); Andre Vida (ss, as, ts, bs); J. D. Parran (ss, bsx, f); Kevin O'Neil (g); Joe Fonda (b); Kevin Norton (d, vib, mar, perc).* 8/97.

**** Ninetet (Yoshi's) 1997: Volume 2

Leo CDLR 382/383 2CD *As above.* 8/97.

Braxton's week-long residency at the Oakland club was his most sustained examination of Ghost Trance Music. These two volumes are among the most satisfying of the saxophonist's larger group records and are warmly recommended to anyone who wants to explore this particular area of enquiry.

What's immediately evident from both sets is how important Kevins Norton and O'Neil have become to Braxton's music, successors you might say to Marilyn Crispell and Gerry Hemingway. The drummer's possibly less important as a kit player than as a vibist and marimba player on these. On 'Composition 209' (Volume 2) he opens up improvising areas that are obviously implicit in Braxton's GTM codes but which no one else seems to be examining. It's reminiscent of what Rashied Ali gave to John Coltrane. Norton's joyous gong-splashes are another delight amid the chatter of the saxophones.

O'Neil is somewhat recessed in the mix but he's also an engagingly modest player who never grandstands and who understands completely how to use dynamics effectively. Whether picking out single note Morse or pulling off complex chords, he's always integral to what is going on. Thirty-three minutes into 'Composition 210' and he's in the spotlight, his guitar bubbling like magma while the horns, Braxton to the fore, low like prehistoric creatures around him. It's one of the highpoints of the whole week.

There are moments on both sets when individual horn voices come to the fore: Braxton's attractive quaver, Fei's pinched, haunted tone, Parran's extremes of pitch. However, it's probably best to stop searching out who is playing what and to concentrate on the totality of these remarkable performances. Writer Steve Days spins out a complicated conceit in his liner-notes, aligning this group with the *Birth Of The Cool* band and Braxton's new music with Miles Davis's innovations of the '50s. Temperamentally, it's probably difficult to imagine two musicians further apart, but it's clear that Miles has become an important resource and quiddity for Braxton in the later '90s and Day's analysis, lateral as it is, ends up absolutely on the money.

Four big pieces, then, played by a biggish group that had the luxury of a whole week to explore this language. The music whirls and winds, unravels ideas only to wrap them up knottily tight again. It's hard to avoid the impression on 'Composition 207' that you're not listening to music but moving inside it.

*** Two Compositions (Trio) 1998

Leo LRCD 327/328 2CD *Braxton; Chris Jonas, Seth Misterka, Jackson Moore, David Novak (sax, etc).* 4/98.

Two separate trios here: Braxton students Jonas and Novak on the first disc and 'Composition 227', the rather more experienced Moore and Misterka on the other, consecutively numbered piece. Performance at Wesleyan has become a regular source of Braxton recordings and these are no more than routine documentations, without much sense of moment or theatre. The range of sounds is, as ever, enormous, from the lowest-pitched saxophones to flute (on which Braxton is uncharacteristically fluttery), from celesta to a strange 'tourist instrument' Novak seems to have picked up in Indonesia. The level of detail is extraordinary but, on the first disc at least, there is little of the pulse and swing one expects from a Braxton performance.

(★★★) Compositions No. 10 & No. 16 (+101)

hatNOW 108 *Braxton; Guillermo Gregorio (as, cl); Gene Coleman (bcl); Jim O'Rourke (g, elec); Michael Cameron (b); Carrie Biolo (vib, perc).* 98.

Not strictly a Braxton record, but a repertory performance of two impotant pieces. 'No. 10' is actually given two separate readings, one dramatically longer than the other, which probably counts as an improvisational 'take', except that the mood here is abstract and somewhat academic, despite the personalities of the performers. Gregorio has a paper-dry tone, not dissimilar to Braxton's and is a proficient technician. It's not likeable music, though and most Braxton fans can overlook it.

★★(★) Four Compositions (Washington, DC) 1998

Braxton House BH 009 *Braxton; Taylor Bynum (t, flhn); Joe Fielder (tb); Chris Olness (btb); Anita Miller (frhn); Chris Washburne (tba); Rob Brown (f); Brandon Evans (sno, c mel, ts, f, bcl); James Fei (ss, as, bcl); Jackson Moor (as, cl); Chris Jonas (ss, as, ts) Richard McGee (ss); Seth Misterka (as); J. D. Parran (ss, bs); Andre Vida (as, ts, bs); Yosuke Oshima (ob); Rafael Cohen (eng hn); David Novak (bsn, cbsn); Eric Ronick (p); Pete Cafarella (acc); Kevin O'Neil (g); Rachel Thompson (vn); Jonathan Zorn (acc, b); Joe Fonda (b); Kevin Norton (perc).* 5/98.

Braxton conducts, adds some unusual sonorities (including F saxophone), and basically curates the now familiar admixture of massive structural hubris, occasional sweetness and overall confusion. Some of the ensemble playing is so erratic that one genuinely has to wonder how accurately performances like these reflect the composer's intentions and to what extent Braxton's followers are now hypnotized by the procession of opus numbers.

★★★ Four Compositions (GTM) 2000

Delmark 544 *Braxton; Kevin Uehlinger (p, melodica); Keith Witty (b); Noah Schatz (perc).* 00.

★★★ Four Compositions (GTM) 2000

CIMP 235 *As above.* 00.

GTM, of course, refers to Ghost Trance Music, Braxton's radical improvisational philosophy which utilizes a highly restricted range of materials in a seemingly infinite number of ways. To what extent these pieces are 'compositions' – numbers 242 to 245 on the Delmark, 280 to 283 on the rawer sounding CIMP – in any recognizable sense is conjectural. The impression given by the Ghost Trance Music sequence is of a vast body of pre-existent music examined from the inside by any number of idiosyncratic performers, each of whom brings personal and musical baggage and a time-specific understanding of the basic code. This could be universalism of the most flabbily mystical sort, were not the discipline of a Braxton performance not so rigorous. His fellow players here are not *naïfs*, but they bring a fresh and uncomplicated perspective to both dates. The Delmark recording interestingly brings the story round almost full circle to 1968's *Three Compositions Of New Jazz.* What an extraordinary musical road Braxton has travelled since then. (As a footnote, helpful as are personnel numbers and dates, there is an inevitable confusion about nomenclature in the Braxton discography. These sets are a good illustration.)

★★★★ Solo (NYC) 2002

Parallactic 53 *Braxton (as solo).* 02.

A generation after *For Alto*, and for all his experimentation with larger ensembles and orchestras, Braxton is still often most compelling when playing alto saxophone solo. This set has a familiar configuration: 12 compositions from all over his career, plus three 'standards'. It's with them that the main interest lies. Braxton has shown an increasing interest in Miles Davis's legacy in recent years and 'Tune Up' is a case in point, a spikier and more academic reading than Miles would have considered possible or desirable, but recognizable and utterly convincing. He makes more of a statement on Ornette's 'Peace', which seems to expose some of the song's naivety, but saves his most profound meditations for a titanic exploration of 'Body And Soul'. Sceptics who think it was mined hollow before Coleman Hawkins hung up his saxophone should listen and think again. A wonderful record, and a salutary reminder that Braxton is an alto man through and through, in the mixed lineage of Hodges, Parker, Desmond and Dolphy.

★(★) Four Compositions (Duets) 2000

CIMP 235 *Braxton; Alex Horowitz (v).* 10/00.

We honestly haven't a clue what this one is about. A series of 15 brief improvisations (the liner only lists half a dozen 'compositions') which act as accompaniments to the 'comic' readings and monologues of Alex Horowitz. He is neither subversive, provocative, nor (most heinous of all) funny or entertaining. There may be some curiosity value for devoted Braxton collectors, but your dollars would be better spent. On almost anything.

★★★(★) Ten Compositions (Quartet) 2000

CIMP 225 *Braxton; Kevin O'Neil (g); Andy Eulau (b); Kevin Norton (d).* 5/00.

★★★(★) Nine Compositions (Hill) 2000

CIMP 236 *Braxton; Paul Smoker (t); Steve Lehman (as); Kevin O'Neil (g); Andy Eulau (b); Kevin Norton (d).* 5/00.

These are two of the most interesting repertoire projects Braxton has ever undertaken. The second album is dedicated entirely to work by Andrew Hill, most of it drawn from his classic Blue Note period; but Hill also dominates the first record, with six compositions covered there as well. Braxton and his (pianoless) group respond to the dark sonorities and restless rhythmic probing of tunes like 'Black Monday' 'The Griots' (both on CIMP 225) and 'New Monasery', 'Euterpe' and 'Tail Feather' (236). Braxton restricts himself to relatively conventional instrumentation, just alto, with flute and soprano on the two records respectively.

The addition of extra horns on the second album is a considerable bonus. Smoker has shown himself to be a sympathetic partner before, and his take on Hill is as interesting as the leader's, though Steve Lehman does little more than fill. The presence of a guitar player gives the harmonic language a looser and more open aspect, and O'Neil is a key performer throughout this three-day project which helped round out an astonishingly busy period for Braxton at Wesleyan, with countless hours of music put on tape during May alone.

★★★ 8 Compositions (Quintet) 2001
CIMP 243 *Braxton; Richard A. McGhee III (ss, ts, f); Abubakar Alvin Benjamin Carter Sr, Babafemi Alvin, Benjamin Carter Jr, Sipho Robert Bellinger (perc).* 3/01.

This, as with much of CIMP's output, is an extremely dry and slightly forbidding set. The lack of any acoustic sweetening and any manipulation beyond the careful placement of the five players with horns bracketing the trio of percussionists, makes it a demanding listen as a continuous performance. Best, we've found, to take it a track at a time and let the rigorous complexities of 'Compositions 293' and '299' work in their own time, and the simpler beauties of '296', with the lowest of the clarinet family and the huskily delicate flute, exert a more immediate charm. It is worth spending time with these recordings. They do not yield up their power at a single, casual sitting.

★★(★) Composition No. 247
Leo CDLR 306 *Braxton; James Fei (ss, as, bcl); Matthew Welch (bagpipes).* 5/00.

★★(★) Composition No. 169 + (186 + 206 + 214)
Leo CDLR 320 321 *Braxton; James Fei (ss, as, bcl); Chris Jonas (ss); Slovenia Radio Orchestra.* 6/00.

It would be tickling to report that Braxton had diversified his instrumentation yet again to include the bagpipes, but such duties are devolved to Matthew Welch and it is he who determines the range of this piece, another of Braxton's Ghost Trance Music projects. As the Scottish half of the *Guide* team could explain through gritted teeth (an emotional response to teenage memories rather than a physiological symptom), the pipes offer a very limited range of notes, and these are the basis of a long, repetitive motif which becomes the backbone for an hour of technically demanding, psychologically wearing music. The two other reed players execute some complex manoeuvres, often at a high level of rhythmic complexity, but the overall impression is one-dimensional and rather static. One wonders how much Highland *piobreachd* Braxton has listened to and how much a composer of his instincts might draw from it. Welch is also the performer on a set of ten bagpipe compositions by Braxton, released on the Parallactic label. *247* suggests some development of the possibilities inscribed on that record but fulfils them only in the most limited way.

Divided over two CDs, *Composition No. 169 + …* is more impressive than genuinely enjoyable. Braxton's liner-note is tediously convoluted and self-defining, and one really wonders whether anyone but the composer himself has any idea what is going on. And yet, that is what they have always said about Ornette Coleman, and his place in the history of the music is almost as problematically secure. Braxton's orchestral language is clotted and murky; the three saxophonists weave some interesting patterns and ideas, but the whole experience is somewhat alienating and unapproachable.

★★★ Composition No. 249
Parallactic 27 *Braxton; Brandon Evans (C ss, Bb ss, ts, bs, cl, bcl, f).* 00.

★★(★) Elliptical Axis 15
Parallactic 28-30 3CD *As above; additional instruments.* 5/00.

★★★ Compositions/Improvisations 2000
Barely Auditable 222 *Braxton; Scott Rosenberg (sno, as, ts, cl, cbcl).* 00.

Much of the music Braxton released in the later '90s was from his Ghost Trance idiom. This group of duet records immediately strikes a contrast, because once again Braxton sounds propulsive and directed, and once again has focused on the idiomatic possibilities of his admittedly preposterous range of instruments. Evans is a Braxton acolyte who shares his mentor's ambition. Strictly credited to him, *Elliptical Axis 15* amounts to almost 165 minutes of music, distributed over three CDs, and all of it delivered on a range of exotic saxophones, including the F soprano and the C melody, clarinets and flutes. Impressive as it is in sheer technical virtuosity, we can say with some sureness that you are unlikely to revisit the whole performance a second time.

Braxton's *Composition No. 249* is a less wearying experience. At less than an hour, it is manageable and logical and the interplay of voices has more direct moment. Evans's work seems like an exercise in parallelism rather than a genuine dialectic. The delivery is also a little crisper all round.

In point of fact, only three very short tracks on *Compositions/Improvisations 2000* are freely improvised, and much of the weight of composition falls to Rosenberg, another Braxton disciple and a very impressive instrumentalist. There are moments here when one might be listening to the master multi-tracked, so sympathetic a collaborator is the younger man. Where Rosenberg differs from Evans is that he seems more obviously rooted in jazz idiom, an anchor that allows him to range even wider musically.

★★★ Eight Standards (Wesleyan) 2001
Barking Hoop 004 *Braxton; Kevin O'Neil (g); Andy Eulau (b); Kevin Norton (d).* 01.

We're increasingly perturbed by Braxton's forays into standards. He often doesn't appear to treat the original theme with much respect, certainly as far as intonation and articulation are concerned, but always manages to find fascinating things to say and do. The choice of material here is quite unexpected: Django Reinhardt's 'Nuages' can rarely have been treated quite so searchingly, while 'Someday My Prince Will Come' is both true to and a light-year away from the Miles Davis version. Much credit here has to go to Norton, a formidable drummer but also the demiurge of Barking Hoop records, and to guitarist O'Neil, who is the most interesting player on the set: committed, intense and fiery on the Django theme, thoughtful and even introspective elsewhere. See if you spot the moment when he almost pulls off a Wes Montgomery octave run under one of Braxton's most unfettered lines.

★★★ Duets (Wesleyan) 2002
Innova 6576 *Braxton; Taylor Ho Bynum (co, t, slide t).* 02.

If you want to confirm the genius of, say, Jackson Pollock, check out some of the forgeries that have been fraudulently attributed to him. If you want to confirm the extraordinary order and discipline of Anthony Braxton's sound-world, check out the hideously chaotic 'improvisation' that nestles unwanted in the midst of this otherwise compelling record. Unusually, in addition to his own pieces, 'Compositions 304/305', Braxton here addresses the work of another composer, and not a standards composer either. Bynum is a Wesleyan pupil of the saxophonist's; his playing style is reminiscent of Joe McPhee's brass; 'Scrabble' might mean the word game rather than the physical activity, and there is a good deal of language improvisation in both players' unusually vocalized tones; 'All Roads Lead To

Middletown' sounds like a throwback. The real value of the set lies in 'Composition No. 305 (+ Language Improvisation 44)', which moves beyond the whirls and four-dimensional spirals of Ghost Trance Music, and back into something spikier, more boppish and in many respects more engaging. How interesting it should happen in the presence of one of his own students.

Joshua Breakstone (born 1955)

GUITAR

Studied at Berklee and then followed a neoclassical path, playing open-toned electric guitar in a conventional bop format.

*****(*) Let's Call This Monk!**
Double-Time DTRCD-121 *Breakstone; Dennis Irwin (b); Mickey Roker (d).* 12/96.

***** This Just In ...**
Double-Time DTRCD-149 *Breakstone; Sid Simmons (p); Dennis Irwin (b); Kenny Washington (d).* 2/99.

***** The Music Of Bud Powell**
Double-Time DTRCD-172 *Breakstone; Earl Sauls (b); Keith Copeland (d).* 6/00.

Breakstone loves the sound of traditional jazz guitar, as in cool, clear, single-note lines delivered with a soft articulation and a tone that insinuates rather than jumps out of his amplifier. He can peel melodies off the frets with little effort, but sometimes his manner is so relaxed that his improvisations go to sleep; with impeccable but deferential rhythm sections on many of his records, that's a small but significant problem.

The discography has taken a bit of a pasting of late. The surprise record in the batch is *Let's Call This Monk!*. Breakstone and Monk may not have much in common, but the lean aspects of the guitarist's style sit comfortably with the ten Monk tunes on display here. Breakstone picks some of the toughest and least tractable tunes from the book – 'Work', 'Let's Call This', 'Brilliant Corners' – and plays them with a kind of deadpan bite that makes one hear the material afresh. Irwin and Roker make an immaculate team, and their unfussy and tersely swinging style suits the occasion perfectly.

This Just In ... is a perfectly plausible continuation but, with so much else going on with the guitar in jazz at present, Breakstone may need to do something startling to gain the attention of new listeners. This is another pacific set of bop material (he even starts with 'Bebop' itself), played skilfully and painlessly. And so is *The Music Of Bud Powell*, though with no piano in the line-up at least Breakstone puts himself under pressure to deliver. Powell's awkward emotions are absent, inevitably, although in his sleevenote the guitarist points out the difference between playful Bud ('Comin' Up') and difficult Bud ('Tempus Fugit'). Solid enough.

***** Tomorrow's Hours**
Capri 74054 *Breakstone; Earl Sauls (b); Keith Copeland (d).* 02.

After Bud Powell, a more obvious source of material for a guitarist. However, Wes Montgomery's more obvious stuff ('Bumpin'', for instance) isn't covered here and apart from a few giveaway octave runs there isn't much to suggest the great one's legacy. In fact, and perhaps encouragingly, the best track on the album is the sole Breakstone original, the title-track, a swinging, delicately balanced idea that the trio despatches with great aplomb. Wes tunes like 'Doujie', 'Jingles' and 'Missile Blues' aren't the most memorable in the canon and one ends the album concluding that, superb player though he was, Montgomery was a bit of a slouch in the composition stakes.

Michael Brecker (born 1949)

TENOR SAXOPHONE, EWI

One of the most admired and emulated saxophonists in contemporary jazz. He began playing in rock and soul bands in the late '60s, worked with Horace Silver and Billy Cobham in the '70s and put together the very successful Steps Ahead group in 1979. His work as a session-man has polished his style into something superbly confident and muscular, a Coltrane without the questing inner turmoil. After many years as a superleague sideman, he finally began making discs under his own name in 1987, and has only infrequently chosen to continue that regimen.

***** Michael Brecker**
GRP 050113-2 *Brecker; Kenny Kirkland (ky); Pat Metheny (g); Charlie Haden (b); Jack DeJohnette (d).* 87.

****(*) Don't Try This At Home**
GRP 050114-2 *Brecker; Don Grolnick, Herbie Hancock, Joey Calderazzo (p); Mark O'Connor (vn); Mike Stern (g); Charlie Haden, Jeff Andrews (b); Jack DeJohnette, Adam Nussbaum, Peter Erskine (d).* 88.

The sax-playing one of the Brecker brothers has appeared on some 500 record dates but has still made only a handful of discs as sole leader. His steely, brilliant sense of structure ensures that almost every solo he plays is impressive; whether he is emotionally involving may depend on the listener's willingness to believe.

Michael Brecker, his 1987 debut, suggested that he had been unreasonably shy about recording as a leader. His own compositions, 'Sea Glass' and 'Syzygy', are attractive if not exactly haunting, while producer Don Grolnick's tunes elicit some suitably herculean solos. The interplay with DeJohnette inevitably recalls something of the Coltrane–Elvin Jones partnership, while Kirkland, Haden and the unusually restrained Metheny combine to create a super-session of genuine commitment. But *Don't Try This At Home* seemed like a too casual follow-up, with several of the pieces sounding like left-overs from the first session, and Brecker cruising through the record in his session-man identity rather than imposing a leader's presence.

***** Now You See It ... (Now You Don't)**
GRP 9622 *Brecker; Jim Beard, Joey Calderazzo (ky); Jon Herington (g); Victor Bailey, Jay Anderson (b); Adam Nussbaum, Omar Hakim (d); Don Alias, Steve Berrios, Milton Cardona (perc).* 90.

Brecker's third record as a leader is a mixed success. Too few of the eight themes are truly memorable or demanding on anything other than a technical level, and some of the synthesizer orchestration is a distraction rather than a benefit. The best jazz comes in the tracks where the saxophonist gets a clear run at the listener: on 'Peep', which turns into a kind of abstract funk, and 'The Meaning Of The Blues', which is unadorned tenor-plus-rhythm. The slow intensification of the saxophonist's improvisation on 'Minsk' is the one moment when Brecker best displays his mastery. Don Grolnick's production is snappy and clean without being as glaring as many fusion records.

***** Tales From The Hudson**

Impulse! 051191-2 *Brecker; Joey Calderazzo, McCoy Tyner (p); Pat Metheny (g); Dave Holland (b); Jack DeJohnette (d); Don Alias (perc).* 96.

***** Two Blocks From The Edge**

Impulse! 051261-2 *Brecker; Joey Calderazzo (p); James Genus (b); Jeff Tain Watts (d); Don Alias (perc).* 98.

Brecker continues to be sparing with his own records. These two are rewarding on their own terms without throwing out a masterpiece. The leader contributes several themes to *Tales From The Hudson* but only three to *Two Blocks From The Edge*, and he seems little interested in composing. There's the expected quota of hard-nosed tenor playing on each disc, and he varies his methods from solo to solo. 'African Skies' on the first is an explosive display of licks, while gentler tempos elicit a longer line. Ballads, though, still seem carved out of an impersonal block, and his reluctance to characterize remains a source of frustration. There's another all-star feel to *Hudson*, with Tyner sitting in on two tracks, but the smaller and less imposing group on *Two Blocks* is really a better situation for Brecker; he can play powerfully without seeming to compete. Enough moments of excitement on both to satisfy his followers, of whom there are many.

*****(*) Time Is Of The Essence**

Verve 547844-2 *Brecker; Larry Goldings (org); Pat Metheny (g); Elvin Jones, Jeff Tain Watts, Bill Stewart (d). n.d.*

Brecker has fronted some fine bands before, and the three different quartets on this disc – each distinguished by a different drummer – are at least as strong as any of them. He chose Larry Goldings as Larry Goldings, rather than as an organ-player for the date, and with Metheny digging into his funky rather than impressionist bag, the results are only occasionally like the world's highest-paid bar band. As a mix of personalities, it's a blend worth sampling, but the main effect may be on Brecker himself. At 50, he was relaxing perhaps as much as he would ever let himself. Chord-sequences are harvested for notes as intensively as ever, but one feels that Brecker wants to throttle back now at moments when he might have gone for broke before. The warm undertow of Goldings's chords and pedal bass and the lyricism of Metheny (however harsh he might want to be, Pat is always going to sound fundamentally lyrical) add up to a disc which, for all its muscle-flexing, a sympathetic listener can almost cosy up to.

***** Nearness Of You: The Ballad Book**

Verve 011030-2 *Brecker; Herbie Hancock (p); Pat Metheny (g); Charlie Haden (b); Jack De Johnette (d); James Taylor (v).* 00.

Brecker's ballad record has the feel of superstars idling in a departure lounge. The most expensive jazz group on Earth (give or take a Marsalis or two) purrs through some standards and pop. Michael's never going to wear his heart on his sleeve, so only on the title-piece, groomed to a fault, does he get close to what could be called feelings. Otherwise, as well played as it obviously is, the music reminds of the romantic interlude in a Jean-Claude Van Damme film – it's only going to get exciting when somebody gets thumped.

***** Wide Angles**

Verve 7614288 *Brecker; Alex Sipiagin (t); Peter Gordon (flhn); Robin Eubanks (tb); Steve Wilson (f, af); Iain Dixon (cl, bcl); Charles Pillow (ob); Mark Feldman, Joyce Hammann (vn); Lois Martin (vla): Erik Friedlander (clo); Adam Rogers (g); John Patitucci (b); Antonio Sanchez (d); Daniel Sadownick (perc).* 1/03.

Brecker's Quindectet work through arrangements by Gil Goldstein, although they're used mostly as vehicles for the saxophonist, who understandably hogs most of the solo limelight. As so often with Brecker, the admirability quotient is high, the warmth uncomfortably low. But he does have a big problem: when you can play anything you want, with anyone you want, what exactly is there to do? The star–sideman rating is relatively low here, and Goldstein has picked the best executants, yet Brecker still feels isolated by his very eminence, and that tells in the music.

Randy Brecker (born 1945)

TRUMPET

The older Brecker sibling left college to go on the road, stayed in Europe for a time, and then returned home to join R&B giants Blood, Sweat And Tears. Unlike Michael, who has devoted himself to a post-Coltrane idiom, Randy still likes to dabble in fusion. He has recorded surprisingly little under his own name.

***** Score**

Koch 51416 *Brecker; Jerry Dodgion (as, f); Michael Brecker (ts); Hal Galper (p); Larry Coryell (g); Eddie Gomez, Chuck Rainey (b); Mickey Roker, Bernard Purdie (d).* 1–2/69.

Recently reissued, Randy's debut album is an amazingly confident and polished effort, devised to demonstrate his skill in both jazz and more popular settings. Unlike most other trumpeters in the field, Brecker has never remotely sounded like a Miles clone. If anything, his tonality comes from Dizzy and Freddie Hubbard, and both influences are still in place today, even though he has developed a strongly individual voice along the way. *Score* features two basic groups but is remarkably consistent in feel. The tone is light and seemingly effortless, with occasional outbreaks of more heated improvisation, though these tend to be short-circuited. Where even the 19-year-old Michael digs deep, Randy tends to tire of an idea before it climaxes naturally. Boldly, the whole set – with the exception of the kids' song 'The Weasel Goes Out To Lunch' – is original material. The elegant Galper contributes three tunes, 'Name Game', 'The Vamp' and the title-track, and is a model of easy swing throughout. Randy's Hubbardisms are evident almost every time he solos, but he already sounds like an original voice.

***** Into The Sun**

Concord Vista CCD 4761-2 *Brecker; Dave Bargeron (tb); David Taylor (btb, tba); David Sanborn (as); Bob Mintzer (bcl); Keith Underwood (af, bf); Lawrence Feldman (bf); Gil Goldstein (ky); Adam Rogers (g); Bakithi Kumalo (b); Jonathan Joseph (d); Café (perc); Maúcha Adnét (v); Richard Sussman (syn prog).* 97.

Unlike his younger brother, who has stayed true to post-bop jazz, Randy has experimented widely in more popular forms. That spirit surfaces on *Into The Sun*. 'The Sleaze Factor' and

'Just Between Us' are the strongest tracks, relying on a careful integration of parts and on strong, concise soloing. One quality Brecker does share with Miles is an ability to make single notes and tiny phrases stand out and represent much. The album depends largely on subtle colorations from an unusual array of horns, mostly favouring lower pitches.

**** Hanging In The City**

ESC 4902 *Brecker; Michael Brecker (ts); George Whitty (ky); Joe Locke (vib); Dean Brown, Hiram Bullock, Joe Caro, Adam Rogers (g); Richard Bona, Christian Minh Doky (b); Will Lee (b, v); Don Alias (perc); Katreese Barnes (v).* 01.

Dear God! What is going on here? Brecker abandons his usual approach, adopts the persona 'Randroid' and raps boastfully about his colourful love life. Mercifully, there is some more than decent playing from a typically strong band who seem eager to maintain regular output, but a few moments – notably 'Then I Came 2 My Senses' – will have you reaching for the sleeve just to make sure. Whenever the trumpet cuts in, you can relax and say Yup, *that* Randy Brecker. But it's not always so obvious. Crisply produced and packaged, it may well win Randy a whole new cohort of fans. We liked the instrumentals but, apart from that: Hey, Randy, *too* much information, man.

****(*) 34th N Lex**

ESC 03684 2 *Brecker; Michael Davis, Fred Wesley (tb); David Sanborn (as); Michael Brecker, Ada Rovatti (ts); Ronnie Cuber (bs); George Whitty (ky); Adam Rogers, Chris Taylor (g); Christian Minh Doky, Gary Haase (b); Clarence Penn (d); Makeeba Mooncycle, J. Phoenix (v).* 5/02.

It would be nice to report that this was a return to form. It is certainly more obviously a jazz record, with some fine soloing from the guests, but it lacks urgency and never really commands attention the way a player of Brecker's quality should. 'Tokyo Freddie' is a tribute to his old mentor Freddie Hubbard, who made the opposite mistake and went for broke too often and too quickly. By the time it comes along, though, the album is almost over and Randy still hasn't imprinted himself on it. The title-track kicks things off promisingly, but it is the peerless Ronnie Cuber (still one of the finest ever exponents of the big horn) who wins the laurels. Michael is in his usual unshakable form, but David Sanborn glides through his spots as if he were playing in a hotel.

There is probably an enormous market for jazz of this stamp. It is expert enough to interest more demanding fans (though disillusion surely lurks) and certainly smooth enough for wallpaper. It really isn't clear whether Randy has tired of the jazz life – he has after all been doing this full time for decades – or whether he feels he's exploring new genres and crossovers. By our mark, a disappointment either way.

The Brecker Brothers

GROUP

Michael and Randy Brecker began working as co-bandleaders in 1975 and scored some very successful albums before they choose to disband the group in 1982. They re-formed as an occasional recording and touring collaboration in the '90s.

***** The Brecker Brothers**

Arista 74321 22103-2 *Randy Brecker (t, flhn); Michael Brecker (ss, ts); David Sanborn (as); Don Grolnick (ky); Bob Mann (g); Will Lee (b); Harvey Mason (d); Ralph MacDonald (perc).* 1/75.

***** Detente**

Arista 74321 31313-2 *As above, except add Steve Khan, Hiram Bullock (g), Steve Gadd (d); omit Sanborn, Mann, Mason.* 77.

***** Heavy Metal Be-Bop**

Arista 74321 19257-2 *Randy Brecker (t, ky); Michael Brecker (ss, ts); Barry Finnerty (g); Neil Jason (b); Terry Bozzio (d); Sammy Figueroa, Rafael Cruz (perc).* 78.

***** Straphangin'**

Arista 74321 31312-2 *Randy Brecker (t, flhn); Michael Brecker (ss, ts); Mary Gray (ky); Barry Finnerty (g); Marcus Miller (b); Richie Morales (d); Sammy Figueroa, Manolo Badrena (perc).* 81.

***** The Brecker Brothers Collection Vol. 1**

RCA ND 90442 *As above Arista discs.* 75–81.

***** The Brecker Brothers Collection Vol. 2**

RCA ND 83076 *As above.* 75–81.

*****(*) Priceless Jazz Collection**

GRP 059948-2 *Randy Brecker (t, flhn); Michael Brecker (ss, ts); David Sanborn (as); Robbie Kilgore, George Whitty, Dean Brown, Mike Stern (g); James Genus, Will Lee, Armand Sabal-Leco (b); Steve Jordan, Max Risenhoover, Dennis Chambers (d); Steve Thornton, Don Alias (perc). n.d.*

***** Return Of The Brecker Brothers**

GRP 059684-2 *Similar to above. n.d.*

***** Out Of The Loop**

GRP 059784-2 *Similar to above. n.d.*

The most popular fusion band of their era: where Weather Report were Zawinul's electro-impressionists, the Breckers were a playing band, overloaded with chops but often creating music of drilled excitement. Michael Brecker, the foremost technician of his era, was a soloist of ferocious power, and the essentially more lyrical Randy made a sometimes piquant contrast to his brother, although that comes through more effectively on their GRP albums. The Arista material will be nostalgic for many who return to it in the CD era: dog-eared copies of the original vinyl must still sit on the dustier shelves of former followers of the style. These records are usually dated by their wah-wah guitars and rhythm sections, which sometimes sound as if they're trying to play a sort of muscle-bound disco music. But a lot of the original excitement remains. Some of the freshness went out of their albums as they neared the end of the band's original life, but the insuperable skills of the players persist, and both the Breckers were seeking a genuine musical result, rather than the confections of smooth jazz. We're grading all the albums the same because, despite any differences in style, they really do all emerge in much the same way. Either of the two RCA collections is a good bet for the curious.

After individual success during the '80s, the Breckers decided to get together again for occasional recording projects. The 1992 *Return* traded slightly more on atmosphere than on punch and made deeper use of studio resources; but most will recognize it all as business as usual, continued on *Out Of The Loop*. But the mid-price *Priceless Jazz Collection*, which is effectively a cheap best-of covering the two GRP discs, is the best single way to put the BBs on your shelf. Some of these CD editions are getting pretty long in the tooth now, but they continue to hold their place in the catalogue: a tribute, perhaps, to the Breckers' enduring fanbase.

Buddy Bregman

COMPOSER, ARRANGER

Bregman worked in Hollywood in the '50s, mostly accompanying and arranging for singers such as Bing Crosby, but he made several records in a contemporary big-band idiom for Verve.

★★★(★) Swinging Kicks

Verve 559514-2 *Conte Candoli, Maynard Ferguson, Ray Linn, Pete Candoli, Conrad Gozzo (t); Milt Bernhart, George Roberts, Frank Rosolino, Lloyd Ulyate (tb); Herb Geller, Bud Shank (as); Georgie Auld, Bob Cooper, Ben Webster, Stan Getz (ts); Jimmy Giuffre (bs); André Previn, Paul Smith (p); Al Hendrickson (g); Joe Mondragon (b); Stan Levey, Alvin Stoller (d).* 12/56.

Bregman is a kibitzer in jazz history, but his few Verve dates as a leader are great fun and this one has kept its sparkle. Seventeen tracks, many of them not even broaching the two-minute barrier, offer tiny episodes of West Coast jazz at its wittiest. The group is split into big-band, quartet, quintet, sextet and septet formations, and the record ends on a duet for Ben Webster and André Previn! 'Mulliganville' is a clever take on the saxophonist's œuvre, 'Terror Ride' seems pretty mild, and elsewhere there are good opportunities for Conte Candoli, Shank and Rosolino to have their say. Getz makes one imperious appearance on 'Honey Chile'. Remastered with superb crispness, and the period cover shot is intact.

John Wolf Brennan

PIANO, KEYBOARDS, ELECTRONICS, COMPOSER

An Irishman who has been based on the continent for many years, Brennan has an utterly distinctive touch at the keyboard and is the composer of complex but intensely beautiful themes which are almost impossible to locate stylistically.

★★★ Text, Context, Co-Text, Co-Co-Text

Creative Works CW 1025 *Brennan (p solo).* 94.

A broodingly thoughtful album containing music as imaginatively self-referential as the title might suggest. Almost every piece seems to be a meditation on its own origins, tightly wrapped into one or two basically simple ideas. There is one piece for prepared piano, deployed intelligently and with great feeling. It comes a little unexpectedly in the middle of the session, which one finds oneself listening to almost in a trance. Delightful music for the mind and the heart.

★★★ Moskau-Petuschki/Felix-Szenen

Leo Lab CD 034 *Brennan; Lars Lindvall (t, flhn); Martin Mayes (hn, v); Marion Namestnik, Tscho Theissing (vn); Daniele Patumi (b); Oscar Bingisser, Liana Schwanja (v).* 7/94, 6/95.

Two superb theatre-pieces inspired by the work of Wenedikt Jerofejew and Robert Walser respectively, *Moskau-Petuschki* and *Felix-Szenen* take Brennan a further step along the road. Jerofejew was an alcoholic who wrote only incidentally, and yet his work has a dreamed magnificence one would simply not find in a writer more literary and aware. Brennan's 'micromonotonal' poem is broodingly beautiful, not so much intense as highly focused, with the heightened perception one might associate with drunkenness (the poet's, not the composer's!).

We find the Walser material less immediately compelling, a somewhat different sound-world despite the similarity of instrumentation – violin, trumpet, piano and bass, as against violin, horn, piano and bass for the Jerofejew piece – and a more openly expressive setting that lacks the prismatic exactness of the earlier piece.

★★★★ The Well Tempered Clavier

Creative Works 1012 *Brennan (p, prepared p solo); Marianne Schroeder (p).* 5/97.

Aside from a brief appearance by the magnificent Schroeder, this is a solo performance and a superb representation of Brennan's extraordinary pianism. There are tributes to both Henry Cowell and John Cage, two of the inspirations behind Brennan's extended technique. There are a number of studies for prepared piano here, coming in sequence in the middle of the session, and they are in some respects definitive of Brennan's attempt to synthesize melody, mathematics and a kind of musical materialism that renders sound insignificant of anything other than itself. If that sounds an increasingly abstract exercise, don't forget that melody is at the beginning and end of it. Also included on the album is a fulsome tribute to the late Russian genius Sergey Kuryokhin, and a wonderful thing called 'Rump-L-Rumba (7/4 for Five Hands)', which is (almost) self-explanatory. A wonderful record.

★★★★ ... Through The Ear Of A Raindrop

Leo CD LR 254 *Brennan; Paul Rutherford (tb); Evan Parker (ts, ss); Peter Whyman (bcl); Chris Cutler (d, perc); Julie Tippetts (v).* 7/97.

And, at last, the record we always knew he would make: a rich and vividly textured marriage of poetry – Shakespeare, Poe, Heaney, Paulin and Paula Meehan, together with a poem by Julie Tippetts – and instruments. The three horns blend together wonderfully and unexpectedly, with Parker working in the quieter and less abrasive style that he occasionally brings to vocal accompaniments. Rutherford is a poet himself and is constantly responsive to the cadence and fall of words. Here he surpasses himself. Someone somewhere down the line should consider prising Julie away from home and a long-standing duo with the old man and getting her to record a duo set with Brennan. He seems the ideal foil, the perfect yin–yang partner for her own wonderful synthesis of the everyday and the magical. On every track here they have things to communicate to one another, and the lilt and flow of Brennan's piano playing is endlessly attractive.

★★★(★) Momentum

Leo CD LR 274 *Brennan; Gene Coleman (bcl, melodica); Christian Wolfarth (perc).* 10/98.

★★★ Momentum 2: The Laws Of Refraction

Leo CD LR 296 *As above, except add Alfred Zimmerlin (clo).* 10/99.

★★★ Momentum 3

Leo CD LR 355 *As above, except omit Coleman and Zimmerlin; add Bertrand Denzler (ts); Christian Weber (b).* 01.

Momentum is a wonderfully confected group and a great outlet for Brennan's distinctive approach. His prepared-piano sounds are very different from those deployed by, say, Keith Tippett; their strangeness is more unsettling. The first album kicks off wonderfully. In conjunction with percussion and then with bass clarinet on 'Robots Don't Cough' and 'Poco Loco', Brennan takes you into a realm which is almost beyond human music; if the record has a running theme, it is the disjunction between the human and the machine – even a machine as familiar as the piano and as humanely vocalized as the melodica. Wonderful stuff again from the Irishman.

The second album is not quite as unearthly. Whether the music really is an attempt to articulate principles of refraction in sound is a moot point and shouldn't distract the listener. The addition of cello gives a richer and, in a curious way, a more percussive sonority to the group. 'Simple Harmonic Motion' and the long 'Standing Wave' are the best tracks on an album that wanders a bit, but which comes across with more energy and heat than the first.

The defection of Coleman was a disappointment and his bass clarinet sound is missed on the third album. However, Brennan has attempted to keep the same basic instrumentation, Weber's bass being played with a lightness and speed that suggests cello. The track titles spell out the word 'syntegration', presumably a hybrid of 'synthesis' and 'integration'. The group members seem intent on each other's speech, listening almost politely and perhaps too consciously avoiding the log-jams of sound that mar some improvised music. On the other hand, the ear sometimes craves a bit more activity and a bit more detail.

****** Flugel**

Creative Works 1037 *Brennan (p solo).* 11/98–1/02.

Brennan returns to the solo vein he explored on *The Well Tempered Clavier*, but with a new confidence and richness of sound. This is intended as a further episode in a grand cycle of piano works and if the quality is maintained it will be one of the most important cycles of its kind in the modern repertoire. *Flugel* is of course the German term for grand piano, but Brennan typically reads it in a more expressive and metaphoric vein as well. Again the titles refer to scientific ideas ('String Theory') or make gentle puns ('You Can't Be Sirius!'), but this time there is a pair of meditations on medieval hymns and one can see Brennan moving further and more boldly in this direction. His technique is jaw-droppingly assured and wonderfully delicate with little of the bravura hammering that afflicts most post-Cecil Taylor piano improvisers.

*****(*) Zero Heroes**

Leo CD LR 373 *Brennan; Peggy Lee (clo); Dylan Van der Schyff (d, perc).* 3/02.

Similar in many respects to the language of *Momentum*, but with yet another fresh new dimension in the wonderful cello playing of Peggy Lee. She is the key element in this set of light and almost skitting improvisations. Brennan is his normal astute and puckish self and Van der Schyff is much more than a third wheel and much more than a colourist. He gives many of the pieces, which are of fairly uniform length and longer than usual for Brennan, a cast-iron structure and logic. Our only hesitation is that the album suffers from a touch *too* much uniformity overall. Further testimony, though, to Brennan's remarkable imaginative scope.

Patrick Brennan (born 1954)

ALTO SAXOPHONE

Detroit-born Brennan won Cadence and Coda accolades with his very first recording, back in 1982, but hasn't broken through to the big time. Roscoe Mitchell and Ornette Coleman are the only obvious influences on saxophone.

***** Which Way What**

Deep Dish 103 *Brennan; Rachim Ausar-Shahu (b); Acacio Cardoso (d).* 95.

One's first reaction on hearing this disc might be to check the recording date. Trio sessions of this type have been around for some time and probably reached their zenith with Ornette's Gyllencirkelt recordings for Blue Note. Brennan is very much in that mould and in Ausar-Shahu and Cardoso he has playing partners who are well versed in their Izenzons and Moffetts. The tracks are mostly brief, pungent and slightly inconsequential. There isn't a piece here that really grabs the attention, and yet cumulatively this is a rather effective record that asks to be heard again.

***** Saunters, Walks, Ambles**

CIMP 187 *Brennan; Lisle Ellis (b).* 9/98.

A rather misleadingly laid-back title for an album of such focus and intensity, unless perhaps Brennan is aware that it was no less an authority than Henry David Thoreau who declared that sauntering and ambling were the key disciplines for an American philosopher. Duos of this kind are always demanding, but Brennan has attempted to lend a bit of familiarity to his slightly esoteric approach by including two Monk tunes, the opening 'Crepuscule With Nellie' and two versions of 'Misterioso'.

'Nellie' is by far the longest thing on the set, and it serves as an introduction and warm-up number. It's only when Brennan and Ellis really get into the meat of their encounter on the four-part 'saunter, walk, amble' that things heat up. Brennan has a rather clenched and inconsistent tone, but Ellis is wise to every harmonic waver and shift and he stays with the line, whatever is going on. The key track is Roscoe Mitchell's composition, 'Nonaah', which brings out the best in both men. 'Bucket-A-Blood' is for unaccompanied saxophone and suggests that Brennan might yet do interesting things in that direction.

*****(*) Sudani**

Deep Dish 109 *Brennan; Nirankar Khalsa (d); M'allim Najib Sudani (guinbri); Tola Cohia Brennan (oud); Bujmaa, M'barak Sudani, Larbi Faud, Yassine Lekuni (v, other instruments).* 5/99.

Patrick fulfils that thought with another interesting unaccompanied number here, 'The Wind and Najib', but this is an exception on a record which finds him again emulating Ornette by collaborating with Gnaouan musicians from Morocco. Again the basic format is a trio, Khalsa and Sudani occupying relatively familiar roles, albeit in unfamiliar metres. A surprising number of the tracks sound like orthodox bebop with a few unexpected textures and tonalities, but there is a genuine attempt at multicultural synthesis. 'Tirarmalia Blues', sung in English, is one example, and the intense 'Around Sidi Hammu' is another, albeit less obviously eclectic.

Brennan's problem is that he is now so securely identified with the Ornette style that one scarcely hears what is original about his work. His mentor once dabbled with the tenor and yet more notoriously switched to trumpet and violin; this might yet be a valid tactic for Patrick, except that we'd just call him a copycat again.

Willem Breuker (born 1944)

SAXOPHONES, CLARINETS, RECORDER

There has been a hint of Year Zero in modern Dutch music, a response to the (in some cases) near total destruction of the cultural infrastructure – buildings, people, Willem Pijper's entire MSS – during the war. Breuker has thrived in its blasted spaces, creating not just a musical 'style' but a new approach to music out of the ashes and remnants. Compounded of jazz, special effects, classical forms, jingles and church tunes, there is nothing else quite like it.

★★★(★) To Remain

BVHAAST CD 8904 *Breuker; Andy Altenfelder, Boy Raaymakers (t); Chris Abelen, Bernard Hunnekink, Garrett List, Gregg Moore (tb); André Goudbeek (as); Peter Barkema, Maarten Van Norden (ts); Henk De Jonge (p, ky); Arjen Gorter (b); Rob Verdurmen (d, perc).* 9/83–4/89.

★★★★ Bob's Gallery

BVHAAST CD 8801 *Breuker; Andy Altenfelder, Boy Raaymakers (t); Chris Abelen (tb); Bernard Hunnekink (tb, tba); André Goudbeek (as); Peter Barkema (ts); Henk De Jonge (p, syn); Arjen Gorter (b); Rob Verdurmen (perc, xyl); Peter Kuit Jr (tapdance).* 12/87.

If the Dutch soccer side of the '70s played 'total football', then this is 'total jazz'. Joachim Berendt likens Breuker's use of Dutch and Low German folk music to Roland Kirk's un-ironic and loving use of the less elevated music of the black tradition. Eclecticism of this sort has been a feature of post-war Dutch music. Composers like Louis Andriessen and Misha Mengelberg have made extensive use of jazz and rock forms as a way of breaking down the tyranny of serialism and of rigid formal structures. Like the late Frank Zappa, whom Breuker in some respects resembles and whose strange critical marginality he shares, the Dutchman was turned on to classical music by hearing Varèse, whose enthusiastic embrace of chaos is very much a part of what Breuker and Mengelberg are about; but Breuker has made a point of guying the more pompous aspects of all the musics he has a hand in. In structural terms, he does so by simple juxtaposition, placing popular melodies alongside quasi-classical themes. In terms of instrumental colour, he relies on the populist associations of saxophones, tubas; sometimes ukuleles and mandolins, elsewhere invented (non)instruments like Toby Rix's. Clearly, a good deal of this music fits only rather uncomfortably into a 'jazz' category. Breuker's Kollektief is a performance band in the fullest sense. Whether the music transfers successfully to record will depend largely on personal taste and on a level of sympathy with what Breuker is about. However, it is necessary to point out that most of the performances, even the concert recordings by the Kollektief, depend to some extent on visual components which the listener at home has no access to.

Breuker has also frequently been likened to Kurt Weill and is as likely to use harmonic devices, structural principles, and occasionally straight quotes from concert music as from popular sources; he is also a fundamentally theatrical composer, and several of his records are of music written for dramatic performance or for films.

Unfortunately, his label BVHaast has been in a somewhat chaotic state in recent years and many of the Kollektief's recordings seem to have disappeared from circulation, even though they may be theoretically still in catalogue. We list *To Remain* (which has definitely been reissued under a new number and in a new digipak format) and *Bob's Gallery*, among older releases, in part because these are two of the best Breuker records and they should be relatively easy to obtain. On the latter, the title-track, which is inspired by a Gary Larson cartoon, features magnificent solos by Goudbeek, Raaymakers and Breuker. 'Morribreuk', with Altenfelder and Raaymakers processing from the back of the hall to the stage, is a dedication to Ennio Morricone. There is also a dedication to the offbeat jazz pianist and composer (has Breuker ever done 'Yellow Waltz'?) Richard Twardzik, and a selection of pieces from the theatre work, *Thanks, Your Majesty*, making this one of the jazzier Kollektief records. That's a factor which may appeal to those who find his media-mixing a turn-off.

★★★(★) Kurt Weill

BVHAAST CD 9808 *As for records above, except add Nico Nijholt (tb); Alex Coke (picc, f); Rena Scholtens, Lorre Lynn Trittel (vn); Aimée Versloot (vla); Loes Luca (v).* 83–97.

A nicely compiled anthology of earlier Weill-inspired recordings, with new interpretations of the 1928 *Ol Musik* which feature the dynamic, theatrical voice of chanteuse Loes Luca. There is also a wonderful 1997 performance of 'My Ship' from *Lady In The Dark*, which highlights the skills of saxophonist and flautist Alex Coke, a relatively recent addition to the Breuker stable. Again, some of the arrangements were made for film and television purposes, but this time they also sound like performance works rather than utility music.

★★★(★) Pakkepapèn

BVHAAST CD 9807 *Breuker; Andy Altenfelder, Boy Raaymakers (t); Bernard Hunnekink (tb, tba); Nico Nijholt (tb); Alex Coke (ts, picc); Henk De Jonge (p, perc); Lorre Trytten (vn); Arjen Gorter (b); Rob Verdurmen (d).* 9/97.

★★★★ Psalm 122

BVHAAST CD 9803 *Breuker; Andy Altenfelder, Boy Raaymakers (t); Nico Nijholt (tb); Bernard Hunnekink (tb, tba); Peter Barkema (as); Alex Coke (ts, f, bf); Henk De Jonge (p, syn); Arjen Gorter (b); Rob Verdurmen (d); Trytten Strings; Koor Nieuwe Muziek.* 2/98.

This batch of Breukeriana includes a now familiar mix of fierce playing, wry satire, genuine emotion and a gift for imaginative packaging. *Pakkepapèn* comes in a textured, semi-transparent slipcase featuring abstract images of instruments. The group interplay is strongly reminiscent of early pre-theatrical Breuker albums. Breuker is scarcely featured, leaving the solo space to some familiar names from the past – Gorter and Raaymakers memorably on 'Pakkepapèn 6' – and relative newcomer Alex Coke, who narrates 'Hello, My Name Is Joe' before turning in a superb tenor solo on 'Worksong Part 2'. This is one of the best Breuker albums for years.

The real stunner is Breuker's meditation on Psalm 122, with its joyous apotheosis of Jerusalem as the refuge and triumph of the scattered tribes. One feels that much of what Breuker has been about down the years is concentrated and focused here. It is very much a piece about arrival.

Something of John Zorn's interrogation of the Judaic tradition with Masada can be heard here and there, but Breuker's approach is actually much more rigorous and daring. Barrel-organ renditions and a wonderfully executed *a cappella* performance of the psalm – more properly, song of degree – punctuate a long and complex suite. The ending is quite breathtaking: another barrel-organ turn gives way to the blessing of 'Peace be within thy walls', with Coke on bass flute and tenor saxophone; and then, breathtakingly, Lorre Lynn Trytten and Breuker on soprano bring the whole work to a climax. Even if you have not previously heard Breuker's music, this should be a priority. Rich, deeply cadenced music.

★★★(★) Hunger!

Bvhaast 9916 *Breuker; Boy Raaymakers (t, uke, v); Andy Altenfelder (t); Nico Nijholt (tb, v); Bernard Hunnekink (tb, tba); Alex Coke (ts, piucc, kaz); Hermine Deurloo (as, hca); Henk De Jonge (p, syn); Lorre Trytten (vn); Arjen Gorter (b); Rob Verdurmen (d); Loes Luca (v).* 6–8/99.

★★★(★) Thirst!

Bvhaast 0300 *As above, except add Peter Barkema (as); Denise Jannah (v); omit Luca.* 9/97–6/00.

The first albums by the Kollektief since the death of long-serving altoist Peter Barkema, who appears only on the final track of *Thirst!*, an arrangement of Ravel's *Pavane Pour Une Infante Défunte*. Otherwise, these are, in a sense, business as usual, if Breuker's non-stop eclecticism and inspirational bridging of sources can be characterized in such a mundane way. *Hunger!* is marginally the pick of the two, with two extended Breuker works, arrangements of Claude Bolling, Rossini, John Roger Thomas and Boris Vian, as well as a Verdurmen original. Luca is the guest vocalist, sounding a bit like Mistinguette, but it's Breuker who takes the vocal on 'Yes We Have No Bananas'. *Thirst!* is rather curiously programmed: Breuker splits the title-piece into three, with the first section inexplicably relegated to the far end of the disc, and there are consecutive versions of 'Lonely Woman', one with and one without vocal. Denise Jannah is a more 'jazzy' vocalist than Breuker normally engages, but she's very good on an old Dutch film tune, 'Telkens Weer'. Henk de Jonge stars in a madcap treatment of Bartók's Bagatelle Op 6. Some hits, some misses, but both discs are as engaging as ever.

★★★ Previously Unreleased Recordings 1969–1994

Bvhaast 0301 *Breuker; Klaas Kos, Boy Raaymakers, Gerard Van der Vist, Andy Altenfelder (t); Jan Wolff (flhn); Harry Dieleman, Willem Van Manen, Bert Koppelaar, Bernard Hunnekink (tb); Harry Bijholt (cl); Rien de Reede, Eleonore Pameijer (f); Peter Bennink (as, bagpipes); André Goudbeek (as); Maarten Van Norden (ts); Frans Baan (bsn); Ruud Bos, Misha Mengelberg (p); Rob Du Bois, Henk De Jonge (ky); Eddie de Windt, Wim Overgaauw, Eef Albers (g); Tony Pels, Toos Van der Meer (mand); Leo Borgart (acc); Ernö Ola, Lorre Trytten (vn); Fons Rats (vla); Hans Boncsel (clo); Dutch Schultz, Maarten van Regteren Altena, Arjen Gorter (b); Han Bennink, Rob Verdurmen (d); studio orchestra.* 69–94.

Scraps, leftovers and unfinished business from Breuker's vault, winkled out by compiler Thomas Schüssler. It starts with three minutes of psychedelic jazz from 1970 and gets as far as a piece in dedication to Bosnia which includes the beginnings and ending of all four Brahms symphonies, although the main body of the disc is given over to 'Koninkrik' (Kingdom), a perhaps typical Breuker theatre-piece. Those who look back fondly at Breuker's free period will enjoy the six minutes of 'Serendipity' with Mengelberg and the Benninks. Like most such collections, it's all over the place, but Breukerphiles won't want to miss it.

Dee Dee Bridgewater (born 1950)

VOCALS

Hailed as a natural successor to Ella Fitzgerald, Dee Dee has the same unfailing swing and instinct for complex harmony. A commanding presence on the stand, she communicates equally well in the studio but has mostly favoured live recordings.

★★(★) Dee Dee Bridgewater

Atlantic 76567 80 760-2 *Bridgewater; Barry Beckett, Tom Hensley, Joe Sample, Harold Wheeler (ky); Pete Carr, Jerry Friedman, Jimmy Johnson, Chris Morris, Ray Parker Jr, Dean Parks, Melvin Ragin, David T Walker (g); Herb Bushler, Wilton Felder, David Hood (b); Henry Davis, Ed Green, Roger Hawkins, Alan Schwartzberg (d); Gary Coleman, Bobby Hall (perc); Vivian Cherry, Gwendolyn Guthrie, Arlene Martell, Linda November (v).* 76.

★★★ Just Family

Elektra Masters 75596 2719-2 *Bridgewater; Chick Corea, George Duke, Ronnie Foster, Bobby Lyle (ky); David T. Walker (g); Scarlet Rivera (vn); Stanley Clarke, Alphonso Johnson, Abraham Laboriel, Ken Wilde (b); Leon Ndugu Chancler, Harvey Mason, Norman Farrington (perc); Airto Moreira (perc).* 10/77.

This Elektra Masters reissue underlies just how far back Dee Dee now goes. The album, produced with bassist Stanley Clarke, is very much of its time, featuring a whole phalanx of fusioneers and a set of soul-infused songs that lack the sophistication of later recordings. The production values may be dated but there is no mistaking the quality of the work. The main question mark seems to be Dee Dee's inability or unwillingness to change pace or dynamic. Even the quieter ballads seem a touch forced, though on something as unexpected as Elton John's 'Sorry Seems To Be The Hardest Word', she genuinely triumphs, bringing power and pathos to what was already an overworked song. The earlier guitar- and keyboard-heavy Atlantic reissue frankly isn't much to our taste and comes across like a bid to relocate Bridgewater in a rock-tinged mainstream. The material featuring Sample and Felder of the Crusaders is top drawer but the album as a whole smacks of commercial compromise.

★★★ Live In Paris

Verve 014137-2 *Bridgewater; Hervé Sellin (p); Antoine Bonfils (b); André Ceccarelli (d).* 11/86.

★★★ Live at Montreux

Verve 511895-2 *Bridgewater; Bert Van den Brink (p); Hein Van De Geyn (b); André Ceccarelli (d).* 7/90.

Dee Dee's best work has been in concert recordings and these are the discs that probably set her back on course as a jazz singer after her spell trying to cut it in soul and pop. A move to Paris put her in touch with competent, like-minded players who were able to bring a touch of sophistication to the material. Sellin has a lovely touch and brings a quieter and less forceful dynamic to songs like 'Misty' and 'There Is No Greater Love', allowing Dee Dee to ease her own tendency to push too hard. The Montreux set has a less relaxed quality, but the choice of material is more challenging, both technically ('A Night In Tunisia') and emotionally (it's tough for singers to take on 'Strange Fruit'). She pays further tribute to Horace Silver on a brightly executed medley, but the outstanding cuts are the bebop classic and an occasionally startling version of Jobim's 'Insensatez'.

★★★(★) Keeping Tradition

Verve 519607-2 *Bridgewater; Thierry Eliez (p); Hein Van De Geyn (b); André Ceccarelli (d).* 92.

★★★★ Love And Peace: A Tribute To Horace Silver

Verve 527470-2 *As above, except add Stéphane Belmondo (t), Lionel Belmondo (ts), Horace Silver (p).* 94.

★★★(★) Dear Ella

Verve 527896-2 *Bridgewater; Cecil Bridgewater, Byron Stripling (t); Bob Flowers (tb); Antonio Hart (as); Lou Levy (p); Milt Jackson (vib); Kenny Burrell (g); Ray Brown (b); Grady Tate (d).* 1–2/97.

A title like *Keeping Tradition* is a strong clue to Dee Dee's musical instincts. Her cool, limber swing works brilliantly on 'Fascinating Rhythm', 'Just One Of Those Things' and a superb medley of 'I'm A Fool To Want You' and 'I Fall In Love Too Easily'. If her debt to Ella weren't obvious from this, it's heavily underscored on the 1997 tribute album, which was recorded with a star-laden band over four nights in New York and Chicago. She starts with a light, buoyant reading of 'A Tisket A Tasket', establishing her voice before reaching for something more in the ballads. Her ability to convey the drama of 'How High The Moon' and 'Stairway To The Stars' while exploring their complex harmonic potential – echoes of bebop in her interchanges with Brown, the former Mr Fitzgerald – is endlessly impressive.

Like the eponymous Atlantic album, *Love And Peace* is a funkier conception, as befits its dedication to the music of Mr Funk himself. Surprisingly, Horace Silver's tunes lend themselves well to vocal performance, and Dee Dee is content to swap tags and allusions with the composer, who has always been a one-man dictionary of musical quotations. Good to hear him playing with such obvious enjoyment.

★★★(★) Live at Yoshi's

Verve 543354 *Bridgewater; Thierry Eliez (p, org); Thomas Bramerie (b); Ali Jackson (d, perc).* 98.

The important thing about this date was the date. Dee Dee's appearance at the Oakland club would have been Ella Fitzgerald's 80th birthday. Her old idol was clearly much in her mind, but so too were some of the other great jazz divas, and Bridgewater takes the opportunity to show what she's learned from Betty, Sassie and here and there Billie as well. 'What A Little Moonlight Can Do' will always seem like Lady's song, but Dee Dee stakes a formidable claim on it here. Her scatting is less mannered than it once threatened to become, and there is a logic and elegance to her improvisational solos now. The band is very good indeed, with some stunning work from Eliez. There is also a video version of this gig.

★★ This Is New

Verve 0168 842 *Bridgewater; Nicolas Folmer (t); Denis Léloup (tb); Antonio Hart (as, f); Daniele Scannapieco (as); Thierry Eliez (ky); Louis Winberg (g); Juan José Mosalini (bandoneon); Ira Coleman (b); André Ceccarelli (d); Minino Garay (perc).* 01.

Kurt Weill isn't the obvious choice of composer for Dee Dee Bridgewater, and this studio album is a major disappointment. Not even a long sojourn in Europe has taught her what this material needs – a kind of knowing irony to temper the overwhelming decadence she pours over 'Alabama Song'. 'Youkali' and 'I'm A Stranger Here Myself' have their pluses but the wacky version of 'Mack The Knife' should be passed over in silence. Since it comes right at the end of the disc, it can easily be omitted. Nice to hear her working with horns, but the premise is so fundamentally flawed that this was never going to work.

Arthur Briggs (c. 1899–1991)

TRUMPET

Born in Charleston, Briggs played in army bands and the Southern Syncopated Orchestra, 1919–21, then travelled through Europe, often leading his own bands through the '30s. Interned during the war, then returned to France and taught.

★★★ Hot Trumpet In Europe

Jazz Archives 158472 *Briggs; George Hirst, Bobby Jones, Theodore Brock (t); Jean Naudin, F. Monetti, Isidore Bassard, Billy Burns (tb); Georges Jacquemont-Brown (cl, as, ts); Peter Duconge, Franz Feith, Billy Barton (cl, as); Carlos Vidal (cl, bs); Mario Scanavino (cl, ts, bs); Alcide Castellanos (as); Francis Giulieri (ts, bs); U. Irrlicht, Marek Weber, Eugen Bermann, Armin Lieberman (vn); Egide Van Gils, Georg Haentzchel, Stephane Mougin, Freddy Johnson (p); Frank 'Big Boy' Goudie (cl, ts); C. B. Hilliom (bs, bsx); Al Bowlly (g, v); Sterling Conaway (g); Harold M. Kirchstein, Mike Danzi, Maceo Jefferson (bj); Hans Holdt, Arthur Brosche (tba); Juan Fernandez (b); Eugene Obendorfer, Dick Stauff, Jean Taylor, Billy Taylor (d); Spencer Williams, Louis Cole (v).* 3/27–7/33.

When Briggs enlisted with Will Marion Cook's orchestra and came to Europe in 1919, he seldom went back. His records are obscure compared with those of Jabbo Smith or Henry Allen, but he could claim to be as convincing an Armstrong disciple as they and he worked in relative jazz isolation in Europe through the '20s and '30s. This disc brings together the sides made by his Savoy Syncopators in 1927, an otherwise all-European band that handled themselves capably enough, although it's only on his solos that the records sit up. The trumpet on 'Ain't She Sweet?' is an interesting blend of styles, and the music works best in the hot-dance vein; when they get to a 'genuine' jazz piece such as King Oliver's 'Snag It', the results are comparatively disappointing. Eight tracks from 1933, rare items, give Briggs his best opportunities, and two duets with pianist Freddy Johnson are a glimpse of what he could really do. He sounds a little too urbane for the blues on 'Grabbin' Blues' since there's a certain sweetness in his manner, but a cultivated, elegant stylist he undoubtedly was. A few of the earlier tracks are a bit rough, but the remastering is mostly strong and clear.

Nick Brignola (1936–2001)

BARITONE, SOPRANO, TENOR AND ALTO SAXOPHONES, CLARINET, ALTO AND BASS CLARINETS, FLUTE, PICCOLO

A reed specialist of wide-ranging abilities, Brignola is first and foremost a baritone man. Originally from New York State, he worked in different settings and different parts of the USA, trying a fusion band in the early '70s and returning to hard bop in the '80s. He favoured the big side of the big horn, playing a hard-bop vocabulary with great power and command. Cancer took him at the end of 2001.

*** Raincheck

Reservoir RSR CD 108 *Brignola; Kenny Barron (p); George Mraz (b); Billy Hart (d).* 9/88.

**** On A Different Level

Reservoir RSR CD 112 *Brignola; Kenny Barron (p); Dave Holland (b); Jack DeJohnette (d).* 9/89.

*** What It Takes

Reservoir RSR CD 117 *Brignola; Randy Brecker (t); Kenny Barron (p); Rufus Reid (b); Dick Berk (d).* 10/90.

Brignola enjoyed a long sojourn with the independent label Reservoir which served him wonderfully well, with a sequence of albums that any saxophonist would envy. Brignola's facility goes hand in hand with a consistently imposing sound – as fluently as he plays, he always makes the baritone sound like the big horn that it is – and the flat-out burners are as tonally effective as the big-bodied ballads which are dotted through these sessions. *Raincheck* is a trifle diffuse, since Brignola turns to clarinet and soprano every so often, and *What It Takes* brings on Randy Brecker for a little variation in the front line, which is bought at the expense of the music's more personal feel (and the leader again doubles on the other reeds). *On A Different Level*, though, is suitably head-and-shoulders above the others. Brignola sticks to baritone, and the solos on 'Tears Inside', 'Hot House' and 'Duke Ellington's Sound Of Love' are sustained with fantastic strength, mirrored in the playing of the rhythm section, which is the kind of team that makes any horn player sound good. Brignola's shrewd choice of tunes here encapsulates a pocket history of jazz baritone – from Carney on 'Sophisticated Lady' to Adams on the Mingus tune – but he puts it all under his own flag, with DeJohnette and Holland marking superb time behind him. A great modern baritone set.

*** It's Time

Reservoir RSR CD 123 *Brignola; Kenny Barron (p); Dave Holland (b).* 2/91.

A singular feat of overdubbing. Brignola brings out not only the baritone but also all of his clarinets, flutes, other saxes and a piccolo. Mike Holober's arrangements create intelligent variations on the standard reed section and introduce all sorts of counterpoint and texture. But producer Mark Feldman doesn't secure a convincing enough mix; there's too much artifice here, as naturally and enthusiastically as Brignola approaches the project. 'Dusk' and 'Renewal' are pleasing scores, and there are a couple of straighter blows on 'Speak Low' and a clarinet treatment of 'I Thought About You'. Holland is marvellous as usual, especially on 'Dusk'.

*** Live At Sweet Basil, First Set

Reservoir RSR CD 125 *Brignola; Mike Holober (p); Rich Syracuse (b); Dick Berk (d).* 8/92.

Given that he deliberately avoided having a drummer on the previous date, there's some irony about this one. All the real dialogue goes on between Brignola and drummer Dick Berk, whose hefty, momentous style is a fine foil for the burliness of the leader's baritone. The soprano comes out on 'Mahjong' and the alto for part of 'Sister Sadie', but otherwise it's all baritone, on a clear-eyed 'Everything Happens To Me', a nicely paced 'I Hear A Rhapsody' and a grandly articulated 'East Of The Sun'. Occasional club-date longueurs, but otherwise this is a fine continuation of possibly the best sequence of baritone records of recent times.

***(*) Like Old Times

Reservoir RSR CD 133 *Brignola; Claudio Roditi (t, flhn); John Hicks (p); George Mraz (b); Dick Berk (d).* 5/94.

***(*) The Flight Of The Eagle

Reservoir RSR CD 145 *Brignola; Kenny Barron (p); Rufus Reid (b); Victor Lewis (d).* 6/96.

The tenets of the blowing date are followed without any suspicion of routine on *Like Old Times*. The two long blow-outs on 'When Lights Are Low' and 'The Night Has A Thousand Eyes' are marked by perfectly controlled dynamics, with no loss of excitement as one solo passes into another. Roditi is in rare form, and Hicks supplies all the right leads. However, the leader surrenders nothing to either of them, with a pointed clarinet meditation on 'More Than You Know' and a terrific solo on 'Thousand Eyes' as particular highlights. Rudy Van Gelder still doesn't put enough air round the horns, and this cuts back on the music's impact to a degree.

No problems with the sound on the impeccably registered *The Flight Of The Eagle*. Brignola returns to a simple quartet setting and sticks to the baritone for eight pieces, measured out with the utmost finesse by all four hands. Barron, Reid and Lewis don't seem to know how to put a foot wrong, and the leader is at his most civilized. 'Gerrylike' is a nod of farewell to Mulligan, the gentlest guying of the older man's methods, while the complex changes of the title-tune are wholly absorbing. There is also a near-perfect ballad in 'My Foolish Heart', where Lewis steps aside. The only quibble might be that the music is at times almost bloodless in its excellence, but it seems folly to carp.

*** Spring Is Here

Koch 3-6905-2 *Brignola; Netherlands Metropole Orchestra.* 94–7.

A dream date for a horn player, this matching with the Netherlands Metropole Orchestra brings out Brignola's sunniest side. He almost gambols through 'Gerrylike' and is just as perky with 'Baubles, Bangles And Beads'. Some of the lushness of 'When You Wish Upon A Star' is a bit lost on such a hearty executant, and the arrangements are rather weeping-waterfall on the ballads. Brignola fans will still want this.

*** Poinciana

Reservoir RSR CD 151 *Brignola; Phil Markowitz (ky); Steve LaSpina (b); Billy Hart (d); Café (perc).* 4/97.

This one's a bit disappointing. Nick sounds a little sleepless on a couple of the tunes, and for once the band doesn't seem to really respond to him. There are still some pieces worth savouring, such as the musing 'What'll I Do', but this isn't among the best of his Reservoirs.

★★★(★) Tour De Force
Reservoir RSR CD 168 *Brignola; Chuck D'Aloia (g); Eddie Gomez (b); Bill Stewart (d); Café (perc).* 12/00.

Nick's farewell is a final paragraph which reprises all his old virtues – great sound, great time, smart tune selection, and a band that cooks at a good temperature. Bebop gets its spotlight in a quick 'Donna Lee'. Dave Holland's 'Backwoods Song' is one Brignola did on his earlier *On A Different Level*, and the new version has an extra scratch of funk. 'Labyrinth' is as free as he was ever going to get, and it's a lesson in a rules player taking what he needs from wide open spaces. Gomez and Stewart make the kind of team that will make most horn players sound good, and the little-known D'Aloia does well. Reservoir's patronage of this fine musician did them great credit.

Alan Broadbent (born 1947)

PIANO

Born in New Zealand, he went to Berklee in 1966 and then joined Woody Herman as pianist-arranger. He's been in demand since in both capacities and is the pianist in the Charlie Haden Quartet West.

★★★(★) Pacific Standard Time
Concord CCD 4664 *Broadbent; Putter Smith (b); Frank Gibson Jr (d).* 1/95.

There's a great clarity of thought about Alan Broadbent's playing: his interpretations of jazz and show standards seem thought through and entire and, while that may suggest a lack of spontaneity, he also manages to make the music sound fresh. These are very satisfying records. The pianist takes his first cues from Parker and Powell, yet one seldom thinks of bop while listening to him: there is much interplay between the hands, a sly but considerate cunning and a striking concern to develop melodies which are entirely faithful to the material. The only drawback here is the choice of material: some of the themes are just a shade too familiar and, since Broadbent's way is to personalize by small, well-chosen gestures, the trio don't quite characterize each piece as strongly as they might. That said, this is still a very fine record. Broadbent's touch is so lucid and refined that he makes one hear every note as a specific choice, and his sense of swing is good enough to lift slow tempos and mediate fast ones. Smith and Gibson are unadventurous but completely in sympathy with him. 'Summer Night', 'Django' and 'Easy To Love' are about as close to perfect as they can be.

★★★★ Personal Standards
Concord CCD 4757-2 *Broadbent; Putter Smith (b); Joe LaBarbera (d).* 10/96.

Words like 'civilized' and 'cultured' are as likely to be disparaging as complimentary when discussing jazz, yet there's simply no avoiding them when considering Broadbent's music. This superlative record continues one of the great sequences of recent times. Here he tackles eight of his own originals, plus one he wishes he'd written himself, Putter Smith's 'North'. As before, the playing is so impeccable, the interplay so refined – surely LaBarbera has never played better than this – and the insights so profound that one is left at a loss for words. Broadbent deserves the highest acclaim. Once again, we have to grumble that the pianist has been getting so much work as an arranger that he doesn't seem to have time to make records of his own!

Bosse Broberg

TRUMPET

Veteran Swedish modernist whose rare records as a leader only commenced when his career was fully mature.

★★★ East Of The Sun
Dragon DRCD 235 *Broberg; Joakim Milder (ts); Gösta Rundqvist (p); Red Mitchell (b); Martin Löfgren (d).* 2/92.

★★(★) A Swede In Copenhagen
Music Mecca 2033-2 *Broberg; Ole Stolle (t); Soren Kristiansen (p); Ole Skipper Mosgaard (b); Leif Johansson (d).* 6/95.

★★★ Regni
Phono Suecia PSCD 93 *Broberg; Peter Asplund, Magnus Broo, Hans Dyvik (t, flhn); Jan Allan (t); Thomas Driving (flhn); Olle Holmquist (tb, tba, euph); Nils Landgren, Bertl Lovgren (tb); Sven Larsson (btb, tba, didjeridu); Krister Andersson (as, ts, cl); Lennart Aberg (as, ts); Dave Wilczewski (ss, ts); Jon Högman (bs); Gösta Rundqvist (p); Dan Berglund (b); Martin Löfgren (d).* 12/95.

It took many years for Broberg to get his name up front on a record marquee, and even then the Dragon album is nominally shared with Red Mitchell, on one of his last sessions before returning to the USA. It's a thoughtful set of post-bop, conservatively styled – even with Milder in the group – but effective for all that. Broberg's Milesian affinities come to the fore when he has the mute in, but he can sometimes go off on wailing, swing-style blasts when he feels he needs to wake himself up. The duet with Mitchell on 'I Cover The Waterfront' is especially fine, but some of the other tunes ramble a bit. *A Swede In Copenhagen* catches Bosse sitting in with a local group, and he is sometimes nearly outplayed by the excellent Stolle, who gets no features to himself but turns in some sturdy solos. Here and there Broberg seems fallible, and some of his forays into very long phrases followed by short ones all but coin a cliché. The set offers seven pretty obvious standards and could perhaps have used more preparation.

No such complaint against the orchestral music on *Regni*. Some of it is so intensely written – nothing more so than the labyrinthine 'Monkey Serenade' – that one applauds the chops of the players for just getting through it. This kind of jazz suggests that Broberg has been storing up his composing for, if anything, too long: it feels overworked. But some of the scores, such as the intriguing 'Portrait Of Uriah' with its astonishing feature for Lennart Aberg's tenor, and the brief reduction of 'Sir Gil Ahead' with a typically shining solo from Jan Allan, hold the attention decisively. The band is first class, too.

Bob Brookmeyer (born 1929)

VALVE TROMBONE, PIANO

The Missourian is the first brass player since Juan Tizol to favour the valve trombone over the slide instrument. He began his career as a pianist and continued to play keyboard for many years, but it was his emergence as Chet Baker's replacement in the Mulligan pianoless quartet that really established his name. Brookmeyer spent many years as a studio musician and in the Jones–Lewis big band, and the experience has strongly coloured his own arranging and composition.

★★★(★) The Dual Role Of Bob Brookmeyer

Original Jazz Classics OJC 1729 *Brookmeyer; Jimmy Raney (g); Teddy Charles (vib); Teddy Kotick (b); Mel Lewis, Ed Shaughnessy (d); Nancy Overton (v).* 1/54, 6/55.

Almost the first sounds to be heard on the classic *Jazz On A Summer's Day* soundtrack are the mellow tones of Bob Brookmeyer's valve trombone interweaving with Jimmy Giuffre's clarinet on 'The Train And The River'. It's a curiously formal sound, almost academic, and initially difficult to place. Valve trombone has a more clipped, drier sound than the slide variety, and Brookmeyer is probably its leading exponent, though Maynard Ferguson, Stu Williamson and Bob Enevoldsen have all made effective use of it.

Brookmeyer has always been keen to share piano duties and is a very considerable keyboard player, as he proves on *The Dual Role.* 'Rocky Scotch' and 'Under The Lilacs' are both readily categorized as 'cool' jazz, but there is a surprising degree of variation in Brookmeyer's tone that anticipates the more inflected and expressive playing of later years.

★★★ Brookmeyer

RCA Victor 74321 59152 2 *Brookmeyer; Al Derisi, Joe Ferrante, Bernie Glow, Louis Oles, Nick Travis (t); Joe Singer (frhn); Don Butterfield (tba); Gene Quill (as); Al Cohn (as, ts, cl); Al Epstein, Eddie Wasserman (ts); Sol Schlinger (bs); Hank Jones (p); Milt Hinton, Buddy Jones (b); Osie Johnson (d).* 9 & 10/56.

This was an attempt to showcase Brookmeyer in three rather different contexts, from large band down to octet. The big-band arrangements, like the opening 'Oh, Jane Snavely', are interestingly pared down, almost folkish in conception, but arranged in the most interesting way with four trumpets, three tenors, baritone and rhythm providing the background for the solitary trombone. The next session was very different, with a pair of trumpets, french horn and tuba, but just two reeds, alto doubling clarinet, and, once again supporting a roomy bottom end, Sol Schlinger's baritone. The results are no less spare and undramatic, but the subtlety and control are equally striking, and these are more compelling performances than the two octets, 'Confusion Blues' and 'Zing Went The Strings Of My Heart', which seem to have been taped a further week later. These sessions represented quite a substantial investment in Brookmeyer's growing reputation. Even given the tastes of the time, which embraced everything from Kentonish swing to the stirrings of the Third Stream, they must have been quite difficult records to sell. Like a lot of material of the same vintage, though, they come up to date very impressively.

★★★(★) Traditionalism Revisited

Blue Note 94847 *Brookmeyer; Jimmy Giuffre (ts, bs, cl); Jim Hall (g); Joe Benjamin, Ralph Pena (b); Dave Bailey (d).* 7/57.

Late-'50s recordings, like *Traditionalism Revisited*, saw Brookmeyer exploring classic material with an augmented version of Giuffre's Newport trio and in an idiom the clarinettist was to christen 'folk jazz'. The aim here was something that almost became the legitimacy in the '90s, playing classic jazz tunes and standards with due respect to the tradition, but with markedly modern harmonies. The effect is most noticeable on 'Sheik Of Araby' and 'Louisiana', which bracket the set, but the entire session is handled with a great consistency of vision, as much to the credit of Jimmy Giuffre as to Brookmeyer. On 'Honeysuckle Rose' there are some choruses on which Bob accompanies himself on piano without double-tracking, a rather extreme example of the 'dual role' he has adopted throughout his performing career.

★★(★) Dreams

Dragon DRCD 169 *Brookmeyer; Gustavo Bargalli, Jan Kohlin, Lars Lindgren, Fredrik Norén, Stig Persson (t, flhn); Mats Hermansson, Mikael Raberg, Bertil Strandberg (tb); Sven Larsson (btb); Dave Castle (as, ss, cl); Håkan Bröstrom (as, ss, f); Johan Alenius, Ulf Andersson (ts, ss, cl); Hans Arktoft (bs, bcl); Anders Widmark (p, ky); Jan Adefeldt (b); Johan Diedelmans (d).* 8/88.

In the later '80s Brookmeyer seemed to be coming to the fore again, both as a player and more particularly as a composer and bandleader. Given what was to come later, *Dreams* is not a particularly inspiring example. It's a dull piece, lifted by one or two passages on 'Cats' and 'Missing Monk', but lacking the coherence and warmth which had become a signature element of his work once the initial cool period was tempered.

★★★ Electricity

ACT 892 192 *Brookmeyer; John Abercrombie (g); Rainer Bruninghaus, Frank Chastenier (ky); Dieter Ilg (b); Danny Gottlieb (d); WDR Big Band.* 3/91.

Based in Europe, Brookmeyer found more opportunities for large-scale sessions than he ever had back home. *Electricity* isn't, to be frank, a particularly wonderful set, but it is immaculately arranged and recorded and, of the soloists, Brookmeyer and Abercrombie are capable of something special, even when the material doesn't appear to be promising. Bob's tone has lightened a touch over the years (unless it is simply modern microphones) and he often now puts more notes into a phrase than he did before.

★★★ Paris Suite

Challenge 70026 *Brookmeyer; Kris Goessens (p); Riccardo Del Frà (b); Dre Pallemaerts (d).* 10/93, 1/94.

With the exception of Berg's 'Chaconne', played in a delicately swinging way, this is entirely dominated by originals. Pianist Goessens is responsible for three of them, including the *déjà-vu* 'Gospel Song', while Brookmeyer contributes 'Chanson' (the longest track) , 'Airport Song' and 'Erik Satie', which may draw its inspiration from one of the *Gnossiennes.* The group interaction is consistently interesting and Goessens's solos are far from negligible.

★★★(★) Old Friends

Storyville STCD 8292 *Brookmeyer; Thomas Clausen (p); Mads Vinding (b); Alex Riel (d).* 11/94.

Brookmeyer's gifts as an arranger have occasionally deflected attention from his skills as a live performer. This was recorded in the Jazzhus, Copenhagen: five long numbers packed with invention, if a little hampered by Brookmeyer's cool, slightly expressionless delivery. Perhaps oddly at this juncture, his phrasing on 'Polka Dots And Moonbeams' recalls no one more than Jimmy Giuffre, though elsewhere on the set he is brassier and more impacted. The closing 'All Blues' is the only track that doesn't quite work – though for reasons which are never entirely clear – and perhaps only because the rhythm section seem to have gone to sleep a bit. Not a great album, but an immensely attractive one.

CORE COLLECTION

★★★★ New Works / Celebration

Challenge CHR 70066 *Brookmeyer; Thorsten Beckenstein, Jorg Engels, Ralf Hesse, Torsten Mass, Sebastian Strempel (t); Christian Jakso, Ludwig Nuss, Ansgar Striepens (tb); Edward Partyka (btb); Marko Lackner, Stefan Pfeifer (as); Nils Van Haften, Paul Heller (ts); Marcus Bartelt, Scott Robinson (bs); Kris Goessens (p); Jurgen Grimm (ky); Ingmar Heller (b); John Hollenbeck (d); Christopher Dell (perc).* 7/97.

The earlier music on this delightful set was written for a festival in Lübeck in 1994, with Gerry Mulligan as guest soloist. Posthumously documented on record, it features the multi-talented Scott Robinson in the solo role, turning the folk- and dance-based material into something at once familiar and strange. Robinson is a formidable soloist and he brings a genuine individuality to the part. Of the other tracks, 'Cameo' is essentially a solo spot for Brookmeyer, while 'Duets', built on one of Bob's minimalist themes, is a great basis for improvisation and includes some inventive drumming from John Hollenbeck. The closing item, 'Boom Boom', is derived from the earlier 'Danish Suite' and provides a light-toned and joyous closer. Brookmeyer has rarely written or played better.

★★(★) Out Of This World

Koch International 6913 *Brookmeyer; Ruud Breuls, Henk Keijink, Jan Hollander (t); Paul Woesthuis (tb); Cor Bakker, Hans Vroomans (p, syn); Peter Tiehuis (g); Jan Hollestelle (b); Eddy Koopman, Cees Kranenburg (d, perc); woodwinds; strings.* 98.

Very much a solo showcase for Brookmeyer, to the detriment sometimes of charts that are intelligently prepared – by Rob Pronk, Lex Jasper, Henl Meutgeert and others – but which need a touch of improvisational tension or at very least some other voices to lend them focus. Brookmeyer has been doing unconventional readings of standard material for years and one might have expected something spikier and more illuminating than these bland settings. Some of the responsibility lies with the arrangers and some with the orchestra, who fail to generate much excitement. Perhaps the session was put together at speed. It seems odd that an arranger of Brookmeyer's gifts should not be represented other than as a player.

★★★(★) Together

Challenge CHR 70068 *Brookmeyer; Mads Vinding (b).* 10/98.

The sonorities are delightful, Brookmeyer's wuffling sound set against Vinding's smart, articulate lines, and the notes are pretty good too. Each of these is a full-on duet, no sense of either man giving much in the way of quarter to the other, yet they're beautifully co-operative, little counter-melodies or riffs emerging as they go, before it's on to the next thing. Brookmeyer turns to the keyboard for three tracks, including his originals, 'New Song' and 'Pretty Song' – not a man to waste time on fancy titles.

★★★ Madly Loving You

Challenge CHR 70097 *Brookmeyer; Thorsten Benkenstein, Sebastien Strempel, Torsten Maas, Thomas Gansch (t, flhn); Dominik Stöger, Ansgar Striepens, Christian Jaksjö (tb); Richard Henry (btb); Christine Chapman, Pip List, Isabelle Van der Wiele (frhn); Marko Lackner, Oliver Leicht, Matthias Erlewein, Frank Delle, Edgar Herzog (reeds); Andy McKreel (tba); Ingmar Heller, John Goldsby (b); John Hollenbeck (d).* 9/99.

Bill Kirchner, in the notes, advises the listener that the CD is too rich for a single sitting, and he's right – it's too long, the pieces (eight compositions from various hands, including Maria Schneider, Bill Holman, Manny Albam and Jim McNeely, in dedication to Brookmeyer) sometimes exhaustingly complex. Brookmeyer is the only principal soloist and he plays with keen interest, though, as with all such projects, some pieces seem more effective than others. It'll do until we have a new set featuring the man's own charts.

★★★ Holiday

Challenge CHR 70103 *Brookmeyer; Mads Vinding (b); Alex Riel (d).* 6/00.

Brookmeyer's piano-playing used to be described, not without affection, as faintly eccentric. It's a little hard to agree with the note-writer who claims 'a rich sound, a dazzling touch and effortless swing feeling'. Brookmeyer's playing is effort*ful*, a ponderous manner which makes his off-kilter voicings and individual way with time all the more characterful. A whole CD of Bob at the piano – which is what this is – may strike some as too much of an interesting thing, which accounts for our moderate rating. But it's a very sweet change from the plentiful, blandly virtuosic piano-trio music which has been made of late. Vinding and Riel enjoyed it, too.

★★★(★) Waltzing With Zoe

Challenge CHR 70081 *Brookmeyer; Torsten Benkenstein, Torsten Maass, Sebastian Strempel, Eric Vloeimans, Angelo Verploegen (t, flhn); Adrian Mears, Jan Oosting, Bert Pfeiffer (tb); Ed Partyka (btb); Marko Lackner, Oliver Liecht (ss, as, f, cl); Matthias Erlewein (ts, cl); Nils van Haften (ts, cl, bcl); Edgar Herzog (bs, bcl, cbcl); Kris Goessens (p); Achim Kaufmann (syn); Ingmar Heller (b); John Hollenbeck (d).* 1/01.

Brookmeyer describes these compositions for the New Art Orchestra as 'character pieces', a term he may have derived from classical practice, but which is richly resonant here. 'For Maria' is dedicated to fellow bandleader Maria Schneider and is a fulsome tribute to her ability to colour an orchestra differently with every composition. Other tracks, like the title-piece, have a more programmatic feel, though not necessarily a restrictive one, and 'American Tragedy' is criss-crossed with ambiguities. The opening 'Seesaw', which features a decidedly old-fashioned drum part, is potentially off-putting, but even casual listeners should stay online; the rest of the album is packed with intrigue.

Brookmeyer's genius as an orchestrator can be gauged from 'Child At Play', in which a sequence of fragmentary melodic shapes suddenly reveals an overall design that, in retrospect, has been there all along. It is a masterly stroke, delivered with grace.

Cecil Brooks III (born 1961)

DRUMS, PERCUSSION

A reliable and inventive player on the New York scene, influenced by bebop masters like Art Blakey and Max Roach, Brooks has recorded extensively as a bandleader over the last decade, without much recognition.

***** For Those Who Love To Groove**
Savant 2023 *Brooks; Riley Mullins (t); Bruce Williams (as); Don Braden (ts); Radam Schwartz (org).* 99.

Packed with short, pugnacious tracks, this is credited to the CB3 Band, and calls on organist Schwartz's arranging skills, as well as Brooks's own confident leadership. The organ accompaniment is effective but a touch one-dimensional. Don Braden is a commanding presence and it's a pity that he isn't cut loose more often. Cecil's tough but relaxed groove is an ideal platform for saxophone players, but none of the solos are given sufficient time to develop. The best are terse and emphatic; the rest are merely rather abbreviated. Brooks makes his own most impressive statement on 'Lakumbe's Theme', but he also bridges a nice medley of standards – 'Body And Soul', 'I Can't Get Started', 'Tenderly' – and he shows an imaginative take on recent repertoire in programming Babyface's 'Can We Talk?'.

***** Live At Sweet Basil**
Savant 2034 *Brooks; Riley Mullins (t); Don Braden (ts); John Hicks (p); Dwayne Dolphin (b).* 8/00.

***** Live at Sweet Basil: Volume 2**
Savant 2039 *As above.* 8/00.

By contrast with the earlier set, these are somewhat drawn-out performances, ponderously long in the case of the opening 'Bounce' and the closing 'Vamp for Cho', but a little more focused and energized in between. 'Chelsea Bridge' and 'But Beautiful' are especially good, and the two horns mesh on the ensemble passages in a way that comes only with familiarity and a shared musical vision. Brooks himself seems ever more confident as a leader. Contrast the recording career as leader of the equally busy Marvin 'Smitty' Smith, which now seems stalled; Cecil meanwhile forges ahead and will be interesting to watch over the next couple of albums.

Good as the first set was, a second tranche from his Sweet Basil residency was a surprise. A pleasant one, as it turns out. Jimmy Heath's 'Voice Of The Saxophone' was an inspired choice for this group, as was Errol Garner's 'Dreamy'. After the opening 'Swamp Run', there's nothing more of Cecil's own until the closing 'Yvette', 'Spontaneous Percussion' and 'Hill District', which end the album on a thoughtful high. Brooks is not exclusively a high-end energy player, as he proves on 'Prelude To Yvette', but his real strength is driving a group along, and he does that cheerfully throughout this set. A two-CD package might have been a better option, but nice to complete the picture this way.

David 'Bubba' Brooks (1923–2002)

TENOR SAXOPHONE

Robust improviser with a deceptively delicate touch under the muscle.

***** The Big Sound Of Bubba Brooks**
Claves 1395 *Brooks; Bross Townsend (p); Michael Howell (g); Bob Cunningham (b); Grady Tate (d).* 8/96.

***** Smooth Sailing**
TCB 97702 *Brooks; Kenny Drew Jr (p); Peter Bernstein (g); Peter Washington (b); Kenny Washington (d).* 2/98.

****** Polka Dots And Moonbeams**
TCB 21212 *Brooks; Jack Wilkins (g); Lonnie Liston Smith (org); Charli Persip (d).* 99.

It's difficult to pin down Bubba's style. Somewhere between Charlie Rouse and Von Freeman makes some sense of it, though he lacks Charlie's early-morning yawn and stretch and Von's sheer eccentricity of sound. *The Big Sound* unveils a pretty familiar roster of tunes – 'Body And Soul', 'Willow, Weep For Me', 'I Let A Song Go Out Of My Heart', 'Moon River' – though not too many tenor men would start a date with a reading of a Tina Brooks blues. The tenor chestnut is despatched with some elegance and a rare understanding of the song's original dynamic. The other players, Tate and to a lesser extent Cunningham apart, are little known, but Townsend is a tidy and unfussy player who knows his chords and isn't afraid to reharmonize when he feels it would be advantageous. He even coaxes something extra out of 'Moon River'.

The second album is in exactly the same mode, though this time it's Arnett Cobb (the title tune) who's lifted out of the B-list and given prominence. There's more emphasis than before on Ellington material. Drew steers the band through 'Cotton Tail' and adds his own increasingly delicate touch to 'In A Mellow Tone' and 'Prelude To A Kiss', where Dave does his husky romantic routine to perfection. The only disappointment is a read of 'Billie's Bounce', the bebop changes coming across a bit clattery and unsubtle.

The third record is in some respects the most interesting of all. Bubba's liking for guitar players inevitably leads him toward the organ-guitar format. Here he's teamed with young Turk Wilkins and the impressively turbaned Dr Smith, who these days looks like a cross between Don King and the Laird of Lesmahagow and plays like he's been doing after-hours gigs in a storefront church for 25 years. The rolling gospelly lines suit Brooks perfectly and he has a chance to stretch out on Errol Garner's 'Perpetual Motion' and another Arnett Cobb number 'Dutch Kitchen Bounce'. Persip is immense, sounding as if he were playing in front of a big band, which is how Dave himself likes to sound.

Tina Brooks (1932–1974)

TENOR SAXOPHONE

Harold Floyd Brooks – known as 'Tiny' or 'Tina' – was a stalwart of the late '50s Blue Note stable but was mysteriously sidelined in the label's release programme. It may be that for all his nimble and clever musicianship his personal problems, and notably a long-standing addiction to heroin, rendered him unbankable. Brooks died unseasonally young, of liver failure exacerbated by drug use. He remains best known for his work on Freddie Redd's live soundtrack to the Jack Gelber play The Connection.

*****(*) Minor Move**
Blue Note 22671 *Brooks; Lee Morgan (t); Sonny Clark (p); Doug Watkins (b); Art Blakey (d).* 58.

***** Back To The Tracks**
Blue Note 21737 *Brooks; Blue Mitchell (t); Jackie McLean (as); Kenny Drew (p); Paul Chambers (b); Art Taylor (d).* 60.

***** The Waiting Game**

Blue Note 40536 2 *Brooks; Johnny Coles (t); Kenny Drew (p); Wilbur Ware (b); Philly Joe Jones (d).* 3/61.

For a considerable time, Tina Brooks's Blue Note work was available only in a Mosaic box set. For reasons that can be only guessed at, his scheduled first album, *Minor Move*, was shelved by label boss Alfred Lion and was only released in Japan two decades later. When its successor also eventually appeared on CD, Blue Note managed to find some alternates not included on the Mosaic roster, but *True Blue* isn't currently available. A similar fate awaited later sessions. All of which makes the Brooks discography intriguingly problematic.

The immediate and obvious reaction is puzzlement. Brooks was a powerful and very able player, whose touch never faltered at faster tempos and whose ballad playing was markedly individual. He was also a more than decent composer, as 'Nutville' and the title track on the first LP suggest. This is a quintessential Blue Note session, tough, professional hard bop with a sophisticated emotional temper. Morgan and Clark are legends in their own way, but there is no mistaking that the debut album belongs wholly to the leader. A transcription of his solo on 'Nutville' would make interesting reading and Tina's reading of 'The Way You Look Tonight' is stunning.

'Back To The Tracks' is also a fine original, and gets the 1960 session up to impressive speed. A pace, alas, that the album doesn't quite sustain. Brooks had a habit of starting strongly and then tailing off. It happens in solos and the habit seems imprinted on the album sessions as well. Mitchell and McLean are less obviously *simpatico* partners, but Jackie is in great voice throughout, and when the two saxophones interlock, the harmonics are intriguing.

Release of *The Waiting Game* in 2002 was a significant moment. It is not necessarily Tina's most satisfying record, but it is certainly his boldest. It starts conventionally enough with the bluesy 'Talkin' About', which sounds like any other Blue Note session of the time, followed by the show-off bebop of 'One For Myrtle', but it also harbours some surprises in minor-key compositions like 'David The King', which has an odd, almost Middle Eastern quality. It's then followed by a weird, south of the border interpretation of 'Stranger In Paradise', which borrows harmonic devices from the original Borodin theme. Once again, throughout the album the saxophonist sounds completely on the case, supremely confident at all tempos and with significant things to say on ballad features.

It may be that Tina Brooks fell victim to Blue Note's marketing 'department'. Alfred Lion never to our knowledge explained why these discs were not released as planned. Fortunately, they are now available to showcase a fleeting but remarkable talent.

Håkan Bröstrom (born 1955)

SOPRANO, ALTO AND TENOR SAXOPHONES

Born in Hotala, Sweden, Bröstrom began playing tenor in blues bands, before switching to alto and going into post-bop. Works on the Stockholm contemporary scene.

***** Dark Light**

Dragon DRCD 190 *Bröstrom; Bobo Stenson (p); Max Schultz (g); Christian Spering (b); Anders Kjellberg (d).* 12/90.

***** Celestial Nights**

Dragon DRCD 257 *As above, except omit Schultz.* 2/94.

***** Still Dreaming**

Dragon DRCD 297 *Bröstrom; Tim Hagans (t); Marc Copland (p); Christian Spering (b); Jeff Hirshfield (d).* 11/95.

Bröstrom's manner sheds a pale (though not pallid) Swedish light on the post-bop vocabulary. He is a fluent and ambitious improviser on all three horns, although the tenor comes out only on the first record, and he isn't shy about his composing since every theme was written by him. Some of the music is merely meandering, and little really compels the attention – yet that isn't really Bröstrom's style anyway: he likes to set up long, drifting pieces which let the players communicate without undue stress. 'Dark Light' and 'Till Cornelis' on the first disc, 'Spring' on the second and the haunting 'Carmilla' on the third are fine examples of the kind of thing he's trying to achieve. The first two discs benefit from Stenson's typically idiosyncratic playing, quick and intelligent yet quirkily shaped. Spering is splendid on all three discs, but there is a change of pace on the third with the arrival of the American players. 'Three-Year-Old Cowboy' suggests a slightly difficult rapprochement between Europe and the USA but, after that one, Bröstrom seems to inveigle the visitors into playing it his way. All three records should appeal to Europhiles of a certain temperament.

***** Do You Remember?**

Dragon DRCD 386 *Bröstrom; Anders Persson (p); Palle Danielsson (b); Bengt Stark (d).* 4/03.

After an eight-year absence, Bröstrom returns to Dragon with eleven originals and a fresh (if scarcely inexperienced) rhythm section. The music's taken on a more purposeful, less dreamy tone, although this arguably undercuts what individuality Bröstrom may have proposed on the earlier discs: here, he tends to sound like many another skilled saxophonist, and titles such as 'Just Another Ballad' and 'Quiet Evening At Home' do tend to make one ask how much he has to say. The rhythm section play with enough graft to make one listen through anyway.

Brotherhood Of Breath

GROUP

Formed in 1970 by SA expatriate Chris McGregor in London. Active mostly in the early '70s, but '80s reunions until McGregor's death kept the name alive.

*****(*) Live At Willisau**

Ogun OGCD 001 *Chris McGregor (p, leader); Harry Beckett, Marc Charig, Mongezi Feza (t); Nick Evans, Radu Malfatti (tb); Dudu Pukwana (as); Evan Parker, Gary Windo (ts); Harry Miller (b); Louis Moholo (d).* 1/73.

The trick was to keep breathing, because Death was always near by. Chris McGregor's passing and Dudu Pukwana's, and before them Johnny Mbizo Dyani's, Harry Miller's and Mongezi Feza's, confirmed that there was a shadow across this music, as if the life that was breathed into it had to be paid for in some way that had nothing to do with technical exactness or acoustic precision. From the opening moments of 'Do It', with its searing Evan Parker solo, to the relative ease of the closing 'Funky Boots', this is affirmative music of a rare sort, bringing together African *kwela*, post-Ellington swing, free jazz, and even touches of classicism in a boiling mix that grips the heart throughout. Pukwana, Charig and Feza are perhaps the dominant soloists, but the two trombone players have their moment in the sun on 'Kongi's Theme' (a McGregor original for Malfatti) and 'Andromeda'. The only player under-represented on this particular occasion is the survivor, Moholo, who carries on the Blue Notes/Brotherhood tradition into the new, post-apartheid age. The other remark to make is that many will be shocked at how poorly this legendary group is represented, even now.

Peter Brötzmann (born 1941)

ALL SAXOPHONES AND CLARINETS, TAROGATO

Studied art in Wuppertal, then played trad jazz as a teenager before moving into free playing in the early '60s, one of the first European saxophonists to do so. Led a trio with Han Bennink and Fred van Hove from 1968. While most renowned at home and in Europe during the '70s, in the '80s he began acquiring an American status and has since become a godfather-figure to more than one generation of free-jazz explorers.

***(*) For Adolphe Sax

Atavistic Unheard Music UMS/ALP 230 *Brötzmann; Fred Van Hove (p); Peter Kowald (b); Sven-Åke Johansson (d).* 6–9/67.

Brötzmann's influence over the European free-music scene is enormous, and many of his pioneering achievements have only recently been acknowledged in the wider domain. He was playing free jazz in the early '60s and by the time of this astounding album – originally pressed and distributed by the saxophonist himself – was a stylist whose intensity and sureness of focus were already established. The huge, screaming sound he makes is among the most exhilarating things in the music and, while he has often been typecast as a kind of sonic terrorist, that does insufficient justice to his mastery of the entire reed family. The only precedents for his early work are to be found in the contemporary records of Albert Ayler, although Brötzmann arrived at his methods independently of the American. His first trio record is of a similar cast to, say, Ayler's *Spiritual Unity* – a raw, ferocious three-way assault, and in this welcome new edition it underlines how far Brötzmann had already come with his ideas and execution. Kowald and Johansson sometimes trail in his wake, but mostly they're right there along for the ride. There's a bonus of a previously-unheard ten-minute piece where Fred Van Hove joined in at a Radio Bremen session.

CORE COLLECTION

♛ **** Machine Gun

FMP CD 24 *Brötzmann; Willem Breuker, Evan Parker (ts); Fred Van Hove (p); Buschi Niebergall, Peter Kowald (b); Han Bennink, Sven Ake Johansson (d).* 5/68.

***Machine Gun* is one of the most significant documents of the European free-jazz underground. The three saxophonists fire off a ceaseless round of blasting, overblown noise, built on the continuous crescendo managed by Bennink and Johansson and, as chaotic as it sounds, the music is informed by an iron purpose and control. Although the recording is crude, the grainy timbre is a fitting medium for the music. In 1990, *Machine Gun* was reissued on CD with two alternative takes which match the original versions in their fearsome power. Whenever we return to it, the power of this amazing record seems as potent as ever.**

***(*) Fuck De Boere

Atavistic Unheard Music ALP211 *Brötzmann; Paul Rutherford, Malcolm Griffiths, Willem Van Manen (tb); Willem Breuker, Evan Parker, Gerd Dudek (ts); Fred Van Hove (p); Derek Bailey (g); Peter Kowald, Buschi Niebergall (b); Han Bennink, Sven-Åke Johansson (d).* 3/68–3/70.

***(*) Nipples

Atavistic Unheard Music ALP205 *Brötzmann; Evan Parker (ts); Fred Van Hove (p, org); Derek Bailey (g); Buschi Niebergall (b); Han Bennink (d).* 4/69.

*** More Nipples

Atavistic Unheard Music UMS/ALP 236 *As above.* 4/69.

Two valuable rediscoveries. *Fuck De Boere*, dedicated to Johnny Dyani, couples a pair of Frankfurt Festival performances two years apart. The first is a live take on 'Machine Gun', which rather inevitably pales beside the original, but the 36-minute title-piece is a typically extravagant opus for ten players which carries all before it, the trombones and saxophones making tumult over the relatively sparse(!) backing of Bailey, Van Hove and Bennink. Sound is pretty good in the circumstances. *Nipples* was originally released on the tiny Calig label (and produced by Manfred Eicher!): only a little over 30 minutes of music, half of it actually recorded elsewhere, by the group minus Parker and Bailey, but this medium-size ensemble is rather rare in the Brötzmann discography and the results are not a little fascinating – for all the leader's kvetching in the new sleeve-note. *More Nipples* turns up further music from the same sessions (since the two discs could have fitted on to one, a new single edition might have been more generous), and offers some quality leftovers, though leftovers is what they are.

*** The Berlin Concert

FMP CD 34/35 2CD *Brötzmann; Albert Mangelsdorff (tb); Fred Van Hove (p); Han Bennink (cl, d, perc).* 8/71.

The Berlin Concert, originally released as three separate albums, was culled from two days of performance at the Berlin Free Music Market, where the (long-standing) trio was augmented by trombonist Albert Mangelsdorff, whose experience in many other areas of jazz left him unintimidated by the demands of this group. Sound is again only average, but the vigour and earthy bravado of the quartet sustain the listener through the unglamorous circumstances of the music-making. There's little to choose among the various improvisations, but there is a long, compelling feature for Mangelsdorff in 'Alberts', and 'Couscouss De La Mauresque' includes some finely detailed playing by van Hove, even though his piano is often obscured.

*** Reserve

FMP CD 17 *Brötzmann; Barre Phillips (b); Gunter Sommer (d).* 11/88.

A big jump forward from 1971, since the deletion of FMP's catalogue on vinyl has decimated this period of the Brötzmann discography, at least for the time being. Here, on relatively conventional turf, with the more gently inclined Phillips at the bass, Brötzmann digs through three long improvisations. Even on CD, sound is still only reasonable in fidelity, but the music has some attractive empathy, particularly between the leader and Phillips.

***** Wie Das Leben So Spielt**

FMP CD 22 *Brötzmann; Werner Lüdi (as).* 9/89.

Lüdi drifted in and out of free playing for many years, but he sounds enthusiastic enough about being added to Brötzmann's pack of sparring partners on record. Playing only alto, while Brötz runs through his whole arsenal of reeds, Lüdi concocts a stuttery romanticism (of sorts) to set against his companion's fields of fire. Highly invigorating, as usual.

*****(*) No Nothing**

FMP CD 34 *Brötzmann.* 8/90.

The saxophonist still has plenty of new things to say on his third solo album, perhaps the most quiescent of the three, yet often exploding into a logical catharsis. He changes between various saxes and clarinets during the 14-track programme and manages to sustain close to 75 minutes of music, all of it faithfully recorded by Jost Gebers.

*****(*) Dare Devil**

DIW 857 *Brötzmann; Haruhiko Gotsu (g); Tetsu Yahauchi (b); Shoji Hano (d).* 10/91.

Yet another sensational – and sensationally effective – blow-out. Recorded live in Tokyo with what sounds like some kind of Japanese hardcore band, Brötzmann sounds completely at home and enjoying every second of the challenge. Hano, who produced the record, beats out minimal but brazenly effective tattoos and Gotsu is a modest master at making riffs into feasible compositions. Brötzmann just goes at it head first.

***** The Marz Combo**

FMP CD 47 *Brötzmann; Toshinori Kondo (t); Paul Rutherford, Hannes Bauer (tb); Werner Lüdi, Larry Stabbins (saxes); Nicky Skopelitis, Caspar Brötzmann (g); William Parker (b); Anton Fier (d).* 2/92.

Not, perhaps, one of the great Brötzmann sessions: the saxophonists are scarcely a match for the leader, or a useful contrast; while Rutherford is as magnificent as ever, few of the others really rise to the challenge of sharing time with Peter himself. Yet there are still moments of incandescence during the 74 minutes of music and the energy level rarely drops below invigorating.

***** Songlines**

FMP CD 53 *Brötzmann; Fred Hopkins (b); Rashied Ali (d).* 10/91.

*****(*) Die Like A Dog**

FMP CD 64 *Brötzmann; Toshinori Kondo (t, elec); William Parker (b); Hamid Drake (d).* 8/93.

***** Sacred Scrape**

Rastascan BRD-015 *Brötzmann; William Parker (b); Gregg Bendian (d).* 92.

As an elder statesman of free playing, Brötzmann is working steadily but not carelessly: his records are still soaked in the intensity which he's been pursuing for 30 years and, like Bailey or Parker, he alights on new situations and turns them to fit some part of an entrenched but flexible aesthetic. *Die Like A Dog* is the starkest, most Gothic of these three discs, a harrowing meditation on the life and work of Albert Ayler, whose earliest work mirrored Brötzmann's own. This is fuming and at times almost intractable stuff, but its spiritual measure is palpable, and the quartet play with stunning commitment. *Songlines* is more a 'traditional' free trio, the American team of Ali and Hopkins playing with a flair and (indeed!) swing which Brötzmann uses for shape and context with his own severe kind of lyricism. *Sacred Scrape* sets him alongside another generation of American improvisers, and this is a more scattershot battle of wits, Bendian's broken mass of rhythm and noise cracking around the reedman's grand oratory. Parker, a veteran of many a Cecil Taylor scrap, calmly finds his own space in the music. Three good ones.

***** Nothing To Say**

FMP CD 73 *Brötzmann (saxes, cl, tarogato solo).* 11/94.

Solo number four is in dedication to Oscar Wilde and is the calmest record of Brötzmann's career. He picks up the tenor only once, is rumbustious on the bass sax for the title-track but delivers an almost sorrowful lament on the same instrument for 'A Heavy Creeping Shade'. The tarogato and the alto sax bring out his most experimental and piercing solos. There is some stasis here and there; for once, a Brötzmann record seems a shade too long.

****** The Dried Rat-Dog**

Okkadisk 12004 *Brötzmann; Hamid Drake (d).* 5/94.

***** The 'WELS' Concert**

Okkadisk 12013 *As above, except add Mahmoud Gania (guembri, v).* 11/96.

Drake is a particularly perceptive and persuasive partner for Brötzmann. The great advantage of *The Dried Rat-Dog* is Bradley Parker-Sparrow's excellent sound, which lets one hear the nuances in both men's playing. Drake's rhythms have a steadier, more momentous pulse than most free-jazz drumming, and his use of frame drums and tablas adds a global touch that sits quite comfortably next to the saxophonist's characteristic energy. There are six pieces, brimful of eloquent interplay, and on 'Trees Have Roots In The Earth' and 'Dark Wings Carry Off The Sky', Brötz uncorks some of his most vivid tenor playing for a long time.

The live record is less impressive, perhaps since Gania's powerful role tends to undercut Brötzmann a little. Much of the dialogue in three long pieces is between Gania and Drake, with the former's shamanic vocals and thunderous vamps lending a Middle-Eastern flavour that Brötzmann tends to decorate rather than find a way into. Still a worthwhile event, though.

***** Sprawl**

Trost 070 *Brötzmann; Alex Buess (reeds, elec); Stephan Wittwer (g); William Parker (b); Michael Wertmüller (d).* 8/96.

This is the group, Sprawl – possibly a one-off for this recording, so we are listing it under Brötzmann's name. Some of the time he's buried underneath a typhoon of electronics – whether engendered by Wittwer or Buess isn't entirely clear – and it's a bit of a sonic mudbath. The spookier textures of 'Martyrdom Und Genuss' are more absorbing. And there is also Parker to listen to – now not only a major individual voice, but a superb exponent of *arco* bass playing. A mysterious recording.

*****(*) Evolving Blush Or Driving Original Sin**

PSFD-79 *Brötzmann; Haino Keiji (v).* 4/96.

It's rare indeed for Brötzmann to be upstaged, yet Haino's vocals – a spectrum of sighs and whispers at one end and unearthly screams at the other – are, if anything, the more striking element here. The Japanese is better known as a guitarist, but he uses his throat exclusively on this extraordinary hour of music. Documented with starkly beautiful clarity, this is spacious, outward-going music, with tracts of silence surrounding the two voices and few hints of mere madness.

**** The Chicago Octet / Tentet

Okkadisk OD12022 3CD *Brötzmann; Joe McPhee (c, vtb, ss); Jeb Bishop (tb); Mars Williams (ts, as, cl); Ken Vandermark (ts, cl, bcl); Mats Gustafsson (bs, fluteophone); Fred Lonberg-Holm (clo); Kent Kessler (b); Michael Zerang, Hamid Drake (d).* 1–9/97.

**** Stone Water

Okkadisk OD 12032 *As above, except add Toshinori Kondo (t, elec), William Parker (b); omit McPhee and Williams.* 5/99.

The three-disc set should be fairly described as a landmark recording on several levels: a major documentation of Brötzmann on an American label, a rare instance of his large-group music, and a definitive meeting of himself with some of the many American masters – from McPhee to Vandermark – who've been influenced by him. (We should also remark that the simple elegance of the design and artwork, also by Brötzmann, makes a mockery of the elaborate and preposterous packaging which major labels such as Verve seem to be investing so much effort in.) There are one and a half discs each of live and studio material, with three compositions appearing in each incarnation. In fact, Brötz himself contributes only two pieces, 'Burning Spirit' and 'Foolish Infinity'; the others come from Bishop, Gustafsson, Zerang, Drake and Lonberg-Holm, so it can fairly be said to be a co-operative effort, even if the saxophonist's name features on the marquee. Of course he plays a huge role as a performer, but so do the other reed players, besides the other participants. The sheer exhilaration of hearing Brötzmann, Williams, Vandermark and Gustafsson piledriving along as a reed section is about as awesome as you'd expect, but there's much else here to surprise and captivate: the worldly groove of 'Makapoor', the sombre granite-block textures of 'Other Brothers' which explode into a fast shuffle. An affecting tribute to the great man and his influence on a world of improvising which is still evolving and expanding – but the players were clearly having too much of a good time to get all weepy and emotional about it. Rah! Rah! Rah!

The sequel, cut at the 1999 Victoriaville Festival by a slightly different line-up, is hardly less exciting and absorbing. For all the extraordinary volume on show, this is a remarkable feat of engineering, which tends to underline that Brötz has only rarely had his music documented with the kind of accuracy suggested by this effort. As before, a celebration of Peter's art and soul by and with kindred spirits, which leaves a listener breathless.

*** Peter Peter Peter Und Johannes

Ninth World Music 013 *Brötzmann; Johannes Bauer (tb); Peter Friis Nielsen (b); Peter Ole Jørgensen (d).* 97.

***(*) Three Rocks And A Pine

Ninth World Music 020 *As above, except Mats Gustafsson (ts, bs) replaces Bauer.* 99.

A rare encounter between Brötzmann and Bauer which is, in the end, somewhat disappointing. The clarinet comes out more often than the tenor, and Bauer settles for an expressionism which sometimes deteriorates into space-filling, even on a CD which only brushes the 40-minute mark.

The exhilarating follow-up suggests at once that the first session was actually in need of more experienced recording: for this one, the same engineer secured a much bigger and more imposing sound. Gustafsson is one of Peter's spiritual offspring and he is a fine partner for the great man. Fourteen tracks range from the perfect 22-second miniature of 'Clearance Sale' to elongated blowouts of the order of 'The Four-Stroke Engine', though all are abetted by the excellent bass-and-drums pairing.

**** Little Birds Have Fast Hearts No. 1

FMP CD 97 *Brötzmann; Toshinori Kondo (t, elec); William Parker (b); Hamid Drake (d).* 11/97.

**** Little Birds Have Fast Hearts No. 2

FMP CD 101 *As above.* 11/97.

A return visit to the 'Die Like A Dog Quartet'. Parker and Drake are the best 'rhythm section' (if they can admit to that limited description) that Brötzmann has had for years. Kondo, one of the most unfettered and genie-like spirits in free playing, is far too seldom encountered in this kind of situation now, and his madcap sounds are the heat-haze high-altitude counter to Peter's massive, earth-rooted oratory. Recorded over three nights at the 1997 Total Music Meeting, these are all of a piece, and without any demerits. We're hoping that there's still enough left for a third volume.

***(*) Live At The Empty Bottle

Okkadisk 10005 *Brötzmann; Kent Kessler (b); Hamid Drake (d).* 7/98.

Kessler may not be William Parker's equal but he does pretty well, and Brötz sounds both passionate and cheery on this set of performances from Chicago. Drake isn't a muscleman drummer, but the leader has had so many of those behind him over the years that Hamid's more tractable, polymorphous sound is a source of refreshment: there's nothing wanting. An hour of top music.

***(*) Noise Of Wings

Slask SLACD 019 *Brötzmann; Peter Friis Nielsen (b); Peeter Uuskyla (d).* 3/99.

***(*) Live At Nefertiti

Ayler aylCD-004 *As above.* 3/99.

Have horn, will travel. Here he is in Kungälv, Sweden (*Noise Of Wings*), and Gothenburg (*Nefertiti*) for two more bouts. Nielsen, also present in 'The Wild Man's Band', plays a juicy electric bass that keeps on bubbling up through the sound of wings beating. Uuskyla keeps hammering on his snare as if he has a Sisyphean requirement to stop it rolling back over him. The saxophonist sets up and goes, and gives it his all. Really nothing to choose between the two sets – although how agreeable to find Peter recording for a label named Ayler.

***(*) From Valley To Valley

Eremite MTE018 *Brötzmann; Roy Campbell (t); William Parker (b); Hamid Drake (d).* 7/98.

***(*) Aoyama Crows

FMP CD 118 *As above, except Toshinori Kondo (t, elec) replaces Campbell.* 11/99.

Roy Campbell, guesting with the Die Like A Dog Quartet in place of Kondo for the day, has no problem with the turbulent environment, but he does bring an almost boppish feeling to some of his parts, which can be viewed as either a smart contrast to or a lessening of the overall impact. Minus Kondo's darkly surreal playing, the quartet feels tamer, but Campbell brings his own kind of intensity and this is a fascinating alternative matrix to the group's other sets.

In any case, Kondo was back in the fold for the FMP session, recorded at the 1999 Total Music Meeting. In the notes, Brötzmann mentions that the set was played in a state of near-exhaustion. Whether that makes this already dark, fierce music any more fierce and dark is a matter for the listener, though one can hardly call it fatigued: troubled by over-exertion, possibly. It's still a thrilling 70 minutes.

***** Fryed Fruit**
Red Toucan RT 9316 *Brötzmann; Sakari Luoma (g); Nikolai Yudanov (d).* 6/99.

From a club gig in Finland. Some might consider Brötzmann an original, pre-electric heavy metal man, but whether he fits in with Luoma's guitars, the 'authentic' article, is another matter. Despite the expected energies, not one of our favourites.

***** Right As Rain**
FMP CD 112 *Brötzmann (cl, ts, bsx, bcl solo).* 8/00.

Dedicated to the memory of Werner Lüdi, this is Brötzmann's gentlest record. The wild man of legend is barely recognizable on a piece such as the long clarinet soliloquy 'There Were Tears In Her Eyes', and the whole record has a melancholy feel different to most of his work. Sometimes very beautiful, but the air of sadness also gives the impression of some uncomfortable eavesdropping.

****** Never Too Late But Always Too Early**
Eremite MTE 037/38 2CD *Brötzmann; William Parker (b); Hamid Drake (d).* 4/01.

Subsequently declared in homage to Peter Kowald, this catches the trio in magnificent form in Montreal. Two long sets have very little that one could call a treading of water and the potential for Parker and Drake to get funky is realized at several points. A high point in a prolific run of work.

*****(*) The Darkest River**
Ninth World Music NWM 027 *Brötzmann; Pierre Dørge (g); Peter Friis Nielsen (b); Peter Ole Jørgenson (d).* 5/01.

Dørge isn't the likeliest candidate to be the latest guest star with this group, but he fits in surprisingly comfortably, shifting between his various rock, jazz and melodious-worldly positions and making most of it work. Broodingly quiet episodes mingle with the expected firestorms, and there's only an occasional trace of disagreement over direction.

***** Flying Feathers**
FMR CD91-10402 *Brötzmann; Peter Friis Nielsen (b); Peeter Uuskyla (d).* n.d.

This particular trio may be running out of steam a little, and Uuskyla especially is starting to seem very much in the shadow of the likes of Hamid Drake in Brötz's other groups. Still a good blow, but not one of the great ones.

Marlon Browden

DRUMS

A young drummer at work in New York, here making his leadership debut.

***** Marlon Browden Trio**
Fresh Sound FSNT 115 *Browden; Pete Rende (p); Matt Pavolka (b).* 12/00.

A modest, almost introspective debut for this powerful player, and in a genre which usually characterizes drummer-led records as big and in-your-face sessions, this is a refreshing outing. The music has a shapeless feel, Browden's four originals rather drifting past, and covers of Björk and Miles Davis – the latter finding Rende on electric piano and the trio nicely approximating the moody, timeless feel of the gentler electric Davis. Browden drums propulsively but he's a thinker at the kit, interested as much in the tone and colour of his drums and cymbals as in pushing the music. An attractive sketch for future work.

Ari Brown (born 1943)

TENOR, ALTO AND SOPRANO SAXOPHONES, FLUTE, PIANO

A veteran of Chicago's AACM, Brown has stayed as a local player and can be spotted with bandleaders such as Kahlil El'Zabar and Malachi Thompson, as well as leading his own group.

***** Ultimate Frontier**
Delmark DE 486 *Brown; Kirk Brown (p); Yosef Ben Israel (b); Ayreeayl Ra (d); Dr Cuz, Enoch (perc).* 1/95.

Brown has been associated with many players in the AACM but he's fundamentally a conservative: the best things on this record come when he delivers a big, beefy ballad performance as on 'One For Luba' and 'Sincerity'. Much of the rest is an unmistakable Chicagoan stew of churning post-bop, 'Big V' and the crashing 'Motherless Child' sending the saxophonist to blaze away over a busy if rather faceless rhythm-section. For all his impetus, Brown is a rather galumphing horn-player, his phrases falling squarely on or around the beat. Taken a piece at a time, this is quite exciting but listeners may find themselves rather weatherbeaten by the end of it.

***** Venus**
Delmark DE 504 *Brown; Kirk Brown (p); Josef Ben Israel, Thaddeus Expose (b); Avreeayl Ra (d); Art Burton, Enoch (perc).* 3/98.

Brown has been steadily working on his Chicago turf and making the occasional appearance on record to remind us that he's still out there. What's more or less the same band as last time finds him musing on some old spirits: Willie Pickens, Roscoe Mitchell, and several unspoken nods towards Coltrane. 'Rahsaan In The Serengeti' has him doing the Kirk thing by playing soprano and alto simultaneously. But it's still the more inward playing that suits him best: his duet with Kirk Brown on 'Oh What A World' is secular gospel of an individual order.

Clifford Brown (1930–56)

TRUMPET

Relative to the length of his career, Clifford Brown perhaps had a greater impact on the music than any comparable instrumentalist. A whole generation of jazz trumpeters were affected by his combination of fast attack and broad, lyrical tone, which sounded like a hybrid of Fats Navarro and Miles Davis. Brownie's early death was a genuine tragedy for the music, its reverberations still felt two generations later.

CORE COLLECTION

★★★★ The Complete Blue Note And Pacific Jazz Recordings

Blue Note 34195-2 4CD *Brown; J. J. Johnson (tb); Stu Williamson (vtb); Gigi Gryce (as, f); Lou Donaldson (as); Charlie Rouse, Zoot Sims (ts); Jimmy Heath (ts, bs); Bobby Gordon (bs); Russ Freeman, Elmo Hope, John Lewis, Horace Silver (p); Percy Heath, Joe Mondragon, Curley Russell, Carson Smith (b); Art Blakey, Kenny Clarke, Philly Joe Jones, Shelly Manne (d).* 6/53–8/54.

This four-CD compilation of all the Blue Note and Capitol recordings is as elegantly remastered and packaged as anyone could possibly wish. Two of these sessions were recorded under the leadership or co-leadership of J.J. Johnson, Art Blakey and Lou Donaldson. The live Birdland sessions of February 1954 are splendidly extended and afford the best possible glimpse of the young genius on the brink of his breakthrough. The rest of the material simply teems with promise and it is almost inconceivable – indeed heartbreaking – listening to the first three discs, to think that none of it would ever come to proper fruition. The sheer fecundity of Brown's musical imagination never fails to amaze.

★★★★ Memorial Album

Blue Note 32141-2 *Brown; Gigi Gryce (as, f); Lou Donaldson (as); Charlie Rouse (ts); Elmo Hope, John Lewis (p); Percy Heath (b); Philly Joe Jones, Art Blakey (d).* 6–8/53.

★★★ Clifford Brown Memorial

Original Jazz Classics OJC 017 *Brown; Art Farmer, Idrees Sulieman (t); Herb Mullins, Ake Persson (tb); Arne Domnérus, Gigi Gryce (as); Benny Golson (ts); Oscar Estell, Lars Gullin (bs); Tadd Dameron, Bengt Hallberg (p); Percy Heath, Gunnar Johnson (b); Philly Joe Jones, Jack Noren (d); collective personnel.* 6–9/53.

★★★(★) Clifford Brown Quartet In Paris

Original Jazz Classics OJC 357 *Brown; Henri Renaud (p); Pierre Michelot (b); Benny Bennett (d).* 10/53.

★★★(★) Clifford Brown Sextet In Paris

Original Jazz Classics OJC 358 *Brown; Gigi Gryce (as); Henri Renaud (p); Jimmy Gourley (g); Pierre Michelot (b); Jean-Louis Viale (d).* 10/53.

★★★(★) Jazz Immortal

Blue Note 32142-2 *Brown; Stu Williamson (vtb); Zoot Sims (ts); Bobby Gordon (bs); Russ Freeman (p); Joe Mondragon, Carson Smith (b); Shelly Manne (d).* 7–8/54.

In the days after Clifford Brown died – Richie Powell with him – and as the news filtered through to clubs and studios up and down the country, hardened jazz musicians put away their horns and quietly went home to grieve. Only 26, Brown was almost universally liked and admired. Free of the self-destructive 'personal problems' that haunted jazz at the time, he had seemed destined for ever greater things when his car skidded off the turnpike.

To this day, his influence on trumpeters is immense, less audibly than Miles Davis's, perhaps, because more pervasive. Though most of his technical devices – long, burnished phrases, enormous melodic and harmonic compression within a chorus, internal divisions of the metre – were introduced by Dizzy Gillespie and Fats Navarro, his two most significant models, it was Brownie who melded them into a distinctive and coherent personal style of great expressive power. Almost every trumpeter who followed, including present-day figures like Wynton Marsalis, has drawn heavily on his example; few though have managed to reproduce the powerful singing grace he took from the ill-starred Navarro.

After a first, near-fatal car accident, Brown gigged in R&B bands and then worked briefly with Tadd Dameron, before touring Europe with Lionel Hampton towards the end of 1953, on which he enjoyed a good-natured and stage-managed rivalry with Art Farmer, and recorded the excellent quartet, sextet and big-band sides now reissued on OJC and sampled on *Blue And Brown*. By this time, he had already recorded the sessions on the confusingly titled *Memorial* (OJC) and *Memorial Album* (Blue Note). The former combined European and American sessions and isn't the most compelling of his recordings, though Dameron's arrangements are as challenging as always, and there are some fine moments from the Scandinavians on the September date.

In their new RVG editions, both *Memorial Album* and *Jazz Immortal* are tempting buys, even if you have the complete edition, since once again the Van Gelder magic has been worked on the sound, which beats any previous issue (even if Mr VG didn't do the original engineering in both cases). The former has been extended to include all alternative takes and would make a fine introduction to Brown for a newcomer. The latter sets Clifford up with a gang of West Coasters in a series of Jack Montrose charts and, while the set might seem 'slick' in comparison with some of Clifford's playing situations, it does bring out the excellence of Brownie originals such as 'Daahoud' and 'Joy Spring' and the playing is handsome.

★★★★ Brownie

Emarcy 838 306-16 10CD *Brown; Maynard Ferguson, Clark Terry (t); Herbie Mann (f); Danny Bank (f, bs); Herb Geller, Joe Maini (as); Walter Benton, Harold Land, Paul Quinichette, Sonny Rollins (ts); Kenny Drew, Jimmy Jones, Junior Mance, Richie Powell (p); Barry Galbraith (g); Joe Benjamin, Keter Betts, Curtis Counce, Milt Hinton, George Morrow (b); Oscar Pettiford (b, clo); Bobby Donaldson, Roy Haynes, Osie Johnson, Max Roach (d); Helen Merrill, Dinah Washington, Sarah Vaughan (v); strings arranged and conducted by Neal Hefti; collective personnels.* 8/54–2/56.

★★★★ Jazz Masters: Clifford Brown

Emarcy 842933 *Brown; as above.* 2/54–2/56.

★★★★ Alone Together

Verve 526373-2 *Brown; Harold Land, Hank Mobley, Paul Quinichette, Sonny Rollins (ts); Danny Bank (bs); Herbie Mann (f); Ray Bryant, Jimmy Jones, Richie Powell (p); Barry Galbraith (g); Joe Benjamin, Milt Hinton, George Morrow (b); Roy Haynes, Osie Johnson, Max Roach (d); Helen Merrill, Sarah Vaughan (v); strings.* 8/54–1/56.

★★★ Study In Brown

Emarcy 814 646 2 *Brown; Harold Land (ts); Richie Powell (p); George Morrow (b); Max Roach (d).* 55.

★★★ More Study In Brown

Emarcy 814637-2 *As above, except add Sonny Rollins (ts).* 56.

Brownie gathers together all the material Brown recorded for Emarcy between 2 August 1954 and 16 February 1956. It includes no fewer than nine previously unreleased takes, together with a number of alternative takes that have appeared in other contexts. The research was done by the indefatigable Kiyoshi

Koyama and the recordings remastered digitally from the originals held at the Polygram Tape Facility at Edison, New Jersey. The liner-notes are by Dan Morgenstern and are impeccably detailed.

Inevitably, the best of the music is in the Roach–Brown sessions. The drummer's generosity in making the younger man co-leader is instantly and awesomely repaid. On the earliest of the sessions (Discs 1 and 2, originally released as *Brown And Roach Incorporated*), there is a brilliantly impressionistic arrangement of Bud Powell's 'Parisian Thoroughfare' (whose onomatopoeic effects are echoed on a 'Take The "A" Train' from February 1955, Disc 9), a superb 'Jordu', and an offcut of Brown soloing on 'Sweet Clifford', a reworking of the 'Sweet Georgia Brown' changes. Whether cup-muted or open, he sounds relaxed and completely confident. Land plays a more than supportive role and is generously featured on 'Darn That Dream'.

The next session (Discs 3 and 4) was a studio jam recorded a week or so later, with Herb Geller, the un-chancy Joe Maini and Walter Benton all on saxophones, and Kenny Drew, Curtis Counce and Roach filling out the band. There are three takes (the first incomplete) of a blues called 'Coronado' (Disc 3), then extended versions of 'You Go To My Head', 'Caravan' – and a fragmentary variant, 'Boss Man' – and 'Autumn In New York'. Posthumously released as *Best Coast Jazz* and *Clifford Brown All Stars*, they contain some of the trumpeter's weakest and most diffuse playing. Always eminently disciplined, his solos lost much of their shape in this context. However, it's worth it for Maini's contribution.

The 14 August jam with Dinah Washington (Discs 5 and 6) includes over-long versions of 'What Is This Thing Called Love', 'Move' and 'I'll Remember April', but there are two fine medleys and Brown is superb on 'It Might As Well Be Spring', which extends his accompanist's role. He has less space round Sarah Vaughan (Disc 7), but he compresses his responses to the vocal line into beautifully polished choruses and half-choruses; Paul Quinichette is magnificent. Brown also accompanies Helen Merrill (Disc 8) on her debut recording; this is slighter, even prettified, and Quincy Jones's arrangements are definitely overcooked, but the trumpeter's contributions are gently effective.

The first quintet sessions for six months (Disc 9) find the group in rattling form. *Study In Brown* marks the trumpeter's emergence as an individual star of formidable magnitude. He takes 'Cherokee' at a dangerous pace and doesn't fudge a single note (there are bootleg recordings of him doggedly alternating and inverting practice phrases). Throughout the album, his entries have real *presence* and his delivery floats over the rhythm section without ever losing contact with Roach's compelling metres. 'Jacqui' is relatively unusual fare, and it may be significant that Land, with his West Coast roots, handles it most comfortably. This was the saxophonist's last studio date with the band. His replacement, Sonny Rollins, has at this point in his career a slightly crude approach. He is nevertheless bursting with ideas that push the group's capabilities to the utmost and his first statement on 'Gertrude's Bounce' may suggest recourse to the review button, so daring is it in conception and execution. Brown himself sounds as though he must be reading off prearranged sequences, firing out eight-, four- and two-bar statements that seem to contain more and more musical information the shorter they get. This is the material released as *At Basin Street.*

Koyama has dug out previously unsuspected masters of 'Love Is A Many Splendored Thing' (taken at a distinctly unslushy pace) and 'Flossie Lou' (which reworks 'Jeepers Creepers'). A rehearsal fragment of the latter is included on a 3-inch bonus CD single, like the cherry on top of the cake. *Brownie* is a bulky and, inevitably, expensive work of documentation. The trumpeter has scarcely a bad moment, but there is a lot of material to digest, and newcomers might prefer to begin with the excellent *Jazz Masters* compilation, which draws from all but the unfeasibly long jam-sessions and consists of 'The Blues Walk', 'I Get A Kick Out Of You', 'Jordu', 'Parisian Thoroughfare', 'Daahoud', 'It's Crazy', 'Stardust', 'I'll Remember April', 'I've Got You Under My Skin', 'Yesterdays' and the original release of 'Flossie Lou'. For accessibility and sheer value it could hardly be bettered. At least some of those who invest will want to move on to the Complete Works. Brown's qualities ring out on every bar.

Alone Together, it should be made clear, consists of one CD of Brownie material (much of it with Roach) and one CD of somewhat later Roach recordings; these latter are discussed in the appropriate place. As a package it makes a very attractive introduction to both artists. Of Brownie, there is the magnificent 'Joy Spring' from August 1954, the February 1955 'Cherokee' from *A Study In Brown*, 'Gertrude's Bounce' from January 1956 with 11 other tracks from the Emarcy sessions. No surprises, but elegantly packaged and very desirable.

Study In Brown and *More* contain material already covered elsewhere but they are also attractive individually. Brown's 'Cherokee' is still one of the most arresting performances in modern jazz and his solo on 'Take The "A" Train' is a masterpiece of organization, holding a typically long line in suspension over many bars.

**** The Ultimate Clifford Brown

Verve 539776-2 *Brown; as for Verve recordings above.* 54–56.

*** Clifford Brown's Finest Hour

Verve 543602-2 *As various Verve albums above.* 8/54–2/55.

Another in Verve's excellent series of *Ultimate* artist-selected compilations. This time, it's Nicholas Payton who chose the tracks, including doubtless a few that had a direct impact on his own playing style. Nearly all standards and covers, in the event, and with perhaps too diplomatic an emphasis on Brownie's work as accompanist to Helen Merrill, Sassie and Dinah Washington, but irreproachable apart from that. Anyone who encounters the opening 'Gertrude's Bounce' and catches the Brown–Roach–Rollins–Richie Powell–Morrow band for the first time is likely to be hooked for the duration. The *Finest Hour* set includes the odd curios, such as Helen Merrill's 'Yesterdays', but with two other Brown compilations on Verve still in the racks this one's docked a point for pointlessness.

***(*) Clifford Brown With Strings

Emarcy 558078-2 *Brown; Richie Powell (p); Barry Galbraith (g); George Morrow (b); Max Roach (d); strings.* 1/55.

Beautifully repackaged and presented, the January 1955 sessions are, in retrospect, most remarkable for Neal Hefti's delicately nuanced arrangements which always seem to deliver up surprises. The 12 tracks are almost perfectly uniform in length and delivery, and it's all the more remarkable that they remain fresh and inventive. Brown sounds as bright as a new pin in this digitally remastered version, but he isn't artificially foregrounded in front of the strings; they receive their due share as well.

Damon Brown

TRUMPET, FLUGELHORN, VOCAL

Young British trumpeter, with experience in pop situations but going straight ahead under his own name.

*****(*) Blues On The Run**

Jazz House JHCD 065 *Brown; Tim Garland, Renato D'Aiello (ts); Jim Watson, Jonathan Gee, Leon Greening (p); Arnie Somogyi, Ben Hazleton (b); Sebastien Rochford, Winston Clifford (d).* 1/00.

*****(*) Good Cop Bad Cop**

33 Jazz 061 *Brown; Jonathan Gee (p); Yorai Oron (b); Yaaki Levy, Shai Zelman (d); Idit Eshel (v).* 5/00–4/01.

The decisive playing on *Blues On The Run* is a pleasure after so much rhetoric on so many standard post-bop records. Brown is a trumpeter who likes to make every part of the line matter. A lot of his improvising is in small, incisive phrases, but when he goes long, he breaks it up with a snarled note or deliberately wayward intonation. The results are clean, but not squeakily so. It helps to have the contrasting tenors of Garland and D'Aiello on hand – pity that they only play together on the smart 'Keep Moving' – and each of the three pianists is an asset too. 'Sky Blue' is a less than enthralling ballad, and 'Mack The Knife' seems like a filler finale, but there's not much wrong with this excellent set.

The follow-up came about following a gig at the Israeli Red Sea Festival, and with Gee getting co-billing there's as much emphasis on piano as trumpet. Jonathan's 'Cicada' and 'Catwoman' are strikingly effective themes in their different ways, and Brown plays some exultant solos. 'Roughneck Blues' begins as a trumpet–drums duo in the earlier album, and in this version that dialogue is extended to full length with Zelman.

Donald Brown (born 1954)

PIANO

Perhaps best known as a composer, Brown grew up in Memphis and had a spell with the Messengers before arthritis forced him to concentrate more on music education and occasional recording.

*****(*) The Sweetest Sounds**

Evidence 22203 *Brown; Steve Nelson (vib); Charnett Moffett (b); Alan Dawson (d).* 6/88.

The title of a later album, *Piano Short Stories*, probably best sums up Brown's art. He is concise, linear and his solo narratives are always beautifully constructed, though more Jean Toomer than Guy de Maupassant. This was originally released on Jazz City and is a valuable record of a player whose career has been somewhat intermittent. It's basically a trio date, but Nelson joins in on four numbers, to somewhat mixed effect. The best of the session can be found on 'Night Mist Blues' (Ahmad Jamal) and the originals 'Affaire D'Amour' and 'Nature's Folk Song'. There are a couple of pop tracks as well, but so transformed by Brown the composer that they come across as well-trodden standards.

***** Piano Short Stories**

Space Time 9601 *Brown (p solo).* 95.

Brown's allusiveness on 'Take The "A" Train' on this his first live solo record shows how steeped he is in the music of the swing era. It affects his writing, originals like 'For Pops' and 'Philippe's Stomp', but it also colours his approach to 'On Green Dolphin Street', which doesn't sound like a hard bop vehicle any longer. With his Muse catalogue out of print this is a valuable reintroduction to Brown, who worked through the early '80s despite health problems. The stand-out tracks are the opening 'I Didn't Know What Time It Was' and a superb, off-beat reading of Herbie Hancock's 'Dolphin Dance'.

***** Enchanté**

Space Time 9910 *Brown; Stephane Belmondo (t, flhn); Bill Easley (as, f, cl); Steve Nelson (vib); Essiet Essiet (b); Billy Higgins (d); Daniel Sadownick (perc).* 99.

***** French Kiss**

Space Time 2012 *Brown; Jerome Barde (g); Essiet Essiet (b); Billy Kilson (d); Anga Diaz (perc).* 00.

Brown's skills as a composer have always been recognized by fellow players and all too infrequently by a wider jazz public. Again here he demonstrates an ability to suggest whole narratives within the span of a relatively conventional song form. The earlier record seems like a poem to life in France, elegant, subtle and ruthlessly modern even where it's steeped in history. The same basic group also figures on *French Kiss*. As well as writing original themes like 'The McGhaw's Place' and 'Poem For Martin', though, Brown shows his class in picking other challenging repertoire. How many piano players have taken on Bobby Hutcherson's 'Pomponio' or given McCoy Tyner's 'Utopia' such an imaginative working? Brown's title-tune is a delight and his version of Charlie Chaplin's 'Smile' is dazzling, typical of his ability to give familiar tunes the most original introductions.

Fans of Brown can also find him on *A Season Of Ballads*, a trio album shared with Harold Mabern and Charles Thomas, also released on Space Time.

****(*) At This Point In My Life**

Space Time 2115 *As above: add Bill Mobley (t, flhn); Jean Toussaint (ss, ts).* 99.

A disappointing record, badly recorded and curiously pretentious. The 'suite' dedicated to bassist Essiet is without obvious rationale and the opening 'Reruns From The Seventies', apparently dedicated to Prince and George Clinton, seems an odd bid for pop credibility. By now, virtually all the material is original, and Brown's touch as a composer is still evident on 'Dear Waddia' and 'What Do You Think Of Me Now?', the latter a powerful ballad. Almost all of these songs would have been better served with slimmer arrangements and a more sensitive engineering job.

***** Autumn In New York**

Space Time 2219 *Brown; Essiet Essiet (b); Billy Kilson (d).* 5/00.

The trio works much better and Brown seems to be back on form here, except that he does seem increasingly inclined to pepper his solos with tags and quotes from contemporary songs, legitimate enough if the allusions are recognizable but pointlessly enigmatic when they aren't, as here. Essiet is in better shape on this one as well and Kilson's crisply precise drumming helps to cement similarities with the classic Ahmad Jamal trio.

Guillermo E. Brown (born 1976)

DRUMS

Brown grew up in New Haven and played rock and hip-hop before launching a jazz career as Susie Ibarra's replacement in the David S. Ware group. A powerful rhythm player, he continues to diversify.

***** Soul At The Hands Of The Machine**
Thirsty Ear 57118 *Brown; Daniel Carter (t, as, cl, f); Andre Vidal (sax); Shahzad Ismaily, Keith Witty (b); Natasha Latasha Diggs (v).* 02.

The 'E.' is to distinguish him from electronica musician Guillermo Barreto Brown but don't be surprised if they turn up on the same record some day. Brown is an eclectic in the proper sense, selecting elements of a dozen musical styles to meld this confident, indeed brazen, debut. It has elements of bebop, free jazz, funk and hip-hop, but the joins don't show. The opening 'If We Can Ever Find A Way', 'Manganese' and the climactic 'Outside Looking In' bespeak a real composer, thinking musically rather than formulaically.

Multi-instrumentalists Carter and Vidal are responsible for a lot of the detail and both play a range of horns magnificently. Brown himself samples an array of beats, turns on the power and occasionally shifts down to create passages of disconcerting quiet and concentration. The two bassists – Witty on acoustic, Ismaily on what sounds like a Fender Jazz – weave complex patterns that never sound like complexity for its own sake. Singer Diggs is an asset, varying the fare rather than providing a distraction.

This may not be the jazz sound of tomorrow, but it won't sound like yesterday's fad either. Brown is hip, current and, above all, a formidable musician.

Jeri Brown (born 1952)

VOCAL

A modern standards singer with an approach somewhere between classic and experimentalist.

*****(*) Mirage**
Justin Time JUST 38 *Brown; Fred Hersch (p); Daniel Lessard (b).* 2 & 3/91.

The big difference between Broadway and opera singers, or between musicals and opera, is that the former always does (or always should) sound conversational. The lovely Jeri Brown has the ability to make every song sound as if spoken directly and without artifice. Even her scatting sounds like a kind of thinking aloud, unhistrionic and much subtler than might at first appear.

The first of her records is certainly the most conventional, and *Mirage* is almost hijacked by Fred Hersch's wonderfully subtle accompaniments. He is credited with the title-tune and with 'A Child's Song', and is co-writer on the ambitious 'Ten Twenty', which may have been kept to last deliberately but seems rather thrown away in that lowly position. Brown is not a confident bopper – 'Good Bait' is not going to catch anything – but she positively glows on the less rhythmic, more through-composed pieces. Very definitely an album that grows.

****** 'Unfolding' The Peacocks**
Justin Time JUST 45 *Brown; Michael Dubeau (ss, shakuhachi); Peter Leitch (g); Kirk Lightsey (p); Rufus Reid (b); Wali Muhammad (d); Suzanne Doucet, Shawn Smith (v).* 2/92.

****** A Timeless Place**
Justin Time JUST 70 *Brown; Jimmy Rowles (p, v); Eric Von Essen (b).* 5/94.

The long-underrated Jimmy Rowles has been a big influence on Ms Brown's work. He is the guiding spirit of *'Unfolding' The Peacocks*, and he appears on the later record, playing and singing. Ms Brown effectively deconstructs Rowles's classic 'The Peacocks', turning it into a rich vocalization somewhat in the manner of Norma Winstone (who provides the lyrics to 'A Timeless Place' on the later record). The mournful yelp of the male peafowl is suggested by Michael Dubeau's shakuhachi part; his only other contribution to the record is a soprano line on 'Jean', but both are clinchers. Lightsey and Reid develop atmospheric, sepia-tinted backdrops, but the attention is constantly on the singer. 'Orange Coloured Sky' is wholly delightful, and Bob Dorough's 'Wouldn't You' sounds freshly minted. The two backing singers appear on the eerie 'Tuang Guru', a Saharan chorale by Abdullah Ibrahim, further evidence of Ms Brown's adventurousness.

The vocal duet with Rowles on 'Don't Quite Know' is glorious, and Jimmy's playing throughout the album has a quietly magisterial quality. He co-wrote 'Morning Star' with the great Johnny Mercer and delivers it many years later as if it had only just risen in his mind.

*****(*) Fresh Start**
Justin Time JUST 78 *Brown; Greg Carter (ss); Cyrus Chestnut (p); Avery Sharpe (b); Wali Muhammad (d).* 5/95.

***** April In Paris**
Justin Time JUST 92 *Brown; Alain Jean-Marie (p); Pierre Michelot (b); John Betsch (d).* 4/96.

Was a fresh start needed? Or did Jeri Brown merely want to explore other dimensions of her vocal talents? Certainly there was nothing to suggest that she wasn't working a fertile and long-lasting seam, but the new record sees her working in a much lower register than before, not always with absolute assurance. The opening 'Come, Come And Play With Me', co-written with Greg Carter, is unexpectedly oblique and seemingly influenced by stuff Cassandra Wilson was doing back in M-BASE days. Brown's scat is dark-toned and angular, pitched just in front of a superb solo from Avery Sharpe, who is the most prominent band member. (Carter is featured on just one track, and it might have been good to have heard a little more from him.) She works approximately the same territory on a wordless version of Oscar Pettiford's 'Harlem After Dark', followed later by Tadd Dameron's expansively boppish 'You're A Joy'. Cyrus Chestnut has backed Betty Carter, and she seems another feasible source for at least some of the material. 'Orange Sky' is mentioned again, obviously a strong personal resonance, and there is a rather unexpected version of 'Shall We Gather By The River', before the title-piece is reprised. A nicely shaped album, but not one that really plays to her strengths.

The death of Jimmy Rowles meant that there were to be no more duets. *April In Paris* includes 'Morning Lovely', a Rowles tune which seems to sit outside either her normal or even her more recent range, but it works beautifully nevertheless. Again, the band is very good. Jean-Marie has more than a hint of Bill Evans about him and John Betsch is exactly the sort of delicate, tuneful drummer singers revel in. It's Michelot, though, who provides most of the drama, light and shade aplenty and seemingly endless invention throughout a rather odd roster of songs: 'Once Upon A Summertime', 'The Twelfth Of Never', 'Summertime', 'Greensleeves' and 'The Windmills Of Your Mind'. Co-written with Kenny Wheeler, 'Gentle Piece' is thrown away in the opening slot; 'When April Comes Again' would have been a better call, both musically and thematically. Dare we say ... a slightly disappointing record. Established Jeri Brown fans will find much to treasure on it, but anyone who hasn't yet been converted should perhaps begin elsewhere.

*****(*) Zaius**

Justin Time JUST 117-2 *Brown; Don Braden, David Murray (ts); John Hicks (p); Curtis Lundy, Avery Sharpe (b); Sangoma Everett (d).* 98.

****** I've Got Your Number**

Justin Time JUST 122-2 *As above, except add Wali Muhammad (d); Leon Thomas (v).* 1 & 11/98.

'I've Got Your Number' is not just an excellent vocal performance. It's also a reference to Jeri's bulging contacts book. The best measure of her growing confidence and reputation is her ability to call together a band like this. For some reason, the chemistry doesn't quite come off on the first of the pair. Hicks and bassists Lundy and Sharpe (who share duties) are superb vocal accompanists, underpinning the spooky drama of 'You Must Believe In Spring' and always leaving lots of space round the singer. They all must have done 'Softly, As In A Morning Sunrise' a thousand times before, but it still comes across as fresh as the new day.

David Murray's interest in song has been more emphatically stated than acted upon. His role on 'Midnight Sun' and on Gerry Niewood's 'Joy' is a revelation. Don Braden makes more of an impact on *Zaius* and only re-emerges for 'As Long As You're Living' on the second record which is well sequenced and comfortably paced. It seems only the day before yesterday that Jeri Brown was a new face and one to watch. Looking at that face has never been arduous, but it's maybe distracted us from the sheer quality, and now the amount, of her recorded output.

***** Image In The Mirror: The Triptych**

Justin Time 151 *Brown; Milton Sealey (p); Avery Sharpe (b); Grady Tate (d, v).* 5–6/00.

Brown continues to plough her own bold furrow with this closely structured concept album. It doesn't so much tell a story as establish a narrative mood, and it's as far away as can be imagined from the usual run of sub-Ella standards/scat albums that clog the shelves. Brown's voice is naturally introspective, not ideal for big dramatic projection, and the material here, self-written or in collaboration with pianist Sealey, is mostly pitched to suit that style and range. 'All At Once' and the closing 'The Dragonfly And The Pearl' are remarkable performances from all concerned. Ms Brown continues to intrigue and enchant.

***** Firm Roots**

Justin Time 184 *Brown; Seamus Blake (ts); Eric Klory (clo); Avery Sharpe (b); Wali Muhammad (d); Andre Martin (perc).* 02.

A less enterprising but not less appealing album than its predecessors, this one finds Jeri exploring some unexpected corners of the songbook. Including Bacharach and David's 'What the World Needs Now Is Love, Sweet Love' is always a risky ploy on a jazz album, but Ms Brown pulls it off with great aplomb. 'Feeling Good' is a Bricusse/Newley classic, but a neglected classic and it's good to hear it in this context. Bill Cosby has a hand in 'With A Child's Heart' and it is one of the most affecting things in the set.

Seamus Blake is as adept and tuneful as ever, but it's that man Sharpe who takes the laurels, building firm harmonic platforms for Jeri Brown to construct her songs. The addition of cello as a harmony instrument brings a new texture and dimension. Another delightful record.

Marion Brown (born 1935)

ALTO SAXOPHONE

Studied music in his native Atlanta, then was caught up in New York's free jazz of the '60s. After some years in Europe, he returned to the USA and has since worked mainly in education, specializing in African musical and linguistic traditions.

***** Marion Brown Quartet**

ESP Disk 1022 *Brown; Alan Shorter (t); Ronnie Boykins, Reggie Johnson (b); Rashied Ali (d).* 65.

*****(*) Three For Shepp**

Impulse! IMPCD 12692 *Brown; Grachan Moncur III (tb); Dave Burrell, Stanley Cowell (p); Norris Jones (b); Bobby Capp, Beaver Harris (d).* 12/66.

***** Afternoon Of A Georgia Faun**

ECM 527710-2 *Brown; Anthony Braxton (as, ss, cl, cbcl, Chinese musette, f, perc); Bennie Maupin (ts, af, acorn, bells, wood f, perc); Chick Corea (p, bells, gong, perc); Larry Curtis (p); Jack Gregg (b, perc); Billy Malone (d); Andrew Cyrille (perc); William Green (top o'lin, perc); Jeanne Lee (v, perc); Gayle Palmore (v, p, perc).* 8/70.

Possessed of a sweet, slightly fragile tone and a seemingly limitless melodic resource, Brown is nevertheless one of the most undervalued of saxophonists. At present, he has a very thin showing in the catalogues. There is a certain poignant irony in the fact that his finest recorded work should be solo saxophone, for he is a dedicated educator with a long-standing commitment to collective – and often untrained or amateur – music-making. Brown's one and only recording for ECM, *Afternoon Of A Georgia Faun*, came out of that ethos, performed by six instrumentalists and three assistants on 'little instruments' like Brown's invented top o'lin (pot lids fixed to a board and bowed like a fiddle). All the performers permutate their instruments at work-stations in fulfilment of Brown's ideal of 'interchangeable discourse'. The results, predictably, are uneven and slightly unkempt, but there is some affecting music on the album. Chick Corea's solo on the title-piece is near perfect, and both Braxton and Maupin produce passages of great beauty.

Brown's ESP recording is pretty typical of the label's output at the time: full-on free jazz with an emphasis on energy and intensity. Brown had survived the maelstrom of Coltrane's *Ascension* and seemed determined here to harness similar energies. The opening 'Capricorn Moon' is the best cut; many listeners may decide not to proceed further.

Archie Shepp famously may or may not have appeared uncredited in the closing moments of John Coltrane's momentous *A Love Supreme*. One certainly expects to hear him on *Three For Shepp*, not least because he glowers out at the listener from the cover, a pose in sharp contrast to Brown's intent and slightly cautious stare. The session consists of three Brown compositions and three – 'Spooks', 'West India' and 'Delicado' – by Shepp. The two had worked together for Impulse! when the alto man played on Shepp's *Fire Music*, and the musical sympathy established there is unmistakable. Brown's 'Fortunato' suggests a direct influence, albeit without Archie's fierce ideological muscle. The contrast between the two rhythm sections is interesting and instructive. Sirone plays on both, but the partnership of Dave Burrell and Bobby Capp works ideally for the leader's own themes, while the more emphatic and blues-influenced Shepp tunes call for players of Cowell's and Harris's authority. The front-row combination of alto and trombone still sounds faintly alien, but Moncur is such an expressive player that the slight mismatch of register – still evident on CD – doesn't jar more than incidentally.

Pete Brown (1906–63)

ALTO SAXOPHONE

Brown grew up in Maryland but came north to New York to start a career that, despite associations with Buster Bailey and John Kirby, never really came to much. He was overtaken by bebop and ill-health and disappeared into obscurity well before his premature death.

*** Pete Brown, 1942–1945

Classics 1029 *Brown; Dizzy Gillespie, Joe Thomas (t); Jimmy Hamilton (cl); Sam Price, Kenny Watts (p); Al Casey, Herman Mitchell, Bill Moore (g); Charlie Drayton, Al Hall, Milt Hinton, John Levy, Al Matthews, Ed Nicholson (b); J. C. Heard (d); Nora Lee King (v).* 42–45.

Brown's swing alto should have been distinctive enough to sustain a more successful solo career, but he remains a relatively unknown figure. Though he continued recording right up to 1961, almost nothing of his work remains in print. These amiable sides are a decent record of his brightly pitched horn and his gift for the kind of easy, bluesy soloing that Captain John Handy made more famous later, possibly influenced by Brown. As titles like 'Pete's Idea', 'Pete Brown's Boogie' and 'Fat Man's Boogie (Big Boy Boogie)' probably suggest, the material is undemanding and aimed at the jukebox market. Nonetheless, he's an engaging soloist with a nice, vocalized tone and anyone interested in the development of pre-bebop alto playing will find the disc fascinating.

Ray Brown (1926–2002)

DOUBLE BASS, CELLO

The most frequently cited artist in our first and subsequent editions was bassist Ray Brown, whose career has spanned the bebop era and a myriad sessions as sideman and leader since then. Brown was born in Pittsburgh, witnessed the birth-pangs of bebop, acted as music director for his wife, Ella Fitzgerald, played with Dizzy Gillespie and as a result was involved in the formation of what became the Modern Jazz Quartet. He also worked with Oscar Peterson and was a founder member of the LA4, whose brand of soft Latin jazz was a perfect vehicle for Brown's uncluttered rhythm and tasteful melodic sense.

*** Jazz Cello

Verve 065395 *Brown; Don Fagerquist (t); Harry Betts (tb); John (Jack) Cave (frhn); Paul Horn, Bob Cooper, Med Flory, Bill Hood (reeds); Jimmy Rowles (p); Joe Mondragon (b); Dick Shanahan (d).* 60.

A fascinating early glimpse of Brown as leader, and doubling on cello to give him a more prominent lead voice. The arrangements are crisp and mellow, even if the balancing is suspect in places. It's all standards material, which is a shame given the amount of arranging skill on show. 'Alice Blue Gown' and 'Rock-A-Bye Your Baby With A Dixie Melody' are tiny pieces but among the most effective. It falters a bit when the duration stretches.

***(*) Much In Common

Verve 533259-2 2CD *Brown; Nat Adderley (c); Joe Newman, Ernie Royal, Clark Terry, Snooky Young (t); Jimmy Cleveland, Paul Faulise, Urbie Green, Melba Liston, Tom McIntosh, Tony Studd, Britt Woodman (tb); Ray Alonge (frhn); Bob Ashton, Danny Bank, Jimmy Heath, Romeo Penque, Phil Woods (reeds); Julian 'Cannonball' Adderley, Earl Warren (as); Seldon Powell (ts); Jerome Richardson (bs, f); Milt Jackson (vib); Tommy Flanagan, Hank Jones (p); Wild Bill Davis (org); Kenny Burrell (g); Sam Jones (b); Albert 'Tootie' Heath, Osie Johnson, Grady Tate (d); Marion Williams (v).* 1/62–1/65.

A valuable compendium of three of Brown's albums for Verve, co-starring with vibist Milt Jackson (his companion on the small-group *Much In Common* from 1964 and the eponymous co-fronted session from the following January) and also Cannonball Adderley, who is the featured soloist on the earliest of the three sessions. This date, credited to Brown's All-Star Big Band, also affords a chance to hear Brown the cellist on three numbers, and the reissue includes valuable alternatives of 'Work Song' and his own 'Cannon Bilt'. The sides with Jackson are the best on the record, though, inventive to the highest degree and brimming with ideas at every turn. Three versions of 'Stella By Starlight' is probably pushing it a bit, but there is more than enough strong music to fill an attractive double CD, and fans of any of the three principals (or indeed of arrangers Ernie Wilkins, Oliver Nelson and Jimmy Heath) will find much to enjoy. Modern sound cleans up the textures considerably and the bassist is properly audible on *Much In Common* at last.

*** Something For Lester

Original Jazz Classics OJC 412 *Brown; Cedar Walton (p); Elvin Jones (d).* 6/77.

Bassists seem to job quite promiscuously, and bassists of Brown's calibre are hard to find. As with Paul Chambers and Ron Carter, the Brown discography is enormous. Unlike the other two, however, his output as a leader is proportionately and qualitatively substantial. The OJC is an old Contemporary release, with that label's openness of sound. Jones isn't perhaps the ideal drummer and he gets in the way on 'Georgia On My

Mind', but all in all this is a very enjoyable session and Brown's introductory statements on 'Love Walked In' are pure class.

***** Duo Sessions**

Concord CCD 4938 *Brown; Jimmy Rowles (p).* 12/77–10/79.

This brings together *As Good As It Gets* and *Tasty!* into an attractive double-CD set. The material is fairly predictable American songbook fare, but between them these two guys have such a deep stake in that repertoire that they are able to sound as if they were standing alongside Harold Arlen and Duke Ellington as they wrote. Vintage stuff, and the pay-off of 'Nancy' and 'Smile' is just exquisite.

*****(*) Soular Energy**

Concord CCD 4268 *Brown; Red Holloway (ts); Gene Harris (p); Emily Remler (g); Gerryck King (d).* 8/84.

A really fine album which only needs Jeff Hamilton in his usual slot behind the drums to lift it into minor-classic status. King is a fine drummer but lacks sparkle and is inclined to hurry the pulse unnecessarily. Perhaps in retaliation, Brown takes the '"A" Train' at a pace which suggests privatization may be around the corner. Slowed down to an almost terminal grind, it uncovers all manner of harmonic quirks which Brown and the attentive Harris exploit with great imagination. Red Holloway and – rather more anonymously – the late Emily Remler sign up for a shortish and slightly inconsequential 'Mistreated But Undefeated Blues'. Brown's counter-melody figures on 'Cry Me A River' and, especially, the closing 'Sweet Georgia Brown' could almost be taped as his calling-card. Exemplary.

**** Don't Forget The Blues**

Concord CCD 4293 *Brown; Al Grey (tb); Ron Eschete (g); Gene Harris (p); Grady Tate (d).* 5/85.

A cheery 'all-star' – so why Eschete? – session that never really amounts to much. Tate is another in a line of first-class drummers to have recorded under Brown's leadership. In some regards he is the most conventional, though Roker is no revolutionary either, and there is a slightly stilted quality to some of the medium-tempo tracks.

***** Summer Wind**

Concord CCD 4426 *Brown; Gene Harris (p); Jeff Hamilton (d).* 12/88.

Superb live sets from an excellent working trio who interweave seamlessly and earn their solo spaces many times over. Brown's blues stylings get more assured with each passing year. Originals like 'The Real Blues' and Milt Jackson's oblique, bebop-flavoured 'Bluesology' all repay careful attention. 'If I Loved You', 'Summertime' and 'Days Of Wine And Roses' all comfortably fit the former Mr Ella Fitzgerald, while 'It Don't Mean A Thing', 'Mona Lisa' and 'Put Your Little Foot Right Out' uncover quite different aspects of Brown's increasingly complex musical persona.

*****(*) Moore Makes 4**

Concord CCD 4477 *Brown; Gene Harris (p); Jeff Hamilton (d); Ralph Moore (ts).* 91.

Does Moore make more? On balance, yes. The cover depicts a saxophone standing in as fourth leg of a tea-table. The Brown trio has stood up on its own for years now and scarcely needs the help. On the other hand, Moore's forceful tenor adds such an effective element to 'My Romance' and the superb 'Stars Fell On Alabama' that one wonders what filled those spaces before. Brown's bass lines are still among the best in the business, and the desk-slide was pushed well up to catch them.

****** The Best Of The Concord Years**

Concord CCD 2164 2CD *Brown; Harry 'Sweets' Edison, Blue Mitchell (t); Bud Shank (as); Red Holloway, Plas Johnson, Richie Kamuca, Ralph Moore (ts); George Duke, Gene Harris, Art Hillery, Hank Jones, Jimmy Rowles (p); Mike Melvoin (ky); Laurindo Almeida, Herb Ellis, Joe Pass (g); Johnny Frigo (vn); John Guerin, Jeff Hamilton, Jake Hanna, Gerryck King, Shelly Manne, Mickey Roker, Jimmie Smith (d).* 73–93.

Two dozen selections drawn from Ray's long and distinguished tenure at Concord. Most of the tracks will be familiar from the listings above, but for anyone who hasn't invested in any of these, this is a very attractive proposition. Fans will quibble with some of the selections – where is 'Bam Bam Bam', for instance – but few will complain that they haven't had value for money. Ironically, the variation of line-up – everything from the LA4 to prestigious festival spots – helps one concentrate on Brown's own contribution, which is all to the good.

*****(*) Bassface**

Telarc CD 83340 *Brown; Benny Green (p); Jeff Hamilton (d).* 93.

***** Don't Get Sassy**

Telarc CD 83368 *As above.* 94.

The shift to Telarc was a positive one for Brown, and it yielded more albums than he had been able to release on Concord. The working trio of the time was to be one of the best he ever assembled, and these two albums are testimony to the understanding that grew between them. There's not much to say about either critically, beyond the obvious point that the sound-quality is the equal of the Concord sessions, but that Brown himself doesn't seem to be stretching and he remains content to leave the spadework to his two younger cohorts.

***** Some Of My Best Friends Are ... The Piano Players**

Telarc CD 83373 *Brown; Benny Green, Ahmad Jamal, Geoff Keezer, Dado Moroni, Oscar Peterson (p).* 94.

*****(*) Some Of My Best Friends Are ... The Sax Players**

Telarc CD 83388 *Brown; Benny Carter, Jesse Davis (as); Joe Lovano, Ralph Moore, Joshua Redman, Stanley Turrentine (ts); Benny Green (p); Gregory Hutchinson (d).* 11/95.

It's axiomatic that Brown adapts to almost any musical company. These two sessions set out to nail the point for ever. The choice of piano players was scarcely controversial, though Moroni perhaps sticks out as the least celebrated of the bunch. Jamal is predictably smooth and over-prepared, and it's Peterson who approaches the session with the most open mind, pitching into his cameos with cheerful good grace.

It's the saxophone album, no less appealing in concept or execution, which stands out; if you wanted to provide someone with a sampler which helped explain how rhythm sections shift their premisses and adapt to a new voice, then this would be the logical primer. Everyone is absolutely in character. Jesse Davis does his now-accomplished Parker impression on 'Moose The Mooche' and a quieter, Hodges-tinged take on 'These Foolish Things'. Carter is featured on 'Love Walked In' and 'Fly Me To The Moon', proving once again that he is indestructible. Redman and Moore are inevitably less assured and they have less experience with standards, and in the event the laurels go to the veteran Turrentine and the younger Lovano, who kicks off with 'How High The Moon' and continues with 'Easy Living', while big Stan contributes the Illinois Jacquet theme, 'Port Of Rico', and 'God Bless The Child'. Programmed into the CD are brief conversation tracks with each guest, which can be cued to play just before the relevant number. After a couple of goes, most listeners will dispense with them, but they're nice to have.

*** Seven Steps To Heaven

Telarc CD 83384 *Brown; Benny Green (p); Ulf Wakenius (g); Gregory Hutchinson (d).* 95.

Wakenius has been making waves in recent years and has proved himself to be a guitarist of genuine initiative and talent. Even so, he's a surprising guest on this trio set, and he melds only rather uneasily with a settled line-up. Green and Hutchinson are both in rather muted form, and much of the emphasis this time out falls to Brown himself.

*** Super Bass

Telarc CD 83393 *Brown; Benny Green (p); John Clayton Jr, Christian McBride (b); Gregory Hutchinson (d).* 10/96.

***(*) Live At Scullers

Telarc 83405 *Brown; Benny Green (p); Gregory Hutchinson (d).* 96.

In fact, both are recorded live at Sculler's nightclub in Boston. *Super Bass* is a feast for bassophiles. Brown and former Basie stalwart Clayton stand for the older generation, but McBride, hip as he is, is well clued-up on the history of his instrument, and most certainly he isn't left standing. After stating the 'SuperBass' theme, the three stringfellows launch into a riveting interpretation of 'Blue Monk'. After very little time, it's easy to separate the voices and determine who's playing what. Brown tends to favour the fast, upper register lines, Clayton the low, gentle throb, and McBride the intermediate harmonic region, never overawed or diffident, but certainly paying his elders due respect. 'Bye Bye Blackbird' has him duetting with the boss, as Clayton does on 'Lullaby Of Birdland'. There are just two tracks from Brown's regular trio of Green and Hutchinson, who sound excellent on both 'Who Cares?' and the specially composed 'Sculler Blues'. Hutchinson appears elsewhere, but Green seems a little underused in the circumstances. McBride's 'Brown Funk' is the closer, a new theme that sounds as if it has been around for generations.

The trio set is terrific, kicking off on a rousing version of 'Freddie Freeloader', following up with 'En Estate', a brilliant 'Bye Bye Blackbird', 'But Not For Me' and 'If You Only Knew', the last of these a titanic performance from Brown who stamps his authority on the group on every track, growling '*My* tempo' if anyone else decides to take the initiative.

*** Some Of My Best Friends Are ... Singers

Telarc 83441 *Brown; Antonio Hart (as); Ralph Moore (ts); Russell Malone (g); Geoff Keezer (p); Gregory Hutchinson (d); Dee Dee Bridgewater, Etta Jones, Nancy King, Kevin Mahogany, Marlena Shaw, Diana Krall (v).* 12/97, 4/98.

Ray's years with Ella must have sensitized him to the needs of singers, and he is all taste and unobtrusive support on these dozen songs featuring the talents of half that number of talented and even idiosyncratic modern vocalists. Rising star Diana Krall is strongly featured in the top half of the record on 'I Thought About You' and 'Little Boy', performances deeply (which is to say not superficially) influenced by Ella's extraordinary musicianship and sense of rhythm. The two tracks with Etta Jones are equally good and 'There Is No Greater Love', with Russell Malone on guitar, is a revelation. The pairing of guest instrumentalists and singers is very subtle, but the key to the whole elegant package is the now seasoned trio.

***(*) Live At Starbucks

Telarc 83502 *Brown; Geoff Keezer (p); Karriem Riggins (d).* 9/99.

Jazz and a good cup of joe is presumably the formula, though a wise management, knowing Brown's volatile temperament, managed to keep the steamer silent for this delightful live set. Ray is in storming form, but it's Riggins, perhaps fuelled by a couple of espressos, who really drives this one along. The main event is a sequence of Ellington tunes in the middle of the set, not a medley but an interesting progression of themes from 'Mainstem' and 'We Love You Madly' to 'Caravan'. Keezer's musical intelligence and wit shine through on every track, but he goes to town on the Tizol tune. 'I Should Care', which is part of a medley, is the most successful of the rest and there's even an encore 'Starbuck's Blues' before everyone went home sleepless.

***(*) Some Of My Best Friends Are ... The Trumpet Players

Telarc 83495 *Brown; Terence Blanchard, Jon Faddis, Roy Hargrove, James Morrison, Nicholas Payton, Clark Terry (t); Geoff Keezer (p); Karriem Riggins (d).* 00.

The series continues with perhaps the most surprising chemistry yet. Australian James Morrison trades some wonderful lines with Ray on 'I Thought About You'. Of the younger guys, it's Nick Payton who slays the rest with his version of Joe Henderson's 'The Kicker', while the ever more seasoned Blanchard makes some lovely contemporary moves on Benny Goodman's curtain-piece, the Gordon Jenkins-composed 'Goodbye'. Ray is, as ever, mixed well forward but not intrusively so. These sets all suffer from a certain diffusion of style, but this time around that works in the album's favour. Nice stuff.

*** Walk On

Telarc 83515 2CD *Brown; Monty Alexander, Benny Green, Geoff Keezer (p); Lewis Nash, Josh Clayton (b); Gregory Hutchinson, Karriem Riggins (d).* 1/00, 94, 96.

Ray's last studio date with the trio would have made a very fine record on its own but Telarc have released what is effectively a memorial volume with live material from the mid '90s and with earlier groups, making this a very attractive double package. The January 2000 set is marked out by the 'Ray Brown Suite', a three part conception that puts the bassist very much in the foreground. However, the strongest things on the record are a lovely reading of 'Honeysuckle Rose' and an unexpected version of Wes Montgomery's 'Fried Pies'. 'Hello Girls' is also a high point, with Keezer and Brown locked tight together, while Riggins picks out all sorts of funky accents, similar to his reading of 'Lined With A Groove', which is pure '50s soul-jazz.

The live cuts are welcome souvenirs of past associations. Alexander and Nash turn in some very fine things on 'In A Mellow Tone' and the sprightly 'Woogie Boogie', and there is a fine strut through 'F.S.R.' (i.e. 'For Sonny Rollins') with Green and Hutchinson but it's the other group, with Keezer, second bassist Clayton and McBride that stands out on disc two, confirming Geoff's telepathic understanding with the boss.

★★★★ Some Of My Best Friends Are ... Guitarists
Telarc CD 83499 *Brown; Geoff Keezer (p); Herb Ellis, John Pizzarelli, Kenny Burrell, Ulf Wakenius, Bruce Forman, Russell Malone (g); Karriem Riggins (d).* 1–2/00.

Released posthumously, and therefore hard to criticize in any case, this is the 'best friends' gig we'll remember most affectionately. There is some great playing on this fifth disc in the series, notably from Kenny Burrell on 'Fly Me To The Moon' and 'Soulful Spirit', a tender eulogy to the late Billy Higgins. John Pizzarelli sets the ball rolling with a bouncy 'Squeeze Me' but it's when the familiar tones of Herb Ellis kick in with 'I Want To Be Happy', returning later with a more workmanlike 'Blues For Junior' that you sense how comfortable Ray is in the company of other string players. Ulf Wakenius is there as a representative of a younger generation and he is magnificent on 'Blues For Ray' and 'My Funny Valentine'. And plaudits too to Russell Malone for one of the most unexpected tracks, a quick-changing 'Heartstrings'.

The little genius himself is in great form throughout, full-voiced, sly, sometimes engagingly brusque. Not a dud phrase from him in the entire session. A record to treasure.

★★★ Super Bass 2
Telarc 68483 *Brown; John Clayton, Christian McBride (b); George Gludas, Larry Fuller (perc).* 12/00.

Pretty much more of the same, but the concept has settled down a bit and the interplay with McBride in particular is spot on. Ray reprises the 'Superbass Theme' before kicking into a brilliant version of 'Get Happy', followed, just for variety, by Monk's 'Misterioso', and then 'Papa Was A Rolling Stone'. Eclectic, or what? The addition of percussion to 'Taco With A Pork Chop' varies the sound nicely, but still a bit one-dimensional for many tastes.

★★★(★) With Monty Alexander And Russell Malone/Producer's Choice
Telarc CD 83562 2CD *Brown; Monty Alexander, Benny Green, Ahmad Jamal, Geoff Keezer (p); Russell Malone (g); John Clayton, Christian McBride (b); Jeff Hamilton, Gregory Hutchinson, Lewis Nash, Karriem Riggins (d).* 93–01, 3/02.

This memorial volume comprises Brown's last recording, made with Alexander and Malone, both in fine form, with a selection of recordings from the last decade of his life, a compilation disc put together by producer Elaine Martone. There are some wonderful gems on the bonus disc, including a duet with young Turk Christian McBride (if describing someone called Christian as a Turk isn't nonsensical) and a superb 'Blue Monk' with Ahmad Jamal. But it's the new and sadly final outing that really commands the attention. Alexander is forceful but respectful, giving the boss lots of room, but insistent enough in his solo spots. Malone gives them both the perfect basis for loose, rhythmic improvisation, but sometimes swamps the mix a little. Instead of 'choosing' older material, the producer might have been better employed tweaking the balance.

Ray Brown's true monument is a body of recorded work that still rivals any in this book. From beginning to end, he was a model of musical intelligence, a living historian of jazz.

Reuben Brown (born 1939)

PIANO

Brown has rarely ventured much further than the local scene afforded by his native Washington, DC, although as a young man he tried a spell in New York and he's occasionally been sighted in touring groups. He learned to play stride as a teenager but is stylistically otherwise in the bop-and-after mainstream.

★★★★ Ice Scape
Steeplechase SCCD 31423 *Brown; Rufus Reid (b); Billy Hart (d).* 1/94.

★★★(★) Blue And Brown
Steeplechase SCCD 31445 *Brown (p solo).* 1/94.

Nils Winther has a knack for finding pianists with an unemphatic but quietly individual touch, and Brown is right in that pocket. *Ice Scape* would earn four stars just for the outstanding version of 'Mack The Knife': played in a very slow three, full of space and low light, it is a brilliant personalization of a very unlikely vehicle. But Brown also comes up with strikingly nuanced treatments of 'A Night In Tunisia' and 'Lush Life', and his own writing reveals a deep thinker: the title-piece is a curious ballet worthy of, say, Ran Blake. Reid and Hart – the latter a high-school pal of Brown's – do sterling work on an unhackneyed and exemplary record.

Sadly, Brown suffered a stroke before the record was released and he is apparently not yet able to play again. *Blue And Brown*, recorded as a solo set at the same sessions, is therefore no more than a postscript to the other disc. Although many of the 15 themes are familiar, Brown goes to great lengths to treat them differently, both from each other and from previous interpretations. He might drop in a staccato right-hand figure, in the manner of Paul Bley, to surprise an otherwise placid momentum, or he may find a unique tempo on a tune that otherwise follows a different drum. Listeners fed up at the prospect of yet another 'Round Midnight' will be startled at how fresh Brown makes this one sound. Just here and there he takes things a shade too slowly, and we might have liked to hear more of his tunes in the programme; only 'Look Away' and the title-piece are Brown's. But this is otherwise a pair of discs that deserve a much wider attention than they've received.

Rob Brown (born 1962)

ALTO SAXOPHONE

Brown began making his mark in the '80s, a free-form altoman whose willingness to go a long way out is tempered by a penchant for lyricism.

★★★ Blink Of An Eye
No More 3 *Brown; Matthew Shipp (p).* 10/96.

Two exhaustively long duets, the second just breasting the half-hour mark, form the body of this disc and, for all their intensities and ingenuities, the players struggle to sustain interest across this length and with this bare instrumentation. Shipp and Brown specifically avoid the obvious Taylor–Lyons comparisons, but they have insufficient material at their fingertips to justify a format which calls for the highest levels of improvisational finesse – at least, on this evening. The brief third piece, which acts as a coda to the first two, is so much more focused and persuasive that one feels all the more disappointed at the longueurs of the first two.

★★★(★) Scratching The Surface
CIMP 161 *Brown; Assif Tsahar (ts); Chris Lightcap (b); Lou Grassi (d).* 10/97.

Bob Rusch's sleeve-note seems to hint at a disappointment that this band is playing in a fundamentally conservative style as far as free music is concerned. Brown does, indeed, even hint at a Konitz influence in the broken ballad, 'Stray Arrow', and Tsahar is a lot more effective in this temperate setting than he is on some of his all-out sessions. Lightcap and Grassi are as happy to play a slow four like 'A Hatful' as they are to be the time-and-motion men of 'Clean Sweep'. The result is surely the best record Brown's put his name on.

Sandy Brown (1929–75)

CLARINET, VOCAL

Born in India, Brown grew up in Edinburgh and was playing clarinet there in rhythm clubs as a teenager. Formed a band with childhood friend Al Fairweather and came to London. Moved from simple trad beginnings to a mainstream style which became increasingly sophisticated, although he recorded little. Also worked as an architect building sound studios and was a gifted writer, but illness curtailed his activities, and he died young in 1975.

****(*) The Historic Usher Hall Concert 1952**
Lake LACD94 *Brown; Al Fairweather (t); Bob Craig (tb); Stan Greig (p, d); Norrie Anderson (b); Dizzy Jackson (b); Jim 'Farrie' Forsyth (d).* 1/52.

*****(*) Sandy's Sideman**
Lake LACD 133 *Brown; Al Fairweather, Spike Mackintosh (t); John R. T. Davies, John Picard (tb); Dick Heckstall-Smith (ss); Alan Thomas, Dave Stephens (p); Bob Clarke (vn); Diz Disley (g); Mo Umansky (bj); Brian Parker (b); Graham Burbidge (d).* 4/55-6/56.

****** McJazz And Friends**
Lake LACD58 *Brown; Al Fairweather (t); Jeremy French (tb); Dick Heckstall-Smith (ss); Ian Armit, Dill Jones, Dave Stephens, Harry Smith (p); Diz Disley (g, bj); Cedric West, Bill Bramwell (g); Tim Mahn, Major Holley, Brian Brocklehurst, Arthur Watts (b); Graham Burbidge, Stan Greig, Don Lawson, Eddie Taylor (d).* 5/56–11/58.

*****(*) Work Song**
Lake LACD 160 *Brown; Kenny Wheeler (t, flhn); Al Fairweather (t); George Chisholm, Tony Milliner (tb); Tony Coe (ts, cl); Ron Rubin, Brian Lemon (p); John McLaughlin (g); Brian Prudence, Bobby Orr (b); Benny Goodman, Terry Cox, Bobby Orr (d).* 7/62–12/68.

*****(*) In The Evening**
Hep 2017 *Brown; Ray Crane (t); John Picard (tb); Bruce Turner (ss, as, ts); Tony Coe (ts); Brian Lemon (p); Tony Archer, Dave Green (b); Bobby Orr (d).* 6/70–5/71.

Brown has assumed almost legendary status among British musicians and fans of a certain age, although the memories are starting to fade, and there is precious little left to remember him by in terms of recordings. The 1952 recording (of fair amateur quality) catches the Brown–Fairweather axis before it moved to London, and while the leaders are already players of some character, the rest of the band aren't. Much stronger is the later Lake disc, which reissues the Nixa LP *McJazz* and adds tracks from various EPs and compilations, four of them under Heckstall-Smith's leadership. Both Brown and Fairweather play beautifully on the *McJazz* tracks, with Brown's interest in high-life music adding a unique tang to many of the ensembles; the result is a worldly British mainstream which still sounds impressively individual. Brown's clarinet had shed most of an early Johnny Dodds influence and had become strikingly his own – fluent, but with a carefully controlled gaspipe edge to it that let him stand out in any ensemble. The original LP is the important material here, but the makeweight tracks all have lots of interest; 'Portrait Of Miles' is a classic quartet performance. An indispensable reissue for anyone interested in this period.

Sandy's Sidemen is a real collectors' piece, tracks recorded for the Tempo label which have been incredibly sought-after on original vinyl. The Brown-Fairweather group is augmented by various guest stars, and there are live tracks from a Festival Hall concert. This is really only a whit behind the *McJazz* music.

Work Song is also valuable, if more of a curiously mixed assemblage. There are three 1962 live tracks (Railway Hotel, Hampstead) from an old Decca various-bands album called *Hot Jazz, Cool Beer* and four from an EP made a year later. Fairweather is on both dates, Tony Coe comes in for the second. The live music is terrific and closes with a rousing take on Mingus's 'Wednesday Night Prayer Meeting'. The 1963 tracks are a shade more ordinary, though still a smart show of British mainstream in rude health. But it's the *Hair At Its Hairiest* session which is unique – a band which brings together Brown, Wheeler, Chisholm and McLaughlin is going to be something unrepeatable. Still, it was a prosaic project. Brian Lemon arranged a set of tunes from the *Hair* musical in a familiar jazzmen-go-pop situation, and nobody really breaks away from the settings, though Brown and Chisholm especially plug in some witty solos. George's farewell is a gem.

Brown's playing never declined, even if his health ultimately did. His final quartet record, from 1971 and originally issued on Doug Dobell's 77 label, is on the Hep CD, plus a few tracks with a larger group, cut a year earlier. The tone is a little more mellifluous but still takes on a tart edge when he wants to make some point, and the lines he plays still seem completely original, even on a blues or a familiar standard. A one-off.

Dave Brubeck (born 1920)

PIANO

Born in Concord, Massachusetts, Brubeck was educated on the West Coast, where he studied composition under Milhaud, a period of study interrupted by a spell in a services band. Brubeck's first trio was augmented to a quartet with the addition of altoist Paul Desmond, whose peerless sound became definitive of Brubeck's music; Desmond was also the composer of the group's best-known theme, 'Take Five'. The pianist's blocky chordal compositions and smooth melodic runs were apt to be dismissed as college or cocktail jazz, but he has continued in the same vein for more than half a century and was still making fine records in his seventies.

*****(*) The Dave Brubeck Octet**
Original Jazz Classics OJC 101 *Brubeck; Dick Collins (t); Bob Collins (tb); Paul Desmond (as); Dave Van Kriedt (ts); Bill Smith (cl, bs); Ron Crotty (b); Cal Tjader (d).* 48–49.

****** Early Concepts**
Proper Pairs 132 2CD *Similar to above.*

Often derided as a white, middle-class formalist with a rather buttoned-down image and an unhealthy obsession with classical parallels and clever-clever time-signatures, Brubeck is actually one of the most significant composer-leaders in modern jazz. Tunes like 'Blue Rondo A La Turk', 'Kathy's Waltz' and Paul Desmond's 'Take Five' (which Brubeck made an enormous hit) insinuated their way into the unconscious of a whole generation of American college students. Though he has contributed very little to the 'standards' gene-pool ('In Your Own Sweet Way' is probably the only Brubeck original that is regularly covered), he has created a remarkable body of jazz and formal music, including orchestral pieces, oratorios and ballet scores. The Brubecks constitute something of a musical dynasty. His elder brother, Howard, is a 'straight' composer in a rather old-fashioned Francophile vein, while his sons, bassist and trombonist Chris, drummer Danny and keyboard player Darius, have all played with him.

It used to be conventional wisdom that the only Brubeck records which mattered were those that featured the liquid alto of Paul Desmond. Such was the closeness – and, one might say, jealousy – of the relationship that it was stated in Desmond's contract that his own recordings had to be pianoless. What no one seemed to notice was that Desmond's best playing was almost always with the Brubeck group. Brubeck himself was not a particularly accomplished soloist, with a rather heavy touch and an unfailing attachment to block chords, but his sense of what could be achieved within the bounds of a conventional jazz quartet allowed him to create an impressive and often startling body of music that demands urgent reassessment.

The early Octet catches Brubeck at the height of his interest in an advanced harmonic language (which he would have learnt from Darius Milhaud, his teacher at Mills College); there are also rhythmic transpositions of a sort that popped up in classic jazz and were subsequently taken as read by the '60s avant-garde, but which in the '50s had been explored thoroughly only by Max Roach. Relative to Gerry Mulligan, Brubeck has been not been widely regarded as a writer-arranger for larger groups, but the better material on this rather indifferently recorded set underlines how confidently he approached the synthesis of jazz with other forms. Tracks like 'Serenades Suite' and 'Schizophrenic Scherzo' are a great deal more swinging than most products of the Third Stream, a movement one doesn't automatically associate with Brubeck's name. *Early Concepts* is a hefty trawl through the early material that yields no fewer than 52 elegantly thoughtful tracks and some intriguing Dave Van Kriedt material that prompts some revisionist thinking about the sources of Brubeck's early style.

*** The Dave Brubeck Trio

Fantasy CDJZD 005 2CD *Brubeck; Ron Crotty (b); Cal Tjader (d, vib, perc).* 48–50.

***(*) Dave Brubeck–Paul Desmond

Fantasy F 24727 *Brubeck; Paul Desmond (as); Ron Crotty, Wyatt Ruther (b); Herb Barman, Lloyd Davis, Joe Dodge (d).* 52, 53, 54.

*** Stardust

Fantasy F 24728 *As above, except add Norman Bates, Fred Dutton (b).* 52–54.

The trios are bubbly and smoothly competent but lack the luminous quality that Desmond brought. Brubeck disbanded the trio after injuring his back in a swimming accident. The lay-off was a significant one and led indirectly to his most creative association. Desmond joined the reconvened group in 1951 (Tjader had gone off to do other things) and immediately transformed it. His duos with Brubeck on the later Fantasy are a measure of their immediate mutual understanding; 'Over The Rainbow' is one of the loveliest improvisations of the period, caught in a whispery close-up. Tjader is still an interestingly varied player at this period, far from the bland stylist he was to become later.

The quartets with Crotty (he succeeded Norman Bates; no, not that one) and Davis aren't considered to be the classic Brubeck groups; that was the later line-up with Wright and Morello, but they were excellent on their own less ambitious terms. *Brubeck–Desmond* compiles two earlier Fantasy LPs, *Jazz At The Black Hawk* and *Jazz At Storyville.* There's an intriguing rehearsal version of the 'Trolley Song' that suggests something of what went into this music. *Stardust* is more of a grab-bag and is perhaps the dullest compilation from this early period; there are, though, fine Desmond performances throughout, and Brubeck fans will want to have some less familiar material collected there.

**** Jazz At Oberlin

Original Jazz Classics OJC 046 *Brubeck; Paul Desmond (as); Ron Crotty (b); Lloyd Davis (d).* 3/53.

*** Jazz At The College Of The Pacific

Original Jazz Classics OJC 047 *As above.* 12/53.

*** In Concert

Fantasy 60-013 *Brubeck; Paul Desmond (as); Ron Crotty (b); Joe Dodge (d).* 53.

Jazz At Oberlin was an enormous success on its first release and is still durable more than 50 years later, with some of Brubeck's and Desmond's finest interaction; one of the pianist's innovations was in getting two musicians to improvise at the same time, and there are good examples of that on the Oberlin College set. It's all standard material, and there are excellent performances of 'Perdido', 'Stardust' and 'How High The Moon' which adumbrate Brubeck's later interest in unconventional time-signatures. The other 1953 set was another of Brubeck's celebrated college gigs, a shrewd promotional move that opened up his music and jazz more generally to a young, well-educated audience. Desmond has a slightly quieter night than usual in Stockton, but Brubeck, back at his alma mater, is in exceptional form, playing well within himself but showing all his class and sophistication.

In Concert is a slightly pointless compression of the two live records. Given that both are still available, there seems little reason for a sampler, though a budget double-CD would be welcome. The repetition of 'Stardust' and 'All The Things You Are' confounds the notion that this was a 'reading' band, too stiff to improvise. The sound is a bit remote and Crotty isn't always clearly audible.

*** Jazz Goes To College

Sony International 9513 *Brubeck; Paul Desmond (as); Bob Bates (b); Joe Dodge (d).* 3/54.

This was the sort of title that raised hackles. Brubeck, though, had broken an important new jazz audience and he was entitled to make hay with it. This is a delightful album, full of clever ideas that would appeal to the music students – a touch of polytonality and some unexpected signatures – and exciting enough to draw in everyone else. 'Balcony Rock' is a stunner, with superb solos from both Desmond and Brubeck, high points for them both. 'The Song Is You' and 'Out Of Nowhere' are probably the best of the rest, though the original 'Le Souk' and 'Take The "A" Train' are fine performances.

***(*) Brubeck Time

Columbia CK 65724 *Brubeck; Paul Desmond (as); Bob Bates (b); Joe Dodge (d).* 10/54.

This was recorded round a film shoot by the celebrated Gjon Mili and George Avakian's brother Aram (who went on to film *Jazz on a Summer's Day*). A purist to his suede shoes, Mili had taken a good deal of convincing that Brubeck was a worthy subject but had relented. There is a story that Mili's dismissiveness spurred Brubeck to angry heights not normally associated with him. Certainly, 'Stompin' For Mili' sounds as if he might have meant the preposition to read 'On'. There is some fabulous music on the disc. Desmond's solo on 'Why Do I Love You' is brilliantly subtle, and 'Audrey' (a soft minor blues intended to counterbalance the thudding Mili piece) is delicate to the point of fragility. This really was Brubeck time. He appeared on the cover of *Time* magazine, and was pushing jazz's demographics into territory no one had anticipated. The music stands up pretty well, too.

*** Jazz; Red, Hot And Cool

Columbia CK 61468 *Brubeck; Paul Desmond (as); Bob Bates (b); Joe Dodge (d).* 10/54, 8/55.

Reissued in 2001, and augmented by two very good tracks, this is a good representation of how much Brubeck was still learning from the example of his teacher, Darius Milhaud. Desmond is still rather raw and uninflected at this point, but Dave is playing with great authority and confidence, and his solo on 'Little Girl Blue' is jaw-dropping. Even remastered, the sound is a bit muddy and one-dimensional, but Brubeck fans will be delighted to have this one back in circulation.

***(*) Brubeck Plays Brubeck

Columbia Legacy CK 65722 *Brubeck (p solo).* 56.

*** Dave Brubeck Plays And Plays And Plays ...

Original Jazz Classics OJC 716 *Brubeck (p solo).* 2/57.

After these, Brubeck more or less gave up solo performance for the next few decades. *Brubeck Plays Brubeck* is distinguished by his most famous composition, 'In Your Own Sweet Way', a gloriously understated performance. 'The Duke' is rarely covered, but it is another of Dave's great conceptions, moving cleverly and logically through the 12 keys. *Plays And Plays ...* is less sparkling but no less packed with ideas.

*** Reunion

Original Jazz Classics OJC 150 *Brubeck; Paul Desmond (as); Dave Van Kriedt (ts); Norman Bates (b); Joe Morello (d).* 2/57.

Following the end of his association with Fantasy (he'd signed for Columbia in 1954) *Reunion* brings back the full-voiced Van Kriedt and Bates from the early bands. There's a greater preponderance of 'classical' tags – 'Pieta', 'Prelude', 'Divertimento', 'Chorale' – most of them interpreted rather loosely. The danger of reunions is that they underline all that has changed in the interim. Brubeck had moved on, assimilating his advanced ideas ever more comfortably; it shows here in Van Kriedt's palpable unsuitability.

*** Dave Digs Disney

Columbia 471250 2 *Brubeck; Paul Desmond (as); Norman Bates (b); Joe Morello (d).* 6 & 8/57.

A brilliant idea, later copied by another piano player. Sun Ra's take on Disney tunes isn't any more way-out than Dave's manipulation of the Dwarves' song 'Heigh Ho!' into a classic Brubeck piece. Other tunes, 'Give A Little Whistle', the CD bonuses 'Very Good Advice' and 'So This Is Love' are more so-so, but as you might expect 'When You Wish Upon A Star' and the Miles-sanctified 'Someday My Prince Will Come' are delicious, packed with romance and a certain wistfulness that occasionally came upon Brubeck as well as Desmond.

*** Jazz Impressions Of Eurasia

Columbia Legacy CT 48531 *Brubeck; Paul Desmond (as); Joe Benjamin (b); Joe Morello (d).* 7 & 8/58.

Somewhat like Duke's *Far East Suite*, this was inspired by a long hike round Asia, where Brubeck was already a bona-fide star. The most famous piece here is 'Brandenburg Gate' (only the gateway to 'the East' if you take a strict Cold War view, but then Isfahan isn't in the Far East either) and deservedly so. It's quintessential Brubeck, with a superb contribution from Desmond, who approaches these charts with effortless grace. 'The Golden Horn' and 'Calcutta Blues' are more generic, though the latter has hidden pitfalls that Brubeck copyists must have stumbled across over the years.

***(*) The Great Concerts

Columbia 462403 *Brubeck; Paul Desmond (as); Eugene Wright (b); Joe Morello (d).* 3/58, 2/63.

This pulls together the double-LP, *At Carnegie Hall*, with *Brubeck In Amsterdam*. 'Great' is pushing it a bit for the earlier of the two, but the Dutch gig is quite special. Morello's easy swing on 'Wonderful Copenhagen' (from 1958) sets the pace and the standard for most of the disc, which is more than usually even in tempo and might have benefited from a more judicious trawl through the material. Good value for money, though.

*** Gone With The Wind

Columbia CT 40627 *Brubeck; Paul Desmond (as); Eugene Wright (b); Joe Morello (d).* 4/59.

Strictly speaking, this is 'Jazz Impressions Of The Deep South', complete with a flying read of 'Camptown Races', and imaginative interpretations of 'Ol' Man River', 'Shortnin' Bread' and 'Basin Street Blues'. It's never been our favourite Brubeck record: something a little forced about the concept and some unintentionally grotesque ideas that don't fit this band. *Southern Scene* actually followed the next year, but it's currently out of circulation.

CORE COLLECTION

**** Time Out

Columbia CK 65122 *Brubeck; Paul Desmond (as); Eugene Wright (b); Joe Morello (d).* 6–8/59.

Catalogued as a 'Historic Reissue' (industry-speak for a golden egg), this is the music everyone associates with Brubeck. So familiar is it that no one actually hears what's going on any more. As the title suggests, Brubeck wanted to explore ways of playing jazz that went a step beyond the basic 4/4 that had remained the norm long after jazz threw off the relentless predictability of B flat. The opening 'Blue Rondo A La

Turk' (with its Mozart echoes) opens in an oddly distributed 9/8, with the count rearranged as 2-2-2-3. It's a relatively conventional classical *rondo* but with an almost raucous blues interior. 'Take Five' is in the most awkward of all key signatures, but what is remarkable about this almost iconic slice of modern jazz is the extent to which it constantly escapes the 5/4 count and swings. Morello's drum solo is perhaps his best work on record (though his brief 'Everybody's Jumpin'' solo is also excellent) and Brubeck's heavy vamp has tremendous force. Though it's almost always identified as a Brubeck tune, 'Take Five' was actually written by Desmond.

Most of the other material is in waltz and double-waltz time. Max Roach had explored the idea thoroughly on *Jazz In 3/4 Time*, but not even Roach had attempted anything as daring and sophisticated as the alternations of beat on 'Three To Get Ready' and 'Kathy's Waltz', which is perhaps the finest single thing on the album. Desmond tends to normalize the count in his solo line, and it's easy to miss what is going on in the rhythm section if one concentrates too exclusively on the saxophone. The Desmond cult may be fading slightly and as it does it may be possible to re-establish the Brubeck Quartet's claim *as a unit* to be considered among the most innovative and adventurous of modern-jazz groups.

***(*) Brubeck & Rushing

Columbia Legacy CK 65727 *As above, except add Jimmy Rushing (v).* 60.

Mr 5/4 meets Mr 5-by-5. One of the unlikelier encounters in modern jazz, but also one of the happiest as Brubeck gets down to some serious blues comping in support of the former Basie vocalist whose compact frame and big voice are a constant delight. 'Ain't Misbehavin'' finds them both on familiar ground and the chemistry is remarkable, confounding any abiding impression of Brubeck as a buttoned-down college boy. As with most of these reissues, there is just one additional track, an engaging if slight version of 'Shine On, Harvest Moon'.

*** Brubeck A La Mode

Original Jazz Classics OJC 200 *Brubeck; Bill Smith (cl); Eugene Wright (b); Joe Morello (d).* 5 & 6/60.

*** Near-Myth

Original Jazz Classics OJC 236 *As above.* 5/60.

A La Mode introduced another regular associate, fellow-Californian Smith, who has a lumpier touch than Desmond and a far less sophisticated improvisational sense. Interesting writing on *Near-Myth*, but both the playing and the reproduction are a shade muted. It may be that Smith is playing literally muted on parts of *Near-Myth*; he's certainly experimenting with different articulations on his horn and though for the most part these were techniques that belonged back in the conservatory they provide an intriguing resonance to the date. We've never considered these essential Brubecks, but they have their qualities and they have their supporters.

*** Time Further Out

Columbia Legacy CK 64668 *As above, except omit Smith; add Paul Desmond (as).* 61, 63.

There weren't many groups of the time or since that included the time-signature of each number beside the title, but so central to Brubeck's idiom had metre become that it was almost expected. The lead-off track here, in a sequence of tunes which constitute a suite dedicated to painter Joan Miró, is 'It's Raggy Waltz', laid in a relatively conventional time. What makes it particularly interesting is the inclusion of a live version, recorded at Carnegie Hall two years later, which suggests how comfortable the group was with non-standard times. 'Unsquare Dance', 'Bru's Boogie Woogie' and 'Blue Shadows In The Street' are all effective ideas, executed with classical authority. Desmond is in sparkling form, rawer and more blues-based than usual.

***(*) Brandenburg Gate: Revisited

Columbia Legacy CK 65725 *Brubeck; Paul Desmond (as); Eugene Wright (b); Joe Morello (d); orchestra.* 8/61.

The title-piece was written for the *Jazz Impressions Of Eurasia* date, and Brubeck reworks it here as a set of 11 orchestral variations in which a string ritornelle provides the 'rhythm section' for small-group improvisation. This includes some impressive work, not just from the leader and Paul Desmond, but also from bassist Wright, who has a firm tone and an impressive array of blues lines at his disposal. Brother Howard Brubeck's arrangements of 'Kathy's Waltz' and 'In Your Own Sweet Way' keep respectfully close to the original performances, augmenting them and rethinking their improvisational course. Howard acknowledges that the interplay between sympathetic soloists – and Dave and Paul Desmond were almost telepathically close – is more sensitive than anything an arranger can pull off, but he has attempted to give the settings the same light, responsive feel, and *Brandenburg Gate: Revisited* is a model for jazz recording with strings.

**(*) The Real Ambassadors

Columbia Legacy 57663 *Brubeck; Louis Armstrong (t, v); Trummy Young (tb); Joe Darensbourg (cl); Billy Kyle (p); Eugene Wright (b); Joe Morello, Danny Barcelona (d); Howard Brubeck (perc); Jon Hendricks, Dave Lambert, Carmen McRae, Annie Ross (v).* 9/61.

A failed experiment but an intriguing attempt at musical theatre. Dave and Iola Brubeck's anti-racism show is marked more by good intentions (and superb booking) than by its musical qualities, which are swamped by star turns. The vocalists are all wonderful but don't have much to work with. A curiosity.

***(*) The Dave Brubeck Quartet At Carnegie Hall

Columbia CK 61455 2CD *As above.* 2/63.

Benny Goodman had transformed the old place 25 years earlier, and this vintage live recording merely adds to the Carnegie Hall's reputation. The quartet play astonishingly well on this cold late winter night. The opening version of Handy's 'St Louis Blues' is amazingly inventive and the old standard 'Pennies From Heaven' is turned inside out. Hits like 'Blue Rondo A La Turk', Desmond's 'Eleven Four' and 'Take Five' are subject to the same inventive re-creation and the climax is held off through more than 12 minutes of 'Castillian Drums', a piece of artful theatre that shows how good Dave was at shaping a show. The original tapes are in good shape and the CD transfer is very faithful and clean.

**** Jazz Impressions Of Japan

Columbia CK 65726 *As above.* 6/64.

**(*) Jazz Impressions Of New York

Columbia CT 46189 *As above.* 6–8/64.

Japan hasn't been available for a while and, like much of Dave's output, it's a revelation. Brubeck and the band had been in the Far East a few months before and they came back infused with new ideas and new harmonies, many of which make their way into these original themes. 'Fujiyama', 'Osaka Blues' and 'The City Is Crying' make inventive use of non-Western harmonies, even where the basic idiom is still familiar. On the last of these, Desmond bears comparison with Johnny Hodges's 'Isfahan' solo for Duke. Wonderful to have it back. What we wouldn't give to be hearing this astonishing record for the first time.

The New York record, by contrast, is a real disappointment. The music was originally written for a television show called *Mr Broadway* but none of it really comes across and what is left is a slightly wishy-washy tone poem chopped into song form. For real collectors only.

***** Bravo! Brubeck!**

Columbia Legacy CK 65723 *As above, except add Benjamin Chamnin Correa (g); Salvador Rabito Agueros (perc).* 5/67.

***** Buried Treasures**

Columbia Legacy CK 65777 *As above, except omit Correa, Agueros.* 5/67.

Brubeck's sold-out tour to Mexico in 1967 opened up to him yet another new range of musical impulses, and they are prominently displayed in this excellent live record. Apart from 'Poinciana', 'Besame Mucho' and his own 'Nostalgia De Mexico', all the songs are drawn from traditional material arranged for the quartet by Brubeck. The anchor of the group is Wright, who seems to revel in this idiom. Desmond is less forthright and expressive than usual and his solos are far short of their usual expressive brilliance. A fine album nevertheless, and interesting to hear the classic group augmented with two local players.

The material on *Buried Treasures* wasn't heard on an official release until 1998. It isn't by any means as compelling as the earlier record, but the central sequence of 'Sweet Georgia Brown', 'Forty Days' and 'You Go To My Head' contains the essence of a Brubeck concert of the time. The sound is also very good, presumably the result of an official recording rather than a mere concert documentation.

*****(*) Greatest Hits**

Columbia CK 65417 *Brubeck; Paul Desmond (as); Eugene Wright (b); Joe Morello (d).*

Fairly predictable packaging of standard fare. For the record: the single-album set includes 'Take Five', 'It's A Raggy Waltz', 'Camptown Races', 'Unsquare Dance', 'Mister Broadway', 'I'm In A Dancing Mood', 'The Trolley Song', 'In Your Own Sweet Way' and 'Blue Rondo A La Turk'.

***** This Is Jazz: Dave Brubeck Plays Standards**

Columbia Legacy CK 65450 *Brubeck; Paul Desmond (as); Gerry Mulligan (bs); Bob Bates, Jack Six, Eugene Wright (b); Alan Dawson, Joe Dodge, Joe Morello (d).* 7/55–10/68.

***** Ballads**

Columbia Legacy 89919 *As above.* 55–68.

A widely scattered trawl of tunes from Brubeck's Columbia catalogue. It was Desmond who insisted that the group write its own material (or hire someone to do so) and it is surprising that nowadays no one thinks of Brubeck as first and foremost a standards performer. These eight tracks give the lie to that, with long live performances of 'St Louis Blues', 'Like Someone In Love' and 'Sometimes I'm Happy', culled from the *Great Concerts* disc (the first two) and *Interchanges* (the Caesar/Youmans tunes). All of this material is available elsewhere, but as a sample of what Dave could do with familiar themes it's a very good introduction, cleanly transferred and with informative sleeve-notes.

****** Live At The Berlin Philharmonie**

Columbia 481415 2CD *Brubeck; Gerry Mulligan (bs); Jack Six (b); Alan Dawson (d).* 11/70.

Considerably augmented with two previously unissued tracks, including the opening 'Out Of Nowhere' and no fewer than six tracks not previously issued in the USA, this double-CD set restores one of the legendary concerts of the period. It catches both Brubeck and Mulligan on top form, playing with great spontaneity and charm. Their exchanges on 'St Louis Blues', 'Limehouse Blues' and 'Basin Street Blues', the middle segment of the second disc and (except for the first) previously unheard in the States, casts a new light on both men's musical background, while on more deliberate material like 'Blessed Are The Poor' and 'Out Of The Way Of The People' Mulligan shows himself to be equal to Brubeck's more reflective side. The trio is competent without being unduly inspired, for this was an evening for the front men and only modest duties were expected from anyone else.

***** Vocal Encounters**

Columbia CK 61551 *Brubeck; Paul Desmond (as); Eugene Wright (b); Joe Morello (d) Louis Armstrong, Tony Bennett, Carmen McRae, Jimmy Rushing, Peter, Paul and Mary; Lambert, Hendricks and Ross (v).* 1/60–3/70.

One certainly doesn't associate Brubeck with singers, but over the years he recorded many vocal encounters and some of the strongest of them are documented here. Louis Armstrong sings 'They Say I Look Like God' but does so with a notable lack of irony, which may be telling. Lambert, Hendricks and Ross and Peter, Paul and Mary put in an appearance, as does Jimmy Rushing. Dave's classical interests emerge on the latter encounter, which is an adaptation – 'Because All Men Are Brothers' – from the *St Matthew Passion.* Tony Bennett fans will enjoy his unrehearsed appearance, but the real delight of the set is Carmen McRae's brilliant, witty attempt on 'Take Five'. A slightly odd compilation – only because the premise is odd; Dave isn't really a singer's piano player – but a thoroughly enjoyable set of tracks. Part of it was previously available as *Summit Sessions.*

***** The Last Set At Newport**

Atlantic 81382 *As above.* 7/71.

***** We're All Together Again For The First Time**

Atlantic 81390 *As above, except add Paul Desmond (as).* 10/72, 11/72.

Brubeck and Desmond teamed up again for one-shot tours all through the early '70s, and they played to huge crowds. Something of the magic had gone, though. Desmond's playing still provokes a thrill, especially when he weaves round Mulligan on 'Rotterdam Blues' on the *All Together Again* European tour compilation. Mulligan fitted perfectly into Brubeck's conception, swinging hard in uneven measures when there was a call for it, caressing a ballad the next moment. The Newport session is mostly upbeat, a show-stopping bravura performance that lacks subtlety but confirms Brubeck's remarkable ability to work a crowd. Desmond, one suspects, was happier in more intimate settings. He often sounds slightly frail on the European dates.

***** Back Home**

Concord CCD 4103 *Brubeck; Jerry Bergonzi (ts); Chris Brubeck (b, tb); Butch Miles (d).* 8/79.

***** Tritonis**

Concord CCD 4129 *As above, except omit Miles; add Randy Jones (d).* 3/80.

Concord would oversee the next phase of Brubeck's career, and this eloquent set is testimony to how modern the group of the time could sound. Bergonzi is the key element after the leader himself, bringing a broad, resonant sound to 'Caravan', 'Yesterdays' and the original 'Two Part Contention'. Miles would shortly give way to Randy Jones, who gave the group a more uniform and swinging feel on *Tritonis*. The title-piece and 'Theme For June' are both outstanding. Nice sound, if a bit uniform and uninflected.

***** Paper Moon**

Concord CCD 4178 *Brubeck; Jerry Bergonzi (ts, b); Chris Brubeck (b, btb); Randy Jones (d).* 9/81.

****(*) Concord On A Summer Night**

Concord CCD 4198 *Brubeck; Bill Smith (cl); Chris Brubeck (b, tb); Randy Jones (d).* 8/82.

****(*) For Iola**

Concord CCD 4259 *As above.* 8/84.

***** Reflections**

Concord CCD 4299 *As above.* 12/85.

****(*) Blue Rondo**

Concord CCD 4317 *As above.* 11/86.

***** Moscow Night**

Concord CCD 4353 *As above.* 3/87.

The Concord years suggest that whatever Brubeck once had has now been thoroughly run to ground. Only the most dedicated fans will find much to get excited about on these albums, though there are lovely things on *Paper Moon* which hark back to the old days. 'We Will All Remember Paul' on *Reflections* is a heartfelt tribute to Desmond (who died in 1977) and the surrounding material seems to be lifted by it. *Moscow Night* also seems to be up a gear and the versions there of 'Three To Get Ready', 'Unsquare Dance' and 'St Louis Blues' are the best for years. Otherwise non-essential. Brubeck *fils* and Jones are curiously stiff and unswinging, and Smith's initial promise seems (temporarily at least) to have evaporated; he is probably a less sophisticated player now than he was in 1960. Jerry Bergonzi was one of a number of young radicals introduced to Dave by Chris and Danny. It's still clear whose record it is, but there are signs that Brubeck was able to take on board new ideas, often far removed from his primary concerns.

****** Time Signatures: A Career Retrospective**

Columbia/Legacy 472776-2 4CD *Brubeck; Dick Collins (t); Bob Collins (tb); Paul Desmond (as); Bobby Militello (as, f); Dave Van Kriedt, Jerry Bergonzi (ts); Gerry Mulligan (bs); Bill Smith, Perry Robinson (cl); Darius Brubeck, Billy Kyle (p); Bob Bates, Norman Bates, Joe Benjamin, Chris Brubeck, Ron Crotty, Charles Mingus, Jack Weeks, Dave Powell, Wyatt Ruther, Jack Six, Eugene Wright (b); Herb Barman, Danny Brubeck, Lloyd Davis, Alan Dawson, Joe Dodge, Randy Jones, Joe Morello (d); Cal Tjader (vib, d, perc); Salvador Rabito Agueros, Howard Brubeck, Teo Macero, John Lee (perc); Louis Armstrong, Carmen McRae, Jimmy Rushing, Lambert, Hendricks and Ross (v); New York Philharmonic Orchestra conducted by Leonard Bernstein.* 46–91.

This is *the* stocking-filler for a Brubeck fan, a magnificently packaged four-CD box with immaculately reproduced liner photographs and a detailed booklet breaking down each and every track. There is also a long biographical essay by Juul Anthonissen. The recordings are drawn from the 1946 *Old Sounds From San Francisco, Trio Featuring Cal Tjader, Octet, Brubeck–Desmond, Jazz At Storyville, Jazz At Oberlin, Jazz Goes To College, Brubeck Time, Jazz: Red, Hot And Cool, Brubeck Plays Brubeck, And Jay And Kai At Newport, Jazz Impressions Of The USA*, the underrated *Dave Digs Disney, In Europe, Newport 58, Jazz Impressions Of Eurasia, Gone With The Wind, Time Out* (of course!), *Southern Scene* (a companion to *Gone*), *The Riddle, Brubeck And Rushing, Bernstein Plays Brubeck Plays Bernstein, Tonight Only!*, the inevitable follow-ups *Time Further Out, Time Changes* and *Time In, Countdown Time In Outer Space, Brandenburg Gate: Revisited, The Real Ambassadors* (with Louis Armstrong), *Summit Sessions, Bossa Nova USA, At Carnegie Hall, Jazz Impressions Of Japan*, and of *New York, Angel Eyes, Anything Goes!, Bravo! Brubeck!, The Last Time We Saw Paris, Compadres* and *In Berlin* (with Mulligan), *Brother, The Great Spirit Made Us All* (with the sons and unexpected Brubeckians, Perry Robinson and Jerry Bergonzi), and the recent *Quiet As The Moon* and *Once When I Was Very Young*. From the collector's point of view, it's a shame that there isn't far more unreleased material; but the point is, as this astonishing list shows, that Brubeck has been unusually well documented over the years. There has undoubtedly been stuff left on the editing-room floor and in the vaults, but there has also been an unusually severe quality-control process.

There are wonderful oddities in the playlist: the duo with Mingus on 'Sectarian Blues', the 12-tone rumba from *Jazz Impressions Of New York*, the vocal items with Pops, Carmen and Jimmy Rushing, the odd 'Lost Waltz' from 1965's *Time In*. What they reveal is not so much an 'experimental' or an unexpected Brubeck as a man propelled by what John Aldridge called 'the energy of new success' into the centre of the musical culture and allowed to pick and choose, and to initiate, the projects which interested him. *Time Signatures* has been selected with the music, not the matrix numbers, in mind, and it offers an ideal introduction to one of the music's most popular and enduring figures.

***** Late Night**

Telarc 83345 *Brubeck; Bobby Militello (as, ts, f); Jack Six (b); Randy Jones (d).* 10/93.

***** Nightshift**

Telarc 33351 *As above, except add Chris Brubeck (btb), Bill Smith (cl).* 10/93.

This was a good spell for Brubeck. *Late Night* was recorded at the Blue Note and is a model for anyone wanting to make a live jazz recording, with every instrument realistically located in the mix and every note and nuance exactly registered. The music isn't as inspiring as the sonics, unfortunately, though Dave's relaxed and quite possibly unrehearsed procession through the Ellington songbook is one of his best performances of the great man's work, so similar and yet so radically different from his own.

Though *Nightshift* is essentially a trio album with guest appearances by the horns, it is the augmented tracks that remain in the ear. Smith is in cracking form on 'You Go To My Head', dizzy and sober at the same time. Militello captures attention almost every time he is featured. His under-employed tenor is very fine on 'Travelin' Blues' and is almost reminiscent of Booker Ervin, while his alto feature on 'Yesterdays' once again had critics and most listeners reaching for comparisons with Paul Desmond.

***** In Their Own Sweet Way**

Telarc 83355 *Brubeck; Darius Brubeck (p); Matthew Brubeck (clo); Chris Brubeck (b, btb); Dan Brubeck (d).* 1/94.

The great snowstorm of January 1994 in New York had a few unintended musical consequences, not least an opportunity for the Brubeck family to make this rare quintet record. Matthew is the obvious outsider, but his cello gives an extra weight to the middle register. Most of the real action takes place between Dave and Darius and their self-titled duet is by far the best thing on the record. Brubeck's only really established standard, of which the album title is an obvious variant, gets the disc off to a good start, but it also confirms just how solidly this is the old man's record. Every tune, except the closing 'Sweet Georgia Brown', is his. As a one-off encounter, *In Their Own Sweet Way* is entertaining enough, but it's by no means a classic.

***** Just You, Just Me**

Telarc 33363 *Brubeck (p solo).* 94.

Remarkably, Dave hadn't recorded solo for nearly 40 years when this was released. He's instantly identifiable from the very first bars but, without a group, the ideas run a little thin. Brubeck's mastery of a certain idiom – chordal, melodic – is unchallengeable, but it is also unchallenged and it would be more interesting to hear him pushed into new situations rather than be allowed to muse like this.

***** Young Lions & Old Tigers**

Telarc CD 83349 *Brubeck; Roy Hargrove (t); Ronnie Butacavolli (flhn); Michael Brecker, Joe Lovano, James Moody, Joshua Redman (ts); Gerry Mulligan (bs); George Shearing (p); Chris Brubeck, Christian McBride, Jack Six (b); Randy Jones (d); Jon Hendricks (v).* 95.

It wasn't a bad idea to pair Brubeck with old and new friends but, as with so many projects of this type, no single relationship is given enough time to establish basic ground-rules, let alone develop into something more substantial. Joe Lovano's conservatism has led him into more than one project of this sort and on the tango specially written for him he sounds respectful and slightly constrained. There are also named dedications to Chris McBride, Roy Hargrove, James Moody, Gerry Mulligan and Michael Brecker, all of them redolent of a relaxed, jamming atmosphere. It might have been more effective if Brubeck had elected to do what he did with George Shearing and play an established tune (in this case his own established repertory piece, 'In Your Own Sweet Way') with whatever wrinkles and variations the youngsters chose to work on it. As things stand, it is quite hard to gauge how securely they are all engaged with his work. A thoroughly enjoyable album up to a point, but something of a wasted opportunity, given the range of talent on offer.

(***) To Hope! A Celebration

Telarc 80430 *Brubeck; Cathedral Society Chorus & Orchestra.* 96.

Brubeck sustained a parallel career writing sacred music. This is the first time one of his masses has been recorded in its entirety. It's a beautiful piece, worth hearing on its own account, but also illuminating as regards some of Brubeck's small-group practices: polytonality, voice-leading and so on. It doesn't require a staunch faith to be moved by *To Hope!*

***** Double Live From The USA And UK**

Telarc 83400 2CD *Brubeck; Bobby Militello (as); Alec Dankworth, Jack Six (b); Randy Jones (d).* 95, 98.

Despite shaky health, Brubeck's activities showed no signs of slackening during the '90s, and this 2001 release brought together material recorded at the National Cathedral in Washington, DC, an occasion on which Brubeck had presented his sacred mass. Some of the playing is astonishing, like his polytonal introduction to 'Cherokee', which reminded us of Ornette Coleman (readers who know Ornette's infamous Croydon recording will understand why). Dave is also stunning on 'Body And Soul' and, with Militello sounding like Desmond reborn on several cuts, this is a vintage record.

The remaining tracks were made during a British tour three years later and from Cardiff and London. This was a more straightforwardly crowd-pleasing affair, and so 'Take Five', 'Take the "A" Train' and 'Take The Tickets At The Door, Please' seemed to be the order of the day. But Dave is incapable of playing cynically and delivers eight strong performances with the band. We just doubt that they belong together on a double CD, though by this stage the stockpile of unreleased sessions was presumably of EU sugar-mountain proportions.

***** A Dave Brubeck Christmas**

Telarc 83410 *Brubeck (p solo).* 6/96.

Bah, humbug, and, yes, God bless us every one also. Santa Brubeck offers more than a few thought-provoking moments on this mostly generic Yuletide record. His own 'To Us Is Given' and 'Run, Run, Run To Bethlehem' are delightful, and his approach to the traditional themes – including 'Silent Night', 'Away In A Manger' and 'Jingle Bells' – is as accomplished as you would expect, mining previously unheard subtleties from the old tunes. But tell us, when do you all listen to Christmas albums? Only when there's snow on the ground? Or with heavy irony in July?

*****(*) So What's New?**

Telarc CD 83434 *Brubeck; Bobby Militello (sax, f); Jack Six (b); Randy Jones (d).* 97.

Issued to coincide with the fortieth anniversary of Brubeck's first visit to Britain in 1958. The writing is as vivid and stretching as ever: 'Fourth Of July' shifts in just that interval with a summery, affirmative sound; 'Her Name Is Nancy' is a dazzlingly clever set of changes and 'Chorale' is another Bach tribute.

Even past his 75th birthday, Brubeck continued to compose with unabated enthusiasm, and this record boldly consisted of brand-new material, seemingly devised to counter any impression that the old man had settled back into sepia-tinted ballad playing. 'It's Déjà Vu All Over Again' is a clever exercise in nostalgia-that-isn't, recapturing the classic group sound, but finding new and challenging things to say in the old block chord style. Three additional tunes stand out: 'Marian McPartland' was written for that lady and featured in a duet version with her in the same spring as this was recorded; 'Thing You Never Remember' is another antidote to the life lived backwards; 'Waltzing' is simply and sheerly beautiful, an instant standard. The 'new' quartet pushes no boundaries but sticks very much to the idiom of its predecessors. Militello has a quiet session, perhaps because in this studio session and with such challenging new compositions he was happier to leave the spotlight to the boss; Bobby's moment was to come on the road.

*****(*) 40th Anniversary Tour Of The UK**

Telarc 83440 *Brubeck; Bobby Militello (as); Alec Dankworth (b); Randy Jones (d).* 11/98.

Anticipation was heightened by rumours that Dave's health was once again causing concern and that he might not be able to fulfil engagements. In the event, the 1998 tour was packed with good material, though most of the exciting playing was from saxophonist Militello, who has established himself as the new Paul Desmond. Alec Dankworth also sounds as if he had listened to a good few early Brubeck records in his mum and dad's collection. What was particularly interesting was how readily Brubeck experimented with the set-list, including unexpected things like his own 'Salmon Strike', the tango-based 'Time Of Our Madness' and 'Oh, You Can Run (But You Can't Hide)', in which the famous Joe Louis line might seem to be an ironic comment on the need to keep down to business: making the date and playing the blues, which Brubeck does with notable darkness and vigour. The closing number is a solo tribute to the departed Gerry Mulligan, 'Goodbye Old Friend'.

***** The Crossing**

Telarc 83520 *Brubeck; Bobby Militello (as, f); Alec Dankworth (b); Randy Jones (d).* 9 & 10/00.

In the late '90s Brubeck seemed to ponder a lot about his transatlantic travels over the years, perhaps recognizing the special warmth with which he was regarded in Britain and Europe. The title-track here – it opens the album – is an evocation of putting out to sea in a big liner. Don't expect Mingus- or Zawinul-style grunts and hoots; this is a cheerful departure, criss-crossed with streamers and ticker tape. Other highlights include 'All My Love', a ballad for Iola Brubeck, and 'Randy Jones' which gives the seasoned sideman a well-deserved feature. The final part, 'Hold Fast To Dreams', reflects Brubeck's literary side as well as his bigger musical ambitions. It comes from a suite of pieces inspired by the poetry of Langston Hughes, another who looked out, sometimes more broodingly, over the Atlantic.

*****(*) One Alone**

Telarc 83510 *Brubeck (p solo).* 00.

Solo records are relatively rare in the Brubeck canon and this is a delight. Dave closes the set with a wonderful revoicing of 'Over The Rainbow', the kind of thing that has prompted gushing reviews for trendier and more 'authentic' jazzmen. There are only two originals on the programme, 'Weep No More' and 'Summer Song', which was originally written for Louis Armstrong; but what this set demonstrates more than anything is Dave's ability to colonize almost any material to his own particular vision. Brilliant, idiosyncratic and acoustically vivid.

***** 80th Birthday Concert: Live With The LSO**

LSO Mode LSO0011 *Brubeck; Bobby Militello (as, f); Darius Brubeck (p); Matthew Brubeck (clo); Chris Brubeck (b, btb); Dan Brubeck (d); London Symphony Orchestra.* 12/00.

A very special occasion which saw Dave's four boys on the stand with him. Veteran manager Russell Gloyd conducted the LSO in a series of arrangements, including some by the late Howard Brubeck, which just filled out the family association further. The long 'Chorale' is mainly for the strings. Matt is featured strongly on cello on 'In Your Own Sweet Way', one of Howard's arrangements, but it's the augmented quartet which steals the show towards the end. Following 'Brandenburg Gate Revisited' (another Howard chart), Bobby Militello kicks into 'Take Five' and sets up a delightfully exuberant and joyous performance of the classic, almost ten minutes in which Dan takes the spotlight for an unexpectedly good drum solo. 'Unsquare Dance' rounds out an extraordinary evening. The old chap must have been beaming.

****** Park Avenue South**

Telarc 83570 *Brubeck; Bobby Militello (as, f); Michael Moore (b); Randy Jones (d).* 7/02.

This was recorded in a Starbuck's in New York City, which might once have prompted cynical comments about Brubeck's cappuccino jazz. There's nothing decaff about the bright opener 'On the Sunny Side of the Street' (funny choice for an after midnight gig), which bounces along on Brubeck's punchy chords and the peerless Moore's astonishingly fluent base. They build up the pace and emotional temperature with a superb 'Love For Sale', before Brubeck slows things down with 'Elegy', a piece written for the Norwegian journalist Randi Hultin, who sadly didn't live to hear it played. 'I Love Vienna' and 'Don't Love Me' are both exquisite jazz waltzes, but the most famous Brubeck piece of all explores a different time signature. 'Take Five' has never belonged to anyone but its composer Paul Desmond, which is maybe why these days it's treated as a feature for drummer Jones, who negotiates the threes and twos brilliantly. After it, 'Show Me The Way To Go Home' rounds out a vintage set.

(****) Classical Brubeck

Telarc 60621 2CD *Brubeck; Bobby Militello (as, f); Michael Moore (b); Randy Jones (d); London Symphony Orchestra; London Voices.* 03.

Following *To Hope!* Telarc set out to document more of Brubeck's sacred/classical scores. There are two main works here: *Pange Lingua Variations* from 1983, which uses Gregorian chant in an inventive way, and *Voice of the Holy Spirit* from two years later, another multi-part piece that miraculously sounds more coherent than its fragmentary structure would suggest. It seems that there was little rehearsal time and that the LSO players were obliged to sight-read their parts. Once or twice, the ensembles are slightly more ragged than presumably written, but had producer/manager Russell Gloyd not revealed the circumstances of a very hurried recording, few listeners would have been any the wiser. Again, this sits apart from Brubeck's jazz work, but anyone interested in him as a man and musician will want to hear these radiant pieces.

Brunies Brothers Dixieland Jazz Band

GROUP

Abbie and Merritt Brunies were two of six brothers who made up one of the most imposing musical families in New Orleans. Merritt (1895–1973) and Albert (1900–1978) worked together until the middle '60s.

***** Brunies Brothers Dixieland Jazz Band**

American Music AMCD-77 *Albert 'Abbie' Brunies (t, v); Merritt Brunies (tb, v); Jules Galle (cl); Eddie James (p); Tony Fountain (b); Joe Wentz (d).* 10/57.

The Brunies Brothers were great figures in their earlier days, with Abbie leading The Halfway House Orchestra on their famous '20s sessions. They were still popular when they made this set at the Buena Vista Hotel in Biloxi: it was a working band, and if the music has more of Dixieland than New Orleans in it, it's still a rousing date. Both brothers play in a tough and unsubtle manner which Galle ducks in and around as if trying to squeak into a confined space. James sounds like he's stuck with a honky-tonk instrument and Wentz's snare sounds more like an upturned washtub but these idiosyncrasies tend to add to the fun. Five alternative takes have been added to the original LP. The brothers carried on working together until their health began to give out in the middle '60s.

Georg Brunis (1902–74)

TROMBONE, VOCAL

Among the most misspelled musicians in jazz, Georg was one of five musician-brothers, and was playing trombone before his tenth birthday. A stalwart of early New Orleans jazz, he was with Ted Lewis for ten years, and later formed associations with Muggsy Spanier and Wild Bill Davison, eventually spending most of the 50s working a regular Chicago gig. He worked in classic Dixieland bands until failing health finally caught up with him.

*****(*) George Brunies And His Rhythm Kings**
Jazzology JCD-12 *Brunis; Dick Baars, Carl Halen (c); Pat Patterson, Frank Powers (cl); Clarence Hall (p, v); Gene Mayl (b, tba); Glenn Kimmel (d).* 6/64–7/65.

Nice to have a record under Brunis's name in the catalogue. This reissues a couple of dates made for Jazzology in the mid-'60s, both recorded in Dayton, Ohio: the tunes are all Dixieland warhorses, but they're played with terrific enthusiasm and it helps that Mayl and Kimmel are a rhythm team who really kick the band along. Patterson is a pretty wayward clarinettist, but since Brunis worked with Ted Lewis for years, perhaps he'd developed a taste for that kind of thing. Baars and Halen are both feisty individuals in the Davison manner, and Brunis tailgates his way through the music, as up for it as ever. If there is a disappointment it's that he only gets two vocals. Remastered sound has plenty of presence, although here and there the balances are a little odd.

Jimmy Bruno

GUITAR

Philadelphia-based guitarist who has played that scene for many years with few concessions to a worldlier jazz résumé. His style is a throwback, but timeless with it.

****(*) Sleight Of Hand**
Concord CCD 4532 *Bruno; Pete Colangelo (b); Bruce Klauber (d); Edgardo Cintron Orchestra.* 4–5/91.

***** Burnin'**
Concord CCD 4612 *Bruno; Craig Thomas (b); Craig Holloway (d).* 2/94.

Bruno is a Philadelphia homebody whose playing sits squarely in the big-toned electric tradition. He's more fond of chords, octave playing and parallel lines than of single-string solos, and it gives his improvisations a meaty texture that fleshes out his simple tunes. That said, the first record is impressively skilful but not very exciting. The 'orchestra' is a Latin rhythm section that sits in on two tracks for a useful change of pace, but otherwise Bruno has to carry everything himself, since Colangelo and Klauber offer anonymous support. *Burnin'* goes up a notch since Thomas and Holloway bring some muscle of their own to the date. Two deft solos by Bruno include a thoughtful revision of Coltrane's 'Central Park West' that's quietly effective.

***** Like That**
Concord CCD 4698 *Bruno; Joey DeFrancesco (org, t); Craig Thomas (b); Steve Holloway (d).* 95.

***** Live At Birdland**
Concord CCD 4768 *Bruno; Bobby Watson (as); Craig Thomas (b); Vince Ector (d).* 12/96.

*****(*) Live At Birdland II**
Concord CCD 4810 *As above, except Scott Hamilton (ts) replaces Watson.* 12/96.

Like That is an agreeable balance. DeFrancesco impresses as much on trumpet as he does on organ – the duet between guitar and horn on 'Stars Fell On Alabama' is a nice surprise – and Bruno finds plenty of ways of varying his own pace, 'Razer's Edge' in particular going some way outside. He has also built up a fruitful relationship with Thomas, who impresses again on the first *Birdland* record. This is more like heartland bebop; if Bruno doesn't quite catch the excitement that Ron Affif found in a similar situation, he plays a theme like 'Move' with a sort of refined fire. Watson joins in for the second half of the programme and turns up the heat on the likes of 'Au Privave'.

The return visit (actually a second helping from the same season) might be Bruno's best calling-card, since the first half has some of his most appealing playing on the likes of 'Poinciana', and the second benefits from the presence of guest Scott Hamilton. Temperamentally, these two are a good match, and something as juicily rhapsodic as 'Lover Man' makes one forget how many times this tune's been done before.

***** Polarity**
Concord CCD-4888-2 *Bruno; Joe Beck (g).* 12/99.

**** Midnight Blue**
Concord CCD-4980-2 *Bruno; Ron Kerber (ss, ts); Dave Hartl (ky); Gerald Veasley (b); Marc Dicciani (d).* 3/01.

With Bruno on seven-string and Beck playing his own invention, the alto guitar, the duets record has an unusual feel. Bruno is the principal improviser, although Beck has a nice solo turn on 'Tenderly'. It has its soporific side, too, as in most such records, but the nimbleness appeals.

Midnight Blue is a deliberate change of direction, after 'five bebop records and that's enough for now'. Instead, lightweight fusion.

Gai Bryant

SOPRANO AND ALTO SAXOPHONES

Australian saxophonist in the post-bop field.

*****(*) High Jinx**
Rufus RF037 *Bryant; Sandy Evans (ts); Lloyd Swanton (b); Martin Highland (d).* 11/97.

A very enjoyable set. The unusual instrumentation makes for free but carefully considered music, working cunning variations on the head-solos-head format. Bryant writes intriguing lines which are structured just enough to provide pointers without laying down too many laws. The saxophonists make no claims for great virtuosity – the fast pace of the title-track comes close to defeating them – but at the mid-tempo lope from which much of the record works, they come up with all sorts of interesting notions, and a piece like the self-explanatory 'Fishing In Thirds' is a puzzle that's handsomely solved. Swanton and Highland accompany – and make their own mark – with great heart.

Ray Bryant (born 1931)

PIANO

A Philadelphia man, Bryant is a major and often undersung player of bebop piano, with blues and gospel subtexts never far away. A frequent leader and record-maker for 40-plus years.

***** Ray Bryant Trio/Dancing The Big Twist**
Collectables 7417 *Bryant; Pat Jenkins, Joe Newman (t); Matthew Gee (tb); Buddy Tate (ts); Ben Richardson (bs); Bill Lee, Jimmy Rowser (b); Gus Johnson, Mickey Roker (d); Ray Barreto (perc).* 56, 62.

***** Ray Bryant Trio**
Original Jazz Classics OJC 793 *Bryant; Ike Isaacs (b); Specs Wright (d).* 4/57.

*****(*) Alone With The Blues**
Original Jazz Classics OJC 249 *Bryant (p solo).* 12/58.

Bryant is not an orthodox bopper in the way Hampton Hawes once was, and his solo performances are even further away from the predominant Bud Powell model of bop piano. Noted for an imaginative and influential alteration of the basic 12-bar-blues sequence on his 'Blues Changes', Bryant is a distinctive pianist who resembles Hawes superficially but who, unlike the older man, has often been content to record solo. The two early OJCs (originally done for Prestige and New Jazz) are both welcome revivals, the solo set in particular a thoroughgoing investigation of Bryant's favourite form.

These days, Bryant has to rely on Collectables to keep his output in circulation. *Trio* (a different, earlier record) and *Dancing the Big Twist* are a few years apart and made with very different line-ups. Both, though, are quintessential Ray Bryant, pungent, boppish but with a decidedly funky swing. He brings something of his own to Monk's 'Well, You Needn't' and sounds surprisingly like Hampton Hawes on 'Cry Me A River'. The 'Twist' album is exactly that, though he might have found a corner for Wardell Gray's 'Twisted'. Not to every taste, but a great party record, we've found.

Original blues compositions are interwoven with an affecting 'Lover Man' and a delicious, gospelly 'Rockin' Chair'. Bryant's coming out as a solo performer could hardly have been more gracefully handled.

***** The Madison Time**
Collectables 9335 *Bryant (p solo).* 3/60.

This was formerly released on Collectables as *The Madison Time With A Hollywood Big Beat* and included a second set of film themes played the Bryant way. Whether copyright problems have prompted its withdrawal we don't know, but even on its own this is an engaging session, featuring the two-part 'Madison Time' from the jukeboxes and a fine version of 'The Hucklebuck', a dance craze of the time. We're told.

***** Cold Turkey**
Collectables Records COL 5749 *Bryant; Jimmy Rowser (b); Ben Riley (d).* 63–4.

****(*) Groove House**
Collectables Records COL 5753 *Bryant; Wally Richardson (g); Tom Bryant (b); Bobby Donaldson, Panama Francis (d).* 5–6/63.

****(*) Soul**
Collectables Records COL 5754 *Bryant; Tom Bryant (b); Sonny Brown, Walter Perkins (d).* 64.

*****(*) Live At Basin Street East**
Collectables Records COL 5755 *Bryant; probably as above.* 64.

These are valuable reissues for Bryant fans, though we might wish for a little more information on their provenance. Some of the sessions at least were made for Sue Records and, while we have no reason to think these CDs are anything but above-board, the presentation is decidedly slipshod.

The most desirable of the bunch is the live set, which opens with a superb 'What Is This Thing Called Love?' and swings in every measure from there to the close. *Cold Turkey* is a more acerbic set, but with some strong points. *Soul* is a disappointment and *Groove House* could do with some variation of pace. A feast for confirmed Bryant fans, but nothing of any real moment for casual listeners.

***** Montreux 77**
Original Jazz Classics OJC 371 *Bryant (p solo).* 12/76.

*****(*) Here's Ray Bryant**
Original Jazz Classics OJC 826 *Bryant; George Duvivier (b); Grady Tate (d).* 1/76.

***** Solo Flight**
Original Jazz Classics OJC 885 *Bryant (p solo).* 12/76.

***** All Blues**
Original Jazz Classics OJC 778 *Bryant; Sam Jones (b); Grady Tate (d).* 4/78.

***** Potpourri**
Original Jazz Classics OJC 936 *Bryant; Jimmy Rowser (b); Mickey Roker (d).* 5/80.

There's still a slight feeling of uncertainty, as if Bryant wasn't yet sure what direction his revived career was going to take. That was to become much clearer over the next few years, with a signing to Pablo; most of these albums have returned via the OJC series. They're a strong, idiomatic sequence of blues-to-bop piano and there's little to choose between them, although our pick if pressed would be the impeccably programmed *Here's Ray Bryant.*

***** Somewhere In France**
Hyena 9315 *Bryant (p solo).* 93.

This was a tape given to Bryant by a soundman on one of his gigs. No one knows exactly where it was recorded, but certainly in France and therefore in 1993. It could have been any time in the previous 25 years, so consistent and recognizable is Bryant's style. Interesting that Dizzy's 'Con Alma' should sound more like a classical etude in this arrangement than on the original. 'Django' and a making-up-time 'Take The "A" Train' are both superlative and make you forget the rather indifferent source.

Bryant apparently has dozens of cassettes of this kind; whether Joel Dorn finds enough worthy of formal release remains to be seen.

The Buck Clayton Legacy

GROUP

A mainstream repertory group dedicated to the music of Buck Clayton.

*****(*) All The Cats Join In**

Nagel-Heyer 006 *Randy Sandke (t); Jerry Tilitz (tb); Antti Sarpila (cl, ss, ts); Harry Allen, Danny Moss (ts); Brian Dee (p); Len Skeat (b); Oliver Jackson (d).* 11/93.

***** Encore Live**

Nagel-Heyer 018 *As above, except add Scott Robinson (bs), Butch Miles (d); omit Jackson.* 11/94.

One of the principal ways in which jazz repertory is enduring is through projects like this. Clayton became a great eminence as composer/bandleader after he had to give up playing, and Sandke's enthusiasm for that legacy has engendered this band, which mixes old-time Clayton staples like 'Buckin' The Blues' with some of his less familiar charts. The first album is studio, the second live; since there are twin versions of nine of the tunes, maybe only a committed fan needs both. Or maybe not: this is awfully good swing-styled jazz. Some of the themes have been done to decrepitude over the years, and still the group summons a freshness about 'Jumpin' At The Woodside' (a quite classic treatment on the studio disc, a trifle winded on the live one), 'Robbins' Nest' and some of the others. The studio set edges ahead on the basis of the stricter ensembles, a thrilling two-tenor workout for Allen and Moss on 'Lester Leaps In' and three previously unknown Clayton scores. But the live set has plenty of atmosphere and Robinson and Sarpila (on only three of the studio tracks) to beef up the front line. Jackson's drumming abets the earlier disc: since he died not long afterwards, Miles takes over for the concert and, if he's hardly a master of subtlety, the extra weight does kick the band along.

Milt Buckner (1915–77)

ORGAN, PIANO

Grew up in Detroit and started his career with McKinney's Cotton Pickers and the Lionel Hampton Band, where his much-imitated locked hands piano style attracted notice. Adept on piano and organ, he recorded a fair amount on his own.

***** And His Alumni**

Black & Blue 909 *Buckner; Wallace Davenport (t); Buster Cooper (tb); Earl Warren (as); Eddie Chamblee, Arnett Cobb (ts); André Persiany (p); Roland Lobligeois (b); Panama Francis (d).* 71.

***** The Definitive Black & Blue Sessions: Pianistically Yours**

Black & Blue 917 *Buckner; André Persiany (p); Roland Lobligeois (b); Sam Woodyard (d).* 11/75.

***** The Definitive Black & Blue Sessions: Green Onions**

Black & Blue 929 *Buckner; André Persiany (p); Roy Gaines (g); Roland Lobligeois (b); Panama Francis, Michael Silva (d).* 2/75.

***** Block Chords Parade**

Black & Blue 953 *Buckner; Major Holley (b); Jo Jones (d).* 2/74.

***** Milt Buckner**

Progressive 7017 *Buckner; Illinois Jacquet, Buddy Tate (ts); Joop Scholten (g); Koos Van der Suils, Chris Smidiger (b); Sonny Payne (d).* 75.

The pickings are thinner than for some time, but the Black & Blues fill in much of the story of Milt's time in Europe. The first session is a brand-new release, having lain in the vaults for some time. Milt's locked hands approach is an acquired taste, riveting over short periods but curiously wearing after a while. 'Hamp's Boogie Woogie' is a good place to start, but even here the greasy solos and blocky chords are less than appealing. 'King Porter Stomp' and the long, indulgent read of 'Green Onions' are better, but apart from flashes of Cobb and some nice licks from Milt, this is a drab piece of work.

The trio, now augmented with extra tracks, is probably the most interesting of the bunch. Milt's chording is less mannered than usual and he allows some of his lines to flow a little rather than producing them in chunks. Holley is a great accompanist at this kind of thing and if he was further forward in the mix it would be possible to hear how good he is.

The late sessions with Jacquet and Tate, who don't appear together, still find Milt in breezy form but it's hard to be excited about his playing, which relies on the same licks and tricks every time. Jacquet squeals righteously and Tate does his own smoother thing. Nothing for the unconverted, though. It's pretty much the same story with *Green Onions* and *Pianistically Yours*, though we're sure to hear from readers who think Milt is a master.

John Bunch (born 1921)

PIANO

Worked on the West Coast in the '50s in big bands and small groups, then often with Benny Goodman during the '60s and '70s, and MD for Tony Bennett. Gradually achieved a wide recognition, but his reputation is largely confined to mainstream musicians' circles.

*****(*) John Bunch Plays Kurt Weill**

Chiaroscuro CD(D) 144 *Bunch (p solo).* 5/75–1/91.

***** Struttin'**

Arbors ARCD 19157 *Bunch; Phil Flanigan (b).* 11/95.

***** Arbors Piano Series At Mike's Place Vol. 1**

Arbors ARCD 19184 *Bunch (p solo).* 11/96.

Despite his seniority, John Bunch was a little-known sideman, accompanist and orchestra pianist until he was in his 50s. In the '70s and '80s he secured wider attention as a member of the mainstream clan championed by Concord. There's nothing demonstrative about his style, which is in the aristocratic swing tradition of Teddy Wilson, but he can play with power when he wants, as well as with fingertip delicacy.

The *Kurt Weill* album is a rare and strikingly imaginative project: only a handful of Weill's tunes have entered the jazz repertoire, and Bunch's thoughtful settings – some at ballad tempo, others with a flavour of stride, some delivered with Monk-like rhythms – make all of them sound like plausible vehicles. The original (1975) sessions have been extended with six tracks cut in 1991, and there's amazingly little to choose between them in terms of both sound and interpretation.

Bunch's other discs have a less decisive quality about them, as if he was prepared to settle for a sort of routine excellence – nice, but nothing really to make one want to return to the music very often. *Struttin'*, a series of duets with the solid Flanigan, points up how bebop touched Bunch's style: he does 'Crazeology' and Oscar Pettiford's 'Laverne Walk' among some standards, but it's bebop down a couple of gears. The later solo session offers 18 pleasant interpretations, with just a bare handful of surprises in the set-list, and, though the pianist's even-handed approach and respect for the melodies is warmly agreeable, it's a bit stately.

Jane Bunnett (born 1956)

SOPRANO SAXOPHONE, FLUTE

Bunnett owed much of her early prominence to the wise tutelage of Don Pullen, with whom she recorded. The young Canadian has specialized in the treacherously pitched soprano saxophone, creating a voice which is as light and fleet as her flute-playing, but with a surprisingly hard edge. Partner Larry Cramer's trumpet helps soften it when they play together. In recent years, Bunnett has concentrated very largely on Cuban music.

**(*) Rendez-Vous Brazil/Cuba

Justin Time 74 *Bunnett; Larry Cramer (t, flhn); Sabine Boyer (af); Hilario Durán Torres (p); Filo Machado (g, v, perc); Carlitos Del Puerto (b); Celso Machado (perc).* 6/95.

The *Brazil/Cuba* project is dominated by Filo Machado compositions, and he is clearly the effective co-leader of a session that almost puts Bunnett's solo skills at a discount in favour of a highly rhythmic and dance-orientated group sound. It's all doubtless very authentic, and Cramer could find work in wedding bands any day of the week, growing a lot more comfortable with this type of material every time he goes out, but one wonders whether it's the most effective direction for the young Canadian.

**(*) Chamalongo

Blue Note 23684 *Bunnett; Larry Cramer (t); Hilario Durán Torres, Frank Emilio (p); Tata Guines, Pancho Quinto (perc); Amado J. Dedeu, Gregorio Hernandez, Pedro Martinez, Merceditás Valdes (v).* 3/98.

A Blue Note contract is supposed to be nothing but good. Unfortunately, on this occasion it seems to have blunted Jane's peerless tone and stilted her phrasing. There is also a heavy emphasis on vocals and, while some of the tracks are fascinating in and of themselves – we specially liked the unusual 'Descarga À La Hindemith' – the overall impact is rather lightweight.

***(*) Ritmo + Soul

Blue Note 24456 *Bunnett; Larry Cramer (t); Hilario Durán Torres (p); Roberto Occhipinti (b); Pacho Quinto (perc); Dean Bowman (v).* 9/99.

A bright and bouncy set that seems less hung up on 'authenticity' than other of Bunnett's records. Her soprano-playing has never been fresher or more eloquent. Jane's own composition 'The River' is outstanding, unravelled at length. 'Francisco's Dream' is co-written with Cramer and receives similarly elaborate treatment. The other long track is the traditional 'Drume Negrita', which comes right at the heart of the record and beats to a rhythm which is as thoughtful as it is infectious. Jeff McCulloch's engineering is pin-sharp and Bunnett produces with admirable even-handedness, mixing herself a little back in the picture. A very attractive record.

*** Alma de Santiago

Blue Note 34273 *Bunnett; Larry Cramer (t, flhn); Carlos Thomas (t); Juan Chacon Gonzalez (ss); Julio Cesar Gonzalez Simon (as); Rey Amaury Burgos Delis (ts); Oscar Galan Ruiz (bs); Geovanis Alcantara, David Virelles (p); Roberto Occhipinti (b); Wilfredo Fuentes Cespedes, Los Conga De Los Hoyos de Santiago de Cuba (perc); Fernando De Maso (tres); Eduardo Tiburon Morales, Los Jubilados de Santiago de Cuba (v).* n.d.

Jane Bunnett's love affair with Cuba has never been so fulsomely consummated. And yet this evocation of musical life in the island's second city has some surprising components. 'Donna Lee' – the Charlie Parker composition – is given an almost Asiatic feel, as if John Coltrane had a hand in its composition and arrangement. The members of the Santiago Jazz Saxophone Quartet add an extra dimension, as they do on the delicious mambo 'Shin Shin' and the ubiquitous 'Almendra' which is said to be the most recorded *danzon* of all time.

The component members of Spirits of Havana are present, and Larry Cramer is as accurate and pungent as usual, but the emphasis here is very much on the local players and singers. Los Jubilados are magnificent on 'Son Satiaguero' and 'Camaroncito Seco', and Eduardo Tiburon Morales rises to the forefront on 'Lagrimas Negras'. Very much a record for Cuban music fans, but a thoroughly convincing and entertaining performance.

*** Spirituals and Dedications

Justin Time 169 *Bunnett; Larry Cramer (t); Dewey Redman (ts); Stanley Cowell (p); Kieran Overs (b); Mark McLean (d); Dean Bowman (v).* 01.

Given the personnel and a vividly eclectic choice of material – Roland Kirk, Charles Mingus, Cowell, traditional spirituals – this is a curiously unmoving and flat set. The musicianship is as good as one might hope and expect, but the players never seem to meld into something greater than the parts. This might be due to Bowman's strong but slightly overpowering presence on the vocal tracks. Redman also seems mismatched with the rest of the group.

Mingus's 'Ecclusiastics' is probably the best single track, but it is wonderful to hear a new version of Cowell's 'Illusion Suite'; Stanley also contributed 'Cal Massey' and 'Powerful Paul Robeson'. Unusual at this juncture to hear Jane in anything other than a Cuban setting, but welcome as that is, this doesn't quite come off.

*** Cuban Odyssey

Blue Note 41992 *Bunnett; Larry Cramer (t); Hilario Duran, Paulo Quinto, Guillermo Rubalcaba (p); Pepi Oviedo (g); Carlos del Puerto (b); Tata Guines, Raul Hernandez, Jose Quintana (perc); other musicians and singers.* 00.

This is one of those records where one wishes one could have been at the recording sessions. The atmosphere is infectious and joyous, but unfortunately some of that is lost when heard cold and this delightful album is unlikely to spend much time in the CD player. The high spots are very good indeed, notably the long 'Suite Matanzas' and 'Ron Con Ron', which was co-written with percussionist Guines. The traditional themes are despatched with obvious affection and a clear understanding of their roots and origins, but one misses being at the party.

Albert Burbank (1902–76)

CLARINET

Played in New Orleans during the '20s and '30s; after war service, was with Herb Morand, Paul Barbarin and Kid Ory. Rarely sighted away from his hometown and was a regular with Preservation Hall groups until his death.

***** Albert Burbank With Kid Ory And His Creole Jazzband**

Storyville STCD 6010 *Burbank; Alvin Alcorn (t); Kid Ory (tb); Don Ewell (p); Ed Garland (b); Minor Hall (d).* 5–7/54.

Burbank scarcely ever left New Orleans, and it's an irony that the only disc currently under his own name should have been recorded elsewhere (he toured briefly with Ory's band and returned home the same year). These tracks, culled from six different 1954 concerts at San Francisco's Club Hangover, were made under Ory's leadership, and it's rather a matter of paying respects that they appear under Burbank's name; Ory and Alcorn have just as major a role in the music. But the clarinettist has much to say, too. He was a dramatic player, switching between long and short phrases and possessing an odd, shrimpy vibrato which gives his high notes a peculiarly affecting quality. There are fine solos on 'Fidgety Feet' and the rest of a frankly ordinary set of material, but the epic 'Blues For Jimmie Noone', which runs for 11 minutes, has a funereal grandeur that is only finally undercut by Garland's disastrous *arco* passage. Alcorn is, as ever, in rousing form, too. Fair recording, given the source material.

John Burgess

TENOR SAXOPHONE, BASS CLARINET, FLUTE

Scots saxophonist, part of a new wave of players based around Edinburgh.

***** The Beautiful Never**

Urge 2 Burge [no number] *Burgess; Theo Saunders (p); Henry Franklin (b); Willie Jones III (d).* 1/97.

***** The Urge To Burge**

Caber 012 *Burgess; Kevin MacKenzie (g); Mario Caribé (b, perc); John Rae (d).* 4/99.

The Edinburgh-based reed man is possessed of a lovely sound and an impressive stock of ideas. The debut disc was made in California with a skilful American group. Saunders and Jones are at the heart of things at all times, freeing Burgess to make his slightly querulous but heartfelt declarations. The more atmospheric numbers go straight on the personal playlist, mostly for late-nite use; the tougher swingers are as challenging as one might hope.

The follow-up is very much a consolidation. Burgess stays well within himself and relaxes enough to create some genuinely beautiful and moving solos, notably on the opening 'Once Upon A Long Ago', which sets out his trademark Webster-influenced saxophone. As before, his bass clarinet work is moody and atmospheric. An oddly sequenced album, *The Urge To Burge* doesn't come to life until the fourth track, 'The North Beach Hi-Life', which ironically is a flute feature. It's also the only shared credit, a co-composition with bassist Caribé, who provides a steady foundation throughout. As often when a guitarist is preferred to a piano-player, the harmonic language is much more ambiguous. MacKenzie probably ought to spend a couple of years in New York to polish up his basic chops, but you can't fault his taste and timing, and his acoustic accompaniment on 'Nine Lives' is impeccable.

Burgess is locked into a mainstream ballad approach that will certainly win him admirers but doesn't challenge him enough. What he needs at this stage is just one raw and rough-edged session of blues and bebop material. He'd come back all the stronger.

Raymond Burke (1904–86)

CLARINET

Began playing home-made instruments as a teenager, then graduated to sax and clarinet. Played in New Orleans for most of his life, through revivalism and beyond, and was closely associated with Preservation Hall from 1960, and with Kid Thomas Valentine.

(***) Raymond Burke's Speakeasy Boys 1937–1949

American Music AMCD-47 *Burke; Wooden Joe Nicholas, Vincent Cass (t); Joe Avery (tb); Louis Gallaud, Woodrow Rousell (p); Johnny St Cyr (g); Austin Young (b); Bob Matthews (d).* 37–5/49.

Burke's clarinet-playing stands squarely in the line of the New Orleans masters: he had the sweet-toned delivery of Willie Humphrey but could be as elaborate and blues-inflected as Johnny Dodds when he wished. Some of this can be gleaned from a very rough CD in the American Music series. Most of the tracks come from 1949 acetates by a band from which Burke stands out: Nicholas sounds terribly weak and shaky when he struggles to the front, and Avery's trombone is inept enough to make one wince (even the sleeve-notes describe him as 'ratty'). The loudest person in the band is St Cyr! Despite all that, Burke still weaves some lovely solos out of the situation. The other tracks are even more obscure: a 1937 'Solitude' with George Hartman's (unknown) band, a couple of duets with Woodrow Rousell, and four dusty tracks with Vincent Cass's (unknown) band. Sound-quality ranges from dire to moderately decent (two final acetates were turned up in a New Orleans flea market in 1993). For New Orleans scholars only.

*****(*) Raymond Burke And Cie Frazier With Butch Thompson In New Orleans**

504 CDS 27 *Burke; Butch Thompson (p); Cie Frazier (d).* 8/79.

This is more like the way Raymond Burke should be remembered. Though already late in life, he was still playing very well in 1979, his understated delivery the mark of a man whose unassuming approach to his art has helped it endure. In itself, the music is nothing much: a battery of tunes, played at more or less the same tempo, with Frazier marking out a steady pulse and Thompson comping and taking easy-going solos. But scarcely any of the 15 tunes are too familiar – there are New Orleans rarities like A. J. Piron's 'I Want Somebody To Love', 'Gypsy Love Song' and 'Oh Daddy' – and each is played with genuine pleasure by the three men. Thompson never pushes too hard, and Burke's musing solos have an eloquence all their own. On a hot day, with a jug of iced tea to hand, this can sound like the very heart of jazz.

Dwayne Burns

TRUMPET, VOCAL

New Orleans trumpeter of a new generation, active in the city since the early '80s and now a regular at the Maison Bourbon and Preservation Hall.

***** Thanks A Million**

504 CDS 90 *Burns; Freddie Lonzo (tb); Daniel Farrow (ts, bs); Jonathan Lecofski (p); Eric Webster (bj); Al Bernard (b); Hurley Blanchard (d).* 4/00.

A recent report from the old city. Burns leads a mix of old-timers and younger hands on this spirited walk through 11 chestnuts. They have lots of fun with the likes of 'Bourbon Street Parade', although a more standard standard such as 'Keepin' Out Of Mischief Now' is less appealing (and the bass intonation is suspect). It's a bit shocking to hear such a date in clean modern sound. Lonzo is reliable, the others about par. But Burns himself is the attraction, a strong, limber soloist and lead horn. He'll be better heard in better company, perhaps.

Ralph Burns (1922–2001)

PIANO, ARRANGER

Burns arrived in New York in 1942 and contributed major pieces to the band books of Charlie Barnet and Woody Herman, particularly the latter, with whom he worked until the '50s. He then did various studio arrangements and by the '70s was working mostly in film and theatre scoring. Absolutely dedicated to music, he continued to work on charts until his death.

***** Bijou**

Original Jazz Classics OJC 1917 *Burns; Tal Farlow (g); Clyde Lombardi (b); Osie Johnson (d).* 55.

Burns's contribution to jazz is as an arranger and composer; his piano-playing is capable but unremarkable. The main point of this set is to hear some of his most renowned pieces – 'Spring Sequence', 'Bijou', 'Autobahn Blues' – in a quartet setting. He points up how the harmonies work, and with Farlow taking a back-seat role, it's good dinner music. 'Perpetual Motion' might be the most interesting piece, since he overdubs a second piano part, and the results have a Tristanoesque feel. His other albums for Decca, which featured larger groups, are somewhat more interesting but have still yet to be reissued.

Dave Burrell (born 1944)

PIANO, KEYBOARDS

Grew up in Hawaii and studied at Berklee, before joining the New York free-jazz movement in the late '60s. Most frequently encountered of late as a David Murray sideman.

***** Esquisses For A Walk**

NTCD 319 *Burrell; Daniel Huck (as, v); Carl Schlosser (ts, f); Ricky Ford (ts); Chris Henderson (d); Laurence Allison (v).* 98.

Burrell has never fallen easily into any stylistic categories. He has worked with Marion Brown, Giuseppi Logan, Archie Shepp and Sonny Sharrock, among many others. In the late '60s, as these associations suggest, he was much involved with the avant-garde while retaining an affection for standards jazz and for non-jazz styles such as ragtime, calypso and, at more of a sceptical distance, elements of the so-called 'Third Stream'. It is only really possible to say that Burrell himself represents a fourth or umpteenth stream. He doesn't have much in the catalogue at present. Jointly led by saxophonist Huck, this rather strange session takes Burrell a step further into his exploration of jazz styles. There is a wonderful reading of 'Honeysuckle Rose', which manages to touch base with Waller and Tatum but nevertheless bears Burrell's signature in every bar. A new approach to 'Trade Winds' isn't quite as successful, but shows how much mileage there is in the material. 'Lush Life' has a kind of defiant melancholy which suits the song, but you won't have heard it performed quite like this before.

Don't be put off by the rather pretentious and enigmatic title. This is a strong, intriguing album with some fine contributions from Ford and the other saxophonists. Not in the front rank of Burrell's output, but well worth hearing and probably a grower.

*****(*) Recital**

CIMP 230 *Burrell; Tyrone Brown (b).* 8/00.

Probably best heard after the Morton/Parker/Coltrane tribute record on Gazell (now deleted), this simply recorded session works yet more variations on 'Giant Steps', finessing that astonishing performance with even greater authority. Brown is an able partner, though he sounds a bit lost on the free-form 'Samba Rondo'. Already known as an eclectic's eclectic, Burrell this time puts Trane upsides with Louis Armstrong's 'Struttin' With Some Barbecue' and makes the switch of source seem the most logical thing in the world, which to a degree it is. Another very fine record from a consistently underrated player.

*****(*) Live At Caramoor**

Sonoris SCD 5161 *Burrell (p solo).* n.d.

As ever, the impressive thing in this solo recital is Burrell's sheer range. Here he does a Coltrane medley (with a fiercely independent yet plausible take on 'Giant Steps') and a Nat Cole-like 'Sweet Georgia Brown' alongside several of his own originals: out of them all, it's his signature piece 'Punaluu Peter' which stands tallest, nine minutes of superbly fresh invention.

Kenny Burrell (born 1931)

GUITAR, VOCAL

Born in Detroit, Burrell had already played with Dizzy Gillespie and Oscar Peterson before moving to New York in 1956. Ever since, he has been the most dependable of sidemen and the most quietly inspiring of leaders, mixing both blues and bebop into a style which remains conservative but genuine and unemphatically direct. He has been closely associated with Jimmy Smith's small groups over the years, and has a penchant for Duke Ellington's music: in both cases, the admiration was mutual.

***** All Night Long**

Original Jazz Classics OJC 427 *Burrell; Donald Byrd (t); Hank Mobley (ts); Jerome Richardson (ts, f); Mal Waldron (p); Doug Watkins (b); Art Taylor (d).* 12/56.

***** All Day Long**

Original Jazz Classics OJC 456 *Burrell; Donald Byrd (t); Frank Foster (ts); Tommy Flanagan (p); Doug Watkins (b); Art Taylor (d).* 1/57.

***** Blue Moods**

Original Jazz Classics OJC 019 *Burrell; Cecil Payne (bs); Tommy Flanagan (p); Doug Watkins (b); Elvin Jones (d).* 2/57.

***** The Cats**

Original Jazz Classics OJC 079 *Burrell; Idrees Sulieman (t); John Coltrane (ts); Tommy Flanagan (p); Doug Watkins (b); Louis Hayes (d).* 4/57.

***** Kenny Burrell & John Coltrane**

Original Jazz Classics OJC 300 *Burrell; John Coltrane (ts); Tommy Flanagan (p); Paul Chambers (b); Jimmy Cobb (d).* 3/58.

Burrell is one of the great enduring lights in the music. He's the most gentlemanly of musicians, never losing his grip on a playing situation and in command of a seemingly inexhaustible supply of interesting licks. He has a tone as lulling as that of Joe Pass, but he shies away from that player's rococo extravagances. It's difficult to pick out the best of Burrell, for his earliest sessions are as maturely formed as his later ones, and while he's played with a vast number of musicians he manages to fit seamlessly into whatever the context happens to be. In the '50s he was a popular man to have on blowing dates, and his early work for Prestige is mostly in that mould. The sessions that were designated as all-day and all-night don't actually go on that long, but some of the solos seem to, and there's little to especially recommend them beyond a few livelier moments. *Blue Moods* is a reflective canter through a typical programme of blues and standards, with a feature for Jones on 'Drum Boogie'. OJC 300 finds Coltrane in his restless early period, but Burrell seems to be a calming influence, and they have a beautifully shaded duet on 'Why Was I Born?'. *The Cats* benefits from Flanagan's leadership, and the pianist's shapely contributions add further lustre to the music, all of it very well engineered.

*****(*) Blue Lights**

Blue Note 57184-2 2CD *Burrell; Louis Smith (t); Tina Brooks, Junior Cook (ts); Duke Jordan, Bobby Timmons (p); Sam Jones (b); Art Blakey (d).* 5/58.

Two blowing dates that have the edge on the Prestige sessions – just that bit sharper and more swinging, and with Smith, Cook and the star-crossed Brooks in attendance, the horns are that bit more interesting too. Blakey lets nobody coast, and even though the material is routine, it doesn't much matter. Originally split across two albums, they're restored to CD with a long look at 'I Never Knew' as the bonus.

****** Bluesy Burrell**

Original Jazz Classics OJC 926 *Burrell; Leo Wright (as); Coleman Hawkins (ts); Tommy Flanagan, Gildo Mahones (p); Major Holley, George Tucker (b); Eddie Locke, Jimmie Smith (d); Ray Barretto (perc).* 9/62–8/63.

What a marvellous session this was. Burrell sounds at his most seductive on 'I Thought About You', at his most suavely blue on 'Montono Blues'; but it's his interplay with the imperious Hawkins, in one of his last great periods, that makes the record special. 'Tres Palabras' is a classic performance, given further weight by Flanagan's wonderfully economical solo, and here and on his three other appearances Hawkins carries all before him. One bonus track from a session made the following year with Wright and Mahones is nothing special, and the remastering seems laden with tape-hiss, but the music comes over with plenty of presence.

*****(*) Midnight Blue**

Blue Note 95335-2 *Burrell; Stanley Turrentine (ts); Major Holley (b); Bill English (d); Ray Barretto (perc).* 1/63.

Many a copy of this was worn smooth on vinyl, and the two new-to-CD tracks, 'Kenny's Sound' and 'K Twist', are a welcome bonus, especially in the handsome sound of the RVG Edition. Somewhat atypically low-flame for a Blue Note date, even if Burrell had already visited these climes on the *Night Lights* sessions, they take the soul-food licks of 'Chitlins Con Carne' some way towards ferocity, but the implacable beat refuses to get too nasty, and the following 'Mule' is more typical. Beautifully paced and as elegant a record as the label ever released, this is still an ideal choice for the time and mood of the title.

*****(*) Blue Bash!**

Verve 557453-2 *Burrell; Jimmy Smith (org); George Duvivier, Milt Hinton (b); Bill English, Mel Lewis (d).* 7/63.

Three days of spare studio time while Smith was at work on a big-band date led to this hugely enjoyable blowing date, meat and potatoes for the two principals. Their interplay on the title-track sums up their whole musical relationship: punchy, bluesy, but soaked in the good humour of playing for kicks. Seven extra takes might have spoiled the balance of the record, but for once the extra music means extra enjoyment.

***** Soul Call**

Original Jazz Classics OJC 846-2 *Burrell; Will Davis (p); Martin Rivera (b); Bill English (d); Ray Barretto (perc).* 4/64.

Burrell's reluctance to assert any special kind of leadership tells against him on a date like this, when the supporting players have little to say by themselves. The title-piece and 'Mark One' are solid slow blues, and all the licks are smoothly executed. Otherwise, little to remember.

*****(*) Guitar Forms**

Verve 521403-2 *Burrell; Johnny Coles, Louis Mucci (t); Jimmy Cleveland, Jimmy Knepper (tb); Andy Fitzgerald, George Marge (cor, f); Ray Alonge, Julius Watkins (frhn); Steve Lacy (ss); Ray Beckenstein (as, f); Lee Konitz (as); Richie Kamuca (ts, ob); Bob Tricarico (bsn, f); Roger Kellaway (p); Bill Barber (tba); Ron Carter, Joe Benjamin (b); Elvin Jones, Charli Persip, Grady Tate (d); Willie Rodriguez (perc).* 12/64–4/65.

This is arguably the closest Burrell has come to a signature achievement, even if it is more by association with Gil Evans, who arranged it. Burrell's sanguine approach might make him a less characterful soloist than those who've handled other of Evans's concerto set-pieces, but in some ways that works to the music's advantage. Without misleading emotional resonances of the kind associated with, say, Miles Davis cracking notes, the purity of Evans's veils of sound emerges the more clearly in the likes of 'Lotus Land'. The new Master Edition issue includes a great many extra and alternative takes which frankly are best programmed out except when one is in an especially scholarly mood.

*** Blues: The Common Ground

Verve 589101-2 *Burrell; Berbie Gow, Thad Jones, Jimmy Nottingham, Jimmy Owens, Ernie Royal, Snooky Young (t); Wayne Andre, Jimmy Cleveland, Paul Faulise, Urbie Green, Tony Studd, Bill Watrous (tb); Jerome Richardson (reeds); Herbie Hancock (p); Don Butterfield, Harvey Phillips (tba); Ron Carter (b); Donald McDonald, Grady Tate (d); Don Sebesky (arr).* 12/67–2/68.

Next to *Guitar Forms* this is slighter stuff, with Sebesky's simplistic charts framing Burrell. Very much of its time – 'The Preacher' has a late-'60s, happy-clappy feel to it, for instance – although there are a few fine moments to salvage, such as a brooding 'Angel Eyes'. Burrell, pro that he is, isn't coasting.

*** Kenny Burrell: Jazz Masters 45

Verve 527652-2 *As Guitar Forms, except add Jimmy Nottingham, Thad Jones, Ernie Royal, Marvin Stamm, Joe Shepley (t), Wayne Andre, Urbie Green, Tony Studd (tb), Jerome Richardson (woodwinds), Harvey Philips (tba), Phil Woods (as), Richard Wyands, Herbie Hancock (p), Jimmy Smith (org), Vince Gambella (g), Ron Carter (b), Mel Lewis, Donald McDonald (d), Johnny Pacheco (perc).* 64–69.

This creams off some of *Guitar Forms* along with tracks from *A Generation Ago Today, Blues: The Common Ground, For Charlie Christian And Benny Goodman, Asphalt Canyon Suite* and *Night Song*, so there's a fair amount of otherwise-unavailable Burrell here. That said, several of those discs weren't among his finest hours, and he sounds as happy here on a single track with Jimmy Smith as he does on his own-name projects. *Guitar Forms* is a better bet as a single disc, but collectors will certainly want this one too.

** God Bless The Child

CTI/Epic 505164-2 *Burrell; Freddie Hubbard (t); Hubert Laws (f); Richard Wyands (p); Ron Carter (b); Billy Cobham (d); Ray Barretto (perc); strings.* 4–11/71.

Another occasion where Burrell has to fight his way past Don Sebesky arrangements. Worse, there is the Creed Taylor CTI production, which softens every virility and makes sure that nothing dares disturb. Two unreleased solos are a compensation, but basically this is an awful relic of its time.

**(*) Stormy Monday Blues

Fantasy 24767-2 *Burrell; Jerome Richardson (ss, ts, f); Richard Wyands, Kirk Lightsey (p); John Heard, Stan Gilbert (b); Lenny McBrowne, Richie Goldberg, Eddie Marshall (d).* 6/74–12/75.

Not a vintage period for Kenny. This couples *Stormy Monday*, an agreeable if unremarkable quartet date, with *Sky Street*, a misguided attempt to bring jazz into the '70s, with soupy electric piano from Lightsey and four rambling tunes. But he was about to get back on track.

CORE COLLECTION

**** Ellington Is Forever Vol. 1

Fantasy FCD-79005-2 *Burrell; Jon Faddis, Snooky Young (t); Thad Jones (c, flhn); Jerome Richardson (ss, ts); Joe Henderson (ts); Jimmy Jones (p); Jimmy Smith (org); Jimmie Smith (d); Mel Lewis, Richie Goldberg (perc); Ernie Andrews (v).* 2/75.

Burrell's greatest album looks unpromising from a distance, after countless tribute records have become such a catch-all theme in the past 25 years. But this salute to Ellington remains one of the great examples of the genre. Cut at a couple of loose-knit sessions over two days, the cast is a shifting one, from 12 men on a hard-hitting 'Caravan' to a Burrell solo on 'Jump For Joy' and Jimmy Jones's moving soliloquy on 'Take The "A" Train'. 'C Jam Blues' sets Faddis and Thad Jones against the rhythm section, a blues medley allows a rare sighting of Snooky Young as a soloist, and Henderson is splendid on 'I Didn't Know About You'. Most affecting of all is the absolutely definitive treatment of 'My Little Brown Book' by Ernie Andrews and Jimmy Jones. Burrell may be just a bystander at times, but he presided over a magnificent session.

*** Ellington Is Forever Vol. 2

Fantasy FCD-79008-2 *As above, except add Nat Adderley (c), Quentin Jackson (tb), Gary Bartz (cl, as), Sir Roland Hanna (p), Stanley Gilbert, George Mraz, Monk Montgomery (b), Philly Joe Jones (d); omit Jimmie Smith, Lewis, Goldberg.* 11–12/75.

The return match was a disappointment, even though there are delightful moments: Smith's lovely glide through 'Solitude', and Thad Jones and Young together on 'Come Sunday'. Too many of the other pieces sound routine or merely good.

*** Stolen Moments

Concord CCD2-2128-2 2CD *Burrell; Reggie Johnson (b); John Heard (b); Carl Burnett, Roy McCurdy (d); Kenneth Nash (perc)* 3/77–12/79.

*** When Lights Are Low

Concord CCD 4083 *Burrell; Larry Gates (b); Carl Burnett (d)* 9/78.

One could complain that Burrell's unflappability and Concord's smooth, welcoming presentation tend to anaesthetize rather than stimulate, and there's little to make one sit up and take notice on these discs. But Burrell was in his prime as an improviser, and if the format doesn't encourage innovation, the solos on, say, 'Tin Tin Deo' or 'It Shouldn't Happen To A Dream' are evidence of his mettle. The trio albums are from a fine vintage and still afford much understated pleasure; the one previously called *Tin Tin Deo* has now been coupled with the slightly later *Moon And Sand* under the heading *Stolen Moments*, and the later date is a shade more disappointing in that the rhythm section seems less happy and Burrell sounds less involved.

*** Togethering

Blue Note 25651-2 *Burrell; Grover Washington Jr (ss, ts); Ron Carter, Reggie Workman (b); Jack DeJohnette, Grady Tate (d); Ralph McDonald (perc).* 4/84–2/85.

Five producers are credited, so there wasn't much danger of things getting out of hand. This was Burrell's and Washington's only studio project together (two tracks from Blue Note's celebrated Town Hall concert of 1985 are a bonus), and it's a friendly encounter. The slightly unkempt feel is provided by DeJohnette, not the sort of drummer to merely hang around and keep time; but the two principals seem to go their own sweet and untroubled way, nevertheless. The live tracks, with Workman and Tate, are 'Summertime' and 'I'm Glad There Is You', and though Washington's soprano sound isn't very ingratiating, he's more energetic than he is in the studio.

****(*) Guiding Spirit**

Contemporary CCD-14058-2 *Burrell; Jay Hoggard (vib); Marcus McLaurine (b); Yoron Israel (d).* 8/89.

Burrell continued to work through the '70s and '80s in his patient, unhurried way. So here he is in 1989, still pretty, still bebop, still no trouble, still fine. Not that great, unless one needs a late-night painkiller.

*****(*) Sunup To Sundown**

Contemporary CCD-14065-2 *Burrell; Cedar Walton (p); Rufus Reid (b); Lewis Nash (d); Ray Mantilla (perc).* 6/91.

A good one. 'Out There' hits a fine groove from the outset, and it's quickly apparent that Walton, Reid and Nash are bringing the best out of the nominal leader, whose solos find an extra pinch of energy and grit without surrendering any of his smoothest moves.

*****(*) Lotus Blossom**

Concord CCD 4668 *Burrell; Ray Drummond (b); Yoron Israel (d).* 6/95.

Lotus Blossom is a patient reminder of Burrell's beguiling excellence. As with his original Concords of almost 20 years earlier, he does little more than tackle a good set of jazz and standard tunes, assign a sensible rhythm section to follow him, and spin thoughtful lines out of them that whisper of the blues and bebop without speaking them out loud. This would be neoclassicism in other hands; with Burrell, it's the real thing.

***** The Best Of Kenny Burrell**

Blue Note 830493-2 *As Blue Note albums above, except add Grover Washington Jr (ss), Frank Foster, Hank Mobley (ts), Seldon Powell (f), Tommy Flanagan, Horace Silver, Herbie Hancock, Hank Jones (p), Bobby Broom, Rodney Jones (g), Ben Tucker, Dave Jackson, Reggie Workman, Doug Watkins, Milt Hinton, Oscar Pettiford (b), Shadow Wilson, Louis Hayes, Osie Johnson, Jack DeJohnette, Kenny Washington (d), Ray Barretto (perc).* 3/56–10/86.

Thirty years (on and off) of Burrell on Blue Note. A couple of rarities – a single release of 'Loie' and a quartet track with Hancock – plus some familiar fodder from the early days, along with tracks from the so-so *Togethering* and *Generation* albums.

***** Kenny Burrell And The Jazz Giants**

Prestige 60-028 *As OJC albums listed above.*

A solid if rather bitty compilation from Burrell's many appearances on Prestige, and the roll-call – from Coleman Hawkins to Stanley Turrentine – is the expected who's who for this nonpareil sideman.

***** Lucky So And So**

Concord CCD-4951-2 *Burrell; Onaje Allan Gumbs (ky); Rufus Reid (b); Akira Tana (d).* 9/00.

Kenny sings! Only on four tracks – and they pass painlessly enough. Most of the record is too nice to really stir any feelings, even if 'The Feeling Of Jazz' is a neatly turned way to start. The pick is probably 'Bluescope', which at least features the guitarist going at his favourite form with his familiar assurance.

Gary Burton (born 1943)

VIBRAPHONE

Unusually for a player and musician of his stature, Burton has mostly preferred to play the compositions of others, notably Carla Bley. A distinguished educator, his groups have long been a proving ground for young talent, while his four-mallet approach and distinctive approach to arrangement create an instantly recognizable sound.

***** Who Is Gary Burton?**

RCA Victor SP 2665 *Burton; Clark Terry (t); Chris Swansen (tb); Bob Brookmeyer (vtb); Phil Woods (as); Tommy Flanagan (p); John Neves, Gene Cherico (b); Joe Morello (d).* 9/62.

****(*) Three In Jazz**

RCA 52725 *Burton; Jack Sheldon (t); Monty Budwig (b); Vernell Fournier (d).* 2/63.

The rhetorical question is not yet comprehensively answered, which is rather in the nature of rhetorical questions. This impressive record affords Burton ample solo space and a chance to show off his skills as a composer, but the real action is devolved to the group. Morello and Cherico are still there from Gary's debut as leader the year before, *New Vibe Man In Town.* 'Fly Time Fly' and 'Storm' are impressive, and Gary is recorded crisply and forcefully enough, but it isn't yet the sort of record that makes you feel in the presence of anything extraordinary.

There are many more musicians than listed here on *Three In Jazz*, but Burton's quartet only features on four tracks. The remainder of the album is taken up with material by Sonny Rollins and his modernist group (Don Cherry included) and Clark Terry. Oddly, the album as a whole in no way jars, but Burton's contribution is quite limited, and the album only has a toehold in the discography.

***** Tennessee Firebird**

Bear Family 14458 *Burton; Chet Atkins, Jim Colvard, Ray Edenton (g); Buddy Emmons (steel g); Charlie McCoy (hca, b); Bobby Osborne (mandola); Sonny Osborne (bj); Norman Spicher (vn); Henry Strzelecki, Steve Swallow (b); Grady Martin (b, g); Kenneth A. Buttrey, Roy Haynes (d).* 9/66.

***** Duster**

Koch Jazz 7846 *Burton; Larry Coryell (g); Steve Swallow (b); Roy Haynes (d).* 4/67.

***** Lofty Fake Anagram**

One Way 34489 *As above, except omit Haynes; add Bob Moses (d).* 8/67.

*****(*) A Genuine Tong Funeral**

RCA Victor 07863 66748 2 *Burton; Michael Mantler (t); Jimmy Knepper (tb, btb); Howard Johnson (tba, bs); Steve Lacy (ss); Gato Barbieri (ts); Carla Bley (p, org); Larry Coryell (g); Steve Swallow (b); Lonesome Dragon, Bob Moses (d).* 67–8.

*****(*) Country Roads And Other Places**

Koch Jazz 7854 *Burton; Jerry Hahn (g); Steve Swallow (b); Roy Haynes (d).* 9/68.

Burton's early recordings were driven by an ambition to synthesize jazz, rock and country music with some elements of classical form. The early *Tennessee Firebird* is almost a country set, as the personnel must suggest, though Burton's own playing points in other directions. The mix of up-tempo tunes like 'Panhandle Rag' with gentler-paced ballads (notably 'Black Is

The Color Of My True Love's Hair') prevents the album, which is rather brief, from settling into a monotonous groove. Perhaps too Nashville for some tastes, but think what Bill Frisell was doing to great critical acclaim three decades later, and most jazz purists will swallow their disdain for a record featuring Chet Atkins and Charlie McCoy.

By contrast, *Duster* was one of the first jazz-rock records, and though it seems rather tame compared to later work by the Mahavishnu Orchestra, Return To Forever, Lifetime and, of course, Weather Report, it undoubtedly had an impact on at least some of those outfits, even if only as permission to mix rock beats and distorted guitar into a jazz performance. Mike Gibbs's 'Sweet Rain' is the outstanding track, a modern classic, but Carla Bley's 'Sing Me Softly Of The Blues' runs a close second. One of his most striking recordings, though, was a performance of Carla Bley's 'dark opera without words', *A Genuine Tong Funeral*. This was intended for full staging with costumes and lights but is really known only as a recorded piece. Bley intended no connection whatsoever with actual Chinese music, and the basic provenance of the album is that same synthesis of modern styles which Burton himself was pursuing at the time. The work has a brooding, processional quality, using suspended harmonies and minor variants to create an atmosphere of loss and, on occasion, inexplicable dread. 'Mother Of The Dead Man' is perhaps the best-known single component, largely because Mike Gibbs included it in concert programmes, but it's the centrepiece, 'Silent Spring' – originally written for Steve Swallow but now dominated by Gato Barbieri, Larry Coryell and Burton – which stands out. Burton's playing is more open and abstract than at any other point in his career. The CD reissue is augmented by a few tracks from *Lofty Fake Anagram* (which you can work out for yourselves). This 1968 disc has also long been out of circulation, and while it lacks the energy and grace of *Country Roads*, it's a valuable comeback and a tremendous showcase for Coryell.

Country Roads is still a joy after more than 30 years – plaudits to Koch for bringing it back. The playing is as fresh and unfettered as it ever seemed, and themes like 'Family Joy', 'And On The Third Day' and 'Country Roads', which may be better known from composer Mike Gibbs's versions, occupy a vivid corner in the memory of anyone who grew up with jazz at this time. The album marked the debut of guitarist Hahn, who keeps his occasional excesses well under control and plays smooth lines with a lot of rhythmic pace. Burton is in excellent form, dancing on the bars, and then suddenly changing pace to accommodate the gracious sweep of 'My Foolish Heart' and 'Wichita Breakdown'. There is even a small Ravel arrangement, handled in a way reminiscent of guitarist Larry Coryell's approach to classical themes.

**** Gary Burton And Keith Jarrett

Rhino 8122 71594 *Burton; Keith Jarrett (p, ss); Sam Brown, Jerry Hahn (g); Richard Greene (vn); Steve Swallow (b); Bill Goodwin (d).* 6/69, 7/70.

**(*) Good Vibes

Koch Jazz 8515 *Burton; Richard Tee (p); Eric Gale, Jerry Hahn (g); Chuck Rainey, Steve Swallow (b); Bill Lavorgna (d, perc).* 9/69.

***(*) Paris Encounter

Atlantic 112783 *Burton; Stéphane Grappelli (vn); Steve Swallow (b); Bill Goodwin (d).* 11/69.

Ever since the late '60s, and the band that established his name and mature style, Burton has shown a marked preference for the quartet format, and for working with guitarists. The 1967 band included Larry Coryell, Steve Swallow and Bob Moses, and it remains perhaps his most consistently inventive unit. Swallow has been a steady presence and provides a consistent but imaginative bottom line for Burton's occasionally fly-away approach. In 1969 and 1970 Burton co-led a group with Keith Jarrett and recorded the magnificent *Throb*, which is also included on the Rhino compilation and is still – for us at least – one of the most evocative records produced at the time. Mike Gibbs's title-track is a *zeitgeist* moment, a wry, innocent thing with an almost European depth of focus.

Good Vibes is an almost forgotten Atlantic release, now rescued from oblivion by the obliging Koch. There is no avoiding the impression of a musician – and a label – trying to rise to the challenge presented by rock. There is too much guitar and too much heavy backbeat, and Burton's own playing dissolves into shapelessness, even on his own material. 'Vibrafinger', 'Boston Marathon' and 'Leroy The Magician' are originals.

The 35-year age gap did nothing to dim Burton's meeting with Hot Club veteran Grappelli. *Paris Encounter* is a delicious set, opening with Django's 'Daphne' and including Mike Gibbs's 'Sweet Rain' (a dedication to Burton) and Steve Swallow's much-covered 'Eiderdown'. Grappelli seems to enjoy the pitch and pace of the vibes and the rhythm section, of which Burton himself is of course a part, laying out bright, buoyant chords even as he develops a melody line. One of the happiest records of his career.

*** The New Quartet

ECM 835002-2 *Burton; Mick Goodrick (g); Abraham Laboriel (b); Harry Blazer (d).* 3/73.

The New Quartet was a more or less self-conscious attempt to synthesize the earlier band; the newcomers are by no means faceless epigoni, and the resulting album is robustly conceived and performed, and is marked by some of the best writing Burton had to work with. There are pieces by Carla Bley, Gordon Beck and Mike Gibbs; 'Olhos De Gato' and Beck's 'Mallet Man' are masterly.

*** Ring

ECM 829191-2 *Burton; Mick Goodrick, Pat Metheny (g); Eberhard Weber (b); Bob Moses (d).* 7/74.

**(*) Dreams So Real

ECM 833329-2 *As above, except Steve Swallow replaces Weber (b).* 12/75.

*** Passengers

ECM 835016-2 *Burton; Pat Metheny (g); Steve Swallow, Eberhard Weber (b); Danny Gottlieb (d).* 11/76.

Burton's mid-'70s albums with rising star Metheny and the distinctive Weber now sound a little tarnished, but their blend of country softness and Weber's slightly eldritch melody-lines still make for interesting listening, even if the group never sounds quite as enterprising as it did live. The three ECM CDs are pretty much of a piece, but *Passengers* – actually co-credited to Weber – is probably the one to go for initially.

Burton makes a considerable virtue out of what might have become an awful clutter of strings and percussion. The themes are open and clearly stated, even when they are relatively complex as on 'The Whopper', and Weber's forceful, wailing sound is strongly contrasted to those of the two guitarists; Swallow as usual plays bass guitar with a pick, getting a clean, exact sound the coloration of which contrasts with Metheny's rock-influenced sustains. Weber's own composition 'Yellow Fields' undergoes an attractive variation.

CORE COLLECTION

**** Hotel Hello

ECM 835586-2 *Burton; Steve Swallow (b).* 5/74.

Hotel Hello is by far the most impressive of Burton's two-handers and an ideal opportunity to examine the vibist in close-up. The overture and vamp to 'Hotel Hello' are worthy of Carla Bley, and the detailed interplay between the co-leaders is often revelatory. This is one of the high points of ECM's distinguished catalogue.

*** Matchbook

ECM 835014-2 *Burton; Ralph Towner (g).* 7/74.

**(*) Duet

ECM 829941-2 *Burton; Chick Corea (p).* 10/78.

At first blush the Burton/Corea partnership looked like a marriage made in heaven, and they toured extensively. In practice, and at least on record, the collaboration fell foul of the inevitable similarity between piano and vibraphone and of the performers' out-of-synch musical personalities. The earlier *Crystal Silence* is more properly credited to Corea, since he is the chief writer. On *Duet* the pianist never seems far from whimsicality, and it is interesting to see how much more positively and forcefully Burton responds to Towner's light but well-anchored style. *Matchbook* is surprisingly disciplined and coherent for all its lacy textures and delicate, almost directionless transitions; Burton's and Towner's other collaboration *Slide Show* (ECM 1306) reversed the performers' names on the cover and so by our ruthlessly alphabetical rubric stops for T. Disappointing, though.

*** Real Life Hits

ECM 825235-2 *Burton; Makoto Ozone (p); Steve Swallow (b); Mike Hyman (d).* 1/82, 11/84.

Real Life Hits is understated and rather inward-looking, but renewed acquaintance reveals a record of unsuspected depth and dimension. As so often, the compositions are from other hands – Carla Bley, John Scofield, Ozone, Swallow, Duke Ellington – but Burton has the gift of transforming them into his own creative idiolect. The interpretation of Duke's 'Fleurette Africaine' is exquisite, and Carla's 'Syndrome' and 'Real Life Hits' give the band something to chew on. We are as guilty as anyone, but an easily underestimated record.

**(*) Whiz Kids

ECM 831110-2 *Burton; Tommy Smith (ts); Makoto Ozone (p); Steve Swallow (b); Martin Richards (d).* 6/86.

Though Ozone (who has a fine CBS album to his credit) resurfaced to great effect on *Whiz Kids*, all the buzz was about the Scottish *wunderkind* Smith, another pupil of Burton's at Berklee, and just at this time beginning to receive serious critical attention. The results (perhaps inevitably, given all the hype) are a shade disappointing. Burton has never been easy with saxophone players (see his two tracks with Michael Brecker on *Times Like These*), and the lead voices clutter and compete furiously, without any logic or drama. Ozone keeps things more or less tidy, but it is an uncomfortable set and definitely missable.

*** Departure

Concord CCD 4749 *Burton; Fred Hersch (p); John Scofield (g); John Patitucci (b); Peter Erskine (d).* 96.

Despite a line-up to die for, this set never manages to ignite and remains stalled in its own good taste and elegance. Burton's playing has reached a level where he no longer thinks instrumentally but musically, using the vibes merely as a way station. Because Hersch is more deliberate and ironic, and Scofield more pressingly emphatic, the expected revelation never quite happens, and though 'Chick's Japanese Waltz' is lovely and 'Poinciana' serves as a reminder of how good a repertory player Burton can be, neither track is able to lift the set as a whole.

*** Astor Piazzolla Reunion: A Tango Excursion

Concord CCD 4793 2 *Burton; Daniel Binelli, Marcelo Nisinman, Astor Piazzolla (bandoneon); Nicholas Ledesma, Makoto Ozone, Pablo Ziegler (p); Horacio Malvicino (g); Fernando Suarez-Paz (vn); Hector Console (b).* 97.

Gary's association with Piazzolla started in 1985 and continued in mutual admiration and respect for the remainder of the brilliant bandoneonist's life. At the end of the record, and probably best consigned to afterthought, there is a 'virtual' duet between the vibist and the late Piazzolla, recorded playing 'Mi Refugio'. It's affecting enough, but there are far more convincing performances elsewhere on the disc that steer away from necrology and pastiche. Burton's arrangements are deft and in keeping with the spirit of the original. 'Soledad' and 'Lunfarno' cover much of the emotional spectrum, dark, intense and throbbing with complex internal rhythms. Daniel Binelli and Marcelo Nisinman stand in place of the great man on a number of tracks, but for the most part Piazzolla's presence is in the music, and any hint of pastiche is avoided.

***(*) Like Minds

Concord CCD 4803 *Burton; Chick Corea (p); Pat Metheny (g); Dave Holland (b); Roy Haynes (d).* 11/98.

The degrees of propinquity are too complicated to work out, but suffice it to say that, while the paths of these five musicians have crossed many times over the years, they have never worked together in the same group. Burton is very much the lead voice, and although both Corea and Metheny, who had not (to our knowledge) worked together before, are accorded plenty of solo space, they indulge it sparingly. The choice of tunes could hardly have been happier, with Metheny getting the lion's share of credits, outstandingly on 'Tears Of Rain'. Chick's 'Windows' is a well-established modern classic and receives a wonderful interpretation from the group. Gary's own solos on 'Country Roads' and 'Like Minds' are models of structure and form. Supergroup albums are hit-and-miss, but this one can be heartily recommended. The individual elements cohere splendidly round a rhythm section to die for, and one hopes this band might some day hit the road. Unlikely, but an enticing thought.

***(*) Libertango

Concord CCD 4938 *Burton; Nicolas Ledesma, Pablo Ziegler (p); Horacio Malvicino (g); Fernando Suarez-Paz (vn); Marcelo Nisinman (bandoneon); Hector Console (b).* 1/99.

Even after Astor Piazzolla's death, Burton continued to explore the language and dynamics of tango, and this lovely record reunites him with some of the musicians who were key players in the Argentinian's group. A little like Ellington, Piazzolla wrote with specific performers in mind and 'Escualo' was intended for Suarez-Paz and 'Contrabajissimo' for Console. The presence of a vibraphonist was always going to be controversial in a tango outfit, but Burton plays down anything that is likely to jar with the basic idiom, creating a sound that is not so much blandly authentic as absolutely true to the spirit of a great world music and a great improvising tradition.

★★★(★) Virtuosi

Concord CCD 2105 *Burton; Makoto Ozone (p).* 8–10/01.

The concept is quite straightforward: a set of classical themes used as the basis for duo improvisations. No Burton compositions at all and just Ozone's 'Something Borrowed, Something Blue' from the players, but the range of material is eclectic and strong, ranging from the opening take on the ever-jazzy Ravel's not especially jazzy 'Le Tombeau De Couperin' to a medley from Delibes' *Lakme*, a couple of fragments by Gershwin and a truly astonishing interpretation of Rachmaninov's Op. 32 Prelude VIII. Ever the teacher, Burton analyses each piece in his liner-note, but there is no real need to know the original material in order to appreciate this remarkable set. It won't be to every taste, and if your taste in jazz requires an input of 'Sweet Sue' or 'All The Things You Are' you might find it a touch recherché. On the other hand the musicianship from a beautifully balanced duo is unexceptionable and hugely impressive and most will find *Virtuosi* a rewarding experience.

★★★(★) For Hamp, Red, Bags And Cal

Concord CCD 4941 *Burton; Mulgrew Miller, Makoto Ozone, Danilo Perez (p); Russell Malone (g); Christian McBride, John Patitucci (b); Lewis Nash (d); Luis Quintero (perc).* 5–6/00.

This is Gary's most explicit tribute to his great ancestors on the vibraphone: Lionel Hampton, Red Norvo, Milt Jackson and Cal Tjader. Each is represented by two or three tunes, and while no special effort is made to pastiche or mimic their style the spirit of these four great ancestors imbues the record. 'Flying Home' is maybe the best example, a breezy, swinging performance that recalls Hamp's classic years. 'Django' and 'Bags' Groove' are for Jackson, of course, and are wonderfully adept, but it is the sheer strangeness of Red Norvo's 'Dance Of The Octopus' at the end of the record that is likely to send even uncommitted listeners back to the start. Gary can rarely have been recorded so well, and the groups are bedded in round him intimately but with enough space to keep the voices individual and strong. Nice contributions from regular partner Ozone, Miller and the redoubtable McBride.

John Butcher

TENOR, SOPRANO AND BARITONE SAXOPHONES

A London-based improviser, Butcher's main instruments are soprano and tenor saxophones, although he is also interested in altering their sound via electronics or studio techniques.

★★★★ Thirteen Friendly Numbers

Unsounds 07 *Butcher (ss, ts, bs solo).* 3–12/91.

A British improviser whose playing is highly accomplished and strikingly individual, Butcher's recital is unlike any other solo-saxophone record. Nine of the 13 tracks are real-time solos on either tenor or soprano, while the other four create some unprecedented sounds and textures through overdubbing. 'Bells And Clappers', for instance, piles up four tenors into a brittle choir of humming overtones that has a chilling, sheet-metal sound, while the amplification introduced into the brief 'Mackle Music' is peculiarly disturbing. On the more conventional solo tracks, Butcher's mastery of the instrument creates a vocabulary which can accommodate pieces as disparate as 'Notelet', which is like a single flow of melody, and the explorations of single aspects of performing technique, as on 'Humours And Vapours' and 'Buccinator's Outing'. Assisted by a clear and suitably neutral recording, this is a masterful record which should be investigated by anyone interested in free playing. It's now been reissued in a new pressing on the Dutch Unsounds label.

★★★(★) Concert Moves

Random Acoustics RA 011 *Butcher; Phil Durrant (vn); John Russell (g).* 11/91–9/92.

A typical Braxton documentation would have had this as at least a three-disc set, and the group is great enough to stand it. Lyrical when you expect frenzy, light and airy when darkness seems about to fall, the trio doesn't confound expectations so much as create freshness from moment to moment. Russell almost always plays quietly, and Durrant prefers a vocabulary of small, scratchy gestures, so it's left to Butcher to use the largest range of techniques, songful high motifs, circular riffs, blatted notes, slap-tongue devices, all sorts of everything. It is as fine a set of free playing as one could encounter in recent times, with a piece such as 'Playfair's Axiom' almost a model of what-can-be-done, though it probably won't convert anyone to this aesthetic. Docked a fraction for the sound-mix – Russell is further away than even he would prefer.

★★★(★) London And Cologne

Rastascan BRD 026 *Butcher (ss, ts solo).* 10/94–4/96.

Perhaps less secure technically than some of his solo-sax peers, Butcher's soliloquizing has a palpable humanity about it. One can almost feel the grain of his playing as he essays it, and this gathering of live solos is suitably involving. He gets a vocalized sound out of the tenor which is nevertheless under quite a stringent control; there's little abandon in his playing, and the rather explosive soprano piece 'Our Man In Acton' (a place in West London) is a surprise after the different rigours of the tenor solos. If this is slightly less absorbing a disc than the earlier *Thirteen Friendly Numbers*, there's still the one studio piece, 'Shrinkdown', a quite amazing treatment for four sopranos which opens another new sound-world.

★★★ Secret Measures

Wobbly Rail WOB 006 *Butcher; Phil Durrant (elec).* 11/97.

★★★(★) The Scenic Route

Emanem 4029 *Butcher; Phil Durrant (vn); John Russell (g).* 3–5/98.

★★★(★) Music On Seven Occasions

Meniscus MNSCS 004 *Butcher; Jeb Bishop (tb); Veryan Weston (p); Thomas Lehn (syn); John Corbett (g); Terri Kapsalis (vn); Fred Lonberg-Holm (clo); Alexander Frangenheim (b); Gino Robair, Michael Zerang (perc).* 6/96–2/98.

*****(*) Light's View**
Nuscope 1004 *Butcher; Georg Graewe (p).* 4/98.

Butcher is beginning to get on record in a big way, though each of these releases will be found with varying degrees of difficulty, depending on where you are. *Secret Measures* is the least appealing for us, since it consists entirely of Butcher's playing undergoing real-time electronic treatment by Durrant, and the results are more like randomized electronic music than free improvisation. Interesting, but for rarefied tastes.

Not that *The Scenic Route* is any less hard-core, a repeat match for the trio of *Concert Moves* which finds them in the same resilient form at two concerts a week apart in London and Paris. The opening 'Heavy Merge', 20 minutes of severely attractive interplay, arguably says everything they have to on the disc, but there are a further 47 minutes of music anyway.

Music On Seven Occasions is a good way to sample Butcher's music. It gathers together 14 duets and four solos from various (mostly brief) encounters in England and America, and stretches from the melodious three minutes with Bishop to the frosty shape-making with Lehn.

Light's View is a surprise encounter with new-music polymath Graewe. With no residual jazz thinking traceable in the work of either man, the playing has a sometimes chilly rigour about it, but Butcher isn't averse to mining at least a melodic motif, and in its rather glacial way the music has plenty of purpose to it.

***** 12 Milagritos**
Spool LINE 9 *Butcher; Matthew Sperry (b); Gino Robair (perc).* 6/98.

*****(*) Intentions**
Nuscope CD 1011 *Butcher; Phil Durrant (vn); Peggy Lee (clo).* 6/00.

***** The Contest Of Pleasures**
Potlatch p201 *Butcher; Axel Dörner (t); Xavier Charles (cl).* 8/00.

Three by three. Whether it would be fair to describe Butcher as a calming influence is moot, but he does seem to pacify noisemaking in the same way that Peter Brötzmann encourages it. Each of these is concentrated and thick with detail, sometimes microtonal, sometimes with the volley of gestures between participants. *12 Milagritos* is the closest Butcher comes to some kind of frenzy, with Sperry and Robair following an almost traditional improvised tack; *The Contest Of Pleasures* is the most 'ambient', recorded in a French chapel, and more concerned with texture than most. Both are a beat behind the excellent *Intentions*, where Lee and regular partner Durrant participate in quick, agile, intense explorations that teeter towards outliving useful life but are quickly called to a halt when they do.

***** Shooters And Bowlers**
Red Toucan RT 9318 *Butcher; Gerry Hemingway (d, vib, hca, sampler).* 2–5/00.

***** Points, Snags And Windings**
Meniscus 010 *Butcher; Dylan Van der Schyff (perc).* 7/00.

Even with a drummer/percussionist at his back, Butcher only rarely considers pushing with excess force, which is why in the encounter with Hemingway the stormier moments are less impressive. The two long tracks are from an American concert, the studio pieces set down in London, and there's some nice cat-and-mouse along the way. 'Shift' is beautifully developed over 17 minutes. Hemingway's ancillary instruments are less appealing. With Van der Schyff the music feels less bitty, and it sometimes suggests an ongoing evolution which proposes the music as a complete matter, maybe even a concept album. Surely not!

*****(*) Vortices And Angels**
Emanem 4049 *Butcher; Derek Bailey (g); Rhodri Davies (hp).* 5/0.

Not a trio – it's Bailey and Butcher for the first two, Davies and Butcher for the other three. While we still miss the Parker–Bailey duets of old, this pairing – which often resounds with comic timing and playfully rude remarks – is a match made up in spirited high jinks, as well as striking notes of proper intensity when necessary. With Davies playing harp (with a few embellishments), Butcher is less involved in yin and yang, and they look for atmospherics of a kind, as well as dialogue. A very entertaining disc.

****** Fixations (14)**
Emanem 4045 *Butcher (ss, ts solo).* 6/97–9/00.

Butcher's return to a solo situation is like a summing-up of recent work, drawn from concerts and a radio recording over a three-year period. 'For improvisation to make sense, sounds must be put to work,' says John in his sleeve-note. In these gentle, fierce and unstintingly thoughtful explorations of the saxophone in its various spaces, it is a pleasure to listen to the process of making fine art.

*****(*) Apples Of Gomorrah**
Grob 429 *Butcher; Phil Minton (v).* 2–8/99.

Recorded in studio conditions and on a couple of gigs, here's Butcher in tandem with that spellbinding maverick Phil Minton. Both are partial to long tones and some of these 17 pieces are akin to taught, highly-strung drones. Others are, inevitably, entirely different. John's fondness for containment sets Phil into an almost conspiratorial, whispery mode. Bizarre and delightful.

***** Requests And Antisongs**
Erstwhile 007 *Butcher; Phil Durrant (elec, feedback).* 1–2/00.

The authors remember seeing Durrant when he was simply bowing and scraping (at the violin): here, he's on 'live electronic manipulation and modular feedback'. Phil does tend to dominate these pieces, with John emerging from electronic hailstorms and nightmares in a damaged brain. One can't complain about the 'human touch' being missing from any of this: if anything, the music's so resolutely tactile that the textures seem almost palpable to the ears. Mercurial one minute, drowning in electronic slurry the next, it's a one-off.

***** Guerrilla Mosaics**
482 Music 482-1013 *Butcher; Miya Masaoka (koto); Gino Robair (perc).* 6/00.

The textures here have a tinselly quality, the pinging of the koto almost bouncing against Butcher's rasps and slap-tongueing. Robair patters underneath. Not one of our favourites – track for track it's strong enough, but there's a thinness across CD length which discourages repeat listenings.

*****(*) Tincture**
Musica Genera MG 004 *Butcher; Fred Lonberg-Holm (clo); Michael Zerang (perc).* 3/01.

After the last few, this one's almost jazzy – Zerang plays his version of kit drums, and the peripatetic Lonberg-Holm plays bass (and cello) on his cello. It's recorded in a hot close-up, the silences having an inky blackness, all of which suits the music. Tough and argumentative.

*****(*) Invisible Ear**

Fringes, no number *Butcher (ss, ts, syn, elec solo).* 02.

Whether close-miking the soprano for what seem to be little more than a few sucking (blowing?) sounds, or building a small cathedral of multi-tracked, amplified and/or feedbacked saxes, Butcher makes fascinating sounds. Whether it's music (let alone jazz) or not is a question some may want to ask. But what extraordinary things come out of the speakers when this set goes on. RC's copy is number 368 out of 600, so if you want one, be quick!

***** Equation**

Spool/Field 3 *Butcher; Mike Hansen (record players); Tomasz Krakowiak (perc).* 5/02.

He's becoming as prolific as Evan Parker – and as interested in every kind of playing situation. Hansen clearly gives his stylus a hard time, although for much of the way he sounds as if he's turning the dial on a staticky radio. The 'Noise Temperature Suite' is long-winded; more diverse and approachable is the 'Standing Wave Suite'.

Jaki Byard (1922–99)

PIANO, TENOR SAXOPHONE, VIBRAPHONE, DRUMS

Born in Worcester, Massachusetts, Jaki started out as a brass player and continued to practise multi-instrumentalism for much of his career, though doubling on saxophone rather than trumpet or trombone. He worked with Earl Bostic, with Maynard Ferguson and, later, with Charles Mingus, a career pattern that usefully hints at his forceful, rootsy approach. Blessed with a powerful left hand and a free approach to harmony, Jaki was able to work in almost any context, from gospelly blues to the avant-garde.

****** Out Front!**

Original Jazz Classics OJCCD 1842 *Byard; Richard Williams (t); Booker Ervin (ts); Ron Carter, Bob Cranshaw, Walter Perkins (b); Roy Haynes (d).* 61.

*****(*) Blues For Smoke**

Candid CCD 79018 *Byard (p solo).* 12/60.

*****(*) Here's Jaki**

Original Jazz Classics OJCCD 1874 *Byard; Ron Carter (b); Roy Haynes (d).* 61.

*****(*) Hi-Fly**

Original Jazz Classics OJCCD 1879 *Byard; Ron Carter (b); Pete LaRoca (d).* 63.

***** Live! At Lennie's On The Turnpike**

Prestige PRCD 24121 *Byard; Joe Farrell (ts, ss, f); George Tucker (b); Alan Dawson (d, vib).* 4/65.

***** The Last From Lennie's**

Prestige PRCD 11029-2 *As above.* 4/65.

Byard's enormous power and versatility are grounded on a thorough knowledge of brass, reeds, drums and guitar, as well as piano, and there are passages in solos which suggest some attempt to replicate the phrasing of a horn rather than a keyboard instrument. On a straight comparison between two solo sets two decades apart, it seems that Byard does now play more pianistically, though the distinctive left- and right-hand articulation of themes – based on a highly personal synthesis of ragtime and stride, bop and free jazz – is still strongly evident in 1981.

The early Prestige and New Jazz sets reissued on OJC are uniformly excellent. *Out Front!* remains our favourite, largely because it shows off Byard's infallible instinct for horn voicings relative to the piano. Tracks like 'European Episode' and a melting 'Lush Life' are well worth studying in some detail. The idiom is much the same, though obviously simplified, on the trio albums, two thoroughly original selections which challenge many of the existing clichés imposed by precedent on this type of group. Byard allows melody lines to swing round the band, exploiting Carter's tremendous fingering on 'Giant Steps' (*Here's Jaki*) and 'Round Midnight' from *Hi-Fly*, which also includes the fascinating 'Excerpts' from *Yamecraw*. LaRoca is a much undervalued drummer, only recently returned to the recording studio; like Haynes, he has a delicate, pattering touch that always makes the beat sound mobile rather than fixed.

Blues For Smoke is a minor classic, with the wonderful 'Aluminium Baby', originally written for trumpeter/bandleader Herb Pomeroy, and 'Diane's Melody'. Recommended, as is the live quartet from 1965, which highlights the seriously underrated Farrell in one of his most attractive and sympathetic settings. The charts are rather sketchy and a couple of them sound like run-throughs; it's the musicianship rather than anything in the writing that makes them work. *The Last From Lennie's* pretty much mops up the useable tapes from Lennie's. There's also what sounds like a rehearsal run-down of a new tune, 'King David'. There are two takes of Byard's dolorous tribute to the recently departed Eric Dolphy, with whom he and Tucker had worked on *Outward Bound* in 1960. The tune is a hard, dissonant blues, very much in the Dolphy mould. The second take is longer and less assured, and may have been a first run-down with this band. Even Farrell sounds less than confident with it, though he's in top form on 'Dolphy #1'. The same tinge of sadness, of something suppressed or lost, is there as well in the oddly titled 'St Mark's Place Among The Sewers', a long, atmospheric piece that might be mistaken for a tone poem about Venice except that it refers to the Lower East Side street where the Five Spot club was located.

***** On The Spot!**

Original Jazz Classics OJCCD 1031 2 *Byard; Jimmy Owens (t, flhn, perc); Paul Chambers, George Tucker (b); Alan Dawson, Billy Higgins (d).* 4/65, 2/67.

The most distinctive track on this rather brief session, augmented for CD only by 'Snow Flakes', is the live version of 'Spanish Tinge', which adds Morton to Tatum and Powell amid Jaki's personal pantheon. The chemistry with trumpeter Owens, long undersung and overlooked, is riveting on most of the tracks, and the other members of the studio rhythm section, Chambers and Higgins, are in absolutely crackling form. Jaki's two forays on alto saxophone won't have scared any ghosts, but they're effective enough. Nicely remastered, and a welcome addition to the man's discography.

***** Freedom Together!**

Original Jazz Classics OJCCD 1898-2 *Byard; Richard Davis (b); Alan Dawson (d); Junior Parker (v).* 1/66.

Byard's eclectic virtuosity is strongly in evidence here. In addition to piano, he plays tenor saxophone, vibes and drums. 'Ode To Prez' is a homage to his great idol and underlines how instinctive an understanding Jaki has of pre-bebop styles. The trio with Davis and Dawson was seasoned and road-hardened, but limited by its own broad remit. A more concentrated programme might have offered a better representation of what all three are about. The closing 'Young At Heart' is a throwaway, amusing enough but out of place. Parker's feature, 'Getting To Know You', has its strengths, but again it doesn't seem entirely in keeping with the rest of the album. A qualified success, this one is an acquired taste.

***** Sunshine Of My Soul**

Original Jazz Classics OJCCD 1946 *Byard; David Izenzon (b); Elvin Jones (d).* 10/67.

A strong-voiced trio that sounds like no other group. Izenzon's unusual take on jazz bass is a key element, as is – inevitably – Elvin's patented polyrhythmic approach, but it's Byard who stars on this recently reissued set, stamping his considerable authority on 'St Louis Blues' as well as on a number of thoughtful originals. The transfers are expertly done and the record adds another important date to the Byard discography.

*****(*) The Jaki Byard Experience**

Original Jazz Classics OJCCD 1913-2 *Byard; Roland Rahsaan Kirk (sax, cl); Richard Davis (b); Alan Dawson (d).* 9/68.

***** Solo/Strings**

Prestige 24246 *Byard; George Benson (g); Ray Nance (vn); Ron Carter (clo); Richard Davis (b); Alan Dawson (d, vib).* 68, 69.

Jaki knew Roland Kirk from the Mingus band and had always found much in common with him, musically and temperamentally. However quirky the two men were, they shared a deep and insightful awareness of the music's history, and Jaki's playing here is a primer of jazz piano styles from the dawn of jazz to the bop revolution. Kirk adds distinctive clarinet, on which he sounds a generation older than his chronological or stylistic age, and Davis and Dawson add their usual intelligent contributions. Too quirky and casual to be entirely satisfactory, this is nevertheless a fascinating jazz record.

Solo/Strings brings together a couple of albums from the end of the '60s; one track from the two original LPs has been dumped for reasons of length. The 'with strings' title of the earlier set was slightly – perhaps deliberately – misleading, because Jaki hadn't convened a full orchestra, but a hand-picked quartet of string players who are unlikely to bathe the music in undifferentiated harmonies. The result is compellingly original, quite unlike anything else you've ever heard.

Jaki's solo performances are an object lesson in jazz piano history as well, everything from the Morton references of 'The Spanish Tinge' to the borders of atonal freedom. For sheer *joie de vivre*, 'The Hollis Stomp' would be hard to beat, but 'New Orleans Stomp' is the test piece for keyboard students of every stamp.

*****(*) To Them, To Us**

Soul Note 121025 *Byard (p solo).* 5/81.

***** Phantasies**

Soul Note 121075 *Byard; The Apollo Stompers: Roger Parrett, Al Bryant, John Eckert, Jim White (t); Steve Wienberg, Steve Swell, Carl Reinlib, Bob Norden (tb); Stephen Calia (btb); Bob Torrence, Manny Boyd (as); Jed Levy, Alan Givens (ts); Preston Trombly (bs); Dan Licht (g); Ralph Hamperian (b); Richard Allen (d); Denyce Byard, Diane Byard (perc, v).* 9/84.

***** Foolin' Myself**

Soul Note 121125 *Byard; Ralph Hamperian (b); Richard Allen (d).* 8/88.

*****(*) Phantasies II**

Soul Note 121175 *Byard; The Apollo Stompers: as above, but omit Eckert, Wienberg, Norden, Boyd, Givens, Trombly, Licht, Denyce Byard; replace with Graham Haynes (t); Rick Davies (tb); Susan Terry (as); Bud Revels (ts), Don Slatoff (bs); Peter Leitch (g); Vincent Lewis (v).* 8/88.

Byard is inclined to swamp sidemen with weather-changes of idiom or mood. No such problems with *Foolin' Myself*. Hamperian and Allen have grown into Byard's music and become confident interpreters. The set's full of oblique harmonies and wonderfully off-centre themes; the CD offers a big sound with a lot of warmth, typical of Giovanni Bonandrini's in-house production at Soul Note.

Working with Maynard Ferguson and then with Mingus gave Byard some insight into how to steer at high speed. Without any doubt, his excellence as a section player fed into his solo and small-group playing as well. *Phantasies* is an uncomfortable big-band excursion with vocals from Byard's Denyce and Diane (she of the melody – see above); though well produced and more than adequately executed, the album runs pastiche a little too close for comfort and lands somewhere between at least three stylistic stools. That said, it contains some great ensemble work on the Ellington material, and some of the modernist things – 'Lonely Woman', 'Impressions' – are excitingly done. A change of heart since the first edition, prompted by the emergence of *Phantasies II*, an altogether better-structured and more together exercise in nostalgia. Byard's skills as a comping pianist and bandleader are seen nowhere better than on 'Concerto Grosso', a playful look at a Baroque form within the context of a jazz band. Vincent Lewis does a convincing job as an Apollo crooner, with a rich baritone that owes something to Eckstine. Musically, though, the most interesting thing is 'II IV I', a title which refers to the cadence minor/dominant/major which dominates the piece. It takes Byard back to the great days of the Harlem stride pianists. He recorded little in the '90s and this is currently the last of his available recordings.

Don Byas (1912–72)

TENOR SAXOPHONE

Born in Muskogee, Oklahoma, Byas served his apprenticeship in a variety of big bands. Often considered to be a bridge between the swing and bebop generations, he often anticipates Charlie Parker's solo development, stringing together whole series of tiny melodic ideas into a coherent line with a challenging harmonic profile. In later life he was a fine ballad player, though his critical standing was much eclipsed by younger players.

***** Midnight At Minton's**

High Note HCD 7044 *Byas; Joe Guy (t); Thelonious Monk (p); Kenny Clarke (d); Helen Humes (v); other personnel unknown.* 41.

***** Don Byas, 1944–1945**

Classics 882 *Byas; Charlie Shavers, Joe Thomas (t); Rudy Williams (as); Johnny Guarnieri, Kenny Watts (p); Clyde Hart (p, cel); John Levy, Slam Stewart, Billy Taylor (b); Cozy Cole, Slick Jones, Jack 'The Bear' Parker (d); Big Bill Broonzy (v).* 7/44–3/45.

***** Don Byas 1945**

Classics 910 *Byas; Buck Clayton, Dizzy Gillespie (t); Gene Sedric (cl); Jimmy Powell (as); Hal Singer (ts); Johnny Guarnieri, Sammy Price (p); Leonard Ware (g); Al Hall, Eddie Safranski, Oscar Smith (b); Denzil Best, Big Sid Catlett, J. C. Heard, Harold 'Doc' West (d); Rubel Blakey, Albinia Jones (v); other personnel unknown.* 4–9/45.

***** Don Byas 1945: Volume 2**

Classics 959 *Byas; Emmett Berry, Benny Harris, Dick Vance (t); Erroll Garner, Johnny Guarnieri, Cyril Haynes, Jimmy Jones, Dave Rivera (p); Al Casey, Milt Hinton, John Levy, Eddie Safranski, Slam Stewart (b); J. C. Heard., Fred Radcliffe, Harold 'Doc' West (d).* 8/44–11/45.

A respectful pause for those figures condemned to the limbo of the 'transitional'. Don Byas dominates the strip of turf mid-way between Coleman Hawkins and Charlie Parker, combining the old man's vibrato and grouchy tone with Bird's limber solo style and fresh, open diction. Hard these days to recognize just how highly regarded Byas once was, until one actually hears him.

The earliest of these recordings was made by a young student at Columbia University, Jerry Newman, who trawled the clubs and taped hours of music for his own satisfaction. These cuts were originally released on Onyx Records in the early '70s, but no one seems able to cast light on who was playing. Monk is already pretty unmistakable on four of the tracks, including a magnificent 'Stardust' and 'Exactly Like You', but the remaining personnels are lost to history. Inevitably, the sound is less than professional, but Byas's tenor cuts through the fog and Malcolm Addey's remastering sharpens the focus considerably.

Byas left the Basie band in 1943 and became one of the unsung heroes of early bebop, matched – for sheer class and undue neglect – only by Lucky Thompson. To a degree, Byas rode his luck for (like one of those actresses said to be 'loved' by the camera) he was always hugely flattered by the microphones of the time. The early material for Savoy, documented on the earlier Classics compilation, captures a polished stylist who is already in command of a vibrant tone and a thoroughly coherent solo approach. Shavers is as abrupt and pugnacious as ever, a wonderful mismatch of temperaments that works to perfection. The July tracks are better than the later session, largely because they are simpler and concentrate on straight major-key exchanges between the two horns.

In January 1945 Byas cut four sides for Jamboree, disappointing because they seem to slip back half a generation to the jump and swing styles that were disappearing, to be replaced by bop. 'Jamboree Jump' is also known as 'Byas-A-Drink', a neat feature for saxophone and Joe Thomas's Eldridge-like trumpet. Later material for Hub is dominated by Big Bill Broonzy vocals and officially credited to Little Sam And Orchestra, which was probably a good idea, given how pedestrian this material now sounds. Later in 1945 Byas recorded for National (backing singer Albinia Jones in a session which included Dizzy Gillespie), Jamboree again (with Buck Clayton), Super Disc with the marvellous group that numbered Garner, Stewart and West, American and Hub, the last an oddly plaintive session with singer Rubel Blakey and an instrumental version of 'Poor Butterfly' with Powell and Singer. Pianist Guarnieri is a much-underrated performer and an ideal accompanist for Byas on three of these dates, matching the saxophonist's smooth transitions between keys with an effortless charm. The September 1945 encounter with Stewart and Heard, which included lovely versions of 'Laura' and 'Stardust', is vintage Byas. The second Classics volume for 1945 also includes some material recorded under the leadership of Emmett Berry and Cyril Haynes, but there is some wonderful material from Don's quartet and quintet, including the variation on 'How High The Moon' that would shortly be transformed by Benny Harris into 'Ornithology'. These are the birth pangs of bebop.

***** Don Byas, 1946**

Classics 1009 *Byas; Peanuts Holland (t, v); Tyree Glenn (tb); Hubert Rostaing (cl); Beryl Booker, Humphrey Brannon, Sanford Gold, Billy Taylor (p); Leonard Gaskin, John Simmons, Frank Skeete, Ted Sturgis (b); Buford Oliver, Fred Radcliffe, Max Roach (d).* 5–12/46.

***** Don Byas, 1947**

Classics 1073 *Byas; Peanuts Holland (t); Tyree Glenn (tb); Hubert Rostaing (as); Jacques Diéval, Gene Schroeder, Billy Taylor (p); Tony Gottuso, Jean-Jacques Tilché (g); Jean Bouchety, Slim Dunham, Lucien Simoens (b); Johnny Blowers, Armand Molinetti, Buford Oliver (d).* 45–6/47.

*****(*) Laura**

Dreyfus FDM 36714-2 *Byas; mostly as discs above.* 6/45–1/49.

In 1946, Byas joined the Don Redman Orchestra for a European tour and, though he returned during the course of the year and recorded sessions for Gotham and Savoy, he was soon to move his base and live away from America for the rest of his life. Some of the 1946 material is less than pristine, but Don's solos are always immaculately judged. The May 1946 session is merely a set of accompaniments for the saxophonist, mostly in ballad form. 'London Donnie' is a curious misreading of 'The Londonderry Air' and Don's solo is flat and unimaginative; but the rest of the set, notably 'Cherokee', points to the bebop revolution that was fomenting elsewhere. The August date is distinguished by a more balanced and responsive band who are required to do more than simply touch in backgrounds. The following month saw him recording for Gotham with Beryl Booker on piano, and then at the end of the year Don was in Paris recording under his own, Peanuts Holland's and Tyree Glenn's leadership.

The 1947 recordings were all made in Paris, and mostly for Blue Star. The key track, almost worth the price of the disc on its own, is a magnificent version of 'Laura', which marks an exception to the concentration on bebop. The groups Don was working with were for the most part competent and highly professional, but they lack the bounce of the Redman alumni who came to France with him. The latest Classics volume is rounded out with a version of 'Annie Laurie', made in New York in 1945 and previously overlooked.

The Dreyfus compilation pulls together Byas appearances from various situations, including some of his Paris dates. If you want only a single example of Byas from this period, this is attractive, and avoids some of the more routine material dotted through the Classics sequence.

***** Autumn Leaves**

Ronnie Scott's Jazz House JHAS 613 *Byas; Stan Tracey (p); Rick Laird (b); Tony Crombie (d).*

Recorded at Ronnie Scott's club with the house rhythm section (Laird subsequently gave up playing for photography) and running down a weel-kent programme of standards and jazz tunes. Byas's deceptively but harmonically exact tone is spot-on for 'Autumn Leaves' itself, a taut and wise reading of one of his favourite standbys. 'I Remember Clifford' and 'All The Things You Are' are sharper and more boppish, full of oblique references to other tunes and unpredictable harmonic shifts, many of them driven by Tracey's percussive attack and lateral imagination. Recording quality isn't of the very best, straight to a machine in the club, but it communicates a lot of presence and the quiet intensity of Byas's well-worked routine.

Charlie Byrd (1925–2000)

GUITAR

Uneventful career until he settled in Washington in the '50s, where he cemented a reputation that eventually led to the hugely successful bossa nova albums with Stan Getz. A gently effective if unremarkable stylist whose methods may have had some influence on the rise of soft, fusion-lite music.

***** Jazz Recital**

Savoy 12095 *Byrd; Tom Newsom (ts, f); Al Lucas (b); Bobby Donaldson (d).* 2/57.

Interesting to hear Byrd before the bossa nova bug bit. One suspects that Jelly Roll Morton meant something a little stronger when he talked about the 'Spanish tinge' in jazz. Certainly, 'Spanish Guitar Blues' here is almost too lightweight and studied to count as jazz at all, though Charlie does turn in lovely versions of 'My Funny Valentine' and 'Spring Is Here'. The group doesn't really balance well with his acoustic sound and one feels the session might have gone better as a series of guitar/bass duets; Lucas at least sounds as though he's listening.

***** Byrd's Word**

Original Jazz Classics OJCCD 1054 *Byrd; Bobby Felden (vtb); Buck Hill (ts); Kenneth Pasmanick (bsn); Joe Carson (p); Keter Betts (b); Bertell Knox, Eddie Phyfe (d); Ginny Byrd (v).* 58.

***** Byrd On The Wind**

Original Jazz Classics OJCCD 1086 *Similar to above; add Rev. Richard White (ob).* 59.

Byrd still sounds like a man looking for his niche. *Word* features some of his fiercest playing, not Sonny Sharrock, but certainly tougher than the gentle Latinist of later years. The best thing on an album somewhat overstocked with guest spots (notably Ginny Byrd's vocals) is a duet, 'Conversation Piece', with the redoubtable Betts, who was to be a loyal exponent of Charlie's music in these years. Also recently reissued on OJC is *Byrd On The Wind*, which teamed him up with woodwind players from the Atlanta Symphony. The results are attractive enough but one consistently hopes for more jazz guitar and less orchestral tableau work.

***** Mr Guitar**

Original Jazz Classics OJC 998 *Byrd; Keter Betts (b); Bertell Knox (d).* 59.

***** The Guitar Artistry Of Charlie Byrd**

Original Jazz Classics OJC 945 *Byrd; Keter Betts (b); Buddy Deppenschmidt (d).* 60.

***** Byrd At The Village Vanguard**

Original Jazz Classics OJC 669 *As above.* 1/61.

***** Latin Byrd**

Milestone 47005 *Byrd; Hal Posey (t); Tommy Gwaltney (vib); Gene Byrd (b, g); Keter Betts (b); Bill Reichenbach (d, perc); additional woodwind and strings.* 61–63.

***** Bossa Nova Pelos Passaros**

Original Jazz Classics OJC 107 *Byrd; Keter Betts (b); Bill Reichenbach (d).* 4/62.

****(*) Byrd At The Gate**

Original Jazz Classics OJC 262 *As above, except add Clark Terry (t), Seldon Powell (ts).* 5/63.

The release in 1962 of the evergreen *Jazz Samba* with Stan Getz, and the legal kerfuffle that followed, put Charlie Byrd firmly on the map. Like all hugely successful products, there was an element of *ersatz* about it, and Byrd's Latin stylings have never sounded entirely authentic and are often quite rheumaticky in articulation. Here, though, is a historically valuable selection of albums, the Village Vanguard set in particular full of that characteristically American syndrome that John Aldridge called 'the energy of new success' and which comes just before what the French call the *crise de quarante*. Byrd sounds full-toned and quick-fingered, and the themes still have a bloom they were to lose all too quickly in the years that followed. There's very little to choose between what is now a pretty comprehensive run of Byrd's early Riverside albums. Betts and the various drummers keep tabs on the leader, who's always musical but only rarely doing something to really make one listen beyond the pleasant drift of what's coming out of the speakers. The horns add very little to the Gate set except extra noise. The problem with Byrd was that, even at the Village Vanguard, he always sounded as if he was preparing for Carnegie Hall.

Latin Byrd shares some material and a cover picture with *Bossa Nova Pelos Passaros*, the one on which Charlie poses in front of a perch of exotic avifauna, wearing the look of a man who fears he's about to be pecked; the toucan has a particularly unpredictable mien. The music inside, which brings together *Latin Impressions* and *Charlie Byrd's Bossa Nova*, could hardly be more relaxed and laid back. Charlie fits in some solos, some quartet tracks and some more elaborate arrangements which include woodwind and string accompaniment. There's quite a bit of folk-derived material, which means that the melodic profile of the set is pretty straightforward; not too much orthodox bebop showing through here. Ed Michel and Orrin Keepnews do an uncomplicated production job on the two original albums respectively.

****(*) Brazilian Byrd**

Columbia 52923 *Byrd; woodwind, strings.* 64.

There were better Jobim sets to come, not least a useful compilation of small-group work for Concord. This is delightful in its way, but it's hard to rescue from the Easy Listening bin.

***** Solo Flight**

Original Jazz Classics OJCCD 1093 *Byrd (g solo).* 65.

We've long been convinced that – Keter Betts, Bill Reichenbach and Bertell Knox aside – Byrd hasn't always been best served by his supporting groups. This unaccompanied record somewhat confirms that. Byrd's softly struck chords, occasional dynamic surprises and sure-fingered picking mean that there is plenty of interest throughout. 'Mood Indigo' and an unexpected 'House Of The Rising Sun' are the outstanding tracks.

★★(★) Byrd Song

Original Jazz Classics OJCCD 1092 *Byrd; Keter Betts (b); Bill Reichenbach (d).* 65.

A puzzling record, billed as 'with voices', but apart from a few tacked-on yodels from an unidentified chorus who don't even trouble to get out the lyric sheet, there is nothing much to appeal to a singing fan. There are some nice moments – 'Who Will Buy?' is appropriately joyous and 'I Left My Heart In San Francisco' properly nostalgic – and a couple of more unexpected spots, like Charlie's solo excursion on 'Action Painting', which is as far from Ornette's take on abstract expressionism as can be imagined.

★★★ Tambu

Fantasy FCD 9453 *Byrd; Cal Tjader (vib); Mike Wolff (p); John Heard (b); Joe Byrd (b); Michael Stephans, Dick Berk (d, perc); Mayoto Correa (perc).* 9/73.

Like a lot of jazz records from around this time, *Tambu* is constrained not by indifferent playing but by certain giveaway tics in the sound. Wolff's electric piano and Joe Byrd's duh-duh-duh bass guitar conspire with an overlit and glaringly contrastive mix to bleach all the character out of Byrd's playing. Tjader was the co-leader on this date, and the vibes, too, are all over the place, jingling like a bead-curtain and then improbably tolling down at the bass end. It all mars some very good playing, from virtually all concerned.

★★★ Byrd By The Sea

Fantasy 24252 *Byrd; Joe Byrd (b); Bertell Knox (d).* 3/74.

The original release was very run of the mill, but the 2000 reissue has added almost as much material again, including a wholly unexpected reading of 'It Don't Mean A Thing ...' which is enough to convince anyone who's previously dismissed Charlie on the premise of that very song. Here, he swings confidently, backed by the redoubtable Knox and by Joe seemingly on an electric instrument. In addition to the rather dull cod-classical 'Fantasy In B Minor', there is a piece of genuine Vivaldi, played with precision and feeling, and a previously overlooked Jobim reading, 'Meditation'. With this to hand, it's easier to forgive the lame versions of pop tunes: 'A Salty Dog', 'Norwegian Wod', 'Killing Me Softly'.

★★★ Three Guitars

Concord 6004 *Byrd; Barney Kessel, Herb Ellis (g); Joe Byrd (b); Johnny Rae (d).* 7/74.

Promoters and A&R men have always recognized that there's an audience for guitar specials like this. Put together any three saxophonists of similar stature, and the take on the door or through the record-shop tills will be significantly smaller. Musically, it's polished and shiny and ever so polite. Kessel and Ellis play a duo, Byrd plays with his own trio, rents it out to the other pair for 'Slow Burn', and then they all get together for 'Undecided', 'Topsy' and 'Benny's Bugle'. Honours just about even.

★★(★) Blue Byrd

Concord CCD 4082 *Byrd; Joe Byrd (b, v); Wayne Phillips (d).* 8/78.

★★ Isn't It Romantic

Concord CCD 4252 *As above, except replace Phillips with Chuck Riggs (d).* 8/79.

Byrd had a dull time for much of the '70s. These discs find him less becalmed than usual and, on *Blue Byrd*, just occasionally inspired. He handles mainstream standards well, surprising now and again with a figure completely out of left field; but the trio format leaves him much too exposed for comfort, and the up-close recording almost parades his stiffness.

★(★) The Charlie Byrd Christmas Album

Concord CCD 42004 *Byrd (g solo).* 6/82.

This is fine for those who like this sort of thing, as Jean Brodie might say. Almost everyone else will hate it with a passion.

★★★ The Bossa Nova Years

Concord CCD 4468 *Byrd; Ken Peplowski (ts, cl); Dennis Irwin (b); Chuck Redd (d); Michael Spiro (perc).* 4/91.

One of the astonishing things about Byrd's career is his relentless conservatism in the choice of material. One would hardly expect an artist of his inclinations or stature to desert an established audience by adopting Jimi Hendrix songs, but one might reasonably expect him to challenge that audience a little more often than he does. *The Bossa Nova Years* contains precisely the roster of soft-centred Jobim/Gilberto themes you probably began whistling as you read the title. What makes it more galling is that they're all played superbly, in the sense that there isn't a hair out of place on any of them. Peplowski can usually be relied on for a bit more than he offers here. As a performance, this is brushed and pomaded to the point of anonymity. A shame, really.

★★★ Charlie Byrd / The Washington Guitar Quintet

Concord CCD 42014 *Byrd; Carlos Barbosa-Lima, Howard Alden, Washington Guitar Quintet: John Marlow, Jeffrey Meyerriecks, Myrna Sislen, Larry Snitzler (g); Joe Byrd (b); Chuck Redd (d).* 4/92.

What's disappointing about this brilliantly arranged and very beautiful record is how numbingly obvious the programme turns out to be: 'Nuages', 'Django', *Concierto De Aranjuez* segued with Chick Corea's 'Spain', Stanley Myers's 'Cavatina' from *The Deerhunter*, another Reinhardt tune, Jobim, Almeida. With a little more imagination this could have been a masterpiece. Instead, it all too swiftly runs aground. Only when Alden's electric guitar is introduced for three numbers before the end – Cole Porter's 'Easy To Love' and Kurt Weill's 'I'm A Stranger Here Myself' and 'Speak Low' – is there much in the way of dramatic variation. The other members of the Washington Guitar Quintet (Byrd himself makes up the five) try to invest the earlier tunes with a bit of percussive spice, but again the material draws them down.

★★★ Moments Like This

Concord CCD 4627 *Byrd; Ken Peplowski (cl); Bill Douglas (b); Chuck Redd (d, vib).* 94.

Immediately and wholly better. The blend of guitar, bass, clarinet and (mostly) vibraphone is very appealing, and Byrd exploits the possibilities to the maximum. His chording on 'Rose Of The Rio Grande' is highly distinctive, often moving outside the natural sequence, and Douglass is a willing assistant in keeping many of the pieces from becoming predictable. A fine record by a musician whose career has taken some odd turns over the years.

*****(*) Du Hot Club De Concord**
Concord CCD 4674 *Byrd; Johnny Frigo (vn); Hendrik Meurkens (hca); Frank Vignola (g); Michael Moore (b).* 6/95.

Better than it might have been, and largely because the Hot Club parallel isn't pushed too far or too long. The sound is very much more Latin, less straightforwardly swinging and melodically more varied. Byrd himself seems to enjoy this line-up and plays with great ease on 'Besame Mucho', 'Old New Orleans Blues' and 'Cottontail', to pick just three outstanding tracks. Delightful in every way.

***** Au Courant**
Concord 4479 *Byrd; Joe Byrd (b); Chuck Redd (vib).* 97.

A most unusual instrumentation, but a very effective set, dominated by Hart/Rodgers themes. It isn't in the first rank of Byrd discs, but it is more than appealing and not just to guitar aficionados. Chuck Redd's switch to vibes widens the idiom considerably. There are a few Latin inflections here and there but this doesn't feel like an out-and-out samba/bossa record, and Charlie's ability to swing standard material has rarely been heard more clearly.

***** My Inspiration: Music Of Brazil**
Concord CCD 4850-2 *Byrd; Scott Hamilton (ts); Romero Lubambo (g); Chuck Redd (vib); Nilson Matta (b) Duduka Fonseca (d); Maúcha Adnét (v).* 1/99.

As so often in the past, Charlie manages to combine a boppish vigour of line with the easy swing of Brazilian jazz. And as ever, he keeps the material fresh and unhackneyed, juxtaposing Brazilian folk melodies with show tunes (specifically 'My Inspiration') and even a Chopin arrangement. Scott Hamilton guests on half the numbers and, with Chuck Redd favouring vibes rather than kit these days, the range of harmonic options is pretty considerable. Byrd's other partners on the set are the Trio Da Paz, who work very confidently in the idiom. Vocalist Maúcha Adnét adds some attractive colours to a thoroughly enjoyable album.

***** For Louis**
Concord CCD 4879-2 *Byrd; Joe Wilder (t); Steve Wilson (ss, as); Robert Redd (p); Dennis Irwin (b); Chuck Redd (d).* 9/99.

Recorded at the end of Byrd's life, this doesn't, though, have any kind of valedictory feel about it. The tracks (except the bizarre choice of 'Petite Fleur', actually a Bechet staple) are all Armstrong associations. Wilder and Wilson drop in and out of the picture, but it remains Byrd's album, and he sounds in pretty good fettle on the improbable likes of 'Struttin' With Some Barbecue' and 'Indian Summer', even if Pops and bossa nova feel sometimes go awkwardly together.

*****(*) Concord Jazz Heritage Series**
Concord Jazz CCD 4816 *As for Concord releases above.* 80–97.

***** Plays Jobim**
Concord CCD 2135 *Byrd; Scott Hamilton (ts); Ken Peplowski (cl, ts); Henrik Meurkens (hca); Allen Farnham (p); Joe Byrd, Romero Lubambo (g); Bill Douglas, Dennis Irwin, Nilson Matta (b); Dudu Da Fonseka (d); Chuck Redd (d, vib); Michael Spiro (perc); Maucha Adnet (v).* 79–99.

The Heritage volume was issued while Charlie was still alive and so omitting material from the last few records, this is a very attractive survey of the guitarist's tenure with Concord. The emphasis is on diversity, so there is as wide a spread of styles as possible, though the emphasis falls largely on Latin material. For anyone not – or not yet – devoted to Byrd's work, this is an ideal introduction.

The Jobim set is an equally predictable compilation, majoring on the big hits like 'Desafinado', 'The Girl From Ipanema', 'Corcovado' and 'Meditation'. Picked from five of Byrd's albums for Concord, it's a set that will probably reduplicate a serious fan's existing holding, but for a newcomer who's arriving in jazz as a Tom Jobim fan, it's well worth picking up.

Donald Byrd (born 1932)

TRUMPET, FLUGELHORN

Born in Detroit, Byrd joined the Jazz Messengers early on and by the end of the '50s had already worked with a wide range of leaders and had recorded prolifically. His tenure with Blue Note continued in this vein, and he became one of the most recorded of the hard-bop trumpeters, although he subsequently became much more heavily involved in teaching. His crossover period of the early '70s yielded the hit album Blackbyrd although this amounted to selling off the bebop family silver. Later years were spent studying law and in more teaching, although he did some recording in the '80s and '90s.

**** First Flight**
Delmark 407 *Byrd; Yusef Lateef (ts); Barry Harris (p); Bernard McKinney (euph); Alvin Jackson (b); Frank Gant (d).* 8/55.

First Flight is the first album under Byrd's own name, recorded at a concert in Detroit, and while it gave a smart indication of his promise it's Lateef's more commanding solos that take the attention. Harris, perhaps the quintessential Detroit pianist, is also imposing, although he has to contend with a poor piano, and the location sound is disappointingly muddy.

*****(*) Jazz Lab / Modern Jazz Perspective**
Collectables COL-5674 *Byrd; Jimmy Cleveland, Benny Powell (tb); Gigi Gryce (as); Julius Watkins (frhn); Don Butterfield (tba); Sahib Shihab (bs); Tommy Flanagan, Wade Legge, Wynton Kelly (p); Wendell Marshall (b); Art Taylor (d); Jackie Paris (v).* 1–8/57.

The easy-going feel of these dates, which were co-credited to Byrd and Gigi Gryce as leaders, did the trumpeter's work a power of good in finding him a persuasive context. Gryce's charts – which on several tracks involve other horns, although they don't solo – create thoughtful but not overly demanding settings, and with the tempos mostly gently swinging rather than burning, Byrd's lyricism is utilized at least as much as his power steering. With Gryce also playing some deftly-turned improvisations, and decent fills from the pianists, these unassuming but decisively focused dates are exemplars of the then-new grammar of hard-bop repertory. Jackie Paris sings wordless vocals on a couple of tunes, which wasn't a great idea.

****(*) Fuego**
Blue Note 46534 *Byrd; Jackie McLean (as); Duke Pearson (p); Sam Jones (b); Lex Humphries (d).* 10/59.

***** At The Half Note Café, Vols 1 & 2**
Blue Note 95959-2 2CD *Byrd; Pepper Adams (bs); Duke Pearson (p); Laymon Jackson (b); Lex Humphries (d).* 11/60.

*** Free Form

Blue Note 84118 *Byrd; Wayne Shorter (ts); Herbie Hancock (p); Butch Warren (b); Billy Higgins (d).* 12/61.

By the time he signed a deal with Blue Note in 1958, Byrd had already made more records than any of the other up-and-coming trumpeters of the day. It was his easy-going proficiency which made him sought-after: like Freddie Hubbard, who was to the early '60s what Byrd had been to the previous five years, he could sound good under any contemporary leader without entirely dominating the situation. His solos were valuable but not disconcertingly personal, dependably elegant but not strikingly memorable. His records as a leader emerged in much the same way: refined and crisp hard bop which seems to look neither forward nor backwards. Choosing from the above selection – all of them available only as US releases at present – is more a matter of which of the accompanying musicians is most appealing, since Byrd's own performances are regularly polished, almost to the point of tedium. *Fuego* has some good McLean, but the tunes are dull. The live sessions at New York's Half Note are impeccably played and atmospherically recorded (coming through nicely in the latest RVG edition), but they tend to show the best and worst of Byrd. On the first number of volume one, 'My Girl Shirl', he peels off chorus after chorus of manicured licks, and this process gets repeated throughout. One is impressed but dissatisfied, and Humphries's less than outstanding drumming is another problem, although Adams is again splendid. The current RGV edition of this set includes some bonus material and is now generously spread across two discs. *Free Form* puts Byrd among altogether more difficult company, and there's an unflattering contrast between his prim solo on the gospel cadences of 'Pentecostal Feeling' and Shorter's bluff intensity. But he plays prettily on Herbie Hancock's 'Night Flower' (which sounds like 'I Left My Heart In San Francisco'), and the more severe leanings of the title-track suit Byrd's punctilious manner well.

** A New Perspective

Blue Note 99006 *Byrd; Hank Mobley (ts); Herbie Hancock (p); Donald Best (vib); Kenny Burrell (g); Butch Warren (b); Lex Humphries (d); choir.* 12/63.

*** Mustang

Blue Note 59963-2 *Byrd; Sonny Red (as); Jimmy Heath, Hank Mobley (ts); McCoy Tyner (p); Walter Booker (b); Freddie Waits, Joe Chambers (d).* 11/64–6/66.

*** Blackjack

Blue Note 21286-2 *Byrd; Sonny Red (as); Hank Mobley, Jimmy Heath (ts); Cedar Walton, Herbie Hancock (p); Walter Booker, Eddie Khan (b); Billy Higgins, Albert 'Tootie' Heath (d).* 5/63–1/67.

After dozens of straightforward hard-bop dates, Byrd branched out with mixed success. *A New Perspective* has remained popular and contains the seeds of Byrd's wider success in the '70s. His own playing is set against large-scale scoring and the use of a choir, and while there was talk at the time of gospel-inspired fusions, it seems clear that the music aimed for an easy-listening crevice somewhere between soul-jazz and mood music. Set against the stricter tenets of the records which came before it, it's dispensable. *Mustang* and *Blackjack* return to more familiar Blue Note blow-outs. Made up from four sessions over three years, the two discs contain a lot of engaging hard bop in the label's almost ritualized manner and if Byrd himself does no more than play graciously, there are worthy statements from each of the other horns at various points – and look at the roll-call of pianists.

*** Kofi

Blue Note 31875-2 *Byrd; William Campbell (tb); Lew Tabackin (ts, f); Frank Foster (ts); Duke Pearson (p); Ron Carter, Bob Cranshaw (b); Mickey Roker (d); Airto Moreira, Dom Um Romao (perc).* 12/69–12/70.

**(*) Electric Byrd

Blue Note 36195-2 *Byrd; Bill Campbell (tb); Jerry Dodgion (as, ss, f); Frank Foster (ts, cl); Lew Tabackin (ts, f); Pepper Adams (bs, cl); Duke Pearson (p); Wally Richardson (g); Ron Carter (b); Mickey Roker (d); Airto Moreira (perc).* 5/70.

*** Blackbyrd

Blue Note 84466 *Byrd; Alan Barnes (ts, ob, f); Kevin Toney (p); Barney Perry (g); Joe Hill (b); Keith Kilgo (d); Perk Jacobs (perc).* 74.

**(*) Street Lady

Blue Note 53923-2 *Byrd; Roger Glenn (f); Fonce Mizell (ky, t); Jerry Peters, Fred Perren (ky); Chuck Rainey (b); Harvey Mason (d); Stephanie Spruill, King Erricson (perc).* 73.

** Places And Spaces

Blue Note 54326-2 *Byrd; Raymond Brown (t); George Bohannon (tb); Tyree Glenn Jr (ts); Larry Mizell, Skip Scarborough (p); Fonce Mizell (ky, t); Craig McMullen, John Rowin (g); Chuck Rainey (b); Harvey Mason (d); Mayoto Correa, King Erricson (perc); James Carter (whistler).* 8/75.

*(*) Caricatures

Blue Note 80732 *Byrd; Fonce Mizell, Oscar Brashear (t); George Bohannon (tb); Gary Bartz, Ernie Watts (saxes); Patrice Rushen, Jerry Peters, Skip Carpenter (ky); John Rowin, David T. Walker, Bernard Taylor (g); James Jameson, Scott Edwards (b); Harvey Mason, Alphonse Mouzon (d); Stephanie Spruill, Mayuto Carrea (perc); Mildred Lane, Kay Haith, Theresa Mitchell, Vernessa Mitchell, Larry Mizell (v).* 4–5/76.

*** The Best Of Donald Byrd

Blue Note 798638-2 *Byrd; various line-ups.* 69–76.

The previously unreleased *Kofi* fares better than some of Byrd's other music from the period, cut at two sessions a year apart but with basically the same band on each occasion. Byrd's four pieces are vague stabs at a modal/African impressionism, but it's the pragmatic Tabackin and Foster who come off best. It sounds as if Byrd had been listening to Miles more than the musicologists he mentions in the self-serving comments on the sleeve, though to no terrific effect. Somehow the innate bustle of these tracks led towards the shinier, mediated soul-grooves of *Blackbyrd* – modishly arranged round a concept that struck a resonantly harmonious note at the time. It sold past the million mark and outdid all of Blue Note's previous releases. Twenty years on, it sounds much the same: simple, lightweight crossover, with Byrd masking his declining powers as an improviser with a busy group. To paraphrase Swamp Dogg, he wasn't selling out, he was buying in.

And he kept on buying. The process had actually begun rather earlier, as the several recently restored albums now demonstrate. It's interesting to speculate on the connection between these albums and the similarly inclined progress of Miles Davis at the same moment. Certainly *Electric Byrd* takes off from *In A Silent Way*, with echoplexed sounds reverberating around a basically timeless pulse; but it's simplistic stuff next to what Davis was setting down. When they get to the groove tune, 'The Dude', it seems as if Byrd is breathing a sigh of relief that he can drop the arty stuff and get on with something he feels comfortable with. *Blackbyrd* was perhaps the logical thinning-out of this sound, and suddenly Byrd found himself a hit-maker.

It was a hard act to follow. *Street Lady* has its moments, but not too many, and, by trading off top-of-the-line jazzmen for skilful funk players, Byrd was to some extent playing swings and roundabouts. There's certainly even less worth keeping on the soupy *Places And Spaces*, soaked in strings and bounced off the supple but strict rhythms of Rainey and Mason. Besides, Byrd's own tootling isn't even a match for Freddie Hubbard on his sappiest outings. *Caricatures* reduces Byrd further to hapless frontman, less and less trumpet, more singing, and – always – more synthesizers. 'Dancing In The Street' is dinkyfied Motown, and dumb. The curious might be satisfied with *The Best Of Donald Byrd*, which goes for his later phase rather than the hard-bop material.

★★ Thank You ... For F.U.M.L.

Elektra 75596 2720-2 *Byrd; Greg Phillinganes (p); Rick Littlefield, Wah Wah Watson, Paul Jackson Jr (g); Ed Watkins (b); Anthony Cox (d); Jim Gilstrap, Syreeta Wright, Maxine Anderson, Art Posey (v).* 78.

'Every day I feel like dancing to the disco beat' is a line that belongs to 1978 all right, and it would be interesting to conjecture on what Miles Davis (if he ever heard it) thought of Donald's final capitulation to commerce. Our rating may strike some as too generous, but in the end it's not a bad funk band; only the lamentable material and glutinous vocals sink the ship. 'Long sought after by collectors', says the sleeve-note.

Don Byron (born 1958)

CLARINET, BASS CLARINET, BARITONE SAXOPHONE

A passionate, articulate and politically engaged artist, Byron has also been associated with a revival of interest in jazz clarinet. At times self-defeatingly eclectic and sometimes wearing his education at the New England Conservatory a little too ostentatiously, he has nevertheless been one of the most potent catalysts to experiment in jazz.

★★★(★) Tuskegee Experiments

Elektra Nonesuch 79280 *Byron; Bill Frisell (g); Joe Berkovitz, Edsel Gomez (p); Kenny Davis, Lonnie Plaxico, Reggie Workman (b); Richie Schwarz (mar); Pheeroan akLaff, Ralph Peterson Jr (d); Sadiq (v).* 11/90, 7/91.

Don Byron's emergence was almost as great a sensation as that of his poetic namesake. The sight of a young black man in dreadlocks playing Duke Ellington tunes on clarinet of all instruments was, even in 1990, astonishing enough; to then find Byron fronting a klezmer band was a little like discovering that fellow-clarinettist Woody Allen had joined the Art Ensemble Of Chicago.

Byron's debut was a robustly eclectic showcase that in hindsight was hoist by its own teeming ambitions. Listening to it twelve years on is a slightly unsatisfactory experience. Though the title-piece, which refers to a cynical 'medical' programme in '30s Alabama in which black syphilitics were denied treatment, is undeniably powerful, dark and threatening, it sits uneasily alongside a straight reading of Robert Schumann's *Auf Einer Burg* and the romantic 'Waltz For Ellen', both solos. What Byron is doing, obviously, is showing off his range, and without doubt it's impressive. On 'Diego Rivera' (not often one finds a name-check of the great Mexican muralist on a jazz record) and 'In Memoriam: Uncle Dan' he shows what a fine bass clarinettist he is, closer to Harry Carney than to Dolphy. Ellington's 'Mainstem' cements the association.

The sound isn't altogether satisfactory, a little too bottom-heavy and one-dimensional, but again obviously aimed at foregrounding the young star. What followed was bound to be interesting ...

★★★ Plays The Music Of Mickey Katz

Elektra Nonesuch 79313 *Byron; Dave Douglas (t, v); Josh Roseman (tb, v); J. D. Parran. (cl, bcl, ss, f); Mark Feldman (vn, v).* 9/92.

The ink was scarcely dry on the reviews for *Tuskegee Experiments* before the backlash hove into view. Perhaps fortunately for his future credibility, Byron was already shapeshifting. The composer John Adams likes to alternate serious and 'trickster' pieces, and Byron seems to have set himself the same course. Even so, nothing quite prepared anyone who didn't know his interests for *The Music Of Mickey Katz*. Byron had played for some time with a klezmer band and, in interview, had been as apt to name-check Katz as George Russell, Ellington or Dolphy. Katz's *schtick* was to yiddishize popular tunes like 'Home On The Range' ('Heim Afen Range') and 'Sabre' – *seder* – 'Dance'. What Byron adds is a virtuosic intelligence that refuses to categorize music hierarchically into 'serious', 'classical', 'popular' or whatever.

★★(★) Bug Music

Nonesuch 7559 79438 *Byron; Steven Bernstein, Charles Lewis, James Zollar (t); Craig Harris (tb); Steve Wilson (as); Bob DeBellis (ts); Uri Caine (p, v); David Gilmore (g); Paul Meyers (bj); Kenny Davis (b); Pheeroan akLaff, Joey Baron, Billy Hart (d); Dean Bowman (v).* 5/96.

As the '90s advanced, Byron quickly established himself as a valuable specialist sideman, much as Marty Ehrlich and Bill Frisell had done. The difference was that the clarinettist's own career seemed stalled in self-consciousness, the intelligence of his aims and ideas never quite borne out by the resulting records.

The premise of *Bug Music* is unimpeachable, the practice not quite so hot. The title comes from an episode of the Flintstones in which the citizenry of Bedrock are assailed by the Stone Age equivalent of the Beatles (Bug Music, Beatles, get it?). Byron sees the cartoon as a small parable of the way music is categorized and marginalized. Having a direct line to the Creator is a handy critical device. 'It matters very little to God', Byron asserts, 'whether or not a piece of music is Jazz, only that it is a compositional act. This is the only universal truth in music and the entirety of musical art.'

God smiles, then, even on such overlooked or kitsch figures as John Kirby, whose chamber jazz is now somewhat overlooked, and Raymond Scott, who enjoys a certain ironic 'downtown' cachet, despite the obvious fact that both are deeply influenced by Duke Ellington's early work. All three are celebrated on the album, 16 tracks which range from jazz repertoire like 'St Louis Blues', 'Royal Garden Blues' and the Ellingtonian 'Cotton Club Stomp', for which Harry Carney and

Johnny Hodges claim a co-credit, to exotica like Scott's 'War Dance For Wooden Indians' and 'Tobacco Auctioneer'.

'Compositional acts' may be one thing; musical performance is another. We're sufficiently at peace with God ourselves to be able to say that Byron's raw and lumpy attempt to recapture the smooth grace of Kirby's underrated band or the sheer physicality of the Ellington orchestra is *not* currently featuring on the heavenly jukebox, or indeed on the Almighty's personal stereo. Like the Katz project, the album is interesting as an idea and makes for an interesting diversion. It certainly does not stand up at this length. We've found that only the promotional edits of the klezmer record have ever made their way back into the machine. That may be the fate of *Bug Music*, too, and if that simply proves Byron's pessimistic point, so much the worse.

***** Romance With The Unseen**

Blue Note 4 99545 2 *Byron; Bill Frisell (g); Drew Gress (b); Jack DeJohnette (d).* 1–3/99.

Difficult to hear this as anything other than a reflexive reaction to the aggressive category-busting of *Nu Blaxploitation*, which has slipped out of print since our last edition. Byron is the weakest link in the chain. His slightly sharp, very linear clarinet-playing (and he sticks with clarinet throughout) rarely catches the attention in the way that his colleagues almost routinely do. Frisell's subtle comping and solo statements are as arresting as ever; DeJohnette creates a swirly but unflagging pulse and even Gress, not previously thought of as a virtuosic soloist, has some fine moments. The opening meditation on Duke's 'Mural From Two Perspectives' is significant, because it catches Byron out so comprehensively; a lame fragmentary solo, studded with tags from bebop themes and even 'Coming Through The Rye'.

The more impressionistic themes, like Byron's own 'Sad Twilight' and 'Basquiat' (a tribute to the talented, self-destructive artist who grew up in Warhol's shadow), are more effective but still sound like special pleading. 'Bernhard Goetz, James Ramseur And Me' has the usual touch of the soapbox; but then, with typical perversity, Byron throws in a reading of the Beatles' 'Here Comes The Sun' which catches the breath and lifts the heart.

The album ends with 'Closer To Home', another touch of beauty, though here again it's hard to judge how much of the credit goes to Bill Frisell. The talent is undoubted, the commitment unquestionable, but it is difficult to foretell in which direction Byron will go in future.

***** A Fine Line: Arias And Lieder**

Blue Note 26801 *Byron; Uri Caine (p); Jerome Harris (g); Paulo Braga (perc, d); Dean Bowman, Mark Ledford, Cassandra Wilson, Patricia O'Callaghan (v).* 00.

The premise here smacks a little of 'jazz is black classical music' or 'if Shakespeare were alive today he'd be writing for *Coronation Street*'. A category error is a category error, though not always a fundamental obstacle to creativity. In keeping with his genre-vaulting instincts, Byron advances the idea that 'Nessun Dorma' and the Four Tops' 'Reach Out (I'll Be There)' are divided only by chronological distance. The new *lieder* writers are Henry Mancini, Stephen Sondheim, Roy Orbison and Stevie Wonder, who are asked to take their place alongside Robert Schumann and Frédéric Chopin. Offering a little frisson to 'The Ladies Who Lunch' (the Sondheim song is one of the outstanding tracks) is a slightly bewildered Ornette, whose 'Check Up' kicks off the set.

As before, Byron does some of his classical schtick solo, playing an unaccompanied version of the Chopin 'Largetto' to close out the album. Elsewhere, he duets with the similarly minded Caine. The vocal contributions are unusual to say the least. Mark Ledford makes the Coleman song sound very airy-fairy indeed, but opts to do the Big O's 'It's Over' very much in the manner of the original. Patricia O'Callaghan brings a hectic energy to Bernstein's 'Glitter And Be Gay'; Cassandra Wilson makes Sondheim funkier than he usually sounds; and the vocalists team up for a wonderful interpretation of 'Soldier In The Rain'. A bold and occasionally illuminating experiment, though Don's own 'Basquiat' is tellingly the most effective single track. More in that vein might have been advisable, and a bit more weight on the clarinet, please.

*****(*) You Are #6**

Blue Note 32231 *Byron; Ralph Alessi (t); James Zollar (t, flhn); Curtis Fowlkes, Josh Roseman (tb); BobDeBellis (as, ts, f, af); J. D. Parran (f, af); Edsel Gomez (p); Hector Martignon (ky); David Gilmore (g); Don Byron Sr (b); Ben Wittman (d, perc); Leo Traversa (b, v); Milton Cardona (perc, v); Johnny Almendra (perc); Designer, Julie Patton, Gwen Snyder (v); DJ Spooky (remix).*

Subtitled 'More Music For Six Musicians', this is a welcome follow-up to the now-deleted album on which Byron began to define his cross-disciplinary approach as a composer. Significantly, the clarinet is again well to the front, pungent on 'Klang', wispier and more wistful elsewhere. A heavy admixture of guest percussion and the rolling swing of Edsel Gomez's accompaniment give the album a strong Latin feel which is slightly unexpected. 'You Are #6' (is this a reference to cult TV series *The Prisoner*?) is reprised as '#6.5' and there is a DJ Spooky remix of 'Belmondo's Lip', the latter, like 'Klang', derived from a soundtrack project. Apart from these, the writing is much more straightahead than usual. Old man Byron takes a turn on 'Shake 'Em Up', a theme that would go down well at a Havana or Tijuana wedding. Vocalist Designer does a little turn to introduce the players; we are a long way from the engaged fury of *Tuskegee Experiments*, but there is no mistaking the common source and Byron's eventual break-out on the next track is as dark as anything he has recorded. As a foil, 'No Whine' is as delicate as filigree, with just piano accompaniment.The clarinettist's grasp of musical order is formidable, and this is his most sheerly entertaining record to date.

George Cables (born 1944)

PIANO

Gained small-group experience with Art Blakey and Max Roach in the '60s, then backed horn-players, notably Freddie Hubbard and Art Pepper. Something of a journeyman, but his stature has been enhanced by the fine solo and trio albums of the '80s and '90s.

***** Circles**

Contemporary C 14105 *Cables; Joe Farrell (f); Ernie Watts (ts); Tony Dumas, Rufus Reid (b); Peter Erskine, Eddie Gladden (d).* 3/79.

***** Cables Vision**

Original Jazz Classics OJCCD 725 *Cables; Freddie Hubbard (t, flhn); Ernie Watts (ts, ss); Bobby Hutcherson (vib); Tony Dumas (b); Peter Erskine (d); Vince Charles (perc).* 12/79.

Cables is a great accompanist, an essentially modest man who has never been an aggressive soloist but who prefers always, always to service the song. He's still probably best known for his duo performances with the late Art Pepper on the marvellous Galaxy, *Goin' Home*. Cables has a slightly sharp touch that adds an unexpected measure of tension. He plays an electric instrument with great taste and economy throughout *Cables Vision* with the exception of a single acoustic duo with Bobby Hutcherson called 'The Stroll', a wonderful, conversational performance which sounds exactly like a companionable wander by old friends.

Circles is very fine, a richly textured and often very sophisticated set to which Farrell's rapid light-winged flute and Watts's mature, unemphatic tenor contribute strongly. These are somewhat different from later sets in that Cables is not the only – or even the main – focus of attention, but a member of an ensemble or, rather, two very good ensembles. Only later did he emerge as a clearly defined piano stylist.

****** Phantom Of The City**

Contemporary C 14014 *Cables; John Heard (b); Tony Williams (d).* 5/85.

A beautifully balanced piano-trio record, and one of the very best recorded appearances by Tony Williams in the '80s. It's the drummer who gives the set much of its character, and on the Cables composition, 'Dark Side, Light Side', a tune that would reappear in years to come, he brings a jaw-dropping musical intelligence, playing the melody as if working on a tuned instrument. Heard benefited hugely from the transfer to CD some years back; he never lets the pace drop, even nudging at Williams on occasion when the drummer seems content to let the tempo ease in the middle choruses.

Cables is completely in command, opposing long, rippling melody-lines with a firm chordal pattern and working a whole spectrum of harmonic variations on the basic shape of the tune. His touch is still lighter than one would expect from a self-confident front-man, but it is hugely attractive and this is an unmissable record.

*****(*) By George**

Original Jazz Classics OJC 1056 *Cables; John Heard (b); Ralph Penland (d).* 2/87.

*****(*) Cables Fables**

Steeplechase SCCD 31287 *Cables; Peter Washington (b); Kenny Washington (d).* 3/91.

The 1987 Gershwin set – a tribute from one George to another – is richly sophisticated, and the solo performances of 'Embraceable You' and 'Someone To Watch Over Me' are excellent examples of his innate rhythmic sense. The new OJC edition has a bonus track in 'Summertime'. *Cables Fables* is a tribute to the intuitive understanding that exists between the (unrelated) Washingtons, but retrospect suggests that this is a less confident set than those on either side of it.

*****(*) Beyond Forever**

Steeplechase SCCD 31305 *Cables; Joe Locke (vib); Santi Debriano (b); Victor Lewis (d).* 12/91.

This was the first time on record that Cables had tried this kind of instrumentation since the gig with Hutcherson in 1979. The absence of horns is the key difference, allowing the two keyboard/percussion instruments to interact and interweave in long, winding, horn-like passages. 'I Fall In Love Too Easily' is moving and intense, and 'Little B's Poem', written by Hutcherson and featuring Locke, obviously enough, is flawlessly executed, packed with those ladder scales the older vibist bequeathed to his successors.

***** I Mean You**

Steeplechase SCCD 31334 *Cables; Jay Anderson (b); Adam Nussbaum (d).* 4/93.

Not the best of the more recent crop, either under-rehearsed or else lacking the instinctive communication that a trio of this type needs. The title-tune, by Monk, is very flat indeed, played literally and without much spin, and, while the rest sounds accurate and often very tuneful, the disc fatally lacks character.

*****(*) Quiet Fire**

Steeplechase SCCD 31357 *Cables; Ron McClure (b); Billy Hart (d).* 4/94.

'Quiet fire' would do very nicely as a characterization of Cables's qualities as a player. This is a fine record, building on an inventive roster of tunes: John Hicks's 'Naima's Love Song' and Freddie Hubbard's seldom-covered 'The Decrepit Fox'. These come at the end of a session which hasn't lacked either pace or expressive variety from the off. McClure and Hart both know the set-up well and respond with performances that are as focused as they are relaxed.

****** Person To Person**

Steeplechase SCCD 31369 *Cables (p solo).* 4/95.

A seemingly unimaginative programme of material – starts with 'My Funny Valentine', ends with 'Body And Soul' – but an immaculate solo performance that has melody at a premium and never for a moment drifts off into chordal side-roads. The only weak link is the original 'Sweet Rita Suite', a very slight idea that significantly outstays its welcome. The piano sounds great and George is in expansive but disciplined form. 'I Remember Clifford' is the outstanding track.

***** Skylark**

Steeplechase SCCD 31381 *Cables; Jay Anderson (b); Albert 'Tootie' Heath (d).* 4/95.

*****(*) Dark Side, Light Side**

Steeplechase SCCD 31405 *Cables; Jay Anderson (b); Billy Hart (d).* 10/96.

Skylark seems to have been an attempt to find a new, Latin-influenced groove. It's an appealing enough record, but it lacks the sheer grace of the 1996 trio, offering bravado rather than imagination. With Hart at the helm, Cables obviously feels he can do anything, and his playing on 'In A Sentimental Mood' is stretched out to ten minutes, and on the closing tribute to George Adams, Don Pullen's 'Ah George, We Hardly Knew You', is as close to piano heaven as you're entitled to expect. The later session opens on a version of Herbie Hancock's 'Dolphin Dance' that should be transcribed and passed on to all young piano players. The original 'Dark Side, Light Side' is exquisitely idiomatic, and thereafter the mix of Herbie, Monk and Duke (with Pullen to come) suggests how carefully Cables is looking back into the jazz piano tradition. A remarkable, endlessly attractive record.

***** One For My Baby**

Steeplechase SCCD 31487 *Cables; Jim Anderson (b); Yoron Israel (d).* 4/00.

One or two expectations confounded as ever by the imaginative Cables – 'My Foolish Heart', for instance, is taken at a rare old clip, and the choosing of Billy Taylor's 'Capricious', which seems to have flown in via St Thomas, was very smart. That said, the set could use one or two really big performances, and much of it seems to amble by without insisting on the listener – when piano-trio dates are so ubiquitous, that won't quite do.

***** Alone Together**

Groove Jazz 110 *Cables; Carlos Barretto (b); Philippe Soirat (d).* 00.

Yet again, George pulls it out of the hat. Working with a virtually unknown rhythm section, he turns in a trio performance that is professional, often genuinely affecting and full of surprise. His reading of the title-piece – now a groaning war-horse – is inventive and harmonically restless and he even manages to get his colleagues to find new things in 'Phantom Of The City', presumably not a tune they are used to playing every night. The other show-stopper is 'Body And Soul', a delicately nuanced performance that makes reference to some of the iconic solos on that piece, but which also restores the shape of the song somewhat.

***** Shared Secrets**

Muse FX 1001 *Cables; Gary Bartz (as); Bennie Maupin (bcl); Alphonso Johnson, Abraham Laboriel (b); Vinny Colaiuta, Peter Erskine (d).* n.d.

This opens strongly with '5 Will Get Ya 10' and 'Blackfoot', just two of nine originals on this interestingly constructed CD, which features two different trios and effective guest spots from Bartz and Maupin. Over the years, George has continued to favour electric keyboards and he is as convincing as ever with what can only be described as a very personal touch on the amplified instrument. 'Phantom Of The City' gets its umpteenth airing, but with each one reveals itself to be a strong and supple tune, with plenty of room for speculative improvisation. For sheer consistency and durability, George Cables takes some beating on the current scene. At 60, he may have his best years ahead of him.

Michael Cain (born 1966)

PIANO

Contemporary American pianist, prominent as a Jack DeJohnette sideman and with these solos to his credit.

****(*) Strange Omen**

Candid CCD 79505 *Cain; Bruce Saunders (g); Glen Velez (perc).* 11/90.

***** What Means This?**

Candid CCD 79529 *Cain; Anthony Cox (b); Marvin 'Smitty' Smith (d); Paul Hannah (perc).* 3/91.

****** Circa**

ECM 537047-2 *Cain; Ralph Alessi (t, flhn); Peter Epstein (ss, ts).* 8/96.

*****(*) Phfew**

M.A. Recordings 30 *As above.* 00.

If we had opened a stud book in 1990, it would have suggested that Mike Cain be picked up by ECM. From the very start, he sounded like a latter-day version of Chick Corea, not a copyist, but someone who was developing a concept very like Chick's thoughtful swing-as-philosophy/philosophy-as-swing. The album with Saunders and Velez is interesting enough, though it's the guitarist who provides the two most interesting pieces. Cain's 'Piano Sketch' sequence is quintessentially Corean.

The 1991 set with Cox and Smith was obviously an attempt to create a more mainstream jazz sound. The problem is that – again – Cain is upstaged by his playing partners. The piano often seems to be addding an accompaniment to what is going on with the bass and drums. It's still all very imprecise and indefinite, though; why invite trouble by calling a piece 'Meander'?

Circa came as a hugely refreshing change. Cain conceives of the piece as a rite of passage, inspired by the landscapes of Nevada and the curious cultural environment of Las Vegas, where he spent part of his childhood. One almost thinks of the Desert d'Or Norman Mailer conjures up in *The Deer Park*, a place compounded of showbiz huckstering and an almost apocalyptic beauty. Cain's own writing is superb, with 'Red Rock Rain', 'And Their White Tigers' and 'Top O' The Dunes', which come in the latter part of a notably coherent set, standing out. The instrumentation is as effective as it is unusual. Lacking a rhythm player and someone to anchor the chords means that the pianist has to work very differently. Cain almost plays as if he is accompanying singers, shadowing a line, shading in its contours, ironizing and reinforcing by turns. Superb.

ECM seem not to have taken up an option on a second album, which is a shame. Inevitably, the second trio record is less expertly engineered and something of the rich texture of *Circa* is lost on *Phfew*. There are, though, some wonderful things here. In a set which includes longer and shorter pieces, it is the developed themes which work best. 'Strange Omen' is terrific and Cain himself is particularly good; 'Egg' and the curiously titled 'Can't Stir Shoes With Spoons' are equally impressive in their way. At this stage, Cain probably needs the patronage of a major label more than ever.

Uri Caine (born 1956)

PIANO

In straight jazz terms, he has more in common with Herbie Hancock than with anyone else, but Caine's musical interests lie much further afield than that, and much of his surviving body of recorded work – the early JMT albums are no longer available – consists of bold reworkings of classical material.

*****(*) Urlicht / Primal Light**

Winter & Winter 910 004 *Caine; Dave Douglas (t); Josh Roseman (tb); Dave Binney (ss); Don Byron (cl); Danny Blume (g, elec); Mark Feldman (vn); Larry Gold (clo); Michael Formanek (b); Joey Baron (d); DJ Olive (turntables); Aaron Bensoussan (v, perc); Dean Bowman, Arto Lindsay (v).* 6/96.

***** Wagner In Venezia / Wagner In Venice**

Winter & Winter 910 013 *Caine; Mark Feldman (vn); Erik Friedlander (clo); Drew Gress (b); Dominic Cortese (acc).* 96.

★★★★ Gustav Mahler In Toblach: I Went Out This Morning Over The Countryside

Winter & Winter 910 046 2 *Caine; Ralph Alessi (t); David Binney (as); Mark Feldman (vn); Aaron Bensoussan (oud, v); Michael Formanek (b); Jim Black (d); DJ Olive (elec, turntables).* 7/98.

Chosen to kick off Winter & Winter's 'New Edition' imprint, *Urlicht* is an extraordinary feat of imaginative projection, and it almost succeeds. The basic concept for the label is clearly modelled on ECM's swing towards new music, though perhaps Stefan Winter is more interested in fusion and crossover experimentation than is Manfred Eicher. The notion that Mahler's music, for much of the last two decades (and certainly before the popular advent of Górecki, Pärt, *et al.*) the only classical composer to appeal to a rock generation, might be adaptable to a jazz aesthetic, is a pretty startling one. For the most part, the studio album works very well. Caine takes themes from the first and second symphonies (including the 'primal light' theme from the *Resurrection Symphony*), as well as songs from *Kindertotenlieder* and *Des Knaben Wunderhorn*, and turns them into open-ended, loose-woven melodic shapes that invite not so much harmonic improvisation as retexturing. This is what Caine does best; it is also the limiting factor on both these records: after a couple of hearings, there is surprisingly little left to chew on.

The live recording of the same material is a revelation, however, and we are irresistibly reminded of how much more successful Mike Westbrook's live recording of his Rossini makeover was than the studio version. From the tightly reined-in piano introduction to the funeral march from the Fifth Symphony, with its wry Beethoven reference and high harmonics from Feldman and the DJ, to the sweeping romanticism of 'The Farewell' from *Das Lied*, the audience is taken along on a journey that has little to do with musicological orthodoxy, but everything to do with thoughtful deconstruction. Caine intuits how much of Mahler's music comes from folk sources and he hands over these famously sonorous themes to a wailing village band. The strange swoops of live electronics are a convincingly alien presence, hinting at birdcalls, spirit-possession, or merely creaking wheels and axles. We are not so very far from Joe Zawinul's 'His Last Journey'.

The two selections from *Kindertotenlieder* are exquisitely done. '*Oft Denk' Ich, Sie Sind Nur Ausgegangen*' is recast as a mournful duet for violin and trumpet, ever more distant and desolated; taped calls of children also recall Zawinul, whose kids patter and call briefly in the background on Weather Report's *Mysterious Traveller*. There are fresh interpretations of 'Urlicht', the Adagietto from the Fifth Symphony and songs from *Des Knaben Wunderhorn* and *Lieder Eines Fahrenden Gesellen*. A remarkable conception, now matched by a completely satisfying performance.

We are not fans of the Wagner project (which was recorded live in the Piazza San Marco), not so much because of any ideological scruples, but because these immensely sophisticated themes, with their indistinct architecture, really do not lend themselves to this sort of manipulation. Ironically, a harder-edged approach, with guitars and electronics very much to the fore, might have worked better.

There are, of course, things to admire but they are episodic, and Caine has not managed to carry over his intuitive understanding of Mahler's small- and large-scale structures into this superficially similar project. There are also some concerns about the recording itself, which is very hard and dry for a live taping.

★★★ The Sidewalks Of New York / Tin Pan Alley

Winter & Winter 910 038 2 *Caine; Ralph Alessi, Dave Douglas (t); Josh Roseman (tb); Bob Stewart (tba); Don Byron (cl); Bob DeBellis (f); Dominic Cortese (acc, v); Eddy Davis (bj); Mark Feldman (vn); James Genus (b); Ben Perowsky (d); Nancy Anderson, Sadiq Bey, Fay Galperin, Saul Galperin, Susan Haefner, Philip Hernandez, Brian D'Arcy Jones, Renae Morway-Baker, Nancy Opel, Stuart Zagnit (v).* 2/99.

A dramatic shift of tone. *Sidewalks* is a bold attempt to create a montage of songs and tunes that evoke turn-of-the-century New York. Songs like 'Has Anyone Here Seen Kelly' (sung with character by Nancy Opel) sit alongside George Cohan's 'Life's A Very Funny Proposition After All' (recited with grim definition by Stuart Zagnit) and a raft of material from Berlin, Joplin, Edward Bert Madden, Ben Shields, Shelton Brooks and others. The best clue to the inspiration for this is the presence of Don Byron in the ensemble and a set of parody lyrics – '*Ver Shlepste Mir Tsu Dem Ball Game*' – to Jack Northworth and Albert von Tilzer's classic. We're very close to Byron's tribute to the klezmer of Mickey Katz, except that Caine is concerned more with atmosphere and very much less with bringing his chosen material up to date. The most personal clue is the dedication to his late grandfather, who presumably grew up in these streets. It's exquisitely done, often very touching.

★★★(★) Blue Wail

Winter & Winter 910 034 2 *Caine; James Genus (b); Ralph Peterson Jr (d).* 2/98.

Bookended by unexpected, jaggy interpretations of 'Honeysuckle Rose', Caine's return to jazz has more continuities with previous projects than might appear. His own writing is very much in an American song tradition, which in turn drew heavily on European classicism. 'Bones Don't Cry' and the title-track are closest to the feel of the blues, but in 'Digature Of The Line' and 'The Face Of Space', Uri explores tonalities which don't normally play much part in jazz. The trio opens out on 'Blue Wail' and 'Sweet Potato', giving room to Genus and the increasingly impressive Peterson to express themselves, but most of the tracks are terse, tightly structured and sound almost fully written out. Winter & Winter are juggling jazz with other styles and genres, so far successfully. Caine may yet prove to be the label's signature artist.

★★★ Love Fugue

Winter & Winter 910 049 2 *Caine; La Gaia Scienza; Mark Ledford, Julie Patton (v).* 99.

Clarinettist Don Byron had already shown what might be done with Robert Schumann's music in a 'jazz' context, but Caine here takes the idea much further in the company of Italian group La Gaia Scienza, poet Julie Patton and vocalist Mark Ledford. The results are imaginative, attractive and in some regards enigmatic, since it is never quite clear what idiom we are dealing with. The W&W aesthetic is now almost as eclectically assured as ECM's at a similar stage, though it is clear that the brothers have moved further from jazz than even Manfred Eicher has ever dared.

★★★(★) Solitaire

Winter & Winter 910 075 2 *Caine (p solo).* 11/00.

This is the purest and most straightforward representation of Caine's keyboard work for some time. Uri plays like a latter-day Bill Evans who has been touched by some skittish technological sprite. Even on acoustic piano one somehow expects him to conjure up exotic FX. In point of fact, the piano-playing is enough in itself, especially when applied to these mostly original themes. Sammy Cahn's 'All The Way' and Lennon/McCartney's 'Blackbird' are the two 'standards' in the roster.

*** **The Goldberg Variations**
Winter & Winter 910054 *Caine; Ralph Alessi (t); Josh Roseman (tb); Bob Stewart (tba); Don Byron (cl); Greg Osby (as); Jorg Reiter (acc); Ernst Reijseger (clo); Reid Anderson, James Genus, Drew Gress, Reggie Washington (b); Ralph Peterson Jr (d); Milton Cardona (perc); Dean Bowman, David Moss (v); other instrumentalist and chorus.* 10/99–1/00.

*** **The Diabelli Variations**
Winter & Winter 910 086 2 *Caine; Concerto Köln.* 2/02.

It's routinely if jokingly claimed that either J. S. Bach or Ludwig van Beethoven invented jazz. There is certainly plenty of scope for improvisation in *The Goldberg Variations* (previously, of course, recorded quite straight by Keith Jarrett and mined for material by Jacques Loussier and others) and Beethoven frequently yields up bluesy nuggets in the piano pieces.

Caine has a difficult task here, making these sessions sound intelligent and respectful but still imaginatively different. He succeeds better with the Bach than with the Beethoven, which is pretty bland, leaving aside the odd Laurel and Hardy moment. The sweep of the Goldbergs is much more engaging and the musicians Caine has chosen to work with are more conducive to inventiveness than the rather mannered and sober approach of Concerto Köln. One feels that he has now been saddled with a reputation for this kind of thing. What can possibly follow? A Shostakovich record? *The Art of the Fugue*? Opera?

Cab Calloway (1907–94)

VOCAL

One of the most extravagant jazz entertainers, Calloway began playing drums in Chicago but switched to singing and being front-man when he took over The Missourians in 1931. A regular gig at the Cotton Club brought them to prominence and they were among the leading American bands during the rest of the '30s and early '40s. Disbanding in 1948, Calloway worked with a small group but thereafter focused largely on theatre work and general showbiz appearances. He was still performing and appearing when in his late 80s.

*** **Cab Calloway 1930–1931**
Classics 516 *Calloway; R. Q. Dickerson, Lamar Wright, Ruben Reeves, Wendell Culley (t); De Priest Wheeler (tb); Thornton Blue, Arville Harris (cl, as); Andrew Brown (bcl, ts); Walter Thomas (as, ts, bs, f); Earres Prince, Benny Payne (p); Morris White (bj); Jimmy Smith (bb, b); Leroy Maxey (d).* 7/30–6/31.

***(*) **Cab Calloway 1931–1932**
Classics 526 *As above, except add Edwin Swayzee, Doc Cheatham (t), Harry White (tb), Eddie Barefield (cl, as, bs), Al Morgan (b); omit Dickerson, Culley, Prince and Blue.* 7/31–6/32.

***(*) **Cab Calloway 1932**
Classics 537 *As above, except add Roy Smeck (g), Chick Bullock (v); omit Reeves and Smith.* 6/32–12/32.

*** **Cab Calloway 1932–1934**
Classics 544 *As above, except omit Smeck and Bullock.* 12/32–9/34.

***(*) **The Early Years 1930–1934**
JSP CD 908 4CD *As above four discs.* 7/30–9/34.

The rough, almost violent playing of The Missourians, a black dance band recording in New York but drawing most of its talent from the Mid-West, was as impassioned as that of any band of the day. Their dozen records are currently unrepresented on CD, but they were then taken over by a flamboyant vocalist and leader, Cab Calloway. At his very first session – in July 1930, with an astonishingly virtuosic vocal on 'St Louis Blues' – he served notice that a major jazz singer was ready to challenge Armstrong with an entirely different style.

It didn't take long for Calloway to sharpen up the band, even though he did it with comparatively few changes in personnel. Unlike the already-tested format of a vocal feature within an instrumental record, Calloway's arrangers varied detail from record to record, Cab appearing throughout some discs, briefly on others, and usually finding space for a fine team of soloists. Some of the discs are eventful to an extraordinary extent: listen, for instance, to the 1935 'I Ain't Got Nobody' or the dazzling 1930 'Some Of These Days' to hear how enthusiastically the band tackled its charts. The lexicon of reefers, Minnie the Moocher and Smokey Joe, kicking gongs around and – of course – the fabulous language of hi-de-ho would soon have become tiresome if it hadn't been for the leader's boundless energy and ingenious invention: his vast range, from a convincing bass to a shrieking falsetto, has remained unsurpassed by any male jazz singer, and he transforms material that isn't so much trite as empty without the investment of his personality. This was a very popular band, long resident at the Cotton Club, and the stability of the personnel says much about the good pay and working conditions. The prodigious number of records they made both during and after the Depression was matched by scarcely any other bandleader, and it has taken the Classics operation no fewer than ten well-filled CDs to cover them all. Unfortunately, reproduction is rather a mixed bag. The earlier sides were made for Banner and other budget labels and suffer from some booming recording; but there is a fair amount of surface noise, too. However, there's nothing unlistenable here and, since Calloway's music is at its freshest, casual listeners may choose one of these earlier discs as representative.

The JSP set offers everything on the Classics CDs and comes in scrupulous, superior sound courtesy of John R. T. Davies. Definitely first choice for this material.

(***) **Cab Calloway 1934–1937**
Classics 554 *As above, except add Shad Collins, Irving Randolph (t), Claude Jones, Keg Johnson (tb), Garvin Bushell, Thornton Blue (cl, as), Ben Webster (ts), Milt Hinton (b).* 9/34–3/37.

***(*) **Cab Calloway 1937–1938**
Classics 568 *As above, except add Chu Berry (ts), Chauncey Haughton (cl, as), Danny Barker (g); omit Swayzee, Culley, Cheatham and Morgan.* 3/37–3/38.

*** **Cab Calloway 1938–1939**
Classics 576 *As above, except add June Richmond (v), Cozy Cole (d); omit Webster and White.* 3/38–2/39.

*****(*) Cab Calloway 1939–1940**
Classics 595 *As above, except add Dizzy Gillespie, Mario Bauza (t), Tyree Glenn (tb, vib), Quentin Jackson (tb), Jerry Blake (cl, as); omit Maxey, Bushell and Richmond.* 3/39–3/40.

***** Cab Calloway 1940**
Classics 614 *As above, except omit Collins, Randolph, Jones and Blue.* 3–8/40.

***** Cab Calloway 1940–1941**
Classics 625 *As above, except add Jonah Jones (t).* 3/40–7/41.

***** The Chu And Dizzy Years**
Hep CD 1079 2CD *As appropriate discs above.* 8/39–3/42.

Calloway progressed through the '30s with unquenchable enthusiasm. He took fewer risks on his vocals and chose to set down some more straightforward ballad interpretations on several of the later sides, but the singing is still exceptional, and there are new points of interest among the soloists: Ben Webster appears on several tracks on the 1934–7 disc, and Chu Berry follows him in as a regular soloist, while Gillespie, Jackson and Jefferson also emerge. The 1940 disc features some arrangements by Benny Carter and the bizarre 'Cupid's Nightmare' score by Don Redman, a mystifying mood-piece. Jonah Jones, the last great soloist to arrive in this era, sparks several of the 1941 tracks. Reproduction is mostly clean if sometimes lacking in sparkle on the later discs, but the 1934–7 disc is marred by preposterously heavy surface-noise on the opening tracks and we must issue a caveat in this regard.

Hep's double-disc set focuses on the best tracks from the era when Gillespie and Berry counted among the band's best soloists. That said, track for track it isn't a great deal better than the Classics discs – although sound-quality is a definite improvement, and if you want later rather than earlier Calloway, this should be a priority buy.

***** Cab Calloway 1942–1947**
Classics 996 *Calloway; Russell Smith, Shad Collins, Jonah Jones, Lamar Wright, Paul Webster, Roger Jones, Johnny Letman (t); Tyree Glenn (tb, vib); Quentin Jackson, Keg Johnson, Fred Robinson, John 'Shorty' Haughton, Earl Hardy, James Buxton (tb); Jerry Blake (cl, as); Hilton Jefferson, Al Gibson (as); Rudy Powell, Andrew Brown (as, bs); Ted McRae, Walter 'Foots' Thomas, Skinny Brown, Ike Quebec, Bob Dorsey, Sam Taylor (ts); Greely Walton (bs); Bennie Payne, Dave Rivera (p); Danny Barker, John Smith (g); Milt Hinton (b); Cozy Cole, Panama Francis, J. C. Heard, Buford Oliver (d); Dotty Salters (v).* 2/42–12/47.

Calloway kept an excellent band together through the '40s, as a look through the personnel suggests, but the records don't give them too many chances to step out and the material had by now fallen into a rut. Even so, Calloway himself was largely undaunted, though some of the time he sounds as if he's trying to compete with Louis Jordan: on the last session, both 'The Calloway Boogie' and 'Everybody Eats When They Come To My House' ('Pass me a pancake, Mandrake') could have come off Jordan's set-list. These are mostly Columbia sessions, though there are also three V-Disc titles. Some of the transfers sound dusty, but they clean up towards the end.

***** The Alternative Takes 1930–1944**
Neatwork RP 2065 *As appropriate discs above.* 7/30–9/44.

Calloway's alternates don't tell us a very different story to that of his issued sides, but as with other discs in Neatwork's series, this is actually an attractive cross-section of Cab's work in its own right. The first eight tracks go up to 1934 and find the band still in its hottest form, with standouts such as 'Sweet Jennie Lee' and 'Strictly Cullud Affair'. Take one of 'Minnie The Moocher' is great fun. The final four tracks are from V-Discs and three of them feature Lena Horne, although they sound as if they're from very scruffy originals.

Michel Camilo (born 1954)

PIANO

Born to a musical family in the Dominican Republic, his song 'Why Not' was a hit for Manhattan Transfer and other artists took it up. Camilo is a bright and busy player who swings easily.

***** Why Not?**
Evidence ECD 22002 *Camilo; Lew Soloff (t); Chris Hunter (as, ts); Anthony Jackson (b); Dave Weckl (d); Guarionex Aquino, Sammy Figueroa (perc).* 2/85.

***** Suntan Evidence**
Evidence ECD 22030 *As above; omit Soloff, Hunter, Guarionex, Figueroa; add Joel Rosenblatt (d).* 6/86.

Michel grins broadly as he plays, almost palpably enjoying the music he makes. The debut was almost grimly determined to convey that passion for the piano and he plays the hell out of it on a variety of hard-swinging themes, mostly with a strong Latin bent. Unlike Gonzalo Rubalcaba, say, he seems to bypass many elements of bebop and restores a roistering swing element. His soon to be hit 'Why Not?' is here, but the best track is the opening 'Just Kiddin''. He picked his band advisedly for the album, which was originally released in Japan only. Soloff sounds as if he just got off a Mexican wedding gig and Hunter, then and now, is one of the most emotive players on the scene.

Suntan was also made for a small Japanese label. Without horns, it's a chance to hear Camilo in full focus. What's immediately evident is how assured his technique is. He's easy in most keys, even the less obviously pianistic ones, and modulates comfortably whenever the drama of a tune calls for it. Some of the sheer flash of the first record has gone and there are reflective moments that suit him very nicely indeed.

*****(*) Thru My Eyes**
RMM 82067 *Camilo; Lincoln Goines, Anthony Jackson, John Patitucci (b); Cliff Almond, Horacio Hernandez (d).* 10 & 11/96.

At last, the standards album. Predictably, Camilo's taste is for the Latin and the unexpected. He kicks off with a wonderful version of 'Poinciana' and clinches another of his obvious influences with a robust reading of Chick Corea's 'Armando's Rumba'. Also in the line-up: Herbie Hancock's 'Watermelon Man', played in an odd metre and key, Parker's 'My Little Suede Shoes', Dizzy's 'A Night In Tunisia', Mongo Santamaria's 'Afro Blue' and Sonny Rollins's 'St Thomas', which might have been written for the pianist. A lovely set, which makes use of more than one trio. Patitucci, who's worked extensively with Chick, gives a busier and more detailed sound than the stalwart Jackson and it's nice to hear how Michel responds to that fresh challenge.

***** Spain**
Verve 561545 *Camilo; Tomatito (g).* 8/99.

If the Spanish tinge is the key sound in jazz, here it is in abundance. These duets are almost too insistently themed and it might have been interesting to have heard something like 'April In Paris' or 'Out Of Nowhere' given the same treatment. As it is, this comes across as an aural soundtrack to a Spanish document: touch of Rodrigo, 'Besame Mucho', Chick's 'Spain' and a generic original from the pianist.

***** Triangulo**

Telarc 83549 *Camilo; Anthony Jackson (b); Horacio El Negro Hernandez (d).* 2/02.

***** Live At The Blue Note**

Telarc 83574 2CD *As above; omit Jackson; add Chuck Flores (b).* 3/03.

Once again, Camilo originals come to the fore, prompting queries as to why they've been sidelined on past dates: writer's block? or labels feeling that only standards sets will sell? Whichever is true, this is a return to writing form. 'Piece Of Cake' opens the set with a naggingly familiar tune that's close to lots of things, but none you could name. 'Mr C.I.' is joyous and rhythmic, but the slightly older Camilo also leaves lots of room for quieter and more expressive numbers, like 'Con Alma', which gives the Dizzy tune a more than usually thoughtful angle.

With the signings of Oscar Peterson and Dave Brubeck as well, Telarc have somewhat cornered a market in contemporary piano jazz. Camilo has yet to establish the kind of market presence those giants claim as a given and it's slightly puzzling why he hasn't made a greater splash. The live date puts him in the frame with other Blue Note residents – Keith Jarrett, Chick Corea – though inevitably this is a more modest representation from what seems to have been a very successful stint. Anthony Jackson had moved on and what one immediately misses is his muscly tone and simplicity of approach. Flores is closer in spirit to Patitucci and on the 'Blue Bossa' section of the medley he's tight in behind Michel's rhythmically complex solo. There's something faintly mechanical and foursquare about the pianist's improvisation even at this late date and this may be the reason for his relatively quiet public profile. He isn't – or isn't yet – a soloist who can make the hairs stand up on the back of your neck.

Brun Campbell (1884–1953)

PIANO

Taught by Scott Joplin, Campbell was one of the few genuine first-generation ragtimers to record. Born in Kansas, he played all over the south-west in the first decades of the 20th century before retiring to run his own barber shop in 1928, a business he kept going until his death.

***** Joplin's Disciple**

Delmark 653 *Campbell (p solo).* 47.

It's miraculous that we are able to hear a man who was taking lessons from Joplin in 1898. Campbell went back to the piano only in the '40s, when he heard that Joplin's widow was living in poverty: he cut a version of 'Maple Leaf Rag' so that she could earn some royalties. Besides the brief interview which opens the disc and some other fragments of talking, there are 31 solos, some of them no more than scraps of music on a poor piano, and none of them very well recorded. Yet the curiously indomitable spirit of original ragtime has kept the music alive, and lively. As Campbell himself said, speaking of his generation of pianists: 'Some played march time, fast time, slow time and some played ragtime blues style, but none of them lost the melody, and if you knew the player and heard him a block away you could name him by his ragtime style.' Given that Campbell had stopped performing before jazz itself had wiped out his brand of music, these may be some of the most authentic survivals of piano ragtime, even more so than those texts left behind by Eubie Blake, Jelly Roll Morton and Willie 'The Lion' Smith.

John Campbell (born 1955)

PIANO

Mainstream-modernist pianist with his own take on a bebop language.

***** After Hours**

Contemporary 14053 *Campbell; Todd Coolman (b); Gerry Gibbs (d).* 89.

***** Turning Point**

Contemporary 14061 2 *Campbell; Clark Terry (t); Jay Anderson (b); Joel Spencer (d).* 90.

*****(*) Workin' Out**

Criss Cross 1098 *Campbell; Jay Anderson (b); Billy Drummond (d).* 01.

Campbell is a fresh-faced Mid-Westerner whose farmboy demeanour may arouse musical expectations closer to his namesake Glen than to the reality of his tough but sophisticated bop playing. The trios with Coolman and Gibbs are uniformly good, especially the partially deconstructed 'Donna Lee', but there isn't enough here to lift the album out of a huge pool of similar records. The presence of Clark Terry on the second album makes a whale of a difference, to the extent that it seems like a side-project for Clark rather than a Campbell record. John does some nice things on 'Shaw Nuff' and 'Tin Tin Deo' and there is an unexpected atmospheric round 'Canadian Sunset' that makes it worth a second listen.

Workin' Out is the best and boldest album yet, marked by an imaginative choice of material. Campbell moves easily between the Freddie Hubbard swinger 'Sky Dive' and Mingus's 'Duke Ellington's Sound Of Love', Herbie Hancock's 'Maiden Voyage' and Chick Corea's lovely 'Fall'. John sounds like a man who's enjoying his exploration of the jazz piano literature and the trio is right behind him all the way. Time he was more widely appreciated.

Roy Campbell (born 1952)

TRUMPET, FLUGELHORN, CORNET, POCKET-TRUMPET

A New Yorker, Campbell studied with Yusef Lateef in the early '70s and has explored jazz in a world-music context. Founder member of Other Dimensions In Music, and as likely to play free as anything boppish. Divides his time between Holland and the USA and collects horror films.

*****(*) New Kingdom**
Delmark DE-456 *Campbell; Zane Massey (ts); Ricardo Strobert (as, f); Bryan Carrott (vib); William Parker (b); Zen Matsuura (d).* 10/91.

***** La Tierra Del Fuego**
Delmark DE-469 *Campbell; Alex Lodico (tb); Ricardo Strobert (as, f); Zane Massey (ts); Klaas Hekman (bs); Rahn Burton (p); Hideji Taninaka (b); Reggie Nicholson (d); Talik Abdullah (perc).* 12/93.

***** Communion**
Silkheart SHCD 139 *Campbell; William Parker (b); Reggie Nicholson (d).* 9/94.

Campbell plays like the offspring of Lee Morgan (who was actually his teacher) but imbued with a hankering to go much further outside than Morgan ever would have. He loves lyrical playing and, on Parker's piece dedicated to Cecil Taylor, 'For C.T.', he counters the inspiration by playing some of his sweetest horn. But the idea of *New Kingdom* is to create music that salutes the tradition and still pays heed to the avant-garde. The three trio pieces for Campbell, Parker and Matsuura are an expertly constructed bridge, and beautifully played by all three men. Massey and Strobert are sound, if relatively unremarkable saxophonists, but Carrott is a fine participant, moving smoothly between roles as colourist, ensemble man and fleet improviser.

La Tierra Del Fuego is an intermittently exciting stew of traditions and new ideas, with nods to Booker Little and various threads of Afro-Cuban jazz and the hottest modal bands of the '60s. Campbell assembles a rather ragtag cast for this one, with the surprising Hekman a wild card, and as a result it comes off hit and miss. He empties out the studio for *Communion*, which spotlights his freest playing, and this time evokes – perhaps all too obviously – some of Don Cherry's small-group recordings. Probably ten or 15 minutes too much here, since the record palls a little over the full stretch; inventively though Parker and Nicholson play, one hears graft and perspiration rather than flair. But Campbell remains a gratifying and lyrical performer, even at his furthest out.

***** It's Krunch Time**
Thirsty Ear 57107-2 *Campbell; Khan Jamal (vib); Wilber Morris (b); Guillermo Brown (d).* 4/00.

*****(*) Ethnic Stew And Brew**
Delmark DE-528 *Campbell; William Parker (b, perc, shaku); Hamid Drake (d).* 10/00.

The Thirsty Ear record is hit-and-miss, with a closing assault on 'The Star Spangled Banner' that feels like rehearsed vandalism and other points where Campbell seems to want to pressurize himself out of his normal areas and into inappropriate violence. Brown's mix of rhythms go from funk to Latin to 4/4, and they work to varying degrees; but in the more thoughtful moments Campbell hits his most effective stride, and the partnership with Jamal is as fruitful as the one with Carrott was on the earlier disc. *Ethnic Stew And Brew* is altogether finer, even if Campbell's decision to whip together reggae and West African grooves could have led to modish disaster. He's calling on more than one tradition here – not just ancient black-music threads, but the developed avant-garde of the past 30-odd years, and with the masterful Parker and Drake on hand to articulate the fusion the results are mature, considered, but not lacking in passion. Here and there the music feels like a misfire, but that's the price one has to pay for a genuinely innovative try at blending – with Campbell's best trumpet commentaries emerging almost as a bonus.

Conte Candoli (1927–2001)

TRUMPET

Born in Mishawaka, Indiana, 'Count' Candoli toured with several big bands from the late '40s onwards and moved to California in 1954, where he became a fixture in the West Coast scene. He basically worked there until his death, maintaining long associations with Shorty Rogers's groups, the Doc Severinsen Orchestra, Supersax and a small group he co-led with his brother Pete (born 1923), another trumpeter.

***** The Five**
RCA Victor ND 74397 *Candoli; Bill Perkins (ts); Pete Jolly (p); Buddy Clark (b); Mel Lewis (d).* 55.

****(*) Double Or Nothin'**
Fresh Sounds FSR CD197 *Candoli; Lee Morgan (t); Frank Rosolino (tb); Benny Golson, Bob Cooper (ts); Dick Shreve, Wynton Kelly (p); Red Mitchell, Wilfred Middlebrooks (b); Stan Levey, Charli Persip (d).* 2/57.

***** Fascinating Rhythm**
Fresh Sound FSR 311 *Candoli; Pete Candoli (t, flhn); Lou Levy (p); Joe Diorio (g); Fred Atwood (b); John Dentz (d).* 11/78.

***** Sweet Simon**
Best Recordings BR 92101-2 *Candoli; Pete Christlieb (ts); Frank Strazzeri (p); Monty Budwig (b); Ralph Penland, Roy McCurdy (d).* 92.

Conte Candoli was one of the great West Coast brassmen. Often as content to be a foot soldier as a leader, he seldom helmed his own dates, and these discs (the second and third at least a generation apart) suggest an unassumingly likeable style. *The Five* offers a dozen Shorty Rogers arrangements for a prototypical Californian quintet of the era. Candoli and Perkins stroll through the situation almost nervelessly at times, but the playing has the customary élan that these groups lived by. *Double Or Nothin'* is a Howard Rumsey date co-credited to Conte and Lee Morgan, but neither man really has much space to shine. Morgan's youthful swashbuckling is penned in by the charts and, though Golson contributes three good tunes, the material is delivered flatly. Golson and Morgan take some good choruses on 'Blues After Dark', but the two-trumpet tracks are disappointingly tame, and this is hardly Candoli's show. Still awaited on CD from this period are his 1954 quartet date for Bethlehem and Atlantic's cracking *West Coast Wailers* with Lou Levy and Bill Holman.

Fascinating Rhythm rescues a couple of sessions made for the Dobre label in 1978, one with brother Pete as sole horn, the other with a two-trumpet front line. Pete has been less visible as a soloist than his brother over the years, and the two dates are recorded and organized rather scruffily, but it's a pleasure to hear them go at a bebop chestnut like 'Ah-Leu-Cha' and shine it into something special.

Sweet Simon is a veteran bopper's notebook. Candoli graciously covers two tunes by his old friend Frank Rosolino, adds a couple of Frank Strazzeri originals and two of his own, picks out a neat Al Cohn piece called 'Travisimo' and turns it all into an hour of good-humoured blowing. 'Lush Life' doesn't really suit the trumpeter, and he probably cedes too much space to the others, especially bluff tenorman Christlieb; but the pleasure he takes in his own playing shows how much Conte enjoyed his work. Impeccable studio sound.

***** The Complete Phoenix Recordings Volumes 1–6**
Woofy WPCD121/6 *Candoli; Carl Fontana (tb); Bill Anderson (p); Warren Jones (b); Robb Wainwright (d).* 5/93.

Bob Lorenz recorded this group led by Count and Carl over three nights at the Royal Palms Inn in Phoenix in May 1993. Having sat on the tapes for several years, and with both horn-players gone in the interim, Lorenz decided to issue everything played. A preposterous indulgence: but that is the privilege of the independent-label owner, and it's nice that the jazz business can accommodate it still. That said, the music doesn't really benefit from the warts-and-all presentation. While we have listened to all six discs with much pleasure, their claims on the uncommitted listener are slight. The biggest problem is with the rhythm section: they do little more than offer perfunctory backdrop, and Anderson is very ordinary indeed – a bad shortcoming when he gets as much solo space as the leaders. It's a tribute to Candoli and Fontana that they still salvage much for the listener. Count tends to wander off-mike, but his playing is still full of felicities. If anything, though, the impeccable Fontana outdoes him, with his huge sound and rich fund of ideas. The discs are each available separately and we find it impossible to pick a winner out of the six; as already noted, even with the longueurs, lots to enjoy.

*****(*) Portrait Of A Count**
Fresh Sound FSR 5015 *Candoli; Jan Lundgren (p); Chuck Berghofer (b); Joe LaBarbera (d).* 9/96.

Some of the best of Conte's early sets are still out of circulation, but this was a very enjoyable session. Lundgren is making a speciality of this kind of date and he gives the trumpeter unselfish support, while the bass and drums have pedigrees far longer than their arms. The leader's phrasing is a drop more deliberate and hefty than before, but what a gorgeously clear sound he gets, nicely caught by Dick Bank and engineer Jim Mooney. Eleven good standards and a blues.

****(*) Live At Capozzoli's**
Woofy WPCD 85 *Candoli; Med Flory (as); Frank Strazzeri (p); Tom Warrington (b); Dick Berk (d).* 10/98.

A rather disappointing live one this time. The playing's amiable enough, but Flory's sour tone is disagreeable and little enough happens to make it a necessary listen.

*****(*) Conte-nuity**
Fresh Sound FSR 5028 *Candoli; Jan Lundgren (p); Chuck Berghofer (b); Joe LaBarbera (d).* 10/99.

Conte was in marvellous form on this date, for which he was sympathetically handled by Dick Bank and supported adeptly by the same trio as on *Portrait*: it salutes 12 different trumpeters – 'These versions are interpretations and are not intended to replicate the original recordings,' it says rather admonishingly on the sleeve, and if these aren't copycat takes, they're in the spirit. Conte gets the huge weight and pitch of Cootie Williams just right on 'Do Nothin'', as well as Harry Edison's muted beep on 'Jive At Five'. It's Candoli underneath, though, and he paces himself sweetly through the dozen tracks. A voice from a glittering age of jazz improvising, which was sadly stilled at the end of 2001.

Domenico Capezzuto

PIANO

Contemporary stylist leading a piano trio in and around Rome.

*****(*) Piccola Luce**
Splasc(h) 759-2 *Capezzuto; Javier Girotto (ss); Andrea Avena (b); Luca Chiaraluce (d).* 3/01.

Yet another promising discovery from Splasc(h), this trio make delightfully fresh and spontaneous-sounding jazz from the familiar piano/bass/drums trinity. Capezzuto has a deft and very musical touch, rarely allows too many notes to intrude into his playing, and has a taste for high, almost music-box-like figures to resolve a solo line. His tunes have a dancing quality which Avena and Chiaraluce pick up on with no little skill, such as on the tango-like 'Come In Un Film'. Girotto arrives for two tracks, one a dedication to Michel Petrucciani, who would surely have enjoyed the lilt in the playing. The title-piece has a lovely melody, which the record reprises at the end, accompanied by some of the sounds of Rome at night: bewitchingly evocative.

Frank Capp (born 1931)

DRUMS

Working in Los Angeles from 1953, Capp spent much of the time in small groups, backing singers and doing TV work. In 1975 he founded the Capp–Pierce Juggernaut, a big band co-led with Nat Pierce, an old-fashioned swing-to-mainstream orchestra.

***** In A Hefti Bag**
Concord CCD 4655 *Capp; Bill Berry, Bob Summers (t), Snooky Young, Frank Szabo, Conte Candoli (t); Andy Martin, Thurman Green, Alan Kaplan (tb), Marshal Royal, Lanny Morgan, Danny House, Rickey Woodard, Pete Christlieb, Jack Nimitz, Bill Green (reeds), Gerald Wiggins (p), Dennis Budimir, John Pisano (g), Chuck Berghofer (b).* 11/94–3/95.

Co-led by Capp, a drummer loaded with big-band experience, and Nat Pierce, Juggernaut is essentially a troupe of sessionmen out for a good time on the stand. Because they're such proficient players, there's nothing casual about the music; but that also means that it never becomes quite as freewheeling as the musicians might imagine. Too many of the arrangements rely on stock devices pulled from the Basie and Herman books, while the section playing is sometimes overwound. Yet so many good players are on hand that the results are seldom less than enjoyable. *In A Hefti Bag*, the sole survivor from the group's Concord sessions, finds Capp's men piling through 'authentic' Basie charts; as a polished piece of repertory – with the sax section now stronger than the band had ever supplied, too – it's an impressive show, with choice moments for Young, Woodard and Candoli, and a farewell blow from Marshal Royal.

Arrigo Cappelletti (born 1949)

PIANO

Contemporary Italian pianist with a broad range of sympathies, his modern bent tempered by romantic leanings.

****** Samadhi**

Splasc(h) 111-2 *Cappelletti; Roberto Ottaviano (ss, as); Piero Leveratto (b); Massimo Pintori (d).* 4/86.

***** Pianure**

Splasc(h) 308-2 *Cappelletti; Giulio Visibelli (ss); Maurizio Deho (vn); Gianni Coscia (acc); Hami Hammerli, Luca Garlaschelli (b).* 3–5/90.

*****(*) Singolari Equilibri**

Splasc(h) 390-2 *Cappelletti; Hami Hammerli (b); Billy Elgart (d).* 4/92.

Cappelletti is scarcely an original voice – his underlying romanticism is tempered by a linear approach to improvised melody which, especially on *Singolari Equilibri*, can make him closely akin to Paul Bley – but he's a skilful and unusually clear thinker at the keyboard. There's little waste in his compositions, which are unfailingly lyrical, and his harmonies are sparsely voiced, as if he's anxious not to obscure the sonority of individual notes. He asks for highly developed interplay from companions, and the quartet and trio sessions are both memorably characterful. Ottaviano has seldom sounded better than he does on *Samadhi*, which includes two good tunes of his own as well as a thoughtful treatment of John Taylor's 'Windfall' and Cappelletti at his composing best in 'Neve' and 'Incipit'. The trio record is over-full at 77 minutes but there is much ingenuity from all three men, with Elgart's improvisations as interesting as those of the others. *Pianure* is a modest departure, with Cappelletti looking to try his hand at the tango music of Astor Piazzolla: there are many fine moments, but it feels relatively polite and tame next to the passions which Piazzolla himself could generate and the other players can't match the leader in the quality of their solos.

***** Todos Los Nombres Del Agua**

Splasc(h) 433-2 *Cappelletti; Gianni Coscia (acc); Gioconda Cilio (v).* 11/94.

*****(*) Ananda**

Splasc(h) 485-2 *Cappelletti (p solo).* 6/96.

Todos Los Nombres Del Agua sets poetry by Octavio Paz to music, as well as some lyrics by Cilio, and the results tend to go the way of such things: sparse, meditative, the music pressed to match the evocations of the words and sometimes getting there. Cilio, Coscia and Cappelletti each bring something interesting to the situation, but this is one for firmly acquired tastes.

The solo record carries great conviction. Cappelletti's debt to Paul Bley comes out in 'Bleyniana' and there is a dedication to Bartók, as well as Ellington and Monk covers. Performed slowly and gracefully and with very little in the way of pretension, this is more enjoyable than many higher-profile piano records.

*****(*) Little Poems**

Splasc(h) 836-2 *Cappelletti; Giulio Visibelli (ss, f); Flavio Minardo (g); Steve Swallow (b); Pascale Charreton (v).* 9/01.

Cappelletti, Visibelli and Swallow make up a most sonorous triumvirate. Almost regardless of the notes, there's a distinct pleasure in following the three-way dialogue which constitutes the meat of most of these pieces, the bite of the soprano inflected against Swallow's resonant electric bounce and the percussive crispness of the pianist's lines. Cappelletti takes most of the composing credits – the pieces are inspired largely by the poetry of Sylvia Plath, although there are revisits to an old favourite or two such as 'Singolari Equilibri' – and there are piano–bass duos, consonant three-way improvs, a single appearance by Minardo on the fetching 'Monte Ventoso' and Charreton gently singing the words of 'Petit Poème'. Beautifully recorded, this is a welcome return to the studios for Cappelletti.

Dave Carey (1914–99)

DRUMS

Carey began leading bands in and around Croydon in the '30s, and after the war played in both jazz and dance bands, running his own Dave Carey Jazz Band between 1954 and 1960. Thereafter he tended to his musical instrument and record business, many collectors making the pilgrimage to his Swing Shop in Streatham, South London.

***** The Complete Sessions 1955–57**

Lake LACD 162 2CD *Carey; Johnny Codd, Johnny Rowden (t); Tony Milliner (tb); Tony Gibbons (cl); Pat Hawes (p, v); Bob Mack (g, bj); Eric Starr, Bob Sinclair (b).* 1/56–3/57.

Lake's two-disc set brings together the complete output of the Dave Carey Jazz Band, originally issued on Tempo. If it's workmanlike rather than inspirational British trad, there are a few quirks in approach. As Pat Hawes suggests in his sleeve-note, the rhythm section looks for more of a mainstream feel in terms of their delivery, although when Bob Mack is on banjo that thwarts intentions somewhat. Some live tracks from 1956 are both rowdier and more expansive than their usual, but otherwise the group performs in an enjoyable steady-as-they-go manner. Gibbons, who plays in a rather quiet, nimble style, is the most interesting player and his solos are the ones to wait for. A nice homage to a leader who was a great stalwart of the scene.

Thomas 'Mutt' Carey (1891–1948)

TRUMPET

Carey played in the teens of the century with Joe Oliver and others, but his main association was with Kid Ory, with whom he worked in California from 1919. He was bypassed in the '30s but became a revivalist star when returning to work with Ory in the '40s.

***** Mutt Carey And Lee Collins**

American Music AMCD-72 *Carey; Lee Collins (t); Hociel Thomas (p, v); Lovie Austin, J. H. Shayne (p); Johnny Lindsay (b); Baby Dodds (d); Bertha 'Chippie' Hill (v).* 2–8/46.

Carey was an early giant of New Orleans trumpet, but his representation on record is relatively slight, certainly in terms of being in the limelight. His contribution to the one CD under his name consists of six accompaniments to the piano and vocals of classic blues singer Thomas, still in good voice even though she'd been living in obscurity for many years at that point. This isn't some of Carey's best work, though. He sounds surprisingly uncomfortable at several points and much of the playing seems hesitant, but there's some superb interplay on

'Go Down Sunshine', and Thomas herself does very well. Collins, another frequently unsung trumpeter, sounds rather better on his eight tracks, where he plays behind another veteran, Chippie Hill. This is all rough music and it gets close to the core. Good restoration from the original Circle masters. Carey's sessions for Savoy are worth bringing back, but so far that label's reissue programme has ignored them.

Rüdiger Carl (born 1944)

CLARINET, TENOR SAXOPHONE, PIANO, CONCERTINA, ACCORDION, PERCUSSION

Carl became involved in free playing in the late '60s as a saxophonist, but from the late '70s onwards he has increasingly turned his attention to the accordion and, when he plays a reed instrument, the clarinet. He has frequently worked with Irène Schweizer and Hans Reichel in duo and group situations and, in the '80s, formed the COWWS Quintet.

***(*) **Buben Plus**
FMP CD 78 *Carl; Hans Reichel (vn, daxophone).* 5/78–2/94.

***(*) **Solo**
FMP CD 86 *Carl (acc, cl solo).* 1/93–7/95.

*** **Grooves 'N' Loops**
FMP CD 59 *Carl; Irène Schweizer (p, perc); Philipp Wachsmann (vn, vla, elec); Stephan Wittwer (g); Jay Oliver (b).* 1/93.

**** **Book / Virtual COWWS**
FMP OWN-90007/9 3CD *As above, except add Maarten van Regteren Altena (c), Lol Coxhill (ss, v), Hans Reichel (vn), Alexander von Schlippenbach (p), Mayo Thompson (g, v), Lars Rudolph, Joe Sachse (g), Matthias Bauer, Johnny Mbizo Dyani, Arjen Gorter (b), Louis Moholo, Paul Lovens, Gunter Sommer, Sven-Ake Johansson, Han Bennink (d), Andrew Unruh (tubing), Lupa Herz (v).* 10/77–11/96.

Carl's early appearances were as a typically fraught and scattershot saxman in the FMP roll-call, but he has subsequently spent at least as much time with the concertina and accordion. These are what he uses exclusively on the splendidly bizarre *Buben Plus*, which reissues the 1978 FMP LP, *Buben*, with a dozen further duets from 1994. On the latter pieces Carl switches from concertina to accordion and Reichel drops his violin in favour of the daxophone, which is something like a more 'vocalized' violin in timbre. The improvisations bridge wheezing and scraping with lovely singing tones and minimalist counterpoint. The feel of both sessions is enduringly spontaneous. Excellent liner-notes by Steve Beresford.

The *Solo* album might be deemed to be for specialist tastes – though Carl's music is never exactly driven by playing to any crowd. There is a 1995 live performance at Frankfurt's Adler-Werke, an enormous, abandoned factory space, and a set of 18 'miniatures' for solo accordion from some two years earlier. At work in the huge acoustic of the place, Carl finds a blend of intimacy and vastness. His clarinet on 'Hungen 609' sounds like a ship's foghorn. A strange record, but if you are attuned to Carl's music you'll find it a fine, absorbing listen.

The COWWS Quintet, to which the next one and one-third albums should properly be credited, seems to be Carl's band in leadership terms, and its instrumentation and temper suggest a chamber ensemble. There are surprisingly conventional notes in the directions taken by the group, but a subtext of a sort of civilized anarchy: maybe it's best exemplified by 'Gunst I', a guitar solo by Wittwer which starts as a string of funk clichés and ends in sonic mayhem. Pieced together from two evenings of live playing, it's hit-and-miss.

If Carl has been somewhat neglected by recordings in recent years, the enormous *Book/Virtual COWWS* made up for it with what amounts to a scrapbook of his progress over 20 years of playing. Jump-cutting between group and solo recordings, live and studio, extracts from *Buben* and *Tuned Boots*, private and concert and rehearsal tracks, this is the autobiography of a charming extremist. The patchwork nature of it can seem pointlessly eccentric at times, particularly as so many of the pieces are fragments from larger works, but it is never boring: nothing else in this book sets Thelonious Monk's 'Misterioso' to a commentary on a chess game (spoken by Mayo Thompson, who does follow the melody).

The COWWS disc (number three of the set) is entirely different from what the quintet had attempted earlier. Carl says that he has seen the group as something 'combining improvised music with a "cool" head and a certain feeling of distance'. For this recording, he went to rather extraordinary lengths to crystallize that aim. A system of notation was devised out of a mix of numerical and diagrammatic series, and the musicians were obliged to play parts which amounted to a series of linear blocks or segments, each with a manner of playing described in no more than three words ('icy', 'very heavy movement', and so on). Each musician worked alone in the studio for some two hours, acting on the notation, Carl himself giving the beginning and end signals with the use of a stopwatch. Six pieces were then made out of these overlaid parts, with a seventh constructed out of loops and edits. The results are, in effect, a series of virtual group improvisations, hence the title. As music, it is certainly fascinating, not least for how often it seems that the players are responding to one another – when they are, in fact, never doing anything of the kind.

Fredrik Carlquist (born 1969)

TENOR SAXOPHONE

Contemporary Swedish saxophonist based in and around Malmö.

***(*) **It's About Time, It's About Love**
Dragon DRCD 337 *Carlquist; Anders Bergcrantz (t); Krister Jonsson (g); Mattias Svensson (b); Peter Nilsson (d).* 10/98.

*** **Opposite**
Dragon DRCD 372 *Carlquist; Johan Leijonhufvud, Krister Jonsson (g); Mattias Svensson, Mulle Holmquist (b); Peter Nilsson (d); Leif Jonsson (perc).* 2–4/01.

The first record is characteristic Swedish post-bop. 'Ten Tons Of Terror' starts the album with an explosive tenor–drums duet, before the title-track mollifies the spirits in an attractive, song-like piece for the full quintet (Bergcrantz is only on three tracks). 'Milos' is a stark ballad, seemingly left hanging in mid-phrase, where the plaintiveness of Carlquist's tone is arresting. New leaders stuffing their debuts with their own writing has become a discouraging weakness in jazz's progress, but Carlquist makes light of the responsibility and his seven originals here make a pleasing, confident impression. Bergcrantz is as fine as usual and one might have wished for more of him here.

From its odd instrumentation inwards, the follow-up is an ambitious if not entirely convincing departure. Split between a sextet for sax, two guitars, acoustic bass, drums and percussion, and trio pieces for tenor, drums and electric bass, it's a curious hybrid. The guitars lend a spacey, '70s-rock feel to the originals, and the leader's sometimes neutral delivery imposes little authority. The trio pieces, though, aim for something harsher. Rather effortful.

Mike Carr (born 1937)

ORGAN, PIANO, VIBES

Born in South Shields, Carr was playing jazz in the Newcastle area from 1960. He moved to London and led several trios, eventually backing Ronnie Scott in the early '70s, and still plays in many small-group situations. A renowned expert on the subject of Hammond organs.

*** Bebop From The East Coast 1960/1962

Birdland MC596 *Carr; Ian Carr (t); Gary Cox (ts); John McLaughlin (g); Midge Pike, John O'Carroll, Spike Heatley (b); Johnny Butts, Ronnie Stephenson, Jackie Denton (d).* 60–62.

A faded but lively memento of a particular part of modern British jazz, the scene around Newcastle in the early '60s. This is monochrome hard bop of surprisingly vivid integrity, Cox's tenor the outstanding voice in a number of quartets/quintets which keyboardist Carr organized, often with his brother Ian on trumpet. The notes suggest a comparison with the Brown–Roach group, which isn't so far-fetched. They must have been even better live – although a few live tracks (one stray one from 1967 with young man McLaughlin on guitar) are actually no stronger than the studio ones.

*** Good Times And The Blues

Cargogold CGCD 191 *Carr; Dick Morrissey (ts); Jim Mullen (g); Mark Taylor (d).* 3/93.

Three British venerables (Mark Taylor isn't quite as senior) having fun on blues and bop lines and getting a good record out of it. While the writing is merely functional, the solos work up a rare head of steam, with Morrissey and Mullen eschewing the politely funky licks of their jazz-funk past and digging in. Carr likes to put the Hammond on a rasping, trebly setting and it gives some of his lightning runs an agreeably spine-tingling quality. An outside producer might have served them better, though, and given Taylor a superior drum sound.

*** Stevenson's Rocket

Birdland MC502 *Carr; Steve Fishwick (t); Steve Kaldestad (ts); Robert Ahwai (g); Matt Fishwick (d); Simon Morton (perc).* 8/02.

A fan's notes on hard bop. Carr wrote ten of the 11 tunes though you'd swear that every one of them came off some half-remembered Blue Note date (must be why he calls this his Blue Note Band). Young Steve Fishwick cops licks off Lee and Freddie while twin brother Matt stokes the traps. Kaldestad is a cooler head. Carr does his usual but adds piano and vibes too. Ahwai adds a few guitar parts late in. Feeling the spirit!

Brian Carrick

CLARINET

The boss of the British Heritage Hall Stompers, Carrick is an English clarinettist in the New Orleans style, here fulfilling a dream gig.

** Brian Carrick With Waldren 'Frog' Joseph And His New Orleans Boys

504 CDS 65 *Carrick; John Simmons (t); Waldren Joseph (tb); Clifford Brown (bj, v); James Prevost (b, v); Gerald French (d).* 4/97.

Recorded on a patio in Dumaine Street, this is Brian Carrick's hope of making a real New Orleans record come true. Alas, it's not very good. Carrick himself is a noble footsoldier in the George Lewis tradition, and John Simmons plays a decent enough lead, but poor Joseph is barely able to play at all, the singing's awful and none of the performances manages to lift off.

Terri Lyne Carrington (born 1965)

DRUMS

A prodigy who was already playing professionally, in heavy company, in her early teens. Infrequently sighted as a leader, in or out of the recording studios, Carrington has nevertheless become recognized as a considerable force on her instrument, and she continues to work with many of today's principal leaders, including Herbie Hancock and Wayne Shorter.

*** Jazz Is A Spirit

ACT 9408-2 *Carrington; Wallace Roney, Terence Blanchard (t); Katisse Buckingham (ss); Gary Thomas (ss, ts, f); Greg Kurstin (ky); Herbie Hancock (p); Kevin Eubanks, Paul Bollenback, Jeff Richman, Danny Robinson (g); Malcolm-Jamal Warner (b, v); Bob Hurst (b); Darryl Jackson, Ed Barguiarena (perc).* 2/01.

Carrington has been in the wilderness for years as far as being a leader on records is concerned: her one previous entry, 1988's *Real Life Story* for Verve, disappeared quickly. But she has been in extraordinary demand as a sidewoman, and this belated follow-up features many friends and associates. Though recorded quickly and in somewhat *ad hoc* circumstances, the music lacks little in the way of preparation, and if the writing is sometimes chilly and thin on melody, in the modern manner, the playing is of a very high calibre. Hancock is on three straightahead tracks and proves that he remains an immense creative force when he's set a decent challenge. But Kurstin is no slouch on the remaining material, Thomas walks his usual line between gothic and extravagant, and tracks such as 'Journey Of Now' and the disarmingly sweet 'Princess' work as compositions as well as food for improvisers. A taped conversation between Jo Jones and 19-year-old Carrington is set to a drum fusillade. Not the classic she may have in her, but it's going the right way.

**** Structure

ACT 9427-2 *Carrington; Greg Osby (as); Adam Rogers (g); Jimmy Haslip (b).* 11/03.

And this is perhaps only a beat or so away from that classic. Stronger material all round: Haslip, Osby and Rogers all contribute good tunes, with typically inscrutable Osbyisms balancing Rogers's unabashed lyricism. Carrington herself puts in three pieces and 'Fire', a slow melody strung out over a fuming beat, is a terrific set piece for the band. But it's the playing which lifts everything, a meeting of four notably individual spirits working in surprising harmony – no waste, nothing crowded. The result is an outstanding example of – why not say it? – modern jazz.

Baikida Carroll (born 1947)

TRUMPET

Based in St Louis, Carroll became a major figure in the Black Artists Group in the '70s but has recorded only rarely. He has remained something of a local figure, while still a skilful and adventurous brass player.

★★★★ Shadows And Reflections

Soul Note 121023 *Carroll; Julius Hemphill (as, ts); Anthony Davis (p); Dave Holland (b); Pheeroan akLaff (d).* 1/82.

★★★(★) Door Of The Cage

Soul Note 121123 *Carroll; Erica Lindsay (ts); Adegoke Steve Colson (p); Santi Debriano (b); Pheeroan akLaff (d).* 3/94.

These are high ratings for a musician who is not generally very well known. He grew up in St Louis and became a leading force in the Black Artists Group, sacrificing a good deal in professional terms to commit himself to radical community music-making when his bright chops and fertile ideas would surely have won him considerable prominence as a leader. As it was, Carroll didn't record on his own account until the late '70s when he cut *Shadows And Reflections*, like so many of his advanced contemporaries, for the Italian IREC group, the umbrella organization for Soul Note and Black Saint. 'This project was born out of sheer dedication.' It has repaid handsomely. Carroll assembled a superb group of musicians for the date. Hemphill was returning the favour of an important solo part on his *Dogon A.D.*, but it is Holland who emerges as the key player, rooting the music in something dark and tremulously substantial, great shadowy bass-lines that seem to push the two horns ever higher on 'Jahi Sundance Lake' and the long Pharoah Sanders-like 'Pyramids'.

It's more than a decade before Carroll emerges as a leader again. *Door Of The Cage* is almost inevitably a slight disappointment after the sheer excellence of its predecessor, but it is still an enormously impressive record. Astonishing that Lindsay hasn't recorded more; it's a rich, warm-toned sound with a hard edge when called for. It's called for less on this second record. In keeping with the times, Carroll favours a more line-driven, melodic approach and a softer, more plangent tone. There is still a brassy bite on numbers like 'King' and 'At Roi', which was originally written for Hemphill (whose chosen name was Roi Boye) in friendly revenge for some of the charts he gave the young trumpeter to play.

★★★ Marionettes On A High Wire

OmniTone 12101 *Carroll; Eric Lindsay (ts); Adegoke Steve Colson (p); Michael Formanek (b); Pheeroan akLaff (d).* 9/00.

The trumpeter pays tribute to a couple of masters here: Don Cherry on 'Griot's Last Dance' and Julius Hemphill on 'Flamboye'. He also includes music written for a production of Strindberg's *Miss Julie*. Unlike the Swede, he is no misogynist and offers a gig to the much underused Lindsay, who solos strongly on the Cherry theme and provides able and effective support elsewhere.

It's hard to locate Carroll on the continuum from traditional blues-based jazz to the free idiom, because he constantly balances elements of the two. 'Our Say', also written for a theatrical production, is both formulaic – a jazz waltz – and genuinely original. Colson is excellent in accompaniment, and akLaff as ever provides powerful rhythmic support.

Bill Carrothers (born 1965)

PIANO

Raised in Minneapolis, Carrothers worked locally as a teenager and moved to New York in 1988. A regular in the city's music and a sideman in numerous situations.

★★★ After Hours Vol. 4

Go Jazz 6037-2 *Carrothers; Billy Peterson (b); Kenny Horst (d).* n.d.

★★★ Duets With Bill Stewart

Birdology FDM 37002 *Carrothers; Bill Stewart (d).* 6/99.

★★★(★) Swing Sing Songs

Birdology 8573-86401-2 *Carrothers; Nicolas Thys (b); Dre Pallemaerts (d).* 5/00.

Carrothers is a class act, already endowed with a formidable breadth of experience, and able to fit in with most contemporary jazz situations. That's often a problem when it comes to helming your own dates, but these records aren't short on confidence or ideas. While the session in Go Jazz's *After Hours* series is a bit one-paced – a dozen ballads all negotiated at a slow walk – Carrothers lays bare the material and breaks it into pristine pieces. One to sample a few tracks at a time. It's rather better recorded than some of the entries in this series.

The *Duets* record reduces the cast to two, although since Stewart and Carrothers have worked together many times there's no sense of anything missing. The material's a good deal more diverse in both source and treatment; not many modern pianists would think of playing 'Puttin' On The Ritz', here played with left-hand boogie figures which pop in and out of the improvising, or 'The Whiffenpoof Song'. Oddest piece might be 'I Apologise', in which Stewart rattles out a tempoless tattoo before Carrothers enters to play the tune almost straight. A lot of the music sounds like a private dialogue, and it's hard to get inside.

Swing Sing Songs is an extraordinary programme. Carrothers seeks out material which even the likes of Mehldau haven't thought about – 'Call Me Irresponsible'? Gordon Jenkins's 'Blue Evening'? Keith Jarrett is a spectre at this feast, in part because the pianist has picked up the older player's annoying singalong habit here and there, but it's Jarrett's acute melodic focus and concentration on the line which Carrothers follows, rather than any devotion to the shrine of Keith. When he does 'Donna Lee', it's tremulously slow, whereas Barry Harris's 'Reets And I' is fast bebop done teasingly straight. The music works a truce between rough-and-ready (Steve Wiese gives them an attractive live sound in the studio) and absolute finesse, and it feels like a real trio at work. More, please.

★★★(★) **Ghost Ships**
Sketch SKE 333030 *Carrothers; Anton Denner (ss, as, ts); Bill Stewart (d).* 9/02.

Another remarkable trio and record, with Carrothers helming material that seems to speak of mysterious past times, the sea, and those who sail on her. There are three tracks here titled 'Ghost Ship', and there's also 'God Bless America' and 'The Navy Hymn'. Carrothers unearths another tune that everyone but him has forgotten in 'Your Hit Parade', and their version of Wayne Shorter's 'Water Babies', all cool lines and spartan dialogue, is another peg in a concept that feels palpable yet entirely elusive. Denner gets into the spirit on his three horns, baleful at times, wistful at others.

Ernie Carson (born 1937)

CORNET, VOCAL

Born in Portland, Oregon, Carson is a brassman who's played in West Coast revivalist circles for many years. He took over the Castle Jazz Band in 1983, but has led many sessions of his own.

★★★★ **Southern Comfort**
GHB BCD-162 *Carson; Charlie Bornemann, Steve Yokum (tb); John Otto, Tom Fischer (cl); Steve Pistorius (p); Bill Rutan (bj, v); Debbie Shreyer (bj); Hal 'Shorty' Johnson, Tom Saunders (tba); Hal Smith, Ken Hall (d).* 1/83–5/93.

★★★ **At The Hookers' Ball**
GHB BCD-125 *Carson; Charlie Bornemann (tb); Herman Foretich, Kim Cusack, Tom Fischer (cl); Steve Pistorius (p); Bill Rutan (bj); Mike Moore, Hal 'Shorty' Johnson (tba); Chuck Chamison, Don Hooker, Hal Smith (d).* 83–99.

★★★(★) **Ernie Carson And The Social Polecats**
GHB BCD-307 *Carson; Tom Bartlett (tb); Kim Cusack (cl); Wally Rose (p); Bill Rutan (bj, v); Debbie Shreyer (bj); Mike Walbridge (tba); Wayne Jones (d).* 5/91.

★★★(★) **One Beer**
GHB BCD-297 *Carson; Charlie Bornemann (tb); Rick Fay (cl, ss); Butch Thompson (p); Bill Rutan (bj, v); Hal 'Shorty' Johnson (tba); Debbie Schreyer (d, bj).* 93.

★★★★ **Every Man A King**
GHB BCD-327 *Carson; Tom Bartlett (tb); Kim Cusack (cl); Pete Clute (p); Debbie Schreyer (bj); Mike Wallbridge (tba); Wayne Jones (d).* 3/93.

★★★★ **If I Had A Talking Picture Of You**
GHB BCD-385 *Carson; Steve Yokum (tb); Tom Fischer (cl); Steve Pistorius (p); Debbie Schreyer (bj); Tom Saunders (bsx); Ken Hall (d).* 6/93.

★★★ **Wher'm I Gonna Live?**
Stomp Off 1277 *Carson; Tom Bartlett (tb); Kim Cusack (cl); Pete Clute (p); Bob Leary (bj); Bill Carroll (tba); Wayne Jones (d).* 3/94.

After going through so many earnest and deadly serious records in the course of our survey, it's something of a relief to unwrap the collected works of Ernie Carson, cornetist, singer (more or less) and custodian of much that would otherwise be forgotten in the annals of old-time hot music and jazz. Carson began as a teenage brassman with his old mentor, Monte Ballou of the Castle Jazz Band. In his prime, which might well be around the time of these sessions, he plays tough-as-nails cornet, recalling the spit and fire of the great Chicagoans more than any revivalist hornman, and he masterminds groups that swing ferociously over such ancient ground as (to pick one from each CD) 'I'm Skipping Rope With A Rainbow', 'You Can Tell Her Anything Under The Sun', 'That Ragtime Minstrel Band', 'Powder Your Face With Sunshine', 'When A Peach From Georgia Weds A Rose From Alabam', 'Melon Time In Dixieland' and 'Honey, I Could Fall In Love'. Each has its share of almost outrageous arcana, going even further than Marty Grosz would. *One Beer* goes back to the English music hall with a knockabout version of Mark Sheridan's 'You Can Do A Lot Of Things', but it also has a fine trio version of 'Maple Leaf Rag' and a ludicrous novelty in 'The Farm Yard Cabaret'. *Every Man A King* is a flawless display of what Carson's gang (many of them borrowed from the Salty Dogs) can do, and it gets the nod in front of the others. Nobody will ever top Sheila Steafel's 'Popsy Wopsy', but Carson's crew get close.

Southern Comfort, dedicated to songs from the South, is pure carnival (beefed up with three extra tracks from 1993). *At The Hookers' Ball* has a rather glaring sound on its earlier tracks which takes some of the gilt off the music, though the music is as bumptious as ever. *Social Polecats* has comparatively restrained material but the band are playing with top gusto. *If I Had A Talking Picture Of You* has a great studio sound, Saunders contributes some fine bass sax, and the best tracks sound as if they're going on rocket fuel. *Wher'm I Gonna Live?* is comparatively disappointing. Maybe it was a bit too cute doing tunes by Billy Ray Cyrus and David Nye, since country music doesn't need wits such as Carson to make it seem ridiculous. The sound of the Stomp Off album is also a shade too nice: this kind of thing needs to be driven right into your face, which is how the GHB records are.

Benny Carter (1907–2003)

ALTO SAXOPHONE, TRUMPET, CLARINET, VOCALS

By 1928 Carter was already arranging for various New York bands, and he led his own group on and off from then until 1936, when he went to London as staff arranger for the BBC Dance Orchestra. Back in the USA, he led his own big band, 1939–41, but had to cut back to a sextet before moving to Hollywood in 1945. Wrote extensively for film and TV thereafter, but also for jazz record dates and singers' albums, while also making records featuring his own playing. The most dapper of saxophonists, an excellent trumpeter, and an arranger with few peers, he was one of the last links to a jazz age now long gone.

★★★(★) **Benny Carter 1929–1933**
Classics 522 *Carter; Louis Bacon, Shad Collins, Leonard Davis, Bill Dillard, Frankie Newton, Howard Scott, Bobby Stark, Rex Stewart (t); J. C. Higginbotham, Wilbur De Paris, George Washington, Dicky Wells (tb); Jimmy Harrison (tb, v); Howard Johnson (as); Don Redman (as, v); Wayman Carver (as, f); Chu Berry, Coleman Hawkins (ts); Horace Henderson, Red Rodriguez, Luis Russell, Fats Waller, Teddy Wilson (p); Benny Jackson, Lawrence Lucie (g); Richard Fulbright, Ernest 'Bass' Hill (b); John Kirby (b, bb); Cyrus St Clair (bb); Big Sid Catlett (d, vib); Kaiser Marshall, George Stafford (d); other personnel unidentified.* 9/29–5/33.

★★★(★) Benny Carter 1933–1936

Classics 530 *Carter; Henry 'Red' Allen (t, v); Dick Clark, Leonard Davis, Bill Dillard, Max Goldberg, Otis Johnson, Max Kaminsky, Eddie Mallory, Tommy McQuater, Irving Randolph, Howard Scott, Russell Smith, Duncan Whyte (t); Ted Heath, Keg Johnson, Benny Morton, Bill Mulraney, Floyd O'Brien, Wilbur De Paris, Fred Robinson, George Washington, Dicky Wells (tb); Howard Johnson, Andy McDevitt (cl, as); Wayman Carver (cl, as, f); Glyn Pacque, E. O. Pogson, Russell Procope, Ben Smith (as); Coleman Hawkins (cl, ts); Chu Berry, Buddy Featherstonehaugh, Johnny Russell, Ben Webster (ts); Pat Dodd, Red Rodriguez, Teddy Wilson (p); George Elliott, Clarence Holiday, Lawrence Lucie (g); Al Burke, Ernest 'Bass' Hill, Elmer James (b); Big Sid Catlett, Ronnie Gubertini, Walter Johnson (d); Charles Holland (v).* 5/33–4/36.

★★★(★) Benny Carter 1936

Classics 541 *Carter; Max Goldberg, Tommy McQuater, Duncan Whyte (t); Leslie Thompson (t, tb); Lew Davis, Ted Heath, Bill Mulraney (tb); Freddie Gardner, Andy McDevitt (cl, as); E. O. Pogson (as); Buddy Featherstonehaugh (ts); Pat Dodd, Billy Munn, Gene Rodgers (p); George Elliott, Albert Harris, Ivor Mairants (g); Al Burke, Wally Morris (b); George Elrick, Ronnie Gubertini (d).* 4–10/36.

★★★(★) Benny Carter 1937–1939

Classics 552 *Carter; Jack Bulterman, Sam Dasberg, Rolf Goldstein, Tommy McQuater, Lincoln Mills, Joe Thomas, Leslie Thompson, George Van Helvoirt, George Woodlen, Cliff Woodridge (t); Jimmy Archey, Lew Davis, George Chisholm, Vic Dickenson, Bill Mulraney, Harry Van Oven, Marcel Thielemans (tb); Tyree Glenn (tb, vib); Freddy Gardner, Andy McDevitt, Andre Van der Ouderaa, Wim Poppink, Jimmy Williams (cl, as); Fletcher Allen, Carl Frye, James Powell, Louis Stephenson (as); Alix Combelle, Sal Doof, George Evans, Buddy Featherstonehaugh, Coleman Hawkins, Bertie King, Castor McCord, Ernie Powell, Jimmy Williams (ts); Eddie Heywood Jr, Freddy Johnson, Eddie Macaulay, Nich De Roy, York De Souza (p); Albert Harris, Ulysses Livingston, Django Reinhardt, Ray Webb (g); Len Harrison, Alvis Hayes, Wally Morris, Jack Pet (b); Al Craig, Kees Kranenburg, Robert Montmarche, Henry Morrison (d).* 1/37–6/39.

★★★★ Benny Carter 1940–1941

Classics 631 *Carter; Emmett Berry, Doc Cheatham, Bill Coleman, Roy Eldridge, Jonah Jones, Lincoln Mills, Sidney De Paris, Rostelle Reese, Russell Smith, Nathaniel Williams (t); Jimmy Archey, Joe Britton, Vic Dickenson, John McConnell, Benny Morton, Milton Robinson, Madison Vaughan (tb); Eddie Barefield, George Dorsey, Chauncey Haughton, Ernie Purce, Bill White (as); George James (as, bs); Georgie Auld, Alfred Gibson, Coleman Hawkins, George Irish, Fred Mitchell, Ernie Powell, Stafford Simon, Fred Williams (ts); Sonny White (p); Bernard Addison, Everett Barksdale, William Lewis, Ulysses Livingston, Herb Thomas (g); Hayes Alvis, Charles Drayton, John Kirby, Wilson Myers, Ted Sturgis (b); Big Sid Catlett, J. C. Heard, Yank Porter, Keg Purnell, Berisford Shepherd, Al Taylor (d); Roy Felton, Maxine Sullivan, Joe Turner, The Mills Brothers (v).* 5/40–10/41.

By 1930, Carter was being widely recognized as a gifted young arranger and multi-instrumentalist. Carter's charts, like his playing, are characteristically open-textured and softly bouncing, but seldom lightweight; though he had a particular feel for the saxophone section, as is often noted, and he pioneered a more modern approach to big-band reeds, his gifts extend throughout the orchestra. As a soloist, he developed in a direction rather different from that of Johnny Hodges, who explored a darker register and a less buoyant sensibility. Carter's earliest recordings with the Chocolate Dandies (the band included Coleman Hawkins) and with McKinney's Cotton Pickers put considerable emphasis on his multi-instrumentalism. Set against trombonist Quentin Jackson's surprisingly effective vocals, he sounds poised and elegant – the essential Carter qualities – whatever his horn; and two takes each of 'Do You Believe In Love At First Sight' and 'Wrap Your Troubles In Dreams' demonstrate how beautifully crafted and custom-made his choruses habitually were.

None of these performances is included on the Classics format which is, on the face of it, rather surprising, since the first two sets include sides Carter recorded with Spike Hughes's Negro Orchestra. In the early '30s Carter's band had been increasingly identified as a proving ground for young talent, and the number of subsequently eminent names appearing in Carter sections increases as the decade advances. In 1936 the urbane young American took up a post as staff arranger for the BBC Dance Orchestra, then under Henry Hall. The London period saw some excellent recording with the local talent, including 'Swingin' At Maida Vale', and there are two separate Vocalion sessions with Elisabeth Welch, the first yielding the classic 'When Lights Are Low', the later and better superb arrangements of 'Poor Butterfly' and 'The Man I Love'.

Later sets with Kai Ewans's orchestra and a variety of European bands are less striking, perhaps because after five well-filled discs Carter's particular mastery does, unjustifiably, begin to pall. There is little tension in a Carter solo, which is presented bright and fresh like a polished apple, and his seemingly effortless approach is rather hard to square with a new construction of jazz improvisation which came in with bebop. However, these sides and those following on in the early '40s are significant because, for much of the next 25 years, Carter concentrated on lucrative film music and small groups.

★★★ When Lights Are Low

Conifer/Happy Days CDHD 131 *Carter; Max Goldberg, Tommy McQuater, Duncan Whyte (t); Leslie Thompson (t, tb); Lew Davis, Ted Heath, Bill Mulraney (tb); Freddie Gardner, Andy McDevitt (cl, as); E. O. Pogson (as); Buddy Featherstonehaugh (ts); Pat Dodd, Billy Munn, Gene Rodgers (p); George Elliott, Albert Harris, Ivor Mairants (g); Al Burke, Wally Morris (b); George Elrick, Ronnie Gubertini (d).* 4–10/36.

A useful abstract of the London sessions Carter made for Vocalion. Conifer have even managed to unearth one track – a rejected take of 'Gin And Jive' – not covered by Classics' completism. Oddly, though, they skip two better tracks, 'Scandal In A Flat' and 'Accent On Swing', from the same session. Carter returned to 'Gin And Jive' in January 1937 and cut a vastly superior version with essentially the same band. Swings and roundabouts again, but the Conifer reissue will appeal to anyone who has a particular interest in the development of hot music in Britain in the '30s.

★★★(★) Benny Carter, 1943–1946

Classics 923 *Carter; Felix Barboza, John Carroll, Paul Cohen, Claude Dunson, Emmett Berry, Lewis Botton, Neal Hefti, Idrees Sulieman, Karl George, Louis Gray, Wallace Jones, William Johnson, Joe Newman, Shorty Rogers, Irving Lewis,*

Fred Trainer, Talib Daawud, Edwin Davis, Milton Fletcher, Jake Porter, Ted Buckner, Loyal Walker, Freddy Webster, Gerald Wilson (t); Alton Moore, J. J. Johnson, Charlie Johnson, Al Grey, John Morris, Henry Coker, John 'Shorty' Haughton, Bart Varsalona, George Washington, Dicky Wells, Andy Williams, Trummy Young (tb); Joe Epps, Jewell Grant, Porter Kilbert, Russell Procope (as); Willard Brown (as, bs); Tony Scott (as, cl); Don Byas, Harold Clark, Dexter Gordon, Eugene Porter, Bumps Myers, Flip Phillips (ts); Humphrey Bannon, Rufus Webster, Sonny White, Gerald Wiggins (p); James Cannady, Al Casey, W. J. Edwards, Freddie Green, Ulysses Livingston, Herman Mitchell (g); Charles Drayton, Thomas Moultrie, Curley Russell, John Simmons (b); Oscar Bradley, Percy Brice, J. C. Heard, Max Roach (d); Savannah Churchill, Dick Gracy, Bixie Harris, Timmie Rogers, Maxine Sullivan (v). 10/43–1/46.

A good vintage for the Carter orchestra, as witness all the stars in the making buried away in its ranks. The session of 21 May 1944 marked the recording debut of 18-year-old Max Roach, but it is also special for a superb Carter alto solo on 'I Can't Get Started', switching to trumpet for 'I Surrender Dear'. A couple of 1945 dates are under the nominal leadership of singers Savannah Churchill and Timmie Rogers, but they are very much in the line of Carter's own style of the time, and the vocals are not much more than a pleasant distraction. In 1945, Carter moved to California but he continued to work and record on the East Coast. A session for Capitol in December yielded 'Prelude To A Kiss' and 'Just You, Just Me', again on alto and trumpet respectively, with some strong soloing from the underrated Bumps Myers. Neal Hefti joined as arranger, with no sign that he made a significant difference to the way the band sounded, and the early 1946 material for De Luxe is a refinement of what Carter had been doing for a decade and more, with just a tiny acknowledgement here and there that bebop was happening. The disc closes with a couple of tracks featuring Maxine Sullivan, still in very good voice. The transfers are patchy throughout the disc, and some listeners may prefer to pick up the better material in other forms.

**(*) The Alternative Takes Vol. 1 1936–1940

Neatwork RP 2019 *As appropriate discs above.* 4/36–5/40.

*** The Alternative Takes Vol. 2 1940–1946

Neatwork RP 2030 *As appropriate discs above.* 5/40–4/46.

*** More Alternative Takes 1936–1937

Neatwork RP 2063 *As appropriate discs above.* 4/36–8/37.

Neatwork's survey starts with five European sessions and then works rather exhaustingly through no fewer than 16 alternates from a January 1940 date, including nine goes at 'Fish Fry'. Not essential. Volume two is mostly Commodore and Keynote stuff, and the third disc rather confusingly goes back to Carter's European sojourn, including many of his London sessions. Tommy McQuater's solo on 'There'll Be Some Changes Made' is a highlight on what is the pick of the three discs.

*** Groovin' High In LA, 1946

Hep CD 15 *Carter; Miles Davis, Fred Trainer (?), Calvin Strickland (?), Walter Williams (?), Ira Pettiford (?) (t); Al Grey, Charlie Johnson, Johnny Morris, Candy Ross (tb); Willard Brown, Joe Epps (as); Harold Clark, Bumps Myers (ts); Bob Graettinger (bs); Sonny White (g); James Cannady, Thomas Moultrie (b); Percy Brice (d).* 7/46.

Carter returned to the United States in 1938, by which time the big-band era was well under way. His sterling talents seem to have appealed more to other musicians than to the public at large and, as the war progressed, he switched coasts. *Metronome* concluded around this time that Carter's bands died so slowly that *rigor mortis* had no chance to set in. From the point of view of the dance floor, he offered little enough, but his arrangements have more than survived transfer to unforgiving CD, and there is some astonishing musicianship. Miles Davis appears on the Hep compilation of Armed Forces Radio Service Jubilee transcriptions, a disc shared with the West Coast bands of Wilbert Branco, Gerald Wilson and Jimmy Mundy. Perhaps of greater historical than musical interest, these capture a very specific moment in jazz, the final flowering of the big swing bands before economic constraints began to bite and before bop took over the running.

**** 3, 4, 5: The Verve Small Group Sessions

Verve 849395 *Carter; Don Abney, Oscar Peterson, Teddy Wilson (p); Herb Ellis (g); Ray Brown, George Duvivier (b); Louie Bellson, Jo Jones, Bobby White (d).* n.d.

***(*) Cosmopolite: The Oscar Peterson Sessions

Verve 521673 *Carter; Bill Harris (tb); Oscar Peterson (p); Herb Ellis, Barney Kessel (g); Ray Brown (b); J. C. Heard, Buddy Rich, Bobby White (d).* 9/52–11/54.

Irritatingly, no exact dates are provided for the sterling *3, 4, 5* sessions for Norman Granz's label. The trio sides with Teddy Wilson and Jo Jones are seeing the light of day only after 40 years in the vaults; mysteriously, because a similar session with Art Tatum and Louie Bellson *was* released. Far from wondering at the absence of a bass player (and Wilson wasn't one of the big left-hand men), one might almost wish that the under-recorded Jones had been left out altogether, so bright is the interplay between alto and piano. Wilson is supreme on 'June In January' and the Parker/Sanicola/Sinatra 'This Love Of Mine', a perfect vehicle for Carter's sinuous para-bop phrasing. An 'audio disclaimer' pointing out 22 seconds of 'slight wow and warbling' on 'Moonglow' has to be considered somewhat diversionary, for the music on the middle quartet section really isn't up to the rest of the album. Originally released as *Moonglow: Love Songs By Benny Carter And His Orchestra* (*sic*), the material is a bit lame, however beautifully played. The final three tracks, also unreleased, come from a super-session with rising star Oscar Peterson. Again, the drummer – added for the date – makes very little mark on the music, which includes the intriguing 'Don't You Think', written by Stuff Smith. Despite some reservations about the middle tracks, this makes a superb introduction to Carter the player (there's not a single writing credit) at a fine stage in his distinguished career.

Cosmopolite brings together material from the LPs *Benny Carter Plays Pretty*, *Alto Saxes* and *New Jazz Sounds*, as well as the one whose title has been recycled. They are by no means as compelling as the earlier reissue, but there are, inevitably, some precious moments, as on 'The Song Is You' with trombonist Harris, Ellis, Brown and Rich, a lovely, centred performance with not a hint of strain. Together these records cover an important period and association in Carter's career. Only the first is obviously essential, but Carter fans will be satisfied only with both.

****** Jazz Giant**

Original Jazz Classics OJC 167 *Carter; Frank Rosolino (tb); Ben Webster (ts); André Previn, Jimmy Rowles (p); Barney Kessel (g); Leroy Vinnegar (b); Shelly Manne (d).* 6/57–4/58.

***** Swingin' The Twenties**

Original Jazz Classics OJC 339 *Carter; Earl Hines (p); Leroy Vinnegar (b); Shelly Manne (d).* 11/58.

Carter's trumpet-playing was still sounding remarkably adept at this stage; it tailed off a bit in later years, though he was still able to maintain what is always thought of as the most difficult instrumental 'double' right into the '90s. The material on *Swingin'* is generally pretty bland, though 'A Monday Date' and 'Laugh, Clown, Laugh' uncover some interesting harmonic wrinkles. The rhythm section was one of the best money could buy at the time, nicely balancing old and new. *Jazz Giant* is one of Carter's best small-group records, full of imagination and invention, and the interchanges with Webster are classic. Originally released on Contemporary, it's very much in line with that label's philosophy of easy swing. The CD of *Swingin'* includes some interesting alternative takes.

CORE COLLECTION

****** Further Definitions**

Impulse! 051229-2 *Carter; Bud Shank, Phil Woods (as); Buddy Collette, Teddy Edwards, Coleman Hawkins, Bill Perkins, Charlie Rouse (ts); Bill Hood (bs); John Collins, Barney Kessel, Mundell Lowe (g); Dick Katz (p); Ray Brown, Jimmy Garrison (b); Jo Jones, Alvin Stoller (d).* 11/61–3/66.

This is the best-known of all Carter's albums, now filled out with material recorded five years after the original sessions, with another mid-size band. Economics may have enjoined this type of ensemble, but Carter's feel for reed voicing is such that loss is turned to gain. The added profit is a spacious but intimate sound. Carter and Hawkins had recorded together in Paris before the war in exactly the same configuration as these sides: four saxophones, piano, bass, drums and guitar (a part that was taken by Django Reinhardt first time around). Johnny Collins isn't quite up to that standard, but he has a sure, subtle touch which is both effective and unobtrusive. All the saxophones solo on 'Cotton Tail', with Benny leading off and Bean bringing things to a magisterial, slyly witty close. 'Crazy Rhythm' is an echo of the first meeting and both the senior men quote from each other's past solo, a nice touch of self-reference. 'Blue Star' is intriguing: a complex, deceptive theme with another effective saxophone interchange.

The later session came after a two-year hiatus in Carter's jazz activities, during which he had concentrated almost entirely on film and television work; the only jazz session he had played in the interim had not been released. The intention was obviously to reduplicate the sound and the success of *Further Definitions.* To a degree, it's a success. Mundell Lowe and Barney Kessel are in a different league from Collins, and the guitar part has a prominence far beyond the earlier date. Shank and Edwards are both in strong, individual form, and Bill Perkins is splendidly Hawksian on a remake of 'Doozy'. This material was originally released as *Additions To Further Definitions,* one of the lamest album-titles ever, and one which belies a crisp, more contemporary-sounding recording. Having them together now is a huge plus. The 20-bit transfers are impeccable and, at more than 70 minutes, it's a good-value purchase.

***** BBB & Co**

Original Jazz Classics OJC 758 *Carter; Shorty Sherock (t); Ben Webster (ts); Barney Bigard (cl); Jimmy Rowles (p); Dave Barbour, Leroy Vinnegar (b); Mel Lewis (d).* 4/62.

A mainstream supergroup with lots of miles on the clock and not a terrific amount to say for itself. The combination of Carter, Webster and Bigard may sound inviting, but it turns into a dry and unforthcoming jam during which everyone defers to everyone else and the fires don't start until the later choruses of 'When The Sun Goes Down Blues'. Carter plays well within himself, elegant as ever but almost diffident in his approach to solos. Interesting for the personnel, but not a wonderful record.

****(*) Tickle Toe**

Vee Jay VJ-024 *Carter; Russ Cheever, William Green, Skeets Herfurt (ss); Wilbur Schwartz, Jack Dumont, Paul Horn, Harry Klee (as); Plas Johnson, Babe Russin, Jewell Grant, Buddy Collette, Carrington Visor (ts); Bill Hood, Chuck Gentry (bs); Gerald Wiggins (p); Joe Comfort (b); Alvin Stoller (d); Fred Aguirre, Emil Richards (perc).* 7/64.

All sax and no brass makes ... for a curious interlude in what was otherwise a busy time for him, writing in Hollywood. Six of the ten charts are by Lalo Schifrin anyway, and at less than 30 minutes there's very little for anyone here but Carter completists.

*****(*) The Three C's**

Sackville SKCD2-2058 *Carter; Bill Coleman (t, v); Jo Gagliardi (t); André Faist (tb); Roger Zufferey (as); Michel Pilet (ts); Marc Erbetta (bs); Henri Chaix (p); Alain Du Bois (g, b); Max Hèdigeur, Bob Jacquillard (b); Pierre Bouru, Romano Cavicchiolo (d)* 12/57–11/68.

Shared with a couple of radio sessions headed by Bill Coleman, this finds Carter in congenial Swiss company on a visit to Baden in 1968 (he was in Europe for a Jazz Expo tour and eager Swiss fans managed to persuade him to do a handful of shows with Henri Chaix's band). As so often, the locals play above themselves, inspired by their famous guest, and the music is quite delightful, with Carter originals such as 'Easy Money' and 'Titmouse' getting space alongside his ballad features on 'I Can't Get Started' and 'Body And Soul'. The Coleman material is from a decade earlier and is scarcely less enjoyable, the trumpeter taking a few laid-back vocals and enjoying the limelight, although Michel Pilet's Hawkish tenor is also good value.

*****(*) The King**

Original Jazz Classics OJC 883 *Carter; Milt Jackson (vib); Joe Pass (g); Tommy Flanagan (p); John B. Williams (b); Jake Hanna (d).* 2/76.

Jackson was another brilliant improviser whose mellifluous approach led detractors to suspect him of giving short weight. Here again, he underlines his genius with a dozen blues choruses of immense sophistication. The closing D-flat blues opens up the kind of harmonic territory on which Carter and Flanagan both thrive, and the set ends with a ringing affirmation. Williams is rather anonymous and Pass seems to miscue slightly on a couple of faster ensembles. Otherwise hard to fault.

***** Carter Gillespie Inc**

Original Jazz Classics OJC 682 *Carter; Dizzy Gillespie (t); Joe Pass (g); Tommy Flanagan (p); Al McKibbon (b); Mickey Roker (d).* 4/76.

*****(*) Wonderland**

Original Jazz Classics OJC 967 *Carter; Harry 'Sweets' Edison (t); Eddie 'Lockjaw' Davis (ts); Ray Bryant (p); Milt Hinton (b); Grady Tate (d).* 11/76.

Remarkable to think that as long ago as 1976 Carter was approaching his 70th birthday. There's a slightly ponderous, aldermanic quality to the AGM with Diz, much polite deference, some cheerful banter but not a great deal of classic music. He sounds in better form on the relaxed *Wonderland*, ably accompanied by Edison (Carter let others handle the brass duties by this stage) and an uncharacteristically cool Lockjaw Davis. 'Misty' was to remain a favourite, played with curious emphases and a wry unsentimentality.

*****(*) Montreux '77**

Original Jazz Classics OJC 374 *Carter; Ray Bryant (p); Niels-Henning Orsted Pedersen (b); Jimmie Smith (d).* 7/77.

*****(*) Live And Well In Japan**

Original Jazz Classics OJC 736 *Carter; Cat Anderson, Joe Newman (t); Britt Woodman (tb); Budd Johnson (ts); Cecil Payne (bs); Nat Pierce (p); Mundell Lowe (g); George Duvivier (b); Harold Jones (d).* 4/77.

1977 was a monster year at Montreux, and a good deal of the music performed over the main weekend has been preserved on live Pablo releases (and subsequently on OJC). The Carter set is one of the best of them. Though his soloing here doesn't quite match up to some choruses on a Count Basie jam from the following day, 'Three Little Words', 'Body And Soul' and 'On Green Dolphin Street' are absolutely sterling. The band swings comfortably and NHOP plays delightful counter-melodies on 'In A Mellow Tone'.

Turning 70, Carter seemed eager to dismiss biblical estimates of an average lifespan by playing like a man half his age. In an all-star line-up in Japan (a country he came to love and where he was treated like a minor deity) he trades superbly crafted licks with all and sundry. The sound is rather cavernous but there's great atmosphere, and the playing makes up for all other deficiencies.

***** Summer Serenade**

Storyville STCD 4047 *Carter; Kenny Drew (p); Jesper Lundgaard (b); Ed Thigpen (d); Richard Boone (v).* 8/80.

Carter's small-group encounters, like this Scandinavian session, were a well-polished act; but it takes a certain genius to make the umpteenth version of quite banal tunes like 'Back Home In Indiana' and 'When Lights Are Low' sound quite as freshly minted as Carter does here. The rhythm section is admirably professional and Boone holds his wheesht for all but one track, which is all to the good.

****(*) The Best Of Benny Carter**

Pablo PACD 2405 *Carter; Cat Anderson, Harry 'Sweets' Edison, Joe Newman (t); Britt Woodman (tb); Eddie 'Lockjaw' Davis, Budd Johnson (ts); Cecil Payne (bs); Ray Bryant (p); Mundell Lowe (g); George Duvivier, Milt Hinton, Niels-Henning Orsted Pedersen (b); Harold Jones, Jimmie Smith, Grady Tate (d).*

Odd and uninspired choice of material. Better to stick to the original Pablos.

***** Meets Oscar Peterson**

Pablo 2310926 *Carter; Oscar Peterson (p); Joe Pass (g); Dave Young (b); Martin Drew (d).* 86

How much more interesting this might have been as a duo. Even allowing for some melodic breaks from Pass, the rhythm backings are bland and undynamic enough to seem superfluous. 'Baubles, Bangles And Beads' moves at the gentle lope both men seem to prefer nowadays, and Peterson's statement of the theme is about as straightforward as he's ever been.

Benny's albums for Musicmasters in the '80s and '90s are now in abeyance, and the gentleman himself enjoyed a quiet retirement until he finally left us in his 96th year.

Betty Carter (1930–98)

VOCALS

Known as 'Betty Bebop' when she sang with Lionel Hampton in the '40s, Carter broke off from performing to raise a family. On her return in 1969 she became the most demanding and virtuosic of jazz singers. Her touring groups were little academies for young players, like a miniature Jazz Messengers, and until her unexpected death she maintained a ferocious appetite for performing both in clubs and on bigger stages.

***** Finally**

Roulette Jazz 53332 *Carter; Norman Simmons (p); Lisle Atkinson (b); Al Harewood (d).* 12/69.

Billie Holiday once said that she didn't feel like she was singin', she felt like she was playin' a horn. So, too, with Betty Carter, who transcended the 'bop vocalist' tag and created a style that combined the fluent, improvisational grace of an alto saxophone with an uncanny accuracy of diction. Even when her weighting of a lyric is almost surreal, its significance is utterly explicit and often sarcastically subversive. The latter quality has allowed her to skate on the thin ice of quite banal standard material, much of which has acquired a veneer of seriousness from nowadays being heard only as instrumentals; 'Body And Soul' is the obvious example, medleyed with 'Heart And Soul' on the 1969 live album, taped at New York's Judson Hall.

Some of the pieces on *Finally* are left deliberately raw. 'Girl Talk' is wild, but what is she thinking about as she sings 'The Sun Died' or 'You're A Sweetheart'? With Carter the charge of emotion isn't always obvious and often requires a certain shift of perspective in the listener. What these sides consistently demonstrate – and this was to remain a stock-in-trade – is the ability to take and reshape a song so radically that it becomes something quite new, a 180° reorientation of something familiar which retains only a few subtle reminders of its original. A process similar, in other words, to the contrafacts on standard material made by the bebop pioneers, but with the added complication of words which also overturn expectations of what female jazz singers might be concerned about or required to say.

***** I'm Yours, You're Mine**

Verve 533182 *Carter; Andre Hayward (tb); Mark Shim (ts); Xavier Davis (p); Matt Hughes, Curtis Lundy (b); Gregory Hutchinson (d).* 96.

For all her eminence, Carter was commercially unsuccessful as a recording artist, even in jazz terms. Most of her Verve albums have lately disappeared from print, which is a tacit hint that, for all her greatness as a performer, she only rarely managed to translate that to a studio situation. Officially a Verve/Bet-Car co-release, *I'm Yours, You're Mine* is frankly a disappointment. But for the title-track and a long performance of 'September Song', and for another first-rate band, this would be ignorable. Carter's ability to invest a song with multiple meanings has for some reason been set aside. The springy rhythm has turned staccato and the humour seems strained. Lundy and Hutchinson perform brilliantly, and there is genuine pleasure in hearing Carter negotiate her course through the accompaniment, but there's not much on *I'm Yours* for the enthusiast.

James Carter (born 1969)

SOPRANO, ALTO, TENOR, BARITONE AND F-MEZZO SAXOPHONES, BASS AND CONTRABASS CLARINETS, FLUTE

From Detroit, Carter has made a great impact with his name records for DIW and Atlantic, blending traditionalism and a near-avant-garde sensibility with self-conscious but charismatic assertion.

*****(*) JC On The Set**

Columbia CK 66149 *Carter; Craig Taborn (p); Jaribu Shahid (b); Tani Tabbal (d).* 4/93.

***** Jurassic Classics**

Columbia CK 67058 *As above.* 4/94.

When you arrive on the scene wearing messianic initials, much is expected; not miracles perhaps, but certainly something special. Carter emerged from a faintly preposterous ensemble known as the Tough Young Tenors, the only one of the bunch who sounded anything like as tough and streetwise as he looked. The basic sound was hard-edged and earthy, but with some of the deconstructive trappings of the avant-garde, and Carter was said to have a practice room at home stuffed full of old horns, the better to explore the untouched registers of his voice. He had worked with the ever under-remarked Frank Lowe, and that was probably as close as anyone was going to get to find a valid comparison. Certainly a very different player from Josh Redman, whose skills were being loudly bruited at the same time.

Carter sounds like a Detroit player through and through: metallic, brisk and not above a quiver of sentiment. The debut album delivered in trumps. Not least, it delved into unexpected corners of the repertoire: Sun Ra's 'Hour Of Parting', the somewhat obscure Texan John Hardee's 'Lunatic', alongside Duke's 'Caravan' and 'Sophisticated Lady'. And Carter demonstrated that he had things of his own to say, whether down in baritone range or squealing and testifying as he did on the original 'Blues For A Nomadic Princess'. Choosing a Don Byas tune, 'Worried And Blue', pointed to a more than fashionable interest in classic jazz and its forgotten warriors. The phrasing is immaculate, the tone youthfully wayward here and there but still authentic.

Jurassic Classics probably came too soon, certainly too soon on top of what had been a tough and busy year. Suddenly the burnish wasn't quite bright enough to blot out some of the weaknesses: a tendency to barge through a tune, shake it painfully by the hand in a mistaken outflow of respect, fail to do it justice. The second album put him ever more clearly in touch with the jazz mainstream, but it found him flailing a bit, not so much out of his depth, but with an inelegant stroke.

****** The Real Quietstorm**

Atlantic 782742 *As above, except add Dave Holland (b); Leon Parker (d).* 10–11/94.

Signing for Atlantic was a positive move. It seemed to impose a certain corporate discipline and 'house style', death to the spirit for some artists but salutary for someone like Carter, who seemed to be going in umpteen directions at once. To some extent, it's a showcase, a chance to try out paces on six different horns, including bass flute on the extraordinary 'Ballad For A Doll', which also features Holland. But it's also an album that demonstrates that Carter is not just a flash multi-instrumentalist but a musician who chooses his persona carefully. The tenor monologue, 'The Stevedore's Serenade', is still one of the most startling saxophone performances of the '90s, and though the title is dismal, 'Intimacy Of My Woman's Beautiful Eyes' is alto-playing that invites comparison with Dolphy's on 'Tenderly'. It's the two baritone duets, with Taborn on 'Round Midnight' and Shahid on 'Eventide', that stand out, and it may be that in years to come Carter will settle on alto and baritone, similarly pitched if not equally weighted, as his two main instruments.

****** Conversin' With The Elders**

Atlantic 7567 82908 *As above, except omit Holland and Parker; add Lester Bowie, Harry 'Sweets' Edison (t); Larry Smith (as); Buddy Tate (ts); Hamiet Bluiett (bs).* 10/95–2/96.

An inspired idea: to throw Carter up against the very ancestral voices that haunt and propel him. Both guests and material come from out of a past not always so very distant, but certainly very different from the scene the young man inherited. Carter's loyalty to Shahid, Tabal and Taborn is exemplary, and they form a unified background for the guest spots.

The most venerable, chronologically speaking, are Edison and Tate, and 'Lester Leaps In' and 'Centrepiece' with Sweets and 'Moten Swing' and 'Blue Creek', the latter with Buddy on clarinet, are convincingly, supremely authentic. The paired altos on 'Parker's Mood' almost cancel each other out, so rigorously do they observe the master's cadence, and Smith – heard, as all the guests are, through the left channel – doesn't seem to want to bust loose. The set kicks off, wonderfully but rather deceptively, with Bowie's 'Freereggaehibop', on which his entire armoury of rips, snorts, smears and impossibly low-register vocalizations are used. Appropriately, he comes back to round off the album with 'Atitled Valse', but by then the honours have already been secured by Bluiett and by two fantastic baritone duets, on Coltrane's 'Naima' and, more boldly, on Anthony Braxton's 'Composition 40Q', one of the more approachable themes in the Braxton canon, but still a startling piece to cover.

Carter is playing with dazzling confidence and restrained power. His early tendency to overblow and over-emphasize the attack has now given way to a breathy, almost intimate sound which can be scaled up or down in keeping with the material.

*****(*) In Carterian Fashion**

Atlantic 83082-2 *Carter; Dwight Adams (t); Cassius Richmond (as); Henry Butler, Cyrus Chestnut, Craig Taborn (org); Kevin Carter (g); Steve Kirby, Jaribu Shahid (b); Alvester Garnett, Leonard King, Tani Tabbal (d).* 98.

Carter faces up to the end of his 20s with a swirling, raucous album, centred on the blues and marked by a choppy, rhythmically agitated organ sound. Oddly, despite featuring three such different players as Taborn, Chestnut and Butler on the Hammond, the sound is rather uniform. The young saxophonist is still conversing with elder spirits, including two arrangements of traditional material, 'Down To The River' and 'Trouble In The World', the latter emerging out of free-form chaos and into one of the most orderly and plain-spoken things on any of the records. 'Skull Grabbin'' is restless and fractured, an uneasy piece that sounds too much like a grab for shock value. Carter's bass clarinet work on 'Odyssey' weaves an illuminating counterpoint with trumpet and alto over a softer than usual Hammond track. 'Frisco Follies' is the somewhat token workout on the other horns, baritone and soprano. Increasingly, though, Carter sounds like a genuine tenor man. The tribute to Lockjaw Davis builds an idiosyncratic solo round two almost subliminal Jaws licks. Yves Beauvais's production is crisp and deliberately unresonant, leaving the horns floating in free space.

****(*) Chasin' The Gypsy**

Atlantic 83310 *Carter; Regina Carter (vn); Jay Berliner, Romero Lubambo (g).* 2/00.

***** Layin' In The Cut**

Atlantic 83305 *Carter; Jeff Lee Johnson, Marc Ribot (g); Jamaaladeen Tacuma (b); G. Calvin Weston (d).* 11/99.

Two very different dates from James to mark the turn of the millennium. *Layin'* is a tough and sometimes abrasive funk project that here and there veers in the direction of Ulmer-school harmolodics. Most of the tracks are credited collectively, which suggests that a certain amount of this material was worked out live in the studio and jammed down. Perhaps predictably, the most successful performances are the two Carter compositions which come right at the end of the record, 'There's A Puddle' and 'GP'. The two guitarists have clearly listened to their share of Prime Time records, but they don't bring that deranged energy to the session and much of the playing sounds stilted and unsure.

The other Atlantic from 2000 was obviously intended to demonstrate Carter's eclecticism, but his take on Django Reinhardt is wholly unsuccessful. He doesn't feel the idiom, however well he understands the harmonic language, and most of the numbers sound too tentative and unfinished for release. As if to compensate, James experiments with some outlandish horn, propping up his bass saxophone on a couple of cuts and turning to the F mezzo horn (most recently associated with the late Thomas Chapin) on 'Oriental Shuffle', which is probably the most appealing number on the date.

***** Live At Baker's Keyboard Lounge**

Warners 9362-48449-2 *Carter; Dwight Adams (t); Larry Smith (as); Franz Jackson (ts, v); Johnny Griffin, David Murray (ts); Kenn Cox (p); Gerard Gibbs (org); Ralph Armstrong (b); Leonard King, Richard 'Pistol' Allen (d).* 6/01.

Carter's farewell to Warners was cut over three days at the Detroit club, with various famous sitters-in. It's really not much more than somebody's raggedy ol' live set. Carter gets almost absurdly far out on the jam staple 'Tricotism' (and that's just track one), and then it's a parade of what almost amount to showbiz cameos. David Murray meets his overblowing match on 'Freedom Jazz Dance' and the veteran Franz Jackson has fun with the lyric on 'I Can't Get Started'. Everybody troops on for the final 'Foot Pattin''. Doubtless a riot if you were there; as a record, it's entertaining enough if you're in the mood.

***** Gardenias For Lady Day**

Columbia 514879 *Carter; John Hicks (p); Peter Washington (b); Victor Lewis (d); Miche Braden (v); strings.* n.d.

Carter goes to Columbia (while his first albums were released on that label in the US, they were actually made by Japanese DIW) and opens his account with a Billie Holiday tribute. A smallish string section is daubed over some of the tracks, and the saxophonist is on relatively restrained form, but he still makes it a long way from a Ben Webster record. Braden sings on three tracks and is notably un-Billie-ish. It's an interesting record and perhaps not much more. 'I'm In A Low-Down Groove', which is just for Carter and rhythm section, hints at a more adventurous session, where he overdubs horns and threads different voicings through a single track.

John Carter (1928–91)

CLARINET, ALTO AND TENOR SAXOPHONES, FLUTE

Born in Fort Worth, where he played with Ornette Coleman in the '40s, he moved West in 1961 and formed a regular partnership with Bobby Bradford four years later. A dedicated teacher, he brought his own studies of clarinet and Afro-American lore together in a rich and detailed style of jazz which was very much his own.

***** Tandem 1**

Emanem 4011 *Carter; Bobby Bradford (c).* 4/82.

***** Tandem 2**

Emanem 4012 *As above.* 4/82.

In 1964 Carter founded the New Art Jazz Ensemble with Bobby Bradford, one of a number of quietly influential groups that give the lie to received notions about West Coast jazz. *Seeking* is the group's debut on disc, and if it precedes the best work the two men were to do in the studio – the extraordinary *Secrets*, made for Revelation in 1971 and 1972 – it is still a powerful record. Alas, both discs are currently unavailable. On *Secrets*, Carter and Bradford anticipated what is arguably the most radical phase of their career, technically speaking, by playing the first section as an unaccompanied duo for clarinet and cornet. 'Circle', the track in question, resurfaces as a live performance on the first volume of *Tandem*, and it underlines as well as anything how close and intuitive the two men's working relationship was. Carter is often the normalizing element, bringing the music back to a more logical and discursive position, tempering Bradford's fieriness and then blowing the whole thing open himself. The tandem principle applies throughout, though. Once one man is in motion, the other is bound to follow.

It should be said that the sound on these recordings is pretty deplorable. The April 1982 concert from Worcester, Massachusetts, which is heard in order on the first album with the final numbers carried over to the sequel, is marred by print-through, a disconcerting pre-echo (the trick is to store music tape tail-out) and traffic noise, while the remaining pieces, recorded three years earlier in Los Angeles, were on cassette. 'Tandem' kicks off both sessions, a warm-up piece with enough unselfconscious showmanship to win round the flintiest sceptic. There are solos on both discs: Bradford's forcefully romantic 'Woman' on *Tandem 2* and 'Portrait Of JBG' on the first disc, Carter's 'Angles' (Emanem 4011), two versions of 'Echoes From Rudolph's' (one on each) and the startling 'Les Masses Jigaboo' on the second volume, which anticipates his ambitious Afro-suite of coming years. All credit to Martin Davidson for deciding that this music was significant enough to overturn doubts about its technical quality.

***** Dauwhe**

Black Saint 120057 *Carter; Bobby Bradford (c); Charles Owens (ss, cl, ob); James Newton (f); Red Callender (tba); Roberto Miguel Miranda (b); William Jeffrey (d); Luis Peralta (perc).* 2–3/82.

In the decade before his death, Carter worked at a multi-part sequence of suites called *Roots And Folklore: Episodes In The Development Of American Folk Music.* But at present *Dauwhe*, which traces the African origins of the music, is the only one still in print. The band realizes Carter's intentions handsomely, and Newton in particular is a strong presence. However, like his frequent partner Bobby Bradford, Carter has not been well served by the CD era so far, and this important musician's work is currently languishing in the margins.

Kent Carter (born 1939)

DOUBLE BASS

The multi-talented Carter, who also plays violin, cello and keyboards, was born in New Hampshire and has often seemed to gravitate to quieter locations; nevertheless he was part of the free revolution in jazz and worked with Paul Bley, Steve Lacy and the Jazz Composers Orchestra. His strong sense of rhythm is matched by an interest in abstraction.

***** Beauvais Cathedral**

Emanem 4061 *Carter; Michala Marcus (f); Richard Marechin (p); Carlos Zingaro (vn).* 3–12/74.

***** The Juillaguet Collection**

Emanem 4033 *Carter; Albrecht Maurer (vn).* 8/96.

There may be some curious musical destiny in names to explain why the Parkers have so taken to the saxophone and why there are so many Carters in jazz, including one other master of the bass. These days, Kent lives somewhat out of the way, in a tiny village in the south of France, where he and his partner run a music, arts and dance studio (MAD).

Beauvais Cathedral was Carter's first album. It isn't quite a solo project, though what sounds like a string quartet on 'Steps' is the result of careful overdubbing of all four parts. Carter worked closely with Emanem's Martin Davidson, using some fairly archaic equipment to create these tracks. The results are warm, resonant, 'live' in feel and consistently fascinating. There are three short double-bass solos, a virtuosic cello solo which uses rhythm and dynamics to create an illusion of overdubbing (or two players) and a number of 'ensemble' pieces. Some of these are created with other players – Zingaro also collaborated on a 1984 record – some as tape collages, and 'Play Time', dedicated to Steve Lacy, is a cello dialogue with a radio receiver. A couple of pieces are for dance works.

A much later string collaboration, *The Juillaguet Collection* was recorded at the Carters' dance centre. Maurer is the bassist's junior by two decades, but their musical understanding is complete and the ten full-length performances and final fragment are each and all worthy of prolonged attention. This is a record that needs some time and application, but it still comes unmistakably from within a modern jazz sensibility.

Regina Carter

VIOLIN

Previously spotted with String Trio Of New York, Carter has made major-label debuts at both Atlantic and Verve.

***** Rhythms Of The Heart**

Verve 547177-2 *Carter; Kenny Barron, Werner 'Vana' Gierig (p); Rodney Jones, Romero Lubambo (g); Richard Bona (g, b, perc, v); Peter Washington (b); Lewis Nash (d); Cassandra Wilson (v); Mayra Casales (perc).* 11 & 12/98.

Some jazz fiddlers never forget getting laughed at on the way home from music lessons and spend a whole career acting out all those fantasies about whipping open the case and producing a Thompson – or these days an Uzi – rather than a Strad. Carter is refreshingly *un*embarrassed about carrying her violin on the block. Her idol is Stuff Smith, unmistakably so on the evidence of the opening 'Lady Be Good'. Like Smith, she cocks a snook at the instrument's canonical status while demonstrating an enviable technical facility.

A natural swinger, she tackles Tadd Dameron's 'Our Delight' with the exuberance of a whole horn section. The only shortcoming in this debut recording is a rather flat and unexpressive approach to ballads. 'Spring Can Really Hang You Up The Most' is way too downbeat and Carter's phrasing goes out of idiom. Verve's habit of propping up new talent with star names works well here, but it also underlines a hint of inexperience. Cassandra Wilson and guitarist Rodney Jones hijack 'Papa Was A Rolling Stone'; an inspired choice of material but perversely handed over to the guests. Kenny Barron checks in with two originals and stamps his authority over 'Spring ...' as well. The descending four-note figure that repeats throughout 'Cook's Bay' is made for the string instrument, but it is Barron's own statement that commands attention. Similarly, Richard Bona dominates his own 'Mandingo Street'. It might have been preferable to offer Carter a bit of tough love and let her grow up a bit more exposed. She is capable of much more than what's on show here.

***** Motor City Moments**

Verve 543927-2 *Carter; Marcus Belgrave (t); James Carter (ts, bcl); Werner 'Vana' Gierig, Barry Harris (p); Russell Malone (g); Daryl Hall (b); Alvester Garnett, Lewis Nash (d); Mayra Casales (perc).* 00.

Good enough, though hardly a star's coming-out – which is as it should be: Carter should be allowed her own time and space. Trouble is, Verve probably won't be that patient, and again this attractively campaigned homage to Detroit is, as so often, a case of a leader being compromised by concept and guest stars. The only one of those who makes real sense is the great Barry Harris, a proper inclusion on any Detroit album, and a man who takes over in even a brief passage on 'Prey Loot'. Otherwise, there's James Carter (at least he's a cousin of the leader), a version of Stevie Wonder's 'Higher Ground' (shouldn't have bothered) and good moments when Carter and her core group dig in and go.

***** Paganini: After A Dream**

Verve 065554-2 *Carter; Werner 'Vana' Gierig (p); Regina Carter (vn, v); Borislav Strulev (clo); Chris Lightcap (b); Alvester Garnett (d, v); Mayra Casales (perc, v); strings.* 11–12/02.

Carter plays an instrument which once belonged to Paganini on this attractive set, and with Ravel, Fauré, Debussy and other such cats listed in the composing credits, the results are predictably gorgeous in tone. 'Predictable' is about it, though: the melodies aren't a springboard to anything special, and it hardly counts as any kind of jazzing the classics. A nice opportunity for any violinist – now, let's have a challenging record next time.

Ron Carter (born 1937)

DOUBLE BASS, CELLO, PICCOLO BASS

Joined Chico Hamilton in 1962, then with Miles Davis, 1963–8. Recognized since as a musicians' musician, and in demand as session-man and teacher, although his own records have often been mixed successes: flirtations with jazz-rock, chamber-music forms and more conventional straightahead playing have yielded little in the way of a masterpiece.

***** Where?**

Original Jazz Classics OJC 432 *Carter; Eric Dolphy (as, bcl, f); Mal Waldron (p); George Duvivier (b); Charli Persip (d).* 6/61.

Doubts that a young black boy could possibly play convincing cello led to the pre-teen Carter switching to bass, and launching a remarkable career. Perhaps only Ray Brown has recorded more on the instrument, but whereas Brown's solo career was rather late in starting, Carter has such innate musicality that he has always been able to sustain progress as a leader in his own right. With *Where?* he is unfortunate in that the record will always be seen as an item in the Eric Dolphy discography, rather than Carter's own. It's dominated by a brilliant bass/clarinet duo of the sort Dolphy created many times with Charles Mingus, and by a fine, unsentimental reading of 'Softly, As In A Morning Sunrise'. Carter plays cello on 'Really' and 'Saucer Eyes' as he had on Dolphy's second album, *Out There*, also originally released on New Jazz. Waldron and (on the two cello tracks) Duvivier give firm support, and Persip once again displays the skills that should have guaranteed him a higher rating than he currently receives in histories of the music.

**** Pastels**

Original Jazz Classics OJCCD 665 *Carter; Kenny Barron (p); Hugh McCracken (g, hca); Harvey Mason (d); strings.* 10/76.

There is nothing inherently wrong with wanting to play with strings, but in this case Carter has done no more than take a competent and uninspired jazz record and pour syrup over it. If the basic tracks were more uplifting, this would scarcely matter, but they're not and the arrangements do nothing to help.

***** Peg Leg**

Original Jazz Classics OJCCD 621 *Carter; Jerry Dodgion, Walter Kane, George Marge (reeds); Jay Berliner (g); Kenny Barron (p); Buster Williams (b); Ben Riley (d).* 11/77.

With almost all of Carter's Blue Note work unavailable in the West, it is quite hard to identify his best recordings on CD. *Peg Leg* is very good indeed, with a first-rate version of Monk's 'Epistrophy', featuring the light, fast sound of his piccolo bass. There remain some doubts about the sound, which even on CD is floaty and indistinct in character. The band is interesting rather than involving or strong-voiced. Dodgion is in good form and has some strong ideas to air, but he never quite gets on top of challenging themes and arrangements, and too often seems to go for obvious ideas and quirky sound, rather than a well-constructed statement.

****** Third Plane**

Original Jazz Classics OJCCD 754 *Carter; Herbie Hancock (p); Tony Williams (d).* 7/77.

A killer band, and easily Carter's most impressive showing under his own name. There is a good deal of solo bass material, as one would expect, but all of it makes sense in context and is so well constructed and executed that it never palls. Commercial pressures being what they were, it wasn't easy for players of Hancock's and Williams's generation to make an acoustic piano record in 1978. Williams doesn't quite get the point and he thrashes about at inopportune moments, but Carter's big gloopy fills on 'Stella By Starlight' and Hancock's 'Dolphin Dance' are absolutely perfect for the job.

***** Uptown Conversation**

Embryo/Rhino 7567 81955 *Carter; Hubert Laws (f); Herbie Hancock (p); Sam Brown (g); Billy Cobham, Grady Tate (d).* 10/69.

A rather odd record, alternating cheesy jazz funk with some brilliant solo bass interludes (indexed but not listed or titled). Laws seems more in place here, and on the long 'Half A Row' and 'Little Waltz' the components of Carter's curiously stretched sound-world start to make sense at last. Produced by Herbie Mann, which may explain why the flute sound is so good, the record has a bright, spacious quality that one didn't often get from Carter. The reissue has been filled out with alternative takes which add little or nothing to the original release.

***** New York Slick**

Original Jazz Classics OJC 916 *Carter; Art Farmer (flhn); J. J. Johnson (tb); Hubert Laws (f); Kenny Barron (p); Jay Berliner (g); Billy Cobham (d); Ralph McDonald (perc).* 12/79.

***** Patrão**

Original Jazz Classics OJCCD 778 *Carter; Chet Baker (t); Amaury Tristao (g); Aloisio Aguiar, Kenny Barron (p); Jack DeJohnette, Edison Machado (d); Nana Vasconcelos (perc).* 5/80.

Smooth, sweet, but not cloying, and not really all that 'slick', either: the 1979 session doesn't exactly have the constituents breaking sweat, but the pleasure of having such a line-up is something that Carter clearly delighted in, and if the results are still on the predictable side it's a handsome effort.

Three tracks featuring just Baker, Carter, Kenny Barron and Jack DeJohnette stand out head and shoulders from the rest on the slightly wet and uninspired *Patrão*. None of the *norteamericanos* (Barron here and there excepted) sounds at ease with the basic idiom and a good deal of the scene-setting is discursive and flat. The trumpeter was playing well around this time, whatever else was going on in his life, and he turns in a couple of beautifully weighted and crafted solos. Barron is rock steady and never less than convincing, but he has been mixed very oddly, with what sounds like a lot of compression, which isn't the case with the other musicians.

*****(*) Telepathy**
Concord CCD 4963 2CD *Carter; Jim Hall (g).* 11/82, 8/84.

Carter's bass is unmistakably a string instrument. He made that clear on his fruitful collaboration with the Kronos Quartet, and he does again on these fine duos with guitarist Hall, which were originally released as two albums, *Live At Village West* and *Telephone*. The sound on the live disc leaves something to be desired, but there are excellent performances of 'All The Things You Are', 'Embraceable You', 'Bags' Groove', 'Baubles, Bangles And Beads' and Sonny Rollins's calypso, 'St Thomas'. Carter's statement on 'Bags' Groove' is one of his best on record, a beautifully shaped and meltingly expressive solo that avoids all the clichés that have attached to the tune. Hall is perhaps heard to better advantage on the studio album, which highlights his unobtrusive and pitch-perfect accompaniment. The mix is pristine and so are the performances, and no surprise that the key track is that old duo standard, 'Alone Together'.

***** The Bass And I**
Blue Note 59698 *Carter; Stephen Scott (p); Lewis Nash (d); Steve Kroon (perc).* 97.

This was the album that set the pace for a flurry of sophisticated Blue Note sessions from Carter. It's the only one of the sequence that is standards-based, which somehow restricts its individuality. On 'You And The Night And The Music', 'Someday My Prince Will Come' and 'The Shadow Of Your Smile' one might be listening to A. N. Other and his All Stars, but then comes a flash of real insight and originality, as in the three subtly multi-dimensional originals which lift the record out of the ordinary. Scott was still finding his feet and there were to be other drummers over the next couple of years, but Steve Kroon booked his place in Ron's working outfit and delivered from the off.

***** Orfeu**
Blue Note 22490 *Carter; Houston Person (ts); Stephen Scott (p); Bill Frisell (g); Payton Crossley (d); Steve Kroon (perc).* 99.

***** When Skies Are Grey**
Blue Note 30754 *Carter; Stephen Scott (p); Harvey Mason Sr (d); Steve Kroon (perc).* 5/00.

Carter's affection for Latin rhythms has never been more clearly expressed than on these recent Blue Notes. *Orfeu* offered up a slightly unexpected personnel, but Person and Frisell meld beautifully. One of the highlights is Carter's arrangement of Dvořák's 'New World' *largo*, here known as 'Goin' Home'. It and the preceding 'Por-Do-Sol' are the key to an elegantly crafted record.

The later set is no less gentle and unassuming, but its occasionally soporific mood camouflages some formidable playing from all concerned. Mason and Kroon mesh beautifully on 'Besame Mucho' and Jobim's 'Corcovado', but the real star of the session is Stephen Scott, whose recording career seemed briefly eclipsed when he left Verve. He's found a niche with Carter. The big man's material clearly appeals and Stephen contributes strong, lyrical choruses to 'Loose Change', 'Caminando' and the formidable closer, 'Mi Tiempo'. Lovely sound.

*****(*) Stardust**
Blue Note 37813 *Carter; Benny Golson (ts); Sir Roland Hanna (p); Joe Locke (vib); Lenny White (d).* 4/01.

The title-track is a lovely duet with Roland Hanna, who is in exceptional form throughout this delightful set. The main theme seems to be the legacy of fellow-bassist Oscar Pettiford. Three of OP's tunes are included, the lazily swinging, latinized 'Tamalpais', the boppish 'Bohemia After Dark', and the simple, endlessly reworkable 'Blues In The Closet'. Golson enjoys the straightforward lines and driving rhythm and Lenny White's drumming has a fresh contemporary feel that brings this session right up to date.

Carter's writing skills are as good as ever, though the best idea on the set is 'That's Deep', a contrefact on 'How Deep Is The Ocean?' He reaches for memories of Eric Dolphy on the blues-based 'Nearly' and swings easily through 'Tail Feathers'. Joe Locke is a vivid presence and when he drops out on 'The Man I Love', one immediately misses his bright, ringing lines.

****(*) Eight Plus**
Dreyfus 36705 *Carter; Carol Buck, Kermit Moore, Chase Morrison (clo); Leon Maleson (b); Lewis Nash (d).* 02.

A fascinating string project that sees Carter concentrate on the piccolo bass, leaving the lower end to the impressive Maleson. Unfortunately, the tonality is somewhat unvaried and the mixture of strings with a conventional rhythm section doesn't come off. One wonders why Ron wasn't happy to take the plunge with the three cellists and worry less about giving the album a more conventional swing metre. His writing is as limber and effective as ever and 'Little Waltz' and the more upbeat 'El Rompe Cabeza' stand out. However, while these might have worked as single tracks, here they are not much more than standouts on a rather one-dimensional record.

Dick Cary (1916–94)

PIANO, TRUMPET

Worked in New York from the early '40s, including stints with Louis Armstrong's All Stars, Jimmy Dorsey, Eddie Condon and Bobby Hackett. Moved to Los Angeles in 1959 and freelanced, with much involvement in rehearsal and with big bands for which he had a vast book of arrangements.

***** Dick Cary And His Tuesday Night Friends**
Arbors ARCD 19132 *Cary; Dick Forrest, Betty O'Hara, Bob Summers (t); Dick Hamilton, Barrett O'Hara, Ernie Tack (tb); Lee Callett, Fred Cooper, Terry Harrington, Abe Most, Tommy Newsom (reeds); Dave Koonse (g); Herb Mickman (b); Gene Estes, Jerry McKenzie (d).* 5–8/93.

A charming discovery. Dick Cary is best remembered as a Condonite and member of Armstrong's All Stars, but he wrote a vast number of arrangements for numerous bands, and his house in Sunland, California, was in his final years a favourite haunt of this rehearsal band. Some of their informal sessions are set down here. There are 14 of Cary's arrangements; dedicated to friends, dogs and streets, they're a wryly ingenious lot, not so much quirky as full of unexpected turns, shafts of light, surprising chords. The band is full of professionals who obviously loved the music, and though every one is a first take and not meant for posterity, there are few fluffs or wrong steps. This sound is home-made too, but that doesn't stop the beauty of 'Bud', 'Henry' or 'Vallen's Waltz' coming through. Think of a gentle West Coast outfit spirited from the '50s to the '90s, and you're some of the way there.

****** Got Swing?**
Arbors ARCD 19253 *Dick Hamilton (t, alto hn, p); Jack Trott (t); Dave Ryan (tb); Ernie Tack (btb); Abe Most (cl); Phil Feather (ss, ts, cl); Terry Harrington (ts); Fred Cooper (bs, f); Dave Koonse, Barry Copper (g); Herb Mickman (b); Jerry White (d).* 4/00.

The man is gone, but the band lives on. Cary's Tuesday Night Gang was brought together for what's effectively a studio re-creation of his rehearsal band (with the chairs set round as they would have been at one of Dick's get-togethers). They played another 19 Cary charts, mixing originals with covers, including plenty of Ellington. The whole thing is absolutely delightful – unpretentiously swinging, peppered with hot solos from the likes of Most and Feather, and this time caught in beautiful sound. For sheer playability this one's out of the top drawer.

Casa Loma Orchestra

GROUP

Formed by saxophonist Glen Gray, they played in New York from 1929 and recorded extensively in 1931–7. Gray fronted the band from 1940 and, although touring ceased around 1950, he continued to lead versions of the group on record.

****(*) Casa Loma Stomp**
Hep 1010 *Bobby Jones, Dub Shoffner, Joe Hostetter, Frankie Martinez (t); Pee Wee Hunt (tb, v); Billy Rauch (tb); Glen Gray (as); Pat Davis (as, ts); Les Arquette (cl, ts); Ray Eberle (as, cl); Howard Hall (p); Mel Jenssen (vn); Gene Gifford (g, bj); Stanley Dennis (b, tba); Tony Briglia (d); Jack Richmond (v).* 10/29–12/30.

***** Maniac's Ball**
Hep 1051 *As above, except add Grady Watts, Sonny Dunham, Frank Zullo (t), Fritz Hummel (tb), Art Ralston (as, ob, bsn), Clarence Hutchenrider (cl, as), Kenny Sargent (as, v), Jack Blanchette (g); omit Martinez, Arquette.* 3/31–2/37.

Glen Gray led this band, originally formed from a group called the Orange Blossoms, and they have a rather odd place in the music's history. The early records sound like no more than competent dance-band fare, although something peculiar happens halfway through a very stodgy 'Happy Days Are Here Again' (the third title on disc one) when it suddenly bursts into a hot performance fired up by Hunt's trombone. Most of the tracks on *Casa Loma Stomp* are pretty uneventful, but there are some exceptions: 'San Sue Strut' seems to be twice as fast as anything else here, and the signature title-tune is at least a fair display of early white swing. But it's the second disc, *Maniac's Ball*, which has all the famous Casa Loma music: Gene Gifford's charts for 'White Jazz', 'Black Jazz' and 'Maniac's Ball' design the orchestra as a precision-driven locomotive, riffs piling one over another, the tempos mercurial yet uncomfortably stiff. If it was Gifford's idea of jazz, it seemed an awkward transition between old-style hot music, the functional dance bands and the swing orchestras that were about to emerge. Aside from Hunt, a genuine personality, the soloists lacked much individuality and the reed-players seem especially unremarkable. There's something exhilarating about their assault on 'Put On Your Old Grey Bonnet', but by the time of their second version of 'Royal Garden Blues' the band sounds anonymous. Larry Clinton took over from Gifford and his 'A Study In Brown' is the farewell track here: it led nowhere. Scholars should welcome these Hep compilations, handsomely prepared and mastered, but the story is not a fascinating one.

Castle Jazz Band

GROUP

West Coast revivalists of long standing, the original band dating back to the early '50s, later line-ups under the direction of Ernie Carson.

**** The Famous Castle Jazz Band**
Good Time Jazz GTCD 10030-2 *Don Kinch (t); George Bruns (tb); Bob Gilbert (cl); Freddie Crews (p); Monte Ballou (bj, v); Bob Short (tba); Homer Welch (d).* 8/57.

**** Plays The Five Pennies**
Good Time Jazz GTCD 10037-2 *As above.* 59.

Stragglers from the Lu Watters-inspired revival of the '40s, these traditionalists re-formed for the purposes of these dates. It might have appeased their original fans, but the music sounds like second-hand revivalism today, and the players perform with a rather gauche humour in their delivery. There is one rarity on the first album in 'I've Been Floating Down The Old Green River', but everything else has been done better elsewhere, both before and since. Covering the Five Pennies, the Red Nichols band which by then was covering itself anyway, was a singularly unpromising idea.

Philip Catherine (born 1942)

GUITAR, ELECTRIC GUITAR, GUITAR SYNTHESIZER

Catherine is of mixed English/Belgian parentage. His first guitar influence, apart from the unavoidable Django Reinhardt, was the brilliant Belgian René Thomas (who died prematurely in 1975), but he was quick to respond to the jazz-rock techniques of both John McLaughlin and Larry Coryell. He has a limpid but by no means languid style, still with strong tinges of Django's easy swing.

*****(*) I Remember You**
Criss Cross 1048 *Catherine; Tom Harrell (flhn); Hein Van de Geyn (b).* 10/90.

*****(*) Moods: Volume 1**
Criss Cross 1060 *As above, except add Michael Herr (ky).* 5/92.

***** Moods: Volume 2**
Criss Cross 1061 *As above.* 5/92.

Recorded as a tribute to the late Chet Baker, *I Remember You* reunites the line-up that made *Chet's Choice* for Criss Cross in

1985, with Tom Harrell's floating melancholic flugelhorn steering dangerously close to Baker's weary, self-denying diction. Harrell contributes two fine originals – the softly swinging 'From This Time, From That Time' and 'Songflower' – Van de Geyn one and Catherine two. The opening 'Nardis' serves as an unintended farewell to Miles. Hank Mobley's 'Funk In Deep Freeze' and the closing 'Blues For G.T.' are slightly unexpected in this context but, drummerless, take on the same slightly enervated quality that is raised only by Catherine's astonishingly accurate rhythm guitar. 'My Funny Valentine'? Well, yes, of course; they could hardly have got away without it. Harrell's statement and subsequent solo are pretty much in the Baker vein, and again it's the guitarist who lifts the performance a notch, using his pedals imaginatively. A beautiful album.

Attractive as they are in many regards, one wonders whether the *Moods* sessions really yielded enough for two full-length discs. As the title doubtless unconsciously hints, there is just a crickle of suspicion that Catherine is drifting towards an elegantly jazzy mood-music. The three interesting tracks on *Volume 2*, significantly, are the Tom Harrell compositions whose rather deprecating titles, 'The Waltz' and 'Twenty Bar Tune', disguise a considerable expenditure of imaginative effort.

*** Live

Dreyfus 36587 *Catherine; Bert Van den Brink (p, ky); Hein Van de Geyn (b); Hans Van Oosterhout (d).* 3/96.

A long and delightfully uncomplicated set from the guitarist and his Dutch quartet, *Live* almost feels like a career summation, with superb versions of 'René Thomas', 'Mingus In The Sky', Hermeto Pascoal's 'Nem Um Talvez', Miles's blues 'Freddie Freeloader', and 'Stella By Starlight'. Catherine's guitar-sound has changed little over the years, but outside the studio it inevitably has a more spiny and percussive quality, and it suits him very well. His solos are immaculately shaped and always expressive. Our own reservation concerns the group. Van de Geyn is a hugely gifted player and brings the same qualities Catherine found in NHOP. The other three, though, sound slightly plodding in comparison.

*** Guitar Groove

Dreyfus 36599 *Catherine; Alphonso Johnson (b); Rodney Holmes (d).* 99.

This is an unusually straightahead trio for Catherine, and it's mostly very convincing. Apart from 'Stardust', all the compositions are by Catherine, some of them evident reworkings of past themes and ideas, many of them written in an upbeat and deliberate style. 'Merci Afrique' and 'Guitar Groove' will be a revelation to anyone who thinks they have Catherine stereotyped as a dreamy impressionist. Holmes and Johnson offer solid if unspectacular support, but the light falls squarely on the guitarist throughout.

***(*) Blue Prince

Dreyfus 36614 *Catherine; Bert Joris (t, bugle); Hein Van de Geyn (b); Hans Van Oosterhout (d).* 6/00.

After the quiet and occasional longueurs of some of the recent albums, this one goes off a storm, kicking in with 'Coffee Groove' and an unexpectedly progressive/fusion sound to the leader's guitar. Much of the set is bop-influenced, as one might expect, but there is little Django in evidence. On 'Global Warming', which comes second in the running order and really defines the shape of the album, Catherine seems to be looking for a much darker and more sombre coloration. Joris and Van de Geyn are extremely able accompanists, but Van Oosterhout doesn't seem to have bought into the idiom and sounds curiously old-fashioned and square.

*** Summer Night

Dreyfus Jazz FDM 36637 2 *Catherine; Bert Joris (t); Philippe Aerts (b); Joost Van Schaik (d).* 5/02.

Again, Joris is an important part of the formula and he and Catherine exchange some interesting ideas on 'Time After Time'. The problem with this record is that it is too bitty and eclectic to cohere. There are moments, as on 'Janet', when Philip returns to something like a jazz-rock idiom, while some of his straight jazz playing, on 'Round About Midnight' for instance, is rather flat and uninflected. On a single track, 'Gilles Et Mirona', he explores double tracking in a 'solo' outing and it's odd – though possibly encouraging for the guitarist – that this is the most compelling thing on the album. Despite the resolutely unswinging Schaik, the jazz component is perhaps higher than usual this time round, but Catherine still seems ambivalent about the idiom and seems to mistake volume and intensity for real improvisational content.

Sid Catlett (1910–51)

DRUMS

Born in Evansville, Indiana, Catlett became a great New York drummer. He worked with Henderson, Goodman, Redman and Armstrong, and eventually joined Armstrong's All Stars in 1947. He took bebop rhythm in his stride. Much loved by other musicians, he became ill at the end of the '40s and died after collapsing at a concert in Chicago.

***(*) Sid Catlett 1944–1946

Classics 974 *Catlett; Charlie Shavers, Joe Guy, Gerald Wilson (t); Barney Bigard, Edmond Hall (cl); Bull Moose Jackson, Willie Smith (as); Eddie 'Lockjaw' Davis, Illinois Jacquet, Frank Socolow, Ben Webster (ts); Art Tatum, Marlowe Morris, Eddie Heywood, Horace Henderson, Pete Johnson (p); Bill Gooden (org); Al Casey, Jimmy Shirley (g); Oscar Pettiford, John Simmons, Gene Ramey (b).* 1/44–46.

Catlett's reputation has increased in recent years with the re-evaluation of many of the swing-era giants, and he will be remembered as one of the great jazz drummers. Dead of a heart attack at 41, his legacy is comparatively small, but he was a complete master of drums and cymbals whose virtuoso technique was unflashy and skilful. He seldom drew attention to himself yet played with fabulous panache and dominated his groups without seeming to overwhelm them. This hotchpotch of small-band dates – for V-Disc, Commodore, Session, Delta, Regis, Capitol and Manor – is fascinating. Most of them were under his nominal leadership. The opening 'Rose Room' is from a V-Disc jam session and is virtually a duet with Barney Bigard, an extraordinary display that brings out the best in each man. Six quartet tracks with Ben Webster and Marlowe Morris are similarly electric, and five more with horns including Shavers, Hall and Socolow, though indifferently recorded, include some splendid moments. The next five sessions are a mixed lot and have rather less interest, but for its first half the CD is close to indispensable. Catlett's mercurial style, with cymbal playing that glistens even through the unsatisfactory recording, unexpected rimshot fusillades and the most detailed snare rhythms, was one of the few swing-based methods that didn't sound passé in the bebop era.

Oscar 'Papa' Celestin (1884–1954)

CORNET, VOCAL

Celestin was in all the early major New Orleans bands, eventually leading the Tuxedo Brass Band in the 1910s. He led some of the few New Orleans recording dates in the '20s but more or less retired in the '30s, coming back to great success in the revival of the late '40s.

♛ ** Papa Celestin & Sam Morgan**

Azure AZ-CD-12 *Celestin; Louis 'Kid Shots' Madison, Ricard Alexis, George McCullum, Guy Kelly (c); Williams Ridgley, August Rousseau, William Matthews, Ernest Kelly (tb); Willard Thoumy, Paul 'Polo' Barnes, Earl Pierson, Sid Carriere, Clarence Hall, Oliver Alcorn (reeds); Manual Manetta, Jeanette Salvant (p); John Marrero, Narvin Kimball (bj); Simon Marrero (b, bb); Abby Foster, Josiah Frazier (d); Charles Gills, Ferdinand Joseph (v).* 1/25–12/28.

Little enough music was actually recorded in New Orleans in the '20s to make any surviving tracks valuable. But the sessions led by Celestin and Morgan (the latter dealt with under his own entry) would be remarkable anyway. Despite the importing of devices from dance-band trends elsewhere, particularly in the later tracks, they really sound like no other jazz of the period. The first three tracks are by the Original Tuxedo Jazz Orchestra, with Madison and Celestin as the front line, and the deliriously exciting 'Original Tuxedo Rag' is a blazing fusion of ragtime, jazz and dance music that makes one ache to hear the band as it might have sounded live. The 13 subsequent titles from 1926–8 are less frantic and are occasionally troubled by the mannerisms of the day, weak vocals in particular. But the reed sections manage their curious blend of sentimentality and shrewd, hot playing – a New Orleans characteristic – with surprising finesse; the ensembles are consistently driving, and the two-cornet leads are frequently as subtle and well ordered as those of King Oliver's band. Celestin himself, a great veteran of the city's music even then, has been undervalued as a soloist: he plays very well on 'My Josephine' and the superb slow piece, 'It's Jam Up'. Taken together with the equally fine Sam Morgan tracks, we rate this as a five-star record, especially given the outstandingly clear and powerful remastering.

***** The 1950s Radio Broadcasts**

Arhoolie CD 7024 *Celestin; Bill Matthews (tb); Alphonse Picou (cl); Octave Crosby (p, v); Ricard Alexis (b, v); Christopher 'Black Happy' Goldston (d).* 7/50–6/51.

These are valuable reminders that Celestin continued to be a force in New Orleans jazz many years after the seminal tracks listed above. Although a car accident and spells of ill-health made his appearances erratic in the '40s, Papa was leading this band regularly on radio in the early '50s, and these surviving airshots show how spirited and uplifting their take on the tradition was. The most surprising thing is how vigorous and hard-knuckled the rhythm section are, especially when one is used to the fairly genteel pulse adopted by most NO revivalists. Mathews is boisterous in the Ory tradition, Picou has some nice moments and Celestin himself obviously enjoys his Indian summer. The sound is boxy and flat, as one might expect from the source material, but collectors will know what to expect.

Celestrial Communication Orchestra

IMPROVISING ENSEMBLE

Founded and led by bassist Alan Silva (see separate entry), this is one of the most durable free improvisation collectives still at work. There is no misprint in the heading to this.

***** Luna Surface**

Sunspot 539*Silva; Bernard Vitet (t, frhn); Grachan Moncur III (tb); Archie Shepp (as); Anthony Braxton (ss, as); Kenneth Terroade (ts); Dave Burrell (p); Leroy Jenkins (vn, vla); Malachi Favors, Beb Guerin (b); Claude Delcloo (d).* 8/69.

***** Alan Silva & The Celestrial Communication Orchestra**

Sunspot 529 2CD *Silva; Bernard Vitet (t, frhn); Alan Shorter (t); Joseph Jarman (sax, f, bsn); Steve Lacy (ss); Ronnie Beer (ss, ts, f); Roscoe Mitchell (sax, f, ob); Robin Kenyatta (as, f); Michel Portal (as, cl); Dieter Gewissler (vn); Jouk Minor (vla); Kent Carter (clo); Irène Aëbi (clo, cel); Dave Burrell, Bobby Few, Joachim Kühn (p); Malachi Favors, Beb Guerin (b); Famoudou Don Moye, Joseph Cooper, Oliver Johnson (d, perc).* 12/70.

An early incarnation of the Orchestra, featuring familiar American avant-gardists and some less well-known free players. Despite some heavyweight saxophone talent, the dominant sound here is that of strings. Silva himself plays both bass and violin, bowing the latter instrument upright as if it were a cello or double bass. Jenkins does his usual scratch-and-wail stuff, and that's not to belittle the dramatic sound he makes. There's not much obvious form to 'From The Luna Surface', the only piece, so if you like your free jazz very free indeed it's a great delight. Otherwise, it'll be a mystifying period piece. The other CCO disc was recorded in Paris just after Christmas 1970 and originally released on BYG Actuel. The cast is somewhat different but the sound-world is immediately identifiable with an emphasis on string sounds and long drones.

***** HR 57 I**

Eremite MTE 039 *Roy Campbell, Baikida Carroll (t, flhn); Itaru Oki (t, oki t); Johannes Bauer, Joseph Bowie, Steve Swell (tb); William Lowe (btb, tba); Joe Daley (tba, thn); Marshall Allen (as, f, EWI); Kidd Jordan (ts); Sabeer Mateen (as, ts, cl, f); Francis Wong (ts, f); J. D. Parran (bs, cl, wooden f); Daniel Carter (as, ts, cl, f, t) Oluyemi Thomas (Cmel, bcl, wooden f); Karen Borca (bsn); Bobby Few (p); Wilber Morris, William Parker (b); Jackson Krall, Warren Smith (d, perc); Ijeoma Thomas (v); Alan Silva (cond, syn).* 5/01.

***** HR 57 II**

Eremite MTE 040 *As above.* 5/01.

***** HR 57 III**

Eremite MTE 041 *As above.* 5/01.

***** HR 57 IV**

Eremite MTE 042 *As above.* 5/01.

(****) HR57 Treasure Box

Eremite no number *As above.* 5/01.

These remarkable albums were recorded over two concerts in May 2001 at the Uncool Festival in Poschiavo, Switzerland. The odd title refers to a 1987 House of Representatives resolution introduced by congressman John Conyers Jr of Michigan 'respecting the designation of jazz as a rare and valuable national American treasure'. The text of the resolution is performed in both concerts by Ijeoma Thomas and establishes a utopian context for these large-scale improvisations.

Silva assembled his orchestra well before the concerts to allow rehearsal time as well as personal space for the members to interact. A measure of the chemistry so developed is the 26½-minute 'Soon' on disc four of the series; this was a spontaneously composed and harmonized composition, and the only non-improvised element of these performances. All the rest were led and conducted live by Silva, who also played synthesizer. His gestures and body movements direct every parameter of the music: pitch, dynamics, tempo and the density of sound. Suffice it to say that with so many players of this temperament, the sound is very dense indeed. These, though, are much better representations of the Orchestra's potential than past recordings. Silva effectively disbanded CCO in 1989 to concentrate on other projects. His Eremite recordings with the Sound Visions Orchestra (see under Silva entry) was a return to this kind of work and clearly reawakened the bassist's interest in such projects.

The ensemble includes musicians who have been closely associated with the leader in other formations: Bobby Few was a member of Center Of The World (a quartet which also numbered Frank Wright and Muhammad Ali); Johannes Bauer had played with the bassist in Traditions; Kidd Jordan knew him from the TTT ensemble; Marshall Allen was a friend from Sun Ra days. Raphe Malik was ill and was replaced by Itaru Oki. Such close associations paid dividends.

Describing the music is almost impossible. So large are the sections of *HR 57* in its various incarnations that any generalization is impossible, but the sound has a strong, almost primitive quality which perhaps recalls Silva's association with Albert Ayler in his later days. The pun on 'celestial' and 'terrestrial' in the ensemble's name is telling; this is not entirely earthly fare, but it is not floating 'space' music either. However, just as Sun Ra learned a great deal from his association with Fletcher Henderson, so Silva isn't so very far from the great bandleaders of a later generation. If one can imagine the Albert Ayler group guesting with the Stan Kenton band, that isn't so very far from the reality. We have found these fascinating sets aurally 'difficult', sometimes frustrating, but packed with moments of majestic power and even a certain frail beauty. As an assertion of jazz's authority and position in American culture, these four hours of music are unequalled, though some may find the whole package a hefty outlay.

An astonishingly beautiful object, even leaving aside the music inside, each copy of the strictly limited *Treasure Box* is unique. All 383 copies are hand-painted, making them instantly collectable artefacts as well as documents of some of the most powerful free music around.

Andrea Centazzo

DRUMS AND PERCUSSION

An Italian drummer-percussionist heavily involved in the free-music scene of the '70s, documenting much music via his Ictus LP label.

***** Trio Live**
New Tone 5027-2 *Centazzo; Steve Lacy (ss); Kent Carter (b).* 12/76.

***** Drops**
New Tone 5037-2 *Centazzo; Derek Bailey (g).* 4/77.

***** Real Time**
New Tone 5029-2 *Centazzo; Evan Parker (ss, ts); Alvin Curran (p, t, syn).* 12/77.

***** Environment For Sextet**
New Tone 5026-2 *Centazzo; Toshinori Kondo (t); John Zorn (reeds); Tom Cora (clo); Polly Bradfield (vn); Eugene Chadbourne (g).* 11/78.

***** USA Concerts West**
New Tone 5028-2 *Centazzo; Vinny Golia (reeds); John Carter (cl); Greg Goodman (p).* 12/78–7/79.

***** The Bay**
New Tone 5037-2 *Centazzo; Bruce Ackley (ss, cl); Jon Raskin (as, cl); Andrew Voigt (ss, as, f); Larry Ochs (ts, as).* 12/78.

These reissues will be a nostalgic reminder for many collectors of the improvised music scene of the '70s. Documented on tiny labels, it was a frail but hardy outcropping which survived in the smallest margin of the industry. Ictus was a label owned and run by percussionist Andrea Centazzo, and he managed to get out a small string of releases in the late '70s which all feature him in various instrumental combinations. Centazzo himself has largely disappeared from recording, but these CDs resuscitate his original efforts. None of them is exactly outstanding from a purely musical point of view, but they're as relevant to their scene as any bunch of Blue Notes or Riversides. Centazzo persuaded many a leading light from the free-playing pantheon to perform with him, and the results chart an episodic adventure in the form. *Trio Live* is a decent Lacy gig from the period – three chunks of his favourite 'The Way', plus a particularly thorny treatment of 'Ducks' – at which Centazzo seems a bit of a bystander. *Drops* has him duelling with Bailey in his most snapping form, although the guitarist seems to go his own way for the most part. *Real Time* is a surprising triologue with Parker and Curran, in which the participants cover some scratchy sonic ground, with analogue synthesizer, saxes and percussion in a sometimes exhilarating muddle. *Environment For Sextet* brings together six free spirits in another rather cloudy situation, emphasizing that the principal difficulty with most of these records is the poor fidelity. Centazzo seems to have favoured a high top end and little bass, which gives his drums a hissing, glassy quality and undercuts many of the textures. This is still a valuable if sometimes naïve glimpse of Zorn, Chadbourne and Co. in their early days, although – then as now – it's Kondo who sounds the most liberated and radical voice. *The Bay* performs a similar function for ROVA, whose other early discs have yet to make it to CD. Centazzo himself still sounds like a kibitzer on his own date, though.

Arguably the most interesting of the six discs is the one offering previously unreleased material, *USA Concerts*. The lengthy duet with Goodman is a disappointing mess, but the piece with Golia and Carter is wonderful. The clarinettist dominates a beautiful improvisation, including a long solo clarinet passage, and the three musicians find a genuine empathy. Centazzo himself does little on any of the discs to suggest that he was any kind of major voice. Perhaps he is more of an Eddie Condon type, a great organizer but a comparatively insignificant contributor in purely instrumental terms.

*****(*) Shock!!**
New Tone RDC 5043-2 *Centazzo; Gianluigi Trovesi (ss, as, bcl, picc cl).* 1/84.

Of a slightly later vintage than the discs listed above, this is a better-recorded and notably vivid encounter. Trovesi and Centazzo had already worked extensively together in the Mitteleuropa Orchestra. The opening title-track is not really so shocking; it's a joyful ride, with soprano sax racing over the drummer's almost conventional kit rhythms. Much of the playing works to preordained structures, such as the march of 'Tro.Ce', and the extraordinary sound of the bass clarinet over lumbering marimba figures in 'A Day In Tunisia'. A strikingly intense set which clearly benefited from pre-match preparation.

Henri Chaix (born 1925)

PIANO

A leading member of the Swiss jazz movement in post-war years, Chaix is a dedicated mainstream pianist whose home-grown recordings have rarely reached a wider audience. He occasionally plays trombone.

***** Jumpin' Punkins**
Sackville SKCD2-2020 *Chaix; Alain Du Bois (b); Romano Cavicchiolo (d).* 10/90.

***** Jive At Five**
Sackville SKCD2-2035 *As above.* 8/93.

***** Just Friends**
Sackville SKCD 2048 *As above.* 4/98.

'A listener could close his eyes and never believe that this is a Swiss playing in Geneva' – thus did Rex Stewart commend Henri Chaix's playing in 1967. Chaix became Switzerland's mainstream leader in the '40s, and he backed many American visitors. But his own circumstances have seldom taken him to international audiences. *Jumpin' Punkins* finds him in vigorous form, touching few intensities but taking a satisfyingly personal route through jazz-piano tradition. His favourite manner is a medium-tempo stride, a variation which is faithful to James P. Johnson's methods, and he makes 'Yesterdays' and 'All God's Chillun Got Rhythm' into believable stride vehicles. Yet his unassumingly romantic treatment of 'Ruby My Dear' suggests that more demanding jazz material holds few terrors for him. Du Bois and Cavicchiolo stay out of his way, and the recording pays handsome regard to the Bösendorfer piano.

Jive At Five is no more and no less than a second helping, three years on. The material is more mainstream than ever, and one could wish that Chaix would look around for one or two more interesting tunes. But this is his style and he's right at home in it. The trio lasted for 30 years and was brought to an end only when Du Bois died shortly after *Just Friends* was recorded. It's another attractive set, though by no means an advance on the previous two. Chaix had his style of playing and had presumably no career ambitions left to exercise.

Serge Chaloff (1923–57)

BARITONE SAXOPHONE

Worked with several big bands before an important spell with Woody Herman, 1947–9. Based himself in his home town of Boston in the '50s, but contracted spinal paralysis which eventually killed him. One of the few baritone men to make a go of bop, his few own-name records are marginalized classics.

*****(*) We The People Bop: Serge Chaloff Memorial**
Cool & Blue C&B CD 102 *Chaloff; Sonny Berman, Miles Davis, Gait Preddy, Red Rodney (t); Ernie Royal (t, v); Mert Goodspeed, Bennie Green, Bill Harris, Earl Swope (tb); Woody Herman (cl, v); Charlie Mariano (as); Al Cohn, Allen Eager, Flip Phillips, Sonny Stitt (ts); Al Haig, Ralph Burns, Barbara Carroll, Lou Levy, Bud Powell, George Wallington (p); Terry Gibbs (vib); Artie Bernstein, Chubby Jackson, Oscar Pettiford, Curley Russell, Frank Vaccaro, Chuck Wayne (b); Denzil Best, Tiny Khan, Don Lamond, Max Roach, Pete DeRosa (d).* 9/46–12/49.

***** The Fable Of Mabel**
1201 Records 9003 *Chaloff; Nick Capazuto, Herb Pomeroy (t); Gene DiStachio (tb); Charlie Mariano, Boots Mussulli (as); Varty Haritounian (ts); Russ Freeman, Richard Twardzik (p); Ray Oliver, Jimmy Woode (b); Buzzy Drootin, Jimmy Zitano (d).* 6 & 9/54.

Hugely talented, but the career was riven by personal problems, and the end was dreadful. Chaloff's approach to the unwieldy baritone was restrained rather than virtuosic (the result of an extended apprenticeship with Jimmy Dorsey, Georgie Auld and Woody Herman) and concentrated on the distinctive timbre of the instrument rather than on outpacing all opposition. Nevertheless, he was an agile improviser who could suddenly transform a sleepy-sounding phrase with a single overblown note.

Chaloff's work has never been easy to find, although those who invested in Mosaic's edition can permit themselves a self-satisfied smile. Two takes of his famous 'Blue Serge' are included on the memorial record, which contains a good selection of Chaloff in the studio and on stage, over some of his most productive years. Some effort has been made to ferret out tracks that feature him strongly, such as 'Serge's Urge' with Red Rodney, and one comes away with a surprisingly clear sense of his stormy musical personality.

The Fable Of Mable has been in and out of circulation over the lifetime of this book. Hearing these tracks afresh prompts no fresh assessment of Chaloff's position but confirms what a fine player he could be. There are two sessions here, one under the leadership of Mussulli, with Russ Freeman in the band and a later nonet session led by Serge himself. The latter includes no fewer than five alternate takes, including three takes of the title-tune which was written by eccentric pianist Richard Twardzik, who's usually described as the composer of 'Yellow Waltz', as if that were the only thing of note he ever did. Those familiar with the Black Lion release of this will be delighted with the extra material.

CORE COLLECTION

****** Blue Serge**
Capitol 94505 *Chaloff; Sonny Clark (p); Leroy Vinnegar (b); Philly Joe Jones (d).* 3/56.

Happily, this classic is still around. Chaloff's masterpiece is both vigorous and moving, not for the knowledge that he was so near to his own death but for the unsentimental rigour of the playing. 'Thanks For The Memory' is overpoweringly beautiful as Chaloff creates a series of melodic variations which match the improviser's ideal of fashioning an entirely

new song. 'Stairway To The Stars' is almost as fine, and the thoughtful 'The Goof And I' and 'Susie's Blues' show that Chaloff still had plenty of ideas about what could be done with a bebopper's basic materials. This important session has retained all its power.

Dennis Chambers (born 1960)

DRUMS

Chambers is an in-demand drummer whose most comfortable range is powerful jazz-fusion of a sort pioneered by Billy Cobham and Alphonse Mouzon.

*** Outbreak

ESC 03682 2 *Chambers; Randy Brecker, Jim Hynes (t); Michael Davis (tb); Aaron Heick (as, ts); Michael Brecker (ts); Bob Malach (ts, bsx); Jim Beard (ky); John Herington, Nick Moroch (g); Dean Brown (g, b); Rodney Skeet Curtis, Matthew Garrison, Will Lee, Gary Willis (b); Danny Sadownick, Arto Tuncboyaciyan (perc).* 2–4/02.

Misleadingly billed as Chambers's debut, this actually comes a decade after his first effort as a leader. *Getting Even*, which may still be available as an import CD, featured Dennis in a funky fusion setting alongside old employers John Scofield, Mike Stern and the late Bob Berg. Keyboard man Jim Beard was also on hand to help with arrangements, as he does here. Chambers isn't either a confident composer or indeed a soloist of Billy Cobham's quality. His role is to drive the music along, whether it's a Sly Stone tune ('In Time') or the Cobham-like 'Groovus Interruptus', which is irrepressibly jolly but also contains some of the most imaginative drumming on the set.

Beard is again the major influence on the sound, mixing small-group tracks with larger arrangements. The album begins with a roar on 'Roll Call', which features some vintage playing from the Breckers. Michael is the star turn on the title-track as well, a wild, wailing sound that builds the excitement steadily. A decade on from *Getting Even*, it's hard to judge whether or how Chambers has developed as a leader. He's certainly much subtler and much more relaxed as a performer. A confident sophomore release.

Joe Chambers (born 1942)

DRUMS, VIBRAPHONE, MARIMBA

Studied and played in Washington, DC, in the early '60s, then moved to New York and played – and wrote – on a wide range of Blue Note and post-bop sessions. Though less often visible now, he's still occasionally sighted on record.

***(*) Phantom Of The City

Candid CCD 79517 *Chambers; Philip Harper (t); Bob Berg (ts); George Cables (p); Santi Debriano (b).* 3/91.

Joe Chambers has featured in post-bop jazz mostly as a drummer, but he is a gifted composer as well, and several of his earlier themes – particularly the four he wrote for Bobby Hutcherson's *Components* (Blue Note) – deserve to be better known than they are. He numbers Jimmy Giuffre as a crucial influence, and there's certainly a parallel between the thinking of both men regarding free and formal structures. That said, only two of the themes on this recent date are Chambers compositions: 'For Miles Davis', a serene yet vaguely ominous *in memoriam*, and the brighter 'Nuevo Mundo'. Chambers the drummer has become a thoughtful, interactive performer, seldom taking a driving-seat initiative and preferring a careful balancing of tonal weights and measures. He has a near-perfect band for his needs here: Berg's tenor is habitually analytical, Cables is a romantic with a terse streak of intelligence, and Harper's Berigan-like low notes and dryly spun lyricism – featured on an extended reading of 'You've Changed' – add further spice. The live recording, from New York's Birdland, is clear and full-bodied.

***(*) Mirrors

Blue Note 96685-2 *Chambers; Eddie Henderson (t); Vincent Herring (as, ts, ss); Mulgrew Miller (p); Ira Coleman (b).* 7/98.

Invited to do a one-off album for Blue Note's anniversary, this rather marginalized but intriguing figure came up with a project which seems to have its most obvious roots in his work with Bobby Hutcherson. Nowhere is this more evident than in 'Circles', which has him multi-tracking himself on drums and vibes to create a shimmering rhythmic and harmonic swirl that is the record's clear highlight. 'Tu-Way-Pock-E-Way' brings New Orleans to New York and 'Caravanserai' does the same thing for unspecified eastern modes. Henderson and Herring give the impression of being less well-travelled and here and there one could have wished for more worldly horn-players, but this is a pleasing entry for Chambers the composer and leader. His drumming remains exemplary.

*** Urban Grooves

441 FFO-0003 *Chambers; Gary Bartz (ss, as); Eric Reed (p, syn); Rufus Reid (b); Bobby Sanabria (perc).* 3/02.

Another unpredictable offering from the enigmatic Chambers. For a record called *Urban Grooves*, the music feels surprisingly dreamy and even pastoral at times. The leader contributes three originals, of which the ballad 'Irina' is the pick, and there are some curious pieces of repertory: Miles Davis's 'Sid's Ahead' remodelled with marimba, congas and synthesizer strokes, 'In A Sentimental Mood' set to an inappropriate slow shuffle. Bartz seems subdued, and some of the best music is in the trio tracks, especially a swinging 'Surrey With The Fringe On Top', where Reed shines.

Paul Chambers (1935–1969)

BASS

Raised in Detroit, Chambers began working as a prominent small-group sideman in 1954, and next year joined Miles Davis, staying until the end of 1962. Then with Wynton Kelly, and sundry other gigs. Narcotics and other health problems led to his early death aged 33. A pioneer of individuality in bass after bebop, Chambers was one of the first to assert a soloist's position on the instrument, as well as introducing arco playing and fashioning an ensemble role which was suitably oblique and modern for the new music.

*** Whims Of Chambers

Blue Note 37647-2 *Chambers; Donald Byrd (t); John Coltrane (ts); Horace Silver (p); Kenny Burrell (g); Philly Joe Jones (d).* 9/56.

Chambers led only a handful of record dates. These were early days to feature the bass in a spotlight role, and the session feels artificially showcased around his solo work. The *arco* passages may have been groundbreaking, but the tone still grates at times. That aside, it's a solid and sometimes sparky hard-bop date, and rather a forgotten item in the Coltrane discography at least; Trane charges at both 'Nita' and 'We Six' in his best 1956 form. But the star soloist overall is probably Burrell. Two other Blue Note albums, *Paul Chambers Quintet* and *Bass On Top*, will have to be sought out as Japanese reissues.

Thomas Chapin (1958–98)

ALTO SAXOPHONE, FLUTE, SOPRANO SAXOPHONE, MEZZO-SOPRANO SAXOPHONE, SOPRANINO SAXOPHONE

Thomas Chapin died of leukaemia aged just 40, but leaving behind a remarkably compressed and expressive body of music that now seems definitive of the New York downtown scene of the '90s. In his final couple of years, Chapin moved towards a more mainstream sound, but dabbling in the unfamiliar sounds of the mezzo-soprano saxophone, he always sounded fresh and radical.

***** Third Force**

Knitting Factory KFWCD 103 *Chapin; Mario Pavone (b); Steve Johns (d).* 11/90, 1/91.

***** Anima**

Knitting Factory KFWCD 121 *As above, except add Michael Sarin (d etc.).* 12/91.

Third Force is gruffer and in some respects less adventurous, adhering to a narrower groove, often trading on rather limited ideas. 'Ahab's Leg' is the strongest individual item, but the set as a whole works well cumulatively. The combination of Pavone and Johns boded well for future projects and, with the involvement of Michael Sarin, established the axis of what was to be Chapin's working group, polished and intuitive when they made a first visit to Europe in 1995.

Anima provides further live performances and offers three unwontedly stretched-out tracks on which the saxophonist solos at length, though with a minimum of actual development, ceding the foreground to the rhythm section for much of the time. Chapin's sound is ever more refined, and certainly by no means as blunt as formerly; but the Dolphy influence is still in place on both versions of 'Lift Off' and has allowed him to explore the limits of harmonic organization, while staying inside essentially jazz structures.

*****(*) Insomnia**

Knitting Factory KFWCD 132 *As above, except add Al Bryant, Frank London (t), Curtis Fowlkes, Peter McEachern (tb), Marcus Roja, Ray Stewart (tba).* 12/92.

***** I've Got Your Number**

Arabesque AJ 0110 *Chapin; Ronnie Mathews (p); Ray Drummond (b); Steve Johns (d); Louis Bauza (perc).* 1/93.

*****(*) You Don't Know Me**

Arabesque AJ 0115 *Chapin; Tom Harrell (t, flhn); Peter Madsen (p); Kyoto Fujiwara (b); Reggie Nicholson (d).* 8/94.

Chapin isn't usually as smoothly accommodating as on *I've Got Your Number*, and it makes one wonder whether he wouldn't have received wider recognition if he had stuck to a mainstream agenda. He sounds superficially like Richie Cole, but on Bud Powell's 'Time Waits' he reverts to a version of his Jackie McLean delivery. It's a most effective record, with a generally able band (though Ray Drummond must have had round shoulders by the end of the afternoon, having carried it throughout). It comes a bare month after the live project documented on *Insomnia*, where Chapin experiments with a larger group for the first time on disc. It's a jolly good record by any standard but, relative to the saxophonist's output, a rather important one, suggesting that he may yet develop into a significant mainstream/modern composer and arranger, full as it is of arresting ideas.

In a very real sense, *You Don't Know Me* is its logical sequel, a beautifully crafted set which finds Chapin at his most expressive and open-hearted. Interesting to hear him working outside the comfort zone of the Pavone/Johns/Sarin axis, and with a piano-player. Far from impeding him, it seems to have broadened his harmonic range considerably. Harrell is masterful, of course, and adapts surprisingly quickly to the opening sequence of numbers identified as 'Safari Notebook', on which Chapin moves into Sonny Fortune territory. The most sympathetic of the records to date though, as we have suggested, not necessarily the most representative or revealing.

*****(*) Menagerie Dreams**

Knitting Factory KFWCD 167 *Chapin; John Zorn (as); Vernon Frazer (g); Mario Pavone (b); Michael Sarin (d).* 94.

****** Haywire**

Knitting Factory KFWCD 176 *Chapin; Mark Feldman (vn); Mario Pavone (b); Michael Sarin (d).* 96.

Chapin was already suffering indifferent health when the second of these two fine albums was recorded at the Knitting Factory. The trio was by this stage functioning like a unit, and Chapin himself was relaxed enough to play as straight or free as circumstances and instinct dictated. Much of the time, perhaps drawing inspiration from the work for Arabesque, he sticks to an inside groove and relatively straightforward harmonics, leaving some of the more extravagant embellishment to Pavone. Every now and then, though, he gives a reminder of his left-field side, and with the like-minded Zorn on hand, *Menagerie Dreams* is one of his most searching records.

****** Sky Piece**

Knitting Factory KFR 208 *Chapin; Mario Pavone (b); Michael Sarin (d).* 7/96.

Doubtless there are other live recordings (and perhaps unreleased studio sessions) still lying in the vaults, but for the moment this exquisite album has to be Thomas Chapin's sign-off and epitaph. Its dominant sounds aren't, curiously, his ever widening array of saxophones and flutes – he adds sopranino saxophone, bass flute and the wooden pinkullo this time – but the sounds of nature and the more sinister cadence of an alarm clock, ticking quietly on 'Just Now', ringing vociferously on 'Alphaville'. It may be that Chapin didn't know or intuit at this point how little time was actually left to him, and he seems to have included the clock (and the Godard title) in a bid to explore ideas of expanded or – as in Dali – melted time. His explorations in nature yield the title-piece, inspired by a trip to Namibia in 1993 and introducing the sombre sound of Chapin's bass flute, perfectly attuned to Pavone's bass figurings; then there is 'Essaouira', evoking the Moroccan coastal town with a shawm-like tone; and 'Night Bird Song', the longest piece, which documents some of the sounds heard on a nature trek in Connecticut. Somewhat unusually, Chapin also includes a repertory tune, Monk's 'Ask Me Now', the second time on the album that the all-important present tense is mentioned in a title.

****** Night Bird Song**

Knitting Factory Works KFR CD 240 *Chapin; Mario Pavone (b); Michael Sarin (d).* 8–9/92.

We include this out of chronological sequence because it is a posthumous release and because it was Thomas's decision to release it as the follow-up to *Sky Piece*. Listening to it now is to return whole to a point in Chapin's career when the future seemed open-ended and full of potential, with few clouds on the horizon. He had put the session aside, waiting for an ideal moment, and had even picked the cover art, a fragment of *mola* cloth from the Blas islands in Panama which he found while touring with Lionel Hampton. The album is as tightly woven as a piece of cloth, a suite of segued themes that is as satisfyingly coherent as anything he ever recorded. Three of the tunes – 'Alphaville', the title-track, and 'Changes Two Tires' – appeared on *Sky Piece*. The former pair are welded together on a dark, almost chordal tone on saxophone, which is picked up by Pavone on bass. 'Cliff Island' is played on sopranino, as is the cartoony 'Tweeter's Last Adventure'. Constantly experimenting with new timbres, he plays (blows? sings?) a reedless alto on 'The Roaring S', a brilliant example of how much Thomas was influenced by natural environments and places.

For those who cherish his work, though, the most deeply moving piece is the flute track, 'Aeolus', which half a decade later was to be the last piece Thomas played in public before his final sickness. Soaring, anchored, paradoxical, it's essentially a duet with Pavone, who emerges more and more clearly as the secret sharer in Chapin's brief, brilliant, foreshortened career. Wonderful stuff; even if it isn't the final word, it has the magisterial confidence of a major statement.

****** Alive**

Knitting Factory KFCD 1196 8CD *As for Knitting Factory records above.* 90–96.

A generous, 68-track compilation celebrating Tom's short life and career. Most fans will have the majority of this material already, but hearing it in concentration simply underlines just what a passionately intense career it was. Issued at a budget price, the eight-CD set also includes a bonus disc recorded at the University of California–Davis in 1992. It's not the greatest of recordings and certainly wouldn't have made the grade had Tom still been working, but it adds to the monumental worth of this release which is highly desirable, especially if you haven't previously sampled Chapin. Given the currently unclear situation regarding the Knitting Factory label, best to get this one soon if it's on your list.

Bill Charlap (born 1966)

PIANO

The son of a songwriter, Moose Charlap, and a singer, Sandy Stewart, Charlap is a young New Yorker with a fundamentally mainstream approach.

***** Along With Me**

Chiaroscuro CRD 326 *Charlap; Sean Smith, Andy Eulau (b); Ron Vincent (d).* 6/91–8/93.

***** Souvenir**

Criss Cross 1108 *Charlap; Scott Colley (b); Dennis Mackrel (d).* 6/95.

***** The Gerry Mulligan Songbook**

Chiaroscuro CRD 349 *Charlap; Ted Rosenthal (p); Dean Johnson (b); Ron Vincent (d).* 6/96.

****(*) Distant Star**

Criss Cross 1131 *Charlap; Sean Smith (b); Bill Stewart (d).* 12/96.

A pupil of Jack Reilly, Charlap has worked under many leaders; his own early records are a confident display of his powers. *Along With Me* is sweetly handled, from Sean Smith's pretty ballad, 'Has This Song Been Written For You Before?', to an almost rhapsodic treatment of Parker's 'Donna Lee', but the record is so even-tempered that it could use a little excitement. *Souvenir* is certainly the pick of the four. The two opening blues, Coleman's 'Roundabout' and Reilly's 'Half Step', are ingenious variations which the pianist relishes, and he plays them with tremendous panache. Colley and Mackrel make a convincing team, and although there are a couple of makeweights – the extended 'Alone Together' is overdone, and Jim Hall's 'Waltz New' is undercooked – it's a good record.

The duets with Rosenthal on Gerry Mulligan material (both men served time under Jeru) are capably done and will appeal to those interested in what remains something of a novelty form in jazz. Something's a little amiss on *Distant Star*, though. The more quiescent material becalms the group, and somehow the spirit which ignited the first Criss Cross date can't get started here.

****** Written In The Stars**

Blue Note 27291-2 *Charlap; Peter Washington (b); Kenny Washington (d).* 3/00.

*****(*) Stardust**

Blue Note 35985-2 *As above, except add Frank Wess (ts), Jim Hall (g), Shirley Horn, Tony Bennett (v).* 01.

Sympathetically produced, these trio sessions (the second has various guest-star turns) put Charlap into his most productive situation. His background seems like an enormous assist. Rather than coming to the standard repertoire as someone who grew up with pop and rock, this kind of material is very much in the family business, and he seems to read melodies such as 'In The Still Of The Night' or 'The Nearness Of You' with intuitive understanding. The debut for Blue Note is close to perfection in this idiom. The songs chosen are familiar without being hackneyed, the Washingtons transcend their working-pro selves, and Charlap plays with the confidence of a man who knows just where he wants to go with each tune. If it's not the sound of surprise, it's the craftsmanship of a thinker whose knowledge of transpositions and melodic possibilities enables him to open a fresh book on the material.

The lightning gallop through 'Jubilee' which opens *Stardust* promises equal bounty, yet it's a pity that Blue Note felt the need to saddle Charlap with the famous names; their seniority is starting to tell on some of them, and it merely distracts from the pianist's own impact. Charlap is an excellent accompanist, but this should be his show. Even so, the trio's work on 'I Walk With Music', 'Georgia' and 'One Morning In May' is worth waiting for.

****** Somewhere: The Songs Of Leonard Bernstein**
Blue Note 94808 *Charlap; Peter Washington (b); Kenny Washington (d).* 10/03.

One-composer recitals are a commonplace, but Leonard Bernstein, for all his perceived jazziness, is a rare contributor to the bandstand. Scarcely any of the tunes the pianist's chosen here are likely to be called, and it's hard to think of many other versions of 'Glitter And Be Gay', 'Jump' or 'A Quiet Girl'. As Charlap remarks, Bernstein was also a lot nearer to our own time than the likes of Kern or Berlin – he's modern, and even though his songs tend to be tougher meat for improvisers used to the familiar terrain of 'Night And Day', there's a case for their greater relevance to players as accomplished and hip as these.

Besides which there is Charlap's family connections with the great Broadway movers, by now well-documented. Like his other records, this one's quiet, considered and full of the peculiar clarity which Charlap brings to the keyboard: even as he's finding fresh routes across the chorus lines, he rarely sounds as if he's dropped in even a note which possibly might not belong. Given that several of these pieces have relatively unfamiliar melodies, that could seem less impressive than it is, yet listen to the new clothes he puts on 'Lucky To Be Me' and 'America'. The Washingtons have a difficult role to undertake, since they need to support a player whose stance hardly tolerates a false step, but they're impeccable. At the end, Charlap plays 'Somewhere' itself as a sort of encore, and it's a serene and beautiful finale.

Teddy Charles (born 1928)

VIBES, MARIMBA, XYLOPHONE, GLOCKENSPIEL, PIANO, PERCUSSION

A vibesman with several big bands at the end of the swing era, Charles turned to composition in the '50s and recorded several albums in a modestly experimental style, forming associations with Miles Davis and Charles Mingus along the way.

*****(*) New Directions**
Original Jazz Classics OJC 1927 *Charles; Hall Overton (p); Don Roberts, Jimmy Raney (g); Kenny O'Brien, Dick Nivison (b); Ed Shaughnessy (d).* 11/51–1/53.

*****(*) Collaboration: West**
Original Jazz Classics OJC 122 *Charles; Shorty Rogers (t); Jimmy Giuffre (ts, bs); Curtis Counce (b); Shelly Manne (d).* 8/53.

***** Evolution**
Original Jazz Classics OJC 1731 *As above, plus J. R. Monterose (ts); Charles Mingus (b); Jerry Segal (d).* 8/53–1/55.

***** Coolin'**
Original Jazz Classics OJC 1866 *Charles; Idrees Sulieman (t); John Jenkins (as); Mal Waldron (p); Addison Farmer (b); Jerry Segal (d).* 4/57.

Charles's sessions as a leader have never progressed beyond a collectors' reputation. He is usually respected as a harbinger of Coleman's free music; the early records aim for an independence of bebop structure which still sounds remarkably fresh. *New Directions* collects the results of three extremely rare ten-inch LPs. The first duplicates the Norvo–Farlow–Mingus instrumentation while securing a quite different result. Here and there Charles almost casually throws out a solo steeped in bop virtuosity – as in the incredible flight on 'Ol' Man River' – but for the most part he's looking to have the trio make sense as an ensemble, carefully balanced in its tones and shapes. Roberts and O'Brien, though, are rather uninspiring partners. Four tracks with Raney, Nivison and Shaughnessy are more encouraging, with Raney's perplexing miniature 'Composition For Four Pieces' and a bumpy, almost abstract treatment of 'A Night In Tunisia'. The final date belongs as much to Hall Overton – who wrote all four pieces – as to Charles, who also plays marimba, vibes and glockenspiel. Ira Gitler's original notes talk about Bartók, Stravinsky and Milhaud, and there's a suitably long-haired feel to the music, which seems rather charmingly experimental a half-century on. However, 'Mobiles' and 'Antiphony' retain their head-turning qualities, even if the remastering has retained an awful lot of tape hiss.

The two 1953 sessions, spread across the two discs, explore contrapuntal textures in a way which only Lennie Tristano had already tried, and there is a wonderful sense of interplay with Rogers and Manne especially. 'Variations On A Theme By Bud' from *Collaboration: West* is a small classic of anticipatory freedom, the music played around key centres rather than a framework of chords. But Charles's interest in harmony and arrangement required larger groups than these, and the quartet session with Mingus, Monterose and Segal is less impressive. *Coolin'* features a surprising line-up of rarely encountered horns in a programme of evenly divided originals. Charles takes a back-seat role, contributing only one tune and taking his turn in the round-robin of solos. This is a more conventional hard-bop session, but the tunes have some piquant interest. Waldron's off-centre 'Staggers' and 'Reiteration', a typical piece of minor-key brooding, are worth reviving. Jenkins plays with splendid intensity, but Sulieman's solos are mere bop convention, quotes and all.

CORE COLLECTION

****** The Teddy Charles Tentet**
Collectables COL-6161 *Charles; Art Farmer (t); Gigi Gryce (as); J. R. Monterose (ts); George Barrow, Sol Schlinger (bs); Mal Waldron (p); Jimmy Raney (g); Don Butterfield (tba); Teddy Kotick (b); Joe Harris (d).* 1/56.

This album remains Charles's masterpiece, and the Collectables edition restores it to the catalogue, although minus the three extra tracks which appeared on Atlantic's earlier CD issue. Full of pungent writing from several hands, the record is almost a showcase for some of the sharpest arranging minds of the day: Giuffre, Brookmeyer, Waldron, Evans and especially George Russell, whose 'Lydian M-1' makes an extraordinary climax to the date. Charles's own 'The Emperor' and the transfiguration of 'Nature Boy' stand as tall as the rest of the scores. A welcome return for a neglected classic.

Charleston Chasers

GROUP

Britishers playing their contemporary version of old hot dance music.

***** Pleasure Mad**
Stomp Off CD 1287 *Ian Hintersley, Sean Colan (c, t); Bob Hunt (tb, c); Claire Murphy (cl, as, cmel, ts, bs); Nik Payton*

(cl, as, cmel, bs, v); Zoltan Sagi (cl, as, ts, bs); Raina Reid (p, v); Tom Langham (bj, g, v); Malcolm Sked (sou); Debbie Arthurs (d, v). 8–9/94.

***** Steaming South**

Stomp Off CD 1314 *As above, except Mike Henry (t), Tony Carter (cl, as, ts), Steve Shaw (tb), Graham Roberts (bj, g) replace Hintersley, Hunt, Murphy, Langham.* 4/96.

***** Smilin' Skies**

Stomp Off CD1376 *Paul Rudeforth (t); Sean Bolan (c); Andy Flaxman (tb); Nik Payton (cl, as, ts, bs, v); Robert Fowler (cl, as, ts); Richard Exall (cl, as, ts, v);, Raina Reid (p, v); Martin Wheatley (bj, uke, g, v); Malcolm Sked (sou); Debbie Arthurs (d, v).* 11/00.

English – *very* English, once you hear the vocals – hot dance music, based around Gloucestershire but recorded in Stratford, Maidstone and London. Their repertoire is virtually all from the bandbooks of the likes of Jean Goldkette, Ted Weems and various pillars of New York society, but they sometimes drop in some Ellington or Beiderbecke, and all of it is performed with much panache and evident pleasure. Payton sounds like the outstanding soloist, although none of them is a slouch; and Raina Reid's arrangements have as much flair as the original charts. That said, there is little reason to listen to their 'Since My Best Girl Turned Me Down' when one can hear the Beiderbecke version, and some of it falls into the metronomic category. It is, though, in good sound – and it might tempt ears unused to the ancient timbres of original hot dance. *Smilin' Skies* is the latest arrival, but despite the turnover in personnel, little changes with this outfit (when Debbie Arthurs signs off with Annette Hanshaw's 'That's all' tagline, she's still as English as they come). Nice work, but very tied to the idiom.

Tommy Chase

DRUMS

Veteran British hard-bopper who likes it done the old-fashioned way.

***** One Way**

Spotlite SPJ 410 *Chase; Jon Eardley (t); Ray Warleigh (as); John Bunch (p); Danny Padmore (b).* 6 & 10/78.

Chase has regularly expressed dismay at the way his beloved music is heading: guys in T-shirts playing synths probably sums it up. His own recorded output hasn't survived its moment by and large, but here is a fine hard-bop set from the '70s, co-led with Warleigh and featuring Jon Eardley as a guest on some tracks. It's also a great place to sample Warleigh's now rather overlooked contribution to British jazz. And make sure you put a suit and tie on.

Doc Cheatham (1905–97)

TRUMPET, VOCALS

Adolphus Cheatham was born in Nashville and started out in burlesque bands, in which he backed Bessie Smith among others. He went on to have one of the longest careers in jazz history, with McKinney's Cotton Pickers, Cab Calloway and, in the '50s following a spell away from the music, with many Latin American bands. In his 80s and 90s he was a revered old master, still playing a weekly gig in Greenwich Village.

***** Hey Doc!**

Black & Blue 887 *Cheatham; Gene Connors (tb); Ted Buckner (as); Sam Price (p); Carl Pruitt (b); J. C. Heard (d).* 5/75.

*****(*) Duets And Solos**

Sackville SKCD-5002 2CD *Cheatham; Sam Price (p).* 11/76–11/79.

Doc Cheatham became one of the most enduring jazz musicians of his time – and his time seemed to span much of the history of the music. He was effectively rediscovered in the '70s after many years of society band work, having been among the most esteemed of lead trumpeters in the big-band era. He was recording in the late '20s, and his studio work of some 60 years later shows amazingly little deterioration in the quality of his technique, while the ideas and appetite for playing remained wholly unaffected by the passage of time. It's not so much that one feels a sentimental attachment to such a veteran, but that Cheatham's sound represents an art which literally died out of modern jazz: the sweet, lyrically hot style of a swing-era man. Prior to his records in the '80s, Cheatham's main work was with Cab Calloway in the '30s, Eddie Heywood in the '40s (often backing Billie Holiday), and in various settings in the '50s and '60s; but it wasn't until these albums that he was heard at length as a leader.

The Black & Blue set is pretty rough and ready, not least because Sam Price's piano is only approximately tuned. However, there's some lovely playing from everyone concerned and the rising-70-year-old Doc blows some lovely solos on 'Ain't Misbehaving' and 'Blues In My Heart', while singing effectively on the ballad 'If I Could Be With You'. His intonation is strong and mostly very correct, though there are a couple of moments when that d***ed piano throws him off.

Duets And Solos is arguably Cheatham's most valuable recording, since it both recalls the earlier age which he seems so much a part of – the trumpet/piano format recalls Armstrong and Hines, and the material mixes rags, stomps, blues and whiskery pop – and sits comfortably in modern sound and with a knowing air of sagacity. Price (whose session of 12 solos fills up spare space on the two-disc set) is fine, and often better than he is on his own featured recordings, although his solo showpieces are less impressive as rather mechanical blues and light boogie.

***** Live At The Windsor Jazz Series**

Jazzology 333 *Cheatham; James Dapogny (p); Daniel Jordan (b); Richard 'Pistol' Allen (d).* 81.

For some reason, these tapes lay unreleased for nearly 20 years. Perhaps they were waiting for the youngster to come good. Doc is in fine form, blowing easily and with conviction on 'Struttin' With Some Barbecue' and doing a fairly outrageous 'Hello Dolly', which previously only Pops could pull off convincingly. The band is nice and tight and Dapogny has some refreshing ideas of his own.

***** At The Bern Festival**

Sackville 2-3045 *Cheatham; Roy Williams (tb); Jim Galloway (ss); Ian Bargh (p); Neil Swainson (b); Terry Clarke (d).* 4/83–1/85.

This live session finds Cheatham unfazed by a hard-swinging and quite modern-sounding band, with Roy Williams sitting in on the first six tracks – he has a delightful feature on 'Polka Dots And Moonbeams' – and Galloway's soprano measuring the distance between Sidney Bechet and Steve Lacy. Three later tracks were taped on more local ground in Toronto. If the rhythm section sometimes crashes rather more than it might for Cheatham's taste, he still sounds invigorated by the setting, and his hand-muted playing on 'Creole Love Call' or the firm, silvery solos on 'Cherry' and 'Love Is Just Around The Corner' are commanding examples of his best work.

***** Live At Sweet Basil**
Jazzology JCD-283 *Cheatham; Jerry Zigmont (tb); Sammy Rimington (cl, as ts); Jon Marks (p); Arvell Shaw (b); John Russell (d).* 4/92.

Much of Doc's latter-day legacy will exist in the form of live albums. This one often has the feel of a Louis Armstrong date, what with old-time All-Stars bassist Shaw in the line-up and several tunes associated with Pops, so it's interesting to hear Cheatham's style on his old rival's material, as well as the versatile Rimington partnering the maestro. The rest of the group is a bit ordinary but there's a pleasing feel of New-Orleans-in-New-York about it all.

***** Swinging Down In New Orleans**
Jazzology JCD-233 *Cheatham; Brian O'Connell (cl); Butch Thompson (p); Les Muscutt (g, bj); Bill Huntington (g, b); Peter Badie (b); Ernest Elly (d).* 92.

****(*) You're A Sweetheart**
Sackville SKCD2-2038 *Cheatham; Sarah McElcheran (t); Jim Galloway (ss, vbs); Jane Fair (cl, ts); Norman Amadio (p); Rosemary Galloway (b, v); Don Vickery (d).* 3–11/92.

Doc seems neither more nor less than his usual self on both of these, so it comes down to the settings as to which is preferable. But there's no real contest. Jazzology's seasoned team of veteran modern traditionalists (if that doesn't sound too absurd) provides a springy, amiable and perfectly appropriate background for the trumpeter's lean, sometimes puffy solos and singing, with Thompson a model of deftness. It plays plenty of tunes from the old town and makes them all sound as if they're worth the attention. The Canadian sessions captured on the Sackville disc are more routine, and though there's a sweet ballad in 'Under The Moonlight Starlight Blue', most of this is rather too ordinary.

***** Meets The Swiss Dixie Stompers Plus Two**
Jazzology 327 *Cheatham; André Racine (t); Willie Glasser (tb); Peter Bariswy (ts, cl); Randy Wirz (cl); Michael Gotz (p); Marcel Lack (bjo); Martin Albrecht (b); Dave Elias (d).* 95.

In a short interview included before the finale 'Struttin' With Some Barbecue', the 90-year-old admits to some backstage jitters before playing with a new and unfamiliar group. He needn't have worried on his own account or theirs. The Swiss manage to sound organized and carefree and Doc himself is playing with a lot of gusto and control, shaping his notes as well as he ever had and only muffing his articulation rarely. He sounded as if he could go on doing this at festivals into the new century. Not in the front rank of Doc albums, but well worth having.

Jeannie Cheatham

PIANO, VOCAL

AND

Jimmy Cheatham (born 1924)

BASS TROMBONE, VOCAL

Husband-and-wife team who take a genial, often gentle route through R&B flavoured by jazz horns and swing rhythms.

***** Sweet Baby Blues**
Concord CCD 42582 *Jimmy Cheatham; Jeannie Cheatham; Snooky Young (t, v); Jimmie Noone (ss, cl); Charles McPherson (as); Curtis Peagler (as, ts); Red Callender (b, tba); John 'Ironman' Harris (d); Danice Tracey, Chris Long (v).* 9/84.

***** The Concord Jazz Heritage Series**
Concord CCD 4837-2 *As above, except add Nolan Smith (t, flhn), Hank Crawford (as), Plas Johnson (ts), Frank Wess (f, ts), Eddie 'Lockjaw' Davis (ts), Dinky Morris (ss, ts, bs), Eddie 'Cleanhead' Vinson (as, v), Rickey Woodard (as, ts, cl), Jimmie Noone (ss, ts, cl), Richard Reid (b).* 84–95.

Like many of their somewhat younger counterparts on Concord, the Cheathams did this kind of record for the label long enough to create their own little genre. Some may find Concord's spotless recording not much in keeping with the rougher spirits of what is a variation on jump-band blues, but the horns are perfectly cast and the material is smartly chosen to get the most out of the formula. Jeannie Cheatham's singing is a nice blend of girlishness and acting tough, and husband Jimmy plays Butterbeans to her Susie. Not much of their lengthy stay at the label is currently in print, but the debut album remains, and the *Jazz Heritage* compilation is a respectable cross-section of their work.

Chris Cheek (born 1968)

TENOR SAXOPHONE

Inside-to-out saxophonist, currently busy in the New York scene.

***** I Wish I Knew**
Fresh Sound FSNT 022 *Cheek; Kurt Rosenwinkel (g); Chris Higgins (b); Jorge Rossy (d).* 10/96–1/97.

****** A Girl Named Joe**
Fresh Sound FSNT 032 *Cheek; Mark Turner (ts); Ben Monder (g); Marc Johnson (b); Jorge Rossy, Dan Rieser (d).* 5/97.

A self-effacing debut from the American saxophonist who's done some accomplished foot-soldiering elsewhere. A solitary original hides in the middle of a programme of standards, quietly thought out at ballad tempos, and although firmly articulated by all hands the music has a melancholy air which seems to crystallize in the tenorman's injured timbre. Rosenwinkel plays limpid lines in counterpoint to Cheek, and they score a kind of reluctant success.

Two tenors, guitar, bass and two drummers. Cheek's hardly chosen a conventional set-up for his second Fresh Sound set. This one is very much about the composing – contrapuntal lines, parallel melodies, close-cropped harmony. He could hardly have a more responsive or tuned-in group to perform a subtle and vivid set of music: Johnson, a supreme hired gun at this point, is the perfect bassman for the job, melodious but inquiring; Monder is an unassuming master; Turner is one of the keenest sax voices of the moment. And Cheek himself stands as tall as anyone on the date. Another exceptional set from the Fresh Sound New Talent imprint.

***** Vine**
Fresh Sound FSNT 086 *Cheek; Brad Mehldau (p); Kurt Rosenwinkel (g); Matt Penman (b); Jorge Rossy (d).* 12/99.

Another stellar line-up, although this time it works less well. Mehldau plays Fender Rhodes, and the complex thematic material feels a little elongated at times, as if Cheek were trying to create a brainy sort of jazz-rock. Cheek's own playing softens the contours a little, but it can sometimes feel as if the band's playing to orders which are wound too tight. The great exception is the finale, a duet for piano and soprano which touches a vein of melody that the rest isn't quite privy to.

*****(*) Guilty**
Fresh Sound FSNT 125 *Cheek; Ethan Iverson (p); Ben Street (b); Jorge Rossy (d).* 3/00.

*****(*) Lazy Afternoon**
Fresh Sound FSNT 126 *As above.* 3/00.

On a visit to Barcelona, here's Cheek with Ethan Iverson, working patiently through two sets of standards at the Jamboree Club. Interestingly, the players make little attempt to be disrespectful of the material: many of the tunes (particularly the ballads) are played disarmingly straight, and even where there's a striking departure – as on the steadily building, bruising epic which is made out of 'All Or Nothing At All' on *Guilty* – each step in the journey is a logical move forward from the last one, rather than some abstracted leap into the void. Cheek's idiosyncratic tone gets its fullest exposure in these sets, and Iverson's compelling pianism is ideal as both platform and independent voice. He also contributes the one original, 'Guilty' itself, subsequently part of The Bad Plus's book. Two fine records.

Don Cherry (1936–95)

POCKET TRUMPET, WOODEN FLUTES, DOUSSN'GOUNI, PIANO, KEYBOARDS, MISCELLANEOUS INSTRUMENTS, VOICE

Born in Oklahoma, Cherry played R&B before meeting Ornette Coleman in 1956. Worked in his quartet, then with John Coltrane and the New York Contemporary Five. Visited Europe and thereafter retained a base there as well as in America. An inveterate traveller, he listened to seemingly all the world's musics. Besides doing his own extravagantly multi-cultural records, gigs and events, he played Coleman's music again (in Old & New Dreams and with his former leader) and turned up in guest situations, though his playing was affected by lip trouble. He succumbed to liver failure in Spain in 1995.

****** Mu: First Part, Second Part**
Varese 061147 *Cherry; Ed Blackwell (d).* 8/69.

This one never fails to astonish and delight. Don moves between trumpet, piano, various flutes and singing. The diversity of idiom establishes an agenda for later, multi-cultural projects, both Cherry's own and a whole raft of so-called world music. His range is astonishing, everything from bright New Orleans vamps and marches to African songs, folksy Americana to totally free passages. Blackwell is the most sympathetic of accompanists. He delivers crisp, ringing lines with a minimum of fuss, but it is his musicality that impresses.

There are a couple of nods along the way to Dollar Brand (Abdullah Ibrahim) and the African roots jazz he pioneered. But the conception is essentially Cherry's, a bold, sweeping synthesis that was hinted at in those remarkable, revolutionary encounters with Ornette Coleman (the trumpeter's role is still undersung) but which is only made explicit here. Though it can sound bitty and tentative in some regards, *Mu* is an astonishing experience and a key modern recording.

***** Orient / Blue Lake**
Charly 513 2CD *Cherry; Johnny Mbizo Dyani (b); Han Bennink (d, perc, acc); Okay Temiz (d); Mocqui Cherry (tambura).* 3/71.

Over a couple of weeks in 1971, Cherry recorded two live double LPs for the BYG Actuel label, using two different groups. These albums have had intermittent circulation since, including some unauthorized issues and bootlegs. Now they're back together again on this double CD, restoring an important part of the Cherry story.

The first group features Cherry's then wife Mocqui on tambura and Dutch master Han Bennink on percussion and accordion. The language is expansive and indefinable, with elements of as many folk traditions as you can name and both long tracks sustain attention and renewed attention amazingly well. The other group is closer to a jazz aesthetic, but still, as on 'Eagle Eye', makes use of ethnic material and procedures. 'Dollar And Okay's Tunes' is a wonderful example of group improvisation. Dyani's sweeping, thunderous bass and Cherry's singing to himself while at the piano lend the set curious echoes of all sorts of modern jazz precedents but it's a unique sound all the same and wonderful to have these recordings back in the library in appropriate form.

**** Actions**
Intuition 3606 *Cherry; Manfred Schoof, Tomasz Stańko, Kenny Wheeler (t, co); Albert Mangelsdorff (tb); Peter Brötzmann (ts, bsx); Willem Breuker (ts, cl); Gerd Dudek (ss, ts); Gunter Hampel (f, bcl); Fred Van Hove (p, org); Terje Rypdal (g); Buschi Niebergall, Peter Warren (b); Han Bennink (d, perc, tabla, thumb p); Krzysztof Penderecki (cond).* 10/71.

A remarkable collaboration with Polish composer Krzysztof Penderecki – who is still best known for his scarifying Hiroshima threnody – *Actions* features the Eternal Rhythm Orchestra in a classic confrontation between free jazz and the new music. There are two large pieces, Cherry's 'Humus: The Life Exploring Force' and Penderecki's graphic 'Actions for Free Jazz Orchestra', and a short encore, based on traditional material. The playing is intense, mostly abstract and not particularly well recorded. Listeners from the classical and new music community were happy to be caught slumming. Jazz fans thought it very highbrow and nourishing. In point of fact, it's a messy and rather disconnected project that hasn't aged very elegantly.

*****(*) The Sonet Recordings**
Verve 533049 2CD *Cherry; Irfan Sumer (ts, perc); Bernt Rosengren (tarogato); Christer Bothen (p); Selcuk Sun (b); Okay Temiz (d, perc); Bengt Berger, Agneta Ernstrom (perc).* 11/69–5/73.

The death of Don Cherry in 1995 imposed a more profound silence than most such passings. In a very real sense, Cherry's recorded output is beside the point. He was a musical gypsy, a kind of planetary *griot*, as someone once put it, who defined his musical art as that of people 'listening and travelling'. He himself never stopped doing either – or, of course, playing. The last time one of the authors met him was at the Jazz Jamboree in Warsaw in 1993. He was as likely to turn up in India, Korea or Latin America. For some time he lived in Scandinavia, and the Sonet compilation brings together two albums, one made in the studio in Stockholm in 1973 and one recorded live in Ankara four years earlier. There is no typical Don Cherry album. Though he adds an unforgettable voice to things like the classic Ornette Coleman Atlantics, he is not primarily an instrumentalist and certainly not a trumpet innovator. The first thing to be registered about these recordings is that Cherry plays no trumpet at all on *Eternal Now*, the Swedish session, but ranges across a bizarre variety of percussion and stringed instruments, piano and harmonium. Aficionados of the Scandinavian scene will cherish a track featuring the great tenorist Bernt Rosengren on *tarogato*, a folksy cousin to the soprano saxophone made of rosewood. 'Love Train' is perhaps the most jazz-based piece on the session. The remaining tracks are squarely in the world-music idiom that Cherry was to make his own in years to come. *Live Ankara* is closer to the work with Ornette: tight, compressed lines on the cheap little Pakistani pocket trumpet Cherry favoured, and two Ornette themes just to cement the connection. Typically, though, much of the material is folk-inspired, arrangements of Turkish tunes by Maffy Falay. Cherry does, though, include two or three of his own pieces and these, 'St John And The Dragon' and 'Man On The Moon' especially, sound more securely within his comfort zone.

*** El Corazon

ECM 829199-2 *Cherry; Ed Blackwell (d).* 2/82.

Like fellow-trumpeter Leo Smith, Cherry had a rather intermittent association with ECM, returning to the label just before the end of his life for the very mixed *Dona Nostra*. Apart from the records with Codona, his ECM output was limited to the 1993 disc and these duos with Blackwell who, after Ornette and Collin Walcott, was probably his closest associate from the jazz end of the spectrum. This encounter lacks the rawness of performance one responds to on *Mu* but gains infinitely in sheer clarity of sound. It also includes what by this stage in his career had become a rare standard item, Thelonious Monk and Denzil Best's 'Bemsha Swing'. Blackwell is immense, as ever, relishing the space and music which is freed from the vertical hierarchies of harmonic jazz. Those who heard the duo workshopping and gigging report that *El Corazon* is only a muted version of what they were capable of. It's a solid but in the end rather uneventful record.

*** Nu – Live At The Bracknell Jazz Festival

BBC Legends BBCJ7004-2 *Cherry; Carlos Ward (as, f); Mark Helias (b); Ed Blackwell (d); Nana Vasconcelos (berimbau, perc, v).* 6/86.

Cherry's world-music interests haven't quite obscured his deep jazz roots on this live appearance at England's much-missed festival. Ward's reeling, bop-tinged solos, which also appealed to Cecil Taylor, are a major feature, and so too is Vasconcelos's party piece 'O Berimbau'. Don squeezes off tight notes and phrases and there is more trumpet-playing than on some occasions. The set was scheduled for release some time ago, but was delayed for contractual reasons.

***(*) Art Deco

A & M 395258-2 *Cherry; James Clay (ts); Charlie Haden (b); Billy Higgins (d).* 8/88.

Signs in the later '80s that Cherry, or those who were signing him up, wanted to mainstream his work, lead him back towards jazz and away from the centrifugal spin of world music. There are moments when this might almost be a later *Ornette On Tenor*; Clay has had a quiet career since the '50s, but he comes from the same Texas soil and brings a refreshingly down-home touch to Coleman tunes like 'The Blessing' and 'Compute'. Again, there are a couple of standards, 'When Will The Blues Leave', 'Body And Soul' (which is really Clay's feature) and a further, indifferent version of 'Bemsha Swing'. Cherry plays mostly muted and seemed to have reverted to a cross between his old, rather tentative self and mid-period Miles Davis, softer and more accommodating than one might like to hear. Along with the Ornette tribute band, Old And New Dreams, this is probably as good as it got until CherryCo enterprises actually got back together again in the early '90s.

***(*) Multi Kulti

A & M 395323 *Cherry; Bill Ortiz (t, v); James Harvey (tb); Jeff Cressman (tb, v); Bob Stewart (tba); Carlos Ward (as); Jessica Jones, Jony Jones (ts); Peter Apfelbaum (ts, ky, perc); Peck Allmond (bs); Will Bernard, Stan Franks (g); David Cherry, Frank Serafine (syn); Karl Berger (mar); Bo Freeman, Mark Loudon Sims (b); Ed Blackwell, Deszon X. Claiborne (d); Joshua Jones V (d, perc, v); John L. Price (d programmes); Frank Ekeh, Robert Buddha Huffman, Nana Vasconcelos (perc); Anthony Hamilton, Ingrid Sertso (v); collective personnel.* 12/88–2/90.

This is the closest Cherry ever came and was ever likely to come to a big crossover hit. Adding a sophisticated studio gloss to his polystylism didn't blunt it in any way, though there are moments when one wants to hear a live equivalent, something a little blunter and more ragged. The horns are consistently excellent, with Ward providing a voice not unlike Ornette's to stir those ancestral memories. The presence of Peter Apfelbaum, who went on to found the Cherry-influenced Hieroglyphics Ensemble, is an indication of his growing impact on a younger generation of players who were kicking against the restrictions of formula bebop and looking for other inputs. Difficult to judge how much Cherry himself was drawing at the time from stepdaughter Neneh Cherry, who had graduated from the James Brown-meets-bop Rip, Rig & Panic and was striking out on her own with a jazzy hybrid of hip-hop and rap styles.

*** Dona Nostra

ECM 521727-2 *Cherry; Lennart Aberg (sax, f); Bobo Stenson (p); Anders Jormin (b); Anders Kjellberg (d); Okay Temiz (perc).* 3/93.

There are sparks of brilliance here, but they are lost in ashpits of compromise. The wind that stirs the coals, significantly, is Ornette Coleman, two of whose pieces are included. The old pairing was to go on the road later the same year, and Cherry seems keen to pack his strong-voiced solos with tags and phrases remembered from years, even decades, before. Restricting himself to trumpet, he eases through 'Race Face' with less fury than the composer brings to it; for 'Fort Cherry' and 'Prayer' (still the outstanding cut), he injects a warmer-than-usual tone, prompting the question whether he has switched to a more conventional horn. The sound is magnificent, and Stenson demonstrates once again what a superbly responsive player he is, and Aberg (still not widely known outside Scandinavia) amply justifies his shared credit. It is not, overall, much of a showing for such a considerable musician, but Cherry never seemed like a man much concerned with his place in posterity, and his elusiveness on record is in some ways appropriate.

Laurie Chescoe (born 1933)

DRUMS

A Londoner who's been in numerous British trad-to-Dixie and revival bands since the late '50s. Latterly he has often worked with Keith Nichols.

****(*) Feeling Good**
Lake LACD 99 *Chescoe; Ian Hunter-Randall (t); Dave Hewitt (tb, c, b horn); Dave Jones (cl, bs); Allan Bradley (p, v); Tony Pitt (g, bj, v); John Rodber (b).* n.d.

***** Now We Are Ten**
Lake LACD 149 *Chescoe; Ben Cohen (c, v); Dave Hewitt (tb, c, b horn); Al Gay (cl, ts); Stan Greig (p); John Stewart (bj, g); Pete Skivington (b).* 9–10/00.

The sleeve-notes call them 'vital and exciting', but no, it's more easy-going and built for comfort. Chescoe's team has been through various incarnations since it was formed in 1990 and here are two of them. The music follows a Condonite model but that tends to ask for outsize personalities to make it work, and these gentlemen often stick to a British reserve. Hunter-Randall is rather fallible on the earlier disc, and the vocals are awful. *Now We Are Ten* (the misleading cover photo suggests that the band is ten strong, but it's a septet) is a notch better – superior sound and a more spirited group. Ben Cohen's vocals aren't much of an improvement, though. The outstanding musician on both dates is Chescoe himself, playing a doughty version of Baby Dodds and George Wettling. Ralph Laing's sleeve-note makes a pitiful plea for more trad and mainstream, which suggests that he's unaware of Lake's many other activities in the field.

Cyrus Chestnut (born 1963)

PIANO

Chestnut grew up, musically speaking, in church, playing gospel music for choirs in his native Baltimore. He studied there and in Boston before working with George Adams and Jon Hendricks and in the Betty Carter group.

*****(*) Nut**
Evidence 22152-2 2CD *Chestnut; Christian McBride (b); Carl Allen (d).* 1/92.

***** Another Direction**
Evidence 22135-2 *As above.* 4/93.

***** Revelations**
Atlantic 82518-2 *Chestnut; Christopher J. Thomas (b); Clarence Penn (d).* 6/93.

Chestnut has settled in as a major part of the jazz mainstream. These albums (the Evidence sets are reissues of records originally released in Japan) are already old enough to be classed as juvenilia, but they're very enjoyable in their own right. *Nut* and *Another Direction* burst with good humour and inventiveness, the pianist assisted by superb back-up from McBride and Allen; although the material is relatively familiar (Ellington, standards and the occasional gospel piece) and the treatments unstartling, the joy in the music is unmistakable.

Chestnut, Thomas and Penn were the members of one of Betty Carter's recent rhythm sections, and the deftness of the *Revelations* trio certainly bespeaks mutual familiarity. The opening 'Blues For Nita' is a beautifully controlled workout in which Chestnut controls the dynamics as sagaciously as any keyboard veteran. Instead of coming from the post-bop piano masters, he looks back to those who bridged swing and bop, in particular Oscar Peterson. 'Little Ditty' features a trademark show of virtuosity, while the gospel inflexions of 'Lord, Lord, Lord' might have come from Ray Bryant. The down-side of this direction is a certain sameness and predictability about some of his solos, as if he'd already fallen into patterns of playing. But the quiet gravity of his solo ballad 'Sweet Hour Of Prayer' suggests that he has other sides to develop, too.

*****(*) Dark Before The Dawn**
Atlantic 82719-2 *As above, except Steve Kirby (b) replaces Thomas.* 8/94.

One of the interesting things about Chestnut is his take on gospel roots. So few modern jazz pianists have tackled the issue of gospel melody and harmony within a post-bop context – beyond the customary 'soulful' clichés – that Chestnut's meditative approach is something of a rarity. Here, on 'It Is Well (Within My Soul)', he plays a beautifully modulated treatment of a traditional hymn, but more important is the way he integrates gospel materials into his overall approach. It lends a distinctive touch to most of the pianism on show here and plays a notable part in his choice of dynamics; he can play remarkably delicately, but – and he's physically a big man – he can really thump the keyboard when he wants to. That range is splendidly exploited by the variety of the themes on display, and Kirby and Penn offer exemplary support. Still, there are contrivances here and there, even if this strong record will do for now.

*****(*) Blessed Quietness**
Atlantic 82948-2 *Chestnut (p solo).* 4/96.

Chestnut goes all the way with an album of hymns, spirituals and carols – 'What you hear is simply my heart'. Rather than playing any of them straight, he creates a gently persuasive form for such commonplace pieces as 'We Three Kings', 'Amazing Grace' and 'Silent Night', delineating melodies with absolute clarity yet fashioning his own framework for each piece. That lends both surprise and familiar warmth to, say, 'The First Noel', a well-worn tune given a delicate new grace. Unbelievers may find a whole disc of this something of a stretch, but the pianism is marvellous. Perhaps Chestnut can do this only once in his career. If so, he's made a near-perfect job of it with this disc.

*****(*) Cyrus Chestnut**
Atlantic 83140-2 *Chestnut; James Carter (as); Joe Lovano (ts); Ron Carter (b); Billy Higgins, Lewis Nash (d); Anita Baker (v).* 98.

Back on the solid ground of post-bop, Chestnut handles this unfrilly session with implacable assurance. Carter sticks to alto and is, for him, on surprisingly bubbly form, leaving some of his importance at home for the date. His extravagant sound on 'The Journey' is infectiously high-spirited. Lovano strolls in for two tracks and trades jabs with Carter on the closing 'Sharp'. Cyrus enjoys being in charge of this set, and he confers a light touch on the whole session. Even the two guest vocals by Anita Baker, who sings 'Summertime' softly and 'My Favourite Things' delicately, don't sit uncomfortably with the other tracks.

★★★(★) Soul Food
Atlantic 83490-2 *Chestnut; Marcus Printup (t); Wycliffe Gordon (tb); Gary Bartz (as); James Carter (ts); Stefon Harris (vib); Christian McBride (b); Lewis Nash (d).* 6/01.

Chestnut shuffles his options here. Three tracks offer horns and rhythm section, three others have the trio plus Stefon Harris, and there are pieces for rhythm section and solo piano too. The tracks with Harris are in some ways the least convincing, since the meeting of musicians seems too politely handled, while those with the horns are a lot ruder. Carter, as usual, ignores barriers of both taste and discretion, and it doesn't half lively up the music. Could be a band to make a great live album. In the meantime, Chestnut returns to the feel of *Blessed Quietness* for a solo 'Swing Low Sweet Chariot'. Major-label politesse intrudes here and there; otherwise, a good continuation of Chestnut's progress.

★★★(★) You Are My Sunshine
Warner Bros 9362-48445-2 *Chestnut; Michael Hawkins (b); Neal Smith (d).* 11/02.

Chestnut's new trio offers him a straightforward vehicle for his playing. The programme is in what's now the familiar Chestnut pocket: gospel tunes and a few originals. His Garner tribute, 'Erroling', is a difficult piece well executed (and it's interesting to learn that he plans a Garner homage for his next project). There's a steady-state feel to Cyrus's playing which perhaps puts him at some remove from the Jason Moran matrix, but he's set fair to become one of the great jazz-piano entertainers if records like this can get him the necessary attention.

Chicago Underground Duo/Trio

GROUP

New music from Chicagoan experimenters.

★★★ 12 Degrees Of Freedom
Thrill Jockey 060 *Robert Mazurek (c, p, f); Jeff Parker (g); Chad Taylor (perc, vib).* 1–6/97.

★★★(★) Possible Cube
Delmark DE-511 *Robert Mazurek (c, elec, vib, mar, org); Jeff Parker (g, org); Noel Kupersmith (b, vib); Chad Taylor (d, vib).* 5/98.

Mazurek (who has more conventional records listed under his own name), Taylor and Kupersmith are the CUT, with Parker seemingly an honorary member. The music is a low-key mix of post-bop and music (or sound) that has drifted in from many other points. Several of the pieces on *Possible Cube* are more-or-less conventional sequences for cornet, bass and drums, but they're interspersed with percussion episodes, wandering improvisations in free time, and electronics. 'Othello', the first track, starts in familiar territory but dissolves into what's almost a dream sequence for synthesizers. Very brief tracks intermingle with pieces like the marathon 'Into Another You', underpinned by the bleating organ-lines that Parker contributes. The Thrill Jockey record is cooler and more abstract, and even has one piece ('Waiting For You Is Like Watching Stillness Grow Into Enormous Wings') that sounds like a self-contained piece of minimalist composition. But both are interesting proposals to blend genuine jazz material with what's coming out of Chicago's avant-garde rock community. Underground, but maybe not for long.

★★★(★) Flamethrower
Delmark DE-521 *As above.* 00.

The Trio – still four-strong for this release – continues to undermine expectations of what can be done with cornet, guitar, acoustic bass and acoustic drums. It continues to use judicious electronic manipulation and some overdubbing – modern stuff like that. So the first three tracks are the trio jam 'Quail' (written by Mazurek, though he doesn't play on it), two minutes of bleep called 'Fahrenheit 451' and the supremely knowing Tristano-ite stroll called 'Warm Marsh', which could have come off *Jazz From The East Village*. Bar for bar, there's probably nothing new here at all, but who else has ever contextualized all these strands quite like this?

★★★(★) Synesthesia
Thrill Jockey 077 *Robert Mazurek (c, elec); Chad Taylor (perc, vib); Sam Prekop (syn).* 99.

★★★(★) Chicago Underground Quartet
Thrill Jockey 093 *As above, except add Jeff Parker (g), Noel Kupersmith (b); omit Prekop.* 8/00.

The Thrill Jockey records continue this intriguing group's progress. *Synesthesia* is attributed to the Duo (Prekop appears on a single track): after the long, strange 'Blue Sparks From Her, And The Scent Of Lightning', much of it is almost conventional cornet–percussion improvising, but very well done, and Mazurek reintroduces electronics whenever you're expecting something else. *Quartet* bows to the inevitable and acknowledges that there are four of them. Dreamy, slippery music, calling up memories of old prog-rock situations but never quite resolving them, it's fusion for the ages, and curiously addictive.

★★★ Axis And Alignment
Thrill Jockey 106 *Robert Mazurek (c, p, elec); Chad Taylor (vib, g, perc).* 01.

Briefly (a little over 40 minutes), Mazurek and Taylor continue their adventure. Again, much of this is a dialogue between Mazurek's cornet and Taylor's drums, the vibes drifting mysteriously between them, electronics used more sparingly than ever, Taylor eventually plucking a guitar part on 'Memoirs Of A Space Traveller'. Maybe this time it's less progress, more marking time. Where to next?

Buddy Childers (born 1926)

TRUMPET, FLUGELHORN

Childers joined Stan Kenton as lead trumpet when only a teenager, and stayed until 1954. Thereafter he worked extensively in Los Angeles and Las Vegas, usually in big bands, a setting which he still loves, although he occasionally plays as a single when a guest at events such as Kenton conventions.

★★★ Just Buddy's
Candid CCD 79761 *Childers; Danny Barber, Mark Thompson, Nipper Murphy, Art Davis, Peter Fleming, Warren*

Kime (t); Scott Belige, Tom Kordus, John Blane, Scott Bentall, Bob Samborski (tb); Mike Smith, John Negus, Peter Ballin, Dave Brandom, Ron Kolber, Jerry Dimusio, Brian Ripp (sax); Bobby Schiff (p); Steve Roberts (g); Larry Gray, Bill Lanphier (b); Joel Spencer (d). 11/83–2/84.

***** West Coast Quintet**
Candid CCD 79722 *Childers; Jimmy Zito (vtb); Brian O'Rourke (p); John Leitham (b); Paul Kreibach (d).* 6/94.

***** It's What's Happening Now!**
Candid CCD 79749 *Childers; Ron King, Ron Stout, Tim Wendt, Gary Halopoff, Jeff Kaye, Brian Schwarz, Dave Trigg, Deborah Bergeron (t, flhn); Andy Martin, Dick Hamilton, Thurman Greene, Charlie Morillas, Randy Alcroft, Jack Redmond (tb); Ken Shroyer, Bryant Byers (btb); Ray Reed, Ann Patterson, Glenn Garrett, George Harper, Charlie Orena, John Stevens, Charles Owens (sax); Brian O'Rourke (p); Paul Murphy, Doug MacDonald (g); Trey Henry, Harvey Newmark (b); Ralph Razze, Jerry White (d); Tierney Sutton (v).* 96.

A lead man of huge experience, Buddy Childers loves to play in a big, swinging band playing smart charts and unpretentious material. That sums up what happens on both of the big-band sets listed here. *Just Buddy's*, first released on Trend, was cobbled together from various sessions but hits the spot from the opening 'Nica's Dream' onwards. *It's What's Happening Now!* was put together in Dick Hamilton's tiny overdub studio – 18 people in a 20 by 26 foot room. The sound is, in the circumstances, very good. Mostly these are top session and orchestral guys playing for the fun of it and while neither date really sounds immortal, there's much pleasure to be had. Some of Buddy's articulation has softened but that means he gets an even sweeter sound out of the flugelhorn, as on an attractive take on Russ Garcia's 'Come Home Again'.

The quintet date is another good blow. There are a few interesting touches, such as the fast clip for 'My Funny Valentine'. Zito has a lovely feature on 'Street Of Dreams' and the rhythm section give the horns a terrific push.

George Chisholm (1915–97)

TROMBONE

Born in Glasgow, Chisholm came to London in 1935 and quickly established himself on the dance-band/jazz scene. He played with Fats Waller three years later and was arranging for the Squadronaires during the war years. In the '50s he became a favourite on radio and subsequently on TV, in commercials and on variety shows, but his credentials as a trad-to-mainstream trombonist were unimpaired, as his occasional recordings showed. In the '80s and '90s he remained a favourite at clubs and in festivals, and his career only faded following the death of his wife in 1995.

*****(*) Early Days 1935–1944**
Timeless CBC 1-044 *Chisholm; Tommy McQuater, Johnny Claes, Dave Wilkins, Kenny Baker, Stan Roderick, Alfie Noakes (t); Eric Breeze, Bruce Campbell, Dave Walters (tb); Jimmy Durant (ss, bs); Dougie Robinson, Harry Hayes (as); Benny Winestone (cl, ts); Danny Polo, Jimmy Williams, Andy McDevitt (cl); Reg Dare, Aubrey Franks, Jimmy Skidmore (ts); Eddie Macauley, Leonard Feather, Jack Penn, Billy Munn (p); Norman Brown, Ivor Mairants, Alan Ferguson, Dick Ball, Jock Reid, Tiny Winters, Charlie Short (b); Dudley Barber, Ben Edwards, Jock Cummings (d).* 1/38–5/44.

***** In A Mellow Tone**
Lake LACD108 *Chisholm; Kenny Baker (t); Tony Coe (cl, as, bs); Tommy Whittle (ts, f); Alan Branscombe (p, vib); Brian Lemon (p); Lennie Bush, Kenny Baldock (b); Bobby Orr, John Richardson (d).* 8/72–5/73.

Chisholm was a marvellous part of British jazz for decades, and the slightness of his legacy on record – at least in the limelight – is to be regretted. The Timeless compilation is both valuable and enjoyable, a twin merit not always encountered in historical surveys. It brings together several dates from the '30s and two from the '40s with Chisholm featured in various London groups. Four titles by Danny Polo's Swing Stars are fine, but the pick is probably the famous Jive Five session of October 1938, with all known takes included. Besides Chisholm proving that he had few peers on the slide horn outside the USA during the period, there are glimpses of the admirable McQuater, as well as an acetate made in Leonard Feather's office in 1935, featuring a jam on 'Pardon Me Pretty Baby' by the 20-year-old trombonist. Aside from this item, which has very rough sound, transfers are very good.

Lake has salvaged an obscure mainstream date for Rediffusion in 1973 which shows the old warrior still in impeccable form, alongside Baker, Coe, Whittle and the rest. 'Walk Right Up Folks', taken at a fearsome tempo, shows what he could do in a hot mainstream situation, and the subsequent 'Star Dust' (the sleeve listings have transposed this title with 'The Boy Next Door') shows off his finely groomed tone. A couple of live tracks with rhythm section alone are the makeweights. Unpretentious music which should make British readers nostalgic about the irrepressible Chis.

Herman Chittison (1909–67)

PIANO, VOCALS

Nicknamed 'Ivory', this gifted pianist from Flemingsburg, Kentucky, had a tendency to perfectionism which may have hampered his career as a recording artist. He worked in Europe and in Egypt until the start of the war, when he returned to America to launch a radio career as Ernie the Blue Note Pianist.

*****(*) Herman Chittison, 1933–1941**
Classics 690 *Chittison; Ikey Robinson (g, v); Arita Day (v).* 7/33–9/41.

***** Herman Chittison, 1944–1945**
Classics 1024 *Chittison; Carl Lynch, Jimmy Shirley (g); Calton Powell, Cedric Wallace (d); Thelma Carpenter (v).* 5/34–5/45.

Chittison's great mistake was to take on Tatum and Waller at their own game, trying to accelerate his ragtime and stride approach to such an extent that he was able to play very fast but only rather vapidly. And yet he was capable of playing with astonishing beauty, as on 'Where Or When', from the second Classics volume. He was also greatly drawn to classical material, and 'Schubert's Serenade' is one of the highlights of the January 1944 session for World Transcriptions.

The earlier volume contains some valuable sides, the bulk of them recorded in France. The solo 'Honeysuckle Rose' is unashamedly Walleresque, and it nearly works. The solo stuff is almost always better, and the album might receive a slightly higher rating if it weren't for the dreary material with Robinson and the two tracks with Day, who shouldn't be confused with Anita O'Day (and wouldn't be if you could hear her sing).

The later trio underlines Chit's preference for playing solo with the most minimal accompaniment. Jimmy Shirley and both Cedric Wallace and Calton Powell are accomplished players but rarely come to the fore. All of this material was recorded back in New York City except 'You Gave Me Everything But Love', which was made for Brunswick in Paris a decade earlier and is included here to fill out an earlier chapter in an extraordinary and still unappreciated career.

**** P.S. With Love**

IAJRC 1006 *Chittison (p solo).* 6/64–67.

Recorded late in Herman's life, this previously unissued group of solos (nine of them cut only weeks before his death from lung cancer) isn't the best introduction to his work. The material is fairly weak, consisting largely of show tunes that don't favour his strengths. 'Jealousy' is interesting, but 'The Sound Of Music' is merely kitsch. Decent recording quality but a lack of substance throughout.

Charlie Christian (1916–42)

GUITAR

Played in touring groups in the early '30s, and was playing an electric guitar by 1937. Heard by Benny Goodman, he joined the Goodman orchestra and small group and was otherwise found jamming at New York's Minton's Club, an early crucible of bebop. Hospitalized for TB in 1941, he died the next year after contracting pneumonia.

****** The Genius Of The Electric Guitar**

Columbia CK 65564 4CD *Christian; Alec Fila, Irving Goodman, Cootie Williams (t); Cutty Cutshall, Lou McGarity (tb); Gus Bivona, Skippy Martin (as); Georgie Auld, Pete Mandello (ts); Bob Snyder (bs); Lionel Hampton (vib); Count Basie, Dudley Brooks, Johnny Guarnieri, Fletcher Henderson (p); Artie Bernstein (b); Nick Fatool, Harry Jaeger, Jo Jones, Dave Tough (d).* 39–41.

***** The Original Guitar Hero**

Columbia 83864 *As above.* 39–41.

***** Complete Studio Recordings**

Definitive 11176 3CD *Similar to above.* 39–41.

****** Solo Flight**

Topaz TPZ 1017 *As above, except add Henry 'Red' Allen, Ziggy Elman, Dizzy Gillespie, Johnny Martell, Jimmy Maxwell (t), Red Ballard, Vernon Brown, J. C. Higginbotham, Ted Vesley (tb), Edmond Hall (cl), Earl Bostic, Benny Carter, Buff Estes, Skippy Martin, Toots Mondello, Hymie Schertzer (as), Bus Basey, Coleman Hawkins, Jerry Jerome, Ben Webster (ts), Clyde Hart, Ken Kersey (p), Meade Lux Lewis (cel), Israel Crosby, Milt Hinton (b), Big Sid Catlett, Cozy Cole (d).* 39–41.

***** Celestial Express**

Definitive 11122 2CD *Similar to above.* 39–41.

***** Radio Broadcasts, 39–41**

Cleopatra 1150 *Similar to above.* 39–41.

****** Swing To Bop**

Dreyfus FDM 36715-2 *As above discs.* 11/39–3/41.

Who actually invented bebop? Parker and Gillespie seemed to arrive at near-identical solutions to the blind alley of jazz harmony. Thelonious Monk was never an orthodox bopper, but he had his two cents' worth. And then there was Charlie Christian, who in some accounts was the first to develop the long lines and ambitious harmonic progressions of bop. Christian's appetite for booze and girls was only ever overtaken by his thirst for music. He once improvised 'Rose Room' for nearly an hour and a half, a feat which prompted Benny Goodman to hire him. Though Christian's greatest contributions, in terms of musical history, were the historic jams at Minton's in New York out of which bebop emerged, his role in the Goodman and Lionel Hampton bands, documented rather well on *Solo Flight*, represent the bulk of what is left to us. There are versions around of the Minton's material, but they enjoy a slightly uncertain existence. Christian's first commercial outings were the September 1939 sides with Hampton. A single track from it ('One Sweet Letter From You') and one from a month later ('Haven't Named It Yet') give a sense of the excitement the bandleader obviously felt at this freshly discovered young voice.

Christian was arguably the first guitarist to make completely convincing use of an electric instrument and, though his style blended Texas blues riffing with Lester Young's long-limbed strolls, he was able to steer a path away from the usual saxophone-dominated idiom and towards something that established guitar as an improvising instrument in its own right. Goodman clearly recognized that and gave him considerable solo space in his sextet. Amplification meant that the guitar could be heard clearly, and Christian's solos on 'Rose Room' and 'Star Dust' remain models for the instrument.

Since our last edition, the Christian discography has mushroomed with the release of at least three important box sets. The Definitives and the Columbia represent a considerable outlay. Are they worth it? We'd say that for all but the most dedicated listeners, prepared to wait some considerable time for a whiff of Charlie's undoubted genius, the Definitive studio set takes second place to the Columbia, while the live box is too rough and ready in places to merit the space it will occupy on your shelf.

The live radio material shows just how much Goodman's swing was part of the wider culture of its day and how much Christian contributed to it. These cuts, recorded at Carnegie Hall and other major venues, including Madison Square Garden, are evidence of Charlie's speed of thought and absolute devotion to a sound which is both electric in its embrace of amplification and organic as well.

The Columbia box set has 98 tracks, including 70 master takes. If that's too much, *The Original Guitar Hero* offers a relatively cheap, single-CD reduction. The sound-quality is exquisite, a model for all reissue programmes. We can't fault it at any level, except perhaps to raise the question of just how important in the history of the music Christian really was. Is there anything here that really merits such an extravagant packaging, or is Christian just another of those artists re-created by a posthumous mythology? *Avocatus diaboli.*

Jodie Christian (born 1932)

PIANO

A veteran of the local Chicago jazz scene, Christian, despite his considerable experience, didn't start recording as a leader until 1992. While broadly based in a hard-bop idiom, he has also worked with Roscoe Mitchell.

★★★(★) Experience
Delmark DE-454 *Christian; Larry Gray (b); Vincent Davis (d).* 5/91–2/92.

★★★ Rain Or Shine
Delmark DE-467 *As above, except add Paul McKee (tb), Roscoe Mitchell (ss, as, ob), Art Porter (as), Ernie Adams (d), George Hughes (d), Francine Griffin (v).* 5/91–12/93.

Christian opens the first record with a Byzantine exploration of the blues on 'Bluesing Around', and it gives the impression that he couldn't wait to get stuck into his first date as a leader, on the cusp of his 60th birthday. A local Chicagoan through and through, he can play for anybody, yet, unlike many such sidemen, he has a distinction of his own. More than half of the CD is solo piano, with a slow 'Mood Indigo' and a lovely original called 'Faith' as particular standouts. Christian's decisive touch and complex but clear voicings bespeak a talent that has absorbed everything it needs from the jazz tradition. Gray and Davis help out assiduously on the four trio tracks.

The follow-up is by comparison a bit disappointing. 'Let's Try' is a fine opener with sterling work by McKee and Porter – who sounds quite different from his Verve Forecast self – and the ballad medley works well, with an especially impressive turn by the trombonist on 'Polka Dots And Moonbeams'. But the tracks with Roscoe Mitchell, who sounds notably sour and argumentative, just don't fit in, no matter how nobly Christian tries to bring them round. Griffin sings on two tracks, and Jodie himself croons one number.

★★★ Soul Fountain
Delmark DE 498 *Christian; Odies Williams (t); Roscoe Mitchell (as, f); Art Porter (as); John Whitfield (b); Ernie Adams (d).* 8/94.

★★★ Front Line
Delmark DE 490 *Christian; Sonny Cohn (t); Norris Turney (as); Eddie Johnson (ts); John Whitfield (b); Ernie Adams, Gerryck King (d); Francine Griffin (v).* 1/96.

Soul Fountain at least integrates Mitchell rather more successfully into Christian's format. However, it's odd to hear him blowing on 'Now's The Time', and the long 'Consequences' doesn't really work, so again there's the feeling that this is a record where too many styles are being jostled together. The piano solos 'Everlasting Life' and 'Blessings' are further evidence of Christian's gifts, and the lovely duet with Porter on 'My One And Only Love' makes a touching farewell to the since-departed altoman.

Front Line assembles a nice group of old-timers for a set of old-time tunes – Ellington, Basie, standards. Turney still has his Hodges and Willie Smith sound beautifully together, but Sonny Cohn sounds a bit shaky, cleverly though he disguises it, and Johnson is merely big and bluff. Christian acts as referee here and gets the best he can out of the team; it's good fun.

★★★(★) Reminiscing
Delmark DE-531 *Christian; Dennis Carroll (b); Tony Walton (d).* 7/00.

Approaching 70, Jodie takes a look back through tunes that mark out some point in his musical past, and it's a delightful session. He likes, as always, to paraphrase melodies, but not so much that you can't tell what they might be, and he has a swinging team behind him; Walton's solo on the opening 'How Insensitive' takes the ear straight away. He makes André Previn's 'It's Good To Have You Near' walk a line between spare and florid, and the blues is played with placid authority on 'Chicago Delta Blues'.

Ian Christie (born 1927)

CLARINET

AND

Keith Christie (1931–80)

TROMBONE

The Christie brothers were a sometimes explosive combination in the combustible years of British trad. Ian retired to the sidelines and worked as a TV critic, returning to occasional playing in the '80s, but Keith took a nomadic path through British jazz, moving from trad to Ted Heath to Tubby Hayes and studio and theatre work. He died in 1980, his last years troubled by alcoholism.

★★★(★) Christie Brothers Stompers
Cadillac SGC/MEL CD 201 *Ian Christie; Keith Christie; Ken Colyer (c); Dickie Hawdon (t); Pat Hawes, Charlie Smith (p); Nevil Skrimshire (g); Ben Marshall (bj); Mickey Ashman, Denny Coffee (b); George Hopkinson, Bernard Saward, Pete Appleby (d); Bill Colyer (wbd); Neva Raphaello (v).* 6/51–8/52.

This captures the sometimes crazed intensity of original British trad better than any of the more renowned Colyer, Lyttelton or Barber reissues. The Christies originally put together the group with players from the Lyttelton and Crane River bands, and the CD collects tracks from various sessions for Melodisc, along with four live tracks from a previously unknown acetate. Though the first few numbers suffer from poor sound, they belt along with bewildering power. Colyer's lead is less self-consciously 'authentic' than he would later become, and Keith Christie delivers some hair-raising solos. The later sessions with Dickie Hawdon in for Colyer are comparatively steady, but the fierce rhythm sections, Ian Christie's gargling but supple solos and the queer blend of high spirits and grim determination that seems to typify this music keeps everything fresh. Remastering has been done very capably from some less than ideal sources. The CD is also beautifully packaged and annotated.

Gunter Christmann (born 1942)

TROMBONE, CELLO

An improviser with a long-standing involvement in European free music, Christmann began recording for FMP in the early '70s. Primarily a trombonist, he now plays cello almost as often. His evolving project, Vario, established in 1979, is the name given to the differing improvising groups that he puts together; it has reached Vario 34 at least. He also works extensively in film and has explored the connections between improvised music and film-making.

★★★(★) Alla Prima

Concepts Of Doing 001 *Christmann; Alexander Frangenheim (b). 1/97.*

★★★★ Here Now

Concepts Of Doing 003 *Christmann; Evan Parker (ss, ts). 1–4/98.*

★★★ Water Always Writes In Plural

Concepts Of Doing 004 *Christmann; Mats Gustafsson (ss); Thomas Lehn (syn); Christian Munthe (g); Alexander Frangenheim (b); Paul Lovens (d). 7/98.*

Welcome back to this maverick spirit, who hasn't been particularly well-served by CD to date. These albums on Concepts Of Doing supplement the issues on Edition Explico, Christmann's own tiny label which issues records in minuscule runs. He is one of the great individualists of the trombone: a vocabulary of gasps, smears, wheezes, etc., etc., but a sensibility that seems to think in long-form as well as in the moment-to-moment strangeness which his music runs by. The duets with Frangenheim will evoke memories of his old FMP albums with Detlef Schonenberg, but this is better recorded and more fully achieved. Though both men work very quietly for much of the way, Christmann's playing in particular is as spontaneous and unpredictable as ever: his trombone will suddenly bark out a note that shocks the listener. With Parker, there's an almost sing-song quality to their interplay. A perfectly rounded disc which starts with two long soprano solos by Parker in his most magisterial style, continues with three duets ('Here Now 2', for tenor and trombone, is especially fine), and finishes with Christmann at his nuttiest in three unfathomable solos.

Water Always Writes In Plural is by Vario 34, a recent incarnation of Christmann's ongoing group music. Considering the players involved, it's a surprisingly low-key event, scissored into nine pieces in which the players appear to be circling rather respectfully round one another.

★★★(★) One To (Two)

Okkadisk 10002 *Christmann; Mats Gustafsson (ss, ts, bs). 8/97.*

A rare American record for Christmann, even if it was recorded in Hanover. Gustafsson is a more incendiary performer than the trombonist (or should we now call him cellist? He plays the string instrument on 12 of the 18 tracks), but he inevitably bows to Gunter's more insidious aesthetic. These pecked-off miniatures are taut, concentrated, eccentric, and often very funny, as well as disquieting: one of those records when you're never sure what will happen next.

★★★(★) (For) Friends And Neighbo(u)rs

Concepts Of Doing 008 *Christmann; Phil Minton (v). 10/01.*

Minton's long gallery of voices makes him an exceptionally appropriate partner for the similarly free-spirited Christmann. These nine duets are both frightening and nonchalantly hilarious. Minton's ability to go from a guttural whisper, which sounds much lower than any note touched by Chaliapin, to an ear-splitting howl – in no more than a heartbeat – keeps the listener in a state of permanent, nervous anticipation. Christmann, never one to indulge in any kind of yin and yang dialogue, somehow finds answering lines which have their own unearthly strangeness. He divides his time between cello and trombone more equally here. Amazing stuff, though if you've never encountered either man before, take fair warning that it's very strange music.

June Christy (1926–90)

VOCAL

Followed Anita O'Day as Stan Kenton's singer in 1945 and sang with him regularly for years while having her own recording career, mostly with Capitol in the '50s and '60s. When her career waned she basically retired, although she recorded a couple of sessions in the '70s. Married to Bob Cooper.

★★★ Original Studio Radio Transcriptions

Swing Factory SWCD66601 *Christy; Stan Kenton Orchestra. 45–46.*

Although there's no real documentation in this package, it's an attractive set of features for Christy from her earliest Kenton period. She sounds amazingly confident and able on even a tricky song such as 'Lullaby In Rhythm'. Transfers are a mixed lot, though there's nothing too rough to spoil enjoyment.

★★★(★) Day Dreams

Capitol 832083-2 *Christy; Stan Kenton (p); orchestras directed by Frank DeVol, Bob Cooper, Pete Rugolo, Shorty Rogers. 3/47–5/55.*

♛ ★★★★ Something Cool: The Complete Mono and Stereo Versions

Capitol 34069-2 *Christy; Pete Rugolo, orchestra. 53–60.*

★★★ Duet

Capitol 89285-2 *Christy; Stan Kenton (p). 55.*

★★★★ The Misty Miss Christy

Capitol 98452-2 *Christy; Pete Rugolo Orchestra. 56.*

★★★(★) Fair And Warmer & Gone For The Day

Capitol 95448-2 *Christy; orchestra. 57.*

★★★★ The Song Is June

Capitol 55455-2 *Christy; Pete Rugolo Orchestra. 7/58–8/60.*

★★★(★) Ballads For Night People & The Intimate Miss Christy

Capitol 96728-2 *Christy; Bud Legge (f); Al Viola (g); Don Bagley (b); orchestra arranged by Bob Cooper. 60–63.*

★★★(★) Big Band Specials

Capitol 498319-2 *Christy; Conte Candoli, Lee Katzman, Al Porcino, Ray Triscari (t); Vern Friley, Lew McCreary, Frank Rosolino, John Haliburton, Ken Shroyer, Dick Nash (tb); Bob Cooper, Joe Maini, Jack Nimitz, Bill Perkins, Bud Legge, Charlie Kennedy (saxes); Jimmy Rowles (p); Joe Mondragon (b); Mel Lewis (d). 10–11/62.*

★★★★ The Best Of The Jazz Sessions

Capitol 53922-2 *Christy; various groups as above. 9/49–8/68.*

June Christy might be the great lost jazz singer of her era, but she is not forgotten – her years with Stan Kenton and several solo hits have sustained her legend. Yet jazz-vocal followers have seemed reluctant to place her in the same league as Ella or Billie or Sarah. We beg to differ. Christy's wholesome but peculiarly sensuous voice is both creative and emotive. Her long, controlled lines and the shading of a fine vibrato suggest both a professional's attention to detail and a tender, solicitous feel for the heart of a song, something which makes the often dark material of her later years the more affecting. Her greatest moments are as close to creating definitive interpretations as any singer can come.

Barely into her 20s she was already a confident and stylish singer, a swing-era canary with a feel for the cooler, more knowing pulse of the years ahead. *Day Dreams* collects various singles and a few unreleased pieces from 1947–50, including a rare scat vehicle on 'The Way You Look Tonight' (just the sort of thing Christy wasn't supposed to be good at, though she handles it superbly), a gorgeous treatment of Gershwin's 'Do It Again', Bob Graettinger's bizarre chart for 'Everything Happens To Me' and a couple of fine Ellington treatments. Two duet tracks with Stan Kenton from 1955 are leftovers from their *Duet* session.

Her best work was done with arranger Pete Rugolo (although numerous charts by her husband, Bob Cooper, shouldn't be forgotten). The masterpieces are certainly *Something Cool* and *The Misty Miss Christy*. The original LPs were perfectly programmed and meticulously tailored to Christy's persona. 'Something Cool' itself is a story that bears endless retelling, but 'Midnight Sun', 'I Should Care' and several others seem like definitive interpretations, a marvel for Christy's technique – perfect breath control and vibrato – as well as for her emotional colouring. It only took EMI/Capitol something like 20 years to finally sort out putting both the original mono version (from 1953–5) with the 1960 stereo remake on one CD. The later interpretations are deeper, more considered, but still beautifully fresh after more than 40 years. In its current incarnation, this disc demands our highest accolade.

The Misty Miss Christy is almost as good. Her version of 'Round Midnight' ought to go down as one of the great treatments of that much-covered song. Rugolo's inventiveness is unstinting throughout, handling the orchestra in surprising ways but doing nothing to unsettle or take the attention away from the singer. *Fair And Warmer* is doubled up with *Gone For The Day*, two further 1957 sessions with Rugolo, and these breezy songs still have a tang of melancholy about them which singer and arranger seem to encourage in each other.

The *Duet* album with her longtime boss, Kenton, is the oddity among her sessions. Kenton clunks away and Christy, exposed as never before, for once seems to falter in her own technique. Though there's a bittersweetness in all of her records, here she sounds fatalistic.

The Song Is June, which couples that album with the later *Off Beat*, is unmissable. While there are some swingers here, including delightful versions of 'A Sleepin' Bee', 'The One I Love (Belongs To Somebody Else)' and 'The Song Is You', the nocturnal brooding of 'Saturday's Children', 'Nobody's Heart' and 'You Say You Care' is more typical. Rugolo never did a better chart than his astonishing arrangement of 'Remind Me', and Christy's mature style blends the sweetness of her youth with a serene melancholy that can be deeply affecting. These have never been famous records; they should be.

The British end of Capitol has issued a double-up of *Ballads For Night People* (arranged by Bob Cooper and featuring his own tenor in a particularly fine 'My Ship', although 'Kissing Bug' and an achingly slow 'Bewitched' are also fine) and *The Intimate Miss Christy*, where June has only a Julie Londonish accompaniment behind her. It's a moot point as to whether her version of 'Ev'ry Time' outdoes Chris Connor's: a close thing. *Big Band Specials* offers her a dozen hits from the swing era, some rarely sung, such as 'Skyliner', 'Swingin' On Nothin'' and 'Until'. Must have been a nostalgic exercise for her in 1962, and charts by Cooper, Bill Holman and Shorty Rogers make the grade. All in all, it's a pleasure to see so many of her Capitol albums back in circulation, though their availability will vary depending on where you are.

Best Of The Jazz Sessions is an astute compilation that goes as far as a small-group session of 1968. One can complain about some of the omissions, but there is more than enough great Christy here to make it essential for those who might prefer to sample some of her work.

***** A Friendly Session Vol. 1**

Jasmine JASCD 341 *Christy; Johnny Guarnieri (p); others unknown.* 50.

****(*) A Lovely Way To Spend An Evening**

Jasmine JASMCD 2528 *Christy; Stu Williamson (t); Herb Geller (as); Russ Freeman (p); Monte Budwig (b); Shelly Manne (d); Jerry Gray Orchestra.* 57–59.

These are shoddy but nevertheless useful survivals. The earlier disc finds Christy on a set of radio transcriptions with a Johnny Guarnieri small group – 20 songs, including at least one tantalizing rarity, 'The Sky Without The Stars'. Sound is one-dimensional but listenable. It is also thin and weakly spread on the later Jasmine disc, too; but the performances find the singer in inventive and bright form, and both the tracks with Manne's group and with the Jerry Gray band are hip and swinging affairs.

Jim Cifelli (born 1961)

TRUMPET, FLUGELHORN

An upstate New Yorker, Cifelli made his name with the Uptown Jazz Orchestra before founding his own nonet, whose repertoire is influenced by Gil Evans's classic arrangements and by the work of Manny Albam, Cifelli's composition teacher.

***** Bullet Trane**

Orchard 3503 *Cifelli; Andy Gravish (t, flhn); Pete McGuinness (tb); Cliff Lyons (ss, as); Joel Frahm (ts); Barbara Cifelli (bs, bcl, f); Pete McCann (g); Mary Ann McSweeney (b); Tim Horner (d).* 98.

***** So You Say**

Challenge 73175 *As above.* 99.

***** Tunnel Vision**

Short Notice Music SNM 002 *As above.* n.d.

Cifelli is more impressive as a leader/arranger than as a soloist, and the real joy of these records is his ability to give a small(ish) group the range and power of an orchestra, while giving a substantial line-up the flexibility of a small group. His compositional interests can be gauged from a bold segue of Wayne Shorter's 'Fee Fi Fo Fum' and 'Speak No Evil' on the most recent record, but it is the originals which are most interesting.

Bullet Trane also includes Herbie Hancock's 'Dolphin Dance', but it has to follow the title-piece, which is an inspired variation on Coltrane's 'Countdown'. It's pretty clear that Cifelli had been listening to *Blue Train* around this time. The line-up of horns suggests that influence, and so does the inclusion of Tadd Dameron's 'Lady Bird', which Trane reworked on his Blue Note session. Here, as elsewhere, it is trombonist McGuinness who really catches the ear, a strong but airy player who delivers a lot of atmosphere and also some clever harmonic ideas.

The second album is every bit as good, and underlines the significance of having a guitar player rather than a pianist as the main harmony instrument. McCann is a driving, propulsive player, but he leaves the harmonic texture wide open. He is particularly good on the unexpected 'Where Is Carmela Going Now?'. The saxophonists come into their own on 'So You Say'. Frahm is magnificent on 'Undercurrent' and Lyons turns in a superb soprano solo on 'Without Changes', which was written by bassist McSweeney. Barbara Cifelli is, of course, the boss's wife and is something of a journeywoman, but easily overlooked. She brings a sonic range and a much-needed change of texture to some of the charts.

The third album is the most accomplished yet, but Cifelli converts may expect something more this time round. The polish is unmistakable, but *Tunnel Vision* is a slightly characterless piece of product. With the exception of the Shorter segment and the delightful Latin 'Cambio De Corazone', there is nothing that surprises. Petty to quibble, though, with such thoughtful and well-executed modern jazz. More power to their collective elbow.

Peter Cincotti (born 1984)

PIANO

At seven years old, he shared a stage with Harry Connick Jr. The rest is history for the precocious New Yorker.

***** Peter Cincotti**

Concord CCD 2159 *Cincotti; Scot Kreitzer (ts); David Finck (b); Kenny Washington (d).* 3/03.

He has the looks, the chops, and the background to make it big, damn him. The debut is as debuts are, an attempt to show off as many facets as possible. Hence, 'Nature Boy' medleyed with the Beatles' 'Fool On The Hill', a jazzed-up version of Blood, Sweat & Tears' 'Spinning Wheel' and, just so we all remember he's barely out of short pants, 'Rainbow Connection' from *The Muppet Show*. In the wake of Harry Connick, who spotted the youngster's talent and invited him to join in at a prestige gig, there are lots of singer–pianists around. Peter will have to work hard to consolidate this promising debut.

Circle

GROUP

A short-lived quartet featuring the four principals, which came together when Braxton joined the already-working trio of Corea, Holland and Altschul.

***** Paris-Concert**

ECM 843163-2 2CD *Anthony Braxton (reeds, perc); Chick Corea (p); Dave Holland (b); Barry Altschul (d).* 2/71.

Something of a historical document at this point, although unsatisfactory in many respects. This was recorded on the group's one European tour, and it was a quartet that wouldn't last long, mainly because of tensions building up between Braxton and Corea. This concert souvenir is full of hustle and bustle, but it doesn't seem to go anywhere in particular. There's a yearning for freedom by all hands, but Corea isn't really interested in following Braxton's approach any more than Braxton is interested in playing 'Nefertiti' and 'There Is No Greater Love', which start and finish the album. Their playful 'Duet', though, is an unexpected highlight. Holland and Altschul play a lot of music, but they are very poorly served by the sound, which is atypically thin and clattery for an ECM session. Scholars of the period have found it fascinating, though.

Soesja Citroen

VOCALS

Leading singer on the Dutch scene.

****** Sings Thelonious Monk**

Timeless 11021 *Citroen; Dusko Goykovich (t); Cees Smal (tb); Ferdinand Povel (as); Ruuel Brink (ts); Herman Schoonderwalt (bs); Cees Slinger (p); Josh Clayton, Jacques Schols (b); Kees Kranenberg, Peter Ypma (d).* 3–4/83.

***** Shall We Dance Or Keep On Moping**

Timeless 11007 *Citroen; Frederic Leeflang (ss, as, ts); Albert Sarko (p); Jan Voogd (b); John Engels (d).* 89.

As non-obvious vocal projects go a Monk album is well up there, but Citroen did this with such intelligence and aplomb that Carmen McRae copied the idea five years later, probably secure in the knowledge that the Dutch woman was little known outside her own country. Soesja's grasp of Monk's off-kilter rhythm and harmonic invention is evident from the opening 'In Walked Bud', which is subtle and sassy. What follows is equally good: 'Round About Midnight' has been done many times before, but what of her version of 'Crepuscule With Nellie' (rechristened 'In Twilight') and 'Let's Cool One' (which comes out as 'Come With Me')? 'Blue Monk' gets a slightly different treatment, but it's also a killer. This is a hugely exciting album, worthy of the widest notice.

The sequel is no less bold in its choice of material, with Randy Weston's 'Little Niles' and a wonderful 'Hi-Fly' in with Ornette's 'Lonely Woman', Fran Landesman's 'Spring Can Really Hang You Up The Most' and the Gershwin title-tune. If it lacks the concentration of the earlier record and its sheer richness of sound, this is the place to take note of Citroen as a vocal stylist. She has a light, attractive head voice, which switches to something more muscular when she tackles low registers. There's not quite enough continuity between the two for purists, but no one will deny its effectiveness or unaffected beauty.

***** Here And Now**

Challenge 70003 *Citroen; Jarmo Hoogendijk (t); Cees Slinger (p); Jan Voogd (b); Arnoud Gerritse (d).* 94.

*****(*) Songs For Lovers And Losers**

Challenge 70034 *Citroen; Ack van Rooyen (flhn); Louis van Dyke (p); Hein van de Geyn (b).* 96.

***** Song For Ma**

Challenge 70056 *Citroen; Michael Moore (cl); Berend van den Berg (p); Hein van de Geyn (b); Joost Kesselaar (d).* 99.

Interestingly, she reprises 'Crepuscule For Nellie'/'In Twilight' for the first of the Challenge records, which was produced by Chris Ellis. The sound is immediately more polished and intimate, and though the change in register isn't especially obvious from the Monk tune, you hear it at once on the opening 'As Long As I Live'. Still eclectic, Soesja has songs by Stix Hooper and David Frishberg in with the standards.

Ellis's instinct in playing Soesja's voice off against a single horn paid dividends on the first of his collaborations, though Hoogendijk only appears on four tracks. He repeats the formula on the drummerless *Songs*, which carries off its bruised romanticism with great conviction, especially on 'Lush Life'. The Monk song appears again on *Song For Ma*, an inclusion perhaps justified by the intention to make this a more autobiographical set, something that became clear when she toured the music to great acclaim. The title-song is magnificent: 'No one can touch me / for this is my kingdom / wrapped in her love / protected but free'. Time she was better known outside her native country.

Sonny Clark (1931–63)

PIANO

Recorded on the West Coast from 1953, on the East from 1957, and recorded constantly for the next six years, though alcohol and heroin ruined him.

***** 1954 Memorial Album**

Jazz Factory JFCD 158 *Clark; Simon Brehm (b); Bobby White (d).* 1/54.

The odd title – given the date of his death – is explained by the fact that this was only released on LP in 1975 by the defunct Xanadu. It is in fact a private recording and of fairly poor quality, but it does give a valuable insight into the development of a short-lived talent who should have done so much more. There are a couple of interesting improvisations and versions of 'Body And Soul', 'All God's Chillun Got Rhythm' and 'Over The Rainbow'. Though primarily of historical value, it does have an undeniable charm that overcomes most of the technical deficiencies.

****(*) Oakland 1955**

Uptown 2740 *Clark; Jerry Good (b); Al Randall (d).* 55.

Not released until 1995, this live recording of a bop-dominated set by the 24-year-old Clark reveals him to be more competent than genuinely visionary at this stage. 'Bags' Groove', 'Ow!' and 'All The Things You Are' are delivered somewhat in the style of Bud Powell, but with a few harmonic devices which point in other, potentially more interesting directions. Randall and Good work manfully, but neither is particularly adventurous, and here and there Sonny is working almost half a measure ahead of his colleagues. Shaky sound-quality doesn't help. The best was yet to come, fortunately.

***** Sonny's Crib**

Blue Note 46819 *Clark; Donald Byrd (t); Curtis Fuller (tb); John Coltrane (ts); Paul Chambers (b); Art Taylor (d).* 10/57.

*****(*) Sonny Clark Trio**

Blue Note 51238-2 *Clark; Paul Chambers (b); Philly Joe Jones (d).* 11/57.

****** Cool Struttin'**

Blue Note 95327-2 *As above, except add Art Farmer (t); Jackie McLean (as).* 1/58.

***** Standards**

Blue Note 21283-2 *Clark; Paul Chambers, Jymie Merritt (b); Wes Landers (d).* 11–12/58.

Clark approached music with a joyous abandon. As long as there was a piano in the corner, a bottle opened and some business to attend to in a back room, he seems to have been content. Perhaps because the darkness of his private life – a pendulum back and forth between alcohol and narcotics – never seems to have impinged on his ability to play, he enjoyed a steady if short-lived tenure as Blue Note's house pianist. Note-perfect, rhythmically bouncy and always ready with a quirky idea, he was an ideal group-player, rather less convincing in the context of a hornless group like the eponymous 1957 date. Chambers, then approaching his heyday, has a greater than usual share of the spotlight, perhaps because Sonny's capacity for solos was never substantial.

Sonny's Crib is something of a transitional record. Its roots are still very much in orthodox bebop, though there are signs already of the shift to a more open approach. Unusually, the set is dominated by standards, from the opening 'With A Song In My Heart' to two versions of 'Speak Low' and 'Come Rain Or Shine'. Byrd is on astonishing form in the opening selection, and though the three-man front line doesn't really work, each of the horns has some effective moments.

Cool Struttin', now reissued in Blue Note's Rudy Van Gelder series, is an immaculately tasteful jazz album and one of the key documents of hard bop. The title-piece is a long-form blues, with room for the horns to stretch out. Sonny's own finest moment is his solo on 'Blue Minor', another original. His three-note trills are almost Monkian and the percussive, spacious attack is reminiscent of the bebop giant at his most capacious. Though Clark rarely strays far from the blues, one can hear Farmer itching to break through into other dimensions. The reissue contains two extra tracks unreleased on LP: his own 'Royal Flush' and a wayward interpretation of Rodgers and Hart's 'Lover'. Easy to see why it was excluded.

The standards album lacks character. Clark's great strength, like Monk's and Powell's, lay in imposing his own personality on algebraically simple materials. Here he is required to play melodically, and he sounds merely workmanlike. Landers is a very pedestrian drummer by the standards set by Philly Joe.

*****(*) My Conception**

Blue Note 22674 *Clark; Hank Mobley, Clifford Jordan (ts); Kenny Burrell (g); Paul Chambers (b); Art Blakey, Pete LaRoca (d).* 3/59.

Appearing as they did in the shadow of *Cool Struttin'*, the March 1959 sessions never gained the reputation of their wonderful predecessor. This is unfortunate, for here again Clark showcases a wonderful set of originals. The title-track and two versions of 'Minor Meeting' are the best measure of his compositional talent and his ability to deploy some very different stylists in his band. The result is an immaculately tasteful and sophisticated modern jazz record; perhaps not quite as individual as other of Clark's Blue Note sessions, but certainly one of the most accomplished. The 2000 reissue includes the long 'Eastern Incident' and 'Little Sonny', which help complete the picture on the now widely recognized Clark.

*****(*) Leapin' And Lopin'**

Blue Note 84091 *Clark; Tommy Turrentine (t); Charlie Rouse (ts); Butch Warren (b); Billy Higgins (d).* 11/61.

Subject to erratic availability, this final recording as a leader is further testimony to Clark's skills as a composer. 'Voodoo' is the signature track, harmonically clever and rhythmically more challenging than the group seem to recognize. Sonny himself is tautly disciplined, showing no signs of the personal problems that would cut short his life just a couple of years later. There are two versions of 'Melody For C' (not 'in C', as is sometimes written) and the variant is a good indication of how exacting he was even at this stage in his career. Even the initially rejected 'Zellmar's Delight', one of the most obscure items in the Clark discography, is restored to the CD reissue. Turrentine contributes 'Midnight Mambo', but the only standard is 'Deep In A Dream', which is thoughtfully, almost introspectively, executed.

Sonny Clark Memorial Quartet

GROUP

One-off project dedicated to the late pianist's music.

***** Voodoo**

Black Saint 120109 *John Zorn (as); Wayne Horvitz (p); Ray Drummond (b); Bobby Previte (d).* 11/85.

John Zorn's enthusiasm for the adventurously simple bop of Sonny Clark surfaced in his News For Lulu group. This, though, was a more sustained homage, seven Clark originals played with real feeling and attention to detail. Zorn himself gets a sound that at moments might recall Jackie McLean, but with a drier edge. It, coupled with Previte's drumming, is the giveaway. It's pretty obvious you're not listening to a period performance but to a latter-day version of Sonny's music. No great surprises in the selection of covers: 'Cool Struttin'', 'Minor Meeting', 'Nicely', 'Something Special', a heroic 'Voodoo', 'Sonia' and, ending as emphatically as it begins, 'Sonny's Crib'. A fascinating disc for anyone interested in the Blue Note diaspora.

Kenny Clarke (1914–85)

DRUMS, XYLOPHONE

Born in Pittsburgh, Clarke came from a musical family and had an early facility on a wide range of instruments, a level of musicianship that suffused everything he did. He is one of the prime movers of the bebop movement but remained in a more swing-orientated idiom than either Art Blakey or Max Roach. Clarke spent his later years in France and was something of a hero in his adoptive country.

***** Complete 1946–1950 Swing Master Takes**

Jazz Factory JFCD22845 *Clarke; Benny Bailey, Dick Collins, Kenny Dorham, Fats Navarro (t); Nat Peck (tb); Joe Brown, Hubert Fol, Michel de Villers, Sonny Stitt (as); Ray Abrams, Jean-Claude Fohrenbach, Dave Kriedt (ts); Cecil Payne, Eddie de Verteuil (bs); Jack Denjean, André Persiany, Bud Powell, Ralph Schecroun, Gerald Wiggins (p); Harry Montaggioni (g); Claude Laurence (vn); John Collins, George Hadjo, Al McKibbon, Alf Messelier, Pierre Michelot (b).* 9/46–6/50.

***** Kenny Clarke, 1946–1948**

Classics 1171 *As above.* 46–48.

***** Kenny Clarke, 1948–1950**

Classics 1233 *As above.* 48–50.

'Klook', so called because of the distinctive 'klook-mop' sound of his favourite cadence, is one of the most influential drummers of all time. There are those who allow him a hand in the invention of bebop, and certainly in recent times the focus of the bebop revolution has shifted away from the horn-men and towards the rhythm section that gave bop its ferocious energy and drive. While working with Dizzy Gillespie in the early '40s, having made his recording debut at 24 in Sweden with the dire James Anderson on vocals, Clarke began to depart from normal practice by marking the count on his top cymbal and using his bass drum only for accents. With his left hand he rattled out the counter-rhythms that weave their way through all his records. It became the distinctive sound of bebop, imitated and adapted by Blakey and Roach, who came to the music with rather different presuppositions about it, and it remains essential background work for drummers even today. Clarke had a strong but also quite delicate sound. The cover of *Plays André Hodeir* (now deleted, more's the pity) shows him wielding extra-long sticks, as he did from time to time throughout his career; they enabled him to get around his kit and to pick out a highly nuanced sound that lesser drummers could never duplicate.

The Jazz Factory set pretty much overlaps with the Classics, but the packaging is much better with the latter and the transfers seem to come across clearer. Apart from the May 1948 date, which is shorn of four not particularly exciting numbers presumably for reasons of duration, it includes all of Kenny's recordings under his own name in the period concerned. Paradoxically, some of the sessions were under the nominal leadership of altoist Michel de Villers, though just to make matters even more complicated 'The Man I Love' from 5 May 1948 was originally credited to tenor saxophonist Jean-Claude Fohrenbach.

As for Kenny's contribution to these, there were fewer bombs dropped by the Luftwaffe in the preceding years. His distinctive accents are evident on every track and given the relative anonymity of the settings, it is Clarke one tends to listen to on most of these tracks. The September 1946 session was recorded in New York City with Fats Navarro (in stunning form), Kenny Dorham, Sonny Stitt and two other saxophonists. It's easily the best date covered by these sets. The Paris sides are professional and often warmly engaging, but they lack the urgency of those 52nd Street Boys.

*****(*) Pieces Of Time**

Soul Note 121078 *Clarke; Andrew Cyrille, Milford Graves, Famoudou Don Moye (d, perc).* 9/83.

Unfortunately, his Savoys are now again awaiting reissue, and there's only this unrepresentative later disc in the catalogue. Though the record was hailed on release as a much-needed reminder that Milford Graves was still alive and functioning, Klook was the elder statesman at this astonishing confrontation, and he more or less steals the show with a seemingly effortless display that has the younger guys diving into their bags for ever more exotic wrinkles on the same basic sound. Not to all tastes, perhaps, but an intriguing and historic record nevertheless.

Clarke–Boland Big Band

GROUP

Co-led by the Belgian pianist and the American drummer, this all-star band ran intermittently but often with a stable personnel over the period 1961–72.

***** Now Hear Our Meanin'**

Collectables 7497 *Kenny Clarke (d); Francy Boland (p); Edmond Arnie, Benny Bailey, Jimmy Deuchar, Maffy Falay,*

Idries Sulieman (t); Erich Kleinschuster, Nat Peck, Ake Persson (tb); Carl Drevo, Billy Mitchell, Ronnie Scott (ts); Sahib Shihab (bs, f); Jimmy Woode (b). 1/63.

***** Handle With Care**

Koch 8534 *As above.* 1/63.

These 1963 recordings were sponsored by producer Gigi Campi and recorded in Germany. The arrangements are spot on, open-ended, relaxed but also germanically precise and the playing from all the soloists (including some great stuff from Ronnie Scott) is marvellous. Clarke and Boland never claimed much solo space, preferring to keep the engine-room turning over, but lovers of big-band music will enjoy these latter-day masters of the craft. There are another couple of Clarke–Boland sessions on Collectables, but always paired with other leaders. The twofer with Jimmy Giuffre, *Western Suite*, is worth looking out for.

***** Jazz In The Movies – More Jazz**

Camjazz 1065 *Clarke; Boland; personnels similar to above.* 68.

No personnels given on some versions of this, but they can probably be extrapolated from other sessions of the time and it's known that Shake Keane was present. The idea is a pretty simple one, though the jazz quotient is disappointingly low. Nino Rota and Ennio Morricone are both strongly represented and this is probably more of interest to film-music fans than to more orthodox jazz collectors.

The Classic Jazz Quartet

GROUP

A quartet of knowing old dogs in the classic-mainstream idiom. Their existence was effectively terminated by Wellstood's death.

****** The Complete Recordings**

Jazzology JCD-138/139 2CD *Dick Sudhalter (c); Joe Muranyi (cl, ss); Dick Wellstood (p); Marty Grosz (g, v).* 11/84–3/86.

The Classic Jazz Quartet – they preferred their original name, The Bourgeois Scum – were one of the pioneer outfits who helped create the renewed taste for old(er) jazz repertory in the '80s and '90s. This package is a comprehensive set of their work – two studio LPs, plus about an LP's worth of previously unreleased, live-without-an-audience music – set down before Wellstood's untimely death ended the group. They resuscitate much-neglected material from the '20s and '30s, fill in with the odd chestnut and sneak by a few originals. The range of arrangement and dynamic which a quartet can touch on is surprising at this length, and the band always surprises, though the Germanic treatment of 'Mississippi Mud' will be tiresome to some. Grosz's wit has become relatively familiar in the last ten years, but the feel of this music has a freshness about it that some subsequent revivalism has missed; Sudhalter does a fine line in neo-Bix, the undervalued Muranyi is consistently strong; and 'the engine, the generator, driving the whole contraption', Wellstood shows why the band went down when he did. The notes in the booklet are rather exhaustingly clever, and the remastered sound is very fine.

The Classical Jazz Quartet

GROUP

New York supergroup assembled to jazz the classics.

*****(*) Tchaikovsky's The Nutcracker**

Recording Arts/Vertical Jazz 5507-2 *Stefon Harris (vib, marim); Kenny Barron (p); Ron Carter (b); Lewis Nash (d).* 8/01.

*****(*) Plays Bach**

Recording Arts/Vertical Jazz 5508-2 *As above.* 4/02.

While these come on more like a marketing concept than records with a pressing need to exist, the playing is so classy and swinging that they're impossible not to enjoy. As a single instance, listen to the tremendous groove the band hit on 'Blues À La Russe' on the Tchaikovsky set. Bob Belden (who arranged both discs) crafts plausible ways for the material to open up to a jazz interpretation. The Tchaikovsky pieces tend to work off Peter's variety of melodic hooks, but tackling Bach is a much tougher proposition (in part because a certain M. Loussier got there a long time ago). Belden chose two bits of Brandenburg, part of the A Major Oboe Concerto, Invention No. 4 and 'Jesu Joy Of Man's Desiring', the unlikeliest cut of all – it works, though. It helps that the players seem completely unselfconscious about the gig, Harris in particular plays exultantly, and the studio sound is superb.

Benn Clatworthy (born 1956)

TENOR SAXOPHONE

London-born but LA-based, Benn is the grandson of music hall legend Gertie Lawrence, an association that has coloured recent work.

***** Gertie, Phil, Theo & Me**

Mainstem MSTCD 0029 *Clatworthy; Theo Saunders (p); Phil Robson (g).* 01.

A remarkable family heritage lies behind this elegant set of music hall and show tunes, done as duos in London with Robson and in Hollywood with Saunders. 'Body And Soul' and 'Someone To Watch Over Me' are the only pieces regularly used as jazz standards, but the remainder of the set reveals some gems, notably 'Shall We Dance?' and Noel Coward's 'Poor Little Rich Girl' and 'Someday I'll Find You'. Clatworthy brings his Coltrane styling to the Rodgers and Hammerstein classic 'I Whistle A Happy Tune'. The guitar tracks work better on balance than the piano ones, but only because the harmonies are more unexpected.

Thomas Clausen (born 1949)

PIANO

Studied at the Copenhagen Academy before making a name for himself in the Danish jazz scene of the '70s, accompanying Dexter Gordon, working with his own trio, and building an international reputation through the '80s and '90s.

****** Psalm**

Storyville STCD 4185 *Clausen; Mads Vinding (b); Alex Riel (d).* 6/94.

We listed a fine solo session in a previous edition and this exemplary trio date affirms Clausen's imaginative powers. It was an audacious idea to open the disc with the slow, dynamically surprising title-piece, and there are more surprises as the session proceeds. 'Dancing In The Dark' hardly refers to its melody at all, and the bare spaces of 'Soft' are beautifully handled. Clausen is at ease at any tempo and refuses to offer too many notes, while Vinding is as much a melodist as a timekeeper. Riel has seldom played better. He is very upfront in the mix, but engineer Hans Nielsen gives him a wonderful sound, and his playing on, say, 'Skygger' gives terrific impetus to what otherwise would have been a mere mood piece.

*****(*) Turn Out The Stars**
Storyville STCD 4215 *Clausen; Severi Pyysalo (vib).* 6/97.

For sheer beauty of sound this pairing makes waves, and the musical interaction is pretty fine too. Pyysalo plays with enough aggression and point to defer suggestions of excess prettiness, and his improvising (such as the astringent solo on Coleman's 'The Turnaround') is similarly tough-minded. But the players don't shy away from making the music sound harmoniously beautiful too. Clausen brought three themes to the session, and 'Green Eyes' lingers in the mind.

****(*) Follow The Moon**
Stunt STUCD 19808 *Clausen; Jan Zum Vohrde (as, f); Fernando de Marco (b); Afonso Correa (d); Caecilie Norby (v).* 9–10/97.

***** Prelude To A Kiss**
Stunt STUCD 00142 *As above, except omit Norby.* 5/00.

These are by Clausen's Brazilian Quartet. Whatever his affinities with this music, it sets him apart from his earlier work, although it's amusing to hear that a Dane sounds just as capable in this genre as, say, Danilo Perez. The earlier set is too bouncy and over-bright with electric keyboards. A revision of 'Desafinado' is charmless, Norby sings on two tracks (and is a 'presence' on a third), and only on 'The Old Man In The Midnight Sea' and the title-piece do Clausen's writing talents make a mark. Jan Zum Vohrde plays much more flute than alto, and at times it all comes dangerously close to chirpy muzak.

The follow-up is better: the rhythm section plays in a cooler, less affected style, the flute and piano duet on 'Prelude To A Kiss' works well, and the piano solo 'Portrait In Black And White' is Clausen at his most persuasive.

*****(*) My Favorite Things**
Stunt STUCD 01242 *Clausen; Jesper Lundgaard (b); Peter Danemo (d).* 10/01.

One day in the studio for Clausen's new trio: 12 tunes (whittled down from 20), all first takes, cut live to two-track. This anti-perfectionist stance offers the usual pros and cons. Danemo is imposing in the mix, and some of the pieces, such as a confused 'Over The Rainbow', could have used more work. But Clausen has a knack for getting the best out of these situations, and much of the music-making is close to sublime. 'My Favorite Things' itself is alive and characterful. Several rare standards – 'Jasmine', 'Deep In Your Heart', 'If You Are But A Dream' – are performed with uncommon grace. And if Danemo is too loud, he's still exciting to hear, in tandem with the quietly masterful Lundgaard.

*****(*) Balacobaco**
Stunt STUCD 03112 *Clausen; Jan Zum Vohrde (as, f); Pia Kaufmanas (f, picc-f); Ida Speyer Gron (vla); Tine Rehling (hp); Mikkel Nordso (g); Fernando De Marco (b); Afonso Correa (d).* 3/03.

The Brazilian Quartet returns, this time augmented by Nordso and the 'Madame Claude Harp Trio'. If the jazz content again seems dispersed, the overall feel of the record really is filled with sunshine: Clausen has written some charming parts for the guest players, and the textures are pretty without becoming cloying. Besides, there's always his own piano to salvage any fears of music-lite taking over. The studio sound is also excellent.

James Clay (1935–95)

TENOR SAXOPHONE

A Texan saxophonist with only a handful of records to account for a big reputation, based on his playing on the local circuit in the late '50s. A brief comeback on record in the '80s led him nowhere.

****(*) The Sound Of The Wide Open Spaces**
Original Jazz Classics OJC 257 *Clay; David 'Fathead' Newman (ts); Wynton Kelly (p); Sam Jones (b); Art Taylor (d).* 4/60.

***** A Double Dose Of Soul**
Original Jazz Classics OJC 1790 *Clay; Nat Adderley (c); Victor Feldman (vib); Gene Harris (p); Sam Jones (b); Louis Hayes (d).* 10/60.

Clay is a semi-legendary figure whose reported influence on Ornette Coleman is interesting but scarcely borne out by these early records. *The Sound* gets into the brawling spirit typical of such two-tenor encounters but offers only a glimpse of Clay as a distinctive force. *A Double Dose* is only marginally more interesting, given that the date is organized as little more than a rote hard-bop affair, but Feldman's vibes are an unusual foil on three tunes, and 'Linda Serene' and 'Lost Tears' are mildly interesting originals.

Buck Clayton (1911–91)

TRUMPET

Though Buck was leading his own big band as early as 1934, it was his time with Basie which established him as a soloist of distinction, a player with a warm, brassy tone and a softness of delivery that was well suited to ballad playing and to accompanying singers. His recording career was long and fruitful, and only towards the end did Buck's standards slip.

***** Buck Clayton 1945–1947**
Classics 968 *Clayton; Dicky Wells, Trummy Young (tb); George Johnson (as); Scoville Browne (as, cl); Ed Hall (cl); Flip Phillips (ts); Lucky Thompson (ts); Sammy Benskin, Johnny Guarnieri, Billy Taylor, Teddy Wilson (p); Brick Fleagle, Freddie Green, Tiny Grimes (g); Al Hall, Milt Hinton, Al McKibbon, Slam Stewart (b); Danny Alvin, Jimmy Crawford, J. C. Heard, Sid Weiss, Shadow Wilson (d); Canada Lee, Sylvia Sims, Kenneth Spencer (v).* 5/45–11/47.

***** The Classic Swing Of Buck Clayton**

Original Jazz Classics OJC 1709 *Clayton; Dicky Wells, Trummy Young (tb); Buster Bailey, Scoville Brown (cl); George Johnson (as); Jimmy Jones, Billy Taylor (p); Brick Fleagle, Tiny Grimes (g); John Levy, Al McKibbon, Sid Weiss (b); Cozy Cole, Jimmy Crawford (d).* 46.

Clayton is one of the great players of mainstream jazz. Responsible for no particular stylistic innovation, he managed to synthesize much of the history of jazz trumpet up to his time with a bright, brassy tone and an apparently limitless facility for melodic improvisation, which made him ideal for the open-ended jams he recorded for Columbia and, latterly, Chiaroscuro. He played with Basie until 1946, the year of the fine *Classic Swing* sessions, and after a stint in the army he struck off on his own again, forming a productive association with shouter Jimmy Rushing which survived long enough for the European tour featured on the Steeplechase set below. The OJC set has much to enjoy. 'Harlem Cradle Song', with Young and Wells, has a lovely, easy swing, and there is a fine instrumental version of 'I Want A Little Girl', normally a Jimmy Rushing feature. The record is, however, now basically a duplication of the Classics set, which has other material too.

Most of Classics 968 was recorded under Buck's own name, though the earliest date, from the day the bomb was dropped on Hiroshima, is under Freddie Green's name, and there is a later session for Keynote led by drummer J. C. Heard. Enough of the *echt* Clayton comes through on the sides for HRS which were recorded in 1946, including classics like 'Harlem Cradle Song' and 'Dawn Dance', tunes which bespeak a gentle artistry and an absolute musical integrity. There is some excellent stuff from Teddy Wilson (originally billed as Theodocius) and from all the reedmen, but the disc could have done without the educational 'Jazz Band', narrated by Canada Lee and sung by Kenneth Spencer, an oddity with a single B-take part for Buck. Clayton was a superb vocal accompanist, and his fills and subtle responses are always tasteful, but he's heard to better effect on the instrumental all-stars tracks from the same occasion, tackling 'Moonglow' with consummate artistry and taste.

*****(*) Copenhagen Concert**

Steeplechase SCCD 36006/7 2CD *Clayton; Emmett Berry (t); Dicky Wells (tb); Earl Warren (as, cl); Buddy Tate (ts); Al Williams (p); Gene Ramey (b); Herbie Lovelle (d); Jimmy Rushing (v).* 9/59.

Plenty of old friends in this band, from the lubricious Wells to the galvanic Rushing, and Clayton sheriffs the ensemble with his expected panache. Eighty-five minutes of music is rather ungenerously spread over two CDs, and since it isn't all deathless stuff, it might have been better reduced to a single disc of the real highlights. But the real problem is the sound, and nobody suffers worse than Buck himself, who is way off mike for many of his solos.

*****(*) Buck & Buddy**

Original Jazz Classics OJCCD 757 *Clayton; Buddy Tate (ts); Sir Charles Thompson (p); Gene Ramey (b); Mousie Alexander (d).* 12/60.

***** Buck & Buddy Blow The Blues**

Original Jazz Classics OJCCD 850 *As above.* 9/61.

These document a happy association. Buddy Tate was a player of similar lineage to Clayton, and all their recordings together have a warmth of genuine understanding. Much of the music on *Buck & Buddy* was formerly on the Prestige double-LP *Kansas City Nights*. Originally recorded for Swingville, it gives a near-perfect sense of where Buck was at the end of his last really productive decade before the trumpeter's curse, persistent lip problems, began to curtail his activity. There's certainly no sign of difficulty here. He trades figures with Tate on 'Birdland Betty' and more romantic shapes on 'When A Woman Loves A Man'.

Blow The Blues is pretty much more of the same, but the heat is off and, with the sterling exception of 'Don't Mind If I Do', the individual numbers fail to catch fire.

*****(*) Buck Clayton All-Stars, 1961**

Storyville STCD 8231 *Clayton; Emmett Berry (t); Dicky Wells (tb); Earl Warren (as); Buddy Tate (ts); Sir Charles Thompson (p); Gene Ramey (b); Oliver Jackson (d).* 4/61.

***** Basel, 1961**

TCB 2072 *As above.* 5/61.

Over in Europe, Buck's brand of swing didn't seem old-fashioned in 1961, and this touring octet was applauded to the rafters right across the continent. Part of TCB's Swiss Radio Days Jazz Series, the album is a typically well-mastered broadcast session. At rising 50 Buck sounds absolutely in command of tone and articulation, and he phrases effectively from the original 'Swinging At The Copper Rail' onwards. 'Robbins' Nest' and 'Night Train' both receive long readings with the horns trading lonely figures on the Jimmy Forrest classic. State-of-the-art swing from a band of past masters, anxious to demonstrate that, away from America at least, they weren't past it. Recorded just a few weeks earlier, the Storyvillle album comes from a Paris show. A similar set, and the band are in equally good heart, but the sound is nothing like as good, Jackson hugely loud, Sir Charles peeking through the cymbals, and the horns sometimes here, sometimes there.

***** Baden, Switzerland, 1966**

Sackville 2028 *Clayton; Michel Pilet (ts); Henri Chaix (p); Isla Eckinger (b); Wallace Bishop (d).* 2/66.

By the mid-'60s Clayton was an international star, and like many jazz musicians of his generation, he found Europe a happier hunting-ground than back home in the States. The Swiss air was obviously good for him and on this amiable set he cuts loose on an array of standards, notably 'Stompin' At The Savoy' and 'One O'Clock Jump', with coltish enthusiasm. These weren't the occasions for softer and more expressive performance, but Buck does also perform well on the slower numbers, and he gets sterling assistance from an experienced Swiss band.

***** Ben And Buck**

Sackville SKCD 22037 *Clayton; Ben Webster (ts); Henri Chaix (p); Alain Du Bois (g); Isla Eckinger (b); Romano Cavicchiolo (d).* 67.

***** A Buck Clayton Jam Session**

Chiaroscuro CRD 132 *Clayton; Doc Cheatham, Joe Newman (t); Urbie Green (tb); Earl Warren (as); Budd Johnson, Zoot Sims (ts); Joe Temperley (bs); Earl Hines (p); Milt Hinton (b); Gus Johnson (d).* 74.

***** A Buck Clayton Jam Session 1975**

Chiaroscuro CRD 143 *Clayton; Joe Newman, Money Johnson (t); Vic Dickenson, George Masso (tb); Lee Konitz, Earl Warren (as); Budd Johnson, Sal Nistico, Buddy Tate (ts); Tommy Flanagan (p); Milt Hinton (b); Mel Lewis (d).* 6/75.

Buck wasn't playing at all towards the end. He suffered a serious collapse immediately after the *Ben and Buck* concert and after that was never up to soloing with any sort of attack or pressure. Clayton doesn't play at all on the Chiaroscuro jams, but conducts an all-star band in a selection of originals. His various jam-session dates for Columbia were great successes in their day, but they're all out of print for now (Mosaic have collected them in one of their boxed editions). The first date was something of a late revival of the form. The band is close to matchless as far as swing-to-mainstream line-ups are concerned, and while nothing much happens that deserves immortality, the session gets by on sheer charisma. The 1975 set is doubly valuable for the inclusion of two rehearsal takes of 'The Duke We Knew' and 'Glassboro Blues', two of the best things he did in later years.

***** The Buck Clayton Swing Band Live From Greenwich Village, NYC**

Nagel Heyer CD 030 *Clayton; John Eckert, Jordan Sandke, Byron Stripling, Warren Vaché (t); Matt Finders, Bobby Pring, Harvey Tibbs (tb); Jerry Dodgion (as); Doug Lawrence, Frank Wess (ts); Scott Robinson, Joe Temperley (bs); James Chirillo, Dick Katz (g); Lynn Seaton (b); Dennis Mackrel (d).* 2/90.

From the moment he laid down his horn, Clayton concentrated on writing and arranging charts with a startling energy and commitment. Though one immediately misses that full-throated voice and the ease with which it negotiated tricky changes and tough expressive transitions, the band is utterly idiomatic and unmistakably the work of Wilbur Clayton. Even as close to the end as this, there isn't a speck of tarnish on the sound, as if Buck had been able to pass on an apostolic blessing. Either oddly or significantly, depending on how you view it, the brasses are played down in the distribution of solos. Guitarist Katz is ludicrously over-featured, and there is more than enough from the one-dimensional Dodgion (though he is very good on 'B.C. Special' and 'Black Sheep Blues'). Vaché comes into his own on 'Cadillac Taxi', a little too late to make his mark on the session as a whole. The real interest, though, lies in the charts, which are as briskly and confidently executed as ever. A fitting memorial to a remarkable survivor.

Jay Clayton (born 1941)

VOCALS

Billie Holiday used to say that she wasn't singing, she was playing a horn. That's true of Jay Clayton as well, a singer who improvises like an instrumentalist, less convincing as an interpreter of emotive lyrics than as a weaver of harmonic spells.

***** The Jazz Alley Tapes**

Hep CD 2046 *Clayton; Jay Thomas (t, as); Jeff Hay (tb); Don Lanphere (ts); Marc Seales (p, ky); Chuck Deardorf (b); Dean Hodges (d).* 9/88.

Clayton is a vividly gifted vocal improviser whose feel for a lyric is perhaps less convincing than her ability to mimic horn lines. Though rooted in bebop, she's also capable of tackling more demanding harmony, like the variations of Coltrane's 'Mr P. C.' on *Tapes*. Oddly, she sounds too close to Don Lanphere's saxophone for that now well-established relationship to work as well as they seem to feel it does. They obviously play comfortably together (Clayton is also featured on his *Go ... Again*), but there's something rather too bland and pat about it.

****** Beautiful Love**

Sunnyside SSC 1066 *Clayton; Fred Hersch (p).* 96.

Exquisitely beautiful. Hersch is one of the genuinely great vocal accompanists, and his playing here is impossible to fault. With delicious perversity, he sticks close to the original song, while Clayton ranges out into unexpected harmonic territory. Wayne Shorter's 'Footprints' and that understated classic 'Blame It On My Youth' are handled with consummate grace and skill. The sound is blushingly intimate, and Clayton throws herself into her various parts with utter abandon.

*****(*) Circle Dancing**

Sunnyside SSC 1076 *Clayton; Jim Knapp (p); Briggan Krauss (as); Randy Halberstadt (p); Phil Sparks (b); Aaron Alexander (d).* 97.

This one comes with a sharp insistence that all the sounds heard are made in real time and unsweetened. Clayton manipulates digital delay with virtuosic skill, and her bluesy, intense delivery, melded with two horns, is as compelling as ever. The material is largely original and is all thoroughly assimilated and personalized. Catch Jay's first entry on the title-tune and her floating, nippy phrasing on 'Sappho' and 'Ditto'. A fine record from a genuine vocal star.

*****(*) Brooklyn 2000**

Sunnyside SSC 1096 *Clayton; Gary Bartz (ss, as); George Cables (p); Anthony Cox (b); Jerry Granelli (d).* 9/00.

In the age of Krall, what place for a singer such as Jay Clayton? Her waywardness with pitch and time won't fall pleasantly on ears that want soothing slices of easy listening, and they won't welcome a band as tough and magisterial as this one. As ever, it's a great group performance which a Clayton record assembles. She'd never worked with some of these guys, but the empathy suggests a regular team, and with Bartz at his most attacking at some moments, and most lyrical at others ('I Told You So'), there's no shortage of jazz, if that's what you're after. The free pieces may split the house. 'Lament For John Coltrane' has some superb playing (not least from Granelli) through which the singer has difficulty making her way. Yet there's an incontestably lovely 'Young And Foolish', performed as a duet with Cables, which will leave any Krall fan speechless.

Kid Clayton

TRUMPET, VOCAL

Although scarcely recorded, Jimmy Clayton was a regular bandleader in New Orleans from the mid-'20s up to the '50s, and played in the deepest style of the local brassmen – George Lewis thought him 'the closest to Shots Madison'.

***** Kid Clayton's Happy Pals**

American Music AMCD-62 *Clayton; Joe Avery, Bill Matthews (tb); Albert Burbank (cl); Emma Barrett (p); George Guesnon, Charlie Hamilton (bj); Sylvester Handy, August Lanoix (b); Alex Bigard, Abbey 'Chinee' Foster (d).* 8/52–9/62.

Four tracks from a 1952 session for Folkways and ten made for an album issued by Icon in 1963 is about all there is of Jimmy Clayton on CD. His playing (and cheerful singing) is deep in the old New Orleans groove, proper, unfancy and careful. He has a brighter tone than Kid Thomas Valentine and he leads the group with evident enjoyment, although the later tracks expose a certain frailty: at this point he hadn't played regularly for some years and had been obliged to make a living in steel mills and road gangs. The best playing comes from Albert Burbank, with his full liquid tone and dapper phrasing. A typical survival in American Music's archive: unsympathetic ears will be baffled by it all, and others will enjoy some of the rootsiest jazz there is.

Dave Cliff (born 1944)

GUITAR

Born in Northumberland, Cliff began as a rock player before studying at Leeds College and switching his sympathies to jazz. He has worked widely with both British and American musicians, mostly in a broad-based mainstream idiom.

***** Sippin' At Bells**
Spotlite SPJ-CD 553 *Cliff; Geoff Simkins (as); Simon Woolf (b); Mark Taylor (d).* 94.

***** Play The Music Of Tadd Dameron**
Spotlite SPJ-CD 560 *Cliff; Geoff Simkins (as); Roy Hilton (p); Simon Woolf (b); Steve Brown, Ron Parry (d).* 3/96.

***** When Lights Are Low**
Zephyr ZECD 18 *Cliff; Howard Alden (g); Dave Green (b); Allan Ganley (d).* 11/96–5/97.

Cliff's unassuming style might be read by some as British diffidence. He is a thinking guitar-player whose cool tone and bebop diction make up a voice of experience and, when paired with the similarly minded Simkins, the irresistible comparison is Billy Bauer with Lee Konitz – particularly when they play some duets on the first Spotlite record. The second is all Dameronia (there is an interesting old interview with Dameron and Benny Golson stuck on the end of the disc) and very persuasively done. The Zephyr album is an off-the-cuff meeting with the on-tour Howard Alden, over thistledown rhythms from Green and Ganley. Nothing to find fault with anywhere, yet the very palpable *politesse* of the music may prove enervating to some.

Alex Cline (born 1956)

DRUMS, PERCUSSION

A California-based drummer with an interest in percussive exotica and a freely focused manner that lets him move between post-bop, free playing and a rockier kind of world music.

***** The Lamp And The Star**
ECM 837112-2 *Cline; Aina Kemanis, Nels Cline (v); Jeff Gauthier (vn, vla, v); Hank Roberts (clo, v); Wayne Peet (p, org); Eric Von Essen (b); Susan Rawcliffe (didjeridu).* 9/87.

***** Montsalvat**
Nine Winds NWCD 0174 *As above, except omit Nels Cline, Roberts and Rawcliffe.* 5/92.

***** Right Of Violet**
Nine Winds NWCD 0184 *Cline; Jeff Gauthier (vn); G. E. Stinson (g etc.).* 4/95.

While his brother Nels has sometimes sought out rockier climes, Alex has pursued a music based around lush textures and thick, harmonic swirls – an unusual course for a percussionist, perhaps, although his vast kit of drums, cymbals, bells and percussive devices is as appropriate to melodic needs as much as to rhythmical ones (there is a double-LP of solo percussion in vinyl history). Both *The Lamp And The Star* and *Montsalvat* have a non-specifically devotional programme, characterized by Cline's imagistic titles – 'A Blue Robe In The Distance', 'Emerald Light', 'The Kiss Of Peace' – but there is nothing mushy or New Age-ish about the music, which has a strong and very individual resonance. Kemanis's wordless singing is neither too wispy nor too overpowering but a logical part of the flow. The later disc is preferred, if only because the long pieces such as 'He Hears The Cry' and 'In The Shadow Of The Mountain' come closest to the kind of transcendence Cline is after.

Right Of Violet has ten collective improvisations by the trio and, while this is tougher music, it still moves off the shimmering base which Cline uses as his touchstone. The opening 'An Elegy Of Waves' says it all, Gauthier's lines spiralling off Stinson's battery of effects, and the formula is set here: the violinist carries most of the melodic parts while Stinson and Cline fashion the atmospherics. The record is rather exhaustingly long but when they get to a piece as eerily beautiful as 'Sophia' there's a proper sense of timelessness.

***** Sparks Fly Upward**
Cryptogramophone 102 *Cline; Wayne Peet (ky); G. E. Stinson (g); Jeff Gauthier (vn); Aina Kemanis (v).* 4/98.

*****(*) The Other Shore**
Cryptogramophone 106 *As above, except omit Peet, Kemanis.* 99.

****** The Constant Flame**
Cryptogramophone 110 *As above; add Vinny Golia (sax); Nels Cline (g); Wayne Peet (ky); Michael Elizondo (b); Brad Dutz (perc); Aina Kemanis (v).* n.d.

Recent years have seen Cline refining his overall musical approach and striking out on a new label that seems to afford him some freedom from generic pigeon-holes. Certainly it is difficult to pin down precisely what musical language these records speak in, beyond the certainty that jazz remains their root and source.

Sparks Fly Upward begins as beautifully as anything in the drummer's output to date, with ethereal overdubbed violins evoking stained-glass imagery in 'Rose Window'. Kemanis is an important element of the group and the powerful closing track, using the text of one of Rilke's most death-haunted poems, the ninth of the *Sonnets To Orpheus*, rounds out the set. The long title-piece is more of a showcase for the leader and its lack of structure makes for slightly difficult listening, certainly on second and subsequent exposure. A fine record nevertheless, and Peter Erskine produces deftly and with feeling for the textural virtues of Cline's approach.

The middle record of the sequence is rightly attributed to the three players individually rather than The – or *an* – Alex Cline Trio. A cursory listen might lead you to conclude that the leader is actually the violinist, since Gauthier is often out front, backed by heavily treated guitar and soft washes of percussion. There is even less rhythmic drive this time, and Cline's percussion devices, which have always included Finnish kantele, autoharp and other exotica, have very little to do with establishing metre and more to do with sustaining an overall mood. 'Froggy's Midnight Cabaret' is something of an exception and stands out a little oddly in this rather ethereal set. The ending is extraordinary, slowing almost to stasis and delivered in a hushed and almost reverential tone: 'Nothing To Teach'.

The addition of saxophone, bass and keyboards and the reintroduction of Kemanis lends *The Constant Flame* a more familiar profile. The title-piece is dedicated to a former boss, clarinettist John Carter, and shows how thoroughly Cline has learned how to combine organized structure with improvisatory freedom. Other tracks are also personal dedications: 'Bridge' is for the adventurous pop vocalist David Sylvian, formerly of Japan; 'Evening Bell' is for Toru Takemitsu and rather literally 'Oriental' in its Zen-like spareness. Cline is at his most urgent on the opening 'Paramita', written for Don Cherry; heavyweight drumming gives way to kantele and synthesized backgrounds. Kemanis is used more sparingly and more dramatically than of yore, and is a key presence again, ending the set with a delightful 'Benediction', which is spiritual but resolutely unsolemn. Cline is on an astonishing roll at the moment.

Nels Cline (born 1956)

GUITAR

Brother of Alex, Cline is a thinking-man's fusion kind of guitar-player.

***** Chest**
Little Brother 006 *Cline; Bob Mair (b); Michael Preussner (d).* 6/93.

Like almost every guitar-player of his generation, Cline trades off rock, but he does so with sufficient sophistication and originality, so that it's possible to think he's made the whole thing up. He makes full use of the electric guitar's expanded repertoire of sounds, distortion, fuzz, bent notes and an aggressive, almost percussive attack.

There's not much easily obtainable at present, at least under his own name. The stripped-down dynamics of the trio suit Cline well, striking a balance between power and subtlety. While superficially reminiscent of Terje Rypdal's trio, the group is more exactingly detailed, and successive albums have opened up more and more areas of interest, not least in Cline's own writing. *Chest* is tightly organized, almost like a suite.

Rosemary Clooney (1928–2002)

VOCAL

She made her name as a Hollywood actress and a musicals star, but her 1956 Duke Ellington album suggested Clooney's aptitude for jazz, and her many albums for Concord dating from the mid-'70s confirmed her talent for the idiom.

***** Swing Around Rosie**
Verve 589485-2 *Clooney; Buddy Cole (org); unknown (p, g, b, d).* 12/58.

***** Rosie Solves The Swinging Riddle!**
Koch 7991 *Clooney; Nelson Riddle Orchestra.* 6/60.

Now that Columbia have managed to delete *Blue Rose*, her pairing with the Ellington orchestra, these are the only early Clooneys in print of relevance (for her more pop-orientated recordings, admirers should look to one of her three exceptionally attractive multi-disc sets issued by the German Bear Family operation). *Swing Around Rosie* is a sort of mid-point between her pop and jazz situations, and she's in lusty voice: 'A Touch Of The Blues' is a vintage performance. Too bad that the accompaniment was entrusted to the Buddy Cole combo, which makes a terribly dinky sound. *Rosie Solves The Swinging Riddle!* is no classic, but it's a superior big-band-meets-singer record. They picked some rather archaic songs, such as 'Angry' and 'Shine On Harvest Moon', some of which seem to hint at the countryish direction Clooney's career was taking at the time: she sounds as if she's putting on a farmgirl twang on 'Get Me To The Church On Time'. But swingers such as an unexpectedly sprightly 'I Get Along Without You Very Well' hit the mark.

***** Everything's Coming Up Rosie**
Concord CCD 4047 *Clooney; Bill Berry (t); Scott Hamilton (ts); Nat Pierce (p); Monty Budwig (b); Jake Hanna (d).* 77.

***** From Bing To Billie**
Concord CCD2-2231-2 4060 2CD *As above, except Warren Vaché (c) replaces Berry; add Cal Collins (g).* 78–9.

*****(*) Sings The Lyrics Of Ira Gershwin**
Concord CCD 4112 *Clooney; Warren Vaché (c, flhn); Scott Hamilton (ts); Roger Glenn (f); Nat Pierce (p); Cal Collins (g); Chris Amberger (b); Jeff Hamilton (d).* 10/79.

***** With Love**
Concord CCD 4144 *Clooney; Warren Vaché (c, flhn); Scott Hamilton (ts); Nat Pierce (p); Cal Tjader (vib); Cal Collins (g); Bob Maize (b); Jake Hanna (d).* 11/80.

***** Sings The Music Of Cole Porter**
Concord CCD 4185 *Clooney; Warren Vaché (c, flhn); Scott Hamilton (ts); David Ladd (f); Nat Pierce (p); Cal Tjader (vib); Cal Collins (g); Bob Maize (b); Jake Hanna (d).* 1/82.

*****(*) Sings Arlen And Berlin**
Concord CCD2-2134-2 2CD *Clooney; Warren Vaché (c); Scott Hamilton (ts); Dave McKenna, John Oddo (p); Ed Bickert, Chris Flory (g); Phil Flanigan, Steve Wallace (b); Gus Johnson, Jake Hanna (d).* 1/83–6/84.

Clooney virtually quit music in the '60s and went through some difficult personal times, but her re-emergence with Concord in the '70s and '80s became a very gratifying return. She became one of the most prolific artists on the label, and the best of these sets, even in a very consistent run, set a very high standard. If she is not, at her own insistence, a jazz singer, she responds to the in-house team with warm informality and the breadth of her voice smooths over any difficulties with some of the more intractable songs. Her voice has a more matronly and less flexible timbre than before, but pacing things suits her style, and good choices of tempo are one of the hallmarks of this series. The 'Songbook' sequence is one of the best of its kind: the Arlen and Gershwin records are particularly fine. *With Love* has some indifferent 'contemporary' tunes from the likes of Billy Joel, but the rest of it more than matches up. Countless cameos from Hamilton, Vaché and the others lend further class. The songbook sets are now available also as a six-CD set, *The Songbook Collection* (CCD-4933-2), and the Arlen and Berlin discs are combined into a two-CD package which is particularly attractive.

*****(*) Rosemary Clooney Sings Ballads**
Concord CCD 4282 *Clooney; Warren Vaché (c, flhn); Scott Hamilton (ts); John Oddo (p); Ed Bickert (g); Chuck Israels (b); Jake Hanna (d).* 4/85.

★★★★ Sings The Lyrics Of Johnny Mercer
Concord CCD 4333 *As above, except Michael Moore (b), Joe Cocuzzo (d) replace Israels and Hanna; add Dan Barrett (tb).* 8/87.

John Oddo began working regularly with Clooney with a Woody Herman album (currently deleted) and has been MD of most of the records since. But the steady, articulate feel of the records is a continuation of what came before. The Johnny Mercer is perhaps the single best record Clooney has ever done: the choice of songs is peerless, and she has the measure of every one. The *Ballads* disc is full of top-rank songs. Very little to choose between these sets, though the Mercer would be our first choice for anyone who wants just a taste of what Rosie can do.

★★(★) For The Duration
Concord CCD 4444 *Clooney; Warren Vaché (c); Scott Hamilton (ts); John Oddo (p); Chuck Berghofer, Jim Hughart (b); Jake Hanna (d); strings.* 10/90.

★★★ Girl Singer
Concord CCD 4496 *Clooney; Warren Luening, George Graham, Larry Hall, Bob Summers (t, flhn); Chauncey Welsh, Bill Booth, Bill Elton, George Roberts (tb); Brad Warnaar (frhn); Dan Higgins (c, as, ts, f); Joe Soldo (cl, as, f); Gary Foster (as, af, f); Pete Christlieb (cl, ts, f); Bob Cooper (ts, f); Bob Tricarico (bs, bcl, f); John Oddo (ky); Tim May (g); Tom Warrington (b); Joe LaBarbera (d); Joe Porcaro (perc); Monica Mancini, Ann White, Mitchel Moore, Earl Brown, Mitch Gordon (v).* 11–12/91.

If anything, these are slightly disappointing. *For The Duration* is a set of wartime songs similar to one attempted by Mel Torme and George Shearing, and Clooney belabours what is occasionally trite (or at least over-exposed) material. *Girl Singer* features an orchestra which has one thinking about the small group of the earlier records: if that formula had perhaps been used to the point of diminishing returns, this one is a top-heavy alternative which suits Clooney's voice less well. Still, Oddo's arrangements leave room for some solos from the horns, and the singer moves from Dave Frishberg to Duke Ellington to Cy Coleman songs with her customary resilience.

★★★(★) Do You Miss New York?
Concord CCD 4537 *Clooney; Warren Vaché (c); Scott Hamilton (ts); John Oddo (p); John Pizzarelli (g, v); Bucky Pizzarelli (g); David Finck (b); Joe Cocuzzo (d).* 9/92.

★★★ Still On The Road
Concord CCD 4590 *Clooney; Warren Luening, Rick Baptist, George Graham, Larry Hall, Larry McGuire (t, flhn); Chauncey Welsh, Bill Elton, Charley Loper, Phil Teele, Lew McCreary (tb); Gary Foster, Nino Tempo, Joe Soldo, Tommy Newsom, Bob Tricarico, Dan Higgins, Don Ashworth (reeds); John Oddo (ky); Tim May, Steve Lukather (g); Chuck Berghofer (b); Jeff Hamilton (d); Joe Porcaro, Dan Greco (perc); Earl Brown, Jack Sheldon (v).* 11/93.

Turning 65, Rosie still sounded in very good form, although some of Concord's production decisions seemed designed to push her towards kitsch rather than great singing situations. *Do You Miss New York?* is an album of Big Apple memories and her best since *Show Tunes* – excellent material, the Concord house-team in strong form and the singer notably relaxed and amiable. 'As Long As I Live' and a duet with John Pizzarelli on 'It's Only A Paper Moon' work out very well. *Still On The Road* is one of those travelogue albums (Rosie did a similar one years ago with Bing Crosby) and benefits from some high-stepping, big-band charts, but Willie Nelson and Paul Simon are composers she shouldn't bother with, and guest spots by Earl Brown and Jack Sheldon were misguided ideas.

★★★ Demi-Centennial
Concord CCD 4633 *As above, except add Wayne Bergeron (t), Fred Simmons (tb), Ron Jannelli, Vince Trombetta (reeds), Thomas Warrington (b), Steve Houghton (d); omit Hall, McCreary, Tempo, Newsom, Tricarico, Lukather, Hamilton, Greco, Brown, Sheldon.* 10–11/94.

★★★ Dedicated To Nelson
Concord CCD 4685 *As above, except add George Roberts (tb), Gene Cipriano (reeds), Dennis Budmir (g), Gregg Field (d); omit Simmons, Jannelli, Warrington, Houghton, Teele, Higgins, Ashworth, May, Porcaro.* 9/95.

Demi-Centennial celebrates Clooney's 50th anniversary as a performer, and all the songs have personal ties. Some of the record comes close to drowning in American schmaltz, but it's hard not to find some of the songs affecting, and the sincerity of the singing is a given. Both this and the subsequent *Dedicated To Nelson* are so sumptuously recorded that it's possible just to enjoy the production values by themselves. For the latter, Clooney goes back to some transcriptions of arrangements which Nelson Riddle did for an old TV series: stretched to recordable length, they're brought to life by Oddo's crack team of studio pros. Very well done, and the singer enjoys herself, though her voice has lost some of the bloom of her earlier Concords.

★★(★) Mothers And Daughters
Concord CCD 4754-2 *Clooney; Warren Luening (t, flhn); Gary Foster (reeds); Vince Trombetta (ts); John Oddo (p); Dennis Budimir (g); Chuck Berghofer (b); Joe LaBarbera (d); Keith Carradine, Betty Clooney (v).* 54–10/96.

Unless one is infatuated with a newborn, this set of songs about, well, mothers and daughters will seem particularly glutinous. Concept albums are hurting jazz: discuss. For undiscriminating fans only.

★★★ At Long Last
Concord CCD 4795-2 *Clooney; Michael Williams, Scotty Barnhart, Shawn Edmonds, Bob Ojeda (t); David Keim, Clarence Banks, Alvin Walker II (tb); William Hughes (btb); John Kelson (as, f); Brad Leali (as); Doug Miller (ts, cl, f); Kenny Hing (ts, cl); Gary Foster (ts); John Williams (bs, bcl); Terence Conley, John Oddo (p); Will Matthews (g); James Leary (b); Butch Miles (d); Barry Manilow (v); Grover Mitchell (cond).* 11/97–6/98.

Back on form with the Basie band, Rosie steers assuredly through this one. John Oddo's charts are shared with three each by Allyn Ferguson and Peter Matz and the programme is all evergreens. Barry Manilow does his credibility some good with a duet on 'How About You' and, though the soloists don't add much, the band is the purring Basie machine for sure. The singer's great records were probably behind her now, but only a churl would dislike this.

★★(★) Sentimental Journey
Concord CCD 4952-2 *Clooney; Dave Scott, Brian Kettlehut, Mike Olmos, Thomas Marriott (t); Doug Beavers, Greg Saul (tb); Matt Catingub (as, ky, v); Albert Alva, Jeff Prinz (as);*

Matt Cowan (ts); Jennifer Lovejoy (bs); Vincent Falcone (ky); John Oddo (p); Dan Parentti, Chuck Berghoffer, Tom Warrington (b); Steve Moretti, Bob Leatherbarrow, Joe LaBarbera (d). 01.

Matt Catingub and his gang, Big Kahuna and The Copa Cat Pack (they're big on Hawaiian shirts) assist Rosie on this recent set, her final entry on record. The playing has lots of heart, and so does the singing, but frankly she was starting to talk her way through songs, and admirers of the vintage Concord dates will be disappointed.

Clusone 3

GROUP

Dutch freely structured trio with expat US reedsman in tow.

***** Clusone 3**

Ramboy 02 *Michael Moore (cl, bcl, as, hca, cel); Ernst Reijseger (clo); Han Bennink (d, perc).* 90.

***** An Hour With**

hatOLOGY 554 *As above.* 3/98.

What began as a one-off group for the 1980 Clusone Festival, and originally as a quartet with pianist and composer Guus Janssen, turned into one of the unlikeliest but most successful *ménages à trois* on the scene. There are moments when the clarinettist and cellist – good, solid, conservatory instruments, both – look as if they might have been detailed to keep a watch on the drummer, whose notion of 'playing the room' is sometimes literally just that: Bennink does a celebrated party piece where he pushes a janitor's broom round the floor to a shuffle rhythm that would do Dave Tough proud. As in the best such dramas, you look and listen again and realize that both Moore and Reijseger have a funny look in their eye, and that behind those proper sounds – the clarinet's melancholy wail and the cello's philosophizing – there are some extremely offbeat ideas at play and that it's Bennink who's keeping it all in check.

The live disc *An Hour With* was the group's swansong and is, like their previous (deleted) live set for Gramavision, a fine record of their freewheeling, associative concert approach. However settled the set-list, their gigs always give the impression of happening spontaneously. Again, it's a series of medleys, this time organized around bird songs – everything from 'Turkey In The Straw' to Saint-Saëns's 'Le Cygne'. It is all full of dash, mockery and a kind of hard-bitten melancholy too, but at the same time there's a transitory quality to the event which suggests that maybe the group was right to call it a day before the whole thing hardened into mere vaudeville repertory.

Arnett Cobb (1918–89)

TENOR SAXOPHONE

Cobb went into Lionel Hampton's band as a replacement for Illinois Jacquet but later made a name as a hard-blowing leader whose Texan honks and wails were tempered with a genuinely feeling touch on the occasional ballad. Having undergone spinal surgery when he was 30, Cobb was seriously injured and disabled less than a decade later. His subsequent career is testament to his great strength of will and unfailing appetite for jazz.

*****(*) The Wild Man Of The Tenor Sax, 1943–1947**

EPM Musique JA 159422 *Cobb; Cat Anderson, Wendell Curley, Duke Garrette, Joe Morris, Jimmy Nottingham, David Page, Leo Shepherd, Joe Wilder, Lamar Wright, Snooky Young (t); Fred Beckett, Sonny Craven, Allan Durham, Al Hayes, Al King, Andrew Penn, Vernon Porter, Booty Wood, Jimmy Wormick (tb); Earl Bostic, George Dorsey, Gus Evans, Ben Kynard, Bobby Plater (as); Johnny Griffin, Al Sears, Fred Simon (ts); Charlie Fowlkes (bs); Herbie Fields, Rudy Rutherford (cl); Dardanelle Breckenridge, Milt Buckner, George Rhodes (p); Lionel Hampton (p, vib); Billy Mackel, Eric Miller (g); Walter Buchanan, Joe Comfort, Charlie Harris, Vernon King, Ted Sinclair (b); Eugene 'Fats' Heard, George Jenkins, George Jones, Fred Radcliffe (d); Wynonie Harris, Milton Larkins, Dinah Washington (v).* 43–47.

*****(*) Arnett Cobb, 1946–1947**

Classics 1071 *Cobb; Wendell Culley, Joe Morris, David Page (t); Al King, Booty Wood (tb); Herbie Fields (ts); Charlie Fowlkes (bs); Milt Buckner, George Rhodes (p); Billy Mackel (g); Walter Buchanan, Charles Harris (b); George Jenkins, George Jones (d); Milton Larkins (v).* 46–8/47.

***** Arnett Blows For 1300**

Delmark 471 *As above, except omit Culley, Fields, Fowlkes, Buckner, Mackel, Harris, Jenkins.* 47.

The most significant recent addition to the Arnett Cobb discography are these compilations of his early work for Apollo and – in the case of the Classics set – for Hamp-Tone, too. While Ellingtonians frequently recorded side-projects, it was relatively rare for members of Hamp's band to record apart from the leader. The EPM compilation basically gathers together solos from the early years under Hampton, Wynonie Harris and Dinah Washington, and then takes the story up to the saxophonist's post-war foray into leadership. The quotient of actual Cobb material is rather low, but for anyone interested in exploring his roots and influences it's invaluable.

Unusually for Classics, the first item included was actually made under Milt Buckner's leadership, but all the rest of the material is by Arnett's first groups after striking out on his own. Old associations die hard, though, and two tracks on the May 1947 date are intended to recall happy days with Hamp. Both 'Still Flyin'' and 'Top Flight' recall Cobb's featured solos on 'Flyin' Home'. Thereafter, Arnett seemed more inclined to strike out on his own and, while some of his compositions are no more than generic themes for blowing, he seems to have found a niche for the early group. The sound is immediately better with Apollo, rich and unmuffled, and generous to the saxophone.

An even longer-standing debt is paid when vocalist Milton Larkins, one of Cobb's first employers, steps up to take three songs as part of the August 1947 recording. It was the session that included the definitive performance of 'Arnett Blows For 1300' which gives the Delmark issue its title. This basically reprises all the tracks the saxophonist made for Apollo. The transfers are crisp and clear.

***** Cobb's Idea**

Ocium 0478 *Cobb; Ed Lewis, Cootie Williams (t); Dicky Harris (tb); Johnny Acea (p); Keter Betts, Walter Buchanan (b); Jimmy Cobb (d); Dinah Washington (v).* 47–52.

Useful round-up of material from Apollo and Okeh, delivered in agreeable packaging and, as with other Ocium reissues, including a small surprise for anyone who plays the disc through a computer.

***** Cobb And His Mob In Concert, Featuring Dinah Washington**

High Note 7068 *As for the above.* 52.

Any glimpses of Dinah Washington in her prime are precious and here she is with a hard-driving, bluesy band who're not prepared to nod out when the singer's on. Though he's not well recorded, Cobb sounds in fantastic form, blowing wonderfully dissonant notes and phrases on many of his choruses, shaping them round an idiosyncratic harmonic sense too rarely acknowledged. 'When I Grow Too Old To Dream' is outstanding. Great work from the Acea–Betts–Cobb trio, who get a lot of prominence here.

***** Blow, Arnett, Blow**

Original Jazz Classics OJC 794 *Cobb; Strethen Davis (p); George Duvivier (b); Arthur Edgehill (d).* 59.

****(*) Party Time**

Original Jazz Classics OJC 219 *Cobb; Ray Bryant (p); Wendell Marshall (b); Art Taylor (d).* 5/59.

***** More Party Time**

Original Jazz Classics OJCCD 979 *Cobb; Tommy Flanagan, Bobby Timmons (p); Sam Jones (b); Art Taylor (d); Danny Barrajanos, Buick Clarke (perc).* 2/60.

***** Smooth Sailing**

Original Jazz Classics OJC 323 *Cobb; Buster Cooper (tb); Austin Mitchell (as); George Duvivier (b); Osie Johnson (d).* 60.

***** Blue And Sentimental**

Prestige PRCD 24122 *Cobb; Red Garland (p, cel); George Duvivier, George Tucker (b); J. C. Heard (d).* 11/60.

Cobb overcame serious illness and a crippling motor accident (several covers picture him propped on his crutches as he plays) to keep his career afloat in the '60s and after. A powerful saxophonist in the so-called 'Texas tenor' tradition, he was an ideal big-band player – with Lionel Hampton mainly – who never scaled down quite enough for small-group work. On *Blow, Arnett, Blow* and the following *Party Time*, he is clearly still suffering the after-effects of the accident, playing awkwardly and doing not much more than going through the motions, however much sheer energy and drive he managed to muster.

As the personnel details confirm, *More Party Time* wasn't further material or out-takes from the May 1959 session but a completely separate recording. Flanagan doesn't seem quite the right piano-player for Arnett at this stage in his career, but the chemistry is pretty good. Bobby Timmons was on hand the following day and 'Down By The Riverside' has the soulful, revivalist energy one expects of him. A thoroughly entertaining record.

The earlier records for Prestige, now available on OJC, are far from sophisticated but there is a delicacy to Cobb's playing which becomes obvious only over time, and we have previously noted an unexpected similarity between some of his slower tunes and Coltrane's early ballad performances, a similarity that points at similar sources rather than any direct influence or crossover.

***** Deep Purple: The Definitive Black & Blue Sessions**

Black & Blue 864 *Cobb; Milt Buckner (org); Clarence 'Gatemouth' Brown (g); Michael Silva (d).* 7 & 8/73.

***** The Wild Man From Texas**

Black & Blue 868 *Cobb; Wallace Davenport (t); Frank Buster Cooper (tb); Eddie Chamblee (ts); Earl Warren (as); Milt Buckner (org, vib); André Persiany (p); Tiny Grimes, Roland Lobligeois (b); Panama Francis (d).* 5/75, 5/76.

***** Jumpin' At The Woodside**

Black & Blue 870 *As above; omit Davenport, Cooper, Chamblee, Warren, Buckner, Persiany.* 5/74.

Cobb's recovery from injury was slow and painful but in the '70s he found himself a minor star in France, where his disability must have seemed like a profound existential statement. These Black & Blue sounds have been around off and on for some time, but the label is now putting out augmented sessions. Buckner was an ideal partner at this stage in Cobb's career, though the organist had ambitions of his own to sustain and often sounds as if he's trying to clear the studio of everyone else. *The Wild Man* is probably overstating the case, for there is more sophistication to these arrangements than one hears at first, and perhaps more than some of the players understood. Cobb's phrasing is wonderful and his ability to adjust the dynamic of individual notes in a phrase is worth looking into. The French-based rhythm sections are very strong but unmistakably not Stateside units, with a curious bounce to the rhythm that Francis cheerfully goes along with. Not much point commenting on individual tracks. The repertoire is pretty standard, and hinted at in the titles. What counts here is the continuity of these performances. When heard in bulk Cobb's stature rises exponentially. Too easily dismissed as a honker, he deserves to be considered alongside, say, Paul Gonsalves as an innovative figure in shaping blues choruses.

***** Arnett Cobb Is Back**

Progressive PCD 7037 *Cobb; Derek Smith (p); George Mraz (b); Billy Hart (d).* 6/78.

***** Tenor Abrupt – The Definitive Black & Blue Sessions**

Black & Blue 958 *Cobb; Guy Lafitte (ts); Sir Roland Hanna (p); Jimmy Woode (b); Eddie Locke (d).* 3/80.

***** Show Time**

Fantasy F 9659 *Cobb; Dizzy Gillespie (t); Clayton Dyess (g); Paul English (p, org); Kenny Andrews, Sammy Price (p); Derrick Lewis (b); Malcolm Pinson, Mike Lefebvre (d).* 8/87.

The material on Fantasy is pretty late and frail. Cobb shares the Houston stage and the disc with Dizzy Gillespie and the singer, Jewel Brown. Two years before his death the tone is still intact, but there really isn't much to say any more and there's a queasy sense of going through the motions once too often. Newcomers might like to start with the 1978 disc, a much more spirited date with the underrated Smith a particularly helpful foil. *Tenor Abrupt* is reissued with bonus tracks, like most of the B&B 'definitives'. It's interesting to hear how much like Cobb Lafitte tries to sound in a couple of places, not so much in tone, but in phrasing, and how thoroughly he misses Arnett's asymmetrical but still powerfully swinging style.

****(*) Tenor Tribute**

Soul Note 121184 *Cobb; Jimmy Heath (ts, ss, f); Joe Henderson (ts); Benny Green (p); Walter Schmocker (b); Doug Hammond (d).* 4/88.

(*) **Tenor Tribute, Volume 2
Soul Note 121194 *As above.* 4/88.

Though this was always conceived as a collective project with a three-saxophone front line, Cobb gets the nod on grounds of alphabetical priority, seniority, and not least because this Nuremberg concert came in the last full year of the Texan's life. Like most similar things, this is full of exciting and entertaining episodes but won't hang together as a whole. Cobb sounds pretty good, considering. His choruses on 'Smooth Sailing' and during a lengthy ballad medley (all on Volume One) are nicely weighted and well – perhaps too well – thought out. However, he's comprehensively blown away by the two youngsters, who both sound full of vim and ideas. He does better on 'Cottontail', which opens Volume Two, but there isn't enough top-flight stuff to support a second disc, and it palls very quickly; even 'Flying Home' at curtain time lacks sparkle. Heath's lighter tone and occasional forays into soprano and flute broaden the range a bit, for this is otherwise pretty heavy fare. Green does his best to push it along, but there's not much manoeuvrability in a band like this, and he has to rein in quite sharply more than once. Avid collectors only.

Junie Cobb (1896–1970)

CLARINET, SOPRANO AND TENOR SAXOPHONES, VIOLIN, PIANO, VOCAL

A multi-instrumentalist who worked in the Chicago scene of the '20s, Cobb was recorded as a reed-player and leader, but he also played banjo and later in life took to the piano. His music is typical of the small-group barrelhouse style of the day which, by the '60s – when he recorded again – was softer but no less energetic.

***(*) **The Junie Cobb Collection, 1926–29**
Collector's Classics COCD-14 *Cobb; Jimmy Cobb (c, t); Cicero Thomas (t); Arnett Nelson (cl, ts); Angelo Fernandez, Johnny Dodds, Darnell Howard (cl); Ernie Smith (bs, bsx); George James (as, bs); Tiny Parham, Jimmy Blythe, Frank Melrose, Alex Hill, Earl Frazier (p); Tampa Red (g); Eustern Woodfork (bj); Walter Wright (tba); Bill Johnson (b); Jimmy Bertrand (d, xy, slide-whistle); Clifford Jones (d, kz); Tommy Taylor, Harry Dial (d); W. E. Burton, Georgia Tom Dorsey (v).* 6/26–10/29.

This is classic Chicago jazz of its period. Cobb's groups – The Hometown Band, The Grains Of Corn and the Kansas City Tin Roof Stompers are three of those here – bounce along in a rough-and-ready barrelhouse manner, never touching the sophistications of Armstrong or Dodds (who turns up as sparring partner for Cobb on two early tracks) but creating their own peculiar exhilaration. Cobb's saxophone style, an idiosyncratic mix of slap-tonguing and the more progressive manner of Hawkins, gets a wild momentum going on some tracks; and reliable stompers such as Blythe, Melrose and Hill keep the music hot in the rhythm section, as does Woodfork's banjo. Jimmy Cobb plays most of the trumpet parts, often surprisingly effectively. There are also (among a generous 24 tracks) three cuts from a hitherto lost 1929 session for Vocalion. The transfers show variable levels of surface noise, but the remastering is lively and vivid throughout.

(*) **Chicago The Living Legends: Junie C. Cobb And His New Hometown Band
Original Jazz Classics OJC 1825-2 *Cobb; Fip Ricard (t); Harlan Floyd (tb); Leon Washington (cl, ts); Ikey Robinson (bj); Walter Hill (b); Red Saunders (d); Annabelle Calhoun (v).* 9/61.

Rediscovered in 1961, Cobb had given up clarinet in favour of piano. The pick-up band assembled for this session is mostly younger hands rather than old-timers (Robinson and Saunders are the exceptions) and some of the music sounds like tourist trad. But Cobb's enthusiasm carries much of the music, even if Washington is a comparatively ordinary substitute as reedsman.

Billy Cobham (born 1944)

DRUMS, PERCUSSION, ELECTRONICS, PIANO

Born in Panama and raised in New York, Cobham was early in the jazz-rock field with Miles Davis and with his own group, Dreams, before forming the Mahavishnu Orchestra with John McLaughlin. The power and complexity of his playing merits comparison with Elvin Jones and Tony Williams, and yet Cobham seems to have been content on occasion to play unimaginative fusion in which mere fireworks overcame his natural gifts.

***(*) **Spectrum**
Atlantic 781428 *Cobham; Jimmy Owens (t, flhn); Joe Farrell (as, ss, f); Jan Hammer (p, ky); Tommy Bolin, John Tropea (g); Ron Carter, Lee Sklar (b); Ray Barretto (perc).* 5/73.

*** **Shabazz**
Atlantic/Wounded Bird 8139 *Cobham; Randy Brecker (t); Glenn Ferris (tb); Michael Brecker (ts); Milcho Leviev (ky); John Abercrombie, John Scofield (g); Alex Blake (b).* 7/74.

*** **Crosswinds**
Atlantic/Wounded Bird 7300 *Cobham; Randy Brecker (t); Garnett Brown (tb); Michael Brecker (ts); George Duke (ky); John Abercrombie (g); John Williams (b); Lee Pastora (perc).* 74.

*** **Total Eclipse**
Atlantic/Wounded Bird 8121 *Cobham; Randy Brecker (t, flhn); Glenn Ferris (tb, btb); Michael Brecker (ts, f); Milcho Leviev (p, ky); Sue Evans (mar); Cornell Dupree (g); Alex Blake (b).* 74.

Billy Cobham could almost qualify these days as the forgotten giant of the fusion era, but for the steady return of some of his earliest solo work and a burgeoning recording schedule in the '90s. A superb technician and clearly a man of great musical intelligence and resource, he has nevertheless committed some awful clunkers to record. Whereas *Spectrum*, his debut as leader, was one of the finest records of the jazz-rock era, a record to set alongside *Birds Of Fire*, *Head Hunters* and the earlier Return To Forever discs, much of what has followed has been remarkably hazy, and a stint with GRP in the mid- to late '80s was decidedly ill-advised. Luckily for his rep, the Atlantic is a survivor and one of the few Cobham albums that still hang around the racks. The cliché about Cobham – that he is all fire and fury and 20-minute drum solos – has never stood up to scrutiny. In actuality, he is a somewhat introspective drummer whose compositions are often blurry and unmemorable. Enjoy

Spectrum for its bravado and some fine contributions from the various hands – not least the drummer himself.

Recorded live in Europe, *Shabazz* reprised a couple of the tunes from *Spectrum* and turned all the dials up to 11. 'Taurian Matador' and 'Red Baron' stand up to the punishment pretty well, and there are also a couple of new tracks, 'Tenth Pin' and the title-piece which were road-tested on Billy's tour. The recording is classic '70s 'in concert' fare, cavernous and booming, with the drums mixed well up. Twenty-five years on, it stands up better than it has any right to.

Crosswinds isn't quite as fresh in retrospect. Billy's solo feature on 'Storm' is the centrepiece of what is virtually a concept album, mood music and tone poems cranked up high. Duke is a key element of the band right from the off, prefiguring the Billy–George encounters of the later '70s. Here, though, the big man has a surprising deftness of touch.

Total Eclipse was the third solo release on Atlantic and, in some respects, the most ambitious and enigmatic. Again somewhat themed round the moon landings and the space programme generally, it begins with 'Solarization', a suite of pieces distinguished by a remarkable solo from Leviev. Billy's own big feature comes at the end of the album and is easily programmed out; five and a half minutes of solo percussion at this intensity constitutes cruel and unusual punishment. He does a Jack DeJohnette on 'The Moon Ain't Made Of Green Cheese', coming out from behind the kit to play piano behind Brecker's gorgeous flugelhorn. Abercrombie's ability to switch from limpid purity to pumped-up aerobatics is consistently impressive, and his solo on 'Moon Germs' is one of the best things he recorded in the '70s. The long 'Sea Of Tranquility' is a loose, band jam and a more fitting end to the record than Billy's clattering 'Last Frontier'.

★★★ A Funky Thide Of Sings

Atlantic 2894/Koch International 8527 *Cobham; Walt Fowler (t); Randy Brecker (t, flhn); Bones Malone (tb); Michael Brecker (ts, f); Larry Schneider (sax); Milcho Leviev (p, ky); John Scofield (g); Alex Blake (b).* 75.

This is the record that marks the transition from Cobham's largely successful post-Mahavishnu recordings to a period of drab, slugging funk. The line-up was pretty well established by now, but the addition of Scofield gives the group a harder-edged blues quality which wasn't always in evidence before. Oddly, the most appealing thing on the album is the drum solo, 'A Funky Kind Of Thing', which immediately precedes the long closing 'Moody Modes' by Leviev. An otherwise rather dull record ends on the most unexpected of highs.

★★ On Tour In Europe

Atlantic 113797 *Cobham; George Duke (ky, v); John Scofield (g, g syn); Alphonso Johnson (b).* 76.

Oh, dear; oh, Lord. This is what we used to groove to in the '70s and it hasn't aged at all well. Billy and fellow-front-man George Duke obviously had a ball with this project, and there are some mildly entertaining moments: Scofield's 'Ivory Tattoo' is very good indeed, but it is valuable mainly as a foretaste of his maturer work; Duke's 'Do Whatcha Wanna' is as embarrassing as a shameless decade ever got. Billy can still generate excitement, as he does on 'Frankenstein Goes To The Disco', but why Atlantic have seen fit to reissue this in preference to far finer material in their back-catalogue is something of a mystery ... unless of course there's a huge Cobham–Duke fanbase we don't know about.

★★(★) Magic / Simplicity Of Expression: Depth Of Thought

Sony International 492526 *Cobham; Mike Lawrence, Marvin Stamm (t, flhn); Wayne Andre, George Quinn, Alan Raph (tb); Daniel Corrado, Brooks Tillotson (frhn); Eddie Daniels (ts, woodwind); Alvin Batiste (cl, bcl, v); Joachim Kühn, Mark Soskin (p, ky); Mike Mainieri (vib); Steve Khan, Ray Mouton, Peter Maunu (g); Randy Jackson (b); Sheila Escovedo (perc); Frank Floyd, Kathleen Kaan, Zachary Sanders, Raymond Simpson (v); strings.* 77.

★★★ Inner Conflicts

Wounded Bird 9174 *Cobham; Randy Brecker (t); Jimmy Owens (t, flhn); Julian Priester (tb); Michael Brecker, Ernie Watts (ts); Dawilli Gonga, Don Grolnick (ky); John Scofield (g); Ruth Underwood (mar, xyl); Alphonso Johnson, John Williams (b); Pete Escovedo, Sheila Escovedo (perc).* 77.

★★★ Alivemutherforya

Sony International 82813 *Cobham; Tom Scott (ts); Mark Soskin (ky); Steve Khan (g); Alphonso Johnson (b).* 11 & 12/77.

This was one of the busiest years of Cobham's career and it yielded markedly variable results. The double-header reissue brings together some of the best and some of the worst of Cobham on record. *Magic* is a fine album; the other 1977 release is as drab as its pretentious title suggests. Kühn and Soskin create some worthwhile patterns on the first record, and there are some fine, funky charts to work off (conducted by Sheila E), but nothing to set the blood racing. Bob Clearmountain did the engineering and got a big, florid sound, built around the drumkit. So much tizz, though, that like a lot of Billy's records of the time it's actually quite hard on the ears.

Alivemutherforya benefits from being a small-group record. There is still a lot of electronic muddling, most egregiously Johnson's bass synth, but the lines of individual tunes are clearer and Tom Scott has the astonishing ability to make something ponderous and clunky take unexpected wings. Billy's quieter than on some of his discs and the subtlety of his cross-figures and fives against fours comes through strongly, or rather, subtly.

The other 1977 disc will appeal more just because of the line-up, which includes some luminaries. In reality, it's hard to hear what anyone is doing beyond the odd break of Brecker, Brecker, Scofield or Watts. Billy experiments with electronics, which are nicely assimilated on the opening title-track. The album tails off after that, though the Afro-Cuban cast of 'El Barrio' is interesting and there are some nice things on the closing 'Arroyo'. Not his best work, but certainly preferable to the disco-fusion of the other two.

★★★(★) Rudiments – The Billy Cobham Anthology

Atlantic 8122-742287-2 2CD *As Atlantic albums above.* 73–78.

A two-disc survey of all the highlights (and some low points) from Cobham's Atlantic career, which outclasses its one-disc predecessor from the same stable. Entirely idiomatic within the context of its era – flash, smoke and brawn – and an entertaining potpourri.

★★ Warning

Cleopatra 510 *Cobham; Onaje Allan Gumbs (p, ky); Gerry Etkins (ky); Dean Brown (g); Sa Davis (perc).* 85.

★★(★) Power Play

Cleopatra 508 *As above.* 86.

Testosterone levels were getting dangerously high on Billy's records of the mid-'80s, originally made for GRP and now reissued on his own imprint. The best measure of the change is a remake of 'Stratus' on the well-named *Warning*, a drably supercharged interpretation of one of the most durable fusion compositions of the time. There's more to enjoy on the slightly later disc; less weight on the keyboards and some fine, imaginative work from Billy on the suite, 'Summit Afrique'.

***** Picture This**
Cleopatra 507 *Cobham; Randy Brecker (flhn); Grover Washington Jr (ss, ts); Tom Scott (lyricon); Michael Abene (p, ky); Gerry Etkins (ky); Abe Laboriel (b); Sa Davis (perc).* 87.

This was an unexpected return to form. Billy built a modest supergroup round his own working band of the period and, with Randy Brecker guesting on 'Taurian Matador' (another fine '70s composition), he pulls one out of the hat. Grover Washington is elegance itself on his featured tracks, and the inclusion of Prince's 'Sign O' The Times' was a cheeky masterstroke. Good to hear Tom Scott, the butt of jazz purists for a decade and a half, making a lyricon sound more expressive than most orthodox saxophone players could manage with an original Adolphe Sax instrument.

****(*) By Design**
Cleopatra 505 *Cobham; Ernie Watts (ts); Joe Chindamo (p); Brian Bromberg (b).* 91.

Billy's return to a more jazz-influenced sound was no great surprise, given shifting market trends at the start of the '90s. The basic conception is still strongly tinged with his fusion work, but Cobham has simplified his drumming to a degree and has overcome his apparent suspicion of common or regular time-signatures. The tunes could come from almost any period in his career. 'Permanent Jet Lag' and 'Mirror's Image', which is reprised as a solo feature, are very much the Cobham of yore, though there are also signs that Billy is interested in a more modulated and song-like approach; 'Slidin' By' and 'Panama' are delightful.

***** Incoming**
Cleopatra 472 *Cobham; Rita Marcotulli (p); Peter Wolpl (g); Ira Coleman (b); Nippy Noya (perc).* 92.

****(*) The Traveler**
Cleopatra 509 *As above, except omit Marcotulli; add Joe Chindamo (ky), Mike Mondesir (b), Gary Husband (d, ky), Carole Rowley (v).* 11/93.

***** Paradox**
Tiptoe 88836 *Cobham; Bill Bickford (g); Wolfgang Schmid (b).* 97.

***** Focused**
Cleopatra 482 *Cobham; Randy Brecker (t, flhn); Gary Husband (ky, perc); Carl Orr (g).* 2/99.

Overlooked on their release, these revealed a new and much gentler side to Cobham. *Incoming* now seems like a turning point in the drummer's career, and it is ironic that all the critics (ourselves included on occasions) who complained about his febrile power drumming, which Billy and Gary Husband spoof on *The Traveler*, should have failed to respond to a more measured approach. The group on *Focused* couldn't be better tailored, and young Carl Orr emerges as a potentially significant player whose composition, 'Nothing Can Hurt Her Now', is one of the high spots of the record, not least for the solo it inspires from Brecker, who seems to respond to working in Billy's groups.

Paradox was a short-lived power trio that allowed Billy to revisit some of his earlier compositions. 'Quadrant 4' is less fiery here than the version made famous by the late Tommy Bolin on *Spectrum*, but it's still quite effective and certainly more appealing than the pig-iron grunge of Bickford's 'Four More Years'. Schmid is a full partner in the trio, contributing some authentically funky tunes and playing in flat-out Jaco/Jack Bruce/Jonas Hellborg mode for most of the set.

***** Nordic**
Cleopatra 506 *Cobham; Tore Brunborg (ts); Bugge Wesseltoft (p); Terje Gewelt (b).* 96.

The Scandinavian line-up isn't in Billy's usual line of things, but the group finds a great deal of common ground to explore, and there is imaginative writing from everyone concerned, Cobham himself taking something of a back seat with just four compositions out of ten. He also moderates his dynamics and attack to accommodate some quite complex ideas going on between Wesseltoft and Gewelt: slight, almost folkish themes woven together into much larger structures. The saxophonist is perhaps the wild card; Brunborg is a very talented player but a guitarist might, as ever in Billy's bands, have offered a more consistent and idiomatic sound.

***** The Art Of Three**
Blowithard BIH 010 *Cobham; Kenny Barron (p); Ron Carter (b).* 01.

All polished refinement, sheer class – but no excitement and, with Kenny doing a routine he's modelled to bland perfection by now, this really goes by without much interest. A superstar encounter and not much more.

Michael Cochrane (born 1948)

PIANO

Post-bop pianist who started working in New York from 1974. An experienced teacher and sideman.

*****(*) Elements**
Soul Note SN 121151-2 *Cochrane; Tom Harrell (t); Bob Malach (ts); Dennis Irwin (b); James Madison (d).* 9/85.

The ensembles are keenly pointed, the solos have great contextual power, and Cochrane's tunes are all just slightly out of the ordinary; in sum, this is a very interesting post-bop record by a leader looking hard for new ground. 'Tone Row Piece No. 2' is the most surprising theme, the melody organized with strict adherence to 12-tone technique, and, although it's a little less fluid than the other pieces, one can't fault Cochrane's ambitions. Or his own playing: he has a terse, improvisational flair, tempered by a romantic streak. Harrell and the fine and underrated Malach sound in very good shape, and the contrast between the boisterous 'Reunion' and the steadily darkening 'Waltz No. 1' shows the extent of the range on offer here.

***** Song Of Change**
Soul Note 121251-2 *Cochrane; Marcus McLaurine (b); Alan Nelson (d).* 11/92.

Not exactly a retreat, but Cochrane's session pulls back on his ambitions to some degree, as the sleeve-notes seem to aver ('no agenda, no ideology, no big ideas'). He still sounds convincing without the cover of horns, and the trio work up some impressive interplay within the ensembles, even in such lightweight material as 'Once I Loved'. But the five standards receive comparatively straightforward piano-trio treatment, and Cochrane's four originals are a shade less compelling than some of his previous writing. It goes out on a very swinging 'Bemsha Swing' indeed.

***** Cutting Edge**
Steeplechase SCCD 31430 *Cochrane; David Gross (as); Ron McClure (b); Yoron Israel (d).* 9/97.

***** Gesture Of Faith**
Steeplechase SCCD 31459 *Cochrane; Eddie Gomez (b); Alan Nelson (d).* 4/98.

Cutting Edge is a solid entry from a gifted musician. There's something almost Tristano-like about his 'Lines Of Reason', and the record finds a good balance between the originals, four standards and pieces by Corea and Powell. Gross is a fluent if somewhat anonymous altoist.

He's back to a trio for *Gesture Of Faith*. Gomez and Nelson are a glittering team, as their fours on 'Baby Steps' make clear, and they give the pianist all he could want in terms of energy and interactivity. But the date still feels a little prosaic in comparison with some of Cochrane's earlier music.

***** Footprints**
Steeplechase SCCD 312476 *Cochrane; Ron McLure (b); Yoron Israel (d).* 11/98.

****(*) Minor Matrix**
Steeplechase SCCD 31494 *Cochrane; Calvin Hill (b); Alan Nelson (d).* 4/00.

***** Quartet Music**
Steeplechase SCCD 31513 *Cochrane; Bob Malach (ts); Calvin Hill (b); Jeff Hirshfield (d).* 3/01.

***** Pathways**
Steeplechase SCCD 31542 *As above.* 11/02.

The first trio set is all Wayne Shorter material, the second a mix of jazz composers; that both have almost exactly the same feel to them suggests that Cochrane is a good executant but not a profound interpreter. He always seems more engaged on his own material, and the quartet record comes to life most on his own tunes, 'Tones For Bones' and 'Simba'. Bill Evans's 'Orbit', for instance, sounds entirely perfunctory. These are respectable and sometimes satisfying sets which could use some injection of surprise. *Pathways* convenes the same quartet for much the same result: if everything engaged the players as much as 'The Line Forms At The End', the closing original, this might be outstanding. As such, it's merely agreeable.

Codona

GROUP

Short-lived but memorable, Codona reinforced what Walcott's other group, Oregon, was doing. This is what might be called 'world jazz', a cosmopolitan free style that, even after 20 years, still sounds fresh and alert.

*****(*) Codona**
ECM 829371-2 *Don Cherry (t, f, doussn'gouni, v); Collin Walcott (sitar, tabla, hammered dulcimer, sanza, v); Nana Vasconcelos (berimbau, perc, v).* 9/78.

***** Codona 2**
ECM 833332-2 *As above.* 5/80.

***** Codona 3**
ECM 827420-2 *As above.* 9/82.

In 1978, at Collin Walcott's behest, three musicians gathered in Tonstudio Bauer, Ludwigsburg, and recorded one of the iconic episodes in so-called (but never better called) 'world music'. Any tendency to regard Codona's music, or Walcott's compositions, as floating impressionism is sheer prejudice, for all these performances are deeply rooted in modern jazz (Coltrane's harmonies and rhythms, Ornette Coleman's melodic and rhythmic primitivism) and in another great and related improvisational tradition from Brazil. Nothing done subsequently quite matches the impact of the original *Codona*. It featured three long Walcott pieces (most notably the closing 'New Light'), the collectively composed title-track, and a brief, witty medley of Ornette Coleman tunes and Stevie Wonder's 'Sir Duke'. The permutations of instrumental sound are astonishing, but rooted in a basic jazz-trio format of horn, harmony and percussion. All three men contribute string accompaniment: Walcott on his sitar, Vasconcelos on the 'bow-and-arrow' berimbau, Cherry on the Malian doussn'gouni. The interplay is precise and often intense. The members' developing interests and careers created a centrifugal spin on the later albums, which are by no means as coherent or satisfying. At their best, though, which is usually when Walcott's writing is at its best, they are still compelling. 'Walking On Eggs' on *Codona 3* is one of his and their best performances. In all, though, perhaps that initial album should stand as a one-off.

Tony Coe (born 1934)

TENOR SAXOPHONE, CLARINET, SOPRANO SAXOPHONE

Possessed of an instantly recognizable sound, whether on tenor or his old rosewood clarinet, Coe had his first major professional stint with Humphrey Lyttelton, before striking out on his own. Canterbury-born, he always has a hint of both folksong and church music in his solo work.

****** Some Other Autumn**
Hep CD 2037 *Coe; Brian Lemon (p); Dave Green (b); Phil Seamen (d).* 1/71.

Tony Coe guaranteed his small – albeit rarely credited – corner of music heaven when he played the lead saxophone part in later versions of Henry Mancini's *Pink Panther* theme; apparently Plas Johnson played on the original. The other oft-told story about him is that he turned down a place in the Count Basie Orchestra – though, given that he was past 30 and already a leader and a writer of some standing, it's perhaps less surprising.

He went on to record the material on *Some Other Autumn* in company that will have aficionados of the British scene of the '60s blinking with nostalgia. A superb personnel and some inspired playing from Coe. If 'Body And Soul' is the tenor saxophonist's Everest – and we're still inclined to insist that it is – then Coe negotiates it without breathlessness and with a grand sweep that is entirely reciprocated by Lemon and Green. Seamen is called upon less here than on other tracks, but throughout the set he shows his extraordinary quality. He was house drummer at Ronnie Scott's at the time and was playing in exceptional company. His wilder touches are kept in check here, though he does some interesting stuff on 'Perdido'.

The three tracks that follow are the real pay-off: a superb 'When Your Lover Has Gone', with Coe leaning into the melody, importunate and mournful, then 'In A Mellow Tone' and the closer, 'Upper Manhattan Medical Group', which is the kind of performance you simply want to re-cue again and again. A superb record and certainly the place to begin. Sadly, the wonderful hat ART album, *Nutty On Willisau*, is now out of print, thus denying a glimpse of Coe in rather more avant-garde mode.

***** British-American Blue**

Between The Lines 007 *Coe; Roger Kellaway (p).* 6/78.

***** Coe-Existence**

Whatmusic CD 004 *Coe; John Horler (p, ky); Ron Rubin, Trevor Tomkins (b); Frank Ricotti (perc).* 78.

These are both recent rescues from oblivion, and – *Coe-Existence* particularly – help to fill out a picture of what Coe was doing in the '70s when British free jazz and creative improvisation were pretty seriously assailed. Some of the usual suspects are there and a special word for the remarkable Frank Riccotti who seems doomed never to receive his due credit. Salvaged by Coe fan Franz Koglmann, the duo session emerged from a day off in the studio for Kellaway, in London to do some film work. Eleven free pieces, nurtured by Kellaway's composer's piano, and decorated by Coe's rationalist take on free space. The results are a kind of free form in the academy, goosed a little here and there by Coe (exclusively on clarinet) but basically calm without being withdrawn or restrained. An interesting little survival.

*****(*) Captain Coe's Famous Racearound**

Storyville STCD 4206 *Coe; Palle Bolvig, Jan Kohlin, Henrik Bolberg Pedersen, Benny Rosenfeld, Lars Togeby (t, flhn); Steen Hansen, Kjeld Ipsen, Vincent Nilsson (tb); Giordano Bellinicampi, Axel Windfeld (btb); Bob Brookmeyer (vtb, cond); Michael Hove, Jan Zum Vorde (as, reeds); Uffe Markussen, Bob Rockwell (ts, reeds); Flemming Madsen (bs, reeds); Nikolaj Bentzon, David Hazeltine (p); Anders Lindvall, Thomas Ovesen (g); Steve Arguëlles, Jonas Johansen (d); Ethan Weisgard (perc).* 3/95.

In 1995, Tony Coe was awarded the prestigious Jazzpar Prize, no small but certainly belated recognition of his gifts. Would that he were as highly regarded back home in Britain. Part of the award is a new composition and performance with the Danish Radio Jazz Orchestra. The title-piece makes a strong and lyrical climax to an album that combines big-band charts and a superb small combo consisting of Pedersen, the mellifluous Brookmeyer, Hazeltine, Ovesen and Arguëlles; the drummer provides two of the compositions, 'Toy Box' and 'Antonia'. There are two further compositions by Brookmeyer and Maria Schneider, 'Nasty Dance' and 'My Lament' respectively, the latter a wonderful orchestral conception.

Unusual for a Jazzpar winner to be so reticent about his own work, but Coe was awarded primarily as a player, one suspects, and it would be a waste if he weren't to play standards. 'Fools Rush In' and 'How Long Has This Been Going On?' (the latter for full orchestra) are both superb. Coe's tone is, as ever, as pure as spring water, with none of the quavering 'oboe' sound that he reacts so badly against, while accepting that it suited Coltrane's purposes perfectly. Brookmeyer has an unerring sense of orchestral dynamics and he conjures some inch-perfect ensembles out of the Danes. A splendid record.

*****(*) Blue Jersey**

AB CD 4 *Coe; Dave Horler (vtb); John Horler (p); Malcolm Creese (b); Allan Ganley (d).* 4/95.

****** In Concert**

AB CD 6 *Coe; John Horler (p); Malcolm Creese (b).* 3/97.

Two exceptional live albums. The earlier was made at the Jersey Jazz Festival, with the Brookmeyer-influenced Dave Horler on valve trombone. He contributes to an unusual arrangement of 'I Got Rhythm', but it's Coe's clarinet solo that blows the whole thing apart, a truly remarkable performance that gets the set off to a great start. To be frank, nothing that follows quite matches up, though 'You Stepped Out Of A Dream' and an unexpectedly paced 'What Is This Thing Called Love?' run it close, with the trombonist playing magnificently again on the latter. The other Horler shows his skills as a composer on two tunes: 'Solid Silver' is inspired by Horace of that ilk, but it ranges far and wide for ideas, with even a hint of Debussy in the middle section; the closing 'Royal Blues' works some unusual wrinkles on a fairly basic idea.

If we've been slightly niggardly with the stars on *Blue Jersey*, that's simply because as a Tony Coe album it sits a little behind the splendid live set recorded a couple of years later at St George's, Brandon Hill, in Bristol. Drummerless, and with no second horn, it's an ideal showcase for Coe, and he responds with near-perfect versions of 'Body And Soul' and 'Re: Person I Knew' which even casual readers will recognize as shibboleths, and a lovely 'You Stepped Out Of A Dream'. St George's has a warm, churchy acoustic and the piano is in excellent shape. Creese (who produced these CDs) is sounding more communicative every time one hears him, and he brings a robust presence both to ballads and to up-tempo songs. If you haven't sampled Tony Coe before, either of these will provide a crash course; the latter is our strong recommendation.

****** Days Of Wine And Roses**

Zephyr ZECD 22 *Coe; Alan Barnes (as, bs, ss, cl, bcl); Brian Lemon (p); Dave Cliff (g); Dave Green (b); Allan Ganley (d).* 1 & 2/97.

This is simply exquisite. The pairing of Coe's tenor and Barnes's alto on the closing choruses of 'My Old Flame' is a high point in recent British jazz. Coe's woody clarinet is featured on the title-track, a virtuosic scatter of notes as the melody is reinvented, re-examined and, finally, heart-stoppingly stated with magnificent simplicity.

The rhythm section could hardly be improved upon, and there is a wonderful tenor/guitar duet on 'Flamingo' which once again highlights Dave Cliff's special talents. *Days* could hardly be bettered, the jewel in Zephyr's already sparkling crown. Coe has also co-starred on other Zephyr recordings, but these we have covered under cornetist Warren Vaché's entry.

*****(*) Ruby**

Zah Zah ZZCD 9802 *Coe; Brian Dee (p); Matt Miles (b); Steve Arguëlles (d).* 98.

Typical of Coe to create a standards album that surprises more than it lulls. The title-piece is an interesting choice, a film tune which has been covered – to our knowledge – only by Ray Charles. The reason for its inclusion becomes clear when Tony plays an additional figure of his own, inspired by the initials of his first granddaughter, Ruby Elizabeth Delaney (Coe), with *Re* generating the first element in the phrase D-E-D-C.

It's just one of a series of tasteful reinventions on the disc. 'My Shining Hour' nods in the direction of John Coltrane but has its own statement to make, and the clarinet and piano conversation of 'More Than You Know' almost remakes the tune. The original 'Backward Tracings', which gives the album much of its character, is a reworking of familiar chords, presumably 'Yesterdays' but possibly combined with another motif.

Of the band, Arguëlles stands out strongly and is given due prominence in the mix. Another exile to France, he has absorbed a great deal of music in the last five years and now sounds entirely in command of his own voice. His solo on 'Love Walked In' is a model, using a bebop diction to suggest the kind of swinging work one might have heard from Dave Tough in the old days. A splendid record from a small but enterprising label.

***** Dreams**
Zephyr ZECD29 *Coe; Gerard Presencer (flhn); Brian Lemon (p); Dave Green (b).* 2/00.

Beautiful session, but it's too samey: the melodies emerge with ravishing elegance, but 13 ballads without much tempo variation turns this into a lovely album of background music. Taken a track at a time, it works fine, and Coe's in splendid voice – check his final cadences on 'Ghost Of A Chance' for a sample.

Jeff Coffin

SOPRANO, ALTO AND TENOR SAXOPHONES, CLARINET, BASS CLARINET, FLUTE

Multi-reedsman, leading his group The Mu-tet and apparently a rare example of a Nashville-based jazzman.

***** Commonality**
Compass 7 4278-2 *Coffin; Rod McGaha (t); Chris Enghauser (b); Tom Giampietro (d).* 7–9/98.

***** Go-Round**
Compass 7 4325-2 *Coffin; Rod McGaha (t); Roy Agee (tb); Chris Walters (p, acc); Tracy Silverman (vla); Pat Bergeson (g, hca); Derek Jones (b); Tom Giampietro (d); Futureman (perc).* 10–11/00.

Coffin's bluesy sound and snappy phrasing are just the right side of slickness, and these are basically fun records, even though he gets a bit self-consciously Trane-like on the title-track of the first album. He does that one on alto, then switches to tenor for the ensuing 'Espoo You', and since this is a dedication to Rollins, maybe there's a certain identity problem. But Enghauser and Giampietro set up enough grooving beats to keep him honest, and McGaha helps out on four tracks. Mainly, this is a good post-bop blow, earnest but unfancy.

Go-Round starts out with a wood-flute fanfare and introduces viola and dumbek into what looks like a worryingly world musical scenario. But the theme's not so exotic, and as the tracks start to go by, it's clear that Coffin has just brought in the odd bit of spice to brighten his mix. He uses five different horns as lead instrument, and if this makes for a sometimes faceless fluency, the other players help to put some interesting wrinkles into the record. Worth a try.

Ryan Cohan

PIANO

Best known as a session arranger and composer, Cohan struck up a strong partnership with Ramsey Lewis before developing his own recording career.

***** Here And Now**
Sirocco 1016 *Cohan; Scott Burns (ss, ts); James Gailloreto (ss, f); James Cammack (b); Tom Hipskind (d); Dede Sampaio (perc).* 9/01.

A debut that at times sounds as if it might be some adventurous but overlooked corner of the Blue Note '60s catalogue. Cohan's skills as a writer are widely recognized, and he is certainly a more impressive composer than he is a soloing pianist, but the real high point of this album is how dextrously he has arranged and voiced his fellow-musicians. The sextet is not fully deployed on every cut, which means that there is considerable flexibility in the sound, with a heavier sonority on some of the tracks than others. Nor do any of the other soloists stand out particularly. What one remembers from this is a coherent, well-drilled group playing fine modern ensemble jazz. Too few records of that type around.

Avishai Cohen (born 1970)

DOUBLE BASS, PIANO, PERCUSSION

Young virtuoso bassist, a Chick Corea sideman and now recording for Corea's own imprint.

*****(*) Adama**
Stretch Records SCD 9015-2 *Cohen; Steve Davis (tb); Steve Wilson (ss); Chick Corea, Jason Lindner, Brad Mehldau, Danilo Perez (p); Amos Hoffman (g, oud); Jeff Ballard, Jordy Rossi (d); Don Alias (perc); Claudio Acuña (v).* 97.

***** Devotion**
Stretch SCD 9021-2 *Cohen; Steve Davis (tb); Jimmy Greene (ss, ts, f); Jason Lindner (p); Amos Hoffman (g, oud); Jeff Ballard (d).* 98.

This young associate of Chick Corea always looked likely to carve his own path. Cohen wasn't so much a virtuoso bassist as a thoroughly musicianly member of Chick's group, the kind of player who does the job at hand with consummate professionalism but who manages to leave you with the feeling that he will need to be checked out subsequently.

His debut is all the more impressive for the skill of the writing. Everything except 'Besame Mucho' is by Cohen. The tunes range from bright swingers like 'Ora' to a pair of items lifted from a 'Bass Suite'. The first is played just by trombone, soprano saxophone and broodingly eloquent bass, an unexpected instrumentation that is more than merely quirky. What emerges might well be a stripped-down section of a big-band piece, and it would be no surprise if this was where Cohen's career heads in years to come. Middle Eastern influences are in evidence here and there, not just in the use of an oud, but also in the writing, which favours non-Western scales. Label-boss Chick Corea pops up to give his blessing on 'Gadu', playing Fender Rhodes alongside Danilo Perez on acoustic piano and sounding as if he might have been called away from something more important. Chick is also the dedicatee of 'The Gift' on the second album; if only he had been around to perform as well.

Trombonist Davis returns for the second album, which is pretty much more of the same. There are two more fragments of 'Bass Suite', though this increasingly looks like a flag of convenience for otherwise untitled material. The stand-out track is 'Ot Kain', inspired by a poem of Shay Yemini, which in turn takes its inspiration from Akhenaten's hymn to the sun.

Two elegantly crafted albums, perhaps not quite differentiated enough to be really special, but far from ordinary nevertheless.

*****(*) Colors**

Stretch 9031 *Cohen; Steve Davis, Avi Lebovich (tb); Jimmy Greene (ss, f); Jason Lindner (p); Amos Hoffman (g, oud); Jeff Ballard (d, perc); Yargil Baras (b); Antonio Sanchez (d); Claudia Acuña (v); string quartet.* 12/00.

This took Cohen's solo career into a new dimension. The writing is bright and thoughtful, the arrangements (with trombones, soprano saxophone and string quartet on the title-track) full-voiced, and the improvisation impressively difficult to separate from written passages. If it's music that appeals to you, the Japanese edition has two extra tracks. Some of the melodies might well be from one of John Zorn's 'radical Jewish culture' projects for Tzadik, though there is nothing ideological about Cohen's work and no special pleading in his own playing, which sounds light and free. Yargil Baras takes over bass-playing duties when Cohen is otherwise engaged. All 13 songs are originals, though 'IB4U' is co-credited to Avi Levobich, who's also the most significant lead voice on the set. This was something of a breakthrough album, though Cohen's wider reputation was soon to be complicated by the emergence of a trumpet player called … Avishai Cohen.

***** Unity**

Stretch 9036 *Cohen; Diego Urcola (t, flhn); Avi Lebovich (tb, v); Yosvany Terry (as, ts, shekere); Yargil Baras, Bryan Keelen (b); Antonio Sanchez (d, v).* n.d.

The recording debut of Cohen's International Vamp Band has an unexpected Latin quality which doesn't quite surface explicitly but remains a background colour. Cohen doubles on piano, which explains why a couple of bassists are listed; Keelen is the leader's pupil and is given his break here. Avishai seems to be looking for a new approach that recasts him as bandleader and writer rather than bassist. He's modestly successful – 'Etude' and 'Vamp' suggest the expressive limitations of the set – but it isn't quite there.

***** Lyla**

Razdaz 4601 *Cohen; Diego Urcola (t, flhn); Alex Norris (flhn); Avi Lebovich (tb, f); Yosvany Terry (as, shekere); Chick Corea (p); Yargil Baras (b); Eric McPherson (d); Mark Giuliana (d, perc, elec); Lola, Jeff Taylor (v).* 9/03.

This is a curious half-step forward, half-step back project, marked by more straight post-bop jazz than its predecessor, but also moving out into a new, song-based territory at the same time. The songs are very effective and brightly executed by a thoroughly sympathetic band, but there are glimpses, too, of a freer, more improvisatory style lurking behind 'Ascension' (emphatically *not* a Coltrane cover), 'Structure In Emotion' and 'Lyla' itself. There are this time a couple of covers. Chick Corea's 'Eternal Child' is a nod to the old boss, who plays well here; the Beatles' 'Come Together' is smartly reinvented and there is even a version, very successful, of rapper Dr Dre's 'The Watcher'. Stand braced for more challenging crossovers on subsequent Cohen albums.

Tom Cohen

DRUMS

Contemporary drummer speaking a mainstream post-bop language.

***** Tom Cohen Trio**

Cadence CJR 1067 *Cohen; Ron Thomas (p); Mike Richmond, Bill Zinno (b).* 2/95–6/96.

Cohen doesn't give himself a lot of solos but he definitely leads from the front. The tracks which bookend the record, 'Things You Were' and 'Motion Potion', are as trenchant as you like, and elsewhere he and Richmond (Zinno comes in for only one track) set up a powerful undertow for Thomas's piano. The music is a scrupulous and swinging essay on the piano-trio style. There are three Bill Evans compositions, but it's the hard-hitting side of Evans's music that they take off from; the other material – mostly originals by Thomas, though 'Things You Were' is a thin disguise for 'All The Things You Are' – is effective if not terribly vivid. John Anthony's studio mix pushes everything to the front, which can make it a little tiring to listen to.

Al Cohn (1925–88)

TENOR SAXOPHONE

Cohn was the consummate jazz professional. His arrangements were foursquare and unpretentious and his saxophone-playing a model of order and accuracy. He was perhaps never more completely himself than as one of the Four Brothers, the legendary Woody Herman saxophone section. Later in life, though, his soloing took on a philosophical authority, unexciting but deeply satisfying.

***** Broadway**

Original Jazz Classics OJC 1812 *Cohn; Hal Stein (as); Harvey Leonard (p); Red Mitchell (b); Christy Febbo (d).* 7/54.

*****(*) You 'N' Me**

Verve 589318-2 *Cohn; Zoot Sims (ts, cl); Mose Allison (p); Major Holley (b) Osie Johnson (d).* 6/60.

***** Either Way**

Evidence ECD 22007 *Cohn; Zoot Sims (ts); Mose Allison (p); Bill Crow (b); Gus Johnson (d); Cecil 'Kid Haffey' Collier (v).* 2/61.

***** From A To Z**

RCA 47790 *Cohn; Dick Sherman (t); Zoot Sims (ts); Hank Jones, Dave McKenna (p); Milt Hinton (b); Osie Johnson (d).* 62.

Virtually all one needs to know about Al and Zoot's long-standing association can be found on the sober-sounding 'Improvisation For Two Unaccompanied Saxophones' on *You 'N' Me*. All the virtues (elegant interplay, silk-smooth textures) and all the vices (inconsequentiality and Sims's tendency to follow his favourite patterns) are firmly in place. A and Z were apt to cover the whole expressive gamut from A to B, as

Dorothy Parker once memorably said about Miss Hepburn. The rest of this set is their all-but-patented, cheerfully swinging one-two, bodacious unisons followed by a thumping good solo out of each horn, and maybe a little cameo from Allison too. It may not dig all that deep, but when you're listening to it you tend to wonder why more jazz records don't have this feel-good factor. The remastered sound has a rather fierce edge to it.

The Evidence set is sparky enough, if only because Allison is such an enlivening presence. Still wholly underrated as a pianist and misplaced in the history of the music – filed under 'vocal', or 'easy listening' in one major store of our acquaintance – Mose brings a touch of acidity to the slightly sweet harmonies Sims for one seems to prefer. Cohn was always a more adventurous player, and he responds well to the pianist's sly, stealthy cues. With the whole Xanadu catalogue currently *hors de combat* and awaiting CD transfer (and how much longer must we wait?), this session becomes all the more valuable.

The *Broadway* disc is exceedingly well behaved, even dull, until Cohn launches into a ballad medley that simply takes one's breath away. Stein is virtually unknown; he's recorded with Teddy Charles and fellow-altoist Phil Woods, and on the basis of this performance might have expected to make more of a splash on his own account. The rest of the band do their jobs like men on an hourly rate.

The RCA compilation is one of a number of Cohn's Victor albums which have had some European release (including *Jazz Workshop, That Old Feeling, Natural Seven* and *East Coast – West Coast Scene*) but remain difficult to find: RCA's back catalogue is in bad need of the kind of refurbishment which has been routinely accorded to Verve and Blue Note. It's pretty standard Al and Zoot material, though above-average production and mastering and a nicely presented package. A handful of extra takes – including 'Tenor For Two, Please, Jack' and 'More Bread' – fill out the picture and will be an additional draw for fans of this long-standing pairing.

***(*) In Concert At East Stroudsberg University

IAJRC 1016 *Cohn; Harry Leahey (g); Steve Gilmore (b); Bill Goodwin (d). 4/86.*

*** Keeper Of The Flame

Jazz House JHCD 022 *Cohn; Dick Pearce (t, flhn); Pete Beachill (tb, vtb); Andy Mackintosh (as); Dave Hartley (p); Chris Laurence (b); Quinny Laurence (d). 5/87.*

With albums for Xanadu and Concord all missing in action, there's shamefully little of Al's later work in circulation. From the fierce Charlie Parker blues which kicks off the disc, the concert set, from a Pennsylvania college gig, is sheer delight. Al had lost Zoot, but his own playing was as tough – mentally and in the firmness of his delivery – as ever. Leahey was a bop guitarist who didn't record much, and he gets in some pretty momentous licks of his own, while Gilmore and Goodwin are old hands Cohn could entirely rely on.

The London recording was made in a studio rather than in concert, but it has the easy flow of a sympathetic gig. The Jazz Seven play 'Keeper Of The Flame' in tribute and Cohn takes a couple of tracks with rhythm only. These are the most effective of all – which is no surprise. He sounds calm, untroubled and completely on top of things. Less than a year later, he was gone.

George 'Kid Sheik' Cola (1908–96)

TRUMPET, PIANO, VOCAL

This New Orleans brassman was fronting bands by the age of 17, and he rambled around the city's music and as an ambassador overseas into the '80s, working in small groups as leader and in the city's most renowned brass bands, the Olympia and the Eureka.

** Kid Sheik With Charlie Love And His Cado Jazz Band – 1960

504 CDS 21 *Cola; Charlie Love (t); Albert Warner (tb); Emil Barnes (cl); Louis Gallaud (p); Emanuel Sayles (bj); Albert Jiles (d). 8/60.*

** Kid Sheik's Swingsters 1961

American Music AMCD-91 *Cola; Eddie Sommers (tb); Harold Dejan (as); John Smith (p); Alcide 'Slow Drag' Pavageau (b); Alex Bigard (d). 2/61.*

** In Boston And Cleveland

American Music AMCD-69 *Cola; Louis Nelson, Albert Warner (tb); John Handy (cl, as); James Sing Miller, Louis Gallaud (p); Fred Minor (bj); Chester Zardis, John Joseph (b); Alex Bigard, Cie Frazier (d). 61–69.*

*** First European Tour

GHB BCD-187 *Cola; Jack Weddell (tb); Sammy Rimington (cl); Paul Sealy (bj); Barry Richardson (b); Barry Martyn (d). 6/63.*

*(*) Kid Sheik & Brother Cornbread In Copenhagen

Jazz Crusade JCCD-3002 *Cola; Peter Goetz (tb); Joe 'Brother Cornbread' Thomas (cl); Peter Nissen (bj); Niels Henrik Ross-Petersen (b); Keith Minter (d). 11/74.*

Kid Sheik Cola was much loved in the ranks of New Orleans brassmen, and the notes to several of these discs detail the affection he inspired on his travels. CD listeners will find his music hard going, though. He plays in the mould of the short-breathed frontman and packs a punch only occasionally. Solos tend to be self-effacing, and he usually lets someone else drive things along. This mixed bag of records doesn't fare too well. The 504 date offers a band which sounds almost enfeebled at times, even as weathered New Orleans music goes. Charlie Love is the bandleader, and Kid Sheik sits out on six tracks. But even when he's there the music flickers into real life only occasionally, as on a rickety but spirited 'Down In Honky Tonk Town'. *Swingsters 1961* was recorded by Barry Martyn and features Cola's regular band of the day, but Martyn's notes reveal all sorts of alarums and excursions before the session was done, and it sounds like a shambles for much of the time. Cola plays a couple of ramshackle blues at the piano for a change of pace. *In Boston And Cleveland* includes two knockabout sessions which are largely dominated by Handy; sound-quality is indifferent and there's some awful singing, but it's listenable. The pick is surely *First European Tour*, in which Kid Sheik was chaperoned by Martyn and Rimington through a spirited session that still sounds good. Recorded at Egham Cricket Club.

The notes to the Jazz Crusade set remember the occasion of the recording with much nostalgia, which makes the fairly awful music a terrible disappointment. The main culprit is Brother Cornbread's clarinet, which flies out of tune at every opportunity, though nobody seems to care much. Obviously a happy night, but you definitely had to be there.

***** New Orleans Stompers**

GHB BCD–76 *Cola; Jim Robinson (tb); Sammy Rimington (cl, as); Dick Griffith (bj); Dick McCarthy (b); Big Bill Bissonnette (d).* 75.

We're not sure about the date, and the GHB documentation is, as often, confusing. Either way, this is Cola and Robinson having fun with some younger confederates. No classic, but it might be the best disc under Cola's name all the same. Rimington sounds a little wayward at times.

Cozy Cole (1909–81)

DRUMS

Cole cut his teeth with Cab Calloway and Stuff Smith and enjoyed a hit with 'Topsy', which kickstarted his career as leader. A bright, energetic player with a few trademark touches.

***** Cozy Cole 1944**

Classics 819 *Cole; Shorty Rogers, Charlie Shavers (t); Hal d'Amico, Aaron Sachs (cl); Walter Thomas (as, ts); Don Byas, Coleman Hawkins (ts); Johnny Guarnieri, Clyde Hart, Billy Rowland (p); Billy Taylor (b, p); Tiny Grimes (g); Slam Stewart, Sid Weiss (b); June Hawkins (v).* 2–9/44.

***** Cozy Cole 1944–1945**

Classics 865 *Cole; Emmett Berry, Shad Collins, Frankie Newton, Joe Thomas (t); Ray Conniff, Tyree Glenn, Trummy Young (tb); Earl Bostic (as); Walter Thomas (as, ts); Don Byas, Bud Johnson (ts); Ernie Caceres (bs); Johnny Guarnieri, Earl Hines (p); Remo Palmieri (g); Mark Shopnick, Slam Stewart, Billy Taylor, Teddy Walters (b).* 11/44–4/45.

****(*) And All That Big Band Jazz**

Orchard 7194 *Cole; Bernie Privin, Ernie Royal, Joe Wilder (t); Henderson Chambers, Urbie Green, Frank Rehak, Hale Rood (tb); Barney Bigard, Peanuts Hucko (cl); Pepper Adams (bs); Dick Hyman (org); Don Abney, Hank Jones, Nat Pierce, Mal Waldron, Al Williams (p); Billy Bauer, Kenny Burrell, Al Caiola, Barry Galbraith, Jimmy Raney, Mundell Lowe (g); George Duvivier, Milt Hinton, Jack Lesberg, Wendell Marshall, Wilbur Ware (b); Kenny Clarke (d); other personnel.* 58.

Engaging rather than essential, Cole nevertheless managed to pack his band with fine soloists who vie for attention on his sides for Continental, Keynote and later Guild. Little of the Classics material offers more than a glimpse of any of them, the leader included, though 'Strictly Drums' is an attractive feature. A few interesting guest spots do stand out, notably from Don Byas and from Coleman Hawkins, who delivers a brusquely brilliant solo on 'When Day Is Done'. There is also an opportunity to catch the still-teenage Shorty Rogers, making his recording debut on the 1944 sides and, so far as can be judged, sounding very confident. Though essentially swing performances, the frantic pace and bomb-dropping bass accents suggest that bebop really is just round the corner.

Cole's longevity was helped greatly by the surprise 1958 hit 'Topsy', which became a staple of his act. It's included, along with 'Turvy' and 'Topsy-Turvy' on the Orchard compilation, which is shared with torch singer Savina. An unlikely pairing, but a perfectly pleasant package for the enthusiast.

Freddy Cole (born 1931)

PIANO, VOCAL

The youngest of the Cole brothers, it took Freddy until the '90s to get himself noticed and on record in a significant way. His piano work is much more modest than Nat's, but his voice certainly makes the most of the family resemblance.

***** Always**

Fantasy FCD-9670-2 *Cole; Byron Stripling (flhn); Robin Eubanks (tb); Jeff Scott (frhn); Frank Perowsky (ss, ts, f); Grover Washington Jr (ss); William Kerr (as, f); Antonio Hart (as, ts); Javon Jackson (ts); Roger Rosenberg (bs); Mel Martin (af); Cyrus Chestnut (p); Lionel Cole (ky); Joe Locke (vib); Tom Hubbard, George Mraz (b); Yoron Israel, Russ Kunkel (d); Steve Berrios (perc); strings.* 12/94.

***** I Want A Smile For Christmas**

Fantasy FCD-9672-2 *Cole; Joe Ford (ss); Larry Willis (p); Joe Locke (vib); Jerry Byrd (g); Tom Hubbard (b); Steve Berrios (d).* 7/94.

*****(*) A Circle Of Love**

Fantasy FCD-9674-2 *As above, except add Danny Moore (t), Don Braden (ss), Mel Martin (f), Cyrus Chestnut (p), George Mraz (b).* 9/93–12/95.

*****(*) To The Ends Of The Earth**

Fantasy FCD-9675-2 *As above, except add Byron Stripling (t), Robin Eubanks (tb), Antonio Hart (as), Javon Jackson (ts), Frank Perowsky (cl), William Kerr (as, f), Roger Rosenburg (bcl), Yoron Israel (b); omit Willis, Byrd, Moore, Braden.* 1/97.

Freddy Cole's fine sequence of Fantasy albums helped set him up as an artist of some stature in his own right. The records make a convincing sequence, prepared with great care and thoughtfulness by producer Todd Barkan. The glittering line-up of names on the first disc sets the precedent, with a programme of meticulously arranged standards. Nobody really has any space to cut loose, but the splendid Chestnut is magisterial at the piano, Washington (especially fine on 'You Must Believe In Spring') and Hart take apposite cameos, and the result is a laid-back but not soporific entry. Cole stays away from the piano and sticks to husking through the lyrics. There are a couple of clinkers; 'The Rose' seems to have strayed in from another project altogether. The Christmas collection is, surprisingly, almost as good, centred round the small group listed in the personnel. Willis plays with quiet dignity, and Ford, a surprise choice for sole horn, traces filigree lines over the sometimes unpromising Yuletide material. It's to Cole's credit that when they get to 'The Christmas Song' he sings it in a way that's nothing like Nat.

A Circle Of Love mixes a session recorded for the Alfa label in 1993 with three newer tracks, one of them a quite immaculate take on an unlikely Paul Williams song, 'You're Nice To Be Around'. This and the subsequent *To The Ends Of The Earth* proceed with and polish a formula with which Cole seems completely at home: older standards mixed with newer pop tunes, the blend brought into focus by the carefully chosen tempos and instrumentation. A slow and thoughtful 'Manha De Carnaval' and a fine 'If I Had You' highlight the first disc, while a shimmering duet with Locke on 'Once You've Been In Love' and a handsome treatment of Abbey Lincoln's 'Should Have Been' stand out on the second. Barkan has assembled what is by now a repertory cast of players, and they work with perfect sensitivity to the way Cole sings.

***** Le Grand Freddy**
Fantasy FCD 9863-2 *Cole; Lew Soloff (t); Lou Marini (ts, f); Grover Washington Jr (ts); Cedar Walton, Cyrus Chestnut, Mike Renzi (p); Joe Locke (vib); George Mraz, David Williams (b); Kenny Washington, Grady Tate, Yoron Israel, Ben Riley (d).* 12/94–2/99.

Ouch! An awful pun for the title of this collection in which Freddy sings Michel Legrand. While much of this is new, some tracks were lifted off Cole's earlier Fantasy sets. There are surprising successes, such as 'Windmills Of Your Mind', and some songs which definitely don't suit him, like a far-too-blasé 'Once Upon A Summertime'.

***** Merry-Go-Round**
Telarc CD-83493 *Cole; Lew Soloff (t); Steve Davis (tb); Lou Marini (as, f); Eric Alexander (ts); Gary Smulyan (bs); Cedar Walton (p); George Mraz, Herman Burney (b); Curtis Boyd (d).* 9/99.

Fetching up at yet another label, Cole turns in what is coming to seem like a scrupulously polished act. Todd Barkan is still producing, and the material is diligently chosen, although here and there one can quarrel with what seemed like a good idea at the time. 'Through A Long And Sleepless Night', for instance, is more suavely rueful than sleepless. You couldn't improve the band, though it's playing to strict orders.

**** In The Name Of Love**
Telarc CD-83545 *Cole; Barry Danielian (t); David Mann (ss, as); Jay Beckenstein (ss); Bette Sussman (p); Jason Miles (ky); Romero Lubambo, Dean Brown, Jeff Mironov (g); Will Lee, Mark Egan (b); Keith Carlock (d); Cyro Baptista, Marc Quinones (perc); Katreese Barnes, Cassandra Reed (v).* 2–8/02.

Oh no – Freddy goes pop. Given a faceless AOR production by Jason Miles and handed songs by Boz Scaggs and Van Morrison (never mind Miles's own dreary 'When It Rains'), all of a sudden he's just another elderly crooner trying to keep up with 'the times'.

Nat Cole (1917–65)

PIANO, VOCAL

Born in Montgomery, Alabama, Cole was equally adept at playing the piano and singing, although it was his voice that brought him stardom. He began leading a piano–guitar–bass trio in 1939, and his keyboard style – much influenced by Earl Hines and Teddy Wilson – suggested a transition between swing and what would become the bebop vocabulary. The trio was so successful that it set the main precedent for piano small groups. Cole became enormously popular as a singer, though, and gradually left the keyboard behind, rarely playing in a jazz setting after 1950. A chain-smoker from morning till night, he died from cancer in 1965. His daughter Natalie and brother Freddy carry on his performing tradition.

***** Nat King Cole 1936–1940**
Classics 757 *Cole; Kenneth Roane (t); Tommy Thompson (as); Bill Wright (ts); Oscar Moore (g); Wesley Prince, Eddie Cole (b); Jimmy Adams, Lee Young (d); Bonnie Lake, Juanelda Carter (v).* 7/36–2/40.

***** Nat King Cole 1940–1941**
Classics 773 *Cole; Oscar Moore (g); Wesley Prince (b); Maxene Johnson (v).* 7/40–3/41.

***** Nat King Cole 1941–1943**
Classics 786 *Cole; Lester Young (ts); Oscar Moore (g); Wesley Prince, Red Callender, Johnny Miller (b).* 7/41–11/43.

***** Nat King Cole 1943–1944**
Classics 804 *Cole; Shad Collins (t); Illinois Jacquet (ts); Oscar Moore (g); Johnny Miller, Gene Englund (b); J. C. Heard (d).* 11/43–3/44.

Cole began with deceptively lightweight, jiving music (sample titles: 'Scotchin' With The Soda', 'Ode To A Wild Clam') which masked the intensity of his piano style to a large extent. Smooth, glittering, skating over melodies, Cole's right-hand lines were breaking free of his original Earl Hines influence and looking towards a dashing improvisational freedom which other players – Powell, Haig, Marmarosa – would turn into the language of bebop. Cole was less inclined towards that jagged-edge approach and preferred the hip constrictions of songs and good-natured jive. With pulsing interjections from Moore and Prince (subsequently replaced by Miller), this was a surprisingly compelling music. Classics starts its usual chronological survey with four obscure 1936 titles by a group led by Eddie Cole. The trio proper begins in 1939 with 12 titles cut in a single day. Next (Classics 773) came a session of transcriptions, where Cole shares vocal duties with Maxene Johnson, for the Davis & Schwegler company – the label went bankrupt before the sides were even issued and Cole ended up with a compensation payment of $7.47 for his trouble. The rest of the CD offers Nat's first two sessions for Decca, and while the trio hadn't yet perfected its dapper formula, there's much to enjoy in the likes of 'Sweet Lorraine' and 'Slow Down'. Classics 786 moves on through a session with Lester Young and Red Callender amid more trio work. There's a single quintet date with horns on Classics 804, but this disc is probably the best single representation of Cole's early music, with hits such as 'Straighten Up And Fly Right' and some deft interpretations of standards. Transfers, from unlisted sources, seem good.

***** The Jazzman**
Topaz TPZ 1012 *As above, except add Wesley Prince (b).* 40–44.

***** The McGregor Years 1941–1945**
Music & Arts CD 911 4CD *Cole; Oscar Moore (g); Wesley Prince, Johnny Miller (b); Anita O'Day, Ida James, Barry Sisters, Anita Boyer (v).* 2/41–5/45.

*****(*) Nat King Cole 1944–1945**
Classics 861 *Cole; Bill Coleman (t); Buster Bailey (cl); Benny Carter (as); Coleman Hawkins (ts); Oscar Moore (g); John Kirby, Johnny Miller (b); Max Roach (d); Kay Starr (v).* 11/44–5/45.

*****(*) Nat King Cole 1945**
Classics 893 *Cole; Charlie Shavers (t); Herbie Haymer (ts); Oscar Moore (g); Johnny Miller, John Simmons (b); Buddy Rich (d).* 5–12/45.

*****(*) Nat King Cole 1946**
Classics 938 *Cole; Willie Smith (as); Oscar Moore (g); Johnny Miller, Red Callender (b); Jackie Mills (d).* 2–6/46.

*****(*) Nat King Cole 1946–1947**
Classics 1005 *As above, except omit Smith, Callender, Mills; add Jack Parker (d), strings.* 8/46–7/47.

★★★(★) Nat King Cole 1947
Classics 1031 *As above, except omit Parker, strings.* 7/47.

★★★(★) Nat King Cole 1947 Vol. 2
Classics 1062 *As above, except add Johnny Mercer (v), strings.* 8/47.

★★★(★) The Vocal Classics 1942–1946
Capitol 833571-2 *Cole; Oscar Moore (g); Johnny Miller, (b).* 42–46.

★★★(★) The Best Of The Trio (Instrumental)
Capitol 798288-2 *As above, except add Irving Ashby (g), Joe Comfort (b), Jack Costanza (perc).* 43–49.

★★★(★) Live At The Circle Room
Capitol 521859-2 *Cole; Oscar Moore (g); Johnny Miller (b).* 9/46.

★★★(★) Jazz Encounters
Capitol 796693-2 *Cole; Dizzy Gillespie, Bill Coleman, Ernie Royal, Ray Linn (t); Bill Harris (tb); Buddy DeFranco, Buster Bailey (cl); Coleman Hawkins, Charlie Barnet, Flip Phillips, Herbie Haymer (ts); Benny Carter (as); Heinie Beau, Fred Stulce, Harry Schuman (reeds); Billy Bauer, Irving Ashby, Oscar Moore, Dave Barbour (g); Eddie Safranski, Johnny Miller, Joe Comfort, Artie Shapiro, John Kirby (b); Buddy Rich, Max Roach, Nick Fatool, Earl Hyde (d); Woody Herman, Jo Stafford, Nellie Lutcher, Johnny Mercer, Kay Starr (v); Stan Kenton Orchestra.* 12/47–1/50.

Cole made a tremendous number of recordings with his trio; Mosaic once issued a comprehensive survey which ran to 18 CDs (currently out of print). Classics's ongoing survey is up to 1950 and offers a sensible way of collecting these tracks. The *1944–1945* set includes one date for V-Disc and has a session by the Capitol International Jazzmen. Carter and Hawkins have starring roles, but the highlights of the session are the two vocals by the young Kay Starr, who handles 'If I Could Be With You' and 'Stormy Weather' quite beautifully. *1945* offers a date where Cole played with the Herbie Haymer Quintet, the saxophonist shining on four engaging titles; the rest is solid Cole trio music. *1946* starts with a Keynote session where Cole sat in with Willie Smith and rhythm section; the rest is nearly all Capitol material and includes his hit, 'Route 66'. All the trio sessions maintain an enviable standard, and there are few duds among all the tracks; only occasionally does a song offer too little for Cole and cohorts to work with. The pianist's luxuriant swing and dextrous touch as well as his intelligently varied arrangements for the trio and its wonderfully responsive following of his leads, all seem inexhaustible. Moore is, indeed, almost Cole's equal on an executive level, and their best playing often runs in dazzling, parallel lines.

Classics 1005, covering 1946–7, has a discouraging preponderance of so-so ballads, but the boppish 'That's What' and a flying 'Honeysuckle Rose' pick matters up towards the end. Not one of the best in this series, though. Classics 1031 shows how hard Cole was working – he cut 19 of these titles in a single week. Song-quality is up here, and with only the three trio members involved it's a good single-disc representation of their music. Classics 1062 calls in Johnny Mercer to sit in on four hip titles, including 'My Baby Likes To Be-Bop', but matters deteriorate from there, with a strings session (including Nat's first 'Nature Boy'), a couple of nursery rhyme novelties and some more forgotten songs, although 'Lament In Chords' is an attractive mood-piece with fine work by Moore.

Music & Arts has expanded its previous set of broadcast transcriptions into a huge, four-disc edition. There are a lot of vocals by Anita Boyer, Anita O'Day and the baby-voiced Ida James, and together with the occasional roughness in the transfers this adds up to a package aimed more at completists than at the general collector; plenty of good jazz, all the same. The Topaz disc covers tracks from Capitol, Decca and seven airchecks and is a capable selection, though the field is starting to get crowded for this material. Capitol's own set of *Vocal Classics* includes all the obvious jive tunes and will please most looking for a single disc of Cole the singer-pianist, as opposed to the other way around, which is catered for by the instrumental disc. Oddly enough, here one keeps waiting for Nat to start singing! Capitol has also recently uncovered a live date from the Circle Room, nothing very different from what Nat was doing in the studio or on the radio, but solid KC Trio fare.

Capitol's *Jazz Encounters* disc is a remarkable demonstration of Cole's versatility, bringing together seven dates in which he acted in the main as a sideman yet still usually dominated the tracks. Two pieces with the Metronome All Stars – which include Gillespie and Harris – are followed by one with Kenton and the session with the swing-styled Capitol International Jazzmen. A beautiful set of Jo Stafford songs, a couple of jive routines with Woody Herman and a date with Capitol boss Johnny Mercer make the record essential for Cole's admirers.

★★★ Nat 'King' Cole 1947 Vol. 3
Classics 1135 *Cole; Irving Ashby (g); Johnny Miller (b).* 10–11/47.

★★★ Nat 'King' Cole 1947–1949
Classics 1155 *As above, except add Dizzy Gillespie, Buddy Childers, Ken Hanna, Al Porcino, Ray Wetzel (t); Bill Harris, Milt Bernhart, Harry Betts, Harry Forbes (tb); Bart Varsalona (btb); Buddy DeFranco (cl); Art Pepper, George Weidler (as); Flip Phillips, Bob Cooper, Warren Weidler (ts); Bob Gioga (bs); Billy Bauer (g); Joe Comfort, Eddie Safranski (b); Buddy Rich, Shelly Manne (d); strings.* 12/47–1/49.

★★★ Nat 'King' Cole 1949
Classics 1196 *Cole; Irving Ashby (g); Joe Comfort (b); Jack Costanzo (perc); Maria Cole, Starlighters, Alyce King's Vokettes (v); strings.* 3–8/49.

Irving Ashby replaced Oscar Moore on guitar towards the end of 1947, and Joe Comfort displaced Johnny Miller the following year; otherwise it was business as usual for the King Cole Trio. Capitol set down session after session – the 24 titles on Classics 1135 were made in less than two weeks – partly because of a threatened union ban on recording, which wiped out much of 1948 for the record labels. Quality control undergoes the occasional blip, but Cole had always had to deal with makeweights as well as good songs, and his own performances are rarely less than impeccable. Ashby gets a little solo limelight here and there, and while the general tenor of the music is smoothing out, there's still the occasional R&B tinge in the likes of 'Money Is Honey'. Classics 1155 rattles off another dozen trio titles before a session where Cole featured with the Metronome All Stars – 'Leap Here' is a bop snapshot, while 'Metronome Riff' puts a 22-piece band through a curious Pete Rugolo chart. More significant, though, is the advent of strings on Nat Cole records. 'Lost April', which became a huge hit backed with 'Nature Boy', and 'Portrait Of Jennie' are charming, but they point to the end of Cole's jazz career.

Classics 1196 starts with another new sound: Jack Costanzo's bongos, from this point a regular with the trio. 'Laugh! Cool Clown' is actually 'Vesti La Giubba', and 'Bop-Kick' is as close as Cole ever came to straight bebop. 'Land Of Love' and 'Lush Life' have more arranging by Rugolo, and 'Etymology' features Nat explaining how Gillespie's bebop language translates for squares, though sadly the record wasn't issued at the time. Of all the discs in this series, this one fluctuates the most. It starts with the 'Bop-Kick' session and ends on Cole with the Starlighters doing 'All I Want For Christmas (Is My Two Front Teeth)'.

***** Nat 'King' Cole 1949–1950**
Classics 1305 *Cole; Ernie Royal (t); Charlie Barnet (ts): Irving Ashby (g); Gene Orloff (vn); Joe Comfort (b); Earl Hyde, Lee Young (d); Jack Costanza (perc); Woody Herman, Nellie Lutcher, The Starlighters, Alice King Vokettes (v); strings.* 9/49–5/50.

Showbiz has almost taken over here, starting with a Hawaiian tune, a novelty called 'The Horse Told Me' (also done by renowned horseplayer Bing Crosby), a couple of jive titles done with Woody Herman, two more with Nellie Lutcher and the undeniably luscious 'Mona Lisa'. But Nat's refusal to either surrender his suave sense of swing or talk down to his audience carries him through situations which would undo most performers. He still earns the stars. Clean transfers.

****** Cool Cole**
Proper PROPERBOX 31 4CD *As various discs above.* 12/40–8/50.

Picking out the highlights from Cole's most prolific (and consistent) period is never going to be easy, but Proper have done a thoughtful job in selecting 104 titles from Nat's long 'trio' tenure with Capitol. The great hits are here alongside some of the superior jazz titles, and there's enough here to propose this as a one-stop selection for anyone wanting the pick of Cole's most jazz-directed recordings.

*****(*) Big Band Cole**
Capitol 796259-2 *Cole; Count Basie Orchestra, Stan Kenton Orchestra.* 50–58.

A compilation of sessions with Basie's band (minus Basie) and two tracks with the Kenton orchestra, plus two other songs with a top-flight studio band. Cole should have made more big-band jazz records than he did – for all the beauty and warmth of his straight records – and this compilation shows the missed opportunity. Cole doesn't swing noticeably harder here than he does normally, but set-pieces such as 'The Blues Don't Care' and 'Wee Baby Blues' establish a different mood from his normal regimen, and he sounds as comfortable and good-humoured as he ever did elsewhere. Beautifully remastered, this is highly recommended.

CORE COLLECTION

*****(*) After Midnight**
Capitol 520087-2 *Cole; Harry 'Sweets' Edison (t); Juan Tizol (vtb); Willie Smith (as); Stuff Smith (vn); John Collins (g); Charlie Harris (b); Lee Young (d); Jack Costanzo (perc).* 8–9/56.

Cole's one latter-day jazz date has a huge reputation, but there are disappointing aspects to it: Cole didn't seem to want to stretch out in the music, and the tracks are all rather short. Tizol was a strange choice as one of the horn soloists, and Edison, while effective enough, tends to stroll through it all, as was often his wont. But the music is still an unblemished and beautifully groomed example of small-group swing, and Cole proves that his piano-playing was undiminished by his career switchover. There are several tracks that were left off the original LP and an alternative take.

Nat's later Capitol albums are without exception dedicated to his singing, and although we have opted not to list them here, they are recommended as examples of great vocal records.

Bill Coleman (1904–81)

TRUMPET, FLUGELHORN

Born in Kentucky, he switched to trumpet from clarinet after hearing Louis Armstrong. Played in New York bands, 1927–35, and then moved to Paris, where he became a celebrity. Returned to New York, 1940, but was summoned back to Paris in 1948 and this time remained there, occasionally travelling but mostly playing 'en France'.

*****(*) Hangin' Around**
Topaz TPZ 1040 *Coleman; Henry 'Red' Allen, John Butler, Shad Collins, Bill Dillard (t); Billy Burns, J. C. Higginbotham, Dicky Wells (tb); George Johnson, Albert Nicholas (cl, as); Andy Fitzgerald, Joe Marsala (cl); Edgar Courance, Frank Goudie (cl, ts); Pete Brown, Willie Lewis, Joe Hayman (as); Charlie Holmes (as, ss); Coleman Hawkins, Teddy Hill (ts); Herman Chittison, Garnet Clark, John Ferrier, Ellis Larkins, Luis Russell (p); Stéphane Grappelli (vn, p); Oscar Aleman (g); Will Johnson (bj, g); Al Casey, Carmen Mastren, John Mitchell, Django Reinhardt, Joseph Reinhardt (g); June Cole, Eugene D'Hellemmes, George 'Pops' Foster, Richard Fulbright, Wilson Myers, Oscar Pettiford, Gene Traxler (b); Paul Barbarin, Bill Beason, Tommy Benford, William Diemer, Ted Fields, Shelly Manne (d).* 9/29–12/43.

***** Bill Coleman, 1936–1938**
Classics 764 *Coleman; Christian Wagner (cl, as); Eddie Brunner, Edgar Courance, Frank Goudie (cl, ts); Alix Combelle, Noel Chiboust (ts); Herman Chittison, John Ferrier, Emile Stern (p); Stéphane Grappelli (vn, p); Oscar Aleman, John Mitchell, Django Reinhardt, Joseph Reinhardt (g); Roger Grasset, Eugene D'Hellemmes, Wilson Myers, Lucien Simoens (b); Tommy Benford, William Diemer, Ted Fields, Jerry Mengo (d).* 1/36–9/38.

*****(*) From Boogie To Funk**
Emarcy 549401-2 *Coleman; Quentin Jackson (tb); Budd Johnson (ts); Patti Brown (p); Les Spann (g); Buddy Catlett (b); Joe Harris (d).* 60.

Many people encounter this fine trumpeter only in the context of sessions with the great Django Reinhardt. Having worked with Don Redman and Luis Russell, he first went to Paris in 1933, and he finally settled there three years after the war. The Topaz includes one early track, recorded under Russell's leadership in 1929. Though his contribution is brief and outclassed by Allen's, it is enough to mark him down as a player to be followed. The next tracks jump on to the Paris sojourns, activity with Garnet Clark's Hot Clubs Four and a duo with Herman Chittison on 'I'm In The Mood For Love', one of the things that overlap with the Classics volume. There is obviously a good deal of overlap between these, though the Classics set kicks off with only a slightly earlier (a week, to be exact) encounter between the pair, with bassist Eugene D'Hellemmes in support on 'What's The Reason' and 'After You've Gone'.

Classics omit the material recorded under the leadership of Dicky Wells and Willie Lewis but for some reason (the quality of the solos presumably) do include five tracks made with clarinettist and tenorman Eddie Brunner, and of course the Topaz extends forward in time to the war years. Of the years in common, the only big loss is a storming version of 'I Got Rhythm' for Dicky Wells, with Django powering the band along. If his is the dominant voice on the instrument in this time period, the Argentinian, Oscar Aleman, suggests a range of alternatives and an arresting solo style on the same January 1936 session as the Chittison/D'Hellemmes cuts.

Coleman has a bright, uncomplicated tone and delivery, and a nice singing voice. He probably reached his peak in the mid- to late '30s, but he had the sort of chops that can go on pretty much for ever, unpressured, distinct and slightly discursive. The Emarcy reissue is a very pleasing discovery: despite the distinctly unpromising title, the music's top-notch mainstream, with Johnson and Jackson abetting Bill's moves and the music going off at a sunny, flexible pace.

***** A Smooth One**

Jasmine 628 2CD *Coleman; Tony Milliner–Alan Littlejohns Sextet; Lew Hooper (p); Mat Mathewson (g); Mark MacCarthy (b); Johnny Richardson (d). 67.*

There's a huge gap in the Coleman discography before this date which was recorded live in Manchester in 1967. These previously unissued performances are decently recorded and fairly well mastered, though there's still quite a lot of snash around the horns that no amount of twiddling with the equalizers will get rid of. The set has a shake-down feel, with one untitled original, the shambolic 'Hollering At The Watkins' and a very wobbly approach to 'Caravan'. There's a lot of music to get through, fine when you consider how few modern Coleman records there are, but a hefty call on your time if you're not a fan. The local band do a decent job.

***** Plus Four**

Jazzology 196 *Coleman; François Guin (tb); Michael Garret (p); Jean-François Cotorie (b); Art Taylor (d). 77.*

The LP original of this is now rare, though it still turns up at British record fairs. Well settled in France, Coleman found enough *sympathique* musical company to keep him busy in later years. What's nice about this session is that there's no saxophone. The two brasses blend together nicely and it's only a pity that the set-list isn't more adventurous. Perhaps the constraint was pianist Garret, who isn't always assured in his chording, as if he isn't quite across the changes. Taylor, also an exile in France, is superbly relaxed and keeps the rhythm taut but not pushy. Not bad sound, though certainly not of the standard you might have expected for the time.

***** Really I Do**

Black & Blue 162 *Coleman; Guy Lafitte (ts); Red Richards (p); Bill Pemberton (b); Panama Francis (d). 5/80.*

Bill Coleman died in Toulouse in August 1981, so this recording is one of his last. Black & Blue were loyal supporters of American visitors and exiles and Bill must have been grateful for the belated attention. Lafitte did some fine work with Arnett Cobb the same year and he's in equally good form on this, clearly enjoying the relaxed pace that Coleman favoured in later years. The opening 'Crazy Rhythm' is about as hectic as it gets. Most of the tracks are of modest duration, with no extended solos and no experimental tacks, though the inclusion of Dicky Wells's seldom covered 'Hello Babe' stands out. Coleman's embouchure still sounds in excellent shape. He hits notes cleanly and accurately and with less vibrato than on some sessions. There's a poignancy to the session none the less.

George Coleman (born 1935)

TENOR, ALTO AND SOPRANO SAXOPHONES

Greatly admired by other players, and once recruited by that peerless talent-spotter, Miles Davis, the Memphis-born saxophonist has rarely enjoyed commensurate public success. His complex harmonic awareness occasionally pushes outside orthodoxy entirely, but even when playing the changes, Coleman is a challenging improviser.

***** Playing Changes**

Ronnie Scott's Jazz House JHCD 002 *Coleman; Hilton Ruiz (p); Ray Drummond (b); Billy Higgins (d). 4/79.*

For anyone who has worn smooth their copy of the old Pye LP, *Ronnie Scott Presents George Coleman 'Live'*, this could be a fair substitute. Recorded during the same 1979 residency at Frith Street, *Playing Changes* consists of just three – two *long*, one shorter – takes. Coleman's attack is typically robust and veined with unexpected harmonic ore. However, anyone whose copy of the original LP survives may feel that they already have the best of the deal. 'Laura' is, at 23 minutes plus, a tad too long and slightly overgenerous to both Ruiz and the still-inexperienced Drummond; by contrast 'Stella By Starlight', which occupies a whole side of the Pye, is a much more coherent performance. The best of the saxophonist's work occurs when he moves sideways of the given changes and into his inventive high harmonic mode. There are either misfingerings or symptoms of a weary reed in the closing ensembles of the end-of-set 'Moment's Notice' which detract a little from an intriguing variation on the Coltrane original. On balance, it might have been better to put together a stronger 65-minute CD integrating the best of the two sessions. Scratches aside, most listeners will be returning to the Pye a lot more often than to this.

*****(*) My Horns Of Plenty**

Birdology FDM 37005 *Coleman; Harold Mabern (p); Ray Drummond (b); Billy Higgins (d). 3/91.*

A welcome return for this set, only fleetingly available in its previous issue. We are slightly bothered by the reverberant studio mix, but the music's top class, an authoritarian player with a rhythm section that respects him but wants to assert itself too. 'Lush Life' goes from a musing, out-of-tempo intro into a grand 12 minutes of playing. The brief 'Sheik Of Araby' rushes along, and the closing 'Old Folks' – performed on alto, a rarity for Coleman – is all bursting melody.

*****(*) Blues Inside Out**

Ronnie Scott's Jazz House 46 *Coleman; Peter King (as); Julian Joseph (p); Dave Green (b); Mark Taylor (d). 97.*

Back at Ronnie's with a later version of the house band and a swinging set of standard and repertory tunes. Only the title-track and 'Venus Flytrap' are originals, the latter a tricksy and sinuous theme that brings out the best in the gifted Joseph. Long versions of 'Never Let Me Go', 'Tune Up' and 'Oleo' are more routine blowing numbers, but 'Nancy (With The Laughing Face)' is a reminder of how expressive George can be playing ballads. The recording, presumably done on the club's desk, is rather boxy and has a few moments of unnecessary distortion, but this is another worthwhile set from a location where Coleman is always an honoured and much-liked visitor.

***** I Could Write A Book: The Music Of Richard Rodgers**
Telarc 83439 *Coleman; Harold Mabern (p); Jamil Nasser (b); Billy Higgins (d).* 5/98.

The initial inspiration for this record seems to have been a guest spot in a Carnegie Hall Jazz Band concert devoted to the music of Rodgers. The material selected is hardly unexpected, but George finds new things to do with 'Lover' and 'My Funny Valentine', roughening up the changes and investing 'Valentine' with a dark sobriety that banishes any hint of winsomeness. The band includes two old friends from Memphis, Mabern and Nasser, and the presence of Higgins at the kit guarantees a pungent swing. 'Thou Swell' is a duet for saxophone and drums, and 'People Will Say We're In Love' is just by the rhythm section. There are echoes here and there of Sonny Rollins, John Coltrane and Joe Henderson, but George never quite stamps his authority on standard material as imaginatively as that great trio.

*****(*) Danger High Voltage**
Two And Four TF-003 *Coleman; Jim Rotondi (t); Adam Brenner (as); Ned Otter (ts); Gary Smulyan (bs); Harold Mabern (p); Ray Drummond (b); George Coleman Jr (d); Daniel Sadownick (perc).* 3/96.

It's little short of outrageous – if not exactly astonishing – that Coleman's great octet charts had gone largely unrecorded, but George's tenor disciple Ned Otter produced this session in 1996 and finally managed to release it on Two And Four in 2000. If there are a couple of minor disappointments – fair enough for Otter to get two of his own charts into the gig, but it's Coleman's stuff we want to hear, and Stevie Wonder's wretched 'Isn't She Lovely' isn't in our list of favourite songs – the fat, swaggering sound of the band is a delight (and it's immaculately set down by Rudy Van Gelder). Bobby Watson's 'Conservation' is all hustling, buzzing horns and works a treat. 'Portrait Of Jennie' is a monumental recasting of the old Nat Cole ballad. Soloists throughout don't disappoint. Next to a David Murray Octet, this is tailored and finessed, but it's not much less exciting.

***** Four Generations Of Miles**
Chesky JF238 *Coleman; Mike Stern (g); Ron Carter (b); Jimmy Cobb (d).* 5/02.

Miles Davis tributes continue to emerge. This one is intriguing in that it showcases guys who worked with the trumpeter at different stages of his long, protean career. The band's quality is self-evident and this is a spontaneous cruise through some of the more obvious Miles repertoire; no 'Time After Time' or 'Human Nature', but lots of stuff from the '50s, like 'There Is No Greater Love', 'On Green Dolphin Street', and 'Freddie Freeloader' and 'All Blues', which Cobb has specially strong memories of creating. Mike Stern is there to add a little contemporary spin to the repertoire but he doesn't insist too much on it and is mostly happy to act as accompanist.

Coleman sounds in good voice, broad and expansive in his theme statements, but interestingly laconic in his solos. Perhaps he nurses a certain ambivalence about Miles. A thoroughly enjoyable record and a useful addition to Coleman's still rather truncated discography.

Ornette Coleman (born 1930)

ALTO SAXOPHONE, TENOR SAXOPHONE, TRUMPET, VIOLIN

Born in Fort Worth, Texas, Coleman began working in R&B bands, frequently attracting derision, before finding players for his own group, including Don Cherry and Charlie Haden. Worked with Paul Bley in Los Angeles and made his recording debut there. Sensational New York debut of his quartet in 1959, and a string of ground-breaking albums for Atlantic followed. In the '60s he learned trumpet and violin, made trio and small-group records for Blue Note, RCA and Columbia, performed orchestral music, and generally went his own way. Developed a theory of 'harmolodics' and played in electric groups in the '70s and '80s, recording only occasionally. In the '90s, signed a new association with Verve, but the records have again been infrequent. The principal godfather of free jazz, Coleman's music is an endlessly reshaped fantasy spun from his mild-mannered, enigmatic self.

***** Something Else!**
Original Jazz Classics OJCCD 163 *Coleman; Don Cherry (t); Walter Norris (p); Don Payne (b); Billy Higgins (d).* 2/58.

***** Tomorrow Is The Question**
Original Jazz Classics OJCCD 342 *Coleman; Don Cherry (t); Percy Heath, Red Mitchell (b); Shelly Manne (d).* 1, 2 & 3/59.

No jazz musician – possibly ever – has so comprehensively and irremediably divided opinion. To some (and the supporters included Gunther Schuller) he is a visionary genius who has changed the shape of modern music; to others he is a fraud, innocent or otherwise, whose grasp of musical theory is at best shaky and for the greater part unbearably pretentious. Long before anyone had heard of 'harmolodics' – and don't search below for a quotable definition – it was thought that Coleman represented the third spur of the modernist revolution, a shift in approach to melody and rhythm to match Coltrane's skyscraping harmonics and Cecil Taylor's introduction of atonality.

Though the 1958 Hillcrest Club residency with Paul Bley represents something of a crux in Coleman's development, it is still startling to hear him with a pianist, and it was to be thirty years before he was inclined to repeat the experiment. Coleman got the first of these sessions at Red Mitchell's behest, and it suffers all the drawbacks of haste; problems that were largely ironed out on the more thoughtful *Tomorrow Is The Question*, a set which includes 'Tears Inside', perhaps the most beautiful single item in the whole Coleman canon. *Tomorrow* is also notable for Shelly Manne's impeccably hip contribution; an unlikely recruitment on the face of it, even given his tenure at Contemporary, but absolutely bang up to the moment.

Forty years have dented the sheer alienating swipe of these discs, but they certainly confound the received view of Coleman as a raucous tent-show turn. The tone is as wayward and raw as could be, but with an intense loneliness at the heart.

****** The Shape Of Jazz To Come**
Atlantic 8122 72398-2 *Coleman; Don Cherry (pkt-t); Charlie Haden (b); Billy Higgins (d).* 10/59, 7/60.

★★★★ **Change Of The Century**
Atlantic 81227 3608-2 *As above.* 10/59.

★★★(★) **This Is Our Music**
Atlantic 7567 80767-2 *As above.* 7/60.

★★★(★) **Art Of The Improvisers**
Atlantic 90978 *As above, except add Jimmy Garrison, Scott LaFaro (b).* 59–60.

★★★★ **Free Jazz**
Atlantic 8122 72397-2 *Coleman; Don Cherry (pkt-t); Freddie Hubbard (t); Eric Dolphy (bcl); Charlie Haden, Scott LaFaro (b); Ed Blackwell, Billy Higgins (d).* 12/60.

★★★ **Ornette!**
Atlantic 81227 3692-2 *Coleman; Don Cherry (t); Scott LaFaro (b); Ed Blackwell (d).* 1/61.

★★★(★) **Ornette On Tenor**
Atlantic 781394 *Coleman; Don Cherry (pkt-t); Jimmy Garrison (b); Ed Blackwell (d).* 3/61.

★★★ **Art Of The Improvisers**
Atlantic 781572 *Coleman; Don Cherry (pkt-t); Jimmy Garrison, Charlie Haden, Scott LaFaro (b); Ed Blackwell, Billy Higgins (d).* 59–61.

★★★ **Twins**
Atlantic 81227 3684-2 *As above.* 5/59–1/61.

Difficult – perhaps impossible – to reconstruct the impact these records had when they first appeared or the frustration that some of the players understandably evinced in trying to get to grips with Coleman's ideas. Bassist Jimmy Garrison is said to have lost his temper on the stand one night, baffled by playing off-notes rather than chords, increasingly convinced that the whole thing was a scam.

These, though, are the classic Coleman albums, even if one retains a degree of scepticism. CD transfer has brought forward the other members of the group, underlining Cherry's role and bringing Haden out of the shadows. Brash as the titles are, the music is surprisingly introspective and thoughtful. The first two in the group were actually released out of chronological sequence, which was major sucks to all the critics who talked – and still do – about 'development' and 'progress'.

Most of the essential Coleman pieces are to be found here, though interestingly only one of them – 'Lonely Woman' – has ever come close to repertory status. Bubbling under are 'Una Muy Bonita' from *Change* (which is now available in a new edition), 'Congeniality' and 'Focus On Sanity' on *Shape*, and things like the alphabetical themes from *Ornette!* (now available separately, but also included in its entirety on the wonderful, indispensable *Beauty Is A Rare Thing*). *This Is Our Music* includes the single standard of this vintage, 'Embraceable You', which takes the theme as far beyond Charlie Parker as Bird was beyond the Gershwin original.

Of the major statements of jazz modernism, *Free Jazz* and Coltrane's *Ascension* are key documents, sharing some personnel. Jimmy Garrison's onstage tantrum had led to his departure from the Coleman group and a switch to Trane's quartet. The difference is exactly what the young bassist identified. No chords here, just gestural splashes of sound which make sense of the Jackson Pollock cover and the Abstract Expressionist aesthetic embodied by the Double Quartet. Oddly, the music was still locked into theme-and-solos conventions (as was *Ascension*, to be fair) and doesn't break free of personality. What redeems it is the sheer variety of sound-colours the group conjures up in its paired soloists: Dolphy's fruity, fraught bass clarinet, contrasted to Ornette's thin tone; Hubbard and Cherry sounding like non-zygotic twins; LaFaro's alchemical transformations sitting still while Haden lopes around like Wilbur Ware in jogging pants. Separating Higgins and Blackwell *is* possible, but largely redundant.

A 'First Take' of *Free Jazz* – shorter, less assured, but arguably more coherent – is the main item on the compilation *Twins*. It also includes 'The Monk And The Nun', an offcut from *The Shape Of Jazz To Come*, two pieces, 'Little Symphony' and 'Joy Of A Toy' from a July 1960 session and 'Check Up' from January 1961. The exact sessionography can be traced in John Litweiler's fine biography of the saxophonist. This was an intensely busy and personally difficult time in Coleman's life. He admitted to exhaustion and disillusionment, and seemed on the verge of giving up; Stuart Nicholson's liner-note quotes him as saying that he only continued because the other members of the quartet depended on him for their livelihood. In the event, Higgins fell foul of personal problems of his own and Haden left as well, which is why they are replaced by Blackwell and LaFaro on 'Check Up', a new sound for the group delivered by two equally talented but rather different players.

The 31 January 1961 date yielded *Ornette!*, which has been out of print for some time. The tune titles, enigmatic initials 'T & T', 'C & D', 'W.R.U', 'R.P.D.D.', were all taken from Sigmund Freud works – *Totem And Taboo, Civilization And Its Discontents*, and so on. This was presumably an attempt to ground himself in the psychoanalysis-obsessed Zeitgeist but of course it also lent weight to those who thought that Ornette's music and musical philosophy were for the couch rather the concert hall or club. LaFaro is not especially prominent on the initially rejected 'Check Up' but throughout the session he drives the group on, a more forceful and harmonically challenging player than Haden, though it has to be said that much of his harmonic challenge, including some strange double-stopped chords on 'R.P.D.D.', is ignored, or at least not taken up. The reissue includes another bonus track, 'Proof Readers', the significance of which title can safely be taken as (mis)read.

Like Bird's one session on tenor, *Ornette On Tenor* has attained a status out of all proportion to its actual merits. It hooks Ornette back into the raw R&B of his Texas roots, but it never sounds like anything other than himself in a lower register and somewhat diminished in pace.

CORE COLLECTION

♛ ★★★★ **Beauty Is A Rare Thing**
Rhino/Atlantic R2 71410 6CD *As above, except add Robert DiDomenica (f); Bill Evans (p); Eddie Costa (vib); Jim Hall (g); George Duvivier (b); Sticks Evans (d); The Contemporary String Quartet.* 5/59–3/61.

A magnificent compilation set which brings together 57 separate tracks, six of which have not been released before, most of them from the July 1960 session which fed into *This Is Our Music*, the most unemphatic of the Atlantics. *Beauty* (and the title comes from a track on the same disc) brings together extra material that has already appeared on compilations like *Twins*, *Art Of The Improvisers* and the Japan-only and ungrammatical *To Whom Who Keeps A Record.* Of the new material, 'Revolving Doors' from July 1960 and the long 'Proof Readers' from January 1961 with Scott LaFaro are perhaps the most interesting. A pity that no one thought to

include or to keep interview material with Ornette for this issue and, of course, we'll all never stop regretting the fire that destroyed so much of the material from this period.

*** Town Hall Concert 1962

Get Back 1006 *Coleman; David Izenzon (b); Charles Moffett (d); Selwart Clarke, Peter Goldstein (vn); Julian Barber (vla); Kermit Moore (clo).* 62.

Coming as it does in a fallow and problematic period in Coleman's career, this ESP live recording is a valuable reissue. The musical philosophy of this particular trio is already well-known from the classic Golden Circle recordings made in Denmark three years later, but here Coleman showcases two of the compositions that dominated his repertoire with Izenzon and Moffett. 'Sadness' is one of his most plangent and affecting themes, not quite the dirge of the later 'Broken Shadows', but very much in the same vein and deeply marked by the blues. 'Doughnuts' is more buoyant and catches Ornette in his most demonstrative form, punching out notes like a bar-walking R&B man. The final trio piece was the LP-proportioned 'The Ark', a seething, troublous piece that refuses to cohere, but which affords bassist and drummer some important feature opportunities.

At this period, Ornette was deeply disillusioned by the vagaries of the jazz world and was dabbling in formal composition. 'Dedication To Poets And Writers' is a terse and schematic string quartet. It has little in common with accepted classical procedures, but the passage work and articulation sound idiomatic, evidence of the composer's interest in stringed instruments. It might have made a more interesting piece had Ornette found a way to integrate his trio into the structure, but it points the way forward to what would be even more troubled projects in the future.

*** Chappaqua Suite

Columbia 480584 2CD *Coleman; Pharoah Sanders (ts); David Izenzon (b); Charles Moffett (d); other personnel unidentified; Joseph Tekula (cond).* 6/65.

This is emphatically not an official Coleman release. It was written and performed as a soundtrack score for a film by avant-garde director Conrad Rooks, who seemed to win over the hesitant Ornette with an unwontedly respectable cash deal. When the music was finished, though, Rooks declined to use it, on the flimsy ground that it was too strong and self-contained for the film (equivalent to telling a woman that she's too beautiful, intelligent and good to marry the likes of you), and then commissioned Ravi Shankar to perform an alternative soundtrack. Whether Rooks seriously meant all this, whether he feared his film would be overpowered, or whether, like many before and after him, he simply hadn't a clue what the hell was going on isn't clear, but with exquisite perversity Columbia, or at least the French and Japanese arms of a company that had been deeply sceptical of Ornette's work, rushed out the one record he didn't want heard.

It's an odd piece, strident boppish figures rising like *T. rex* out of swampy orchestral textures. Ornette's keening sound is as evocative as ever, but there's no context for it. Sanders is credited but pretty anonymous, and the sound is distant and spatially uncertain. The unusual circumstances of its creation, its slightly shadowy, almost bootleg, emergence, and some wonderful cover photography have conspired to give *Chappaqua Suite* a cachet out of all proportion to its real merits. It remains a curiosity, almost paradigmatic of Coleman's wayward progress.

CORE COLLECTION

**** At The Golden Circle, Stockholm: Volume 1

Blue Note 35518 *Coleman; David Izenzon (b); Charles Moffett (d).* 12/65.

**** At The Golden Circle, Stockholm: Volume 2

Blue Note 35519 *As above.* 12/65.

Blue Note's purchase on the modernist movement was uncomfortably peripheral: a single Coltrane release, a brief skirmish with Cecil Taylor's fierce atonality, and a tentative, but in the event patiently sustained, engagement with Ornette. These sessions from Sweden catch the trio at its peak: densely textured, dark-toned and fierce. Much has been made of Ornette's lack of reliance on pianos, but it's obvious from these sessions that Izenzon fulfils that function. The leader may not lean on chords and progressions, may even 'hear' the changes differently, but, as with Dewey Redman later, he needs an anchor.

Coleman plays superbly throughout. Guess-the-next-note pieces like 'European Echoes' work less well than 'Morning Song' and 'The Riddle', and the obligatory fiddle-and-trumpet feature, 'Snowflakes And Sunshine', is unusually bland. 'Faces And Places' is typical of the way Ornette built a theme out of seemingly unrelated melodic cells, a honeycomb of sound without undue sweetness and without conventional symmetry. The sound is good for a club recording, faithful to the bass and to Moffett's restless overdrive.

The release in 2002 of the new editions of the Gyllencirkelt date was the only really significant moment in an otherwise very quiet discography. The addition of five alternatives makes this a highly desirable purchase for Coleman fans. In reality, the versions are not so very different. Perhaps the alternatives (not strictly such, but taken from other sets during the residency) are a little flabbier; Ornette misfingers a couple of times and Izenzon has a couple of knocks on his fretboard which might easily have been ironed out. But these are historically significant performances and help round out our picture of one of the great modern innovators.

*** New York Is Now

Blue Note 84287 *Coleman; Dewey Redman (ts); Jimmy Garrison (b); Elvin Jones (d).* 4–5/68.

*** Love Call

Blue Note 84356 *As above.* 4–5/68.

Coltrane was dead a little under a year. As there was to be in American poetry on the death of Robert Frost, there was a palpable unease in jazz as to who was the titular head of the pack. Teaming Ornette with Trane's old rhythm section was something of a misalliance, not least given Jimmy Garrison's stated misgivings. Perhaps because they're on hand, Coleman relies on some unwonted vertical improvisation, building on chords that are never quite explicit. Redman, like Izenzon before him, does the foundation work. As he was to do on the magnificent live *Crisis*, he offers capacious pedal-points and comfortably contoured lower-register figures. Whatever else they do, these reduce the dynamism of Coleman's solos, turning them into long, spun-out noodles.

The two opening tracks ('The Garden Of Souls' on *NY Is Now* and 'Airborne' on *Love Call*) might have made a respectable single album. Much of the rest is makeweight. An alternative take of the already tedious R&B 'Broad Way Blues' constitutes an ambiguous 'bonus' and 'We Now Interrupt For A Commercial' (pointlessly stripped of a small morsel of satirical actuality for the CD version) is plain silly, though it may well have inspired Redman's later 'Funcitydues'.

A pity that Coleman's association with this label and its resources could not have developed further.

★★★(★) Friends And Neighbours: Live At Prince Street

RCA Victor 47795 *Coleman; Dewey Redman (ts); Charlie Haden (b); Ed Blackwell (d).* 2/70.

Recorded almost a year after the apocalyptic set at New York University's Loeb Center, a set which yielded the still-deleted *Crisis* album, this catches Ornette in his NY loft. The audience does community singing on the opening 'Friends And Neighbours' which finds Ornette sawing joyously on fiddle. An instrumental version of the same track follows, before he switches to alto for the beautiful, subtly crafted 'Long Time No See'. There is a single trumpet track, 'Let's Play', before the set ends with 'Forgotten Songs', which seems to be related to some of the *Skies Of America* themes, and the long 'Tomorrow', which includes the most substantial Ornette solo of the record.

Friends And Neighbours seems to have been an unofficial release, unauthorized at the time, even though Bob Thiele is listed as co-producer. It catches Ornette in particularly laid-back form, sounding relaxed even in the squalls of violin on the title-track and creating blues progressions of astonishing originality on the alto tracks. Whatever its standing, it's a more than worthwhile addition to the catalogue.

★★★ The Complete Science Fiction Sessions

Columbia/Legacy 63569 2CD *Coleman; Bobby Bradford, Gerard Schwarz (t); Don Cherry (pkt-t); Dewey Redman (ts); Cedar Walton (p); Jim Hall (g); Charlie Haden (b); Ed Blackwell (d); Billy Higgins (tymp); Webster Armstrong, David Henderson, Asha Puthli (v).* 9/71.

This issue more or less rounds out Coleman's often troubled association with Columbia. There seems little likelihood for the foreseeable future of sumptuous boxed sets of alternate takes and other materials. For the moment, at least, the picture is complete.

Science Fiction has never been one of the saxophonist's best-known or -liked dates. The large ensemble, a basic septet plus guest musicians, has a very different function to the *Free Jazz* Double Quartet and in some respects anticipates the orchestral experiments of *Skies Of America*. 'Science Fiction' itself is pure nonsense, as is the ludicrous 'Good Girl Blues' and the bitingly ironic 'Civilization' (discontents come as standard). The narration by David Henderson doesn't really add much that is illuminating and the real interest of these sessions is the emergence of themes like the dirge 'Broken Shadows' (heard in superb live performance on the long-deleted *Crisis!*) and 'Happy House'. 'Rock The Clock' anticipates the electric Prime Time period, though for the most part, this is a muddled and patchy set, likely to be of interest only to established Coleman fans who can hear past the sheer oddity of Jim Hall's role and who're able to identify anticipations of future innovations. Anyone who tells you that Ornette didn't work with a piano-player for 30 years should simply utter the words 'Cedar' and 'Walton'; Cedar probably still wonders what this was all about.

★★★(★) Skies Of America

Columbia/Legacy 63568 *Coleman; David Measham (cond); London Symphony Orchestra.* 5/72.

There is still no more controversial item in the whole Coleman discography. Legends abound about this recording. That it represents Ornette's first orchestral composition; not so, earlier works were performed but went unrecorded. That the musicians of the LSO were so disgusted by the score that they deliberately played wrong notes; unlikely, but a useful sideswipe at Ornette, by suggesting his music was unplayable, even by professionals. That Ornette did not authorize release of the edited version Columbia mastered; the composer was clearly unhappy, but he recognized that this was the only way his new music was going to be heard.

One reliable fact colours the whole story of *Skies Of America*. The original conception was for something like a Baroque *concerto grosso*, with the saxophonist's band playing a concertante part, while the orchestra played the *ripieno* or 'replenishing' passages. A Musicians' Union ban meant that the group could not be included. Ornette is there, though, and appears through the later stages of the recording – soaring, searing alto lines that transform the performance utterly.

Skies is conceived as a single, continuous piece, but most releases have identified individual themes and passages. Some of these are quite familiar. 'The Good Life', which comes four minutes in, is a reworking of the earlier 'School Work' and is unmistakably the germ of 'Dancing In Your Head', the definitive theme of Ornette's upcoming 'electric period'. There is a subversively scrambled version of 'The Star Spangled Banner' aka 'The New Anthem' and there are echoes of other Coleman tunes from every stage of his career.

The LSO may not have encountered music like this before and may not have understood the early adumbrations of harmolodics, but it does them no credit to say that they played badly or, worse still, deliberately fluffed. The ensembles sound rich and ambiguous and the instrumental texture is attractively varied. *Skies Of America* has been caricatured as the place where Ornette finally offered a pitched battle with the music industry. Thirty years on, it sounds like a gentler compromise than that, an honest attempt by all concerned to get a challenging piece of music off the page and into the air.

★★★★ Body Meta

Verve/Harmolodic 531916 *Coleman; Charles Ellerbee, Bern Nix (g); Jamaaladeen Tacuma (b); Ronald Shannon Jackson (d).* 12/75.

★★★ Dancing In Your Head

Verve 543519-2 *As above, except add Robert Palmer (cl); Master Musicians of Joujouka.* 1/73, 12/75.

It was a shock to the system in 1975, hearing Coleman with what initially sounded like a rock band and then continued to sound like a rock band, except that repeated exposure reveals how many layers and subtleties this music camouflages. Purists were appalled by the relentlessly thudding rhythm of the two long 'variations' on 'Theme From A Symphony' from *Dancing*; but even they can't pretend that the music doesn't have dimensions that by-the-yard orchestral writing lacks. The harmolodic method, which applied a radical democracy to every parameter of the music – rhythm, melody, harmony – was by no means new at this point. Theoretically, everything was already in place on the Town Hall gig; the means of expression were still old-fashioned, though.

Ornette's alto playing is fiercely linear but jumps up and down the levels like some pixilated hero in an arcade game. The 'rock' influence is largely superficial, since the rhythmic approach is the opposite to rock's relentless emphasis on strong beats. The Grateful Dead (with whose guitarist, Jerry Garcia, Ornette was to record towards the end of the '80s) were doing something like this in their long-form jams, but with a blissed-out insouciance which is the opposite of Ornette's drivenness and urgency. Rhythmically, almost everything is there: march cadences, rags, swing, stop-time, hints of reggae and long passages in the bass.

There is another track from 1973, with Coleman in the company of the Master Musicians of Joujouka, who had been 'discovered' by Brian Jones of the Rolling Stones. Herbally enhanced harmolodics, anyone? This was recorded in 1973. *Pace* the liner-note, the main session was taped in 1975, not 1976, and this is confirmed by John Litweiler's book, *The Harmolodic Life.* The session also included the material released as *Body Meta* on Ornette's own label, Artist's House. Its reappearance on Harmolodic (Ornette's imprint within the Polygram empire) is hugely welcome.

The five tracks include a reworking of 'European Echoes' (already heard on the Gyllenecirkelt records). Its performance here underlines once again the continuity of Coleman's enterprise at this time; what had seemed satirical first time around, this time is played rather straighter. The presence of guitars, and the fibrillating groove set up by the former Rudy McDaniel (Tacuma), is the only real difference, but it's largely a superficial one, and we still maintain that it was Izenzon who – consciously or not – pushed Ornette ever further in this direction.

Chronologically earlier in the sessionography, *Body Meta* is the better record, more concentrated and intense, less rambling. It was also the first time Ornette had been allowed decent rehearsal time before a recording. The ballad, 'Fou Amour', is magnificent, and 'Macho Woman' is wincingly powerful, with Shannon Jackson in some sort of overdrive. A key moment in Coleman's progress.

***** Sound Museum: Three Women**
Verve/Harmolodic 531657 *Coleman; Geri Allen (p); Charnett Moffett (b); Denardo Coleman (d); Lauren Kinhan, Chris Walker (v).* 96.

***** Sound Museum: Hidden Man**
Verve/Harmolodic 531914 *As above, except omit Kinhan and Walker.* 96.

A curious, indeed typically perverse undertaking: two albums of almost identical material, performed back to back by the same band. The only real difference in sequence is that *Three Women* includes a song performed by Kinhan and Walker, while *Hidden Man* has a variation on 'What A Friend We Have In Jesus' and a slightly altered running order. Ornette's insistence on an absolute democracy of listening and response is carried to extraordinary lengths here; it is often difficult to gauge how these performances actually vary, and to what extent the two albums are supposed to have a consistent identity. To take just the most familiar item, 'European Echoes' is no more than incidentally reworked, while 'Mob Job' and 'Macho Woman' are much of a muchness, tempo changes notwithstanding.

Allen's role is broadly similar to what the guitarists were doing on earlier records. Her M-Base background hasn't been so thoroughly sloughed that she isn't responsive to this kind of thing; that whole project drew much of its inspiration, consciously or otherwise, from Ornette, and she (more than most) responded to the historical antecedents. Denardo's skill as a producer becomes more evident with almost every release. The sound here is immaculate, with lots of space round the piano and drums.

****** Colors**
Verve/Harmolodic 537789 *Coleman; Joachim Kühn (p).* 8/96.

On the face of it an unlikely combination, but one which yielded Ornette's most evocative album of recent years. Interesting to compare it with another, almost contemporary Verve release, the *1 + 1* duo by Herbie Hancock and Wayne Shorter. It's pipe and slippers compared to this restless, searching set, recorded live in Germany, at the Leipzig Opera. The worst thing about it is a slightly cavernous sound. The performances are extraordinary.

Kühn has recorded in a duo context before, with CMP in-house genius Walter Quintus, and with guitarist (and former front man with Focus) Jan Akkerman. Both times he has demonstrated a responsive intelligence that thrives on harmonic ambiguity and on a suspension of conventional harmonic resolutions. All the pieces, quite short by live-performance standards, were written specially for the date. 'Refills', 'Story Writing' and 'Night Plans' are the most substantial pieces, though most of the detail comes from Kühn rather than Ornette. A wholly unexpected meeting of minds, and one of the happiest dates Ornette has put on record in years.

Steve Coleman (born 1956)

ALTO AND SOPRANO SAXOPHONES, VOCALS

Steve Coleman's approach to jazz is thoroughly mystical, believing that music is a symbolic language that probes deeper than rational ideas and expresses both the order and the chaos of the universe. Given that dual status, his arrangements are either whirlingly chaotic or disconcertingly four-square, an ambiguity that he exploits much as Sun Ra did. Coleman's saxophone lines are long and discursive, a long way removed from classic bebop.

***** Motherland Pulse**
Winter & Winter 919001 *Coleman; Graham Haynes (c); Geri Allen (p); Lonnie Plaxico (b); Marvin 'Smitty' Smith (d); Cassandra Wilson (v).* 3/85.

***** On The Edge Of Tomorrow**
Winter & Winter 919005 *As above; omit Plaxico; add Kelvyn Bell (g); Kevin Bruce Harris (b); Mark Johnson (d).* 1 & 2/86.

***** World Expansion**
Winter & Winter 919010 *As above; add Robin Eubanks (tb, v); Jimmy Cozier, D. K. Dyson (v).* 11/86.

Coleman's debut marked the first broad acceptance of what became known as the M-Base school of music. The immediate impression is of a looser and more harmonically conventional version of his namesake Ornette's earlier years. Steve's alto has a keening insistence that carries a lot of weight and information on these fine cuts. The songs are mostly short and well-structured, if a little too similar in conception. The exceptions are the middle pair 'Wights Waits For Weights' and 'No Good Time Fairies', on which Cassandra Wilson sings.

The follow-up record has also reappeared on Winter & Winter, who are in the process of reissuing the JMT catalogue. This time the funk seems a little more programmed, partly because the level of electricity is well up (Allen is on synth throughout and Bell plugs in for the set) but also because the sheer novelty of Coleman's approach wore off quite quickly and it wasn't until his later, denser records that he achieved a proper synthesis between streety immediacy and musical sophistication. '(In Order To Form A) More Perfect Union' boils with irony, and if you know where the quote comes from, you'll know why.

The third record seems to mark time, but the introduction of Eubanks brings in a vivid new solo voice who does something of what Haynes had delivered on the earlier disc, but more warmly.

*** Sonic Language Of Myth: Believing, Learning, Knowing

RCA Victor 64123 *Coleman; Ralph Alessi, Shane Endsley (t); Tim Albright (tb); Ravi Coltrane, Craig Handy (ts); Vijay Lyer, Robert Mitchell, Jason Moran (p); Stefon Harris (vib); Sara Parkins, Todd Reynolds, Mary Rowell (vn); Dave Gold (vla); Dorothy Lawson (clo); Reggie Washington, Anthony Tidd (b); Sean Rickman (d); Miguel Diaz (perc); Earl Charlston, Karen McVoy, Eugene Palmore, Jeanne Ricks, Rosangela Silvestre (v).* 5/99.

The twin poles of Coleman's musical language are evident here, with stately, almost swing-based arrangements giving way to some of the most hectic group improvisation since Coltrane's *Ascension.* The use of strings is imaginative and unexpected, featuring players who obviously understand the language of this difficult music. The leader's voice is ever more emphatic and discursive, but just occasionally Coleman drifts off line and into long footnotes and digressions. Generally, though, he treats this as a collective endeavour and leaves considerable room for band members to bear witness of their own. The set consists of five long compositions and two brief interludes. 'Precession' is highly involved and bewilderingly structured, but it stands as overture to the album as a whole and establishes a mood of dark wisdom; Handy is superb on it. One of the most intriguing passages is 'The Gate', with Ravi Coltrane and Albright joining the leader for a mysterious transition that is over almost before one quite understands what is going on. Coleman's pantonality and his ability to have several voices working simultaneously is evident on the final two sections – 'Ausar (Reincarnation)' and 'Heru (Redemption)' – which represent the climax and dénouement of the whole ritual. This is the kind of music Anthony Braxton has long striven to create. It may be that Coleman, coming from his direction, has created a body of work every bit as thoughtful and philosophically entire as the great man's.

*** The Ascension To Light

RCA 74321 74219-2 *Coleman; Ralph Alessi, Shane Endsley (t); Gary Thomas (ts); Gregoire Maret (hca); Vijay Iyer (p); David Gilmore (g); Min Xiao-Fen (pipa); Anthony Tidd (b); Sean Rickman (d); Cassandra Wilson, Sophia Wong (v); The Imami Winds.* 2–6/99.

Coleman's final RCA set restores his Five Elements set-up, plus a wind ensemble. The sense that the saxophonist is building his own vast archive of music and associated resources, for a jazz-derived individual culture that might bear comparison with Ellington or Sun Ra, is hard to evade, with the orchestral 'Reciprocity', the horns-only 'Instantaneous' and the music-with-text of '42 Assessors' each suggesting avenues of exploration which Coleman is determined to build on, and won't quit till he does. Big- or small-scale, it's all huge in ambition and design. As a record, it feels, as so often, overweighted and too dense to assimilate fully: one feels that these are just parts of something which so far is eluding the simple codification a CD offers.

***(*) Resistance Is Futile

Label Bleu LBLC 6643/4 2CD *Coleman; Jonathan Finlayson, Ambrose Campbell-Akinmusire (t); Geoffrey De Masure (tb); Andy Milne (ky); Anthony Tidd (b); Sean Rickman (d); Jesus Diaz (perc, v).* 7/01.

*** On The Rising Of The 64 Paths

Label Bleu 6653 *Coleman; Jonathan Finlayson (t); Malik Mezzadri (f, v); Anthony Tidd, Reggie Washington (b); Sean Rickman (d).* 3–4/02.

Coleman's progress is such that he can now review some of his own history, hence the presence on this live-in-Montpellier double-CD of old Five Elements favourites such as 'Wheel Of Nature' and 'Change The Guard', which go all the way back to 1986's *On The Edge Of Tomorrow.* He seems able to usher new spirits into his fold – scarcely a name in the personnel will be familiar, even to seasoned Five Elements fans – and have them execute his intentions with unblinking assurance. Every man-jack of them is quick, precise, and able to solo on cryptic materials without a stumble. On long pieces such as 'Wheel Of Nature' and '9 To 5', Coleman is overseeing ensemble performances that personify the sculpted astringency of his own saxophone playing.

Here and there he touches on 'the tradition'. Parker's 'Ah-Leu-Cha' is barely recognizable, and entirely unbopped. A ballad treatment of 'Easy Living' isn't so much cool as neutral, the saxophonist working it out almost mathematically. Yet Mal Waldron's 'Straight Ahead' emerges as an oddly poignant performance. When they tag 'Straight No Chaser' on to the end of 'Hits', it's like a bizarre echo of another time and place. This is rather warmer than many of Coleman's later albums. He orchestrates horns like nobody else and, while there isn't much humour in Steve's music, he's a passionate musician.

There's certainly not much humour on *Rising Of The 64 Paths,* but there is extraordinary beauty. The meaning of the title isn't absolutely clear, except that it refers to points of convergence and completion describing processes in nature.The opening track is angular M-Base jazz. The leader's alto line sounds like the kind of thing Braxton was doing in the early days and has an immediately dramatic presence, abetted by Rickman. 'Mist And Counterpoise' follows and takes the breath away. It's more of a unison line, a stately processional that disappears into the distance without ever really declaring itself; misty, certainly, but only ambiguously counterpoised. Where bassist Tidd had played electric on the opening track, here his opposite number Washington plays upright.

It gets slightly weirder from here on. Mezzadri opens 'Call For Transformation' with an eldritch wail but then switches to flute for a stop-time theme that falls between Kenton and Dolphy. Coleman hasn't been heard much of since the opening track but he's back in mournful form for 'The Movement In Self', a duet with the brilliant Rickman, and is very much at the helm for 'Dizzy Atmosphere', the Gillespie tune much transformed. The alternate of this track, lighter and more buoyant, doesn't make much sense beyond that shift in texture. Enigmatic and sometimes troubling, Steve Coleman continues to make challenging music.

Collective Identity

GROUP

Founded in New York City and inspired by the World Saxophone Quartet, the group aims for a melting pot of styles.

★★★(★) The Mass

Palmetto PM2062 *Sam Newsome (ss); Jorge Sylvester (as); Aaron Stewart (ts); Alex Harding (bs).* 99.

The aim was to create a flexible group sound that would sound greater than the sum of its parts. To a large extent, they have succeeded, largely because the members' wider cultural concerns are directed the same way. The opening number, Newsome's 'The World According To Shaquana Lee-Maria Goldstein' is intended as a portrait of someone so polycultural her name is impossible to pin down ethnically, 'the world's first Afrasian-Jewyorican'. It's a piece worthy of the WSQ, full of dense ensembles and spirited solo passages. 'Young Lions (In The Meat Market)' is a long meditation of the fate of creative musicians in an entertainment economy. It's perhaps over-long, but Stewart's basic structure is sound and solid. 'Remembranza' recalls Sylvester's Panamanian roots, an origin he interestingly shares with Eric Dolphy; it's a swinging, dance-like piece and with Harding's closing 'Spirit Take My Hand', a gospelly swinger, the closest thing to song form on the record. Harding's other composition is the title-tune, which presumably has less to do with Catholic liturgy than with the collectivist ethos of the group. The remaining track, and the only non-original, is an arrangement by Amadou Diallo of Wayne Shorter's classic 'Nefertiti', which has become something of a test piece for adventurous young players. They meet the challenge superbly. Nothing since 2000 from this fine quartet, which suggests the project may be in abeyance. A pity; this is a strong, thoughtful debut which merits repeated hearings.

Buddy Collette (born 1921)

REEDS AND WOODWINDS

Born in Los Angeles, Collette worked with Charles Mingus in 1946, but made his mark as a prominent member of the LA session fraternity in the '50s. With Chico Hamilton, 1955–6, but otherwise led his own bands and freelanced, later doing much teaching, and organizing big bands for the Monterey Festival.

★★(★) Man Of Many Parts

Original Jazz Classics OJC 239 *Collette; Gerald Wilson (t); Dave Wells (tb); Bill Green (as); Jewell Grant (bs); Gerald Wiggins, Ernie Freeman (p); Barney Kessel (g); Gene Wright, Red Callender, Joe Comfort (b); Max Alright, Bill Richmond, Larry Bunker (d).* 2–4/56.

★★★ Nice Day With Buddy Collette

Original Jazz Classics OJC 747 *Collette; Don Friedman, Dick Shreve, Calvin Jackson (p); John Goodman, Leroy Vinnegar (b); Bill Dolney, Shelly Manne (d).* 11/56–2/57.

★★(★) Jazz Loves Paris

Original Jazz Classics OJC 1764 *Collette; Frank Rosolino (tb); Howard Roberts (g); Red Mitchell (b); Red Callender (tba); Bill Douglass (d).* 1/58.

Buddy Collette had the misfortune to be a pioneer on an instrument whose jazz credentials remain in doubt: though he was a capable performer on alto, tenor and clarinet, he became renowned as a flautist and consequently got stuck in the role of novelty session-man in the West Coast scene of the mid-'50s. On his own dates, at least, he got to handle the rest of the instruments from his music room. *Man Of Many Parts*, originally issued on Contemporary, is gimcracked around his multi-instrumentalism and is mildly enjoyable without catching much fire. A shade better is the entertaining *Nice Day*: his prime instrument here is clarinet, his woodsy sound isn't so far from Jimmy Giuffre's, and it makes an interesting gambit on the minor blues, 'Minor Deviation' (on which the little-known Shreve plays an outstanding solo), and the queer arrangement of 'Moten Swing'. The record is let down a little by switching between three different rhythm sections, but it ends usefully on the tenor feature, 'Buddy Boo'. Excellent remastering. The players can't do very much with *Jazz Loves Paris*, a pretty thin concept, based round songs about, er, Paris. Callender's tuba introduces a novelty element and all the tracks are too short to let the players breathe, but there are still a few nice moments: Roberts on 'La Vie En Rose', the hopped-up reading of 'The Last Time I Saw Paris' and any of Rosolino's brief turns out front. Four alternative takes beef up the CD reissue.

★★★ Flute Talk

Soul Note 121165 *Collette; James Newton (f); Geri Allen (p); Jaribu Shahid (b); Giampiero Prina (d).* 7/88.

Collette's return to the studios, recorded on an Italian tour, is hurried but agreeable enough, and this could be the best group he's ever led on record. The meeting with Newton is more respectful than combative, and Allen is her usual unpredictable self, alert in places, asleep in others. The recording could be sharper.

★★★ Big Band In Concert

Bridge 9096 *Collette; Al Aarons, Ronald Barrows, Anne King, Nolan Shaheed (t); Leslie Benedict, George Bohannon, Garnett Brown, Maurice Spears, Brett Woodman (tb); Steven Carr, Jackie Kelson, Ann Patterson, John D. Stephens, Louis V. Taylor, Ernie Fields (reeds); Gerald Wiggins (p); Fred Katz (clo); Al Viola (g); Richard Simon (b); Leon Ndugu Chancler, Chico Hamilton (d).* 6/96.

A slightly belated release for this enjoyable big-band date, in which Collette doesn't play but directs and generally has fun. There are plenty of old friends from LA's glory days in the band, and Chico Hamilton arrives at the end to play drums on 'Buddy Boo'. Against the formidable standards of contemporary American big bands, this one's probably no more than so-so, but the music's feisty and entertaining.

Scott Colley (born 1963)

BASS

Born in Los Angeles, Colley came up through the local scene and worked with Carmen McRae among others. Based in New York since the beginning of the '90s.

★★★(★) This Place

Steeplechase SCCD 31443 *Colley; Chris Potter (ts, bcl); Bill Stewart (d).* 9/97.

★★(★) Subliminal ...

Criss Cross 1157 *As above, except add Bill Carrothers (p).* 12/97.

***** The Magic Line**
Arabesque 153 *As above, except omit Carrothers.* 8/00.

Colley's pedigree as a first-call bassist is unquestioned and it's no surprise that he should have made such a successful transition to leadership. His favoured format so far has been a pianoless trio, though the presence of Carrothers on *Subliminal* broadens the palette considerably. The Steeplechase record isn't Scott's debut. *Portable Universe* was released on Freelance the same year, but didn't leave much of a mark. The first available trio session has much to enjoy, nicely balanced between a few pleasing originals (especially 'Long Lake' and 'This Place') and jazz themes. Potter can sometimes seem a bit mechanical in a trio setting – 'Airegin' has none of Rollins's charisma in it – but he makes a gorgeous matter out of 'The Peacocks', and the Coltrane blues, 'Mr Day', is very good. Colley has a graceful feel to his playing, lithe without sounding too rubbery, and though he gives himself space he realizes that the listener's unlikely to want one bass feature after another.

The Criss Cross date isn't as good. Bill Stewart's 'Don't Ever Call Me Again' is the kind of tune that's more interesting to play than to listen to, and this time Colley's own originals fill up the record, and they're sometimes inscrutable in the modern manner. Carrothers is curiously reticent: he sits out some tracks and, even when there, plays diffidently. Things get back to normal on the third record, which is something of a breakthrough in creative terms. The trio sounds like a long-established unit and the writing – 'Trip To Williamsburg' and 'Dog Logic' in particular – is terse, energetic and strong. Stewart and Potter each chip in with a track, but these seem like token acknowledgements this time. Colley is very much in command and playing with Pettiford-like authority.

***** Initial Wisdom**
Palmetto PM 2080 *Colley; Ravi Coltrane (ts); Adam Rogers (g); Bill Stewart (d).* 02.

Apart from a short, freely improvised track, Camelio's 'Rubber Clock', Ornette's 'Alpha' and Evans's 'Barracudas', all the compositions are by Colley. With a somewhat different line-up, he's thrown back on to more conventional bass duties, though the vigorous comping of Adam Rogers, a fine and distinctive player whether soloing or sitting behind the front line, frees him up considerably. Coltrane Jr has never quite settled into a style. There are days when he sounds like his father, like Michael Brecker and even like Wayne Shorter. It's the last of these who impinges here, especially on 'Barracudas', though that may just be an association of ideas, since Shorter covered it on his *The Collector*. The free-form track apart, all the tracks are disciplined and to the point. Colley doesn't mess about but cuts to the funk whenever possible.

Max Collie (born 1931)

TROMBONE, VOCALS

Born in Melbourne, Collie arrived in London in 1962 and four years later formed his own Dixieland outfit. Character and determination saw the band build up a big audience, even when that music was completely out of public favour. He's still out there playing.

***** Live At The Strathallan**
Raymer Sound RSCD 754 *Collie; Phil Mason (c); Jack Gilbert (as, cl); Jim McIntosh (bj); Trefor Williams (b); Ron McKay (d, v).* 5/78.

This sort of music doesn't really sound right on a CD and, if there is such an entity as the 'CD generation', they probably don't buy it anyway. Collie works at the blue-collar, Transit van end of the Bilk–Ball–Barber spectrum, a rough-diamond revivalist with a big strong tone, notably tight and well-schooled bands and an entertainment potential that goes off the scale. His albums do little more than provide tasters of the live act: cheerfully unfashionable and utterly untroubled by any recent rethink of traditionalism in jazz. There are no fiery solos, no fancy arrangements. Songs are simply counted off and played. Full stop.

This is a perfect illustration of what the Collie band does best, captured live and formerly a cassette-only release. Phil Mason's cornet is bright and peppy, Collie plays with his usual warmth and humour and the set-list is as varied as ever, with an emphasis on blues and blues-toned tunes. 'Aunt Hagar Blues' and 'Milenberg Joys' are highpoints in the Collie discography.

***** Latest And Greatest**
Reality RCD 113 *Collie; Denny Ilett (c); Steve Mellor (cl); Lord Arsenal (p); Chris Marney (bj); Trefor Williams (b); Peter Cotterill (d); Pauline Pearce, Marilyn Middleton Pollock (v).* 9/93.

***** The Thrill Of Jazz**
Reality RCD 109 *As above.* 89.

***** New Orleans Mardi Gras: Volume 2**
Reality RCD 111 *As above.* 91.

***** Live In Stuttgart 1998**
Reality RCD 115 *Collie; Denny Ilett (c); Gabe Essian (cl); David Bashford (bj); Count John McCormick (b); Alan 'Slim' Poston (d).* 98.

***** Hot Jazz Celebration**
Reality RCD 116 *As above.* 2/01.

Interestingly, the rationale behind *Latest And Greatest* was to provide a representative CD sampling of Collie material for fans who had just bought a player. Simple enough formula: just turn up and play lots of the old stuff. The inclusion of Pearce and Middleton Pollock was doubtless intended as a plus but, unlike Ottilie Paterson's contribution to Chris Barber records, it doesn't work out quite like that. 'Dippermouth Blues', 'Fidgety Feet', 'When You And I Were Young, Maggie', 'Shimmee Sha Wabble', and so on, and so forth. Wholly undisturbing fun.

The earlier discs, listed out of chronological sequence for convenience of personnel listing, do more of the same and it's some kind of tribute to Max's persistence and quality control that 'more of the same' doesn't imply anything negative or condescending. The Stuttgart date is a reminder of how popular this kind of jazz is in Germany and particularly in former East Germany where it was seen as authentically proletarian and untroubled by bourgeois artiness, though not many of its fans would have subscribed to that dialectic; they just liked the sound of jazz along with a litre of beer. The band is one of the most stable in the business, not necessarily as individuals but certainly as a unit and they play up a storm before an enthusiastic audience.

Recorded by German radio, *Hot Jazz Celebration* marks Max's 70th birthday in grand style (the first seven tracks were recorded on the day itself), and illustrates just how inexhaustible even this supposedly dead-and-buried end of the jazz spectrum actually is. The old fellow sounds very sprightly indeed and his trombone tone is as full of rude health as ever.

New bugs Essian and Bashford do well, and it's good to find Count John McCormick is being gainfully employed.

Graham Collier (born 1937)

COMPOSER, DOUBLE BASS

Collier's '60s groups were consistently fascinating, but always hinted at even more ambitious musics waiting in the wings. In later years, and now a retired bass-player, Collier has had some opportunities to showcase those ideas. A gifted composer and educator, he has continued to make interesting and compelling music.

*****(*) Deep Dark Blue Centre**
Disconforme 1957 *Collier; Harry Beckett, Kenny Wheeler (t, flhn); Michael Gibbs (tb); Dave Aaron (ts, f); Karl Jenkins (bs, ob); Phil Lee (g); John Marshall (d).* 1/67.

***** Down Another Road**
Disconforme 1958 *Collier; Harry Beckett (t, flhn); Nick Evans (tb); Stan Sulzmann (ss, as); Karl Jenkins (ob, p); John Marshall (d).* 3/69.

***** Songs For My Father**
Disconforme 1959 *Collier; Harry Beckett (t, flhn); Derek Wadsworth (tb); Tony Roberts, Alan Skidmore, Brian Smith, Alan Wakeman, Bob Sydor (ts); Geoff Castle, John Taylor (p); Philip Lee (g); Chick Webb (d).* 1–2/70.

***** Mosaics**
Disconforme 1960 *As above, except omit Taylor; add Geoff Castle (p).* 12/70.

Collier's early records were of surpassing thoughtfulness – which is perhaps why they won fulsome critical plaudits and then disappeared. These welcome reissues restore an important chapter in the story of British jazz and underline Collier's subtle appropriation of compositional ideas as far afield as Charles Mingus (the most profound influence) and Miles Davis's collaborations with Gil Evans, which have an impact on the sound-world of these remarkable recordings. *Deep Dark Blue Centre* takes its name from a comment of Hoagy Carmichael's about the essence of jazz. Collier plumbs those places in every track of this, and especially on the understated 'Blue Walls', 'Hirayoshi Suite' and the long, closing title-track, which once took up most of an LP side but here sits logically at the end of a sequence of shorter pieces that nudge at the same basic ideas. Of the soloists, Wheeler and Beckett are the most significant, on alternate tracks, while the other horns take a less substantial role. Collier himself is featured sparingly, as was his modest wont, but he remains at the heart of every track, steering them into that mysterious place called jazz.

Songs For My Father is the most accessible. The seven 'songs' are identified only by time-signature or other marking – 7/4, ballad, 9/8, a waltz in 4/4, rubato, dirge and 4/4 figured – but they are much more expressive than that suggests. Collier has always had a gift for writing charts which are both demandingly complex and open-ended enough to give soloists space to express themselves. Harry Beckett is the main soloist on the album, though Skidmore and the rather more anonymous Wakeman each receive generous space. Tenorist Bob Sydor was a regular in Collier groups, but then he seemed to drift out of the limelight; a pity, since he has an engaging presence.

Down Another Road suggests that maybe there was to be a major change of direction. It doesn't emerge, beyond an ever more comfortable assimilation of advanced jazz harmonic ideas to the prevailing rock rhythm of the day. John Marshall's ability to blend those two seemingly inimical concepts can't be exaggerated. He's been a giant presence in modern British jazz, all too often rendered invisible. Jenkins plays a lot of piano on this disc, but is also effective on oboe. It's Beckett who commands in the solo space, though. 'Danish Blue' is the most engaging track on a set of slightly anonymous material.

Beckett has the true bluesman's gift of combining hard times and melancholy with absolute unfettered joy, and he touches both ends of the spectrum on *Songs For My Father*. His phrasing on 'Song Four', that 4/4 waltz, is immaculate and his ability to play expressively and at speed in unusual time-signatures is a mark of his talent. Two additional tracks were recorded live (glorious mono!) in Brighton in May 1970. (Incidentally, the Chick Webb credited here is *not* the Chick Webb of the swing era. Just in case you wondered.)

Mosaics was more ambitious but also much looser in structure, a sequence of themes, variations and instrumental cadenzas, somewhat Mingusian in cast, but marked by Eastern themes and modalities which played no part in Mingus's work. There was a lot of writing of this kind around in Britain at the time – Neil Ardley's now overlooked work is a good point of comparison – but no one explored it more fully and more intelligently than Collier. Again the soloing is less impressive than the overall conception of these pieces, but given the prominence given to solo excursions on *Mosaics*, it's a less coherent work.

*****(*) Darius**
Disconforme 1971 *Collier; Harry Beckett (t, flhn); Derek Wadsworth (tb); Geoff Castle (p); Ed Speight (g); John Webb (d).* 3/74.

***** Midnight Blue**
Disconforme 1972 *As above, except omit Castle; add Roger Dean (p).* 2/75.

The promised Collier reissue programme has now kicked in, offering a chance to hear his ambitious '70s work. These albums are unmistakably in a modern-jazz idiom, however boldly stretched out. *Darius* came out at a time when many bandleaders were experimenting with Miles Davis's abstract expressionist approach. Most, however, offered little other than paintball copies of *Jack Johnson* and *Live/Evil*. Where Collier differs is that every instrumental voice is clearly registered and is invested with expressive personality. Beckett and Wadsworth are two of the finest and most individual brass-players of the time, and both are magnificent on 'Darius' itself, one of two long tracks that made up the original LP. The sound transfer is very faithful, if a little soft-edged, but this suits the temper of the music very well.

The change of emphasis marked by *Midnight Blue* is subtle and gradual. The replacement of Castle by Dean adds a measure of abstraction to the accompaniments, and Collier himself seems to be looking for a long line on which to hang his increasingly advanced compositional ideas. The absence of saxophones was unusual at the time, but in keeping with the composer's characteristic sound-world.

*****(*) New Conditions**
Disconforme 1973 *Collier; Harry Beckett (t, flhn); Henry Lowther, Pete Duncan (t); Malcolm Griffiths (tb); Alan*

Wakeman (ss); Mike Page (as); Roger Dean (g); Ed Speight (g); John Webb (d); John Mitchell (perc). 6/76.

*****(*) Symphony Of Scorpions**

Disconforme 1974 *As above, except omit Wakeman; add Art Themen (ss, ts); Tony Roberts (ts).* 11/76.

***** The Day Of The Dead**

Disconforme 1975 2CD *As above, except omit Webb; add Roy Babbington (b); Ashley Brown, Alan Jackson (d).* 3/77, 4/78.

As he approached 40, Collier made enormous compositional advances. *New Conditions* is a quantum step beyond the relatively conventional blowing language of the earlier records. Though there is plenty of opportunity for conventional soloing, with Lowther and Wakeman particularly effective, the real logic of the piece is a steady journey through a virtual geography which includes some intriguing ethnic flourishes towards the titanic climax of what was conceived and written as a single, coherent work.

It may sound as though *Symphony Of Scorpions* is a more explicitly architectonic work, but the truth is that this record marked a partial – and wholly successful – step back towards a 'jazz' approach. It relies heavily on the thoughtful fire of Art Themen's Coltrane-tinged tenor and soprano. Art has seldom played better and fully merits his central position in an ambitious four-part structure. The advanced harmonic ideas of George Russell were much discussed at this time, and Collier seems to have been influenced by them, creating richly ambiguous backdrops for his solo players. The finale is curious, beginning with a powerful, rocking theme which then dissolves into uncertainty, only to be reprised, perhaps as an afterthought, in a beautiful Themen/Speight duet. A deeply satisfying work.

The third record from this period is inspired by the work of novelist Malcolm Lowry. One can see why the author of *Under The Volcano* might appeal to a composer of Collier's instincts: not for his hectic intoxication but for his multi-layered discourse and ability to dissolve figure and ground into one headlong stream of consciousness. Collier has by this point given up bass-playing in favour of synths and conducting. He adds important colours to the ensemble, stark primaries and acid tones which reflect the theme. The recitation of Lowry texts is more lulling than anything else and doesn't really add significantly to the impact of a work which already seems quite in tune with the novelist's aesthetic. More than a curiosity, but even with the inclusion of the previously unissued 'Triptych' certainly not an essential Collier record.

**** Something British Made In Hong Kong**

Disconforme 1976 *Collier; Geoff Warren (ss, as, f, af); Roger Dean (p, syn); Ed Speight (g); Paul Bridge (b); Ashley Brown (d).* 12/85.

We were unable to determine first time round whether or how much irony was at play here, and we are none the wiser now. This is an odd dip in Collier's thoughtful output, an album of near pastiche or misguided trendiness. The writing is one-dimensional and the production, revolving round synths and guitar, very messy and unappealing. Completists – and ironists – only.

***** Charles River Fragments**

Boathouse BHR 004 *Collier; Henry Lowther, Steve Waterman, Patrick White (t); Hugh Fraser (tb); Bill Mee (btb); Andy Grappy (tba); Art Themen (ts, ss, bsx); Mark Lockheart (ts, ss); Geoff Warren (as, af); Chris Biscoe (bs, acl); Pete Saberton (p); Ed Speight (g); Dudley Phillips (b); John Marshall (d).* 95.

Fifteen years ago Collier organized a jazz orchestra called Hoarded Dreams which was responsible for some of the most vividly creative music ever performed in the British Isles under the umbrella of 'jazz'.

The main piece on this CD was commissioned by the BBC for performance at the London Jazz Festival. Dedicated to Herb Pomeroy, with whom Collier had studied at Berklee College, and to Charles Mingus, it's a large, sprawling work for improvising ensemble which relies heavily on the gifts of the players. Fraser, Lowther, Themen and Lockheart are the most important front-line players. The ideas are, as ever, expansive, and the balance between big shapes and small details is maintained with great consistency.

The only other item on the set is the (relatively) short 'The Hackney Five', on which Waterman is prominently featured. It's a mere prelude, though, to the longer work. Some of Collier's earlier, small-group records are tabled for reissue, but at time of writing are still not available. When they do reappear, they may well prompt a serious reassessment of this important British artist, out of whom much of the most inventive latter-day British jazz, including that anarchic collective Loose Tubes, has emerged.

***** The Third Colour**

ASC CD 28 *Collier; Simon Finch, Steve Waterman (t); Ed Sarath (flhn); Mat Colman, Hugh Fraser (tb); Oren Marshall (tba); Steve Main, Karlheinz Miklin, Art Themen, Geoff Warren (sax); Roger Dean (ky); Ed Speight (g); Andy Cleyndert (b); John Marshall (d).* 11/97.

One of the marks of Collier's great strength as a composer is that he regards music as a medium in which performers express themselves, not one in which the composer attempts to make a mark. Hence 'Three Simple Pieces', hence 'Shapes, Colours, Energies', 'The Third Colour' and 'The Miró Tile', all performed at Collier's 60th birthday celebration. It was one of a sequence of special events in 1997. 'Three Simple Pieces' was written for a birthday concert at the Guildhall, where he taught, and is a generous invitation to solo elaboration. The band is somewhat lacking in punch, but Themen and John Marshall bring real power to the third of the sequence.

The drummer's tubist namesake is strongly featured on 'Energy Squared', part of 'Shapes …' and he shows up again on the opening 'Groove' of 'The Third Colour', testimony to Collier's interest in writing for low horns. The title-piece takes its inspiration from art theorist Clement Greenberg's suggestion that line is the 'third colour', a reflection of Collier's interest in the space between composition and improvisation.

***** Winter Oranges**

Jazzprint 126 *Collier; Danish Radio Jazz Orchestra.* 11/00.

***** Bread And Circuses**

Jazzprint 131 *Collier; 15-piece ensemble.* 9/01.

These are both ambitious projects, recorded with two very different orchestras. The Collective on *Bread And Circuses* is a group of Western Australians, presumably young, since the playing sounds precociously accurate and a tiny bit soulless; the Danish group is one of the most effective big bands on the scene, capable of a roar of noise and delicate *piano* within a few bars, and certainly capable of giving complex charts a rich emotional inflection. The structure of *Bread And Circuses* is typical Collier: an introduction followed by a series of 'patterns', ballads and blues, with clapping segments and solos that sound like instrumental cadenzas. His young players might well have taken our earlier advice and spent an hour or two in the listening booth with *Mosaics* or *Songs For My Father*. They certainly seem to know what's expected of them.

The other disc is more weighty and more classically structured. The set consists of the title-suite, commissioned by the band, and parts of 'Three Simple Songs' from *The Third Colour*. These are all impeccably done and delivered with a richness of vision that suggests many hours of rehearsal, but is probably the result of accurate sight-reading combined with Collier's generously insistent personality. This is the man who helped transform British jazz in the '80s by his sponsorship of what became Loose Tubes. He has been a dogged presence on the scene, even when in exile in Spain, and his music deserves to be heard more widely.

George Colligan (born 1970)

PIANO, ORGAN, SYNTHESIZER, TRUMPET, DRUMS

Born in Maryland, Colligan is one of the leading younger pianists in New York. He leads his own groups and has frequently worked as accompanist to Vanessa Rubin and with Gary Thomas.

***** Activism**
Steeplechase SCCD 31382 *Colligan; Dwayne Burno (b); Ralph Peterson (d).* 11/95.

*****(*) The Newcomer**
Steeplechase SCCD 31414 *Colligan; Ingrid Jensen (t, flhn); Mark Turner (ts); Dwayne Burno (b); Billy Drummond (d).* 4/97.

Colligan is exciting to hear, even if the records don't always impress as complete entities; give him time. The trio session has some head-turning playing from all hands. Colligan contributes only one original, the title-piece, and for the rest chooses tunes by Monk, Silver, Shorter, Pearson and others. Some of his playing is brilliant enough to find the results a bit oversmart, even cruel: his take on Waller's 'Jitterbug Waltz' seems almost sarcastic. There's a lot to enjoy here, but several tracks go on too long, as often happens on Steeplechase sessions; Burno, not a terribly interesting soloist, is given too much space; and Peterson, enjoyably overplaying as usual, might not be the ideal drummer for the situation. On a relatively restrained piece such as 'Estate' the pianist comes into his own.

The Newcomer suggests that Colligan feels comfortable in a band situation, and maybe this will always be his best context. It certainly puts improvisations like that on Shorter's 'The Big Push' into useful perspective: mercurial blocks, trills, bebop lines, locked-hands, Colligan can find a use for every device in jazz piano. He brought three interesting themes to the date and the band is excellent, with Jensen and Turner both surpassingly thoughtful in their improvisations.

*****(*) Stomping Ground**
Steeplechase SCCD 31441 *Colligan; Drew Gress (b); Billy Hart (d).* 9/97.

*****(*) Constant Source**
Steeplechase SCCD 31462 *Colligan; Jon Gordon (as, ss); Mark Turner (ts); Ed Howard (b); Howard Curtis (d).* 4/98.

*****(*) Small Room**
Steeplechase SCCD 31470 *Colligan (p solo).* 9/98.

The trio record is a clear advance on Colligan's first Steeplechase in this format. He had only rarely played with Gress and Hart and there was little preparation, so the results are formidably well-shaped and the playing on a very high level. Colligan restricts himself to a single original and his tune choices are a fan's notes on modern jazz: Billy Harper's 'Priestess', Kenny Wheeler's 'For Jan', Charles Tolliver's 'Right Now'. Here and there Colligan overcooks a tune: 'What Are You Doing The Rest Of Your Life' meanders into a remote and not terribly interesting place. Mostly, though, his vigour and salty aggression, tempered by an innately fine touch, bring these pieces vividly to life, abetted by top work from the other two men.

There is one standard, a fairly drastic revision of 'I'm Getting Sentimental Over You', but otherwise the quintet record, *Constant Source*, concentrates on Colligan's own material. 'Void' is a somewhat amazing bridge between emptiness and form. 'Pitchrider' has a remote connection with blues changes but goes somewhere quite different and was inspired by Gary Thomas's music. Considering that he leads from the piano, Colligan shows a surprising penchant for evading tone centres and encouraging his horn players to take a journey into clear space. He harmonizes them in sometimes discomforting ways, as in the title-track, which seems ready to spiral off into abstract Konitz–Marsh counterpoint before it falls into place. Lucky to have Gordon and Turner, who can extemporize their way out of whatever trouble he's plotted. Brimful of ideas.

The solo record is no premature indulgence. If anything, it's a rather sober effort after the previous two. Some of the material, such as Gary Thomas's 'Exile's Gate', is used to investigate what he can wring out of a specific formula, in that case the piling of structure on to an unchanging left hand. 'Elves' is Chick Corea impressionism without the whimsicality. 'When Your Lover Has Gone' is a ballad treatment in which the melody (of both verse and chorus) is ingeniously recast and it should be compared with 'Some Other Time', which banishes memories of the Bill Evans version. A tough and decidedly idiosyncratic effort.

***** Unresolved**
Fresh Sound FSNT 054 *Colligan; Jon Gordon (as); Mark Turner (ss, ts); Kurt Rosenwinkel (g); Drew Gress (b); Howard Curtis (d).* 98.

***** Desire**
Fresh Sound FSNT 071 *Colligan; Perico Sambeat (as, ss, f); Mario Rossy (b); Marc Miralta (d).* 2/99.

Unresolved is Colligan's most multifarious and ambitious record so far. Besides piano, he plays organ, synth, trumpet and even drums on one track. Turner is present throughout, Gordon and Rosenwinkel appear twice each. If anything, there's a sense that Colligan may be trying a shade too hard with this one. The electric keyboards cloud the picture more than they introduce useful colour, and the opportunity to use Gordon and Turner together consistently, as he did on *Constant Source*, is rejected. 'Evil Ambition' feels over-written; 'Unresolved' is as inconclusive as its title. But there are still enough ideas in the best of it to compel the attention: 'Modeidi's Modalities' is a menacing development out of 'Donna Lee', 'Nebulosity' gets a great performance out of Turner, and when he gives himself some open space Colligan injects some inspirational touches.

Desire focuses on a quartet once again. Colligan pleads for this to be heard as something other than a blowing session: having seen the chart for the opening 'Battle Cry', we doubt if the musicians would have entertained that thought for a moment. Fine as Sambeat is, he doesn't overturn memories of Gordon and Turner on the earlier records, and Rossy and Miralta are similarly not quite as powerful as some of their predecessors. As considerable as Colligan's composing and playing is, it can at times seem a shade cryptic unless it has interpreters who can really open it up, and to that extent we prefer the Steeplechase records. But even here there are memorable things: the pianist's compact, ingenious solo on the title-track, the askew balladry of 'Last November'.

****** Agent 99**

Steeplechase SCCD 31498 *Colligan; Doug Weiss (b); Darren Beckett (d).* 11/99.

***** Como La Vida Puede Ser**

Fresh Sound FSNT 102 *Colligan; Perico Sambeat (ss, as, ts); Antonio Serrano (hca); Tom Guarna (g); Mario Rossy (b); Marc Miralta (d); Guillermo Magil (perc).* 5/00.

*****(*) Twins**

Steeplechase SCCD 31485 *Colligan; Jesper Bodilsen (b).* 2/00.

*****(*) A Wish**

Steeplechase SCCD 31507 *As above.* 3/01.

Agent 99 is a tremendous trio record, first choice among Colligan sets to date: the opening 'You Do Something To Me' is an eventful reharmonization which entirely transforms an unremarkable song, and from then on the trio come up with something fresh and detailed on every tune. The title-piece proves their hard-bop chops, a Blue Note copy that's performed with great panache, and 'Poor Butterfly' is classic ballad playing. A vivid use of an overworked idiom.

The Fresh Sound album revisits the territory of *Desire* and, while interesting enough, and building on Colligan's Latin inclinations, it's not our favourite demonstration of his powers. Oddly enough, his interest in rhythm gets a more provocative and productive exposure on the fine duo records, where he addresses samba pulses, the varied time of 'Up Jumped Spring' – and even comes up with an original called 'Scandinavian Rhythm'. Both sets feel a little off-the-cuff (as is often the Steeplechase way, perhaps) but the playing has so many ideas as it goes forward that its uncluttered feel and ripe invention are a typical Colligan tonic. As a sample, go to the steadily evolving transformation of Jerome Kern's 'Nobody Else But Me' on *Twins*, which has you hanging on till the very last note. Great stuff!

Alice Coltrane (born 1937)

PIANO, HARP

Also known as Turiya and Sagittananda, Alice McLeod grew up in Detroit, studied classical music and took piano lessons with Bud Powell. Her highly distinctive style is based on long, rippling arpeggios, very much in keeping with husband John's advanced harmonics, though debate still continues sporadically as to how much she contributed to his thinking in later years. Prayerful and intense, Alice Coltrane's albums are not for the cynically disposed.

***** A Monastic Trio**

Impulse! 051267-2 *Coltrane; Pharoah Sanders (ts); Jimmy Garrison (b); Rashied Ali, Ben Riley (d).* 67–68.

***** Ptah, The El Daoud**

Impulse! 051201-2 *Coltrane; Joe Henderson, Pharoah Sanders (ts, af); Ron Carter (b); Ben Riley (d).* 1/70.

****(*) Journey In Satchidananda**

Impulse! 051228-2 *Coltrane; Pharoah Sanders (ss, perc); Vishnu Wood (oud); Charlie Haden, Cecil McBee (b); Tulsi (tamboura); Rashied Ali (d); Majid Shabazz (perc).* 11/70.

***** Astral Meditations**

Impulse! 051242-2 *Coltrane; Frank Lowe, Pharoah Sanders, Joe Henderson, John Coltrane (ts); Reggie Workman, Cecil McBee, Ron Carter (b); Ben Riley, Elvin Jones, Jack DeJohnette (d); Elaine Jones (timp); strings.* 66–71.

***** Alice Coltrane: Priceless Jazz**

GRP/Universal GRT 1345 *As for discs above, except add Jimmy Garrison (b), Clifford Jarvis (d), Tuksi (perc); strings inc. John Blair, Leroy Jenkins (vn).* 68–72.

Alice McLeod was introduced to John Coltrane by, of all people, Terry Gibbs, with whom she had recorded *Jewish Melodies In Jazztime*. She became a member of the Coltrane group, attracting a sour later analogy with Yoko Ono. Increasingly after Trane's death in 1967, his widow was drawn into quite another religious tradition – or, rather, an eclectic synthesis of Egyptian, Indian and Oriental systems. Her first solo record is a pretty straightforward tribute to her late husband, and very much bound up with the music they were making together over the last couple of years. It also establishes Pharoah Sanders as her most responsive and sympathetic playing companion, at this stage a shriller and more acerbic performer than Coltrane but occasionally capable, as on 'Ohnedaruth' and 'The Sun', of reaching the heights Trane aspired to. The American edition of the CD has two extra tracks, but it isn't for our money as good a mastering. Opt for the slightly shorter Japanese version if you get the chance.

Ptah is the highest avatar of God in Egyptian religion, and the title-piece is a rippling essay in transcendence, the paired horns coming from quite different directions (though one questions whether Mrs Coltrane's suggestion that Henderson is 'intellectual' and Sanders 'abstract, more transcendental' quite hits the mark). Their doubling on alto flute on 'Blue Nile' is magnificent, a perfect complement to piano and harp. By the time this record was made, Alice Coltrane had already recorded for Impulse! without horns. 'Turiya & Ramakrishna' retreads that sound, a simple three-note cell expanded into a huge meditation that is the triple-distilled spirit of lightness. Carter is a hugely important component at this stage, though one does wonder whether Ben Riley was the right drummer for the gig.

Unfortunately, the second of Alice Coltrane's 1970 recordings (also made at the home studio at Dix Hills, New York) is a rather lumpy affair, the spirit of sinking. 'Something About John Coltrane' is a drab workshop version of a D minor idea that had recurred throughout Trane's later work. 'Isis And Osiris', which follows and ends the album, is a good illustration of Mrs Coltrane's growing interest in non-European scales (represented by the North African oud), just as elsewhere the tamboura evokes drones that have – or had then – no accepted part in Western music. Sanders limits himself to soprano – not his natural horn and a not entirely comfortable sound. McBee, Haden and Ali are more obviously attuned to this music, but somehow the chemistry obstinately fails to work. It might be thought that preferring the more conventional of these two sets is itself a failure to understand and accept Alice Coltrane's more radical experiments. The ideas are clearly more sophisticated on *Journey*; the execution falls some way short.

Astral Meditations finds Alice in the company of another Trane disciple, Frank Lowe, a strong and in some ways more challenging voice than Pharoah Sanders. Lowe is interested in things which Alice tends to pass over, melody most obviously, and the encounter is a fruitful one. Touring again towards the end of the '90s, Alice Coltrane sounded strong and individual and still capable of surprise.

The Priceless compilation includes material from two other Impulse! records which have not been reissued: *Hunting Ashram Monastery* and *Universal Consciousness.* The latter is pretty way out but includes some strong jazz-based material, and the string arrangements are by Ornette Coleman, of all people.

***** Eternity**

Sepia Tone 5 *Coltrane; Oscar Brashear, Paul Hubinon (t); George Bohannon, Charles Loper (tb); Jerome Richardson (as, f); Terry Harrington (ts, cl); Louise di Tullio (picc); Hubert Laws (f); Charlie Haden (b); Ben Riley (d); Armando Peraza (perc); woodwinds, strings, vocals.* 8–10/75.

This is a very good introduction to Alice Coltrane's ambitious – or rather, self-denyingly universal – musical vision. She closes the set with a remarkably faithful rendition of a passage from Stravinsky's *Rite Of Spring,* and throughout pitches herself somewhere between neo-classicism and the most extravagant romanticism. The opening 'Spiritual Eternal' is a fine representation of her organ-playing, much of it jaggedly dissonant, which suddenly breaks through into a massive orchestral passage which sweeps the soloist up into something much larger and more embracing. Nothing else on the album quite comes up to the quality of its opening and closing, though 'Om Supreme' and 'Morning Worship' are both very moving and 'Los Caballos' touches on an unsuspected Afro-Cuban side to her aesthetic. Given her surname and background in religious practice, it is difficult to locate Alice Coltrane in jazz history. Sets like this confirm her authority and importance. This and two of the albums that follow were originally on Warners, but have been reissued on Sepia Tone.

**** Radha-Krisna Nama Sankirtana**

Warner Bros 9362 48182-2 *Coltrane; with percussion, voices.* 8/76.

**** Transcendence**

Sepia Tone 6 *Coltrane; Satori String Quartet; percussion, voices.* 5/77.

***** Transfiguration**

Sepia Tone 1 *Coltrane; Reggie Workman (b); Roy Haynes (d); strings.* 4/78.

The difficult call here is whether Alice has abandoned jazz altogether in favour of some new 'Eastern' idiom that is primarily devotional. The first two albums really don't belong in a 'jazz' guide except in so far as they seem to draw some of their language from gospel and blues. Largely thanks to Haynes and Workman, both of whom of course worked with her late husband, *Transfiguration* has some fine playing, but Alice's free-form chording and extended vamps make for rather dry and effortful listening. The set was recorded live at Schoenberg Hall, UCLA. We wouldn't dream of knocking these records or the profound sensibility behind them, but we admit to being unequal to any confident assessment of their worth.

John Coltrane (1926–67)

TENOR, SOPRANO AND ALTO SAXOPHONES, FLUTE

Arguably the most influential musician in modern jazz, both technically and spiritually, Coltrane had a relatively conventional and unspectacular apprenticeship in R&B, working with the likes of King Kolax, Earl Bostic and Eddie 'Cleanhead' Vinson. By 1949, though, he had become involved in bebop and recorded for the first time with Dizzy Gillespie, before signalling a shift towards a more open-ended experimentalism in Miles Davis's remarkable quintet which introduced modalism to his work. A brief period with Thelonious Monk in 1957 effectively signalled the start of Coltrane's career as leader; over the next ten years his quartet – particularly with McCoy Tyner, Jimmy Garrison, Elvin Jones and later Rashied Ali – brought about a seismic shift in jazz harmony. The group's ever longer improvisations seemed bent on packing in every conceivable variation and inversion of an often conventional pop theme, and it made use of ever greater tonal distortion and timbral effects. In 1960, inspired by Sidney Bechet and Steve Lacy, Coltrane added soprano saxophone to his repertoire. Problems with narcotics and then alcohol addiction were left behind when Coltrane began to espouse an intense, somewhat personalized version of Judaeo-Christianity, with a few elements of African animism and Eastern mysticism thrown in. It sustained him through the latter phase of his foreshortened career. Coltrane died of liver cancer at the age of 40.

***** John Coltrane And The Jazz Giants**

Prestige 60014 *Coltrane; Donald Byrd, Miles Davis, Wilbur Harden (t); Tadd Dameron, Red Garland, Thelonious Monk (p); Paul Chambers, George Joyner, Earl May, Jamil Nasser, John Simmons, Wilbur Ware (b); Jimmy Cobb, Louis Hayes, Philly Joe Jones, Art Taylor, Shadow Wilson (d).* 56–58.

****(*) Dakar**

Original Jazz Classics OJCCD 393 *Coltrane; Pepper Adams, Cecil Payne (bs); Mal Waldron (p); Doug Watkins (b); Art Taylor (d).* 4/57.

***** Coltrane**

Original Jazz Classics OJCCD 020 *Coltrane; Johnny Splawn (t); Sahib Shihab (bs); Mal Waldron (p); Paul Chambers (b); Albert 'Tootie' Heath (d).* 5/57.

If this was, as is often claimed, the most influential player in modern jazz, then his turbulent achievement was all the more remarkable in being packed into a single decade of music-making. Almost exactly ten years separate the first records as leader and the dark, sometimes anguished curtain-call of *Expression,* made weeks before Trane's death in 1967.

If Coltrane's career had ended with the closure of his Prestige contract, how would we understand and rate him now? As a major innovator? Probably not, though there are signs from the beginning that he was pushing for something beyond the existing conventions of hard bop. As a distinctive saxophone stylist? Yes, to a degree. The biting tone had been burnished in numerous big bands, and more than a year in Miles Davis's group (the apotheosis of which was to come in March and April 1959 with *Kind Of Blue*) had promoted a restless, tumbling solo style. In fairness, though, it is hard to hear any of these early albums as anything other than way-stations to greatness. The Jazz Giants sessions are a worthwhile sampling of what Trane was doing with various leaders around the time of his first recordings as leader. It's a shambolic compilation in some ways with some questionable choices of material, but it provides a context for what was to follow.

Dakar was supervised by vibraharpist Teddy Charles, who included three of his own tunes in the session and presumably negotiated the unusual tenor-and-two-baritones front line. Transfer to CD helped the sound enormously, ungluing some of the ensembles and putting a little needed space between Coltrane and the other two reeds. Adams's relatively straightforward 'Mary's Blues' and Mal Waldron's 'Velvet Scene' are probably the best tracks, as simple and direct as the minor feel allows. Charles's own 'Dakar' and 'Cat Walk' are too fanciful and sound under-rehearsed. *Coltrane* redeems the bottom-heaviness of the earlier session by building in Johnny Splawn, who always sounds as if he's just rushed in with a telegram. Chambers is on excellent form, dancing lightly through the changes. Trane himself sounds a good deal more assured than even a month before.

★★ Tenor Conclave

Original Jazz Classics OJCCD 127 *Coltrane; Al Cohn, Hank Mobley, Paul Quinichette, Zoot Sims (ts); Red Garland (p); Paul Chambers (b); Art Taylor (d). 9/56.*

★★★ Cattin' With Coltrane And Quinichette

Original Jazz Classics OJCCD 460 *Coltrane; Paul Quinichette (ts); Mal Waldron (p); Julian Euell (b); Ed Thigpen (d). 5/57.*

★★(★) Wheelin' And Dealin'

Original Jazz Classics OJCCD 672 *Coltrane; Paul Quinichette, Frank Wess (ts); Mal Waldron (p); Doug Watkins (b); Art Taylor (d). 57.*

This was a time when American recording executives tended to regard the tenor saxophone in much the same way as the post-Korea military regarded atomic bombs and missiles. One awesomely powerful weapon of destruction and control: good. Lots of ditto: very good. Listening to these records, though, is a little closer to how Beethoven must have felt during the French bombardment of Vienna, intimidated, a little deafened, and desperate for a waltz to break up the lockstep of 4/4s. The difference is that the French cannon were state-of-the-art and these tenorists simply sound old-fashioned. Inevitably, Coltrane stands out. No one else, then or since, has ever sounded like that, and a combination of law-of-averages and the competitive ethos that was part of such multi-horn sessions guarantees some excellent moments. The pairing with Quinichette is the most relaxed. *Cattin'* is an underrated album with a light, almost joyous feel, two guys of markedly different temperament discovering a companionable middle ground.

★★★ Lush Life

Original Jazz Classics OJCCD 131 *Coltrane; Donald Byrd (t); Red Garland (p); Earl May (b); Louis Hayes, Albert 'Tootie' Heath, Art Taylor (d). 5/57–1/58.*

An album of oddments, really, garnered from three distinct sessions over a six-month period. This was the time when Sonny Rollins was experimenting at the Village Vanguard with a pianoless trio. Coltrane's more tentative step in the same direction – which was to be repeated only sporadically in years to come – was actually enforced when Garland failed to show for the date. May is too anonymous a player to go the extra yard required for this exacting discipline. There are unexpected inconsistencies of register and articulation in Coltrane's own performances, perhaps suggesting reed, mouthpiece or (even at this stage) dental problems. The title-piece has the rugged grandeur of many of Trane's ballad meditations, but the often remarked resemblance to Stan Getz is already fading fast.

★★★(★) Traneing In

Original Jazz Classics OJCCD 189 *Coltrane; Red Garland (p); Paul Chambers (b); Art Taylor (d). 8/57.*

This is more like it – Coltrane and rhythm. This is the first group that sounds as if it might contain the germ of the later classic quartets. And not just any old off-the-peg rhythm section either, but Miles Davis's current line-up. The title-piece is one of the first of the saxophonist's open-form blowing themes, a progression of chords which doesn't so much propel the scant melody as catapult it across the changes. Trane's solo is fiery and committed to the hilt, the sound of a virile pretender not yet rising to the majesty of later years. He also shows a remarkably delicate touch with a ballad; 'You Leave Me Breathless' is also a key moment, and a valuable reference point when one compares it with *Soultrane*, recorded with the same group six months later.

★★★(★) The Ultimate Blue Train

Blue Note 53428 *Coltrane; Lee Morgan (t); Curtis Fuller (tb); Kenny Drew (p); Paul Chambers (b); Philly Joe Jones (d). 9/57.*

★★★★ Blue Train

Blue Note 95326 *As above. 9/57.*

A perfect example of the Blue Note effect, an over-valued record which bathes in the cachet of what turned out to be a fleeting association with the most glamorous label of its time. Michael Cuscuna has explained that, during the winter of 1956–7, it seems Coltrane visited the Blue Note offices because he wanted to get hold of some Sidney Bechet records, though apparently not yet to study soprano saxophone technique. Alfred Lion was present and mooted the possibility of the saxophonist recording for the label. It was Lion's partner, Francis Wolff, who handled contracts, and, though some money seems to have changed hands, Wolff was not in the office on the day concerned and the agreement to record for Blue Note was settled on a handshake. It was almost a year later that Coltrane remembered the commitment and the good-faith payment and insisted on honouring it. That there was to be no follow-up is a shame, one of the most intriguing might-have-beens and what-ifs of recent musical history.

That aside, the unavoidable conclusion is that *Blue Train* is not an unalloyed masterpiece. It certainly wasn't recorded on the fly. Part of the Blue Note ethos was paid rehearsal, and there seems to have been ample studio time. The band fulfil their responsibilities perfectly well, but this was far from an ideal line-up for Coltrane. The rhythm section had already recorded together for Blue Note under Chambers's leadership, and Chambers and Jones were already familiar to Coltrane from Miles's band. Though Drew sounds out of sympathy with the charts, the real question marks are against the names of

Morgan and Fuller, both gifted players, but both locked on stylistic trolley-lines. Morgan seems content with a subsidiary role, but Fuller blusters and registers a positive presence only on 'Locomotion'. The opening is still where it all happens; the title-tune is a starkly powerful blues which propels Coltrane into his first unquestionably major recorded solo. Once heard, it's a sound that is not easily forgotten, at once plaintive and urgent, hard-edged but also vulnerable. The rest of the album falls away. 'Moment's Notice' was to become a staple in years to come; here, it is repertory hard bop. 'Lazy Bird' is based on a Tadd Dameron theme and is quite effective; 'I'm Old Fashioned' is a slightly formulaic ballad which would have been more appropriate as a quartet item, just tenor and rhythm.

Coltrane is said to have spoken of *Blue Train* as his own favourite among his records. Needless to say, Blue Note has a stake in reinforcing the point. Many wondered whether anything further was taped and preserved at the session of 15 September 1957. Forty years later – and also to mark the 30th anniversary of Coltrane's death – Capitol released an 'enhanced' CD-ROM of the session, including two alternative takes, an extra 17 minutes of music in all, as well as documentary footage and interviews. Interestingly, controversy broke out within the ranks. Rudy Van Gelder, who had engineered the session, referred to release of some of the material as a 'desecration', objecting to the issue of an earlier, unsatisfactory take of 'Blue Train'. What Blue Note had originally done was to issue take number nine of that famous opening track, but to issue it with the better piano solo from take eight spliced in. On *The Ultimate Blue Train* take eight can be heard for the first time entire, and with the same piano solo restored to its original position. The rights and wrongs of this would occupy much of this section; most listeners who know 'Blue Train' well will be fascinated and probably reassured to know that, whatever chemistry takes place between takes, the definitive version is the one they already know (Coltrane was to have problems along these same lines later in his career, with 'Ascension'). Neither the alternative of 'Lazy Bird' nor, indeed, the CD-ROM material on the final track adds very much, though the outer packaging of *The Ultimate* features a much better crop of Francis Wolff's famous cover portrait of Trane. Perhaps only diehard purists will insist on sticking to the original version.

***** The Believer**

Original Jazz Classics OJCCD 876 *Coltrane; Donald Byrd, Freddie Hubbard (t); Ray Draper (tba); Gil Coggins, Red Garland (p); Spanky DeBrest, Paul Chambers (b); Louis Hayes, Larry Ritchie, Art Taylor (d).* 12/57–12/58.

A fascinating compilation for early sight and sound of young talent. McCoy Tyner is composer of the title-piece, two years before he joined Coltrane's group. Hubbard, who solos to startling effect on 'Do I Love You Because You're Beautiful?', is already a monster. Two tracks are under the joint leadership of tuba-player Draper, a figure always destined to be marginal but capable of some fine and emotive playing on a cumbersome horn.

*****(*) Soultrane**

Original Jazz Classics OJCCD 021 *Coltrane; Red Garland (p); Paul Chambers (b); Art Taylor (d).* 2/58.

***** Settin' The Pace**

Original Jazz Classics OJCCD 078 *As above.* 3/58.

What a difference it must have been turning back to Prestige, where there was scant rehearsal time and a consequent need to stick with familiar material. One senses that this is the point in Coltrane's career when he should be opening up and exploring his own ideas. Of course, in a sense he was. Even now, some enthusiastic supporters mislocate the much-cited 'sheets of sound' period, assuming that the phrase refers to the teeming wails and seemingly endless solos of later years. In fact, it relates to the work Trane was doing through the extended public woodshed that was 1958. *Soultrane*, to be fair, is an excellent record. One can quickly hear how much further the saxophonist was able to push the harmonic language than he had been doing with the same group in August 1957. 'I Want To Talk About You' was to become another of Coltrane's favourite standards, and this is a hugely thoughtful and technically adroit reading, ranging without strain across two-and-a-half octaves. *Settin' The Pace* is much less venturesome and might easily be mistaken for a second-string selection from the same date, except that it was recorded a month later. The outstanding track is the Jackie McLean composition, 'Little Melonae', which the rhythm section seems to know inside out.

***** The Last Trane**

Original Jazz Classics OJCCD 394 *Coltrane; Donald Byrd (t); Red Garland (p); Paul Chambers, Earl May (b); Louis Hayes, Art Taylor (d).* 8/57, 3/58.

'Last' not quite in the barrel-scraping sense, for the out-takes from the Garland, Chambers and Taylor date are actually very good indeed, and for anyone who finds this period of Coltrane's career more appealing than later work 'Come Rain Or Come Shine' is likely to be a welcome addition to the collection.

**** Black Pearls**

Original Jazz Classics OJCCD 352. *As above, except add Donald Byrd (t).* 5/58.

For our money, one of the drabbest sessions in the whole Coltrane canon. Even Homer nods, but the problem here is that no one seems prepared to nod out, opting to grind away pretty remorselessly. Byrd can be an engaging player, but this certainly wasn't his natural gig.

***** Plays The Blues**

Prestige 11005 *Coltrane; Donald Byrd (t); Gene Ammons, Paul Quinichette (ts); Pepper Adams (bs); Jerome Richardson (f); Tommy Flanagan, Red Garland, Mal Waldron (p); Kenny Burrell (g); Paul Chambers, George Joyner, Earl May, Jamil Nasser (b); Jimmy Cobb, Art Taylor (d).* 57–58.

Further salami-slicing from Prestige and issued as part of a roots series in which major artists concentrate on the blues. No more surprising than announcing 'Lawrence Welk Plays Polkas', and much better sampled on the original releases.

***** Trane's Blues**

Blue Note 98240 *Coltrane; Donald Byrd, Kenny Dorham, Lee Morgan (t); Curtis Fuller (tb); Hank Mobley (ts); Sonny Clark, Kenny Drew, Wynton Kelly, Horace Silver, Cecil Taylor, McCoy Tyner (p); Kenny Burrell (g); Paul Chambers, Steve Davis (b); Art Blakey, Louis Hayes, Elvin Jones, Philly Joe Jones (d).* 57–60.

***** The Art of Coltrane**

Blue Note 98645 *Similar to above.*

Another pair of compilations, one devoted entirely to the blues, the other to a somewhat more rounded picture of Trane's development; both of them from the stable that really missed out on Trane's great years, hence some desire to capitalize on what they do have. 'Blue Train' is, of course, the outstanding performance, but Clark's 'Sonny's Crib' and Dorham's 'Shifting Down' are both excellent performances, and the inclusion of Cecil Taylor on one of these provides a rare chance to hear the two giants together, comparable in significance to Parker's encounter with Monk. Nicely packaged, but hard to know who this is for.

***** Like Sonny**

Capitol 93901 *Coltrane; Ray Draper (tba); John Maher, McCoy Tyner (p); Steve Davis, Spanky DeBrest (b); Billy Higgins, Larry Ritchie (d).* 58, 60.

Valuable for that first glimpse of Coltrane in the company of McCoy Tyner, the pianist whose instinctive grasp of modal principles was to be a key factor in the saxophonist's spectacular progress over the next few years. This basically puts together two quite different sessions, one of them featuring the tuba-player Ray Draper and his anonymous rhythm section. It includes some interesting material, including Draper's own 'Essii's Dance', but it's the nascent quartet with Steve Davis and Billy Higgins which really points the way forward.

***** The Standard Coltrane**

Original Jazz Classics OJCCD 246 *Coltrane; Wilbur Harden (t, flhn); Red Garland (p); Paul Chambers (b); Jimmy Cobb (d).* 7/58.

***** Bahia**

Original Jazz Classics OJCCD 415 *As above, except add Art Taylor (d).* 7 & 12/58.

***** The Stardust Session**

Prestige 24056 *As above.* 7 & 12/58.

It takes a certain wishful attitude to think of these as transitional records, except in the rather general sense that everything Coltrane did was in transit to some other spiritual or musical reality. It's easy enough to untangle these three late releases from the Prestige period. *The Standard* pretty much explains itself, a low-intensity operation with the emphasis on ballads. Two tracks from the same session plus 'My Ideal', 'Something I Dreamed Last Night' and 'I'm A Dreamer (Aren't We All)' are included on *Bahia*, though the liner details inconsistently imply that the middle item was taped on the December date, which seems unlikely. Harden's warm, unemphatic trumpet-playing is perfectly appropriate to the setting, and it rarely attempts anything that will scare the horses. He and the leader seem to have worked out the approach only rather notionally, and each of their improvisations has an informal, loose-limbed quality that is attractive but hardly dynamic. *The Stardust Session* is a Prestige compilation including all of *The Standard Coltrane* and a couple of items from *Bahia*; it's reasonable value if you can find it.

*****(*) The Prestige Recordings**

Prestige 25104 6CD *As above.* 11/56–7/58.

**** Jazz Showcase**

Original Jazz Classics 6015 *As for Prestige recordings above.* 11/56–7/58.

The boxed set offers the most comprehensive and, for most listeners, exhaustive documentation of Trane's time with the label, which as always in these matters was shorter than it seems in retrospect. It reveals the saxophonist still in larval stage and not yet the compellingly beautiful imago of the Atlantic years. The single CD sampler is unsatisfactory in almost every respect.

***** Coltrane Time**

Blue Note 7 84461 *Coltrane; Cecil Taylor (p); Chuck Israels (b); Louis Hayes (d).* 10/58.

No inconsistency: *Blue Train* was indeed Trane's only session for Blue Note. *Coltrane Time* – or *Coltranetime*, cover and spine differ – was a United Artists release, reissued by Capitol much later. Chanced upon, and especially when Coltrane is not soloing, the session sounds rather anonymous. Its importance – like the mid-1957 dates under Thelonious Monk's leadership – is the unique opportunity to hear two of the great modernist pioneers together. Unfortunately, they seem to cancel one another out. Both are playing rather circumspectly, perhaps in deference to the other, and the real star of the session, his contribution greatly enhanced by CD, turns out to be Israels, composer of the excellent final tune, 'Double Clutching', which mirrors Dorham's opening 'Shifting Down'. Neither of the two leaders contributes any writing. If part of the intention was to widen Taylor's appeal (and this seems to have been the aim), it is done at the expense of his most distinctive characteristics. Coltrane comes out of it rather better, but he is still constrained by the two standards, 'Just Friends' and 'Like Someone In Love', which allow him to do little more than hang out a few more sheets of sound before stepping back to allow Taylor some solo space of his own, in which he seems disinclined to indulge.

CORE COLLECTION

****** Giant Steps**

Atlantic 781337 *Coltrane; Tommy Flanagan, Wynton Kelly, Cedar Walton (p); Paul Chambers (b); Jimmy Cobb, Lex Humphries, Art Taylor (d).* 3, 5 & 12/59.

****** Giant Steps: Deluxe Edition**

Rhino 75203 *As above.*

Moving from Prestige to Atlantic had the same effect on Coltrane as a more extended association with Blue Note might have done. The first album is the product of time and preparation, and it cements its status as Trane's first genuinely iconic record, with no fewer than seven original compositions, most of them now squarely established in the repertory. The big stylistic shift is the move away from chordal jazz, and a seemingly obsessive need to cross-hatch every feasible subdivision before moving on to the next in the sequence. In its place, a faster-moving, scalar approach that was to achieve its (in the event) brief apotheosis in the title-track. That this was a technically exacting theme is underlined by the false starts and alternative takes included on *The Heavyweight Champion* set (below), but there is a chance to sample an earlier version of the tune on this CD reissue, performed with another group a month and a half before the issued recording (which featured Flanagan, Chambers and Taylor). Cedar Walton just about goes through the motions at the 26 March session. He finds the beautiful ballad 'Naima' a more approachable proposition, though this time the released version was actually from a later session still, with Wynton Kelly and Jimmy Cobb. It remains one of Trane's best-loved themes, a million miles away from the pitiless drive of many of his solos. Dedicated to the bassist, 'Mr P.C.' is a delightful original blues which has become part of most

contemporary horn-players' repertoire. 'Syeeda's Song Flute' is a long, spun-out melody for Trane's daughter. The remaining tracks are 'Spiral', 'Countdown' and the funky, homely 'Cousin Mary'. *Giant Steps* was released on the cusp of a new decade, in January 1960. It threw down a quiet, unaggressive challenge. Once again, it is difficult to see it as anything other than a transitional record. Flanagan doesn't sound much more confident with the new idiom than Walton had been on the dry run, though he is a more intuitively lyrical player.

The 'deluxe edition' includes alternates of most of the tunes; these variants have been available before, of course, but they still help to build a picture of what was going on during this remarkable session. Having them isolated in the context of the issued album is of some merit, though perhaps only newcomers to the Coltrane diaspora will be unaware of the extraordinary enterprise that had such seasoned and intelligent players wrestling with a new conception in jazz.

**** Coltrane Jazz

Atlantic 781344 *Coltrane; Wynton Kelly, McCoy Tyner (p); Paul Chambers, Steve Davis (b); Jimmy Cobb, Elvin Jones (d).* 11–12/59, 10/60.

Again, sessions overlap. Much of this comes from the date that yielded the issued 'Naima', but there is also a later track, 'Village Blues', which features Tyner and Jones, meaning that the classic quartet is just around the corner. At this point, four years after picking up those Bechet records from Alfred Lion (but seemingly inspired by having heard straight-horn specialist Steve Lacy), Trane was deliberating on what was to be his only significant 'double', the querulously pitched soprano saxophone. Even when he is playing tenor, though, there are signs that he is looking for new pitch relationships, and he can be heard exploring split tones on 'Harmonique'. With the exception of Johnny Mercer's 'My Shining Hour', all the material is original, a consolidation and in some regards a slight retreat from the innovations of *Giant Steps*. However, by this point 'Coltrane Jazz' does begin to sound like a distinct stylistic subspecies.

*** The Avant-Garde

Rhino 79892 *Coltrane; Don Cherry (t); Charlie Haden, Percy Heath (b); Ed Blackwell (d).* 6–7/60.

A needlessly, perhaps off-puttingly self-conscious title for an album which was intended to square the circle by putting Coltrane in contact with the third of the modernist triumvirate, Ornette Coleman, or at least his group and his music. Three of the numbers played are Ornette's 'The Blessing', 'Focus On Sanity' and 'The Invisible'; 'Cherryco' is the trumpeter's; and 'Bemsha Swing' is by Monk and Denzil Best. Except on the last – and presumably most familiar – of these, Trane sounds untypically awkward. His soprano-playing is not yet either idiomatic or nimble, and on 'The Blessing' he makes even Ornette's eccentric pitching sound dead centre. A curiosity rather than a major recording.

**** My Favorite Things

Atlantic 8122 75350-2 *Coltrane; McCoy Tyner (p); Steve Davis (b); Elvin Jones (d).* 10/60.

**** Coltrane's Sound

Rhino/Atlantic R2 75588 *As above.* 10/60.

**** Coltrane Plays The Blues

Rhino 79966 *As above.* 10/60.

The Avant-Garde didn't appear until rather later, and Coltrane's real coming out as a soprano player was disguised behind the unthreatening banner of a Rodgers and Hammerstein tune. Yet who could have anticipated the sheer strangeness of his take on 'My Favorite Things'? Call it what you will, a radical subversion of American popular song, the quintessence of the scalar approach, a new synthesis of Western and Eastern idioms (and all of these have been advanced and substantiated), it is a remarkable, unsettling performance. In later years, 'My Favorite Things' was to become a regular feature of Coltrane's live sets, often spun out to several times the length of this relatively controlled, 13-minute version. Here, it has all the freshness and innocence of the original song, and though Tyner follows his boss in largely ignoring its chord structure, he still manages to retain the familiar contours.

A year and a half after *Kind Of Blue*, Trane still sounds as if he is hearing versions of the Miles Davis group in his head. 'Summertime', 'Every Time We Say Goodbye' and 'But Not For Me' are all marked by Miles's cool modality. The two Gershwin songs are taken on tenor, and 'Summertime' points forward to some of the things Coltrane was to be doing on the larger horn over the next couple of years, with basically this group. (Davis was shortly to be replaced.)

The all-standards programme was a marketing strategy as much as anything, for there was to be a good deal of very mixed material, including some originals, in the extended session that ran from 20 to 26 October. *Colrane's Sound* was programmed to deliver a much darker sound and was issued in a sleeve on which Coltrane's calm face was reduced to smears of paint; he is reported to have been distressed by it. The album starts as dramatically as anything since *Blue Train* with a roiling interpretation of 'The Night Has A Thousand Eyes' which is both in the spirit of and dramatically different from his treatment of 'My Favorite Things'. Coltrane merely states the theme of 'Central Park West' on his soprano; otherwise it is a feature for Tyner. The leader is back with a vengeance on 'Liberia', as blackly intense as anything he was to do in the Atlantic period. Nothing else on the album (that is, nothing on the original second LP-side) quite matches up. Trane's Afro-excursion on that tenor-player's rite of passage, 'Body And Soul', sounds rather predictable in the context; though, given that the saxophonist was redefining the parameters almost session by session, that's a highly relative judgement.

The blues album, made over the same long session as most of the *Coltrane's Sound* tracks, is often overlooked or reviewed as if it were a separate and distinct project. Much of the interest lies in Tyner's withdrawal from some of the numbers, a first experiment with a pianoless trio since Prestige days. Here once again simplicity of statement and sophistication of harmonic structure lie in fertile balance. Worth dusting off. The new edition has four alternates of 'Blues To Elvin'.

*** Olé Coltrane

Atlantic 8122 75351-2 *Coltrane; Freddie Hubbard (t); Eric Dolphy (as, f); McCoy Tyner (p); Art Davis, Reggie Workman (b); Elvin Jones (d).* 5/61.

The end of Coltrane's time with Atlantic and already overlapping with the *Africa/Brass* project, which was to be his first Impulse! recording. There has always been debate about Trane's influences and associations: how much he learnt from Monk, how much he understood or appreciated what Cecil Taylor and Ornette Coleman were doing, and to what extent he was influenced by Eric Dolphy, or Dolphy by him. The difference was that he enjoyed a warm personal association with the younger man, who was to bring his own distinctive touch to some of Coltrane's greatest compositions and contrafacts when they toured Europe later in 1961, following the Village Vanguard residency. It seems increasingly clear that Dolphy's role in 'arranging' *Africa/Brass* was less central than once thought. His part in *Olé Coltrane* was also supportive rather than central. Dolphy was even obliged for contractual reasons to appear as George Lane. His flute shadows Coltrane's soprano on the title-track, switching to alto for 'Dahomey Dance' and for McCoy Tyner's prescient 'Aisha'. These are the only three tracks on the original release, though an inititally untitled ballad, known as 'To Her Ladyship' and credited to Billy Frazier, was also recorded. The presence of Hubbard also helped expand the timbral range, pointing to the new, more orchestrated sound Coltrane was interested in developing at the time. Interesting as it is episodically, *Olé* never quite holds the attention.

****** The Heavyweight Champion**

Atlantic/Rhino 8122 71984 7CD *Personnel as for Atlantic recordings above.* 1/59–5/61.

We have not previously felt moved to demote a coronetted item, though in this case we did make threatening noises on the grounds that this capacious box and the artist it celebrates deserved a more appropriate title. Given that all the Atlantic records are available singly, and that some of the more important alternatives and rejected material have been released on two still widely available compilations, *The Coltrane Legacy* and *Alternate Takes*, only the most dedicated and well-heeled of fans will feel the need to have this set.

There will always be disagreement between those who want to understand the archaeology of a classic session – in this case, *Giant Steps* – and to be able to track back through umpteen false starts and breakdowns, and those who simply want to have the pristine performances. There are no fewer than ten alternatives of 'Giant Steps' itself, most of them grouped on the last CD of the set, a collection of out-takes packaged in a mock-up of an old tape-box. The evolution of the definitive performance, and of a piece that Coltrane was not to perform in concert or to re-record, is of course part of the history of the music, and we are privileged to have access to it; the studio banter is relaxed and funny, underlining most musicians' recollection of Coltrane as a gentle, easy-going man who was only obdurate when it came to writing playable themes. For anyone who has none of the Atlantics, this is a worthwhile buy, though we'd still recommend them in their issued form.

****** The Very Best Of John Coltrane**

Rhino 79778 *As for Atlantic/Rhino releases above.* 59–61.

We are not great lovers of compilations and best-of collections, but should a young nephew or niece ever betray complete ignorance of Coltrane and his work, this would be the ideal introduction, to the middle, gentler phase of his career at least. It begins boldly with 'Giant Steps' and includes 'Cousin Mary', 'Naima', 'My Favorite Things', 'Central Park West' and 'Summertime', along with a couple of blues and standards. And when they say, 'Uncle/Aunt, this has changed my life,' you can reminisce about how it changed yours as well.

*****(*) The Last Giant: The John Coltrane Anthology**

Rhino 71255 2CD *As for Atlantic/Rhino releases, above; additional personnel.* 46–67.

There are probably people out there who think 'anthology' means something different from 'best of' or 'compilation'; but not even the prospect of having a glimpse of Trane playing bebop in 1946, doing a radio session with Dizzy Gillespie, or accompanying Gay Crosse's 'Good Humor Six' in 1952 will be enough to persuade hardened collectors to part with their cash for this retread of the formula. All the obvious Altantic benchmarks are there, as they'd have to be, and there are two hours plus of music; but as an introduction, it's a poorer bet than others.

****** The Complete Africa/Brass Sessions**

Impulse! 052168-2 2CD *Coltrane; Freddie Hubbard, Booker Little (t); Britt Woodman (tb); Carl Bowman, Charles Greenlee, Julian Priester (euph); Jimmy Buffington, Donald Corrado, Bob Northern, Robert Swisshelm, Julius Watkins (frhn); Bill Barber (tba); Eric Dolphy (as, f, bcl); Garvin Bushell (picc, reeds); Pat Patrick (bs); McCoy Tyner (p); Paul Chambers, Art Davis, Reggie Workman (b); Elvin Jones (d).* 5–6/61.

Coltrane's debut for Impulse! was to have, like some of the masterworks that followed, a slightly muddled history. Only with the release of this properly annotated double-CD is it possible to gain an accurate understanding of what was going on. Still with some effort, unfortunately, for even after two CD generations there are still inaccuracies. The first and obvious point to make about the music is that, while Trane clearly was becoming interested in large-scale ensemble playing and in a bigger, more collective sound, this is essentially a quartet album with a fairly minimal – though undeniably powerful – orchestration done by Coltrane, Tyner, Dolphy (who has previously had too much of the credit) and – on one track, the initially rejected 'The Damned Don't Cry' – Romulus Franceschini.

As before, chord structures are left implicit at best and time-signatures are never as clear-cut as they might appear. Even the waltz-time – or 6/8 – feel Coltrane had begun to favour for long-form soprano improvisations is breaking up into constituent subdivisions. The impact of African music on the title-piece is difficult to pin down or quantify, but it is unmistakably there, and it was to mark a new departure for Coltrane. The original *Africa/Brass* CD consisted of just three tracks: 'Africa' itself, a huge conception generated by the simplest of two-note bass figures; 'Greensleeves', another soprano deconstruction of a familiar tune; and 'Blues Minor'. (The notes here suggest that it consisted of 'Greensleeves' and two takes of 'Africa': nonsense.) In the mid-'70s, Impulse! released *Africa/Brass Sessions: Volume 2*, which consisted of 'Song Of The Underground Railroad' and alternatives of 'Greensleeves' and 'Africa', while a further version of the title-piece and a Cal Massey composition called 'The Damned Don't Cry' emerged on the double-LP compilation, *Trane's Modes*. This is still garbled, and there are still some question marks over the exact composition of the orchestra (a previous CD release claims Jimmy Garrison was involved, in advance of his signing as the Coltrane Quartet's regular bassist) but the above is our best effort.

The music is extraordinary. Coltrane sounds exalted on 'Africa' and turns in performances of markedly different emotional temperature on each of the three available versions. For students of his soprano work, the two versions of 'Greensleeves' are equally a revelation. A bright, swinging idea, 'Blues Minor' is in some respects a throwback to the Atlantic years, but 'Song

Of The Underground Railroad' looks defiantly forward, indeed is perhaps the most prescient thing on the entire set, anticipating the saxophone/drums axis of work with Elvin Jones and, still more, Rashied Ali.

**** The Complete 1961 Village Vanguard Recordings

Impulse! IMPCD 054232-2 4CD *Coltrane; Eric Dolphy (bcl); Garvin Bushell (ob, cbsn); McCoy Tyner (p); Jimmy Garrison, Reggie Workman (b); Ahmed Abdul-Malik (oud); Elvin Jones, Roy Haynes (d).* 11/61.

It was seemingly Coltrane's decision to record material in a club setting where a measure of direct communication with the audience was possible. For the better part of four decades, these performances at one of New York's premier jazz spots were available in scattered form and with uncertain identification of personnel. The situation seemed to be eased considerably when reissue producer Michael Cuscuna played the surviving tapes to Reggie Workman, who was able to nail the question of who played on which track.

The original *Live At The Village Vanguard* included 'Spiritual', a half-remembered song from long before, taped on the night of 3 November and featuring an extraordinary vocalized bass-clarinet solo from Dolphy; after this comes 'Softly As In A Morning Sunrise' without Dolphy. Taped the night before, the torrential tenor outpouring of 'Chasin' The Trane' comes with an almost physical shock; it is a trio piece on which Tyner sits out but which, like a couple of other tracks, includes Dolphy in the final cadence. There had been nothing quite like this in jazz; no one had dared to create a solo as freely stressed, polytonal and downright ugly since the days of the early bluesmen, except that Coltrane was sustaining this level of invention for more than a quarter of an hour. It was an approach that sparked off instant controversy. It is now confirmed that Garrison was the bassist on 'Chasin' The Trane' and, with all the benefit of hindsight, it does have a more urgent and percussive sound than Workman's.

Other material from the November 1961 residency first appeared on *Impressions*, which was released two years later and included the mysterious 'India', on which Trane's soprano floated over twinned basses; it could almost be shawm and drones, were it not so hard-edged. The solo on 'Impressions', which was recorded on the same night as 'India' and 'Spiritual', is one of the most important in Coltrane's whole career, a staggering edifice which looks disorderly only from a certain aesthetic distance. Internally, it is as rigidly watertight and non-impressionistic as it is possible to imagine.

The 1963 release was augmented with two studio tracks recorded that year, 'Up 'Gainst The Wall' and the intensely beautiful 'After The Rain'. Thereafter, material from the 1961 Vanguard stint was to appear on compilation discs: six tracks, including another 'Greensleeves', another 'India' and 'Spiritual' from Sunday, 5 November (with guest musicians Bushell and Abdul-Malik), a version of 'Chasin' The Trane' with Dolphy in tow, and 'Brasilia', which had previously been known as 'Untitled Original', were released on a 1977 compilation, *The Other Village Vanguard Tapes.* There was more material on the previously mentioned *Trane's Modes* (including yet another 'Chasin' The Trane' on which Tyner *does* briefly appear but on which Jones is replaced by Roy Haynes) and two further items, variants on 'India' and 'Spiritual', were released on *From The Original Master Tapes* (now deleted).

It is now clear that only numbers that were thought likely to be worthy of release were actually taped at the Vanguard, so the remaining material is not as wearisomely exhaustive as might have been feared. Even so, *The Complete 1961 Village Vanguard Recordings* is a formidable document, a body of work which, like Miles's Plugged Nickel sessions, allows the devoted listener to graph changes in emphasis, temper, pitching and approach, night on night. A measure of devotion is certainly required. The set amounts to four and a half hours of concentrated music. David A. Wild's archiving work and commentary are as useful a path through it as one could wish for. One of the points he is at pains to make is how integral Dolphy was to this group, a prominence that seemed to be minimized in the original releases. This doesn't seem to have arisen from any hostility or suspicion regarding the younger man's work, simply a desire to foreground and enhance an Impulse! artist instead. Whether the quartet 'Chasin' The Trane' is better or not, it certainly is less securely Coltrane's. Just to muddy the water further, there is also 'Chasin' Another Trane' with Dolphy and (very briefly) Tyner as well. It has now surfaced on *Newport '63* (below).

In the event, there are only three previously unissued items, which may sway the final decision whether to purchase or not. All three, interestingly, feature Dolphy on bass clarinet. Wild suggests that it was Dolphy who wrote 'Miles's Mode', which is back-titled as such after its appearance on *Coltrane* the next year, but which is referred to in the Vanguard tapes as 'The Red Planet'. 'Naima' is always to be treasured, and again Dolphy almost steals the show with his solo.

**** Live At The Village Vanguard: The Master Takes

Impulse! 051251-2 *Coltrane; Eric Dolphy (bcl); McCoy Tyner (p); Jimmy Garrison, Reggie Workman (b); Elvin Jones (d).* 11/61.

The budget option for those who can't or won't shell out for the whole schtick. This reunites 'Spiritual', 'Softly, As In A Morning Sunrise' and 'Chasin' The Trane' from the original *Live*, with 'India' and 'Impressions' from the later *Impressions.* We can't argue with the music, but we do wonder how many more ways GRP will find to slice this particular salami.

***(*) Coltrane

Impulse! 589567 *Coltrane; McCoy Tyner (p); Jimmy Garrison (b); Elvin Jones (d).* 4 & 6/62.

*** Coltrane

Impulse! 589567 2CD *As above.* 4–6/62.

This is the classic quartet's first manifestation in the studio, and it is a slightly odd, even rather formulaic, record. The requisite show-tune feature for soprano this time falls to 'The Inch Worm', a rather irritating Frank Loesser song from the film, *Hans Christian Andersen.* 'Miles's Mode' (aka 'The Red Planet') is dealt with rather briskly, and 'Tunji' is one of the more forgettable items in Trane's book. Ultimately, the album stands or falls on a truly dramatic reading of the Arlen/Mercer song, 'Out Of This World'. It's an inspired if unexpected first item; it's then followed by Mal Waldron's 'Soul Eyes', a tune of grace and elegant emotion. The album's worth having for those two alone. The 2002 reissue spreads over two discs and includes extra cuts of 'Tunji' and other material, including 'Big Nick' and 'Up 'Gainst the Wall'. Not essential and in some ways out of place.

*** The European Tour

Pablo Live 2208222 *Coltrane; McCoy Tyner (p); Jimmy Garrison (b); Elvin Jones (d).* 62.

***(*) Bye Bye Blackbird

Original Jazz Classics OJCCD 681 *As above.* 62.

*** The Paris Concert

Original Jazz Classics OJCCD 781 *As above.* 62.

A year after the visit with Dolphy, Trane and the quartet were back in Europe and pulling down extraordinary reviews. There are, in addition to these records, several more of questionable or indeterminate provenance. *Bye Bye Blackbird* is probably the best of the bunch, consisting of just two mammoth performances, the title-track and another 'Traneing In'. There is some valuable material on the Pablo disc, and one rarity, 'The Promise'. The Paris date has also appeared in other forms and with very mixed sound-quality; the blues, 'Mr P.C.', is terrific, the rest less so.

**** Live Trane: The European Tours

Pablo 84433 7CD *As above.* 61–63.

A titanic collection. The statistics alone are impressive: an astonishing 37 tracks of which 19 are previously unreleased, most invitingly a 1961 concert performance in Hamburg with Eric Dolphy as guest star. This is comprehensively bootlegged territory, but these are nicely cleaned-up recordings and though not up to contemporary standards – Garrison is still poorly served throughout – sufficient to their purpose. Inevitably, given the nature of Coltrane's performances at the time, there is a good deal of repetition of themes: six versions of 'My Favorite Things', five of 'Impressions' and 'Mr P.C.', and four of 'Naima'. A thunderous 'Blue Train' is one of the best of the less familiar cuts.

Basically, the set brings together all of *Afro Blue Impressions, The Paris Concert, Bye Bye Blackbird* and *The European Tour.* Anyone who already has these discs and doesn't feel the need for sometimes slightly generic performances (and there is no getting away from this – Trane wasn't infallibly inventive) may want to hang on to their cash. But for anyone who is just beginning to explore the Coltrane canon, this is a valuable resource, albeit an expensive one.

***(*) Ballads

Impulse! 589548 2CD *Coltrane; McCoy Tyner (p); Jimmy Garrison (b); Elvin Jones (d).* 9–11/62.

*** John Coltrane And Johnny Hartman

Impulse! 051157-2 *As above, except add Johnny Hartman (v).* 3/63.

America in 1962 was no place to be black and angry. LeRoi Jones's play *Dutchman* is susceptible of a good many readings, but among other things it is about white America's ambivalent willingness to let black anger discharge itself, in order to destroy and negate it. In John Coltrane, there was a constant war between rage and beauty. Compounded by personal pain and not yet redeemed by the great spiritual awakening celebrated on *A Love Supreme,* it often saw him zig-zag between celebration and an almost nihilistic ferocity. In the second half of 1962 Coltrane had been experiencing further dental problems and was having difficulty with his articulation. Partly to work around that limitation, partly no doubt to generate some market-friendly product, Bob Thiele suggested the *Ballads* project, and also the session with singer Johnny Hartman; he had also managed to arrange the historic encounter with Duke Ellington. Coltrane had always been an exquisite ballad-player and the material he chose for the date was guaranteed to please: 'Too Young To Go Steady', 'I Fall In Love Too Easily' and a brief, flawless 'Nancy (With The Laughing Face)'. The bonus track on the original CD was 'Vilia', but the augmented edition includes further versions of 'All Or Nothing At All', 'It's Easy To Remember' and 'Greensleeves'. We remain unconvinced that these add much.

The slightly frustrating thing about the session with Hartman is that, with the exception of 'Lush Life', there isn't a vocal performance of one of the standard songs Trane had made his own. How interesting it would have been to hear Hartman singing 'I Want To Talk About You' ('My Favorite Things' sounds less probable). Ironically, too, Trane's tone seems to have hardened up again by the spring of 1963 and is obviously being kept in check, whereas on the *Ballads* date he is not quite coasting but is certainly holding back a little, ceding a lot of the foreground to Tyner, who fills the air with rolling chords and delicate right-hand fills. Garrison also seems to relish the pace and the space, producing cello-line tones that are reminiscent of Oscar Pettiford or, closer at hand, Paul Chambers. These are now available as part of the Impulse! Reissue Series, with enhanced audio, 20-bit super-mapping, gatefold design (we're quoting now, you understand), rare photos and original liner-notes. The sound *is* good, but probably not good enough to make you want to throw away your old copy and who really wants to hear five versions of 'Greensleeves' and seven of 'It's Easy To Remember'?

*** Live At Birdland And The Half Note

Cool & Blue C&B CD 101 *Coltrane; McCoy Tyner (p); Jimmy Garrison (b); Elvin Jones (d).* 5/62–5/65.

***(*) Coltrane Live At Birdland

Impulse! 051198-2 *As above.* 10–11/63.

Despite his hostility towards more or less everything that happened after bebop, Philip Larkin rather liked *Live At Birdland.* He did, however, suggest that Coltrane spent too much time 'rocking backwards and forwards as if in pain between two chords'. By the end of 1962, it would have taken a well-schooled musician to identify those chords reliably, but in a sense Larkin is right. LeRoi Jones's typically hyped-up liner-note to the same record points once again to the anomaly of so much beauty existing amid so much pain. The early '60s were a strange time for black Americans. The club tracks on the album – and, despite the title, there are a couple of studio items as well – were recorded a month before JFK's assassination, with the country poised between hope and violence. The end of 'Afro-Blue' is an intense cry of pain and blame, commingled with defiance; and 'The Promise', the soprano feature heard on the European tour the autumn before, has a more ironic sound in an American setting. By this stage Trane was able to play the more familiar standard tunes in his bag with a trance-like freedom. 'I Want To Talk About You', which appears in different versions on both discs, is a million miles from the Billy Eckstine song; on the Impulse! version, it ends with a fiercely intense, unaccompanied coda. Jones perceptively describes the way Coltrane's music of this period seems to break through an impenetrable fog of sound with a sudden, almost miraculous directness of statement. The two studio tracks are powerful examples; 'Alabama' was, as is well known, inspired by the death of schoolchildren in a bomb outrage in Birmingham, and 'Your Lady' was a love poem to Alice McLeod, shortly to be his wife; a less celebrated theme than 'Naima', but no less beautiful.

The Cool & Blue disc brings together performances from quite a long span of time – and then includes them out of chronological sequence. 'My Favorite Things' and 'Body And Soul' come from June 1962, and it is surely not fanciful to note the dramatic darkening of intent between these performances and the album's closing 'Song Of Praise' from May 1965. Along with the Eckstine tune, the other item from 1963 is 'One Up And One Down', a tune which somehow seems made for Eric Dolphy, who was off at the time making his own next – and, as it turned out, next-to-last – jump forward.

***(*) Newport '63

Impulse! GRP 11282 *Coltrane; Eric Dolphy (as); McCoy Tyner (p); Jimmy Garrison, Reggie Workman (b); Roy Haynes (d).* 11/61, 7/63.

Not to be confused with *New Thing At Newport*, which was recorded at the Festival two years later and is shared with Archie Shepp. All the tracks from 1963 had been available before, on the Impulse! albums, *Selflessness* and *To The Beat Of A Different Drummer*. The different drummer in this case was Haynes, who was standing in for the increasingly erratic Jones, a heroin-user. Haynes has a lighter, springier sound and consequently these three very familiar themes – 'I Want To Talk About You', 'My Favorite Things' and 'Impressions' – are rather differently channelled. Coltrane seems to shadow-box with the drummer, placing his notes differently. Tyner and Garrison aren't well served by the recording, but they're audible and both seem to be playing well.

The anomaly of a 1961 reference and the unquoted presence of Dolphy and Workman is explained by the makeweight track, 'Chasin' Another Trane', a reworking of the big blowing theme from the Village Vanguard residency. It has previously been issued on *Trane's Modes* and also now on the Vanguard *Complete* set. Just to confirm that we are awake, McCoy Tyner is not listed in the track credits on this CD. He *is* there, but just for two choruses; then he makes his excuses and leaves.

**** Afro-Blue Impressions

Pablo Live 2620101 2CD *Coltrane; McCoy Tyner (p); Jimmy Garrison (b); Elvin Jones (d).* 63.

It may seem strange to describe a Coltrane record as 'professional', but this is one of the most polished performances in the canon. No real screaming highs, no dark inscapes, but rugged, straightforward versions of 'Naima', 'Impressions' and, not much represented in the live discography, 'Cousin Mary' from *Giant Steps*. There is also a foretaste of 'Lonnie's Lament', which was to be included on *Crescent* the following spring. The 1963 European tour has always been regarded as something of an anti-climax after the remarkable tours of '61 and '62. Not so, we find.

***(*) Crescent

Impulse! 051200-2 *Coltrane; McCoy Tyner (p); Jimmy Garrison (b); Elvin Jones (d).* 4 & 6/64.

Of all the new-generation CDs, this is the one which seems to have gained most from 20-bit super-mapping, yielding a brighter sound and opening up a silver lining in what has always seemed to be Coltrane's most melancholy record. *Crescent* is often seen as the dark hour that comes just before the spiritual dawning of *A Love Supreme*. 'Wise One' and 'Lonnie's Lament' are certainly among the least effusive of his tunes, drawn once again from memories of field calls, spirituals and spontaneous blues; but 'Bessie's Blues' emerges ever more vividly, a flash of light like a morning star. We are not sure what the exact circumstances were, but *Crescent* seems to have had a troubled birth. The band recorded versions of all five numbers on the album – and a head arrangement of 'Song Of Praise' – at a session on 27 April 1964. Two of those masters no longer exist, 'Crescent' and 'Bessie's Blues' being replaced with shorter versions on the LP. Unless purely technical concerns intervened, it's possible that Jones was the factor. He seems wildly inconsistent on the record, out of focus and removed one minute, but also claiming his first significant written feature on 'The Drum Thing'. Either way, a very significant record.

CORE COLLECTION

♛ **** A Love Supreme

Impulse! 051155-2 *Coltrane; McCoy Tyner (p); Jimmy Garrison (b); Elvin Jones (d).* 12/64.

**** A Love Supreme: Deluxe Edition

Impulse! 589945 2CD *As above; add Archie Shepp (ts); Art Davis (b).* 12/64, 7/65.

The first records in Coltrane's career as a leader were the work of a man who had submerged himself in heroin and alcohol and who had mortgaged his physical health as a result. If, as superstition and a measure of biological science suggest, people are transformed every seven years, then Coltrane is something like proof positive. Few spiritual breakthroughs have been so hard won, but he had also reinvented himself technically in that time, creating a body of music in which simplicity of materials generates an almost absurd complexity of harmonic and expressive detail. This is quintessentially true of *A Love Supreme*. Its foundations seem almost childishly slight, and yet what one hears is a majestic outpouring of sound, couched in a language that is often brutally violent, replete with split notes, multiphonics and toneless breath noises.

It is not a piece that can be separated from the creator's intentions and programme. Coltrane explicitly stated that the final movement, 'Psalm', should be understood as an instrumental expression of the text that was printed on the sleeve. The rest has the pace of a liturgical act of the kind that might have been encountered in a field mission. 'Acknowledgement' begins with a sweeping fanfare that will return at the close. A sonorous eight-bar theme creates the background to the four simple notes – 'A love su-preme' – which have become some of the most familiar in modern jazz. Stated by Garrison, they are reworked and varied through the scale by Coltrane, whose solo defies categorization. The chant is husky, strangely moving, and seems to occupy a different space and imprint from the hectic movement of the rhythm section. If this was to be Garrison's finest hour with the group, it is probably Jones's as well. He plays figures of great complexity that seem to change shape and direction every time one listens to the record.

They are slightly simpler on 'Resolution', but only in the interest of piling up the emotional pressure still more. Coltrane's entry has an almost violent impact, and in LP days it was difficult to find the resolve to flip the disc over and essay the other side, even though it is clear that the music is left hanging, still bereft of the other sort of resolution. 'Pursuance' takes us into the dark wood, a troubled, mid-life

moment. From now until the end, the rhythms are anxious, fractured, unsure. Horn and piano stagger like pilgrims from one brief point of rest to another. The closing 'Psalm' has an almost symphonic richness, culminating in a final 'Amen', a two-note figure in which a second saxophone (said to be Archie Shepp's) joins Coltrane. A partial restatement of the opening fanfare provides a reminder of the road travelled and also of the circularity of all such journeys.

The story of the making of *A Love Supreme* has been told in Ashley Kahn's fine book, which coincided with the release of the long-awaited deluxe edition. This provides a further insight into what went on in the studio during the making of the studio album, including two sextet cuts with Shepp and Davis who are thanked on the original album but aren't heard. These are alternate versions of 'Resolution' and 'Acknowledgement'. The larger group doesn't bring anything significant to light that isn't in the original piece. More interesting is the inclusion of the Quartet's performance of *A Love Supreme* at the much-bootlegged Antibes Festival of July 1965. This was a relatively rare occurrence. What militates against the centrality of the suite to Coltrane's spiritual mission is how rarely he returned to this material in subsequent years. There have been more 'tribute' run-downs of the album by young followers than there were performances by the original players, an irony worth pondering when the album's real importance is put in the scales.

Even extreme familiarity fails to tarnish *A Love Supreme.* It is without precedent and parallel, and though it must also be one of the best-known jazz records of all time, it somehow remains remote from critical pigeonholing. Having awaited the revelation of the deluxe edition, we find no epiphanies in it, just a certain anecdotal interest. Most casual listeners would be best advised to stick with the original issue, and cling on to that vinyl copy if you have. There is no cooler album to tuck under your arm as you cross the campus.

We have suggested before that the record documents a group at that moment of maximum energy before it sunders. Certainly, Tyner no longer seems at ease, and Jones is almost too forceful, too over-determining. The original release credited Coltrane alone and mentioned Tyner, Garrison and Jones only by their first names, reinforcing the idea that *A Love Supreme* was a great personal testament rather than a group effort. That's no longer seen to be the case. If all great art is the product of grace under pressure, then here the music seems to emerge out of several atmospheres, heavy, almost choking, but immensely concentrated and rich.

*** The Very Best of John Coltrane

Impulse! 549113 *As above.* 61–64.

*** Standards

Impulse! 549914 *As above.* 61–65.

*** Spiritual

Impulse! 589099 *As above.* 61–67.

'The Very Safest Of John Coltrane' might have been a better title for the first of these catchpenny compilations. Excluding the ferocious work that came in the latter part of his time with the label and relying on familiar material like Ellington's 'In A Sentimental Mood' and live versions of 'My Favorite Things' and 'Naima' (which were both originally on Atlantic releases), this might well serve as a useful introduction to Trane's output, but its limitations outweigh its value.

Spiritual is a fairly lame concept in the circumstances. Hearing these tunes out of context is potentially misleading, and not just because 'Acknowledgement' from *A Love Supreme* is only part of a much larger work. The problem is that Trane's spirituality, which was palpably genuine and deeply felt, worked best in relation to angrier, more abstract and sometimes just plain pretty ideas. Lifting all of these pieces out of their original settings and grouping them as if they represented a sacred concert does a little violence to their true character. Not much, it has to be said. 'Dear Lord' is still magnificent, 'Tunji' and 'Spiritual' itself are consistently inventive and Impulse! has even seen fit to include something from that 'difficult' later period: 'Ogunde' from *Expression.*

Standards has some value as a representation of how Coltrane alternately caressed and subverted traditional and repertory themes. The inclusions are in no way surprising: 'Greensleeves', 'Softly, As In Morning Sunrise' from the Vanguard Sessions, 'Lush Life' with Johnny Hartman, 'The Inch Worm', Eckstine's 'I Want To Talk About You' and five others. We're not the first to register surprise that the most significant standards performance of his career, indeed in the development of contemporary jazz *isn't* there. You guess which one, but yes, it's sung by a naughty nun-turned-nanny.

***(*) The John Coltrane Quartet Plays

Impulse! 051214-2 *Coltrane; McCoy Tyner (p); Art Davis, Jimmy Garrison (b); Elvin Jones (d).* 2 & 5/65.

A bare two months after completing *A Love Supreme*, Coltrane was back in the studio. Not surprisingly, the intention seems to have been to record another standards package. There was to be something of a hiatus before the set was completed, and in the event it included the original theme, 'Brasilia' (spelt with a 'z' in this version), from the Village Vanguard days, as well as a complete version of 'Song Of Praise' which had been tabled and recorded as a head on the *Crescent* date. What problems Coltrane was experiencing or what degree of emotional and creative burn-out he might have felt after *A Love Supreme*, we don't know. It's clear that, as ever, his mind is searching in new directions. The first session on *Plays* yielded a version of 'Nature Boy' with two bass players. The following day, a master version was cut, along with the Bricusse/Newley 'Feelin' Good', on which Davis also appears. It wasn't until 17 May that the remaining tracks were recorded, though in the meantime Coltrane and the quartet (without Davis) had included 'Nature Boy' in a set at the Village Gate. All three versions are now included on the CD, along with 'Feelin' Good', which was rejected. The obligatory show-tune this time out is the odious 'Chim Chim Cheree', another soprano essay, but this time inexplicably truncated, the shortest thing on the album; it may be that Coltrane decided to narrow his parameters slightly or it may simply be that he was now tiring of this long-standing formula. *Plays* is a fine record and the interaction of the group, both standard and augmented, is faultless. It is, however, a difficult item to place personally and artistically.

***(*) The Gentle Side Of John Coltrane

Impulse! 051107-2 *Coltrane; Duke Ellington, McCoy Tyner (p); Aaron Bell, Jimmy Garrison (b); Roy Haynes, Elvin Jones, Sam Woodyard (d); Johnny Hartman (v).* 62–65.

The Gentle Side is one of those records which – like *Mellow Miles* – seems to miss the point. It is, however, eminently approachable, even by those who are unpersuaded by Trane's more incendiary side, and it offers a pleasant, late-night option for those who've found *Ascension* to be a little abrasive for dinner parties. In addition to material from *Ballads* and the Hartman date, and the eternal 'Soul Eyes', there is 'After The Rain' from *Impressions*, 'Wise One' from *Crescent*, and 'Dear Lord' from *Transition*. Good value.

* Coltrane For Lovers

Impulse! 549361 *As above.* 61–64.

* Plays For Lovers

Prestige 6020 *As for Prestige dates above.* 57–61.

Oh, for goodness' sake! We're tempted to tell you that this contains a previously unreleased rehearsal of 'Ascension', which we have long regarded as excellent make-out music, but it does not. Needless to say, the music is fine: 'Soul Eyes', 'Nancy', 'My One And Only Love', 'After The Rain', 'In A Sentimental Mood'. It's the concept we have problems with. Avoid.

And, for god's sake, part two, *Plays For Lovers*, is just barrel scraping. It's desperate. Play her some Chet Baker instead.

♛ **** Ascension

Impulse! 543413-2 *Coltrane; Freddie Hubbard, Dewey Johnson (t); Marion Brown, John Tchicai (as); Pharoah Sanders, Archie Shepp (ts); Donald Garrett (bcl, b); Joe Brazil (b, perc); McCoy Tyner (p); Art Davis, Jimmy Garrison (b); Frank Butler, Elvin Jones (d); Juno Lewis (perc, v).* 6/65, 10/65.

There is nothing else like *Ascension* in Coltrane's work; indeed, there is nothing quite like *Ascension* in the history of jazz. Ornette Coleman's *Free Jazz* experiment is almost mannerly and formal by comparison. By the middle of 1965, Coltrane had done as much with the quartet, technically speaking, as he seemed likely to. Even so, no one could have foreseen what was to emerge from the session of 28 June. If ever Eric Dolphy was missed, it must have been on this occasion, but Dolphy had died in Berlin the previous year and the one player who might have wholly understood what Coltrane was about was no more.

In the simplest way, *Ascension* continues what Coltrane had been doing on *A Love Supreme*. The pattern of notes which begins the piece is a clear reference to the fanfare to 'Acknowledgement', but the vast collective improvisation which follows is almost antithetical to the highly personal, almost confessional quality of the earlier piece. The group was similarly constituted to the double quartet which recorded *Free Jazz*, though much less schematic. Coltrane devised a situation in which signals – from Hubbard and Tyner, in the main – could be given to switch modes, introducing new scalar and harmonic patterns. Soloists had a measure of freedom, and distinct ideas do seem to emerge within a broken field of gestural sounds. Everything is determined by the first few bars; nothing is determined entirely. It is a work that synthesizes the rules of classic jazz with the freedoms of the New Thing. Its success is difficult to gauge; its impact is total, overwhelming.

As with much of Coltrane's association with Impulse!, the circumstances of release are now hopelessly confused. It seems that Coltrane had originally authorized the release of the first version recorded, and this was issued in late 1965 as Impulse! AS-95. Then the saxophonist decided that the 'wrong' master had been used, and the second take was substituted, leaving 'Ascension – Edition I' as a piece of jazz apocrypha. Hearing them on this compilation, it is difficult to argue with Marion Brown's support of Coltrane's position. The second take is more cohesive and more expressive. The involvement of players like Brown and Tchicai – and Shepp and Sanders in particular – afforded a first chance to hear the 'school of Coltrane' in action. Predictably, no one sounds anything like the master, but the overall impact of the piece does suggest that warriors were gathering round the standard.

Individual performances serve a very different purpose here than on previous records and on other large-scale projects of the time like Coleman's. On *Free Jazz*, solos emerge out of the ensemble and impose a rather normative structure. Here, they provide an internal commentary that does not even threaten to disrupt the integrity of the piece. The main obvious difference between the two versions is the order of play. On the revised release (Edition II) the solos run: Coltrane, Johnson, Sanders, Hubbard, Brown, Shepp, Tchicai, Tyner and a bass duet (try to imagine the impact of *that*), while on Edition I Shepp and Tchicai are in front of Brown, and Elvin Jones solos near the end. Coltrane must have had reasons for his preference (though even he seems to have been uncertain), but there is not so very much separating the two versions qualitatively. After a time, they resemble a rock formation seen from a subtly different angle, but still unchangeably the same outcrop.

If Coltrane had not reached his 40th birthday, if his already diminishing lifespan had gone no further than the end of 1965, he would still have been guaranteed greatness on the strength of *A Love Supreme* and *Ascension* alone. There is no doubt which of the two is more approachable. Probably ten times more people own *A Love Supreme* than have even heard of the later masterpiece. That is one measure. The sheer scale and range of Coltrane's vision and ambition is another, no less important.

*** New Thing At Newport

Impulse! 543414-2 *Coltrane; McCoy Tyner (p); Jimmy Garrison (b); Elvin Jones (d); other material by the Archie Shepp Quartet.* 7/65.

Ascension was recorded on 28 June. Less than a week later, the quartet appeared on stage at Newport. Introduced by Fr Norman O'Connor, who seems to think that Elvin Jones is a newcomer to jazz, they kick into 'One Down, One Up', the same theme as 'One Up And One Down' on the Cool & Blue Birdland disc, and not so very different from the reading there. The piece that reveals the proximity of *Ascension* is a barbed version of 'My Favorite Things', which was originally released on the *Mastery Of John Coltrane* compilation and was added to this two-header only when it was transferred to CD. Just the two tracks by Coltrane; the remainder of the material is by Archie Shepp, whose discipleship was already paying rich dividends.

**** Sun Ship

Impulse! 051167-2 *Coltrane; McCoy Tyner (p); Jimmy Garrison (b); Elvin Jones (d).* 8/65.

This remains one of the least known of Coltrane's albums, recorded in between *Ascension* and the *Om* and *Kulu Se Mama* sessions. There is a short nugget of conversation before 'Dearly Beloved', a minor-key ballad which sees Coltrane working on top of a gently unfolding, continuous rhythm. The angle of attack is much sharper on the title-piece, and it is tempting to wonder (not just because of the title) whether Trane was once again listening to his lost creative twin, John Gilmore. Certainly the resemblance here is quite overt. The solo, pitched very high in the *altissimo* range, is based on a four-note figure that might suggest any number of genealogies. 'Attaining' is quieter, a freely pulsed minor blues which, as the sterling David Wild suggests, is generically related to several other of Coltrane's folk-tradition pieces. Its climax is extraordinary. A fourth star may seem extravagant, but it's high time this fine record was better known.

***(*) Live In Seattle

Impulse! 21462 2CD *Coltrane; Pharoah Sanders (ts); Donald Garrett (bcl); McCoy Tyner (p); Jimmy Garrison (b); Elvin Jones (d).* 9/65.

It is tempting to suggest that the whole grunge movement, fomented by those who reached their majority in the mid-'80s, represented the genetic fall-out of Coltrane's visit to Washington State 20 years earlier. From now to the end of his life, Coltrane's live performances were to be at times agonizingly protracted. 'Evolution' lasts more than half an hour and is oddly uninvolving for much of its length, save for a wonderful moment when the three horns demonstrate the kind of interweaving line and block texture that was attempted on *Ascension*. Garrett is not Dolphy, but he has certainly learned something of Dolphy's idiom. Sanders is not quite flat out yet, perhaps saving himself for the Vanguard and Japanese dates of the following year. By this stage, Tyner is lost. He plays manfully both in Seattle and in the subsequent studio set (which is included in *The Major Works*), but this is no longer his music. Even Jones, once so ubiquitously evident, has dropped into the shadows.

**** First Meditations

Impulse! GRP 11182 *Coltrane; McCoy Tyner (p); Jimmy Garrison (b); Elvin Jones (d).* 2/65.

***(*) Meditations

Impulse! 051199-2 *As above, except add Pharoah Sanders (ts), Rashied Ali (d).* 11/65.

These two related sessions, which cover essentially the same material, bridge the end of the classic quartet and the opening phase of the new, augmented group with Sanders and Ali. This is music that emerges directly out of *A Love Supreme*, tiny, motivic ideas, often stated by Garrison, generating huge, sprawling improvisations, scalar segments proliferating into enormous harmonic fissions. In February 1965 (which, remember, is the same month as the preliminary sessions for *Plays*) Coltrane and the quartet recorded a version of a new five-part suite consisting of 'Love', 'Compassion', 'Joy', 'Consequences' and 'Serenity'. When he returned to the studio in November, the saxophonist substituted the unbelievably turbulent 'The Father And The Son And The Holy Ghost' for the original opening movement, and moved 'Love' to what was the start of the continuous second side of the released LP.

The most important difference, apart from the addition of a second horn (an initiative that almost began on *A Love Supreme*) and of Ali's almost unpulsed, pure-sound drumming, is that the movements are run together almost seamlessly, whereas on *First Meditations* the breaks are quite distinct even though the sections are played without pause. On grounds of simple beauty and perhaps out of sentimental attachment to the group that was breaking up, the early version is to be preferred, though it clearly no longer represented what Coltrane wanted to do.

The CD of the February session includes an alternative version of 'Joy', the piece that sets in motion the final, multi-part movement. It's obvious that Coltrane is already trying to escape the sticky webs which Jones had woven for him. Had the old and new drummers been able to play together, 'Father/Son/Holy Ghost' suggests that something quite out of the ordinary might have occurred. As it is, *Meditations* and its Ur-text represent the final – and this time absolute – split between Coltrane and the rhythm of bebop.

**** Live At The Village Vanguard Again!

Impulse! 051213-2 *Coltrane; Pharoah Sanders (ts); Alice Coltrane (p); Jimmy Garrison (b); Rashied Ali (d); Emmanuel Rahid (perc).* 5/66.

That arch-conservative critic of jazz, Philip Larkin, was disposed to like elements of *Live At Birdland*; he considered this set, taped five years after the exhaustive 1961 sessions, to represent in triple-distilled form the 'blended insolence and ugliness' of the New Wave. Ugliness is debatable; there is not a scrap of insolence about it, unless it be to play such a passionate and beautiful poem to one wife while another is playing piano behind you. Much has been said about what the one-time Alice McLeod brought to the group. Like her harp and organ playing, she tends to work in blocks of sound-colour rather than linear developments. That is partially evident on 'Naima', but it comes out most strikingly on a huge deconstruction of what had been *the* Coltrane standard. This 'My Favorite Things' is almost the *reductio ad absurdum*. The version in Japan (see below) is almost the equivalent, if this isn't too unfortunate an analogy, of bombing Nagasaki just days after laying waste to Hiroshima. The point has been made, even if Jimmy Garrison's long, rambling introduction threatens never to clear the floor. Ali is already a key element, though here he has a percussionist as foil. It is easy to make the mistake of thinking that this is from the earlier Vanguard sessions – easy, that is, if one doesn't check personnel or listen to any of the music. It is drastically, diametrically different. There is no forward motion, no predetermined resolution; there is only music, always and eternally at the ear. Its insistence is both its triumph and, at those few moments when concentration lapses, yes, its hint of insolence.

*** Living Space

Impulse! 051246-2 *Coltrane; McCoy Tyner (p); Jimmy Garrison (b); Elvin Jones (d).* 65.

The last word from the classic quartet, and not much more than a selection of largely untitled and generic oddments. Easy to romanticize a piece called 'The Last Blues' when there was in fact still a mile or two left on the extraordinary journey of John Coltrane, but it brings an intriguing and often very beautiful album to a satisfying end. Once again, the label has tried and failed to capture the quality of the original Impulse! covers.

**** The Classic Quartet: The Complete Impulse! Studio Recordings

GRP 280 8CD *Coltrane; McCoy Tyner (p); Jimmy Garrison (b); Elvin Jones (p); plus Art Davis (b); Roy Haynes (d).* 61–65.

Important to register that this is *not* the complete Coltrane on Impulse!. The 66 cuts do include alternatives and some other unissued material, but only of the quartet itself and not of those augmented sessions when other players were recruited, so look in vain for *Ascension*, and for the sets with Duke Ellington and Johnny Hartman. The only exceptions are when Roy Haynes was standing in for the troubled Jones and some extra bass from Art Davis. The sessions are organized chronologically and almost symbolically from the residual prettiness of 'Greensleeves' to the fractured intensity of 'Living Space', and there is obviously considerable merit in hearing the music develop (and occasionally regress) rather than in the issued form, which often jumped out of or mixed the actual sequence of recording. However, the original releases are so much a part of the mind-set of a whole musical generation that it is hard to forget them, and most committed Coltrane fans will probably quickly return to the individual LPs. That said, this is a magnificently packaged and organized document, and it stands as a memorial to one of the truly great groups in the history of jazz.

★★★★ Interstellar Space

Impulse! 543414-2 *Coltrane; Rashied Ali (d, perc). 2/67.*

The final masterpiece. Only long after Coltrane's death did Andrew Cyrille start to explore in detail the rhythmic implications of some of Coltrane's late work. It had been axiomatic that he had taken bebop harmony as far as humanly possible, and then some. The records after *Africa/Brass* are largely devoted to a search for the time beyond time, an uncountable pulse which would represent a pure musical experience not chopped into bars and choruses. Only with the induction of the unconventionally tutored Rashied Ali did such a thing become practically possible. With Coltrane on tenor and Ali running a gamut of percussion, this is the purest sound-experience of all the records. 'Mars', the first of the planetary sequence, is characterized as the 'battlefield of the cosmic giants', and that is exactly how it sounds, with huge, clashing brass tones and a dense clangour from the drum kit. 'Venus' is appropriately quieter, amorous and almost delicate, with Ali barely scuffing his cymbals with wire brushes. 'Jupiter (Variation)' was known to Coltrane fans even when *Interstellar Space* was out of catalogue, being included on one of the *Mastery Of John Coltrane* compilations of out-takes and ephemera. The release version is the shortest item on the set, a stately expression of 'supreme wisdom', coming immediately before the climactic evocation of joy that is 'Saturn'. 'Leo' is known in a live version from the Tokyo concerts but wasn't on the original album.

★★★ Expression

Impulse! 11312 *Coltrane; Pharoah Sanders (ts, picc, perc); Alice Coltrane (p); Jimmy Garrison (b); Rashied Ali (d). 2–3/67.*

★★(★) Stellar Regions

Impulse! 051169-2 *As above.*

It would be wonderful if the final studio sessions really had represented the final wisdom of the greatest saxophonist since Parker, but *Expression* and the additional material issued as *Stellar Regions* (like the track titles, named long afterwards by Alice Coltrane) is a murky, often undistinguished work. There's some interest in hearing Coltrane on flute ('To Be', this from a man born in Hamlet, North Carolina) and there are a couple more instrumental quiddities, but what little of the music really convinces occurs on 'Offering' and 'Expression' itself, both of which are notably becalmed, almost resigned. 'Number One' is a new addition on CD. The suspicious thing about *Stellar Regions* is that the best track is 'Offering' again, not an alternative but the identical version which appears on *Expression*. This isn't so much sharp practice (God knows, GRP must have enough stuff salted away) as desperation, an attempt to rescue an otherwise dud album which even falls down on the typography of a pastiche cover. The talking point is 'Tranesonic', which appears in two takes. Though credited with tenor only (and there are no further flute tracks), the sound seems smaller, fatter, more tightly focused and, though most of the pitching is comfortably within tenor range, the positioning suggests a different horn, presumably an alto. This was confirmed on BBC Radio 3 by Evan Parker, though at least one correspondent vehemently denies it, as if alto-playing were an unforgivable offence. Oddly, and quite unlike much of the Impulse! catalogue, *Expression* manages to sound worse on CD than on the notoriously muddy LP. *Stellar Regions* is an improvement, though back-to-back auditions of 'Offering' suggest that the difference is too slight even to be cosmetic. An achievement as great as this somehow calls for a better conclusion, but life and art both conform to an inexorable logic of decline. Coltrane might still have been playing in the '70s, '80s, '90s; might, even as you read, be shuffling out to play 'My Favorite Things' for the hundred-and-umpteenth time. The fact is that he isn't; but what he did during that extraordinary, packed decade cannot be changed or gainsaid or diluted by slow, inevitable compromise.

(★★★) The Olatunji Concert: The Last Live Recording

Impulse! 589120-2 *Coltrane; Pharoah Sanders (ts); Alice Coltrane (p); Jimmy Garrison (b); Rashied Ali (d); Jumma Santos (d). 4/67.*

Recorded just three months before Coltrane's death from liver cancer, this has an obvious historical importance, and yet nothing can disguise the impression of a rather bad bootleg. The recording seems to have been made privately and with no thought of release, and so inevitably the sound of scraping barrels accompanied its release in 2001, anticipating the 35th anniversary of Trane's passing. Comprising just two long performances, 'Ogunde' and yet another reprise of 'My Favorite Things', it is a ferocious performance, largely dominated by Sanders, who already seems ready to take up his friend's mantle. The poor sound-quality, appallingly bad relative to the Village Vanguard tapes and even the airshots of Trane in Europe three years earlier, means that most of the textural detail is lost. Garrison is audible but his articulation is muddied in the transfer, and the percussion is hideously splashy and indistinct. One also feels halfway through 'My Favorite Things' that a seam has been mined almost to exhaustion. Impulse! has an obvious interest in releasing material like this; how well it reflects on a major artist is open to question.

★★★★ Legacy

Impulse! 314 589 295 2 *As for many of the above. 57–67.*

A decade of superb music-making and spiritual quest, boiled down to four CDs. The man who curated it was born two years before the saxophonist's death and never heard him play. Ravi Coltrane has been able to do what compilers and anthologists are rarely able to and draw material from a number of labels. The set starts back in 1957, with 'Straight Street' from the Prestige *Coltrane* and ends up in stellar regions with Rashied Ali. The four discs are awkwardly themed – 'Harmonic and Melodic', 'Rhythmic', 'Elvin and Trane' and 'Live'. There's only one previously unissued track and that is 'One Down, One Up', edited from the tail of 'Nature Boy' on *The John Coltrane Quartet Plays*. It might seem odd to single out Elvin Jones, but it's pretty clear that of the classic quartet members it was he who fuelled Trane's evolving and often misunderstood rhythmic vision; however much John relied on Rashied Ali towards the end, it was Jones who shaped his most important recordings. Given that there is so little new material, it's unlikely that this is going to appeal to any but completist collectors. Its value as an introduction is equally debatable, but it's probably the best of an indifferent bunch.

Ravi Coltrane (born 1965)

TENOR AND SOPRANO SAXOPHONES

John Coltrane's son – who was two when his father died – has taken his time about establishing himself on record, with numerous sideman appearances prior to his first American albums as a leader.

***** Moving Pictures**
RCA 74321 55887-2 *Coltrane; Ralph Alessi (t); Steve Coleman (as); Michael Cain (p); Lonnie Plaxico (b); Jeff 'Tain' Watts (d); Junior Gabu Wedderburn, Jeremiah McFarlane, Clyde Wedderburn (perc).* 10/97.

****(*) From The Round Box**
RCA 74321 73923-2 *Coltrane; Ralph Alessi (t, flhn); Geri Allen, Andy Milne (p); James Genus (b); Eric Harland (d).* 9–12/99.

Coltrane's patient progress is interesting if not exactly compelling to observe. Whatever expectations may have been heaped on his shoulders, the music and the man are clearly not in the business of major statements. While that may be admirable enough, the records are so far nothing special. *Moving Pictures* works under a thoughtful Steve Coleman production and is a measured, often inward-looking set of performances by the players. The Ancient Vibrations percussion trio makes three appearances and is notably effective on McCoy Tyner's 'Search For Peace'. Coleman and Coltrane each take a charge through Joe Henderson's 'Inner Urge', which brings a spark that the rest of the record turns away from.

As so often in this situation, Coltrane's originals both here and on *From The Round Box* seem pale next to the imported material. On the second disc, Wayne Shorter's 'Blues A La Carte' and Ornette Coleman's 'The Blessing' outclass the rest, and it seems almost perverse to begin a record with three originals as dreary as 'Social Drones' (by Alessi), 'The Chartreuse Mean' and 'Word Order'. 'Monk's Mood' is taken at a crawl. It could use some swinging. The closing doodle of 'Between Lines' sums up a disappointing record.

***** Mad 6**
Eighty-Eight's/Columbia 510884 2 *Coltrane; George Colligan, Andy Milne (p); James Genus, Darryl Hall (b); Steve Hass (d).* 5/02.

Coltrane Jr still sounds more like Joe Henderson and, in some moods, Dexter Gordon than he does his father. He certainly hasn't yet learned to harness the soprano's demons as John did. The choice of material here is suspect. The music hardly needs another version of 'Round Midnight' and there is not enough architecture to Ravi's version of 'Self-Portrait In Three Colours' to justify its inclusion. The opening '26-2' and the closing 'Fifth House' are much more promising vehicles and they prompt the best from all concerned. George Colligan demonstrates anew what a gifted and thoughtful player he can be and we could have done with more of him on this. The title-track is a brief oddity, its inclusion a sign of uncertainty more than of confidence. Ravi is a fine player, hampered by an impossible weight of expectation. All he lacks is a vision and a story to tell. The passing years may provide the latter.

Ken Colyer (1928–88)

CORNET, TRUMPET, GUITAR, VOCAL

The purist's purist, Colyer was born in Great Yarmouth and taught himself the cornet. He co-founded the Crane River Jazz Band, before joining the merchant navy and deserting in New Orleans, where he met idols like George Lewis. In 1953 he began bandleading in Britain with Chris Barber and subsequently led numerous bands based around the New Orleans sound. For a time in the '50s he also played guitar in a skiffle offshoot. His Studio 51 Club was an important traditional venue. Ill-health dogged his later years, but he stuck to his musical principles, always.

***** Vintage Ken Colyer**
Lake LACD 190 *Colyer; Chris Barber (tb, b); Monty Sunshine (cl); Lonnie Donegan (bj, v); Jim Bray (b, sou); Ron Bowden (d).* 5/53.

***** In The Beginning**
Lake LACD 014 *Colyer; Chris Barber, Ed O'Donnell (tb); Acker Bilk, Monty Sunshine (cl); Lonnie Donegan, Diz Disley (bj); Jim Bray, Dick Smith (b); Stan Greig, Ron Bowden (d).* 9/53–9/54.

***** The Unknown New Orleans Sessions**
504 CD 23 *Colyer; Albert Artigues (t); Jack Delaney (tb); Raymond Burke (cl); Stanley Mendelson (p); Edmond Souchon (g, v); Bill Huntington, Lawrence Marrero (bj); Dick Allen (tba); Alcide 'Slow Drag' Pavageau (b); Harold 'Katz' Maestri, Charles Merriweather, Abbie Brunies (d).* 12/52–2/53.

(***) The Complete 1953 Recordings
504 CD 53 *Colyer; Jarrison Brazlee (tb); Emil Barnes (cl); Bill Huntington (bj); Albert Glenny, George Fortier (b); Albert Jiles (d).* 2/53.

Colyer has a unique place in British jazz. Nobody has ever been more revered than he in local circles, and few were so righteously dogmatic about their music. At a time when the trad boom of the '50s was just getting under way, he abjured such 'modern' role models as Armstrong and Morton and insisted on the earlier New Orleans methods of George Lewis and Bunk Johnson. Colyer's records from the period emerge as an intriguing muddle of stiff British orthodoxy and something that finds a genuine accord with the music that obsessed him. The 504 sessions were made on Colyer's fabled visit to New Orleans – where he even spent time in the local jail for breaking immigration laws – and find the young cornetist sitting in with various local players. The tracks on *Unknown New Orleans Sessions* were lost for years and this is the first appearance for most of them: there's a real vitality and a bluff panache about the playing, with Colyer's deliberately primitive lead firmed up by the sheer force of his obsessions. Listeners should be warned, though, that the sound is inevitably pretty dingy. It's even worse on *The Complete 1953 Recordings*, which has all the music from two evenings spent at Emile Barnes's house on La Harpe Street. Colyer plays well with some of his spiritual forebears but it's hard to hear what's going on for much of the time. The two Lake records stand as an important document for British jazz, if only for the musicians involved – Barber, whose subsequent disagreements with the trumpeter led him to assume command of a different edition of the band; Bilk, whose erratic clarinet had yet to acquire the distinctive glow of his later records; Sunshine, who stayed with Barber and has since enjoyed an immortal reputation with European trad audiences; and Donegan, who became the major name in skiffle. If the music is comparatively stilted, its formal strictness pays off in the music's terseness.The tracks on the newly issued *Vintage Ken Colyer* were actually made in Copenhagen (or most were), and while the sound is a bit on and off, the original Colyer line-up is full of energy and the leader's own kind of bravado. The so-called skiffle tracks at the end are, though, pretty awful.

***** Studio 51 Revisited**
Lake LACD 25 *Colyer; Mac Duncan (tb); Ian Wheeler (cl); Ray Foxley (p); Johnny Bastable (bj); Ron Ward (b); Colin Bowden (d).* 58.

Studio 51 Revisited is a documentary of a typical night at Colyer's London headquarters, an echo now nearly 50 years old. The sound is surprisingly good, considering it was captured by one microphone slung from the ceiling, and again the music is all of a piece – tough, committed, rather unsmiling but rewarding on its own terms. Everything interlocks, everything works, and the band is all of a piece.

**** The Decca Skiffle Sessions**
Lake LACD 07 *Colyer; Bob Kelly (p); Alexis Korner (g, mand); Johnny Bastable (g, bj); Mickey Ashman, Ron Ward (b); Bill Colyer, Colin Bowden (wbd).* 6/54–11/57.

***** Captured Moments**
Upbeat URCD 165 *Colyer, Mac Duncan (tb); Ian Wheeler (cl); Peter Hunck, Diz Disley (bj); Dick Smith, Mukki Herman (b); Stan Greig (d, p); Bill Colyer (wbd).* 3/55.

***** Sensation!**
Lake LACD 1 *Colyer; Mac Duncan (tb); Ian Wheeler (cl); Ray Foxley (p); Johnny Bastable (bj); Dick Smith, Ron Ward (b); Stan Greig, Colin Bowden (d).* 4/55–5/59.

***** Marching Back To New Orleans**
Lake LACD 21 *As above, except add Bob Wallis, Sunny Murray (t), Mick Clift (tb), Dave Keir (as), Derek Easton (ts), Maurice Benn (tba), Neil Millet, Stan Greig (d).* 4/55–9/57.

*****(*) The Classic Years Vol. 2**
Upbeat YRCD 189 *Colyer; Mac Duncan (tb); Ian Wheeler (cl); Johnny Bastable (bj); Ron Ward (b); Colin Bowden (d).* 5/57.

***** Up Jumped The Devil**
Upbeat URCD114 *Colyer; Mac Duncan (tb); Ian Wheeler (cl); Ray Foxley (p); Johnny Bastable (bj); Ron Ward (b); Colin Bowden (d).* 57–58.

***** The Famous Manchester Free Trade Hall Concert 1957**
504 CD51/2 *As above, except add George Lewis (cl).* 4/57.

***** Serenading Auntie**
Upbeat URCD 111 *As above, except add Graham Stewart (tb), Sammy Rimington (cl), Dick Smith (b), Bill Colyer (wbd).* 6/55–8/60.

Colyer worked hard at his subject and, as the '50s progressed, his music became a genre unto itself. The most useful reissues include *Lonesome Road*, *Marching Back To New Orleans* and *Sensation!*, effectively an alternative live version of *Colyer Plays Standards*, although much of the material – 'Underneath The Bamboo Tree' and 'Bluebells Goodbye', to name two – would hardly be classed as standards in most band books. *Marching Back To New Orleans* opens with seven tracks from the session which produced *Sensation!* – including an uproarious 'Red Wing' – and then includes the entire date by the Omega Brass Band, where Colyer tried his hand at an 'authentic' New Orleans parade band: shambling, stentorian, it's a bizarre sound, and actually surprisingly close to the genuine article. Typically, Colyer refused to pick obvious tunes, and chose instead 'Isle Of Capri', 'Tiger Rag' and 'Gettysburg March', which occasionally rise in an almost hysterical crescendo. *Sensation!* collects various single and EP tracks, including all four from the sought-after *They All Played Ragtime* EP, which is in some ways Colyer's most distinctive achievement: it includes such rarities as 'Kinklets' (recorded by Bunk Johnson at his final session), 'Fig Leaf Rag' and what might be the first jazz version of 'The Entertainer', many years before Joshua Rifkin and *The Sting*. This is an ensemble music: Colyer was a reluctant soloist, and although Wheeler and Duncan are lively they struggle a bit when left on their own. Foxley is actually the most impressive improviser on the basis of *Lonesome Road*, reissued on LP some years ago but still to reach CD. Colyer's steady, unflashy lead, and the four-square but oddly hypnotic beat of the rhythm section (using a banjo to the end), still manage to add their own character. The one avoidable disc is *Skiffle Sessions*, which enshrines Colyer's heartfelt if bizarre interest in that movement. His own guitar-playing goes on like a machine, and though Korner, who at least knew how to play feasible blues, is also on hand, this is for the curious only.

Captured Moments is mostly from an NDR radio broadcast and benefits from the clear, if slightly thin, sound. All of Colyer's lugubrious announcements are left intact (he also patronizes what was even then a knowledgeable crowd). There are five further tracks from a set in a Dusseldorf bar. *The Classic Years Vol. 2* offers a set from Eel Pie Island, and the band sound is in rather better heart on home turf. Mostly familiar material, but this was something of a purple patch for Colyer and the playing is consistently good.

Up Jumped The Devil documents various live sessions at Studio 51. This was one of the best Colyer bands and, though the sound is rather muffled, their hard-won vitality breaks through to surprising effect. They manage to sustain 'Milneburg Joys' for chorus after chorus and, as sometimes happens in this kind of jazz, the sheer determination of the music becomes almost hypnotic. The concert tour with George Lewis was another legendary moment, and 504's documentation of their Manchester show, spread across two CDs, reeks of authenticity. The enthusiasm of the audience is infectious, and Lewis himself responds with his best form, even on chestnuts he'd played countless times. The sound is sometimes distant but mostly quite clear and clean.

Serenading Auntie splices together material from five different Colyer dates for the BBC (radio and even one TV session) over a five-year period. Some of the music seems a bit thin, as if they were cutting some of the tunes short, but on the ragtime material particularly the spirit abides, and there is one of Colyer's most wistful vocals on 'In The Evening'. One of the sessions sounds as if it's on a radio that's drifting on- and off-station, but the rest are all right.

CORE COLLECTION

***(*) Club Session With Colyer

Lake LACD 6 *Colyer; Mac Duncan (tb); Ian Wheeler (cl); Johnny Bastable (bj); Ron Ward (b); Colin Bowden (d).* 10–11/56.

Perhaps the essential Colyer record, and certainly his most famous single album, this catches the Colyer band at its most persuasive. The playing isn't noticeably superior to other Colyer records – consistency was the man's long suit, after all – but in its balance of blues, gospel and standards, its driving rhythms and clipped solos, it is as close to perfect as Colyer would get at a recording (actually made at the Railway Hotel in West Hampstead, and not at the regular haunt of Studio 51).

***(*) Colyer Plays Standards

Lake LACD 144 *Colyer; Mac Duncan (tb); Ian Wheeler (cl); Ray Foxley (p); Johnny Bastable (bj); Ron Ward (b); Colin Bowden (d).* 8/58.

The last great record by what some would have as the great Colyer line-up. Foxley's arrival may have dented the band's purism for some, but he certainly steadied the ensembles and the rhythm section. Excellent set-list, and everything well played.

*** In The Sweet Bye And Bye

Upbeat URCD 167 *Colyer; Mac Duncan (tb); Ian Wheeler (cl); Ray Foxley (p); Johnny Bastable (bj); Ron Ward (b); Colin Bowden (d).* 8/58.

*** Live At The 51 Club – 1960

Dine-A-Mite Jazz DJCD-003 *As above, except Graham Stewart (tb) and Sammy Rimington (cl) replace Duncan and Wheeler.* 7/60.

Call it Studio 51 or 51 Club, Colyer's Great Newport Street residency is one of the things that inscribed him in trad history in Britain, and these further survivals from their numberless nights there will presumably delight Colyer collectors; the less committed may wonder what the fuss is all about. Neither is exactly a hi-fi experience, although we've heard worse. The 1958 line-up is classic, some say the best Colyer had, but the brasher, lippier sound of the 1960 set may appeal more to some, with the 18-year-old Rimington already in hot form. If neither is a musical masterpiece, both reek of righteous atmosphere.

***(*) This Is The Blues

Lake LACD 188 *Colyer; Graham Stewart, Geoff Cole (tb); Sammy Rimington (cl); Little Brother Montgomery (p, v); Johnny Bastable (bj); Ron Ward (b); Colin Bowden, Pete Ridge (d).* 12/60–11/61.

A Denis Preston production, this all-blues programme has been handsomely remastered and makes a strong claim on even Colyer sceptics. A new line-up was finding its feet and Rimington's tone needed oiling, but the music is played with a fine dedication and everything sounds unexpectedly fresh. A bonus track features Colyer in duet with Little Brother Montgomery on 'Buddy Bolden's Blues', although Ken sounds a bit overawed.

**(*) When I Leave The World Behind

Lake LACD 19 *Colyer; Geoff Cole (tb); Sammy Rimington (cl); Johnny Bastable (bj); Ron Ward (b); Pete Ridge (d).* 3/63.

***(*) Colyer's Pleasure

Lake LACD 34 *As above.* 62–63.

*** On Tour

GHB BCD-16 *As above, except Bill Cole (b), Brian Hetherington (d) replace Ward and Ridge.* 65.

If everything on *When I Leave The World Behind* was as good as a terrifically swinging account of J. C. Higginbotham's 'Give Me Your Telephone Number', this would be a classic record. As it is, it's an interesting memento of Colyer's '60s band, playing a broad range of rags, King Oliver tunes, and other odds and ends. Rimington weaves interesting lines all through the music, Cole is a strong, hard-bitten trombonist; only the rhythm section, bothered by the pedestrian Ridge, is weaker. The recording, salvaged by Paul Adams from some private tapes, is variable and rather boomy, but it's listenable enough.

Much superior is *Colyer's Pleasure.* The band never sounded better in a studio (actually a pub back room), with Colyer and Rimington loud and clear, and the excellent set-list gets a varied and inventive treatment: 'Dardanella' is a classic performance. The original LP (once issued on the old budget label, Society) is augmented by five previously unissued acetates by the same band.

On Tour finds them in Malmö, Sweden, before a small but keen audience. It's a particularly interesting programme – 'Minstrel Man', 'Hilarity Rag', 'Swipsey Cakewalk', 'Ghost Soldier' – and the band sound in fine shape, although Hetherington's drums are on the brash side. Another surviving amateur tape: Colyer's archivists have always been a diligent crowd.

*** The Real Ken Colyer

Cadillac SGC 77 CD 02 *Colyer; Geoff Cole; Sammy Rimington (cl); Pat Hawes (p, v); Johnny Bastable (bj); Ron Ward (b); Pete Ridge (d).* 2/64.

Once issued on Doug Dobell's 77 label, this reappears with seven extra tracks, and is another good one, following a similar set-list to *When I Leave The World Behind* and making the most of it. Rimington, especially, sounds in top gear.

**(*) More Of Ken Colyer And His Handpicked Jazzmen

Ken Colyer Trust KCT3CD *Colyer; Mike Sherbourne (tb); Jack Gilbert (cl); Jim McIntosh (bj); Ray Holland (b); Tony Scriven (d).* 1/72.

*** Boston Church Service

GHB BCD-351 *Colyer; Barry Palser (tb); Sammy Rimington (cl); Ray Smith (p); Pete Morcom (bj); Alan Jones (b); Colin Bowden (d).* 6/72.

** Very Very Live At The 100 Club

Upbeat URCD 130 *Colyer; Keith Avison (tb); Sammy Rimington (cl); Ron Weatherburn (p); John Griffith (bj); Annie Hawkins (b); Colin Bowden (d).* 6/72.

*** Won't You Come Along With Me

Ken Colyer Trust KCT5CD *Colyer; Dale Vickers (tb); Chris Blount (cl); Pete Trevor (p); John Bly, Dave Brennan (bj); Harry Slater (b); Mike Ellis (d).* 10/73–12/77.

*** Ken Colyer In Holland

Music Mecca 1032-2 *Colyer; Cor Fabrie (tb); Butch Thompson (cl); Jos Koster (bj); Ad Van Beerendonk (b); Emiel Leybaert (d).* 11/76.

**(*) Urgent Request

GHB BCD-184 *Colyer; Dale Vickers (tb); Chris Blount (cl); Ray Smith (p); Dave Brennan (bj); Harry Slater (b); Mick Ellis (d).* 11/78.

Colyer disbanded his regular group in 1971, partly due to illness, and these are mementoes of the motley situations he found himself in after that. *Boston Church Service* is one of his most interesting latter-day discs. The church was actually an enormous gothic-looking pile in Lincolnshire; the band play mostly sacred tunes and they are blessed by an unexpectedly fine concert sound: a good one. The earlier KCT disc comes in clean sound and the band sound very enthusiastic, but this is a ragbag affair which could use a little finesse. Colyer played with Chris Blount's pro-am group many times in the early to mid-'70s and *Won't You Come Along With Me* is a collection of scraps from various surviving live tapes. Much of the playing is pretty shambolic but there are some queerly affecting moments, such as the wistful singing by Colyer on 'Basin Street Blues' and the atmosphere of the East Midlands in the '70s which seems to permeate tracks that were cut in pubs in Derby, Ilkeston and Fadler Gate. *Very Very Live At The 100 Club* has plenty of atmosphere and Colyer and Rimington play soundly, but Avison's grotesque trombone doesn't help and the sound is pretty scruffy. *Urgent Request* is from a date in Derby where Ken sat in with Chris Blount's band and, if the music goes off well enough, there's little to remember. *In Holland* finds Ken joining the long-established Storyville Jazzband, who sound rather better than he does: much of his trumpet work from this period seems to get by on irascibility alone. A solid programme, in listenable sound.

****(*) A Boston Concert**

Upbeat URCD 167 *Colyer; Barry Palser (tb); Sammy Rimington (cl, as); Ray Smith (p); Pete Morcom (bj); Alan Jones (b); Colin Bowden (d).* 6/72.

***** Once More For Auntie**

Upbeat URCD 137 *Colyer; Sonny Morris (t); Len Baldwin (tb); John Wurr, Gerry Turnham, Monty Sunshine (cl); John R. T. Davies (as, bs, tb); Ray Smith, Pat Hawes (p); Stu Morrison, Bill Stotesbury, Ben Marshall (bj); Mickey Ashman, Arthur Bird, Julian Davies (b); Colin Bowden, Paul Rosenberg (d).* 8/72–3/75.

The raft of Colyer discoveries seems to sail on and on. Mike Pointon must be pulling our legs when he claims that Colyer's music 'is as controversial today ... as it ever was during his lifetime' in the *Boston Concert* notes. That aside, the band were in good spirits at Boston's Montmartre Club, although much is carried on the shoulders of the rhythm section and Rimington: Palser isn't much help and Ken sounds as if he's having an off day.

The main interest in the BBC sessions on *Once More For Auntie* are the five titles by the re-formed (for the occasion) Crane River Jazz Band, featuring Colyer and Morris as a two-horn front line, Sunshine, Davies, Hawes and the rest. Unfortunately this comes in the poorest sound of the three sessions, for some reason, but their assault on King Oliver's 'Wa Wa Wa' (a bit modern for Ken) has plenty of go in it. The two earlier dates are more routine, although the material does suggest how big Colyer's book had grown over the years: 'Daddy's Little Girl', 'It's Only A Paper Moon' and 'Cataract Rag' among the titles.

****(*) Jazz At The Strathallen**

Raymer Sound RSCD778 *Colyer; Len Baldwin (tb); Gerry Turnham (cl); Ray Smith (p); Bill Stotesbury (bj); Arthur Bird (b); Paul Rosenberg (d).* 1/78.

***** Winter Wonderland**

GHB BCD-435 *Colyer; Dave Vickers (tb); Chris Blount (cl); Ray Smith (p); Dave Brennan (bj); Harry Slater (b); Paul Rosenberg (d).* 12/79.

And still they keep coming. The Strathallen line-up wasn't all that good, with some decrepit-sounding trombone from Len Baldwin, but the music's cheerful enough and there's an interesting choice in Sam Morgan's 'Short Dress Gal'. *Winter Wonderland* has better playing all round, although some tunes do ramble on – 'Winter Wonderland' itself goes over the ten-minute mark and for some reason Colyer sings the entire lyric twice over. Respectable sound on both discs.

***** Blame It On The Blues**

Azure AZ-CD-33 *Colyer; Jean-François Bonnel (cl); Paul Sealey (bj, g); Ken Ames (b).* 1/85.

***** Wrap Your Troubles In Dreams**

Azure AZ-CD-34 *As above.* 1/85.

**** Too Busy**

CMJ 008 *Colyer; Les Hanscombe (tb); Dave Bailey (cl); Tim Phillips (bj); Keith Donald (b); John Petters (d).* 2/85.

****(*) Together Again**

Lake LACD 53 *Colyer; Les Hanscombe (tb); Acker Bilk (cl); Pat Hawes (p); Brian Mitchell (bj); Julian Davies (b); Pete Lay (d).* 7/85.

Colyer's illness cut him down in the end, and his later recordings are a mix of sad decline and a reflective, almost introspective approach as he adapted his circumstances to his music. There's no better example than *Blame It On The Blues*, which features a gentle, airy quartet working patiently through ten favourites at London's Pizza Express. Bonnel is a deferential partner and the sound is lovely. *Wrap Your Troubles In Dreams* is a second helping from the same occasion, and really is just as good: Colyer's playing on the closing 'Trouble In Mind' is more specifically emotive than he usually allowed himself to be, and it makes a rather poignant valediction. *Too Busy* is missable: Colyer guests with the John Petters group, and he is clearly taking things very gingerly. The band plays decent, fat-free trad, but the trumpeter's own contribution is unexceptional. He is, alas, also the weak link on *Together Again*, a surprise reunion with Bilk, again at the Pizza Express. Hawes has a bad time with the awful 'old' PE piano and Colyer's lead sounds very shaky; the stars are for Acker, returning to some heartland repertoire and again proving himself one of our best jazzmen.

Company

FLEXIBLE IMPROVISING ENSEMBLE

First organized by Derek Bailey as a week of 1977 concerts in London, where a pool of improvisers played together over the course of an evening in a series of more or less ad hoc groupings. It grew into a sequence of such events stretching over many years, until Bailey called a halt in the '90s. Probably most of them were recorded, but only a small number have actually emerged in CD form; several vinyl-only records are long since gone.

****** Company 6 & 7**

Incus CD07 *Derek Bailey (g); Wadada Leo Smith (t, f); Anthony Braxton (as, ss, f, cl); Evan Parker (ts, ss); Lol*

Coxhill, Steve Lacy (ss); Steve Beresford (p, g); Tristan Honsinger (clo); Maarten van Regteren Altena (b). 5/77.

****** Once**

Incus CD04 *Derek Bailey (g); Lee Konitz (as, ss); Richard Teitelbaum (ky); Carlos Zingaro (vn); Tristan Honsinger (clo); Barre Phillips (b); Steve Noble (perc, bugle). 5/87.*

****** Company 91**

Incus CD16 *Yves Robert (tb); John Zorn (as); Derek Bailey, Buckethead (g); Alexander Balanescu (vn); Paul Rogers (b); Paul Lovens (perc); Pat Thomas (elec, ky); Vanessa Mackness (v). 91.*

****** Company 91**

Incus CD17 *As above. 91.*

*****(*) Company 91**

Incus CD18 *As above. 91.*

Incus, the label Derek Bailey co-founded in 1970 with saxophonist Evan Parker and drummer Tony Oxley, has dedicated part of its catalogue to the documentation of the occasions when Bailey brought together groups of British and international improvisers, some with a free-jazz background, some coming more from a classical environment, for a weekend or week of unstructured improvisation. Company was founded in 1977 and became the most important locus of free improvisation in Britain during its existence. It is, of course, moot whether existential performances which admit of no gap between conception and execution and which are completely conditioned by intuition really belong on record. What is remarkable about the above records (and the vanished LPs recorded at other events) is the extent to which they remain compellingly listenable long after the occasion of their performance is past; newcomers are directed particularly to *Once* and *6 & 7* which seem to encapsulate the challenges and beauties of Company in equal measure.

The music is extremely difficult to quantify or categorize. It was clear from the earlier encounters that it was necessary to negotiate a divide between free music which owned to no generic ties and a deep structure drawn from jazz. The first Company Week proper was in 1977, and it is fondly remembered for the then rare chance to see important overseas players like Braxton, Smith and Lacy playing with the Europeans. However, the visiting Americans (notably Braxton) appeared to find the radical and collective freedom on which Bailey quietly insisted rather unsettling; against that, both Steve Lacy and, much more surprisingly, former Tristano disciple Lee Konitz (who took part in the 1987 Company documented on *Once*) have managed to assimilate their notably dry approach to Bailey's. It's very instructive to compare what Parker does with Braxton here and on their 1993 London duo released on Leo (for which, see under Braxton's entry). As so often, it's the smaller combinations that stick in the mind. Tristan Honsinger's duo with Leo Smith on the same record is a tiny masterpiece.

Perhaps because Company Weeks are no longer annual events, the 1991 gathering is remembered with special clarity and affection and amply merits such full documentation. As always, the line-up included players not usually associated with the free-music scene, and the set begins, appropriately, with a duo by the classically trained Vanessa Mackness and classical violinist Alex Balanescu who, having got the remaining starch out of his instrument, simply goes for it. His duo with Bailey on Volume 2 is almost equally good. One of the oddities of 1991 was the inclusion of the heavy metal guitarist, Buckethead, who performs in mask and costume. The trio on Volume 2 which features him with Zorn and the young British improviser, Pat Thomas, was one of the high points of the week, though the chemistry didn't work quite so well when the guitarist joined Rogers and Balanescu (a duo would have been good) at the end of that same disc. The final part documents the Friday and Saturday. Historically, musical relationships are expected to develop as the week advances. There were signs in 1991, though, that some were unravelling. The performances on Volume 3 are by no means so well calibrated, and there are signs of weariness in the American ranks. That said, this disc is dominated by Zorn, first in duo with Robert (a quirky and unpredictable performer) and then with various larger combinations. The set ends with a noisy exchange between Bailey and Buckethead to which the audience makes an equally noisy contribution.

Eddie Condon (1905–73)

GUITAR

Born in Indiana, Condon became the quintessential Chicago jazzman, though he actually spent relatively little of his career there. A ringleader of the gang of young white players in Chicago in the '20s, he arrived in New York in 1928 and hustled his way to prominence, forming famous associations with the Commodore record label, Nick's club and eventually his own place, on West Third Street. He appeared frequently on radio and later on TV. He toured extensively in the '50s and '60s but was finally slowed up by illness. As a rhythm guitarist, he was often barely audible, but he was unassumingly talented.

CORE COLLECTION

****** Eddie Condon 1927–1938**

Classics 742*Condon; Jimmy McPartland, Bobby Hackett (c); Max Kaminsky, Leonard Davis (t); George Brunies, Floyd O'Brien, Jack Teagarden (tb); Mezz Mezzrow, Frank Teschemacher, Pee Wee Russell (cl); Bud Freeman, Happy Caldwell (ts); Alex Hill, Jess Stacy, Joe Sullivan (p); Jim Lannigan, Artie Bernstein, Artie Shapiro, Art Miller (b); George Wettling, Gene Krupa, Johnny Powell, George Stafford, Big Sid Catlett (d). 12/27–4/38.*

Condon was the focus of Chicago jazz from the '20s to the '40s, garnering a personal reputation that far exceeds his actual musical significance. He is now best seen as a catalyst, a man who made things happen and in the process significantly heightened the profile of Dixieland jazz in America. He was rarely anything more than a straightforward rhythm guitarist, generally avoiding solos, but he had a clear sense of what his role ought to be and frequently laid out to give the piano-player more room. His chords have a rather melancholy ring, but are always played dead centre.

The Classics discs offer a chronological overview of a career that didn't get seriously under way on record until the '40s. The five sessions from the '20s are key staging-posts in the evolution of Chicago jazz, starting with the four classic titles cut by the McKenzie–Condon Chicagoans in 1927, in which McPartland and the ill-fated Teschemacher made up a superbly vibrant front line. Two 1929 sessions feature some top-notch early Teagarden, and the 1933 band date includes the original versions of Freeman's famous turn on 'The Eel'.

But it then goes quiet until the first sessions for Commodore in 1938, the start of another classic Condon era.

****** Eddie Condon 1938–1940**

Classics 759 *As above, except add Muggsy Spanier (c), Marty Marsala (t), Miff Mole, Vernon Brown (tb), Brad Gowans (vtb), Joe Bushkin, Fats Waller (p), Clyde Newcombe (b), Lionel Hampton, Dave Tough (d); omit McPartland, Davis, O'Brien, Mezzrow, Teschemacher, Caldwell, Hill, Lannigan, Bernstein, Miller, Krupa, Powell, Stafford, Catlett.* 4/38–11/40.

*****(*) Eddie Condon 1942–1943**

Classics 772 *As above, except add Yank Lawson (t), Benny Morton (tb), Gene Schroeder (p), Al Morgan, Bob Casey (b), Tony Sbarbaro (d); omit Spanier, Marsala, Mole, Brown, Waller, Newcombe, Hackett, Hampton, Tough, Teagarden.* 1/42–12/43.

***** Chicago Style**

ASV AJA 5192 *As above discs.* 27–40.

*****(*) Eddie Condon 1944–1946**

Classics 1033 *Condon; Bobby Hackett, Wild Bill Davison (c); Hot Lips Page (t, v); Sterling Bose, Billy Butterfield, Max Kaminsky, Yank Lawson (t); Lou McGarity, Miff Mole, Jack Teagarden, Fred Ohms (tb); Brad Gowans (vtb); Pee Wee Russell, Edmond Hall, Tony Parenti (cl); Joe Dixon (cl, bs); Bud Freeman (ts); Ernie Caceres (bs); Gene Schroeder, Joe Bushkin, Jess Stacy, James P. Johnson (p); Bob Casey, Bob Haggart, Sid Weiss, Jack Lesberg (b); Dave Tough, Joe Grauso, George Wettling, Johnny Blowers (d); Lee Wiley, Bubbles Sublett (v).* 3/44–7/46.

****(*) Eddie Condon In Japan**

Chiaroscuro GRD 154 *Condon; Buck Clayton (t); Vic Dickenson (tb); Bud Freeman (ts); Pee Wee Russell (cl); Dick Cary (p, ahn); Jack Lesberg (b); Cliff Leeman (d); Jimmy Rushing (v).*

The MCA compilation of studio sessions from the early '40s has been dumped, so follow the story on Classics 772 and 1033. Here are most of the Condon stalwarts playing to three-minute, 78-r.p.m. length, tucking small, gem-like solos into otherwise powerhouse ensembles – the rhythm sections were always good – and making all the choruses count. They may have had dubious reputations off the bandstand, but Condon's men were disciplined about their kind of jazz. Classics 1033 features three V-Disc titles (Lips Page sings 'Uncle Sam's Blues' on one of them), but the sessions otherwise originate from Decca. The mysterious Bubbles Sublett sings on 'Atlanta Blues' (which is misnumbered on the sleeve).

The Commodore dates take up most of the next two Classics CDs. Relaxed but smart, graceful and hot at the same time, Condon's various bands made eloquent jazz out of what were already becoming Dixieland warhorses. The four-part version of 'A Good Man Is Hard To Find' from 1940 is a little masterpiece, but almost anything from these sessions has its memorable moments, and players like Kaminsky, Brunies and Bushkin never found a better context to work in. All these discs are recommended, but transfers (from unlisted sources) are, as usual, a mixed bunch – though Commodore's own recording could vary from session to session. The ASV compilation is a good bet for anyone wanting a single disc from the period, covering most of the early dates and adding some titles by Billy Banks, Joe Marsala and Bud Freeman.

Condon enjoyed a long and successful association with Columbia, which released a substantial body of work in the '50s; some of it has come back in the Collectables releases listed below. The live set from Japan is rather poorly balanced and a little makeshift, but still worthwhile for Condonites.

*****(*) The Town Hall Concerts Vol. 1**

Jazzology JCD 1001/2 2CD *Collective personnel for this and following ten discs: Condon; Muggsy Spanier, Dick Cary (c); Billy Butterfield, Sterling Bose, Bobby Hackett, Jonah Jones, Hot Lips Page, Max Kaminsky, Wingy Manone, Yank Lawson (t); Jack Teagarden, Bill Harris, Benny Morton, Miff Mole, Lou McGarity, Tommy Dorsey, Vernon Brown (tb); Pee Wee Russell, Joe Marsala, Edmond Hall, Jimmy Dorsey, Hank D'Amico (cl); Sidney Bechet (ss); Ernie Caceres (bs, cl); Gene Schroeder, James P. Johnson, Willie 'The Lion' Smith, Norma Teagarden, Jess Stacy, Cliff Jackson, Dave Bowman (p); Carl Kress (g); Bob Haggart, Bob Casey, Jack Lesberg, Johnny Williams, Sid Weiss (b); George Wettling, Joe Grauso, Cozy Cole, Gene Krupa, Rolo Layon, Johnny Blowers, Danny Alvin, Big Sid Catlett (d); Lee Wiley, Red McKenzie, Harry The Hipster Gibson (v).* 6/44.

*****(*) The Town Hall Concerts Vol. 2**

Jazzology JCD 1003/4 2CD *As above.* 6/44.

****** The Town Hall Concerts Vol. 3**

Jazzology JCD 1005/6 2CD *As above.* 7/44.

*****(*) The Town Hall Concerts Vol. 4**

Jazzology JCD 1007/8 2CD *As above.* 8/44.

*****(*) The Town Hall Concerts Vol. 5**

Jazzology JCD 1009/1010 2CD *As above.* 9/44.

***** The Town Hall Concerts Vol. 6**

Jazzology JCD 1011/2 2CD *As above.* 10/44.

****** The Town Hall Concerts Vol. 7**

Jazzology JCD 1013/4 2CD *As above.* 11/44.

***** The Town Hall Concerts Vol. 8**

Jazzology JCD 1015/6 2CD *As above.* 12/44.

*****(*) The Town Hall Concerts Vol. 9**

Jazzology JCD 1017/8 2CD *As above.* 1/45.

*****(*) The Town Hall Concerts Vol. 10**

Jazzology JCD 1019/20 2CD *As above.* 2–3/45.

*****(*) The Town Hall Concerts Vol. 11**

Jazzology JCD 1021/2/3 3CD *As above.* 3–4/45.

Condon's Town Hall concerts became an institution on radio during 1944–5, and Jazzology's superb edition has put together all 46 of them. Each of these packages contains four half-hour shows, compèred with a mixture of genial bonhomie and irascibility by Condon himself. He credits every player, sets the beat up for every number, kids around at the expense of most of the others (but especially the benighted Pee Wee Russell) and makes sure that proper standards of Dixieland are maintained at all times. Choosing among the discs is a little invidious since all of them are patchy, all are occasionally troubled by the sound (which is, though, usually quite listenable) and each falls back on routine instead of inspiration at some point. But the general standard of music is surprisingly high, given the show-biz feel of some of the situations. The second volume has a tribute to Fats Waller, the third a tribute to Bix Beiderbecke. If Russell is consistently the star player, there are often precious glimpses of men who would seldom make much more music in the studios: Spanier, Mole, Marsala, Manone. *Volume 7*, which features Jack and Norma Teagarden as guest stars, is a very good one, and perhaps the best to sample. *Volume 10* brings in regular guest Sidney Bechet, who usually gets a feature or two to himself, and has the coup of getting both Dorsey brothers into one of the bands. *Volume 11* is extended to a third disc and includes two try-out shows for a Chesterfield sponsorshop which ultimately never happened. All of them have period feel and excellent music in great measure, a lasting tribute to Condon's bluff expertise and an incomparably valuable document of a particular moment in the music's course.

***** Eddie Condon 1947–1950**

Classics 1177 *Condon; Wild Bill Davison (c); Bobby Hackett, Max Kaminsky, Yank Lawson, Johnny Windhurst (t); Jack Teagarden, Cutty Cutshall (tb, v); Will Bradley (tb); Dick Cary (ahn); Peanuts Hucko (cl, ts); Pee Wee Russell, Edmond Hall (cl); Ernie Caceres (bs); Gene Schroeder (p, cel); Joe Bushkin, Ralph Sutton (p); Jack Lesberg, Bill Goodall (b); George Wettling, Johnny Blowers, Big Sid Catlett, Buzzy Drootin (d); Jimmy Atkins, Peggy Ann Ellis (v).* 8/47–10/50.

There's a single date for Atlantic in 1949, but otherwise these titles were all made for Decca. The first six tracks feature Teagarden vocals and range from the feeble 'Tulip Time In Holland' to a great here's-the-band routine on 'We Called It Music'. Any gathering of Condon tracks is going to offer a striking variety of styles, even within his own conventions, and here there's the ferocious Davison, the elegant Hackett, and the contrasting clarinets of Hucko, Russell and Hall. There are rag features for Sutton (on what sounds like a tack piano), Atkins sings the rarely-heard lyrics to both 'At The Jazz Band Ball' and 'Jazz Me Blues' and Peggy Ann Ellis croons 'Black Bottom'. Some of the later pieces have a more commercial bent and sound more like Dixieland routine than is usual with Condon, but it remains an engaging set. Transfers seem fair, though the Atlantic tracks have a lot of hiss.

***** Dr Jazz Vol. 1: Eddie Condon With Johnny Windhurst, No. 1**

Storyville STCD 6041 *Johnny Windhurst (t); Cutty Cutshall (tb); Edmond Hall (cl); Gene Schroeder (p); Bob Casey, Bill Goodall (b); Cliff Leeman, Buzzy Drootin, Monk Herbert (d).* 1–6/52.

***** Dr Jazz Vol. 8: Eddie Condon With Johnny Windhurst No. 2**

Storyville STCD 6048 *As above, except add Condon; omit Goodall, Herbert.* 1–5/52.

***** Dr Jazz Vol. 5: Eddie Condon With Wild Bill Davison**

Storyville STCD 6045 *As above, except add Wild Bill Davison (c), Ralph Sutton (p), Bill Goodall (b), Don Lamond, George Wettling (d); omit Windhurst.* 12/51–3/52.

Radio broadcasts from Eddie's club, dating from the early '50s. Sound is occasionally scruffy but decent enough. The main point of the first two discs is to hear the seldom-recorded Windhurst whose blend of Armstrong and Hackett gave his playing a lovely dancing quality that still manages to power a front line. Obvious material, but worth a listen; as is the disc with Davison, though given his ubiquitous discography, this scarcely goes down as essential. Condon doesn't play on the first disc, but he turns up here and there on the other two.

***** Eddie Condon 1951–1953**

Classics 1354 *Condon; Wild Bill Davison (c); Dick Cary (t); Cutty Cutshall (tb); Ed Hall, Peanuts Hucko (cl); Gene Schroeder (p); Bob Casey, Walter Page (b); Buzzy Drootin, Cliff Leeman (d).* 12/51–11/53.

Most of this is made up of the Savoy *Ringside At Condon's* sessions, which seemed designed to re-create the experience of a night at Eddie's place (with dubbed-in applause) for home-body listeners. The sound is rather scruffy and it puts a less than flattering spin on the solos by Davison, Cutshall and Hall. The last four tracks are from Columbia's *Jam Session Coast-To-Coast*, but that duplicates with the Collectables issue listed below.

*****(*) Jam Session Coast-To-Coast / Jammin' At Condon's**

Collectables 7526 *Condon; Wild Bill Davison (c); Billy Butterfield (t); Cutty Cutshall, Lou McGarity (tb); Dick Cary (ahn); Ed Hall, Peanuts Hucko (cl); Bud Freeman (ts); Gene Schroeder (p); Walter Page, Al Hall (b); Cliff Leeman (d).* 11/53–7/54.

****** Bixieland / Treasury Of Jazz**

Collectables 7526 *As above, except add Bobby Hackett (c), Pee Wee Russell (cl), George Wettling (d), omit McGarity.* 4/55–1/56.

***** Midnight In Moscow / The Roaring Twenties**

Collectables 7517 *Condon; Billy Butterfield, Bobby Hackett, Wild Bill Davison (t); Cutty Cutshall, Vic Dickenson, Lou McGarity (tb); Bob Wilber, Peanuts Hucko (cl); Dick Cary (p, ahn); Gene Schroeder (p); Leonard Gaskin, Jack Lesberg (b); George Wettling, Buzzy Drootin (d).* 6/57–1/62.

At last some of the Condon sessions from the LP era have made it to CD, via these Collectables reissues, originally released on Columbia. The classic LP out of this group is certainly *Bixieland*, a rare example of a Condon concept album, devoted to tunes associated with Bix Beiderbecke. The cornet role is shared between Bill Davison and Bobby Hackett, and both acquit themselves admirably, in part because they see no need to try and copy Bix – in fact, none of these renditions makes any effort to duplicate the originals. It's in the spirit, but it's Condonian. The *Treasury Of Jazz* sessions introduce Russell back into the fold, and he is outstanding on 'Three-Two-One Blues'. In clean sound, this is a classic Condon collection.

Although the other two aren't far behind. *Jam Session* is nicely informal, but the band are right on their toes; *Jammin' At Condon's* doubles the normal size of the group and features twice as many horns as usual, with 'How Come You Do Me Like You Do' full to bursting at nearly 13 minutes in length. *The Roaring Twenties*, from 1957, has the felicitous front line of Davison, Dickenson and Wilber, and Wettling stokes them along at a terrific pace on the likes of 'Wolverine Blues', 'China Boy' and 'That's A Plenty'. The strange set here is the 1962 *Midnight In Moscow* (and it seems odd hearing anyone but Kenny Ball tackling the title tune). Besides that track, the rest make up a kind of travelogue, with 'Loch Lomond', 'Londonderry Air' and 'Theme From Swan Lake' all included; not very Condonian at all.

Chris Connor (born 1929)

VOCAL

Born in Kansas, she started out with Claude Thornhill, then joined Stan Kenton in 1952. Thereafter she worked as a soloist, recording many albums for Bethlehem and Atlantic. Only occasional records in the '60s and '70s, but she was more visible in the '80s.

CORE COLLECTION

****** Chris Connor**

Atlantic 7567-80769-2 *Connor; Nick Travis (t); Sam Marowitz, Ray Beckenstein (as); Zoot Sims (ts); Danny Bank (bs); John Lewis, Moe Wechsler (p); Barry Galbraith (g); Oscar Pettiford, Milt Hinton (b); Connie Kay, Osie Johnson (d).* 1–2/56.

The cool vocalist *par excellence*. Connor's records for Bethlehem and Atlantic showcased the ex-Kenton singer in a way that led to some definitive interpretations; her versions of 'Ev'ry Time', 'It's All Right With Me', 'I Wonder What Became Of Me' and several more are unlikely to be bettered. She has remained something of a cult figure, but in her prime she sold records to a wide audience and several of her Atlantics were considerable hits in their way. The debut, *Chris Connor*, is a welcome revival in Atlantic's 50th anniversary programme. Four tracks with the quartet of Lewis, Galbraith, Pettiford and Kay – a band that should have made its own record – are a marvel, and so is 'When The Wind Was Green'. Her open-vowel sounds have an oddly yearning quality which is heightened by the way she can sing low notes very softly, yet make them emphatic.

*****(*) Chris Connor / He Loves Me, He Loves Me Not**

Collectables COL-CD-6239 *As above, except add Ralph Burns Orchestra.* 56.

Collectables have coupled Chris's first two Atlantics in a very attractive two-on-one, although the stereo mix is rather glaring on the first disc and there seems to be an unwonted amount of echo on some tracks. For some unexplained reason, they also leave off two tracks from the debut (one of which is the sublime 'When The Wind Was Green') and substitute two alternatives. Still, it's good to have all of the fine *He Loves Me, He Loves Me Not* in one place, with its oustanding versions of 'Angel Eyes' and 'About The Blues'.

*****(*) I Miss You So / Witchcraft**

Collectables COL-CD-6814 *Connor; orchestras led by Ray Ellis and Richard Wess.* 7/56–9/59.

Connor cut a third LP in 1956, *I Miss You So*, and here it's coupled with the later *Witchcraft*. The earlier record is mostly ballads, and mostly given a more MOR treatment, although the singing remains superbly involving. *Witchcraft* is in more of a high-stepping vein, courtesy of Richard Wess's bouncy charts, but there are some very good songs, which Connor does well with – 'Baltimore Oriole', 'Like A Woman' and an excellent 'Lady Sings The Blues'.

****** Sings The George Gershwin Almanac Of Song**

Atlantic 2-601 2CD *Connor; Joe Newman, Doc Severinsen (t); Eddie Bert, Jimmy Cleveland, Jim Thompson, Warren Covington (tb); Sam Most, Peanuts Hucko (cl); Herbie Mann (f); Eddie Wasserman, Al Cohn (ts); Danny Bank (bs); Ralph Sharon, Stan Free, Hank Jones (p); Barry Galbraith, Joe Puma, Mundell Lowe (g); Milt Jackson (vib); Wendell Marshall, Milt Hinton, Oscar Pettiford, Vinnie Burke (b); Osie Johnson, Ed Shaughnessy, Ronnie Free (d); Johnny Rodriguez (perc).* 7/57.

Connor's Gershwin collection is almost as comprehensive as Fitzgerald's, in the company of seven different instrumental groups. Trifles such as 'Bla Bla Bla' or 'I Can't Be Bothered Now' are graced with thoughtful readings, the swingers dispatched unhurriedly, the ballads lingered over; despite the size of the project, there's no sense of routine. A much-neglected songbook project.

***** Two's Company**

Roulette 37201-2 *Connor; Maynard Ferguson, Chet Ferretti, Rolf Ericson, Bill Berry (t); Ray Winslow, Kenny Rupp (tb); Lanny Morgan (as, f); Joe Farrell (ts, ss, cl); Willie Maiden (ts); Frank Hittner (bs); Jaki Byard (p); John Neves (b); Rufus Jones (d).* 61.

One of two albums Connor made with the Maynard Ferguson orchestra. There are haunting versions of Alec Wilder's 'Where Do You Go' and 'The Wind', but some of the swingers go off the scale in the Ferguson manner, and 'Guess Who I Saw Today' belongs to Nancy Wilson.

***** Haunted Heart**

High Note HCD 7079 *Connor; Ingrid Jensen (t, flhn); Bill Easley (ts); Michael Abene (p); Chip Jackson, Steve LaSpina (b); Dennis Mackrel (d).* 3/01.

****(*) I Walk With Music**

High Note HCD 7095 *As above, except add Jack Wilkins (g), Memo Acevedo (v); omit Jensen and LaSpina; add strings.* 5/02.

Connor in the new century. Michael Abene's sympathetic arrangements set out to take care of Chris, and while some of the quicker pieces are risky business ('By Myself' was a wrong step as the opener), she does better by the more quiescent tunes, like 'Stairway To the Stars'. 'Drinking Again' is a hurtful place to finish. It's a sometimes eerie record, which lives on its memories a little, although Connor's artistry carries her through.

I Walk With Music is a return visit with much the same band. Chris never seems to have had much luck with 'contemporary' songs, and some of these weren't inspired picks. It works best when she gets to place her trust in classic virtues, such as the slow version of 'How High The Moon' and 'Shall We Dance' (the Gershwin one).

Bill Connors (born 1949)

GUITAR

Second-generation fusion guitarist with a sequence of moody records from the '70s and mid-'80s.

***** Theme To The Guardian**

ECM 829387-2 *Connors (g solo).* 11/74.

***** Of Mist And Melting**

ECM 847324-2 *Connors; Jan Garbarek (ts, ss); Gary Peacock (b); Jack DeJohnette (d).* 12/77.

***** Swimming With A Hole In My Body**

ECM 849078-2 *Connors (g solo).* 8/79.

Once Chick Corea's guitarist in Return To Forever, Connors shares his old boss's galling tendency to short-change exceptional technical ability with rather bland and self-indulgent ideas. The later trios have a certain energy and immediacy, but they're crude in comparison to the Corea-influenced solo projects. Connors's acoustic work is finely detailed and there are some interesting things on *Swimming*, albeit worked out in a shut-off, self-absorbed way that, like a lot of Allan Holdsworth's work, may appeal to guitar technicians but which can be curiously off-putting for everyone else. *Theme*, long in the tooth now, was probably the most satisfactory of the bunch until *Of Mist And Melting* reappeared on CD; the presence of Garbarek and of a rhythm section that cooks along in a dark strain adds quantifiably to the range, yielding more of his typically tense atmospheric pieces.

Contraband

GROUP

Organized and led by trombonist Willem van Manen, this Dutch big band follows a line somewhere between the Willem Breuker Kollektief and the more strait-laced jazz orchestras of middle Europe.

*****(*) Live At The Bimhuis**

Bvhaast 8906 *Toon De Gouw, Louis Lanzing, Ad Gruter (t); Willem van Manen, Hans Sparla, Hans Visser (tb); Theo Jörgensmann, Paul van Kamenade, Rutger van Otterloo, Maarten van Norden, Eckard Koltermann (reeds); Ron van Rossum (p); Hein Offermans (b); Martin van Duynhoven (d).* 11/88.

*****(*) De Ruyter Suite**

Bvhaast 9104 *As above, except Chris Abelen (tb), Jeroen van Vliet (p), Eric van der Westen (b) replace Sparla, Van Rossum and Offermans.* 4/91.

***** Boy Edgar Suite**

VPRO EW 9412 *As above, except Frans Vermeersen (reeds), Charles Huffstadt (d) replace Van Norden and Van Duynhoven.* 5/94.

Contraband is Willem van Manen's 'occasional' big band. The trombonist and veteran of Holland's post-bop and free-music scene is a skilled and dynamic composer-arranger, and the first two records – the first live, the second studio, and both written almost entirely by van Manen – are packed with incident. The group delivers all the power and finesse of the great big bands, and it glories in soloists who crackle their way out of complex charts. But sometimes there are hints of strain or of over-familiar effects – clustering muted trumpets or high reeds, for instance, or fast cutting from passages of rigid orthodoxy to all-out freedom – which suggest that it's a best-of-both-worlds which the band can't quite grasp. It would be churlish, though, to deny the vividness, sweep and panache of a band which ought to be far better known than it is. 'Contra-Suit' from the live record, and the three-part title-piece of *De Ruyter Suite*, dedicated to Dutch critic Michiel de Ruyter, are grand yet wholly coherent big-scale structures, and the soloists – especially Jörgensmann on clarinet and Van Kamenade on alto – refuse to dilute the intensity of the whole band.

Boy Edgar Suite may disappoint some in that Van Manen's two pieces are presented rather soberly, one a tribute to the Dutch jazz eminence, Boy Edgar, the other a threnody for Miles Davis. The other composition, Eckard Koltermann's two-part 'Constant Pictures', is rather more boisterous and has a particularly fine solo from Chris Abelen. All that said, Contraband 94 (as they are billed) are in fine shape, with the brass sections colouring Van Manen's scores with characteristic aplomb; and the composer's own improvisation in Part Three of the 'Edgar Suite' is especially gripping.

*****(*) Hitit**

Bvhaast 9802 *Toon De Gouw, Louis Lanzing, Willem Schoenmaker (t); Willem van Manen, Chris Abelen, Hans Visser (tb); Theo Jörgensmann, Paul van Kamenade, Rutger van Otterloo, Frans Vermeersen, Eckard Koltermann (reeds); Stevko Busch (p); Arnold Dooyeweerd (b); Charles Huffstadt (d).* 12/97.

Contraband have grown into a complex entity. Willem van Manen seems to have an awkward relationship with the prevailing mummery of big-band music: he likes to make things swing, and he leaves necessary space for jazz solos in all his pieces, but his scores have the intricacy and flavour of different composing traditions, and sometimes one can hear him wrestling with his various angels. His four pieces here (there is a fifth by Chris Abelen) refer to jazz rather than revelling in it, and it's a progression which can be traced from *Live At The Bimhuis* to here. There is also little in the way of theatre, satire or some of the other staples which this school is supposed to dwell on. In its undemonstrative way, this is the kind of ensemble which is pointing a way out of the impasse of the big-band tradition.

****** Pale Fire**

Bvhaast 0401 *As above except Willem Schoenmaker (t), Patrick Hagen (reeds), Gerco Aerts (b) replace, Jörgensmann and Dooyeweerd.* 12/00.

Nothing more or less than a grandly accomplished continuation of Contraband's music. Willem van Manen should take a bow for his marvellous composing here, from the superbly realized reconciliation of form and free in the title-piece, through the spirited *in memoriam* to trumpeter Willem Schoenmaker, 'So Long S.', to an appealingly stark feature for Koltermann's bass clarinet in 'Herne'. Where Matthias Ruegg would turn this material into a deafening culture-lesson, Van Manen finds fun, grit and an unabashed lyricism. The other records may be no less fine, but this does feel like the best place to make their acquaintance.

Carla Cook

VOCAL

Raised in Detroit, Cook studied in Boston and has subsequently worked in a wide range of situations, spending some time in Europe.

***** It's All About Love**

Maxjazz MXJ 106 *Cook; Regina Carter (vn); Cyrus Chestnut, Andy Milne (p); Kenny Davis, Darryl Hall (b); George Gray, Billy Kilson (d); Jeffrey Haynes (perc).* 3/99.

***** Dem Bones**

Maxjazz MXJ 111 *Cook; Fred Wesley, Craig Harris, Tyrone Jefferson (tb); Cyrus Chestnut (p, org); James Genus (b); Billy Kilson (d); Jeffrey Haynes (perc).* 8/00.

Cook mixes up jazz, soul and gospel strains in what is termed the contemporary manner. If her voice isn't especially distinctive, it's a focused instrument: she hits all the notes she wants, and if she occasionally overdoes it – as on 'Salt Song', a Spanish vamp on the first disc – that's just the occasional fate of this kind of singing. The tough part is reconciling these bits and pieces into a coherent record, and *It's All About Love* is in the end a likeable jumble. The title-track is a fair stab at a soul tune, which inevitably sounds weedily produced in jazz surroundings, while the gospel invocation of 'Hold To God's Unchanging Hand' is po-faced. She's best on the more comfortable standards, such as 'The Way You Look Tonight'. Regina Carter steals the show with a couple of guest solos.

Disc two sounds as if it's going to be gospel all the way, but the title actually refers to the surprising idea of using a three-man trombone section on several tracks. Nice notion, but the bones aren't really given quite enough to do: the flatulent workout on the title-track sounds like a novelty piece, while the crisper use of the horns on such as 'The More I See You' works better. Carla sounds in good heart, and she does very well with 'Just A Sittin' And A Rockin''. Not such a good idea was 'Ode To Billie Joe'. As with so many of the newer singers, material is an issue she hasn't managed to resolve.

Junior Cook (1934–92)

TENOR SAXOPHONE

Joined Horace Silver in 1958 and stayed with front-line partner Blue Mitchell until 1969. Taught and led small groups through the '80s.

*** Junior's Cookin'

Original Jazz Classics 1002 *Cook; Blue Mitchell (t); Ronnie Mathews, Dolo Coker (p); Gene Taylor (b); Roy Brooks (d).* 4–12/61.

*** The Place To Be

Steeplechase CCD 31240 *Cook; Mickey Tucker (p); Wayne Dockery (b); Leroy Williams (d).* 11/88.

*** On A Misty Night

Steeplechase SCCD 31266 *As above, except Walter Booker (b) replaces Dockery.* 6/89.

*** You Leave Me Breathless

Steeplechase SCCD 31304 *Cook; Valery Ponomarev (t); Mickey Tucker (p); John Webber (b); Joe Farnsworth (d).* 12/91.

Junior Cook's work with Horace Silver and a few other leaders revealed a tenorman of staunch loyalty to the hard-bop language, and though he never quite broke through to the front rank, he left many inventive solos on record. As a leader, he was rather less successful. There was only a solitary date for Jazzland in 1961, with his frequent partner Blue Mitchell, and with a sturdy rather than inspiring rhythm section (the record was cut at two sessions, Mathews coming in for Coker on the second) the music is dependably warm, but finally forgettable.

Cook came into his own again during the final decade of his oddly underachieving career. Steeplechase has been a profitable home for many a journeyman hard-bopper, with the label's comfortable house-sound and familiar menus making plenty of otherwise disenfranchised musicians feel comfortable. Cook's records for the company worked out rather well, even though none of them can claim classic status. If the saxophonist's dependability was his strongest suit, he nevertheless manages to find enough in the way of ear-catching ideas to give his up-tempo workouts an edge of involvement which grants even something as simple as 'Cedar's Blues' on *The Place To Be* a tough credibility. His powers were also in decline to some extent, but that tends to lend such a professional player a further challenge: how does he deal with it? Cook's answer seems to be to shy away from over-familiar material and to turn to more timbral variation than he would have bothered with as a younger man. *On A Misty Night* is marked by a considered choice of material – 'By Myself', 'Make The Girl Love Me', 'My Sweet Pumpkin' – and the leader's thoughts on the title-tune, once associated with Coltrane, stake his place in the grand tenor lineage. *You Leave Me Breathless* was his last date, made a few months before his death, and although there is some rambling – a few solos have one chorus too many, for instance – Cook's playing has a candid, clear-eyed quality which is quite affecting. Ponomarev is rather ordinary; but all three records are greatly assisted by the presence of Tucker, who is sympathetic, and driving when he has to be.

Bob Cooper (1925–93)

TENOR SAXOPHONE, OBOE

One of the major West Coast saxophonists of the '50s, Cooper's utter professionalism and consistency suggest a kinship with like-minded players such as Zoot Sims, although his light tone and unemphatic phrasing were in close harmony with the Californian playing of the period. A former sideman with Stan Kenton (he was also married to Kenton vocalist June Christy), he worked extensively with Shorty Rogers and Howard Rumsey, as a partnership with Bud Shank, in various big bands and in the prolific studio-session work of the '60s. He remained a versatile and swinging player up until his death from a heart attack in 1993.

*** Coop! The Music Of Bob Cooper

Original Jazz Classics OJC 161 *Cooper; Conte Candoli, Pete Candoli, Don Fagerquist (t); Frank Rosolino, John Halliburton (tb); Lou Levy (p); Victor Feldman (vib); Max Bennett (b); Mel Lewis (d).* 8/57.

Because he chose to spend much of his career away from any leadership role, Cooper's light has been a little dim next to many of the West Coast players of the '50s, especially since he often worked as an accompanist to his wife, vocalist June Christy. His flute-and-oboe sessions with Bud Shank are out of print, but this sole feature album, recorded for Contemporary, displays a light, appealing tenor style and arrangements which match rather than surpass the West Coast conventions of the day. The drily effective recording is typical of the studios of the period.

*** Milano Blues

Fresh Sound FSR-CD 179 *Cooper; Hans Hammerschmid, Pim Jacobs (p); Rudolf Hansen, Ruud Jacobs (b); Victor Plasil, Wessel Ilcken (d).* 3–4/57.

Two sessions from a European visit, both with local rhythm sections, a studio date in Milan and a live show in Holland. Cooper sounds a little over-relaxed on the Italian date, but the livelier 'Cappuccino Time' is sinuously done, and the live tracks feature a fine tenor blow on 'Indiana'. A couple of oboe features don't assert a great jazz role for the instrument. Goodish sound throughout, though the drums are a bit thin on the studio date.

*** For All We Know

Fresh Sound FSR-CD 167 *Cooper; Lou Levy (p); Monty Budwig (b); Ralph Penland (d).* 8/90.

*** The Bob Cooper–Conte Candoli Quintet

VSOP 93 *Cooper; Conte Candoli (t); Ross Tompkins (p); John Leitham (b); Paul Kreibich (d).* 6/93.

Cooper made rather sporadic returns to the studios in the '80s and '90s but he remained a guileful player, his tone deceptively languid: when the tempo picks up, the mastery of the horn asserts itself, and he gets the same kind of even-handed swing which the more demonstrative Zoot Sims or Al Cohn could muster. The wistful *For All We Know* stands as an honest studio farewell: typically thoughtful preparation by Cooper and Levy, on good and unhackneyed standards and with quartet arrangements that make the most of the various combinations of players. But Coop worked until he died, and the VSOP live album was done just weeks before his passing. Recorded at the Hyatt Newporter on Newport Beach, this is a vigorous set of old pro's bebop, longish solos for all hands, but good humour and skill prevail. Cooper's ballad feature on 'We'll Be Together Again' says his goodbyes.

Keith Copeland (born 1947)

DRUMS

Son of trumpeter Ray Copeland, Keith is a drummer who has played professionally since the age of 15 and is equally active as an educator, holding professorships in Germany and other posts in both the USA and Ireland.

***** The Irish Connection**

Steeplechase SCCD 31469 *Copeland; Tommy Halferty (g); Ronan Guilfoyle (b).* 95.

***** Round Trip**

Steeplechase SCCD 31425 *As above.* 9/96–2/97.

***** Postcard From Vancouver**

Jazz Focus JFCD 023 *Copeland; Miles Black (p); Rick Kilburn (b).* 97.

***** Live In Limerick**

Steeplechase SCCD 31469. *As Steeplechase albums.* 2/98.

Halferty's thick tone and juicy blend of bebop lines and fat, resonant chords tend to dominate the first two records, though Copeland and Guilfoyle are no slouches and the resultant trio music has plenty of grip. Highlights would be a somewhat Latinized 'You Don't Know What Love Is' and a very gritty blues called 'Minor Infringement', both on the second record. A rare example of Steeplechase recording in Ireland!

The Canadian date is with players from another local scene, not much known of outside Vancouver, although Kilburn in particular has done a great deal of sideman work. This is another spirited date, pushed hard by the drummer, with a good set of bop and hard-bop covers in the programme. Black is gifted with a good piano sound (he plays electric sometimes too) and his variations on three different Monk tunes are particularly incisive.

Back to Ireland for the third record by that trio. They repeat their arrangement of 'You Don't Know What Love Is', among others, and these versions are looser and funkier, though soundwise a whit less focused than they were in the studio. John Scofield's 'Chariots' is a neat sublimation of the master's style by Halferty.

Marc Copland

PIANO, KEYBOARDS

Copland arrived in New York in the early '70s, spent a period in the Chico Hamilton group, and has since been a regular presence in the area, although his records as a leader have been intermittent.

***** Never At All**

Future Music FMR CD05 28193 *Copland; Stan Sulzmann (as, ss, f).* 2/92.

*****(*) That's For Sure**

Challenge CHR 70098 *Copland; Kenny Wheeler (t, flhn); John Abercrombie (g).* 10/00.

*****(*) Lunar**

hatOLOGY 583 *Copland; David Liebman (ss, ts); Mike McGurk (b); Tony Martucci (d).* 10/01.

***** Poetic Motion**

Sketch SKE 333020 *Copland (p solo).* 10/01.

Copland isn't well-known as a leader, but he's been around the block, and these sessions are strong enough to stand pretty tall in a competitive environment. The session with Sulzmann was an old pals encounter, and the pieces were put down more or less spontaneously. Predictably, Copland's use of synthesizers is both individual and tasteful. The highlight perhaps is the flute chase on 'Phobos And Demos', though Copland's 'Guinevere', which closes the album, is lovely, too.

His Savoy albums are away for the moment, but with Abercrombie (his old bandmate in the Chico Hamilton group) and Wheeler, Copland taps a rich vein of lyricism. The opening 'When We Met' is intoxicatingly fine, the harmonic material throwing out hooks which hang in the memory. From there, on a programme of originals from each hand (the only exception is 'How Deep Is The Ocean'), the trio works responsively and with absolute finesse, Abercrombie introducing notes of intensity just when you think the project might get too sweet and nice. Perhaps Wheeler has done one chamber-jazz situation too many, for we feel we've listened to some of his solos before, but otherwise it's very fine.

Lunar is shared under Liebman's name, and again the originals – from both leaders – carry much of the day although Werner Uehlinger's request that they start with Jimmy Giuffre's 'Cry, Want' was a brilliant notion. Copland's 'All That's Left' brings on an exceptionally fine group performance (for once, the fade device used here and elsewhere suggests an elusiveness rather than bafflement over an ending). Liebman goes for the Great White Whale of the modern book by tackling 'Naima' to close, and his delicacy with the theme is very affecting.

Copland has a go at it on the solo record, too, though as with the rest of the album he seems to be afflicted by a touch of excess reverence. 'Spartacus Love Theme' comes off well in this style, but for all the fineness of the playing one feels this set could use a sniff of iodine to go with all the gracious handiwork.

*****(*) Double Play**

Steeplechase SCCD 31509 *Copland; Vic Juris (g).* 3/01.

***** What It Says**

Sketch SKE 333040 *Copland; Gary Peacock (b).* 9/02.

*****(*) Round And Round**

Nagel Heyer 2035 *Copland; Greg Osby (as).* 11/02.

It looks as if Copland is making a speciality out of the duet form. With Peacock, he's coolly accomplished, but the record feels very limited in range, lacking dynamism, variety and juice, although each piece is an effective pastel.

The other two work to a similar agenda, yet feel entirely different. With Juris, the pianist manages to evoke some mind-reading act, the pair moving so cleverly and gracefully in tandem that the toughness of the improvising – as in a demandingly exacting performance of 'Stella By Starlight' – is all but concealed by the melodious nature of the playing. Juris certainly takes equal honours in what is a detailed yet warmly played set.

With Osby, it's less about simpatico than a mildly confrontational situation. Osby's astringent outlook is somewhat at odds with the kind of softer lyricism which Copland purveys; in turn, Copland is less lush than he is in some of his dialogues with other improvisers and, though he takes the lion's share of the writing, he tends to throttle back a little in the actual playing. The result is music which is melodically rich in a concentrated and wasteless way, both men restrained in their different ways. This is certainly one which cries out for a repeat match.

Chick Corea (born 1941)

PIANO, KEYBOARDS, COMPOSER

Over the years, Chick Corea has created a body of music that has embraced Latin funk, a strong Bartók influence, free jazz, extended rock and, more recently, classical forms as well. A consummately expressive player with a complex intellectual stance, he has not been afraid to flirt with banality, a sure sign of creative greatness.

****** Tones For Joan's Bones**

Atlantic 75352 *Corea; Stuart Blumberg, Woody Shaw (t); Joe Farrell (ts, f); Steve Swallow (b); Joe Chambers (d).* 11–12/66.

***** Inner Space**

Atlantic 305 *As above, except add Hubert Laws (f); Ron Carter (b); Grady Tate (d).* 66.

Corea is a pianist and composer of remarkable range and energy, combining a free-ish jazz idiom with a heavy Latin component and an interest in more formal structures. The obvious parallel is with his ECM stable-mate, Keith Jarrett, an even more prolific keyboard improviser with a similar facility for melodic invention within relatively conventional popular forms or in more loosely conceived improvisatory settings; they also share a certain ambivalence about audiences. Corea's stated ambition is to assimilate the 'dancing' qualities of jazz and folk musics to the more disciplined structures of classical music. He has written a half-dozen classic melodies, notably the much-covered 'La Fiesta', 'Return To Forever' and 'Tones For Joan's Bones'.

Given that he had already been playing for 20 years, there is no reason to regard *Tones* as the work of a prodigy. Chick has said in interview that he felt under no particular pressure to record as a leader and approached the first session, which was produced by Herbie Mann, with a very relaxed attitude. That is evident in every track. The title-piece is a jazz classic and the opening 'Litha' deserves to be better known. Corea's classical interests are evident in the brief 'Trio For Flute, Bassoon And Piano', which is very different from the extended hard-bop idiom of the rest of the set, but well worth hearing all the same. Chick already sounds very much his own man and in possession of every resource that he was to exploit in future years. The writing is crisp and assured, with a gutsy swing. Tunes like 'Sundance', 'Converge' and 'The Brain' are embryonic Corea, but far from undeveloped. The band is brilliantly coloured, deep blues and shouting reds, and the remainder of the rhythm section as effective as any on the scene. *Inner Space* merely compiles *Tones* with some Hubert Laws material featuring Chick from the same period.

****** The Complete 'Is' Sessions**

Blue Note 40532 2CD *Corea; Woody Shaw (t); Bennie Maupin (ts); Hubert Laws (f, perc); Dave Holland (b); Jack DeJohnette (d); Horace Arnold (d, perc).* 5/69.

Corea was working with Miles Davis and was shortly to take part in the *In A Silent Way* and *Bitches Brew* sessions, when these remarkable recordings were made in May 1969. They are the work of a developing and diversifying composer. The opening 'It', a duet with flautist Laws, is almost a classical étude and tinged with Debussyan harmonies. The track that follows could hardly be more different. 'The Brain' is sturdy hard bop that features Bennie Maupin's underrated tenor saxophone playing. (And if that 'underrated' sounds like rote praise for an obscure musician, it's worth noting that his name was strangely omitted from the original LPs of *Is* and *Sundance*.)

There are alternate takes of six of the tracks. 'Sundance' itself is a superb idea, graced by Shaw playing muted, an effect that reinforces the closeness of this to Miles's sessions of the time. 'Song Of The Wind' is also known as 'Waltz For Bill Evans', elegant and free-flowing and very much better on the issued take than the alternate. 'This' has Chick on Fender Rhodes, again sounding like the artist from the Davis band. DeJohnette is in fine form here and elsewhere. The only non-Corea piece is by another Miles recruit, Dave Holland, who brought in the testing 'Jamala'.

The title-piece picks up some of the energy of Chick's free-jazz work with Circle and with Anthony Braxton. There's a danger of sounding like a Three Stooges routine here, but while 'It' is pseudo-classical, 'Is' is a free-form piece that seems to (no pun intended) circle round certain ambiguous modalities, but basically allows the musicians to float clear of chords, melody or progressions of any sort and explore their own musical natures. Therapeutically, it might have worked. Musically, it's quite dull after the opening few minutes.

*****(*) Piano Improvisations Vols. 1 & 2**

ECM 811979-2 & 829190-2 *Corea (p solo); Ida Kavafian (vn); Fred Sherry (clo).* 4/71.

****(*) Children's Songs**

ECM 815680-2 *As above.* 7/83.

Valid as the comparison with Jarrett is, there is a world of difference between the miniatures on *Piano Improvisations* and Jarrett's hugely rambling excursions. Corea is superficially less demanding, but he still repays detailed attention. If his taste was to lapse in the following years, he was surely never more decorously apt than in these 1971 sessions, which after 20 years are still wearing well. *Children's Songs* is a much less compelling set.

****** Now He Sings, Now He Sobs**

Blue Note 38265 *Corea; Miroslav Vitous (b); Roy Haynes (d).* 3/68.

★★★★ The Song Of Singing
Blue Note 84353 *Corea; Dave Holland (b); Barry Altschul (d).* 4/70.

★★★ A.R.C.
ECM 833678-2 *Corea; Dave Holland (b); Barry Altschul (d).* 1/71.

★★★ Trio Music
ECM 827702-2 2CD *Corea; Miroslav Vitous (b); Roy Haynes (d).* 11/81.

★★(★) Trio Music, Live In Europe
ECM 827769-2 *As above.* 9/84.

The trios offer the best internal evidence of Corea's musical and philosophical trajectory. *Sings/Sobs* is a fine, solid jazz set with some intelligently handled standard material, but at this point Chick was dabbling in free music and much of the material sounds collectively improvised.

A bare three years later, Corea, falling under the influence of the Scientology movement, was playing altogether more experimentally, with a searching, restless quality that he lost in later years. *The Song Of Singing*, which is probably the best of the trio records, is marked by fine melodic invention and some remarkably sophisticated group interplay which demands that the record be heard as a trio performance, not just as Corea plus rhythm. The two 'Ballads', numbered I and III, are credited to the three musicians and are presumably improvised over predetermined structures; one wonders how many were left on the editing-room floor. Corea's two compositions, 'Rhymes' and 'Flesh', are slightly vapid but sharpen up on familiarity. 'Nefertiti' is a modern jazz classic and this bare version should be compared with the Circle version.

A.R.C. isn't entirely successful, but the quality of Holland and Altschul renders it a credible essay that Corea was never fully to develop. He left the demanding Circle (whose single record contained versions of Holland's 'Toy Room' and Wayne Shorter's 'Nefertiti', both covered on *The Song Of Singing*) later in 1971, convinced that the music was losing touch with its audience. This is the beginning of the pianist's awkward populism, which was to lead him to a commercially successful but artistically null flirtation with fusion music of various sorts.

The reconvened Vitous/Haynes trio perfectly illustrates Corea's change in attitude. Vitous and Haynes are both superbly gifted players, but they take no discernible chances, sticking close to a conception laden with Corea's increasingly vapid philosophizing. By 1984, there isn't much left on Old Mother Hubbard's shelves.

★★★★ Return To Forever
ECM 811978-2 *Corea; Joe Farrell (ss, f); Stanley Clarke (b); Airto Moreira (d, perc); Flora Purim (v, perc).* 2/72.

★★★★ Light As A Feather
Verve 557115-2 2CD *As above.* 10/72.

Lightweight it may be in some regards, but *Light As A Feather* is a perennial favourite. Repackaged with extra tracks from the sessions, including several versions of 'What Games Shall We Play?', it is one of Chick's most engaging and approachable records. The leaders bounces joyously and unself-consciously throughout, transforming relatively simple themes like '500 Miles High', 'Captain Marvel' and the ubiquitous 'Children's Song' into grand dancing processions. The earlier record is in some respects better still, more improvisational in cast but still constructed around song forms. Purim's voice was never better, and Clarke keeps his lead guitarist ambitions to himself for the present. Moreira is rarely heard on a regular drum kit, and he offers an unconventional pulse that gives both sets a distinctive tilt. He plays a particularly strong role on 'Return To Forever' and on the long, buoyant 'Sometime Ago/La Fiesta'.

★★★ Hymn Of The Seventh Galaxy
Polydor 825 336 *Corea; Bill Connors (g); Stanley Clarke (b); Lenny White (d, perc).* 8/73.

★★(★) Where Have I Known You Before
Polydor 825206 *Corea; Al DiMeola (g); Stanley Clarke (b); Lenny White (d, perc).* 7–8/74.

★★★(★) Return To The Seventh Galaxy
Verve 533108-2 2CD *As for Light As A Feather, Hymn Of The Seventh Galaxy, Where Have I Known You Before, except add Steve Gadd (d), Mingo Lewis (perc).* 10/72–3/75.

★★★ The Best Of Return To Forever
Columbia CK 36359 *As for the above, except add Jim Pugh (tb), Gayle Moran (v).* 72–75.

The following year, Corea formed an electric group called Return To Forever. Not to be confused with the group that made the ECM record; only Clarke remains. There's something very '70s about *Hymn Of The Seventh Galaxy* and *Where Have I Known You Before*. Compared to the Mahavishnu Orchestra, which was very cheeseclothy and intense, Return To Forever was rather closer to a dance group, and the very buoyancy of the music often glossed over its subtleties. Though both records are painfully dated, certainly in technical terms and even despite careful remastering, they do retain some of the freshness and energy of the earlier, acoustic band, and it's perfectly possible to shut one's eyes to Corea's quasi-mystical titles.

The best of the group's material, plus some tapes from Chick's personal archive, are included on the two-CD Verve set, which is a more than adequate memorial to the group. 'Hymn Of The Seventh Galaxy', 'Captain Senor Mouse' and 'Theme To The Mothership' are all there, as well as '500 Miles High', 'Captain Marvel' and 'Light As A Feather' from the earlier group. The bonus is three tracks from a live radio broadcast from Quiet Village, Long Island, a long version of 'Spain' and two Stanley Clarke numbers, 'After The Cosmic Rain' and 'Bass Folk Song'.

The material on disc two, which includes two tracks from the 1975 *No Mystery*, documents the decline and end of what was undeniably a highly inventive band. In this form, the material is very welcome, though most listeners will find themselves returning to the first set very much more often.

The Columbia 'best of' isn't strictly that but a rock-orientated survey of some of the band's most full-on playing. It may yet bring in new listeners to Corea's music, but most initiates will find this selection one-dimensional.

★★(★) The Leprechaun
Polydor/Verve 519798-2 *Corea; Danny Cahn, John Gatchell, Bob Millikan (t); Wayne Andre, Bill Watrous (tb); Joe Farrell (reeds); Annie Kavafian, Ida Kavafian (vn); Louise Shulman (vla); Fred Sherry (clo); Eddie Gomez, Anthony Jackson (b); Steve Gadd (d); Gayle Moran (v).* 75.

★★ My Spanish Heart
Polydor 2669034 2CD *Corea; 17-piece band, including strings; Jean-Luc Ponty (vn); one track of Corea; Stanley Clarke (b); Narada Michael Walden (perc).* 10/76.

****(*) The Mad Hatter**

Verve 519799-2 *Corea; John Thomas, Stuart Blumberg, John Rosenberg (t); Ron Moss (tb); Charles Veal, Kenneth Yerke (vn); Denyse Buffum, Michael Nowack (vla); Dennis Karmazyn (clo); Herbie Hancock (ky); Joe Farrell (ts, f, picc); Eddie Gomez, Jamie Faunt (b); Steve Gadd, Harvey Mason (d); Gayle Moran (v).* 78.

***** Friends**

Polydor 849 071 *Corea; Joe Farrell (ts, ss, f); Eddie Gomez (b); Steve Gadd (d).* 78.

Things went a little awry thereafter. *The Leprechaun* was so intent on being charming that it ended up deeply charmless. It marked some sort of a return to acoustic jazz, though Corea himself lined up a bank of then state-of-the-art keyboards, most of which now sound no more contemporary than a clavichord might. He added horns and a few strings and tied himself up in a drab fantasy realm that muffled even the sub-Bartókian melodies which had emerged from time to time in Corea's work and had their apotheosis in the *Children's Songs* (above, and – numbers five and fifteen – on *Friends*). *The Mad Hatter* was in the same dismal vein, with horns and strings clogging up some of the most promising material. The one bright spot is Joe Farrell's part on 'Humpty Dumpty', a typically elegant and feeling tenor break.

Friends was the one with the embarrassing Smurfs cover which must have put off hundreds of potential buyers. Perversely, it's better than the two previous items. The long 'Smaba Song' and the title-track are close to his best for this vintage, and Farrell and Gomez give the session a considerable boost. Corea was still publicly thanking L. Ron Hubbard for his 'continual inspiration', but it was never clear how exactly the fantasy realm into which these works dipped was the product of a clear – or Clear – vision that went beyond verbalized or abstract concepts and to what extent they were a sign of creative exhaustion.

My Spanish Heart was a rare instance of Corea working with a large band. It gives every impression of having been got up for the tourists. It's a rather ersatz Latin concoction that never seems to earn its climaxes or justify the band's rather strained enthusiasm.

****** Jazz Masters 3**

Verve 5198202-2 *As above.* 72–78.

A cracking anthology, ideal as a portable or automobile backup. Includes 'Spain', 'Light As A Feather', 'My Spanish Heart', 'Captain Marvel' and more. Next time someone says, 'Chick Corea? Never heard of him,' this is your natural recourse.

**** Corea Hancock**

Polydor 835360 *Corea; Herbie Hancock (p).* 2/78.

***** Crystal Silence**

ECM 831331-2 *Corea; Gary Burton (vib).* 10/79.

****(*) In Concert, Zurich, October 28, 1979**

ECM 821415-2 2CD *As above.* 10/79.

****(*) Lyric Suite For Sextet**

ECM 815274-2 *As above, except add string quartet.* 9/82.

Interesting duo performances of 'La Fiesta' and 'Maiden Voyage' on *Corea Hancock* (a compositional credit apiece), but by no means a compelling album, with some of Hancock's notions baffling in the extreme. *Crystal Silence* is a lot more substantial than it initially sounds and the music holds up well on the subsequent concert performance, which for a time was a worthwhile substitute, though CD has given the sound a cleaner and more distinctive edge. 'Senor Mouse' and 'Crystal Silence' reappear from the studio disc and there is a fine eponymous Bud Powell tribute that is well worth the admission price.

The *Lyric Suite* recalls Ravel more readily than Alban Berg, which is no bad thing. It's delicate, attractive music, sensibly limited in scope, firmly and, as always, beautifully executed. Less baroquely ambitious than Jarrett's classical compositions, it comes across as something of a by-blow.

***** Tap Step**

Stretch GRS 00092 *Corea; Alan Vizutti (t, flhn); Joe Henderson (ts); Joe Farrell (ts, ss); Hubert Laws (f, picc); Bunny Brunel, Stanley Clarke, Jamie Faunt (b); Tommy Brechtlein (d); Don Alias, Airto Moreira, Laudir Oliveira (perc); Nani Vila Brunel, Shelby Flint, Flora Purim, Gayle Moran (v).* 12/79, 1/80.

The Stretch Collector series was planned as a way of releasing previously unheard or unavailable Corea material, partly (as in the case of the item below) to offset bootleg issues, partly, one suspects, as a reaction to the pianist's rather difficult relationship with the recording industry.

The stuff on *Tap Step* is pretty much of a muchness; a heavy emphasis on electric piano, synth and clavinet, a fondness for rock settings, Latin percussion and, here and there, voices. Only on 'Grandpa Blues' with Bunny Brunel on fretless bass and Stanley Clarke on his piccolo bass is there anything that really grabs the attention. The few glimpses of Joe Farrell are welcome as always, and Joe Henderson, who in these years was quite close to Corea (see below), contributes a typically unstuffy and intelligent part to 'Flamenco', which belongs in the *Light As A Feather* league. Other than these two tracks, little of distinction to report.

*****(*) Live In Montreux**

Stretch GRS 00122 *Corea; Joe Henderson (ts); Gary Peacock (b); Roy Haynes (d).* 81.

Chick wore a T-shirt emblazoned with the legend 'EAT CARROTS'. Haynes played throughout as if on a diet of raw steak. Henderson and Peacock just snacked away happily. This is a further dip into the Corea archive for Stretch, a supergroup encounter introduced with due sense of occasion by Montreux organizer Claude Nobs, who just about gets off-stage quick enough before the fireworks begin. Though things like 'Folk Song' and 'Psalm' are not in themselves demanding, the standard of musicianship required to last in this company is awesome. On 'Hairy Canary' (which may be an oblique reference to Charlie Parker's music), the four jostle a bit and generally check one another out. The main weight of the session falls to the two tracks already mentioned and an extended improvisation on 'Trinkle Tinkle', a version of Chick's 'Quintet No. 2' and Peacock's 'Up, Up, And …' Even though the horn sound is often rather uncertain and indistinct, Henderson remains the key to the whole proceedings, an improviser of undimmed resource and patience, required to work in a notably floaty and uncertain harmonic landscape. Not a great recording, but a splendid record all the same.

***** Works**

ECM 825426-2 *Corea (p solo and with various bands).* 71–83.

***** :rarum: Selected Recordings**

ECM 066 578 2 *As for Return To Forever and Crystal Silence, except add Gary Burton (vib); Miroslav Vitous (b); Roy Haynes (d).* 72–81.

Works is a well-selected sample of the pianist's decade-plus with ECM. Not many surprises, though it's interesting how thin the short piano improvisations from ECM 1014 and 1020 sound when heard out of context. It's now been superseded by the first volume of a promised two in the *:rarum* series from ECM, which are selected by the artists themselves. It's interesting how rigorously Chick has restricted his selection to just a few projects and associations. The trio with Haynes and Vitous is classic and so too is the material from *Return To Forever.*

**** Voyage**

ECM 823468-2 *Corea; Steve Kujala (f).* 7/84.

**** Septet**

ECM 827258-2 *As above, except add strings and french horn.* 7/84, 10/84.

Voyage is a flimsy confection that is very difficult to take entirely seriously. Part of the problem is that the two players take it very seriously indeed, when what it cries out for is a little lightness of touch. *Septet* is no more pulse-quickening, but it has the benefit of a certain variation of register and timbre that is episodically quite interesting.

***** Akoustic Band**

GRP 059 582 2 *Corea; John Patitucci (b); Dave Weckl (d).* 89.

***** Alive**

GRP 059 627 2 *As above.* 91.

From the very first notes of 'My One And Only Love' and 'Bessie's Blues' on the first of these, Corea is unmistakable. For better or worse, he still has perhaps the most distinctive stylistic signature in contemporary jazz piano, a rippling fulness of sound that cloys very quickly. Here, then, the promised Akoustic Band and a mainly standards set. Compared to what Keith Jarrett has done with similar repertoire, the thinness of Corea's conception becomes clearer. *Akoustic Band* has its moments, mostly on original material, and *Alive* is an uncomplicated, entertaining set; the pianos both sound first-rate and the production is spot-on.

***** Three Quartets**

Stretch GRS 00032 *Corea; Michael Brecker (ts); Eddie Gomez (b); Steve Gadd (d).* 1 & 2/81.

Stretch is Corea's own imprint, devoted not just to archive material like the Montreux concert (above) but to new recording as well. The *Three Quartets* were structured jazz compositions with a wide range of classical influences, and they see Corea exploring some of the territory Bill Evans (who had died prematurely the year before) left uncolonized. 'Quartet No. 2' is the only one broken down into parts – dedications, respectively, to Duke Ellington and John Coltrane – and it is harmonically the most varied. The other two are unmistakable Corea, mixing funky lines with a floating, very classical sound which the Bösendorfer Grand richly accentuates.

After the main session ended, the band filled in studio time with a few untried originals and an off-the-cuff run-through of Charlie Parker's 'Confirmation'. Though they don't quite fit in with the three main items for the original LP, they contain (perversely enough) some of the leader's best playing on the record. Michael Brecker was still developing what has since become the most ubiquitous contemporary tenor sound after John Coltrane and Jan Garbarek, and he still sounds adventurous and forceful.

****(*) The Chick Corea Elektric Band**

GRP 059 535 2 *Corea; Scott Henderson, Carlos Rios (g); John Patitucci (b); Dave Weckl (d, perc).* 86.

***** Inside Out**

GRP 059 6012 *As above, except omit Henderson, Rios; add Eric Marienthal (sax), Frank Gambale (g).* 90.

****(*) Beneath The Mask**

GRP 059 649 2 *As above.* 8/91.

****(*) Eye Of The Beholder**

GRP 059 564 2 *Corea; Eric Marienthal (sax); John Novello (syn); Frank Gambale (g); John Patitucci (b); Dave Weckl (d).* 88.

****(*) Paint The World**

GRP 059 741 2 *Corea; Eric Marienthal (sax); Mike Miller (g); Jimmy Earl (b); Gary Novak (d).* 93.

***** Priceless Jazz**

GRP 059 878 2 *As for the above.* 86–93.

We've never been convinced by the Elektric Band but, given Chick's almost incurable inventiveness, there is always something to ponder and enjoy. The first album is disconcertingly crude, but with the introduction of Marienthal the textures are softened and there are several moments even sceptical visitors would be happy to revisit. *Paint The World* was credited to Elektric Band II; the formula is very much the same. The compilation disc is a very decent compromise, though we'd quibble with the specific choice of tracks.

****(*) Touchstone**

Stretch 00042 *Corea; Alan Vizutti (t); Lee Konitz (as); Steve Kujala (ts, f); Al DiMeola, Paco De Lucia (g); Carlos Benavent, Stanley Clarke, Bob Magnusson (b); Lenny White (d); Carol Shrive (vn); Greg Gottlieb (vla); Alex Acuña, Don Alias, Laudir Oliveira (perc); Gayle Moran (v).* 82.

Prefaced by a nutty fable about the Singing Woman and Rivera, 'Touchstone' itself has the same soapy unreality as Hollywood fantasies like *Legend.* Scored for keys, guitar, voice, bass and percussion, it is no more than a couple of slight themes, lent a papier-mâché superstructure and then vaguely jazzed up. There are more interesting things on the record. Lee Konitz's contribution to 'Duende' is a reminder of Getz's *Sweet Rain,* and 'Compadres' reunites Return To Forever for an overlong but attractive blow. The main problem with *Touchstone* is its bittiness. There is more musical substance than on *The Mad Hatter,* but as a disc it's all over the place and can really be seen only as a haphazard sampler.

*****(*) Expressions**

GRP 900732 *Corea (p solo).* 93.

Significant on two counts: the first solo record for some time, and a very welcome return to standards. Corea includes only two of his own compositions (a wonderful reading of 'Armando's Rhumba'), but he scans the history of modern piano jazz with a typically eclectic range of vision. The second original is a 'Blues For Art' and the whole session is dedicated to Tatum. There are tunes by Strayhorn, Monk and Bud Powell, but in each case it's the Tatum strand that is most evident. It's beautifully recorded (Corea is listed as both producer and 'recordist') with a full, old-fashioned sound, pleasantly different from GRP's usual glitter.

★★★(★) Time Warp

Stretch GRS 00152 *Corea; Bob Berg (ts, ss); John Patitucci (b); Gary Novak (d).* 4/95.

A quasi-narrative suite with a sci-fi storyline, bog-standard stuff: purplish glows, names with too few vowels, unbidden transitions from place to place, a little philosophy and dogma ... and yet, one of the best and straightest Corea albums for some time. There is little obvious musical connection between the numbers, nor needs there to be, but Corea has woven the whole package into a suite with interpolated cadenzas from saxophone – bridging 'The Wish' and 'Terrain', his own intro to 'New Life', by far the most important track on the disc – and Patitucci's switch to Garrison mode to set 'Discovery' in motion.

'New Life' is as boldly optimistic and as quietly chastened as anything since *Song Of Singing* on Blue Note. It was a trio, and in some ways this record has the feel of a trio performance with Berg superadded, mostly effectively as here, but sometimes more jarringly where it seems clear that he is working his own agenda. The mystery – other than what exactly is going on in the story of Arndok – is why Corea should have felt drawn to a drummer as leaden and hostile as Novak. But for him, and a few raw edges elsewhere, this would be up with Corea's very best, rather than teetering problematically on the fringes.

★★★(★) Remembering Bud Powell

Stretch SCD 9012 *Corea; Wallace Roney (t); Kenny Garrett (as); Joshua Redman (ts); Christian McBride (b); Roy Haynes (d).* 96.

Bud in his last days was as troubled as Chick has been Clear, and on the face of it this seems an unlikely permutation. It also seems surprising that Corea should have put together such a substantial line-up for a tribute to Powell, when a basic piano trio might have seemed the better and more likely option. In the event, *Remembering* is a small triumph, an understated and affectionate album that gives a clear impression of its subject – as understood by a follower – but without succumbing to sycophancy. Apart from a specially written tribute, all the tracks are credited to Powell. There is a superb quintet version of the brooding, problematic 'Glass Enclosure', a brisk, almost antagonistic version of 'Oblivion', and more thoughtful renditions of 'Tempus Fugit' (didn't it just?) and 'I'll Keep Loving You'. Corea's touch is exquisite and one has the sense that he has steeped himself in the literature before tackling the session.

★★★★ Music Forever And Beyond: The Selected Works Of Chick Corea – 1964–1996

GRP GRD 5 9819 5CD *Selected from the above.* 64–96.

A sumptuously packaged, sensibly chronicled and themed set that will keep any Corea fan happy for weeks. The first three discs are chronological, followed by two which cover standards (with Berg, Patitucci and Novak), solos, duets and 'surprises'. Of these last, the most appealing is a 1949 78-r.p.m. recording made by indulgent parents of the boy wonder playing 'I Don't See Me In Your Eyes Anymore'. There are also unreleased tracks from a Montreux concert in 1982 with John McLaughlin, and a specially recorded version of 'Round Midnight' with string quartet, made for this release. It may feel that some of the material on offer has been round the track once too often, most particularly the stuff on disc two, but there is more than enough new material to keep the fussiest collector happy, though bootleggers may have beaten GRP to the punch on some of the live tracks. Hard to fault on any count.

★★★(★) Native Sense: The New Duets

Stretch SCD 9014 *Corea; Gary Burton (vib).* 97.

An old partnership, to be sure, but one which never sounded as if it had exhausted all the ideas. This latter-day set is more robustly recorded than previous encounters, with a plain, unadorned sound that does neither man any harm. It's quite a long record and, aside from a couple of brief 'Bagatelles' and a short, delightful 'Armando's Rhumba', the tracks are played out at length, with plenty of time and space to exchange ideas. The two outstanding performances are 'No Mystery' (which of course contains at least one, a harmonic puzzle) and the more free-floating 'Rhumbata', which is a joyous dance theme.

★★★★ Origin: Live At The Blue Note

Stretch 9018 *Corea; Steve Davis (tb); Steve Wilson (ss, as, f, cl); Bob Sheppard (ss, ts, bcl, f); Avishai Cohen (b); Adam Cruz (d).* 1/98.

★★★(★) A Week At The Blue Note

Stretch 9020 6CD *As above.* 1/98.

Anything Miles and Keith Jarrett can do, Chick can do every bit as well. To deal with business matters first, the material on these CDs was all recorded during a residency at the Blue Note club in New York. The single album is not a sampler or taster; none of the tracks is reduplicated on the complete set, which is inevitably going to have a limited shelf-life. Taped over three nights at the very start of the year, the sets have pretty much the same configuration. The joy is in hearing how Chick and the horns approach them differently set to set.

The single disc showcased what was obviously an important new band for Corea, one that offered him a chance to experiment with complex voicings but also still swing like crazy. The closing version of the Van Heusen classic, 'It Could Happen To You', is magnificent and far ahead of the single version on the boxed set, and there are stunning versions of originals like 'Dreamless', 'Molecules' and 'Soul Mates'. We can't but conclude that the very best material was selected for the original release and that the rest was expected to gain in force by sheer bulk and repetition. To be clear, there are three versions of 'Bewitched, Bothered And Bewildered', two of 'Molecules' and 'Sifu', three of the blues, 'Matrix', and five of the brief 'Say It Again', which comes in two parts. *A Week* also includes three Monk tunes and Charlie Parker's 'Bird Feathers'. Completism is almost always excessive and only serious students of Chick's pianism will find themselves working through the box more than once. Some of the themes are quite ragged and 'Molecules' in particular doesn't quite come off, though it does point to a growing Ellington influence on Chick's thinking. We say plump for the single album and, if you're lucky enough to find the Japanese release, you should find an extra version of 'Sifu', run down at home with just the trio, which should have you purring all the louder.

★★★(★) Change

Stretch 9023 *As above, except replace Cruz with Jeff Ballard (d).* 98.

Having debuted Origin on the Blue Note sets, Corea took the slightly altered line-up into the studio for a relaxed, swinging set that seems to restore the Latin emphasis. 'Little Flamenco' is a joyous thing, with fine flute work from Wilson and authentic handclaps from the drummer. 'Early Afternoon Blues' might almost be Horace Silver, and there are a couple of moments when Chick seems to namecheck Dr Funk. 'Armando's Tango' is now almost a repertory piece, but it has rarely sounded as fresh and alert, and 'Awakening' which closes the set is as near as you'll get to a career summation in six and a quarter elegant minutes. The only surprise of the set, apart from Cohen's lovely original 'Lylah', is Chick's recorded debut on marimba on 'Wigwam'. He plays with mallets like he plays with his fingers, but the extra percussive edge is delightful and sets the tone for a fresh, inventive record that really does mark a change of direction as well as consolidation of 40 years on the job.

***** Solo Piano – Originals**
Stretch 9028 *Corea (p solo).* 11/99.

***** Solo Piano – Standards**
Stretch 9029 *As above.* 11/99.

By this stage of a distinguished career, there is an air of monumentality about almost everything Corea issues. This, following the release of his *Concerto*, a classical work, is no exception: two discs containing exactly (or very nearly) what the titles suggest. The opening set is a mostly brisk career survey, taking in such hits as 'Armando's Rhumba', 'Brasilia' and the ubiquitous 'Spain', but also including a long improvisation on 'Children's Song #12' and arrangements of two Scriabin preludes (which don't strictly qualify as 'originals'). Chick also invites audience members to throw him titles and then delivers four brief, clever improvisations – 'The Chase', 'The Falcon', 'Swedish Landscape' and 'April Snow' – which serve as a reminder of what a quick-witted instant composer he can be.

The Scriabin pieces apart, it's a fairly predictable roster. What's odd about the *Standards* volume is that it quickly turns into a tribute to Thelonious Monk, who is represented by no fewer than four tracks; two more are by Bud Powell, so bop repertory features more strongly than one might have expected. Chick is recognizable in every phrase, but there is something slightly distanced about the playing; in retrospect, his attack on *Originals* isn't quite as committed as it might be, leaving one with the impression that these two discs were cut rather with the market in mind than as documentations of vivid performance.

*****(*) Past, Present & Futures**
Stretch 9035 *Corea; Avishai Cohen (b); Jeff Ballard (d).* n.d.

This is much more like the real thing, a genuinely creative and thoughtful Corea album that unites the best of his old experimentalism with the structural grandeur of recent years. Apart from 'Jitterburg Waltz', which may contain two tiny Dolphy quotes – possibly unconscious – all the material is original and yet it nods insistently in the direction of Chick's peers. 'Fingerprints', for instance, is both nominally and harmonically a gesture towards Wayne Shorter's classic, and the astonishing climax of 'Life Line' is a summation of much of the harmonic language of recent jazz. 'Dignity', 'Anna's Tango' and 'The Chelsea Shuffle' are all outstanding concepts and the trio plays instinctively and with great control on each of them, allowing the emotion to come through without sacrificing the pace or the structure of the theme. Cohen is in astonishing form, creating some entirely unexpected multi-metres which will have ordinary fans and bass players alike scrolling back to check out his technique. Ballard is slightly more passive and supportive, but he is the ideal man for this trio, and a far cry from some of the bashers Chick has employed in the recent past. A wonderful record, and a great return to form.

****** Rendezvous In New York**
Stretch 038 023 2 2CD *Corea; Terence Blanchard (t); Steve Davis (tb); Steve Wilson (ss, as); Michael Brecker, Tim Garland, Joshua Redman (ts); Gonzalo Rubalcaba (p); Avishai Cohen, Eddie Gomez, Christian McBride, John Patitucci, Miroslav Vitous (b); Jeff Ballard, Steve Gadd, Roy Haynes, Dave Weckl (d); Bobby McFerrin (v).* 9/01.

Chick celebrated 60 years young with a special event at the Blue Note in New York that reunited him with some of the musicians who have played a role in his extraordinary career. There are nine different bands and pairings represented here, and thus nine different aspects of his playing personality. It all begins joyously enough with three duets with Bobby McFerrin, who kicks straight into 'Armando's Blues' followed by a fine version of 'Blue Monk' and an astonishing medley of 'Concierto De Aranjuez' and Chick's own 'Spain'. Even if it was rehearsed, it sounds totally spontaneous and utterly wonderful.

What follows is more sombre – 'Matrix' from the *Now He Sings, Now He Sobs* trio of Miroslav Vitous and Roy Haynes, ten minutes of restlessly exploratory piano trio. The *Remembering Bud Powell* band does its stuff on 'Glass Enclosure' and 'Tempus Fugit' before Chick and Gary Burton renew their acquaintance on 'Crystal Silence'. The Akoustic Band and Origin are both strongly featured on disc two, as is the New Trio with Avishai Cohen and Jeff Ballard and the *Three Quartets* band with Mike Brecker, Eddie Gomez and Steve Gadd. The real highpoint of the second disc, though, is a wonderful second read of 'Concierto De Aranjuez' with fellow-pianist Gonzalo Rubalcaba; breathtaking.

Julian Coryell

GUITAR

Chip off old block, but quite a polished chip.

***** Duality**
N2K 10011 *Coryell; Donald Harris (t); Bob Mintzer (ts, bcl); Lafayette Harris Jr (p, ky); Mark Sherman (vib); Eugene Moye (clo); Scott Colley, Jonathan Sanborn (b); Billy Hart, Steve Wolf (d); Daniel Sadownick (perc).* 7/97.

Julian's later work seemed even further away from a jazz idiom. Here, though, he's working through the same kind of cross-influence as his father in earlier days. There are a number of rock songs among the originals – Elvis Costello's 'Shipbuilding', Steely Dan's 'Deacon Blues' and Joni Mitchell's 'River' along with the Dylan tune (in this case 'All I Really Want To Do') which seemed *de rigueur* in 1997 – but there are enough wise jazz heads in the line-up to keep the thing from pastiche. It may be that ten years down the line Julian turns to bebop like his father did. It may be that by then we're no longer making the comparison.

Larry Coryell (born 1943)

GUITAR

Coryell was born and raised in Galveston, Texas. He played in pianist Mike Mandel's group before joining Chico Hamilton and Gary Burton, where his rock-tinged sound came to wide notice. In later years, he formed the group Eleventh House which, along with Return To Forever and the Mahavishnu Orchestra, was definitive of the jazz-rock boom of the early '70s. In more recent years, Coryell has moved between pure bop, fusion and Latin styles. His limpid delivery and almost classically accurate lines conceal real power, most evident in his early, Hendrix-influenced days, but still evident in the later, Latin-inspired work.

***** Coryell**

Universe 21 *Coryell; Jim Pepper (ts, f); Mike Mandel (p, ky); Melvin Bronson, Ron Carter, Chuck Rainey (b); Bernard Purdie (d).* 69.

Coryell played with Sonny Sharrock on Herbie Mann's *Memphis Underground* and was quickly aware that the excitements of rock could be married with the subtleties and intellectual sophistication of jazz. It was inevitably going to be some time before he made that equation securely and with a degree of elegance, but all the lineaments are present here. Tracks like 'Sex' and 'Morning Sickness' are less provocative than their titles suggest and the guitarist's musicianship is exemplary. It's on 'The Jam With Albert' that one recognizes just what an extraordinary musician we are dealing with: still young, still raw, but bursting with talent. To his credit, Coryell would go off in the very near future and construct his own band. He could very easily have kept falling back on seasoned and big-name pros, but there was a sound in his head and he wanted to shape it his way. A very valuable rescue from the vaults, reissued in 2001.

***** Lady Coryell**

Vanguard VCD 6509 *Coryell; Jimmy Garrison, Miroslav Vitous (b); Elvin Jones, Bob Moses (d).* 69.

*****(*) Spaces**

Vanguard 79345 *Coryell; Michael Lawrence (t); Chick Corea (p, ky); John McLaughlin (g); Miroslav Vitous (b); Billy Cobham (d).* 7/70.

***** Live At The Village Gate**

Universe 22 *Coryell; Melvin Bronson (b); Harry Wilkinson (d); Julie Coryell (v).* 1/71.

**** Barefoot Boy**

One Way 71001 *Coryell; Steve Marcus (ss); Melvin Bronson (b); Roy Haynes, Harry Wilkinson (d); Lawrence Killian (perc).* 71.

**** The Real Great Escape**

Vanguard VSD 79329 *Coryell; Michael Brecker (ts); Steve Marcus (ss, ts); Mike Mandel (p, syn, ky); Melvin Bronson (b); Harry Wilkinson (d); Earl DeRouen (perc); Julie Coryell (v).* 73.

***** At Montreux**

Vanguard 79410 *Coryell; Michael Lawrence (t); Mike Mandel (ky); Danny Trifan (b); Alphonse Mouzon (d, perc).* 7/74.

****(*) Planet End**

Vanguard VCD 79367 *Coryell; Michael Lawrence (t); Chick Corea, Mike Mandel (p, ky); Steve Khan, John McLaughlin (g); Will Lee, Danny Trifan, Miroslav Vitous (b); Billy Cobham, Alphonse Mouzon (d).* 75.

'Schizophrenic' is a wildly misused critical adjective, but if there was ever a split musical personality, it is Coryell. The guitarist never seemed able to make up his mind whether he wanted to be Chet Atkins, Jimi Hendrix or Segovia; and there were always doubts about his chops as an improviser. Nevertheless, Coryell is the unsung hero of the fusion movement, who sometimes sailed too close to actual rock and roll. *Live At The Village Gate* was recorded very soon after Hendrix's death and it was hard to tell whether guitarists were queueing up to bury or to praise him. Larry was certainly one of the most faithful copyists and this is an exciting record, marred by a waffly version of the Jack Bruce song, 'Can You Follow?', and a drab vocal from Julie on 'Beyond These Chilling Winds'.

Barefoot Boy reintroduces Steve Marcus and was to set the pattern of Coryell's groups for some time thereafter. The key element here, though, is Roy Haynes, who *blazes* through the set as if the devil were on his tail. Gabor Szabo's 'Gypsy Queen' is the opening and best cut, while the pretentiously named 'Call To The Higher Consciousness' meanders through some powerful episodes and some extremely drab passage-work for a tad over 20 minutes. A difficult album to judge now because so much astonishing work came out of it, but very much a transitional record.

The Real Great Escape is the major disappointment in this batch, a noisy, macho mess of a record that has its excitements but never quite manages to marry energy with a measure of thought.

Perhaps better to go back to the original albums, of which *Spaces* is the most celebrated, a floaty, meditative disc with a solid core of invention and some formidable interaction between the two very different guitarists. McLaughlin so often worked best in dialogue with another guitar player, whether Coryell, Santana or Paco De Lucia and Al DiMeola in later years, and on *Spaces* he is thoughtful and intense. The stereo separation is a bit drastic by later standards, but it contributes to the nostalgic appeal of the record. The inclusion of Scott LaFaro's 'Gloria's Step' and René Thomas's 'René's Theme' was an obvious signal that this was not another rock group but an outfit schooled in the modern jazz tradition.

Lady Coryell was more obviously influenced by rock. The title-track, dedicated to Julie, is a fusion classic and has rather eclipsed the rest of a fine and thoughtful album, which saw the aesthetic of the John Coltrane Quartet and of the MC5 (who always claimed to have been influenced by Trane) brought full circle. 'You Don't Know What Love Is' sounds like a token standard.

Planet End was Larry's last album for Vanguard and is little more than a series of loose and rather sloppy jams. The Eleventh House formula was well established by this stage but one can almost hear the guitarist coasting towards the end of a contract, and the only track which combines the excitement and elegance of earlier days is Larry Young's 'Tyrone'.

***** The Essential Larry Coryell**

Vanguard VCD 79575/6 2CD *Coryell; Randy Brecker (t); Steve Marcus (ss); Mike Mandel (p, syn); John McLaughlin (g); Mervin Bronson, Chuck Rainey, Albert Stinson, Danny Trifan, Miroslav Vitous (b); Billy Cobham, Elvin Jones, Bob Moses, Alphonse Mouzon, Bernard Pretty Purdie, Harry Wilkinson (d); Julie Coryell (v).* 68–75.

★★★(★) Improvisations: The Best Of The Vanguard Years

Vanguard VCD 79614/5 2CD *As above, except add Michael Lawrence (t), Darius Brubeck (p), Steve Khan (g), Chris Brubeck, Ron Carter, Jimmy Garrison (b), Danny Brubeck (d), Ray Mantilla (perc).* 68–75.

★★ Basics

Universe 20 *Similar to above.* 68–69.

These samplers in their different ways pretty much cover the waterfront in terms of the Vanguard years. *Improvisations* is longer and much more detailed and has probably superseded the sketchier sampling on *Essential.* The two-CD set includes all the obvious things: 'Lady Coryell', 'René's Theme', 'Spaces (Infinite)' with McLaughlin, the fiery 'Jam With Albert', 'Low-Lee-Tah' and the enigmatic 'Scotland 1', which was inspired by Larry's visit to the Buddhist community at Eskdalemuir. All in all, a fitting summation of a highly creative period that wouldn't be matched for sheer energy until the mid-'80s. *Basics,* however, is anything but that and only Coryell collectors will be interested in these studio off-cuts; it's also pretty thin value for money at just over half an hour.

★★★★ The Restful Mind

Universe 33 *Coryell; Ralph Towner (g); Glen Moore (b); Collin Walcott (perc).* 74.

A very special record that manages to avoid all the pitfalls usually associated with crossover projects that aim to marry jazz and classical music. Ravel has always appealed to improvisers and he is represented here by 'Pavane For A Dead Princess' (a misleading translation of *défunte,* by the way; a pavane is by no means a mourning dance and 'a princess of olden times' might be a better rendition). This is Coryell at his thoughtful best and a long way removed from the Hendrix-inspired wailer of former years.

The real pay-off comes in two pieces after Robert de Visée, both of them originally written for the theorbo. These are magnificently crafted and paced, especially the opening menuet. The Coryell originals are all equally well adapted to the setting which saw the guitarist in the company of three-quarters of Oregon, who were also recording for Vanguard at this time. Towner is an excellent partner, and a very different kind of guitarist from John McLaughlin. Oregon were determinedly acoustic, but Larry employs synth effects and some measure of amplification as well as his beautifully toned Lo Prinzi guitar. 'Ann Arbor', 'Song For Jim Webb' and the title-piece all manage to avoid that familiar dreary slither into New Age drabness. This one is more than 25 years old, but it comes across as fresh and as inventive as ever.

★★★ Twin House

ACT 9202 *Coryell: Philip Catherine (g); Joachim Kühn (p).* 76, 77.

Indifferently recorded in London and Hamburg, these are mainly guitar duets, with just one opening for Kühn. Coryell leads off a great version of 'The Train And The River', and there's a companionable 'Nuages'; but for the most part the material is original and very fresh. The two guitars are rather crudely separated and could do with narrowing a bit, but there are passages where it's impossible to judge who's playing what, though generally Catherine plays with a fuller, less rhythmic intonation.

★★★ A Quiet Day In Spring

Steeplechase SCCD 31187 *Coryell; Michal Urbaniak (vn); Jesper Lundgaard (b).* 11/83.

This was an interesting pairing. The Polish-born fusion violinist has had a fairly up-and-down career and can sound rather sentimental in a more intimate setting like this. However, Coryell gets him going on tunes like his own 'Polish Reggae' and two lovely waltzes on which he combines delicate open-string passages with rich, triple-stopped chords that conjure up the Polish Romantic composers. Coryell takes a back seat where necessary, as on the violinist's feature, 'Stuff's Stuff', but is at his expressive best on 'Rue Gregoire Du Tour', picking out soft, sustained variations on the melody.

★★★ Dragon Gate

Shanachie 97005 *Coryell; Stefan Grossman (g).* 89.

Coryell credits Ellis Marsalis with the revelation that allowed him to play Coltrane's 'Giant Steps' as a solo guitar piece: recast the piece in waltz time and slow it right down, and the changes would make sense ... and so they do. Throughout the album, Coryell pays tribute to the masters who made him want to be a musician, and his version of Wes Montgomery's 'West Coast Blues' has to be heard in that light. Coryell plays alone, overdubbed, and in duet with Grossman. *Dragon Gate* is beautifully textured, well paced, but perhaps a little too technical for the casual listener.

★★★(★) Twelve Frets To One Octave

Shanachie 97015 *Coryell (g solo).* 91.

Covering everything from raw, rootsy blues to the sober, classical shapes of 'Bartók Eleven' to the lovely lilt of 'Transparence' (not to be confused with the Philip Catherine tune of the same name). Technically, Coryell has it all taped. His single-note runs are fleet and dexterous, his chording has harmonic mass and bulk, and his rhythms and counter-rhythms frequently create the impression that more than one musician must be involved. We have re-examined at least half-a-dozen spots on this album, persuaded that some sort of overdubbing was used, but apparently and convincingly not.

★★★ Live From Bahia

Past Perfect 205710 *Coryell; Marcio Montarroyos (t); Donald Harrison (as); Luiz Avellar (ky); Romero Lubambo (g); Nico Assumpção, Francisco Centeno (b); Billy Cobham (d); Bashiri Johnson, Monica Millet, Tiao Oliveira (perc); Dori Caymmi (v).* 92.

Repackaged and now missing the rather poignant and misleading dead fish cover of the 1992 CTI release, this gentle Latin set still comes across well. Coryell plays acoustic throughout and at times – on 'The Harbor' and 'The Crab Peddler' – might be there just as an accompanist to Dori Caymmi who sings her own songs. Harrison also brings in 'Oshun, Goddess Of Love', so there's much less emphasis on Coryell writing this time out. There are some fine players in the line-up and some fine playing, but with Coryell in relaxed and unemphatic mood this isn't one of his best records.

★★★ Sketches Of Coryell

Shanachie 5024 *Coryell; Alex Sipiagin (t); Dave Mann (ss, ts); Bob Berg (ts); Julian Coryell, Peter Moffitt, Mark Sherman (ky); Rodney Jones (g, ky); Kennan Keating (b, ky); Kenwood Dennard (d); Jonathan Abrams, Emedin Rivera (perc).* 96.

This mixed and patchy album includes compositions by Moffitt, Sherman and Keating, as well as Stevie Wonder's 'I Am Singing' and an arrangement of the Miles-endorsed 'Concierto De Aranjuez'. Coryell's playing long since reached a peak of confidence, but one misses the energy and freshness of his early fusion work and his first dabbling in classical repertoire. These days, he seems more bent on affirming his eclecticism and range.

★★★ Spaces Revisited

Shanachie 5033 *Coryell; Bireli Lagrene (g); Richard Bona (b); Billy Cobham (d).* 2/97.

It had been rumoured for some time that the group which made *Spaces* at the turn of the '70s, one of the finest fusion records of all time, might reconvene for a recording. In the event, Lagrene is an interesting replacement for John McLaughlin and Camerounian Richard Bona makes a very different sound from Miroslav Vitous. Coryell's 'Variations On Pork Pie Hat' and his introduction to an interpretation of 'Ruby My Dear' are of the highest calibre. This is not so much a nostalgic re-creation of the original group as an entirely new working of a sound that might otherwise be rather dated and time-warped. Bona's funky bass sits just as well with Cobham's percussion, but it also has a percussive edge its predecessor lacked. A remarkable record in its own right.

★★★(★) Monk, Trane, Miles & Me

High Note HCD 7028 *Coryell; Willie Williams (ts); John Hicks (p); Santi Debriano (b); Yoron Israel (d).* 5/98.

For all his interest in classical, Latin and fusion music, Coryell has remained very much devoted to straight, bop-based jazz, and this tough, funky album is a testament to his ongoing engagement with modern jazz and its great masters. Larry kicks off with two brisk standards, 'Star Eyes' and 'Alone Together', and starts to engage with his ancestors in an interpretation of Monk's 'Trinkle Tinkle'. Coltrane is represented by 'Naima', which is obvious fare for the guitarist, but also the more aggressive 'Up Against The Wall'. Miles is limited to a rather dull version of 'All Blues', while 'me' is represented in two originals, 'Fairfield County Blues', generic and rather bland, and the closing 'Almost A Waltz'. Oddly, the most effective composition and performance of the set is down to bassist Santi Debriano; 'Patience' is a moody waltz and Larry admits that he had to go back to the Van Gelder studio to re-record his part and master the strange, slashing chords the bassist had written for him.

★★★ Cause & Effect

Tone Center 40022 *Coryell; Tom Coster (org, ky); Victor Wooten (b); Steve Smith (d).* 8/98.

Given the revival of interest in '70s fusion towards the end of the century, it wasn't so very surprising to hear Coryell return to the idiom. Coster and Smith are veterans of Carlos Santana's jazz-orientated rock band. The session consisted largely of open-ended jams, created with a freshness that couldn't have been guaranteed had Coryell insisted on recording old tunes from the Eleventh House days. Coryell's 'Bubba' is as greasy and funky as anything he has ever done and the finale, 'Wes And Jimi', a heartfelt tribute to two profound influences. The obvious source for all this is Tony Williams's Lifetime, but we were also reminded of the trio reconvened in the '90s by former Lifetime man, Jack Bruce, with saxophonist Dick Heckstall-Smith and drummer John Stevens. Terrific stuff. Pure nostalgia for those who remember the first generation; a treat even for those who don't.

★★★ Private Concert

Acoustic Music 1159 *Coryell (g solo).* 4/99.

Smoothly elegant and thoughtful jazz but the 'private' side of it is perhaps overstated. Always given to introspection, even in his more furious moments, Coryell sounds as though he is playing for his own entertainment rather than ours.

★★★ Coryells

Chesky 192 *Coryell; Julian Coryell (g); Murali Coryell (g, v); Brian Torff (b); Alphonse Mouzon (perc).* 8/99.

Larry and Julie were long-time collaborators, but this disc features a new generation of Coryells, the first time that fellow-guitarists Julian and Murali have joined dad on record. It's a project that includes material like 'Low-Lee-Tah', which was written before they were born. The best interaction between the three comes on Larry's classic 'Transparence' and on Julian's composition, 'Sink Or Swim', which suggests that in future years he will also be an impressive writer. Murali additionally sings on a couple of cuts and Julian has a couple of numbers to himself, accompanied only by bassist Brian Torff, whose touch is impeccable. Mouzon sticks to hand drums throughout, occasionally recalling his role in Larry's fusion band, Eleventh House, but also suggesting just how inventive a musician he has always been in his own right.

★★★(★) New High

High Note 7052 *Coryell (g solo).* 10/99.

Effortlessly swinging, packed with ideas and very much in a jazz idiom, *New High* saw Coryell enter a new decade and a new age with supreme confidence. His solo on 'Bags' Groove' is almost arrogantly straightforward and unfussy, and the dying falls of 'Old Folks' are tempered by a wise and sanguine major key theme. Cracking stuff.

★★★(★) Inner Urge

High Note 7064 *Coryell; Don Sickler (t); John Hicks (p); Santi Debriano (b); Yoron Israel (d).* 2/00.

Picking up where he left off with *New High*, Coryell continues to reposition himself as a jazz guitarist first and foremost with this powerful set of repertory tunes. Unusually, the guitarist only programmes two originals, 'Allegra's Ballerine Song' and 'Turkish Coffee', preferring to work imaginative variations on a range of relatively unfamiliar material. 'Dolphin Dance' and 'In A Sentimental Mood' are, of course, pretty well established, but who else has had the vision to programme Harold Land's 'Compulsion and 'Terrain' (that's how the album begins and ends) and who else is exploring Ray Bryant's 'Tonk'? The real pay-off, though, is a cracking interpretation of Joe Henderson's 'Inner Urge'. Our only quibble is that it might have been more effectively placed later in the album.

All of the group are in fine form. Hicks loves this kind of format and plays wonderfully on the Ellington. Debriano, whose 'Abra Cadabra' is the other track on the set, is a firm presence, working in an around Coryell's lower tones with instinctive ease. Sickler also produces and Rudy van Gelder's gives *Inner Urge* its clear, ringing sound, flattering to Coryell and spot on for the others as well.

***** Cedars Of Avalon**

High Note 7093 *Coryell; Cedar Walton (p); Buster Williams (b); Billy Drummond (d).* 12/01.

There probably isn't a better jazz rhythm section on the planet than this one, three guys who understand the architecture of a tune like 'Bemsha Swing', 'What's New' or even 'Limehouse Blues' but who could each of them enhance it at the drop of a hat. Walton and Williams both play like composers, even their seemingly off-the-cuff drop-ins are fresh melodic ideas. All of which isn't to deny Coryell his due of praise, merely to set it up with appropriate context and accompaniment. The company would be flattering to any player, but the guitarist is in superb form here, a jazz player to his toes, putting out some of the best music of his career. The fusion player and power-chord monger of past years is still evident from time to time, as when he flips the switch for his solo on the Monk tune, but Coryell has learned the necessary lessons from that period of his life and is in no mind to repeat them or it. Fine stuff.

***** The Power Trio: Live In Chicago**

High Note 7109 *Coryell; Larry Gray (b); Paul Wertico (d).* 02.

Lest anyone fears a second coming for the likes of West, Bruce & Laing, this is a rather subtler kind of power trio than that. The opening 'Autumn Leaves' is breathtakingly bold, starting in fast bop mode and quickly going outside. 'Star Eyes' is handled somewhat the same way. Coryell only includes one original but programmes some challenging fare, from George Harrison's 'Something', which the audience may or may not have recognized, to 'Bags' Groove', which ends the set on a high. The sound isn't great and Gray and Wertico are not of the leader's quality. And yet the ideas are strong and their relative simplicity of accompaniment (think somewhere between a Warne Marsh trio and the Jimi Hendrix Experience) is their greatest strength.

***** Birdfingers**

Universe 55 *Coryell; Randy Brecker, Mike Lawrence (t); Steve Marcus (ss, ts); Jim Pepper (f); Darius Brubeck (p); Mike Mandel (p, org, ky); Mervin Bronson, Chris Brubeck, Ron Carter, Glen Moore, Chuck Rainey, Danny Triffan (b); Dan Brubeck, Steve Haas, Bob Moses, Alphonse Mouzon, Bernard 'Pretty' Purdie, Harry Wilkinson (d); Ray Mantilla, Earl DeRouen, Collin Walcott (perc); Julie Coryell (v).*

The cover has the younger Coryell in rock-star mode, though still toting a jazzman's guitar. There you have the delightful paradox of the career that's sketched out on this odd compilation. It covers the ground from live versions of 'Eleventh House Blues' and 'Beyond These Chilling Winds' (with Julie, from the Village Gate disc) to a Robert de Visee sarabande from *The Restful Mind* to Latin stuff and the turn to post-bop jazz. As an introduction, it's probably as confusing as it is helpful. As an illustration of Coryell's eclecticism, it's hard to beat.

Eddie Costa (1930–62)

VIBES, PIANO

Costa made some impact on the New York scene of the middle '50s, but at the beginning of the next decade his star was in the ascendant, and he was equally adept on both vibes and piano. The end came suddenly in a car accident in 1962.

*****(*) Guys And Dolls Like Vibes**

Verve 549366-2 *Costa; Bill Evans (p); Wendell Marshall (b); Paul Motian (d).* 1/58.

Costa's legacy as a leader consists of only four albums, and this is the first to make it to CD. Although the programme is a typical Broadway-goes-jazz session of its day, the stellar line-up (though nobody recognized it as such at the time of the original Coral LP issue) will raise a browser's eyebrows. Evans is still in his tough, boppish salad days and when paired with Costa's equally brisk and searching solos the six themes from *Guys And Dolls* come in for some productive scrutiny. While hardly a lost masterpiece, this is a rare survival, and hopefully Verve will keep it in print long enough to reach a wider audience than it ever enjoyed in its vinyl form.

Louis Cottrell (1911–78)

CLARINET

A student of Lorenzo Tio and Barney Bigard, Cottrell was working with the Young Tuxedo Band while still a teenager, and he toured and recorded with Don Albert in the '30s. He played the old-fashioned French Albert system clarinet.

***** The Louis Cottrell Trio**

Original Jazz Classics OJC 1836-2 *Cottrell; Emanuel Sayles (g); McNeal Breaux, Alcide 'Slow Drag' Pavageau (b).* 1/61.

One of the least-known albums in Riverside's *New Orleans: The Living Legends* series featured this charming trio music by a clarinettist far less remembered than most of the city's favourite sons on this horn. Cottrell's style has none of the harshness of the George Lewis manner: he preferred the soft tone and modest vibrato that typified the old-fashioned elegance of the Lorenzo Tio style. He never had a better showcase than this one, with the spirited strum of Sayles and the no-frills line of Breaux alongside (Pavageau appears on only one brief track). On some songs he seems careless about his phrasing and falters here and there, but on others – 'Rose Room' is a good instance – the purling variations on the tune secure a surprising intensity. Two tracks, previously available only on an anthology LP, have been added to the original programme for the CD reissue.

Dunstan Coulber

CLARINET, TENOR SAXOPHONE

Perrier Award winner in 2000 and a rising star on an unfashionable instrument, which he intersperses with some Scott Hamilton-like tenor.

***** Standards For A New Century**

Nagel Heyer NH CD 081 *Coulber; John Pearce (p); Steve Brown (b); Nik Preston (d).* 9/01.

There is a feeling of reinventing the wheel when someone like Dunstan Coulber comes along – not because jazz is such a novelty-obsessed, shark-like form that dies if it doesn't keep moving relentlessly forward, rather because the critics go through entirely predictable contortions at the sound of a young man playing in the idiom of a past era or decade. They did the same when Scott Hamilton, whom Dunstan resembles somewhat on tenor, began his career at Concord. Coulber isn't an instrumentalist of quite that calibre and it has to be said that the title of this release promises rather more than it delivers. What you get is crisp, deliberately old-fashioned jazz clarinet and swing tenor ranging across a predictable roster of standards. You know from the first bar that he's not going to be doing Radiohead covers, but Porter, Duke, Gershwin, Harry Barris and Rodgers & Hart seem somewhat unadventurous for such a young man. Is there nothing since that era that's captured his heart? Coulber's caught between a hard place and the blandishments of rock. He'll do well, but many seasoned jazz fans picking this up will wish they were listening to the 'real thing', whatever that is.

Curtis Counce (1926–63)

DOUBLE BASS

Counce moved from Kansas City, where he had won some experience with one of the last territory bands, to join the best of the West Coast boppers in Los Angeles. Reminiscent of other West Coasters like Red Mitchell and Monty Budwig, he had a big, swinging delivery which suited solo exposure.

***** You Get More Bounce**

Original Jazz Classics OJC 159 *Counce; Jack Sheldon, Gerald Wilson (t); Harold Land (ts); Carl Perkins (p); Frank Butler (d).* 10/56.

*****(*) Landslide**

Original Jazz Classics OJC 606 *As above.* 4/57.

***** Carl's Blues**

Original Jazz Classics OJC 423 *As above.* 8/57.

***** Sonority**

Contemporary C 7655 *As above.* 1/58.

*****(*) Exploring The Future**

Boplicity CD 7 *Counce; Rolf Ericson (t); Harold Land (ts); Elmo Hope (p); Frank Butler (d).* 4/58.

'More bounce' promised, more bounce delivered. Elasticity aplenty in Counce's late-'50s quintet, one of the better and more resilient bands working the West Coast scene at the time. Perhaps the best of the albums is *Exploring The Future*, but *Landslide* is a fine one too, showcasing Land's beefy tenor and Sheldon's very underrated soloing. Perkins, remembered best for his weird, crab-wise technique, was probably on better form with this band than anywhere else on record, but the real star – a point recognized by the drum solo 'The Butler Did It' on *Carl's Blues* and 'A Drum Conversation' on the bin-end *Sonority* – was Frank Butler, a powerful technician who shared Counce's own instinctive swing. He is also the dedicatee of 'A Fifth For Frank' (do they mean the interval or the measure of whisky?) on *Landslide*. Most of the material stems from the same half-dozen sessions but is none the worse for that, given the quality of the material. *Sonority* initially sounded like the makeweight, but repeated hearings suggest it's a stronger statement than we originally thought. Counce's own contribution to 'A Night In Tunisia' and 'How Long Has This Been Going On' is worthy of anyone's notice.

Though he lived for another few years and certainly recorded again, this is his last record as leader. The original Dootone release of *Exploring The Future* is now a considerable rarity and it's good to have the music back in circulation. This is hard bop without the strut and the sneer, just laid-back, swinging music, played to challenging charts and arrangements (largely) by Elmo Hope. The pianist's 'Race For Space' and 'Countdown' are both quite advanced and the titles suggest how much these guys wanted to be seen as part of something new rather than a music that was beginning to sound dated. The transfers are very good, with Counce settled into the middle of the ensemble. Ericson and Land are sometimes a touch off-mic, but not to any troubling extent. This band has drifted into the margins of jazz history now, but inquisitive listeners will find an adventurous and exciting group whose legacy is well worth reviving again.

Stanley Cowell (born 1941)

PIANO

Cowell's vocation was decided when at the age of six he saw Art Tatum. College-educated, his real apprenticeship was with Roland Kirk; but it was the association with Charles Tolliver, with whom he founded the Strata East label, that really shaped his dark, complex style which draws on Bud Powell and Monk as well as Tatum.

****** Sienna**

Steeplechase SCCD 31253 *Cowell; Ron McClure (b); Keith Copeland (d).* 7/89.

This may well be Cowell's finest moment on record, a tightly marshalled, endlessly inventive trio session that comes at the beginning of a period of intense creativity. The two opening tracks, 'Cal Massey' and the gentle ballad 'I Think It's Time To Say Goodbye', take the measure of Cowell's extraordinarily expressive range. Copeland seems a little out of place on slower tracks, which might well have been done as duos with the excellent McClure, but the drummer's abrupt unison accents on 'Evidence' are startlingly effective. This is quite the best version of Monk's tune since the master's own and it represents a peak from which the album can only decline. A long 'I Concentrate On You' adds nothing to the hundreds that have gone before, waffling round the chords in an almost detached way. It's only with the title-track, just one of a cycle of 'Sienna'-related compositions, and with the closing 'Dis Place' that Cowell lets loose his remarkable harmonic and rhythmic intelligence. An excellent album, recorded in an odd, rather claustrophobic acoustic.

*****(*) Departure No. 2**

Steeplechase SCCD 31275 *Cowell; Walter Booker (b); Billy Higgins (d).* 10/90.

***** Games**

Steeplechase SCCD 31293 *Cowell; Cheyney Thomas (b); Wardell Thomas (d).* 8/91.

***** Bright Passion**

Steeplechase SCCD 31328 *As above.* 4/93.

Turning 50, Cowell had acquired a new creative momentum. Recorded in Denmark and marking a new and fruitful association with Steeplechase, *Departure* is his most jagged and pugnacious recording for some time. 'Photon In The Paper World' (or is it 'A Paper World'?) reappears from 1969, and 'Splintered Ice' has the same harmonic virtuosity as 'Softly' on the Maybeck disc. In both cases, though, Cowell manages to combine technical mastery with genuine expressiveness. 'Four Harmonizations Of The Blues' is almost as mechanical as it sounds. There has always been a strain of sheer cleverness in Cowell's playing, games with false symmetries and weird harmonic regresses; when it breaks through as obviously as this, it's decidedly tiresome.

The later dates are hampered by an inexperienced and below-par rhythm section, and one has to ask what the motivation was. Cowell transcends it triumphantly on *Games*, playing with huge authority and often without seeming reference to his colleagues. There are some majestic episodes on 'From The Rivers Of Our Father', but they fail to add up to anything larger. 'Sienna: Welcome To The New World' is perfunctory and bland, and the new material fails to get things moving. The trio is a lot tighter and more responsive on the later set, but Cowell is muted and workaday, and there's an odd, perfunctory air to the date. After the triumphs of the last couple of years, we can readily spare him an off-day. These last two are for resolute collectors only.

★★★(★) Live

Steeplechase SCCD 31359 *Cowell; Cheyney Thomas (b); Wardell Thomas (d).* 4/93.

As purple patches go, this was of the deepest mauve, Cowell and his young trio at the Copenhagen Jazz House. The piano certainly isn't of studio quality and there are a couple of notes that sound dead here and there (on early tracks, so perhaps we aren't hearing them in real-time order), but it has enough presence to lift the set. Cowell sticks mainly to standards and jazz tunes, opening with 'Anthropology' and closing with 'In Walked Bud', but mostly staying away from bebop in between. The three originals, 'Bright Passion', 'Brilliant Circles' and a long 'Prayer For Peace', are easily the most interesting things on the record, and perhaps it was merely in deference to the rhythm section that Cowell didn't include more of his own compositions. Nils Winther produces with a sure touch, delivering a set that is both atmospheric and (but for that piano) technically spot-on.

★★★★ Angel Eyes

Steeplechase SCCD 31339 *Cowell (p solo).* 4/93.

How very different he sounds without the constraint (as it often seems) of a group. *Angel Eyes* offers a solid hour of flawless piano jazz. From the opening, Coltrane-tinged 'The Night Has A Thousand Eyes' to the small group of more demanding originals at the close – 'Akua', 'The Ladder', 'Abscretion' – Cowell grips the attention. Following his harmonic logic is beyond most listeners and certainly most of his fellow-players, but it's none the less impressive. The house piano at Steeplechase sounds rather light in this solo context; it's certainly not one of those great woofing concert things, nor has it the purring, woody resonance of the piano at Maybeck. But it's responsive enough for Cowell to weave a subtly inflected spell. Even John Lennon's 'Imagine', a fairly unpromising theme, is woven into something of genuine grandeur.

★★★(★) Setup

Steeplechase SCCD 31349 *Cowell; Eddie Henderson (t); Dick Griffin (tb); Rick Margitza (ts); Peter Washington (b); Billy Hart (d).* 10/93.

Cowell has never seemed an excessively brooding player, but this is joyously upbeat by any standard. It had been some considerable time since he released a group record with horns and it does the old heart good. The key track is 'Sendai Sendoff', featured in solo form on *Angel Eyes* but here arranged for an excellent and thoroughly sympathetic band. Henderson is in sterling form, always at his best when relieved of the responsibilities of leadership. A word, too, for the unsung Griffin, who gives the ensemble passages a rich, caramelly texture. The saxophonist is less well adapted to Cowell's idiom, and there are a few moments of uncertainty there. The Steeplechase sound is flawless and Nils Winther has managed to create a *simpatico* environment in which the musicians are encouraged to play as they feel, rather than keeping their eye on the clock and an ominously clicking metre. Cowell has rarely sounded more relaxed than over these past few years and, even allowing for a philosophical change of pace that comes with age, the label set-up has to take much of the credit.

★★★(★) Mandara Blossoms

Steeplechase SCCD 331386 *Cowell; Billy Pierce (ts); Jeff Halsey (b); Ralph Peterson (d); Karen Francis (v).* 11/95.

A wholly unexpected departure. Debby Randolph's lyric to 'Equipoise' sounds as if it was always intended to be there, and Karen Francis's rich, well-trained voice lifts the song up out of the ordinary. With the strongly vocalized Pierce on the session, this has a rich, choral feel that is quite startling and it is certainly not readily identified as a Cowell set. He writes his own lyrics for 'This Life' (the best of the bunch) and the title-track. Randolph and John Scott are responsible for the remaining words. 'Mandara Blossoms' is the briefest thing on the set, a haunting watercolour built on a falling figure, and intended to suggest a moment of philosophical calm. Difficult to say why and where the elements don't quite cohere, but we have some misgivings. The sound isn't always balanced very persuasively and it's occasionally difficult to hear what Cowell himself is doing. The best (and longest) track of all is Billy Strayhorn's 'Daydream', complete with extra verse, and it succeeds largely because it pitches Karen and Stanley against each other, with saxophone coming in at exactly the right juncture.

★★★(★) Hear Me One

Steeplechase SCCD 31407 *Cowell; Bruce Williams (as); Dwayne Burno (b); Keith Copeland (d).* 10/96.

The unexpected inclusions here are Monk's 'Ruby My Dear' and that bebop groaner, 'Anthropology'. Neither is within Cowell's normal spectrum. He is by no means a devoted Monkian, and so handles this one with more respect and fidelity than one would expect. He tells the story of having met Monk and telling him that he had written some tunes in his style. 'How can you write tunes in my style when all my songs are different?' Fair point, and that more than anything Cowell has taken on board. There is no Cowell style. Each song is the 'cry of its occasion', as the poet said. 'Banana Pudding' is an Eastern-sounding idea, constructed round a non-jazz scale. 'Tinged' is new, and apparently intended to be played with some electronic and vocal elements. As a straight group piece, it lacks for nothing. 'Photon In A Paper World' (and it does seem to be 'a', not 'the') is revived, one of his durable originals. A dramatic reworking of 'Anthropology' is successful up to a point, though Williams's Parkerisms are unconvincing; the saxophonist contributes one original, the closing track 'Ferrell', and he sounds like a promising writer. Cowell's recording career now spans more than 30 years. There have, inevitably, been highs and lows; there has also been an impressive consistency of purpose and the highest level of musical thought.

Anthony Cox

DOUBLE BASS

Vastly experienced bassman with a long list of credits. The solo career has been more variable.

*** That And This

Sketch 333029 *Cox (b solo). 02.*

Solo bass records are tough, even when studio overdubbing, octave splitting and other effects are employed. Cox likes to do it fairly straight, as is his wont as a sideman, but he has the range and the warmth of tone to carry it off. There are some lovely things here like a co-composition with Dino Saluzzi and Don Friedman and the moving 'Mr Cox High School Band Leader', but for the most part, this is a record for bass addicts, unlikely to be of interest to many general listeners, for all its musicality. No sign of a return for Anthony's *Dark Metals* or *Factor Of Faces*, his previous forays as leader.

Norrie Cox

CLARINET

An Englishman in America, Cox led British bands during the trad boom but decamped to the US – in his capacity as an engineer – in 1966. Returned to music in the '80s and is heavily involved in authentic revivalism.

*** Dance Hall Days

Delmark DE-236 *Cox; Charlie DeVore (c); Jim Klippert (tb); Mike Carroll (g, bj); Bill Evans (b); Donald 'Doggie' Berg (d). 11/98.*

Recorded in a wooden-floored dance hall in Wisconsin (the Park Ponderosa Ballroom), the sound is beautifully authentic even if the playing is frequently rickety. Cox's New Orleans Stompers seems like a motley bunch, even if it drinks deep of the spirit. The music is a pretty mixed bag: often Cox himself is the weak link, with 'Jerusalem Blues' (which sounds like 'Burgundy Street Blues') showing how far off his model George Lewis he can be. But the music has its own raggedy gumption, and it feels honest.

Lol Coxhill (born 1932)

SOPRANO, TENOR AND SOPRANINO SAXOPHONES

Deeply rooted in jazz, but ranging over free music, instrumental chanson and an idiosyncratic quasi-folk, Lol is a vastly talented soprano specialist with an utterly individual tone; it ranges from aching sweetness to hard-edged multiphonics. Lol on record isn't quite the point, but there is now at least a representative selection on offer.

*** Spectral Soprano: Solo And Group Improvisations, 1954–1999

Emanem 4204 2CD *Coxhill; Mat Davis, Pete Kempster, Roland Ramanan (t); Donald Manson, Annie Whitehead (tb); Paul Rutherford (euph); Alex Ward (cl); Tony Coe (cl, v); Harrison Smith (bcl); Neil Metcalfe (f); Evan Parker (ss); Caroline Kraabel, Bruce Turner (as); Terry Day (home-made wind instruments); Steve Miller (p); Dave G. Holland (p); Veryan Weston (p, ky); Steve Beresford (p, v); Pat Thomas (ky, elec); Lu Edmonds (3-string bj); Hugh Metcalfe (g, v); Mike Cooper (slide g, elec); Rhodri Davies (hp); Orphy Robinson (mar); Nigel Coombes, Philipp Wachsmann (vn); Mark Wastell, Colin Wood (clo); Olly Blanchflower, John Edwards, Dave Green, Simon H. Fell, Peter Love (b); Laurie Allan, Steve Noble, Roger Turner (d); Ansuman Biswas, Jeff Griffin (perc); Paul Schutze (elec); Rik Rue (samples); Adam Bohman (amp objects); Bob Cobbing (v, bodhran); Tony Knight's Chessmen. 54–99.*

**(*) Ear Of Beholder

See For Miles SEECD 414 *Coxhill; Burton Greene, Jasper Van't Hof (p); Pierre Courbois (d); David Bedford (p, v); various walk-ons, environments. 7/70, 1/71.*

*** Toverbal Sweet ... Plus

See For Miles SEECD 480 *Coxhill; Jasper Van't Hof (p); Pierre Courbois (d). 72.*

There is no one quite like Lol Coxhill, which may be why he has been neglected, relegated to the role of festival MC and resident clown of the British free scene. The only musician one might feasibly liken him to, however improbable it may sound, is Lee Konitz. Coxhill has carved a path from straight standards playing to abstract improvisation, taking in rock groups (like Kevin Ayers's proto-slacker Whole World outfit) along the way. If that is the point at which he deviates from jazz loyalist Konitz, the resemblance is reinforced again by Lol's fragile, endlessly lyrical soprano tone.

Spectral Soprano is a wonderful primer, a grab-bag of material from the beginning of Lol's professional career onwards. As such, it doesn't have much structure or principle of order, but it dramatizes his personal take on both jazz and free music. An early recording – made at a lo-fi 3¾ i.p.s – has him running the changes on 'Autumn In New York' and already demonstrating his preference for melody over mere harmonic variation. There are cuts featuring the young saxophonist, still then basically a Pres-influenced tenor man, with Tony Knight's Chessmen who toured with visiting American R&B artists; there are solo performances from throughout his career, most notably 'Magic Buffalo', which has him ranging between tenor, soprano and piano; and there are duos and group pieces, with Steve Miller, bassist John Edwards, with the so-called Melody Four (a trio, naturally) and with the London Improvisers Orchestra. A predictably eclectic *dramatis personae* includes alto saxophonist Bruce Turner, 'the Dirty Bopper', Lu Edmonds of punk band the Damned and poet Bob Cobbing. Lol also checks the acoustics of a Danish swimming pool with a slide saxophone. As a compilation, it isn't faultless and there are some frankly bad recordings included, however good the music, but it builds a picture of a remarkable and remarkably protean musician; Lol's spoof saxophone tuition tape at the start of CD2 is a delight.

It has been said that Coxhill is not so much an improviser as an instant composer. This is only half true, for his grasp of vertical harmony is impeccable, as can be heard on 'Lover Man', included on *Ear*. (This disc was released much earlier but picks up the story at a somewhat later stage.) His great strength, though, is the busker's ability to turn out simple, effective tunes, seemingly by the yard. *Ear Of Beholder* was recorded for BBC DJ John Peel's Dandelion label. It consists of a few studio tracks, some festival material – like the tenor 'Deviation Dance', on which the sound is pushed through a Gibson Maestro – and some tunes busked out on London streets; the opening 'Hungerford' was recorded where Lol used to have a regular pitch on the pedestrian bridge outside Charing Cross railway station. A double LP has been compressed on to a single CD with the omission of just one track. It could have been cropped and edited further. The long 'Rasa Moods' with Van't Hof, Courbois and Greene was recorded in Utrecht; the sound is grim but the playing is fascinating, with some effective use of the Maestro again. A whimsical grab-bag (there's even a track of kids singing 'I Am The Walrus'), very much in the spirit of Peel's own wayward enthusiasms, it doesn't wear particularly well and will be of most interest to those who've lost their (now very tradeable) vinyl and want to recapture something of those faraway years.

The trio material on *Toverbal Sweet* is more consistent. A club recording, it is more evenly proportioned, representing the mid-ground between jazz and free music all three were exploring in their different ways at the time. Van't Hof uses both electric and acoustic piano, but much of the action comes from Courbois's expanded kit. Very much a group effort, harder-edged than Lol's work with the Johnny Rondo Duo and the Melody Four.

**** Coxhill On Ogun

Ogun OGCD 008 *Coxhill; Michael Garrick (electric p); Veryan Weston (p); Ken Shaw, Richard Wright (g); Dave Green, Paul Mitchell-Davidson (b); Colin Wood (clo); John Mitchell (perc). 77–8.*

Glorious. Bringing together two of Lol's best records, *The Joy Of Paranoia* and *Diverse*, from the later '70s, this is the place to start if you've never encountered him before. *Joy* began with a live group improvisation recorded in Yorkshire; 'The Wakefield Capers' is the perfect illustration of Lol's ability to play free forms with all the sweetness of a Johnny Hodges and little of fellow-soprano specialist Steve Lacy's acidulous attack. Accompanied by the three guitars of 'Paws For Thought' – with Mitchell-Davidson on a wibbly bass – he weaves two long, thoughtful solos full of long, bent notes, sliding intervals and little melodic ideas which seem to rise up out of nowhere. 'The Cluck Variations' is a collaboration with pianist Weston, quite formally cast but full of anarchic invention. 'The Joy Of Paranoia Waltz' should be played at all wedding receptions just at the moment when new in-laws start to eye one another across the dance floor; it uses inventive overdubs on a simple riff. The clinching joy of the 1978 album for us, though, was the pair of standards, 'Lover Man' and 'Perdido', played as duets with Michael Garrick on electric piano. These offer further strong evidence of Lol's gifts as a standards player. The Tizol tune is a revelation, reinvented wholesale.

Diverse is not so immediately appealing, but it is a strong and inventive set consisting of one solo piece and a quartet. 'Diver' is more strictly a duet with a loose floorboard at Seven Dials in London; the quartet consists of cello, bass and percussion. Played entirely free, these pieces come from a jaggier end of the idiom than 'Wakefield Capers'.

*** Digswell Duets

Emanem 4052 *Coxhill; Veryan Weston (p); Simon Emmerson (elec). 5/78.*

Recorded at Digswell House in Welwyn Garden City, the earlier set of duets featured an experimental pairing. Coxhill's saxophone sound was processed by Emmerson's electronics, leaving Lol to respond in turn to the transformed sound. The recording doesn't do complete justice to the music, which is a pity, because there is always a lot of detail in Lol's playing, and this is already somewhat compromised by the processing, though not to its detriment. Some of the resulting soundscape is just that – a rather bland abstract wash without much drama or incident. However, Lol is far too shrewd a player and Emmerson too sensitive an accompanist to allow attention to fade, and the most effective moments are when fragments of melody, sometimes familiar enough to seem like standard material, creep through the mix.

The remaining tracks document an early stage in what was to be a profoundly fruitful association with Weston. The duo's approach to two standard themes, 'Embraceable You' and 'I Can't Get Started', is typical of Lol's improvisation-first-then-the-tune approach, which makes complete sense here. There are other, related segments included in the Oxford set. Lol is playing with great clarity and with tremendous speed and ease, and some of his lines will startle mainstream jazz players who've written him off as a novelty act. Like much of this label's output, a valuable document that could have done with some studio sweetening, though that runs against both Coxhill's and Emanem's ethos.

*** Termite One

Bruce's Fingers 32 *Coxhill; Paul Rutherford (tb); George Haslam (bs); Simon H. Fell (b); Paul Hession (d). 89.*

Recorded at the Termite Festival in 1989 and only released on the bassist's own label a decade later. The combination of Coxhill, Haslam and the peerless Rutherford is intoxicating, but the presence of a rhythm section somehow seems to constrain the music, even though neither Hession nor Fell plays conventional metre. Lol's playing isn't well served by a shaky recording, which dips and distorts at will, but as a document of five important British improvisers this is a very worthwhile issue.

***(*) Three Blokes

FMP CD 63 *Coxhill; Steve Lacy, Evan Parker (ss). 94.*

Stylistically Coxhill is very different from either fellow-Briton Evan Parker or Steve Lacy, the other main soprano specialists. His first influence seems to have been Charlie Parker, though he had a solo apprenticeship in R&B groups as well. He plays a curious part in these sessions. The concept was a mixture of solos, duos and trios, and Lol finds himself playing something like the Dewey Redman role in the Ornette Coleman band of the '70s, rationalizing, normalizing, finding a middle ground and occasionally injecting a moment of gruff humour into some fairly dry and dour proceedings. No reason to say that this is his record rather than theirs, except that his is by some way the smallest extant discography of the three, and he does seem to occupy an important middle ground that makes him the fulcrum and the catalyst.

*** Solos East/West

Slam CD 308 *Coxhill; George Haslam (bs).* 90, 95.

Unfortunately, Lol and George don't play together at any point; the title is strictly accurate. Interesting to compare the two approaches. Haslam comes to free jazz from an interest in West Coast cool, and though he has never sounded like a Mulligan acolyte (Chaloff is perhaps more his speed), he shares something of Gerry's awareness of large-scale modal structure. Lol is much more of a vertical improviser, albeit one who is highly sensitive to melody as well as harmonics. His solos are a cross between advanced changes-playing and spontaneous composition. Occasionally here, one senses the imminence of a familiar standards idea, but these rarely announce themselves unambiguously. The rating is based solely on Coxhill's contribution and doesn't reflect on a high-quality album.

***(*) Boundless

Emanem 4021 *Coxhill; Veryan Weston (p).* 1/98.

They recorded before, in 1978, with a superb performance on Lol's *The Joy Of Paranoia.* Like Lol, Weston is a brilliant miniaturist, and the combination of the two is exquisite. Not that many of these 15 tracks are particularly short. The longest are over six minutes and are developed in the saxophonist's familiar, jazz-based style. Weston is no less lateral a thinker, but his sources are very different, and part of the joy of the session is the combination of two seemingly unlike personalities who find huge areas of common enthusiasm, almost against the odds. Though Coxhill concentrates almost entirely on soprano these days, it might have been preferable to vary the colours a little bit. It's a long record – almost 70 minutes of music – and the tonality remains light and sharp throughout, an impression reinforced by a rather severe digital recording. Great stuff, though, and further reminder of Coxhill's improvisational skills.

*** Alone And Together

Emanem 4034 *Coxhill; Stevie Wishart (vn, hurdy-gurdy); Marcio Mattos (clo, elec).* 10/91–5/99.

Emanem's Martin Davidson is still sourcing an extraordinary range of overlooked tape material documenting Britain's free scene. This disc brackets almost a decade of material, but though the settings are very different the basic rules of engagement remain Lol's own. The big difference here is that for the first four tracks he doubles on sopranino, a tough horn to discipline and a rather piercing sound when heard at any length. 'A Rare Sopranino Solo' confirms that it holds no terrors, but it's not the easiest of listens. Three of the four are duets with Wishart, who brings along her hurdy-gurdy as well, creating a witch's kettle of bagpipe drones; very effective. The duet with Mattos is characteristically thoughtful and again constructed over a drone background, this time using live and gently responsive electronics. The remainder of the set, not so comfortably recorded, consists of a solo soprano recital at the Queen Elizabeth Hall (and presumably in the lobby). A continuous 20-minute improvisation, with a tiny encore tacked on the end, it's just one of a thousand such gigs Lol must have played over the years, but no less valuable for that.

**** Worms Organising Archdukes

Emanem 4074 *Coxhill; Veryan Weston (p, org).* 01, 02.

Lol and Veryan Weston have been playing partners for a quarter of a century, and it shows. These are riveting duo performances, full of surprise and tender beauty. The curious title comes from the provenance of the recordings, the Worm in Rotterdam and the Archiduc, a new music venue in Brussels; the 'organising' part is a chamber organ interlude recorded at the Red Rose in London.

'The Second Duet Of Worms' features some of Coxhill's best playing on record, an expressive, jazzy introduction that builds into something genuinely capacious. Weston's piano style is best characterized as romantic and though these titles are almost always added after the fact, he might well have been aware of the historical resonance of an 'Archduke Duo'. Both these pieces are virtuosic, with Coxhill exploring the upper range of his saxophone and his now familiar, but by no means hackneyed, repertoire of multiphonics and other effects. This is a valuable documentation of a creative friendship, accessible and intimate.

*** Out To Launch

Emanem 4086 *Coxhill (ss solo) and with: Ian Smith (t); Paul Rutherford (tb); Neil Metcalfe (f); Alex Ward (cl); Veryan Weston (p); Lu Edmonds (amplified bass bj); Olly Blanchflower (b); Steve Noble (perc); Michael Kosmides (theremins); Knut Aufermann, Steve Beresford, Pat Thomas (elec).* 10/01, 3 & 4/02.

The title is label boss Martin Davidson's joke, a reference to what he claims is his least favourite Eric Dolphy album. Most of the music is solo performance, recorded in Chicago and London, but with the addition of a group improvisation with members of the London Improvisers Orchestra who had convened to play a special launch concert for Lol's *Spectral Soprano* retrospective. The CD had to be delayed but the gig went ahead; hence, Unlaunched Orchestra. It seems Coxhill was unwilling to start the music himself, which explains a degree of hilarity at the start of the piece, which is the shortest and least appealing element of another very strong record. The longest track is the Chicago set, named 'Music For Feathery Fronds'. It's a virtuosic performance, full of jazz references and extended technique on the saxophone. The two other improvisations 'Relaunch One And Two' are denser and darker in mood, but no less effective and no one should be so fooled by Lol's jovial festival MC persona as to mistake the depth of feeling which permeates his work. Again, very warmly recommended.

*** Mouth

Fragile Noise CD 01FN52 *Coxhill; Mick Walter (ts).* n.d.

Sixteen challenging improvisations from this unfamiliar partnership in rather strange but effective packaging. Lol's ability to weave in and out of someone else's lines or simply to lay down textures for a fellow-improviser is well on show here. A couple of times you might almost be listening to Lee Konitz and Warne Marsh on a particularly crazed afternoon, and Lol simply can't help his jazz roots showing. Mostly, though, it's free if notionally songlike and very effective.

*** Milwaukee 2002

Emanem 4097 *Coxill; Paul Rutherford (tb); Torsten Muller (b).* 4/02.

It isn't clear who should get the attribution on this set of solos, duos and one trio but Lol gets the nod on alphabetical grounds. A year or two back, we might have given it to Paul Rutherford, but his discography has grown exponentially and while his opening 'Woodland Bone Patterns' (the items were recorded at the Woodland Pattern Book Center in Milwaukee) is the longest piece on the album it's also much less focused than we expect of Paul. Lol's 'Sax Patterns' and his following duos with Rutherford and Muller are the heart of the set and then the three are together for a closing improvisation that shows how much common ground they share, but also what yawning gaps there are between Muller's strenuous adherence to freedom and Coxhill's and Rutherford's genetic adherence to jazz.

Crane River Jazz Band

GROUP

One of the seminal British traditional groups, the CRJB was formed by Ken and Bill Colyer in 1949, and went through various incarnations before the Colyers left in 1951, whereupon Sonny Morris kept it going until 1957.

***** The Crane River Jazz Band**
Cadillac SGC/MEL CD 202 *Ken Colyer (c, t, g, v); Sonny Morris (c); John R. T. Davies (tb, org, g); Ray Orpwood (tb); Monty Sunshine (cl); Pat Hawes (p, wbd, v); John Shipcott (p); Ben Marshall (bj); Julian Davies (b); Ron Bowden, Cyril Louth, George Hopkinson, John Westwood (d); Bill Colyer (perc).* 50–53.

***** Vintage Crane River Jazz Band 1950–1952**
Lake LACD 182 *As above except add Phil Dearne (p), Les Page (bj), Denny Coffee, Stan Pearcy (b), Pete Appleby (d), omit Louth, Westwood.* 50–52.

The first track on the Cadillac set, a version of 'Muddy Old River' by Ken Colyer and John R. T. Davies (on guitars!), sounds as ancient and mysterious as a Ma Rainey discovery, and in a way the whole CD offers that kind of experience: eavesdropping on the primeval stirrings of British traditional jazz. The material is an eccentric mix of ragtime, blues, music-hall songs, New Orleans staples and Creole melodies, all of it played by impressionable young Londoners in the early '50s. The sound is suitably dusty and sometimes so is the playing, but these memories of the Metro Club and various exotic Home Counties locations have their own peculiar charisma.

The Lake set adds to our knowledge. Much of the first half is made up of more practice sessions from 1950, and as earnest as they were to get sound and feel right, they weren't there yet. The later music from 1951-2 is a bit smarter and more fluent, although it's still Ken Colyer (even though he was about to depart for his own band) whose playing one waits to hear. Little to choose between either of these discs, perhaps, although only a diehard specialist will really want both of them.

Hank Crawford (born 1934)

ALTO AND BARITONE SAXOPHONES

Like David Newman, Crawford had long experience in the Ray Charles touring band and made a string of bluesy soul-jazz recordings for Atlantic in the '60s. Born in Memphis, he started on baritone but took up alto in 1959. Spells in commercial music took him away from jazz but Milestone's albums have reasserted his roots in R&B and small-group jazz.

***** More Soul**
Atlantic 8122-73709-2 *Crawford; Phillip Guilbeau (t); John Hunt (t, flhn); David Newman (ts); Leroy Cooper (bs); Edgar Willis (b); Milt Turner (d).* 3/61.

***** Midnight Ramble**
Milestone MCD-9112-2 *Crawford; Waymon Reed, Charlie Miller (t); Dick Griffin (tb); David 'Fathead' Newman (ts); Howard Johnson (bs); Dr John (ky); Calvin Newborn (g); Charles Greene (b); Bernard Purdie (d).* 11/82.

****(*) Indigo Blue**
Milestone MCD-9119-2 *Crawford; Martin Banks, Danny Moore (t); David 'Fathead' Newman (ts); Howard Johnson (bs); Melvin Sparks (g); Wilbur Bascomb (b); Bernard Purdie (d).* 8/83.

**** Mr Chips**
Milestone MCD-9149-2 *Crawford; Randy Brecker, Alan Rubin (t); David 'Fathead' Newman (ts); Howard Johnson (bs); Richard Tee (ky); Cornell Dupree (g); Wilbur Bascomb (b); Bernard Purdie (d).* 11/86.

***** Night Beat**
Milestone MCD-9168-2 *Crawford; Lew Soloff, Alan Rubin (t); David 'Fathead' Newman (ts, f); Howard Johnson (bs); Dr John (ky); Melvin Sparks (g); Wilbur Bascomb (b); Bernard Purdie (d).* 9–10/88.

***** Groove Master**
Milestone MCD-9182-2 *As above, except Lou Marini (ts) replaces Newman; add Gloria Coleman (org).* 2–3/90.

Hank Crawford says that he tries 'to keep the melody so far in front that you can almost sing along', and that irresistibly vocal style lends his simple approach to the alto a deep-rooted conviction. His best records are swinging parties built on the blues, southern R&B – Crawford apprenticed in the bands of Ike and Tina Turner and Ray Charles – and enough bebop to keep a more hardened jazz listener involved.

More Soul is one of his vintage Atlantics, actually his first as leader, and minus a piano he gets the horns to act as the harmonic carpet. The result is a sonorous, churchy kind of record (the band is basically Ray Charles's unit), with Hank and Fathead Newman taking solo honours.

Following his long spell at Atlantic, he renewed his career with Milestone, which began by providing him with consistently sympathetic settings – in the end, too consistent. There's little to choose among the albums listed above, all of them are smartly organized around Crawford's libidinous wail. *Mr Chips* gets lower marks for a mundane choice of material, while *Midnight Ramble*, *Night Beat* and *Groove Master* are enlivened by the inspiring presence of Dr John on piano and organ. Typical of Crawford's mature command is the way he empowers Whitney Houston's 'Saving All My Love For You' on *Groove Master* with a real authority.

****(*) Soul Survivors**
Milestone MCD-9142-2 *Crawford; Jimmy McGriff (ky); George Benson, Jim Pittsburg (g); Mel Lewis, Bernard Purdie (d).* 1/86.

****(*) Steppin' Up**
Milestone MCD-9153-2 *Crawford; Jimmy McGriff (ky); Billy Preston (p); Jimmy Ponder (g); Vance James (d).* 6/87.

****(*) On The Blue Side**
Milestone MCD-9177-2 *As above.* 7/89.

Crawford shares leadership duties with McGriff on these small-group albums, and between them they try to update the sound of the '60s organ combo without surrendering the juice and fire of the original music. *Soul Survivors* is the best of the three because the renewed partnership is at its freshest, and Benson is for once employed in a worthwhile jazz context; but, taken a few tracks at a time, all three discs are enjoyable if lightweight.

****(*) Portrait**
Milestone MCD-9192-2 *Crawford; David 'Fathead' Newman (ts); Johnny Hammond (org); Jimmy Ponder (g); Vance James (d).* 90.

***** South-Central**
Milestone MCD-9201-2 *Crawford; Stan Hope, Dr John (p); Gloria Coleman (org); Melvin Sparks (g); Peter Martin Weiss, Wilbur Bascomb (b); Grady Tate, Bernard Purdie (d).* 2/90–8/92.

**** Tight**
Milestone MCD-9529-2 *Crawford; Earl Gardner, David Rubin (t); David 'Fathead' Newman (ts, f); Howard Johnson (bs); Danny Mixon (p, org); Melvin Sparks (g); Stanley Banks (b); Idris Muhammad (d).* 4–5/96.

Crawford's more recent records are basically disappointing. *South-Central* has its moments, especially on a rollicking 'Splanky', but elsewhere Crawford sounds like he's starting to take it easy, and perhaps one can't altogether blame him. *Tight*, though, does no credit to anyone. 'Breezin'' is thin and hapless in this incarnation and, while the band is full of old pros, they sound like they're staggering through this date. Bob Porter's production also hides Hank somewhere in the back row. What happened to that sound?

*****(*) Heart And Soul**
Rhino/Atlantic R2 71673 2CD *As above Milestone albums, except add Marcus Belgrave, Lee Harper, Phil Guilbeau, John Hunt, Fielder Floyd, Joe Newman, Ernie Royal, Bernie Glow, Snooky Young (t); Jimmy Cleveland, Benny Powell, Tom Malone (tb); Frank Wess (as); Seldon Powell, James Clay, Harvey Thompson, Abdul Baari, Wendell Harrison (ts); Leroy Cooper, Howard Johnson, Pepper Adams, Alonzo Shaw, Ronnie Cuber, Jim Horn (bs); Ray Charles, Richard Tee, Clayton Ivey (p); Lucky Peterson (org); Frankie Crawford (ky); B. B. King (g, v); Steve Cropper, Will McFarlane, Sonny Forrest, Eric Gale, Hugh McCracken (g); Edgar Willis, Charlie Green, Ron Carter, Gary King, Willie Weeks (b); Richie Goldberg, Milt Turner, Bruno Carr, Bernard Purdie, Roger Hawkins (d); Etta James (v).* 7/58–5/92.

Another handsome package in the Rhino/Atlantic series gives us something close to the definitive Hank Crawford retrospective. It starts, fittingly, with the Ray Charles band at Newport, but the key early tracks on disc one are those from the *More Soul*, *Soul Clinic* and *From The Heart* albums. The Atlantic material works to a grand formula, but a formula none the less, and it palls a little over two long CDs. So the second disc, after a few Creed Taylor rhapsodies from the '70s, turns to the Milestone albums for the rest of the compilation. Tracks with B. B. King and Etta James restore to Crawford his righteous role as a signifying sideman and pretty much close the circle on this middleweight's gratifying career. Re-mastering is exemplary throughout, with the Atlantic tracks sounding as good as new.

****(*) Road Tested**
Milestone MCD-9274-2 *Crawford; Jimmy McGriff (org); Wayne Boyd (g); Bernard Purdie (d).* 7/97.

****(*) After Dark**
Milestone MCD-9279-2 *Crawford; Danny Mixon (p, org); Melvin Sparks (g); Stanley Banks, Wilbur Bascomb (b); Bernard Purdie (d).* 2/98.

***** Crunch Time**
Milestone MCD-9287-2 *Crawford; Jimmy McGriff (org); Melvin Sparks, Cornell Dupree (g); Bernard Purdie (d).* 11/98.

The old firm of Crawford and McGriff share the billing on the first and third of these. If you have any of their earlier collaborations, it's hard to see why you'd want these to go with them, since there's nothing new, and nothing much worth re-visiting on either of them. These are seasoned pros who can turn out these records to order and, while there's nothing amiss, what is there to remember? Wayne Boyd is a busy guitarist on the first date, which also has an overly reverberant sound, as if they were trying to make the band sound bigger. Bob Porter tightens that up on *Crunch Time*, and this makes the band sound leaner and fitter so it's a marginally better record. Bernard Purdie is not the world's subtlest drummer, but that's what they want.

Hard to see the point of the interim *After Dark*. It's meant to show off Hank's worldliness as a bluesman, but tunes such as 'My Babe' and 'Git It!' are the kinds of thing he's been playing all his life anyway. Bernard Purdie is not the world's bluesiest drummer, either, but he's still giving them what they want.

***** The World Of Hank Crawford**
Milestone MCD-9304-2 *Crawford; Marcus Belgrave (t, flhn); Ronnie Cuber (bs); Danny Mixon (p, org); Melvin Sparks (g); Stanley Banks (b); Kenny Washington (d).* 2/00.

What a wonderful world? Well, it's fair enough, and if this seems like arid professionalism at times, taken a few minutes at a time – jukebox-length, possibly – it beats any smooth jazz one could cite. Ronnie Cuber's a soulful addition to the band, and if Mixon does tend to come on like Liberace at the piano, at least he's better behaved on organ. Hank just does his usual thing.

Marilyn Crispell (born 1947)

PIANO

Famously, Crispell was turned on to modern jazz when she heard a John Coltrane record. Her classical training and very exact, flowing style were uniquely well suited to a transition to polytonal jazz. Crispell's improvisations are always densely detailed and powerfully emoted. Her association with Anthony Braxton in another classic quartet was yet another key relationship.

***** Live In Berlin**
Black Saint 120069 *Crispell; Billy Bang (vn); Peter Kowald (b); John Betsch (d).* 11/82.

Crispell was, in retrospect, probably overdocumented for a number of years; more recently, things have gone rather quieter on the disc front, but she has been one of the most significant piano improvisers of the last two decades. When all is said and done, the Coltrane and Cecil Taylor influences weighed much less heavily on her earliest recordings than was routinely thought and, though she has regularly returned to Coltrane in particular as a kind of guiding spirit (see below), she is certainly not a slavish imitator. She holds up strongly in some pretty rugged company in this early set from the Total Music Meeting. The shift to CD has lifted the piano considerably and effects a bit of separation and space in the background. The set is dominated by a huge piece, 'ABC', dedicated to her next most important influence, Anthony Braxton, with whom she has worked very profitably for many years. Her background in classical, particularly Baroque, music is still clearly audible as she negotiates oblique contrapuntal passages and wild, seamless fugues. The two string-players seem worlds apart and don't interact very effectively. Kowald replaced guitarist Wes Brown, who had appeared on an earlier Cadence LP called *Spirit Music* and seemed much more in tune with Crispell's conception.

**** Selected Works: 1983–1986, Solo Duo Quartet

Leo Golden Years of New Jazz 11 2CD *Crispell; Doug James (perc); Didier Petit (clo) Marcio Mattos (b); Yoval Mincemacher (d, perc).* 83–86.

A most valuable recovery from the LP archive, this brings together the solo *Rhythms Hung In Undrawn Sky*, the duo set with Doug James, *And Your Ivory Voice Sings*, and a somewhat less satisfactory album of quartet improvisations with strings and percussion. We have long canvassed for the return of the first two records, and they sound as fresh and compelling as ever. Crispell's supposed Taylor influence is never as evident in reality as it threatens to be in theory, and the solo record is much more obviously influenced by Coltrane's piled harmonies and increasingly inventive rhythmic language. The duo with the relatively unknown James has enormous strength as well and comes across with renewed vigour on CD. We remain unconvinced by the quartet with Petit and the equally uncelebrated Mincemacher, though the extraordinary Mattos holds the set together.

**** For Coltrane

Leo CDLR 195 *Crispell (p solo).* 7/87.

Solo performances by Crispell are dramatic, harmonically tense and wholly absorbing. The first of these was a remarkable concert given in London in the summer of 1987, when Crispell supported Alice Coltrane and the two Coltrane boys, Ravi and Omar, with a solo set dedicated to Alice's late husband. Opening with a torrid 'Dear Lord' and closing with the billowing 'After The Rain', she improvised a series of 'collages' in memory of the great saxophonist. She also performed a piece called 'Coltrane Time', a title of convenience for a sequence of rhythmic cells on which the saxophonist had been experimenting in the period immediately before his death. A beautiful record, *For Coltrane* is a companion-piece to *Labyrinths* on Victo, recently restored to the catalogue.

**** Gaia

Leo Records LR 152 *Crispell; Reggie Workman (b); Doug James (d, perc).* 3/87.

Gaia is one of the finest composition/improvisation records of the '80s, a hymn to the planet that is neither mawkish nor sentimental, but tough-minded, coherent and entire. Spared conventional rhythm-section duties, Workman and James combine extremely well, producing both a dense *ripieno* for Crispell's dramatic *concertante* effects and a powerful drama of their own.

**** Labyrinths

Victo 6 *Crispell (p solo).* 10/87.

Those who overstate the Cecil Taylor connection were thrown their best piece of evidence here where Crispell pays explicit tribute in 'Au Chanteur Qui Danse', a long improvisation dedicated to Taylor. It's neither homage nor pastiche, but a very personal improvisation which uses some of Taylor's familiar dancing rhythms, firecracker phrasing and dervish concentration.

Equally significant in modelling Crispell's musical universe is the presence of two John Coltrane themes, the Tadd Dameron-derived 'Lazy Bird' and an absolutely magnificent reading of 'After The Rain', which was a signature concert piece of Crispell's at this period. Brief as the former is, it underlines her instinctive understanding of jazz harmony and song form; Crispell rarely excavates material like this for its purely technical dimensions. What she creates here is logically formed, expressively coherent and quietly perfect. Recorded live in Quebec during the annual Festival de Musique Actuelle, this is one of her best records of the '80s and certainly one of the best of the solo recordings.

*** Live In Zurich

Leo LRCD 122 *Crispell; Reggie Workman (b); Paul Motian (d).* 4/89.

It's interesting to compare Motian's role here with his work behind Geri Allen and Charlie Haden in their trio. He seems busier than usual, louder and more emphatic, except when the spotlight falls on him, as it does on the second long improvisation, and he reverts to a more familiar articulation. There are moments of clutter on this set, taken from a European tour, but also signs that Crispell had found a group that allowed her to extend her rhythmic ideas still further. Signing off with Coltrane's 'Dear Lord' was a familiar enough tactic by this stage, but listen to how she relocates the song's harmonies by subtly distorting its metre. A fine and affecting performance and a very enjoyable record.

**** Overlapping Hands: Eight Segments

FMP CD30 *Crispell; Irène Schweizer (p).* 90.

Like much of Crispell's best work, *Overlapping Hands* is a concert performance, and a duo at that. There are moments when it might almost be one person playing, so close is the understanding between the two women, but for the fact that they do sound very different. Schweizer's sound is sharper and more Europeanized; Crispell's draws deeper on an American tradition and constantly refers to tonal centres that her collaborator wants to push away to the very boundaries of the music. The recording is near perfect, and a tremendous advance on some of FMP's more Heath Robinsonish concert efforts; the music is a joy.

*** Circles

Victo 12 *Crispell; Oliver Lake (ss, as); Peter Buettner (ts); Reggie Workman (b); Gerry Hemingway (d).* 10/90.

Four long compositions which move into free territory before revealing their structure. Unusual at this period to hear Crispell work with horns and unfortunately she sounds a little overpowered by them. Some of this is an artefact of the live mix, which is hopeless, but one also senses something between a hesitancy and a more conscious desire to keep out of the front line and concentrate on shaping the inner contours of an otherwise turbulent piece, as she does on the very long opening

'Rituel'. Too long, arguably, since it seems to explode prematurely and then spend the rest of its 24-minute duration smouldering like ammunition cooking off in a wrecked tank. 'Chant' and 'Circles' are better, still with roots in the ritualized music theatre of the '60s avant-garde but with a strangely redemptive quality. Judicious editing and a more sympathetic mic set-up would have yielded a better record, but we also have doubts about this line-up. The chemistry with Workman and Hemingway is as fresh and fissile as ever, but neither Lake nor Buettner seems involved with the main action.

(★★★★) **Stellar Pulsations / Three Composers**

Leo CD LR 194 *Crispell; Don Byron (cl); Ellen Polansky (p); Gerry Hemingway (d); WDR Radio Orchestra, David de Villiers (cond).* 7/92.

A further step away from the immediate concerns of this *Guide*, the marvellous *Stellar Pulsations* represents the work of three composers who are exploring the borderlines of improvisation and formally scored music. Manfred Niehaus's *Concerto For Marilyn* has a wholly scored and fixed orchestral part, with partial notation for the piano-player in the first movement. This part is called 'Concerto For Chico'; movements three and four also refer to the Marx Brothers. The second movement is a swaying 'unhoused tango' in which piano and orchestra conjoin in open-ended tempo. 'Concerto For Harpo' is a piano/harp duet. A timpanist joins in for 'Concerto To Provoke Groucho', leading to a final cadenza for Crispell.

Pozzi Eschot's *Mirabilis II* draws on music by Mother Hildegard (a figure much admired by both Crispell and Anthony Braxton) to create a framework for trio improvisation. As before, Crispell and Hemingway seem to be in complete communication, but Don Byron's part is a little less sure-footed and often sounds as if he's merely reading off. The balance of composition and improvisation is clearer in Robert Cogan's *Costellar Pulsations*, which starts the disc. Here Crispell improvises over Ellen Polansky's notated (but not immutable) score, from which the performer can select and reorder elements. Echoing the language and ideas of *Overlapping Hands* (above), Crispell allows the piece to divide naturally into expressive segments, some of which strongly suggest tonality, others the orderly but indefinable progress of natural (or cosmic) events. Though less likely to appeal to straight jazz fans, this is another beautiful record and, in its way, another important stage in Crispell's development as an artist.

★★★★ **Spring Tour 1994**

Alice ALCD 13 *Crispell; Anders Jormin (b); Raymond Strid (d).* 94.

Well, the season seems completely apposite for music as fresh and affirmative as this. There used to be – probably still is – an awful test-piece for pianists by Christian Sinding called 'Rustle Of Spring'. No one need ever perform or listen to it again ... Where often Crispell can sound slightly dense and introspective, here she dares to play somewhat more simply and directly. She is undoubtedly encouraged by her two colleagues. Strid has a brisk, beery exuberance (and does a famous line in home-brew, incidentally) which doesn't invite tortured, existential dramatics, while the bassist is quite simply one of the most beautiful stylists currently working on the instrument. Heady, uplifting stuff, perhaps more immediately winning than the excellent things below.

★★★★ **Band On The Wall**

Matchless MRCD 25 *Crispell; Eddie Prévost (d, perc).* 5/94.

★★★(★) **Destiny**

Okkadisk OD 12003 *Crispell: Fred Anderson (ts); Hamid Drake (d, perc).* 8/94.

Recorded live during the Women Of New Music festival in Chicago, the Okkadisk set is marred – Crispell-wise – only by having the piano mixed down too low and occasionally swamped by saxophone and percussion. Otherwise it finds her in thoroughly sympathetic company. Anderson's diction is Coltrane-influenced but generously varied and thoroughly personalized. As with Braxton and Prévost (below), this seems like a relationship written in the stars, and it allows them to build up whole areas of interaction in which the exchange of ideas is almost too fast to follow. Drake provides sterling accompaniment and, like Prévost, often takes the initiative in breaking up Crispell's long, suspended lines into shorter, more discursive sections.

The Matchless disc was also recorded live, at the Manchester venue called Band On The Wall. It's a fiery, sometimes almost violent performance in which ideas are run together with a challenging insouciance. Extravagant as she often is, Crispell has rarely sounded so thoroughly unfettered; oddly, perhaps, because Prévost is a highly disciplined drummer and certainly one of the most swinging in a free idiom. One slight oddity of the set is the inclusion of the Denny Zeitlin composition, 'Quiet Now', towards the end. How many repertory pieces has this pairing explored?

★★★ **MGM Trio**

Ramboy 9 *Crispell; Michael Moore (cl); Gerry Hemingway (d).* 94–95.

Difficult to know whether this is legitimately a Crispell release since it's very much a group of equals (named after their initials) and this project is devoted to compositions by label-owner Moore. However, it's Crispell who one hears first and last, teasing out the mysterious beauty of songs like 'Temperamental Annie', 'The Pound Fell Down' and 'The Bigger The Dot, The Better The Fishing', which seems to allude (musically, at least) to some of the classic texts of German improv. What's interesting above all is hearing Crispell in a relatively formal setting. Composition has always been one of her main interests, though it has tended to be hidden behind free-form improvisation. Here she shifts the micro–macro balance subtly and reveals new aspects of her pianism.

★★★★ **Nothing Ever Was, Anyway**

ECM 537222-2 2CD *Crispell; Gary Peacock (b); Paul Motian (d).* 96.

Crispell included Annette Peacock's 'Gesture Without Plot' on each of the two sets documented above, and this exquisitely recorded tribute marks a more extended engagement with the finest female jazz composer of recent times, Carla notwithstanding. The choice of material scarcely matters, because the album becomes a type of mini-opera without words, an extended portrait of one fine artist's engagement with another. There are moments when the Peacock/Motian partnership is almost too strong-voiced and runs some risk of overpowering the piano, which occupies a now familiar spectrum of dynamics. Crispell has seldom (if ever) played as elegantly and with such control. Perhaps the discipline of staying within the bounds set by another composer – and one with a much more melodic approach than Coltrane, say – allowed her to free up one hitherto suppressed aspect of her musical personality. Suffice it to say that we consider this a contemporary masterpiece. To miss it would be to overlook a piano trio the equal of anything since the late Bill Evans.

***** Dark Night and Luminous**

Musica Secreta 7 *Crispell; Agusti Fernandez (p).* 98.

There have been many significant Catalan improvisers down the years, from sometime Braxton associate Tete Montoliu to Pedro Iturralde and now Agusti Fernandez. The pianist has also worked successfully with Derek Bailey. This duo recording is less satisfactory, largely because the sound isn't very good. It isn't so much that one can't tell who is playing what as that there is a significant level of distortion when the signal becomes fuller or the dynamics shift. None the less, it is interesting to hear Crispell working with another keyboard player and to compare this with the much more muscular collaboration with Irene Schweizer. *Dark Night And Luminous* is almost sentimental by comparison.

***** Red**

Black Saint 120199 *Crispell; Stefano Maltese (reeds).* 9/99.

***** Blue**

Black Saint 120230 *As above ; add Gioconda Cilio (v)* 9/99.

At moments, this is uncannily similar to Marilyn's work with Anthony Braxton, except that the clarinettist (which is how we feel he's best characterized) is rhythmically much less open than the American. Most of these pieces find her playing almost second fiddle and sounding unusually dry. Technically, the standard of performance is very high indeed, but there is little of Crispell's fierce passion and energetic commitment, and when she does cut loose at moments on *Red* the effect is rather strained. Cilio joins the duo for a couple of vocalized pieces at the end of *Blue*, immediately prompting the query why she wasn't more fully absorbed into these sessions.

****** Amaryllis**

ECM 013400-2 *Crispell; Gary Peacock (b); Paul Motian (d).* 2/00.

Brilliantly curated by label boss Manfred Eicher, this trio session allows Crispell and her colleagues to play some old compositions alongside trio improvisations. Motian's 'Conception Vessel' has some of the hallmarks of a modern classic, but it is Crispell's brief, intense 'Rounds' which defines a lovely set, intense and languid by turns and full of wonderful invention. The piano tone is gorgeous and Peacock is playing with a fuller voice than ever. A record to absorb yourself in many times over.

Sonny Criss (1927–77)

ALTO AND SOPRANO SAXOPHONES

Born in Memphis, he played in R&B bands before recording as a bebop leader. Latterly worked in rehabilitating young offenders but became afflicted by depression and took his own life.

***** California Boppin'**

Fresh Sound FSR CD 156 *Criss; Al Killian, Howard McGhee (t); Teddy Edwards, Wardell Gray (ts); Charles Fox, Russ Freeman, Hampton Hawes, Michael 'Dodo' Marmarosa (p); Barney Kessel (g); Harry Babasin, Red Callender, Addison Farmer (b); Tim Kennedy, Jackie Mills, Roy Porter (d).* 4, 6, 7 & 10/47.

*****(*) Memorial Album**

DIW 302 *Criss; Al Killian, Clark Terry (t); Dexter Gordon, Wardell Gray (ts); Gil Barrios, Jimmy Bunn, Charles Fox, Hampton Hawes (p); Dave Bryant, Billy Hadnott, Shifty Henry, Clarence Johnson (b); Frank Butler, Tim Kennedy, Billy Snyder, Chuck Thompson (d); Damita Jo (v).* 10/47, 8/50, 9/52, 6/65.

*****(*) Sonny Criss Quartet, 1949–1957**

Fresh Sound FSRCD 64 *Criss; Hampton Hawes (p); Iggy Shevack, Buddy Woodson (b); Chuck Thompson (d).* 9/49, 11/57.

Criss was perhaps a little too tightly wrapped for the destiny that seemed to await him. Though it was the altogether more robust Sonny Stitt – with whom Criss is occasionally confused – to whom Charlie Parker promised 'the keys of the Kingdom', it was Criss out on the West Coast who inherited most of the ambiguities of Parker's legacy.

California wasn't a happy place for Bird, by and large, and there's something hectic, almost desperate, in Criss's super-fast runs and soaring, high-register figures. The earliest of the material is rather derivative but provides several excellent opportunities to hear Criss's pure, urgent tone and delivery; he comes in behind Wardell Gray on 'Groovin' High' almost impatiently, with a little flurry of notes, before stretching out and shaping those distinctive wailing passages and held notes. The June 1947 material, with the rhythm section that backed Parker at the Hi-De-Ho in Los Angeles earlier that year (Hawes, Farmer, Porter), is probably the best on the disc, with a particularly fine version of 'The Man I Love' that also features Teddy Edwards and Howard McGhee. Two long jam-sessions have lots of episodic interest but are marred by Al Killian's dreary high-note work.

The DIW memorial is an excellent buy, offering a bitty but reasonably comprehensive survey of the whole career with the exception of Criss's brief Indian summer of the mid-'70s. Unfortunately, there's an overlap with *California Boppin'*, and quite a substantial one; doubly unfortunately, it's the October 1947 Portland jam with Killian and Wardell Gray. However, the record's worth having for the 1965 material with Hampton Hawes (see below), and a one-off track from 1950 ('I Can't Give You Anything But Love') with Clark Terry and Dexter Gordon, on which Criss more than holds his own. Hawes spurs him.

He's on hand for both the sessions on the other Fresh Sound, playing a little neatly on the 1949 tracks, which have a brittle politeness suggestive of buried tensions in the studio, but opening out majestically on the two standards which start the November 1957 session. On 'Willow Weep For Me', Criss delivers a gently sorrowful solo, spoken with manly regret and without a wasted gesture. Hawes matches him, and bassist Woodson – an unremarked player – comes in with a fluent statement of his own. In this still small discography, this has to be considered a significant release.

*****(*) Intermission Riff**

Original Jazz Classics OJCCD 961-2 *Criss; Joe Newman (t); Bennie Green (tb); Eddie 'Lockjaw' Davis (ts); Bobby Tucker (p); Tommy Potter (b); Kenny Clarke (d).* 10/51.

These tapes were hidden away from 1951 until 1987. Criss's talent had been spotted early on and, when he was still in his teens, he was asked to join Norman Granz's Jazz at the Philharmonic collective on a nationwide tour. This was a return fixture and any hint of diffidence or uncertainty has long since evaporated. Still flaunting his Parker influence with superb insouciance, Criss creates some breathtaking solos, notably on 'Perdido', which rubberstamps his bebop visa, but also on a lovely version of 'Body And Soul', on which he doffs his cap to Benny Carter and Johnny Hodges as well.

Davis and the underrated Green play a full part and they and the splendid rhythm section come through superbly on an overdue CD transfer that plugs a significant gap in the Criss discography.

*** The Complete Imperial Sessions

Blue Note 24564 2CD *Criss; Sonny Clark, Kenny Drew (p); Barney Kessel (g); Larry Bunker (vib); Leroy Vinnegar, Buddy Clark, Bill Woodson (b); Larance Marable, Chuck Thompson (d).* 2 & 8/56.

This plain and unvarnished compilation brings together the three records Criss made for Imperial: *Jazz USA*, *Go Man* and *Plays Cole Porter*. The last of the group is a perfect illustration of what Harold Bloom calls the anxiety of influence, a session reeking of the late Charlie Parker's influence, precisely because it attempts to throw off Bird's manner. 'I Get A Kick Out Of You', right at the end, balances respect and a declaration of independence just about perfectly.

The other material is very strong, with Sonny playing workaday themes with a relaxed authority that he was rarely to equal again. His rhythmic and harmonic mannerisms are occasionally evident and sometimes intrusive, but this is probably not a set to listen to continuously, but to be sampled from time to time. Every expense has been spared in the remastering, and the sound comes across raw, fresh and authentic.

*** Sonny Criss Quartet Featuring Wynton Kelly

Fresh Sound FSRCD 318 *Criss; Ole Hansen (tb); Wynton Kelly (p); Bob Cranshaw (b); Walter Perkins (d).* 1/59.

Wynton isn't really featured at all on this pick-up session recorded in Chicago while Criss and trombonist Hansen were touring with Buddy Rich's band. The playing is workmanlike and none too enterprising, though Sonny gets in some very elegant solos, using Hansen as his foil whenever the temperature goes up. Sets like this were bread and butter to a player of Criss's character, and here he shows what a pro he was, ever ready to rise to a modest challenge and entertain whoever was on hand to listen.

*** Mr Blues Pour Flirter

Verve 549231 *Criss; George Arvanitas (p, org); Pierre Michelot (b); Philippe Combelle (d).* 4/63.

Oddly missing the near-contemporary track which gives the session its title, this reissue is part of Verve's Francophile reissue programme and it adds some nice standards performances to the Criss list. Nothing too dramatic here but, following the death of Bird, this was as close as most Europeans were likely to get to the real thing and Sonny frames some delightful solos, not least on 'Don't Get Around Much Anymore' and 'God Bless The Child'. It would be good to hear more from Criss's fruitful time in France.

***(*) This Is Criss!

Original Jazz Classics OJCCD 430-2 *Criss; Walter Davis (p); Paul Chambers (b); Alan Dawson (d).* 66.

**** Portrait Of Sonny Criss

Original Jazz Classics OJCCD 655-2 *As above.* 67.

These are two of the best Criss albums currently available. His ability to invest banal tunes with real feeling (see *I'll Catch The Sun!*, below, for real alchemy) is evident on 'Sunrise, Sunset', a tune from *Fiddler On The Roof* given a brief but intense reading on *This Is Criss!*. Criss does something similar, though at greater length, to 'Days Of Wine And Roses', adjusting his timbre subtly throughout the opening choruses.

'Wee' on *Portrait* takes him back to bop days, an astonishing performance that manages to skate over a lack of solid ideas with sheer virtuosity. 'Smile' bears comparison with Jackie McLean's readings, but the real stand-out tracks are 'On A Clear Day', which is hugely emotional, and 'God Bless The Child'. The CD also offers a bonus 'Love For Sale', which probably deserved to be left out first time round. The band is good and Davis (who wrote 'Greasy' on *This Is Criss!* and 'A Million Or More Times' on *Portrait*) is the mainstay.

*** The Beat Goes On!

Original Jazz Classics OJCCD 1051 *Criss; Cedar Walton (p); Bob Cranshaw (b); Alan Dawson (d).* 1/68.

Reissued in 2000, this provides a bit of context for what was to follow. Criss was still in a bebop riff at this point in his career, but also keen to push out beyond it into something altogether more relaxed rhythmically. His delicate metrical hesitations work nicely on the title-piece, which is much subtler than at first appears, and there is some lovely playing on 'Yesterdays' and 'Ode To Billie Joe'. Deftly remastered, this is a welcome addition to the Criss discography.

CORE COLLECTION

**** Sonny's Dream

Original Jazz Classics OJCCD 707-2 *Criss; Conte Candoli (t); Dick Nash (tb); Ray Draper (tba); David Sherr (as); Teddy Edwards (ts); Pete Christlieb (bs); Tommy Flanagan (p); Al McKibbon (b); Everett Brown Jr (d).* 68.

This is a most welcome CD reissue of a project subtitled 'Birth Of The New Cool' and featuring six Horace Tapscott compositions and arrangements. Though he has only recently begun to receive wider recognition, Tapscott's influence on the West Coast has been enormous, and this was a rare chance for Criss to play in front of a carefully orchestrated mid-size band.

'Sonny's Dream' is an astonishing opener, with luminous solos from both Criss and Tommy Flanagan. Criss switches to soprano for the brief 'Ballad For Samuel', dedicated to a respected teacher, but profoundly marked by Coltrane (who had recently died). Tapscott's inventiveness and political sensibilities are equally engaged on 'Daughter Of Cochise' (an unusually relaxed solo from Criss) and 'Black Apostles', originally dedicated to Arthur Blythe (another Angeleno saxophonist who made a personal accommodation with Bird's idiom) but transformed into a brooding and ferocious lament for the three martyrs of the black liberationist movement.

A remarkable album that lapses only to the extent that the band is sometimes reduced to providing highly coloured backdrops for Tapscott's American history lessons and Criss's soloing (which bears comparison with Evan Parker's on the *With Strings* sessions).

***** Up, Up And Away**

Original Jazz Classics OJCCD 982-2 *Criss; Cedar Walton (p); Tal Farlow (g); Bob Cranshaw (b); Lenny McBrowne (d).*

***** Rockin' In Rhythm**

Original Jazz Classics OJCCD 1022-2 *Criss; Walter Davis, Eddie Green (p); Paul Chambers, Bob Cranshaw (b); Alan Dawson (d).*

Like many jazz players of the time, Criss felt he had to respond to the challenge of pop. 'Up, Up And Away' was a gift for his soaring, risky, joyous tone, and the partnership with Farlow gives the material a taut, swinging excitement. Cedar Walton is disappointing by his own high standard and seems to do little more than mark time when he's not actually soloing. 'Scrapple From The Apple' plights Sonny's troth with bebop afresh, though by this point in the story it's clear that he's aware the chapter is over. There's a touch of pastiche in his solo choruses.

Rockin' In Rhythm returns to pop rather more circumspectly. 'Misty Roses' is delightful and 'Eleanor Rigby' preserves much of that song's melancholy poetry. The real bonus on this CD reissue, though, is a previously unissued 'All The Things You Are', with Walter Davis in exceptional form. Two lovely, undemanding records.

*****(*) I'll Catch The Sun!**

Prestige PR 7628 *Criss; Hampton Hawes (p); Monty Budwig (b); Shelly Manne (d).* 1/69.

Something of a comeback for Criss, and perhaps the most amenable and sympathetic band he ever had, reuniting him with Hawes. The material is vile, but players like these made a living out of turning sows' ears into silken purses, and both 'California Dreaming' and 'Cry Me A River' have a genuine depth of focus. Criss sounds composed and confident in this company, and solos with impressive logic and considerable emotion.

***** Live In Italy**

Fresh Sound FSRCD 337 *Criss; Georges Arvanitas (p); Jacky Samson (b); Charles Saudrais (d).* 1/74.

Criss's deutero-bop was still a market force in Europe when gigs back home were becoming scarce and the crowd here applaud the musicians (or themselves) with fanatical abandon every time they hear something they like. Sonny's approach to 'Summertime' is enough to convince the most jaded listener that, even with a European section and even when this close to the end of his life, he is able to turn in a delightful and well-structured solo, managing to namecheck other Gerwshin material along the way. 'Tin Tin Deo' and 'Lover Man' are equally good, though the band have heard the latter on record too many times and don't seem to be playing to the leader's tempo. Arvanitas is superb, though even he can't cope with the obligatory pop tune – here, 'Sunny' – and lapses into some weird version of prog rock on his solo. Criss saves the day, as he often did, and the record as a whole scores unexpectedly high, though don't expect much by way of sound quality.

Bob Crosby (1913–93)

VOCAL, LEADER

Bing's brother was a decent light vocalist and something of a figurehead for his band. When he left the Tommy Dorsey group in 1935, he became frontman for an orchestra that was a rarity: a big band that preferred Dixieland to the smoother side of swing. It was very successful until its disbandment in 1942. Crosby kept his solo career going and presided over many reunions of his old colleagues.

***** You Can Call It Swing**

Halcyon DHDL121 *Crosby; Yank Lawson, Phil Hart, Zeke Zarchy, Andy Ferretti (t); Ward Silloway, Art Foster, Warren Smith, Mark Bennett (tb); Gil Rodin, Matty Matlock (cl, as); Noni Bernardi (as); Eddie Miller (cl, ts); Dean Kincaide (ts); Bob Zurke, Gil Bowers, Joe Sullivan (p); Nappy Lamare (g); Bob Haggart (b); Ray Bauduc (d); Judy Garland, Connie Boswell (v).* 4/36–2/37.

***** A Strange New Rhythm In My Heart**

Halcyon DHDL122 *As above, except add Billy Butterfield (t), Bill DePew, Joe Kearns (as), Kay Weber (v); omit Hart, Foster, Bowers, Sullivan, Garland and Boswell.* 2–11/37.

***** You're Driving Me Crazy**

Halcyon DHDL123 *As above, except add Charlie Spivak (t), Connie Boswell (v); omit Ferretti, Bennett, Bernardi, Kincaide.* 11/37–2/38.

***** How Can You Forget?**

Halcyon DHDL125 *As above, except add Irving Fazola (cl); omit Boswell.* 2–3/38.

***** The Big Noise**

Halcyon DHDL 126 *Crosby; Yank Lawson, Charlie Spivak, Billy Butterfield, Zeke Zarchy (t); Ward Silloway, Warren Smith (tb); Irving Fazola (cl); Matty Matlock (cl, as); Joe Kearns (as); Eddie Miller (cl, ts); Gil Rodin, Dean Kincaide (ts); Bob Zurke (p); Nappy Lamare (g); Bob Haggart (b); Ray Bauduc (d); Bing Crosby (v).* 3–10/38.

***** Strange Enchantment**

Halcyon DHDL 127 *As above, except add Sterling Bose, Bill Graham (t), Jimmy Emmert (tb), Bill Stegmeyer (cl, as), Marion Mann, The Andrews Sisters (v); omit Spivak, Silloway, Kincaide, Lawson, Bing Crosby.* 10/38–3/39.

***** Them There Eyes**

Halcyon DHDL 128 *As above, except add Shorty Sherock (t), Ray Conniff (tb), Joe Sullivan, Floyd Bean (p), Teddy Grace (v); omit Bose, Graham, Matlock.* 3–11/39.

***** High Society**

Halcyon DHDL 130 *As above, except add Max Herman (t), George Koenig (as), Jess Stacy (p), Helen Ward (v); omit Bean, Emmert, Mann, Zurke.* 7–10/39.

***** Reminiscing Time**

Halcyon DHDL 131 *As above, except add Eddie Wade (t), Marion Mann (v); omit Sullivan.* 10/39–2/40.

A charming vocalist, if hardly a jazz singer, Bob Crosby fronted a band which ploughed an unusual furrow among the swing-era groups. The small-group sides, under the name the Bob Cats, were cast in a tempestuous Dixieland style. The music was a throwback to the best hot music of a decade before, and many of the full band's best sides – 'South Rampart Street Parade', 'Royal Garden Blues', 'Wolverine Blues' – were made from the same mould. The fuming trumpet of Yank Lawson, Eddie Miller's fluently hot tenor, the New Orleans-styled clarinets of Irving Fazola and Matty Matlock, all created an authenticity which, say, Tommy Dorsey's Clambake Seven could only hint at. The Crosby orchestra was almost unique among its contemporaries in that it carried the small-group Dixieland style into the bigger format. Haggart's adept arrangements, the timbre of the soloists – they sounded tough even when filling in eight or sixteen bars relatively straight – and the rhythm section's genuine swing all made the big band surprisingly hot when given their head. Yet, as usual, so many of the full orchestra's records were tainted by schmaltz and novelty that the integrity of the best music is always compromised in any chronological survey. Crosby was game enough to give his men their share of solo space, on the lesser tracks as well as the jazz-directed ones, which means that all is seldom lost. But in the end even the Bob Cats were playing the miserable likes of 'Adios Americano', 'Oh Mistress Mine' and 'You Oughta Hang Your Heart In Shame'.

The Halcyon discs are a complete ongoing survey in chronological order, but that means that the best sides are mixed with the mediocre, and the shoddy packaging and sometimes dull remastering are often discouraging. The earlier material tends to be the more interesting but the remastering is sounding better as it has gone on. It would be good to have the Bob Cats material sensibly compiled by itself, but the Australian Swaggie issues which managed that feat are now hard to find.

**(*) So Far So Good

Halcyon DHDL 132 *Crosby; Eddie Wade, Max Herman, Billy Butterfield, Bob Peck (t); Warren Smith, Ray Coniff (tb); Irving Fazola (cl); George Koenig, Bill Stegmeyer (as); Eddie Miller (cl, ts); Gil Rodin (ts); Jess Stacy (p); Nappy Lamare (g); Bob Haggart (b); Ray Bauduc (d); Marion Mann (v).* 2–3/40.

** From Another World

Halcyon DHDL 133 *As above, except add Muggsy Spanier (c), Al King (t), Floyd O'Brien (tb), Hank D'Amico (cl), Doc Rando, Matty Matlock (cl, as), Bonnie King, Bob-O-Links (v); omit Wade.* 3–9/40.

** Gone, But Not Forgotten

Halcyon DHDL 135 *As above, except add Elmer Smithers (tb), Bing Crosby, Connie Boswell, Merry Macs (v); omit Butterfield, Peck, Smith, Koenig, Stegmeyer, Mann.* 9–12/40.

**(*) Far Away Music

Halcyon DHDL 136 *As above, except add Bob Goodrich (t), Bonnie King, Liz Tilton (v); omit Bing Crosby, Boswell, Merry Macs.* 1–6/41.

*** Something New

Halcyon DHDL 137 *As above, except add Yank Lawson, Lyman Vunk (t), Buddy Morrow (tb), Art Mendelsohn (as); omit Goodrich, D'Amico, Spanier, King.* 5/41–1/42.

The Crosby story continued apace. This group made a huge number of records and, with the Halcyon series close to its conclusion, they take up a lot of shelf space. But this was a dreary period for the band on record. Despite the arrival of Spanier – who's mostly wasted, although he gets the occasional few bars – the orchestra's records were flabby with bad songs, routine charts and a marked absence of the Dixie-to-swing feel which made them popular in the first place. There's also the usual quota of vocals to get through. Very little worth keeping on four of the above discs, but matters perked up with the return of Yank Lawson in 1941, and *Something New* goes out on a session where the band was back with its original hot material. Remastering is clean enough throughout, although it doesn't seem to have much sparkle.

*** Ecstasy

Halcyon DHDL 138 *Crosby; Yank Lawson, Max Herman, Lyman Vunk (t); Floyd O'Brien, Buddy Morrow, Elmer Smithers (tb); Matty Matlock, Doc Rando, Art Mendelsohn (cl, as); Eddie Miller (ts, cl, v); Gil Rodin (bs, ts); Jess Stacy (p); Nappy Lamare (g); Bob Haggart (b); Ray Bauduc (d); Muriel Lane, Fred Astaire, Bing Crosby, Margaret Lenhart (v).* 1–5/42.

*** Where Do We Go From Here?

Halcyon DHDL 140 *As above, except add Pete Carpenter, Bruce Squires (tb), Ted Klein (cl, as), Cody Sandifer (d), Mary Lee, Wilde Twins (v); omit Lane, Lenhart.* 5–7/42.

These two discs finally complete Halcyon's marathon documentation of the Crosby band. Since both include a generous showing of Bob Cats titles (eight on the first, ten on the second) the jazz content is in the ascendancy again and both discs sport decent remastering. Brother Bing and Fred Astaire show up in guest spots on both discs. The band was about to be silenced by the Petrillo recording ban of 1942, but more serious was the draft, which was spiriting away many leading players, and in the end Bob's band broke up in the week before Christmas 1942. As usual, the orchestral numbers often fall prey to poor material and sweetness overruling heat, but *Ecstasy* in particular includes a good proportion of tracks where Lawson, Miller and Matlock can blow off some steam.

*** Associated Transcriptions Vol. 1

Nostalgia Arts 301 3018 *Crosby; Phil Hart, Yank Lawson (t); Ward Silloway, Artie Foster (tb); Matty Matlock (cl, as); Gil Rodin, Noni Bernard (as); Eddie Miller (cl, ts); Dean Kincaide (ts); Gil Bowers (p); Nappy Lamare (g); Bob Haggart (b); Ray Bauduc (d); Kay Weber (v).* 2–3/36.

*** Associated Transcriptions Vol. 2

Nostalgia Arts 301 3028 *As above, except Zeke Zarchy (t), Warren Smith (tb), Bob Zurke (p) replace Hart, Foster and Bowers.* 9/38.

These two discs of transcription performances for radio broadcast catch the Crosby band early in its life. The formula was already pretty much in place, with sweet tunes and vocal features mostly taking precedence, although when a hot number comes along the band don't muff their opportunity. Many of these tunes have barely survived the years – does anyone remember the likes of 'You Dropped Me Like A Red Hot Penny'? – yet the performances are well turned and when they get the chance to go at the likes of 'Fidgety Feet', they swing. Surprisingly clean and agreeable sound on both discs.

(***) 1937/40 Broadcasts

Soundcraft SC-5009 *Personnel unlisted but likely as for contemporaneous discs above.* 4/37–40.

The sound quality of these airshots is ragged, but it's fascinating material. The 1937 tracks come from a concert where Crosby split the bill with groups led by Johnny Dodds (!) and Roy Eldridge – though, alas, only the Crosby material has survived. The orchestra is in swinging form and they get the chance to stretch out: 'Dogtown Blues' runs for almost seven minutes. A pair of tracks from a 1938 film-short soundtrack are unexceptional, and then come six tracks from a 1940 broadcast from Chicago's Blackhawk. Surprisingly, all the material is very much in the Dixieland idiom, and The Bob Cats get to play too. The restricted sound is unfortunate, but fans of the group will find plenty to enjoy here.

Connie Crothers (born 1941)

PIANO

A former student of Lennie Tristano, Crothers is a leading figure in a group of improvisers who are keeping the Tristano-ite tradition alive and are building on his compositions and methods as repertory.

****(*) Perception**
Steeplechase SCCD 31022 *Crothers; Joe Solomon (b); Roger Mancuso (d).* 74.

***** Swish**
New Artists NA1001 *Crothers; Max Roach (d).*

***** Concert At Cooper Union**
New Artists NA1002 *Crothers (p solo).* 1/84.

***** Duo Dimension**
New Artists NA1003 *Crothers; Richard Tabnik (as).* 85.

Crothers is immersed in the language and lore of Lennie Tristano, intensely enough to generate a feeling – at least among her early records – that she is merely following in his footsteps (intimidating though that might be). But just as the best of the young hard-boppers found new wrinkles in that currency, Crothers has much of her own to say and, given the still-unexplored expanse of Tristano's methods, it still sounds fresh, even as repertory music. The Steeplechase album finds her taking tentative steps towards her own style, with a preponderance of literal translations of themes such as 'Perception'. Solomon and Mancuso are a functional assist. But the start of a sequence of records for the New Artists label marks a much more interesting documentation. The meeting with Roach finds the pianist far from overwhelmed by her illustrious partner on six improvised duets; the solo record is an open-handed display of thoughtful virtuosity; and the duets with the (inevitably) Konitz-like Tabnik run along probing paths. Crothers plays with the familiar evenness and uses the long, steady, deliberate lines of the style, but her dynamics offer unexpected contrasts of touch and her chordings can build to massive weight and intensity.

*****(*) Love Energy**
New Artists NA1005 *Crothers; Lenny Popkin (ts); Cameron Brown (b); Carol Tristano (d).* 4/88.

*****(*) New York Night**
New Artists NA1008 *As above.* 12/89.

***** In Motion**
New Artists NA1013 *As above.* 11/89.

*****(*) Jazz Spring**
New Artists NA1017 *As above.* 3/93.

The formation of this excellent quartet, little known though it is, has been a valuable means of exploring Tristano's music as repertory. Lenny Popkin builds on Warne Marsh's grey, scratchy tone with fretful cadences of his own, Carol Tristano secures a quietly propulsive swing, and Brown's unobtrusively forceful lines eliminate any sense that the music could grow static, either rhythmically or harmonically. Crothers plays for the band yet manages to make her best improvisations distinctive and freely developed, while still minding the essential logic of the form. This is tough, serious jazz, a little self-regarding in its selflessness, but none the worse for that. If Popkin is – so far – never quite the individual voice that he might be, he's still a determined improviser. *In Motion* gets a fractionally lower score for the foreshortened delivery of most of the pieces; but any of the discs offers a fine portrait of the group.

***** Deep Into The Center**
New Artists NA1020 *Crothers; Roger Mancuso (d).* 12/93–12/94.

***** Music From Everyday Life**
New Artists NA1025 *Crothers (p solo).* 3/93–6/96.

The duets with Mancuso, taken from 'informal sessions' over a period of a year, are hard work – all but two are severe improvisations, and 'I'll Remember April' is left as something of a corpse. The performers tend to run in parallel rather than interact, with Mancuso particularly oblique in his responses, and the monochrome sound may leave some listeners discouraged. But such deliberately unglamorous jazz has its rewards, and others will find the concentration in the playing absorbing enough. So too with *Music From Everyday Life*. 'Good Morning Heartache' is spare and intense, 'Star Eyes' cut entirely adrift from its body. The improvisation on a Bartók folk dance is a charmer, though, and the miniature 'Be' which starts the disc is a near-perfect improvised composition. It's a patchwork of sessions over three years, and suits eavesdroppers.

*****(*) Session**
New Artists NA1027 *Crothers; Lenny Popkin (ts); Rich Califano (b); Carol Tristano (d).* 96.

Califano is a new recruit, but otherwise it's music as usual from this remarkable quartet. Eight fastidiously shaped tracks, with the melodies of 'I Remember You' and 'Easy Living' dismissed from view, the unfathomably long line of 'Starline' a breathing test for Popkin, and the eternal, selfless pulse set down by bass and drums. In one sense, a pointless music, delivered as a seamless, smooth, yet unpredictable line.

***** Ontology**
New Artists NA 1035 *Crothers; Richard Tabnik (as); Sean Smith (b); Roger Mancuso (d).* 12/98–4/99.

Crothers and her group play as intensely and unbendingly as ever. 'My Shining Hour' is witheringly taken apart, and 'Come Rain Or Come Shine' is only slightly less startling, given the quiescent tempo. Smith and Mancuso play more pushily than any of the previous rhythm teams have and the title-piece, with its rolling thunder of chords from the piano, is almost Tayloresque in its delivery. Tabnik's return shows his curious range of tones getting ever more freakish. For music which some characterize as excessively cool and cerebral, it's extraordinarily harsh at times. But the sound, with a very muddy mid-range, doesn't do them full justice.

Pat Crumly

ALTO, TENOR AND SOPRANO SAXOPHONES, FLUTE

Stalwart saxophonist of the British Home Counties scene since the '60s, Crumly has played behind singers such as Jack Jones and in pop and blues bands, but as a leader his aspirations are more towards a wordly kind of post-bop.

***(*) Third World Sketches**
Spotlite SPJ-CD 431 *Crumly; Dick Pearce (t, flhn); Pete Saberton (p); Dave Green (b); Trevor Tomkins (d); Simon Morton (perc).* 5/84.

****(*) Behind The Mask**
Spotlite SPJ-CD 549 *Crumly; Richard Edwards (tb); John Pearce (p); Phil Lee (g); Simon Woolf (b); Simon Morton (d); Bosco D'Oliveira (perc).* 8/93.

***** Flamingo**
Spotlite SPJ-CD 550 *Crumly; Guy Barker (t); Richard Edwards (tb); John Pearce (p); Alec Dankworth (b); Simon Woolk (b); Simon Morton (d); Bosco D'Oliveira (perc).* 8/93.

***** Weaver Of Dreams**
33 Jazz 886 *Crumly; Nick Weldon (p); Tim Wells (b); Mark Fletcher (d).* 3/03.

As well meant as it undoubtedly was at that time, *Third World Sketches* sounds like an ill-advised dry run for the fusion of jazz and world music. Crumly's tunes offer various dedications to various parts of the world called Third, but the shoddy production, under-rehearsed band and thinly constructed situations don't exactly encourage the listener to investigate what sounds like a very dated record. At its most cheerful, as on the opening 'Urban Urchins', there's some enjoyable music, but mostly this record casts some talented players into a very poor light.

The other two Spotlite albums are in a much more straight-ahead vein. The pace is continuously varied between standards and originals, ballads and quicker tunes, and unfortunately nothing really settles down or sticks in the mind, capable as much of the playing is. *Behind The Mask* is somewhat blighted by a thoroughly disagreeable and echoey sound-mix; *Flamingo* is better, though still less than ideal. Barker puts in some of the best playing.

Weaver Of Dreams updates Crumly's discography and is probably the best of these. Pat picks up the tenor (for 'Anthropology'!) and otherwise changes timbral pace across what is mostly a set of standards, although there's a nicely wistful dedication to Spike Robinson. The rhythm section are keen to make their mark, and Weldon gets usefully restless with some of the chord sequences. Not a notably special record but satisfying enough.

The Crusaders

GROUP

The group's personnel came together out of a group of players working together at a high school in Houston. They made many albums for Pacific Jazz in the '60s, polishing a soulful variation on the small-group West Coast jazz of the time, before making a long sequence of successful soul-funk-jazz albums in the '70s.

***** Chile Con Soul**
Pacific Jazz 90957 *Wayne Henderson (tb); Wilton Felder (ts); Hubert Laws (f); Joe Sample (ky); Clare Fischer (org); Al McKibbon (b); Stix Hooper (d); Carlos Vidal, Hungaria 'Carmelo' Garcia (perc).* 7/65.

***** Live At The Lighthouse '66**
Pacific Jazz 37988 *Wayne Henderson (tb); Wilton Felder (ts); Joe Sample (ky); Stix Hooper (d).* 1/66.

*****(*) Lighthouse '68**
Pacific Jazz 76851 *As above, except add Buster Williams (b).* 11/67.

***** Scratch**
GRP 050115-2 *As above, except add Larry Carlton (g), Max Bennett (b); omit Williams.* 74.

*****(*) Southern Comfort**
GRP 6016 *As above, except omit Bennett.* 74.

*****(*) Those Southern Knights**
GRP 050117-2 *As above.* 76.

***** Street Life**
MCA 101815-2 *As above, except add Robert O Bryant (t), Garnett Brown (tb), Maurice Spears (btb), Jerome Richardson (as), Oscar Brashear, Robert Bryant Jr (ts), Bill Green (bs), Arthur Adams, Billy Rogers, Roland Bautista, Barry Finnerty, Paul Jackson, David T. Walker (g), Alphonso Johnson, James Jamerson (b), Randy Crawford (v); omit Henderson and Carlton.* 79.

***** Live In Japan**
GRP 059746-2 *Wilton Felder (ts); Joe Sample (ky); Barry Finnerty, Roland Bautista (g); Alphonso Johnson (b); Stix Hooper (d); Rafael Cruz (perc).* 81.

Dropping the word 'jazz' from the name was, of course, a form of critical suicide; it happened in 1971, and since then the Crusaders have for some been a byword for commercial compromise. Despite which, the group has maintained a consistency and occasionally a perverse integrity of purpose since first emerging in 1961 out of a Houston high-school band. The basic line-up – Felder, Hooper, Sample, Henderson – has been in place from the start, despite individual projects and excursions, fallings-out and Star Chamber reshuffles. The Crusaders offer a solidly funky combo music which might almost have been programmed by a computer; it hinges on Sample's bar-room piano, Felder's and Henderson's uncomplicated horn lines, and Hooper's accurate but curiously undynamic drumming. No less, and seldom any more; but the group has made some very good records along the way and the chaotic state of its discography is a pity.

Of some 15 albums made for Pacific Jazz between 1961 and 1969, there are still only a handful in print in remastered versions. *Chile Con Soul* is one of the earlier sets and features an augmented Crusaders with Laws, Fischer, McKibbon and a percussion section added to beef up the chilli. Though it sits a little awkwardly between the group's usual soul-bop and the prevailing appetite for a garnish of Latin rhythm, this isn't bad, just untypical.

The live date from Hermosa Beach in 1966 offers what is presumably a pretty faithful version of what the band sounded like in concert around this time: slick, capable and unshakeably jazz-centred, doing versions of 'Round Midnight', Trane's 'Some Other Blues', 'Milestones' and 'You Don't Know What Love Is', alongside the originals. These include Sample's 'Blues Up Tight', Felder's 'Miss It', Henderson's 'Scratch' and Vinnegar's rootsier 'Doin' That Thing'. Sixteen minutes are added to the original LP release.

The Lighthouse was a regular live gig for the band, and the 1968 set made there was one of their best for the label. Buster Williams added compositional as well as bass weight, and the group's signature version of 'Eleanor Rigby' holds up well. Four previously unissued tracks add 27 minutes of new music, and at mid-price this is a fine introduction to this period of the group.

The addition of outside players (guitarists and bassists most obviously) seldom disrupted the basic formula; Larry Carlton was the *de facto* 'fifth Crusader' for many years. That period was set down by Blue Thumb during the '70s, although several of the better albums are still missing in action. Of those easily obtainable, *Scratch*, which is live, *Southern Comfort* and *Those*

Southern Knights, which are studio, are fine – the latter two in particular showing how a pop-funk-jazz album could still be committed and based around creative playing.

Street Life, spotlit by Randy Crawford's vocal, was their commercial breakthrough but largely their undoing as a close-knit ensemble. The big-band arrangement and the drafting in of a raft of guitarists to replace Carlton gnawed through the group's hard-won independence, and their music increasingly drifted towards a lite-soul feel. The Japanese live album shows some sparks still flying, all the same.

Recent years have seen the band's legend tarnished by all manner of litigious uproar. Some of the members are still working together, but Sample, for so long their compositional backbone, is not involved. A couple of '90s albums are too sad to list here.

Ronnie Cuber (born 1941)

BARITONE, ALTO AND TENOR SAXOPHONES, FLUTE

Born in Brooklyn, Cuber started on baritone in 1959 at the behest of Marshall Brown, and it became his main horn. He worked with Maynard Ferguson and Woody Herman, as well as with numerous Latin groups and in support of soul artists. He is an in-demand clinician all over the USA.

***** Cubism**
Fresh Sound FSRCD 188 *Cuber; Joe Locke (vib, ky); Bobby Broom (g); Michael Formanek (b); Ben Perowsky (d); Carlos Patato Valdes (perc).* 12/91.

***** Airplay**
Steeplechase SCCD 31309 *Cuber; Geoff Keezer (p); Chip Jackson (b); Ben Perowsky (d).* 4/92.

*****(*) The Scene Is Clean**
Milestone 9218 *Cuber; Lawrence Feldman (f); Geoff Keezer (ky); Joey DeFrancesco (org); George Wadenius (g); Tom Barney, Reggie Washington (b); Victor Jones (d); Manolo Badrena, Milton Cardona (perc).* 12/93.

***** In A New York Minute**
Steeplechase SCCD 31372 *Cuber; Kenny Drew Jr (p); Andy McKee (b); Adam Cruz (d).* 4/95.

***** NY Cats**
Steeplechase SCCD 31394 *Cuber; Ryan Kisor (t); Michael Weiss (p); Andy McKee (b); Tony Reedus (d).* 3/96.

Cuber has played on a great many sessions as a sideman, but his records as leader are down to a handful. He gets a light, limber feel out of the baritone when he wants to, though he can make it sound gruff and monstrous. His odd adaptability to Latin rhythms means that his own discs usually have more than a few traces of Brazilian bop about them. The feel on *Cubism* is directed towards a 'lite' kind of jazz-funk, but Locke's typically shrewd playing and a few worthwhile licks from the valuable Broom lift it out of the rut that Cuber was in on some of his earlier releases. *Airplay*, despite the somewhat ironic title, puts Cuber back into hard bop with Keezer's fine work as his line to earth. Most of the tunes work a rather old-fashioned groove, as if this were a tribute to the great days of Blue Note and Prestige, but the baritone work is as forthright and full-bodied as Cuber has ever sounded. *The Scene Is Clean* is another blend of styles. The Dameron title-tune, the modal jazz theme 'Song For Pharoah' and the winsome 'Flamingo' are more traditionally sewn, but the bristling Latin tunes again carry an infectious spirit, and it's obvious that the leader feels right at home here. Although Cuber picks up tenor and alto here and there, the big horn is what holds his soul, and he sounds appreciative on this date.

In A New York Minute is good enough. Drew is an elegant foil, Cuber brought five originals to the date, and the playing is felicitous. By the end, though, the record's run out of steam, and 'Sophisticated Lady' and 'Caravan', the most overworked pieces of Ellingtonia, are unwelcome choices.

NY Cats is something of a misfire, despite the promising line-up and some pleasing tunes. George Benson's 'Mimosa' is an engaging piece, 'Do Nothin' Till You Hear From Me' is a smart baritone vehicle, and there's some tremendous blowing on the closing 'Better Git It In Your Soul'. But the band sounds loose – Reedus is all over the place – and for once the Steeplechase sound is unpleasing, with Cuber given an unfortunately flat timbre. Remaining honours go to Kisor.

Bill Cunliffe (born 1956)

PIANO

A former classical student won over by an Oscar Peterson record, Cunliffe works from a swing-to-bop axis

***** Bill Plays Bud**
Naxos 86024 2 *Cunliffe; Ralph Moore (ts); Dave Carpenter (b); Joe LaBarbera (d); Papo Rodriguez (perc).* 10/96.

Previous sightings of Cunliffe with the Clayton–Hamilton Orchestra and with the Minnesotan brassman Bruce Paulson suggested a competent, unspectacular player. As leader, he is much more emphatic and he brings an authentic flavour to these more- and less-familiar Bud Powell themes. His phrasing on 'Comin' Up' can't be faulted: terse, slightly off-centre and robustly percussive. Familiar material is reworked, including a substantial rethink of '52nd Street Theme' and 'Un Poco Loco'. He also digs out a couple of rarities, 'Willowgrove', an effusive bop blues theme, and the strange 'Dusk At Saudi', which seems to be a version of 'Midnight Sun'. The set is nicely framed by Cunliffe's own composition, 'Melancholia', and a closing essay on 'Glass Enclosure'.

Moore's contribution is restricted to 'Polka Dots And Moonbeams' and '52nd Street' but, as ever, he finds things to say in that still-hard-to-place economical delivery. Like Cunliffe, Moore sounds as if he has skipped the Coltrane–Tyner generation entirely. It's very much the leader's set, though.

*****(*) Live At Bernie's**
Groove Note GRV 2009-2 *Cunliffe; Darek Oleszkiewicz (b); Joe LaBarbera (d).* 2/01.

*****(*) How My Heart Sings**
Torii, no number *Cunliffe; Bobby Shew (t, flhn); Justin Ray (flhn); Bruce Paulson (tb); Bob Sheppard (ss, as, ts, cl, f, af); Jeff D'Angelo (b); Joe LaBarbera (d).* 03.

The trio date comes off very well (the first ever to be recorded at Bernie Grundman's, usually a studio reserved for mastering). In beautiful sound, the group work through a frankly unpromising programme – including such tired pieces as 'Satin Doll' and 'Waltz For Debby' – with a surprising freshness. The Bill Evans tune gets a dancing, heady workout and even 'Satin Doll' – structured as a Petersonesque homage – is full of ideas.

His originals are a thoughtful lot, including 'Ireland' (a dedication to the English composer) and 'Amusing Paramours', and he even makes something of Rod McKuen's 'Jean'. Unfussy and fine work from the rhythm section.

The curious Torii label (which refuses to issue catalogue numbers with their discs, apparently) seems dedicated to esoteric projects and Cunliffe leads a sextet (Ray is present on only two tracks) through a programme of music by Earl Zindars. The only really familiar pieces (courtesy of Bill Evans's patronage) are 'How My Heart Sings' and 'Elsa', but Cunliffe is a very persuasive advocate for the writing. His charts for the horns give the band plenty to do and the music is several steps up on the usual round-robin of head and solos. 'Here's To Neil' and 'City Tune' especially have the range and substance of full orchestrations. Shew, Paulson and Sheppard are impeccable rather than dangerous soloists and their improvising adds to a cultured air which in context is very satisfying.

Ted Curson (born 1935)

TRUMPET, POCKET TRUMPET

He moved from Philadelphia to New York in the '50s and had an important spell wih Charles Mingus, 1959–60. Co-led a small group with Bill Barron, before moving to Europe in the late '60s, and has since divided his time between Europe and the USA. A prominent educator and a rare example of an American who has pushed European jazz back home, Curson moves easily between hard bop and more free areas in his own playing.

***** Plays Fire Down Below**
Original Jazz Classics OJC 1744 *Curson; Gildo Mahones (p); George Tucker (b); Roy Haynes (d); Montego Joe (perc).* 12/62.

****** The New Thing & The Blue Thing**
Koch CD 8531 *Curson; Bill Barron (ts); George Arvanitas (p); Herb Bushler (b); Dick Berk (d).* 65.

Thin representation for a highly significant innovator who came to prominence with Mingus, wrote the beautiful 'Tears For Dolphy' and then spent much of his time in Europe. A radical with a strong interest in classic jazz, Curson's work on piccolo trumpet often resembles Rex Stewart's, though he's closer to Fats Navarro on the concert horn. *Fire Down Below* is a reasonable representation of his pungent, unsentimental style. Mahones laces a basically conventional approach with figures reminiscent of Carl Perkins. Tucker and Haynes might explain a resemblance to Eric Dolphy's debut album on New Jazz, on which they played, and they're equally impressive here. The drummer is quietly forceful on the two quartet tracks 'The Very Young' and 'Only Forever', but he sounds slightly cramped by the addition of congas on the remainder.

Koch's rescue programme has had few worthier objects than Curson's 1965 Atlantic, *The New Thing & The Blue Thing*, which is not two albums stuck together but a reference to the stylistic poles of Curson's work. It teams him with the like-minded Barron, who plays brightly on two Curson originals 'Straight Ice' and 'Elephant Walk', but wanders off course a bit elsewhere. Arvanitas is a fascinating player, with a robustly lyrical touch, tracking Curson's maverick line on 'Star Eyes' with real imagination. Ted sticks to concert trumpet throughout, or so it sounds, but even here he manages to squeeze out tight, high tones that suggest a piccolo instrument. His phrasing on 'Reava's Waltz', an early appearance of what was to become a long-standing favourite, is precise and expressive. Arvanitas sits this one out.

Leo Cuypers (born 1947)

PIANO

Expelled from Maastricht Conservatory 'due to his views on art and life', Cuypers came to attention at the 1969 Loosdrecht jazz competition and later joined the Willem Breuker Kollektief, staying until 1980. His 1995 album marked a return after some years away from music.

***** Zeeland Suite & Johnny Rep Suite**
Bvhaast 9307 *Cuypers; Willem Van Manen (tb); Bob Driessen (ss, as, bs); Willem Breuker (ss, as, ts, bcl); Piet Noordijk (as); Hans Dulfer (ts); Harry Miller, Arjen Gorter (b); Martin Van Duynhoven, Rob Verdurmen (d).* 9/74–9/77.

Cuypers is known internationally only as one of Willem Breuker's cronies, but these two vintage sessions from the Bvhaast catalogue, usefully reissued on a single CD, give him some modest limelight as a leader. That said, the 'Zeeland Suite' in particular is much like a Breuker cross-section of riffs and ideas and is more impressive as a framework for the players – Gorter and Miller on 'Two Bass Shit', Breuker and Driessen on 'Bach II And Bach ' – than as any thematic sequence. The 'Johnny Rep Suite' is again dominated by Breuker himself, delivering 'Kirk' as a roaring tribute to the eponymous Roland; but at least Cuypers gets a couple of pieces more or less to himself at the end. The original recording is rather rough and a little unkind to the piano.

***** 'Songbook'**
Bvhaast 9502 *Cuypers (p solo).* 8/95.

A comeback after a number of years of retreat. Cuypers prepared a studio album, but on hearing the tape of this informal recital preferred this off-the-cuff session. There are 17 original tunes, some little more than embellished vamps but others showing the most acute and inventive harmonic thinking. A handful seem like flawless gems, such as the haunting 'Joplin' or 'Bouquet Mélancholique'; others have a nearly throwaway air about them. Cuypers seems rusty at some moments, virtuosic at others; one follows the record through, wondering what will emerge next.

Andrew Cyrille (born 1939)

DRUMS

Born in Brooklyn, Cyrille played with leaders from Nellie Lutcher to Roland Kirk, before starring in Cecil Taylor's mid-'60s trio, staying until 1975. His own groups push a colourful and lively blend of post-bop with other musical vernaculars, fuelled by his own virtuosic playing.

*****(*) Metamusicians' Stomp**
Black Saint 120025-2 *Cyrille; Ted Daniel (t, flhn, wood f); David S. Ware (ts, f); Nick DiGeronimo (b).* 9/78.

****** Nuba**
Black Saint 120030-2 *Cyrille; Jimmy Lyons (as); Jeanne Lee (v).* 6/79.

****** The Navigator**
Soul Note 121062-2 *Cyrille; Ted Daniel (t, flhn); Sonelius Smith (p); Nick DiGeronimo (b).* 9/82.

Many years ago, Cyrille took part in a series of concerts entitled 'Dialogue Of The Drums'. Somewhat behind the great wave of the avant-garde – or the 'New Thing' – he, Milford Graves and Rashied Ali demonstrated what they had brought to it. What was immediately evident was that though he seemed a quieter and more accommodating player, less addicted to the free-form thrash, Cyrille was the most instinctively musical of the trio. The only other name that ought to have been there was Sunny Murray, whom Cyrille replaced in the Cecil Taylor Trio in 1964, staying with the pianist for just over a decade and playing on the apocalyptic *Unit Structures.*

Something of Taylor's turbulent language creeps into *Nuba,* which also features Taylor's loyal saxophonist, Jimmy Lyons. Including a setting from Jeanne Lee's *The Valley Of Astonishment And Bewilderment,* this highly lyrical album is almost a miniature opera, developing the ideas on Cyrille's astonishing solo record, *What About?,* which finds him vocalizing – albeit without words – the pain and frustration of the black experience in America. Lyons's calm and stoical approach is the perfect conduit for this music, and both men seem to be working at the opposite extreme from the fierce abstractions of the Taylor group.

Metamusicians' Stomp and *The Navigator* feature the group Cyrille called Maono, and they signal his increasing interest in an Africanized language for jazz. On the latter record, each of the players introduces a section, adding bearings and compass points to a collective navigation back to the source. As with many of Cyrille's records, it asserts the jazz tradition by seeming to shed it, layer by layer. What this and the earlier *Metamusicians' Stomp* seem to suggest is that, the further jazz goes back towards its point of ancestral departure, the more completely it is itself.

*****(*) The X-Man**
Soul Note 121262-2 *Cyrille; James Newton (f); Alex Tit Pascal (g); Anthony Cox (b).* 5/93.

****** Good To Go, With A Tribute To Bu**
Soul Note 121292-2 *Cyrille; James Newton (f); Lisle Atkinson (b).* 10/95.

Flute and guitar add a new spectrum to *X-Man,* one that seems closer to Cyrille's basic understanding of melody. Newton's 'E-Squat' is a strong, clearly stated idea from a player who seems to understand Cyrille's intentions from the bottom up, and the drummer responds with some of his simplest and least cluttered playing on record. 'Simple Melody' is extraordinary, something out of a far-off place that yet seems as familiar and immediate as the most overworked standard.

Atkinson had alternated with Nick DiGeronimo in Maono and he's a welcome addition to the later trio. The set is bracketed by two takes of Cyrille's brilliant impersonation of Art Blakey *in excelsis.* They and the other title-piece are essays in freedom and responsiveness. The surprises on this album are a version of John Carter's 'Enter From The East' (how one thirsts for a chance to hear the composer's clarinet cutting into this), a reading of Andrew Hill's 'Nicodemus', with Atkinson touching in the chords, John B. Gordon's 'Aftermath', and, more surprising yet, a standard, 'The Inch Worm', done as if another JC hadn't thought of it yet. If you have yet to sample Cyrille's work on record, meet a master in his pomp.

*****(*) C/D/E**
Jazz Magnet 2007 *Cyrille; Marty Ehrlich (f, cl, ss, as); Mark Dresser (b).* 10/98.

This marvellous group seems to draw at least some of its inspiration from Ornette Coleman, but Ornette in a quiet and tender mood. The album is surprisingly quiet and delicate, featuring short songs and very little full-on group improvisation.

Cyrille shows what a delicate touch he has on 'Aubade', and the version of the late Thomas Chapin's 'Aeolus' is equally tender. Dresser contributes a homage to Bobby Bradford which, apart from another Ornettish idea – 'BBJC' – is his only input as a writer. The rest is shared between drummer and saxophonist, and it's Marty who catches the attention with 'View From The Point' and '2 For Cyrille'. A lovely record, unexpectedly pitched but infinitely rewarding.

Daniele D'Agaro (born 1958)

TENOR SAXOPHONE, BASS CLARINET

Italian reedman resident in the Netherlands who mixes traditional jazz standards with taut originals.

***** Strandjutters**
hatOLOGY 590 *D'Agaro; Ernest Glerum (b); Han Bennink (d).* 6/02.

Better known in northern Europe than in his native Italy, D'Agaro has still to break through to wider recognition. Unlike his countryman Gianni Beggia, he has conjured up a somewhat American tone in his saxophone playing, though his clarinet still has residues of classical technique. These are mostly shortish pieces, around the six-minute mark, suggesting that D'Agaro prefers to concentrate on melody, for which he has a definite if perverse talent, than on vertical harmonic improvisation. The title-piece is definitive of the style and also of its limitations. What might have been profound ends up sounding crabby and cross-grained. The exception, in terms of length and harmonics, is 'Old Folks', which comes in at nearly ten minutes. In addition to his free jazz and music-theatre side, Bennink is a fine standards player and this material suits him very well indeed. However, it's the strong-toned Glerum who is the star of this intriguing but for the moment tentative set.

Carsten Dahl (born 1967)

PIANO, ORGAN

Danish pianist, putting a contemporary spin on bebop piano.

***** Will You Make My Soup Hot And Silver**
Storyville STCD 4203 *Dahl; Lennart Ginman (b); Frands Rifbjerg (d).* 12/96.

***** Message From Bud**
Storyville STCD4232 *As above.* 12/98.

From the brisk momentum of 'Autumn Leaves' onwards on the first disc, it's clear that Dahl is minded to take an unhackneyed path through this set of often very familiar material: 'Giant Steps', 'Take Five', 'Caravan', and others. He plays several pieces associated with Miles Davis and not one of them is quite what you'd expect. 'Freddie The Freeloader' is done over a choppy, bustling rhythm, 'I Thought About You' is unrecognizably slow and distant. He frequently has his rhythm players set up a groove of some sort while he lays elliptical comments over the top; melodies are left alone or reharmonized. It keeps you listening in a whatever-next way, although sometimes the approach seems almost deliberately and unconvincingly cute. His only originals are a blues and a bluesy vamp tune.

Carsten says that the title-piece of *Message From Bud* came to him in a dream in which he was drinking with Bud Powell. It sounds like a clever Powell copy, for sure. This second disc is slightly less arch than the first one, and there's a Garneresque twist to the two-fisted way he swings some of the standards. 'Blue In Green' is effective because he doesn't sound like Bill Evans, preferring a heavier, more deliberate touch.

****(*) The Butterfly Dream**
Storyville STCD 4243 *Dahl (p solo).* 2–10/99.

***** Jazzpar 2000 Quintet**
Storyville STCD 4248 *Dahl; Jörg Huke (tb); Tony Coe (ss, ts, cl); Lars Danielsson (clo, b); Aage Tanggaard (d).* 3/00.

Dahl was the 2000 Danish prize-winner in the annual Jazzpar competition, and as usual played a series of concerts with a group of his choosing. Although the six tunes included here (from two different gigs) sometimes suffer from solo longeurs, there's a nice piquancy about the pairing of Coe and the lesser-known Huke, whose playing has a broadband technique without resorting to flamboyance. Danielsson is asked to bring out his cello as often as the bass, and instead of celebration, the concerts are rather thoughtful, self-effacing features for the leader's writing. 'Crazy Folks', for instance, is a sewing together of folk themes from England, Sweden, Germany and Denmark, a nod to each man's roots. Very good, but not the place to come first if it's Dahl the instrumentalist you wish to hear.

For that, inevitably, the solo record is the answer. Dahl characterizes it as 'landscapes from my mind', and the geography is made up of 14 first-take improvisations. The unavoidable comparison is with the first Jarrett and Corea solo records for ECM. This is nice, but lacks their charismatic sense of discovery, and is akin to eavesdropping on a session in the practice room. Aside from the rumbustious number four, it's all at much the same ruminative pace, too.

Albert Dailey (1939–84)

PIANO

Born and classically trained in Baltimore, Dailey never enjoyed the prominence that his skills seemed to call for. He worked with a wide variety of leaders, including Charles Mingus and conspicuously Stan Getz, but made very few recordings of his own.

***** That Old Feeling**
SteepleChase 31107 *Dailey; Buster Williams (b); Billy Hart (d).* 7/78.

Albert's sole surviving record as leader is ample cause to wonder why he isn't better known. Working with two blue chip sidemen obviously makes a difference, but his solos here are elegant and thoughtful, perhaps on reflection too thoughtful in a market where dexterity and a certain fulsomeness of expression are often preferred. There is nothing filigree about Dailey's ballad playing, but his quiet modulations and intricate passage work are maybe too abstract for some listeners. The long version of the title track and an equally developed 'Yesterdays' are the best things here, though Albert also shows how responsive he is to song form with briefer interpretations of 'Loverman' and the Beatles' 'Michelle'.

No sign of a return to catalogue for *The Day After The Dawn*, released on Columbia a year before this disc, though there is also a later Muse record, which might stand better chance of reissue. We can hope.

Meredith D'Ambrosio (born 1941)

VOCAL, PIANO

A Bostonian, D'Ambrosio has been recording since 1978, often in the company of her husband, pianist Eddie Higgins. A speciality is her melding of a standard with a newly composed variation of both the words and the melody.

***** Lost In His Arms**
Sunnyside SSC 1081D *D'Ambrosio; Ray Santisi (p); Norman Coles (g); Chris Rathbun (b).* 7–10/78.

***** Another Time**
Sunnyside SSC 1017D *D'Ambrosio.* 2/81.

*****(*) Little Jazz Bird**
Sunnyside SSC 1040D *D'Ambrosio; Phil Woods (cl, as); Hank Jones (p); Gene Orloff, Fred Buldrini (vn); Julian Barber (vla); Fred Slatkin (clo); Steve Gilmore (b); Bill Goodwin (d).* 3/82.

****** It's Your Dance**
Sunnyside SSC 1011 *D'Ambrosio; Harold Danko (p); Kevin Eubanks (g).* 3/85.

****(*) The Cove**
Sunnyside SSC 1028D *D'Ambrosio; Lee Konitz (as); Fred Hersch (p); Michael Formanek (b); Keith Copeland (d).*

*****(*) South To A Warmer Place**
Sunnyside SSC 1039D *D'Ambrosio; Lou Colombo (t); Eddie Higgins (p); Don Coffman (b); Danny Berger (d).* 2/89.

*****(*) Love Is Not A Game**
Sunnyside SSC 1051D *D'Ambrosio; Eddie Higgins (p); Rufus Reid (b); Keith Copeland (d).* 12/90.

***** Shadowland**
Sunnyside SSC 1060D *D'Ambrosio; Ron Kozak (f, bcl); Blair Tindall (cor, ob); Eddie Higgins (p); Johnny Frigo (vn); Erik Friedlander (clo); Jay Leonhart (b); Ben Riley (d).* 7/92.

*****(*) Sleep Warm**
Sunnyside SSC 1063D *D'Ambrosio (p, v).* 2/91.

A vocalist whose approach is so soft and unemphatic that sometimes she barely seems to be present at all. But her choice of songs is so creative and the treatments so consistently refined that the records are unexpectedly absorbing. *Another Time* is a reissue of a privately produced session, and its bare-bones approach is perhaps a little too austere, but it's still an impressive recital of 18 songs. Another reappearance is the 1978 session, *Lost In His Arms*, which unfolds at the steady, thoughtful pace of all of her music. *Little Jazz Bird*, despite an eccentric studio production by Rudy van Gelder, is ingeniously programmed to accommodate Woods and the string quartet, and the songs encompass Dave Frishberg, Gene Lees, Loonis McGloohan and two exceptional pieces by Deborah Henson-Conant, 'How Is Your Wife' and 'When The End Comes'. *It's Your Dance* is arguably D'Ambrosio's most fully realized record: with only Danko and Eubanks (who's never played better) in support, D'Ambrosio maintains a supernal glow throughout the record. Almost all the songs are unusual, from her own lyrics to 'Giant Steps' and Dave Brubeck's 'Strange Meadowlark' to Al Cohn's 'The Underdog', the title-track's reworking of John Carisi's 'Israel' and the lovely Burke–Van Heusen rarity, 'Humpty Dumpty Heart'. The vocalist's choice of material and the hip understatement of her singing create the core of her work. Her voice is too small and unambitious to make any play for jazz virtuosity, but she achieves a different authenticity through economies of scale.

That said, it goes a little wrong on *The Cove*, which is too composed and sleepy, the playing sounding fatigued rather than laid-back. But *South To A Warmer Place* restores her run: Colombo plays a Bobby Hackett-like role and, since many of the songs are relatively familiar, this may be the best place to start hearing D'Ambrosio's enchanting work. *Love Is Not A Game* has some more memorable treatments: 'Autumn Serenade', J. J. Johnson's 'Lament', Denny Zeitlin's 'Quiet Now'. On 'Oh Look At Me Now', she extends the song into a coda which has her composing new lyrics for a variation on the tune, and that approach is carried over into 5 of the 12 tunes on *Shadowland*, perhaps with mixed success. She still sounds at her best on the introspective, soliloquy-like material, such as Burton Lane's 'A Rainy Afternoon', and Noël Coward's 'Zigeuner' is another surprising and successful choice. Eddie Higgins, her husband, provides sympathetic piano throughout, although her own playing isn't negligible. *Sleep Warm* is for more specialized tastes, perhaps, since it is mainly a set of modern and old-fashioned lullabies for a child.

***** Because Of Spring**
Sunnyside SSC 1069D *D'Ambrosio; Eddie Higgins (p); George Mraz (b); Jeff Hirshfield (d).* 9/94.

***** Silent Passion**
Sunnyside SSC 1075D *D'Ambrosio; Gene Bertoncini (g).* 1/96.

***** Echo Of A Kiss**
Sunnyside SSC 1078 *D'Ambrosio; Mike Renzi (p); Jay Leonhart (b); Terry Clarke (d).* 8/97.

D'Ambrosio extends her placid progress with more albums. *Because Of Spring* continues her songs-out-of-other-songs method on four tracks, and her strong suit continues to be her song selection: 'Moon Dreams' and 'Through A Long And Sleepless Night' were two good ideas, but, as so often with her records, it often teeters into a quiet, quiet margin that makes no impression. Although *Silent Passion* reduces the cast to two – and Meredith handles the piano duties – it's a degree more intense and an ounce more involving, with Bertoncini making elegant work out of his dialogue and the singer a shade more assertive. *Echo Of A Kiss* tries her out with a new line-up, although she's settled so deeply into her meditative groove that there's now a danger that she's going to make the same record each time with slowly diminishing returns. 'April Fooled Me' and 'Snowfall' are the rediscoveries, to go with her own originals.

Tadd Dameron (1917–65)

COMPOSER, BANDLEADER, PIANO

Born in Cleveland, Dameron was writing arrangements from the mid-'30s and worked for Harlan Leonard in New York from 1939. Soon got caught up in bebop and wrote for the Gillespie band, before leading his own small groups in the late '40s with Fats Navarro and Miles Davis. Drug problems slowed him down in the '50s and he was imprisoned for three years from 1957. Returned for a few further projects but died from cancer at a time when jazz had basically left him behind.

***** Cool Boppin'**
Fresh Sound FSCD 1008 *Dameron; Miles Davis (t); Kai Winding (tb); Sahib Shihab (as); Benjamin Lundy (ts); Cecil Payne (bs); John Collins (g); Curley Russell (b); Kenny Clarke (d); Carlos Vidal (perc).* 2/49.

*****(*) Fontainebleau**
Original Jazz Classics OJC 055 *Dameron; Kenny Dorham (t); Henry Coker (tb); Sahib Shihab (as); Joe Alexander (ts); Cecil Payne (bs); John Simmons (b); Shadow Wilson (d).* 3/56.

***** Mating Call**
Original Jazz Classics OJC 212 *Dameron; John Coltrane (ts); John Simmons (b); Philly Joe Jones (d).* 11/56.

****(*) The Magic Touch**
Original Jazz Classics OJC 143 *Dameron; Ernie Royal, Charlie Shavers, Clark Terry, Joe Wilder (t); Jimmy Cleveland, Britt Woodman (tb); Julius Watkins (frhn); Jerry Dodgion, Leo Wright (as, f); Jerome Richardson (ts, f); Johnny Griffin (ts); Tate Houston (bs); Bill Evans (p); Ron Carter (b); Philly Joe Jones (d); Barbara Winfield (v).* 2–4/62.

It's Dameron's fate to be remembered now largely for a handful of compositions – 'Hot House' and 'Lady Bird' pre-eminently – which became standards. As such, Dameron is a much-underrated performer who stands at the fulcrum of modern jazz, midway between swing and bebop. Combining the broad-brush arrangements of the big band and the advanced harmonic language of bop, his own recordings are difficult to date blind. The title of one of the most renowned tunes, 'On A Misty Night', catches the sense of evanescence which seems to surround both the man and the music.

Fats Navarro played as well with Dameron as he did with anyone; the Blue Note sets issued as *The Fabulous Fats Navarro* should strictly be credited to the Tadd Dameron Sextet/Septet and to Bud Powell's Modernists, but became known as a posthumous tribute to the brilliant young trumpeter who died in 1950. Navarro's big, ringing brass-tone is superb on a second take of 'Anthropology' (Dameron features on the first), two takes of 'Good Bait' and a witty 'Oh! Lady Be Good'.

Another young genius took a significant stride forward under Dameron's wing. John Coltrane's solo on 'Soultrane' and the ballad construction on 'On A Misty Night' are among the best things in his early career. Though *Mating Call* is often discussed as if it were a Coltrane album, it's the pianist who's firmly in the driving seat, directing an ensemble sound subtly different from anything else that was coming out of bebop. Though dedicated to the memory of another ill-fated trumpet genius, Clifford Brown's *Memorial* set (listed under his name) is also valuable for insights into Dameron's methods. 'Theme Of No Repeat', 'Dial "B" For Beauty' and 'Philly J.J.' are relatively little known compared to 'Lady Bird' and 'Good Bait', but they evidence a consummate grasp of instrumental voicing; the last of the three also stands up well on the Dameronia recording reviewed below. Also shared is *Cool Boppin'*, which fuels debate about the real parentage of Cool School jazz by pairing Dameron's Royal Roost session of February 1949 with Miles Davis's residency there the previous autumn and winter; Miles also plays with Dameron's group. 'Good Bait' isn't a vintage performance, but the treatments of 'April In Paris' and 'Webb's Delight' point in interesting directions that help refocus appreciation of Dameron's art.

Fontainebleau originates from Dameron's last full year of freedom before the term of imprisonment that more or less ended his career. It's a fine set, with no clutter in the horns. The title-piece is wholly written out, with no scope for improvising, but there is plenty of individual work elsewhere, notably from Dorham. Never a virtuoso soloist, Dameron prefers to work within the very distinct chord-progressions of his tunes, big, lush confections that are too sharp-edged ever to cloy. The final record, *The Magic Touch*, was a great disappointment at the time. It revisits signature pieces such as 'On A Misty Night' and even 'Fontainebleau', but in foreshortened and even glib versions which, while not without interest, suggest that Dameron himself had perhaps lost interest in his own music.

Paolo Damiani (born 1952)

BASS, CELLO, VOCAL

Italian bassist and bandleader trying different post-bop directions.

***** Poor Memory**

Splasc(h) HP 07 *Damiani; Paolo Fresu (t, flhn); Gianluigi Trovesi (ss, as, bcl); Claude Barthelemy (g); Aldo Romano (d).* 7/87.

***** Eso**

Splasc(h) H 404-2 *As above, except Danilo Rea (p), Antonio Iasevoli (g), Roberto Gatto (d), Raffaela Siniscalchi, Sabina Macculi (v) replace Barthelemy and Romano.* 93.

Poor Memory is a fine concert recording, featuring several of the brightest contemporary talents in Italian jazz. Fresu continues to impress as a lyrical voice, but Trovesi's hard-hitting reed solos and Barthelemy's harsh, rock-directed guitar provide piquant contrast. Damiani's compositions find a suitable middle ground between hard bop and freer modes, and the live recording is agreeably rough-edged and human-sounding.

Eso has a few unexpected vocal contributions, including those by the leader, although Siniscalchi is the one with the outstanding voice. In the main, this is the mix as before, with Fresu and Trovesi both in excellent voice.

*****(*) Song Tong**

Splasc(h) H 460-2 *Damiani; Kenny Wheeler (flhn, t); Gianluigi Trovesi (as, acl); Maurizio Giammarco (ss, ts); Stefano Battaglia (p); Jean Marc Montera (g); Joel Allouche (d); Fulvio Maras (perc); Maria Pia De Vito, Tiziana Simona Vigni (v).* 8/91.

Actually recorded before *Eso* but getting a rather belated CD release, this must be Damiani's best work. A terrific group make vivid work out of a rather fanciful set of charts: the title-tune moves from lament to percussion fantasia to neo-African vamp. Each musician has an important part without anyone dominating, and the way Damiani makes the most of Wheeler's vulnerable tone and Trovesi's and Giammarco's contrasting styles is superbly effective. Just occasionally the music sounds a trifle arch but it's sustained in the most accomplished way.

***** Mediana**

EGEA SCA 067 *Damiani; Carlo Marianni (launeddas); Sandro Satta (as); Carlo Rizzo, Michele Rabbia (perc).* 1/99.

Damiani and cohorts try their hand at a style previously investigated by Paolo Carrus, the Sardinian folk music played on such instruments as the *launeddas*. It's joyful music and far from the untempered, unsophisticated feel one might expect: Damiani brings the skirl of the pipes and the 'local' percussion into a brimmingly modern improvisational context. Satta's quicksilver alto works well in this situation. The record isn't really sustained to the end, and there's still an inescapable feeling of worldly novelty, but it will please adventurous tastes.

Franco D'Andrea (born 1941)

PIANO, KEYBOARDS

Worked on radio in Rome in the early '60s and spent much of that decade in free forms – with Gato Barbieri, the Modern Art Trio and the jazz-rock Perigeo. Later turned to more conservative post-bop forms, but he remains a restless stylist and has roamed far and wide in his recording activities.

***** Kick Off**

Red 123225-2 *D'Andrea; Giovanni Tommaso (b); Roberto Gatto (d).* 4/88.

***** Earthcake**

Label Bleu LBLC 6539 *D'Andrea; Enrico Rava (t, bugle); Miroslav Vitous (b); Daniel Humair (d).* 1/91.

***(*) Enrosadira**

Red 123243-2 *D'Andrea; Luis Agudo (perc).* 91.

****** Airegin**

Red 123252-2 *D'Andrea; Giovanni Tommaso (b); Roberto Gatto (d).* 4/91.

D'Andrea is a senior figure among Italy's post-bop musicians; his playing has a scholar's penchant for irony and dramatic construction and, while there's plenty of Mediterranean fire in his music, he's just as partial to a meditative frame of expression. Either of the two trio sessions for Red, with two of his favourite partners, will make a good place to start hearing D'Andrea's jazz. *Kick Off* offers comparatively short measure with only five tunes, and the sound-balance isn't too kind to the piano, but the trio demonstrate a very refined empathy, the balance of initiative shifting almost from measure to measure. *Airegin*, though, is even better. There are some superb reworkings of the jazz repertoire on 'Epistrophy', 'Doxy', 'Airegin' and 'Blue In Green', as well as some fine originals, with Tommaso's 'My Dear One' and D'Andrea's own 'Things Called'. The pianist takes a lot of trouble to reharmonize or otherwise vary the delivery of the familiar pieces without making it seem effortful.

The Label Bleu disc is something of an all-star session and, while nothing extraordinary happens, it's a significantly democratic affair, with compositions from each man and the title-piece standing as a highly articulate and detailed improvisation. *Enrosadira*, though, is eminently avoidable, a muddle of electronic keyboards pitched against Agudo's splashy percussion: good therapy for D'Andrea, perhaps, but tedious to listen to.

****** Chromatic Phrygian**

YVP 3057 *D'Andrea; Stephan Schertler (b); Billy Elgart (d).* 10/89.

A belated release, but what a great one! The trio format always seems to bring out the best in this fundamentally reluctant player who would rather defer to his *politesse* in a solo situation. Schertler and Elgart are having none of that. Elgart's way of swinging the music is a marvel: he fills up every space without getting in anybody's way and has all kinds of business to offer without seeming to overplay. It's a pity, in a way, that the programme is mostly originals from either D'Andrea or Schertler (and there is one item which is seemingly improvised by all three men), since they do so well with the opening take on 'This Can't Be Love', full of shadows and sudden lights, that one wishes that the programme was all made up of familiar standards, to be suddenly invigorated. But this is still a quite splendid record.

***** 3 Lines**
Philology 77-2 *D'Andrea (p solo).* 3/96.

*****(*) Jobim**
Philology 125-2 *D'Andrea; Andrea Ayace Ayassot (as); Aldo Mella (b); Alex Rolle (d).* 1/97.

***** Ballads And Rituals**
Philology 127-2 *As above.* 5/97.

3 Lines is an exercise in overdubbing meant to evoke the Bill Evans of *Conversations With Myself.* It feels like an album out of its time: Evans made his enlightened experiment in a pre-digital age, and D'Andrea's constructions say little that he might not have said with a single piano track. That said, the best tracks have a judicious and sometimes clever deployment of resources that makes, say, 'Tango In Three Colours' rather fetching. The homage, if such it is, to Jobim is fair enough, but the butterfly delicacy of the composer's best melodies is rather taken to the cleaners by this group and D'Andrea seems to be presiding over an ill-conceived event.

The same group reconvenes for *Ballads And Rituals.* Mella and Rolle get into all sorts of interesting rhythms from the start, with the clumping stomp of 'Dancing Colors' suggesting a kind of dub-like atmosphere. Ayassot is a difficult player to warm to, sounding at times as if he'd rather be heading into the eye of some freely formed hurricane, and his tart playing is a sometimes grating contrast to D'Andrea's romantic bent – something he can't entirely leave behind, no matter how far afield he looks. But the pianist gets in some fine moments when nobody seems to be looking, as in the lovely piano intro to 'Shifting Melody'.

***** Solo 1 – Standards**
Philology 401.2 *D'Andrea (p solo).* 4/01.

***** Solo 2 – Abstractions**
Philology 402.2 *D'Andrea (p solo).* 4/01.

***** Solo 3 – Woods**
Philology 403.2 *D'Andrea (p solo).* 4/01.

***** Solo 4 – Gato**
Philology 404.2 *D'Andrea (p solo).* 4/01.

*****(*) Solo 5 – Duke**
Philology 405.2 *D'Andrea (p solo).* 4.01.

***** Solo 6 – Valzer, Opera, Natale**
Philology 406.2 *D'Andrea (p solo).* 4/01.

****(*) Solo 7 – Napoli**
Philology 407.2 *D'Andrea (p solo).* 4/01.

***** Solo 8 – Classic Jazz**
Philology 408.2 *D'Andrea (p solo).* 4/01.

With characteristic extravagance, Paolo Piangiarelli invited D'Andrea to set down eight solo albums, over the course of a few days. The pianist felt unsure, but in the end executed the entire project over three mornings and two afternoons. Each set had a concept, but D'Andrea decided to shift continuously from one to another during the course of the recording. Most of the titles are more or less self-explanatory: compositions by (Phil) Woods, Gato (Barbieri) and Duke (Ellington), jazz and other standards, traditional jazz pieces, a set of free pieces, and another of Christmas and operatic themes. As with many extended solo projects, if the set has an Achilles' heel, it's tempo: in more than nine hours of music, a great deal of it unfolds at the same ruminative mid-tempo gait, and given D'Andrea's thoughtful, thoughtful manner, a good many of the pieces get rather sleepy. Countering this are many pleasurable aspects: the way D'Andrea will sometimes get into a rolling momentum, his equivalent of a Ducal locomotive design; his judgement of voicings and sonorities; his sudden ignition at a moment when a piece seems to be drying out; and his sheer knowledge of what the acoustic keyboard can create. It would be stretching it to call this in any way essential, and maybe the whole thing could have been boiled down to an excellent disc or two, but compared to some of the indulgences in the modern record industry this one's very benign. If we have to make a token choice, as a single favourite, it would be the Ellington set: though it looks like an unpromisingly hackneyed choice of tunes, D'Andrea's approach is particularly bright and craftily inventive.

*****(*) Magicians At Work**
Philology 214.2 *D'Andrea; Renato Sellani (p).* 5/02.

An extended and delightful game of cat and mouse between two old foxes. When the idea for a duets album was put to Sellani, he remarked, 'I hope that Franco will not fire on the Red Cross'; he needn't have worried. For a sample, try 'There Is No Greater Love', where the two pianists send out all sorts of smoke signals and teasing leads over ten minutes or so.

***** Round Riff & More**
Philology 241.2 *D'Andrea; Massimo Morriconi, Ares Tavolazzi (b).* 5/02.

This time it's piano in the middle and a bassist in each channel. They choose some pleasing originals from the D'Andrea book to play, and mostly the three men work sympathetically, although there's an underlying sense that it's a bit of an extended novelty rather than a valid musical situation.

Putney Dandridge (1902–46)

PIANO, VOCALS

A vaudeville singer and pianist, Dandridge led a string of sessions over two years which included some fine players behind him; a brief but interesting career on record.

****(*) Putney Dandridge 1935–1936**
Classics 846 *Dandridge; Henry 'Red' Allen, Richard Clarke, Shirley Clay (t); Buster Bailey (cl, as); Tom Mace, Gene Sedric (cl, ts); Chu Berry, Kenneth Hollon, Johnny Russell (ts); Harry Grey, Teddy Wilson (p); Arnold Adams, Dave Barbour, Clarence Holiday, Nappy Lamare (g); Artie Bernstein, Ernest 'Bass' Hill, John Kirby, Grachan Moncur (b); Bill Beason, Cozy Cole, Walter Johnson, Manzie Johnson (d).* 3/35–3/36.

***** Putney Dandridge 1936**

Classics 869 *Dandridge; Henry 'Red' Allen, Doc Cheatham, Wallace Jones, Bobby Stark (t); Tom Mace (cl); Joe Marsala (cl, as); Charles Frazier, Teddy McRae (ts); Clyde Hart, Roger 'Ram' Ramirez, James Sherman, Teddy Wilson (p); Arnold Adams, Eddie Condon, Allan Reuss, John Trueheart (g); Ernest 'Bass' Hill, John Kirby, Wilson Myers, Mack Walker (b); Big Sid Catlett, Cozy Cole, Slick Jones (d).* 6–12/36.

Fame is notoriously fickle, but she seems to have treated Putney Dandridge with more than her typical disdain. There can be few recording careers so abruptly foreshortened. Dandridge cut his first sides for Vocalion in March 1935 and stopped recording for good with the last of these sessions, taped with Doc Cheatham, Teddy Wilson and Sid Catlett on 10 December 1936. Not quite a mainstream jazz singer, he should have been able to dicker a natural vaudevillean's facility with a lyric into a sustainable career. There was certainly no shortage of able players on the few records he did make. His piano playing would never have set the room on fire, and for all but the first two tracks on the earlier volume he was able to rely on Teddy Wilson's calm professionalism. The earliest track is 'You're A Heavenly Thing', which is enlivened by a chorus or two on celeste; nothing is known about the other musicians involved but theories abound as to who they might be. Three months later, an impeccably pedigreed group backed him on a totally hokey 'Nagasaki' (complete with pre-war stage Japanese), 'Chasing Shadows' (a lovely break from Berry) and 'When I Grow Too Old To Dream'. After that, or maybe after 'I'm In The Mood For Love' with Red Allen (a.k.a. 'Gabriel') and Buster Bailey, all but the most resilient fans will have drifted off.

The 1936 sessions drift ever further into novelty singing. 'Mary Had A Little Lamb' and 'Here Comes Your Pappy (With The Wrong Kind Of Load)' are a waste of Allen, Marsala and Cole, though the drummer gets off an excellent break on 'If We Never Meet Again'. A month earlier, Dandridge had defied all reasonable expectation with back-to-back readings of 'These Foolish Things' and 'Cross Patch' which touch something deeper. The smooth arrangements are marred by some ropy solo work. Allen and Doc Cheatham are, needless to say, consistently good, but Bobby Stark surely wasn't up to a professional date in this company. The curtain falls with 'Gee! But You're Swell' in December 1936.

Dave D'Angelo

ALTO SAXOPHONE

D'Angelo's Section 8 is one of the strongest saxophone ensembles around.

***** In A Minute**

Double Time 160 *D'Angelo; Steve Marcus (ss, ts); Andy Fusco (as); Walt Weiskopf (ts); Jack Stuckey (bs); Joel Weiskopf, Tardo Hammer (p); Phil Palombi (b); Steve Davis (d).* 3/00.

The line-up gives the best clue to the quality of D'Angelo's Section 8. There are five leaders on the stand. That can sometimes lead to mayhem, but here the arrangements are as tightly organized as anyone could wish for and most of the tracks are compact and to the point. Because there are five saxophonists to accommodate, opportunities to hear D'Angelo at any length are rare, but he has a bright, attractively shrill tone, somewhat reminiscent of Bobby Watson, though less obviously steeped in the blues. Marcus and Walt Weiskopf also shine. Check out the excellent final sequence: a long read of 'Lazy Afternoon', a delightful 'All My Tomorrows' (the best ballad of the set) and the superb title track. Excellent ensemble jazz.

Eddie Daniels (born 1941)

CLARINET, TENOR SAXOPHONE, ALTO FLUTE

Daniels studied at Brooklyn College, joined the Thad Jones–Mel Lewis Orchestra, staying for six years, then freelanced and led his own record dates as a leader. He is a rare example of a post-bop musician specializing on clarinet.

****(*) First Prize!**

Original Jazz Classics OJC 771 *Daniels; Roland Hanna (p); Richard Davis (b); Mel Lewis (d).* 9/66.

Daniels was allegedly once told by Tony Scott to stick to the tenor saxophone, advice he subsequently ignored, as his many clarinet records bear witness to. Even on tenor, though, he wasn't terribly exciting. Five tracks on sax, three on clarinet, and the scarcity of the original album suggests that Daniels wouldn't have been all that missed on either instrument in the long run. Competent but uninvolving playing.

****(*) Beautiful Love**

Shanachie 5029 *Daniels; Ron Odrich (bcl); Lawrence Feldman (af); Bob James (p); Chuck Loeb (g); David Finck, Tim LeFebvre (b); Wolfgang Haffner (d); David Charles (perc).* 10/96.

****(*) Swing Low Sweet Clarinet**

Shanachie 5073 *Daniels; Frankfurt Radio Big Band.* 11/99.

Daniels's move from GRP has depleted his catalogue. These entries from Shanachie suggest no dramatic new departures. The arrangements of Bach, Satie and Rachmaninov on *Beautiful Love* are about as innovative as one would expect, and the presence of mood-jazz supremo James underlines the conception. Very pretty, and about as substantial as marshmallow. The big-band record is a bit better, with a few interesting scores from various hands (although we are not fond of the way Peter Reiter clobbers 'Stardust'). Even then, Daniels plays with a faceless kind of skill, which makes one wonder why this is on instead of Goodman, Shaw or DeFranco.

Dee Daniels

VOCALS

Elegant singer with blues and gospel influences. Lived in Europe for many years.

***** Let's Talk Business**

Capri 74027 2 *Daniels; Jeff Clayton (saxes); Larry Fuller (p); John Clayton (b); Jeff Hamilton (d); Joanie Bye, Cecile Larochelle (v).* 90.

****(*) Close Encounter Of The Swingin' Kind**

Timeless 312 *Daniels; Johan Clement (p); Koos Wiltenberg (b); Fred Krens (d).* 91.

*****(*) Wish Me Love**

Mons 874769 *Daniels; Metropole Orchestra.* 3/96.

The debut record is probably the strongest from this blues-flavoured vocalist. The band is first rate, drawn from the ranks of the Clayton/Hamilton orchestra, and knows exactly how to support a singer of Daniels's full-voiced quality. Some of the material is questionable, in that cutesy songs like 'The Inch Worm' don't suit her persona. She can, though, carry off 'The Battle Hymn Of The Republic' without sounding as if she's starting a football game. Her original 'Let Me Love You Tonight' points to a modestly developing talent as a writer, but the best stuff is from other hands, notably an unusual version of Jimmy Reed's 'Baby, What You Want Me To Do'.

The trio accompaniment on the Timeless is too mechanical for a singer of Daniels's disposition. She needs a warmer and more responsive sound than this. Nonetheless, there are some good things on the album, including a wholly unexpected arrangement of Oscar Peterson's 'Nigerian Market Place'. Also impressive are 'On Green Dolphin Street' (which like 'Body And Soul' has become a 'standard' rather than the lovely song it is) and a straightish version of 'Lover Man'.

With the weight and authority of the Metropole Orchestra behind her, she sounds magnificent on *Wish Me Love*. Here, the gospelly strain (and Daniels's brother is a pastor, we believe) comes through forcefully. 'Sometimes I Feel Like A Motherless Child', 'God Bless The Child', 'Tonight I Won't Be Singing No Blues' and 'Here's That Rainy Day' all call on the arranging skills of Jeff Clayton and Rob Pronk and the ensembles are one of the high points of the album. Daniels's phrasing is occasionally suspect but she carries enough emotional power to smooth over technical hitches.

Lars Danielsson (born 1958)

BASS, KEYBOARDS

He came to prominence as a sideman on the Swedish scene in the early '80s and worked with many American players before leading small groups of his own. Recently he has been in demand as a producer as well as player.

*****(*) New Hands**

Dragon DRCD 125 *Danielsson; David Liebman (ss); Bobo Stenson (p); Goran Klinghagen (g, ky); Jon Christensen (d).* 12/85.

****** Poems**

Dragon DRCD 209 *As above, except omit Klinghagen.* 4/91.

This is a very fine group, and *New Hands* is certainly the equal of any of Liebman's records with Quest. The bassist's six compositions range from a mysterious electronic lament on 'Chrass' to the memorable ballads of 'It's Your Choice' and 'Johan', the former featuring a bass solo of astonishing virtuosity. Stenson and Christensen live up to their reputation as two of the most outstanding Europeans on their respective instruments, and Liebman's work is typically broad in its sympathies, from gnarled volleys of notes to long-breathed lines of high lyrical beauty.

Poems, recorded after a brief 'reunion' tour by the band, is a degree finer even than *New Hands*. Liebman contributes the funky, brittle 'Little Peanut' and two other tunes, while the bassist turns in some of his best writing for the haunting 'Crystalline' and 'Suite'; but it's the interaction of four master-musicians which engenders the magic here: there really are no joins to be seen and, with Christensen at his most robustly inventive, the rhythmic layers are as songful as those created by Liebman and Stenson. Richly recorded and highly recommended.

***** European Voices**

Dragon DRCD 268 2CD *Danielsson; Niels-Petter Molvaer (t); Nils Lindgren (tb); Sven Fridolfsson (as); Joakim Milder (saxes); Michael Riessler (cl, bcl, sno); Lars Jansson (p); Tobias Sjogren, Eivind Aarset (g); Marilyn Mazur (d).* 12/93.

European Voices is two discs of various groupings, improvisations and compositions, boiled down from seven hours of material. Perhaps surprisingly, the range of moods is actually more limited than on some of Danielsson's other discs – the tone stretches from pastel calm to craggy, restless discord, but rhythmically it's rather flat and unmoving. There are some beautiful passages, such as the carefully wrought 'Eden' or the vigorous 'Falling Down'; but overall this feels like a project that's of more importance to its maker than to his audience.

***** Live At Visiones**

Dragon DRCD 309 *Danielsson; David Liebman (ss); Bobo Stenson (p); Jon Christensen (d).* 3/96.

The quartet's live album is a pleasing souvenir of one gig, though it doesn't stand the closest comparison with their studio efforts. Five tunes from their book get an expanded treatment, not always to advantage: the ramblings which open and close 'Folk Song', for instance, detract from the gripping middle section. But this is such a talented group that there are many felicities to enjoy, with Liebman very fine on 'Little Peanut' and Stenson affirming his mastery in virtually every phrase. Danielsson has been very busy as an in-demand sideman and producer of late, which has left him perhaps too busy to add to this listing.

*****(*) Origo**

Curling Legs CLP CD 32 *Danielsson; John Abercrombie (g); Adam Nussbaum (d).* 12/95.

Danielsson has been doing much work as sideman and producer and this obscure effort for the Oslo label Curling Legs is the only 'new' thing we could find to add to his listing. If some of Abercrombie's latter-day music has tended towards delicacy, this set fields a good deal more muscle, even hinting at the guitarist's Gateway work at some points. All three of them relish the reggae groove of 'Daze Off' and 'Kyrie' starts off in moody filigree and ends up close to heavy metal. Aside from a characteristic scamper through Porter's 'I Love You', the originals are shared creditwise between Danielsson and Abercrombie and the trio find a nicely diverse series of approaches.

Harold Danko (born 1947)

PIANO

One of Danko's most successful playing associations has been with Lee Konitz, and he shares the saxophonist's idiosyncratic mix of cool and intense emotion. There is an almost classical correctness to his pianism, which borrows somewhat from Ellington.

***** Next Age**

Steeplechase SCCD 31350 *Danko; Rich Perry (ts); Scott Colley (b); Jeff Hirshfield (d).* 10/93.

A first recorded glimpse of what was to become a fairly regular line-up. The move to Steeplechase has been nothing but positive for Danko. Producer Nils Winther has an intuitive feel for piano players and he gives Harold a well-rounded, spacious sound that enhances his increasingly positive and resonant playing. A pity in some ways that this wasn't a trio set, but the circumstances of the recording were that it was a return fixture for a group who had recorded under saxophonist Perry's leadership some weeks before. 'Next Age' is optimistically dedicated to Bill Clinton, and the saxophone part is wet and undefined enough to have been performed by the Pres himself. Perry, to be fair, is a fine player, soft and yielding as the original President, but less thoughtful. He sounds perfectly in keeping on 'For Bud', but he seems (to our ears) less appropriate on the more adventurous contrafacts like 'Gregarious Solitude' and 'Silk Lady'. There is another tribute to Edison Machado in 'Subindo' – rising, ascending – which is paired with another, originally 'straight' concert-piece called 'Luz Caverna'. Characteristically intelligent, and straightly beguiling.

****** After The Rain**

Steeplechase SCCD 31356 *Danko (p solo).* 8/94.

The obvious point of comparison here is another record of Coltrane tributes by Tommy Flanagan (who did actually play with the great man, and on one of his most significant dates). Where Flanagan treats the date as an occasion for fulsomely abstract meditations on the basic material, Danko approaches them both more modestly and more radically. He tackles no fewer than 14 Coltrane compositions, ranging from 'After The Rain' (the most obviously pianistic), 'Lonnie's Lament' and 'Syeeda's Song Flute', but moving on to less obvious material like 'Dahomey Dance', 'Mr Day' and 'Straight Street'. What is remarkable is that Danko makes these tunes sound ideally suited to the piano, and also utterly his own. Though clearly intended as a homage, there is no obstacle to wholesale reinvention, and Danko recasts songs like 'Mr Sims', a deep blues, and 'Wise One', a brooding meditation on the tradition, with a free hand. The sound is entirely suited to the material, open and spacious without being cavernous, exact without the close-miked over-definition that some labels favour for sets of this kind.

***** New Autumn**

Steeplechase SCCD 31377 *Danko; Rich Perry (ts); Scott Colley (b); Jeff Hirshfield (d).* 4/95.

****** Tidal Breeze**

Steeplechase SCCD 31411 *As above.* 4/95, 10/96.

*****(*) The Feeling Of Jazz**

Steeplechase SCCD 31392 *As above.* 3/96.

They stride towards the camera on the cover of *Tidal Breeze* like the cast of some benign adaptation of *Reservoir Dogs*: Mr Blues, Mr Blues, Mr Blues and Mr White. Perry's bleached tone isn't to all tastes, and here he sounds best on the Ellington and Strayhorn tribute, *The Feeling Of Jazz*, though this is the record on which Danko cedes more of the foreground to his colleagues, aiming for a more rounded group sound.

The originals on *New Autumn* and *Tidal Breeze*, both of them all-Danko sets, are more and more idiosyncratic. Just one track from April 1995 turns up on the later record, but it ('Personal Cornucopia') is so good that one can't quite understand why it wasn't included in the original set. Danko writes with a dark and sometimes impenetrable authority. On the most recent album he reprises 'Wayne Shorter' and follows it with 'McCoy's Passion', two numbers which underscore two of the most obvious (make that the least and then the most obvious) influences on his playing and writing style. 'Pastoral Landing' on the same record is a fascinatingly extended work-out, and one minor quibble regarding this body of work as a whole is that Danko seldom takes the option to stretch out and really develop ideas.

That is what he allows himself to do on the Ellington album, just seven numbers which (to be strictly accurate) consist of compositions of Ellington, Strayhorn and one ('Big Nick') by John Coltrane. These are the same tunes and in the same sequence as on Duke's 1962 encounter with the saxophonist for Impulse!. It may be that Danko has exhausted this particular line and may have to revert on future discs to solo or trio formats. For the moment, though, this is the combination which seems to engage his talents most fully. Strong statements, immaculately performed.

*****(*) This Isn't Maybe**

Steeplechase SCCD 31471 *Danko (p solo).* 7/98.

It's typical of Danko that he should have conceived this tribute to Chet Baker without the inclusion of 'My Funny Valentine'. There isn't an obvious or conventional gesture on the whole album, which breathes with the trumpeter's spirit, but in dialogue with an admirer who clearly learnt much from it. Most of the tracks are quite short and melodic and, apart from 'These Foolish Things' and 'The Touch Of Your Lips', aren't obvious choices. Jimmy Heath's 'D's Dilemma', two Dameron tunes and Phil Urso's 'Way To Go' give an idea of how carefully Harold has thought out his approach to Chet, his influences, associations and legacy.

*****(*) Stable Mates**

Steeplechase SCCD 31451 *Danko; Rich Perry (ts); Scott Colley (b); Jeff Hirshfield (d).* 4/97.

***** Nightscapes**

Steeplechase SCCD 31490 *As above.* 00.

*****(*) Prestigious**

Steeplechase SCCD 31508 *As above, except add Dave Ballou (t), Michael Formanek (b); omit Colley.* 3/01.

A careful variation in methods and material has made this group's sequence of albums sufficiently diverse to hold the attention, even given the often inward-looking feel of the music. *Stable Mates* is an essay on jazz composition from (roughly) the period 1956–66, with Gillespie, Heath, Hancock, Mulligan, Feldman, Mingus, Golson, Miles Davis and Thad Jones all covered. As ever, there's an interesting tension between Perry's softly insinuating solos and Danko's more dramatic reinvention of the material. As a sample, follow the opening minutes of Corea's 'Windows', which feels like a direct tussle between piano and tenor for the upper hand – though in the end realization dawns that Danko was being supportive all along (and this is also a fascinating parallel world to that of the Getz–Corea original). 'Dolphin Dance', another tune Getz favoured, gets a lovely reading, and 'Nostalgia In Times Square' does the cerebral blues rather well.

Nightscapes is a series of original nocturnes which earn a mark for being interesting rather than fully engaging, and it suggests that the quartet does best when they're working in a repertorial role – which is immediately reconvened with *Prestigious*, a homage to Eric Dolphy's composing. Ballou and Perry are hardly the likeliest first choices to cover Booker Little and Eric Dolphy, but their remoteness from plagiarism works in the record's favour, and these are very much group performances, the result of hours of study by Danko on material which even now has rarely been sighted in the modern idiom. 'Serene', 'Miss Ann' and 'Les' are entirely recast without obliterating Dolphy's various matrices. A fascinating set.

*****(*) Fantasy Exit**
Steeplechase SCCD 31530 *Danko; Michael Formanek (b); Jeff Hirshfield (d).* 3/02.

*****(*) Trilix**
Steeplechase SCCD 31551 *As above.* 4/03.

Danko's happy to admit that he prefers to cede melodic responsibilities to a horn player and, given the huge modern lumber-room of piano-trio records, setting down two more at the label where hitherto his best work has been mostly with horns does seem like a show of risk-taking. Where both sets score is in the kind of connoisseurship which has often served pianists well at Steeplechase: Danko assumes his audience to be knowledgeable and literate, and he chooses material (across both dates) from Jaki Byard, Randy Weston, Tony Williams and Freddie Redd, among others, while using only two originals of his own. Fittingly enough for an experienced educator, this has an air of masterclass about it. Fortunately, Formanek (who dominates Duke Jordan's 'Flight To Jordan' at the start of *Trilix*) and the supremely dependable Hirshfield play as full partners, helping to draw both discs out of the merely competent category. Danko's never going to win awards for exciting records; these graceful, tough entries are much more his style.

Alec and John Dankworth Generation Band

GROUP

An occasional project featuring the father-and-son team which is a central dynasty in British modern jazz.

***** Nebuchadnezzar**
Jazz House JHCD 029 *Guy Barker, Gerard Presencer, John Barclay (t, flhn); Mark Nightingale (tb); Keith Riby (frhn); John Dankworth (ss, as, Cmel, f); Andy Panayi (as, f); Tim Garland (ss, ts, f); Jimmy Hastings (bs, cl, f); Robin Aspland (p); John Parricelli (g); Christian Garrick (vn); Dave Powell (tba); Alec Dankworth (b); Ralph Salmins (d).* 10/93.

***** Rhythm Changes**
Jazz House JHCD 043 *As above, except add Noel Langley (t, flhn), Dave Laurence (frhn), Stuart Hall (vn, g); omit Barclay, Riby, Garrick.* 7/95.

The family firm in fine fettle. John Dankworth's representation on CD is disappointingly thin at present, considering his stature in postwar British jazz, but at least these two absorbing discs of big-band music – where he shares leadership duties with son Alec – are readily available. *Nebuchadnezzar*, recorded in a single day at the Ronnie Scott Club (though not in front of an audience), packs a dozen scores by various hands into its duration. The results are somewhat mixed, but the successes – Alec's take on 'Ida Lupino', Andy Panayi's treatment of 'Black Narcissus' and John's waltz-time blues, 'Nebuchadnezzar' – are performed with great panache and attention to dynamics: the band is often at its best when playing on the softest tones. *Rhythm Changes* was cut during a 'proper' set at the club (and a fine sound engineer Chris Lewis secured, too), and is inevitably more shouting – but better played all round. 'I Got Rheumatics' is a flag-waver in which the obvious prototype gets a glittering respray; 'Around The Track' is another refined show of dynamics; and throughout, as with the earlier disc, one is struck by the band's notably adept use of the sonorities of the brass section, with the tuba parts a crucial note of individuality. The soloists are a stellar lot in British terms, but the band's the thing.

Jacqui Dankworth

VOCALS

Daughter of Cleo Laine and John Dankworth; accomplished singer, songwriter and actress.

*****(*) As The Sun Shines Down On Me**
Candid CCD 79753 *Dankworth; Mike Outram (g, thumb p); Alec Dankworth, Tim Harries (b); Roy Dodds (d); Martin Brunsden (musical saw).* 02.

It is mysterious why Jacqui Dankworth is not better known. Certainly relatively to other female singers on the British scene who are far more noisily bruited in the press, she is a class act. Her mostly standards performance on the Candid is the best thing yet, ably supported by brother Alec and the consistently underrated Roy Dodds. Jacqui is sharp enough to include James Taylor, Stevie Wonder, Joni Mitchell and Bob Dylan songs amongst the show tunes, but it's her reading of things like 'You Must Believe In Spring', 'Teach Me Tonight' and 'In A Sentimental Mood' that clinches her jazz credentials. The album starts on an unusual note with a faintly surreal 'Blue Moon', featuring Mike Outram on thumb piano (he uses it again on Joni's 'Man From Mars') and Martin Brunsden's musical saw. Anyone interested in Jacqui Dankworth's work should sample the jazz-flavoured A. E. Housman settings on her earlier Spotlite disc.

John Dankworth (born 1927)

ALTO AND SOPRANO SAXOPHONES, CLARINET

A Londoner, Dankworth is one of the major figures in British postwar jazz. One of the bop pioneers at Club 11 in the late '40s, his Dankworth Seven and big bands were important groups in the '50s and '60s, and the orchestra played at Newport in 1959. He has scored numerous films and become a force in music education from his base in Wavendon. Married to the singer Cleo Laine.

***** Moon Valley**
Audio B ABCD 7 *Dankworth; John Horler (p); Malcolm Creese (b); Allan Ganley (d).* 2/98.

Dankworth's back-catalogue is full of fine music, but scarcely any of it has been made available on CD – at least, outside of some various-artists compilations – and he has often been too busy with concert work to rectify the situation. But at least there's this pleasing quartet date for Malcolm Creese's label. It's one day in the studio, and the pieces have a slightly too casual feel, but John's title-piece is a lovely melody in three and 'Spooks', done on clarinet, is a typical Dankworth lark. His tone has dried out a little and 'Son Of Sparky' almost goes wrong, but not quite. The rhythm section, with the admirable Ganley, are happy to join in the fun.

***** JD5**

Q-Note QNT 10101 *Dankworth; Mark Nightingale (tb); John Horler (p); Alec Dankworth (b); Allan Ganley (d).* 12/02–2/03.

Establishing a new imprint for his own music will hopefully see a lot more Dankworth material becoming available again – as well as new stuff, like this likeable quintet session. The impeccable Mark Nightingale takes some of the pressure off John's shoulders by helping out with horn duties, and the other three know the leader's moves inside out. Perhaps too much so – in some ways it's a bit of a rerun of the Audio B date, with 'Son Of Sparky' reappearing. The orchestral Dankworth is what needs to arrive on CD.

Stefano D'Anna (born 1959)

TENOR SAXOPHONE

Contemporary Italian saxophonist in a 'classic' post-bop idiom.

****** Leapin' In**

Splasc(h) H 374-2 *D'Anna; Enzo Pietropaoli (b); Fabrizio Sferra (d).* 12/91.

***** Carousel**

Splasc(h) H 666-2 *D'Anna; Fabio Zeppetella (g); Pietro Ciancaglini (b); Roberto Gatto (d).* 2/98.

*****(*) Runa**

Splasc(h) H 912-2 *D'Anna; Pietro Ciancaglini (b); Mimmo Cafiero (d).* 3/03.

D'Anna says that he admires the 'sculpture-like clarity' of Sonny Rollins's improvising, and his own playing strives to secure the same lucidity. If he is in Rollins's debt, though, he also goes to exceptional lengths to evade modern saxophone cliché. Rhythmically he eschews easy double-time passages or tonal distortions: there's an evenness to his line which gives his solos an irresistible flow, and a steely clarity to his tone that doesn't detract from his lyricism. His seven compositions here all differ from one another, and three standards are scrupulously remodelled: 'I've Grown Accustomed To Her Face' is strikingly different from the classic Rollins reading, 'Be-Bop' is fantastically fast and biting, and 'Body And Soul', done as a duo for tenor and uncredited soprano, refers to the melody hardly at all and reminds us of a Konitz–Marsh collaboration. A stunning recital all round.

Carousel isn't a bad record, but after its predecessor it feels like a severe disappointment. The biting energy which made the first record so compelling has been displaced by a more considered delivery (as well as by a soft-edged studio sound), and Zeppetella takes up plenty of space. D'Anna does all the writing himself, and there are no familiar tunes to centre the record. What comes out is merely a sound, accomplished set of post-bop improvising.

Runa marks a welcome return to form on record. With the power-packed Cafiero at the drums, the music is excitable, while it still takes succour from D'Anna's rigorous delivery. At the same time, it's looser and more free-flowing than the first record. Several of D'Anna's seven originals refer to aspects of his native Palermo, although there's little here which nods towards the folkish feel of some Sicilian records – these players are maybe too worldly for that. 'I Should Care' and ''S Wonderful' are hard-bitten ballad readings and there's a somewhat surprising dedication to Stan Getz, not a tenorman whose influence sounds apparent on D'Anna.

Olu Dara (born 1941)

CORNET, GUITAR, VOCALS

Born Charles Jones, Dara adopted his Yoruba name in the '70s, after his move to New York City and immersion in the jazz avant-garde. He has seen service with a disparate array of leaders – David Murray, Philip Wilson, Henry Threadgill and Cassandra Wilson among them – but surprised many when he eventually recorded under his own name by playing and singing blues- and gospel-tinged songs.

***** In The World: From Natchez To New York**

Atlantic 83077 *Dara; Rudy Herbet (org); Ivan Ramirez (g); Kwatei Jones-Quartey (g, perc); Alonzo Gardner (b); Greg Bandy (d, perc); Richard James (perc); Cantrese Allaway, Darada David, Melba Joyce, Mayanna Lee, Joyce Malone, Nas (v).* 99.

****(*) Neighborhoods**

Atlantic 83391 *Dara; Dr John (p); Rod Williams (p, org); Ivan Ramirez, Kwatei Jones-Quartey (g); Alonzo Gardner (b); Greg Bandy (d, perc); Cantrese Allaway, Cassandra Wilson (v).* 00.

No one expected Dara's belated debut to take this course. He sings country blues and accompanies himself on guitar over eleven strikingly original, if neo-traditional, songs. Liner notes by Ntozake Shange give a measure of where Dara is coming from in an African-American tradition. Listeners might be surprised not to hear his tight, Pops-influenced trumpet, but shouldn't be put off an intriguing record.

Despite the stellar guests, the follow-up was quite disappointing, formulaic and generic where the first album was fresh and unusual. The cornet puts in a welcome appearance again, though Dara seems to have given up playing much guitar.

Carlo Actis Dato (born 1952)

REEDS

Co-founder of the pioneer Italian post-bop band Art Studio, Dato has been active since the early '70s and is involved with several groups, of which his quartet is the principal focus.

*****(*) Ankara Twist**

Splasc(h) H 302 *Dato; Piero Ponzo (cl, bcl, as, bs, f); Enrico Fazio (b); Fiorenzo Sordini (d).* 10/89.

Though Dato plays some tenor, he is most at home on baritone and bass clarinet, and he's a volatile and unpredictable player with a compensating brilliance of timing: just when one thinks he's gone too far in a solo, he pulls it around and returns to the structure. As a composer, he writes themes that suggest some bridging-point between jazz and Balkan folk music, and the bucolic air of, say, 'Moonlight In Budapest' on *Oltremare* (currently still on LP only and in need of CD transfer) is counterpointed by the very next tune on the record, 'Portorico Smog'. The tracks on this quartet album are rather brief and have a programmatic feel to them, but they're played with great verve and enthusiasm by the group: Ponzo is a useful foil to the leader, Fazio is authoritative, Sordini full of bustle.

*****(*) Dune**

Splasc(h) H 354-2 *Dato; Laura Culver (ss, clo, berim); Alex Rolle (xy, perc); Massimo Barbiero (d, mar).* 2/91.

Rolle and Barbiero join in the fun and the quartet take some aspects of 'world music' to the cleaners: march and tango rhythms are mischievously undercut by Carlo's tendency to jump into bawling improvisations – he lets off another almost brutal baritone assault on 'Ketchup' – and by Laura's deadpan drones and vamps on the cello. The two percussionists are pressed into subsidiary roles, leavening the sometimes sparse arrangements, and sometimes the action seems a little too contrived on a very long (74 minutes) CD: 'Mar Del Plata' is delivered rather stiffly. But the crackerjack liveliness of the best playing is a delight.

***** Urartu**

Leo 220 *Dato (bs, bcl, ts solo).* 3/94.

Dato's first solo set is a typically mercurial and imaginative effort. He caricatures his reeds and loves to make excessive, elaborate noise with them, using circular breathing, slap-tonguing and whatever else he can think of and, though he plays a couple of standards, they come out rather cold. Most of the pieces seem like lightning sketches and, once he's finished with the idea, it's done. Maybe not an important Dato record but another very enjoyable one.

*****(*) Blue Cairo**

Splasc(h) 454-2 *Dato; Piero Ponzo (as, cl, bcl); Enrico Fazio (b); Fiorenzo Sordini (d).* 7/95.

Back with his original quartet, Dato picks up where he left off and draws out a personal synthesis of musics which are looking eastwards again – this time to Katmandu (where an element of 'A Night In Nepal' was recorded), Egypt, and maybe some points unspecified which the market-place overtones and snake-charmer solos on offer in many of the tracks seem to celebrate. This is funny, sentimental music that can suddenly shock you with a heartbreaking melody or a burst of anger; for all its globalism it's quite one-dimensionally simple in feel, dependent often on a tune curling up like smoke from the horns, but it's vibrantly alive. Ponzo, Fazio and Sordini know the moves and have them covered.

*****(*) Pasodoble**

Splasc(h) 642 *Dato; Enzo Rocco (g).* 6/97.

May they have this dance? Dato shows off some jazz roots here – he might make you think of classic hard-bop tenor on the likes of 'Ordinary Bus' – and Rocco can be Jim Hall or Billy Bauer when he wants to be. Yet they both throw in dissonance, timbral contrasts, odd mixed matches of style and tempo – it's a typically extravagant Dato date, even if there's only two of them playing the music. And with 19 tracks dispatched inside the hour, boredom thresholds are never once flirted with.

***** Son Para El Che**

Splasc(h) 675 *Dato; Massimo Rossi (ss, as); Antonio Fontana (g); Frederico Marchesano (b); Dario Bruna (d).* 10/97.

A new band for Dato, but the agenda's a familiar one for him: if this is a dedication to Che Guevara, it goes to the Argentine via the most convoluted of routes. Fontana is probably the key man and frankly he often overdoes it, taking his effects pedals to the cleaners on the final 'Last Blow' and generally trying to push his way to the front. The genre-hopping, for once in Dato's music, at times seems exaggerated beyond its effectiveness. But some of the leader's own solos break through and grip.

****** Delhi Mambo**

yvp 3065 *Dato; Piero Ponzo (as, bcl, cl, picc); Enrico Fazio (b); Fiorenzo Sordini (d).* 2/98.

On holiday from Splasc(h) for a moment, Dato calls back the quartet and they dash off their best record. 'Et Voilà' introduces the band one at a time, before their footsteps are heard beating a hasty retreat. But they come back for another hour or so of music. As ever, the tunes are full of Eastern promise, but the travelogue elements have fused into the collective spirit of the band so solidly that there's no sense of distances flippantly travelled. They're at home wherever they are, and whatever they're playing, be it bossa, bop or something they heard at the local café. A great one.

*****(*) Wake Up With The Birds**

Leo LR 285 *Dato; Kazutoki Umezu (ss, as, cl, bcl).* 11/98.

*****(*) Paella & Norimaki**

Splasc(h) 730-2 *Dato; Enzo Rocco (g).* 7/00.

Dato and Umezu make a tremendous sound together, two guys who can get plenty of air into and out of their lungs: the opening ten minutes of 'Mad Chickens' is a great display of a kind of barking sonority. They're not really screamers on the horns. The interplay's more about running loops around each other, whether on groaning bass clarinets or swooning saxes. Very romantic. Like most solo reeds records, there are times when you feel you've had enough, but it's a fine show.

Yum yum! The return match with Rocco features their recipe for paella in the sleeve-notes. While you're making that, Carlo and Enzo can supply another hour of sparky, sometimes mournful duets. A little more careful than their previous entry, perhaps, but again they create a broad gallery of styles and forms within an hour of music, which sometimes ('Haba-blanca') reaches a serene plateau inscribed with only a few notes.

*****(*) The Moonwalker**

Leo LR 311 *Dato (bs, ts, bcl solo).* n.d.

Dato's second solo for Leo is great fun. His playing would be called 'angry' or 'passionate' if these notes were played by any another saxophonist, but Carlo always seems to be ready to give the listener a wink that it all shouldn't be taken too seriously. Again, the solos are brief and absolutely to the point, and there's all sorts of field recordings interspersed between them – schoolchildren singing, and a pretty disgruntled fellow speaking on Malian radio.

***** Ginosa Jungle**

Splasc(h) 710-2 *Dato; Piero Ponzo (as, cl); Enrico Fazio (b); Fiorenzo Sordini (d).* 4/98.

*****(*) Fes Montuno**

yvp 3081 *As above.* 1/00.

We don't get out much, so we've yet to hear the quartet on stage, but at least there's now a souvenir of one of their live shows in *Ginosa Jungle*, recorded in Belgium. Since they don't have any difficulty in reaching top gear in the studio, there's no special frisson about a live recording, and there's definitely an ingredient missing for the homebody listener (what's the laughter about?). Actually, entertaining though it is, this isn't our favourite by the group.

Back in the studio for *Fes Montuno*. As ever, Dato has no difficulty in rustling up a dozen new tunes, with all the usual global supermarket flavours in them, and as ever they're played with gusto and top chops. But maybe this music won't go too much further before it starts to parody itself. The end of this CD is rather odd.

***** Don Quijote**
Splasc(h) 769.2 *Dato; Massimo Rossi (ss, as); Antonio Fontana (g, marranzano); Federico Marchesano (b); Dario Bruna (d).* 9/01.

*****(*) Istanbul Rap**
yvp 3112 *Dato; Piero Ponzo (as, sop-cl, picc); Enrico Fazio (b); Fiorenzo Sordini (d, perc).* 10/02.

The Dato band and the quartet may have very different personnel, but the results aren't so dissimilar. The band is noisier, perhaps a shade more anarchic; the quartet is jazzier, perhaps a shade more showbiz. Both flirt with silliness, only to have Dato or one of his trusted gangs turn everything right with a spot-on solo or a heartbreaking melody. *Don Quijote* is entertaining, like all of Dato's discs, but the keeper is *Istanbul Rap*, which finds Fazio and Sordini in great form, helping to stabilize the bounce and merriment in the horns. It remains a moot point how much longer Dato can sustain this tack, and how many more caravanserais he'll send us on.

****(*) USA Tour/April 2001/Live**
Splasc(h) 520.2 *Dato; Ken Vandermark (ts, cl, bcl); Wayne Horvitz (ky); Reuben Radding, Clyde Reed, Damon Smith (b); Dave Storrs, Gino Robair (d).* 4/01.

***** American Tour**
Splasc(h) 534.2 *Dato; Taylor Ho Bynum (t); David Mott (bs); Fred Lonberg-Holm (clo); Ron Samworth (g); Dylan Van Der Schyff (d); Glenn Kotche (perc).* 2/02.

Souvenirs of two visits to America. The first disc has quite a few sound problems and often seems like a glorified bootleg. Mostly it's free solos, with the occasional star guest joining in – Vandermark sits in at the Empty Bottle in Chicago and for once doesn't dominate. Interesting in bits, but far from essential Dato. The second trip is a little more effective as a kind of diary of the tour. Trio tracks with Samworth and Van Der Schyff work out particularly well and suggest that, for all his skills as a soloist, Dato likes good company best.

Kenny Davern (born 1935)

CLARINET

Born on Long Island, Davern began playing in New York's traditional jazz circles in the '50s. He was known as a sideman until the '70s, when his association with Soprano Summit, with Bob Wilber, brought him wider recognition. Has investigated the avant-garde, but he plays mostly in a swing-mainstream idiom, and these days sticks exclusively to clarinet.

***** A Night With Eddie Condon**
Arbors ARCD 19238 *Davern; Bernie Privin (t); Lou McGarity (tb); Dill Jones (p); Eddie Condon (g); Jack Lesberg (b); Cliff Leeman (d).* 4/71.

Not exactly pre-history for Davern, but this rowdy tape of a gig at Syracuse by a latter-day Condon gang is his earliest featured set at present. A slight speed wobble here and there isn't too intrusive. Whether you hear this as a vintage Condon group is up to the listener, but the playing is very strong – if Privin overchalks it at times, Davern and McGarity are both splendid – and the atmosphere of Condon's bandleading is unique (he brings Dill Jones up sharply for starting 'Rosetta' too quickly). Good fun.

*****(*) Stretchin' Out**
Jazzology JCD-187 *Davern; Dick Wellstood (p); Chuck Riggs (d).* 12/83.

*****(*) Never In A Million Years**
Challenge CHR 70019 *As above, except omit Riggs.* 1/84.

*****(*) Playing For Kicks**
Jazzology JCD-197 *Davern; Martin Litton (p); John Petters (d).* 11/85.

***** East Side, West Side**
Arbors ARCD 19137 *Davern; Dan Barrett (c, tb); Joel Helleny (tb); Bucky Pizzarelli (g); Bob Haggart (b); Tony DeNicola (d).* 6/94.

***** Kenny Davern & The Rhythm Men**
Arbors ARCD 19147 *As above, except omit Barrett and Helleny; add John Bunch (p).* 6/95.

****** Breezin' Along**
Arbors ARCD 19170 *Davern; Bucky Pizzarelli, Howard Alden (g); Greg Cohen (b); Tony DeNicola (d).* 6/96.

In his sixties, Kenny Davern has claims to being the major clarinettist in jazz, having now forsaken the soprano sax ('I play soprano once a year and it takes only a few moments to confirm that I made the right decision'). He had little in the catalogue under his own name until the '80s, but recent years have seen him setting down several fine records. There's little waste in his execution, garrulous though his phrasing often is, and he succeeds in playing in what is essentially a swing-based clarinet style while suggesting that he's also perfectly aware of every jazz development that has taken place since (he once recorded with Steve Lacy, Steve Swallow and Paul Motian on *Unexpected*, Kharma PK-7, still not on CD).

Stretchin' Out is one of the best showcases for his own playing, starting with a mellifluous and perfectly paced 'The Man I Love' and proceeding through five more standards with unflagging inventiveness. Wellstood is a superb partner, harrying and supporting him in equal measure, but the drawback is the presence of Riggs, who's not only too loud in the mix but superfluous to what should have been a duo session. *Never In A Million Years* finds Davern and Wellstood alone together at New York's Vineyard Theatre and, though the bare format is a little dry across CD length, there is some marvellous sparring between the two men. *Playing For Kicks* goes back to the trio and, while Litton isn't remotely up to Wellstood's standard, it's another great clarinet set, with the ancient ('Willie The Weeper') and the comparatively modern ('Lullaby Of The Leaves') on the agenda. *East Side, West Side* and *Rhythm Men* are two recent Davern sessions for Arbors. Barrett is a valuable front-line partner, playing cornet for the most part, though he picks up his slide for a very ripe duet with Helleny on 'Sidewalks Of New York'. Davern seems in good spirits on both sessions, and the rhythm section fits like a comfortable shoe. In the end, though, both dates sound a little hindered by their lack of preparation – expert playing, fine solos, but nothing to lift them a notch above what is now a bulging bracket of mainstream records.

If that seems a bit harsh, we have stopped sitting on the fence and given an unqualified fourth star to *Breezin' Along*. The band is a peach: Pizzarelli and Alden are a great team, driving the fast numbers along and softly suggesting all the harmonic detail in the slower ones, while Cohen and DeNicola are strong without seeming obtrusive. Davern himself measures the material with an almost insouciant virtuosity: two Beiderbecke chestnuts, 'Since My Best Girl Turned Me Down' and 'Jazz Me Blues', are super, but we'd single out the gorgeous variations on 'Baby Won't You Please Come Home' as Davern at his peak.

*****(*) Spanish Eyes**
Chiaroscuro CD(D) 344 *Davern; Phil Woods (as); Flip Phillips (ts); Derek Smith (p); Howard Alden (g); Milt Hinton (b); Joe Ascione (d).* 11/95.

Whatever else was played at the 1995 Floating Jazz Festival, it can't have outswung or otherwise smoked this set. Davern seems to be at the top of his game from the off – his 'Elsa's Dream' solo is both far out and inside – and Flip, as ever, defied Father Time. The rhythm section are completely in the groove – Smith risks some things which a more stoic pianist wouldn't have thought about, and Alden is as ever a man for all seasons – and, to cap it all, Phil Woods strolls in for a final 'Lover Come Back To Me'. There are one or two vagaries in the sound, but nothing too serious.

***** Smiles**
Arbors ARCD 19207 *Davern; Howard Alden, Bucky Pizzarelli (g); Greg Cohen (b); Tony DeNicola (d).* 98.

In Ira Gitler's words, 'easy listening jazz from the Irish-Jewish soul of a story-telling reedsman'. This re-run of *Breezin' Along* isn't as consistently fine as its predecessor. The choice of tunes is less interesting, and Davern sounds a whit less involved. But this is still mainstream jazz of tremendous calibre, and Alden and Pizzarelli are again a marvellous team.

***** The Jazz Kennection**
Arbors ARCD 19246 *Davern; Ken Peplowski (cl, as); John Bunch (p); Howard Alden (g); Greg Cohen (b); Tony DeNicola (d).* 10/00.

Not bad, but this doesn't feel like vintage work by either of the two Kens, though maybe it's just that they're let down a little by Cohen and DeNicola, who could give them more of a lift. Peps is mainly on alto, while Davern sticks to the stick.

Ben Davis

CELLO

Britain's answer to David Darling.

***** Double Dares Are Sometimes Different**
FMR CD 48 *Davis; Chris Biscoe (ss, as, acl); Tim Wells (b); Martin France (d); Paul Clarvis (perc).* 01.

Attractive set of compositions and arrangements for this unusual instrumentation. Occasionally recalls Eric Dolphy's work with Ron Carter on cello, but Davis has a lighter, almost folkier sound and his harmonic ideas are more open and genial. Biscoe is always an attractive player, more than a colourist, and Wells, France and Clarvis do their bit toward making this a vivid debut.

Eddie 'Lockjaw' Davis (1922–86)

TENOR SAXOPHONE

Born in New York, Davis made his name with Cootie Williams, before joining Count Basie in 1952; he stayed, on and off, until 1960. Frequently paired with Shirley Scott or Johnny Griffin in the '60s, he spent seven further years with Basie before working as a solo through the late '70s and '80s; died unexpectedly in Las Vegas.

*****(*) Eddie 'Lockjaw' Davis 1946–1947**
Classics 1012 *Davis; Fats Navarro (t); Sadik Hakim, Al Haig, Johnny Acea (p); Bill De Arabngo, John Collins, Huey Long (g); Gene Ramey (b); Denzil Best, Butch Ballard (d).* 5/46–4/47.

This is almost pre-history for the Davis most familiar to LP collectors. The most important tracks are the eight sides for Savoy, with Fats Navarro, by Eddie Davis And His Be Boppers. Davis straddles bop and swing in his phrasing; if anything, with his swallowed notes, sandpapery tone and sudden shrieks, he's already a genre unto himself. Navarro is not quite the budding genius he would shortly become, but he's budding nevertheless, and this is exciting music. The rest of the disc is made up of sessions for Haven, Apollo, Lenox and three tracks which later turned up on a Plymouth LP. Some of the material is obscure enough to have an unidentified personnel, and recording quality is, as with many indie labels of the '40s, often indifferent; but Davis barrels through all these dates with the boldness that would characterize his career. A very enjoyable set.

*****(*) The Cookbook Vol. 1**
Original Jazz Classics OJC 652 *Davis; Jerome Richardson (ts, f); Shirley Scott (org); George Duvivier (b); Arthur Edgehill (d).* 6/58.

***** Jaws With Shirley Scott**
Original Jazz Classics OJC 218 *As above, except omit Richardson.* 9/58.

***** Smokin'**
Original Jazz Classics OJC 705 *As above, except Richardson returns.* 9–12/58.

***** The Cookbook Vol. 2**
Original Jazz Classics OJC 653 *As above.* 12/58.

***** The Cookbook Vol. 3**
Original Jazz Classics OJC 756 *As above.* 12/58.

***** Jaws In Orbit**
Original Jazz Classics 322 *As above, except add Steve Pulliam (tb); omit Richardson.* 5/59.

***** Bacalao**
Original Jazz Classics OJC 1090 *As above except omit Pulliam, add Ray Barretto, Luis Perez (perc).* 12/59.

***** Gentle Jaws**
Prestige PRCD-24160-2 *As above, except add Red Garland (p), Sam Jones (b), Art Taylor (d); omit Barretto and Perez.* 60.

By the time he got to the LP era, Davis had become one of the most honest, no-nonsense soloists in the music. He hardly changed his methods from one date to another. Whatever else is going on around him, he gives it his best shot. His apprenticeship in New York big bands in the '40s led him towards rhythm-and-blues rather than bebop, but it was as either a section soloist with Basie or a jazz combo leader that Jaws functioned best. His sound was, on reflection, a surprisingly complex matter. Unlike many of the players working in the organ-combo format, where Jaws made his biggest impact, his phrasing had an elongated quality that he broke up only with his matter-of-fact brusqueness: as if he was masking emotion with a temperament that told him to get on with it.

He spent the late '50s leading the group which made the OJC reissues listed above. The records are formulaic – blustering solos over bluesy organ riffs – but endowed with a spirit that makes the discs highly enjoyable, taken one at a time. All three *Cookbook* albums are entertaining displays of good-natured fisticuffs, with the food theme followed through in all the titles ('The Chef', 'Skillet', 'In The Kitchen' and so on) and Jaws taking the roof off on 'Have Horn, Will Blow', which garners an extra notch for the first disc. Richardson's flute is a needless cooling-off device on most of the tracks, but these are fun records. *Bacalao* is a new arrival: a little bit of Latin bustle is added courtesy of Barretto and Perez, but mostly it's good business as usual with Jaws and Shirley. *Gentle Jaws*, if that title doesn't sound like a contradiction, puts together a couple of small-hours sessions where the man huffs and hustles his way through a selection of top-notch ballads, sentiment without slop.

CORE COLLECTION

★★★★ Very Saxy

Original Jazz Classics OJC 458 *Davis; Coleman Hawkins, Arnett Cobb, Buddy Tate (ts); Shirley Scott (org); George Duvivier (b); Arthur Edgehill (d).* 4/59.

Prestige called in three other tenormen on their books to sit in with the Davis–Scott combo, and the results were barnstorming. The programme is all simple blues, but the flat-out exuberance of the playing is so exhilarating that it would be churlish to give it anything less than top marks, particularly in the excellent remastered sound. As competitive as it might appear, nobody is bested, and the clout of Davis and Cobb is matched by the suaver Tate and the grandiloquent Hawkins. Their 'Lester Leaps In' is a peerless display of saxophone sound.

★★(★) Afro-Jaws

Original Jazz Classics OJC 403 *Davis; Clark Terry, Ernie Royal, Phil Sunkel, John Bello (t); Lloyd Mayers (p); Larry Gales (b); Ben Riley (d); Ray Barretto (perc).*

★★★(★) Trane Whistle

Original Jazz Classics OJC 429 *Davis; Clark Terry, Richard Williams, Bob Bryant (t); Melba Liston, Jimmy Cleveland (tb); Jerome Richardson, Oliver Nelson, Eric Dolphy, George Barrow, Bob Ashton (reeds); Richard Wyands (p); Wendell Marshall (b); Roy Haynes (d).* 9/60.

★★★ Streetlights

Prestige PRCD 24150-2 *Davis; Don Patterson (org); George Duvivier (b); Paul Weedon, Billy James (d).* 11/62.

Afro-Jaws puts the saxophonist in front of brass and percussion to no very telling effect. But *Trane Whistle*, a set of Oliver Nelson arrangements for a cracking big band, puts him in his element and, though the charts are perhaps too functional to make the record a classic, the knock-out power of Davis's blowing is thrilling. An Ernie Wilkins arrangement of 'You Are Too Beautiful' shows off his skills with a ballad, too. *Streetlights* puts him back in the organ-combo setting with the slightly more 'modern' style of Patterson. Nobody puts himself out particularly, and the tunes are mostly obvious, but the playing is hard to fault.

★★★★ The Tenor Scene

Original Jazz Classics OJC 940 *Davis; Johnny Griffin (ts); Junior Mance (p); Larry Gales (b); Ben Riley (d).* 1/61.

★★★(★) Live At Minton's

Prestige 24206 *As above.* 1/61.

★★★(★) Blues Up And Down

Milestone 47084 *As above, except add Lloyd Mayers (p).* 11/60–6/61.

Griff and Lock were a famous team, and rightly so. The important thing was that neither man approached their collaboration as a mere blowing situation: Davis remembers that they rehearsed regularly and never let the set-list atrophy. Both *The Tenor Scene* and *Live At Minton's* emanate from the same marathon session at Minton's in 1961 (originally spread across four separate LPs – not all the tracks are here). *The Tenor Scene* has nothing fancy about it in terms of the tunes, but the playing has whipcrack impact, the rhythm section are right on top of it, and the light work made of a difficult tune such as 'Straight No Chaser' shows how masterful these tenormen were. A classic jazz record. We slightly prefer it to *Live At Minton's*, though there's scarcely a notch in it, and the second set is more focused around Monk and bebop material. *Blues Up And Down* couples two studio dates, the LP of the same title and the slightly earlier *Griff And Lock* (Mayers replaces Mance on the later session). They're a shade cooler in the studio, but it's still a piquant match.

★★★ Goin' To The Meetin'

Prestige 24259 *Davis; Shirley Scott (org); Horace Parlan (p); George Duvivier, Buddy Catlett (b); Arthur Edgehill, Art Taylor (d); Ray Barretto, Willie Bobo (perc).* 4/60–5/62.

Coupling *Goin' To The Meetin'* with *Misty*, this one feels a little more of a potboiler, since the tracks on the later session (with Parlan) are rather brief and over too fast. The session with Shirley still gets up to a good temperature.

★★★(★) Straight Blues

Prestige 11014-2 *As OJC albums listed above, plus Harry 'Sweets' Edison (t), Count Basie (p), John Heard (b), Jimmie Smith (d).* 12/58–5/76.

An enjoyable compilation of some of Jaws's bluesiest moments from his Prestige years, with the 'Untitled Blues' from a Harry Edison Pablo date tacked on for extra measure. Not a second wasted.

★★★ Lock, The Fox / The Fox And The Hounds

Collectables COL-2182 *Davis; Ernie Royal, Joe Newman, Thad Jones, Snooky Young, Bert Collins (t); Urbie Green, Wayne Andre, Jimmy Cleveland, J. J. Johnson (tb); Tony Studd (btb); Jerome Richardson, Bobby Plater (as); Frank Wess, Billy Mitchell, Frank Foster (ts); Danny Bank (bs); Hank Jones, Sir Roland Hanna, Ross Tompkins (p); Gene Bertoncini, Billy Butler, Les Spann (g); Russell George, George Duvivier (b); Chuck Lampkin, Grady Tate (d); Ray Barretto (perc).* 6–11/66.

These albums were previously reissued (minus a few tracks) as *Save Your Love For Me* on Bluebird, but here's the pair in their entirety. The band on *Lock, The Fox* sets up some good grooves for Jaws to get his teeth in to, and Spann plays some ear-tickling fills. As with the second, big-band, set though, the tracks are all rather curtly tailored, possibly with radio-play in mind. Plater's charts for the orchestra (and what a line-up!) are less than sensational. Even with these reservations, though, Davis remains inimitable, and the music has mostly worn better than we remembered.

*****(*) Eddie 'Lockjaw' Davis With Michel Attenoux**
Storyville STCD 5009 *Davis; Patrick Artero (t); Claude Gousset (tb); Michel Attenoux (as); Gabriel Garvanoff (p); Jean-Pierre Mulot (b); Teddy Martin (d).* 7/75.

*****(*) Leapin' On Lenox**
Black & Blue 926.2 *Davis; Eddie 'Cleanhead' Vinson (as); Milt Buckner (p); Bill Doggett (org); Jimmy Leary, Milt Hinton (b); Gus Johnson, J. C. Heard (d).* 7/74–7/78.

****(*) Swingin' Till The Girls Come Home**
Steeplechase SCCD 31058 *Davis; Thomas Clausen (p); Bo Stief (b); Alex Riel (d).* 3/76.

***** Straight Ahead**
Original Jazz Classics OJC 629-2 *Davis; Tommy Flanagan (p); Keter Betts (b); Bobby Durham (d).* 5/76.

***** Montreux '77**
Original Jazz Classics OJC 384 *Davis; Oscar Peterson (p); Ray Brown (b); Jimmie Smith (d).* 7/77.

Davis went the journeyman route of wandering freelance through the '70s and '80s. The Black & Blue disc is a superior repackaging of two sessions, one with Buckner, and a second (though only three tracks long) with Vinson and Doggett. The first is more like straight-ahead, the second has something of a soul-jazz feel, with Vinson wailing in on 'Double Eddie', but they make a fine match and it's a pleasure to hear Buckner in particular get some individual space. The real stars of the Montreux concert recording are Peterson and Brown, whose hard clarity creates a formidable platform for the nominal leader; but Davis himself sounds somewhat below par, his solos overwrought, and the music is exciting only inconsistently.

The pick of the rest is certainly the Storyville session with a team of French mainstreamers. Impromptu as the session was – Davis simply harmonized his parts with Attenoux on the scores – it's played with enormous gusto by all seven men, the horns matching Jaws in their surly attack, and rollicking events like Neal Hefti's 'Midnite Blue' get a good thrashing. Yet there are three terrific ballad solos by the tenorman on 'Moonlight In Vermont', 'What's New?' and 'Lush Life'. Excellent sound. The Steeplechase set seems much more ordinary, and even the OJC disc with Flanagan rarely gets much above professional expertise.

***** All Of Me**
Steeplechase SCCD 31181 *Davis; Kenny Drew (p); Jesper Lundgaard (b); Svend-Erik Norregaard (d).* 8/83.

Davis was still a commanding player up until his unexpected death in 1986. His recording regimen was a casual one, and his later discs have a pot-luck quality, but the leader himself secures an unusual level of commitment: all his records manage to be recommendable for his own tenor playing. The Steeplechase date is accomplished and genial. He was always good value.

Jesse Davis (born 1965)

ALTO SAXOPHONE

A New Orleans man, Davis studied with Ellis Marsalis and then in New Jersey and New York. Basically a hard-bop player, with traces of what came before and after sifted in. The influences are clear: Cannonball Adderley and Phil Woods.

***** Second Nature**
Concord CCD 4883 *Davis; Massimo Farao (p); Aldo Zunino (b); Massimo Dall'omo (d).* 6/99.

Concord's founder, the late Carl Jefferson, spoke of Davis with profound affection and clearly regarded him, after Scott Hamilton, as one of his own most prescient signings. Since 1991, the albums came just about once a year and they bespeak a steadily maturing player. However, the entire sequence has now been deleted, bar the final entry. Farao is another hugely gifted Italian who combines a genuine jazz feel with a plangent lyricism. The pianist is credited with a couple of compositions – 'Marta's Samba' and 'Tommaso' – and comps extremely well. His soloing is brisk, melodic and uncomplicated. Davis sounds good in this company, though he coasts rather too often for comfort. A more challenging environment might tempt Jesse to leave behind his failsafe licks and harmonic devices and strike out for new territory. Looks like he's going to have to find a new label to make that happen, but on the basis of some Scottish club appearances early in 2004, he's currently in fine form.

Miles Davis (1926–91)

TRUMPET, FLUGELHORN, ORGAN

One of the pivotal artists of the twentieth century, Miles was a shapeshifting imp of the perverse, capable of extraordinary beauty and a kind of self-negating ugliness almost by turns. He grew up in comfortable circumstances in Alton, Illinois, and never once, even at the zenith of the Black Power movement, affected any plantation or ghetto poses. He went to New York to study and to follow in the footsteps of Charlie Parker, with whom he worked, not entirely at ease with the rapid, declamatory language of bebop. After the war, he began to experiment with Gerry Mulligan and others, using cooler modalities and larger groups. This eventually brought him within the orbit of one of the two men who were to exert the greatest influence on his recording career. Gil Evans worked with Miles in workshop sessions and later arranged some of his greatest big-band recordings. In the mid-'50s the trumpeter formed a quintet and recorded classic discs for Prestige, culminating in Kind Of Blue. He also dabbled in film music, an experience which led him in a new direction and a new, more floating approach to harmony and structure. This became most evident in the fierce, loosely organized jams which producer Teo Macero, his other éminence grise, transformed into releasable albums. Ill-health, disenchantment and scrapes with the law and corporate politics led Miles to withdraw from music-making for some time, emerging only to play organ on some of the darkest and most troublous music he or any artist ever recorded. Late years brought a measure of renewed and belated superstardom and, though he showed signs of returning to blues-based jazz, he was required to play pop-derived hits to festival audiences who worshipped him as a natural rebel and an icon of style.

★★★ Complete Savoy And Dial Recordings

Definitive 11158 *Davis; Dizzy Gillespie (t); J. J. Johnson (tb); Charlie Parker (as); Lucky Thompson (ts); Duke Jordan, John Lewis, Dodo Marmarosa, Bud Powell (p); Arv Garrison (g); Vic McMillan, Tommy Potter, Curley Russell (b); Roy Porter, Max Roach (d).* 45, 46.

If one were to pick two figures to encapsulate the diversity, continuity within change, and the sheer artistic grace of jazz, then one could only point to Duke Ellington and to a figure who in some ways is Duke's dark opposite, in other ways his equal, but who grew to distrust the very name 'jazz' as a white commercial construct. In his lifetime, Miles Davis experienced a curious combination of adulation and disdain; endlessly changing yet never sounding like anyone other than himself, endlessly experimenting yet innately hostile to the self-conscious experimentalism of the avant-garde; an enigma wrapped up in a conundrum, yet expressed by a voice of fragile purity. And never was the epithet 'vocal' better applied to a horn player, for even after he had scoured his own voice down to the famous husky growl of later years (against medical insistence, he shouted at an agent following throat surgery), his trumpet-playing was pristine.

It should be understood from the start that Miles Davis was not a virtuoso trumpeter. There were plenty of other slim black men (and some heftier ones, like Dizzy) around at the end of the war who could blow him offstage without effort. Even so, the early bebop sets suggest that he knew his way round the complex harmonics and rapid metres of the time and could hold his own in the company of Charlie Parker and others. Repackaging this early material as if under Miles's leadership is pretty sharp practice, though some of those dates were nominally his and so their reissue as such is perfectly if nominally justified. His real forte was elsewhere Miles's great gift was musical rather than technical. He could place a note with the precision and accuracy of the painters he admired, and he was a total musician in that everything that happened within his orbit somehow came to sound like part of his own conception.

★★★★ The Complete Birth Of The Cool

Blue Note 94550 *Davis; Kai Winding, J. J. Johnson (tb); Junior Collins, Gunther Schuller, Sandy Siegelstein (frhn); John Barber (tba); Lee Konitz (as); Gerry Mulligan (bs); Al Haig, John Lewis (p); Nelson Boyd, Al McKibbon, Joe Shulman (b); Kenny Clarke, Max Roach (d); Kenny Hagood (v); Mike Zwerin (tb); Sahib Shihab (as); Benjamin Lundy (ts); Cecil Payne (bs); Tadd Dameron (p); John Collins (g); Carlos Vidal (perc).* 9/48–3/50.

★★★(★) Cool Boppin'

Fresh Sound FSCD 1008 *As above.* 9/48–2/49

... and then suddenly we are in the presence of a major innovator. But who? Since Miles's death, Gerry Mulligan has gone on record, without rancour but with unmistakable emphasis, to claim a much larger hand in these astonishing performances than the attribution of *Birth Of The Cool* to Miles alone has ever allowed. It had been clear, even from his tenure with Charlie Parker, that Miles was not a natural bebopper, favouring a much cooler, less abrasive sound. As the released tracks all demonstrate, Miles and his collaborators were more interested in texture and structure than in stratospheric soloing and cutting contests. Whoever was the main creative force, Miles was certainly the enabler, bringing together like-minded players in New York City, and, though the results (recorded at three sessions over the span of a year) were a commercial failure at the time, these pioneering efforts by arrangers Mulligan, Gil Evans and John Carisi are allusive, magical scores that channelled the irresistible energy of bebop into suprising textures and piquant settings for improvisation.

Davis and Konitz play as if in sight of some new musical world. One can almost share in their delight and surprise as unexpected harmonic fragrances waft off the landscape in front of them. Airshot material by a different line-up has been available as *The Real Birth Of The Cool* on Bandstand. This was taped before the now-classic studio sessions and shows the same music – 'Jeru', 'Budo', 'Godchild' – in evolution rather than finished and definitive. Nine of the same tracks appear on *Cool Boppin'*, which is valuable for some great early solos by the leader. The sound, recorded at the Royal Roost club, is no better than average for this kind of material, but there is sufficient of interest in the performances to make it a worthwhile buy, and there is some fine material under Tadd Dameron's leadership on the same disc, including some glorious moments when Davis lifts Dameron's wonky lyricism to new heights. The *Complete* brings together all the available material from this historic experiment, beautifully remastered and nicely packaged.

★★★ Young Miles

Properbox 1017 4CD *As above; other personnels, including Charlie Parker group.* 45–49.

Unlike many of the Proper sets, this one seems a touch redundant, given that there are better and more authoritative releases of all this material. The packaging and documentation is average, and the remastering leaves the sound a bit flat and unexpressive, which may suit some of the 'Birth of the Cool' tracks, but dims the wattage on Miles's work with Charlie Parker. OK, but pretty unispiring, even at the price.

★★★ All Stars Recordings

Definitive 11164 *Davis; Marion Hazel, Fats Navarro, Joe Newman (t); Ted Kelly, Fred Robinson, Dicky Wells, Kai Winding (tb); Howard Johnson, Ray Perry, Jimmy Powell, Sahib Shihab (as); Stan Getz, Coleman Hawkins, Illinois Jacquet, Benjamin Lundy, Big Nick Nicholas (ts); Leo Parker, Cecil Payne (bs); Tadd Dameron, Bill Doggett, Leonard Feather, Hank Jones (p); John Collins (b); Al Lucas, Gene Ramey, Curley Russell (b); Art Blakey, Kenny Clarke, Max Roach, Shadow Wilson (d); Carlos Vidal (perc); Kay Penton (v).* 45–52.

★★(★) Complete Vocalists Sessions

Definitive 11160 *Davis; Hobart Dotson, Leonard Hawkins, King Kolax (t); Herbie Fields (t, cl); Bennie Green, Walter Knox, Chips Outcalt, Gerald Valentine (tb); Billy Eckstine (tb, v); John Cobbs, Sonny Stitt (as); Gene Ammons, Budd Johnson, Arthur Simmons (ts); Cecil Payne (bs); Tony Scott (cl); Teddy Brannon, Linton Garner, Jimmy Jones (p); Freddie Green, Mundell Lowe, Connie Wainwright (g); Leonard Gaskin, Tommy Potter, Billy Taylor Sr (b); Art Blakey, J. C. Heard, Ed Nicholson (d); Ann Baxter, Earl Coleman, Sarah Vaughan, Rubberlegs Williams (v).* 45–52.

Two very average compilations of early material that casts little light on Miles's subsequent development. It's interesting enough to hear snippets of Miles in and around Sassie, Rubberlegs Williams, Earl Coleman and the now largely forgotten Ann Baxter, and of course a stint in the Eckstine band was a virtual finishing school for musicians of this generation, but like the other volume of historical and archival value only and not an urgent purchase even for enthusiastic collectors of Milesiana.

*** Quintet With Lee Konitz; Sextet With Jackie McLean

Fresh Sound FSCD 1000 *Davis; Don Elliott (mel, vib); Lee Konitz, Jackie McLean (as); Gil Coggins, John Lewis (p); Connie Henry, Curley Russell (b); Connie Kay, Max Roach (d); Kenny Hagood (v).* 9/48–5/52.

Things were moving rather slowly for Miles on the recording front, but these sessions, which straddle the *Birth Of The Cool* period, are a useful guide to what he was doing round the scene. The 1948 session finds him in company with Konitz on four titles, most of them unwontedly upbeat and ebullient. The only change of pace is for 'You Go To My Head', which is kept to a lugubrious meander for the benefit of Kenny Hagood. Rare to hear Miles going for high notes with quite this enthusiasm, though absolutely no mistaking, even at this early date, the sinuous grace of Konitz's improvising; and in retrospect what an influence – sometimes literal, sometimes negative – it was to have on Miles's own approach.

The sextet date is rather disappointing, cluttered and somewhat regressive in idiom. Certainly much less sign of the Davis of the future; more of the querulous bopper he was leaving behind. Also airshot recordings, these share the technical limitations of the quintet date, but more damagingly, since it's much harder to pick out the detail. Miles is soloing confidently. His own 'Out Of The Blue' is confident, clean-limbed and strong, and McLean is beginning to sound like a star in the making.

**(*) Miles Davis With Horns

Original Jazz Classics OJCCD 053 *Davis; Bennie Green, Sonny Truitt (tb); Al Cohn, Sonny Rollins, Zoot Sims (ts); John Lewis (p); Leonard Gaskin, Percy Heath (b); Kenny Clarke, Roy Haynes (d).* 1/51–2/53.

*** Dig

Original Jazz Classics OJCCD 005 *Davis; Jackie McLean (as); Sonny Rollins (ts); Walter Bishop Jr (p); Tommy Potter (b); Art Blakey (d).* 10/51.

It would be some while before Miles repaid Prestige's confidence in him with a completely authoritative and satisfying record. Had one done an end-of-year audit in December 1951, would he have seemed a likely contender? The earlier set is almost dreary and ill-defined and, though Miles solos with great confidence on 'My Old Flame' and 'Blueing', there isn't much else to write home about. *Dig* is most obviously questionable on technical grounds. Whatever has happened to players as forceful as Potter and Blakey, lost in a disagreeable mix? 'Conception' appears in a less than challenging form, and there is a positively banal approach to 'It's Only A Paper Moon'. If the story hadn't gone a great deal further than this, Miles might have been a footnote. *Birth Of The Cool* notwithstanding, he had still to produce a work of real individuality.

*** Conception

Original Jazz Classics OJCCD 1726 2 *Davis; J. J. Johnson, Kai Winding (tb); Charlie Kennedy, Lee Konitz, Jackie McLean (as); Stan Getz, Sonny Rollins, Zoot Sims (ts); Gerry Mulligan (bs); Tony Aless, Walter Bishop Jr, Al Haig, Sal Mosca (p); Billy Bauer (g); Arnold Fishkin, Chubby Jackson, Tommy Potter, Gene Ramey (b); Art Blakey, Roy Haynes, Don Lamond, Stan Levey, Max Roach (d).* 3/51.

A largely forgotten and overlooked album, featuring Miles in the company of Stan Getz and Lee Konitz, three graceful exponents of cool improvisation together at the threshold of the '50s and each destined to make a very different impact on the music of the next two decades. The arrangements are somewhat too big and fussy to suit the soloists, but there is no mistaking how professional they are. Most of the tracks are very short indeed, but 'My Old Flame' offers an opportunity to stretch out a touch more generously. This was intended as a limited-edition reissue, but copies have been widely available.

*** Miles Davis: Volume 1

Blue Note 32610 *Davis; J. J. Johnson (tb); Jackie McLean (as); Jimmy Heath (ts); Gil Coggins, Horace Silver (p); Percy Heath, Oscar Pettiford (b); Art Blakey, Kenny Clarke (d).* 5/52–3/54.

***(*) Miles Davis: Volume 2

Blue Note 32611 *As above.*

*** The Best Of Miles Davis

Blue Note 7982872 *As above and Capitol sessions, except add Julian 'Cannonball' Adderley (as), Hank Jones (p), Sam Jones (b).* 1/49–3/58.

Time, strength, cash and patience; Herman Melville said these were the key to an artistic career. When Blue Note picked up Miles, he was an artist who needed all four, temperamentally and creatively. These are inconsistent records, but they are also the first tokens of a genuinely personal vision and a solo style that could never be mistaken for anyone else. Although still addicted to heroin when the first two sessions were made, and with his professional life in some disarray, Davis was beginning to move beyond the confines of small-group bebop and explore the more expansive musical language he had sketched in with the *Birth Of The Cool* ensemble. Nothing quite as ambitious here; but definite signs, even in these rather brief and pithy tracks, that he has changed gear. The music is intense yet restrained, cool yet plangent. The first date seems comparatively hurried, but the second, with fine compositions from Johnson, Heath and Bud Powell, is indispensable, the first Davis record since *Birth* that *must* be in your collection. The third features Davis with rhythm, and as sole horn it properly includes some very strong playing, with fast, eventful solos on 'Take Off' and 'The Leap', as well as an idiosyncratic reading of Monk's 'Well, You Needn't'.

The jumbled sequencing of the original LPs has been corrected on CD; the first and third sessions are complete on the first volume and the second is on Volume 2. Remastering has perked up the rhythm section no end, but otherwise there is no appreciable gain. *The Best Of* collection covers the Blue Note albums, *Birth Of The Cool* and 20 minutes of material from Cannonball Adderley's 1958 *Somethin' Else*. A pleasant enough introduction, but nothing here that could replace the original records.

*** Birdland 1951

Blue Note 4177 *Davis; J. J. Johnson (tb); Eddie 'Lockjaw' Davis, Sonny Rollins, Big Nick Nicholas (ts); Kenny Drew, Billy Taylor (p); Charles Mingus, Tommy Potter (b); Art Blakey (d).* 2, 6 & 9/51.

*** Complete Birdland Performances

Definitive 11165 *As above; add Jackie McLean (as); Connie Henry (b).* 51, 52.

Genuine Miles rarities are rarer than rare things these days when most of the action is rehash and repackaging, so these live dates are doubly welcome, especially given that the February 51 cuts haven't been issued before. The sound is uniformly awful, but no worse than other honoured texts, and Miles is audible throughout, often sounding perfunctory and slightly bored by the context, but capable of delivering moments of great beauty, as he does on the second of two versions of 'Half Nelson' and an inspired 'Tempus Fugit', on which he gives the Bud Powell composition a whole new aspect. The Definitive set introduces McLean in an early appearance but fine form. Otherwise, pretty much of a muchness.

*** Complete Sessions

Jazz Factory JFCD 22583 *Davis; Jimmy Forrest (ts); Charles Fox (p); John Hixon (b); Oscar Oldham (d); unknown (perc).* 52.

Like Miles, Jimmy Forrest of 'Night Train' fame was from St Louis. In the early '50s, Miles was scuffling a bit, not showing up for gigs and then turning in surprise sessions. Back home for a spell, he sat in with Forrest at the Barrelhouse Club. Even in retrospect, not much can be expected of the session, given the vast temperamental and aesthetic difference between trumpeter and saxophonist, and yet these are thoroughly enjoyable and vital sessions, again pointing to Miles's relative comfort with bebop and Forrest's ability to show subtlety when called upon. 'All The Things You Are' and 'What's New' are fine performances, but it's the bop stalwarts like 'A Night In Tunisia' which attract the most notice, solid and dependable performances which flatter Forrest somewhat and show Miles in a better light than his physical and mental state at the time might suggest. The recording is remarkably clean and clear, and this is a worthwhile acquisition for anyone with a developing collection of the great man's work.

*** Collectors' Items

Original Jazz Classics OJCCD 071 *Davis; Charlie Parker, Sonny Rollins (ts); Walter Bishop Jr, Tommy Flanagan (p); Paul Chambers, Percy Heath (b); Philly Joe Jones, Art Taylor (d).* 1/53–3/56.

*(*) At Last! Miles Davis And the Lighthouse All Stars

Original Jazz Classics OJCCD 480 *Davis; Chet Baker, Rolf Ericson (t); Bud Shank (as); Bob Cooper (ts); Russ Freeman, Lorraine Geller (p); Howard Rumsey (b); Max Roach (d).* 9/53.

The 1953 session with Parker on tenor is a curio and it makes an odd makeweight for the accompanying later quintet with Rollins, which includes a skilful solo by the saxophonist on 'Vierd Blues' and a fine investigation of Brubeck's 'In Your Own Sweet Way' by Davis. The session, along with *Blue Moods* (for which, see below), may also still be available as the double-LP, *Collectors' Items*, on Prestige. The live jam session recorded at the Lighthouse is best forgotten by admirers of the trumpeter whose desultory playing was hardly worth preserving on ponderous versions of 'Infinity Promenade' and 'Round Midnight'. Interesting to hear him in company with 'the white Miles Davis', and we must concede that the sound-quality is very good for a club date.

*** Blue Haze

Original Jazz Classics OJCCD 093 *Davis; Dave Schildkraut (as); John Lewis, Charles Mingus, Horace Silver (p); Percy Heath (b); Art Blakey, Kenny Clarke, Max Roach (d).* 5/53–4/54.

**** Walkin'

Original Jazz Classics OJCCD 213 *Davis; J. J. Johnson (tb); Dave Schildkraut (as); Lucky Thompson (ts); Horace Silver (p); Percy Heath (b); Kenny Clarke (d).* 4/54.

***(*) Bags' Groove

Original Jazz Classics OJCCD 245 *Davis; Sonny Rollins (ts); Milt Jackson (vib); Thelonious Monk, Horace Silver (p); Percy Heath (b); Kenny Clarke (d).* 6/54, 12/54.

**** Miles Davis And The Modern Jazz Giants

Original Jazz Classics OJC 347 *Davis; John Coltrane (ts); Milt Jackson (vib); Red Garland, Thelonious Monk (p); Paul Chambers, Percy Heath (b); Kenny Clarke, Philly Joe Jones (d).* 12/54–10/56.

Things are beginning to take shape. Though none of these dates is by itself a classic, an impression is beginning to consolidate of a formidable artist with the capacity to reinvent his language wholesale, while remaining demonstrably within a tradition. The *Blue Haze* set is split between a merely good quartet date from 1953 and three altogether excellent tracks from the following March, by the same quartet that cut the final date for Blue Note. Few will even know Dave Schildkraut's name, but he makes a positive contribution to a single track from the April 1954 session, which is more fully covered on *Walkin'*.

Here and on *Bags' Groove* Davis hits stride at last. The earlier session includes two clear-cut masterpieces in the title-track and 'Blue'N'Boogie'; the solos are diamond-sharp, absolutely without fat or verbiage, and elegantly executed. Most of *Bags' Groove* features a quintet with Rollins, a group which produced fine if slightly less than exalted music. It's marked out as the first occasion – and 'Oleo' the first track – on which he used the Harmon mute which was to define his sound in future years. Two compelling takes of the title-track round out a solid performance; these actually come from a Christmas Eve 1954 date which is otherwise contained in *Meets The Modern Jazz Giants* and documents the only official encounter between Davis, Monk and Jackson. The clash between the vibrapharpist's typically fleet lines and the different kinds of astringency represented by Monk and Davis made for a tense and compelling situation. This disc is, in turn, completed by a very fine 'Round Midnight' by the quintet with John Coltrane.

**(*) The Musings Of Miles

Original Jazz Classics OJCCD 004 *Davis; Red Garland (p); Oscar Pettiford (b); Philly Joe Jones (d).* 6/55.

*** Blue Moods

Original Jazz Classics OJCCD 043 *Davis; Britt Woodman (tb); Teddy Charles (vib); Charles Mingus (b); Elvin Jones (d).* 7/55.

***(*) Quintet / Sextet

Original Jazz Classics OJCCD 012 *Davis; Jackie McLean (as); Milt Jackson (vib); Ray Bryant (p); Percy Heath (b); Art Taylor (d).* 8/55.

Davis's final quartet session prior to the formation of his famous quartet is surprisingly lacklustre. Jones and Pettiford were allegedly exhausted, though this has in other contexts been a euphemism for other problems, and it does seem that

Pettiford was drunk. He certainly sounds less than on the case, and Davis is left to hold the music together, playing rather grimly.

The brief *Blue Moods* session, though poor value on a single disc, is interesting for using an instrumentation he was never to experiment with again. The outstanding track, and one of the best things he did in these years, is a deeply melancholy version of 'Nature Boy' that points forward to the lorn poetry of future years. 'Alone Together', 'There's No You' and 'Easy Living' complete a very attractive session. Given how much padding has gone on elsewhere, it's strange that nothing could have been found to add a bit of value to this one, though we're not wedded to the practice of padding for padding's sake.

The August 1955 session is something of a farewell to Davis's most carefree music, with four pacey and involving workouts on mainly blues material – though, at little over half an hour, this is also particularly poor value for a single CD. McLean plays on 'Dr Jackle' and 'Minor March', and these are all the better for his brash, blustery presence.

***** Plays For Lovers**

Prestige 6019 *Davis; Britt Woodman (tb); Dave Schildkraut (as); John Coltrane (ts); Red Garland, Horace Silver (p); Teddy Charles (vib); Paul Chambers, Percy Heath, Charles Mingus (b); Kenny Clarke, Elvin Jones, Philly Joe Jones, Max Roach (d).* 53–56.

Not such a crass idea, given the quality of the music on display here. Miles's ballad-playing, punctuated with space and silence, was already a miracle, and these assorted tracks have an appropriately romantic feel without overdoing the schmaltz. Classics include 'Round Midnight' and a stunning 'When I Fall In Love', which closes out the set. His version of 'My Funny Valentine' makes Chet Baker's efforts seem even slighter.

****(*) Hi-Hat All Stars**

Fresh Sound FSRCD 13 *Davis; Jay Migliori (ts); Bob Freeman, Al Walcott (p); Jimmy Woode (b); Johnny Zitano (d).* 55.

Eavesdroppings from the bootleg capital of America. By the time this was recorded, Miles had moved far beyond an idiom his colleagues at the Hi-Hat were only just learning to cope with. They give him no help whatsoever and, though it fills in a tiny corner of the story, it's of little more than specialist documentary detail. As might be expected, the sound doesn't gladden the ear.

***** Miles**

Original Jazz Classics OJCCD 006 *Davis; John Coltrane (ts); Red Garland (p); Paul Chambers (b); Philly Joe Jones (d).* 11/55.

****** Relaxin'**

Original Jazz Classics OJC 190 *As above.* 5/56–10/56.

*****(*) Workin'**

Original Jazz Classics OJCCD 296 2 *As above.* 5/56–10/56.

****** Steamin'**

Original Jazz Classics OJCCD 391 2 *As above.* 5/56–10/56.

****** Cookin'**

Original Jazz Classics OJCCD 128 2 *As above.* 11/55, 10/56.

****** The Complete Prestige Recordings (1951–1956)**

Prestige 8PCD 012 2 8CD *As for Prestige recordings above.* 51–56.

Great music is sometimes made in inauspicious circumstances. Another 'Quintet of the Year' two years earlier showed a marked disinclination to tear themselves away from sport on television and play a concert, and yet Bird, Dizzy, Bud Powell, Mingus and Max Roach turned in one of the great performances of all time. Miles's 1956 quintet cut these records to round out a contract before moving on to Columbia, and yet they represent a purple patch in his output. As far as the jazz of the time is concerned, they are time-capsule material, though gallingly it is impossible to pick out a single outstanding disc. They are uneven in inspiration, but at their greatest they bespeak an extraordinary sense of spontaneity, a brilliant assemblage of players in creative flux. The greatest contrast, much discussed, is between Davis – spare, introverted, guileful – and the leonine, blistering Coltrane, who was still at a somewhat chaotic stage in his development. But equally telling are the members of the rhythm section, who contrive to create a different climate behind each soloist and sustain the logical flow of the tunes. Recorded at just a handful of marathon sessions, each record has its special rewards: a slow, pierced 'My Funny Valentine', on *Cookin'*, the supple swing of 'I Could Write A Book' and revitalized bebop of 'Woody'N'You' from *Relaxin'*, a haunted version of 'It Never Entered My Mind' on *Workin'*. It would be possible to throw up another half-dozen contenders, and everyone will have particular favourites. One further unlikely contender is 'Surrey With The Fringe On Top' and the following track, the bebop classic, 'Salt Peanuts', on *Steamin'*.

The message remains the same: these records should be in every serious jazz collection. Whether or not one wants to plump for the exhaustive Prestige box containing them all will depend on bank balance and individual appetite for such all-in-one packages. As will be seen, the box preserves material from much earlier in the trumpeter's association with Prestige, but there is much to be said for sampling all these records in something close to their original form. Rudy van Gelder's splendid engineering and Bob Weinstock's production have ensured that the music has survived in excellent condition, and the CD reissues sound well enough, if a little compressed. The English company Ace has released *Cookin'* and *Relaxin'* on a single CD, which is superb value and may well still be available.

***** Round About Midnight**

Columbia CK 85201 *As above.* 10/55–9/56.

Released on the new label but recorded for the old, this inevitably sounds like a footnote. The material is fine but somehow fails to cast quite the consistent spell which the Prestige sessions do.

****** Miles Ahead**

Columbia CK 65121 *Davis; John Carisi, Bernie Glow, Taft Jordan, Louis Mucci, Ernie Royal (t); Joe Bennett, Jimmy Cleveland, Frank Rehak (tb); Tom Mitchell (btb); Tony Miranda, Willie Ruff (frhn); Lee Konitz (as); Sid Cooper, Romeo Penque (woodwinds); Danny Bank (bcl); Paul Chambers (b); Art Taylor (d); Gil Evans (cond).* 5/57.

Miles had worked with Gil Evans before, of course, but this first full-length collaboration highlighted their like-mindedness and an illuminating reciprocity of vision. Curiously, given the reputation that these records have garnered, they aren't always well played (excepting the soloist, of course), with fluffs aplenty and shaky ensembles, though this first outing is pristine compared to the shaky passage-work on *Porgy And Bess*, later. *Miles Ahead* was rightly identified as a concerto for Miles, a work of classical ambitions, and though some thought that condemned it to some pale beyond jazz, it is absolutely central to what Miles and Gil were about. Recorded over four sessions in May 1957, it has great internal consistency. It no longer makes much sense to talk about 'tracks', for the internal subdivisions here are effectively moments in a long, continuous work. Even so, certain things do stand out: 'The Maids Of Cadiz', 'My Ship', the title-track and a lovely version of Ahmad Jamal's 'New Rhumba'. Frailties of performance apart, Evans gave the music a great depth of focus, doubling up bass lines and creating distance and tension between upper and lower lines in a way that was to affect Miles for the rest of his career, even after he had given up using unamplified orchestrations. Though it is far from being expressively one-dimensional – there are moments of playful humour – the pervading tone is a melancholy lyricism. This was the first time Miles was to record with flugelhorn, an experiment which added an instrumental 'double' to just about every horn-player's bag but which the initiator was to repeat only very briefly. The flugelhorn's sound isn't so very different from his trumpet soloing, though palpably softer-edged. Though he plays open all the time, as he was to do again on *Milestones*, some of the burnish seems to be lost. A quiet masterpiece, all the same, and one with a guaranteed place in the top flight of Miles albums.

**** L'Ascenseur Pour L'Échafaud

Fontana 836305 *Davis; Barney Wilen (ts); René Urtreger (p); Pierre Michelot (b); Kenny Clarke (d).* 12/57.

One of the most discussed items in the entire canon, strangely enough, given that it was written as soundtrack music. It did, though, provide Miles with his first real compositional challenge, something more than blowing themes, and it helped steer him in the direction of the abstract, themeless experiments of the following decade. Interesting as it is on record, the music makes complete sense only when combined with the images of Louis Malle's bleak thriller, ostensibly a murder story, but actually about the claustrophobic impact of social technology. Most of the fragments – and the requirements of the medium also steered Miles towards a more open-ended and unresolved approach – are slow and moody, though inevitably there is a motorway number. So successful was Miles's scoring that he effectively redraws the movie's inner landscape, accentuating its psychological elements and the philosophical reserve of its somewhat fugitive subtext. The other players contribute a good deal to the whole, with the late Barney Wilen particularly prominent.

CORE COLLECTION

**** Milestones

Columbia CK 85203 *Davis; Julian 'Cannonball' Adderley (as); John Coltrane (ts); Red Garland (p); Paul Chambers (b); Philly Joe Jones (d).* 4/58.

Sometimes sidelined as a 'transitional' record, a pause at the portals before entering into the magnificence of *Kind Of Blue* a year later. Retrospect suggests that the distance between them isn't so very great, either musically or qualitatively. In April 1958, Miles hadn't recorded a small-group date for more than a year. A lot of thinking, woodshedding, a lot of hard conceptual work had been done in the interim. On *Milestones* the trumpeter is certainly still working out ideas that were adumbrated on *L'Ascenseur*, but there is no sense whatever that this is anything other than a completely achieved performance, and a highly accomplished one. There are no standards, and all the material is harmonically and rhythmically challenging, sometimes simply by suspending conventional harmony and by constraining complex ideas within a deceptively simple 4/4. One of the profound differences between Miles and the saxophonists is that, while they tend to play on the beat, he is almost always across it. Adderley isn't always right for the music, and he sounds awkward and shuffling on 'Sid's Ahead', one of the album's truly great tracks. Standing alongside two of the greatest soloists in the music, then and ever, one understands his slight discomfiture. He is much more to the fore on 'Straight, No Chaser', but again it is Miles's solo which commands attention, actually quoting 'When The Saints Go Marching In' without obvious irony, a gesture that confounds all those who accused him of being a scorched-earth modernist with no interest in the past. If 'Sid's Ahead' is brooding and mournful, then 'Milestones' itself, on which he returns briefly to flugelhorn, is sharply ambiguous in its dancing exuberance, a truly startling performance. This is one of the very great modern-jazz albums.

***(*) Miles And Coltrane

Columbia 460824 *Davis; John Coltrane (ts); Julian 'Cannonball' Adderley (as); Bill Evans, Red Garland (p); Paul Chambers (b); Jimmy Cobb, Philly Joe Jones (d).* 10/55–7/58.

***(*) '58 Miles

Columbia CK 47835 *As above, except omit Garland, Jones.* 58.

**** Miles Davis & Thelonious Monk: Live At Newport 1958 & 1963

Columbia/Legacy C2K 53585 2CD *As above, except add Charlie Rouse (ts), Pee Wee Russell (cl), Thelonious Monk (p), Butch Warren (b), Frankie Dunlop (d).* 7/58, 7/63.

The historic Newport Festival appearance of July 1958 has been available in rather scattered form for some time, and it is very good to have it complete on the double-CD Legacy set, albeit rather awkwardly paired with a much later Monk set. Any impression that the two giants are playing together should be quickly corrected. The only connection here is Newport. Miles and Coltrane are playing brilliantly throughout, with the saxophonist firing on all cylinders, and sounding lighter-hearted than he often does, on 'Ah-Leu-Cha' and 'Bye Bye Blackbird'. Once again, the contrast with Miles's spare and angular approach is very striking. The 1958 compilation brings together material that was formerly issued on *Black Giants* and *Jazz At The Plaza* (of which, a little more below). 'Oleo' and 'My Funny Valentine' were the best things on that fine set, which is now restored to catalogue. *Miles And Coltrane* is filled out by two much earlier items, 'Little Melonae' and 'Budo', from 1955. We can but recommend the budget-priced Davis/Monk double.

**** Porgy And Bess

Columbia CK 65141 *Davis; John Coles, Bernie Glow, Louis Mucci, Ernie Royal (t); Joseph Bennett, Jimmy Cleveland, Richard Hixon, Frank Rehak (tb); Willie Ruff, Gunther Schuller, Julius Watkins (frhn); Bill Barber (tba); Julian 'Cannonball' Adderley, Danny Bank (as); Phil Bodner, Romeo Penque, Jerome Richardson (f); Paul Chambers (b); Jimmy Cobb, Philly Joe Jones (d).* 7–8/58.

In his biography of Miles, Ian Carr very accurately attributes the difference between this album and the similarly constituted *Miles Ahead* to Miles's own role as preacher, engaged in a call-and-response dialogue with the congregation/ensemble. While 'Summertime' and 'It Ain't Necessarily So' are straightforward solo features, albeit very remarkable ones, 'Prayer' is an astounding *tour de force*, harmonically suspended, and with Miles's most extraordinary recorded solo to date punctuated by agonized screams and shouts, whether of affirmation or suffering it isn't always easy to judge. Miles was not in good physical condition during the making of the record, which perhaps explains the twisting intensity, the bent notes and slurs which seem to express some inner pain. It is less easy in the circumstances to explain the simple grandeur of 'The Buzzard Song' or indeed of the two solos mentioned above; 'Summertime' has an aura of calm that was seldom again to enter into his playing. We have already pointed to shortcomings in the playing of the ensemble. These frankly are as nothing compared to the sheer quality of the music performed.

*** Jazz At The Plaza Vol. 1

Columbia CK 85245 *Davis; Julian 'Cannonball' Adderley (as); John Coltrane (ts); Bill Evans (p); Paul Chambers (b); Philly Joe Jones (d).* 9/58.

Only released as late as 1973 and out of circulation for quite a long time, this one has struggled to maintain profile among the superb sessions that surround it. It owes its reputation largely and properly to its status as a dry run for the *Kind Of Blue* sessions that were to follow not much later, but the sound quality is very poor and the provenance is compromised, a company party that was never meant to be released as a record. Probably the stand-out track recorded at the New York City hotel is 'My Funny Valentine', which features just Miles and rhythm. Adderley sits out 'If I Were A Bell'; but this isn't one of Trane's better nights, and the interplay between the two giants isn't as earth-shaking as one by now (selfishly) feels it ought to be. Unlike some of the official live sessions, this doesn't have an in-built aura of history, but it comes across as rather more than just another date. Perhaps this band was incapable of 'just another date'. With what was to come within the year, though, it inevitably palls into relative insignificance.

CORE COLLECTION

♛ **** Kind Of Blue

Columbia CK 64935 *Davis; Julian 'Cannonball' Adderley (as); John Coltrane (ts); Bill Evans, Wynton Kelly (p); Paul Chambers (b); Jimmy Cobb (d).* 3–4/59.

In the summer of 1997 Jimmy Cobb described this celebrated album, one of the most famous of all time, as 'just another date for us'. So history is made, unnoticed and perhaps unappreciated by the participants. There is no other record with quite the general appeal of *Kind Of Blue*, and modern sampling has now delivered up what must be considered the definitive version of it. The key presence may be that of Evans (Wynton Kelly plays only on the blues, 'Freddie Freeloader') and it is his allusive, almost impressionistic accompaniments which provide the ideal platform for the spacious solos created by the horns. This was the first widely acknowledged 'modal jazz' date, and it is interesting how thoroughly it has now been absorbed into mainstream language. Presumably it once sounded a good deal less familiar. Tension is consistently established within the ensembles, only for Davis and Coltrane especially to resolve it in songful, declamatory solos. The steady mid-tempos and the now familiar plaintive voicings on 'So What' and 'All Blues' reinforce the weightless, haunting qualities Miles was bringing to his music. If you have anything approximating to a jazz collection, you will already have this record, on some format and with one or other of the issued numbers. Even if you do, you may want to consider investing in this impeccable version.

***(*) Sketches Of Spain

Columbia CK 65142 *Davis; John Coles, Bernie Glow, Taft Jordan, Louis Mucci, Ernie Royal (t); Dick Hixon, Frank Rehak (tb); John Barrows, Jimmy Buffington, Earl Chapin, Tony Miranda, Joe Singer (frhn); Bill Barber (tba); Albert Block, Eddie Caine, Harold Feldman, Romeo Penque (woodwinds); Jack Knitzer (bsn); Danny Bank (bcl); Janet Putnam (hp); Paul Chambers (b); Jimmy Cobb, Elvin Jones (d).* 11/59–3/60.

Similarly improved by CD transfer and enhanced sampling, but still in our view overrated. Though it has moments of luminous beauty, it's hard to escape the feeling that this is a record which has acquired a mystique over and above its musical virtues. Despite – or perhaps because of – far more time in the studios than on the earlier collaborations with Gil Evans, the whole is poorly focused, with the ambitious 'Concierto De Aranjuez' sometimes (heresy!) sounding like inflated light music, with only Miles's occasional intensities driving energy into the whole.

The dialogue between trumpet and ensemble on 'Solea' is the best sequence on the session, raising the improvisational stakes more than a little. Although the trumpeter is giving of his best throughout, the sometimes haphazard percussion tracks and muzzy ensembles suggest a harbinger of some of the trance music Miles would later delve into in the '70s. Curiously, extra time in the studio failed to deliver good sound, and the CD transfer is very dry.

***(*) Miles Davis In Stockholm Complete

Dragon DRCD 228 4CD *Davis; John Coltrane (ts); Sonny Stitt (as, ts); Wynton Kelly (p); Paul Chambers (b); Jimmy Cobb (d).* 3 & 10/60.

A number of live recordings exist from this period, away from Miles's officially sanctioned releases, and the material on Dragon – excellently recorded by Swedish Radio – affords valuable glimpses of two European sojourns in 1960. The concert with Coltrane (which includes a six-minute interview with the saxophonist) suggests a battle of giants: Trane piles in with all his most abandoned lines, while Davis remains – especially in a nearly anguished 'All Blues' – almost aloof. The rhythm section play with impervious jauntiness, and it adds up to a tremendous concert recording. The concert with Stitt is only slightly less effective. Stitt, admittedly, wrestles with no dark demons, but his plangency and itch to play are scarcely less powerful than Coltrane's, and his switching between alto and tenor offers more light and shade. Davis is again bitingly inventive, even on material which by this stage he must have played many, many times.

*** Live In Zurich 1960

Jazz Unlimited JUCD 2031 *Davis; John Coltrane (ts); Wynton Kelly (p); Paul Chambers (b); Jimmy Cobb (d).* 4/60.

Stuff that has been available before, but done quite professionally here and showing the band at relaxed medium pace, neither stretching unduly nor merely coasting. 'If I Were A Bell' is the most impressive of the four numbers. 'So What' sounds a little shrugged off, and Miles and Trane seem to get their wires crossed once or twice.

***** Some Day My Prince Will Come**

Columbia 466312 *Davis; John Coltrane, Hank Mobley (ts); Wynton Kelly (p); Paul Chambers (b); Jimmy Cobb, Philly Joe Jones (d).* 3/61.

*****(*) In Person – Friday Night At The Blackhawk: Volume 1**

Columbia 87097 2CD *As above, except omit Coltrane, Jones.* 4/61.

*****(*) In Person – Saturday Night At The Blackhawk: Volume 2**

Columbia 87100 2CD *As above.* 4/61.

****** In Person – Friday And Saturday Night At The Blackhawk – Complete**

Columbia 87106 4CD *As above.* 4/61.

In April 1961, Miles Davis was just a few weeks short of his 35th birthday. That spring was to be an odd mix of fresh starts and deceptively routine business for the trumpeter. The following month, Miles was on stage with Gil Evans' big band at Carnegie Hall and recorded what would become the third of his albums to reach the pop charts. He had, though, already made a studio album with a new quintet. Coltrane's 'guest' appearance on the somewhat lethargic *Some Day My Prince Will Come* is astonishing; he plays two solos, on the title-track and on 'Teo', which put everything else in the shade.

Release of the album was delayed and it wasn't until the following spring that *Someday My Prince Will Come* started selling briskly. By then, though, it had been overtaken by something new for Miles, the release of a first official live album.

It was taped on 21 and 22 April at the Blackhawk club in San Francisco, a decision that turned two ordinary evenings at work into a document. Like many a historical text before it, *In Person … At the Blackhawk* was left full of lacunae and inconsistencies. Different release versions featured different songs; bootlegs circulated with incorrect titles; completist collectors were obliged to make do with Japanese liner-notes. Now, though, after more than 40 years, it is possible to hear all the music played on those two spring nights, spread over four ear-opening CDs.

The perfectionist Miles had hitherto resisted making a club recording, but in several respects this was a period of new initiatives for the trumpeter. Miles had recently ended a fruitful but often troubled working relationship with Coltrane. Though he was initially replaced by Sonny Stitt, he probably sounded too much of a throwback for the progressive Miles and, in the event, Coltrane's permanent successor was the funky hard-bop tenor Hank Mobley. Despite an impressive pedigree of Blue Note releases, and despite the obvious attraction to Miles of a terser and more succinct approach than the increasingly elaborate Coltrane, Mobley seemed an improbable choice.

It was, however, consistent with other changes in the band. Miles had also replaced his pianist, Bill Evans, with the 30-year-old Jamaica-born Wynton Kelly, a rhythmic, blues-based player who worked in sharp contrast to Evans's thoughtful lyricism and who could be expected to fit in with the new saxophonist's curiously hybrid tough-tender sound. The other members of the rhythm section had been on the best-selling *Kind of Blue* date a couple of years before. Even so, the overall sound of the group had changed significantly and in a way that challenges the consensus view of Miles's development in the '60s.

'Change' is one of the weasel words that have stalked Davis's reputation. 'Transitional' is as far as most critics are prepared to go and 'transitional' *In Person … At the Blackhawk* has remained for much of its erratic existence. The April 1961 sessions are still the least studied and to that degree least controversial in the trumpeter's canon. To some degree, their neglect is circumstantial and due to that shaky release history. Compared to the dates recorded with a different band four years later at the Plugged Nickel in Chicago and released on no fewer than seven CDs, this seems a relatively modest package. Or at least it did until Sony released these complete versions of both dates with no fewer than 13 previously unreleased performances, including an entire late set from the Saturday night.

Modest as they seem, these are revelatory recordings and they prompt a pretty wholesale reassessment of Miles's mid-career. With supreme irony, almost the first thing one hears at the start of the first Friday night is Miles fluffing his intro to a bebop classic, Sonny Rollins's 'Oleo'. He makes up for it immediately and delivers a blazing solo that must count as one of his best of the period.

The new edition is slightly awkward in that in order to preserve the integrity of each set it places the first and third from the Friday night on one CD and the second on disc two. It's a minor quibble, relative to the importance of the music. The opening set is dominated by a reading of the staple 'No Blues', which comes in at more than 17 minutes. Here again both Miles and Hank Mobley are in their element, but it also becomes clear that the key to this band is the pianist. Kelly has extraordinary hand speed, even greater quickness of thought and exactly the kind of spatial awareness Miles must have looked for in an accompanist. His fast, bluesy piano runs anticipate the horns, support them and pick up their cues almost telepathically. Kelly almost never cuts across the leader or the rather more lumbering saxophonist and never plays a facile or merely workmanlike phrase. It all counts.

After a long and fiery interpretation of Cole Porter's 'All Of You', the second set continues with another of the previously unreleased tracks, a theme previously known as 'Teo', after Miles's producer, but here unaccountably entitled 'Neo'. How new it is in this interpretation is hard to gauge. It is not so much reharmonized as industrially strengthened. Kelly puts unbreakable spider-wires across the chords, Cobb and Chambers rev up the pulse and Miles fires off strings of notes that are as elaborate in construction as anything he had committed to record. It's a tune that turns up again on the Saturday night, along with versions of 'No Blues', 'If I Were A Bell', 'On Green Dolphin Street', 'I Thought About You' and the little set-closer 'Love, I've Found You', which functions much like 'The Theme' and rounds things off. After his uneasy pick-up, Miles doesn't choose to revisit 'Oleo' but starts off at rather more familiar velocity with the release version of 'If I Were A Bell'. The contrast between the two versions of the Frank Loesser would be hard to exaggerate. Whereas on Friday, starting off the third set, the trumpeter attacks the tune as if it were an air-raid warning, on Saturday he takes it with a much easier swing and bounce and relies on Kelly to fill in the harmony. He's back on the attack for an unbelievably fast version of 'So What', which almost doubles the tempo of the version on *Kind of Blue*. Kelly's open chords leave the field wide open for both Davis and Mobley.

Richard Carpenter's 'Walkin'' had been the centrepiece of the previous night's second set, despite being marred by articulation problems and a couple of missed cues. The Saturday version is more than a *tour de force* performance. In 12 astonishing minutes, Miles deconstructs the tune. Five minutes in, he remakes it again as Kelly and Mobley join him in new harmonic territory. The intensity of Miles's playing is remarkable. His solo is rich, maximal and far from introverted; he sounds almost malevolently focused.

There is nothing else quite as good on any of the four CDs. From a historical point of view, the inclusion of a complete late set from the Saturday night – 'I Thought About You', 'Someday My Prince Will Come' and a double time 'Softly, As In a Morning Sunrise' – is very important, not least because it fails to confound the unexpectedly hard-swinging nature of this line-up. Leaving aside a few bad cues, miscounts (on Miles's part, largely) and a foreshortened 'Autumn Leaves', which starts a little late because the tape machine wasn't switched on, it is hard to see why all of this material has not been released sooner. Even fans who have spent years with the original Blackhawk releases will find these tracks thought-provoking and in some respects genuinely revelatory. However much he may have spoken about change, Miles Davis's career was remarkably of a piece. His playing, late and early, was grounded in bebop, which is grounded in the blues. These are the two main influences on the Blackhawk line-up, but they did not appear with that group and they did not vanish with its disbandment. Though he seldom in his final years even hinted at bebop, Miles's last years were dominated by the blues, a recognition that still hasn't filtered through his dabblement with pop and hip-hop. The Blackhawk sessions are among his purest jazz performances. There is little of the orchestral impressionism that came with his association with Gil Evans, and nothing of the studio collage he pioneered with Teo Macero (which might explain the renaming of that tune). These are the proof that Miles could cut it as a hard-blowing and straightahead jazz musician, terms which he probably regarded as demeaning even as he picked up his campaign medals. His seeming lack of interest in this kind of improvisation in later years didn't disguise his lack of ability at it, but rather his desire to take its basic elements and refine out some of the cruder elements. The Blackhawk sessions do not present a great jazz musician as ambitious auteur, but as a passionate exponent of a great vernacular art form. The 1961 band spoke with a common plainness of purpose. Mobley and Kelly were important factors in that, but it was Miles's own strong utterance that makes these restored performances so compelling. They don't mark a transition in Miles's career so much as reassert some basic principles that for much of the rest of his long and productive life were left unspoken and too often went unheard.

**** The Complete Columbia Recordings: Miles Davis With John Coltrane, 1955–1961

Columbia 65833 6CD *As for Round About Midnight, Milestones, Kind Of Blue, Some Day My Prince Will Come.* 55–61.

*** The Best Of Miles Davis And John Coltrane: 1955–1961

Columbia Legacy 61090 *As above.*

Miles's rate of progress from the cautious modal idiom of *Round About Midnight* to the majestic credo of *Kind Of Blue* is one of the great transitions in the whole of jazz. It doesn't represent any great epiphany, analogous to those which were supposed to herald the coming of bebop, nor does it correspond to any great spiritual reawakening. It is, much more impressively, the result of steady and concentrated application to the transformation of American song.

What makes this set valuable to collectors is the inclusion of 18 unreleased alternatives from the period. As ever, though, our recommendation is that you experience these albums in their released forms, certainly before closing with the complexities of issued and rejected takes. The albums are here intact in any case, with the exception of *Someday My Prince Will Come* and the original order is easy enough to programme. An essential purchase for the Miles completist and a fantastic gift for anyone falling in love with his work of this period, but a pricey and perhaps over-glamorous piece of product that fails to disguise the fact that the real action is already out there.

The sampler includes just one alternative take of 'Straight No Chaser' and is otherwise a very predictable and unexceptionable mix of release material. The narrative is inevitably sketchier, but one can still hear the evolution of Miles's group through this critical half-decade. Sorry to be repetitive, but our advice is still to concentrate on the released albums.

***(*) Miles Davis At Carnegie Hall 1961

Columbia CK 65027 2CD *Davis; Johnny Coles, Bernie Glow, Louis Mucci, Ernie Royal (t); Dick Hixon, Jimmy Knepper, Frank Rehak (tb); Paul Ingraham, Bob Swisshelm, Julius Watkins (frhn); Bill Barber (tba); Hank Mobley (ts); Danny Bank, Eddie Caine, Romeo Penque, Jerome Richardson, Bob Tricarico (reeds, woodwinds); Wynton Kelly (p); Paul Chambers (b); Janet Putnam (hp); Bobby Rosengarden (perc).* 5/61.

Davis's Carnegie Hall concert of 1961 set the seal on his emergence as a jazz superstar over the preceding five years. Split between music by the quintet and Gil Evans's arrangements of some of the material from their albums together, the night was distinguished by the leader's own playing, executed with more incisiveness on the Evans material than on the studio versions. 'Teo' and 'No Blues' include compelling solos, as alert and packed with attitude as anything he was to do throughout his career. On the down side, Mobley is still no match for the departed Coltrane, and 'Concierto De Aranjuez' is not dignified by the setting. Time was when this material was rather scattered. One quickly gets used to having it properly marshalled, and it is difficult to get past the sheer grandeur of the conception. Even in 1961, at what must be considered the peak of his career, no jazz musician could possibly have expected a setting as sumptuous as Gil gives him. When our last edition appeared, the complete CBS box was still in the making; it rounded out the picture on the Miles and Gil association. Few places sum it up better than this, though.

**(*) Quiet Nights

Columbia CK 65293 *Davis; Johnny Coles, Bernie Glow, Louis Mucci, Ernie Royal (t); Dick Hixon, Jimmy Knepper, Frank Rehak (tb); John Barrows, Paul Ingraham, Robert Swisshelm (frhn); Bill Barber (tba); Steve Lacy (ss); Bob Banks, Eddie Caine, Romeo Penque, Jerome Richardson, Bob Tricarico (reeds); George Coleman (ts); Janet Putnam (hp); Victor Feldman (p); Ron Carter, Paul Chambers (b); Frank Butler, Jimmy Cobb, Elvin Jones (d); Bobby Rosengarden (perc).* 7, 8 & 11/62.

Miles was furious when this record was released, accusing Teo Macero of working behind his back. It is pretty thin stuff, anonymous, big-band arrangements with just one small-group track, 'Summer Night', recorded in Los Angeles with the *Seven Steps To Heaven* sextet. Some of the tunes, 'Corcovado' and 'Slow Samba' in particular, are very beautiful, but it's hard to get the notion of easy listening out of one's head.

***** Seven Steps To Heaven**

Columbia 466970 *Davis; George Coleman (ts); Victor Feldman, Herbie Hancock (p); Ron Carter (b); Frank Butler, Tony Williams (d).* 4 & 5/63.

Two oddities on this: Miles playing with a West Coast band and including such classic jazz pieces as 'Basin Street Blues' and 'Baby, Won't You Please Come Home'. The later session unveiled his new group, with Herbie Hancock and the very young Tony Williams. They sound relatively sure-footed on 'Seven Steps' and Hancock certainly understands the need for subtler harmonic – or, rather, chromatic – shading in the music. As so predictably often with Miles, it's possible to hear in this record the seeds of change, but it's an album that is much more illuminating retrospectively, once Miles's later and more revolutionary work has been absorbed.

****** Miles In Antibes**

Columbia 462960 *Davis; George Coleman (ts); Herbie Hancock (p); Ron Carter, Richard Davis (b); Tony Williams (d).* 6/63, 5/66.

*****(*) My Funny Valentine**

Columbia 471276 *As above, except omit Richard Davis.* 2/64.

****** The Complete Concert, 1964**

Columbia 471246 2CD *As above.* 2/64.

Coleman is the unsung hero of the Davis discography. Indeed, for our money he is one of the unsung heroes of modern jazz. His scouring, muscular style is very different from that of Coltrane: less intense, more straightforward and yet not without subtlety. *In Antibes* is a very fine concert set, recorded just weeks after this band had been formed. 'Autumn Leaves' is the kind of jazz performance that gets the music a good name: sleek, tough and unsentimental, but not unfeeling, and powered by the young prodigy at the drum-kit. All of the music is unpredictable and exciting, unpredictable largely because familiar material is shone through a prism that mixes abstraction with a genuine delight in melody.

Recorded at the Philharmonic Hall in Lincoln Center, *My Funny Valentine* has a moody and elegiac quality which Miles attributed to President Kennedy's death the previous November. The group plays with almost ritual stateliness, and there is a plangent, wounded quality to the trumpet-sound that was to emerge less frequently thereafter. The double-CD set brings together *My Funny Valentine* with *Four & More*. Excellent value.

*****(*) Miles In Berlin**

Columbia CK 62976 *As above, except Wayne Shorter (ts) replaces Coleman.* 9/64.

Wayne Shorter's arrival stabilized the new group, since Shorter was a major composer as well as soloist. Although the set in Berlin is the standard one of 'So What' and so on, the pungency of Davis's solos is matched by a new depth of interplay with the rhythm section, as well as by Shorter's phenomenally harsh-sounding parts. The highlight is a superbly intense reading of 'Autumn Leaves'. There is a huge amount of bootleg material from this period – not as much as for the '80s band, but still in distracting quantities. We have long since given up noting even the better of these issues. This is how the group should be heard: unmistakably live and present, but professionally recorded and mastered.

****** E.S.P.**

Columbia 467899 *As above.* 1/65.

****** Miles Smiles**

Columbia CK 65683 *As above.* 10/66.

*****(*) Sorcerer**

Columbia CK 65680 *As above.* 5/67.

*****(*) Nefertiti**

Columbia CK 65681 *As above.* 6–7/67.

***** Miles In The Sky**

Columbia CK 65684 *As above, except add George Benson (g).* 1 & 5/68.

***** Filles De Kilimanjaro**

Columbia CK 46116 *As above, except omit Benson; add Chick Corea (ky), Dave Holland (b).* 6–9/68.

This has always been an enigmatic period in Miles's career, a band and a set of relationships which didn't so much develop as go through a looping sequence of self-discoveries and estrangements. The leader himself often sounds almost disengaged from the music, perhaps even alienated from it, though one always senses him there, listening. *Miles Smiles* opens up areas that were to be his main performing territory for the next few years, arguably for the rest of his career. The synthesis of complete abstraction with more or less straightforward blues-playing (Shorter's 'Footprints' is the obvious example of that) was to sustain him right through the darkness of the '70s bands to the later period when 'New Blues' became a staple of his programmes. After *Smiles*, *E.S.P.* is probably the best album, with seven excellent original themes and the players building a huge creative tension between Shorter's oblique, churning solos and the leader's private musings, and within a rhythm section that is bursting to fly free while still playing time. Miles returns to his old tactic with Coltrane of paring away steadily, often sitting out for long periods or not soloing at all. It is simply that with Shorter he has a saxophonist who is capable of matching that enigmatic stance, rather than rushing off on his own. He does not solo on 'Nefertiti', one of the great compositions from this time, on which the horns simply pace away over Williams's boiling rhythm. The album which bears its name is cool and strong, again largely due to the writing. As on its predecessor, Miles cedes compositional duties to Shorter and only starts writing again with *Miles In The Sky*, which is ironically the weakest of the bunch. It is also unmistakably a transitional work, and the arrival of Corea and Holland for two tracks on *Filles De Kilimanjaro* points forward to the next phase in this extraordinary story. As always, though, Miles is looking back as well as forward. The standard treatments on the live albums, things like an exhaustive 'Stella By Starlight' and (what almost counts as a standard) 'All Blues', are occasionally rambling but always have something of importance to register, no matter when and in what mood one hears them.

♛ **** **The Complete Live At The Plugged Nickel**
Columbia CXK 66955 7CD *Davis; Wayne Shorter (ts); Herbie Hancock (p); Ron Carter (b); Tony Williams (d).* 12/65.

***(*) **Highlights From The Plugged Nickel**
Columbia CK 67377 *As above.* 12/65.

The Rosetta Stone of modern jazz: a monumental document written in five subtly and sometimes starkly different dialects but within which much of the music of the post-bop period has been defined and demarcated. When future histories of the music are written – and it would be possible to write a convincing version of the story from 1945 to 1990 merely by reference to Miles's part in it – these sessions will be adduced as a turning point. Arguably Miles's best ever group – dispute it if you will – working its way out of one phase and into another in which time and harmony, melody and dynamics were radically rethought. The improvisations here would have been inconceivable a mere couple of years earlier; they don't so much float on the chords as react against them like phosphorus. Three years later, they fed directly into Miles's electric revolution and the beginning of what was to be the long dramatic coda.

To set the time and place, these were recorded (officially, by Columbia engineers) at the Plugged Nickel Club in Chicago. Though the Blackhawk sessions are better than most, the registration here is superb, not much different from what one would hope for in a studio. At first glance, and with an eye to the predictably high price, one might wonder whether so repetitive a documentation would be worth either the cash or the patience (or the time and strength, just to complete Herman Melville's sequence). The short answer is an emphatic yes and unambiguously so, because here it is possible to observe at the closest quarters Miles and his musicians working through their ideas set by set in ways that make the named material, the songs, more or less irrelevant. Even when it is clear he is working from 'Stella By Starlight' or 'My Funny Valentine', Miles is moving out into areas of harmonic/melodic invention and performance dynamics which were unprecedented in the music, and doing so within the concentrated span of two nights at the club.

Unlike the two original LPs, on which Columbia had forgivably presumed to deliver up the 'best' of the sessions, it is now possible to hear Carter clearly. His role is absolutely crucial and there are times when one can almost visualize Miles flicking from one solid outcrop to another like a caddis fly. Hancock occasionally sounds diffident and detached, and he is the only one of the group who resorts to repeated licks as the sets progress. He may have been tired, but he may also, as McCoy Tyner was to do at almost exactly the same time, have realized that he was to some extent external to the real drama of this extraordinary music.

The sampler album is a perfectly decent representation of the whole, but in most cases it will do no more than whet an appetite for the complete box. These are genuinely historic recordings. It would be better to go without a dozen – make that two dozen – run-of-the-mill jazz records to finance this glorious package.

*** **Circle In The Round**
Columbia C2K 46862 *Davis; Julian 'Cannonball' Adderley (as); John Coltrane, Hank Mobley, Wayne Shorter (ts); Chick Corea, Bill Evans, Red Garland, Herbie Hancock, Wynton Kelly, Joe Zawinul (p); Joe Beck, George Benson (g); Ron Carter, Paul Chambers, Dave Holland (b); Jimmy Cobb, Philly Joe Jones, Tony Williams (d).* 10/55–1/70.

An interesting (if seldom very involving) compilation of outtakes from Davis's Columbia albums over a 25-year period. The long title-track is an attempt at a mesmerizing mood-piece which works for some of the time, but fades in and out of focus. Earlier pieces with the great quintet are more vital and include a marvellous 'Love For Sale' from 1958. The CD omits some of the music from the original double-LP.

♛ **** **Miles Davis And Gil Evans: The Complete Columbia Studio Sessions**
Columbia CXK 67397 6CD *As for Columbia recordings above, except add Dick Leith (btb), Bill Hinshaw, Art Maebe, Richard Perissi (frhn), Buddy Collette, Paul Horn (f), Gene Cipriano (ob), Fred Dutton (bsn), Herbie Hancock (p), Ron Carter (b), Tony Williams (d).* 57–68.

Utterly, sandbaggingly wonderful – and, alas, expensive as well. This is the kind of set into which one can disappear for weeks at a time. Most of the material has been around for a long time, but there is a mass of studio interaction, alternative takes and two previously unreleased suites, *The Time Of The Barracudas* and *Falling Water*, both retrospectively titled, but from 1963 and 1968 respectively. The figures speak for themselves; six hours of music on 116 selections, all of them remixed from the original masters using super bit sampling. How much more, and how much more pristine, could anyone possibly want?

CORE COLLECTION

**** **In A Silent Way**
Columbia 450982 *Davis; Wayne Shorter (ts); Chick Corea (p); Joe Zawinul (p, org); John McLaughlin (g); Dave Holland (b); Tony Williams (d).* 2/69.

*** **The Complete In A Silent Way Sessions**
Columbia Legacy 65632 3CD *As above, except add Joe Chambers, Jack DeJohnette (d); Teo Macero (perc).* 69.

One feels a touch self-conscious describing yet another Miles Davis record as 'transitional'. As an artefact, *In A Silent Way* is already a long way even from the increasingly abstract work of the previous couple of years. It was in every sense a collage using 'found objects', put together with a view to the minimum detail and coloration required to make an impact. Two of the 'objects' were John McLaughlin, recruited on the nod and apparently unheard by the trumpeter, and Joe Zawinul, whose 'In A Silent Way' became a centrepiece of the album. Three electric instruments give the band a sound completely unlike the previous incarnation, though it is clear that there are very significant continuities between this record and *Miles Smiles* or *E.S.P.*, and these should not be overlooked. In order to bring the performances up to LP length, Teo Macero stitched repeats of certain passages back into the fabric of the music, giving it continuity and a certain hypnotic circularity. Once again, a practical contingency (Miles was apparently happy with the short chunks that had been recorded) resulted in a new creative development, no less significant than Charles Mingus's overdubbing on *The Black Saint And The Sinner Lady*. Even if one had no inkling of what had gone before, *In A Silent Way* is a very beautiful album, touching

and centred. The title-piece and 'Shhh/Peaceful' are among the most atmospheric recordings in modern jazz.

On the assumption that 'more is better', the *Complete In A Silent Way Sessions* were awaited with as much hushed anticipation as must have preceded the opening of the Dead Sea Scrolls. In the event, the experience is almost as enigmatic and troubling. To stumble over a conclusion first, hearing the raw material in its entirety makes one give thanks for the genius of Miles and Teo Macero in seeing what was essential in these extraordinary recordings and what was of less significance. There is nothing here that improves on the released version. Some of the material here, like 'Mademoiselle Mabry', 'Frelon Brun' and 'Dual Mr Anthony Tillman', was used to pad out *Filles De Kilimanjaro* and *Water Babies*; some other material found its way on to *Circle In The Round*. The brooding minor-key 'It's About That Time' was to become known as an anchor for important live sets by the 'lost' Davis band.

The real interest lies in the alternative takes of the title-piece and of 'Shhh/Peaceful'. These are good enough, though one cannot quibble with the decision as to issued takes. The album versions are supplemented on disc three by 'The Ghetto Walk', a genuine rarity and perhaps the only thing on the set that in any way significantly alters one's view of Miles at this period. In many ways it presages the trumpeter's return to the blues towards the end of his life. That was seen as a late, almost deathbed, return to the fold; this amazing track, which features sterling work from McLaughlin and Shorter as well as from the leader, is ample confirmation that Miles was never far from the blues.

Collectors and genuine scholars will find much to ponder here. The rest of us can merely marvel at how many marble chips have to be left on the studio floor to create one *David* or one *Balzac*. Miles carved out this material from the most obdurate of material. The albums he created and curated with Macero's help are timeless masterpieces. Insights into their genesis are fascinating but ultimately unnecessary. You'll listen to *In A Silent Way* a hundred times; you might listen to these tracks thrice, and then only to wonder how the miracle was achieved.

**** Sketches Of Spain / Kind Of Blue / In A Silent Way

Sony 65604 *As for the original albums.* 59–69.

Easy for us to be slightly cynical about repackaging like this, but try to imagine you are a 17-year-old who has never heard of Miles Davis and receiving the gift of this wonderfully priced budget set of three of his greatest records. What an incomparable thrill to hear 'Concierto De Aranjuez' and 'Freddie Freeloader' and 'In A Silent Way' for the very first time.

**** Bitches Brew

Columbia 460602 2CD *Davis; Wayne Shorter (ts); Bennie Maupin (bcl); Chick Corea, Larry Young, Joe Zawinul (p); John McLaughlin (g); Harvey Brooks, Dave Holland (b); Charles Alias, Jack DeJohnette, Lenny White (d); Jim Riley (perc).* 8/69.

*** The Complete Bitches Brew Sessions

Columbia C4K 65570 4CD *As above.* 8/69.

Much less beautiful than *In A Silent Way* and far more unremittingly abstract, this is one of the most remarkable creative statements of the last half-century, in any artistic form. It is also profoundly flawed, a gigantic torso of burstingly noisy music that absolutely refuses to resolve itself under any recognized guise. There are stories (authenticated by Teo Macero) that the recordings were made under the cloud of an enormous dust-up between producer and star. Certainly Miles plays with a dour aggression but also, on 'Sanctuary' (apparently the first item to be recorded), with an odd vulnerability which surfaced only occasionally during his later career. Though there had been experiments before with tape editing, *Bitches Brew* was made in an unprecedented way. Basically, the tapes were set to roll and the musicians improvised in the studio, creating a huge body of music which would later be assembled by Miles and Macero. There being no question of alternative or rejected 'takes', the complete sessions contain a huge body of music not used and unrelated to anything on the now repackaged and remastered release edition.

Listening to the complete sessions underlines what an intuitive genius Macero was. Far from augmenting the reputation of the album, the full picture tends to deplete it. Individually, there are some lovely themes, like the Latin 'Yaphet' and 'Corrado' on disc two, but most of the unused material, like 'Trevere' on the next disc, is extremely tentative and lacks focus and engagement. Valuable as it doubtless is to gain some insight into how this extraordinary album was made, it is evident that attention wavers after the first disc, not because attention spans are getting shorter, but quite simply because the quality of the music is not up to scratch. The most significant change in personnel from previous bands was the replacement of Williams and his very linear approach with the more sculptural DeJohnette. The rhythms are immediately more shifting and uncertain, matching the complete polytonality of much of the music. It is rarely possible to decide what key the pieces are in, once they are under way, and there is never much consistency between the key of a 'solo', if such they are, and what the rest of the band is about. The electric keyboards (with Young drafted in to play his distinctive clusters) create a shimmer out of which Miles stabs out some of his most maximal trumpet-playing on record, hordes of ideas packed together into a relatively small space on 'Miles Runs The Voodoo Down' and 'Bitches Brew'. Zawinul and McLaughlin don't play on every track, but the naming of a piece after the guitarist suggests how important he became to this sound. Again, the whole package is less of a performance in the old-fashioned sense than an artefact, the details of which are secondary to the overall effect. And that – for all the sheer awkwardness of some passages and the internal inconsistency of the music – is shattering.

***(*) Big Fun

Columbia CK 63973 2CD *Davis; Carlos Garnett, Steve Grossman, Wayne Shorter (ss); Bennie Maupin (bcl); Chick Corea, Herbie Hancock, Lonnie Liston Smith (p); Joe Zawinul (p, org); John McLaughlin (g); Khalil Balakrishna, Bihari Sharma (sitar, tambura); Harvey Brooks, Ron Carter, Michael Henderson, Dave Holland (b); Billy Cobham, Jack DeJohnette, Al Foster (d); Airto Moreira (perc).* 11/69–6/72.

Recorded during what was perhaps the most intensely productive period of his life, this wasn't released until four years after the earliest of the sessions, by which time Miles had declared himself bored with the music, stating with unmistakable emphasis that he was already somewhere else. The period after *Bitches Brew* wasn't so much a time of consolidation as one of further exploration and redefinition. The elements of the music are firmly in place, and if this is a less powerful set than its predecessor that is merely because it lacks the sudden, alienating wallop, already seems almost familiar. The key elements of the sound are in place: a distorted, almost pain-racked trumpet, the dissonant bleat of soprano saxophone, electric keyboards, thumping, funk-laden bass and a great slew of percussion. The medley of 'Great Expectations'/'Muhler Laranja' is titanic, a huge slab of electric sound. 'Go Ahead John' is again focused on the British guitarist who landed on Miles's world and found himself at home there. 'Ife' is an African tapestry, brightly coloured but also dark and dangerous. This may very well be the least-known item in the whole Miles Davis discography. It certainly isn't the best thing he ever did, but it is absolutely of its moment, and hard to overlook.

****** Jack Johnson**

Columbia 471003 *Davis; Steve Grossman (ss); Herbie Hancock (ky); John McLaughlin (g); Michael Henderson (b); Billy Cobham (d); Brock Peters (v).* 1 & 11/70.

****** The Complete Jack Johnson Sessions**

Columbia 86359 5CD *As above; add Wayne Shorter (ss); Bennie Maupin (bcl); Chick Corea, Keith Jarrett (ky); Herbie Hancock (org); Sonny Sharrock (g); Ron Carter, Dave Holland, Gene Perla (b); Jack DeJohnette (d); Airto Moreira (perc); Hermeto Pascoal (v, d).* 2, 3, 5 & 6/70.

A hugely underrated item in the canon, to a large extent it resolves some of the unfinished business of *Bitches Brew.* Made for a movie soundtrack, like *L'Ascenseur Pour L'Échafaud* before it, *Jack Johnson* offers a perfect example of Miles's imagination being channelled and focused by a project.

Warts-and-all collections of major jazz figures are nothing new. Verve's box of Charlie Parker's later studio recordings and concert appearances is packed not just with the reissue compiler's staple of 'alternate' (i.e. rejected) takes but also with false starts, rundowns for level, studio chatter. True fans are always archaeologists and these are the potsherds of genius. The recent run of Miles Davis reissues is different in that it doesn't offer scattered variants on canonically familiar themes and performances. What makes it unique is the (then) unique way the albums of the late '60s and early '70s were created.

There is a basic consensus that the reissue programme has been only intermittently illuminating, and sometimes a triumph of commercial packaging over musical insight. The much-trumpeted *Complete Bitches Brew Sessions* was actually no such thing, but a bland collage of complete and unedited takes that offered little insight into how Davis and his team actually worked. A similar approach to the earlier *In A Silent Way* was more fruitful but left most listeners feeling that the original album edit was as near to perfect as any Miles Davis fan might wish.

The picture changed sharply in 2003 with the release of *The Complete Jack Johnson Sessions,* an exhaustive documentation of how an apparently minor soundtrack project led to one of Miles's most dramatic stylistic and demographic shifts, a moment in his career where his and his audience's understanding of 'jazz' was robustly challenged. By 1970, conscious that studio-confected rock was fast encroaching on his audience, Miles was already dabbling in the same technique while attempting to remain an improviser. The making of *A Tribute to Jack Johnson* was the key text in that effort. It's an album that has until now been frequently overlooked in the Miles Davis canon. Even the recording company paid it scant attention, putting their marketing effort squarely behind the next set, *Miles Davis At Fillmore: Live At The Fillmore East.*

At the end of the decade, he was reaching out to a new audience and reaching out with a very new sound. On 6 and 7 March 1970, Miles and what has been called the 'lost quintet' appeared at Bill Graham's New York rock barn as part of a strange bedfellows billing with Neil Young and Crazy Horse and the Steve Miller Band. On those nights, they played material mainly from *In A Silent Way* and *Bitches Brew.* During the days, though, something new was being run down at Columbia's Studio B on West 52nd Street, a classic jazz address for such unexpected music. In 1970, though, he was also experimenting with newcomers. Soprano saxophonist Steve Grossman was just 19, while electric bassist Michael Henderson, recruited or some would say poached from Stevie Wonder's group, was also still a teenager. These were the Young Turks who would help steer the next revolution in Miles Davis's music.

During that spring, Miles's basic group consisted of Grossman (who replaced Wayne Shorter), pianist Chick Corea, English bassist Dave Holland, drummer Jack DeJohnette and percussionist Airto Moreira. Over the course of four months, though, Miles would draft in other players, many of them already veterans of the *Bitches Brew* sessions. Though not a charter member of the working group, almost the most important voice of all was another Englishman. John McLaughlin's guitar, often distorted, is the driving force on many of these wild, open-ended improvisations.

Along with McLaughlin's guitar, Henderson's almost simplistically locked-in bass was the new signature sound, anchoring the funky, day-glo ostinati that Miles now wanted as backgrounds for his increasingly free improvisations. The dense keyboard textures and multiple percussion which had created the *Bitches Brew* sound now gave way to something leaner, darker and faster on its feet.

Unlike the Malle film, the 1970 project was on a subject very close to Miles's heart, William Cayton's documentary on the life of boxer Jack Johnson, who won the world heavyweight title in controversial circumstances in 1908 and lost it again equally controversially seven years later. Johnson's flamboyance, conspicuous success and clashes with the white establishment seemed to prefigure Miles's own. The trumpeter also liked to hang out in boxing gyms and spar, helping to build the image of a sharply combative little cat always ready to fight his corner. Many of the tracks are named after great boxers: 'Ali', 'Duran', 'Archie Moore'.

The original *Tribute To Jack Johnson* released in February 1971 (with some success despite the down-key marketing by Columbia) consisted of just two LP-side pieces, 'Yesternow' and 'Right Off', assembled after the fact by Teo Macero, but the basic performances remain surprisingly intact. At the 7 April session 'Right Off' began as a vague studio jam. McLaughlin, presumably bored with waiting while Miles and Teo talked shop in the booth, started to play a shuffle vamp in E. Henderson and Cobham picked up on it and started to play. Herbie Hancock had been passing and was drafted in on organ. After a few minutes, the red light was on, and Miles was in the studio playing some of the fiercest trumpet of his career.

The issued 'Right Off' consisted of edits from three takes of the theme recorded that day, together with an unaccompanied trumpet solo Miles had taped for Macero in November 1969. These takes are now available in full. 'Yesternow' was compiled in a similar way, using takes of 'Willie Nelson' recorded back in February with a different band. This line-up included Chick Corea on electric piano, Bennie Maupin on bass clarinet, and a second guitarist, the heavily echoplexed Sonny Sharrock. Again, Macero reverted to the 1969 solo trumpet tape and to an orchestral accompaniment underneath actor Brock Peters's narration. It's a less sheerly surprising track, but no less powerful than 'Right Off' and driven by the same visceral intensity. Its motor is a 12-minute bass riff pinched directly from James Brown and Sly Stone.

The archaeology of these sessions will occupy Miles Davis fans for years. Owners of the appropriate software will be able to follow Macero's processes for themselves and reassemble the original release version. Others will trace the appearance of material from February to June 1970 on a string of later releases and compilations. They might also wonder whether, already owning *Live-Evil, Big Fun, Get Up With It* and even the afterthought *Directions*, their investment was worthwhile. Columbia certainly didn't seem to feel any sense of real urgency about the set, moving swiftly on to the release of two live albums, *Black Beauty* and *Miles Davis At Fillmore*, which symbolized Miles's rock revolution by being recorded at Bill Graham's legendary West and East rock venues. The label also downgraded the special nature of *A Tribute To Jack Johnson* by reissuing the second run without the original graphic of the boxer in his roadster surrounded by gals but with a photo of the white-vested Miles in that familiar, soon-to-be-branded pose.

After June 1970, it was to be two years before Miles Davis played again in a recording studio. When he did, *On the Corner* was an even more blatant bid for a new rock constituency, with doubled guitars and an even skimpier bass line. Perhaps the message of the *Jack Johnson* project hadn't yet got across to the trumpeter's satisfaction. It remains, in parts and in whole, the roughest, rawest electric-jazz record ever. It stands at the head of what was to be Miles Davis's most difficult decade, artistically and personally.

*****(*) Live At The Fillmore East, March 6 1970: It's About That Time**

Columbia/Legacy C2K 85191 2CD *Davis; Wayne Shorter (ss, ts); Chick Corea (p); Dave Holland (b); Jack DeJohnette (d); Airto Moreira (perc).* 3/70.

This is an important Miles issue, and it is an issue, not a re-release. Bootleg copies of this extraordinary concert have been around for some time and Columbia have wisely followed their unedited, as-it-happened approach. Historically the 6/3/70 gig was critical because it documents Miles's electric concept live for the first time and also catches one of the last handful of gigs by a classic line-up. The occasion was curious in that the Davis group was warming up for Neil Young and Crazy Horse and for the Steve Miller Band, so the audience was certainly youthful, rock-orientated; if they knew Miles at all, it was either from recent things like *In A Silent Way* or else the cool modal sound they'd heard in their 'hip' dad's record collection.

We are used to describing situations where Miles is absent, reticent, utterly minimalist or seemingly diffident. From the very beginning of 'Directions', which kicks off the first set, he is stabbing out notes with fire and purpose and his trumpet-playing through the evening is exemplary. Both sets also end with 'It's About That Time', and here Miles goes into overdrive, pushing incredibly hard. First time out, he segues into 'The Theme', as it can't ever have been heard before; for the second set, the subsidiary theme is 'Willie Nelson'. Both feature 'Spanish Key', given a harder and more antagonistic reading the second time. Otherwise, the sets differ. The remaining element at first house is 'Masqualero', which seems to bridge old-style Miles to the new, rock version. Later in the evening, he moves more uncompromisingly to new material: 'Miles Runs The Voodoo Down' and 'Bitches Brew'.

The main action falls between Davis and Corea, with the trumpeter constantly attempting to trump Chick's harmonic shifts. The addition of Airto Moreira on percussion broadens the rhythmic language considerably and creates a wonderfully open metre. Shorter would very soon head off to form the central axis of Weather Report, reverting to a quiet and introspective style that is the antithesis of his burning intensity here. Anyone who knows him only from 'Orange Lady' or 'Vertical Invader' would do well to listen to his soloing here.

A genuinely important release, the Fillmore East gig is one of those rare occasions when one can hear the course of a genre change direction during the course of a concert. Miles has had an excess of historical and pseudo-historical baggage piled on him; he has also been saddled with a Warholian reputation as a man who made expansive gestures and left others to craft the finished product. This extraordinary document confirms the former and totally confounds the latter: a master musican totally in command of his art, and – possibly for the last time – a forceful maximalist in performance.

****** Live-Evil**

Columbia C2K 65135 2CD *Davis; Gary Bartz (as, ss); Steve Grossman (ss); John McLaughlin (g); Chick Corea, Herbie Hancock, Joe Zawinul (p); Keith Jarrett (p, org); Ron Carter, Michael Henderson, Dave Holland (b); Khalil Balakrishna (sitar); Billy Cobham, Jack DeJohnette (d); Airto Moreira (perc); Hermeto Pascoal (p, v); Conrad Roberts (v).* 2, 6 & 12/70.

There was the slim, centred aesthete called Miles Davis, and there was the dark monster from the id called Selim Sivad, presiding deity of this boilingly intense, unremitting record. 'What I Say', which dominates the latter part of the first disc, is perhaps the most extreme performance Miles was ever to record, one of four tracks on this double set recorded at the Cellar Door in Washington, DC. Some have suggested that the presence of John McLaughlin, not at this time part of the regular gigging group, had a negative impact. Certainly the studio tracks without the Englishman's presence have a very different feel, a quieter and more centred sound on 'Selim' and 'Nem Um Talvez' (albeit both very brief) which makes one wonder if this is the case. Davis looks for a dense, almost sculptural sound in which layers of keyboard clusters generate a shifting, swampy undertow, difficult to penetrate, hard to resist. Abdul Mati's disturbing, surreal cover-art contributes more than a little to the impact of this record, its juxtaposition of affirmative beauty and perverse ugliness. Not many records of the time remain so compulsively disturbing, and so unexpectedly beautiful.

*****(*) Black Beauty**

C2K 65138 2CD *Davis; Steve Grossman (ss); Chick Corea (p); Dave Holland (b); Jack DeJohnette (d); Airto Moreira (perc).* 4/70.

*****(*) At Fillmore**

C2K 65139 2CD *As above, except add Keith Jarrett (org).* 6/70.

Miles found himself – and jazz – a new audience in 1969 and 1970, appearing on stages more familiarly graced by Jefferson Airplane and the Grateful Dead. These two sets, from the Fillmores West and East respectively, extended the *Bitches Brew* formula: churning rhythm, staccato trumpet stabs, swirling harmonic colours and splashes. The material is repetitive, the treatments constantly shifting. 'Bitches Brew', 'Sanctuary', 'It's About That Time' and, less expectedly, the standard 'I Fall In Love Too Easily' appear several times across both albums. The big difference is the recruitment of Jarrett as an organist between April and June, a richness of texture that enhances the music enormously, though in every other respect the West Coast date is better.

***(*) Get Up With It

Columbia C2K 63970 2CD *Davis; Sonny Fortune (as, f); Carlos Garnett, John Stubblefield (as); Steve Grossman (ss); David Liebman (f); Wally Chambers (hca); Cedric Lawson (p, org); Herbie Hancock, Keith Jarrett (ky); Pete Cosey, Cornell Dupree, Dominique Gaumont, Reggie Lucas, John McLaughlin (g); Khalil Balakrishna (sitar); Michael Henderson (b); Billy Cobham, Al Foster, Bernard Purdie (d); Airto Moreira, Mutume, Badal Roy (perc); additional brass and rhythm arrangements by Wade Jarcus and Billy Jackson.* 70–74.

Miles's first attempt to make Ellington dance with Stockhausen. Dedicated to the recently deceased Duke and dominated by a huge, mournful tribute, *Get Up With It* is more coherent than its immediate predecessors and very much more challenging than its marginal reputation would suggest. Recorded over a period of four years, and put together very much after the fact, it traces Miles's growing interest in a whole range of apparently irreconcilable musics. In his ghosted autobiography, he explains his attachment to Sly Stone's technologized Afro-funk on the one hand and Stockhausen's brooding music-as-process on the other. What united the two, beyond an obvious conclusion that pieces no longer needed to end or be resolved, was the idea that instrumental sound could be transformed or mutated almost infinitely and that the interest of a performance could be relocated from harmonic 'changes' and settled on the manipulation of sound textures over a moving carpet of rhythm. Since *Bitches Brew*, and very noticeably on an album like *Jack Johnson*, Miles had been willing to consider the studio and the editing suite a further instrumental resource. With *Get Up With It* and the two live albums that follow, Miles went a step further, putting together bands that create similar phases and process-dominated 'improvisations' in real time.

There is a conventional wisdom that Miles's trumpet-playing was at a low ebb during this period: health problems are adduced to shore up the myth of a tortured genius robbed of his truest talent, clutching at even the most minimal musical opportunities. Even those who *had* heard the mid-'70s albums, which acquired an added mystique by being the last before Miles's five-year 'retirement', were apt to say that he 'no longer played trumpet'. Though distorted by wah-wah pedals and constantly treading water in its own echo, Miles's horn was still doing precisely what the music required of it; the same applied to his resort to organ ('Rated X') and piano ('Calypso Frelimo'). The poorer tracks ('Maishya' and 'Red China Blues' start off very late-nite) give only a misleading representation of how finely balanced Miles's radical populism actually was; a live version of 'Maishya' from the infamous Osaka gig is altogether tougher. The essence of the 'new' Miles is to be found on the Duke composition, 'He Loved Him Madly', a swarthy theme that sounds spontaneously developed, only gradually establishing a common pulse and tone-centre but replete with semi-conscious, almost dreamed references to Ellington's work. 'Honky Tonk', by contrast, is an actual throwback to the style and personnel of *Jack Johnson*. Though put together piecemeal and with Miles apparently willing to let Teo Macero edit greater or lesser chunks out of extended performances, *Get Up With It* is of considerable historical importance, looking forward not just to the apocalyptic live performances of 1975 but to the more polished and ironic pop-jazz of the comeback years.

**(*) On The Corner

Columbia CK 63980 *Davis; Teo Macero (as); David Liebman, Carlos Garnett (ts); Chick Corea, Herbie Hancock, Harold I. Williams (ky); David Creamer, John McLaughlin (g); Collin Walcott (sitar); Michael Henderson (b); Badal Roy (tabla); Jack DeJohnette (d); William W. Hart (d, perc); Don Alias, Mtume (perc).* 72.

*** In Concert: Live At Philharmonic Hall

Columbia/Legacy 65174 *Davis; Carlos Garnett (as, ts); Cedric Lawson (syn, ky); Reggie Lucas (g); Khalil Balakrishna (sitar); Michael Henderson (b); Al Foster (d); James Mtume Heath, Badal Roy (perc).* 72.

On The Corner featured the notorious Corky McCoy cover, featuring Miles's new constituency of latter-day zoot-suiters, Afros, gays, steatopygous chicks in hot-pants, and Willie The Pimp look-alikes. The trumpet has a flex and plug. The wah-wah pedal remains firmly depressed throughout. The critics hated it. Mostly they were right. *On The Corner* is pretty unrelieved, chugging funk, and one has to dig a little bit for the experimental subtleties that lie in Miles's most unpromising records. Where electronics gave him a sinister, underground sound at the apocalyptic Osaka concert documented on *Agharta* and *Pangaea*, here the sound is tinny and unfocused. The supporting cast is also questionable. Garnett was to have something of a solo career on the back of his association with the great man, but he never convinces in this company.

The Philharmonic Hall set is the obvious companion-piece. By this stage, Miles has more or less completely abandoned the concept of themes-and-solos and clearly differentiated instruments or instrumental groups in favour of a thick, percussion-heavy substrate through which Miles's trumpet surges like a sand-worm. Acoustically, it's a mess. Michael Henderson's bass saws around out of control, and the addition of sitar and tabla adds a thickness to the mix that some will find deeply unpalatable. 'Rated X' is already way out in rock territory, but it's the transformation of the theme from *Jack Johnson* that most clearly signals the distance Miles has come over that short time.

***(*) Dark Magus

Columbia C2K 65137 2CD *Davis; David Liebman (ts, ss); Azar Lawrence (ts); Peter Cosey, Dominique Gaumont, Reggie Lucas (g); Michael Henderson (b); Al Foster (d); Mtume (perc).* 3/74.

Recorded in Carnegie Hall – but, oh, how very different from 13 years earlier. This was a further variation. *Out* the electric sitar, *in* a third guitarist, *out* every last vestige of the cool poet who had recorded *In A Silent Way*, and *in* the dark abstractionist who was to turn in *Agharta* and *Pangaea*, both recorded and released in Japan a year later. *Dark Magus* is divided into four parts, thematically non-identical but so closely related that they sound, and should sound, like aspects of some great granitic slab. Nothing to separate 'Moja', 'Wili', 'Tatu' and 'Nne' but shadings and striations of sound and, as one gets to know these recordings better, one becomes almost fixated on the tiniest inflexions. Which is where Miles enthusiasts will find meat and drink in this.

★★★★ Agharta

Columbia 467897 2CD *Davis; Sonny Fortune (as, ss, f); Pete Cosey (g, syn, perc); Reggie Lucas (g); Michael Henderson (b); Al Foster (d); Mtume (perc).* 2/75.

★★★(★) Pangaea

Columbia 467087 2CD *As above.*

It bears repeating: Miles's trumpet-playing on these bruising, unconscionable records is of the highest and most adventurous order, not the desperate posturing of a sick and cynical man. The use of a wah-wah pedal – routinely interpreted as a sign of creative failure – is often fantastically subtle, creating surges and ebbs in a harmonically static line, allowing Miles to build huge melismatic variations on a single note. The truth is that the band, Fortune apart, aren't fully understanding of the leader's conception; Henderson ought to be on the case by this stage but he tends to plod, and the two guitarists are apt to get off on long, spotlit solos that are almost laughably tame and blustery when set alongside Miles's knife-fighter reserve and reticence.

A re-run 'Maishya' and a long edit from the *Jack Johnson* theme (miscredited on the original release of *Agharta*) underline the importance of two underestimated earlier albums, *Live–Evil* and *Get Up With It.* The idiom scarcely touches any longer on European norms, adding Stockhausen's conception of a 'world music' that moves like creeping tectonic plates ('Pangaea' and 'Gondwana', the other great slab of sound, are the names palaeo-geographers give to the primeval super-continents) to Afro-American popular forms, though it should be pretty clear that Sly Stone has by this stage been left as far behind as bebop. 'Gondwana' is the most coherent performance on either album. It opens on Fortune's suprisingly delicate flute and proceeds trance-like, with Miles's central trumpet episode bracketed by shimmering organ outlines and sullen, percussive stabs. It is difficult music to cut into slices and wrap. Key centres are only notional and deceptive; most of the rhythmic activity – unlike Ornette's Prime Time bands, which were revving up around this time – takes place along a single axis, but with considerable variation in the intensity and coloration of the pulse; the solos – like Weather Report's – are constant but also inseparable from the main thrust of the music. There is a growing appreciation of these admittedly problematic recordings (which were originally considered worthy of release only in Japan) but time will tell how significant they are in the overall trajectory of Miles's music.

★★★(★) The Man With The Horn

Columbia 468701 *Davis; Bill Evans (ss); Barry Finnerty (g); Rod Hill (g, v, ky); Robert Irving III (p, ky); Felton Crews, Marcus Miller (b); Al Foster, Vince Mendoza (d); Sammy Figueroa (perc).* 81.

★★★ We Want Miles

Columbia 469402 *Davis; Bill Evans (ss); Mike Stern (g); Marcus Miller (b); Al Foster (d); Mino Cinelu (perc).* 6 & 7/81.

★★★ Star People

Columbia 25395 *As above, except add John Scofield (g), Tom Barney (b).* 83.

This is perhaps the period in Miles's career that most urgently requires reassessment. Yes, he had been ill and out of circulation. No, these are not classic records. In retrospect, though, they sound much closer in spirit to the Miles of 1960 than to the Miles of 1970. Selim Sivad has been exorcized and, though at moments his remnant sounds like a mere husk, there is a lot going on musically even in Miles's foreshortened, almost minimal statements. 'Back Street Betty' sounds as if it might have been around for more than a decade, and the cheeky 'Jean-Pierre' which accompanies it on *The Man With The Horn* was to become a concert staple in these years, reappearing on the live *We Want Miles.* There's a bravura pastiche on a theme from *Aida,* apparently a remnant of a plan to make a full-scale operatic record on the lines of the great suites with Gil. In addition, and rarely for this period, a standard, too, a feeling interpretation of 'My Man's Gone Now' which gives the lie to the notion that the trumpeter had lost his jazz chops along the way.

Star People has long been a favourite of ours. Though never a big critical or commercial success, it stands out in this period as one of the first unambiguous signs that Miles was trying to re-inscribe himself in a jazz tradition. Punctuated by pre-recorded organ interludes, it mixes swing-era choruses over Motown riffs, dark blues shapes and passages that seem to hark all the way back to Buddy Bolden. An astonishing performance, marred by cluttered arrangements and a fuzzy mix.

★★(★) Decoy

Columbia 468702 *Davis; Branford Marsalis (ss); John Scofield (g); Darryl Jones (b); Robert Irving III (syn); Al Foster (d); Mino Cinelu (perc).* 84.

Something of a dud. *Decoy* was recorded up in Canada, where Davis had sensationally snubbed the trumpet star of the new generation, Wynton Marsalis. Miles's curiously ambivalent attitude to saxophonists (perhaps less curious from a man who had played with Charlie Parker and John Coltrane) is underlined by the insulting underuse of the elder Marsalis brother. The sound is hard, brittle and unlovely, and there are passages when almost anyone might be playing, or even no one, so programmed and preset is the sound. One has to listen long and hard for brief glimpses of what had made Miles great, and when they come they are lost in a drab electronic landscape as featureless as a neon arcade.

★★★(★) You're Under Arrest

Columbia 468703 *Davis; Bob Berg (ss); Robert Irving III (ky); John McLaughlin, John Scofield (g); Darryl Jones (b); Al Foster (d); Steve Thornton (perc); Marek Olko, Sting (v).* 85.

The final studio release with Columbia (issued with a preposterous cover shot of a sick-looking Miles posing grouchily with what looks like a toy long-stock pistol) has acquired classic status on the strength of his loveliest latter-day transformations of pop material. His version of Cyndi Lauper's 'Time After Time', a medium-tempo waltz, is straightforwardly lovely, etched in melting top notes and passionate sours; but the finest performance on the record is the version of Michael Jackson's 'Human Nature'. The title-track is set up with some engaging 'read him his rights' / 'you got one phone call' nonsense from the guest vocalists and there's some steaming funk on 'Katia'.

McLaughlin and Scofield vie for attention, but the dominant sound is the solid whoomph of Darryl 'The Munch' Jones's thumb-slap bass. Not jazz as we know it, Jim, but a hugely entertaining record and a happier end to the long, tempestuous association with Columbia than *Decoy* would have been.

**** Aura

Columbia CK 63962 *Davis; Palle Bolvig, Perry Knudsen, Palle Mikkelborg, Benny Rosenfeld, Idrees Sulieman, Jens Winther (t, flhn); Jens Engel, Ture Larsen, Vincent Nilsson (tb); Ole Kurt Jensen (btb); Axel Windfeld (tba, btb); Niels Eje (ob, eng hn); Per Carsten, Bent Jaedig, Uffe Karskov, Flemming Madsen, Jesper Thilo (reeds); Thomas Clausen, Ole Koch-Hansen, Kenneth Knudsen (ky); John McLaughlin, Bjarne Rouype (g); Lillian Tbernqvist (hp); Niels-Henning Orsted Pedersen, Bo Stief (b); Lennart Grustvedt, Vince Wilburn (d); Marilyn Mazur, Ethan Weisgard (perc); Eva Thaysen (v).* 85.

Miles's first big-band record since the Gil Evans projects of the later '50s. In 1984 he had been awarded the prestigious Sonning Prize by the Danish government, an accolade normally accorded only to 'straight' composers. In recognition, and as a personal tribute to the influence of Miles's music, Palle Mikkelborg composed 'Aura' and persuaded the trumpeter to appear as soloist. CBS promptly sat on it for three years, further evidence of their cavalier treatment of one of the unquestionably great artists of the twentieth century. A suite of eight 'colour poems' with an introduction and wonderful variation on 'Red', the piece is built up out of a slightly bizarre ten-tone scale – stated by John McLaughlin in a brief 'Intro' – derived from the letters of Miles's name. This in turn yields a chord and a basic theme, which is then transformed by all the usual processes of serial composition, inversion, retrograde inversion and so on, and also by Miles's familiar colouristic alchemy. Miles's inclusion clearly lent the music a considerable fillip and some much-needed critical cachet, and Mikkelborg (a gifted trumpeter with a particular expertise in electronic shadings and transformations) might just as readily have taken the lead role himself. It is, though, marvellous to have Miles ranged against a large group again, and Mikkelborg's arrangements (particularly on 'Green', which is an explicit attempt to recapture his classic sound) are clearly influenced by Gil Evans's grouping of instruments and interest in pitching top and bottom lines against one another in unusual sonorities.

Miles's duet with NHOP on 'Green' is one of the finest moments on the record, spacious and delicately executed. He's almost as good on 'Orange', which makes specific references to the *Bitches Brew* period, and on the two versions of 'Red'/ 'Electric Red', where he tries out the theme a second time, muted, and moves outside the structure entirely to lay bright watercolour washes over the insistent riff. Mikkelborg's intention seems to have been to inscribe Davis yet more firmly into the history of American music. The solitary musings of 'White' are repeated with Mikkelborg's carefully stacked horns on 'Yellow' (which also restates the M.I.L.E.S D.A.V.I.S row) drawing the trumpeter into the musical community that he helped to create. There are more or less explicit references to such touchstones as *Kind Of Blue* and *Sketches Of Spain*. There are also plenty of generic references: hints of bebop harmony, subtle modes and, on 'Blue', reggae. The closing 'Violet' is a blues, an idiom to which Miles returned more and more frequently in his last years. It's also, though, a tribute to two former Sonning winners, Igor Stravinsky and Olivier Messiaen (whose colour mysticism seems to have made an impact on Mikkelborg). In referring to them, and to Charles Ives on the pivotal 'Green', the Dane also allows Miles to take his place in a broader musical continuum, not just in the condescending by-way that came to be known (though not by Miles) as jazz. Unique among the later records, and all the more precious for it, *Aura* has an unexpected power to move.

**** The Essential Miles Davis

Columbia Legacy 85475 2CD *As for Columbia recordings above.*

All the way from Bird's 'Now's The Time' to Marcus Miller's 'Portia'. We are apt to be cynical and dismissive of compilations, but this one is exemplary. Featuring not more than one or two tracks from any one album, and including no 'bonus' material or previously unreleased rehearsal takes, this double-CD set offers as cogent a summation of Miles's Columbia career as anyone might wish. There are 23 cuts; not one is a dud and some of the specific selections, like 'Generique' and 'Little Church', aren't the ones you're instinctively jotting down as you make your own parallel, virtual list. Sometimes the big labels restore your faith, and this time Columbia have offered a genuinely effective and worthwhile anthology from a body of work they have on occasion been accused of treating cavalierly.

*** Tutu

Warner Brothers 925 490 *Davis; George Duke, (p, ky); Adam Holzman, Bernard Wright (ky); Michal Urbaniak (vn); Marcus Miller (b, ky); Omar Hakim (d, perc); Paulinho Da Costa, Steve Reid (perc).* 86.

***(*) Amandla

Warner Brothers 925 873 *Davis; Kenny Garrett (as); Rick Margitza (ts); Jean-Paul Bourelly, Michael Landau, Foley McCreary, Billy Spaceman Watson (g); Joe Sample (p); Joey DeFrancesco, George Duke (ky); Marcus Miller (ky, b, etc.); Al Foster, Omar Hakim, Ricky Wellman (d); Don Alias, John Bigham, Mino Cinelu, Paulinho Da Costa, Bashiri Johnson (perc).* 89.

You know the feeling when some favourite movie or TV series is reincarnated as an animated cartoon: somehow something quite essential isn't there. Nothing to do with Warner Brothers, who probably couldn't quite believe their luck, picking up Miles at this point in his career, but there is something of that about these records. The first post-CBS records were an uneasy blend of exquisite trumpet miniaturism and drab cop-show funk, put together with a high production gloss that camouflaged a lack of real musical substance. Though he was acutely sensitive to any perceived put-down by middle-class whites, little was known about Miles's specific political beliefs at this or any previous time. The Jack Johnson tribute – written for someone else's project – was as close as he came to an explicit statement of solidarity. Talking to a French interviewer, he said that naming albums for Bishop Desmond Tutu and after the African National Congress rallying cry – 'Amandla' – was the only contribution he felt he could make to the liberation struggle in South Africa; Miles also namechecks Mandela on 'Full Nelson', though this is also a reference to his own earlier 'Half Nelson' and simultaneously signals a reawakening interest in blues and bop harmonies which was to occupy him for much of the rest of his life.

The horn sounds as deceptively fragile as ever, but it's made to dance in front of shifting sonic backdrops, put together in a cut-and-paste way that succeeds very much better on *Amandla* than on the earlier set. 'Big Time' and 'Jilli' have a hectic, thudding energy, while at the other end of the spectrum Miles's dedication to the late 'Mr Pastorius' catches him in convincingly lyrical form. There's no mistaking the ultimate provenance of Marcus Miller's vivid techno-arranging. In particular, his use of synthesized percussion on 'Hannibal' recalls 'La Nevada' on Gil Evans's *Out Of The Cool*, an influence that became explicit to the point of pastiche later.

*** Music From Siesta

Warner Brothers 925 655 *Davis; Marcus Miller (ky, b, etc).*

The film, based on a novel by Patrice Chaplin, has long been forgotten (though it isn't anything like as bad as was suggested at the time) but the music survives and stands up very convincingly on its own. By this time, Miller had taken over writing and arranging duties almost completely and Miles was beginning to take on an unaccustomed Grand Old Man demeanour and series of guest appearances. The trumpeter's free-hand Spanish sketches inevitably conjure up an earlier attempt to evoke that 'tinge'. In many respects, this is a tighter, more focused and more imaginatively marshalled project than *Sketches Of Spain*, though one obviously misses the blood-orange richness of Evans's orchestrations. Appealingly abstract, if a little undemanding; we think better of this one every time we hear it.

*** Dingo

Warner Brothers 7599 26438 *Davis; Chuck Findley, Oscar Brashear, Ray Brown, George Graham (t); George Bohannon, Thurman Green, Jimmy Cleveland, Lew McGreary, Dick Nash (tb); David Duke, Marnie Johnson, Vince De Rosa, Richard Todd (frhn); Buddy Collette, Kenny Garrett, Bill Green, Jackie Kelso, Marty Krystall, Charles Owens, John Stephens (reeds); Kei Akagi, Michel Legrand, Alan Oldfield (ky); Mark Rivett (g); Foley McCreary, Abraham Laboriel, Benny Rietveld (b); John Bigham, Harvey Mason, Alphonse Mouzon, Ricky Wellman (d, perc).* 91.

Though Rolf de Heer's movie will undoubtedly draw a little extra resonance from the casting of Miles as trumpeter/shaman 'Billy Cross', the music may again be a little more vital than the images it was written to accompany, as with *Siesta.* Michel Legrand's scores and orchestrations are predictably slick and rather empty, but there are some nice touches and a couple of sly echoes (presumably intentional) of Miles's work for Louis Malle's *L'Ascenseur Pour L'Échafaud.* Lest anyone be alarmed at what has happened to Miles's lip on the opening 'Kimberley Trumpet', solo duties are shared with Chuck Findley in the role of 'Dingo Anderson'. Attractive, but a slightly sad memorial of a dying man. This was Miles's last year on the planet, and it seems a pity to begin it so far from home, at the opposite side of the world from Alton, Illinois.

*** Doo-Bop

Warner Brothers 7599 26938 *Davis; Easy Mo Bee, J. R., A. B. Money (v); other personnel unspecified.* 91.

Almost the end. Perhaps inevitably, it isn't of earth-shaking significance but, equally predictably, it finds Miles taking another ostensibly rejuvenating stylistic turn. Unfortunately, Easy Mo Bee's doo-wop/rap stylings are so soft-centred and so lyrically banal as to deny 'The Doo-Bop' and almost anything else on the record any real credibility: 'Let's kick a verse for man called Miles / Seems to me his music's gonna be around for a long while / 'Cuz he's a multi-talented and gifted musician / Who can play any position'. Right.

Neither 'Blow' nor the 'posthumous' 'Fantasy', compiled after Miles's death, offer much in the way of succour. It seems that Miles brought in material recorded in the late '80s and known as the RubberBand session, so this final set might be likened to the grab-bag approach of *Get Up With It*, or indeed to the *ex post facto* constructions of Teo Macero, except that in this case no discernible musical nous is in evidence, no real creative energy expended. Miles plays well and with surprising aggression in places, but the backgrounds are uniformly trite and the samples (from Kool & The Gang, James Brown, Donald Byrd's 'Street Lady', Gene Ammons's 'Jungle Strut', among others) are used with an almost perverse lack of imagination. As a farewell to the studio, it's a severe disappointment.

*** Miles Davis & Quincy Jones Live At Montreux

Warner Brothers 45221 *Davis; Miles Evans, Lew Soloff (t); Benny Bailey, John D'Earth, Wallace Roney, Ack Van Rooyen, Marvin Stamm, Jack Walrath (t, flhn); Roland Dahinden, Conrad Herwig, Tom Malone (tb); Dave Bargeron, Earl McIntyre (tb, euph); Dave Taylor (btb); Alex Brofsky, John Clark, Claudio Pontiggia, Tom Varner (frhn); Howard Johnson (tba, bs); Sal Giorgianni (as); Bob Malach (ts, f, cl); Larry Schneider (ts, ob, f, cl); Jerry Bergonzi (ts); Alex Weber (cl); Christian Gavillet, Roger Rosenberg (bcl, bs); Xavier Duss, Judith Wenziker (ob); Reiner Erb, Christian Rabe (bsn); Xenia Schindler (hp); George Gruntz, Dave Seghezzo, Tilman Zahn (p); Delmar Brown, Gil Goldstein (ky); Carlos Benavent, Mike Richmond (b); Kenwood Dennard, Grady Tate (d).* 7/91.

*** Montreux Highlights

Warners 46324 *As above.*

His last bow. Miles and Quincy had never worked together. For years the trumpeter had refused to retread his great material. Presto! The ultimate wish-list booking for a 25th anniversary event, something that would galvanize Montreux like nothing else. It was clear that Miles was ailing at the time, and his solos often find him out of breath (though not of ideas) and lacking in any real physical or creative stamina. The arrangements are grandly overdone, but there's no mistaking the rapturous nature of the reception from the Montreux crowd. It was a career retrospective up to *Sketches Of Spain.* After 'Boplicity' from *Birth Of The Cool*, the band launches into medleys from *Miles Ahead* and *Porgy And Bess.* It doesn't take long to recognize that Quincy Jones is no Gil Evans, and it's a pity that the smaller Evans group (a ghost band by this stage, alas) couldn't have been entrusted with the music instead of the huge George Gruntz Concert Jazz Band (*and* guests), who play with typical precision but with the sort of dead-centredness one expects of studio house-bands. Jones hails Miles Davis as a 'great painter' and that is exactly what he was. He left some masterpieces, some puzzling abstracts, and a pile of fascinating sketches. The Leonardo of our time.

*** Highlights From Complete Miles Davis At Montreux

WEA International 89895 *As for many of the above.* 73-91.

This is a reasonable sampling of Miles's appearances at the toney summer festival. The emphasis is very much on recent things: 'Code MD', 'Jean-Pierre', 'Heavy Metal Prelude' and the like. There's some fine florid playing from the trumpeter here and there but mostly he's locked into his minimalist mode, laying tone colours like abstract brushstrokes, rarely saying more than he absolutely needs to. For live recordings, the tapes are of superb quality and the post-production is expertly done. Perhaps a misleading summary of what was a long and fruitful association, but worth having if the budget didn't stretch to the complete set.

***** Heard Around The World**
WEA 73612 *Davis; Kenny Garrett (as, f); Rick Margitza (ts); Kei Akagi, John Beasley, Joey de Francesco, Adam Holzman, Robert Irving III, Deron Johnson (ky); Foley, Richard Patterson, Benny Rietveld (b); Ricky Wellman (d); Erin Davis, Munyungo Jackson, Marilyn Mazur (perc).* 88–91.

For a time, the favourite accessory for the Miles fan was a row of privately recorded C-90s taped at one of the trumpeter's annual tours. This set dispenses with most of those, offering a properly recorded sampling of the late bands and of favoured themes like Michael Jackson's 'Human Nature', 'Time After Time', as well as 'In A Silent Way', 'Amandla' and the often overlooked 'New Blues'. These groups may have been keyboard-heavy, with perhaps too much attention on Foley's lead bass, but it's Garrett who consistently impresses, even if Miles did suspect him of 'wearing Sonny Stitt's dirty drawers'.

****** Panthalassa: The Music Of Miles Davis, 1969–74**
Columbia CK 67909 *Personnels as for Columbia albums, 1969–74; assembled by Bill Laswell.* 97.

***** Panthalassa: The Remixes**
Columbia 69897 *As above; remixes by various hands.* 98–99.

There was every good reason to fear the heresies of the epigoni, and yet in the event this is a classic Miles Davis album, created not as pastiche but out of the material he left behind, and according to methods that he and Teo Macero had pioneered. Laswell was given access to the original masters – and who knows what must have gone on in smoky rooms before the final signature was given? – and assembled a magnificent collage out of the work of the electric period. 'In A Silent Way' begins mysteriously and majestically, only slowly coming into focus as the theme one remembers and loves. There are huge, stretched passages which bear only tangential relation to the original, but they are unmistakable for all that. The material from *Agharta*, transformed into a vast chthonic dub, is magnificent and must have had Miles smiling in whatever heaven he currently occupies. Similarly, 'He Loved Him Madly', the trumpeter's tribute to the only other jazz musician who rivals him for sheer grace and inventiveness, Duke Ellington, is definitively reconstructed. Some were sceptical and suggested that this was a catchpenny gimmick, designed to wring a few more dollars out of Columbia's holding. In fact, it is a record that Miles would have been proud to make. For a score of reasons, and not least because there is a technical coolness about it which no amount of reverberant production will mitigate, it will never win the affection that the source material attracts. It is, however, absolutely central to the story, and no Miles Davis fan should be without it.

Given the music culture of the time, and the kind of aesthetic Miles himself was gravitating towards in his last years, and given further the origin of many of his works as studio artefacts, it's not surprising to see Miles accorded the remix treatment. We are not on the strongest ground here, but most of these makeovers are firmly in the spirit of the original. The work of Doc Scott and Jamie Myerson on some of Miles's darkest electric musings does little more than underscore their intensity. DJ Cam should be horsewhipped for what he does to 'In A Silent Way' but, by and large, taste and good sense prevail and, this being very much a vinyl culture, there is an LP edition, with extra tracks.

Richard Davis (born 1930)

BASS

Played in Chicago classical orchestras as well as with Ahmad Jamal, before touring and then freelancing in New York from 1960. He had associations with artists as diverse as Eric Dolphy and Van Morrison before a long stint with the Jones–Lewis band, followed by teaching, which has only occasionally been interrupted with new recordings.

*****(*) Persia My Dear**
DIW 805 *Davis; Sir Roland Hanna (p); Frederick Waits (d).* 8/87.

*****(*) One For Frederick**
Hep CD 2047 *Davis; Cecil Bridgewater (t); Ricky Ford (ts); Sir Roland Hanna (p); Frederick Waits (d).* 7/89.

Stravinsky's favourite bass player, Davis draws heavily on the example of fellow-Chicagoan Wilbur Ware, bringing considerable rhythmic virtuosity and a tremendous range of pitches and timbres to solo performances. Whatever the merits of his pizzicato work (and there are those who find him much too mannered, relative to Ray Brown and Ron Carter), there is no one to touch him as a soloist with the bow. His *arco* statements on 'Manhattan Safari', the opening track of the excellent studio *Persia My Dear*, rather take the sting out of Hanna's funky lines, but Hanna too shares an ability to mix dark-toned swing with a sort of classical propriety, as he shows on three compositions. On the later set, recorded live at Sweet Basil, bass and piano combine particularly well for 'Misako', a Monk-influenced Davis original which also appears on the excellent *Four Play*, with Clifford Jordan, James Williams, Ronnie Burrage and Davis. The same influence is even more explicit on 'De Javu Monk', which offers probably the best representation on record of Davis's unaccompanied style, all weird intervals and changes of metre. As on the closing 'Strange Vibes' (a Horace Silver tune), Hanna comes in to balance the bassist's tendency to abstraction. The Hep album is dedicated to drummer Waits, who died four months after the recording. His introduction to 'City Bound' (and to the album) is very strong, and he turns in a fine, accelerated solo on 'Brownie Speaks', one of the stronger tracks on *Persia My Dear*.

***** The Bassist: Homage To Diversity**
Palmetto 2071 *Davis; John Hicks (p).* n.d.

Somewhat reminiscent of Charlie Haden's essays in Americana, this lovely set mixes gospel, blues and jazz with a gentle confidence. Davis's unaccompanied 'Go Down Moses' and recitation on 'C.C. Rider' are interesting accents, but the real meat of the record is to be found in the duets with Hicks. 'Come Sunday', 'A Flower Is A Lovesome Thing' and the Carmichael/Mercer classic, 'Skylark', are all well-chosen themes. Davis's 'diversity' isn't a bland eclecticism but a rooted expression of a life spent at the service of creative music.

Steve Davis (born 1967)

TROMBONE

Began on trumpet but switched to trombone and studied at Hartford with Jackie McLean. The last-ever new recruit to The Jazz Messengers in 1989. Since then, a regular face in post-bop playing situations.

***** The Jaunt**
Criss Cross 1113 *Davis; Mike DiRubbo (as); Eric Alexander (ts); Bruce Barth (p); Ugonna Okegwo (b); Eric McPherson (d).* 6/95.

***** Dig Deep**
Criss Cross 1136 *Davis; Jim Rotondi (t, flhn); Eric Alexander (ts); David Hazeltine (p); Nat Reeves (b); Joe Farnsworth (d).* 12/96.

*****(*) Crossfire**
Criss Cross 1152 *Davis; Mike DiRubbo (as); Eric Alexander (ts); Harold Mabern (p); Nat Reeves (b); Joe Farnsworth (d).* 12/97.

*****(*) Portrait In Sound**
Stretch 9027-2 *Davis; Steve Wilson (as, af); David Hazeltine, Brad Mehldau (p); Steve Nelson (vib); Nat Reeves, Avishai Cohen (b); Joe Farnsworth, Jeff Ballard (d).* 3–4/00.

Davis is an adept, declarative player, always indebted to his work with Jackie McLean and Art Blakey, a hard-bop grounding which gives his playing unarguable strength and articulacy. He doesn't overplay, but he's generous with his lines and he gets a sound which often has a shouting intensity while keeping well clear of obvious expressionism. That makes his albums conventional but full and satisfying. Like many such sessions, the quality – or at least the memorability – of each may depend on one's own taste for the tunes and the instrumentations. *Crossfire* is our favourite of the Criss Crosses: Davis makes full use of the front line for some voicings in the classic Messengers manner; there are a couple of terrific blowouts in 'From The Inside Out' and 'Cousin Mary', and the songful treatment of 'Old Folks' is very appealing. Both *The Jaunt* and *Dig Deep* are tough and enjoyable, if thinner with the kind of moments which really pick up such dates and make the listener want to cling on. Alexander, as usual, is a force for good.

Portrait In Sound has a somewhat more ambitious feel, with Davis the sole horn on most tracks and a couple of pieces where Mehldau, Cohen and Ballard replace his more regular rhythm section – although neither the rambling 'Shadows' nor the doleful 'I Found You' are highlights. Davis does better in the interplay with Nelson, an asset to most situations, and they work well at strong tempos.

Wild Bill Davis (1918–1995)

ORGAN, PIANO

Davis studied music in Texas and joined the Louis Jordan band in 1945, before switching to the electric organ and doing some freelance arranging. He was one of the first of the R&B school of organ players and worked as a soloist until his death.

****(*) In The Groove!**
Fresh Sound FSR-CD 308 *Davis; George Clarke (ts); Bill Jennings (g); Grady Tate (d).* 59–60.

****(*) In the Mellow Tone**
Fresh Sound FSR-CD 309 *As above.* 59–60.

Fair representations of the kind of music Davis was making at the time, small-combo tracks which are more like instrumental pop than anything with much jazz in it – they give themselves the occasional solo, but mostly these are simple renditions of familiar tunes from 'Satin Doll' on down. Despite the titles of this pair, which are drawn from the same sessions, each is a mixture of up-tempo and ballad set-pieces. Davis's most worthwhile records remain the albums he cut with Johnny Hodges in the '60s, but these remain out of favour so far as reissues are concerned.

Xavier Davis (born 1971)

PIANO

Born in Grand Rapids, Michigan, Davis studied jazz trombone but ended up as a pianist and was one of the last to work with Betty Carter. He is also a regular in the Tom Harrell group, as is his bassist brother Quincy.

***** Innocence Of Youth**
Fresh Sound FSNT 128 *Davis; Brandon Owens (b); E. J. Strickland (d).* 7/01.

This is Davis's second session as a leader. It's a briskly delivered set, some attractive originals (although Harrell's composition 'Bell' sounds to have a lot more to it than most of the pianist's own tunes), some engaging ideas: the blues 'Milk With A Koolaid Chaser' scarcely sits up as a blues at all. Davis is at his best when playing at an easy tempo: several of the tunes intensify too quickly and the trio start to sound like a McCoy Tyner pastiche, although that may be down to a lack of familiarity with each other's playing. 'Milestones' (the John Lewis one) is neatly turned out with some altered chords. Owens shines in his solos. Overall, a strong effort, not quite out of the top drawer.

Wild Bill Davison (1906–90)

CORNET

Davison worked in Ohio and Chicago in the '20s and was in Milwaukee for most of the '30s, before arriving in New York in 1941. He was quickly associated with the Condon circle and made strings albums in the '50s. From 1960 he freelanced, touring and recording relentlessly almost until his death.

*****(*) The Commodore Master Takes**
Commodore CMD 14052 *Davison; George Brunies, Lou McGarity, Vernon Brown, George Lugg (tb); Pee Wee Russell, Ed Hall, Joe Marsala, Albert Nicholas (cl); Bill Miles (bs); Gene Schroder, Dick Cary, Joe Sullivan (p); Eddie Condon (g); Bob Casey, Jack Lesberg (b); Danny Alvin, George Wettling, Dave Tough (d).* 11/43–1/46.

***** This Is Jazz**
Jazzology JCD-42 *Davison; Jimmy Archey (tb); Albert Nicholas, Edmond Hall (cl); Ralph Sutton, James P. Johnson. (p); Danny Barker (g); George 'Pops' Foster (b); Baby Dodds (d).* 47.

***** Showcase**

Jazzology JCD-83 *Davison; Jiri Pechar (t); Jimmy Archey, Miloslav Havranek (tb); Garvin Bushell (cl, bsn); Josef Reiman (as, cl); Karel Mezera (ts); Ivor Kratky (bs); Ralph Sutton, Pavel Klikar (p); Miroslav Klimes (g, bj); Zdenek Fibrish (tba); Sid Weiss (b); Morey Feld, Ales Sladek (d).* 12/47–10/76.

Born in Defiance, Ohio, Wild Bill Davison looks to have slung the town sign round his neck as a badge of identity. His Commodore sessions – all 24 titles neatly gathered on the recent CD – show that he was both at home and slightly uncomfortable as a Condonite. These are typically strong, no-frills Dixieland dates with notably fine work from the undersung Brunies and Wettling, among the many sidemen, and Davison's punchy lead fits well; but you can tell, at times, that he'd rather be going his own way than acting as a purely nominal leader of a gang that really belonged to Eddie Condon.

There's more early stuff on JCD-42 and JCD-83, typical This Is Jazz fare, with a good if workmanlike band (Sutton is the outstanding player) and a frowsy Davison vocal on 'Ghost Of A Chance'. Clean sound on both releases; the second is shared with a curious 1976 session, made in a Czech castle with a local team who aren't up to the challenge, even if Davison sounds in good spirits.

*****(*) Wild Bill Davison & His Jazzologists**

Jazzology JCD-2 *Davison; Lou McGarity (tb); Tony Parenti (cl); Hank Duncan (p); George 'Pops' Foster (b); Zutty Singleton (d).*

****(*) Rompin' And Stompin'**

Jazzology JCD-14 *Davison; Bruce Gerletti (tb); John McDonald (cl, ts); Bob Butler (p); Eddie Collins (g); Jim Joseph (tba); Frank Foguth (d).* 10/64.

***** Surfside Jazz**

Jazzology JCD-25 *Davison; Tom Saunders (c); Guy Roth (tb); Jim Wyse (cl); George Melczek (p); Frank Harrison (b); Gene Flood (d).* 8/65.

***** After Hours**

Jazzology JCD-22 *Davison; Kenny Davern (cl); Charlie Queener (p); George Wettling (d).* 66.

****(*) Jazz On A Saturday Afternoon Vol. 1**

Jazzology JCD-37 *Davison; Wray Thomas (tb); Herman Foretich (cl); Ernie Carson, Eustis Tompkins (p); Jerry Rousseau (b); Mike Hein (d).* 6/70.

****(*) Jazz On A Saturday Afternoon Vol. 2**

Jazzology JCD-38 *As above.* 6/70.

**** Just A Gig**

Jazzology JCD-191 *Davison; Slide Harris (tb, v); Tom Gwaltney (cl); John Eaton (p); Van Perry (b); Tom Martin (d); Johnson McRee (kz, v).* 11/73.

*****(*) 'S Wonderful**

Jazzology JCD-181 *As above, except add Vic Dickenson (tb), Buster Bailey (cl), Dick Wellstood (p), Willie Wayman (b), Cliff Leeman (d).*

***** Lady Of The Evening**

Jazzology JCD-143 Davison; various groups as above, 65–81.

***** Solo Flight**

Jazzology JCD-114 *Davison; Paul Sealey, Denny Wright (g); Harvey Weston (b).* 10/81.

Davison took every chance he had to make records, it seems, and the big run of Jazzology records contains a rather mixed bag of work. McGarity and Parenti are admirable and underrated players, and they make up a very good front line with Bill on the Jazzologists date: as righteous Dixieland goes, this is arguably the best record of the bunch. The Surf Side Six were a local band working in Detroit when Davison muscled in on their gig (a habitual occurrence) and shook the rafters on a few tunes. Nothing fancy, but some nice music. Much the same scenario with the *After Hours* date, where Bill drove by a gig where George Wettling was in charge, sat in, taped it, and counted his royalties. The footwork with Davern is rather good. *Rompin' And Stompin'* is another of his hired-gun sessions with a crew of local (as in Detroit) Dixielanders of little distinction. This one is definitely for Davison completists.

The two *Saturday Afternoon* gigs aren't very exciting either, an Atlanta group providing the backdrop for the Davison horn, and the following *Just A Gig* is just as it says, this time hailing from downtown Manassas, Virginia. Some very shaky sidemen on this one (and we don't just mean their vibrato). A couple of leftovers turn up on *'S Wonderful*, which is by a much superior group: Davison and Dickenson are a dream front line, the snarling bite of the one with the droll, loping gait of the other; if neither is quite at his best, it's a tonic after some of the other playing on these CDs. *Lady Of The Evening* is a hotchpotch collection of one session with rhythm section from 1971 and several out-takes from some of the prior dates: some strong, bruising horn on the main date, though.

Solo Flight finds him in London in 1981. Wright, Sealey and Weston make so much reverberant noise that at times even Davison has to struggle to make himself heard. It's worth the effort, though, since, despite some fluffs, he battles on with the kind of fierce licks that, rasp by rasp, made up an unrepeatable jazz persona.

***** Swinging Wild**

Jazzology JCD-219 *Davison; Bert Murray (tb); Bruce Turner (cl, as); Ronnie Gleves (p, vib); Dave Murphy (b); Tony Allen (d). circa* 66.

*****(*) With Freddy Randall**

Jazology JCD-160 *As above, except add Freddy Randall (t), George Chisholm (tb), Lennie Felix (p), Dave Markee (b); omit Murray and Murphy. circa* 66.

***** Memories**

Jazzology JCD-201 *Davison; Alex Welsh (t); Roy Williams (tb); John Barnes (cl, ts, bs); Fred Hunt (p); Jim Douglas (g); Ron Mathewson (b); Lennie Hastings (d).* 12/66.

Davison enjoyed British company, and these dates (from roughly the same period) are a congenial setting for him. *Swinging Wild* was cut live at the Nottingham Dancing Slipper and the sound is dusty, but the playing has plenty of vinegar in it. Better, though, is the meeting with Randall's band. Interesting to hear Freddy alongside one of his great influences and, although he defers to Bill most of the way, they have a great scrap over 'Royal Garden Blues'. Chisholm, in excellent fettle, is a further bonus. The final four tracks are from an unidentified gig by a similar line-up. *Memories* sets Bill up with the Alex Welsh band, at a gig in Deansgate. Nothing immortal, but Barnes and Williams are always worth waiting for, and Davison obviously found the occasion to his liking.

***** Jazz Ultimate**

Jazzology JCD-241 *Davison; Lou McGarity (tb); Joe Muranyi (cl); Chuck Folds (p); Jack Lesberg (b); Cliff Leeman (d).* 12/70.

★★★ Wild Bill In New Orleans
Jazzology JCD-170 *Davison; George Masso (tb); Noel Kalet (ss, cl); David Paquette (p); Ed Garland (b); Bob Bequillard (d).* 4/75.
★★(★) Live At The Memphis Jazz Festival
Jazzology JCD-133 *Davison; George 'Doc' Ryan (c); Jim Beebee (tb); Chuck Hedges (cl); Joe Johnson (p); Milt Hinton (b); Barrett Deems (d); Sherri Connor (v).* 6/82.

Still more Wild Bill from Jazzology. *Jazz Ultimate* is a good-natured, ambling set from a club in Connecticut with a band co-led by Lou McGarity. *In New Orleans* includes the reliable Masso and has explosive soprano from the little-known Kalet, which resulted in Davison ordering him to get back to the clarinet, since he didn't like the horn! The set from Memphis isn't very well balanced in terms of sound, the microphones apparently right next to the drum set, and Sherri Connor is more like Mae West than Bessie Smith, but Davison comes blasting through regardless. Although these are all good in their way, Davison wasn't a great one for varying his material, and all but the most intent followers of the man may feel that these are each several notches below essential.

★★(★) With Fessor's Big City Jazz Band
Storyville STCD 5525 *Davison; Otto Hansen, Verner Nielsen (t); Ole Fessor Lindgreen (tb); Elith Nykjaer (cl, as); Steen Vig (ss, ts); Jesper Thilo (ts); Ralph Sutton, Torben Petersen, Hans Kjaerby (p); Lars Blach (g); Preben Lindhart, Hugo Rasmussen, Ole Mosgaard (b); Thorkild Moller, Svend Erik Norregaard (d).* 12/73–12/78.
★★★ But Beautiful
Storyville STCD 8233 *Davison; Per Carsten Petersen (as); Jesper Thilo (ts, cl); Uffe Karskov, Steen Vig (ts); Flemming Madsen (bs); Niels Jorgen Steen, Torben Munk (g); Hugo Rasmussen (b); Ove Rex (d).* 2/74.
★★★ Wild Bill In Denmark Vol. 1
Storyville STCD 5523 *Davison; Ole Stolle (t); Arne Bue Jensen (tb); Jorgen Svare (cl); Bent Jaedig (ts); Jorn Jensen (p); Lars Blach (g); Jens Solund (b); Knud Ryskov Madsen (d).* 2/74–1/77.
★★★ Wild Bill In Denmark Vol. 2
Storyville STCD 5524 *As above, except omit Stolle.* 2/74–7/75.
★★★ Wild Bill Davison With Papa Bue
Storyville STCD 5526 *Davison; Ole Stolle (t); Arne Bue Jensen (tb); Jorgen Svare (cl, ts); Jorn Jensen (p); Lars Blach (g); Jens Solund (b); Knud Ryskov Madsen (d).* 5/75–1/77.
★★★ Sweet And Lovely
Storyville STCD 4060 *Davison; strings.* 8/76.
★★(★) Together Again!
Storyville STCD 8216 *Davison; Ole Fessor Lindgreen (tb); Jesper Thilo (cl, ss, ts); Ralph Sutton (p); Lars Blach (g); Hugo Rasmussen (b); Svend Erik Norregaard (d).* 5/77.

Storyville have been trawling through their archives for some more Davison. The first four listed above all date from a similar period in Copenhagen, where he was a frequent visitor, and there's actually little to choose between them. The tracks with Fessor Lindgreen are rather more ordinary, despite the presence of Sutton (and an uncredited harmonica player), and this merits a slightly lower rating. All three discs with Papa Bue cover several sessions and there are some excellent things in 'When It's Sleepy Time Down South', 'You Are Too Beautiful' and 'Driftin' Down The River', Bill sounding much more at home here than he did with many home-grown Dixielanders. The rhythm section in particular is good enough to keep everyone on the straight and narrow. *But Beautiful* features a similar crew and the reed team shine in particular. Davison's patented rasp and fat-free phrasing have become a little blurred by time but he seems unbothered by that issue. The inimitable snarl is present and sounds intermittently correct on the album with strings, a blissful carpet of violins that Davison, well, spits on. This, indeed, is jazz.

Which leaves the Storyville reunion with Ralph Sutton – pity, though, that this wasn't a great moment for either man. Bill sounds a bit out of sorts, the material is a little too sloppy for his tastes, and Sutton is poorly recorded. Still a few good blasts in the locker, and four alternative takes as a bonus.

Ernest Dawkins (born 1953)

ALTO SAXOPHONE, TENOR SAXOPHONE

An alumnus of AACM, Dawkins was a childhood neighbour of Anthony Braxton and shares his multi-instrumentalism without sharing the more high-flown aspects of Anthony's musical philosophy. Dawkins's New Horizons Ensemble follows a path between post-bop and free music.

★★★ South Side Street Songs
Silkheart 132 *Dawkins; Ameen A. C. Muhammad (t); Steve Berry (tb); Jeff Parker (g); Yosef Ben Israel (b); Avreeayl Ra (d).* 5/94.
★★★ Chicago Now – Thirty Years Of Great Black Music
Silkheart 140 *As above; omit Ra; add Reggie Nicholson (d).* 97.
★★★ Jo'burg Jump
Delmark DG 524 *As for South Side Street Songs.* 97.
★★★★ Cape Town Shuffle
Delmark DG 545 *As above: add Khari B (v).* 8/02.

The influence of the Art Ensemble of Chicago weighs heavily on the first of Dawkins's New Horizons Ensemble records. There are two tributes to bassist Malachi Favors, but the most arresting moment is the long opening track, 'Whence To Whither', which gets the album off to a start that promises without ever quite delivering. 'Just Is Me' is equally long, but doesn't have the fire or the coherence and the record peters out prematurely.

The second album is also patchy, but the addition of Nicholson adds some fire and focus to the overall mix and Dawkins himself seems more contained. The group's basic schooling in the blues comes out on 'Improvisation No. 2' but here and there Dawkins's imperfect pitching and articulation become an issue.

The third record is the first for an American label, a belated homecoming that speaks for itself. In so far as there is a 'Chicago sound' associated with the AACM, this is it. The longer cuts, 'The Gist of It', 'Shorter Suite' and 'Jo'burg Jump' itself are the most successful representation of the Ensemble's increasingly confident balance of freedom and structure. 'Transcension' may well be intended as a reference to John Coltrane's most adventurous experiment in that direction, but it benefits from a further generation of radical ideas and is attractively compressed.

The African connection is even more evident on *Cape Town Shuffle*, a live recording taped at Hothouse. It kicks off in strident vein with a powerful tenor solo from Dawkins over an intriguing Senegalese rhythm known as 'wango'. 'Third Line And The Cape Town Shuffle' is a joyous, defiant processional that might have come from the pen of Abdullah Ibrahim. Ernest then pays tribute to another source figure, the Eric Dolphy of Mingus band days, in a piece called 'Dolphy And The Monk Dance'. The saxophonist's hand-over to Muhammad is (literally) breathtaking, as exciting a passage as this group has ever delivered. The only quibble is directed at the drab rap that comes with 'Jazz To Hip Hop' but it would be churlish to deny Khari B his moment in the spotlight. This is easily the most compelling NHE record yet.

Day & Taxi

GROUP

Swiss trio exploring the ruins of post-bop and after.

***(*) About

Percaso 17 *Christoph Gallio (ss, as); Dominique Girod (b); Diter Ulrich (d).* 8/97.

***(*) Less And More

Unit UTR 4121 *As above.* 8/97.

Both discs were recorded at the same sessions. Gallio is a saxophonist who goes in for a kind of grouchy lyricism – dry, like Steve Lacy, whom he can sound like on both alto and soprano in the way he testily gets through a solo, and mean with melody. It's music which the three men seem to give up only grudgingly, slow tempos suiting them more than fast ones, with Ulrich's uncluttered drumming useful to the style. They're not afraid of using traditional props like heads and grooves for Gallio to work over. A piece can change character, suddenly loosening up and flying, and then return to being earthbound. They have some beautiful originals, nearly all from Gallio, though Ulrich is allowed two and Girod one across the pair of records. Less freedom than you'd expect, and not much convention either. Good.

***(*) Private

Percaso 20 *Christoph Gallio (ss, as); Daniel Studer (b); Marco Käppeli (d).* 12/01.

One could complain that there's no 'advance'. There are the same hard-won rewards, the same gruelling explorations of a small, tight area. But new drummer Käppeli is more expansive (they hit a real groove on 'Peter Zorro H'), and that feel extends into the rest of the music-making, which feels a shade more liberated. The recording is a bit brighter and some of the epigrammatic qualities have been softened. Otherwise, though, Gallio's astringent notions endure, satisfyingly.

Elton Dean (born 1945)

ALTO SAXOPHONE, SAXELLO

Began with blues bands and then with Soft Machine, 1968–72, since when he has led various bands of his own and had particular associations with pianists Keith Tippett and Howard Riley. A great inside-to-outside player with a passionate sound, at ease in most jazz situations.

*** Just Us

Cuneiform 103 *Dean; Marc Charig (c); Nick Evans (tb); Mike Ratledge (p, org); Roy Babbington, Jeff Green, Neville Whitehead (b); Phil Howard, Louis Moholo (d).* 71, 72.

He gifted his name to Elton John (honestly!) and took his inspiration from the saxophone heavyweights like Trane and Joe Henderson. Along the way, assisted by a now 75-year-old King saxello, a sort of curvy soprano, he has created a sound all his own, tight-toned and highly expressive.

The debut album was recorded while Dean was still with Soft Machine, and made largely with fellow-Softs, though it is clear he was already interested in exploring new territory. 'Oogleno-vastrome' is reminiscent of the nonsense of misheard words – like 'Klactoveesedstene' – favoured by Charlie Parker and Dizzy Gillespie, and the track, running at more than 15 minutes, comes across like fierce post-bop. The washes of electric piano are reminiscent of what was happening across the Atlantic in Miles Davis's studios, and there is a hint of the new fusion sound in pieces like 'Neo-Caliban Grides' (the word is a Dean discovery) and 'Part: The Last'. Charig's cornet clinches the lineage.

Deservedly rescued from oblivion by Cuneiform, *Just Us* is a great introduction to a compelling voice. Fantastic cover, too.

*** Ninesense – Live At The BBC

Hux 046 *Dean; Harry Beckett, Marc Charig, Mongezi Feza (t); Nick Evans, Radu Malfatti, Paul Neiman (tb); Alan Skidmore (ss, ts); Keith Tippett (p); Harry Miller (b); Louis Moholo (d).* 5/75, 3/78.

Tapes from the heyday of the BBC's sponsorship of jazz in Britain and taken from the programme of that name. This valuable and intermittently exciting release catches the group at the beginning of its career, with the ill-fated South African trumpeter Mongezi Feza in the line-up, and at the end, when Harry Beckett had replaced Mongs (who died later in 1975) and Nick Evans was in for Paul Neiman. The format is self-explantory, three pairs of horns and a rhythm section dominated by Tippett's romantic piano and Moholo's committed drumming. The music ranges from edgy bop to more romantic charts like 'Sweet Francesca'. Feza is the star of the opening 'Dance', which shows how swinging and funky an outfit this was in its early days. The first Ninesense album was still some time off but the May 1975 session gells wonderfully.

The later session is dominated by the extraordinary 'Nicra', a title which also lent itself to the trombonists' own project and which is dominated by Nick and Radu. 'Seven For Me' is Dean's own best spot, though Harry Beckett runs him close, as does the late Harry Miller, whose bass playing is richly rhythmic. These will be nostalgic sounds for anyone who loves British jazz of the period. Let's hope the BBC vaults are raided more regularly.

*** El Skid

Voiceprint 230 *Dean; Alan Skidmore (ss, ts); Chris Laurence (b); John Marshall (d).* 77.

Co-led (hence the name) by fellow-saxophonist Skidmore, but Dean's two compositions, 'First in the Attic' and the slightly shorter and quieter 'That's For Cha', dominate the record. Where Skidmore seems to want to blow fiercely, Dean takes time and space to make the whole group sing. Not to say that

Alan's writing isn't up to snuff, but it is certainly much less adventurous than his colleague's and the closing 'K and A Blues' palls rapidly. Laurence and Marshall are one of the best rhythm sections Europe ever produced and the record is worth having just for them. Another nice reissue, though, thanks to the other label dedicated to rescuing British jazz of the '70s from the vaults.

***** Unlimited Saxophone Company**

Ogun OGCD 002 *Dean; Trevor Watts (as); Paul Dunmall, Simon Picard (ts); Paul Rogers (b); Tony Levin (d).* 89.

*****(*) The Vortex Tapes**

Slam CD 203 *Dean; Nick Evans (tb); Simon Picard, Jerry Underwood, Trevor Watts (sax); Howard Riley, Keith Tippett (p); Marcio Mattos, Paul Rogers (b); Tony Levin, Louis Moholo, Nigel Morris, Mark Sanders (d).* 9/90.

***** All The Tradition**

Slam 201 *Dean; Howard Riley (p); Paul Rogers (b); Mark Sanders (d).* 90.

All through his career, perhaps beginning with Ninesense in the '70s, Dean has attempted to put together larger-scale groups. The USC is a recent incarnation, a big reed front line with tremendous depth of focus and lots of light and shade.

The Vortex sessions are inevitably more varied. They come from a short season of improvisational encounters at the north London club and they're distinguished for bringing together younger and less well-documented players with veterans like Tippett, Moholo, Rogers and Riley. They are the real stars, not to diminish the achievement of the less-experienced men. Some may feel that the language used is anachronistic rather than forward-looking but, with players of such quality, almost everything played is of interest.

Dean was never averse to including standard or repertory material in his sets. The long-missing Ogun LP *They All Be On This Old Road* began with a superb reading of Coltrane's 'Naima' and Elton returns to the Trane canon on *All The Tradition* with a fine version of 'Crescent'. More unexpectedly, he takes a group of free-jazz players through the changes of 'Darn That Dream' and rounds out the set with 'I Remember Clifford'. Whatever the intention, it flags up a player well able to hold his own in a straightahead context. His own playing is forceful and endlessly inventive, while Riley, effectively co-leader, is his usual quietly magisterial self. Rogers makes the bass sing and Sanders plays with great invention, though he's perhaps prone to wilful subversions of familiar counts and metres. Sometimes a less ironic approach works better for him. Fine stuff, though.

****** Rumours Of An Incident**

Slam SLAMCD 223 *Dean; Roswell Rudd (tb); Alex Maguire (p); Marcio Mattos (b); Mark Sanders (d).* 10/96.

***** Bladik**

Cuneiform RUNE 92 *Dean; Roswell Rudd (tb); Paul Dunmall (ts); Keith Tippett (p); Paul Rogers (b); Tony Levin (d).* 10/96.

Not the least of Dean's achievements in recent years has been to provide a new platform for one of the great outsiders of modern jazz, trombonist Roswell Rudd. They had met almost 20 years before in Carla Bley's touring band and had maintained some contact since, even though Rudd was no longer working very regularly. These encounters were recorded, two days apart, during Rudd's trip to London in the autumn of 1996. Two very different-sounding bands, and if we give the nod to the live Slam session, it's simply because the less familiar rhythm section has a fascination and a quality all its own. Maguire and Mattos establish an immediate rapport, and drummer Sanders, who has yet to receive proper recognition, is in magnificent form. The disc documents the beginning of the first set (nothing tentative, straight into the action) and the end of the last, by which time things are beginning to unravel a little, though the intensity is still there.

Dean positively revels and it's a shame that he sounds so much less assured two days later for the studio session. The middle track of three, of dramatically increasing length, is called 'Too Suchmuchness', and it's tempting to say that this is the problem, a faint sense of time being marked and ideas being reprocessed to fill out the session. Rudd certainly sounds less engaged than at the Vortex club two nights before and on a radio session broadcast after the trip, and the constituent elements don't cohere as one would expect, given the personnel.

****** Newsense**

Slam CD 229 *Dean; Jim Dvorak (t); Roswell Rudd, Paul Rutherford, Annie Whitehead (tb); Alex Maguire (p); Marcio Mattos (clo); Roberto Bellatalla (b); Mark Sanders (d).* 11/97.

The title is a pun, of course, but it also refers back to Dean's superb Ninesense, six paired horns and rhythm, which gigged and recorded for Ogun in the late '70s. The new outfit is further fruit of Dean's association with Roswell Rudd. This is a superb band. The brass are excellent, with American-born Dvorak more than holding his own against the trombones. The paired bass and cello is very effective with Mattos's wailing, almost mystical sound pushed well to the fore. He and Dean are the two most provocative and moving voices in the ensemble. Dean has rarely sounded as exuberant and joyous, and the improvised 'Snap, Crackle And Pop' with Rudd and Whitehead is a delight from start to finish.

****** Into The Nierika**

Slam 201 *Dean; Roberto Bellatalla (b); Mark Sanders (d).* 98.

Dean in full cry on a free date and sounding in thoroughly impressive voice. The trio setting, though not particularly well recorded, is an ideal context for the saxophonist, who develops his ideas at length over three long tracks. The opening 'Following Through' is spell-binding, reflecting the visionary quality hinted at in the title; 'Nierika' appears to refer to some kind of wormhole between ordinary and heightened reality. The saxello is still sufficiently unfamiliar in pitch to give the music a mysterious and evanescent quality, one which Bellatalla and Sanders both enter into willingly.

The thematic material is both strongly developed and ultimately irrelevant, almost as if its function is to serve as a catalyst. This is somewhat similar to the earlier practice of British groups like Amalgam, who would take a folkish theme and then effectively leave it behind as they moved into pure abstraction. Dean updates the idiom powerfully and produces a thoroughly compelling record.

***** QED**

Blueprint 274 *Dean; Jim Dvorak (t); Paul Dunmall, Simon Picard, Jason Yarde (ts); Alex Maguire (org); Roberto Bellatalla, Paul Rogers (b); Tony Bianco, Mark Sanders (d).* 1/00.

★★★ **Moorsong**

Cuneiform 143 *Dean; Alex Maguire (org); Mark Hewins (g); Fred T. Baker (b); Liam Genockey, Mark Sanders (d).* 01.

These records present Dean in a number of working contexts, more and less successful. *QED* introduces fine pianist Maguire on Hammond organ. Teamed with free-jazz drummer Bianco on 'Hammond X', the trio makes a stirring and evocative sound, but evocative of precisely what is harder to say. The influence seems to be American, but the off-kilter rhythms and lyrical passages unmistakably suggest a British group and Dean's use of electric piano will recall his time with Soft Machine. The same trio closes out the record with a less successful piece, 'New Roads'.

Maguire is also on hand for a drummerless trio with bassist Bellatalla, but Roberto is upstaged by Paul Rogers in his 'Sheepdogs' duet with Elton, one of the briefer things on the record, but the one we'll remember longest. Dunmall, Picard and Yarde join the leader on an iffy saxophone quartet (not a genre we generally admire if it isn't up to Rova or WSQ standard) and there is a fine, if somewhat predictable quintet with Dvorak and underrecorded trombonist Nick Evans. An agreeable album but packed with tracks that suggest either dead ends, like the all-saxophone group, or else directions that need deeper exploration, as in the duet with Rogers.

Moorsong is an equally bitty but interesting album that features three separate groups. The quartet with Baker, Genockey and the formidable Maguire (on organ again) is the most compelling. 'Bedrock Ruse' and 'Baker's Treat' (the latter a feature for Fred T.) are unexpectedly funky and might remind some listeners of Trevor Watts's later, more rhythmic projects, except that the Hammond sound consistently conjures up American comparisons. Certainly don't expect anyone not attuned to Dean's alto and saxello sound to pick up the provenance straight away.

The other effective group is a collaboration with guitarist Hewins, a regular Dean colleague, and drummer Mark Sanders, who for us is one of the true stars of British improv. 'Soldering On' is stunning. Sanders plays kettle drums at the climax and it's a chillingly beautiful sound.

★★(★) **Bar Torque**

Moonjune 101 *Dean; Mark Hewins (g).* 01.

Three long improvisations recorded at the Jazz Café in London. Impressive as they might have been on the night, they don't transfer to record well and the disc will seem a bit of a slog to some listeners. The middle piece, 'Sylvan', is probably the most interesting, in that it explores Dean's more lyrical side in the context of free playing. Hewins conjures some interesting sounds and textures from his guitar synth and one comes away from the session more in admiration for his resource than genuinely moved. Not a major item in what is now a pretty (deservedly) generous discography.

John D'Earth (born 1950)

TRUMPET

Still not a breakthrough artist, D'Earth plays pungent modern jazz with an individual spin.

★★★ **Restoration Comedy**

Double Time 176 *D'Earth; Jerry Bergonzi (ts); Mulgrew Miller (p); Mike Richmond (b); Howard Curtis (d).* 5/00.

The trumpeter has assembled a quality band and the pace isn't allowed to flag for a moment. D'Earth's preference is for brisk, rhythmically complex themes which demand very controlled playing. 'Ooboo Way' is the most intriguing of these, but 'Restoration Comedy' and the opening 'In Media Res' are well constructed, too. Not much standard fare for comparison, but 'There Will Never Be Another You' is sufficient to suggest that John can tackle most material in most registers. A little more light and shade would be good, but this is a fine album, featuring a very able band.

Joey DeFrancesco (born 1971)

ORGAN, PIANO, SYNTHESIZER, TRUMPET, VOCAL

Himself the son of a Hammond B3 player, DeFrancesco grew up in Philadelphia and came to wider attention following the 1987 Thelonious Monk Contest. He signed to Columbia after that, but five albums for the label are already out of the catalogue. He has since worked in a John McLaughlin group and has recorded for smaller labels.

★★ **All In The Family**

High Note HCD 7021 *DeFrancesco; Bootsie Barnes, Houston Person (ts); Papa John DeFrancesco (org); Melvin Sparks (g); Byron Landham (d).* 8/97.

★★★(★) **Goodfellas**

Concord CCD-4845-2 *DeFrancesco; Frank Vignola (g); Joe Ascione (d).* 3/98.

★★★ **The Champ**

High Note HCD 7032 *DeFrancesco; Randy Johnston (g); Billy Hart (d).* 5/98.

DeFrancesco, now just past 30, is still a young man, but already he seems like a veteran of the scene, having numerous albums and associations already behind him. He plays respectable trumpet and handles piano with equal facility, but it's his organ-playing (he actually uses a modified C-3) which is his calling-card. His albums tend to be cheery, excitable affairs which are an entertaining listen but rarely call for regular returns to the CD system, and his tenure with Columbia doesn't seem to have led him anywhere special.

On the evidence of his recent albums, DeFrancesco is searching for context. The meeting with his dad has its moments, but the record is sonically unkempt (a surprisingly poor Rudy Van Gelder engineering job) and pretty shabby as an album. *The Champ* benefits from Johnston's supercharged solos (he sounds a sight livelier than Kenny Burrell ever did in this role) and Joey works up the appropriate heads of steam on a straightforward homage to Jimmy Smith. But there's an air of pointlessness about it all.

The most characterful of these is *Goodfellas*, from its great cover photo inwards. It celebrates Italian-American pop with such pasta-sauce-stirrers as 'Volare', 'All The Way' and 'Fly Me To The Moon' (as well as, peculiarly, Monk's 'Evidence'!) done by a trio of popular Italian-Americans. This is a good little band and DeFrancesco, clearly enjoying the rapport, plays with a nice mix of boisterousness and sensitivity.

★★★ **Incredible!**

Concord CCD 4890-2 *DeFrancesco; Jimmy Smith (org); Paul Bollenback, Phil Upchurch (g); Byron Landham, Frank Wilson (d).* 10/99.

***** Singin' And Swingin'**

Concord CCD 4861-2 *DeFrancesco; Frank Szabo, Wayne Bergeron, Conte Candoli, Carl Saunders (t); Andy Martin, George Bohannon, Bob McChesney, Mike Millar (tb); Sal Lozano, Don Shelton (as); Pete Christlieb, Rickey Woodard (ts); Jack Nimitz (bs); Paul Bollenback, Mike Howard (g); Ray Brown (b); Byron Landham, Dave Cook, Paul Liebelshon (d); strings.* 1/99.

The meeting between Joey and Jimmy was inevitable enough, although the old maestro and the young one share the keyboard duties on only two medleys – the other four tracks have DeFrancesco by himself. Smith gives the pretender a bit of a lesson on 'Yesterdays' (the intro is classic Jimmy) and 'The Reverend', which gets away from both of them a bit. It's an amiable release.

But Concord are still trying everything to make DeFrancesco click in the jazz charts, and for *Singin' And Swingin'* he steps up to the microphone. 'The concept was Sinatra with the Basie band, flat-out,' says the artist in the notes and, while it's not that good, it's not that bad either. Basie didn't use strings, we should remind him, but then Frank didn't play organ, and in this context Joey's very crisp fingerings work particularly well in smart, contained solos. Christlieb and Woodard have a few nice moments.

***** Plays Sinatra His Way**

High Note HCD 7105 *DeFrancesco; Houston Person (org); Melvin Sparks (g); Byron Landham (d).* 8/98.

***** Ballads And Blues**

Concord CCD 2108-2 *DeFrancesco; Gary Bartz (as); Papa John DeFrancesco (org); Pat Martino, Paul Bollenback, John DeFrancesco (g); Byron Landham (d).* 00.

Joey's High Note and Concord releases seem to be competing with each other, although the latest High Note seems to have sat on the shelf for some five years. The band is a slight mismatch for a project based around Sinatra tunes: Sparks is more of a blues player, and while Joey likes the high-stepping Frank, he's less happy with the balladeer, which in turn is more Houston's style. It's okay.

Ballads And Blues sounds more like what the High Note band should have been doing. As in the past, Joey can't resist bringing in some family members, although Bartz and Martino lend useful muscle. The curious thing about DeFrancesco's records, given his outsize personality, is their lack of notable individuality: there's little about them which seems like a signature touch.

Buddy DeFranco (born 1923)

CLARINET

With several swing bands in the '40s, on alto and clarinet, he then worked with small groups through the '50s. In California from the early '60s, leading a Glenn Miller ghost band from 1966 and later teaching extensively. Returned to more active recording and performing duties in the '80s. The master technician of the clarinet, but his best work is out of print and he is in much need of reputation-restoration.

***** Mr Clarinet**

Verve 847408-2 *DeFranco; Kenny Drew (p); Milt Hinton (b); Art Blakey (d).* 4/53.

Nobody has seriously challenged DeFranco's status as the greatest post-swing clarinettist, although the instrument's desertion by reed players has tended to disenfranchise its few exponents (and Tony Scott might have a say in the argument, too). DeFranco's incredibly smooth phrasing and seemingly effortless command are unfailingly impressive on all his records. But the challenge of translating this virtuosity into a relevant post-bop environment hasn't been easy, and he has relatively few records to account for literally decades of fine work. He's also had to contend with the usual dismissals of coldness, lack of feeling etc.

His early records with Sonny Clark remain in limbo and should surely see wider release before much longer, although we are starting to have our doubts on that: a whole raft of excellent Verve material, amounting to some 15 albums, seems to be permanently out of favour with that label (those who acquired Mosaic's edition of those dates, also no longer available, are fortunate indeed). At least this session has made a recent return, in Verve's LPR series of attractively packaged 'LP-sleeve' discs. The material isn't much more than three standards and some blues, and Drew is rather less interesting than Clark, but for the clarinet-playing alone the record is mighty attractive, DeFranco blowing with superb authority on 'Buddy's Blues' and putting a coolly songful spin on 'Autumn In New York'.

***** Free Fall**

Candid CHCD 71008 *DeFranco; Victor Feldman (p); John Chiodini (g); Victor Sproles (b); Joe Cocuzzo (d).* 7/74.

***** Gone With The Wind**

Storyville STCD 8220 *DeFranco; Willie Pickens (p); Todd Coolman (b); Jerry Coleman (d).* 77.

***** The Buenos Aires Concerts**

Hep CD 2014 *DeFranco; Jorge Navarro (p); Richard Lew (g); Jorge López-Ruiz (b); Osvaldo López (d).* 11/80.

***** Mr Lucky**

Original Jazz Classics OJC 938 *DeFranco; Albert Dailey (p); Joe Cohn (g); George Duvivier (b); Ronnie Bedford (d).* 82.

***** Hark**

Original Jazz Classics OJC 867 *DeFranco; Oscar Peterson (p); Joe Pass (g); Niels-Henning Orsted Pedersen (b); Martin Drew (d).* 4/85.

***** Holiday For Swing**

Contemporary 14047 *DeFranco; Terry Gibbs (vib); John Campbell (p); Todd Coolman (b); Gerry Gibbs (d).* 8/88.

*****(*) Like Someone In Love**

Progressive PCD-7014 *DeFranco; Derek Smith (p); Tal Farlow (g); George Duvivier (b); Ronnie Bedford (d).* 3/89.

***** Five Notes Of Blues**

Musidisc 500302 *DeFranco; Alain Jean-Marie (p); Michel Gaudry (b); Philippe Cobelle (d).* 12/91.

Until some more of the Verve sets return, DeFranco seems destined to be a marginalized figure. He issued little in the '60s and '70s while teaching and bandleading, but the reappearance of *Free Fall* offers a glimpse of him in 1974. Nice to be reminded of Feldman's pianism, and there is a great workout on the title-track, but hints elsewhere of a modish tinge date the music. *Gone With The Wind* catches him on the hoof in Chicago with a local rhythm section, and it has its moments, but this is obviously just another gig. Pablo took DeFranco on board for a while in the '80s. *Hark* and *Mr Lucky*, both now back in the OJC programme, are spit-polished recitals which earn their stars just for the calibre of the clarinettist's impeccable delivery and musical rigour, although neither is exactly exciting. The association with the exuberant Terry Gibbs has given him a better focus and, although there are better things listed under Gibbs's own name, *Holiday For Swing* bounces through a well-chosen programme in which DeFranco creates some febrile improvisations.

Like Someone In Love is, by a squeak, perhaps the best of the more recent studio dates. The rhythm section is guided in the main by the effortless Duvivier and, with Farlow at his most beguiling in a guest role, DeFranco sounds perfectly relaxed and on top of the programme. The fast pieces show the expected flair, but it's the almost honeyed interpretations of the title-tune and 'How Long Has This Been Going On?' which impress the most.

The live concerts caught on the Hep and Musidisc releases offer lively music, and DeFranco tends to take more chances in this situation: he really takes apart 'Billie's Bounce' in Buenos Aires and responds vigorously to a pushy rhythm-section. In Paris, with the local rhythm-section, he plays a more quiescent set which includes a finely caressed 'Early Autumn'. Neither disc is ideally recorded, though, and the Argentinian players probably get more space than is comfortable.

*****(*) You Must Believe In Swing**
Concord CCD 4756 *DeFranco; Dave McKenna (p).* 10/96.
*****(*) Do Nothing Till You Hear From Us!**
Concord CCD 4851 *As above, except add Joe Cohn (g).* 7/98.

Concord threw a line to players of DeFranco's sensibilities. His first, *Chip Off The Old Bop* has been deleted, but the one to get is the magisterial encounter with Dave McKenna, still as fiercely full-blooded as ever at the keyboard, and musician enough to have DeFranco working at his top level. 'Poor Butterfly', 'The Song Is You' and 'Invitation' are worth the admission price, and there are seven others.

There's a return match on the newest Concord, with Joe Cohn sitting in. DeFranco is sounding immortal: there's no lessening in the technique, and he even brought a couple of originals to the date. Cohn is a respectful bystander, but his chording adds an extra layer of rhythmic propulsion which adds to the swing. We hear that, in his 80s, Mr DeFranco is still practising for several hours every day!

***** Cookin' The Books**
Arbors ARCD 19298 *DeFranco; John Pizzarelli (g, v); Martin Pizzarelli (b); Ray Kennedy (p); Butch Miles (d).* 6/03.

Sounds like the practice is paying off. Buddy's in as spry and breezy form as ever in this meeting with the Pizzarelli Trio plus Butch Miles. The material's obvious, but these guys know every song in the book anyway, and they basically just dig in and blow, everything reaching a hot climax with 'Scrapple From The Apple'. Unlikely that a set like this will convert anyone to DeFranco's cause, but at this point he's unlikely to be bothered either way.

Eli Degibri

TENOR SAXOPHONE

Israeli saxophonist with New York experience, making his leadership debut here.

***** In The Beginning**
Fresh Sound FSNT 170 *Degibri; Aaron Goldberg (p); Kurt Rosenwinkel (g); Ben Street (b); Jeff Ballard (d).* 1/03.

A strong, slightly aloof player – he often sounds as if he's talking to himself, even as he's working hard on a solo – Degibri's difficulty on this set is that he's surrounded himself with outstanding players. As one instance, try 'Shoohoo', where the band really start to burn during a solo by that fine individualist Rosenwinkel, yet the temperature recedes when the saxophonist takes centre stage. All bar two pieces are by the leader, and he writes rather slow, effortful melodies which are delivered as declamatory statements. Even when he does 'Cherokee' all by himself there's a sense of plodding. But it's a great band.

Jack DeJohnette (born 1942)

DRUMS, PIANO, KEYBOARDS, MELODICA

Studied piano in Chicago and kept pace with that on drums too. Joined Charles Lloyd in 1966 and was with Miles Davis, 1969–71; since then has basically freelanced at the highest levels, including Jarrett Standards Trio, and led his own diverse groups, touching on fusion and worldly music but mostly in a driven personalization of post-bop language.

***** The DeJohnette Complex**
Original Jazz Classics OJCCD 617 *DeJohnette; Bennie Maupin (ts); Stanley Cowell (p); Eddie Gomez, Miroslav Vitous (b); Roy Haynes (d).* 12/68.

In past editions, bassists Ray Brown and Milt Hinton and drummer Billy Higgins have seemed to be the most frequently recorded jazz performers of all time. Every evidence is that Jack DeJohnette, now just sixty, is going to overtake them in the outside lane and with time and room to spare. What sets this extraordinary musician apart, though, isn't the sheer bulk of his output but its vivid musicality. Everything he does is marked with intelligence, controlled fire and an enviable instinct for both texture and form.

This early album was recorded a mere month after his first studio date with Miles Davis, for whom he played on *Bitches Brew*, having played with Coltrane and Jackie McLean. It's a fine band he's assembled, fairly conventional in emphasis, but with Cowell and Vitous the maverick component. DeJohnette reverted to piano, on which he'd started out, playing rock'n'roll, for the first day's session. On the second, he reverts to the kit, showing a cymbal technique that owes something to Tony Williams, but much more to earlier masters like Philly Joe. Not a classic album, but an impressive start to the discography and certainly a pointer to what was to come later.

***** Sorcery**
Original Jazz Classics OJCCD 1838-2 *DeJohnette; Bennie Maupin (ts, bcl); John Abercrombie, Mick Goodrick (g); Michael Fellerman, Dave Holland (b).*

Dominated by DeJohnette's 'Reverend King Suite', this is an awkwardly paced album that never quite makes sense as a totality. Whatever the circumstances of its creation, it smacks of hesitancy. Even the passionate tribute to Black America's martyr-saint fails to lift it above the ordinary. That said, Maupin and Holland are both superb, and the title-piece – part of a sequence – and 'Four Levels Of Joy' offer useful pointers to where DeJohnette wanted to go with his music.

***** Pictures**
ECM 519284-2 *DeJohnette; John Abercrombie (g).* 2/76.

With typical prescience, Manfred Eicher signed DeJohnette up for ECM, recognizing the kind of totalizing musical imagination he is always drawn to. Abercrombie was a highly effective partner, and the duos are more satisfying than the solo performances with piano, organ and drums. The guitarist is typically light, fleet and subtle, spinning off lines that are both lyrical and tightly woven, even when moving with deliberation. DeJohnette himself was clearly wrestling at this time with the tension between his own sterling musicianship and the need to be a good group player, a more obviously functional sideman. Whether he has ever entirely solved this knotty equation remains unclear, but on this record he shows both sides of his creative personality very clearly.

***** New Directions**

ECM 829374-2 *DeJohnette; Lester Bowie (t); John Abercrombie (g, mand g); Eddie Gomez (b).* 6/78.

Caught live on a record now deleted, this group demonstrates what an extraordinary and exciting player DeJohnette can be. He has never sounded as convincing in the studio – or at least never under his own name. The thinnish air of Willisau hasn't cut his wind, or Bowie's, though Abercrombie sounds oddly out of condition. Apart from the final, improvised 'Multi Spiliagio', where he stutters out a nervous cross-beat to DeJohnette's hissing cymbal and free-ish tom-tom accents, he remains pretty much in the background. His solos are caught a lot more cleanly in the studio, and some may well prefer the subtler sound-mix. DeJohnette himself is well recorded on the earlier record, clean and detailed but lacking the rich musicality of the live date.

*****(*) Special Edition**

ECM 827694-2 *DeJohnette; David Murray (ts, bcl); Arthur Blythe (as); Peter Warren (b, clo).* 3/79.

*****(*) Tin Can Alley**

ECM 517754-2 *DeJohnette; Chico Freeman (ts, f, bcl); John Purcell (as, bs, f); Peter Warren (b, clo).*

***** Album Album**

ECM 823467-2 *DeJohnette; David Murray (ts); John Purcell (as, ss); Howard Johnson (tba); Rufus Reid (b).* 84.

DeJohnette didn't so much suffer an identity crisis in these years as an ongoing difficulty in establishing a clear market identity for his music. Band and album names (and there was even one called *Untitled*) were almost deliberately flat and uninflected, all the odder when DeJohnette was trying to create a new and different group approach, marked by an interest in quite extreme instrumental sonorities – tuba, bass, piccolo, alto clarinet – and relatively complex charts. He was also able to call on some highly inventive players. Murray, who sounds wonderful on the original *Special Edition*, was just coming into his own, and Arthur Blythe, who spent the next few years in a creative trough, is still at this point playing out of his skin. 'One For Eric' is a richly inventive tribute to Dolphy, but it might have been better for a little brass; it's certainly our strong feeling that these groups – like New Directions before them – were better for the addition of a horn player, and Carroll's blunt, pugnacious approach is just right.

Purcell's multi-instrumentalism, kept in check on the two late recordings, works well in the context of the more experimental *Inflation Blues* (not available at present), softening Carroll's attack and complementing Freeman's rather linear approach. One of the least known of DeJohnette's albums, *Tin Can Alley* is certainly one of the very best, with an increasingly rock- and funk-coloured approach balancing Purcell's rather more abstract styling and Warren's imaginative, off-line patterns and rich timbre. DeJohnette's solo spot – a peril of drummer-led albums – is the vivid 'Gri Gri Man'.

*****(*) Dancing With Nature Spirits**

ECM 531024-2 *DeJohnette; Steve Gorn (ss, cl, f); Michael Cain (p, ky).* 5/95.

The big gap in the discography is explained by the deletion of several records for Impulse! and Blue Note, none of which lasted long in the catalogues. Instead, Jack went back to ECM. So much potential for misty mysticism here, elegantly avoided by DeJohnette's beautifully modulated new trio. Judicious use of keyboards and Gorn's horns (including the rich tone of a Bansuri flute) gives the group a generous range of sounds, and all three contribute compositional materials. Gorn's main input is 'Anatolia', the most self-consciously 'ethnic' piece in the set; Cain's 'Emanations' is, as it sounds, more abstract, but the main bulk of the record is taken up with two long, largely improvised pieces. The title-track is richly textured and surprisingly logical in its development, not at all impressionistic; 'Healing Song For Mother Earth' is a little longer, and feels more so, tailing off into reworked ideas. Again, DeJohnette concentrates on percussion, and the music gains immeasurably.

****** Oneness**

ECM 537343-2 *DeJohnette; Jerome Harris (g); Michael Cain (p); Don Alias (perc).* 1/97.

An unexpected sound-world for DeJohnette, partly a return to the early ECM days but also striking out into new territory. Cain seems an increasingly significant component, and on the two collectively composed tracks, 'Free Above Sea' and 'From The Heart', he becomes the dominant voice. DeJohnette and Alias share the opening 'Welcome Blessing', a brief, delightful introduction to an album that manages to plug into something profound and stay with it from start to finish. The closing track is almost half an hour long, seguing from a collective improvisation into DeJohnette's 'C.M.A.' and rounding out the set with a flash of passion and fire sometimes missing from his music. Our only hesitation concerns the atmospheric 'Priestesses Of The Mist', who outstay their welcome by a few minutes. It's now several years since Jack's recorded a new set of his own, and the time has surely come for another.

Lea DeLaria

VOCAL

Herself a stand-up comedienne with a jazz-musician father, DeLaria eventually followed in the family tradition and has commenced with a couple of startling collections of surprising material.

*****(*) Play It Cool**

Warner Bros 9362-47993-2 *DeLaria; Scott Wendholt (t); Keith O'Quinn (tb); Tom Varner (frhn); John Gordon, Vincent Herring (as); Seamus Blake (ts); Roger Rosenberg (bs); Gil Goldstein (p, acc); Larry Goldings, Brad Mehldau (p); Howard Alden (g); Bob Stewart (tba); Larry Grenadier (b); Gregory Hutchinson (d).* n.d.

*****(*) Double Standards**

Warner Bros 9362-48274-2 *DeLaria; Seamus Blake (ts); Bill Hayes (glass hca); Gil Goldstein (p, acc); Adam Rogers (g); Stefon Harris (mar); Christian McBride (b); Bill Stewart (d); Bashiri Johnson (perc).* 11/02.

DeLaria is surely a breath of cool air in a scene now over-crowded with soundalike standards singers. *Plays It Cool* is all standards, but very much out of the hardcore show-tune end of the book, with numbers from *Sweeney Todd, Chicago, Follies* and *Little Me* rather than the usual string of well-worn tunes. Abetted by smart New York charts and players, she sashays through the material with sublime irreverence – her 'All That Jazz' makes Ute Lemper sound as stiff as Nellie Melba. She skirts with kitsch, but it's a sexy, insolent record – the arrangements by Goldstein and Goldings (sounds like a firm of tailors) are slick, but she's a lot looser and more lascivious than Streisand.

Even so, it sounds polite next to *Double Standards*, which is a jazzwoman's juicy assault on the rock songbook of the past 30 years or so – Blondie's 'Call Me', No Doubt's 'Just A Girl', Soundgarden's 'Black Hole Sun' (unbelievably turned into a sweet ballad), The Pretenders' 'Tattooed Love Boys' and Jane's Addiction's 'Been Caught Stealing' among them. What saves her from mere cabaret or satire is that she can really walk the walk – she has a strengthening voice, her chops have quickly improved from record one to record two, and she's young and smart enough to relate to the material from both sides of the fence. So it's glamorous, lewd, yet on the solid ground of jazz musicianship.

Barbara Dennerlein (born 1964)

ORGAN, KEYBOARDS

Born in Munich, Dennerlein began playing organ at 11 and was already working in clubs at 16. She is very well known in her home country, frequently appearing on the broadcast media, and since signing to Verve has begun to build an international audience.

*****(*) Straight Ahead!**

Enja 5077 *Dennerlein; Ray Anderson (tb); Mitch Watkins (g); Ronnie Burrage (d).* 7/88.

*****(*) Hot Stuff**

Enja 6050 *Dennerlein; Andy Sheppard (ts); Mitch Watkins (g); Mark Mondesir (d).* 6/90.

Straight Ahead! belies its title with some unexpectedly adventurous music. The blues accounts for three of the compositions, but they're blues blown open by Anderson's yawning trombone expressionism, Watkins's post-modernist funk and Burrage's wide range of rhythms. Dennerlein sounds happiest on the up-tempo numbers, such as the heroically delivered title-piece, but her use of organ colour maximizes the potential of a cumbrous instrument.

Hot Stuff is in some ways more conventional, with Sheppard a less wayward spirit than Anderson, but the band cooks harder than before and the compositions – especially 'Wow!', 'Birthday Blues' and 'Polar Lights' – take organ-band clichés and turn them on their head. Mondesir's excitable drumming adds to the intensity. These are still Dennerlein's most swinging and least self-conscious records.

***** That's Me**

Enja 7043-2 *Dennerlein; Ray Anderson (tb); Bob Berg (ts); Mitch Watkins (g); Dennis Chambers (d).* 3/92.

With some of the cast of *Straight Ahead!* coming back into the frame, this is a good but non-committal album from Dennerlein. The presence of Berg and Chambers tends to up the testosterone count at the expense of some of the freewheeling exuberance which marks the organist's best music; they beef up the tempos and the sonic weight without adding anything else of much moment. Anderson grows ever more outlandish – his 'One For Miss D' is over the top, even for him – and a finale like 'Downtown N.Y.' hints that Dennerlein might have been looking towards cop-show themes as her next forte. But there is still much gutsy, entertaining playing here.

***** Take Off!**

Verve 527664-2 *Dennerlein; Roy Hargrove (t, flhn); Ray Anderson (tb); Mike Sim (ss, as, ts, bs); Mitch Watkins (g); Joe Locke (vib); Lonnie Plaxico (b); Dennis Chambers (d); Don Alias (perc).* 3/95.

With another illustrious band, Dennerlein made her major-label move. It's to her credit that she remains the centre of the music and the main force behind it; as prodigious as her colleagues here are, nobody outplays her. On the other hand, there are times on some of the longer, up-tempo themes, where one wishes that someone would step forward and dominate what are otherwise cheerful workouts. The most vivid piece is 'Purple', in which Dennerlein's sense of line and texture elevates an otherwise conventional ballad.

***** Junkanoo**

Verve 537122-2 *Dennerlein; Randy Brecker (t, flhn); Frank Lacy (tb); David Murray (ts, bcl); David Sanchez (ts, ss); Thomas Chapin (f); Howard Johnson (bs, tba); Joe Locke (vib); Mitch Watkins (g); Lonnie Plaxico (b); Dennis Chambers (d); Don Alias (perc).* 10/96.

Another entertaining and colourful record in which Dennerlein assembles an even more formidable line-up for nine original charts. The expected cameos by the likes of Murray and Sanchez again don't overpower the leader's own quick-witted playing; and again the music is rarely more than the sum of its parts, bubbling along but never quite finding the ignition which fired some of her earlier music.

*****(*) Outhipped**

Verve 547503-2 *Dennerlein; Darren Barrett (t); Alex Sipiagin (flhn); Ray Anderson (tb); Antonio Hart (ss); Craig Handy (ts, bs); Steve Slagle (f, af, picc-f); Steve Nelson (vib, mar); Mitch Watkins (g); James Genus (b); Jeff Tain Watts (d); Don Alias (perc); Ada Dyer, André Smith (v).* 99.

Kudos to Dennerlein for varying the sound and style of her records. This sounds like the best of her Verve entries – good tunes, apposite charts, another terrific line-up, and some witty transformations, such as 'Satisfaction' turned into a New Orleans shuffle. Out of the gang, it's her old chums Anderson and Watkins who turn in the best solos.

Ted Des Plantes

PIANO, VOCAL

Des Plantes and his Washboard Wizards are a studio band formed to play the classic jazz of the '20s in modern sound and with a soupçon of modern style.

**** Midnight Stomp

Stomp Off CD 1231 *Des Plantes; Leon Oakley (c); Jim Snyder (tb, v); Larry Wright (cl, as, ts, ocarina, v); John Otto (cl, as, v); Frank Powers (cl, as); Mike Bezin (tba, v); Jack Meilahn (bj); Hal Smith (wbd, d).* 3–4/91.

Never a dull moment with this superb traditional outfit, barrelling through a connoisseur's choice of classic material in Ohio. They have the measure of all 18 tracks, and even at over 70 minutes the record never runs out of puff. Individually, each man has the right blend of chops and enthusiasm: nobody pretends to outright virtuosity, but there are no painful mistakes either. Oakley is a properly salty cornet lead, Snyder is a ripe 'bone man, but it's Wright and Otto, their styles harking back to the oldest Chicago masters as if bebop had never happened, who lend a rare authenticity. Smith's washboard (the group is actually called The Washboard Wizards, though Des Plantes is the affable leader) lends a rare crispness to the rhythms, and even the singing is more than passable. Des Plantes chooses real obscurities from the oldest days of the music, including tunes from the books of Bennie Moten, Perry Bradford, Doc Cook, Alex Hill and The Pods of Pepper, and everything sounds fresh-minted in outstanding studio sound.

*** Ain't Cha Got Music?

Jazzology JCD-225 *Des Plantes; Chris Tyle (t, v); David Sager (tb); Tom Fischer (cl, as, ts); Barry Wratten (cl); John Gill (bj); Tom Saunders (b, tba); Hal Smith (d, wbd, v).* 5/92.

The time-frame moves forward about eight years to the early swing-era styles here, with Des Plantes's Louisiana Swingers re-creating the manner of that day on another 17 songs. If this one seems more ordinary, it's because the material is sometimes more familiar and the approach already mined: Marty Grosz does this kind of thing with perhaps an ounce more character and, while the New Orleans-based group have the measure of Henry Allen's 'Algiers Stomp' and James P. Johnson's title-track, they don't do so well by 'The Touch Of Your Lips'. That aside, the playing is still pleasantly hot and swinging.

***(*) Ohio River Blues

Stomp Off CD 1290 *Des Plantes; Leon Oakley (c); John Otto (cl, as); Larry Wright (cl, as, ts); Ken Keeler (g, bj); Ray Cadd (tba); Hal Smith (d, wbd).* 10/94.

Des Plantes strikes again with a fresh team and another set of archaeological discoveries: King Oliver's repertoire gets a shakedown (though none of the obvious titles), and there's even a nod to our own Fred Elizalde in 'Stomp Your Feet'. Back at home in the '20s, Ted's team sound in great nick, and the only disappointment is that there isn't more of his ridiculous singing.

** Christmas Night In Harlem Stride

Solo Art SACS-125 *Des Plantes (p solo).* 11/95–2/96.

Des Plantes roams around the Christmas songbook on this solo date. It would have been better as an EP, since 'Christmas Night In Harlem' and a few others are fine, but there are some awful misjudgements too, such as two dreadful versions of 'God Rest Ye, Merry Gentlemen', one done in ragtime, the other as a misbegotten blues fantasy.

***(*) Shim Sham Shimmy Dance

Stomp Off CD 1325 *As Ohio River Blues, except John Gill (bj, v) replaces Keeler.* 8/97.

Ted has another go at the Clarence Williams songbook this time, something of a homecoming since this was the material The Washboard Wizards were first formed to play. The 19 tunes are dispatched with the band's familiar geniality; we especially liked the ensemble singing and Larry Wright's ocarina solo on 'Pile Of Logs And Stones (Called Home)', but it's idle to single out any one track in a consistently enjoyable set. Ted has taken us to task in his sleeve-note for calling his singing 'ridiculous'. All right, then; how about 'warm-hearted'?

***(*) Railroad Man

Stomp Off CD1357 *As above.* 6/00.

Still locked into the '20s as a source of material, and it suits them just fine. This time Ted has picked out 18 tunes which have hardly been covered since – everything from Henry Allen's great 'Make A Country Bird Fly Wild' to the New Orleans Owls' 'White Ghost Shivers' (the one 'modern' exception is a tune from the book of the top German trad outfit the Barrelhouse Jazz Band – a nice nod across the sea to some old-world veterans). The sound is superbly crisp, the arrangements foot-perfect, the solos hot. Perhaps if you don't cotton on to this kind of thing now you never will, and maybe the Wizards don't do much to please an audience which wants to hear 'The Saints'. Everyone else should do as we do, and just tune in and enjoy.

Paul Desmond (1924–77)

ALTO SAXOPHONE

Desmond's warm, glowing tone and melodic ease are almost definitive of the cool saxophone, and he has had a large if unexpected impact on modernists like Anthony Braxton. Such was the Californian's importance to pianist Dave Brubeck, for whom Desmond wrote the classic 'Take Five', that there was a contract stipulation insisting Desmond never recorded on his own account with another piano player. Premature death denied him and us what would surely have been a maturing and ever wiser performer.

*** Quintet / Quartet Featuring Don Elliott

Original Jazz Classics OJC 712 *Desmond; Don Elliott (t, mellophone); Dave Van Kriedt (ts); Jack Weeks, Barney Kessel (g); Norman Bates, Bob Bates (b); Joe Chevrolet, Joe Dodge (d); Bill Bates Singers.* 2/56, 57.

It's still fashionable among the more categorical sort of jazz enthusiast to anathematize anything committed to record by Dave Brubeck *unless* it also features Paul Desmond. In addition to downplaying Brubeck's considerable significance, this rather overplays Desmond's occasionally self-conscious style and rather begs the question why most of his better performances tended to be with Brubeck in any case. Desmond did, however, strike up a fruitful association with the members of the MJQ and made some excellent recordings with them, of which some good samples remain. Desmond's own-name outings were, by verbal agreement with Brubeck, always made without piano.

There are hints on the sessions with Don Elliott of Gerry Mulligan's pianoless quartets. There was also the added (later) plus of Jim Hall, who perfectly fitted Desmond's legato approach and interest in top harmonics (an approach that improbably influenced Anthony Braxton).

***** Desmond Blue**
RCA Victor 7432 137751 *Desmond; Tony Miranda, Albert Richman (frhn); Phil Bodner, Robert Doty, George Marge, Romeo Penque, Stan Webb (reeds); Jim Hall (g); Gloria Agostini, Gene Bianco (hp); Gene Cherico, Milt Hinton (b); Connie Kay, Osie Johnson, Bobby Thomas (d); strings.* 9 & 10/61, 3/62.

*****(*) Glad To Be Unhappy**
RCA Victor 7432 131311 *Desmond; Jim Hall (g); Gene Cherico, Gene Wright (b); Connie Kay (d).* 6/63–9/64.

****** Two Of A Mind**
RCA Victor 7432 125764 *Desmond; Gerry Mulligan (bs); John Beal, John Benjamin, Wendell Marshall (b); Connie Kay, Mel Lewis (d).* 6–8/62.

***** Take Ten**
RCA Victor 7432 125760 *Desmond; Jim Hall (g); Gene Cherico, Gene Wright (b); Connie Kay (d).* 6/63.

****** Easy Living**
RCA Victor 7432 131393 *As above, except add Percy Heath (b).* 6/63–6/65.

***** Bossa Antigua**
RCA Victor 7432 122110 *As above, except omit Cherico, Heath.* 7–9/64.

Desmond's recordings for RCA Victor are the pinnacle of his career. If contractual promises meant he was unable to record with a piano player, Desmond found the perfect alternative in Hall and, as will be seen, managed to maintain a consistent line-up for nearly all of his time with the label. He also sustained an extraordinary consistency of performance. It is difficult in all conscience to make distinctions between these sessions. Desmond's tone and quiet, lyrical delivery almost never vary from date to date. Occasionally, he will throw in a discordant interval or roughen up his timbre to add a measure of drama. It is astonishing, listening to this music in bulk, to discover how modern, even avant-garde, it is in impact. For all Anthony Braxton's insistence on Desmond as a primary influence, no one has ever quite taken the point at face value. These extraordinary sides point up how immensely thoughtful Desmond was, less cerebral than Braxton's other bellwether, Warne Marsh, but brimming with harmonic intelligence.

***** From The Hot Afternoon**
Verve 543487-2 *Desmond; Irwin Markowitz, Marvin Stamm (t, flhn); Paul Faulise (btb); Jimmy Buffington (frhn); Phil Bodner, George Marge (as, cl, ob); Don Hammond, Hubert Laws (f, af); Stan Webb (f, af, perc); Pat Rebillot (ky); Dorio Ferreira, Edú Lobo (g); Ron Carter (b); Airto Moreira (d, perc); Jack Jennings (perc); Wanda De Sah (v); strings.* 6–8/69.

One of the few occasions when Desmond seemed in some peril of bowing to market pressure and making a pop album. At first hearing, this is somewhat similar to the bouncy Latin style that Charles Lloyd was making a commercial success of at around the same time. The obvious difference is Paul himself. Not by any means a natural Latin player – even a soft bossa doesn't quite sit right for his phrasing – he is more thoughtful than rhythmic, and the short tracks don't really allow him to develop ideas fully. A beautiful record, though, sensitively arranged and immaculately produced and engineered. By no means merely a 'summer of '69' curiosity.

***** Skylark**
CTI ZK 65133 *Desmond; Gene Bertoncini, Gabor Szabo (g); Bob James (p); George Ricci (clo); Ron Carter (b); Jack DeJohnette (d); Ralph MacDonald (perc).* 12/73.

***** Like Someone In Love**
Telarc 83319 *Desmond; Ed Bickert (g); Don Thompson (b); Jerry Fuller (d).* 3/75.

The '70s were a period of retrenchment rather than decline for Desmond. His health was already suspect by the turn of the decade, and those who dealt with him at close hand seem to have been aware that not all was well. Qualitatively, there is not much to choose between these records, though the settings are very different and the technical quality ranges from pristine to documentary roughness. The Telarc session was recorded live in Toronto and pitches the saxophonist up against a sympathetic but rather passive group who do everything they can to back him but conspicuously fail to challenge or beguile him.

Skylark puts him in company with younger players who have swallowed the rock and roll potion. Carter and DeJohnette remain true believers but, even at this stage, both were experimenting with rock grooves. The long 'Romance De Amor' is pretty free of any such posturing, and a retake of the title-track suggests how much Desmond himself was resisting the drift. The setting is not conducive to his best work, though, and of all his records, and for all the fine playing on it, this is the one which seems most seriously time-locked.

Jimmy Deuchar (1930–93)

TRUMPET

Born in Dundee, Deuchar arrived in London at the beginning of the '50s, and was soon established as a leading modern trumpeter. Important spells with Ronnie Scott and Tubby Hayes, then the Clarke–Boland Orchestra. In the '70s and '80s he divided his time between London and Scotland, a fine soloist to the end.

***** Showcase**
Jasmine JASCD 616 *Deuchar; Ken Wray (tb); Derek Humble (as); Tubby Hayes, Don Rendell (ts); Dill Jones, Victor Feldman (p); Sammy Stokes, Lennie Bush (b); Phil Seamen (d).* 1/53–4/55.

*****(*) Opus De Funk**
Jasmine JASCD 621 *As above, except add Ronnie Scott (ts), Stan Tracey, Terry Shannon (p), Kenny Napper (b), Allan Ganley, Tony Crombie (d); omit Rendell, Jones, Stokes, Feldman.* 4/56–3/57.

*****(*) Pal Jimmy!**
Jasmine JASCD 624 *Deuchar; Ken Wray (tb); Derek Humble (as); Tubby Hayes (ts); Eddie Harvey, Harry South (p); Kenny Napper (b); Phil Seamen (d).* 3/57–3/58.

These are welcome reminders of the great Scot, whose sound sometimes seemed like a hybrid of Bunny Berigan and Fats Navarro, and who is usually recognizable within a few bars – taut, hot, but capable of bursts of great lyricism. Some of his best work is with Tubby Hayes, who himself pops up in various of these dates; but these precious survivals of the British scene of the '50s – which exist solely through the dedication and enthusiasm of Tony Hall, who oversaw all the sessions – are fine too. The first two discs are bothered by the boxy and inadequate sound (and the remastering, which may not be from the original tapes, is less than first class), but the playing is of a standard which may surprise those unfamiliar with this period of British jazz. There are excellent contributions from Humble, Hayes, the very neglected Shannon and the redoubtable Seamen; but Deuchar, as is proper, takes the ear most readily: punchily conversational, sometimes overly clipped, but then throwing in a long, graceful line when you don't expect it, he was a distinctive stylist. These sets are made up from EPs and ten-inch LPs, but the third reissues all of the splendid *Pal Jimmy!* plus a stray track from a compilation. The trumpeter's solo on the title-track blues is a classic statement. Again, less than ideal remastering, but with original vinyl copies of these extremely rare records costing a king's ransom, they're very welcome indeed.

***** The Anglo/American/Scottish Connection**

Hep CD 2006 *Deuchar; Colin Steele (t, flhn); Nicol Thomson (tb); Bob Martin (as); Gary Cox, Frank Griffith (ts); Jay Craig (bs); Johnny Patrick, Tom Cawley (p); Dave Cliff (g); Dave Lynane, Dave Chamberlain (b); Jack Parnell, Matt Fishwick (d).* 4/79–2/03.

This reissues the original 1979 date *The Scots Connection* with five extra tracks recorded in 2003, when a suitably multinational group played five previously unrecorded Deuchar arrangements. Likeable as the original session was, it's attracted more attention as one of Deuchar's very few later featured appearances and anyone coming to it expecting some kind of neglected classic is likely to be disappointed. Deuchar and Cox both play with a lot of grace and invention, but the rhythm section is frankly very tame and the music could use more of a lift than it gets. The main point of interest is hearing Deuchar play on some of his own pieces, and the 'new' tracks offer a contemporary band with Steele slipping easily into Jimmy's shoes. Martin plays an attractive lead on 'Daydream' and the score for 'Israel' is especially effective.

Furio Di Castri (born 1955)

BASS, PIANO

A prolific contributor to the modern Italian movement, Di Castri has worked frequently as both leader and sideman.

***** What Colour For A Tale**

Splasc(h) H 351-2 *Di Castri; Stefano Cantini (ss, perc); Ramberto Ciammarughi (ky); Manhu Roche (d).* 4/91.

***** Urlo**

YVP 3035 *Di Castri; Paolo Fresu (t, flhn, elec).* 1–2/93.

*****(*) Mythscapes**

Soul Note 121257-2 *As above, except add Jon Balke (p), Pierre Favre (d).* 1/95.

The bassist is an inquisitive stalwart of the contemporary Italian scene. Across the very long *What Colour For A Tale*, Di Castri displays a fine ear for nuance and interplay in a quartet that features the most delicate electronic additions from the mainly acoustic Ciammarughi and pert, fiery soprano from Cantini. One standard, Jimmy Van Heusen's 'Nancy', turns up in the middle, but otherwise the tunes are mostly penned by the leader.

He has frequently worked with Paolo Fresu, and the duo record, *Urlo*, is an absorbing account of their partnership, sketched across 27 miniatures (some no more than a few seconds long), embellished by occasional electronics and the merest touch of overdubbing. Perhaps inevitably, this comes out as piecemeal: they develop an immaculate interplay on longer pieces such as 'Blind Streets', but at other times the tunes seem like props for the two players to show off the exquisite sound they get. Not that that's unpleasant.

The quartet record, *Mythscapes*, is democratically credited, though the two Italians take the lion's share of the composing credits. Di Castri's strong ear for melody breaks through on his tunes, especially the very fetching 'Suenos', which sounds like a sketch straight from Spain. Fresu, naturally, does his Miles impersonation here and there, though Balke's incisive piano parts and Favre's ingenious drums avert any idea of pastiche. Formless here and there, but all beautifully done.

*****(*) Wooden You**

Splasc(h) 694-2 *Di Castri; Mauro Negri (cl, bcl); Andrea Dulbecco (mar); Billy Elgart (d).* 3/99.

Di Castri's idea was to have a group of 'wooden' instruments playing Monk's music, though by the time of the record only two tunes by the master remained and the rest was original. The nimble Negri and the thoughtful Dulbecco make a satisfyingly full-textured sound, with Di Castri's tunes a strong platform. There's an occasional tendency towards lugubriousness, but we may be mistaking that for Italian romanticism.

*****(*) Fellini**

Audion CD 2 *Di Castri; Paolo Fresu (t, flhn).* 99.

Their second duo exchange is another celebration of beautiful sound, whether bathed in reverb, dappled with electronics, or simply in the inbuilt tone of two great players. Yet there's plenty of hard-nosed improvising too: the fierce give-and-take of 'Open Trio', for instance. Recorded live at Le Carrozze Record, it's sustained across more than 70 minutes with surprising intensity: only rarely does the combination fall back on mere rhapsodizing.

Stefano di Battista (born 1968)

ALTO AND SOPRANO SAXOPHONES

Italian saxman based in Paris, given an international shot by recording for Blue Note.

*****(*) A Prima Vista**

Blue Note 97945-2 *di Battista; Flavio Boltro (t); Eric Legnini (p); Rosario Bonaccorso (b); Benjamin Henocq (d).* 8/98.

*****(*) Stefano di Battista**

Blue Note 28417-2 *di Battista; Flavio Boltro (t); Jacky Terrasson (p); Rosario Bonaccorso (b); Elvin Jones (d).* 7/00.

***** Round About Roma**

Blue Note 542406-2 *di Battista; Eric Legnini (p); Rosario Bonaccorso (b); Andre Ceccarelli (d); Les Archets De Paris Orchestra.* 7/02.

European post-bop rarely reaches American shores, so it was agreeable to find Blue Note releasing the second of these two sets in America. US readers might also like to ask their importer for the first one, which is a splendid session, brimming over with joyful playing: it's hard bop softened by Italian sunshine (even though recorded in Amiens), and both horn players have a brush of Mediterranean charm to go with the bristling energy. If in doubt, simply try the opening three minutes of 'Spirit Of Messengers'.

Di Battista gives himself a bit more limelight on the quartet set (Boltro is kept to three appearances). He has a way of finding a sweetly melodic hook in an otherwise conventional theme, as in the opening 'Elvin's Tune', and 'Johnny's Time' is soaked in lyricism. On alto he has an oddly vocalised sound which goes with a vibrato that he likes to use for dynamic variation. Jones and Terrasson are the star guests, but they're not coasting; if anything, Terrasson sounds more convincing here than he does on many of his own records.

Bookended by the two most vigorous pieces, the orchestral setting of *Round About Roma* suits di Battista handsomely, without ever quite suggesting that what's on offer – bedecked in lavish Vince Mendoza arrangements – is much more than high-octane mood music. 'Anastasia' and the closing 'The Next Nine Hours' are both given a lift by Ceccarelli, who otherwise has the least interesting job on the record, and di Battista plays vivid soprano on the former, bruising alto on the latter. In between is a lot of very pretty music.

Robert Dick (born 1950)

FLUTES

Dick is an avant-garde concert flautist who has also found a niche in improvisation and the outer reaches of jazz. He is also a member of eclectic trio New Winds. A superb performer on all the flutes (he can even make the F contrabass instrument sound feasible), he has a huge tonal and timbral range, which he uses to maximum effect on these records.

*****(*) The Other Flute**
GM Recordings GM 2013 *Dick (f solo).* 86.

***** Venturi Shadows**
O.O Records 7 *Dick; Mary K. Fink (f); Ned Rothenberg (shakuhachi); Steve Gorn (bansuri); Neil B. Rolnick (elec).* 91.

***** Steel And Bamboo**
O.O Records 12 *Dick; Steve Gorn (bansuri).* 92.

*****(*) Third Stone From The Sun**
New World 80435 *Dick; Marty Ehrlich (bcl); Jerome Harris (b, g); Jim Black (d); Shelley Hirsch (v); Soldier String Quartet: Laura Seaton, Dave Soldier (vn); Ron Lawrence (vla); Mary Wooten (clo).* 1/93.

****** Worlds Of If**
Leo CDLR 224 *Dick; Ned Rothenberg (as).* 2/94.

Dick is a latter day Gazzeloni, the flautist who inspired Eric Dolphy and who lies behind one of Eric's best-loved improvisations. It is featured on *The Other Flute*, an album dominated by Edgard Varèse's 'Density 21.5', one of the real classics of the modern flute repertoire. Its presence alongside Paganini's 'Caprice in E Minor, Op. 1' might suggest that this is essentially a classical project and inappropriate to this book. And yet everything Dick tackles has a tense, improvisational edge.

The material on *Venturi Shadows* is closer to his 'straight' repertoire. Rolnick's sampling locates 'A Black Lake With A Blue Coat In It' in the midst of a huge sonic landscape. By contrast, 'Further Down' and 'Heart Of Light' are unaccompanied solo pieces on flute and piccolo respectively. Dick duets with Steve Gorn on 'Bassbamboo', with Mary K. Fink on 'Recombinant Landscapes' and with Rothenberg on 'Daytime'. The final track is a mish-mash of overdubbed sounds, disconcertingly undisciplined from a player of Dick's taste and precision.

The duets with *bansuri* master Gorn on *Steel And Bamboo* are interesting rather than involving. The contrast in timbre palls rather quickly and there are passages when the two participants seem be thinking and working in entirely opposite directions. Students of flute will undoubtedly be fascinated and should be aware that all of Dick's scores and transcriptions are available from his publishing house, Multiple Breath.

There have been many jazz-centred Hendrix tributes over the last few years, but *Third Stone From The Sun* is one of the most unexpected and imaginative. Dick and arranger Dave Soldier give 'Pali Gap', 'Purple Haze' and 'Voodoo Chile' workouts that are obviously influenced by the Kronos Quartet's tongue-in-cheek approach but which are far more inventive musically. Producer Marty Ehrlich and Shelley Hirsch play on the title-track only, giving it an extra dimension the whole album could do with. Not to be missed, though.

For sheer, astonishing impact, *Worlds Of If* is the Dick record to start with. It begins with percussive, hollow sounds on the F bass flute (it might almost be some sort of marimba), stalking a range a full octave beyond a conventional bass instrument. 'Sea Of Stories', dedicated to novelist Salman Rushdie, shows how far Dick has come with the concept of overdubbing. Here, he weaves a mysterious carpet of sound in which threads of melody pop up in unexpected places, like characters returning from some distant enchantment. 'Eleven In Use' is a duo with Ned Rothenberg, the man Dick describes as the 'Jules Verne of the saxophone'; whatever it means, great music comes of it. There are other literary inspirations, as well, ideas from science-fiction writers Philip K. Dick and Ron Goulart (*Worlds Of If* was the name of an influential SF magazine), but there is no mistaking the absolute musicality of Dick's approach. He makes a palimpsest of Edgar Varèse's 'Density 21.5', playing it straight but multi-tracking additional interpretations, written as if Varèse himself had lived long enough to hear (and doubtless appreciate) Hendrix. That influence, with substantial input from Ornette Coleman, comes out on 'Lapis Blues', scored for 'harmolodic flute ensemble'. To borrow a tag from some other SF comics, *Astounding, Amazing* and *Fantastic*!

***** Irrefragable Dreams**
Random Acoustics RA 018 *Dick; Mari Kimura (vn).* 96.

A taut and remarkably disciplined set of improvised duets with a Japanese violinist who shares the same eclectic background in jazz and new music. Some of these pieces sound fully written out, most obviously when Dick plays his concert flute, but as ever the bulk of the set explores extreme sonorities and unconventional technique, and there is an obvious responsiveness in the exchanges which suggests that the dozen tracks really are spontaneously created. Kimura has a lovely tone, balanced and carefully inflected, and Dick as recorded is right close up, punctuated with breaths and occasional mouth noises. Very authentic.

*****(*) Aurealis**
Victo CD 052 *Dick; John Wolf Brennan (p, prepared p); Daniele Patumi (b).* 97.

Strictly speaking, this is credited to Trio Aurealis, which joins the ADD Trio and New Winds in Dick's roster of associations; but, unlike the last of these at least, it sounds very much like his own group. Brennan is himself a gifted and enormously expressive performer and a brilliant composer, but this is a context which induces him to set aside some of his characteristic mix of complexity and lyricism in order to improvise in a more linear way. Dick's familiar quiver of flutes has rarely been deployed so sensitively. The sequence of astronomical pieces grouped as 'Stellar Nursery' is particularly effective.

*****(*) Jazz Standards On Mars**

Enja ENJ 9327-2 *Dick; Regina Carter (vn); Dave Soldier (vn, metal vn); Judith Insell (vla); Dawn Buckholz (clo); Richard Bona, Mark Dresser, Kermit Driscoll (b); Steve Arguëlles, Ben Perowsky (d); Valerie Naranjo (perc, v).* 98.

Perhaps the most immediately accessible Dick album to date, featuring arrangements of material by John Coltrane ('India'), Eric Dolphy again ('Gazzeloni' and 'Something Sweet, Something Tender'), Jimi Hendrix ('Machine Gun') and Wayne Shorter ('Water Babies'). Arranged for the Soldier String Quartet and rhythm section by violinist Dave Soldier, it's a record that straddles Dick's interest in jazz and new music. The pace is necessarily slower than one might expect from some of the material, but Carter is an impressive front-line player and Dresser, playing upright bass rather than electric, gives the group a taut, propulsive rhythm. Some of the tracks sound a touch over-arranged and 'Machine Gun' is probably too close to Kronos's now clichéd approach to Hendrix for comfort. All the same, a very good, very listenable record that will win Dick new listeners.

***** Sic Bisquitus Disintegrat**

Enja ENJ 9361 *Dick; Christy Doran (g); Steve Arguëlles (d, perc).* 8/98.

The title is dog Latin for 'that's the way the cookie crumbles' and there is a kind of ironic pomposity about some of the music on this delightful disc. Dick's classical approach gives gravitas to otherwise simple ideas and the album as a whole has an almost solemn quality that belies its materials entirely. Doran is a magic box of effects as always and Arguelles underlines his status as one of the most intelligent percussionists on the European scene.

Vic Dickenson (1906–84)

TROMBONE

Raised in Ohio, Dickenson started out with territory bands before working with Bennie Moten and Claude Hopkins. He worked in and around Boston in the '40s and '50s and later played with the revivalist swing outfit, Saints And Sinners, in New York, as well as with his great friend, Bobby Hackett, in many groups. A much-liked and admired figure among fellow musicians, Dickenson was also an accomplished songwriter, although comparatively few of his songs were ever puiblished.

CORE COLLECTION

****** Gentleman Of The Trombone**

Storyville STCD 5008 *Dickenson; Johnny Guarnieri (p); Bill Pemberton (b); Oliver Jackson (d).* 7/75.

Much of the contemporary trombone vocabulary comes from the playing of Vic Dickenson. His bravura range of sounds on the horn laid the groundwork for everything that players such as Ray Anderson and Craig Harris do. After spending many years hidden away in trombone sections, he came into his own in the '50s, although records under his own leadership are comparatively rare and he fronted only a handful of dates during the entire LP era. His early '50s sessions for Vanguard frustratingly drift in and out of availability, and the sensible thing is to get them if you see them.

It's a big jump from there to the Storyville dates. On *Gentleman Of The Trombone*, the tunes are nearly all standards or blues, but Dickenson liked a wide repertoire and, even when one of the tunes might seem a dull choice, he makes it new: there are few versions of 'Bye Bye Blackbird' that can stand next to this one. The peppery delivery, unpredictable accents, huffing low notes and barking high ones, even his charmingly doleful singing: all are essential parts of a great jazzman who always gave his best. For all the humour in his work, there's an underlying feeling for blues that deepens all his solos, and his own composing is represented by the typically wistful 'Just Too Late'. Guarnieri's rococo touches get a bit much at times, but the record is all about Dickenson.

***** Ding Dong**

Storyville STCD 8229 *Dickenson; Buddy Tate (ts, bs); Red Richards (p); George Duvivier (b); Oliver Jackson (d).* 4/76.

Ding Dong has all the expected good spirits, but the music is rather lumbered by the presence of Tate, who isn't having an especially good day. Vic and the rhythm section by themselves offer the best value, as in a lusciously blathery 'Blue And Brokenhearted'.

Walt Dickerson (born 1931)

VIBRAPHONE

Philadelphia-born, he worked on both coasts in the late '50s and early '60s, gaining much attention as a new voice on vibes; but he faded from view until a long sequence of records for Steeplechase in the '70s. A deep thinker on the instrument, with a style that steps aside from the inherent prettiness of the vibes.

***** This Is Walt Dickerson**

Original Jazz Classics OJC 1817 *Dickerson; Austin Crowe (p); Bob Lewis (b); Andrew Cyrille (d).* 3/61.

****(*) A Sense Of Direction**

Original Jazz Classics OJC 1794 *Dickerson; Austin Crowe (p); Edgar Bateman (b); Ernest Guillemet (d).* 5/61.

*****(*) Relativity**

Original Jazz Classics OJCCD 1867 *Dickerson; Austin Crowe (p); Ahmed Abdul-Malik (b); Andrew Cyrille (d).* 1/62.

****** To My Queen**

Original Jazz Classics OJCCD 1880 *Dickerson; Andrew Hill (p); George Tucker (b); Andrew Cyrille (d).* 9/62.

Walt Dickerson has never enjoyed the kind of critical praise heaped on Bobby Hutcherson's head. While Hutcherson is unquestionably the more innovative player, with a direction that diverges sharply from the orthodoxy laid down in the late '40s and early '50s by Milt Jackson, Dickerson can be seen as the more interesting player, with a style that combines something of Jackson's piano-based approach with Lionel Hampton's exuberantly percussive sound and an ear for tunes that head off in unexpected directions like the wonderful 'Time' and 'Death And Taxes' on *This Is*.

To My Queen is his best record, not least for the pairing of Hill and Cyrille, and for the beautiful title-track, dedicated to the vibist's wife Elizabeth. A duet with Tucker on 'God Bless The Child' bespeaks a close understanding that is also evident on the title-piece. We resolutely refuse to be put off fine records by the absence of additional material, but this weighs in at just a fraction over half an hour, and with the best will in the world it's hard not to want more.

Cyrille was a stalwart of Dickerson groups until he went off to join Cecil Taylor. On *Relativity*, alongside Abdul-Malik and the little-known Crowe, he gets his teeth into a this time mostly standards programme, sounding less immediately identifiable than in future years, but certainly not a formula player. Seven tracks give an illusion of greater duration, though this disc is also under 35 minutes.

***** Serendipity**
Steeplechase SCCD 31070 *Dickerson; Rudy McDaniels (b); Edgar Bateman (d). 8/76.*

*****(*) Peace**
Steeplechase SCCD 31042 *Dickerson; Lisle Atkinson (b); Andrew Cyrille (d). 11/76.*

****(*) To My Queen Revisited**
Steeplechase SCCD 31112 *Dickerson; Albert Dailey (p); Andy McKee (b); Jimmy Johnson (d). 7/78.*

***** To My Son**
Steeplechase SCCD 31130 *As above, except omit Dailey. 9/78.*

On the best of the Steeplechases, *Peace*, Cyrille drives things along with great generosity of spirit. The addition of Albert Dailey, a pianist of comparatively limited conceptual range, to an already successful trio was a tactical error. Vibes and piano are apt to cancel each other out; when they don't on *To My Queen Revisited*, they merely sound mismatched.

On *To My Son*, working without a piano, Dickerson sounds both edgier and more uncomplicatedly expressive. This is a throwback to the work of the '60s, and a much more convincing version of that style than the previous item.

***** Divine Gemini**
Steeplechase SCCD 31089 *Dickerson; Richard Davis (b). 2/77.*

***** Tenderness**
Steeplechase SCCD 31213 *As above. 2/77.*

*****(*) Dialogue**
Steeplechase SCCD 31345 2 CD *As for Divine Gemini and Tenderness. 2/77.*

***** Shades Of Love**
Steeplechase SCCD 14889 *Dickerson (vib solo). 11/77.*

****(*) Visions**
Steeplechase SCCD 31126 *Dickerson; Sun Ra (p). 7/78.*

***** I Hear You John**
Steeplechase SCCD 31146 *Dickerson; Jimmy Johnson (d). 10/78.*

We have just caught up with Dickerson's solo record from this period, the beautiful *Shades Of Love*. Working alone presented no terrors for a musician of such dexterity and fullness of vision. The original LP consisted of just three tracks, 'Infinite Love', the short 'Love Is You' and the rather unromantic sounding 'Interim Love'. The reissue includes a second take of 'Infinite Love', which will be of interest to anyone who is intrigued by Dickerson's full-on approach to improvisation and to anyone who follows the history of the vibraphone in jazz. Tinged by Hamptonisms and some licks lifted straight from Milt Jackson, the bulk of the set is more open and abstract than either of those great masters would have attempted. A fine (re)discovery.

Shades Of Love notwithstanding, the duo was probably Dickerson's ideal performing context. A busy player, he nevertheless revelled in space (and not always the kind of space that a collaboration with Sun Ra implies). For all its cosmic subtexts, *Visions* is remarkably restrained, with Ra playing some of his most intimate and earthbound piano. Once considered a minor classic (and certainly Dickerson's most play-listed recording), it has lost a lot of its original sheen.

Richard Davis is a well-practised duo improviser – most notably with Eric Dolphy – and he falls in at once with Dickerson's conception, giving the whole session a rich, almost symphonic depth of tone and breadth of development. The two albums have been compiled as *Dialogue*, though for the time being they may be found separately. *I Hear You John* is rather prosaic, though there is no mistaking the amount of emotion that has gone into it. As an attempt to make a record with another percussionist, it is fascinating.

***** Life Rays**
Soul Note 121028 *Dickerson; Sirone (b); Andrew Cyrille (d). 82.*

Another Dickerson we haven't got around to before now and another pleasant surprise. In the dynamically abstract company of Norris Jones (aka Sirone) and hyperactive Andrew Cyrille, he emerges as a particular kind of modernist, still very much rooted in the tradition. Most of the tracks are quite long, but the original 'Good Relationship' and a titanic version of 'It Ain't Necessarily So' give the set epic dimensions. Dickerson seems to have hardened up his mallets or to be striking harder than usual. Perhaps because of Cyrille's presence, the music has a percussive quality not heard on most of the Steeplechases. Sirone is magnificent whenever he steps forward to take a spot, but rather anonymous when simply accompanying. Cyrille is faultless and deserves a joint credit.

Whit Dickey (born 1954)

DRUMS

Dickey initially studied with Milford Graves, and has been associated with Davis S. Ware and Matthew Shipp. He is very much in the line of the 'New Thing' percussionists, almost 'classically' free. In 2001 he recorded with Nommonsemble.

*****(*) Transonic**
AUM Fidelity 005-2 *Dickey; Rob Brown (as); Chris Lightcap (b). 1/98.*

***** Big Top**
Wobbly Rail 10 *As above, except add Joe Morris (g). 00.*

Dickey and Brown are frequent workmates, and Lightcap does a sound job in finding a way between them: *Transonic* is flaring and exciting trio free-jazz, much of it played at full tilt, yet never so chaotically noisy that you feel the players are blowing just for the hell of it. Dickey notes, interestingly, that several of the eight themes were inspired by a couple of Monk tunes, 'Off Minor' and 'Criss Cross', and that grounding in a central jazz language suggests how they keep sight of a solid form behind the spontaneities. Virile and volatile.

Big Top builds on its predecessor. Morris adds a layer of sound which helps the accessibility of this music. Dickey's two originals bracket Dolphy's 'Prophet' and Monk's lively 'Skippy', played very freely. The leader can sound hyperactive and unreflective, but there is no mistaking the power of his playing.

***** Life Cycle**
AUM Fidelity AUM020 *Dickey; Rob Brown (as, f); Mat Maneri (vla); Matthew Shipp (p).* 9/00.

Dickey calls this band 'The Nommonsemble', and it works best when the music has the clean lines and precise responses of carefully composed chamber music: the fifth piece (part?), 'Acceptance', runs to that agenda. They're a highly compatible quartet, four thinkers who prefer the dryer end of free jazz and, while the record isn't exactly exciting, it certainly makes its own space.

Neville Dickie (born 1937)

PIANO

Born in County Durham, Dickie was playing professionally in his teens. He has a huge knowledge of pre-swing piano styles and is particularly devoted to Fats Waller and the stride masters.

*****(*) Shout For Joy**
Southland SCD-31 *Dickie; Dick Morrisey (ts); Al Casey (g); Mickey Ashman (b); Terry Jenkins (d).* 5/89.

This is a lot of fun, and up to this point Dickie had never had a better sound on a record – cut at the Bull's Head in Barnes, the very close-up sound gives the group a real physicality which, when they dig in on the stompers, is enormously effective. Fifteen favourites from various books – Albert Ammons, Freddie Shayne, Leroy Carr, plus various standards – give Britain's answer to Don Ewell and Ralph Sutton the chance to execute some of the steadiest of his steady-rolling blues-to-boogie lines. Al Casey is on hand to add a smiling authenticity, but the real surprise is the presence of Morrisey, spreading around his best R&B licks at a period when he was doing the soft-funk of Morrisey Mullen. When they pile into 'Swanee River', it's sheer joyful abandon.

***** The Piano Has It**
Stomp Off CD1269 *Dickie; Mickey Ashman (b); John Petters (d).* 4–9/93.

Dickie gets one of his most sympathetic outings here, though the concept is a mite dusty: 21 treatments of piano-roll solos, all played in faithful approximation to the originals, often solo but sometimes with the support of Ashman and Petters. This is a scholar's record and it stands up well on that count, with Dickie obviously enjoying himself and the best of the pieces – James P. Johnson's 'Modernistic', for instance – securing a strong virtuosity. It *is* all rather samey, though, and, capable though he is, Dickie doesn't quite have the bullish impact of his heroes. This kind of piano needs a soupçon of bluster to make it come fully alive.

***** Oh! Play That Thing**
Stomp Off CD1309 *Dickie; Mickey Ashman (b); Norman Emberson (d).* 8–9/95.

As before, really, although this time Dickie goes for the most sacred institution of revivalists, the King Oliver Creole Jazz Band. Nearly all of these pieces are out of Oliver's 1923 repertoire, and this time Dickie has some more provocative points to make. His version of 'Snake Rag', for instance, points up the crossover between early jazz and ragtime with startling clarity, as well as underlining how ragtime *had* to turn itself into jazz. The few later pieces, such as a terrific version of 'Wa Wa Wa' (from the Dixie Syncopators' repertoire), are a valuable addendum to the basic list, and Ashman and Emberson embellish (to no special advantage) on eight tracks; but once again the record runs aground on its sameness, for all the energy and dedication on show.

*****(*) Charleston Mad**
Stomp Off CD1324 *Dickie (p); Martin Wheatley(bj, g).* 6–7/96.

*****(*) Don't Forget To Mess Around**
Stomp Off CD1341 *Dickie; Alex Revell (cl); Martin Wheatley (bj).* 8/98–1/99.

Dickie and producer Bob Erdos have been shrewd in varying the settings for his sometimes steamrollering style. It's hard to imagine anyone wanting all of his records, but each of them has bountiful rewards, and this latest pair might be his best – although the usual Stomp Off generosity (these two are 77:00 and 77:52 respectively!) can be a bit exhausting. *Charleston Mad* arose out of the idea to do numbers by the classic (female) blues singers of the vaudeville era, and there are some terrific obscurities along with more familiar tunes. Dickie essays his customary striding for much of the disc, but he tempers the momentum with barrelhousing of a less pugilistic sort, and there is the excellent Wheatley, who underscores (and solos) with banjo or guitar on ten tracks.

Don't Forget To Mess Around re-creates the Armstrong repertoire of the '20s. Dickie is obviously at home on fast, stomping tunes like 'Struttin' With Some Barbecue' but the record is cleverly paced, with Revell and Wheatley adding piquancy in their several walk-on roles. Dickie will never tap into any kind of delicacy, but on a tune such as 'I'm Goin' Huntin'' at least he tricks a certain daintiness out of his right-hand figures. It's merry music.

***** Never Heard Of Such Stuff!**
Stomp Off CD 1397 *Dickie; Norman Emberson (d).* 4/03.

This isn't the first time a CD has been specifically devoted to Fats Waller's rarer material – Stomp Off themselves have done it before with Marty Grosz's *Unsaturated Fats*, and that one was better than this. Dickie's difficulty is that many of Waller's lesser-known tunes are unfamiliar for the good reason that they're not up to his best, and while Neville strides through the programme with his usual enthusiasm, a long CD is pushing it a bit. Still, there are a few genuinely attractive rarities here, which receive a suitable elevation.

Danny D'Imperio (born 1945)

DRUMS

Veteran New York-area drummer, dedicated to hardcore hard bop and leading groups, whose style is unflinching and straight to the point. Much big-band experience, culminating in a tour with the Buddy Rich band after the leader's death.

***** Danny D'Imperio Sextet**

VSOP 71 *D'Imperio; Steve Lampert (t); Andy Fusco (as); Ralph Lalama (ts); Mike Pellera (p); Chuck Bergeron (b).* 5/88.

****** Blues For Philly Joe**

VSOP 81 *D'Imperio; Greg Gisbert (t); Gary Pribek (as); Ralph Lalama (ts); Hod O'Brien (p); Steve Brown (g); Dave Shapiro (b).* 9/91.

*****(*) Hip To It**

VSOP 86 *As above, except add Jimmy Johns (tb), Andy Fusco (as); omit Pribek.* 10/92.

*****(*) Glass Enclosure**

VSOP 96 *D'Imperio; Andy Gravish (t); Gary Pribek (as); Ralph Lalama (ts); Hod O'Brien (p); Steve Brown (g); Dave Shapiro (b).* 9/91.

*****(*) The Outlaw**

Sackville SKCD2-3060 *D'Imperio; Greg Gisbert, Andy Gravish (t); Chris Persad (flhn); Gary Pribek (as); Ralph Lalama, John Rohde (ts); Joe Carello (bs); Hod O'Brien (p); Dave Shapiro (b); Steve Brown (perc).* 8/94–8/96.

Superbly accomplished hard bop without frills, bluster or wasted space, despite the repertorial tunes and long running-times. D'Imperio originally called the band the Metropolitan Bopera House but got into a famous spat with the Met itself and had to stand down. The bruising quality of the music suggests that he couldn't have given up without a fight. Each set-list admits no originals, just classic or neglected set-pieces from the golden years of hard bop, and the band, in whichever incarnation, plays the hell out of them. The individual soloists have their standout moments, although Gisbert, then virtually unknown, makes a remarkable appearance on *Blues For Philly Joe* and Lalama is consistently fine across all five records. Away from any leadership or compositional duties, the horns seem entirely relaxed while still able to burn, and perhaps the most notable element is how crisp the ensemble work is: unison lines have the crisp intensity of great big-band section playing. With everything coming democratically from the past, the formula also lets obscurer pieces stand as tall as obvious chestnuts like 'Nica's Tempo'. D'Imperio himself is commanding without trying to take over: he keeps himself to fills and breaks and, if he seems entirely in thrall to Art Blakey (listen to how he drives the band on the Wayne Shorter arrangement of 'One By One' from *The Outlaw*), so be it. With no agenda beyond playing the music, the band actually sound more in keeping with this tradition than many a more self-consciously respectful unit.

Maybe the first record is a trifle routine, but by the time of the second the group sounds almost imperious. *Blues For Philly Joe* remains our favourite – for Gisbert, and for the beautiful studio sound – and we award it a token extra point; but the next three are almost as fine, and Gravish is a very exciting import on the most recent records.

***** Danny D'Imperio And The Bloviators**

Rompin' 045 *D'Imperio; Chris Persad (t); Gary Pribek (as); Ralph Lalama (ts); Joe Carello (bs); Dino Losito (p); Peter Mack (b).* 9/00.

***** Big Band Bloviation**

Rompin' 046 *D'Imperio; Dave Stahl, Greg Gisbert, Joe Magnarelli, Chris Persad, Glenn Drewes (t); John Mosca, Larry Farrell, Bruce Eidem (tb); Jim Daniels (btb); Joe Carello (as, f); Gary Pribek (as); Eric Alexander, John Rohde (ts); Barry Harris, Dino Losito (p); Peter Bernstein (g); Peter Mack (b).* 10/01.

Still out there, keeping the hard-bop flame, and now on a new label. The septet record is, surprisingly, a little disappointing, in part because the placid studio sound tames the spirit of the band and makes them sound like the very thing which D'Imperio has managed to avoid in the past, an everyday hard-bop group. There's still plenty to enjoy, with the usual set of vintage tunes (plus, shockingly, an original by Losito!), and the horns inevitably step out for some accomplished solos. The big band set sounds tougher, although again there's an unwonted hint of routine in performances which for once lose some of their impetus with the strings of solos. Even so, the three-trumpet chase on 'Three More Foxes', Eric Alexander on Wes Montgomery's 'Four On Six' and a grooving 'Adam's Apple' (by Alan Broadbent, not Wayne Shorter) are worthy flashpoints.

Gene DiNovi (born 1928)

PIANO

Worked with Lester Young and Benny Goodman, flirted with bebop in Joe Marsala's group and then came to the notice of Duke Ellington and Billy Strayhorn, of whom he became an accomplished interpreter. Later worked largely with singers before a belated renaissance as a solo star.

***** Renaissance Of A Jazz Master**

Candid 79708 *DiNovi; Terry Clarke (b); Dave Young (d).* 93.

***** Live At The Montreal Bistro**

Candid 79726 *As above.* 93.

The first Candid title says it all. DiNovi had been working for 52 years when this was made. There were earlier sets on Marshmallow, but these are pretty obscure. Unusually, no Ellington or Strayhorn in the set list, but a nice mix of familiar and less familiar standards, played with Gene's usual songful touch. 'Right As The Rain', by Harold Arlen and Yip Harburg, is something of a rarity, 'Bill' was originally a P. G. Wodehouse lyric and 'Have A Heart' was a collaboration between Gene and Johnny Mercer. Apart from these, he includes two originals, including 'Budding Memories', which has a boppish cast, and the gentle 'Elegy'. The other outstanding track, which taxes Clarke and Young a little, but productively, is John Carisi's also rarely covered 'Springsville'.

The live set was dedicated by DiNovi to drummer and composer Tiny Kahn who had recently passed away. 'Tiny's Blues' and 'TNT' are just two of the bright originals in a well-paced set that stays pretty much away from familiar standards. 'The Things We Did Last Summer' isn't too frequently performed in this context and DiNovi has the gift of delivering the song unexpectedly straight within an elaborate harmonic package. As before, Clarke and Young are stalwart supporters, but the emphasis is always and rightly on the piano man. A welcome return by a neglected figure.

***** Plays The Music Of Benny Carter**
Hep 2076 *DiNovi (p solo). 99.*

The value of Clarke and Young becomes most obvious when they aren't there. There's a slightly shapeless quality to DiNovi's solo performances, not because he's an undisciplined performer but rather because he tries to pack so much into a song like 'Blues In My Heart' that the structure seems in danger of falling apart. The other obvious tunes are included, with 'When Lights Are Low' a particular highlight. The piano sound is captured well, with lots of light and shade.

*****(*) Plays Duke Ellington And Billy Strayhorn**
Baldwin Street 205 *DiNovi; Dave Young (b). 02.*

Back at the Montreal Bistro, where each April, around Duke's birthday, DiNovi plays a residency devoted to the music of Ellington and Strayhorn. It's a wonderful idea and DiNovi's spoken introductions give the event and the CD a special cast. Working without a drummer, but with the all-important anchor provided by Dave Young, he sounds in great form. 'Isfahan' is meltingly beautiful, though played with more muscle than most horn players give it, and the two medleys, 'Chelsea Bridge/Warm Valley' and 'Single Petal Of A Rose/A Flower Is A Lovesome Thing' are impeccably constructed. 'Lady Mac' and 'Tomorrow Mountain' are less well known and all the more welcome for that. With any luck, a second volume is lurking in the wings somewhere.

Joe Diorio (born 1936)

GUITAR

A veteran modernist in jazz guitar, Diorio is a noted teacher and theorist who didn't get on record under his own name in a serious way until the '90s.

***** Double Take**
RAM RMCD 4502 *Diorio; Riccardo Del Frà (b). 4/92.*

*****(*) We Will Meet Again**
RAM RMCD 4501 *Diorio (g solo). 5/92.*

***** The Breeze And I**
RAM RMCD 4508 *Diorio; Ira Sullivan (f, af, ss, as, perc). 6/93.*

*****(*) More Than Friends**
RAM RMCD 514 *Diorio; Steve LaSpina (b); Steve Bagby (d). 6/93.*

He knows all the tunes, obviously loves them immoderately, but still manages always to impart a little personal spin and variation to even the most hackneyed warhorse standard. These recordings are all supremely elegant, affectionate and mainly thoughtful, and it is immensely difficult to draw qualitative distinctions between subtly different sessions. In our judgement, the duos with Mick Goodrick (listed under Goodrick's name) are less appetizing than the trio discs or the pairing with Sullivan, a player who trades up a limited stock of ideas by the sheer variety of sounds he can command on his horns. The other duo session, with Del Frà, is alternately exquisite and drab (two takes of 'Summertime' isn't quite gilding the lily). Like it, most of the sessions consist of standards, but graced with so much intelligence that almost all sound as if they have just been written. And then there are the unexpected coups, like 'The Summer Knows' on *The Breeze And I*, which jolt the whole thing into a new dimension. Diorio keeps going in and out of focus as a solo artist. This batch of reissues is a pretty good sample of the vintage, an artist who has a very personal take on harmonic improvisation (see his book, *Intervallic Designs*) and who has managed to reconcile it comfortably with straight chordal accompaniment, polyphonic ideas and some carefully selected aspects of free improvisation.

****** To Jobim With Love**
RAM 4529 *Diorio (g solo). 9/95.*

A delicious set of bossa classics preceded by Joe's short title tribute to the Brazilian master. All the usual suspects are there: a certain young lady from Ipanema, a night of quiet stars, a samba built round one note, and other sweetly melancholy tunes. Diorio's phrasing is effortlessly exact but manages to swing beautifully. Even when he appears to have minor problems of articulation, as on a couple of tracks, he covers with a wryly tolerant smile. Lovely stuff and a must for lovers of jazz guitar and bossa nova.

*****(*) I Remember You: A Tribute To Wes Montgomery**
RAM 4523 *Diorio; Steve LaSpina (b); Steve Bagby (d). 98.*

Joe apparently knew Wes and obviously knows the classic trios inside out. Given that Montgomery wasn't much of a composer, almost all the material here is repertory stuff, though the trio include some original things as well, notably 'The Two Faces Of Steve'. LaSpina is wonderful on his own 'When You're Away' and lays down a memorable solo. Bagby is superb on his brushes and the whole set reeks of class. The most appealing tracks, for both Wes and Joe fans, are the opening 'I Remember You' and a wonderfully prolonged version of 'In A Sentimental Mood'. Nice, crisp sound that combines a live feel with studio polish.

***** Stateside**
Diorio Jazz 1729 *Diorio; Bob Magnusson (b); Jim Plank (d). 00.*

Diorio hasn't found it easy to gain the interest of American labels, so this is a first issue on his own imprint. It follows the now familiar pattern of apparent predictability – eight fairly conventional standards – despatched with considerable invention. 'Alone Together' is a wonderful exercise in group co-ordination; Magnusson and Plank sound as if they've played this one with Joe dozens of times, but they're still finding new angles. 'Corcovado' is given an edgier quality than is usual, as is 'You And The Night And The Music'. But the album saves its greatest delight for last. Thad Jones's 'A Child Is Born' is a genuine modern classic and this is a definitive performance, close to perfection.

Mark Diorio

GUITAR

Breezy bop guitar with an idiosyncratic spin.

***** Once Upon A Guitar**
Zinnia 106 *Diorio (g solo). 99.*

It's testimony to Diorio's skill and vision that 15 unaccompanied pieces, compressed into not much more than three-quarters of an hour, pass by in what seems like a quarter of the time and yet leave the listener thirsting for more. Most of the pieces are very short, sometimes almost gnomic, but whether originals like 'Schleppfuss', the most substantial single piece, bop favourites like Tristano's 'All About You', Parker's 'Au Privave' and 'Billie's Bounce' (confidently medleyed) or standards like 'There Will Never Be Another You' they are played with considerable personality. Nicely recorded, too.

Mike DiRubbo (born 1970)

ALTO SAXOPHONE

Studied with Jackie McLean at the Hartt School of Music and still clings to that style of playing.

***** From The Inside Out**
Sharp Nine 1013 *DiRubbo; Steve Davis (tb); Bruce Barth (p); Nat Reeves (b); Carl Allen (d).* 10/94.

DiRubbo's debut cemented his Jackie-isms by teaming him with players who had worked with McLean. It's an influence lightly enough worn, though, and for this album Mike ranges more widely for his material. Sahib Shihab's 'Rue De La Harpe' is outstanding, a deceptively detailed line, and there is a nice version of Dizzy Gillespie's generic 'Bebop'. The original themes begin with the title track, which gets the set off to a brisk start, but one starts to sit up and take notice with the subtly paced 'Role Reversal' and 'Blues To Your Old Country', which features European chords within an expanded 12-bar format. Allen's drumming is, as ever, sharply on the money, and the relatively unusual front line of saxophone and trombone gives the set a distinctive timbre that guarantees most listeners will want to hear more of DiRubbo.

*****(*) Keep Steppin'**
Criss Cross 1205 *DiRubbo; Joe Rotondi (t); Mike LeDonne (p); Dwayne Burno (b); Joe Farnsworth (d).* 1/01.

*****(*) Human Spirit**
Criss Cross 1231 *As above; omit LeDonne, Burno; add David Hazeltine (p); Peter Washington (b).* 5/02.

DiRubbo gravitated as naturally to Criss Cross at the end of the '90s as he would have to Blue Note three decades earlier. His style is still firmly locked into that period of hard bop and in some respects this is a more straightahead set than its predecessor. The title track is very much in period and very effective on its own terms, building on the group awareness established on Mike LeDonne's opening 'Encounter', a fairly orthodox variation on familiar chord changes. 'Introspection' is in relaxed waltz time and the saxophonist's solo contains subtle nods to Stan Getz and Joe Henderson. LeDonne is usually the allusive one, and scarcely a chorus of his goes by without one or two sneaky tips of the hat to great and less celebrated piano players. McCoy Tyner's 'Sunset' is for saxophone and rhythm only and it's good to hear DiRubbo featured so prominently. He has a warm and emphatic tone, pitched lower than McLean and at times almost sounding like the middle register of a tenor saxophone.

That distinctive timbre is even more evident on the second Criss Cross date. The basic elements of the group sound are still in place and the replacement of LeDonne, such a crucial element on the first record, is handled seamlessly. Hazeltine favours a less allusive and less oblique approach, as can be heard on 'Minor March' and the intriguing 'Throwback'. DiRubbo's terse theme statements are again heard to good effect and his soloing goes from strength to strength. Another fine record by a rising star.

Bill Dixon (born 1925)

TRUMPET

A major figure in modern jazz, Dixon started out in music after leaving the military at the end of the Second World War. His first important associations were with Cecil Taylor and Archie Shepp, but in 1964 the trumpeter organized the October Revolution in Jazz, the New Thing's equivalent of the Armoury Show. He has been an important educator, largely at the Bennington College in Vermont.

***** 7-Tette/New York Contemporary Five**
Savoy Jazz 73008 *Dixon; Don Cherry, Ted Curson (t); Ken McIntyre (as, f); George Barrow, Archie Shepp (ts); Howard Johnson (bs, tba); Ronnie Boykins, David Izenzon (b); Sunny Murray (d).* 2/64.

This is Dixon's important first statement, released on the label he was helping to run, and paired here with a set by Archie Shepp's New York Contemporary Five, who claimed the second side of the original LP. Dixon's piece is the five-part 'Winter Song', a gently flowing, semi-abstract suite of ideas that are reminiscent in places of some of Mingus's late '50s pieces, but marked throughout by Dixon's melancholy lyricism and fine sense of structure. The Shepp material is worth having as well, though inevitably one wishes there were more material by both groups. Two alternate takes of 'Winter Song: Section III, Letter F' appear on the CD and add somewhat to our understanding of the genesis of the album, but it's still a thin representation of Dixon's work at this time.

****** Solo Works (Odyssey)**
no label/no number 6CD *Dixon (t solo, speech).* 70–90.

*****(*) Collection: Music for Solo Trumpet**
Cadence 3712 *Dixon; add Lawrence Cook, David Moss (perc).* 70–76.

Dixon's mellow tone, mournful delivery and preference for short, asymmetrical phrases sometimes recall Miles Davis. His is a very different line of development, though. These mostly lo-fi recordings are a valuable record of his progress as a solo performer. The box set, carefully compiled by the trumpeter himself and issued with examples of his fine artwork, is for specialists only but it's a rewarding experience, even at five hours' duration, for anyone interested in his self-determined and sometimes lonely career.

It's difficult to trace any obvious line of evolution from the earliest pieces – the tiny 'Mosaic', 'Albert Ayler' and longer 'Fortunata' from 1970 – to epic conceptions like 'Jerusalem' from 1990, which is one of the most important Dixon pieces currently available. Some of the pieces are dedicated to fellow-artists and friends, Booker Little in a gorgeous piece from 1975-6, 'For Wallace Thurman' and 'Umbra e Luce – For Sid Makay' both from 1973. Remarkably few come across merely as technical exercises, even when that is the presumed intention, and it's to Dixon's eternal credit that every piece, however shakily recorded, seems to have its own logic and purpose. The final disc consists of a valuable interview with the trumpeter, talking about his art, the vagaries of a career as a creative musician and the genesis of these beautiful, dramatic way-stations on his long artistic odyssey.

Realistically, most listeners will be satisfied with the Cadence set which includes much of this material on two rather brief CDs. The Little requiem, 'Mosaic', 'Albert Ayler' and the three part 'I See Your Fancy Footwork' are all there. Like the main set, it isn't an easy listen, as solo horn projects never are, but it's hugely satisfying.

***(*) Opium

Between the Lines btl 011 *Dixon; Franz Koglmann (flhn); Steve Lacy (ss); Stephen Horenstein (ts); Alan Silva (b); Aldo Romano (d); Gerd Geier (elec).* 74, 75.

This is not really a Dixon record, since he appears on only one track, but it helps to fill in an important missing part of his discography. These sessions were originally released on LP on Pipe Records and have only recently been issued on Koglmann's own label. 'For Franz' is Dixon's track and it is the best thing on the record. Dixon and the no less reticent Koglmann sound fine together and Alan Silva has always seemed to be one of the trumpeter's most sympathetic collaborators. The other tracks, all of which feature label boss Koglmann, are less exciting, though Steve Lacy collectors will welcome the return of material from *Flaps*.

*** Bill Dixon In Italy: Volume 1

Soul Note 121008 *Dixon; Arthur Brooks, Stephen Haynes (t); Stephen Horenstein (ts, bs); Alan Silva (b); Freddie Waits (d).* 7/80.

*** Bill Dixon In Italy: Volume 2

Soul Note 12011 *As above.* 7/80.

Having made a substantial mark with Cecil Taylor – notably on *Conquistador* – Dixon's own work seemed to languish during the '70s and it was only the enthusiasm of Giovanni Bonandrini (blessings rain on him) that gave the trumpeter an outlet commensurate with his gifts.

The 1980 disc – a studio recording despite what the title might imply – is very much in the Taylor line and the closing track on Volume 1 is dedicated to the pianist. Dixon doesn't feature himself that prominently, preferring to spread much of the higher voicing round the three-trumpet front line. Horenstein has an unenviable task trying to keep up and is much more effective when he switches to baritone, a role taken by Howard Johnson on the first LP. Remarkably these were only Dixon's third sessions as a leader in nearly twenty years.

**** November 1981

Soul Note 121038 *Dixon; Mario Pavone, Alan Silva (b); Laurence Cook (d).* 11/81.

*** Thoughts

Soul Note 121111 *As above; add Marco Eneidi (as); John Buckingham (tba); Peter Kowald, William Parker (b).* 5/85.

***(*) Sons Of Sisyphus

Soul Note 121138 *As above; omit Eneidi, Kowald, Parker.* 6/88.

November 1981 may be considered Dixon's small-group masterpiece, patiently conceived and executed, and generously proportioned. Dixon likes to build his ideas around silence, but these statuesque themes also use rich drones provided by the bass player (a device even more noticeable on *Thoughts*, which has three of them). As ever, the trumpet is used quite sparingly, with the opening 'Webern' (less than a minute and a half) there to underline his use of the *Klangfarbenmelodie* device whereby different instruments play different parts of the line and in which timbre and colour are structural principles and not just decoration. Music as concentrated as 'Penthesilea' or the 'Llaattiinnoo Suite', performed live, requires certain adjustments of musical expectation, but they are consistently satisfying and Bonandrini provides a generous, albeit intimate, sound which suits Dixon very well indeed.

Pavone and Cook survive from the earlier group, but *Thoughts* lacks its impact and drifts off into inconsequential and sometimes pretentious ramblings (for which, see 'For Nelson and Winnie: A Suite in Four Parts', which sounds like random studio ideas cobbled together to meet an important public moment). Again, Dixon's playing is at a discount, though by now it is clear that it is as important when he is not playing as when he is. Listeners familiar with his approach will be aware of familiar techniques, different air pressures through the horn, subtle dynamics and, always, an imaginative structural use of silence.

Sons Of Sisyphus (the title refers to an earlier, large-scale composition) is superior in almost every regard. It begins with a brooding duo for bass and Dixon on piano. 'Silences For Jack Moore' is a threnody for a dancer friend, always an important source of inspiration for Dixon, cast in the familiar bass range he favours. The sonorities are even darker on the long title-tracks, where Buckingham's tuba fills the role accorded the trio of bassists on *Thoughts*. The overriding impression is of space and movement and there's a sense in which Dixon's melancholically graceful soloing follows Cecil Taylor's much-quoted assertion that his own improvisations imitate the leaps that a dancer makes in space. As before, the cover features one of Dixon's own canvases, an abstraction based on an intelligently restricted palette.

*** Vade Mecum

Soul Note 121208 *Dixon; Barry Guy, William Parker (b); Tony Oxley (d).* 8/93.

***(*) Vade Mecum II

Soul Note 121211 *As above.* 96.

*** Papyrus

Soul Note 121308 *Dixon; Tony Oxley (d).* 9/00.

*** Papyrus: Volume 2

Soul Note 121338 *As above.* 9/00.

Inside almost all of Dixon's small group recordings, there is a dark pressure, like the imprint of a much larger composition that has been denied full expression. That is profoundly evident on *Vade Mecum*, which begins Dixon's association with British percussionist Tony Oxley. It might be argued that both Oxley and compatriot Guy are too 'strong' in conception to conform easily to Dixon's exceptionally disciplined approach, and there is a hint that this may have resulted in conflict when one finds Oxley's role dismissed as 'background' on the later duo records. The two bassists take very different parts: Parker is sonorous and inward, while Guy, possibly playing a chamber bass in places, flitters rapidly and sometimes sounds as if he's being played at double speed. 'Anamorphosis' on the first record is one of Dixon's most thoughtful conceptions, but if anything the second disc is a more coherent and cogent representation of what this remarkable group was capable of.

We've wrestled with the Dixon/Oxley duos long enough to be able to say honestly that we don't quite know what to make of the relationship. There are certainly moments when trumpeter and percussionist seem to be working on different ideas and possibly playing at different times. And yet, there is such a stirring thoughtfulness to Dixon's spacious solo lines that the logic carries each piece forward to a satisfactory conclusion.

*** Berlin Abbozzi

FMP CD 110 *Dixon; Matthias Bauer, Klaus Koch (b); Tony Oxley (d).* 7/00.

Again, Dixon experiments with this quartet formation and again the impression is of players working at some remove from each other, or rather that Dixon works at some distance from the ensemble. His horn lines are as open and gnomic as ever, though there is a quality to the sound which is new, possibly a studio artefact and certainly not a desirable one. Bauer and Koch are sometimes in the way, of each other if not of Dixon and Oxley, who seem to reprise the same slightly guarded and touchy relationship one hears on *Papyrus*. The long suite which constitutes the main element of the programme is based on melodic ideas, resonant pedal points and slow, softly shifting accompaniments that have run through Dixon's work since the '60s.

Marcio Doctor (born 1965)

PERCUSSION

Born in Buenos Aires, Doctor came to Europe in 1989 after a successful touring career with Comedia. He studied percussion with Mark Nauseef and others and combines a variety of ethnic styles. Restless World is one of several affiliations. He is currently percussionist with the NDR Big Band in Germany.

*** Restless World

Provocateur PVC 1024 *Doctor; Christof Lauer (as, ts); members of NDR Big Band.* 01.

Doctor's European debut is remarkably conventional. Billed as 'music for winds and percussion' it explores exotic grooves in much the way an Ellington band might have dabbled in unfamiliar time signatures. 'Restless World' itself is a rousing and exhilarating rallying call for Doctor's kind of pan-global music, but its roots seem firmly laid in jazz's ongoing tension between 4/4 and 6/8. 'Primal Soils' is more atmospheric. Lauer is as strong-voiced and expressive as ever, but it's Doctor's own sharply intelligent and rigorously sustained percussion which catches the ear on Restless World. Perhaps we'll have a chance to hear him soon in a small-group context.

Baby Dodds (1898–1959)

DRUMS, VOCAL

Johnny's brother was playing drums at sixteen and developing great showmanship. With King Oliver in 1922, then in Chicago for 20 years, before playing in New York with Bunk Johnson. Exemplifying the New Orleans style while remaining at a tangent from it, Dodds finally slowed down in the '50s when suffering a series of strokes.

(****) Baby Dodds

American Music AMCD-17 *Dodds; Bunk Johnson, Louis 'Kid Shots' Madison, Wooden Joe Nicholas (t); Jim Robinson, Joe Petit (tb); George Lewis, Albert Burbank (cl); Adolphe Alexander Jr (bhn); Isidore Barbarin (ahn); Lawrence Marrero (bj); Red Clark, Sidney Brown (tba); Alcide 'Slow Drag' Pavageau (b).* 44–45.

One of the best examples of living history in the catalogue, *Baby Dodds* features the leading drummer of New Orleans jazz talking at some length about his traps, his cymbals, his style and how it all comes together – for jazz bands, marching bands, funeral parades and whatever else a drummer had to play for. Most of the music is actually lifted from other records, notably Bunk Johnson's American Music CDs, but this is the place to hear Baby's history lesson. Some of it is horse sense that still holds good – 'Tiger Rag is played too fast,' he grumbles, and then we hear the tempo he liked to play for it – and when he talks us through a lesson in technique, the good-natured generosity of the man comes alive again, four decades after his death. Remastering of all the speech/drum tracks is excellent, and though the music comes in mainly for illustration the compilers have chosen some fine slices of New Orleans to go with the talk.

***(*) Jazz A La Creole

GHB BCD-50 *Dodds; Albert Nicholas (cl); Don Ewell, James P. Johnson, Don Kirkpatrick (p); Danny Barker (g); Pops Foster, Haywood Henry (b); Freddy Moore, Johnny Williams (d).* 1/46–6/47.

Although Baby's style is all over this CD, he actually appears on only nine of the 18 tracks. Priceless are the two 'Drum Improvisation' pieces, where he demonstrates the full range of his kit and what a New Orleans man could and should do with it. There are trio pieces with Ewell and Nicholas, a piano/drums duet, and a single track where Danny Barker and Pops Foster join Baby. Otherwise there are pieces which feature Nicholas alongside James P. Johnson and four Creole songs where Danny Barker takes the lead. All of these numbers come from the very earliest days of Rudi Blesh's Circle label, and the sleevenotes include Blesh's reminiscences of how the initiative came into being. There seem to be quite a few audio problems with the original masters, but listeners should put up with that and tune in to some very deep music, full of Louisiana spirit, even when it was being set down in New York City.

Johnny Dodds (1892–1940)

CLARINET, ALTO SAXOPHONE

Dodds and his brother Baby grew up in New Orleans and took the archetypal route north to Chicago, where jazz flourished in its new environment. Though he did take some lessons with Lorenzo Tio Jr, the clarinettist was mainly self-taught and this may account for some idiosyncrasies of technique, matters of articulation and pitching which, though not strictly correct, contributed very considerably to Dodds's distinctive sound on a blues. He was one of the great early soloists of jazz.

**** Johnny Dodds 1926

Classics 589 *Dodds; Freddie Keppard, George Mitchell (c); Kid Ory, Eddie Vincent (tb); Junie Cobb (cl); Joe Clark (as); Lockwood Lewis (as, v); Lil Hardin Armstrong, Jimmy Blythe, Arthur Campbell, Tiny Parham (p); Curtis Hayes, Cal Smith, Freddy Smith (bj); Eustern Woodfork, Johnny St Cyr (bj, v); Clifford Hayes (vn); W. E. Burton (wbd, v); Earl McDonald (jug, v); Jimmy Bertrand, Jasper Taylor (d, perc); Papa Charlie Jackson, Trixie Smith (v).* 5–12/26.

****** Johnny Dodds 1927**

Classics 603 *Dodds; Freddie Keppard (c); Eddie Ellis (tb); Lil Hardin Armstrong, Jimmy Blythe, Tiny Parham (p); Jasper Taylor (d); Baby Dodds (wbd).* 1–10/27.

****** Johnny Dodds 1927–8**

Classics 617 *Dodds; Natty Dominique, George Mitchell (c); R. Q. Dickerson (t); Honoré Dutrey, Kid Ory, John Thomas (tb); Charlie Alexander, Jimmy Blythe (p); Bud Scott (bj); Bill Johnson (b); Baby Dodds (d); W. E. Burton (wbd, v); Julia Davis (v).* 10/27–7/28.

***** Johnny Dodds 1928–40**

Classics 635 *Dodds; Natty Dominique, Herb Morand (c); Charlie Shavers (t); Honoré Dutrey, Preston Jackson (tb); Charlie Alexander, Lil Hardin Armstrong, Jimmy Blythe, Richard M. Jones, Frank Melrose (p); Teddy Bunn, Lonnie Johnson (g); Junie Cobb (g, v); Bill Johnson, John Kirby, John Lindsay (b); O'Neil Spencer (d, wbd, v); Baby Dodds (d, wbd).* 7/28–5/40.

***** 1926-1929: The Alternative Takes**

Neatwork RP 2012 *As for Classics above.* 26-29.

****** Johnny Dodds & Jimmy Blythe, 1926–1928**

Timeless CBC 015 *Dodds; Louis Armstrong, Natty Dominique, Freddie Keppard (t); Punch Miller (c); Roy Palmer (tb); Jimmy Blythe (p); Bud Scott (bj); Jimmy Bertrand (wbd); W. E. Burton (wbd, v); Jasper Taylor (d, wbd); Trixie Smith (v).* 5/26–3/28.

*****(*) New Orleans Stomp**

Frog DGF39 *Dodds; Louis Armstrong (c, t); Natty Dominique, George Mitchell (c); James Tate (t); Fayette Williams, Roy Palmer, John Thomas (tb); Stump Evans (as, bs); Norval Morton, Barney Bigard (ts); Lovie Austin, Teddy Weatherford, Lil Hardin Armstrong, Earl Hines, Charlie Alexander (p); Johnny St Cyr, Bud Scott (bj); John Hare (tba); Jimmy Bertrand (d, wbd); Baby Dodds (d).* 3/26–10/27.

Johnny Dodds was the model professional musician. He rehearsed his men, frowned on alcohol and drugs, and watched the cents. In 1922 he was a member of King Oliver's Creole Jazz Band at Lincoln's Garden in Chicago, the band that included Louis Armstrong, Lil Hardin Armstrong, trombonist Honoré Dutrey, and Dodds's wayward younger brother, Warren 'Baby' Dodds. The clarinettist left in 1924, after a quarrel about money, and set out on a highly successful recording career of his own that faltered only with the beginnings of the swing boom. Dodds died in 1940 and was promptly canonized by the revivalists.

His tone was intense and sometimes fierce, rather removed from the soft introspections of Jimmie Noone or George Lewis's folksy wobble. Like Jimmy Giuffre two generations later, Dodds favoured the lower – chalumeau – register of the instrument in preference to the piercing *coloratura.* He doubles briefly on alto saxophone on July 1926 cuts (Timeless CD above) with Jimmy Blythe. The switch may have been an attempt to get some change out of Paramount's insensitive microphones for, unlike Sidney Bechet, Dodds never seriously considered a full turn to the saxophones.

Though much of his most renowned work was with Louis Armstrong's Hot Five and Seven, the Classics compilations are the essential Dodds documents. They contain work for Brunswick, Columbia, Gennet, the ropey Paramount, Victor and Vocalion. The real classics are the cuts made for Columbia with the New Orleans Wanderers/Bootblacks, a line-up that included George Mitchell, Kid Ory, Joe Clark, Johnny St Cyr and Lil Hardin Armstrong. There are fine clarinet duets with Junie Cobb (and without brass) from 26 August 1926 which have been rather overlooked in the rush of enthusiasm for the Wanderers/Bootblacks performances of the previous month. Inevitably, very little matches up to these classics, but Dodds's reconciliation with King Oliver in September for a single track ('Someday Sweetheart') underlines the great might-have-been of their interrupted association. Dodds by this time was making too much regular money in Burt Kelly's Stables, a South Side club much frequented by Italian businessmen (if you follow), to pursue or accept a longer recruitment. A pity, because there's a definite falling-off after 1926. The duets with Tiny Parham are interesting, and there are excellent things on the Vocalion trios of April 1927; too many pick-up bands, though, and on a lot of the material Dodds is overpowered by other voices, notably Louis Armstrong (in for a Black Bottom Stompers session that also included Barney Bigard and Earl Hines) and Jelly Roll Morton. The Classics format omits the two Morton tracks but does reinstate a number, 'Cootie Stomp', from the State Street Ramblers session of August 1927 and includes a rare June 1928 session with the vocalist Julia Davis (allegedly half her entire recorded output) and trumpeter R. Q. Dickerson. The 1927–8 disc does, though, include some of the material excerpted on *Blue Clarinet Stomp*, below. The final Classics volume ends with a bit of a rush and there really isn't much in it that even those who love Dodds's music will greatly treasure, beyond a trio 'Indigo Stomp' with Lil Hardin Armstrong and Bill Johnson from February 1929 – although the 1938 session with the young Shavers includes one quite beautiful piece in '29th And Dearborn'.

We're ambivalent about the Neatwork volumes, which at best are only likely to be of interest to the serious collector and share the usual problems of Classics sound-quality, though there are signs that this has been addressed. There are some good things here, of course, starting with the very early 'What A Man' with Teddy Peters and an unknown pianist from March 1926, and a raucous 'Salty Dog' with Freddie Keppard's Jazz Cardinals from September of that same year. Under his own name, the best things are a test pressing of 'Blue Clarinet Stomp' (slightly slower than expected) from 1928 and another Victor test of 'Indigo Stomp' with Lil Hardin and Bill Johnson from February 1929.

While the Classics discs remain the most comprehensive, they are steadily being overtaken by other issues. The Timeless and Frog compilations cover the same ground in different permutations. *New Orleans Stomp* is particularly attractive – excellent sound, and though these aren't the sessions which really find Dodds at his best, there are some rarities to tempt collectors: the swinging Teddy Peters vocal record of 'What A Man!', the alternative takes of the Lil's Hot Shots and Black Bottom Stompers sessions, and the Erskine Tate date with Armstrong where Dodds's presence is uncertain. Neither disc will disappoint anyone who isn't interested in following the Classics sequence right through to its heartbreakingly banal end with the feeble 1940 session. The personnel and dates attached to each disc are the best guide to possible overlaps.

***** Paramount Recordings**

Black Swan BSCD 32 *Dodds; Natty Dominique, Freddie Keppard, Tommy Ladnier (c); Kid Ory, Eddie Vincent (tb);*

Lovie Austin, Jimmy Blythe, Arthur Campbell, Tiny Parham (p); Blind Blake (g); Eustern Woodfork (bj); Jasper Taylor (perc); Jasper Taylor (wbd); Buddy Burton (wbd, v); W. E. Burton (d); Baby Dodds (d, wbd); Viola Bartlette, Edmonia Henderson, Charlie Jackson, Elzadie Robinson, Trixie Smith, Henry Williams (v). 10/24–12/27.

A collection of oddments from the Paramount label, almost all of them recorded under other leaders, often singers. The earliest of them is a session with Edmonia Henderson, back in October 1924. Sometimes this was exactly what brought out the best in the clarinettist, as in his dazzling solo behind Lovie Austin on the August 1926 session, when he turns 'Chicago Mess Around' into a miniature epic. Three tracks recorded the next year feature Dodds in a happy-sounding duo with Tiny Parham; '19th Street Blues' and 'Loveless Love' are well worth savouring. Many of the personnels listed are best guesses, since Paramount's ledgers were all destroyed during the Depression, but for the most part these sound accurate and are consistent with known activity. Not much more than a footnote on the Dodds story, but a valuable purchase for collectors of early Chicago jazz.

*****(*) Blue Clarinet Stomp**

Frog DGF 3 *Dodds; Natty Dominique (c); Honoré Dutrey (tb); Charlie Alexander, Lil Hardin Armstrong (p); Bill Johnson (b); Baby Dodds (d, wbd).* 7/28–2/29.

There are several things which make the Frog desirable: having the Victor sessions together, having them relatively untinkered with, and having the (seemingly) correct discographical story of 'Pencil Papa' for which dates and sessions seem to have been transposed. All to the good. Collectors will be satisfied; newcomers can feel they have a reasonable sampling of the classic material; and the remastering is top-notch. Dodds is one of those jazzmen who may be in danger of slipping into history, and a reissue as meticulous as this does play its part in keeping a crucial memory of early jazz alive.

Chris Minh Doky (born 1969)

DOUBLE BASS

Younger brother of Niels Lan Doky, Chris learned music at home and at the Royal Danish Conservatory before taking up bass. Moved to the US in 1989 and played extensively on the fringes of jazz before signing to Blue Note. He has also recorded with his brother.

***** Cinematique**

Blue Note 26121 *Doky; Joey Calderazzo, Larry Goldings (org); Makoto Ozone (p); Toots Thielemans (hca); Clarence Penn, Bill Stewart, Jeff Tain Watts (d).* 02.

An intriguing idea to record with three very different trios and to do the sessions in 'live' form, with just single takes crammed into two hours of studio time for each line-up. The 'New York' trio of Calderazzo and Watts is high-energy, that with Larry Goldings and Bill Stewart more laid-back and reflective and the third configuration, Ozone and Penn and piano instead of organ, a hybrid of the two. Ozone interestingly began his career on Hammond and only later switched to piano. Whether it's reflected in his touch or not is a matter for conjecture, but the album's emphasis is clear. Chris has assembled some intriguing material to reflect the different characters of his constituent trios, but it's a measure of the album's slightly anonymous character that the show is stolen comprehensively by Thielemans's guest spot on 'Goldfinger'.

Niels Lan Doky (born 1963)

PIANO

Of Danish–Vietnamese parentage, Doky started on guitar and switched to piano at 12. Went to the USA and Berklee in 1978 and settled in New York afterwards. Has recorded for Storyville, Milestone and Blue Note, and is now signed to Verve. Also produces a wide range of other jazz artists.

*****(*) Here Or There**

Storyville STCD 4117 *Doky; Niels-Henning Orsted Pedersen (b); Alvin Queen (d).* 1/86.

***** The Target**

Storyville STCD 4140 *Doky; Niels-Henning Orsted Pedersen (b); Jack DeJohnette (d).* 11/86.

*****(*) The Truth**

Storyville STCD 4144 *Doky; Bob Berg (ts); Bo Stief (b); Terri Lyne Carrington (d).* 6/87.

***** Daybreak**

Storyville STCD 4160 *Doky; John Scofield (g); Niels-Henning Orsted Pedersen (b); Terri Lyne Carrington (d).* 9/88.

*****(*) Close Encounter**

Storyville STCD 4173 *Doky; Gary Peacock (b); Alex Riel (d).* 7/89.

Doky's early records might have created more of a stir than they did and, looking back at them even now, this already seems like his best and most undervalued work. He plays with dazzling fluency, has a biting, percussive touch, relishes fast tempos and has a decisive, linear manner. He writes terrific riff tunes, too. Storyville's five albums are all strong examples of what he can do, brusquely recorded to show off his sound. While there's little to choose among the three trio dates, all of which are made up of originals plus a favourite standard or two, we've given the edge to the debut record for the sheer excitement that seems to energize every minute of the music. *The Truth*, a live session, loses some immediacy over the course of four long pieces, but it's an accomplished quartet, even if Berg's occasionally faceless tenor isn't an ideal match. *Daybreak* adds Scofield's dependably handsome guitar to the proceedings, and 'Jet Lag' and 'Natural' find Doky's writing at its wittiest.

***** Paris By Night**

Soul Note 121206-2 *Doky; Randy Brecker (t); Christian Minh Doky (b); Daniel Humair (d).* 2/92.

Something of a holding operation, this on-the-hoof live date from Paris is nothing more or less than an accomplished blow on some jazz standards, with Brecker in firm voice, and the brothers displaying their usual seamless drive.

**** Haitek Haiku**

Emarcy 548410-2 *Doky; Gino Vannelli (v).* 00.

Doky's '90s music has now largely left the catalogue, and this effort for Emarcy seems to remain as his only surviving album from his tenure with Emarcy/Verve. It's a disappointment. Not very *haiku*-like at all, this keyboard noodling is an indulgence. What next?

Eric Dolphy (1928–64)

ALTO SAXOPHONE, BASS CLARINET, FLUTE, CLARINET

Born in Los Angeles, Dolphy made his first recordings with the bebop-based Roy Porter band as early as 1949. His own recording career, though, was packed into just four hectic years. A definitive multi-instrumentalist, Dolphy pioneered use of the bass clarinet as a solo improvising instrument. His Parker-derived alto saxophone was strongly identified with advances in post-bop harmony, but Dolphy was also involved in the jazz/classical synthesis of the Third Stream. Much of his best work as performer and arranger was in the company of John Coltrane and Charles Mingus, and there was clearly a reciprocal influence in both cases. Unable to find sufficient challenging work in the United States, and anxious to prove himself before his forthcoming marriage, Dolphy travelled Europe as a 'single' but died of undiagnosed diabetes in Berlin. Though much loved, he remains a classic outsider whose real impact is only slowly being assimilated.

*** Outward Bound

Original Jazz Classics OJCCD 022 *Dolphy; Freddie Hubbard (t); Jaki Byard (p); George Tucker (b); Roy Haynes (d).* 4/60.

Since his tragically premature death, Eric Dolphy has acquired an almost saintly reputation. His generosity of spirit is well attested by almost everyone who ever worked with him, and in his short performing and recording career he worked with Charles Mingus and John Coltrane, as well as with Oliver Nelson, Ron Carter and Ken McIntyre.

Dolphy's mastery of alto saxophone is undoubted, a sound and idiom that marked a definite step forward from the prevailing Charlie Parker style, but combining elements of Ornette Coleman's radicalism as well. What makes him unique, though, is the ability to improvise with equal ease on the seemingly unwieldy bass clarinet, the first player to give it a convincing solo voice, and to a somewhat lesser extent on flute. His debut as leader also found him playing straight clarinet as well.

It was to be more than a decade after his studio debut with Roy Porter before Dolphy made a record of his own. *Outward Bound* was taped on April Fool's Day, 1960. Dolphy had been working in the band of another drummer, Chico Hamilton, and it's thought that bassist George Tucker arranged the session which led to this disc. By later standards it's a fairly cautious initiative and, if Dolphy had never made anything else, it seems unlikely that he would have been regarded as anything other than a footnote to bebop, and perhaps a bystander in the revolution of the early '60s. However, there are enough points of interest to suggest that something interesting was happening.

'G.W.' is dedicated to the Californian bandleader, Gerald Wilson, who had taught Dolphy something about arranging. It's in an unorthodox, slightly top-heavy form. '245', apparently the number of Dolphy's house, is an equally heterodox blues, while 'Les', named for trombonist Lester Robinson, is a 14-bar theme which establishes an unsettling harmonic tension between melody-line and accompaniment. Dolphy's bass clarinet is heard on 'Miss Toni' and 'On Green Dolphin Street', and his flute on 'Glad To Be Unhappy' and, while all three are confident, even original, there's not yet the alienating originality that was to come later.

Hubbard's role is interesting, not least because he was to appear much later on Dolphy's epoch-making *Out To Lunch!*, but there are signs already that the band don't quite understand what the leader is about. The new edition includes three alternates: nothing revelatory, but meat and drink to Dolphy admirers

**(*) Other Aspects

Blue Note CDP 7 48041 *Dolphy; Ron Carter (b); Gina Lalli (tabla); Roger Mason (tamboura); other musicians unidentified.* 7/60–62.

The tapes represented here were kept for almost 20 years by Dolphy's close friends, Juanita and Hale Smith, when he left for Europe to work with Charles Mingus. After his death in Berlin, they remained in Hale Smith's care, and it was only after a memorial concert in 1985 that they were unearthed and considered for release.

It remains unclear whether Dolphy himself ever saw these five performances, of which he named only two, 'Jim Crow' and 'Improvisations And Tukras', as being suitable for commercial release. They were, however, studio performances and the sound is certainly more than adequate. The most substantial piece is the 15-minute 'Jim Crow', on which Dolphy plays all three of his horns over a backing of piano, bass, percussion and a strangely affecting female vocal, obviously intended to recall a mournful spiritual, but with the same Indian cast as the flute 'Improvisations And Tukras'. Two pieces now known as 'Inner Flight #1 & 2' are also for flute, albeit much less convincingly voiced, and 'Dolphy-N' is a duet with Carter. Whoever the bassist is on the November 1960 session, it certainly *isn't* Carter and, though some circumstances and some aspects of the sound point to its being George Duvivier, there is no way of confirming this.

In a sense, the provenance doesn't matter. These are candid snapshots of a master musician caught at the point of creative take-off in his career. Even if they are less than wholly satisfying, they add to a disconcertingly small and compressed discography, and one can see why Blue Note, who were responsible for Dolphy's one acknowledged masterpiece, wanted to release them.

***(*) Out There

Original Jazz Classics OJCCD 023 *Dolphy; Ron Carter (clo); George Duvivier (b); Roy Haynes (d).* 8/60.

This is where the promise begins to pay dividends. Since recording *Outward Bound*, Dolphy had appeared on five albums under the leadership of Charles Mingus, Oliver Nelson and Ken McIntyre, and he was to work with John Lewis, Eddie 'Lockjaw' Davis, Mingus again, Abbey Lincoln, Gunther Schuller, his stylistic nemesis Ornette Coleman and even the Latin Jazz Quintet before the year was over. Of them all, it was to be Mingus and Coleman who exerted the greatest influence, though Dolphy also had an important role in Schuller's 'Third Stream' experiments.

It's Mingus who lurks in the background of *Out There*. Dolphy's decision to dispense with piano and replace it with Ron Carter's cello might well have been inspired by Nathan Gershman in the Chico Hamilton group, but the language is much closer to what Mingus was doing at the time, the tonal centre pitched low. 'Eclipse' was one of the very first Mingus compositions to be picked up by another bandleader, and it affords a rare glimpse of Dolphy playing a regular, concert-pitched clarinet. The E-flat blues, 'Serene', is outwardly about as conventional as anything he ever did, but already Dolphy is hearing new and unexpected dimensions to chords and is experimenting with unconventionally subdivided structures, as on the title-track and the modified 12-bar blues, '7 West'.

As with its predecessor, *Out There* was issued with a drably surreal cover obviously intended to suggest that Dolphy and his music were pretty wacky. One suspects that most potential purchasers who hadn't heard of his reputation wouldn't have been buying on the strength of the cover.

** Caribe

Original Jazz Classics OJCCD 819 *Dolphy; Gene Casey (p); Charlie Simons (vib); Bill Ellington (b); Manny Ramos (d, perc); Juan Amalbert (perc).* 8/60.

It's come to something when even the record company makes apologies about the music inside. The Latin Jazz Quintet was a south-of-the-border, poor man's MJQ. Though hardly in John Lewis's league, Casey was a pretty decent bop pianist and the session is confident if scarcely effortful or particularly involving. One wonders why, other than the chance of a paying gig, Dolphy was drawn to it. The only other explanation is some ancestral loyalty to Caribbean music; Dolphy's father was intensely proud of his Panamanian origins.

As might be expected, Dolphy Jr devotes himself mainly to alto and flute, with the bass clarinet featuring only briefly on 'First Bass Line', and there it has a rather functional role. The two flute numbers, 'Sunday Go Meetin'' and 'Spring Is Here', are quite delicately shaded, and there are flashes of invention on 'Blues In 6/8' and the title-track. Otherwise, this is a fallow episode. Confusingly, Dolphy recorded with another, entirely different group known as the Latin Jazz Quintet less than a year later, a mostly standards set which was released on United Artists, but which has never (as far as we are aware) appeared on CD.

**** Far Cry

Original Jazz Classics OJCCD 400 *Dolphy; Booker Little (t); Jaki Byard (p); Ron Carter (b); Roy Haynes (d).* 12/60.

The week before Christmas 1960 was a quite astonishing one in Dolphy's career. On Tuesday, 20 December, he took part in Gunther Schuller's *Jazz Abstractions* project, taping two Third Stream pieces in the company of Ornette Coleman, Scott LaFaro, Bill Evans and Jim Hall. The following day he played in Ornette's ambitious double quartet, the sessions that were to yield one of the definitive statements of the jazz avant-garde, *Free Jazz.* The very same day, he went over the river to Hackensack, New Jersey, and recorded *Far Cry*, his one studio recording with the brilliant and ill-fated Booker Little.

Interestingly – and it's not clear whether he simply wanted to rework them or that he simply needed a couple of more familiar themes – he decided to re-record two items from *Out There.* The title-piece of the August album becomes the title-piece of this, tougher and boppish in style, while 'Serene' remains essentially the same, which is perhaps why it was dropped from the original release. Byard brought in two pieces which helped turn side one of the LP into an extended tribute to Dolphy's most obvious creative forerunner: 'Mrs Parker Of K.C. (Bird's Mother)' and 'Ode To Charlie Parker'.

The record is most remarkable for the first recorded appearance of what was to be Dolphy's most celebrated composition, 'Miss Ann', a delightful 14-bar theme that he was to play until the very end of his life. Little drops out for 'It's Magic', one of the first times one feels Dolphy is doing something really special on bass clarinet, and the whole band sits out 'Tenderly', leaving Dolphy to carve an astonishing, unaccompanied alto solo, a piece of work that bridges Coleman Hawkins's pioneering 'Picasso' and Dolphy's own later solo bass clarinet excursions on 'God Bless The Child', except that here the tune is still very much in evidence. Some have suggested that he was influenced by Sonny Rollins's unaccompanied 'Body And Soul', recorded just two years earlier. Doubtless he knew it, but whether the influence is direct and deliberate, coincidental or semi-conscious is difficult to tell.

**** At The Five Spot: Volume 1

Original Jazz Classics OJCCD 133 *Dolphy; Booker Little (t); Mal Waldron (p); Richard Davis (b); Ed Blackwell (d).* 7/61.

***(*) At The Five Spot: Volume 2

Original Jazz Classics OJCCD 247 *As above.* 7/61.

**** Memorial Album

Original Jazz Classics OJCCD 353 *As above.* 7/61.

Dolphy's working association with Little was to be tragically short-lived. The two-week residency at the Five Spot in New York was the group's major point of exposure, and it's immensely frustrating that only one night, 16 July 1961, was documented. It's often been suggested that this was a group in rapid transition, and it would be of immense value to document that happening, night on night.

Even so, the music that was recorded is exceptional. Interesting how often Dolphy albums are defined by unaccompanied performances, and the Five Spot dates include a first recorded outing for 'God Bless The Child', which was to become Dolphy's bass clarinet feature, a sinuous, untranscribable harmonic exercise that leaves the source material miles behind. Dolphy had recently recorded *The Quest* under Waldron's leadership and the pianist's two compositions, 'Fire Waltz' and 'Status Seeking'. Here Dolphy takes the initiative, roughening the texture of 'Fire Waltz' and suggesting a more joyous take on Waldron's typically dark writing. Little contributes 'Aggression', 'Booker's Waltz' and the splendid 'Bee Vamp', a tough, off-centre theme that was to fall only rather uncomfortably under the horn-player's fingers.

Perhaps the finest thing of all is Dolphy's own 'The Prophet', which was directed to Richard Jennings, who had designed those slightly half-baked covers for *Outward Bound* and *Out There.* It's also quite clearly an autobiographical piece, an insight into Dolphy's own quicksilver personality and forward-looking intelligence. No flute, incidentally, on these cuts, perhaps because Dolphy was becoming aware that the bass clarinet – and most particularly its unfettered soliloquy on 'God Bless The Child' – had become a voice of equal weight.

A mere matter of weeks after the Five Spot residency ended, Booker Little was dead, felled by uraemia. Speculation about what might have been is as fascinating as it is futile, but the thought that this group might have gone on and grown is hugely beguiling.

*** Berlin Concerts

Enja ENJ 3007 2CD *Dolphy; Benny Bailey (t); Pepsi Auer (p); Jamil Nasser (b); Buster Smith (d).* 8/61.

Less than three years after these (seemingly televised) performances from the Deutschlandshalle in Berlin, Dolphy was dead. They're poignant as a first sign of Dolphy 'going single', working the more open European scene with pick-up bands. This one was better than most, not just because Bailey's tense, boppish sound occasionally recalls Little, but also because Auer and Smith lean hard on the beat and push things along briskly. 'G.W.' is remarkably similar to the version on *Outward Bound*, Bailey tends to dominate on 'Hot House' (not surprisingly) and 'I'll Remember April', on which he is unsentimentally lyrical. He sits out 'When Lights Are Low' by namesake Benny Carter, and Dolphy thrives on the extra space. Even so, he sounds constrained on these tracks, not even opening up on the now obligatory 'God Bless The Child'. A curiosity, and a significant one in the foreshortened Dolphy canon, but certainly not one for casual buyers.

★★★(★) In Europe: Volume 1

Original Jazz Classics OJCCD 413 *Dolphy; Bent Axen (p); Chuck Israels, Erik Moseholm (b); Jorn Elniff (d).* 9/61.

★★★ In Europe: Volume 2

Original Jazz Classics OJCCD 414 *As above.*

★★★ In Europe: Volume 3

Original Jazz Classics OJCCD 416 *As above.*

★★★ Stockholm Sessions

Enja ENJ 3055 *Dolphy; Idrees Sulieman (t); Knud Jorgensen, Rune Ofwerman (p); Jimmy Woode (b); Sture Kalin (d).* 9/61.

The *In Europe* dates were recorded in Copenhagen two days apart in September 1961. We were probably too negative about these in previous editions. The Danish players are certainly not even close to Dolphy's standard, and clearly they don't understand his more advanced ideas, but they are all decent, time-served players and, while some of their accompaniments are callow in the extreme, they don't really seem to affect the blissfully tolerant Dolphy all that much. Two versions of 'Don't Blame Me' are taped on 6 September. Moseholm bungles his bass solo and Dolphy simply says, 'Let's try it again.' It's the drummer who makes a mess of 'When Lights Are Low', but there are no retakes, and Dolphy opts for the revised bridge popularized by Miles Davis, rather than Carter's original.

The second date, recorded in a more generous acoustic at the Studenterforeningens Foredragssal, a lecture theatre rather than a concert hall, is altogether better. 'Les' is played again, though for some reason it was mistitled 'Miss Ann' when the discs were first released. Dolphy seems content to settle back into the bebop idiom that the Danish players are comfortable with. 'Laura' is a tremendous alto performance, laced with Parker quotes; 'Oleo' is one of the most effective bass clarinet outings documented to this point, and this must be considered the definitive recording of 'God Bless The Child', Dolphy's innate creativity suddenly freed from the constraints of playing down and breaking loose in an extraordinary outpouring of ideas.

The other intriguing item from Copenhagen is a duet version of 'Hi Fly', recorded on flute and bass; Chuck Israels was in Scandinavia with the Jerome Robbins dance company and obviously came and sat in. The *Stockholm Sessions* were released much later. The Swedes are arguably more adventurous but technically less adept, and here and there Dolphy seems to be having problems with reed, mouthpiece or articulation. Perhaps he was simply tired. 'Miss Ann' is lacklustre, and even 'God Bless The Child' lacks the emotional clout he was bringing to it earlier in the month. These were the last recordings that Dolphy was to make for Prestige. It had been an important experience for him, though the circumstances of the final year suggest that he wasn't entirely at ease.

★★★ Here And There

Original Jazz Classics OJCCD 673 *Dolphy; Booker Little (t); Jaki Byard, Mal Waldron (p); Richard Davis, Erik Moseholm, George Tucker (b); Ed Blackwell, Jorn Elniff, Roy Haynes (d).* 1/60–8/61.

A rag-bag of oddments from the Prestige years. Most interesting is 'April Fool' from the session which yielded *Outward Bound*, a quartet track without Hubbard. 'Status Seeking' and 'Don't Blame Me' are also out-takes, and there is a version (almost inevitably) of 'God Bless The Child'. The total discography is thin enough to make any survivals interesting and worth having, but the appearance of the complete Prestige sessions renders this compilation pretty redundant.

★★★★ The Complete Prestige Recordings

Prestige 9PRCD 418 9CD *Dolphy; other personnel as for the above, plus Bobby Bryant, Clark Terry, Richard Williams (t); Jimmy Cleveland, Melba Liston (tb); Oliver Nelson (as); Ken McIntyre (as, f); Bob Ashton, Eddie 'Lockjaw' Davis, Jerome Richardson (ts); George Barrow (bs); Walter Bishop Jr, Richard Wyands (p); Joe Benjamin, Sam Jones, Wendell Marshall (b); Charli Persip, Art Taylor (d).* 4/60–9/61.

Dolphy's association with Prestige spanned the period 1 April 1960 to 8 September 1961, when he recorded the second of the Copenhagen sessions. During his contract, he made records under the leadership of Oliver Nelson, Ron Carter, Mal Waldron and, often forgotten, Eddie 'Lockjaw' Davis; the record with the Latin Jazz Quintet was also, strictly speaking, a sideman gig.

Screamin' The Blues was his first recording with Nelson, made in late May 1960. Dolphy played bass clarinet on the title-track but otherwise stuck to alto. Nelson plays tenor, except on 'Alto-itis', which is the best point of comparison for their work on the E-flat horn. This is fairly basic bebop material. On 23 February, Dolphy joined Nelson again to play on *Blues And The Abstract Truth* for another label, Impulse!. He had the call again for what was to be Nelson's *Straight Ahead*, made on 1 March for Prestige. Dolphy cut three tracks on alto, three on bass clarinet, including the extraordinary 'Ralph's New Blues', easily his best solo of the session.

In late June, Dolphy played on sessions for Ron Carter's *Where?* and Mal Waldron's *The Quest*. On the latter, Dolphy encountered the notably abrasive Booker Ervin, a pairing that resulted in some tough and pliant solos. Harmonically and rhythmically, this was a challenging set. For the first time on record since *Outward Bound*, Dolphy plays only alto and clarinet. Waldron was in some respects the ideal foil at this point in Dolphy's career. Earlier, in June 1960, multi-instrumentalist Ken McIntyre had offered him a chance to play with a top-flight rhythm section and with a degree of freedom he would have been hard pressed to find elsewhere. The result, originally released on *Looking Ahead*, is more interesting than genuinely involving, and the session with Lockjaw Davis is more of a curiosity than anything, a set released as *Trane Whistle* on which Dolphy does not solo.

Having this material in a single-box set, chronologically organized, properly documented and complete with alternatives, adds something to the Dolphy story. Expensive as it is, most genuine fans will find it revealing and full of unexpected insights.

★★(★) Candid Dolphy

Candid 9033 *Dolphy; Benny Bailey, Ted Curson, Kenny Dorham, Roy Eldridge, Lonnie Hillyer, Booker Little (t);*

Jimmy Knepper, Julian Priester (tb); Charles McPherson (as); Walter Benton, Coleman Hawkins (ts); Nico Bunink, Tommy Flanagan, Don Friedman, Mal Waldron (p); Ron Carter, Art Davis, Charles Mingus, Peck Morrison (b); Jo Jones, Dannie Richmond, Max Roach (d); Roger Sanders, Robert Whitley (perc); Abbey Lincoln (v). 10/60–4/61.

Though Dolphy worked exclusively for Prestige as a leader, he did work for other labels during 1960 and 1961. His involvement with Charles Mingus was one of the most intense creative relationships of his life; by comparison, his work with Coltrane is off-centre, creating an impression of two men on parallel but quite separate courses. The first take of 'Stormy Weather' with Mingus is extraordinary. Other tracks catch him with Little, under the trumpeter's leadership in March 1961, and with Abbey Lincoln, under the auspices of the Jazz Artists' Guild. A compilation of this sort is inevitably patchy. Without context, it probably won't mean much to anyone.

**(*) Vintage Dolphy

Enja ENJ 505 *Dolphy; Edward Amour, Don Ellis, Nick Travis (t); Jimmy Knepper (tb); Phil Woods (as); Benny Golson (ts); Lalo Schifrin (p); Barry Galbraith, Jim Hall (g); Warren Chiasson (vib); Art Davis, Richard Davis, Chuck Israels, Barre Phillips (b); Gloria Agostini (hp); Sticks Evans, J. C. Moses, Charli Persip (d); string quartet.* 3/62–4/63.

Almost worth it for Charles Stewart's sleeve photograph alone: Dolphy in profile, beard jutting, lips pursed, his bass clarinet looped over his shoulder and neck like a serpent. Musically, it's not such a big deal, a slightly uneasy combination of jazz and Third Stream material. 'Iron Man' is fine, but there isn't much else that suggests an urgent reassessment and, as with the Candid compilation, it never quite tots up to more than the sum of its parts.

***(*) The Illinois Concert

Blue Note 4 99826 2 *Dolphy; Cecil Bridgewater (t, frhn); Larry Franklin, Joe Kennon, Dick Montz, Roman Popowycz, Bruce Scafe (t); Bob Barthelmy, Bob Edmondson, Jon English, Dick Sporny (tb); Carol Holden, Ralph Woodward (frhn); Aaron Johnson (tba); Nick Henson, Bob Huffington, Vince Johnson, Kim Richmond, Ron Scalise (reeds); Herbie Hancock (p); Eddie Khan (b); J. C. Moses (d).* 3/63.

So tiny is the official discography that every addition is welcome. This live recording from the last full year of Dolphy's life isn't an attic discovery. It has been known about for years, played on radio by Brian Saunders, and available in low-quality bootlegs, but only in 1996 was it brought to the direct attention of discographer Alan Saul and to Dolphy's aunt, Luzmilda Thomas, who authorized its issue through the services of Michael Cuscuna.

Dolphy attended a seminar/workshop on improvisation at the University of Illinois in March 1963 as part of the 11th Festival of Contemporary Arts. He performed an evening concert with his working quartet, and with a brass ensemble drawn from the studentship. The recording quality is far from pristine, particularly on the flute feature, 'South Street Exit', a tune also recorded on *Last Date*, but this belated release is a key step in building a more complete picture of Dolphy's foreshortened development.

The great delight of this recording is, of course, the chance to hear two of the great composer/performers of modern jazz working together. Hancock was already beginning to make his own way in 1963, but this is clearly Dolphy's project. The set opens with 'Softly, As In A Morning Sunrise', with the leader on bass clarinet. The interplay between horn and piano is hypnotic and extraordinarily extended, and really the meat of the session is in this first track. The pianist resists the temptation to go outside conventional tonality altogether but, by his present and later standard, this is an 'outside' performance which dispenses with direct melodic statement until the final measures.

What follows is a brief statement of a theme, 'Something Sweet, Something Tender', which was to figure strongly on Dolphy's culminating Blue Note album, *Out To Lunch!*. Almost as soon as it is has been registered, it gives way to Dolphy's trademark meditation on 'God Bless The Child', again and as ever played on bass clarinet. There is probably a musicology Ph.D. waiting for someone with the analytical nous to compare the half-dozen existing versions. Our feeling is that this was a slightly constrained performance, with a hint of bitterness that isn't typical of Dolphy. Those present in March 1963 say that Dolphy was upset by some rather offhand treatment by academics and academic composers at the symposium component of the arts festival; perhaps something of that affront spilled over into his playing.

'South Street Exit' is marred by technical shortcomings, as mentioned above, but it is a vigorous and astute performance on what was always Dolphy's least assured horn. He switches to alto for 'Iron Man', which was to be recorded in studio later in the year. A review at the time seems to have referred to this piece as 'Bombs', which is just one of a couple of titular puzzles. For the second half of the recital, he stays on alto but now in the company of an *ad hoc* brass ensemble including then student Cecil Bridgewater and with the university big band. The final track is a reworked arrangement of *Outward Bound*'s 'G.W.' (which presumably had always been intended for a large group), but the really interesting one is 'Red Planet', a composition essentially identical to 'Miles's Mode', which has always been attributed to John Coltrane. Given the closeness of the two saxophonists, the piece may well have been co-composed, but it seems pretty likely that Dolphy at least had a hand in it.

'G.W.' recalls the large-scale brass arrangements Dolphy had done for Coltrane on *Africa/Brass*. The Illinois recital shows how close his thinking still was to Trane's, even though he seemed to be moving in other directions. By our calculation, the entire known Dolphy catalogue is only about 10 per cent of the total known discography of John Coltrane; given such a quantification, almost anything that survives is going to seem of disproportionate value, but *The Illinois Concert*, officially sanctioned, professionally mastered and elegantly produced, is a real find. There are stories that more material from the same period will shortly be forthcoming. We look forward to hearing it.

*** Music Matador

Fresh Sound FSR-CD 304 *Dolphy; Woody Shaw (t); Clifford Jordan (ss); Sonny Simmons (as); Prince Lasha (f); Bobby Hutcherson (vib); Richard Davis, Eddie Khan (b); Charles Moffett, J. C. Moses (d).* 6/63.

***(*) Conversations

Celluloid CELD 5014 *As above.* 6/63.

Producer Alan Douglas had almost barometric intuitions about what was happening in jazz and new music. He supervised five consecutive nights of recordings with Dolphy in the spring of

1963. Unattractively packaged and of less than pristine sound-quality, they have often been overlooked or treated as subsidiary items in the Dolphy canon. They are, however, key works, paving the way towards his great late masterpiece and important in setting him in some larger-than-usual ensembles.

'Iron Man' is a strong, muscular theme, and Dolphy's alto-playing is replete with wild overtone surges and unexpected harmonic outbreaks. Fats Waller's 'Jitterbug Waltz' (on *Conversations*) is a lively flute feature, arguably his most effective performance on the instrument to date. Woody Shaw is perfect on 'Burning Spear' (*Music Matador*), perhaps a more appropriate brass sound than Hubbard had been and was to be again. Jordan (mis-identified as 'Clifford Jarvis' on some early releases) sounds unfamiliar on soprano, but is tightly marshalled on his solo spot. Jaki Byard's 'Ode To C.P.' is a version of the piece Dolphy first recorded back in 1960, but here, one of three duets with Richard Davis (the other two on bass clarinet), it has a wry, haunted character. 'Love Me' (*Conversations*) is the first unaccompanied alto solo since 'Tenderly' for Prestige, a poignant, tender ballad.

The subsidiary players are uniformly impressive. Sonny Simmons is one of the unsung heroes of the avant-garde, and Prince Lasha – pronounced 'le-shay' – is Dolphy's musical twin on flute. The key addition, though, is Hutcherson on vibraphone, soon to be a mainstay of the *Out To Lunch!* band, offering a very different, percussive sound to the ensembles.

Tantalizingly, it is thought that more material exists from these sessions – not surprisingly, given that they took place over several nights – but so far none of it has surfaced. It is a great pity that the sound is not more generous, but Dolphy himself is usually quite well served, and the quality of the music sustains both records.

CORE COLLECTION

♛ **** Out To Lunch!

Blue Note 98793 *Dolphy; Freddie Hubbard (t); Bobby Hutcherson (vib); Richard Davis (b); Tony Williams (d).* 2/64.

This was the third time Dolphy had used the word 'out' in an album title. Oddly, perhaps even paradoxically, *Out To Lunch!* now seems both more outside and more mainstream than his earlier work. It also stands in a slightly curious relation to what is already a quite small and concentrated recording output. When the readers of a British music magazine voted it the finest jazz of all time, how many of them would have been familiar with *Outward Bound* or with the *Iron Man/Conversations* sessions? How much of their response was conditioned by the commonplace tragedy of Dolphy's imminent death (not in a car wreck, a shooting or by an overdose, but simply from an untreated riot of sugar in the blood), by Reid Miles's brilliant cover imagery, and indeed by the enormous cachet of Blue Note.

This was a unique association, Dolphy's only other release for the label the posthumous *Other Aspects*, though a month later he was to have a major role in Andrew Hill's *Point Of Departure*. How high does *Out To Lunch!* stand? If it is a masterpiece, then it is not so much a flawed as a slightly tentative masterpiece. Since the spring 1963 sessions for Alan Douglas, Dolphy had quite audibly been working towards a new compositional sophistication. The session of 25 February 1964 was engineered by Rudy Van Gelder. The sound is strong and very centred, and the new band (with Tony Williams in for J. C. Moses and the incendiary Freddie Hubbard in for the rather more measured Woody Shaw) was better suited to Dolphy's increasingly dissonant and fractured conception. Even so, however wayward these five tunes look and occasionally sound, every one of them is anchored in tradition, to some degree, and there is a shifting equipoise – track by track – between harmonic, rhythmic and timbral elements.

The solitary flute track is inspired by the great modernist, Severiano Gazelloni, and might be expected to be a quasi-concert piece reminiscent of Varèse's 'Density 21.5', which Dolphy had played. Not so. In fact, 'Gazelloni' is a relatively conventional bop theme, but one distinguished by Dolphy's virtuosic articulation and biting attack. In the same way, 'Straight Up And Down' and 'Out To Lunch' itself, the two alto pieces, are bordering on complete harmonic freedom, but again anchored in a rhythmic groove that could support heavy rail transport. Transfer to CD was good for bass players generally, but in this case it particularly underlined the role of Richard Davis (a fine orchestral player, of course, indeed Stravinsky's favourite) in touching in harmonies that would otherwise be unstated or tacit. Hutcherson doesn't function much like a piano player, but unleashes percussive and often polytonal lines that allow Dolphy maximum freedom of invention.

Long exposure suggests that the real, radical core of *Out To Lunch!* lies in the two opening numbers. 'Hat And Beard', a tribute to Monk, and 'Something Sweet, Something Tender' are both taken on bass clarinet, and the sheer physicality and dynamic cohesion of Dolphy's entry on the first tune is the key moment in his entire output. It is 'angular', as the cliché runs, but it is also profoundly lyrical and unmistakably thoughtful. The later tracks are by no means a falling away, but they certainly represent a consolidation rather than an advance on what Dolphy does in those opening moments. The irony of *Out To Lunch!* is that there was to be no sequel and that, precisely as Dolphy found his voice, he was prepared to submerge it (to a degree) in a responsive ensemble. This is not yet a great group record, but the lineaments were there.

*** Last Date

Emarcy 5101242 *Dolphy; Misha Mengelberg (p); Jacques Schols (b); Han Bennink (d).* 6/64.

Following *Out To Lunch!*, Dolphy recorded with Andrew Hill, then he rejoined the Charles Mingus Jazz Workshop for an eventful Town Hall concert and then a European tour, which was to be the most densely documented period of his career, a slew of live recordings (some of them unauthorized) issued under Mingus's name. The late spring found Dolphy on his own in Paris and the Netherlands, going single as he had three years earlier. In the last week of June he was in Berlin, to play at a new club called The Tangent, but he was unwell and managed only one or two sets. On the 29th he died in the Achenbach Hospital, having suffered a cardiac and circulatory collapse brought on by diabetes.

An unfortunate aura of glamour surrounds the last words of the great. Because there will be nothing more, they have a certain finality and definitiveness. *Last Date*, recorded in Hilversum on 2 June, is certainly not the last time Dolphy played. There are bits and pieces from later on in the month, and there are inevitable rumours of other tapes. However, this is the last formal recording available, made in front of record executives and guests, who supply the 'live' applause. The performances are very good indeed and Misha Mengelberg's trio are sympathetic and responsive foils. Dolphy opens with Monk's 'Epistrophy', an interesting kick-off point after the Monk-inspired opening of *Out To Lunch!*. Inevitably, this is milder, but the bass clarinet sound is as urgent and alien as ever. 'Hypochrismutreefuzz' is a Mengelberg original, very much in the bebop idiom, which dominates the session and is somewhat old-fashioned sounding. 'The Madrig Speaks, The Panther Walks' is actually a reworking of 'Mandrake' from the Douglas sessions, and a slightly conventional containment of it. The real delights on this disc are the two flute themes, 'South Street Exit', in which Dolphy conjures up a light, joyous sound, and a 'conference of the birds' theme. The key performance, unusually at this stage, is the standard, 'You Don't Know What Love Is', a masterpiece of construction and expression which prompts an audible sigh of delight from one of the audience (said to be actor Hans Veerman) at the end of its 11-minute span.

Which leaves just 'Miss Ann', a plain and unfussy alto theme which was probably as close as possible to triple-distilled Dolphy, the affectionate, generous spirit everyone who came close to him remembers. A certain mythology surrounds this track, which ends the album. The Philips release – and this Emarcy reissue – appended Dolphy's own voice, a statement that has become his curtain-call: 'When you hear music, after it's over, it's gone in the air. You can never recapture it again.' This wasn't said at the recording, but during an interview with jazz historian Michiel de Ruyter, some time earlier in the spring of 1964. There is much of Dolphy that can never be recaptured, which is what makes that which survives so precious. Even as he experimented, even as he overthrew the rules, he managed to maintain a solidity of presence, a foothold in the tradition, which meant that his music, however fleeting, would never be gone in the air.

Sophia Domancich

PIANO

French pianist who has sometimes worked with fusion and art-rock groups, occasionally making music in more of a free-bop style.

★★★(★) Funerals
Gimini GM 1001 *Domancich; Yvon Guillard (t); Jérome Naulais (tb); Alain Guillard (ts); Paul Rogers (b); Bruno Toccane (d); John Greaves (v).* 7/91.

★★★ L'Année Des Treize Lunes
Seventh A XV *Domancich; Paul Rogers (b); Tony Levin (d).* 12/94.

★★★(★) La Part Des Anges
Gimini GM 1008 *As above.* 7/97.

The music might not fit Rainer Werner Fassbinder's film, but it's a fine essay on the piano trio form. Domancich seems eager to involve her superb rhythm section as much as possible, and they give ideal support to her propulsive and clear-headed playing. Rogers, arguably, does the most impressive things here: 'Parrots', which starts out like a stately Charlie Haden kind of melody, is rousted by his explosive bass solo and evolves into a gripping three-way conversation. He also has one entire piece to himself ('Min'). But sometimes, as on the very long centre-piece 'Annie, Pierre Et Les Enfants', the music settles into a kind of beautiful lassitude, interesting from moment to moment but not quite convincing in the long run. Excellent studio sound provided by Gérard Lhomme.

La Part Des Anges is a sequel in very much the same mould. Domancich is again more interesting for her writing and group sound than for her improvising, and there's a dramatic cast to the music which makes a long track such as 'Sur Les Traces ...' seem like a carefully wrought set-piece. With the pianist's foursquare delivery contrasting with the free play of Rogers and Levin, it's an oddly intriguing result.

We have just caught up with the earlier *Funerals*. Though this is primarily a trio date too, the horns make mournful declamations on the title-track and 'B. Rubatto'. John Greaves sings a lyric inspired by John Donne. It's gloomily played out, a little in the manner of Michael Mantler, but in its steady, wasteless way the music has real power, with Rogers superb as usual.

Natty Dominique (1896–1982)

TRUMPET

Anatole Dominique was born in New Orleans but went to Chicago in 1913 and did most of his playing there. He recorded often with Johnny Dodds in the '20s, but his later appearances on record were very few.

★★(★) Natty Dominique's Creole Dance Band
American Music AMCD-18 *Dominique; Preston Jackson (tb); Darnell Howard (cl); Ralph Tervalon (p); Sam Casimir (g); Bill Settles (b); Baby Dodds, Bob Mathews (d).* 9/53.

Recorded at a hotel gig in 1953, this is an interesting discovery of some obscure Chicago jazz of its day. Dominique recorded little after the '20s and his trademark – a vibrato shake that makes his horn sound like it's constantly trembling – is hardly ideal stuff to lead a band with. But it's not a bad group: Howard plays some sly solos, Jackson is good, and Baby Dodds, whose beat Dominique always thought unsurpassable, keeps the band honest. Natty reminisces about his glory days on a couple of tracks.

Arne Domnérus (born 1924)

ALTO SAXOPHONE, CLARINET, BARITONE SAXOPHONE

The 25-year-old Domnérus's appearance at the Paris Jazz Fair wakened an interest in Swedish jazz. He honed his technique as a member of the Swedish Radio Big Band, but it was Dompan's small-group playing, influenced by bop but also by Scandinavian folk forms, which established a reputation that has lasted for almost half a century. On saxophone and clarinet, he is crisp, light-toned and nimble.

★★★(★) Portrait
Phontastic PHONT CD 9313 *Domnérus; other personnel includes Clifford Brown, Rolf Ericson, Art Farmer, Clark Terry (t), Putte Wickman (cl), Benny Carter (as), Rolf Blomqvist, Jerome Richardson (ts, f), Lars Gullin (bs), Bengt Hallberg (p, org), Lars Estrand (vib), Sture Akerberg, George Mraz, Georg Reidel (b), Rune Carlsson, Oliver Jackson, Johan Lofcrantz (d).* 46–93.

*** Favourite Groups: 1949–1950

Dragon DRCD 358 *Domnérus; Leppe Sundevall (t, thn, b); James Moody (ts); Per-Arne Croona, Lars Gullin (bs); Bengt Hallberg, Gunnar Svensson, Gösta Theselius (p); Ulf Linde (vib); Yngve Akerberg, Simon Brehm, Gunnar Almstedt, Thore Jederby (b); Sven Bollhem, Anders Burham, Jack Noren (d).* 49–50.

*** Arne Domnérus And His Orchestra 1950–1951 With Rolf Ericson Dragon

DRCD 381 *Domnérus; Rolf Ericson (t); Rolf Blomqvist (ts); Lars Gullin (bs, d); Gunnar Svensson (p); Yngve Akerberg (b); Jack Noren, Gunnar Nyberg (d); Harry Arnold, Sonya Hedenbratt, Bibbi Johnson (v).* 50–51.

'Jazz is Melody, Swing and Vitality.' That is the legend and the promise that surrounds the photograph of Dompan. One of the finest Scandinavian jazz musicians of his generation, Domnérus oversaw a shift away from the heavily bop-influenced Scandinavian idiom of the early '50s towards something more straightforwardly romantic and impressionistic. The early sessions are not presently available, but they reveal Domnérus sounding closer to Benny Carter than to Parker in his phrasing, with a wan, meditative quality that frequently refers to diatonic folk themes and hymn tunes. (It may be Domnérus whom the ageing bopper is thinking about in the great jazz movie, *Sven Klangs Kvintett* (purportedly a fictionalized biography of Lars Gullin), when he says that the only places you could hear jazz in Scandinavia in the '70s were churches. For a time at least, Domnérus performed in 'sacred concerts' that combined jazz and liturgical materials.)

Portrait, as it suggests, is a career profile, 18 tracks covering the period from the end of the war (a single cut from a Sonora disc called *Ben's Music*, 1946) right up to *Sugar Fingers*. There's a quite extraordinary performance of Strayhorn's 'Blood Count', played as a duet with long-term associate Hallberg at the organ of the Stockholm Konserthus, and there is a single track from their New York trip, *Downtown Meeting*, where they recorded with Clark Terry, George Mraz and Oliver Jackson. There's return traffic on the Quincy Jones-conducted Swedish All-Stars session of 1953, an Art Farmer vehicle also featuring Clifford Brown and the great Swede, Lars Gullin. There's also a Swedamerican summit from 1982 with the veteran, Benny Carter, originally released as *Skyline Drive And Towards*.

Useful as *Portrait* is for a career summary, it makes for unsatisfactory listening as a continuous whole. It's a slightly ramshackle sampling, put together more with an eye to coverage than to the creation of a well-balanced CD; an aircheck from the Salle Pleyel in Paris, May 1949, makes it in only as a historical oddity and, second track in, it's a touch off-putting. These misgivings apart, it's still the best Domnérus album, or we should say *surviving* album. The best of all is the 1977 duo with Hallberg, *Hypertoni*. Enthusiasts can have fun looking for that.

Favourite Groups is no less of a ragbag, but a valuable set to have. In 1949, brothers Lars and Anders Burman founded the Metronome label and signed the 25-year-old Domnérus as their first star. Bebop had just made an impact and the opening 'Conversation', written by the gifted Theselius is built round the same chords as 'Cherokee'. The track which follows from that first session is slower and freer in structure, but also more individual in tonality. The set includes some rarities, like 'Running A Temperature', which has not previously been released, and a version of Duke's 'Everything But You' from October 1949, which features Arne on baritone, anticipating later sessions with the peerless Gullin.

Arne's clarinet playing, inspired by Buddy DeFranco, is featured on 'I Surrender Dear' and 'Night And Day' from the same session, and throughout the February 1950 date, which is co-led by Theselius. The pianist is little known outside Scandinavia, but here he fully merits Domnérus's description of him as an unsung genius. Whenever he plays, the energy level seems to soar. Gullin is wonderful on 'Body And Soul' and 'Out Of Nowhere' from the latest of the dates, a broadcast from October 1950. The former is on a Caprice LP but the latter is, as far as we know, previously unissued. Another important corner of the picture filled in.

For all the young Swede's enthusiasm for bebop, melody, swing and vitality are still very much the order of the day and there is little sign that Domnérus was influenced by Charlie Parker. His solo on 'Out Of Nowhere', one of the best cuts on the 1950/1951 compilation, suggests that he was listening thoughtfully to Bird, but possibly unconvinced that this was the way forward. Lars Gullin will be the main draw for most listeners to this, though Rolf Ericson is clearly a mover and shaker at this period, already experimenting with the cooler, drier sound that was to take over after bebop. The trumpeter certainly merits his featured status but Gullin's whispery baritone is a constant delight and his work on 'Lullaby In Rhythm' is stunning.

As with most of these sets, the sound isn't absolutely pristine and there are some ugly moments in the remastering. Historically, though, and for the sheer pleasure of hearing two great saxophonists in their heyday, all are worth considering.

*** Jump For Joy, 1959–1961

Dragon 196 *Domnérus; Jan Allan (t); Rolf Blomqvist (ts, f); Rune Falk (bs); Rune Gustafsson (g); Bengt Hallberg, Gunnar Svensson, Bengt-Arne Wallin (p); Georg Reidel (b); Egil Johansen (d).* 59–61.

Jump For Joy feels like a more coherent set than the earlier compilations. Dompan is heard on clarinet throughout and is particularly strong on material like Mingus's 'Boogie Stop Shuffle' and Monk's 'Friday The 13th', not the kind of thing you'd automatically associate with the Swede. Arne was, however, listening to just about everything at this time and his ears were never closed to anything, however new or challenging.

Hallberg and (less emphatically) Svensson are important collaborators in this period. Bengt's sheer musical intelligence strikes sparks whenever he and Arne get together and some listeners may find themselves cueing back to the start of tracks just to follow the pianist's thoughtful logic. A recommended set.

*** Antiphone Blues

Proprius PRCD 7744 *Domnérus; Gustaf Sjokvist (org).* 8/74.

Inspired by Duke Ellington's sacred concerts, and recorded in Spånga Church, these moving duets draw heavily on Ellington compositions, alongside spirituals, Russian and Swedish vespers, Schumann's 'Träumerei', and an arrangement of a Vivaldi largo. The Ellington themes – 'Almighty God', 'Come Sunday' and 'Heaven' – are deeply moving, but the real measure of Domnérus's brilliance is the improvisation, 'Antiphone Blues', a thoughtful and beautifully constructed piece that lends a shape to the whole, otherwise logically constructed, record.

***** Dompan At The Savoy**

Phontastic PHONT CD 8806 *Domnérus; Ulf Johansson (p, tb, v); Sture Akerberg (b); Aage Tanggaard (d).* 9/90.

*****(*) Sugar Fingers**

Phontastic PHONT CD 8831 *Domnérus; Jan Lundgren (p); Lars Estrand (vib); Sture Akerberg (b); Johan Lofcrantz (d).* 7/93.

His typical sound, even on the alto and clarinet, is low, soft and somewhat undynamic. In later life, this has become even more pronounced – though, like Lee Konitz, Domnérus is occasionally able to surprise with brief episodes of dissonance. *Sugar Fingers*, recorded at the Swedish Academy of Music rather than in church, has a politely respectful, elder-statesman feel, and the band hover round him like courtiers. Pianist Lundgren's title-track sounds almost tailor-made for the leader but, ironically, it's the one number he sits out.

Dompan At The Savoy is unusual in that Hallberg is absent. In his place is Ulf Johansson, who came in to jam and show off his multi-instrumentalism by contributing trombone solos to 'Honeysuckle Rose' and 'Solitude'. It's a relaxed, affectionate session ('Dompan' is the saxophonist's nickname in Sweden) that doesn't purport to offer much more than easy, mid-paced swing. No sign at all of Domnérus's more acerbic, Konitz-influenced side, and as such not a particularly representative or flattering point of contact.

*****(*) Happy Together**

Ladybird LBCD 0019 *Domnérus; Putte Wickman (cl); Rune Gustafsson (g); Jan Lundgren (p); Jesper Lundgaard (b); Aage Tanggaard (d).* 12/95.

Recorded, you'll not be surprised to learn, at the Royal Academy of Music in Stockholm, over two nights, this contains no real surprises. Both Wickman and Domnérus had been awarded the Swedish Gold Medal Illis Quorum the previous year for their services to music, and much of the music that followed had a faintly ritual, almost honorific quality, roughened up here and there by association with younger players, as on these sessions. Lundgaard is the main culprit, pushing the pace along faster than the two veterans might like and then holding back maddeningly on the slower tunes. It's all very good-natured jockeying and the frontmen are absolutely in control of the situation. Dompan's tone has broadened a little with the passing years. The resemblance to Benny Carter is more pronounced, though occasionally nods to Johnny Hodges still flicker through. The choice of material is as eclectic as ever: two Ellington tunes, Thad Jones's 'Three And One', Roger Kellaway's seldom covered 'I Have The Feeling I've Been Here Before', Bobby Timmons's 'Moanin'' and a misspelt Horace 'Parland''s tune, a surprise package for the very end of a hugely enjoyable if a little formal performance.

*****(*) In Concert: Live '96**

Caprice CAP 21526 *Domnérus; Bosse Broberg (t); Lennart Aberg (ts, f); Bengt Hallberg (p); Rune Gustafsson (g); Georg Riedel (b); Egil Johansen (d).* 10/96.

A typically eclectic and well-paced septet date which ranges from original, blues-based material by Riedel and Hallberg to folkloric explorations arranged by Jan Johansson and others. Domnérus was quick to spot the potential of traditional Scandinavian musics in a jazz context, and what is striking here is that the 'trad' format conceals a powerful measure of experiment. The leader is less emphatic than in years gone by, his tone blurry and ill-defined, but the flow of ideas is unstaunchable. Aberg and Hallberg are inventive partners, and the rhythm section has a springy, buoyant quality that lifts what might have been a rather ponderous date.

CORE COLLECTION

****** Face To Face**

Dragon DRCD 344 *Domnérus; Bernt Rosengren (ts, f); Jan Lundgren (p); Hans Backenroth (b); Aage Tanggaard (d).* 99.

Two great masters of European jazz playing a set of relaxed standards with an expert and unobtrusive rhythm section. There is more to the story than that, not least Arne and Bernt's clever referencing of jazz history, notably moments from the recorded collaborations of Lee Konitz and Warne Marsh. Kicking off with Warne's curtain-piece, 'Out Of Nowhere', was just a gentle warm-up, and in the event the horns leave much of the passage-work to the piano player. The really interesting stuff begins with 'Body And Soul', which is taken on clarinet and flute, overturning expectations and giving the old groaner a new and quietly vivid life. 'That Tired Old Routine Called Love' is a feature for the trio, 'St Louis Blues' and 'Just One Of Those Things' are spots for Rosengren out on his own, while Arne takes the spotlight on 'Stardust' and, back on clarinet, 'What Kind Of Fool Am I?', a duet with Lundgren. This is a wonderful jazz record, clearly thought out and articulated, packed with relaxed invention and some genuinely moving moments. Thoroughly recommended.

***** Dompan!**

Fresh Sound 5032 *Domnérus; Jan Lundgren (p); Tom Warrington (b); Paul Kreibich (d).* 9/00.

In the late summer of 2000, Dompan played a residency at the Jazz Bakery near Los Angeles. The concept was a tribute to Duke, Rabbit and Sweet Pea, and the material is ideally suited to the clarinettist's swinging approach. He doesn't make any effort to pastiche Johnny Hodges or to take liberties with Ellington's compositions, which are mostly bright swingers – no 'Isfahan' this time, interestingly – and require a singing tone and great rhythmic awareness. The band is very good, too. Lundgren leads from the back, with powerful, accurate chords and a deft touch in his solo spots. Warrington is little known outside his locale, but he anchors the harmony very well and contributes some original ideas when called upon.

Lou Donaldson (born 1926)

ALTO SAXOPHONE

Arrived in NYC in the early '50s and worked with Monk, Blakey and Mingus, as well as leading his own groups. An unreconstituted bebopper, he played enough blues and gospel licks in his solos to forge the path towards soul-jazz in the '60s. Still performing in Europe and the USA.

****(*) Blues Walk**

Blue Note 46525-2 *Donaldson; Herman Foster (p); Peck Morrison (b); Dave Bailey (d); Ray Barretto (perc).* 7/58.

***** Good Gracious!**

Blue Note 54325-2 *Donaldson; John Patton (org); Grant Green (g); Ben Dixon (d).* 1/63.

*****(*) Alligator Boogaloo**
Blue Note 84263-2 *Donaldson; Melvin Lastie Sr (c); Lonnie Liston Smith (org); George Benson (g); Leo Morris (d).* 4/67.

***** The Midnight Creeper**
Blue Note 24549-2 *Donaldson; Blue Mitchell (t); Lonnie Smith (org); George Benson (g); Leo Morris (d).* 3/68.

***** Everything I Play Is Funky**
Blue Note 31248-2 *Donaldson; Eddie Williams, Blue Mitchell (t); Charles Earland, Lonnie Liston Smith (org); Melvin Sparks (g); Jimmy Lewis (b); Idris Muhammad (d).* 8/69–1/70.

Lou Donaldson has remained among the most diligent of Charlie Parker's disciples. His playing hardly altered course in 40 years of work: the fierce tone and familiar blues colourings remain constant through the '50s and '60s and, if he's as unadventurous as he is assured, at least his records guarantee a solid level of well-executed improvising. He replaces Parker's acidity with a certain sweetness which can make his work pall over extended listening and, considering his reputation, his albums seem to add up to a disappointing lot.

Donaldson's stack of Blue Note albums has drifted in and out of circulation. There isn't all that much around at present. *Blues Walk*, true to its title, is Donaldson at his bluesiest, and Bailey and Barretto make a propulsive combination; the material, though, is rather dull. *Good Gracious!* looks like another rote Blue Note affair, but with Patton and Green present and in rattling good spirits, both of them outplaying the leader, it comes off as one of his best. *Alligator Boogaloo* comes from the period when the saxophonist was trying to make the best of the soul-jazz trend, without much success on this occasion – routine playing on lightweight back-beat music, though the album was a hit in its day and has remained popular. Both *Midnight Creeper* and *Everything I Play Is Funky*, though dating from a fallow period in Blue Note's fortunes, stay on the right side of righteous. The former includes rising star Benson in its ranks, and the latter lives out the title convincingly enough, the record drawn from a brace of sessions a few months apart (Mitchell and Smith sub for Williams and Earland on the second). No masterwork, but the funky side of soul-jazz hadn't yet lost its edge and it grooves along.

**** Birdseed**
Milestone MCD 9198-2 *Donaldson; David Braham (org); Peter Bernstein (g); Fukushi Tainaka (d); Ralph Dorsey (perc).* 4/92.

****(*) Caracas**
Milestone MCD 9217-2 *Donaldson; Lonnie Liston Smith (org); Peter Bernstein (g); Kenny Washington (d); Ralph Dorsey (perc).*

Lou's Milestone albums were a disappointing lot: he sounds plain tired a lot of the time, and digital glare doesn't suit him. His old chum Smith is often a pretty feeble prop and Bernstein plays many of the best licks. Everyone sounds all-in on *Birdseed*, which is something Parker wouldn't have tolerated; but matters perk up a degree on *Caracas*. There's no shape to the albums, though, just casual blowing.

***** Live On The QE2**
Chiaroscuro CR(D) 366 *Donaldson; Nicholas Payton (t); Lonnie Liston Smith (org); Randy Johnston (g); Danny Burger (d).* 11/99.

Lou's first album in years is an enjoyable stroll through some of his old favourites – 'Harlem Nocturne', 'Marmaduke', 'I Can't Get Started', 'The Midnight Creeper', the set-list writes itself. He's assembled a fine little outfit, though: Johnston has had lots of practice at this kind of gig, and a rejuvenated Smith works up a few new wrinkles at the Hammond. Payton turns up for a couple of blows, and Lou warns 'fusion or con-fusion musicians' against playing anything as tricky as original bebop. Sound advice!

Michel Doneda

SOPRANO AND SOPRANINO SAXOPHONES

French improviser, specializing in the highest saxophone frequencies and investigating multi-national partnerships.

***** Open Paper Tree**
FMP CD 68 *Doneda; Paul Rogers (b); Le Quan Ninh (perc).* 5/94.

This must have been a remarkable set – performed at Berlin's Free Music Workshop in 1994 – but, as so often with great improvisations, something's been lost in the translation. For once, Jost Gebers doesn't seem to have secured a very faithful sound, and the grand range of Le Quan's percussion parts has been withheld. Rogers also suffers. The surviving document still has a raw, wound-up quality, which makes for unsettling listening over a long disc. Doneda's soprano begs no great virtuosity and he makes an awkward voice with the others, yet this makes the music the more intense and hard-won. There's little obvious textural interest, more a drawn-out struggle among three rather disparate voices, or entities. Tough work, and absorbing stuff for those who like a challenge.

***** Ce N'est Pourtant ...**
L'Empreinte Digitale 13056 *Doneda; Benat Achiary (v, perc).* 4/95.

*****(*) M'Uoaz**
Scissors 002 *Doneda; Tetsu Saitoh (b); Alain Joule (d); Antonella Talamonti (v).* 11/95.

The magical moments on *Ce N'est Pourtant ...* come when the duettists are recorded in the open air, and the chime of bells and birdsong intersperse their improvisations. Achiary is something between noise-maker and lieder virtuoso and between them they create some spellbinding moments, lusty bawling underpinned by the hectoring saxophone. But it's a tough act to sustain over 70 minutes, and the three long pieces get tired before they're done.

M'Uoaz includes another singer, although she appears only on the second of four long pieces. The only musician common to all four tracks is Saitoh, since there are two duets, a trio and a quartet improvisation. It's fitting, since much of the music overall seeks an unspecified but clear Japanese feel, Joule's percussion sounding like the backdrop for a kabuki theatre-band and Talamonti singing almost in a ritual tongue. 'T'Zane', the trio piece, which runs for close to half an hour, is full of sparkle and colour.

****(*) Anatomie Des Clefs**
Potlatch 598 *Doneda (ss solo).* 98.

The solo album, a nettle which Doneda grasps to only intermittent reward. 'Intermittent' is one way of describing the music, too, since much of it (especially the half-hour opening track) seems to have as much silence as sound in it. Elsewhere he recalls some of Roscoe Mitchell's more therapeutic pieces for saxophone players, mustering every outlandish technique he can think of to get a result out of the fish horn. This needs a lot of tolerance.

**** Not**
Victo 068 *Doneda; Jean-Marc Montera (g, elec); Erik M (turntables, records etc).* 5/99.

Doneda has his name on some interesting records, but he rarely seems to be the outstanding player. Montera and Erik M set the agenda for this live record, while the saxophonist is left to squeak and squiggle over the top. This kind of situation often seems to devolve into random electronic music, and frankly this is tiresome to listen to, oddly humourless for much of its dank duration.

Dorothy Donegan (1922–98)

PIANO, VOCAL

Born in Chicago, Donegan was playing in church at 11. Performed in clubs and studied informally with Art Tatum. Despite a formidable technique, she was more of an all-round entertainer, and appeared regularly in films and shows from the '40s and at clubs and festivals in her later years, singing and doing impersonations as well as playing piano.

***** The Many Faces Of Dorothy Donegan**
Storyville 101 8362 *Donegan; Arvell Shaw, unknown (b); Panama Francis, unknown (d).* 61–6/75.

***** Dorothy Donegan**
Four Leaf Clover FLC CD 121 *Donegan; Jan Allan (t); Red Mitchell (b); Lars Bejbom (d).* 11/75.

***** Live In Copenhagen 1980**
Storyville STCD 8262 *Donegan; Mads Vinding (b); Ed Thigpen (d).* 5/80.

**** The Explosive Dorothy Donegan**
Audiophile ACD-209 *Donegan; Jerome Hunter (b); Ray Mosca (d).* 3/80.

**** I Just Want To Sing**
Audiophile ACD-281 *As above.* 3/80.

****(*) Live At The 1990 Floating Jazz Festival**
Chiaroscuro CD(D) 312 *Donegan; Jon Burr (b); Ray Mosca (d).* 10–11/90.

****(*) Live At The 1991 Floating Jazz Festival**
Chiaroscuro CR(D) 318 *As above, except add Dizzy Gillespie (t).* 10/91.

***** Live At the Floating Jazz Festival 1992**
Chiaroscuro CR(D) 323 *As above, except Clark Terry (t) replaces Gillespie.* 10/92.

A veteran whose greatest fame came very late in her career, Donegan was a pianist whose exuberance and sometimes hysterical virtuosity make her difficult to assess. The Four Leaf Clover set, cut live in Stockholm, asserts her position as the female Tatum from the off, with a typically garrulous 'It Could Happen To You', and if you want to hear Donegan the cabaret entertainer, 'A Good Man Is Hard To Find' is just about definitive. Red Mitchell is an invaluable prop, and Jan Allan steps up to blow on 'Memories Of You'. It's a strong helping of Donegan fun, and the Storyville set from a gig in Copenhagen is another good one, with excellent support from Vinding and Thigpen, the latter proving himself to be Donegan's most swinging drummer. 'The Best Things In Life Are Free' and 'Take The "A" Train' are attacking set-pieces which turn out particularly well. The two Audiophiles, both taken from one session, are much less successful, gathering together a muddle of standards and medleys in unattractive sound on a day when Donegan's least sensitive instincts were in charge.

Her show-stopping appearances on Hank O'Neal's Floating Jazz cruises brought her some useful notoriety in the '90s. The 1990 session includes her celebrated impersonations of Lena Horne, Pearl Bailey, Eartha Kitt and (dead on) Billie Holiday, which are worth hearing once. But there's also some strong piano, and this rhythm section knows her well enough to make the music swing and stay together. Gillespie makes only the most desultory appearance on the 1991 date, which also has a very engaging 'Tea For Two'. Terry is more generously featured on his guest role the following year, and this is probably the one to get out of the three, although her spoken reminiscences at the end of the previous two discs make an interesting postscript. She was a phenomenon, whatever one thinks about the music, and a sensible best-of culled from all these recordings would be something to hear.

Donegan fans should welcome the appearance of *The Many Faces Of*. The first half is a session done for the small French label Mahogany in 1975, with Shaw and Francis, and although the piano's not very good and the balance is off, the music is in a rollicking humour. She tackles everything from 'You Are The Sunshine Of My Life' to Beethoven's 'Minuet In G', and there's a ten-minute 'Donegan's Blues' which is definitive in its way. The fill-up offers nine tracks drawn from London House broadcasts dated to 1961. Bass and drums (whoever they are) swing alongside and Dorothy is in high-energy mode.

Christy Doran (born 1949)

GUITARS, EFFECTS

Guitarist-improviser whose technique and range of interests let him wander, with mixed results, through most areas of contemporary music.

***** Musik Für Zwei Kontrabasse, Elektrische Gitarre Und Schlagzeug**
ECM 847941-2 *Doran; Bobby Burri, Oliver Magnenat (b); Fredy Studer (d).* 5/90.

Doran's second ECM album is an uncomfortable and ultimately unsatisfactory affair which veers between hard, almost industrial sound and a nervous, algebraic discourse. The formal 'new music' title isn't really reflected in the eight tracks (one of which is by Burri and only two of which, 'Chemistries I/II', are related – by name only). Doran's sound is as pumped up as usual, and it's tempting to speculate whether the music would have had greater impact had the *zwei Kontrabasse* been stood down for the afternoon. Recording twin basses is an engineer's nightmare; but for a rather crude channel separation, they are virtually indistinguishable. Production is credited to the band; one wonders how ECM chief Manfred Eicher might have handled it.

****** Race The Time**
MGB CD 973 *Doran; Jamaaladeen Tacuma (b); Fredy Studer (d).* 5/97.

It would be stretching a point to suggest that here is a trio which interacts with the subtlety and sophistication of Bill Evans's classic Village Vanguard group. Not far off, but not quite there. Doran's elegant chordal approach and delay-laden melody lines are the next step on, but this is a sound that also draws on the Jimi Hendrix Experience and Cream, the rock power trio pacified enough to accommodate the guitarist's elemental sound. Apart from the title-track and 'New Outline', all the tunes are by Doran and they re-affirm his gift for sweet, untroubled themes that open out on to vast landscapes of sound. The opening 'Circumstances' is deceptively brief, and it's only with the middle sequence of 'Race The Time', 'No Matter Where You Roam' and 'Incognito' that the real flavour of the set comes through. Doran has rarely played better and never (so far) had playing partners who so completely echo his intentions.

★★★ **Black Box**
Double Moon DMCHR 00710022 *Doran; Wolfgang Zwiauer (b); Fabian Kuratli (d, perc); Muthuswamy Balasubramoniam (mridangam, v); Bruno Amstad (v).* 01.

★★★ **Heaven Is In The Streets**
Double Moon DMCHR 0071032 *As above; omit Balasubramoniam; add Hans-Petter Pfammatter (p, ky).* 02.

Doran's New Bag group draws on a wide range of modern fusion styles. Kuratli has a strong background in hip-hop and other forms, while Amstad is a singer who has explored ethnic techniques like throat-singing. Zwiauer is the most sought-after Swiss bass player of his generation, a solid but consistently unpredictable presence at the heart of the group. There isn't much jazz on these two recordings, but the sheer inventiveness of the music puts it closer in spirit to jazz than to rock, even when the rhythm and energy suggest the latter. Balasubramoniam's contributions on the double-headed mridangam are strongly featured on *Black Box*, making the album reminiscent of some of Trilok Gurtu's crossover experiments. The second album (actually the group's third release) is distinguished by the fine 'Albino', a space-age rock theme with a lot of electronic detail, and by 'Bastard', which builds in a version of 'Strange Fruit' in a mini-suite of admirably condensed music. Doran's familiar electric style is most accurately captured on 'No Rest For The Wicked'. He's less impressive on *Black Box*, but the group is strong and tight and it's very much in line with his consistently eclectic approach.

Pierre Dørge (born 1946)

GUITAR

A Danish guitarist whose conventional start in modal bop and fusion settings didn't prepare one for his sometimes outlandish adventures in his New Jungle Orchestra.

★★★ **Landscape With Open Door**
Steeplechase SCCD 31115 *Dørge; Walt Dickerson (vib).* 8/78.

★★★ **Ballad Round The Left Corner**
Steeplechase SCCD 31132 *Dørge; John Tchicai (ss, as); Niels-Henning Orsted Pedersen (b); Billy Hart (d).* 10/79.

The Dane is an experienced performer in jazz-rock and free settings, although his guitar tone is bright and clear, almost in a mainstream jazz tradition. But these small-group settings don't suit him very well. The duo session with Dickerson blends counterpoint almost too cleanly and tends to pall rather quickly, while the quartet date, despite the promising line-up – Tchicai has been a frequent collaborator with the guitarist – is depressingly low in vitality, the compositions given only a perfunctory treatment.

★★★ **Brikama**
Steeplechase SCCD 31188 *Dørge; Michael Marre (t, euph); Kenneth Agerholm, Niels Neergaard (tb); John Tchicai (ts, bcl); Jesper Zeuthen (as); Morten Carlsen (ts, bcl, bsx, ney, tarogato); Doudou Gouirand (as, ss); Bent Clausen (vib, perc); Irene Becker (ky); Johnny Mbizo Dyani (perc, v); Hugo Rasmussen (b); Thomas Akuru Dyani (perc); Marilyn Mazur (d, perc).* 3/84.

★★★(★) **Very Hot – Even The Moon Is Dancing**
Steeplechase SCCD 31208 *Dørge; Harry Beckett (t, flhn); Kenneth Agerholm, Niels Neergaard (tb); Soren Eriksen, Doudou Gouirand (ss, as); Jesper Zeuthen (as); John Tchicai (ts, v); Morten Carlsen (ts, bsx, f, tara, cl, zurna); Irene Becker (ky, perc, v); Bent Clausen (vib, perc); Johnny Mbizo Dyani (b, p, v); Hugo Rasmussen (b); Marilyn Mazur (d); Ahmadu Jarr (perc).* 7/85.

★★★(★) **Johnny Lives**
Steeplechase SCCD 31228 *As above, except omit Neergaard, Eriksen, Gouirand, Dyani and Jarr; add Hamid Drake (d), Thomas Akuru Dyani (perc).* 4/87.

These albums are by New Jungle Orchestra, the nearly-big band under Dørge's leadership, which has by now been going long enough to count as an institution itself. Dørge explores the idea of a global jazz village by pushing what is basically a post-bop orchestra into African, European and any other climes he can assimilate: roistering horn parts might emerge from a lush percussive undergrowth, or heartbreaking ballads may be brightened by Dørge's own sparkling high-life guitar solos. Inevitably there are moments on the records that sound misconceived or cluttered, but these are surprisingly few: what one remembers is the joyful swing of the ensembles, the swirling tone-colours and rhythmic pep. There are fine soloists too in Tchicai, Carlsen and Beckett. *Brikama* is absolutely stunning, with vivid voicings and a bewildering range of instrumental characters. *Very Hot* is slightly fresher, with a winning reworking of Ellington's 'The Mooche' and two very long yet convincing pan-global jams; but it would be unwise to pass up *Johnny Lives*, dedicated to the late Johnny Dyani, which has some beautiful writing and playing in such as 'Lilli Goes To Town' and 'Mbizo Mbizo'.

★★★(★) **Zig Zag Zimfoni**
Stunt STUCD 01022 *Dørge; Kasper Tranberg (c); Kenneth Agerholm (tb, darbuka); Mads Hyhne (tb); Jakob Mygind, Anders Banke (ss, ts); Morten Carlsen (ts, f, taro); Peter Fuglsang (cl, bcl, f); Irene Becker (ky); Hugo Rasmussen (b); Bent Clausen (d); Ayi Solomon (perc); Josefine Cronholm (v).* 9–10/00.

Dørge's records are frustratingly difficult to find and we have to admit that we've missed a few releases from the '90s for ULO, DaCapo and Olufsen, all of which have now disappeared anyway. But here's his first for the new century, and it finds the New Jungle Orchestra in rude health. As ever, this Jungle music is more about the Middle East than anything tropical, from the worldly rave-up of 'Arab Klap' which starts proceedings, on through the polyrhythmic hothouse of 'Bahrain'. Jazz keeps its hand in with the solos: as with the Sun Ra Arkestra, a more ruthless setting would expose weaknesses, but the NJO look after their own and there's always a huge support mechanism surrounding every improvisation. Exhilarating, and just occasionally exhausting.

Kenny Dorham (1924–72)

TRUMPET, VOCALS

His given name was McKinley, which is why it's sometimes given as 'Kinny' Dorham. Born in Fairfield, Texas, and a veteran of local bands, he seemed to pop up at the all major points of change in modern jazz, with Billy Eckstine's band, with Dizzy Gillespie, with Charlie Parker, and as founding trumpeter of the Jazz Messengers. Later in his career he spent considerable time in Europe, where his classically tinged modernist ideas gained a more sympathetic hearing. Dorham was also an effective singer.

*****(*) Kenny Dorham Quintet**

Original Jazz Classics OJC 113 *Dorham; Jimmy Heath (as, bs); Walter Bishop Jr (p); Percy Heath (b); Kenny Clarke (d).* 12/53.

***** Afro-Cuban**

Blue Note 7468152 *Dorham; J. J. Johnson (tb); Hank Mobley (ts); Cecil Payne (bs); Horace Silver (p); Oscar Pettiford (b); Art Blakey (d); Carlos Patato Valdes (congas).* 1/55, 3/55.

Dorham never sounded more like Dizzy Gillespie than on *Afro-Cuban*, punching out single-note statements across the rhythm. The marvellous 1953 quintet features gulping blues passages that manage to thrive on the thinnest harmonic oxygen; never a mere showman, it is Dorham's mental stamina that impresses, a concentration and attention to detail that make him one of the most coherent and structurally aware of the bebop players. He is also one of the better composers, a point – 'Blue Bossa' apart – which is generally overlooked.

*****(*) Kenny Dorham And The Jazz Prophets: Volume 1**

Chess GRP 18202 *Dorham; J. R. Monterose (ts); Dick Katz (p); Sam Jones (b); Arthur Edgehill (d).* 4/56.

At the turn of 1956, Dorham left the Messengers to form his own group, which in a less than coincidental echo of his former employ he called the Prophets. The minor-key theme-piece, 'The Prophet', makes for an arresting opening, with Dorham and an in-form Monterose swapping tiny phrases. 'Blues Elegante' opens with Katz and Jones, followed by Dorham playing muted and coming as close as he ever did to the Miles Davis sound, which he flirts with again on the Billie Holiday ballad, 'Don't Explain'. The transfers are far from perfect, with occasional distortions and some noise which is presumably explained by tape wear. However, these are valuable enough sides to overcome any technical quibbles. Fans of Dorham's now underrated and certainly understated approach will welcome this reissue.

CORE COLLECTION

*****(*) 'Round About Midnight At The Café Bohemia Vol. 2**

Blue Note 46542 *Dorham; J. R. Monterose (ts); Kenny Burrell (g); Bobby Timmons (p); Sam Jones (b); Arthur Edgehill (d).* 5/56.

****** 'Round About Midnight At The Café Bohemia**

Blue Note 33775 2CD *As above.* 5/56.

... and at around midnight a sequence of minor keys would seem to be in order. Whatever else, Dorham always had a predilection for a unified mood, and this session, combining the Monk tune, 'Autumn In New York', and 'A Night In Tunisia' with three originals (more fuel to our conviction that he is a neglected writer), manages to sustain a slightly brooding, intensely thoughtful atmosphere. As a foil, Monterose was an excellent recruitment. Burrell swings with the usual horn-like attack and Timmons vamps righteously, though without ever really showing his mettle. Dorham's own solos are models of grace and tact, always giving an impression of careful construction and development, and an unfailing sense of texture. Francis Wolff's subtly doctored cover shot offers an intriguing impression of the man, showing Dorham in a bright check jacket, but with a faraway look in his eyes as he clutches the microphone; above him, a ghostly image of an American townscape, vivid but also fleeting.

The reissue is a double set that includes four valuable alternatives, sensibly programmed to garner maximum drama and the fullest understanding of what Dorham was going through at the time.

***** Jazz Contrasts**

Original Jazz Classics OJC 028 *Dorham; Sonny Rollins (ts); Hank Jones (p); Oscar Pettiford (b); Max Roach (d); Betty Glamann (hp).* 5/57.

***** Two Horns / Two Rhythm**

Original Jazz Classics OJC 463 *Dorham; Ernie Henry (as); Wilbur Ware (b); Granville T. Hogan (d).* 11/57–12/57.

The pianoless horn-and-rhythm experiment posed interesting problems for Dorham. Ware's big bass almost fills in the gap; but what is interesting about the set as a whole is how Dorham adjusts his delivery, counting rests much more carefully, filling in with a broader intonation on ensemble passages. Henry and Hogan are by no means passengers, but the real drama of the recording is played out across the three octaves that divide trumpet and bass on some of the bridging passages. Rollins wasn't at first glance the ideal partner for Dorham, but he began to steer him in the direction of an altogether different approach to thematic variation which really became evident only towards the end of the decade. *Horns/Rhythm* gains a star for boldness; *Jazz Contrast* drops back one for the wishy-washy sound.

***** This Is The Moment**

Original Jazz Classics OJC 812 *Dorham; Curtis Fuller (tb); Cedar Walton (p); Sam Jones (b); G. T. Hogan, Charli Persip (d).* 7 & 8/58.

Like Chet Baker, Dorham always considered his singing to be an integral part of what he was and did as a musician. He had sung with Dizzy's band in the '40s but had made the decision to concentrate on his horn. Even here, it's his 15 July 1958 playing that counts and, while it's tempting to reverse the emphasis and say that it's as lyrical as his singing is improvisatory and horn-like, almost the reverse is the case. Dorham doesn't sing like a horn man but he gives the lyric almost deliberate weight and emphasis, closer to speech rhythms than to top-line jazz. Unlike many hyphenate players, he makes a hard and fast distinction between the two 'voices'. 'From This Moment On' is done as an instrumental but 'I Remember Clifford' is adorned with the Jon Hendricks lyric, when it might have been more interesting the other way round. Both horns are muted throughout, lending the whole a soft, staccato bounce that is no less attractive for being determinedly understated. Historically, the album is significant for being Cedar Walton's first recording. He's not yet the presence he was to be in future years, a sapling rather than the solidly rooted sideman-for-all-seasons that he was to become. Nevertheless his soloing is adroit and unclichéd and his accompaniment firm without being domineering. A telling debut.

***** Blue Spring**

Original Jazz Classics OJC 134 *Dorham; David Amram (frhn); Julian 'Cannonball' Adderley (as); Cecil Payne (bs); Cedar Walton (p); Paul Chambers (b); Jimmy Cobb, Philly Joe Jones (d).* 1–2/59.

*****(*) Quiet Kenny**

Original Jazz Classics OJC 250 *Dorham; Tommy Flanagan (p); Paul Chambers (b); Art Taylor (d).* 11/59.

***** The Arrival Of Kenny Dorham**

Fresh Sound FSRCD 200 *Dorham; Charles Davis (bs); Tommy Flanagan (p); Butch Warren (b); Buddy Enlow (d).* 1/60.

Dorham enjoyed a brief resurgence towards the end of the '50s, and any of the above would serve as a reasonable introduction to his more deliberate, Miles-influenced approach of that period. *Quiet Kenny* is a minor masterpiece. The blues-playing is still as emotional as ever but there is a more relaxed approach to the basic metres, and Tommy Flanagan in particular invites a quieter and more sustained articulation of themes. *Arrival* sees him in good voice, tooting through a light but demanding programme that includes Rollins's favourite 'I'm An Old Cowhand' and 'Stella By Starlight' with the most open tone he'd produced.

***** Whistle Stop**

Blue Note 25646 *Dorham; Hank Mobley (ts); Kenny Drew (p); Paul Chambers (b); Philly Joe Jones (d).* 1/61.

***** Una Mas**

Blue Note 21228 *Dorham; Joe Henderson (ts); Herbie Hancock (p); Butch Warren (b); Tony Williams (d).* 4/63.

Despite the sustained energy of *Una Mas*, the title-track of which is one of Dorham's finest moments, and of *Trompeta Toccata* (both of which paired the trumpeter's brightly burnished tone with the muscular tenor of Joe Henderson), Dorham seemed to be running out of steam in 1963; 'one more time' was beginning to sound like once too often.

Whistle Stop made a reappearance in 2000. It's a bright and bubbly record, packed with great writing – 'Buffalo', 'Philly Twist' and 'Sunrise in Mexico' – and robust playing from all concerned. The album closes with the disturbingly titled 'Dorham's Epitaph', but it was far from that. Kenny had a long way to go.

***** The Art Of The Ballad**

Prestige 11013 *Dorham; David Amram (frhn); Julian 'Cannonball' Adderley, Ernie Henry (as); Harold Land, Oliver Nelson, Sonny Rollins (ts); Jimmy Heath (ts, bs); Cecil Payne (bs); Walter Bishop, Ray Bryant, Kenny Drew, Tommy Flanagan, Amos Trice, Cedar Walton (p); Betty Glamann (hp); Paul Chambers, Percy Heath, Clarence Jones, Wendell Marshall, Eddie Mathias, Oscar Pettiford, Wilbur Ware (b); Kenny Clarke, Jimmy Cobb, G.T Hogan, Max Roach, Art Taylor (d).* 53–59.

Good to see Kenny represented alongside more obvious players in this budget series. The trumpeter was a finely sensitive interpreter of ballads. And yet the album represents somewhat thin pickings for anyone eager to hear Kenny highlighted at length. Rightly, in our view, Prestige have gone for great performances rather than for tunes which highlight Dorham to the exclusion of others. Many of the tracks were made for other leaders, Ernie Henry, Harold Land and Oliver Nelson, and with Cannonball Adderley as co-leader. And yet it's the very quietness and almost reticence of Kenny's solo on 'Passion Flower' for Nelson that steals the record. That, and Cannonball Adderley's glorious, blues-drenched choruses on 'It Might As Well Be Spring'. An attractive package, and one that may well send newcomers in search of Dorham's original LPs.

Jimmy Dorsey (1904–57)

ALTO AND BARITONE SAXOPHONES, CLARINET, TRUMPET

The elder, reed-playing Dorsey brother worked with his sibling on the New York session-scene of the '20s before co-leading a band which he eventually took over after a quarrel with Tommy. A superb technician on his horns, admired by Charlie Parker and others, Dorsey's music matched his basically mild-mannered demeanour. He was reconciled with his brother, and their final venture as co-leaders ended with Tommy's death, followed by Jimmy's passing only months later.

****(*) Pennies From Heaven**

ASV AJA 5052 *Dorsey; George Thow, Toots Camarata, Joe Meyer (t); Don Mattison (tb, v); Bobby Byrne, Joe Yukl, Bruce Squires (tb); Fud Livingston (as, ts); Jack Stacey, Len Whitney (as); Skeets Hurfurt, Charles Frazier (ts); Bobby Van Eps, Freddy Slack (p); Roc Hillman (g, v); Slim Taft, Jack Ryan (b); Ray McKinley (d, v); Bob Eberle, Frances Langford (v).* 3/36–6/37.

***** Amapola**

ASV AJA 5287 *As above, except add W. C. Clark, Shorty Sherock, Ralph Muzillo, Nate Kazabier, Johnny Napton, Shorty Solomon, Jimmy Campbell, Ray Anthony, Paul McCoy, Bob Alexy, Ray Linn, Marky Markowitz, Phil Napoleon (t), Sonny Lee, Jerry Rosa, Al Jordan, Phil Washburne, Andy Russo, Nick Di Maio (tb); Noni Bernard, Dave Matthews, Sam Rubinowich, Milt Yaner, Frank Langone, Bill Covey (as), Leonard Whitner, Herbie Haymer, Don Hammond, Babe Russin (ts); Chuck Gentry, Bob Lawson (bs); Freddy Slack, Joe Lippman, Johnny Guarnieri, Dave Mann (p), Guy Smith, Allan Reuss, Tommy Kay (g), Jack Ryan, Bill Miller (b), Buddy Schutz (d), Bing Crosby, The Andrews Sisters, Helen O'Connell, Kitty Kallen (v).* 7/36–10/43.

★★(★) At The 400 Restaurant 1946

Hep CD 41 *Dorsey; Bob Avery, Claude Bowen, Ray Linn, Tonny Picciotto, Nathan Solomon, Seymour Baker, Irving Goodman, Louis Mucci (t); Si Zentner, Thomas Lee, Nick Di Maio, Anthony Russo, Fred Mancusi, Don Mattison, Bob Alexander (tb); Jack Aiken, Frank Langone, Bill Covey, Cliff Jackson (as); Bobby Dukoff, Charles Frazier, Charles Travis, Gill Koerner (ts); Bob Lawson, Johnny Dee (bs); Marvin Wright, Lou Carter (p); Herb Ellis, Teddy Walters (g); Jimmy Middleton, Norman Bates (b); Adolf Shutz, Karl Kiffe (d); Dee Parker, Paul Chapman (v).* 1/46.

★★★ Original Studio Radio Transcriptions

Swing Factory SWCD66612 *Dorsey; other personnel unlisted.* 39–49.

The elder Dorsey brother was a saxophonist of the highest technical accomplishment, though it tended to lead him to merely show off on many of the records he made as a session-man in the '20s. The band he formed in 1935 after splitting up with his brother was a commercial dance unit rather than any kind of jazz orchestra, but the group could swing when Dorsey wanted it to, and there was some impeccable section-playing, particularly from the trombones. The first ASV disc pulls together 18 tracks from this period, a mixture of vocal features for Eberle, Langford and McKinley and more jazz-orientated titles. 'Dorsey Dervish' harks back to the leader's technical exercises of the decade before, but 'Stompin' At The Savoy' is creditable enough, and Bobby Byrne's beautiful lead trombone on 'In A Sentimental Mood' (contrary to the sleeve-notes, Byrne doesn't sing on this tune) outdoes even Tommy Dorsey for mellifluousness. It's a pity, though, that titles such as 'Swamp Fire', 'Major And Minor Stomp' and 'Cherokee' are omitted. The remastering is rather lifeless.

Amapola collects 24 of the biggest hits by Dorsey's band over a seven-year period. The emphasis here is on the ballad and vocal-feature side of Dorsey's discography, and if this is what you want, it's an ideal record – from the title-track, Helen O'Connell's signature rendition of 'Green Eyes' and Kitty Kallen's 'Besame Mucho' to the somewhat more swinging 'I Fall In Love With You Every Day' and the novelty 'Six Lessons From Madame La Zonga', these are the memories which Dorsey's amen corner will probably remember best. The odd soloist pops up here and there to remind us that it was basically a good band. Better transfers than on the earlier ASV CD.

The Hep CD is a lot more modernistic: among the opening four tracks, which date from 1944, is a Dizzy Gillespie arrangement of 'Grand Central Getaway'. The remainder are airshots taken from a New York engagement two years later and, while the band has nothing very outstanding about it, there are one or two worthwhile solos from Bob Avery and the leader whose attractive score, 'Contrasts', hints at directions which he never really followed. Generally, though, there is rather more jazz-inflected material here than on the earlier CD, and remastering makes the best of the broadcast recording. The Swing Factory issue is in good sound, but the lack of any documentation leaves one guessing as to provenance and identity of the players: all one seems to hear is a good though anonymous swing band. Dorsey's is one of the last major swing-era bands still awaiting a full CD documentation, and these bits and pieces are all there is to hand.

Tommy Dorsey (1905–56)

TROMBONE, TRUMPET

A ubiquitous figure on the New York dance-band circuit of the '20s, Dorsey went on to lead one of the most successful swing-era big bands, although the jazz content of the records was often in doubt. The 'Sentimental Gentleman' of swing was a martinet of a leader, but he kept his band going through the ups and downs of the post-swing era, eventually reuniting with his brother Jimmy in their final orchestra. His perfect legato trombone style and singing high tone were his signature, something which heavily influenced his band singer, Frank Sinatra. In 1956, he choked to death in his sleep.

★★★ Tommy Dorsey 1928–1935

Classics 833 *Dorsey; Manny Klein, Andy Ferretti, Sterling Bose, Bill Graham (t); Joe Ortolano, Ben Pickering, Dave Jacobs (tb); Jimmy Dorsey, Sid Stoneburn (cl, as); Noni Bernardi (as); Clyde Rounds (as, ts); Johnny Van Eps (ts); Paul Mitchell, Fulton McGrath, Frank Signorelli (p); Arthur Schutt (harmonium); Eddie Lang, Mac Cheikes (g); Gene Traxler, Jimmy Williams (b); Sam Rosen, Sam Weiss, Stan King (d); Edythe Wright, Eleanor Powell (v).* 11/28–11/35.

Classics' opening disc takes in Dorsey's great 1928–9 dates where he plays trumpet – a bit shaky, but tremendously fierce, with terrific Eddie Lang support. These sound very clean and bright, which is why the rotten quality of the 1935 orchestra dates is so disappointing. These can't have been direct transfers. Either way, Dorsey got off to a modest start with five fairly nondescript sessions – though the fourth released his hit theme, 'I'm Getting Sentimental Over You'.

★★(★) Tommy Dorsey 1935–1936

Classics 854 *Dorsey; Sterling Bose, Andy Ferretti, Joe Bauer, Max Kaminsky, Sam Skolnick (t); Ben Pickering, Joe Ortolano, Walter Mercurio (tb); Joe Dixon (cl, as, v); Sid Stoneburn (cl, as); Fred Stulce, Noni Bernardi (as); Clyde Rounds (as, ts); Sid Block, Johnny Van Eps (ts); Dick Jones (p); Bill Schaffer (g); Gene Traxler, Dave Tough, Sam Weiss (d); Edythe Wright, Buddy Gately, Jack Leonard (v).* 12/35–3/36.

★★★ Tommy Dorsey 1936

Classics 878 *As above, except add Steve Lipkins (t), Red Bone, Les Jenkins (tb), Bud Freeman (ts), Carmen Mastren (g), The Three Esquires (v); omit Bose, Ferretti, Ortolano, Stoneburn, Bernardi, Block, Van Eps, Weiss, Gately.* 4–10/36.

★★★ Tommy Dorsey 1936–1937

Classics 916 *As above, except add Bunny Berigan, Bob Cusumano, Andy Ferretti, Jimmy Welch (t), Artie Foster (tb), Slats Long (cl, ts); omit Skolnick, Pickering, Schaffer.* 11/36–2/37.

★★★ Tommy Dorsey 1937

Classics 955 *As above, except add Pee Wee Erwin (t), Mike Doty, Johnny Mince (cl, as), Howard Smith (p); omit Berigan, Lipkins, Cusumano, Foster, Three Esquires.* 2–5/37.

Like all the great swing orchestras, Dorsey's band was as much about dance music as it was about jazz, and listening through these tracks may disappoint some expectations. Relatively few of the songs can be called survivors of the era since there is a lot of forgettable chaff among the material. Many of the arrangements are more functional than challenging, solos are usually kept to a minimum, and the feel of the orchestra harks back to Dorsey's earlier days as often as it looks ahead. All that said, the trombonist could claim several virtues. While he was the principal soloist, he could call on several fine jazzmen: Freeman, Dixon, Mince and – above all – Berigan, whose tantalizing first stint with the band (a mere five sessions) resulted in 'Song Of India', 'Marie', 'Mr Ghost Goes To Town' and 'The Goona Goo', to cite four memorable solos (all on Classics 916). Dorsey also had one of the best band singers of the era, Edythe Wright, as well as his Clambake Seven small group (discussed below). Sometimes an unpromising title will turn out surprisingly well, and on a piece like 'Keepin' Out Of Mischief Now' (Classics 916) the whole band shows what it could do. There is also the splendid swing drumming of Dave Tough to listen to.

Of these four discs, the first gets lower marks for a low ration of worthwhile tracks and some very sloppy remastering, the quality of which seems to vary from track to track. The standard improves on the next three, although a listen to the Retrieval CD listed below against the Clambake Seven tracks on Classics 955 shows how much better a job can be done with a little care and some mint originals. Classics 916 is probably the pick for the tracks with Berigan.

***** Tommy Dorsey 1937 Vol. 2**

Classics 995 *Dorsey; Pee Wee Erwin, Joe Bauer, Andy Ferretti (t); Les Jenkins, Red Bone (tb); Johnny Mince, Mike Doty (cl, as); Fred Stulce, Skeets Herfurt (as); Bud Freeman, Tony Antonelli (ts); Howard Smith (p); Carmen Mastren (g); Gene Traxler (b); Dave Tough (d); Edythe Wright, Jack Leonard (v).* 5–7/37.

***** Tommy Dorsey 1937 Vol. 3**

Classics 1035 *As above, except Walter Mercurio (tb) replaces Bone; omit Antonelli and Doty; add Lee Castle (t).* 7–9/37.

***** Tommy Dorsey 1937–1938**

Classics 1078 *As above, except add Earle Hagen (tb), Maurice Purtill (d); omit Bauer, Mercurio.* 10/37–3/38.

Dorsey was making records at an incredible pace: he cut 22 sessions in 1937 alone, proof of the band's popularity. As usual, though, the results are the swing-era mix of worthwhile music and softcore ballads and schmaltz. When the vocalist sits out and Dorsey gives the soloists some space, the full band delivers something fine, such as 'Canadian Capers' (Classics 1035), but for the most part the jazz content is left to the Clambake Seven sessions, where Dorsey, Freeman and the underrated Mince especially put some real heat into the proceedings. But there are also other compensations: Edythe Wright's singing is always a pleasure, and the mellifluous sound of the leader is frequently parlayed into similarly graceful playing by the whole band. There is the quota of jazzed classics, from such unlikely sources as Dvořák and Rimsky-Korsakov, on Classics 995; and Classics 1078 has his big hit, 'The Dipsy Doodle', arranged by Larry Clinton, although the second half of the disc is let down by some particularly bland material. Transfers aren't startling, but the music comes through cleanly enough.

***** Tommy Dorsey 1938**

Classics 1117 *Dorsey; Pee Wee Erwin, Lee Castle, Andy Ferretti (t); Les Jenkins, Frank D'Annolfo, Earle Hagen (tb); Johnny Mince (cl, as); Fred Stulce, Skeets Hurfurt, Hymie Schertzer (as); Bud Freeman, Deane Kincaide (ts); Howard Smith (p); Carmen Mastren (g); Artie Shapiro, Gene Traxler (b); Maurice Purtill (d); Edythe Wright, Jack Leonard, The Three Esquires (v).* 2–5/38.

***** Tommy Dorsey 1938 Vol. 2**

Classics 1156 *As above, except add Charlie Spivak, Yank Lawson, Max Kaminsky (t), Buddy Morrow (tb); omit D'Annolfo, Freeman, Shapiro.* 7–9/38.

***** Tommy Dorsey 1938–1939**

Classics 1197 *As above, except add Sam Shapiro (t), Dave Jacobs, Buddy Morrow, Elmer Smithers, Ward Silloway (tb), Babe Russin (ts); omit Erwin, Hagen, The Three Esquires.* 9/38–1/39.

Not really a banner year for Dorsey, whose biggest success still lay ahead of him. These three discs are, as before, a mix of sessions for the orchestra and for The Clambake Seven, and though the small-group sides are the warmest, some of the best playing is still in the music by the big band. Dorsey lost one of his best soloists when Bud Freeman departed (midway through Classics 1117). His replacement, Deane Kincaide, brought some charts into the band's book – although these were a curious set of throwbacks to '20s hits such as 'Copenhagen', 'Washboard Blues' and 'Panama' (all on Classics 1156), and 'Tin Roof Blues' and 'Down Home Rag' (Classics 1197). Spirited playing by the band, though, and Lawson and Russin were new recruits who could turn in a useful 16 bars. Even Dorsey himself, though sometimes maligned as a soloist, has some fine moments along with his usual rich lead lines. The material has its share of forgotten non-hits of the day, although in general Dorsey managed to avoid some of the worst of the pop fillers which blighted many a swing band's book. Transfers are all right, though not exactly bright.

***** The Song Is You**

Bluebird 66353-2 5CD *Dorsey; Bunny Berigan, Jimmy Blake, Ray Linn, Clyde Hurley, Ziggy Elman, Chuck Peterson, Al Stearns, Manny Klein, Jimmy Zito, Roger Ellick, Mickey Mangano, Dale Pierce, George Seaberg, Charlie Shavers, Gerald Goff (t); Dave Jacobs, Elmer Smithers, Ward Silloway, Lowell Martin, George Arus, Les Jenkins, Walter Mercurio, James Skiles, Walt Benson, Nelson Riddle, Tex Satterwhite, Karle De Karske, William Haller, Richard Noel (tb); Johnny Mince, Fred Stulce, Skeets Herfurt, Dean Kincaide, Babe Russin, Hymie Schertzer, Paul Mason, Don Lodice, Heinie Beau, Manny Gershman, Bruce Snyder, Harry Schuchman, Buddy DeFranco, Sid Cooper, Gale Curtis, Al Klink, Bruce Branson, Babe Fresk, Dave Harris, Gus Bivona, Vido Musso, Bill Shine (saxes); Howard Smith, Joe Bushkin, Milt Raskin, Milt Golden, John Potoker (p); Carmen Mastren, Clark Yocum, Bob Bain, Sam Herman (g); Joe Park (tba); Gene Traxler, Sid Weiss, Phil Stevens, Sid Block (b); Cliff Leeman, Buddy Rich (d); Frank Sinatra (v).* 2/40–7/42.

*****(*) The Best Of Tommy Dorsey And His Clambake Seven 1936–1938**

Retrieval RTR 79012 *Dorsey; Max Kaminsky, Pee Wee Irwin (t); Joe Dixon, Johnny Mince (cl); Bud Freeman (ts); Dick Jones (p); Bill Schaffer, Carmen Mastren (g); Gene Traxler (b); Dave Tough, Maurice Purtill, (d); Edythe Wright (v).* 12/35–2/47.

*****(*) The Music Goes 'Round & Around**

ASV AJA 5497 *Dorsey; Sterling Bose, Pee Wee Erwin, Max Kaminsky, Yank Lawson, Ziggy Elman, Charlie Shavers, Bobby Hackett, Jimmy Blake, Billy Butterfield (t); Joe Dixon, Johnny Mince, Buddy DeFranco, Peanuts Hucko (cl); Sid Block, Bud Freeman, Skeets Herfurt, Babe Russin, Bommie Richman, Arthur Rollini (ts); Paul Mitchell, Dick Jones, Howard Smith, John Potoker, Gene Schroeder, Rocky Coluccio (p); Mac*

Chiekes, Carmen Mastren, Sam Herman (g); Gene Traxler, Sid Bloch, Jack Lesberg (b); Sam Weiss, Dave Tough, Russ Isaacs, Graham Stevenson, Cliff Leeman, Alvin Stoller, Buzzy Drootin, Moe Purtill (d); Edythe Wright, Hughie Prince, Sy Oliver (v). 12/35–12/50.

Dorsey's small group was an initiative he began almost as soon as the bigger band became successful, and he ran it on and off alongside the main orchestra for the rest of his career. As with the big band, though, the group's material is often thin and prone to the occasional novelty tune which spoils what should have been a definitive small-group swing outfit. Retrieval's 21-track selection mystifyingly leaves out some very good Sevens (including our favourite, 'Rhythm Saved The World', which at least is on Classics 854), but otherwise offers a vivid portrait of some of Dorsey's best playing – his own solos a marriage of urbanity and heat – and excellent spots for Freeman, Erwin and Dixon. The best thing, though, is the superlative remastering by John R. T. Davies, which lets one hear what Carmen Mastren and Dave Tough were doing for the first time in any reissue and makes one aware of what a swinging rhythm section this was.

The alternative disc on ASV is pretty good too. Inevitably there are duplications, but it also offers five much later tracks from 1950, which include some smart Bobby Hackett work.

***** Tommy Dorsey 1939**

Classics 1237 *Dorsey; Yank Lawson, Andy Ferretti, Lee Castle, Pee Wee Erwin (t); Dave Jacobs, Ward Silloway, Elmer Smithers (tb); Johnny Mince (cl, as); Fred Stulce (as); Skeets Herfurt (as, v); Deane Kincaide, Babe Russin (ts); Howard Smith (p); Carmen Mastren (g); Gene Traxler (b); Dave Tough (d); Edythe Wright, Jack Leonard (v).* 1–5/39.

***** Tommy Dorsey 1939 Vol. 2**

Classics 1278 *As above, except add Mickey Bloom (t), Hymie Schertzer (as), Charles Carroll, Cliff Leeman (d); omit Castle.* 5–7/39.

****(*) Tommy Dorsey 1939 Vol. 3**

Classics 1327 *As above, except add Jimmy Blake (t), Noni Bernardi (as), Anita Boyer (v); omit Erwin.* 8–10/39.

For sheer prolificacy, Dorsey was practically unmatched at this point: these discs include 67 different titles, and they don't even cover a full year's output. And Dorsey's greatest music was arguably still ahead of him. Classics 1237 has some plain material, as usual, but the band make the absolute most of 'Tea For Two'; 'By The River Sainte Marie' gets an unexpectedly fine performance, and 'Milenberg Joys' nods back to an older hot style. Classics 1278 follows a similar pattern and has more of the dance band than the swing orchestra in it, although there are some excellent things - Sy Oliver's two-part arrangement of 'Lonesome Road', Edythe Wright on 'Well, All Right', and another good Oliver chart in 'Stomp It Off', even if the band could have played it with a little more vigour. Classics 1327 is easily the weakest of the three, despite including a Clambake Seven date (one of their mildest): lots of dull Jack Leonard vocals, and precious little swing.

****(*) Palladium 1940 & Raleigh Show 1943**

Jazz Hour JH-1035 *Personnel unlisted.* 40–43.

****(*) 1942 War Bond Broadcast**

Jazz Hour JH-1013 *Personnel unlisted.* 7–10/42.

Both these discs of airshots are for hardcore followers only. The earlier set has some good if rusty 1940 material with Sinatra and, though the 1943 show is in surprisingly bright and clear hi-fi, the band sounds jolted and there's a lot of irrelevant speech-making. The 1942 disc starts off in poor sound, which gets increasingly worse until halfway through, when the October programme cleans up and works off a couple of nice if familiar Sy Oliver arrangements.

***** The Carnegie Hall V-Disc Session April 1944**

Hep CD 40 *Dorsey; Pete Candoli, George Seaberg, Sal La Perche, Dale Pearce, Bob Price, Ralph Santangelo, Mickey Mangano (t); Walter Benson, Tommy Pederson, Tex Satterwhite, Nelson Riddle (tb); Buddy DeFranco, Hank D'Amico (cl, as); Sid Cooper, Leonard Kaye (as); Gail Curtis, Al Klink, Don Lodice, Mickey Sabol (ts); Bruce Branson, Manny Gershman (bs); Michael 'Dodo' Marmarosa, Milt Raskin (p); Dennis Sandole, Bob Bain (g); Joe Park (tba); Sid Block (b); Gene Krupa, Maurice Purtill, Buddy Rich (d); Bing Crosby, Frances Langford, Georgia Gibbs, Bob Allen, The Sentimentalists, Bonnie Lou Williams (v); plus string section.* 10/43–9/44.

****(*) The All Time Hit Parade Rehearsals**

Hep CD 39 *As above, except omit Candoli, Price, Santangelo, D'Amico, Kaye, Klink, Gershman, Raskin, Sandole, Krupa and Purtill, Crosby and Gibbs; add Judy Garland, Frank Sinatra (v).* 6–9/44.

Although there isn't a great deal of jazz on these records, they give a clearer idea of the sound of Dorsey's band since John R. T. Davies's superb remastering puts many reissues to shame. *All Time Hit Parade* is drawn from acetate transcriptions of rehearsals for a radio show of that name and, while they tend to display the sweeter side of Dorsey's band, the smooth power of the sections is put across smartly by the sound. Sinatra has a couple of fine features in 'I'll Walk Alone' and 'If You Are But A Dream', and there's a showcase for Marmarosa on 'Boogie Woogie'. The V-Disc material, again in splendid restoration, is rather more exciting, with a number of spots for La Perche, DeFranco and Klink. Crosby and Langford deliver a couple of messages to the troops as a bonus.

***** Live In Hi-Fi At Casino Gardens**

Jazz Hour JH-1018 *Personnel unlisted.* 6–8/46.

The first show here is OK but nothing special, with Charlie Shavers's feature on 'At The Fat Man' the only standout; but the second, with extended workouts on six good charts by Bill Finegan and others, is much more like it. There's a lot of badinage between Tom and the announcer, which will either charm or repel, but the music's strong and the sound, if not exactly 'hi-fi', is quite listenable.

*****(*) At The Fat Man's 1946–1948**

Hep CD 43 *Dorsey; Jack Dougherty, Mickey Mangano, George Seaburg, Ziggy Elman, Charlie Shavers, Claude Bowen, Vern Arslan, Chuck Peterson (t); Larry Hall, Tex Satterwhite, Greg Philips, John Youngman, Charles La Rue, Red Benson, Nick Di Maio, Dick Noel (tb); Buddy DeFranco, Billy Ainsworth, Marshall Hawk, Louis Prisby (cl, as); Sid Cooper, Bruce Branson (as); Boomie Richman, Don Lodice, Babe Fresk, Corky Corcoran, Marty Berman (ts); Joe Koch (bs); John Potoker, Rocky Coluccio, Paul Smith (p); Sam Herman, Tony Rizzi (g); Sid Block, Sam Cheifetz, Norman Seelig (b); Alvin Stoller, Louie Bellson (d); Stuart Foster, Denny Dennis, Lucy Ann Polk, Gordon Polk, The Sentimentalists (v).* 5/46–12/48.

*****(*) The Post-War Era**

Bluebird 66156-2 *Similar to above, except add Charlie Shavers, Paul McCoy, Cy Baker, Irving Goodman, Johnny Martel, Bernie Glow, Hal Ableser, Chris Griffin, Stan Stout, Doc Severinsen, Ray Wetzel, Billy Butterfield, Art Depew, Johnny Amoroso (t), Bill Siegel, Sam Levine, Bill Schallen, Larry Hall, Sol Train, Al Mastren, Buddy Morrow, Dean Kincaide, Will Bradley, Bill Pritchard, Ange Callea (tb), Abe Most, John Rotella, Billy Ainsworth, George Kennon, Walt Levinsky, Hugo Lowenstein, Sol Schlinger, Danny Bank, Jerry Winner (reeds), Gene Kutch, Lou Levy (p), Ward Erwin, Bob Baldwin (b), Buddy Rich (d).* 1/46–6/50.

Dorsey's later records deserve a wider hearing than they've been given by posterity. He had no more hits on the scale of 'Marie' or 'Song Of India', but he remained – as then-new arranger Bill Finegan, responsible for the best arrangements on the Bluebird CD, asserts in the sleeve-note – a keen-eared musician and less conservative than many of his contemporaries. *The Post-War Era* is a splendid cross-section of the pick of Dorsey in the '40s, with smart scores such as 'Hollywood Hat', with its amazing brass figures, or 'Tom Foolery' sounding as good as anything in his earlier work. There are some previously unissued tracks among the 22 on offer, and the sound, though dry, is clean and sharp. The Hep compilation suffers from some very variable sound-sources and, though these airchecks feature some fine alternative versions of some of the scores on the Bluebird disc (as well as a couple of delicious vocals by Lucy Ann Polk), it stands very much in the shadow of the studio disc.

Dorsey Brothers Orchestra

GROUP

As bandleaders, the brothers put aside their many differences for a while at least. While their early bands were studio-only outfits, they formed a 'real' Dorsey Brothers Orchestra in 1934, but it lasted only a year before Jimmy took it over after a quarrel with his sibling. Their last co-led band ran from 1953 until Tommy's death.

***** The Dorsey Brothers' Orchestra Vol. 1**

Jazz Oracle BDW 8004 *Leo McConville, Fuzzy Farrar, Mickey Bloom, Nat Natoli, Mannie Klein (t); Tommy Dorsey (t, tb); Jack Teagarden, Carl Loffler, Glenn Miller (tb); Jimmy Dorsey (cl, as); Arnold Brilhart (cl, as, f); Frank Teschemacher (cl, ts); Herbert Spencer, Bill Green (ts); Adrian Rollini (bsx); Frank Signorelli, Arthur Schutt (p); Charles Dondron (vib); Carl Kress (g, bj); Eddie Lang (g); Tony Colucci (bj); Jimmy Williams (b); Joe Tarto, Hank Stern, Jack Hansen (tba); Stan King, Chauncey Morehouse (d); Smith Ballew, Hal Kemp, Nye Mayhew, Saxie Dowell, Skinny Ennis, Irving Kaufman (v).* 2–11/28.

***** The Dorsey Brothers' Orchestra Vol. 2**

Jazz Oracle BDW 8005 *Similar to above, except add Phil Napoleon, Muggsy Spanier, Frank Guarente (t), Joe Yukl (tb), Ollie Boyd (cl), Max Farley (as, f), Alfie Evans, Larry Abbott (as), Lucien Smith (ts, v), Jim Crossan, Paul Mason (ts), Phil Raines (bsn), Irving Brodsky (p), Al Duffy, Leo Kroucrick, Murray Kellner, Sam Rates, Nat Brusiloff, Sam Freed (vn), Emil Stark (clo), Jimmy Mullen (b), Ray Bauduc (d); Bing Crosby (v).* 1/29–1/30.

***** The Dorsey Brothers' Orchestra Vol. 3**

Jazz Oracle BDW 8006 *Similar to above, except add Bunny Berigan, Bill Moore, Louis Gracia, Charles Margulis (t), Foster Morehouse, Larry Binyon, Bud Freeman (ts), Fulton McGrath (p), Tony Sacco (g, bj, v), Dick McDonough (g), Artie Bernstein (b), Scrappy Lambert, Wes Vaughan, Elmer Feldkamp (v).* 11/30–4/33.

***** Harlem Lullaby**

Hep CD 1006 *Manny Klein, Sterling Bose, Bunny Berigan (t); Tommy Dorsey (tb); Larry Binyon (cl, as, ts); Jimmy Dorsey (cl, as); Joe Venuti, Harry Hoffman, Walter Edelstein, Lou Kosloff (vn); Joe Meresco, Fulton McGrath (p); Dick McDonough (g); Artie Bernstein (b); Stan King, Chauncey Morehouse, Larry Gomar (d); Bing Crosby, Mae West, Ethel Waters, Mildred Bailey, Lee Wiley (v).* 2–7/33.

The Dorseys could call on their best pals for their many studio dates, even before the 'official' formation of their orchestra in 1934. A string of sessions for OKeh (and a couple for other labels) are comprehensively covered by the nicely presented Jazz Oracle CDs, which include numerous alternative takes, a few rare tests and the various 'solo' sessions which the brothers undertook in the period. Considering how often they threw in 8 or 16 hot bars into the many conventional dance records they played on, it's a bit surprising that their own bands were not much more jazz-orientated than their bread-and-butter dates. The pickings on both of the first two discs are regrettably slim. The January 1929 date has some fine vocals by Bing Crosby, but too many of the tracks are troubled by feeble singing and only a few brief glimpses of a soloist (despite the often stellar line-ups, it's only Tommy and Jimmy who do the real improvising). A track such as 'Breakaway' on the second volume is a comparative corker. But the solo sessions that were features for each Dorsey separately are still fondly remembered by collectors, and they're presented in admirable sound here: Jimmy's clarinet feature on 'Prayin' The Blues' still sounds terrific, and it reminds one of why Charlie Parker and Dexter Gordon both held him in high esteem.

The third volume is arguably the best, since Berigan shows up and has some excellent solo spots of his own, along with those of the brothers: sample the rollicking 'Parkin' In The Moonlight' as a choice example. The disc closes five more feature-sessions for the Dorseys as individual soloists. Tommy's turn on 'Maybe' doesn't have much jazz in it, but this rare pair of test-takes shows just why he was the greatest smooth-man of his day. First-rate transfers, although the January 1930 date for Cameo has taxed even John R. T. Davies to the limit as far as getting something out of the shellac goes.

Hep's compilation offers the chance to hear the brothers and their men backing four vocalists of the day. Mae West's pair of titles are little more than a not especially tuneful extension of her man-eating persona, and Wiley's session shows the singer still in raw shape, but the four tracks with Crosby show how much the singer had learnt from jazz players, and the eight featuring Mildred Bailey are delightful, her light and limber voice gliding over the music with little effort. There are brief solos for the Dorseys and Berigan here and there, but the record belongs mainly to the singers. First-class remastering throughout.

****(*) The Dorsey Brothers Orchestra – 1935**

Circle CCD-20 *George Thow, Jerry Neary, Charlie Spivak (t); Tommy Dorsey, Joe Yukl, Don Matteson (tb); Jimmy Dorsey (cl, as); Jack Stacey (as); Skeets Herfurt (ts); Bobby Van Eps (p); Roc Hillman (g); Delmar Kaplan (b); Ray McKinley (d); Bob Crosby (v).* 1/35.

Thirteen transcriptions for WBC, with the orchestra in fine fettle. Crosby is restricted to four vocals and the emphasis is on the band, but the charts tend towards the sweet rather than the hot, and when they do tackle a fast one – as with 'Sugar Foot Stomp' or 'Eccentric' – the ensemble sound and a certain rhythmic squareness suggest that the Dorseys hadn't yet got their feet out of the '20s. The sound is clean if a little muffled. The rest of the CD is given over to 12 tracks by Arnold Johnson's orchestra.

***** Casino Gardens Ballroom 1946**

Hep 59 *Bob Alexy, Ray Linn, Irving Goodman, Tony Picciotto, Shorty Solomon, Cy Baker, Tony Faso, George Seaburg, Mickey Mangano, John Dougherty, Ziggy Elman, Charlie Shavers, Claude Bowen, Hal Ableser (t); Tommy Dorsey, Mickey Iannone, Sonny Lee, Andy Russo, Nick Di Maio, Bob Alexander, Don Matteson, Fred Mancusi, Chauncey Welsh, Larry Hall, Tex Satterwhite, Greg Philips, John Youngman, Charles La Rue, Walt Benson (tb); Jimmy Dorsey, Jack Aiken, Frank Langone, Tino Isgrow, Buddy Williams, Bob Lawson, Norman Stern, Cliff Jackson, Gilbert Koerner, Vince Francis, Serge Chaloff, Buddy De Franco, Sid Cooper, Don Lodice, Babe Fresk, Boomie Richman, Abe Most, Bob Dawes, Louis Prisby, Bruce Branson, Marty Berman, Corky Corcoran, Joe Koch (reeds); Marvin Wright, Rocky Coluccio, Joe Potoker, Lou Carter (p); Herb Ellis, Tony Rizzi, Bob Bain (g); Joe Stutz, Sid Block, Sam Chiefitz, John Frigo (b); Buddy Schutz, Karl Kiffe, Alvin Stoller, Louie Bellson (d); Dee Parker, Stuart Foster, Bob Carroll (v).* 1/45–7/47.

Strictly speaking, not the brothers together at all, but their respective orchestras featured together in a number of 'battles of the bands' broadcasts. The music is the typical late-swing mix of flag-wavers and crooner ballads. Not much to get excited about, but both bands are as well-heeled as you'd expect, and there are nice glimpses of Herb Ellis and Serge Chaloff with Jimmy's band on a genial treatment of 'Perdido'.

Dave Douglas (born 1963)

TRUMPET

In less than a decade, Douglas has established himself as a key figure in modern jazz, an individualistic stylist whose grasp of history is apparent mainly in elision and omission rather than homage. A seasoned and responsive performer on other leaders' records, he now has a substantial body of work under his own name.

*****(*) Parallel Worlds**

Soul Note 121226 *Douglas; Mark Feldman (vn); Erik Friedlander (clo); Mark Dresser (b); Michael Sarin (d).* 93.

None other than Gunther Schuller turns up in the sleeve-notes to drop names like Stravinsky, Bartók, Berg and Lutoslawski, as well as Don Ellis, Bob Graettinger and Leo Smith, and to say how much 'I like the Webernesque textures'. Unlike, say, Paul Smoker or Franz Koglmann, two other trumpeters who have attempted some confluence between free jazz and twentieth-century classical forms (and both to be stablemates of Douglas on hat ART), the now ubiquitous Douglas actually includes some canonical material in this quietly ambitious programme. There can't be many more startling openings to a 'jazz' record than 'Sehr Bewegt', an arrangement of the third of Webern's Op. 5, *Five Movements For String Quartet.*

Elsewhere on the album, alongside half a dozen highly idiosyncratic originals, Douglas includes a 'Grand Choral' by Stravinsky (part of *L'Histoire Du Soldat*) as well as Weill's 'Ballad In Which MacHeath Asks Everyone To Forgive Him', and Ellington's 'Loco Madi'. This, plus an unconventional instrumentation in jazz terms, makes for an interesting prospect. By the turn of the '90s, Douglas was being touted as the coming thing – like Bill Frisell a stylist sufficiently unimprisoned by style to make a significant intervention on almost anyone's disc. Membership of John Zorn's ridiculously prolific Masada group cemented perceptions of him as a strong, dry, essentially melodic player whose sound fell somewhere between Booker Little, Miles and Don Ellis. The release of *Parallel Worlds* suggested strongly that Douglas wasn't going to be imprisoned by generalities, either. It's a generously eclectic set, very much within a jazz idiom. The long title-piece and 'For Every Action' are beautifully structured, with crisp, responsive writing for the strings, loaded bass-lines and acres of free space for (mostly) mid-paced improvisation.

As was to become obvious on later records, not least in songs about Bosnian children on the *The Tiny Bell Trio*, Douglas often seems as much inspired by humanitarian and political concerns as by purely musical ones, and there is no mistaking the passion and the commitment he brings to his evocation of 'Parallel Worlds', lives lived under conditions that fall far short of ideal. However academic his influences might sound – and it is Schuller, rather than Douglas, who does that – he is far from uncommunicative, far from unemotional.

*****(*) The Tiny Bell Trio**

Songlines SGL 1504 *Douglas; Brad Schoeppach (g); Jim Black (d).* 12/93.

***** Tiny Bell Trio**

Arabesque Jazz AJ 0126 *As above.* 96.

With the formation of the Tiny Bell Trio, Douglas cemented his interest in European song form. The first of these two extraordinary records includes arrangements of pieces by Joseph Kosma ('La Belle Saison' and 'Fille d'Acier'), Weill again ('Drowned Girl'), a piece by Germaine Tailleferre, the only female member of Les Six, and a traditional Hungarian *csárdás* (all on the Songlines disc).

A setting like this would be too exacting for a less than supremely confident player. Douglas floats almost unconcernedly over Schoeppach's guitar chords, often in a key which is relative to the implied location of the piece. His attack seems a little brighter and sharper than on the Soul Note, but this may be a function of better recording.

The live set on Arabesque is a touch disappointing, and certainly not up to some of the performances the group turned in over this period. Interestingly, Douglas seems to lean more heavily on chord structures in a setting like this, but there is ample evidence of his left-field approach, and committed enthusiasts will be delighted with further evidence of his talents.

****** In Our Lifetime**

New World/Countercurrents 80471 *Douglas; Josh Roseman (tb); Chris Speed (cl, ts); Marty Ehrlich (bcl); Uri Caine (p); James Genus (b); Joey Baron (d).* 12/94.

★★★★ Five

Soul Note 121276 *As for Parallel Worlds, except Drew Gress (b) replaces Dresser.* 8/95.

Reconvening the band which made *Parallel Worlds* was an interesting initiative in the context of the progress Douglas seemed to have made with *In Our Lifetime*. The second of the pair has a broader, more orchestral sound, the supplementary horns deployed for depth of focus rather than for surface detail, and that is perhaps the big change in the string group. Feldman, Friedlander and Gress are treated much less as solo strings than as members of an ensemble (admittedly more autonomous than one might usually expect).

The presence of a piano on the earlier disc appears to restrict Douglas somewhat, though Caine is hardly unaware of the musical language being explored. The diversions into atonality seem less doctrinaire and there are signs that Douglas is taking a more mainstream tack on jazz harmonies. Both albums are heavily tinged with a Booker Little influence; 'Strength And Sanity' (on *In Our Lifetime*) is a Little composition, rapidly followed by four miniatures in the spirit of his playing. On the later disc, Woody Shaw, composer of 'Actualities', is an additional influence, and immediately one hears a new and significant facet of what Douglas is about.

★★★★ Constellations

hatOLOGY 673*Douglas; Brad Schoeppach (g); Jim Black (d, perc).*

★★★(★) Tiny Bell Trio Live In Europe

Arabesque AJ 0126 *As above.* 10/96.

The best of the earlier Tiny Bell records, *Constellations*, was recorded off-road but mid-tour. One hears immediately that this is a working unit, with a considerable mutual understanding. Douglas's Balkan interests – both musical and political – come through strongly on the now-reissued disc. 'Taking Sides' is inspired by the brutal civil war in former Yugoslavia, a raw, powerful expression of anger and mourning that stands with the best work he has committed to record. In an entirely different vein, 'Maquiladoras' takes up cudgels for low-paid migrant workers. 'Scriabin' is a thoughtful essay in extreme chromaticism, almost serial in quality, and 'Hope Ring True' sounds like '60s agit-prop jazz put through several filters of irony, or it may just mean what it says. To underline his eclecticism and sense of history Douglas hands the pianoless group a forgotten Herbie Nichols theme, 'The Gig', and makes it sound utterly contemporary as well.

Douglas seems confident in his partners, allowing Black in particular to stretch out and express himself. As accordionist Guy Klucevesek was to do in later groups, Schoeppach throws deliciously complex harmonic shapes, a crushed-velvet foil to the trumpeter's bright lines. As before, 'Csárdás' is something of an encore piece, but the real glory of the set is an almost 12-minute 'Zeno', which opens a central section of compelling modern jazz that is bookended by Douglas's trademark Schumann arrangement. There is some makeweight material, but Douglas fans will find much to ponder in the shorter pieces as well.

★★★ Stargazer

Arabesque AJ 0132 *Douglas; Josh Roseman (tb); Uri Caine (p); Joey Baron (d).* 12/96.

At first blush the most conventional set Douglas has yet recorded, this is still sufficiently original to command attention. The leader leans more heavily than usual on chords and a straightforward count, albeit dressed up in Baron's usual skittery style. Strong, confident, but, by the standard of Douglas's recent output, somewhat pedestrian.

★★★ Magic Triangle

Arabesque AJ 0139 *Douglas; Chris Potter (ts); James Genus (b); Ben Perowsky (d).* 5/97.

A rather conventional and only occasionally teasing set. The leader's tone is limpid and softly burnished, and Potter gives further notice of a broad musical capacity. The compositions are all original and the real interest of the album lies in the writing, which shows what a brilliant touch Douglas has with rather more straightforward jazz heads and themes: 'Padded Cell', 'Odalisque' and 'The Ghost' suggest a kinship with an unexpected array of mostly keyboard-based composers, Herbie Nichols, Herbie Hancock, Horace Tapscott.

The absence of a harmony instrument is the most radical departure from Douglas's usual practice and sharply distinguishes this record from what was to follow, but Genus covers the ground admirably and provides enough rhythmic punch to allow Perowsky the kind of expressive freedom Jim Black claimed in the Tiny Bell Trio.

★★★★ Charms Of The Night Sky

Winter & Winter 910 015-2 *Douglas; Guy Klucevesek (acc); Mark Feldman (vn); Greg Cohen (d).* 9/97.

A line-up calculated to combine musical complexity with the purest aesthetic grace. The language is very similar to that of the Tiny Bell Trio but, with Klucevesek and Feldman in the group and no drummer, the pace is slower and more deliberate, a musingly graceful album that never subordinates musicality to mere effect.

'Dance In Thy Soul' is a long tribute to Charlie Haden, conceived somewhere between a classical sonata and one of Haden's beloved torch songs of the '40s. Klucevesek's touch with shorter, song-like forms can be heard in a sequence of three 'Mug Shots', tiny sketches that would gladden the heart of any lyricist and possibly drive him to despair at the same time.

For a change, there is a jazz standard, Herbie Hancock's 'Little One', and a version of Francesco Cilea's 'Poveri Fiori', a performance that squares perfectly with Winter & Winter's intriguing hybrid of jazz, folk and classical idioms. Where the label catalogue keeps them apart and compartmentalized, Douglas likes to hear them cross-pollinate. This is a record beyond category, full of jazz but something else as well, the kind of record which points forward to new directions for the music's second century.

★★★(★) Moving Portraits

DIW 934 *Douglas; Bill Carrothers (p); James Genus (b); Billy Hart (d).* 12/97.

Once again an intriguing blend of idiomatic jazz-writing and some unexpected borrowed material, like the two Joni Mitchell songs which begin the album's final section. The closing track, 'Romero', is one of Douglas's most substantial jazz performances, and 'Moving Portrait' is the best evidence yet of how thoroughly he has absorbed modern classical procedures, rather than just importing *ad hoc* themes and ideas.

The presence of Hart is interesting. Jabali has been a constant source of inspiration over the years and he plays here with a calm, swinging authority, all the while responsive to the demands of Douglas's music. Carrothers is not the sort of player to set the heather on fire, but he has a nice touch, sounds as if he might have played the odd bit of Schumann in his youth, and clearly enjoys the challenge of these inventive compositions.

CORE COLLECTION

★★★★ Convergence

Soul Note 121316-2 *Douglas; Mark Feldman (vn); Erik Friedlander (clo); Drew Gress (b); Michael Sarin (d).* 1/98.

This, of course, is the same band that made *Parallel Worlds* and *Five*, with the single change of Drew Gress for Mark Dresser. The latter album was so named because the leader didn't want the project to be thought of as Douglas-and-strings. Five years on, it's a well-proven point. The quintet plays like a unit and puts down roots, throws out shoots all over the place.

No surprise by this stage in the game to find Douglas programming 'Desseins Eternels' from Olivier Messiaen's organ work *La Nativité Du Seigneur*, and following it with Weill's 'Bilbao Song'. The trumpeter claims he first heard the Messiaen piece in a blindfold test set by a friend, and thought it was 'Joe Zawinul, early Weather Report', which attests not to musical illiteracy but to a grasp of the basic seamlessness of musical styles, for the French composer's strong bass pedals are very similar to Zawinul's signature procedure.

The two key tracks here are a farewell to drummer Tony Williams, a perfect illustration of Douglas's ability to invest long form with real significance, and 'Meeting At Infinity', which indirectly gives the album its title and underlines how Douglas likes to have separate musical lines converge only virtually, leaving them to their own instrumental logic. Anyone who has those early records and nothing else will feel on familiar ground and will sense that there's been a fair amount of musical progress along the way. Anyone who's kept pace with the Dave Douglas story will be well satisfied with the synthesis he makes.

★★★(★) Songs For Wandering Souls

Winter & Winter 910 042-2 *Douglas; Brad Shepik (g); Jim Black (d, perc).* 12/98.

The guitarist has either changed his name or is the victim of an egregious typo. He certainly hasn't changed his approach, though on occasion there is something slightly blunter and more guttural in his attack. Along with the obligatory Schumann 'standard' and a group of new compositions, Douglas unexpectedly includes Roland Kirk's 'Breath-A-Thon', which was originally a solo piece on Rahsaan's *Natural Black Inventions: Roots Strata*. By this stage, though, expectations of Douglas are pretty open-ended anyway.

The sound is very good, engineered by Joe Perla, with the educated ears of Stefan Winter guaranteeing the quality control. Not the most compelling item in the Douglas canon, but a marvellous representation of his gifts, all the same.

★★★★ Leap Of Faith

Arabesque 145 *Douglas; Chris Potter (ts); James Genus (b); Ben Perowsky (d).* 9/98.

Stunningly good modern jazz, performed with a seriousness that never dips into solemnity. 'Mistaken Identity' and the oddly (possibly mistakenly) titled 'Igenous' are dazzlingly original. 'Western Haiku' suggests that Douglas is already inventing his own idiom, while 'Guido's High Note' suggests that he can tackle just about anything technically. Potter is more than along for the ride, he is a genuine sharer in this music; and the relatively mainstream pairing of Genus and Perowsky guarantees that the music stays straightforward and swinging, even when the source material points away from jazz strictly conceived and towards some as yet unnamed and undefined synthesis of styles.

★★★(★) Soul On Soul

RCA 63603 *Douglas; Josh Roseman (tb); Chris Speed, Greg Tardy (ts, cl); Uri Caine (p); James Genus (b); Joey Baron (d).* 8/99.

Mary Lou Williams is still more honoured in the breach – or at least the oversight – than the observance, so it is doubly pleasurable to hear her receive the tributes of a younger-generation player of Douglas's instincts. He combines Williams themes – most of them fairly familiar, like 'Mary's Idea' and 'Aries' from the *Zodiac Suite* – with things of his own. The unifying factor is Dave's intelligent, soulful voice and his ability to frame bands which convey a bigger idea without sounding pretentious or strained. Tardy is a valuable addition to the basic line-up, but it is the now semi-regular group who carry most of the music. Roseman is in fine form, Caine is virtually unstoppable and Genus and Baron create take-off runways and landing strips that manage to sound both completely reliable and stimulatingly bumpy. Glorious stuff from a master musician.

★★★(★) A Thousand Evenings

RCA 63698 *Douglas; Mark Feldman (vn); Guy Klucevesek (acc); Greg Cohen (b).* 8/00.

Astonishing that Douglas should have the confidence and the sheer moxie to programme the 'Goldfinger' theme alongside his own 'In So Many Worlds' suite, and to hand over the reins to Klucevesek for a solo performance on 'Variety'. The accordionist is a remarkable musician, as individual on his instrument as Douglas is on trumpet, and with something of the same diversity of idiom. There are almost too many inputs at work here: classical music, tango, folk from East and West, and of course avant-garde jazz as well. And yet Douglas is able to contrive a synthesis of them all that neither sounds strained nor feels overwrought.

★★★(★) Witness

RCA 63763 *Douglas; Josh Roseman (tb); Joe Daley (tba); Chris Speed (ts, cl); Bryan Carrott (vib, mar, glock); Mark Feldman (vn); Erik Friedlander (clo); Drew Gress (b); Michael Sarin (d); Ikue Mori (elec p); Yuka Honda (samples); Tom Waits (v).* 12/00.

This, for the record, is the one that features rock icon Tom Waits, in spoken-word mode on 'Mahfouz'. Douglas has the imagination and the clout to pull off tricks like that and to do it with complete aplomb. *Witness* is a remarkably coherent and unified set. For all its eclectic sourcing of materials – Middle Eastern, African, Jewish, mainstream American – it sounds like nothing but itself, and it stands up to a lot of active listening. Dave gets inside his sources, understands how they work and then sets about making them his own. The sound is rich and subtly inflected, with the trumpet drifting in just above the rest of the ensemble. Clever and compelling stuff from an artist who seems capable of taking on any challenge and making something original and personal from it.

***** The Infinite**

RCA 63918 *Douglas; Chris Potter (ts, bcl); Uri Caine (p); James Genus (b); Clarence Penn (d).* 12/01.

The line-up will strike seasoned Douglasites as unusual, and indeed this does mark a certain change of direction for the trumpeter. Despite the fulsome thank you to Miles Davis on the sleeve, that influence is now more spiritual than audible. If Douglas sounds like anyone else, it is Tomasz Stańko, who has the same brittle lyricism and almost classical severity of purpose.

Among the themes tackled here are soul diva Mary J. Blige's 'Crazy Games' and Björk's 'Unison'. Like Miles, Douglas is delving into contemporary pop for material. Neither of these tracks is a 'Time After Time' or a 'Human Nature', but it may be that Dave is not interested in scoring hits. He feels like an artist who is biding his time and waiting for the business to come round to his way of thinking.

****** Freak In**

Bluebird 64008 *Douglas; Chris Speed (cl); Seamus Blake (ts); Craig Taborn (p); Jamie Saft (ky); Romero Lubambo, Marc Ribot (g); Joey Baron, Michael Sarin (d); Karsh Kale (d, perc); Ikue Mori (elec p).* 6/02.

It seems unlikely that future jazz histories will identify this as Douglas's *Bitches Brew*, largely because that particular revolution took place in 1969, but also partly because in tone and range it's closer to both *In A Silent Way* and the later, darker *Agharta* and *Pangaea*. Douglas has employed electronic processing to give *Freak In* a whirling, beat-driven quality that remains entirely consistent with his more usual energies. His playing has never been more prominent and never stronger, as he shows on 'Culver City Park' and 'Traveller, There Is No Road'. His tone is strong, slightly sharper than usual in the presence of electronics, and his line still very much affected by other musics, rock and Balkan folk, but also contemporary classical performance. Ribot's guitar, producer Saft's keys and Taborn's Fender Rhodes all help provide rich settings for the trumpet. 'November' is a ballad form worthy of Miles Davis, while the opening title-piece builds something wild round the most basic of rhythmic shapes. Douglas's rate of production slowed noticeably around this time, not because of any dearth of ideas, but because he was touring incessantly and still absorbing new musical languages.

****** Strange Liberation**

RCA 50818 *Douglas; Chris Potter (ts, bcl); Uri Caine (p); Bill Frisell (g); James Genus (b); Clarence Penn (d, perc).* 8/03.

The purple patch continues. The title comes from Martin Luther King's wry comment about how the Vietnamese populace must regard American intervention. In 2003, with American troops dying in 'liberated' Iraq, it must have seemed ever more pertinent.

Strange Liberation is less electronically driven than its predecessor, though the introduction of Bill Frisell on guitar (apparently a long-held ambition) gives the record an equally distinctive character. 'Frisell's Dream' is a witty jazz piece, nodding to Monk and others, but marked by Douglas's now ultra-confident eclecticism. 'The Jones' also seems to allude to Monk, though less obliquely. Easily the best track on a notably quiet and unemphatic album is 'A Single Sky', a minor-key idea established by Caine and elaborated brilliantly by Potter and Douglas in canons. It's brief, but, by hell, it's effective. Another wonderful record, albeit one that requires a more careful listen than its predecessor.

Down Home Jazz Band

GROUP

A West Coast revivalist institution, run for many years by brassman Chris Tyle.

***** Dawn Club Joys**

Stomp Off CD1241 *Bob Schulz (c, v); Chris Tyle (c); Tom Bartlett (tb, v); Bob Helm (cl, v); Ray Skjelbred (p); Jack Meilahn (bj); Mike Bezin (tba); Hal Smith (d).* 7/91.

***** Back To Bodega**

Stomp Off CD1273 *Chris Tyle (t, v); Bob Mielke (tb); Bob Helm (cl, ss, bcl, v); Wally Rose (p); Carl Lunsford (bj, v); Mike Walbridge (tba); Hal Smith (d); Barbara Dane (v).* 8/93.

***** Dancing The Jelly Roll**

Stomp Off CD1316 *Chris Tyle (c, v); John Gill (tb, v); Frank Powers (cl); Steve Pistorius (p, v); Leah Bezin (bj); Mike Walbridge (tba); Hal Smith (d).* 10/96.

Chris Tyle's group has been a fixture in West Coast traditional circles for many years, though there was a ten-year disbandment in the '70s, and he has more recently been engaged with other projects. The first two discs pay tribute to the Lu Watters Yerba Buena sound, which had a huge impact on revivalists in the USA. There are a few oddities – such as 'When Ragtime Rufus Rags The Humoresque' on *Back To Bodega!* – but much of the material is from a relatively familiar pocket. The distinction comes in the tight syncopation of the ensembles, the particular jig-jog rhythm and the blend of knowingness and genuine enthusiasm which American trad relies on. It helps that original Yerba Buena man Helm is on hand for an extra drop of authenticity. *Dancing The Jelly Roll* is all ragtime – of sorts – even though the Down Home style of rag is less formally 'right' and more in the Turk Murphy style. They go far enough forward to dip into the Bennie Moten repertoire for items like 'Goofy Dust' and generally make a valid case for all 21 pieces.

Arthur Doyle

TENOR SAXOPHONE, FLUTE, RECORDER, VOCAL

Originally from Birmingham, Alabama, Doyle played in R&B bands in the '60s before joining New York's avant-garde. He moved in 'underground' circles before spending five years in prison in the '80s. In the '90s he returned to the free scene and began recording again.

**** Do The Breakdown**

Ainsoph Lamed *Doyle (ts, f, v solo).* 4/97.

****(*) Dawn Of A New Vibration**

Fractal 009 *Doyle; Sunny Murray (d).* 3/00

***** Live At Glenn Miller Café**

Ayler CD-002 *As above, except add Bengt Frippe Nordström (as).* 3/00.

** The Basement Tapes

Durtro 062 *Doyle; Dan Warburton (vn); Edward Perraud (d).* 6/01.

Doyle tends to come across as an exhausted version of Charles Gayle. His tenor-playing has the same kind of bludgeoning power, but where Gayle's music has a passionate and religious intensity, Doyle often sounds merely bleary. He sings in a manner which suggests an inebriated shaman, and his flute-playing is pretty unlovely. Records have so far brought forth very mixed results. *Do The Breakdown* has the lo-fi feel of a field recording, and has a certain shambolic power. With Murray, at least he has a motor, and the drummer very much carries the next two records. The Fractal disc is salvaged by Murray's usual level of inventiveness, and while Doyle has the audacity to claim a composer credit on the most corroded 'Nature Boy' ever recorded, he does strike some sparks. The Glenn Miller date has the poignant presence of Nordström on three tracks (he died later that year). For the rest, it's much as the previous set, although better recorded, and 'Two Free Jazz Men Speak' apotheosizes their duet manner. *The Basement Tapes* is a trio session where Warburton's negligible violin scrapes quietly below some of Doyle's most rootless musings. He has quite a grand reputation, but even adventurous listeners may find that it's all very much an acquired taste.

Hamid Drake (born 1955)

DRUMS, PERCUSSION

Born in Louisiana, Drake moved with his family to Chicago, where he took drum lessons from Fred Anderson's son, later taking over his role in Fred's regular group. Since then, Drake has established himself as one of the leading players on the free-jazz scene, with a host of sideman credits.

*** Ask The Sun

Okka Disc 12008 *Drake; Michael Zerang (d, perc).* 5/91, 9/95.

All percussion dates are something of an acquired taste but this is an unexpectedly accessible and groove-driven date that shows Drake (where he can be separated from his partner) in a different light to the free player. Only the rather brief 'The Wisdom Sisters' sounds abstract. Of the rest, the live 'The Black Basement' is dramatic and richly textured, while 'Sacred Womb (For Oshun)' and the reassuringly un-Irish 'River Dance' have a playful, ritual quality. The duo play standard kits but also use hand drums, other percussion and didjeridus.

*** The Atlanta Concert

Okka Disc ODL 1006 LP *Drake; Peter Brötzmann (ts, cl, tarogato); Fred Hopkins (b).* 5/97.

Like Drake, Brötzmann has the ability to combine scarifying power with surprising delicacy and it is this beguiling concert that makes the trio album so delightful. For some listeners, though, its real value will be as a record of the late Fred Hopkins, who died in January 1999, robbing the jazz scene of one of its most eloquent voices and one of its most engaging personalities. Fred's bouts of catch-as-catch-can with the drummer are brimful of mischief and razor-sharp wit. This isn't one of Drake's better showings in that he is frequently consigned to accompaniment rather than an equal role, but he does it with such authority that all one hears is a unified and highly expressive musical unit.

**** Emancipation Proclamation: A Real Statement of Freedom

Okka Disc 12036 *Drake; Joe McPhee (pocket t, ts).* 00.

*** Soul Bodies: Volume 1

Ayler 024 *Drake; Assif Tsahar (ts, bcl).* 5/01.

***(*) Brothers Together

Eremite 35 *Drake; Sabir Mateen (as, ts, cl, bcl, f, v).* 4/01.

Emancipation Proclamation is a markedly thoughtful set, and a wonderful showcase for both players. McPhee's pocket trumpet is as primordial as the dawn and conjures up whole histories. Drake is remarkably quiet and restrained, happy to play a supportive role on the tribute to Miriam Makeba ('Mother Africa'), elsewhere leading and shaping the music. His touch is extraordinary. Rolling patterns lead into freer passages which rely on the momentum of what has gone before, giving many of these pieces a stronger metrical feel than is actually present. McPhee is as single-minded and enigmatic as ever and the opening 'Cries And Whispers', which introduces this live recital, has a majestic presence that belies its rather tentative origins.

The gig with Tsahar is not so satisfying, largely because Tsahar is a more impatient player, less of a listener. However, it's very much Drake's gig again. The long title-piece and 'Heart's Mind' find the drummer developing the language of Elvin Jones, Andrew Cyrille, Sunny Murray and Milford Graves, though there are moments when he sounds more like Ed Blackwell than any of them, creating complexities with the most basic of sonic materials. No sign – so far as we know – of volume 2, though our instinct is that a single strong CD edited from this performance would have been sufficient.

The title-piece of *Brothers Together* also suffers from a tentative quality, but by the time Mateen and Drake are firing on all cylinders, this is a scorching session and the closing piece, 'New Life Dance', makes half an hour pass by in seeming seconds. Mateen is a versatile reedman and his clarinet playing in particular deserves attention, full of dark power and illuminated with a quality the much-heralded Don Byron can only dream of. His role on 'Knowing Oneself' is absolutely central, though again Drake takes a hold of the music and pushes it into new and unexpected shapes.

Mark Dresser (born 1952)

DOUBLE BASS

Dresser is often assumed to be a lifelong New Yorker, but he actually cut his musical teeth in his native Los Angeles, where he studied with Bertram Turetzky and worked with an array of figures on the West Coast free scene, including David Murray and Arthur Blythe. His membership of the Anthony Braxton Quartet was important in steering him towards leadership.

*** Later

Victo 79 *Dresser; Fred Frith (g, p, org, vn); Ikue Mori (d machines).* 9/94.

**** Force Green

Soul Note 121273 *As above, except add Phil Haynes (d), Theo Bleckmann (v).* 9/94.

Though Dresser uses the bow rather sparingly, there is something very proper and legitimate about his plucked lines, even when they are free form. The Victoriaville set with Frith and Mori is an unusual one in the Dresser canon, but as one of his freest outings, it's interesting to compare it with more structured work. Pitched against Mori's drum machines and Frith's complex guitar wizardry, Dresser threshes and bashes at his bass, conjuring up a storm of sound that manages to be both more subversive and more warmly human than his partners'. When Frith switches to organ and violin that impression is less obvious and it's miraculous how much character Mori gives to her electronic kit. A fine record, though probably a misleading place to begin Dresser studies.

On 'Bosnia', one of the tracks on *Force Green*, Douglas utters despairing, pain-racked cries over Dresser's harmonic squeaks and rumbles, an intense evocation of both men's (Dresser is the composer) humanitarian reaction; Bleckmann, who is used as a second horn rather than a lyric vocalist, comes in with muezzin cries and wails that reinforce the Balkan/Middle Eastern tonality. The previous track, 'Ediface', is a more obviously jazz-based structure and allows Douglas to stretch out, counterpointed by Bleckmann's slightly nasal scats. The long 'Castles For Carter' is an elaborate fantasy for the late clarinettist, John Carter, and a passing reference to his *Castles Of Ghana* album. Tightly organized round a series of pan-tonal themes, it never sounds like a blowing piece, nor as if it is wholly written out; and it's here for the first time on the set that the young Moroney and Haynes come into their own. Up to that point it could almost have been another trio. Douglas blows a thoughtful remembrance of his great predecessor on 'For Miles', with a sly quote from a famous solo, before Bleckmann reverts to falsetto for a gorgeous dialogue that consigns Dresser to the background for a few minutes. Moroney experiments with preparation again, creating a strange, sitar-like tone. This is otherwise very much the bassist's record, but only in the proper sense that he steers the music. Co-producer Tim Berne keeps him properly located in the mix – even the unaccompanied intro to 'Castles' is naturally balanced – and the total effect is of an ensemble rather than a loose coalition of individuals, which is what this music requires.

*** Banquet

Tzadik 7027 *Dresser; Mathias Ziegler (f, cl); Marcus Roja (tba); string quartet.* 11/97.

Dominated by a passionate mourning song for the victims of TWA Flight 800, *Banquet* is one of Dresser's most beautiful and unusual projects to date. 'Loss Of The Innocents' is scored for cello, tuba and clarinet, while the remainder of the album is a species of mini double concerto for flute and bass with string quartet, a piece which allows Dresser to explore extremes of sonority and pitch with great sophistication. A most unusual record, but a highly effective one that embraces expressiveness and formal control.

*** Sonomondo

Cryptogramophone 104 *Dresser; Frances-Marie Uitti (clo).* 99.

Uitti is best known as an exponent of extended cello technique and an interpreter of challenging contemporary composition, such as the work of Giacinto Scelsi. In this (presumably improvised) setting, she is no less impressive, coaxing everything from great motorcycle revs to bat-squeak harmonics from her instrument. Dresser may well have experimented with settings like this during his time with Bert Turetzky. The results are variable as a listening experience, and we found our enjoyment waning after 'Sonomondo' and 'Grati'. What follows is sketchier and less achieved, but this is still a very intriguing and worthwhile album, and string players of all complexions will find it an endless source of ideas.

*** Marinade

Tzadik 7063 *Dresser; Marcus Weiss (as); Matthias Ziegler (cbf); Denman Maroney (p); Mary Rowell (vn); Stefania Verita (clo); Gerry Hemingway, Michael Sarin (d).* 00.

Some of Dresser's most challenging ensemble writing went into this record and it is a shame that *Marinade* isn't more successful as a passage. Not to play too much with titles, this seems like the preparatory work for something larger. There is a tentative quality to long pieces like 'Air To Mir', 'Althaus', 'Subtonium X' and the title-track which will leave the listener a little unsatisfied and possibly perplexed. Dresser plays with structural ideas which don't in the end go anywhere but seem to take a long time to realize that they are, if not lost, then at least off course. The sheer richness of musical thought is, as ever, a delight, but one expects something more from Mark.

*** Reunion: Live At The Guelph Jazz Festival

Intrepid Ear 002 *Dresser; David Mott (bs); Gerry Hemingway (d).* 01.

Dresser and Hemingway anchored the rhythm section of one of the most important groups in contemporary jazz, Anthony Braxton's early '80s quartet. This reunion underlines the depth of understanding that always prevailed between them, whether in the context of Braxton's music or their own. The bulk of the set is a long, rather shapeless improvisation titled 'Deep Into The Unfathomable'. Were it not for the lightness of touch and level of detail, we might be inclined to say that that is exactly how it feels. The two principals are well versed in each other's language and seem to have certain routines pretty much worked out. Mott works a lonelier furrow, but finds his way pretty intuitively. The sound doesn't flatter any of them but it's Gerry who's least well served, sounding splashy and blurred in the more dynamic passages; Mark, by contrast, is well to the front and mostly clear. An interesting document, but largely for dedicated fans of these guys.

***(*) The Marks Brothers

Dewerf 22 *Dresser; Mark Helias (b).* 4–8/00.

**** Duologues

Victo 73 *Dresser; Denman Moroney (p).* 11/00.

**** Aquifer

Cryptogramophone 111 *As above, except add Matthias Ziegler (fl).* 3/01.

These are remarkable records and they repay the closest attention. *The Marks Brothers* snuck into 20th place on 2001's poll of *Cadence* editors' choices and you can see why it's there: a fine record, full of beguiling detail, but not the kind of thing you'd listen to as often as you thought it deserved. Dresser's partner on *Duologues* is a pianist of considerable invention, one who works as much inside the instrument as on the keyboard but with a unity of sound and approach that runs counter to the often haphazard feel of 'prepared piano'. Some of Dresser's work almost sounds like conventional jazz phrasing, but on

'Fanfare For The Rare Woman' he explores the outer reaches of his own instrument's sound, and together the two performers create a sequence of pieces which go well beyond conventional instrumentalism.

The conception is extended on *Aquifer* with the addition of Ziegler, who brings an element of electronic processing to his flute work. What is surprising is how much of the music comes directly out of a jazz tradition. There is a strong blues coloration to 'Digestivo' which contrasts sharply with the near abstraction of 'Sonomatopoeia' and Maroney's 'Pulse Fields', which come right at the centre of the record. A couple of the pieces have been around for long enough to seem almost like repertory items, but for the most part this is a highly original and challenging record. Like its predecessor, it is best to approach it with no preconceptions and merely surrender to its captivating sound-world. We warmly recommend you try it.

★★★(★) Nine Songs Together
CIMP 295 *Dresser; Ray Anderson (tb).* 9/03.

Anderson was the first player Dresser met on his arrival in New York city in 1975. That their association is a long and warm one is evident on this fine set of duos, recorded in the usual unadorned CIMP way and presented in the order played. The opening improvisation is very much a renewal of acquaintance; 'One Plate' refers to an Oliver Lake poem, 'I Want All My Food On One Plate' – in other words, no musical boundaries of any sort; it also reinforces Dresser's foodie theme. The long 'Taps For Jackie' is a threnody to the trombonist's late wife, Jackie Raven, a poet and tapdancer. It's a moving piece, but not just a song of mourning. The most substantial element of the set is a new (outer) *Planets Suite*, which has less to do with Holst than with John Coltrane and Rashied Ali. Anderson plays the percussionist on this one, while Dresser teases out long, folkish lines. They chuck in a couple of standards: Billy Taylor's 'I Wish I Knew How It Would Feel To Be Free' and just for fun a closing version of 'I'm Confessin' That I Love You'. A delightful record that touches a whole gamut of emotions.

Kenny Drew (1928–93)

PIANO

Drew's first influences were Art Tatum and Fats Waller, and these were so deeply inscribed that later contact with Bud Powell and Thelonious Monk didn't have quite the overwhelming impact it had on some players of that generation. The gracious New Yorker spent many years in Europe, first in Paris, and later in Copenhagen in a long lasting and well-documented residency with Niels-Henning Orsted Pedersen at the Jazzhus Montmartre. Drew's expressive talent has been passed on to his son, Kenny Jr.

★★(★) The Kenny Drew Trio
Original Jazz Classics OJCCD 065 *Drew; Paul Chambers (b); Philly Joe Jones (d).* 9/56.

Kenny Drew's death still seems untimely, though it wasn't a career that lacked fulfilment. He began recording in 1949 with Howard McGhee's orchestra, in which he was, by all accounts, a rock of reliability. The first of the Riversides is no better or worse than many another piano-trio date of the day: light, bluesy variations on a flock of standards. Chambers and Jones are typically strong in support, but the material is under-characterized. 'Ruby My Dear' never quite makes it to the starting line and the better tracks are lighter-weight material like 'It's Only A Paper Moon' and 'Caravan', where Drew's elegant, deceptive swing has an opportunity to unfold without pressure.

★★(★) This Is New
Original Jazz Classics OJC 483 *Drew; Donald Byrd (t); Hank Mobley (ts); Wilbur Ware (b); G. T. Hogan (d).* 3–4/57.

★★★ Pal Joey
Original Jazz Classics OJC 1809 *Drew; Wilbur Ware (b); Philly Joe Jones (d).* 10/57.

★★★ Trio/Quartet/Quintet
Original Jazz Classics OJC 6007 *As above.* 57.

Nothing very new here, despite both the title and the period; this sort of hard-bop fare was already becoming a standard repast in 1957. It may say something for the principals involved that the most interesting presence appears to be Ware, who is constantly inventive. The recording is somewhat reticent in dealing with the horns. *Pal Joey* is a typical jazz-goes-to-Broadway album of the day: it earns an extra notch, though, for Ware's hungry, probing lines and the crisper lines that this trio secures.

Trio/Quartet/Quintet is a compilation of tracks from this early Riverside contract. It's probably the best representation of the period, missing out most of the chaff and including a good smattering of the better tracks.

★★★★ Trio/Quartet/Quintet: The Riverside Collection
Original Jazz Classics OJCCD 6007 2 *As for the above.* 56–57.

A first-rate sampling of Kenny's work for Riverside, this includes tracks from *Trio, Pal Joey* and *This Is New*. The emphasis, though, is very much as it was throughout Drew's career, on trio work and there are a couple of bonus tracks to please collectors. Time now – surely? - for Blue Note to do the decent thing and issue a similar set of Kenny's earlier – 1953 – trio with Art Blakey and Curley Russell.

★★★ Plays The Music Of Harry Warren And Harold Arlen
Milestone 47070 *Drew; Wilbur Ware (b).*

An evocative and elegant compilation of tunes by two of America's finest songwriters. Supported by the broad-toned and responsive Ware, Drew plays most of these themes pretty straight. Items like 'The Boulevard Of Broken Dreams' are more or less melodic transcriptions; elsewhere he probes a little deeper into the chords, attempting to realign rather than rewrite. Little real jazz action, but an unfailingly attractive record with a full, unmuddied sound.

★★★ Solo–Duo
Storyville STCD 8274 *Drew; Niels-Henning Orsted Pedersen, Bo Stief (b).* 66, 12/78, 9/83.

Two blocks of duo material, recorded a decade and a half apart, with a solo set from 1978 wedged in between. The four unaccompanied tracks are brief and relatively uninspired. Drew seems to draw sustenance from the two bassists, and on the live tracks with Stief from 1983 he hits a wonderful groove. 'There Is No Greater Love' is the most finished performance of the set, though the opening 'Everything I Love' with NHOP has an emphatic presence as well, a clear studio sound which renders every tiny detail audible.

***** Duo**
Steeplechase SCCD 31002 *Drew; Ole Molin (g); Niels-Henning Orsted Pedersen (b). 4/73.*
***** Duo 2**
Steeplechase SCCD 31010 *As above, except omit Molin. 2/74.*
***** Duo Live In Concert**
Steeplechase SCCD 31031 *As above. 6/74.*
****(*) Everything I Love**
Steeplechase SCCD 31007 *Drew (p solo). 10–12/73.*

Drew left America for Europe in 1961 and worked and recorded there until his death. His numerous records for Steeplechase are modest successes, but the pianist's very consistency is perhaps his undoing: it's frequently hard to tell one disc – or even one performance – from another. The three duo sessions with NHOP are the best, if only because there is a fine clarity of interplay and the bassist doesn't settle for Drew's plainer modes of expression. The solo date is rather too quiescent.

***** If You Could See Me Now**
Steeplechase SCCD 31034 *Drew; Niels-Henning Orsted Pedersen (b); Albert 'Tootie' Heath (d). 5/74.*
***** Dark Beauty**
Steeplechase SCCD 31016 *As above.*
*****(*) Dark And Beautiful**
Steeplechase SCCD 37011/12 2CD *As above.*

Drew went to Copenhagen in 1966 and became a stalwart of the jazz scene there, playing a long residency at the legendary Jazzhus Montmartre with NHOP, Tootie Heath and whatever guests were in town. We've previously accused these discs of blandness, but of course there are subtleties as well, and perhaps the best place to start, and to take a measure of Drew's pianism, is the two-CD set, *Dark And Beautiful*. Here, stretched out over a generous playing time, are Drew's patient exposition and almost conversational phrasing.

Dark Beauty is distinguished by a more than usually varied array of song-writing credits, as if Drew were deliberately casting his net wide and then moulding each song – from his old favourite Harry Warren's 'Summernight' to Thomas Clausen's 'Silk Bossa' – to the particular character of this group. He also programmes Miles's 'All Blues' and Brubeck's 'In Your Own Sweet Way', and he closes with a version of 'Stranger In Paradise' which suggests he knows his Borodin as well as he knows his Broadway songbook.

***** Morning**
Steeplechase SCCD 31048 *Drew; Philip Catherine (g); Niels-Henning Orsted Pedersen (b). 9/75.*
***** Lite Flite**
Steeplechase SCCD 31077 *Drew; Thad Jones (c); Bob Berg (ts); George Mraz (b); Jimmy Cobb (d). 2/77.*
***** In Concert**
Steeplechase SCCD 31106 *Drew; Philip Catherine (g); Niels-Henning Orsted Pedersen (b). 2/77.*
***** Ruby My Dear**
Steeplechase SCCD 31129 *Drew; David Friesen (b); Clifford Jarvis (d). 8/77.*

A further group of Steeplechases in rather more varied company. The obvious comparison is between the NHOP trio and the one on *Ruby My Dear*. Friesen is a similarly cultivated bass-player with a very large and handsome tone. On the title-track, one of Drew's relatively infrequent nods to Monk, he sounds amazingly like Wilbur Ware. Jarvis's sound is perhaps the closest Drew has found to the drummers of the classic swing era and the set skates along on his unfailing beat. There are three originals, a version of Austin Wells's rarely covered 'Sunspots' and, more surprisingly, a version of Jobim's 'Gentle Rain'.

Lite Flite doesn't have the most probable of line-ups, but it works. Berg is in good form, obviously straining every sinew to make the grade in this company. He certainly sounds less relaxed than his seniors. The gracious Thad Jones glides through his solos as if he were sitting in an armchair, and he even allows himself a couple of subtly corrected fluffs – though it's a pity none of Thad's tunes were included on the list. Mraz and Cobb are very much the kind of rhythm section Drew has always relied on, big-toned and very straightforward.

Morning and *In Concert* are an intriguing extension of the familiar Montmartre partnership. Catherine is perhaps over-indulged on the live album with his own 'Twice A Week', which seems too frequent or, rather, too long. For the rest, it's a mild-mannered run-through of material that would have been familiar to all three: John Lewis's 'Django', 'Here's That Rainy Day', Pettiford's 'Blues In The Closet' and a breezy closing 'On Green Dolphin Street'. Certainly worth a listen but, like *Morning*, perhaps a little too mild and unemphatic for many tastes.

***** Your Soft Eyes**
Soul Note 121040 *Drew; Mads Vinding (b); Ed Thigpen (d). 11/81.*

Vinding and Thigpen are swinging enough, but there is not much substance to this record. Good to have it on CD, which improves the sound no end, but nothing to get excited about.

****(*) And Far Away**
Soul Note 121081 *Drew; Philip Catherine (g); Niels-Henning Orsted Pedersen (b); Barry Altschul (d). 2/83.*

Drew made several records for the Japanese Baystate company in the early '80s, as well as this session for Soul Note: his compositions continue to work a slight, pretty seam to rather soporific ends, but the record benefits from the presence of Altschul, whose ear for texture helps to create a more integrated and purposeful sound for such Drew originals as 'Rianne'.

*****(*) At the Brewhouse**
Storyville 8318 VHS Storyville 6963/DVD 1140 *Drew; Niels-Henning Orsted Pedersen (b); Alvin Queen (d). 93.*

Very near the end, Kenny still plays with magisterial calm and youthful energy. He kicks off the Brewhouse set with a storming version of Dave Brubeck's 'In Your Own Sweet Way' and then delivers a completely original and unexpected arrangement of the Jewish folk theme 'Hush-A-Bye'. The opening measures of 'It Could Happen To You' are brilliant, original jazz piano, totally unexpected. The climax of the set, 'You Don't Know What Love Is' and 'All Blues', showcases a trio at the very peak of its powers. This was a flurry of unexpected drama towards the end of a long and dignified career. The video and DVD options don't add much; Drew was never a showy or histrionic player, but he was always curiously reassuring and restful to watch, a man very much absorbed in a job he enjoyed. Even by this stage, it looked as if Kenny Drew could go on for ever playing music of this quality and it was a genuine surprise when one day that calm voice was silenced.

Kenny Drew Jr (born 1958)

PIANO

There are few signs of son-of-a-famous-father syndrome round Kenny Drew Jr. His dad graced the jazz world quietly and without arrogance and he seems to have cast no overpowering shadow; indeed, Kenny Jr was brought up by his grandparents and an aunt. His development has been very individual, often drawing on musics outside jazz.

***** Portraits Of Mingus And Monk**
Claves 50 1194 *Drew; Lynn Seaton (b); Marvin 'Smitty' Smith (d).* 94.

****** Secrets**
TCB 98502 *As above.* 95.

This was a wonderful working group, packed with dynamism and full of ideas. Kenny does 'Light Blue' and 'Weird Nightmare' as solo pieces on the *Portraits* album, both of them subtly modulated and multi-dimensional. But it's really the trios that catch the ear. Kenny includes his own arrangement of a piece by Mompou which is subtle and swinging and irresistibly recalls Chick Corea. His playing more and more resembles Chick's as well, an outpouring of lyricism that seems to have no limit, and it's fascinating to compare the two versions of 'Serial Blues' and hear how comprehensively he revises his approach from one take to another.

There is only one Corea composition on *Secrets*, the highly concentrated and structurally challenging 'Mirror Mirror', but his distinctive voicings seem to invest the album from start to finish. Also in the programme, Steve Swallow's 'Falling Grace' with its rippling, rhapsodic feel, two tunes by Kenny Sr, both lovingly executed, and an arrangement of Vince Guaraldi's 'Great Pumpkin Waltz'.

The earlier album, also astutely produced by Aleardo G. Buzzi, is less to our taste but is still a fine jazz album. A touch too busy in places, as if Smitty is eager to get off to his next gig, but the full sound has enough space around it not to sound crowded.

*****(*) This One's For Bill**
TCB 99352 *Drew (p solo).* 11/95.

Kenny recorded 'This One's For Bill', almost a decade ago on his Antilles album, but it obviously has a place again here in this meditation on Evans and his influence. The piece kicks off this thoughtful and expressive set, which touches on some forgotten corners of the Evans canon, pieces like 'Remembering The Rain' and 'The Two Lonely People' with its long, elaborate form. Kenny also plays a stretched-out version of Miles's 'Nardis', one of the trumpeter's most pianistic ideas, and the Johnny Mandel theme for *M*A*S*H*, 'Suicide Is Painless'. The recording was made in a Masonic Hall on West 25th Street in New York City, a woody, responsive space which brings out the very best in the big Hamburg Steinway Kenny opted to play for the gig. Its tone is just right for him, and the set flows sweetly from the very first bars.

***** Crystal River**
TCB 98202 *Drew; Michael Philip Mossman (t, flhn); Ravi Coltrane (ss, ts); Steve Nelson (vib); Lynn Seaton (b); Tony Reedus (d).* 97.

Conceived on a larger-than-usual scale, but somehow less than the sum of its parts. Drew's sextet is almost like a scaled-down big band and the sound is very full, very generously arranged. Mossman and Coltrane Jr are slightly anonymous as soloists, but the pianist carries the day. Of all Drew's albums, this is the least kindly recorded. The piano is very forward and the other trio members with him, and their prominence isn't properly balanced by a strong enough register from horns and vibes. Disappointing.

***** The Rainbow Connection**
Evidence 22158 *Drew; Terence Blanchard (t); Charnett Moffett (b); Cody Moffett (d).* 98.

*****(*) Passionata**
Arkadia 70561 *Drew; Peter Washington (b); Lewis Nash (d); strings.* 98.

It was around this time that Kenny Jr started to programme his father's work prominently. Sensitive and moving, *Passionata* is a full-scale tribute, titled after the unfinished song which he completes and records here for the first time. The set also includes Drew Sr material like 'Dark Beauty', one of the old man's finest compositions, and standards that he must have played a thousand times. Young Kenny's gift is to take them on a stage again, and his interpretation of 'Summertime' has a classical feel that distances it a little from the average jazz reading. This is certainly the most accommodating and inventive trio Kenny has worked with since the days of Lynn Seaton and Smitty Smith. Washington has an enormous range and a capacity for free, fulsome melody that doesn't get in the way of a strong, sure beat, leaving Nash to embellish and elaborate more freely than usual in such a context. The strings are arranged by Bob Belden, unobtrusive, idiomatic and very cleanly registered.

The other set is marked by a superb reading of Drew Sr's 'Serenity', another of his gently understated themes. The presence of Blanchard on the date gives the group sound an almost orchestral quality in places, something that Kenny was to toy with whenever he got the chance. The other delight of this fine set is a reading of Monk's little-played 'Boo Boo's Birthday', a finger-breaking theme that Kenny pulls off with ease. The rhythm section is as tight and sympathetic as a band of brothers ought to be, and the sound is very sharp and detailed.

***** Follow The Spirit**
Sirocco FJL 1004 *Drew; Steve Wilson (ss, as); Lynn Seaton (b); Tony Jefferson (d).* 98.

*****(*) Winter Flower**
Milestone MCD 9289-2 *As above, except omit Wilson.* 6/98.

Two delightful albums from a now fully mature talent, a musician with his own distinctive vision. It's no longer possible to tease apart the influences that go to make Kenny Drew Jr. Increasingly, he sounds like himself. The session with Wilson is rather flatly recorded, which means that the horn parts are more prominent than they ought to be and the all-important rhythm work of Seaton is rather dull and recessed. However, the band does wonderful things on tunes like 'Serial Blues' (now an established item in Drew's repertoire), 'Soldier In The Rain' and a delightful standard, 'Wrap Your Troubles In Dreams'.

The Milestone disc is certainly to be preferred. Jefferson has established a place in Drew's employ and sounds more confident with his role every time out. This time, Kenny nods to Chopin in a lilting A minor waltz, to Ellington in 'Isfahan', which is not just a horn player's song, and to the great Astor

Piazzolla in 'Argentine Rhapsody', which opens up the group's rhythmic language considerably. Nicely recorded and packaged; a significant further step in the pianist's career.

★★★(★) Remembrance

TCB 20202 *Drew; Wallace Roney (t); Stefon Harris (vib); Santi Debriano (b); Tony Jefferson (d).* 12/99.

A memorial concert to the recently departed Milt Jackson, Art Farmer and bossa composer Manfredo Fest. Though basically conceived as a trio date, the presence of Roney and Harris brings in the most obvious echos of the great vibist and flugelhornist. Kenny Drew Sr made the first recording of 'With Prestige' with Art's group, so it was an obvious inclusion here, a strong, rolling theme with lots of harmonic potential. There is also a stunning version of 'Blame It On My Youth', on which Roney mutes his horn without drifting into the ubiquitous Miles Davis style. Harris is properly front and centre for 'Bags' Groove', a brilliant tearing version, only matched for sheer power on *Remembrance* by a stunning version of 'Epistrophy', one of Kenny's favourite Monk tunes. There are tributes to Fest as well, an original 'Song for Manfredo', a gentle reading of Jobim's 'Children's Games' and a brief take on 'Bossa Blues'.

Once again, Kenny has assembled a fine trio and augmented it with appropriate flair. It's hard to take this record off and not reach for something by Art or Bags, and that's tribute enough to its quality.

★★★ Live At Montreux

TCB 21152 *Drew (p solo).* 7/99.

For this relatively rare solo set – there hasn't been one that we're aware of since the Maybeck recital – he mixes familiar material like 'Nardis' and 'Solar', 'There Is No Greater Love', 'Alone Together' and an Ellington medley with relatively unusual things. The most striking is Steve Swallow's 'Radio', which is given a playful treatment. There is also an Astor Piazzolla composition, more obviously pianistic and every bit as good. Drew's originality surfaces on his reading of 'Alone Together'; here the old groaner takes on a fresh and almost ironic quality. In contrast he delivers Duke's 'Single Petal Of A Rose' and 'Prelude To A Kiss' without much embellishment.

Paquito D'Rivera (born 1948)

ALTO, SOPRANO AND TENOR SAXOPHONES, CLARINET

A prodigy in Havana, playing in his father's band at six, D'Rivera was a founder (with Chucho Valdes and Arturo Sandoval) of Irakere. He defected to the USA in 1980. Since then he's been involved in bop and Cuban music in about equal measure.

★★★ The Best Of Paquito D'Rivera

Columbia 507611-2 *D'Rivera; others unlisted, but including Hilton Ruiz (p), Eddie Gomez (b), Ignacio Berroa (d).* 81–88.

★★★ Tico! Tico!

Chesky 034 *D'Rivera; Danilo Perez (p); Fareed Haque, Romero Lobambo, Tibero Nascimiento (g); David Finck, Nilsson Matta (b); Portinho, Mark Walker (d).* 7–8/89.

D'Rivera was the first of the recent wave of Cuban musicians to defect to the USA, and his intensely hot, infectiously runaway style on alto has enlivened a number of sessions. He has the same difficulty which besets his compadre, Arturo Sandoval – finding a consistently productive context for a talent which is liable to blow away on the winds of its own virtuosity. D'Rivera is never short of a string of firecracker phrases, but they can often be as enervating to a listener as the most laid-back of jazz easy-listening dates. His Columbia albums tended to end up as Latinized hard bop, no better or worse than a typical neo-classic session, if a little more sparky than most. Columbia's new best-of set tidies up seven albums which by themselves were weakened by too many indifferent moments. D'Rivera still blows far too much smoke when working on the likes of 'On Green Dolphin Street', but at least when rationalized into a greatest hits, the music does not pretend to be more than a sequence of highlights, which suits his style.

The Chesky album suggested ways that D'Rivera could make a more convincing kind of fusion. The bolero, waltz and bossa-nova rhythms are integrated into a setting which sifts bebop into an authentic South American stew, and the leader turns to the clarinet as well as the alto (and a little tenor) to decorate the pulse. Chesky's brilliant sound only heightens the sunny qualities of Paquito's music.

★★★ Havana Café

Chesky JD 80 *D'Rivera; Danilo Perez (p); Fareed Haque, Ed Cherry (g); David Finck (b); Jorge Rossy (d); Sammy Figueroa (perc).*

More of the same, really. But the very quick tempos tend to underline D'Rivera's difficulty in finding a context. He can handle these rapid-fire speeds, but other members of the band – Perez and Haque in particular – find it difficult both to sustain the pace and to have anything interesting to say. Two classical pieces, 'Improvisation' and 'Contradanza', offer a little more variety, and this time D'Rivera brings out his soprano rather than his tenor.

★★★ Who's Smoking?

Candid CCD79523 *D'Rivera; Claudio Roditi (t, flhn); Mark Morganelli (flhn); James Moody (ts); Danilo Perez, Pedriot Lopez (p); Harvie Swartz (b); Al Foster (d).* 5/91.

Lots more gilt-edged hard bop, heavy on smoke, glitter and flash but short on anything beyond the showmanship. D'Rivera and Roditi strike sparks off each other until they're practically smouldering, and there is a rather good 'Giant Steps' which emerges out of it all. Taken moment by moment, fair game.

★★★(★) Live At Manchester Craftsmen's Guild

Blue Jackel MCG 1003 *D'Rivera; Diego Urcola, Mike Ponella (t); Conrad Herwig (tb); William Cepeda (tb, conch); Scott Robinson (as); Andres Boiarsky (ts, ss); Marshall McDonald (bs, ts); Dario Eskenazi (p); Fareed Haque (g); Oscar Stagnaro (b); Mark Walker (d).* 2/97.

That's Manchester, Pennsylvania, British readers should note. The band is the United Nation Orchestra, as founded by Dizzy Gillespie and now passed on to D'Rivera, and the rhythmic subtexts come not only from Brazil and Cuba but also from Uruguay, Puerto Rico and Argentina. Dishevelled and seemingly under-rehearsed, the band's jostling, rather fractious delivery proves more effective than that of many a better-drilled and more confident outfit. Several of the tunes have the teeming, shouting quality which one feels this music should aspire to, and for once D'Rivera's solos have to simply take their place in a rich, tempestuous fabric. His duet with bassist

Stagnaro, on which he plays clarinet, is a real surprise, almost melancholy in timbre even as the virtuosity abides. A fine live souvenir.

***** 100 Years Of Latin Love Songs**

Inak 30452 *D'Rivera; Dario Eskenazi (p); Roberto Perera (hp); Aquiles Baez (g, cuatro); Fareed Haque, David Oquendo (g); Oscar Stagnaro (b); Mark Walker (d); Luis Conte (perc); strings.* 9/98.

***** Tropicana Nights**

Chesky JD 186 *D'Rivera; Mike Ponella, Diego Urcola, Gustavo Bergalli, Adalberto Lara, Alejandro Odio (t); Noah Bless, Luis Bonilla, Jimmy Bosch, William Cepeda (tb); Manuel Valera (as); Andres Boiarsky, Ocar Feldman (ts); Marshall McDonald (bs); Oriente Lopez, Daniel Eskenazi (p); David Oquendo (g); Joe Santiago (b); Mark Walker (d); Ralph Irizarry, Joe Gonzalez, Mailton Cardona (perc); Brenda Feliciano, Lucrecia (v).* 99.

D'Rivera is looking for contexts and these showbiz situations suit him as well as anything. *100 Years Of Latin Love Songs* takes us decade by decade through a century of South American music, although frankly it's all treated in much the same way by Paquito's band and Bob Belden's sweet-natured string charts. Charming light music, shaken into wakefulness now and then by D'Rivera's solos. *Tropicana Nights* puts him in front of another show band, too big to attain any great jazz mobility or personality, but loaded with fine players out for a good time. Plenty of Latin kitsch, with some more pointed improvising from the leader.

*****(*) Habanera**

Enja 9395-2 *D'Rivera; David Taylor (btb); Kenny Drew (p); Michael Formanek (b); Clarence Penn (d); Mino Cinelu (perc); Absolute Ensemble with Kristjan Järvi (cond).* 9/99.

This time D'Rivera goes back to roots his admirers may have never realized that he had. Producer Daniel Schnyder's classics-meets-jazz projects have often sounded too arch, but he gets the tone just right as a setting for D'Rivera's romantic ebullience on clarinet and alto sax. A crack rhythm section plays expertly where required, but the most gorgeous music comes in miniatures such as the title-piece, a feelingful original for clarinet and strings, and the Euro-Cuban exotica of 'Wapango'. The Absolute Ensemble brings old-world dignity and finesse to the proceedings – enough to ensure that D'Rivera doesn't ham things up too much – and he in return punctures the hubris of Schnyder's 'Variations On I Got Rhythm And Cuban Overture' and lets it swing and have fun. The closing clarinet soliloquy of 'Lecuonerias' makes a delightful farewell. Paquito's best record by a country mile.

****(*) The Clarinetist Volume One**

Peregrina PM50221 *D'Rivera; Pablo Zinger, Frank Chastenier (p); Gustavo Tavares (clo); Niels-Henning Orsted Pedersen (b); Wolfgang Haffner (d); Pernel Saturino (perc); European Art Orchestra.* 7–10/00.

***** Brazilian Dreams**

MCGJ 1010 *D'Rivera; Claudio Roditi (t); Jay Ashby (tb); Helio Alves (p); Mart Ashby (g); Oscar Stagnaro (b); Paulo Braga (d); New York Voices (v).* 4/01.

A pity that the Peregrina album falls flat. Putting D'Rivera on clarinet only in a variety of settings was an interesting idea, but the fare on offer is insubstantial and everything bar the final 'Trio No 1' is set against the cloying backdrop of the European Art Orchestra. Pieces by Carlos Franzetti and Astor Piazolla are reduced to light-music interludes and it's almost a relief when the rhythm section go into four on Ray Tico's 'Habana'. The closing trio is chamber music.

Recorded live, there's an enjoyable fizz about much of *Brazilian Dreams*. D'Rivera has assembled a band that know his moves and the showbiz snap of New York Voices brings plenty of fun to the party. They're a lot slicker and smarter than the average Brazilian vocal-on-a-jazz-record and will annoy as many ears as they please, but as we've remarked above, this is the kind of turf D'Rivera seems to enjoy the most.

Billy Drummond (born 1959)

DRUMS

Born in Virginia, he followed his father's footsteps in becoming a drummer, arriving in New York in 1988. Joined the OTB band and has since freelanced with many groups, leading occasional dates of his own.

***** Native Colours**

Criss Cross 1057 *Drummond; Steve Wilson (as, ss); Steve Nelson (vib); Renee Rosnes (p); Ray Drummond (b).* 3/91.

*****(*) The Gift**

Criss Cross 1083 *Drummond; Seamus Blake (ts, ss); Renee Rosnes (p); Peter Washington (b).* 12/93.

****** Dubai**

Criss Cross 1120 *Drummond; Chris Potter (ts, ss, bcl); Walt Weiskopf (ts); Peter Washington (b).* 12/95.

Drummond's relaxed facility and knack of piling on the pace as and when required made him a first-call player in the '90s. Much of the action takes place on the cymbals, a light, fast, highly tuneful sound punctuated with sudden dramatic accents and edgy metallic chimes.

He's now recorded three times for Criss Cross and has sounded steadily more confident and self-possessed. The debut is rather muddled, with vibes and piano getting in each other's way and Wilson fighting a rather congested sound. Blake is better on *The Gift* because he has the power and determination to make his presence felt. Rosnes, who is also Mrs Drummond, is never quite as assured as on her own dates, but she contributes to a well-balanced programme which includes Harold Land's 'Ode To Angela' and Charles Lloyd's unexpected and very beautiful 'Apex'.

Dubai dispenses with a harmony instrument altogether, and the result is quite startling. Drummond's closeness to Max Roach suddenly becomes evident, and the originals – his own 'Dubai', Potter's 'Bananfish' and Weiskopf's 'Invisible Sun' and 'Drumhead' – take on a stark but intensely melodic quality. As well as his original compositions, Weiskopf is strongly featured on Strayhorn's gruffly romantic 'Daydream'. Potter shines particularly on Pat Metheny's 'The Bat', another number where Drummond leaves his traps alone and concentrates entirely on cymbals, a most effective trademark. He also figures strongly on the closing 'Mushi Mushi', a Dewey Redman theme which should be heard more often. The albums are now rather old, and perhaps Billy's lost his place as a potential leader.

The Dry Throat Fellows

GROUP

Swiss jazz jokers quite capable of playing it serious and straight.

***** Do Something**

Stomp Off CD 1226 *René Hagmann (c, tb, cl, as, bsx); Jacques Ducrot (cl, ss, as, v); Bertrand Neyroud (cl, ts, gfs, v); Pierre-Alain Maret (g, bj); Michel Rudaz (tba); Raymond Graisier (wbd, perc, v).* 11–12/90.

Since trad has long since colonized Europe, it should come as no surprise that this wry troupe of Swiss players should be as adept as they are. If this is the humorous side of traditional playing, though, how come their version of Clarence Williams's 'Red River Blues' cuts anyone else's? Secret weapon René Hagmann, who does most of the arranging, is equally at home with brass or reeds; Bertrand Neyroud plays the most vibrant clarinet this side of Don Byron; and new recruit Jacques Ducrot (there are two earlier LPs on Stomp Off) sounds right at home with an alto style that seems to have heard of nothing after 1932. He also puts a ridiculous vocal on 'Sweet Sue (Just You)'. Sounds daft on a CD player, but sounds pretty good anywhere else. A shame we've heard nothing more from them in over a decade now.

Marc Ducret (born 1957)

GUITAR, GUITAR-SYNTHESIZER

A Parisian, Ducret came to international notice via his stint in the Orchestre National Du Jazz. Later associated with Louis Sclavis and more recently with Tim Berne.

***** (detail)**

Winter & Winter 910003-2 *Ducret (g solo).* 1/96.

***** Un Certain Malaise**

Screwgun 70005 *Ducret (g solo).* 6–7/97.

Ducret is still rather more familiar as sideman than as leader, but these solo records mark out a tiny niche in the current scheme of things. Performed with chiming clarity and precision, *(detail)* features Ducret alone on acoustic six- and twelve-string guitars. *Un Certain Malaise* is a live album where the guitarist is again by himself, though this time on electric. His virtuosity, inventiveness of thought from moment to moment and skilful blending of genres are never in question. Neither disc, though, entirely escapes from a certain *ennui*. The scrawling treatment of 'What Did I Forget?/Old Brown Shoe' which opens *Un Certain Malaise* is an impressive show of chopsmanship, but it's not so different from listening to Edward van Halen and, deprived of anything but his own context, Ducret seems landlocked. *(detail)* sometimes sounds like mere strumming, for all his refinements.

***** In The Grass**

Enja 9343-2 *Ducret; Bobby Previte (d, ky).* 9/96.

Two knowing practitioners stir together an hour or so of sparring on guitars, drums and keyboards. Plenty of interesting bits and pieces which add up to the usual mixed result.

***** Qui Parle?**

Sketch SKE 333038 *Ducret; Alain Vankenhove (t); Michel Massot (tba, tb); Yves Robert, Thierry Madiot (tb); Christophe Monniot (as, bs); Dominic Pifarely (vn); Benoit Delbeq, Allie Delfau (p, sampler); Bruno Chevillon, Helene Labarriere (b); Francois Verly, Eric Echampard (d); Anne Magouet (v).* n.d.

Writers and poets inspire this long set, which features a more lavishly orchestrated setting than Ducret has worked in on previous projects. Needs more time to digest, but on first blush this feels – like so many such projects – weighed down by its eclecticism, musical as well as textual, with Ducret keen to work in neo-industrial settings as well as melodious acoustic ones.

Mac Duncan (1931–81)

TROMBONE, VOCAL

A hard-nosed Yorkshireman, Duncan played trombone for several years with Ken Colyer before leading trad groups of his own in the '60s and '70s. His suicide in 1981 shocked his community.

***** Live At The Lord Napier 1973**

Upbeat URCD 188 *Duncan; Sonny Morris (t, v); Dave Bailey, Jack Gilbert (cl); Jim MacIntosh (bj); Eddie Edwards, Ray Holland (b); Brian Duddy (d).* 4/73.

Duncan left very little to remember him by – at least under his own leadership – and this souvenir of a typical gig at The Lord Napier pub in Thornton Heath is a pretty splendid blast of unreconstructed British trad. Morton's 'The Chant' taxes them a bit, but otherwise the group barnstorm their way through a set of familiar numbers from the repertoire with a good deal of bad-mannered aplomb. Morris, sometimes a degree more debonair with other players, joins in with Duncan's salty temperament and at its best – which, admittedly, is not on every tune – the group really charge along. Bailey and Gilbert get together on the last four tracks for some two-clarinet fun. The recording isn't bad for the period.

Paul Dunmall (born 1953)

SAXOPHONES, CLARINET

Bebop, free jazz, folk forms and increasingly large-scale composition all play a part in Dunmall's thinking. He is a charter member of free group Mujician, but increasingly follows his own demanding star.

*****(*) Soliloquy**

Matchless MRCD 15 *Dunmall (solo).* 10 & 12/86.

The only obvious comparison – in terms of instrumentation, sound and basic conception – is John Surman, who has similarly experimented with solo performance and with multi-tracking. However, a more valid comparison might be Evan Parker's tense, complex improvisations, though Dunmall has a folk-influenced side which is far removed from Parker's usual territory. The most remarkable piece on this excellent set is 'Voyage', solo soprano playing which finds a route and a niche midway between those fellow-Brits and fellow-reedmen. 'Human Atmospheres' is a more extreme performance, exploring the limits of pitch, while 'Holocaust', which opens with huge unison siren effects, becomes a sober, extended meditation on destructiveness and loss. Intimately and often viscerally recorded, this isn't music to put on and walk away from. Some will find it a tough listen, but Dunmall's music pays big aesthetic dividends.

*** Folks

Slam CD 212 *Dunmall; Paul Rogers (b); Polly Bolton (v).* 12/89, 9/93.

*** Essential Expressions

Cadence Jazz Records CJR 1079 *Dunmall; Tony Levin (d).* 1/96.

Rogers was – and still occasionally plays as – a member of Mujician, a superb improvising ensemble comprising Dunmall, Keith Tippett and Tony Levin, who partners Paul on *Essential Expressions.* Hearing the group's bassist and reed player in isolation helps unpack one – albeit secondary – element of Mujician's distinctive language, which is a folky melodism, traditionless and quite abstract, almost like the bare skeleton of a tune, thrown up as if in X-ray.

Rogers's fierce, almost competitive style is down a notch in this more intimate setting and there is less of his percussive strumming than usual. Alternating four- and five-string basses, though, he still produces a powerful sound, providing an effective bed for Dunmall's full range of clarinets and saxophones. The presence of Polly Bolton on a single track suggests there may be some future mileage in a vocal disc, an area of interest which has been increasingly important to Slam over the last few years.

The duos with Levin sound more spontaneous and less deliberate. Levin is a treasure. Like Eddie Prévost, he combines freedom with unmistakable swing and, on the evidence of the title-track, it would be hard to distinguish him from some of the American masters whose idiom he has absorbed and colonized. The admixture of jazz is less obvious here, though the soprano feature ('I Found An Angel') touches on a couple of standard themes. Dunmall otherwise sticks to a blunt tenor sound that is frequently reminiscent of session producer Evan Parker. Technically, *Essential Expressions* is more impressive, but most listeners will find *Folks* the more approachable of the pair.

***(*) Quartet And Sextet / Babu

Slam CD 207 2CD *Dunmall; John Corbett (c); Simon Picard (ts); John Adams (g); Paul Rogers (b); Tony Levin (d).* 9/93.

Mujician has functioned as a trio without Rogers; Babu is a trio without Keith Tippett. Inevitably, it is less harmonically rich and on occasions sounds rather stark, an effect heightened by a rather unresponsive acoustic. However, the two larger groups seem to occupy a bigger space and Dunmall's voice is proportionately stronger and more obviously sensitized to its surroundings. The one sextet track, 'Apocalypse Now And Then', is the only one to feature a harmony instrument, and Dunmall responds fulsomely, broadening his tone and attacking the line with vigour. The quartet with Picard, bass and drums is very intense and yields some of Dunmall's best music on record.

**** Ghostly Thoughts

hatOLOGY 503 *Dunmall; John Adams (g); Mark Sanders (d).* 7/96.

A tremendous record, pay-off for years of effort. As an example of small-group playing, the closing 'Up And Down The Back', with its internal symmetry and straightforward logic, is hard to beat; after a percussion introduction, Adams joins Sanders for a while before Dunmall, who concentrates on tenor and baritone this time out, sweeps in to gather the music up into a great peak before letting it settle again. As on the longest item, 'Abit Of Rice, Nice', the pace is more thoughtful than frenetic. 'Human Machines' is the big baritone feature, dark and ruggedly textured. Sanders is heroic throughout the session, playing with great concentration and – if this doesn't sound like hyperbole – recalling not so much fellow-Briton Eddie Prévost as Prévost's great precursors, Max Roach and Ed Blackwell. Adams is less well known but he, too, contributes his full.

*** Desire And Liberation

Slam SLAMCD 225 *Dunmall; Gethin Liddington (t); Chris Bridges, Annie Whitehead (tb); Simon Picard (ts); Keith Tippett (p); Paul Rogers (b); Tony Levin (d).* 11/96.

Early fruit of Dunmall's growing interest in large-scale composition for improvising groups. Inspired by the thinking of Shri Ramakrishna, *Desire And Liberation* is a free-flowing suite compounded of Dunmall's now familiarly folkish themes and some fine jazz blowing. Though essentially continuous, each of the sections is dominated by one instrument or, in one case, by a duet for trombones. The obvious model is Coltrane's *Ascension.* The basic material is more complex, the responses less frenetic, but the set-up is much the same. Dunmall leads with great authority, followed by bass, the trombones, Picard, Levin, Liddington (the least known of the group but making a strong showing) and finally Tippett in less than expansive form, keeping things much tighter than usual. The BBC live recording is good, though the clarity of the horns is compromised a little here and there.

**** Bebop Starburst

Cuneiform RUNE 112 *As above.* 6/97.

An even more assured performance by the octet and by Dunmall the composer, digging back into the music which first got him involved in jazz. *Bebop Starburst* is a five-part suite which sounds both thoroughly written out and also free. There are occasional hints here and there of 'I Got Rhythm' and 'How High The Moon'; but this isn't a memorial quilt of contrafacts and standards, but an effort to write in the spirit of the originators. Once again, Liddington is in strong form, showing that he can 'do' Dizzy *and* Howard McGhee. Annie Whitehead is as expressive as ever, and the two saxophonists, neither of them Bird clones, blend very effectively indeed. The octet's anchor is, of course, the now almost telepathically responsive Mujician. Tippett's sense of structure is second to none, and Rogers and Levin are always right on the case. This is music that deserves the widest exposure, the kind of thing that the Founding Fathers of bop would love to have done but lacked either the wherewithal or the final jump of imagination. Excellent modern music, with ties to the past.

***(*) Totally Fried Up

Slam CD 235 *Dunmall; John Adams (g); Mark Sanders (d).* 3/98.

The second outing from Dunmall's free-bop trio doesn't have quite the slapping impact of its predecessor, but it's still a powerful record. The defining sound is Adams's hard-scrabble guitar, which is also capable of great delicacy, as at the end of 'Samskaras'. Perhaps in deference to label boss George Haslam, himself a distinguished baritonist, Dunmall leaves the big horn at home. A pity; what these five tracks could do with is just a touch of timbral and harmonic variation. Sanders is as compelling a drummer as ever, with a limitless rhythmic facility and a fine judgement for the placing of more abstract accents. Good stuff all round.

★★★★ The Great Divide

Cuneiform Rune 142 *Dunmall; Gethin Liddington (t); Paul Rutherford, Hilary Jeffries (tb); Elton Dean (as); Evan Parker (ss, ts); Keith Tippett (p); John Adams (g); Paul Rogers (b); Tony Levin, Mark Sanders (d).* 99.

A remarkable achievement. The augmented personnel appears on only the final track. The rest of the set is for Paul's now well-established octet and treads a fine line between composition and free improvisation. The six parts of the main piece are beautifully modulated but leave ample room for some of the most spirited improvisation Dunmall has put on record. Paul Rutherford, easily the most underrated player of his generation, is in astonishingly good form, blocking out huge sounds in the ensemble passages and playing solo with fire and passion. The core personnel of Mujician know one another so well that they anticipate every turn in the music.

★★★(★) East West North South

FMR 72 *Dunmall; John Adams, Philip Gibbs (g); Mark Sanders (d).* 98.

A fine quartet recording that sees Dunmall diversify again into bagpipe playing, a sure sign of his desire to break out of the still relatively restrictive practice of multi-intrumentalism. These are strong group sessions, with the guitars acting as a sonic trampoline for some of the saxophonist's more extravagant but also most carefully controlled flights. Away from Mujician, Dunmall comes across as a very organized player, interested in diatonic melody but also concerned with microtonal procedures, overtone playing and high harmonics. The beauty of these tracks is that most of this happens organically and seemingly unconsciously, unforced.

★★★(★) I You

FMR CD 97 *Dunmall; Tony Bianco (d, perc).* 99.

★★★ Out From The Cage

FMR CD 102 *As above; add John Adams (g); John Edwards (b).* 99.

★★★ Hit And Run

FMP CD 116 *Dunmall; John Butcher (ts); John Edwards (b).* 99.

★★★ Utoma Trio

Emanem 4040 *Dunmall; Simon Picard (ts); Tony Bianco (d).* 7/99.

Comparable at moments to John Coltrane's duets with Rashied Ali on *Interstellar Space*, *I You* is a magnificent exploration of identity, communication, the bizarre mathematics of one and the only even prime number, places, people and the ideas that animate them. Dunmall has never sounded better on a range of horns and Bianco, an American percussionist still to make the impact he deserves, is the ideal accompanist. Rhythmically, he is astute and highly focused, but also has the ability to give his percussion waves of overtone which act as a drone (significant, given Dunmall's later dabbling with bagpipes) behind the saxophone.

The group record is an extension of Dunmall's regular freebop trio and thus in some regards closer to his work with Mujician. Bianco is again the anchor, but Edwards – consistently Britain's most underrated improviser – is the star turn here, as he is on the fine *Hit And Run*, brokering most of the action between guitar and saxophones. Another terrific record, though oddly recorded and slightly flat acoustically.

Hit And Run also features markedly abstract interplay with Butcher. These are not Dunmall's most engaging sessions but Butcher is an immensely powerful and thoughtful player who explores the farthest reaches of saxophone playing and anyone brave enough to work in his company finds it a stimulating experience.

The Emanem trio is also superb, with two tenor saxophones pitched against the drum kit. It might legitimately be listed as Bianco's record, both alphabetically and because his contribution is so critical, but it falls into a continuum of Dunmall records that represents one of the most stimulating saxophone documents of recent times.

★★★ Master Musicians of MU

Slam CD 241 *Dunmall; Philip Gibbs (g).* 11/99, 1/00.

Dunmall was beginning to refine his armoury at this period, steadily dropping his trademark multi-instrumentalism in favour of the tenor saxophone, plus bagpipes. This is one of the few occasions around this time when he did deploy multiple horns, including some rather exotic items like the *comemeuse*. Gibbs has been a long-term collaborator; he plays electric on the November 1999 session, acoustic two months later. The opening 'Tom O'Bedlam' is in Dunmall's familiar folk idiom. The long 'Beyond The Black Stump' sees him switch uneasily to soprano, but it's the powerful 'Dweller On The Threshold' and a move to the bigger horn that really cements Paul's decision to switch to tenor. He sounds assured, individual and absolutely controlled. A wonderful track in the midst of an eclectically middling album.

★★★ Solo Bagpipes

FMR CD 118 *Dunmall (pipes).* 01.

After Rufus Harley, Tony Roberts and Courtney Pine, pipe major Paul Dunmall. The pipes exert a powerful attraction for creative jazz players, offering drones and quarter-tones and a shifting pitch that has been very much part of saxophonists' language for years. How successful a set this is depends very much whether you apply to it more orthodox standards of pipe-playing (in which case it isn't) or if you accept Dunmall's generous premises and listen to it on its own terms. It's a moving and very beautiful set that only severe pipeophobes will dislike, though we notice with grim satisfaction that he isn't yet prepared to take on the 'great pipes' of the *ceol-mhor*, the terrifying Highland bagpipe.

Over the past couple of years, Paul Dunmall has released a lot of material on CD-R. This is available direct from the artist, but properly falls outside our remit in this book. But do make contact with him; there is some remarkable music to be heard.

★★★★ Hour Glass

Emanem 4208 2CD *Dunmall; Paul Rogers (b); Marcio Mattos (b, elec); Tony Bianco (d, perc).* 2 & 4/02.

★★★★ Rylickolum: For Your Pleasure

Creative Improvised 289 *Dunmall; Paul Rogers (b); Kevin Norton (d, vib).* 3/03.

★★★★ Awareness Response

Emanem 4101 *As above; omit Norton.* 3/03.

Dunmall was in a purple patch in 2002/2003. His albums of this period mark the fruition of a long-developing vision, music that comfortably transcends (rather than aggressively transgressing) the boundaries of free, composed, jazz and folk forms. The trio with Mattos and Bianco is marked by the bassist's creative manipulation of electronics, creating the kind of expansive drones and sonic environments that Dunmall likes to work within. He plays tenor throughout the continuous one hour piece, a feat of physical control that equals some of Evan Parker's titanic performances. The other set finds him working with Paul Rogers on his A.L.L. bass (see below). It's a more familiar partnership but no less stimulating and the even longer 'The Teepees Dive Deeply' is a wrenching, joyous experience.

Rylickolum is a stunning album, caught live on a spring 2003 tour. Norton is one of the most important figures on the American scene; his contributions to Anthony Braxton's work have overshadowed his own development, but he remains perpetually creative and restless and his vibraphone playing here is perhaps the key element on the album. As he shows again on the duo set, Rogers is a master bass player, forcefully declaring a pulse that resonates through the free passages that follow. Restricting himself to soprano and tenor this time, Dunmall shows how far beyond his freebop roots he has gone, peppering his solos with what sound like fragmentary folk melodies, abstract exercises and pure-sound passages which have no relation to melody or harmonic changes. The title is dialect for a damn' good time and if the Roxy Music subtitle puts you off, don't be. One of the best records of 2003, and well matched by the Emanem release that followed.

The duo album sees Rogers playing an A.L.L. bass built by Antoine Leducq and featuring six playing strings that give him access to most of the cello range, as well as twelve drone strings that help to boost the power of the instrument. It's a magnificent sound, and sits well with Dunmall's pipes and saxophones. The level of empathy here is extraordinary and the long 'Priceless Response' must rank among both musicians' best recorded performances, tense, taut and emotionally draining creative music.

Johnny Dunn (1897–1937)

TRUMPET

Born in Memphis, Dunn was a sensation in the New York of the very early '20s. He subsequently visited Europe and eventually spent most of his professional time there in the '30s, though he died young, in Paris.

*** Cornet Blues

Frog DGF33 *Dunn; Pike Davis (t); Herb Flemming, Earl Granstaff, Calvin Jones (tb); Garvin Bushell, Herschel Brassfield, Rudolph Dunbar, Nelson Kincaid (cl, as); Ernest Elliott (cl); Rollin Smith (as, ts); Alonzo Williams (cl, ts); Dan Wilson, George Rickson, Leroy Tibbs, Jelly Roll Morton, James P. Johnson, Fats Waller (p); George Smith (vn); John Mitchell, Sam Speed, Maceo Jefferson (bj); Harry Hull, Bill Benford, (tba); Jesse Baltimore (d).* 12/21–3/28.

Dunn is a throwback to the first era of jazz on record, an entertainer who was eventually eclipsed by the fast pace at which black music evolved in the '20s. He arrived in New York in 1919 and seems to have been a trumpet kingpin in the city until Louis Armstrong blew into town five years later. Like Freddie Keppard, Dunn played hard and loud, and his records have never enjoyed much vogue. Some 80 years on, this superb reissue reopens the book. In another extraordinarily fine remastering, we can at least get close to what Dunn and his Original Jazz Hounds (later just his Original Jazz Band) sounded like. Whether he ever had army experience isn't clear, but 'Sergeant' Dunn seemed to have a penchant for bugle motifs in both his titles and his style of playing. Although the 1921 'Bugle Blues' is entirely different from the 1928 'Original Bugle Blues' which closes the record (with Fats Waller and James P. Johnson on two pianos!), Dunn still blasts the ears in the same way. He must have come from some kind of brass band tradition, like so many of the pre-jazz hornmen: there's that familiar stern vibrato and 'proper' phrasing which Armstrong and his followers eventually dismissed. 'Hawaiian Blues' and 'Four O'Clock Blues' aren't very exciting tracks, but as a coupling they sold 700,000 copies in 1922, and Dunn's playing actually shines out of his surroundings. If the rest of the Jazz Hounds had been up to his level – as Oliver's band were to their leader in 1923 – these sides would have had a far higher reputation.

Dunn played in London in 1923 and 1926 and recorded with C. B. Cochran's Plantation Orchestra, although he is rather outdone by Pike Davis on the four existing tracks. The Columbia date of March 1928 has the somewhat extraordinary presence of Jelly Roll Morton on piano (what was he doing there?) and is an important survival, with the master inimitable on his own 'Ham And Eggs' and Dunn playing some of his best open horn. An important reissue, though on strictly musical terms non-specialists will find it hard work.

Phil Durrant

VIOLIN, ELECTRONICS

A Londoner who has worked extensively in the home-grown improvisation scene, Durrant has moved from mainly group work to the solo environments suggested by the first record, which explore the violin's possibilities as an amorphous sound-source via electronic treatments.

*** Sowari

Acta 10 *Durrant (vn, elec solo).* 11/96–2/97.

As fiercely demanding a disc as one could expect in improvised music, this solo effort compiles Durrant's various adventures with acoustic and electronically altered violin. The four untreated pieces are pretty hard work, often seeming like plays on the barest of structural themes, while the electronic episodes give rise to the occasional doubt, as in the funny, alarming 'Chew 3': is he actually in control of all the squelch and zap that's coming out of the speakers? Detailed exposure is more reassuring: this isn't trance music or any kind of minimalism, rather a refined exploration of a very particular playing medium.

*** Further Lock

Concepts Of Doing 002 *Durrant; Alexander Frangenheim (b).* 3/97.

Durrant sticks to an unamplified and otherwise untreated instrument here, with Frangenheim doing the same, and the results are sometimes dry to the point of desiccation: this is dour, unexciting music, but it is played with a severe concentration which in its way is compelling. Because both men tend to deny any sweetness in the playing, it feels like hard work, but the best of these 14 mostly quite brief duets stand up to the closest scrutiny.

***(*) **Dach**

Erstwhile 014 *Durrant; Radu Malfatti (tb); Thomas Lehn (syn).* 2/01.

Malfatti's interest in improvisation of the quietest and most evanescent sort dominates this fascinating trio session. The title – 'roof' – refers to the sounds one hears at the beginning of the session as wind and rain creak and patter at the roof of the auditorium. The continuous, one-hour performance has the quiet concentration of an AMM concert, high praise for music like this. It's not a demanding listen in the sense that dynamics and dissonance are high, but it requires a level of evenly suspended attention to appreciate such delicate art.

Dutch Swing College Band

GROUP

One of the world's longest-serving jazz groups, the DSCB were founded by Peter Schilperoot in 1945, and are still playing the European circuit with undiminished enthusiasm.

**** **Back In Time**

Philips 842045-2 *Peter Schilperoot (c, cl, bs, d); Rod Mason, Sytze Van Duin (c); Joost Van Os, Ray Kaart, Kees Van Dorsser, Wybe Buma, Oscar Klein, Billy Butterfield (t); Bill Brant, Wim Kolstee, Dick Kaart, Bert Boeren (tb); Dim Kesher (cl, as); Jan Morks (cl); Bob Kaper (as); Bud Freeman (ts); Joop Schrier, Frans Vink, Teddy Wilson, Fred McMurray (p); Arie Ligthart, Jaap Van Kempen (g); Joop Van Leeuwen, Dick Bakker (bj); Henny Frohwein, Chris Bender, Bob Van Oven, Koos Serierse, Henk Bosch Van Drakestein (b); Arie Merkt, Tony Nüsser, André Westendorp, Martin Beenan, Louis De Lussanet, Peter Ypma, Huub Janssen (d).* 45–10/87.

***(*) **Live In 1960**

Philips 838765-2 *Oscar Klein (c); Dick Kaart (tb); Peter Schilperoot (cl, bs); Jan Morks (cl); Arie Ligthart (g); Bob Van Oven (b); Martin Beenen (d).* 60.

*** **Swinging Studio Sessions**

Philips 824256-2 *As above, except add Ray Kaart (t), Chris Smildiger (b), Peter Ypma, Hub Janssen, Louis De Lussanet (d).* 6/60-6/69.

*** **Digital Anniversary**

Philips 824585-2 *Sytze Van Duin (c); Bert Boeren (tb); Bob Kaper (cl); Peter Schilperoot (ss, ts, bs, cl); Fred McMurray (p); Henk Bosch Van Drakestein (b); Huub Janssen (d).* 10/85.

*** **Digital Jubilee**

Philips 845090-2 *As above, except add Adrie Braat (b); Wybe Buma (t); Wim Kolstee (tb); Dim Kesber (cl); Joop Schrier (p); Eddie Hamm (b); Martin Beenen (d).* 5/90.

*** **Collectors Items**

Philips 514100-2 *As various discs above.* 6/61–7/66.

*** **Live On Stage**

Timeless CDTTD 645 *Bert De Kort (c, v); George Kaatee (tb); Bob Kaper (cl, as, v); Frits Kaatee (cl, ss, bs); Rob Agerbeek (p); Adrie Braat (b); Bob Dekker (d).* 3/01.

This remarkable institution finally makes it into our pages, and about time too – they've only been going since 1945. Peter Schilperoot founded the group and led it until his death in 1990, and it has survived him in handsome style. Originally an enthusiastic if uneventful trad group, the band quickly matured into a unit with its own take on the bridge between the classic traditional style and a more swing-styled mainstream, although in the end the 'classic' side of the band has always held sway. There were always good soloists on hand, some of the best including clarinettist Jan Morks, trumpeter Oscar Klein and the long-serving Bert De Koort, and the rhythm players avoided the mechanical thud of much trad. A regimen of constant touring kept their professionalism polished, and over the years they have made dozens of records.

The Philips discs cover some of their glory years. First choice for those who want a single example of the band must surely be *Back In Time*, which covers every era of the band up to 1987 and includes some of their collaborations with the likes of Billy Butterfield, Bud Freeman and Teddy Wilson. But all of the Philips discs are strong in their way. *Swinging Studio Sessions* is a neat cross-section of their early and mid-'60s work. The 1960 live set goes with a real punch and, with Morks and Klein in top form, is one of their liveliest records. *Collectors Items* is bits and pieces from the '60s, inessential but plenty of fun in its own right. *Digital Anniversary* marked their 40th anniversary, and it's not one of their brightest sets; *Digital Jubilee* was their 45th, although the concert recording is poignant for the knowledge that Schilperoot was only months away from his death.

Bob Kaper carries the DSCB torch these days, and they still, as he says 'have a ball!'. The live album on Timeless starts, as always, with their signature tune 'Way Down Yonder In New Orleans', and thereafter it's entertaining business as usual for these diehard jazz lovers.

Dominic Duval

BASS

Duval has been at work on the edges of jazz since the '60s, although he has got on to record only recently. He has been closely connected with the Cadence/CIMP nexus of players, and it wouldn't be unreasonable to see him as an East Coast 'undergrounder' of his day, which is roughly right now.

*** **Nightbird Inventions**

Cadence CJR 1072 *Duval (b solo).* 12/96–1/97.

*** **The Wedding Band**

CIMP 137 *Duval; Jay Rosen (d).* 1/97.

Duval is a prodigiously skilled player who likes working on the broadest canvas. His solo album finds his bass doctored in numerous ways – with long echo, stereo panning, chorusing and more – for 13 pieces; and for once the comparative brevity of the individual tracks is a slight disadvantage: fewer, longer expositions might have effected a more convincing whole. But his inventiveness is undeniable, his use of his effects board subtle and persuasive, and here and there he comes up with a sonically ravishing idea, such as the closing 'Final Thoughts – Look Through Windows In Rain'.

The duets with Rosen feature the bass unadorned, and with the drummer playing with restraint on a modest kit the music has an evenly modulated flow – effective in small doses yet, as so often, monotonal over almost 70 minutes of music. Recorded at an astonishingly low level, this is a disc to sample as a series of brief encounters, which is how it works best.

(*) **The Navigator

Leo LR 257 *Duval; Jason Hwang (vn); Ron Lawrence (vla); Tomas Ulrich (clo).* n.d.

***** Equinox**

Leo LR 267 *As above, except Michael Jefry Stevens (p, perc) replaces Hwang and Lawrence.* 8/97.

***** State Of The Art**

CIMP 141 *Duval; Mark Whitecage (ss, as, cl); Jason Hwang (vn); Tomas Ulrich (clo).* 2/97.

***** Live In Concert**

Cadence CJR 1097 *As above, except add Joe McPhee (t, ts).* 8/98.

Variously credited to The C.T. String Quartet, The Equinox Trio and Duval's String Ensemble, these quite difficult records extend the approach of the earlier discs in different ways: they're heavier, gloomier, louder, more complex, and ultimately quite exhausting to get through. *The Navigator* is so elephantine in feel – the resonant sound is no help at all – that the interesting textures are hard work to decipher, never mind appreciate. Much of this is closer to formal chamber music than to any kind of jazz, and the improvisations, if such they be, are set to what seem to be specifically controlled energy levels. *Equinox* is a good deal easier to follow and Stevens is a good alternative to the other two, but this is still rather mysteriously cryptic music-making.

State Of The Art benefits enormously from CIMP's famously dry and naturalistic recording. You can hear every microtone and string-squeak, and the busy interaction recalls Incus's famous *Company 1* LP. But Duval's interest in very low, groaning *arco* chords does tend to bog the music down just when it seems like an improvisation should be flying. The concert recording was done at New York's Knitting Factory, in decent enough sound, although again the ensembles tend to congeal a bit. McPhee walks into this situation with his usual fearlessness, and his saxophone parts, alternately sonorous and barkingly aggressive, are powerful enough, although he tends to sit on top of the group rather than work within it. For hardy souls!

***** Asylem**

Leo LR 316 *Duval; Herb Robertson (t, whistle, f hp, v); Bob Hovey (tb, v); Jay Rosen (d, etc).* n.d.

Often funny (if you're going to take a title such as 'Rectal Parasites' seriously, you've been watching too many Dario Argento films), this quartet's music suffers from the want of focus and editing which such freely formed occasions frequently encounter, but there are structures, and they're pillaged for ideas with some sort of aplomb. Robertson, usually at his best on other people's records, is a gutsy frontman, though Hovey – who takes a composer credit on each track – may be the bigger influence.

***** Cries And Whispers**

Cadence CJR 1111 *Duval; Joe McPhee (flhn, ts); Mark Whitecage (acl, as); Jason Hwang (vn); Tomas Ulrich (clo).* 8/99.

The quintet of *Live In Concert* returns. It's scarcely less oppressive as a piece of music-making but, a year further on, the ensemble has assumed a less *ad hoc* presence, and gothic episodes such as 'Cries And Whispers II' (which gets a cheer from the audience) have a more genuine impact. But the cloudiness of many of the ensembles is more frustrating than anything else.

*****(*) The Experiment**

Blue Jackel 5036-2 *Duval; Jason Kao Hwang (vn).* 4/99.

****(*) Undersound**

Leo LR 295 *Duval; Joe McPhee (ss, ts); John Heward (d, v).* n.d.

The duet record with Hwang is likely for specialist tastes, but there are some genuinely extraordinary moments, none more so than in the captivating dedication to Messiaen, 'Speaking Of Birds', where the combination of bass and violin and Dave Kowolski's 'implemented recording techniques' creates a dissonantly beautiful racket, not unlike a flocking of birds in a threatening sky. Not everything is as good – nothing like, perhaps – but there are lovely passages to go with the expected scratching and scraping.

Undersound is in more of a straightforward free-playing vein. McPhee is mostly on soprano and Heward isn't a great asset. Duval bookends with two bass solos, and the rest is pretty average.

Johnny Mbizo Dyani (1945–86)

BASS

Joined Chris McGregor's Blue Notes in 1962 and came to London with them in 1965. Settled there for five years before eventually moving to Denmark and playing with John Tchicai, Don Cherry, the trio, Detail, and others.

*****(*) Witchdoctor's Son**

Steeplechase SCCD 31098 *Dyani; John Tchicai (as, ss); Dudu Pukwana (as, ts); Alfredo Do Nascimento (g); Luiz Carlos De Sequeira (d); Mohamed Al-Jabry (perc).* 3/78.

***** Song For Biko**

Steeplechase SCCD 31109 *Dyani; Dudu Pukwana (as); Don Cherry (c); Makaya Ntoshko (d).* 7/78.

***** Mbizo**

Steeplechase SCCD 31163 *Dyani; Dudu Pukwana (as, ss); Ed Epstein (as, bs); Churchill Jolobe (d).* 2/81.

The late Johnny Dyani was calmly visionary, with a deep swelling of anger and irony underneath; technically robust; stylistically various. More than any of the South African exiles, Dyani absorbed and assimilated a wide variety of styles and procedures. He spent much of his active life in Scandinavia, where he forged close artistic relationships with John Tchicai, Don Cherry and with Dollar Brand (Abdullah Ibrahim) with whom he shared a particular vision of Africa. The music is strongly politicized but never programmatic. *Witchdoctor's Son* and *Song For Biko* come from Dyani's most consistently inventive period. Some of the early '80s material is a little more diffuse and, though Pukwana – another who has since re-entered Azania beyond life – is a powerfully compelling solo voice, he always seemed to mute Dyani's more inventive progressions as if there could only be one strong voice at a time.

The self-named *Mbizo* is certainly the starkest and darkest of Dyani's records, with Pukwana wailing and shouting on both his horns and Epstein filling in behind with full-chested baritone and a more measured alto sound which is reminiscent of Tchicai. It's an unsettling record, unmistakably personal and stressed, glowing with dark anger.

***** Afrika**

Steeplechase SCCD 31186 *Dyani; Ed Epstein (as, bs); Charles Davis (as); Thomas Ostergren (b); Gilbert Matthews (d); Rudy Smith (steel d); Thomas Akuru Dyani (congas).* 10/83.

***** Born Under The Heat**

Dragon DRCD 288 *Dyani; Mosa Gwangwa (tb); Charles Davis (as); Ulf Adaker (t); Krister Andersson, Ed Epstein, Peter Shimi Radise (ts); Pierre Dørge (g); Thomas Ostergren (b); Gilbert Matthews (d).* 11/83–5/85.

*****(*) Angolian Cry**

Steeplechase SCCD 31209 *Dyani; Harry Beckett (t, flhn); John Tchicai (ts, bcl); Billy Hart (d).* 7/85.

Afrika is probably the weakest of Dyani's records, marred by an ill-matched rhythm-section and out-of-character horns. Dyani never found another drummer with Ntoshko's instincts and empathy, but he came briefly close with Churchill Jolobe and then again towards the end of his life with Billy Hart. *Angolian Cry* is a strong record, brimming with the pathos and joy that marked *Song For Biko*. Beckett is an uncut national treasure and it's interesting to hear Tchicai on the less familiar tenor. *Born Under The Heat* reappeared with two new live tracks, quartet performances recorded at the Lund Museum of Art with Epstein, Dørge and Matthews, a glimpse of Mbizo in the last year of his life. Not all the horns play together on the other tracks. Gwangwa appears only on 'The Boys From Somafco' and 'Song For The Workers', two of the more obviously political compositions. Johnny plays piano on 'Wish You Sunshine', 'Portrait Of Tete Mbambisa' and 'Song Of The Workers' and, as ever, one wonders what he might have done on a solo piano disc. The absence of a harmony instrument elsewhere isn't a problem, but it occasionally leaves the sound unanchored and hard to get a purchase on. Dyani's short life was packed with music, but listening back to these discs forces the inevitable conclusion that his best work never made it on to record. Almost always, the atmosphere of the studio and the lack of an audience to warm the air leaves one of the most distinctive bass players since Charles Mingus uninspired by comparison with his own extraordinary standard.

The Dynamite Vikings

GROUP

Fronted by Estonian guitarist Matt Soo, this eclectic trio covers a remarkable range from near-rock grooves to free jazz.

***** Vikingology**

Cope CD 057 *Matt Soo (g, g syn); Pierre Dorge (g); Thommy Andersson (b); Karsten Mathiesen (d, elec).* 2/01.

Soo is a born surrealist with a wicked gift for guitar mimicry and the kind of strong rhythmic sense that saves a project like this from degenerating into pseudo-film music. Given how similar the two are in temperament, it is a pity that Dorge, a master of this kind of thing, isn't around for the whole album. He features on four group improvisations and shows Soo a thing or two about what can be done with*out* a guitar synthesiser. Difficult to define exactly what the Dynamite Vikings do, but Baltic bebop with a backbeat should get you past any awkward questions. Hugely entertaining and thoughtful as well.

Allen Eager (1927–2003)

TENOR SAXOPHONE

Someone will one day make a film of Allen Eager's life, the racing cars, drugs, girls, curious obsessions, but for the purposes of this book he was a fine, Lester Young-influenced tenorist who failed to pursue his musical career with any urgency.

***** In The Land Of Oo-Bla-Dee, 1947–1953**

Uptown 2749 *Eager; Johnny Carisi, Miles Davis, Dizzy Gillespie, Red Rodney (t); Charlie Parker (as, ts); Serge Chaloff (bs, ts); Mike Coluccio, Bud Powell, Richard Twardzik (p); Specs Goldberg, Bernie Griggs, Jimmy Johnson, Eddie Safranski (b); Gene Glennon, Freddy Gruber, Buddy Rich, Max Roach, Morty Yoss (d).* 47–53.

The fun of this – and it's hardly a major document – is Eager's apparent predilection for persuading his colleagues to swap horns. 'Serge Swings Allen's Axe' is just about self-explanatory, with the great baritonist dabbling on Eager's own horn. He does something similar with Charlie Parker. Bird plays tenor on 'Swapping Horns' and then they do the same theme all over again on 'Original Horns'. 'All The Things You Are' from the same all-star session doesn't feature Eager at all, but does include some fine collectable playing by Charlie Parker and Bud Powell. One of the delights of a set that majors on period detail is the set of photographs by Milton Greene, at whose place some of the jam material was recorded. Musically, the best thing is a version of Al Cohn's 'The Goof And I', but there are some good live numbers recorded at the Hi Hat in Boston, with Symphony Sid Torin emceeing. Finally (the tracks go against chronological sequence, so why shouldn't we?) there is a rare airshot of Eager's own 'Some Blues', recorded for CBS's *Adventures In Music* programme in 1949.

The Eagle Brass Band

GROUP

A 'modern' group led by drummer Barry Martyn, created to uphold the disappearing tradition of old-style New Orleans brass bands.

***** The Last Of The Line**

GHB BCD-170 *Leo Dejan, Herbert Permillion, Andrew Blakeney, Emery Thompson, Milton Batiste, Dan Pawson (t); John Ewing, Alex Iles, Wendell Eugene, Mike Owen (tb); Al Carson (bs horn); Joe Darensbourg, Chris Burke (cl); Floyd Turnham, Harold Dejan (as); Sam Lee, Fred Kemp (ts); Teddy Edwards, Emile Martin, Barry Martyn (d).* 1/83–5/89.

Barry Martyn's notes espouse a kind of New Orleans fundamentalism which the music echoes as a mix of battle-cry and last hurrah. Martyn formed his Eagle Brass Band as a final rallying point of the old brass-band tradition of the city, and these late recordings – one session was actually cut in Los Angeles in 1983, but the second was made in New Orleans – are a defiant staring-down of pretenders like The Dirty Dozen Brass Band. Whether old pros or young believers, the players in the two bands which Martyn assembled, six years apart, seem to have the authentic style in their bones, and they can crack notes and wobble their vibratos on the tattered likes of 'Just A Little While To Stay Here', 'Eureka March' and 'Bourbon Street Parade' without a shred of self-consciousness. The raw, fragile music is certainly unlike virtually anything else in jazz, while seemingly central to the music's existence. That said, many will find a CD's worth of this group a very long haul.

Charles Earland (1941–2000)

ORGAN

Organ combo leader from Philadelphia, who actually began as a saxophonist and played with the Jimmy McGriff group. He switched to organ in 1963. Black Talk!, his definitive album, was a considerable hit in its day, though he never recaptured the same measure of success.

*****(*) Black Talk!**
Original Jazz Classics OJC 335 *Earland; Virgil Jones (t); Houston Person (ts); Melvin Sparks (g); Idris Muhammad (d); Buddy Caldwell (perc).* 12/69.

****(*) Black Drops**
Original Jazz Classics OJC 1078 *Earland; Virgil Jones (t); Clayton Pruden (tb); Jimmy Heath (ss, ts); Maynard Parker (g); Jimmy Turner (d).* 6/70.

***** Leaving This Planet**
Prestige PRCD-66002-2 *Earland; Freddie Hubbard (t, flhn); Eddie Henderson (t); Joe Henderson (ts); Dave Hubbard (ss, ts, af); Patrick Gleeson (ky); Eddie Arkin, Greg Crockett (g); Brian Brake, Harvey Mason (d); Larry Killian (perc); Rudy Copeland (v).* 12/73–1/74.

The recent revival of interest in 'traditional' jazz organ rekindled Earland's career. He made a key album, *Black Talk!*, at the very end of the '60s. Earland updated the heavier style of players such as Jack McDuff and Jimmy Smith, chose more pop-orientated material and delivered it with a percussive attack. Jones and Person are useful props, but Earland drives the music – even an unpromising piece like 'Aquarius' becomes a convincing, bluesy groove piece. *Black Drops* was the follow-up, but is nothing like as good – only 'Early Bird' and 'Buck Green' emerge from a generally polite situation. *Leaving This Planet*, though it comes with some of the excess baggage of the era – dopey space effects, wah-wah guitars and the like – isn't far behind the debut, though, and summons a first-rate cast to hammer through what's really a blowing session with some space-age debris. Hubbard's own set-piece, 'Red Clay', also features.

***** Front Burner**
Milestone M 9165 *Earland; Virgil Jones (t); Bill Easley (ts); Bobby Broom (g); Rudy Williams (d); Frank Colon (perc).* 6/88.

****(*) Third Degree Burn**
Milestone MCD-9174-2 *Earland; Lew Soloff (t); David 'Fathead' Newman, Grover Washington Jr (ss, ts); Bobby Broom (g); Buddy Williams (d); Ralph Dorsey (perc).* 5/89.

****(*) Blowing The Blues Away**
High Note HCD 70109 *Earland; James Rotundi (t); Eric Alexander (ts); Bob De Vos (g); Greg Rockingham (d).* 2/97.

***** Slammin' And Jammin'**
Savant SCD 2008 *Earland; Carlos Garnett (ts); Melvin Sparks (g); Eric Sealls (b); Bernard Purdie (d); Gary Fritz (perc).* 5/97.

****(*) If Only For One Night**
High Note HCD 7092 *Earland; Najee (ss, ts, f); Melvin Sparks (g); Buddy Williams (d); Gary Fritz (perc).* 10/99.

The second wave of Earland's career was largely respectable rather than eventful so far as records were concerned. The Milestone albums have a degree of freshness which a couple of subsequent efforts for Muse missed altogether. *Blowing The Blues Away* is a smidgeon sharper and livelier, with Rotundi and Alexander playing the faithful horn disciples, and *Slammin' And Jammin'*, though not much more subtle than its title (and its cover art), has a straightahead simplicity and power that works nicely a couple of tracks at a time. *If Only For One Night*, which turned out to be his final album, is very routine, and Najee (on vacation from his smooth-jazz chores) is a weak lead voice. Maybe 'The Mighty Burner', who died at the start of the new century, found little new in a genre which has probably reached the end of its creative journey; but he played good repertory.

Echoes Of Ellington Orchestra

ENSEMBLE

Imaginative and faithful arrangements of the great man's oeuvre, and lacking only genuine star soloists.

***** Rockin' In Ronnie's**
Ronnie Scott's Jazz House 50 *Bruce Adams, Gavin Mallett, Jon Lee, Graham Russell (t); Bob Hunt, Mike Innes (tb); Peter Ripper (as, Cmel, cl); Colin Skinner (as); Jay Craig (as, bs, cl, bcl); Iain Dixon (ts); Ray Gelato (ts, v); Peter Walton (g, bj); John Francis (vn); Dave Olney (b); Mike Smith (d).* 97.

The Echoes outfit doesn't have the cachet of a ghost band but the charts are the genuine article, bearing the thumbprint of Mary Lou Williams and Billy Strayhorn as well as Duke himself. Most of the themes are despatched briskly, but 'Mood Indigo', 'Take The "A" Train' and 'Diminuendo And Crescendo In Blue' are given long and detailed readings with ample space for soloing. No latter-day Hodges or Gonsalves steps forward, but there are strong spots from Bruce Adams and the hugely underrated Ray Gelato, and the famous London jazz spot echoes to the rafters.

Peter Ecklund (born 1945)

TRUMPET, CORNET, BUGLE

Formerly a Boston schoolteacher, Ecklund turned pro in the '70s and began playing in pop and American folk-jazz settings. Later studio work led to a reputation for his repertory skills, and he is in demand in that situation; he has also published studies of Armstrong and Beiderbecke.

*****(*) Ecklund At Elkhart**
Jazzology JCD-246 *Ecklund; Dan Barrett (tb); Bobby Gordon (cl); Mark Shane (p); Marty Grosz (g, v); Greg Cohen (b); Hal Smith (d).* 7/94.

*****(*) Strings Attached**
Arbors ARCD 19149 *Ecklund; Scott Robinson (cl, ss, as, bs); Jay Ungar (vn); Lenny Pickett (cl, srspn); Kenny Kosek*

(mand); Chris Flory, Frank Vignola, Marty Grosz, Molly Mason (g); Cynthia Sayer (bj); Greg Cohen, Murray Wall (b); Richard Crooks (d). 4/92–3/95.

Ecklund began to come into his own after some years of excellent foot-soldiering. Though under his nominal leadership, *Ecklund At Elkhart* is really nothing more or less than another of the ineffably hot and good-humoured jazz parties which always seem to take place when Marty Grosz and his pals are on hand. Another 15 chestnuts from 1918 to 1939, some of which only the Grosz gang would dare go near these days, especially the once-frightful 'Trees', here given a peppery rendition. Barrett and Gordon have plenty of good solos and Shane is a model of light-fingered swing, but Ecklund does take marginal honours with cornet-playing of finesse and pukka good cheer.

Pieced together from six sessions over three years, *Strings Attached* ranges from duos to septets and is often awfully good: try 'Try A Little Tenderness', completely shorn of its Otis Redding bathos and turned into a lilting lament, or a tune we've waited to hear in jazz for a long time, the lovable novelty, 'Wedding Of The Painted Doll'. There are winning vignettes from Robinson and Ungar and, when Ecklund simply plays a classic standard such as 'Too Marvelous For Words', it's just marvelous (*sic*). But titles like 'All-Purpose Cowboy Melody' give away the one weakness: there's an in-joke feel that lays the dead hand of kitsch on some of this stuff.

***** Gigs – Reminiscing In Music**

Arbors ARCD 19230 *Ecklund; Dan Block (cl, as, bs); Bobby Gordon (cl); Joel Martin, Warren Bernhardt (p); Keith Ingham (cel); Jay Ungar (vn); Peter Davis (g, bj, cl); Steve Cardenas, Madeleine Peyroux, Molly Mason, Frank Vignola (g); Guy Fischetti (pedal steel); Cynthia Sayer (bj); Howard Johnson (tba); Greg Cohen, Pete Toigo, Marty Grosz, Murray Wall, Kelly Friesen, Harry Aceto (b); Richard Crooks (d).* 1/98–1/99.

Tunes and musicians who remind Ecklund of places he's played and jobs he's worked. He can hardly escape the charge of self-indulgence with an agenda like that but, good-natured fellow that he is, he makes this a charming set of performances. A lot of it has the feel of folk music – from barn dances or back porches – but the players are anything but Saturday-night amateurs. If they were, they might have summoned a bit of useful hamfistedness here and there – for the most part, the music's so polite it's almost perfumed. But that's the price of being a pro. Highlight: Leroy Carr's 'Midnight Hour Blues'.

Billy Eckstine (1914–93)

VOCAL, TRUMPET, VALVE TROMBONE

Though a competent brass-player, it was Eckstine's voice that was his fortune. When he arrived in Chicago in 1938, he found success as a vocalist with the Earl Hines band, and he subsequently ran his own big band during 1944–7, giving employment to many of the sharpest young talents in the nascent bebop scene. He turned to small-group work in 1947 and spent the rest of his career as a soloist, finding much MOR success but usually with a jazz flavour somewhere.

***** Billy Eckstine 1944–1946**

Classics 914 *Eckstine; Dizzy Gillespie, Freddy Webster, Shorty McConnell, Al Killian, Gail Brockman, Boonie Hazel, Fats Navarro, Raymond Orr (t); Trummy Young, Howard Scott, Claude Jones, Jerry Valentine, Taswell Baird, Alfred 'Chippie' Outcalt, Walter Knox (tb); Budd Johnson, Jimmy Powell, John Jackson, Bill Frazier, Sonny Stitt, John Cobbs (as); Gene Ammons, Dexter Gordon, Wardell Gray, Thomas Crump, Arthur Sammons (ts); Rudy Rutherford, Leo Parker, Teddy Cypron (bs); John Malachi, Clyde Hart, Richard Ellington (p); Connie Wainwright (g); Oscar Pettiford, Tommy Potter (b); Shadow Wilson, Art Blakey (d); Sarah Vaughan (v).* 4/44–10/45.

Eckstine's orchestra was a legendary incubator for young bebop talent, as a glance at the personnel shows, and it's a pity that the band's surviving performances are mostly of ballads and features for the leader. Not that one should decry anything that Eckstine himself does. His massive, smooth, sumptuous voice has its own virtues, and on the rare occasion when he handles an up-tempo piece – 'I Love The Rhythm In A Riff' – he is just as adept. There are glimmers of Gordon, Ammons, Gillespie and Navarro here, as well as Vaughan's debut on 'I'll Wait And Pray' but it's the power of the band as a whole, the lift given by the young Art Blakey and the rapt power of Eckstine's balladeering which are the merits of these tracks. Docked a point for the sound which is never good off the original masters for De Luxe and National, but it probably ought to be better than this.

*****(*) Together**

Spotlite SPJ-CD 200 *Eckstine; Gail Brockman, Boonie Hazel, Shorty McConnell, Fats Navarro (t); Taswell Baird, Alfred 'Chippie' Outcalt, Howard Scott, Jerry Valentine (tb); John Jackson, Bill Frazier (as); Gene Ammons, Budd Johnson (ts); Leo Parker (bs); John Malachi (p); Connie Wainwright (g); Tommy Potter (b); Art Blakey (d); Lena Horne, Sarah Vaughan (v).* 2–3/45.

These Jubilee broadcast transcriptions, mostly with excellent sound, offer arguably the best evidence of the calibre of the Eckstine orchestra. Johnson, already a veteran at 35, is one of the most impressive soloists, but there are precious glimpses of Navarro and features for Horne and Vaughan, and the power of the sections – especially the trumpets – comes bursting through. Great hipster announcements too by MC Bubbles Whitman!

***** Billy Eckstine 1946–1947**

Classics 1022 *Eckstine; Boonie Hazel, Shorty McConnell, Raymond Orr, Kenny Dorham, Fats Navarro, Miles Davis, Hobart Dotson, Leonard Hawkins, King Kolax, Ray Linn (t); Alfred 'Chippie' Outcalt, Robert Scott, Jerry Valentine, Walter Knox (tb); Norris Turney, Junior Williams, Sonny Stitt, John Cobbs, Sonny Criss (as); Gene Ammons, Arthur Sammons, Josh Jackson, Wardell Gray (ts); Tate Houston, Leo Parker, Cecil Payne (bs); Richard Ellington, Jimmy Golden, Linton Garner, Warren Bracken (p); Connie Wainwright (g); Bill McMahon, Tommy Potter, Shifty Henry (b); Art Blakey, Tim Kennedy (d); strings.* 1/46–4/47.

These six sessions for National are again dominated by ballads and the incomparable Eckstine voice, but a glance through the personnels show what an abundance of jazz talent there was on hand: Blakey is always booting the band along; Navarro breaks through here and there; and the final date is a small-group session which offers Wardell Gray soloing on 'She's Got The

Blues For Sale'. The original sound is still poor, although the later sessions show National improving their microphones to some extent.

***** Billy Eckstine 1947**

Classics 1142 *Eckstine; Ray Linn (t); Gerald Valentine (tb); Sonny Criss (as); Wardell Gray (ts); Warren Bracken (p, g); Shifty Henry (b); Tim Kennedy (d); orchestras led by Sonny Burke, Hugo Winterhalter.* 4/47–8/47.

By this point, Eckstine had had enough of his 'legendary' band – 'The legendary Billy Eckstine was about to starve,' he later remarked. Though there's a single small-group date for National to start proceedings, the rest of the disc has him fronting studio bands and the 24-piece Hugo Winterhalter Orchestra. The material is all in the mould of 'Just An Old Love Of Mine' and 'On The Boulevard Of Memories', and the tempos rarely hitch up their skirts. On its own terms there is some sumptuous singing, but don't expect much more than a flicker of jazz in here.

*****(*) Billy's Best!**

Verve 526440-2 *Eckstine; orchestras of Hal Mooney, Bobby Tucker.* 8/57–9/58.

***** Imagination**

Emarcy 848162-2 *Eckstine; Pete Rugolo Orchestra.* 58.

***** At Basin Street East**

Emarcy 832592 *Eckstine; Benny Bailey, Clark Terry, Ernie Royal (t); Curtis Fuller (tb); Julius Watkins (frhn); Phil Woods (as); Jerome Richardson, Eric Dixon (ts, f); Sahib Shihab (bs); Patti Bown (p); Don Elliott (vib); Don Arnone (g); Stu Martin (d).* 61.

****** Everything I Have Is Yours**

Verve 819442-2 2CD *Eckstine; various groups.* 47–57.

*****(*) Verve Jazz Masters: Billy Eckstine**

Verve 519693-2 *Eckstine; various groups.* 49–58.

Eckstine's was the ripest, most luxurious voice in black music, and though his later records suggest he was fundamentally a conservative one shouldn't forget how radical a role it was for a black singer to adopt such a romantic persona in the '40s. Eckstine's many records for Mercury from the '50s and '60s are still relatively scarce in the reissue racks. One of the surviving 'original' albums, *At Basin Street East* is a rousing encounter with Quincy Jones's big band. The contrast here is between Eckstine's opulent, take-my-time delivery and the scintillating punch of what was a fierce, slick, note-perfect organization. *Imagination* is more in the slicked-down ballad mode, and some of these tunes have never oozed quite so much; Rugolo provides limousine-class charts. *Billy's Best!* is a beauty which we have petitioned for reissue in the past, so it is a special pleasure to welcome it in such splendid remastering. 'When The Sun Comes Out' shows how Eckstine could handle a high-stepping arrangement without seeming to require any exertion of his own, and the following 'I Got Lost In Her Arms' presents ardour as the most gentlemanly of emotions. The arrangements walk a line between vigour and schmooze, and there are six bonus tracks added to the original LP programme.

First choice here, though, must go to the two-disc set, *Everything I Have Is Yours,* which charts Eckstine's course with all his hits and a few plum rarities in the order of 'Mister You've Gone And Got The Blues'. The *Jazz Masters* disc boils it down to 16 tracks and throws in a previously unissued obscurity, 'I Lost My Sugar In Salt Lake City' to tempt diehard collectors.

*****(*) Once More With Feeling**

Roulette 81862 *Eckstine; orchestras conducted by Billy May and Joe Reisman.* 7/59–1/60.

He's cool, he's romantic, but he knows about the blues, and even if he does have an expensive orchestra behind him, he's made sure he's got the likes of Buddy Collette, Benny Carter, Jimmy Rowles and Red Callender in the band. Just luxurious. The sound is, too, in this remastering, and there's the bonus of two sides of a single which wasn't on the original album.

****** No Cover No Minimum**

Roulette 98583-2 *Eckstine; Charlie Walp (t); Bucky Manieri (tb); Charlie McLean, Buddy Balboa (saxes); Bobby Tucker (p); Buddy Grievey (d).* 8/60.

A superlative example of Eckstine's art, and surely still his best record in print. Recorded at a Las Vegas lounge, the 21 tracks (12 of them previously unissued) luxuriate in Bobby Tucker's simple arrangements and bask in the grandeur of Eckstine's voice and phrasing. 'Moonlight In Vermont' has never sounded more richly expansive, 'Lush Life' is a proper ode to barfly poetry, and the swingers are delivered with an insouciance and a perfect mastery of metre that creates shivers of delight. The remastering is very full and vivid on what is an indispensable issue.

***** Now Singing In 12 Great Movies**

Verve 589307-2 *Eckstine; orchestras arranged by Bill Byers and Hal Mooney.* 61–7/63.

The backings have started to turn vanilla, although it makes no difference to Eckstine, and if anything he revels in the extra bank or two of strings which seem to be on hand here. Agreeable songs, from various hit films of the day, but the jazz quotient is melting away.

Harry 'Sweets' Edison (1915–99)

TRUMPET

Born in Columbus, Ohio, Edison worked in territory groups before joining Count Basie in 1938, staying until 1950. After that there were countless studio dates (with Sinatra and many other singers), all-star sessions and the like; Sweets became the most revered of elder statesmen and was playing right up until his death in 1999.

*****(*) 'Sweets' At The Haig**

Definitive DRCD *Edison; Georgie Auld, Benny Carter, Bob Lawson (sax); Arnold Ross, Jimmy Rowles (p); Joe Comfort (b); Buddy Rich, Alvin Stoller (d).* 7/53.

A valuable recovery, since this period of Sweets's career isn't well represented. Recorded shortly after his arrival in Los Angeles, the main part of the set consists of quartet tracks made with Ross, Comfort and Stoller. 'Pennies From Heaven' and 'Tea For Two' are both solid performances and Harry's solos are mellifluous, nicely structured and of perfect length. The sound isn't bad, though Comfort's bass sounds a touch artificial, as if boosted in the remastering. The remaining tracks were made with an octet. Rowles is superb but Sweets rises to the occasion and sounds powerful on 'Just Blues'.

***** Jawbreakers**

Original Jazz Classics OJC 487 *Edison; Eddie 'Lockjaw' Davis (ts); Hugh Lawson (p); Ike Isaacs (g); Clarence Johnston (d).* 4/62.

★★ Sweets For The Sweet

Collectables 5718 *Edison; Don Abney, Gerry Wiggins (p); Red Callender, Leroy Vinnegar (b); Jackie Mills (d). 7/65.*

Jawbreakers comes highly recommended, a big, raw session that springs a romantic version of 'A Gal In Calico' which contrasts well with the tough funk of 'Oo-ee!'. It has a good, full sound. *Sweets For The Sweet*, originally on Sue (compare *Sweets For The Sweet Taste of Love* on Vee-Jay), is a slushy and sentimental wallow, with very little genuine jazz playing. Nice enough as a background, but with little to move the jazz fan.

★★★ Just Friends

Black & Blue 918 *Edison; Eddie 'Lockjaw' Davis (ts); Gerry Wiggins (p); Major Holley (b); Oliver Jackson (d). 7/75.*

★★★ Just You, Just Me

Black & Blue 885 *Edison; Earl Hines (p). 78.*

Sweets hadn't made an album under his own name for nearly ten years, when he cut these attractive sets for Black & Blue in France. Davis had become a regular partner and the perfect foil to Harry's softly burnished tone and they blend together wonderfully here. 'There Is No Greater Love' is the stand-out track on a fairly predictable roster of material, which includes a couple of run-through originals got together for the session. Wiggins, Holley and Jackson do their business briskly and without fuss and there's a job-well-done feel to the whole proceedings. The Hines material is exactly as you would expect: jovial, steely with technique and thoroughly enjoyable without ruffling too many feathers.

★★★ Edison's Lights

Original Jazz Classics OJC 804 *Edison; Eddie 'Lockjaw' Davis (ts); Count Basie, Dolo Coker (p); John Heard (b); Jimmie Smith (d). 5/76.*

★★(★) Simply Sweets

Original Jazz Classics OJC 903 *Edison; Eddie 'Lockjaw' Davis (ts); Dolo Coker (p); Harvey Newmark (b); Jimmie Smith (d). 9/77.*

Ubiquitous as an accompanist/soloist, Edison made surprisingly few records of his own, given the length of his career. Like many players of his type, he often sounds better on other people's sessions, though the presence of Basie on *Edison's Lights* audibly inspires him (compare the rather lacklustre tracks made on the same day with Coker). The '70s association with Lockjaw Davis produced some of the best of his work, a bright, bursting sound which can also be quite reserved and contemplative. The sound is good and full.

★★★ Harry 'Sweets' Edison/Eddie 'Lockjaw' Davis

Storyville 8225 *Edison; Mogens Eghjort (t); John Darville, John Larson, Bjarne Thanning (tb); Hans Leonardo Pedersen, Jens Sondergard (as); Eddie 'Lockjaw' Davis (ts); Kenny Drew (p); Hugo Rasmussen (b); Svend Erik Norregaard (d); Richard Boone (v). 2 & 12/76.*

★★★ Harry 'Sweets' Edison/Eddie 'Lockjaw' Davis & Richard Boone

Storyville 1025536 *As above. 2 & 12/76.*

These sets, with Davis, the cheerfully eccentric Richard Boone and the well-drilled Pedersen Jazzkapel are delightful from start to finish. A slick but responsive medium-size band provides both a solid foundation and a fast-moving engine for the two front-men. Boone plays no trombone on this occasion, but sings with his usual unabashed oddity. Lockjaw punches into his solos with great vigour and it's nice to hear the two main horns doing their good cop/bad cop routine so unselfconsciously. Nice stuff; however, be aware that Sweets appears on about half the cuts only.

★★(★) There Will Never Be Another You

Nagel Heyer 83 *Edison; Henrik Meurkens (vib); Torsten Zwingenberger Quartet. 86.*

Sweets was past his 70th birthday when this was recorded and there is a clear decline in powers, not so much in his ability to shape a solo as in basic technique. Even some of the middle-register tones seem to be hit only approximately, and while he remains in tune most of the time, there is just an edge that suggests it could all go wrong any second. He's not helped particularly by the band, who seem a little unsure here and there, even on fairly basic material like 'Cotton Tail' and 'In A Mellotone', which are the best things on the set. Sweets's own 'Centrepiece', originally a collaboration with Jon Hendricks, ends proceedings on a high, but it's thinnish pickings from so great a player. Newcomers won't be beguiled and settled fans will feel short-changed.

★★★(★) For My Pals

Pablo 2310934 *Edison; Buster Cooper (tb); Curtis Peagler (as, ts); Art Hillery (p, org); Andy Simpkins (b); Albert 'Tootie' Heath (d). 12/88.*

★★★ Swing Summit

Candid CCD 79050 *Edison; Buddy Tate (cl, ts); Frank Wess (ts, f); Hugh Lawson (p); Ray Drummond (b); Bobby Durham (d). 4/90.*

Edison's artistic longevity was remarkable. *For My Pals*, with a larger than usual group, marked a welcome return to form: 'Lover Man' and 'There Is No Greater Love' are both top-notch performances and the sound is immaculate. *Swing Summit* contains less interesting material, but is brightly and faithfully recorded, and excellent value.

★★★ Live At The Iridium

Telarc 83425 *Edison; Clark Terry (t, flhn); Frank Wess (ts, f); Junior Mance (p); Marcus McLaurine (b); Dave Gibson (d). 4/97.*

His very last bow was at New York's Iridium, with a gang of old friends: nothing's said that wasn't said before, often enough, but for the pleasure of hearing these wily veterans together for a final time it's a record worth having.

Teddy Edwards (1924–2003)

TENOR SAXOPHONE, CLARINET

Arrived in Los Angeles in 1944 after working in territory bands, and has basically remained there since, active through the '50s and '60s and then making guest appearances in the '80s and '90s. A blend of southwestern blues and West Coast cool informs his sound.

★★★(★) Steady With Teddy

Cool N' Blue C & B CD 115 *Edwards; Benny Bailey, Howard McGhee (t); Iggy Shevack (tb); Dexter Gordon (ts); Duke Brooks, Hampton Hawes, Michael 'Dodo' Marmarosa, Jimmy Rowles (p); Arvin Garrison (g); Red Callender, Addison Farmer, Bob Kesterson (b); Roy Porter (d). 10/46–8/48.*

These are the earliest glimpses of Edwards on record, with boppers who put a lyrical spin on the familiar changes. Tracks like 'Dilated Pupils' from the 1946 session (a McGhee composition, significantly) suggest the sort of background he was working against. Though he has had his ups and downs, Edwards's relaxed, imperturbable manner has sustained him well; 'steady with Teddy' has been the watchword.

***** Sunset Eyes**

Blue Note 948488 *Edwards; Ronnie Ball, Joe Castro, Amos Trice, Ben Tucker, Leroy Vinnegar (p); Billy Higgins, Al Levitt (d).* 8/59.

Right from the beginning, Edwards's recordings have been of a consistently high quality, testimony to his likeable and no-nonsense approach. All of these tracks, which feature a varying personnel, are well worked out and smoothly executed and most feature a personable solo from the leader. There is little out of the ordinary about any of them. 'Teddy's Tune' and Vinnegar's 'Vintage '57' are given somewhat longer readings, but for the most part the cuts are brief and song-like. The CD reissue includes three extra tracks, but these add nothing of moment to the original.

*****(*) Teddy's Ready**

Original Jazz Classics OJC 1785 *Edwards; Joe Castro (p); Leroy Vinnegar (b); Billy Higgins (d).* 8/60.

***** Back To Avalon**

Contemporary CCD 14074 *Edwards; Nathaniel Meeks (t); Lester Robertson (tb); Jimmy Woods (as); Modesto Brisenio (bs); Danny Horton (p); Roger Alderson (b); Lawrence Marable (d).* 12/60.

Recorded in 1960, *Back To Avalon* was an interesting attempt at arrangement for a mid-size band. The problem is that the octet doesn't generate quite the head of steam the blandness of these charts requires in compensation, and there isn't enough going on on the solo front, with Edwards rather subdued and preoccupied. Even the workhorse, 'Good Gravy', fails to raise a cheer. Lester Koenig's recording can't shoulder any significant blame, and the remix for CD restores a lot of detail. Nothing quite compares, then, to the session with McGhee listed below, though *Teddy's Ready* (originally on Contemporary) has a timeless vigour that makes it endlessly repeatable. It followed a period of ill-health – unrelated, it should be said, to the usual perils of a jazzman's life in those days – and one can hear the relief and delight in the slightly too hasty attack on 'Scrapple From The Apple' and 'Take The "A" Train'. In later years, Edwards was reliably to be found *behind* the beat. Not a great deal is known nowadays about Arizonan Castro; he tends to be thought of as an accomplished accompanist (Anita O'Day and June Christy) who never quite made it as a straight jazz player. On this showing he's more than worthy, and the support of his two colleagues here goes without saying.

****** Together Again!**

Original Jazz Classics OJC 424 *Edwards; Howard McGhee (t); Phineas Newborn Jr (p); Ray Brown (b); Ed Thigpen (d).* 5/61.

*****(*) Good Gravy**

Original Jazz Classics OJC 661 *Edwards; Danny Horton, Phineas Newborn Jr (p); Leroy Vinnegar (b); Milton Turner (d).* 8/61.

Edwards's reunion with a cleaned-up Howard McGhee in 1962 led to one of the best mainstream albums of its day. *Together Again!* is beautifully and almost effortlessly crafted. The ultra-straight 'Misty' showcases Edwards's moody ballad approach, and there is a fine 'You Stepped Out Of A Dream'. Three months later, and without a second horn, Edwards waffles and digresses engagingly but doesn't quite get into the frame. Horton depped for Newborn for much of the three-day session; he's a bright enough lad, but lacks horsepower and swing. Vinnegar is as surefire as ever.

***** Heart And Soul**

Original Jazz Classics OJC 177 *Edwards; Gerald Wiggins (org); Leroy Vinnegar (b); Milton Turner (d).* 62.

***** Nothin' But The Truth**

Original Jazz Classics OJC 813 *Edwards; Walter Davis Jr (p); Phil Orlando (g); Paul Chambers (b); Billy Higgins (d); Montego Joe (perc).* 12/66.

***** It's All Right**

Original Jazz Classics OJCCD 944 *Edwards; Jimmy Owens (t, flhn); Garnett Brown (tb); Cedar Walton (p); Ben Tucker (b); Lennie McBrowne (d).* 5/67.

***** Out Of This World**

Steeplechase SCCD 1147 *Edwards; Kenny Drew (p); Jesper Lundgaard (b); Billy Hart (d).* 12/80.

Heart And Soul is warm enough, but there's a hint that Teddy would like some company in the front line, and for all the guileful support he gets from Wig and the others, it's a bit routine in parts. The rather later *Nothin' But The Truth* is well-mannered, but with the exception of 'But Beautiful' and the title-track (to but no more buts than that), it's a rather average set. Even with a rhythm section of this quality, Edwards doesn't sound inclined to hurry or be infused with anything more dynamic than his usual step-up-and-play approach.

It's All Right is an unusual set in that some of the material points in the direction of Coltrane and even Ornette Coleman; though never remotely avant-garde, Teddy knew what was happening on the scene, and on 'The Cellar Dweller' and 'Mamacita Lisa' he was able to combine his usual easy, blues-inflected swing with something harder and darker.

*****(*) Midnight Creeper**

High Note Records HCD 7011 *Edwards; Virgil Jones (t); Richard Wyands (p); Buster Williams (b); Chip White (d).* 3/97.

A new label for Edwards – his several Verve albums of the '90s have all been axed – and for former Muse-man Houston Person, who produces with his usual skill, letting the music work rather than trying to sweeten it artificially. If Edwards's recording activities were less in evidence in the '90s, despite the renaissance with Polygram, there's certainly nothing wrong with either his technique or his enthusiasm. The album opens with the eponymous nocturnal wanderer, a thing of shadows with a ghostly wail. There are two other originals, 'Walkin' In The Rain', which sounds as if it might have been written for a larger group, and the medium ballad 'Sensitive'. Jones plays only on these three and 'Sunday', and the remainder of the set consists of standards, which is perhaps a pity, though the quality of playing on 'Tenderly' (the longest track), and the closing 'Almost Like Being In Love' makes up for everything. Williams is in cracking form throughout the album, and along with Wyands and White he creates the kind of relaxed but positive vibe on which Edwards thrives. Not a classic album, but a damn fine one from the oldster.

***** Close Encounters**

High Note 7002 *Edwards; Houston Person (ts); Stan Hope (p); Ray Drummond (b); Kenny Washington (d).* 99.

Person plays and produces on this mostly effective two-header. Edwards's style contrasts subtly with his fellow tenorman's, easy and uncomplicated where his confrère tries to be sophisticated. This is probably as much Houston's set as Teddy's but the shared leads are compelling, and the individual features suggest that the plaudits go Edwards's way. Standout track is the unhurried 'Pennies From Heaven'.

***** Ladies Man**

High Note 7067 *Edwards; Eddie E. J. Allen (t); Ronnie Mathews (p); Chip Jackson (b); Chip White (d).* 5/00.

***** The Legend Of Teddy Edwards**

Cope 16/Image 1504 DVD *Edwards; Larry Nash (p); Wendell Williams (b); Gerryck King (d).* 01.

Teddy pays court to ten lovely ladies, some of them – like 'Donna Lee' and 'Laura' – familiar from the canon, some – like 'Saskia' – more recent debutantes. The group could hardly be more responsive but it is Mathews who holds proceedings together with wit, intelligence and courtly good humour. Teddy solos briefly but well, and fans of his easy brand of modern jazz will find this Houston Person-produced set more than satisfying.

The Cope CD is musically less interesting, though Edwards is such an elegant soloist than almost anything of his is bound to have some interest. There are some bonus tracks which add to the picture of a player who was shortly to depart the scene. There is also a DVD of the same name, which we haven't seen but sounds like a welcome souvenir of Teddy's stay.

***** Smooth Sailing**

High Note 7088 *Edwards; Richard Wyands (p); Ray Drummond (b); Chip White (d).* 12/01.

He was battling failing health when this was made, but you wouldn't know it. Edwards's easy swing, generous solo development and ability to inject some gentle humour into otherwise sober performances (as he does on 'Robbins' Nest') is endlessly infectious. Wyands is a formidable accompanist and Drummond and White don't attempt to patronize the old man by keeping the pace down. Even at this age and even seriously ill, Teddy is able to swing a line with the best of them. Hank Mobley's 'Hank's Tune' and the Arnett Cobb title-track are among the highlights, and smooth sailing is what we'd wish Teddy Edwards: calm seas and a prosperous voyage.

Marty Ehrlich (born 1955)

REEDS, FLUTES

Studied in Boston in the '70s with Ran Blake, among others, then moved to New York in 1978, and has been at the centre of the jazz and new music scene ever since.

*****(*) Can You Hear A Motion?**

Enja 8052-2 *Ehrlich; Stan Strickland (ts, f); Michael Formanek (b); Bobby Previte (d).* 9/93.

***** Just Before The Dawn**

New World/CounterCurrents 80474 *Ehrlich; Vincent Chancey (frhn); Erik Friedlander (clo); Mark Helias (b); Don Alias (perc).* 94.

Ehrlich invites many comparisons in his playing, but the spirit which is starting to seem closest to his is Anthony Braxton's. While the opening clarinet tune on *Can You Hear A Motion?* is a dedication to John Carter, it's Braxtonian tone and logic one hears. Ehrlich humanizes the approach: he gets bite and swing out of this woodsy-sounding quartet and inculcates a rural feel into a team which includes such urbanites as Formanek and Previte. 'The Welcome' pivots on a township-like melody, while 'Ode To Charlie Parker' is a chamber-piece for clarinet, flute and bass, and a lovely one too. This probably counts as Ehrlich's best disc since *Pliant Plaint.* The next Dark Woods Ensemble record, *Just Before The Dawn,* is as highly coloured but a shade less vivacious in the playing. Sometimes the group gets a little hung up on its own sounds and shadings, perhaps.

****** New York Child**

Enja 9025-2 *Ehrlich; Stan Strickland (ts); Michael Cain (p); Michael Formanek (b); Bill Stewart (d).* 2/95.

Assured, vibrant and intensely beautiful for much of its duration, this is surely Ehrlich's finest hour to date. His sound goes so well with Strickland's that they invite comparisons with Konitz and Marsh. Each has a pliable, unshowy tone, ideal for the plaiting of timbres which the unisons seek to achieve. Cain has seldom played better than here – his improvised duet with Ehrlich on 'Prelude' and the luminous solo on Julius Hemphill's 'Georgia Blue' are gorgeous – and Stewart and Formanek are entirely admirable. Ehrlich's writing follows a patient course. 'I always find it easier to play within the context of a melody,' he says, 'and I always look for what is specific about the language of a given piece.' That peaceable logic gives Ehrlich's outside-isms complete conviction.

*****(*) Light At The Crossroads**

Songlines SGL 1511-2 *Ehrlich; Ben Goldberg (cl, bcl); Trevor Dunn (b); Kenny Wollesen (d).* 97.

The pleasures here are in the jousting between Ehrlich and Goldberg and the subtle, almost sneakily swinging rhythms set down by Dunn and Wollesen. On a clever piece like Wayne Horvitz's Monk inversion, 'Ask Me Later', they find a humorous counterpoint which touches a comic aspect in their reeds without resorting to pastiche or clowning. Elsewhere they're irreproachably sober. Light, and dark.

*****(*) Relativity**

Enja 9341-2 *Ehrlich; Michael Formanek (b); Peter Erskine (d).* 2/98.

Ehrlich's name comes first, but this is really a co-operative trio, and if there's a dominant personality, it's Erskine, whose constant creativity within free and time playing is a wonderful resource for any group. As Ehrlich says: 'The harmony moves through the drums, the melody spins a long line from the bass, and I can feel free to make my horn into a ride cymbal.' Ten compositions are shared round the group, with a nice reminder of Don Grolnick (in whose band Ehrlich and Erskine played together) with his 'Taglioni'. Spontaneous but cultured and cultivated playing by all three sets of hands.

***** Song**

Enja 9396 *Ehrlich; Ray Anderson (tb); Uri Caine (p); Michael Formanek (b); Billy Drummond (d).* 10/99.

*****(*) Malinke's Dance**

Omnitone 12003 *Ehrlich; Tony Malaby (ss, ts); Jerome Harris (b); Bobby Previte (d).* 12/99.

Song feels disappointingly conventional, an album of interpretations (Bob Dylan is one contributor) which feels almost like a gang of post-modernists trying to play unaffected mainstream. Ray Anderson's cameo on 'Blue Boye's Blues' livens things up a bit, but for all the refinement of the playing this has a pointless feel to it.

Malinke's Dance is the record of a Knitting Factory gig and is altogether sharper and more satisfying. Malaby is an effective new partner for the leader and the set has a detailed, worked-out but not over-polished feel to it, driven along by the superb Previte – listen to him constantly prodding, poking and changing the pace on 'Rhymes'.

★★★(★) The Long View
Enja ENJ 9452 *Ehrlich; Eddie Allen, James Zollar (t); Ray Anderson, Clark Gayton (tb); John Clark (frhn); Marcus Rojas (tba); Ned Rothenberg (as, bcl); Sam Furnace (as, f); Robert DeBellis (ss, ts, cl); H. D. Parran (ts, bcl); Andy Laster (bs, cl); Wayne Horvitz (p); Mark Feldman (vn); Ralph Farris (vla); Erik Friedlander (clo); Mark Dresser, Mark Helias (b); Pheeroan AkLaff, Bobby Previte, Michael Sarin (d); Eddie Bobe (perc).* 4/02.

Easily overlooked. The episodic structure and the fact that these six 'movements' and postlude were written in response to paintings by Oliver Jackson might lead some listeners to conclude that this is not a proper Ehrlich album but some sort of side-project. Ten minutes with these carefully constructed and – for all his protestations to the contrary – quite painterly pieces should dispel any such doubt. Helias conducts and has to hold together some quite complex voicings and some intriguingly layered passages. Marty is in great form, not just as main soloist, but also as writer; in fact it is remarkable, given the talent assembled in the orchestra, that he should have shouldered so much playing responsibility. Every exposure to this fine album yields new insights. There is some excellent brass and string work that suggest orchestral writing on an ever grander scale may be part of the Ehrlich agenda for the next few years.

Thore Ehrling (born 1912)

TRUMPET, VOCAL

Born in Stockholm, Ehrling played in Frank Vernon's dance band from 1930, then formed his own small group in 1938 and developed it into a successful big band, which endured until 1957. He also worked extensively in music publishing.

★★★ Jazz Highlights
Dragon DRCD 236 *Ehrling; Gosta Redlig, Gosta Pettersson, Gosta Torner, Rune Ander, Yngve Nilsson, Olle Jacobson, Arnold Johansson, Putte Bjorn, John Linder, Nisse Skoog (t); George Vernon, Sverre Oredsson, Sven Hedberg, Andreas Skjold (tb); Ove Ronn, Curt Blomqvist, Erik Andersson, John Bjorling, Carl-Henrik Noren, Casper Hjukstrom, Stig Gabrielsson, Gunnar Lunden-Velden, Arne Domnérus, Harry Arnold, Fritz Fust, Rolf Londell, Georg Bjorklund, Mats Borgstrom (reeds); Stig Holm, Mats Olsson (p); Folke Eriksberg, Sven Stiberg (g); Thore Jederby, Hasse Tellemar (b); Anders Solden, Gosta Heden, Uffe Baadh, Henry Wallin, Bertil Frylmark (d).* 1/39–12/55.

★★★(★) Swedish Swing 1945–1947
Ancha ANC 9503-2 *Similar to above.* 3/45–7/47.

A sizeable slice of Swedish jazz history is packed on to the 26-track Dragon CD, decently remastered from some rare originals. Ehrling had already worked in dance bands for many years before forming his first orchestra in 1938 – he had been a Benny Carter sideman two years earlier – and, although his band made as many concessions to popular taste as did Basie and Ellington, they made enough good jazz-directed records to grant this retrospective more than a passing interest. Among the early tracks, a very swinging 'Roses Of Picardy' and a Dorsey-like 'Meditation' are impressive. Carl-Henrik Noren's arrival brought his interesting tunes to the book, including the Ellingtonian 'Mississippi Mood'; but the later tracks suggest that Ehrling never got much further than the solidly competitive swing style that was established by the early '40s. Soloists are more functional than inspiring, although Ove Ronn's Hodges-like alto is always worth catching, as is Noren, and Domnérus appears on one track. A pleasing tribute to a great name in Swedish jazz.

The Ancha disc is for more dedicated tastes, since it covers a couple of broadcasts from the mid-'40s. The first is all-Ellington, done with a surprising amount of panache, though the arrangements seem like slavish copies. The second is by a nonet, with Bjorling's clarinet taking a significant role and a couple of kitsch items betraying the music's dance-hall origins. The second set is a bit crackly, but sound is otherwise clear enough.

Dietrich Eichmann (born 1966)

PIANO

A Berliner, Eichmann is a composer who has lately turned to improvising.

★★★ The Temperature Dropped Again
Leo LR 390 *Eichmann; Jeff Arnal (perc).* 12/02.

A busy set of duet performances. Eichmann studied with Alex von Schlippenbach at one point, and with Arnal a quickfire percussionist much versed in the Paul Lovens style, the music sounds to be in a grand tradition of middle-European improvising. The pianist takes a very different line to the Cecil Taylor school, mixing prepared-piano sparseness with needling runs and delicate, almost lacy decorations.

Bruce Eisenbeil (born 1963)

GUITAR

A subtle young Chicagoan, Eisenbeil is a rather 'pure' technician in the Derek Bailey mould. He sounds more like a cross between Sonny Sharrock and David Moss, though.

★★★ Nine Wings
CIMP 144 *Eisenbeil; Rob Brown (as); Lou Grassi (d).* 3/97.

★★★(★) Mural
CIMP 194 *Eisenbeil; J. Brunka (b); Ryan Sawyer (d).* 2/99.

Eisenbeil sounds like a wild man in spite of himself. He plays unadorned electric guitar, without effects or accoutrements, in a simple open tone that's bent into service as an avant-garde instrument. With the peripatetic Brown, something of a free-playing veteran by now, and the tinkering Grassi, he leads the trio through eight compositions (and one brief improv) that break down structure into bloody three-way confrontations. 'Hermitage Of Xzeng Xzu' and 'Mercury' are especially all out. Brown's experience comes to the fore and he makes light of his exposed position, but Eisenbeil is arguably the more interesting performer since he tries to reconcile his melodicism with playing out.

The CIMP no-tricks sound isn't much help on this occasion, but it has certainly been tweaked for the second album, which is an arresting panel of soundscapes, shaped round two long tracks, 'Caesar' and 'Woman With A Handful Of Rain'. Sawyer's fast-decay cymbal sound is a key element, but Eisenbeil himself has extended his range of articulations, and he creates a new vocabulary of 'natural' effects which broadens and deepens the musical discourse considerably.

***** Opium**

CIMP 241 *Eisenbeil; David Taylor (btb); Michael Attias (as, bsx); Jay Rosen (d). 2/01.*

The downright peculiar instrumentation is matched by the often bizarre music-making. Eisenbeil's deliberately stringy sound, twanging between the mooing low notes of Attias's bass sax and Taylor's bass trombone, will nonplus many listeners. Here and there it's almost akin to Eddie Lang and Adrian Rollini meeting in a nightmare. Refreshing, though, when applied in very small doses, maybe no more than a track at a time. 'Ode To Blind Joe Death' might be a nod to John Fahey. But looking for meanings here is likely to induce bafflement.

Either/Orchestra

GROUP

Led and organized by Russ Gershon and based in and around Massachusetts, this big contemporary ensemble now has a nearly two-decade history, playing material from jazz, rock and other modern-music sources.

***** Dial E**

Accurate AC-2222 *Tom Halter, Dave Ballou, Bob Sealy, Dan Drexter (t); Russell Jewell, Josh Roseman (tb); Rob Rawlings, Bob Sinfonia (as); Russ Gershon (ts); Steve Norton (bs); Kenny Freundlich (ky); John Dirac (g); Mike Rivard (b); Jerome Deupree (d). 7/86.*

*****(*) Radium**

Accurate AC-3232 *Tom Halter, John Carlson (t, flhn); Russell Jewell, Curtis Hasselbring (tb); Rob Rawlings (as); Russ Gershon (ss, ts); Charlie Kohlhase (bs); Kenny Freundlich (ky); John Dirac (g); Mike Rivard (b); Jerome Deupree (d). 8/87–1/88.*

*****(*) The Half-Life Of Desire**

Accurate AC-3242 *As above, except add Douglas Yates (ss, as), Dave Finucane (bcl), John Medeski (ky), Mark Sandman (g, v). 89.*

****** The Calculus Of Pleasure**

Accurate AC-3252 *As above, except add Bob Nieske (b), Matt Wilson (d); omit Freundlich, Dirac, Rivard, Deupree, Finucane, Sandman. 4–6/90.*

****** The Brunt**

Accurate AC-3262 *As above, except add Dan Fox (tb), Andrew D'Angelo (as, bcl, cl), Chris Taylor (ky), John Turner (b); omit Hasselbring, Yates, Medeski, Nieske. 5/93.*

A modest-sized big band full of outsize talents, Either/Orchestra has made scarcely any international impact. Leader Russ Gershon has squeezed these CDs out of the impossible restrictions that modern budgets have set for this kind of band if it wants to work and make records. It's a heroic accomplishment that the group is as swinging, exciting and cheerfully cutting-edge as it is. All the first three records are a rag-bag of favourite cover versions, bristling originals and complexities with which only the most skilful and hungry players could go for broke. *Dial E*, its debut, has made it to CD only recently; comparatively rough-and-ready compared with the finesse of the later discs, it's still an exciting and unpredictable record. Rollins's 'Doxy' is turned into an outlandish shuffle, they have the chutzpah to take apart 'Brilliant Corners', and the extravagantly extended '17 December' is an early manifesto of what the band could do. *Radium* is all live and runs the gamut from a tragedian's version of 'Willow Weep For Me' to a madcap distillation of 'Nutty' and 'Ode To Billie Joe', with Roscoe Mitchell's 'Odwallah' as a bonus. *The Half-Life Of Desire* expands the palette a little with Medeski's arrival; this brilliant keyboardist has a sure grasp of which electronics will and which won't work in a neo-trad context, and on Gershon's 'Strange Meridian' he blends acoustic and electric parts with perfect aplomb. Rock and 'world' musics get only a modest look-in in this group's work; its material comes largely from within jazz language itself, which sets it a little apart from such groups as Peter Apfelbaum's ensemble. Yet it still manages to cover the King Crimson metal blow-out, 'Red', and tamper with Miles Davis's 'Circle In The Round' on the same record.

The Calculus Of Pleasure, part live and part studio in origin, is arguably the group's best to date. There is an astonishing arrangement of Horace Silver's 'Ecaroh', previously a piano-trio tune, and a sour, lavish update of Benny Golson's 'Whisper Not' which is an object lesson in renewing stale jazz repertory. Julius Hemphill's 'The Hard Blues' also comes in for a grandly decadent interpretation, with brass and reeds fattening up the harmonies as never before. This leaves five originals from within the band's own ranks. Mention should also be made of soloists such as Medeski, Hasselbring, Yates and Kohlhase, foot-soldiers and front-liners alike.

There is no falling off in quality with *The Brunt*. Though both Hasselbring and Medeski have departed, the team remains terrifically strong as a playing unit. The complexities of 'Notes On A Cliff' and the swaggering 'Permit Blues' are shrugged off, and the title-piece, a bequest by Hasselbring, is a feast of overlapping ideas. One of their most dramatic repertory adventures takes place in Mal Waldron's 'Hard Talk', and only the Ellington piece, 'Blues For New Orleans', disappoints – but that is classic Ellington. The charming retread of Bob Dylan's 'Lay Lady Lay' is a fitting finale and reminds that the band's secret may lie in acting good-humoured rather than merely being humorous. This is also their best-recorded CD.

*****(*) Across The Omniverse**

Accurate AC-3272 2CD *As above discs. 7/86–9/95.*

Two packed discs of out-takes from their first five albums. Some good Ellington/Hodges, some Sonny Simmons, and the usual slew of maverick originals. If there's an air of second choice about some of it, the E/O spirit abides and it would take a churl not to enjoy the music and the sleeve-note stories, such as the wedding gig they played where the bride asked for something by Philip Glass.

*** More Beautiful Than Death

Accurate AC-3282 *Tom Halter, Colin Fisher (t, flhn); Joel Yennior (tb); Jaleel Shaw, Miguel Zenon (as); Russ Gershon (ss, ts); Charlie Kohlhase (bs); Dan Kaufman (ky); Rick McLaughlin, Atemu Aton (b); Harvey Wirht (d); Vicente Lebron (perc).* 5/98–8/99.

Probably their best and worst album at the same moment. Gershon wrote all this material, bar the three tracks which comprise 'Ethiopian Suite', and it's a more private, more melancholy Either/Orchestra which results. 'Number Three' and the title-track are dense, meditative pieces which have brought the repeat button into play. Some of the fun seems to have gone out of the band, yet it has taken on a more singular collective cast. Or maybe it's Gershon asserting himself more thoroughly. Either way, the soloists make less impression, the ensembles sound more important, and where the band might once have found itself in the kind of category in which groups such as Mingus Dynasty reside, it suddenly sounds a good deal more idiosyncratic than that. Admirers of the earlier records may be unsure whether to feel good or bad about what is assuredly a progression.

*** Neo-Modernism

Accurate AC-3284 *As above; omit Zenon, Kaufman, Shaw; add Jeremy Udden (as); Gregory Burk (p, ky).* 6/01.

The new disc is very similar in mood to its predecessor. Again all the material – but for Bob Nieske's 'Fast Edd' – is by Gershon and again the mood is mostly dark and speculative. The most obvious and regrettable change is the plodding accompaniment provided by Gregory Burk, who stands in for the more mercurial Dan Kaufman. On the opening 'Los Olivados', the pianist seems to be reading off his chords rather too deliberately. Given that Wirht keeps the metre strong but open, he could have afforded to relax things a bit.

'Baby Invents Monk' is a more skittish thing, and to that extent closer to the original Either/Orchestra concept, which might be said to be Kenton with a sense of humour. Here, Burk redeems himself amply with a jaggy and Monk-inspired solo that swings in its own unexpected way. The 'modernist' slant, made explicit on the next track, is of the gentler and more accommodating sort. This is not a group interested in alienation effects. On 'The Modernist', the horns march in ragged procession, but it has to be said that the Nieske tune is the best thing on the record, a setting for Gershon's wailing soprano solo. 'Heavily Amplified Hairpiece' is the kind of title one might have expected of Britain's Loose Tubes and there is a kinship in the deliberately rocked-up pace of the closing piece.

Mats Eklöf

BARITONE SAXOPHONE, CLARINET

Contemporary Swedish saxophonist with a satirical bent, formerly in Position Alpha.

*** Get Stupid

Dragon DRCD 317 *Eklöf; Staffan Svensson (t); Niclas Rydh (tb); Thomas Jäderlund (ss, as, bcl); Thomas Gustafson (ts, ss); Jonny Axelsson (vib, mar, perc); Johannes Lundberg (b); Goran Kron (d).* 5/97.

Anything but stupid. Eklöf's sleeve-note betrays a peculiar sense of humour, and this extravagant record, which sews together 15 compositions in a virtually unbroken whole, is deadpan-funny in a way that only Swedish jazz can be (one might wish to consult the penultimate track, 'The Swedish Way', for further discussion on that note). Impenetrable harmonies, solos that bounce between brooding and hilarious, off-colour carnival melodies and the strange use of Axelsson's vibes as a sort of narrative-thread make this as individual as anything in this *Guide*. Eklöf stakes his place in a great tradition of European mavericks, but the record will strike many as a particularly acquired taste. Still, we'd like to hear more from him!

Roy Eldridge (1911–88)

TRUMPET, VOCAL, PIANO

Roy Eldridge is the marker between swing trumpet and the bebop revolution, and it's no accident that his theme, 'I Remember Harlem', should also have appeared on one of Ornette Coleman's breakthrough performances. The archetypal high-note artist, Little Jazz became an all too enthusiastic participant in cutting contests, sometimes neglecting expression in favour of excitement and competition. And yet he remains perhaps the greatest brass player of the generation after Louis Armstrong and put an indelible stamp on modern jazz.

***(*) The Big Sound Of Little Jazz

Topaz TPZ 1021 *Eldridge; Al Beck, Bill Coleman, Torg Halten, Mickey Mangano, Norman Murphy, Joe Thomas, Dick Vance, Graham Young (t); Fernando Arbello, Joe Conigliaro, Ed Cuffee, John Grassi, Jay Kelliher, Babe Wagner, Dicky Wells (tb); Buster Bailey, Benny Goodman, Cecil Scott (cl); Omer Simeon (cl, as, bs); Russell Procope (cl, as); Sam Musiker (cl, ts); Scoops Carey, Benny Carter, Joe Eldridge, Ben Feman, Andrew Gardner, Hilton Jefferson, Howard Johnson, Rex Kittig, Jimmy Migliore, Clint Neagley, Mascagni Ruffo (as); Tom Archia, Walter Bates, Chu Berry, Don Brassfield, Coleman Hawkins, Teddy Hill, Ike Quebec, Ben Webster, Elmer Williams, Dave Young (ts); Sam Allen, Teddy Cole, Rozelle Gayle, Clyde Hart, Horace Henderson, Bob Kitsis, Joe Springer, Jess Stacy, Teddy Wilson (p); Bernard Addison, Danny Barker, Ray Biondi, John Collins, Bob Lessey, Lawrence Lucie, Allan Reuss, John Smith (g); Biddy Bastien, Israel Crosby, Richard Fulbright, John Kirby, Ed Mihelich, Truck Parham, Artie Shapiro, Ted Sturgis (b); Bill Beason, Big Sid Catlett, Cozy Cole, Gene Krupa, Zutty Singleton, Harold 'Doc' West (d).* 2/35–11/43.

*** Roy Eldridge, 1935–1940

Classics 766 *Similar to above.* 35–40.

Roy Eldridge has been widely acknowledged as the bridge between swing and bebop trumpet. Listening to Dizzy Gillespie at the (in)famous Massey Hall concert with Charlie Parker, Charles Mingus, Bud Powell and Max Roach, there is little doubt about the ancestry of the trumpeter's high-register accents. However, Eldridge can't just be seen as Moses who led his people out of the desert of late swing and up to the borders of bop's promised land. He did his thing longer and more consistently than the modernists' version of the story would have you believe.

Eldridge moved to New York in 1934 and was quickly recognized as a new star. The introductory bars of '(Lookie, Lookie, Lookie) Here Comes Cookie', first item on the valuable Topaz compilation, offer a glimpse of the excitement the youngster must have caused. His ability to displace accents and play questionable intervals with perfect confidence and logic is immediately evident. More than just a high-note man, Eldridge combined remarkable rhythmic intuition with an ability to play intensely exciting music in the middle and lower register, often the acid test that separates the musicians from the instrumentalists. His solo on 'Blue Lou' – recorded with the Fletcher Henderson band in March 1936 – is a perfect case in point. He does the same kind of thing with the Teddy Wilson band on 'Blues In C Sharp Minor', fitting his improvisation perfectly to the moody key; Chu Berry's follow-up and Israel Crosby's tensely throbbing bass complete a masterful performance. At the other end of the emotional spectrum, there are the starburst top Cs (and beyond) of 'Heckler's Hop', high point of an excellent set as leader with a band anchored on Zutty Singleton's tight drumming. The vocal tracks with Mildred Bailey are often quite appealing and show how responsive an accompanist Eldridge was, again able to play quietly and in contralto range when called upon. A solitary Billie Holiday track – 'Falling In Love Again' – gives a flavour only of that association, which is more fully documented under her name.

The sound is less crystalline on the Topaz (and decidedly muddy in places on the weirdly inconsistent Classics), but both of these cover pretty much the same material. As the massed personnels will again suggest, it selects from the broadest range of bands and sessions, starting with Teddy Hill, taking in Krupa, Henderson, the Little Jazz Ensemble with Chu, the Chocolate Dandies with Carter, and the other Teddy, the urbane Wilson. In just over an hour it offers a pretty straightforward and representative account of the first decade of activity.

CORE COLLECTION

**** Heckler's Hop

Hep CD 1030 *Similar to above, except add Prince Robinson, Franz Jackson (ts), Panama Francis (d), Mildred Bailey, Helen Ward, Gladys Palmer, Laurel Watson (v).* 36–39.

There is much to recommend the Hep selection, not least a high-quality transfer that renders such notes with absolute clarity and minimum distortion. Though it covers a shorter chronological span and puts undue emphasis on less than startling singers, its immediacy and presence (check out the end of 'After You've Gone', a classic Eldridge moment) make it the item of choice for us.

Given the dominance of Dizzy and the alternative direction opened up by Miles, Eldridge's work has been at something of a premium in recent years. These, though, are essential – and usefully complementary – documents of modern jazz and offer a salutary lesson for anyone who still tends to think of the music as a sequence of upper-case historical styles.

*** Live At The Three Deuces Club

Archives of Jazz 3801242 *Eldridge; Joe Eldridge (as); Scoops Carey (as, cl); Dave Young (ts); Teddy Cole (p); John Collins (g); Truck Parham (b); Zutty Singleton (d).* 1/37?

*** Arcadia Shuffle: Live At The Arcadia Ballroom

Archives of Jazz 3801142 *Eldridge; Robert Williams (t); Eli Robinson (tb); Joe Eldridge (as); Prince Robinson (ts, cl); Franz Jackson (ts); Clyde Hart (p); John Collins (g); Ted Sturgis (b); Panama Francis (d); Laurel Watson (v).* 8/39.

The Three Deuces cuts aren't securely dated but reissue producer Jerry Valburn believes February 1937 is a safe bet, right in the middle of Roy's long residency at the Chicago club, a legendary after-hours joint where musicians gathered to see what was new. 'Little Jazz' is done as a smooth theme tune and at a gentler pace than usual. It follows 'Minor Jive' featuring Roy with a mute so far inside the bell the air must have had difficulty getting out. 'Mr Ghost Goes To Town' is a curiosity, written by Will Hudson. The highlight of the set is a 'Deuces Medley' made up of 'I Surrender Dear' and other material strung together by Zutty Singleton's delightfully nailed-down accompaniment.

The Arcadia material also includes 'Little Jazz' (two takes from the same evening) 'Heckler's Hop' and 'Minor Jive'. The last of these is terrific, with Prince Robinson and Roy's ill-fated brother setting the leader up for a beautifully judged solo that cops a couple of ideas from earlier performances but still manages to find new angles on Pops' original Hot Five theme. Some of the cuts are pretty generic, like a stock version of 'Woodchopper's Ball', and some are heads worked up as blowing vehicles: 'Roy's Riffin' Now', 'Arcadia Shuffle' and the durable 'Swinging At The Deuces', which obviously passed its road test. Eldridge is hitting his top notes with ease, but seems mostly content to stay in a lyrical middle register and concentrate on the melody. His choruses are nicely shaped and deceptively paced, with more notes and more expressive variation than their length might suggest. Two valuable documents from a busy and mostly happy period in the trumpeter's long career.

***(*) Roy Eldridge, 1943–1944

Classics 920 *Eldridge; Thomas Aiken, Emmett Berry, John 'Bugs' Hamilton, Cookie Mason, Joe Thomas, Clarence Wheeler (t); Ted Kelly, Jack Teagarden, Andrew Williams, George Wilson (tb); Barney Bigard (cl); Joe Eldridge, Andrew Gardner, Sam Lee (as); Tom Archia, Franz Jackson, Ike Quebec, Hal Singer (ts); Dave McRae (bs); Ted Brannon, Rozelle Gayle, Johnny Guarnieri, Art Tatum (p); Napoleon Allen, Al Casey (g); Lionel Hampton (vib); Israel Crosby, Oscar Pettiford, Ted Sturgis, Billy Taylor (b); Big Sid Catlett, Cozy Cole, Harold 'Doc' West (d).* 11/43–10/44.

After leaving Gene Krupa, Eldridge recorded some sides for Brunswick in the late autumn of 1943. Later he was pitched into the free-for-all atmosphere of the jam sessions for V-Disc which prefigured the Jazz At The Philharmonic summits. An *Esquire* jam at the Metropolitan Opera House yielded 'Tea For Two' with Jack Teagarden, Barney Bigard, Hamp and Oscar Pettiford, the beginning of a sequence of loose jams which pressurized Eldridge into stratospheric high-note-playing at the expense of the delicacy he amply demonstrates on the earlier 'Stardust'. Early 1944 saw the Little Jazz Trumpet Ensemble with Thomas and Berry recording four sides for Keynote, of which 'I Want To Be Happy' and 'St Louis Blues' illustrate much the same tendency. Eldridge's harmonic brilliance and absolutely assured technique mean that these, like later discs, are of the highest quality; but one does wonder whether his talents were best deployed in this very limited way. A later session for Decca has him giving a vocal rendition of 'St Louis Blues' at the front of a big, well-drilled orchestra. By the end of the war, Little Jazz had cornered the market in a certain style of trumpet-playing. If Dizzy Gillespie was more fashionable and seemingly more in touch with cutting-edge developments, Eldridge remained vital and persuasive, maintaining an edge which was to last until the end of his life.

★★★ Roy Eldridge, 1945–1947

Classics 983 *Eldridge; Henry Clay, Andy Ferretti, Bill Graham, Thomas 'Sleepy' Grider, Marion Hazel, Elton Hill, Yank Lawson, Sylvester Lewis, Jimmy Maxwell, Dave Page, Jim Thomas, Elmon Wright (t); Nat Atkins, Will Bradley, Mort Bulman, Richard Dunlap, Charlie Greenlea, John McConnell, Hal Matthews, Fred Ohms, Al Riding, Fred Robinson, George Robinson, Ward Silloway, Sandy Watson (tb); Ray Ekstrand, Mike Doty, Joe Eldridge, Chris Johnson, Porter Kilbert, Sahib Shihab (as); Ernie Caceres (cl); Tom Archia, Charles Bowen, Nick Caiazza, Al Green, George Lawson, Walt Lockhart, Flip Phillips, Harold Webster (ts); Cecil Payne, Don Purvance, Hank Ross, Al Townsend (bs); Dave Bowman, Mike Coluchio, Buster Harding, Duke Jordan, Billy Roland (p); Napoleon Allen, Mike Bryan, Al Casey, Luke Fowler, Allan Hanlon (g); Trigger Alpert, Louis Carrington, Carl Pruitt, Rodney Richardson, Eddie Safranski, Ted Sturgis (b); Lee Abrams, Cozy Cole, Earl Phillips, Specs Powell, Melvin Saunders (d).* 3/45–5/47.

Roy had worked with Artie Shaw for a time in the last two years of the war, before going out with his own small groups again. The third Classics volume brings together the big-band sides he made for Decca, Coral and Vox, and three fascinating V-Discs cut just after the war; the first of them 'Roy Meets Horn' features a spoken introduction by Eddie 'Rochester' Anderson. The two early Deccas catch Eldridge at opposite extremes, buoyantly walking the high wire on 'Little Jazz Boogie' and doing tough'n'tender on 'Embraceable You', both of them superb arrangements by Buster Harding. The 1946 dates are evenly spaced through the year and find Roy on a high, punching out terse, evocative choruses with a minimum of fuss. His playing on these sides is almost always more satisfying than any of his Jazz At The Philharmonic spots. Of the later tracks 'Lover Come To Me' from September is an excellent example of how Eldridge's control of dynamics was his most powerful tool. 'Tippin' Out' and 'Yard Dog' from the May session are marred by an odd imbalance between soloist and ensemble, the latter sounding very distant. The WNEW Saturday Night Swing Session with fellow JATP stalwart Flip Phillips includes two tracks on which Eldridge clearly doesn't play, unusual practice for Classics. There is still too much distortion at the top end on these reissues. With some artists, that isn't too serious a problem, but Eldridge's rips and smears are too often reduced to noise.

★★★ Wild Driver

Ocium OCM 0020 *Eldridge; Zoot Sims, Buddy Tate (ts); Teddy Brannon, Dick Hyman, Gerry Wiggins (p); Oscar Peterson (org); Barney Kessel (g); Clyde Lombardi (g); Ray Brown, Pierre Michelot (b); Kenny Clarke, J. C. Heard, Ed Shaughnessy, Charlie Smith (d); Anita Love (v); strings.* 50–51.

★★★ Roy Eldridge, 1951

Classics 1311 *Eldridge; Lennart Sundeval (t); Ove Lind (cl); Don Byas, Carl-Henrik Norin, Buddy Tate (ts); Claude Bolling, Teddy Brannon (p); Charles Norman (p, hpd); Rolf Berg, Clyde Lombardi (g); Gunnar Almstedt, Guy de Fatto, Thore Jederby (b); Anders Burman, Armand Molinetti, Charlie Smith (d); strings.* 1, 3, 8, 12/51.

Eldridge came to Europe with Benny Goodman's sextet in 1950 and spent a very productive year away from most of the politicking and jockeying that seemed to be going on in American jazz. These sides, and there is considerable overlap between the two records, find him in bright and jovial form, and certainly less combative than he felt it necessary to be back home.

The earliest cuts on the Ocium set were made in Paris with Zoot Sims and vocalist Anita Love. They're slight enough pieces, though 'The Man I Love' is delightful. Love's singing isn't epochal, but she's a foil to Roy's more lascivious delivery, heard to best effect on the two sides of 'Saturday Night Fish Fry' from January 1951 that open the Classics set. The Ocium continues with a lovely quartet session recorded less than a week after the Sims encounter. 'Wild Driver' and 'Someone To Watch Over Me' are superb cuts, balancing lyricism with power. Gerry Wiggins accompanies sagely and Michelot and Clarke had a telepathic rapport.

Much of the remaining material also features on the Classics set, and for once there isn't much to choose between them as far as sound is concerned. Compiler Tomas Gonzalez for some reason omits 'I See Everybody's Baby' from the August 1951 Verve session, recorded with strings back in New York for Verve where Roy was taken up by kingmaker Norman Granz. These were plush surroundings for the trumpeter and he makes the most of them with a big ripe sound and some lovely, unhurried phrasing on his own 'I Remember Harlem'.

The tracks cut in Stockholm for Metronome at the start of the year are pretty workmanlike. Roy's used more as a vocalist than trumpeter and apart from some nice breaks on 'Hoppin' John' the session of 29 January with clarinet and harpsichord in the group is pretty strange. There are also four cuts from a Vogue session made in Paris in March 1951 with Don Byas and Claude Bolling, and two delightful duets with Bolling on 'Wild Man Blues' and 'Fireworks'. Some nice things here, but nothing of the quality that shines through the rest of that busy year, which also included a fine session with Buddy Tate in August. Too much singing, not enough horn, but Roy knew which side his bread was buttered.

The Ocium is probably the better buy and what may clinch it for most purchasers is the inclusion of four tracks for Verve from December 1952 (shortly to appear on Classics, to be sure, but here first) which pitch Roy in with Oscar Peterson on organ, with Barney Kessel, Ray Brown and J. C. Heard. 'Rockin' Chair' and 'Little Jazz' are possibly the best things on either disc.

★★★(★) Roy And Diz

Verve 521647-2 *Eldridge; Dizzy Gillespie (t, v); Oscar Peterson (p); Herb Ellis (g); Ray Brown (b); Louie Bellson (d).* 10/54.

They enjoyed this. A little friendly sparring, with just enough edge to get the juices on the move. Alongside the man who influenced his style more than any other, Dizzy sounds comfortable and in good humour. On 'Pretty Eyed Baby' they take turns at accompanying the other's scat chorus, but the gloves are off for 'Limehouse Blues', where they try to cut one another like a pair of teenagers. Though thoroughly bested, Gillespie gets off a sarky quote from Eldridge's 'Heckler's Hop', only to find it taken up, turned around and thrown back with interest. Despite the obvious kinship, it's interesting to compare their styles. Gillespie gets cornered on the long blues only because he's taken some chances with the sequence. Eldridge, by contrast, stays as close as possible to the original melody, embroidering it and turning it around, but not veering off into distant keys as the bop-nurtured Diz does almost as a matter of course. Peterson gives both hornmen a solid leg-up from time to time, but it's clear that his sympathies are mainly with Little Jazz. An old-fashioned, unpretentious session, and a good one.

****** The Nifty Cat**
New World 80349 *Eldridge; Benny Morton (tb); Budd Johnson (ts, ss); Nat Pierce (p); Tommy Bryant (b); Oliver Jackson (d).* 11/70.

****(*) Little Jazz & The Jimmy Ryan All Stars**
Original Jazz Classics OJC 1058 *Eldridge; Bobby Pratt (tb); Joe Muranyi (ts); Dick Katz (p); Major Holley (b); Eddie Locke (d).* 4/75.

***** Happy Time**
Original Jazz Classics OJC 628 *Eldridge; Oscar Peterson (p); Joe Pass (g); Ray Brown (b); Eddie Locke (d).* 6/75.

***** Jazz Maturity ... Where It's Coming From**
Original Jazz Classics OJC 807 *Eldridge; Dizzy Gillespie (t); Oscar Peterson (p); Ray Brown (b); Mickey Roker (d).* 6/75.

***** What It's All About**
Original Jazz Classics OJC 853 *Eldridge; Budd Johnson, Norris Turney (sax); Milt Jackson (vib); Norman Simmons (p); Ted Sturgis (b); Eddie Locke (d).* 1/76.

*****(*) Montreux '77**
Original Jazz Classics OJC 373 *Eldridge; Oscar Peterson (p); Niels-Henning Orsted Pedersen (b); Bobby Durham (d).* 7/77.

***** Roy Eldridge & Vic Dickenson**
Storyville STCD 8239 *Eldridge; Vic Dickenson (tb); Budd Johnson (ts); Tommy Flanagan (p); Major Holley (b); Eddie Locke (d).* 5/78.

Much of Eldridge's recorded output was for a time tucked away on trumpet compilations and festival albums. The major compilations above have done much to improve the situation; perhaps only the Benny Carter discography has been so comprehensively turned around in the same period. Even so, there is quite a lot of valuable Eldridge to be found on one-off sessions from later years. *Jazz Maturity* with Diz and Peterson is pretty much a reworking of studio associations, but there were occasions in later years when the trumpeter found himself not so much reliving his old amities as reinventing them. The connection with Budd Johnson was a good case in point. The concert in St Peter's Church on Storyville is very relaxed and mild, but there are moments on the New World disc (an unexpected place to find Eldridge material) which are quite startling in their harmonic language, a further sign that Roy was always prepared to try new angles. Johnson doesn't hustle and bluster as Hawkins tended to do at this period, so there is every encouragement for the wee guy to proceed with some interestingly wayward stuff.

What It's All About is disappointing in that Eldridge seems content to do little more than punch out high notes and then swoop down to swoony ballad territory, then up, then down. By this stage in his career it had all got too easy and predictable, though one or two articulation problems seem to have crept in and were certainly affecting his attack on material like 'The Heat's On', which needs to be pretty exact if it isn't to sound banal. The album with some of the regulars from what was then still a living institution, Jimmy Ryan's, is too sloppy to strike any sparks.

Along with the New World album, perhaps the best of the later stuff is the Montreux set, part of a good series documenting what was considered to be a vintage year. The trumpeter appears to have regained some of his fire and sparkle and doesn't seem to require much notice for the upper-register stabs. The 1978 concert from St Peter's Church in New York is as laid-back and comradely as could be, with some wise musicianship but not much excitement. A decade from the end of his life, Roy had won all the bouts he cared about; merely playing seemed to be reward enough.

Mark Elf

GUITAR

New York guitarist who's busily documenting his own work in the field of post-bop improvising.

***** Live At Smalls**
Jen Bay Jazz JBR 0007 *Elf; Neal Miner (b); Joe Strausser (d).* 10/95.

***** New York Cats**
Jen Bay Jazz JBR 0005 *Elf; Jay Leonhart (b); Dennis Mackrel (d); Kevin Burrell (perc).* 11/98.

***** Swingin'**
Jen Bay Jazz JBR 0008 *Elf; Aaron Goldberg (p); Robert Hurst (b); Winard Harper (d).* 8–12/00.

***** Dream Steppin'**
Jen Bay Jazz JBR 0009 *Elf; Neal Miner (b); Lewis Nash (d).* 12/00–11/01.

Elf is a guitarist set in the tradition of Farlow, Raney and the rest of the bebop masters. He's quick, he bites off every note so you can almost feel it, and he has the plangent inevitability of someone who lives by eighth notes. In other words he's set in his ways, but it's an accomplished style. His own Jen Bay Jazz label runs to something like ten records; these are the ones we've heard. Elf never varies his delivery; and the choice between discs which are cut from the same cloth is going to depend on things like tune preferences and sidemen. The Smalls record is a bit rougher than the others and has a nice, curt feel to it. Elf gives himself some overdubbed rhythm on parts of *New York Cats*, which can help a bit – his articulation is sometimes so deliberate that it can border on the mechanical. There's a bit of variety on *Swingin'*, with Goldberg arriving for two tracks and the record closing with two guitar solos. Of the four, this is probably our favourite. *Dream Steppin'* has the highest proportion of originals, although Elf loves to solo and it often hardly seems to matter what the subject matter is. He says he's not bothered about sales, but is at pains to point out that several of the albums have featured highly on American jazz radio. 'I record because I love to play this music and hope that others will enjoy my life's work.' Go, Mark!

Eliane Elias (born 1960)

PIANO, VOCAL

Born in São Paolo, Brazil, she worked in big bands before moving to New York in 1981. Briefly with Steps Ahead and

Randy Brecker (to whom she was married) and since then she worked as a leader and recorded in a light but effective fusion of Brazilian and post-bop forms.

★★★(★) The Three Americas

Blue Note 53328-2 *Elias; Dave Valentin (f); Gil Goldstein (acc); Mark Feldman (vn); Oscar Castro-Nueves (g); Marc Johnson (b, v); Satoshi Takeishi (d); Cafe (perc, v); Manolo Badrena (perc); Amanda Elias Brecker (v).* 96.

★★★(★) Sings Jobim

Blue Note 95236-2 *Elias; Michael Brecker (ts); Oscar Castro-Nueves (g); Marc Johnson (b); Paulo Braga (d); Cafe (perc).* 97.

In her quiet and uncomplicated way, Elias has created a more genuine and affecting synthesis of American music than many a more self-consciously pioneering type. *The Three Americas* seeks to align North, South and Central American rhythms, harmonies and melodies in a seamless whole, and with the chamberish instrumentation, folkish tunes and soft, settled textures she makes the fusion a plausible and generous creation that's beautifully sustained across themes like 'Chorango', 'Caipora' and 'Jungle Journey'. There are just a few dips into mere light-music pleasantry, but this is mostly a convincing entry.

Sings Jobim might have been crashingly obvious, yet Elias manages to take an unpredictable course through most of the tunes. Even with tenor and rhythm on hand, she makes 'Desafinado' sound nothing like the Getz–Gilberto version. 'So Danco Samba' is quirkily crisp and precise. 'Samba De Uma Nota So' is as gentle as featherfall. Her voice would win no prizes at jazz singing school, but neither would Astrud Gilberto's. Johnson, as always, is a little giant in these situations and he's an indispensable presence on both discs.

★★★(★) Impulsive!

Stunt STUCD 00102 *Elias; Benny Rosenfeld, Jesper Riis, Palle Bolvig, Henrik Bolberg Pedersen, Jens Winther (t, flhn); Bob Brookmeyer (vtb); Vincent Nilsson, Steen Hansen (tb, bhn); Kjeld Ipsen (b); Klaus Löhrer (btb); Axel Windfeld (btb, tba); Michael Hove (as, ss, cl, f); Nicolai Schultz (as, ss, f, af); Uffe Markussen (ts, ss, cl, bcl); Tomas Franck (ss, ts, cl); Flemming Madsen (bs, cl, bcl); Nikolaj Bentzon (ky); Anders Lindval (g); Thomas Ovesen (b, v); Jonas Johansen (d); Ethan Eweisgard (perc).* 2/97.

Composed by Elias, arranged by Bob Brookmeyer, and played by the Danish Radio Jazz Orchestra, this gets the most out of Eliane's lyrical side. There's a tenor battle-royal on the title-track, but what Brookmeyer looks for is to underscore and counterpoint her melodies with his inimitable brass scoring: particularly effective on 'So In Love', to take just one instance. 'It's not world music, it's jazz with a capital J,' says band boss Peter Larsen. Amen to that.

★★★(★) Everything I Love

Blue Note 520827-2 *Elias; Rodney Jones (g); Marc Johnson, Christian McBride (b); Jack DeJohnette, Carl Allen (d).* 99.

This time the focus is squarely on bebop material and its encumbrances: can anything new be wrought out of 'Woody 'N You', 'Nostalgia In Times Square' and a string of standards that would have been regulation fare on 52nd Street bandstands? What she does is look for the sweetness and the lyricism in the tunes, without sacrificing improvisational finesse. It helps that she's become a characterful singer, a small voice but not an unsteady or shy one. The accompaniments are as high-grade as the names suggest, and this is altogether as pleasing a 'repertory' record as one could envisage in this field.

★★★ Kissed By Nature

RCA Bluebird 09026-63914-2 *Elias; Randy Brecker (t); Rick Margitza (ts); Paulo André Tavares (g); Marc Johnson (b); Joey Baron, Paulo Braga (perc).* n.d.

A new label, and they clearly want Eliane to become a singing star. The obvious comparison – given her background, and the kind of material on offer – is with Astrud Gilberto, but she's better than that. The vocalist she most reminds us of is actually Françoise Hardy, whose light, sing-song delivery is not so different to Elias's half-sung, half-spoken way with some of the lyrics. At least many of these tunes are relatively unfamiliar, given that most come from her own pen; and she's clearly taken care not to reduce her piano-playing to a mere added attraction. Still, it's a step in a direction in which she will do well to resist capitulation to commercial imperatives.

The Elite Syncopators

GROUP

Group dedicated to performing original ragtime repertory in ensemble form.

★★★ Ragtime Special

Stomp Off CD1286 *Terry Parrish (p); James Marshall (bj); Steve Ley (tba); Mike Schwimmer (wbd, v).* 4–5/94.

Ragtime piano as a singleton enterprise is specialized enough, but placing it in the context of a repertory group was quite something in the '90s. Of the 26 tracks here, all but three are original rags, two-steps or cakewalks of differing vintages, and it's some tribute to the expertise of the quartet – and that of the composers – that the music doesn't go stale across the duration of a long CD. The sometimes unvarying jollity of ragtime is tempered by intelligent programming – an occasional vocal, or the juxtaposition of reflectively melodic as opposed to pop-tune rags – and the graceful syncopation of the playing. Parrish's liner-notes offer useful background on all the tunes for hardcore scholars and, though this is a lot to take in at one sitting, determined cakewalkers will find it an indispensable primer.

Kurt Elling (born 1967)

VOCALS

A Chicagoan, Elling sent a demo tape to Blue Note and won a deal. He's a sophisticated beat vocalist for the '90s and beyond.

★★★(★) Close Your Eyes

Blue Note 30645 2 *Elling; Von Freeman, Edward Petersen (ts); Laurence Hobgood (p); Dave Onderdonk (g); Rob Amster, Erich Hochberg (b); Paul Wertico (d, perc).* 2–11/94.

★★★★ The Messenger

Blue Note 52727 2 *As above, except omit Freeman; add Orbert Davis (t, flhn); Eddie Johnson (ts); Jim Widlowski (perc); Cassandra Wilson (v).* 7–12/96.

★★★(★) This Time It's Love

Blue Note 93543 2 *Elling; Brad Wheeler (ss); Eddie Johnson (ts); Laurence Hobgood (p); Dave Onderdonk (g); Johnny Frigo (vn); Rob Amster (b); Michael Raynor, Paul Wertico (d, perc).* 12/97–1/98.

It's easy to see Elling as a younger, more contemporary version of Mark Murphy, but the death of Frank Sinatra and subsequent reassessment of his extraordinary output suggests that Frank was a powerful influence as well. Elling shares Murphy's poetic understanding, and *Close Your Eyes* includes two poems by Rainer Maria Rilke, including 'Now It Is Time That Gods Came Walking Out', in which he manages to hint at the Charlie Parker title as well. Elling is one of the last great exponents of vocalese – setting specially written words to recorded jazz solos – though it is now clear that many of his most demanding pieces in this idiom have still to be recorded. It's perhaps a style which is waiting to be fully rediscovered. The other Rilke text is 'How The Thimble Came To Be God', which is part of a vocalese reading of Paul Desmond's solo on Brubeck's 'Balcony Rock'. He also provides a vocal introduction and coda to 'Dolores' Dream', based on Wayne Shorter's solo intro on the 1977 VSOP version. The other poet, the American anarchist Kenneth Rexroth, is represented by 'Married Blues'.

One of the great joys of vocalese has always been the ability to tell a story, and Elling blends a narrative by Jim Heynen into 'Storyteller Experiencing Total Confusion'. He makes Fran Landesman's 'Ballad Of The Sad Young Men' sound as fresh as the day it was written. The guest spots – by Von Freeman on the punning '(Hide The) Salome' and Edward Petersen on 'Storyteller' and Herbie Hancock's 'Hurricane' – are nicely judged, and the basic band, which provides most of the musical arrangements, is impossible to fault. It sounds much less like a working band than the line-up on *The Messenger*, which is a studio album divided into two sets that one can imagine the group performing in a club setting. It briefly brings together the two finest jazz singers of the '90s. An unexpected choice of repertoire, but Rod Argent's 'Time Of The Season' teams Kurt Elling and Cassandra Wilson, an exquisite blending of voices that combines an absolutely authentic jazz sensibility with the power and inflexion of rock and soul singers. Elling opens with a glorious version of 'Nature Boy' that brings it back from the abstractions of John Coltrane and restores some of the fragile melancholy of the Nat Cole hit. 'April In Paris' is a little routine, but the suite that follows – 'The Beauty Of All Things', 'The Dance' and 'Prayer For Mr Davis' – is superb, three strong Hobgood/Elling compositions that top anything on the first album. 'Gingerbread Boy' and a melting 'Prelude To A Kiss' set up a virtuosic climax, 'Time Of The Season', followed by the long 'The Messenger', a composition by Edward Petersen into which Elling builds a spontaneous narrative on the death of his brother. Subtle and deeply moving.

The highlight of *This Time It's Love* is a superb vocalese based on Lester Young's solo on 'She's Funny That Way', but it's almost topped by 'Freddie's Yen For Jen', which takes its inspiration from Freddie Hubbard and is one of the most compelling vocal performances of recent times. Irving Berlin's 'The Best Things Happen When You're Dancing' receives a notably straight and melodic reading, but 'Every Time We Say Goodbye' is slyly recast with altered chords. Frigo's violin and Onderdonk's acoustic strumming add an old-fashioned swing and shimmer to 'I Feel So Smoochie'. A bittier album than its predecessors, it works triumphantly in individual episodes but may perhaps disappoint as a whole.

★★★★ Live in Chicago

Blue Note 22211 *Elling; Von Freeman, Eddie Johnson, Ed Petersen (ts); Laurence Hobgood (p); Rob Amster (b); Michael Raynor (d); Kahil El'Zabar (perc); Jon Hendricks (v).* 99.

What an electrifying live performer Elling is! This marvellous set is drawn from a three-night residency at the Green Mill club in Chicago. The set has a hometown, gala feel, and the guest appearances by local hero El'Zabar and the veteran Hendricks add the final touch to an excellent disc. 'My Foolish Heart' is a titanic performance, brilliantly inflected and packed with invention. Elling thinks musically, but never loses sight of a song's emotional freight. Backed with three powerful tenors, he produces a tone of horn-like strength and purity, and there are moments when one doesn't automatically think 'singer' as some phrases ring out across a slightly noisy ambience.

The technical quality is actually very good indeed, though there are couple of slightly dead moments on Shorter's 'Night Dream' (lyrics by Elling himself), but the engineering manages to balance a lot of live presence with a commendable level of musical detail. Very strongly recommended, even if you only have it for Mr Hendricks's walk-on. Such moments are rare and to be savoured.

★★★★ Flirting With Twilight

Blue Note 31113 *Elling; Clay Jenkins (t); Bob Sheppard (ss, ts); Jeff Clayton (as); Laurence Hobgood (p); Marc Johnson (b); Peter Erskine (d).* 1–2/01.

This confirms Elling as the finest singer of his generation. His technique is formidably assured and his range of material is now quite extraordinary. He opens on Glenn Miller's 'Moonlight Serenade' and turns it into a complex modernist epic, condensed into just under four and a half minutes. As usual, he takes on less familiar material; Curtis Lundy's 'Orange Blossoms in Summertime' becomes a compelling jazz poem that honours the bassist's art (Elling seems well aware of what goes on down in the engine room) and builds into something bigger and more ambitious. Jazz singers have rarely been drawn to Stephen Sondheim, but Kurt sees the merit in 'Not While I'm Around' (from *Sweeney Todd*). Though he comes across the perennial problem with Sondheim – that the songs don't entirely work outside their dramatic context – he makes a strong case for it as a new standard.

The accompanists are in cracking form. Johnson is huge, and in combination with Peter Erskine he drives the music along, enriching the harmonic palette with every phrase. He is sole accompanist on the Dietrich classic 'Je Tire Ma Reverence'. The horns aren't quite as compelling or vigorous this time, but Sheppard emerges as a figure who commands closer inspection. First-class vocal jazz.

★★★★ Man In The Air

Blue Note 80834 *Elling; Jim Gailloreto (ss); Laurence Hobgood (p); Stefon Harris (vib); Rob Amster (b); Frank Parker Jr (d).* 03.

This is perhaps *the* jazz vocal album of the last decade. Almost ten years on from his debut, Elling delivers a bold and accomplished performance, marked by a highly original choice of material and some devastating playing from his regular band. Elling's scat and his delivery of a ballad are now so confident that he is able to take on material like John Coltrane's 'Resolution' and bring to it a genuine philosophical understanding as well as a musically coherent performance. He also includes Joe Zawinul's lovely ballad 'Time To Say Goodbye' and Herbie Hancock's 'A Secret I', both of them thoroughly original and intelligent interpretations.

Hobgood is the key to the record, a master of subtle harmonic shifts and rhythmic changes. Harris's contribution is more dramatic, but less thoughtful and Gailloreto is more a useful foil to Elling's rich voice than a completely successful soloist. All quibbles apart, though, this is a remarkable record, as accessible as it is challenging.

Duke Ellington (1899–1974)

PIANO

Born in Washington, DC, to a middle-class family, Ellington learned piano as a child, became interested in the local ragtime players, and started leading his own groups around 1918. Duke Ellington & his Washingtonians worked in New York from 1924, and a residency at the Cotton Club from 1927 sealed its breakthrough. Long tours followed, with trips to Europe in the '30s, and an almost continuous presence in the recording studios. In the '40s he played a series of annual Carnegie Hall concerts, wrote for the stage and briefly dispersed the big band, but reassembled it in 1949 with 18 players. Although the '50s saw a decline in his fortunes at home, his Newport appearance in 1956 reasserted his eminence. He also wrote for film and TV, and in the '60s he continued to tour relentlessly, in every part of the world. His final illness slowed him down, but he was working up until his hospitalization for cancer early in 1974. Besides his major works, his individual compositions – with and without his frequent collaborator, Billy Strayhorn – number in the thousands, and his recorded legacy is surely the largest and grandest that jazz will ever be able to boast. He recorded for every major American label over a 50-year period, and there are in addition countless broadcast and concert recordings of his music.

*** Duke Ellington 1924–1927

Classics 539 *Ellington; Bubber Miley, Pike Davis, Harry Cooper, Leroy Rutledge, Louis Metcalf, June Clark (t); Jimmy Harrison (tb, v); Charlie Irvis, Joe 'Tricky Sam' Nanton (tb); Don Redman (cl, as); Otto Hardwick (Cmel, as, ss, bs); George Thomas (as, v); Edgar Sampson (as); Prince Robinson, Rudy Jackson (ts, cl); Harry Carney (cl, ts, bs); George Francis, Fred Guy (bj); Mack Shaw, Henry 'Bass' Edwards (bb); Sonny Greer (d, v); Alberta Jones, Irving Mills, Adelaide Hall (v).* 11/24–11/26.

Ellington still bestrides the history of jazz on record, some 30 years after his passing. The sheer volume of recorded works – authorized and otherwise – continues to enrich our understanding of the music, while offering many frustrations and disappointments to go with the numberless masterworks. After the enormous and comprehensive LP reissues of the '70s – specifically the multiple-disc sets issued by French RCA and CBS, as well as numerous and lengthy sequences of broadcast material from private labels – the industry has made plenty of headway in reissuing all this material on CD. With the copyright lapsed on all the pre-1954 records, smaller labels have taken up the challenge of chronological reissues. The Classics sequence, meanwhile, currently stands at over 30 discs, and goes as far as 1952; more will doubtless be available by the time we are in print.

Classics is content to stick to the band sides leading up to the Victor version of 'Black And Tan Fantasy' in 1927; it has omitted a handful of obscure early accompaniments to singers. However, the early material will be of interest only to scholars and the merely curious. Poor recording – the mastering of several tracks is rough, and in the absence of hearing high-quality originals ourselves, we're unsure as to how good a job has been done on some of the items – and a primitive, clumsy ensemble will be almost shocking to any who've never been acquainted with the earliest Ellington. Certainly the stiff rhythms and feeble attempts at solos on all the pre-1926 records are sometimes painful to hear and, if it weren't for Bubber Miley, the man who made Ellington 'forget all about the sweet music', there'd be nothing to detain anyone here. Yet Miley is already distinctive and powerful on his solo on the Washingtonians' 'Choo Choo' from November 1924. With 'East St Louis Toodle-oo', from the first important Ellington session, the music demands the attention. Any comprehensive edition will include much duplication, since Ellington spread himself around many different record labels: he recorded for Broadway, Vocalion, Gennett, Columbia, Harmony, Pathé, Brunswick, OKeh and Victor in the space of a little over three years. It also includes the debut versions of 'Black And Tan Fantasy', Ellington's first masterpiece, and Adelaide Hall's vocal on 'Creole Love Call'. Remastering is occasionally indifferent.

***(*) Duke Ellington 1927–1928

Classics 542 *Ellington; Bubber Miley, Jabbo Smith, Louis Metcalf, Arthur Whetsol (t); Joe 'Tricky Sam' Nanton (tb); Otto Hardwick (ss, as, bs, bsx); Rudy Jackson, Barney Bigard (cl, ts); Harry Carney (bs, as, ss, cl); Fred Guy (bj); Wellman Braud (b); Sonny Greer (d); Adelaide Hall (v).* 10/27–3/28.

***(*) Duke Ellington 1928

Classics 550 *As above, except add Lonnie Johnson (g), Baby Cox, Palmer Brothers(v); omit Jackson, Smith.* 3–10/28.

*** Duke Ellington 1928–29

Classics 559 *As above, except add Freddy Jenkins (t), Johnny Hodges (cl, ss, as), Ozie Ware, Irving Mills (v); omit Metcalf, Cox and Palmer Brothers.* 10/28–3/29.

Ellington progressed quickly from routine hot dance records to sophisticated and complex three-minute works which showed a rare grasp of the possibilities of the 78-r.p.m. disc, a trait which he developed and exemplified better than anyone else in jazz from then until the '50s. Yet during these years both Ellington and his band were still seeking a style that would turn them into a genuinely distinctive group. Having set down one or two individual pieces such as 'Black And Tan Fantasy' it didn't mean that Duke was fully on his way. The 1926–8 records are still dominated to a high degree by the playing of Bubber Miley, and on a track such as 'Flaming Youth' (Classics 559), which was made as late as 1929, it is only Miley's superb work that makes the record of much interest. Arthur Whetsol made an intriguing contrast to Miley, his style being far more wistful and fragile; the way he plays 'The Mooche' on the 1928 Victor version is in striking contrast to Miley's delivery (all versions are on Classics 550), and his treatment of the theme to 'Black Beauty' (also on Classics 550) is similarly poignant. Joe Nanton was a shouting trombonist with a limited stock of phrases, but he was starting to work on the muted technique which would make him into one of Duke's most indispensable players. It was already a great brass team. But the reeds were weaker, with Carney taking a low-key role (not always literally: he played as much alto and clarinet as baritone in this era), and until Bigard's arrival in 1928 it lacked a distinctive soloist. Hodges also didn't arrive until October 1928. When the Ellington band went into the Cotton Club at the end of 1927, the theatricality which had begun asserting itself with 'Black And Tan Fantasy' became a more important asset, and though most of the 'Jungle' scores were to emerge on record around 1929–30, 'The Mooche' and 'East St Louis Toodle-oo' show how set-piece effects were becoming important to Ellington. The best and most Ellingtonian records of the period would include 'Blue Bubbles' (Classics 542), 'Take It Easy' and 'Jubilee Stomp' (1928 versions, on Classics 550), and 'Misty Mornin'' and 'Doin' The Voom Voom' (both Classics 559). But even on the lesser tunes or those tracks where Ellington seems to be doing little more than copying Fletcher Henderson, there are usually fine moments from Miley or one of the others. The Classics CDs offer admirable coverage, with a fairly consistent standard of remastering, and though they ignore alternative takes Ellington's promiscuous attitude towards the various record companies means that there are often several versions of a single theme on one disc (Classics 542, for instance, has three versions of 'Take It Easy').

*****(*) Duke Ellington 1929**
Classics 569 *Ellington; Cootie Williams (t, v); Arthur Whetsol, Freddy Jenkins (t); Joe 'Tricky Sam' Nanton (tb); Barney Bigard (cl, ts); Johnny Hodges (ss, as, cl); Harry Carney (bs, cl, as); Fred Guy (bj); Wellman Braud (b); Sonny Greer (d, v); Ozie Ware (v).* 3–7/29.

***** Duke Ellington 1929–1930**
Classics 577 *As above, except add Juan Tizol (vtb), Teddy Bunn (g), Bruce Johnson (wbd), Harold Randolph, Irving Mills (v); omit Ware.* 8/29–1/30.

***** Duke Ellington 1930**
Classics 586 *As above, except add Cornell Smelser (acc), Dick Robertson (v); omit Bunn, Johnson and Randolph.* 1–6/30.

***** Duke Ellington 1930 Vol. 2**
Classics 596 *As above, except add Charlie Barnet (chimes), Sid Garry, Jimmy Miller, Emanuel Paul (v); omit Smelser.* 6–11/30.

***** Duke Ellington 1930–1931**
Classics 605 *As above, except add Benny Paine (v, p), Chick Bullock, Frank Marvin, Smith Ballew (v); omit Barnet, Robertson, Miller and Paul.* 11/30–1/31.

The replacement of Bubber Miley by Cootie Williams was the key personnel change in this period. Williams was a leaner, less outwardly expressive version of Miley, but equally fiery. His scat singing was a fast development of Armstrong's vocal style, and he gave the brass section a new bite and brightness, even if he lacked Miley's ability to growl quite so intently. Hodges and Carney, too, were coming into their own, and along with Ellington's increasing mastery in handling his players, the band was now growing in assurance almost from session to session. The Victor recording of 7 March 1929 (Classics 569) exemplifies many of the new powers of the orchestra. 'Hot Feet' includes a superb Hodges solo, Williams singing and playing with great authority, and the band moving out of the older hot style without sacrificing any drive. It was the now extraordinarily powerful swing of the rhythm section that was responsible for much of this advance. The same session is a fine instance of what it could do, from Braud's subtly propulsive drive on the excellently scored 'The Dicty Glide' to his outright stomping line on 'Hot Feet', with Greer taking a showman's role on his cymbals and traps and the remarkable Guy strumming a quick-witted counterpoint that made the banjo seem far from outdated (he would, though, soon switch to guitar). The two important Victor sessions on this disc (a third, two parts of a Cotton Club medley, is less substantial) make this a valuable issue; there are two fascinatingly different versions of the small-group blues, 'Saratoga Swing', as well as little-known Ellington attempts at 'I Must Have That Man' and an accompaniment to singer Ozie Ware.

Ellington was recording at a prodigious pace – surprisingly so, given the state of the industry at that time – and there are some three CDs' worth of material from 1930. Classics 586 includes some tunes that reek of Cotton Club set-pieces – 'Jungle Nights In Harlem', 'Jungle Blues' – and some thin novelty tunes, but new versions of 'The Mooche' and 'East St Louis Toodle-oo' and new originals like 'Shout 'Em Aunt Tillie', 'Hot And Bothered' and 'Cotton Club Stomp' are more substantial. Classics 596 has three different versions of 'Ring Dem Bells' with outstanding solos by Williams, three of 'Old Man Blues', and a first try at 'Mood Indigo'. Classics 605 has three versions of 'Rockin' In Rhythm', each showing a slight advance on the one before, the tempo brightening and the reeds becoming smarter, and a slightly ironic reading of 'Twelfth Street Rag' which hints at Duke's later treatment of other people's jazz standards. But the record closes with his first lengthy work, the two-part 'Creole Rhapsody', where for perhaps the first time the soloists have to take a firm second place to the arrangement. (This is the 10-inch 78 version; the subsequent 12-inch version is on the next disc in the Classics sequence.) Remastering is mainly good and full-bodied; some of the records from more obscure companies sound a little rougher, there are some tracks in which bass boom overcomes mid-range brightness, and frequent hints that these are not first-hand dubbings. Still, only more demanding ears may be particularly troubled by the mixed transfer quality.

***** Duke Ellington 1931–1932**
Classics 616 *Ellington; Arthur Whetsol, Freddy Jenkins, Cootie Williams (t); Joe 'Tricky Sam' Nanton, Lawrence Brown (tb); Juan Tizol (vtb); Johnny Hodges (as, ss, cl); Barney Bigard (cl, ts); Harry Carney (bs, cl); Fred Guy (bj, g); Wellman Braud (b); Sonny Greer (d); Frank Marvin, Ivie Anderson, Bing Crosby (v).* 1/31–2/32.

***** Duke Ellington 1932–1933**
Classics 626 *As above, except add Ray Mitchell, Adelaide Hall, Mills Brothers, Ethel Waters (v); omit Crosby.* 5/32–1/33.

*****(*) Duke Ellington 1933**
Classics 637 *Similar to above.* 2–8/33.

*****(*) Duke Ellington 1933–1935**
Classics 646 *Similar to above.* 9/33–3/35.

The second 'Creole Rhapsody' opens Classics 616, a longer and better-played though still imperfect version, but the rest of the disc is more conventional Ellington, with 'It Don't Mean A Thing' and 'Lazy Rhapsody' the highlights in a programme which is mainly made up of other writers' songs. The arrival of both Lawrence Brown and Ivie Anderson is more important: Brown gave the brass section a new mellifluousness, and Anderson was probably the best regular singer Duke ever employed. Classics 626 has ten Ellington themes out of 23 tracks and loses impetus at the end with sundry accompaniments to singers, but there are four substantial pieces in 'Slippery Horn', 'Blue Harlem', 'Ducky Wucky' and especially 'Lightnin'', though the orchestra often sounds sloppy here.

Classics 637 and 646 divide the fine Brunswick material (previously on the now-deleted Jazz Information sequence) between them, and 646 covers a number of important Victor sessions as well: 'Stompy Jones', the locomotive classic, 'Daybreak Express' and 'Blue Feeling'.

***(*) **Cotton Club Stomp**
Naxos Jazz Legends 8.120509 *As above.* 27–31.
*** **It Don't Mean A Thing**
Naxos Jazz Legends 8.120526 *As above.* 30–34.
*** **Jazz Cocktail**
ASV AJA 5024 *As appropriate discs above.* 10/28–9/32.
(*) **Rockin' In Rhythm
ASV AJA 5057 *As appropriate discs above.* 3/27–7/36.
**** **Early Ellington**
GRP 053640-2 3CD *As appropriate discs above.* 3/27–5/32.

The various compilations of early Ellington offer a considerable choice. The pair of Naxos discs are very enjoyable, although the second has a slightly idiosyncratic track selection. The two ASV albums aren't really competitive since the remastering is rather grey and undefined, especially on ASV AJA 5057. GRP's three-disc set covers all of Ellington's Brunswick material up to 1932 and makes a particularly enjoyable and welcome package.

***(*) **Duke Ellington 1935–1936**
Classics 659 *Ellington; Charlie Allen, Cootie Williams, Arthur Whetsol (t); Rex Stewart (c); Joe 'Tricky Sam' Nanton, Lawrence Brown (tb); Juan Tizol (vtb); Johnny Hodges (cl, ss, as); Harry Carney (cl, as, bs); Otto Hardwick (as); Barney Bigard (cl, ts); Ben Webster (ts); Fred Guy (g); Hayes Alvis, Billy Taylor (b); Fred Avendorf, Sonny Greer (d); Ivie Anderson (v).* 4/35–2/36.
***(*) **Duke Ellington 1936–1937**
Classics 666 *As above, except add Pete Clark (as), Brick Fleagle (g); omit Allen, Avendorf.* 2/36–3/37.
***(*) **Duke Ellington 1937**
Classics 675 *As above, except add Wallace Jones (t), Sandy Williams (tb), Bernard Addison (g), Chick Webb (d); omit Whetsol, Clark and Fleagle.* 3–5/37.
**** **Duke Ellington 1937 Vol. 2**
Classics 687 *As above, except add Freddy Jenkins (t), Jack Maisel (d); omit Sandy Williams, Webb.* 5–10/37.
**** **Duke Ellington 1938**
Classics 700 *As above, except add Harold 'Shorty' Baker (t), Mary McHugh, Jerry Kruger (v); omit Jenkins and Maisel.* 1–4/38.
**** **Duke Ellington 1938 Vol. 2**
Classics 717 *As above, except add Scat Powell (v).* 4–8/38.
***(*) **Duke Ellington 1938 Vol. 3**
Classics 726 *As above, except omit Anderson, Kruger, McHugh and Powell.* 8–12/38.

Ellington's mid- and late-'30s output is a blend of commerce and art, as in most of his work; but it's astonishing how seldom he lets a duff track slip through. Even the most trifling pieces usually have something to commend them. Classics 659 is important for the four-part original recording of 'Reminiscing In Tempo', a dedication to Ellington's mother that was one of the first of his extended works; but it also has the joyful 'Truckin'' and two early 'concerto' pieces in 'Clarinet Lament' for Bigard and 'Echoes Of Harlem' for Cootie Williams. Classics 666 starts with some unpromising material magically illuminated: Rex Stewart's filigree touches on 'Kissin' My Baby Goodnight', the lovely scoring on 'Maybe Someday'. Several tracks here are small-group crossovers with the Columbia discs (see below), but there are top-drawer records by the full group, including 'In A Jam', 'Uptown Downbeat', the rollicking 'Scattin' At The Kit Cat' and 'The New East St Louis Toodle-oo', an example of Ellington's revisionism. One of the best in this sequence.

In contrast, Classics 675 is a bit thin so far as the full-band tracks are concerned, though two versions of 'Azure' shouldn't be missed. Much stronger is Classics 687, which peaks on the still remarkable first recording of 'Diminuendo And Crescendo In Blue' but which also has the tremendous 'Harmony In Harlem', 'Chatterbox' and 'Jubilesta', as well as several of the small-group sessions. Classics 700 includes a lot of distinctive Ellingtonia that has been obscured by some of his obvious hits: 'Braggin' In Brass', 'The Gal From Joe's', the new version of 'Black And Tan Fantasy', superbly played by the band which transforms itself from dance orchestra to complex jazz ensemble – and back again. Though seldom commented on, the rhythm section of Guy, Taylor or Alvis and Greer is unobtrusively fine. There are more neglected winners on Classics 717, including 'I'm Slappin' Seventh Avenue' (which Cecil Taylor always admired), 'Dinah's In A Jam', the lovely treatment of 'Rose Of The Rio Grande' and the very fine 'The Stevedore's Serenade'. The next disc might be a little behind in class, but there are more fine small-group sides led by Hodges (see below) and further lesser-known Ellington originals. The remastering in this series is inconsistent but, for the most part, very listenable; as a sequence of records, it's of a very high calibre.

***(*) **Duke Ellington 1938–1939**
Classics 747 *Ellington; Wallace Jones, Cootie Williams, Louis Bacon (t); Rex Stewart (c); Lawrence Brown, Joe 'Tricky Sam' Nanton (tb); Juan Tizol (vtb); Barney Bigard (cl, ts); Johnny Hodges (ss, as, cl); Otto Hardwick (as); Harry Carney (bs, as, cl); Fred Guy, Brick Fleagle (g); Billy Taylor Sr (b); Sonny Greer (d); Jean Eldridge (v).* 12/38–3/39.
***(*) **Duke Ellington 1939**
Classics 765 *As above, except add Billy Strayhorn (p); omit Bacon, Fleagle and Eldridge.* 3–6/39.
***(*) **Duke Ellington 1939 Vol. 2**
Classics 780 *As above.* 6–10/39.
**** **Duke Ellington 1939–1940**
Classics 790 *As above, except add Ben Webster (ts), Jimmy Blanton (b); Ivie Anderson (v).* 10/39–2/40.
**** **Duke Ellington 1940**
Classics 805 *As above.* 2–8/40.
**** **Duke Ellington 1940 Vol. 2**
Classics 820 *As above, except add Herb Jeffries (v).* 9–11/40.
**** **Duke Ellington 1940–1941**
Classics 837 *As above, except Ray Nance (t) replaces Williams.* 11/40–7/41.
**** **Duke Ellington 1941**
Classics 851 *As above, except add Junior Raglin (b).* 7–12/41.
***(*) **Ko-Ko**
Dreyfus FDM 36717-2 *As above.* 3–10/40.

With all of the late-'30s Ellington now back in print, it's easier to see that he had been working towards this exceptional period for the band for a long time. Ellington had been building a matchless team of soloists, his own composing was taking on a finer degree of personal creativity and sophistication, and with the arrival of bassist Jimmy Blanton, who gave the rhythm section an unparalleled eloquence in the way it swung, the final piece fell into place. The 6 May 1940 session, which opens *Never No Lament* (below), is one of the great occasions in jazz history, when Ellington recorded both 'Jack The Bear' (a feature for Blanton) and the unqualified masterpiece 'Ko-Ko'. From there, literally dozens of classics tumbled out of the band, from originals such as 'Harlem Air Shaft' and 'Main Stem' and 'Take The "A" Train' to brilliant Ellingtonizations of standard material such as 'The Sidewalks Of New York' and 'Clementine'. The arrival of Billy Strayhorn, Ellington's closest collaborator until Strayhorn's death in 1967, is another important element in the music's success.

The four Classics discs covering 1939 include many of the small-group dates led by Bigard, Hodges and Williams, and those who have the Columbia sets may not want to duplicate this material. (However, followers of Duke's piano solos will want Classics 747, which includes a couple of little-known 1939 items, 'Just Good Fun' and 'Informal Blues'.) Classics 790 includes some important stuff: the Ducal solo 'Blues' and the duets with Blanton, 'Blues' and 'Plucked Again'. Thereafter, the 1940–41 discs cover much the same ground as the three-disc RCA Bluebird set. All this is four-star material, and for those who would prefer to have it a disc at a time, this isn't a bad way forward. Transfers are all right, though certainly no than Bluebird's, and sources are as usual unlisted.

The Dreyfus compilation selects 19 tracks from the banner year of 1940. In fine sound and properly presented, this would make a good introduction for any Ellington tyro.

CORE COLLECTION

★★★★ Never No Lament

RCA Bluebird 82876-50857-2 3CD *Ellington; Wallace Jones, Cootie Williams, Ray Nance (t); Rex Stewart (c); Joe 'Tricky Sam' Nanton, Lawrence Brown (tb); Juan Tizol (vtb); Barney Bigard, Chauncey Haughton (cl); Johnny Hodges (ss, as, cl); Harry Carney (bs, cl, as); Otto Hardwick (as, bsx); Ben Webster (ts); Billy Strayhorn (p); Fred Guy (g); Jimmy Blanton, Junior Raglin (b); Sonny Greer (d); Ivie Anderson, Herb Jeffries (v).* 3/40–7/42.

Bluebird's set collects 70 tracks (and five alternative takes) from a two-year period which many hold as Ellington's greatest on record, and it's certainly the summation of his work within the three-minute confines of the 78-r.p.m. disc. This latest remastering, drawn from the huge complete RCA Ellington edition of a few years back, is in stunning sound and is a delight from first to last. Our only complaint is in the cheap and shoddy packaging, which does no justice to the music. But what music!

★★★(★) Reminiscing In Tempo

Naxos 8.120589 *As various discs above.* 32–35.

★★★(★) Echoes Of Harlem

Naxos 8.120682 *As various discs above.* 36–38.

★★★(★) Braggin' In Brass

Naxos 8.120706 *As various discs above.* 38.

★★★★ Tootin' Through The Roof

Naxos 8.120729. *As various discs above.* 39–40.

While pre-war Ellington is now open house for anyone who fancies putting together their own compilation, at least Naxos have gone about it in a sensible way, and these excellent compilations choose to pick only the best tracks from each period rather than offer exhaustive coverage. In clean sound, with excellent notes and documentation and at a bargain price, these would be a worthy introduction for anyone who wants to investigate this music for the first time.

★★★ Duke Ellington Presents Ivie Anderson

Columbia 501654-2 2CD *As various discs above.* 2/32–2/40.

It was a good idea to collect some of the best records featuring Ellington's finest singer, and with 32 tracks, full personnels and even all the lyrics to the songs, this looks like a fine effort. But once again this is a straight copy of a late-'60s vinyl edition, and the remastering is poor, doing Ivie an injustice. Even so, listening through all her vocals reminds us why she was such a loss to the band when she departed, and Bobby Short's acknowledgement of her as an influence suddenly seems obvious – he really does sound as if he took many of her mannerisms for himself.

♛ ★★★★ The Duke At Fargo 1940

Storyville STCD 8316/7 2CD *As above, except omit Haughton, Strayhorn and Raglin.* 11/40.

Of the many surviving location recordings of the Ellington band, this is one of the very best, catching over two hours of material from a single dance date in North Dakota, part of it broadcast but most of it simply taken down by some amateur enthusiasts. Storyville, the Swedish label which has done so much to nurture the documentation of mainstream American jazz, released a 60th-anniversary edition of the music in 2000, in an exceptionally handsome presentation. The sound is probably as fine as it will ever be. Here is one of the greatest Ellington orchestras on a typical night, with many of the best numbers in the band's book and the most rousing version of 'St Louis Blues' to climax the evening. The sound is inevitably well below the quality of the studio sessions, but it's a fine supplement to them, and an almost definitive glimpse into a working day in the life of one of the great swing orchestras. An essential swing-era document and an indispensable piece of Ellingtonia.

★★★(★) At The Hurricane

Storyville 101 8359 *Ellington, Ray Nance (t, vn); Rex Stewart, Taft Jordan, Harold 'Shorty' Baker, Wallace Jones (t); Lawrence Brown, Joe 'Tricky Sam' Nanton, Sandy Williams, Juan Tizol (tb); Johnny Hodges (as); Sax Mallard, Nat Jones(as, cl); Chauncey Haughton (cl); Jimmy Hamilton (cl, ts); Ben Webster (ts); Harry Carney (bs, bcl); Fred Guy (g); Alvin 'Junior' Raglin (b); Sonny Greer (d); Betty Roche (v).* 4–6/43.

Three radio shows from The Hurricane, a swank eaterie at 49th and Broadway. Sound is decent, although technical problems meant losing some of the material from the third show. Betty Roche gets one of her largest features in the Ducal discography and sounds impressive. The expected good showing by Hodges and Webster here, and the odd surprise, such as Juan Tizol doing a piece out of the Tommy Dorsey book, 'Nevada'.

★★★(★) Duke Ellington 1942–1944

Classics 867 *Ellington; Wallace Jones, Harold 'Shorty' Baker, Dizzy Gillespie, Scad Hemphill, Taft Jordan, Cootie Williams (t); Ray Nance (t, vn); Rex Stewart (c); Joe 'Tricky Sam' Nanton, Lawrence Brown, Claude Jones, Juan Tizol (tb); Barney Bigard, Chauncey Haughton, Jimmy Hamilton (cl); Johnny Hodges (as); Otto Hardwick (as, bsx); Ben Webster, Skippy Williams, Al Sears (ts); Harry Carney (cl, bs); Billy Strayhorn (p); Fred Guy (g); Junior Raglin, Jimmy Blanton, Wilson Myers (b); Sonny Greer (d); Ivie Anderson, Herb Jeffries, Al Hibbler (v).* 11/39–5/44.

★★★★ Duke Ellington 1944–1945

Classics 881 *As above, except add Cat Anderson (t), Duke Brooks (p), Red Callender (b), Hilliard Brown (d), Joya Sherrill, Kay Davis (v); omit Jones, Baker, Gillespie, Cootie Williams, Stewart, Webster, Skippy Williams, Blanton, Jeffries, Anderson.* 12/44–4/45.

★★★ Duke Ellington 1945

Classics 915 *As above, except add Bob Haggart (b), Marie Ellington (v), Tommy Dorsey (tb) and his orchestra.* 4–5/45.

★★★★ Duke Ellington 1945 Vol. 2

Classics 951 *As above, except omit Haggart, Marie Ellington and Dorsey and orchestra.* 5–7/45.

Classics brings together a mix of studio dates and V-Discs for these releases. Classics 867 starts with the final Victor sessions before the recording ban, and there are masterpieces of the order of 'What Am I Here For?' and 'Main Stem' before four sessions for V-Disc from 1943–4: some excellent Hodges, and there's an extended 'Boy Meets Horn' for Rex Stewart. Peculiarly, they fill up the disc with two 1939 V-Disc tracks that were missed off an earlier disc. Classics 881 returns to Victor for four pop tunes before the studio version of 'Black, Brown And Beige', a Capitol small-group date led by Sonny Greer which has Jordan and Bigard in top form, and the delightful V-Disc debut of 'Perfume Suite', including Duke's dapper piano treatment of 'Dancers In Love'. A splendid issue. Classics 915 looks promising but is let down by very poor sound on a V-Disc version of 'Black, Brown And Beige' (a subsequent 'Harlem Air Shaft' sounds much better). Some of the Victor material is relatively lightweight, although the disc does include the famous occasion when the Duke sat in with the Tommy Dorsey band and the trombonist returned the favour by sitting in with the Ellington band on the following day. Classics 951 includes ten further titles from V-Disc and there are some beauties among them, including excellent takes on 'Hollywood Hangover' (actually a Buck Clayton composition) and 'Ring Dem Bells', and a masterly treatment of 'New World A-Comin''. For the rest, more Victor sessions, including the studio version of 'Perfume Suite' (which mystifyingly omits 'Dancers In Love') and the debut of 'Diminuendo And Crescendo In Blue'.

★★★(★) Duke Ellington & His Orchestra Vols 1–5

Circle CCD-101/2/3/4/5 (5CD, only available separately) *Basically as above discs in this period.* 43–45.

Since the American recording ban was in full swing, Ellington's studio work was limited to material like this, transcriptions in the World Broadcast Series. Circle has included what seems to be every available fragment from these sessions, which means multiple takes and many false starts. If this detracts from a general recommendation, it ought to be remembered that this was the greatest Ellington orchestra in top form, and there are countless things to marvel at in the likes of (to pick a few of our personal favourites) 'Air Conditioned Jungle', 'Let The Zoomers Drool', 'Blues On The Double', 'In A Jam', 'Blue Cellophane' and 'Three Cent Stomp'. Besides, the many breaks allow an intriguing insight into Duke's way of working. Excellent notes and impressive remastering.

★★★★ Black, Brown And Beige

RCA Bluebird 86641 3CD *Ellington; Taft Jordan, Cat Anderson, Shelton Hemphill, Ray Nance, Rex Stewart, Francis Williams, Harold 'Shorty' Baker (t); Claude Jones, Lawrence Brown, Joe 'Tricky Sam' Nanton, Tommy Dorsey, Wilbur De Paris (tb); Jimmy Hamilton (cl, ts); Otto Hardwick (as); Johnny Hodges (as); Al Sears (ts); Russell Procope (cl, ts); Harry Carney (bs); Fred Guy (g); Junior Raglin, Sid Weiss, Oscar Pettiford, Al Lucas, Bob Haggart (b); Sonny Greer, Big Sid Catlett (d); Al Hibbler, Joya Sherrill, Kay Davis, Marie Ellington, Marian Cox (v).* 12/44–9/46.

While this ultimately stands a notch below the music on *Never No Lament*, it is still an essential Ellington collection. Besides numerous further examples of the composer's mastery of the three-minute form, there are the first of his suites to make it to the studios, including most of 'Black, Brown And Beige' – which was never finally recorded in its entirety in the studio – and 'The Perfume Suite'. New Ellingtonians include Cat Anderson and Taft Jordan – two brilliantly individual members of the brass section – as well as the lyrical Shorty Baker, Al Sears and Russell Procope. Ellington's confidence may have been sagging a little from the loss of major soloists – Webster, Williams – and the indifference to some of his higher ambitions as a composer, but the orchestra itself is still inimitable. Remastering is kind enough, even if not always wholly respectful of the music, but most will find it acceptable.

★★★(★) The Duke Ellington Carnegie Hall Concerts January 1943

Prestige 34004 2CD *Ellington; Rex Stewart, Harold 'Shorty' Baker, Wallace Jones (t); Ray Nance (t, vn); Joe 'Tricky Sam' Nanton, Lawrence Brown (tb); Juan Tizol (vtb); Johnny Hodges, Ben Webster, Harry Carney, Otto Hardwick, Chauncey Haughton (reeds); Fred Guy (g); Junior Raglin (b); Sonny Greer (d); Betty Roche (v).* 1/43.

★★★ Live At Carnegie Hall Dec. 11 1943

Storyville 1038341 2CD *As above, except add Taft Jordan (t), Jimmy Hamilton (cl, ts), Skippy Williams (ts), Al Hibbler (v); omit Webster, Roche.* 12/43.

★★★(★) The Duke Ellington Carnegie Hall Concerts December 1944

Prestige 24073 2CD *As above, except add Shelton Hemphill, Cat Anderson (t), Claude Jones (tb), Al Sears, (reeds), Hilliard Brown (d), Kay Davis, Marie Ellington (v); omit Baker, Jones, Williams, Haughton, Greer.* 12/44.

★★★(★) The Duke Ellington Carnegie Hall Concerts January 1946

Prestige 24074 2CD *As above, except add Francis Williams (t), Wilbur De Paris (tb), Al Lucas (g), Oscar Pettiford (b), Sonny Greer (d), Joya Sherrill (v); omit Stewart, Nanton, Guy, Raglin, Brown, Marie Ellington.* 1/46.

★★★(★) The Duke Ellington Carnegie Hall Concerts December 1947

Prestige 24075 2CD *As above, except add Harold 'Shorty' Baker, Al Killian (t), Tyree Glenn (tb, vib), Russell Procope (reeds), Fred Guy (g), Junior Raglin (b); omit Jordan, Anderson, De Paris, Hamilton, Lucas, Sherrill.* 12/47.

Ellington's Carnegie Hall appearances began in 1943 and continued on an annual basis. The only surviving recordings are mainly in indifferent condition, and none of the Prestige CDs can really be called hi-fi, despite extensive remastering work. Nevertheless, Ellington scholars will find them essential, and even casual listeners should find much to enjoy. The 1943 concert premièred 'Black, Brown And Beige' and its lukewarm reception became a notorious snub that reduced Ellington's confidence in the work. These surviving extracts are fascinating but inconclusive. The rest of the programme includes many greatest hits and one or two scarcer pieces. The missing concert from the Prestige series was the December 1943 event, now restored via the Storyville set: sound on vinyl editions was always poor, and this really isn't much better, but there are still some characteristic glories such as 'Black And Tan Fantasy'. The 1944 concert includes many less-familiar tunes – 'Blutopia', 'Suddenly It Jumped', 'Blue Cellophane' – plus more 'Black, Brown And Beige' and the debut of 'The Perfume Suite', as well as a glorious finale showcase for Nanton on 'Frankie And Johnny'. Notable in the next concert were a reworking of 'Diminuendo And Crescendo In Blue' and some fine miniatures, including 'Magenta Haze', Joya Sherrill's fine interpretation of 'The Blues' and a euphoric treatment of 'Solid Old Man'. The 'Liberian Suite' is one of the principal items of the 1947 set, but the Ray Nance feature in 'Bakiff', Duke's own spot on 'The Clothed Woman' and Carney on 'Mella Brava' are of equal interest. While all the concerts have their weak spots, each has enough fine Ellington to make it more than worthwhile.

***** The Treasury Shows Vol. 1**
D.E.T.S. 903 9001 2CD *Collective personnel for this and next seven discs: Ellington; Rex Stewart, Taft Jordan, Shelton Hemphill, Wallace Jones, Harold 'Shorty' Baker, Cat Anderson (t); Ray Nance (t, vn, v); Joe 'Tricky Sam' Nanton, Lawrence Brown, Juan Tizol (tb); Jimmy Hamilton (cl, ts); Johnny Hodges, Otto Hardwick (as); Ben Webster, Al Sears (ts); Harry Carney (bs); Billy Strayhorn (p); Fred Guy (g); Junior Raglin, Oscar Pettiford (b); Sonny Greer (d); Al Hibbler, Joya Sherrill, Kay Davis, Marie Ellington (v).* 6/43–4/45.

*****(*) The Treasury Shows Vol. 2**
D.E.T.S. 903 9002 2CD *As above.* 4–5/45.

*****(*) The Treasury Shows Vol. 3**
D.E.T.S. 903 9003 2CD *As above.* 5/45.

*****(*) The Treasury Shows Vol. 4**
D.E.T.S. 903 9004 2CD *As above.* 5–10/45.

*****(*) The Treasury Shows Vol. 5**
D.E.T.S. 903 9005 2CD *As above.* 6–9/45.

*****(*) The Treasury Shows Vol. 6**
D.E.T.S. 903 9006 2CD *As above.* 7/45.

*****(*) The Treasury Shows Vol. 7**
D.E.T.S. 903 9007 2CD *As above.* 6–10/45.

*****(*) The Treasury Shows Vol. 8**
D.E.T.S. 903 9008 2CD *As above.* 7–9/45.

The US Treasury Department hired Ellington to perform public service broadcasts as part of their remaining war effort in 1945, and the band worked on these sessions throughout most of 1945 and much of 1946. Many of them have survived as airshots and the music was extensively reissued during the vinyl era, in a series which ran to more than 50 LPs. Now the D.E.T.S. label (via Storyville) is putting the material on to CD for the first time, and these first eight two-disc sets are the result. Besides station breaks and Duke reading out war bond promotional messages, there's a lot of vintage Ellington. Our ratings may seem on the generous side, given that sound-quality is variable and there is a lot of repetition, but as with so many of the major swing orchestras, away from the studios the band's treatments of even familiar fare were looser and more expansive. In addition, there are extra broadcasts from New Zanzibar and Birdland (New York), Meadowbrook Gardens (California) and the Blue Note (Chicago). When complete, this will be an exceptional archive of Ellington at work. For the initial release, it is hard to pick out highlights; each set has its merits, and they await fuller and more detailed listening. The latest volumes have such choice pieces as 'Blue Belles Of Harlem' and 'The Perfume Suite' (Volume 7) and 'The Magazine Suite' (Volume 8). But we doubt that any committed Ellingtonian will be disappointed by any of them.

*****(*) Duke Ellington 1946**
Classics 1015 *Ellington; Ray Nance (t, vn, v); Taft Jordan, Shelton Hemphill, Cat Anderson, Francis Williams, Harold 'Shorty' Baker (t); Lawrence Brown, Claude Jones, Wilbur De Paris (tb); Jimmy Hamilton (cl, ts); Johnny Hodges (as); Russell Procope (as, cl); Al Sears (ts); Harry Carney (bs, cl); Fred Guy (g); Oscar Pettiford (b); Sonny Greer (d); Marion Cox, Kay Davis (v).* 8–11/46.

A mixed bag; the final sessions for Victor, two tracks that were issued only in France on the Swing label, the first of several dates for Musicraft and six V-Discs drawn from the November Carnegie Hall Concert, including the four-part 'Deep South Suite'. Sound on the latter isn't so good, but the other transfers are fine. The Victor material includes some of Ellington's ingenious transformations of other material, such as 'Beale Street Blues' and 'My Honey's Lovin' Arms', and 'Magenta Haze' is a typically gorgeous Hodges feature.

*****(*) Duke Ellington 1946–1947**
Classics 1051 *As above, except add Dud Bascomb (t), Tyree Glenn (tb), Al Hibbler, Chester Crumpler (v); omit Cox.* 11/46–9/47.

Thirteen more titles for Musicraft, a V-Disc session and seven titles celebrating Duke's return to the Columbia label. The Musicrafts have been in and out of the catalogue, and this edition seems to be about as good as any other in terms of the sound. Memorable moments include the raucous 'Happy-Go-Lucky Local', Al Sears buzzing through 'Hiawatha (The Beautiful Indians)', the four-horn concerto, 'Jam-A-Ditty', and a vintage Ellington pastel in 'Lady Of The Lavender Mist'.

***** Duke Ellington 1947**
Classics 1086 *As above, except add Billy Strayhorn (p), Woody Herman, Delores Parker (v); omit Anderson, De Paris and Crumpler.* 9–11/47.

All these were Columbia sessions, though several tracks were not heard until the LP era. There is some commercial flab here, including versions of 'Singin' In The Rain', 'Cowboy Rhumba' (with guest vocalist Woody Herman!), 'Put Yourself In My Place' and 'I Fell And Broke My Heart'. The only really characteristic Ellington date is from November 1947, with 'Stomp, Look And Listen', 'Air Conditioned Jungle' and 'Three Cent Stomp'.

★★★★ The Complete Duke Ellington & His World Famous Orchestra

Hindsight HBCD501 3CD *Ellington; Shelton Hemphill, Francis Williams, Harold 'Shorty' Baker, Ray Nance, Dud Bascomb, Bernard Flood, Cat Anderson (t); Lawrence Brown, Claude Jones, Tyree Glenn, Joe 'Tricky Sam' Nanton (tb); Russell Procope, Johnny Hodges, Jimmy Hamilton, Al Sears, Harry Carney, Otto Hardwick (reeds); Billy Strayhorn (p); Fred Guy (g); Oscar Pettiford, Wilson Myers (b); Sonny Greer (d).* 3/46–6/47.

These transcriptions have drifted in and out of circulation over many years, but this fine three-disc set brings them all together in mostly clean and quite lively sound. There are a host of rarities – 'Violet Blue', 'Park At 106th', Ray Nance doing 'St Louis Blues', Al Sears tearing up 'The Suburbanite', Harry Carney's 'Jennie' … and so on. Quite a feast, and a fine addendum to the studio tracks of the period.

★★★(★) Take The 'A' Train

Dreyfus FDM 36732-2 *As various discs above.* 3/38–12/50.

An interesting cross-section of big Ellington hits, often in less familiar broadcast and transcription versions, though sound-quality remains strong throughout. A good way to reacquaint yourself with pieces that you may have thought you knew only too well.

★★★(★) Duke Ellington 1947–1948

Classics 1119 *Ellington; Shelton Hemphill, Francis Williams, Dud Bascomb, Herman Grimes, Al Killian, Harold 'Shorty' Baker (t); Ray Nance (t, vn); Lawrence Brown, Claude Jones, Quentin Jackson (tb); Tyree Glenn (tb, vib); Jimmy Hamilton (cl, ts); Johnny Hodges (as); Russell Procope (as, cl); Al Sears (ts); Harry Carney (bs); Billy Strayhorn (p); Fred Guy (g); Edgar Brown, Junior Raglin, Oscar Pettiford (clo, b); Sonny Greer (d); Elayne Jones (perc); Al Hibbler, Dolores Parker, Kay Davis (v).* 11/47–11/48.

★★★ Duke Ellington 1949–1950

Classics 1191 *As above except add Nelson Williams (t), Jimmy Forrest (ts), Wendell Marshall, Lloyd Trotman (b), Jo Jones (d), Chubby Kemp, Lu Elliott, Sara Forde (v), omit Hemphill, Francis Williams, Grimes, Bascomb, Jones, Sears, Guy, Brown, Davis.* 10/49–10/50.

★★★(★) Duke Ellington 1950

Classics 1217 *As above except add Cat Anderson, Andres Merenguito (t), Mercer Ellington (flhn), Paul Gonsalves (ts), Wild Bill Davis (org), John Collins (g), Joe Shulman (b), Yvonne Lanauze (v), omit Killian, Forrest, Trotman, Pettiford, Kemp, Elliott, Forde.* 10–12/50.

An awkward period for Ellington. With the new LP format waiting in the wings, he could begin to think more about his extended works. But Columbia, which suspended his contract in 1950, wasn't so enchanted. Classics 1119 includes the 'Liberian Suite' (including the V-Disc instrumental version of 'I Like The Sunrise'), a few lesser-known nuggets ('New York City Blues', 'On A Turquoise Cloud'), and ends on another V-Disc recording of 'The Tattooed Bride'. Typical Ellington in its mixing of the commercial and the aspirational. Classics 1191 is much more of a hotch potch and features the first sessions on the Mercer label, while the Columbia situation was in abeyance. The final Columbia sessions are mostly vocal features (though there is wonderful Hodges in 'On The Sunny Side Of The Street'), and the first Mercer sessions are routine vocal settings for Chubby Kemp and Sara Forde, plus the debut of Pettiford on cello in a strange quintet date. For specialists only.

Classics 1217 has the intriguing Ellington–Strayhorn piano duets, although these are listed separately as an OJC reissue under Strayhorn's name. In November, Duke returned to Columbia for one three-song session (which marked the debut of Paul Gonsalves) and a second date that offered extended studio versions of 'The Tattooed Bride' and 'Mood Indigo'. Excellent Ellingtonia.

★★★ Duke Ellington 1950–1951

Classics 1258 *Ellington; Harold 'Shorty' Baker, Nelson Williams, Cat Anderson, Andres Merenguito, Ray Nance (t); Mercer Ellington (flhn); Lawrence Brown, Quentin Jackson, Tyree Glenn, Juan Tizol, Britt Woodman (tb); Johnny Hodges, Willie Smith (as); Russell Procope (cl, as); Jimmy Hamilton (cl, ts); Paul Gonsalves (ts); Harry Carney (bs); Billy Strayhorn (p); Wendell Marshall (b); Sonny Greer, Louie Bellson (d); Yvonne Lanauze (v).* 12/50–5/51.

★★★(★) Duke Ellington 1951

Classics 1282 *As above, except add Willie Cook, Clark Terry, Dick Vance, Francis Williams (t), Lloyd Oldham (v); omit Merenguito, Mercer Ellington, Glenn, Hodges, Greer, Lanauze.* 6–12/51.

★★★ Duke Ellington 1952

Classics 1320 *As above, except add Hilton Jefferson (as), Jimmy Grissom, Betty Roche (v); omit Vance, Williams, Strayhorn.* 3–7/52.

Here the Classics sequence (now up to 42 CDs!) enters the LP era in earnest. Classics 1258 starts with extended versons of 'Sophisticated Lady' and 'Solitude', both made for Columbia (and notable as Sonny Greer's last appearance with the orchestra), then goes into four little-known tracks by The Coronets, one of the small groups which recorded for Mercer Ellington's label. Cat Anderson almost out-Cooties Cootie Williams on 'Night Walk'. However, ensuing sessions for Columbia (marking Louie Bellson's debut on 'The Hawk Talks') and Mercer are in very average sound and lose marks for presentation. The final date, for Columbia again, is better, although the three tracks (two of which were only issued in the UK) are nothing special.

Classics 1282 starts with four more titles for Mercer. There's an almost funky 'Caravan' by a sextet (Duke on piano, Strayhorn on organ!) and Willie Smith is superb on 'Alternate'. The remaining four sessions were made for Columbia and include two extended pieces: 'A Tone Parallel To Harlem' and the almost forgotten 'Controversial Suite', which pokes gentle fun at the traditional versus modern argument which was stirring up jazz at the time.

Most of Classics 1320 is taken up with the live programme which made up RCA's *Seattle Concert* LP. It's a relatively routine set, in unexceptional sound, but as always there are moments to savour – not least Duke's introduction of Britt Woodman prior to 'Sultry Serenade'. After that, four tracks for Columbia, including an extended '"A" Train' where Betty Roche takes the vocal.

★★★(★) Ellington Uptown

Columbia 512917-2 *Ellington; Cat Anderson, Willie Cook, Clark Terry, Ray Nance, Francis Williams, Harold 'Shorty' Baker, Shelton Hemphill, Al Killian (t); Quentin Jackson, Britt Woodman, Juan Tizol, Lawrence Brown, Claude Jones (tb); Tyree Glenn (tb, vib); Johnny Hodges (ss, as, cl); Russell Procope (as, cl); Hilton Jefferson, Willie Smith (as); Jimmy*

Hamilton (ts, cl); Al Sears, Paul Gonsalves (ts); Harry Carney (bs, cl); Billy Strayhorn (p); Wendell Marshall, Junior Raglin (b); Sonny Greer, Louie Bellson (d); Al Hibbler, Betty Roche (v). 5/47–6/52.

*** Masterpieces By Ellington

Columbia 512918–2 *Ellington; Harold 'Shorty' Baker, Nelson Williams, Cat Anderson, Andres Merenguito, Ray Nance, Willie Cook, Clark Terry, Dick Vance, Francis Williams (t); Mercer Ellington (flhn); Lawrence Brown, Quentin Jackson, Tyree Glenn, Juan Tizol, Britt Woodman (tb); Johnny Hodges, Willie Smith (as); Russell Procope (cl, as); Jimmy Hamilton (cl, ts); Paul Gonsalves (ts); Harry Carney (bs); Billy Strayhorn (p); Wendell Marshall (b); Sonny Greer, Louie Bellson (d); Yvonne Lanauze. Lloyd Oldham (v).* 12/50–8/51.

Ellington Uptown was always a patched-up job, bringing together the 1947 recording of 'Liberian Suite' with what were dignified as 'concert versions' of '"A" Train', 'Harlem Suite' and 'Perdido', with Louie Bellson's feature 'Skin Deep' and another look at 'The Mooche'. It all comes up very clean in this fresh remastering, especially 'Liberian Suite'. If you're collecting the Classics sequence (above) you'll already have all this, but Columbia's package is certainly attractive.

Masterpieces was another project to debut Ellington in the LP era, with the long versions of 'Mood Indigo', 'Sophisticated Lady', 'The Tattooed Bride' and 'Solitude'. Given the somewhat droopy feel to the music, this isn't one of our favourites, although again the new Columbia packaging is appealing.

***(*) Live At Birdland 1952

Jazz Unlimited JUCD 2036 *Ellington; Clark Terry, Willie Cook, Ray Nance, Cat Anderson (t); Quentin Jackson, Britt Woodman (tb); Juan Tizol (vtb); Hilton Jefferson, Jimmy Hamilton, Russell Procope, Harry Carney (reeds); Wendell Marshall (b); Louie Bellson (d); Betty Roche, Billy Grissom (v).* 11/52.

A complete Birdland broadcast, marred by intrusive announcements (it was a programme in honour of Duke's 25th anniversary, and they never let us forget it) and repetitive material. But 'Monologue' and 'The Tattooed Bride' seldom turn up in live recordings. Clear sound for the period.

***(*) Piano Reflections

Capitol 92863-2 *Ellington; Wendell Marshall (b); Butch Ballard, Dave Black (d); Ralph Colier (perc).* 4–12/53.

Ellington's apparent reluctance to document himself extensively as a pianist must be a source of regret, but these 1953 sessions find him pondering on 14 of his own tunes (and Mercer's 'Things Ain't What They Used To Be'). Most of them are too short to show any great development from the original themes, and Duke's habitual cat-and-mouse with the listener takes some of the pith out of the session; but it shows how distinctive his touch had become, how mannerism could become even more inimitable than Basie's minimalism, and how Ellington could fashion moving little episodes out of mere fragments.

*** Ellington '55

Capitol 520135-2 *Ellington; Clark Terry, Cat Anderson, Willie Cook (t); Ray Nance (t, vn, v); Quentin Jackson, Britt Woodman, Alfred Cobbs, George Jean, John Sanders (tb); Russell Procope (as, cl); Rick Henderson (as); Paul Gonsalves (ts); Jimmy Hamilton (cl, ts); Harry Carney (bs, bcl); Billy Strayhorn (cel); Wendell Marshall, Jimmy Woode (b); Dave Black (d).* 12/53.

Ellington's first 12-inch album, but not his most auspicious. The bland mix of old favourites and standards like 'Body And Soul' suggests the impasse the band was in prior to its Newport comeback. Gonsalves gets a blow on 'Body And Soul' and there is a marathon 'It Don't Mean A Thing', previously unissued.

CORE COLLECTION

**** Ellington At Newport 1956 (Complete)

Columbia C2K 64932 2CD *Ellington; Cat Anderson, Willie Cook, Ray Nance, Clark Terry (t); Quentin Jackson, John Sanders, Britt Woodman (tb); Johnny Hodges, Russell Procope (as); Paul Gonsalves, Jimmy Hamilton (ts); Harry Carney (bs); Jimmy Woode (b); Sam Woodyard (d).* 7/56.

The 1956 Newport Festival marked a significant upswing in Duke's critical and commercial fortunes. In large part, the triumph can be laid to Paul Gonsalves's extraordinary 27 blues choruses on 'Diminuendo And Crescendo In Blue', which CBS producer George Avakian placed out of sequence at the end of what was to be Ellington's best-selling record. Gonsalves's unprecedented improvisation (which opened up possibilities and set standards for later tenor saxophonists from John Coltrane to David Murray) was clearly spontaneous, yet in a way it dogged him for the rest of his life, and Ellington continued to introduce him, years later, as 'the star of Newport'.

Gonsalves himself suggested that a particularly competitive edge to the band that night was the real reason for his playing. Johnny Hodges had just returned to the fold after a brief stint as an independent bandleader. His beautiful, almost stately solo on 'Jeep's Blues' was intended to be the climax to the concert, but Hodges found himself upstaged in the subsequent notices, and the concert firmly established Gonsalves as one of the leading soloists in jazz. Unfortunately, much of the solo was played badly off-mike (of which more later) and in the past it was slightly difficult to get a complete sense of its extraordinary impact. It does, nevertheless, dominate the album, overshadowing Hodges and, more significantly, the three-part 'Festival Suite' – heard in its original live form for the first time here – which Ellington and Strayhorn had put together for the occasion. The first part, 'Festival Junction', is more or less a blowing theme for a parade of soloists, including a first excursion by Gonsalves, who gives notice of what's to come with some blistering choruses (though not 27) on the third part, 'Newport Up'.

Columbia's new edition of the music puts an entirely fresh slant on the occasion. The circumstances of how a 'virtual' stereo production came about are too complex to detail here (go to Phil Schaap's notes in the booklet for that), but essentially Columbia's mono tape was combined with a *second* mono recording of the music, made by Voice Of America. It was their microphone which Gonsalves was mistakenly playing into, thereby making him seem remote in the original Columbia mono mix! Instead, VOA's recording (rediscovered at the Library of Congress in the '90s) is on one channel and Columbia's on the other, meticulously synchronized.

The result is certainly an astonishing advance on previous versions of this famous event. The attempted 're-creations' of the live event on the following Monday, such as the repeat of 'I Got It Bad And That Ain't Good' with two notes repaired and canned applause added, are here, as is the studio 'Newport Jazz Festival Suite' with Norman O'Connor's remarks

from the live event spliced in. There are no fewer than ten new tracks too, mostly from the concert itself. The overall sound is excellent and fully conveys the near-pandemonium of the occasion! Absolutely essential Ellington.

*** Duke And Friends, Connecticut Jazz Festival 1956

IAJRC 1005 *As above, except add Buck Clayton (t), Willie 'The Lion' Smith, Hank Jones (p), Jimmy Grissom (v). 7/56.*

The Connecticut set was played 22 days later. Ellington's 'Newport Jazz Festival Suite' gets another airing, but the rest is a bit of a mess, with throwaway versions of some of the hits and some blues, plus a fairly uproarious Nance feature of 'Her Cherie'. Of some interest are extra tracks with Clayton fronting a small Ellington group and three numbers by the Lion. Good concert sound.

**** Such Sweet Thunder

Columbia CK 655684 *Ellington; Cat Anderson, Willie Cook, Ray Nance, Clark Terry (t); Quentin Jackson, John Sanders, Britt Woodman (tb); Johnny Hodges, Russell Procope (as); Paul Gonsalves, Jimmy Hamilton (ts); Harry Carney (bs); Jimmy Woode (b); Sam Woodyard (d). 8/56–5/57.*

The wit and sagacity of his nod to Will Shakespeare makes for one of the most delightful of all Ellington records. Hard to choose between the pleasures of hearing Clark Terry cough out the words (or so it seems) 'Lord, what fools these mortals be' through his horn at the end of 'Up And Down'; or Britt Woodman's remarkable solo on 'Sonnet To Hank Cinq'; or Hodges's heartbreaking delineation of 'Star-Crossed Lovers'. Sweet, swinging, perfect Ellingtonia. This new edition sounds terrific, with the music all in stereo for the first time, and there are an extra ten tracks of alternative takes, a few associated pieces from nearby sessions, and the huge (nine-minute) first version of 'Star-Crossed Lovers'.

**(*) Ellington Indigos

Columbia CK 44444 *As above, except add Harold 'Shorty' Baker (t), Rick Henderson (as), Ozzie Bailey (v). 10/57.*

This sounds like a chore for the company. Ten smoochy ballads, only three of them by Duke, with the band set on snooze. The players play themselves rather than playing, so to speak. But Shorty Baker is still a marvel on 'Willow Weep For Me'.

*** A Drum Is A Woman

Columbia CK 65567 *As above, except add Betty Glamann (hp), Candido Camero, Terry Snyder (perc), Margaret Tynes, Joya Sherrill (v). 57.*

Ellington's 'history of jazz' is a sly oratorio with virtuoso singing by Tynes and Sherrill, as well as an amusing commentary on jazz history by Duke as narrator and composer. Somewhat dated, perhaps, though not a bad antidote to the earnest history-mongering of the '90s from one of the music's sharpest intellects.

**** Black, Brown And Beige

Columbia CK 65566 *Ellington; Cat Anderson, Harold 'Shorty' Baker, Clark Terry (t); Ray Nance (t, vn); Quentin Jackson, John Sanders, Britt Woodman (tb); Jimmy Hamilton (cl); Bill Graham (as); Russell Procope (cl, as); Paul Gonsalves (ts); Harry Carney (bs); Jimmy Woode (b); Sam Woodyard (d); Mahalia Jackson (v). 2/58.*

This is one of the worthiest of Columbia's Ellington centenary reissues. Duke was hurt by the indifferent reception that his great work received on its debut, and this truncated version was his only full-scale studio treatment of it. Even this was coolly received, but it sounds like vintage and often glorious Ellington now. Mahalia Jackson's magisterial presence adds to what now seems like the first sacred concert. There is what amounts to an entire alternative take of the suite via a number of extra tracks, and all of it is in beautifully remastered sound, with great notes. Bravo!

***(*) Live At Newport 1958

Columbia C2K53584 2CD *Ellington; Harold 'Shorty' Baker, Clark Terry, Cat Anderson (t); Ray Nance (t, v); Quentin Jackson, John Sanders, Britt Woodman (tb); Harry Carney, Paul Gonsalves, Jimmy Hamilton, Johnny Hodges, Russell Procope, Gerry Mulligan (reeds); Mildred Falls (p); Jimmy Woode (b); Sam Woodyard (d); Lil Greenwood, Mahalia Jackson, Ozzie Bailey (v). 7/58.*

The original *Newport 1958* LP was actually a studio re-creation, cut a few weeks later. This set restores the original performances and covers plenty of extra ground. Some useful rarities such as 'Princess Blue', the Clark Terry feature 'Juniflip', and a track where the guesting Mulligan spars with Harry Carney, 'Prima Bara Dubla'. Mahalia Jackson is another unlikely drop-in and she belts out an impressive 'Come Sunday'. There are plenty of loose ends, as with most festival shows, but this is a good one to have restored.

***(*) At The Alhambra

Pablo 5313-2 *As above, except omit Greenwood, Jackson, Bailey and Mulligan. 10/58.*

In excellent sound, this is the band at Paris's Alhambra Theatre. It's a happy blend of old and new, from the '20s staples to then-current tunes like 'Juniflip', 'Jam With Sam' and 'Hi Fi Fo Fum'. Hodges gets three luxuriant features and Harry Carney makes light work of the difficult 'Frustration', although Jimmy Hamilton nearly falls over his feet on 'Newport Up'. Another night with the Duke.

**** Back To Back

Verve 521404-2 *Ellington; Johnny Hodges (as); Harry 'Sweets' Edison (t); Les Spann (g); Al Hall, Sam Jones (b); Jo Jones (d). 2/59.*

**** Side By Side

Verve 521405-2 *As above, except add Roy Eldridge (t), Lawrence Brown (tb), Ben Webster (ts), Billy Strayhorn (p), Wendell Marshall (b). 58–59.*

Back To Back is a small-group (and small-hours) classic, now given a new remastering in Verve's Master Edition series. The opening 'Wabash Blues' sets an attractive 32-bar theme over an initially disconcerting Latin rhythm that goes all the way back to W. C. Handy's experiments with tango measures in a blues context. Hodges and Edison take contrasting approaches on their solos, with the trumpeter working the changes in fairly orthodox fashion, Hodges sticking much closer to the melody. 'Basin Street Blues' features Spann in a slightly wavering but completely authentic solo, after which Hodges comes in with two delightfully varied choruses. Ellington's own solo is a curious affair, with a slightly wistful quality but also marked by repeated references to his own youthful style, in particular the descending arpeggios that became something of a tic.

The varied 12-bar form of 'St Louis Blues' is further developed in Ellington's fast, accurate introduction. The two horns do a call-and-response routine that further underlines their different approaches. Duke is the featured soloist again on 'Loveless Love' ('Careless Love'), a traditional tune with some kinship to the blues, but not a strict blues at all. Fittingly, though, the set ends with 'Royal Garden Blues', an orthodox 12-bar structure given a deliberately basic (Basie-like?) treatment.

The companion piece, *Side By Side*, brings Strayhorn in for Ellington at the piano and enlists Webster, Eldridge and Brown. Hodges dominates again, but his friends all have some pertinent remarks, and although the material is jam-session stuff as usual, it falls open to the expertise on show here. Three tracks from the session with Duke, including a classic 'Stompy Jones', are carried over to this one.

**** The Duke D.J. Special**

Fresh Sound 141 *Ellington; Cat Anderson, Harold 'Shorty' Baker, Clark Terry (t); Ray Nance (t, vn); Quentin Jackson, John Sanders, Britt Woodman (tb); Jimmy Hamilton (cl,ts); Russell Procope (cl, as); Johnny Hodges (as); Paul Gonsalves (ts); Harry Carney (bs); Jimmy Woode (b); Jimmy Johnson (d).* 3/59.

***** Live At The Newport Jazz Festival '59**

Emarcy 842071-2 *Ellington; Cat Anderson, Harold 'Shorty' Baker, Fats Ford, Clark Terry (t); Ray Nance (t, vn); Quentin Jackson, John Sanders, Britt Woodman (tb); Jimmy Hamilton (cl, ts); Russell Procope (cl, as); Johnny Hodges (as); Paul Gonsalves (ts); Harry Carney (bs); Jimmy Woode (b); Sam Woodyard (d).* 7/59.

*****(*) Live At The Blue Note**

Roulette 828637-2 2CD *As above, except add Billy Strayhorn (p), Johnny Pate (b), Jimmy Johnson (d).* 8/59.

The Emarcy is a lively concert performance with the trumpets in particularly good throat. Juan Tizol's 'Perdido' makes a welcome return to the band-book. The CD transfers are good, with very little dirt. The slightly earlier *Special* has a near-identical band in lower gear and with an occasionally slipping clutch. While it's comforting to know that Homer nods, there's no compelling need to have him doing it on your stereo.

The session at Chicago's Blue Note is drawn from three sets on a single night. Overhead mikes caught the performances, which consequently have a live but slightly askew feel, as if we're listening from the gods. Four tunes from the *Anatomy Of A Murder* score get a welcome outing, Strayhorn comes on to do a duet, Stan Kenton and June Christy drop by to say hello ... a typical night's work for the master. Best moment: the perennially underrated Shorty Baker blowing as sweet as he could on 'Almost Cried'.

*****(*) Blues In Orbit**

Columbia CK 44051 *Ellington; Cat Anderson, Harold 'Shorty' Baker, Clark Terry (t); Ray Nance (t, vn); Quentin Jackson, John Sanders, Britt Woodman, Booty Wood (tb); Matthew Gee (bhn); Harry Carney, Paul Gonsalves, Bill Graham, Jimmy Hamilton, Johnny Hodges, Russell Procope (reeds); Billy Strayhorn (p); Jimmy Woode (b); Jimmy Johnson, Sam Woodyard (d).* 2/58, 2/59.

If 'Blues In Orbit' was some sort of Ducal welcome to the age of Sputnik, the previously unreleased 'Track 360' is an elegant train-ride, Pullman-class and with a nod in the direction of Honegger's popular concert-opener, 'Pacific 231', swaying over a track laid down by Sam Woodyard; the drummer fell ill shortly afterwards and isn't heard on the rest of the album.

There are two more tracks which weren't on the original release. 'Brown Penny' is a state-of-the-art Hodges solo, played in imitation of Kay Davis's earlier vocal version and sounding as if it is being poured out of a bottle. The other also features Hodges on a slightly too syrupy reading of 'Sentimental Lady' (aka 'I Didn't Know About You'). Hodges rather dominates the album, soloing even on 'Smada', which was usually a Hamilton spot. Hamilton himself has mixed fortunes, sounding anonymous on tenor on his own 'Three J's Blues' and 'Pie Eye's Blues'. The latter is a rackety 12-bar that compares badly with the subsequent 'C Jam Blues', where Hamilton goes back to clarinet and rounds off a sequence of solos that includes excellent work by Gonsalves, the little-known Matthew Gee and Booty Wood. A very fine album, with just enough new compositional input – 'Blues In Blueprint' and 'The Swinger's Jump' – to vary a slightly predictable profile.

*****(*) Festival Session**

Columbia 512916-2 *Ellington; Cat Anderson, Harold 'Shorty' Baker, Clark Terry, Ray Nance, Willie Cook, Andres Merenguito (t); Quentin Jackson (tb, b); Britt Woodman, John Sanders (tb); Johnny Hodges (as); Russell Procope (as, cl); Jimmy Hamilton (ts, cl); Paul Gonsalves (ts); Harry Carney (bs, bcl); Jimmy Woode, Joe Benjamin (b); Sam Woodyard, Jimmy Johnson (d).* 9/59.

Not a live session, but a studio date meant to collect some of the pieces Duke had played on his spin through the summer's festivals. One curiosity is that there were three bassists playing: Woode was late, Quentin Jackson subbed on the first tune, Joe Benjamin on another, and then Woode turned up. The Gonsalves feature 'Cop-Out Extension' was recorded several times, but much of the rest – including the three-part 'Duael (*sic*) Fuel' and four-part 'Idiom '59' – were hardly touched again. 'Launching Pad' (aka 'Blues In the Round') is the finale, and in the notes, Clark Terry says 'I wrote the whole damn thing. Duke orchestrated it'. Clark was further miffed that Duke gave the trumpet solo to Ray Nance! As ever, Ellington and band working at top speed, before it was on to the next thing.

***** Anatomy Of A Murder**

Columbia CK 65569 *As above, except add Gerald Wilson (t); omit Gee and Woodyard.* 5–6/59.

Ellington's score for Otto Preminger's film strikes a moderate number of sparks. The title-theme shows he could write thriller material as strong as anything Pete Rugolo and Shorty Rogers were turning out for Hollywood, but the more impressionistic music tends to sound like middleweight Ellington. Columbia's fresh edition adds a lot of odd bits and pieces – the single version of the title-piece, an interview with Ellington, and so forth – interesting stuff, but really for scholars only.

*****(*) Live At Monterey 1960**

Status DSTS 1008

***** Live At Monterey 1960 Part Two**

Status DSTS 1009 *Ellington; Willie Cook, Andres Meringuito, Eddie Mullins (t); Ray Nance (t, v); Quentin Jackson, Booty Wood, Britt Woodman (tb); Juan Tizol (vtb); Jimmy Hamilton, Russell Procope (cl, as); Johnny Hodges (as); Paul Gonsalves (ts); Harry Carney (bs, cl); Aaron Bell (b); Sam Woodyard (d); Lil Greenwood, Jimmy Rushing (v).* 9/60.

In fine concert sound, here's some previously unheard Ellington from 1960. Volume one has several seldom-encountered tunes; the second disc is slighter stuff, with Rushing doing three amiable turns and a run across 'Red Carpet' (the rest of the disc features the Cannonball Adderley group). Wally Heider did the original recording, and though some of the soloists drift off, the clout of the band comes over very well.

*** The Ellington Suites

Original Jazz Classics OJC 446 *Ellington; Cat Anderson, Harold 'Shorty' Baker, Mercer Ellington, Money Johnson, Eddie Preston, Clark Terry (t); Ray Nance (t, vn); Quentin Jackson, Vince Prudente, John Sanders, Malcolm Taylor, Booty Wood, Britt Woodman (tb); Johnny Hodges, Harold Minerve, Norris Turney (as); Russell Procope (as, cl); Jimmy Hamilton (ts, cl); Russ Andrews, Harold Ashby, Paul Gonsalves (ts); Harry Carney (bs, bcl); Joe Benjamin, Wulf Freedman, Jimmy Woode (b); Jimmy Johnson, Rufus Jones (d).* 2/59–10/72.

An interesting collection of extended and medley pieces from the 1959 'Queen's Suite' to the late and indifferent 'Uwis Suite'. Significantly or not, the most arresting track on the whole album, which has good sound-quality throughout, is 'The Single Petal Of A Rose', a duo for Ellington and bassist Jimmy Woode.

*** First Time!

Columbia CK 65571 *Ellington; Cat Anderson, Thad Jones, Willie Cook, Sonny Cohn (t); Ray Nance (c, vn); Quentin Jackson, Louis Blackburn, Lawrence Brown (tb); Frank Foster, Paul Gonsalves, Harry Carney, Frank Wess, Johnny Hodges, Jimmy Hamilton (reeds); Count Basie, Billy Strayhorn (p); Freddie Green (g); Eddie Jones, Aaron Bell (b); Sam Woodyard, Sonny Payne (d).* 7/61.

Never highly regarded, but if one approaches this meeting of the Basie and Ellington bands in a spirit of undemanding fun, that's what comes out. There is a share of over-the-top blitzkrieg, as in the preposterous 'Battle Royal', but several nimble little touches – the sonorous trombone backdrop for Jackson on 'To You', the extended Basie blues, 'Segue In C', which offers chances for both pianists, and the jovial 'BDB' by Strayhorn – keep the scale of the occasion under control, and a feeling of grand good humour prevails. The new edition comes in handsome sound and adds six alternative takes or rehearsals.

**** The Duke

Columbia C3K 65841 3CD *Ellington with various groups.* 27–62.

This is the place to consider Columbia's Centenary compilation from their Ellington holdings. It starts with 1927's 'Hot And Bothered' and ends on the titanic 'Battle Royal' bust-up with Basie. There are plenty of interesting and unobvious choices, particularly on disc two, which covers the period 1947–52 and is otherwise largely missed by Columbia's other reissues. A detailed booklet is a pleasing extra, with many photographs, and the remastering is up to the new standards which the majors have lately been setting. An excellent buy.

*** Featuring Paul Gonsalves

Original Jazz Classics OJC 623 *Ellington; Cat Anderson, Bill Berry, Roy Burrowes, Ray Nance (t); Lawrence Brown, Chuck Connors, Leon Cox (tb); Russell Procope (cl, as); Johnny Hodges (as); Paul Gonsalves (ts); Jimmy Hamilton (cl, ts); Harry Carney (bs); Aaron Bell (b); Sam Woodyard (d).* 5/62.

A deserved album feature for a saxophonist who contributed enormously to the Ellington sound and who has made a considerable impact on contemporary players like David Murray, but whose reputation has been somewhat eclipsed by that of Johnny Hodges. The tenorist's solo material is typically extended and supremely logical, and his tone, sometimes a little muffled and lacking in individuality, is razor-sharp here. Whether the 'name' ranking was planned beforehand or was awarded in recognition of particularly inspired playing isn't clear, but this is a significant set by one of the unsung geniuses of the saxophone, who joins Warne Marsh and Richie Kamuca in the ranks of those who have been passed over in favour of noisier talents.

*** Duke Ellington Meets Coleman Hawkins

Impulse! 051162-2 *Ellington; Ray Nance (c, vn); Lawrence Brown (tb); Johnny Hodges (as); Coleman Hawkins (ts); Harry Carney (bs, bcl); Aaron Bell (b); Sam Woodyard (d).* 8/62.

The sketchy nature of this meeting of giants finally tells against it. The good-natured fun of 'Limbo Jazz' is the tonic note of the date, and while there is much entertaining playing by the small band on hand, one wishes for some of the gravitas which at least got into the date with Coltrane (see below). 'Solitude' is added to the original LP programme.

***(*) Duke Ellington And John Coltrane

Impulse! 051166-2 *Ellington; John Coltrane (ts, ss); Aaron Bell, Jimmy Garrison (b); Elvin Jones, Sam Woodyard (d).* 9/62.

It's known that Coltrane was going through a difficult transitional phase when this remarkable opportunity was presented to him. Six months before, he had recorded the simply titled *Coltrane* with what was to be the classic quartet. He was, though, stretching for something beyond its surprisingly relaxed lyricism and had managed to wreck his mouthpiece (no minor loss for a saxophonist) trying to improve its lay. His work around this time is, in retrospect, quite conventional, certainly in relation to what was to follow, and it's often Ellington, as so often in the past, who sounds the 'younger' and more adventurous player. It is, for all that, a slightly disappointing record which peaks early with a brilliant reading of 'In A Sentimental Mood' but never reaches such heights again.

***(*) Money Jungle

Blue Note 46398 *Ellington; Charles Mingus (b); Max Roach (d).* 9/62.

Set up by United Artists, this was intended to put Duke in the company of two modernists of the next generation, both of whom (Mingus especially) had drawn particular sustenance from his example. It was the first trio recording the bassist had made since the 1957 Jubilee sessions with Hampton Hawes and Dannie Richmond. Despite his apparent misgivings before and during the session, Mingus completely steals the show, playing complicated countermelodies and dizzying, out-of-tempo runs in every register. Much of the material seems to have been put together at speed and inevitably relies quite heavily on the blues. 'Money Jungle' itself and 'Very Special' are both reasonably orthodox 12-bars and both sound improvised. 'La Fleurette Africaine' is clearly developed from a simple melodic conception, stated at the beginning by the piano. Long-standing Ellington staples, 'Warm Valley' and 'Caravan', are rather less successful, and it isn't clear on the former whether a rather agitated Mingus is unfamiliar with the changes or whether he is suffering one of the minor huffs Ellington recounted later.

*** Recollections Of The Big Band Era

Atlantic 790043-2 *Ellington; Cat Anderson, Bill Berry, Roy Burrowes, Eddie Preston, Cootie Williams (t); Ray Nance (t, vn); Lawrence Brown, Chuck Connors, Buster Cooper (tb); Russell Procope (cl, as); Jimmy Hamilton (cl, ts); Johnny Hodges (as); Paul Gonsalves (ts); Harry Carney (bs, cl, bcl); Ernie Shepard (b); Sam Woodyard (d).* 11/62.

Something of a novelty set, bringing together some of the most famous theme- and signature-tunes of the pre- and immediately post-war bands. Billy Strayhorn's arrangement of Don Redman's 'The Chant Of The Weed' and piano part on the Harry James-associated 'Ciribiribin' are noteworthy, but there are also name-checks for Woody Herman ('The Woodchopper's Ball'), Erskine Hawkins ('Tuxedo Junction'), Louis Armstrong ('When It's Sleepy Time Down South'), Paul Whiteman (Gershwin's 'Rhapsody In Blue') and, inevitably, Basie's 'One O'Clock Jump' and Cab Calloway's 'Minnie The Moocher'. Thoroughly enjoyable, and something more than just a nostalgic wallow. Some of Ellington's own arrangements are strikingly original, virtually reconceiving the material.

***(*) The Reprise Studio Recordings 1962–1965

Warners/Rhino 8122-73658–2 5CD *Ellington; Cootie Williams, Cat Anderson, Roy Burrowes, Bill Berry, Eddie Preston, Herbie Jones, Nat Woodard, Mercer Ellington, Howard McGhee, Rolf Ericson (t); Ray Nance (t, c, vn); Lawrence Brown, Chuck Connors, Buster Cooper (tb); Russell Procope (cl, as); Johnny Hodges (as); Jimmy Hamilton (cl, ts); Paul Gonsalves (ts); Harry Carney (cl, bcl, bs); Billy Strayhorn (p); Stéphane Grappelli (vn); Svend Asmussen (vla); Ernie Shepard, Major Holley, Peck Morrison, John Lamb (b); Sam Woodyard (d); Paris/Hamburg/Stockholm Symphony Orchestras.* 11/62–4/65.

Warners have solved the problem of putting together an expensive and time-consuming reissue project by getting someone else to do all the work, since this is a completely unembellished reprint of Mosaic's Ellington-on-Reprise box – mastering, artwork, sleeve-notes, it's all the same. Given that Mosaic do this kind of thing better than anyone else – if you like their black-and-white design minimalism, that is – it's a sensible enough decision.

How much one welcomes this set depends on how dedicated an Ellingtonian you are. The late Mark Tucker contributed an extensive essay to the Mosaic package, and though he suggests that the Reprise sessions 'received scant acclaim and little critical scrutiny', even his notes betray the feeling that a lot of the music in the ten album-length sessions which Ellington set down is of secondary Ducal importance. The one masterwork is *Afro-Bossa*, a beautiful set of a dozen Ellington and Strayhorn miniatures – only five of the 12 pieces break the three-minute mark – which might almost hark back to the dazzling early-'40s era in their compact ingenuity. *The Symphonic Ellington* realizes one of Duke's ambitions in presenting 'Harlem' and 'Night Creature' in a form which twins the band with three different symphony orchestras, and the final *Concert In The Virgin Islands* is a live-in-the-studio re-creation of a typical mid-'60s Ellington programme, old favourites mixed with new entries.

After this, though, we get two albums of pop covers, one of music from *Mary Poppins*, a greatest-hits package and two sessions which weren't even released during the Reprise years: one collection of big-band covers and the unlikely *Jazz Violin Session*, where Svend Asmussen and Stéphane Grappelli joined Ray Nance for a lot of bowing and scraping. Ellington's knack for teasing great performances out of unpromising material was always an intergral part of his own tradition: here, for instance, one can find 'I Can't Stop Loving You' and 'Feed The Birds', treatments which can stand alongside such earlier masterpieces as 'The Sidewalks Of New York'. But the great moments are scattered, and most of these sessions feel much more dated than *Afro-Bossa*. Given Ellington's habitual masking of his true feelings, it's hard to divine what his priorities really were at this point. As achievements to be proud of, the great works of the '60s were surely the big-scale pieces, yet Duke hankered after being on jukeboxes and the radio, and a lot of his touring was still playing for dancers.

What Frank Sinatra expected from Ellington when he signed him to Reprise is even harder to figure out. The ballyhoo at the outset suggested that Duke would have carte blanche over what he wanted to record and would take on a wider A&R role for the label. Yet the association lasted less than three years, Reprise never really got going in jazz terms, and surely some of these dates were the product of 'suggestions' from outside Duke's own camp. One valuable thing, though, was the *sound* of Ellington's Reprise sessions: finally, the sonic richness of the Ellington ensemble was set down in consistent, high fidelity, and perhaps the greatest pleasure of these five discs is sitting back and basking in it...

***(*) The Great Paris Concert

Atlantic SD 2-304 *Ellington; Cat Anderson, Roy Burrowes, Cootie Williams (t); Ray Nance (c, v); Lawrence Brown, Chuck Connors, Buster Cooper (tb); Johnny Hodges (as); Russell Procope (cl, as); Jimmy Hamilton (cl, ts); Paul Gonsalves (ts); Harry Carney (bs, cl); Ernie Shepard (b); Sam Woodyard (d).* 2/63.

Great? Very nearly. Oddly, perhaps, the quality of this set doesn't lie so much in the solos as in the ensembles, which are rousing to an almost unprecedented degree. 'Suite Thursday' is an unexpected gem for anyone who hasn't encountered it before, and there are lovely settings of 'Rose Of The Rio Grande' and the *Asphalt Jungle* theme. The sound is big and resonant, as it presumably was in the hall, and more than almost any of the live recordings of the time it conveys something of the excitement of a concert performance.

*** Harlem

Pablo 2308-245 *Ellington; Cat Anderson, Rolf Ericson, Herbie Jones, Cootie Williams (t); Lawrence Brown, Buster Cooper, Chuck Connors (tb); Russell Procope (as, cl); Johnny Hodges (as); Jimmy Hamilton (cl, ts); Paul Gonsalves (ts); Harry Carney (bs, bcl, cl); Major Holley, Jimmy Woode (b); Sam Woodyard (d).* 64.

In 1964 Ellington made a triumphal return to Carnegie Hall, the scene of the famous wartime concerts. The title-piece remains one of Duke's most effective big-scale works, and the rest is a useful mix of standard hits and well-turned features for the band's good guys.

***(*) In The Uncommon Market

Pablo 2308-247 *Ellington; Cat Anderson, Roy Burrowes, Cootie Williams (t); Ray Nance (t, vn); Lawrence Brown, Chuck Connors, Buster Cooper (tb); Johnny Hodges (as); Russell Procope (as, cl); Jimmy Hamilton (ts, cl); Paul Gonsalves (ts); Harry Carney (bs); Ernie Shepard (b); Sam Woodyard (d).* n.d.

Undated, but this probably comes from the same period as the above. Challengingly unfamiliar scores – 'Bula', 'E.S.P.', 'Silk Lace' – and trio performances of two concepts of 'The Shepherd' make this a valuable session. The soloing is not so much below par as clearly subordinated to collective values, and the ensembles repay the closest attention.

**(*) Yale Concert

Original Jazz Classics OJC 664 *Ellington; Cat Anderson, Herbie Jones, Cootie Williams, Mercer Ellington, Ray Nance (t); Lawrence Brown, Chuck Connors, Buster Cooper (tb); Russell Procope (as, cl); Johnny Hodges (as); Jimmy Hamilton (ts, cl); Paul Gonsalves (ts); Harry Carney (bs); Jeff Castleman (b); Sam Woodyard (d).* 4/65.

This has its moments but suffers from the surfeit of available Duke-in-concert. Apart from 'A Chromatic Love Affair' and a beautiful Hodges medley, there's nothing worth cutting classes for.

***(*) Berlin '65 Paris '67

Pablo 5304-2 *As above, except add Ray Nance, Money Johnson (t), John Lamb (b), Rufus Jones (d); omit Castleman.* 65–67.

Echoes from a couple of European stopovers, although smartly chosen and with numerous highlights. The great set-piece of 'Ad Lib On Nippon' features Ellington playing cat-and-mouse with John Lamb; but it's the features for Gonsalves and Hodges, each at their most magnetic and songful, that raise the enjoyment level to the maximum. A pleasing new discovery.

***(*) Soul Call

Verve 539785-2 *As above, except omit Nance and Johnson.* 7/66.

The vast amount of music on Verve's eight-disc box *Complete Côte d'Azur Concerts* includes a lot of Ellington, but we are discussing it under Ella Fitzgerald's name. This Verve LP originally appeared as a stand-alone disc, and it's been extended to CD length with music from four different festival sets at Juan-Les-Pins. The important pieces are a vivacious reading of 'La Plus Belle Africaine', deliciously lit up by Woodyard's skittering rhythms and Carney's stately solo, the bubbling near-calypso 'West Indian Pancake', and a couple of *Such Sweet Thunder* excerpts. Loaded with atmosphere.

*** A Concert Of Sacred Music

Status DSTS 1015 *As above, except add Louie Bellson (d), Bunny Briggs (tap), Tony Watkins, Jon Hendricks, Jimmy McPhail, Esther Merrill, Herman McCoy Choir (v); omit Rufus Jones, Woodyard.* 66.

Although not all of this is new material as such – it includes both 'New World A-Comin'' and 'Come Sunday' – this live set from Grace Cathedral in Los Angeles is effectively the first Sacred Concert. The band is often peripheral to the various singers and choirs engaged for the concert: Hendricks has four showcases, the effulgent Tony Watkins and Esther Merrill have three, Bunny Briggs taps his way through 'David Danced Before The Lord' and the Herman McCoy Choir handles three pieces in the spirit. Ellington's own principal involvement comes in his piano solo version of 'New World A-Comin'', an impressive treatment. If this is more a collection of interesting bits and pieces, it's an inconclusive part of the composer's rather awkward sacred canon. Salvaged from damaged tapes, and in really quite respectable sound.

*** The Popular Duke Ellington

RCA Victor Gold 09026 638802 *As above, except Sam Woodyard (d) replaces Bellson; omit vocalists.* 66.

Dave Hassinger secured a big, almost voluptuous sound for the band at RCA's Music Center Of The World studio, and serving it well on this session of remakes, 11 venerable nuggets from the book plus a new blues called 'The Twitch'. The performances are in some ways nothing special, but somehow the band summoned considerable heart on tunes they must have done thousands of times. Hodges is almost lubricious on 'I Got It Bad And That Ain't Good' and Williams is sublime in 'The Mooche' and 'Creole Love Call'.

**(*) Live At The Greek Theatre

Status DSTS 10143 *As above, except add Jimmy Jones (p), Jim Hughart, John Lamb (b), Ed Thigpen (d), Ella Fitzgerald (v).* 9/66.

Duke's spoken intros sound as if he's broadcasting from Mars, but the band sounds all right, and it does a typical tour of service for the period. Ella sings a short set with her trio and does 'Cotton Tail' with the band. Hardly a deathless discovery.

**(*) Masters Of Jazz – Volume 6

Storyville STCD 4106 *Ellington; Cat Anderson, Harold 'Shorty' Baker, Bill Berry, Eddie Mullens, Ray Nance (t); Lawrence Brown, Chuck Connors, Leon Cox (tb); Jimmy Hamilton (cl, ts); Russell Procope (as, cl); Johnny Hodges (as); Paul Gonsalves (ts); Harry Carney (bs, cl, bcl); Aaron Bell (b); Sam Woodyard (d).* 62–66.

The performances here are pretty much *comme il faut*, but again it's Ellington's solo medley, recorded somewhat later than the rest, which really catches the ear. The complexity of his delivery is quite astonishing, even when it is clearly calculated to beguile. Not a great album, but enthusiasts will want the solo spot.

**** The Far East Suite

Bluebird 82876-55614-2 *Ellington; Cat Anderson, Mercer Ellington, Herbie Jones, Cootie Williams (t); Lawrence Brown, Chuck Connors, Buster Cooper (tb); Harry Carney, Paul Gonsalves, Jimmy Hamilton, Johnny Hodges, Russell Procope (reeds); John Lamb (b); Rufus Jones (d).* 12/66.

It should really have been *The Near East Suite*. In 1963, the State Department sent the Ellington band on a tour that took in Ceylon, India and Pakistan, most of the Middle East, and Persia. The tour was eventually interrupted by the assassination of JFK, but Duke and co-writer Strayhorn slowly absorbed the sights and tone-colours of those weeks, and nearly three years later went into the studio to record the suite. Typical of Ellington's interpretation of the genre, it is really little more than a well-balanced programme of individual songs but with a greater-than-usual degree of overall coherence, summed up at the end by 'Amad'. 'The Tourist Point Of View' serves as an overture and a reminder of the Duke's characteristic sound, and it introduces two of the most important solo voices, Anderson and Gonsalves. 'Bluebird Of Delhi' relates to a mynah that mocked Billy Strayhorn with a beautiful song (played by Jimmy Hamilton) and then brought him down with the resounding raspberry one hears at the end of the piece.

What follows is arguably the most beautiful single item in Ellington's and Strayhorn's entire output. Hodges's solo on 'Isfahan' is like attar of roses, almost (but not quite) *too* sweet and, once smelt, impossible to forget. Critical attention has almost always focused on Hodges, but it's important to be aware of the role of the backing arrangements, a line for the saxophones that seems as monumental as the place it celebrates. The other unquestionable masterpiece of the set is 'Mount Harissa', a soft, almost spiritual opening from Ellington, building up into a sinuous Gonsalves solo over a compulsive drum-and-cymbal pattern and huge orchestral interjections. An evocation of Agra, location of the Taj Mahal, is quite properly assigned to Harry Carney, in superb voice.

Ellington's ability to communicate points of contact and conflict between cultures, assimilating the blues to Eastern modes in tracks like 'Blue Pepper (Far East Of The Blues)', never sounds editorialized or excessively self-conscious. This remains one of the peaks of post-war Ellington. It has recently been remastered yet again and is now on the Bluebird label!

***(*) The Intimacy Of The Blues

Original Jazz Classics OJC 624 *Ellington; Cat Anderson, Willie Cook (t); Lawrence Brown (tb); Norris Turney (f); Johnny Hodges (as); Harold Ashby, Paul Gonsalves (ts); Harry Carney (bs); Wild Bill Davis (org); Joe Benjamin, Victor Gaskin, Paul Kondziela, John Lamb (b); Rufus Jones (d).* 3/67–6/70.

Delightful small-group settings, of which the 1967 'Combo Suite' (incorporating the title-piece, 'Out South', 'Near North' and 'Soul Country') is far and away the best. Even in restricted settings like this, Ellington manages to get a tremendous depth of sound, and the disposition of horns is such that Carney's line often suggests that a whole section is at work. The tenor is contrastingly quieter and less forceful, which has the same effect.

**** ... And His Mother Called Him Bill

RCA Victor 74321851512 *Ellington; Cat Anderson, Mercer Ellington, Herbie Jones, Cootie Williams (t); Clark Terry (flhn); Lawrence Brown, Chuck Connors, Buster Cooper, John Sanders (tb); Harry Carney, Johnny Hodges, Paul Gonsalves, Jimmy Hamilton, Russell Procope (reeds); Aaron Bell, Jeff Castleman (b); Steve Little, Sam Woodyard (d).* 8–11/67.

This is Ellington's tribute to Billy Strayhorn, who died in May 1967. The mood is primarily one of loss and yearning, and Strayhorn titles like 'U.M.M.G.', standing for 'Upper Manhattan Medical Group', and 'Blood Count' bear poignant witness to his prolonged final illness. Hodges's solo on the latter is almost unbearable and it is surpassed in creative terms only by the later 'Day-Dream'. 'U.M.M.G.' has an urgent, ambulance-ride quality, largely conveyed by Ellington's clattering piano that sets it in sharp opposition to the easy swing of the opening 'Boo-Dah'.

The CD has four previously unreleased tracks, including 'Smada', 'My Little Brown Book' and (another Hodges feature) 'Lotus Blossom'; but the main interest focuses on the tracks mentioned above and on the astonishing 'All Day Long', which counts as one of Duke's most devastating orchestral conceptions, as daring as anything in the modern movement.

**(*) The Intimate Ellington

Original Jazz Classics OJC 730 *Ellington; various line-ups.* 69–71.

Definitions of intimacy must vary. This isn't an obvious choice for last thing at night with a glass of malt and the dimmer turned down. Apart from the feeble 'Moon Maiden', on which Ellington plays celeste, it's an averagely appealing album with some assured big-band playing and a useful sample of Ellington's still-underrated trio performances (which may yet come to seem more significant than essays on the scale of 'Symphonette'). The sound wobbles a bit from track to track, an almost inevitable problem on compilations for quite various forces, and there is a problem with the bass register.

*** Second Sacred Concert

Prestige P 24045 *Ellington; Cat Anderson, Mercer Ellington, Cootie Williams (t); Lawrence Brown, Buster Cooper (tb); Harry Carney, Paul Gonsalves, Johnny Hodges, Russell Procope (reeds); Jeff Castleman (b); Sam Woodyard (d); voices.* 68.

Ellington's last few years were often spent writing liturgical music. The first of the sacred concerts has now appeared on Status (listed above). The second is a blend of jazz, classical and black gospel materials, profoundly influenced by the large-scale Masses and praises of Mary Lou Williams, Ellington's only serious rival in jazz composition on the large scale. Despite the dimensions of the piece and the joyous, ringing concords, it is a surprisingly dark work, with a tragic sub-theme that constantly threatens to break through. Non-believers will still appreciate the extraordinary part-writing; for Christians of whatever persuasion, it remains an overwhelming musical experience.

***(*) Latin American Suite

Original Jazz Classics OJC 469 *Ellington; Lawrence Brown, Buster Cooper (tb); Johnny Hodges (as); Paul Gonsalves (ts); Harry Carney (bs); only soloists identified.* n.d.

Typically, this late suite is not an attempt to duplicate the sounds and rhythms Ellington and his band heard on their first trans-equatorial trip in 1968 (surprisingly late in his career, on the face of it). Rather, it records the very personal impressions the southern half of the Americas made on a mind so fine that it was never violated by anything as vulgar as a new influence, and never so closed-off as to reject any new stimulus. Where most composer/bandleaders would have packed the rhythm section with congas, shakers and timbales, as Stanley Dance points out, Ellington conveys a strong Latin feel with his regular rhythm section. On the short 'Tina', an impression of Argentina, he uses a small rhythm group with two bassists and works a bluesy variation on the tango. The bass is again important on the jovial 'Latin American Sunshine', paired with Ellington on a rather untypical theme statement. The opening 'Oclupaca', a title that follows the jazz cliché of reversing names, is a bright, danceable theme that recalls the Latin-influenced big bands of the '30s and '40s. And that is the overall impression of the set. Perhaps fittingly, there is a nostalgic feel underneath its typically adventurous arrangements and voicings. There's a wistful quality to 'The Sleeping Lady And The Giant Who Watches Over Her', ostensibly the two mountains overlooking Mexico City; but one wonders if Ellington wasn't thinking about Latin America and the neo-colonial United States, with its cultural dominance and magpie eclecticism, and expressing a tinge of regret that he hadn't plunged into the music of the southern continent earlier in his career.

*** The Duke In Washington

Storyville STCD 8310 *Ellington; Wallace Jones, Rex Stewart, Taft Jordan, Shelton Hemphill, Francis Williams, Cat Anderson, Reunald Jones, Clark Terry, Willie Cook (t); Ray Nance (t, vn); Joe 'Tricky Sam' Nanton, Juan Tizol, Lawrence Brown, Claude Jones, Wilbur De Paris, Quentin Jackson, Britt Woodman, John Sanders (tb); Jimmy Hamilton, Skippy*

Williams (cl, ts); Otto Hardwick, Johnny Hodges, Rick Henderson (as); Paul Gonsalves (ts); Harry Carney (bs); Fred Guy (g); Aaron Bell, Junior Raglin, Oscar Pettiford, Jimmy Woode (b); Sonny Greer, Dave Black, Sam Woodyard (d); Betty Roche, Kay Davis (v). 12/43–4/69.

Hard to know exactly where to place this entertaining compilation of Ellington live material, all from his home town, and spread across a quarter-century or so. He gets an astonishing reception at the Naval Training Center (1944), where Rex Stewart does a terrific 'Amor, Amor'. Harry Carney is luxurious on 'Sono' (1946), and there's a full-scale reading of 'Harlem' (1955). Duke, Aaron Bell and Sam Woodyard run through a couple of numbers in a rather poorly recorded 1962 festival episode, and finally there is his piano-solo dedication to the First Lady from the 1969 birthday party at the White House. Very mixed sound, but most of it's great fun.

***(*) Up In Duke's Workshop

Original Jazz Classics OJC 633 *Ellington; Johnny Coles, Willie Cook, Mercer Ellington, Money Johnson, Jimmy Owens, Eddie Preston, Alan Rubin, Fred Stone, Cootie Williams (t); Tyree Glenn, Bennie Green, Benny Powell, Julian Priester, Vince Prudente, Malcolm Taylor, Booty Wood (tb); Russell Procope (as, cl); Johnny Hodges, Harold Minerve, Buddy Pearson, Norris Turney (as); Harold Ashby, Paul Gonsalves (ts); Harry Carney (bs); Joe Benjamin, Victor Gaskin, Paul Kondziela (b); Rufus Jones (d).* 4/69–12/72.

The line-ups don't actually vary very much, but there are a number of relatively unfamiliar names, notably those trying to fill Johnny Hodges's shoes, for which they should have been assigned rabbits' feet. As the title implies, these are working sessions – and slightly tentative ones at that. The early 'Black Butterfly' and the interesting 'Neo-Creole' are significant pieces, but in only eight cuts there's a fair bit of slack.

CORE COLLECTION

**** New Orleans Suite

Atlantic 81227-3670-2 *Ellington; Cootie Williams, Money Johnson, Al Rubin, Fred Stone (t); Booty Wood, Julian Priester, Chuck Connors (tb); Dave Taylor (btb); Johnny Hodges, Russell Procope, Norris Turney, Harry Carney, Paul Gonsalves (reeds); Wild Bill Davis (org); Joe Benjamin (b); Rufus Jones (d).* 4–5/70.

This remains our favourite among the later big-scale works. Ellington looked to create another of his quasi-historical overviews here, but there was no commentary, just a sequence of intensely beautiful vignettes. The rollicking 'Blues For New Orleans' which opens the set features Davis in a very effective cameo, but the wellspring of this album is the sound of the orchestra rather than individual soloists; the reed section is truly on song for the last time (Hodges died during the making of the album and is absent from the final tracks). Gonsalves and Carney abide, though, and the scoring for 'Second Line', 'Bourbon Street Jingling Jollies' and 'Portrait Of Mahalia Jackson' is sadly beautiful, exceptionally expressive. 'Portrait Of Wellman Braud' is also a fascinating rhythmic exercise. Atlantic have finally done a new mastering, and it sounds terrific.

**** The Afro-Eurasian Eclipse

Original Jazz Classics OJC 645 *Ellington; Mercer Ellington, Money Johnson, Eddie Preston, Cootie Williams (t); Chuck Connors, Malcolm Taylor, Booty Wood (tb); Russell Procope (cl, as); Norris Turney (as); Harold Ashby, Paul Gonsalves (ts); Harry Carney (bs); Joe Benjamin (b); Rufus Jones (d).* 71.

World music of a very high order. Ellington's understanding of non-Western forms was often limited to a grasp of unusual tone-colours, but here, on 'Chinoiserie', 'Didjeridoo' and 'Afrique', he produces something that sounds genuinely alien. The original Fantasy release sounded veiled and mysterious, but the CD reissue is quite bright, perhaps too much so for music of this sort. However, sharper resolution does confirm a strong impression that, far from being a by-blow, these pieces are essential items in the Ellington canon.

*** Togo Brava Suite

Blue Note 30082-2 *Ellington; Cootie Williams, Johnny Coles, Mercer Ellington, Eddie Preston, Harold 'Money' Johnson (t); Chuck Connors, Malcolm Taylor, Booty Wood (tb); Russell Procope (as, cl); Harold Minerve (as); Norris Turney (as, f); Paul Gonsalves, Harold Ashby (ts); Harry Carney (bs); Joe Benjamin (b); Rufus Jones (d); Nell Brookshire (v).* 10/71.

Recorded on tour in England, this finds the band starting to slip into its final phase, with Hodges, Brown and Anderson all gone and Ellington's own health in decline. This is nevertheless a spirited and often absorbing set. 'Togo Brava Suite' and 'La Plus Belle Africaine' don't have the feel of major Ellingtonia, but they're delivered with great brio, and there are good turns elsewhere for Turney (whose flute was new to Duke's palette), Gonsalves and the ageless Carney.

**(*) Live At The Witney

Impulse! 11732 *Ellington; Joe Benjamin (b); Rufus Jones (d).* 4/72.

Another rare concert featuring the piano-player – entirely by himself on many of the tunes. Nine rambling minutes of 'New World A-Comin'' and a tune called 'A Mural From Two Perspectives', which is so clumsily played that it seems even Duke doesn't know it, are rather discouraging. There is much kidding around with the audience on the up-tempo pieces and the hits, and he even chucks in a minute or so of 'Soda Fountain Rag', his first composition. The piano-sound is bass-heavy and there is an audible hum during quiet passages.

*** This One's For Blanton

Original Jazz Classics OJC 810 *Ellington; Ray Brown (b).* 12/72.

An inventive idea of Norman Granz, to pay tribute to Blanton via his boss and a later disciple. It's no great masterwork, though, since Ellington seems to have gone at it with the usual throwaway elegance that he invested in all of his spotlight piano work; but the interesting piece is the 'Fragmented Suite For Piano And Bass'. Probably the best of the later albums starring Duke's piano, all the same.

**(*) Duke's Big 4

Pablo 2310703 *Ellington; Joe Pass (g); Ray Brown (b); Louie Bellson (d).* 73.

A joshing sort of set that put little demand on the improvisational instincts of any of the participants. This was the kind of stuff they could all do blindfold at festivals, and apart from some of Duke's chording, which is typically unpredictable, there's not much to listen to.

***** In Sweden 1973**

Caprice 21599 *Ellington; Money Johnson, Johnny Coles, Barry Lee Hall, Mercer Ellington, Rolf Ericson (t, flhn); Vince Prudente, Art Baron, Chuck Connors, Ake Persson (tb); Russell Procope (as, cl); Harold Minerve (as, f, picc); Harold Ashby (ts, cl); Percy Msrion (ts); Harry Carney (bsm bcl); George Wein, Nils Lindberg (p); Joe Benjamin (b); Rocky White (d); Alice Babs, Anita Moore, Tony Watkins (v).* 10/73.

****(*) Eastbourne Performance**

RCA Victor Gold 74321 303162 *As above, except omit Ericson, Persson, Wein, Lindberg, Babs.* 12/73.

The Swedish concert was clearly a happy occasion, with the final Ellington band augmented by old hand Ericson, trombone master Persson and Alice Babs, a singer Duke held in high esteem. All three have their moments but Alice is especially fine on 'Serenade To Sweden' and 'Checkered Hat'. Lindberg and Wein sit in on a couple of encores and some of the poorer sides of this edition of the orchestra have been left out of the concert tapes, which are in good, clear sound.

The Eastbourne set is not quite as bad as its admittedly awful reputation. There are dreadful moments for Moore and Watkins, and some of the features seem redundant, an admission that the band as much as its master was living on borrowed time. But a final 'Creole Love Call' retains its elegance, and Ellington himself, with his characteristic ability to shrug off illness and fatigue for a performance, sounds very good on 'Pitter, Panther, Patter' – his very last officially recorded feature.

****(*) Continuum**

Fantasy 24765-2 *Cootie Williams, James 'Buddy' Bolden, Money Johnson, Barry Lee Hall, Calvin Ladner (t); Chuck Connors, Vince Prudente, Art Baron (tb); Harold Minerve, Maurice Simon, James Spaulding (as); Harold Ashby, Ricky Ford, Anatole Gerasimov (ts); Harry Carney, Joe Temperley (bs); Lloyd Mayers (p); Edward Ellington II (g); J. J. Wiggins, Larry Ridley (b); Freddie Waits, Rocky White (d).* 6/74–5/75.

Mercer did his best to keep the Ellington orchestra alive, but perhaps it was already fading away, even before its boss did. Cootie Williams returned, but he was an old man, too, and Harry Carney passed away between sessions for this album. Mercer put together a set-list which mixed chestnuts with a few neglected pieces, but the performances sound tame or tired: four previously unreleased tracks in this new edition include a 'Harlem Air Shaft' which is a pale shadow of the original. Rather a melancholy farewell.

Don Ellis (1934–78)

TRUMPET

Though born in Los Angeles, Ellis studied in Boston and worked in New York big bands in the late '50s. Played with George Russell in 1961 and cut three experimental albums of his own before forming a big band that won festival and crossover popularity, despite the music's complexity. Film-score work took up the early '70s, but a heart attack in 1975 slowed him and he died three years later.

***** ... How Time Passes ...**

Candid 9004 *Ellis; Jaki Byard (p, as); Ron Carter (b); Charli Persip (d).* 10/60.

***** Out Of Nowhere**

Candid 9032 *Ellis; Paul Bley (p); Steve Swallow (b).* 4/61.

***** New Ideas**

Original Jazz Classics OJC 431 *Ellis; Al Francis (vib); Jaki Byard (p); Ron Carter (b); Charli Persip (d).* 6/61.

*****(*) 'Live' At Monterey**

Pacific Jazz 94766-2 *Ellis; Bob Harmon, Paul Lopez, Glenn Stuart, Ed Warren, Alan Weight (t); Ron Meyers, Dave Wells (tb); Terry Woodson (btb); Reuben Leon (ss, as, f); Tom Scott (as, saxello, f); Ira Schulman (as, ts, cl); Ron Starr (ts, cl); John Magruder (bs, cl); Dave Mackay (p, org); Chuck Domanico, Ray Neapolitan, Frank De La Rosa (b); Steve Bohannon, Alan Estes (d); Chino Valdes (perc).* 9 & 10/66.

***** Live In 3⅔/4 Time**

Pacific Jazz 23996 *Very similar to above.* 10/66.

'I believe in making use of as wide a range of expressive techniques as possible,' said Ellis, who never lost sight of his own artistic credo, and made some of the most challenging music of recent times. Draw a line from Jimmy Giuffre to Maynard Ferguson, and somewhere around its imaginary midpoint you might find Don Ellis; he has been alternately praised and decried as a latter-day Kenton, but he actually belongs to a much older and more jazz-centred tradition. *How Time Passes* was made before the Third Stream finally ran dry. Half the album is devoted to 'Improvisational Suite No. 1', in which the soloists are asked to extemporize, not on chord progressions or standard melodies, but on a relatively orthodox 12-tone row, distributed among the instruments and out of which chords can be built. The material is less reminiscent of Arnold Schoenberg, who'd spent his last years in Ellis's native California, than of Ernst Krenek, another European exile to the West Coast. Miraculously, it still swings.

The title-track is loosely inspired by Stockhausen's views on musical duration. The extraordinary accelerations and decelerations of tempo are initially almost laughable; but it's a highly significant piece, and Ellis's own solo (with Byard following less convincingly on his alto saxophone 'double') is superbly structured. The ballad 'Sallie' has a more straightforward modal theme.

Out Of Nowhere is much more conventional and standards-based, but Ellis plays lines and melodic inversions of considerable inventiveness, always striking out for the microtonal terrain he was to colonize later in the '60s when he began to work on a four-valve quarter-tone trumpet. 'All The Things You Are' – a fifth take, incidentally – is quite extraordinary, running from free abstract patterns round the subdominant to fast, almost Delta-ish runs in quadruple time. The two versions of 'I Love You' show how he miscues occasionally here – but always in pursuit of metrical accents no one else was attempting at the time. Bley plays superbly, though unfortunately Swallow is a bit far back in the mix.

On *New Ideas* Ellis moves effortlessly between the D-flat blues of 'Uh Huh', the atonal 'Tragedy', the strict canon of 'Imitation' and the stark, improvisational approach of 'Despair To Hope' and a piece for unaccompanied trumpet. Even with a more conventional jazz context, the opening 'Natural H' and 'Cock And Bull' are strikingly original, with Ellis demonstrating an ability to assimilate advanced harmonic ideas to jazz. Challenging, provocative music, sympathetically recorded by Rudy Van Gelder. The band is on the case from start to finish, with a particular word of praise for Francis, who has a demanding role. Ellis's own liner-notes are very informative about his methods.

Ellis helpfully pops up with a breakdown of the 19-beat figure at the start of his big band's legendary 1966 Monterey appearance: '33 222 1 222 ... of course, that's just the area code!' Everything about Ellis's band was distinctive. He fielded three basses and three percussionists, played a four-valve, quarter-tone trumpet, and performed programmed jazz tunes with names like 'Passacaglia And Fugue' and 'Concerto For Trumpet'. All of which could seem like mere gimmickry, except that Ellis's solo on the opening track and his statements throughout the album sound absolutely like the real thing. Monterey MC Jimmy Lyons compares the impact of the band to that of the Stan Kenton Orchestra. That to some ears might sound two-edged, but, like Kenton, Ellis manages to combine intellectual sophistication and visceral impact. Hank Levy's 'Passacaglia And Fugue' is a perfect example. Tom Scott's funky solo never once diverts from classical forms but still manages to swing its butt off.

The original album also included the concerto, which was recorded a month later at the Pacific Jazz Festival; apparently the Monterey version of the same piece did not satisfy Ellis. His playing on the issued version isn't flawless, but it has great power. The reissue includes three previously unissued cuts: a short thing called 'Crete Idea', featuring trombonist Ron Meyers, the swing pastiche of 'Beat Me Daddy, Seven To The Bar' and another rhythmic exercise called – and in – '27/16'. To put this last into context, Ellis mildly notes on the album sleeve that the longest metre he had attempted to date was 85, though he modestly defers to folk forms where the count is well into three figures!

The title of the other 1966 album is difficult to render in print – three-and-two-thirds over four – but the same fascination with complex time-signatures is in evidence. Recorded at Shelly's Manne Hole and at Monterey, it now comes with extra cuts of some tracks, including a fantastic 'Freedom Jazz Dance'. 'Barnum's Revenge' and the original 'Orientation' (which some players would dis-) are the most entertaining and provocative cuts and the remastered sound is very good indeed.

★★★★ Electric Bath

Columbia CK 65522 *Ellis; Bob Harmon, Glenn Stuart, Ed Warren, Alan Weight (t); Ron Meyers, David Sanchez, Terry Woodson (tb); Reuben Leon, Joe Roccisano (as, ss, f); Ira Schulman (ts, f, picc, cl); Ron Starr (ts, f, cl); John Magruder (bs, f, bcl); Mike Lang (p, ky); Ray Neapolitan (b, sitar); Frank De La Rosa (b); Dave Parlato (b); Steve Bohannon (d); Alan Estes, Mark Stevens, Chino Valdes (perc).* 9/67.

In 1966 the world of music seemed a much bigger place. The Beatles were still reinventing the popular song, John Coltrane, Ornette Coleman and Cecil Taylor were rethinking harmony and melody, and Ravi Shankar was teaching the West that Western music was just one among many. Don Ellis had already staked his place in that great experiment; but with *Electric Bath*, recorded at the high-water mark of the rock revolution, he showed that jazz – albeit unorthodox – could still generate the level of excitement youngsters had come to expect as of right. To hear it from another perspective, *Electric Bath* was recorded in the same year as John Coltrane's death and doesn't for a moment cede priority to Trane's harmonic and rhythmic innovations.

As with earlier work, what immediately strikes the listener is a whole slew of unexpected time-signatures, but by this stage in his career Ellis had no difficulty in combining metrical complexity with hot blowing. His own solos on 'Indian Lady' and 'Turkish Bath' are endlessly fascinating. Even seasoned brass players, perhaps forgetting that four-valve horn, still wonder how some of the phrases were articulated. The orchestra isn't quite up to speed all the time. Asking a working band to play and swing in 17/4 is asking a lot, and yet the lineaments of the music are as clear today as they must have seemed baffling 30 years ago. The new issue is superbly remastered, with a ripe, fruity bass. Rounding out an entrancing album are the single versions of both the compositions mentioned above. What happened when 'Turkish Bath' or 'Indian Lady' came on the jukebox or the car radio? How many listeners stopped dancing or wondered if they were on the brink of a Roswell moment? No one else sounded like this. Tough as it sometimes is, Ellis's music is never less than exhilarating.

★★★ Shock Treatment

Koch 8590 *Very similar to above.* 2/68.

★★★ Live At Montreux

Koch Jazz 51410 *Ellis; Jack Coanm, Gil Rathel, Glenn Stuart (t); Alan Kaplan (tb); Richard Bullock (btb); Sidney Muldrow (frhn); Jim Self (tba); James Coile, Ann Patterson, Jim Snodgrass (reeds); Randy Kerber (p, ky); Laurie Badessa, Pam Tompkins (vn); Jimbo Ross (vla); Paula Hochhalter (clo); Darrell Clayborn (b); Leon Gaer (b, elec); Dave Crigger (d, perc); Mike Englander, Ruth Ritchie (perc).* 7/77.

Originally on Columbia, *Shock Treatment* is now available with half a dozen bonus tracks, including the mysterious 'Zim' and 'Rasty' and a fine, if unorthodox, version of 'I Remember Clifford'. There are signs that Ellis was moving in a more commercial direction at this point, perhaps aware that jazz was still losing ground to pop and rock, though he must also have known that as long as popular music is dance-driven, it was unlikely that his work would ever have a major market presence. His playing is still adventurous and bright, but the band misses Tom Scott, who seemed to buy into the Ellis philosophy more comfortably than any of the other soloists.

The Montreux set (not to be confused with the Monterey gig) has only recently reappeared, and it comes with three bonus tracks, including the long, extraordinary 'Arcturus'. Newcomers to Ellis Island will find that their usual compass bearings are overthrown and may find the complex time-signatures and weird harmonies a little hard to take. 'Open Wide' and 'Niner Two' are worth sampling, but if you haven't experienced the trumpeter's work before, *Electric Bath* (above) is a much more comfortable place to soak.

Herb Ellis (born 1921)

GUITAR

Studied at North Texas State and played with Jimmy Dorsey in the '40s. Major association was with the Oscar Peterson Trio, 1953–8, and as an accompanist to singers. Much studio work and subsequent club dates as a senior swing-to-bop stylist.

★★★★ Nothin' But The Blues

Verve 521674-2 *Ellis; Roy Eldridge, Dizzy Gillespie (t); Stan Getz, Coleman Hawkins (ts); Oscar Peterson (p); Ray Brown (b); Stan Levey, Gus Johnson (d).* 10/57–5/58.

This is the classic Ellis album, cut in 1957 with a small group of Eldridge, Getz, Brown and Levey in tow. Despite the magisterial presence of the horns – Eldridge is absolutely commanding, peeling off some scalding open-horn choruses and a lovely, stealthy one with the mute on 'Tin Roof Blues', and Getz does his stomping-tenorman bit as well as the lyrical one – it's the guitarist who sets the tone. Soft-spoken but swinging, artfully pushing the music forward, colouring the harmonies and opening up the pianoless group's sound, Ellis leads from behind and takes some of his best solos too. There are eight terrific tracks like this, with four makeweights from a session for some film music in which Gillespie and Hawkins also have brief cameos. In beautiful remastered sound.

***** In The Pocket**

Concord CCD2-2154-2 2CD *Ellis; Harry 'Sweets' Edison (t); Plas Johnson (ts); Mike Melvoin; George Duke (ky); Ray Brown (b); Jake Hanna (d).* 75–76.

Ellis was one of the early members of the Concord stable and his first discs for the label set something of the house style: tempos at an easy jog, standard programmes with one or two eccentric choices, and bands that are like an assembly of old rogues joshing one another about old glories. The two albums with Edison and Brown have now been reissued as the twofer *In The Pocket*, and while there's nothing exactly surprising here, it's all thoroughly enjoyable in its comforting way: Ellis digs in, the trumpeter turns in some of his wryest solos, and Brown is insuperably masterful as always.

***** An Evening With Herb Ellis**

Jazz Focus JFCD019 *Ellis; Bill MacDonough (p); Chuck Israels (b); John Nolan (d).* 2/95.

Not a bad way to spend an evening. The Ellis trademarks – a gutsy, physical style of playing, with his south-west twanging delivery, independence of single-string lines and bluesy chording – are intact and well to the fore. But it does seem like a simple pick-up date, with the rhythm section doing little more than their duty.

Liberty Ellman (born 1971)

GUITAR

Born in London, raised in the Bay Area, Ellman had a solid grounding as a member of Greg Osby's group, but has made his own associations and after moving to New York in 1998 has been an increasingly visible presence with an approach to style that blends M-Base jazz, hip-hop and other styles.

***** Orthodox**

Noir 12 *Ellman; Eric Crystal (ts); Vijay Iyer (g); Brad Hargreaves (d); Babou Sagne (djembe); DJ Pause (turntables).* 98

***** Tactiles**

Pi 108 *Ellman; Greg Osby (as); Mark Shim (ts); Stephan Crump (b); Eric Harland (d).* 02.

An angular but refreshingly understated player, Ellman does not hog the foreground on either of these releases. His funk and hip-hop mannerisms are more than that, components of a genuinely original attack and language. The debut album starts with turntable effects on 'Translator' and closes with a lovely guitar/piano duet on Billy Strayhorn's haunting 'Blood Count'. It's a spectrum that gives an important measure of how important jazz is to Ellman. His funk stylings on a piece like 'Psi Missing' are still open and improvisational, his grooves consistently unpredictable, and in Iyer he is joined by one of the rising stars of the new music.

The sophomore effort is a lot more polished than the designation makes it sound. Working with saxophonists – Shim mainly, but with three guest spots from Osby – strongly reinforces the jazz lineage. The opening is tentative but with the second track, 'Clean is Rich', the group's blowing potential becomes obvious, Ellman lays down an elegantly asymmetrical solo before giving way to Shim's attractively staccato feature, A repetitive scale sets the music off in a different direction entirely.

Old boss Osby comes in on the moody 'Temporary Aid', floating in behind the guitarist's softly stated chords and sounding disconcertingly like Johnny Hodges for a phrase or two. Greg is also back for 'How Many Texts' and 'Ultraviolet', which are closer to the M-Base idiom. A special word, too, for drummer Harland, who cements these cuts with a brilliantly varied pulse and a lovely range of timbres and sonorities.

Ziggy Elman (1914–68)

TRUMPET

Joined Benny Goodman in 1936, then was with Tommy Dorsey, 1940–47, before leading own (unsuccessful) big band. After that, worked mostly in TV and radio, though alcohol troubled his later years. His 1938–9 sessions were feature dates with a studio band.

***** Ziggy Elman 1938–39**

Classics 900 *Elman; Noni Bernardi, Toots Mondello, Hymie Schertzer (as); Jerry Jerome, Arthur Rollini, Babe Russin (ts); Milt Raskin, Jess Stacy (p); Ben Heller (g); Artie Bernstein, Harry Goodman, Joe Schwartzman (b); Nick Fatool, Al Kendis (d).* 12/38–12/39.

***** Ziggy Elman And His Orchestra, 1947**

Circle CCD 70 *Elman; Harry DeVito (tb); Clint Garvin (cl); Johnny Hayes (ts); Virginia Maxey, Bob Manning (v); other personnel unidentified.* 3–4/47.

The man born Harry Finkelman played trumpet with enormous power, but he has somehow been dismissed in recent years as a *Schmaltzmeister* with no real jazz feel. Ziggy's image was set in stone by his appearance as himself in *The Benny Goodman Story*, though by then he was too ill to play his own solos, and his parts had to be dubbed in by Mannie Klein. Goodman had hired him in 1936, impressed by his adaptability and tone (and not put off by the weird embouchure; Ziggy played, literally, out of the side of his mouth). The post-war material is better known, but it is never much more than routine. Johnny Hayes is a similarly underrated player, but he was to do more interesting things elsewhere, and DeVito always had fascinating ideas to share. What made the pre-war band interesting was the unusual front line of single trumpet and saxophone section. 'Fralich In Swing' is a Jewish wedding-dance tune which Goodman had turned into a hit song, 'And The Angels Sing'. It loses none of its freshness with Elman blaring away in front. The remaining material for Bluebird sticks to the basic formula and relies on essentially the same pool of Goodman-trained players, which may account for the tightness of the section work. The absence of Goodman may account for the joyous, just-let-out-of-jail quality of some of the playing. Noni Bernardi is exceptional, immediately distinguishable from his fellow-altoists, and Jess Stacy and Milt Raskin hold down the chords with calm precision. The sound-quality on the whole is good, though there is some distortion on the December 1938 session, which may be an artefact on the transfers or, more likely, a result of engineers unused to Elman's bravura style.

Kahil El'Zabar

DRUMS, PERCUSSION, FLUTE

A prime mover in contemporary Chicago jazz, and a leading light among the spirits who emerged from the '70s period of the AACM, El'Zabar is a drummer-percussionist who uses individual hand drums as often as the regular kit. His small-scale groups, such as the Ethnic Heritage Ensemble and the Ritual Trio, seek big-scale results in terms of creating new Afro-American fusions.

***** Big Cliff**
Delmark DE-477 *El'Zabar; Ari Brown (ts, p); Billy Bang (vn); Malachi Favors (b). 9/94.*

*****(*) 21st Century Union March**
Silkheart SHCD 142 *El'Zabar; Joseph Bowie (tb, perc); Edward Wilkerson (ts, acl, perc). 6/95.*

*****(*) Love Outside Of Dreams**
Delmark DG-541 *El'Zabar; David Murray (ts, bcl); Fred Hopkins (b). 5/97.*

***** Jitterbug Junction**
CIMP 150 *El'Zabar; Ari Brown (ts, ss); Malachi Favors (b). 6/97.*

El'Zabar is a percussionist with a knack for creating exciting musical situations out of elemental materials. His most long-standing group is the Ethnic Heritage Ensemble, although their early records are all currently unavailable. The team has an almost chamberish feel on *21st Century Union March.* Bowie takes a prominent soloist's role, Wilkerson seems reserved, and the music has a gentle way of unfolding, even when El'Zabar works up some thunder at his various drums. There is some merely filled-in time, but the best of it has all the group's qualities on show and it remains a unique ensemble.

The Ritual Trio is responsible for the CIMP session, which is generally more volatile and loudly spoken. Brown isn't as strong a player as Wilkerson, and the attempted masterwork in 'The Sweet Nectar Of Cacophony' is finally unconvincing, but the dedication to Coltrane miniaturizes the quartet's passions rather effectively, and the trio plays with great enthusiasm.

Big Cliff gets its biggest kicks out of the title-piece, in which Bang and Brown take boiling solos, and the funky fun of 'Another Kind Of Groove', where the sawing violin over the bomp rhythms starts to get a hypnotic happening under way. Though the music is dedicated to El'Zabar's late father, it is celebratory; scarcely a new take either on what he's done before or on Chicago jazz itself, it's nevertheless a very satisfying record.

Love Outside Of Dreams appeared only recently. El'Zabar and Murray clearly get on well in musical terms (as the final disc in this entry suggests) and this free-flowing date recalls some of the saxophonist's exciting early records, particularly in the likes of 'The Ebullient Duke'.

*****(*) Papa's Bounce**
CIMP 167 *El'Zabar; Joseph Bowie (tb, perc); Ernest Dawkins (as, ts); Atu Harold Murray (perc, f). 2/98.*

****** Freedom Jazz Dance**
Delmark DE-517 *As above, except Fareed Haque (g, perc) replaces Murray. 3/99.*

CIMP's dry, 'real' sound suits the EHE just fine, and it's seldom made a record that sounds as lucid and spontaneous as *Papa's Bounce.* Dawkins is an excellent recruit, the whole tradition of Chicago saxophone running through his greasy, gritty yet perversely romantic sound, and Bowie's range of trombone effects seems to have been extended. When El'Zabar hits on a multi-kulti groove like 'Blue Rwanda', he gets as close as anyone has to blending the different deltas of Afro-American sound with an ancestral tinge.

The addition of Haque gives the band yet another sound, even while working off the same simple formula of two horns and a drum. The title-piece nods towards El'Zabar's Chicagoan mentor, Eddie Harris, and allows Dawkins to uncork one of his most sweeping solos, starting out in bebop and pulsing in and out of the tradition from there. Haque doesn't get in the way of the horns, here or elsewhere, but he provides a new, lean textural ground for them to work from in addition to the leader's colourful beats. That gives an extra pinch of harmonic spice to tracks such as 'Katon' and 'So Low But Not Alone'. And Bowie seems to progress with every record. The result is arguably the best EHE album to date.

***** Spirits Entering**
Delmark DE-533 *El'Zabar; Billy Bang (vn). 7/99.*

****(*) The Power**
CIMP 205 *As above, except add Hamiet Bluiett (f, bsx, cbsx). 7/99.*

The duo set with Bang has some splendid music, though it's compromised a little by the dry and thin tone the violinist has in the mix. El'Zabar makes enough noise to drown out Bang at times, but in the more mellifluous passages it's a fine match.

Not so the trio date for CIMP. The notes refer evasively to some arguments among the musicians and the producers, and whatever waffle there is about anger transmuting into musical power, this was clearly not a happy session. Bluiett seems like a dead weight for much of the way (and despite the instrumental credits, he sounds as if he's playing his usual baritone rather than bass sax, at least some of the time), although that said there are still a few beautiful moments, such as the fingertip delicacy of 'Moment's Resolution'.

**** Conversations**
Delmark DE-514 *El'Zabar; Archie Shepp (ts); Ari Brown (ts, p); Malachi Favors (b). 1/99.*

**** Africa N'Da Blues**
Delmark DE-519 *As above, except Pharoah Sanders (ts) replaces Shepp. 12/99.*

Oh dear – no, no, and again we say, no. Not a bad idea of El'Zabar to harness some fine old spirits of the vintage Chicago avant-garde, but he made the forgivable – though disastrous – mistake of asking Archie Shepp to be one of them. Shepp's ludicrous, fumbling playing is all wrong, and when poor Ari Brown (who has to settle for the piano for much of the date) was allowed to get his saxophone out, the results should have made Shepp pack up and go home. El'Zabar and Favors still manage to get some grooves going, so two stars for them anyway.

Frankly, the collaboration with Sanders is hardly any improvement. Pharoah does some reasonable work, although he largely continues to coast on his reputation, and again having Brown at the piano is a mistake; he's not a very good piano-player, and the trio feature of 'Autumn Leaves' is a waste of time. All of this might sound all right live in some funky basement, but as a record it's not much better than feeble.

*****(*) One World Family**

CIMP 220 *El'Zabar; David Murray (ts, bcl).* 3/00.

A lovely session, from the quietly ruminative discourse of 'Ryan's Groove' to the closing optimism of the title-track. While it ties in with Murray's increasing immersion in a kind of global jazz, it also looks back to the sparse textures and open feel of his early recordings. El'Zabar inevitably comes off as a second banana in these duets, but he gives Murray a juicy collection of beats and pulses to work from.

James Emery (born 1951)

GUITAR

An innovative and imaginative guitarist who took his cue from Charlie Parker, Emery quickly made his own synthesis of modern jazz styles. He is perhaps still best known as a member of the String Trio Of New York, but his own recording career has taken off with a number of highly distinctive albums.

****** Standing On A Whale Fishing For Minnows**

Enja ENJ 9312-2 *Emery; Marty Ehrlich (as, cl, f); Michael Formanek (b); Gerry Hemingway (d, mar, vib).* 9–10/96.

****** Spectral Domains**

Enja ENJ 9344-2 *Emery; Marty Ehrlich (ss, as, f); Chris Speed (ts, cl); Kevin Norton (vib, mar, perc); Mark Feldman (vn); Michael Formanek (b); Gerry Hemingway (d).* 9/97.

Emery had recorded once or twice before, but even if this isn't a CD debut, *Standing ...* is a cracking achievement for a player who hadn't yet made much impact as a leader. The group is perfectly poised and balanced and, with Ehrlich's usual range of horns and voices and Hemingway's superb touch on marimbas and vibes as well as the kit, the range of sound is quite startling.

The title-track is a turbulent, angular thing, with Hemingway strongly featured. Ehrlich understandably takes the lead voice on most tracks, though it's often what Emery himself is doing underneath which merits attention, and his deployment of guitar and soprano guitar, and the hard-to-pin-down sounds on the downhome 'Texas Koto Blues' are continuously interesting. Just one standard, a throwaway 'Crepuscule With Nellie'; otherwise all the songs are Emery's own, combining power and wit, a straightahead feel and subtle inflexions from outside jazz altogether. Great name, great record.

Monk features again on the second record, where one of the key tracks is a crisp version of 'Trinkle Tinkle'. Equally briefly, Emery attacks Ornette's 'Kathelin Gray' and comes up with a version that knocks the composer's into a cocked hat. His own interest in the interface between jazz and modern composition is most obvious on 'Chromosphere' and the long – perhaps overlong – 'Sound Action Seven', where he manages to balance open-form improvisation with subtle writing. A version of 'Standing On A Whale ...' suggests how far he has stretched even in a year. Hemingway and Formanek are magnificent and the horns and violin fill out a hugely expansive sound.

*****(*) Luminous Cycles**

Between the Lines btl 015 *As above, except omit Formanek; add Drew Gress (b).* 10/00.

The now familiar sextet configuration continues to yield results. Emery cleverly pairs the clarinets on the title-track, a nervy, stop-start theme that has its feet in bebop and its ambitions elsewhere entirely. That also goes for the following 'One Red Thread', a slowly weaving idea that has connections with Eric Dolphy's *Out To Lunch* session. Emery ranges between hard-scrabble riffs in complex time and more delicate picked rubato lines, like the introduction to 'Beyond Words'. Speed's clarinet solo is an old-fashioned delight, almost swing era in its shaping. As ever, Hemingway and Norton provide thoroughly musical accompaniment. Not a significant advance in Emery's musical language, but a confident consolidation.

****** Transformations**

Between the Lines btl 027 *Emery; Franz Koglmann (flhn); Tony Coe (ts, cl); Peter Herbert (b); Emilio Pomarico (cond); Klangforum Wien.* 9/01.

This is an extremely impressive achievement, a large-scale work for orchestra and improvising musicians. There is every ground for suspicion of projects of this stamp. All too often either the orchestration is a bland and dispensable backdrop for the improvisers, or looked at the other way, the improvisers are there to add some figure and detail to a fairly dull orchestral conception. The miracle of 'Transformations' is that Emery has managed to create a strong musical architecture *and* a context for improvisation. The pairing of Coe and Koglmann reflects his own ambivalent take on jazz, a mixture of deep, romantic commitment and a certain scepticism. Koglmann's solos frequently draw attention to jazz history, but they ironize it at the same time. Coe is more of a fundamentalist and his lovely tone imparts a warmth and intensity to the most abstract passages. Emery starts the whole thing off with a movement called 'Archai', which might refer to both strings and the distant past.

Arranged in five connected sections with three interludes, 'Transformations' is the pinnacle of Emery's career so far, a work of real depth and resonance and one which repays frequent hearings. Under Emilio Pomarico, the Klangforum Wien plays with confident gusto and precision. The set is rounded out by a sequence of quartets on which Peter Herbert is the additional soloist. 'Down Home Tone Poem' and 'Bird's Nest' are further interesting reflections on what jazz is about in the 21st century. A perfect match of artist and label.

Giuseppe Emmanuele

PIANO

Catanian pianist, with a Bill Evans character, but exploring the wider reaches of the jazz tradition too.

***** A Waltz For Debby**

Splasc(h) H 200 *Emmanuele; Paolo Fresu (t, flhn); Pietro Tonolo (ss, ts); Nello Toscano (b); Pucci Nicosia (d).* 1/90.

***** Reflections In Jazz**

Splasc(h) H 389-2 *As above, except Orazio Maugeri (as), Paolo Mappa (d) replace Fresu and Nicosia.* 12/91.

A Waltz For Debby is a lovely record. Emmanuele is a Bill Evans admirer, and the quintet's version of the title-song pays suitable homage to its composer; but the four originals by the pianist show a light but clear watermark of his own, and he plays with strength as well as delicacy: the solo on an unusually sunny reading of Lennie Tristano's 'Wow' even suggests some of the energy of the young Tristano himself. Fresu and Tonolo, though, are probably the most accomplished players here and both have plenty of chances to shine. *Reflections In Jazz* is perhaps a degree less involving: Maugeri is a bustling player, but Fresu's elegance is missed and, though there is a limpid version of Ellington's 'On A Turquoise Cloud' to commence with, Emmanuele's music seems a fraction less beguiling this time. Tonolo, though, continues to impress.

***** Into The Tradition**

Splasc(h) H 458-2 *Emmanuele; Giovanni La Ferlita, Maurizio Agosta, Giuseppe Privitera, Enzo Gulizia, Vito Giordano (t); Camillo Pavone, Antonio Caldarella, Filippo Nascone Pistone, Matteo Miraglia (tb); Salvo Famiani, Ercole Tringale, Carlo Cattano, Umberto Di Pietro, Salvo Arena, Giancarlo Cutuli, Larry Smith (reeds); Claudio Cusmano (g); Nello Toscano (b); Pucci Nicosia (d); Maria Patti (v).* 3/95.

Emmanuele arranges ten pieces, most of them standards, for the City Brass Orkestra. The occasional wobble in the section-work wouldn't be tolerated in American big bands but there's a compensating sense of Mediterranean sun in the melodic fabric and Emmanuele likes to keep them busy in his charts – there's always something interesting to listen to, even if the soloists aren't especially arresting. Guest Larry Smith does the most ear-grabbing things on alto.

***** From USA To Mediterraneo**

Splasc(h) 486-2 *Emmanuele; Alberto Amato (b); Pucci Nicosia (d).* 5/96.

*****(*) Reflection No. 2**

Splasc(h) 673-2 *As above, except add Vito Giordano (t, flhn), Pietro Tonolo (ss, ts); strings.* 7/96–7/98.

The trio record is nicely titled: it starts with three American tunes and, for the rest, relies on Emmanuele himself and other Italians for the compositions. On this showing, though, America's ahead. Bix Beiderbecke's 'In A Mist' is an audacious choice, and it's handsomely transformed into a modern vehicle; 'All The Things You Are' and Ellington's 'Reflection In D' are just as good. But the unfamiliar pieces are less strongly characterized and the playing is gracious but not always involving.

The quintet date is stronger, with a new version of 'Fine Stagione' from the previous record, and flavoursome treatments of 'Time Remembered' and 'Israel'. The use of strings adds a further element; though they were recorded two years after the quintet set down their music, Emmanuele has cleverly integrated the scoring and they're used to darken rather than sweeten the situation.

Buddie Emmons

STEEL GUITAR

Country music session-man makes jazz album!

****(*) Steel Guitar Jazz**

Verve 542536-2 *Emmons; Jerome Richardson (ss, ts); Bobby Scott (p); Art Davis (b); Charli Persip (d).* 7/63.

'The birth of a new instrument in jazz' trumpeted the sleeve of this 1963 Mercury album, but the results weren't so much stillborn as quickly sent away for adoption. Buddie plays the blues capably enough on 'Bluemmons', but a lot of this is plain silly, and Jerome Richardson must have been shaking his head when they did 'Oleo' and 'The Preacher'. The sleeve-notes describe the steel guitar's antics as 'tasteful and judicious', which is about as damning a bit of faint praise as one could wish for. Thereafter, Emmons went back to more Nashville-oriented work.

Johannes Enders (born 1967)

TENOR AND SOPRANO SAXOPHONES

A Bavarian by birth, Enders studied in Munich and Graz before spending time in the USA. Back in Munich he's played in both straightahead and fusion-led outfits such as Mars Mobil.

***** Bright Nights**

Enja 9352-2 *Enders; Ingrid Jensen (t, flhn); George Colligan (p); Dwayne Burno (b); Howard Curtis (d).* 11/97.

***** Quiet Fire**

Enja 9390-2 *Enders; Vincent Herring (ss, as); Roberto Di Gioia (p); Marc Abrams (b); Rick Hollander (d).* 4/99.

Enders doesn't impose himself enough to dominate *Bright Nights*, though considering the calibre of the band that's hardly severe criticism. The four originals are meaty enough to feed the soloists and '400 Years Ago Tomorrow' (Walter Davis) and 'Butterfly' (Hancock) are expert picks from the jazz book. It's all solid, purposeful work. Having Colligan play electric piano – and he's busy with it – lends a different stroke to the ensembles, and the long 'Brooklyn Blue' works itself up to a fine, controlled intensity.

Vincent Herring contributed an admiring sleeve-note to the first record, and he's on board for *Quiet Fire*. Where Enders had more of a visitor status on the New York date, *Quiet Fire* was cut on home German turf, and there's a more punctilious feel to material and delivery, even as both horns are prone to prodigious heat. The marathon opener, 'Day Number One', works off a relentless vamp which the saxophonists relish, and it feels as if it could usefully go on for even longer than it does. But the later parts of the session have a more prosaic turn to them. 'Norwegian Wood' sounds like the Coltrane quartet doing 'Chim Chim Cheree', and the sense that the two horns are standing in for Trane and Adderley is sometimes uncomfortable, as energetic as the playing is.

***** Monolith**

Enja 9433-2 *Enders; Micha Acher (flhn); Roberto Di Gioia (p); Joe Locke (vib); Wolfgang Muthspiel (g); Ed Howard, Thomas Stabenow, Patrick Scales (b); Christian Salfellner, Markus Acher (d); Rebekka Bakken (v).* n.d.

Enders has been working with members of the 'Weilheim underground', yet another European 'scene', and this record is mostly about electronic textures, beats and harmonies. At least he puts his reed instruments right at the front of the mix, and plays some attractive solos intermingling with various juicy synthetic sounds. It's actually quite a pretty record, even if the occasional beat does threaten to blow out the speakers. Guests such as Muthspiel, Bakken and Locke contribute the usual interesting bits and pieces.

Sidsel Endresen (born 1952)

VOCALS

Norwegian vocalist starting in folk parameters and moving towards a free expression.

***** So I Write**
ECM 841776-2 *Endresen; Nils Petter Molvaer (t, flhn, perc); Django Bates (p); Jon Christensen (d).* 6/90.

*****(*) Exile**
ECM 521721-2 *As above, except add Bugge Wesseltoft (ky); David Darling (clo).* 8/93.

***** Nightsong**
ACT 9004-2 *Endresen; Bugge Wesseltoft (p, syn).* 94.

*****(*) Duplex Ride**
ACT 9000-2 *As above, except add Jon Bang (v).* 97–98.

***** Undertow**
Jazzland 548195-2 *Endresen; Nils Petter Molvaer (t); Patrick Shaw Iversen (f); Roger Ludvigsen (g, perc); Audun Klieve (d); Bugge Wesseltoft (perc).* 00.

*****(*) Out Here, In There**
Jazzland 017368-2 *Endresen; Bugge Wesseltoft (ky, elec).* 01.

Working rather obliquely outwards from a jazz/folk/ improvised idiom, Endresen sings with a deceptive range that pushes her up into the lyric-soprano register and down into contralto accents on the more sombre songs. Jon Balke's settings on the first record, to 'So I Write', 'This Is The Movie' and 'Dreamland', perfectly suit her slightly prosaic lyrics. There are no up-tempo tracks but, whether singing exactly on the beat or drawing out the words without any pretext of verse-metre, Endresen seems completely confident, and the accompanying group is superb though often minimal in gesture. Bates – who's credited with the two weakest compositions – plays beautifully: no electronics, no horn, no additional percussion, just beautifully modulated stylings which accord with the accompanist's duty to point up the words without swamping them.

The second record has a much richer instrumental palette. Bates takes along his tenor horn. Endresen's singing is stronger and more pointedly articulated, so there is no risk of her being overpowered. The songs are interspersed with instrumental variations in which Darling plays a big part, and the overall impact is of a much more musicianly product, carefully thought out and immaculately performed.

Endresen's relationship with Wesseltoft has yielded some classic live performances. The later album is a better measure of what they have done together. It combines some entirely improvised pieces with repertory material like the classic Paul Simon song, 'Fifty Ways To Leave Your Lover', which Endresen turns into a slow, bleached lament. Following it is 'And Later, The Rain', a quiet narrative of loss accompanied by soft, aggrieved percussion. 'Duplex Ride' itself combines recitative with abstract vocal sounds, synth patterns and an uneasy journey across London. 'Six Minutes Or So' is a scarifying inscape, anxious, stressed, moving and completely musical.

Nightsong is more conventional, not because it contains standard material like 'The Lady Is A Tramp' and 'I Think It's Gonna Rain Today', but because the relation between vocal line and accompaniment is so much less challenging. Even so, both of these albums are fascinating extensions of what Endresen has done before. The two Jazzland releases find Endresen again getting the Svengali treatment from Bugge Wesseltoft. Fortunately, she has her own way to go too. Both discs are portfolios of lyrics and soundscapes rather than collections of songs, and making her whispery progress through them, Sidsel has never sounded more distinctive. There are some misconceived things on *Undertow*, but the more allusive second record has much to intrigue.

Enten Eller

GROUP

Piedmontese bop-to-fusion band, formed in the late '80s.

***** Antigone**
Splasc(h) H 352-2 *Mario Simeoni (ts, f); Carlo Actis Dato (ts, bs, bcl); Ugo Boscain (p); Giovanni Maier (b); Massimo Barbiero (d); Alex Rolle, Andrea Stracuzzi (perc).* 1/91.

***** Medea**
CMC 9961-2 *Alberto Mandarini (t, flhn, v); Maurizio Brunod (g); Rocco de Lucia (b); Massimo Barbiero (d).* 1–2/96.

****(*) Trait D'Union**
Splasc(h) 623 *Alberto Mandarini (t, flhn); Maurizio Brunod (g); Giovanni Maier (b); Massimo Barbiero (d, mar).* 4/97.

***** Melquiades**
Splasc(h) 805 *As above, except add Tim Berne (as).* 5/99.

***** Auto Da Fe**
Splasc(h) 819-2 *As above.* 00.

This band is from Piedmont, which has spawned several of the best of the newer Italian groups (Enrico Fazio, Claudio Lodati, Carlo Actis Dato). *Antigone* is their second album and is, if anything, even more brawling than their rough-and-ready earlier set, with the opening tracks, 'Il Mago' and 'Pragma', blown open by Actis Dato and Simeoni; but a lengthy set also includes ballads, and the basic quintet know each other's moves to make this blend of modal, bop and fusion leanings into an entertaining whole.

Medea and *Trait D'Union* pick up the thread a full six years on, with a very different line-up. Brunod's guitar tends to set the tone, which leans towards out-and-out fusion, although Mandarini makes sure that some bop vernacular survives. There are stabs at completely free playing and both sets are altogether more temperate, sometimes moving towards sound-painting. For all its frequent energy, this is rather bland stuff.

Melquiades brings in Tim Berne as surprise guest star. As if under threat, Brunod doubles his assault and introduces more loops, effects and whatever else he can think of to keep the attention; even so, there are still moments of quiet such as 'Per Emmanuela'. Berne seems content to be a band member but still gets in some imposing remarks. There is a return match for the pairing on *Auto Da Fe*, with rather mixed results. The group seem to be increasingly moving towards a free (or at least an open-ended) preference, but bassist and drummer seem unsure of which way to play it, and some interesting improvising could use a better anchor.

***** Euclide**
Splasc(h) CDH 919.2 *Alberto Mandarini (t, flhn); Lauro Rossi (tb); Achille Succi (as, cl); Maurizio Brunod (g); Giovanni Maier (b); Massimo Barbiero (d).* 7/03.

Another new line-up for the band. Rossi's mournful trombone makes an early impression on 'Cruna', and the group sounds at its most effective in this kind of processional piece. But the funk-into-free of 'Funkhit', up next, is another false step. Thereafter the music's distinctly hit and miss, veering from thoughtful formality to crusty free playing, Brunod again alternating as hero and villain. They clearly like a mixed palette, but settling for one style over another seems to be a struggle.

Hannes Enzlberger

DOUBLE BASS

Gifted Austrian bassist and composer. Has Carla Bley fixation.

***** Songs To Anything That Moves**

Between the Lines btl 022 *Enzlberger; Thomas Berghammer (flhn); Oskar Aichinger (p).* 00.

*****(*) Tango 1–8**

Between the Lines btl 030 *Enzlberger; Thomas Berghammer (flhn); Otto Lechner (acc).* 2/01.

Despite the title, which is taken from her *Escalator Over The Hill*, the first album has nothing to do with Carla Bley beyond a certain level of creative inspiration. In company with Berghammer and fellow BTL artist Aichinger, Enzlberger creates delicately nuanced chamber jazz of a pleasingly abstract sort. After three long opening tracks, of which 'Heisse Nacht' is the most successful, the bassist presents a suite of short pieces under the generic title 'Sieben Versatzstücke'. These are not quite miniatures and not quite songs either, and it is not entirely clear what thematic relationship there is between the elements. They do, however, eventually cohere convincingly.

The Bley influence is more overt (though unstated) on *Tango 1–8*, a project suffused with the sardonic spirit of her 'Reactionary Tango'. Eight tangos are interspersed by improvised solos and duos, again featuring the delicate, Koglmann-like flugelhorn of Thomas Berghammer but this time instead of piano the accordion of Otto Lechner. Fine as he is on his instrument, Enzlberger is more interesting as a composer. His ideas develop logically but also laterally and he takes the source material into some unexpectedly fruitful areas. Almost inevitably, Berghammer is the dominant voice. His delicacy conceals a toughness as he reveals in duo with the leader and when he energizes the music with hot rips and runs.

Rolf Ericson (1922–97)

TRUMPET

Born in Stockholm, he learned trumpet as a child and, after playing with local groups, went to the USA in 1947. Acquired experience with a wide range of leaders, from Charlie Barnet and Woody Herman to Charles Mingus, eventually joining Ellington in 1963. Also returned home to tour, lead his own Swedish big band and take a sojourn in Berlin. One of the Europeans who made most international impact in the '40s and '50s.

***** Rolf Ericson & The American Stars 1956**

Dragon DRCD 255 *Ericson; Lars Gullin, Cecil Payne (bs); Duke Jordan, Freddie Redd (p); Tommy Potter, John Simmons (b); Joe Harris, Art Taylor (d); Ernestine Anderson (v).* 6 & 7/56.

***** Stockholm Sweetnin'**

Dragon DRCD 256 *Ericson; Nisse Sandström (ts, p); Claes Crona (p); Goran Lindberg (b); Mel Lewis (d).* 8/84–7/85.

***** Ellington & Strayhorn**

Sittel SITCD 9223 *Ericson; Lennart Aberg (ss, ts, f); Bobo Stenson (p); Goran Klinghagen, Max Schultz (g); Dan Berglund (b); Egil Johansen (d); Rose-Marie Aberg (v).* 1/95.

****** I Love You So ...**

Amigo AMCD 879 *Ericson; Bernt Rosengren (ts); Lars Sjøsten (p); Bjorn Alke (b); Fredrik Norén (d).* 97.

The gifted and likeable Ericson left a very fine legacy on record, though comparatively little is under his own name. A totally reliable section-player – Lew Soloff or Jack Walrath would be obvious current parallels – he tended to hide away a gentler and more lyrical side, and it's this which comes out on *I Love You So* ... which reached us, bizarrely, the day Ericson's death was announced.

The 1956 recordings date from a tour when Rolf was asked to front a band of Americans for a Swedish visit. The first tour was wrecked by the narcotic problems of two of the visitors, and only four tracks by this sextet survive. The bulk of this disc has Ericson and Gullin in the front line, with Redd, Potter and Harris in the rhythm section. Despite the problems, the tour was instrumental in bringing a wave of hard bop to Sweden, previously drawn more to American cool. Ericson and Gullin are in brimming form, though the live recording isn't ideal. Anderson sings on six tracks.

Ericson was still in fine fettle on the 1984 date for Dragon: a good, juicy selection of jazz tunes and standards by an accomplished band, with Sandstrom's Lestorian tenor a fine foil for the trumpet; there are four previously unreleased trumpet–piano duets as a bonus on the CD. Ericson takes things a little more gingerly on the set of Ellington and Strayhorn tunes for Sittel, but it's an even better band – Aberg's solemn tenor, Stenson's unfailingly intelligent piano, the light, deep rhythm section. One or two too-obvious choices, but a couple of nice rarities – and the studio sound is gorgeous: try Rolf's muted work on 'Star-Crossed Lovers'.

The title-piece on *I Love You So* ... is the only Ericson composition on a set of surpassing elegance and sophistication, the leader's own gifts more than matched by the peerless Rosengren and by a hugely experienced rhythm section. 'I Had The Craziest Dream' is the most substantial single piece, a long exploration of those slightly wayward chords and offbeat melody line. Harold Ashby's 'Ashes' is an intriguing choice, not often covered, but Ericson saves his most pungent statement for 'Brownie Speaks', written by the superb Clifford B. but rarely heard to better effect than here. Ericson's clean, unfussy delivery works well in just about every mood from flat-out blowing to the most delicate and Chet Baker-like of ballads. *I Love You So* ... was intended to celebrate Ericson's return to Sweden from a long stay in Germany. Sadly, but appropriately, it turned into his memorial.

Peter Erskine (born 1954)

DRUMS

After starting out with Stan Kenton, Erskine has become one of the most sought-after drummers in American jazz, taking the occasional rock gig for fun. Stints with Weather Report and John Abercrombie were crucial to his developing outlook, and he has created a considerable body of work as a composer.

***** Peter Erskine**

Original Jazz Classics OJC 610 *Erskine; Randy Brecker (t, flhn); Michael Brecker (ts); Bob Mintzer (ts, bcl); Don Grolnick, Kenny Kirkland (p); Mike Mainieri (vib); Eddie Gomez (b); Don Alias (perc).* 6/82.

Erskine is (justifiably) among the most admired drummers of the contemporary American circuit: besides his formidable technique, he's gregarious enough to handle virtually any musical situation and is a thoughtful composer to boot. His first record as a leader found him in charge of a relatively straightforward post-bop session; but, with such a heavyweight gathering of studio craftsmen all on their toes, the results are impressive if a little too brawny here and there.

***** You Never Know**

ECM 517353-2 *Erskine; John Taylor (p); Palle Danielsson (b).* 7/92.

*****(*) Time Being**

ECM 521719-2 *As above.* 11/93.

This has become a trio of considerable stature. *You Never Know* seemed disappointing, perhaps, in that Erskine himself deferred so much to Taylor. There is only one composition by the leader, with four by Taylor and three (very good) by Vince Mendoza; this is really a piano album in which Erskine does conscientious time and duty. A less fully realized record than the later discs, it's still a strong set, although it relies on Taylor's lean pastoralisms, which are always interesting, seldom compelling. *Time Being* follows the same path but is more involving. One reason is a greater sense of group identity, with the three men finding a teetering balance between their parts; another is the wider variation in material, with Staffan Linton's 'Liten Visa Till Karin' a particularly delightful choice; another is Danielsson's increasing involvement, his bass parts securing an eminent voice inside the trio. Impeccable.

*****(*) As It Is**

ECM 529085-2 *As above.* 9/95.

Ever more impeccable. Where DeJohnette never quite gives up on a drummer's muscle, even in the midst of a set of the balmiest, sweetest tunes, Erskine is prepared to lie back and stroke the gentlest rhythms out of the kit. Since Taylor and Danielsson are the kind of players who glove their intensities anyway, pieces like 'Glebe Ascending' and 'For Ruth' emerge as a distinctive blend of rural impressionism and sophisticated strength. Here also is another version of 'Touch Her Soft Lips And Part', memorably recorded on the drummer's 1991 date for Novus. Maybe Erskine can't get the tune out of his mind, but when the results are as gorgeous as this, who can blame him?

*****(*) Juni**

ECM 539726-2 *As above.* 7/97.

Diminishing returns may set in at some point, but not yet. None of these eight themes really stands out, but they're treated as vehicles for group chemistry and are arguably best heard as a single interconnected piece. Erskine continues to do a tremendous amount at the kit without once sounding intrusive or overbearing; Taylor and Danielsson pace thoughtfully around him. This kind of trio music won't be to all tastes, but it's exceedingly well done.

*****(*) Behind Closed Doors Vol. 1**

Fuzzy Music PEPCD 005 *Erskine; Randy Brecker (t); Bob Mintzer, Joe Lovano (ts); Alan Pasqua, Kenny Werner (p); Mike Mainieri (vib); Anand Bennet (vn); John Scofield (g); Marc Johnson, Dante Pascuzzo (b); Alex Acuña, Zakir Hussain (perc); WDR Big Band.* 3/91–3/96.

Released on Erskine's own label, this is an absorbing collection of outtakes and leftovers from a number of sessions, apparently dating as far back as the date which produced his *Sweet Soul* set for BMG. Some of this is outstanding. Kenny Werner's 'Herbie Nichols', with Erskine, Lovano and Johnson, is strong enough to make one want to hear the whole date, and the worldly 'A To Z' is an offbeat but intriguing meeting with Bennet, Hussain, Pascuzzo and Acuña. There's a couple of less impressive outings with the WDR Big Band and a typically self-effacing solo (if a drum solo can ever be self-effacing) from Peter himself.

*****(*) Live At Rocco**

Fuzzy Music PEPCD 007 2CD *Erskine; Alan Pasqua (p); Dave Carpenter (b).* 10/99.

Pasqua's forceful, sometimes gushing lyricism dominates this live trio date, and maybe it's too much, stretched across two hours and two CDs. But after the more severe beauties of the ECM trio with Taylor, this feels like a kind of release – a more generous, big-sounding, more American date. The playing is so disarmingly songful and radiant that it would take a curmudgeon not to enjoy it. If you like the younger, less rambling Jarrett, Pasqua's your man, and since Carpenter and Erskine aren't given to merely leaning back and letting him wander, we get the melody-making without the indulgence. Here and there, as in an overlong 'How About You?', the music loses its grip – but not for long, and Erskine himself, while content to stay as a support, calmly makes his presence felt throughout. For a live set, the music is also beautifully registered in the recording.

***** Side Man Blue**

Fuzzy Music PEPCD010 *Erskine; Andy Haderer (t); Rolf Römer (cl, ts); Frank Chastenier (p); John Goldsby (b).* 3/01.

If the names aren't all that familiar, that may be because they're from the WDR Big Band, an orchestra Erskine loves to play with, and the music's drawn from a score the drummer prepared for a play by Warren Light. Like any soundtrack, it doesn't transfer straightforwardly to a stand-alone CD, given that there are different versions of several of the pieces, and its true function is as programme music. That said, Erskine again shows that he's no mean composer, even for a conventional quintet.

Lars Erstrand (born 1936)

VIBRAPHONE

Born in Uppsala, Erstrand tried piano, tuba and trombone before taking up vibes after hearing Lionel Hampton. He worked with Ove Lind in the '60s, played with Benny Goodman in 1972 and has been a sideman and leader in numerous situations since.

*** **Two Sides Of Lars Erstrand**
Opus 3 8302 *Erstrand; Roland Jivelid (ts); Knud Jorgenson (p); Bertil Fernqvist (g); Arne Wilhelmsson (b); Pelle Hulten (d).* 5–6/83.

*** **Lars Erstrand And Four Brothers**
Opus 3 8402 *As above.* 6/84.

*** **Tribute To Benny Goodman Quartet**
Opus 3 8603 *Erstrand; Ove Lind (cl); Rolf Larsson (p); Pelle Hulten (b).* 12/86.

(*) **Dream Dancing
Opus 3 9101 *Erstrand; Kjell Ohman (org); Tommy Johnson (b); Gus Dhalberg (d).* 2/91.

*** **Beautiful Friendship – The First Set**
Sittel SITCD 9204 *As above, except add Ken Peplowski (cl, ts), Frank Vignola (g).* 6/92.

*** **Beautiful Friendship – The Second Set**
Sittel SITCD 9205 *As above.* 6/92.

***(*) **International All Stars – Live At Uttersberg '98**
Gemini GMCD 98 *Erstrand; Roy Williams (tb); Jan Lundgren (p); Hans Backenroth (b); Joe Ascione (d).* 8/98.

Erstrand's enduring admiration for the Lionel Hampton style – as best evidenced in their meeting on *Two Generations*, Phontastic 8807 – disguises a rather broader range of interests. *Two Sides* also touches on bebop in 'Sweet And Hot Mop' and even traces of European echoes of the MJQ in such as the Bach 'Invention In C Major'. This and the *Four Brothers* disc feature an entertaining band – Jivelid's nicely Lestorian tenor floats agreeably over the rhythm-players, and Jorgenson unobtrusively steals the show on several tracks with some quick-witted improvisations. The Goodman tribute is an accurate-sounding evocation, with Lind's wonderfully supple lines twining round the vibes apparently effortlessly. The organ band with Ohman puts the pots on, at least compared with the other discs, and it encourages the vibesman to dig in more wholeheartedly than he does on some of the other records. *Dream Dancing* suffers from a few more laid-back and almost sleepwalking ballads, but the two live albums on Sittel have some genuine fire in the belly on the up-tempo tunes: 'Jim Dawgs' is almost over the top in its energies and 'Lady Be Good' personifies the swinging small combo. Peplowski is an unlikely man for a grooving organ/tenor band, but he puts his romantic hat on for the ballads and 'I Thought About You' on the first disc is a charmer. Second guest Vignola prefers strumming over single notes. But both discs have a sound-problem: the organ sounds either tinny or buzzy at different moments, and the overall mix seems rougher than it should have been. Erstrand enjoys it all, though.

The 1998 concert set from Uttersberg is a notch ahead of the other discs because everyone's on his mettle and the band is an intriguing mix of personalities. Young lions such as Lundgren and Backenroth blow alongside an enthusiastic Erstrand and the admirable Williams, who often ends up in soporific mainstream situations but here is asked a few questions and comes up swinging mightily. A great session.

***(*) **Lars Erstrand Meets Rebecca Kilgore**
Gemini GMCD 116 *Erstrand; Jan Lundgren (p); Hans Backenroth (b); Joe Ascione (d); Rebecca Kilgore (v).* 8/03.

Joyous high spirits here, despite the fact that the music – again from an Uttersberg festival – was played over two days, one in torrential rain, the other in the face of a plague of mosquitoes. Becky Kilgore raises the spirits as she seems to on all of her appearances, and her signature version of 'The Lady's In Love With You' is a beauty. Lundgren is smart without being too clever, Ascione keeps the tempos as chipper as they should be, and Erstrand himself is in fine fettle. An enduring language, caught on the hoof and proving its durability.

Booker Ervin (1930–70)

TENOR SAXOPHONE

Originally a trombone-player, Ervin taught himself saxophone while in the services and instinctively veered towards the kind of blunt, blues-soaked sound of fellow-Texans like Arnett Cobb and Illinois Jacquet. He had his big break with Mingus, who liked his raw, unaffected approach. The career was painfully short, but Booker packed a lot in. He's still missed.

*** **The Book Cooks**
Rhino 76691 *Ervin; Tommy Turrentine (t); Zoot Sims (ts); Tommy Flanagan (p); George Tucker (b); Dannie Richmond (d).* 6/60.

***(*) **That's It**
Candid CCD 79014 *Ervin; Horace Parlan (p); George Tucker (b); Al Harewood (d).* 1/61.

Texan tenor of a rather special sort. Booker started out on trombone and carried over some of the brass instrument's broad portamento effects into his reed work. He made his name with the Charles Mingus group and has only rather slowly established a reputation as a solo recording star, despite an impressive range of records. Recently reissued, the debut album finds him in strong and confident voice, but with a certain guardedness in his soloing. Zoot Sims was there for moral support and there could hardly be a greater contrast in tenor styles, the one bluff and reticent, the other cool and open-hearted. 'The Blue Book' and the title-track are generic Ervin performances, but stick around for the delightful brief 'Poor Butterfly' which closes the album.

On the Candid disc, Ervin is in full, fierce voice, blending elements of Don Byas and John Coltrane into a typical Texan shout. 'Uranus' is his finest ballad performance. George Tucker's deliberate introduction to 'Booker's Blues' takes the music down into some south-western storm cellar, where it spins out its unhurried message. To avoid contractual problems, Parlan was originally credited (with rather arcane literary humour) as 'Felix Krull', but there is nothing fraudulent about his playing on the album.

*** **Exultation**
Original Jazz Classics OJCCD 835 *Ervin; Frank Strozier (as); Horace Parlan (p); Butch Warren (b); Walter Perkins (d).* 6/63.

***(*) **The Song Book**
Original Jazz Classics OJC 779 *Ervin; Tommy Flanagan (p); Richard Davis (b); Alan Dawson (d).* 2/64.

***(*) **The Blues Book**
Original Jazz Classics OJC 780 *Ervin; Carmell Jones (t); Gildo Mahones (p); Richard Davis (b); Alan Dawson (d).* 6/64.

***** Groovin' High**
Original Jazz Classics OJCCD 919 *As above.* 12/63–10/64.

****** The Freedom Book**
Original Jazz Classics OJC 891 *As above, except omit Mahones, Jones; add Jaki Byard (p).* 12/63.

*****(*) The Space Book**
Original Jazz Classics OJCCD 896 *As above.* 10/64.

With the inclusion of *Groovin' High*, a further round-up of material from the prolific 'Book' sessions, most of Ervin's recordings for Prestige are available again. These are consistently excellent discs, marking the core of Ervin's output as a solo artist. Davis and Dawson are strong rhythm-players of the kind the saxophonist needed, and their ability to play gently on the ballad album is as impressive as their driving beat on 'No Booze Blooze'. *The Freedom Book*, with its wider remit, is probably the best of the lot, with Byard a more robustly percussive and blues-aware pianist. *The Space Book* serves as reminder of just how concentrated these sessions were and how ideas from one take and tune inevitably spilled over into the next. Reading the 'books' in sequence is an instructive exercise, the kind of in-depth coverage a label like Prestige and producer Bob Weinstock were able to give a developing artist in those days. We can only suggest that you try the experiment yourselves or, if in doubt about the investment, plump for *The Freedom Book* first, that way avoiding some of the more formulaic bop. *Exultation* was more of a loose jam, a rather uncentred and shapeless record that never seemed like good value for money and which isn't much improved by the addition of extra tracks.

*****(*) Settin' The Pace**
Prestige PRCD 24123 *Ervin; Dexter Gordon (ts); Jaki Byard (p); Reggie Workman (b); Alan Dawson (d).* 10/65.

***** The Trance**
Original Jazz Classics OJCCD 943-2 *As above, except omit Gordon.* 10/65.

***** Heavy!!!**
Original Jazz Classics OJCCD 981-2 *As above, except add Jimmy Owens (t), Garnett Brown (tb).* 66.

The conjunction of Ervin and the not-too-dissimilar Dexter Gordon on *Settin' The Pace* makes for interesting listening, though it's Dexter who establishes the ground-rules and sets the pace for most of the tunes. 'The Trance' is included, and there is a bouncing, fiery workout on 'Dexter's Deck', the kind of theme he drank by the gallon and played by the hour.

The Trance was recorded at the same session in Munich. It's a lean and straightforward jazz album, not without its subtleties. 'Groovin' At The Jamboree' is a blowing blues, nothing fancy but powerfully argued. 'Speak Low' is handled with a gruff grace, but the real emotional weight of the album is concentrated in the title-track, a memorial to the bassist George Tucker. Appropriate that a player who would not so very long after attract such a moving tribute himself should have written such an effective threnody to a fellow-player.

Heavy!!! is an odd record. Including some of Ervin's most exploratory playing, it is also one of his most unvarnished performances. The material is decidedly left-field, opening with 'Bachafillen', including 'Bei Mir Bist Du Schön' and Byard's weirdly wonderful 'Aluminum Baby' and closing with 'Ode To Charlie Parker'. The three-horn front line is reminiscent of Coltrane's *Blue Train* session, with a similar mismatch of voices and styles, but on the whole it works.

****** Booker'N'Brass**
Pacific Jazz 7243 4 94509 2 *Ervin; Martin Banks, Johnny Coles, Ray Copeland, Freddie Hubbard, Charles Tolliver, Richard Williams (t); Garnett Brown, Bennie Green (tb); Benny Powell (btb); Kenny Barron (p); Reggie Johnson (b); Lenny McBrowne (d).* 9/67.

Teddy Edwards arranged and conducted this often-overlooked large-ensemble record on which Ervin is plonked in front of a superbly crafted horn section and plays his heart out. The tracks were recorded over three days at Webster Hall in New York City. For a time a shoddy bootleg purporting to document additional material from the same session went the rounds; listening carefully to Bob Belden's remastered issue, we're convinced that this was at very best a rehearsal tape. There are still flaws here and there on the issued version, not least a clinker towards the end of his solo on 'I Left My Heart In San Francisco', but it's a set that works when it's relaxed and expressive. Alternative takes of 'LA After Dark' suggest how assiduously Teddy worked to get the band to sound loose and unfussy while hitting the beats and pitches square on.

Ervin pays tribute to Duke Ellington on 'East Dallas Special', which is rich enough to prompt a feeling that he might have gone on to become a brilliant big-band composer and performer. 'Do You Know What It Means To Miss New Orleans' and 'St Louis Blues' are unexpected inclusions, but Ervin brings a contemporary flavour to both. Good to see this Pacific release back in the catalogue. It's an ideal showcase for Ervin's still-underrated talents.

Pee Wee Erwin (1913–81)

TRUMPET

George Erwin was playing trumpet on American radio when still a boy. He worked with Benny Goodman and Ray Noble in New York, and helped Glenn Miller to create his celebrated sound. Extensive studio work in the '40s, before a ten-year gig at Nick's through the '50s. Latterly, he taught and did more studio playing, a master technician to the end.

*****(*) Dr Jazz Vol. 14: Pee Wee Erwin**
Storyville STCD 6059 *Erwin; Vic Dickenson (tb); Gene Sedric (cl); Teddy Roy (p); Johnny Giuffrida (b); Morey Feld (d).* 4–5/52.

***** ... Swingin' That Music**
Jazzology JCD-80 *Erwin; Herman Foretich (tb, v); Herb Gardner (tb); Harry Hagan, Mason 'Country' Thomas (cl); Freddie Deland, Al Stevens (p); Steve Jordan (g); Ike Isaacs, Van Perry (b); Hal Smith, Chuck Redd (d).* 3/80.

The material is a stable-full of Dixieland warhorses and the sound is no better than broadcast quality, but the *Dr Jazz* session is a marvellous set. Erwin was a great jazz trumpeter whose handful of LPs under his own name have had no luck with CD reissue. This is a welcome, if inadequate, remedying of that situation. Recorded from four different broadcasts at Lou Terassi's Club on West 47th Street – the gig was really Bobby Hackett's, but Pee Wee depped for him three nights a week – the music is sheer good fun, though without sloppiness or untucked shirt-tails. Erwin's poise as a trumpeter is akin to

Hackett's, but he was a hotter player, and in a fast piece like 'Clarinet Marmalade' he gets off a solo which is as embroidered as vintage Hackett, but feistier too. While the rhythm section is perhaps no more than good enough, both Dickenson and the undervalued Sedric play in top gear.

The Jazzology set was made the year before Pee Wee's death. The band play regulation Dixieland and do it capably. But even here, it's Erwin's beautiful trumpet which makes the record. There is a stray festival track to round things off, with a different band.

Wayne Escoffery (born 1975)

TENOR SAXOPHONE

Strong-voiced young player who made a quiet stir with his debut release.

***** Times Change**

Nagel Heyer 2015 *Escoffery; Aaron Goldberg (p); Joel Forbes (b); Carl Allen (d).* 1/01.

In a scene still packed with Trane-spotters and Brecker step-brothers, it's nice to come across a saxophonist who nods to Sam Rivers and Yusef Lateef on his debut disc. Wayne's reading of Rivers's lovely 'Beatrice' is a high point of the record, but before it comes along he has already got things going with a hard-swinging original, 'Come Back Lucky'. Escoffery doubles on soprano on 'Dawn', which exposes some of his weakness as a soloist: lots of technique, not yet much in the way of drama. His take on Jobim's 'Triste' has promise and he does a great job with the Lateef piece, 'Water Pistol', which is a pianoless trio. When Goldberg is around, he does great work and the group as a whole sounds tight and sympathetic. Escoffery is a man to watch.

Ellery Eskelin (born 1959)

TENOR SAXOPHONE

Raised in Baltimore, where his mother played the Hammond B-3, Eskelin has moved on to be an experienced figure in New York's new jazz of the '90s and beyond. His principal group is a trio with Jim Black and Andrea Parkins.

****** Figure Of Speech**

Soul Note 121232-2 *Eskelin; Joe Daley (tba); Arto Tuncboyaciyan (perc).* 7/91.

*****(*) Premonition**

Prime Source 2010 *Eskelin (ts solo).* 7/92.

***** Jazz Trash**

Songlines SGL 1506-2 *Eskelin; Andrea Parkins (acc, sampler); Jim Black (d).* 10/94.

Eskelin is a tenor player who stands some way apart from the throng. The saxophonist has a querulous tone and likes to stretch phrases into elongated shapes that push against what are otherwise fairly conventional parameters; he chooses standards or simple thematic constructions to play on, and is good at moving in and out of familiar tonalities. There are a couple of unavailable earlier records, but *Figure Of Speech* was the real breakthrough. Eskelin's purposeful avoidance of the obvious routes of improvisation – specifically, theme-and-variation structures – brings a rare sense of something new to this project in particular. Daley's tuba and Tuncboyaciyan's quiet, pattering percussion are important voices, but their essentially simple figures throw the detail and complexity of Eskelin's own playing into very sharp relief. The tunes revolve round carefully coded motifs or structural ideas without depending on them, and the improvisations usually form separate entities of their own, contrasting with (rather than commenting on) the written material. This is a rare kind of freedom, negotiated with superb assurance by all three men.

The solo album *Premonition* might be for more rarefied tastes, but there's no doubting Eskelin's mastery of the horn or his ingenuity in dealing with the chosen material here. While there are three improvisations that deal with timbral extremes, wide intervals and rhythmic variations, the three further solos based on standard tunes are even more remarkable, culminating in a bizarre demolition of 'Besame Mucho'. Much is reminiscent here of an early David Murray solo album, particularly Eskelin's big tone and busker's vibrato, but this is less obviously experimental, more achieved.

Jazz Trash has 'interesting' writ large, but goes little further. Eskelin skirmishes with Parkins and Black rather than creating any tangible interplay, and while there are numerous intriguing moments – 'Rain' is a nicely abstruse essay on ballad form, for instance – there's a certain paucity to the textures which makes it hard to sustain over the 70-odd minutes.

***** The Sun Died**

Soul Note 121282-2 *Eskelin; Marc Ribot (g); Kenny Wolleson (d).* 2/96.

Recorded in New York but steeped in Chicago, which is where John Corbett's entertaining travelogue/sleeve-note takes us, this is some kind of tribute from a man who grew up in Baltimore. The tunes are all bar-b-q specials from the greasy cookbooks of Gene Ammons, Harold Vick, and Jack McDuff, but especially Ammons, whose homage comes specifically in Eskelin's gruff, grizzled tone and buzzsaw licks. It takes two or three tracks to acclimatize, but the trio kicks this material around good-naturedly until one feels at home in a distorted language. Problematically, though, the record seems to run short of steam by the end, and Ribot sounds a tad too self-conscious about it all to support Eskelin to the best. But Wolleson is great; how did he get those sounds on 'The People's Choice'?

***** Green Bermudas**

Eremite MTE02 *Eskelin; Andrea Parkins (sampler).* 6/96.

****** One Great Day**

hatOLOGY 502 *As above, except add Jim Black (d).* 9/96.

Green Bermudas is Eskelin's most abstract disc, in which he decorates Parkins's oddball array of sampled sounds (bland singalong pop, varispeed drums, even chunks of Eskelin himself from *Premonition*) with some of his sparsest playing. A lot of it feels like experimental bits and bites of music, at least until the two long tracks which close the record, each a testing dialogue between the two performers. *One Great Day*, though, feels like a huge advance over the trio's previous *Jazz Trash*. This time there's a palpable interplay between the trio and the duos which emerge when somebody sits out. Black's compendium of jazz, rock and free rhythms is spontaneously exciting, just as Parkins conjures unpredictable shapes out of her instrument. Eskelin himself has never sounded stronger or more figurative about the physicality of the sax; he often seems to be grabbing and twisting the sounds as they emerge.

***** Dissonant Characters**
hatOLOGY 534 *Eskelin; Han Bennink (d).* 12/98.

More or less positioned by jazz time, these friendly and generous duets are entertaining if somewhat dashed-off in feel. Bennink enjoys Eskelin's evasiveness – 'Just when you think you've got him, he gets away' – and the two of them gambit and counter-gambit with each other. Sometimes the playfulness can be a bit irritating to us bystanders, and you wish they'd settle into something; but that's hardly the point of what's a fun exercise. A bonus is the excellent sound which Peter Pfister creates for them.

*****(*) Kulak 29 & 30**
hatOLOGY 521 *Eskelin; Andrea Parkins (acc, sampler); Jim Black (d).* 10/97.

*****(*) Five Other Pieces (+2)**
hatOLOGY 533 *As above.* 10/98.

Two and a quarter hours of non-stop invention. Eskelin takes a very considered approach to the music of his trio, both in his originals – *Kulak 29 & 30* – and in the pieces he chooses to cover – *Five Other Pieces (+2)*. Parkins, who might be the key individual in the group, continues to use her sampler most frequently to sound like a gothic Hammond, which might be taking Eskelin back to his salad days; either way, the music here is less self-consciously eclectic than in some of their earlier collaborations. There's a droll side to pieces such as 'Fifty Nine' and 'Visionary Of The Week' and it lightens what might otherwise be an occasionally dour palette. Courtesy of Black's lurching rhythms, the music sways rather than swings. When they tackle a piece such as the old Mahavishnu Orchestra chestnut 'The Dance Of Maya' the result is blackly comic, without giving the impression that they're playing it for laughs. Eskelin himself refuses to settle into familiar free licks and sounds – some of his solos are huge slices of saxophone oratory, scaled down to fit the dimensions of what remains an intimate group, focusing on details. One has the impression that their records may never quite measure up to what they can communicate in a live performance. But that's an old saw anyway.

***** Ramifications**
hatOLOGY 551 *Eskelin; Andrea Parkins (acc, sampler); Erik Friedlander (clo); Joe Daley (tba); Jim Black (d).* 9/99.

*****(*) The Secret Museum**
hatOLOGY 552 *As above except omit Friedlander and Daley.* 11/99.

*****(*) Vanishing Point**
hatOLOGY 577 *Eskelin; Matt Moran (vib); Mat Maneri (vla); Erik Friedlander (clo); Mark Dresser (b).* 12/00.

***** 12 (+1) Imaginary Views**
hatOLOGY 584 *Eskelin; Andrea Parkins (acc, p, sampler); Jim Black (d).* 4/01.

***** Arcanum Moderne**
hatOLOGY 588 *As above.* 5/02.

Ramifications debuts Eskelin's writing for a five-piece group. As with his smaller unit, it's tightly coherent, the details matter, and parts interconnect with a kind of severity, while managing to steer a path away from po-faced posturing. There's space, and intensity levels are moved around (or up and down) very methodically. The title-piece opens on a fluttering tenor improvisation, then settles into a dead-slow blues march which finally crawls to a halt. Friedlander then picks up on the theme as the introduction to the next piece, though it develops differently after that – a process of alignment, rather than thematic evolution, which Eskelin likens to film-making. What's troublesome is the air of gloom which seems to hang over the set, something which even Black's vigorous rhythms to 'Title Piece' can't dispel. 'Transister' is a rousing resolution, but it's an awfully sombre journey.

The trio work through a sort of suite on *The Secret Museum*, and if it's hard work for the listener, at least they offer a kind of modern-jazz respite in Monk's 'We See', placed more or less at the centre. It's a strange and difficult record which we are somewhat divided on, but if the listener takes to it then they will do so very strongly.

Vanishing Point is entirely improvised, cut at a six-hour session. Eskelin notes that 'the inevitable comparisons with classical music will be made with respect to this one', but it doesn't much sound like any classical music we know. The chamber-music instrumentation may yield one set of expectations, but the bustle of the opening 'Scatter Brain' should dispel them straight away. Three strings, vibes and tenor is a striking combination and the players deal with it imaginatively, although one feels that there may be more direction by Eskelin than the premise of the date implies – the strings often fall into what sound like orchestrated sections (though the music's none the worse for it).

The 12 'ideas' of the fourth record in this sequence each offer a 'concept containing some specific element that characterizes an open improvisation' – pretty old hat to European improvisers, maybe, and in a sense it harks back (in a more simplified way) to *Figure Of Speech* from ten years before. But it suits Eskelin, who seems like the kind of player who wants freedom but can't bring himself to abandon most of his structural principles. Some of it is power-trio, some atmospheres, and as before Parkins often takes the key decision inside a piece. Perhaps it distils some of the more madcap music off *Green Bermudas*, too. By the end – a reading of the Monk obscurity 'Oskar T' which might be deliberately crude – the music's beginning to sound tired.

Arcanum Moderne closes the circle for now. It seems almost cruel to do to the samba form what the trio do in the opening 'It's A Samba', and Eskelin's astonishing saxophone part marks some kind of high point for his own playing. Thick with knowledge, hung up on procedural matters, scientific and emotive in even-steven quantities, it's quite likely a group like no other.

John Etheridge (born 1948)

GUITAR

A self-taught guitarist, in the '70s he became one of the most noted and technically adept British jazz-rock players with Soft Machine. Has since worked for himself and a variety of leaders, in situations ranging from duos to Nigel Kennedy's fusion orchestra.

***** Second Vision**
Voiceprint BP 341 *Etheridge; Ric Saunders (vn); Dave Bristow (ky); Jonathan Davey (b); Micky Barker (d).* 80.

... or Soft Machine meets Fairport Convention. Long languishing unheard, this 1980 recording underlines the guitarist's love of working with violin players. Saunders is a formidable technician, and on tracks like 'Ice Bells', 'First Steps' and 'Wynsmead', the two front men weave a magic compounded of jazz, folk and contemporary fusion which by 1980 had begun to lapse towards tired orthodoxy but sounds very strong here.

***** Ash**

JazzPrint JPVP 102 *Etheridge; Steve Franklin (ky); Henry Thomas (b); Mark Fletcher (d).* 92.

A welcome reissue almost a decade on. *Ash* sounds a little tired and dated on its second appearance, largely because the sound is a bit flat and uninspired, but John is in cracking form on 'In Your Own Sweet Way', 'Ugetsu' and on the Hendrix standard 'Little Wing' which has always been a favourite with jazz musicians. The band works away manfully, though without doing much more than supporting John's excellent front lines.

***** Sweet Chorus: A Tribute To Stéphane Grappelli**

Dyad DY001 *Etheridge; Christian Garrick (vn); Dave Kelbie (g); Malcolm Creese (b).* 6–7/98.

*****(*) Chasing Shadows**

Dyad DY004 *As above.* 2/01.

The obvious point of comparison for *Sweet Chorus* is fellow-guitarist Martin Taylor's now well-established Spirit Of Django project. Both men had the privilege of working with the late Stéphane Grappelli, but seem to have learnt rather different things. Whereas Taylor is above all a melodist, Etheridge has a more analytical, sometimes a more schematic approach to the material. Not all of it is directly associated with Grappelli, though the performances are in the right spirit and don't lack for authenticity.

It takes something special now to invest 'Nuages' with any degree of originality and conviction, but the group sounds so completely sensitized to the Hot Club aesthetic that even this tired old warhorse sounds completely fresh. The same is true of Jobim's 'How Insensitive' and the Reinhardt/Grappelli title-tune. Young Christian Garrick is a chip off the old block, though it's hard to tell where the bloodlines are strongest: his dad Michael's intense harmonic awareness or Grappelli's transformation of the fiddle into a singing, expressive jazz voice. Malcolm Creese can do this stuff standing on his head, and his contribution is significant on things like 'Rhythm Futur' and 'Shine', two of the strongest tracks. Others break down the basic group into trios, duos and Etheridge solos. The last of these lack something. Not technique, not expressiveness, but perhaps a basic confidence. The guitarist has, after all, worked a roundabout path from the shoe-gazing English avant-rock of Soft Machine to the much cleaner sound of this record. He pulls it off without strain, but still sounds like a man who expects to break loose at any second and crank up some feedback or smash a guitar. He's always sounded fine without stadium histrionics, and these cuts are a welcome reintroduction to his manifold talents.

Chasing Shadows is a marvellous record, a confident performance from a now well-established band. They tackle 'Giant Steps' with a gleeful confidence and Garrick's playing now seems tightly melded to the leader's. 'Moment's Notice' continues that particular seam. The real surprises are earlier in the disc, with glorious versions of 'Do You Know What It Means To Miss New Orleans' and 'Someone To Watch Over Me', the latter an ideal vehicle for Etheridge's lyrical side.

***** The Music of Frank Zappa: Absolutely Live**

JazzPrint JPVP 122 *Etheridge; Paul Jayasinha (t); Annie Whitehead (tb); Ben Castle (sax, f); Steve Lodder (ky); Rob Statham (b); Mike Bradley (d); Teena Lyle (perc).* 00.

After nodding to Grappelli, Etheridge pays homage to the guitarist who, after John McLaughlin, has probably had the biggest impact on his own playing. Zappa's compositions have yet to find a secure place in the jazz repertory (slower for some reason than Jimi Hendrix's), but 'The Grand Wazoo', 'Big Swifty' and 'King Kong' (previously canonized, of course, by Jean-Luc Ponty) are all given vivid and mostly authentic workouts. Whitehead is in stunningly good form. Her tone is so rich and resonant that there are moments when she almost sounds paired in the mix with a second horn. Etheridge himself fires off licks like the composer himself, constructing solos out of found material, natural blues and rock progressions and sometimes by a highly idiosyncratic harmonic leap into the unknown.

Charles Eubanks (born 1948)

PIANO

Elder brother of Robin and Kevin. Has worked with modernist luminaries Rashied Ali, Archie Shepp and Oliver Lake but was late making his debut as leader.

***** New Beginnings**

CIMP 250 *Eubanks (p solo).* 6/01.

***** Birds Of Baghdad**

CIMP 290 *As above.* 6/03.

With a style firmly rooted in tradition, Eubanks's belated solo ventures are harmonically strong and rhythmically less varied than one might like on a solo disc. Very much a left-hand man, he constructs strong foundations for Parker's 'Donna Lee' and 'Sippin' At Bells' and Coltrane's 'Countdown', and these familiar tunes are the best way of sampling how Eubanks constructs his own originals. 'Ra-Shied', dedicated to a former boss, is a darkly swinging thing, with a powerful bass and lots of cross-detail. 'Sand Prints' and 'Fortune Teller' have a more mysterious quality.

There is one Monk tune on each of the albums. 'Tell Me Why' on *New Beginnings* is a less taxing piece than 'Trinkle Tinkle' on *Birds Of Baghdad* but Charles despatches them both with delightful calm. The second record pretty much reprises the mood and feel of the first. There are the same elements of stride and gospel, boogie and bop, in pretty much the same permutations. But there is also a slight darkening of mood. Titles like 'Roadmap To Swing' and 'Birds Of Baghdad' hint at big themes and the title-piece is a swirl of impressions. The three-movement 'Making Overtures' also sounds like an autobiographical sketch and is certainly the most substantial thing on the set. Again, though, Eubanks shows he can give a standard like 'How Deep Is The Ocean' a fresh spin.

Robin Eubanks (born 1959)

TROMBONE, BASS TROMBONE, KEYBOARDS

The Eubanks family is the Philadelphia equivalent of the Marsalises. Robin is a versatile, expressive player, with a distinctively flowing line which lends itself to straight jazz settings, while brother Kevin has always flirted with jazz-rock. Busy as a sideman, Eubanks has nevertheless been able to record fairly regularly on his own account, although most of it is currently deleted.

★★★(★) Different Perspectives

Winter & Winter 919023 *Eubanks; Michael Mossman (flhn); Clifton Anderson, Slide Hampton (tb); Doug Purviance (btb); James Weidman (p, ky); Kevin Eubanks (g); Rael Wesley Grant, Peter Washington (b); Teri Lyne Carrington, Jeff Tain Watts (d).* 88.

★★★★ Dedication

Winter & Winter 919032 *Eubanks; Steve Turre (tb); Mulgrew Miller (p, syn); Charnett Moffett (b); Tony Reedus (d); Jimmy Delgado (perc).* 4/89.

The trombonist's debut was originally released on JMT and has been out of circulation for some time. A pity, because it's a corking record, full of clever writing, subtle arrangement and some very good playing indeed. Younger brother Kevin (whose own career seems to have faltered) is on hand to crank up the funk element on such things as Stevie Wonder's 'Overjoyed', but for the most part the set is dominated by Eubanks themes. These are responsive to what was going on in pop music, but they are unmistakably the work of a man steeped in classic jazz. 'Midtown' sets the agenda at a tempo that suits Robin and he sticks to it for most of the set, phrasing accurately and with great feeling. The guest trombonists are there for more than moral support and the whole disc comes across as a 'bone makeover, a primer for a new slide dialect.

The second album is, if anything, even better. Turre is a master in his own right and while they're anxious to avoid too many Jay and Kai clichés, he and Robin do draw on that very successful example. Some of the writing is straight jazz, like the swinging 'Koncepts', but the more successful tracks trade high energy for expression, like the moody dedication to Woody Shaw.

★★★ Wake Up Call

Sirocco SJL 1001 *Eubanks; Duane Eubanks (t); Antonio Hart (as); Eric Lewis (p); Lonnie Plaxico (b); Gene Jackson (d).* 2/97.

Wake Up Call was the first release on John Priestley's Sirocco label. It's a quiet, thoughtful record, mixing standard material – the Rodgers and Hart standard 'You Are Too Beautiful', Lee Morgan's 'Ceora' and Bird's bebop classic 'Scrapple From The Apple' – with a group of well-crafted originals. 'Soliloquy' is the best, a gently rocking ballad which immediately sounds familiar. There are two Wayne Shorter tunes, pointing to one of Eubanks's less obvious influences. A shame that he simply fades out on 'Oriental Love Long', which somehow deserves a more considered ending. However, it does give way to the brisk and breezy title-track, which restores a measure of shape and urgency.

★★★(★) 4:JJ/Slide/Curtis and Al

TCB 97802 *Eubanks; Antonio Hart (as, ts); Mike Cain (p); Lonnie Plaxico (b); Gene Jackson (d).* 98.

Robin continues his mission to the great trombone stars of the past with this set named after four of them, to wit Johnson, Hampton, Fuller and Grey. It's another vivid demonstration of the Philly man's combination of fresh imagination and some scholarship in the music. Apart from Wayne Shorter's 'Black Nile' (an intriguing choice), Thad Jones's 'A Child Is Born', and a lovely soulful version of 'Speak Low', all the material is by Eubanks and is well up to his very high standard. These days he has traded in high-energy playing pretty much for a more romantic approach. It suits his tone perfectly, especially on the tenor trombone. Interesting to hear him work with a saxophone rather than other brass players. Less clotted with keyboards and guitars than earlier albums, the mix is a bit muddy and ungenerous and one wishes the leader were allowed to cut through the band a bit more urgently.

Eureka Brass Band

GROUP

Augmented by George Lewis for the day, this is the Eureka BB as it stood in 1951, one of the city's leading parade bands of the day.

(★★★★) New Orleans Funeral And Parade

American Music AMCD-70 *Percy Humphrey, Willie Pajeaud, Edie Richardson (t); Albert Warner, Sunny Henry (tb); George Lewis (cl); Ruben Roddy (as); Emmanuel Paul (ts); Joseph 'Red' Clark (sou); Arthur Ogle, Robert 'Son' Lewis (d).* 8/51.

Probably the most authentic example of old New Orleans music in its original environment, even if this recording of traditional funeral and parade music was recorded in a French Quarter alleyway rather than actually on the job. The regulars of the Brass Band, as it was then, were augmented by Lewis for the day, although he plays flat, and the brass are similarly wayward in their intonation. The recording is musty, the tempos ragged, the extra takes of four of the numbers come as an anti-climax and some of the dirges threaten to dissolve altogether. But many will find this a moving, rather magnificent recording. Seldom has the old music sounded so affecting, the workmanlike attitude of the players lending something like nobility to it all. The remastering has actually been done very well, considering the source material, and the superb documentation – by Alden Ashforth, the teenage enthusiast who recorded the session – adds to the undeniable mystique.

★★★(★) In Rehearsal, 1956

American Music AMCD-110/111 2CD *Percy Humphrey, Willie Pajeaud, George 'Kid Sheik' Cola (t); Sonny Henry, Albert Warner (tb); Ruben Roddy (as); Emmanuel Paul (ts); Joe Clark (tba); Cie Frazier, Robert Lewis, Alfred Williams (d).* 1/56.

Samuel Charters managed to record the Eureka again in 1956, for Moe Asch's Folkways label, and some 80 minutes of rehearsal music has also survived. Here it is, rather extravagantly spread across two CDs. Given that some of this is chatter, tune-ups and breakdowns, it's scarcely an essential way into this kind of music. But Charters's vivid notes bring the occasion back to life, and since it presents the Eureka players at their most typical (this time without Lewis) it may even be more valuable as a document than *New Orleans Funeral And Parade.* Since these were one-microphone rehearsals, it's inevitably wanting in high fidelity. But that will scarcely trouble anyone who comes to this with sympathetic ears.

Bill Evans (born 1958)

TENOR AND SOPRANO SAXOPHONES

Studied in north Texas and New Jersey, then with Dave Liebman, who recommended him to Miles Davis. With Davis, 1980–84, then worked with his own groups and in various fusion-orientated situations.

*** Escape

Escapade ESC 03650-2 *Evans; Wallace Roney (t); Jim Beard (ky); Lee Ritenour, Jon Herington, Gary Poulson, Nick Moroch (g); Victor Bailey, Marcus Miller, Mark Egan, Ron Jenkins (b); Billy Kilson, Steve Ferrone (d); Manolo Badrena (perc); MC 900 Ft Jesus, Mark Ledford, Ahmed Best (v).* 12/95–1/96.

Evans got off to a high-profile start with his work in the Miles Davis band of the early '80s. His star has remained reasonably bright since then, although a stint with Blue Note led him nowhere in particular and his earlier group records for Jazz City and Lipstick have been mixed successes. He seems to enjoy the fusion-blowing context while wishing to keep at least one foot in a boppish environment. Jim Beard's artful production enhances *Escape*, which is typical of the new breed of art-jazz that's starting to come out of what used to be straightahead fusion dates. Beard adds lots of touches to the mix, cocooning Evans and the other soloists in glittering keyboard and percussion surrounds. A piece such as 'Coravilas' is pure studio dreamtime, and Evans decorates the environment very prettily. That said, it's difficult to hear this as either deep or enduring.

*** Modern Days And Nights

Double-Time DTRCD-120 *Evans; Andy LaVerne (p); John Patitucci (b); Steve Davis (d).* 11/96.

*** Starfish And The Moon

Escapade 03654-2 *Evans; Jim Beard, Henry Hey (ky); Adam Rogers (g, mand); Jon Herington (g, b); James Genus (b); Vinnie Colaiuta (d); Arto Tuncboyaciyan (perc, v); David Blamires, Caroline Leonhart (v).* 97.

Modern Days And Nights, a slow-burning set of Cole Porter pieces, is by a co-operative group for which LaVerne seems to have taken most of the arranging decisions. Some of the tunes are clever in the slightly exasperating way that LaVerne often enjoys, melodies reharmonized and rhythms destabilized as if to make sure that players of this accomplishment aren't just going over standards they know backwards. The environment suits Evans, who finds his most plaintive tone for 'Every Time We Say Goodbye' in particular, but the record has an air of calculation that undercuts its appeal. *Starfish And The Moon* continues with the feel of *Escape*, Beard handling the textural elements again, and Evans certainly seems as much at home here as in the unadorned fusion camp. The two sides of the story are told by 'It's Only History', close to an electronic pastorale, and 'Red Dog', a trim, forceful blow.

*** Soul Inside

ESC 03668-2 *Evans; Lew Soloff (t); Conrad Herwig (tb); Ricky Peterson (p, org); John Scofield, Dean Brown (g); James Genus, Tim LeFebvre (b); Steve Jordan (d); Don Alias (perc); Les McCann, Vaneese Thomas (v).* 6/00.

An entertaining simulation of a top-drawer R&B band, just about pushed into the jazz zone by Evans's own solos and the odd 'interesting' chord here and there. Les McCann turns in some throaty vocals on a couple of tracks, though whether that adds or detracts from the jazz side of things may be up to the listener. This gang of top-class session-men (doubtless engaged at top rates, too) will never really sound loose or uncomplicatedly funky, but they can play – and unlike some of his other own-name efforts, Evans sounds as if he feels at home.

**(*) Big Fun

ESC 03681 *Evans; Randy Brecker, Lew Soloff (t); Conrad Herwig (tb); Mickey Raphael (hca); Robben Ford, Hiram Bullock (g); Ricky Peterson (org); Clifford Carter (p); James Genus (b); Vinnie Colaiuta (d); Manolo Badrena (perc); Les McCann, Willie Nelson, Bruce Hornsby (v).* 1–5/02.

Same again, and if the tougher tracks hit pretty hard, the less appealing ones are, well, even less appealing. Hiring Willie Nelson to sing 'For What It's Worth' must have seemed like a good idea to somebody. Docked a notch for basically going nowhere.

Bill Evans (1929–80)

PIANO

Evans's first notable gig was with the Tony Scott group, in 1956, and his most important early liaison was with Miles Davis, with whom he recorded the Kind Of Blue album. Thereafter he worked more or less continuously in the trio format for the rest of his life, although there are solo sessions, records with singers and a few with horns or orchestral arrangements. Prolific in the studio and in being recorded in concert, Evans's enormous influence may have happened in two ways: his records were widely disseminated and listened to by musicians, and their attractive surface also appealed to an audience seeking sophisticated but easy-going new jazz. He suggested to more than one generation of pianists a way of dealing with modality, and his harmonic thinking showed a subtle way out of the dead-end of bebop changes. A difficult personal life was exacerbated by his dependence on various drugs, which ultimately ruined his health and led to an early death.

*** New Jazz Conceptions

Original Jazz Classics OJC 035 *Evans; Teddy Kotick (b); Paul Motian (d).* 9/56.

Evans's discography is extensive anyway, but he is in such demand by fans and collectors that almost everything he did is now available on CD again, which few of the major artists in this book can claim. Taken altogether, it is an incredible body of work, flawed and even repetitive though much of it may be, and it is particularly rewarding to work through it chronologically. Evans began modestly enough with a fine, comfortable set of boppish trio performances which created little stir at the time (the record sold some 800 copies over the course of one year). Orrin Keepnews, the producer, was convinced he should record Evans by hearing a demo tape played over the telephone, and the pianist's distinctive touch and lovely tone are already apparent. He makes bop material such as Tadd Dameron's 'Our Delight' into comprehensive structures, and the three tiny solos – including the very first 'Waltz For Debby', his most renowned original – hint at what was to come. But it's clearly a talent in its early stages.

*** Tenderly

Milestone MCD-9317-2 *Evans; Don Elliott (vib, perc).* 56–57.

Evans fanatics will certainly want to hear this, though whether they'll feel they have to return to it much is another matter. Don Elliott recorded some informal home sessions where he and Evans played duets, and here's a CD's worth of two guys having fun with 'Tenderly', 'Airegin', 'Laura', some blues, and whatever else came into their heads. There's chatter, prompting, some laughs, the odd car horn and telephone bell. Nothing's 'finished' – it's all rather charming. At the very end is a prototype version of the Evans original 'Funkallero', which he wouldn't record until 1962. Elliott's vibes (he's shown with his french horn on the cover, but doesn't pick it up) tend to take the subservient role, but that's partly because the pianist is so strong, and it's a palpable reminder of what a driving player the young Evans was, even in such off-the-cuff situations. Home-grown sound, naturally, though that adds to the charisma.

****** Everybody Digs Bill Evans**

Original Jazz Classics OJC 068 *Evans; Sam Jones (b); Philly Joe Jones (d).* 12/58.

Perennially reluctant, busy with the Miles Davis group, Evans didn't record as a leader until two years after *New Jazz Conceptions.* This superb record was worth the wait, though. Jones and Jones back him with enough spirit to bring out his most energetic delivery, and the assertiveness he'd found with Davis lent Evans an assurance that makes 'Night And Day' and 'Oleo' into driving performances. But 'Peace Piece', a translucent reshaping of the opening phrases of 'Some Other Time', which Evans came up with in the studio, is one of his most affecting soliloquies, and the ballad reading of 'Young And Foolish' makes an almost astonishing contrast to the up-tempo pieces. 'Some Other Time', which was omitted from the original LP, is present on the CD version of the reissue.

****** Portrait In Jazz**

Original Jazz Classics OJC 088 *Evans; Scott LaFaro (b); Paul Motian (d).* 12/59.

****** Explorations**

Original Jazz Classics OJC 037 *As above.* 2/61.

♛ ** Sunday At The Village Vanguard**

Original Jazz Classics OJC 140 *As above.* 6/61.

♛ ** Waltz For Debby**

Original Jazz Classics OJC 210 *As above.* 6/61.

****** At The Village Vanguard**

Riverside 60-017 *As above.* 6/61.

Evans was having trouble finding good bassists, but LaFaro's arrival precipitated the advent of one of the finest piano trios jazz has ever documented. The bassist's melodic sensitivity and insinuating sound flowed between Evans and Motian like water and, while notions of group empathy have sometimes been exaggerated in discussion of this music – it was still very much directed by Evans himself – the playing of the three men is so sympathetic that it set a universal standard for the piano–bass–drums set-up which has persisted to this day. Both *Portrait In Jazz* and *Explorations* have their small imperfections: there's an occasional brittleness in the latter, possibly a result of the quarrel which LaFaro and Evans had had just before the session, and the recording of both does less justice to LaFaro's tone and delivery than it might. But 'Autumn Leaves', 'Blue In Green', 'Beautiful Love' and the transformation of John Carisi's 'Israel' to the trio format are as sublimely integrated and inspiring as this kind of jazz can be. Yet the two records culled from a day's work at the Village Vanguard are even finer. Evans's own playing is elevated by the immediacy of the occasion. His contributions seem all of a piece, lines spreading through and across the melodies and harmonies of the tune, pointing the way towards modality yet retaining the singing, rapturous qualities which the pianist heard in his material (Evans retained a relatively small repertoire of favourite pieces throughout his career). All the Vanguard music is informed by an extra sense of discovery, as if the musicians were suddenly aware of what they were on to and were celebrating the achievement. They didn't have much time. LaFaro was killed in a car accident ten days later. There are extra tracks and alternative takes on the CD editions of all the above and, because the trio finally left very little music behind them, they are indispensable. *At The Village Vanguard* offers nothing new, simply ten tracks culled from the other two records; a nice single-disc representation, but the others must be heard in their entirety. This is music which, more than most in the jazz literature, continues to provoke marvel and endless study by listeners and musicians alike.

Audiophiles should note that three of the albums are now also available as 20-Bit remastered editions, as follows: *Portrait In Jazz* (RCD-1162-2), *Sunday At The Village Vanguard* (RCD-9376-2) and *Waltz For Debby* (RCD-9399-2).

CORE COLLECTION

****** The Complete Live At The Village Vanguard 1961**

Riverside 3RCD 1961–2 3CD *As above.* 6/61.

As we went to press, Riverside released this three-disc set of absolutely everything from the Vanguard tapes. For once in such enterprises, there's nothing that's not worth having – the breakdown on the opening 'Gloria's Step' is the only 'new' thing here – and as a set of piano-trio music it is virtually peerless. The latest mastering brings the music into its clearest perspective.

*****(*) Moon Beams**

Original Jazz Classics OJC 434 *Evans; Chuck Israels (b); Paul Motian (d).* 5–6/62.

****** How My Heart Sings!**

Original Jazz Classics OJC 369 *As above.* 5–6/62.

Chuck Israels replaced LaFaro, although Evans was at first so upset by the bassist's death that he stopped playing for a while. After some months of work, the pianist felt they were ready to record, and Keepnews, who'd wanted to get an all-ballad album out of Evans, cut both the above discs at the same sessions, alternating slow and up-tempo pieces and saving the ballads for *Moon Beams.* There are five Evans originals – 'Very Early' and 'Re: Person I Knew' on *Moon Beams*, 'Walking Up', 'Show-Type Tune' and '34 Skidoo' on *How My Heart Sings!* – and the slightly unfocused readings by the trio can be accounted for by the fact that the pianist revealed them to the others only at the dates. But this was otherwise a superb continuation of Evans's work. Israels plays pushy, hard-bitten lines and meshes very capably with Motian, and it spurs Evans into a sometimes pugnacious mood. 'Summertime' numbers among the more dramatic revisions of this standard, and 'In Your Own Sweet Way', present on the CD of *How My Heart Sings!* in two different takes, negotiates Brubeck's theme with a hint of asperity. Not that the ballads are wispy; 'Stairway To The Stars', for instance, is a model of firm melodic variation.

★★★★ Undercurrent
Blue Note 790538-2 *Evans; Jim Hall (g).* 4–5/62.

★★★ Interplay
Original Jazz Classics OJC 308 *Evans; Freddie Hubbard (t); Jim Hall (g); Percy Heath (b); Philly Joe Jones (d).* 7/62.

Temperamentally, Evans and Hall hit it off perfectly in the studios. Their duet album is a masterpiece of quiet shadings, drifting melancholy and – perhaps surprisingly – hard swinging, the latter quality emerging on a particularly full-blooded 'I'm Getting Sentimental Over You'. But it's the nearly hallucinatory ballads, 'Dream Gypsy' and 'Romain', which stick in the mind, where harp-like tones and gently fingered refrains establish a rare climate of introspection. The *Interplay* session, organized by Keepnews to keep Evans in funds, is comparatively desultory, but Hubbard plays rather well, and 'When You Wish Upon A Star' retains its powdery charm.

★★★(★) At Shelly's Manne Hole
Original Jazz Classics OJC 263 *Evans; Chuck Israels (b); Larry Bunker (d).* 5/63.

An understated yet tremendously intense 'Round Midnight' is among the highlights of this considerable club recording. Bunker and Israels were again given sight of some of the material only on the night of the recording, and their concentration adds to the tense lyricism which Evans was spinning out at the piano. A couple of rare excursions into the major blues, 'Swedish Pastry' and 'Blues in F/Five', complete a very strong programme, and the recording is particularly fine and well balanced.

★★★★ The Solo Sessions Vol. 1
Milestone M 9170 *Evans.* 1/63.

★★★(★) The Solo Sessions Vol. 2
Milestone M 9195 *Evans.* 1/63.

These solo records were both made on the same evening, as part of a contract-fulfilling exercise, and they lay unreleased for over 20 years. The music finds Evans at his most exposed (the tunes include 'Why Was I Born?' and 'What Kind Of Fool Am I?'), and there's an underlying tone of aggressive disquiet, which has to be set against some deliriously lyrical passages. Two medleys – of 'My Favourite Things/Easy To Love/Baubles, Bangles And Beads' and 'Love Theme From Spartacus/Nardis' – are particularly revealing (both are on *Volume 1*), and there's a reading of 'Ornithology' on the second disc which sounds as vital and energized as anything that Evans recorded for Riverside.

★★★★ The Complete Riverside Recordings
Riverside 018 12CD *Personnel collected from all above-listed OJC records.* 56–63.

This huge collection is certainly a breathtaking monument to Evans's art, and it would merit coronation if the individual albums weren't so easily available. It includes all the music listed on the OJC albums above, as well as the two solo discs on Milestone, which originally made their first appearance in this boxed set.

★★★(★) Empathy / A Simple Matter Of Conviction
Verve 837757-2 *Evans; Monty Budwig, Eddie Gomez (b); Shelly Manne (d).* 8/62–10/66.

Although Budwig is excellent and Gomez, making his debut with Evans, is superb, it's the partnership with Manne which is the most interesting thing about these records. Evans seldom responded to a hard-driving drummer – a meeting with Tony Oxley in the '70s was fairly disastrous – but Manne's canny momentum creates sparks of interplay without disturbing the pianist's equilibrium. That said, the high spontaneity of these sessions sometimes misses the clarity of thought which is at the core of Evans's music, and although there's a flashing ingenuity in their playing on, say, 'With A Song In My Heart' with its mischievous coda, the more considered strengths of the pianist's regular trios are finally more satisfying. But Evans fans mustn't miss it.

★★★(★) Conversations With Myself
Verve 521409-2 *Evans (p solo).* 1–2/63.

★★★(★) Trio '64
Verve 539058-2 *Evans; Gary Peacock (b); Paul Motian (d).* 12/63.

These discs show how much music Evans was coming up with in this period. An entire album of overdubbed three-way piano, something only Tristano had tried before, and another new trio taking on a striking set of fresh material. *Conversations* has aroused sometimes fierce views both for and against its approach, but in an age where overdubbing is more or less the norm in record-making, its musicality is more important. Carefully graded, each line sifted against the others, this is occasionally too studied a record, and the follow-up *Further Conversations With Myself* is arguably more graciously realized. But 'Theme From Spartacus' and a fine-grained 'Round Midnight' are pieces where Evans seems to gaze at his own work and find it compelling. The trio record features Peacock's only official appearance with Evans, and the empathy is stunningly adventurous. On 'Little Lulu', for instance, the reach of the bassist's lines and his almost flamenco-like rhythms score brilliant points against the pianist's own energetic choruses. Motian, for once, seems subdued. Both of these are now available in Verve's Master Edition series, and *Trio '64* has been expanded to include seven alternatives and one 'new' piece, 'My Heart Stood Still'.

★★★ Trio '65
Verve 519808-2 *Evans; Chuck Israels (b); Larry Bunker (d).* 2/65.

★★★ Bill Evans Trio With Symphony Orchestra
Verve 821983-2 *Evans; Chuck Israels (b); Larry Bunker, Grady Tate (d); strings, directed by Claus Ogerman.* 9–12/65.

Trio '65 documents a good rather than a great edition of the trio on a middling day in the studios, although it still sounds better than most piano-trio dates. The tempos sound rather brusque – this is a good one to play to people who still think Evans was pure marshmallow – and some of the tracks seem to be curtly dismissed, but there is still a good 'Round Midnight' and a fine 'If You Could See Me Now'. The album with arrangements by Claus Ogerman is very pretty, if hardly a milestone in jazz meets the symphony. Ogerman's charts are sweetly romantic rather than overbearing, and this gives the trio some space in which to work; if the confections which the arranger makes out of Bach, Chopin, Fauré and Granados are scarcely challenging, he manages to make it sound a plausible backdrop to the pianist's musings, and 'Time Remembered' and 'My Bells' sound fine, too.

★★★(★) At Town Hall
Verve 831271-2 *Evans; Chuck Israels (b); Arnold Wise (d). 2/66.*
★★★(★) Intermodulation
Verve 833771-2 *Evans; Jim Hall (g). 66.*
★★★(★) Further Conversations With Myself
Verve 559832-2 *Evans (p solo). 8/67.*
★★★(★) At The Montreux Jazz Festival
Verve 827844-2 *Evans; Eddie Gomez (b); Jack DeJohnette (d). 6/68.*
★★★ Alone
Verve 833801-2 *Evans (p solo). 9–10/68.*
★★★ The Best Of Bill Evans On Verve
Verve 527906-2 *As above Verve discs. 5/63–12/69.*

Evans's period with Verve went on to produce two further in-concert albums and his first officially released solo record, aside from the multi-tracked albums. *At Town Hall* includes some exquisite playing on his favourite standards, together with the long 'Solo – In Memory Of His Father', a requiem that includes 'Turn Out The Stars'. Wise makes his only appearance in the Evans canon and keeps out of the way. The Montreux disc was a Grammy winner in its day and is another one-time-only appearance for DeJohnette – hardly the ideal man for the position – but, along with fellow recruit Gomez, he pushes Evans into his most tigerish form. 'Nardis' and 'A Sleepin' Bee' sound particularly strong. Much of the solo album's music sounds low-voltage, even for Evans, but the very long (over 14 minutes) exploration of 'Never Let Me Go' investigates what would become Keith Jarrett territory, with both prowess and resource to spare. The CD includes alternative takes of three of the pieces. *Intermodulation* is maybe not quite as perfect as was *Undercurrent*, their earlier disc; the choice of material encourages a slightly less ethereal feel. But this is still Evans and Hall together, which ought to be commendation enough.

Further Conversations With Myself repeats the trick of his earlier overdubbed solo set and, though this one is far less well known, we prefer it for its more complete picture of Evans as a soloist, talking to himself. 'Emily' is played almost friskily, 'The Shadow Of Your Smile' is meticulously prepared from its simple beginnings. Sometimes he takes a wrong turning, but it remains a rather endearing kind of record. The sound, though, is still not very kind, even in this Verve Master Edition.

The Best Of Bill Evans On Verve is a taster for the complete edition of 18 CDs listed below. This picks a dozen tracks from 12 albums to make a very playable sampler. If one returns to his Riverside albums as the best of Evans, the Verve sequence has plenty of treasure, usefully dipped into here.

★★★(★) The Complete Bill Evans On Verve
Verve 527953-2 18CD *Evans; Don Elliott (mel, vib, perc); Phil Woods (cl); Stan Getz (ts); Jeremy Steig (f); Sam Brown, Jim Hall (g); Monty Budwig, Eddie Gomez, Chuck Israels, Ron Carter, Richard Davis, Gary Peacock, Ernie Furtado (b); Shelly Manne, Ed Shaughnessy, Elvin Jones, Philly Joe Jones, Larry Bunker, Grady Tate, Arnold Wise, Jack DeJohnette, Marty Morell, Al Beldini (d); Monica Zetterlund (v); strings and brass. 7/57–3/70.*

The size and packaging of this set, one of the biggest single-artist reissues of all time, originally excited much comment – it comes in a slowly oxidizing metal container, which one has to get used to, since it's no straightforward matter getting the CDs out. What, though, of the music? It collects all of Evans's sessions for Verve, with a lot of previously unheard material included, starting with an obscure set from the 1957 Newport Festival with Don Elliott (dispensable) and going as far as Mickey Leonard's arrangements for strings and Evans's electric piano (uneventful). In between are all the Verve discs discussed above, and much else.

The most significant prize is surely the full collection of tracks by Evans with Gomez and Philly Joe Jones from the Village Vanguard in August 1967. The original double-LP of 14 tracks is expanded to an astonishing 46 tunes on three discs. Evans liked to play with Jones, with whom he had worked in the Miles Davis band years before, and the drummer's prodding, restless manner brought out a rare kind of intensity in the pianist. Instead of his collected self, there's a more improvisatory – almost daredevil – manner at certain moments which few other performers seemed to find in him. For these items alone the set is valuable.

The session with Monica Zetterlund is a favourite of ours, although one has to have a certain sympathy with this idiosyncratic singer, and as graciously as Evans plays he could hardly have seen this as an essential part of his work. Most of the remaining material is discussed above, although it's good to have the often-forgotten album with Gary McFarland arrangements from 1963. Several sessions have extra takes and the final couple of discs offer various offcuts, including a complete deconstruction of the MGM album, *From Left To Right*, with numerous alternatives. Aside from the material with Jones, which will surely be released separately in the fullness of time, there's actually little here to truly excite any re-evaluation, although the remastered sound seems very well handled throughout. The accompanying booklet (more like a book) includes all documentation and several interviews. It is a tempting package, although good as the best of it is, there is enough middling material to warrant our withholding a top recommendation. Evans scholars will want it anyway; the rest of us may be more inclined to pull the individual discs off the shelf.

★★★ From Left To Right
Verve 557451-2 *Evans; Sam Brown (g); Eddie Gomez (b); Marty Morell (d); orchestra. 69–70.*

Originally released on MGM, this is one of Evans's most obscure records (though it also appears in the set listed above). Evans plays acoustic and electric pianos, there are some not especially edifying arrangements by Mickey Leonard, and there's a hint of Creed Taylor in the overall feel. For completists only.

★★★ You're Gonna Hear From Me
Milestone 9164 *Evans; Eddie Gomez (b); Marty Morell (d). 11/69.*
★★★ Montreux II
Columbia 481264-2 *As above. 6/70.*
★★(★) The Bill Evans Album
Columbia CK 30855/480989-2 *As above. 5/71.*
★★★ The Tokyo Concert
Original Jazz Classics OJC 345 *As above. 1/73.*
★★★ Live In Tokyo
Columbia 481265-2 *As above. 1/73.*

Some of the steam had gone out of Evans's career on record at this point, after the astonishing consistency of his first ten years in the studio. Gomez, a great technician, has an immediately identifiable 'soulful' sound which tends to colour his lines a mite too highly: his interplay with the leader assumes a routine excellence which Morell, a fine if self-effacing drummer, tends to play alongside rather than inside; and bass and piano take more conspicuously solo turns rather than seeking out the three-way interplay of the earlier trios. On their own terms, the individual albums are still usually very good and highly enjoyable. *You're Gonna Hear From Me*, cut live at Copenhagen's Montmartre, is a lively date, with 'Waltz For Debby' taken at possibly its fastest-ever tempo, a surprisingly light-hearted 'Round Midnight' and an excellent 'Nardis' in a generally bountiful session. Evans dabbles with a little electric piano on *Album*, but both Japanese concerts are straightahead and flow with ideas; 'Up With The Lark' on the OJC is a marvellous piece, and the Columbia version is almost as good. *The Bill Evans Album* was always a weak note in the Evans discography and the latest edition sounds no better. *Montreux II* is fine on its own terms, but this is a very familiar programme and nothing especially stands out.

***** The Secret Sessions**

Milestone 4421-2 8CD *Evans; Teddy Kotick, Eddie Gomez (b); Arnie Wise, Philly Joe Jones, Jack DeJohnette, John Dentz, Marty Morell, Eliot Zigmund (d).* 3/66–1/75.

Evans was the kind of musician to create disciples in listeners as well as musicians, and there was none more diligent than Mike Harris, who lugged in a semi-portable tape-machine to the Village Vanguard over a period of ten years to catch Evans at work. The tapes have been cleaned up by Milestone and feature various incarnations of the trio over a decade of jazz. Aside from the earliest date, where Teddy Kotick does a good job, it's Eddie Gomez all the way, with six different drummers. The sessions with Philly Joe Jones are especially interesting, although Verve's big box elicits much similar material in better sound. It's the fidelity which is the real problem with these eight discs. Perhaps it's better than most amateur recordings, but not much: the bass booms and always seems over-prominent, the crowd chatters, and finely though Evans often plays, he's never done justice by the equipment. One feels that only the most hungry of admirers won't be disappointed. Still, besides the obvious linchpins of the Evans repertoire, there are a number of tunes he seldom looked at and, for all the dustiness of the sound, Milestone have clearly done their best to create a singular document, which this is.

***** Since We Met**

Original Jazz Classics OJC 622 *Evans; Eddie Gomez (b); Marty Morell (d).* 1/74.

***** Re: Person I Knew**

Original Jazz Classics OJC 749 *As above.* 1/74.

***** Jazzhouse**

Milestone M 9151 *As above.* 74.

***** Blue In Green**

Milestone M 9185 *As above.* 74.

***** Intuition**

Original Jazz Classics OJC 470 *As above, except omit Morell.* 11/74.

***** Montreux III**

Original Jazz Classics OJC 644 *As above.* 7/75.

***** From The 70's**

Original Jazz Classics 1069 *As above.* 73–74.

Evans signed to Fantasy (the source of the OJC material listed above) and with his assiduous producer, Helen Keane, created a big body of work that lasted through the '70s. *Since We Met* and *Re: Person I Knew* both come from a single Village Vanguard engagement and, though Gomez and Morell don't erode memories of LaFaro and Motian, the music speaks with as much eloquence as this trio could muster. *Jazzhouse* and *Blue In Green* are more recent 'discoveries' of Evans concerts, which tell us nothing new about him and must be considered for collectors only, even if the playing is mostly impeccable. Consistency had become Evans's long suit, and he seemed content to tinker endlessly with his favourite pieces, disclosing little beyond the beauty of his touch, which by now was one of the most admired and imitated methods in piano jazz. *From The 70's* salvages two duets with Gomez and a live set from The Manne Hole. The two albums with Gomez as sole partner explore a wider range of material – *Montreux III* is a particularly well-turned concert set – but one still misses the extra impetus of a drummer.

*****(*) Alone (Again)**

Original Jazz Classics OJC 795 *Evans (p solo).* 12/75.

***** Crosscurrents**

Original Jazz Classics OJC 718 *Evans; Lee Konitz (as); Warne Marsh (ts); Eddie Gomez (b); Eliot Zigmund (d).* 2–3/77.

****(*) Quintessence**

Original Jazz Classics OJC 698 *Evans; Harold Land (ts); Kenny Burrell (g); Ray Brown (b); Philly Joe Jones (d).* 5/76.

***** I Will Say Goodbye**

Original Jazz Classics OJC 761 *Evans; Eddie Gomez (b); Eliot Zigmund (d).* 5/79.

***** Eloquence**

Original Jazz Classics OJC 814 *Evans; Eddie Gomez (b).* 11/73–12/75.

***** The Complete Fantasy Recordings**

Fantasy 1012 9CD *As all Fantasy/OJC sessions listed above.* 73–79.

The Fantasy material isn't on a par with the magnificent complete Riverside set, but it has many rewards and the complete edition includes two bonuses: an interview with Marian McPartland from her *Piano Jazz* radio series, and a 1976 date in Paris. A few recent reissues have brought some other Fantasy sessions back into general circulation. *Crosscurrents* is another interesting if ultimately unremarkable meeting with two great horn players. *I Will Say Goodbye* finds the trio tackling some relatively unfamiliar material in 'A House Is Not A Home', 'Quiet Light' and 'Seascape'. But it's good to have the neglected *Alone (Again)* as a separate release. This features some very fine Evans on five favourite standards, with a long and wide-ranging exploration of 'People' as the highlight. *Quintessence* provided some answer as to what Evans would have done if he'd recorded more frequently with a bigger group in his later years – he would have made an amiable and not especially interesting Evans-plus-horns date. *Eloquence* is a mixture of solos and duets with Eddie Gomez, some studio, some live. Losing the drummer doesn't do anything special for the situation, but two ballads, 'In A Sentimental Mood' and 'But Beautiful', are notably effective.

****** The Tony Bennett/Bill Evans Album**
Original Jazz Classics OJC 439 *Evans; Tony Bennett (v).* 6/75.

***** Together Again**
Concord CCD-2198-2 *As above.* 9/76.

Pairing Evans with Tony Bennett was an inspired idea that pays off in a session which has an illustrious kind of after-hours feel to it. Bennett, as big-hearted as always, lives out the helpless-Romeo lyrics of such as 'When In Rome', and sounds filled with wonder when working through a gorgeous 'The Touch Of Your Lips'. He also sings what's surely the definitive vocal version of 'Waltz For Debby', where the corn of Gene Lees's lyric suddenly sounds entirely right. Evans plays deferentially but creates some lovely accompaniments and seems to read every mood with complete accuracy.

For some reason the follow-up album was nothing like as good. There's nothing as sly and lively as 'When In Rome' here, and the session has a droopy feel that the preponderance of doleful lyrics only accentuates, even though, one track at a time, there are still some lovely episodes.

***** You Must Believe In Spring**
Warner Bros 8122-73719-2 *Evans; Eddie Gomez (b); Eliot Zigmund (d).* 8/77.

***** New Conversations**
Warner Bros 7559-27505-2 *Evans (p solo).* 1–2/78.

***** Affinity**
Warner Bros 7599-27387-2 *Evans; Larry Schneider (ss, ts, f); Toots Thielemans (hca); Marc Johnson (b); Eliot Zigmund (d).* 10–11/78.

***** We Will Meet Again**
Warner Bros 7599-27504-2 *Evans; Tom Harrell (t); Larry Schneider (ts, ss, f); Marc Johnson (b); Joe LaBarbera (d).* 8/79.

*****(*) The Paris Concert Edition One**
Warner Bros 7559-60311-2 *As above, except omit Harrell and Schneider.* 11/79.

*****(*) The Paris Concert Edition Two**
Warner Bros 7599-60311-2 *As above.* 11/79.

Evans's Warners albums are comparatively neglected and little talked-of. *Affinity*, co-credited with Toots Thielemans, was the first album to feature his final bassist, Marc Johnson, and some of the music is heartbreakingly lovely, although Thielemans, when tuned in to the typical Evans wavelength, can often sound helplessly doleful on his horn. There are some tunes which Evans was trying out as new elements of his set, such as Paul Simon's 'I Do It For Your Love', and even Schneider contributes 'Tomato Kiss'. Somehow it feels a bit stiff and produced, though, and 'The Other Side Of Midnight' and one or two others come out sounding like mere mood music. *We Will Meet Again*, in dedication to Bill's late brother, Harry Evans, brings in Harrell and LaBarbera. Once one gets past the idea that a two-horns-plus-rhythm quintet is simply not Evans's natural environment at this point, the playing seems fine but, despite some more new tunes and Harrell's flowing solos, the music lacks focus – or particularity, even – which is rather discouraging.

New Conversations restores the multiple-overdubbing technique which Evans had tackled during his Verve years. He uses acoustic and electric pianos for some extra tonal variation, and the results are very pleasing rather than compelling. 'Remembering The Rain', for instance, is characteristically beautiful in the pianistic touch, but more of a pretty-pastel piece than anything.

The live albums are both from the same Paris concert. Though the trio was still quite new, it was already forging new momentum out of the pianist's favourite pieces, and there are some very fine things here: 'Re: Person I Knew', 'Laurie' and 'Quiet Now' are good enough to stand with the best of his many versions of these, and he has another go at 'I Did It For Your Love' on the first record. The sound is mostly good, though Johnson's bass – less 'pneumatic' than Gomez – isn't quite focused in the mix.

The appearance of *You Must Believe In Spring*, actually the earliest of this group, pretty much completes this part of the story. Evans introduced his rather annoying obsession with 'Theme From MASH' here, and some of the other tunes pander to ideas of the pianist as romantic misery, but a bonus version of 'Freddie Freeloader' makes a nice compensation.

***** Half Moon Bay**
Milestone 9282-2 *Evans; Eddie Gomez (b); Mary Morell (d).* 11/73.

***** Getting Sentimental**
Milestone 9336-2 *Evans; Michael Moore (b); Philly Joe Jones (d).* 1/78.

***** Homecoming**
Milestone 9291-2 *Evans; Marc Johnson (b); Joe LaBarbera (d).* 11/79.

In the search for fresh and unheard Evans, Milestone has uncovered these three dates. *Half Moon Bay* was done at a favourite little beach-house club in California and finds the 1973 trio in rare form, the usual set but played with particular intensity. *Getting Sentimental* has real rarity value (it's another one of the private recordings made by Mike Harris) and catches Michael Moore auditioning for the trio, with Philly Joe on drums. As a set of trio music it's perhaps nothing all that special, and the sound is only average, but Evans collectors will certainly want to hear it. *Homecoming* is from the days of the final trio and was done at Bill's old Alma Mater in Hammond, Louisiana – hence the title. Again, the music is played with considerable gutsiness – hear the almost thunderous ending to 'But Beautiful' – and is personalized by the pianist's many spoken introductions, a rarity in the Evans discography. We award only moderate ratings, though, since each is an amateur recording and well short of the accustomed standard. Admirers will certainly want to hear them, but casual followers may be disappointed.

***** Letter To Evan**
Dreyfus 191064-2 *Evans; Marc Johnson (b); Joe LaBarbera (d).* 7/80.

*****(*) The Brilliant**
Timeless CDSJP 329 *As above.* 8–9/80.

*****(*) Consecration 1**
Timeless SJP 331 *As above.* 8–9/80.

*****(*) Consecration 2**
Timeless SJP 332 *As above.* 8–9/80.

Evans was still being almost obsessively documented by concert microphones. Several months with Philly Joe Jones at the drums seem to have gone undocumented, but Johnson and LaBarbera eventually proved to be a challenging team which propelled the pianist through a remarkable burst of creativity. He compared this group to his original band with LaFaro and Motian, and there's certainly a sense of an evolving music, with the three men playing as a close-knit ensemble and Evans stretching out in improvisations which were roaming much more freely than before. Even long solos had hitherto kept a relatively tight hold of the thematic material underpinning them but, in all the concerts which these discs cover, Evans sounds unencumbered by frameworks, and such pieces as 'Letter To Evan' (*The Brilliant*) are as close to clear freedom as he ever came. The Timeless records all come from an engagement at San Francisco's Keystone Korner and chart a very high level of playing, with Johnson especially challenging memories of the many great bassmen who had worked with Evans. Fine recording. They have now also been combined as a three-disc box (Timeless SJP 009). *Letter To Evan* is marred by confused sound, but there's still some very committed and powerful music here.

*****(*) Turn Out The Stars**
Warner Bros 45925-2 6CD *Evans; Marc Johnson (b); Joe LaBarbera (d).* 6/80.

***** The Last Waltz**
Milestone 4430-2 8CD *As above.* 9/80.

***** Consecration**
Milestone 4436-2 8CD *As above.* 8–9/80.

Here is the final Evans group in an extended series of performances, from a Village Vanguard residency for *Turn Out The Stars*. It is in many ways a great set of performances. Evans was clearly prepared to try new things with this group, and although one sometimes feels the music is struggling rather aimlessly with form, as if reluctant to seek a freedom that would ultimately be more confining, the group feels vital in a way that Evans's trios hadn't touched on in some time. There are the expected tunes, present and correct, and in the best of them – 'Nardis', for instance – Evans, Johnson and LaBarbera find genuine new ground in repertoire that the pianist might otherwise have done to death.

The only drawback may be a sense of loss which long-time Evans admirers might feel is palpable in the music. The seraphic glow in Evans's early and middle period is sometimes glimpsed here, but seldom; for all the ingenuities on show, some of the songlike beauty which enlightens his most affecting music has vanished. In its place is a certain heaviness of hand and probably heart. Johnson and LaBarbera, team players of a different disposition, in some ways seem more at home in these expanded settings than Evans does. Either way, devotees will want to decide for themselves.

And now they also have an even more close-to-the-bone farewell in *The Last Waltz*, no fewer than eight discs of Evans from his final completed residency, at San Francisco's Keystone Korner. These performances were made only days before the pianist's death. Evans students will certainly want to study the six versions of 'Nardis', and his final thoughts on 'new' pieces such as 'I Do It For Your Love', as well as the familiar watermarks. As with *Turn Out The Stars*, there's an impression of energy being forced through the fingers, and working through the music seems like a much tougher assignment than following the playing of the younger Evans. That said, there remain passages which would be the envy of most other pianists in jazz. This has now been joined by yet another eight-disc set, which is mostly the first sets taken down on the same evenings. Without wishing to opt out of a more considered discussion, it's hard to think of much else to add. As before, certain tunes get several treatments (six of 'My Romance', although this is one of the most interesting vehicles for the pianist's thinking, five each of 'Tiffany' and 'Your Story' and five of 'Re: Person I Knew'). While he plays some tunes at an overfast pace, others are slowly unfolded in a vintage Evans manner. No musician should be asked to stand up to this kind of obsessive scrutiny, but it should be said that for all their idiosyncrasies, there's much fine music in all of these sets.

Gil Evans (1912–88)

PIANO, ARRANGER, COMPOSER

His name is famously an anagram of Svengali and Gil spent much of his career shaping the sounds and musical philosophies of younger musicians. His association with Miles Davis was definitive of one strain of modern jazz, but Gil went on to rewrite the musical legacy of Jimi Hendrix as well. Born in Canada, and serving a hard-knocks apprenticeship in Claude Thornhill's band (which also had a big impact on Miles), Gil drew heavily on Duke Ellington as both composer and arranger. His peerless voicings are instantly recognizable.

***** Gil Evans And Ten**
Original Jazz Classics OJC 346 *Evans; John Carisi, Jack Loven, Louis Mucci (t); Jimmy Cleveland, Bart Varsalona (tb); Willie Ruff (hn); Lee Konitz (as); Steve Lacy (ss); Dave Kurtzer (bsn); Paul Chambers (b); Jo Jones, Nick Stabulas (d).* 9–10/57

The sessions on *Gil Evans And Ten*, recorded four months after his epochal arrangements for *Miles Ahead*, are oblique, intelligent modern jazz, with Carisi's trumpet prominent, Lee Konitz and Steve Lacy lending the reed parts the floating feel typical of an Evans chart. It's a record somewhat overshadowed by the Impulse! and Verve sessions below, but there's still plenty to listen to and enjoy.

CORE COLLECTION

****** Out Of The Cool**
Impulse! 051186-2 *Evans; Johnny Coles, Phil Sunkel (t); Keg Johnson, Jimmy Knepper (tb); Tony Studd (btb); Bill Barber (tba); Ray Beckenstein, Eddie Cane (as, f, picc); Budd Johnson (ts, ss); Bob Tricarico (f, picc, bsn); Ray Crawford (g); Ron Carter (b); Elvin Jones, Charli Persip (d).* 12/60.

***Out Of The Cool* is Evans's masterpiece under his own name (some might want to claim the accolade for some of his work with Miles) and one of the best examples of jazz orchestration since the early Ellington bands. It's the soloists – Coles on the eerie 'Sunken Treasure', a lonely-sounding Knepper on 'Where Flamingoes Fly' – that immediately catch the ear, but repeated hearings reveal the relaxed sophistication of Evans's settings, which give a hefty band the immediacy and elasticity of a quintet. Evans's sense of time allows Coles to double the metre on George Russell's 'Stratusphunk', which ends palindromically, with a clever inversion of the opening measures. 'La Nevada' is one of his best and most neglected scores, typically built up out of quite simple materials. The sound, already good, has been enhanced by digital transfer, revealing yet more timbral detail.**

★★★(★) The Individualism Of Gil Evans

Verve 833804-2 *Evans; Ernie Royal, Johnny Coles, Bernie Glow, Louis Mucci (t); Jimmy Cleveland, Tony Studd (tb); Ray Alonge, Jimmy Buffington, Gil Cohen, Don Corado, Bob Northern, Julius Watkins (frhn); Bill Barber (tba); Al Block, Garvin Bushell, Eric Dolphy, Andy Fitzgerald, Steve Lacy, George Marge, Jerome Richardson, Wayne Shorter, Bob Tricarico (reeds); Kenny Burrell, Barry Galbraith (g); Bob Maxwell, Margaret Ross (hp); Paul Chambers, Richard Davis, Milt Hinton, Gary Peacock, Ben Tucker (b); Osie Johnson, Elvin Jones (d).* 9/63, 4 & 7/64.

★★★ Verve Jazz Masters 23: Gil Evans

Verve 516728-2 *Similar to above.* 63–64

Individualism is a looser album, made with a pool of overlapping ensembles, perfectly tailored to the compositions and all securely grounded in the bass. The solos are now mainly improvised rather than written, and stray more freely from the original composition, in anticipation of the '80s bands. 'Hotel Me' is an extraordinary performance, basically very simple but marked by throaty shouts from the brass that set up Evans's own churchy solo. 'El Toreador' again features Coles, less certain-sounding than on *Out Of The Cool*, but still a soloist of considerable imagination. Remarkable as the music is, there's an oddly unfinished feel to the record, as if it had been put together out of previously rejected bits and pieces. It isn't just a CD round-up, though. The *Jazz Masters* album doesn't pretend to be anything else, but it's actually a well-paced and wholly convincing survey, ideal for anyone coming at Gil's music with no previous acquaintance or no stock of old vinyl.

★★★(★) Svengali

ACT 9207 *Evans; Tex Allan, Hannibal Marvin Peterson, Richard Williams (t); Joseph Daley (tb, tba); Sharon Freeman, Peter Levin (frhn); David Sanborn (as); Billy Harper (ts, f); Trevor Koehler (ss, bs, f); Howard Johnson (bs, tba, flhn); David Horowitz (syn); Ted Dunbar (g); Herb Bushler (b); Bruce Ditmas (d); Sue Evans (perc).* 73.

'Zee Zee' reappears on *Svengali* as a feature for the incendiary Peterson, who turns it into a prolonged cry of anger, exhilaration and commanding abstraction, surprisingly different from his usual run of things. The other big number is Harper's own 'Cry Of Hunger', a companion piece on this concert recording, prominently featuring the composer and apparently reassembled at the production stage by Evans, who thus becomes an *ex post facto* composer in the way that he and Teo Macero often were on Miles projects. The sound is very good, given the live provenance, and the horns all come through with striking clarity. Not so some aspects of the extended rhythm section, which often sounds distant and out of focus.

★★★(★) Plays The Music Of Jimi Hendrix

RCA Victor 09026 638722 *Evans; Hannibal Marvin Peterson, Lew Soloff (t, flhn); Tom Malone (tb, btb, f, syn); Peter Gordon (frhn); Pete Levin (frhn, syn); Howard Johnson (tba, bcl, b); David Sanborn (ss, as, f); Billy Harper (ts, f); Trevor Koehler (as, ts, f); David Horovitz (p, syn); Paul Metzke (syn, b); Joe Gallivan (syn, perc); John Abercrombie, Ryo Kawasaki, Keith Loving (g); Warren Smith (vib, mar); Don Pate, Michael Moore (b); Bruce Ditmas (d); Sue Evans (perc).* 6/74, 4/75.

A title like that probably did raise eyebrows in 1974. Evans's championing of Hendrix's compositions – 'Little Wing' most immortally – was a controversial but ultimately career-stoking decision. It's a little difficult to tell, while listening to these powerful tracks, whether the quality of the music is testimony to Hendrix's genius as a composer or Evans's as an arranger, or to some strange posthumous communication between the two. Some of the tunes are inevitably moved a long way from source; '1983 A Merman I Should Turn To Be' takes on a new character, as does 'Up From The Skies', two takes of which are included. 'Little Wing' remains the touchstone, though, and the recording, from spring 1975, is superb. Now reissued with extra tracks, the Hendrix set is essential listening.

★★(★) Live At The Public Theater Volume 1

Storyville STCD 5003 *Evans; Jon Faddis, Hannibal Marvin Peterson, Lew Soloff (t); George E. Lewis (tb); Dave Bargeron (tb, tba); Arthur Blythe (as, ss); Hamiet Bluiett (bs, a f); John Clark (hn); Masabumi Kikuchi, Pete Levin (syn); Tim Landers (b); Billy Cobham (d).* 2/80.

★★(★) Live At The Public Theater Volume 2

Storyville STCD 5005 *As above.* 2/80.

A transitional band in most regards, with all the lags and hesitancies that implies. Individual performances are generally good, but there's a lack of excitement about the music and a greater abstraction than in preceding and later line-ups. Hendrix sits very comfortably alongside Evans's favourite Mingus tune, 'Orange Was The Color Of Her Dress ...'.

★★★ Live At Umbria Jazz: Volume 1

Appaloosa 1002 *Evans; Miles Evans, Tom Malone, Shunzu Ohno, Lew Soloff (t); George E. Lewis (tb); John Clark (frhn); Dave Bargeron (btb, tba); Chris Hunter (ss, as); John Surman (bs, ky); Gil Goldstein, Pete Levin (ky); Delmar Brown (ky, v); Emily Mitchell (hp); Mark Egan (b); Danny Gottlieb (d); Anita Evans (perc); Urszula Dudziak (v).* 87.

★★★ Live At Umbria Jazz: Volume 2

Appaloosa 1003 *As above.* 87.

These recordings from late in the career of Evans's touring band seem to be available under a number of imprints, which may raise some questions about the exact provenance. However, these are fine, fiery performances from a time-served band. They cover the now familiar range of composers with Hendrix and Mingus very much to the fore, and if you have a need for another version of 'Little Wing', here it is (volume 2). Pete Levin's 'Subway' on the first disc and Urszula Dudziak's 'Wake Up' on the second are well worth having; there is also some interest in hearing John Surman with the Evans band, but by this stage in the game, you either know what this outfit was about or you probably don't care.

★★★ Paris Blues

Owl 013429-2 *Evans; Steve Lacy (ss).* 12/87.

Rather nice to have this back in print, although it's scarcely a momentous occasion, musically speaking, for either man. Mingus themes predominate, and Gil takes yet another look at 'Orange Was The Color Of Her Dress', which was likely the last thing on his music-stand. Interesting to hear Lacy at work on this music, but in the end the results are merely light and agreeable.

★★★ 75th Birthday Concert

BBC Legends 7007 *Evans; Miles Evans, Palle Mikkelborg, Lew Soloff (t); Dave Bargeron (btb, tba); Steve Lacy (ss); Chris Hunter (ss, as); John Surman (ss, bs); Don Weller (ts); Delmar*

Brown (ky, v); Hiram Bullock (g); Mark Egan (b); Danny Gottlieb (d); Anita Evans, Airto Moreira (perc). 87.

Gil's 75th birthday was marked by a special concert at the Hammersmith Odeon in London, recorded for broadcast by the BBC and now available on disc. The occasion was distinguished by a brief walk-on from Van Morrison, who delivered an excruciating version of 'Moondance' before disappearing again; mercifully it is not included in the recording. What is, is a valuable interview with Evans, conducted by the late Charles Fox. Musically, it's very much of its time and period, with cuts from two houses in the big hall, which was shamefully underfilled. Both versions of 'Stone Free' are very good and there are a couple of cracking Mingus interpretations, but it's the surprise elements – 'Murder By Numbers' and 'Synchronicity' – that really catch the ear. The recording is as good as you'd expect, with lots of presence in the orchestra and plenty of detail round individual horns.

***** The Honey Man**

Newtone 5022 *Evans; Stanton Davis, Miles Evans, Shunzu Ohno (t); George E. Lewis (tb); John Clark (frhn); Howard Johnson (tba, bs, bcl); Chris Hunter (ss, as, f); Hiram Bullock (g); Mark Egan (b); Danny Gottlieb (d).* n.d.

Released in 2000, this fills in our picture of the Monday Night Orchestra only somewhat. There are versions of Mingus's 'Boogie Stop Shuffle' and 'Goodbye Pork Pie Hat' and of Hendrix's 'Voodoo Chile', but these are relatively bland and crowd-pleasing. The one surprise is the title-track 'Here Comes De Honey Man', a rarely covered Gershwin composition delivered here with raw passion and considerable commitment.

***** A Tribute To Gil**

Soul Note 121209 *Miles Evans (t, perc); Lew Soloff (t); Dave Bargeron, Tom Malone (tb, tba); Chris Hunter (as, f); Alex Foster (ts); Gil Goldstein (ky); Bireli Lagrene (g); Michal Urbaniak (vn); Mark Egan (b); Danny Gottlieb (d); Urszula Dudziak (v, elec).* 7/88.

Gil's death came along with the band's festival diary pretty full, and not surprisingly, the decision was taken to fulfil as many engagements as possible, with Gil Goldstein as concertmaster. These performances were recorded in Italy during July 1988. The two main items selected are long versions of 'Orgone' and 'London' with, by comparison, very short, almost schematic readings of 'Moonstruck One' and 'Eleven', neither of which goes over the two-minute mark. It's to be wondered why and how these selections were made, for they don't seem to answer any obvious logic. Urszula Dudziak is characteristically dramatic in her feature, 'Duet', and the horn, violin and synth solos are all sharp, emphatic and to the point. Even so, we are left to wonder what else was recorded on the tour and why we haven't heard more of it.

Orrin Evans (born 1975)

PIANO

Born in New Jersey, Evans has subsequently worked extensively in and around the Philadelphia scene before moving to New York (and back again): a contemporary pianist-composer with plenty to say.

*****(*) Justin Time**

Criss Cross 1125 *Evans; John Swana (t); Tim Warfield (ts); Rodney Whitaker (b); Byron Landham (d).* 12/96.

*****(*) Captain Black**

Criss Cross 1154 *Evans; Sam Newsome (ss); Antonio Hart (as); Ralph Bowen (ts, ss, as); Tim Warfield (ts); Avishai Cohen (b); Ralph Peterson (d).* 10/97–6/98.

***** Grown Folk Bizness**

Criss Cross 1175 *Evans; Sam Newsome (ss); Ralph Bowen (ts, as); Rodney Whitaker (b); Ralph Peterson (d).* 6/98.

****** Listen To The Band**

Criss Cross 1195 *Evans; Duane Eubanks (t); Sam Newsome (ss); Ralph Bowen (ts, as); Reid Anderson (b); Nasheet Waits (d).* 6/99.

*****(*) Blessed Ones**

Criss Cross 1213 *Evans; Eric Revis (b); Edgar Bateman, Nasheet Waits (d).* 1/01.

Five outstanding records from a very gifted pianist. As a group of projects, they work on several levels: as evidence of the leader's own powers as a player and soloist; as examples of the way standards and familiar repertory are being recharged through a new generation's ideas; and as a showcase for some of the Criss Cross cast of post-bop characters who include a number of tremendous talents.

All of this was obvious from the opener, *Justin Time*, where Evans mixes four originals, four standards and 'Tune Up'. The key player on the date is Tim Warfield, who brings an almost livid colour to Evans's music: their duet on 'My Shining Hour' is in a great tradition of duo virtuosity; but just as impressive is the wonderfully tender examination of 'It Had To Be You' at a daringly slow tempo. Evans's writing has a pleasingly lyrical bent, which his suitably affectionate 'Mom', voiced by Swana's trumpet, makes clear.

Captain Black depends more heavily on Evans's originals, which here and there put ingenuity above communicability – some of the writing sets up high-level challenges for the horn-players, such as the ferociously quick 'Big Jimmy', which they inevitably master while the listener is left a bit short-winded. That said, Bowen and Warfield especially turn in some astonishing solos. Peterson, as is his wont, overplays all through while giving everybody out front enough feeds to let them go wherever. There's a surprising solo version of 'Calvary' which certainly tries new threads on the gospel axis.

Grown Folk Bizness starts with another solo, on 'Rocking Chair', which seems a fussy bit of revisionism, but from there the trio (Bowen and Newsome arrive only for the final three tracks) work through an interesting set of choices – Richie Beirach's 'Elm', 'Bernie's Tune', Ralph Peterson's 'Volition'. Here and there – as in 'Bernie's Tune', for instance – Evans uses his talents to almost nihilistic ends, the tune rendered all but meaningless by his playing. His version of Monk in 'Rhythm-A-Ning' sounds flippant, and the piece is uplifted by Bowen's alto solo. Overall, this set's the weakest of the five.

In contrast, *Listen To The Band* is out of the very top drawer. 'I Want To Be Happy' is this time a dramatically effective standard reworking, apparently from a standing start where the tune wasn't even called. From there, the sextet play mostly originals from within the group, although 'In His Place' is another absorbing variation on a gospel touch, and Evans's solo on 'There Is A Quiet Place' is pensively beautiful. Throughout, the playing is less obviously flashy, better integrated, yet still sounding fresh and contemporary.

No originals, but everything from a couple of Coltrane tunes to the warhorse 'Autumn Leaves' on the all-trio date, *Blessed Ones* – although, as with some earlier standards, you'd be pressed to spot the tune, since he starts from the changes and puts the minor-key feel into the background, so it's much more jaunty and assertive than usual. Pat Metheny's 'Bright Size Life' is treated as a 'breathing-together' tune, a real trio piece. 'I Will Wait For You' gets a thorough demolition. Evans isn't a destructive pianist, but he does like to use only those parts of the material which he thinks are best placed to offer up something new. In contrast, 'The Inchworm' circles regularly around the melody. But some of the most impressive playing comes in the two versions of Trudy Pitts's 'Anysha', done as an undeniably romantic ballad, but with a complexity of feeling that calls for patient and repeated listenings to both versions.

***** Meant To Shine**
Palmetto PM-2087 *Evans; Ralph Bowen (ss, ts, bcl, f); Sam Newsome (ss); Eric Revis (b); Gene Jackson (d).* 1/02.

Evans's debut for Palmetto is perhaps slightly marred by a tendency to earnestness. The tunes are all originals (Bowen and Revis contribute one apiece) and the preponderance of slow to mid-tempos in a tight programme (less than 50 minutes of music, which makes the Criss Cross sessions seem almost verbose) adds to a sense of droopiness. That said, the band play with real power, and in the horn lines on 'Elevation' and 'Commitment' there are glimmers which make one long to hear what Evans might do in a big-band situation. He gives so much frontage to Bowen and Newsome that his own playing sometimes feels set to one side, but in 'Don't Write No Shit About Me' and 'Commitment' there is some mighty playing from the piano. A mixed bag, though Evans admirers will surely want to hear it.

Douglas Ewart (born 1946)

MULTIPLE WIND INSTRUMENTS

Born in Jamaica, Ewart was part of the AACM experience in Chicago and continues to experiment with self-made instruments and an entirely individual aesthetic.

***** Bamboo Meditations At Banff**
Aarawak 003 *Ewart (flutes solo).* 01.

*****(*) Angles Of Entrance**
Aarawak 004 *Ewart; Mwata Bowen, Edward Wilkerson (cl); Anthony Braxton (b flat cbcl, E flat sno cl); Don Byron (ss, bcl); Roscoe Mitchell (scl, bcl); J. D. Parran (cacl, acl); Henry Threadgill (scl); Malachi Favors Mahgostut (b, perc).* 01.

Ewart's rare appearances on record, notably with trombonist George Lewis, have been insufficient to give more than a flavour of his remarkable gifts. These self-produced items are more like the thing and represent the apotheosis of the Ewart endblown flute (basically a kind of recorder) and of part of the clarinet family not even known to Anthony Braxton.

The two CDs offer an ideal introduction to Ewart's soundworld. The solo flute record is virtuosic and very beautiful, while the clarinet choir goes to the heart of the ensemble language that was at the heart of the AACM experience. *Angles Of Entrance* is a rare chance to hear an ensemble of contemporary reed luminaries all together. 'Migrations Of Whales' revisits a long-standing concern and is perhaps too literal to be entirely easy, though if it were called 'Compostion #24' no one would be any the wiser. Apart from a few recognizable Byron licks (he rather stands out from the choir) and some familiar Braxton devices, it's an admirably collective project. Ewart does not push himself forward, which is why the solo record is such an important addition to his limited discography

Don Ewell (1916–83)

PIANO

Born in Baltimore, Ewell was working in the city from the mid-'30s onwards, playing in a style that harked back to the New Orleans fashion of Morton, from a decade earlier. He later played regularly with New Orleans musicians such as Bunk Johnson and George Lewis and worked with Jack Teagarden from 1956 to 1962, before returning to New Orleans. He toured Europe in the years leading up to his death, but he suffered, first through his daughter's illness and then his own, dying at 66.

***** Music To Listen To Don Ewell By**
Good Time Jazz 12021-2 *Ewell; Darnell Howard (cl); Minor Hall (d).* 3/56.

***** Man Here Plays Fine Piano!**
Good Time Jazz 10043-2 *Ewell; George 'Pops' Foster (b); Minor Hall (d).* 2/57.

***** Free 'N' Easy!**
Good Time Jazz 10046 *Ewell; Darnell Howard (cl); George 'Pops' Foster (b); Minor Hall (d).* 6/57.

The much-recorded Ewell hasn't been well served by CD so far, but the recent GTJ reissues restore some of his eminence. A structured, disciplined practitioner of stride piano, Ewell took his cues from New Orleans musicians – his early sessions in the '40s were with Bunk Johnson and George Lewis – without succumbing to any raggedly 'authentic' mannerisms. One hears an almost prim sense of detail in his playing, the tempos unerringly consistent, the left hand a meticulous counterpoint to the right, the variations as refined and logical as in ragtime. The pair of GTJ reissues find him with the great New Orleans drummer, Minor Hall, and between them they offer a seasoned kind of classic jazz piano, without the music ever losing its balance. *Free 'N' Easy!* is more from the same sessions, with Howard more generously featured. It's unpretentious, amiable traditionalism.

***** Live At The 100 Club**
Solo Art SACD-89 *Ewell (p solo).* 2/71.

**** Don Ewell With The Yarra Yarra Band – Nicholas Hall Concert**
GHB BCD-378/9 2CD *Ewell; Maurie Garbutt (t); Roger Janes (tb); Paul Martin (cl, ts); Paul Finerty (g, bj); Don Heap (b); Peter Clowsey (d).* 10/75.

The solo format was arguably not Ewell's natural métier, and the Solo Art session is solid but oddly wearisome over CD duration. His treatment of Fats Waller was somewhere between fanciful and respectful; 'Keepin' Out Of Mischief Now' is almost rococo in some of its designs, while the following 'Handful Of Keys' is very fast and seems to pirouette on tiptoe.

Nicholas Hall Concert finds him on tour in Australia. The Yarra Yarra Band are doughty but not exactly outstanding local players, and this is a pretty average chunk of trad on the road. Docked an extra notch for being released as an expensive double-CD – the best of this could easily have been boiled down to a single disc, with no loss to posterity. There is a lot more of Ewell on LP which has so far not made it to the modern medium.

Excelsior Brass Band

GROUP

One of the most long-standing New Orleans brass bands, the EBB traces its roots back to the 19th century and maintains a venerable tradition.

*****(*) Jolly Reeds And Steamin' Horns**
GHB BCD-290 *Teddy Riley, James May (t); Gregory Stafford (c); Fred Lonzo, Clement Tervalon (tb); Michael White (cl); Oscar Rouzan (as); David Grillier (ts); Walter Payton (bb); Freddie Kohlman, Calvin Spears, Stanley Stephens (d).* 10/83.

The rich yet carefully 'restricted' tradition of New Orleans brass bands made a cautious and piecemeal transition to CD, and this disc by perhaps the oldest institution in the genre – the EBB was originally formed in 1880 – is a very fine example of the tradition as it stands in modern times (or at least in 1983). The digital sound allows one to hear all the detail which scrappy old recordings eliminated, and the ineffable bounce of the drummers (two on snare, one on bass), the old-fashioned tremble of the reeds and the sheer brassiness of the brass create some sense of a living tradition on material which is profoundly historical – 'Just A Closer Walk With Thee', 'Amazing Grace', 'Down In Honky Tonk Town', 'Just A Little While To Stay Here' and so on. At the same time the primitivism of the band can only be affected. Players such as White, Lonzo and Riley could probably go bebop if they wanted to, which one could never say about original brass-band stalwarts. Whether that matters may depend on the ear of the behearer. It still makes for a very spirited and enjoyable session.

Face To Face

GROUP

Lyrical trio with more than one-off potential.

***** Canossa**
Intuition 3238 *Ernie Watts (ts); Jasper van't Hof (p, organ, ky); Bo Stief (b).* 9/99.

This doesn't look the most promising partnership on paper, but both Watts and van't Hof are highly expressive players with their own compositional ideas, while Stief is one of the most underrated bass-players around, and not just in Europe. The chemistry is strong and immediate, audible on the pianist's long title-track, on Stief's 'First Day' and Watts's only contribution this time, 'On The Border'. They do a wonderful version of Charlie Mariano's 'Pink Lady', but other than that do standards or repertory pieces. Van't Hof is the featured composer with four titles but it's Watts's flowing, mellifluous saxophone that dominates the sound-world of a trio that sounds like no other group around. A pity there's been no follow-up on record.

Peter Fairclough

DRUMS, PERCUSSION

British drummer and composer, playing contemporary jazz with a touch of English pastoral.

***** Shepherd Wheel**
ASC CD 1 *Fairclough; Paul Dunmall (ts, ss, Cmel); Peter Whyman (as, ss, cl); Pete Saberton (p); Rick Bolton (g); Tim Harries, Tim Holmes (b); Richard Newby (d, perc); Christine Tobin (v).* 1/95.

***** Wild Silk**
ASC CD 8 *Fairclough; Keith Tippett (p, perc, zither).* 12/95.

*****(*) Permission**
ASC CD 18 *Fairclough; Tim Whitehead (ts); Mike Walker (g); Dudley Phillips (b).* 3/97.

The great strength of a musician like Peter Fairclough is that he never sounds as though he's hitting anything, even when he is playing forcefully. Keith Tippett is, in this regard, a perfect partner and foil. How many times have reviewers attempted to describe his piano-playing as 'percussive but lyrical', or words to that effect? Often, on *Wild Silk*, Fairclough sounds to be playing a melody line to one of Tippett's flowing, multi-layered accompaniments. In addition to keyboard, Tippett also leans deep into the piano interior, using his favoured woodblocks and pebbles on the strings, always sounding fresh and spontaneous, never 'prepared'. The two long tracks, 'The Emerald Tree' and 'In The Glade Of The Woodstone Bird' (titles courtesy of Mrs Tippett), call on a huge array of sounds which need not be identified and sourced to enjoy this music. Indeed, it's probably better that they aren't. As with Ovary Lodge, in which the Tippetts were joined by Harry Miller and Frank Perry, it is positively beneficial to forget who might be playing what.

Unfortunately, that isn't the case with *Shepherd Wheel*, a sincere but rather forced attempt to forge a synthesis between English folk forms and jazz improvisation. The main interest here lies with the solo material, and in particular the contrasting performances of Whyman and Dunmall, both of whom are highly idiosyncratic players. Fairclough's long indenture to the Mike Westbrook group has paid dividends in terms of structure, voicing and pace, but the record as a whole doesn't quite satisfy and comes out a little less than the sum of its parts.

Permission is a relaxed, thoroughly competent contemporary-jazz record, thoughtful rather than powerfully engaged, and marked by attention to basics rather than more ambitious ends. Fairclough's writing has acquired a Latinate feel, almost as if influenced by Chick Corea's *Light As A Feather* period. The opening 'Relic' and 'Misnomer' are heavily marked by Phillips's Stanley Clarke-inspired electric bass lines, less prominent – or perhaps merely easier to overlook – later on the record. There are a couple of collectively written or improvised pieces, of which 'Sandscribe' is the more interesting, and a couple credited to Fairclough and guitarist Walker, who turns in his usual eclectic performance. Of these, 'Wildlife' is the most arresting: big, squally chords laid over a multi-layered percussion figure. Whitehead hasn't the most attractive tone, but it somehow suits this repertoire perfectly, its slight sharpness holding it just ahead of Walker's rather prosaic chords and runs. Fairclough himself plays very quietly and with a lot of space. A good record, easy to overlook.

★★ Imago

Jazzprint JPVP 132 *Fairclough; Keith Tippett (p, perc).* 10/01.

Basically, this is everything that was said on *Wild Silk*, reiterated. Tippett's reluctance to play beyond a small circle of confrères does suggest a narrowing of horizons which seems palpable here, and it does Fairclough few favours to be playing second fiddle in this context.

Richard Fairhurst

PIANO

Started piano at the relatively late age of 15, but quickly emerged as a major force in British jazz composition.

★★★ Hungry Ants

Babel BDV 9404 *Fairhurst; Iain Ballamy, Osian Robert (ss, ts); Steve Watts (b); Tim Giles (d).* 95.

★★★ Formic

Babel BDV 9824 *Fairhurst; Rob Townsend (ss, ts, perc); Tim Harries (b); Tim Giles (d, perc).* 98.

★★★ Myrmidons

Babel BDV 2133 *As above; add Stuart Hall (g).* 02.

Fairhurst's debut, recorded when he was still in his early 20s, bespeaks an older, more mature talent. Some of the writing, or perhaps more accurately some of the track titles, suggest the laddish humour of the Loose Tubes crowd (and former LT saxophonist Iain Ballamy has a similar food obsession), but the content of tunes like 'Lo-Ganberries' and 'Rat On Stilts' bespeaks a wise and thoughtful talent. His playing is not so distinctive, but it doesn't (yet) need to be. Ballamy is the lead voice in Hungry Ants (band name as well as album title), as you'd expect given his experience, and his arrangement of 'Mad About The Boy' is superb and unexpected. They also do a version of Mingus's 'Self Portrait In Three Colours' which rivals the original for sheer verve and perceptiveness.

The second album – and formic acid is the bitter stuff ants secrete when small boys poke sticks and fingers into their nests – is a strong consolidation. Apart from 'Sludge' and the two parts of 'Mandibles', which are collectively composed, and Harries's attractive 'Whenever', all the tunes are by Fairhurst. He doubles on Hammond this time, but shows no particular individuality on the organ. 'Fish Magic' borders on whimsy but is too solid an idea ever to seem merely clever. His playing has developed steadily and on 'Fetish' and 'Growth In An Old Garden' he combines a briskly modern style with a tinge of English pastoralism that is very attractive.

The third album was delayed when Giles suffered an attack of RSI and was sidelined for a period. The classical tinge is still there and so too is a generous range of reference – 'The Twittering Machine' is inspired by a Paul Klee work – that never sounds pretentious or irrelevant.

Al Fairweather (1927–93)

TRUMPET

Born in Edinburgh, Fairweather co-led groups with his frequent partner, Sandy Brown, from the early '50s and helped pioneer the development of the British mainstream sound. He worked with Acker Bilk in the '60s, but thereafter became a full-time teacher and played less often.

★★★(★) Fairweather Friends Made To Measure

Lake LACD75 *Fairweather; Kenny Ball (t); Tony Milliner (tb, btb); John Picard, Chris Barber (tb); Sandy Brown (cl); Bruce Turner, Tony Coe (as); Red Price, Dick Heckstall-Smith (ts); Ian Armit, Stan Greig (p); Bill Bramwell (bj); Tim Mahn (b); Graham Burbidge, Allan Ganley (d).* 11/57–11/61.

This will be nostalgic for readers who were around when the British mainstream was just coming into being, as trad gave way to a more settled idea of small-group swing. *Fairweather Friends* was made for Pye, and the extremely rare *Made To Measure*, issued originally as a limited edition of 100 copies, came out on Ristic. The latter set has the surprise of Kenny Ball sharing front-line duties with Fairweather's big sound, remaining under the Armstrong spell but starting to lean, as was Humphrey Lyttelton, in the direction of Buck Clayton. Solid, but more inventive, is the excellent *Fairweather Friends*, which has the 22-year-old Coe playing handsome alto and the trumpeter turning in some of his best performances. There is a peculiar bonus in the shape of a B-side by the Laurie Johnson Orchestra with Fairweather, Barber and Brown playing 'Doin' The Racoon', an old '20s hot dance number.

Digby Fairweather (born 1946)

TRUMPET, CORNET, MELLOPHONE, VOCALS

Not to be confused with the Scottish cornetist Al Fairweather, Digby turned professional in the '70s – though he continues to write and broadcast – and played with a variety of traditional groups. He has an accurate and expressive tone and solos strongly. We're also happy to report that he is co-author of a jazz reference book almost as distinguished as this one.

★★★ Songs For Sandy

Hep CD 2016 *Fairweather; Roy Crane, Al Fairweather (t); John Picard (tb); Tony Coe (ts); John Barnes (as, cl, bcl); Alan Cooper (bcl); Brian Lemon (p); Dave Green (b); Tony Allen, Bobby Orr (d).* 70, 82.

★★★ With Nat In Mind

Jazzology JCD 247 *Fairweather; Pete Strange (tb); John Barnes (cl, as, bs); Pat Smuts (ts); Dave Lee (p); Paul Sealey (g); Jack Fallon (b); Johnny Armatage (d); Wild Bill Davison, Lisa Lincoln (v).* 94.

★★★(★) Squeezin' The Blues Away

Spirit Of Jazz SOJ CD 10 *Fairweather; Tony Compton (acc, d machine); Lisa Lincoln (v).*

Digby Fairweather's embouchure has been baffling fans and trumpet students for years. Like Ziggy Elman's, it appears to project from just under his right ear. However odd the angle, though, it hasn't adversely affected Fairweather's sound, which is richly toned and curiously delicate, especially at slower tempos.

There are still some who think that it was Digby, not Al Fairweather, who was the great Sandy Brown's playing partner. Dig stands in very comfortably for his namesake on the 1982 *Songs*, a superb convocation of British talent and songs with Brian Lemon and Prudence and Terry Cox, recorded privately. A fitting and heartfelt tribute. The bulk of the record, though, is

Digby's suite of songs, which tell Brown's life in music. 'Singing Away The Cold In Edinburgh' is a legendary anecdote of Sandy and Al still making music even when their horns have been hocked. The other material is equally intense and idiomatic.

Fairweather's tribute to the veteran Nat Gonella is eloquent, nicely paced and includes some of his most characteristic playing. The guest stars span the generations, establishing a link back to Nat's Georgians and their origins in the Lew Stone orchestra. Nat's theme 'Georgia On My Mind' is given a fulsome airing, with Wild Bill taking the vocal. 'I Must See Annie Tonight' carries references of the old master's association with American greats like Benny Carter, and it's treated with due respect. There are less-expected things as well; 'I'm Feelin' Like A Million' is arranged from Nat's original solo, and 'September Song', which Nat never actually recorded, offers him an opportunity to express his satisfaction with the proceedings.

The duos with Compton take a moment or two to get used to, but they are consistently fascinating thereafter. Fairweather plays with a breezy, unfussy clarity, and the accordion wheezes and chugs after its manner, an undersubscribed sound in jazz but one with plenty of untapped potential. Lisa Lincoln, also featured on the Nat tribute, contributes two lovely vocals. (We could, frankly, have done without the drum machine.)

***** Something To Remember Us By**

Jazzology JCD 288/289 2CD *Fairweather; Stan Barker (p).* 84.

***** The Mick Potts Tribute Concert**

Flat Five GBHCD02 *Fairweather; Roy Williams (tb); Dave Shepherd (cl); Kathy Stobart (ts); Brian Lemon (p); Norman Fisk (b); Brian Rogerson (d).* 11/93.

Memories of two lost friends and colleagues. Digby worked with pianist and educator Stan Barker many times and recorded an LP, *Let's Duet*, with him. This is included here, along with a dozen tracks recorded at an arts centre bar in Southport. The live cuts are pretty decently registered, but the studio sound is very flat and unresponsive, and there's probably no more than one good CD spread over the time. It does, though, celebrate an association and the interplay of instruments on 'Lover Man' (two versions), and 'Something To Remember Us By' is definitive of the best of British traditional jazz.

Potts was a fine trumpeter in much the same mould as Digby. Founder of Britain's Greatest Jazz Band, he died unseasonally young, leaving a hole in British jazz. A measure of the affection in which he was held is this BBC-recorded live session from Carlisle. Highlights of a brisk and celebratory evening include Kathy Stobart's feature on 'Emily' and the Fairweather/Lemon duet on 'I Can't Give You Anything But Love'.

***** Recorded Delivery**

Loose Tie Records LOTCD 4310 *Fairweather; Roy Williams (tb, v); Dave Shepherd (cl); Al Gay (ts, cl); Brian Lemon (p); Jim Douglas (g); Len Skeat (b); Allan Ganley (d).* 10/97.

Sponsored by the Post Office, so no surprise to find 'Airmail Special', 'Penny Black Blues', 'I'm Gonna Sit Right Down And Write Myself A Letter' and, of course, 'My Funny Valentine' in this bright, attractive session by some of Britain's senior traditionalists. Fairweather's arrangements are as taut and amiable as ever, and his playing and singing are full of *bonhomie*.

***** Twelve Feet Off The Ground**

Flat Five GBHCD03 *Fairweather; Malcolm Earle Smith (tb, v); Julian Marc Stringle (cl, as, v); Craig Milverton (p, ky, v); Len Skeat (b); Bobby Worth (d).* 99.

***** Moon Country**

A AL73192 *As above, except add Pete Strange (tb), John Barnes (as, bs, bsx, cl, v), Martin Litton (p), Paul Sealey (g, bj), Chris Ellis (v), Bloomfield String Quartet.* 00.

The second of these is, as the title hints, a tribute to the music of Hoagy Carmichael. Digby doubles on piano and penny whistle as well as vocals, and sounds as if he's having a thoroughly good time in the Fairweather's Friends format. Litton is a wonderful accompanist and obviously knows the Carmichael songbook inside out and upside down. The arrangements are generous and generally faithful to the originals, except where Digby has added a more old-fashioned revivalist spin to things like 'Lazybones' and 'Baltimore Oriole'. Other outstanding tracks include 'Manhattan Rag', played at interesting speed, and the closing 'Serenade To Gabriel', which should guarantee Dig his spot in the heavenly chorus. When the time comes.

Twelve Feet is a more conventionally swinging set from the established band. 'Pink Champagne' is segued with 'Sister Kate' and there is a rollicking, salacious version of 'The Blues My Naughty Sweetie Gave To Me'. Digby's tone is strong, but there is a new warmth in the recording, a closeness that suits his style well.

***** Things Ain't What They Used To Be**

Robinwood Productions RWP 0020 *Fairweather; Chris Gower (tb); Julian Marc Stringle (cl, as, v); Craig Milverton (p, ky, v); Dominic Ashworth (g, v); Len Skeat (b); Bobby Worth (d).* 4/03.

The Fairweather Half-Dozen sound more alert and adventurous than ever. There are 18 tracks here and every one of them is sharply crafted and despatched. George Melly turns up for a vocal on 'When My Ship Comes In', sounding as if the vessel in question might have been a rum runner from Barbados. The Ellington/Bigard classic 'Saturday Night Function' is a great vehicle for all concerned and Digby's phrasing is exquisite, reminiscent of the co-composer's own. Indeed, there is a reed-like smoothness to some of his choruses now that is beguiling and unexpected, and not at all at odds with the utterly idiomatic brass sound he gets with that notorious embouchure.

Dalia Faitelson

GUITAR, VOICE

Born in Israel and based in Denmark, Faitelson is a guitarist of mild fusion temperament and a singer of idiosyncratic bent.

***** Common Ground**

Storyville STCD 4196 *Faitelson; Susi Hyldgaard (ky, acc); Johannes Lundberg (b); Niels Werner Larsen (d); Marilyn Mazur (perc).* 4–5/94.

It would be a pity to pass by this thoughtful, measured record on account of its unfamiliar names. Faitelson's pitch is a kind of impressionist fusion and, while there are a couple of misplaced attempts at rocking out, most of the music is quiet and intelligent. The leader is shy about putting herself out front, and there is at least as much improvising space for the effective Hyldgaard and the agile Lundberg, who closes the record with a fine solo over Faitelson's calm strumming. The production is somewhat flat, though that may be in keeping with the players' intentions.

*** Diamond Of The Day

Stunt STUCD 19908 *Faitelson; Randy Brecker (t); Jerry Bergonzi (ts); Lelo Nika (acc); Thommy Andersson (b); Adam Nussbaum (d); Manolo Badrena (perc); Susi Hyldgaard, Maya Faitelson Larsen (v).* 1/99.

*** Point Of No Return

Stunt STUCD 01152 *As above, except add Chris Cheek (ss, ts), Ayi Solomon (perc); omit Bergonzi, Badrena, Hyldgaard and Larsen.* 3/01.

Ambitious, heavy company for Faitelson to be playing in, and there are times on the first record when she seems like a sidewoman on her own gig. But the music is a lot tougher and more upfront than the previous disc, and the world-music zestiness of 'Facing South' and 'Advancing Hours' is convincingly transmitted. Star player here is the startling Nika, whose accordion crosses most effectively the various genres hinted at in the overall mix. Brecker and Bergonzi play with commitment, though it's clearly a chance gig for them, and the modest vocals are a painless intrusion.

Singing plays a more prominent role, on five of nine tracks, in *Point Of No Return*, which reunites most of the same personnel, and given that Faitelson's vocals are often hoarse and awkward, this will scare away the uncommitted. Some echoes of the likes of Mari Boine here, and jazz is taking a back seat to Faitelson's worldly groove. But the instrumental passages are more striking than before. Cheek fits right in, and both he and Brecker sound in tune with the leader's spare composing; try the elegant harmonizing of 'Secrets'.

Giovanni Falzone (born 1974)

TRUMPET, FLUGELHORN

Sicilian trumpeter, with experience in several musical disciplines, here working in a vein between hard bop and free stylings.

*** Music For Five

Splasc(h) 766.2 *Falzone; Tino Tracanna (ts); Francesco Pinetti (vib, marim); Tito Mangialajo Rantzer (b); Ferdinando Faraò (d).* 7/01.

Falzone declares that he most enjoys switching between instinctual playing and working on specific structures, which is pretty much the terrain inhabited by *Music For Five*. The ensemble has an attractively loose-knit feel, with the glassiness of Pinetti's vibes adding timbral interest, and the compositions give the players plenty to chew on, particularly in their varied approach to tempo. As an improviser, Falzone seems to have rather less to say, and the weight falls mostly on Tracanna's shoulders. In the end, this gets a perhaps inevitable mark of 'interesting'.

Charles Fambrough (born 1950)

BASS

When the Philadelphia-born bassist first recorded under his own name, he was already 41. By then, though, he had a substantial CV, including stints with the Messengers and with McCoy Tyner's band.

*** City Tribes

Evidence ECD 22149 *Fambrough; John Swana (t); Craig Handy (ss, ts, bcl); Dave Valentin (f); Billy O'Connell (ky); Ricky Sebastian (d); Cafe, Marlon Simon (perc).* 95.

**(*) Keeper Of The Spirit

Audioquest AQ 1033 *Fambrough; John Swana (t); Grover Washington Jr (ss); Ralph Bowen (ts, ss, f); Art Webb (f); Joel Levine (recs); Edward Simon (p); Adam Holzman, Jason Shatill (ky); Lenny White (d); Marlon Simon (d, perc); Joe Gonzalez (perc).* 12/94.

Fambrough favours a solid, lower-register sound that sometimes recalls Paul Chambers, sometimes Mingus. His earlier albums for CTI are worth searching for in the cut-out and secondhand bins, but the reissue of *City Tribes* helps to fill in the picture a little. Like *Keeper Of The Spirit*, it's a slightly disappointing record, given Fambrough's track record. Swana and guest player Valentin are well featured, as is the bassist himself, but the impression is of parts rather than anything coherent. Only Craig Handy seems willing to take things up and on. The later album also embraces some unlikely sounds, including tenor recorder on 'Save That Time'. In some respects this is a more ambitious album than its predecessors, but it lacks the straightforwardness and precision that make the others such compelling listening. Washington, a much underrated soloist, provides the leaven, but there is also a drabness and lack of vitality which is depressing after earlier highs.

**(*) Upright Citizen

Random Chance 7 *Fambrough; Poogie Bell (t, perc); John Swana (t); Gerald Albright (as); Joe Ford, Grover Washington (ss); Vincent Budesa (p); Bruce Barth, Alex Bugnon, George Duke, Mulgrew Miller, Bill O'Connell (p, ky); Jon Lucien (b, v); Gerald Brown, Pete Vinson (d); Munyungo Jackson, Marlon Simon (perc).* 97.

Originally issued on Nu Groove, this is an augmented release with the same tracks in a different order. This seems wise, since it brings 'Fun City', easily the best thing on the set, up to first place, rather than buried among the also-rans. For some obscure reason, Fambrough has added drum programmes to his bass lines, creating a curiously mechanical clank which sits oddly with the floating soprano lines of guests Washington and Ford. Another of the walk-ups, George Duke confirms what a great piano-player he can be, and what a complete klutz as well, deliberately ironizing some of his solos so that the most affecting passages seem like a put-on. A collaboration with Swana, 'Disguises', is one of the few hits here, but the attempt to make smooth jazz seem rugged simply doesn't work and some promising ideas are thrown away in foggy arrangements and muddled sound.

**(*) Charles Fambrough Live At Zanzibar Blue

Random Chance 6 *Fambrough; Sean Jones (t); Joe Ford (ss); Bill O'Connell (p); Wilby Fletcher, Lenny White (d); Roland Guerrero (perc); Dolores Fambrough (v).* 02.

An obscurity, but a welcome opportunity to catch a Fambrough unit on the stand. The sound is frankly awful but the playing is consistently good on a set of inventive charts, mostly despatched quickly. White and Fletcher share drumming responsibilities and offer Charles rather different approaches to the metre.There are no long jams, even when, as on 'Bossa For Grover' and Miles's 'All Blues', one might have appreciated more of a stretch. The opening 'K-Mac' is perhaps the best of the originals and it's a pity it comes first, because there is a definite slackening of attention thereafter. Ford and young trumpeter Jones are star turns and Mrs Fambrough turns out to have a lovely voice on her single spot; Charles himself is still something of an underachiever, not because the ideas are not there but because the execution is still wanting.

Antonio Farao

PIANO

Italian pianist working in a familiar post-bop idiom.

*****(*) Far Out**
CAM 7757-2 *Farao; Bob Berg (ts); Martin Gjankovski (b); Dejan Terzic (d).* 10/02.

Basically, this is a good Italian piano-trio situation which Berg walked into as hired gun (in what turned out to be one of his final studio sessions). The results are impressively muscular, precise and virtuosic, the kind of settings which always brought out the best in Berg, and consequently this is likely to go down as one of his better showings on record. The opening pelt through 'Seven Steps To Heaven' is registered quite flawlessly, a real helter-skelter ride, and from there the session is a fine show of chopsmanship. Farao's tunes have enough musical interest to humanize the situation, and there's a bruised quality to some of Berg's declamations that lends a streak of vulnerability to otherwise ironclad playing. At full length, a little exhausting – but you don't have to play it all the way through.

Tal Farlow (1921–98)

GUITAR

Self-taught, Farlow got his first break by working with the Red Norvo Trio in 1949. Norvo's dexterity inspired Farlow to accelerate his own technique. It was a very popular group, and after he left it, Farlow worked as a leader in his own right, although following his marriage in 1958 he went into a kind of semi-retirement and spent much of his time as a sign painter. He was seen more frequently in the '80s and '90s, his technique intact.

*****(*) Complete 1956 Private Recordings**
Definitive DRCD 11263 2CD *Farlow; Eddie Costa (p); Vinnie Burke (b); Gene Williams (d).* 12/56.

****** The Swinging Guitar Of Tal Farlow**
Verve 559515-2 *Farlow; Eddie Costa (p); Vinnie Burke (b).* 56.

****** Tal Farlow: Jazz Masters 41**
Verve 527365-2 *Farlow; Bob Enevoldsen (vtb); Bill Perkins (ts); Bobby Gordon (bs); Claude Williamson, Eddie Costa, Gerald Wiggins (p); Red Mitchell, Ray Brown, Monty Budwig, Oscar Pettiford, Vinnie Burke, Bill Tackus, Knobby Totah (b); Stan Levey, Chico Hamilton, Joe Morello, Jimmy Campbell (d).* 1/55–3/58.

***** Finest Hour**
Verve 549677-2 *Farlow; Claude Williamson, Eddie Costa, Gerald Wiggins (p); Red Norvo (vib); Barry Galbraith (g); Red Mitchell, Ray Brown, Oscar Pettiford, Vinnie Burke (b); Stan Levey, Chico Hamilton (d).* 52–56.

*****(*) The Return Of Tal Farlow**
Original Jazz Classics OJC 356 *Farlow; John Scully (p); Jack Six (b); Alan Dawson (d).* 9/69.

One could hardly tell from the catalogue that Farlow is one of the major jazz guitarists, since most of his records – as both leader and sideman – still languish out of print. Perhaps, in the age of Bill Frisell and Pat Metheny, his plain-speaking is simply out of favour. His reticence as a performer belied his breathtaking speed, melodic inventiveness and pleasingly gentle touch as a bop-orientated improviser. His tenure at Verve included some marvellous sessions and at least *The Swinging Guitar Of Tal Farlow* has returned; there are plenty more that could be reinstated in the catalogue. Farlow's virtuosity and the quality of his thinking, even at top speed, inspired more than one generation of guitarists, and given the instrument's current popularity in jazz, his neglect is mystifying.

The *Jazz Masters* compilation remains an excellent introduction to his work, creaming off the pick of seven albums at Verve. Trios with Eddie Costa and Vinnie Burke are especially fine, but so is the date with Gerry Wiggins, Ray Brown and Chico Hamilton, which features one of the fastest treatments of 'Cherokee' ever recorded. Unassumingly though he plays, one never feels intimidated by Farlow's virtuosity, even when he takes the trouble to reharmonize a sequence entirely or to blitz a melody with single-note flourishes. An indispensable compilation. *Finest Hour* is good too, and duplicates none of the tracks on the JM selection, although it does rather beg the question that if this were his finest hour, why weren't these tracks used before? Docked a notch for releasing this instead of restoring the original albums in full, which would be the proper course of action. *The Return* is hardly less fine than the Verve sessions, and Farlow plays just as quickly, with comparable insight; try the lovely variations on 'My Romance'.

The Definitive set reissues two albums originally issued on Xanadu in the '70s, private recordings made at the apartment of a jazz fan named Ed Fuerst. The sound is surprisingly good, and it's precious also for an extended glimpse at the playing of Eddie Costa. The quartet luxuriate their way through eight standards, some around the 15-minute mark, and freed from studio and audience expectations, the music's notably unselfconscious and falters only occasionally.

***** A Sign Of The Times**
Concord CCD 4026 *Farlow; Hank Jones (p); Ray Brown (b).* 77.

***** On Stage**
Concord CCD 4143 *As above, except add Red Norvo (vib), Jake Hanna (d).* 8/76.

*****(*) Chromatic Palette**
Concord CCD 4154 *Farlow; Tommy Flanagan (p); Gary Mazzaroppi (b).* 1/81.

***** Cookin' On All Burners**
Concord CCD 4204 *Farlow; James Williams (p); Gary Mazzaroppi (b); Vinnie Johnson (d).* 8/82.

***** Autumn Leaves**

Concord CCD2-2133-2 2CD *Farlow; Sam Most (ts, f); Frank Strazzeri (p); Gary Mazzaroppi, Bob Maize (b); Tom Sayek, Albert 'Tootie' Heath (d).* 9/77–84.

On *A Sign Of The Times* the music is delivered with pristine accuracy and brightness by these infallible pros, but somehow there's a spark missing. Even though they've gone to the trouble of arranging a dark, contrapuntal framework for 'You Don't Know What Love Is', for instance, or treating 'Stompin' At The Savoy' in a unique way, one misses the sizzle of Farlow's older work. Sumptuously recorded and balanced among the three players, though, and hard not to enjoy. *On Stage* was cut the year before, and the presence of Norvo and Hanna, as well as the concert setting, puts a bit more zip into the situation, but again this isn't more than the sum of its parts. The onstage mix is somewhat wayward (Norvo's vibes sound prissy), and the music tends towards strings of solos, graceful though they are.

Chromatic Palette is just a shade better than the first two. Flanagan digs in a little harder than he often does, and Farlow's own playing has a majestic breadth to it on some of the tunes, all of which are dispatched quickly and with few frills. Mazzaroppi sounds somewhat like a more youthful Red Mitchell on the bass. Try the hard-bitten 'Nuages' as a sample.

Cookin' On All Burners was nearly the last of Tal's Concord sessions. Williams doesn't quite have the aristocratic touch of Flanagan, but it's a solid enough date, with some of the guitarist's favourite standards given a characteristically quick-fire treatment. The very last of them, *The Legendary*, has now been coupled with the other 'missing' record, *Tal Farlow '78*, into the two-disc reissue *Autumn Leaves*. The 1978 date was a trio session and arguably not one of Tal's best: with no piano to assist, Mazzaroppi is sometimes found wanting, and some of the quicker tempos leave Farlow in occasional trouble. The later set has fine support from Strazzeri and Most and is a better bet.

Art Farmer (1928–99)

FLUGELHORN, TRUMPET

Born in Iowa and raised in Phoenix, Arizona, Farmer had a long and distinguished career. He settled in Los Angeles in the late '40s and did not make the inevitable move to New York until the mid-'50s. Associations with Gigi Gryce, Horace Silver and Gerry Mulligan followed, and he co-led The Jazztet with Benny Golson from 1959. He worked extensively in Europe through the '60s and '70s, and by the '80s was an admired elder statesman of bebop trumpet, though his soft and persuasive style found him playing flugelhorn or the hybrid 'flumpet' more often than not. His twin brother, Addison (1928–63), was a bassist.

***** Art Farmer Septet**

Original Jazz Classics OJC 054 *Farmer; Jimmy Cleveland (tb); Clifford Solomon, Charlie Rouse (ts); Oscar Estell, Danny Bank (bs); Quincy Jones, Horace Silver (p); Monk Montgomery, Percy Heath (b); Art Taylor, Sonny Johnson (d).* 7/53–6/54.

*****(*) When Farmer Met Gryce**

Original Jazz Classics OJC 072 *Farmer; Gigi Gryce (as); Freddie Redd, Horace Silver (p); Addison Farmer, Percy Heath (b); Kenny Clarke, Art Taylor (d).* 5/54–5/55.

****** The Art Farmer Quintet**

Original Jazz Classics OJC 241 *Farmer; Gigi Gryce (as); Duke Jordan (p); Addison Farmer (b); Philly Joe Jones (d).* 10/55.

****(*) Two Trumpets**

Original Jazz Classics OJC 018 *Farmer; Donald Byrd (t); Jackie McLean (as); Barry Harris (p); Doug Watkins (b); Art Taylor (d).* 8/56.

***** Farmer's Market**

Original Jazz Classics OJC 398 *Farmer; Hank Mobley (ts); Kenny Drew (p); Addison Farmer (b); Elvin Jones (d).* 11/56.

Art Farmer began his recording career with the ten-inch album, *Work Of Art*, the contents of which are on OJC 054. Although pitched around Farmer's trumpet solos, the music is as much in debt to the composing and arranging of Jones and Gryce, and witty originals such as 'Elephant Walk', 'The Little Band Master' and 'Wildwood' make up the programme. Yet Farmer's skilful contributions elevate the scores; and it's clear that his style was already firmly in place: a pensive restraint on ballads, a fleet yet soberly controlled attack on up-tempo tunes, and a concern for tonal manipulation within a small range of inflexions. If he was comparatively unadventurous, then as later, it didn't stop him from developing an individual style.

This begins to come clear in the small-group work of the mid-'50s. The outfit he led with Gigi Gryce has often been overlooked, but the two OJC reissues are both impeccable examples of a more considered approach to hard-bop forms. While *When Farmer Met Gryce* is the better known, it's slightly the lesser of the two. *Art Farmer Quintet* has some of Gryce's best writing in the unusual structures of 'Evening In Casablanca' and 'Satellite', while 'Nica's Tempo', constructed more from key centres than from chords, might be his masterpiece; in the sequence of long solos, Farmer turns in an improvisation good enough to stand with the best of Miles Davis from the same period. The rhythm section, too, is the most sympathetic of the three involved.

The two-trumpet meeting with Byrd is capable but routine, a typical Prestige blowing session of the period, while *Farmer's Market* suffers slightly from unexpectedly heavy tempos and an erratic performance from Mobley, although Kenny Drew takes some crisp solos.

CORE COLLECTION

****** Portrait Of Art**

Original Jazz Classics OJC 166 *Farmer; Hank Jones (p); Addison Farmer (b); Roy Haynes (d).* 4–5/58.

Though as unassumingly handled as everything in Farmer's discography, this one has long been signposted as a classic. The rhythm section is beautifully balanced and offers exemplary support to the leader, whose playing summons elegance, fire and craftsmansip in almost perfect accord, with his ballad-playing particularly refined. Never as fêted as any comparable session by Miles Davis, this is still jazz trumpet-playing on an exalted level and should be acknowledged as such.

****** Modern Art**

Blue Note 84459-2 *Farmer; Benny Golson (ts); Bill Evans (p); Addison Farmer (b); Dave Bailey (d).* 9/58.

This Blue Note album, originally on United Artists and finely remastered, is one of Farmer's most successful records of the period. Golson contributes one excellent theme, 'Fair Weather', but most of the others involve subtle reworkings of familiar standards: a surprisingly jaunty 'The Touch Of Your Lips', a beguilingly smooth reading of Junior Mance's 'Jubilation', a stately 'Like Someone In Love'. The presence of Evans makes a telling difference – his solos are so finely thought out that it makes one wish he'd become the regular man in The Jazztet.

★★★(★) Blues On Down

Chess GRP 18022 *Farmer; Tom McIntosh (tb); Benny Golson (ts); Cedar Walton (p); Tommy Williams (b); Albert 'Tootie' Heath (d).* 9/60–5/61.

The balance of two albums by The Jazztet, *Big City Sounds* and *The Jazztet At Birdhouse*. If Golson was the prime mover as far as arranging and material were concerned, Farmer's soft, insinuating lines and long-form view of a solo remain the most absorbing elements in the group's sound, and they balance Golson's more obviously powerful delivery. McIntosh is a somewhat subservient third voice but he does nothing wrong, and the rhythm section is fine – hear the often-forgotten Williams especially, with his superb playing on 'Five Spot After Dark'. These were excellent small-group albums, as good in their way as anything by the Messengers in the same era.

★★★★ Out Of The Past

Chess GRP 18092 *Farmer; Tommy Flanagan, Harold Mabern (p); Tommy Williams (b); Roy McCurdy, Albert 'Tootie' Heath (d).* 9/60–10/61.

Another peerless example of Farmer plus rhythm section, this draws together most of two Argo LPs, *Art* and *Perception*; for an unexplained reason, producer Orrin Keepnews has left off one track from each disc, despite there being room enough on the CD. The earlier date with Flanagan is close to perfect, a measured, unflashy but deeply felt reading of seven tunes that peaks on 'Goodbye, Old Girl' and 'I'm A Fool To Want You'. The second date, with Mabern, was done on flugelhorn and is only a whit behind. Quite essential.

★★★(★) Live At The Half Note

Atlantic 90666 *Farmer; Jim Hall (g); Steve Swallow (b); Walter Perkins (d).* 12/63.

Not much of Farmer's work as a leader in the '60s remains easy to find. The empathy between Farmer and Jim Hall makes the live Half Note session a compelling occasion. Long and unflagging renditions of 'I Want To Be Happy' and 'Stompin' At The Savoy' feature both men in vibrant improvisations, and each has an engaging ballad feature. Discographies list a sheaf of unissued tracks from these sessions – when will we hear them?

★★★(★) To Sweden With Love

Koch KOC CD 8510 *Farmer; Jim Hall (g); Steve Swallow (b); Pete LaRoca (d).* 4/64.

Recorded in Stockholm during a Swedish tour, the only record by this quartet features improvisations based around six traditional Swedish folk tunes. Though some of the playing is a little cautious, possibly due to the unfamiliarity of the material, Farmer and Hall are again sparkling in their solos and interplay, and Swallow and LaRoca support so well that one regrets there was nothing further from this band. Some 32 minutes makes the running-time miserly.

★★★(★) Sing Me Softly Of The Blues

Atlantic 7567-80773-2 *Farmer; Steve Kuhn (p); Steve Swallow (b); Pete LaRoca (d).* 3/65.

★★★(★) Interaction / Sing Me Softly Of The Blues

Collectables COL-CD-6235 *As above except add Jim Hall (g), Walter Perkins (d).* 7/63–3/65.

Kuhn displaces Hall, and though one immediately misses the deftness and subtlety of the master guitarist, the pianist is far from an unworthy substitute. Basically ballad-directed, with Farmer keeping to the flugelhorn, the playing is immaculate and slow-burning as only Farmer's records can be – although the fast closing blues, 'One For Majid', is played with fine energy. Collectables have coupled the same album with the earlier *Interaction*, which still has Jim Hall in the band. Although the studio sound isn't very ingratiating, the playing is again exemplary after a surprisingly stiff start with 'Days Of Wine And Roses'. What a partnership Farmer and Hall were!

★★★ Baroque Sketches / The Time And The Place

Collectables COL-CD-6870 *Farmer; Jimmy Heath (ts); Cedar Walton (p); Walter Booker (b); Mickey Roker (d); orchestra arranged by Benny Golson, including George Duvivier (b).* 9/66–2/67.

Baroque Sketches is a mix of genuine and pastiche baroque (from Bach to John Lewis), hepped up with what amount to boogaloo rhythms. Benny Golson was smart enough to make the charts straddle kitsch and a more proper jazz feeling and Farmer, the consummate pro, plays seriously enough. Meatier is the quintet session – purportedly live at New York's Museum Of Modern Art, though the applause sounds suspiciously dubbed-in – where trumpet and tenor blow expansive solos over Cedar Walton's artful comping. A worthwhile survival.

★★★ What Happens?

CAM 498377-2 *Farmer; Phil Woods (as); Martial Solal (p); Henri Texier (b); Daniel Humair (d).* 10/68.

This Italian date has some prodigious playing, but the problem is in the sound-mix. Humair is so loud (particularly his cymbals) that he all but buries both Texier and Solal. That said, Farmer and Woods play some terrifically hot solos: Woods is spectacular on Kenny Dorham's 'Blue Bossa'. If you can tune out the drums, this is a worthwhile listen.

★★★ On The Road

Original Jazz Classics OJC 478 *Farmer; Art Pepper (as); Hampton Hawes (p); Ray Brown (b); Shelly Manne, Steve Ellington (d).* 7–8/76.

Farmer undertook a long stay in Europe at the end of the '60s and most of his '70s work is out of print. This one has an exceptional band, although the music is not quite as good as one might have hoped. The sole outstanding group performance is 'Namely You', where Farmer and Pepper both turn in superb solos, while 'Will You Still Be Mine?' and 'What Am I Here For?' are merely very good. Pepper, entering his Indian summer in the studios, was still a little unfocused, and Hawes is not quite at his best. But Farmer is as consistently fine as ever, by now using the flugelhorn almost exclusively, and the recording captures much of the quality of his tone.

★★★(★) Manhattan

Soul Note 121026-2 *Farmer; Sahib Shihab (ss, bs); Kenny Drew (p); Mads Vinding (b); Ed Thigpen (d).* 11/81.

★★★(★) Mirage

Soul Note 121046-2 *Farmer; Clifford Jordan (ts); Fred Hersch (p); Ray Drummond (b); Akira Tana (d).* 9/82.

***** ARTistry**

Concord CCD2-4974-2 2CD *Farmer; Fred Hersch (p); Bob Bodley, Ray Drummond (b); Billy Hart, Akira Tana (d).*

Farmer spent the early part of the '80s recording, like so many of his colleagues, for European rather than American companies. *Manhattan* blends excellent original material from Drew, Horace Parlan and Bennie Wallace with a jaunty reading of Charlie Parker's 'Passport', and Shihab is an unexpected but rumbustious partner in the front line. *Mirage* is perhaps a shade better, with Jordan at his most fluent, Hersch numbering among Farmer's most sympathetic accompanists and another Parker tune, 'Barbados', taken at an ideal tempo. Drummond and Tana are also splendid. The Concord issue couples two albums, *A Work Of Art* and *Warm Valley*, dates that miss only the stimulation of another front-line horn to set off Farmer's most introspective playing, although Hersch's finely wrought ballad, 'And Now There's You', is the kind of track that makes any record worth keeping for that alone.

***** The Jazztet: Moment To Moment**

Soul Note 121066-2 *Farmer; Curtis Fuller (tb); Benny Golson (ts); Mickey Tucker (p); Ray Drummond (b); Albert 'Tootie' Heath (d).* 5/83.

*****(*) Real Time**

Contemporary 14034-2 *As above, except Marvin 'Smitty' Smith (d) replaces Heath.* 2/86.

*****(*) Back To The City**

Original Jazz Classics OJC 842 *As above.* 2/86.

The occasionally re-formed Jazztet was rather more of a showcase for Golson – as both composer and performer – than it was for Farmer. Their Soul Note session is a somewhat perfunctory return, with the six themes passing in prescribed fashion; but the Contemporary album, recorded live at a single residency at New York's Sweet Basil, gives a vivid idea of the group's continued spirit. *Real Time* offers lengthy readings of Golson staples such as 'Whisper Not' and 'Are You Real'. There's also an expansive treatment of 'Autumn Leaves' which finds all the soloists at their best. Coltrane's influence on Golson is arguably never more clear than in this music. Farmer is keenly incisive with the muted horn, romantically ebullient with it open, and Tucker emerges as a considerable soloist and accompanist; his solo on 'Autumn Leaves' is sweepingly inventive. Smith, the most audacious drummer of his generation, is the ideal occupant of the drum stool. *Back To The City* is now back on CD and features some lesser-known items from the band's book, including a rare outing for Farmer as composer, 'Write Soon'.

****(*) Azure**

Soul Note 121126-2 *Farmer; Fritz Pauer (p).* 9/87.

Although Farmer clearly enjoys the company of Pauer, these nine duets are not very compelling listening. One can't avoid the feeling that Farmer relaxes more in the company of a full rhythm section and, adept as Pauer is at filling the rhythmic and harmonic backdrops, the results seem a little stiff here and there, despite showcasing Farmer's flugelhorn tone at its most beguiling.

****** Something To Live For**

Contemporary CCD-14029-2 *Farmer; Clifford Jordan (ts); James Williams (p); Rufus Reid (b); Marvin 'Smitty' Smith (d).* 1/87.

♛ ** Blame It On My Youth**

Contemporary CCD-14042-2 *As above, except Victor Lewis (d) replaces Smith.* 2/88.

****** Ph. D**

Contemporary CCD-14055-2 *As above, except Marvin 'Smitty' Smith (d) replaces Lewis; add Kenny Burrell (g).* 4/89.

As he entered his 60s, Art Farmer was playing better than ever. The three albums by this wonderful group speak as eloquently as any record can on behalf of the generation of players who followed the first boppers (Farmer, Jordan) yet can still make modern music with a contemporary rhythm section (Williams, Reid, Lewis, Smith). The first record, dedicated to Billy Strayhorn's music, is a little doleful on the ballads but is otherwise perfectly pitched. *Blame It On My Youth*, though, is a discreet masterpiece. Art's reading of the title-track is one of his very finest ballad interpretations, even by his standards. Jordan plays with outstanding subtlety and guarded power throughout and has a memorable feature of his own on 'I'll Be Around', and Williams leads the rhythm section with consummate craft and decisiveness. But it's Lewis who, like Smith, shows amazing versatility and who really makes the music fall together, finding an extra ounce of power and crispness in every rhythm he has to mark out. *Ph. D* doesn't quite maintain this exalted level but, with Burrell guesting in jovial mood, it's as good-humoured and fluent as the others. Outstanding production work from Helen Keane.

***** Central Avenue Reunion**

Contemporary CCD-14057-2 *Farmer; Frank Morgan (as); Lou Levy (p); Eric Von Essen (b); Albert 'Tootie' Heath (d).* 5/89.

The reunion is between Farmer and Morgan, friends from the Los Angeles scene of the early '50s, yet never together on record before. The music, from a live engagement at Kimball's East in California, is finally disappointing: Morgan's keening and late-flowering interest in what extremes he can reach on his horn isn't a very apposite partner for Farmer's unflappable flugelhorn, and the rhythm section have few ambitions beyond comping. Some fine moments amid a generally routine record.

***** Art Farmer And The Jazz Giants**

Prestige 60-027 *Farmer; various line-ups as on OJC and Contemporary albums listed above.* 55–87.

Only those with very limited shelf-space will settle for a compilation from Farmer's many Prestige and Contemporary albums, since so many of the originals boast so much fine music. This does the job, though.

***** The Company I Keep**

Arabesque AJ0112 *Farmer; Tom Harrell (t, flhn); Ron Blake (ss, ts); Geoff Keezer (p); Kenny Davis (b); Carl Allen (d).* 1/94.

The title is appropriate in a slightly discomforting way. Farmer sounds like the senior citizen of this party, and virtually all the best strokes are pulled by his much younger companions. Harrell takes most of the brass honours, Blake is fleet and incisive, and Keezer is masterful; his harmonically intriguing 'Song Of The Canopy' is certainly the best original here. Art takes measured, dark solos, but he sounds more like a patron than a leader.

***** Live At Stanford Jazz Workshop**

Monarch MR1013 *Farmer; Harold Land (ts); Bill Bell (p); Rufus Reid (b); Albert 'Tootie' Heath (d).* 8/96.

A seasoned team of five old pros offers a more settled and perhaps more congenial home for Farmer here. Three Monk tunes are on offer, and Art gets the flumpet to work on 'If You Could See Me Now' to cockle-warming effect. Land's similarly unfancy approach sits smilingly alongside.

*****(*) Silk Road**

Arabesque AJ0130 *Farmer; Ron Blake, Don Braden (ss, ts); Geoff Keezer (p); Kenny Davis (b); Carl Allen (d).* 6/96.

If this proves to be Farmer's last studio date, it's a splendid farewell. He sounds stronger and more involved than he did on *The Company I Keep*, and the band is terrific, Keezer acting more or less as MD and coming up with a cracking chart for Ray Bryant's 'Tonk' to start the disc. Keezer's own two tunes are very effective, there is a rare glimpse of Farmer's own writing in 'Flashback', and the two saxophonists are a piquant contrast to each other and to the brassman. A version of 'Stardust', which is thoughtful but steely, is Art's parting nod to the ballad form he put so much trust in.

Joe Farnsworth

DRUMMER

Joe comes from a musical family. Dad was trumpeter and bandleader Roger Farnsworth, and all the brothers have been involved in music. Studied with Arthur Taylor and Harold Mabern and has recorded with Mabern, Cecil Payne, Junior Cook and stable-mate Eric Alexander, who returns the favour on Joe's debut.

***** Beautiful Friendship**

Criss Cross 1166 *Farnsworth; Eddie Henderson (t, flhn); Steve Davis (tb); Eric Alexander (ts); Cedar Walton (p); Nat Reeves (b).* 99.

Bright, strong, revivalist hard bop from a thoroughly musical percussionist whose roots in the music run deep. The debut album is haunted by the death of Joe's brother, baritone saxophonist James Farnsworth, who is remembered on his own, long 'I See You, Brother', as well as regular partner Alexander's fine 'Joobie'. The presence of Henderson and Walton obviously lends distinction to the session and the standard of playing is predictably high. Farnsworth is not himself a composer and the overall impression is of material drawn from hither and yon, though Lee Morgan's 'Melancholee' is the only repertory piece on the set. Walton's two tunes, 'I'm Not So Sure' and 'Something In Common', are the most assured, while Alexander's closing 'Joe's Tempo' is a basic blowing theme, probably better heard in a live context. A fine start, though as yet no sign of a follow-up.

Joe Farrell (1937–86)

TENOR AND SOPRANO SAXOPHONES, FLUTE

Arrived in New York from Chicago in 1960 and worked with many of the leading outfits there – Mingus, Byard, Russell – in that decade. Founder member of the Jones–Lewis Orchestra and later with Chick Corea in the original Return To Forever. Turned mostly to West Coast session-work in the '70s, before returning to touring in his final years.

***** Moongerms**

CTI/Epic *Farrell; Herbie Hancock (p); Stanley Clarke (b); Jack DeJohnette (d).* 11/72.

*****(*) Sonic Text**

Original Jazz Classics OJC 777 *Farrell; Freddie Hubbard (t, flhn); George Cables (p); Tony Dumas (b); Peter Erskine (d).* 11/79.

There is still little enough Farrell in the catalogue, but his CTI session is a deserved revival. He plays only soprano and flute, and it's blighted by Creed Taylor's emasculating production values, but there's still some terrific playing by a quartet that here sounded as adventurous as a Taylor session was likely to allow.

Farrell's best album, *Sonic Text*, originally on Contemporary, has appeared only belatedly on CD. It captures perfectly his adventurous modal approach and his interest in pure sound. His flute part on Cables's 'Sweet Rita Suite' is both effective and unusual. He was perhaps a better flautist than saxophonist, but his soprano work always had what one-time colleague Flora Purim describes as a 'singing' quality that eliminates the horn's often rather shrill character. Hubbard may be too assertive a player for Farrell's music – the trumpeter's own 'Jazz Crunch' is slightly out of character for the set as a whole – but when he switches to flugelhorn for 'When You're Awake' and the slightly melancholy 'If I Knew Where You're At', which might almost be by Chick Corea, he sounds spot on. The closing 'Malibu', reminiscent of some of the things with Corea, is Farrell's best testament.

***** Darn That Dream**

Drive Archive 41038 *Farrell; Art Pepper (as); George Cables (p); Tony Dumas (b); John Dentz (d).* 3/82.

Darn That Dream is almost guaranteed an audience, given that it affords a late glimpse of Art Pepper, who died just three months after these sides were recorded for Real Time. Art appears alongside Farrell on three longish tracks, 'Section 8 Blues', 'Mode For Joe' and a superb reading of the title-track. Nothing else on the album quite matches up to these, though we have some quibbles about how well Art and Joe tuned up before they started playing. A couple of passages sound a little out.

Claudio Fasoli (born 1939)

TENOR AND SOPRANO SAXOPHONES

Italian post-bop saxophonist, frequent sideman, occasional leader.

*****(*) Welcome**

Soul Note 101171-2 *Fasoli; Kenny Wheeler (t, flhn); Jean-François Jenny-Clark (b); Daniel Humair (d).* 3/86.

***** Cities**

RAM RMCD4503 *Fasoli; Mick Goodrick (g); Paolino Dalla Porta (b); Billy Elgart (d).* 93.

***** Ten Tributes**

RAM RMCD4517 *As above, except add Kenny Wheeler (t, flhn), Henri Texier (b); omit Dalla Porta.* 4/94.

***** Mirror**

RAM RMCD4522 *Fasoli; Stefano Battaglia (p); Jay Clayton (v, elec).* 5/94–5/95.

Fasoli's various discs under his own leadership have dipped a toe into the water of differing jazz styles without sounding especially at ease in any one of them. Most conventional is probably the Soul Note, which finds Wheeler playing with unusual aggression, spurred perhaps by the tough underpinnings of Jenny-Clark and Humair. Track for track, with a few excellent originals and each man playing and listening hard, this has claims to be Fasoli's best set, even if it is only a one-day-in-the-studio quickie.

When he tries to go outside familiar parameters, as on the edgy 'Surfaces' on *Cities*, Fasoli's broken phrasing can sound contrived. But otherwise this is an interesting session, made up of dedications to different metropolises. Goodrick's versatile range is a more authoritative force than the leader's playing, binding the parts together and taking liquid, affably lyrical solos in his own time. Dalla Porta and Elgart play restlessly, unwilling to settle into any simple groove; yet when the four of them find the same pulse – '20121' is a good example – the results are very pleasing. *Ten Tributes* is slow and thoughtful and just a bit heavy-going; Fasoli blends five standards and five originals and takes the trouble slightly to alter the fabric of each of the familiar tunes. It's interesting – 'Yesterdays' adds a bar of silence to each eight measures, like a regular pause for thought – but some may find it a degree too painstaking to enjoy.

One feels, again, that Clayton's stream-of-larynx style of singing isn't especially congenial for either Fasoli or Battaglia. Yet despite some merely meandering passages, the best of *Mirror* is very good indeed. The writing is shared among the three of them, and there is a dry and – in the context – quite fetching demeanour to the title-piece and 'Within', both by the saxophonist. The most charming moment comes, though, when Fasoli steps aside and lets singer and pianist uncover the most unlikely lyricism in Kermit the Frog's 'Bein' Green'.

Riccardo Fassi (born 1955)

KEYBOARDS

Italian keyboard-player, adept in small-group and orchestral settings as both composer and performer.

****(*) Notte**

Splasc(h) H 345-2 *Fassi; Claudio Corvini, Aldo Bassi, Flavio Boltro (t); Roberto Rossi (tb, shells); Mario Corvini (tb); Michel Audisso (ss); Sandro Satta (as); Torquato Sdrucia (bs); Antonello Salis (acc); Fabio Zeppetella (g); Luca Pirozzi, Francesco Puglisi (b); Massimo D'Agostino, Alberto D'Anna, John Arnold (d); Alfredo Minotti (perc, v).* 2/91.

****(*) Toast Man**

Splasc(h) H 307 *Fassi; Flavio Boltro (t, flhn); Dario La Penna (g); Massimo Moriconi (b); Alberto D'Anna (d); Massimo Rocci, Alfredo Minotti (perc).* 2–4/90.

***** One For Leonardo**

Splasc(h) H 379-2 *Fassi; Flavio Boltro (t, flhn); Riccardo Luppi (ss, ts, f, af); Sandro Cerino (bcl, cbcl); Massimo Moriconi, Paolino Dalla Porta (b); Alberto D'Anna (d); Alfredo Minotti (perc).* 4/92.

Fassi works both in small-group settings and with his big Tankio Band, which is responsible for *Notte*. His orchestral scores are colourful and fluent if not always individual and, as so often, it's the soloists who make *Notte* catch fire, even if only here and there. British readers will be reminded of Kenny Wheeler with John Taylor when they hear 'Octopus' and 'La Foresta' on *Toast Man*. Some of the other tracks here, though, aim for a studious kind of fusion, Fassi turning to synthesizer over piano, and his lyrical bent is obscured by those settings, although Boltro is attractively elegant throughout. The trumpeter gets even more space on *One For Leonardo*, which is probably Fassi's best work with the big group. There is only a dash of electronics this time and the soundscape is widened by the bass reeds of Cerino; not all the sonic effects are convincingly integrated into Fassi's arrangements, and he seems short on real melodic invention, but Boltro and the useful Luppi play with great purpose on the date.

***** New York Trio**

YVP 3036 *Fassi; Rufus Reid (b); Marvin 'Smitty' Smith (d).* 12/92.

***** Plays The Music Of Frank Zappa**

Splasc(h) 428 *Fassi; Claudio Corvini, Mike Applebaum, Giancarlo Ciminelli, Flavio Boltro (t); Massimo Pirone (tb, tba); Mario Corvini (tb); Sandro Satta, Michel Audisso, Torquato Sdrucia, Francesco Marini, Riccardo Luppi (reeds); Fabio Zeppetella (g); Francesco Lo Cascio (vib, mar); Antonello Salis (acc); Luca Pirozzi (b); Alberto D'Anna (d).* 5/94.

The New York album is unexpectedly straightahead, lean, immediate: Fassi brought a portfolio of strong themes to the studio, and Reid and Smith play up to their best form in support. The Zappa tribute-album returns Fassi to the Tankio Band format. He chooses a group of Zappa favourites – all from the '60s output, though – and sets them up as something between blowing vehicles and smartly arranged pastiches. As homage, it's probably too respectful, but it does get a lot of good jazz out of the likes of 'Twenty Small Cigars'.

*****(*) L'Amico Immaginario**

Splasc(h) 630.2 *Fassi; Gary Smulyan (bs); Massimo Moriconi (b); Giampaolo Ascolese (d).* 3–12/94.

Much of this is a straightforward duet with Smulyan, on the shelf for six years before release, but surely among Fassi's most successful recordings. The lovely harmonies of 'Why Buddha' are given a thoroughgoing exploration which is nevertheless simply and benignly affecting. Free from any heavyweight agenda, both men play in their breeziest and most generous manner. There are two trio tracks without Smulyan and only a single quartet piece, the brisk 'Near The River'.

*****(*) Walkabout**

Splasc(h) DH 475-2 *Fassi; Paolino Dalla Porta (b); Billy Elgart (d).* 1/96.

Fassi's latest trio session is another strong effort, less direct than the New York record, more elusive and at times – especially Dalla Porta's mysterious 'Game 1' – openly free. Yet there is still plenty of bebop in 'Di Coccio' and 'What Cosa?', and Fassi and his team sit very comfortably in both milieus. Elgart is crucially effective, constantly busy without seeming intrusive, and Dalla Porta offers some lovely countermelodies: his 'Message From The Earth' is one of the prettiest things on any of Fassi's records.

*****(*) Belleville (Vite In Sospeso)**

Splasc(h) 810-2 *Fassi; Steve Lacy (ss); Antonello Salis (acc); Ruben Chaviano (vn); Steve Cantanaro (b); Alfredo Minotti (perc).* 4/98.

***** Serial Killer**

Splasc(h) 826-2 *Fassi; Enrico Rava, Claudio Corvini, Giancarlo Ciminelli (t); Mario Corvini (tb); Massimo Pirone (btb, tba); Michel Audisso (ss, as); Sandro Satta (as); Riccardo Luppi (f, picc); Torquato Sdrucia (bs); Antonello Salis (acc); Ruben Chaviano (vn); Luca Pirozzi, Gianluca Renzi (b); Pietro Iodice, Ettore Fioravanti (d); Alfredo Minotti (perc).* 3/01.

The first of these two is a soundtrack album, though the 16 episodes are quite able to stand on their own, and the instrumentation – offered as varying permutations of the sextet – has an affecting overall timbre which transcends its chamberish look. There are only four themes, which are replayed under different circumstances, with varying degrees of improvisation permitted. The overall mood is wistful and faintly melancholy (a mood which for once seems to infect even the unsentimental Lacy). An unexpectedly lyrical effort from the often ebullient Fassi.

The Tankio Band return for *Serial Killer*. Some of Fassi's beloved influences (especially Frank Zappa) pervade a little too strongly at times, the title-track sounding like big-band rock, and a few of the pieces have the feel of a kind of aimless ingenuity. More effective are 'Solstizio D'Estate', with guest Rava in high form, and the smart reworking of Morricone's 'Indagine', which features Fioravanti in a sequence of five duets.

Nick Fatool (1915–2000)

DRUMS

A great veteran of swing-era drumming, Fatool went the route of several dedicated craftsmen and ended up playing good Dixieland when good swing bands faded away. Early work with Goodman, Shaw and others is listed elsewhere in the book. He later enjoyed many Dixieland associations, especially around the Lawson–Haggart circle.

***** Nick Fatool's Jazz Band**

Jazzology JCD-158 *Fatool; Ernie Carson (c); Johnny Mince (cl); Eddie Miller, Bud Freeman (ts); Lou Stein, Ray Sherman (p); Bill Rutan (g, v); Howard Alden (g); Bob Haggart, Phil Stevens (b).* 1/82–3/87.

This rare outing as a leader for the grand old swing drummer is very good fun. The band are all veteran campaigners and though some of the playing isn't exactly light on its feet they get up a good head of steam on 'Shine', 'Hotter Than That' and similar chestnuts. Carson provides the fireworks while Miller, Mince and Stein take joshing solos. Fatool gives himself some breaks but otherwise lets the others take the limelight. Lively and full-blooded sound, which is somewhat diminished on two 1982 tracks with Freeman and Alden, cut live at a club engagement, which fill out the disc. This is likely to remain as Nick's only entry in the CD era.

Dan Faulk (born 1969)

TENOR AND SOPRANO SAXOPHONES

From Philadelphia, Faulk is a post-bopper with a few strong sideman credits to his name and these confident leadership sets.

*****(*) Focusing In**

Criss Cross 1076 *Faulk; Barry Harris (p); Rufus Reid (b); Carl Allen (d).* 12/92.

Benny Golson contributes an appreciative liner-note, and at first hearing Faulk might well be a player of Golson's generation and experience. He has a big, slightly old-fashioned tone to go with his racy delivery of new and standard material. His own 'Quintagon' quickly demonstrates his ability to push bebop chords a step further. Faulk frequently departs from the basic harmonic structure but in ways that give even 'wrong' notes an aura of relatedness. Harris is, of course, an ideal collaborator in this, and the partnership comes into its own on two Monk tunes, 'Nutty' and 'Epistrophy'; 'Barry's Tune' is offered by way of thanks. Though the liner details list only tenor, Faulk shifts to the straight horn for one of the oddest takes on 'I Love Paris' ever committed to disc. Allen is at his best here and on 'Lover', laying off threes against fours, speeding up, then softening the count. If, as Golson suggests, ballads offer the most accurate index of a young player's chops, then Faulk is definitely on the up, with a long and flawless version of Horace Silver's 'Peace' that constantly finds new things to do with the tune. This is an excellent album. The only quibble with it is that the sound is a little too condensed and central, an arrangement that masks Reid's contribution and frequently finds Harris and the leader right on top of each other.

***** Spirits In The Night**

Fresh Sound New Talent FSNT 024 *Faulk; Myron Walden (as); Joe Martin (b); Jorge Rossy (d).* 10/96.

Jordi Pujol's New Talent imprint is offering valuable studio time to developing players and Faulk has created a strong and individual statement here. His Coltrane influence is most in evidence on 'The Night Has A Thousand Eyes', the opening cut, and it emerges here and there in the originals which follow, not least 'Three Cheers For Paul Chambers', which is less breathless than it sounds. The basic trio is competent if unspectacular, and Walden, who is special guest on five tracks, has some interesting things to say on 'The Heath Blues', his own 'Stop'N'Go' and the Chambers song. The session could have done with a sprinkle of producerly magic dust; competent but lacking an extra dimension.

***** The Dan Faulk Songbook, Volume 1**

Uglifruit UFP 012 *Faulk; Carlton Holmes (p); Ugonna Ukegwo (b); Will Terrill III (d).* 03.

Faulk's coming-of-age seems complete with the first volume of this set. As so often with two-part teasers of this sort, we're already inclined to feel that a single, solid CD of original material might be a better judgement than a two-parter. There are longueurs on Volume 1, though the best of the material is excellent and the group is well suited to Dan's concept. Tunes like 'Crawfish' and 'Hopscotch' seem a touch programmatic and don't deliver much punch. The opening sequence of 'Look For The Sun' and 'Violets For Tuesday' (influenced by 'Violets For Your Furs') is beautiful and there are excellent solo spots throughout from the leader and the accomplished Holmes. A patchy record, which means that unless he is keeping the best stuff for Volume 2, our anxieties may be borne out.

Pierre Favre (born 1937)

DRUMS, PERCUSSION

Favre's career has embraced almost every style from Dixieland (while still in his teens he had gigs with Albert Nicholas and Lil Armstrong) to bebop and the avant-garde. An instrument-maker as well as a percussionist, he is interested in how sound functions and the relationship between sound and substance.

***** Singing Drums**
ECM 823639-2 *Favre; Paul Motian (d, gongs, crotales, calabashes, rodbrushes); Fredy Studer (d, gongs, log d, cym); Nana Vasconcelos (berimbau, tim, congas, water pot, shakers, bells, voice).* 5/84.

*****(*) Window Steps**
ECM 529348-2 *Favre; Kenny Wheeler (t, flhn); Roberto Ottaviano (ss); David Darling (clo); Steve Swallow (b).* 6/95.

Singing Drums rapidly degenerates into an acoustically pristine sampling of effects and devices with no sense of centre and very little coherent development. Ironically, on such a crowded canvas, the music seems to call out for horns or strings to draw the various strands together. There is a slight feeling that the participants are working from very different cultural and technical premises, which don't quite manage to communicate as they should. If the first of this pair appeals only to rather specialist tastes, the second is accessible to all. The presence of Wheeler and the much-admired Ottaviano guarantees music of interest, and this session has to be considered one of Darling's most focused and aware albums. Favre himself is seldom out of focus, but he is never intrusive and he holds the long 'Lea' together with great intelligence.

***** Portrait**
Unit UTR 5004 *Favre (perc solo).* 97.

Portrait is a fairly chewy listen, but a rewarding one, given a degree of patience. Percussionists will doubtless have a field day trying to identify the sources of the sounds, which are admirably varied and unclichéd, but for most listeners it will be a case of cautious sampling a track or two at a time. The basic pulse is almost impossible to track without recourse to quite complex mathematical procedures. Whether unconsciously or deliberately, Favre seems to like experimenting with prime numbers – 1, 2, 3, 5, 7, 11 – and with the Fibonacci sequence – 0, 1, 1, 2, 3, 5, 8 – as he builds patterns within patterns. The recording is of a very high quality, sounding 'live' without compromising on detail.

****** Soufflés**
Intakt CD 049 *Favre; Michel Godard (tba, serpent); Roberto Ottaviano (ss); Lucas Niggli (perc).* 6/97.

The dynamism of this fascinating group takes a moment or two to sink in. As often as not, what is happening is that the two horns fulfil an accompanying role to the two percussionists. Aside from that, the whole ethos of the group is rhythmic, interlocking patterns, phased metres and that same dark pulse. Niggli comes from Cameroon and currently lives in Uster, near to Favre's base in Zurich. He is the Swiss's dark twin, a robust performer with his own ideas, but with a sound which is familiar to anyone who has followed Favre's work. In conjunction, they create a music of some complexity, not always easy to absorb at a single hearing, as on the deceptive 'Felix Dancing In Own Space', but always yielding new dimensions each time it is heard ... and this is a record that should be listened to often. Favre at his very best.

***** Punctus**
Splasc(h) 817-2 *Favre; Tino Tracanna (sno, ss, bs).* 6/00.

On the face of it, one of Favre's most jazz-orientated sessions, with Tracanna following conventional saxophone vocabularies much of the way. Only two of the 14 pieces break the four-minute barrier, and they're even (gasp!) playing the blues on 'Line Blues Line', with Monk ('Misterioso') not far behind. As ever, Favre atomizes various aspects of the drummer's doctrine and comes up with numerous diversions, although Tracanna's response is to play with meditative reserve himself. Probably not the most compelling record either man has made.

****** European Chamber Ensemble**
Intakt 062 *Favre; Michel Godard (tba, serpent); Roberto Ottaviano (sax); Phillipe Schaufelberger (g); Karen Boeschoten (vn); Marius Ungureanu (vla); Pierre-François Massy (b); Lucas Niggli (perc).* 02.

It's the blandest and most unpromising of album titles, but it delivers an exquisite impact right from the opening 'Amarcord D'Un Rose'. The Singing Drums group has been expanded to an octet, and with an instrumentation that perhaps justifies the title, but there is nothing remotely academic or formulaic about Favre's writing here. It is as limpidly beautiful as ever and his percussion is wonderfully focused and communicative, never merely functional. As the leader suggests in his liner-note, there is a mixture of delight and profound melancholy about these tracks. They are mostly short, certainly shorter than the opening piece, and almost songlike in structure, though without recourse to strophic shapes or resolutions. Some, like 'Casa Di Nebbia', 'Colonel Sorbet' and 'Le Scorpion' are not much more than miniatures, but repeated hearings reveal their subtlety and depth and both Ottaviano and Godard find ways of expanding their remit whenever solo space opens for them.

Wally Fawkes (born 1924)

CLARINET, SOPRANO SAXOPHONE

A British trad veteran – though born in Vancouver – Fawkes is still best known for his long association with Humphrey Lyttelton. Strongly influenced by Sidney Bechet and some of the New Orleans masters, his big tone and aggressive phrasing are a contrast to his self-deprecating approach to his jazz career. Daily Mail readers know him better as the artist of the long-running Flook comic strip, under the name Trog.

***** Flook Digs Jazz**
Lake LACD 143 *Fawkes; Spike Mackintosh (t); Eddie Harvey, Keith Christie, Jeremy French, John Mumford (tb); Ian Armit, Lennie Felix, Colin Bates (p); Lennie Bush, Tom Mahn, Russ Allen (b); Eddie Taylor, Jackie Turner, Dave Pearson, John Armatage (d).* 3/57–4/59.

A welcome gathering-in of 21 tracks originally spread across one ten-inch LP and four EPs, which accounts for Fawkes's '50s output under his own modest leadership. Although the line-ups are subject to continuous change from the trombonist backwards, Fawkes and Spike Mackintosh – a fondly remembered trumpeter who hardly made any other records – are a constant in the front line. The music has more to do with a genteel kind of small-band swing than trad, with Mackintosh's skilful take on mid-period Louis Armstrong leading the way. Wally himself plays the most worthwhile solos, with the trombonists each trying some interesting things. As is often the case with British bands in this idiom, nothing really stands out enough to make a deathless impression, but very enjoyable taken a few tracks at a time – as the original formats suggested!

***** Fidgety Feet**

Stomp Off CD1248 *Fawkes; Tony Davis (t, v); Alan Bradley (tb); Roy Hubbard (cl, v); Ken Freeman (p); Brian Mellor (bj); Phil Matthews (tba); Brian Lawrence (b); Derek Bennett (d).* 1–2/92.

'Trog' has seldom taken leadership duties in the recording studios, but he gets top billing here as guest with the Zenith Hot Stompers. The band don't exactly break into a muck sweat, but there's plenty of vim on the upbeat numbers and Fawkes forms a neat partnership with Hubbard on several of the tunes. The clarinettist gargles the odd note, but for the most part he is still in great nick and this 'Trog's Blues' is probably as good as any he's given of late. Recorded in dry but lively sound at the Bull's Head by the redoubtable Dave Bennett.

***** Jazz Jurassics**

Macjazz 003610 *Fawkes; Colin Smith (t); Stan Greig (p); Pete Skivington (b); Ritchie Bryant (d).* 9/99–1/00.

Wally shares the nominal leadership here with Stan Greig, and Smith comes in for half the tracks to add some extra piquancy. The playing sometimes has a cheese-paring quality which listeners used to Coltrane-length solos may not appreciate, but it's more like a shrewd husbanding of resources by these venerable veterans, and with Bechet specifically invoked here and there – via 'Revolutionary Blues' and 'Bechet's Wedding Day' – there's a trace of homage from the clarinettist to some of his old mentors.

Enrico Fazio

BASS

A frequent sideman, but also an ambitious composer-arranger – especially for large groups – Fazio is characteristic of the broad sweep of the Italian modern-mainstream.

*****(*) Euphoria!**

Splasc(h) H 327-2 *Fazio; Alberto Mandarini (t); Lauro Rossi (tb); Francesco Vigone (ss, as); Carlo Actis Dato (ts, bs, bcl); Fiorenzo Sordini (d, vib, mar); Franca Silveri (v).* 7/89.

***** Favola**

CMC 9921-2 *Fazio; Alberto Mandarini (t); Floriano Rosini (tb); Sergei Letov (ss); Francesco Vigone (ss, as); Piero Ponzo (as, bs, cl, bcl); Andrea Chenna (ob); Eleonora Nervi (tba); Giuliano Palmieri (elec); Fiorenzo Sordini (d); Vittorio Bestoso (v).* 11/90.

***** Gracias!**

CMC 9951-2 *Fazio; Alberto Mandarini (t, flhn); Gianpiero Malfatto (tb, tba); Francesco Vigone, Pablo Ledesma (ss, as); Carlo Actis Dato (ts, bs, bcl); Luis Nacht (f, ss); Fiorenzo Sordini (d); Pini Levalle, Marcelo Garcia, Pablo Rodriguez (perc).* 3/91–7/95.

Fazio loves an exciting, kinetic band, full of carnival colours and offbeat energies. While the longest section of *Euphoria!* is a tribute to Charles Mingus which incorporates four Mingus themes, it doesn't sound much like a Mingus band: trombone, bassoon and oboe make only fleeting appearances, but the central unit of three horns, bass and drums swarms all over Fazio's pleasing melodies enough to convince that there's a bigger band at work here than the numbers suggest. Mandarini is very different from the cool trumpeters who set today's brass norm: notes seem to topple out of his horn, and long, barely controlled lines spiral crazily over the ensemble. Actis Dato's typically zesty ripostes and Vigone's brusque, pinchy alto lines fill in the rest. *Favola* is a festival commission, a 12-part suite with vocal commentary by Bestoso and some more strong writing by the leader. Ponzo and Letov are worthy substitutes for Actis Dato, but the music is a little more constrained and less freewheeling this time. *Gracias!* has a very long title-track, a short piece dedicated to Raymond Burr and Dmitri Shostakovich, an even shorter studio coda and two live tracks that go back to a 1991 Buenos Aires concert. The live items, for which the group goes up to ten pieces, feel like fillers, and it's the other music which works. Fazio still gets his men to give their all and, despite the occasional wrong turning, it remains head-turning music.

***** Zapping!**

Leo LR 372 *Fazio; Alberto Mandarini, Fabrizio Bosso (t, flhn); Gianpiero Malfatto (tb, tba, f); Francesco Vigone (ss, as); Carlo Actis Dato (ts, bs, bcl); Angelina Perrotta (vln, vla, ky); Fiorenzo Sordini (d).* 6/01–4/02.

Fazio explains that his intentions as a composer here were to 'zap' between 'hundreds of excerpts from many styles of music and [use] them out of context'. It takes an expert team and a very strong directorial hand to make such eclecticism seem anything but shallow, and most of the way Fazio and his players seem up to the task. One might question, though, if there really are hundreds of jumpcuts here: most of the pieces seem to have very little illogic to them. Essentially the record continues the bright, inventive work of the previous discs. 'Kitsch' is one of two very big pieces, and here and in the final 'In Vino Veritas' one might complain that Fazio is simply overcrowding the stage, as enthusiastically and evocatively as his musicians perform. The notebooks of a particularly inquisitive mind.

Leonard Feather (1914–94)

PIANO, CELESTE

One of the great voices to speak up for jazz for many decades, Feather was a Londoner in love with the music who went to America in the mid-'30s and continued to be fiercely involved for the rest of his long life. Though he worked extensively as a producer, often as a composer, and occasionally as a performer, it's as a commentator on the music and a distinguished historian-critic that he will be best remembered.

***** Leonard Feather 1937–1945**

Classics 901 *Feather; Bobby Hackett (c, g); Dave Wilkins (t, v); Buck Clayton, Archie Craig (t); Benny Carter (t, as);*

Edmond Hall, Andy McDevitt (cl); Pete Brown (as); Joe Marsala (cl, ts); Buddy Featherstonehaugh, Bertie King, Coleman Hawkins (ts); Joe Bushkin (p, cel); Dan Burley, Eddie Macaulay, Billy Kyle (p); Alan Ferguson, Eddie Freeman, Remo Palmieri, Tiny Grimes (g); Wally Morris, Len Harrison, Artie Shapiro, Hayes Alvis, Carl Powell, Oscar Pettiford, Jack Lesberg (b); Al Craig, George Wettling, Hymie Schneider, Cozy Cole, Specs Powell, Morey Feld (d); Leo Watson (v). 5/37–1/45.

Pleasing to have a CD available under the nominal leadership of this great proselytizer, journalist and general man-about-jazz. Although Feather went to the USA as a young man and remained there most of his life, there are two London sessions here by some of his British friends under the name Ye Olde English Swynge Band. On such wholly unpromising material as 'Colonel Bogey' they actually sound pretty good, given that they basically dispense with the melodies as quickly as possible. More substantial are three All-Star Jam Band dates which Feather organized, including such luminaries as Hackett, Carter, Clayton and Hawkins. Nobody really excels, but there is some fine small-band swing and Hawk gets a feature to himself on the 1944 date, 'Thanks For The Memory'. The disc closes on the rare session when Leonard and fellow-scribe Dan Burley sat at two pianos alongside Tiny Grimes, Jack Lesberg and Morey Feld for some blues and boogie fun. Transfers are from clean originals, but there is some turntable rumble and other flaws that a little care could have eradicated.

John Fedchock (born 1957)

TROMBONE

Fedchock's strong experience in modern big bands, which included a long stint with Woody Herman as his MD, stands him in the very best stead for these albums of modern big-band music.

**** New York Big Band

Reservoir RSRCD 138 *Fedchock; Tony Kadleck, Greg Gisbert, Barry Ries, Tim Hagans (t, flhn); Keith O'Quinn, Clark Gayton, George Flynn (tb); Jon Gordon (ss, as); Mark Vinci (as); Rich Perry, Rick Margitza (ts); Scott Robinson (bs); Joel Weiskopf (p); Lynn Seaton (b); Dave Ratajczak (d); Jerry Gonzalez (perc).* 9/92.

***(*) On The Edge

Reservoir RSR CD 153 *As above, except add Scott Wendholt (t, flhn), Charles Pillow (ss, as, cl), David Taylor (btb), Allan Farnham (p), Bobby Sanabria, Emedin Rivera (perc).* 10/97.

A glance through the personnel shows immediately that this is far from being another anonymous studio big band: Fedchock has creamed off some of the sharpest of New York's contemporary players and created a meticulous and skilful, yet passionate orchestra. The leader spent seven years with Woody Herman and knows his trade: he has a sonorous if not especially distinctive style as a soloist, which gives the featured treatment of 'Ruby, My Dear' a glistening quality, but he leaves the showstopping moments to players such as Perry, Robinson, Hagans, Margitza and Gisbert. 'Limehouse Blues' is a brilliant flag-waver, tempestuous but perfectly controlled; 'La Parguera' is melodically lovely, far more than the typical Latin potboiler; and when they end on the dreaded *Flintstones* theme, Fedchock takes the trouble to reharmonize it and actually takes the parodic element out. Glittering digital recording lends extra attack.

We grade the follow-up, *On The Edge*, a notch lower, although it's still a splendid record. Fedchock mixes his own writing with another expert choice of jazz themes – Oliver Nelson's '111-44', Pastorius's 'Teen Town' and more – and the orchestra, present as before but with even a few extra names, still sounds Rolls-Royce. Maybe the sheer freshness of the debut has been dissipated but, on a flag-waver such as Thad Jones's 'Ain't Nothin' Nu', this still sounds like one of the great orchestras in jazz.

***(*) Hit The Bricks

Reservoir RSR CD 163 *Fedchock; Scott Wendholt (t); Chris Potter (ss, ts); Allen Farnham (p); Rufus Redd (b); Dave Ratajczak (d); Adrian D'Souza (perc).* 1/00.

A small-group set is inevitably going to seem like an anti-climax after the previous two, though on its own terms this does more than well enough, and it does throw greater light on Fedchock the instrumentalist: his solo beginning to 'Twilight' demonstrates a lovely sound on the horn, and he spots notes with the sort of accuracy which displays a great section-man's skills. The band has some familiar spirits in it – perhaps too familiar, in the case of Wendholt and Potter – but they make appropriately light work of the music and it's a warm result all round.

***(*) No Nonsense

Reservoir RSR CD 170 *Fedchock; Tony Kadleck, Craig Johnson, Scott Wendholt, Barry Ries (t, flhn); Keith O'Quinn, Clark Gayton (tb); George Flynn (btb); Mark Vinci (ss, as, f, af); Charles Pillow (ss, as, cl); Rick Margitza (ts); Rich Perry (ts, f); Scott Robinson (bs); Allen Farnham (p); Lynn Seaton (b); Dave Ratajczak (d); Bobby Sanabria (perc).* 5/02.

Back with the big band, Fedchock delivers a set which the title amiably sums up. Given that they meet and record rarely enough, the group doesn't have the chance to settle into mere routine; on the other hand, there isn't quite the unified snap and sparkle that a more regular team might use to transform Fedchock's originals, which are fine if a little on the workman-like side. They make a terrific big sound, though.

Avram Fefer (born 1965)

SOPRANO, ALTO AND TENOR SAXOPHONES, CLARINET, BASS CLARINET

A native of San Francisco, Fefer is a free-bop saxophonist who spent time in France in the early '90s but has otherwise been based on the American East Coast.

**(*) Lucille's Gemini Dream

CIMP 237 *Fefer; Steve Swell (tb); Wilber Morris (b); Igal Foni (d).* 1/01.

**(*) Shades Of The Muse

CIMP 286 *Fefer; Tomas Ulrich (clo); Ken Filiano (b); Jay Rosen (d).* 4/03.

Fefer's heavy, almost bleary sound on the tenor is the main expressive force in this music, and it's not exactly uplifting. The tunes on *Lucille's Gemini Dream* are a dour lot, and only Swell's 'Cycle Of Fits', which has a superb duet between sax and trombone, really engages the ear (the producer's suggestion that Fefer's tunes 'could work their way into the book of jazz standards' is surely hubris). For all that, when they hit a more urgent pace, as they do on the title-piece, the quartet strike some sparks. *Shades Of The Muse* obliges Fefer to hold down the horn parts by himself and there are some interesting ruminations from the string-players. On clarinet, the leader is almost perky on 'Oblique Departures' and he takes 'BC Reverie' as a solo for bass clarinet. Still, the music often seems so effortful that enjoyment is very sporadic.

Mark Feldman (born 1955)

VIOLIN

Feldman learned violin in his native Chicago and was playing the bar circuit as a teenager, before moving to Nashville in 1980 and playing on hundreds of country-music sessions. He later moved to New York and became heavily involved in the downtown scene.

***** Music For Violin Alone**

Tzadik TZ 7006 *Feldman (vn solo).* 4/94.

His sideman work has been so consistently provocative and exciting that in some ways Feldman's solo record is a shade disappointing. In part, it's because this is more a record of violin music than a jazz or an improviser's set. Several of the 11 pieces demonstrate his brimming virtuosity and catholic range, but the symmetry and neatness of much of it means that the electric excitement he brings to his group playing is diminished. Only on the very last piece, '4 Spiker', does one hear the kind of free-flowing invention which dominated Leroy Jenkins's solo violin record (still awaited on CD). That said, the sheer mastery which Feldman displays throughout will delight any who admire the instrument, in a jazz context or any other.

Victor Feldman (1934–87)

PIANO, VIBRAPHONE, DRUMS

Originally a drummer, the Londoner switched to vibes and piano just before the first of these records was recorded, a time when he was working with Ronnie Scott. His career took off in America and he was guaranteed his moment in jazz Valhalla when Miles Davis recorded 'Seven Steps To Heaven'. In later years, Feldman dabbled in rock and with electric keyboards. His acoustic style was far more distinctive.

*****(*) Departure Dates**

Jasmine JASCD 609 *Feldman; Dizzy Reece, Jimmy Deuchar (t); Ken Wray (b-t); John Burden (frhn); Derek Humble (as); Ronnie Scott, Tubby Hayes (ts); Harry Klein (bs); Tommy Pollard, Norman Stenfalt (p); Eric Peter, Lennie Bush (b); Phil Seamen, Tony Crombie (d).* 12/56.

*****(*) In London Vol. 1**

Jasmine JASCD 622 *Feldman; Dizzy Reece, Jimmy Deuchar (t); Ken Wray (b-t); Derek Humble (as); Ronnie Scott (ts); Tubby Hayes (bs); Terry Shannon, Norman Stenfalt (p); Pete Blannin, Lennie Bush (b); Phil Seamen (d).* 12/56.

*****(*) In London Vol. 2**

Jasmine JASCD 625 *As above discs, except add Bobby Pratt (t), Joe Temperley, Pete King (bs), Kenny Napper (b), Benny Goodman (d).* 12/56–1/57.

These reissues bring together Feldman's various sessions for the Tempo label, the lone outpost of British modernism in the '50s, and offer an intriguing glimpse into an emerging and vivid new doctrine. As British jazz emerged from the swing era (more like the dance-band era, actually) a fresh generation of players began finding an identity out of American trends, and Feldman, then in his early 20s, was clearly one of the sharpest talents. He's heard mostly on vibes, sometimes at the piano, and occasionally on drums. Though this music was originally spread across various 12- and ten-inch LPs and EPs, it's brought together in one place for the first time. On quartet sessions where Feldman plays vibes, there are inevitable echoes of American models – 'You Are Too Beautiful' from *In London Vol. 1* could be a vintage MJQ standard reading – yet the players have their own things to say, especially in originals such as Crombie's 'The Toff' and 'Time Will Tell'. *Departure Dates* features a septet of two trumpets, alto, vibes and rhythm and is as tonally surprising as the line-up suggests, while there's also a somewhat extraordinary big-band session which ransacks every kind of arranging style. The second *In London* is again split between big band, sextet and quintet, with famously effective cameos from the likes of Reece, Hayes, Scott and Deuchar. If it's Feldman's vibes you most want to hear, the earlier *In London* is the one to have, dedicated mainly to quartet music, though Dizzy Reece arrives for the leisurely original, 'Wilbert's Tune', and there are two more rowdily exciting charts for a nonet. While there are some secondhand touches, it's striking how smart much of this music still sounds, with near-forgotten figures such as Pollard, Shannon and Humble also registering strongly. Remastering is generally so-so, although the packaging has a cheap feel to it.

*****(*) Suite Sixteen**

Original Jazz Classics OJC 1768 *Feldman; Jimmy Deuchar, Dizzy Reece, Jimmy Watson (t); Ken Wray (t, bt); John Burden (frhn); Jim Powell (tba); Derek Humble (as); Tubby Hayes, Ronnie Scott (ts); Harry Klein (bs); Tommy Pollard, Norman Stenfalt (p); Lennie Bush, Eric Peter (b); Tony Crombie (d, p); Phil Seamen (d).* 8 & 9/55.

*****(*) With Mallets A Fore Thought**

VSOP 13 *Feldman; Frank Rosolino (tb); Harold Land (ts); Carl Perkins (p); Leroy Vinnegar (b); Stan Levey (d).* 9/57.

****** The Arrival Of Victor Feldman**

Original Jazz Classics OJCCD 268 *Feldman; Scott LaFaro (b); Stan Levey (d).* 1/58.

It was probably inevitable that Feldman would move to America, but there's enough fine musicianship on *Suite Sixteen* to suggest that he might equally easily have stayed and played at home had London just offered enough adventurous paying gigs. Divided into big-band, septet and quartet tracks, *Suite Sixteen* was cut just prior to his first American trip. It isn't a classic like *Arrival*, which is also remembered as a precious addition to the brief Scott LaFaro discography, but it's a fine record all the same. As a cross-section of the local talent – Deuchar, Scott, Hayes, Crombie, Seamen, Reece – it's a remarkable document. Musically, it doesn't come up to some of the later, American sessions, but it features four excellent Feldman originals (the ambitious title-piece was actually written by Tony Crombie), Allan Ganley's 'Duffle Coat', Dizzy Reece's exuberant 'Maenya', which makes a fine closer, and Kenny Clarke's and Gerald Wiggins's 'Sonar'.

Feldman plays all three of his instruments but concentrates on vibes, with excellent solos on his own brief 'Elegy', where he follows the fiercely melancholic Deuchar, and on 'Maenya'. It's an interesting aspect of his solo work that its quality always seems to be in inverse proportion to its length. Feldman was a master of compression who often lost his way beyond a couple of choruses. The septet and quartet tracks are less buoyant, though 'Brawl For All', which features the leader's only piano contribution, is excellent. The sound is good but needs to be adjusted according to personnel.

Mallets (as bad a pun as you get) is reissued from a long-gone Interlude LP. Feldman concentrates on vibes, and the mesh with pianist Perkins, possessor of that famous crablike technique, is very good indeed. Rosolino and Land are featured on only half the tracks, but they bring to the session a breezy bounce that is engaging and endlessly refreshing. As always, Vinnegar and Levey generate a brisk, propulsive context for the band.

Arrival is a marvellous record, completed just after Victor had settled in Los Angeles. LaFaro's role in extending the vocabulary of the piano trio is well documented in his association with Bill Evans but, given how tragically foreshortened his career was, it's surprising that these sides haven't received more attention. As ever, the young bassist is firm-toned, melodic and endlessly inventive, and the interplay with the piano is stunning: long, highly wrought lines round a basic bop figuration. Levey's accents are quietly insistent and the whole recording seems to have been miked very close, as was the practice at the time. 'Serpent's Tooth', 'Satin Doll' and 'There Is No Greater Love' are the outstanding tracks. This should certainly be in the collection of anyone interested in the evolution of the piano trio in jazz, and it's good to see it in CD format at last.

*** Merry Olde Soul

Original Jazz Classics OJC 402 *Feldman; Hank Jones (p); Sam Jones, Andy Simpkins (b); Louis Hayes (d).* 60, 61.

Altogether more predictable than *Arrival* – and perhaps an indication of the toll exacted by Feldman's time as an in-demand session player. 'Bloke's Blues' contains flashes of originality (though Hank Jones didn't seem to know what it was all about) and there's a wonderful shimmering quality to the vibes on 'Serenity'. Otherwise, it's rather bland standards fare.

*** His Own Sweet Way

Ronnie Scott's Jazz House JHAS 605 *Feldman; Rick Laird (b); Ronnie Stephenson (d).* 2/65.

Caught live at Ronnie Scott's old premises in London's Gerrard Street, this was a happy homecoming for the exiled Feldman, a residency with real warmth and class. Feldman plays piano on all but three tracks, and the only pity is that there isn't rather more of his glittering vibraphone playing. The recording quality is only so-so and doesn't help numbers like a long and rambling version of Liszt's 'Liebestraum' or the Brubeck-written title-piece. Laird and Stephenson show their class as accompanists from the very start and, on originals like 'Azul Serape' and 'Too Blue', show how responsive they were to what clearly were not familiar themes. Much of London's jazz community turned out to see these gigs and the *bonhomie* and warm rivalry are palpable, even on disc.

Simon H. Fell (born 1959)

BASS, KEYBOARDS, ELECTRONICS

Working out of Haverhill, Suffolk, Fell proposes a mature and fully thought-out synthesis of improvisation and composition in his work. While many of his small-group recordings are of uncompromised free music, he is also very interested in large-scale composition, and how its processes can be applied to the improvising group.

**** Composition No. 12.5

Bruce's Fingers BF 26 *Fell; Alan Leggett (t); Martin Jones (flhn); Tim Brooks (tb); Charles Wharf (cl, ss, bcl); Alan Wilkinson (as, bs); Pete Minns (ts); Bruce Godfrey (vn); Helen Godfrey (clo); Paul Hession (d).* 2–7/90.

Remastered for CD in 1999, this was a minor legend in its vinyl format: here it comes with extra sections from a subsequent cassette release and an amended finale. Recorded in Royston, it features a remarkable ensemble who seem utterly committed to Fell's dramatic forms: the playing is superb. Some of it already has a kind of period charm, such as the phoney piano and squiggly electronics, but the music seems as fresh and intense as it did on its first release. Combining free playing, jazz improvisation, densely structured composition and studio manipulation (such as the drum solo accompanied by reverse-electronics), the agenda for the piece sounds intimidating, yet the results are enough to sweep any open-eared listener along. Fell's retrospective notes fill in some of the detail. He has gone on to do more powerful all-round achievements, but the bite and energy of this music still sound phenomenal. Sad to reflect that several of these players have since dropped from sight.

***(*) Bogey's

Bruce's Fingers BF 31 *Fell; Alan Wilkinson (ss, as, bs); Paul Hession (d).* 6/91.

**** Foom! Foom!

Bruce's Fingers BF 5 *As above.* 2/92.

***(*) The Horrors Of Darmstadt

Shock SX025 *As above.* 6/93.

*** Music For 10(0)

Leo Lab 013 *Fell; Guy Llewellyn (frhn); Charles Wharf, Pete Minns, Mick Beck, Alan Wilkinson (reeds); Mary Schwarz (vla); Paul Buckton (g); John McMillan (b); Paul Hession (d); Ben Watson (v).* 11/93.

The best precedent for this music is the old Brötzmann trio with van Hove and Bennink: exploding, tumultuous, improvised sound. There is little point in cold analysis of Wilkinson's saxophones (primarily baritone, for which he is creating a valuable new outlook) as they roar over the top of Fell's bass and Hession's drums, or the amazing internal dialogues which the trio manage to create even as they break the sound barrier. It's a welcome, cold-shower experience at a time when acoustic free jazz has dropped many of its confrontational aspects: these men revivify the intensities of Ayler, Brötzmann and others in the small but noble tradition of great noise. A CD is a poor substitute for a live performance, but *Foom! Foom!* (six pieces, from the lengthy 'Ballad Of Otis Twelvepersons' to the almost snapshot-like 'The Alphabet Poised Like Twenty-Six Frozen Ducklings') is a fine place to start, and the live *The Horrors Of Darmstadt* (recorded at the legendary Leeds Termite Club) is the essential in-concert aftermath, opening on the 32-minute mayhem of the title-track. Recording on the live CD is indifferent, but both are splendid records. *Bogey's* is a revival of a 1991 set at the Huddersfield club celebrated in the title: sound is again less than ideal, but anything the group was doing in this period is worth keeping.

Music For 10(0) celebrates a decade of achievement at the Termite Club with a symphony for ten improvisers and one poet. Though close listening reveals much scrupulous organization by Fell, the music writhes in ways that sound utterly spontaneous, and many of the textures and juxtapositions are as dramatic and undiscovered as anything free music can throw out. Though the full-scale version of the work runs for about 90 minutes, this one works perfectly well at some 75 minutes. The libretto is provided (and shouted) by Ben Watson, a sequence of love letters to or tirades about the various record shops which exist in the city. Watson's bellowing may discourage repeat plays, but it's all pretty hilarious and great and ludicrous in roughly equal measure.

***(*) Frankenstein

Bruce's Fingers BF 25 *Fell; Charles Wharf (ss, ts, cl, bcl, ky).* 3/92–10/96.

If there's one thing Fell enjoys, it's density. This is a long-standing duo (there are some previous records now in vinyl heaven) and their music is a great boiling soup of sound, treated and mistreated either in real time or by the studio. Fell also takes to keyboards and electronics for these eight multi-part pieces, recorded over six sessions across four years. A flowchart usefully explains how the music was put together, although a basic grasp of atomic physics may be of some use in deciphering it. Bach and 'Here's That Rainy Day' put in guest appearances and there are several versions of Fell's underground hit, 'Crammed With Distressing Brain'. It is also, *en passant*, a concept album based around James Whale's *Frankenstein.*

*** Registered Firm

Incus CD33 *Fell; Alan Wilkinson (as, bs); Joe Morris (g); Paul Hession (d).* 6/96.

Joe Morris walks into the lion's den with eyes open and plectrum at the ready. Recorded at yet another Leeds celebrity hangout, The Blizzard Condition, this is an amiable blow, but it's hard to avoid the feeling that Morris is either kibitzing from the sidelines or holding the others back. That said, 'Bows And Buttons' is as juicily violent as it should be.

*** 9 Points In Ascent

Bruce's Fingers BF 24 *Fell; Graham Halliwell (as).* 7/97.

Fifty-two minutes of improvising by Fell and altoman Halliwell. The saxophonist is an anti-virtuoso, the bassist a virtuoso who makes light of that skill. Awkward, edgy, full of sudden squalls, or very occasional shafts of light.

**** Composition No. 30: Compilation III

Bruce's Fingers BF 27 2CD *Fell; Gary Farr, Tom Rees-Roberts, Joanne Baker (t); Paul Wright, Carol Jarvis, Matthew Harrison (tb); David Tollington, Tim Page (frhn); Becky Smith (cl); John Butcher (ss, ts); Carl Raven (ss, cl); Simon Willescroft (as); Hayley Cornick (as, f); Mick Beck, Katy Hird (ts); Jo Luckhurst (bs, bcl); Alan Wilkinson (bs); Nikki Dyer (f, picc); Charles Wharf (cbcl); Sam Koczy (ob); Jeremy Webster (bsn); Jon Halton (contrabass bsn); James Cuthill (p); Fardijah Freedman (hpd); Orphy Robinson (vib); Thanea Stevens (dulcichord); Justin Quinn, Stefan Jaworzyn, Colin Medlock, Damien Bowskill, Andrew Stewart (g); Mark Wastell, Matthew Wilkes, Kate Hurst (clo); Rhodri Davies (hp); John Preston (b); Paul Hession, Mark Sanders (d).* 1–4/98.

'As a piece based almost entirely on the principles of total serialisation, *Compilation III* has an unnecessarily complex, ornate and mathematical basis to every aspect of its existence' – this composer pulls no punches. For further enlightenment, ask for a copy of Fell's 136-page score. Recorded at numerous sessions involving the RNCM Big Band, the Anglia X Ensemble and sundry (and many familiar) improvisers, the result is a mighty two-disc work which, despite its rigorous structural undertow, nevertheless seems like a phantasmagoric improvisation from end to end, where the performers arrive and depart in predestined but spontaneous ways. Many of the 'constructs' which exist within the piece are clearly organized to the last letter, but only if you want to hear them that way. We prefer to hear it as the lifetime masterpiece by a major contemporary musician – except, of course, Fell is hopefully going to be delivering much more music to us yet.

We would also recommend to adventurous ears the excellent *Pure Water Construction* (Discus 11), an electroacoustic suite masterminded by Fell and another maverick composer-organizer, Martin Archer. Just outside this book's parameters, but it will appeal to any who enjoy the above discs.

***(*) Ghost Notes

Bruce's Fingers BF 28 *Fell; Rhodri Davies (hp); Mark Wastell (clo).* 11/97–9/98.

Fell's mistrust of 'tasteful' improvising ensures straight away that a meeting of cello, harp and bass isn't going to get itself hung up in pretty, tinkling textures. It's all rough-and-tumble, scrubbing and scraping – which doesn't mean that there aren't moments of space, delicacy and quiet along the way. Recorded on three different occasions, it is not, in fact, an entirely free record: seven of the 11 pieces start from a composition, by such hands as Phil Durrant and Guto Pryderi Puw, as well as Fell and Wastell, and for those interested enough to follow the detailed notes, this might as well be a small masterclass in the art of bridging the fabled improv–composing gap. Everyone else can merely enjoy a fine trio playing for its life.

*** Kaleidozyklein

Bruce's Fingers BF 46 *Fell; Rachel Cocks (cl); Paul Koschiecha (d); LSTwo Ensemble.* 11/00.

Another monster undertaking from Fell, which attempts to create 'a "classical" music realized with the sensibility, techniques and flexibility associated with experimental jazz and improvisation'. The five-part composition stretches across 70-odd minutes, but for once in Fell's oeuvre the music is often more interesting to read about – via his usual engrossing sleeve-note commentary – than listen to: the classical overpowers the jazz elements for much of the way, and with a sometimes cloudy recording, the necessary details are often obscured. Even the closing 'Intensity' never seems quite as intense as it should be. That said, there is still plenty to mull over in what's been set down here – it's just not the first place to make Fell's acquaintance.

*** Friendly Faces: Live-Tempera

ArtPart 02 *Fell; Lol Coxhill (ss); Marcus Heesch (painting).* 4/02.

We think this is the only CD in this volume which includes a painter (working in jute, albumen and eggtempera) at work simultaneously with the musicians. Fell and Heesch (who is audible) work together in the first half, and they are subsequently joined by Coxhill. It's a fine opportunity to hear Fell in solo close-up and in some ways the second half is a pressure-drop after the intensities the bassist works through at the beginning. There's also some frustration in not witnessing the painting, although you can see the finished work on the CD sleeve. Recorded at Sound 323 on London's Archway Road (the doorbell can be heard along with some traffic noise!).

Helen Fenton

VOCALS

Hails from Sydney. Yet to make much impact farther afield.

****(*) After Dark**
La Brava 9812 *Fenton; large band.* 98.

A fairly predictable roster of jazz classics from the Australian songbird. The orchestrations are warm and resonant, but in no way exceptional. The one original, 'Standing In The Light', is tucked away rather unambitiously at the end. It wakened us up, but too late to rescue a dull record.

Lionel Ferbos

TRUMPET, VOCAL

It's not unfair to call Ferbos a lesser light of New Orleans jazz, and his recorded appearances have been comparatively few. But since his emergence at the beginning of the '50s he's been a reliable if unassertive presence in the city's traditional music.

****(*) The Mighty Four – Dancing At The Melody Inn**
American Music AMCD-99 *Ferbos; Harold Dejan (as, v); George Guesnon (bj, v); Alex Bigard (d).* 11/63.

***** At The Jazz Band Ball**
504 CDS 18 *Ferbos; Lester Caliste (tb); Sammy Rimington (cl, as); David Grillier (cl, ts); Les Muscutt (g, bj); McNeal Breaux, Bill Huntington (b); John Robichaux, Frank Oxley (d).* 11/87–1/98.

The Mighty Four were really Bigard's group, assembled at short notice to play a regular gig at the Melody Inn, which lasted for several years from 1953. The spare format didn't bother the crowds, who packed the place, and for this 1963 reunion the quartet went through some of their old book. Ferbos is a trumpeter in the short-breathed New Orleans line, jabbing at phrases and faithful to melody lines, and in what's a co-operative sound he refuses to dominate or play too hard. Spirited work from Guesnon and Bigard, who speeds up in his enthusiasm, and the recording has survived in clear condition, though in the end this is a minor offering.

The 504 CD comes from the other end of Ferbos's career, with two dates cut 12 years apart. The first is by a five-piece given some throttle by Robichaux's drums, although both Ferbos and Grillier are reluctant to do much more than decorate the likes of 'Cherry Pink And Apple Blossom White'. The later date, from the end of the century, has the reliable Rimington and trombonist Caliste on hand, and is very enjoyable, although Lionel's vocals make one long to hear his trumpet.

Maynard Ferguson (born 1928)

TRUMPET, FLUGELHORN, VALVE TROMBONE, BARITONE HORN, BANDLEADER

Born in Verdun, Canada, and an alumnus of the big bands of Boyd Raeburn and Charlie Barnet, Ferguson combined a fiery tone and fast articulation with a structure influenced by Count Basie and Stan Kenton. MF has always been receptive to new repertoire and many of his most distinctive themes are derived from recent pop music.

*****(*) Jazz Masters 52: Maynard Ferguson**
Verve 529905-2 *Ferguson; Buddy Childers, Don Palladino, Ray Linn, Pete Candoli, Tom Slaney, John Bello, Joe Burnett (t); Milt Bernhart, Bob Burgess, Jimmy Cleveland, Herbie Harper (tb); Jimmy Ford, Anthony Ortega (as, ts); Bud Shank (as, f); Benny Carter, Herb Geller (as); Bob Cooper (ts, ob); Georgie Auld, Bill Holman, Ben Webster, Al Cohn, Ernie Wilkins, Willie Maiden, Nino Tempo, Willie Maiden (ts); Bobby Gordon (bs, bcl); Tate Houston (bs); Russ Freeman, Lorraine Geller, Bobby Timmons, Gerald Wiggins (p); Howard Roberts (g); Ray Brown, Curtis Counce, Richard Evans, John Kirby, Red Mitchell, Joe Mondragon (b); Gary Frommer, George Jenkins, Shelly Manne, Alvin Stoller (d); Larry Bunker (d, vib); Irene Kral (v).* 12/51–8/57.

***** The Birdland Dream Band**
RCA Bluebird 6455 *Ferguson; personnel includes Jimmy Cleveland (tb); Herb Geller (as); Al Cohn (ts); others as above.* 9–12/56.

***** Live At Peacock Lane, Hollywood**
Jazz Hour JH 1030 *Ferguson; personnel includes Herb Geller (as); Richie Kamuca (ts); Mel Lewis (d); others not indicated.* 1/57.

There are few sights more impressive in animal physiology than the muscles in Maynard Ferguson's upper thorax straining for a top C. Unfortunately, on record there are no such distractions; putting a Ferguson disc on the turntable evokes sensations ranging from walking into a high wind to being run down by a truck. The Verve compilation fills in what until recently had been a missing part of the story, the early stuff for Emarcy on *Dimensions*, *Round The Horn* and *Boy With Lots Of Brass*. The earliest item of all is actually from a Ben Webster session arranged by Benny Carter, in whose august company Ferguson sounds a touch too brassy and brash. There is also a track, 'Can't We Talk It Over?', from a Mercury album by arranger Pete Rugolo. The rest, though, is pure double-smelted Ferguson.

The Birdland Dream Band's material is exciting, with some fine solos from Cleveland and Geller in particular. Ferguson was juggling business and playing responsibilities at this time and occasionally the strain seems to show. Yet he had a roster of fantastic arrangements from some of the best in the business (including Jimmy Giuffre, Marty Paich, Bob Brookmeyer and Bill Holman) so he could hardly go wrong.

The material on Jazz Hour gives a fairly reliable account of what the MF Orchestra sounded like (to change the metaphor yet again) at its hormonal peak: brash, brazen, curiously likeable even when it is slapping the listener jovially round the mouth. There is as little point commenting analytically on these tracks – say, for example, 'Stand Up And Preach' – as analysing a rainstorm or the tide: it's just there, and you have to deal with it or not. What may be slower to register is the sheer grace and elegance of some of the leader's gentler features, like 'My Funny Valentine'.

*** The New Sounds Of Maynard Ferguson And His Orchestra

Fresh Sound FSRCD 2010 *Ferguson; Rick Kiefer, Dusko Goykovich, Harry Hall, Nat Pavone (t); Don Roane, Kenny Rupp (tb); Lanny Morgan (f, as); Willie Maiden, Frank Vicari (ts); Ronnie Cuber (bs); Michael Abene, Roger Kellaway (p); Linc Milliman (b); Tony Inzalaco, Rufus Jones (d); Willie Rodriguez (perc); other percussionists unidentified.* 64.

This was a smaller, rather subtler and more coherently inflected Ferguson outfit than many before or since. Benefiting from arrangements by Don Sebesky, Oliver Nelson, Bill Holman and others, and sticking to short, pungent durations (rather than the blowsier format of the live act), it packs 20 tracks into a generous 75 minutes that will delight converts and leave the uninitiated still a little winded. It's the usual blend of contemporary material (Hancock's 'Watermelon Man' and Alex North's 'Antony And Cleopatra Theme') with jazz staples like Golson's 'Whisper Not' and Basie's 'One O'Clock Jump', together with non-mainstream items like 'The Londonderry Air'.

*** Live At The Great American Music Hall

Status DSTS 1004 *Ferguson; Lyn Biviano, Wayne Naus, John DeFlon, Bob Summers (t); Billy Graham (tb, vtb); Eddie Byrne (vtb, btb); Andy Mackintosh (as); Tony Buchanan (ts); Bruce Johnstone (bs); Pete Jackson (ky); Joe DiBartolo (b); Randy Jones (d).* 3/73.

*** Live At The Great American Music Hall: Volume 2

Status DSTS 1007 *As above.* 3/73.

This was the period when it was virtually *de rigueur* to cover pop hits, so 'MacArthur Park' (a big hit for Ferguson) and 'Hey Jude' take their place alongside 'Take The "A" Train'. The energy level is as high as always on this closely but accurately recorded live record which is high on atmosphere, if occasionally wanting in respect of subtle improvisational activity. Interestingly, even at this point a good deal of the solo space is devolved to other players, notably the ecclesiastically named but decidedly unpriestly Billy Graham and Brubeck's one-time standby, drummer Randy Jones.

**(*) Chameleon

Columbia Legacy 46112 *Ferguson; Bob Summers (t, flhn, perc); Stan Mark, Lynn Nicholson, Dennis Noday (t, flhn); Jerry Johnson, Randy Purcell (tb); Andy Mackintosh (ss, as, f, perc); Brian Smith (ts, f, perc); Bruce Johnston (bs, f, perc); Allan Zavod (p); Rick Petrone (b); Danny D'Imperio (d).* 4/74.

An odd mix of jazz classics and pop tunes, *Chameleon* was one of MF's less successful bids for crossover appeal. His version of Herbie Hancock's 'Chameleon' is full of charm and he makes a wonderful job of Chick Corea's 'Fiesta', bringing a joyous, bright-toned bounce to both. But Wings' 'Jet' and Stevie Wonder's 'Living For The City' are pretty drab. A short interpretation of 'I Can't Get Started' sounds like a sop to more mainstream jazz fans, and the only surprise of the set is the trumpet/baritone duet on 'Superbone Meets The Bad Man', a theme written for the session by arranger Jay Chattaway. Should anyone ever tell you that Teo Macero never produced a dodgy record, this is the one to pull out.

*** Conquistador

Columbia 34457 *Ferguson; James Bossy, Randy Brecker, Jon Faddis, Bernie Glow, Stan Mark, Irvin Markowitz, Dennis Noday, Alan Rubin, Marvin Stamm, Ron Tooley (t); Wayne Andre, Roger Homefield, Julian Priester, Randy Purcell, David Taylor (tb); Donald Corrado, Brooks Tillotson (frhn); Mark Colby (ss, as, ts); Mike Migliore (ss, as); George Young (as); Joe Farrell (ts); Bobby Militello (bs, f); Bob James (p, ky); Kenny Ascher, Biff Hannon (ky); George Benson, Eric Gale, Jeff Layton, Lance Quinn (g); Gordon Johnson, Gary King, Will Lee (b); Peter Erskine, Phil Kraus, Harvey Mason Sr, Alan Schwatzberg (d); Ralph MacDonald (perc); Patti Austin, Richard Berg, Ellen Bernfield, Ernie Bernfield, Vivian Cherry, Lani Groves, Gwen Guthrie, Martin Nelson, Linda November (v); strings.* 77.

Dominated by the themes from *Rocky* (which had some chart success) and from *Star Trek*, this is an easy album to overlook so long after its release, but it was a second turning-point in the trumpeter's career, propelling him into new prominence. The bands he put together in those days were a notable mix of brilliant instrumentalists and poppy session-men. The vocal component on 'Mister Mellow' is likely to prompt second thoughts from anyone who was captured by the sheer bravura of 'Gonna Fly Now', Bill Conti's theme-song for *Rocky*, but there is enough strong playing right across the board to win over the most sceptical of listeners. A typically over-egged production – by Jay Chattaway – significantly dates the sound, but *Conquistador* was a strong indication of how determined Maynard was to win new audiences and to keep the mettle of his playing well up to the mark. His playing would get stronger still in the following decade, but as a band record this one is still hard to beat.

*** This Is Jazz: Volume 16

Columbia CK 649790 *As for Columbia records above.*

Very much a chart-dominated compilation, with 'Birdland', 'Gonna Fly Now' and, of course, 'MacArthur Park' taking up most of the space. Not much for Ferguson specialists, but presumably intended as a user-friendly introduction to the trumpeter's work.

*** Live From San Francisco

Rhino 71704 *Ferguson; Hoby Freeman, Hugh Ragin, Alan Wise (t); Chris Braymen, Steve Wiest (tb); Tim Ries (ss, as); Daniel Jordon (ts); Denis DiBlasio (bs, v); Ron Pedley (p, ky); Gregg Bissonette (b, d).* 8/83.

Recorded at the Great American Music Hall in San Francisco, the set is centred on the allusive and cleverly structured 'Bebop Buffet', which does exactly what the title suggests, sampling the tastiest bop themes. Trombonist Steve Wiest's 'South 21 Street Shuffle' is generic bop, but the mix of originals and standards keeps the texture nicely varied. MF is in unusually moody form on 'Lush Life'; though he doesn't seem likely to settle back into a moody, ballad-playing old age, he can turn on the schmaltz with the best of them. Interesting, too, to see the name of Hugh Ragin, usually very much a modernist, in this line-up.

**(*) Body And Soul

Jazz Alliance 10027 *Ferguson; Wayne Bergeron, Alan Wise (t, flhn); Alexander Iles (btb, ts); Rick Margitza (ss, ts); Tim Ries (ss, as, ts, f); Denis DiBlasio (f); Todd Carlon (ky); Dave Carpenter (b); Dave Miller (d); Chad Wackerman (d prog); Steve Fisher (perc).* 1/86.

Sauced with cheesy electronics and lethally overproduced by Jim Exon and Chad Wackerman, this is far from vintage Ferguson. The high-note work is as impressive as ever and Bergeron, Margitza and Ries are strong in support. 'Body And Soul' is a striking performance; more usually associated with the tenor saxophone, it responds to the brass treatment very well indeed. Matt Harris's themes and arrangements are spot-on for the group, if a little formulaic.

***** These Cats Can Swing**
Concord CCD 4669 *Ferguson; Carl Fischer, Jon Owens, Joey Tartell (t); Tom Garling (tb); Chip McNeill (ss, ts); Matt Wallace (ss, ts); Ron Oswanski (p, org, ky); Chris Berger (b); Jason Harnell (d); Lorenzo Martinez, Sandea (perc).* 94.

***** One More Trip To Birdland**
Concord CCD 4729 *Ferguson; Scott Englebright, Carl Fischer, Larry Foyen (t); Tom Garling (tb, g); Christopher Farr (ss, as, ts); Matt Wallace (as, ts, v); Dan Zank (p, ky); Paul Palombi (b); Marko Marcinko (d, perc).* 6/96.

Pumped up and fiery, Maynard puts together latter-day bebop, much of it composed by the resourceful Tom Garling and by arrangers Denis DiBlasio and Alan Baylock with a more measured and harmonically subtle approach. As a live outfit Big Bop Nouveau were one of the most exciting around in the mid-'90s and, though some of it can be dismissed as mere excitement, overheated and overloud, there is more lyricism on *These Cats* than on earlier projects. 'Caravan' is wonderful, and so too is the long 'Sweet Baba Suite (Bai Rav)', which underlines how good MF can be when he stretches out over a long line rather than shorter bebop phrases. Here and on *One More Trip* the weight of the arrangements still falls pretty heavily on the trumpets, but Matt Wallace more than holds his own on alto and could be one of the finds of the last few years. A cover of Joe Zawinul's 'Birdland' manages to avoid most of the hackneyed mannerisms.

***** Brass Attitude**
Concord CCD 4848 *Ferguson; Wayne Bergeron, Carl Fischer, Frank Greene (t); Tom Garling (tb); Sal Giorgianni, Matt Wallace (as, ts); Denis DiBlasio (bs, v); Paul Thompson (b); Dave Throckmorton (d).* 10/98.

More restrained and lyrical than in years gone by, MF is still capable of risky high-wire acrobatics and the odd touch of experimentalism, as on the Indian 'Misra-Dhenuka'. Here as elsewhere, Maynard seems torn between styles and traditions, and the strain is perhaps greater than the synthesis. Nicely recorded, the album suggests that the old fellow hasn't yet finished growing.

Bobby Few (born 1935)

PIANO

Few was a childhood friend of Albert Ayler in Cleveland and played on some of Albert's last recordings. He emigrated to Paris at the end of the '60s and formed Centre Of The World to play free jazz. Later he was closely associated with fellow-exile Steve Lacy. His recordings as leader are few and far between but none the less welcome.

***** Continental Jazz Express**
Boxholder BXH 026 *Few (p solo).* 5/00.

***** Few And Far Between**
Boxholder BXH 029 *Few; Avram Fefer (ts); Wilbur Morris (b).* 6/00.

Few's eclectic piano style draws on influences from right across the jazz spectrum. Like Dave Burrell, he incorporates elements of stride and boogie-woogie, some seemingly classical flourishes and many aspects of pure freedom. At its best, it is exhilarating; at its occasional worst, it is merely confusing. The solo record is an attempt to boil down the history of jazz piano into a single performance; played continuously, it leaves the listener a little giddy and trying to catch up with the last set of references. Vigorous and attractive stuff, all the same.

The trio package is reminiscent of Few's debut disc *More Or Less*, recorded back in 1973 with fellow Centre Of The World members Alan Silva and Muhammad Ali, but where that was outwardly a conventional piano trio (in reality, anything but) this puts an unusual set of tonalities in place of genuine radicalism. 'Continental Jazz Express' is again the main theme, but the set is distinguished by a remarkable version of 'Nostalgia In Times Square'. Few is an intriguing player but as a solo artist he rarely reaches the heights he attained with Steve Lacy and his sessions for the saxophonist are perhaps his best representation on record.

Scott Fields

GUITAR

Fields is a veteran of the Chicago free-jazz scene of the '60s who quit in 1975 and returned to active duty from a new base in Madison, Wisconsin, in the '90s.

****(*) 48 Motives**
Cadence CJR 1064 *Fields; Joseph Jarman (as); Marilyn Crispell (p); Matt Turner (clo); John Padden, Hans Sturm (b); Vincent Davis, Geoff Brady (perc); Stephen Dembski (cond).* 1/96.

***** Disaster At Sea**
Music & Arts CD-961 *Fields; Matt Turner (clo); Vincent Davis (d).* 5/96.

***** Five Frozen Eggs**
Music & Arts CD-987 *Fields; Marilyn Crispell (p); Hans Sturm (b); Hamid Drake (d).* 10/96.

***** Sonotropism**
Music & Arts CD-1007 *Fields; Larry Ochs (sno, ts); Marilyn Crispell (p); Matt Turner (clo).* 10/96.

****(*) Mamet**
Delmark DE-527 *Fields; Michael Formanek (b); Michael Zerang (d).* 8/00.

These albums mark the re-emergence of an interesting talent. Each disc has its moments, although none strikes us as indispensable and they give the impression of a man with a lot to say, trying to get it all out as fast as possible. *48 Motives* and *Sonotropism* both experiment specifically with long-form ideas. The Cadence disc sets the ensemble a structure of 48 eight-bar melodic fragments, subdivided and shared among the ensemble with various rhythmic motives stirred in. The result is a continuous piece lasting almost an hour, the sound ebbing and flowing among the players. Somehow the music sounds far less structured than one expects, often resolving into a kind of drone, and although everyone is clearly giving their all, the piece is troubled by a muzzy sound-mix which badly affects the overall impression. Dembski is cast here in a Butch Morris-like role, and he steps further into the limelight on *Sonotropism*, which is a 50-minute composition/improvisation which he notated and directed. The feel here is of an exquisite piece of chamber jazz just sufficiently dirtied to keep it lively. Crispell, who's done so much of this kind of playing with Anthony Braxton, is perfect for the job, and Ochs is equally capable. Three brief improvisations by the quartet fill out the playing time.

Fields himself is content to be a busy ensemble player on those two, but he is more forward on *Disaster At Sea*, which he describes as an *opera seria* based around a seafaring tragedy. The trio hits an extraordinary level of intensity on 'Sputter', which seems like a vivid evocation of panic, and the subsequent pieces carry the story through. Yet there is a sameness about the dynamics which fails to sustain the attention through what is ultimately a rather dry piece of music-making.

Five Frozen Eggs – the sleeve-notes explain the title – strikes something of a balance among the various styles Fields is investigating, loosening the chamberish qualities of some of the pieces without surrendering the rather formal, almost courtly kind of free organization he seems to be interested in. His own playing here eschews much in the way of effects (employed more extensively on *Disaster At Sea*) and there is a sense of contrapuntalism among the four musicians which makes this record perhaps the best place to sample Fields's music – energetic, occasionally volatile, but fundamentally about form and its effect on content.

Mamet is another one which shrieks 'concept!'. This time, a musical pendant to the eponymous playwright's work. Slow, dense and effortful, it's hardly an enlightening or even very involving listen.

***** From The Diary Of Dog Drexel**

Rossbin 008 *Fields; Greg Kelley (t); Kyle Bruckmann (ob, cor); Guillermo Gregorio (cl, as); Carrie Biolo (vib, mar, perc).* 4/02.

Recorded in a strange, hollow ambience, this is a spirited if ill-tempered sequence of group pieces, with a coda where the ensemble members each played solos which were then doctored by Gregory Taylor's software into a droning, rattling track that sounds somewhat like old *musique concrète*. Unfathomable.

Ken Filiano

DOUBLE BASS, BELLS

A brilliant bass-player and respected educator, Filiano has worked with Paul Smoker, Bobby Bradford and Vinny Golia but has only belatedly emerged as a solo performer.

*****(*) Subvenire**

Nine Winds NECD 0223Q *Filiano (b solo).* 01/02.

Solo bass performance is a very tough discipline. There is, of course, some remarkable work in this form, by the likes of Peter Kowald, Barre Phillips, Barry Guy and Bertram Turetzky. Until now, Ken Filiano has modestly avoided the spotlight, thereby denying more adventurous listeners a remarkable instrumental voice. His bowed playing on the opening 'water down stone' – trendy lower-case and a misspelt album title are our only quibbles – is poetic and effective, but Filiano is more than a musical water-colourist. There is the same genuine jazz feel to these rather abstract cuts as one finds on his work with producer Vinny Golia (who runs the label) and with Paul Smoker. Another fruitful association is marked by a cover of Bobby Bradford's 'woman', segued with the original 'crucible'. This is the penultimate track to an album that ends on a jazzy high with the lovely 'dancing shadows' and guarantees a return visit. Bold and splendid.

Milo Fine (born 1952)

PIANO, DRUMS, PERCUSSION

Minneapolis-based and thus free from fashionable concerns, Fine runs his own Free Jazz Ensemble (often an SME-like duo with guitarist Steve Gnitka) and writes on music.

*** Precision In Inexactitude**

Lotus Sound 04 *Fine; Steve Gnitka (g).* 97.

**** Surges/Suspensions, Comme Toujours**

Shihshihwuai 7-9 3CD *As above, except add John O'Brien (t, flhn); Jason Hale Shapiro (p, syn); Elliott Fine (perc).* 98.

***** Koi/Klops**

Emanem 4060 *As above, except omit O'Brien, Elliott Fine; add Nathan Smith (b, g, bcl); Scott Newell (ts, v).* 12/00–4/01.

Depending on how it initially strikes you, Fine's brand of improvisation can seem like the radical purity of a child's view of the world – obsessive repetition of water drip or farting sounds – or it can seem like an extended tantrum. Fine extends the *idiot savant* approach to his groups as well and their nursery-like confusion either enchants or enrages, again depending on your initial disposition.

Most of Fine's discography is on LP and on his own Shihshihwuai label. The Lotus Sound CD is the first survivor, a drab fingerpainting session that seems to have been edited randomly, so there isn't any logic to the improvisations in the long as well as short term. One wonders not so much at why Fine continues in this vein – many a neglected genius has stuck to his last through ridicule and oversight – but how he has managed to win round Gnitka to his cause. For part of its history at least, the Ensemble was just the two of them.

The main document here is *Surges/Suspensions, Comme Toujours*, an exhaustive(ing) three-CD documentation of two nights at Augsburg Hall in Fine's native Minneapolis. There are no track titles, just details of who played on each piece. Most are delivered at length, but some seem arbitrarily edited, which is either a further statement of Fine's mischievous aesthetic, or else a sign that tapes ran out. It scarcely matters. Fascinating as his procedures are, we can't imagine anyone spending the time to listen to these sides, certainly not more than once. Contrary to our usual stance on free-improvised music, you surely had to be there.

The Emanem set features two different configurations of the group: one a quartet with Smith and Shapiro, the other a trio with Newell, but it's Fine and Gnitka who take the stage alone on the first two improvisations. Milo sticks to his modified drumkit, but at this vintage the group was experimenting with electronics, including Shapiro's confident exploration of synthesizer, and the expanded sound palette is a refreshing change. Hearing the Ensemble in this context, it's hard not to compare them to Emanem's archived Spontaneous Music Ensemble recordings. The comparison illustrates a seemingly radical split between American and European approaches to free improvisation: the colonials go out of their way to avoid melody, harmony, a groove; the Europeans simply deem them irrelevant and get on with it. Divided, you might say, by a common language.

Firehouse Five Plus Two

GROUP

Formed by trombonist Ward Kimball, this semi-pro revivalist band of the '50s and '60s was originally drawn from the staff at Walt Disney Studios. They proved to be unexpectedly popular and made many records.

**** The Firehouse Five Plus Two Story**

Good Time Jazz 2GTJCD-22055-2 2CD *Johnny Lucas, Danny Alguire (t); Ward Kimball (tb); Clark Mallory, Tom Sharpsteen, George Probert (cl); Ed Penner (bs, tba); Frank Thomas (p); Dick Roberts (g, bj); Harper Goff (bj); Jim McDonald, Monte Mountjoy, Jerry Hamm (d).* 5/49–3/54.

****(*) Goes South!**

Good Time Jazz GTJCD-12018-2 *Danny Alguire (t); Ward Kimball (tb); George Probert (cl, ss); Frank Thomas (p); Dick Roberts, Harper Goff (bj); Ed Penner (tba, b); Jim McDonald, Monte Mountjoy (d).* 1/54–11/56.

****(*) Plays For Lovers**

Good Time Jazz GTJCD-12014 *Danny Alguire (t); Ward Kimball (tb); George Probert (cl, ss); Frank Thomas (p); Dick Roberts (bj); Ed Penner (tba, b); Jim McDonald (d).* 9–12/55.

**** Goes To Sea**

Good Time Jazz GTJCD-10028-2 *As above, except Ralph Ball, George Bruns (tba, b) replace Penner.* 2–11/57.

**** Crashes A Party**

Good Time Jazz GTJCD-10038 *As above, except Don Kinch (tba, b) replaces Ball and Bruns; Eddie Forrest (d) replaces McDonald.* 9/58–11/59.

****(*) Dixieland Favourites**

Good Time Jazz GTJCD-10040-2 *As above.* 9/59–3/60.

**** Around The World**

Good Time Jazz GTJCD-10044 *As above.* 3/60.

**** At Disneyland**

Good Time Jazz GTJCD-10049-2 *As above.* 7/62.

**** Goes To A Fire!**

Good Time Jazz GTJCD-10052 *As above.* 4–6/64.

**** Twenty Years Later**

Good Time Jazz GTJCD-10054-2 *As above, except K. O. Ecklund (p) replaces Thomas; Bill Newman (uke) replaces Roberts; add George Bruns (tba).* 10/69.

It's difficult to offer a serious criticism of this group who played their good-time jazz mainly for the fun of it yet became mystifyingly popular. The music seldom varies from record to record, even from track to track – it's Dixieland done with vigorous enthusiasm rather than panache, and it's as formulaic as anything done by British trad groups. Yet there's a certain degree of authenticity which the group conferred on itself, largely through sheer persistence. The earlier versions of the band play with clockwork momentum, and there is an almost Spike Jones-like feel to their music, occasionally underlined by Kimball's use of sirens and washboards to point up what was already a kitsch act. The personnel which settled down in the later '50s, though, made some rather more personal and quite successful records, notably the *Dixieland Favourites* set, although our favourite title (and sleeve) is surely *Plays For Lovers!*. The brass-players were often rather reticent about taking solos and it was left mainly to Probert to be the chief improviser: his playing is often sour and he can't sustain solos for very long, but there's at least an interestingly quirky edge to his best moments, and that tends to go for the band as a whole, too.

Ella Fitzgerald (1917–96)

VOCAL

Moved to New York as a child, and after several attempts at singing work, won a Harlem talent contest and began working with Chick Webb, achieving much success. Took over his band after his death, then worked as a soloist in the '40s. Managed by Norman Granz, she became America's favourite jazz singer, and her Verve albums in the mid-'50s established both the label and her eminence as a songbook interpreter. Toured throughout the '60s and '70s, recording latterly for Granz's Pablo label; but spells of poor health slowed her down in the '80s and her final years were spent in seclusion.

(***) Ella Fitzgerald

ASV AJD 055 2CD *Fitzgerald; Taft Jordan, Mario Bauza, Bobby Stark, Gordon Griffin, Zeke Zarchy, Ziggy Elman (t); Sandy Williams, Nat Story, Claude Jones, Murray McEachern, Red Ballard (tb); Benny Goodman (cl); Teddy McRae, Louis Jordan, Pete Clark, Edgar Sampson, Elmer Williams, Wayman Carver, Garvin Bushell, Chauncey Haughton, Hymie Schertzer, Bill DePew, Arthur Rollini, Vido Musso (reeds); Tommy Fulford, Joe Steele, Jess Stacy (p); John Trueheart, Allan Reuss, Bobby Johnson (g); Beverley Peer, Bill Thomas, Harry Goodman (b); Chick Webb, Gene Krupa (d).* 10/35–12/37.

****(*) The Early Years Part 1**

GRP 052618-2 2CD *As above.* 35–37.

****(*) Ella Fitzgerald 1935–1937**

Classics 500 *As above, plus Frankie Newton (t), Benny Morton (tb), Chu Berry (ts), Teddy Wilson (p), Leemie Stanfield (b), Cozy Cole (d).* 6/35–1/37.

*****(*) Ella Fitzgerald 1937–1938**

Classics 506 *As above, except omit Griffin, Zarchy, Elman, McEachern, Ballard, Goodman, Schertzer, DePew, Rollini, Musso, Stacy, Reuss, Goodman, Newton, Morton, Berry, Wilson, Stanfield and Cole; add George Matthews (tb), Mills Brothers (v).* 1/37–5/38.

***** Ella Fitzgerald 1938–1939**

Classics 518 *As above, except add Dick Vance (t), Hilton Jefferson (as); omit Mills Brothers.* 5/38–2/39.

**** Ella Fitzgerald 1939**

Classics 525 *As above, except add Bill Beason (d).* 2–6/39.

***** Ella Fitzgerald 1939–1940**

Classics 566 *As above, except add Irving Randolph (t), John 'Shorty' Haughton, Jimmy Archey, Floyd Brady, John McConnell (tb), Sam Simmons (ts), Roger 'Ram' Ramirez (p); omit Webb.* 8/39–5/40.

***** Ella Fitzgerald 1940–1941**

Classics 644 *Similar to above, except add John McConnell, Earl Hardy (tb), George Dorsey (as), Elmer Williams (ts), Ulysses Livingston (g), Jesse Price (d); omit Sandy Williams and Ramirez.* 5/40–7/41.

***** The Early Years Part 2**

GRP 052623-2 2CD *As appropriate discs above.* 39–41.

**** Live From The Roseland Ballroom New York 1940**

Jazz Anthology 550032 *Fitzgerald; Dick Vance, Taft Jordan, Bobby Stark (t); George Matthews, Nat Story, Sandy Williams (tb); Garvin Bushell (cl, ss); Hilton Jefferson (as); Wayman Carver (as, ts, f); Teddy McRae (ts, bs); Tommy Fulford (p); John Trueheart (g); Beverley Peer (b); Bill Beason (d).* 40.

***** A-Tisket, A-Tasket**

Naxos Jazz Legends 8.120540 *As various discs above.* 36–41.

Fitzgerald's fabled break came when she won an Apollo Theatre talent contest in 1934, aged only 17, and by the following year she was singing for Chick Webb's band. When Webb died in 1939, the singer inherited leadership of his band; by this time she was its undoubted star. But her recordings of the period are often hard to take because the material is sometimes insufferably trite. After Ella had a major hit with the nursery-rhyme tune, 'A-Tisket, A-Tasket', she was doomed – at least, until the break-up of the band – to seek out similar songs. The Classics CDs offer a chronological survey of her work up to 1941, and while the calibre of her singing is consistent enough – the voice at its freshest, her phrasing straightforward but sincerely dedicated to making the most of the melody – the tracks seem to spell the decline of what was, in the mid-'30s, one of the most swinging of big bands. The arrangements are often blandly supportive of the singer rather than creating any kind of partnership, and when the material is of the standard of 'Swinging On The Reservation' it's difficult to summon up much enthusiasm. Still, there are many minor successes. The 1937–8 CD includes the session which produced Webb's only 12-inch 78, 'I Want To Be Happy' and 'Halleleujah', arranged by Turk Van Lake, and 'Rock It For Me' and 'Bei Mir Bist Du Schön' look forward to the authority which Fitzgerald would bestow on her later records. The 1939–40 disc, although it sports 'My Wubba Dolly', has a number of swinging features such as 'After I Say I'm Sorry', 'I'm Not Complainin'' and a fine 'Baby, Won't You Please Come Home?'. Fitzgerald tends to treat all the songs the same – there's little of Billie Holiday's creative approach to the beat – but the lightness of her voice lets her float a lyric without losing her grip on it.

The remastering of all these discs is very mixed. The earlier discs vary almost from track to track, some laden with hiss, some foggy, others crisp. 'A-Tisket A-Tasket', on the 1937–8 volume, is dreadfully brassy. Only the 1939–40 set has consistently clear transfers. The ASV two-disc set offers a cross-section from Ella's earliest sessions, but the remastering is bass-heavy and listening isn't much fun. The best bets are the two GRP anthologies, which come in reasonably consistent sound at least. With all this material out of copyright, there are other sets on the market, too: a double-set on Memoria, *Savoy Ambassadors*, and a single-disc ASV release called *Rhythm And Romance*. Collectors can choose at their leisure, but we commend the GRP set for completists. We also issue a warning that there are numerous cheap multi-disc sets which mix out-of-copyright studio dates of this period with indifferent broadcast material, often packaged to suggest the Ella of later years. Buyers beware.

The Jazz Anthology set captures a 1940 airshot which mixes superior material – 'Royal Garden Blues', 'Sugar Blues' – with tunes of the order of 'Chewin' Gum', but it's not without period charm, though the sound is indifferent.

The Naxos compilation rounds up some of the better items from the Webb years, plus 'Goodnight, My Love' with Benny Goodman.

***** Ella Fitzgerald 1941–1944**

Classics 840 *Fitzgerald; John McGhee (t); Eddie Barefield (as); Teddy McRae (ts); Tommy Fulford, Bill Furness, Bill Doggett (p); Ulysses Livingston, Slim Furness, Bernie Mackey (g); Peck Furness, Beverley Peer, Bob Haggart (b); Bill Beason, Kenny Clarke, Ernie Hatfield, Johnny Blowers (d); Ink Spots (v).* 10/41–11/44.

The beginning of Ella's solo career, away from the Chick Webb band. It starts with a lovely version of 'Jim', and the first three sessions have some excellent material, but the 1942 dates with the Four Keys are more novelty-orientated, and two sessions with the Ink Spots are missable. The 1944 tracks see her with an orchestra again. Transfers are from unlisted sources and are good enough.

***** Ella Fitzgerald 1945–1947**

Classics 998 *Fitzgerald; Louis Armstrong (t, v); Charlie Shavers (t); Lou McGarity (tb); Peanuts Hucko (cl); Al Sears (ts); Buddy Weed, Renee Knight, Billy Kyle, Nick Tagg, Eddie Heywood (p); Joe Mooney (acc); Jimmy Shirley, Remo Palmieri, Hy White (g); Trigger Alpert, Junior Raglin, Billy Taylor, Haig Stephens, Lemont Moten (b); Buddy Rich (d, v); George Wettling, Big Sid Catlett, Sylvester Paine, Keg Purnell, Eddie Bourne (d); Ink Spots (v); plus groups led by Randy Brooks, Vic Schoen, Louis Jordan, Bob Haggart.* 2/45–3/47.

***** Ella Fitzgerald 1947–1948**

Classics 1049 *Fitzgerald; Idrees Sulieman (t); Illinois Jacquet (ts); Sir Charles Thompson (org); Hank Jones (p); Hy White (g); Ray Brown, John Simmons (b); J. C. Heard (d); plus group led by Bob Haggart.* 3/47–11/48.

All but a few of these tracks are from sessions for Decca, the exceptions being a handful of titles on Classics 998 made for V-Disc (including an entertaining dust-up with Buddy Rich on 'Blue Skies'). Ella was still getting very thin material – her exuberant scat showcase on the 1945 'Flying Home' was followed by a ludicrous 'Stone Cold Dead In De Market' with Louis Jordan – but the voice was starting to bloom into its full maturity and there are some lovely things scattered amid the lesser pieces: 'I'm Just A Lucky So And So', 'A Sunday Kind Of Love', 'That Old Feeling' and a hip and convincingly boppish 'How High The Moon'.

*****(*) Lady Be Good**

Dreyfus FDM 36718-2 *As various discs above.* 10/45–9/49.

A strong compilation of Ella's '40s work. Nineteen tracks cover both her work on standards and some of the most jazz-oriented material, in excellent sound.

***** Ella Fitzgerald 1949**

Classics 1153 *Fitzgerald; orchestras led by Sy Oliver, Gordon Jenkins, Sonny Burke; Louis Jordan; Mills Brothers (v).* 1–11/49.

*****(*) Ella Fitzgerald 1950**

Classics 1195 *Fitzgerald; Louis Armstrong (t, v); Charlie Shavers (t); Hank Jones (p); John Collins (g); Ray Brown (b);*

Charlie Smith (d); Four Hits & A Miss (v); Sy Oliver Orchestra; Louis Jordan Tympany Five. 2–12/50.

Decca sessions throughout. Since the label had still not really figured out how to present her, like many of her contemporaries Fitzgerald was stuck with good and bad material alike, often within the same session. Classics 1153 has some delightful collaborating with both Louis Jordan and the Mills Brothers, although both sessions tend to present her as a novelty singer. 'I Couldn't Stay Away From You' is a superior ballad, and the Sy Oliver charts for 'In The Evening' and 'Basin Street Blues' set her up as an almost vaudevillian belter. Classics 1195 bounces between sublime and ridiculous. There are some appealing duets with Jordan, Armstrong and even Sy Oliver ('Don'cha Go Way Mad'), and the eight Gershwin titles with Ellis Larkins (also see below). Yet the latter session is followed by 'Santa Claus Got Stuck In My Chimney' and two feeble Ink Spots titles. If you're collecting this series rather than Universal's various compilations, this one is a must; but, of course, the Gershwin material is also available on *Pure Ella* (below).

***(*) The Enchanting Ella Fitzgerald: Live At Birdland 1950–1952

Baldwin Street Music VBJH 309 *Fitzgerald; Don Elliott (mel); Hank Jones, Raymond Tunia, Don Abney (p); Terry Gibbs (vib); Ray Brown (b); Charlie Smith, Jimmy Crawford, Roy Haynes (d).* 12/50–8/55.

Four Birdland broadcasts, plus 'I Can't Get Started' from the Apollo and a couple of tracks from a Basin Street show from 1955. Besides all the usual period charm, these are rare examples of the improvising Fitzgerald in her prime. She scats her way through such set-pieces as 'Air Mail Special', 'Lemon Drop' and 'Preview', and when she's on song she's breathtaking. Plus the expected mix of ballads and whatever her new release on Decca was at the time ('We hope you'll buy it'). Pretty good airshot sound for the most part.

*** 75th Birthday Celebration

MCA GRP 26192 2CD *Fitzgerald; Louis Armstrong (t, v); Taft Jordan, Aaron Izenhall, Leonard Graham (t); Sandy Williams (tb); Louis Jordan (as, v); Josh Jackson, Hilton Jefferson, Teddy McRae (reeds); Bill Doggett (p, org); Billy Kyle, Bill Davis, Ellis Larkins, Don Abney, René Knight, Hank Jones, John Lewis (p); Carl Hogan, John Trueheart, Bill Jennings, Hy White, Bernie Mackay, Jimmy Shirley (g); Arnold Fishkind, Jesse Simpkins, Ray Brown, Haig Stephens, Bob Bushnell, Joe Mondragon, Beverley Peer, Bob Haggart, Junior Raglin (b); Larry Bunker, Sylvester Payne, George Wettling, Chick Webb, Johnny Blowers, Eddie Byrd, Joe Harris, Rudy Taylor (d); Dick Jacobs, Harry Dial, Vic Lourie (perc); Ink Spots (v); orchestras led by Bob Haggart, Chick Webb, Vic Schoen, Sy Oliver, Gordon Jenkins, Benny Carter and Toots Camarata.* 5/38–8/55.

*** The War Years 1941–1947

GRP 052268-2 2CD *Similar to above.* 41–47.

*** The Last Decca Years 1949–1954

Decca/GRP 050668-2 *Fitzgerald; Louis Armstrong (v, t); orchestra led by Sy Oliver.* 49–54.

**** Pure Ella

GRP 051636-2 *Fitzgerald; Ellis Larkins (p).* 9/50–3/54.

Universal's Ella holdings are now vast, since they bring together both the Decca and the Verve material. The birthday collection (although packaged more like a wedding album, and now a bit dated since she's passed on) is an intermittently convincing cross-section of her best for Decca over some 17 years. The early tracks are given short shrift since there are only two tracks with Webb, and accurate though it may be as a portrait of her Decca period, there's too much pap chosen from the '40s – rubbish with the Song Spinners and the Ink Spots. Premium scat on 'Lady Be Good' and a gorgeous duet with Pops on 'Dream A Little Dream Of Me' salvage the day; the '50s stuff is better, with a full session of Benny Carter charts and one track from the collaboration with Larkins. *The War Years* covers her uncertain early period at Decca more comprehensively, while *The Last Decca Years 1949–1954* is devoted mostly to Sy Oliver arrangements and is a sometimes frustrating mixed bag. Some of Oliver's charts are mysteriously banal – he makes 'I've Got The World On A String', to choose one promising piece, almost vaudevillian – and 'Goody Goody' wasn't the sort of song to bring Ella any grown-up appeal. But her singing is approaching its great period, and she does some wonderful things with 'You'll Have To Swing It (Mr Paganini)', 'In The Evening' and 'Angel Eyes', among others. Whether collectors will want this or the chronological survey offered by Classics is up to them, since neither cherrypicks as it might.

Pure Ella is a masterpiece, her first great album (*Ella Sings Gershwin*) coupled with *Songs In A Mellow Mood*, all of it with Larkins's gentle, persuasive accompaniments. Her voice bridges the girlish timbre of her early days with the grander delivery she moved on to for her Verve albums; and on this almost ideal programme of standards nothing is out of place. Fine remastering and an essential Fitzgerald item.

CORE COLLECTION

**** The Cole Porter Songbook

Verve 537257-2 2CD *Fitzgerald; Buddy Bregman Orchestra.* 2/56.

In January 1956, Fitzgerald began recording for Norman Granz's Verve label, and the first release *The Cole Porter Songbook* became the commercial rock on which Verve was built. It was so successful that Granz set Ella to work on all the great American songwriters, and her series of songbook albums are an unrivalled sequence of their kind. The records work consistently well for a number of reasons. Fitzgerald herself was at a vocal peak, strong yet flexible, and her position as a lyric interpreter was perfectly in tune with records dense with lyrical detail; each disc carefully programmes familiar with lesser-known material; the arrangers all work to their strengths, Bregman and May delivering hard-hitting big-band sounds, Riddle the suavest of grown-up orchestrations; and the quality of the studio recordings was and remains outstandingly lifelike and wide-ranging on most of the discs. The Porter set is a sentimental favourite of many, in the jazz audience and beyond, and it's one of the records which typifies the first great era of the long-playing record.

**** The Rodgers And Hart Songbook

Verve 537258-2 2CD *Fitzgerald; Buddy Bregman Orchestra.* 8/56.

**** Sings The Duke Ellington Songbook

Verve 559248-2 3CD *Fitzgerald; Cat Anderson, Willie Cook, Clark Terry, Harold 'Shorty' Baker (t); Quentin Jackson, Britt Woodman, John Sanders (tb); Jimmy Hamilton (cl, ts); Johnny Hodges (as); Russell Procope (cl, as); Ben Webster, Paul*

Gonsalves, Frank Foster (ts); Harry Carney (bs, bcl, cl); Duke Ellington, Paul Smith, Oscar Peterson (p); Stuff Smith (vn); Barney Kessel, Herb Ellis (g); Jimmy Woode, Joe Mondragon, Ray Brown (b); Alvin Stoller, Sam Woodyard (d). 9/56–10/57.

*****(*) The Irving Berlin Songbook**
Verve 543830-2 2CD *Fitzgerald; Paul Weston Orchestra.* 3/58.

****** The George & Ira Gershwin Songbook**
Verve 539759-2 4CD *Fitzgerald; Nelson Riddle Orchestra.* 1–3/59.

****** Ella Sings The Harold Arlen Songbook**
Verve 589108-2 *Fitzgerald; Billy May Orchestra.* 8/60–1/61.

***** The Jerome Kern Songbook**
Verve 821669-2 *Fitzgerald; Nelson Riddle Orchestra.* 63.

***** The Johnny Mercer Songbook**
Verve 539057-2 *Fitzgerald; Nelson Riddle Orchestra.* 10/64.

***** The Songbooks**
Verve 823445-2 *As above discs.* 56–64.

****** Best Of The Songbooks**
Verve 519804-2 *As above discs.* 56–64.

*****(*) Best Of The Songbooks – The Ballads**
Verve 521867-2 *As above discs.* 56–64.

***** Day Dream: Best Of The Duke Ellington Songbook**
Verve 527223-2 *As Ellington set above.* 9/56–10/57.

***** Oh, Lady Be Good! Best Of The Gershwin Songbook**
Verve 529581-2 *As Gershwin set above.* 3/59.

****** The Complete Songbooks**
Verve 519832-2 16CD *As above discs.* 56–64.

Arguably the greatest achievement is the Gershwin set, once a five-LP box, now a resplendent four-CD set, which works patiently through 53 songs without any suspicion of going through the motions. The delight in listening to these discs one after another lies in hearing some almost forgotten tunes – 'The Half Of It, Dearie, Blues', 'You've Got What Gets Me', even 'Just Another Rhumba' – alongside the premier Gershwin melodies, and Fitzgerald's concentration is such that a formidable standard is maintained. Verve's new Master Edition adds a fourth disc to the original three and includes the only surviving alternative takes (Ella complains on take eight of 'Oh, Lady Be Good' that she may never get it – she does) as well as ten songs in their mono mixes – quite a revelation, since the voice actually comes through more clearly on these tracks, and it makes one wish to hear the whole set that way on CD as well. Listening through this great archive, one notices here and there how even Ella was discomfited by some of Ira's more pernickety lyrics but, pro that she is, it doesn't dismay the singer.

We have listened again to the other discs, some in the light of their Master Edition formats. It now seems clear that our reservations about the Rodgers and Hart set were largely unfair. Ella is so supremely effective on the best tracks that one forgives the occasional blandness in handling Lorenz Hart's wit. The Harold Arlen and Cole Porter sets remain singular masterpieces, too. Arlen's songs are among a jazz singer's most challenging material, though, and Fitzgerald is ebulliently partnered by Billy May, who sounds more pertinent here than he did on some of the sessions he did with Sinatra. The two separate discs have now been combined as a double-disc package in the Master Edition series. The Mercer record is slightly disappointing after the previous Gershwin triumph with Riddle, and the Kern collection, though fine enough, is also a secondary choice. The two discs dedicated to Berlin (now combined as a single two-CD set) are a bit patchy, but the first volume starts off with a quite unsurpassable reading of 'Let's Face The Music And Dance', in which Ella negotiates all the changes in backdrop without the slightest hint of discomfort and goes on to wonderfully tender versions of 'Russian Lullaby' and 'How Deep Is The Ocean'. The second disc works further miracles with 'Isn't This A Lovely Day' and 'Heat Wave'.

The collection made with Duke Ellington is a somewhat different matter, with the composer himself working with the singer. It's been an undervalued record in the past, with charges of under-rehearsal flying about, and there's certainly a major difference between these sessions and the others. Riddle would surely never have tolerated the looseness of some of the playing, or Sam Woodyard in any circumstances. Yet the best of the disc finds Ellington inspired, with such tunes as 'Caravan' evoking entirely new treatments and swingers like 'Drop Me Off In Harlem' fusing Ella's imperturbable time with the rough-and-ready movement of the band in full cry. Some of the tracks feature her with a small group, and there is an 'I Got It Bad And That Ain't Good' which finds Johnny Hodges almost oozing out of the speakers. Highly recommended, although we are a little disappointed with the new remastering, which makes the Ellington band sound improbably fierce at times.

The best-of pick on *The Songbooks* isn't bad, with 19 tracks and a little over an hour of music, but it emphasizes how little fat there is in the original albums. The more recent *Best Of The Songbooks* is a neat pocket-edition, with some lesser-known tracks alongside the obvious winners. There are also the subsequent *The Ballads* and single-disc editions filleted from the Ellington and Gershwin sets. But the addictive qualities of these albums often leave one hankering for more, and the solution to that problem is the 16-CD set which collects the whole lot.

***** One O'Clock Jump**
Verve 359806-2 *Fitzgerald; Count Basie Orchestra; Joe Williams (v).* 1/56–4/57.

***** At Newport**
Verve 559809-2 *Fitzgerald; Don Abney, Mal Waldron, Junior Mance, Ray Bryant (p); Wendell Marshall, Joe Benjamin, Ike Isaacs (b); Jo Jones, Jimmy Cobb, Specs Wright (d); Carmen McRae (v, p); Billie Holiday (v).* 7/57.

***** Get Happy!**
Verve 523321-2 *Fitzgerald; orchestras led by Frank DeVol, Russell Garcia, Marty Paich, Nelson Riddle, Paul Weston.* 7/57–10/59.

Three more recent additions to the catalogue which mostly round up what there is left of Ella that still hasn't been reissued. She gets top billing on *One O'Clock Jump*, which is an outrage since she sings only on the first of 13 tracks, and even that is a duet with Joe Williams! The rest of the disc is a middleweight Basie date of the period, somewhat R&B in feel, with Williams showcased extensively. The Newport album brings together the sets sung at the 1957 festival by Ella, Billie and Carmen, and is at times close to a shambles. Fitzgerald has a difficult time with her trio and is fighting them over the tempos of more than one song, although 'Air Mail Special' is a stunning scat showcase. Holiday is in awful shape and struggles through her set. McRae gets off to a dreadful start, since half of her group didn't show up until three numbers in (she sounds as if she's cheering when they do arrive) and she gets barely any time onstage anyway.

Fascinating documentary record, but whether listeners would want to return to it very often is debatable.

Get Happy! is an unhappy set of songs – 'Beat Me Daddy Eight To The Bar', 'Like Young', 'Cheerful Little Earful' – strung together from five different sessions under five different leaders. In the circumstances, consummate pro that she is, Ella still turns in some fine work.

★★★★ Like Someone In Love
Verve 511524-2 *Fitzgerald; Ted Nash (as); Stan Getz (ts); Frank DeVol Orchestra.* 10/57.

★★★ At The Opera House
Verve 831269-2 *Fitzgerald; Roy Eldridge (t); J. J. Johnson (tb); Sonny Stitt (as); Coleman Hawkins, Stan Getz, Flip Phillips (ts); Oscar Peterson (p); Herb Ellis (g); Ray Brown (b); Connie Kay (d).* 9–10/57.

★★★★ Ella Swings Lightly
Verve 517535-2 *Fitzgerald; Don Fagerquist, Al Porcino (t); Bob Enevoldsen (vtb); Bud Shank (as); Bill Holman (ts); Lou Levy (p); Mel Lewis (d).* 58.

★★★ Ella In Rome (The Birthday Concert)
Verve 835454-2 *Fitzgerald; Oscar Peterson, Lou Levy (p); Herb Ellis (g); Ray Brown, Max Bennett (b); Gus Johnson (d).* 4/58.

★★★(★) Sings Sweet Songs For Swingers
Verve 0602498604175 *Fitzgerald; Frank deVol Orchestra.* 11/58–7/59.

★★★(★) The Intimate Ella
Verve 829838-2 *Fitzgerald; Paul Smith (p).* 60.

★★★ Mack The Knife (Ella In Berlin)
Verve 519564-2 *Fitzgerald; Paul Smith (p); Jim Hall (g); Wilfred Middlebrooks (b); Gus Johnson (d).* 2/60.

★★★ Ella Returns To Berlin
Verve 837758-2 *Fitzgerald; Lou Levy, Oscar Peterson (p); Herb Ellis (g); Wilfred Middlebrooks, Ray Brown (b); Gus Johnson, Ed Thigpen (d).* 2/61.

★★★(★) Ella Wishes You A Swinging Christmas
Verve 827150-2 *Fitzgerald; Frank DeVol Orchestra.* 60.

★★★ Clap Hands, Here Comes Charlie!
Verve 835646-2 *Fitzgerald; Lou Levy (p); Herb Ellis (g); Joe Mondragon, Wilfred Middlebrooks (b); Stan Levey, Gus Johnson (d).* 1–6/61.

★★★(★) Ella Swings Brightly With Nelson
Verve 519347-2 *Fitzgerald; Nelson Riddle Orchestra.* 59–61.

★★★ Ella Swings Gently With Nelson
Verve 519348-2 *Fitzgerald; Nelson Riddle Orchestra.* 61–62.

★★★ Rhythm Is Our Business
Verve 559513-2 *Fitzgerald; Bill Doggett Orchestra.* 1/62.

★★★(★) Ella And Basie
Verve 539059-2 *Fitzgerald; Joe Newman, Al Aarons, Sonny Cohn, Don Rader, Fip Ricard (t); Henry Coker, Grover Mitchell, Benny Powell, Urbie Green (tb); Marshal Royal (as, cl); Eric Dixon (ts, f); Frank Wess (ts, as, f); Frank Foster (ts); Charlie Fowlkes (bs); Freddie Green (g); Buddy Catlett (b); Sonny Payne (d).* 7/63.

★★★ These Are The Blues
Verve 829536-2 *Fitzgerald; Roy Eldridge (t); Wild Bill Davis (org); Herb Ellis (g); Ray Brown (b); Gus Johnson (d).* 10/63.

★★★(★) Verve Jazz Masters: Ella Fitzgerald
Verve 519822-2 *Fitzgerald; various groups.* 55–62.

The songbook albums may be Fitzgerald's best-remembered at Verve, but there were many more good ones, and most of them are now on CD. Essential: *Like Someone In Love*, a very fine programme of major standards and rarities, with Getz taking solos on four tracks; *Ella Swings Lightly*, arranged by Marty Paich with his West Coast band handling the backings; the meeting with Basie, which is a little more fun than her encounters with Ellington, brash and exciting but tempered by the invulnerable machine that was Basie's band; *The Intimate Ella*, a one-on-one meeting with underrated pianist Paul Smith, and a good instance of the big voice being shaded down; and the Christmas album, the least affected and most swinging seasonal jazz album ever made. Good ones: *At The Opera House*, which is a bit of a typical JATP rave-up but has its moments; *Clap Hands, Here Comes Charlie!*, a swinging small-group encounter, and something of a rarity in her record dates from this period; *Sings Sweet Songs For Swingers*, with a great set of charts by Frank DeVol, a neglected and only recently reissued record; and *Returns To Berlin*, which comes in excellent sound. The original *Berlin* set has been beefed up with some extra tracks in its latest incarnation and includes the famous version of 'Mack The Knife'.

Disappointing, but still worth hearing, are *These Are The Blues*, which tends to prove that Ella is no great queen of the idiom, despite the nicely simmering back-ups from Davis and Eldridge, and the Rome concert. *Rhythm Is Our Business* seems like a shot at some kind of youth market, with Doggett's R&B-flavoured scores and material like 'Hallelujah I Love Him So'. Ella sings gamely enough, but this isn't really her thing. The *Swings Brightly/Swings Gently* albums with Riddle are welcome appearances on CD. The *Brightly* set is the superior one, if only for the irresistible treatment of 'Don't Be That Way'; but the ballads disc is fine, too. The Verve Jazz Masters disc picks its way past some of the other Ella compilations and delivers an interesting summary for those who don't want to trawl through the whole Verve catalogue. Her albums with Louis Armstrong are listed under his name.

★★★ Ella Sings Broadway
Verve 549373-2 *Fitzgerald; orchestra led by Marty Paich.* 62.

We'll single out this recent addition to Verve's now gigantic Ella catalogue. Unusual because it has a Marty Paich West Coast sound to it, and the songs are an interesting collection from various Broadway hits of the time. A few duffers, but don't miss 'Hernando's Hideaway', 'Whatever Lola Wants' and 'Almost Like Being In Love'.

★★★ Ella At Duke's Place
Verve 529700-2 *Fitzgerald; Cat Anderson, Herbie Jones, Cootie Williams (t); Lawrence Brown, Buster Cooper, Chuck Connors (tb); Jimmy Hamilton (cl, ts); Russell Procope (cl, as); Johnny Hodges (as); Paul Gonsalves (ts); Harry Carney (bs); Duke Ellington (p); John Lamb (b); Sam Woodyard (d).* 10/65.

If only the whole album had been as good as the opening, a wonderful reading of 'Something To Live For'. The other ballads in the first half are nearly as good. But the up-tempo pieces show both singer and band at something less than their best, Ellington's notorious weakness for inappropriate speeds getting the better of him and Ella not quite on top of the situation, even if the good things were worth salvaging.

***** Ella And Duke At The Côte D'Azur**

Verve 539030-2 2CD *As above, except add Dud Bascomb, Mercer Ellington (t), Ben Webster (ts), Jimmy Jones (p), Jim Hughart (b), Grady Tate (d). 7/66.*

*****(*) Côte D'Azur Concerts**

Verve 539033-2 8CD *As above. 7/66.*

This is the original double-LP set with just a few extra tracks, whetting the appetite for the eight-disc set that covers all the concerts from this occasion by Fitzgerald and Ellington. In what is effectively a truncated form, this seems like little more than a patchwork of some pieces by Ellington and some by Ella with her trio (Jones, Hughart and Tate). Since neither situation finds the artists at their greatest heights, this goes down as an enjoyable but familiar sampling of festival routine. Highlight: Ella's serenely effective 'The More I See You'.

The big set is more about Ellington than Ella, and it includes on the final disc a full-scale rehearsal of three pieces which will intrigue Ducal scholars. Our grading may be on the generous side. There's much to enjoy on each of the discs, but presenting what is effectively four days of work, with all the various repetitions and routines of the artists exposed, is a demystification which many will not particularly welcome. It's symptomatic of the size-matters philosophy which the CD era and reissue programmes have almost obsessively encouraged in recent years.

***** Whisper Not**

Verve 589478-2 *Fitzgerald; Marty Paich Orchestra. 7/66.*

A rematch with Marty Paich. 'Old Macdonald' is enough to have anyone pushing the reject button (what on earth was Norman Granz thinking of?) but Ella is in gorgeous form for several songs, particularly 'Thanks For The Memory', 'Time After Time' and 'Lover Man'.

***** Jukebox Ella: The Singles Vol. 1**

Verve 0044007605820 2CD *Fitzgerald, with various groups and orchestras, as in Verve sessions listed above. 1/56–10/67.*

Fitzgerald recorded plenty of sides meant for single consumption during her Verve reign, and they've been gathered in for this 36-track double-disc set. Anyone expecting a lot of buried treasure is going to be disappointed, because Granz seems to have reserved some of Ella's most teeth-grinding material for such occasions: here are such immortal tunes as 'Hotta Chocolatta', 'Dreams Are Made For Children', 'I'm A Poached Egg (Without Toast)' and the German version of 'You're Driving Me Crazy'. There are good things too: a swinging 'Beale Street Blues', a smooth 'Desafinado'. Mostly, though, for Ella completists only. The packaging is super.

*****(*) Something To Live For**

Verve 547800-2 2CD *Fitzgerald; various accompanists, most listed above. 35–66.*

In the overcrowded marketplace of Fitzgerald compilations, at least this one breaks new ground, covering both her Decca and Verve material in one package and two CDs. Excellent sound throughout and fine documentation will make this a worthwhile choice for many, but the track listing seems to have been closely tied in with a PBS documentary and in consequence feels compromised; any Ella admirer will be disappointed at some of the omissions.

****(*) In Budapest**

Pablo 5308-2 *Fitzgerald; Tommy Flanagan (p); Frank De La Rosa (b); Ed Thigpen (d). 5/70.*

A rare sighting of Ella in Eastern Europe, from a period when she wasn't making many records. The concert set has many of the usual pieces, and she has a go at 'Spinning Wheel', one of the worst songs of the era (and she says as much). There's a lovely Cole Porter medley, and she manages to make the most of 'Raindrops Keep Falling On My Head' and even 'I'll Never Fall In Love Again'. For completists.

***** Take Love Easy**

Pablo 2310-702 *Fitzgerald; Joe Pass (g). 73.*

****(*) Fine And Mellow**

Pablo 2310-829 *Fitzgerald; Clark Terry (t, flhn); Harry 'Sweets' Edison (t); Eddie 'Lockjaw' Davis, Zoot Sims (ts); Tommy Flanagan (p); Joe Pass (g); Ray Brown (b); Louie Bellson (d). 1/74.*

*****(*) Ella In London**

Pablo 2310-711 *Fitzgerald; Tommy Flanagan (p); Joe Pass (g); Keter Betts (b); Bobby Durham (d). 4/74.*

***** Montreux 1975**

Pablo 2310-751 *As above, except omit Pass. 7/75.*

*****(*) Ella And Oscar**

Pablo 2310-759 *Fitzgerald; Oscar Peterson (p); Ray Brown (b). 5/75.*

***** Fitzgerald And Pass ... Again**

Pablo 2310-772 *Fitzgerald; Joe Pass (g). 1–2/76.*

**** Dream Dancing**

Original Jazz Classics OJC 1072 *Fitzgerald; Nelson Riddle Orchestra. 6/72–2/78.*

****(*) Lady Time**

Pablo 2310-825 D *Fitzgerald; Jackie Davis (org); Louie Bellson (d). 6/78.*

***** A Perfect Match**

Pablo 231-2110 *Fitzgerald; Pete Minger, Sonny Cohn, Paul Cohen, Raymond Brown (t); Booty Wood, Bill Hughes, Mel Wanzo, Dennis Wilson (tb); Kenny Hing, Danny Turner (ts); Eric Dixon, Bobby Plater (as); Charlie Fowlkes (bs); Count Basie (p); Freddie Green (g); Keter Betts (b); Mickey Roker (d). 7/79.*

***** A Classy Pair**

Pablo 2310 132 *As above, except add Nolan Smith (t), John Clayton (b), Butch Miles (d); omit Cohen, Betts and Roker. 2/79.*

***** Digital III At Montreux**

Original Jazz Classics OJC 996 *Similar to above, except add Paul Smith (p), Joe Pass (g), Niels-Henning Orsted Pedersen (b). 7/79.*

Back with Norman Granz again, Ella recorded steadily through the '70s, but there was little to suggest she would either repeat or surpass the best of her earlier music. If encroaching age is supposed to impart a greater wisdom to a singer of songs, and hence into the interpretation of those songs, it's a more complex matter with Fitzgerald. While her respectful delivery of lyrics honours the wordsmithing, she brought little of the personal gravitas to the American songbook which was Sinatra's trademark. Her scatting grew less fluent and more exaggerated, if no less creative in its construction; her manipulation of time and melody became more obvious because she had to push herself harder to make it happen. There are still many good records here, but no really great ones, and all of them miss a little of the grace and instinctive improvisation which float off her older records.

Granz recorded her in several settings. With Joe Pass, the bare-strings accompaniment is initially intimate but finally dull. Pass can't devise enough variation to make the music stay awake, and Fitzgerald isn't always sure how strongly she's able to come on. Their duet albums are nice enough, but one is enough. *Fine And Mellow* is a rather noisy and brash session, but the title-track is a very good version of the Holiday favourite, which sounds just as good in Ella's hands. The Montreux and Nice live sets are merely OK, and much better is the London date from 1974. Probably the final chance to hear Ella in a club setting, and it's a racy and sometimes virtuosic display by the singer, a fine souvenir of what was a memorable visit. The 1979 Montreux set is unexciting. Most of it is average Basie or Pass, and Ella does only one ballad and a lumber through 'Flying Home'. Of the big-band dates, *Dream Dancing* features Nelson Riddle at his sententious worst and is missable, while the two sets with Basie are boisterous if comparatively uneventful. *Lady Time* is an unusual setting which tries Ella out as a kind of club-class blueswoman; she makes a game go of it. The other must-hear record, though, is the duet (almost – Ray Brown offers discreet support) with Oscar Peterson, *Ella And Oscar.* The pianist plays as hard as usual, but instrumentalist and vocalist bring out the best in each other, and there are at least three near-classics in 'Mean To Me', 'How Long Has This Been Going On?' and 'Midnight Sun'.

****(*) Ella Abraça Jobim**

Pablo 2630-201 *Fitzgerald; Clark Terry (t); Zoot Sims (ts); Toots Thielemans (hca); Mike Lang, Clarence McDonald, Terry Trotter (ky); Joe Pass, Oscar Castro-Nueves, Paul Jackson, Mitch Holder, Roland Bautista (g); Abe Laboriel (b); Alex Acuña (d); Paulinho Da Costa (perc).* 9/80.

****(*) The Best Is Yet To Come**

Original Jazz Classics 889 *Fitzgerald; Al Aarons (t); Bill Watrous (tb); Marshal Royal (as); Bob Cooper (ts); Jimmy Rowles (p); Art Hillery (org); Joe Pass, Tony Tedesco (g); Jim Hughart (b); Shelly Manne (d); strings and woodwind.* 2/82.

****(*) Nice Work If You Can Get It**

Pablo 2312-140 *Fitzgerald; André Previn (p).* 5/83.

***** Speak Love**

Pablo 2310-888 *Fitzgerald; Joe Pass (g).* 3/83.

***** Easy Living**

Pablo 2310-921 *As above.*

**** All That Jazz**

Pablo 2310-938 *Fitzgerald; Clark Terry, Harry 'Sweets' Edison (t); Al Grey (tb); Benny Carter (as); Mike Wofford, Kenny Barron (p); Ray Brown (b); Bobby Durham (d).* 3/89.

***** The Best Of Ella Fitzgerald**

Pablo 2405-421 *As various Pablo discs above.*

***** Bluella: Ella Fitzgerald Sings The Blues**

Pablo 2310-960 *As various Pablo discs above.*

The '80s saw Fitzgerald slackening off her workload as illness and perhaps sheer tiredness intervened. The Jobim collection came too late, since every other singer had already had their shot at this kind of thing; *The Best* was another tiresome set of Nelson Riddle arrangements; and the duo album with Previn was a pointless bit of star-matching. Which left two more albums with Pass and what proved to be a farewell set in the strained and unconvincing *All That Jazz.* At least the best-of is a good selection from the pick of the above. *Bluella* tackles the thorny issue of Fitzgerald in her most vulnerable idiom by settling for pseudo-blues items such as 'C-Jam Blues', 'Duke's Place' and 'Smooth Sailing'. Not bad.

*****(*) The Concert Years**

Pablo 4414-2 4CD *Basically as Pablo albums above.* 53–83.

Distilled from Fizgerald's live appearances as a headliner and with JATP, this is a very strong four-disc set which should be the first stopping-point for those who want to hear Ella the improviser and jazz musician. Starting with JATP material from the '50s, it takes in three different shows with Ellington, the 1974 set at Ronnie Scott's club, three Montreux appearances from the '70s, and a final (1983) show in Tokyo. If there are occasional lapses in judgement, where her scatting or phrasing can become almost parodic, the quality of her musicianship wins through. Cameos from many famous names add to the interest.

Paul Flaherty

ALTO AND TENOR SAXOPHONES

Based in and around Connecticut, Flaherty is the nominal leader of a gang of unreconstituted free-jazzers, most of whom appear on these records.

***** Prana**

Zaabway 2007 *Flaherty; Froc (g); Richard Downs (b); Randall Colbourne (d).* 4/89.

***** Ottawa**

Zaabway 2006 *Flaherty; Randall Colbourne (d).* 7/91.

*****(*) Fat Onions**

Cadence CJR 1054 *Flaherty; James 'Chumly' Hunt (t, pkt-t); Stephen Scholz (vn); Mike Murray (g); Richard Downs (b); Randall Colbourne (d).* 11/93.

***** Visitants**

Zaabway 2001 *As above, except omit Hunt and Scholz.* 3/94.

Flaherty is an irascible-sounding saxophonist who takes his cues from the unadorned energy playing of the '60s and early '70s. He co-leads these groups with drummer Colbourne, and together they marshal a music which forms around dense, braying collectives, sometimes recalling the heterophony of the Ayler ensemble, sometimes a golden-age FMP session, and sometimes creating something peculiarly their own. It's an exhilarating experience – and an exhausting one, handled over CD length; but endemic to this kind of listening is a sense of shared work-experience with the players.

Flaherty has uncovered some old history with the release of *Prana* and *Ottawa.* The quartet session is slightly more easy-going than some of their subsequent music, though Flaherty himself offers no quarter, as usual. Froc (that seems to be his entire name) is more reserved on the guitar. The duo set, from the 1991 Ottawa Festival, is intense, if at times rather pinched, with only two players involved.

Fat Onions, with its bigger ensemble and heavier, cloudier music, is still our favourite from this batch. There are moments of lyricism and quiet, though these are annihilated soon enough, and the group breaks into a kind of hymnal mode when it wants to sound celebratory. For the committed only, perhaps, but it's pleasing to know that this kind of jazz is still being explored and created. Recording is all right, if on the dry side.

***** Third Rail**

Zaabway 2002 *Flaherty; Richard Downs (b, sou); Randall Colbourne (d, v). 9/95.*

*****(*) Ringtaw**

Zaabway 2004 *As above, except add James 'Chumly' Hunt (t, perc); Matt Moran (vib, perc); Mike Murray (g). 9/96.*

***** Resonance**

Zaabway 2005 *Flaherty; Raphe Malik (t, p); Daniel Carter (t, cl, as, ts, f, p); Sabir Mateen (as, ts, cl, f, p, v); Randall Colbourne (d, p). 5/97.*

Flaherty and Colbourne soldier on, from the 'hotbed of free jazz', Connecticut. *Third Rail* is the axis at its most pure: Flaherty simply roars on and on, with the other two scuttling about below, though Downs gets off a bit of a surprise when he starts parping on a sousaphone on 'Rosebud Ricochet'. *Ringtaw* is surely their finest hour so far, three long but dourly beautiful improvisations in which the sextet achieve a genuinely conspiratorial music at the same moment as each one is blowing his head off. Or so it seems. 'Part 1' is a modest triumph, though some unexpected lyricism blossoms in 'Part 2'. They could use a better studio-sound, though – Colbourne especially gets short-changed with the mix on offer.

Resonance is a souvenir of a let's-walk-on-and-see-what-happens kind of concert, where Connecticut's finest met with Malik, Mateen and Carter, apparently shouldering an Art Ensemble's worth of instruments among them. Exhilarating as usual and a nice mix of voices, though again the rough live sound hinders appreciation at times.

*****(*) Anahad**

Cadence CJR 1107 *Flaherty; James 'Chumly' Hunt (t, flhn, pkt-t); Mike Murray (g); Richard Downs (b); Randall Colbourne (d). 11/98.*

The team return for another freewheeling, free-ranging and freely formed set of free jazz (only the record is not free – you'll have to pay for it). As usual, they open with a tremendous blow on 'Smokeshop', almost 29 minutes long, and follow it with three more which are more or less more of the same, only different. The sound is never going to get crystal-clear, but it works. As ever, hugely enjoyable if you like this kind of music; if you don't, you'll relate to the 26 put-downs which Flaherty cheerfully lists in the sleeve-note, the kind of thing these guys and many like them must have heard their whole playing lives. Our favourite is 'My wife said to get your record outta the house'.

***** The Ilya Tree**

Boxholder BXH016 *Flaherty; Greg Kelley (t); John Voigt (b); Laurence Cook (d). 11/99.*

***** The Hated Music**

Ecstatic Yod e#1b/fypc16 *Flaherty; Chris Corsano (d). 6/00.*

Flaherty away from some of his usual gang. *The Ilya Tree* is, next to some of the customary uproar, almost chamberish in feel. Kelley brings a certain sobriety to the occasion, even tossing in a boppish phrase or two, and there's more light and shade than usual; although in some ways that denies Flaherty his usual individuality. *The Hated Music* (methinks thou dost ...) is back on merciless territory, sax and drums locked in argument. A bit better recorded than some of the saxophonist's previous entries. But Flaherty can use the contrast offered by a bigger band.

***** Sannyasi**

Wet Paint 3001 *Flaherty; Greg Kelley (t); Chris Corsano (d). 5/01.*

***** Voices**

Wet Paint 3002 *Flaherty (as, ts solo). 9/01.*

Back with the gang. They caught a good one with *Sannyasi*, in decent studio sound, and a great blow by all hands. 'This music isn't for everyone – but it should be', says Paul. Well, give them time!

Voices finds him alone at last. He sounds to be in a thoughtful mood, and there are passages of unaffected sweetness to go along with lung-clearing outbursts. He never stays away from the extreme stuff for very long, although Flaherty's idea of 'extremes' probably isn't like most people's. Like many solo records, this isn't truly sustained, but it's strong.

Tommy Flanagan (1930–2001)

PIANO

One of the piano masters of Detroit, he played on many major recordings in the late '50s but thereafter sought an accompanist's security behind Ella Fitzgerald and Tony Bennett. Emerged as an undimmed creative spirit in the '70s and '80s, a bebopper of gentlemanly distinction.

***** The Cats**

Original Jazz Classics OJC 079 *Flanagan; Idrees Sulieman (t); John Coltrane (ts); Kenny Burrell (g); Doug Watkins (b); Louis Hayes (d). 4/57.*

If it's difficult to make fine qualitative distinctions within Tommy Flanagan's discography, it isn't difficult to distinguish his output from the average piano trio of the last 30 years. The earlier albums date from a period before he became known as one of the finest accompanists in the business, backing Tony Bennett and, more memorably, Ella Fitzgerald in her great late-'60s resurgence. *The Cats* is officially a Prestige All Stars session, but it is Flanagan's stewardship of the house rhythm section that makes the gig his own, and there is a wonderful 'How Long Has This Been Going On' for trio which clinches the deal. He is always at the heart of the action, helping out the hornmen when they lose their way, once or twice cutting through the verbiage to get back to the song. There is also material from this period and from similar line-ups on other discs.

*****(*) Overseas**

Original Jazz Classics OJC 1033 *Flanagan; Wilbur Little (b); Elvin Jones (d). 8/57.*

Made in Stockholm, this was rather a collectors' piece when issued by Prestige the first time, with a clever cover design that read *Over CCCCCC* etc. It is interesting to compare Flanagan's 'Relaxin' At Camarillo' and 'Eclipso' with the versions he made 20 years later on Enja's *Eclipso*: a remarkable constancy of energy and trim melodic ideas. Jones does some fine work, nowhere more so than in the odd introduction to 'Eclipso' and the fiercely effective 'Beat's Up'. As ever, Flanagan's bop vocabulary is uplifted by his beautiful touch.

***** The Tommy Flanagan Trio**

Original Jazz Classics OJC 183 *Flanagan; Tommy Potter (b); Roy Haynes (d). 5/60.*

This plain-label session is as blunt and straightforward as the title suggests and helps plug a longish gap in the available documentation. Flanagan rolls his sleeves up and wades straight into a nicely judged programme of standards with an emphasis on medium-paced ballads. He's at his best on 'In The Blue Of The Evening' and 'In A Sentimental Mood', the opening and closing numbers, while 'You Go To My Head' underlines his determination to stay in sight of the lyric at all times.

***** The Tokyo Recital**
Original Jazz Classics OJC 737 *Flanagan; Keter Betts (b); Bobby Durham (d).* 2/75.

***** Montreux '77**
Original Jazz Classics OJC 372 *As above.* 7/77.

*****(*) The Best Of Tommy Flanagan**
Pablo PACD 2405 410 *As above.* 2/75 & 7/77.

***** Something Borrowed, Something Blue**
Original Jazz Classics OJC 473 *As above, except Jimmie Smith (d) replaces Durham.* 1/78.

*****(*) Eclypso**
Enja ENJ 2088 *Flanagan; George Mraz (b); Elvin Jones (d).* 2/77.

*****(*) Our Delights**
Original Jazz Classics OJC 752 *Flanagan; Hank Jones (p).* 1/78.

*****(*) Super Session**
Enja ENJ 3059 *Flanagan; Red Mitchell (b); Elvin Jones (d).* 2/80.

***** The Magnificent Tommy Flanagan**
Progressive 7059 *Flanagan; George Mraz (b); Al Foster (d).* 81.

***** Thelonica**
Enja ENJ 4052 *Flanagan; George Mraz (b); Art Taylor (d).* 12/82.

Throughout the '70s and early '80s, Flanagan explored aspects of harmony most closely associated with the late John Coltrane, often stretching his solos very far from the tonal centre but without lapsing into the tuneless abstractions that were such a depressing aspect of Coltrane's legacy.

Elvin Jones's presence and multidirectional approach are always a plus on Flanagan dates. *Eclypso* develops the relationship further; *Super Session* brings it to a peak, recorded three years later. The only real drawback with these Enja dates is the less than attractive piano-sound, which one has to listen through. *Our Delights* has all the signs of a real meeting of minds. As usual, not a particularly adventurous roster of tunes: 'Our Delight', 'Jordu', 'Lady Bird', two takes of 'Robbins' Nest', 'Autumn Leaves' – but beautifully crafted all the same.

The Best Of ..., which brings together much of the preceding *Tokyo Recital* with the live session from *Montreux '77*, might more usefully have been labelled a Strayhorn tribute, since he is the main composer represented. Flanagan sounds bright and airy but also a little empty of ideas, and some of his colleagues' work is decidedly pedestrian and uninspired.

Throughout these dates, Flanagan's a wonderfully lyrical performer, with the widest imaginable range of diction and association. There is not a dull or fudged set in the bunch.

***** Jazz Poet**
Timeless 301 *Flanagan; George Mraz (b); Kenny Washington (d).* 1/89.

'Jazz poet' would be a fair passport entry for what Flanagan does. A beautifully judged and perfectly performed record you'll find yourself playing often. Though a studio session, it has the relaxed but subtly challenging feel of one of Flanagan's club dates. Outstanding tracks include the opening 'Raincheck', 'Caravan' and an unexpected version of 'St Louis Blues'. Mraz is at the top of his powers and Washington doesn't attempt to muscle in but keeps to his business patiently and accurately. Lovely.

*****(*) Let's**
Enja ENJ 8040 *Flanagan; Jesper Lundgaard (b); Lewis Nash (d).* 4/93.

***** Flanagan's Shenanigans**
Storyville 41928 *As above; add Jesper Thilo (ts); Steen Hansen (hn); Vincent Nilsson (baritone hn); Jan Zum Vohrde (as, bcl); Flemming Madsen (bcl); Uffe Markussen (ss, ts, bcl).* 93.

Flanagan was the 1993 winner of the prestigious Jazzpar Prize and this music was recorded as part of those celebrations. The trio date is a celebration of Thad Jones's music; much of it, most famously 'A Child Is Born', has been well covered by big bands and by horn groups, but never before by a piano trio. (Mal Waldron has covered Jones tunes on club dates, but never with this degree of concentration.) Flanagan knew Thad years ago when they were both starting out. One suspects that they were temperamentally similar,and these treatments bespeak a warm sympathy. It's a generous programme; as well as the title-piece and 'Child', there are performances of 'Mean What You Say', 'To You', 'Bird Song' and 'Scratch' (Nash standing out prominently on these), 'Thadrack', 'Three In One', 'Quietude', 'Zec' and, finally, 'Elusive', which closes the record on a high.

The Storyville set features the same trio working with the Jazzpar Windtet. They provide some lovely moments, particularly on the opening track, Flanagan's own 'Eclypso', where Vincent Nilsson turns in a lovely baritone horn solo. 'Beyond The Bluebird' is also covered, as is the clever and devious 'Minor Mishap'. Most of the rest is standard or repertoire material, but including the title-piece, written for him by James Williams. Tommy's solo on 'But Beautiful' is one of the best of his career and Jesper Thilo's feature on 'For Lena and Lennie' is worth the price of admission alone. A lovely album all round and a worthy souvenir of an overdue accolade.

*****(*) Sunset And The Mockingbird: The Birthday Concert**
Blue Note 93155 *Flanagan; Peter Washington (b); Lewis Nash (d).* 98.

To mark his 67th birthday, Flanagan took over the Village Vanguard and delivered one of his trademark performances. As ever, the material is chosen with intelligence and delivered with real expression. He kicks off with a superb rendition of Thad Jones's 'Birdsong'. Another Thad tune, 'Let's', comes along later, as does Dizzy's 'Tin Tin Deo', both of them songs Tommy had made very much his own in recent years. He's also done a lot to promote the work of Tom McIntosh, whose 'Balance Scales' featured on the Jazzpar disc and is reprised here along with 'The Cupbearers' and 'With Malice Toward None'. Tommy's piano sounds in good heart and his technique well up to scratch. Washington and Nash are ideal collaborators, unobtrusive but effortlessly creative. A fine set and a worthy memorial to an artist who passed away just a couple of years later.

Ingebrigt Haker Flaten

BASS

Flaten is a leading member of the Norwegian free division which has been making some international waves alongside Ken Vandermark and others.

***** Double Bass**

SOFA 511 *Flaten (b solo).* 12/02–5/03.

Flaten uses two instruments on what is basically a brief collection of mostly brief improvisations, ranging from 'The Joy Of German Bowing', which sounds like two minutes of grunting, to the more melodic application of 'Slides'. Two pieces have 'random overdubs done without playback'. As so often on a solo record, the bassist takes the chance to isolate certain technical considerations and use those as the basis for a piece's structure or overall sound, although here he usually ends the piece as soon as – or even before – he thinks the idea's even beginning to flag. While there sounds to be little in the way of prepared-instrument techniques, he certainly gets some curious timbres out of the big fiddle, as in the tough strumming of 'Gghame-shu'. In the end, not a record to stand tall next to soliloquies by Kowald or Guy, but sometimes striking enough.

Bob Florence (born 1932)

PIANO, ARRANGER

Active since the late '50s as an arranger in the Los Angeles area, Florence has provided scores and playing situations for many Californian groups, and his own big-band records are unambiguously complex and modernistic playing situations for the best musicians he can find.

***** Name Band – 1959**

Fresh Sound FSCD 2008 *Florence; Johnny Audino, Tony Terran, Jules Chaikin, Irv Bush (t); Bob Edmondson, Bobby Pring, Don Nelligan, Herbie Harper (tb); Bob Enevoldsen (vtb); Herb Geller, Bernie Fleischer (as); Bob Hardaway (ts); Don Shelton (ts, cl); Dennis Budimir (g); Mel Pollan (b); Jack Davenport (d).* 11/58.

*****(*) Funupmanship**

Mama MMF 1006 *Florence; Larry Ford, Warren Luening, Steve Huffsteter, Wayne Bergeron, Charlie Davis, (t, flhn); Rick Culver, Don Waldrop, Alex Iles (tb); Bob Efford, John Lowe, Dick Mitchell, Lanny Morgan, Kim Richmond, Lee Callett (reeds); Tom Warrington (b); Steve Houghton (d).* 92.

***** With All The Bells And Whistles**

Mama MMF 1011 *As above, except add Carl Saunders (t, flhn), Bob McChesney (tb), Terry Harrington, Bob Carr (woodwinds), Brian Kilgore (perc); omit Ford, Culver.* 2/95.

****** Earth**

Mama MMF 1016 *As above, except add George Graham (t, flhn), Charlie Loper (tb), Trey Henry (b), Gregg Field (d); omit Lowe, Morgan, Callet, Warrington, Houghton, Kilgore.* 4/96.

*****(*) Serendipity 18**

Mama MMF 1025 *As above, except add Rick Baptist, Ron Stout (t), Jeff Driskill (ts, cl, f), Dick Weller (d); omit Davis, Mitchell, Carr, Field.* 8/98.

Florence has done sterling work as a big-band arranger, leader and performer over 40 years. His bread has been buttered in Los Angeles studio work, but none of these records sounds compromised by that background: he likes big, swinging, powerful bands, and his charts are stuffed with activity. Soloists seldom get by without counterpoint or some other sort of support, and – unusually for the Californian orchestral tradition – he's as interested in long-form writing as he is in punchy three- and four-minute numbers. His bands are usually staffed by the best executants, with two or three knockout soloists as a bonus, and the Fresh Sound reissue shows that that's been the case from the start. There are marvellous turns by Herb Geller and Bob Enevoldsen here, but the section-work, though filled with unfamiliar names, lacks nothing in polish and attack. The disc is stuffed with alternative takes, but there's plenty of interest throughout.

Florence resumed his recording in the late '70s with seven albums for Discovery, but they all seem to be missing in action for now. His albums for Mama bring the story up to date. *Funupmanship* gains an extra ounce of energy from the live recording, and here Florence really puts the band on its mettle: 'Slimehouse' comes out of the stalls ferociously, and 'Come Rain Or Come Shine' is smart enough to have would-be arrangers scratching their heads. Among the soloists, Kim Richmond plays a key role: a modernist with sufficient tradition in him to uphold and transcend his surroundings. After that, *With All The Bells And Whistles* seems like a pressure drop, and 'Teach Me Tonight' is too arch to convince. Compensations include the rough-housing by the two saxes of Mitchell and Harrington on 'Tenors, Anyone?', which just about makes up for its title. *Earth*, though, finds Florence and team back to top form. These are some of his most challenging and head-turning charts, with 'Straight No Chaser' an extraordinary example of a transformation of a jazz standard. As ever, the soloists seem compelled to give of their best – too many excitements in this department to catalogue here – and if Florence perhaps doesn't quite edge out the peerless Bill Holman in creative terms, he's one of the few arrangers fit to walk in Holman's steps.

No real drop in intensity on *Serendipity 18*, which undergoes a few changes in personnel (Weller is a powerhouse addition to the rhythm section) and finds Florence at his most feisty: 'I haven't simplified anything.' As ever his scores are extravagant with detail and complexity, at times to the point of super-abundance, but the impact of the band in delivering these scores is little short of awesome and, on a more mediated piece such as 'Tres Palabras', the wit of the scoring comes through more clearly. A tremendous sequence of big-band records.

Chuck Folds

PIANO

Brilliant but underrated stride and classic jazz specialist, best known for his association with Doc Cheatham.

****** Hitting His Stride**

Arbors 19117 *Folds (p solo).* 96.

***** Remember Doc Cheatham**

Arbors 19218 *Folds; Spanky Davis, Irving Stokes (t); Frank Tate (b); Jackie Williams (d).* 11/98.

Even for students of jazz piano, Folds may be an undiscovered treasure. In style, he's not so much rumbustious as muscularly intelligent, which makes his moments of pathos and episodes of romance all the more effective. Though in different moods he superficially resembles a number of classic players, comparison isn't helpful since Chuck is very much his own man, with a strong, equal-handed approach and a very distinctive approach to rhythmic phrasing.

The solo album is probably the best place to start listening, 21 fine unaccompanied performances, some of them material associated with Fats Waller and James P. Johnson (the latter's 'Mule Walk' and 'Keep Off The Grass') but ranging as far afield as Strayhorn's 'Johnny Come Lately'. There are some nice obscurities lurking in the programme as well. Good sound on the piano, though the dynamics aren't quite as well observed as one might have hoped.

Folds first worked with Doc Cheatham in 1972 and the association continued for a quarter of a century, most prominently in a regular Sunday gig at Sweet Basil in New York. Here Chuck and his 'Sweet Basil Friends' compile a tribute to Cheatham, who died in 1997. The trumpeters are both seasoned players but even two of them don't make up for Doc's absence, and the best moments are again when Chuck is at the piano alone, as on 'A Kiss To Build A Dream On' and the even better 'Sweet Lorraine'. It's a nice group, though, and their collective efforts shape a very attractive album

Joe Fonda

BASS, VOICE

Bassist and co-leader with Michael Jefry Stevens of a regular free-bop group, as well as exploring other free-thinking projects.

***** The Wish**
Music & Arts CD 916 *Fonda; Herb Robertson (t, flhn); Mark Whitecage (as, ss); Michael Jefry Stevens (p); Harvey Sorgen (d); Laura Arbuckle (v).* 6/93–8/95.

***** Parallel Lines**
Music & Arts CD 979 *As above, except omit Arbuckle.* 96.

***** Live From Brugge**
Dwerf 010 *As above.* 4/97.

***** Evolution**
Leo CD LR 260 *As above.* 4–10/97.

***** Live At The Bunker**
Leo CD LR 301 *As above, except omit Robertson; add Paul Smoker (t).* 00.

These are all by the Fonda–Stevens Group, a band of largely 'unfashionable' improvisers exploring the parameters of free bop on a likeable set of records. Robertson and Whitecage are both conservative radicals whose most splenetic moments wouldn't cause an earthquake disturbance. It's their solos and dialogues with different members of the rhythm section that tend to direct the music, even though the writing is all by Fonda and Stevens. The compositions tend to be either open-ended sketches or Coleman-like melodies counterpointed between the instruments, and if the latter carry less conviction it's because the playing seems to run ragged when it should be pointed. Whitecage in particular is a wayward voice who's at his best when least fettered by his surroundings. Of the first three albums here, *The Wish* is the least focused, *Parallel Lines* the most specific, *Live From Brugge* the liveliest (and the one that admits of a collective sense of humour, as in 'The Money Thing' and 'Down On The Delta'). But there is so little to choose qualitatively between the three that it seems unwise to make a clear distinction.

Evolution is well titled, because it sees the group move back and forth in musical time. 'Birdtalk' is a clear reference to the bop roots of most of the players. Robertson's solo is superb, somewhere between Dizzy Gillespie and Booker Little, while 'Song For My Mother' breathes poetry. The balance of voices isn't quite right, perhaps in the interests of group democracy, but the music comes across fine and strong. The replacement of Robertson with the drier-toned and more academic Smoker might seem to threaten a reduction in pace and excitement, but this isn't the case. In fact, *Live At The Bunker* is one of the group's very best showings. The closing 'Oh Lord, It's Nice To Sit On Your Porch Today', complete with vocals, is a good summing up of the group's strengths and idiosyncrasies. Better sound, but still not pristine.

***** What We're Hearing**
De Werf 007 *Fonda; Carl Morena (p); Jeff Hirshfield (d).* 94.

A strong collaborative group that is as different from the conventional piano trio as one might imagine. Fonda is the lead voice for a good deal of the way, much as Ray Brown has tended to lead his trios, and certainly shapes and propels the most interesting lines of enquiry. Morena will be a new voice for some; he's certainly jazz-based, but seems aware of other musics as well, giving him a flexible vocabulary of phrases and accents. Hirshfield can't be faulted, either as a time-keeper or, here, as a colourist who augments his colleagues' lines with beautifully placed strokes.

***** When It's Time**
Jazz'halo TS 011 *Fonda (b solo).* 5/99.

Albums of solo bass are difficult to assess because they are rarely of more than specialist interest. This is an honourable exception. Because Fonda is such a thoroughly musical player, his solo excursions are always logical, expressive and never merely technical exercises. Playing mostly original material (the title-track is by Attila Zoller) Joe constructs elegant shapes and architectures with each piece, drawing on a number of techniques, including *sul ponticello* at one point, or so it sounds, to vary the sonority of his instrument. The recording is quite good but apt to distort at higher volumes.

***** Full Circle Suite**
CIMP 198 *Fonda; Taylor Ho Bynum (t, conch); Chris Jonas (ss); Gebhard Ullman (bcl); Kevin Norton (d).* 3/99.

****(*) Distance**
Leo Lab 069 *Fonda; Xu Fengxia (guzheng, v).* 5/99.

***** The Healing**
Leo LR 338 *Fonda; Herb Robertson (t); Michael Jefry Stevens (p); Harvey Sorgen (d).* 10–12/00.

The opening track on *Full Circle Suite*, 'Next Step', which is based in part on a Kevin Norton arrangement of 'Brilliant Corners', is a very fine piece of work, evolving naturally out of its thematic materials into some clear-headed and creative improvising. The opening section sets an Ayler-like slow theme over fast rhythms, before a series of improvisations around a second theme and finally a frantic stop-on-a-dime conclusion. From there, though, the record gets bogged down into the familiar CIMP style of overlong tracks and lack of self-restraint. Fonda gets a coherent sound out of a group of strong-willed players, but even they don't sustain the 27′44″ of the title-track, and a potentially great record is a merely good one.

The duos with guzheng player Xu Fengxia are interesting, but they suggest two worlds not really meeting, and the best music comes in the first part of 'Underwater Market Selling Clocks', where Fonda executes the simplest of accompaniments to the other player's natural virtuosity.

The Healing brings back the Fonda–Stevens Group. Not particularly well recorded – Fonda himself gets a rather muzzy sound – and, while the brief 'Fast' is an excellent collective piece, the almost conventional ballad, 'Tania's Deam', seems like an unsatisfactory departure. A mixed bag.

***** Blisters**
Jazz'halo TS 016 *Fonda; Gilbert Isbin (g).* 5/02.

And blisters is what they presumably both had after this hard-picking, percussive duo session. Isbin is a new name to us, but he earns immediate respect for his witty, dancing guitar lines. Fonda weaves in and out, detuning his bass on several occasions and seeming to do it mid-performance on a couple of the longer cuts. The music pales slightly as the set goes on, but only because the listener finds it hard to keep pace with such a brisk set in which so many different techniques are being deployed.

Ricky Ford (born 1954)

TENOR SAXOPHONE

Began recording in the '70s and had spells with Mercer Ellington, Charles Mingus and Dannie Richmond, before leading his own dates. A considerable technician and hearty player, yet to achieve much wider recognition.

***** Manhattan Blues**
Candid CCD 79036 *Ford; Jaki Byard (p); Milt Hinton (b); Ben Riley (d).* 3/89.

*****(*) Ebony Rhapsody**
Candid CCD 79053 *As above.* 6/90.

An erratic but occasionally brilliant player, Ford is best known for his work with Mingus and Abdullah Ibrahim. His own records are ambitious in extent, covering a range of idioms from bop, modal-to-free harmony, and back to a broad swing style. On the 1989 *Manhattan Blues* Ford's breadth of reference is instantaneously answered by the eclectic Byard and by the bassist and drummer; Ford's soloing is thoughtful but still curiously uninvolving. *Ebony Rhapsody*, with the same line-up, irons out the occasional awkwardnesses and finds Ford with a band that seems increasingly responsive to his changes of direction; 'Mirror Man', a duet with Milt 'The Judge' Hinton, has an authority worthy of Coleman Hawkins, and the other originals bespeak a growing compositional talent.

*****(*) Hot Brass**
Candid CCD 79518 *Ford; Lew Soloff, Claudio Roditi (t); Steve Turre (tb); Danilo Perez (p); Christian McBride (b); Carl Allen (d).* 4/91.

The arrangements here are sharp and pungent. 'Banging, Bashing, Bowing and Blowing' is a superb band workout, and '11/15/91' is a chromatic lament for Martin Luther King Jr, written at the time of the Gulf War, while 'Carbon 14' draws its inspiration from Ford's interest in Afro-Americana and the theory that black Africans may have discovered America long before Columbus. Digging ever deeper into those roots, the resulting music is mightily impressive.

Michael Formanek (born 1958)

DOUBLE BASS

Solo bass performance is one of the toughest of all musical disciplines within the embrace of jazz. Formanek is one of the few around – one thinks also of Barre Phillips and Mark Dresser – who is capable of sustaining interest at length. Most of his recording under his own name has been with sympathetic small groups, but Formanek has also been able to go out alone.

***** Loose Cannon**
Soul Note 121261 *Formanek; Tim Berne (as, bs); Jeff Hirshfield (d).* 10/92.

Formanek is a musician of considerable intelligence and range, with ideas that probably need more extended exposure. Mingus is probably the main source, though Formanek rarely leads from the front, preferring a more unassuming role (*Low Profile*, title of a later disc, gets it about right). What makes all his records distinctive in their surprisingly different ways is his approach to texture and space, and his ability to give individual voicings a thoroughly idiomatic cast.

Berne is a sourer and more acerbic player than Greg Osby (who played on Formanek's deleted debut set) and occasionally he seems pushed too far forward in the mix. What he brings, though, is a solid, blocky presence around which Formanek's own natural lyricism flows like water round a splintery rock. Berne also contributes much of the writing to *Loose Cannon* and, while it's easy to see where the bassist sees fruitful common ground, it would have been good to hear more of his own ideas.

***** Am I Bothering You?**
Screwgun SCRU U 70006 *Formanek (b solo).* 12/97.

In a previous edition we suggested that it would be good to find Formanek a commission for big band or orchestra. It speaks volumes about our prescience – and about the realities of jazz performance – that the next disc should be in that chewiest of all improvising forms: solo bass. Michael's Lowinsky bass sings through the whole session. Whether playing pizzicato or with bow, as he does at the start of 'Overhead Justice', he brings a terrific momentum and charge to what might otherwise be bleakly abstract music. Ending with a flourish on Muddy Waters's 'Rollin' Stone' was a masterstroke.

Jimmy Forrest (1920–80)

TENOR SAXOPHONE

Forrest will always be associated with the mournful swinger, 'Night Train', which was inspired by Duke Ellington. The saxophonist worked with Jay McShann (alongside Charlie Parker) and Andy Kirk, before establishing himself as a leader. Though by no means an innovator, he had a thoroughly individual voice on tenor, raw and tender by turns.

*****(*) Night Train**
Delmark 435 *Forrest; Chauncey Locke (t); Bart Dabney (tb); Charles Fox, Bunky Parker (p); Herschel Harris, John Mixon (b); Oscar Oldham (d); Percy James, Bob Reagan (perc).* 11/51–9/53.

***** All The Gin Is Gone**
Delmark 404 *Forrest; Harold Mabern (p); Grant Green (g); Gene Ramey (b); Elvin Jones (d).* 12/59.

***** Black Forrest**
Delmark 427 *As above.* 12/59.

Forrest is the mid-point, stylistically if not quite geographically, between Charlie Parker and Ornette Coleman. His early R&B experience invested his work with a strong, funky sound, which evolved into something richer and more complex, but always straight down the line rhythmically. After leaving the Ellington orchestra, he scored a big hit with 'Night Train', an R&B classic based on Duke's 'Happy Go Lucky Local'. It's the leading item on the eponymous Delmark, an album packed with short, funky themes that really ought to be heard on a jukebox rather than a home hi-fi. It's still a hugely engaging session and confirms that, even in his pop days, Forrest was never merely a honker and wailer but a fine melodist.

Just as later sessions are treasure for glimpses of cult heroes like Joe Zawinul and Larry Young, so the presence of Grant Green on these early sessions has both attracted notice and deflected it away from Jimmy's own melodic hard-bop approach. *All The Gin Is Gone* predates the better-known sessions for New Jazz and Prestige, but it has great strengths and the version of 'Caravan' is masterly. Here, too, the documentation is now complete with the release of *Black Forrest*, a 1972 release drawn from the same sessions as *All The Gin Is Gone.* The date saw the saxophonist lined up with the massive Mabern and precocious youngster Green on a beefy set of blues and ballads. Typically tough and direct playing from all hands.

***** Forrest Fire**
Original Jazz Classics OJC 199 *Forrest; Larry Young (org); Thornel Schwartz (g); Jimmie Smith (d).* 8/60.

***** Out Of The Forrest**
Original Jazz Classics OJC 097 *Forrest; Joe Zawinul (p); Tommy Potter (b); Clarence Johnston (d).* 4/61.

***** Sit Down And Relax With Jimmy Forrest**
Original Jazz Classics OJC 895 *Forrest; Hugh Lawson (p); Calvin Newborn (g); Tommy Potter (b); Clarence Johnston (d).* 9/61.

***** Most Much!**
Original Jazz Classics OJC 350 *As above, except omit Newborn; add Ray Barretto (perc).* 10/61.

***** Soul Street**
Original Jazz Classics 987 *As above, plus Art Farmer, Idries Sulieman (t), Jimmy Cleveland, George Cooper (tb), Jerome Richardson (as, f), George Barrow, King Curtis, Oliver Nelson, Seldon Powell (ts), Pepper Adams (bs), Ray Bryant, Gene Casey, Chris Woods (p), Tiny Grimes, Mundell Lowe (g), George Duvivier, Wendell Marshall (b), Roy Haynes, Osie Johnson, Ed Shaughnessy (d).* 61.

Understandably, much of the interest of these centres on a pre-Weather Report Zawinul and the late, great Larry Young, but Forrest is an intriguing performer in his own right. For reasons never satisfactorily explained, there weren't that many tenor saxophonists in the bebop revolutions. Like Big Nick Nicholas and Lucky Thompson, Forrest was something of a players' player, with only a rather marginal following now. That's a pity for, as these sets amply demonstrate, his playing was full of character, a little rough-hewn in places but capable of greater subtlety than his big hit, 'Night Train', might suggest.

Forrest Fire pits him against the brimstone stomp of Young's Hammond; between them, they roll up the floor. It's the biggest possible contrast to the lighter and more detailed sound of *Out Of The Forrest*, but in most respects this is the right context for the saxophonist, who had no desire to play delicately detailed changes. *Sit Down And Relax* sounds like a ballad date but there is the expected ration of slowly burning groovers, and the Detroit pianist, Hugh Lawson, arrives to underline the soulful side of the group.

Most Much! is a fine set, restoring two tracks from the same session previously released only as part of *Soul Street* on New Jazz: all of Forrest's work for Prestige and New Jazz is in catalogue. The final CD includes material by an Oliver Nelson-led octet, but it also features Nelson and King Curtis on the superb 'Soul Street', which may be the definitive Forrest cut after 'Night Train', ear candy for tenor enthusiasts. A slightly bitty compilation, it's still greater than the sum of the parts. *Most Much!* demonstrates what a developed time-feel Forrest had. The first three tracks could hardly be more different in emphasis. 'Matilda' is a traditional calypso, given a forceful reading, with the saxophonist closely backed by the unsung Lawson. 'Annie Laurie' is similarly upbeat but seldom departs from the melody. 'Autumn Leaves' is full of glassy harmonies and a first taste of the curious rhythmic displacements and imaginative harmonic inflexions that make him such a significant way-station between bop and the New Thing. The closing 'Most Much' is a tough rocker, with strong upper-register effects. The recording isn't really up to standard but, as usual, it's 'only' Tommy Potter who suffers unduly.

Arne Forsén (born 1960)

PIANO

Contemporary Swedish pianist, with experience in free music and theatre work as well as post bop.

***** Where Is The Moon?**
Dragon DRCD 253 *Forsén (p solo).* 6/00.

Forsén doesn't do anything dramatically personal here, but this is a very likeable and shrewdly collected programme of solos. Three Monk tunes are calmly but insightfully measured out, four improvisations are put down with considerable grace, and two tracks played on a tack piano are a mildly startling change of tone. A reluctance to prepare – or at least a faith in the immediacy of the moment – means that he falls back on familiar kinds of spontaneity here and there. Still, it's sweetly done.

Sonny Fortune (born 1939)

ALTO AND SOPRANO SAXOPHONES, FLUTE

Fortune has never been a prolific composer, and he is in some respects a very straightforward saxophone stylist, retaining elements of the R&B style, in which he originally worked. Employment with Elvin Jones, McCoy Tyner, Miles Davis and Buddy Rich broadened his horizons and in the '90s he entered a second, very effective period as a leader in his own right.

*****(*) In The Spirit Of John Coltrane**
Shanachie 5063 *Fortune; John Hicks (p); Reggie Workman (b); Rashied Ali, Steve Berrios, Ronnie Burrage, Julio Collazo (d).* 99.

Past contact with both McCoy Tyner and Elvin Jones may have given Fortune a clearer than usual insight into the legacy of John Coltrane. Interestingly, despite superficial similarities of timbre and attack, and coming from the same home-town, he has never sounded like a Trane disciple. Significantly, too, this tribute record consists largely of originals. The only Coltrane tunes are 'Olé' and 'Africa', not by any means obvious choices. Two more former associates of Trane's – Reggie Workman and Rashied Ali – turn up on this dark-hued and mostly reflective disc, which has an old-fashioned sound and might well be some lost session from the '60s. Sonny's three main horns are all heard, and there is a nice variation of approach, though almost every track makes some reference to the great man (or to 'Mr Jones'). Ali is in fine form on his appearance, but Ronnie Burrage is the revelation, quoting figures from the classic Quartet records, often against the metre of the song. Fortune's phrasing has become more exact over the years, and there is a stiffness about his delivery on 'Hangin' Out With JC Again' which is at odds with its relaxed, comradely feel. An attractive record, rather than a great one, but certainly different from the usual run of Trane memorials.

Clare Foster

VOCALS

Fine standards singer, working an overcrowded market.

*** Believing In Angels

33 Jazz 058 *Foster; Paul Jayasinha (t, flhn); Pete Jacobsen (p).* 01.

There's much to admire here: the brightness of Foster's delivery, the simplicity and appropriateness of her improvised passages, Jacobsen's sharply thoughtful accompaniment and Jayasinha's unexpected contribution. Unfortunately, with so many vocal albums around in the market-place she's going to find it difficult to be heard over the crowd. The label has a sample of 'I'm Old Fashioned' on its website. Try it, and if the voice moves out of the ordinary, you'll like the rest.

Frank Foster (born 1928)

TENOR AND SOPRANO SAXOPHONES

Like Jimmy Heath, Cincinnati-born Foster turned to the tenor saxophone largely to free himself of the all-pervasive influence of Charlie Parker. He has remained profoundly influenced by bop, even when experimenting with large-scale composition, and even as leader of the Basie band, a responsibility he took on in the mid-'80s and which he handled with great skill for a decade.

*** Fearless

Original Jazz Classics OJCCD 923 *Foster; Virgil Jones (t); Albert Dailey (p); Bob Cunningham (b); Alan Dawson (d).* 1/65.

***(*) Soul Outing!

Original Jazz Classics OJCCD 984 *Foster; Virgil Jones (t); Pat Rebillot (p); Billy Butler (g); Richard Davis (b); Bob Cunningham (b, d); Alan Dawson (d, perc).* 66.

Although Frank Foster made his name with Basie in the '50s – and a less bop-orientated band one couldn't wish to find – he had assimilated enough of the music of Charlie Parker into his playing to make him stand out as a particularly vivid soloist in that tightly integrated unit.

Fearless is one of a couple of dates he made for Prestige in the mid-'60s, and it's a solid, if formulaic, example of what the label managed to eke out of its various signings during the period. Foster opts for five originals and a long, joyous version of 'Jitterbug Waltz'. There are signs that he has been listening to John Coltrane, though the disciplined bop of the early records is still the dominant impression. The group sounds rigorously prepared but not so note-perfect that the playing loses freshness, and Jones and Dailey in particular respond with great alacrity to the challenge of the new material.

Soul Outing! was the second release as leader after leaving the Basie camp, and it's a step on in terms of style and conception. This time, Foster keeps it very tight and disciplined, and he modulates his own new material with two songs from the Adams/Strouse musical, *Golden Boy*, neither of them songs that have otherwise had much place in jazz repertory. His own 'Chiquito Loco' is an engaging swinger and 'Skanaroony' a look back to bebop. The contributions of guitarist Butler are kept to a minimum and are all the more effective for that.

*** The House That Love Built

Steeplechase SCCD 31170 *Foster; Horace Parlan (p); Jesper Lundgaard (b); Aage Tanggaard (d).* 9/82.

The early-'80s sessions are entertaining examples of Foster's mighty swing and full-blooded improvising, yet the settings somehow don't demand enough of him to make him give of his absolute best. Despite comprising mainly original material, the Steeplechase quartet date emerges as much like any other modern tenor-plus-rhythm session, although 'I Remember Sonny Stitt' is an imposing tribute to the then recently departed saxophonist.

*** Two For The Blues

Original Jazz Classics OJCCD 788 *Foster; Frank Wess (as, ts, f); Kenny Barron (p); Rufus Reid (b); Marvin 'Smitty' Smith (d).* 10/83.

These meetings with Frank Wess, another Basie colleague to whom Foster seems wedded through all eternity, are rather carefully conceived, as if the players were trying too hard to avoid the blowing clichés which sometimes dominate such records. Wess is a subtler and more varied player, but Foster is a crafty character and often has the last word.

The first album includes three Wess originals and just one composition by Foster, but the real surprises come in the opening ten minutes. The brisk, bright title-track, with some nice harmonic reworkings by both hornmen, is followed by a galloping 'Send In The Clowns', a most surprising rendition of the Sondheim classic and probably the high point of the album, though the paired readings of 'Nancy (With The Laughing Face)' and 'Spring Can Really Hang You Up The Most' are delightful too.

*** Swing

Challenge 70051 *Foster; Mickey Tucker (p); Earl May (b); Billy Hart (d).*

Caught live, Foster's quartet delivers an hour of tough, sensitive jazz. Frank signs off with Coltrane's 'Giant Steps', just to show that he can play those hallowed changes every bit as well as the younger guys, and do it at a stroll. There's a fine version of

'Chiquito Loco' and a long 'Shiny Stockings', which he's been doing since God was a small boy. Not the most elegant of albums, but an accurate representation of the man at work and sounding full of life.

★★★(★) Leo Rising
Arabesque 0124 *Foster; Derrick Gardner (t); Stephen Scott (p); Christian McBride (b); Lewis Nash (d).* 8/96.

Having shrugged off the responsibility of the Basie band, Foster concentrated on an Indian summer as a soloist and small-group leader. His soprano work has never been more individual than on 'Leo Rising' itself, which is a hard track to identity, heard out of context. Now approaching 70, Foster sounds poised and mature, and the group is full of wise heads on young shoulders. Scott and McBride trade quips and quotations while keeping a weather eye on the oldtimer. He knows they're at it but never wavers for a moment. The years have been kind to Foster in that his kind of tenor playing is a virtual orthodoxy, and yet he always manages to pack a lot of history into his solos, not by quotation, as the younger men do, but rather in sheer range of expression. Trumpeter Gardner joins in for a single track, enough to register a presence and suggest that he, too, may be a voice to listen up for in years to come.

★★★(★) We Do It Diff'rent
Mapleshade 9532 *Foster; Kenyata Beasley, Cecil Bridgewater, Jon Faddis, Derrick Gardner, Frank Greene, Jeremy Pelt (t, flhn); Vince Gardner, Stanford Hunter (tb); Bill Lowe (btb, tba); Bill Saxton, Bruce Williams (as); Joe Ford (ts); James Stewart (bs); Danny Mixon (p); Earl May (b); Sylvia Cuenca (d); Dennis Rowland (v).* 6/02.

Credited to Foster's Loud Minority Big Band, this is a rousingly entertaining set that brings a new contemporary edge of the sophisticated minimalism of the Basie band. Arranging is very much Frank's thing now and the charts on things like 'Stella By Starlight' and a magnificent 'Shiny Stockings' are inch perfect and for once on projects like this the main appeal is the ensemble playing rather than the soloing. None the less, there are fine statements from most of the senior brass-players, from baritonist Stewart and drummer Cuenca. Danny Mixon holds the band together from the keyboard and if there is an occasional slackness elsewhere in the rhythm section it's of an attractive rather than a troubling sort.

The live recording is full and detailed, though there are one or two slight distortions on the higher horns which might briefly discomfort the listener who's playing this as it should be, at 8 or 9 on the dial. Great stuff.

George 'Pops' Foster (1892–1969)

BASS

He began on cello but had changed to string bass by his teens. He worked on riverboats and with all the major New Orleans bandleaders, before moving to St Louis and eventually New York, where he worked through the '30s. A celebrated figure in the '40s revival, he carried on until his death, always rock-solid in the New Orleans style.

★★★ George 'Pops' Foster
American Music ASMCD-105 *Foster; Art Hodes (p).* 68.

Pops and Art chat about the bassman's long life and career, and intersperse the dialogue with whichever tunes come up in the conversation. Privately recorded by Hodes, it's eavesdropping on old friends. Pops plays in his elemental style, grumbling away with the bow on 'Closer Walk With Thee', slapping on the others, and they open and close with 'Mahogany Hall Stomp'. Only 37 minutes and musically slight, it's a precious survival all the same.

Lem Fowler

PIANO, VOCAL

A Chicagoan pianist working in the local studios during the early and middle '20s.

★★(★) Complete Recorded Works 1923–1927
RST JPCD-1520-2 *Fowler; Sidney De Paris, Seymour Trick, Clarence Wheeler (t); Ernest Elliott (ss, cl); Percy Glascoe (cl, as); Charlie Holmes (as); Stanley Harding, Al Brunson (wbd); Helen Baxter, Mae Scott, George Williams, Helen McDonald (v).* 5/23–7/27.

Lemuel Fowler is a shadowy figure about whom almost nothing is known, but he made a fair number of records as accompanist and bandleader, and all of the earlier sides are here. A capable writer – there are three versions of his hit 'You've Got Ev'ry Thing A Sweet Mama Needs But Me' included here – he had a confident and somewhat Mortonesque manner at the piano: interesting to hear a version of 'Jelly Roll Blues' among the band sides. The accompaniments number ten and are the usual somewhat dour lot for the period, but the tracks by Lem's Washboard Wonders have a lot more go in them. A pity, though, that the sidemen – especially Wheeler, Trick and the clownish Glascoe – are an awful lot. Only on the last few tracks, where De Paris and a larger band come in (there are several unknowns among the personnel), is everyone playing properly and together. Knockabout stuff, not without appeal, although the transfers are a rum effort: one of the early couplings, from an OKeh original, has a bad speed wobble.

Joel Frahm

TENOR SAXOPHONE

Vigorous hard-bopper who cut his teeth with fellow-Palmetto star, drummer Matt Wilson.

★★★ Sorry, No Decaf
Palmetto 2043 *Frahm; David Berkman (p); Doug Weiss (b); Matt Wilson (d).* 9/98.

★★★(★) The Navigator
Palmetto 2063 *Frahm; David Berkman (p); Scott Colley (b); Billy Drummond (d).* 3/00.

The debut title is probably the Starbucks generation equivalent of 'No Jamfs Allowed', but Joel delivers on the ironic apology with some strong, high-caffeine playing. He presumably encountered Dewey Redman while working with Matt Wilson and there is a definite touch of Dewey's angular approach on the nicely titled 'Interesting Perhaps, But Hardly Fascinating Rhythm'. The tunes are all originals, except for Berkman's 'Interesting Perhaps ...', Mal Waldron's peerless 'Soul Eyes' and on the standards front a nice revisit with Johnny Mercer's 'Laura' and a trio version of 'Pennies From Heaven' that must be Rollins-inspired.

The strong debut was followed by an even more confident sequel. Having paid off a debt to Wilson, Joel teams up with a rhythm section that actually suits his approach much better, even if Drummond's swing doesn't entirely suit the idiom of 'The Navigator' and 'Fort Wayne'. Significantly, Berkman gets much more of the action this time round and is composer of four tracks, including the fine opener 'White Bear Speaks' and the edgy 'Ants'. The only standard is 'My One And Only Love', but it's an epic performance, with the best saxophone solo on the disc. A new duo album with Brad Mehldau arrived too late for this edition.

Tomas Franck (born 1958)

TENOR SAXOPHONE

Swedish saxophonist who studied at Malmö, now living in Copenhagen. Greatly influenced by Dexter Gordon in particular.

***** Bewitched**

Stunt STUCD 18905 *Franck; Thomas Clausen (p); Jesper Lundgaard (b); Leroy Lowe (d).* 11/88.

***** Tomas Franck In New York**

Criss Cross Jazz Criss 1052 *Franck; Mulgrew Miller (p); Kenny Washington (b); Billy Drummond (d).* 12/90.

***** Crystal Ball**

Stunt STUCD 19408 *Franck; Jorgen Emborg (p); Lennart Ginman (b); Jonas Johansen (d).* 9/94.

A stalwart of the Danish Radio Big Band, Franck sounds much like many another hard-bop tenorman, heavily in hock to Coltrane, Gordon and so forth. But it must be admitted that he has the style down as well as most, and these three discs are an expansive fund of music from an enthusiastic performer. *Bewitched* was his debut and, though the seven originals are nothing special, the playing has weight and guts to it, with Clausen providing typically inventive accompaniment and the musing version of the title-piece particularly effective. The studio sound is a bit glassy, though. The prospect of recording a quartet date on a first trip to New York seems to have held no terrors for Franck at all. Miller is his usual courteous and thoughtful self, and Washington and Drummond keep good time. The writing is again unremarkable, but Franck knows how to get the best out of himself as an improviser; the long solo on the opening 'Triton' shows no lack of ideas. *Crystal Ball* is the pick of the three. Back almost on home turf – Franck may be based in Copenhagen, but he's actually a Swede – the saxophonist plays some of his most intense music. The extended improvisation on 'Fahrenheit 451' is a prodigious display of how commanding he can be on the horn and, if it touches no startling new ground, the authority is impressive by itself.

***** At The Circus**

Stunt STUCD 01192 *Franck; Carsten Dahl (p); Lennart Ginman (b); Ole Streetberg (d).* 5–7/99.

Cut live at Copenhagen's Circus-Building (there is a stray track from a slightly earlier date at Copenhagen Jazz House), Franck and his latest team trawl through a standard, some Ellington, a couple of blues themes and a ballad. Coltrane as a big, expansive soul. Nothing fancy, but nothing much wasted.

Bud Freeman (1906–91)

TENOR SAXOPHONE, CLARINET

One of the legendary Austin High School Gang, the elegant Chicagoan was the first significant tenor saxophonist, a lighter but certainly not pallid Coleman Hawkins. It was a long career, and Freeman continued to sound like no one but himself right to the end. 'The Eel' was a classic performance, almost a novelty tune, but at the same time bespeaking a brilliant improvisational talent.

***** Bud Freeman, 1928–1938**

Classics 781 *Freeman; Bobby Hackett (c); Bunny Berigan, Johnny Mendel (t); Joe Bushkin (t, p); Floyd O'Brien (tb); Bud Jacobson, Pee Wee Russell (cl); Dave Matthews (as); Dave North, Jess Stacy, Claude Thornhill (p); Eddie Condon (g); Norman Foster (bj); Grachan Moncur, John Mueller, Artie Shapiro (b); Cozy Cole, Gene Krupa, Marty Marsala, Dave Tough, George Wettling (d); Red McKenzie, Minerva Pious (v).* 12/28–11/38.

***** Bud Freeman, 1939–1940**

Classics 811 *Freeman; Max Kaminsky (t); Jack Teagarden (tb, v); Brad Gowans (vtb); Pee Wee Russell (cl); Dave Bowman (p); Eddie Condon (g); Clyde Newcomb, Pete Peterson, Mort Stuhlmaker (b); Danny Alvin, Morey Feld, Al Sidell, Dave Tough (d).* 7/39–7/40.

*****(*) Swingin' With 'The Eel'**

ASV AJA 5280 *As above, except add Muggsy Spanier (c), Joe Bauer, Pee Wee Erwin, Andy Ferretti (t), Les Jenkins, Earle Hagen, Walter Mercurio (tb), Peanuts Hucko (cl), Skeets Hurfurt, Fred Stulce (as, cl), Johnny Mince (ts), Howard Smith (p), Carmen Mastren, Hy White (g), Trigger Alpert, Gene Traxler (b), George Wettling (d).* 10/33–7/39.

Freeman was perhaps the first truly significant white tenor player. If he looked, and chose to behave, like the secretary of some golf club in the Home Counties – episode one of his autobiography was called 'You don't look like a musician' – his saxophone walked all over the carpets in spikes, a rawer sound than Lester Young's (to which it is often likened) and with a tougher articulation.

Classics (*1928–1938*) includes one astonishing oddity, a piece of ham acting by Freeman and the bizarrely named Minerva Pious; no verbal description will quite suffice ... The 1938 trio with Stacy and Wettling is excellent evidence for Freeman's gifts as a highly focused improviser. His harmonic shifts and deceptively easy chromatic transitions on 'I Got Rhythm' (January of that year and an astonishing performance) and 'Three Little Words' (a later session, in November) have a cut-out-and-keep quality that will endear them to all saxophone-players.

The 1939 recording of 'The Eel' is the final track on the ASV compilation which, unlike Classics, includes work for other leaders – Eddie Condon, Tommy Dorsey and Muggsy Spanier. The real collectables are Bud's own cuts, though, and the November 1938 trios with Stacy and Wettling are among the best of his small-group statements, stripped down, muscular but still urbane. The sound is much better than on the French label which further recommends this sampling of half a decade's material.

(*) **1935–1945: The Alternate Takes
Neatwork RP 2044 *As above.* 12/35–11/45.

One senses Bud's own frustration when a take broke down. Quite why anyone would want to listen to it happen over again 60 years on is beyond us. Here they all are, though, in glorious whatever it's supposed to be. Had we but world enough and time ...

*** **Bud Freeman, 1945–1946**
Classics 942 *Freeman; Yank Lawson (t); Lou McGarity, Bill Mustarde (tb); Edmond Hall, Peanuts Hucko (cl); Gene Schroeder, Buddy Weed (p); Carmen Mastren (g); Herman Alpert, Bob Haggart (b); Ray McKinley (d); Five De Marco Sisters (v); other personnel unidentified.* 8/45–46.

(*) **Bud Freeman, 1946
Classics 975 *Freeman; Wild Bill Davison (c); Billy Butterfield, Charlie Shavers(t); Will Bradley, Vernon Brown (tb); Ernie Caceres, Edmond Hall, Peanuts Hucko (cl); Bill Dohler(as); Bus Davis, Jack Gardner, Gene Schroeder, Paul Jordan, Tut Soper, Joe Sullivan (p); Carl Kress, Carmen Mastren (g); Bob Casey, Bob Haggart, Al Hall, Jim Lanigan, Mike Rubin, John Simmons, Sid Weiss (b); Jim Barnes, Frank Rullo, George Wettling (d); Marilyn Hall, Five De Marco Sisters (v).* 11–12/45, 9/46.

Following Freeman's release from the army, he signed up for the Majestic, though he made some additional recordings for V-Disc in October 1945. Unlike Lester Young, he didn't re-enter civilian life bearing a sackful of woe, but he was certainly not as sharp as he had been in pre-war days. Versions of 'I'm Just Wild About Harry' and 'I Got Rhythm', cut in September, have some of the old grace and agility, but almost everything else on the set seems stuffy by comparison. The V-Disc material is sourly ironic; 'For Musicians Only (A Musical Treatise On Jazz)' fails to convince, even as satire, and the later tracks, recorded with an unknown band, are oddly drab. The only other curiosity in this set is 'The Atomic Era', a duet with drummer McKinley.

The follow-up is unusual in being largely from 1945 rather than the given date. The quality material is the set of cuts made for Emarcy and Keynote in December, with Peanuts Hucko, Wild Bill Davison, and the rapidly developing Charlie Shavers all in attendance The three-point front line on 'You Took Advantage Of Me', 'Sentimental Baby' and 'You're My Everything' is just about all anyone needs from this disc, which is padded out with some pretty feeble vocal material and a few tracks under pianist Paul Jordan's nominal leadership.

*** **All Star Swing Sessions**
Prestige 24286 *Freeman; Herman Autrey, Harold 'Shorty' Baker, Bunny Berigan, Pee Wee Erwin (t); Big Chief Russell Moore, Dicky Wells (tb); Herb Hall (cl); Claude Hopkins, Red Richards, Claude Thornhill (p); Eddie Condon (g); George Duvivier, Leonard Gaskin, Grachan Moncur III (b); Cozy Cole, J. C. Heard, Herbie Lovelle (d).* 35, 60, 62.

A nice selection of material that spans enough time to confirm that basically Freeman didn't change, just kept doing his own self-confident thing. The best of the set is the 1960 material with Harold 'Shorty' Baker and Claude Hopkins, pungent swing with a sophisticated edge. The remainder is more historically minded, with glimpses of Berigan and Condon, but not much of real substance. A good introduction for anyone who has nothing of Bud's on the shelf already.

*** **Superbud**
Jazzology 185 *Freeman; Keith Ingham (p); Pete Chapman (b); Johnny Armitage (d).* 74, 92.

Originally released on the British 77 label, this has now been enhanced by half a dozen rare Freeman compositions, performed solo by pianist Ingham. The group material from the original record is greatly entertaining, with Bud in strong and confident voice, and his improvisations on ''S Wonderful' and 'Tea For Two' (the latter long a favourite) are both excellent. Decent sound, and the 1992 tracks are an unexpected bonus.

*** **California Session**
Jazzology 277 *Freeman; Dick Cathcart (t); Betty O'Hara (tb, euph); Bob Reitmeier (cl); Ray Sherman (p); Howard Alden (g); Phil Stephens (b); Nick Fatool (d).* 82.

Unreleased until 1997, this remarkable session was supposed to have been a cameo walk-on by the 75-year-old Freeman. But, when he turned up at an LA concert put on by the Poor Angel Hot Jazz Society, he decided that it would be entertaining to sit in for the whole set. He sounds a little unprepared and there are awkwardnesses along the way, even on the surprisingly brisk version of 'Body And Soul', but Bud sounds in excellent spirits and form, tackling familiar material like 'Just A Closer Walk With Thee' and 'Tea For Two'. Howard Alden was new on the scene, but he immediately establishes himself as a deft and clever soloist, spinning alert counter-melodies and showing no sign of being intimidated by appearing – unexpectedly in the event – on the same stage as the great man.

*** **The Dolphin Has A Message**
JSP CD 882 *Freeman; Brian Lemon (p); Len Skeat (b); Allan Ganley (d).* 5/80.

The old master in relaxed and elegant form with a contingent of capable Brits. This was Freeman's natural turf and he plays these dozen themes, ranging from 'Satin Doll' and 'Tangerine' to 'Here's That Rainy Day' and 'I Cover The Waterfront', with a quiet wisdom that instantly garners respect. It's not the most exciting or pulse-racing of records, but to expect that would be missing the point.

*** **The Real Bud Freeman**
Principally Jazz 01 *Freeman; Stuart Katz (p); Bob Roberts (g); John Bany (b); Barrett Deems (d).* 12/83.

Bud's recorded swansong was made on his return to Chicago after a long stint in Britain. The home band rolls out the carpet for him, and guitarist Roberts is a particularly responsive partner, trading some lovely ideas with the leader on 'I Cover The Waterfront'. Deems is one of the best mainstream drummers located in the Windy City and it's he as much as anyone who gives the set its perky swing, certainly belying the saxophonist's advanced age. There are couple of fluffs and a few moments when Bud doesn't seem to know quite where he's going with a solo, as on 'My Romance', where he drifts off in another melodic direction entirely, thinks better of it, and then doesn't quite get back in the groove. Otherwise, though, a wholly attractive set and a decent farewell to the studio. The CD includes a bonus three tracks that weren't on the original release.

Chico Freeman (born 1949)

TENOR AND SOPRANO SAXOPHONES, BASS CLARINET, CLARINET, FLUTE

Von Freeman's son and occasional collaborator audibly belongs to a different jazz generation. And yet, behind the Coltrane-influenced harmonics and advanced techniques like circular breathing, Chico has remained loyal to the basic principles of Chicago blues and jazz. Over the years, he has flirted with free jazz and with funk and fusion in his Brainstorm group. He is at his best, though, in front of a small group with a programme of challenging modern themes.

***** Beyond The Rain**

Original Jazz Classics OJCCD 479 *Freeman; Hilton Ruiz (p); Juni Booth (b); Elvin Jones (d).* 6/77.

Freeman was one of the first to demonstrate the indisputable but not always obvious point that radicalism and an awareness of tradition were not incompatible. His playing always sounds entirely of the moment, technically adroit, rooted in the past but always searching for something beyond. What may seem an ill-matched personnel actually delivers a very responsive ensemble. Freeman himself is hard-edged but lyrical, highly focused but also relaxed and unforced. Jones and Booth sound rather old-fashioned in this context, and one wonders whether Ruiz was the right piano player; but in the last analysis it is the product that counts and one can't argue with the quality of this early record.

*****(*) Chico**

India Navigation IN 1031 *Freeman; Muhal Richard Abrams (p); Cecil McBee (b); Steve McCall (d); Tito Sampa (perc).* 77.

****** Chico Freeman Quartet**

India Navigation IN 1042 *Freeman; John Hicks (p); Cecil McBee (b); Jack DeJohnette (d).* 78.

The titles just about say it all. While the first of these, fine as it is, now seems like a rather self-indulgent exercise in self-discovery, a first real foray into the avant-garde, the second is an absolutely cracking group-record. In it, Freeman finds a way of using the intense and compacted technique which was rapidly coming under his command to create some first-rate modern jazz, cutting-edge stuff which doesn't advertise its own cleverness. We're still greatly drawn to the earlier disc, not least because McBee and McCall sound so good on CD. This was a key period for Chico, a time of consolidation and advance. This pair of discs perfectly demonstrates the sources he was working through, some of them unfashionable at the time, like Paul Gonsalves, and the distinct personality he was beginning to stamp on them.

*****(*) The Outside Within**

India Navigation IN 1042 *As above.* 78.

Restored to the catalogue in 1992, this is pretty much in the same line: a confident, tough-minded set of three Freeman originals and one, 'Undercurrent', by McBee. The leader's bass-clarinet-playing seems particularly vivid on this occasion for some reason, strong angular ideas with a lot of detail thrown in on 'The Search', which is also a high point for McBee, playing with his bow, and for Hicks, who lifts it and turns it into something philosophical, full of blues grandeur. 'Luna' is very different, an almost Oriental scale which doesn't go the way one expects it to, but which fuels a truly extraordinary solo from the leader, who is consistently up to form, albeit in darker mood than on some of the albums.

***** Spirit Sensitive**

India Navigation IN 1070 *Freeman; John Hicks (p); Jay Hoggard (vib); Cecil McBee (b); Billy Hart, Famoudou Don Moye (d).* 78.

*****(*) Still Sensitive**

India Navigation IN 1071 *Freeman; John Hicks (p); Cecil McBee (b); Winard Harper (d).* n.d.

*****(*) No Time Left**

Black Saint 120036 *Freeman; Jay Hoggard (vib); Rick Rozie (b); Famoudou Don Moye (d).* 6/79.

Take our greybeard word for it, this was a surprise when *Spirit Sensitive* came out: players of Freeman's radical disposition were not expected to make records of standards. In a roundabout way this release did more to encourage the Young Turks to look back into the tradition, to get out their Ellington and Strayhorn charts, than anything else going on at the time. This is the direct ancestor of David Murray's repertoire projects and as such is a very important document. Passing time has, we feel bound to report, blunted its listenability more than somewhat. The performances are a little raggedy here and there and the addition of Hoggard to the line-up does nothing to clean up the ensembles, but nor does it add a measure of fruitful ambiguity either. Why have a player as richly gifted as Hicks on hand and then muddy what he's best at? These are quibbles, and pretty meaningless at this distance, but they may explain a less sanguine rating.

We are honestly not clear about the dating of *Still Sensitive*. The disc is undated, but it is billed as a 'sequel' and it bears a consecutive release number, though it re-emerged on CD only in 1995. We must work on the assumption that it is roughly contemporary, an assumption made with some resistance, it has to be said, because in many respects this feels like a later, maturer recording. Again standards-based, it has a more obviously romantic slant and in some ways is less subtle, less tempered with occasional moments of irony. When Chico plays 'Nature Boy' and 'Someone To Watch Over Me', you get the strong feeling that he isn't playing games but is telling it from the heart. Not the most obvious of ballad-players, he has done something very special here.

The first of the Black Saint albums is actually little known compared to its predecessor. It immediately makes sense of Hoggard's involvement. Without a piano-player, the sound is much more open, more scurrying and complex and also, at this stage, when Chico seemed to be concerned with speeding his delivery on up-tempo numbers, much more responsive. Otherwise, it's a tight and accurate little group, and the Italian label's sound-quality is more than a match for anything Chico got at India Navigation.

***** Freeman & Freeman**

India Navigation IN 1069 *Freeman; Von Freeman (ts); Muhal Richard Abrams, Kenny Barron (p); Cecil McBee (b); Jack DeJohnette (d).* 4/81.

The family firm. The Freemans play well together, with Von's sliding tonalities closing the gap between his more mainstream approach and Chico's pure-toned modernism. Their gruff partnership on 'The Shadow Of Your Smile' invests a hokey tune with considerable dignity, and 'I Can't Get Started' is an excellent performance from both. A fascinating band, familiar enough in this context by now and held together by DeJohnette's endlessly interesting figures and powerful surges; the two keyboard men undertake a concise exercise in comparative pianistics, Chicago *v.* Philly, with Barron coming out fractionally ahead on points.

CORE COLLECTION

**** Destiny's Dance

Original Jazz Classics OJCCD 799 *Freeman; Wynton Marsalis (t); Bobby Hutcherson (vib); Dennis Moorman (p); Cecil McBee (b); Ronnie Burrage (d); Paulinho Da Costa (perc).* 10/81.

One of the great jazz records of the '80s, it has remained in our premier league ever since its release, and it shows no signs of dating or tarnishing. The presence of Hutcherson, the premier vibraharpist of the day and a giant of an improviser, is a huge part of it, and Wynton is playing straightforwardly and with all his fire. Once again – and apologies if this is becoming a rant – it seems odd to pitch Hutcherson up against a piano-player, and one of limited if perfectly serviceable talent, except that Moorman respects his space and the sound is so smoothly crafted that there is a lot of room around both, good separation and none of the muddiness that ruins such encounters. The material is all original and all strongly idiomatic, allowing Freeman to air his growing repertoire of circular breathing, extended harmonics and overblown notes; again, though, as on *Chico Freeman Quartet*, technique never takes the place of musicality. A marvellous record that has given us consistent pleasure for nearly 20 years, and of how many can that be said?

**(*) You'll Know When You Get There

Black Saint 120128 *Freeman; Eddie E. J. Allen (t, flhn); Von Freeman (ts, p); Geri Allen (p, ky); Don Pate (b); Victor Jones (d); Norman Hedman (perc); Joel Brandon (whistling).* 8/88.

The only real disappointment in the catalogue, though still more than worthy of a listen. It's a curiously muted record with no real centre of gravity and none of the character of its predecessors. Freeman was already involved in the fusion project known as Brainstorm, and this seemed to send him off in a new, electrically supercharged direction which didn't always allow him as much creative freedom as he seemed to think. Hearing him perform with Dad again was well worthwhile but Geri Allen seems rather wasted, and the ancillary players don't bring a lot of genuine interest.

***(*) Luminous

Jazz House JHCD 010 *Freeman; Arthur Blythe (as); John Hicks (p, ky); Don Pate (b); Victor Jones (d); Norman Hedman (perc).* 2/89.

***(*) The Unspoken Word

Jazz House JHCD 017 *Freeman; Arthur Blythe (as); Julian Joseph (p); Curtis Lundy (b); Idris Muhammad (d).* 9 & 10/93.

Freeman's association with the erratic and frustratingly inconsistent Blythe has been a fruitful one for both, and Freeman's occasional sojourns at Ronnie Scott's Club in London have always been the cue for some of his fieriest and most committedly engaged music. Monk's 'Rhythm-A-Ning' is common to both discs, as is Cecil McBee's 'Peacemaker' and an original 'Playpen'. More than four years separate the sessions, and the second features a very different group, anchored by the young British pianist, but the quality is consistent and consistently high. Freeman still indulges his now quite seamless circular breathing and there are moments when he seems to be indulging technical facility for its own sake; but for the most part these are highly musical performances, with some great ensemble playing and an almost routine delivery of virtuosic solos from both front-men. Hard to separate them, but with a gun at our temple we'd grudgingly plump for the earlier of the two. However, the option's made easier now by the fact that both have been reissued as a double-set (JHDE 204).

*** Up And Down

Black Saint 120136 *Freeman; Mal Waldron (p); Rocky Knauer (b); Tiziana Ghiglioni (v).* 7/89.

The interplay between Freeman and Waldron, who is one of the great jazz colourists, is consistently fascinating and would have made a fine duo album. The other two participants in this drummerless session are more questionable. Knauer never stamps his personality on the music, and Ghiglioni (an excellent vocalist on her own turf) is completely wrong for this relatively straight context. Something of an oddity in the Freeman catalogue, it hasn't been seen or heard much of since its release.

***(*) Focus

Contemporary CCD 14073 *Freeman; Arthur Blythe (as); George Cables (p); Santi Debriano (b); Yoron Israel (d).* 5/94.

Another shift of label, and a more mainstream sound. There is an almost magisterial calm to some of the playing of this vintage. It is certainly hard to fault his articulation and his shaping of a solo, and at least part of the excitement of this highly accomplished record is hearing how Freeman, even with a very gifted harmonic improviser at his back in the person of George Cables, is able to bring himself back to some point of rest at the end of a solo. But he always does, and it is exhilarating to take to the air with him. Freeman has made the odd appearance on record since, but it seems terribly disappointing that for the past decade the record industry has largely – for whatever reason – sidelined this very talented musician.

George Freeman (born 1927)

GUITAR

Von Freeman's brother hasn't enjoyed quite the same resurgence as his sibling, but is once again coming to notice. Associated with Gene Ammons and later with Richard Groove Holmes, George's funky soul-jazz is undemandingly enjoyable.

*** Birth Sign

Delmark 424 *Freeman; Lester Lashley (tb); Von Freeman, Kalaparusha Maurice McIntyre (ts); Sonny Burke, Robert Pierce (org); Billy Mitchell (d).* 3/69.

George's debut was an album of easy-going guitar/tenor/organ jazz, with some funky contributions from brother Von. 'Mama, Papa, Brother' and 'Cough It Up' are generic but great fun. The only variation is the larger ensemble – including McIntyre – which plays on 'Must Be, Must Be'. More from that line-up would have been intriguing.

****(*) Rebellion**

Orchard 6364 *Freeman; Von Freeman (ts); Penny Pendleton (b); Michael Raynor (d).* 95.

***** George Burns!**

Orchard 6365 *Freeman; Von Freeman (ts); Eldee Young (b); Phil Thomas (d); Ronald Cooper (v).* 99.

***** At Long Last George**

Savant 2035 *Freeman; Maurice Brown (t); Von Freeman (ts); Gerey Johnson (g); Curtis Prince (d); Kevin Patrick (perc); Rene Marie (v).* 10/00.

Three more resolutely cheerful and undemanding records from the old timer – who wasn't quite as venerable as *the* George Burns, but getting there. The mix is pretty much as before, though the emphasis falls more squarely on George's licks and fills. On balance, *Rebellion* is the weakest of the group, though a rousing version of the traditional 'Joshua Fit The Battle Of Jericho' recommends it. Other outstanding tracks: 'I've Grown Accustomed To Her Face' and 'Surrey With The Fringe On Top' on *At Long Last* and a group of swinging originals, including 'Vonski', on *George Burns!*

Russ Freeman (1926–2002)

PIANO

Though born in Chicago, Freeman was working with the boppers in California as early as 1946. Stints with Chet Baker and Shelly Manne in the '50s and early '60s settled a West Coast cool mantle on him, though he was a tougher exponent of the style than many. Thereafter mostly involved in TV as an MD.

*****(*) One On One**

Contemporary 14090-2 *Freeman; Shelly Manne (d).* 6/82.

Freeman and Manne had cut a duo session 28 years earlier, but this is otherwise a rare glimpse of Freeman in the latter-day spotlight, when he rarely made jazz sessions. The pianist's strong left hand makes up for the absence of a bassist, and the session has a nice, freewheeling sound to it without straying too far from the cool kind of bop which both men made their own. It's a treat to be reminded of Manne's complete mastery of the kit, the sticks and the brushes, and if Freeman was in any way rusty it seldom shows. Four alternates and an unissued original pad out to CD length, and Russ contributed an affectionate sleeve-note to a reissue which, sadly, emerged only months before his death.

Von Freeman (born 1922)

TENOR SAXOPHONE

Von has had an oddly shaped career. For a long time he was very much in the shadow of his son, Chico, and he spent a lot of time away from jazz altogether. In his 50s, though, he returned to the fold and since then has created a body of eccentrically clustered but virile swing.

***** Doin' It Right Now**

Koch 8536 *Freeman; John Young (p); Sam Jones (b); Jimmy Cobb (d).* 72.

***** Serenade And Blues**

Chief CD 3 *Freeman; John Young (p); David Shipp (b); Wilbur Campbell (d).* 6/75.

***** Young And Foolish**

Challenge 75017 *Freeman; John Young (p); David Shipp (b); Wilbur Campbell, Charles Walton (d).* 8/77.

While his son and fellow tenorist, Chico, has explored sometimes baffling extremes of free jazz and neo-funk, Von Freeman has stuck with a curious down-home style that occasionally makes his saxophone sound as if it is held together with rubber bands and sealing wax. Stylistically it is closer to Ornette Coleman (or Roland Kirk) than to Lester Young and it fitted quite seamlessly into Chico's band in the '80s, but in the sense that Ornette is himself a maverick traditionalist.

Von was 50 before he made his debut as leader. Roland Kirk produced it. In some respects, it's an odd set. Kicking off with 'The First Time Ever I Saw Your Face' seems an unlikely stratagem for a Chicago bluesman, but Von makes it sound like something written a stone's throw from Lakeshore Drive. The originals included a 'Portrait' of pianist Young who is the unsung hero of the date, as well as the title-tune and the enigmatic 'White Sand'. Originally issued on Atlantic, it's recently been made available on Koch.

Serenade And Blues is a relaxed and wholly untroubled set of standards, cut with a friendly rhythm section; the session was originally released, shorn of a track, on the parent Nessa as *Have No Fear.* The decision to stay back in Chicago did nothing for Freeman's recording schedule. 'Von Freeman's Blues' and the strong closing 'I'll Close My Eyes' were, for long enough, the closest thing on record to a Freeman set at the Enterprise Lounge.

Young And Foolish falls into that category. It consists of just three long, but steadily decreasing tracks, of which the opener 'I'll Close My Eyes', is positively epic. Von's unusual tone and relaxed phrasing work surprisingly well at this length, but the high point of the set is the much shorter (though still nine minutes plus) take of 'Bye Bye Blackbird', on which Young (who's regularly namechecked in Freeman titles) is heroic, a neglected master of jazz piano.

***** Walkin' Tuff**

Southport S-SSD 0010 *Freeman; Jon Logan, Kenny Prince (p); Carroll Crouch, Dennis Carroll (b); Wilbur Campbell, Mike Raynor (d).* 89.

***** Fire With Von Freeman**

Southport S-SSD 0014 *As above.* 91.

*****(*) Never Let Me Go**

Steeplechase SCCD 31310 *Freeman; Jodie Christian (p); Eddie De Haas (b); Wilbur Campbell (d).* 5/92.

*****(*) Lester Leaps In**

Steeplechase SCCD 31320 *As above.* 5/92.

***** Dedicated To You**

Steeplechase SCCD 31351 *As above.* 5/92.

The studio selections on the two Southports are obviously meant to sound as in-yer-face and immediate as a club date. Logan/Crouch/Campbell are the first-string linebackers: punchy, up-front and slightly cavalier about the rule book. When the pace slows a bit, and the *dee*-fence is called on, Messrs Prince, Carroll and Raynor take the field. They claim an assist on both 'Nature Boy' and 'But Beautiful', but get a bit waylaid on 'Blues For Sunnyland'. Halfway through, the saxophonist goes on a long solo run, playing 'How Deep Is The Ocean' completely unaccompanied. Very effective, too.

Any fears that Freeman was going to be John Lee Hookered – turned into an overnite sensation just in time for his bus-pass –

failed to materialize. His more recent career has been a self-confident demonstration that a recording contract is a spoonful of jam, but not necessarily bread and butter to a jazz musician. However, for his 70th birthday, the old boy treated himself to a Paris trip, on which *Never Let Me Go* and *Lester Leaps In* were recorded. Both discs have a resolutely old-fashioned air and might easily have been recorded in 1975. This has something to do with the sound of Christian's electric piano, but also the very foursquare beat that Campbell favours. The Rollins accents that Freeman brings to 'The End Of A Love Affair' and 'I'll Remember April' on *Never*, and still more noticeably to 'A Nightingale Sang In Berkeley Square' on *Lester Leaps In*, haven't been so much in evidence before. The delicacy that used to be dusted only sparsely over ballads is now a major component of the sound, and there are touches of near-genius on the chestnut 'Alone Together' and the heart-on-sleeve Cole Porter 'I Love You', which alone make this a vintage performance. 'Dedicated To You' is a bit lacking in punch, a further example of Steeplechase's tendency to squeeze every last drop out of a recording session.

***** Inside Chicago: Volume 3**

Steeplechase 31531 *Freeman; Brad Goode (t); Paul McKee (tb); Ron Perillo (p); Stewart Miller (b); Bob Rummage (d).* 1–2/93.

***** Inside Chicago: Volume 4**

Steeplechase 31532 *As above.* 1–2/93.

These are out of apparent sequence because volume three is an earlier session than the dates below. Teamed with Brad Goode, one of the livewires of Chicago jazz, Freeman sounds in great shape at the Green Mill club, over by Lawrence Avenue, scene of many triumphs. There's a strong bop feel to the set-list, with 'A Night In Tunisia' and 'Star Eyes' (the latter a favourite of the first boppers) both outstanding on the first album, but it's Von's distinctive timbre and loosely swinging ideas that carry the day. The sound isn't too bad, though there seem to be some dips in dynamic, presumably because Freeman has moved off-mic. The second set is, if anything, better, but only because it features 'Bye Bye Blackbird', a theme that always seems to get the best out of Von. As with volumes one and two, it's not certain that there's enough top-quality material to make two full CDs out of the date; one well-packed album might have sufficed.

****(*) Inside Chicago: Volume 1**

Steeplechase 31500 *Freeman; Brad Goode (t); Joan Hickey (p); Sherman Davis (b); Michael Raynor (d).* 95.

****(*) Inside Chicago: Volume 2**

Steeplechase 31501 *As above.* 95.

This certainly doesn't merit two CDs, being just a fairly average club date from Von. He programmes Shorter's 'Footprints', which had been a favourite of son Chico (who played it with his Brainstorm outfit) but the tape runs out after just six minutes, which is slightly frustrating. Von also includes his own 'Blues For Sunnyland Slim' on volume 2, along with a couple of bebop staples, 'Oleo' and 'Anthropology'. Goode is a very fine player and it's relatively unusual to hear Von in company with a trumpeter, so there is some merit in that, but we can't really see why this was released in this form. With some judicious editing this might have made a very strong single CD rather than a flabby pair.

***** Live At The Dakota**

Premonition 90750 *Freeman; Bobby Peterson (p); Terry Burns (b); Phil Hey (d).* 4–5/96.

An equally delayed release for this 1996 date at the club in St Paul, Minnesota, where Von was teamed with a very enthusiastic and highly competent house band. Its talents notwithstanding, Freeman does 'My Little Brown Book' unaccompanied and makes a fascinating job of it. He also includes Wayne Shorter's 'Footprints'. He kicks off, though, with a long reading of 'Bye Bye Blackbird' which demonstrates just how much he carries in his bag, melodically and harmonically. Peterson isn't a rapid-fire soloist like his great namesake, but he constructs nice ideas and keeps the shape of a song beautifully. The tape's been lying around for quite a while. Nice to see it released at last.

*****(*) 75th Birthday Celebration**

Half Note Records 4903 2 *Freeman; Chico Freeman (ts); Willie Pickens (p); Brian Sandstrom (b); Robert Shy (d); Dianne Reeves (v).* 7/98.

*****(*) Von & Ed**

Delmark 508 *As above, except add Ed Petersen (ts); omit C. Freeman, Reeves.* 98.

As the date suggests, the 75th birthday album was actually a year late, but the idea was sparked by an appearance by Von and Chico, Von's guitarist brother George at the Chicago Jazz Festival the year before; drummer Bruz Freeman, another brother, stayed home in Hawaii, but remarkably Von's mother, almost 100, is there in spirit, listening to the show go out on radio.

Having honoured the old man back home, Chico's idea was to give him a further party in New York and at the Blue Note, and the record is a document of two spring nights with Chico's group there. The material is pretty much out of the book – 'Softly, As In A Morning Sunrise', 'There Is No Greater Love' and 'Lover Man' – but they also do Chico's delightful 'To Hear A Teardrop In The Rain'. It's great to hear the Freemans playing together, as it always is, the lad all fabulous technique and gleaming speed, the dad content with pedal power and guile, but still getting there ahead as often as not. Dianne Reeves does a pretty guest spot on 'Comes Love', but since it's placed early in the set, it doesn't really change its character, which is thoughtful, driving saxophone improvisation, culminating in Newk's 'Tenor Madness'.

A very different second horn on the set with Petersen. The only piece in common in a rather boppish set is 'Lover Man', and this more than anything exposes differences in the respective rhythm sections. Ed and Von have much in common, not least the kind of sweetness that boils dangerously, like overheated caramel. There are touches of that on the opening 'Mr P. C.', which brings a rootsy but exploratory quality to Trane's blues theme. Miles's 'Four' is more straightforwardly interpreted, though Von, coming through the left channel and from left-field, to a large degree ignores the modes. The rest of the set is a dip back into the bop bag, with 'Lover Man' followed by 'A Night In Tunisia' and a long, closing version of 'Lover', which lets the two horns loose on the Rodgers theme in a real explosion of ideas. Studio-recorded, Von sometimes sounds a bit ropey, but Riverside in Chicago is on the back doorstep; Von obviously has a rapport with engineer Paul Serrano and supervising producer Robert Koester, and he treats the gig pretty much as if it were a club set. Not quite as compelling as the birthday party, but possibly of more interest to hardcore Vonskians.

*****(*) You Talkin' To Me?**

Delmark 525 *Freeman; Frank Catalano (ts); Larry Novak (p); Larry Kohut (b); Joel Spender (d).* 8/99.

Catalano is almost two generations younger than Freeman, but he holds his own magnificently on this hard-blowing session. 'I Could Write A Book' is the outstanding performance; it underlines Von's ability to be hard-edged and romantic in a single cut. Catalano is no mere copyist. He has carved out a tone and solo style that is already his own and already compelling, though he tends to rely on formula phrases and harmonic devices. On 'Summertime' he creates something genuinely new in his statement. You won't trace this back to any source in the jazz library. The rhythm section gives good, if slightly uninspired support.

*****(*) The Improvisor**

Premonition 90757 *Freeman; Jason Moran (p); Mark Helias (b); Michael Raynor, Nasheet Waits (d).* 12/01–1/02.

As he approached his 80th birthday, Freeman showed no signs of slowing up or losing his touch. These sides were cut in and around Chicago in the months before the big day and they feature a top-drawer young band who were presumably thrilled skinny to be working with the old guy. The material here is fascinatingly varied, from Kenny Dorham's 'Blue Bossa' to Duke Ellington's little-known 'I Like The Sunrise'; Von also includes a couple of originals, 'Ski-Wee' and 'Blues For Billie', both of which are more than just blowing vehicles. Though the tone is as erratic and eccentric as ever, he sounds in great voice and his phrasing and chorus-shaping on 'If I Should Lose You' are impeccable, if deliberately rough-hewn. We won't tempt providence by saying Von Freeman sounds as if he could go on for ever, but …

Paolo Fresu (born 1961)

TRUMPET, FLUGELHORN, CORNET, ELECTRONICS, PERCUSSION

Grew up in Sardinia and played as a teenager in the town band. Moved towards jazz and began recording in the '80s; he has since become one of the highest-profile new-school Italian players. Heavily involved in education, theatre music and some contemporary composition.

***** Ostinato**

Splasc(h) 106-2 *Fresu; Tino Tracanna (ss, ts); Roberto Cipelli (p); Attilio Zanchi (b); Ettore Fioravanti (d).* 1/85.

***** Inner Voices**

Splasc(h) H 110-2 *As above, plus David Liebman (ss, f).* 4/86.

*****(*) Mamut: Music For A Mime**

Splasc(h) H 127-2 *As above, except omit Liebman; add Mimmo Cafiero (perc).* 11/85–5/86.

***** Quatro**

Splasc(h) H 160-2 *As above, except omit Cafiero.* 4–6/88.

***** Live In Montpellier**

Splasc(h) H 301-2 *As above.* 7/88.

An outstanding exponent of the new Italian jazz, Fresu is in much demand as a sideman, but his records as a leader offer some of the best views of his music. Fresu's early quintet included the agile Tracanna and the expert bassist Zanchi, and together they follow an energetic yet introspective kind of jazz that suggests a remote modern echo of an early Miles Davis group – the trumpeter does, indeed, sound like the Davis of the mid-'50s often enough to bother some ears. Most of the time the resulting music is engaging rather than compelling: the soloists have more to say than the compositions and, although the group works together very sympathetically, the records never quite take off. Liebman is soon at home on the session he guests on; the live record from Montpellier is scrappy yet often more exciting than the others; and *Quatro* has some bright originals. *Mamut*, though, is the best of these records: although the programme is a collection of fragments for the theatre, the miniatures include some of Fresu's most vivid writing, and the title-piece and 'Pa' are themes which hang in the memory. Fresu even finds something new to say on a solo reading of 'Round Midnight'.

***** Evening Song**

Owl 014733-2 *Fresu; Michele Eletto (frhn); Alessandra Giura Longo (f); Mario Nobile (clo); Furio Di Castri (b, elec, perc).* 4/91.

*****(*) Contos**

EGEA CSA 039 *Fresu; John Taylor (p); Furio Di Castri (b).* 93.

The Fresu–Di Castri partnership now extends to several records (some are listed under Di Castri's name through our alphabetical tyranny) and, while the music has its merely pretty side to it, there's underlying sinew: the electronics are used with an often miserly restraint, and though something like 'Una Notte Sul Divano' seems like a bag of effects, it's immediately countered by the noble melody of 'Ossi Di Seppia', one of two tracks where flute, horn and cello join in. This isn't the best of their records, but it's still a stimulating listen.

Contos is a concert recording. Taylor's cultured playing gloves some of the sharper directions which Fresu and Di Castri like to pursue, but the playing wants nothing in the way of steady-going lyricism, and the piano's harmonic weight builds on the originals – try, for instance, Di Castri's 'Evening Song' to see how much Taylor finds in the material.

***** Night On The City**

Owl 013425-2 *Fresu; Tino Tracanna (ss, ts); Roberto Cipelli (p); Attilio Zanchi (b); Ettore Fioravanti (d).* 5/94.

*****(*) Ensalada Mistica**

Splasc(h) 415 *As above, except add Gianluigi Trovesi (as, cl, bcl).* 5/94.

A decade of work made this into a very confident, imposing group. Fresu is generous about sharing space, but his is still the most impressive single voice: luxurious brass sound, firm delivery, staunchless flow of ideas. Still, Trovesi and Tracanna make a formidable front line, and the rhythm section continue to grow. Both sets were made at, apparently, the same sessions, but *Night On The City* was conceived, as Fresu puts it, 'almost as a game': a set of new music which band members had brought in, played immediately after one of the sessions for *Ensalada Mistica*, all done in one two-hour, after-midnight stretch, 'the emotion of a single night in the city'. Given that nothing had been played in, the results say much about the group's empathy, even if sometimes the music feels more like a reading than a performance. The Splasc(h) date brings in Trovesi (no explanation for his absence from the other set), and he typically adds an extra, rumbustious dimension to an already considerable band. Neither record has much of the blowing session in it:

speeds rarely get above a mid-tempo stroll, and improvisations are put squarely at the service of the composition. It won't be to all tastes, but Fresu's exacting kind of post-bop sounds like a notably personal idiom.

***** Wanderlust**
BMG 74321 46435-2 *As above, except Erwin Vann (ts) replaces Trovesi.* 5/96.

Somewhat of a disappointment, though it's hard to say exactly why. There are some typically elegant originals and the closing 'Touch Her Soft Lips And Part' suits the leader so well that it might have been written for him. A drooping spirit seems to hang over some of the music, though, as if the band were actually tired (it was recorded on a single day on a tour stop-off) and, while one doesn't expect bebop fireworks from this band, the preponderance of slow tempos lends a rather lachrymose feel.

*****(*) Metamorfosi**
RCA Victor 74321 65202-2 *Fresu; Nguyen Lê (g); Antonello Salis (fisarmonica, whistle, v); Furio Di Castri (b); Roberto Gatto (d).* 12/98.

For sheer songful beauty, Fresu's writing is hard to over-value and, although he's generous in also allowing his sidemen composing space, it's his own writing – 'Elogio Del Discount', 'Nightly' and 'Nymphéas' in particular – which hangs in the mind. His Angel Quartet are full of seraphic souls and Lê is brilliantly appropriate for the leader, modernist enough to bring in all his effects pedals but sensitive to his surroundings and reluctant to overpower the unadorned jazz language which the leader is so adept with (even if he, too, adds a smidgen of electronics to his own tone here and there). Di Castri and Gatto, veterans of this scene by now, play bruisingly fast at times, as in Gatto's own 'Giravolta', but they can create what's needed for subtle acoustic music as well. Against expectations, this also owes very little to any Miles Davis music – even if they do end on 1 minute 11 seconds of Davis's ancient bebop script, 'Little Willie Leaps'.

*****(*) Melos**
RCA Victor 74321 782982 *Fresu; Tino Tracanna (ss, ts); Roberto Cipelli (p); Attilio Zanchi (b); Ettore Fioravanti (d).* 5/00.

Fresu's gorgeous sound has never been captured better. The first notes on the record are the delicate, half-choked wispiness of the trumpet reaching for its star, and with the mute firmly in for much of the way the Miles comparisons are something which even this individualist can't complain too much about. After the ambitious group records, this might seem like a retrenchment: much of the music is paced at a slow tempo, and 15 tunes are crammed into a little over 50 minutes. The trumpet–piano 'Luiza' is over before they've barely started. The quick, boppish 'Tutto E Il Contrario Di Tutto' is a delightful exception, and the record might have used more like it; but this kind of miniaturist sound-painting is something Fresu has done before, and nobody can touch him at it when it goes as well as this does.

*****(*) Scores!**
CAM 7758-2 *Fresu; Diederik Wissels (p); Dhafer Youssef (oud, v); Nguyen Lê (g); Furio Di Castri (b); Federico Sanesi (perc); Quartetto Alborada (strings).* 6–12/02.

Film-score records are problematic as stand-alone pieces, with their emphasis on visual cues, sudden stops and starts, and the miniaturization of pieces that would normally receive expansive treatment. But they are their own world, too, and Fresu inhabits this place with great skill. He uses a colourful ensemble – Sanesi has a vast array of percussive devices at his disposal – but roots much of the music around the very solid Wissels (who did the string arrangements) and his own playing has rarely been so precise and feelingful, even within confined spaces. The music was done for *Il Piu Crudele Dei Giorni* and *L'isola*.

Erik Friedlander (born 1960)

CELLO

A regular on many a New York new-music session, Friedlander uses the cello as a stand-alone instrument, equally happy as soloist or ensemble player, and he seems unbothered by its few jazz credentials.

***** The Watchman**
Tzadik TZ 7107 *Friedlander; Chris Speed (cl); Andrew D'Angelo (bcl); Drew Gress (b).* 1/96.

This is by Chimera, the quartet which had earlier made its debut on the Japan-only *Chimera* (Avant 057). Issued as part of Tzadik's Radical Jewish Culture series, the music is grave, stately and ceremonial, with very little resorting to extended techniques. The blurb which comes with the CD says that the melody lines are 'reminiscent of cantorial singing', but that rather facile suggestion overlooks Friedlander's carefully weighted ensemble writing, which is the abiding feature. Maybe they say all they have to in the 12 minutes of 'Elisha', but the CD is refreshingly lacking in excess baggage at 46 minutes.

***** Topaz**
Siam SMD-50003 *Friedlander; Andy Laster (as); Stomu Takeishi (b); Satoshi Takeishi (perc).* 12/97.

***** Skin**
Siam SMD-50008 *As above, except add Alexander Fedoriouk (cimbalom), Atlas Cello Quartet.* 6/99.

Friedlander's tunes are abetted in *Topaz* by two Eric Dolphy numbers and Miles Davis's 'Tout De Suite', all three of which receive quiet transformations into what is essentially a chamber-music language. Laster's melodious playing, the incisive but not overbearing thrum of Stomu Takeishi's electric bass and the spare patterns of Satoshi Takeishi's percussion instruments are intermingled with a simple generosity. Since each man is seemingly reluctant to step out, the music comes across as all of a piece, although one occasionally wishes for an outburst to enliven a rather monochromatic palette (a title like 'Three Desperate Men' doesn't live up to its billing). But the improvising has the polish of experience and high craft.

The follow-up opens its viewfinder just a little more. Besides the originals, there are covers of Henry Mancini, Googoosh, Mingus, Hemphill and Carlos Santana, and we have to say that a strong melody (Mancini's 'Susan') does provide an assist. It remains an intriguing instrumentation, but there's an odd pop-fusion feel to some of the music where one expects a deeper intensity. Fedoriouk and the quartet lend exoticism and weight respectively.

★★(★) Grains Of Paradise

Tzadik TZ 7154 *Friedlander; Bruce Dessner (g); Joyce Hammann, Karen Milne, Peter Rovit (vn); Trevor Dunn (b); Satoshi Takeishi (perc).* 6/01.

A disappointing return to Tzadik's 'Radical' sequence, this feels like anything but. The string writing has an unfortunate mood-music feel to it and Friedlander holds his own playing back, perhaps as a consequence, or maybe in deference to the label's manners. Rather than focusing on his writing and leadership, we'd like to hear the cellist cutting out more space as a solo force.

Dave Friedman (born 1944)

VIBRAPHONE, MARIMBA, PERCUSSION

Studied percussion at Juilliard and worked in New York classical circles before moving into jazz with Wayne Shorter and other leaders. Formed a duo with Dave Samuels in the '70s; later led his own small groups.

★★★ Other Worlds

Intuition 3210-2 *Friedman; Jean-Louis Matinier (p acc); Anthony Cox (b); François Verly (perc).* 97.

Friedman's methods are unusual among vibes-players in that he seems at least as interested in the percussive and rhythmic qualities of the instrument as he is in harmony and melody. He also uses the marimba as often as he does the vibraphone. There's not much under his own name at present. The most singular voice here is Matinier, who makes light of the accordion's café connotations. Friedman plays a rather subdued role, working more closely with Cox than in the front line, and the music that results has an ethereal feel which doesn't quite evade the blandness that often troubles the leader's work. The Jobim tune 'O Grande Amor' is typical of the tuneful if slender repast on offer.

Don Friedman (born 1935)

PIANO

Studied classical piano before working in and around San Francisco, '50s–'60s; played with Jimmy Giuffre, Herbie Mann, Ornette Coleman and Charles Lloyd, then slipped from view until a recent revival with the Steeplechase label.

★★★ A Day In The City

Original Jazz Classics OJCCD 1775 *Friedman; Chuck Israels (b); Joe Hunt (d).* 6/61.

★★★(★) Circle Waltz

Original Jazz Classics OJCCD 1885 *Friedman; Chuck Israels (b); Pete LaRoca (d).*

★★★ Flashback

Original Jazz Classics OJCCD 1903 *Friedman; Dick Kniss (b); Dick Berk (d).* 63.

Friedman's experimentalism is of a relaxed, Californian sort. He started out as a relatively orthodox West Coaster, bringing aspects of the Bill Evans style to work with Shorty Rogers, Jimmy Giuffre and others, but increasingly he has incorporated elements of classical composition and 12-tone technique, as well as abstraction, to his playing. The *leitmotif* that governs *A Day In The City* is actually kept well disguised. Subtitled 'Six Variations On A Theme' and devoted to the hours from dawn through rush hour to the mildly threatening hush of the night, it isn't so much a theme-with-variations as a piece that never quite declares its central subject but toys with several possibilities. Elegantly and atmospherically played, it could almost be a Bill Evans session; certainly the nocturne has that feel.

Flashback also courted the inevitable comparison with Evans but was sufficiently original to survive and thrive. Friedman's bebop skills were evident from the opening 'Alone Together' and the brisk 'News Blues', but the real substance of the sessions, which featured a little-known rhythm section, was on 'Ochre' (subdivided theme–solo–duet–theme), the original 'Ballade In C Sharp Minor' and the elegant title-track which ends the set. Perhaps too many stylistic influences jockeying for position, but a fine record all the same.

Circle Waltz introduces LaRoca, a more beguiling presence than Hunt, and it is probably his brisk, tuneful cymbal work which makes the difference between the two sets. Typically, Friedman sticks largely to familiar material, a superb rendition of 'I Hear A Rhapsody' which almost conjures up the lyric, so expressive is it, and a forceful, unsentimental intepretation of Dave Brubeck's 'In Your Own Sweet Way'. A splendid record.

★★★(★) Dreams And Explorations

Original Jazz Classics OJC 1907 *Friedman; Attila Zoller (g); Dick Kniss (b); Dick Berk (d).* 64.

★★★(★) Metamorphosis

Original Jazz Classics OJC 1914 *Friedman; Attila Zoller (g); Richard Davis (b); Joe Chambers (d).* 2/66.

Credit to Fantasy for bringing back so much of the work of an unfashionable and, in the end, rather obscure figure. These two sets are notable for the introduction into the group of Zoller, who takes some of the pressure off Friedman as far as being the main improvisational voice is concerned and who establishes a surprising and progressive dialogue with the pianist as well as with the rest of the group. Although there are a couple of standards on the first disc, most of the music is based around originals by both Friedman and Zoller (the latter even gets three to the pianist's two pieces on the second set). Between them, and with the sympathetic if slightly distanced rhythm sections, they create a jazz which flirts with freedom, often runs on contrapuntal or even confrontational lines, and recollects something of the Tristano-ite doctrine, even if the results seem much hotter and less inward-looking than any Tristano record. After four intense, unsparing originals on *Dreams And Explorations*, it comes almost as a relief when they tackle the melody of John Carisi's 'Israel', which would be the most demanding piece on many a record. The later *Metamorphosis* seems to be pitched as the masterpiece; although there are some fascinating pieces – Giuffre's 'Drive' and Zoller's 'Troubadours Groovedour' in particular – there's a certain fussiness which holds the group back (Berk is, curiously enough, a better drummer for the group than the outwardly more adventurous Chambers). These obscure and all-but-forgotten records are well worth a revival, but don't expect an unjustly neglected masterwork.

★★★ Hot Pepper And Knepper

Progressive PCD 7036 *Friedman; Jimmy Knepper (tb); Pepper Adams (bs); George Mraz (b); Billy Hart (d).* 6/78.

This is not entirely characteristic and has to be co-credited to the hornmen name-checked. Adams brings the original 'Hellure', there is a cover of Rollins's 'Audubon' (plus a very good alternative take) and a long medley that strings together 'Alfie', 'Laura', 'Prelude To A Kiss' (another Friedman enthusiasm) and 'I Got It Bad (And That Ain't Good)'. In addition, two takes of 'I'm Getting Sentimental Over You' and 'Beautiful Love', both of which show how restless an improviser Friedman can be, and how fettered he patently is by the conventional round of themes and solos. Halfway through the longer first take of 'Beautiful Love' he sounds as if he is going to take the whole thing off in an entirely new direction, but the inertia of the band holds him back, and the B-minor tonality reasserts itself.

*****(*) Almost Everything**
Steeplechase SCCD 31468 *Friedman; Ron McClure (b); Matt Wilson (d).* 4/95.

At 60, Friedman seemed disinclined to ease up on the pace. This is one of his most upbeat and joyful sessions ever, a resilient demonstration of his multifarious skills. Even 'On Green Dolphin Street', which sometimes seems to have yielded up all its secrets, receives a fresh interpretation. There is a brief group of originals, most impressively 'Before The Rain', which presumably name-checks the Coltrane tune beloved of pianists, and 'Waltz For Marilyn', the longest thing on the set. McClure is sterling in support and the little-known Wilson goes about his business with assurance.

*****(*) The Days Of Wine And Roses**
Soul Note 121277-2 *Friedman; Marco Ricci (b); Giampiero Prina (d).* 3/95.

Definitely in the middle of a purple patch. Balanced between five standards and four (interleaved) originals, this is a poised and richly sophisticated set. The originals are worked out freely from barely sketched structures (one title, 'Hi Low Fast Low Hi', gives up the idea in itself) while the standards depart from convention without departing too dramatically from the originals, the melody rarely far away – and the harmonies never clothed too heavily. Prina and Ricci came to this date unprepared, but they acquit themselves well.

****** My Romance**
Steeplechase SCCD 31403 *Friedman (p solo).* 11/96.

Sounding like a man with nothing to prove, Friedman works through some of his favourite songs. Beginning with 'How Deep Is The Ocean', he nails the usual Evans analogy from the off. Yes, it is and no, it isn't. The harmonic understanding is the same, but underneath there is a tense, rhythmic restlessness which was not part of Bill's bag at all. He continues with 'These Foolish Things', 'My Foolish Heart' (is he trying to make a point here?), 'I Can't Get Started', 'My Romance', 'My Funny Valentine', 'Angel Eyes', 'Sophisticated Lady' and 'Darn That Dream', as self-deprecating a roster of songs as you could assemble and yet united by the same ironic intelligence Friedman brings to everything he does. Piano jazz of a high order.

*****(*) Invitation**
Progressive 7043 *Friedman; George Mraz (b); Ronnie Bedford (d).* 98.

***** Opus D'Amour**
Sackville SKCD 2-3058 *Friedman; Don Thompson (b).* 99.

***** Match Point**
TBR 109576 *Friedman; Tom Butts (ts); Garry Mazzaroppi (b); Alyse Levy (v).* 99.

Friedman hit a purple patch at the end of the '90s. Approaching 70, he plays with magisterial calm, wit and a constant sense of adventure. *Invitation* is a delicious record, graced by the elegant Mraz and driven along by the less well-known but impressive Bedford. Some of the harmonic elision on 'Little Boat' and during his solo on 'You Stepped Out Of A Dream' serves as a reminder that the man once played with Ornette Coleman, when the saxophonist still had a use for piano-players. For the most part, though, Don attends to the dynamic and drama of the song and glides through the changes as if they were part of the original idea. What is impressive about his playing here is that there is no self-conscious switch from structure to improvisation. Theme statements sound fresh and spontaneous; solos sound as if they were precision engineered by someone in love with his materials.

The duets with Thompson are in very much the same vein, but more spacious and laid-back in delivery. That Friedman once roomed with Scott LaFaro (dedicatee of 'Memory Of Scotty') perhaps explains his affection for bass-players. There should probably be cliché warning signs round duo recordings of 'Alone Together' but this one manages to coax new ideas from the old groaner, while 'My Funny Valentine' is fragile and wry by turns. Thompson has lovely articulation and is recorded in intimate close-up.

Match Point is our least favourite of the group, just because there is less room for Friedman to shine. Alyse Levy performs on only four tracks, including a delightfully relaxed 'Time After Time', but the saxophone is occasionally dominant and Don seems to have more basic comping to do than normal.

*****(*) Attila's Dreams**

Ephemeris Jazz 023 *Friedman; Andrew Cheshire (g); Ron McClure (b); Joey Baron (d).* 99.

A wonderful group and a wonderful memorial to the late Attila Zoller. The guitarist was a friend of Friedman's but it is Cheshire who contributes the most explicit tribute, along with two other fine compositions, 'Joe Dream' and 'Silent Sorrow'. Don is in fine form from the start with a magnificent reading of John Carisi's 'Israel'. His originals 'Flamands' and 'SAFT' are expertly conceived and beautifully played, with less of the once intrusive Bill Evans influence. McClure is of course a master in this kind of setting and there is an excellent, reharmonized version of his fine composition 'Pink Cloud'. A lovely album from start to finish, marred only by a rather blocky and unsubtle sound mix. Well worth hunting down.

***** My Foolish Heart**

Steeplechase SCCD 31534 *Friedman; Jed Levy (ss, ts); Tim Ferguson (b); Tony Jefferson (d).* 4/00.

Delightful as Levy is in his way (more Bobby Jaspar than Lester Young), he isn't quite right for this session. His soprano work on 'Petite Fleur' is absolutely idiomatic but has none of his leader's inventiveness. 'Desafinado' is a much more successful reading, lithe and limber and full of cheerful guile. Levy's finest moment comes in a beautifully constructed solo on 'Memory Of Scotty', Don's moving tribute to the lost genius of jazz bass. The saxophone drops out for 'Bye Bye Blackbird' and the title-piece and here Don is able to stretch out in his favoured setting and explore the less obvious dimensions of these familiar themes.

David Friesen (born 1942)

DOUBLE BASS

Friesen studied music while with the US Army in Germany and subsequently worked with John Handy and Joe Henderson. His output is very varied, including many projects in a New Age style. Friesen also favours the Oregon bass, an amplified acoustic instrument.

***** Amber Skies**
Quicksilver 4005 *Friesen; Joe Henderson (ts); Paul Horn (f); Chick Corea (p); Paul Motian (d).* 1–4/83.

***** Two For The Show**
Summit 258 *Friesen; Clark Terry (t, flh); Bud Shank (as); Michael Brecker (ts); Uwe Kropinski, John Scofield (g); Denny Zeitlin (p).* 8/92–7/93.

****(*) Returning**
Burnside 13 *Friesen; Glen Moore (b).* 95.

***** Live At Jazz Bakery**
Intuition 1999 *Friesen; Denny Zeitlin (p).* 5/96.

**** With You In Mind**
Summit 290 *Friesen; Gary Versace (p).* 7/00.

**** Grace**
Khaeon 200203 *Friesen; Jeff Gardner (p).* 12/99.

Much of the bassist's work falls outside the remit of this book. Nevertheless, he has issued some fine jazz recordings. The best of them is *Amber Skies*, which calls on former employer Henderson (in fine form) and a very fine rhythm section led by Chick Corea. The record is also notable for some jazz flute from Paul Horn, who is best known as a fusion player. Miles Davis's 'Blue In Green' stands up to a robust examination, a much better direction for Friesen's talents than lame originals like 'In The Place Of Calling'.

The leader's bass style is modelled loosely on Scott LaFaro but without Scottie's rhythmic and harmonic subtleties. It isn't always possible to tell when Friesen is playing his amplified instrument, but his tendency is to play loudly and with a lot of vibrato. Wilbur Ware might be another possible influence.

Three To Get Ready was to come along a little later, but perhaps a title like *One For The Money* was too harshly materialistic for a musician of Friesen's refined sensibilities, for it doesn't seem to figure in his work-list. The middle part of the 'trilogy' is a series of striking duets. There are some lovely moments in the pieces with Zeitlin, which are taken from a 1992 Jazz Bakery gig, but the piece that cements the bassist's credentials as a viable jazz player is Sonny Rollins's bebop classic 'Airegin'. It's taken at breakneck speed, with Michael Brecker hanging on like a rodeo rider. Bud Shank joins Friesen on a more predictable and stately 'Alone Together', which makes up for its lack of adventure with sheer beauty of sound. The guitar duets are less effective but all else is swept away by the appearance of Clark Terry, who rips into 'I Want To Be Happy' with palpable delight. A fine and unexpected album.

The duo format clearly appeals to Friesen, who prefers the intimacy of conversation to the more complex dynamics of group performance. The Jazz Bakery dates with Zeitlin are beautifully crafted, possibly a bit soft-centred, but eminently listenable. Material as challenging as Shorter's 'Nefertiti' and Coltrane's 'Equinox' don't usually turn up in supper club jazz, and this set shouldn't be overlooked. The partnerships with Jeff Gardner and Gary Versace are less evenly balanced. Friesen is clearly a better technician and a faster musical brain than either of his partners, though Gardner writes most of the material on their set, which was recorded live in Belgium.

Favoured items of repertoire included 'All The Things You Are', 'My Funny Valentine' and, above all, Miles Davis's 'Blue In Green', which also turns up on the double bass summit *Returning*. Oregon's Glen Moore is another performer who has flirted with New Age stylings, but here the two men avoid any such embarrassments with some strong interplay on the self-explanatory 'Free Bowing' and lovely versions of those favourite standards. Stand-out track from *With You In Mind* is a lithe 'You And The Night And The Music'.

The Fringe

GROUP

A long-standing trio of free-boppers, formed in 1978 and still going strong.

*****(*) It's Time For The Fringe**
Soul Note 121205 *George Garzone (sax); John Lockwood (b); Bob Gullotti (d); Nick Racheotes (v).* 4/92.

***** Live**
A.V. Arts ADJ CD 004 *As above, except omit Racheotes.* 3/93.

*****(*) Live In Israel**
Soul Note 121305 *As above.* 97.

***** Live At Iseo**
Soul Note 121375 *As above.* 8/02.

The Fringe plays a pleasantly old-fashioned variety of free bop that is rather reminiscent of '60s British bands like Trevor Watts's Amalgam trio. Garzone is probably a more diverse player in the sense that he gravitates much less to fixed tonalities. The caveman poses on the cover of *It's Time For* are doubly ironic, since this is such civilized improvisation, polite even when Garzone is screeching up in the false register. (The cover shot is, incidentally, a reference to 'Neanderthal Man', on which guest performer Racheotes delivers an, ahem, recitation.) It isn't clear why *Live* is attributed to the George Garzone Trio, since the personnels are identical and the Fringe is still functioning as a unit. Taped at Catania, it offers the group's sunnier side, as well as a standard, 'My One And Only Love', which is interpreted with just enough eccentricity to save it from tedium.

The Israel set, taped at the Red Sea Jazz Festival, has some fabulous playing and is pretty decently recorded. There is a long version of 'Body And Soul', freely interpreted, and a splendid thing called simply 'Response', but it's the sheer array of sound conjured up by the trio which is so impressive. The Iseo date consists of a single long suite, nicely paced and cogently structured but ultimately not much more than a few scattered themes knitted into the free jazz equivalent of a long scarf, fun but impracticable. Garzone's ideas are always entertaining, but sometimes what one craves from The Fringe is music that comes from the heart, without further agenda. There's a chill over the most recent set that doesn't endear it.

Bill Frisell (born 1951)

GUITAR, ELECTRIC GUITAR, BANJO, GUITAR SYNTHESIZER, EFFECTS

Raised in Denver, studied at Berklee and began recording at the beginning of the '80s. Associated with downtown New York jazz of that period, but he has since touched numerous other bases and has a vast discography. One of the first jazz-based guitarists to build an aesthetic around an electronic-effects system.

*** In Line

ECM 837019-2 *Frisell; Arild Andersen (b).* 8/82.

Frisell is the first-call guitar man of the contemporary scene, a player who, within a few short years of his emergence as a countrified Hendrix with robust jazz chops, became one of the most widely recorded guitarists of his generation. A simplifier rather than an embellisher, he builds ideas out of the simplest materials, though often very basic and stripped-down ideas disguise harmonic experiments of great sophistication.

In Line was effectively a solo album, with some quiet and unassertive bass-line support from the redoubtable Andersen. The basic ideas could be jotted down on a couple of sides of manuscript paper, and yet one feels Frisell could have spun ideas out of this material all day and most of the following night. The best track, 'Throughout', so appealed to the British composer Gavin Bryars that he turned it into an atmospheric concert piece, 'Sub Rosa'. For the most part, though, Frisell's free modal themes are geared to open-ended improvisation.

*** Rambler

ECM 825234-2 *Frisell; Kenny Wheeler (t, c, flhn); Bob Stewart (tba); Jerome Harris (b); Paul Motian (d).* 8/84.

***(*) Lookout For Hope

ECM 833495-2 *Frisell; Hank Roberts (clo, v); Kermit Driscoll (b); Joey Baron (d).* 3/87.

Frisell's emergence as a convincing leader was, not unexpectedly, slow in coming. Both of these albums suffer from a certain waywardness of focus and a lack of real drive and centre, though *Lookout For Hope* is certainly one of the strongest things he has done. Much of the credit has to go to the combination of Driscoll and Baron, a dream team for a player of Frisell's sensibilities. *Rambler* certainly doesn't succeed at every level and lacks a real acoustic punch, but it is a beautifully structured record with a fascinating instrumental blend, and it was to establish a pattern of ambitious instrumentation which Frisell was to sustain over the next few years.

On *Lookout* he samples a wide variety of styles, including an interest in country that was to become dominant in later years. Some of it recalls work by Larry Coryell at a similar stage in his career; whereas Coryell was a quick-change artiste rather than a genuine synthesizer, Frisell does seem bent on creating something new and unprecedented out of disparate resources.

*** Before We Were Born

Elektra Musician 960843 *Frisell; Billy Drewes, Julius Hemphill (as); Doug Wieselman (bs); Arto Lindsay (g, v); Peter Scherer (ky); Hank Roberts (clo, v); Kermit Driscoll (b); Joey Baron (d, perc); Cyro Baptista (perc).*

Frisell's Elektra debut trades almost too self-consciously on his eclecticism and on the seeming divide between his gentle, country-boy personality and occasional bad-boy grandstanding. The supporting cast is well distributed and each member is allowed to make his mark, though it's a rare session that has Hemphill sounding as anodyne as he does here. The Driscoll/Baron axis comes up trumps yet again, though, and Roberts and Lindsay are their usual idiosyncratic selves.

*** Is That You?

Elektra Musician 960596 *Frisell; Dave Hofstra (t, tba); Wayne Horvitz (ky, b); Joey Baron (d).* 8/89.

**(*) Where In The World?

Elektra Nonesuch 7559 61181 *As above.* 91.

Is That You? was a rather self-conscious dive down into the guitarist's roots, taking its country trashing, big generous sweeps of abstract sound, jazz and a touch of free-form improv. By contrast, the follow-up sounds curiously self-absorbed and anything but interactive. All the usual infusion of country and folk themes (though these are turned head over heels on 'Rob Roy'), bludgeoning blues and abstractionist devices, but there's a polymorphous New Age quality to much of the music that from a player of Frisell's gifts seems downright perverse.

*** Live

Gramavision 79504 *Frisell; Kermit Driscoll (b); Joey Baron (d).* 91.

Distinguished by a fine version of 'Throughout', the theme which so moved Gavin Bryars, this is a good representation of the working trio in action. The version of 'Hangdog' is a little less manic than the original and despatched at a relatively leisurely three and a half minutes. Also delightful versions of 'Child At Heart' (almost epic in sweep) and 'Strange Meeting'. Nicely captured sound, with lots of bass definition.

***(*) This Land

Elektra Nonesuch 79316 *Frisell; Curtis Fowlkes (tb); Don Byron (cl, bcl); Billy Drewes (as); Kermit Driscoll (b); Joey Baron (d).* 10/92.

On *This Land*, Frisell experiments further with stylistic hybrids, putting together elements of jazz and country music, abstract shapes and tuneful miniatures that have the resonant familiarity of the melodies in Aaron Copland's *Appalachian Spring* and *Billy The Kid*. Sonically, it's a fascinating combination, with Fowlkes and Byron often combining to provide elegant dissonances (as on 'Jimmy Carter, Part 1') that are taken over by accordion master Klucevesek on *Have A Little Faith* (below).

CORE COLLECTION

**** Have A Little Faith

Elektra Nonesuch 79301 *As above, except omit Fowlkes, Drewes; add Guy Klucevesek (acc).* 3/93.

Frisell's marvellous examination of Americana takes in Stephen Foster, Sousa, Ives, Copland, Sonny Rollins, Bob Dylan and, most controversially, Madonna. There's no attempt to debunk or satirize, and even Madonna's 'Live To Tell', despite a heavily distorted cadenza with all Frisell's switches and pedals on, sticks pretty close to the original. As was noted on their tour of Britain, Byron's role was rather marginal, and it's Klucevesek and Baron whom one particularly remembers, both enjoying themselves mightily.

Perhaps the only reservation about its predecessor is a slight sententiousness that seems at odds with most of Frisell's compositions. The repertoire and pop pieces on *Faith* encourage a more playful approach and make for a less coherent but far more varied record.

***(*) Go West: Music For The Films Of Buster Keaton

Elektra Nonesuch 79350 *Frisell; Kermit Driscoll (b); Joey Baron (d).* 95.

***** The High Sign / One Week: Music For The Films Of Buster Keaton**

Elektra Nonesuch 79351 *As above.* 95.

Like Don Byron, Frisell has become increasingly interested in the preterite corners of American popular music, the inaudible backwash of the demotic. Nowhere is that better *seen* than in the movies of Buster Keaton, who makes Chaplin seem like a superficial sentimentalist. Unfortunately, much of the music Frisell has to work with is pretty tatty, and though the trio play superbly from start to finish (with Driscoll better favoured in the mix than on *Live*) there is not much to chew on here beyond a bittersweet kitsch. Frisell sounds wonderful, of course, but only in short bursts.

****(*) Nashville**

Elektra Nonesuch 79415 *Frisell; Pat Bergeson (hca); Jerry Douglas (dobro); Ron Block (bj, g); Adam Steffey (mandolin); Viktor Krauss (b); Robin Holcomb (v).* 9/95, 10 & 11/96.

A weak and watery collage of country themes. The instrumentation is not quite as Nashville in effect as it looks on the page, and Robin Holcomb's vocal presence on two tracks serves as pretty irrefutable evidence that this isn't an entirely straight project. Interesting to compare this, though, with some of the things Pat Metheny has done in similar vein. Frisell now sounds more *faux-naïf* than genuinely innocent, and one spends much of *Nashville* waiting for a joke to be sprung which simply isn't there.

On the positive side, it's played freshly enough and there are sufficient ideas floating around to keep the mind engaged. Even so, it is perhaps the most one-dimensional record Frisell has ever made.

****** Quartet**

Elektra Nonesuch 79401 *Frisell; Ron Miles (t, picc t); Curtis Fowlkes (tb); Eyvind Kang (vn, tba).* 96.

A stunningly beautiful album featuring the most enterprising instrumentation Frisell has deployed since the earlier ECMs. Some of the material again derives from a Keaton film, this time *Convict 13*, but the bulk of the themes were written for a Gary '*Far Side*' Larson television special, and they have that sweetly illogical, uncomplicatedly lyrical slant that Larson himself always brings.

The combination of guitar with two – and sometimes three – brass is irresistible, and the pairing of guitar and violin against trumpet and trombone is hard to argue with. Frisell is playing quite simply but at a high level of invention, and in Miles he has a player of markedly similar temperament: quiet, unassertive, but capable of caustic blasts and sudden dark turns.

The cover reproduces American regionalist Thomas Hart Benton's *The Boy*, a slightly sentimental but unalloyed image of a farm kid heading off, leaving the homestead for the city or some other unknown future. Hard not to think of this as Frisell himself, and hard not to feel that he shares the ambiguity. This is the album he was born to make.

***** :rarum: Bill Frisell Selected Recordings**

ECM 014198 2 *Frisell; Kenny Wheeler (t, flhn); Bob Stewart (tba); Jan Garbarek, John Surman (ss); Billy Drewes, Lee Konitz (as); Joe Lovano (ts); Paul Bley (p); Hank Roberts (clo); Kermit Driscoll, Jerome Harris, Dave Holland, Ed Schuller (b); Joey Baron, Paul Motian (d); Gavin Bryars Ensemble.* 81–96.

Even after Frisell stopped making records for ECM under his own name, he still popped up on occasional sessions, like Kenny Wheeler's lovely *Angel Song*, which explains the chronology here. This sampling of material – part of a new archive series – covers recordings made under the leadership of Jan Garbarek and Paul Motian as well, and it includes Gavin Bryars's 'Sub Rosa', which was developed from a Frisell solo. But it's built round tracks from Bill's *In Line* (on which Bryars heard 'Throughout', though it's the title-track that is sampled), *Rambler* and *Lookout For Hope*.

*****(*) Gone, Just Like A Train**

Elektra Nonesuch 79479 *Frisell; Viktor Krauss (b); Jim Keltner (d).* 97.

Surreal power-trio pop-jazz by a new group, with the experienced Keltner offering a great deal more than the solid backbeat that runs through the record. He is a musician of great subtlety, and while somewhat disconcerting at first, this album repays careful listening.

We are less sanguine about Krauss, certainly as a replacement for the wonderful Driscoll, although on most of these tracks he makes his presence felt and creates rich counter-lines to the guitar. Odd, but nudging its way up towards the front rank.

*****(*) Good Dog, Happy Man**

Elektra Nonesuch 79536 *Frisell; Ry Cooder, Greg Leisz (g); Wayne Horvitz (ky); Victor Krauss (b); Jim Keltner (d).* 99.

Flawlessly executed and almost ridiculously beautiful, this takes Frisell nowhere musically, but must surely have won him new fans. The presence of Cooder on the traditional 'Shenandoah', reshaped much like Madonna's 'Live To Tell' on *Have A Little Faith*, will intrigue many who have no interest in 'jazz guitar'. Those who do will have long concluded that Frisell now has little to do with conventional jazz picking and rhythm play and has moved into a new and self-defining realm which reintegrates jazz with a whole slew of other popular forms.

Keltner has made his greatest impact on the rock and blues scene, but here he shows himself to be a responsive and often subtle player, blending a steady backbeat with a more sophisticated time feel. His work on 'Cadillac 1959' initially sounds at odds with Frisell's concept, but it soon becomes clear that he is the anchorman.

It would probably be refreshing at this juncture to hear Bill either shelve some of the technology or else push it to the maximum. Recent albums have done everything except surprise.

*****(*) Ghost Town**

Nonesuch 79583 *Frisell (g solo).* 99.

It's the choice of material rather than the playing that marks this down immediately as Bill's work. His actual execution has seldom been more varied, from the soft, jazz-guitar sound of 'My Man's Gone Now' to authentic Nashville accompaniment to the wacky banjo picking of 'Fingers Snappin' and Toes Tappin'' which comes in at 50 busy seconds. Frisell plays both acoustic and electric, and includes a bit of bass and sampling as well.

He's in softly elegiac mode for much of the record, though there are odd surreal moments like 'Big Bob', which may or may not be named after David Lynch's monstrous id figure in *Twin Peaks*. Certainly, Bill's take on country does also verge on the sinister. He programmes Hank Williams's 'I'm So Lonesome I

Could Cry' and the Carter classic 'Wildwood Flower' and dabbles in a weird hybrid of Californian rock in 'Variation On A Theme'. A lovely, atmospheric record.

**** With Dave Holland And Elvin Jones**

Nonesuch 79624 *Frisell; Dave Holland (b); Elvin Jones (d).* 01.

The bald title says it all. The trio turned up, looked over some original charts (or rather what sound like sketches), ran them down, added a couple of standards and then packed up. Any illusion you might nurse of Jones adding his trademark polyrhythms and usually inexhaustible energy to a Frisell set will immediately be dispelled; Elvin has rarely sounded so lacklustre. Holland plays some lovely things, but seems inclined to rewrite some of the tracks as he goes along; 'Tell Your Ma, Tell Your Pa' figured on the solo album and here it receives a full-out, nine-minute reading, but it's overextended and rather dull. A version of 'Moon River' is quite nice, but this is by no means a successful album by Bill's usual standards.

***** Blues Dream**

Nonesuch 79615 *Frisell; Ron Miles (t); Greg Leisz (pedal steel).* 01.

Frisell and Miles have much common ground and Bill was the young trumpeter's partner on the lovely *Heaven*. Here, the association is taken a step further with the help of Leisz's unidiomatically dynamic pedal steel. The short title-track gives way to a moody tribute to 'Ron Carter', which as others have noted might just as easily be some lost sketch of Miles Davis's. 'Pretty Stars Were Made To Shine' and 'Like Dreamers Do' are constructed almost like old jukebox singles, 'Greg Leisz' is another Miles-like dedication to a group member, and 'Blues Dream' is reprised at the end to give the whole set an unexpectedly coherent, suite-like quality.

***** The Willies**

Nonesuch 79652 *Frisell; Danny Barnes (g, bjo, org); Keith Lowe (b).* 01.

This is virtually a country album, and while it's entirely consistent with one of Bill's major lines of enquiry over the last few years, it seems ever more remote from jazz. And yet, it contains some wonderful improvised moments from many of the players involved, the guitarist most prominently. Barnes will be known as a member of the Bad Livers and Lowe has worked with Wayne Horvitz, so their musical horizons are wide and varied. If you've been beguiled by Frisell's earlier experiments in Americana, this will be appealing, too.

*****(*) The Intercontinentals**

Nonesuch 79661 2 *Frisell; Jenny Scheinman (vn); Vinicius Cantuaria (g, d, perc, v); Greg Leisz (g, pedal steel); Christos Govetas (oud, bouzouki, v); Sidiki Camara (perc, v).* 02.

Brazil, Greece and Mali make contact with the American heartland. Frisell's folk-country improvisations interweave with new rhythms and new harmonic possibilities on this beautiful, low-key record. Cantuaria is the other star, and while it is often difficult to disentangle the guitar parts, the Brazilian's distinctive voice is the most effective counterpoint to Frisell's. In many respects, this completes a cycle of activity for Bill, all the way back to *Have A Little Faith*. If it belongs in any bin at all, it is 'creative world fusion jazz', but set 'Boubacar' alongside the traditional 'The Young Monk' alongside Cantuaria's 'Perritos' and you could be dealing with many traditions, or none.

David Frishberg (born 1933)

PIANO, VOCAL

Originally a journalist, Frishberg worked as an intermission pianist in the '50s, then began playing in small groups with Bud Freeman and Gene Krupa. His songwriting, witty and literate, has been more successful than his performing career. But he is a clever, accomplished player, a fine no-voice singer and a good MD of small groups.

*****(*) You're A Lucky Guy**

Concord CCD 4074-2 *Frishberg; Bob Brookmeyer (vtb); Al Cohn (ts); Jim Hughart (b); Nik Ceroli (d).* 78.

****** Classics**

Concord CCD 4462 *Frishberg; Steve Gilmore (b); Bill Goodwin (d).* 12/82–3/83.

*****(*) Live At Vine Street**

Original Jazz Classics OJC 832 *Frishberg (p, v solo).* 10/84.

***** Can't Take You Nowhere**

Fantasy FCD 9651 *Frishberg (p solo).* 87.

***** Double Play**

Arbors ARCD 19118 *Frishberg; Jim Goodwin (c).* 10/92.

***** Do You Miss New York ?**

Arbors ARCD 19291 *Frishberg (p, v solo).* 12/02.

Although Frishberg himself notes that a supply sergeant once told him that 'Jazz is OK, but it ain't got no words,' he has done his best to deliver hip songwriting in a form that fits with his individual brand of mainstream piano. If he's become best known as a cabaret recitalist, Frishberg nevertheless has a strong, swinging keyboard style that borrows from the swing masters without making him seem like a slavish copyist. He has worked extensively as a sideman – check, for instance, his discs with Rebecca Kilgore – and seems most suited to swing-styled groups with enough space for him to let loose his favourite rolling, two-fisted solos. Of those recordings under his own name currently in print, *Classics* is the best, since it gathers all his best-known songs together on a single CD (which is a reissue of two LPs made for Omnisound). Sparsely but crisply presented by the trio, here are the prototype versions of such Frishberg favourites as 'My Attorney Bernie', 'Dodger Blue' and 'Do You Miss New York?', bittersweet odes which he is very good at investing with both warmth and wryness. The sound has been dried out by CD remastering but isn't disagreeable.

The return of his Concord debut pushes that one very close, though. Nicely balanced between songs and jazz, the music gets a huge fillip from the presence of in-form horns Cohn and Brookmeyer; Frishberg himself purveys a kind of delicate jauntiness on his solo 'That Old Feeling', and as a record it's beautifully programmed. A fine live set for Fantasy has made it to CD in the OJC series. It's a useful souvenir of an evening with Frishberg, featuring some of his smartest songs, a Johnny Hodges medley where he gets to show off his pianism, and the corncrake voice put to work on his wryest lyrics. A special favourite of ours is the opener, 'You Would Rather Have The Blues', but any of his nine songs here sound good.

Double Play is one where he keeps his voice down and plays alongside the salty cornet of Jim Goodwin. They make a good fist of a fine clutch of old songs ('One, Two, Button My Shoe' was an inspired choice) and Goodwin's thick, rasping tone is unfailingly entertaining; however, for once Frishberg's piano parts are a bit samey from track to track. Something new from

Frishberg would be welcome. A fine duet session with Becky Kilgore is listed under her name.

The problem with *Do You Miss New York?*, another live solo-set, is the feeling that we've heard it all before (not exactly a rare phenomenon in jazz repertory). The tunes are different in the main, but there's little here – in terms of tone, timing and pianism – that wasn't done better on the Vine Street record, nearly 20 years earlier. If you've never heard Frishberg in person, though, a perfectly amiable introduction.

Tony Fruscella (1927–69)

TRUMPET

Grew up in an orphanage and after military service played a sideman role with Lester Young, Stan Getz and others. Made a modest impact on the late bop scene, but drink and narcotics ruined him, and his last years featured no music.

***** The Complete Recordings**
Jazz Factory JFCD 22808/9 4CD *Fruscella; Chauncey Welsh (tb); Phil Woods, Chick Maures, Herb Geller (as); Phil Urso, Allen Eager, Stan Getz (ts); Gene Allen, Danny Bank (bs); Bill Truglia, Hank Jones, Johnny Williams (p); Bill Keck (g); Red Mitchell, Teddy Kotick, Wendell Marshall, Bill Anthony, Paul Chambers (b); Art Madigan, Shadow Wilson, Frank Isola, Howie Mann, Junior Bradley, Roy Hall (d).* 12/48–8/59.

*****(*) Tony Fruscella**
Atlantic 8122-75354-2 *Fruscella; Chauncey Welsh (tb); Allen Eager (ts); Danny Bank (bs); Bill Triglia (p); Bill Anthony (b); Junior Bradley (d).* 3–4/55.

Despite a formidable reputation among some collectors, Fruscella has remained an obscure figure. Jazz Factory's set collects absolutely everything that he did: surviving airshots, live tapes and studio sessions. Much of it is desperate. Most of the live music (in mainly indifferent sound) has very little going for it, including a set from New York's Open Door Club (previously on a Spotlite LP) where the players wind up drunk, and a high school concert with Phil Woods effortlessly outplaying the trumpeter. The studio session with Chick Maures (previously on Spotlite SPJ 126) is a bit better: pale, interesting bebop with a glance towards Tristano, and the two horns play carefully spun improvisations that at least take a different tack from bop convention. But across four CDs, discouragingly slim pickings.

Fruscella's great moment was his 1955 date for Atlantic, and this is easily the best music on offer. All his idiosyncrasies – the undemonstrative tone, laid-back dynamics, penchant for the low register and thin but insistent melodicism – came almost accidentally together into an apologetic whole. It's a very interesting record. But the entire session has been reissued by Atlantic themselves, and this is the one to get as his best legacy.

Wolfgang Fuchs (born 1949)

SOPRANINO SAXOPHONE, CLARINET, BASS AND CONTRABASS CLARINETS

German multi-instrumentalist and reed specialist, playing in the further reaches of improvisation.

****(*) FinkFarker**
FMP CD 26 *Fuchs; Georg Katzer (elec).* 6/89.

*****(*) Binaurality**
FMP CD 49 *Fuchs; Gunter Christmann, Radu Malfatti (tb); Peter Van Bergen (ts, bcl, cbcl); Luc Houtkamp (as, ts, cl); Philipp Wachsmann (vn, elec); Melvyn Poore (tba); Torsten Muller (b); Paul Lytton (d, elec); Georg Katzer (elec, computer).* 6/92.

***** Bits & Pieces**
FMP OWN-90004 *Fuchs; Evan Parker (ss); Jean-Marc Montera (g).* 9/95.

Fuchs is an improviser who's especially interested – as his choice of instruments suggests – in timbral extremes. He extracts a cruel vocabulary of sounds out of the sopranino and the bass clarinet, phrases diced into the smallest fragments, and, while one can construe lines out of the sonic splinters, deconstruction is Fuchs's speciality. *FinkFarker* operates across wide soundscapes, the reed-player combating Katzer's electronics in pieces entitled 'Vicious', 'Confrontation' and so on. Interesting but rarefied.

Binaurality is by Fuchs's larger group, King Ubu Orchestra. Big though the ensemble is, Fuchs has clearly thought very carefully about the balance of instruments and the differing nature of the players, and the result is a free group of unusually specific empathies. The cloudy nature of the brass instruments contrasts with the filigree, pecking lines of the reed-players, with Wachsmann's elegance and the surprise elements of Lytton and Katzer adding to the flavour without distorting any lines of communication. As always with this kind of music, there are dead ends and disappointments as well as achievements: 'Translation No. 4', for instance, loses its way at the halfway mark after an utterly riveting development – it peters out into typical free-jazz crescendo and diminuendo. Yet there are so many fascinating passages here that the record deserves a full hearing.

Half of *Bits & Pieces* is solo, with Fuchs putting his reed family through their most extreme paces. John Corbett's suggestion that Fuchs gets a sound akin to an analogue synthesizer out of the contrabass clarinet is about right, and setting these primeval rumbles next to the sharp, splintery chips of the sopranino is an interesting exercise in contrasts. Whether listeners will feel enjoined to follow what seems like a technical inquiry is another matter. No such issue arises, though, with the duets with Parker and Montera which make up the rest of the disc. The two saxophonists strike explosive sparks, while Montera's unpredictable soundboard makes for a satisfying confrontation.

*****(*) Trigger Zone**
FMP CD 117 *Fuchs; Axel Dörner (t); Radu Malfatti (tb); Peter Van Bergen (ts); Philipp Wachsmann (vn, elec); Jean-Marc Montera (g); Melvyn Poore (tba); Fernando Grillo (b); Paul Lytton (perc, elec).* 11/98.

Peter Niklas Wilson's sleeve-note suggests that this was a difficult, argumentative version of King Ubu, with Fuchs deliberately avoiding any kind of preordained empathy (in contrast to that of *Binaurality*, surely) in his choice of players. Since the record offers what are presumably highlights of two different sets three days apart, the full picture is difficult to follow. 'Area 1' trades almost in subsonics much of the time, and if the dynamics change as the music goes forward, the volume levels remain parsimoniously low for a ten-piece group almost throughout. As a document of an improvised event, this may have more shortcomings than many, but Fuchs is certainly several steps removed from any improvisation norm, and there's much to ponder and indeed argue over here.

***** Three October Meetings**
Balance Point Acoustics 003 *Fuchs; Damon Smith (b); Jerome Bryerton (d).* 10/01.

A relatively straightforward meeting between three improvisers. In a small-combo context, Fuchs is obliged to stress his individuality and sounds unnervingly, here, like Evan Parker, at least on the high horn (and Bryerton and Smith follow set precedents themselves, however vividly). The result is excellent improv-repertory, with no new ground broken.

***** The New Flags**
AII 007 *Fuchs; Xu Fengxia (guzheng, v); Roger Turner (d).* 11/02.

A nuttily unfamiliar instrumentation (and Turner is a past master at making kit drums sound like anything but themselves). But some of the sting is taken out of the music by the length of the pieces (two at around 25 minutes, one much shorter), and Xu's guzheng-playing is rather more involving than her singing. Some passages lost in translation from live to recording.

Curtis Fuller (born 1934)

TROMBONE

Detroit-born Fuller owes much to Kai Winding's modernization of trombone technique (he later worked with the Dane in a version of the Jay & Kai format) and to J. J.'s demonstration of the instrument's solo potential. However, it was the harmonic language of John Coltrane and Miles Davis that marked him most profoundly.

***** New Trombone**
Original Jazz Classics OJC 077 *Fuller; Sonny Red (as); Hank Jones (p); Doug Watkins (b); Louis Hayes (d).* 5/57.

*****(*) With Red Garland**
Original Jazz Classics OJC 1862 *As above, except omit Jones, Watkins; add Red Garland (p), Paul Chambers (b).* 5/57.

***** Curtis Fuller And Hampton Hawes With French Horns**
Original Jazz Classics OJC 1942 *Fuller; Sahib Shihab (as); Julius Watkins, David Amram (fr hn); Hampton Hawes, Teddy Charles (p); Addison Farmer (b); Jerry Segal (d).* 5/57.

Curtis Fuller made his mark on one of the most memorable intros in modern jazz, the opening bars of Coltrane's 'Blue Train'. For many the story stops there, ironically so, since the Blue Note session with Trane was hardly representative of what this mellifluous trombonist was about. Possessed of an excellent technique, slightly derivative of J. J. Johnson, he occasionally found it difficult to develop ideas at speed and tended to lapse, as he had on 'Blue Train', into either repetition or sequences of bitten-off phrases that sounded either diffident or aggressive, depending on the context. The saxophone-influenced delivery, mixed in with rich bell-notes and a trademark enharmonic slide, helped create an ambiguity not accessible to valved or keyed horn players.

There was some excitement about Fuller in 1957, and these two sessions for Prestige, supervised by the redoubtable Teddy Charles, promised much. Sonny Red was the working name of one Sylvester Kyner, a slightly raw player who isn't the obvious choice to work opposite Fuller but who acquits himself on both sets with enthusiasm and some ruggedly straightforward ideas. He's better on the later set, kicking off Garland's cleaner-cut blues chords. The rhythm section is much stronger on the latter disc. Chambers comes through powerfully and the mix of material – including a big saxophone feature on 'Slenderella' and a gorgeous original from Fuller, 'Cashmere' – gives Mr PC all the space he could want to develop his own solid, singing lines. The attempt to integrate two french horns into an otherwise straightahead quintet is the notable feature of the third set. The idea was perhaps a little premature since the horns tend to parp in the background a little disconsolately, not quite invited to the party, although Amram's brief piece 'Five Spot' is a neat miniature. Shihab, like Red before him, is tart and biting, and makes a nice contrast to the rest of the tonally bluff setting.

Andy Fusco

ALTO SAXOPHONE

Fusco wavered between music and pro-football: the sax eventually won. He's a tough, accomplished hard-bop altoman.

***** Out Of The Dark**
Criss Cross 1171 *Fusco; Joe Magnarelli (t); Joel Weiskopf (p); Peter Washington (b); Billy Drummond (d).* 12/98.

Slightly more ragged and flaring than the typical Criss Cross date, this has some exciting music, although the mollifying ballad, 'Epitaph For Sal Amico', and Walt Weiskopf's chart for 'Lament' lack nothing in finesse. But it's probably the pianoless 'It's You Or No One', on a direct current from Charlie Parker, that sums up Fusco's hearty, amiably aggressive playing. Everyone plays to their strengths and it's a satisfying hour of music.

Slim Gaillard (1916–91)

PIANO, GUITAR, VOCALS

In latter years, Gaillard was the perennial guest MC and hipster-about-town, but his impact on the bop'n'beat generation of the '40s and early '50s is hard to exaggerate. The inventor of 'Vout' – a hipster slang generated by adding '-oroonie' to every significant word – was born in Detroit and spent many of his later years in London. Larger than life, he comes across on record only in diluted form.

***** Slim Gaillard 1937–1938**
Classics 705 *Gaillard; Kenneth Hollon (ts); Sam Allen (p); Slam Stewart (b); Pompey Dobson (d).* 37–38.

*****(*) Slim Gaillard 1939–1940**
Classics 724 *Gaillard; Henry Goodwin, Al Killian, Cyril Newman (t); Garvin Bushell (cl); Herman Flintall (as), Kenneth Hollon (ts); Loumell Morgan (p), William Smith (b), Herbert Pettaway (d).* 9/39–8/40.

***** Slim Gaillard, 1940–1942**
Classics 787 *Similar to above.* 40–42.

He always looked gorgeous: an ice-cream suit, shoes that looked as if you could get into them and drive away, a big slob cap tipped over one delightedly un-ironic eye, and the coolest pepper-and-salt beard ever, out of which came a constant stream of song, anecdote and – above all – the hip, nonsensical patois known as 'Vout'. Hard as it may be to recognize this now, Slim was a key personality in the bebop movement. His presence on the Savoy Parkers underlines that. As such, he is a valuable corrective to the notion that bop was hard, serious and antagonistic; above all it was about play and playfulness, and a title like 'Klactoveeseedstene' was not so very far from the kind of semantic juggling Slim loved to indulge in. A long involvement with Slam Stewart, trading as Slim'n'Slam, remains his most memorable, but Gaillard was around for long enough and was personable enough to have worked with most of the greats in some capacity. It's hard to maintain equanimity in the face of something like 'Laughing In Rhythm', which is just that.

Not everyone is a fan of the Classics approach, and almost everyone has some misgivings about transfer quality. However, the French label is certainly the place to turn to if you are a devoted collector of Gaillard, not because it covers the same material better (there is surprisingly little overlap) but because it has better stuff to offer. The basic material is all there, is mostly pristine (by the standards of the label at least), and all, all of it is hugely entertaining. You either buy into this man's sound or you don't. If you don't, no one will ever explain it to you.

***** Slim Gaillard 1945**
Classics 864 *Gaillard; Karl George, Howard McGhee (t); Vic Dickenson (tb); Teddy Edwards, Wild Bill Moore, Lucky Thompson (ts); Michael 'Dodo' Marmarosa, Fletcher Smith (p); Bam Brown (b); Zutty Singleton, Leo Watson (d).* 45.

*****(*) Slim Gaillard 1945: Volume 2**
Classics 911 *Gaillard; Dizzy Gillespie (t); Charlie Parker (as); Jack McVea (ts); Michael 'Dodo' Marmarosa (p); Bam Brown (b, v); Zutty Singleton (d).* 12/45.

Slim spent the early part of America's war in the forces. He wouldn't have been doing much recording anyway, since there was a ban in operation; but it's clear that, once he was out of uniform and ensconced in Los Angeles, he started recording for as many of the new labels springing up on the Coast as would have him; all the items in Volume Two were made within a single winter month. Just to keep up the pace, Slim also appeared in the manic jive movie, *Hellzapoppin*, which makes tiring viewing even 50 years on.

The first of the 1945 groups was the Boogiereeners, with Howard McGhee, Teddy Edwards and Wild Bill Mooore all among the horns, and Lucky Thompson taking the bulk of the solos, notably on 'Slim Gaillard's Boogie' and 'Harlem Hunch', both from September. Later still in the year, he would record with Charlie Parker, a session just after Christmas which yielded the immortal 'Flat Foot Floogie'. That same session also included Diz, Dodo Marmarosa and Zutty Singleton. Some of the earlier stuff has him doubling on harpsichord and novachord, constantly on the look-out for a new and unexpected sound, but it is always the lyrics that catch the attention, especially when they are as surreally arresting as those of 'Atomic Cocktail', made for the label of that name. The trio stuff puts his voice at centre, with not much more than accompaniment, but there should be no mistaking the quality of Slim's musicality. If he was a novelty act, he was a very good one.

***** Slim Gaillard 1946**
Classics 962 *Gaillard; Howard McGhee (t); Marshal Royal (cl); Lucky Thompson (ts); Bill Early, Michael 'Dodo' Marmarosa (p); Wini Beatty (p, v); Bam Brown (b, v); Oscar Bradley, Scatman Crothers, Zutty Singleton (d); Leo Watson (d, v).* 1–5/46.

***** The Legendary McVouty**
Hep CD 6 *Similar to above; except add Jack McVea (ts); Harry 'The Hipster' Gibson (p, v).* 46.

***** The Absolute Voutest, '46**
Hep CD 28 *Similar to above; except add Willie Smith (as); Papa John Creach (vn).* 46.

Including the deathless 'Opera In Vout' and some of the V-Discs Slim made at the end of the war, the Classics set is an extremely attractive package. The January material for Bel-Tone, recorded in Los Angeles, stands up well after more than half a century and, with the likes of Howard McGhee, Marshal Royal, Lucky Thomson, Dodo Marmarosa and Zutty Singleton on the strength, the cuts are musically interesting as well as entertaining. Dodo is the probable pianist as well on an uncertainly dated session for Savoy towards the end of the year which includes the unusual sound of Slim on piano, playing the line of 'Oxydol Highball'. Good stuff, and a must for the Gaillard collector. The Hep set is nicely remastered and at least gives the material a chance to be heard in flattering reproduction. 'Four O'Clock Vout' is an epic reworking of Basie's 'One O'Clock Jump' and there are wonderful versions of 'C Jam Blues' and 'Take The "A" Train' alongside more familiar Gaillard pieces like 'Cement Mixer' and 'Gaillard Special' (nos 1 and 2). Some of the material comes from movie soundtracks, but the bulk is live cuts from Billy Berg's.

***** Slim Gaillard 1947–1951**
Classics 1221 *Gaillard; Buddy Tate (ts); Cyril Haynes, Dick Hyman, Michael 'Dodo' Marmarosa, Maceo Williams (p); Clyde Lombardi (b); Ernie Shepard (b, v); Bam Brown (b, d, v); Herbie Lovelle, Charlie Smith (d); Armando Peraza (perc); Jim Hawthorne (barking).* 47–51.

Slim wasn't just recording for Verve and this rounds up stuff from other labels. The humour is forced – try 'Serenade To A Poodle' if you don't believe it – and the bouncing bebop rhythms increasingly formulaic. However, no one can question Slim's energy or the resilience of his audience. He was still very much the star.

****(*) At Birdland 1951**
Hep CD 21 *Gaillard; Eddie 'Lockjaw' Davis, Brew Moore (ts); Billy Taylor (p); Terry Gibbs (vib); Clyde Lombardi, Slam Stewart (b); Art Blakey, Charlie Smith (d).* 2–9/51.

Rounded out by one track from the Apollo, this documents what became a self-parodying stint at the legendary club. Gaillard has so fallen in love with his own persona that his innate musicality and stage sense have deserted him. The editing of live intros and asides is brilliantly done and there's no faulting this as a piece of product. Musically, though, it's pretty drab and only likely to be of interest to devoted Gaillard collectors. Some nice playing from Gibbs and Jaws, and valuable glimpses of Billy Taylor and Art Blakey as well, but not enough to entice non-initiates.

**** Slim Gaillard Rides Again!**
Verve 589761 *Gaillard; unknown (b) & (d).* 11/59.

This is one of Verve's limited-duration reissues, on sale only until December 2005. We'd say it was past its sell-by date already. Slim's comeback was an uneasy business. He'd abandoned the Vout argot in favour of a whimsical approach to jazz standards, backed here by an unknown group. The results are patchy to put it mildly, marred by a forced humour and a dearth of real musical ideas.

***** Anytime, Anyplace, Anywhere**

Hep CD 2020 *Gaillard; Jay Thomas (t, as, ts); Digby Fairweather (c); Buddy Tate, Jay McShann (p); Peter Ind (b); Allan Ganley (d).* 10/82.

The 1982 sessions reintroduced Gaillard, who had become a festival favourite, to a new audience of young and hip fans who were turning on to a new generation of young British players. Gaillard had eventually settled in London, and this is a mainly British line-up, drawn from established players. The man's energy is unflagging and his inventiveness unstinting; though by this stage listening to Gaillard on record seemed almost redundant when he might very likely turn up at your club on a Friday night, he always makes for an entertaining listen.

****** Laughing In Rhythm**

Properbox 62 4CD *Gaillard; Karl George, Dizzy Gillespie, Henry Goodwin, Al Killian, Howard McGhee, Cyril Newman, Frankie Newton (t); Vic Dickenson (tb); Garvin Bushell, Marshall Royal (cl); Edmond Hall (cl, bs); Pete Brown, Herman Flintall, Charlie Parker, Russell Procope (as); Teddy Edwards (as, ts); Kenneth Hollon, Jack McVea, Wild Bill Moore, Lucky Thompson, Ben Webster (ts); Cecil Scott (ts, cl); Sam Allen, Don Frye, Tommy Fulford, Cyril Haynes, Michael 'Dodo' Marmarosa, Loumell Morgan, Jimmy Rowles (p); Fletcher Smith (p, hpd); B. J. John Smith (g); Wini Beatty (g, v); Ray Brown, Dick Fullbright, William McLeish Smith, Slam Stewart (b); Cozy Cole, Kenny Clarke, Pompey Dobson, Chico Hamilton, Milt Jackson, Hubert Pettaway, Zutty Singleton, Leo Watson (d); Jim Hawthorne (barking).* 37–52.

This is the only Slim Gaillard set anyone really needs. It covers the story from 1937 and the first Slim'n'Slam recordings right through to the rather tired work for Verve in 1952. As ever with boxed sets, the basic stats help to tell (and sell) the story: 15 years of music-making, 102 tracks on four CDs. Even given our affection for the man, it's a prospect to daunt the most dogged of reviewers. However, the packaging and remastering are both good and the classic tracks – 'Flat Foot Floogie', 'Yep Roc Heresay', 'Tutti Frutti', 'Chicken Rhythm', 'Opera In Vout', 'Sabroso' (with Terry Gibbs and Billy Taylor) – are all here. Fantastic value if this is your bag.

Richard Galliano (born 1950)

ACCORDION, PIANO, KEYBOARDS, TROMBONE

Galliano is a compelling improviser with a wonderfully expressive sound and a subtle swing, mostly in 3/4 time and tango rhythms. In smaller ensembles he uses the harmonic richness of the accordion to create an almost orchestral effect, but he is also content to create sparse single-note melodies with minimum harmonization when surrounded by like-minded players.

*****(*) Spleen**

Dreyfus Jazz Line FDM 36513 *Galliano; Eric Giausserand (flhn); Denis Leloup (tb); Franck Stibon (p, syn, v); Jean-Marc Jafet (b); Luiz Augusto (d, perc).* 6/85.

***** Coloriage**

Quadrivium SCA 031 *Galliano; Gabriele Mirabassi (cl).* 7/92.

***** Viagio**

Dreyfus Jazz Line FDM 36562 *Galliano; Bireli Lagrene (g); Pierre Michelot (b); Charles Bellonzi (d).* 6/93.

****** Laurita**

Dreyfus Jazz Line FDM 36572 *Galliano; Michel Portal (bcl); Didier Lockwood (vn); Toots Thielemans (hca); Palle Danielsson (b); Joey Baron (d).* 11/94.

*****(*) Blow Up**

Dreyfus Jazz Line FDM 36589 *Galliano; Michel Portal (bcl, cl, ss, bandoneon, jazzophone).* 5/96.

Astor Piazzolla and, more recently, Dino Saluzzi are the presiding geniuses of modern accordion and bandoneon playing. Galliano is by no means in thrall to either, but like any accordion player he draws heavily on Piazzolla themes, notably 'Libertango' on the wonderful *Laurita*. This is the only Galliano album you really need to have – though if you love it as much as we do, the set of duos with the multi-faceted Portal will surely follow. Original material like 'Spleen' and 'Il Viaggio' is already well trodden, and the pared-down instrumentation on the Quadrivium disc is a good place (if you can find it) to sample both these pieces and to get a measure on Galliano's style. The early album is something of a collage, pieced together in a ramshackle way that has distinct charm but lacks an element of finish. The group with Lagrene, on the contrary, is a blowing gig, with plenty of solo space for all concerned.

What we like about *Laurita* and *Blow Up* is that they combine spontaneity with polish and a wonderfully rich sound-spectrum. Portal's brooding sound lifts both records immeasurably; Toots Thielemans is mistily beautiful on 'Laurita', and then Lockwood has his moment in the spotlight with 'Decisione', whirling it away like a cross between Grappelli and a New Orleans clarinet-player. On *Blow Up*, there are once again a couple of Hermeto Pascoal numbers, a retread of 'Libertango' and a number of originals by Galliano and Portal, including the excellent 'Little Tango' and the tiny closing-piece, both of them credited to the saxophonist but both absolutely suited to this pairing.

*****(*) New York Tango**

Dreyfus 36581 *Galliano; Bireli Lagrene (g); George Mraz (b); Al Foster (d).* 2/97.

A beautiful record from a stellar quartet who each bring something unique to the date. Lagrene and Galliano share a huge amount of musical history, but Mraz's lyrical, almost folkish approach is a vital ingredient and Al Foster's drumming is delicately nuanced and insistently propulsive. Apart from an opening piece by Astor Piazzolla and the closing 'Three Views Of A Secret' by Jaco Pastorius, all the writing is by Galliano. The title-piece and 'Ten Years Ago' are strong ideas, flecked with the blues but with a completely authentic tango feel. Galliano's phrasing is as light and delicately articulated as an acoustic guitar on some tracks, as wheezily brooding as an organ on others. Lagrene and Mraz blend wonderfully behind him when he plays fast lines. 'To Django' is a small masterpiece. The repertoire is perhaps a little unvaried, but anyone who warms to the accordionist's work will love this record.

★★★ French Touch

Dreyfus 36596 *Galliano; Michel Portal (ss); Jean-Marie Ecay (g); Jean-François Jenny-Clark, Jean-François Rouge Remi Vignolo (b); André Ceccarelli, Daniel Humair (d).* 5/99.

Another wonderful record from Galliano, who has rarely swung with more authority. Once again, much of the record's power comes from the sheer quality of the players the accordionist is able to recruit. The late Jenny-Clark and Humair are huge presences in their own right and wonderful group players as well. Their tracks are probably a cut above the other rhythm section of Vignolo and Ceccarelli. The saxophonist has an important guest spot on the waltz-time 'J.F.', presumably dedicated to the great bassist who also partners Galliano on the beautiful 'Sanguine'. Vignolo plays contrabass guitar, a different sound and rhythmic feel to the upright instrument, but only marginally less effective. A great place to start if you haven't encountered Galliano before.

★★★ Passatori

Dreyfus 36601 *Galliano; Stefano Bollani (p); Cinzia Conte (hp); Solisti dell'Orchestra della Toscana (strings, perc).* 99.

This lovely set consists of two multi-movement works by Galliano and Astor Piazzolla respectively, sandwiching a group of shorter themes by both men. Galliano's 'Opale Concerto' is wonderfully varied, switching between hectic activity in complex time-signatures and the dark waltz of the second movement. Piazzolla's 'Concerto Pour Bandoneon' is equally vibrant at the outset and then still markedly in the central movement before accelerating away to a pulse-quickening climax. The shorter pieces make for an attractive foil, with 'Habanerando' outstandingly beautiful and Piazzolla's tiny 'Oblivion' a gem. A lovely record, but as far away from bebop as it gets.

★★★★ Concerts/Inedits

Dreyfus 36606 3CD *Galliano; Michel Portal (cl); Jean-François Jenny-Clark (b); Daniel Humair (d).* 96–00.

This is a wonderful introduction to Galliano and his art. The solo set is the purest and most straightforward but to hear what Galliano is capable of as an improviser, it is best to start with the duos with Michel Portal and the trio tracks with Humair and Jenny-Clark. These latter were recorded at the Montreux Jazz Festival in 1996 and are amazingly good, telepathically responsive, effortlessly melodic and packed with ideas. The bassist is a brilliant accompanist, harmonically aware and rhythmically complex. Galliano combines horn-like lines with big, orchestral chords and almost percussive figures, and one feels that all three players are doing each other's work at times, not competitively but with a genuine awareness of where the music might go next. Splendid and near-essential.

★★★★ Gallianissimo: The Best Of Richard Galliano

Dreyfus 36616 *Galliano; Michel Portal (cl); Toots Thielemans (hca); Steffano Bollani, Franck Sibon (p); Bireli Lagrene (g); Palle Danielsson, Jean-Marc Jafet, Jean-François Jenny-Clark, Pierre Michelot, George Mraz (b); Joey Baron, Charles Bellonzi, Al Foster, Daniel Humair (d).* 93–00.

A lot of material on this and much to ponder. If Richard Galliano were a saxophone-player or pianist, would he enjoy a higher standing in the annals of modern jazz? We increasingly think so and this sampling provides the best of introductions, including collaborations with Toots Thielemans and Bireli Lagrene, as well as now familiar work with Portal, Humair and Jenny-Clark. The technique is dazzling, the recording quality is fine and tracks like Piazzolla's 'Inverno Porteno' and his own 'Viaggio' and 'Spleen' are marvellous beyond words.

★★★ Face To Face

Dreyfus 36627 *Galliano; Eddy Louiss (org).* 5/01.

A most unusual instrumentation, but no less effective for that. The material is pretty much as you would expect at this juncture, with an emphasis on tango and French chanson, though there is a wonderfully unexpected version of 'I Remember Clifford' as well. Nicely engineered to make the most of the two instruments while keeping the balance right, and often most successful when Galliano plays big, wheezy chords and Louiss takes the faster top lines. Enchanting.

★★★ Piazzolla Forever

Dreyfus 36642 *Galliano; Hervé Sellin (p); Jean-Marc Phillips-Varbadejian, Lionel Schmit (vn); Jean-Marc Apap (vn, vla); Raphael Pidou (clo); Stephane Logerot (b).* 8/02.

Recorded in concert at Willisau, this pays homage to Galliano's most obvious mentor and to the most significant composer of tango and accordion music of the last 50 years. Piazzolla's reputation is now so widespread that it hardly needs reinforcement, but few players understand his idiom better than Galliano. The septet format gives the music a formal gravitas that it doesn't really need and in some places it might have been more successful with just a single fiddle, bass and drums. However, Galliano arranges these themes with loving care and every note and phrase is shaped to maximum effect. His own playing moves between joy and sorrow, virtuosic fingering and mournful blocked-in chords.

Hal Galper (born 1938)

PIANO, KEYBOARDS

One of the most responsive of piano-players, Galper received a classical training and established himself early as a persuasive and sophisticated soloist, having worked with a range of leaders from Herb Pomeroy and Chet Baker to Cannonball Adderley and Anita O'Day. His solo work is inclined to the florid, but with a solid foundation of blues harmony, even if he rarely plays a straight blues.

★★★(★) Reach Out

Steeplechase CCD 31067 *Galper; Randy Brecker (t); Michael Brecker (ts, f); Wayne Dockery (b); Billy Hart (d).* 11/76.

★★★(★) Children Of The Night

DoubleTime Records DTRCD *Galper; Randy Brecker (t); Michael Brecker (ts); Wayne Dockery (b); Bob Moses (d).* 2/78.

Galper's wide, sweeping keyboard style needs bass and drums to temper occasional sugariness. *Reach Out* is a vivid, hard-hitting set. The Brecker brothers have seldom combined so effectively under anyone else's leadership, and the arrangements are razor-fine. The later *Speak With A Single Voice* has now been reissued as *Children Of The Night.* Hearing it again after an absence of some years, we find it a stronger and more coherent performance than we originally thought. Twenty years on, it sounds as if it was ahead of its time, combining a Coltrane-like intensity (guaranteed by Mike Brecker's presence) with the richness of Galper's Tyner-influenced piano. Recorded live, the sound was all over the place on vinyl, but it sounds much better on these careful transfers. The reissue takes its title from a long, previously unissued track, probably from early in the session at Rosy's in New Orleans. Neither of the horns sounds convincingly played in. A welcome addition to the catalogue, though.

*****(*) Fugue State**

Blue Chip Jazz 74005 *Galper; Jeff Johnson (b); Steve Ellington (d).* 2/97.

Released on a relatively obscure label and recorded in Manchester's Craftsmen's Guild, this is nevertheless a fine record, with a more than usually imaginative take on the basic piano trio. Unusually, there are no original compositions, but Galper seems determined to push tunes like 'End Of A Love Affair', 'Fascinatin' Rhythm' and 'If You Are But A Dream' to the limits. The trio is consistently supportive and Johnson makes an impression with his crisp stopping on 'Small Feats' and 'Cottontail', ending an impressive session on a personal high. Good luck finding it, and don't be afraid to ask.

***** Let's Call This That**

Double Time *Galper; Tim Hagans (t); Jerry Bergonzi (ts); Jeff Johnson (b); Steve Ellington (d).* 99.

Another thoroughly enjoyable and utterly professional set with not much more to recommend it than that. Galper's touch is possibly a little cruder than of yore, but he always stiffens his attack when working with horns and most of this set is devoted to strenuous blowing. Hagans is impressive and Bergonzi never fails to please. The sound is a bit one-dimensional in places and it's Galper who suffers.

Ganelin Trio

GROUP

The Soviet threesome which created a great stir in the West in the early '80s, following the release of records made from smuggled tapes and their subsequent appearances in Berlin, Italy and London. Disbanded in 1987 when Ganelin left the USSR for Israel.

***** Con Anima / Concerto Grosso**

Leo Golden Years of New Jazz 23 *Vyacheslav (Slava) Ganelin (p, g, basset, perc); Vladimir Chekasin (as, ts, cl, ob, v); Vladimir Tarasov (d, perc).* 76, 78.

***** Poco A Poco**

Leo CD LR 101 *As above.* n.d.

****** Catalogue: Live In East Germany**

Leo CD LR 102 *As above.* 4/79.

♛ ** Ancora Da Capo**

Leo CD LR 108 *As above.* 10–11/80.

*****(*) Con Affetto**

Leo Golden Years GY 2 *As above.* 11/83.

****** Ttaango ... In Nickelsdorf**

Leo Golden Years GY 18/19 2CD *As above.* 10/85.

***** San Francisco Holidays**

Leo CD LR 208/209 2CD *As above, except add Larry Ochs (ts); Bruce Ackley (ss); Jon Raskin (bs); Andrew Voigt (as).* 6/86.

History has moved, and moved in unexpected ways, since our first edition. By far the most significant single event has been the collapse of the Soviet Union, never more than a vast, improbable federation, punctured and leaking at almost every point, but enormously powerful even if only as an idea. Inevitably, its demise has prompted serious questioning of almost every aspect of its politics and culture.

The Ganelin Trio can now perhaps be seen as an expression of that culture's final phase. The group's was a *fin de siècle* music, a mysterious, provocative collage that drew on jazz, on 20th-century composition, on primitive technologies and, to a degree, on the ironic theatrics of the *yurodivy*, the Holy Fool. To what extent their music was genuinely subversive, to what extent a kind of licensed jestering remains as difficult to untangle as the question of what Shostakovich really intended to say in the Fifth Symphony. The music remains, and it remains one of the most significant bodies of work of the last 20 years.

A certain romantic mythology would have you believe that the trio's first recordings were mysterious samizdat documents, smuggled and clandestine, and coming through the speakers with all the crackly mystery of a radio message from the resistance. In point of fact *Con Anima*, originally released by the official Soviet label Melodiya, is a decent recording, though there are shadow sounds on the second session, either the result of print-through (music tape should usually be stored tail-out) or because the stock has been reused and the previous session wiped incompletely. The whole sequence, and the materials that went to the making of *Concerto Grosso* as well, have been organized into two huge tracks, without the fades and functional bridges of the original release. The language is instantly identifiable, eclectic and dramatic, with fragments of jazz, the Baroque, folk song and atonal modernism all melding into something larger. Ganelin plays a lot of guitar on the second LP, which was first released in 1980, some time after its recording, and he invents his own language for the instrument.

Catalogue: Live In East Germany still seems an immensely powerful record, not simply because of its associations, but because of the music itself. It stands up as strongly now as ever before. In the last edition, however, we revised our valuation of the record in the light of one significant development. Confusion has remained about the titling of the group's large-scale suites, though Leo Feigin has done sterling work in sorting out the problem. He has brought out a CD of *Ancora Da Capo* which brings together a recording of part one, made in Leningrad at the famous Autumn Rhythms Festival, of which the trio were the only home stars, with a recording of part two, made a few weeks earlier in Berlin.

This was a breakthrough occasion for the Ganelin Trio. Their work was publicly hailed by the German critic, Joachim Ernst Berendt, and their reputation in the West was established. Two years later they were to appear at the extraordinary event in London we have described in previous editions. Though Leo Feigin was present at the Berlin event, he only subsequently received a tape of it, and the first release of this music was therefore two LPs documenting successive nights at the Leningrad event. Feigin replaced the second of these with the Berlin performance of part two, and this is the Ganelin Trio's definitive performance. Even though somewhat separated by geography and time, and by significant changes in acoustic, this two-part suite has a monolithic intensity which condenses everything the group was about at its best: a shining expressiveness, dense, passionate playing, humour and, underlying it all, an ironclad discipline. It is, quite simply, a masterpiece, and we strongly recommend it to your attention.

This is not in any way to denigrate or downgrade *Catalogue.* It is a continuous cycle, alternating quiet, formal sections with occasional explosions of improvisational frenzy in which Chekasin's saxophone is the main voice. Like much of the trio's work, the mood is predominantly dark and tragic, but with a redemptive quality. If the idiom seems far removed from the usual theme-and-variations, harmonic approach of jazz, it does play an important role, albeit in reverse, with melodic and sometimes standard material serving as the culmination rather than the starting point.

One of the definitive characteristics of the trio's sound is a dry, unpropulsive rhythm, an aspect that can make their work seem remote to listeners schooled on jazz. Tarasov deliberately avoids any settled groove in favour of a light, springy metre that can move in almost any direction or in none. There is no conventional bass, though Ganelin makes distinctive use of the basset. (This mustn't be confused with the basset horn or with the basset clarinet which Chekasin plays; it is in fact a small keyboard instrument which mimics the sound of a string bass, but in a flat and uninflected way, giving the trio its distinctively unswinging feel.)

We make no apology for grouping all these records together, confusing as it may seem. The only reasonable approach to this music is to work through the records patiently, learning how the suites interrelate and learning to identify what elements belong to each. Liner-notes by Leo Feigin, Efim Barban (on *Catalogue*) and Alexander Kan (on *Ancora Da Capo*) help sort out the story, which is a complex and intertextual one.

Feigin's achievement in bringing the group to Western ears cannot be overestimated, even if the relationship has not always been an easy or a wholly comprehending one. After 1980 the Ganelin Trio were able to perform on a world stage; whether what they did was to be accounted jazz or not, jazz musicians were required to take notice, as Rova did in 1986 when a notably relaxed trio played with them in San Francisco. That occasion may now seem like the beginning of the end. Much of the tension has gone out of the music, and Ganelin in particular sounds discursive. There is a long, lifeless version of 'New Wine' and a very long piece called 'Ritardando', which is too persistently evasive and reticent to sustain interest over its 45-minute span. There should be no surprise hearing them do a standard, 'Mack The Knife' (there are more standards on *Encores*), but the qualities that made earlier references to the tradition so powerful have gone, and it almost sounds kitsch.

In 2002, Leo Feigin released an important recording of the group on tour in Nickelsdorf, Austria. This was the first time the Trio had been allowed to travel abroad without a KGB minder and the freedom and confidence it gave them is palpable moment to moment. These performances are also the first occasion on which Vyacheslav Ganelin played a Yamaha synthesizer, taking it onstage less than half an hour after first seeing it and producing an astonishing range of sound that prefigures his later work in electronic synthesis. The two suites included see the group shifting as before between bop, folk tunes and almost martial themes, classical structures and completely free elements. It is as exhilarating as anything in the Ganelin Trio discography.

The Ganelin Trio belong to a particular phase in modern music. They failed to outlive that phase as a group, and though the members continue to experiment, they inevitably do so apart. A reunion seems unthinkable, and given how much water has passed under the bridges of the Neva, the Dnieper and the Don, it is probably undesirable as well.

Jan Garbarek (born 1947)

TENOR, SOPRANO AND BASS SAXOPHONES, FLUTES, KEYBOARD, PERCUSSION

Turned to jazz after hearing John Coltrane records in his native Norway. Studied with George Russell in the late '60s and began recording as a post-bop leader in 1971 for ECM, his label ever since. Has gone deeper into native Norwegian music since 1980's Eventyr, and has increasingly turned to material and settings remote from jazz; popular and successful despite the esoteric nature of his music.

*****(*) Afric Pepperbird**
ECM 843475-2 *Garbarek; Terje Rypdal (g, bugle); Arild Andersen (b); Jon Christensen (d). 9/70.*

***** Sart**
ECM 839305-2 *As above, except add Bobo Stenson (p). 4/71.*

In 1997 Jan Garbarek celebrated his 50th birthday as one of the best-known, and certainly one of the most easily identified, improvising musicians anywhere in the world. His high, keening saxophone, with the cathedral echo ECM have habitually given it, is one of the most readily universalized instrumental sounds in contemporary music. If you know it is Garbarek, it will evoke Nordic landscapes; if not, it suggests nothing more than somewhere far off, desert rather than tundra, the wastes of Africa rather than the northern lands. Few artists of his stature have stayed loyal to a single record label throughout their careers, so much so that it is difficult to tell whether ECM shaped Garbarek or whether he gave definitive voice to that much-discussed chimera, the 'ECM sound'. With the release of *Officium* in the mid-'90s, a non-jazz work made in collaboration with the Hilliard Ensemble, Garbarek followed another ECM artist, Keith Jarrett, into immense crossover appeal. Critical response to *Officium* has already been enormous and it has turned into one of ECM's most lucrative releases, but we do take leave to wonder what this artist might have done in a more promiscuous career, and with more concentration on jazz playing, for he has extraordinary gifts here as well, not just as a colourizing instrumentalist.

Afric Pepperbird was an astonishing debut, and it certainly makes the point that the reflex response to Garbarek's playing would, at this stage at least, have been 'cool', 'impressionistic', 'unmistakably Nordic'. This is by far his most 'out' recording, influenced by Coltrane, but also by Ayler's multiphonic intensity and with strong elements of Dexter Gordon's phrasing. Garbarek's flute, not much heard in later years, has a thin, folksy timbre that is particularly effective when overblown. The rhythm partnership of Andersen and Christensen was hard to beat at the time (though Eberhard Weber and Palle Danielsson became the bassists of choice in future) and Rypdal's abstract, unmetrical chording is more or less perfect for the gig.

Sart is a typical second album, trying to reduplicate the first and show how much the leader has 'developed' at the same time. Though Stenson is a wonderful player and we won't hear a word said against him, this is one of his least impressive showings ever. Garbarek again uses flute and, this time out, bass saxophone, though not yet the Wayne Shorter-influenced soprano that was to be such a trademark in years to come.

★★★(★) Triptykon

ECM 847321-2 *Garbarek; Arild Andersen (b); Edward Vesala (d, perc).* 11/72.

In an admittedly unfair and skewed blindfold test conducted during the preparation of a previous edition, three avowed Garbarek fans failed to recognize their hero on this. Certainly, anyone who climbed on board with or after *Dis* would have difficulty recognizing the hard tone and the free-form language. There are signs that both saxophonist and drummer are dissatisfied with free music, and Andersen is hesitant, breaking up his rhythm shapes with the deliberateness of a man swearing in a foreign language. This is also the last real appearance of Garbarek the multi-instrumentalist, doubling on soprano, baritone (a hint of Lars Gullin there, perhaps) and flute. In the final analysis, it's the Finn who wins the day, playing brilliantly from start to finish. From the point of view of future projects, *Triptykon* says more about him than about Garbarek.

★★★(★) Witchi-Tai-To

ECM 833330-2 *Garbarek; Bobo Stenson (p); Palle Danielsson (b); Jon Christensen (d).* 11/73.

★★★(★) Dansere

ECM 829193-2 *As above.* 11/75.

Things were beginning to come together for Garbarek at this point, both critically and commercially, and *Witchi-Tai-To* was probably the first of his records about which it was possible to say that it was both characteristic and surprising, both impressionistic and funky, European and jazz-based. The saxophone tone is more relaxed, indeed more relaxed than it would be very often again, with a less pressurized embouchure and more sense of playing in distinct breath-groups or verses. The folk element was not so much a departure as a logical extension of what he'd been doing up to this point. The title-piece is a version of Jim Pepper's surprise hit, a delightful performance that is as fresh now as ever.

Dansere was a quieter session for the saxophonist, but it plays now almost as a co-led session with the steadily developing Stenson, who commands much of the attention and who might have been worthy of a couple of trio tracks. Indeed, had this session been taped in the '90s, that is probably what ECM would have done.

CORE COLLECTION

★★★★ Dis

ECM 827408-2 *Garbarek; Ralph Towner (g, 12-string g); wind harp; brass sextet.* 12/76.

Few modern jazz records have been as thoroughly plundered for atmospheric cameos as *Dis*. From wildlife movies about the snowy owl, to more threatening jeremiads on the effects of Chernobyl on Sami reindeer herds, it has been the soundtrack. The copyright kickbacks notwithstanding, it's a beautiful album, quintessential Garbarek pitched against a wind harp (recorded at the top of a fjord, with the winds from the North Sea eternally gusting in) and the softly articulated sound of a brass ensemble. It established a style which the saxophonist was to return to many times in years ahead, spells and riddles on soprano saxophone (and wood flute) and a deep, mourning tone that floats and drifts over the rhythm.

★★★★ Places

ECM 829195-2 *Garbarek; Bill Connors (g); John Taylor (org); Jack DeJohnette (d).* 12/77.

★★★ Photo With Blue Sky

ECM 843168-2 *Garbarek; Bill Connors (g); Eberhard Weber (b); Jon Christensen (d).* 12/78.

The end of the '70s saw a pattern established whereby Garbarek went into the studio at each year's end to consolidate and capture what had been learnt in performance and to send out new feelers for the year ahead. It is what a village bard might have done in winter quarters, spin tales about the year past and boast about what would come when the sun returned. *Dis* was also the first of a group of records with a guitarist, on which Garbarek experimented with more open and ambiguous harmonies and textures. *Places* has never been as highly regarded as *Dis*, but it is a small masterpiece, dominated by one long track, a pattern that repeats itself throughout Garbarek's output. 'Passing' begins with misterioso organ from Taylor, tense drum rips from DeJohnette, and an unresolved, questioning figure on the guitar. Garbarek's entry picks it up without variation; for much of the record, similar or identical ideas are distributed round the band. There is no real linear argument to a Garbarek solo by this stage. Ideas are static, unpropulsive and almost sculptural in impact. It is a style that served him well but also proved to be something of a straitjacket.

★★ Aftenland

ECM 839304-2 *Garbarek; Kjell Johnsen (org).* 12/79.

On a checklist of ECM and Garbarek clichés, this scores highly: 'Nordic', 'moody', 'atmospheric', and resolutely unfunky. Reminiscent of some of Keith Jarrett's experiments of the same time, but lacking Jarrett's insouciant arrogance, it proves to be a very difficult record to listen to and like. Some of the material might well have been interesting in a concert setting, but as a commercial release this is the closest the estimably disciplined Norwegian has ever come to self-indulgence.

★★★ Eventyr

ECM 829384-2 *Garbarek; John Abercrombie (g, 12-string g, mand); Nana Vasconcelos (talking d, perc, v).* 12/80.

★★★ Paths, Prints

ECM 829377-2 *Garbarek; Bill Frisell (g); Eberhard Weber (b); Jon Christensen (d).* 12/81.

★★★ Wayfarer

ECM 811968-2 *As above, except omit Christensen; add Michael DiPasqua (d, perc).* 3/83.

This is the only stage in Garbarek's career when he seems to be marking time. These are formulaic records, clearly intended to capitalize on the success of *Dis*, but rarely rising to its splendours. Each of the three has its merits, and Abercrombie and Frisell are more appropriate players for the context than the unpredictable Connors who can be great or unutterably bland. Vasconcelos is probably too much of a one-man band to fit into anyone else's concept, but he is a great entertainer and records featuring him are never dull. A word for DiPasqua as well, a big heart and the chops to give *Wayfarer* the sort of swing and thrust it deserves.

★★★ It's OK To Listen To The Gray Voice

ECM 825406-2 *Garbarek; David Torn (g); Eberhard Weber (b); Michael DiPasqua (d).* 84.

The title reference is to a poem by Tomas Tranströmer, one of the great voices of modern European literature. It's refreshing to hear Garbarek tackling something new, and this is certainly a departure for him. How the poetry of Tranströmer relates to the music Garbarek is playing is never made entirely explicit and sometimes isn't an entirely convincing source of inspiration, but what one hears is tough and strong, and without a shred of self-indulgence.

** All Those Born With Wings

ECM 831394-2 *Garbarek (sax solo).* 8/86.

This was a disappointment, albeit a not unexpected exercise at this stage in his career. Garbarek was working through a number of personal and stylistic changes, and was bound to miscue on occasion. We've never found this to be anything other than dully introspective and unemphatic.

*** Legend Of The Seven Dreams

ECM 837344-2 *Garbarek; Rainer Bruninghaus (ky); Eberhard Weber (b); Manu Katché (d); Nana Vasconcelos (perc, v).* 7/88.

*** Rosensfole

ECM 839293-2 *Garbarek; Agnes Buen Garnås (v).* 88.

*** I Took Up The Runes

ECM 843850-2 *As for Legend Of The Seven Dreams, except add Bugge Wesseltoft (syn); Annte Ailu Gaup (v).* 8/90.

Towards the end of the '80s, Garbarek began to explore Nordic folk musics and myth in a more structured way, thus turning the casually unsubstantiated generalizations about his Nordic style back on themselves. *Rosensfole* is really Garnås's album and is none the worse for that, Garbarek limited in the main to providing a shifting, minimal stage for her dramatic singing. The opening 'He Comes From The North' on *Legend* is based on a Lappish *joik*, converted into state-of-the-art 'world music' by Vasconcelos's unplaceable percussion and vocal. There are also three brief, unaccompanied tracks, two on soprano saxophone, one on flute, to demonstrate how Garbarek has pared down his playing once again to the barest bones of melody.

Runes is in the same vein, but the experiment of adding a rock drummer and synthesizer player to the core trio was an inspired one, and the long central track is one of Garberek's most ambitious works. The energy of the live performance doesn't quite come across on record, but there is more than enough of interest to bridge occasional lapses of pace.

***(*) Star

ECM 849649-2 *Garbarek; Miroslav Vitous (b); Peter Erskine (d).* 1/91.

This was widely thought to be Garbarek's return to straight jazz playing, but any such expectation is confounded at the first fence, a rather woolly number which is the saxophonist's only composition of the set. What the piece does is lay out an array of tone colours that are imaginatively deployed by the trio throughout the album, which has a stripped-down and business-like feel. Garbarek's tone is still his unique selling point and he manages to infuse his tenor-playing with a brittle-edged fragility one would normally associate with the soprano horn. There is still a tendency to place long notes like personal monograms, but the signature is in a new, bolder sans-serif which reads as freshly as *Triptykon* did 20 years ago.

Vitous is purposive and surely grounded; the clouds are in the mountains now, not vice versa. Erskine doesn't seem the obvious choice, but the obvious alternative – Christensen – hasn't the simplicity and directness the session seems to call for. The improvised 'Snowman' is indicative of how far Garbarek has progressed during his folksy sabbatical from blowing jazz, and it may even be a satirical response to all the editorial blah about his cool and stiffness. In Wallace Stevens's words, it takes a 'mind of winter' to make music like this; that doesn't mean it lacks passion.

***(*) Ragas And Sagas

ECM 511263-2 *Garbarek; Manu Katché (d); Ustad Shaukat Hussain (tabla); Ustad Nazim Ali Khan (sarangi); Ustad Fateh Ali Khan, Deepika Thathaal (v).* 5/90.

*** Madar

ECM 519075-2 *Garbarek; Anouar Brahem (oud); Ustad Shaukat Hussain (tabla).* 8/92.

These two records are 'world music' in the most positive sense. They demonstrate the essential irreducibility of what Garbarek is about. Karnatic ideas had cropped up in his work before and there are certain raga-like sequences even in the early albums, harmonically static, rhythmically mobile but not conventionally swinging. *Ragas And Sagas* was a perfectly logical step. It succeeds for the most part a good deal better than the collaboration with oud-player Brahem (on whose own records Garbarek has also recorded), but only because Garbarek himself is in better voice. Though the combination of Norwegian and non-European styles is every bit as seamless on both, Garbarek simply plays better with Hussain and his colleagues.

**** Twelve Moons

ECM 519500-2 *Garbarek; Rainer Bruninghaus (ky); Eberhard Weber (b); Manu Katché (d); Marilyn Mazur (perc); Mari Boine, Agnes Buen Garnås (v).* 9/93.

Appropriately, it was Garbarek who was chosen to front ECM's 500th release with this magnificently packaged offering. It finds him at an interesting point of development, still exploring folklore but also easing his way back into a more jazz-orientated programme. There's a very heavy emphasis on soprano saxophone, perhaps to blend better with the voices, but even here the tone is stronger and heavier than of yore, and on occasions almost sounding full enough to be an alto.

Katché is essentially a rock drummer, with a crude but immensely vibrant delivery. One thinks occasionally of Ginger Baker, but among previous associates he is closer to Edward Vesala than to Jon Christensen. This time around, in addition to Sami *joiks*, Garbarek includes an arrangement of national composer Edvard Grieg's gentle 'Arietta', and a new version of the late Jim Pepper's 'Witchi-Tai-To', which has been a staple piece much of his career. A beautiful record, by far the best of the later releases.

(***) Officium

ECM 445369-2 *Garbarek; Hilliard Ensemble (v).* 9/93.

So much critical copy has been directed at this, and so many copies sold, that it seems redundant to add to the chorus. An anthology of 14th- and 15th-century church music, arranged for vocal ensemble and saxophone, it has hooked into a vast appetite for 'faith minimalism' and for music of spiritual uplift. Immaculately recorded and featuring some exquisite saxophone-playing, it makes no pretence to being jazz or even some close cognate. Listening to it now, in the context of the later (and, in our view, very much more accomplished) *Mnemosyne*, it is clear how Garbarek and his colleagues are feeling their way towards a shared musical language that will take account of both written and improvised elements. The problem for us is that the composed elements are too literally interpreted, while the improvisations drift free of any sure anchor.

***** Visible World**

ECM 529086-2 *Garbarek; Rainer Bruninghaus (p, ky); Eberhard Weber (b); Marilyn Mazur (d, perc); Manu Katché (d); Trilok Gurtu (perc); Mari Boine (v).* 6/95.

Officium was always going to be a tough act to follow, and Garbarek wisely chose to go with what was effectively his working group of the moment. The majority of these tracks are for trio, with either Bruninghaus or Weber and Katché or Mazur. There are also some searching duos, including the 'The Creek' with Katché, in which Garbarek seems to be experimenting in a quiet way with new rhythmic ideas. The longest track, 'Aftenlandet', was originally written as a music–video collaboration; featuring Boine and Mazur, it has a delicately mysterious quality. Garbarek briefly plays clarinet on this disc, suggesting that he may also be interested in hearing new colours and sounds. No sign yet of those occupying the foreground, but lots of possibilities sketched into this essentially consolidating record.

***** Rites**

ECM 559006-2 2CD *Garbarek; Bugge Wesseltoft (syn, acc, elec); Rainer Bruninghaus (p, ky); Eberhard Weber (b); Marilyn Mazur (d, perc); Jansug Kakhidze (v); Tbilisi Symphony Orchestra; Sølvguttene Boys' Choir.* 3/98.

Rites is at once over-extended and too busy. It is also curiously programmed. The title-track might almost be an out-take by pop band Enigma, who combine dance beats with Gregorian chant. Wesseltoft is very adept at this kind of synthesis, and it's interesting as an extension of the work Garbarek has been doing with the Hilliard Ensemble. Generally, though, the tracks are the familiar mixture of acoustic jazz and folk themes. Bruninghaus is a secure technician but one who doesn't alter his approach when he plays electronic keyboards, even analogue types, and so he manages to lose his passage-work on 'Vast Plain, Clouds' between idioms. He is closer to the mark on an interesting version of 'It's OK To Listen To The Gray Voice', an unexpected but welcome reappearance of a Garbarek composition that always seemed to have more mileage than it got on the album of that name.

The second disc is a mirror of the first. Wesseltoft's electronics establish the mood for 'It's High Time', and he contributes some effective and moving accordion to a version of Don Cherry's 'Malinye'. Elsewhere, though, it's the interplay of Weber and Mazur which creates the dramatic interest. 'Pan' is solo Garbarek. What follows is both intriguing and slightly enigmatic. First, the saxophonist is joined by a boys' choir in 'We Are The Stars', and then, for no very solid reason, he includes a recording of the 62-year-old Georgian singer and composer performing his own 'The Moon Over Mtatsminda'. Garbarek has no hand whatever in the composition.

The album peters out with two further electronics-driven pieces, 'Evenly They Danced' and 'Last Rite'. The second is obviously intended to give the set as a whole some symmetry and a sense of ending, but most listeners will have flagged and switched off by then. As so often, a fine single CD has been lost in an excess of uncompelling material.

*****(*) Mnemosyne**

ECM 465122-2 2CD *Garbarek; Hilliard Ensemble.* 4/98.

Garbarek and the Hilliards returned to the monastery of St Gerold five years on with a considerable body of shared experience. Many performances of *Officium* had opened up a rich palette of musical connections. Inspired by a poem of Friedrich Hölderlin which is about chaos and loss and the reach towards the abyss, it is a more turbulent but also more accepting conception than *Officium*.

Drawing on church music – by Tallis, the Abbess of the Paraclete, Orthodox psalm- and hymn-composer William Billings – as well as Native American themes, a Scottish love song, and a second-century Greek invocation of the sun, it becomes a complex tapestry of musical associations, woven together by some mercurial improvisation and the Hilliards' trademark note-perfect ensembles. The cover imagery is drawn from Ingmar Bergman's film, *The Seventh Seal*, but anyone dismayed at the prospect of Baltic gloom can be reassured that *Mnemosyne* is a much more joyous and open-hearted work than the art-work might suggest. It has light and shade, a genuine sense of drama and a warmth that has been harder to find in Garbarek's recent work.

****** :rarum**

ECM 440 014 165-2 2CD *As various discs above.* 11/75–6/95.

Garbarek's choice from 30 years of recording for the label is actually telescoped into the 'middle' 20 years, with, disappointingly, nothing from his vivid, earliest work. Whatever claims Keith Jarrett may have on it, it's clear that this is the key testament in ECM's catalogue, with a clear and logical progression of achievement, from the quartet music of 'Skrik & Hyl' through to 'Parce Mihi Domine' from his work with the Hilliard Ensemble. There can be no perfect sampler of Garbarek's music, given his inquisitive outreach, but this is surely close to an ideal introduction.

Red Garland (1923–84)

PIANO

Born in Dallas, Garland was a minor figure in the first phase of bebop, but he became eminent through his association with the great Miles Davis group of the mid-'50s; the leader was very taken with his light but hip style. He made a long sequence of records for Prestige but gradually faded from prominence, eventually returning to Dallas.

***** A Garland Of Red**

Original Jazz Classics OJC 126 *Garland; Paul Chambers (b); Art Taylor (d).* 8/56.

***** Groovy**

Original Jazz Classics OJC 061 *As above.* 12/56–8/57.

***** Red Garland's Piano**

Original Jazz Classics OJC 073 *As above.* 3/57.

***** The P.C. Blues**

Original Jazz Classics OJC 898 *As above, except add Philly Joe Jones (d).* 3/56–8/57.

*****(*) Red Garland Revisited!**
Original Jazz Classics OJC 985 *As above, except add Kenny Burrell (g); omit Jones.* 5/57.

***** It's A Blue World**
Original Jazz Classics OJC 1028 *As above, except omit Burrell.* 2/58.

***** Manteca**
Original Jazz Classics OJC 428 *As above, except add Ray Barretto (perc).* 4/58.

***** Rediscovered Masters Vol. 1**
Original Jazz Classics OJC 768 *As above.* 6/58.

***** Can't See For Lookin'**
Original Jazz Classics OJC 918 *As above, except omit Barretto.* 6/58.

***** All Kinds Of Weather**
Original Jazz Classics OJC 193 *As above.* 11/58.

***** Red In Bluesville**
Original Jazz Classics OJC 295 *As above, except Sam Jones (b) replaces Chambers.* 4/59.

***** Rojo**
Original Jazz Classics OJC 772 *Garland; George Joyner (b); Charli Persip (d); Ray Barretto (perc).* 8/58.

***** Stretching Out**
Prestige 24272-2 *Garland; Jimmy Rowser, Doug Watkins (b); Specs Wright (d).* 8–10/59.

***** At The Prelude Vol. 1**
Prestige 24132 *Garland; Jimmy Rowser (b); Specs Wright (d).* 10/59.

Graceful yet unaffectedly bluesy, Red Garland's manner was flexible enough to accommodate the contrasting styles of both Miles Davis and John Coltrane in the Davis quintet of the mid-'50s. His many records as a leader, beginning at about the same period, display exactly the same qualities. His confessed influences of Tatum, Powell and Nat Cole seem less obvious than his debts to Erroll Garner and Ahmad Jamal, whose hit recording of 'Billy Boy' from the early '50s seems to sum up everything that Garland would later go on to explore.

All of the listed trio sessions feature the same virtues: deftly fingered left-hand runs over bouncy rhythms, coupled with block-chord phrasing which coloured melodies in such a way that Garland saw no need to depart from them. Medium–up-tempo treatments alternate with stately ballads, and Chambers and Taylor are unfailingly swinging, if often constrained, partners. The later sessions feature a slightly greater empathy, but we find it very hard to choose a favourite among these records. The choice may depend on the tunes on each record, some of which are presented thematically (*All Kinds Of Weather*, for instance, is made up of 'Rain', 'Summertime', and so on). The guest role for Barretto on *Manteca* is a mostly peripheral one – he plays a quiet second line of percussion – although he's given a couple of lively features with Taylor on the title-tune and 'Lady Be Good'. The remastering is clean, although Chambers, while conspicuously present, is seldom awarded anything better than a dull bass sound. *At The Prelude* is a snapshot of Garland at work in a New York club, though he doesn't sound appreciably different away from the studios.

Of the newer arrivals on CD, *Can't See For Lookin'* is a solid workout with a particularly pleasing treatment of the Gershwin standard 'Soon', and *It's A Blue World*, though it features an interminable *arco* solo by Chambers on 'This Can't Be Love', is much brighter than its title suggests, with a lightning canter through 'Crazy Rhythm'. *The P.C. Blues*, originally conceived as a tribute to Chambers, starts with the Miles Davis-session 'Ahmad's Blues' and goes through two exemplary ballads before reaching the absurd – though impeccably handled – 'Tweedle Dee Dee'. Line for line, this is one of our favourite Garlands. *Revisited!*, though, is our first choice for any who want a single Garland set fom the period. His own version of 'Billy Boy' is here, there are two classic slow-burners in 'Everybody's Somebody's Fool' and 'The Masquerade Is Over', and Burrell shows up to spar on 'Four' and 'Walkin''.

A recent release is *Stretching Out*, which combines the LPs *Satin Doll* and most of *Lil' Darlin'*, itself drawn from the same sessions as *At The Prelude*. Nice work, but business as usual.

***** All Mornin' Long**
Original Jazz Classics OJC 293 *Garland; Donald Byrd (t); John Coltrane (ts); George Joyner (b); Art Taylor (d).* 11/57.

*****(*) Soul Junction**
Original Jazz Classics OJC 481 *As above.* 11/57.

*****(*) High Pressure**
Original Jazz Classics OJC 349 *As above.* 11–12/57.

****(*) Dig It!**
Original Jazz Classics OJC 392 *As above, except add Paul Chambers (b).* 3/57–2/58.

Garland's recordings with Coltrane are typical of the long, relaxed blowing sessions which Prestige were recording at the time, and some of the tracks are very long indeed: 'All Mornin' Long' runs for 20 minutes, 'Soul Junction' and 'Lazy Mae' from *Dig It!* for 16 apiece. There are inevitable *longueurs* in this approach, and Byrd, though accomplished, lacks the greater authority which he would bring to his later, Blue Note albums. But there are some solos of immense power from the tenor saxophonist, and the playing on *Soul Junction* and *High Pressure* especially is as purposeful as the format allows (all the recordings from November 1957 were made on the same day). *Dig It!*, patched together from three sessions and including a fairly routine trio version of 'Crazy Rhythm', is slightly inferior.

*****(*) Rediscovered Masters Vol. 2**
Original Jazz Classics OJC 769 *Garland; Richard Williams (t); Oliver Nelson (as, ts); Doug Watkins, Peck Morrison (b); Specs Wright, Charli Persip (d).* 8/59–3/61.

***** Soul Burnin'**
Original Jazz Classics OJC 921 *As above, except add Sam Jones (b), Art Taylor (d).* 8/59–3/61.

***** Red Garland Trio With Eddie 'Lockjaw' Davis Vol. 1**
Original Jazz Classics OJC 360 *Garland; Eddie 'Lockjaw' Davis (ts); Sam Jones (b); Art Taylor (d).* 12/59.

***** The Nearness Of You**
Original Jazz Classics OJC 1003 *Garland; Larry Ridley (b); Frank Grant (d).* 12/61.

****(*) Solar**
Original Jazz Classics OJC 755 *Garland; Les Spann (g, f); Sam Jones (b); Frank Grant (d).* 1/62.

****(*) Red's Good Groove**
Original Jazz Classics OJC 1064 *Garland; Blue Mitchell (t); Pepper Adams (bs); Sam Jones (b); Philly Joe Jones (d).* 3/62.

***** When There Are Grey Skies**
Original Jazz Classics OJC 704 *Garland; Wendell Marshall (b); Charli Persip (d).* 9/62.

Davis appears on only three tracks of OJC 360, but it's enough to enliven an otherwise somnolent disc of ballads, originally issued in Prestige's Moodsville series; a stentorian reading of 'When Your Lover Has Gone' works especially well. The second volume of *Rediscovered Masters* couples a very good session by Red's favourite trio, with Watkins and Wright, strolling through a quickfire 'Blues In The Closet' and a long, languorous 'Mr Wonderful', with a scarce quintet date featuring Williams and Nelson in the front line. The latter is nothing extraordinary, since both men sometimes sound as if they've strolled into the date by accident, but Nelson's sombre tenor makes a pleasing foil to Williams's more elegant horn. Two more tracks from this date are on *Soul Burnin'*, including a particularly pretty 'If You Could See Me Now', and four characteristic trio tracks round out an enjoyable disc. *Red's Good Groove* is a Prestige potboiler, and only Pepper Adams, who didn't like being bored, really makes an effort. *Solar* returns Garland to a rhythm format, although Les Spann's presence isn't very useful; *The Nearness Of You* is another enjoyable stroll through eight standards; and *When There Are Grey Skies* was to be Red's last album for nearly ten years. He delivers one of his most considered interpretations here in the almost painstaking exploration of 'Nobody Knows The Trouble I've Seen', beautifully sustained over some 12 minutes.

***** Crossings**
Original Jazz Classics OJC 472 *Garland; Ron Carter (b); Philly Joe Jones (d).* 12/77.

****(*) Red Alert**
Original Jazz Classics OJC 647 *Garland; Nat Adderley (c); Harold Land, Ira Sullivan (ts); Ron Carter (b); Frank Butler (d).* 12/77.

Garland continued to make records in the '70s and '80s, and those that remain show his style unchanged, although some of the litheness went out of his touch. *Red Alert* is a decent if impersonal attempt at recapturing one of Red's old Prestige blowing dates. Nice enough cameos by the horns, but the prettiest music is when they sit out and let the pianist play 'It's Impossible'. *Crossings* features such fine support from the rhythm section that the music gathers its own momentum.

Tim Garland

TENOR AND SOPRANO SAXOPHONES, BASS CLARINET

Born in Ilford, Garland was already making records ony a few years after taking up the saxophone. His subsequent progress, with bands such as the folk-jazz group Lammas, has been somewhat slower.

****(*) Made By Walking**
Stretch SCD 98030-2 *Garland; Gerard Presencer (t, flhn); Geoff Keezer, Chick Corea (p); Joe Locke (vib, marim); Avishai Cohen (b); Jorge Rossy (d).* 2–5/00.

***** Storms/Nocturnes**
Sirocco SJL 1017 *Garland; Geoff Keezer (p); Joe Locke (vib, marim).* 8/01.

***** Rising Tide**
Sirocco SJL 1022 *As above.* 12/02.

***** Soho Story**
DNSTCD 2001 *Garland; Henry Lowther, Martin Shaw (t); Gerard Presencer (t, flhn); Barnaby Dickinson (tb); Gareth Williams (p); John Parricelli (g); Orlando Le Fleming (b); Sebastiaan de Krom, Jeff Ballard (d).* 9/01.

Garland's progress has actually been rather slow: pushing 40, he's only recently received much general attention. The Stretch album marks an attempt to pitch him on to a world stage, after years of worthy if unremarkable work with groups such as Lammas, but despite some agreeable music there's little to really collar the attention of an international audience here. He may have won some recent spurs in the Chick Corea group, but for all its energy the music here lacks much in the way of striking individuality. If anything, he's outplayed by the excellent Presencer.

The trio with Keezer and Locke (they seem to have adopted the name Storms/Nocturnes following the first album) is a kind of internationalized version of what the Lammas group created – English pastoralism toughened by hints of blues and a more robust, worldly outeach. They achieve it some of the time, although for every passage of genuinely assertive music, there's another which sounds introverted and self-conscious. Garland's difficulty is that he can't seem able to translate his good-natured delivery into something which commands the attention.

Soho Story is by the Dean Street Underground Orchestra, which is the London equivalent of the several New York Monday-night big bands. It's a good group, and the record has plenty of smart moments, but there's little of the effortless class which their American counterparts bring to this kind of thing: it's more effortful, the directions and charts almost slavishly followed, the freewheeling feel which would make this kind of project really cut loose notably absent. They probably need to make a few more records yet.

Erroll Garner (1926–77)

PIANO, HARPSICHORD

Moved from Pittsburgh to New York in 1944 and was quickly established as a nightclub pianist, working for the rest of his career as a soloist or in trios. After the huge success of the Concert By The Sea album for Columbia, he became an enduring international star. A unique stylist, somewhat like a mix of Earl Hines, the stride players and the boppers, his self-taught mastery – he never learned to read and other pianists were sometimes engaged to teach him songs – only seemed to increase his likeability with his many admirers.

**** Erroll Garner 1944**
Classics 802 *Garner (p solo).* 11–12/44.

****(*) Erroll Garner 1944 Vol. 2**
Classics 818 *Garner (p); John Simmons (b); Harold 'Doc' West (d).* 12/44.

**** Erroll Garner 1944 Vol. 3**
Classics 850 *Garner; Inez Cavanaugh (v).* 12/44.

*****(*) Erroll Garner 1944–1945**
Classics 873 *Garner; Charlie Shavers (t); Vic Dickenson (tb); Hank D'Amico (cl); Lem Davis (as); Slam Stewart, Eddie Brown (b); Cliff Leeman, Harold 'Doc' West (d).* 12/44–3/45.

***** Erroll Garner 1945–1946**
Classics 924 *Garner; John Levy Jr (b); George DeHart (d).* 9/45–2/46.

*** Erroll Garner 1946–1947
Classics 1004 *Garner; Red Callender (b); Nick Fatool, Lou Singer, Harold 'Doc' West (d).* 4/46–6/47.

Erroll Garner was one of a kind. He was as *outré* as the great beboppers, yet bop was alien to him, even though he recorded with Charlie Parker. He swung mightily, yet he stood outside the swing tradition; he played orchestrally, and his style was swooningly romantic, yet he could be as merciless on a tune as Fats Waller. He never read music, but he could play a piece in any key, and delighted in deceiving his rhythm sections from night to night. His tumbling, percussive, humorous style was entirely his own.

Garner's earliest recordings were done semi-privately, and though issued on Blue Note in the '50s, they're in often atrocious sound, and one has to be either a scholar or devoted fan to get much out of them. Most of his style is in place, and one can hear his debt to Tatum already. The first three Classics discs include what there is of these survivals, and it's a difficult listen.

The next two discs in its sequence are rather more interesting. *1944–1945* puts together a session which has been a collectors' piece for many years: a jam with Shavers, Dickenson, D'Amico and Davis which includes extended versions of 'Gaslight' and some impromptu blues. Lovely stuff, with the principals all in good fettle, and a very rare glimpse of Garner with horns. A trio date with Brown and West (for Black And White) and a solo session for Signature fill up the disc. *1945–1946* includes a scruffy-sounding solo date for Disc before a pithy if unmomentous string of solos recorded for Mercury in 1945. Two solos for V-Disc round things off, but the spoken intro by Bob Hope sounds as if he was auditioning for the Chipmunks and there's clearly a speed problem here. Classics 1004 includes two trio dates for Mercury and one for Dial, then four solos for Victor and an eight-title solo date for Dial. The Victor coupling of 'Erroll's Bounce' and 'Erroll's Blues' is one of Garner's most characteristic pieces up to this point in the discography, and it sounds good in this transfer; some of the other titles are rather foggy, but even the originals aren't so good.

*** Erroll Garner 1947–1949
Classics 1109 *Garner; Howard McGhee (t); Benny Carter (as); Wardell Gray (ts); Ulysses Livingston, Oscar Moore (g); John Simmons, Nelson Boyd (b); Jackie Mills, Teddy Stewart, Alvin Stoller (d).* 4/47–3/49.

*** Erroll Garner 1949
Classics 1138 *Garner; Teddy Edwards (ts); John Simmons (b); Alvin Stoller (d); Dave Lambert (v).* 49.

*** Erroll Garner 1949 Vol. 2
Classics 1182 *Garner; John Simmons, Leonard Gaskin (b); Chuck Thompson, Alvin Stoller, Charlie Smith (d).* 6–7/49.

*** Erroll Garner 1949–1950
Classics 1205 *As above, except add Harold 'Doc' West (d), Johnny Hartman (v); omit Thompson.* 8/49–4/50.

These four CDs cover sessions for Savoy, Modern, Vogue, Atlantic, Portrait, Mercury, 3 Deuces and Roost, which hints at how prolific Garner already was. Classics 1109 has a couple of jam-session survivals in 'One O'Clock Jump' and 'Blue Lou', with some fine Wardell Gray; the rest is trio music, with four solo titles made on a trip to Paris. Erroll cut 13 titles for Savoy in one session (all on Classics 1138), and though there's a preponderance of slowish tempos, there are some characteristic Garner touches. An airshot of 'Cherokee' from a *Just Jazz* show (with Teddy Edwards and a scatting Dave Lambert) leads to a couple of solo sessions. He turns Duke's voicings inside out on a fascinating stride-styled 'Take The "A" Train', and 'My Old Kentucky Home' is delicately prised open to a rocking pulse. Classics 1182 begins with a couple of solos, goes into two fuzzy live tracks, then runs through two long trio sessions for Savoy and Atlantic. Although constrained a little by the 78 r.p.m. duration, these are some of the most particular Garner sessions to date, bouncing and bustling through the songs at quicker tempos and luxuriating in the ballad arpeggios. The Atlantic date has an almost impressionistic feel, with titles such as 'Reverie', 'Turquoise' and 'Twilight' – Garner as mood-music maestro. Classics 1205 offers three trio dates, a single solo of 'Love Is The Thing', and a session with Johnny Hartman breezing through four ballads. Slow tempos predominate at most of these dates (even 'Jitterbug Waltz' is played very kindly), although the final session for Roost has more go in it on the likes of 'Tippin' Out With Erroll'. Given the distinctly average sound throughout most of these sets (matters do improve a little towards the end, though not that much), these are all really for Garner nuts only, though you are unlikely to be disappointed with the music unless you expect high fidelity.

*** Erroll Garner 1950
Classics 1240 *Garner; John Simmons (b); Harold 'Doc' West, Shadow Wilson (d); Florence Wright (v).* 5–6/50.

***(*) Erroll Garner 1950–1951
Classics 1310 *As above except omit West.* 6/50–7/51.

Classics 1240 includes Erroll's last tracks for Atlantic and his first for Columbia, where he immediately gets a much better sound, although there's no concession to LP-length: virtually everything is still around the three-minute mark. But at least we get to hear Erroll in decent sound for the first time, and on Classics 1310 that really comes to the forefront: 'Poor Butterfly', a thrilling 'Honeysuckle Rose' and the mix of gaiety and wistfulness in 'Play Piano Play' which must be deemed a Garner trademark. The disc ends with three rather mysterious Garner solos for a label named Recorded In Hollywood (though not all that well).

*** Erroll Garner Collection Vol. 3: Too Marvellous For Words
Emarcy 824419-2 *Garner; Wyatt Ruther (b); Eugene 'Fats' Heard (d).* 5/54.

***(*) Contrasts
Verve 558077-2 *As above.* 7/54.

By this period Garner had settled into his format as well as his style – swashbuckling trios which plundered standards with cavalier abandon. Bass and drums have only to keep up with Garner, but they provide a deceptively important anchor, for otherwise his treatments might simply wander off. The drummer's role is particularly important. As percussive as the pianist is, he leaves many accents to the man with the traps, and Heard has to concentrate hard to keep up. Garner's heartiness, his fondness for extravagantly arpeggiated ballads and knockabout transformations of standards can grow wearisome over the length of an album, and his favourite mannerisms become irritating. But there are undervalued aspects to these records. He is a quirky but resonant blues-player; he keeps the melody sacrosanct, even at his most mischievous; he always swings. *The Original Misty* has now been supplanted by a Master Edition version of its original album, *Contrasts*, in better sound and with the famous track cleaned up effectively. The *Collection* albums are all of previously unreleased material.

****** The Erroll Garner Collection Vols 4 & 5: Solo Time!**
Emarcy 511821-2 2CD *Garner (p solo).* 7/54.

*****(*) Solitaire**
Mercury 518279-2 *Garner (p solo).* 3/55.

Garner made few solo records, but these sessions are among his finest. The *Solo Time!* collection was set down in a single afternoon of one-take performances at a Detroit radio station. Garner indulges himself in long, immoderate performances that show his imagination at its most free-spirited and abundant. The treatment of 'It Might As Well Be Spring' is archetypal: over 8¼ minutes he changes keys, builds huge orchestral crescendos, throws in a waltz-time passage, mocks and cherishes the melody, and finishes with an edifice that stands alone. Most of the tracks are variations on that manner, to a greater or lesser degree, and even when he falls back on Garnerisms the energy and spontaneity are something to marvel at. Only a shade behind is the 'proper' studio session which produced *Solitaire.* Here are ten minutes of 'Over The Rainbow', and perhaps the only jazz treatment of 'When A Gypsy Makes His Violin Cry'. Excellent remastering in both cases, the piano sounding a shade harder on *Solitaire.*

CORE COLLECTION

*****(*) Concert By The Sea**
Columbia CK 40589 *Garner; Eddie Calhoun (b); Denzil Best (d).* 9/55.

Garner's most famous album and one of the biggest-selling jazz records ever made, *Concert By The Sea* is essentially neither more nor less than a characteristic set by the trio in an amenable setting. Moments such as the teasing introduction to 'I'll Remember April', the flippant blues of 'Red Top' and the pell-mell 'Where Or When' find Garner at his most buoyant; but rather more interesting is his well-shaped treatment of 'How Could You Do A Thing Like That To Me'. The recording was never outstanding but the reissue serves it well enough.

***** Close Up In Swing / A New Kind Of Love**
Telarc CD-83383 *Garner; Eddie Calhoun (b); Kelly Martin (d); strings, brass, woodwind; Leith Stevens (cond).* 7/61–7/63.

***** Dreamstreet / One World Concert**
Telarc CD-83350 *Garner; Eddie Calhoun (b); Kelly Martin (d).* 59–8/63.

***** That's My Kick / Gemini**
Telarc CD-83332 *Garner; Arthur Ryerson, Wally Richardson (g); Ernest McCarty, Milt Hinton (b); George Jenkins, Herbie Lovelle, Jimmie Smith (d); Johnny Pacheco, Jose Mangual (perc).* 66–72.

Telarc has pulled these out of the lengthy list of Garner albums lying in the back-catalogue; as two-for-one deals on CD, they're decent value. That said, most of these sessions are unlikely to stir much excitement except among hardcore devotees. *Dreamstreet* is nice, the *One World* show notably lively, *That's My Kick* has a slightly augmented band with guitar and percussion, and *Gemini* found Erroll taking a turn at the harpsichord. Garner remains interesting from moment to moment, but over CD length his style's limitations tend to show up on ordinary albums, which is basically what these are.

The exception is *Close Up In Swing / A New Kind Of Love.* The first album is another regulation trio date, but the second is a film score which Garner, despite his illiteracy, put together via block arrangements that were subsequently orchestrated and left open for him to improvise the piano parts. The results say little that's profound about his music, but it's an interesting diversion to hear him magnified via a full orchestra.

*****(*) Erroll Garner Collection Vol. 1: Easy To Love**
Emarcy 832994-2 *Garner; Eddie Calhoun (b); Kelly Martin (d).* 6/61–8/65.

***** Erroll Garner Collection Vol. 2: Dancing On The Ceiling**
Emarcy 834935-2 *As above.* 6/61–8/65.

Previously unreleased material, but this is quality Garner. Both discs round up nuggets from various early-'60s sessions, and there are some fine things on both, such as the dizzying opening to 'It Had To Be You' or the prime after-hours Garner of 'Like Home'.

***** Plays Gershwin & Kern**
Mercury 826224-2 *Garner; Eddie Calhoun, Ike Isaacs (b); Kelly Martin, Jimmie Smith (d).* 8/64–2/68.

***** Jazz Around Midnight – Erroll Garner**
Verve 846191-2 *Garner; Red Callender, John Simmons, Leonard Gaskin, Wyatt Ruther (b); Lou Singer, Harold 'Doc' West, Charlie Smith, Eugene 'Fats' Heard (d).* 12/45–48.

***** Erroll Garner: Jazz Masters 7**
Verve 518197-2 *Garner; Wyatt Ruther (b); Eugene 'Fats' Heard (d); Candido Camero (perc).* 54–55.

*****(*) This Is Jazz**
Columbia CK 64968 *Garner; John Simmons, Wyatt Ruther, Al Hall (b); Shadow Wilson, Specs Powell, Eugene 'Fats' Heard (d).* 6/50–2/57.

Many of Garner's albums from the late '50s and '60s have been lost from the catalogue, and the Gershwin and Kern set is no more than typical of the period. But Garner is well served by the *Around Midnight* compilation, which closes with the very long and unpredictable 'Over The Rainbow' from *Solitaire*; and the *Jazz Masters* disc is sound value, a smart choice of solo and trio pieces from the Mercury sessions. Columbia's *This Is Jazz* is a pleasing set drawn from its various holdings; 'Moonglow' is a particularly fine treatment.

Carlos Garnett (born 1938)

TENOR, ALTO, SOPRANO AND BARITONE SAXOPHONES

Born in Panama, Garnett is a self-taught saxophonist. He arrived in New York in 1962 and worked with various leaders in the '60s and '70s, culminating in a spell with the Miles Davis electric group. In the '70s he made a string of albums which fused Panamanian music, jazz and soul, a style he called Universal Black Force. After a period of inactivity, Garnett returned to music, seemingly stronger than ever.

***** Fuego En Mi Alma**
High Note HCD 7001 *Garnett; Carlton Holmes (p); Brad Jones (b); Shingo Okudaira (d); Neil Clarke (perc).* 9/96.

*****(*) Under Nubian Skies**
High Note HCD 7023 *As above, except add Russell Gunn (t); omit Clarke.* 9/97.

Garnett's Muse albums had a bit of a cult following within the so-called acid jazz movement, but they've once again gone back into limbo. His return to active duty in the late '90s is very welcome, if the excellent *Under Nubian Skies* in particular is anything to go by. 'I feel I'm doing better soloing than I did back in my earlier days,' Garnett says, and he's right, sticking to the tenor and thinning out the verbiage of the old music. *Fuego En Mi Alma* could have used a little more contrast (supplied by Gunn on the later date), and here and there Garnett sounds just a tad rusty, but it's spirited and generous music, which the deferential rhythm section is particulary well suited to. Garnett is coming straight out of classic-period Coltrane for much of *Under Nubian Skies* and, since again the rhythm section is supportive rather than combative, it throws his sound into a sharper relief. Gunn is happy to be a good-natured foil, and there are some useful, boppish originals for them to work out on. An enjoyable surprise.

*****(*) Moon Shadow**

Savant 2011 *Garnett; Derrick Gardner (t); Robert Trowers (tb); Alvin Flythe (ts); Carlton Holmes (p); George Marshall (b); Shingo Okudaira (d); Neil Clarke (perc).* 12/99.

The renaissance continues with this fine Trane-tinged set. As usual, though, Garnett manages to avoid slavish influence. His 'Giant Steps' might well be one of the Neptune's ladders that makes up the Panama Canal. It's a briskly Latin interpretation, harmonically exact, but rhythmically much more supple than the original. The same is true of 'My Favorite Things' and also 'Softly, As In A Morning Sunrise', which hints at the Coltrane of the legendary Village Vanguard sessions.

The other horns solo only sparingly, a pity in the case of Robert Trowers, who is always worth hearing, but they do a fine job of articulating Garnett's larger vision of a pan-Afro-American musical language. Drummer Okudaira is particularly impressive and is credited with the clever modal 'McCoy On The Block'. This is another fine record from a resurgent musician.

Kenny Garrett (born 1960)

ALTO SAXOPHONE, FLUTE, OTHER INSTRUMENTS

Arrived in New York in 1980, and his stint as a sideman with Miles Davis lifted his reputation. Has since worked prolifically as both leader and sideman, close to hard-bop foundation but with an awareness of funk and everything else.

***** Introducing Kenny Garrett**

Criss Cross CRISS 1014 *Garrett; Woody Shaw (t, flhn); Mulgrew Miller (p); Nat Reeves (b); Tony Reedus (d).* 11/84.

Garrett's old boss Miles Davis once accused him of wearing 'Sonny Stitt's dirty drawers', which is a typically acute if slightly bitchy way of characterizing the youngster's plangent, blues-soaked style. Garrett was one of the more successful of Miles's later saxophonists, and he has gone on to carve a distinctive and successful career for himself as leader.

The debut on Criss Cross – Gerry Teekens has proved to be almost as prescient as Miles himself at spotting talent – is a more than decent effort. The inclusion of Woody Shaw was a powerful stroke. Woody is a far more sympathetic partner than the bustling, somewhat aggressive Roney on a subsequently deleted Paddle Wheel disc, although four years on Garrett sounds more than ready to cope with the extra octane. Roney is of course the closest thing around to Miles in his prime; Shaw is a very different stylist, superficially closer to the great man's softly enunciated tone but utterly different in his phrasing and in his approach to solos.

Garrett tackles all the material with a freshness and lack of prejudice that is instantly appealing. His bluesy phrasing is very exact, for all its relaxed delivery, and his habit of lingering on low tones just a fraction longer than you expect gives his solos a very solid, anchored presence, which has allowed him to work on occasion without a harmony instrument. It is always clear that he *hears* the bottom line very clearly, and it may even have been that facility which recommended him to Miles.

***** Prisoner Of Love**

Atlantic 82046 *Garrett; Miles Davis, Barry Lee Hall Jr (t); Muhammad Abdul Al-Khabyyr (tb); Sayydah Garrett (cl); Foley McCreary, Darryl Jones, Marcus Miller (b); Ricky Wellman (d); Rudy Bird, Mino Cinelu (perc); vocal choir.* 89.

Graced by an appearance from Miles Davis, and featuring much of the great man's working band of the time, this was Garrett's testimonial for good service. It's a well-crafted and somewhat ambitious record. Taking his cue from Marcus Miller, who plays everything going, Garrett plays all the instruments on three tracks, including an affecting and rather powerful version of 'Lift Ev'ry Voice And Sing'. Otherwise, it's pretty squarely in late Miles mode and, but for the prominence of the saxophone, many will guess that they're listening to out-takes from some otherwise undocumented session. This isn't to decry Garrett's contribution, but there is a faint sense that he is swamped by more dominant partners, guests who've hijacked his party.

***** African Exchange Student**

Atlantic 82156 *Garrett; Mulgrew Miller (p); Ron Carter, Charnett Moffett (b); Elvin Jones, Tony Reedus (d); Rudy Bird, Tito Ocasio, Steve Thornton (perc).* 90.

*****(*) Black Hope**

Warner Bros 9362 45017 *Garrett; Joe Henderson (ts); Kenny Kirkland (p, syn); Donald Brown (syn); Charnett Moffett (b); Brian Blade, Ricky Wellman (d); Don Alias (perc).* 92.

Straddling a change of label, and also something of a shift in Garrett's approach to things, these are both convincing statements by a young man still coming to terms with his artistic inheritance. The difference between them is that on *Black Hope* he is no longer processing influences but responding to predecessors as an equal. He certainly isn't put off by the presence of Henderson on 'Transit Dance' and 'Bye Bye Blackbird' on the later disc. Joe's solo construction is so magisterial that any partner runs the risk of sounding banal, but Garrett more than holds his own, and the lessons absorbed pay huge dividends on future projects. Kirkland is a more naturally lyrical player than Mulgrew Miller and provides a wider and more vivid range of colours.

As before, Garrett shows himself capable of working without a harmony instrument, and *African Exchange Student* includes a pianoless trio with Carter and Jones, good enough to make one wish for a whole album of it. Pure greed, for it's an excellent enough album as it stands, marked down only a notch for lacking overall shape and construction, too much like a hotchpotch of sessions, not enough like a coherent project.

★★★★ Triology

Warner Bros 9 45731 *Garrett; Kiyoshi Kitagawa, Charnett Moffett (b); Brian Blade (d).* 95.

This is a very special record, made with Garrett's working trio (and with a couple of tracks featuring old pal Moffett). Garrett is still content to play standards and repertoire pieces, and he brings fresh angles to Brubeck's 'In Your Own Sweet Way' and the old warhorse 'Giant Steps' which he plays with a respectful insouciance as if it really doesn't matter if he stumbles. His major encounter with Coltrane was still to come, but it is clear that Trane's music and presence are increasingly important to him at this time.

There's refreshingly little ego on any of these discs, and *Triology* above all suggests the work of a young master musician who clearly recognizes the way he has to go relative to the towering achievement that has gone before him. The dedication to Henderson and Rollins is perhaps a sign of where his thinking now lies; *pace* 'Giant Steps', Garrett doesn't sound like a Coltrane disciple, but does obviously recognize that until he confronts this giant in his lair, he cannot quite claim to have won his sword.

★★★★ Pursuance

Warner Bros 9 46209 *Garrett; Pat Metheny (g); Rodney Whitaker (b); Brian Blade (d).* 96.

Perhaps, as he worked his way through the tortuous chords of 'Giant Steps' on *Trilogy*, Kenny Garrett recognized this album would have to be made sooner or later. Coltrane tributes were ten a penny over a couple of years surrounding the 30th anniversary of his death, but this is one of the best. Having a guitarist on board, and a guitarist of Metheny's undersold gifts, opened up the structure of almost all the songs included, and Garrett's ability to second-guess harmonic progressions and a straight chordal accompaniment make this a very free interpretation indeed.

They kick off with 'Countdown' and 'Equinox', continue with 'Liberia' and 'Dear Lord', and really hit pace with a terse and wonderful version of 'After The Rain'. The title-piece begins a gigantic coda which includes a very brief, almost throwaway version of 'Giant Steps' again. The other Trane compositions included are 'Lonnie's Lament', 'Like Sonny', 'Alabama' and 'Latifa', each of them intelligently rethought and reworked.

★★★(★) Songbook

Warner Bros 9 4651 *Garrett; Kenny Kirkland (p); Nat Reeves (b); Jeff Tain Watts (d).* 97.

Almost inevitably, Garrett followed up the Coltrane project with a set entirely of originals. The big statements – 'Brother Hubbard', 'November 15' and 'She Waits For The New Sun' – all sound as if they have been gestating for some time, and are brilliantly worked by the band. Garrett at this stage could easily have gone for an augmented unit with extra horns, but it's refreshing hearing him with just rhythm again, and Kirkland responds to what was presumably new and unfamiliar material with a great deal of imagination.

The sound is very immediate, and though there are a couple of edits here and there which don't sound quite right – as if the pitch has shifted a little from one take to the next – the finished product is about as good as it could be.

★★★(★) Simply Said

Warner Bros 9 8759 *Garrett; Sheldrick Mitchell (p, org); Mulgrew Miller (p, v); Pat Metheny (g); Marcus Miller, Nat Reeves (b, v); Chris Dave, Jeff Tain Watts (d, v); Bashiri Johnson (d); Raymond Harris (v).* 98.

The absent guest here is Kenny Kirkland, who died shortly before and whose loss perhaps adds to rather than explains a rather melancholic sound to the album as a whole. Even upbeat, Garrett sounds thoughtful and even guarded. Always a player who takes time to process the lessons of the recent past, he can sound repetitive. Here, though, he cheerfully recaps and compresses solos from *Trilogy* and *Songbook*, without seeming to play musical leftovers.

Garrett's new band is fresh and unaffected. Mitchell is an interesting organ player and a decent writer as well, claiming a single but valuable credit with 'Words Can't Express'. The only question mark hangs over Dave's unvarying count. Metheny is in for only two tunes and Marcus Miller for three. Big Mulgrew has a guest spot alongside Jeff Watts, helping to keep the sound varied and subtly weighted. Pointless to expect a dramatic step forward from this patient and hard-working artist. By now, though, reasonable to expect an effective and professional statement, which is exactly what *Simply Said* is.

★★★ Happy People

Warner Bros 9362 47754-2 *Garrett; Michael Stewart (t, flhn); Vernell Brown (p); Randy Razz (g); Bobby Hutcherson (vib); Marcus Miller, Charnett Moffett (b); Chris Dave (d), Jean Norris (v).* 9/01.

★★★★ Standard Of Language

Warners 48404 *Garrett; Vernell Brown (p); Charnett Moffett (b); Chris Dave, Eric Harland (d).* 9/01, 02.

For all the shadow cast by the World Trade Center attacks, this is a happy, funky recording, almost a throwback to the kind of thing Carlos Garnett was doing back in the '70s; Grover Washington fans would find much to appreciate in it as well. The best tracks are, almost inevitably, those that feature Hutcherson, who seems to invest the whole album with his personality. Stewart brings a warm and soulful tone to the two opening tracks and Marcus Miller gives 'Song For DiFang' his usual snappy touch, punching in a wonderfully inventive countermelody. The other guests are less significant, though Randy Razz's guitar does bring an extra dimension to 'Ain't Nothing But The Blues'. We could have lived without Jean Norris's vocal contributions, but doubtless they will help pitch the record towards the club and dance market that Warners are hoping for.

Some of the tracks on the magnificent *Standard Of Language* were originally intended for the earlier album but were not deemed suitable given its tragic connotations. It's not entirely clear why. Whatever the strategic thinking, this is the album that finally clinches Warners' investment in Garrett. The long, three-part title-track is a virtual summation of all he has learned from the greats of the saxophone – Parker, Coleman, Coltrane – and a strong declaration of independence from them as well. 'XYZ' is stunning neo-bop with an old-fashioned swing. The band perform magnificently throughout and the trimmed-down personnel allows Garrett's luminous alto to shine through. Unmissable.

Michael Garrick (born 1933)

PIANO

Best known for his Jazz Praises project, Enfield-born Garrick has taken Duke's 'sacred' music on a step, using jazz as the basis for a body of liturgical music which swings with the gift of tongues. An able and dexterous soloist, he is one of the finest jazz pianists to come out of Britain since the war.

★★★★ A Lady In Waiting

Jazz Academy JAZA 1 *Garrick; Dave Green (b); Alan Jackson (d).* 93.

When the Big Audit is completed, Britain will find itself in trouble for not having disclosed a national asset on the scale of Michael Garrick, or for not having found an appropriate outlet for his talents. Even though his extra-curricular activities as teacher, writer and administrator have occasionally intruded, Garrick's fleet, uncomplacent keyboard style and elegant compositional touch have not been fully appreciated. Though perhaps best understood as a big-band composer in the tradition of Ellington, Garrick is also a formidable small-group player, and this seasoned trio plays scaled-down versions of pieces originally conceived for orchestra. The most accurate measure of the leader's skills is his approach to repertory material like Hancock's 'Dolphin's Dance' and John Lewis's wonderfully pianistic 'Two Degrees East, Three Degrees West'. The group is recorded clearly and uncomplicatedly, and the album as a whole is both exhilarating and moving.

★★★(★) Meteors Close At Hand

Jazz Academy JAZA 2 *Garrick; Andy Bush, Mike Diprose, Ollie Preece, Martin Shaw, Steve Waterman, Ian Wood (t, flhn); Brian Archer, Matt Coleman, Pat Hartley, Bill Mee, Mark D'Silva (tb); Scott Garland, Jimmy Hastings, Mike Hall, Martin Hathaway, Bob McKay, Mike Page, Jim Tomlinson, Matt Wates (sax); Phil Lee, Colin Oxley (g); Paul Moylan (b); Alan Jackson (d).* 6 & 7/94.

A generous studio sampling of material from Garrick's *Royal Box* (a reaction to tabloid mayhem) and from his Thomas Hardy, J. R. R. Tolkien and jazz character suites. Just to establish continuity with the small-group album, there is a lovely version of 'A Lady In Waiting', with solos from Bill Mee and Pat Hartley on trombones (each differently voiced), Martin Hathaway and Steve Waterman. The *Hardy Country* tunes include some of Garrick's best writing. Waterman is the star turn again on 'Middle Piddlecombe', though Garrick himself turns in a relatively rare solo on the lovely 'Blues As An Autumn Mist', which could hardly be more Ellingtonian if it tried. Portraits of Dizzy Gillespie, Arturo Sandoval and Lester Young exercise a gifted and beautifully balanced band, and the Tolkien obsession which has yielded up some of Garrick's quirkiest and most memorable writing emerges in 'River Running', a delicately phrased theme for bass clarinet, tenor saxophone and the leader's piano. Old-stagers like Jimmy Hastings and younger guys like Matt Wates and Scott Garland fill out a superb reed section. The horns aren't quite so compelling, but the arrangements are so good that the absence of fiery front-line playing isn't missed. Some quibbles about the recording, but a genial and thoroughly entertaining album.

★★★ Parting Is Such

Jazz Academy JAZA 3 *Garrick; Don Rendell (ts); Chris Garrick (vn); Dave Green (b); Alan Jackson (d).* 95.

The addition of Christian Garrick and the urbane Rendell lifts an otherwise rather one-dimensional record. In addition to nine originals, the trio tackles the famous Canteloube 'Baïlero', Lennon/McCartney's 'Here, There And Everywhere' and 'My Funny Valentine'. Garrick is on excellent and relaxed form, phrasing less formally than usual but with great expressiveness.

★★★★ For Love Of Duke ... And Ronnie

Jazz Academy JAZA 4 *Garrick; Gabriel Garrick, Ollie Preece, Steve Waterman, Ian Wood (t); Brian Archer, Bill Mee, Mark D'Silva (tb); Mike Hall, Martin Hathaway, Bob McKay, Jim Tomlinson, Matt Wates (sax); Colin Oxley (g); Paul Moylan (b); Alan Jackson (d); Jacqui Dankworth (v).* 95, 96.

★★★(★) Down On Your Knees

Jazz Academy JAZA 5 *Garrick; Mark Armstrong, Gabriel Garrick, Paul Jayasinha, Martin Shaw, Steve Waterman (t); Brian Archer, Matt Coleman, Dave Holt, Bill Mee, Mark Nightingale, Malcolm Earl Smith (tb); Paul Booth, Ben Castle, Mike Hall, Bob McKay, Jim Tomlinson, Matt Wates (sax); Dominic Ashworth (g); Paul Moylan (b); Alan Jackson (d); Anita Wardell (v).* 99.

Garrick is gradually assembling a full documentation of his output as a big-band composer. It seems on the face of it perverse that works like 'Jazz Praises' should be recorded piecemeal – another two pieces are recorded on *For Love Of ...* – except that they fit perfectly well into the broader context of his work. Equally, more of the *Hardy Country* material – 'The Storm (Was Its Lover)' – juxtaposes nicely with tunes dedicated to Ellington and written in memory of altoist Joe Harriott, whose free-form writing and playing had such a huge impact on the British scene. The final dedication is, of course, to the late Ronnie Scott, with whom Garrick worked only very rarely but for whom he shares a widespread affection and debt.

The use of Jacqui Dankworth to fill in what would have been a whole choir on the original score is underlined once again in Anita Wardell's work on the recent *Down On Your Knees*. Anita's ability to inflect songs with apposite and accurate emotion represents an important dramatic resource to Garrick, who can concentrate on leading a band of undoubted technical sophistication and iron-clad swing. The live version of 'Take The "A" Train', recorded at the Vortex club in London, is a joyous curtain-piece, but the mood overall is more thoughtful, even when the pace is intense. As ever, Garrick is mining material that goes back to the Rendell–Carr quintet of the '60s and its reaction to the advanced harmonics of the John Coltrane Quartet, while 'Torrent' is lifted from a 1970 Garrick LP, *The Heart Is A Lotus.*

Both albums are recorded quite plainly but with lots of instrumental colour and, taken together with *Meteors*, should help relocate Garrick as a major catalytic force in British jazz, a lighter-voiced but in some respects more compelling figure than the more obviously combustible Stan Tracey.

★★★(★) The New Quartet

Jazz Academy JAZA 7 *Garrick; Martin Hathaway (ss, as); Paul Moylan (b); Alan Jackson (d).* 10–11/01.

What a deliciously surprising record this is, and only those who haven't bothered to keep up with Michael *will* be surprised. He sounds playful and almost skittish, but then delivers a line of such emotional sonority that the heart skips a beat. The range of influences is now so broad-reaching that the idea that he should be influenced by anyone outside his own head almost seems absurd, except that Thelonious Monk is the presiding deity of this record, Monk and the Tatum who would also take a turn at the organ.

Hathaway is rather light-voiced and sometimes awkwardly cool when a little emotion might seem called for, but he plays beautifully on his own 'That-u-be-a Good Idea', and elsewhere makes effective and poignant entrances. 'Cappuccino Gabrieli' is a small marvel, and Garrick's ballad style is in evidence once again on 'Little Girl'. Some of the music sounds under-rehearsed and the recorded sound isn't entirely perfect, but make time for this record if you possibly can.

***** Green And Pleasant Land**

Jazz Academy JAZA 8 *Garrick; Dominic Ashworth (g); Christian Garrick (vn); Paul Moylan (b).* 10/02.

A beautiful set recorded live in the gentle acoustic of Missenden Church in Buckinghamshire, a place with important associations in Anglican life. Garrick's String Quartet is a beautifully balanced group with lots to do for all four players and no overemphasis on the piano, except as the orchestral heart of proceedings. The new writing is beautifully inflected but requires a reading of Garrick's liner-note for full appreciation, ideally beforehand because the music merits some concentration. A quiet delight, but not one you'll want to sample very often.

****(*) Peter Pan – Jazz Dance Suite**

Jazz Academy JAZA 9 *Garrick; Mark Armstrong, Quentin Collins, Gabriel Garrick, Dave Priseman, Nick Smart (t); James Adams, Dave Eaglestone, Mark D'Silva (tb); Jamie Anderson, Paul Booth, Mick Foster, Martin Hathaway, Bob McKay, Matt Wates (reeds); Dominic Ashworth, Pete Callard (g); Paul Moylan (b); Alan Jackson (d); Anita Wardell (v).* 7/03.

Written as part of his 70th birthday celebrations, this large-scale piece is wordy rather than worthy and a touch bland in its orchestration and voicing. Garrick's ability to write some of the most devastating big-band music ever heard in Europe in a jazz context seems quite far away here. *Peter Pan* draws on some elements of English pastoralism, and imports a little of the whimsy one occasionally gets from Kate and Mike Westbrook, but without their irony and savagery. Apart from 'The Lost Boys' and 'Hook' themes, it's a rather dull listen.

George Garzone (born 1950)

TENOR AND SOPRANO SAXOPHONES

Garzone is one of the most articulate and passionate educators in jazz, and his Coltrane-influenced approach is always fascinating, though scantily represented on record. He is leader of modern group The Fringe.

***** Alone**

NYC 6018 *Garzone; David Kikoski (p); Chuck Loeb (g); Mike Mainieri (vib); Eddie Gomez (b); Lenny White (d); Bashiri Johnson (perc); Luciana Souza (v).* 95.

Garzone is one of those rare players who always seem to be hovering on the brink of abandoning the chordal structure altogether, while remaining essentially faithful to it. He does that time and again here, abetted by a fine and responsive band built around Kikoski and Gomez. The leader's tenor sound is big and confident without being in any way brash, and he transforms some very familiar and rather romantic thematic material – 'Nature Boy', 'Lush Life', 'Insensatez', 'What Is This Thing Called Love?' – into strong, Trane-tinged jazz. One is constantly reminded of transitional periods in Coltrane's career while listening to this. Garzone's gift is in letting you hear how such changes took place, not just delivering a pre-set outcome. His deconstruction of 'Nature Boy' is an excellent example.

Mainieri produces and guests on vibes; Loeb provides one song, 'Anytime Tomorrow'; Souza's attractive vocals are limited to just two tracks. A strong set from a frequently overlooked performer.

***** Fours And Twos**

NYC 6024-2 *Garzone; Joe Lovano (ts); Joey Calderazzo (p); John Lockwood (b); Bill Stewart (d).* 4/96.

*****(*) Moodiology**

NYC 6031 2 *Garzone; Douglas Yates (as, bcl); Claire Daly (bs); Kenny Werner (p); Mike Mainieri (vib); John Lockwood (b); Bob Gullotti (d).* 11/98.

Garzone plays with a notably hard edge and with an unfailingly logical solo development. His great strength is the articulation and unravelling of fast-paced melody lines with a very open-ended chord-structure. Any feeling that he is trapped at the same evolutionary point as the Coltrane of the classic Atlantic sessions is easily confounded, but those albums are the best point of comparison.

Fours And Twos is the kind of thing that ends up being called a 'connoisseurs' record'. Garzone may be less renowned than front-line partner Lovano but he plays with as much authority and heft, and hearing the two tenors carve up some of these pieces – even in the oblique way that they do – is a fine example of nonconformist exhilaration. The tenor solos tend to be split up by contributions from the rhythm section so there's no sense of a cutting contest, anyway. Because there's no conscious effort at variety in the make-up of the record, it stands on the quality of thinking and execution and, abetted by a terrific trio, the saxophonists deliver royally on that count. The originals are good enough, the standards (a powerhouse 'Have You Met Miss Jones' and a sax duo on 'In A Sentimental Mood') beguiling, and they're further blessed by a vivid sound in the studio.

Moodiology is very much a tribute to friends and influences. The prelude is a dark, Trane-influenced blues, and the great man's influence is also reflected in 'Naima', though for some mysterious reason that wonderful love poem is credited as a Garzone composition. George's fragile soprano statement certainly isn't enough to wrest it from the real creator. The other repertory pieces, 'I'll Remember April', 'Summertime' and 'Soul Eyes', are handled with grace and real authority.

***** The Fringe In New York**

NYC 6034 *Garzone; Mike Mainieri (vib); John Lockwood (b); Bob Bullotti (d).* 99.

Heart-on-sleeve time again, as Garzone pays tribute to the influence of John Coltrane. He opens the album with an original 'Tribute' and closes it with a quiet, soprano interpretation of 'Central Park West', one of the few tracks on which Coltrane himself did not solo. Joe Lovano had done the same thing a year or two before on alto, but George keeps his alto in reserve to overdub lines to the free-flowing melodies of 'Anthony Goes To Mardi Gras' and 'A Fox In The Woods'.

Mainieri is again present for the majority of numbers, though he wisely sits out the breakneck 'Ultra Tempo', which is clearly improvised by the basic group but presumably required some careful training beforehand. Mainieri's 'Plus One' is an attractive blues. Garzone generally sticks to tenor but shows signs here of wanting to vary his sound; the soprano lines of 'Between Two Cities' suggest he may do more in that gentler direction.

Geoff Gascoyne

BASS

British bassist with a wide range of stylistic experience. An occasional leader with a number of high-profile associations.

★★★(★) **Voices Of Spring**
Jazzizit JITCD 9605 *Gascoyne; Gerard Presencer (flhn); Andy Panayi (ts, f); Tim Garland, Mark Lockheart (ts); Gareth Williams (p); Jim Mullen (g); Jeremy Stacey (d); Claire Martin, Ian Shaw (v).* 9/95.

★★★ **Winter Wonderland**
Jazzizit JITCD 9710 *Gascoyne; Andy Panayi (ss, af); Pete Churchill (p); Adam Glasser (hca).* 3–7/97.

★★★(★) **Autumn**
Jazzizit JITCD 0026 *Gascoyne; Ben Castle (ss, ts); Jim Watson (p); Steve Brown (d).* 99.

Voices Of Spring showcases both Gascoyne's elegant playing and writing and the smart, unfussy methods of a stalwart group of British performers. The four horns each make excellent cameos, with the saxophonists in particular showing strong individual colours, and Martin and Shaw have a distinctive song apiece. Old salt Mullen lends some nonchalant fire, and the leader has the wit to feature himself sparingly. The excellent studio sound ices the cake.

Winter Wonderland is a Christmas album and among the prettiest of its genre. It is mostly duets between Churchill and Gascoyne, with the melodies surviving a modest element of improvisation.

If you wanted to sample something of what was going on in British jazz as it stood at the end of the 20th century, you could do a great deal worse than going to *Autumn*. There are nine originals by Geoff and two unexpected choices of cover performed by a top-drawer group. Castle's slippery, unpredictable phrasing and the admirable work done by two rising 'stars' – Watson and Brown – make the most of the opportunities in the writing, which is both catchy and musically substantial. A very satisfying hour of jazz.

Giorgio Gaslini (born 1929)

PIANO, KEYBOARDS

Studied composition in Milan, and composed and conducted into the early '60s, before forming a jazz quartet, which he performed with in factories and hospitals in an effort to bring jazz to a new audience. Has written operas and large-scale works, along with striking revisions of familiar composers. One of the most distinguished players in the Italian jazz lineage.

★★★ **L'Integrale No. 1, No. 2**
Soul Note 121350/1-2 2CD *Gaslini; Nino Impallomeni, Giulio Libano (t); Raoul Ceroni (tb); Gino Stefani (cl); Lorenzo Nardini (cl, as); Gianni Bedori (as, bs, f); Marcello Boschi (as); Eraldo Volonté (ts); Gastone Tassinari (f); Mario Loschi (ob); Antonio De Serio, Bruno Crovetto, Alceo Guatelli (b); Gil Cuppini, Ettore Ulivelli, Franco Tonani (d).* 48–64.

★★★(★) **L'Integrale No. 3, No. 4**
Soul Note 121352/3-2 2CD *Gaslini; Don Cherry, Enrico Rava (t); Dino Piana (tb); Lorenzo Nardini (sno); Steve Lacy (ss); Gianni Bedori (as, ts, bs, f, picc); Gato Barbieri (ts); Eros Ferraresi, Mario Macchio (vn); Enrico Fiorini (vla); Dino Bazzano (clo); Bruno Crovetto, Kent Carter, Jean-François Jenny-Clark (b); Franco Tonani, Gianni Cazzola (d); orchestra, choir.* 64–68.

The years roll back for Giorgio Gaslini. In a rare example of a reissue retrospective on Soul Note, the pianist's early chapters are dusted off for this four-CD archive. If the first two discs seem for the most part to be 'prentice work, they're not without interest. As early as 1948, still in his teens, Gaslini was arranging 'Night In Tunisia' and writing his own 'Bop-Bop' and 'Drums Be-Bop' for Gil Cuppini's sextet. From there, it's a jump to 1957 and a five-part piece for octet; then his quartet music for Antonioni's *La Notte*; and finally the formation of his famous quartet with Gianni Bedori, Bruno Crovetto and Franco Tonani. The entire second disc is given over to his 'Dall'Alba All'Alba' suite for the group. Rather dustily recorded, most of this music is for Gaslini specialists, but even here there's plenty of material for the most elegant kind of crossovers – of jazz with a series of Italian musical traditions.

The third and fourth discs continue the matter. 'Dodici Canzoni D'Amore' sets a dozen Italian love-songs to a treatment by Gaslini's group and a small string ensemble. The shabby recording doesn't help, and there are a few curious touches, such as an uncredited organ which makes theremin-like sounds here and there. Gaslini says that he gave the piano the responsibility for pathos, while the others handled the atmosphere. It's a curious but beguiling piece. His score for another film, *Un Amore*, takes up the rest of disc three: the quartet with orchestra and choir. If the orchestral parts sound very like vintage Morricone, that may be because they're men of like mind; either way, this is lightweight.

The fourth disc revives his most celebrated piece of the period, 'New Feelings', with Cherry, Lacy, Barbieri, Jenny-Clark and some Italian homeboys. As a clash of serialism and free playing, it has its awkward moments and, since Gaslini wrote the basic score only the night before, it's scarcely a well-prepared scenario: but all the players must have embraced the occasion, since the enthusiasm of the playing endures. Back to the quartet for 'La Stagione Incantata', a four-seasons suite: Bedori in particular sounds as if he's been liberated by his work on 'New Feelings', and in long form Gaslini makes increasing use of space, texture and astringent melodic variation. Newcomers should start with some of the later records, but the pianist's admirers will welcome these adventurous reissues.

★★★★ **Gaslini Plays Monk**
Soul Note 121020 *Gaslini (p solo).* 5/81.

★★★ **Schumann Reflections**
Soul Note 121120 *Gaslini; Piero Leveratto (b); Paolo Pellegatti (d).* 7/84.

Only a performer and composer whose stated aim is 'total music', a grand unified synthesis of jazz, serialism, pop, classical forms and electro-acoustic procedures, could possibly relate with equal ease to Thelonious Monk, Robert Schumann and Albert Ayler. This, though, is what the remarkable Milanese has done. Playing and writing since his early teens, he has combined jazz with orchestral music, and he is an experienced conductor. As the Monk album clearly demonstrates, his sense of form is rock solid, and what may be surprising about these tracks is how little he attempts to subvert the basic outlines. He remains faithful to the outlines of the piece from first to last but is obviously intrigued by internal consistencies, rhymes and chimes, and he blends individual songs into an elegantly crafted suite which ought to be listened to as a whole if possible.

The Schumann material is less obviously tractable to this kind of performance, and there are moments when one will have the impression of listening to a Bill Evans record put through some strange diffraction grid. The harmonic richness of the original leaves an improviser with less to do than when dealing with the bone and sinew of a Monk tune, but at the same time with an infinity of possibilities that may trip up even a subtle improviser. The trio setting doesn't seem quite right for this material, and Pellegatti is a rather lumpish player for jazz.

*** Multiple

Soul Note 121220 *Gaslini; Roberto Ottaviano (as, ss, sno, bcl); Claudio Fasoli (ts, ss); Bruno Tommaso (b); Giampiero Prina (d).* 10/87.

This is an interesting group. Ottaviano is more than just a utility player, but he has certainly traded in soloistic virtuosity in favour of an ability to create a spectrum of sound-textures. Fasoli is more obviously straightahead and, as the spearhead of the group with Gaslini, he makes for a convincing front-man. The rhythm section sounds terribly European, not because it doesn't swing but because the swing is so terribly exact and unvaried. A little bend and stretch here and there would improve this session immeasurably, and yet it's a record one goes back to, more out of curiosity than affection, but often enough to suggest that it has its virtues.

***(*) Ayler's Wings

Soul Note 121270 *Gaslini (p solo).* 7/90.

An extraordinary undertaking. Transcribing Albert Ayler, seemingly the most anti-pianistic of improvisers, would appear to be an almost absurdly quixotic task. So much of what Ayler was about fell between the conventional pitches that it would seem impossible to render it on a piano, and yet Gaslini converts that fierce microtonality into ripples and arpeggios that are as provocative as they are unexpectedly appealing. There is not as much darkness and passion as one would expect to hear, given the source material, but in its place there is a sort of grandeur that Albert never quite achieved. Superimposing 'Omega Is The Alpha' over 'Bells' is an oddity that works against the odds, and the versions of 'Ghosts' and 'Truth Is Marching In' have a Bachian simplicity. A genuine homage, profoundly felt and wholly successful. Some question marks about the recording; none about the music therein.

**** Lampi

Soul Note 121290 *Gaslini; Daniele Di Gregorio (vib, mar, perc); Roberto Bonati (b); Giampiero Prina (d).* 1/94.

One of Gaslini's most characteristic devices is a sudden dead halt over a heavy drum-beat. On *Lampi* it stands for the shocked pause that comes between a bolt of lightning (which is what the word means) and the rumble of thunder. In that flashbulb silence, nothing but the sound of the heart, and Gaslini plays strange tricks with the pulse rate on this remarkable record, pushing and stretching the beat, setting one instrument against the others, bending time. Never before has he made such imaginative use of percussion; Di Gregorio is a more than able second lead, a player with ideas of his own and a technique that recalls Bobby Hutcherson. Bonati and Prina fulfil their roles more modestly, but neither sounds out of sympathy with this demanding music.

***(*) Jelly's Back In Town

DDQ 128020 *Gaslini; Paolo Fresu, Umberto Marcandalli, Sergio Orlandi (t); Luca Begonia, Pierluigi Salvi (tb); Oscar Gelmi (hn); Tino Tracanna (ts, ss); Gianluigi Trovesi (as, bcl); Guido Bombardieri, Maurizio Moraschini (as, cl); Alberto Nacci (ts); Roger Rota (bs); Maurizio Beltrami (f, picc); Ugo Gelmi (bsn); Adelio Leoni (g); Fabrizio Garofoli (p); Sandro Massazza (b); Vittorio Marinoni (d); Stefano Bertoli (perc); Silvia Infascelli (v).* 2/96.

Monk, Schumann, Ayler ... and now Jelly Roll Morton. Gaslini's arrangements are embedded into a suite which in the pale, bleached light of the city at dawn – 'La citta all'alba' – allows Morton to move freely between past and present, between the roots of jazz and its uncertain future. After 'Billy Goat Stomp', there are three Creole and French songs from Louisiana, tiny and exquisitely played. After that, 'Spanish Swat', 'Wolverine Blues' and 'Freakish', and then a real shock, the 'Miserere' from *Trovatore*, a shock because it serves as a further reminder of the sheer diversity of Morton's sources. The remainder of the set is less compelling, though Gaslini's original material is superb. The Ensemble Mobile was convened for the festival at Bergamo, and the three guest soloists – Fresu, Tracanna (a revelation) and Trovesi – provide an appealing diversity of approach.

***(*) Mister O

Soul Note 121300 *Gaslini; Livio Simone Ramasso (c); Luca Calabrese, Sergio Casesi, Alberto Mandarini (t); Gianpiero Malfatto, Lauro Rossi (tb); Erik Zavaroni (tba); Giulio Visibelli (f); Gianluigi Trovesi (as, ss); Maurizio Moraschini, Guido Bombardieri (as, cl); Riccardo Luppi (ts, ss); Carlo Actis Dato (bs, bcl); Michelangelo Cagnetta, Vitaliano De Rossi (vn); Stefano Montaldo (vla); Andrea Anzalone (clo); Vittorio Rabagliati (p); Daniele Di Gregorio (vib, xyl, perc); Roberto Bonati (b); Giampiero Prina (d); Arturo Testa, Paolo Lorenzi, Bernardo Lanzetti, Maurizio Sciuto, Laura Conti, Marco Radaelli, Cristiano Pecchio, Piero Lucarelli, Luca La Penna, Lucia Minetti, Rosella Liberti, Daniela Panetta (v).* 7/96.

Mister O is the Moor Othello, transposed and transformed in this ambitious jazz-opera. Gaslini has experimented with theatrical and staged performances for many years, including an early attempt at an operatic event based on the life of Malcolm X, but this is the most ambitious thing he has written to date. To a large extent, it falls outside the strict remit of this *Guide*, but there is enough of a jazz element, and it is close enough to past work – notably the 'Miserere' on the last record – for it to be of interest to anyone who has kept pace this far. Arturo Testa is superb as Mister O, and Paolo Lorenzi is convincingly frail as 'Des' (Desdemona), but the key performance is, as it should be, Bernardo Lanzetti's as Jago. He is some distance from Verdi's villain, a more moderate and humane creation with a defence of forgivable weakness on his side. Also in the mix, three rappers and young people of the New Village, who bring a contemporary slant to the story. Vittorio Franchini has been a collaborator with Gaslini for some time; he excels himself here. The jazz orchestra performs magnificently. With solo space at a premium, individual voicings become ever more important. Every instrument is registered cleanly and vividly; every bar and phrase is made to count.

*****(*) Enigma**
Soul Note 121390-2 *Gaslini; Alberto Mandarini, Mario Cavallaro, Warner Borgia (t); Gianpiero Malfatto, Beppe Caruso (tb); Gavino Mele (frhn); Achille Succi, Alessandro Benassi (as, cl, bcl); Riccardo Luppi (ts, f); Rossano Emili (bs); Daniele Di Gregorio (vib, perc); Erik Zavaroni (tba); Roberto Bonati (b); Giampiero Prina (d).* 9/00–3/01.

Gaslini's latest group, Proxima Centauri Orchestra, at work on two new compositions and a theme borrowed from Sun Ra. 'Enigma' itself is three 'sets' and an aria to close. The Ra piece, 'Lanquidity', opens with a beautiful piano solo on the theme, before the rhythm section join in, and some of the horns arrive, sparingly, before the close: a lovely homage to the Saturnian. The big piece is the ten-part 'Planets Promenade Suite', at just over 30 minutes. As ever, the composer introduces all shadings of his musical interests, yet in the main this is Gaslini's most conventional large-scale music: anyone familiar with modern big-band procedure will find nothing intimidating here, just excellent playing by a picked team on imaginative material.

Gaslini admirers may also like to investigate *Song Book Vol. 1* (Agora AG 261), a collection of what might be described as his art-song work, performed by three singers with the composer accompanying.

***** Sacred Concert/Jazz Te Deum**
Soul Note 121420-2 *Gaslini; Paolo Fresu (t); Orchestra Jazz della Sardegna; Coro Polifonico.* 6/00.

Both like and unlike an Ellington Sacred Concert, this is testing ground for Gaslini. The 'Sacred Concert' itself lasts some 23 minutes and has both text and music by Gaslini; the 'Te Deum' is in three parts (music by Gaslini, Gabriele Verdinelli and Bruno Tommaso) and runs for 50 minutes. Mostly it's a convincing mix of disciplines. The 'Concert' is more of a concert piece, but the solo voices have a freedom of expression which is different from most liturgical music, and the discreet use of a rhythm section adds an alternative pulse. There's the odd echo of something like *Jesus Christ Superstar*, perhaps, and like Ellington, Gaslini is too urbane to settle for creative humility. The 'Te Deum' uses the orchestra more vividly, although ultimately the piece can't quite transcend its episodic nature (and Tommaso's music is some of the most interesting). The live recording is all right, although a classical producer would likely find it less than acceptable.

Gateway

GROUP

Convened for a single ECM date in 1975, the group subsequently reconvened for a second set in 1977 and then for a belated revisitation in 1994.

***** Gateway**
ECM 829192-2 *John Abercrombie (g); Dave Holland (b); Jack DeJohnette (d).* 3/75.

***** Gateway 2**
ECM 847323-2 *As above.* 7/77.

*****(*) Homecoming**
ECM 527637-2 *As above.* 12/94.

*****(*) In The Moment**
ECM 529346-2 *As above.* 12/94.

It's part of the mythology of American culture that there are no second acts and that you can't go home again. The appearance in 1995 of a new Gateway record confounded all that. An almost two-decade gap had cemented the instinctive understanding of three players who, one way and another, had pegged out much of the territory of modern jazz. Abercrombie's gently arpeggiated and almost countrified picking had been one of the definitive sounds of ECM's early years. Holland and DeJohnette came with more baggage than it seemed possible to carry and, predictably, the first album didn't quite gel. The bassist sounds almost pedestrian in places, seemingly not fired by Abercrombie's writing, and it's interesting that, when the group reconvenes in 1994, the title-piece of *Homecoming* is a long Holland composition that addresses exactly the shortcomings of the first disc. *Gateway 2* was an engaging enough follow-up, but it has all the hallmarks of an obligatory sequel. Still, the group's early-'90s live appearances were revelatory and sent fans scurrying back to the original records; whatever their shortcomings, they retained a freshness that is as engaging as it is unexpected. *In The Moment* is supergroup playing of a high order, three hugely experienced musicians interacting without anxiety and with dazzling ease. The long 'Shrubberies' is probably the best single item in the Gateway catalogue, and if anyone has yet to sample the group, this is the place to start. Since the tenth anniversary of that reunion is already upon us, wouldn't it be nice to have to do it all one more time?

Jacques Gauthé (born 1939)

CLARINET, SOPRANO SAXOPHONE

Gauthé is a Frenchman who heard Bechet in Paris in the '50s and has been trying to follow in those footsteps ever since. His Creole Rice Yerba Buena Jazz Band also draws inspiration from the Lu Watters–Monte Ballou style of Californian revivalism.

*****(*) Someday, Sweetheart**
GHB BCD-299 *Gauthé; Scott Black, Chris Tyle (c, v); Tom Ebbert (tb); John Royen (p); Amy Sharpe (bj); Tom Saunders (tba, v); Trevor Richards (d).* 7/89.

***** Paris Blues**
Stomp Off 1216 *Gauthé; Daniel Barda (tb); Alain Marquet (cl); Louis Mazetier (p); Enzo Mucci (bj, g); Michel Marcheteau (sou).* 2/90.

*****(*) Creole Jazz**
Stomp Off 1256 *Gauthé; Chris Tyle (t); Duke Heitger (c); John Gill (tb, ky, d, v); Tom Ebbert (tb); Steve Pistorius (p); Amy Sharpe (bj); Tom Saunders (tba); Hal Smith (d).* 7/92.

*****(*) Yerba Buena Style**
GHB BCD-331 *Gauthé; Duke Heitger, Chris Tyle (t); John Gill (tb, v); Bob Helm (cl, as); Steve Pistorius (p); Tom Saunders (b, tba); Jeff Hamilton, Kenny Hall (d).* 4/94.

***** Echoes Of Sidney Bechet**
Good Time Jazz 15006 *Gauthé; Duke Heitger (t); Mike Owen (tb); Steve Pistorius (p); Lars Edegran (g); Tom Saunders (b); Chris Tyle (d).* 1/97.

Gauthé has been leading the Creole Rice Jazz Band in New Orleans for many years. His passionate dedication to Sidney Bechet gets full rein on the Good Time Jazz disc, which sounds as if the old master has walked into the '90s without blinking and set down his favourite pieces in modern sound. Gauthé walks a slightly awkward line between homage and pure re-creation here, playing soprano almost throughout, but the sheer intensity of his mission is rather inspiring – after all, in a world full of Coltrane disciples, Bechet's followers aren't exactly swarming all over the bandstands. The band tends to play second fiddle here – a further step towards authenticity.

On the other discs, Gauthé grants more space all round. *Paris Blues*, cut on a return visit home to France, is meant as a two-clarinet showcase with Marquet, yet the quickfire Mazetier and the barking Barda get in plenty of shots of their own. Gauthé sticks to clarinet on both this and *Creole Jazz*, finding as much Dodds as Bechet.

We would pick *Creole Jazz* as just about the best of these, since the material is a cheerful set of crusty antiques such as 'Auntie Skinner's Chicken Dinner', revivalist set-pieces like the Claude Luter tunes and silvery memories of Armstrong, Morton and Oliver. But the earlier *Someday, Sweetheart* is only a whisker behind – lots of Oliver and Armstrong performed modestly but with no little skill and warmth. And *Yerba Buena Style*, on which Bob Helm, the venerable sideman of Lu Watters, joins in, has many roaring moments, especially on the first session with eight pieces and a two-trumpet front line; try the tempestuous assault on 'Flat Foot'.

***** Bechet Summit**

GHB BCD-397 *Gauthé; Claude Luter (cl, ss); Bob Wilber (cl); Steve Pistorius (p); Lars Edegran (g); Tom Saunders (b); Chris Tyle (d).* 5/97.

Gauthé, Luter and Wilber have all been playing long enough to assert themselves over Bechet's looming influence, and if this is mostly material associated with the master, they play it as themselves. Wilber is present on only the first two tracks, and thereafter Gauthé and Luter perform a gentlemanly joust, with the rhythm team in jolly support. Undemanding fun.

Charles Gayle (born 1939)

TENOR AND SOPRANO SAXOPHONES, BASS CLARINET, PIANO, VIOLA

Born in Buffalo, Gayle had a shadowy jazz presence prior to the late '80s, when he was suddenly lionized as a master of unadorned free playing in a style after Albert Ayler. Often playing as a street musician, and sometimes allegedly homeless or without material possessions, he is a mix of folkloric savant and nurtured star-performer.

****(*) Always Born**

Silkheart 115 *Gayle; John Tchicai (as, ts); Sirone (b); Reggie Nicholson (d).* 4/88.

***** Homeless**

Silkheart 116 *Gayle; Sirone (b); Dave Pleasant (d).* 4/88.

*****(*) Spirits Before**

Silkheart 117 *As above.* 4/88.

Gayle's early music seems like mere sketchwork for what was to come. He lived the life of a street musician in Manhattan for some years, and these three records were all recorded in the same week on what was effectively a field trip by Silkheart. Gayle is like a folk musician in other ways: he harks back to unreconstructed energy music of the '60s, blowing wild, themeless lines with an abandon that sometimes sounds neurotic, sometimes pleading, occasionally euphoric. He seems oblivious to all fashions in jazz, keeps faith with only a few players – drummer Pleasant, whose fractured and weirdly illogical time is a prime feature, and bassist Sirone appear to be two of them – and questions the status quo with unblinking certainty. *Always Born* is a well-meaning failure through Tchicai's efforts. Gayle wasn't really meant to play with another saxophonist, even a venerable veteran of the wave which he harks back to. *Homeless* and, especially, *Spirits Before* are the real, hard stuff, with 'Give' a particularly knotty and troubling performance.

CORE COLLECTION

♛ ** Touchin' On Trane**

FMP CD 48 *Gayle; William Parker (b); Rashied Ali (d).* 10–11/91.

Gayle's subsequent records still seem like an astonishing outburst, even in the aftermath of so many kinds of free-jazz outrage. Perhaps it is Gayle's starkness and simplicity which are so disturbing. He has clearly developed the iron chops that go with playing in the open for hours on end, but the conception and realization of these records is monumental. His holy, holy delivery inevitably makes one think of both Coltrane and Ayler in their most consciously spiritual guise, and a performance like 'Jesus Christ And Scripture' (on *Repent*, below) has all the biblical intensity that one might imagine; but there is also Gayle's own superbly harsh lyricism to go with that. He is unusually adept at both the highest register of the tenor and control of the most outlandish overblowing. Solos are not so much fashioned as drawn straight from the moment; all that seems to be created in advance is an instantaneous planning of a performance that might run on seemingly without end.

The outright masterpiece is the FMP album, which seems likely to be a central document in the free music of the decade. The three men touch on Coltrane from moment to moment (and Ali renews his old relationship in triumph) but this is new, brilliant, eloquent free playing.

****** Repent**

Knitting Factory Works KFWCD 122 *Gayle; Vattel Cherry, Hilliard Greene (b); David Pleasant (d).* 1–3/92.

****** More Live**

Knitting Factory Works KFWCD 137 2CD *As above, except add William Parker (b, cel, vn), Michael Wimberley, Marc Edwards (d); omit Greene and Pleasant.* 1–2/93.

****** Consecration**

Black Saint 120138-2 *As above, except omit Edwards.* 4/93.

*****(*) Translations**

Silkheart SHCD 134 *As above.* 1/93.

*****(*) Raining Fire**

Silkheart SHCD 137 *As above.* 1/93.

***** Kingdom Come**

Knitting Factory Works KFW157 *Gayle; William Parker (b); Sunny Murray (d). n.d.*

*****(*) Unto I Am**

Victo CD032 *Gayle (ts, p, bcl, d solo).* 9/94.

The rhythm-players on the Knitting Factory and Black Saint records are all little known, apart from the admirable Parker, who is as central to events as he is with Cecil Taylor; but they are wonderfully behind Gayle all the way. The opening of 'Deliverance' (*More Live*) suggests that they would be quite an ensemble even without him. The two records cut live at New York's Knitting Factory are exhausting manifestos (particularly the double-disc set) which struggle towards ecstasy or chaos, depending on one's own tolerance. A piece such as 'Sanctification' (*More Live*) certainly goes further in building on Ayler's legacy than even Brötzmann ever has. *Consecration* catches them in the studio and shows only the slightest scaling-down, with 'Justified' another *tour de force*.

It might seem as if Gayle was suddenly being too widely documented, and it's true that his records tend to follow similar patterns. But so far they are still unlike one another. The two newer Silkheart releases feature more by his working quartet, and though two discs without much relief is probably too much even for Gayle addicts, it can't be denied that there's some awesomely powerful interaction here. The only weak spot is Gayle's taste for instruments which don't really suit him; he fiddles away on a viola for some of the time, and it's no more enlightening than Ornette Coleman's violin-playing.

Kingdom Come gets its power from three serene, muscular encounters with Murray and Parker. The drummer doesn't seem to be quite the force of old but he does well enough, and Gayle marches almost obliviously on. Two piano solos and a trio are less inspiring. The all-solo Victo release has a dispensable drum solo and a middling work-out on piano again; but the two tenor solos and the bass-clarinet item are astoundingly heavyweight pieces. Gayle has never sounded as close-up and direct as he does here, the saxophone terrorizing the microphone. And the quality of his thinking is remarkable, even as he appears to lose himself in the music.

***** Berlin Movement From Future Years**
FMP CD 90 *Gayle; Vattel Cherry (b); Michael Wimberley (d).* 8/93.

***** Abiding Variations**
FMP CD 100 *As above.* 8/93.

*****(*) Testaments**
Knitting Factory KFW 174 *Gayle; Wilber Morris (b); Michael Wimberley (d).* 7/95.

***** Delivered**
2.13.61 21324-2 *Gayle; James Jones (p); Gerald Benson (b); Kalil Madi (d). n.d.*

*****(*) Daily Bread**
Black Saint 120158-2 *Gayle; William Parker (clo, p); Wilber Morris (b); Michael Wimberly (d, vn).* 10/95.

****** Solo In Japan**
PSF PSFD-94 *Gayle (ss, ts, p solo).* 7/97.

Recent Gayle records have been somewhat mixed in their impact, even diffuse at times. The *Berlin* date on FMP is disappointingly cloudy, and for all its strength-sapping length, this is a merely middling performance from the trio. *Abiding Variations* offers a second helping from the same period. On Henry Rollins's 2.13.61 label, *Delivered* is similarly underachieved; Jones, Benson and Madi make an unremarkable crew who don't do enough to take the ear but won't stay entirely out of Gayle's way. Only a fierce medley of spirituals makes an impression. *Testaments* is much more severe and reaches its apogee in the monolith of 'Faith Evermore', a tenor saxophone outburst that can stand with any of Gayle's great moments. He still defuses the overall impact with bass clarinet and piano, though.

Daily Bread is another great one. This time, Gayle's doubling lends context and breadth, and when all four men are playing strings (on 'Our Sins' and 'Offering To Christ') the results turn string-quartet music inside out. 'Earthly Things' and 'Shout Merrily' are terrific group performances as well as signature Gayle.

The second all-solo album is an unrelieved masterpiece, the sound tattooed on the air, each phrase carved and sculpted with the cruel intensity of an artist utterly driven. Unglamorous but truthful, the studio sound catches a musician with his guard down but with his delivery unflinching. Gayle still insists on picking up the soprano or turning to the piano, yet when alone with the tenor he creates some of the most disturbingly powerful music jazz has yet borne witness to.

***** Ancient Of Days**
Knitting Factory KFW 263 *Gayle; Hank Johnson (p); Juni Booth (b); Michael Wimberley (d).* 9/99.

With a stack of albums behind him in a short space of time, suddenly Gayle almost seems like an artist with his own repertory, his own 'expected' record. So he does some surprising things here: enlist a pianist and keep himself within a relatively tractable orbit, not so much diminishing the great sound but rationalizing it ('Draw Me Nearer' is still close to overpowering, nevertheless). By the standards of other Gayle records, he sounds almost tamed. It's still a considerable passion.

***** Jazz Solo Piano**
Knitting Factory KFW 288 *Gayle (p solo).* 00.

Not so much a departure – Gayle has, after all, played piano on numerous sets already – but the cover photo alone, of a very dapper gentleman looking as if he's ready to take his place at the hotel lobby's keyboard, is a surprise, and this set amounts to an idiosyncratic conflation of jazz-piano lore. 'Cherokee' and 'All The Things You Are' have certainly not been sighted in a Gayle set-list hitherto.

Gianni Gebbia (born 1961)

SOPRANO, ALTO AND BARITONE SAXOPHONES

Italian saxophonist who is a determined exponent of free improvisation in extremis.

***** Cappuccini Klang**
Splasc(h) CDH 383 *Gebbia; Peter Kowald (b); Gunter Sommer (d).* 3/92.

The Italian improvisation scene is one which remains all too little known in the rest of Europe. A somewhat abstract performer, Gebbia has won the respect and the unflagging support of players of Peter Kowald's stature. This tireless promoter of new talent, ably abetted by Sommer, gives the young man exactly the platform he needs for a fierce, undogmatic programme of improvisations. It might be argued that he errs on the side of abstraction, especially on soprano, where he exploits the treacherous pitching to the full, and there are moments on the Splasc(h) when one hankers after a measure of straightforward lyricism. The 'Cappuccini Suite', though, is exemplary, with some wry pseudo-classical gestures that recall his fellow-countryman, Giorgio Gaslini.

*****(*) Body Limits**
Splasc(h) CDH 462 *Gebbia (as solo).* 95.

The spirit of Braxton's pioneering *For Alto* shouldn't be far away from this, and yet Gebbia seems to come from an entirely different sound-world, one in which Lee Konitz and Ornette Coleman battle without much conviction for his soul. There are 17 tracks, most of them not unexpectedly very short, and Gebbia gets a sound from his 1961 Selmer Mark VI (so we are told) which is both classical and utterly contemporary, idiosyncratic and squarely in the tradition.

***** Il Libro Degli Eroi**
Victo CD 051 *Gebbia; Vittorio Villa (d, perc, didjeridu, v); Miriam Palma (v, perc).* 5/97.

The combination of saxophone (including the eldritch sopranino on this occasion), percussion and voice gives this live set from the Musique Actuelle Festival at Victoriaville an unexpected power and presence. As the title suggests, Gebbia is dealing with strong psychic presences, and his playing suggests exorcism as well as straightforward expressiveness. There are ugly aspects to this record, not just technically but also in the music itself. Not everyone will be convinced, and our advice is to start with the solo saxophone pieces and then perhaps forage a little further afield.

***** H Portraits**
Rastascan 37 *Gebbia (as solo).* 98.

***** People In Motion**
Rastascan 44 *Gebbia; Damon Smith (b); Garth Powell (d, perc).* 99.

Intense as he is, Gebbia is also capable of wit and humour, and there is plenty on these two recent issues. The earlier record is a series of improvisations, all inspired by someone or something beginning with the letter H: anyone from Heisenberg to Humpty Dumpty to Houdini to Hemphill. The delivery is much as usual: cracked, slightly forced but consistently inventive.

The trio record is more conventional, though it is still some way removed from a conventional jazz idiom. Between the cover, showing police restraining (anti-war) demonstrators, and the wailing themes developed on tunes like 'All Across The Nation' and 'There's A Whole Generation', it may be that Gebbia is gently guying the American jazz of the '60s. There are certainly hints of Coltrane, Ayler, Coleman and, perhaps above all, Sanders in his delivery. Smith and Powell play a pretty supportive role and are occasionally surplus to requirements altogether, though the percussionist does a nice line in whirlophones.

Jonathan Gee

PIANO, VOCAL

Young British pianist working in the homegrown post-bop environment.

***** Closer To**
ASC CD14 *Gee; Steve Rose (b); Winston Clifford (d).* 7/95–9/96.

***** Your Shining Heart**
ASC CD21 *As above.* 9/97.

Gee is a strong and imaginative pianist whose progress has been a pleasure to observe for British gig-goers over recent years. These outings as a trio-leader aren't so much premature as slightly compromised by the homebrew limitations of record-making in local jazz. Patched together from three sessions, *Closer To* has an unglamorous sound which does the players few favours and detracts from some interesting writing and a couple of shrewd covers – 'Bye Bye Blackbird' has an almost Tristano-ish feel, and Kenny Wheeler's 'Everybody's Song But My Own' is tersely lyrical. *Your Shining Heart* is much stronger – better recorded (though still less than ideal), better played and, with eight originals by Gee, an intelligent showcase for his composing. Listen to the ingenious climax of 'The Frevo Dreaming' or the pellucid feel of the melodies he draws out of the title-piece. Besides his own playing, the record is a fine opportunity to hear Winston Clifford, another national treasure, and a brilliant exponent of kit-playing that draws the ear without unsettling the group. They will make better records yet, but this one's worth auditioning.

*****(*) Chez Auguste**
Jazz House JHCD 064 *As above.* 4/00.

Still no more than a live set from a night – actually three – at Ronnie's, but the trio gets stronger, smarter and more stylishly inventive every time. Gee's not afraid to keep pieces to sometimes astringent durations – here, 'Catwoman' and 'Velvet Cloud' don't even break the four-minute barrier – and though he's the dominant force, he wants the music to sound like trio music, and a solo philosophy is integrated into a bigger, more outward-looking design. Some passages still sound sketched rather than inked-in, and Gee's use of repetition is sometimes, well, repetitious, but that's the prerogative of musicians with plenty of capacity to progress.

***** Wishbone**
33 Jazz 088 *Gee; Steve Rose (b); Winston Clifford (d).* 10/99–7/03.

Just one track by the trio, from a live gig in Azerbaijan, of all places; then it's the solo Gee – as well as the singing Gee, a progression whose merits we are rather undecided on. Give him his due, he recorded it all before the Jamie Cullum phenomenon took hold. But the Ellington tunes he chose as vocal vehicles are quite a tough ask for a singer making his debut. The solo pieces work an effective line between structure and some free-thinking solos, but the trio track is good enough to make one wish for more from that gig.

Matthew Gee (1925–79)

TROMBONE

Born in Houston, Gee played with Dizzy Gillespie, Illinois Jacquet and Count Basie in the '50s, but his most important association was with Duke Ellington, 1959–63. He slipped away from view after that, though he continued to perform in clubs.

***** Jazz By Gee**
Original Jazz Classics OJC 1884 *Gee; Kenny Dorham (t); Ernie Henry (as); Frank Foster (ts); Cecil Payne (bs); Joe Knight (p); John Simmons, Wilbur Ware (b); Art Taylor (d).* 7–8/56.

The notes contain a verdict that Gee was one of the best bop-influenced trombonists, but he seems ill-suited to leadership duties on this pair of serviceable but sloppy sessions. He shares the front line with Henry on one and with Dorham,

Foster and Payne on the other, and the record seems rowdy and ill-judged. Gee's solos veer between a barking delivery and a much more subtle, almost inward-looking manner: listen to his solo on, of all things, 'Sweet Georgia Brown'. There's a rare chance to hear Henry on the quintet titles, but he doesn't seem at his most interesting. The septet titles are better, more organized, and if nobody exactly covers themselves with glory, at least the music has a curious vividness to it: it sounds more interesting than some of the more efficient records of the period.

Geisser-Mazzola Quartet

GROUP

American improvisers seeking to be 'urban, fast and hypersensitive'.

★★ Maze

Quixotic 5002 *Guerino Mazzola (p); Scott Fields (g); Matt Turner (clo); Heinz Geisser (perc, valiha).* 10/97.

★★(★) Heliopolis

Cadence CJR 1122 *As above, except Mat Maneri (vn, vla) replaces Turner.* 10/99.

The group's interactive intentions are honourable, but it's let down by its collective imagination, or lack of it. The pieces on the first disc feel thick and gloomy, and though Maneri does his best to inject a little light and energy into the second, they're not much better. The main culprit seems to be Geisser, who lumbers around his kit and restricts the group to earthbound status.

Herb Geller (born 1928)

ALTO AND SOPRANO SAXOPHONES, FLUTE, VOCALS

Geller has told his own musical life-story of late (see below), but the bare bones of it are encompassed by an early sojourn in New York, where he met his wife, pianist Lorraine Walsh, and a long stint on the West Coast with the likes of Shorty Rogers and Maynard Ferguson. Herb and Lorraine co-led their own small group, and after her untimely death he has continued to work mostly with young and adventurous bands.

★★★★ That Geller Feller

Fresh Sound FSR CD 91 *Geller; Kenny Dorham (t); Harold Land (ts); Lou Levy (p); Ray Brown (b); Lawrence Marable (d).* 3/57.

★★★(★) Birdland Stomp

Fresh Sound FSRCD 174 *Geller; Kenny Drew (p); Niels-Henning Orsted Pedersen (b); Mark Taylor (d).* 5/90.

★★★★ The Herb Geller Quartet

VSOP 89 *Geller; Tom Ranier, Jimmy Rowles (p); John Leitham (b); Louie Bellson (d).* 8/93.

Relatively untroubled by fashion, Geller set out as an orthodox, Parker-influenced bopper – *rara avis* on the West Coast in those days – before turning towards a more broadly based and decidedly cooler style which incorporated elements of Paul Desmond, Johnny Hodges and even Benny Goodman, with whom he worked in the later '50s. Until recent years, he's been hard to spot, buried in a German radio big band and other groups. He is, though, a brilliant songwriter in the tradition of Berlin, Gershwin and Porter, and he has also written musicals.

That Geller Feller is the best of the available sets. The originals – 'S'Pacific View', 'Marable Eyes', 'An Air For The Heir' and 'Melrose And Sam' – are tightly organized and demand considerable inventiveness from a group that frequently sounds much bigger than a sextet. Dorham plays a lovely, crackling solo on the opening track but is otherwise rather anonymous when out on his own. Geller's own introduction to 'Jitterbug Waltz' is wonderfully delicate, with more than a hint of Benny Carter in the tone and phrasing. He also does a fine version of the Arlen–Gershwin rarity, 'Here's What I'm Here For', which John Williams picked up on later in 1957 on the excellent *Plays The Music Of Harold Arlen*.

Confusingly titled, given the existence of an Enja record of the same name, *Birdland Stomp* is way ahead on quality. At 62, Geller has a beautiful tone and the Ellington–Strayhorn medley with which the Spanish-recorded session ends suggests he has renewed his debt to Hodges. His articulation on Parker's 'Cheryl' isn't all it might be, and even the capable Drew sounds a bit sticky, but both are magnificent on the title-tune and 'Autumn Nocturne'. Recorded with a heavy emphasis on NHOP's bass, this is nevertheless one of Geller's best latter-day recordings, topped only by the VSOP.

Ruby Braff calls one CD *Controlled Nonchalance*. It's a title that would double very happily for the 1993 Geller release. At 65 he sounds utterly relaxed and in command of his craft. Of the originals, 'Chromatic Cry' and 'Stand-Up Comic' stand out. The first, an exquisite ballad, sounds like something that may have popped into his head during a solo or else in the rehearsal room; the second is a wry look at another group of improvising entertainers – 'Comedy is not the same / social critic is the game' – a vocal tribute topped by a piquant soprano solo. Geller's forte these days is the evocative ballad. 'Isfahan' is totally restructured in the middle section, otherwise played *à la* Hodges. Jimmy Rowles guests on his own evergreen, 'The Peacocks', with its softly eldritch cries and brooding mystery. A wonderful record by a seldom acknowledged master who charted his own course out of orthodox bebop.

★★★(★) Plays The Al Cohn Songbook

Hep CD 2066 *Geller; Tom Ranier (ts, cl, bcl, p); John Leitham (b); Paul Kreibich (d); Ruth Price (v).* 7/94.

Blessed by Flo Cohn, this is an imaginative sample of Al's capacious catalogue of tunes. The addition of multi-instrumentalist Ranier adds a whole range of colours and allows a reprise of Cohn's writing for Zoot Sims. 'Halley's Comet' is the best of these (Zoot's real name was John Haley), though interestingly it's played on alto and clarinet. Ranier's bass clarinet is deployed to superb effect on ''T Ain't No Use', a low, mournful sound that conveys a wealth of emotion. Herb transforms the sinuous line of 'Infinity', and plays a remarkable unaccompanied chorus that underlines how thoughtful an improviser he remains. His late wife Lorraine had once told him that jazz was neither an Olympic sport nor a fashion show, and this solo is entirely true to that principle, relying on basic musicality rather than technique and on felt experience rather than stylistic vogue. A fine record, and a fitting tribute to a great jazz composer.

★★★ Playing Jazz: The Musical Autobiography Of Herb Geller

Fresh Sound FSR 5011 *Geller; Tom Ranier (p); John Leitham (b); Paul Kreibich (d); Lothar Atwell, Mike Campbell, Rich Crystal, Stephanie Haynes, Chuck Niles, Polly Podewell (v).* 1/95.

This is a most extraordinary record. Essentially it is a stage musical without images, a journey through Herb's life from the day he gets his first saxophone, to playing opposite Lenny Bruce with Lorraine, to her death and his subsequent attempt to 'Pick Up The Pieces'. His own younger self is portrayed by Lothar Atwell, Lorraine by Stephanie Haynes, with the other singers taking the other roles, held together with a narration by Chuck Niles. Like all musicals, it is an uneasy mix of rather prosaic recitative (Herb's jazz lecture is a particularly embarrassing example) and some glorious songs and playing. His solo on 'My Favorite Songs', a tribute to the great songwriters who are just about to be assailed by rock'n'roll, is as good as he has recorded in years, and Tom Ranier's following chorus is all simplicity and grace. Sometimes it's unconsciously funny, sometimes more effectively so, as when his first teacher, Max Flack, tells Pop Geller: 'One day, listen to Max / A *President* will play the sax'. Indeed. 'Playing jazz is telling your life story' has always been Herb's motto and this one-off record makes that explicit. Not the easiest of listens and unlikely to find its way back to your CD player very often, but an intriguing idea beautifully executed.

***(*) I'll Be Back

Hep CD 2074 *Geller; Edward Harris (g); Thomas Biller (b); Heinrich Koebberling (d).* 8/96.

*** You're Looking At Me

Fresh Sound FSR 5018 *Geller; Jan Lundgren (p); Dave Carpenter (b); Joe LaBarbera (d).* 2/97

The line-up on *I'll Be Back* was the working group of the mid-'90s, and Herb's communication with his young players is consistently impressive. Unusually, he favours guitar over piano in this line-up, and the more open harmonies suit Herb's strongly melodic approach. Most of the original material comes from a musical he wrote about the great Josephine Baker, *La Bakair*. 'A Bitter Dream' and 'Too Little Time' are darkly mature compositions; sandwiching Hoagy Carmichael's 'One Morning In May', they bring the album to a wholly satisfying climax. It begins with Porter's 'Dream Dancing', and one can hear how subtly Geller programmes this and, indeed, all his records, modulating keys, rhythms and emotional pitch, constructing a musical drama rather than a procession of song. Three of the Baker tunes appear on *You're Looking At Me* and the contrast is very striking. It's a long album, perhaps overlong, and very much more conventional in outlook. As he has done consistently over the last decade, Geller uses it as an opportunity to revisit his own musical education and growth – the album even features a photograph of himself at ten, playing his first alto – and to air some favourite melodies, like Strayhorn's 'Orson' and Earle Warren's '9:20 Special'. Herb's tone is tighter and more staccato than usual and his pitching on soprano isn't entirely secure.

***(*) Hollywood Portraits

Hep CD 2078 *Geller; Brian Kellock (p).* 10/99.

The real star here is Scottish virtuoso Kellock, who turns what is effectively an abstract session (the naming of tunes after movie sirens seems a slightly arbitrary joke) into a sweeping procession of duets that just gets more inventive as it progresses. In fact, the major distraction comes from working out exactly what private association has inspired a piece on Judy Holliday or Claudette Colbert, Marilyn, Garbo, or any of 16 others. Herb doubles on soprano for about half a dozen tracks, but it's his swinging alto which dominates, and Kellock is right behind him every step of the way, rhythmically solid, harmonically inventive and constantly alert to changes in direction. A fine record and further testimony to producer and label owner Alastair Robertson's curatorial skills.

***(*) To Benny and Johnny – With Love From Herb Geller

Hep CD 2084 *Geller; Hod O'Brien (p); Chuck Berghofer (b); Paul Kreibich (d).* 6/01.

The Hep association continues with this lovely tribute album. Herb probably doesn't have quite the beauty of tone or graceful delivery of either Johnny Hodges or Benny Carter on either horn, but he clearly loves playing these familiar themes. 'Isfahan' and 'Warm Valley' stand out and Herb's touch on 'Ballad For Very Tired And Very Sad Lotus Eaters' is immaculate. He also rescues 'When Lights Are Low' from the pervasive Miles Davis version which, as Doug Ramsey points out, is a very strange take on such a beautiful song, leaving out the melody altogether. 'Johnny Come Lately' is intense and fiery, almost bebop. The set ends with Carter's 'Summer Serenade' which plays it out on a gentle high.

The band is on point throughout, easing just ahead of Herb much of the time but in the unhurried, endlessly accommodating manner that O'Brien has made his own; listen to his phrasing when bass and drums sit out 'I Didn't Know About You'. Berghofer is a model of musicianship throughout, particularity on the duo piece 'Twelve By Two With Squatty Roo' and when the tonality is complex.

The Georgia Melodians

GROUP

Early example of the 'territory' band, although their records were made in New York in the '20s.

** Georgia Melodians 1924–1926

Timeless Historical CBC 1-031 *Ernie Intlehouse, Red Nichols (c); Herb Winfield, Abe Lincoln (tb); Merrit Kenworthy (cl, as, bsx); Clarence Hutchins (cl, ts, bs); Oscar Young (p); Elmer Merry (bj, g); Carl Gerrold (d); Vernon Dlahart (v).* 7/24–4/26.

They came from Savannah, Georgia, to New York City, where the Edison Company recorded them on numerous occasions – although Joe Moore's notes reveal that the band broke up at the end of 1924, they continued to record until 1926, and the personnel listed is somewhat uncertain. Players like Intlehouse, Kenworthy and Hutchins are about as obscure as jazz history can provide, and listening to the music reveals why. This is hot dance music with a generous ration of solos (Edison's vertical-cut discs allowed for much longer playing time than normal 78s) and an honourable intention to swing, but it's poker-stiff at times and disheartening to hear how little the band improved over two years (the very earliest tracks, once available on a Retrieval LP, are missing from this otherwise complete edition, which adds three previously unissued cuts). Staple numbers such as 'Spanish Shawl' and 'Everybody Loves My Baby' can be heard better elsewhere, although they do a respectable job on 'San'. Beautifully clean transfers, though.

The Georgians

GROUP

Early small group of white jazzmen, drawn from the Paul Specht band and led by trumpeter Frank Guarente.

***** The Georgians 1922–23**

Retrieval RTR 79003 *Frank Guarente (t); Ray Stilwell, Russ Morgan, Archie Jones (tb); Johnny O'Donnell, Frank Smith, Dick Johnson, Harold 'Red' Sailiers (reeds); Arthur Schutt (p); Russell Deppe (bj); Joe Tarto (tba); Chauncey Morehouse (d).* 11/22–11/23.

***** The Georgians 1923–1924**

Retrieval RTR 79036 *As above except add Elwood Boyer (t), Charlie Butterfield (tb), Henry Wade, Al Monquin (reeds), Roy Smeck (bj), Billy Jones, Eddie Cantor, Dolly Kay, Blossom Seeley (v).* 6/22–5/24.

The Georgians were originally a contingent from Paul Specht's more strait-laced dance orchestra, working at New York's Hotel Alamac. With the excellent Guarente leading the group it stood at a point somewhere between the simple ensemble style of the Original Memphis Five and the looser, more inventive methods of the early black Chicago bands. Guarente, a white Italian-American, even took some lessons from Joe Oliver in New Orleans. He was the only improviser of any special merit in the band, but Arthur Schutt, hitherto largely ignored by jazz history, contributed an increasingly sophisticated book of arrangements. The later tracks on the first CD, especially the likes of 'Land Of Cotton Blues' and 'Old Fashioned Love', show real finesse coupled with a proper sense of swing. Most of the tunes have something to commend them, and even novelty pieces like 'Barney Google' are sustained by Guarente's work, although here and there (as in the plodding treatment of 'Farewell Blues') the group fails to make much out of the music.

The second disc takes the story up to Guarente's departure, in May 1924. The best of The Georgians' music is here , in such sides as 'Big Boy' (with a great vocal by Dolly Kay) and the pair of titles which turned out to be Guarente's swansong, 'Savannah' and 'Doodle Doo Doo'. Eddie Cantor turns up to sing at one session and the disc is padded with four titles by the full Specht orchestra. As before, it's Guarente's work which takes the ear and lets this music survive, despite everything that's happened since. Excellent transfers.

Bruce Gertz (born 1952)

BASS

Based in Boston, the bassist leads a regular group through close to a decade's worth of work.

*****(*) Red Handed**

Double Time DTRCD-155 *Gertz; Jerry Bergonzi (ts); Bruce Barth, John Abercrombie (g); Adam Nussbaum (d).* 10/98.

Red Handed is the work of a by-now-settled and substantial group (there are a couple of discs from the early '90s), even if they do rarely get out of their Boston stamping ground. Gertz has thought carefully about his materials, his players and his sources, and has come up with a detailed and absorbing set which is rather like an essay on what a skilful and chops-heavy band like this could do in 1998. 'Giant Steps' is refreshingly cast as a reflective bass-and-drums duet. 'Sun Flash' is tough and assertive and full of appropriate heat. The title-track looks south towards New Orleans, and 'Big Heart' is an open modal sketch which men like Bergonzi and Abercrombie were made to fill in and out. A fine piece of work which surpasses the early stuff by a long way.

Jane Getter

GUITAR

Grew up in New Jersey, but went West before settling in New York. Scofield is a big influence, but she also knows her classic jazz guitarists. Basically a fusioneer, though.

***** Jane**

Lipstick 8958 *Getter; Aaron Heick (sax); Adam Holzman (ky); Jerry Barnes, Victor Bailey, James Genus (b); Rodney Holmes (d); Ju Ju House, Abdou Mboup (perc); Katreese Barnes (v).* 98.

Not often Jeff Beck gets a mention in this book, but he's the dedicatee of 'Beck & Forth', one of the stronger originals on Getter's debut set. It's pretty formulaic fusion work all the way, but she's a decent technician with a lot of road miles under her belt and the standard of playing is high, even if the ideas are a bit hackneyed. 'Little Hands' and 'Riza' are both interesting compositions, but Jane's notion of a cover standard is the Gap Band's 'Outstanding'. Stand in the corner, lassie.

Stan Getz (1927–91)

TENOR, SOPRANO AND BARITONE SAXOPHONES

After various big-band engagements, Getz made his name with the Woody Herman Orchestra (1947–9). A group leader himself thereafter, he recorded for Roost and Verve in the '50s, though often working in Europe. Won enormous popular acclaim with his albums of bossa nova material 1962–4, then returned to his own small groups. Financial success allowed him to work as and when he pleased in the '70s and '80s. Toyed with fusion but quickly returned to straightahead playing. Though troubled by terminal cancer, he continued to play into the final year of his life. A peerless sound on the saxophone, total fluency of phrasing and a lovely way with every melody he played made him perhaps the most widely admired saxophonist of those who followed in Lester Young's footsteps.

***** Early Stan**

Original Jazz Classics OJC 654 *Getz; Shorty Rogers (t); Earl Swope (tb); George Wallington, Hall Overton (p); Jimmy Raney (g); Curley Russell, Red Mitchell (b); Shadow Wilson, Frank Isola (d).* 3/49–4/53.

****(*) The Brothers**

Original Jazz Classics OJC 008 *Getz; Zoot Sims, Al Cohn, Allen Eager, Brew Moore (ts); Walter Bishop Jr (p); Gene Ramey (b); Charlie Perry (d).* 4/49.

***** Prezervation**

Original Jazz Classics OJC 706 *Getz; Kai Winding (tb); Al Haig (p); Gene Ramey, Tommy Potter (b); Roy Haynes, Stan Levey (d); Junior Parker, Blossom Dearie, Jimmy Raney (v).* 6/49–2/50.

*** Stan Getz Quartets

Original Jazz Classics OJC 121 *Getz; Al Haig, Tony Aless (p); Gene Ramey, Tommy Potter, Percy Heath (b); Stan Levey, Roy Haynes, Don Lamond (d).* 6/49–4/50.

After starring as one of Woody Herman's 'Four Brothers' sax section, and delivering a luminous ballad solo on the 1948 'Early Autumn', Getz went out on his own and at first seemed much like the rest of the Lester Young-influenced tenormen: a fast, cool stylist with a sleek tone and a delivery that soothed nerves jangled by bebop. The 'Brothers' idea was pursued in the session on OJC 008 (the rest of the disc is devoted to a Zoot Sims–Al Cohn date): the five tenors trade punches with panache and it's a fun session, if hardly an important one (the CD includes three alternative takes not on the LP issue). *Early Stan* finds Getz as a sideman with a septet led by Terry Gibbs and a quartet under Jimmy Raney's direction. Bright, appealing cool-bop on the Gibbs date, but the Raney session, from 1953, is more substantial, the quartet whisking through four stretching exercises, including 'Round Midnight'.

Prezervation rounds up some odds and ends, including an improbable alliance with Junior Parker on two tracks and a Haig sextet date with Winding and two vocal duets by Jimmy Raney and Blossom Dearie! Not very important. But the *Quartets* set is an attractive dry run for the upcoming four-piece sessions for Roost, and it features the tenorman in very lithe form. The sound on most of these issues was fairly indifferent to start with, and these latest editions emerge well enough.

♛ **** The Complete Roost Recordings

Roost 859622-2 3CD *Getz; Sanford Gold, Duke Jordan, Horace Silver, Al Haig (p); Jimmy Raney, Johnny Smith (g); Eddie Safranski, Teddy Kotick, Bill Crow, Leonard Gaskin, Bob Carter (b); Frank Isola, Tiny Kahn, Roy Haynes, Don Lamond, Morey Feld (d); Count Basie Orchestra.* 5/50–12/54.

So much attention has fallen on Getz's later work that these magnificent sessions are sometimes overlooked. No longer any need for that, now the complete works have been gathered across three generously filled CDs, with three new tunes. The earliest tracks, from a session in May 1950, catch a young man with his head full of bebop and his heart heavy with swing-era romanticism. Those contrary strains sometimes come together, such as in the headily beautiful 'Yesterdays', in a marriage of intellect and emotion that is rare not only in Getz's work but in jazz itself. These two early dates, one with Al Haig, one with Horace Silver, are little short of electrifying. By 1951, he already sounds like the more settled, invincible Getz, but the short track-lengths (a relic of the 78 era) give the music considerable point and direction. The live session from Boston's Storyville Club with Jimmy Raney has long been a prized classic, both musicians unreeling one great solo after another. Two studio dates with a similar band are at a lower voltage but are scarcely less impressive. Eight tracks with Johnny Smith, including the achingly lovely 'Moonlight In Vermont', offer Getz the lyricist in fullest flow, while the three with Basie at Birdland are like a fun bonus. There is so much top-flight jazz in this set that it's quite indispensable, and brought together in one place and remastered to a consistent standard, it's breathtaking.

*** Stan Getz 1951

Classics 1299 *Getz; Lars Gullin (bs); Horace Silver, Bengt Hallberg, Al Haig (p); Jimmy Raney (g); Joe Calloway, Gunnar Johnson, Yngve Akerberg, Leonard Gaskin, Teddy Kotick (b); Walter Bolden, Jack Noren, Kenneth Fagerlund, Roy Haynes, Tiny Kahn (d).* 3–10/51.

As usual, Classics go their chronological way with no deference to any other logic, so this mixes up various Roost recordings with eight titles made in Stockholm with the likes of Gullin and Hallberg. As these aren't easily available elsewhere this one merits a listing. That said, they're not terribly exciting pieces, even though Getz doesn't dip below his customary skilfulness, and his first version of 'Ack, Värmeland Du Sköna' is charming. In somewhat dusty sound.

(***) At Carnegie Hall

Fresh Sound FSCD 1003 *Getz; Kai Winding (tb); Al Haig, Duke Jordan (p); Jimmy Raney (g); Bill Crow, Tommy Potter (b); Frank Isola, Roy Haynes (d).* 12/49–11/52.

(***) Birdland Sessions

Fresh Sound FSR-CD 149 *Getz; Horace Silver, Duke Jordan (p); Jimmy Raney (g); Nelson Boyd, Charles Mingus, Gene Ramey (b); Phil Brown, Connie Kay (d).* 4–8/52.

There's some excellent Getz on both these discs, but we have to withhold a firm recommendation because of the sound-quality. He sounds in prime form at both of the two Carnegie Hall concerts on FSCD 1003, but the sound deteriorates (frustratingly, after a good start) to complete muddiness by the end of the 1952 show. Jordan tends to toss out clichés, but the interplay with Raney is as subtle as usual. The Birdland recordings have been available on various pirate LPs over the years, and this edition is about as listenable as the others. For Getz addicts only.

*** Together For The First Time

Fresh Sound FSCD-1022 *Getz; Chet Baker (t); Russ Freeman, Don Trenner (p); Carson Smith, Joe Mondragon, Gene Englund (b); Larry Bunker, Shelly Manne, Jimmy Pratt (d).* 9/52–12/53.

An interesting discovery: the Mulligan quartet at the Haig with Getz subbing for the leader. He sounds perfectly at home with Baker, Smith and Bunker, and there are some forthright variations on six tunes, including 'Half Nelson' and 'Yardbird Suite'. A subsequent quintet version of 'All The Things You Are' is a lot more dispirited, and there are four quartet airshots from 1952 to fill up the disc, which is in surprisingly good sound for the most part, the Haig titles having been apparently recorded by Richard Bock.

***(*) Stan Getz Plays

Verve 833535-2 *Getz; Jimmy Rowles, Duke Jordan (p); Jimmy Raney (g); Bob Whitlock, Bill Crow (b); Frank Isola, Max Roach (d).* 12/52–1/54.

**** At The Shrine

Verve 513753-2 *Getz; Bob Brookmeyer (vtb); John Williams (p); Bill Anthony (b); Art Madigan, Frank Isola (d).* 11/54.

Getz's long association with Norman Granz and Verve starts here. *Plays* features some of the best recording he was given in the period, and much of the playing is as fine as it is on the Roost dates, with the 1954 quartet session with Rowles particularly pretty. But it's the live sessions from the Shrine in Los Angeles, long a collectors'-item album, which stand out. Getz plays with unstinting invention throughout, Brookmeyer is a witty and unfailingly apposite partner, and the remastered sound is fine.

★★★(★) Stan Getz And The Cool Sounds

Verve 547317-2 *Getz; Tony Fruscella (t); Bob Brookmeyer (vtb); John Williams, Jimmy Rowles, Lou Levy (p); Bob Whitlock, Bill Crow, Leroy Vinnegar, Bill Anthony (b); Shelly Manne, Frank Isola, Max Roach, Al Levitt (d).* 5/53–1/55.

Although the album's packaging suggested this was some kind of new Getz group, it's actually a set of leftovers from various sessions for Granz. The two surviving tracks with Tony Fruscella, from a date which looks as if it was never completed, are interesting, but the notoriously unreliable Fruscella bumbles through his solos. The first four quartet tracks with Lou Levy are, though, gorgeous, and 'Flamingo' and 'Rustic Hop' are two further collaborations with Brookmeyer. Two other tracks have Rowles at the piano, and it was likely his idea to do 'Down By The Sycamore Tree'. Bits and pieces, but this is vintage Getz all the same.

★★★★ The West Coast Sessions

Verve 531935-2 3CD *Getz; Conte Candoli (t); Lou Levy (p); Leroy Vinnegar (b); Stan Levey, Shelly Manne (d).* 8/55–8/57.

★★★★ West Coast Jazz

Verve 557549-2 *As above, except omit Levey.* 8/55.

★★★★ The Steamer

Verve 547771-2 *As above, except add Stan Levey (d); omit Candoli and Manne.* 11/56.

★★★(★) Award Winner

Verve 543320-2 *As above.* 8/57.

What a great period for tenor-saxophone-playing this was, with Rollins laying down his masterpieces on one coast and Getz on the other. Given that Getz is scarcely the prototypical West Coast player, there's a certain irony in the situation. With this distinctively Californian group, though, he set down a classic series of sessions, once issued as three LPs, now expanded to three discs with a number of alternative takes. Candoli, present on the original *West Coast Jazz* date, plays handsomely and is an excellent foil, but it's Getz and the rhythm sections who unfurl the most gorgeous colours: stomping on 'Shine', profoundly inventive on the blues in 'Blues For Mary Jane', winsomely beautiful in ballads like 'You're Blasé'. Relatively unprepared, and programmed around tunes they all knew, the records are, like Art Pepper's rather different sessions for Contemporary, sax/rhythm dates of intuitive greatness. For those who'd prefer a pocket edition of highlights, Verve also has *Best Of The West Coast Sessions* (537084-2). It has also brought back the three original albums in its Master Edition series, which makes a handsome substitute since each has the various alternative takes added to the programmes. Our favourite remains *The Steamer*, but all three offer a string of great rewards.

★★★ Stan Meets Chet

Verve 837436-2 *Getz; Chet Baker (t); Jodie Christian (p); Victor Sproles (b); Marshall Thompson (d).* 2/57.

★★★ Stan Getz And The Oscar Peterson Trio

Verve 827826-2 *Getz; Oscar Peterson (p); Herb Ellis (g); Ray Brown (b).* 10/57.

★★★ At The Opera House

Verve 831272-2 *Getz; J. J. Johnson (tb); Oscar Peterson (p); Herb Ellis (g); Ray Brown (b); Connie Kay (d).* 10/57.

★★★ Getz Meets Mulligan In Hi-Fi

Verve 849392-2 *Getz; Gerry Mulligan (bs, ts); Lou Levy (p); Ray Brown (b); Stan Levey (d).* 10/57.

★★★ Stan Getz & Dizzy Gillespie: Jazz Masters 25

Verve 521852-2 *Getz; Dizzy Gillespie (t); J. J. Johnson (tb); Paul Gonsalves, Coleman Hawkins (ts); John Lewis, Lalo Schifrin, Wynton Kelly (p); Herb Ellis (g); Ray Brown, Art Davis, Wendell Marshall (b); Max Roach, Stan Levey, Chuck Lampkin, J. C. Heard (d); Candido Camero (perc).* 12/53–11/60.

Getz's '50s tracks are still incomplete as far as current CD representation is concerned, but they're getting there. As a body of records, curiously few stand out; there's certainly nothing here on a par with the West Coast dates listed above. The meeting with Baker was recorded in Chicago with a local rhythm section and it feels like an on-the-hoof event: they simply blow together. Next to Getz's meetings with Dizzy Gillespie, this is pale stuff. The session with Peterson is as ebullient as expected, and the Opera House concert with J. J. Johnson includes some extrovert playing from everyone, especially on a snorting romp through Bud Powell's 'Blues In The Closet'. Listening to this kind of playing makes one wonder at Getz's reputation for being a featherlight stylist (he preferred 'stomping tenorman'). The session with Mulligan is beautifully dovetailed: although they notoriously chose to swap instruments for part of the session, the sound of the two horns speaks of a tonal fraternity which sounds rare and entrancing. The *Jazz Masters* disc picks four tracks from two studio dates with Gillespie, plus a JATP piece and a jovial meeting with Gonsalves and Hawkins in 1957.

★★★(★) In Sweden 1958–60

Dragon DRCD 263 2CD *Getz; Benny Bailey (t); Ake Persson (tb); Erik Norström, Bjarne Nerem (ts); Lars Gullin (bs); Jan Johansson, Bengt Hallberg (p); Gunnar Johnson, Ray Brown, Torbjørn Hultcrantz, Georg Riedel (b); William Schiopffe, Sune Spångberg, Joe Harris (d).* 8–9/58, 60.

A spell in Stockholm led to some recording with Swedish musicians and these admirable sessions were the result, a Swedish variation on the cool manner with Getz sounding perfectly comfortable in Hallberg's and Johansson's charts. Gullin and Hallberg shine too, and so does the remarkable Johansson, whose status as the lost master of Swedish jazz is further enhanced by his playing here. The previous edition of this music has now been beefed up with some concert and radio material from 1960 and it's a close-to-indispensable package.

★★★ Stan Getz With Cal Tjader

Original Jazz Classics OJC 275 *Getz; Cal Tjader (vib); Vince Guaraldi (p); Eddie Duran (g); Scott LaFaro (b); Billy Higgins (d).* 2/58.

A one-off session with Cal Tjader which looks forward with some prescience to the bossa nova records that were to come. Certainly the coolly pleasant backings of Tjader's rhythm section make up a cordial meeting-ground for tenor and vibes to play lightly appealing solos, and the charming version of 'I've Grown Accustomed To Her Face' is a winner.

★★★(★) Stan Getz At Large Plus! Vol. 1

Jazz Unlimited JUCD 2001 *Getz; Jan Johanssen (p); Daniel Jordan (b); William Schiopffe (d).* 1/60.

★★★(★) Stan Getz At Large Plus! Vol. 2

Jazz Unlimited JUCD 2002 *As above.* 1/60.

Two very rare Getz albums, recorded in Copenhagen with a local team, and he sounds in wonderful form throughout. The opening 'Night And Day' on the first disc is delivered with heavenly grace and is sustained over chorus after chorus at a perfect tempo. There are some interesting choices of material – by Johnny Mandel, Al Cohn, Harold Land – and though both albums are weighted towards slow to mid-tempos, Getz stays concentrated and inspired throughout. The rhythm section is capable rather than challenging, and the sound is slightly less than ideal, but the music is terrific.

*** Cool Velvet / Voices

Verve 527773-2 *Getz; Herbie Hancock, Hank Jones (p); Dave Hildinger (vib); Jim Hall (g); Blanchie Birdsong (hp); Freddy Dutton, Ron Carter (b); Sperie Karas, Grady Tate (d); Artie Butler, Bobby Rosengarden, Bill Horwath (perc); strings, voices.* 3/60–12/66.

It was inevitable that Getz would do a full-blown encounter with strings, and Russ Garcia's arrangements for the *Cool Velvet* album are workmanlike settings for the lovely sound. *Voices* was arranged by Claus Ogerman, and in the brief frameworks he devises, Getz sounds professionally involved though not much more. Pleasant music, but hardly a competitor to the indispensable *Focus* (see below).

**** Recorded Fall 1961

Verve 549369-2 *Getz; Bob Brookmeyer (vtb); Steve Kuhn (p); John Neves (b); Roy Haynes (d).* 9/61.

A little-known Getz session by a band which the leader had put together for an American tour, this belongs at least as much to Brookmeyer (who penned three of the six tunes) as to the saxophonist. The similarities between the horns are best heard at the quick tempo of 'Minuet Circa '61', where Getz, more than Brookmeyer, has to fall back on some of his favourite licks; their contrasts come out on the following ballad, 'Who Could Care', where the tenor is breathily beautiful and the valve trombone hard and choleric. Getz is sublime again on 'A Nightingale Sang In Berkeley Square' but Buck Clayton's 'Love Jumped Out' brings out the best in both. Throughout, Roy Haynes keeps things crisp and swinging, every accent felt as a particular. Welcome back to a terrific session.

CORE COLLECTION

**** Focus

Verve 521419-2 *Getz; orchestra led by Eddie Sauter* 7–10/61.

Nobody ever arranged for Getz as well as this, and Sauter's luminous and shimmering scores continue to bewitch. This isn't art-jazz scoring: Sauter had little of Gil Evans's *misterioso* power, and he was shameless about tugging at heartstrings. But within those parameters – and Getz, the most pragmatic of soloists, was only too happy to work within them – he made up the most emotive of frameworks. It doesn't make much sense as a suite, or a concerto; just as a series of episodes with the tenor gliding over and across them. In 'Her', the tune dedicated to Getz's mother, the soloist describes a pattern which is resolved in the most heartstopping of codas. This was surely Getz's finest hour. The latest version is in Verve's Master Edition series, and the previously spotty CD edition has been significantly improved, though there's still a degree of tape hiss if you're listening for it.

***(*) Jazz Samba

Verve 521413-2 *Getz; Charlie Byrd (g); Keter Betts (b); Gene Byrd (g, b); Buddy Deppenschmidt, Bill Reichenbach (d).* 2/62.

*** Big Band Bossa Nova

Verve 825771-2 *Getz; Doc Severinsen, Bernie Glow, Joe Ferrante, Clark Terry (t); Tony Studd, Bob Brookmeyer, Willie Dennis (tb); Ray Alonge (frhn); Jerry Sanfino, Ray Beckenstein (f); Eddie Caine (af); Babe Clark, Walt Levinsky (cl); Romeo Penque (bcl); Hank Jones (p); Jim Hall (g); Tommy Williams (b); Johnny Rae (d); Jose Paulo, Carmen Cossa (perc).* 8/62.

***(*) Jazz Samba Encore

Verve 823613-2 *Getz; Antonio Carlos Jobim (g, p); Luiz Bonfa (g); George Duvivier, Tommy Williams, Don Payne (b); Paulo Ferreira, Jose Carlos, Dave Bailey (d); Maria Toledo (v).* 2/63.

**** Getz/Gilberto

Verve 521414-2 *Getz; Antonio Carlos Jobim (p); João Gilberto (g, v); Tommy Williams (b); Milton Banana (d); Astrud Gilberto (v).* 3/63.

*** Getz Au Go Go

Verve 821725-2 *Getz; Gary Burton (vib); Kenny Burrell (g); Gene Cherico (b); Joe Hunt, Helcio Milito (d); Astrud Gilberto (v).* 64.

***(*) The Girl From Ipanema

Verve 823611-2 4CD *As above discs, except add Steve Kuhn (p), Laurindo Almeida (g), Edison Machado, Jose Soorez, Luiz Parga (perc).* 62–64.

***(*) Round Midnight: Stan Getz

Verve 841445 *As above.* 62–64.

Getz's big commercial break. However much he protested that he played other stuff besides the bossa nova in later years, his most lucrative records – and some of his best playing – were triggered by the hit versions of first 'Desafinado' from the first album and then 'The Girl From Ipanema' with Gilberto, the tune that a thousand wine-bar bands have had to play nightly ever since. The original albums still hold up very well. Getz actually plays with as much pungency and alertness as anywhere else, and even though the backings sometimes threaten to slip into a sleepwalk, there's always an interesting tickle from the guitar or the bass to keep the music alive; and the melodies, by Bonfa, Gilberto and Jobim, have proved their quality by how well they've endured. *Jazz Samba* and *Jazz Samba Encore* are excellent, but the famous *Getz/Gilberto*, which has hummed seductively round cafés, wine-bars and bedrooms for over 30 years, remains peerless. Both the latter and *Jazz Samba* have been remastered in Verve's Master Edition series.

The big-band set has some clever arrangements by Gary McFarland, but sundering the intimacy of these whispery settings seems a fairly pointless exercise. And *Getz Au Go Go*, which had the vocals by Gilberto dubbed in subsequently, sounds just a mite too forceful, as though Getz were hurrying to push on to something else. Astrud Gilberto's singing isn't so much an acquired taste as a languid, ghostly sound on the breeze; many will prefer Maria Toledo on the third record listed. *The Girl From Ipanema* collects all the music plus the session for *Stan Getz/Laurindo Almeida*. The *Round Midnight* disc is a functional one-volume sampler with all the hits.

*** Reflections

Verve 523322-2 *Getz; orchestra arranged by Claus Ogerman and Lalo Schifrin.* 10/63.

Besides the bossa, Stan kept one eye on his with-strings audience. Next to Eddie Sauter's work, these are very ordinary settings, cushioned further by a cooing choir almost in the Conniff manner. Which doesn't stop Stan from unfurling some lovely solos, all the same.

★★★★ Nobody Else But Me

Verve 521660-2 *Getz; Gary Burton (vib); Gene Cherico (b); Joe Hunt (d).* 3/64.

Unreleased for 30 years, this one's a marvel. Supposedly put on the shelf so as not to cause any distraction from Getz's bossa nova hit-making, the music here – amazingly, the only studio recording by a group that was a popular concert attraction – is lush and romantic, with the backbone of a master improviser's intelligence. Burton contributes '6-Nix-Pix-Flix' and opens up the harmonic base just enough to give Stan clear, lucid space for his solos. 'Summertime' is a classic, 'Waltz For A Lovely Wife' is rapture, but there's nothing less than great here.

★★★ Stan Getz & Bill Evans

Verve 833802-2 *Getz; Bill Evans (p); Richard Davis (b); Elvin Jones (d).* 5/64.

A curiously unsatisfying match. If one expected feathery ballads and lavishly romantic music, the results were the complete opposite. The only real ballad is 'But Beautiful', the rest go from mid-tempo to stomp, and Davis and Jones break up the beat and harry the two nominal leaders. Both can handle it, but it's disappointing that something on the level of the almost telepathic Evans–Jim Hall records wasn't secured. The CD has several alternative and unissued takes.

★★★(★) Mickey One

Verve 531232-2 *Getz; Clark Terry (t, flhn); Al DeRisi, Ernie Difalco, Joe Ferrante, Bobby Nichols (t); Eddie Bert, John Messner, Ephie Resnick, Sonny Russo (tb); Tom Mitchell (btb); Bob Abernathy, Ray Alonge, Richard Berg, Jimmy Buffington, Earl Chapin (frhn); Harvey Estrin, Al Block, Ray Shiner, Wally Kane, Eli Carmen, Don Ashworth, Charles Russo, (woodwind, reeds); Roger Kellaway (p); Barry Galbraith (g); Richard Davis (b); Mel Lewis (d); Elden Bailey, Phil Kraus, Walter Rosenberger, Joe Venuti (perc); strings.* 8/65.

This time Sauter's arrangements were for the soundtrack to *Mickey One*, with Getz as featured soloist. While this has never had the favour or currency accorded to *Focus*, it's still a formidable piece of work, especially in this excellent remastering, which sorts out the complex textures pretty well. It's film music, which means that minus its context it's always going to lose something, but for all the inherent bittiness a powerful extended work lies within, and Getz rarely played with such consuming force as in some of this music.

★★★ Quartet In Paris

Emarcy 517049-2 *Getz; Gary Burton (vib); Steve Swallow (b); Roy Haynes (d).* 11/66.

The remote concert sound from the Salle Pleyel is a letdown. The music's full of grace and charm, though, especially on a diaphanous-sounding 'When The World Was Young', where Burton's indistinct vibes drift around Getz, who blows a couple of fierce bell-notes as if to disperse them. One for the completist.

★★★(★) Sweet Rain

Verve 815054-2 *Getz; Chick Corea (p); Ron Carter (b); Grady Tate (d).* 3/67.

This was an excellent group, and the youthful Corea proved to be a sympathetic and encouraging partner for the cantankerous leader. Maybe the pianist is too sweet and noodling at times, but 'O Grande Amor' and 'Windows' blend the brightness of Getz's bossa nova years with a spare, precise lyricism, and Carter and Tate have the measure of the situation.

★★★ What The World Needs Now

Verve 557450-2 *Getz; Chick Corea, Herbie Hancock (p); Jim Hall, Phil Upchurch (g); Walter Booker, Ron Carter (b); Roy Haynes, Curtis Prince, Grady Tate (d); Bill Horwath (cymbalom); Artie Butler, Bobby Rosengarden (perc); strings, brass, choir.* 12/66–1/68.

An album of Burt Bacharach tunes, arranged by Richard Evans, which Getz strolls through, sometimes all but overpowered by the surrounding players (the remastering does nothing to diminish their role, either). As if to compensate, he plays more fiercely than usual in places, and there are some surprising stretches of tonal distortion. 'The Look Of Love' finds his sound magnified by studio reverb. A period piece, worth reviving, but hardly a Getzian milestone.

★★★(★) Dynasty

Verve 839117-2 2CD *Getz; Eddy Louiss (org); René Thomas (g); Bernard Lubat (d).* 1–3/71.

Recorded at a live engagement in London, Getz was in happy and swinging form here, and the quartet stretch out as far as they want on the material. Louiss is far more flexible and discreet than most jazz organists and Getz is untroubled by anything the instrument produces, while the reliable Thomas takes some excellent solos.

★★★(★) The Best Of The Verve Years Vol. 2

Verve 517330-2 2CD *Getz; various groups, as above.* 52–71.

★★★(★) Verve Jazz Masters: Stan Getz

Verve 519823-2 *Getz; various groups, as above.*

The double-CD compilation goes for a wide-ranging, packed retrospective, from the earliest Verve material up to *Dynasty*; the VJM disc is more modest but includes 'Her', 'Desafinado', 'Shine' and 'Ipanema'. Each would be a fine introduction to this big period of Getz's music.

★★(★) Captain Marvel

Columbia 468412-2 *Getz; Chick Corea (p); Stanley Clarke (b); Tony Williams (d); Airto Moreira (perc).* 3/72.

★★ Best Of Two Worlds

Columbia CK 33703 *Getz; Albert Dailey (p); João Gilberto (g, perc, v); Oscar Castro-Nueves (g); Clint Houston, Steve Swallow (b); Billy Hart, Grady Tate (d); Airto Moreira, Ruben Bassini, Ray Armando, Sonny Carr (perc); Heloisa Buarque De Hollanda (v).* 5/75.

★★★ Live At Montmartre

Steeplechase SCS 1073 2CD *Getz; JoAnne Brackeen (p); Niels-Henning Orsted Pedersen (b); Billy Hart (d).* 1/77.

This wasn't a vintage period for Getz. The Columbia albums range from perfunctory to mildly engaging. Nothing wrong with the settings (aside from *Best Of Two Worlds*, which is a very pallid re-run of the bossa nova years), but Getz's own playing has taken on a wayward, purposeless quality, and the licks he sometimes fell back on when bored recur frequently enough to be troublesome. *Captain Marvel* was meant to be an energetic new beginning, but the noise created by Moreira drowns out even Williams at times, and Getz never sounds at ease, despite some of his old gumption breaking through. The Montmartre set suffers from a rhythm section that doesn't really work with him.

*** Empty Shells (The Complete Cannes Concert)

Universe UV 074 *Getz; Andy LaVerne (ky); Chuck Loeb (g); Brian Bromberg (b); Victor Jones (d).* 1/80.

This live set sits a little awkwardly between Getz's fusion phase and his return to mainstream values. Electric keyboards, guitar, and Jones here and there switching to – gasp! – a disco hi-hat beat belong to the former, but Stan's clearly on his way back to the hard stuff. Some of the material is unworthy, but by the time they get to Wayne Shorter's 'Lady Day', 'Autumn Leaves' and 'Time After Time' things are looking up. The sound isn't all that good and this is surely one for completists only.

***(*) Billy Highstreet Samba

Emarcy 838771-2 *Getz; Mitchel Forman (ky); Chuck Loeb (g); Mark Egan (b); Victor Lewis (d); Bobby Thomas (perc).* 11/81.

***(*) My Old Flame

Concord CCD 4955-2 *Getz; Lou Levy (p); Monty Budwig (b); Victor Lewis (d).* 5/81.

**** Pure Getz

Concord CCD 4188 *Getz; Jim McNeely (p); Marc Johnson (b); Victor Lewis (d).* 1/82.

***(*) Blue Skies

Concord CCD 4676 *As above.* 1/82.

***(*) Live In Paris

Dreyfus FDM 36577-9 *As above.* 82.

Not so much a miraculous return to form as an artist reasserting his artistry. Getz passed fusion leanings by and moved back to his greatest strength, tenor and rhythm section, of which the Concord albums are triumphant illustrations. *My Old Flame* couples the two originals *The Dolphin* and its companion, *Spring Is Here*, live sessions with a first-class band. Getz is at his most expansive here, reeling off very long but consistently expressive and well-argued solos, his tone a shade harder but still with a misty elegance that softens phrases at key moments. *Pure Getz*, recorded in the studio, is perhaps even better. There is a celebrated version of Billy Strayhorn's 'Blood Count', which alternates between harsh cries and soft murmurings and which became a staple part of Getz's live set at the time; but the variations on 'Come Rain Or Come Shine' and a terse 'Sippin' At Bells' are probably even more masterful. *Billy Highstreet Samba* is by no means a second-rate Getz album; here, for once, he adapted well to what could have been a fusion-led project. The material (by Loeb and Forman) is unusually perspicacious, and Getz responds with bright and committed playing against a group more concerned with playing music than licks. There is also a strong 'Body And Soul' and a couple of rare outings for Getz on soprano.

Blue Skies is a later discovery, dating from the same sessions as *Pure Getz*, and though we have given it a fractionally lower rating there is still some transcendent playing, especially on the slower pieces; Getz's gravitas on a ballad was never more perfectly revealed than in the likes of 'How Long Has This Been Going On?'. The live date is a valuable pendant to the studio sessions, and this was clearly a band in top gear. The only slight drawback is some extra reverb added to the remix, with McNeely's piano also sounding imperfect.

*** The Stockholm Concerts

Verve 537555-2 3CD *Getz; Chet Baker (t, v); Jim McNeely (p); George Mraz (b); Victor Lewis (d).* 2/83.

***(*) Quintessence Vol. 1

Concord CD 4807-2 *As above.* 2/83.

Stan meets Chet, again, but in very unfortunate circumstances. The saxophonist at times almost bullies Baker offstage during these concerts, and the trumpeter often responds by literally quaking through his parts. The Verve set is a somewhat gloomy encounter, not helped by McNeely playing almost on autopilot (he had got off a plane from Australia only hours before!). And yet ... Getz himself plays some magnificent things, such as the first show's quite wonderful 'We'll Be Together Again' and 'How Long Has This Been Going On?'. The original pair of Sonet LPs has been expanded to a full three-CD set, and while the blemishes will trouble some, for Getz's playing alone many will prioritize this one. The Concord album sees the group travelling to Norway for the next stop on the tour. Maybe it had settled down a bit; either way, Baker sounds considerably happier and in stronger voice, and even Stan thaws a bit. Excellent concert sound.

**** Anniversary

Emarcy 838769-2 *Getz; Kenny Barron (p); Rufus Reid (b); Victor Lewis (d).* 7/87.

**** Serenity

Emarcy 838770-2 *As above.* 7/87.

Pristine examples of his art. Sometimes it seems as if there is nothing there but his sound, the 'incredibly lovely sound', as he once murmured to himself, and it's possible to find a strange, inward-looking emptiness at the heart of this music. Certainly he had no pretence to playing anything but long, self-regarding lines that had little to do with anything going on around him. Impeccably though both of these rhythm sections play, their function is purely to sketch in as painless a backdrop as possible for the unfurling of Getz's sound. But it is such a breathtaking beauty he creates that these might be the most sheerly pretty jazz albums of their day. These Emarcy sets are splendidly recorded and let the listener bathe in the rapturous sound of the tenor.

***(*) Yours And Mine

Concord CCD 4740 *Getz; Kenny Barron (p); Ray Drummond (b); Ben Riley (d).* 6/89.

***(*) Soul Eyes

Concord CCD 4783 *As above, except add Yasuito Mori (b).* 6–7/89.

What a trouper. Here's the old man in never-say-die fettle on some of his favourite standards, plus a nice Kenny Barron tune and Thad Jones's title-song. Caught live at Glasgow's Jazz Festival, the sound isn't ideally close, but you can catch most of the nuances and hear enough to tell that Getz was still the man. The rest of the concert appears on *Soul Eyes*, together with three tracks from a Copenhagen show a week later, with Mori in for Drummond. Getz sounds a bit sour on 'Slow Boat To China', but the following 'Warm Valley' is divine. Two excellent additions to the canon.

*** Apasionado

A&M 395297-2 *Getz; orchestra.* 89.

Though already troubled by his terminal illness, Getz still plays handsomely on this superior example of mood music. This has been a maligned record in the past, but we certainly prefer it to Stan's adventures in fusion for Columbia. With keyboards substituting for the string parts and a mélange of soft rhythms and whispering brass in support, this might be deemed an apposite illustration of the most soothing side of his art.

***** The Final Concert Recording**
Eagle EDL EAG 272-2 *Getz; Kenny Barron (p); Eddie Del Barrio (ky); unidentified rhythm section.* 90.

*****(*) People Time**
Emarcy 510134-2 2CD *Getz; Kenny Barron (p).* 3/91.

***** Café Montmartre**
Emarcy 586755-2 *Getz; Kenny Barron (p); Rufus Reid (b); Victor Lewis (d).* 7/87–3/91.

Aside from the point that the title's inaccurate, *The Final Concert Recording* is a mild disappointment, given that the more 'classic' material is interleaved with tunes from the quasi-smooth *Apasionado* session for A&M. Better to go to the pared-down setting of *People Time.* This was cut not long before his death, and Getz has his moments of struggle on the imposing, double-length series of duets with Kenny Barron, his last keyboard partner. Some of the butter has run out of his tone, and unlike many valedictory recordings there isn't a compensating ardour of delivery to go with it: he sounds as if he's just trying to be the same old Getz. But knowledge of his impending death still, inevitably, lends a poignancy to this music which even those previously unmoved by the saxophonist's work may find themselves responding to. Nor should Barron be relegated to the role of mere accompanist: he is a full-fledged partner in these pieces and turns in some of the best improvising. *Café Montmartre* cherrypicks tracks from *People Time, Anniversary* and *Serenity.* Fine music, of course, but docked a notch for pointlessness (and for more on that, see below).

***** A Life In Jazz: A Musical Biography**
Verve 535119-2 *Getz; various groups from Verve albums listed above.* 1/52–3/91.

Released to tie in with a Getz biography, this is an interesting hotchpotch rather than a definitive sampler. It rescues a few rarities – 'Hymn To The Orient' from *Plays,* a solo with Ella Fitzgerald from her *Like Someone In Love* album, and the sultry backing to Abbey Lincoln on 'I'm In Love' from her *You Gotta Pay The Band.* For someone who doesn't have too much Stan, this is a nice variation on the normal hits selection.

***** The Very Best Of Stan Getz**
Verve 584210-2 *Getz; various groups from Verve albums listed above.* 53–81.

***** Getz Plays Jobim: The Girl From Ipanema**
Verve 589361-2 *Getz; various groups from Verve albums listed above.* 2/62–10/64.

If ever there were a case to answer that major labels prefer recycling to fresh initiatives, the Verve Group's relentless repackaging of Stan Getz would rate as prime evidence for the prosecution. With 13 compilations of various kinds listed in the current catalogue (we do not include all of them here), most of them duplicating each other, consumers may feel bewildered. Both of these are well enough chosen (though we disagree with *The Very Best Of*), but each is docked a notch – again – for pointlessness.

Terje Gewelt (born 1960)

BASS

Has done sterling service as a sideman with the likes of Tommy Smith, and this is a somewhat belated leadership bow for the experienced Norwegian.

*****(*) Hide And Seek**
Resonant RM2-2 *Gewelt; Jason Rebello (p); Jon Eberson, Staffan William-Olsson (g); Päl Thowsen, Billy Cobham (d).* 11/98.

Fresh, lively but considered music from a group which Gewelt leads from the front, while suggesting that he has the sense to know that bassist-leaders can also be crashing bores. There's no boring modal blowing, nothing pushed past its useful lifespan – only four of the ten tracks even break the five-minute barrier. Some of it is memorably beautiful. 'End Off ...' is a Metheny-like ballad with unemphatic but gorgeous chord-changes that Rebello and Eberson shape to beguiling effect. But the record works through a broad stylistic range without making it seem like a shopping-list. There's free playing, nostalgically old-fashioned fusion ('Hide And Seek' itself, which has guest Billy Cobham sitting in), even a coolly mediated blues in Carla Bley's 'Sing Me Softly Of The Blues', which is followed by an almost countrified track featuring William-Olsson. It's a sampler of what Gewelt can do and what kind of things he's interested in and, though that recipe often turns into self-indulgence and waste, here it's refreshing.

Tiziana Ghiglioni (born 1956)

VOCALS

Based in Milan, Ghiglioni is an Italian whose dedication to jazz singing begins with the classic style, yet goes far further, taking in the songs of Steve Lacy, Monk and Giorgio Gaslini.

****(*) Streams**
Splasc(h) H 104 *Ghiglioni; Luca Bonvini (tb); Maurizio Caldura Nunez (ss, ts); Luca Flores (p); Franco Nesti (b); Alessandro Fabbri (d).* 12/84.

***** Onde**
Splasc(h) H 133 *Ghiglioni; Carlo Actis Dato (ts, bs, bcl); Claudio Lodati (g); Enrico Fazio (b); Fiorenzo Sordini (d, perc, mar).* 6/87.

***** Yet Time**
Splasc(h) H 150 *Ghiglioni; Roberto Ottaviano (ss); Stefano Battaglia (p); Paolino Dalla Porta (b); Tiziano Tononi (d).* 3/88.

***** Lyrics**
Splasc(h) H 348 *Ghiglioni; Paul Bley (p).* 3/91.

***** Something Old, Something New, Something Borrowed, Something Blue**
Splasc(h) H 370 *Ghiglioni; Enrico Rava (t); Giancarlo Schiaffini (tb); Steve Lacy (ss); Umberto Petrin (p); Attilio Zanchi (b); Tiziano Tononi (d, perc).* 4–5/92.

Since she seems to appear in a quite different setting almost from record to record, it's a little difficult to focus on the merits of Tiziana Ghiglioni's singing. Her albums for Splasc(h) find her both fronting groups and working as an integral element within them: she is almost peripheral to *Onde,* where she guests with Actis Dato's Art Studio band, yet her singing on 'Rosso Di Sera' and 'Voci' is a striking wordless invention. *Streams* and *Yet Time* find her taking a Norma Winstone-like role of alternating pastoral scat with cool readings of lyrics. She has a big, rangy voice which she's reluctant to use in a big way, so many of her vocal improvisations sound restrained; fluency doesn't come easy to her, either. Yet the improvisation on Ornette Coleman's 'Round Trip' on *Yet Time* is sustained with great skill, and her meeting with Schiaffini, which includes bare-bones readings of 'When I Fall In Love' and 'All Blues' as well as more *outré* material, shows her unfazed by working alone with an improvising trombonist. Her enunciation always makes one aware that she's not singing in her native language, and her self-written lyrics are awkward, but she's a charismatic performer.

***** Somebody Special**

Soul Note 121156-2 *Ghiglioni; Steve Lacy (ss); Franco D'Andrea (p); Jean-Jacques Avenel (b); Oliver Johnson (d).* 4/86.

***** I'll Be Around**

Soul Note 121256-2 *Ghiglioni; Enrico Rava (t); Mal Waldron (p).* 7–8/89.

Ghiglioni's albums for Soul Note seek out a more conservative context, with mixed results. Steve Lacy's iron presence is the dominant feature of *Somebody Special* and, while Ghiglioni is a better singer than Irene Aebi, and the quartet are in excellent form, the vocalist doesn't make a strong case for besting Lacy's sometimes intractable forms. *I'll Be Around* is dedicated to Billie Holiday, an inspiration rather than an influence, and in this collection of deathly slow ballads the singer does surprisingly well with Waldron and Rava, the latter especially at his most hauntingly poignant.

***** Sings Gaslini**

Soul Note 121297-2 *Ghiglioni; Renato Geremia (vn); Roberto Bonati (b); Giampiero Prina (d); string ensemble.* 1–2/95.

The songs, lyrics and arrangements are all by Giorgio Gaslini, and they elicit Ghiglioni's most measured, thoughtful work. Sometimes one wishes that she'd let go a little, in the manner of some of her less formal records: the singing is beautifully done, and the arrangements are impeccable, but this is a very temperate climate, and across a CD's length it's a little becalmed. The most *outré* moments are actually provided by the eccentric violin of Geremia.

****(*) Spellbound**

YVP 3058 *Ghiglioni; Gianluigi Trovesi (ss, as, picc-cl, bcl); Guido Di Leone (g); Attilio Zanchi (b); Gianni Cazzola (d).* 2/96.

A typically uncompromised project from the singer, with originals primarily by Zanchi and words by the vocalist. Trovesi acts as her front-line partner. There are several fine pieces, with the curious reworking of 'Cheek To Cheek' particularly good; yet there's a somewhat bizarre tendency for Ghiglioni to try to adopt a hipsterish persona which doesn't really suit her at all. Disappointingly, this discography has stood still for several years now, and we await something new from Tiziana.

Joe Giardullo

SOPRANO AND ALTO SAXOPHONES, BASS CLARINET, FLUTE

A sideman with Marilyn Crispell and Joe McPhee, Giardullo seems fondest of the high end of the reed family and perhaps prefers a temperate side to free playing.

****(*) Art Spirit**

Boxholder BXH 028 *Giardullo; Sangeeta Michael Berardi (g).* 10/97.

**** Language Of Swans**

Drimala 02-347-05 *Giardullo; Chris Sullivan (b); Michael Thompson (d, p).* 9/98.

***** Now Is**

Drimala 03-347-02 *Giardullo; Joe McPhee (t, flhn, ss); Michael Bisio (b); Tani Tabbal (d).* 10/02.

Despite the pretentious and off-putting sleevenotes on all of these releases, Giardullo is a capable if not especially enthralling player. The duet record with Berardi suffers from a certain aimlessness, as the pieces sound impressionistic and lacking in any backbone or solid foundation, a dangerous setting for a reed player with a guitarist who has multiple effects at his disposal. 'Pietrasanta' does a nice line in wistfulness, though. *Language Of Swans* is plain boring for much of the way, not very well recorded and again without any real sense of purpose. Easily the pick of the three is *Now Is*, which benefits from putting Giardullo into a strong and skilled group of improvisers who don't simply go down dead ends.

Michael Gibbs (born 1937)

TROMBONE, PIANO, BANDLEADER

Born in Rhodesia, Gibbs studied at Berklee and Lenox in the USA and came to London in 1965, where he worked as a leader and a studio musician. Went back to teach at Berklee in 1974 but returned to London in 1985. Long list of credits with many orchestras and ensembles around the jazz world, and one of the most noted composer-arrangers of his era, which continues.

****** Michael Gibbs**

Deram 844 907-2 *Gibbs; John Wilbraham (picc t); Nigel Carter, Ian Hamer, Maurice Miller, Derek Watkins, Kenny Wheeler (t, flhn); Cliff Hardie, David Horler, Bobby Lambe, Chris Pyne (tb); Maurice Gee, Ken Goldy, Ray Premru (btb); Jim Buck Jr, Nicholas Busch, Alan Civil, Valerie Smith (frhn); Martin Fry, Dick Hart (tba); Duncan Lamont, Mike Osborne, Tony Roberts, Alan Skidmore, John Surman, Barbara Thompson, Ray Warleigh (reeds); Bob Cornford, Mike Pyne (ky); Ray Russell, Chris Spedding (g); Fred Alexander, Alan Ford (clo); Jack Bruce, Brian Odges (b); John Marshall, Tony Oxley (d).* 70.

*****(*) Tanglewood 63**

Deram 844 906-2 *Gibbs; Harry Beckett, Nigel Carter, Henry Lowther, Kenny Wheeler (t, flhn); Malcolm Griffiths, David Horler, Chris Pyne (tb); Dick Hart, Alf Reece (tba); Tony Roberts, Alan Skidmore, Brian Smith, Stan Sulzmann, John Surman (reeds); Gordon Beck, Mike Pyne, John Taylor (ky); Chris Spedding (g); Bill Armon, Hugh Bean, George French, Tony Gilbert, Raymond Moseley, Michael Rennie, George Wakefield (vn); Fred Alexander, Allen Ford (clo); Roy*

Babbington, Jeff Clyne (b); John Marshall, Clive Thacker (d, perc); Frank Ricotti (perc, vib). 11–12/70.

Few recording careers have got off to such a glorious start as Mike Gibbs's. The opening moments of 'Family Joy, Oh Boy!' on the eponymous debut could split clouds and ripen grain. Gibbs had come to Britain from his native Rhodesia via a spell at Berklee. A very few gigs later he was being talked about as the most vibrant new talent on the scene. Gibbs has the gift that all great leaders of big bands seem to require: that of making complex and daring ideas seem natural and inevitable. In these early records he fused advanced harmonic ideas with a groove that drew on Ellington, Gil and Miles, and rock. As he demonstrated on *Tanglewood 63*, he could move from sun-kissed delight to moonstruck melancholy in a moment. Something about the voicing of the horns – and Gibbs was and is a reluctant trombonist – marked him down as an individualist. He rarely asks for stratospheric playing, concentrating on the middle register. 'Sojourn', which follows 'Tanglewood 63' and the appended 'functional' fanfare, is a lonely stroll through a musical landscape whose topography is rich in associations.

The first album pays some dues – to Stan Getz, John Dankworth, Bob Moses and Gary Burton – but it is utterly individual in conception and execution. Gibbs's charts look challenging, but he has the gift of making difficult passage-work sound coherent and expressive. 'Sweet Rain', 'Throb' and 'And On The Third Day' are classics of British jazz. Surman, Warleigh and Skidmore solo on the first and last, joined on 'Third Day' by Mike Osborne and trombonist Chris Pyne for an exuberant finale that brings a wonderful album to a climax.

The end of *Tanglewood 63* is no less joyous, a long feature for guitarist Spedding over a richly textured rhythm, held together by Roy Babbington's bass guitar, a near-perfect marriage of rock and jazz that was to be Gibbs's staple for years to come, even when the idea of fusion was in retreat. A whole generation of British jazz fans cut their teeth on these records. It's wonderful to have them back.

****** Big Music**

ACT 9231 *Gibbs; Ian Carr, Earl Gardner, Alan Rubin, Lew Soloff (t); John Clark (frhn); Dave Bargeron (tb); David Taylor (btb); Julian Arguëlles (ss); Jim Odgren (as); Chris Hunter (as, ss, ts, f); Lou Marini (ts, ss, f); Bob Mintzer (ts, f, bcl); Dave Tofani (f, af, picc); Dave Bristow, Brad Hatfield (ky); Django Bates (p); Kevin Eubanks, David Fiuczynski, Bill Frisell, Duke Levine, John Scofield (g); Kai Eckhardt (b); Bob Moses (d, d prog); Bad Bill Martin, Ben Wittman (d prog, perc).* 88, 9/90.

Gibbs was and remains a pioneer of a 'pure' kind of fusion: rock instruments and rhythms used to extend rather than diminish the scope of the improvisations. He always makes one feel the breadth and power of a big band, though, insisting on its weight and sonic force rather than breaking it down or using simple solo/accompaniment strategies.

Big Music was assembled in a latter-day Teo Macero style, building up heads, solos, intros and overdubs in the studio to produce the rich and multidimensional style which Gibbs's work demands. It is due to the efforts of John L. Walters that the project happened at all, and it took eight years to get it on to CD. Walters explains that he was looking for 'a missing link between *Out Of The Cool* and *Bitches Brew*, between Charles Ives and Salif Keita' and he points to Bob Moses' band, Mozamba, as a key moment in determining the actual sound. Moses is certainly the crucial element. His rhythmic brilliance makes 'Wall To Wall' the ideal opening track, a madly brilliant dance-floor jam with Jim Odgren's solo an additional bonus. The most obvious nod in the direction of the old Svengali – Gil Evans – is 'Mopsus', which includes overdubbed solos by Bill Frisell and Dave Bargeron. Gil's spirit is also on hand in 'Almost Ev'ry Day', a feature for Chris Hunter's strong, bluesy alto and a piece that might have been around for ever, so strong a hold does it take on first hearing. 'Pride Aside' is the coda, with an immaculate, Miles-influenced solo from Ian Carr. 'Waterfront' is a bonus track featuring Julian Arguëlles on soprano and Django Bates on piano, recorded some time after the main sessions and not originally available for the record. This is a glorious album which entirely merits its place at the start of ACT's 'World's Greatest Jazz Orchestras' series.

*****(*) Europeana**

ACT 9220 *Gibbs; Markus Stockhausen (t); Albert Mangelsdorff (tb); Django Bates (thn); Douglas Boyd (ob); Christof Lauer (ts, ss); Klaus Doldinger (ss); Joachim Kühn (p); Richard Galliano (acc); Jean-François Jenny-Clark (b); Jon Christensen (d); Radio Philharmonie Hannover NDR.* 95.

Gibbs has been characteristically modest about his part in this moody, beautifully evoked 'Jazzphony', which is intended to express European unity by drawing material from the constitutent nations of the EU. The folky material is much simpler, less layered and dense than most of Gibbs's work, and this may explain his faint unease with the results (which are unabashedly beautiful, by the way).

Kühn is the chief soloist, providing a coherence that might otherwise have been impossible to sustain. 'Black Is The Colour' is a feature for the peerless oboe work of Douglas Boyd, paired with Django Bates on tenor horn. 'Stevtone', a Norwegian psalm, is a feature for Markus Stockhausen, who also leads on piccolo trumpet on 'Lo Ceu N'A Creat'. Klaus Doldinger's soprano saxophone turns 'She Moved Through The Fair' into a brooding lament, and Ireland, like France, has a second bite with a moving version of the 'Londonderry Air', with concertmaster Volker Worlitzsch providing the violin solo. A strange, very beautiful record, somewhat difficult to place in the overall schema of Gibbs's work, but bearing his stamp at every turn. Not for every taste, but impeccably tasteful.

*****(*) Nonsequence**

Provocateur 82002-2 *Gibbs; Ingolf Burkhardt, Lennart Axelsson, Michael Leuchsner, Claus Stötter, Dick Lentschat, Reiner Winterschladen, Lew Soloff, Randy Brecker, Earl Gardner, Alex Sipiagin (t); Joe Gallardo, Michael Danner, Dan Gottshall, Stefan Lotterman, Ingo Lahme, Jim Pugh, Dave Bargeron, Dave Taylor (tb); Fiete Felsch, Lutz Buchner, Peter Bolte, Christof Lauer, Frank Delle, Chris Hunter, Alex Foster (saxes); John Clark, Richard Rieves, Karyn Dobbs (frhn); Gil Goldstein (p, acc); Vladyslaw Sendecki (p); Stephan Diez, Hiram Bullock (g); Lucas Lindholm, Steve Swallow (b); Billy Kilson, Mark Mondesir, Ian Thomas (d); Marcia Doctor (perc).* 2–5/01.

One ensemble from the NDR, one from New York's session scene, and Gibbs turning in some sparklingly fresh scores, from an unexpected respray given to 'Moonlight Serenade' to the new African optimism of 'Now Listen Here'. Soloists charge out of these structures with aplomb, but in a sense they're a distraction, since it's the dense yet joyful writing which is the point of this music. Our only reservation is that the New Yorkers can seem almost blasé about their work, certainly next to the Germans. But it's great Gibbs.

Terry Gibbs (born 1924)

VIBRAPHONE, DRUMS

Born in Brooklyn, Gibbs had a relatively uneventful time of it in late swing bands before settling in Los Angeles in 1957 and running a part-time big band of studio pros, as well as recording for Mercury. Worked extensively in TV in the '60s and '70s, but was still touring and performing in the '80s and '90s.

***** Dream Band**
Contemporary CCD 7647-2 *Gibbs; Conte Candoli, Al Porcino, Ray Triscari, Stu Williamson (t); Bob Enevoldsen (vtb); Vernon Friley (tb); Joe Cadena, Med Flory, Bill Holman (ts); Joe Maini, Charlie Kennedy (as); Jack Schwartz (bs); Pete Jolly (p); Max Bennett (b); Mel Lewis (d).* 3–11/59.

***** The Sundown Sessions**
Contemporary CCD 7562-2 *As above, except add Johnny Audino (t), Bob Burgess (tb).* 11/59.

***** Flying Home**
Contemporary CCD 7654-2 *As above, except add Frank Higgins (t), Lou Levy (p), Buddy Clark (b).* 3–11/59.

****** One More Time**
Contemporary CCD 7658-2 *As above, except add Irene Kral (v).* 3–11/59.

The Gibbs bands combined the high-energy swing of Lionel Hampton with the sophistication of the Thad Jones/Mel Lewis outfits (Mel Lewis straddled the drum stool during Gibbs's most productive period). The arrangements, by Marty Paich, Lennie Niehaus and others, are all good, but with a sometimes uneasy emphasis on the higher horns. Gibbs's playing is closer to Hampton's percussive bounce than to any of the competing influences, and he solos with considerable verve; unfortunately the excellent *Main Stem*, one of the best of this sequence, is currently out of print. It's a style that draws a great deal from bop and it's no less well adapted to the small-group performances which he has been focusing on more recently, at least on record (he still runs editions of The Dream Band today, but says he won't record them, in order not to spoil the memory of this great outfit).

One More Time has arrived as the result of Terry finding another box of tapes at home, and what a fine discovery. It's as loaded with atmosphere as anything in this series, and for sheer zing it sounds like the pick of the sequence to us. Irene Kral takes a couple of vocals, Conte Candoli has a couple of lovely features, and Gibbs himself has the audacity to out-Hamp the master on an 11-minute 'Flying Home'. The sound is amazingly good.

***** Jewish Melodies In Jazztime**
Verve 589673-2 *Gibbs; Sam Kutcher (tb); Ramon Musiker (cl); Alan Logan, Alice McLeod (p); Herman Wright (b); Sol Gage (d, marim); Bobby Pike (d).* 1–3/63.

It seems bizarre that Verve have chosen to reissue this set ahead of the 18 other Gibbs albums they have the rights to. On each track, the horns fanfare the melody in a kind of cartoon-klezmer style before the Gibbs quartet step in and do their swinging stuff. It seems strange to think that Alice McLeod was only three years away from playing on some of the most turbulent and difficult jazz records of the day, as Alice Coltrane. Perfectly amiable, but let's have the other Gibbs albums on Mercury next.

***** Chicago Fire**
Contemporary 14036 *Gibbs; Buddy DeFranco (cl); John Campbell II (p); Todd Coolman (b); Gerry Gibbs (d).* 7/87.

***** Air Mail Special**
Contemporary 14056 *Gibbs; Buddy DeFranco (cl); Frank Collett (p); Andy Simpkins (b); Jimmie Smith (d).* 10/81.

***** The Latin Connection**
Contemporary 140222 *Gibbs; Frank Morgan (as); Sonny Bravo (p); Bobby Rodriguez, Jose Madera, Tito Puente, Orestes Vilato (perc).* 5/86.

*****(*) Memories Of You**
Contemporary 14066 *Gibbs; Buddy DeFranco (cl); Herb Ellis (g); Larry Novak (p); Milt Hinton (b); Butch Miles (d).* 4/91.

***** Kings Of Swing**
Contemporary CCD 14067 *As above.* 4/91.

Lively latter-day sets from a player who must be taking multivitamins. All of these feature him in the company of DeFranco in a series of friendly but competitive sets, which were also repeated with the clarinettist as (strictly nominal) leader, but what's a credit among friends? *Memories Of You* is perhaps the best all-round set, with an excellent reading of 'Flying Home' and a romantic but un-schmaltzy 'Poor Butterfly'. *Kings Of Swing* is the poorer half of the same sessions. Of the remainder, *Air Mail Special* ('Love For Sale', 'Blues For Brody', 'Body And Soul') is particularly recommended, with *Chicago Fire* (unexpected versions of 'Giant Steps' and the '52nd Street Theme'). The big-band stuff is the most wholly authentic, but Gibbs's small groups are perhaps more in tune with prevailing tastes.

Some great south-of-the-border bop on *The Latin Connection*, which features great playing from the rehabilitated Frank Morgan and some typically exuberant percussion from Puente. Gibbs is in great form on Parker's 'Scrapple From The Apple' but, even if the pace drops off a bit later in the set, the first half should be enough to put a smile on anyone's face.

***** Play That Song**
Chiaroscuro 337 *Gibbs; Uri Caine (p); Boris Koslov (b); Gerry Gibbs (d).* 94.

***** Wham**
Chiaroscuro 356 *Gibbs; Buddy DeFranco (cl); Flip Phillips (ts); Aaron Goldberg (p); Darek Oleskiewicz (b); Gerry Gibbs (d).* 99.

***** Plays Steve Allen**
Contemporary 14089 *Gibbs; Buddy DeFranco (cl); Tom Ranier (p); Dave Carpenter (b); Gerry Gibbs (d).* 99.

Allen's comedy songs have always been something of an acquired taste, but here they form the basis of a brightly swinging mainstream session that pairs old friends Gibbs and DeFranco in an entirely *simpatico* way. Tunes like 'I Used To Think I Was Crazy' and 'Playing The Field' are hardly classics, but they have their charms and the two front-men have a ball with them, doubtless kvetching all sorts of routines in addition when the microphones were off. Ranier is an excellent accompanist who's presumably boned up on his Steve Allen as well. A nice, warm-hearted set with some surprisingly robust material like the boppish 'South Dakota', which may have a more familiar melodic basis.

The other session with DeFranco maintains the same warm rapport, and the long versions of 'Take Your Time' (well named), 'Please Let Me Play The Blues' and 'Sweet and Lovely' are beautifully crafted. Gibbs still takes such evident delight in playing that it is hard not to respond to these sessions, even if your idea of jazz is a little more modern and advanced.

Son Gerry has been a great addition to the Gibbs sound, and he really catches the mood on *Play That Song*, which was recorded live at the 1994 Floating Jazz Festival on board SS *Norway*. Lots of good feeling on stage and some stunning playing from Terry in the climactic sequence of Artie Shaw's 'Moonray' and the originals 'The Fat Man' and 'The Beautiful People'. Uri Caine has been associated with more serious stuff of late, but he shows here what an inventive swinger he can be.

***** From Me To You**
Mack Avenue MAC 1008 *Gibbs; Pete Christlieb (ts); Mike Melvoin (p); Joey DeFrancesco (org); Dave Carpenter (b); Jeff Hamilton (d); Franz Pusch (perc); Barbara Morrison (v).* 1/02.

A good-natured nod from one master to another, as Terry offers a homage to Lionel Hampton with this set of tunes associated with Hamp. Gibbs still sounds in excellent fettle and can't resist the double-time runs, even on the slower pieces, which were a mark of both men. Professional if not especially exciting support from the others, and Barbara Morrison does Dinah Washington's feature on 'Evil Gal Blues'.

The Gibson Brass Band

GROUP

Formed in 1946, the GBB worked regularly in New Orleans up until the late '60s, by which time many of the musicians had passed on.

***** The Gibson Brass Band Of New Orleans 1963/64**
American Music AMCD–96 *Eddie Richardson, Johnny Wimberley, John Henry McNeil, Joseph Bentley (t); Cal Blunt, Eddie Noble, Roland Cayette (tb); Robert Davis (as); Alphonse Spears (ts); George Sterling, Dave Bailey (d).* 11/63–4/64.

Barry Martyn recorded this group of old-timers 'before they faded into history', setting down the first ten tracks here at an open-air session; five more were subsequently cut in a studio some months later. Once past the very shaky warm-up of 'Come Ye Disconsolate', the music goes with a real swing, and as tattered and off-centre as some of the playing is, this is another worthy survival from American Music's deep archive of pre-jazz roots music. Some of the older members of the band were born as far back as the 1880s and could remember Bolden's era: a strange thought to modern ears.

John Gill

BANJO, TROMBONE, VOCAL

Californian revivalist with multi-thread credentials as trombonist, banjo strummer, bandleader and arranger. Sometimes he sings too.

****(*) Smile, Darn Ya, Smile**
Stomp Off CD 1227 *Gill; Charles Fardella (t); David Sager (tb, v); Lynn Zimmer (ss, ts, cl); Tom Fischer (as, cl); Steve Pistorius (p, v); Debbie Markow, Elliot Markow (vn); Tom Saunders (tba); Hal Smith (d).* 12/90.

***** Headin' For Better Times**
Stomp Off CD 1270 *As above, except add Dan Levinson (ts, cl).* 7/91–12/92.

Shading between revivalism and a straight and strict re-creation of hot dance music, Gill's outfit errs on the side of the latter, which will tend to switch off all but the more dedicated archivists. There are two or three tunes on both discs that build up a bigger head of steam, and both ride out on a hot one: 'Here Comes The Hot Tamale Man', which Freddie Keppard once blew on, was a good idea for the second record. For the rest, though, it's often re-created schmaltz. Which still sounds like schmaltz, however much ironic salt and pepper gets milled over the melodies.

****** Looking For A Little Bluebird**
Stomp Off CD 1295 *Gill; Chris Tyle, Duke Heitger (t); Frank Powers (cl, v); Steve Pistorius (p); Eddy Davis (bj, v); Vince Giordano (tba); Hal Smith (d).* 12/94.

*****(*) Take Me To The Midnight Cakewalk Ball**
Stomp Off CD 1304 *As above.* 8/95.

*****(*) Listen To That Dixie Band**
Stomp Off CD 1321 *As above, except add Lavay Smith (v).* 5/97.

Gill plays trombone rather than banjo here, calls the group The Dixieland Serenaders, and has them play the stuffing out of a repertoire brimful of Oliver, Morton, Dodds – and the Lu Watters/Turk Murphy axis of revivalism. Except that this group actually sounds better than the old-timers of San Franciscan jazz usually did. The two-trumpet front line blows over the rest of the band like a particularly cussed zephyr, and Giordano and Smith give the group a terrific lift even when they're playing a simple two-beat. The result is a shakedown of a lot of mothballed tunes that puts a new lease on almost all of them. We fractionally prefer *Looking For A Little Bluebird* for its maniacal 'Alligator Hop' and the beautiful extended treatment of 'Farewell To Storyville', and for Richard Bird's sound, which shoves the band right in your face while still giving them a full and clear balance. The subsequent *Take Me To The Midnight Cakewalk Ball* is barely a step behind, though, with notable treatments of 'Wa Wa Wa' and 'Grandpa's Spells' ... and 16 more.

The fun continues on *Listen To That Dixie Band*. Quite a ration of blues this time, with four Bessie Smith numbers sung by guest Lavay Smith (on vacation from the Red Hot Skillet Lickers) and the band still sounding in their most flavoursome form. All highly recommended!

Dizzy Gillespie (1917–93)

TRUMPET, PERCUSSION, PIANO, VOCAL

Born in Cheraw, South Carolina, Gillespie started on trumpet at 13. Moved to Philadelphia in 1935 and joined Teddy Hill in 1937, then Cab Calloway in 1939. Formed coterie of after-hours players with Parker, Monk and Kenny Clarke in the early '40s, then began leading his own small groups from 1945, playing the new music of bebop. Led his own big band, 1946–50, and during that time pioneered the fusion of jazz with Latin and Afro-Cuban music. Then returned to small-group work, though he toured with big bands for the State Department, 1956–8. A small group featuring James Moody was his main vehicle in the early

'60s, but occasional big-band work and a campaign to run for the presidency also intervened (he failed to be elected). In the '70s and '80s, he assumed the role of elder statesman of modern jazz and was the focal point for the re-evaluation of bop during that time. Celebrated his 75th birthday with a season of New York concerts, but was diagnosed with cancer shortly afterwards. The guiding theoretician behind bop, the supreme virtuoso of jazz trumpet in the '40s and '50s, a profound teacher, a visionary with regard to jazz and its capacity to fraternize with other musics, and the great entertainer of his era, which lasted 50 years.

***** Dizzy Gillespie 1945**

Classics 888 *Gillespie; Trummy Young (tb, v); Tony Scott (cl); Charlie Parker, Johnny Bothwell (as); Dexter Gordon, Don Byas (ts); Clyde Hart, Jimmy Jones, Frank Paparelli (p); Mike Bryan, Remo Palmieri (g); Oscar Pettiford, Gene Ramey, Slam Stewart, Al Hall, Murray Shipinski (b); Specs Powell, Ed Nicholson, Cozy Cole, Irv Kluger, Shelly Manne (d); Rubberlegs Williams, Sarah Vaughan (v).* 1–2/45.

*****(*) Dizzy Gillespie 1945–1946**

Classics 935 *Gillespie; Howard McGhee, Karl George, Snooky Young (t); Vic Dickenson, George Washington, Ralph Bledsoe, Henry Coker (tb); Charlie Parker, Willie Smith, Marvin Johnson (as); Don Byas, Lucky Thompson, Fred Simon (ts); Gene Porter (bs); Al Haig, George Handy, Wilbert Baranco (p); Bill De Arango, Buddy Harper (g); Curley Russell, Charles Mingus, Ray Brown, Al McKibbon (b); Big Sid Catlett, Earl Watkins, Stan Levey, J. C. Heard, Roy Haynes (d); The Three Angels, Sarah Vaughan (v).* 5/45–4/46.

♛ ** The Complete RCA Victor Recordings**

Bluebird 66528-2 2CD *As above, except add Bill Dillard, Shad Collins, Lamar Wright, Willie Cook, Benny Harris, Miles Davis, Fats Navarro (t), Dicky Wells, Ted Kelly, J. J. Johnson, Kai Winding (tb), Buddy DeFranco (cl), Benny Carter, Russell Procope, Ernie Henry (as), Yusef Lateef, Coleman Hawkins, Ben Webster, Charlie Ventura, Don Byas, Robert Carroll, Teddy Hill (ts), Al Gibson, Ernie Caceres (bs), Lionel Hampton (vib), Lennie Tristano, Sam Allen, James Foreman (p), Charlie Christian, Billy Bauer (g), Milt Hinton, Richard Fulbright, Al McKibbon, Eddie Safranski (b), Bill Beason, Teddy Stewart (d), Vince Guerra, Sabu Martinez, Chano Pozo (perc), Johnny Hartman (v).* 5/37–1/49.

*****(*) Dizzy Gillespie 1947–1949**

Classics 1102 *As discs above.* 12/47–6/49.

*****(*) Dizzy Gillespie 1949–1950**

Classics 1168 *Gillespie; Don Slaughter, Elmon Wright, Willie Cook (t); Matthew Gee, Sam Hurt, Charles Greenlee, Henry Coker, Richard Kenny, Harold Smith (tb); Jimmy Heath, John Coltrane (as); Jesse Powell, Paul Gonsalves (ts); Al Gibson (bs); Milt Jackson (vib); Johnny Acea, Paul Smith (p); John Collins, Floyd Smith (g); Al McKibbon, Jack Cascales (b); Specs Wright (d); Carlos Duchesne, Francisco Pozo, Carlos Vidal (perc); Joe Carroll, Tiny Irvin (v); strings, woodwinds.* 11/49–9/50.

****** The Dizzy Gillespie Story 1939–1950**

Proper PROPERBOX 30 4CD *As various discs above, plus groups led by Teddy Hill, Cab Calloway, Lionel Hampton, Lucky Millinder, Billy Eckstine and Coleman Hawkins.* 5/37–11/50.

*****(*) Night In Tunisia**

Dreyfus FDM 36734-2 *As various discs above.* 1/45–9/47.

*****(*) Cubana Be, Cubana Bop**

Dreyfus FDM 36720-2 *As various discs above.* 6/46–7/49.

John Birks Gillespie had already been recording for almost a decade when he made the earliest of these tracks, and in the Cab Calloway and Teddy Hill bands he cut the outline of a promising Roy Eldridge disciple. His associations with Thelonious Monk and Charlie Parker, though, took him into hitherto uncharted realms. While he continued to credit Parker as the real inspirational force behind bebop, Gillespie was the movement's scholar, straw boss, sartorial figurehead and organizer: his love of big-band sound led him into attempts to orchestrate the new music that resulted in some of the most towering jazz records, particularly (among those here) 'Things To Come' and 'Cubana Be'/'Cubana Bop'. But his own playing is at least as powerful a reason to listen to these tracks. Gillespie brought a new virtuosity to jazz trumpet just as Parker created a matchless vocabulary for the alto sax. It scarcely seems possible that the music could have moved on from Louis Armstrong's 'Cornet Chop Suey' to Gillespie's astonishing flight on 'Dizzy Atmosphere' in only 20 years. A dazzling tone, solo construction that was as logical as it was unremittingly daring, and a harmonic grasp which was built out of countless nights of study and experimentation: Gillespie showed the way for every trumpeter in post-war jazz. His Guild and Musicraft recordings include a single sextet track with Dexter Gordon ('Blue 'N' Boogie'), seven with Parker, four with Sonny Stitt and Milt Jackson, and the balance with his big band.

The RCA set sweeps the board as the cream of Gillespie's studio work in the period. The big-band tracks are complete and in good sound, all the Victor small-group sessions are here, there are pre-history tracks with Teddy Hill and Lionel Hampton as a taster of things to come, and four tracks with the Metronome All-Star bebop group, where Dizzy lines up with Miles, Bird, Fats and J.J. Absolutely indispensable and some of the most exciting jazz of the era.

Classics have rounded up some useful obscurities in their survey. Classics 888 mixes bebop's earliest sounds – a January 1945 date with the first versions of 'Good Bait' and 'Be-Bop' itself – along with dates under the leadership of either Clyde Hart or Trummy Young (who somehow manages to get himself on five of the seven sessions here!). Three dates are almost ruined by the vocals, including the bizarre and inebriated warblings of Rubberlegs Williams; but Gillespie, Byas and Parker (a little restrained) salvage something out of it. Three tracks with Tony Scott and Ben Webster are interesting. Classics 935 includes the first seven titles for Dial (with Parker absent on the second date), adds the first small-band date for Victor, offers four very cloudy and speed-wobbled tracks with a Johnny Richards orchestra and four all-star big-band tracks led by Wilbert Baranco: 'Night And Day' is a great one, even though Gillespie (masquerading as 'John Burk') doesn't solo. This is a scrappy way to hear this music, but diehard Gillespie collectors will want these discs.

Classics 1102 carries on with the Gillespie big-band sides: if you don't have the RCA set, this will fill in gaps such as 'Dizzier And Dizzier' and the immortal 'Cubana Be' and 'Cubana Bop'. Classics 1168 brings this big-band era to a close, adds some sextet sides with Jimmy Heath and Milt Jackson, and then goes into eight titles where Johnny Richards arranged material for strings and woodwinds, with Gillespie firing over the top. The trumpet parts are terrific, even if Richards was scarcely the most daring of arrangers. A few duds in this set, but even here there is sufficient Gillespie to make the disc an attractive buy.

The four-disc *Dizzy Gillespie Story* is a very appealing set: early appearances as a sideman, then many of the key sides from the '40s. If Proper's presentation is to your liking, this will work well as a Gillespie primer. But the two Dreyfus compilations, one of small groups, one of big-band titles, are excellent single-disc overviews of the period too.

★★★(★) Pleyel 48

Arpeggio ARJ017 *Gillespie; Dave Burns, Benny Bailey, Lamar Wright, Elmon Wright (t); Ted Kelly, Bill Shepherd (tb); Howard Johnson, John Brown (as); George Gales, Big Nick Nicholas (ts); Cecil Payne (bs); John Lewis (p); Al McKibbon (b); Kenny Clarke (d); Chano Pozo (perc); Kenny Hagood (v).* 2/48.

★★★(★) Dizzy Gillespie & His Big Band In Concert

GNP Crescendo GNPD 23 *As above, except add Willie Cook (t), Cindy Duryea, Jesse Tarrant (tb), Ernie Henry, James Moody (reeds), James Foreman (p); Nelson Boyd (b), Teddy Stewart (d); omit Bailey, Lamar Wright, Kelly, Johnson, Nicholas, Lewis, McKibbon, Clarke, Hagood.* 48.

Although the big band made only a small number of studio records, it was caught on the wing at a number of concerts, even if seldom in hi-fi conditions. These, though, are two splendid gigs, and only the exasperatingly imperfect sound holds them back from top ratings. Although much of the material is duplicated across the two concerts, some of it is strikingly different: the Pasadena (GNP) concert has a three-minute 'Round Midnight' while the one from Paris runs to almost nine minutes. Gillespie's interest in Latin rhythms brought semi-legendary percussionist Pozo (killed not long after these concerts) into the fold, and there is typically exciting stuff on 'Manteca'. If the orchestra never moves with the neurotic immediacy of small-group bebop, it's still a remarkable sound. The Paris concert has now been issued in yet another edition, on the Arpeggio label (part of the British Magnum group), and the 'digital remastering' doesn't seem to have made much difference to the sound.

★★★ Cognac Blues

Emarcy 014064-2 *Gillespie; Don Byas (ts); Art Simmons, Arnold Ross, Wade Legge (p); Jean-Jacques Tilché (g); Joe Benjamin, Lou Hackney (b); Bill Clark, Al Jones (d); Humberto Canto Morales (perc).* 3/52–2/53.

When economics required Gillespie to dissolve the big band, he carried on with small groups. Operating at something of a tangent to bop – he still performed with Parker on a few occasions, and there is a superb session for Verve with Monk and Bird, as well as the famous Massey Hall concert of 1953 – his playing began to take on a grandeur that sounded even more ravishing than Parker's alto did when confronted with strings. Made in Paris for the Blue Star label, these sessions have a moth-eaten sound and the groups offer very average rhythm sections and Don Byas at his bleariest and least sensitive. The rough sound on the opening date grants Gillespie's vocal on 'Sabla Y Blu' the quality of a field recording. But this was still a vintage period for Dizzy and he does something worth hearing on each of these tracks, the solos either tightly packed with detail or bursting with grand gestures.

★★★(★) Afro

Verve 517052-2 *Gillespie; Quincy Jones, Jimmy Nottingham, Ernie Royal (t); Leon Comegys, J. J. Johnson, George Matthews (tb); George Dorsey, Hilton Jefferson (as); Hank Mobley, Lucky Thompson (ts); Danny Bank (bs, f); Gilberto Valdez (f); Ray Conception, Wade Legge, Alejandro Hernandez (p); Lou Hackney, Robert Rodriguez (b); Charli Persip (d); Candido Camero, Mongo Santamaria, Jose Manguel, Ubaldo Nietes, Rafael Miranda (perc).* 5/54.

Split between a four-part 'Manteca Suite', written by Chico O'Farrill for big band, and a session where Gillespie fronts an Afro-Cuban rhythm section, there's some heady stuff here. 'Jungla', which is mostly trumpet over the five-man drum section, practically steams, and while some of the music might not gel as purposefully as the creators intended, the exhilaration of hearing Gillespie in full flight over all this metropolitan hustle and bustle is thrilling. The small-group tracks have a lot of great trumpet too, although flautist Gilberto Valdes is a rather cheesy foil.

★★★ Diz And Getz

Verve 549749-2 *Gillespie; Stan Getz, Hank Mobley (ts); Oscar Peterson, Wade Legge (p); Herb Ellis (g); Ray Brown, Lou Hackney (b); Max Roach, Charli Persip (d).* 12/53–5/54.

★★(★) For Musicians Only

Verve 837435-2 *As above, except add Sonny Stitt (as), John Lewis (p), Stan Levey (d); omit Peterson and Roach.* 10/56.

★★★ Sonny Side Up

Verve 521426-2 *Gillespie; Sonny Stitt, Sonny Rollins (ts); Ray Bryant (p); Tommy Potter (b); Charli Persip (d).* 12/57.

These all-star encounters have perhaps been overrated. It's interesting to hear Gillespie on what was effectively mainstream material on *Diz And Getz* – two Ellington tunes, three standards and a single Latin theme – but the group strike a surprisingly shambolic note in places, seldom managing to play together, and the superfast blues, 'Impromptu', is a virtual disaster. Worth salvaging are a lovely trumpet treatment of 'It's The Talk Of The Town', some moments from the otherwise audibly ruffled Getz, and a version of 'It Don't Mean A Thing' in which the tempo is actually matched by the intensity of the playing. The music has never sounded like a great feat of engineering: the latest version is another Verve Master Edition and sounds a good deal better than we remember. There is a stray three-minute track from a later session with Hank Mobley as a somewhat dubious bonus. *For Musicians Only* is even more of a blow-out, with 'Be-Bop' and 'Dark Eyes' running over 12 minutes each and Stitt treating it as a carving session: the tempos are almost uniformly hell-for-leather. Exhilarating in small doses, but it's hardly as significant a date as it might have been with a little preparation. *Sonny Side Up* is pretty desultory stuff, too, but with Rollins in his greatest period and Stitt as combative as usual, the two long blues tracks strike some sparks, and Rollins's solo on the brief 'I Know That You Know' is prime cut. Dizzy referees with aplomb.

★★★(★) Dizzy In South America

Consolidated Artists CAP 933 *Gillespie; Quincy Jones, Ermit Perry, Carl Warwick (t); Rod Levitt, Melba Liston, Frank Rehak (tb); Jimmy Powell, Phil Woods (as); Benny Golson, Billy Mitchell (ts); Marty Flax (bs); Walter Davis Jr (p); Nelson Boyd (b); Charli Persip (d); Austin Cromer (v).* 7–8/56.

*** Dizzy In South America Vol. 2

Consolidated Artists CAP 934 *As above.* 7–8/56.

***(*) Live, 1957

Jazz Unlimited JUCD 2040 *Gillespie; Lee Morgan, Ermit Perry, Carl Warwick, Talib Daawud (t); Melba Liston, Al Grey, Ray Connor (tb); Jimmy Powell, Ernie Henry (as); Benny Golson, Billy Mitchell (ts); Pee Wee Moore (bs); Wynton Kelly (p); Tom Bryant (b); Charli Persip (d).* 6/57.

All three of these location recordings are in decent fidelity, and they're valuable survivals of Gillespie's big band, convened in the first instance for a State Department tour of the region. There's no duplication of material across the first two sets; the first, in particular, catches band and leader in close to top form. Besides Gillespie, there are good moments for Woods, Golson and Mitchell in particular. The second volume is a shade less good, if only for the odd dud such as the show-off set-piece, 'The Champ'. But the Jazz Unlimited disc, made in Chesterfield, PA, the following year, shouldn't be missed either. There's the opportunity to compare the different versions of 'Jessica's Day' and Melba Liston's feature, 'My Reverie', but there are several pieces not heard on the South America discs: a crackling 'Autumn Leaves', Ernie Henry featured in 'Dizzy's Business', Golson's 'I Remember Clifford' and 'Whisper Not', and the 18-year-old Lee Morgan featured on 'A Night In Tunisia'. But the driving impression throughout is of how good Gillespie was sounding in front of a fiery big band.

CORE COLLECTION

**** Birks Works

Verve 527900-2 2CD *Gillespie; Joe Gordon, Quincy Jones, Ermit Perry, Carl Warwick, Talib Daawud, Lee Morgan (t); Melba Liston, Frank Rehak (tb); Rod Levitt, Ray Connor (btb); Jimmy Powell, Phil Woods, Ernie Henry (as); Billy Mitchell, Benny Golson, Ernie Wilkins (ts); Marty Flax, Billy Root, Pee Wee Moore (bs); Walter Davis Jr, Wynton Kelly (p); Paul West, Nelson Boyd (b); Charli Persip (d); Austin Comer (v).* 6/56–7/57.

Long awaited in a comprehensive edition, these tracks cover the work of a band that Gillespie toured with as a cultural ambassador, though this is all studio work. Studded with great players, the orchestra also benefits from some of the most perceptive scoring of the day – by Liston, Wilkins, Jones, Golson and other hands – and, with Gillespie in stratospheric form as soloist, the band could hardly have failed. Yet the three original albums remain comparatively forgotten, or at least neglected, which makes the reissue even more welcome.

*** At Newport

Verve 513754-2 *Gillespie; Lee Morgan, Ermit Perry, Carl Warwick, Talib Daawud (t); Melba Liston, Al Grey, Chuck Connors (tb); Ernie Henry, Jimmy Powell (as); Billy Mitchell, Benny Golson (ts); Pee Wee Moore (bs); Wynton Kelly, Mary Lou Williams (p); Paul West (b); Charli Persip (d).* 7/57.

*** Have Trumpet, Will Excite!

Verve 549744-2 *Gillespie; Junior Mance (p); Les Spann (g, f); Sam Jones (b); Lex Humphries (d); Carlos Patato Valdes (perc).* 2/59.

**** Gillespiana / Carnegie Hall Concert

Verve 519809-2 *Gillespie; John Frosk, Clark Terry, Nick Travis, Carl Warwick, Ernie Royal, Joe Wilder (t); Urbie Green, Frank Rehak, Britt Woodman, George Matthews, Arnette Sparrow, Paul Faulise (tb); Jimmy Buffington, Al Richman, Gunther Schuller, Julius Watkins, John Barrows, Richard Berg (frhn); Leo Wright (f, as); Lalo Schifrin (p); Don Butterfield (tba); Art Davis (b); Chuck Lampkin (d); Candido Camero, Willie Rodriguez, Ray Barretto, Julio Collazo, Jose Mangual (perc); Joe Carroll (v).* 11/60–3/61.

***(*) Ultimate Dizzy Gillespie

Verve 557535-2 *Gillespie; various groups.* 6/54–11/64.

Gillespie's Verve contract was arguably a little disappointing in that it produced no single indispensable record. The big- and small-band dates were pot-pourris of dazzling breaks and solos that never quite gelled into the long-playing masterpiece Gillespie surely had in him at this time. Having already outlived many of his key contemporaries in bebop, he was beginning to be a player in search of a context. The best single disc is certainly the one that couples *Gillespiana* – a marvellous assemblage of orchestral charts by Lalo Schifrin, some of his finest work on record, to which Gillespie rises superbly – and the subsequent *Carnegie Hall Concert* of a few months later, not quite so memorable, though this 'Manteca' and the extravagant 'Tunisian Fantasy' are exhilarating. The Newport set from 1957 has some great moments – a fine 'I Remember Clifford', the chunks from Mary Lou Williams's 'Zodiac Suite' with the composer sitting in – and some concert schtick.

Have Trumpet, Will Excite! is a recent revival of the rhythm section via the Cannonball Adderley group, who tend to do little more than vamp away behind the maestro and, given that most of the material is made up of standards, with only 'Woody 'N' You' from Gillespie's usual bag, it may disappoint any who expect unfiltered bebop fireworks. But there's a case for saying that this is one of the best of all Gillespie's small-group albums: the playing has a steely refinement that makes the audacious moments stand out even further, the relatively neutral setting puts a more decisive face on the trumpet choruses, and it's a rare chance to hear Gillespie work through what might have been a hard-bop programme of standard tunes. His 'Moonglow' solo can stand with anything the next wave of trumpeters were coming up with. There are four bonus alternative takes in this new edition.

Roy Hargrove's choice for *Ultimate* focuses on the small-group Gillespie, from 'Bloomdido' with Monk and Bird onwards.

*** An Electrifying Evening With The Dizzy Gillespie Quintet

Verve 557544-2 *Gillespie; Leo Wright (as, f); Lalo Schifrin (p); Bob Cunningham (b); Chuck Lampkin (d).* 2/61.

Not really electrifying, but there's the odd flash of lightning along the way. Dizzy sounds in good spirits and makes his own play for The Famous Trumpet Break on 'A Night In Tunisia', which is pretty superb. Lampkin is very loud in the mix and perhaps not the greatest drummer ever to sit behind Gillespie. Leo Wright, another name not much spoken of these days, plays some tough, even abrasive alto along the way.

***(*) Dizzy Gillespie And The Double Six Of Paris

Philips 830224-2 *Gillespie; James Moody (as); Kenny Barron, Bud Powell (p); Chris White, Pierre Michelot (b); Kenny Clarke, Rudy Collins (d); The Double Six Of Paris (v).* 7–9/63.

This almost-forgotten record doesn't deserve its obscurity. The tracks are small-group bop, with the Double Six group dubbing in supremely athletic vocals later – normally a recipe for aesthetic disaster, but it's done with such stunning virtuosity that it blends credibly with the music, and the interweaving is done with some restraint. Gillespie himself takes some superb solos – the tracks are compressed into a very short duration, harking back to original bop constraints, and it seems to focus all the energies – and even Powell, in his twilight, sounds respectable on the ten tracks he plays on.

***** Dizzy For President**
Knit Classics KCR-3001 *Gillespie; James Moody (ts, as, f); Sleepy Matsumoto (ts); Kenny Barron (p); Chris White (b); Rudy Collins (d); Jon Hendricks (v).* 63.

***** Something Old – Something New**
Verve 558079-2 *As above, except omit Matsumoto and Hendricks.* 63.

***** Jamboo Caribe**
Verve 557492-2 *As above, except add Kansas Fields (perc), Ann Henry (v).* 64.

***** The Cool World / Dizzy Goes Hollywood**
Verve 531230-2 *Gillespie; James Moody (ts, as, f); Kenny Barron (p); Chris White (b); Rudy Collins (d); strings.* 9/63–4/64.

Gillespie's quintet of the early '60s has been largely eclipsed by other, more renowned small groups of the period. It's not so much a miscarriage of justice as a fact of documented jazz life: they didn't do much recording, and what there is is relatively unremarkable. Moody was a splendid presence, garrulous foil or straightman as the occasion required, and with the young Kenny Barron in the rhythm section the group had unusual strength in depth. Yet they never did much of great consequence on record. *Dizzy For President* is a recent discovery of their Monterey Jazz Festival set from 1963. Surviving great moments have to compete with a lot of horseplay (the routine prior to 'Morning Of The Carnival' is priceless), including Dizzy's presidential campaign-song which a guesting Jon Hendricks delivers. Excellent live sound catches the occasion very well, but it may not stand up to many repeat plays. *Something Old – Something New* revisits nuggets such as 'Bebop' and 'Good Bait', along with newer pieces such as 'November Afternoon', but the temperature seems low and the playing inexplicably cautious. *Jamboo Caribe* is described as a 'sensuous calypso adventure', but this was one area of world music which Dizzy never conquered, and a lot of it is trivial. Even so, he gets a beautifully considered solo into 'And Then She Stopped', and the closing 'Trinidad, Goodbye' is a fast, attacking piece that Gillespie and Moody plunder very effectively.

The Cool World, Mal Waldron's score for Shirley Clarke's film, is coupled with the set of movie themes on *Dizzy Goes Hollywood* – some vivid and exciting playing by all hands, but the tracks seem deliberately short and predigested, and the music-making feels contained.

*****(*) The Monterey Festival Jazz Orchestra**
Blue Note 80370-2 *Gillespie; Harry 'Sweets' Edison, Melvin Moore, Fred Hill, Johnny Audino (t); Lester Robinson, Francis Fitzpatrick, Jim Amlotte (tb); Herman Lebow, Sam Cassano, David Burke, Alan Robinson (frhn); Buddy Collette, Gabe Baltazar, Bill Green, Carrington Visor Jr, Jack Nimitz (reeds); Phil Moore (p); Bobby Hutcherson (vib); Dennis Budimir (g); Jimmy Bond (b); Earl Palmer (d).* 65.

Gil Fuller's charts for this band miss some of the freewheeling excitement he gave to the first Gillespie big band in the '40s, but there's real glitter and polish in the playing that the trumpeter responds to with some acrid, pinpoint improvising. It's over too soon.

***** Swing Low, Sweet Cadillac**
Impulse! 051178-2 *Gillespie; James Moody (ts, as, f); Mike Longo (p); Frank Schifano (b); Otis Finch (d).* 67.

After his Verve and Limelight records, Impulse! had a go at getting a record out of Dizzy. It has its moments, for both Gillespie and Moody, but as before there's a sense that the leader simply wasn't much interested in making records and wanted to get on to the next gig.

***** Live At The Village Vanguard**
Blue Note 80507-2 2CD *Gillespie; Garnett Brown (tb); Pepper Adams (bs); Chick Corea (p); Ray Nance (vn); Richard Davis (b); Mel Lewis, Elvin Jones (d).* 10/67.

One of the oddest line-ups Gillespie ever figured in – Nance and Brown swap places, Jones sits in on two tunes, but otherwise the band is as listed. These are club jams rather than thought-out situations, and there are the usual dead spots; but Gillespie takes some magisterial solos – his thoughts on the blues in 'Blues For Max' are worth a close listen – and Adams in particular is in tough, no-nonsense form.

**** The Giant**
Emarcy 159734-2 *Gillespie; Johnny Griffin (ts); Kenny Drew (p); Niels-Henning Orsted Pedersen (b); Kenny Clarke (d); Humberto Canto (perc).* 4/73.

This was a very disappointing meeting. For some reason, Kenny Clarke is overpoweringly loud in the mix, so much so that even Griffin is for once muffled, and the playing droops a lot of the way.

*****(*) Dizzy Gillespie's Big 4**
Original Jazz Classics OJC 443 *Gillespie; Joe Pass (g); Ray Brown (b); Mickey Roker (d).* 9/74.

****(*) The Trumpet Kings Meet Joe Turner**
Original Jazz Classics OJC 497 *Gillespie; Roy Eldridge, Clark Terry, Harry 'Sweets' Edison (t); Connie Crayton (g); Jimmy Robbins (b); Washington Rucker (d); Joe Turner (v).* 9/74.

**** The Trumpet Kings At Montreux '75**
Original Jazz Classics OJC 445 *Gillespie; Roy Eldridge, Clark Terry (t); Oscar Peterson (p); Niels-Henning Orsted Pedersen (b); Louie Bellson (d).* 7/75.

****(*) At The Montreux Jazz Festival 1975**
Original Jazz Classics OJC 739 *Gillespie; Eddie 'Lockjaw' Davis, Johnny Griffin (ts); Milt Jackson (vib); Tommy Flanagan (p); Niels-Henning Orsted Pedersen (b); Mickey Roker (d).* 7/75.

***** Bahiana**
Pablo 2625-708 *Gillespie; Roger Glenn (f, bf, vib); Al Gafa, Michael Howell (vib); Earl May (b); Mickey Roker (d); Paulinho Da Costa (perc).* 11/75.

**** Dizzy's Party**
Original Jazz Classics OJC 823 *Gillespie; Rodney Jones (g); Benjamin Franklin Brown (b); Mickey Roker (d); Paulinho Da Costa (perc).* 9/76.

*****(*) Montreux '77**

Original Jazz Classics OJC 381 *Gillespie; Jon Faddis (t); Milt Jackson (vib); Monty Alexander (p); Ray Brown (b); Jimmie Smith (d).* 7/77.

***(*) Free Ride**

Original Jazz Classics OJC 740 *Gillespie; band arranged by Lalo Schifrin.* 2/77.

****(*) The Trumpet Summit Meets The Oscar Peterson Big 4**

Original Jazz Classics OJC 603 *Gillespie; Freddie Hubbard, Clark Terry (t); Oscar Peterson (p); Joe Pass (g); Ray Brown (b); Bobby Durham (d).* 3/80.

***** The Alternate Blues**

Original Jazz Classics OJC 744 *As above.* 3/80.

****(*) Digital At Montreux 1980**

Original Jazz Classics 882 *Gillespie; Toots Thielemans (hca); Bernard Purdie (d).* 7/80.

***** Musician Composer Raconteur**

Pablo 2620-116 2CD *Gillespie; James Moody (ts, as, f); Milt Jackson (vib); Ed Cherry (g); Michael Howell (b); George Hughes (d).* 7/81.

**** The Best Of Dizzy Gillespie**

Pablo 2405-411

Gillespie's Pablo period marked a return to regular recording after some years of neglect in the studios. The *Big 4* album was the first session he did, and it remains perhaps the best. There is a superb display of trumpet chops in 'Be Bop', a very good ballad in 'Hurry Home' and an intriguing revision of 'Jitterbug Waltz' in which Pass and Gillespie push each other into their best form. *Bahiana* rambles on a bit and the supporting group are unworthy, but Gillespie plays with fire and decision and he elevates his surroundings with some distinction. The other records seem to betray Norman Granz's indecision as to how best to employ Dizzy's talents. The four Trumpet Kings/Summit encounters are typical of their kind: brilliant flashes of virtuosity interspersed with rhetoric and mere showing-off. The best is probably the Joe Turner meeting, where the great R&B singer puts everyone through their paces. *Montreux '77* is Gillespie featuring his young protégé, Jon Faddis, who xeroxes the young Gillespie style but comes up with a remark or two of his own. The earlier set, from 1975, includes some righteous jousting with Davis and Griffin, though it tends to go the way of all such festival showdowns. The best-of set is weak, picking some tracks off records that have thankfully disappeared. *Free Ride* is a hopeless collaboration with Lalo Schifrin that comes as a nasty shock after the great *Gillespiana* from 25 years earlier. *Dizzy's Party* is another one where there's no need to weep over a lost invite. *Musician Composer Raconteur* is a further Montreux appearance and, although Jackson and Moody are made into somewhat hapless guest stars, the grand good humour of the occasion will please those who remember Gillespie's latter-day concerts, and he plays some fine trumpet at various points. *Digital At Montreux 1980* is even more of a one-man show, Thielemans and Purdie excepting. There is something to enjoy on all these records, but they stretch Gillespie's legend very thin at times.

***(*) Closer To The Source**

Atlantic 7567-80776-2 *Gillespie; Sonny Fortune (as); Branford Marsalis (ts); Stevie Wonder (hca, syn); Kenny Kirkland, Barry Eastmore (ky); Hiram Bullock (g); Tom Barney (b); Marcus Miller (b, syn); Buddy Williams, Tony Cintron Jr (d); Mino Cinelu, Marty Bracey (perc); Angel Rogers (v).* 84.

The haphazard nature of Gillespie's recording regimen in the '80s brings home how much the industry wasted the opportunity to provide a meaningful context for such a creative musician. Perpetually on the road, perhaps Dizzy simply wasn't so interested in making records; but the point remains that his legacy of genuinely great records is disappointingly small and is mainly concentrated at the other end of his career. *Closer To The Source* is a hopeless bit of softcore fusion, almost an insult to Gillespie. Other '80s appearances now need to be sought out in the secondhand racks.

****(*) To Bird With Love**

Telarc CD-83316 *Gillespie; Paquito D'Rivera (as, cl); Jackie McLean, Antonio Hart (as); Clifford Jordan, David Sanchez, Benny Golson (ts); Danilo Perez (p); George Mraz (b); Lewis Nash (d); Bobby McFerrin (v).* 1/92.

****(*) Bird Songs**

Telarc CD-83421 *As above, except add Kenny Washington (d).* 1/92.

***** To Diz With Love**

Telarc CD-83307 *Gillespie; Wynton Marsalis, Charlie Sepulveda, Claudio Roditi, Red Rodney, Wallace Roney, Jon Faddis, Doc Cheatham, Lew Soloff (t); Junior Mance (p); Peter Washington (b); Kenny Washington (d).* 1–2/92.

From the concerts which were meant to inaugurate a year of celebration for Dizzy's 75th birthday and which instead turned out to be his final appearances. The trumpet feast on the third disc has the edge, with a hint of a cutting contest in the air, whereas some of the sax-players burn each other out on the first two records. Diz sounds frail but unprepared to admit it.

George Girard (1930–57)

TRUMPET, VOCAL

New Orleans trumpeter who emerged at the tail-end of the '40s revival and whose brief career was terminated by cancer.

***** George Girard**

Storyville STCD 6013 *Girard; Santo Pecora, Bob Havens (tb); Raymond Burke, Harry Shields (cl); Lester Bouchon (ts); Jeff Riddick (p, v); Bob Discon (p); Emil Christian, Chink Martin (b); Monk Hazel, Paul Edwards (d).* 9/54–7/56.

Girard, who died young after contracting cancer, was a very fine trumpeter. He made his name in the Basin Street Six with Pete Fountain, but these recordings – one session made at the Municipal Auditorium in 1954, the other at the Parisian Room in 1956, only a few months before his death – offer formidable evidence of a great, idiosyncratic New Orleans hornman, somewhat in the manner (if not the style) of Henry Allen. Girard's firm lead is countered by his unpredictable solos which may suddenly flare up into wild high notes or stay in a sober middle range: he's hard to second-guess, even on warhorse material such as the tunes played at the 1956 session, which also has excellent work from Havens and Shields. The earlier date is marred by the recording, which is poorly balanced and muffled, and by the feeble tenor work of Bouchon; but Girard and Pecora are both very good: the trumpeter's brilliant solo on 'A Good Man Is Hard To Find' is a small masterpiece of controlled tension. The 1956 recordings are more than adequate, and it's hard to believe that Girard's playing is the work of a man who was already very ill.

Greg Gisbert (born 1966)

TRUMPET, FLUGELHORN

Gisbert spent some years playing lead trumpet with Buddy Rich and Woody Herman, and in the '90s he freelanced in the New York area.

***** Harcology**
Criss Cross Criss 1084 *Gisbert; Chris Potter (ts, ss); John Campbell (p); Dwayne Burno (b); Gregory Hutchinson (d).* 12/92.

***** On Second Thought**
Criss Cross 1116 *Gisbert; Steve Wilson (as); Chris Potter (ts); Peter Washington (b); Billy Drummond (d).* 95.

***** The Court Jester**
Criss Cross 1161 *Gisbert; Conrad Herwig (tb); Jon Gordon (ss, as); Tim Ries (ss, ts, f); Janice Friedman (p); Jay Anderson (b); Gregory Hutchinson (d).* 12/96.

The Criss Cross debut is a bright, unfussy date, strongly marked by the example of Clark Terry, Thad Jones and Tom Harrell, the most obvious influences on Gisbert's trumpet style. He plays clean, uncomplicated lines in a frankly old-fashioned style. Over almost exactly an hour there is nothing that will frighten the horses, and nothing that is not resolutely tasteful and coherent. His big solos are on the title-piece (a solitary Gisbert original), Campbell's 'Turning Point' and the standard, 'Autumn In New York'. For much of the remainder he is happy to sit back and let colleagues take front stage.

A nice strong consolidation on the second album. Potter is once again a full sharer in proceedings, and his composition 'The Green Dress' is one of the highlights of the set. Gisbert's tone has lost some of its old-fashioned quality and now sounds resolutely contemporary. The closing sequence of Tyner's 'Effendi', Parker's 'Segment' and Monk's 'Played Twice' is particularly well judged. Gisbert solos with authority but doesn't outstay his welcome pontificating, preferring to keep his choruses fairly neat and tidy.

The Court Jester is a trifle more ambitious than its predecessors, with the neatly orchestrated 'Robyn Song' getting it off to a coolly impressive start. Friedman is a strong presence, contributing a couple of originals, and the ensemble play is pretty much step-perfect, although again it's a set marked more by consistency than daring. Gisbert comes into his own on a clear-eyed treatment of 'My Ideal'.

Jimmy Giuffre (born 1921)

CLARINET, TENOR AND SOPRANO SAXOPHONES, FLUTE, BASS FLUTE

Born in Dallas, Giuffre studied in his home state, played in an army band and then worked with a series of big bands, before working with Howard Rumsey and Shorty Rogers. Later, Giuffre formed the first of two extraordinary trios which were to transform one branch of jazz. Originally with Jim Hall and Ralph Pena, then with Bob Brookmeyer, and then with Paul Bley and Steve Swallow, Jimmy moved from a kind of organic folk jazz to something approaching free jazz. Later years saw Giuffre concentrate on arranging and teaching, but in the late '80s his playing career was revived just as his early recordings were revived and reassessed.

***** The Complete 1947–1953 Small Group Sessions**
Blue Moon 99951 4CD *Giuffre; Boots Brown, Conte Candoli, Maynard Ferguson, Ray Linn, Shorty Rogers (t); John Graas (flhn); Milt Bernhart (tb); Bob Enevoldsen, Gene Englund (tba); Art Pepper (as); Bud Shank (as, bs, f); Dexter Gordon, Dave Pell (ts); Bob Cooper (ts, bs); Gerry Mulligan (bs); Russ Freeman, Hampton Hawes, Dodo Marmarosa, Marty Paich, Frank Patchen (p); Red Norvo (p, vib); Teddy Charles (vib); Barney Kessel (g); Don Bagley, Red Callender, Curtis Counce, Bob Manners, Joe Mondragon, Howard Rumsey, Carson Smith (b); Roy Harte, Jackie Mills (d); Shelly Manne (d, v); Carlos Vidal (perc); Joe Johnson (v).* 47–53.

These are the 'prentice years, when the 26-year-old was working as sideman, occasional composer and arranger, with a variety of West Coast bands. Like most such 'early years' recordings, there's an element of bad faith about the issue, since there is precious little identifiable Giuffre to be heard on many of the tracks, though even the ensembles tell you something about the musician he was going to turn into. For the record, the set includes 'I'll Follow You' and 'Bop' with Red Norvo, two tunes with Jesse Price and his band, performances by Shorty Rogers And His Giants (including 'Four Mothers' and, from later, 'The Pesky Serpent'), the Shelly Manne Sextet ('Deep Purple' and 'The Princess of Evil' among others), the Teddy Charles Quintet, Howard Rumsey and the Lighthouse All-Stars (familiar enough material), John Graas's Octet and arranger Leith Stevens' All Stars (less so), and some very un-Giuffre work with Boots Brown and his Blockbusters. Sixty-two tracks in all and so a feast for anyone who enjoys the by-ways of West Coast music or who wants more detailed understanding of Jimmy's roots. It was to be another three years, though, before that distinctive voice came through for the first time.

****** The Jimmy Giuffre Clarinet**
Collectables 6162 *Giuffre; Harry 'Sweets' Edison, Short Rogers, Jack Sheldon (t); Bob Cooper (ts, ob); Dave Pell (ts, eng hn); Buddy Collette (acl, f); Harry Klee (bcl, bf); Bud Shank (af); Jimmy Rowles (p, cel); Ralph Pena (b); Shelly Manne (d).* 3/56.

*****(*) The Jimmy Giuffre 3**
Atlantic 90981 *Giuffre; Jim Hall (g); Jim Atlas, Ralph Pena (b).* 12/56.

***** The Jimmy Giuffre 3 / The Music Man**
Collectables 6248 *As above.* 12/56, 1/58.

*****(*) Hollywood & Newport, 1957–1958**
Fresh Sound FSCD 1026 *Giuffre; Bob Brookmeyer (vtb); Jim Hall (g); Ralph Pena (b).* 1/57–10/58.

Cultivating a brown chalumeau register on his clarinet and defending the aesthetic benefits of simple quietness, Giuffre created what he liked to call 'folk jazz'. *The Jimmy Giuffre Clarinet* and *The Music Man*, recorded for Atlantic in the '50s, evoked a middle America which had hitherto played little part in jazz. Giuffre's soft meditations and homely foot-tapping on the earlier album suggested a man playing out on his front porch, sufficiently solitary and unselfconscious to forget the rules and try out unfamiliar tonalities.

Now available on Collectables again *Clarinet* is a delightful experience. For a sample of Giuffre unaccompanied and in that mellifluous lower register he made his own, spin to 'So Low'. At the opposite extreme, there's a nonet track, the closing 'Down Home', which is so-so. In between, lots of unusual duos and trios, including a bandful of clarinets and a pairing with Rowles on celeste for 'Deep Purple'. 'The Side Pipers' is almost Third Stream in its flirtation with atonality, but if you find that too chewy, there's a stunning 'My Funny Valentine' which makes use of all those unusual woodwinds listed above. A very welcome addition to JG's catalogue.

The Jimmy Giuffre 3 contains some of the essential early material, notably a fine version of 'The Train And The River', on which Giuffre moves between baritone and tenor saxophones and clarinet, and the long 'Crawdad Suite', which intelligently combines blues and folk materials. Giuffre's out-of-tempo playing recalls the great jazz singers. Jim Hall was his longest-standing and most sympathetic cohort; they were partnered either by trombonist Bob Brookmeyer or a bassist, most successfully Ralph Pena or Buddy Clark (Jim Atlas plays on only two bonus tracks on the Atlantic CD). The Collectables option adds the 1958 *The Music Man* featuring the nonet and some rather anonymous arrangements. It's a reasonable purchase, but most will be satisfied with the trio album on its own

The Giuffre–Brookmeyer–Hall trio appears behind the credits on the great movie *Jazz On A Summer's Day* (the top of Hall's head is just about visible), playing 'The Train And The River'. The Fresh Sound captures that whole set, together with earlier and later material from the West Coast, where this kind of jazz seemed to have a more natural home. Brookmeyer's slightly lazy, wall-eyed delivery was an ideal foil for Giuffre. He kept to the same end of the tonal spectrum and shared a love of easy tempos.

*** Trav'lin' Light / Merely Marvellous

Collectables 6248 *Giuffre; Bob Brookmeyer (vtb); Jim Hall (g).* 1/58.

These eight tracks are all resolutely tuneful. Giuffre's folksy style of the time is heard at its best on 'The Green Country (New England Mood)', which suggests a familiarity with Charles Ives, and comes through strongly on the standards as well: the title-piece, 'California, Here I Come' and 'Show Me The Way To Go Home', a rare jazz cover and one full of wonky charm. The other half of the Collectables set is a Mabel Mercer record, which may or may not be an attraction.

*** The Easy Way

Verve 065508 *Giuffre; Jim Hall (g); Ray Brown (b).* 8/59.

Reissued in 2003 under Verve's policy of fixed-period releases, this will be available till 2006. There's unlikely to be a rush on the stores, as it's a pleasing but mild set, marked by some fantastic playing from Hall, but only occasionally showing Giuffre in his best light. He switches to tenor for the longest track, 'Ray's Time', and though the dedicatee makes much of the compliment, Jimmy's playing is decidedly unattractive. The baritone track 'Time Enough' is better because it's shorter. The clarinet tracks are much better and he gets off his best work on the first three tracks, 'The Easy Way', 'Mack The Knife' and a delicious 'Come Rain Or Come Shine'.

*** Olympia 23 Fevrier 1960 – 27 Fevrier 1965

Laserlight 710586 *Giuffre; Don Friedman (p); Jim Hall (g); Barre Phillips (b).* 2/60, 2/65.

The earlier set is all standards material, with a typically brilliant interpretation of 'Mack The Knife' and 'The Boy Next Door'. Friedman is prominent, though badly recorded. The familiar Giuffre trio format – clarinet, guitar, bass – works superbly on Jimmy's own compositions and the closing version of Carla Bley's 'Ictus' is worth the price of the record, which makes the best of a very average source tape. Not an essential buy, but fascinating for students of Giuffre as he moved into his most abstract phase.

**** 1961

ECM 849644-2 2CD *Giuffre; Paul Bley (p); Steve Swallow (b).* 3 & 8/61.

**** Emphasis & Flight 1961

hatOLOGY 2-595 2CD *As above.* 11/61.

♛ **** Free Fall

Columbia CK 65446 *As above.* 62.

Giuffre's subsequent drummerless trios and cool, almost abstract tonality created nearly as much stir as Gerry Mulligan's pianoless quintets and encountered considerable critical resistance at the end of the '50s. Nothing that had come along before quite prepares us for the astonishing work that Giuffre created with Paul Bley and Steve Swallow in two 1961 albums called *Fusion* (a term which hadn't yet taken on its '70s associations) and *Thesis* (which seemed equally unpromising as the title of a jazz album). Paired and remastered as *1961*, they constitute ECM's first-ever reissue; it's interesting, first, how modern the music sounds after 40 years (compare it with the Owl set, below) and then how closely it seems to conform to ECM's familiar aesthetics of great formal precision and limpid sound. Herb Snitzer's session photographs have often been commented on. In deeply shadowed and evocatively focused black and white, they say something about the music. It's arguable that Giuffre's playing is equally monochrome and its basic orientation uncomfortably abstract; but again one notices its sometimes urgent but always compelling swing. The slightly earlier *Fusion* is perhaps the more daring of the two sets, balancing starkly simple ideas, as on 'Jesus Maria' and 'Scootin' About', with some complex harmonic conceptions (to which all three contribute). *Thesis*, though, is tighter and more fully realized, and tunes like 'Ictus' and 'Carla' (the former written by the dedicatee of the latter, Bley's then wife, Carla) have been an inexhaustible element of the pianist's concert improvisations ever since. By contrast, the music on *Fusion* seems fixed in and of its moment.

Free Fall, by contrast, is a trickier and more insidious sound altogether. A mixture of Giuffre solos (including some of his most piercing and antagonistic recorded statements) with duos and trios, it catches the group late on in its brief initial history. Remarkable to think of Columbia taking on a project like this in 1962 but, whatever the exact intention of the title, it was clear that the studiousness and philosophical calm which overlaid the previous discs was no longer to be expected. What you're hearing is something that has almost run its course in practical terms but which creatively is far from exhausted. Swallow's fiery scrabbles and sharply plucked single-note runs lend the music a new momentum and the sort of energy to be found in free jazz. Bley may be the most least comfortable of the three by this stage, but he has always been a restless experimenter and by 1962 his eye was probably on the next step. Giuffre often sounds as if he is in a world of his own, intensely focused, totally aware, but communicating ideas for which there was no ready-made language or critical rhetoric.

These – and *Free Fall* especially – are essential documents in the development of a broader jazz idiom that refused to see bop as the only recourse. Giuffre's pioneering has only slowly been recognized.

The live dates that make up *Emphasis & Flight* were recorded a couple of weeks apart in Stuttgart and Bremen. It's interesting to note near-identical durations for the repeated tracks 'Cry, Want', 'Sonic' and 'Stretching Out', though the Stuttgart version of 'Whirrr', which starts the set, is double the length of the Bremen take, which ends it. In each case, though, what's done with a theme varies dramatically. The Bremen stretching out is more supple and harmonically adventurous and indeed the second disc is musically much more satisfying. This rounds out the picture of this extraordinary group in a year of concentrated creativity. Most collections won't support all these discs, but everyone interested in modern jazz should have at least one of them.

★★★(★) The Train And The River
Candid Choice CHCD 1011 *Giuffre; Kiyoshi Tokunaga (b); Randy Kaye (perc).* 4/75.

A long quote from Herman Hesse's *Siddhartha* on the inner sleeve might stir a few warning doubts, which are in the end not necessary at all. Giuffre throws himself 'lovingly' into the 'river' of this music, but does so with an absolute lack of self-consciousness. The very fact that he should be willing to kick off with 'The Train And The River' after so many years is an indication that he hasn't overthrown his folk-jazz loyalties. However, tunes like 'Elephant', 'Tibetan Sun', 'The Listening' and 'Om' which follow do suggest an extra dimension in his work. Increased use of flute and bass flute invests some of these tunes with a fugitive, misterioso quality. Tokunaga and Kaye have interesting playing backgrounds, ranging from the Paul Winter Consort and Howard McGhee in the bassist's case, and Roswell Rudd to Jimi Hendrix in the drummer's. Here and there, such eclecticism becomes too obvious a dimension of their playing, but for the most part they are solid, responsive partners, completely in tune with what Giuffre is doing.

★★★ Quasar
Soul Note 121108 *Giuffre; Pete Levin (ky); Bob Nieske (b); Randy Kaye (d).* 5/85.

★★★ Liquid Dancers
Soul Note 121158 *As above.* 4/89.

For much of the later '60s and '70s, the most intuitive improviser of his generation was obliged to teach improvisation to college students, gigging only in relative obscurity. Randy Kaye was a loyal and dependable supporter in those days, and he adds just the right kind of softly enunciated percussion to Giuffre's '80s quartet albums (a third Soul Note, *Dragonfly*, is currently unavailable). Bob Nieske's 'The Teacher', on *Liquid Dancers*, pays no less a tribute. Scored for Giuffre's bass flute, it has a crepuscular, meditative quality that isn't altogether typical of a lively and almost self-consciously ('Move With The Times') contemporary set. Levin's keyboard stylings are perhaps a little too blandly atmospheric, but they open up the texture for Giuffre's familiar chalumeau clarinet and a surprisingly agile soprano saxophone. The earlier *Quasar* is equally fine and the writing may even be a little better.

★★★(★) Eiffel
CELP C6 *Giuffre; André Jaume (bcl, sax).* 11/87.

★★★ Momentum: Willisau, 1988
hatOLOGY 508 *As above.* 88.

The best of these thoughtful, often delicate duos recall the best of Giuffre's work with Brookmeyer. Jaume has the same intensity and dry wit, and the register of his bass clarinet is not so far from that of the trombone. Recorded in concert, *Eiffel* consists of scored and improvised duets, none longer than five minutes, most around three. Jaume's saxophone on 'Stand Point' tends to break the mood a little but the studied, contemplative tone otherwise remains intact, and Giuffre's articulation and tone have seldom been more compelling. The Willisau set is gently floating, thoughtful and in some respects a little dull, unless you're prepared to give it the attention it deserves. Jaume is happy to play second fiddle, even as Giuffre defers and hesitates, and the best of the set is when the two voices are interwoven.

★★★(★) River Station
CELP C 26 *Giuffre; Joe McPhee (tb); André Jaume (ts, bcl).* 9/91.

Repeating the triumphs of 30 years before, Giuffre found himself an honoured elder in Europe. With the exception of Bley and Swallow, it was nearly always Frenchmen who wanted to perform with him. This session has an air of relaxed preparedness. Some of the duos recall the Giuffre/Konitz encounter of 1978 (now deleted) and the walk-on contribution of Joe McPhee with his trombone on 'Three Way Split' sounds like a long after-echo of the classic Brookmeyer trio. Giuffre's wife had been writing a good deal of music before this time, and she contributes the outstanding 'When Things Go Wrong'. The only thing that has gone wrong with the recording is that the players seem to be placed at opposite ends of the studio. A little 'false mono' might actually have helped.

★★★ Fly Away Little Bird
Owl 3504 *Giuffre; Paul Bley (p); Steve Swallow (b).* 6/92.

The legendary trio reconvened in 1992 with a new agenda. The standards are all radically unfamiliar. 'I Can't Get Started' is totally transformed, similar structurally to what the first beboppers did with show tunes but harmonically much more complex. The three instruments work contrapuntally and in ever tighter circles, sometimes to the detriment of musical logic. The freer pieces and the individual compositions, Swallow's 'Fits' and Bley's suitably drowsy 'Qualude' very much to the fore, are exquisitely conceived and executed. Sometimes, as on the opening title-track, one hears echoes of old songs, but for the most part this is quite abstract and free-flowing. Giuffre's articulation is still remarkable but it's Swallow who emerges as the genius of these tracks, lyrical and tough by turns, always listening and never short of an idea.

Frode Gjerstad

ALTO AND TENOR SAXOPHONES, CLARINET

Norwegian improviser who came to some prominence with a John Stevens group in the '80s and has since worked variously across two continents, with a burst of recent recording.

★★★(★) Hello, Goodbye
Emanem 4065 *Gjerstad; Derek Bailey (g); John Stevens (t, perc).* 10/92.

Gjerstad made a DAT recording of one of three gigs with Bailey and Stevens in Norway during the autumn of 1992. Although Stevens plays, for once, a full-size kit rather than the small version he often used when working with Bailey, the music still has the scuttling animation of intense chamber music. Gjerstad and Stevens work lightly and quickly, never upsetting any balance, while Bailey seems the most aggressive of the three: he ends 'Three Two Three Two One' with one of the longest notes on record. An excellent survival.

*****(*) Seeing New York From The Ear**
Cadence CJR 1069 *Gjerstad; William Parker (b); Rashid Bakr (d).* 3/96.

***** Ikosa Mura**
Cadence CJR 1089 *Gjerstad; Bobby Bradford (t); Borah Bergman (p); Pheeroan akLaff (d).* 9/97.

***** Through The Woods**
CIMP 159 *Gjerstad; Bobby Bradford (t); Wilber Morris (b); Newman Baker (d).* 9/97.

***** Ultima**
Cadence CJR 1108 *Gjerstad; William Parker (b); Hamid Drake (d).* 10/97.

***** Borealis**
Cadence CJR 1091 *Gjerstad; Didrik Ingvaldesen (t); Oyvind Torvund (g); Oyvind Storesund, John Lilja (b); Endre Landsnes, Paal Nilssen-Love (d).* 2/98.

*****(*) Invisible Touch**
Cadence CJR 1099 *Gjerstad; Peter Brötzmann (ts, cl, tarogato).* 7/98.

Gjerstad will be remembered by British audiences for his work in the band Detail, with John Stevens and John Dyani, in the mid-'80s. He's been less frequently heard from since then but has rather suddenly become much more ubiquitous with a flurry of releases on the Cadence and CIMP labels. Spending what seem to be equal amounts of time on alto and tenor, he's a blustery, energy-filled improviser whose playing rarely makes a profound impact but whose ideas thrive on sheer momentum and intensity; he's carried exultantly along by a thunderous groove or a dense stew of voices. *Seeing New York From The Ear* is much like a vintage Jimmy Lyons performance, Gjerstad's alto borne aloft on Bakr's splendid tumult, with Parker's ferocious lines binding it together. It may be music in a familiar mould, but the playing has staunch self-belief and inventiveness.

The two quartet records with Bobby Bradford are something of a reunion, since the trumpeter had previously played with Detail. *Ikosa Mura* is at times so dense and clotted with sound that the music all but congeals. If there's a culprit, it's the fulsome Bergman, who rarely does anything other than overplay; even so, the group often fuses into an exhilarating and rumbustious collective roar. *Through The Woods*, cut in the no-frills surroundings of the CIMP studio, seems very different. Faced with the noisy situation of the previous record, Bradford falls back on a kind of pattern-playing, but on this lighter stage his songful bent emerges. Morris and Baker create a softer, more scuffling rhythmic base. Lyrical moments such as the opening section of 'Frodiodi' are worth waiting for, but there's plenty of little consequence and Gjerstad is often the least impressive player.

Ultima is a single festival set which runs just under an hour. Drake doesn't make such a strong impression as Bakr did on the earlier trio date; for that reason this comes in as an also-ran, though the playing still has its momentous passages. *Borealis* is by Gjerstad's Norwegian crew, the Circulasione Totale Orchestra. Though a studio recording, it seems rather thin and stringy in sonic terms, which mitigates the sense of 'the wind blowing from the North', and the squalls are diminished more than they might be. Nevertheless, a welcome change of pace from the other records, with Torvund's electric whine howling through the core of the band's sound.

The meeting with Brötzmann is from a club gig in Stavanger. Gjerstad is far from overawed by his great contemporary, and if anything is the more ferocious competitor, sticking to alto on this occasion. The final movements are rather peaceable, resolute and collaborative while still in the raw.

***** The Blessing Light**
Cadence CJR 1126 *Gjerstad; Oyvind Storesund (b); Paal Nilssen-Love.* 9/00.

***** Sharp Knives Cut Deeper**
Splasc(h) 850 *As above; add Peter Brötzmann (ts, cl, tarogato).* 12/01.

Slimming the big cast of the Circulasione Totale group down to three, the live three-part dedication to John Stevens, clearly the most important figure in the saxophonist's musical life, makes an interesting sequel, in a way, to the Emanem disc above. Nilssen-Love, for instance, often follows the fundamentalist paths suggested by Stevens, and Gjerstad builds on the deferential alto style of the earlier date with a more forceful and expressionist bent – the final part digs in very hard. He plays some clarinet, too, though this is less impressive. Some occasional dryness takes a bit of the edge off the record's impact.

The follow-up disc benefits immeasurably from the rugged presence of Peter Brötzmann. As well as throwing down his usual gauntlet, the guest turns in some passages of real beauty, reminiscent (as is the album title) of some of his FMP masterpieces of the '70s. Gjerstad raises his game in response but for once the remaining members of the trio seem a bit lacklustre.

***** Nearly A D**
Emanem 4087 *Gjerstad; Derek Bailey (g).* 8/02.

Gjerstad hadn't worked with Bailey for a decade, not since the Stavanger concert documented on *Hello, Goodbye*, when he rolled up at the guitarist's London flat to record this cheerfully informal session. Punctuated by tea-breaks and moments of banter, the album has a relaxed and conversational feel, both players' occasional bouts of sonic aggression notwithstanding. Perhaps as a guest, perhaps out of deference to the senior player, Gjerstad seems more reticent and restrained than usual, but he creates some very beautiful music on his alto, sounding not unlike the early Trevor Watts in places.

*****(*) The Welsh Chapel**
Cadence Jazz CJR1 161 *Gjerstad; John Edwards (b); Mark Sanders (d).* 8/02.

A very different outfit from his Scandinavian trio, the London rhythm section heard on *The Welsh Chapel* offers Gjerstad a whole new range of possibilities. Where Nilssen-Love is a Stevens soundalike, Sanders is a busy, intricate drummer, while Edwards matches the energy of a funkster with a brilliant grasp of line and harmonics. The chemistry makes for one of Gjerstad's most impressive performances on record: keening, intense, still full of grief for the vanished Stevens, but also very much his own man.

Globe Unity Orchestra

GROUP

Formed in 1966 by Alex von Schlippenbach to perform his 'Globe Unity' composition, the Orchestra is a pan-European band of improvisers whose occasional appearances over some 40 years have been rare, but worth waiting for.

****** Globe Unity 67 & 70**
Atavistic Unheard Music Series 223 *Manfred Schoof (c, t, flhn); Kenny Wheeler (t, flhn); Jürg Grau, Claude Deron, Tomasz Stańko, Bernard Vitet (t); Paul Rutherford (tb, thn); Jiggs Wigham, Albert Mangelsdorff, Malcolm Griffiths (tb); Kris Wanders (as, bcl); Gerd Dudek (ts, ss, cl, f); Evan Parker (ts, ss); Michel Pilz (ss, bcl, f); Peter Brötzmann (ts, as, bs); Heinz Sauer (bs, ts, as); Willem Breuker (bs, cl); Alexander von Schlippenbach (p, perc); Karl Berger (vib); Derek Bailey (g); Willy Lietzmann (tba); Buschi Niebergall (b, btb); Peter Kowald (b, tba); Han Bennink (d, perc, shellhorn); Jaki Liebezeit, Mani Neumeier, Sven-Ake Johansson, Paul Lovens (d).* 10/67–11/70.

*****(*) Rumbling**
FMP CD 40 *Manfred Schoof, Kenny Wheeler (t); Gunter Christmann, Paul Rutherford (tb); Peter Brötzmann, Rüdiger Carl, Gerd Dudek, Evan Parker, Michel Pilz (reeds); Alexander von Schlippenbach (p); Derek Bailey (g); Peter Kowald (b, tba); Han Bennink (d, perc, cl); Paul Lovens (d).* 3/75.

****** 20th Anniversary**
FMP CD 45 *Kenny Wheeler (t); Paul Rutherford, Albert Mangelsdorff (tb); Evan Parker (ss, ts); Steve Lacy (ss); Gerd Dudek (bs, bcl, f); Alexander von Schlippenbach (p); Peter Kowald (b); Paul Lovens (d).* 11/86.

****** Globe Unity Orchestra 2002**
Intakt 086 *Manfred Schoof (t, flhn); Paul Rutherford, Hannes Bauer (tb); Ernst-Ludwig Petrowsky (as, cl, f); Peter Brötzmann (ts, cl, tarogato); Evan Parker (ss, ts); Alexander von Schlippenbach (p); Paul Lovens, Paul Lytton (d).* 1/02.

Not too much to show for an incomparable free-music institution. Formed in 1966, the Globe Unity Orchestra has had to sustain itself with rare concerts and even rarer records, an unworthy fate for arguably the finest group to attempt to reconcile big-band forms with free improvisation. Although there has been a revolving cast of players throughout the group's existence, a few hardy spirits (notably Alex Schlippenbach, the original organizer) act as a point of reference. What a great find *67 & 70* is, two sets by two huge editions of the Orchestra, one from Donaueschingen, the other from Berlin, both recorded by German radio. 'Globe Unity 67', which runs for 34 minutes, is one of the most pandemonious pieces of free music we can recall hearing, the 19-strong group (including three drummers) making a magnificent racket which scarcely lets up – and which, on careful listening, revolves around a relatively harmonious structure. The 1970 performance seems almost tame in comparison (Bailey, who would have been inaudible in the 1967 recording, is very much in the front line), yet in formal terms this is the more freewheeling, perhaps the more radical piece. Either way, a disc which is a must-have for admirers of free playing. The radio engineers were obviously taxed by both occasions, but the *Rumbling* CD is by what is more like a contingent from the orchestra. There is Monk's 'Evidence', a march by Misha Mengelberg and a tune by Lacy, while 'Into The Valley' is a nearly continuous 38-minute piece. The latter is the best demonstration of the group's powers, moving through solo and duet passages between the horns to thunderous all-in tussles. Problematically, the original LP editions of this music sounded grey and boxy, but the sound is much bigger and more convincing here.

To celebrate their 20th anniversary, the Orchestra held a Berlin concert at which the 66-minute work on FMP CD 45 was played. While a shade below their 1977 masterpiece, *Pearls*, this is still a vivid, bristling assemblage of ideas and individual spontaneities: Schlippenbach's hand is on the tiller, but each man asserts his individual mastery in his personal way. A very good way of making acquaintance with many of the great modernists of the past 30 years.

Intensely vivid and alive, yet at the same time ghostly and poignant, the performance captured on *Globe Unity Orchestra 2002* is hard to listen to. The Orchestra had not been convened for some 15 years, and it came together for a memorial concert in Aachen for its dedicated fan, Robert Wenseler. Time has wrought changes on GUO, as with everything else: reduced to only nine members, with spirits such as Niebergall and Kowald gone in the interim, there is a palpable sense of raging against the dying of the light. When playing at full tilt, as they do in many passages across the 73 minutes of the performance, it seems barely credible that only nine men are responsible for this superb cacophony. The distinctions between the players have become more specific and cogent as time has gone on: the lilting, lyrical sound of Schoof matched against the fuming uproar of Brötzmann, the unfathomable strangeness of Rutherford next to the simple melodies essayed by Bauer. As the world has grown smaller and even less likely to achieve unity, in its queer way the GUO has become an even more truthful depiction of an idea whose time may never come. If the recording has some shortcomings – what engineer could ever capture an unblemished picture of this extraordinary ensemble? – it hardly detracts from a deeply moving, uplifting experience.

Victor Goines (born 1961)

SAXOPHONES, CLARINETS

One of the generation of New Orleans players taught by Ellis Marsalis, Goines has often featured in musical situations with the Marsalis family and has proved himself a dependable figure in the kind of ensemble which has come to typify the Marsalis kind of traditionalism.

***** Joe's Blues**
Rosemary Joseph RJR 1961 *Goines; Eric Reed, Victor Atkins (p); Reginald Veal, David Pulphus (b); Herlin Riley, Leon Anderson Jr (d).* 1/96–1/97.

****(*) To Those We Love So Dearly**
Rosemary Joseph RJR 1933 *As above except add Nicholas Payton (t), Wycliffe Gordon (tb), Rodney Whitaker (b), omit Atkins, Veal, Pulphus.* 1/99.

***** Sunrise To Midnight**
Rosemary Joseph RJR 1962 *Goines; Wycliffe Gordon (tb); Wessell Anderson (as); Peter Martin (p); Roland Guerin, David Pulphus (b); Herlin Riley, Leon Anderson Jr (d).* 3–6/00.

Goines has tended to perform somewhat in the shadows of the Marsalis clan, in and out of Lincoln Center, but he is a capable and talented player whose records for this tiny Louisiana label make an almost shy case for his qualities. *Joe's Blues* puts him through his paces on four different horns and with two different quartets. He gets a rounded sound out of both saxophones and clarinets, and the bass clarinet feature 'Ballad For Beanie' inculcates a mellowness into that difficult horn which one very rarely encounters. If there's a problem with this impeccable technique, it's that it doesn't exactly grab the listener, and the record tends to pass by too amiably to really keep the attention. Still, the fast virtuosities of 'Stop 'N' Go' and the thoughtful blues 'As We Mature' are worth waiting for towards the end of the set.

The audacious move on *To Those We Love So Dearly* is for Goines to stick exclusively to clarinet – admittedly, four different kinds – for the entire record. What disappoints about it is the lack of strength in the material: too much is based around simple devices such as blues licks, and it suggests Goines has little to say as a writer. By themselves, episodes such as 'Just You Wait' with Gordon in good form are more than listenable, but the record hardly makes a pressing case for itself.

Goines does better by *Sunrise To Midnight.* Six pieces for saxophone and rhythm section evoke the passing of a single day, and the leader takes care to differentiate his approaches, back to using various saxes and clarinets. Good as Reed was on the earlier sets, Martin is a tower of strength here, underlining and pointing up the best of Goines's ideas, and again one admires the immaculate sound the leader gets. The final pieces, featuring Gordon and Anderson, are less impressive, though.

Ben Goldberg (born 1959)

CLARINET, BASS CLARINET

New York-based improviser, aligning his work around the clarinet family.

*****(*) Eight Phrases For Jefferson Rubin**
Victo 057 *Goldberg; Larry Ochs (sno, ts); John Schott (g); Trevor Dunn, Lisle Ellis (b); Michael Sarin (d).* 11/96.

***** Ghost Of Electricity**
Songlines SGL 1525-2 *Goldberg; John Schott (g); Trevor Dunn (b); Kenny Wollesen (d).* 2/99.

Goldberg is an experienced voice in and out of jazz; one of his groups was called the New Klezmer Trio. He plays somewhat proper clarinet, unwilling to make much out of tonal adventures. *Eight Phrases For Jefferson Rubin,* in dedication to a childhood friend who had recently been killed in an accident, is his most personal and effective record. Some of the 'phrases' are rather ponderously long, such as 'Plain Of Jars', but the intriguing instrumentation and pensive, slightly ominous feel of the music are surprisingly powerful, often recalling the feel of Dave Holland's great *Conference Of The Birds* album. Goldberg frequently defers to his fellow players, and the result is a democratic but quite powerfully realized group record of some moment.

Ghost Of Electricity reconvenes the group from the debut record, with five years of growth in between. Strains of old, lost musics – 'hymns, stomps, hollers, anarchic strum-alongs' – are what the record seems to be after. With Schott taking the Frisell route of conjuring every kind of Americana out of the electric guitar's resources, he tends to dominate the soundscaping here, leaving Goldberg to take a rather lonely course over the top. Dunn and Wollesen play what they think will work. The results are often striking – and, just as often, almost arbitrary.

Larry Goldings (born 1968)

ORGAN

Born in Massachusetts, Goldings became a principal on the New York scene in the early '90s, specializing in Hammond organ and adaptable to many kinds of playing situation. Spent a period with John Scofield and he has also featured on piano on one of his own dates.

*****(*) Moonbird**
Palmetto PM 2045 *Goldings; Peter Bernstein (g); Bill Stewart (d).* 2/99

*****(*) As One**
Palmetto PM 2068 *As above.* 5/00.

*****(*) Sweet Science**
Palmetto PM 2084 *As above.* 2/02.

We have been a bit sniffy about some of Goldings's organ albums in the past, and perhaps unfairly: these Palmetto outings sit comfortably in the genre, but it is clearly the work of a musician who's moved on some way from the classic Smith–McDuff–McGriff axis, and the trio has developed into a group of high if self-effacing skill. Now that the leader's albums on Minor Music and Warners have gone into limbo, these at least makes an excellent introduction to the trio's approach. Goldings doesn't want a jam band, and he's always looking for a melodious, even a mellifluous result: even the up-tempo originals, such as 'Mixed Message' and 'Going To Meet The Man' on *As One,* have an innate delicacy to them, as if Goldings were unconvinced by the static histrionics of many organ-band records. On the first record, Joni Mitchell's 'Woodstock' is given a long, brooding, slightly mysterious performance, with Stewart's small cymbals playing a cowbell-like role. Bernstein and Goldings treat each session as an almost continuous dialogue, melodically and harmonically, while Stewart – another player who can make an urgent delivery into something deft and light – is very, very good. No change, really, with *Sweet Science* – same almost pure organ/guitar/drums trinity, same smart pacing, comparable bag of clever and persuasive originals. If none of the records leaps out as a classic, maybe that's just not their style – they'd rather you just came along for the ride, in good-natured appreciation.

Per Goldschmidt

BARITONE AND TENOR SAXOPHONES

Danish saxophonist with international experience, specializing in baritone.

***** Frankly**
Milestone MCD-9224-2 *Goldschmidt; Tom Harrell (t, flhn), Niels Lan Doky (p); Niels-Henning Orsted Pedersen (b), Alvin Queen (d).* 12/93.

****(*) Loneliness**
Stunt STUCD 0042 *Goldschmidt; Carsten Dahl (p); Thomas Ovesen (b); Frands Rifbjerg (d).* 10–12/99.

Goldschmidt is no romantic fool on the baritone. He loves its weight and impact and powers along with few concessions to its size. Even on ballads he prefers to take a terser line than Mulligan or Chaloff ever would have done. Structurally, he's a hard-bopper who can't abide the clichés of the genre. Unfortunately, there is not much by him in the catalogue at present. Lan Doky produces the Milestone session, which sounds terrific, and there are some marvellous moments here. 'Theme For Eve', for baritone, bass and drums only, is exquisitely modulated, and Goldschmidt plays with extra swagger and resilience on the up-tempo tracks. But the concept – playing songs associated with Frank Sinatra – seems intended to tame the leader's most adventurous side, and Harrell, if dependable, seems a notch below his best.

The Stunt album marks a comeback after an illness, and to be blunt Goldschmidt seems to have lost some of his old fire, even if this is an all-ballad programme. On tenor, to which he returned for the first time in many years, he sounds quavery, and even the baritone features have lost some of their vigour. Yet the leader makes no concessions to sentimentality, and there's a leathery poignancy about the music, with the rhythm section's sympathetic touch a definite plus.

Vinny Golia (born 1946)

CLARINETS, FLUTES, SAXOPHONES, SHAKUHACHI, ETC.

Based in the Los Angeles area, Golia and his Nine Winds label are at the heart of the Californian free-playing community. He came to attention in the '70s as a multi-instrumentalist and has led numerous sessions, from solo to big-ensemble performance. His arsenal of wind instruments is vast and he delights in exploring every timbral register.

***** Worldwide And Portable**
Nine Winds NWCD 0143 *Golia; Wayne Peet (p); Ken Filiano (b).* 2/86.

****** Regards From Norma Desmond**
Fresh Sound FSNT 008 *Golia; John Fumo (t); Wayne Peet (p); Ken Filiano (b); Alex Cline (d).* 10/86.

***** Haunting The Spirits Inside Them ...**
Music & Arts CD-893 *Golia; Joelle Léandre, Ken Filiano (b).* 4/92.

*****(*) Against The Grain**
Nine Winds NWCD 0159 *Golia; Rob Blakeslee (t); Nels Cline (g); Ken Filiano (b); Billy Mintz (d).* 10/93.

Vinny Golia has been a central figure in the West Coast avant-garde for many years, and with his Nine Winds label he's been undertaking virtually a one-man documentation of the improvising underground of California – far less 'fashionable' than anything out of New York, but no less significant in the grain of American free jazz. By himself, in the small-group context, Golia reveals an obsession with doubling on numerous instruments: he plays 11 different woodwinds on *Worldwide And Portable*, changing the weave with each different reed. He calls this group The Chamber Trio, and the mood is assuredly sober, the ambitions of the group seemingly based around texture rather than individual lines. The most swinging piece, peculiarly enough, is a dedication to Kafka! But Golia, Peet and Filiano know each other's work very well, and there is much subtlety of interaction. *Against The Grain* is another admirable outing for his quintet: Golia's fascination with long form comes out in the 24-minute 'Presents To Savages/Alternation', and there is some superb contrapuntalism in 'SBB-CFF'. He sticks to sopranino and soprano saxes and two clarinets here; on the meeting with Filiano and Léandre, a chance session following a concert, he plays only flutes, clarinets, piccolo, ocarina, shakuhachi and sheng. This is a whispery, introverted music, the two basses somewhat distant in the sound-mix and Golia laying out as often as pitching in, with sometimes mixed results.

It might seem perverse to pick out a rare record for another label as one of Golia's best. But the recently issued 1986 session for Fresh Sound is a corker. Golia sticks to baritone sax throughout *Regards From Norma Desmond*, and with one of his favourite line-ups they blaze through 50 minutes of free bop that's gripping from first to last, with the outstanding threnody for Booker Little, 'The Cry', particularly fine.

*****(*) Razor**
Nine Winds 0169 *Golia; Michael Vlatkovich (tb); Nels Cline (g); Joel Hamilton (b); Billy Mintz (d).* 4/95.

*****(*) Dante No Longer Repents**
Music & Arts C-992 *Golia; Rob Blakeslee (c, t, flhn); Tad Weed (p); Michael Bisio (b); Billy Mintz (d).* 4/96.

*****(*) Nation Of Laws**
Nine Winds NWCD 0189 *Golia; Rob Blakeslee (c, t, flhn); Nels Cline (g); Joel Hamilton (b); Alex Cline (d).* 7/96.

Three different editions of Golia's quintet. Because Golia himself is partial to such a wide range of horns, the textural possibilities of his groups seem limitless but, just to make sure, there are crucial changes in line-up across the three discs. Vlatkovich uses plenty of variation by himself, mutes and open tones constantly under review, and with Cline changing his own set-up and Mintz and Hamilton booting the group along, this is a restless occasion, provocatively delivered. *Dante No Longer Repents* has some striking contributions from Weed: if Wayne Peet is a more frequent confederate, Weed still summons some beautiful commentaries on the rest of the music, and his harmonic balancing stops the music going too wayward at a few critical moments. Golia is at his most spontaneously inventive on some of these tracks, picking up the piccolo at one point for a startling solo, and although a few pieces outstay their welcome – one often feels that Golia and his various bands love to play so much that it's hard to get them to stop – it's a fine record. *Nation Of Laws* carries on the sequence in good style. The Cline brothers bring their own strengths, and in some ways Nels is the star of the date: listen to his contrasting solos on 'Not Very Pleasance' (crazily mercurial) and 'Perfect In The Pocket' (quickfire post-bop). Golia and Blakeslee push their way forward with a constant exploratory air, as if trying out their front-line sounds and changing their tone and dynamic just to see what new wrinkles they can negotiate. All three, even with their occasional blind turnings, objectify the ways this kind of freeish but already-formulated language can be kept fresh.

***** The Art Of Negotiation**
CIMP 111 *Golia; Ken Filiano (b).* 3/96.

Golia isn't one to parade his technique, but for once – playing clarinet, bass clarinet and sopranino – he takes a stance of aggressive virtuosity, which Filiano sometimes follows (and sometimes not). Though some of these duos run dry before their chops do, there's plenty to listen to.

★★★ Halloween '96

CIMP 129 *Golia; Paul Smoker (t); Ken Filiano (b); Phil Haynes (d).* 10/96.

Cut as a long, loud blow, this kind of date isn't really Smoker's ideal situation, his lines dispersing into a buzz, and with Golia sticking to baritone sax the music's rather grainy and unrelievedly dark (maybe the season played its part). That said, the quartet give their all to the situation, and on the less intense moments some of Smoker's patient lyricism gleams through.

★★(★) 11 Reasons To Begin

Music & Arts CD-966 *Golia; Bertram Turetzky (b).* 3/96.

★★★ Prataksis

Nine Winds NWCD 0199 *As above, except add Wadada Leo Smith (t).* 4/97.

A previous collaboration between Golia and Turetzky is listed under the bassist's name. For *11 Reasons*, Golia brings out his most worldly instruments – sheng, cor anglais, double clay flute, Ghanaian and Chinese flutes, nagaswaram, moxena, Mexican clay ocarina and bon-di – and the results are a curious blend of the exotic and the ascetic. Turetzky's skills as an improviser remain somewhat in doubt, but the best of these duets are as vividly strange as they aspire to be.

When Smith joins in for *Prataksis*, the music becomes altogether more declamatory without exactly raising its voice. The trumpeter's signature gravitas lends an authority to the occasion which raises the music-making to a higher level, although the uncommitted will probably find this something of a meander. Golia himself has a more decorative role: he never quite has a counter for Smith's stoic melody lines.

★★★ Duets

Nine Winds NWCD 0204 *Golia; Susan Allen (hp).* 5/98.

★★★(★) Lineage

Nine Winds NWCD 0214 *Golia; Bobby Bradford (t); Ken Filiano (b); Alex Cline (d).* 8/98.

The duo record with harpist Susan Allen is a good example of Golia's instrumental range: he goes from piccolo to contrabassoon, with seven other instruments in between. Allen is a new-music and classical performer and, while she's played with many jazz musicians, her own methods tend towards a sympathetic formality: her responses to Golia depend primarily on her harmonic imagination. It's a record best sampled two or three duets at a time, since over the long haul it tends to follow a repetitious pattern.

Lineage is an encounter with that distinguished West Coast eminence, Bobby Bradford. They know each other's playing well and, with Filiano and Cline veterans of this music too, the record is a generous conversation among old friends. The cadences of the playing have a well-worn and settled quality: it's a music not of surprise but of supportive empathy. The pleasures come in the skill and grace which these experts use as they go into free space – something not unlike a band of veteran beboppers sifting a chord sequence for a fresh result.

★★★(★) Pilgrimage To Obscurity

Nine Winds NWCD 0130 *Golia; John Fumo, Ralf Rickert, Sal Cracchiolo (t, flhn); Michael Vlatkovich, Doug Wintz, John Rapson (tb); David Stout (btb); Mike Acosta, Steve Fowler, Wynell Montgomery, David Ocker (reeds); David Johnson (vib, mar); Eric Messerschmidt (tba); Ken Filiano, Roberto Miranda (b); Billy Mintz (d); Alex Cline (perc).* 12/85.

★★★(★) Decennium Dans Axlan

Nine Winds NWCD 0140 *Golia; Mark Underwood, John Fumo, Rob Blakeslee (t, flhn); Bruce Fowler, George McMullen (tb); Phil Teele (btb); Emily Hay, Steve Fowler, Bill Plake, David Ocker (reeds); Wayne Peet (ky); Jeff Gauthier (vn); Jonathan Golove, Dion Sorell (clo); Ken Filiano, Joel Hamilton (b); Alex Cline (d); Brad Dutz (perc).* 4/92.

★★★(★) Commemoration

Nine Winds NWCD 0150/0160 2CD *As above, except add Marissa Benedict (t), Michael Vlatkovich (tb), Kim Richmond (reeds), Harry Scorzo (vn), Greg Adamson, Matt Cooker (clo), William Roper (tba), David Johnson (perc).* 91–92.

★★★ Tutto Contare

Nine Winds NWCD 0170 *As above, except add Eric Jorgensen, Joey Sellars (tb), Charles Fernandez (bsn), Steve Adams (reeds), Michael Jacobsen (clo); omit Bruce Fowler, Hay, Gauthier, Benedict, Golove, Adamson, Sorell.* 11/95.

★★★(★) Portland 1996

Nine Winds NWCD 0180 *As above, except add Sal Cracchiolo (t, flhn), Robie Hioki (btb), Kim Richmond (reeds), Jeff Gauthier (vn), Jonathan Golove, Peggy Lee (clo); omit Jorgensen, Sellars, Jacobsen, Ocker.* 2/96.

Golia's Large Ensemble stands apart from his small-group work. The records are fragments from ten years of work with this vast orchestra which Golia apparently keeps going out of his own pocket; with several CDs now available, however, their grand, purposely monumental repertoire is starting to get a fair showing. The group moves like some sea-going leviathan: ponderous, sluggish at times, but suddenly raising itself and achieving grace and beauty. Golia always insists on the weight and thick sonority of the orchestra: sections call and respond to one another somewhat in the big-band tradition, but there is little that one can call swinging, more the contrast of great blocks of sound, the emergence of a soloist to say his piece, the chattering of brass or lowering of a bass reed section. *Pilgrimage To Obscurity* – self-effacing to be sure – alternates between rousing all-hands-on pieces and thinned-out, dirge-like textures. *Decennium Dans Axlan* starts even more slowly, with the gradually accumulating power of 'Tapestry Of Things Before', and ends on the similarly inclined 'Man In A Bottle'; in between, there are some beautiful solos by Rob Blakeslee, Bruce Fowler and Steve Fowler from the round-robin of improvisers. *Commemoration*, though a more recent release, was in part recorded prior to *Decennium Dans Axlan*. Again, Golia marshals his forces around key points, waving in some instruments, keeping others under wraps, and only rarely going for the big climax – though when he does, as on the towering 'Tumulus Or Griffin', it's mightily impressive. *Tutto Contare* is for some reason just slightly less involving: 'Chromazoid', with a superb solo by Rob Blakeslee, is exceptional, but the other pieces are neither more nor less than interesting pieces from the repertory of an imposing orchestra. Their set from Portland finds them back to form immediately in the beautiful 'Surrounded By Assassins', which has some ingenious textural points to make even before the gripping solos by Fernandez (bassoon) and Gauthier (violin). This leads into the mighty sprawl of 'Blue Hawk', a discrete homage to Hawkins, Young and Webster. Golia has long since been using the Ensemble to explore a world that lies somewhere between jazz, improvisation and formal composition: in some of this music especially, he seems close to alighting on a unique world. But the problem which troubles the earlier discs seems just as intrusive on these later ones: the recording quality simply isn't good enough; in a group with two bassists and three percussionists, playing scores of this much complexity, it has to be a lot closer to standard to make the music come fully to life on record.

★★★(★) The Other Bridge (Oakland 1999)
Nine Winds NWCD 0210/0220 2CD *Golia; John Fumo, Jeff Kaiser, Rob Blakeslee (t); Mike Vlatkovich, Danny Hemwall, Scott Ray (tb); Kim Richmond, Paul Sherman, Bill Plake, Eric Barber, Steve Adams, Alan Lechusza, Tara Speiser, Sarah Shoenbeck (woodwind); Wayne Peet (ky); Harry Scorzo, Jeff Gauthier (vn); Jonathan Golove, Guenevere Measham, Colin Pearson (clo); Bill Roper (tba); Ken Filiano (b); David Johnson, Brad Dutz, Alex Cline (perc); Stephanie Henry (cond).* 8/99.

Golia thinks big for his large-scale recordings, and here's another two and a half hours of music for the Large Ensemble. He may have written and scored all the music, but it's scarcely a setting for personal grandstanding: he gives himself just one solo across the entire two discs. The bustling, ebullient 'Thread For Fred' should silence any who feel that jazz is only a modest part of the Large Ensemble's direction, and the soloists – out of the stellar cast, Kim Richmond, Jeff Kaiser and John Fumo merit a particular huzzah – honour the composer's intentions. We feel there is little to add, though, to our judgement on the Ensemble's earlier records. It still sounds like a decent amateur recording rather than the kind of document the Ensemble deserves, but the quality of the music manages to overcome the presentation shortcomings.

★★★ Music For Electronics And Woodwinds
Nine Winds 243 *Golia; Mark Trayle (elec).* n.d.

★★★ Nine Pieces For Solo B♭ Clarinet
Meniscus MNSCS 080 *Golia (cl solo).* 11/00.

Less studied and more mercurial than, say, Braxton's work with Richard Teitelbaum, Golia's duets with electronics man Trayle have a sense of fun to go with the inevitable sonic questing. The woodwinder takes along some of his fun horns (piccolo, for instance) to the date and has a high old time when both sides start twittering. Trayle also plays Vinny back to himself via a direct processing input. It doesn't feel very profound, but it rarely palls.

In a heroic act of self-denial, Golia was obliged to play the solo record on only one horn, an 'ordinary' clarinet. There is a deleted solo album in the Nine Winds back-catalogue, but that was cut 20 years earlier and it's a departure for Golia. Impressive though the playing is, it feels as if it's in search of a context: several of the pieces sound either like exercises or the corralling of a certain idea. The free play of a genuine improvisation can be elusive, even in this open space.

★★★ Music For Like Instruments – The E♭ Saxophones
Nine Winds NWCD 2049 *Golia; Beth Schenck, Jason Mears, Nathan Herrera (as).* 12/02.

Episode one in an 'ongoing project' – music by woodwind ensemble groups which share a common characteristic. Golia here enlists three alto-players while he picks up the baritone, the stritch, the sopranino and the contrabass sax (the latter sounding especially good against the brooding altos on 'Chronos'). Some pieces are barely a minute long, others run for seven or eight, and there's an inconsistent success rate. The deliberate vagaries of pitch in 'Would It Bother You?' bother us a lot. The attention on timbral and harmonic matters does leave some of the pieces a bit bereft from a rhythmical standpoint. Vinny has, though, come up with some of his best titles (we especially like 'Trilled To Be Here'!).

★★★(★) Birdology
Leo LR 389 *Golia; Peter A. Schmid (sno, bs, tubax, bf, b-rec, f, taragot, cl, bcl, cbcl).* 3/03.

If nothing else, this is a feast of reed and woodwind sound, created by two specialists in the extremes of these families of instruments. But what's particularly attractive is the songful way they approach their improvisations: a piece such as 'Blackbirds', for two bass clarinets, or 'Taubenbalz', for alto and bass flutes, really does have the quality of birdsong. A few pieces feature overdubs, some contrast very high and very low reeds – and a few are not much more than a racket. But even non-specialists may enjoy this record.

Mac Gollehon

TRUMPET

Contemporary American brassman, playing in and around New York and New Jersey.

★★★(★) In The Spirit Of Fats Navarro
Half Note 4206 *Gollehon; Frank Lacy (tb); Bill Holloman (ts, org); Ronnie Cuber (bs); James Hurt (p); Lonnie Plaxico (b); Ronnie Burrage (d); Tamm E. Hunt (v).* 00.

Navarro is a tough act to follow, either as homage or inspiration, and Gollehon may not have the young master's most scintillating chops, but he's not bad, and this rowdy, rambunctious date is a splendid and genuine effort. By having Ronnie Burrage play with thumping, thunderous abandon and encouraging the likes of Cuber and Lacy into their most blustering form, he has this set function almost as a bebop party. There's nothing trim or polite about it, and if the shirt-tails aren't quite hanging out, they're not tucked in tight. Navarro's tunes are rarely called these days, even on bop-oriented bandstands, and it's interesting to hear the likes of 'EB-POB', 'Fats Blows' and 'Nostalgia' alongside the more expected 'Our Delight' and 'Dance Of The Infidels', as well as a few functional Gollehon originals. With Tamm E. Hunt's jive monologue the closing 'Bebop Revolution' is, er, in the spirit.

Benny Golson (born 1929)

TENOR SAXOPHONE

A Philadelphian, Golson went from jazz and R&B combos in the early '50s to arranging for Dizzy Gillespie in 1956; then a stint with Art Blakey, and the formation of the Jazztet with Art Farmer in 1959. In the '60s and '70s his main work was as a composer for film and TV, but in the '80s he returned to regular jazz gigs and has recorded frequently since. His book of jazz compositions is one of the most enduring of its kind, with several pieces among the most-played in the hard-bop repertoire.

★★★ Benny Golson's New York Scene
Original Jazz Classics OJC 164 *Golson; Art Farmer (t); Jimmy Cleveland (tb); Julius Watkins (frhn); Gigi Gryce (as); Sahib Shihab (bs); Wynton Kelly (p); Paul Chambers (b); Charli Persip (d).* 10/57.

***** The Modern Touch**

Original Jazz Classics OJC 1797 *Golson; Kenny Dorham (t); J. J. Johnson (tb); Wynton Kelly (p); Paul Chambers (b); Max Roach (d).* 12/57.

***** Benny Golson And The Philadelphians**

Blue Note 494104-2 *Golson; Lee Morgan, Roger Guerin (t); Ray Bryant, Bobby Timmons (p); Percy Heath, Pierre Michelot (b); Philly Joe Jones, Christian Garros (d).* 11–12/58.

*****(*) Gone With Golson**

Original Jazz Classics OJC 1850 *Golson; Curtis Fuller (tb); Ray Bryant (p); Tom Bryant (b); Al Harewood (d).* 6/59.

****** Groovin' With Golson**

Original Jazz Classics OJC 226 *Golson; Curtis Fuller (tb); Ray Bryant (p); Paul Chambers (b); Art Blakey (d).* 8/59.

***** Gettin' With It**

Original Jazz Classics OJC 1873 *Golson; Curtis Fuller (tb); Tommy Flanagan (p); Doug Watkins (b); Art Taylor (d).* 12/59.

***** The Other Side Of Benny Golson**

Original Jazz Classics OJC 1750 *Golson; Curtis Fuller (tb); Barry Harris (p); Jymie Merritt (b); Philly Joe Jones (d).* 11/58.

***** Stockholm Sojourn**

Original Jazz Classics OJC 1894 *Golson; Benny Bailey, Bo Broberg, Bengt-Arne Wallin (t); Grachan Moncur III, Eje Thelin (tb); Cecil Payne (bs); Roman Dylag (b); others. n.d.*

Golson will always be considered, primarily, as a composer and arranger, producing such standards as 'I Remember Clifford', 'Whisper Not' and 'Stablemates'. His powers as a saxophonist have tended to be overshadowed, although his still-growing discography has reasserted the stature of his own playing. Despite contributing several of the staple pieces in the hard-bop repertoire, his own playing style originally owed rather more to such swing masters as Hawkins and Lucky Thompson; a big, crusty tone and a fierce momentum sustain his solos, and they can take surprising and exciting turns, even if the unpredictability sometimes leads to a loss of focus. The earlier of the two 1957 sessions concentrates on the more reflective side of his work, with three tracks by a nonet, three by a quintet with Farmer, and a ballad interpretation of 'You're Mine You' with the rhythm section alone; all well played but comparatively reserved. *The Modern Touch* is impeccably tailored hard bop, bedecked with good writing by the leader and suave playing by the sextet, but it's uneventful rather than exciting.

The later discs contain the seeds of the group which would, when joined full time by Farmer, become the Jazztet. The best is *Groovin'*, titled appropriately since the band hit a splendid pace from the start, and Golson and Fuller turn in inspired solos. *Gone With Golson* is only a notch behind; Golson fashions a catchy arrangement of Bryant's 'Staccato Swing', takes an impassioned course through 'Autumn Leaves' and turns in a fine 'Blues After Dark'. *Gettin' With It* is rather too casual here and there, starting with a 'Baubles, Bangles And Beads' which is so relaxed it scarcely comes off the starting blocks. There's consolation in 'Tippin' On Thru' and a very slow and consummately controlled 'April In Paris'. *The Other Side* is also at a lower temperature but is still very worthwhile. *Stockholm Sojourn* is more about Golson the arranger than the player, and features a Swedish ensemble with various expatriate guests. The scores seem a little restricted by LP playing-time but there are some interesting touches, and Benny Bailey makes a moving statement out of this version of 'I Remember Clifford'.

Benny Golson And The Philadelphians, is now a Blue Note CD but was originally a United Artists LP. The original album is a fine and characteristic set of hard bop, with 'Thursday's Theme' one of the best of Golson's less-remembered tunes, and he and Morgan hit it off as well as they ever did. Four tracks made in France with a local group a few weeks later are less involving and water down the programme somewhat, though Golson's playing is as committed as always.

*****(*) Three Little Words**

Jazz House JHAS 609 *Golson; Stan Tracey (p); Rick Laird (b); Ronnie Stephenson, Billy Hart (d).* 11/65.

A fascinating discovery and a rare example of Golson captured live in his prime, during a residency at Ronnie Scott's Club. Seven long pieces chronicle an evening's work and even though the CD runs a whisker under 80 minutes it's consistently gripping. The intensities which Golson finds in his favourite 'Stablemates' or in a marathon 'Stella By Starlight' are almost shocking. When the former is followed by a caressing treatment of the melody of 'My Foolish Heart' it's a disturbing change of mood. Golson always insists that Coltrane never really influenced his methods and it's intriguing to hear how he is both like and unlike his illustrious contemporary. This is tenor playing of controlled but formidable power and it makes a strong case for reconsidering Golson the saxophonist. The disc also affords a chance to hear Tracey at length, and splendid he is too (Hart replaces Stephenson on the final three numbers). One has to make allowances for the scruffy recording, which is why we have to take off a point.

**** Tune In, Turn On**

Verve 559793-2 *Golson; Art Farmer (t, flhn); Richard Tee (p); Eric Gale (g); James Tyrell (b); Bernard Purdie (d); Warren Smith (perc).* 4/67.

It's not Golson's fault that rubbish like this has returned to the racks – some record companies will stop at nothing to make the most of their back pages. This set of 'the hippest commercials of the '60s' is suitably cheesy: oboes, harpsichords and dub-dub-dah-dah singers vying for attention on jingle-based pieces such as 'Music To Think By'(!). The miracle is that Golson himself still manages to inject a few soulful solos into this situation. The whole is probably not really kitsch enough for some tastes.

***** Up Jumped Benny**

Arkadia 70741 *Golson; Kevin Hays (p); Dwayne Burno (b); Carl Allen (d).* 5/86.

*****(*) Live**

Dreyfus 191057-2 *Golson; Mulgrew Miller (p); Peter Washington (b); Tony Reedus (d).* 2/89.

*****(*) Domingo**

Dreyfus 191132-2 *Golson; Jean-Loup Longnon (t); Curtis Fuller (tb); Kevin Hays (p); James Genus (b); Tony Reedus (d).* 11/91.

Back in a playing milieu after many years in studio work, Golson cut an interesting figure. Though his tone has weakened a little and taken on a querulous edge, his playing hasn't so much declined in stature as changed its impact. He had traded his swing influences for Coltrane 20 years earlier, and by the '80s – after a sabbatical in film and TV scoring – it had resulted in the kind of introspective passion which marks out some of Coltrane's music, even if Golson chose a more conservative set of aims. He sounds in wonderful voice on *Live*, captured on a European stopover in Porto Maggiore. There's a feathery, rippling treatment of 'I Remember Clifford' which makes it clear that, although there have been countless versions of this ballad, the composer himself still has fresh things to say about it. 'Jam The Avenue' is the kind of blow-out that has to have everyone's chops in good order, and Golson has no trouble there. 'Sweet And Lovely' shows that he is still learning from Coltrane, too. The studio date features an impressive quintet (Longnon turns up only for 'Blues March') and continues the long and intriguing partnership between Golson and Fuller, a dialogue seldom remarked on but as productive as any in the post-bop era. The title-track was originally arranged for Lee Morgan in the '50s and has hardly been heard since, but Golson comes up with a fine new arrangement, and it's a pity that he otherwise contributes only one new piece, 'Thinking Mode'; the rest are staples from his book, as well as Fuller's spirited 'A La Mode' and Brubeck's 'In Your Own Sweet Way'.

Up Jumped Benny is an appearance with a young rhythm section, recently issued, in which Golson again makes the running on some of his favourites, along with the nice touch of including Clifford Brown's 'Tiny Capers'. The Swiss audience tends to be a bit noisy, but Golson again impresses with his no-nonsense approach to the material.

***** I Remember Miles**

Evidence ECD 22141-2 *Golson; Eddie Henderson (t); Curtis Fuller (tb); Mulgrew Miller (p); Ray Drummond (b); Tony Reedus (d).* 10/92.

Rather an obvious premise, with Golson leading a seasoned troupe through six Davis staples and a couple of originals, and with Henderson putting in his mute and donning the mantle; by the time they get to 'So What' one wonders at the point of it all. But this is such a great band that it's hard not to enjoy the motions they're going through.

*****(*) Tenor Legacy**

Arkadia Jazz 0742 *Golson; Branford Marsalis, James Carter, Harold Ashby (ts); Geoff Keezer (p); Dwayne Burno (b); Joe Farnsworth (d).* 1/96.

What at first seems like a mismatch blossoms into a compelling, cross-generational recital that blends old spirits like Golson and Ashby with young firebrands such as Carter and the rhythm section. Each track is in dedication to a tenorman of yore (bar Sonny Rollins, still with us) and the treatments are apposite and surprising too. 'Cry Me A River', for instance, catches much of Dexter Gordon's lonesome wit, but is updated by Carter's lightning insights. Ashby sounds a bit frail on his five appearances, but there's no denying his character, and it's a strong counter to Carter's explosive cameos on his feature tracks. Branford arrives only to share 'Body And Soul' with Benny, a cryptic, fascinating version. Golson's thick, foggy sound fittingly wraps things up with a poignant 'In Memory Of', dedicated to his first great influence, Don Byas. Not without its flaws, but a deep and memorable record.

***** Remembering Clifford**

Milestone 9728-2 *Golson; John Swana (t); Ron Blake (ts); Mike LeDonne (p); Peter Washington (b); Joe Farnsworth (d); Tito Puente, Carlos Patato Valdes (perc).* 2/97.

Golson leads a team of youngish boppers through some new originals, a couple of old favourites and a surprising take on 'Lullaby Of Birdland'. Pushing 70, the maestro still sounds in great nick: compared to Ron Blake, he has a chestier and less mobile sound, but he surrenders nothing in expressiveness on the ballad 'You're The First To Know'. The pick of the others, perhaps surprisingly, is LeDonne, whose fills and solos have a jaunty and quick-witted edge that makes plenty of appeal.

*****(*) That's Funky**

Arkadia 70743 *Golson; Nat Adderley (t); Monty Alexander (p); Ray Drummond (b); Marvin 'Smitty' Smith (d).* 9/99.

Old friends revisiting old friends. Nat and Benny were in great heart, taking a fresh look at 'The Sidewinder', 'Moritat', 'Blues March', 'Moanin'' and a few others. Golson calls it his Funky Quintet, but he's taken the trouble to rethink the tunes as well, so we get to hear 'Blues March' at its original thumping Blakey tempo, but with the theme played slower than usual, while the reverse happens on 'Moanin''. Nat has everybody do 'Work Song' – maybe his final recorded version and he still sounds like he loves it. Alexander behaves better than he does on some of his own records, and bass and drums know the language to perfection.

Nat Gonella (1908–98)

TRUMPET, VOCALS

Began playing in minor dance bands before joining Billy Cotton in 1929. In the '30s, with his Georgians, he became a star performer, broadcaster and recording artist. Tried bop briefly after the war, then worked in music hall and variety, with a career revival in 1959, subsequently eclipsed by rock. An honoured elder statesman, he was still singing in the last year of his life.

***** Nat Gonella And His Georgians**

Flapper PAST CD 9750 *Gonella; Bruts Gonella, Johnny Morrison, Chas Oughton, Jack Wallace (t); Miff King (tb); Jack Bonser, Jock Middleton, Joe Moore, Ernest Morris, Mickey Seidman, Albert Torrance (cl, as, bs); Pat Smuts, Don Barigo (ts); Harold Hood, Monia Liter, Norman Stenfalt (p); Roy Dexter, Jimmy Mesene (g); Will Hemmings (b); Bob Dryden, Johnny Roland (d).* 1/35–10/40.

Nat's Georgians – in which brother Bruts played Joe Oliver to his Pops – was one of the most successful British hot bands of the pre-war years. There have been various 'Georgian' revivals (the title was taken from his big hit, 'Georgia On My Mind') since that time and in the '80s Nat was still singing, though no longer playing his horn. The Armstrong influence is so overt as to be unarguable, and yet Gonella brought something of his own as well, a wry, philosophical shrug as he threw off neat aphoristic solos with the biting tone and earthy humour his fans loved. The Flapper disc is a very good selection of early material. Nat spent a little time in America at the end of the decade, and its influence can be heard in the bluesier and more relaxedly rhythmic swing of the later cuts. The New Georgians stuff from 1940 is – heretical though it may be – superior to the original band's output. There's a novelty edge to many of the tracks, but Nat's vocal on 'The Flat Foot Floogie' and even 'Ol' Man River' is never less than musical and in the latter case quite moving. A bit of an institution, who will be fondly remembered by anyone over the age of 60 and who may prove mystifying to anyone under. Gonella has been unfairly neglected in the CD era, and it would be nice for EMI (or someone) to resurrect his marvellous album of reminiscences, *The Nat Gonella Story*, from 1961.

Paul Gonsalves (1920–74)

TENOR SAXOPHONE

'Mex' was a Bostonian who started with Basie but joined Ellington in 1950 and stayed for the rest of his life. Drink and narcotics troubled his career, but Ellington stood by him and coaxed out countless great performances: Newport 1956 was his apotheosis.

***** Ellingtonia Moods And Blues**

RCA Victor 7432 147793-2 *Gonsalves; Ray Nance (t); Booty Wood (tb); Johnny Hodges (as); Jimmy Jones (p); Al Hall (b); Oliver Jackson (d).* 2/60.

****** Gettin' Together**

Original Jazz Classics OJC 203 *Gonsalves; Nat Adderley (t); Wynton Kelly (p); Sam Jones (p); Jimmy Cobb (d).* 12/60.

*****(*) Tell It The Way It Is**

Impulse! 547 960-2 *Gonsalves; Rolf Ericson (t); Ray Nance (c, vn); Johnny Hodges (as); Walter Bishop Jr (p); Dick Hyman (org); Kenny Burrell (g); George Duvivier (b); Ernie Shepard (b, v); Roy Haynes, Osie Johnson (d); Manny Albam (bell tree).* 5 & 9/63.

***** Jazz Till Midnight**

Storyville STCD 4123 *Gonsalves; Jan Johansson (p, org); Bob Cranshaw (b); Albert 'Tootie' Heath (d).* 1/67.

****(*) Mexican Bandit Meets Pittsburg Pirate**

Original Jazz Classics OJC 751 *Gonsalves; Roy Eldridge (t, v); Cliff Smalls (p); Sam Jones (b); Eddie Locke (d).* 8/73.

Almost 30 years after his premature death, it's probably past time for a reassessment of Gonsalves's work. We were privileged to have a glimpse of the mouthpiece he used over the last few years of his life, a gnarled, snaggly thing, almost bitten through, testimony to a foreshortened lifetime of intense improvisation and an unflinching technique. Gonsalves stands in a direct line with earlier masters like Chu Berry and Don Byas, and with (once) young Turks like Frank Lowe and David Murray. It would be absurd to compare his influence with Coltrane's, but it's now clear that he was experimenting with tonalities remarkably similar to Coltrane's famous 'sheets of sound' long before Coltrane; it's also unarguably true that more people heard Gonsalves (albeit in his more straight-ahead role as an Ellington stalwart). His fabled 27 choruses on 'Diminuendo And Crescendo In Blue' at the Newport Jazz Festival in 1956 can be considered the first important extended saxophone solo in modern jazz.

The '60s Ellingtonia session is – unfortunately for Gonsalves – hijacked by Hodges, who claims composer or co-composer credits on four of the tracks, including the closing 'D A Blues'. The tenor man is listed as author of 'Chocataw' and 'The Line-Up', but his main feature is 'Daydreams', a solo statement worthy of Coleman Hawkins, but also anticipating something of Sonny Rollins's later melodic style. The scaled-down orchestral sound smacks a little of Ellington-and-water, but that was the price Duke exacted of all his sidemen's groups. Had he been present, instead of the workmanlike but pedestrian Jones, a rather ordinary session might have been raised a notch, but Ducal spin-offs without the great man were somehow always contrived to sound like second-division affairs.

Hodges again tends to dominate on *Tell It The Way It Is*, which is now repackaged with the slightly earlier *Cleopatra – Feelin' Jazzy*, a slightly odd concept album inspired by Elizabeth Taylor's pyramidal epic. Hodges's arrangements on *Tell It* are more subtly crafted than any he ever recorded on his own account, and Bob Thiele's production gives the individual horns generous space while allowing the sound to meld and blend. A valuable reissue.

Gettin' Together is a remarkable album, beautifully played and recorded. Wynton Kelly's piano playing on 'Walkin'' and 'I Cover The Waterfront' (a Gonsalves favourite) is of the highest quality, and Adderley's slightly fragile, over-confident tone fits in perfectly. Most strongly recommended.

The last of the group makes sad listening after the earlier sessions or any of the great Ellington occasions. Gonsalves at this point had less than a year to live and, while a meeting with the incendiary trumpeter might have been marvellous 15 years earlier, the tenor-playing sounds fractious and tired. Eldridge has a few characteristic squalls to deliver, but seam out the other discs first.

Virgil Gonsalves (born 1931)

BARITONE SAXOPHONE

Somewhat obscure baritonist, who never made the impact of a Chaloff or a Mulligan, but has his merits.

***** Jazz In Hollywood**

Original Jazz Classics OJCCD 1889 *Gonsalves; Bob Enevoldsen, Herbie Harper (tb); Buddy Wise (ts); Steve White (ts, v); Lou Levy, Jimmy Rowles (p); Harry Babasin (b); Larry Bunker, Roy Harte (d).* 9/54.

This interesting set pairs two ten-inch LPs featuring Gonsalves's slightly lumbering style on a sextet date alongside a disc by off-beat saxophonist White, who also merits rediscovery. Virgil's playing is far from revelatory, but his robust delivery, often played in tenor range, is always attractive and the partnership with Enevoldsen and Wise in a three-horn front line with Levy, Babasin and Bunker is expertly and often expressively done, with the trombonist in top form throughout. White's material is mostly out of whack, but entertaining enough. Perhaps one to fish out of the bargain bin rather than make a substantial investment.

Babs Gonzales (1919–80)

VOCALS

Irrepressibly hip and a fine musician, the man from Newark was among the first to give bebop a vocal dimension. Partly because of his colourful autobiographies, he became a cult figure.

***** Babs Gonzales, 1947–1949**

Classics 1124 *Gonzales; Dave Burns (t); Julius Watkins (frhn); Tony Scott (cl); Jordan Fordin, Art Pepper, Don Redman, Rudy Williams (as); James Moody, Sonny Rollins (ts); Tadd Dameron, Linton Garner, Wynton Kelly, Bobby*

Tucker (p); Nelson Boyd, Bruce Lawrence (b); Roy Haynes, Jack Parker, Charles Simmons (d). 47–49.

Babs was the odd man out in Valerie Wilmer's *As Serious As Your Life*, her study of the new avant-garde of the '60s. And yet, corny as some of the work here doubtless now seems, what he did was colonize the rapid transitions and complex harmonies of bebop for singers. The sessions here are variable in quality, but there are some delightful cuts and some intriguing experiments as well. The early work with Three Bips And A Bop is probably among the best. 'Oop-Pop-A-Da' and 'Professor Bop' are both good representations of Babs's vocalese and lyrical approach. 'Weird Lullaby' was another of his hits and became a kind of signature tune after its Capitol release. Babs isn't to every taste, but he was a significant figure on the scene and the line-up shown above should offer some reassurance that the musical quality is not lacking either.

Dennis González (born 1954)

TRUMPET, POCKET TRUMPET, FLUGELHORN, OTHER INSTRUMENTS

Learned trumpet as a teenager and arrived in Dallas in 1977, where he started the Daagnim label, broadcast and acted as a focus for the somewhat embattled new-music community of the area.

★★★★ Stefan

Silkheart SHCD 101 *González; John Purcell (bcl, bf, eng hn, syn, v); Henry Franklin (b, v); W. A. Richardson (d).* 4/86.

★★★(★) Namesake

Silkheart SHCD 106 *González; Ahmed Abdullah (t, flhn, balafon); Charles Brackeen (ts, perc); Douglas Ewart (bcl, as, f); Malachi Favors (b); Alvin Fielder (d).* 2/87.

★★★★ Debenge, Debenge

Silkheart SHCD 112 *González; Marlon Jordan (t); Charles Brackeen (ts); Kidd Jordan (sno, as, bcl); Malachi Favors, Henry Franklin (b); Alvin Fielder, W. A. Richardson (d).* 2/88.

González's recordings for the Silkheart label were part of a determined effort to wrest initiative back from New York and the West Coast and to restore the South's, and particularly the Delta's, slightly marginal standing in the new jazz. The band assembled for *Debenge, Debenge* goes under the uncomfortably agglutinative name New Dallasorleanssippi, that for (the now deleted) *Desert Wind* New Dallasangeles, formulae which give no sense at all of their coherence and directness of statement. González's other great achievement is to have tempted the great tenor player Charles Brackeen out of a self-imposed semi-retirement.

Stefan is probably the trumpeter's masterpiece. The opening 'Enrico', dedicated to the Italian trumpeter Enrico Rava, opens a path for magnificent flugelhorn figurations over a bass/bass-clarinet accompaniment. 'Fortuity' is calm and enigmatic, like the title-track (a dedication to González's son) a simple theme on open chords, but with a strange, dramatic interlude for voices. 'Hymn For Don Cherry' is based on 'At The Cross' and reflects two more of Gonzalez's influences. 'Boi Fuba', the briefest and least successful track, explores Brazilian materials, while John Purcell's closing 'Deacon John Ray' features his Dolphy-ish alto, and the trumpeter is superbly instinctive on the borders of total harmonic abstraction. A masterful record.

Namesake only suffers by comparison, but it shouldn't be missed. The long title-piece is a complex 7/4 figure that manages to sound completely coherent and also as if it were being played by a very much larger band, as if González had been listening to Mingus's appropriations of Ellington on *The Black Saint And The Sinner Lady*. 'Separation Of Stones' is tranced and dreamy, and the solos are softly enunciated, with González muted and the Armstrong-influenced Abdullah on flugelhorn. A percussion overture sets up a mood of combined grief and triumph in anticipation of 'Hymn For Mbizo', a threnody for South African bassist Johnny Dyani, but is interrupted by the lightweight 'Four Pigs And A Bird's Nest', on which González plays his Cherry-patented pocket trumpet, muted on this occasion.

Debenge, Debenge, along with Brackeen's own *Banaar* and *Worshippers Come Nigh* (Silkheart 105 & 111), quickly consolidated the label's quality and confirmed González's considerable musical intelligence. The multi-talented Kidd Jordan builds a bridge between González's ringing, sometimes slightly sharp-toned trumpet and Brackeen's powerful tenor; his son, Marlon Jordan, is a fresh new voice and the Art Ensemble of Chicago veteran, Favors, shows more of his formidable technique than for some time. A superb record, beautifully engineered and produced.

★★ Home

Daagnim CD 6 *González; Tim Green (ts); Scott Bucklin (p); Shane Cooper (g); Aaron González (b); Stefan González (d).* 1–4/01.

★★★ Home Away From Home

Daagnim CD-R 2/CD 7 *González; Douglas Ewart (sno, as, didjeridu); George Cartwright, Tim Green (ts); Kim Corbet, Frank LoCascio (ky); Aaron González (b); Stefan González (d).* 11/01–3/02.

Back after a long spell away from the scene, González calls his family band Yells At Eels (we don't know either) and here the basic trio is augmented for a set of mostly downbeat and rather gentle tunes that find the trumpeter multi-tracked and processed in various ways that do little to preserve his distinctively clear and bright tone. This is a very curious set, not something that is likely to excite Dennis's existing fans or to lasso any new ones. However, the grab-bag of live tracks which is *Home Away From Home* is much more like the real González. He plays a beautiful solo on 'Who You Gonna Call?', the 'Hymn For Julius Hemphill' is attractive, and a long piece dedicated to Leo Smith manages to overcome the presence of a didjeridu. It's all rather diffuse and parts of it ('Nils Petter's Foxtrot') are really no good, but at least some of Dennis's signature lyricism comes through.

Benny Goodman (1909–86)

CLARINET, VOCAL

Studied clarinet from age of 11, began working two years later, and joined the Ben Pollack band in Chicago. Studio work in New York followed until he began bandleading in 1934. Indifferent results until a sensational gig in Los Angeles, then he built the band that became one of the most popular in America, hiring Harry James, Lionel Hampton, Teddy Wilson and Gene Krupa. Survived the big-band decline and toyed with bebop, though with little commitment, as well as occasionally playing the classical repertoire. Continued to tour with big bands (occasionally) and small groups (more frequently) into the '70s and '80s. Despite his martinet reputation, Goodman remained a hugely successful leader. The early hot style matured into an impeccable if calmer manner, and his approach to his own instrumentalism was of unflinching dedication.

***** Benny Goodman 1928–1931**

Classics 693 *Goodman; Wingy Manone (t); Jimmy McPartland (c); Tommy Dorsey, Glenn Miller (tb); Fud Livingston, Larry Binyon (cl, ts); Sid Stoneburn (cl, as); Bud Freeman (ts); Vic Breidis, Joe Sullivan, Mel Stitzel (p); Eddie Lang, Dick Morgan (g); Herman Foster (bj); Harry Goodman (b); Bob Conselman, Gene Krupa (d); Harold Arlen, Grace Johnston, Scrappy Lambert, Paul Small (v).* 1/28–2/31.

***** Benny Goodman 1931–1933**

Classics 719 *Goodman; Charlie Teagarden, Manny Klein, Shirley Clay, Bunny Berigan (t); Jack Teagarden, Tommy Dorsey, Glenn Miller (tb); Sid Stoneburn (cl, as); Larry Binyon (cl, ts, f); Art Karle (ts); Irving Brodsky, Joe Sullivan (p); Eddie Lang, Dick McDonough (g); Artie Bernstein (b); Gene Krupa, Ray Bauduc, Johnny Williams (d); Billie Holiday, Smith Ballew, Paul Small, Dick Robertson (v).* 3/31–12/33.

Goodman's earliest dates as a leader are rough-and-ready New York jazz, with McPartland's gruff lead adding to the grit and Benny doubling on alto and baritone. The notorious 'Shirt Tail Stomp', in which the group lampooned the jazz clichés of the time, became a minor hit. Goodman's two solos, 'That's A Plenty' and 'Clarinetitis', are virtuoso stuff, and a subsequent date in Chicago yielded two more gutsy small-group titles with Manone and Freeman. After that, though, his New York sessions, which take up the rest of Classics 693 and all of 719, are polite, inconsequential dance music. Elements of swing start to creep in as time goes on, but the often stellar personnel have trouble getting any jazz into the records, and the most notable thing is the arrival of young Billie Holiday on two of the final tracks. Sound is mixed – very rough and scratchy on some of the transfers, particularly on the latter sessions on Classics 693.

****(*) Benny Goodman 1934–1935**

Classics 744 *Goodman; Manny Klein, Charles Margulis, Charlie Teagarden, George Thow, Russ Case, Jerry Neary, Sam Shapiro, Pee Wee Irwin, Art Sylvester, Ralph Muzillo (t); Sonny Lee, Jack Teagarden, Red Ballard, Jack Lacey (tb); Hymie Schertzer, Ben Kantor, Toots Mondello (as); Coleman Hawkins, Hank Ross, Arthur Rollini, Dick Clark (ts); Claude Thornhill, Arthur Schutt, Frank Froeba, Teddy Wilson (p); Dick McDonough, George Van Eps, Benny Martel (g); Artie Bernstein, Harry Goodman, Hank Wayland (b); Ray McKinley, Sammy Weiss, Gene Krupa (d); Mildred Bailey, Ann Graham, Helen Ward, Buddy Clark (v).* 2/34–1/35.

***** Benny Goodman 1935**

Classics 769 *Goodman; Jerry Neary, Pee Wee Irwin, Bunny Berigan, Nate Kazebier, Ralph Muzillo (t); Red Ballard, Jack Lacey, Jack Teagarden, Joe Harris (tb); Toots Mondello, Hymie Schertzer (as); Arthur Rollini, Dick Clark (ts); Frank Froeba (p); Allan Reuss, George Van Eps (g); Harry Goodman (b); Gene Krupa (d); Helen Ward, Ray Hendricks, Buddy Clark (v).* 1–7/35.

***** Benny Goodman 1935–1936**

Classics 789 *As above, except add Harry Geller (t), Bill De Pew (as), Teddy Wilson, Jess Stacy (p); omit Neary, Lacey, Teagarden, Van Eps, Hendricks, Clark.* 7/35–4/36.

***** Benny Goodman 1936**

Classics 817 *As above, except add Chris Griffin, Manny Klein (t), Murray McEachern (tb); omit Mondello, Froeba.* 4–8/36.

*****(*) Benny Goodman 1936 Vol. 2**

Classics 836 *As above, except add Sterling Bose, Zeke Zarchy, Ziggy Elman (t), Vido Musso (ts), Lionel Hampton (vib); omit Klein, Geller.* 8–11/36.

*****(*) Benny Goodman 1936–1937**

Classics 858 *As above, except add Irving Goodman, Harry James (t), George Koenig (as), Margaret McCrae, Jimmy Rushing, Frances Hunt (v); omit Bose, Zarchy.* 12/36–7/37.

Goodman was struggling as a bandleader until the mystical night of 21 August 1935 when the swing era apparently began, following his broadcast from Los Angeles. He already had a good band: the reed section was skilful, the trumpets – boosted by the arrival of Bunny Berigan, who had a terrific impact on Goodman himself – strong, and the book was bulging with material. There were Fletcher Henderson arrangements which would help to make Goodman's fortune – 'Blue Skies', 'King Porter Stomp', 'Basin Street Blues' – and Jimmy Mundy and Edgar Sampson charts of a similar calibre. There was Gene Krupa at the drums and Goodman, perhaps the first great virtuoso of the swing era, himself.

It may surprise some, at this distance, to hear how Goodman actually played more of an ensemble role than that of a star leader – at least in terms of the sound of his clarinet and its place on the records. Solos are usually quite short and pithy, and though he takes the lion's share, that was only right and proper; he was far and away the best improviser (Berigan aside, who didn't last very long) in his own band. What one notes about the records is their smooth, almost ineluctable power and fleetness. Krupa's drumming energized the orchestra, but its brass and reed sections were such fine executants (only Lunceford's band could have matched them) that they generated their own kind of inner swing. Henderson, Mundy and Sampson all supplied arrangements which, in a gesture that has dominated big-band writing to this day, pointed up those strengths without looking for fancy textures or subtleties.

The Classics series, moving chronologically through the Columbia and Victor sessions, offers a comprehensive overview. Classics 744 finds the band still in an awkward, transitory phase, which is more or less resolved by the end of Classics 769, which has the first Henderson arrangements, the classic reading of 'King Porter Stomp' and the big hit 'Blue Skies'. The sound of the band, comparatively muffled on the Columbia sessions (though the erratic Classics remastering doesn't help), is smoother, bigger and more sophisticated by the time the Victor dates were properly under way. Classics 789 also includes the first tracks by the BG trio, and though this disc also marks Berigan's departure – leaving Goodman short of a major trumpeter until the arrival of Harry James – one can hear the orchestra growing in stature. Classics 817 and 836 see Jimmy Mundy coming on board as arranger; Ziggy Elman's arrival in the trumpet section in October 1936 adds some extra firepower to the brass. Classics 858 sees Harry James coming into the band, and the record ends on the studio version of 'Sing, Sing, Sing', one of the most familiar set-pieces of the whole swing era. There is the occasional clinker in terms of material, but for the most part Goodman was able to record songs and charts of a consistently high quality, and even where Helen Ward's vocals dominate a record, the band's eminence is obvious. Transfers of the Victor material are usually strong and without much surface noise.

*****(*) Benny Goodman 1937**
Classics 879 *Goodman; Harry James, Ziggy Elman, Gordon Griffin (t); Red Ballard, Murray McEachern, Vernon Brown (tb); Hymie Schertzer, Bill De Pew, George Koenig (as); Babe Russin, Arthur Rollini, Vido Musso (ts); Jess Stacy (p); Allan Reuss (g); Harry Goodman (b); Gene Krupa (d).* 7–11/37.

*****(*) Benny Goodman 1937–1938**
Classics 899 *Similar to above.* 11/37–3/38.

***** Benny Goodman 1938**
Classics 925 *As above, except add Irving Goodman, Corky Cornelius (t), Bruce Squires (tb), Noni Bernardi, Dave Matthews, Milt Yaner (as), Lester Young, Jerry Jerome, Bud Freeman (ts), Freddie Green, Ben Heller (g), Walter Page (b), Dave Tough, Buddy Shutz (d), Martha Tilton (v); omit McEachern, Koenig.* 3–8/38.

***** Benny Goodman 1938 Vol. 2**
Classics 961 *Similar to above.* 11/38.

The arrangements are by Henderson, Mundy, James, Sampson, Basie and even Mary Lou Williams – Goodman took them from many hands. It's a chronological survey, which also mixes in the trio and quartet sessions. The drawback is that the refusal to cherrypick means that Goodman's more routine material is here too. Still, the quality on both Classics 879 and 899 is consistently high; the two 1938 CDs just slip back a notch in terms of the material. Transfers, from unlisted sources, seem fair. But for a more thoughtful and better-transferred study of Goodman's prime years, best to turn to the Hep CDs listed below.

CORE COLLECTION

****** At Carnegie Hall 1938 – Complete**
Columbia C2K 65143 2CD *Goodman; Ziggy Elman, Buck Clayton, Harry James, Gordon Griffin (t); Bobby Hackett (c); Red Ballard, Vernon Brown (tb); Hymie Schertzer, George Koenig, Johnny Hodges (as); Arthur Rollini, Lester Young, Babe Russin (ts); Harry Carney (bs); Jess Stacy, Teddy Wilson, Count Basie (p); Lionel Hampton (vib); Allan Reuss, Freddie Green (g); Harry Goodman, Walter Page (b); Gene Krupa (d).* 1/38.

A famous occasion, and the music still stands up extraordinarily well. This was one of those events – like Ellington at Newport nearly two decades later – when jazz history is spontaneously changed, even if Goodman had clearly planned the whole thing as a crowning manoeuvre. Unmissable points: Krupa's fantastically energetic drumming throughout, leading to the roof coming off on 'Sing, Sing, Sing'; an Ellington tribute and a jam on 'Honeysuckle Rose' with various guests from other bands (George Simon called it 'ineffectual', but it's very exciting); Ziggy Elman powering through 'Swingtime In The Rockies'; and the original quartet going through its best paces. But the whole affair is atmospheric with the sense of a man and a band taking hold of their moment.

Columbia's new edition of this music is a model effort, masterminded by Phil Schapp, whose indomitable detective work finally tracked down the original acetates and gave us the music in the best sound we'll ever get. Most of the previously unheard material is limited to introductions and the like, but there is some new music, and the ambience of the occasion is powerful, even thrilling.

*****(*) Benny Goodman 1938–1939**
Classics 990 *Goodman; Harry James, Ziggy Elman, Gordon Griffin, Charlie Spivak, Bunny Berigan, Sonny Dunham, Irving Goodman (t); Red Ballard, Vernon Brown, Jack Teagarden, Tommy Dorsey (tb); Dave Matthews, Noni Bernardi, Hymie Schertzer (as); Arthur Rollini, Jerry Jerome, Eddie Miller (ts); Jess Stacy, Teddy Wilson, Bob Zurke (p); Lionel Hampton (vib, d); Ben Heller, Carmen Mastren (g); John Kirby, Bob Haggart, Harry Goodman (b); Buddy Schutz; Ray Bauduc (d); Martha Tilton, Johnny Mercer (v).* 12/38–4/49.

*****(*) Benny Goodman 1939**
Classics 1025 *As above, except add Corky Cornelius, Jimmy Maxwell, Johnny Martell (t), Bruce Squires, Ted Vesly (tb), Toots Mondello, Buff Estes (as), Bus Bassey (ts), Fletcher Henderson (p), Arnold Covey, Charlie Christian (g), Artie Bernstein (b), Nick Fatool (d), Louis Tobin (v); omit James, Spivak, Dunham, Irving Goodman, Teagarden, Dorsey, Miller, Wilson, Zurke, Hampton, Mastren, Kirby, Haggart, Bauduc.* 4–9/39.

*****(*) Benny Goodman 1939 Vol. 2**
Classics 1064 *As above, except add Johnny Guarnieri (p), Lionel Hampton (vib), Mildred Bailey (v); omit Cornelius, Griffin, Rollini, Stacey, Cover, Tilton, Mercer.* 9–12/39.

The band sounds invincibly handsome and powerful in these sessions, in spite of some personnel fluctuations. James departs halfway through Classics 990, as does Jess Stacy, with Fletcher Henderson taking over at the piano and adding several more arrangements to the band's book. Christian's arrival is also a matter of celebration. Goodman had his share of indifferent material, but he seemed to get less ephemera than, say, the Dorseys had to handle, and every session has at least one good opportunity for band and soloist. Among the highlights are 'Blue Lou' and 'The Blues', made by an all-star Victor entourage at a one-off session (Classics 990); 'The Kingdom Of Swing' and 'Jumpin' At The Woodside' (Classics 1025, the latter title from Goodman's first session for Columbia); Christian's first small-group date, and Goodman's theme, 'Let's Dance' (Classics 1064). The Victor tracks are in excellent sound but the Columbia sessions are less predictable in transfer quality.

****** Plays Fletcher Henderson**
Hep 1038 *As appropriate discs above.* 4/35–4/39.

****** Plays Jimmy Mundy**
Hep 1039 *As appropriate discs above.* 9/35–11/37.

These two excellently remastered discs offer a good way of exploring the key points of Benny's music in the '30s. It was Henderson's arrangements, still rooted in his favourite call-and-response patterns, that gave Goodman's band its first real identity, and the best of them are collected here. Mundy's charts follow on from Henderson's and are scarcely more subtle. His favourite riff devices occur again and again, and only in some of his saxophone-writing is there any genuine freshness. Nevertheless, the band's superb craftsmanship makes the arrangements fit snugly into what Goodman wanted. None of this music challenges the best of Ellington, Basie or Lunceford, but the particular crispness of Goodman's band is undeniable.

***** More Camel Caravans Vol. 1**
Phontastic PHONTCD 8841/2 2CD *Goodman; Harry James, Ziggy Elman, Chris Griffin (t); Red Ballard, Vernon Brown (tb); Hymie Schertzer, George Koenig (as); Arthur Rollini, Vido Musso (ts); Jess Stacy, Teddy Wilson (p); Lionel Hampton (vib); Allan Reuss (g); Harry Goodman (b); Gene Krupa (d); Martha Tilton (v).* 8/37.

***** More Camel Caravans Vol. 2**
Phontastic PHONTCD 8843/4 2CD *As above, except Brown returns, add Will Bradley (tb), Dave Matthews, Noni Bernardi (as), Ben Heller (g), Dave Tough (d); omit Schertzer, Koenig, McEachern.* 11/37–9/38.

***** More Camel Caravans Vol. 3**
Phontastic PHONTCD 8845/6 2CD *As above, except add Corky Cornelius (t), Bruce Squires (tb), Toots Mondello, Buff Estes (as), Bus Bassey, Jerry Jerome, Bud Freeman (ts), Fletcher Henderson (p), Arnold Coivey (g), Artie Bernstein (b), Nick Fatool (d), Louise Tobin (v); omit Bradley, Musso, Reuss, Tilton.* 9/38–9/39.

***** Camel Caravan Broadcasts Vol. 1**
Phontastic 8817 *As above, except add Cy Baker (t), Jack Teagarden (tb, v), Joseph Szigeti (vn), Johnny Mercer, Billie Holiday, Leo Watson (v).* 1/39.

***** Camel Caravan Broadcasts Vol. 2**
Phontastic 8818 *As above, except omit Baker, Teagarden, Szigeti, Mercer, Holiday and Watson.* 2–3/39.

***** Camel Caravan Broadcasts Vol. 3**
Phontastic 8819 *Similar to above.* 3–4/39.

Airshots have survived in copious quantities as far as the Goodman band is concerned, and these hefty reissues ought to satisfy the most diligent devotee. They are taken from broadcasts sponsored by Camel on the three Phontastic CDs. The sound on the Phontastic discs is clean, if rather fusty. These call for a lot of patience since there are frequent interruptions from the sponsor, dialogue and other distractions; that aside, the group plays handsomely, though there's the usual quota of feeble titles. Phontastic has recently dug up three more two-disc sets which cover the earlier years of this Camel-sponsored show, and though there are numerous exhortations to smoke, the music more or less wins through.

CORE COLLECTION

****** The Complete Small Group Sessions**
RCA Victor 68764 3CD *Goodman; Lionel Hampton (vib); Teddy Wilson, Jess Stacy (p); John Kirby (b); Buddy Schutz, Dave Tough, Gene Krupa (d).* 7/35–4/39.

Goodman's small groups set a new standard for 'chamber jazz', the kind of thing Red Nichols had tried in the '20s, but informed with a more disciplined – and blacker – sensibility. That said, Goodman's own playing, for all its fineness of line and tonal elegance, could be blisteringly hot, and he is by far the strongest personality on all their records, the presence of domineering figures like Hampton and Krupa notwithstanding. This comprehensive edition is a timely addition to the Goodman discography; these tracks have been out many times over the years, but this is a notably handsome and genuine presentation of them, all in one place. Perhaps the trio sessions, made before Hampton's arrival, are the most satisfying, since the brilliant empathy between Goodman and Wilson – one of the great unspoken jazz partnerships – is allowed its clearest expression. Certainly the likes of 'After You've Gone' and 'Body And Soul' express a smooth yet spontaneously refined kind of improvisation. Hampton made the music swing a little more obtrusively, yet he often plays a rather quiet and contained ensemble role, the vibes shimmering alongside Wilson's playing, and it created a fascinating platform for Goodman's lithest playing. While this quickly became formulaic jazz, it was a very good formula.

*****(*) Benny Goodman 1939–1940**
Classics 1098 *Goodman; Ziggy Elman, Jimmy Maxwell, Johnny Martel, Irving Goodman (t); Red Ballard, Vernon Brown, Ted Vesley (tb): Toots Mondello, Buff Estes, Les Robinson (as); Bus Bassey, Jerry Jerome (ts); Count Basie, Johnny Guarnieri (p); Arnold Covey, Charlie Christian (g); Artie Bernstein (b); Nick Fatool (d); Helen Forrest (v).* 12/39–4/40.

*****(*) Benny Goodman 1940**
Classics 1131 *As above, except add Cootie Williams (t), Dudley Brooks (p), Lionel Hampton (vib), Fred Astaire (v).* 4–11/40.

*****(*) Benny Goodman 1940–1941**
Classics 1154 *Basically as above.* 12/40-1/41

*****(*) Benny Goodman 1941**
Classics 1202 *Goodman; Alec Fila, Jimmy Maxwell, Cootie Williams, Irving Goodman (t); Lou McGarity, Cutty Cutshall (tb); Skippy Martin, Gus Bivona, Bob Snyder, Les Robinson (as); Georgie Auld, Jack Henderson, Pete Mondello (ts) Teddy Wilson, Count Basie (p); Mike Bryan, Charlie Christian (g); Artie Bernstein (b); Dave Tough, Jo Jones (d); Helen Forrest (v).* 1–3/41.

Goodman's orchestral recordings were evolving subtly and with some interesting consequences. Eddie Sauter's involvement with the band's book began introducing all kinds of interest in the scores. His charts for 'Zaggin' With Zig' (for Ziggy Elman) and a particularly fine 'How High The Moon' (both on Classics 1098) brought new refinements to the orchestra's approach, and even more telling were his many settings for Goodman's new vocalist, Helen Forrest, clearly one of the best big-band singers. Even seemingly unpromising material such as 'The Fable Of The Rose' and 'Perfidia' were turned into excellent records. Fans of the sextet with Williams, Basie and Christian are catered for by such tunes as 'Till Tom Special' (Classics 1098) and a personal favourite of ours, 'Breakfast Feud' (Classics 1202). And the loyal Henderson was still much involved; 'Henderson Stomp' (Classics 1131) is outstanding, with superb Williams. In short, even when the band was paying its commercial dues, there was always something interesting going on, and Goodman's own mastery of his horn was complete. Less happy are the circumstances of these Classics CDs. We give them high marks for the music, not the remastering, which isn't so much plain bad as annoyingly inconsistent, almost from track to track. It really is time that Goodman was given the box-set treatment by RCA.

****** Sextet Featuring Charlie Christian**
Columbia CK 40379 *Goodman; Cootie Williams (t); Georgie Auld (ts); Fletcher Henderson, Johnny Guarnieri, Count Basie (p); Lionel Hampton (vib); Charlie Christian (g); Artie Bernstein (b); Nick Fatool, Jo Jones, Dave Tough (d).* 39–41.

***** The Rehearsal Sessions 1940–1941**
Jazz Unlimited JUCD 2013 *As above, except add Ken Kersey (p), Harry Jaeger (d); omit Henderson, Guarnieri, Hampton, Fatool, Tough.* 11/40–1/41.

★★★ Small Groups 1941–1945

Columbia CK 44437 *Goodman; Lou McGarity, Cutty Cutshall (tb); Red Norvo (vib); Teddy Wilson, Mel Powell (p); Tom Morgan, Mike Bryan (g); Slam Stewart, Sid Weiss (b); Morey Feld, Ralph Collier (d); Peggy Lee (v).* 10/41–2/45.

Christian was a once-in-a-lifetime collaborator with Goodman, who had bad luck with some of his best sidemen (Christian, Berigan, Hasselgård – all of whom came to untimely ends). The first *Sextet* compilation is full of finely pointed small-group jazz, hinting every now and then at bop, but not so much as to give anyone any trouble. Equally interesting is the mixture of personalities – Williams, Goodman, Auld, Basie – which gives the sextet performances a blend of coolness and resilience that seems to be a direct extension of the leader's own ambitions. Goodman had led a nearly perfect double-life with the small groups and the big band, balancing dance material and 'listening' jazz and making both commercially and artistically successful; and part of that freshness which the small groups created may be due to the fact that several participants – Wilson, Hampton, Christian – weren't regular members of the big band. But after a reorganization in 1941 he started using regular band-members, who turn up on the *Small Groups 1941–1945* compilation. While this is a less impressive set than the earlier small-band discs – Cutshall and McGarity being curious choices and the timbre of most of the tracks sounding like a slightly paler echo of what had gone before – Goodman still plays very well. Respectable remastering on both discs. The *Rehearsal Sessions* brings together multiple takes on four tunes plus a remarkable 27-minute track that details the sextet working towards a finished version of 'Benny's Bugle' (where Cootie Williams eventually has to play the intro 23 times). For Goodman scholars rather than the general collector, but intriguing stuff.

★★★(★) Benny Goodman 1941 Vol. 2

Classics 1236 *Goodman; Cootie Williams, Billy Butterfield, Jimmy Maxwell, Irving Goodman, Gordon Griffin (t) Lou McGarity, Cutty Cutshall (tb); Les Robinson, Gus Bivona, Gene Kinsey, Clint Neagley (as); Georgie Auld, Pete Mondello, Vido Musso, George Berg (ts); Skippy Martin (bs); Johnny Guarnieri, Teddy Wilson, Mel Powell (p); Charlie Christian, Mike Bryan, Tom Morgan (g); Artie Bernstein, Walter Looss, John Simmons (b); Dave Tough, Jo Jones, J. C. Heard, Sid Catlett (d); Helen Forrest, Tommy Taylor (v).* 3-8/41.

★★★(★) Benny Goodman 1941 Vol. 3

Classics 1271 *As above, except add Al Davis (t), Chuck Gentry (bs), Mort Stuhlmaker, Sid Weiss (b) Ralph Collier (d), Peggy Lee (v); omit Irving Goodman, Griffin, Robinson, Bivona, Auld, Mondello, Guarnieri, Wilson, Bryan, Bernstein, Looss, Tough, Jones, Heard, Forrest.* 8–10/41.

★★★(★) Benny Goodman 1941–1942

Classics 1303 *As above, except add Johnny Ferrante, Bernie Privin (t), Julie Schwartz (as), Art Lund, Tommy Dix (v); omit Stuhlmaker, Taylor.* 10/41–1/42.

The quality of Goodman's material, his arrangers and his refusal to let his vocalists dominate recording sessions helped set his band aside from the other white swing orchestras. The occasional bit of fluff slips through, but there isn't a single session without at least one outstanding performance all through these discs. Among the highlights: the unrehearsed warm-up 'Waitin' For Benny' by the sextet (minus Goodman!) and Jimmy Mundy's charts for 'Fiesta In Blue' and 'Air Mail Special' (Classics 1236); the first two takes of Sauter's astonishing 'Clarinet A La King' , Mel Powell's thrilling 'The Earl' and the arrival of Peggy Lee (Classics 1271); the sextet doing 'If I Had You' and 'Limehouse Blues', Lee on 'Blues In The Night' and the V-Disc (unfortunately sonding a bit scruffy) of 'Jersey Bounce'. As before, irritatingly inconsistent mastering on all three discs.

★★★ Benny Goodman 1942

Classics 1324 *Goodman; Bernie Privin, Jimmy Maxwell, Al Davis, John Napton (t); Lou McGarity, Cutty Cutshall, Charlie Castaldo (tb); Clint Neagley, Sol Kane, Bud Shiffman (as); Vido Musso, George Berg (ts); Chuck Gentry, Art Ralston (bs); Mel Powell (p); Tom Morgan (g); Sid Weiss (b); Ralph Collier, Alvin Stoller (d); Peggy Lee, Art Lund (v).* 1–5/42.

★★★(★) Benny Goodman 1942–1944

Classics 1335 *Goodman; Bernie Privin, Cootie Williams, Tony Faso, Lawrence Stearns, Lee Castle, Charlie Frankhauser, Frank Berardi, Johnny Dee, Billy Butterfield, Charlie Shavers, Mickey McMickle (t); Lou McGarity, Charlie Castaldo, H. Collins, Bill Harris, Al Mastren, Vernon Brown, Jack Satterfield (tb); Hymie Schertzer, Bud Shiffman, Clint Neagley, Leonard Kaye, Heinie Beau, Eddie Rosa, Jules Rubin (as); Jerry Jerome, George Berg, Jon Walton, Leonard Sims, Al Klink, Zoot Sims, Jack Simms, Art Rollini, Don Byas (ts); Johnny McAfee, Bob Poland, Eddie Beau, Ernie Caceres (bs); Mel Powell, Jess Stacy, Teddy Wilson (p); Dave Barbour, Allan Reuss (g); Sid Weiss, Cliff Hill (b); Alvin Stoller, Howard Daviesa, Gene Krupa, Morey Feld, Cozy Cole, Specs Powell (d); Dick Haymes, Peggy Lee, Buzz Alston (v).* 2/42–7/44.

It's interesting to hear Goodman tackle 'A String Of Pearls' (Classics 1324), and it underscores how his band was much more of a jazz orchestra than Glenn Miller's tame dance band was – even if there's nothing as individual about that performance as Bobby Hackett's solo for Miller. On the same disc there's a quartet/sextet date with BG at his best on 'St Louis Blues', and another host of Peggy Lee features. Classics 1335 features three sessions squeezed in before the recording ban and most of the rest is V-Disc material. Dick Haymes gets his first features with the band and the studio sides for Columbia close on Mel Powell's fizzing chart for 'Mission To Moscow'. The V-Discs are nearly all instrumental (the exception is Benny himself singing on 'Dinah'!) and have a good share of clarinet. There are also quartet and trio sides which mark a reunion with Teddy Wilson.

★★★(★) Plays Mel Powell

Hep 1055 *Goodman; Alec Fila, Jimmy Maxwell, Cootie Williams, Irving Goodman, Laurence Stearns, Tony Faso, Vince Badale, Al Cuozzo, Frank LePinto, Chris Griffin, John Best, Conrad Gozzo, Bernie Privin, Billy Butterfield, Nate Kazebier, Jimmy Blake (t); Lou McGarity, Cutty Cutshall, Charlie Castaldo, Trummy Young, Chauncey Welsh, Eddie Aulinoi, Kai Winding, Dick LeFave (tb); Skip Martin, Gus Bivona, Bob Snyder, Clint Neagley, Hymie Schertzer, Aaron Sachs, Bill Shine, Jerry Sanfino, Jimmy Horvath, Gene Kinsey, Les Robinson, John Prager (as); Georgie Auld, Jack Henderson, George Berg, Vido Musso, John Walton, Leonard Sims, Al Epstein, Stan Getz, Peanuts Hucko, Pete Mondello, Gish Gilberston, Cliff Strickland (ts); Danny Bank, Bob Poland, Chuck Gentry, Art Ralston (bs); Mel Powell, Count Basie, Johnny Guarnieri, Teddy Wilson, Charlie Queener (p); Johnny White (vib); Mike Bryan, Dave Barbour (g); Artie Bernstein,*

Cliff Hill, Barney Spieler, Clyde Lombardi, Walter Looss (b); Morey Feld, Louie Bellson, Buddy Rich, Dave Tough, Big Sid Catlett, Ralph Ciollier, Jo Jones, Howard Davies (d). 1/41–5/46.

Not quite the twilight years, even if Goodman eventually disbanded his orchestra in December 1946. This is a strong and thoughtfully chosen set of tracks from a relatively unconsidered period in the Goodman discography. Besides Mel Powell's arrangements, there are charts by Jimmy Mundy (an excellent feature for Cootie Williams on 'Fiesta In Blue'), Edgar Sampson, Margie Gibson, Skip Martin and Buster Harding, although Powell's scores are arguably the most interesting – 'Jersey Bounce', 'Mission To Moscow', 'Clarinade' and, above all, his early pieces 'The Count' and 'The Earl'. Besides Williams, there are one or two surprise soloists, including Stan Getz on 'Lucky'. A useful issue.

*****(*) Goodman – The Different Version Vol. 1**
Phontastic NCD 8821 2CD *As discs above.* 39–40.

*****(*) Goodman – The Different Version Vol. 2**
Phontastic NCD 8822 2CD *As above.* 41.

*****(*) Goodman – The Different Version Vol. 3**
Phontastic NCD 8823 2CD *As above.* 41–2.

*****(*) Goodman – The Different Version Vol. 4**
Phontastic NCD 8824 2CD *As above.* 42–5.

*****(*) Goodman – The Different Version Vol. 5**
Phontastic NCD 8825 2CD *As above.* 45–7.

***** The Permanent Goodman Vol. 1**
Phontastic CD 7659 *As above.* 26–38.

*****(*) The Permanent Goodman Vol. 2**
Phontastic 7660 *As above.* 39–45.

There is some irony in that, while no comprehensive edition of Goodman's proper studio releases exists quite yet (though Classics will be there soon), enterprises like this have appeared instead. The five-volume Phontastic set covers ten CDs of alternative takes to the more familiar studio sides, virtually all of it from legitimate, V-Disc or transcription sessions, so the sound-quality is consistently good, if not quite as lively as some reissue projects. The documentation is detailed and superbly organized, and although the alternative takes themselves seldom tell anything strikingly new about Goodman's work – changes amount to matters of precise detail, rather than glaring contrasts – it makes a very impressive series of programmes. So, too, are the alternatives offered up on the other two *Permanent Goodman* discs, which follow a similar course but go back to 1926 (some of the early Ben Pollack sessions) and somehow avoid any duplication with these other sets. A remarkable undertaking, previously released as a long series of LPs but welcome in the newer format.

****** Plays Eddie Sauter**
Hep CD 1053 *As various discs above.* 9/39–1/46.

In exemplary sound and documentation, this collects 23 of Sauter's best charts for Goodman, from the 1939 'Love Never Went To College' to a 1946 transcription of 'Moonlight On the Ganges'. One of the best single-disc representations of vintage BG.

***** Benny's Bop**
Hep CD 36 *Goodman; Howard Reich, Doug Mettome, Al Stewart, Nick Travis (t); Milt Bernhart, Eddie Bert, George Monte (tb); Ake 'Stan' Hasselgård (cl); Mitch Goldberg, Angelo Cicalese (as); Wardell Gray, Eddie Wasserman (ts); Larry Molinelli (bs); Mary Lou Williams, Buddy Greco, Barbara Carroll (p); Billy Bauer, Francis Beecher (g); Clyde Lombardi (b); Mel Zelnick, Sonny Igoe (d); Louis Martinez (perc); Jackie Searle, Terry Swope (v).* 7/48–3/49.

Goodman was interested by the new music but he never felt very comfortable with it, and Hasselgård, present on three tracks here, was much more at home in bop's surroundings. There isn't anything here that would have troubled Parker and Gillespie. More involving is some superb playing from Wardell Gray. This is V-Disc and broadcast material, conscientiously remastered, and the leader (aside from one clinker) plays imperturbably well.

****** B.G. In Hi-Fi**
Capitol 92684-2 *Goodman; Ruby Braff, Charlie Shavers, Chris Griffin, Carl Poole, Bernie Privin (t); Will Bradley, Vernon Brown, Cutty Cutshall (tb); Al Klink, Paul Ricci, Boomie Richman, Hymie Schertzer, Sol Schlinger (saxes); Mel Powell (p); Steve Jordan (g); George Duvivier (b); Bobby Donaldson, Jo Jones (d).* 11/54.

Goodman left the big-band era with his finances and his technique intact, and although this was a more or less anachronistic programme of trio, quintet and big-band sides in 1954, the playing is so good that it's a resounding success. A few Goodman staples are mixed with Basie material such as 'Jumpin' At The Woodside', and Benny's readings are by no means outdone by the originals. Shavers, Braff, Richman and Powell all have fine moments, but Goodman himself is peerless. The sound is a trifle dry but otherwise excellent, and the CD reissue adds four tracks, including a beautiful trio version of 'Rose Room', to the original LP.

****** The Complete Capitol Trios**
Capitol 521225-2 *Goodman; Teddy Wilson, Jimmy Rowles, Mel Powell (p); Jimmy Crawford, Tom Romersa, Eddie Grady, Bobby Donaldson (d).* 11/47–11/54.

Ten tracks from 1947, with Wilson and Crawford, then ten more from 1954, four with Rowles and six with Powell. No evidence that Goodman saw the LP format as an excuse to stretch out; only two of the later pieces break the 3½-minute barrier. Throughout all these sessions, he plays marvellous things, often in ways he wasn't supposed to be so good at; try the blues solo on 'After Hours'. Wilson, Rowles and Powell are all excellent in their different ways, Powell arguably taking the honours. Indispensable Goodman.

*****(*) The Benny Goodman Story**
Capitol 833569-2 *Goodman; Chris Griffin, Billy Butterfield, Doc Severinsen, Jimmy Maxwell, Carl Poole, Harry James, Bernie Glow, Jon Durante, Bernie Privin, Ruby Braff (t); Urbie Green, Will Bradley, Lou McGarity (tb); Hymie Schertzer, Phil Bodner, Milt Yaner (as); Al Klink, Peanuts Hucko, Boomie Richman (ts); Dick Hyman, Morris Wechsler, Mel Powell (p); Lionel Hampton (vib); Tony Mottola, Al Caiola (g); George Duvivier, Milt Hinton (b); Bobby Donaldson, Don Lamond (d); Martha Tilton (v).* 12/55.

Occasioned by his film life-story, this remodelling of some old favourites was well done. 'Sing Sing Sing' was a necessary chore, 'And The Angels Sing' didn't improve with time, and there is some other so-so music; but the sound of the orchestra was handsomely caught by the Capitol engineers, and the small-group tracks at the end are handled with stinging aplomb. Excellent remastering.

**(*) Bangkok 1956

TCB 43042 *Goodman; Mel Davis, John Frosk, Billy Hodges (t); Peanuts Hucko, Al Bock (as); Budd Johnson, Bill Slapin (ts); Hank Jones (p); Steve Jordan (g); Israel Crosby (b); Mousie Alexander (d).* 12/56.

***(*) Basel 1959

TCB 43032 *Goodman; Jack Sheldon (t); Bill Harris (tb); Jerry Dodgion (as, f); Flip Phillips (ts); Red Norvo (vib); Russ Freeman (p); Jimmy Wyble (g); Red Wootten (b); John Marksham (d).* 10/59.

*** An Airmail Special From Berlin

Jasmine JASCD 402 2CD *As above, except add Anita O'Day (v).* 10/59.

European souvenirs. The 1956 band was a good rather than a great Goodman outfit, and what with playing two numbers by the King of Thailand, the Bangkok date has the flavour of a group on its best behaviour rather than a fired-up ensemble. The Basel date is another matter. Goodman is clearly in good heart here, with a pellucid clarinet treatment of 'Memories Of You' one of several highlights, and with favoured sideman Sheldon and the inimitable Harris both in top fettle, this set generates some real heat. The sound is a bit fusty in parts, but not too bad. The Jasmine set offers the Berlin date from the same tour and spreads the whole concert over two CDs (some 95 minutes of music). Anita O'Day is on four tunes. The sound rather wavers in and out of focus at times like a recalcitrant radio dial, and the drums suffer a bit, but not so much that it spoils the music.

***(*) Benny In Brussels Volumes 1 & 2

Collectables COL-CD-6897 *Goodman; Taft Jordan, John Frosk, Billy Hodges, E. V. Perry (t); Vernon Brown, Rex Peer, Willie Dennis (tb); Al Block (as); Zoot Sims, Seldon Powell (ts); Gene Allen (bs); Roland Hanna (p); Arvell Shaw (b); Roy Burnes (d); Jimmy Rushing (v).* 5/58.

Two Columbia albums on one disc. Goodman played this gig at the Brussels World's Fair (that quaint phenomenon of the post-war world) and the reception was rapturous. This was Roland Hanna's 'big-time debut' and Goodman seems to like his playing on 'Hallelujah'. Jimmy Rushing was on the tour but he gets only two miserly appearances on a blues and a 'Mr Five By Five' which lasts barely a minute and a half. The sound is surprisingly full and clear.

*** In Stockholm 1959

Phontastic NCD 8801 *Goodman; Jack Sheldon (t); Bill Harris (tb); Jerry Dodgion (as, f); Flip Phillips (ts); Red Norvo (vib); Russ Freeman (p); Jimmy Wyble (g); Red Wootten (b); John Markham, John Poole (d); Anita O'Day (v).* 10/59.

Although the leader plays very well on this memento of a European tour which Goodman scholars credit as a peak period in his later work, the rather desultory presentation of the music – too many offhand introductions by Benny, and the inclusion of crowd-pleasing pieces like 'Sing Sing Sing' and the hits medley – take some of the fizz out of the record. The band isn't granted too much individual space, which is frustrating, since Sheldon, Norvo and Freeman all sound excellent. Goodman's habit of whistling through other people's solos is caught by the mostly very clear recording, which suffers from only occasional drop-outs.

*** Live In The Sixties

Jasmine JASCD 394 *Goodman; Bobby Hackett (c); Jack Sheldon, Jimmy Maxwell, Clark Terry, John Rosk, Doc Severinsen (t); Rex Peer, Murray McEachern, Willie Dennis, Jimmy Knepper, Bob Alexander (tb); Jerry Dodgion (as, f); Phil Woods (as); Modesto Bresano (ts, f); Flip Phillips, Zoot Sims, Tommy Newsom (ts); Gene Allen (bs); Red Norvo (vib); John Bunch, Russ Freeman, Dave Grusin (p); Turk Van Lake, Jimmy Wyble (g); Steve Swallow, Jimmy Rowser, Red Wootten, Bill Crow (b); Ray Mosca, John Markham, Karl Kiffe, Mel Lewis (d); Charles DeForrest (v).* 9/60–4/62.

Most of this is from a broadcast of a sextet date with Bobby Hackett. Both he and Goodman play well and John Bunch is also on hand, although the stylings of Charles DeForrest are pretty gruesome. There's just a few big-band tracks and one where BG sat in with the band on the Ed Sullivan Show. Audio quality is only fair to middling, but a decent souvenir of a Goodman period not currently well represented.

*** Together Again

RCA Victor 68593-2 *Goodman; Lionel Hampton (vib); Teddy Wilson (p); Gene Krupa (d).* 2–8/63.

Although the quartet was together again, most of the tunes it played didn't come from its original book. The result is rather placid and amiable, lacking nothing in finesse but considerably short on the kind of cumulative power which the original sessions touched on.

*** Hello Benny! / Made In Japan

Capitol 581345-2 *Goodman; Tony Terran, Roy Triscari, Jimmy Zito (t); Bob Edmondson, Vern Friley (tb); Skeets Herfurt, Herb Steward (as); Teddy Edwards, Bob Hardaway (ts); Pete Jolly, Dick Shreve (p); Benny Garcia (g); Monty Budwig (b); Colin Bailey (d).* 65.

A pair of Capitol sessions. *Hello Benny!* put Goodman with a studio orchestra and some then-current tunes. Pro that he was, he plays 'The Pink Panther Theme' and 'Hallelujah, I Love Her So' as if they are at least worthy of his time. The second session is a Japanese concert by the quartet, with Dick Shreve on piano, and they work through a characteristic programme with rather more enjoyment.

*** Jazz Masters 33

Verve 844410-2 *Goodman; Warren Vaché (t); George Young (as); Scott Hamilton, Zoot Sims, Buddy Tate, Frank Wess (ts); Mary Lou Williams (p); Lionel Hampton (vib); Percy Heath (b); Connie Kay (d).* 70–78.

*** 40th Anniversary Concert – Live At Carnegie Hall

London 820349-2 2CD *Goodman; Victor Paz, Warren Vaché, Jack Sheldon (t); Wayne Andre, George Masso, John Messner (tb); George Young, Mel Rodnon (as); Buddy Tate, Frank Wess (ts); Sol Schlinger (bs); Mary Lou Williams, Jimmy Rowles, John Bunch (p); Lionel Hampton (vib); Cal Collins, Wayne Wright (g); Michael Moore (b); Connie Kay (d); Martha Tilton, Debi Craig (v).* 1/78.

Currently, LP-era Goodman is poorly represented in the catalogues, and with the departure of many records to the deletions file, he seems to belong conclusively to the swing era, as far as reissue programmes go. A pity, since there is much of his 'senior' work which is well worth hearing. Goodman's enduring facility as a clarinettist is the most absorbing thing about these sessions, on both sets. The Jazz Masters disc collates material from various appearances during the '70s, including a number of different generations involved, and makes a worthwhile sampler of Goodman's final period. At Carnegie Hall the band played a functional rather than challenging role, the job being to replicate standard scores as flawlessly as the leader wished, and although there are many fine players involved, Goodman's iron hand stifles anything freewheeling which might have emerged. But he drives himself as hard as the others, and the clarinet still sounds august, refined, imperious.

Bobby Gordon (born 1941)

CLARINET

Studied with Joe Marsala, then was a regular at Eddie Condon's in the late '70s, followed by a variety of mainstream work. Now based in San Diego and leading his own group there.

***** Bobby Gordon/Keith Ingham/Hal Smith Trio**
Jump JCD12-17 *Gordon; Keith Ingham (p); Hal Smith (d).* 8/90.

***** Don't Let It End**
Arbors ARCD 19112 *Gordon; Adele Girard Marsala (hp); Ray Sherman (p); Morty Corb (b); Gene Estes (d).* 7/92.

***** Bobby Gordon Plays Bing**
Arbors ARCD 19172 *Gordon; Peter Ecklund, Randy Reinhart (c, t); Dan Barrett (tb); Scott Robinson (ts, bs, bsx); Keith Ingham (p, cel); Marty Grosz (g); Greg Cohen (b); Hal Smith (d).* 6/96.

***** Clarinet Blue**
Arbors ARCD 19223 *Gordon; Dave McKenna (p); Frank Tate (b); Joe Ascione (d).* 5/99.

***** Yearnings**
Arbors ARCD 19277 *Gordon; Bob Wilber (cl, ss); John Sheridan (p); David Stone (b); Tony DeNicola (d).* 03.

Mellow fruitfulness is the sound of Gordon's clarinet. A veteran mainstreamer, he was once a pupil of Joe Marsala, so it was a nice idea to have him record the charming *Don't Let It End* with Adele Girard Marsala. Quiet tempos and gentle embellishments characterize the date. The tunes are all museum-pieces of the order of 'Love Nest' and 'Emaline'. It's done with enough grace to make it work: in its mannerly way, it's a little unique.

The trio session with Ingham and Smith benefits from the pianist's canny playing and deep knowledge of old and often sidelined standards. As sole horn, Gordon sometimes sounds reluctant to play a leading role, and Ingham has to josh him along at times. There are still enough rare pleasures in the song-list to make it worth a look.

The Bing tribute offers a stack of Crosby tunes from the earlier part of the singer's career, going as far back as 'There Ain't No Sweet Man Worth The Salt Of My Tears', which he did with Whiteman and Beiderbecke. A gang of the usual suspects is on best behaviour here, sticking closely, and tenderly, to Keith Ingham's arrangements. Gordon comes out as a bit of a bystander. If not exactly stiff, it's hardly the liveliest record these players have ever delivered.

Gordon often sounds like a calmer, less brazen version of Pee Wee Russell on *Clarinet Blue*. McKenna downsizes his own methods to accommodate him, and the music is genteel but not without its rewards. Gordon's homey sound grows on you. Highlight: an almost suave 'I Wish I Could Shimmy Like My Sister Kate'.

The main point of interest in the meeting with Wilber is the material. 'Doodle Doo Doo', 'Yearnings', 'In A Little Spanish Town' and 'Song Of The Islands' rarely turn up on bandstands now, and they fit the gently noodling interplay very sweetly.

Dexter Gordon (1923–89)

TENOR AND SOPRANO SAXOPHONES

Dexter's own life achieved mythical proportions when he appeared in Bernard Tavernier's Round Midnight, playing a hybrid of himself and Bud Powell. Originally influenced by Lester Young, Gordon favoured easy, behind-the-beat phrasing which could be turned to more confrontational use when required. In 1962, having gone through all too familiar difficulties with narcotics, he moved his base to Europe and stayed for the next decade and a half. In later years, having become a star under Tavernier, he started returning to the USA.

***** Dexter Gordon 1943–1947**
Classics 999 *Gordon; Harry 'Sweets' Edison, Leonard Hawkins (t); Melba Liston (tb); Wardell Gray (ts); Bud Powell, Jimmy Rowles, Argonne Thornton (p); Jimmy Bunn (g); Red Callender, Gene Ramey (b); Johnny Miller, Ed Nicholson, Roy Porter, Chuck Thompson (d).* 43–7.

One of the giants (literally) of modern jazz, Gordon made an impact on players as dissimilar as Sonny Rollins and John Coltrane, but himself remained comparatively unrecognized until a comeback in the '60s (Gordon had lived and worked in Scandinavia in the early half of the decade), by which time many of the post-Lester Young stylistic devices he had introduced were firmly in place under others' patents. Classics now have a firm foot in the bebop era as well, and this first Gordon volume picks up the story while he is working with Fletcher Henderson and just beginning to strike out on his own account. Most of the later material is available in other – and mostly better-quality – configurations, but for early material like 'I've Found A New Baby' and 'Rosetta', which were recorded when the saxophonist was just 20, it's a useful insight. To a degree, Gordon had outgrown his strength; his solo spots sound strained and overblown, and the microphones don't capture much of the breathy resonance that was to be a feature of his mature style. The other personnel are, of course, fascinating, but many of these associations can be picked up again later in the story; despite the issue number, this needn't be considered a priority purchase.

****** Dexter Gordon On Dial: The Complete Sessions**
Spotlite SPJ CD 130 *Gordon; Melba Liston (tb); Teddy Edwards, Wardell Gray (ts); Jimmy Bunn, Charles Fox, Jimmy Rowles (p); Red Callender (b); Roy Porter, Chuck Thompson (d).* 6/47.

Gordon's on–off partnership with fellow-tenorist Wardell Gray was consistently productive, pairing him for much of the late '40s with another Lester Young disciple who had taken on board most of the modernist idiom without abandoning Young's mellifluously extended solo style. The Dial sessions – with Gray and, at Christmas 1947, Teddy Edwards – are pretty definitive of what was going on on the West Coast at the time. Spotlite brings together all the material, including a track with just Edwards up front. 'The Chase' was a studio version of the saxophone contests that Dexter and Gray had been conducting night after night in LA's Little Harlem. The earliest of the sessions features Melba Liston, who was presumably recruited for her skill as an arranger. The charts to 'Mischievous Lady' and 'Lullaby In Rhythm' sound tight and well organized, more coherent than the ultimately rather tiresome 'Chase'. On the same day, Gordon also laid down three tracks with just rhythm, of which 'Chromatic Aberration' is perhaps the most interesting vis-à-vis the development of bebop, but 'It's The Talk Of The Town' is the occasion for one of his most expressive ballad solos of these years. The final Dial session, with Rowles at the piano, was made just before the AFM recording ban began the brief eclipse which skews our perception of what was going on stylistically at this point.

*** Dexter Gordon, 1947–1952

Classics 1295 *Gordon; Teddy Edwards (ts); Jimmy Rowles (p); Red Callender (b); Roy Porter (d).* 12/47–6/52.

The second volume of Classics' Gordon documentation opens with heavy artillery, Dexter outgunning the more laid-back Teddy Edwards on 'The Duel', part of a session for Dial. A week later, he was back in the studio with Leo Parker making some sides for Savoy, with whom he made a further four relatively bland and generic cuts just before Christmas 1947. There's then a substantial jump to February 1952 and 'The Chase' with Wardell Gray. So the dating here is slightly misleading: 1947 and 1952 might be more true to type. Nothing here of any note that isn't otherwise available.

*** The Bethlehem Years

Fresh Sound FSR 154 *Gordon; Conte Candoli (t); Frank Rosolino (tb); Kenny Drew (p); Leroy Vinnegar (b); Lawrence Marable (d).* 9/55.

Not normally thought of as a West Coast man in the stylistic sense, Gordon enjoyed his sojourn back in California during 1955. Charlie Parker's death in March created a vacuum at the head of the saxophone rankings and Gordon looked like an ideal contender. *The Bethlehem Years* compilation is good value for money. Neither Candoli nor Rosolino is a charismatic soloist but they spur Gordon on and lend 'Ruby My Dear' a beefy resonance. Drew and Vinnegar play exceptionally well, and the CD transfer is generally good. In 1955 Gordon had already cemented the style he was to utilize virtually to the end of his career. Its easy, but never shallow, expressiveness and light, springy time-feel were directly related to Lester Young. He was, though, playing in the interim between two drug-related prison sentences that more or less wound up the '50s, which should have been his decade.

**(*) The Resurgence Of Dexter Gordon

Original Jazz Classics OJC 929 *Gordon; Martin Banks (t); Richard Boone (tb); Dolo Coker (p); Charles Green (b); Lawrence Marable (d).* 10/60.

Sometimes known as *Pulsation*, this is a little-known Jazzland date which didn't quite live up to its title: that would happen with the Blue Note sequence which comes next. Gordon seems more like a sideman here than anything, with a cool and no more than proficient team of Angelenos supporting him, and its obscurity is probably deserved.

**** Doin' Alright

Blue Note 784077 *Gordon; Freddie Hubbard (t); Horace Parlan (p); George Tucker (b); Al Harewood (d).* 5/61.

Back in the world and doing all right. Gordon's first recording after a long and painful break is one of his best. Critics divide on whether Gordon was influenced by Coltrane at this period or whether it was simply a case of the original being obscured by his followers. Gordon's phrasing on *Doin' Alright* certainly suggests a connection of some sort, but the opening statement of 'I Was Doin' Alright' is completely individual and quite distinct, and Gordon's solo development is nothing like the younger man's. This is one of Gordon's best records and should on no account be missed.

*** Dexter Calling

Blue Note 46544 *Gordon; Kenny Drew (p); Paul Chambers (b); Philly Joe Jones (d).* 5/61.

Recorded three days later and reflecting the same virtues. With a better-drilled but slightly more conventional band, Gordon is pushed a little wider on the solos, ranging much further away from the stated key (as on a memorable mid-chorus break on 'Ernie's Tune') and varying his timbre much more than he used to. As indicators of how his harmonic language and distinctive accent were to develop, these two 1961 Blue Notes are particularly valuable. The sound is a little better on the later one.

*** Go!

Blue Note 98794 *Gordon; Sonny Clark (p); Butch Warren (b); Billy Higgins (d).* 8/62.

*** A Swingin' Affair

Blue Note 84133 *As above.* 8/62.

Typically good husbandry on the part of Blue Note to get two albums from this not altogether riveting date, one of the first since his return to normal circulation. *Swingin' Affair* stands and falls on a lovely version of 'You Stepped Out Of A Dream'. *Go!*, now available in a crisp new edition, includes Gordon's simplest and finest reading of 'Where Are You', a relatively little-used standard with interesting changes and a strong turn in the middle. The hipsters' motto (pinched from novelist John Clellon Holmes) was meant to suggest relentless improvisatory progress. Gordon was to play better, but rarely with such directness, and it's not entirely idle to ask whether he felt himself hampered by a rhythm section that was not always responsive. 'I Guess I'll Hang My Tears Out To Dry' has him soaring away on his own, almost out of touch with the rest of the band.

** Cry Me A River

Steeplechase SCCD 36004 *Gordon; Atli Bjorn (p); Benny Nielsen, Marcel Rigot (b); Finn Frederiksen, William Schiopffe (d).* 11/62, 6/64.

A pretty dismal album by any standard, much of it is given over to Bjorn's own trio. The title-track receives a predictably fulsome and emotive reading, but Bjorn seems to be all over his keyboard in contrast to Gordon's discipline and reserve. Not an album for the A-list.

CORE COLLECTION

**** Our Man In Paris

Blue Note 746394 *Gordon; Bud Powell (p); Pierre Michelot (b); Kenny Clarke (d).* 5/63.

Gordon's 'purest' bebop album since the early '50s, *Our Man* also shows how much he had continued to absorb of the pre-bop sound of Lester Young and Johnny Hodges. There are hints of both in his ballad-playing and in the winding, almost incantatory solo on 'Night In Tunisia', which is one of his finest performances on record. A classic.

***** One Flight Up**

Blue Note 84176 *Gordon; Donald Byrd (t); Kenny Drew (p); Niels-Henning Orsted Pedersen (b); Art Taylor (d).* 6/64.

Three extended performances, dominated by 'Darn That Dream' (see also *Ballads*, below) and the turned-sideways 'Coppin' The Haven' theme. Byrd was still an impressive player at this period, though he's rarely as adventurous as Hubbard, and Drew is a brilliant accompanist. It's easy to see, particularly on 'Darn', how Gordon continued to influence John Coltrane's harmonic development.

*****(*) Gettin' Around**

Blue Note 46681 *Gordon; Bobby Hutcherson (vib); Barry Harris (p); Bob Cranshaw (b); Billy Higgins (d).* 5/65.

One of the most engaging of Gordon's Blue Note recordings, *Gettin' Around* is also a showcase for the burgeoning talent of Bobby Hutcherson. Though the charts are relatively scant and unchallenging, the standard of performance is very high; Bobby's starburst patterns, executed round Harris's quiet and definite comping, are full of detail and excitement. The material is fairly basic and familiar, with just three Gordon compositions – not much more than blowing themes – tucked away at the end of the album. 'Manhã de Carnaval' gets the record off to a breezy start, and the ensembles here are worthy of study: clean-lined, joyous and absolutely exact, yet with the spontaneity of a first take. Frank Foster's 'Shiny Stockings' was a favourite of the time with tenor-players, and Dexter milks it enthusiastically.

***** The Complete Blue Note Sessions**

Blue Note 834200 6CD *Gordon; Freddie Hubbard, Donald Byrd (t); Bobby Hutcherson (vib); Barry Harris, Kenny Drew, Horace Parlan, Sonny Clark, Bud Powell (p); Bob Cranshaw, Butch Warren, George Tucker, Paul Chambers, Pierre Michelot, Niels-Henning Orsted Pedersen (b); Philly Joe Jones, Al Harewood, Kenny Clarke, Art Taylor, Billy Higgins (d).* 61–5.

Gordon's Blue Notes make a worthy entry in the boxed-set constituency, although exposure at length does tend to show up his vulnerabilities at least as much as his strengths, so our rating is relatively stingy. The woozy relationship with the beat is one problem, and his liking for well-trodden phrases and quotes does tend to pall over the long haul. Collectors will welcome the inclusion of scarcer sessions such as *Clubhouse*, otherwise unavailable.

****(*) Cheese Cake**

Steeplechase SCCD 36008 *Gordon; Tete Montoliu (p); Benny Nielsen, Niels-Henning Orsted Pedersen (b); Alex Riel (d).* 6/64.

***** King Neptune**

Steeplechase SCCD 36012 *As above.* 6/64.

***** I Want More**

Steeplechase SCCD 36015 *As above.* 7/64.

***** Love For Sale**

Steeplechase SCCD 36018 *As above.* 7/64.

****(*) It's You Or No One**

Steeplechase SCCD 36022 *As above.* 8/64.

****(*) Billie's Bounce**

Steeplechase SCCD 36028 *As above.* 8/64.

***** Stable Mable**

Steeplechase SCCD 31040 *Gordon; Tete Montoliu, Horace Parlan (p); Benny Nielsen, Niels-Henning Orsted Pedersen (b); Alex Riel, Tony Inzalaco (d).* 11/74.

***** Bouncin' With Dex**

Steeplechase SCCD 31060 *Gordon; Tete Montoliu (p); Benny Nielsen, Niels-Henning Orsted Pedersen (b); Alex Riel, Billy Higgins (d).* 3/75–9/75.

***** Something Different**

Steeplechase SCCD 31136 *Gordon; Philip Catherine (g); Niels-Henning Orsted Pedersen (b); Billy Higgins (d).* 9/75.

Newly settled in Scandinavia, Gordon turns the tap on full. There's still the emotional equivalent of an airlock, slightly spluttering hesitations alternating with sudden, scalding flows, but it all starts to fit together as this fascinating if very spotty sequence of albums progresses. A more comprehensive pianist, Parlan or Flanagan, might have varied the structures a little, but Montoliu is sympathetic and very lyrical.

The touchstone 'Body And Soul' is beautifully enunciated on *King Neptune* and the band gels in the ensemble passages with little of the slightly mechanistic pulse that afflicted the earlier *Cheese Cake* session. *I Want More* and *Love For Sale* are the best of this group. Gordon's understanding with the players seems increasingly telepathic and his approach to themes correspondingly inventive. *It's You Or No One* and *Billie's Bounce* suffer from *longueurs* which this somewhat obsessive documentation is wont to fall prey to.

Bouncin' With Dex takes essentially the same band forward a decade. By the time of *Swiss Nights* (below), the act is consummately polished. Montoliu sounds relaxed and confident and plays with considerable authority. The addition of guitarist Catherine adds a new band of the spectrum on *Something Different*. From the opening 'Freddie Freeloader' till it closes with 'Polka Dots And Moonbeams' and 'Yesterday's Mood', it exudes *bonhomie* and relaxed invention.

***** The Tower Of Power!**

Original Jazz Classics OJCCD 299 *Gordon; James Moody (ts); Barry Harris (p); Buster Williams (b); Albert 'Tootie' Heath (d).* 4/69.

****(*) More Power**

Original Jazz Classics OJCCD 815 *As above.* 4/69.

Dexter was beginning to visit the USA slightly more frequently again, and this was made on one of his trips. He still sounds tentative on American soil, and not even the presence of James Moody on 'Montmartre' sets things alight, partly because the two tenors manage to cancel one another out. Beware the use of exclamation marks in jazz album titles. It usually indicates that the contents are less exciting than the label would have you believe. As if to prove the point, the sequel turns out to be more interesting than the original release, with a strong version of 'Lady Bird' (which again features Moody) and a brisk dispatch of Dexter's own 'Fried Bananas', part of his staple diet at this period. From the perspective of 30 years later, these sound like diplomatic soundings, preparatory to Gordon's triumphal return; but in themselves they are far from essential additions to a Gordon collection.

*** L.T.D. Live At The Left Bank

Prestige 11018 *Gordon; Bobby Timmons (p); Victor Gaskin (b); Percy Brice (d).* 69.

There is some stunning saxophone work on this recently discovered live session from 1969. Much of the excitement rests with the opening track, an absolutely steaming version of 'Broadway', which Dexter had previously recorded on *Our Man In Paris.* It's a bold and in some respects radical performance that suggests some rethinking of Gordon's position vis-à-vis Coltrane might be in order, even though Trane was long off the scene by this time.

The other three performances are less compelling. 'Boston Bernie' is an original based on quite orthodox bebop changes ('All The Things You Are', it sounds like) but spun out to inordinate length, and it's the only number where the unfamiliarity of the pick-up band (good as they are) impacts on the music. 'In A Sentimental Mood' is taken slow, and quite briefly, before a rousing interpretation of 'Blues Up And Down' takes the set down and out. One from the vaults but definitely food for thought.

*** Tenor Titans

Storyville 8288 *Gordon; Palle Mikkelborg, Lars Togeby (t); Kjeld Ipsen (tb); Jesper Nehammer, Ben Webster (ts); Thomas Clausen, Kenny Drew (p); Bo Steif (b); Alex Riel, Bjarne Rostvold, Kasper Winding (d).* 69, 72.

A confrontation across the generations and, though unexpected, a more logical conjunction than perhaps it appears. Dexter is heard with his quartet and orchestra from a live concert in 1972; Webster is on the same bill, but the two tenor tracks are from a rather earlier set, when they share the lead on three Ellington tunes (if 'Perdido' can be so attributed). Dexter actually takes the initiative on all three and is certainly not minded to defer to the old master.

*** Blue Dex

Prestige 11003 *Gordon; various line-ups as above OJC albums.* 69–72.

A playable compilation of Gordon blowing on the blues from his various Prestige albums. The main point of interest to Dexter specialists will be the inclusion of alternative takes of 'Sticky Wicket' and 'The Jumpin' Blues'.

*** The Art Of The Ballad

Prestige 11009 *Gordon; Thad Jones (t); Tommy Flanagan, Barry Harris, Hampton Hawes, Hank Jones, Wynton Kelly, Junior Mance, Cedar Walton (p); Stanley Clarke, Bob Cranshaw, Sam Jones, Larry Ridley, Martin Rivera, Buster Williams (b); Roy Brooks, Kenny Clarke, Alan Dawson, Louis Hayes, Albert 'Tootie' Heath, Billy Higgins, Oliver Jackson (d).* 4/69–7/73.

One doesn't automatically think of Dexter as a ballad-performer, but this compilation, part of a Fantasy series, finds him in brilliant form on a wide range of material from 'Days Of Wine And Roses', 'Sophisticated Lady' and the old tenor saxophone groaner 'Body And Soul', to unexpectedly folkish material. Mary Hopkin's 'Those Were The Days' and 'The First Time Ever I Saw Your Face' are exquisite and worth the price on their own.

*** At Montreux

Prestige PCD 7861 2 *Gordon; Junior Mance (p); Martin Rivera (b); Oliver Jackson (d).* 7/70.

***(*) The Panther!

Original Jazz Classics OJCCD 770 *Gordon; Tommy Flanagan (p); Larry Ridley (b); Alan Dawson (d).* 7/70.

*** Jumpin' Blues

Original Jazz Classics OJCCD 899 *Gordon; Wynton Kelly (p); Sam Jones (b); Roy Brooks (d).* 8/70.

Dexter's visit to the USA in 1970 confirmed his growing critical stature. He played at Newport, an appearance documented on *At Montreux*, and managed to sound accommodating and almost deferential. For once, a guest player might have lent the proceedings some edge and bite, but as it stands Dexter doesn't sound willing to rock the boat.

Following the modest success of *The Tower Of Power!*, Dex recorded *The Panther!* and, a little later, *Jumpin' Blues* in the USA. It is generally thought that one of the panther's most effective characteristics is its silence, which makes the exclamation mark slightly redundant. In point of fact, the 1970 record marks a stage in Gordon's development in which he was able and willing to play more quietly, using fewer notes, a greater dynamic range and a willingness to dwell on effective phrases rather than rush them past like trolleybuses. 'Body And Soul' is, almost inevitably, the touchstone here again, a delicate, almost kaleidoscopic reading, with Flanagan's immaculate accompaniment using altered chords. 'Mrs Miniver' is an original and is one of the saxophonist's most interesting and little-known tunes; medium tempo and song-like, it has a brilliantly simple bridge and coda that confirms the strength of Gordon's conception at this point in his career.

The August session is notable for one of the last recorded performances by Wynton Kelly, who gives the session a solid blues foundation to originals 'Evergreenish' and the title-track, as well as a group of standard and bebop themes. Dexter is in fine form and plays exquisitely on 'For Sentimental Reasons'. A worthy group of records, though only serious collectors will find room for all three on the shelf.

*** The Jumpin' Blues

Original Jazz Classics OJC 899 *Gordon; Wynton Kelly (p); Sam Jones (b); Roy Brooks (d).* 8/70.

*** Generation

Original Jazz Classics OJC 836 *Gordon; Freddie Hubbard (t); Cedar Walton (p); Buster Williams (b); Billy Higgins (d).* 7/72.

Cut for Prestige on two of Gordon's occasional visits home, these were more like reminders to the jazz audience that the old lion was still out there rather than meaningful statements. Both bands are studded with formidable talents, but the obvious lack of specific preparation makes both seem like mere pick-up dates, capable though the playing often is.

** The Shadow Of Your Smile

Steeplechase SCCD 31206 *Gordon; Lars Sjøsten (p); Sture Nordin (b); Fredrik Norén (d).* 4/71.

**(*) After Hours

Steeplechase SCCD 31226 *As above, except add Rolf Ericson (t).* 4/71.

These are weak performances. 'Polka Dots And Moonbeams' on *Shadow* suffers some difficulties in the first dozen measures, mostly down to the Danish rhythm section. Not usually lacking in proportion, Gordon sounds merely grandstanding on 'Secret Love' and never quite gets hold of 'Shadow Of Your Smile'. Ericson has a bold, swinging tone, but it cuts across Gordon's development on 'All The Things You Are' quite disconcertingly. Two to miss with a clear conscience.

★★★(★) Ça'Purange

Original Jazz Classics OJCCD 1005 *Gordon; Thad Jones (c, t); James Moody (ts); Barry Harris (p); Stanley Clarke, Buster Williams (b); Louis Hayes, Albert 'Tootie' Heath (d).* 6/72.

We had forgotten how good this almost-forgotten Prestige LP was until OJC revived it. The partnership with Thad Jones was a gift from the gods, and it is slightly surprising that none of Thad's compositions made it to the record. It is a rare jazz disc that includes a Ewan MacColl song, but 'The First Time Ever I Saw Your Face' is exquisitely shaped and Dexter's solo is intense and formally perfect. Always a brief album, it has been boosted by a second take of Sonny Rollins's 'Airegin', but we are disinclined to dismiss it for short measure; anyone who has fallen under Dexter's gruff spell will be captivated; anyone who has yet to be convinced can scarcely resist.

★★★ Generation

Original Jazz Classics OJCCD 836 *Gordon; Freddie Hubbard (t); Cedar Walton (p); Buster Williams (b); Billy Higgins (d).* 7/72.

★★★ Tangerine

Original Jazz Classics OJCCD 1041 *Gordon; Thad Jones (t, flhn); Hank Jones, Cedar Walton (p); Stanley Clarke, Buster Williams (b); Louis Hayes, Billy Higgins (d).* 72.

Two CDs originally recorded for Prestige. *Generation* keeps up the quality of the early-'70s albums. Hubbard imparts an urgency and snap to the session and he cheekily ups the ante on 'Milestones' with a brisk and rhythmic statement that is as different as possible from the composer's sanctified version. The CD reissue includes an alternative take of the same tune with, if anything, a better Hubbard feature, though Dexter's solo is flat and off-balance. Monk's 'We See' was a favourite of Dexter's and is sensitively handled; but the surprise hit of the album is André Previn's 'Scared To Be Alone', a tune that sits perfectly for the saxophone.

Tangerine marks an interesting change of pace, a faster delivery and a more pungent attack. Fuelled by two very different rhythm sections, Dexter declines to veer very far from his usual delivery, but it's interesting to hear how differently he phrases in front of Walton and the more lyrical but less challenging Jones.

★★★(★) Round Midnight

Steeplechase SCCD 31290 *Gordon; Benny Bailey (t); Lars Sjøsten (p); Torbjørn Hultcrantz (b); Jual Curtis (d).* 74.

Bailey was a terrific partner: tight, energetic and unfailingly lyrical. To a large extent they ignore the well-intentioned accompaniment of the Swedish trio (Sjøsten is an able player, the others not) and head off on a companionable jaunt round a set of themes that fall easily under their respective approaches. Gordon is completely at home on 'Round About Midnight' and 'Stella By Starlight'; Bailey takes the initiative on 'Blue 'N' Boogie' and 'What's New', and fans of the little trumpeter (one wonders what they must have looked like, side by side on the stand) will find this one of the most profitable of his live recordings.

★★★★ More Than You Know

Steeplechase SCCD 31030 *Gordon; Palle Mikkelborg, Allan Botschinsky, Benny Rosenfeld, Idrees Sulieman (t, flhn); Richard Boone, Vincent Nilsson (tb); Axel Windfeld (btb); Ole Molin (g); Thomas Clausen (p, electric p); Kenneth Knudsen (syn); Niels-Henning Orsted Pedersen (b); Alex Riel, Ed Thigpen (d); Klaus Nordsoe (perc); chamber winds and strings.* 2–3/75.

★★ Strings And Things

Steeplechase SCCD 31145 *Gordon; Allan Botschinsky, Markku Johansson (t); Eero Koivistoinen, Pekka Poyry (reeds); George Wadenius, Ole Molin (g); Niels-Henning Orsted Pedersen (b); unknown ensemble.* 2/65, 5/76.

★★★ Something Different

Steeplechase SCCD 31136 *Gordon; Philip Catherine (g); Niels-Henning Orsted Pedersen (b); Billy Hart (d).* 9/75.

★★(★) Sophisticated Giant

Columbia CK 65295 *Gordon; Benny Bailey, Woody Shaw (t, flhn); Wayne Andre, Slide Hampton (tb); Frank Wess (f, as, picc); Howard Johnson (tba, bs); Bobby Hutcherson (vib); George Cables (p); Rufus Reid (b); Victor Lewis (d).* 6/77.

Beautifully arranged and orchestrated (by Mikkelborg), *More Than You Know* sets Gordon in the middle (as it sounds) of a rich ensemble of textures which are every bit as creatively unresolved and undogmatic as his solo approach. 'Naima' rarely works with a large band, but this is near perfect and Gordon responds with considerable emotion and inventiveness.

Gordon rarely played with a guitarist, but Catherine was an inspired choice for the September 1975 session, alternating warm, flowing lines with more staccato, accented figures towards the top of his range. NHOP responds with firmly plucked and strummed figures and Gordon rides on top in a relatively unfamiliar programme for him – Miles's 'Freddie Freeloader', 'When Sunny Gets Blue', 'Polka Dots And Moonbeams'.

Sophisticated Giant is an energetic but occasionally oblique album that shows off more of Gordon's Coltrane mannerisms. The arrangements (by Slide Hampton) and the overmixed Columbia sound mask some of the subtlety of Gordon's soloing and the true sound of his soprano. The trumpets are a trifle brittle, and this might be considered a later gap-filler rather than an essential buy.

Strings And Things is a diffident, rather shapeless compilation of material with none of the bite of Mikkelborg's usually intelligent orchestration.

★★ The Apartment

Steeplechase SCCD 31025 *Gordon; Kenny Drew (p); Niels-Henning Orsted Pedersen (b); Alex Riel (d).* 8/75.

★★★ Swiss Nights – Volume 1

Steeplechase SCCD 31050 *As above.* 8/75.

★★★ Swiss Nights – Volume 2

Steeplechase SCCD 31090 *As above.* 8/75.

★★(★) Swiss Nights – Volume 3

Steeplechase SCCD 31110 *As above.* 8/75.

★★(★) Lullaby For A Monster

Steeplechase SCCD 31156 *As above, except omit Drew.* 6/76.

The Apartment isn't one of Gordon's best records; it sounds curiously timebound now, far more than anything else he did, and there's a flatness to some of the solo work. Whatever the reason, the three volumes of *Swiss Nights* sound vigorous, pumped-up and highly coherent. There probably wasn't enough material for three albums, though the last is just about justified by 'Sophisticated Lady'. Together, they make a good summation of what this quartet was about.

Lullaby, a pianoless trio and thus unusual for Gordon, sees him trying rather unsuccessfully to bridge the gaps that Drew's absence leaves. It contains some of his freest solos, notably 'On Green Dolphin Street', but there's an element of constancy lacking.

****(*) Swedish Nights**

Steeplechase SCCD 37017/18 2CD *Gordon; Rolf Ericson (t); Lars Sjøsten (p); Sture Nordin (b); Per Hulten (d).* 86.

Mid-price; but more than mid-career and in only middling form, Dexter waffles and meanders far more than usual on seven stretched-out themes and never gets to the knock-out. Miles's 'Prancin'' is desperately verbose and lacks punch. The best of the playing comes early on, with versions of 'All The Things You Are' and 'Darn That Dream'; the second half limps desperately and, cheap as it is, this really doesn't merit the double-CD format.

*****(*) Biting The Apple**

Steeplechase SCCD 31080 *Gordon; Barry Harris (p); Sam Jones (b); Al Foster (d).* 11/76.

****(*) Featuring Joe Newman**

Monad 806 *Gordon; Joe Newman (t); Jodie Christian (p); Sam Jones (b); Wilbur Campbell (d).* 11/76.

Prodigal comes home. In 1976, Gordon made a rare return visit to the States. The response was so overwhelmingly positive that he decided to end his exile permanently. 'Apple Jump' is a joyous homecoming and 'I'll Remember April' one of his loveliest performances. Harris, Jones and Foster fit in comfortably, and the sound is good.

The record with Joe Newman is almost as interesting for the trumpeter's contributions as it is for Dexter's. Unfortunately, the quality of the source tape is so poor that only incomplete performances are available, which means that this remains a fascinating, collectable rarity, but not by any means an essential Gordon album.

***** Live At Carnegie Hall: Complete**

Sony CK 65312 *Gordon; Johnny Griffin (ts); George Cables (p); Rufus Reid (b); Eddie Gladden (d).* 9/78.

A prestigious venue, but a drab blowing session that has Dex and Griff vying for the limelight. The material is a mixture of the old-fashioned themes – 'Blues Up And Down' – and pop tunes, and Dexter makes sure that he is the leading voice on all tracks, though Griffin, playing as fast and furious as he had a decade earlier, holds his own. We've found this a pretty unsatisfying set, diffuse and unfocused, but Gordon fanatics will treasure some elongated solos and able sparring with a fellow tenorman.

***** Settin' The Pace**

Proper 2016 4CD *As various '40s sessions above.*

The sound-quality won't exactly have you quivering in your chair, but 55 tracks of classic Gordon material spread over four discs at a budget price can't be bad and we have to assume that the licensing is all kosher and above board. Dexter fans will have almost all of this material already, but for a newcomer for whom the big man is a recent revelation, this is a very attractive purchase. Classics include 'Hornin' In', 'Wee Dot', 'Long Tall Dexter' and the quirky 'Chromatic Aberration'. Decently packaged, though the supporting material isn't too hot.

Joe Gordon (1928–63)

TRUMPET

With impeccable credentials from the New England Conservatory and an extended apprenticeship with Georgie Auld, Lionel Hampton and Charlie Parker, Gordon was a considerable trumpeter. He was a Jazz Messenger for a short time and appeared in the film The Proper Time, with Shelly Manne. Like Woody Shaw, he mismanaged – or failed to manage – his solo career and his life; at the age of 35 he burned to death in a rooming-house fire that was apparently started by a cigarette on his mattress.

***** West Coast Days**

Fresh Sound FSCD 1030 *Gordon; Richie Kamuca (ts); Russ Freeman (p); Monty Budwig (b); Shelly Manne (d).* 7/58.

***** Lookin' Good**

Original Jazz Classics OJCCD 1934 *Gordon; Jimmy Woods (as); Dick Whittington (p); Jimmy Bond (b); Milt Turner (d).* 61.

A slightly brittle tone, always pitched a little sharp, but affectingly vocalized and never less than expressive: Gordon was an individualist. The recorded legacy is thin but impressive. In the scrappy Fresh Sound (which is in any case shared with Scott LaFaro material) Gordon takes second place to Kamuca and Freeman and never quite settles to the task. The recordings are average for the time (1958) and place (the legendary Lighthouse), though 'Poinciana' finds him several hundred yards off-mike.

There is better sound and music, if a little smoothed out, on the OJC, which was obviously an attempt to market Gordon as the new cool cat on the block. All the tracks are originals, including such unlikely compositions as 'Terra Firma Irma' and 'Non-Viennese Waltz Blues'. Altoist Woods, who made little impact on jazz history, is in good form and the rhythm section stays tight without crowding the front men. Nicely put together, but not much more than a footnote to a sadly short life. Joe was dead less than two years later, enjoying exactly a half a biblical lifespan.

Jon Gordon (born 1966)

ALTO AND SOPRANO SAXOPHONES

Bobby Watson has publicly wondered why Gordon hasn't been pounced on and head-hunted by one of the majors. On the strength of these, it is surprising, but Jon has continued to forge his own determined path. Unlike many players of his type, he communicates brilliantly on record and uses the studio with great imagination.

***** The Jon Gordon Quartet**

Chiaroscuro CR (D) 316 *Gordon; Phil Woods (as); Kevin Hays (p); Scott Holley (b); Bill Stewart (d).* 3/92.

***** Spark**

Chiaroscuro CR (D) 330 *Gordon; Benny Carter, Phil Woods (as); Bill Charlap (p); Sean Smith (b); Tim Horner (d).* 4/94.

When Benny Carter and Phil Woods are lining up to play on your record and Joe Lovano's on hand to write an enthusiastic liner-note, it's pretty clear that something is happening. Gordon is young, bright and effortlessly accomplished, with none of the brashness and over-confidence that often come with 'effortless' talent (which of course it ain't). He handles tricky material with a naturalness born of considerable application, as when he negotiates the curves of Lovano's 'Land Of Ephysus' on the first record.

Predictably, the two Chiaroscuros were sold largely on the strength of the guest artists; but, excellent as Woods and (on the second disc) Carter are, they never quite steal the show from Gordon himself. If, as is now often suggested, the label he was soon to join, Criss Cross, is the Blue Note of the '90s, who does he most resemble? Woods is the main inspiration, but one might also be tempted to point to Jackie McLean; not the obvious parallel in terms of sound, but for sheer joyous involvement in the music, as both performer and writer, it's close. 'Spark' clinches it: a strong, simple idea that is both robust enough for the road and delicate enough to lay claims to real beauty.

*****(*) Ask Me Now**

Criss Cross 1099 *Gordon; Tim Hagans (t); Bill Charlap (p); Larry Grenadier (b); Billy Drummond (d).* 12/94.

*****(*) Witness**

Criss Cross 1121 *Gordon; Tim Hagans (t); Mark Turner (ts); Bill Charlap (p); Sean Smith (b); Tim Horner (d).* 12/95.

The move to Criss Cross was good for Gordon, putting him in the way of a growing pool of young, relatively like-minded musicians who are not constrained by fashion, or indeed by retro ideologies, but who are simply dedicated to mainstream jazz. Gordon makes an early statement of intent with an effortless (that weasel word again!) ride through the scarifying changes of 'Giant Steps' and a showing for his own (presumably Lovano-inspired) 'Joe Said So', as well as the Monk tune that gives *Ask Me Now* its title. The follow-up record is, if anything, less settled, more ambitious. 'Individuation' is an exercise in group counterpoint that slightly outstays its welcome, though it does establish the parameters of the group. 'Interlude' and 'Waking Dream' are a linked pair, the latter a study in complex harmonic organization. 'House Of Mirrors' is by the bassist and features Smith in a solo outing that plucks some of its ideas straight out of Gordon's soprano improvisation, in itself a strong reminder that he has this second voice in reserve.

****** Along The Way**

Criss Cross 1138 *Gordon; Mark Turner (ts); Kevin Hays (p); Joe Martin (b); Billy Drummond (d).* 6/97.

*****(*) Currents**

Double Time DTRCD 136 *Gordon; Ed Simon (p); Ben Monder (g); Larry Grenadier (b); Bill Stewart (d); Adam Cruz (perc).* 2/98.

Gordon continues to consolidate. The final Criss Cross album is a delightfully confident combination of original material and standards. As a winner of the Thelonious Monk Competition, Gordon has every right to tackle 'Friday The 13th' with the insouciant confidence he brings to the jagged theme. He also understands the internal rhythms of a tune like Joe Henderson's 'Inner Urge' and he has incorporated much of that thinking into his own writing. A richly textured 'Body And Soul' sounds like an attempt to write himself into a long saxophone tradition.

On *Currents*, Jon is more concerned to let his own voice come through as a writer. Apart from a couple of repertory pieces, all the compositions are by the saxophonist and they suggest an artist on the brink of great things, though not yet with the maturity to execute his ideas convincingly. 'Twilight Soul' is profoundly influenced by Wayne Shorter, while 'Intention' draws in elements of reggae and ska as well as jazz. The real eye-opener, though, is 'Shape Up', a dense and complex piece which requires many hearings to unravel, and even then resists analysis. Though the band doesn't quite pull it off, Jon is absolutely assured and convincing.

***** The Things We Need**

Double Time 156 *Gordon; Mike LeDonne, Ronnie Mathews (p); Peter Bernstein (g); Dennis Irwin (b); Eddie Locke, Kenny Washington (d); children's choir.* 1–2/99.

*****(*) Possibilities**

Double Time 171 *Gordon; John Scofield (g); Kevin Hays (p); Peter Washingon (b); Bill Stewart (d).* 00.

Despite our prolonged canvassing, Gordon still hasn't attracted the attention – or, rather, the cash investment – of a major label. It doesn't seem to be troubling him, but it may have persuaded him to take the more straightforward and potentially commercial route suggested by *The Things We Need*. This is his most accessible work to date and in some ways his least individual. The playing and writing are as strong as ever, but Jon has softened the edges a bit, even when returning to Monk, as he does here in the company of guest pianist Mathews on 'Monk's Dream' and 'Ugly Beauty'. LeDonne is the main accompanist, but these tracks do stand out. Jon's two long compositions, 'Minor Dues' and 'Stapleton', suggest a shift towards the mainstream, but both are harmonically rich and packed with incident and detail. Milt Jackson's 'SKJ' is an interesting choice, purposeful, upbeat and effortlessly rhythmic, as it needs to be. The oddity of the album is the inclusion of a kids' choir on 'Without A Song', a personal association that brings nothing to the album.

A child appears on the cover of *Possibilities*, underlining how strong such associations are for the saxophonist. This is a return to form, with a strong line-up anchored on Scofield, often without piano (Sco's 'Camp-Out' is the opening number) and driven solidly by drummer Stewart, who has an edgier approach than Kenny Washington; Stewart also chips in with the closing 'Soul's Harbor', a fascinating theme that deserves wider exposure. A trio of original compositions – 'Paradox', 'Riddle' and 'Contemplation' – mark a partial reprise of Gordon's exploratory style. Monk is again represented, this time by 'Misterioso', and there is a version of Trane's 'Moment's Notice', intriguingly without bass.

Wycliffe Gordon (born 1967)

TROMBONE, DIDJERIDU, VOCAL

From Waynesboro, GA, Gordon is one of the musicians whose tenure in the Lincoln Center Jazz Orchestra has helped establish his name – although he is reluctant to relinquish his Michigan base, where he teaches and arranges.

***** Slidin' Home**

Nagel-Heyer 2001 *Gordon; Randy Sandke (t); Victor Goines (ts, cl); Joe Temperley (ss, bs); Eric Reed (p); Rodney Whitaker (b); Herlin Riley (d); Milt Grayson (v).* 12/98.

★★★ The Search

Nagel-Heyer 2007 *Gordon; Marcus Printup (t); Dave Gibson, Jennifer Krupa, Delfeayo Marsalis, Ron Westray (tb); Roger Floreska (btb); Ted Nash (as, f); Walter Blanding Jr, Victor Goines (ts); Eric Reed (p); Rodney Whitaker (b); Winard Harper, Herlin Riley (d).* 11–12/99.

★★★ The Gospel Truth

Criss Cross 1192 *Gordon; Marcus Printup (t, v); Jennifer Krupa, Dion Tucker (tb); Victor Goines (ts, bs, cl); Kurt Stockdale (as); Eric Reed (p); Reuben Rogers (b); Winard Harper (d); Carrie Smith (v).* 5/00.

★★★★ What You Dealin' With

Criss Cross 1212 *Gordon; Ryan Kisor (t); Victor Goines (ss, ts); Herb Harris (ts); Zach Pride (b); Rodney Green (d).* 1/01.

Gordon's albums are a step in the necessary direction of pushing the trombone forward into contemporary prominence. *Slidin' Home* perhaps touches too many bases a little too rapidly – New Orleans, blues, Monk, Ellington, gospel – but already the ebullient transformation of 'Mood Indigo' into an extravagant trombone feature suggests what Gordon can do. Given that his instrument is so often relegated to secondary status, perhaps expectation is bothered by having a trombone so precipitously taking precedence.

Both *The Search* and *The Gospel Truth* slightly bury that difficulty in concepts. The former looks to be laden with slide horns, but the trombone 'choir' is used deftly and with some fine results, particularly in the superfast 'Frantic Flight' and a lovely 'Stardust'. Some of this material feels too smartly worked, though, such as a rather silly reading of Monk's 'Ba-Lue Bolivar Ba-Lues-Are', and perhaps – in the inevitable rush to meet modestly resourced small-label deadlines – the music could have stood a little further research and rehearsal. *The Gospel Truth* goes, inevitably, for sacred material, but again Gordon doesn't quite judge the feel right: there are too many vocals (if that doesn't sound daft in describing a gospel record) and some misguided attempts to sanctify the didjeridu, all of which undercuts some superb playing by Gordon: try 'The Hallelujah Scat'.

What You Dealin' With is easily the best of these, because it's the most freewheeling, the least yoked to context, and it's packed with great playing. The programme of Ellington, Gillespie, 'Cherokee', 'Mr PC' and sundry originals is slyly set up to subvert expectations all the way. 'Blue 'N' Boogie' uproots bebop slickness by strolling in and out of double-time on the theme, with superb nonchalance. 'Cotton Tail' shows that Wycliffe's scatting chops are in pretty good order, too. 'Cherokee' is sheer virtuoso high spirits – after they've hoodwinked us with a stately beginning. 'Bone Abstractions' lets you know just what the man can do with his unruly slide horn, a phantasmagoric throw of the dice. And he has another go at 'Mood Indigo', this time a harmonious mix of sharp improvising and daring high-jinks. All the way through to the funky swing of the closing title-track, Gordon not only leads from the front, he imparts heroic good humour to go with the crackling invention of the playing, from all hands.

★★★(★) United Soul Experience

Criss Cross 1224 *Gordon; Seamus Blake (ts); David Kikoski (p); Larry Grenadier (b); Bill Stewart (d).* 12/01.

★★★(★) Dig This!

Criss Cross 1238 *Gordon; Seamus Blake (ts); Sam Yahel (org); Peter Bernstein (g); Bill Stewart (d).* 12/02.

United Soul Experience pitched Gordon into the thick of an unfamiliar team at more or less a moment's notice, and it's a tribute to his chutzpah that he still got a great result out of it. He and Blake make a handsome front line, the thicker, more expressive sound of the trombonist matched with the lean agility of the tenor. Kikoski colours in the harmonies under each man, rapidly and unstintingly. The closing steal from Ellington's *Anatomy Of A Murder* score, 'Low Key Lightly', is a delicious duet between Gordon and Grenadier.

Dig This! rings a few changes, with Blake and Stewart retained but Yahel and Bernstein coming in. It's still a Criss Cross repertory act, and none the worse for it. 'Limehouse Blues', 'Lonnie's Lament' and 'I Can't Get Started' (a duo with Bernstein) are the core repertoire; the rest are originals. If it feels more like a settling-in for this talented musician, he still imparts enough individuality to suggest that he's setting the pace for the aspiring trombonist.

Mike Gorman

PIANO

Sheffield-born pianist, performing in the familiar modern idiom.

★★★ The Maze

33Jazz 065 *Gorman; Jeremy Brown (b); Matt Skelton (d).* 4–6/01.

Gorman works briskly through nine tunes with a carefree air that touches few depths but similarly stands refreshingly free of pretension. One piece which shows him at his best is 'Quasimodo', a Charlie Parker line that he plays at a jaunty mid-tempo, trying new melodic lines on what's a standard chord sequence and referring back to Bird's melody in deft ways. The five covers do, indeed, elicit the most satisfying music, including 'Airegin' played over a stop-start tempo and 'Mona Lisa' done as a solo flourish to end the date, but the originals are rather less interesting.

Frank Goudie (1899–1964)

CLARINET, VOCAL

Goudie started on trumpet and worked in New Orleans in the 1910s and early '20s, before spending 15 years in Europe with many bandleaders. Worked in France and Berlin after the war and returned to San Francisco in the late '50s.

★★(★) Frank 'Big Boy' Goudie With Amos White

American Music AMCD-50 *Goudie; Amos White (t); J.D Banton (ts); Jimmy Simpson, Burt Bales (p, v); Al Levy (g); Al Conger (b); James Carter (d).* 9/60–3/61.

Goudie is an obscure figure, even among New Orleans musicians, but he was much admired by Albert Nicholas, and these somewhat grimy recordings reveal an idiosyncratic, vigorous clarinettist (his previous spell in the limelight came with a date in Paris in 1937 with Bill Coleman and Django Reinhardt which produced 'Big Boy Blues'). Five tracks with White, Banton, Simpson, Levy and Carter are unexceptional New Orleans dance-hall music (though recorded, like all the tracks, in San Francisco) but the four duets and three trios with Bales and Conger are more substantial. Goudie chews over the melody lines rather than elaborating on them, and there's a folkish lilt to some of his ideas. Recommended, though to New Orleans specialists only.

Dusko Goykovich (born 1931)

TRUMPET, FLUGELHORN

The Bosnian trumpeter is a disciple of Miles Davis, but the infusion of folk forms adds an extra dimension to his music, which is characteristically swinging, though often with an unexpected balance to outwardly familiar metres.

**(*) Belgrade Blues

Cosmic Sounds 16 *Goykovich; Carl Fontana (tb); Derek Humble (as); Karl Drewo, Sal Nistico (ts); Francy Boland, Nat Pierce (p); Jean Warland, Michael Moore (b); Kenny Clarke (d).* 61, 66.

This is an interesting reissue from fairly early in Goykovich's career, though he was already 30 when *Dusko Goykovich International Jazz Octet* was issued. The Miles Davis influence isn't so much a matter of horn sound as of the pace and register of these mainly mid-tempo tunes. The playing is rather unemphatic, though the date and Goykovich's background must be underlined in this context; he must have seemed quite advanced at home. Some of the material is by Francy Boland, who employed the young Yugoslav and brought on his potential. Other tracks are standards, though there is a fine version of Max Roach's 'Mr X', which doesn't often turn up. The remaining four tracks are from a later sextet featuring Sal Nistico and Nat Pierce, who wrote the titular 'Belgrade Blues'. Fairly routine stuff, but of value to anyone who has followed Goykovich's career.

***(*) Swinging Macedonia

Enja 4048 *Goykovich; Eddie Busnello (as); Nathan Davis (ts, ss, f); Mal Waldron (p); Peter Trunk (b); Cees See (d).* 8/66.

One of the most convincing attempts to synthesize jazz and the curious scalar progressions of Balkan folk music. Born in the former Yugoslavia, Goykovich studied at Berklee and saw action with Maynard Ferguson, Woody Herman and with the Clarke–Boland Big Band. His most characteristic work, though, has been with smaller groups. He is a bright, rhythmic player, with a full, rather folksy sound that draws somewhat selectively on the bop trumpet tradition. *Swinging Macedonia* was a bold stroke, with an impact akin to that of Ivo Papasov's much-hyped Bulgarian Wedding Band. Goykovich, though, is more purely a jazz player, and a more adventurous improviser. He's ably supported by an international line-up that hinges on the two American exiles. Waldron deals splendidly with some unfamiliar chord changes, Davis sounds authentically Slavonic (indeed, much like Papasov) and the little-known Busnello makes three or four very effective interventions. More than just an oddity, this deserves to be known more widely.

*** Balkan Blue

Enja 9320 2CD *Goykovich; Gianni Basso (ts); Bora Rokovic (p); Bruno Castellucci (d); Wolfgang Schluter (perc).* 98.

What looks and occasionally sounds like a conventional hard-bop unit is turned to much more adventurous purpose in this long and heartfelt sequence of pieces inspired by Goykovich's native corner of the planet. It is in a sense a musical autobiography, with influences – swing, bebop – acknowledged on the way. Some of the music is merely colouristic and slightly bland in conception, and two CDs-worth is asking a lot of the uncommitted or unconvinced listener. And yet at moments, as in the long 'Bosnia Calling' and 'Macedonia', the blend of folk melodies with jazz harmony and the obvious intensity of expression is very effective indeed. Basso is one of a generation of terse, adventurous Italian saxophonists, little known outside his own country but utterly individual in every note.

*** In My Dreams

Enja ENJ 9408 *Goykovich; Bob Degen (p); Isla Eckinger (b); Jarrod Cagwin (d).* 9/00.

Essentially a ballad album, this is as laid back and lyrical as Goykovich has ever sounded on record. As he approaches 70, he has acquired a philosophical stance that comes through strongly and emphatically here on tracks like 'St Germain des Prés' (a near-perfect tone poem) and 'Skylark', which has rarely sounded so gently melancholy. Degen is an astonishing musician, still largely overlooked, but responsible for the lovely 'Sequoia Song' which provides the album with its high point, as measured and expressive a performance as you'd hope to find. As an album, perhaps a little one-dimensional, but hard to fault track by track.

**** Portrait

Enja ENJ 9427 *Goykovich; Steve Gut (t); Abraham Burton (as); Jimmy Heath, Tony Lakatos, Lucky Thompson (ts); Ferdinand Povel (ts, f); Kenny Barron, Tommy Flanagan, Hans Hammerschmid, Bora Rokovic, Larry Vuckovich (p); Oscar Pettiford (b, clo); Ray Drummond, Fred Dutton, Isla Eckinger, Eddie Gomez, Branko Pejakovic (b); Hartwig Bartz, Clarence Becton, Alvin Queen, Mickey Roker, Dejan Terzic (d); Monica Zetterlund (v).* 59–99.

Released on the occasion of his 70th birthday, this lovely set is an ideal career summary for someone who wants a quick appraisal of who Dusko is and where he's come from musically. It goes back to 1959 and Goykovich's return from the Newport Festival to record with Oscar Pettiford (a fine duet on 'But Not For Me') and with Lucky Thompson and Monica Zetterlund ('Love For Sale', which also features Pettiford on cello). 'I Remember Clifford' and a couple of other tracks were taped live in 1970 at Domicile in Munich with his working group. This period finds the trumpeter clearly under the spell of Miles Davis but with his own folkish influence working in the background.

Paul Grabowsky (born 1958)

PIANO, SYNTHESIZER

Australian post-bop pianist who has moved into soundtrack composition.

***(*) Ringing The Bell Backwards

Origin OR 008 *Grabowsky; Bob Coassin, Scott Tinkller (t, flhn); Stephen Grant (c, acc, g); Simon Kent (tb); Adrian Sherriff (btb, didg); Ian Chaplin (ss, as); Peter Harper (as, f, bcl); Tim Hopkins (ts, bcl); Jim Glasson (ts, f, picc, cl); Elliot Dalgleish (bs); Stuart Campbell (ky); John Rodgers (vn); Steve Magnusson, Shane O'Mara (g); Gary Costello, Philip Rex (b); Niko Schauble, Scott Lambie (d).* 94.

★★★(★) PG3

Origin 058 *Grabowsky; Gary Costello (b); Niko Schauble (d).* 00.

★★★ Shiner

Decca 470183-2 *Grabowsky; Phil Slater (t); Lachlan Davidson (as, bcl); Ren Walters (g); Mike Grabowsky (b); Niko Schauble (d); Alex Pertout (perc); choir and strings.* 5–7/00.

We have previously fretted that Grabowsky's ambitions in film music and suchlike have been set to take him away from jazz, but this crop of recordings tends to allay such fears. The imposing scores in *Ringing The Bell Backwards* propose a powerful fusion, separate from European 'concert music' (they're played, with considerable skill, by an all-Oz group named Australian Art Orchestra), while dwelling on material which belongs to the old world – transformations of 'La Vie En Rose' and 'We'll Meet Again', and pop songs from Weimar's golden age. These are chilling, rather than chilled, classics: 'Spectre Of A Rose' has the aura of a march to the gallows, and 'Unregrettable' (alias 'Je Ne Regrette Rien') is one ingenious allusion after another, integrated into a shouting big-band performance. Some of it is sometimes pointlessly clever, perhaps, and the soloists tend to intrude on passages where one wants to hear how Grabowsky is going to resolve a direction in the scoring; but top marks for ambition and intensity. There's also some particularly surprising use of sampling and studio effects, which for once add real sparks to the recording.

PG3 commences with another of the Australian's pop-song treatments, this time a slow but bright interpretation of 'Make It Easy On Yourself'. Instead of vandalizing such material, Grabowsky all but honours it, and the results are coolly agreeable, though no more so than his originals, which make up most of this musing, unorthodox trio record. Schauble is never a man for simply swinging from the kit, and his playing is full of dramatic pauses, colouristic effects and stark changes of dynamics. This is all manifest in 'Beyond The Black Suit', a remarkable performance, meriting the repeat button on a regular basis. The pianist reshapes 'Straight No Chaser' without ever resorting to the Monk clunk, and 'Star Crossed Lovers' makes for a glowing finale. But the record is a shade too long, with a couple of less than compelling pieces – like the overly introspective 'A Quiet Place' – slackening its grip.

The film score *Shiner* sounds like many such CDs – a good collection of cues, but nothing that really develops beyond its functional base. That said, Grabowsky marshals his small team – Slater offers some good Miles Davis copy, almost as good as Chris Botti's version – effectively, and if you want to have some dinner guests asking, 'What's that?', it's a good talking point.

We should also mention *Sita* (Australian Art Orchestra, no number), a collaboration between Grabowsky, the Indonesian composer–performer Wayan Gde Yudane, members of the AAO and five Balinese musicians. But, it is, frankly, quite beyond the scope of this book.

★★★(★) Tales Of Time And Space

Warner Music Australia 50467 17062 *Grabowsky; Scott Tinkler (t); Branford Marsalis (ss); Joe Lovano (ts); Ed Schuller (b); Jeff Tain Watts (d).* 4/03.

At this point in a lengthy and busy career, Grabowsky has little to prove by making the fabled stopover record in New York with a hired gang of all stars. The cover is all moody, monochrome shots of the city and music is...New York Jazz, but definitely timed to fit Grabowsky's own space. No standards, riff tunes, blues or jams, just nine pointed and substantial compositions, which ask the illustrious team to be very sharp about their business. If Grabowski brings anything 'Australian' to this situation, it's hard to divine what it is, but the pungency of his writing has lost nothing in the round trip: 'Tailfin', 'Silverland' and 'Angel' are destined to be classics in his book, although there's nothing which sounds like he was trying too hard to set a challenge for the players. It's vintage Grabowsky, unusual melodies, tricky rhythmical touches, and the coolly melancholy lyricism, which he often spatters over a ballad. Tinkler, surprisingly, takes star solo honours, Marsalis is obliged to sidestep the sometimes glib brilliance of many of his records, and though Lovano sounds sleepy, he does well enough too. The pianist's own playing isn't especially grabbing, but he should be very proud of the overall result.

Georg Graewe (born 1956)

PIANO, BANDLEADER, COMPOSER

Pianist-composer much in the new tradition of classical study mixed with free improvisation, and seemingly equally content in both idioms.

★★★(★) Flex 27

Random Acoustics RA 007 *Graewe; Ernst Reijseger (clo); Gerry Hemingway (d, perc).* 12/93.

In addition to a duo with the drummer, Willi Kellers, Graewe has worked regularly with two very different improvising trios: well-received work with tubist Melvyn Poore and GrubenKlangOrchester member Phil Wachsmann (see below), and the trio captured in striking form on this disc (two for Music & Arts seem to have been deleted). These are three players of markedly different temperaments, united by a resistance to the fixed resolutions of both 'jazz' and 'New Music'. They play undogmatically and with great exactness, as if they have been rehearsing these pieces for years. Like Eddie Prévost, Hemingway manages to swing even when playing completely free, and his range of articulation is quite extraordinary. Graewe, one of the most enterprising of the post-Schlippenbach pianists, is apt to dissolve his own most acute observations in a flood of repetitions and curious evasions, but the ideas are strong enough to resist corrosion. Reijseger, by contrast, knows how to enjoy an idea and when to dispense with it. The Random Acoustics set is immensely detailed, full of exactitudes and tiny, outwardly meaningless gestures that seem to propel things forward to the next crux.

★★★ Chamber Works

Random Acoustics 003 *Graewe; Horst Grabosch (t); Melvyn Poore (tba); Michael Moore (cl, bcl); Philipp Wachsmann (vn); Ernst Reijseger (clo); Anne LeBaron, Hans Schneider (hp); Gerry Hemingway (d); Phil Minton (v).* 91–2.

Random Acoustics, Graewe's own label, now has a rather impressive list of new music. This is the boss's day in court, a run-down of some of his more adventurous projects at the turn of the decade. The trio is represented again, but so, too, are some of Graewe's more formal pieces and the celebrated trio with Poore and Wachsmann in which nothing sounds as one would expect it to and there is no obvious heading or trajectory for the music, just a concentrated sense of immediacy and presence as the players feed off one another.

★★★★ Melodie Und Rhythmus

Okkadisk OD 12016 *Graewe; Frank Gratkowski (as, cl); Kent Kessler (b); Hamid Drake (d, perc).* 96.

Just melody and rhythm, and a carefully bracketed emphasis on these dimensions. It may be that Graewe has been thinking about Ornette Coleman's groups. Certainly he avoids much emphasis on vertical improvisation, driving the group along the flat with a punchy, one-idea-at-a-time impetus. Drake is a very different kind of player from Hemingway, coming from a different percussion school and lacking either the rock-pumped force or the ability to drift out of time altogether. Kessler is now almost as ubiquitous as William Parker and he has much of Parker's generous intelligence and ability to seed himself at the centre of big, busy structures and still maintain his function, a skill bequeathed to jazz by the great Charles Mingus. Listeners who have previously found that Graewe is lacking in jazz content may enjoy better fortunes with this one.

★★★ Other Songs

Nuscope 1008 *Graewe; Peter Van Bergen (ts, cbcl); Barre Phillips (b).* 6/99.

An unpredictable trio. Van Bergen plays the earlier pieces on contrabass clarinet, turns to tenor for the later ones; and the various pieces are quite short, partly resolved, and heavy on the bass frequencies. It seems like a very 'democratic' situation, although some of the music feels as if it's asking for a lead which never arrives.

★★★★ Fantasiestücke I – XIII

Nuscope 1014 *Graewe (p solo).* 10/00.

We can do little better than quote part of Fred Van Hove's sleeve-note: 'George's fantasy pieces – one seven minutes long, the others between two and five minutes – all seem to end abruptly. They could stop there; they could have been longer or shorter; their length is indefinite. Like life itself, which stops unexpectedly most of the time, it is always unfinished.' Sumptuously recorded, these improvisations are like all of Graewe's work: exact, detailed, unhurried, finessed yet still breathing and spontaneous. As a record of piano music, whatever its supposed genre, it's formidably beautiful – even when unfinished.

Michel Graillier

PIANO, SYNTHESIZER

A regular on the French scene for many years, Graillier backed visiting Americans during the '70s and '80s and has subsequently worked with Simon Goubert and others, working in a dreamy post-bop style.

★★★ Dream Drops

Owl 013434-2 *Graillier; Chet Baker (t); Michel Petrucciani (p); Jean-François Jenny-Clark (b); Ado Romano (d).* 4–11/81.

★★★ It Was A Very Good Night

Seventh XII *Graillier; Alby Cullaz (b); Simon Goubert (d).* 3/90.

★★★ Soft Talk

Sketch SKE 333014 *Graillier; Riccardo Del Fra (b).* 6/00.

Graillier's music isn't likely to collar the attention and his records are likeable if inessential. The Owl disc reissues a 1981 date which he mostly played solo, orchestrating piano parts with synthesizer backdrops into what sounds like pleasantly impressionistic music. Baker and Petrucciani do a single duet apiece. The live gig on *It Was A Very Good Night* introduced his new trio, and while the music isn't as immortal as the title suggests, it's a spirited set. *Soft Talk* works through a set of originals by both men (though they end with a version of 'I'm A Fool To Want You'). The tranquil programme could use one track that really kicks. Mostly, Graillier's thoughtful lines are echoed or amplified by Del Fra, and that's about it.

Grand Dominion Jazz Band

GROUP

Together since the early '80s, the GDJB's members are based in the Pacific North-West and include British emigrants and Americans, playing in a George Lewis–Ken Colyer style.

★★★ Half And Half

Stomp Off CD3989 *Bob Jackson (t); Jim Armstrong (tb, v); Gerry Green (cl, as); Bob Pelland (p); Mike Cox (bj, v); Mike Duffy (b); Stephen Joseph (d).* 3/86–6/88.

★★★ San Jacinto Stomp

Stomp Off CD1268 *As above, except Mike McCombe (d) replaces Joseph.* 1/93.

★★★ The Spiritual Album

Stomp Off CD1291 *As above.* 10/94.

★★★ Smiles

Stomp Off CD1330 *As above, except Jim Marsh (bj) replaces Cox.* 8/97.

★★★ Daddy's Little Girl

Stomp Off CD1337 *As above.* 8/97.

Somewhat in the style of Ken Colyer's revivalism, this is a sturdy and impressive group of (mainly) trad veterans. Two of their earlier LPs were reissued on *Half And Half*: a bit livelier and more, er, virile than their later CDs, this has an interestingly catholic choice of material, with music-hall tunes such as Joe O'Gorman's 'Bedelia' rubbing shoulders with Wally Fawkes's 'Trog's Blues' and Joe Oliver's 'Snag It'. *San Jacinto Stomp* brought them into the CD era. With most of the tracks rolling expansively past the six- and seven-minute mark, they generate a steadily building momentum that's very effective on the likes of 'Bugle Boy March' and Adrian Rollini's 'Old Fashioned Swing'. Jackson is a rather wiry, short-breathed soloist, but Green's wide-bodied alto is nice and the rhythm section play with great heart.

The Spiritual Album is played with respect rather than any deep feeling and will appeal most to dedicated fans. *Smiles* brings in newcomer Jim Marsh on banjo (he has more hair than the others, but it's just as grey) and it wobbles between the sacred ('Oh Lord, Is It I?') and the secular (Ma Rainey's 'Oh My Babe Blues'), though there's nothing that could qualify as the profane. This is the point at which to mention that their vocals are in the trad-band disaster area.

Daddy's Little Girl keeps up the old tradition. 'Spanish Shawl' is a favourite that will never go stale. 'Shout 'Em Aunt Tillie' has a lot more life in it (her?) than when Marcus Roberts played it. They end with Joe Jordan and his 'Teasin' Rag'. The singing is, alas, as before, but there is, hooray, not too much of it. Good show!

Jerry Granelli (born 1940)

DRUMS, SOUND SCULPTURES, BASS

Experienced drummer with a knack for assembling surprising line-ups and forging some fresh fusions of jazz with other styles of improvisation.

★★★★ Broken Circle

Songline/Tonefield INT 3501 *Granelli; Kai Bruckner, Christian Kogel (g); Andreas Walter (b).* 96.

Granelli's most obvious influence would seem to be Paul Motian, a delicate but never lightweight approach that caught the attention of guitarist/pianist Ralph Towner, who recruited him and at one point (or so it is rumoured) considered him to replace Collin Walcott in Oregon. Some of his earlier records are now gone, but the most intriguing of them is *Broken Circle*, an original suite called 'Song Of A Good Name' inspired by the history of Native Americans, together with an imaginative trawl of jazz and popular material, including Prince's 'Sign O' The Times', Peter Gabriel's 'Washing Of The Water', Mingus's 'Boogie Stop Shuffle' and Coltrane's 'Lonnie's Lament'. The two-guitar sound is occasionally reminiscent of Prime Time, more often of Pat Metheny's pastel-and-wash collaborations with Lyle Mays, particularly when Bruckner and Kogel are required to add slide, 'textural' or 'atmospheric' guitar. The Native American suite is very powerful, touching here and there on the folksy sound of Jim Pepper, but by and large more straightforward acoustically than the earlier tracks. A very beautiful record that deserves to be much better known.

★★★(★) Enter, A Dragon

Songlines SGL 1521-2 *Granelli; Curtis Hasselbring (tb); Peter Epstein (ss, as); Briggan Krauss (as); Chris Speed (cl, ts); Jamie Saft (ky, acc, g); J. Anthony Granelli (b).* 9/97.

★★★(★) Crowd Theory

Songlines SGL 1526-2 *As above.* 9/98.

The titles on *Enter, A Dragon*, as well as the longer pieces being interspersed by six so-called 'Haikus', suggest an Eastern concept, but the only real line to that is in Granelli's own exotica of bells, cymbals and chimes. It's otherwise an ensemble of New Yorkers creating a sound that seeks to be hard-hitting but sensuous, big on texture – from the swells of percussion to accordion, fat electric bass and scratchy slide guitar – over which the horns march in and out of earshot. It's often rather pretty, pictorial music from which episodes like the disjointed funk of 'Sting Thing' emerge as strange surprise packages. A very entertaining show. *Crowd Theory* is, suitably enough, thicker and with a heftier ensemble sound. A broader range of material brings in such as Wayne Horvitz's 'The Front', but Granelli's own themes, including the raddled terpsichorea of 'Tango', still have much to captivate.

Darrell Grant (born 1962)

PIANO

Born in Philadelphia, he's had a remarkable career, academically and professionally, working in pop music and in the working groups of both Betty Carter and Tony Williams before striking out on his own. He's also a talented fiction writer.

★★★ Black Art

Criss Cross 1087 *Grant; Wallace Roney (t); Christian McBride (b); Brian Blade (d).* 93.

★★★(★) New Bop

Criss Cross 1106 *Grant; Scott Wendholt (t); Seamus Blake (ts); Calvin Jones (b); Brian Blade (d).* 12/94.

His range of work, which includes stints with Chico Freeman and Roy Haynes as well, and the sheer confidence of his delivery speak for themselves. This confident debut, now a decade old, is relatively conventional in idiom and might be mistaken for something from the Blue Note back catalogue, were it not for Roney's brightly contemporary sound and McBride's now familiar bass work. Grant himself shines on the opening 'Freedom Dance', but tends to replicate a smallish roster of ideas thereafter. 'What Is This Thing Called Love?' exposes some of his weaknesses, but still, no excuse for having overlooked him this long.

The second disc is both more of the same and better. More of the same because Grant's spectrum is comfortably narrow; better largely because of his guests. Blake and Wendholt, both Criss Cross veterans, are in fine form and absolutely at ease with the modernized hard bop Grant writes. His seeming inspiration here is Horace Silver, who contributes a liner-note, but there is less easy swing than on a Silver date and Grant's quotations tend to be more camouflaged than the old name-dropper's. 'Don't Stray' and 'Struttin' To Tangiers' are excellent, but the highlight is a soulful, almost gospelly reading of Duke's 'Come Sunday'.

★★★(★) Smokin' Java

Lair Hill 1 *Grant; Donald Harrison (as); Joe Locke (vib); Bob Stata (b); Brian Blade (d).* 00.

Grant recorded another disc for Joel Dorn's 32 Jazz before it went under, but this is how he should be heard, in a live context with a thoughtfully soulful group. Apart from 'Spring Skylight' and the title-track, all the tunes are by other hands. Gordon Jenkins's 'Goodbye' is magnificent and Joe Locke's intro to the classic 'If I Should Lose You' takes it into a different realm. Locke's own 'Slander' has a nice rhythmic and harmonic twist. The opening 'Little Jimmy Fiddler' establishes the kind of groove you'd expect from a Horace Silver record and Grant and Harrison establish a rapport that lasts for the whole album. Grant also contributes a bright, insightful liner-note that reveals his skill as a writer. Great stuff, and apologies for missing him out in previous editions. Nice to catch up now.

Stéphane Grappelli (1908–97)

VIOLIN

A more complex and enigmatic figure than first appears, Grappelli's apparent affability and lightness of touch seemed to mask a boiling personality, full of contradictions. It makes little sense to think of him simply as the temperamental opposite of his great partner in the Quintet du Hot Club de France, Django Reinhardt. Grappelli was born in Paris and was largely self-taught, which is perhaps why his approach to jazz violin (and along with Stuff Smith and Joe Venuti he more or less invented its use as a jazz instrument) is so idiomatic. A typical Grappelli line is fast, fleet and accurate, but with grace notes and embellishments which suggest a darker tonality as well.

★★★★ Grappelli Story

Verve 515807-2 2CD *Grappelli; Django Reinhardt, Philip Catherine, Larry Coryell, Pierre Cavalli, Diz Disley, Leo Petit,*

Roger Chaput, René Duchaussoir, Joe Deniz, Dave Wilkins, Alan Hodgkiss, Ike Isaacs, Eugène Vées, Jack Llewellyn, Sid Jacobson, Chappie D'Amato (g); Stan Andrews (t, vn); Bill Shakespeare (t); Frank Weir (cl); Dennis Moonan (cl, ts, vla); Stanley Andrews (vn); Harry Chapman (hp); Reg Conroy, Roy Marsh, Michel Hausser (vib); Frank Baron, Raymond Fol, Charlie Pude, George Shearing, Yorke De Sousa, Marc Hemmeler, Maurice Vander (p); George Gibbs, Hank Hobson, Joe Nussbaum, George Senior, Louis Vola, Benoît Quersin, Guy Pedersen, Lennie Bush, Coleridge Goode, Pierre Michelot, Isla Eckinger, Niels-Henning Orsted Pedersen, Eberhard Weber (b); Arthur Young (novachord); Tony Spurgin, Dave Fullerton, Kenny Clarke, Rusty Jones, Alan Levitt, Jack Jacobson, Daniel Humair, Jean-Baptiste Reilles, Jean-Louis Viale, John Spooner (d); Beryl Davis (v); orchestra conducted by Michel Legrand. 1/38–5/92.

*** **Stéphane Grappelli 1935–1940**
Classics 708 *Similar to above.*

*** **Stéphane's Tune: Original Recordings, 1938–1942**
Naxos Jazz Legends 8.120570 *Similar to above.* 38–42.

***(*) **Stéphane Grappelli 1941–1943**
Classics 779 *Similar to above.*

***(*) **Special Stéphane Grappelli, 1947–1961**
Jazz Time 794481 *Grappelli; Joseph Reinhardt, Roger Chaput, Henri Crolla, Jimmy Gourley, Georges Megalos (g); Jack Dieval (p); Pierre Spiers (hp); Pierre Michelot, Benoît Quersin, Emmanuel Soudieux (b); Armand Molinetti, Baptiste Reilles (d).* 10/47–3/61.

***(*) **Jazz Masters 11: Stéphane Grappelli**
Verve 516758-2 *As above, except add Alex Riel (d).* 9/66–5/92.

*** **Special**
Jazztime 251286 *Grappelli; Roger Chaput, Henri Crolla, Jimmy Gourley, Georges Megalos, Joseph Reinhardt (g); Jack Dieval (p); Pierre Spiers; (hp); Pierre Michelot, Benoît Quersin, Emmanuel Soudieux (b); Armand Molinetti, Baptiste Reilles (d).* 47–61.

Grappelli's association with Django Reinhardt and the Quintet du Hot Club de France is one of the legendary stories of jazz. It was Grappelli's pleasure and burden equally to carry that legend forward into one decade after another, a player of enormous range and facility linked by a mystical band to another artist who, by all accounts, made his life extremely difficult. Grappelli's limber, graceful style is so familiar that it hardly needs to be described. Because jazz fiddlers are relatively thin on the ground, he may be the most instantly recognizable jazz musician in the world – an astonishing situation if true. The Classics volumes do their usual good job of dotting 'i's and crossing 't's without worrying too much about the quality of recording or transfer, and there can be no better way of familiarizing oneself with that legacy than the Verve double-CD set which covers everything from the pre-war years to a high-budget recording session with Michel Legrand in 1992, Grappelli's 85th year. It's almost pointless to rehearse the treasures within: 'Nuages', 'Body And Soul', 'Fascinating Rhythm', the 'Nocturne' with Django. There is nothing that will disappoint.

The Jazz Masters compilation is a quicker fix, but again a perfectly acceptable one, with the label's usual scrupulous detailing of sessions and previous releases. The Jazztime *Special* is an excellent and well-transferred sampler of non-Django material, covering the period from their post-war reunion to the great guitarist's death in 1953 and beyond. Grappelli once said somewhat wearily that he would rather play with lesser musicians than ever again have to suffer Django's 'monkey business'. There's enough evidence here to confirm both the violinist's independent stature as an improviser and the plentiful supply of like-minded players. Half a dozen tracks locate Grappelli in harpist Spiers's fine, standards-based quartet. Earlier – 1954 – sets find him alongside the excellent pianist Dieval, yielding a lovely 'The World Is Waiting For The Sunrise', and the guitarist Henri Crolla, who plays in an idiom intriguingly removed from Django's. A single track from the immediately post-war Hot Four, which included Hot Club veterans Chaput and Django's brother, Joseph Reinhardt, marks it unmistakably as Grappelli's band, with a less ambitious improvisatory focus than the great original. 'Tea For Two' is a charmingly slight piano solo from Grappelli.

New since our last edition is the Naxos Jazz Legends compilation. Competitively priced and respectably packaged, it offers a good representation of the violinist's work with Django, Arthur Young and Hatchell's Swingtette. A nice buy for the more general collector.

***(*) **Jazz In Paris: Improvisations**
Emarcy 549 242 2 *Grappelli; Maurice Vander (p, hpd); Pierre Michelot (b); Baptiste Reilles (d).* 2 & 4/56.

No one belongs more securely in Emarcy's *Jazz In Paris* series than Stéphane, and this lively set, originally released on Barclay, is textbook Grappelli. Right from the opening 'The Lady Is A Tramp' you suspect he's going to stick very closely to the melody and show his stuff merely by playing it very fast. Once he's into his solo, though, it's a very different matter: daring harmonic modulations, whole countermelodies and endless grace notes – typical post Hot Club stuff. He does the same thing on 'A Nightingale Sang In Berkeley Square'. Michelot and Vander (who doubles harpsichord unexpectedly on 'Someone To Watch Over Me') keep the accompaniment from becoming too chuggingly obvious and a word for the colourful Mac Kac Reilles, not the greatest drummer in the world – or even Paris – but a character and practical joker who would have put even that arch-trickster violinist Joe Venuti in the shade.

***(*) **Violins No End**
Original Jazz Classics OJCCD 890 *Grappelli; Stuff Smith (vn); Oscar Peterson (p); Herb Ellis (g); Ray Brown (b); Jo Jones (d).* 5/57.

How different they sound, these two masters of an instrument that is still problematic in jazz, still not quite *echt*. Grappelli is all stratocirrus and clear skies; Smith always carries within his line a hint of storms to come. They don't break out on this occasion, but the hint of friendly threat and the insouciance that greets it from the other side of the stage is what makes this such an appealing record. Peterson gets less than his usual due of the limelight and seems happy to do accompanying duties, firing off fewer notes than usual and digging into his memories of stride and blues playing here and there with a procession of mischievous quotes that piano fans can have fun identifying.

(*) **Le Toit De Paris
RCA 88717 *Grappelli; Raymond Fol (p, cel); Tony Ovio (g); Jack Sewing (b); André Hartmann (d).* 69.

This is a so-so date from a period where Stéphane was being groomed for stardom, obviously bringing with him the cachet of having worked with the legendary Django. The drummer does him no favours, but there is something pedestrian about many of the blues and standards themes. Compared to Fol's compositions, though, they're masterworks. There are a couple of attempts to vary the sound: Fol switches to celeste, rarely a good idea; and Stéphane plays some effective plucked figures at the very start of 'What Am I Here For?', which gives it a jangling energy. Little sign of the greatness that was to come.

*** I Hear Music

RCA Victor 74321 79624 2 *Grappelli; Marc Hemmeler (p, hpd); Jack Sewing (b); Kenny Clarke (d, p).* 12/70.

The interesting thing about this one is that Grappelli, Hemmeler and Kenny Clarke all take a turn at the piano. The drummer shows himself to be no mean accompanist on 'Body And Soul' and Stéphane spells the useful Hemmeler on a couple of other cuts, including 'Flower For Kenny', where the pianist shifts to organ. It's a curious set in other ways, faintly mournful for all the affability and quite dark in tonality. 'Danny Boy' (strictly the 'Londonderry Air') and the original 'Coltrane' put that mood in context, but you hear it too on 'Smoke Gets In Your Eyes' and 'Body And Soul'. The recording levels are quite high and the remastering very good, so there's a lot of detail in the sound and a real sense of four men communicating intuitively and intimately. A curiosity in the Grappelli catalogue, but still a very enjoyable CD.

*** Live At Corby Festival Hall

Storyville 8345 *Grappelli; Diz Disley, Denny Wright (g); Len Skeat (b).* 5/75.

'Not jazz', the promoters muttered; and Grappelli's ultimately successful 1972 British tour made a round of folk clubs and small theatres, thereby reinforcing a growing popular appeal (certainly much more effectively than if he had remained on the jazz circuit). The Corby date is dominated by a superb Gershwin medley that shows how thoroughly Stéphane was taken up by the American's Ur-jazz chords and bouncing tunes. Disley was a loyal servant but here he and the group rarely get a meaningful look-in, seemingly happy to lean back and let the master take the spotlight and the plaudits. It's a happier gig than the earlier one, and better recorded as well.

*** Live In Dublin, Ohio

Starburst 1014 *Grappelli; Phil Woods (as); Marc Fosset (g); John Burr (b); Louie Bellson (d).* n.d.

A most unexpected line-up, but a thoroughly entertaining set, and interesting to hear Stéphane in the company of men like Bellson and Woods, who were on hand to guest on this otherwise fairly predictable date. The violinist manages to dominate even these two quite formidable personalities. Woods isn't in the greatest form and Bellson has to rein himself in quite a bit to fit the style of the music. None of the tracks is very long, though there is an extended version of 'Caravan' that even uncommitted listeners will find impressive.

*** Jazz In Paris: Plays Cole Porter

Emarcy 014 061 2 *Grappelli; Marc Hemmeler, Maurice Vander (p); Eddy Louiss (org); Guy Pedersen, Luigi Trussardi (b); Daniel Humair (d).* 5/75, 2/76.

Like Porter himself, Grappelli managed to balance a surface amiability with an iron will and a volcanic temperament. Some of the nastiness and amoral chill of these songs comes across on this set. That's despite the best efforts of a band who seem keen to make it as happy an occasion as possible. Hemmeler had been working with Grappelli off and on for a while and was thoroughly in tune with him, but even he seems to miss the cue on occasions. Louiss and Vander do a good job as well, though it's still odd to hear Stéphane working with keyboard players rather than guitarists. 'I've Got You Under My Skin', from the May 1975 date with Hemmeler, Louiss, Trussardi and Humair is an epic, one of the best things in Stéphane's capacious '70s catalogue.

*** Live At Carnegie Hall / June Night

Collectables 6658 *Grappelli; Diz Disley, John Etheridge (g); Brian Torff (b).* 4/78.

Originally on Sony, this has been picked up by Collectables, who've so far been very restrained where Grappelli is concerned. Disley and Etheridge gave him a very mellow but still propulsive accompaniment and Stéphane sounds in very good form for this blue-chip gig. The other album is by fellow-fiddler Svend Asmussen, and if you're at all interested in other aspects of jazz violin this might be a worthwhile purchase, given that Sony show no sign of restoring the disc to catalogue.

*** London Meeting

Black & Blue 852 *Grappelli; Sir Roland Hanna, Hank Jones (p); Bucky Pizzarelli (g); George Duvivier, Jimmy Woode (b); Alan Dawson, Oliver Jackson (d).* 7/78, 7/79.

*** Sweet Chorus

Black & Blue 900 *As above.* n.d.

The main event here is Grappelli's London encounter with Hank Jones, as elegant a piano accompanist as he ever found, and one of the most challenging as well. It's interesting to hear how Jones cranks up the speed of his delivery to suit Grappelli's normal onrush, building up sixteenth and thirty-second notes in places where you'd normally expect him to play much more spaciously. The other material is good as well, and the second disc fills out the Hanna session quite convincingly, but it's Stéphane and Hank who carry the day here and fully merit their joint billing.

***(*) Young Django

MPS 815672 *Grappelli; Philip Catherine, Larry Coryell (g); Niels-Henning Orsted Pedersen (b).* 1/79.

This is such a gift of a pairing that it's almost a surprise it works so well. Coryell is mannered and rather pretentious in places, but Catherine has this repertoire in his bloodstream and responds to the situation with alacrity, purring beautiful streams of notes and soft, chiming chords. The recording is very good indeed, but it might have been better expended on a slightly more adventurous programme of material. This one suffers slightly from obviousness.

*** Duet

Black & Blue 916 *Grappelli; Bucky Pizzarelli (g).* 7/79.

Pizzarelli was one of Stéphane's most loyal accompanists, able to do what Martin Taylor did later and create some inventive space for himself round the violin without attempting to 'do a Django'. There are lots of alternate takes on this reissue, and yes, they're all very different and inventive, but it would require a devoted Grappelli fan to wade through this more than once in a while. If you have the old Ahead LP (in which case, congratulations), stick to that.

CORE COLLECTION

**** Tivoli Gardens, Copenhagen, Denmark

Original Jazz Classics OJC 441 *Grappelli; Joe Pass (g); Niels-Henning Orsted Pedersen (b).* 7/79.

A superb set, marred only slightly by variable sound. Grappelli's interpretations of 'Paper Moon', 'I Can't Get Started', 'I'll Remember April', 'Crazy Rhythm', 'How Deep Is The Ocean?', 'Let's Fall In Love', 'I Get A Kick Out Of You' reaffirm his genius as an improviser and also his ability to counter slightly saccharine themes with the right hint of tartness. Pass, who occasionally errs on the side of sweetness, plays beautifully, and NHOP is, as always, both monumental and delicate.

***(*) Happy Reunion

Owl 013 430 2 *Grappelli; Martial Solal (p).* 2/80.

Two of the most individual musicians France and her colonies ever produced, united in a set of gracefully intelligent improvisations. They kick off with a brisk, skittish reading of 'Shine' before immediately dropping the pace for Solal's 'Valsitude', where Stéphane executes skater's twirls above the piano's suspended chords. 'Sing For Your Supper' is almost cute, or would be if it weren't for Martial's out-of-tempo accompaniment, almost ignoring what the violinist is doing. 'God Bless The Child' is suitably emotional. That's the way it goes – slow after fast, sad after happy – and that in a sense is the only problem with the set, it seems too schematic in its expressive calendar. We'd reprogramme it, though of course you can do that very readily at home.

***(*) Vintage Grappelli

Concord CCD 4977 2CD *Grappelli; John Etheridge, Mike Gari, Martin Taylor (g); Jack Sewing (b).* 9/80, 7/81.

Taylor has been Grappelli's most sympathetic latter-day collaborator, and they complement each other near-perfectly on these live sets, originally separately issued in 1981 as *At The Winery* and *Vintage 1981*. Taylor's amplified sound adds a little sting to Grappelli's playing, which is always more robust live than in an acoustically 'dead' and feedback-free studio situation. Better known as a jazz-rock player in one of the many later versions of the protean Soft Machine, Etheridge nevertheless fits in well with Grappelli's conception on *At The Winery*, though he is a player whose instincts seem closer to rock and blues than to classic swing. We are not clear whether the single albums have been discontinued although there is some sign that at least the first is still available.

*** Live In San Francisco

Storyville 8297 *Grappelli; Diz Disley, Martin Taylor (g); Dave Grisman, Mike Marshall (mand); Darol Anger (vn); Jack Sewing, Rob Wasserman (b).* 82.

**(*) Live

Warner Brothers 3550 *Grappelli; David Grisman, Tiny Moore (mand); Mike Marshall (g, mand); Mark O'Connor (g, vn); Rob Wasserman (b).* 82.

Previously issued in part on LP, the San Francisco date is a fairly standard Grappelli live set. Taylor is now an integral part of the set-up and already showing Disley how it's possible to be responsive and individually creative at the same time. Stéphane takes his turn at the piano and the basic group is joined by the two mandolinists (horrible noise), Anger and Wasserman, for a final blast that most listeners could do without. And as if that wasn't enough, Grappelli and Grisman headed another mandolin-heavy live date on Warners. Dave is a brilliant exponent of a kind of Americana that you'll either love or hate. The folksy jangle of the mandolin is not one that has established much of a place in jazz, though there are exponents. This one has to be down to personal taste and prejudice.

*** Live At The Cambridge Folk Festival: The BBC Sessions

Varese 061059 *Grappelli; Diz Disley, Marc Fosset, Martin Taylor (g); Patrice Caratini, Dave Etheridge (b).* 83, 73.

Apparently only rediscovered rather recently, this valuable set consists mainly of a group performance from 1983 with Martin Taylor on guitar. The rest comes from a decade earlier and is at best not much more than a filler, especially given the fact that the tape runs out during 'I Can't Give You Anything But Love'.

The sound from the Cambridge event is pretty good. Taylor is well recorded, though there are a few glitches in the registration of Stéphane, which may be why these tapes have not surfaced before now. Oddly, the label misidentifies Django's 'Are You In The Mood?' as the quite different and unrelated 'I'm In The Mood For Love'. Stéphane announces the song to the audience, so it must be that an over-zealous producer decided to overrule the violinist; worrying, since he obviously didn't listen too hard to what follows. The songs are mostly very brief and taken at a brisk and sometimes hurried tempo. 'Them There Eyes' and 'Honeysuckle Rose' are excellent, but it's Taylor's deft work on the opening 'Cheek To Cheek' and 'Love For Sale' (the most extended track) that really catches the ear.

*** One On One

Milestone M 9181 *Grappelli; McCoy Tyner (p).* 4/90.

The outwardly improbable duo with McCoy Tyner works astonishingly well, including Coltrane's 'Mr P.C.' and the Coltrane-associated 'I Want To Talk About You', alongside more familiar repertoire like 'I Got Rhythm' and 'St Louis Blues'. Ever the romantic stylist, Tyner plays with impeccable taste, never losing contact with the basic structure of a tune. Recommended.

***(*) Stéphane Grappelli: 1992 Live

Birdology FDM 370062 *Grappelli; Philip Catherine, Marc Fosset (g); Niels-Henning Orsted Pedersen (b).* 3/92.

And so it went on, seemingly unstoppable. Grappelli's association with Catherine became, remarkably, of longer standing than that with Reinhardt and, as one might expect, their understanding is considerable. This is a joyous disc, recorded in concert at Colombes. 'Oh, Lady Be Good' has the light bounce and unaffected grace that you'd expect, but there are unprecedented depths to 'Blues For Django And Stéphane', which Catherine brought forward for the session. For a live recording, the sound is very good indeed, though there are moments when Grappelli almost sounds detuned: a tape problem? heat?

**** Reunion

Linn AKH 022 *Grappelli; Martin Taylor (g).* 1/93.

One of the happiest new partnerships of more recent years was with the brilliant young British guitarist Taylor, whose solo career was taking off at the time of this utterly enjoyable record. It has the relaxed feel of something put down between lunch and dinner, but there is a steely precision behind the guitarist's relaxed mien and Grappelli is, of course, no pushover. 'Drop

Me Off At Harlem' and 'La Dame Du Lac' are the most taxing workouts, but 'Paper Moon' takes the biscuit for sheer charm, if charm is indeed awarded with biscuits.

★★(★) Live

Justin Time 8469 *Grappelli; Bucky Pizzarelli (g); Jon Burr (b).* 94.

Given how many live sets there are around, from this period and earlier, this is a disappointing issue, largely because the sound is so uninviting and boxy. Whether Stéphane was on auto-pilot in his later years or still using that steel-trap mind to its fullest extent is difficult to gauge. Some of the cuts – like the opening 'All God's Chillun ...' – are very fine indeed; others never quite reach take-off.

★★★★ Flamingo

Dreyfus FDM 36580 *Grappelli; Michel Petrucciani (p); George Mraz (b); Roy Haynes (d).* 6/95.

Who would ever have expected to hear Grappelli in company like this? If at first glance it seems a startling engagement, it is immediately clear that these are players ideally suited to his light, swinging approach. Haynes has the most delicate touch of all the bebop drummers and in recent years has shown how much he responds to song-settings. Mraz almost defines modern swing bass accompaniment, adding his own counterlines under Petrucciani, who seems to be enjoying himself hugely. Rightly, for the most part they stick to standard material. 'Misty' is the closest it all comes to hokiness, but it is done with such open-hearted delight and lack of self-consciousness that it runs no very serious risks. 'I Can't Get Started' and 'I Got Rhythm' between them demonstrate a good change of pace, with Haynes and Petrucciani seeming to dictate the rhythmic course within each track, so that the former has an almost symphonic logic and structure. Very impressive indeed.

★★★ Cosmopolite Concert

Hot Club 101 *Grappeli; Marc Fosset (g); Jean-Phillipe Viret (b).* 96.

Attractive trio set. You could write the running order yourself, from 'All God's Chillun ...' to 'Oh, Lady Be Good'. Not a priority buy, but one that collectors will enjoy.

★★★ Live At The Blue Note

Telarc CD 83397 *Grappelli; Bucky Pizzarelli, John Pizzarelli (g); Jon Burr (b).* 10/95.

Two years away from the end, Grappelli was as much institution as he was musician. Or at least that's what many people thought when they went to see him. Once they *heard* him, though, any such distinction collapsed. He plays here with the same clamped-jaw concentration and 'effortless' agility he'd brought to his work for more than 50 years. The material is predictable enough: 'All God's Chillun Got Rhythm', 'I Got Rhythm', 'Nuages', and then when Bucky's son joins them on stage for the final three numbers, they indulge some fancy work on 'Lady Be Good', 'Sweet Georgia Brown' and a whole medley of well-loved standards. It's a lovely night for Grappelli collectors.

★★★(★) Celebrating Grappelli

Linn AKD 094 *Grappelli; Gerard Presencer (t, flhn); Jack Emblow (acc); John Goldie, Martin Taylor (g); Terry Gregory (b); Claire Martin (v).* 93, 96.

A posthumous tribute drawn from *Reunion* and from Martin Taylor's Spirit of Django record, *Years Apart.* As a souvenir of the guitarist's long and happy association with Grappelli, it's hard to beat: a relaxed, swinging 50 minutes that manage to seem very much shorter. Anyone who has the original albums won't find it very useful, but it's a nicely judged selection of the best of both. Grappelli's technique stands out all the more for the miracle that it was in younger company like this. There is even a moment on 'Jive At Five', not noticed by us before, when he makes a mistake and instantly turns it to advantage, an improvised mend that he converts into an embellishment. The celebration closes with 'Manoir De Mes Rêves', which seems entirely appropriate.

Lou Grassi (born 1947)

DRUMS

New Jersey drummer–bandleader with several projects in the freebop and outwards field.

★★(★) Quick Wits

CIMP 123 *Grassi; Chris Kelsey (ss); Philip Johnston (as); Joe Ruddick (bs); Dave Hofstra (b).* 8/96.

★★★ Mo' Po

CIMP 155 *Grassi; Herb Robertson (c, t); Steve Swell (tb); Perry Robinson (cl, ocarina); Wilber Morris (b).* 7/97.

★★★ Neo Neo

CIMP 201 *Grassi; Ron Horton (t); Tom Varner (tb); Tomas Ulrich (clo).* 4/99.

★★★ PoZest

CIMP 207 *Grassi; Paul Smoker (t); Steve Swell (tb); Perry Robinson (cl, oc); Marshall Allen (as); Wilber Morris (b).* 5/99.

★★★ The Joy Of Being

CIMP 227 *As above, except Joseph Jarman (as, f) replaces Allen.* 6/00.

★★★ ComPOsed

CIMP 262 *Grassi; Paul Smoker (t); Art Baron (tb, f, oc, didjeridu); Perry Robinson (cl, oc); John Tchicai (ts, bcl, f); Wilber Morris (b).* 1/02.

Grassi's various groups – Saxtet, PoBand and quartet – each play with great spirit, but the results are almost always very mixed across the course of a CD. The Saxtet of *Quick Wits* is pretty dreary for much of the way, the horns babbling in less than productive ways, and most of the pieces are too long. The PoBand fares better, and while the two sessions with respective star guests Allen and Jarman have their moments, the best of the three might be *Mo' Po.* 'Air Play' and 'Train Ride' are inventive long-form improvisations which mix well around the three-horn front-line. While we always enjoy Smoker's playing, it's a pity that Robertson moved on, since he makes the most distinctive impression here.

Allen certainly has amazing energy for a 75-year-old, but the problem with both *PoZest* and *The Joy Of Being* is the overabundance of horns. The two sextets throw out too many lines, and given CIMP's resolutely unsweetened style of production, the music can be discouragingly tiring to follow in a piece like the enormous 'Bird Symphony' (from *PoZest,* running for almost 33 minutes). The blues which follows it seems like welcome relief, but you feel that the band's merely guying the form. Jarman arrives like an honoured guest, and when he gets some space for his alto ('Airplay') his old mastery is manifest soon enough. These are powerful sets in their way, but they ask for a lot of work.

The quartet of *Neo Neo* feels subdued for much of the way, and the interesting writing receives a sometimes underbaked reading; but maybe Grassi wasn't the right drummer for this gig, since the front line of Horton and Varner works to an agenda that calls for more refined playing.

The slight reshuffle of the PoBand line-up for *ComPOsed* brings in Baron for Swell and this time the star cameo is from John Tchicai, who also contributed all of the material bar two free pieces. Tchicai's alfresco melodies and sober presence (though he is not, perhaps surprisingly, the most imposing soloist – that distinction goes to an on-form Smoker) confer a certain dignity on what still often sounds like a ragtag band. There is a certain amount of timewasting noodling on did-jeridu and ocarina, as well as more productive dialogue on the likes of 'Tidens Tand'.

Frank Gratkowski (born 1963)

ALTO SAXOPHONE, CLARINET, BASS AND CONTRABASS CLARINETS

Born in Hamburg, Gratkowski is a composer who has also explored free improvisation. He carries over his fiery saxophone approach into the clarinet family.

***** Gestalten**

Jazz Haus Musik 83 *Gratkowski; Dieter Manderscheid (b); Gerry Hemingway (d).* 95.

***** Quicksand**

Meniscus 007 *Gratkowski; George Graewe (p); Paul Lovens (d, perc).* 11/00.

Though Gratkowski has done some of his most effective work in an entirely improvised context, he is perhaps best considered a free jazz composer. The earlier of these albums places the emphasis squarely on group interplay and it is the four collective pieces – 'Dancing Derwish', 'Blazing', 'Gloaming' and 'Duck Hunt' – which stand out most strongly. Hemingway's typically detailed approach, half-way between timekeeping and a lead voice, gives the music its dynamism. By contrast, Manderscheid is less compelling but he is a strong instrumentalist who delivers interesting ideas at a steadier pace. Gratkowski's raw alto sound is reminiscent of Dolphy and, in freer sections, Peter Brötzmann as well. The group that made *Quicksand* is more obviously melodic and one striking dimension of the music here is how structured some of it appears to be. 'Second Coming' is a mournful theme that explores dissonance very carefully. One almost expects a companion piece to return from the cemetery in celebration, but that had to wait for a later occasion.

****** Kollaps**

Red Toucan 9317 *Gratkowski; Wolter Wierbos (tb); Dieter Manderscheid (b); Gerry Hemingway (d).* 5/01.

One of the best free jazz records of recent times, this is the best introduction to Gratkowski's music. 'Annaherungen' has to reappear on record a little later, a boiling, joyous idea that fizzes with thoughtful procedures and some delightfully unfettered playing. 'De Profundis' again casts the saxophonist as a grievous angel, full of lament and some bitterness. The addition of Wolter Wierbos, who has a great empathy with Hemingway in particular, was a master stroke. His full, vocalized sound is a strong foil to Gratkowski's eldritch wailing. Very strongly recommended.

*****(*) GratHovOx**

Nuscope 1012 *Gratkowski; Fred Van Hove (p); Tony Oxley (d, elec).* 11/00.

***** Arrears**

Cactus RT9320 *Gratkowski; George Graewe (p); John Lindberg (b).* 01.

Gratkowski continued to experiment with his favourite and most successful format. The radio broadcast preserved on *GratHovOx* is one of his best appearances on record. Much of the credit has to go to Oxley, whose pioneering integration of electronics is strongly but subtly in evidence here, while Van Hove is an undersung master. Where Graewe continually hints at jazz themes, even occasionally standards, Van Hove seems to fire off instant compositions at quantum speed. He also brings his accordion along and deploys it brilliantly on 'Vorspiel/Foreplay'. Gratkowski has by this period switched his loyalties very largely to the clarinets, even finding room for some of the more subterranean accents of the contrabass clarinet. On the Nuscope record his alto makes only a single appearance, on 'Tranches/Trenches'.

Abandoning percussion on *Arrears* opens up the texture somewhat and gives the music a more flowing and resonant quality, but one feels it lacks an anchor. Lindberg is also a formidable composer but the only problem with this record is that some of its most interesting moves are implicit rather than clearly stated, as if the trio were working to an obscure agenda in which the listener isn't fully complicit.

*****(*) Spectral Reflections**

Leo CDLR 374 *As for Kollaps.* 02.

Featuring the same line-up as Gratkowski's best album, this only fails to live up to its predecessor in that the element of surprise has been lost. Recorded in Cologne and very crisply recorded too, it underlines once again how close to a jazz feel Gratkowski works. 'Homage' is bright, upbeat and almost swinging, and features some extraordinary extended technique on clarinet. As before, Hemingway is a key element in the equation, driving along the faster tracks and contributing his full to the almost Webernian 'Blonk'. By this stage in his career, the saxophonist is able to work with relatively familiar materials, and 'Annaherungen' gets a fresh work-out, its third according to the suffixed number. 'Loom' is the other track worth noting, a complex ensemble chart that lurches back and forth in a manner very typical of Gratkowski's written work. He likes to explore asymmetrical structures, radical shifts of time and pulse, and complex dynamics, but does so in a way that feels organic and integral. Even at their freest, his groups never sound as if they're merely workshopping.

As a pair with *Kollaps*, this establishes the quartet as one of the most adventurous and most accomplished on the European free scene.

***** The Voice Imitator**

Balance Point Acoustics bpa 006 *Gratkowski; Damon Smith (b); Jerome Bryerton (d).* 10/02.

In 2002, Gratkowski travelled to the West Coast, not to learn surfing, but to explore the free scene there. This collaboration with a section (they deny they're a 'rhythm section') little known outside California is a splendid example of his freer work. As often, the poetic import of the album title isn't clear but the pieces included, especially the so-called 'Character Attacks', are exemplary in execution and all of them highly evocative.

Milford Graves (born 1941)

DRUMS, PERCUSSION

Along with Sunny Murray, Rashied Ali and Andrew Cyrille, New Yorker Graves was the man who recalibrated the rhythms of jazz in the avant-garde revolution. A dedicated solo performer, Graves has – partly in consequence – not recorded much under his own name.

**** Milford Graves Percussion Ensemble**
ESP 1015 *Graves; Sonny Morgan (perc).* 7/65.

A disappointing – and disappointingly brief – reissue of an oddly titled 1965 set. These are in fact percussion duos, and particularly obtuse ones. Graves and the little-known Morgan appear to compete rather than communicate and both are recorded poorly. As a curiosity, and as a historical artefact, it will win listeners, but be warned, sometimes 35 minutes can seem like an eternity.

***** Grand Unification**
Tzadik 7030 *Graves (d, perc, v solo).* 2/98.

*****(*) Stories**
Tzadik 7062 *As above.* 10/00.

Like a number of senior avant-gardists, Graves has recently been taken up by John Zorn's eclectic label. For almost the first time in a long career, the drummer can be heard clearly and with definition. The eight items on *Grand Unification* range from epic statements which combine percussion with chanting to relatively brief improvisations which all, curiously, come in at almost exactly the same duration, as if Graves had set himself a certain time-frame as a creative discipline. These are much more effective than 'Gathering', 'Decisive Moments' and 'Intuitive Transformations', which may temper nostalgia for the good old days with the feeling that the good old days might have been a tad self-indulgent.

The second Tzadik release does however climax with a half-hour perormance – 'Evolving Pathways' – which is one of the most powerful statements the drummer has yet to make on record. Here, and throughout this fine record, he seems beyond genre, working in an area that transcends jazz percussion. Again, he chants, murmurs spells and moves between a bewildering array of percussion instruments. The rest of the record is very good and very well recorded again, but it is that last track (almost as long as the whole of the tooth-grindingly dull ESP) which makes it. Graves has at last created a work the equal of his colossal talent.

Wardell Gray (1921–55)

TENOR SAXOPHONE

Gray was born in Oklahoma but grew up in Detroit, where he played in a variety of local groups. His professional breakthrough was with Earl Hines, but he is best remembered for an exhilarating two-tenor project with Dexter Gordon, The Chase. Like Lester Young and Don Byas, Gray maintained a foot in a pre-bop idiom and favoured a loose, eloquent style with few jagged edges. He died young, some believe at the hands of drug dealers to whom he was in debt. This is now questioned.

****(*) Way Out Wardell**
Boplicity CDBOP 014 *Gray; Ernie Royal, Howard McGhee (t); Vic Dickenson (tb); Vido Musso (ts); Erroll Garner, Arnold Ross (p); Red Callender, Harry Babasin (b); Irving Ashby, Barney Kessel (g); Jackie Mills, Don Lamond (d).* 48.

****** Memorial: Volume 1**
Original Jazz Classics OJC 050 *Gray; Frank Morgan (as); Sonny Clark, Al Haig, Phil Hill (p); Teddy Charles (vib); Dick Nivison, Tommy Potter, Johnny Richardson (b); Roy Haynes, Lawrence Marable, Art Mardigan (d).* 11/49, 4/50, 2/53.

****** Memorial: Volume 2**
Original Jazz Classics OJC 051 *Gray; Art Farmer, Clark Terry (t); Sonny Criss (as); Dexter Gordon (ts); Jimmy Bunn, Hampton Hawes (p); Harper Crosby, Billy Hadnott (b); Lawrence Marable, Chuck Thompson (d); Robert Collier (perc).* 8/50, 1/52.

Like his friend and collaborator, Dexter Gordon, Wardell Gray often had to look to Europe for recognition. His first recordings, made just after the war, were not released in the United States. There were not to be very many more, for Gray died in rather mysterious circumstances in 1955, three months after Charlie Parker. The shadow cast by Bird's passing largely shrouded Gray's no less untimely departure. Unlike Gordon, Gray was less than wholly convinced by orthodox bebop, and he continued to explore the swing style of bop's immediate ancestor, Lester Young.

The jams on *Way Out Wardell* were originally issued as a Crown LP. They're interesting but scarcely overwhelming. Gray is obviously in difficulties here and there, though the reason for this isn't clear. Several of his solo choruses resort to exactly identical ideas and/or mechanical inversions of them. He was capable of very much more.

The two-volume *Memorial* remains the best representation of his gifts. The earliest of the sessions is a quartet consisting of Haig, Potter and Haynes, and it includes 'Twisted', a wry blues since covered and vocalized by Annie Ross and, much later, by Joni Mitchell. Ross's version has tended to overshadow the original, which is a perfect place to gauge Gray's Prez-influenced style and his softly angular approach to the basic changes. The CDs include some alternative takes that are frankly pretty redundant both interpretatively and acoustically. Too often Gray tries to reduplicate what he feels are successful ideas rather than wiping the slate clean and trying again from scratch. The best of the rest is a 1952 session with Hawes and Farmer, who do interesting things with 'Farmer's Market' and that Parker shibboleth, 'Lover Man'. The second volume is also notable for the first recorded performances by Frank Morgan, who copied not just Bird's articulation but also some of his offstage habits and found himself in San Quentin for his pains.

****** Wardell Gray Properbox**
Properbox 55 4CD *As for selections above; some additional personnel.* 46–52.

*****(*) Complete Sunset And New Jazz Masters**
Jazz Factory 22810 *Similar to above.* 46–50.

*** **Wardell Gray, 1946–1950**
Classics *Similar to above.* 46–50.

The Wardell Gray discography took a giant leap forward with the issue of these three sets. The question is: which one to go for? Obviously, the completist and the ardent fan will want to go for the exhaustive Properbox, nicely packaged with an informative booklet and full session details, but there is much to recommend the Jazz Factory compilation (not least the price) and anyone who is assembling an inexpensive shelfload of Classics will want the Gray volume as well. The Properbox volumes – *Blue Lou, The Chase, Twisted* and *Farmer's Market* – seem also to be available singly, though there's no reason not to go the whole hog. One of the best parts of the set comes on disc two with a private recording of a session in Portland Oregon from October 1947 with the Sonny Criss group, but there's good music to be had throughout and the sound is very respectable, certainly better than the mushy Classics and more faithful than Jazz Factory's rather brittle remastering.

*** **Live At The Haig 1952**
Fresh Sound FSR CD 157 *Gray; Art Farmer (t); Hampton Hawes, Amos Trice (p); Howard Roberts (g); Joe Mondragon (b); Shelly Manne (d).* 9/52.

He was no less fortunate in having the gloriously expressive Hampton Hawes on all but one track of this fine 1952 date (one Amos Trice, better known for his work with Harold Land, plays on 'Lady Bird'). Gray had been working with Count Basie before these sessions and his conception is significantly pared down, even from the uncluttered approach of *One For Prez.* There is, though, a creeping weariness and inwardness in the voice, sadly reminiscent of Young's own rather paranoid decline, and it's left to Hawes and a pre-flugelhorn Art Farmer to keep spirits up. The mix of styles is just about right and the sound perfectly respectable for material five decades old.

Bennie Green (1923–77)

TROMBONE

A Chicagoan, Green worked with Earl Hines in the '40s and '50s, then led hard-bop groups in the '50s and early '60s. His final years were spent in hotel bands.

*** **Blows His Horn**
Original Jazz Classics OJC 1728 *Green; Charlie Rouse (ts); Cliff Smalls (p); Paul Chambers (b); Osie Johnson (d); Candido (perc).* 6–9/55.

(*) **Walking Down
Original Jazz Classics OJC 1752 *Green; Eric Dixon (ts); Lloyd Mayers (p); Sonny Wellesley (b); Bill English (d).* 6/56.

*** **Bennie Green With Art Farmer**
Original Jazz Classics OJC 1800-2 *Green; Art Farmer (t); Cliff Smalls (p); Addison Farmer (b); Philly Joe Jones (d).* 4/56.

*** **The Swingin'est**
Collectables 7171 *Green; Nat Adderley (t); Gene Ammons, Frank Foster (ts); Frank Wess (ts, f); Tommy Flanagan (p); Eddie Jones (b); Albert 'Tootie' Heath (d).* 60.

*** **Bennie Green**
Time 1046 *Green; Jimmy Forrest (ts); Sonny Clark (p); George Tucker (b); Al Dreares (d); Joe Gorgas (perc).* 9/60.

*** **Glidin' Along**
Original Jazz Classics OJC 1869-2 *Green; Johnny Griffin (ts); Junior Mance (p); Paul Chambers (b); Larry Gales, Ben Riley (d).* 3/61.

*** **Go Ahead And Blow!**
Ocium 23 *Green; Norman Faye (t); Eddie 'Lockjaw' Davis, Coleman Hawkins, Budd Johnson, Big Nick Nicholas, Billy Root (ts); Frank Wess (ts, f); Charlie Ventura (ts, bs); Cecil Payne, Ben Ventura, Rudy Williams (bs); Ted Brannon, Al Haig, Ike Isaacs, Jimmy Jones, John Malachi, Cliff Smalls (p); Roy Kral (p, v); John Collins (g); Nelson Boyd, Chubby Jackson, Kenny O'Brien, Tommy Potter (b); Art Blakey, Roy Haynes, Osie Johnson, Ed Shaughnessy, Shadow Wilson (d); Candido Camero (perc); Jackie Cain (v).* 10/48–4/54.

While these are good records, they rate some way below the discs Green made for Blue Note in 1958–9 (*Soul Stirrin'* has been available briefly as a Blue Note Connoisseur edition: 859381-2). Albums for Bethlehem and Jazzland, all from the early '60s, would also be welcome in reissue form, though *Glidin' Along* has reappeared: a good-natured blow with Griffin, with a set of scrappy originals betraying the lack of preparation.

The Swingin'est, a loose jam with Ammons and two other horns is pleasant but by no means earth-shaking, which means that the alternate takes, included as 'bonus' tracks, are actually more of a liability. The Time has had a chequered history, on that label and Bainbridge. It's a rollicking set, with quite a strong emphasis on Forrest's soulful tenor.

Although he was one of the first trombonists to fraternize with bop – as a teenager, he was in the Earl Hines orchestra that included Parker and Gillespie – Green's personal allegiance remained with a less demanding approach. The 1955 session highlights his singing tone and straightforward phrasing on attractive versions of 'Travellin' Light' and 'Body And Soul'. The band is a congenial one and Rouse's solos are an ounce more interesting than the leader's. *Walking Down* features a less impressive group and as a result is slightly less interesting, though Green is again in swinging form. Best of the four is the edition of the Prestige session which matched Green with Art Farmer, whose affable and calmly intense playing is a piquant complement to the somewhat more boisterous leader: compare their solos on Farmer's 'Skycoach', the trombonist a louche performer.

The material on *Go Ahead And Blow!* was made with Charlie Ventura and with his own septet. It's a mixed bag of tracks, of which the opening 'Euphoria' and 'Platinum', the latter with Coleman Hawkins's group, are outstanding. Ocium are newcomers to the scene, specializing in enhanced CDs with archive images. While Green seems an unlikely priority for this treatment, it's a welcome inclusion. As his decline in later years suggests, Bennie was never forceful enough, either as a soloist or as a business manager, really to make it in the business. His current standing and the present discography just about has it right.

Benny Green (born 1965)

PIANO

Early experience with Betty Carter set this skilful pianist on his way. Though only in his late 30s, he is something of a veteran of the contemporary scene, having cut a raft of albums for Blue

Note in particular. His style is relatively conservative – he professes to want to entertain audiences with the most swinging music he can – and he comes from a school that counts Horace Silver, Wynton Kelly and other midstream boppers among its influences, though Oscar Peterson is his main man.

***** Prelude**

Criss Cross 1036 *Green; Terence Blanchard (t); Javon Jackson (ts); Peter Washington (b); Tony Reedus (d).* 2/88

***** In This Direction**

Criss Cross 1038 *Green; Buster Williams (b); Lewis Nash (d).* 12/88–1/89.

Green came to prominence as pianist with Betty Carter's group, and his mastery of bebop piano – particularly the chunky rhythms of Horace Silver – was leavened by an apparent interest in swing styles as well. Green hits the keyboard hard on up-tempo tunes, and has a preference for beefy chords and straightahead swing. These albums for Criss Cross feature a lot of piano, but there's nothing particularly outstanding about them. The quintet date sounds too much like a mere blowing session for any of the players to make a distinctive mark, and the trio set seems hastily prepared, although the rhythm section lends impressive support.

*****(*) Kaleidoscope**

Blue Note 852037-2 *Green; Stanley Turrentine (ts); Antonio Hart (as); Russell Malone (g); Ron Carter (b); Lewis Nash (d).* 6/96.

*****(*) These Are Soulful Days**

Blue Note 499527-2 *Green; Russell Malone (g); Christian McBride (b).* 1/99.

With a lot of records behind him, some might be tempted to take Green for granted, and his departure from Blue Note (and its culling of much of his back-catalogue) seems a pity since his two final albums were surely his best to this point. *Kaleidoscope* features eight Green originals and there's not a duff one among them. 'Patience' and 'You're My Melody' are charming ballads, transparently beautiful and played with great feeling, while 'My Girl Bill' and 'The Sexy Mexy' take a new look at Green's penchant for funky piano; underlined by Malone's attentive guitar and shrewdly covered by the rhythm section, these are insidious rather than bumptious. Since Nash sits out on three tracks, Green is placed under a softer light at crucial moments, and it suits him. His improvisations throughout are some of his best work. The only slight letdown lies in the contributions of Hart and Turrentine; their various appearances are uneventful enough to make one wonder why they were booked.

These Are Soulful Days is as ferociously swinging as ever, but without a drummer and, with the snapping rhythms of both Malone and McBride wiring the forward momentum, Green sounds at his most carefree and daring. The three men are caught up in a whirl of multi-levelled lines on tracks such as 'Virgo', but the cooling-off that takes place on Elmo Hope's 'Bellarosa' (a beautiful choice) and Cal Massey's title-piece is just as absorbing. The eight tunes are all connoisseur-choices from the Blue Note book, and the only regret must be that there wasn't room for one of Benny's own hits; he's come up with some great, catchy themes, after all, which is right in the BN tradition.

*****(*) Naturally**

Telarc CD-83498 *As above.* 1/00.

A label change hasn't done Green any harm. *Naturally* is mostly delightful. Though there are three solos – including a rationalization of Wayne Shorter's often misbegotten 'Lester Left Town' – the trio tracks are seasoned by an interplay which by now has become intuitive between these three. Carl Perkins's 'Grooveyard', taken at a considerate pace, and Benny's original 'Beg Your Parlan' are quite irresistible. Since Green has been all but anointed as principal heir to Oscar Peterson's legacy, the mantle of jazz communicator, where a joyfulness predominates more than any sense of striving, fits him well.

***** Green's Blues**

Telarc CD-83539 *Green (p solo).* 1/01.

Benny's such a master of the trio idiom that to find him by himself for a whole album brings on the feeling that something's missing. As if to compensate, there's a degree of overplaying, and the record works best a few tracks at a time. But Green remains a pleasure to hear.

****** Jazz At The Bistro**

Telarc CD-83560 *Green; Russell Malone (g).* 6/02.

Two guys with major-label associations behind them, nothing to prove, here on a gig at a St Louis club. It helps that they're both natural showmen, jazz entertainers and communicators. And nobody expects a classic from a piano/guitar duo (huh?) on some small-time live gig. So they settle down and create it anyway: good tunes from jazz composers (Benny Carter, Paul Chambers, Cannonball Adderley), a bit of pop ('How Deep Is Your Love'). Chopsmanship is here, but not too much, and they know when to be funny, and are secure in the knowledge that their audience – that's us, jazz fans – will get the joke, and laugh along with them. In its modest way, this is a classic set for the new century, even as it dwells in and celebrates values which have succoured jazz for decades.

Bunky Green (born 1935)

ALTO SAXOPHONE

His native Milwaukee isn't a famous jazz town but Green's relative invisibility is better explained by a career in jazz education. A thoughtful and often adventurous player, working both outside and inside, he has had a strong impact on younger-generation saxophonists.

***** My Baby (Step High)**

Collectables 7143 *Green; Donald Byrd (t); Jimmy Heath (ts); Wynton Kelly (p); Larry Ridley (b); Jimmy Cobb (d).* 60.

Green's recorded output was never very large, but was certainly more than recent availability might have suggested. This valuable reissue, previously on Vee-Jay and intermittently on Fresh Sound as well, was originally released as *Step High* and without Wynton Kelly's name as co-leader. It may have seemed a good marketing decision to the Collectables people but this is unmistakably Green's date. His alto sound is fluid but hard-edged, somewhere between Eric Dolphy and Jimmy Lyons and his attack places him somewhere between the soul-jazz honkers and the avant-garde, which may be why he has such a betwixt-and-between reputation.

His originals here, 'Counterpunch' and 'Step High', are both strong bop ideas with a lot of harmonic detail and plenty of scope for blowing right through the band. Kelly is his usual bluesy self, but Byrd has some revelatory moments, not least on the ballad 'Don't Blame Me', which is by far the longest cut. Listening to Green in this company makes it obvious why he's had such an impact on some of the younger players, particularly the M-Base crowd, but it also makes you wonder why he still gets the 'Who he?' reaction from the majority of modern jazz fans.

***** Transformations**

Universe 62 *Green; Jeff Bova (syn); Carl Lynch (g); Wilbur Bascomb (b); Jimmy Johnson (d); Al Chalk (perc).* 11/76.

It had been almost a decade since Green was last in the studio. The market had moved on a bit and this set of pop songs and originals, the first of Green's dates for Vanguard, is very much a document of its times. The leader is at his best on originals like 'The Lady From Ancona', but he makes a decent fist of the pop material as well, sounding oddly like Sonny Criss on some of his chart-aware sessions. The band is sublimely anonymous, apart from the excellent Johnson. A pity that the later Vanguards have still to see light of day.

*****(*) Healing The Pain**

Delos 4020 *Green; Billy Childs (p); Art Davis (b); Ralph Penland (d).* 89.

Remarkable that Green's three surviving albums should come from three different decades. This is the best of all, and the album that confirms his importance as a model for the younger generation. The tone is darker and more burnished than of yore, though an occasional switch to soprano restores the sharp, bluesy quality heard on earlier discs. Again, much of the material is original, the tone decidedly sombre. There is no track called 'Healing The Pain', but Bunky does seem to be working out some mournful personal agenda. He starts with a fine interpretation of 'The Thrill Is Gone' and works through a programme that includes titles like 'Who Can I Turn To', 'Wild Life' and 'Goodbye', interspersed with a beautiful 'Love Theme' that has some of the same menace as the love theme from *The Godfather*. This time out, he has a more subtle and accommodating band than for some records and the difference is evident in the rhythm, which is both relaxed and fraught with possibility. A remarkable record and an excellent place to make belated acquaintance.

Grant Green (1931–79)

GUITAR

Deeply rooted in the blues, St Louis-born Green brought a devastating simplicity to the basic guitar–organ trio. He spent much of his career, and still is in hindsight, in the shadow of Wes Montgomery, but he is an altogether different player; less subtle harmonically, he had the ability to drive a melody line and shape a solo as if he were telling a quietly urgent solo. His legacy is complex and arguably more far-reaching than Wes's.

***** Grant's First Stand**

Blue Note 21959 *Green; Baby Face Willette (org); Ben Dixon (d).* 1/61.

****(*) Reaching Out**

1201 Music 9026 *Green; Frank Haynes (ts); Billy Gardner (p); Ben Tucker (b); Dave Bailey (d).* 3/61.

***** Green Street**

Blue Note 40032 *As above, except omit Haynes and Gardner.* 61.

***** Sunday Mornin'**

Blue Note 52434 *Green; Kenny Drew (p); Ben Tucker (b); Ben Dixon (d).* 7/61.

He began, as he was to end in the post-detox '70s, chugging out a bland hybrid of funk and jazz. Yet Green was to be an influential figure, helping to pioneer what was soon to be the familiar guitar, organ, drums sound that later would excite the acid-jazz generation. His has been an impressive posthumous comeback. At the end of his life, and for a time thereafter, Green was consigned to that ironic fate which awaits certain kinds of poet: the 'anthology artist'. It was perfectly possible to assemble a reasonable amount of his work on CD, but only if you were prepared to fork out for an array of themed compilations, usually with some permutation of *Cool*, *Blue* and *Funk* in the title. There was an obvious pun on Green's name, of course, and it usefully conveyed how fresh-voiced he could sound, with his linear approach (derived from saxophone players) and his almost total disregard for chromatic harmony – qualities and choices which in the right company could make a Green tune seem as new and uncomplicated as a spring shoot. The first Blue Note has been a considerable rarity but is now available on CD. Kicking off with 'Miss Ann's Tempo', an original composition, Grant impresses as a bright, uncomplicated player who has delved deeply into the tradition without being in thrall to any one voice. The blues dominate throughout.

Reaching Out is a bit of an oddity and certainly no more than a footnote to the Grant Green story. It was originally available on Black Lion and is only interesting for a brief insight into the forgotten Frank Haynes, a strong-voiced tenor who never seemed to make it to the A-list. The extra takes of 'Our Miss Brooks' and 'One For Elena' are just repetitive. Not a priority purchase.

Nor is *Green Street*, which first came out in 1995 and comes now with a couple of (pretty uninspiring) bonus tracks. Interesting all the same to hear Green in a trio, unsupported by organ or by a second front-line instrument. The originals, 'No. 1 Green St', 'Green With Envy' and 'Grant's Dimensions', are generic and slightly dull with it, though there are nice interpretations of 'Alone Together' and 'Round About Midnight' which lift the pace a little.

Long out of print was *Sunday Mornin'*, which unusually had Green working with a piano player. As ever, the guitarist favours clean-picked single-note runs, fleet and expressive but somehow missing a dimension which, fortunately, Drew is on hand to supply. 'God Bless The Child' and 'So What' are exceptional performances that would have an influence on a whole generation of soul-jazz and later acid-jazz performers.

*****(*) Standards**

Blue Note 21284 *Green; Wilbur Ware (b); Al Harewood (d).* 8/61.

Not technically perfect – there is a curious phrasing on Harewood's cymbals on a couple of tracks – but a most valuable release, helping to bring up to date some more Green material not previously available in the Occident. By the standards of the time, these are complex readings of familiar material. 'I'll Remember April' is a typical call-and-response solo, but entirely unpredictable in cast. Green had on occasion expressed a special preference for the uncluttered sound of a guitar, bass, drums trio, rather than one with organ, and one sees what he means here. The pace is light, fast and dancing, and Ware's solos are models of invention. A pity about anomalies in the sound, which seem to have arisen when the tapes were remastered in 1980. Save for the most fastidious of listeners, these won't diminish the pleasure.

*** Grantstand

Blue Note 46430 *Green; Yusef Lateef (ts, f); Jack McDuff (org); Al Harewood (d).* 8/61.

**** Born To Be Blue

Blue Note 84432 *Green; Ike Quebec (ts); Sonny Clark (p); Sam Jones (b); Louis Hayes (d).* 12/61, 3/62.

Grantstand established the sound and the approach that was to make Green – and Blue Note – a good deal of money over the next few years, to the dubious benefit of the former, who had narcotic problems for some time as a result of both fame and career pressure. The combination of Green's smooth lines, Lateef's simple but inventive tenor and delicate flute tone, and McDuff's swirling lines and choked-off probings is very effective indeed, even if the balance is sometimes off, even on CD. 'Old Folks' and 'My Funny Valentine' give the horn-man lots to do, and he responds with some of the best recorded playing from this stage in his career.

We've always liked *Born To Be Blue* best of all the Blue Notes, along with the splendid *Idle Moments* and *Street Of Dreams*. Quebec, who was the label's musical director at the time, is still not widely admired, but he's on cracking form here, and his pitch and phrasing on 'Someday My Prince Will Come' should be a lesson to all young jazz players. Green has, for us, his finest hour, rippling through 'My One And Only Love' and 'If I Should Love You' with a ruggedness of emotion that goes hand in hand with the simplicity of diction. Not a single note is wasted. 'Count Every Star' actually comes from an earlier session, but it too is judged to perfection, toned down just as it threatens to get schmaltzy. Sonny Clark, another Blue Note signing who has only recently been rediscovered and reassessed, is also in sparkling form, with just enough light and shade to temper his colleagues' bluff romanticism.

CORE COLLECTION

**** The Complete Quartets With Sonny Clark

Blue Note 571924 2CD *Green; Sonny Clark (p); Sam Jones (b); Art Blakey, Louis Hayes (d).* 12/61, 1/62.

The first five items on disc one were available for a time as *Nigeria*, a re-reversal of the Sonny Rollins staple, 'Airegin', which kicked off the set. Everything else on this valuable reintroduction has been issued previously only in Japan. Blue Note completists will know the material from *Gooden's Corner* and *Oleo*. There are alternative takes of both Rollins tunes (the rejected 'Oleo' had already been heard on a 1989 Mosaic box), a superb pre-Coltrane interpretation of 'My Favorite Things', an exquisite 'Moon River', and an equally beautiful 'Nancy (With The Laughing Face)'. If all this suggests sessions heavy on lyricism rather than swinging pace, this is partly true. The presence of the long-neglected, now canonized Clark guarantees that the tempo never slackens, even on the gentlest ballads, and that the harmonic configuration is always adventurous. Hayes is the drummer on all the 1962 cuts, though Blakey's work on *Nigeria* is inventive first to last. The key performance of the set is a ten-minute workout on 'It Ain't Necessarily So', which is completely reworked melodically and marked out by Green's long winding phrases which cut across Blakey's 12/8 pattern. A remarkable performance, and a highly valuable addition to the Green canon.

*** The Latin Bit

Blue Note 37645 *Green; Ike Quebec (ts); Johnny Acea (p); Wendell Marshall (b); Willie Bobo (d); Carlos Patato Valdes (perc); Garvin Maseaux (shekere).* 4 & 9/62.

Once Blue Note recognized that they were dealing with a marketable talent, there was increasing pressure on Green to make themed records. This is the 'south of the border' session. Quebec is featured only on the two tracks recorded in September 1962, both of them pretty dispensable, as unfortunately is most of the record. Despite Green's fleet invention, there is a plodding obviousness to much of the setting. Acea was probably fine as a straight Latin player, but he understands too little of the subtler side of Green to be a genuinely creative partner.

***(*) Feelin' The Spirit

Blue Note 84682 *Green; Herbie Hancock (p); Butch Warren (b); Billy Higgins (d); Garvin Maseaux (tamb).* 12/62.

Blue Note A&R thought it would be a good idea to have Green record an album of gospel tunes. Nobody else at this juncture would have thought it a winning idea, but what emerges is a superbly balanced and movingly performed set that never troubles to up or change the pace, but just keeps on bearing soulful witness. 'Just A Closer Walk With Thee' sounds momentarily as if it might break into a closer jogtrot, and 'Go Down Moses' – or 'Go *Down!* Moses' – pushes the ecstatic button a little too firmly. However, these are excellent performances and Herbie seems to be enjoying himself, sounding a little like a mischievous choirboy with flattened-down hair who's going to add some rolls and scats to every hymn.

**(*) Am I Blue?

Blue Note 35564 *Green; Johnny Coles (t); Joe Henderson (ts); John Patton (org); Ben Dixon (d).* 5/63.

This is one of Grant's duller albums and the reissue doesn't contain any surprises. Henderson is obviously the main draw and his solos always contain something of interest. Perhaps aware of that, Green seems to be musing on something else, not quite engaged with the material, except perhaps on 'Take These Chains From My Heart', which he wakens to halfway through and produces a very thoughtful statement. There's a nearly quarter-hour version of 'For All We Know' at the end, but no additional tracks, so no opportunity for a major rethink.

*** Blues For Lou

Blue Note 21438 *Green; John Patton (org); Ben Dixon (d).* 63.

This trio was one of Green's most durable associations. Issued for the first time in 1999 as part of Blue Note's bandwagon-jumping rare groove/acid-jazz programme, *Blues For Lou* is definitive organ–guitar jazz. Patton is strictly no-nonsense and stamps his personality on the album right from the start, a swirling, voluptuous reading of 'Surrey With The Fringe On Top'. Patton's own composition, 'Big John', isn't merely an organ feature. It also includes one of Green's most effective solos, not to be topped until the trio of tracks at the end of the album which represent his most direct but also most subtle approach to the blues. Dixon is something of a bystander and occasionally overcompensates with unnecessary power, but as a group it hangs together very well and this is a welcome reappearance.

**** Idle Moments

Blue Note 99003 *Green; Joe Henderson (ts); Bobby Hutcherson (vib); Duke Pearson (p); Bob Cranshaw (b); Al Harewood (d).* 11/63.

Strange how much happened in America in November 1963. This vies with *Born To Be Blue* as Green's finest session. Perhaps the former is more securely *his* date. This one featured three other men – Henderson, Hutcherson and Pearson – who were also trying to make a mark of one sort or another at Blue Note, and Green is sometimes eclipsed by the vibist. He holds his own on John Lewis's 'Django' and turns the song around with a lovely, uncomplicated solo. Henderson is rather remote in the mix, and one can see why Rudy van Gelder might have wanted him held back a notch. A lighter-voiced reed player would have been better sonically, but Joe's intelligence and grave humour would have been missed.

*** Matador

Blue Note 78444 *Green; McCoy Tyner (p); Bob Cranshaw (b); Elvin Jones (d).* 5/64.

*** Solid

Blue Note 33580 *As above, except add James Spaulding (ss, as), Joe Henderson (ts).* 5/64.

The Blue Note sessions were coming thick and fast by this stage, and Green seemed inclined to experiment. So counter to both market trend and his own recent output was *Solid* that it wasn't allowed to see the light of day for another 15 years. It's certainly one of the boldest of the guitarist's albums, and the presence of Joe Henderson ups the improvisational ante quite considerably. 'Ezz-Thetic' and 'The Kicker' occupy the opposite musical poles here, but both are hauled into shape by a very strong group.

It was a bold stroke to programme 'My Favorite Things' with two-thirds of John Coltrane's rhythm section working behind him as they did on *Matador*, but it served to illustrate first how adventurous Green could be, even within his harmonically uncomplicated idiom, and also how very different that modernist staple could be made to sound. Cranshaw is a funkier bassist than Jimmy Garrison and he probably makes the biggest overall difference to the sound. Tyner provides a near-perfect pianistic echo of Green's combination of delicacy, structural awareness and understated power. The guitarist already knew Jones from Chicago and from a 1959 Jimmy Forrest session, which was Green's recording debut. A fine album that shouldn't just be valued for the contributions of the supporting cast. Green himself is still very much at his peak.

***(*) Talkin' About

Blue Note 21958 *Green; Larry Young (org); Elvin Jones (d).* 9/64.

There is a mild discographical anomaly attached to this record because, though definitely led by Green, it was included in Mosaic's complete set of Larry Young's Blue Note sessions. Inevitably, Larry captures much of the attention, with huge, swirly figures on 'Talkin' About J.C.', 'Luny Tune' and 'I'm An Old Cowhand', but Green is also in fine form, spinning out some unusually complex lines for him. We've always loved the sound on this record, like fudge ice-cream sitting on ice cubes. Green plays rich and simple by turns, and even Elvin Jones is cool and abstract under all the intensity.

**** Street Of Dreams

Blue Note 21290 *Green; Bobby Hutcherson (vib); Larry Young (org); Elvin Jones (d).* 11/64.

Another exceptional record, though this time it is very much the group set-up that makes the difference. Though hooked into that easily overcooked guitar, organ, drums format, the personnel is such that one can reasonably expect a blend of power grooves and subtlety. Young is exceptional, very much on form, and Hutcherson makes an enormous contribution to a slower-paced and more meditative session than he'd normally favour. There are no originals, but the choice of material, from Charles Trenet's 'I Wish You Love', the staple 'Lazy Afternoon', the Victor Young-written title-track and the closing 'Somewhere In The Night' (often referred to as 'The *Naked City* Theme'), is spot-on. The alternation of solos on the title-track, with Green springing off from Larry Young's ever more intense chord-patterns, is the most impressive, but the quality never drops for an instant. Unusually, Capitol haven't added any alternatives or unreleased material. Perhaps there was none suitable; 35 minutes is short rations by present-day standards, though.

***(*) I Want To Hold Your Hand

Blue Note 59962 *Green; Hank Mobley (ts); Larry Young (org); Elvin Jones (d).* 3/65.

The reintroduction of a horn makes the music seem very linear and a touch unvaried. Coupled to a less enterprising programme of songs, the impact is much reduced. Leading off with a Beatles tune – the title-track – was pretty much par for the course at this time, and it's a strong enough idea to feed Green and Young with some interesting lines. 'Stella By Starlight' is rather weak, sounding as if it's been round the circuit too many times, but Steve Allen's 'This Could Be The Start Of Something' (Allen was a favourite of Green's) is excellently done. Mobley isn't deficient in ideas, but he does seem surplus to requirements for much of the set, and it would have been interesting to hear just Green, Young and Jones tackle exactly the same material. Again, the total duration seems stingy at less than 45 minutes. What has happened to all the stuff that wasn't released?

*** His Majesty King Funk

Verve 527474-2 *Green; Harold Vick (ts, f); Larry Young (org); Ben Dixon (d); Candido Camero (perc).* 5/65.

This compiles Green's record and *Up With Donald Byrd*, a joyous swinger from the trumpeter. 'The Cantaloupe Woman' was a hit for Green, but his section of the album is dominated by a wonderful, long 'Willow Weep For Me' and a cracking original called 'The Selma March'. Vick may not be known to many people. He is very much in the same mould as Mobley, though at moments he might almost be mistaken for Stanley Turrentine as well. He pretty much falls in with what's expected of him, neither surprising nor disappointing. By this stage, though, Young sounds as if he might want to be doing other things, and on 'That Lucky Old Sun (Just Rolls Around Heaven All Day)' he is positively lethargic. Dixon is a less than satisfactory replacement for Jones, who at this point was having 'personal problems' and was otherwise committed to the Coltrane group.

*** Iron City

Savoy Jazz 17227 *Green; Big John Patton (org); Ben Dixon (d).* 67.

Easy to assume that away from Blue Note Green wasn't worth a button. Whatever the shortcomings of his brief association with Verve, *Iron City*, made for Savoy, confounds the suggestion. It's a richly funky date, with some fine playing from a well-established group. Patton's soulful grind works beautifully on 'High Heeled Sneakers' and Nat Adderley's 'Work Song' and Green's title-track suggests he was still able to make original themes out of familiar resources. If you're a Green fan, this one, reissued in 2003, shouldn't be overlooked.

** Carryin' On

Blue Note 31247 2 *Green; Claude Bartee (ts); Neal Creque, Clarence Palmer (p); Billy Bivens (vib); Jimmy Lewis (b); Idris Muhammad (d).* 9/69.

** Green Is Beautiful

Blue Note 28265 2 *As above, except omit Palmer, Bivens; add Blue Mitchell (t); Emmanuel Riggins (org); Candido Camero, Richard Landrum (perc).* 1/70.

A particularly dull spot. Green arguably suffered more than most of his peers from the growing dominance of rock, and his response to the challenge wasn't convincing. Nevertheless, these discs saw him return to the Blue Note fold. Both discs are very repetitive, tunes built on long, unvarying vamps and little imagination. *Beautiful* opens strongly enough with 'Ain't I Funky Now', which at least has some strong work from the horns, but there is little else to stir any excitement and the horns sound like men whistling in a wind. These albums have their admirers (and all of Green's Blue Notes have a certain cult standing) but these are hardly priority purchases.

***(*) Alive!

Blue Note 25650 *Green; Claude Bartee (ts); Ronnie Foster (org); Billy Bivens (vib); Idris Muhammad (d); Joseph Armstrong (perc).* 70.

It seems remarkable that Blue Note weren't more enthusiastic sooner about recording Green in his natural setting. This, from the Cliché Lounge in Newark, is almost his best recording for the label, a burning, sweaty club that might rely a bit on the very commodity it was named for, but none the worse for that. The bigger band adds exponentially to the richness of the sound, and on tunes like 'Sookie Sookie' they get into the deepest and bluest of grooves. Green's opening shot, Kool and the Gang's 'Let The Music Take Your Mind', was a brilliant coup but the reissue includes rather more challenging fare than that, and anyone who has the original LP will want the bonus tracks, which include the Isley Brothers' 'It's Your Thing' and Herbie Hancock's 'Maiden Voyage'. The bonus material adds another 27 minutes to the running time, every second of it worthwhile.

*** Live At The Lighthouse

Blue Note 4 93381 *Green; Claude Bartee (ts, ss); Gary Coleman (vib); Shelton Laster (org); Wilton Felder (b); Greg Williams (d); Bobbye Porter Hall (perc).* 4/72.

Green spent his last few years playing on autopilot, but he was occasionally capable of turning in a gig that combined the old class with a sufficiently contemporary spin to fill a house. This Hermosa Beach session is a case in point. He sounds in excellent fettle and, while he isn't doing anything either new or special, the group-sound is exactly what the punters have come to hear. On the original LP there were a number of disc-jockey announcements which have been eliminated here, but for an introduction by Hank Stewart. The live feel is maintained, though, and a long version of Donald Byrd's 'Fancy Free' is worth the wait. Laster's 'Flood In Franklin Park' contains no surprises, but it's an entertaining enough piece. Unlike some recent reissues, there is at least some value for money here, a solid hour of uncomplicated funk.

** The Main Attraction

CTI/Epic 5051672 *Green; Burt Collins, Jon Faddis (t); Sam Burtis (tb); Michael Brecker, Joe Farrell (ts); Ronnie Cuber (bs); Hubert Laws (f); Don Grolnick (ky); Steve Khan (g); Will Lee (b); Andy Newman (d); Sye Evans, Carlos Martin (perc).* 3/76.

Despite the starry sessionman line-up, this was a dispiriting farewell for Grant, lost in the middle of Creed Taylor's softcore production. In the pathetic attempt to rehabilitate CTI as a valid enterprise, this is a notably low point.

***(*) Street Funk & Jazz Grooves: The Best Of Grant Green

Blue Note 789622 *As for Blue Note releases above.* 64–72.

*** The Best Of Grant Green: Volume Two

Blue Note 37741 *Green; Blue Mitchell, Lee Morgan, Joe Newman, Victor Paz, Jimmy Sedlar, Joe Wilder (t); Harry DiVito (tb); Dick Hickson (btb); Phil Bodner, John Leone, George Marge, Romeo Penque, Jimmy Buffington (frhn); Claude Bartee, George Coleman (ts); Willie Bivens, Billy Wooten (vib); Neal Creque (p); Emmanuel Riggins, Reuben Wilson (org); Wilton Felder, Jimmy Lewis, Chuck Rainey (b); Stix Hooper, Idris Muhammad (d); Ray Armando, Candido Camero, King Ericson, Richard Landrum (perc).* 3/69–4/72.

*** Blue Breakbeats

Blue Note 94705 *Green; Irwin Markowitz, Blue Mitchell, Marvin Stamm (t); Harold Vick (ss); Phil Bodner (woodwind); Claude Bartee (ts); Clarence Palmer, Emmanuel Riggins (p); Richard Tee (ky); Neal Creque, Ronnie Foster (org); William Bivens, Billy Wooten (vib); Cornell Dupree (g); Gordon Edwards, Jimmy Lewis, Chuck Rainey (b); Idris Muhammad, Grady Tate (d); Ray Armando, Joseph Armstrong, Candido Camero, Richard Landrum, Ralph MacDonald (perc).* 69–72.

The first of these was unashamedly targeted at the club dance scene and won Green some new admirers when it was released. The second volume is a touch more jazz-orientated, and it usefully includes material from unavailable records (or expensive Japanese imports) like *Carryin' On, Green Is Beautiful, Visions, Shades Of Green* and *The Final Comedown.* Only 'Sookie Sookie' from *Alive!* and 'Windjammer' from *Live At The Lighthouse* can be found among the records above. So, from a purely practical point of view, this is a useful compilation, arranged chronologically, which helps the continuity considerably. A couple of songs are reduplicated from the first volume, 'Sookie Sookie' and shorter, studio versions of 'The Final Comedown' and 'Windjammer', but for the most part these are separate releases. *Street Funk & Jazz Grooves* has the more obvious stuff, like 'Grantstand' and 'A Walk In The Night', but now that more material has returned to the catalogue it's a less appealing purchase. The second volume brings in one track from a Reuben Wilson album on which Green featured strongly.

Breakbeats is equally pitched at a young, dance-orientated audience. Compiled by DJ Smash, it's intended to cement Green's standing as one of the presiding deities of the club scene. As such, it's a very persuasive set indeed, including the long version of 'Sookie Sookie' and one of 'Ain't I Funky Now'. The shorter tracks, including 'Final Comedown', are less convincing in this context, but it's easy to see why Green has been so respectfully sampled by hip-hoppers.

***** Ballads**
Blue Note 36560 *As for Blue Note recordings above.* 61–72.

***** Retrospective**
Blue Note 40851 2CD *As above.* 61–72.

Two more repackaging jobs, attractive if you haven't any of the Blue Notes already, but otherwise unremarkable.

Jesse Green (born 1973)

PIANO

Son of trombonist Urbie Green and singer Kathy Preston, Jesse started on trombone before switching to piano under the influence of Oscar Peterson.

***** Lift Off**
Chiaroscuro 319 *Green; Joe Cohn (g); Paul Rostock (b); Bobby Durham (d).* 9/92.

***** Sea Journey**
Chiaroscuro 328 *Green; Gary Burton (vib); Gene Bertoncini, Joe Cohn (g); Michael Moore (b); Jackie Williams (d).* 93.

*****(*) Sylvan Treasure**
Chiaroscuro 221 *Green; Patrick Doran (flhn); Phil Woods (as); Chris Potter (ss, ts); Dave Liebman (ts); Frank Hauch (b); Bruce Cox (d); Jerry Davis (v).* 5/02.

Green has made a very useful living playing shipboard gigs on jazz cruises. The 1993 album is a record of one of those, from the *SS Norway*, and it's probably the better by a whisker of the first pair, not least because of the guest appearances by former teacher Burton and guitarist Bertoncini. Jesse seems to like working with guitarists. The duets with Cohn on *Lift Off* (which has a Space Shuttle cover both Jesse and his label probably now regret) are the best parts of that album, which is a rather bland mix of standards done *à la* Chick Corea and even blander originals. Chick's 'Sea Journey' is, of course, prominent on the second disc, which putters out around that point after a cracking opening on 'Softly, As In A Morning Sunrise', 'All The Things You Are' (where he trades ideas with Bertoncini) and 'Billie's Bounce'. The third album is the most inventive of the three. Again, it leans quite heavily on guest spots (notably Woods, but also singer Davis on 'I've Got You Under My Skin') but the originals have much more prominence and the opening 'Extreme Sporting' (apparently about Jesse's knuckle-threatening love of the skateboard) is excellent. Doran is superb on 'PorpDog'; the brighter attack of brass horns suits Green's approach very well indeed. 'Sylvan Treasure' probably hints at something floaty and bucolic but this is a tough-minded and hard-edged disc which asks for and gives no quarter.

Urbie Green (born 1926)

TROMBONE

Green worked with Gene Krupa in the '40s, before taking over from Bill Harris with Woody Herman, and in the '50s he was fronting studio sessions which mixed cool and hard-bop stylings. Less visible subsequently, he often fronted recreation orchestras and in recent years has played more or less as he's pleased.

***** East Coast Jazz Series 6**
Bethlehem R2 76686 *Green; Doug Mettome (t); Al Cohn (ts, f, bcl); Danny Bank (bs, cl, f); Jimmy Lyon (p); Oscar Pettiford (b); Jimmy Campbell, Osie Johnson (d).* 55.

Characteristic of the several sessions which Green helmed for jazz labels in the '50s: standards, plus four originals by arranger Marion Evans which deploy a small group through brief though interesting paces. Most of the arrangements are over before they've had the chance to get started, but in their neat, careful way they work very sweetly, and there are good moments for Green, the all-but-forgotten Mettome (who died in 1964) and Cohn, here appearing under the pseudonym 'Al Horowitz'.

***** Sea Jam Blues**
Chiaroscuro CR(D) 338 *Green; Chris Potter (ss, ts); Jesse Green (p); Paul Rostock (b); Glenn Davis (d).* 5–6/95.

Sea Jam Blues is taken from a jazz cruise where the Green family (Jesse is Urbie's son) were in residence. Potter's presence adds some extra spice to the occasion (he chews up the opening Ellington blues before Urbie even gets started), but it's an altogether congenial setting, and 'You've Changed', rich and ripe, soon affirms Green's well-being. Potter storms through 'Giant Steps' almost by himself, but here it seems like a rather fractious interlude on what is, after all, Urbie's date. A nice memento if you were there.

Rowland Greenberg (1920–96)

TRUMPET

Based in and around Oslo for most of his working life, Greenberg played in an uncomplicated swing style, despite being among those who backed Charlie Parker on his celebrated Swedish tour. He played dance music for much of the '50s and '60s but his recordings show an uncompromised swing trumpeter.

***** Portrait Of A Norwegian Jazz Artist**
Gemini GMOJCD 9504 *Greenberg; Jack Butler (t); Ivan Jacobsen (tb); Per Nilsen (as); Arvid Gram Paulsen, Bjarne Nerem, Erling Andersen, Ben Webster (ts); Jan Fredrik Dahl, Rolf Larsson, Oistein Ringstad, Carsten Klouman, Sigurd Jansen, Arne Klette, Willy Andresen (p); Per Byhaug, Eilif Holm, Arno Guilberg (vib); Robert Normann, Finn Westbye (g); Fred Lange-Nielsen, Frank Cook, Bjorn Pedersen, Hakon Nilsen, Arne Wilhelmsson, Tore Nordlie (b); Stein Lorentzen, Edgar Vestgard, Hans Jarnefeldt, Egil Johansen, Omar Heide Midtsaeter, Per Nyhaug, Kenneth Greenberg, Kurt Falk (d).* 2/40-87.

Greenberg played good swing trumpet with a rasp that can sometimes catch out a listener expecting something much sweeter: his 1960 reading of 'Lover Man' is tough and even vehement. A 1969 'Perdido', where he stands next to Ben Webster, is forceful enough to bring the tenorman out of his indolent shell. This hotchpotch of tracks, unearthed from various obscure sources by the Oslo Jazz Circle, is hardly the album to stand as a true memorial to a capable musician, but it's the only one Greenberg has got at the moment. If he gave bop a grudging respect, it left his style largely untouched, and such influences as Roy Eldridge and Nat Gonella coloured most of what he did. The sound is often dusty, but Greenberg's playing is consistently smart, and the disc will appeal to admirers of swing trumpet.

Burton Greene (born 1937)

PIANO

Studied classical music in Chicago, then with Dick Marx, going to New York in the early '60s and forming the Free Form Improvisation Ensemble in 1963. Joined the Jazz Composers Guild and recorded for ESP. Moved to Paris in 1969, then divided his time between Europe and America, while also studying Indian music.

****(*) Shades Of Greene**
Cadence CJR 1087 *Greene (p solo).* 4/92–12/97.

***** Throptics**
CIMP 182 *Greene; Wilber Morris (b); Lou Grassi (d).* 7/98.

Greene has had a strange time of it in jazz, to say the least: a pioneer spirit in the free jazz of the early '60s, his ESP quartet album ('uninformed by any apparent communicative purpose' – Max Harrison) was reviled and applauded in about equal proportion, though it was ignored altogether in far greater numbers. Subsequent bulletins have been spasmodic and not much more enlightening. *Shades Of Greene* collects material from three solo concerts, two long pieces in Toronto, seven from Hilversum and a much earlier version of 'Off Minor' from a 1992 Amsterdam broadcast. As ever, Greene rambles away to some strange agenda of his own – he can be as long-winded as the most bloody-minded of improvisers, but he can also be pithy and almost epigrammatic when he wants to be – and it's this unpredictability which makes him either intriguing or exasperating, according to taste. We are somewhere in the middle.

The trio set at least allows Wilber and Grassi to centre him to some extent. 'Lennie Lives', for Tristano, and 'Tilo Akandita Brikama', by Pierre Dørge, for Johnny Dyani, are characterful excursions which Greene hurls himself into, but there is a good deal of chaos as well: the opening 'Light Blue' may well finish off some listeners at the first hurdle. A maverick spirit, to be sure!

****(*) Peace Beyond Conflict**
CIMP 251 *Greene; Mark Dresser (b).* 7/01.

As unclassifiable as always, though we don't necessarily mean that as a compliment. Greene's tunes are a curious lot, and the title-track for one sounds very much like 'A Lot Of Living To Do'. Dresser, never a man to waste time or effort, plays with tremendous commitment, surely more than his partner deserves: he's the real focus behind what would otherwise be another example of Greene noodling away to himself. The CIMP sound is not at its best with pianos, which doesn't assist. The sleeve-notes by Burton are an entertaining read, where he talks about being 'stoned from the subtlety' of Sam Woodyard's playing!

Everett Greene (born 1934)

VOCALS

Indianapolis crooner, making his recording debut at bus-pass age.

***** My Foolish Heart**
Savant 2014 *Greene; Houston Person (ts); Norman Simmons (p); Ray Drummond (b); Kenny Washington (d).* 98.

This one is for lovers of some of the old big-band singers, guys like Billy Eckstine and Al Hibbler. Greene has a less individual voice than either of those, and might well be swamped by a heavier accompaniment than producer Person gives him here, but he has a nice sound and a good touch with a song. Opening on 'When Did You Leave Heaven?', he carves out a solidly dependable set for his first disc and saves best to last with 'Hello, Young Lovers' and 'The Very Thought Of You'.

Jimmy Greene (born 1975)

TENOR AND SOPRANO SAXOPHONES, FLUTE

Born in Connecticut, Green studied at Hartford and has played in the Boston area and in New York. He seemed set for great things following a signing to RCA, but his career has subsequently gone a bit quiet.

***** Introducing Jimmy Greene**
Criss Cross 1181 *Greene; John Swana (t, flhn); Steve Davis (tb); Aaron Goldberg (p); Darrell Hall (b); Eric McPherson (d).* 10/97.

***** Brand New World**
RCA 09026-63564-2 *As above, except add Darren Barrett (t, flhn), Dwayne Burns (b), Khalil Kwame Bell (perc); omit Swana and Hall.* 6/99.

Greene made a few waves as a runner-up in one of the Monk Institute competitions and his stint with Horace Silver has given him some dues. Neither of these records is going to have hats thrown in the air, but they're a solid enough start. The RCA debut had its teeth drawn slightly by the simultaneous appearance of the Criss Cross set, actually recorded some two years earlier. *Introducing* feels like just another Criss Cross record for the most part, although here and there Greene is a degree more personal: with the rather dark and sidelong arrangement of 'I Love You', for instance. Swana and Davis sound as if they've just turned up to do the date and they don't add very much.

The RCA set is stronger, but not so much as to make a huge difference. Greene has an attractively light and unemphatic sound on tenor, but this makes it more difficult for him to create a whizz-bang impression over a single set. The band is much the same and the leader's composing takes more prominence, which seems to fuse the front line into a more characterful sound. Future releases may see Greene in a more purposeful light.

*****(*) Forever**

Criss Cross 1245 *Greene; Xavier Davis (p); John Benitez (b); Jeff 'Tain' Watts (d).* 11/03.

It would be flippant to suggest that Greene has turned to the Lord for assistance in his career direction, but this is a full-on album of spirituals, cast in five originals, Ellington's 'Come Sunday', 'Old Rugged Cross' and Thom Bell's 'You Make Me Feel Brand New'. The suggestion that we're in for an hour of sombre testifying is, though, undercut by the brightly grooving treatment of 'Rugged Cross' which opens – and thereafter, Greene keeps energy levels high and the band on its toes. The Coltrane spin he puts on 'In Many Tongues' is deftly personalized by his comparatively light tone and popping articulation. Two soprano and piano duets, 'Forever' and 'He Is Lord', have enough dryness in them to keep simpering at arm's length. It's a fine rhythm section, Watts piling in with his usual fervour, though he's not quite as musclebound as he can be, and Davis has plenty to say here.

Sonny Greenwich (born 1936)

GUITAR

Canadian guitarist looking for challenging turf in an otherwise broad-based post-bop idiom.

***** Standard Idioms**

Kleo 1 *Greenwich (g solo).* 11/91, 9/92.

Greenwich's approach veers between guitar-driven jazz in a contemporary vein and an attempt to capture the sound of the late John Coltrane Quartet. This is not quite as misguided as it might sound, but it works only intermittently. The debut recording on Sonny's own label finds him in pretty familiar form, knocking out big, blocky sounds on a set of originals and tributes that have nothing obviously to do with standards jazz at all, and which are not strictly idiomatic in terms of conventional jazz guitar. Which may be the point. 'Memories of Miles', 'Let Your Heart Sing' and the opening 'Sunshower' are all long, slowly developing improvisations, which don't deliver too quickly. Good recorded sound, if a little intense at higher dynamics.

**** Hymn To The Earth**

Kleo 2 *Greenwich; Jim Hillman (p, d); Jim Gelfand (ky); Ernie Nelson (v).* 10/94.

****(*) Spirit In The Air**

Kleo 3 *As above, except add Ron Seguin (b); Guy Thouin (tabla).* 11/95.

Sonny makes a move into a kind of creative New Age music with these curious projects. There is mercifully just one vocal from Ernie Nelson (in 'Serengeti', on *Hymn*) and he figures as sound-colour in the early stages of 'Black Beauty' on *Spirit*. Any more and we might have shut up shop. On the earlier record, Sonny moves easily from guitar to baritone guitar and keyboards, and Gelfand makes some interesting sounds, reminiscent of the heyday of Lonnie Liston Smith. These will win their admirers, but there probably isn't enough substance for most mainstream jazz fans here.

****(*) Days Gone By**

Sackville 2052 *Greenwich; Ed Bickert (g); Don Thompson (b); Terry Clarke (d).* 6/79.

A more accommodating and gentler side of Greenwich comes out on this archive release with fellow-Canadian Bickert. Whether the setting leaves enough scope for Sonny's usual idiom is a moot point. He sounds a touch constrained and at half-throttle for a good deal of this record and, while he has the chops to deliver, almost no matter what the setting, it is Bickert who takes the plaudits. Sonny asserts himself most forcefully on 'Nica's Dream', the Horace Silver classic, affording him time and space to soar away on some inventive ideas. An even longer improvisation ends the album, with some friendly duelling between the two guitarists. For the most part, though, this is a lacklustre performance from Sonny.

*****(*) Fragments Of A Memory**

Cornerstone 116 *Greenwich; Charles Ellison (t); Mike Allen (ts); Don Thompson (p); Jim Vivian (b); Barry Elmes (d).* 4/01.

At first glance this looks and sounds like another rather straight-ahead date. That's deceptive. Drummer Elmes and pianist Thompson break up the rhythm and the harmony in a most arresting and interesting way. The title-piece, which has a curiously classical bent, is full of odd time-shifts and breaks in line which make it one of Sonny's most challenging conceptions to date. The set actually opens with a looping waltz, 'Fontainebleau', that gives the band plenty to work with. There is a delicious reading of Joplin's 'The Entertainer' – meat and drink to Thompson – and a lovely version of 'Where Is Love'. The horns aren't always right for the music, but apart from a couple of wayward solos by Allen they do sterling work.

Sonny's tone is rich and forceful, with a suggestion here and there that he might either have retuned or switched to baritone guitar. His phrasing on 'Fragments Of A Memory' manages to be both terse and expansive. Very impressive stuff and a return to form that prompts a more thoughtful look at some of the earlier material. We stand by our reservations regarding *Days Gone By* but in the light of this record it's easier to hear a bolder and more innovative album struggling to get out.

***** Special Angel**

CBC 3006 *Greenwich; Marilyn Lerner (p).* 01.

Sonny has shown before how much he enjoys working with piano-players and with the rich harmonic palette they bring to his compositions. This collaboration with the classically inclined Lerner is a case in point. The pieces are mostly impressionistic and heavy on texture, with less going on in the line. Titles are as brief and brisk – 'Domino', 'Spiritual', 'Mosaic' – as the ideas, though that isn't to the detriment of the music. One only wishes for a second CD of more relaxed live performances of these pieces, which seem to call for a stretched-out approach rather than the disciplined reading they get. Far less blues tonality than usual in Greenwich's guitar-playing, making him harder to identify blindfold this time out.

Guillermo Gregorio

SAXOPHONES, CLARINET

A saxophonist of understated brilliance, this inspired Argentinian has taken striking liberties with the harmonic language of classic jazz and swing. His approach is less ironic than that of others in the field, but is no less successful for that.

***** Otra Music**

Atavistic 209 *Gregorio; various personnels.* 63–70.

Almost a new music record, this documents Gregorio's involvement with Fluxus and with tape music, as well as including examples of his free improvisation. Somewhat specialist in scope, it is only included here as an indication of the language he draws on in later years.

*** Background Music

hatOLOGY 526 *Gregorio; Mats Gustafsson (ts, bs); Kjell Nordeson (d). 96.*

*** Ellipsis

hatOLOGY 511 *Gregorio; Gene Coleman (bcl); Jim O'Rourke (g, acc); Carrie Biolo (vib); Michael Cameron (b). 2/97.*

*** Red Cube(d)

hatOLOGY 531 *Gregorio; Mat Maneri (vn); Pandelis Karayorgis (p). 3/98.*

The language of these records will not seem strange to anyone who has experienced the avant-cool of Franz Koglmann, another one-time hat ART recording artist, with whom Gregorio has worked in the past. At first blush, *Ellipsis* is more directly influenced by the Fluxus group and by modernist composers such as Earle Brown and Giacinto Scelsi, with whose pure-sound approach Gregorio has something in common.

After a little exposure, and certainly after one hears what he does with jazz-based material on *Red Cube(d)*, it becomes evident that he has roots in that tradition as well. The later album was seemingly inspired by a batch of lost Red Norvo discs from the '40s. Vibes played a part in the earlier album, though paradoxically not in the second, but their presence on *Ellipsis* and Gregorio's reworkings of Fletcher Henderson's 'Red Dust', 'Ghost Of A Chance' (or 'Chu's Spectre') and 'These Foolish Things' suggest just how much he has tried to combine jazz and other harmonic languages within a rhythmic conception which is not drum-led. The most remarkable piece of all is 'Woodchopper's Nightmare', a veritable palimpsest of themes by Norvo, Shorty Rogers, Woody Herman, Flip Phillips and others. Its concentration is highly impressive and the interplay of saxophone, piano and violin is virtuosic.

Background Music runs some risk of being taken as just that, but anyone who knows the recorded work of the Swedish Gustafsson will be taken by his reflective and low-intensity work here. It's a very quiet record, understated in places almost to the point of disappearance and calling for considerable patience on the listener's part. Gregorio is unlikely to be for every taste. Some of his work veers perilously close to navel-gazing, but like Koglmann he has important things to say about the jazz tradition – things which we ignore at our peril.

*** Degrees Of Iconicity

hatNOW 134 *Gregorio; Carrie Biolo (vib, mar); Fred Lonberg-Holm (clo); Michael Cameron, Kent Kessler (b). 99.*

Once again, Gregorio's music seems rooted in 20th-century modernism and doesn't bear much relationship to jazz. One track here is dedicated to Schoenberg's son-in-law, the Italian composer Luigi Nono, and it just about establishes the tone of the set as a whole. The instrumentation is very unusual but often very effective and Gregorio himself plays with a notable lack of dryness and abstraction. The saxophonist has a later record on the related hat(now)ART label which is devoted to new music; though *Faktura* includes performances from jazz players like François Houle, it falls outside our ambit.

Stan Greig (born 1930)

PIANO

Edinburgh-born, Greig worked as a teenager with Sandy Brown and joined the Ken Colyer band as a drummer in 1954. He worked extensively with Humphrey Lyttelton, the Fairweather–Brown group and, for most of the '60s, Acker Bilk, before rejoining Lyttelton in the '80s and leading his own Harlem Blues and Jazz Band.

*** Boogie Woogie

Lake LACD97 *Greig; Johnny Hawksworth (b); Richie Bryant (d). 71–97.*

Though Greig's main calling is as the archetypal mainstream-band pianist, this set features him in boogie mode. For the most part it's a reissue of an obscure 1971 set for Rediffusion. The piano sound is rather hard, but the playing – of chestnuts such as 'Shout For Joy' and 'Death Ray Boogie', as well as a few appropriate originals – is delightfully bright and bumptious. We are not sure that we agree with the sleeve-note assertion that there aren't many players left who can play 'authentic' boogie woogie, since it's more that the style has simply gone out of fashion. In a way, this set explains why: well done though it is, it tends to pall over album length through the repetitiveness of the idiom. Three 'new' tracks, featuring Greig solo in 1997, are more sedate and even surprisingly hesitant.

Drew Gress (born 1959)

DOUBLE BASS, PEDAL STEEL GUITAR

The bassist has been closely associated with such contemporary luminaries as Dave Douglas and Don Byron. His own projects have included Jagged Sky and Joint Venture and have tended to be resolutely experimental.

*** Heyday

Soul Note121314 *Gress; David Binney (as); Ben Monder (g); Kenny Wollesen (d). 98.*

*** Spin & Drift

Premonition 90752 *Gress; Tim Berne (as, bs); Uri Caine (p); Tom Rainey (d). 6/00.*

Apart from a couple of themes from Bartok's 'Mikrokosmos', all of the material on *Heyday* is by Gress himself and reveals a complex musical personality that's hard to pin down. The bassist can sound fairly jagged – to borrow an adjective from one of his groups – but can also write and play very sweetly indeed, and the pedal steel (heard on *Spin & Drift*) is an unexpected instrument to find in an avant-garde jazz setting. Or it was.

'Devil in the Details' and 'Beeline – Back in the Cage' are big, ambitious pieces, but there is nothing on this rather straightforward group set to suggest the technical experimentalism heard on *Spin & Drift*. Similar line-up, though replacing guitar with piano enriches the harmonic possibilities somewhat. Here Gress provides a running bass commentary in the interstices, and he employs multi-tracking on the opening 'Disappearing, Act I', in which Berne becomes a whole saxophone choir. It's an amazing, arresting start and though nothing else on the record quite comes up to that pitch of drama, it guarantees you keep listening. Caine is instinctively responsive to the polytonal approach Gress favours. Tunes occasionally drift in the direction of Dave Douglas's post-post-modal jazz but there are also classical references (less explicit than the Bartoks) and some more straightforward grooves.

Al Grey (1925–2000)

TROMBONE, VOCAL

Joined Benny Carter after military service, then was with various groups until a key period with Count Basie, 1957–61. Afterwards freelanced, often with old friends Jimmy Forrest and Buddy Tate, and led some record dates of his own.

***** Snap Your Fingers**
Verve 0602498603079 *Grey; David Burns, Donald Byrd (t); Billy Mitchell (ts); Floyd Morris, Herbie Hancock (p); Bobby Hutcherson (vib); Herman Wright (b); Eddie Williams (d).* 1–2/62.

Al Grey will always be remembered as a Basie sideman, even though he spent more years away from the Count's band than with it. His humorous, fierce style of improvising is more in the tradition of such colleagues as saxophonist Lockjaw Davis than in the rather more restrained trombone lineage, although Grey is especially accomplished with the plunger mute. He came to seem like he was assuming Vic Dickenson's mantle as the great trombone individualist.

This rather surprising reappearance brings back a little-known Argo album made just after he left Basie. The first five tracks are a studio date for a sextet, quite tightly arranged around gospel and blues themes; the next three are from a live date at Birdland, where Byrd and Hancock came in for Burns and Morris, although neither is featured much. The surprise presence here is Hutcherson, in a very early appearance, who gets quite a bit of space. Grey's solos are in a rather more modern line than his Basie work would have suggested. It's a satisfying time-waster rather than a great record, but the curious shouldn't be disappointed.

*****(*) Night Train Revisited**
Storyville STCD 8293 *Grey; Jimmy Forrest (ts); Shirley Scott (p); John Duke (b); Bobby Durham (d).* 7/78.

***** Al Grey–Jesper Thilo Quintet**
Storyville STCD 4136 *Grey; Jesper Thilo (ts); Ole Kock Hansen (p); Hugo Rasmussen (b); Alex Riel (d).* 8/86.

The 1978 session catches a good band – at a very unfashionable time for this kind of jazz – enjoying themselves regardless in a few sets from Rick's Café Américain in Chicago. Forrest and Grey sound terrific and they get rambunctious support from Shirley and the rhythm section. The later Storyville session, made on one of his many European sojourns, is typical of his usual manner: brisk mainstream with some sterling blues-playing, although Thilo and the rhythm section accommodate rather than compel Grey into his best form.

***** The New Al Grey Quintet**
Chiaroscuro CD 305 *Grey; Mike Grey (tb); Joe Cohn (t, g); J. J. Wiggins (b); Bobby Durham (d).* 5/88.

*****(*) Al Meets Bjarne**
Gemini GM 62 *Grey; Bjarne Nerem (ts); Norman Simmons (p); Paul West (b); Gerryck King (d).* 8/88.

***** Fab**
Capri 74038-2 *Grey; Clark Terry (t, flhn, v); Don Sickler (t); Mike Grey, Delfeayo Marsalis (tb); Virginia Mayhew (as); Norman Simmons (p); Joe Cohn (g); J. J. Wiggins (b); Bobby Durham (d); Jon Hendricks (v).* 2/90.

The quintet date for Chiaroscuro features a 'family band': Mike is Al's son, Joe is Al Cohn's son, and J. J. Wiggins is pianist Gerald's offspring. Although the group sound a little rough-and-ready at times, and the absence of a pianist is probably not quite as useful a freedom as it might have been, it works out to be a very entertaining record. Mike is almost as ripe a soloist as his father, and the sound of the two trombones together leads to a few agreeably toe-curling moments; but Joe Cohn's playing is equally spirited, and Wiggins and Durham sound fine. The set-list includes some standards and a few pleasingly obscure choices, such as Hank Mobley's 'Syrup And Biscuits' and Art Farmer's 'Rue Prevail'.

The session with Nerem was cut on a visit to Norway. The title-blues is almost indecently ripe, and 'I'm In The Mood For Love' is taken at surely the slowest tempo on record, but there are meaty blowing tunes as well and Nerem, a player in the kind of swaggering swing tradition that Grey enjoys, has the measure of the trombonist. Outstandingly good studio sound.

The Capri record is a bit self-consciously 'produced' around Grey, with a number of guessable routines in place – mumbling duet with Clark Terry, all-bones-together blues, and so on. Al still sounds robust and comfortably on top of the situation. Capri also have a seasonal album featuring Grey, *Christmas Stocking Stuffer* (Capri 74039-2 CD), for those with a taste for yuletide jazz.

***** Matzoh And Grits**
Arbors ARCD 19167 *Grey; Cleave E. Guyton (as, f); Randolph Noel (p); Joe Cohn (g); J. J. Wiggins (b); Bobby Durham (d).* 4/96.

*****(*) Me 'N' Jack**
Pullen PULL 2350 *Grey; Jerry Weldon (ts); Jack McDuff (org); Joe Cohn (g); Jerome Hunker (b); Bobby Durham (d).* 96.

Al seemed ageless, even when he was playing the sly old man, and these two show no falling-off in quality. *Matzoh And Grits* is let down a bit by the band: Cohn and Durham are favourite stagers with Grey and they're fine, but Guyton and Noel are a little ordinary and here and there the music droops, although the Ellington tunes are very good value. *Me 'N' Jack* is much more like it. Pairing Grey with McDuff was an inspired move. The organist refuses to do any showboating and instead takes his turn in the ensembles while offering support to anyone who needs it. Weldon has some good turns, Cohn is terrific, and Grey is in marvellous heart, with his ballad showpiece on 'God Bless The Child' a treat. The rest of the material is nearly all blues, but it doesn't hurt.

Johnny Griffin (born 1928)

TENOR SAXOPHONE

If saxophone playing had a Formula One division, Johnny Griffin would have pole position every start – or he would have had before he discovered a gentler and more lyrical side to his musical personality. Born in Chicago, the Little Giant was part of the first bebop generation, but he only really found his true voice in the '50s, often in partnership with Eddie 'Lockjaw' Davis, with whom he duelled to often spectacular effect. Griffin spent some time in Europe in the '60s but has enjoyed a resurgence back home in more recent years.

***** A Blowing Session**

Blue Note 99009 *Griffin; Lee Morgan (t); John Coltrane, Hank Mobley (ts); Wynton Kelly (p); Paul Chambers (b); Art Blakey (d).* 5/57.

This is the period when Griffin's youthful rep as the fastest tenor on the block was made official. In the company of Coltrane and Mobley, neither of them slouches, he rattles through 'The Way You Look Tonight' like some love-on-the-run hustler with his mates waiting out in the car. Only Trane seems inclined to serenade, and it's interesting to speculate how the track might have sounded had they taken it at conventional ballad tempo. 'All The Things You Are' begins with what sounds like Reveille from Wynton Kelly and then lopes off with almost adolescent awkwardness. This was a typical Griffin strategy. For much of his most productive period Griffin more or less bypassed ballad-playing and only really adjusted his idiom to the medium and slower tempos as he aged. 'It's All Right With Me' is way over the speed limit, as if Griffin is trying to erase all memory of Sonny Rollins's magisterial reading of a deceptively difficult tune. *Blowing Session* is oddly unsettling and by no means the most appealing thing Griffin put his name to. The new special edition is nicely packaged but doesn't overcome our unease.

*****(*) Way Out**

Original Jazz Classics OJCCD 1855 *Griffin; Kenny Drew (p); Wilbur Ware (b); Philly Joe Jones (d).* 2/58.

Recorded by Orrin Keepnews in New York City, this is a set that nevertheless breathes Chicago. In some respects, it isn't the 'person we knew'; Griffin sounds quieter, more measured and contained, and apart from a blaze through 'Cherokee' at high tempo he is content to play a much gentler set. Items like 'Where's Your Overcoat, Boy?' and 'Teri's Tune' centre on Ware's hugely expansive bass line, with Drew in close proximity, leaving Griff to develop and embellish. 'Little John' is distinctive for Drew's solid chording and interchanges with the drummer. The rhythm section could hardly be faulted, and CD transfer has improved sound quality tenfold.

****** Johnny Griffin Sextet**

Original Jazz Classics OJC 1827 *Griffin; Donald Byrd (t); Pepper Adams (bs); Kenny Drew (p); Wilbur Ware (b); Philly Joe Jones (d).* 2/58.

Despite the drummer's name, this was a Chicago group *par excellence*. Everything seems just a little magnified, and tunes like 'Stix' Trix' and 'Woody 'N' You' are gloriously pumped-up and brazen. A pity that Griffin didn't record more with this line-up. They sound like they're just about to hit proper stride when the record ends. Ware is magnificent as always, and Kenny Drew stretches himself ambitiously.

***** The Little Giant**

Original Jazz Classics OJC 136 *Griffin; Blue Mitchell (t); Julian Priester (tb); Wynton Kelly (p); Sam Jones (b); Albert 'Tootie' Heath (d).* 8/59.

This isn't the only album bearing this title (which refers to the diminutive saxophonist's nickname), so it might be worth checking that you're getting the right one. Heath finds it harder than Blakey to keep up, but the rhythm section gets it just about right, opening up the throttle for Griffin and two rather underrated brass soloists with just the right amount of brassiness in their tone to match the leader's.

***** The Big Soul-Band**

Original Jazz Classics OJC 485 *Griffin; Clark Terry, Bob Bryant (t); Julian Priester, Matthew Gee (tb); Pat Patrick, Frank Strozier, Edwin Williams, Charles Davis (sax); Harold Mabern, Bobby Timmons (p); Bob Cranshaw, Vic Sproles (b); Charli Persip (d).* 5–6/60.

A little like standing out in a high wind. Griffin wasn't necessarily the most subtle of bandleaders but he knew how to make a group swing, and that's what he brings to this. An alternative version of 'Wade In The Water' on the CD suggests that this was a group always teetering on the brink of self-destruction, in the musical if not the personal sense. Griffin's frontmanship was pretty tenuous, but when it worked, it worked wonderfully.

***** Studio Jazz Party**

Original Jazz Classics OJCCD 1902 *Griffin; Dave Burns (t); Norman Simmons (b); Vic Sproles (b); Ben Riley (d).* 9/60.

The deal here was that the band would play live, not in a club, but before an invited studio audience. The atmosphere is loose and relaxed, and Babs Gonzales MCs in an attempt to authenticate the live atmosphere, but the freshness and novelty wear off very quickly after 'Good Bait' and 'There Will Never Be Another You'. The band is rather anonymous, but with Griff occupying the spotlight throughout, that isn't so much of an issue. One simply hankers after something a little subtler and more modulated.

****(*) Lookin' At Monk**

Original Jazz Classics OJCCD 1911 *Griffin; Eddie 'Lockjaw' Davis (ts); Junior Mance (p); Larry Gales (b); Ben Riley (d).* 2/61.

There is something amiss here. Much as the latter history of ragtime piano was ruined by a refusal to look even cursorily at Scott Joplin's intended tempi, so Griffin and Lockjaw race through a set of Monk compositions with lights blazing and tyres squealing, and with no real indication that they have a feel for a tune as delicately nuanced as 'Ruby, My Dear' or 'Well, You Needn't', let alone that old warhorse, 'Round Midnight'. The two saxophones attack each tune like a pair of drag-racers, and there's not much more satisfaction to be had from the performances, unless you have an appetite for empty displays of virtuosity. Not, in our view, any great surprise that this 1999 reissue has taken so long to reappear.

***** The Kerry Dancers And Other Swinging Folk**

JVD 60102 *Griffin; Barry Harris (p); Ron Carter (b); Ben Riley (d).* 12/61, 1/62.

Griffin has always been interested in folk themes. Like Stan Getz, he favours the Scandinavian lullaby 'Hush-A-Bye', which figures here alongside some old British and Appalachian themes: 'The Londonderry Air (Danny Boy)', 'Green Grow The Rushes' and 'Black Is The Colour Of My True Love's Hair' as well as original themes like '25½ Daze' and 'Oh, Now I See'. He's in spanking form, wherever the material comes from, and some of his solos here rank with his very best for pace, logic and control. There's also warmth and humour in the playing, which is a nice relief from the headlong stuff that used to be demanded of him.

★★★ White Gardenia

Original Jazz Classics OJCCD 1877 *Griffin; Ernie Royal, Clark Terry (t); Nat Adderley (c); Jimmy Cleveland, Paul Faulise, Urbie Green (tb); Ray Alonge (frhn); Barry Harris (p); Ron Carter, Barry Galbraith, Jimmy Jones (b); Ben Riley (d); strings.* 7/61.

A delightful, smoothly orchestrated tribute to Lady Day that manages to be more than just pastiche. Griff is no Lester Young, and he isn't perhaps the obvious soloist for a gig of this sort. Even so, he makes a wonderful job of 'God Bless The Child' and 'Left Alone', though it's 'That Old Devil Called Love' which allows him to be most fully and obviously himself. The band is not so smooth as to blur some real jazz feel, and the strings are there mainly for depth of focus and harmony, rather than as emotional treacle.

★★(★) Tough Tenor Favourites

Original Jazz Classics OJCCD 1861 *Griffin; Eddie 'Lockjaw' Davis (ts); Horace Parlan (p); Buddy Catlett (b); Ben Riley (d).* 2/62.

A drably generic two-tenors duel, without a shard of sophistication. For some, that will be the highest possible recommendation and 'Ow!' and 'Tin Tin Deo' will be meat and drink. For us, though, this is a dispiriting low in the Little Giant's career, redeemed by Parlan's mournful chords and sudden scampers into the light. This was Griff's last full year in America before beginning his European exile and it's hard to avoid the impression of a man who thinks that something is closing in on him.

★★(★) Do Nothing 'Til You Hear From Me

Original Jazz Classics OJCCD 1908 *Griffin; Buddy Montgomery (p, vib); Monk Montgomery (b); Art Taylor (d).* 63.

At the tag end of his Riverside contract, Griffin seemed to be marking time, and while there was some comfort in the realization that the time in question was less hectic than of yore, it was still outside most saxophonists' comfort zone. The blowing themes are less convincing than they once were and less convincingly executed. The Montgomery brothers, with Monk (unusually for the time) on an upright bass, do a manful job, and Buddy's switch to vibes is very effective, but it's hard to avoid the feeling of creative stalemate that surrounds this session.

★★★ Live In London

Harkit 024 *Griffin; Stan Tracey (p); Malcolm Cecil (b); Jackie Dougan (d).* 12/63.

Griff gives a brief interview on this one, recorded with the house band at Ronnie Scott's during a British visit. Americans were in mostly muted form following the assassination of John F. Kennedy, but Griffin's bustling, multi-note style is still very much to the fore, even if some of the lines seem a little down-turned and blued at the edges. Fine stuff, if not a spectacularly good recording.

★★★ Live At The Jazzhus Montmartre, Copenhagen: Volume 1

DA Music 1047 *Griffin; Kenny Drew (p); Niels-Henning Orsted Pedersen (b); Albert 'Tootie' Heath (d).* 3/67.

★★★ Live At The Jazzhus Montmartre, Copenhagen: Volume 2

DA Music 1048 *As above.* 3/67.

In the Black Lion catalogue this immediately followed Wardell Gray's *One For Prez,* which includes three takes of 'The Man I Love'. There could hardly be a sharper contrast. Where Gray's tone and delivery drew heavily on Lester Young's pre-bop idiom, Griffin swoops on the same material with an almost delinquent energy that comes direct from Charlie Parker. It isn't the most settling of sounds, but the technical control is superb and only a rhythm section of the quality of this one could keep the tune on the road. The new issue adds more material, but the sound isn't as bright.

★★ Blues For Harvey

Steeplechase SCCD 31004 *Griffin; Kenny Drew (p); Mads Vinding (b); Ed Thigpen (d).* 7/73.

★★ The Jamfs Are Coming

Timeless SJP 121 *Griffin; Rein De Graaff (p); Henk Haverhoek, Koos Serierse (b); Art Taylor (d).* 12/75, 10/77.

Both these sessions mark something of a low point in Griffin's generally even output. There's something slightly numbed about the solos on *Blues For Harvey* (compare the title-track with the lovely version on *The Man I Love,* above) and some questionable material which includes a mercifully rare jazz reading of Gilbert O'Sullivan's 'Alone Again (Naturally)'. Griffin takes the theme at his natural clip but makes nothing significant of it. He constantly overshoots the measure on 'Rhythm-A-Ning', another slightly surprising choice which wrong-foots the band on a couple of measures. De Graaff is an interesting player with a steady supply of unhackneyed ideas, but he's only a questionable partner for Griffin and the two never catch light on *The Jamfs Are Coming.* Griffin fans with some practice in mentally editing out dodgy backgrounds might well want to have both of these, but everyone else might as well hang on to their cash.

★★★(★) The Return Of The Griffin

Original Jazz Classics OJCCD 1882 *Griffin; Ronnie Mathews (p); Ray Drummond (b); Keith Copeland (d).* 10/78.

★★★(★) Live / Autumn Leaves

Verve 523261-2 *As above, except Kenny Washington (d) replaces Copeland.* 7/80, 5/81.

The Griffin returned without ever really having been away. The 1978 album was, though, the product of his first visit to the USA since 1963. Griffin's brand of saxophonics had been at something of a discount Stateside for a time, and the Galaxy recording was understandably intended to revive his fortunes. Mathews is a bright and responsive accompanist, and 'A Monk's Dream' and 'Autumn Leaves' are both strong performances, with a slightly altered melody statement on the latter which gives it a wry ambiguity. Copeland has never been a highly regarded player, except by other musicians, and this is further proof of his considerable powers. He is replaced by Washington on the live set, carefully selected from a week-long residency at the New Morning in Paris – except for 'Autumn Leaves' itself, which was recorded the summer before at the Antibes–Juan-les-Pins festival, where the song has had an iconic status since Miles's band gave a near-definitive version there. Griffin's attack is more abrasive on the live version, but he softens his delivery considerably for 'Prelude To A Kiss', a melting performance which again significantly reworks the melody in places.

★★(★) Tough Tenors Back Again!

Storyville 8298 *Griffin: Eddie 'Lockjaw' Davis (ts); Harry Pickens (p); Curtis Lundy (b); Kenny Washington (d).* 7/84.

As far as we can tell, this is the last recorded encounter between Johnny and Locks. It's pretty much par for the course. Any slowing of pace in Griffin's case over recent years is effectively cancelled out in a programme of straight – some would say unrelieved – blowing themes. There are a few entertaining moments, though unfortunately the best of them is the conversational rap on 'Blues Up And Down'. An excellent rhythm section almost saves the day, with the little-known Pickens in decent if unspectacular form, but we remain unconvinced. On the night, in the Jazzhus Montmartre, it must have been exciting. As a recording, it's very one-dimensional.

***** Johnny Griffin And The Great Danes**

Stunt 2012 *Griffin; Jesper Thilo (ts); Thomas Clausen (p); Mads Vinding (b); Alex Riel (d).* 7/96.

Not Griff and a troupe of singing hounds but teamed with one of the best house bands in the business at the Molde Jazz Festival in 1996. Very much business as usual on the playing front. He's forthright on 'Just Friends' and achingly delicate in places on 'All The Things You Are'. Clausen and Thilo make their own strong statements while Vinding and Riel hold the whole package together without constraining anybody. 'Rhythm-A-Ning' is a superb climax, punchy but expressive. A fine date from a top-drawer band.

***** In And Out**

Dreyfus 36610 *Griffin; Martial Solal (p).* 6–7/99.

These two old stagers are a near perfect match, able to balance laconic power with genuine romanticism. The opening and closing tracks are 'You Stepped Out of a Dream' and Monk's 'Well, You Needn't' and both are magnificent. Little of the rest matches up, but the playing is good and Solal's slightly grouchy, sour delivery is a perfect foil for the – these days – laid-back Griff. 'Hey, Now' is another strong performance, but one probably starts to look for a little more variety than the set has to offer.

***** In Copenhagen**

Storyville 8300 *Griffin; Kenny Drew (p); Niels-Henning Orsted Pedersen (b); Art Taylor (d).* n.d.

***** Catharsis!**

Storyville 8306 *Griffin; Kenny Drew (p); Jens Melgaard (b); Ole Streenberg (d).* 00.

Griffin wasn't the only American exile working in Copenhagen. Kenny Drew proved to be an able and sympathetic partner and their dates at the Jazzhus Montmartre were widely admired. We like the first of these records a lot. 'What Is This Thing Called Love?' and 'Body And Soul' are good, but there are persistent problems with the source tape. The playing is generally very good and the band is in cracking form on 'Wee Dot' and 'A Night In Tunisia' which begins with a strange, almost warlike chant. NHOP is his reliable and inventive self, and Taylor's crackling cymbal figures and furious cross-rhythms seem to mark a bridge between classic bebop and the complexities of the Coltrane quartet.

Catharsis! only appeared in 2000. It's every bit as good as the other album, though one or two of the tracks – notably 'Slukefter Blues' and the folk song 'Hush-A-Bye' – are unnecessarily extended. 'Rhythm-A-Ning' is, as always, brisk and evocative. Drew isn't having one of his very best days and may be held back a bit by the second-string rhythm section. But a good reflection of both the front men in their Scandinavian fastness, and 'Isfahan' is just delightful.

***** Johnny Griffin And Steve Grossman Quintet**

Dreyfus 36615 *Griffin; Steve Grossman (ss, ts); Michael Weiss (p); Pierre Michelot (b); Alvin Queen (d).* 00.

Nine hard-blowing tunes from the co-led quintet. Grossman lends the sound some much-needed variety and texture, doubling on soprano, but it's Queen who gives the set its slightly manic energy, playing at the kind of pace Griff used to boast of but these days rarely attains. Johnny's 'Waltzswing' and Gigi Gryce's 'Nica's Tempo' are two of the highlights of an album that has delivered most of its promise before halfway. The remaining tracks are somewhat conventional and trite, and only Grossman's intelligence and ability to vary pace, tone and attack saves it from tedium.

***** Close Your Eyes**

Minor Music 801085 *Griffin; Horace Parlan (p).* 2/00.

Recorded in Hamburg, this is a delicately nuanced set of duets: robustly lyrical on 'Pannonica', more subtly inflected on 'Someone To Watch Over Me' and a delightful 'My Little Brown Book'. Both veterans are on top form and the close-up, intimate recording gives the music a real presence.

Frank Griffith (born 1959)

TENOR SAXOPHONE

Grew up in Eugene, Oregon, studied at Manhattan School of Music and with Bob Brookmeyer and in recent years has been based in England. A fine technician and able composer/arranger.

*****(*) The Suspect**

Hep 2077 *Griffith; Tom Harrell, Chris Rogers (t, flhn); Joel Weiskopf (p); John Hart (g); James Genus (b); Billy Drummond (d).* 11/90.

***** 'Live' Ealing Jazz Festival 2000**

Hep 2081 *Griffith; Henry Lowther, Steve Fishwick (t); Malcolm Earle Smith (tb); Bob Martin (as); Duncan Lamont Jr (bs); Tom Cawley (p); Dominick Howles (b); Matt Fishwick (d).* 8/00.

The debut album has the confidence and poise of a much more established career. Label boss Alastair Robertson's coup was to team Griffith up with a top-notch rhythm section and with Tom Harrell on the first four tracks. Not to do down Chris Rogers, who takes over for the remaining cuts, but Harrell's genius shines through every track. His solo on the first cut, otherwise marked by a brilliant exchange between Genus and Drummond, is the first inkling that something special is taking place. On the slower 'Afterthoughts' it's Hart, also a Hep artist, who catches the attention with a smooth but thoughtful solo, somewhat in the manner of Philip Catherine.

So far, significantly, no word of the leader, who is the most anonymous element of the session. His own statement on 'Afterthoughts' is attractive enough, but sandwiched between Hart and Harrell on flugelhorn he has little chance to shine. Frank gets stronger as the session continues and by the final cut, 'Ricochet', he's in blazing form. His gifts seem to lie more in the direction of writing and arranging than as a soloist.

That's borne out strongly on the live set, which features a 'Birth Of The Cool'-proportioned band and some very inventive arrangements. Apart from 'The Barnes Bull' which closes the set, all the themes are by other hands, but Griffith's voicings are infinitely subtle. The veteran Lowther is on spanking form and on 'Save Your Love For Me', an old Buddy Johnson tune and a genuine rarity, he delivers an almost perfect solo. Like Griffith, altoist Martin is now based in Britain; he shines on 'Young And Foolish'. Other tracks include Blue Mitchell's Carib-funky 'Funji Mama', Gil Evans's drum-centred 'Gone' (originally written for Philly Joe Jones, but here featuring one of the Fishwick brothers) and Jimmy Deuchar's superb 'Here We Are'. Like the first album what strikes is not Griffith's virtuosity on the saxophone but as a leader. These are strong and compelling statements by a musician who will deliver better work still in years to come.

Tiny Grimes (1916–89)

PIANO, VOCAL

A four-string guitar player, Grimes was a sensation in the Art Tatum Trio and then elsewhere in New York clubs of the '40s. Later he tried his luck with rock'n'roll. Illness slowed him in the '60s, but he recovered and was on the festival circuit again in the '70s and '80s.

*** Tiny Grimes, 1944–1949

Classics 5048 *Grimes; James Young (tb); Charlie Parker, Red Prysock (as); John Hardee (ts); George Kelly (p, cel); Clyde Hart, Marlowe Morris, Joe Springer (p); Lucille Dixon, Charles Isaacs (b); Clyde Butts (b, v); Ed Nicholson, Sonny Payne, Jerry Potter, Harold West (d).* 9/44–49.

Fame with Tatum spurred Grimes into a solo career, first of all with a group featuring Charlie Parker, later with an outfit called the Rocking Highlanders which featured another altoist Red Prysock. This unvarnished compilation brings together all the material he recorded under his own name over the period concerned, including a date for Blue Note, still very much in its R&B phase. The tracks with Bird are obviously the most desirable for less committed listeners, but 'Red Cross' is exceptional and some of the later cuts, including versions of 'See See Rider' and the notorious 'Annie Laurie' are worth having as well. One of the best of the early vocals is 'Romance Without Finance'. A nice introduction to a singular talent. Some of this material is also available on Collectables sets at an equally decent price, but this is the option we'd recommend.

*** Callin' The Blues

Original Jazz Classics OJC 191 *Grimes; J. C. Higginbotham (tb); Eddie 'Lockjaw' Davis (ts); Ray Bryant (p); Wendell Marshall (b); Osie Johnson (d).* 7/58.

*** Blues Groove

Original Jazz Classics OJC 817 *Grimes; Coleman Hawkins, Musa Kaleem (ts); Ray Bryant (p); Earl Wormack (b); Teagle Fleming Jr (d).*

*** Tiny In Swingville

Original Jazz Classics OJC 1796 *Grimes; Jerome Richardson (ts, bs, f); Ray Bryant (p); Wendell Marshall (b); Art Taylor (d).* 8/59.

At one time Grimes's standing with fans and fellow-musicians utterly confounded his diminutive nickname. One of the midwives of popular music, he attended bebop's first contractions (the earliest of the legendary Charlie Parker Savoy sessions were under Grimes's leadership) and then, in the early '50s, slapped rock'n'roll firmly on the bottom with his bizarrely kilted (*sic!*) Rocking Highlanders, who can be heard on the now-deleted *Rock The House.*

In Swingville dispenses with the theatricals. Though there's still a novelty element to the music, which includes 'Annie Laurie' (hoots, mon!) and 'Frankie And Johnnie', frontman Richardson is a completely convincing player and Grimes himself glides through some parallel sections that would do Kenny Burrell proud. The earlier *Callin' The Blues* has the improbable pairing of Higginbotham and Davis for the front line, while *Blues Groove* summons the great Hawkins to the studio (as well as Kaleem, a Blakey sideman back in 1947). The material is either blues or obvious standards on both occasions, and nothing feels very substantial, but Grimes likes being in charge and he gets sterling work out of all hands on each occasion.

**(*) Some Groovy Fours

Black & Blue 874 *Grimes; Lloyd Glenn (p); Roland Lobligeois (b); Panama Francis (d).* 5/74.

Grimes enjoyed something of a resurgence in the '70s and this is a perfectly enjoyable, if lightweight, quartet session. 'Lester Leaps In' should be enough to convince anyone that Tiny was never just a novelty act. He still has great chops and his soloing was often surprisingly sophisticated, even on a basic blues. There was to be just one more LP from Grimes before his death. It's currently out of print, but more regrettably so is *Profoundly Blue*, the Muse set he recorded a year before this one in the company of Houston Person and Harold Mabern. It would be nice to see it reissued.

Griot Galaxy

ENSEMBLE

Detroit-based, they were billed as 'the Sci-Fi Band' and dressed accordingly. Activities were suspended when saxophonist Faruq Z. Bey suffered a serious motorcycle accident in 1989.

*** Live At The DIA 1983

Entropy Stereo ESR 001 2CD *Faruq Z. Bey, Anthony Holland, David McMurray (ss, as, ts); Jaribu Shahid (b, cl); Tani Tabbal (d).* 1/83.

In the group's 17-year history, only two Griot Galaxy records were released, the belated debut *Kins* and the later *Opus Krampus*. Given GG's theatrical aesthetic, which derived much from Sun Ra (though the face paint was copped from the Art Ensemble), it was unsurprising that they avoided the studios. This rare hometown performance, taped at the Detroit Institute of Arts, offers a welcome glimpse of the group's often complex, polyrhythmic pieces. Bassist Shahid's long 'Necrophilia' (also heard in live performance on *Opus Krampus*) weaves together a dark Afro-funk with some powerful free playing. The same recipe is slightly overcooked on 'Marz Society', which calls in the two guest percussionists. The best tracks are Bey's 'After Death', a mournful processional, and the blues-soaked 'Fosters', which demonstrates the kind of excitement GG could generate. As a tribute to their most important influence, Sun Ra's

'Shadow World' and 'Spectrum' are covered, five players sounding like a complete Arkestra. Though longevity was not rewarded with commercial or critical success, the individual members have continued to make a contribution. McMurray worked with George Clinton's surreal Funkadelic, Shahid and Tabbal (astonishing on 'Necrophilia') are a first-call rhythm section, and Bey has sufficiently recovered to – unfortunate term in the circumstances – kickstart his career. This rare release is a welcome reminder of a largely forgotten outfit.

Don Grolnick (1947–96)

PIANO, KEYBOARDS

Grolnick became one of the most creative figures on the American studio scene of the '80s and '90s, working with many of his peers as an arranger–performer and blending interests and influences from rock, jazz and South American music. His early death was a sad end to a career which should have had much great music in its future.

★★★★ **The Complete Blue Note Recordings**
Blue Note 57197-2 2CD *Grolnick; Randy Brecker (t); Barry Rogers, Steve Turre (tb); Michael Brecker, Joe Lovano (ts); Marty Ehrlich, Bob Mintzer (bcl); Dave Holland (b); Bill Stewart, Peter Erskine (d).* 92.

★★★ **Medianoche**
Warners 946287-2 *Grolnick; Michael Brecker (ts); Dave Valentin (f); Mike Mainieri (vib); Andy Gonzalez (b); Don Alias, Steve Berrios, Milton Cardona (perc).* n.d.

★★★(★) **The London Concert**
Fuzzy Music PEPCD008 *Grolnick; Randy Brecker (t); Robin Eubanks (tb); Marty Ehrlich (as, bcl); Michael Brecker (ts); Peter Washington (b); Peter Erskine (d); Don Alias (perc).* 1/95.

Grolnick's standing as producer/arranger/Svengali to some of the leading lights of the studio circuit obscured his own music to some extent, but these very fine records ought to have a wider hearing. Grolnick's two Blue Note albums, *Weaver Of Dreams* and *Nighttown*, have been repackaged as a two-disc set. These are superb sessions, utilizing a starry personnel with exemplary finesse, sharing out duties with democratic insight but letting each man test the weight of the music. Grolnick might have been saving his best writing for the second date, since the compelling 'Heart Of Darkness', for one, cuts anything on his previous records, good though they are, and the brilliant update on 'What Is This Thing Called Love' is a recurring surprise. Brecker, Turre and Lovano play to their best, but it's Ehrlich's bass clarinet which is the key voice in the ensemble. Grolnick himself plays shrewd composer's piano as the icing on a considerable cake.

Medianoche reshapes some of Grolnick's material (there is a new version of 'Heart Of Darkness') in a more Latinized environment. The three percussionists and the light timbres of flute and vibes which predominate give the music a deceptively slight and sunny air. Actually, there is a good deal more going on than at first seems apparent, with Grolnick finding all sorts of harmonic and textural nuances in the situation. Brecker, almost the faithful disciple at this point, plays some gracefully measured solos. An intriguing continuation; but Grolnick's early death from lymphoma has left his discography sadly unfinished.

At least Peter Erskine's Fuzzy Music label has brought back memories of the British tour which Grolnick's ensemble undertook in 1995. *The London Concert* is a fine souvenir (with excellent sound, courtesy of Derek Drescher's BBC team) of one of the gigs. While the impeccable finesse of the studio recordings goes by the board to a degree and there is inevitably a lot of chest-beating Michael Brecker, it's a momentous delivery of five Grolnick classics.

Richard Grossman (1937–92)

PIANO

Though he recorded comparatively little, Grossman was an influential figure in the West Coast tradition of free improvisation, and his reputation has increased since his death in 1992.

★★★★ **Trio In Real Time**
Nine Winds NWCD 0134 *Grossman; Ken Filiano (b); Alex Cline (d).* 10/89–1/90.

★★★★ **In The Air**
Nine Winds NWCD 0146 *As above, except add Vinny Golia (sno, ss, bcl), John Carter (cl).* 10–12/89.

Grossman's death silenced a valuable piano voice too soon. He managed the rare feat of distilling structure and freedom, lyricism and astringency, in a tough yet profoundly sensitive way. His playing from moment to moment evokes most of the post-Taylor masters without ever sounding much like any of them, and he secures a very fine interplay with Filiano (who suffers a bit here and there on these recordings, all done at various concerts) and the virtuosic Cline, who really does run the gamut from whispered skin-strokes to screaming clatter. The trio album revises piano-trio dimensions, taking in a pulsing, Evans-like quietness along with the more customary energetics, ideas appearing and evolving with formidable speed. Seventy minutes are sustained here without much trouble. The quintet date is even longer and is cleverly programmed around one theme, an opening improvisation, a very long sequence of overlapping solos and a sardonic encore entitled 'Henny Youngman's Bird Imitation'. Golia and Carter are wonderfully loquacious in their playing, which acts as a neat contrast to the more rigorous piquancy of Grossman's manner: his solo passage on 'Everything Else Is Away' merits close attention.

★★★(★) **Even Your Ears**
hatOLOGY 515 *Grossman; Ken Filiano (b); Alex Cline (d).* 1/90–3/92.

★★★ **Where The Sky Ended**
hatOLOGY 541 *As above.* 12/89–3/92.

These survivals from various Californian concerts are a valuable addition to Grossman's meagre discography. The first hatOLOGY disc is the superior one. 'Fresh Vegetables' and 'The Switchbacks At Big Sur' are piano solos which underline his originality. A flinty, decisive touch and a reluctance to use much sustain spell out how prodigious his imagination was, each phrase a complete entity while still a building-block in a bigger conception. The four trio tracks are slightly less interesting since Cline is for once a bit too loud and fierce for the balance of the group to hold together. But these are still way, way ahead of most piano–bass–drums situations, as the supernal glow of 'Rubidoux Twilight' suggests.

The Magnatone disc which we listed in a previous edition has now been reissued on hatOLOGY, with a little extra music. 'Afternoon Full Of Hummingbirds' is a typically fascinating solo, laden with Grossman's unique harmonic thinking, and the delicate piano–drums tracery of 'Green Of The East' matches it. The long trio piece 'Like Godzilla' is less interesting, and the recording quality is far from terrific.

Steve Grossman (born 1951)

SOPRANO AND TENOR SAXOPHONES

New Yorker Grossman's precocious start found him playing with Miles Davis as early as 1969. He worked with different leaders during the '70s and has operated mostly as a freelance since, often basing himself in Europe.

***** Way Out East Vol. 1**
Red 123176-2 *Grossman; Juni Booth (b); Joe Chambers (d). 7/84.*

***** Way Out East Vol. 2**
Red 123183-2 *As above. 7/84.*

***** Love Is The Thing**
Red 123189-2 *Grossman; Cedar Walton (p); David Williams (b); Billy Higgins (d). 5/85.*

****(*) Bouncing With Mr A.T.**
Dreyfus 36579-2 *Grossman; Tyler Mitchell (b); Art Taylor (d). 10/89.*

Grossman was working with Miles Davis when still only a teenager, and it's tempting to suggest that his career peaked too early. He has a prodigious command of the saxophone and a fearless energy, which puts him in the same class as Michael Brecker and Bill Evans. But Grossman's sometimes faceless facility can also make him appear as just another Coltrane/Rollins disciple. Most of these entries from the '80s make no attempt to evade the appropriate comparisons, since they all stand as hired-gun blowing dates, Grossman peeling off suitably muscular solos against a conventional post-bop rhythm section. The two trio sessions for Red offer perhaps the most exciting music, since Grossman gets more space to work in, and *Vol. 1* provides some impressively characterized standards. *Love Is The Thing*, though, has the players setting themselves a few challenges by turning a ballad recital upside down in a couple of places with, for instance, an almost brutal 'I Didn't Know What Time It Was'. *Bouncing With Mr A.T.* could have been a great one: trouble is, the sound abominably mistreats both Mitchell and Taylor, the result of a club setting in Genoa. Grossman sounds terrific here, and his beautiful treatment of 'Soultrane' should be heard.

***** My Second Prime**
Red 123246-2 *Grossman; Fred Henke (p); Gilbert Rovere (b); Charles Bellonzi (d). 12/90.*

The Red album is another grandstanding festival set, with the time of year marked by Grossman's choice of 'The Christmas Song' as one of the tunes. His tone has a dusky, almost chargrilled feel to it, and there are some improvisations of expansive power, but the rhythm section merely marks time.

***** Do It**
Dreyfus 191032-2 *Grossman; Barry Harris (p); Reggie Johnson (b); Art Taylor (d). 4/91.*

*****(*) In New York**
Dreyfus 1910867-2 *Grossman; McCoy Tyner (p); Avery Sharpe (b); Art Taylor (d). 9/91.*

*****(*) A Small Hotel**
Dreyfus FDM 36561-2 *Grossman; Cedar Walton (p); David Williams (b); Billy Higgins (d). 3/93.*

*****(*) Time To Smile**
Dreyfus 36566-2 *Grossman; Tom Harrell (t, flhn); Willie Pickens (p); Cecil McBee (b); Elvin Jones (d). 2/93.*

Persistence made Grossman into an impressive character. He still doesn't seem ambitious in this period so far as record-making is concerned. *In New York* is live, the other three are studio dates, but all four seem cursorily organized and find him reeling off standards and easily picked jazz themes, seemingly at a moment's notice. For consistency, he's hard to beat. But if the sheer strength of his playing usually transcends any banalities, he seldom goes for broke either. The difference with these records is in the calibre of his accompanists. *Do It* is all heartland bebop – 'Cherokee', 'Dance Of The Infidels', 'Oblivion', 'Chi Chi' – possibly at Harris's request. The pianist doesn't seem quite at his best, though, and it's Taylor's incisive work that stimulates Grossman into his best moments. Though at times it suffers from club-set *longueurs*, the session with McCoy Tyner is on a more intense level; when they dig into 'Impressions', it's as if Tyner has found the man to replace his old boss after all this time. Some great playing here. *A Small Hotel* is more mediated, civilized by Walton's urbane playing and the more rounded feel to the performances; but again Grossman plays with real purpose and feel. *Time To Smile* sets up a meeting with another great drummer, and with Harrell sitting in on some tracks and a smart set-list to work with, the music is mature and satisfying. If these are all, in the end, further chapters in a hard-bopper's blowing book and little more, it's still exhilarating jazz.

***** Quartet**
Dreyfus FDM 236602-2 *Grossman; Michel Petrucciani (p); Andy McKee (b); Joe Farnsworth (d). 1/98.*

One of Petrucciani's last dates, and he surely brings a note of distinction to the event. So much so, actually, that Grossman himself sounds oddly heavy and even fatigued here and there, his solos often leading down some strange by-ways. 'Body And Soul' is positively laboured. Petrucciani shines as always, and even though he often plays more circumspectly than he would in a solo or trio situation, his solos are worth attention.

Marty Grosz (born 1930)

GUITAR, BANJO, VOCAL

Born in Berlin, Grosz began making a name for himself as a rhythm guitarist and sometime group-leader in Chicago in the '50s, playing in an old-fashioned style formed out of a balance of the '20s and the '30s. In recent years he has become a great favourite on the club circuit, working with a variety of mainstreamers, singing, strumming and playing his favourite role, raconteur.

***** Hooray For Bix!**
Good Time Jazz 10065-2 *Grosz; Carl Halen (c); Turk Santos (c, g); Harry Budd (tb); Frank Chace (cl, bs); Bob Skiver (ts, cl); Tut Soper (p); Chuck Neilson (b); Pepper Boggs (d). 12/57.*

*****(*) Sings Of Love And Other Matters**
Jazzology JCD-210 *Grosz; Dan Barrett (c, tb); Dick Meldonian (ss, as, ts); Keith Ingham (p); Phil Flanigan (b).* 5/86.

*****(*) Swing It!**
Jazzology JCD-180 *Grosz; Peter Ecklund (t); Dan Barrett (tb); Bobby Gordon (cl); Loren Schoenberg (ts); Keith Ingham (p); Murray Wall (b); Hal Smith (d).* 6–7/88.

***** Extra!**
Jazzology JCD-190 *Grosz; Peter Ecklund (c); Bobby Gordon (cl, v); Ken Peplowski (cl, as); Murray Wall, Greg Cohen (b).* 8–9/89.

****** Unsaturated Fats**
Stomp Off CD1214 *Grosz; Peter Ecklund (c); Dan Barrett (tb); Joe Muranyi (cl, ss); Keith Ingham (p); Greg Cohen (b); Arnie Kinsella (d).* 1–2/90.

***** Songs I Learned At My Mother's Knee And Other Low Joints**
Jazzology JCD-220 *Grosz; Randy Sandke (t); Peter Ecklund (c); Bob Pring, Joel Helleny (tb); Ken Peplowski (as, cl); Dick Meldonian (cl, ts); Keith Ingham (p); Greg Cohen (b); Chuck Riggs (d).* 3–6/92.

***** Live At The L.A. Classic**
Jazzology JCD-230 *Grosz; Peter Ecklund (c); Bobby Gordon (cl); Greg Cohen (b); Hal Smith (d).* 6/92.

***** Thanks**
J&M CD 502 *Grosz; Peter Ecklund (c); Dan Barrett (tb); Bobby Gordon (cl); Scott Robinson (ts, bs, bsx); Mark Shane, Keith Ingham (p); Murray Wall, Greg Cohen (b); Hal Smith (d).* 4–5/93.

*****(*) Keep A Song In Your Soul**
Jazzology JCD-250 *As above, except add Dan Levinson (as, C-mel), Joel Helleny (tb), Dan Block (cl, as), Chris Dawson (p), Arnie Kinsella (d); omit Barrett, Shane, Wall.* 10/94.

*****(*) Ring Dem Bells**
Nagel-Heyer 022 *Grosz; Jon-Erik Kellso (t); Scott Robinson (cl, ss, bs); Martin Litton (p); Greg Cohen (b); Chuck Riggs (d).* 2/95.

*****(*) Rhythm For Sale!**
Jazzology JCD-280 *Grosz; Peter Ecklund (t, c); Dan Block (cl, as); Bobby Gordon (cl); Scott Robinson (ts, bs); Jack Stuckey (cl, as, bs); Vince Giordano (bsx, b); Pierre Calligaris (p); Keith Ingham (cel); Greg Cohen, Murray Wall (b); Hal Smith, Arnie Kinsella (d).* 5/93–1/96.

***** Just For Fun!**
Nagel-Heyer 039 *Grosz; Alan Elsdon (t, v); John Barnes (cl, as, bs, v); Murray Wall (b).* 4/96.

Grosz has been industriously documenting hot and sweet tunes of pre-war vintage on the basis that they don't write 'em like that any more. He is a master jazz entertainer who takes everything – and nothing – seriously, so even the corniest relics in his set-list are usually funny and convincingly hot at the same time. His genuine affection for this kind of music takes it out of the museum bracket, and it is all performed with much aplomb. Grosz has assembled a favourite repertory of players, and some or all of them are guaranteed an appearance on all of these records. The hot, wistful Ecklund, the charming Gordon, the ineffable Barrett and the mysteriously versatile Robinson chime in with playing that has freshness and bloom. The above discs are variously credited to the Orphan Newsboys, The Collectors Item Cats and Destiny's Tots; but the best of them is probably *Unsaturated Fats*, by the Grosz–Ingham Paswonky Serenaders. This is dedicated entirely to Fats Waller tunes, all but one of them obscurities which Waller himself never recorded: Ingham's spry arrangements put new life into melodies unheard for decades, and there are some real discoveries such as 'Dixie Cinderella' and 'Asbestos'.

Of the others, *Swing It!* is a shade hotter, and *Songs I Learned At My Mother's Knee* has the best title. We've been a while catching up with the early *Sings Of Love And Other Matters*, but this one's fresh and Marty sings on most tracks, with his classic 'The English Blues' to round matters off. The Jazzology live album might have been the most fun but the sound is less than ideal and Grosz has suppressed all his between-song patter (probably so that he can recycle it at future gigs). *Ring Dem Bells* is completely fired up from the opening 'Rose Of The Rio Grande'. The occasionally restrained Robinson really lets himself go on the likes of 'Old Man Blues', Kellso plays livelier horn than he ever has, and Grosz seems to relish every moment. *Keep A Song In Your Soul* and *Rhythm For Sale!* are the most recent studio sets and include everything from 'Satan Takes A Holiday' to 'Sentimental Gentleman From Georgia'. Since Grosz never changes his act much, one could argue that this is starting to seem like a lot of records in a similar guise; on the other hand, one could say the same about Coltrane.

Just For Fun! is a bit different, anyway. Marty's on stage with Elsdon and Barnes from the old country and favourite bass confederate Murray Wall. Some lovely stuff, though they play more familiar standards than usual, and docked a notch for letting both Elsdon and Barnes have a vocal each.

Hooray For Bix! is Grosz pre-history, a rare documentation of his '50s gang, playing Bix tunes with youthful enthusiasm and not a great deal of finesse. At least it's nice to feature a record in the book which has Bob Skiver and Pepper Boggs on it.

***** Left To His Own Devices**
Jazzology JCD-330 *Grosz; Randy Reinhart (c); Dan Block (cl, bs); Scott Robinson (cl, ss, Cmel, bs); Mike Peters (g); Greg Cohen (b).* 1–6/99.

*****(*) At Bob Barnard's Jazz Party**
Nif Nuf 43/002 *Grosz; Bob Barnard (c); John McCarthy (cl); Howard Cairns (b); Len Barnard (d).* 4/99.

Left To His Own Devices is business as usual for Marty, but it's not really one of our favourites: although everything is in place as usual, a few of the performances feel routine, and after the first two tracks – 'The New Yorker', overdue for a revival, and a delicious 'It's A Sin To Tell A Lie' – it settles down a little too comfortably. But the live album (from St Kilda, Australia) is essential for Groszphiles, since it finds him solo on most tracks and enshrines a lot of his in-concert schtick – finally, a proper documenting of one of the premier jazz entertainers. Barnard and friends join in on a few tracks and there's a new version of the immortal 'English Blues'.

*****(*) Remembering Louis**
Jump JCD 12-25 *Grosz; Jon-Erik Kellso (t); Ken Peplowski (cl); Vince Giordano (bsx, b).* 10/01.

This quartet came together out of a performance at the Chautauqua Jazz Party. It's just plain old jazz repertory, even if it is made up of tunes with an Armstrong link, though in some cases a little tenuous – 'The Song Is Ended' and 'In The Land Of

Beginning Again' are hardly staples of the Pops hitbook, though we'd rather hear those than yet another 'Sleepy Time Down South'. And the gang play great.

George Gruntz (born 1932)

PIANO, BANDLEADER

Gruntz studied in his native Basle and Zurich, and worked in European obscurity – though a spell with Phil Woods brought him wider exposure – until forming The Band, an orchestra which he co-led with fellow Swiss players. It became the Gruntz Concert Jazz Band in 1978, a large orchestra which is still active via an annual touring schedule.

**(*) Theatre

ECM 1265 *Gruntz; Marcus Belgrave, Tom Harrell, Palle Mikkelborg (t, flhn); Julian Priester (tb); Dave Bargeron (tb, euph); Dave Taylor (btb); Ernst-Ludwig Petrowsky, Charlie Mariano, Seppo Paakkunainen (reeds); Howard Johnson (bs, bcl, tba); Dino Saluzzi (band); Mark Egan (b); Bob Moses (d); Sheila Jordan (v).* 7/83.

Gruntz has been running his gigantic Concert Jazz Band since 1972. Formidably weighted with famous names in each of its editions, the group is a live phenomenon which perhaps hasn't translated quite so well to record, since none of their albums is well known – although the excellent MPS best-of, culled from several discs for that label, is a fine introduction. Gruntz's persona as writer/arranger is difficult to perceive, since he cheerfully plunders various aspects of big-band tradition for his charts, but he has an unusual way of bridging the kind of freedoms one associates with, say, the Globe Unity Orchestra and the grand language of Ellington and Kenton. Perhaps the CJB is most like a liberated successor to the Clarke–Boland Big Band.

The ECM album catches them in 1983, but the programme is a bit portentous – a long and rather worthy 'The Holy Grail Of Jazz And Joy' takes up the bulk of it – and the results are disappointing.

***(*) Beyond Another Wall

TCB 94102 *Gruntz; Lew Soloff, John D'Earth, Tim Hagans, Jack Walrath (t); Ray Anderson, Art Baron, Dave Taylor (tb); Chris Hunter, Sal Giorgianni, Bob Malach, Larry Schneider (reeds); Howard Johnson (bs, tba); Carl Weathersby (g); Mike Richmond (b); Danny Gottlieb (d); Billy Branch (v, hca).* 11/92.

***(*) Sins 'N' Wins 'N' Funs

TCB 96602 *Full personnel unlisted, but similar to discs above, plus Tim Berne (as), Seamus Blake (ts), Django Bates (whistle).* 3/81–4/95.

Although more inclined towards modern big-band convention than the MPS music, these are still vivid examples of Gruntz's music-making. *Beyond Another Wall* was made on a ground-breaking (if not epoch-busting) tour of China. The concerts seem to have brought out the best in the band: the playing has terrific energy and élan, standouts including Ray Anderson's 'Literary Lizard', once a quartet piece but here brilliantly realized by the brass section, and Mike Richmond's 'Giuseppi', much more electric than it was on the Enja album. Bluesmen Billy Branch and Carl Weathersby are unlikely imports for the occasion, but they fit right in.

Sins 'N' Wins 'N' Funs collects tracks from some 15 years' worth of concerts, in New York, Rome, Israel, Tokyo and wherever else they've hung their collective hat. Although the collective peronnel isn't listed, the soloists by themselves – from Eje Thelin and Sheila Jordan to Tim Berne and Seamus Blake – are testament to the kind of groups Gruntz has managed to put together down the years, the kind of wish-lists which even George Russell and Gil Evans couldn't have matched. As a record, it doesn't really hang together but, as a jumble of mightily entertaining bits and pieces, it's fine.

*** Mock-Lo-Motion

TCB 95552 *Gruntz; Franco Ambrosetti (flhn); Mike Richmond (b); Adam Nussbaum (d).* 5/95.

Gruntz in much more modest surroundings. He takes only a deferential role as an instrumentalist on the orchestral records, and here he's a much more garrulous presence. The music has a splashy quality, not without charm, and when Ambrosetti sits in on three tunes the results are a melodious kind of post-bop, never as original as the band records but pleasing enough.

***(*) Liebermann

TCB 99452 *Gruntz; Marvin Stamm, Alexander Sipiagin, Scott Wendholt, Matthieu Michel (t, flhn); Luis Bonilla, Clark Gayton (tb); Chris Hunter (as, ss, f); Sal Giorgianni (as, ts, f); Larry Schneider (ss, ts, f); Donny McCaslin (ts, f); Steffen Schorn (bs, bsx, bcl); Mike Richmond (b); John Riley (d).* 11/98.

Here they go again, this time at the 1998 Berlin Jazz Festival. The dedicatee is Rolf Liebermann, composer and polymath, whose 1954 'Symphony For Jazz Ensemble' is the centrepiece of this set (and who died just as the record was being prepared for release). Besides this, there are three new pieces and a version of Wayne Shorter's 'Footprints'. The band are in great heart. Among the soloists, none surpasses Marvin Stamm, usually deemed a pro's pro among sessionmen but rarely acknowledged as an improviser. Blessed also by an excellent location recording, this is a fine place to make the group's acquaintance.

*** Merryteria

TCB 99502 *As above, except add Kenny Rampton, Terell Stafford, Jens Winther (t, flhn), Ray Anderson, Art Baron (tb), Dave Bargeron (tb, euph), Earl McIntyre, Christoph Schweizer (btb), Raphael Wall (d); omit Michel.* 3–11/98.

***(*) Global Excellence

TCB 21172 *As above, except add Matthieu Michel (t), Scott Robinson (bcl, bs, bsx, cbsx), Mark Egan (b), Danny Gottlieb (d); omit Stafford, Winther, Anderson, Baron, Schweizer, Schorn, Wall, Riley.* 12/01.

Two more boisterous entries by the Gruntz gang. As ever, the appeal may depend on how much you take to Gruntz's composing and which of the soloists appeals. We slightly prefer the second of these, for Marvin Stamm's exceptionally gilded playing in 'Two As One', the raving showcase for the tenor section in 'Steam Passage' and having Scott Robinson get out his contrabass saxophone on 'Brain Play'. The earlier set doesn't slouch and Sipiagin's feature, 'Novgorod Bells', works well, but it's just behind.

Gigi Gryce (1927–83)

ALTO SAXOPHONE, FLUTE

Worked with Tadd Dameron and Lionel Hampton in 1953, then with Oscar Pettiford, the Jazz Lab Quintet and his own small group; but it was his writing which established his reputation. Drifted from sight in the early '60s and didn't record again.

***** And The Jazz Lab Quintet**
Original Jazz Classics OJCCD 1774 *Gryce; Donald Byrd (t); Wade Legge (p); Wendell Marshall (b); Art Taylor (d).* 2–3/57.

***** Sayin' Somethin'**
Original Jazz Classics OJCCD 1851 *Gryce; Richard Williams (t); Richard Wyands (p); Reggie Workman (b); Mickey Roker (d).* 3/60.

***** The Hap'nin's**
Original Jazz Classics OJCCD 1868 *As above, except replace Workman with Julian Euell (b).* 5/60.

*****(*) The Rat Race Blues**
Original Jazz Classics OJCCD 081 *As above.* 6/60.

Joe Goldberg's liner-note for *The Hap'nin's* makes the perceptive point that, however good a player Gryce was, his real talent and contribution was as a leader, a figure who catalysed talent in others. He is certainly a victim of what might be called Rodin's Syndrome, an artist recognized for just one or two not necessarily representative works. Of the many pieces he wrote for a variety of ambitiously proportioned projects – not big in numbers, but in conception – the only ones which have really entered the jazz mainstream are 'Nica's Tempo' and, to a lesser extent, 'Speculation' and 'Minority'. The former was given a definitive statement in a group that also included Thelonious Monk and Art Blakey, which gave it something of a leg-up into the mainstream. In the year of Charlie Parker's death, the pretenders to the throne were thrown into unusually high profile. Gryce was never a virtuosic player, but these sessions suggest that he was more interesting than is often supposed, certainly not a Bird copyist. His tone was darker and with a broader vibrato, the phrasing less supple but with an emphatic, vocal quality that carries over into his flute playing. 'Laboratory' and 'workshop' have always been weasel terms, useful camouflage for the well-founded jazz tradition of rehearsing – or experimenting – at the public's expense. Gryce, though, was a genuine experimenter, even if a relatively modest one. He never stopped trying to find new colorations and new ways of voicing chords, and the set from 1957 is no exception. No great revelations, but Byrd is a responsive partner in the front line and the rhythm section is less hung-up on its own ideas, more aware, one suspects, of what Gryce himself is looking for.

Hard to put any real distance between the later dates. As before, the writing is often a good deal more interesting than the playing. Gryce is often overshadowed by Williams, and the rhythm section boil away as if on their own private date. We still find *The Rat Race Blues* the best set, track by track, from this rather crowded vintage, but there are good things, too, on *The Hap'nin's* (love that punctuation!), including an excellent 'Nica's Tempo', which was originally written for the Messengers, and two lovely standards in 'Lover Man' and 'Summertime'. The picture is now a good deal fuller than it was, though it's unlikely that any but convinced enthusiasts will find space for more than one of these.

Vince Guaraldi (1928–76)

PIANO

Born in San Francisco, and working there for most of his career, Guaraldi had an uneventful time with various leaders in the '50s but found his niche as a pop-jazz composer in the '60s. His Charlie Brown music won him a big audience. A smooth jazzer, ahead of his time.

****(*) Vince Guaraldi Trio**
Original Jazz Classics OJC 149 *Guaraldi; Eddie Duran (g); Dean Reilly (b).* 4/56.

****(*) Jazz Impressions**
Original Jazz Classics OJC 287 *As above.* 4/56.

****(*) A Flower Is A Lovesome Thing**
Original Jazz Classics OJC 235 *As above.* 4/57.

**** Jazz Impressions Of Black Orpheus**
Original Jazz Classics OJC 437 *Guaraldi; Monty Budwig (b); Colin Bailey (d).* 62.

****(*) In Person**
Original Jazz Classics OJC 951 *Guaraldi; Eddie Duran (g); Fred Marshall (b); Colin Bailey (d); Benny Valarde (perc).* 5/63.

****(*) The Latin Side Of Vince Guaraldi**
Original Jazz Classics OJC 878 *Guaraldi; Eddie Duran (g); Fred Marshall (b); Jerry Granelli (d); Bill Fitch, Benny Valarde (perc); string quartet.* 64.

**** The Grace Cathedral Concert**
Fantasy 9678 *Guaraldi; Tom Beeson (b); Lee Charlton (d); St Paul's Church Of San Rafael Choir.* 5/65.

****(*) From All Sides**
Original Jazz Classics OJC 989 *Guaraldi; Bola Sete (g); Fred Marshall, Monte Budwig (b); Jerry Granelli, Nick Martinez (d).* 65.

***** Greatest Hits**
Fantasy FCD-7706-2 *Guaraldi; various groups as above.* n.d.

***** A Boy Named Charlie Brown**
Fantasy FCD-8430-2 *Guaraldi; Monty Budwig (b); Colin Bailey (d).* n.d.

****(*) A Charlie Brown Christmas**
Fantasy FCD-8431-2 *As above, except add Fred Marshall (b), Jerry Granelli (d).* n.d.

Guaraldi was a harmless pop-jazz pianist, not as profound as Dave Brubeck, not as swinging as Ramsey Lewis, but capable of fashioning catchy tunes from favourite licks; the most famous example remains his Grammy-winning 'Cast Your Fate To The Wind'. If this kind of music appeals, the best way to sample it is through the *Greatest Hits* collection, which gathers together his most characteristic moments. The earlier trio dates offer mild, unambitious variations on standards, with Eddie Duran figuring rather more strongly than Guaraldi himself. The *Black Orpheus* set is marked by the seemingly relentless triviality of the material. *In Person* is live, and at a slightly higher temperature than the studio dates, while *The Latin Side* is about as hot-blooded as a game of dominoes. *The Grace Cathedral Concert* finds him jazzing the liturgy to a less than holy-rolling effect.

As a composer, Guaraldi will always be best represented by his music for the Charlie Brown TV-cartoon series (it certainly made an impact on Wynton Marsalis, who has himself done what is effectively a tribute album). The first record in particular includes some charming miniatures, performed with surprising delicacy. The second is merely more of the same with less of the freshness, though it is stuck with Yuletide material. One might dismiss Guaraldi as the lightest of lightweights, but look how many records he has in print.

Johnny Guarnieri (1917–85)

PIANO

Took up jazz piano after hearing some of the stride players in New York, then worked with Benny Goodman and Artie Shaw at the end of the '30s. Various associations, including staff job at NBC, and solo recordings, during the '40s. Much studio work until a move to California in the '60s. Occasional later appearances and non-stop composing: he reckoned to have written 5,000 tunes in his lifetime.

***** Johnny Guarnieri 1944–1946**

Classics 956 *Guarnieri; Billy Butterfield (t); Hank D'Amico (cl); Lester Young, Don Byas (ts); Dexter Hall (g); Billy Taylor, Slam Stewart, Leo Guarnieri, Bob Haggart (b); Cozy Cole, Sammy Weiss, J. C. Heard (d).* 4/44–1/46.

***** Johnny Guarnieri 1946–1947**

Classics 1063 *Guarnieri; Tony Mottola (g); Bob Haggart, Trigger Alpert, Leo Guarnieri (b); Cozy Cole, Morey Feld (d); Rosemary Calvin (v).* 5/46–47.

The kind of musician whose name is drifting into obscurity, not through wilful neglect but because he never had his name on any significant recordings. Guarnieri's consummate professionalism, unselfish attitude (he became a generous and much-liked teacher later in life) and robust energy made him a fixture in his milieu – New York club jazz of the '40s – although various big-band leaders tried to squirrel his talent away in the confines of their own orchestra. His own-name LP recordings are minor works which have never been reissued, and at present these Classics compilations of various and mostly minor-league dates are all that will be found under his stamp. His 1944 Savoy trio sessions form the bulk of Classics 956, and they show how much of his right hand came from Waller and Tatum: these are frothy, mischievous dates which also highlight Slam Stewart's hokum. But the first session has Lester Young hiding in the shadows, and a later one has some splendid work by Don Byas. Aside from a couple of vocals by Rosemary Calvin, Classics 1063 is all solo, trio or (with Mottola's guitar) quartet material. There's a novelty element to much of this music: the pianist isn't interested in touching great depths of feeling, preferring to make his point through a precise, almost dainty paraphrase of his melodic material. He sings on 'Bobo, The Bowery Barber', which makes one glad that he didn't do it too often. The transfers are no more than adequate and there's very little sparkle in the sound.

Gul 3

GROUP

Stockholm-based trio, working in a free but carefully organized terrain.

***** Soul**

Crazy Wisdom 159072-2 *Johan Arrias (as, bs, v); Leo Svensson (clo, perc, vb); Henrik Olsson (ky, g, d, v).* 2/00.

A pretty extraordinary record to emerge from a major label (Crazy Wisdom is a part of the Universal group) and a tribute to Mats Gustafsson's powers of persuasion for his Crazy Wisdom imprint. Nothing tops the opener, 'Opener', which has activity going on behind high, grating held notes from what seem to be overdubbed saxophones. Thereafter, the trio explore sober, sparse, open textures which are so slow and methodical that, by the time of the closing 'Rainbows And Speeding Motorbikes', the music threatens to come to a dead halt, which it eventually does. Recorded with gritty immediacy, the deadpan interplay (Olsson works more as a soundscaper than any kind of rhythm player) is coldly interesting. Likely to stand as a strange one-off.

Friedrich Gulda (1930–2000)

PIANO

Notorious for eccentric behaviour, including faking his own obituary, Gulda began as a classical performer before becoming involved in jazz. Considered an influence on the young Joe Zawinul, he combines a similar interest in classical form with an impressive swing.

***** Friedrich Gulda At Birdland**

RCA Victor PM 1355 *Gulda; Idrees Sulieman (t); Jimmy Cleveland (tb); Phil Woods (as); Seldon Powell (ts); Aaron Bell (b); Nick Stabulas (d).* 6/56.

Gulda was exotic fruit when he arrived in the United States, somewhat as Joe Zawinul was to be, but no one could deny his ability to play modern jazz. Contrary to the title, this isn't a live gig but a studio session. Here, along with 'A Night In Tunisia' and the Leiber/Stoller 'Bernie's Tune', his band swings through a set of somewhat sombre originals, including 'Dark Glow' and 'Air From Other Planets' (which is an indirect reference to Schoenberg, via Stefan George). The piano sound isn't great, but Gulda's comping is absolutely spot on and there is enough solo action from the horns to make this a worthwhile sample of a musical one-off.

Lars Gullin (1928–76)

BARITONE SAXOPHONE, PIANO

A major figure in Scandinavian modernism as a player, leader and composer, Gullin is eminent in European circles, but is still little known elsewhere. His career tailed off somewhat in the '70s and his early death denied him the chance to enjoy the retrospective acclaim which has gone to several of his generation.

***** Lars Gullin Vol. 1 1955–56**

Dragon DRCD 224 *Gullin; Chet Baker (t); George Olsson (tb); Arne Domnérus (cl, as); Rolf Berg, Bjarne Nerem (ts); Lennart Jansson (bs); Richard Twardzik, Gunnar Svensson (p); Georg Riedel, Jimmy Bond (b); Peter Littman, Bosse Stoor, Egil Johansen (d); Caterina Valente (v).* 4/55–5/56.

Gullin has been gone for over 25 years now, but he remains among the most creative of European voices. After working in big bands as an alto player, he took up the baritone at the age of 21, and his utterly distinctive sound – delicate, wistful, pensively controlled – is the linchpin of his music. When he wrote for six or more instruments he made the band sound like a direct extension of that big, tender tone. He seems like neither a bopper nor a swing stylist. The first volume in Dragon's reissue programme includes a meeting with Baker's quartet, with a few precious glimpses of Twardzik, a melancholy 'Lover Man' and Caterina Valente vocalizing on 'I'll Remember April'; there are also three charming octet pieces.

CORE COLLECTION

★★★★ Lars Gullin Vol. 2 1953

Dragon DRCD 234 *Gullin; Weine Renliden, Conte Candoli (t); Frank Rosolino (tb); Lee Konitz (as); Zoot Sims (ts); Kettil Ohlsson (bs); Putte Lindblom, Bob Laine, Mats Olsson (p); Yngve Akerberg, Georg Riedel, Simon Brehm, Lars Petersson, Tauno Suojärvi, Don Bagley (b); Jack Noren, Bosse Stoor, Stan Levey (d); Rita Reys (v).* 3–12/53.

This second volume includes the superb tracks that were issued as a ten-inch album by Contemporary in the USA. Gullin sustains a steady, effortless flow of ideas on all his solos and plays alto on two tunes. The rest of the disc includes various studio sessions with other leaders and three tracks with the visiting Americans, in which Gullin holds his own comfortably.

★★★ 1954/55 Vol. 3 Late Date

Dragon DRCD 244 *Gullin; Leppe Sundevall (bt); Kurt Jarnberg (tb); Rolf Billberg (ts); Jutta Hipp, Bengt Hallberg, Claes-Goran Fagerstadt (p); Rolf Berg (g); Georg Riedel, Simon Brehm (b); William Schiopffe, Bosse Stoor (d); Moretone Singers (v).* 9/54–6/55.

Lower marks only because the seven tracks with the cooing Moretone Singers may disenchant some supporters, even though Gullin's own playing remains impeccable (the fine improvisation on 'Lover Man', for example). Four brief tracks with Hipp's trio are unremarkable, but two tracks by the Gullin sextet, 'Late Summer' and 'For F. J. Fans Only', are superb.

★★★(★) In Germany 1955 And 1956 Vol. 1

Anagram CD 2 *Gullin; Lee Konitz (as); Hans Koller (ts); Willi Sanner (bs); Attila Zoller (g); Roland Kovac (p); Johnny Fischer (b); Karl Sanner, Rudi Sehring (d); Erwin Lehn Orchestra.* 11/55–1/56.

★★★(★) In Germany 1955, 1956 And 1959 Vol. 2

Anagram CD 5 *As above except add Horst Jankowski (p), Peter Witte (b), Hermann Mutschler (d), Kurt Edelhagen Orchestra.* 1/56–3/59.

Olle Lind has been collecting Gullin recordings for many years and these two discs are the projected beginning of a ten-CD series which opens his archive for the first time. The recordings are of various provenance – live, studio, radio – and are mostly in excellent sound. The highlight of the first volume is a wonderfully expansive 'Too Marvellous For Words', which really demonstrates Gullin's powers as a melodist. On the second, there's a fine chart for 'Yesterdays' by Gösta Theselius, and some delicious sparring with Konitz, particularly on two versions of 'Ablution' (Lee plays baritone on the second!). Four different versions of the lovely 'Late Summer' are spread across the two discs. The discs are designed more for Gullin collectors than the general audience, but most will respond to some excellent jazz.

★★★(★) Vol. 4 Stockholm Street

Dragon DRCD 264 *Gullin; Bengt-Arne Wallin (t, flhn); Andreas Skjold, Eje Thelin (tb); Putte Wickman (cl); Rolf Billberg (as); Harry Bäcklund (ts); Lars Bagge (p); Sune Larsson (g); Lars Pettersson, Claes Lindroth, Erik Lundborg (b); Sture Kallin, Bosse Skoglund, Robert Edman (d).* 1/59–9/60.

The series picks up again with the contents of four EP sessions plus four other tracks from the same period. The brief playing-time afforded by the medium concentrates Gullin's writing, the harmonic weight offset by the plain rhythmic language. Arguably not his best work as a player – there is a bonus in two tracks from an abandoned session, including a longer treatment of 'Darn That Dream', which have extended but somewhat desultory solos by the leader – but some of these miniatures are hauntingly effective, especially 'Nightshade' and the bittersweet gem 'The Yellow Leaves' Love To The Earth'.

★★★(★) Portrait Of My Pals

EMI (Swed) 792429-2 *Gullin; Jan Allan, Torgny Nilsson (tb); Rolf Billberg (as); Harry Bäcklund (ts); Lars Sjøsten (p); Bjorn Alke, Kurt Lindgren (b); Bo Skoglund (d); strings.* 6/64.

★★★(★) Aeros Aromatic Atomica Suite

EMI (Swed) 750752-2 *Gullin; Bertil Lövgren, Leif Hallden, Jan Allan, Maffy Falay (t); Håkan Nyqvist (t, frhn); Bertil Strandberg (tb); Sven Larsson (btb, tba); Arne Domnérus, Claes Rosendahl, Lennart Aberg, Erik Nilsson (woodwinds); Bengt Hallberg (p); Rune Gustafsson (g); Stefan Brolund, Georg Riedel (b); Egil Johansen (d).* 72–3.

★★★ Like Grass

EMI/Odeon 475206-2 *Gullin; Lee Konitz (as); Bernt Rosengren (ts, f); Gunnar Lundqvist (f); Red Mitchell (b); Island Ostlund (d).* 8/73.

★★★ Bluesport

EMI (Swed) 1364612 *Gullin; Maffy Falay (t, flhn); Bertil Strandberg (tb); Lennart Aberg (ss); Lennart Jansson (as); Bernt Rosengren (ts); Gunnar Lindqvist (f); Lars Sjøsten (p); Amadeo Nicoletti (g); Jan Bergman, Bjorn Alke (b); Fredrik Norén, Rune Carlsson (d); Ahmadu Jarr, Okay Temiz (perc).* 9/74.

Though released only in Sweden, these reissues are essential parts of the Gullin canon. *Portrait Of My Pals* includes some of Gullin's most skilful writing, with strings appended to six tracks; the versions of 'Prima Vera' (alias 'Manchester Fog') and 'Decent Eyes' are among his best work, the timbres of the ensemble beautifully handled. Remastering hasn't helped the original sound, which was never very clear, and the presence of two basses in the rhythm section imparts a rather odd, off-centre feel to the rhythms. The CD includes three alternative takes and one newly issued tune.

Aeros Aromatica Atomica Suite was a project close to Gullin's heart, and this fine performance by a team of Swedish mainstays must be counted one of his strongest records. If one isn't always convinced that the composer truly has hold of the thematic thread running through the three parts, the textures and contrasts are still absorbing, and there is always the solo work by the horns (and the perennially undervalued Gustafsson). Excellent sound this time. *Bluesport*, though recorded later, has an inferior mix, and this time some of the music sounds only half finished. But the vibrant title-track alone is compelling and Gullin's own powers as an improviser, if less sharp than in his youth, remained a notable force.

Like Grass is disappointing in that it features Gullin on piano rather than baritone. The music was mostly new, but there are also new visits to 'Silhouette' from 1951 and 'Blue Mail' and 'Subway' from 1960. It's a bitty, rather misshapen set. The long pieces 'The Carousel' and 'Like Grass' are surrounded by trio, duo and solo pieces which are little more than fragments. Konitz and Rosengren are together on only two tracks, and they make a rather strange contrast to each other on 'The Carousel', the alto pinchy and the tenor full of bluster. Designed as Gullin's piano record, it's an oddity.

Peter Gullin (1959–2003)

BARITONE AND TENOR SAXOPHONES

The son of Lars is no mean saxophonist himself, playing able post-bop horn in these contemporary settings.

***** Tenderness**

Dragon DRCD 222 *Gullin; Jacob Fischer (g); Ole Rasmussen (b).* 2/92.

***** Transformed Evergreen**

Dragon DRCD 266 *As above, except replace Fischer with Morten Kaargard (g).* 3/94.

*****(*) Untold Story**

Dragon DRCD 315 *As above.* 3/97.

It's somewhat brave for a son to follow quite so closely in the parental footsteps, though a couple of Coltranes have tried it. Peter's baritone sound was fuller and throatier, though something of the difference must surely be explained by modern recording techniques. What the old man wouldn't have given for the bright top-notes and rich bottom-end Peter (whose birth was celebrated in 'Peter Of April') gets on *Tenderness* and its two sequels. The classical references pall after a while, but they are handled with some taste both on the first album and on *Untold Story*, where Prokofiev and Rimsky-Korsakov are both namechecked on 'Incognito'. Gullin Jr stuck with the same drummerless concept from the beginning. With a piece like 'Men Stig In' on the same record he showed that he had begun to write themes which sit comfortably with it. Kaargard (a Dane, like Rasmussen) is also a gifted writer, and his three pieces include the title-track. Gullin himself only latterly began to develop convincingly in this direction. The three 'Fantasias' on the previous disc border on the pedestrian, while 'The Hollow Clown' (and we still think it ought to be 'crown') suggests he'd been listening to Mingus. There isn't a note here that isn't played with taste and conviction, but it may yet be a touch too dry and accommodating for some tastes. Sadly, like his father, Peter was taken much too soon.

Russell Gunn (born 1971)

TRUMPET, FLUGELHORN, KEYBOARDS, PERCUSSION

Raised in St Louis, Gunn was a trumpet-competition winner in 1989 and a rapper in high school. He played with the Oliver Lake group before going to New York and featuring in Buckshot LaFonque and the Lincoln Center Jazz Orchestra.

****(*) Gunn Fu**

High Note HCD 7003 *Gunn; Gregory Tardy (ts, f); Sherman Irby (f); James Hurt (p); Stefon Harris (vib); Eric Revis (b); Ali Jackson (d).* 12/96.

****(*) Love Requiem**

High Note HCD 7020 *Gunn; Myron Walden (as); Mark Turner (ts); Gregory Tardy (f, ts); James Hurt, Shedrick Mitchell (p); Stefon Harris (vib); Eric Revis (b); Cindy Blackman (d).* 8/97.

***** Ethnomusicology Vol. 1**

Atlantic 7567-83165-2 *Gunn; Andre Heyward (tb); Bruce Williams (as, cl); Gregory Tardy (ts, f, bcl); James Hurt (ky); Chieli Minucci (g); Rodney Jordan (b); Woody Williams (d); Khalil Kwame Bell (perc); DJ Apollo (turntables).* 7/98.

Gunn looks destined to go places and will look back on his early discs as 'prentice work. His debut record for Muse, *Young Gunn*, was a cautious, promising start, but the record has already disappeared. *Gunn Fu* seems like much more Gunn's own situation, with a young band and arrangements that belong to his own experience, such as the surprising version of 'Invitation' sprung off Revis's compelling bass vamp. Gunn has a big, almost noisy style on up-tempo tunes and there's an interesting gambit in Harris, whose vibratoless vibes are an unpredictable colour. However, the record seems sabotaged by its sound-mix; which muddles and takes the edge off all the sharpest aspects of Gunn's music.

Love Requiem is much more achieved, though it has a curiously inappropriate aura for a set coming out of the usually down-home High Note label. Structured as a nine-part sequence on the rise and fall of a relationship, it does feel ponderously solemn, underscored by episodes such as 'Torment' and 'Psychosis'. Walden, Tardy and Turner make the best of it, but this is another one that the leader may look back on with a little embarrassment when he's no longer young Gunn.

Signed to Warners, Gunn came up with the modish, wiseguy stew of this and that which is *Ethnomusicology Vol. 1*. He's a lively player, and this variation on the styles of Branford Marsalis's *Buckshot LaFonque* has much to entertain, the horns strutting over hip-hop beats, playing rasping R&B charts against turntable scratching, or putting a contrastingly sweet line over a stone-faced funk beat. But it doesn't feel like a record that's built to last.

*****(*) Smokin' Gunn**

High Note HDCD 7056 *Gunn; Bruce Williams (as); Marc Cary (p); Eric Revis (b); Terreon Gully (d).* 12/99.

***** Mood Swings**

High Note HCD 7107 *Gunn (t); Radam Schwartz (org); Eric Johnson (g); Cecil Brooks III (d).* 12/99.

Back, for a moment, in a no-fuss acoustic setting, Gunn and cohorts make a much stronger statement here. It looks forward, but takes its basic grammar from the period when hard bop was opening out into wider forms: so Gunn and Williams bring to mind several past stylists while doing their best to assert themselves on the interesting material. In covering 'Delfeayo's Dilemma', they also start the process of entering modern tunes into a new modern repertory. Gunn's own playing sounds more assured and more adventurous too, and the chameleonic Williams sounds like he'll fit into all kinds of situations.

The follow-up (recorded the same month!) drops him down into an organ/guitar combo situation, but his playing is a constant – tough, gritty, elegant when he wants. 'Blues To Lee', a Morgan homage, more or less apotheosizes his approach in this setting. But docked a notch for sheer calculation. How much does he really invest of himself in any playing situation? Because look what's up next...

***** Ethnomusicology Volume 3**
Justin Time JUST 189-2 *Gunn; Duane Eubanks (t); Antoine Drye (flhn, t);Vincent Chancey (fr hn); Dorian Perriot (tba); Gregory Tardy (bcl); Oliver Lake (as); Kebbi Williams (ts); Stefon Harris (vib); Carl Burnett (g); Nick Rolfe (ky); Marc Cary (p); James Hurt (syn); Carlos Henderson (b); Dana Murray, Rocky Bryant (d); Kahlil Kwame Bell (perc); DJ Neil Armstrong (turntables); Dave Darlington (neve, pro tools); Gunn Fu, Jody Merriday (v).* n.d.

The huge cast-list suggests that it might be a big-band date, but Russell's just varying the pace. It's an angry, uptight record, railing at critics (as if most listeners care about that), prejudice and intolerance, but even without the issues the music has a taut, almost incendiary quality, and it's hard to fault the trumpeter's own contributions. Problem is, context is so dense and riled-up that ethnomusicology starts to sound like as much of a mouthful as it is to say.

John Gunther (born 1966)

ALTO, TENOR AND SOPRANO SAXOPHONES, BASS CLARINET

Contemporary free-bop multi-instrumentalist and composer.

***** Permission Granted**
CIMP 136 *Gunther; Leo Huppert (b); Jay Rosen (d).* 1/97.

Melodious free-bop of an unassuming disposition. This is the kind of record CIMP has set its stall up to accommodate. Gunther is a thinker's saxophonist, almost a Tristano-ite in his reluctance to plumb false registers or end up on a squeal. With Huppert often hidden in the music, the propulsion all comes from Rosen, whose drum parts, for all their invention, often overwhelm everything else. The tunes are quirky things, but the record seems to get quieter and more remote as it goes on, with the rather lonesome 'Lines' and the bass–tenor duet, 'Us', particularly well focused. Gunther ends on a tenor solo of 'Stardust', played with the minimum of elaboration: an affecting coda.

*****(*) Healing Song**
CIMP 163 *As above, except add Ron Miles (t).* 9/97.

*****(*) Above Now Below**
CIMP 176 *As above, except add Rob Thomas (vn).* 6/98.

Better and better. Gunther's composing is the thread that makes these discs work, with 21 pieces across the two discs – and scarcely one of them less than memorable – as well as useful provocation for the improvisers. He's helped greatly by the arrival of the admirable Miles, who can get all over the horn (especially the lowest register, out of which he gets an unearthly growl) and, on the second disc, Thomas, who bides his time between barn-dance figures and a Stuff Smith-like swing. There's a lot of humour in this music (not a commodity this label trades in much), and pieces such as 'BooBoo Joins The Circus', 'The Collective' or several of the episodes in the three 'suites' which fill the second disc should provoke a grin. He's in hock to Ornette Coleman some of the time – 'Sound Byte' is pure Coleman, and 'Colemanation' makes a homage out of it – but there's nothing wrong with that. Very engaging music altogether.

***** Gone Fishin'**
CIMP 232 *As above.* 9/00.

With tunes supplied by Monk, West Africa, Native America (and Gunther), the music is a cheerful mix of urban, urbane and rural. Gunther scores highly on charm and songfulness, two qualities which tend to set him apart from the CIMP roster. Miles is dependably excellent. But the record's bitty, and too long. Some of the shorter pieces such as 'Mbira Music' seem like distracting interludes. Fifty minutes of the best, most focused music would have been enough.

Gush

GROUP

Swedish improvisers at work in a group context, from which the peripatetic Gustafsson has since moved on.

*****(*) ... From Sounds To Things**
Dragon DRCD 204 *Mats Gustafsson (sax); Sten Sandell (p, ky, v); Raymond Strid (d, perc).* 5 & 10/90.

*****(*) Gushwachs**
Bead 002 *As above, except add Philipp Wachsmann (vn, vla, elec).* 5/94.

*****(*) Live At Fasching**
Dragon DRCD 313 *As above, except omit Wachsmann.* 6/96.

Presumably not a coincidence that this trio should bear a name alphabetically very close to saxophonist Mats Gustafsson's. Given that this is very much a collaborative trio, it seems only proper to list it separately. Much of the impetus comes from Strid's big-hearted approach to the kit and associated percussion; the drummer has the rare capacity to suggest a pulse without laying down the rhythmic law. Sandell is a suprisingly fleeting and fugitive figure in this context, often seeming to come in at the last moment to smooth the music into a more finished shape. He is more prominent (or perhaps easier to identify) on the first record. On *Gushwachs*, he blends into the electronic soundscape established by Wachsmann. The addition of the violinist brings an extra dimension to the music. Interesting to compare it with the less successful addition of Marilyn Crispell to the Barry Guy/Gustafsson/Strid trio which has been working concurrently. Whereas Crispell brought an over-the-top expressionism to what was already a very tight-knit group, Wachsmann alters the emphasis dramatically and creates a dark *mise-en-abîme* effect, like a multiple reflection in a hall of cracked mirrors. The live record is in some ways the most disturbing of the three. Sandell sets a fierce agenda on, for instance, 'And Any Warranty Otherwise', which Gustafsson finds himself decorating rather than getting inside. Sometimes it feels like a group coming to the end of its tether, but at other points there's unexpected humour and flight. An altogether admirable trio of records.

Mats Gustafsson (born 1965)

BARITONE, TENOR, SOPRANO, AND SOPRANINO SAXOPHONES, FLUTEOPHONE, OTHER INSTRUMENTS

A Swedish improviser, playing in comparative obscurity at the beginning of the '90s, but latterly becoming more familiar

through work with the group Gush, Barry Guy and Ken Vandermark. Currently has his own imprint, Crazy Wisdom, distributed through Swedish Universal.

***** Nothing To Read**

Blue Tower Records BTCD 03 *Gustafsson; Paul Lovens (d, perc, saw). 3/90.*

****** Mouth Eating Trees And Related Activities**

Okkadisk OD 12010 *As above, except add Barry Guy (b). 12/92.*

*****(*) Parrot Fish Eye**

Okkadisk OD 12006 *Gustafsson; Gene Coleman (bcl); Jim O'Rourke (g, acc, perc); Michael Zerang (perc). 10/94.*

*****(*) The Education Of Lars Jerry**

Xeric XER-CD-100 *Gustafsson (bs solo). 10/95.*

*****(*) Impropositions**

Phono Suecia PSCD 99 *Gustafsson (sax solo). 6/96.*

*****(*) Frogging**

Maya 9702 *Gustafsson; Barry Guy (b). 6/97.*

Gustafsson has the capacity to become one of the giants of European improvisation. Blessed with a seemingly effortless technique, a wittily deconstructive approach to his instrument(s), and a generous intelligence, he never produces work that is less than thoughtful or other than exuberant. The duos with Lovens are not very well recorded but there is some terrific playing from both men, and the CD case is a first example of Gustafsson's interest in design; the session was recorded at the Blatornet antiquarian bookshop in Stockholm's Rorstrandsgatan, but, apart from five pictures of the setting, there is not a single word to read, just thick, blank card.

Impropositions is just the opposite. Released on the (mainly) classical label, Phono Suecia, this enhanced CD, suitable for Mac or PC, also has a beautifully designed book, containing notes on each of 13 solo improvisations and a collection of elegant abstract paintings. The emphasis as ever is on baritone. Gustafsson's lineage is now clear, though Serge Chaloff seems to have been a greater influence than the young Swede's compatriot, Lars Gullin. On 'Just A Slice Of Acoustic Car', the horn is modified with a beer-can inside the bell. 'Out Of IF' is dedicated to Lovens and has an edgy, percussive attack, flurries of notes and pungent, stabbing phrases. 'Long Titles – NO WAY!' sees him shift to tenor, changing the sound by pressing the bell against his knee. One of the most interesting pieces, particularly given what Gustafsson and Barry Guy have discussed regarding the place that movement has in their collaborations, is 'Bevllohallat Hhu/o', which introduces the fluteophone as well as baritone, intended to accompany an improvised dance by choreographer Lotta Melin. The fluteophone is basically a normal flute played through a saxophone mouthpiece and part-muted by a clarinet stand wedged in the other end. It's not an immediately identifiable sound, except in so far as it has become an integral part of Gustafsson's work.

His duo with Guy is celebrated on *Frogging*. Like Gustafsson, the bassist has a great interest in the visual arts, using a drawing by a Scottish abstract expressionist and mythological painter on the cover; Guy is also very interested in the relationship between player and instrument, which seems to be a major concern of Gustafsson's as well. The title of the CD and of individual tracks makes reference to a metaphor on the pair's trio record with drummer Raymond Strid, *You Forget To Answer*, on the same label (now deleted). The long 'Hyla Gratiosa' is memorable for Guy's exquisitely balanced long-form line and his delicacy of touch, even when playing with some force. There is nothing remotely aggressive, though, about either man.

Mouth Eating Trees rather squares the circle, a trio performance of great concentration and one which, despite the extraordinary title, gives away little more about itself, creating a sequence of five enigmatic numbered canvases, each with a sweep out of all proportion to actual size. Numbers one and five are tiny and yet seem to contain an extraordinary amount of musical information. The very long part four, on the other hand, makes a whole out of tiny elements, almost like a mosaic, but with much less sense of developing, unfolding structure. *Parrot Fish Eye*, recorded on an early visit to Chicago, is perhaps the most fun of all his records and might be the easiest place to start with Gustafsson. There's an almost zoological feel to eight duos with percussionist Zerang, whistles, chitterings and unidentified sounds creating an aura of animal-house nuttiness. Five trios with Coleman and O'Rourke are more stealthy in the way they unfold and, if Gustafsson is comparatively reserved here, he and Coleman make an interesting 'front line', if that term's appropriate.

The Education Of Lars Jerry finds him alone at The Renaissance Society in Chicago. The capacious reverberation in the room becomes integral to the recording: Gustafsson's baritone assumes almost gargantuan proportions in this ferocious cavern, yet he can scale it back to clicks and chirrups which just border on audibility. It's one of the more frightening records in this book.

****(*) Improvisers**

Kontrans 143 *Gustafsson; Michael Zerang (perc); Jaap Blonk (v). 3/96.*

***** Hidros One**

Caprice 21566 *Gustafsson; Axel Dörner (t); Gunter Christmann (tb, clo); Fredrik Ljungkvist (ts, bs, cl); Sten Sandell (p); Fred Longberg-Holm (clo); Per-Ake Holmlander (tba); Barry Guy (b); Raymond Strid (d). 10/97.*

*****(*) Windows**

Blue Chopsticks BC 4 *Gustafsson (ts, bs, fluteophone solo). 1/99.*

***** Sticky Tongues And Kitchen Knives**

Xeric-CD-101 *Gustafsson; John Corbett (g, turntables, CD players). 1/99.*

*****(*) Port Huron Picnic**

Spool Line 10 *Gustafsson; Kurt Newman (g); Mike Gennaro (d). 5/99.*

***** Xylophonen Virtuosen**

Incus 38 *Gustafsson; Jim O'Rourke (g, junk). 9/99.*

It can safely be said that Gustafsson is in a prolific period. The *Improvisers* trio with Blonk and Zerang may interest minimalists, but for once we found Gustafsson's relentless pointillism, coupled with Blonk's vocal sounds, dislikeable. *Hidros One* is a big-scale piece (for nine improvisers, tape and conductor), conducted and 'composed' by the leader; away from any visual sense of the performance, though, it's hard to hear it as anything other than a multi-part improv which has its dead spots as well as highs. The one extraordinary moment arrives in the use of the tape at a point halfway through, a subterranean electronic rustling which certainly disturbs the balances.

Windows is a fascinating homage to Steve Lacy. The Lacy tunes are 'Deadline', 'Prospectus' and 'Retreat'; there's a Cecil Taylor piece from the period when Lacy was working with the pianist, 'Louise'; and two Gustafsson originals. As with the earlier *Impropositions*, much play is made of extended techniques (even Lacy, who adds a few comments to the package, admits that 'there are some sounds he makes, you wouldn't even know it's a saxophone, it's just some new sounds'). 'Retreat' is sonorously performed as a baritone dirge. 'Deadline' is a long, completely deconstructed revision. The original 'Outline' is often little more than breath and finger flutterings, yet it holds a fragment of Lacy's inspiration somewhere inside. As ever in this field, not to all tastes, but a remarkable set.

Gustafsson's refusal to submit to saxophone screaming makes much of his small-group work depend on sometimes infinitesimal detail. *Port Huron Picnic* sounds very like an edition of Spontaneous Music Ensemble, built around momentous, even furious scrabblings which teem with tiny incidents. *Xylophonen Virtuosen*'s appeal may depend on how much one takes to O'Rourke's methods, which include lots of open-toned country-blues picking. It certainly makes for an unlikely contrast with Gustafsson's guttural explosions on 'Calling Patti'.

Sticky Tongues And Kitchen Knives is often unabashed mayhem. The first half sets Gustafsson's extremes of tenor saxophone technique against whatever sounds Corbett can produce from turntables and CD players; the second is a more conventional application of baritone sax against Corbett's post-Bailey electric guitar, rather less interesting than his manipulations in the first half, which are sometimes startling. On the basis of the first half here, orchestration suits Gustafsson better as a context.

****** The Thing**
Crazy Wisdom 001/159073-2 *Gustafsson; Ingebrigt Håker Flaten (b); Paal Nilssen-Love (d).* 2/00.

***** Diskaholics Anonymous Trio**
Crazy Wisdom 005/014788-2 *Gustafsson; Jim O'Rourke (syn, computer); Thurston Moore (g).* 00.

The trio with Flaten and Nilssen-Love is Gustafsson in power mode. *The Thing*, aside from two brief items, is made up of extended rampages through four Don Cherry pieces, the saxophonist sticking to alto and tenor. They make a joyful noise out of the likes of 'Cherryco', a black squall out of 'Awake Nu' and a grand show-piece out of 'Trans-Love Airways' that runs from stately bass intro to all-out power-play. It all feels like a great modern free-jazz record, with Gustafsson complemented by superb work from both Flaten and the amazingly energetic Nilssen-Love.

The other trio starts with wall-of-sound guitar, drifts away into more familiar Gustafsson small-group territory of whisperings and grumbling, then dies away in another guitar diminuendo. Not our favourite, but it tickles to know that one of the world's largest record companies is responsible for selling this stuff.

Rigmor Gustafsson

VOCAL, GUITAR

Raised in the Swedish countryside, where the nearest building was 'a barn and not a jazz club', Gustafsson nevertheless decided to dedicate herself to jazz. She moved to New York in her middle 20s after studying in Stockholm and there took up singing.

***** In The Light Of Day**
Prophone PCD 034 *Gustafsson; Gabriel Coburger (ts); Tino Derado (p); Hans Glawischnig (b); Roland Schneider (d).* 4/96.

***** Live**
Prophone PCD 054 *Gustafsson; Karl-Martin Almqvist (ts); Jakob Karlzon (p); Hans Andersson (b); Jonas Holgersson (d).* 10/99.

**** I Will Wait For You**
ACT 9418-2 *Gustafsson; Staffan Svensson (t); Nils Landgren (tb, v); Magnus Lindgren (af); Roberto Di Gioia (p); Lars Danielsson (b); Wolfgang Haffner (d); strings.* 1–4/03.

The debut has plenty of distinctly gauche charm: Gustafsson offers wayward enunciation and 'interesting' pitching at times, but she also tackles some stiff material head on, including 'Very Early', 'Freedom Jazz Dance', 'Infant Eyes' and Chick Corea's 'You're Everything', and her girlishly light tone actually takes some of the weight out of a few of the lyrics to beneficial effect – 'In The Light Of Day', where she duets affectingly with Coburger, works notably well in that regard. Derado, who has a Corea-like touch, contributes a couple of originals, though these don't do so well. The band is, however, a pretty capable unit, putting skates under her without pushing her too fast or too far. Rigmor can often sound like a Scandinavian Rickie Lee Jones here. The live set, recorded back home in Sweden, is tougher and more accomplished, although some may find that there's a consequent loss of that sweetness which helped get the debut across. 'Over The Rainbow' is nicely handled, emotive without getting sentimental, and if the originals aren't especially involving the singer puts them over with a good deal of power. Holgersson is sometimes far too loud and he does obscure some of what Karlzon, an excellent accompanist, is playing.

Produced and musically directed by Nils Landgren, the ACT album is a disappointing continuation. Gustafsson turns in her most polished performances, but the whole project feels far too studied, like a grown-up pop project with a lick or two of jazz. She does alright by 'Fever' but there are misconceived settings of such disparate material as 'Makin' Whoopee' and James Taylor's 'Fire And Rain', and all the freshness of the first record seems to have been largely smothered.

Tord Gustavsen (born 1970)

PIANO

Young Norwegian pianist, very much in the vanguard of the country's new jazz.

*****(*) Aire & Angels**
Bergland 008 *Gustavsen; Siri Gjaere (v).* 5/02.

****** Changing Places**
ECM 016397-2 *Gustavsen; Harald Johnsen (b); Jarle Vespestad (d).* 11/01–6/02.

Gustavsen's style is all simplicity – aphoristic melodies, gently syncopating rhythms (he's played a good share of traditional jazz), blues figures, rocking sequences. Somehow he puts this together into a style which is utterly captivating. The duet record with Gjaere is like some modern *Lieder* recital, with settings of Rupert Brooke and John Donne as well as some original pieces ('Incantation' is a signature piece for young city-dwellers everywhere), but Gustavsen's piano parts put real substance into the slim settings. Gjaere has a small voice which she speaks in as much as she sings with it, and while this is unlikely to be a record for all tastes, it succeeds beautifully on its own terms.

Changing Places carries that sense of nuance and timing over into a trio situation. It helps that one of the modern masters of kit-drumming, Jarle Vespestad, is in the group, although he is obliged to play very differently from his normal power-packed style. The group work through 13 pieces that feel all alike, yet are without any suspicion of routine or preset pattern-playing. The melodies stick immediately in the mind. It should be fascinating to hear Gustavsen's further adventures from this point.

Barry Guy (born 1947)

DOUBLE BASS

The London-born bassist has kept up a parallel career in classical and new-music work and in improvisation. He was a pioneer figure in SME, Amalgam and Iskra 1903, and is the motivating force behind the London Jazz Composers' Orchestra.

*** Improvisations Are Forever Now

Emanem 4070 *Guy; Howard Riley (p); Philipp Wachsmann (vn, elec).* 12/77, 1/79.

It seems strange that until this material resurfaced we were not able to list a small group or solo record under Guy's name earlier than 1990. Some of this material has previously been issued on LP, but a large part of it has not been heard until now. It is an abrasive sound, electronically manipulated by both bassist and violinist, and physically changed by the pianist's inside work. There are no harmonic or melodic reference points and no obvious rhythmic markers either. Sometimes, as on the second improvisation, it appears confused and inchoate, but there are moments of astonishing beauty, as when Riley plays softly with just a minimal string accompaniment on the sixth track. 'Trio Ten' is previously unreleased, a quarter hour of hardcore improvisation that is as off-putting as anything Guy has done and probably not sufficiently realized or complete to warrant CD release. Even so, this is a valuable document that offers a strong picture of where British improvisation was in the late '70s.

***(*) Arcus

Maya MCD 9101 *Guy; Barre Phillips (b).* 90.

Guy's activities in recent years have been largely focused on composition for the London Jazz Composers' Orchestra, which is listed separately. He has, however, kept up his improvisational work, and the items here are well worth pursuing, even if they prove difficult to track down. Though recorded as if on the other side of the veil of Maya, *Arcus* is improvised music of the very highest order. Guy's productive trade-off of freedom against more formal structures is constantly in evidence, and there is enough music of straightforward, digestible beauty to sustain listeners who might otherwise find an hour and a quarter of contrabass duos more than a little taxing. It ends, appropriately enough, on the quiet majesty of 'New Earth', where Phillips's purged simplicity and dancer's grace sound out ahead of Guy's more formal and sculpted delivery. Twice wonderful, but may call for patience.

***(*) Fizzles

Maya MCD 9301 Guy (*b* solo) 9/91.

Fizzles is not so immediately appealing, but it has a quiet charm that reveals itself over repeated listenings and it is certainly better recorded than its predecessor. Guy uses a conventional contrabass on only three tracks, switching for the others to a small chamber bass. In his liner-note, John Corbett relates this to Guy's stated desire to make his instrument as small as possible while he is improvising. One can hear this effect on 'Five Fizzles', a sequence dedicated to Samuel Beckett in which, using both his basses, Guy concentrates on the tiniest details with an almost hallucinatory intensity, much as Beckett would concentrate on a single word, sound or gesture. Pitched higher than a conventional bass, the concert instrument has a cello-like warmth of tone and speed of response that is very attractive, and the drone-like effects in 'Afar' and 'Tout Rouge' are reminiscent of devices in the work of cult Italian composer Giacinto Scelsi. Significantly or not, the most compelling track is for double bass. Dedicated to a Native-American friend, 'She Took The Sacred Rattle And Used It' is one of Guy's finest moments as an instrumentalist.

***(*) Study – Witch Gong Game 11/10

Maya MCD 9402 *Guy; John Korsrud (t); Ralph Eppel (tb); Saul Berson (as); Coat Cooke (ts, bs, f); Graham Ord (ts, ss, picc); Bruce Freedman (ss); Paul Plimley (p); Ron Samworth (g); Peggy Lee (clo); Paul Blaney, Clyde Read (b); Dylan Van der Schyff (d); Kate Hammett-Vaughan (v).* 2/94.

This is a project that takes Guy back closer to the kind of formal-free experiment promulgated and sustained with the London Jazz Composers' Orchestra. Recorded in Canada, *Witch Gong Game 11/10* is a musical realization of certain signs and symbols in paintings by Alan Davie, another of the visual artists to have provided Guy with a rich vein of inspiration in recent years. Guy reads Davie's work as a floating, by no means determinant, system of archetypes which can be interpreted so as to create dense polyphonies, lighter, more textural passages, or else entirely free improvisational areas. The music is as vividly present as Davie's curiously totemic images, and the young orchestra respond to it very openly and sympathetically.

**** You Forget To Answer

Maya MCD 9601 *Guy; Mats Gustafsson (ss, ts, bs, fluteophone); Raymond Strid (d, perc).* 11/94, 7/95.

***(*) gryffgryffgryffs

Music & Arts CD 1003 *As above, except add Marilyn Crispell (p).* 1/96.

A tremendous trio which helped to bring the brilliant young Swedish saxophonist to attention outside his native country. Gustafsson, who has also established a strong recording career of his own, is the obvious star, using his whole range of saxophones, adding devices like a crumpled beer-can in the bell of his baritone, and pioneering the fluteophone, which is basically a flute with a saxophone mouthpiece stuck on one end, and a clarinet stand jammed in the other (the latter a device he discovered by accident, as you may have guessed). His sound is very strong and, in partnership with the barrel-chested Strid, who always plays as if he's having a whale of a time, he generates considerable excitement. It takes a couple of hearings before one realizes that Guy is the fulcrum and the driving force of this group, creating a complex fabric of sound and pushing the two younger men out into areas that don't so much suggest total abstraction as a kind of mathematical abstractness, a rapid computation of possibilities that is, as mathematics always is, deeply exciting. 'Schrödinger's Cat' (named after a philosophical puzzle which seems to intrigue improvising musicians) is the most vibrant track: playful, wry and not taking itself too seriously. All but three short tracks on *You Forget To Answer* were recorded by the BBC in London for the now defunct *Impressions* programme. There are slight problems here and there with the balance of Strid's drums, but the sound-quality is excellent and every tiny buzz and resonance on both bass and saxophone can be heard clearly.

The Swedish Broadcasting Corporation take a more conventional approach on *gryffgryffgryffs*, a broader and less detailed group sound. Admittedly, the inclusion of Crispell makes a significant difference to the sheer density of the group but, even so, this is a blunter, denser product. The key sequence consists of three tracks, 'Org', 'Ghast', 'Orghast', which seem to explore a carefully delimited range of ideas, except that Crispell is never content to remain within narrow harmonic or rhythmic bounds. It works, despite her overblown expressionism.

***** Gudira**

Nuscope 06 *Guy; Robert Dick (picc, f, af, bf); Randy Raine-Reusch (zither, perc).* 5/97.

The title comes from the participants' names, of course, but it somehow fits the hard-to-pin-down, almost Eastern aesthetic created by this instrumentation. Guy's softly percussive thrums and slow arco passages have an exotic quality that is amply reflected by the masterful Dick's range of flutes (most successfully those at the extremes of pitch) and Raine-Reusch's zither, which introduces an attractive alien range of harmonies. Some of the pieces are too long, too conversational or insufficiently realized to be worthy of CD release, but there is more than enough good music and one suspects that had this been issued on Guy's own Maya label the quality control would have been better.

*****(*) Inscape – Tableaux**

Intakt 066 *Guy; Herb Robertson (t); Johannes Bauer (tb); Per Ake Holmlander (tba); Evan Parker (ss, ts); Mats Gustafsson (ss, ts, bs); Hans Koch (ts, cl); Marilyn Crispell (p); Raymond Strid (d, perc); Paul Lytton (perc).* 98.

This might look like a cut-down version of the London Jazz Composers' Orchestra, with European and American stand-ins, but in fact this beautifully constructed piece is perfectly weighted for these forces and, in the event, for these players. The emphasis lies very solidly on Guy's writing, but with soloists as individual as Robertson, Parker and Crispell (not to belittle the others) it is clear that considerable freedom remains at the music's disposal. And that is how it feels listening to *Inscape – Tableaux*, Guy's conception unfolds organically and with an internal logic that has little to do with either the composer's or the performers' will. It's an intensely powerful experience, perhaps lacking the sheer intellectual beauty of some of the LJCO recordings, but with an intimacy and immediacy which they cannot hope to emulate.

****** Odyssey**

Intakt 070 *Guy; Marilyn Crispell (p); Paul Lytton (perc).* 99.

No one will by this stage be expecting a conventional jazz piano trio, and yet this is closer to that discipline than one might expect in that a number of the pieces – 'Harmos', 'Double Trouble', 'Odyssey' – are Guy compositions, more or less familiar from other projects, and only four tracks are collectively improvised. The tonality is mostly quite sombre, though 'Rags' is a loud and skittish idea, and after the bass–percussion introduction 'Harmos' turns into a brooding processional that brings out the very darkest colours in Crispell's recently discovered lyricism. The level of interaction is very high and there is constant empathy between the players. How much of this is down to Guy's scores and direction is difficult to gauge from the outside. These don't sound like dot-driven pieces; the emphasis is still very much on improvisation, but within very definite structures and trajectories. It's not without humour: 'Heavy Metal' gives Lytton a chance to explore his expanded kit and for the others to lean back a bit as well. A superb demonstration of what it's possible to do creatively with the most hackneyed of instrumentations.

*****(*) Birds & Blades, Studio & Live**

Intakt 080 2CD *Guy; Evan Parker (ss, ts).* 9/01.

The usual practice is to do a gig the night before, run down the material and then take it into the studio. This reverses that procedure. Over two nights in Zurich, Guy and Parker recorded a studio session, followed by a live set at Spheres Bar-Buch-Bühne. There's no obvious carry-over of ideas from the one to the other. Both of these musicians are capable of an extraordinary spectrum of sounds and musical vocabularies. On the first disc, they exploit the studio intelligently and affectingly, creating a language that seems to belong to the moment but also to a much wider experience. In a revealing liner interview, Parker says of his playing partner that he turns sunlight into music, that Guy always knows where the sun is, even when it's cloudy. This might sound pretentious or sentimental, except there is a strong feeling in Guy's writing and playing that he keeps a numinous musical energy constantly in view, no matter what he's playing. That comes across very strongly on the live set in the Zurich book-bar. Parker's intense improvisations have their own emotional temperature, but one can hear him orbiting his old friend's boiling fusion of ideas, drawing heat and light from it. This is a remarkable encounter, new ground, a new intensity of expression from a pair of musicians who after 30 years might be thought to have exhausted each other's creative hydrogen entirely.

****** Symmetries**

Maya MCD0201 *Guy (b solo).* 01.

The presence of a Mingus composition ('Weird Nightmare' and 'Eclipse', in fact) on a Barry Guy solo record shouldn't be all that surprising. The bassist's interest in jazz composition has always been implicit in his work. More interesting is its appearance alongside an unaccompanied version of Guy's 'Odyssey' and another set of 'Fizzles' (see the album of that name above). Barry's compositional touch and mastery of his instrument are now part of the same sweeping vision. He seems to deal in archetypes and universals, and painter Alan Davie is the ideal artist for the cover of this remarkable record.

Bobby Hackett (1915–76)

CORNET

One of the best-liked men in the business, Hackett was born in Providence, Rhode Island, and began as a guitarist on the local scene. Influenced by Bix Beiderbecke and Louis Armstrong, he eventually formed his own group in 1938 and played at Benny Goodman's celebrated Carnegie Hall concert. He worked with

Glenn Miller in addition and then disappeared into the studio for almost a decade, making occasional appearances thereafter and almost up to his death.

*** Bobby Hackett, 1938–1940

Classics 890 *Hackett; Sterling Bose, Harry Genders, Joe Lucas, Bernie Mattison, Jack Thompson, Stan Wilson (t); Jerry Borshard, George Brunies, Cappy Crouse, John Grassi, George Troup (tb); Brad Gowans (vtb, as); Bob Riedel (cl); Pee Wee Russell (cl, ts); Jerry Caplan, Louis Colombo (as); Bernie Billings, George Dessinger, Hank Kusen, Hammond Rusen (ts); Jim Beitus, Ernie Caceres (bs); Dave Bowman, Frankie Carle (p); Eddie Condon, Bob Julian, Bob Knight (g); Sid Jacobs, Eddie McKinney, Clyde Newcombe (b); Johnny Blowers, Don Carter, Andy Picard (d); Lola Bard, Linda Keene, Claire Martin, The Tempo Twisters (v).* 2/38–2/40.

Louis Armstrong liked to keep the opposition under the closest observation and so, for much of the '40s, Bobby Hackett played second trumpet under the wing of the man who had influenced his style almost as much as Bix. Hackett was probably too modest for leadership, but in 1938 he made the first recordings under his own name for the Vocalion label, with whom he stayed for the next two years, typically when there were more lucrative possibilities elsewhere.

Hackett had worked in a trio with Pee Wee Russell in the early days and, though temperamentally they were very different indeed, to put it mildly, the clarinettist and guitarist Eddie Condon were first-call recruitments to the Hackett orchestra which recorded four sides in February 1938. Of these the best is the pairing of 'At The Jazz Band Ball' and 'If Dreams Come true', the latter a vehicle for vocalist Lola Bard. A different band but the same formula for the November session that same year, with 'Poor Butterfly' the best showing for Hackett's sweetly melancholy cornet.

Thereafter he tended to use slightly larger bands with augmented saxophones. The sound is closer to the easy swing of the Miller Orchestra he would shortly join, and the romantic tension seems to have deserted the leader for a time. Here and there, there are flashes of brilliance, as on 'Bugle Call Rag' and 'I Surrender, Dear' from July 1939, the latter with a vocal by an earlier-generation Claire Martin, but the latter half of the disc is disappointing and a little flat.

*** 1943 World Broadcasting Jam Session

Jazzology JCD 111 *Hackett; Ray Conniff (tb); John Pepper (cl); Nick Caizza (ts); Frank Signorelli (p); Eddie Condon (g); Bob Casey (b); Maurice Purtill (d).* 12/43.

The title is more or less self-explanatory, a recording set up by Milt Gabler for the WBS Inc. Though not a vintage band, the playing is of a high order, even if some may find the false starts and incompletes irritating. Coniff is a robust presence and some of his fills and countermelodies are worth studying, but it's very much Bobby's gig and, while he doesn't grandstand or posture, he makes the most of the spotlight.

*** Dr Jazz: Volume 2 – 1951–1952

Storyville STCD 6042 *Hackett; Vic Dickenson (tb); Gene Sedric (cl); Teddy Roy (p); John Giuffrida, Irv Manning (b); Buzzy Drootin, Morey Feld, Kenny John (d).* 2/52.

The Dr Jazz sessions were originally broadcast from Lou Terassi's on West 47th Street as part of a WMGM series. Again, it's very much Hackett's gig, though Dickenson is also a strong presence, underlining how much Bobby liked the cornet and trombone to interweave at the front, using the reeds for depth of focus and sometimes merely as wallpaper.

***(*) Bobby Hackett Sextet & Quintet

Storyville STCD 8230 *Hackett; Vic Dickenson, Urbie Green (tb); Bob Wilber (cl); Dave McKenna, John Ulrich (p); Franklin Skeets, Nabil Totah (b); Morey Feld, John Mead (d).* 1/61–62, 1–2/70.

The first six tracks on this fine CD were originally made for a film by the Goodyear Rubber Company. Along with a further half-dozen they were released on a Storyville LP, now augmented with sessions from 1970 with Dickenson back on board as trombonist. Green is a fine player, but it is clear from the very simple themes chosen for the programme (perhaps a sop to the sponsors) that Hackett is playing more notes and relying less on Green for elaborated material than he would on the more formidable Dickenson. Vic is astounding on 'Wolverine Blues', which is very much pitched at his range, and then Bobby comes in with strength and delicacy and makes a small masterpiece of 'Satin Doll'. Why these tracks, along with 'I Can't Get Started' and 'Original Dixieland One-Step', weren't released at the time is something of a mystery. To be sure, they aren't flawless technically, but musically they seem well up to scratch. Good to hear big Dave McKenna making an early appearance on the 1962 session and already playing with his trademark two-handed style. Bob Wilber is also instantly recognizable, with that faintly hollow-toned, very reedy sound coming through on 'Sentimental Blues' and 'When The Saints', where he sounds like one of the old-time New Orleans guys.

*** Milton Jazz Concert 1963

IAJRC 1004 *Hackett; Vic Dickenson (tb); Edmond Hall (cl); Evans Schwartz (p); Champlin Jones (b); Mickey Sheen (d).* 4/63.

The Milton Concert was released by the International Association of Jazz Record Collectors, which has done a great service to Hackett fans and to jazz by making this Massachusetts gig available. The tape-quality isn't tip-top and there are moments when Hall drifts way out of picture but, given the circumstances, the record is very good indeed. Hackett and Dickenson play out of their respective skins, and the rhythm section, which we failed to note before, is in splendid supportive form.

**(*) Plays The Great Music Of Henry Mancini / Plays The Music Of Bert Kaempfert

Collectables COL-CD-7411 *Hackett; Dick Hyman, (p, org, hpchd); rest unknown.* 5–11/63.

**(*) The Swingin'est Gals In Town / Jazz Impressions Of Lionel Bart's 'Oliver!'

Collectables COL-CD-7410 *Hackett; Dick Hyman (org); Don Friedman, (p); George Barnes, Carmen Mastren (g); Jimmy Mitchell (b, g); Vinnie Burke (b); Ray Mosca (d).* 2/63–3/66.

*** Hello Louis! / Plays Tony Bennett's Greatest Hits

Collectables COL-CD-6697 *Hackett; Sonny Russo (tb); Steve Lacy (ss); Roger Kellaway (p); Al Chernet (bj); Harvey Phillips (tba); Ronny Bedford (d); orchestra arranged by Frank Hunter.* 4/64–7/66.

It was a kind initiative of Collectables to restore some of the easy-listening albums Hackett made for Columbia in the '60s, on these two-on-one discs. The pity is that Bobby's best work is so scattered through each of them. The Mancini and Kaempfert collections feature bouncy Dick Hyman arrangements for a dreary small group, and although Hackett's musings on the likes of 'Days Of Wine And Roses' are worth waiting for, the up-tempo pieces are throwaway and the Kaempfert tunes often feeble. *The Swingin'est Gals* comprises hits from *Mame* and *Sweet Charity*, and the *Oliver!* material is played by another small group. Again, it's the ballads which are the keepers – 'Where Is Love?' is a gorgeous Hackett feature – but the rest is often silly. Predictably, it's the third disc which comes out best. The set dedicated to Armstrong uses mostly '20s material and a curiously styled dixieland sextet, but there's the extraordinary chance to hear Lacy playing his last 'traditional' session alongside Hackett, and Bobby is superb on 'Wild Man Blues'. The other record is the other end of the scale, Hackett with lush orchestral charts on songs associated with Tony Bennett, and is luvverly.

*****(*) Butterfly Airs**
Storyville 101 8344 *Hackett; Sir Charles Thompson (p); Benny Wheeler (b); Ed Polito (d).* 64–67.

Club recordings, with Sir Charles in good fettle and the boppish Polito really giving the group a good kick on the quicker tunes. It's Hackett's show, though, and he plays a mix of quality jazz material and the show tunes he was buttering his bread with at this point. As an unadorned display of his powers, this might be his best record in print.

***** Melody Is A Must: Live At The Roosevelt Grill**
Phontastic PHONT 7571 *Hackett; Vic Dickenson (tb); Dave McKenna (p); Jack Lesberg (b); Cliff Leeman (d).* 3–4/69.

This actually predates the later material on *Sextet & Quintet*, but it feels very much of the same vintage. McKenna is still in the band and the association with Dickenson seems tighter than ever. *Melody Is A Must* is a perfect example of Hackett's grace-without-pressure. There are no steam-valve emotional tantrums; nor is there casual verbosity. According to Whitney Balliett, Duke Ellington once spoke, apparently in approval, of Dickenson's 'three tones'. Like the trombonist, Hackett kept the music simple and direct, remarkably uncluttered by ego or undue embellishment. There is still not enough of him around on CD.

Charlie Haden (born 1937)

DOUBLE BASS

Born in Shenandoah, Haden was a child performer who began working in Los Angeles circles in 1957. Joined Paul Bley and then Ornette Coleman in 1958. In the '60s, was associated with Keith Jarrett and his own Liberation Music Orchestra. Since 1980 he has been a free-jazz eminence who has worked mainly in post-bop, particularly with his own Quartet West. His daughters perform rock music.

*****(*) Liberation Music Orchestra**
Impulse! 051188-2 *Haden; Don Cherry (c, f); Michael Mantler (t); Roswell Rudd (tb); Bob Northern (frhn, perc); Howard Johnson (tba); Perry Robinson (cl); Gato Barbieri (ts, cl); Dewey Redman (as, ts); Sam Brown (g, thumb p); Carla Bley (p, perc); Andrew Cyrille, Paul Motian (d, perc).* 69.

The man from Shenandoah, Indiana, helped redefine modern jazz with Ornette Coleman's quartet, and gave a new impetus to jazz bass without ever once pretending that he was playing a horn. Haden is the ultimate timekeeper, bending and stretching the pulse like a true relativist, but never once forgetting his duties. This, coupled with a heartbeat tone, has placed him at the centre of literally hundreds of important sessions.

Ten years after making *The Shape Of Jazz To Come*, his best performance with Coleman, Haden recorded under the collectivist banner of the Liberation Music Orchestra a suite of revolutionary songs from the Spanish Civil War (arranged by Carla Bley), Ornette's 'War Orphans' and Haden's own 'Song For Che'. Everything else on the record is transitional, gateposts and entryways. Like the almost contemporary Jazz Composers' Orchestra (of which most of these players were members), the LMO was a blend of collectivism and radical individualism. Ensemble was everything – but solos were everything, too. On the long suite of anarchist songs begun by 'El Quinto Regimiento', Brown, Cherry and Haden himself are featured, followed by Rudd in the middle section and the almost caustically toned Barbieri in the conclusion, 'Viva La Quince Brigada'. The bassist dominates the brooding 'Song For Che', with Cherry and Redman in support.

Recording quality has been improved immeasurably, and the ensembles now sound open-grained and present, not lost in a backwash of overtones. The orchestra, or a descendant of it, was to return in the early '80s with *The Ballad Of The Fallen* and *Dream Keeper*. They are certainly more polished, but this has the ring of truth.

***** Closeness**
A & M 397000-2 *Haden; Ornette Coleman (as); Keith Jarrett (p); Alice Coltrane (hp); Paul Motian (d).* 76.

***** As Long As There's Music**
Verve 513534-2 *Haden; Hampton Hawes (p).* 1–8/76.

Perhaps only Eddie Gomez, Gary Peacock and George Mraz, all of whom draw something from Haden's example, sound as convincing in duo performance. These are all head-to-head pairings with musicians who have been close to the bassist in one form or another.

Jarrett is a challenging partner, but one already feels that the relationship is competitive rather than collaborative, and when the Jarrett material is set against the session with Hawes the difference is almost flagrantly evident. In the last months of his life, the pianist was moving back towards a more radical conception, having exhausted his interest in fusion. The partnership on Ornette's 'Turnaround' is a high point from this period in Haden's career, and there is a further version on *As Long As There's Music*. The title-track of the last record includes one of the best solos of Haden's recorded career: everything one needs to know about him is there in miniature: hand-speed, strength, delicacy and an innate musicality.

****(*) Duo**
Dreyfus Jazz Line 365052 *Haden; Christian Escoudé (g).* 9/78.

This would be entirely forgettable if it didn't afford advance notice of Haden's gentler side. Though he could be pretty combustible in other contexts, there was always a romantic core to his playing, a fondness for dipping, minor-key themes and meltingly ambiguous cadences. The material is unimaginative, including a drab version of 'Nuages', and only some clever lyrical interplay spares it the 'Reject' button.

★★★ Magico

ECM 823474-2 *Haden; Jan Garbarek (ts, ss); Egberto Gismonti (g, p).* 6/79.

★★★(★) Folk Songs

ECM 827705-2 *As above.* 11/79.

This trio was presumably a going concern for a time. One of the authors was present at some of the sessions for *Folk Songs* and what was obvious there was that, though Garbarek tends to dominate the sound on almost every record he is involved with, it was Haden who called the shots musically. He sounds more sombre than usual, perhaps in reaction to Gismonti and the saxophonist swooping like gulls overhead. *Folk Songs* endures, retaining an uncomplicated charm that wasn't to surface again until Haden's Quartet West records.

★★★(★) The Ballad Of The Fallen

ECM 811546-2 *Haden; Don Cherry (pkt-t); Michael Mantler (t); Gary Valente (tb); Sharon Freeman (frhn); Jack Jeffers (tba); Jim Pepper (ts, ss, f); Dewey Redman (ts); Steve Slagle (as, ss, cl, f); Mick Goodrick (g); Carla Bley (p, glock); Paul Motian (d).* 11/82.

There were seismic shifts in both music and politics between 1969 and 1982, an entire decade of retrenchment and renewed attachment to order. The reconvened Liberation Music Orchestra was never going to sound as it had. What's immediately clear from this is that the LMO was in essence a small group, Redman, Bley, Haden and Motian, augmented *ad hoc* by low brass, additional horns and percussion. Almost all the energy comes from that axis and, if this time around the solo spots are less vibrant, even inflammatory, the big difference is that the arrangements are structural rather than decorative.

As before, and as again on *Dream Keeper* in 1990, the arrangements are by Bley. Most of the tracks are extremely short, building towards 'Too Late' (a superb bass–piano duet), 'La Pasionaria' and 'La Santa Espina'. The climax is as fiery as it has been long in coming.

★★★(★) Quartet West

Verve 831673-2 *Haden; Ernie Watts (as, ts, ss); Alan Broadbent (p); Billy Higgins (d).* 12/86.

★★★(★) Charlie Haden's Private Collection: Volume 1

Naim CD 005 *As above.* 8/87.

The Liberation Music Orchestra was an ambitious *ad hoc* venture. Haden's diary had long been packed with dates for other leaders. The one thing seemingly not catered for was a regular, working small group. That changed with the formation of Quartet West, a lyrical – sometimes almost sentimentally so – ensemble featuring two unsung heroes of the mainstream and, with the recruitment of Larance Marable later, a third; one must assume that Billy Higgins's credentials are unimpeachable.

The first of the Quartet West discs is still the best. Haden wanted to recapture something of the musical atmosphere he had soaked up in childhood, when he had starred in a family radio show. The later *Haunted Heart* was a rather mannered exercise in nostalgia. The 1986 record is in the style of the '40s, beautifully and idiomatically played. Watts and Broadbent are as aware of contemporary harmonics as one would expect, but they aren't prepared to dismiss an older language either. Haden himself straddles the broad highway that runs from Jimmy Blanton to Jimmy Garrison, and some of the phrase shapes irresistibly recall Wilbur Ware. Even allowing for the crystalline quality of the record, who could with confidence have dated these performances of 'Body And Soul' or 'My Foolish Heart'? 'Taney County' is a solo feature, an evocation of the days when he played and sang on the family show; the playing is firm, sure and very expressive.

The *Private Collection* disc, first of a pair, celebrates the bassist's 50th birthday. Not a bad way to notch up the start of a new decade in the business than to call in a few friends for a jam. The recording sounds as if it was made on the fly, but the playing is good enough to make up for any technical insufficiencies. Haden programmes future associate Pat Metheny's 'Hermitage' and 'Farmer's Trust' (which also surfaces on Volume Two) with two little-known Parker tunes, 'Passport' and 'Segment', Miles Davis's 'Nardis' and Tony Scott's 'Misery'.

★★ Silence

Soul Note 121172 *Haden; Chet Baker (t, v); Enrico Pieranunzi (p); Billy Higgins (d).* 11/87.

Not so very surprising, given the context of the Quartet West material, but still a surprise and something of a blip in Haden's recorded progress. By this stage in his slow downward spiral, Chet was playing with just about everyone who'd have him. There's a strange enervation and lack of focus to most of the material, and it's Pieranunzi (a strong and creative presence on the European scene) who wins out. Haden is poorly recorded, recessed and muffled.

★★★(★) Charlie Haden's Private Collection: Volume 2

Naim CD 006 *Haden; Ernie Watts (ts); Alan Broadbent (p); Paul Motian (d).* 4/88.

★★★ In Angel City

Verve 873031-2 *As above, except omit Motian; add Alex Cline, Larance Marable (d).* 6/88.

This time the 'private' tapes come from a public event, and a stirring version of Quartet West reuniting Haden with Motian. Drummer and live setting affect the music more than a little, and Watts responds with an angular, sometimes almost caustic approach that diverges sharply from the other recordings by this group.

Angel City is a mannered pastiche, an attempt to paint in sound the city of Raymond Chandler. The best is very good indeed. The less successful flirts with kitsch. Marable is an excellent foil, in character moody and unforced. Cline actually plays on only one track.

★★★(★) The Montreal Tapes: Volume 1

Verve 523260-2 *Haden; Don Cherry (pkt-t); Ed Blackwell (d).* 7/89.

★★★★ The Montreal Tapes: Volume 2

Verve 523295-2 *Haden; Paul Bley (p); Paul Motian (d).* 7/89.

★★★(★) The Montreal Tapes: Volume 3

Verve 537486-2 *Haden; Geri Allen (p); Paul Motian (d).* 7/89.

★★★★ The Montreal Tapes: Volume 4

Verve 537670-2 *Haden; Gonzalo Rubalcaba (p); Paul Motian (d).* 7/89.

★★★★ In Montreal

ECM 843813-2 *Haden; Egberto Gismonti (g, p).* 7/89.

Over eight nights, straddling the end of June and the first week of July 1989, the Montreal International Jazz Festival in collaboration with Canadian Radio pitched Haden in some wonderfully creative settings, mainly trios but also including a duo with Egberto Gismonti and a final-night reunion with the Liberation Music Orchestra, who were to return to the studio the following April.

Of the trios, that with Cherry is the only one which isn't uniformly excellent. There is a touch of Hamlet-without-the-Prince in what otherwise sounds like a version of the classic Ornette Coleman quartet, a seam Haden had already mined in the Old and New Dreams group. These are stirring performances, but there is something lacking, and it becomes more and more obvious on repeated hearings. Cherry is certainly the weak link, plunging off on his own. 'The Sphinx', 'The Blessing' and 'Lonely Woman' have great strengths, and the other covers are clean-limbed and unfussy: 'Art Deco' and 'Mopti' are excellent.

One of the fascinating aspects of this superb series is the opportunity to hear Haden reworking the same material with different piano players. 'When Will The Blues Leave' misfires with Cherry, but the version with Bley is sterling. 'The Blessing' is the star track on the disc with Rubalcaba, which is an absolute cracker, also including long versions of Haden originals, 'Bay City', 'Silence' and 'La Pasionaria', and a slightly tentative working of fellow-bassist Gary Peacock's 'Vignette'.

The trio with Geri Allen is already well attested, but one suspects that here competing conceptions and some awkward shifts of impetus between the pianist and her older partners have compromised the music somewhat. 'Dolphy's Dance' is excellent, but most of the rest seems bracketed with self-consciousness, even a touch of irony. Bley, by contrast, is in his element: relaxed, magisterial, wry and funny. The version of 'Turnaround', Ornette's masterpiece despite itself and himself, is glorious.

We've felt for some time that the best of that amazing week was probably still to come. The duos with Gismonti were released only in 2001 but they were well worth waiting for. The guitarist is in inspired form, from his own opening 'Salvador' onwards, and responds with typical intelligence and grace to Latin-tinged Haden compositions like 'First Song' and 'Silence'. He also reveals himself to be a more than competent pianist; the phrasing on his own 'Maracatu' is formidable, though here the tape-quality isn't quite as pristine as one might like. A delightful record, nevertheless; but a boxed set of that Montreal week looks ever more desirable.

***(*) First Song

Soul Note 121222-2 *Haden; Enrico Pieranunzi (p); Billy Higgins (d).* 4/90.

No Chet this time, for the saddest and most obvious of reasons, but a set that grows in stature almost every time it's heard. Pieranunzi stakes an ever stronger claim for major league status with a well-structured and resonant performance, dark-toned lyricism that chimes with Haden's romantic attack and with the clipped swing dictated by the drummer. Lennie Tristano doesn't look to be the most obvious source for any of these players, but 'Lennie's Pennies' focuses the entire set.

*** Haunted Heart

Verve 513078-2 *Haden; Ernie Watts (ts); Alan Broadbent (p); Billy Higgins (d); Billie Holiday, Jeri Southern, Jo Stafford (v on record).* 90.

*** Always Say Goodbye

Verve 521501-2 *As above, except omit vocalists; add Stéphane Grappelli (vn).* 7 & 8/93.

Flagrant exercises in nostalgia, utterly beyond the pale, but for the complete lack of irony and detachment. *Haunted Heart* is Haden's 'Radio Days' set, a reconstruction that uses old vocal recordings as scene-setting. *Always Say Goodbye* further underlines Haden's passion for Jo Stafford, adding material by Duke, Coleman Hawkins, Chet Baker and Django Reinhardt, which helps explain the charmingly unexpected addition of the late Stéphane Grappelli. Watts is in very good form.

The palimpsests on Lady's 'Deep Song' and Jeri Southern's 'Every Time We Say Goodbye' – and indeed Jo Stafford's 'Haunted Heart' – are cleverly conceived and executed, but the idea is a trifle overcooked and one almost yearns for some interactive medium which allows performance with or without the archive material, and at will.

*** Steal Away: Spirituals, Hymns And Folk Songs

Verve 527249-2 *Haden; Hank Jones (p).* 7/94.

Depending on your point of view, Jones is either an elegant master of standards jazz, an expressive balladeer with the delivery of an urbane, big-city preacher, or he's an increasingly formulaic purveyor of catechistic ideas. Any way, this recording doesn't comfortably stand the test of time.

Behind the record is the recent loss of Haden's mother, Virginia May, and also his desire to rescue from historical oblivion the makers of spirituals and vernacular hymns. In performance terms, though, this is the start of a slide into a worryingly complacent New Age sensibility, a jazz equivalent of so-called 'faith minimalism'. Done with as much calm professionalism as you would expect, it palls with distance.

*** Now Is The Hour

Verve 529827-2 *Haden; Ernie Watts (ts); Alan Broadbent (p); Larance Marable (d).* 95.

Vintage product from a settled band, perhaps a little anonymous and lacking in focus, but pulling things together with an excellent closing sequence: 'Palo Alto', 'Marable's Parable' and the title-piece. As a Haden performance it isn't so very outstanding, but it reaffirms our growing conviction that this is the Ernie Watts group under an alias.

CORE COLLECTION

**** Beyond The Missouri Sky

Verve 537130-2 *Haden; Pat Metheny (g, sitar).* 96.

This has sold like SnoCones in the desert, a record that obviously appeals to Metheny fans first and foremost, but also to a cohort of New Agers who are hipped to the unguarded frontiers of jazz. The original intention was to record a set of acoustic duets, but these have been embellished with guitar overdubs and with Metheny's previously unveiled acoustic guitar/sitar.

At the heart of the set, two tunes dedicated to Haden's late parents: Roy Acuff's country classic, 'The Precious Jewel', and the traditional 'He's Gone Away'. Also in the line-up, Jim Webb's 'The Moon Is A Harsh Mistress' and two themes from the movie *Cinema Paradiso*. It's easy enough to dismiss this music as undemanding, pastelly and soft-focus. As ever, it's also formidably disciplined, and there's a hint of rock only just under the surface.

*****(*) Night And The City**

Verve 539961-2 *Haden; Kenny Barron (p).* 9/96.

Liner-notes by novelist Rafi Zabor, author of *The Bear Comes Home*, one of the finest fictional creations ever with jazz as its background. That alone will recommend it to some, but it's an imprimatur that is hardly needed. Haden is playing exquisitely and in Barron he has a partner who knows the repertoire with the intimacy of a genuine creator. Dedicated to Manhattan, it's another atmospheric album built around luminous versions of 'For Heaven's Sake', 'Spring Is Here' and a slow, ardent 'Body And Soul'. Each man has an original, Barron's lovely 'Twilight Song', which gets the sun down and the lights on at the start of the set, and Haden's often-covered 'Waltz For Ruth' towards the end.

If it has a downside, it is that the artistry often seems too easy, too unflustered. There is not much risk in any of these tracks. At this stage in both careers that may not be surprising, but it is a little disappointing.

****** None But The Lonely Heart**

Naim CD022 *Haden; Chris Anderson (p).* 7/97.

Anderson is not only blind but a victim of the same brittle-bone ailment that afflicted Michel Petrucciani. A veteran of the Chicago scene, he has played with everyone from Bird to Sonny Rollins and along the way has acquired a formidable grasp of jazz harmonics. There isn't a single track on this magnificently recorded album of standards that doesn't bring something new to the original melody. Even 'Alone Together', that tiredest of all duo chestnuts, takes on a new resonance, while 'Body And Soul' and 'The Things We Did Last Summer' should henceforward be in the study file of every young jazz pianist.

Both voices are recorded in a big, alert acoustic (Cami Hall in New York City) which brings out every detail in both bass and piano. Hard to fault on any count.

*****(*) The Art Of The Song**

Verve 547403-2 *Haden; Ernie Watts (ts); Alan Broadbent (p); Larance Marable (d); Bill Henderson, Shirley Horn (v); orchestra, Murray Adler (cond).* 2/99.

Brave to lay down a first public vocal recording for 45 years (aside from the scarcely noticed cameo on Carla Bley's *Escalator Over The Hill*); braver still to do it in the company of Shirley Horn and Bill Henderson. Shirley's opening reading of Bernstein's 'Lonely Town' establishes the note of nostalgic longing that has surrounded Haden's work for some years. Concert master Murray Adler's violin solo offers the perfect balance to her breathy intimacy. Adler returns as soloist on Haden's own composition, 'Ruth's Waltz'; Henderson delivers the lyric with a sardonic poise which never sounds remotely cynical. His reading of 'Why Did I Choose You?' from *The Yearling* is no less arresting, a song that requires great maturity if it isn't to sound either immature or off-hand. There follows a remarkable arrangement of Rachmaninov's 'Moment musical, Opus 16' which features just Haden (stately, precise and full-voiced) and Watts over strings. The other classical arrangement is Ravel's 'Prelude in A minor', a perfect tonality for Haden.

Broadbent and Watts team up with the orchestra on Jeri Southern's 'Theme For Charlie', which is thereby recast as a tribute to the leader and a prelude to his first recording vocal since the Haden family show days. Interesting that his choice should be the traditional 'Wayfaring Stranger', with its mournfully upbeat 'going over Jordan' conclusion. Another deftly crafted album from a great romantic.

***** Nocturne**

Verve 013611 *Haden; Joe Lovano, David Sanchez (ts); Gonzalo Rubalcaba (p); Pat Metheny (g); Federico Britos Ruiz (vn); Ignacio Berroa (d, perc).* 99.

Haden has long since cornered the market in a brand of melancholy lyricism. This is a curiously one-dimensional album, pinned to a single mood by Berroa's oddly inflexible rhythm. Using mostly Cuban and Mexican standards, and with Rubalcaba strongly featured, Haden has shaped an atmospheric and thoroughly attractive record. All it lacks is a touch of fire. Metheny is laid back on his solitary feature, and even Lovano and Sanchez seem content to play mood music.

***** American Dreams**

Verve 064096 *Haden; Michael Brecker (ts); Brad Mehldau (p); Brian Blade (d); orchestra.* 02.

It sounds here as if the American Dreamer set himself the task of soothing the country's post-9/11 woes with an album of soothingly hopeful songs. Given the quality of the band he assembled, the sliding strings (arranged by Alan Broadbent) seem like an overdose of unguent. The best of the material is, almost inevitably, jazz-based: Keith Jarrett's lovely 'Prism', Mehldau's 'Ron's Place' and Haden's own 'Nightfall' and the title-track. Pieces like 'America the Beautiful' and the soft-pop of Stephen Bishop's 'It Might Be You' need something more. Not irony, since that isn't part of Haden's self-remit, but certainly a more robust rethink.

The principals all play beautifully. Brecker is in comparatively reticent form, doubtless aware of what Haden got from Ernie Watts in Quartet West days. His phrasing is sparer and less emphatic than usual and Mehldau and Blade conribute to an open-textured performance that isn't so much 'jazz lite' as needlessly soft focus.

Tim Hagans (born 1954)

TRUMPET

Although his profile as a leader has come about only recently, Hagans has been in jazz for many years. He worked with Stan Kenton and Woody Herman in the '70s, before moving to Sweden, playing and teaching there until his return to the USA in 1981. He played in Cincinnati and Boston before becoming a fixture on the New York scene.

****(*) Future Miles**

ACT 9235-2 *Hagans; Bo Strandberg, Dan Johansson, Magnus Ekholm, Taunuvaara (t, flhn); P. O. Svanstrom, Magnus Ouls, Peter Dahlgren (tb); Bjorn Hangsel (btb, tba); Hakam Bröstrom, (ss, as, f); John Horlen (as, bcl); Mats Garberg (ts, f); Bengt Ek (ts, cl); Per Moberg (bs, f); Scott Kinsey (ky); Ion Baciu (p); Fredrik Jonsson (b); Jonas Holgersson (d).* 6/00.

Hagans's Blue Note albums seem to have all slipped away for now, and though he's likely to be found extensively elsewhere as a sideman, the own-name albums are down to this guest shot with the formidable Norrbotten Big Band, a Scandinavian situation which the trumpeter at least knows well. If the programme sets out to guess what a 'new' Miles Davis project might have sounded like, it's a fair enough stab but a largely unconvincing one. Some of the originals are overplayed or too long, others seem too tightly constructed: Davis would have frowned at such tutored performances. Hagans plays some respectably in-the-spirit solos and there are good spots for some of the local men, but this isn't a great record.

Al Haig (1924–82)

PIANO

Acknowledged as a master of bebop piano, Haig has nevertheless suffered in comparison to many of his peers through his neglect as a recording artist in later years; he never made a single album for a major label. His work with Parker, Gillespie, Getz and others shows how fine an accompanist and group pianist he was, but his 'name' work is even finer and implies a rare mastery: he was effectively an understated, 'cool' stylist inside the hot medium of bebop. He enjoyed a revival of interest in the '70s but died before he could reap any great rewards from it.

♛ **** **The Al Haig Trio Esoteric**
Fresh Sound FSR-CD 38 *Haig; Bill Crow (b); Lee Abrams (d).* 3/54.

**** **Al Haig Trio**
Fresh Sound FSR-CD 45 *As above.* 3/54.

*** **Al Haig Quartet**
Fresh Sound FSR-CD 12 *Haig; Benny Weeks (g); Teddy Kotick (b); Phil Brown (d).* 9/54.

*** **Al Haig Today!**
Fresh Sound FSR-CD 6 *Haig; Eddie De Haas (b); Jim Kappes (d).* 65.

Al Haig was deplorably served by records in the earlier part of his career, and as a result he is almost the forgotten man of bebop piano. Yet he was as great a figure as any of the bebop masters. If he denied himself the high passion of Bud Powell's music, he was still a force of eloquence and intensity, and his refined touch lent him a striking individuality within his milieu. The first trio album, originally released on the Esoteric label, is a masterpiece that can stand with any of the work of Powell or Monk. Haig's elegance of touch and line, his virtually perfect delivery, links him with a pianist such as Teddy Wilson rather than with any of his immediate contemporaries, and certainly his delivery of an unlikely tune such as 'Mighty Like A Rose' (on FSR-CD 45) has a kinship with the language of Wilson's generation. Yet his complexity of tone and the occasionally cryptic delivery are unequivocally modern, absolutely of the bop lineage. Voicings and touch have a symmetry and refinement that other boppers, from Powell and Duke Jordan to Joe Albany and Dodo Marmarosa, seldom approached. The second *Trio* album, originally released on Period, dates from the same day of recording and is virtually as good – but it could just as easily have fitted on to the same CD as its companion-piece. Still, Haig's bittersweet reduction of 'Round Midnight', present here, is unmissable, even among the many versions of that tune.

The *Quartet* and *Today!* albums are flawed by their circumstances. On *Quartet*, his accompanists are no more than adequate, even though the pianist's subtle touch on a typical programme of standards is impeccable. The sound, though, is inadequate. *Today!* is a stray bulletin from the mid-'60s, originally very rare on vinyl, and several of the tunes sound foreshortened. 'Bluesette' and 'Polka Dots And Moonbeams' still show that Haig's powers were undimmed.

**** **Invitation**
Spotlite SPJ-CD 604 *Haig; Gilbert Rovere (b); Kenny Clarke (d).* 1/74.

It's poorly recorded (even in this remastering), the piano is unexceptional, and Rovere and Clarke do little more than accompany in the most basic manner. But Haig's playing is superb, in a favourite we have long awaited on CD. If ever there was a peformance to assert Haig's complete mastery of not just bebop but the wider refinements of piano jazz, this is it. He makes elaborate but entirely logical fantasias out of the likes of 'Invitation' and 'If You Could See Me Now', both hands engaged in immensely detailed yet extraordinarily graceful lines. His touch and nuance are sublimely effective. Unlucky throughout his career with the circumstances of recording, Haig never made a better 'modern' record than this, and it's a source of frustration that, first, even this one isn't so well framed and second, that he so seldom had the chance to do so much more.

*** **Ornithology**
Progressive PCD 7024 *Haig; Jamil Nasser (b); Frank Gant (d).* 77.

Haig went through a burst of recording late in his life, and he remained a marvellous musician to the end. So far, though, most of the vinyl has yet to make it to CD, outside of Japanese issues. This one is so-so. Nasser and Gant are no more than workmanlike, and Haig himself is sometimes content to take it easy, though his version of Strayhorn's 'Daydream' reminds us how he might have been the premier poet of bebop.

*** **Bebop Live**
Spotlite SPJ-CD 623 *Haig; Peter King (as); Art Themen (ts); Kenny Baldock (b); Allan Ganley (d).* 5/82.

A scruffy recording of a 1982 gig in Hampstead. King and Themen play their own strong bebop variations, but it's Haig we wait to hear, and his greatness glimmers through, just about.

The Halfway House Orchestra

GROUP

Pioneer New Orleans band, one of the few such bands to be recorded in the city during the '20s.

*** **The Halfway House Orchestra 1925–1928**
Jazz Oracle BDW 8001 *Albert Brunies (c); Joe Loyacano (tb); Sidney Arodin, Leon Roppolo (cl, as); Charlie Cordella (cl, ts); Red Long, Mickie Marcour, Bill Whitmore (p); Bill Eastwood; Angelo Palmisano (bj); Chink Martin (tba, b); Leo Adde; Emmett Rogers (d).* 25–28.

The Halfway House was a supper club, the name deriving from its point midway between New Orleans and Lake Pontchartrain, and the patrons were entertained by the (white) band led by Albie Brunies, a strong cornet-player who is the one musician to play throughout all these sessions. Roppolo (from the New Orleans Rhythm Kings) is on the rowdy first session for OKeh, but the later sides (for Columbia) use either Cordella or the excellent Arodin. The band is sometimes polite, but at their best they bridge a gap between jazz and dance music and are hot enough to impress, despite some unpromising material. They're probably best remembered as a vehicle for Brunies, whose playing is consistently engaging. Excellent transfers of the 22 tracks which are their legacy.

Edmond Hall (1901–67)

CLARINET

A native New Orleans man, Hall has often been unfairly eclipsed in discussions of jazz clarinettists. His three brothers all played clarinet too, but it was Ed who took most of the jazz-playing honours, spending several years with Claude Hopkins in the '30s and then freelancing, mostly around New York, for the rest of his life.

****** Edmond Hall 1936–1944**
Classics 830 *Hall; Billy Hicks (t, v); Sidney De Paris, Emmett Berry (t); Vic Dickenson, Fernando Arbello (tb); Meade Lux Lewis (cel); Cyril Haynes, Teddy Wilson, Eddie Heywood, James P. Johnson (p); Red Norvo (vib); Leroy Jones, Jimmy Shirley, Al Casey, Carl Kress (g); Al Hall, Israel Crosby, Billy Taylor, Johnny Williams (b); Arnold Boling, Big Sid Catlett (d); Henry Nemo (v).* 6/37–1/44.

***** Edmond Hall 1944–1945**
Classics 872 *Hall; Irving Randolph (t); Benny Morton, Henderson Chambers (tb); Harry Carney (bs); Teddy Wilson, Don Frye, Ellis Larkins (p); Everett Barksdale (g); Johnny Williams, Alvin Raglin, Billy Taylor (b); Big Sid Catlett, Arthur Trappier, Jimmy Crawford (d).* 5/44–45.

***** The Alternative Takes, Volume 1**
Neatwork RP 2043 *Similar to above discs, plus Bill Coleman (t), Bud Freeman (ts), Charlie Christian (g), Yank Porter (d); Teddy Howard (v).* 10/40–7/44.

***** The Alternative Takes, Volume 2**
Neatwork RP 2052 *As above.* 7–12/44.

****** Profoundly Blue**
Blue Note 821260-2 *Similar to above discs.* 2/41–5/44.

Hall was one of the most popular musicians in the Eddie Condon circle, but his experience – with big bands in the '20s and '30s and with Louis Armstrong's All Stars – was much wider than that. He played in a driving manner that married the character of his New Orleans background with the more fleet methods of the swing clarinettists. Classics 830 starts off with an obscure session by Billy Hicks and his Sizzlin' Six, with Hall as a sideman, but the meat of it is in Hall's first three sessions for Blue Note and a stray Commodore date. This is outstandingly fine midstream swing, with superb contributions from de Paris, Berry, the incomparably refined Wilson, Lewis (on celeste), James P. Johnson and, above all, the magnificent Dickenson, whose solos on the blues are masterful statements of jazz trombone. And there is Hall himself. Sound is mainly excellent, but the final Blue Note date is a bit scruffy. The next Classics disc is less involving: the first session, with Morton and Carney, is more fine small-group swing, but eight tracks in a quartet with Wilson are comparatively sedate and the two final band sessions merely agreeable.

Collectors will surely welcome Blue Note's own edition of their three Ed Hall sessions on *Profoundly Blue*. The sound is, surprisingly, not much better than on the Classics discs, with a lot of surface noise on several tracks, but the music stands tall and three alternative takes are well worth having. The May 1944 session is especially pleasing here, with Carney and Morton getting turns in the spotlight which are as rare as Hall's own.

Neatwork go somewhat laboriously through the various alternative takes from the Blue Note and Commodore sessions on their two CDs. There is the bonus of four tracks from a Columbia date of 1940 where Hall and a group including Bill Coleman and Bud Freeman backed the smoochy singer Teddy Howard. Whether you want these discs or not depends on your taste for having everything from a single session, second-string efforts and all: that said, even on supposedly inferior takes there's still some beautiful playing, and we're very happy to keep these on our shelves, even if seven seconds of a false start on 'Besame Mucho' is hardly a keeper.

***** Edmond Hall With Alan Elsdon**
Jazzology JCD-240 *Hall; Alan Elsdon (t); Phil Rhodes (tb); Andy Cooper (cl); Colin Bates (p); John Barton (g); Mick Gilligan (b); Billy Law (d).* 66.

***** Edmond Hall Quartet**
Jazzology JCD-207 *Hall; Colin Bates (p); Mick Gilligan (b); Billy Law (d).* 11/66.

****** Edmond Hall In Copenhagen**
Storyville STCD 6022 *Hall; Finn Otto Hansen (t); Arne Bue Jensen (tb); Jorgen Svare (cl); Jorn Jensen (p); Bjarne 'Liller' Petersen (bj); Jens Solund (b); Knud Ryskov Madsen (d).* 12/66.

***** Edmond Hall's Last Concert**
Jazzology JCD-223 *Hall; Bobby Hackett, George Poor (c); Joe Robertson (tb); Joe Battaglia, Evans Schwartz, Marie Marcus (p); Wally Livingston, Russell Best (b); Dale Pearman, Bob Saltmarsh (d).* 4/64–3/67.

Hall toured in the '60s until he died, and there is a rash of recordings from his final year or so. The first two Jazzology discs come from a British tour with Elsdon's band: one with the horns, one without. The date with horns just has it for the better variety, though this is in the main an unremarkable line-up of performers, and Hall's careful heat and elegant, supple parts outclass his surroundings, even in his final year. *Last Concert* comes from only days before he died. Sitting in with Hackett and some local players from South Byfield, MA, Hall still sounds in great shape. So does Hackett: but the indifferent band and low-fi sound make this for fans only. Three stray tracks from another occasion fill it out.

The Copenhagen date makes the best memorial to him. 'I like to work in different contexts, but I can only play one style': hot, fluent, swinging, pinching the odd note here and there, but mostly displaying a remarkably clean and supple line, here is Ed Hall at his best. The Papa Bue band play on two tracks, the rhythm section and Hall on most of the others and, while the Swedish players are no great masters, they know how to respect a player who is. Hall even turns in a lovely *a cappella* treatment of 'It Ain't Necessarily So'. Splendid remastering of a beautiful record.

Jim Hall (born 1930)

GUITAR

Played on the West Coast with Chico Hamilton and Jimmy Giuffre in the '50s, then returned east to work with Sonny Rollins and Art Farmer. Many years were spent in studio work, but in his 50s and 60s Hall became much more prominent as a leader, and is now recognized as a subtle master of his instrument.

★★★ Where Would I Be?

Original Jazz Classics OJC 649 *Hall; Ben Aronov (p); Malcolm Cecil (b); Airto Moreira (d).* 7/71.

Hall's smooth, gentlemanly approach got seriously interesting only once he had passed his 60th birthday and started to work with larger groups. The problem with these early sessions boils down, as the title implies, to their unvarying niceness. Totally professional, Hall delivers reliably every time, with no apparent difference in approach between live and studio sessions. He can certainly never be accused of pointless redundancy, for his solos are always unimpeachably controlled.

★★(★) Alone Together

Original Jazz Classics OJC 467 *Hall; Ron Carter (b).* 8/72.

A live set without a single rough edge or corner, and with almost no improvisational tension either. The slight surprise of Rollins's 'St Thomas' quickly evaporates as Hall negotiates its contours with almost cynical ease – is there really no more to it than that? The rest is more caressingly familiar. There are moments of genuine beauty, notably on 'Softly As In A Morning Sunrise' and 'Autumn Leaves', but there's something fatally lacking in the conception.

CORE COLLECTION

★★★★ Concierto

CTI 65132 *Hall; Chet Baker (t); Paul Desmond (as); Sir Roland Hanna (p); Ron Carter (b); Steve Gadd (d).* 4/75.

The title comes from Hall's delicate arrangement of Rodrigo's magnificent *Concierto De Aranjuez*, or rather part of it. The arrangement by Don Sebesky owes little or nothing to Gil Evans and has a more swinging and balanced quality than Gil's idiosyncratic classicism. Much of the rest is original material and arrangements of standard or jazz repertory material. The addition of Chet Baker and Paul Desmond to the line-up gives the record a stellar quality that comes through not just in the promise but also in the delivery. Chet is refined, delicate and less remote than he could be at this time. Desmond is melodic sophistication itself.

The reissue introduces alternatives of the Ellington/Strayhorn tune 'Rock Skippin'', 'You'd Be So Nice To Come Home To' and Jim's own 'The Answer Is Yes'. A magnificent record that must stand as one of his best recordings. It was also one of Creed Taylor's finest moments.

★★★ Live!

Verve 065428 *Hall; Don Thompson (b); Terry Clarke (d).* 75.

Recorded in concert in Toronto, this is a great chance to hear the '70s Hall stretching out on some sympathetic material. The 11-minute 'Angel Eyes' and a slightly shorter but no less effective 'Round Midnight' start the set, and pretty much climax it there, though there are fine moments on 'The Way You Look Tonight' and 'I Hear A Rhapsody'. The Charlie Parker tune is 'Scrapple From The Apple' and as ever Jim takes the bebop changes in his stride. Nicely recorded, with a generous sound from the bass.

★★★(★) Live At The North Sea Jazz Festival

Challenge 70063 *Hall; Bob Brookmeyer (vtb).* 79.

You saw these guys in the opening frames of *Jazz On A Summer's Day*, playing 'The Train And The River' as part of the Jimmy Giuffre 3. It would have been wonderful if they had reprised Jimmy's tune here, but there is much else to admire, from the wonderful opening arrangement of John Lewis's 'Skating In Central Park' to Ellington's 'In A Sentimental Mood', to 'St Thomas', 'Body And Soul' and an improvised duet, 'Sweet Basil'. Brookmeyer's soft, elegant sound blends wonderfully with Hall's effortless harmonic sense, and even sceptical listeners will find much to divert them on these eight tracks.

★★★ The Storyteller (Circles / All Across The City)

Concord CCD 2131 2CD *Hall; Gil Goldstein (p, ky); Don Thompson (p, b); Steve LaSpina, Rufus Reid (b); Terry Clarke (d).* 3/81, 5/89.

There's still a big gap in Hall's discography, accounting for much of the '70s, an admittedly fallow period for the guitarist. *Circles* finds him more conventionally swinging than for some time, but in a rather oddly weighted group in which Thompson doubles on piano and bass (Reid's only in for the fine 'All Of A Sudden My Heart Sings' – did he show up late?). There's not a lot of substance to it, and it would be as flat as a pancake if it weren't for Clarke's peppy drumming, a feature of most Hall records from here on.

All Across The City contains some of Hall's most innovatively 'contemporary' playing. Certainly, no one thrown into the deep end of 'R.E.M. Movement' – a Gil Goldstein composition with free passages from all the players – would suspect the provenance. Elsewhere the material is more familiar. 'Young One (For Debra)' consciously recalls Bill Evans and 'Waltz For Debby'. Of the other originals, the gentle 'Jane' is dedicated to Mrs Hall, composer in turn of 'Something Tells Me'; 'Drop Shot' and 'Big Blues' are tougher but also more humorous in conception, the former featuring Goldstein's electronic keyboards to good effect, the latter an unexpected tribute to Stanley Turrentine. The title-track, a gentle and slightly wondering cityscape, also recalls Hall's association with Bill Evans. Hall, though, is much more than an impressionistic colourist. His reading of Monk's 'Bemsha Swing' confirms his stature as one of the most significant harmonic improvisers on his instrument.

Nice to have these two albums together, even if they don't seem the most obvious pairing from the steadily rationalized Concord catalogue.

★★★ The Concord Jazz Heritage Series

Concord CCD 4831 *Hall; George Shearing (p); Gil Goldstein (ky); Ron Carter, Steve LaSpina, Rufus Reid, Don Thompson (b); Terry Clarke (d).* 81–89.

Jim moved on to other labels in the '90s, most successfully to Telarc, but some of his very best playing was for Concord and this set draws on some of the best work he did for Carl Jefferson. There are some good solo performances, but it is the duos with Carter (especially the Mandel/Mercer 'Emily') and with Shearing that stand out. Not perhaps the most balanced sampling of Jim's work during the '80s, but a very valid introduction nevertheless.

★★★(★) Dedications & Inspirations

Telarc CD 8365 *Hall (g solo).* 10/93.

... or not entirely solo, since on this fascinating record he experiments with a multi-playback system that allows him to overlay rich contrapuntal patterns and often surprisingly austere textures in a set that reflects his love of the visual arts as much as his lifelong passion for jazz. The telling thing is that at no point does the technology ever render it difficult to recognize Jim Hall in there. The voice is his from start to finish, and what he does with 'Bluesography' (which might have made a good alternative title for this session) and 'In A Sentimental Mood' could bear no other stylistic signature. It's perhaps a little too much sheer technical virtuosity to absorb at album length, but track by track it's hard to beat in this superb player's output.

**** Dialogues

Telarc CD 83369 *Hall; Tom Harrell (flhn); Joe Lovano (ts); Bill Frisell, Mike Stern (g); Gil Goldstein (acc); Scott Colley (b); Andy Watson (d).* 2/95.

Something of a dream-team package. There are actually only two duet tracks, both with Goldstein on his regular and bass accordion; the rest are small-group performances designed to highlight horns and guitar, and with Colley and Watson taking pretty much a back seat. With the exception of the closing 'Skylark', which features Harrell in exquisite form, all the tunes are Hall originals, written with a playing partner in mind – 'Frisell Frazzle', 'Calypso Joe', and 'Stern Stuff' – and it is Mike Stern who delivers the surprise of the session with an offbeat blues sound on 'Uncle Ed'. Frisell is in typically playful form on the opening dedication, reappearing on 'Simple Things', which has more of a country feel. The saxophonist has had more convincing days, but he manages to give his two appearances enough of a personal slant to distinguish him from A. N. Other guest hornman. Telarc recordings are famously good, but on this occasion John Snyder and Jane Hall have outdone themselves. Holding back a notch on the rhythm section was a risky stratagem, but what they have produced has near-perfect balance and no loss of definition. Plaudits all round.

***(*) Textures

Telarc CD 83402 *Hall; James Finegan, Ryan Kisor (t); Claudio Roditi (flhn); Conrad Herwig, Jim Pugh (tb); Alex Brofsky (frhn); Marcus Roja (tba); Joe Lovano (ss); Louis Schulman (vla); Myron Lutzke (clo); Scott Colley (b); Terry Clarke (d); Derek DiCenzo (steel d); Gordon Gottlieb (perc); strings.* 9/96.

As he neared 70, Hall grew ever more adventurous, rather than less. The main drawback of this record – easily as well crafted as its predecessor – is that it attempts too much in too short a span. A brass-dominated 'Fanfare' with Hall, Roditi and Pugh all featured; a couple of tracks with strings; a 'string quartet'; and the curious multi-cultural 'Sazanami', with its steel pans part. 'Ragman' is a further dialogue with Lovano, a plaintive evocation of urban loneliness and decay, beautifully constructed. 'Quadrologue', with Hall's electric standing in for first violin and Scott Colley's bass shifting the tonality downward, is a piece of latter-day Third Stream, while 'Passacaglia' is in near-classical form, a little soft-centred on repeated hearings, but an elegant line. Jim's daughter, Devra, contributes an illuminating liner-note.

***(*) Panorama

Telarc CD 83408 *Hall; Art Farmer (flhn); Slide Hampton (tb); Greg Osby (as); Kenny Barron, Geoff Keezer (p); Scott Colley (b); Terry Clarke (d).* 12/96.

Cut live at the Village Vanguard, Hall invites various masters to sit in with his own trio. It makes for a bitty album, but there are some specific highlights, most particularly Osby's two turns: his blues-playing on 'Furnished Flats' is as fine as anything he's set down on record (and paved the way for Hall to feature on one of Osby's own sets). All-original material keeps the situation from turning into a series of walk-on cameos and the results are more than pleasing.

*** Jim Hall And Pat Metheny

Telarc CD 83442 *Hall; Pat Metheny (g).* 7–8/98.

Nothing untoward about this collaboration: Hall is an obvious reference-point for much of Metheny's methods, and the pairing is as *simpatico* as one would expect. Probably too much so: the tracks are so sweetly choreographed, every affinity carefully underscored, that in the end it's little more than a pleasant distraction, and unlikely to make much appeal to anyone who isn't a dedicated guitar-follower.

*** Jazzpar Quartet + 4

Storyville 4230 *Hall; Chris Potter (ts); Thomas Ovesen (b); Terry Clarke (d); Zaploski String Quartet.* 98.

No one has deserved the Jazzpar accolade more, and Jim's musical reaction to the prestigious Danish music prize is a fine set of originals and standards, performed by his own group and – '+ 4' – by the Zaploski String Quartet, who deliver a well-read performance of his early classical piece, 'Thesis'. The strings are also present for a run-through of Hendrix's 'Purple Haze' which owes a good deal to the Kronos concept; but the real highlights of this record are the more straightforward jazz performances: a duo with saxophonist Potter on 'Chelsea Bridge' and a wonderfully paced 'Stella By Starlight'. Congratulations, Jim; recognition of this sort was long overdue.

***(*) By Arrangement

Telarc 83436 *Hall; Jamie Finegan, Lew Soloff (t); Tom Harrell (t, flhn); Conrad Herwig, Jim Pugh (tb); Joe Lovano (ss, cl); Greg Osby (as); Pat Metheny (g); Scott Colley (b); Terry Clarke (d); New York Voices; strings.* 98.

There are some real treasures on this set which, as the title suggests, is arranged by as well as featuring the guitarist. All the settings are extremely imaginative. 'Waltz For Debby' has the New York Voices singing Gene Lees's words to the Bill Evans classic; a string-section backs Hall and Metheny on Gordon Jenkins's 'Goodbye', and Harrell contributes a magnificent solo on Paul Desmond's all too rarely covered 'Wendy'. The larger-scale arrangements are consistently excellent, but it is Hall's ability to invest a small group, even a duo, with an almost orchestral quality that makes him stand out. Lovely stuff.

***(*) Grand Slam: Live At The Regattabar

Telarc 83485 *Hall; Joe Lovano (ts); George Mraz (b); Lewis Nash (d).* 1/00.

What a night this must have been at the Cambridge, Massachusetts, nightspot. Hall was in great form and his companions for the evening are well up to the challenge. Lovano contributed his own 'Chelsea Rendez-Vous', which kicks in straight off the back of Jim's own extended 'Slam' and gets the set off to a belting start. Joe's second composition, 'Blackwell's Message', is in a relatively unfamiliar idiom for Jim, but he rises to it magnificently, as he has to every challenge throughout his career, and the playing is great throughout the group. Nash and Mraz are masters at this kind of thing, giving the rhythm section edge as well as a profound lyricism. Hall's 'All Across The City', now an established favourite, tees up the ending, which, surprisingly, is another Lovano tune, the joyous 'Feel Free'. An almost faultless set and straight up there with Hall's best. We'd be tempted to give Joe joint credit, which is why the star rating is fairly modest.

*****(*) Jim Hall & Basses**
Telarc 83506 *Hall; Scott Colley, Charlie Haden, Dave Holland, Christian McBride, George Mraz (b).* 2/01.

The title is pretty much self-explanatory, a series of duets with some of the finest bass-players on the scene. Much of the material is original, and a good deal is improvised, like the set of 'Abstracts' that draw in Haden, Colley and Mraz during the course of the set. The standard of playing is exemplary throughout, but it is Jim who commands attention with his subtle harmonics, sly shifts of metre and command of sound colour. Another highly successful record from a master who seems to go from strength to strength.

Rob Hall

SOPRANO AND TENOR SAXOPHONES, CLARINET

Cool-toned Scot.

***** Open Up**
FMR UG CD 0110697 *Hall; Dave Frankel (p); Jim Mullen (g); Alex Keen (b); Paul Cavaciuti, Joachim Leyh (d).* 97.

***** Heading North**
FMR CD 06 0898 *As above; omit Mullen, Leyh.* 99.

*****(*) Free-World Music**
FMR CD 97 J0502 *Hall; Chris Greive (tb); Mike Hall (b); Paul Mills (d).* 02.

Hall's light touch and floating delivery are deceptive. He has strong ideas and a playful sense of form. Until the third album, his favoured horns were soprano and clarinet, with a keening sound that suggests a double-reeded instrument or bagpipe chanter. Enjoyable as the first two records are, it's the third – attributed to Hall's Freewheelers – that clinches his growing stature. Not only are the original compositions worth hearing, but his treatment of repertory material by Clifford Brown, John Scofield and Steve Swallow is exacting and far from cravenly respectful. Listen out, too, for guitarist Mullen's guest spots on the first record, confirmation of his remarkable powers.

Bengt Hallberg (born 1932)

PIANO, ORGAN, ACCORDION

Born in Gothenburg, Hallberg was playing on the Swedish swing scene when a teenager, before adapting to bop styles and working with Stan Getz and other Americans. While familiar to foreign audiences, his local status endures as one of the major figures in Swedish jazz, with numerous composing duties, soundtracks and other credits, along with a big discography and a style that seems to encompass most of jazz piano history.

***** Hallberg's Happiness**
Phontastic PHONT 7544 *Hallberg (p solo).* 3/77.

*****(*) The Hallberg Treasure Chest: A Bouquet From '78**
Phontastic NCD 8828 *Hallberg (p solo).* 8–10/78.

***** The Hallberg Touch**
Phontastic PHONT 7525 *Hallberg (p solo).* 8/79.

Bengt Hallberg is a major part of Swedish jazz and has been active since the '40s; not much of his earlier work is currently in print, though. The pianist made only a few albums under his own name in the '60s and '70s, and most of those have disappeared; but these three solo sessions are engaging, if a little lightweight compared to some of his earlier discs. *Happiness* is a packed collection of miniatures, some dispatched in a few breaths, others lingered over: there is a measured look at 'Sophisticated Lady' as well as a couple of jolly, faintly ludicrous ragtime pieces. The presence of the traditional 'Herdesang' is a reminder that Hallberg looked into the possibilities of improvising on native Scandinavian tunes before many more publicized attempts. *Touch* is another mix of unpredictable choices – 'In A Little Spanish Town', 'Charleston' – but plays out with a more thoughtful élan overall. The 1978 *Treasure Chest* set includes an 'Erroll Garner Joke', some judiciously picked standards and a couple of particularly fine ballads – 'I Couldn't Sleep A Wink Last Night' is one.

***** Hallberg's Yellow Blues**
Phontastic PHONT 7583 *Hallberg (p solo).* 84.

*****(*) Hallberg's Surprise**
Phontastic PHONT 7581 *Hallberg (p solo).* 3–5/87.

Few would credit Hallberg with leading the march from jazz to any kind of 'world music'. Yet the sleeve-note author for *Surprise* opines that it 'is not a jazz record', and the other disc consists of traditional folk material. Hallberg has studied and composed in the European tradition, and he moves through non-jazz mediums with the same ease with which he slips from swing to bop and after. These records feature him improvising on music remote from conventional jazz repertory, but they sound unequivocally comfortable, the familiar songful touch brought to bear on a surprising range of themes. The folk pieces are dealt with a little more discreetly, and the pianist trusts the inner lights of the material rather than imposing too much of himself on it; but the *Surprise* record is considerably more adventurous, with 'Take The "A" Train' sandwiched between Paganini's 'Caprice No. 24' and Handel's 'Sarabande', and Neal Hefti lining up with Corelli and Chopin. Hallberg plays on and around each of the pieces, never unduly respectful but sticking to his essential thriftiness and grace as an improviser: some pieces work superbly, others sound curiously abstracted, yet it's an altogether intriguing record.

***** Improvisation**
MPD CD 1 *Hallberg (p solo).* 5–8/88.

'Jazz, klassiskt, folkton? Nej, musik!' Thus go the sleeve-notes for this typically wide-ranging solo recital, mixing traditional airs, Hallberg originals and compositions from such as Evert Taube and Carl Mikael Bellman. As the quotation suggests, this is more of a piano record than any kind of jazz translation (and the recording, drawn from four different concerts, has a classical resonance to it), but it's full of Hallbergian charm and dexterity.

(***) Skansen In Our Hearts
Aquila CD 3 *Hallberg; Gustaf Sjokvist (p); Gavleborg Symphony Orchestra.* 91.

(***) 5×100
Improkomp IKCD 1 *Hallberg; Ad Libitum Choir.* 6/94.

Two of Hallberg's 'outside' projects, touched by jazz but primary examples of how far afield he's explored. *Skansen In Our Hearts* collects five of his orchestral pieces, some concerto-like in form (he sees little reason to exclude himself from any of his own works) and all firmly in a Scandinavian symphonic tradition. Some might wish for some extra gravitas, but there's no questioning the sonority and inventiveness of the composer's writing. *5 × 100* features his writing for choir – psalm settings, Shakespeare, Schubert, Swedish folksong and something of himself. He can't resist the occasional bit of mischief but some of the music is disarmingly lovely, and admirers of his piano will be partial to the four solo interludes. Rather remote recording from the Linkoping Cathedral School.

***** The Tapdancing Butterfly**

Aquila CD 4 *Hallberg; Ronnie Gardiner (b); Sture Akerberg (d).* 92.

Hallberg's trio music has an element of kitsch about it: he likes tempos and rhythms that suggest a kind of jazz vaudeville at times, and the queer setting chosen for 'Poor Butterfly', for instance, will raise either a smile or a wince of irritation. The butterfly theme drifts through these pieces, and the best of them are vintage Hallberg, but it's as well to be tuned in on his wavelength.

CORE COLLECTION

****** Time On My Hands**

Improkomp IKCD 2-3 2CD *Hallberg (p solo).* 2/94–4/95.

Hallberg played a radio concert in which he performed nothing but written requests from the audience, and he liked it so much that he repeated the method at two subsequent sessions. This two-disc set takes the pick of the three occasions. Non-Swedish speakers are denied the chance to savour the pianist's amusing introductions (his first number is the theme from *Dallas*!), but nobody will mistake the elegance, wit and lucidity on show in the playing itself. This is vintage Hallberg, and probably the ideal introduction to one of Europe's most eminent masters.

***** In A Mellow Tone**

Improkomp IKCD 5 *Hallberg; Hans Backenroth (b).* 3/96.

This time Hallberg is in conversation with a young bassist, and they tackle a typical programme for the pianist: three traditional Scandinavian pieces, three originals and a group of standards. In case one expected Hallberg to take a perfunctory route, have a listen to what he does with 'Out Of Nowhere'. Maybe this isn't one of his great ones – the sound is a bit reverberant, and some of the tunes are dispatched almost too quickly – but admirers will enjoy all the same.

***** Stardust In My Heart**

Improkomp IKCD 6 *Hallberg (p solo).* 6/99.

The agenda here was to play 20 standards in as steady and unfussy a way as possible, so there's very little improvising and much respect for the melodies. Bengt takes most of them at a sedate, jogging pace. It's more like a recital than a jazz set, although even here Hallberg can't resist tickling a few embellishments into the situation, and there is a lovely version of his waltz 'In My Heart'. Now semi-retired, maybe he feels he has little left to say for re-recordings, and there's been nothing new since our last edition.

Rich Halley

TENOR AND SOPRANO SAXOPHONES, FLUTE, PERCUSSION

Based in Portland, Oregon, Halley is an experienced freebop saxman with a circle of playing acquaintances that include some notable 'regional' players.

*****(*) Live At Beanbenders**

Nine Winds NWCD 0215 *Halley; Rob Blakeslee (t, c); Michael Vlatkovich (tb); Troy Grugett (as, bs, perc); Phil Sparks (b); William Thomas (d).* 5/98.

***** Objects**

Louie 025 *Halley; Clyde Reed (b); Dave Storrs (d).* 12/01.

*****(*) The Blue Rims**

Louie 030 *As above, except add Bobby Bradford (c, perc).* 12/02.

The tenor-toting computer programmer and zoologist from Portland was in some of our early editions and it's a pleasure to welcome him back with this recent work. The set from Beanbenders in Berkeley is rich with sonorous horns and nicely varied between solos with counterpoint, wailing chorales and sparsely textured improvisations. Blakeslee is particularly strong but the whole record is absorbing. *Objects* is a good example of this regular trio at work, although the record perhaps falls short of a truly memorable statement. Halley's big, Rollinsesque sound is strong by itself, yet he does seem to gain an extra ounce of power and impetus from the presence of other horns, and there's a degree of spacefilling here.

The guest presence of Bradford on *The Blue Rims* surely makes the difference. This is gracious and muscular freebop with excellent playing by all hands.

Jimmy Halperin

TENOR SAXOPHONE

Young American saxophonist working in the Tristano idiom of improvising.

*****(*) Psalm**

Zinnia 110 *Halperin; Sal Mosca (p).* 1/97.

This is the Tristano doctrine in its coolest and most concentrated form. The disc consists of seven lines written by Halperin, played as a series of formal duets and followed by improvisations on six of them: it runs as 49 minutes of uninterrupted music. The lines are utterly remote from their standard chords, as serpentine as any composing in this manner, and the improvising is enacted completely in the spirit of the occasion: oblique, far-sighted, completely self-absorbed yet drily compelling. Halperin suggests an unswerving dedication to the idiom and Mosca is the ideal partner. Scarcely to every jazz taste, and all the better for it.

*****(*) Cycle Logical**

Cadence CJR 1142 *Halperin; Don Messina (b); Bill Chattin (d).* 4/01.

A beautiful continuation of Halperin's slim discography. Messina and Chatti are regular workmates (and also play together in the Larry Bluth group) and their lightly earnest accompaniments are a hand-in-glove platform for the saxophonist to work from. This is a live gig (from the Rahway Arts

Guild in New Jersey) and Halperin purls his way through some originals and tunes by Konitz and Tristano – ideal fodder, naturally, and he is consummately relaxed without sounding in any way becalmed. Some of the improvising is as close to immaculate as this form will ever get – rounded, free-flowing, but purged of cliché or the easy route and the simple resolution. There's also the matter of the tenorman's tone, which has a downy lustre which even Warne Marsh might have envied. If there's a complaint, it's that the live recording is just a little too monochromatic – suits the music in a way, and recalls the unglamorous sound of the great Tristano sessions, but a little more presence in the group wouldn't have hurt. Otherwise unmissable.

Chico Hamilton (born 1921)

DRUMS

A native Los Angeles man, Hamilton played in the city through the '40s and '50s, forming his own band in 1955, which won much acclaim. Studio credits as writer and performer took up much of his time until the '80s, when he began touring and recording with his own groups again. An undervalued and considerable influence and performer.

***** With Strings Attached / The Three Faces Of Chico**

Warners 124534 *Hamilton; Eric Dolphy (as, bcl, f); Dennis Budimir (g); Nate Gershman (clo); Wyatt Ruther (b).* 10/58.

***** Featuring Eric Dolphy**

Fresh Sound FSCD 1004 *Hamilton; Eric Dolphy (as, f, bcl); Dennis Budimir (g); Nathan Gershman (clo); Wyatt Ruther, Ralph Pena (b).* 5/59.

***** The Original Ellington Suite**

Blue Note 24567 *Hamilton; Eric Dolphy (as, bcl, f); John Pisano (g); Nate Gershman (clo); Hal Gaylor (b).* 8/58.

A less celebrated drum-led academy than Art Blakey's, and yet Hamilton has always surrounded himself with gifted young musicians and has helped bring forward players as inventive as Eric Dolphy, Larry Coryell, Charles Lloyd and, much later, Eric Person as well. Hamilton has always taken an inventive and even idiosyncratic approach to the constitution of his groups, and often the only identifying mark is his own rolling lyricism and unceasing swing. Anyone who has seen the classic festival movie, *Jazz On A Summer's Day*, will remember the almost hypnotic concentration of his mallet solo.

Recent years have seen the rediscovery and reissue of some important early work. The compilation of *Three Faces* and *With Strings Attached* is a significant contribution to the discography and a valuable addition to the amount of Eric Dolphy material available, but it was the uncovering (by chance and in England) of test pressings that have now yielded *The Original Ellington Suite* that has really excited collectors and students of the period. Dolphy's alto, clarinet and flute are prominently featured throughout the recording, notably on 'Everything But You' (flute) and 'In A Sentimental Mood' (alto). His phrasing and tone are still relatively conventional, though it seems too advanced for the producer, Richard Bock.

The other reissued set is more familiar and closer in mood to the Hamilton appearance at Newport, but collectors may well already be in possession of these sides. The generally quiet and unemphatic chamber-jazz approach still hasn't won over everyone conditioned by bebop, but these are eminently listenable recordings and Chico's own playing is magnificently controlled and seemingly effortless.

The May 1959 session – previously released as *That Hamilton Man* – is darker and more angular. On his last studio appearance with the Quintet, Dolphy chips in with his first recorded composition; the moody 'Lady E' largely avoids the folkish sentimentality of parts of *Gongs East* and helps sustain the later album's prevailing air of appealing melancholy.

*****(*) The Dealer**

Impulse! 547 958-2 *Hamilton; George Bohannon (tb); Arnie Lawrence (as); Jimmy Woods (ts); Charles Lloyd (ts, f); Archie Shepp (p); Ernie Hayes (org); Larry Coryell, Gabor Szabo (g); Richard Davis (b); Albert Stinson (b, v); Willie Bobo (perc).* 9/62–9/66.

There is still a huge gap, several decades wide, in the Hamilton discography, but at least the reappearance of this fine set signals an intent to backfill some of his excellent work for Bob Thiele at Impulse!. The CD includes the original album, with earlier material from *Chic Chic Chico* and *Passin' Thru*, as well as a single track – the not entirely representative 'Big Noise From Winnetka' – from the label compilation, *Definitive Jazz Scene: Volume 3*.

As ever, much of the emphasis falls on young and relatively untried players. Coryell is treated as the remarkable discovery he undoubtedly was, with generous solo space on almost every track. His soulful blues line and rock intensity are best sampled on 'Thoughts', which begins with an echoed vocal from Chico himself; Larry's spot is punctuated with sharp, pots-and-pans accents from the leader, before giving way to arguably Richard Davis's best solo on record, a wonderfully constructed thing. On his jazz debut Coryell also makes his presence felt with his first recorded jazz composition; 'Larry Of Arabia' is a pretty basic rise-and-fall idea, but it spurs the drummer into a fabulous solo. Too bad the track fades away so lamely; so much so that one suspects there must have been a tape problem.

Shepp stops by to add a piano line to his own 'For Mods Only', as quirky and self-possessed as ever. There is uncredited percussion on the closing 'Jim-Jeannie', a tribute to the Cheathams. Jimmy provides the arrangements for 'The Dealer' and 'Baby, You Know' and conducts 'A Trip', so it's not inconceivable that he was persuaded to shake a tambourine as well. Arnie Lawrence is virtually unknown. A Brooklynite who moved to the West Coast in search of work, he sounds superficially like Charlie Parker, but has a rawer tonality and an almost eccentric approach to phrasing that could never be confused with Bird.

The additional material is marked by the very different guitar-sound of Gabor Szabo, and Charles Lloyd's floatier saxophone and flute. Good as it is to have these things back in circulation, the real weight falls on *The Dealer* itself. Heard afresh, it confirms Hamilton's standing as one of the most original bandleaders around. A few more reissues will perhaps speed up the process of rediscovery.

***** Reunion**

Soul Note 121191 *Hamilton; Buddy Collette (f, cl, as); Fred Katz (clo); John Pisano (g); Carson Smith (b).* 6/89.

No longer 110 lb, the latter-day Hamilton packs an impressive punch. This was a brief album-and-tour reunion of the original Hamilton Quintet, with Pisano in for the otherwise-engaged

Jim Hall, and it reveals Hamilton as one of the most underrated and possibly influential jazz percussionists of recent times. Rather than keeping up with any of the Joneses, he sustains a highly original idiom which is retrospectively reminiscent of Paul Motian's but is altogether more abstract. The spontaneously improvised 'Five Friends' might have worked better as a duet with Collette (like 'Brushing With B' and 'Conversation'), but the immediately preceding 'Dreams Of Youth', dedicated by its composer, Fred Katz, to the dead and betrayed of Tiananmen Square, is one of the most moving jazz pieces of recent years, drawing out Hamilton's non-Western accents. *Reunion* is confidently exploratory and powerfully effective.

***(*) Arroyo

Soul Note 121241 *Hamilton; Eric Person (as, ss); Cary DeNigris (g); Reggie Washington (b).* 12/90.

That Hamilton should christen this band Euphoria is testimony to his continued appetite for music-making. Though it's as far in style as it is in years from the '50s Quintet, there are clear lines of continuity. Hamilton's preference for a guitarist over a piano player helps free up the drums, allowing Hamilton to experiment with melodic improvisation. Typically, DeNigris is given considerable prominence – much as Jim Hall, Larry Coryell and John Abercrombie were at different times – with Person assigned a colourist's role.

The long opening 'Alone Together' is a vibrantly inventive version of a wearying warhorse. Hamilton's polyrhythms open the tune to half a dozen new directions and Washington produces some of his best work of the set. The other standard, Lester Young's and Jon Hendricks's 'Tickle Toe', has the drummer scatting with the same relaxed abandon he applies to his kit. His writing on 'Sorta New', 'Cosa Succede?' and the intriguingly titled 'Taunts Of An Indian Maiden' is still full of ideas, exploiting band textures to the full. DeNigris and Person both claim at least one writing credit, and the guitarist's 'Stop' is ambitious and unsettling. The mix doesn't favour the leader unduly, but Washington is slightly submerged on some of the up-tempo numbers. Hamilton's inventiveness seems unstinted; this is impressive stuff.

***(*) Trio!

Soul Note 121246 *Hamilton; Eric Person (as, ss, sno); Cary DeNigris (g).* 5/92.

At 71, Hamilton still produces a beefy sound and still refuses to stay rooted in the styles of his youth. The 'heavy metal' mannerisms of his late-'80s bands have mellowed a bit, though both Person and DeNigris let rip when the need arises. The trio had been around for some time when the record was cut, and they play as if they're used to one another. DeNigris and Hamilton combine effectively on 'C & C' but the outstanding track is Person's long '10th Vision', which calls in M-Base mannerisms, the oozing funk of old-time organ trios, and hints of a free-ish idiom.

Hamilton simply can't stay still and has obviously decided to play until he drops. Be assured, there's plenty more to come.

***(*) My Panamanian Friend

Soul Note 121265 *As for Arroyo, except omit Washington; add Kenny Davis (b).* 8/92.

To mark the 30th anniversary of the saxophonist's death, this is a tribute to former employee Eric Dolphy, whose tragically foreshortened career after leaving the Hamilton band is still one of the major, if unassimilated, achievements of contemporary jazz. Predictably, perhaps, Hamilton selects from among the least wiggy areas of Dolphy's output: 'South Street Exit', 'Springtime', the blues 'Serene', the inevitable 'Miss Ann' (perhaps Dolphy's best-known composition), 'Mandrake', 'Miss Movement' and, from *Out To Lunch*, 'Something Sweet, Something Tender'. Dolphy's young namesake plays decently, but a lot of the emphasis falls on Hamilton, whose rather enigmatic title relates to Dolphy's Panamanian ancestry, of which Eric Dolphy senior was so proud.

*** Dancing To A Different Drummer

Soul Note 121291 *Hamilton (solo perc).* 3–4/93.

There haven't been many drummers who could sustain this level of interest unaccompanied. Hamilton has always been a highly melodic player and, though there are moments among these ten tracks when he seems to be striving *too* hard for that effect, there is no mistaking the innate musicality of his approach. Some of the tracks – like 'Dance Of The Tympanies' and 'The Snare Drum' – would be mere technical exercises in other hands, but Chico carries them through, logically, smilingly and lovingly. Not perhaps the most instantly accessible of his records, but certainly one for Hamilton enthusiasts.

*** Timely

All Points Jazz 3001 *Hamilton; Eric Person (ss, as, f); Cary DeNigris (g); Paul Ramsey (b).* 99.

As if to mock us for our premature obituary of a couple of editions back, Hamilton continues to create vivid, tireless jazz. Having enjoyed his moment in the foreground on *Different Drummer*, he holds back from the foreground to provide a potent accompaniment to Person and DeNigris. 'Malletdonia' is the exception, but it comes right at the end of the album. The switch to electric jazz and funk is a surprise, given the times and given Hamilton's recent recorded output, but these tracks are every bit as idiomatic and personalized as the more conventional acoustic tunes. We particularly liked 'Cheeks' Groove' and the two-part 'These Are The Dues'. The Salvador Dalí cover (melting watches, predictably) is perhaps a bit of a false note. Hamilton isn't so much bending and distorting time as taking the hurry out of it.

*** Forestorn

Koch 7870 *Hamilton; Steve Turre (tb); Eric Person (ss); Erik Lawrence (ss, as, f); Arthur Blythe (as); Evan Schwam (ts); John Popper (hca); Cary DeNigris, Erik Schenkman (g); Akua Dixon (clo); Paul Ramsey (b); Charlie Watts (d).* 10/00–1/01.

The drummer's first recording for a new label ropes in an impressive roster of guest performers. Husband-and-wife team Turre and Dixon are included on the self-named 'Bone Cello', and 'Black' Arthur Blythe makes a powerful noise on 'Eleven Bars For Arthur'. Person and DeNigris are again compelling, as they tend to be in Chico's company. There are a couple of tracks which drift close to rock or 'nu' blues; Charlie Watts of the Rolling Stones (but a devoted bebopper) is on hand, one of a number of guest appearances.

For the most part this fine tribute to Hamilton's late son (after whom the set and a reprised lament are named) is well up to scratch. Check his performance on 'Here Comes Charlie Now' and the following 'When The Saints Go Marchin' In'.

***** Thoughts Of ...**

Koch International 51009 *Hamilton; Evan Schwam (ts); Karolina Strassmayer (ss, as, f); Erik Lawrence (ss, as); Joe Beck, Larry Coryell, Rodney Jones, Cary DeNigris (g); Paul Ramsey (b).* 02.

Outwardly a series of tributes to great musicians who influenced Hamilton – Lester Young, John Coltrane, Miles Davis – but in reality no more than an excuse for a vaguely themed set of otherwise unremarkable originals and for a couple of guest spots. The reunion with Coryell closes an almost 40-year gap, but the empathy is still there. Beck and Jones are also given prominence, which fortunately gives the saxophones somewhat less to do. Best track is probably 'Thoughts of Miles', which cleverly weaves in a reading of 'Freddie Freeloader'. Though this doesn't rank as a vintage line-up, at 82, Chico still knows how to swing.

Ed Hamilton

GUITAR, KEYBOARDS

Smooth fusion from a talented player who could yet surprise with more straightahead work.

****(*) Planet Jazz**

Telarc 83387 *Hamilton; Charles Howard (ss); Stanley Clarke, Charles Fambrough (b); Lenny White (d).* 96.

****(*) Path To The Heartland**

Telarc 83404 *Hamilton; Dave Falciani (p, ky); Vincent Fay (b); Pat Petrillo (d); Jorge Rossy (perc).* 97.

Hamilton is something of an enigma. Right from the beginning of his recording career, it was clear that he was a player of great technical proficiency and some imagination. However, most of these albums are bogged down in commercial cul-de-sacs, good enough to suggest they should be better, tedious enough to wonder whether the problem is with Hamilton or those who are steering his career.

Planet Jazz is a pleasant enough disc and the presence of fusion legends Clarke and White (and to a lesser extent Fambrough) must have guaranteed it some attention. It's hard, though, to recall a single track on it and all one takes away is an impression of good chops gone somewhat awry. On *Path To The Heartland* Hamilton again seems to be promising something that he's not quite ready to deliver; the heartland of *what*? one is tempted to ask. The group here is actually less anonymous than the roster of names might suggest and there are signs that Hamilton is beginning to shape the kind of sound he wants with what is presumably a working band. It's an amalgam of rock, bop, soul and impressionistic modernism, but the pay-off is a record that asks to be heard again, if only for the bravura of 'Monsters In The Closet' and the not-quite-saccharine sweetness of 'September Solitude', which closes it out on a misleadingly elegiac note.

***** Groovology**

Shanachie 5047 *As above, except add Tim Ries (ss).* 98.

A new record and a new label. Hamilton tries to beguile the fanbase with a smoothly funky opener, 'Fly Like An Eagle', but then cuts loose with probably his most jazz-based session to date. Ries is an important component of the sound, as far from Kenny G as it's decent to get in this idiom and a very thoughtful soloist. 'On My Way' and 'JJ's Groove' are hopeful signs that Hamilton is shaping up as a composer, but one wonders why he feels moved to drape most tracks with synth figures that only muddle the line and add nothing but filler. Again, he opts to close with something soft and squishy, 'Song For A Princess', which is either a personal dedication or a threnody for Diana; we didn't check ...

***** Hear In The Now**

Fahrenheit 2002 *As above, except omit Ries; add Warren Hill (sax).* 99.

'JJ's Groove' makes a welcome return, in a tougher and more accomplished version, and Hamilton seems to have ironed out some of his competing influences to make an album that has a bit of bite as well as some lovely moments. Hill isn't a particularly interesting saxophone player, and certainly not in Ries's class, but he fits the bill here perfectly, even if only as a foil to the leader. Ed himself is on great form and listening to this starts to make sense of some of his more self-consciously eclectic gestures on past records. Recommended.

Jeff Hamilton (born 1953)

DRUMS

Born in Richmond, Indiana, Hamilton held down many big-band and small-group gigs alike through the '70s and '80s, with particular associations with The L.A. Four and Gene Harris. He continues to be in demand for diverse situations and also leads the trio on show here.

***** Hamilton House**

Mons MR 874-316 *Hamilton; Larry Fuller (p); Lynn Seaton (b).* 2/99.

Hamilton has been around and in high-profile gigs for so long that it's almost a surprise to learn that he's still only in his early 50s. A drummer routinely categorized as 'musicianly' (which tended to mean that he didn't just thrash away), he's unusually adept both at sensitive small-band settings and in orchestral situations which call for plenty of brawn. This trio has been a regular item in his schedule since 1994, and Fuller and Seaton are lively, responsive partners. A nice, inventive choice of material – one Hamilton original, a couple from regular confederate John Clayton's book, plus song picks as diverse as 'See See Rider' and 'Here, There And Everywhere' – keeps what is a live set from the Los Angeles club Steamer's bubbling along. Seventy-two minutes is too much music, and in the crowded repertory of piano-trio records this stakes only a minor position, but Fuller's clean, clear playing suits the gig and the leader plays with much evident enjoyment.

Jimmy Hamilton (1917–1994)

CLARINET, TENOR SAXOPHONE

Worked around Philadelphia in the late '30s, then with Teddy Wilson, but his main professional association was with Duke Ellington, whom he worked with for 25 years from 1943. Thereafter he was mostly in teaching, but he made occasional appearances into the '90s.

***** Jimmy Hamilton And The New York Jazz Quintet**

Fresh Sound 2002 *Hamilton; Clark Terry (t); Kenny Kersey, Earl Knight (p); Barry Galbraith, Sidney Gross (g); Oscar Pettiford, Jimmy Woode (b); Osie Johnson, Sam Woodyard (d).* 54.

These tracks were originally released on the Urania label as *Accent On Clarinet* and *Clarinet In High-Fi*, and they're the earliest representation of Hamilton as a leader still in catalogue. The clarinet sound is still sweet rather than hot, but Jimmy knows how to swing even a rather saccharine line. The first of the dates is a pianoless group with two guitars, which is an interesting touch; presumably when you've worked with the Duke, it's difficult to settle for anything less. 'I Get A Kick Out Of You' inspires one of Jimmy's best solos of the period. He's also heard at length on 'Tea For Two' and 'Easy Living' from the slightly later *Clarinet In High-Fi* date.

*** Swing Low Sweet Clarinet

Everest 5100 *Hamilton; John Anderson (t); Britt Woodman, Dave Wells, Booty Wood (bhn); Paul Gonsalves (ts); Jimmy Rowles (p); Aaron Bell (b); Sam Woodyard (d).* 60.

*** Can't Help Swingin'

Prestige PRCD 24214-2 *Hamilton; Clark Terry (t, flhn); Britt Woodman (tb); Tommy Flanagan (p); Wendell Marshall (b); Mel Lewis, Earl Williams (d).* 3–4/61.

The best of Jimmy Hamilton is with Ellington, of course, but the pair of dates for Prestige – originally issued as *It's About Time* and *Can't Help Swinging* – will appeal to collectors of small-group Ellingtonia. For once, there's no Ducal tune in the setlist, but with four fellow Ellingtonians in the band and most of the 'originals' being dressed-up variations on the blues, it's not hard to imagine how the music turns out. Terry and Woodman are only on the first session, and while both sometimes defer to the nominal leader as far as solo impact goes, it's all very gentlemanly. The second date, with Hamilton as the sole horn, is rather more interesting. The famous contrast between his sweetly amiable clarinet and rasping, almost R&B-styled tenor is less pronounced, since he actually plays more saxophone than usual ('Six months may go by before I get a chance to pick it up,' he says in the notes), and at ballad tempo he affects a Websterian approach. It's all mild enough, but gracious.

Even more appealing in some regards is *Swing Low Sweet Clarinet*. Again, the players are nearly all Ellingtonians, and the interesting twist is that Woodman, Wood and incomer Wells are playing baritone horns instead of their familiar trombones (and not baritone saxophones as noted in some sources). It's a rich and capacious sound which Hamilton exploits to the full on a set that's pretty well stocked with Duke's compositions: 'In A Sentimental Mood', 'Do Nothing Till You Hear From Me' and 'The Nearness Of You'. Jimmy contributes two ideas of his own, 'Tempo De Brazilia' and the fun 'Taj Mahal'. Gonsalves is in fine voice, though slightly restrained on a couple of his spots as if trying not to shade the leader.

*** Rediscovered Live At The Buccaneer

Who's Who In Jazz D2-72216 *Hamilton; Gary Mayone (p); Joe Straws (b); Delroy Thomas (d).* 85.

An obscurity, but worth hunting down if you're a fan of Jimmy's. Working with a pick-up band in a St Croix, Virginia club, the 68-year-old works through a set of pretty familiar themes, devoting the whole second half of the night to Ellington tunes. There's nothing outstanding here and nothing that prompts a radical rethink of Hamilton's work, but it's a thoroughly enjoyable disc. The same material seems to be available on a Jazz Time disc as well but we have not had an opportunity to compare.

Scott Hamilton (born 1954)

TENOR SAXOPHONE

Born and raised in Providence, Rhode Island, Hamilton has helped redefine mainstream jazz for two decades. To say that he plays like Ben Webster or Don Byas is to miss the point, for Hamilton has always been more resolutely contemporary than conservative.

**** From The Beginning

Concord CCD 2117 2CD *Hamilton; Bill Berry (t); Nat Pierce (p); Monty Budwig (b); Jake Hanna (d); Cal Collins (g).* 77–78.

***(*) Tenorshoes

Concord CCD 4127 *Hamilton; Dave McKenna (p); Phil Flanigan (b); Jeff Hamilton (d).* 12/79.

He doesn't double on soprano, bass clarinet or flute. He probably doesn't know what multiphonics are. He has never been described as 'angular', and if he was ever 'influenced by Coltrane' it certainly never extended to his saxophone playing. And yet Scott Hamilton is the real thing, a tenor player of the old school who was born only after most of the old school were dead or drawing bus-passes. His wuffly delivery and clear-edged tone are definitive of mainstream jazz, and the affection in which Hamilton is held on both sides of the Atlantic is not hard to understand. And yet what he does is utterly original and un-slavish, not in thrall to anyone.

Concord boss the late Carl Jefferson remembers Hamilton turning up for his first session for the label looking 'like a character in Scott Fitzgerald', with a fifth of gin tucked into his jacket, and playing, as it turned out, like a veteran of the first Jazz Age, a style which drew on Coleman Hawkins, Chu Berry, Lester Young, Don Byas and Zoot Sims, resolutely unfashionable in 1977 but completely authentic and unfeigned.

Hamilton's Concord debut, named after Leonard Feather's enthusiastic imprimatur, wasn't perhaps quite forceful enough to be described in terms of wind but it was certainly a breath of fresh air, and it refocused attention almost immediately on the undischarged possibilities of jazz before the bebop revolution. From the opening lines of 'That's All', it was clear that a special new talent was at work. At 22 Hamilton had the poise and the patience of a much more experienced player. Quite how he had learnt so much so quickly remains something of a mystery and, though there are one or two instances of him coltishly running ahead of the group, what is most impressive is the sheer discipline of his playing.

As the unimaginative title suggests, the follow-up was recorded almost immediately afterwards, given the enthusiasm for the first record. It was perhaps too soon for Hamilton to have settled down and thought about what he was going to do. The absence of Berry was unfortunate, and the addition of guitar makes for a rather smoother and less pungent product. For once, Hamilton seems content to fall back on predetermined ideas. Though everything on the record is played with exemplary professionalism, it never seems to get beyond that point and remains rather formulaic.

These two first shots are now available together as *From The Beginning*, another good value twofer from Concord as it rationalizes a catalogue that has needed overhauling for some time.

The cover of *Tenorshoes* features a pair of basketball boots (a Hamilton signature at the time) bronzed like a baby's first shoes, and beside them a dish of chocolates. However tired Hamilton must have been about constant references to his age – a veteran at 25 – he might usefully have sued over the sweets, because his saxophone playing is fat-free and low-cholesterol. However saccharine some of the tunes – 'I Should Care', 'The Shadow Of Your Smile' and 'The Nearness Of You' might all have come from the confectionery counter – Hamilton explores the changes with a fine, probing intelligence that is every bit as intellectually satisfying as it is emotionally fulsome. The unaccompanied intro to 'I Should Care' and an energetic reading of 'How High The Moon' bespeak a rapidly developing sense of structure and dynamics. McKenna is superb (a duo album would have been a worthwhile investment) and the recording is bright and unfussy, even if Hamilton seems a little too forward on occasion.

*** The Grand Appearance

Progressive 7026 *Hamilton; Tommy Flanagan, Hank Jones (p); George Mraz (b); Connie Kay (d).* 1–2/78.

We're not clear how this non-Concord set came to be recorded, but it's pretty familiar Hamilton fare, a set of mid-tempo swingers mixed in with ballads. The love theme from *The Sandpiper* ('The Shadow Of Your Smile') and the Mercer/VanHeusen classic 'I Thought About You' are both outstanding, but with a group like this, and with Flanagan and Jones alternating on piano, it's pretty hard to go wrong. The sound is somewhat flat and one-dimensional, even by the standard of the time, but the playing more than makes up for any minor technical shortcomings.

*** Major League

Concord CCD 4305 *Hamilton; Dave McKenna (p); Jake Hanna (d).* 5/86.

A grower, and one we feel much more sanguine about this time round. Our anxiety stemmed from the more fiery pace Hanna brought to the set. The trio had played together under McKenna's leadership on *No Bass Hit* for Concord, one of big Dave's themed projects, and it may be that he wriggled slightly at the thought of handing over the reins to the youngster. He's certainly still the playing star of this set, turning in a magnificent solo on 'It All Depends On You' and running a powerful, low-register left-hand line that more than amply takes up any slack from the missing bassist. And remember that this is the configuration Cecil Taylor liked to work with.

CORE COLLECTION

**** Plays Ballads

Concord 4386 *Hamilton; John Bunch (p); Chris Flory (g); Phil Flanigan (b); Chuck Riggs (d).* 3/89.

Still for some Hamilton's best record, not because the ballad programme allows him any paths of least resistance but simply because this is the sort of material which allows him to show off his strengths: harmonic subtlety at slow tempos, delicate, almost seamless transitions between ideas, and an ability to invest a simple, familiar melody with maximum expression. 'Round Midnight' and 'In A Sentimental Mood' are read with an intriguing slant which freshens up the Monk tune considerably. 'Two Eighteen', dedicated to Hamilton's wife (and we suspect it may refer to the number of a honeymoon suite), is surprisingly his first recorded composition; at first blush, it doesn't suggest a writing talent commensurate with his playing skills, but it's a fine piece nevertheless. The Don Byas-associated 'Laura' and an oblique 'Body And Soul' (also considerably freshened) were added only when *Ballads* was transferred to CD. This seems odd, because these are the outstanding performances on the record and, we hear, are much enjoyed by Don and Bean up in heaven.

**** East Of The Sun

Concord CCD 4583 *Hamilton; Brian Lemon (p); Dave Green (b); Allan Ganley (d).* 8/93.

Perhaps a touch of cross-Atlantic pride in our rating for these. A devoted Anglophile, Hamilton was spending more and more time playing in the UK, where he has a more-than-loyal following and where in this group he has found like-minded players of great experience. Just to complicate the geography a little, the tunes on *East Of The Sun* were the result of a readers' poll in the Japanese *Swing Journal.* Hamilton had long wished to record with a British group, and one can see why. Lemon is one of the finest accompanists around, and he solos with such bluff confidence that he often masks the subtlety of what he is playing. Ganley and Green combine effectively, and both of them are accurately caught.

***(*) The Red Door

Concord CCD 4799 *Hamilton; Bucky Pizzarelli (g).* 3/95.

Ah, but who's playing the bass? The answer is Bucky himself, whose seven-string guitar – with low A string – and nimble technique make it sound as if there is at least a trio at work here. The idea of the album was a tribute to Zoot Sims and it includes material that would have been familiar to the great saxophonist. Zoot and Bucky appeared in this configuration on a 1975 album for Classic Jazz; we can't comment on it, but there is no doubt that each and every item on this set has Zoot's signature all over it, and Bucky frequently quotes his distinctive phrases. There are some fascinating moments on this. 'Gee Baby, Ain't I Good To You' is astonishing, pitched high and fast, but it's a subtly transposed interpretation of 'Jitterbug Waltz' that really catches the attention; virtuosic, intelligent jazz, played at a very high level. Buy and enjoy this record.

***(*) After Hours

Concord CCD 4755 *Hamilton; Tommy Flanagan (p); Bob Cranshaw (b); Lewis Nash (d).* 96.

So effortless and smooth that it could almost pass by unnoticed. To our eternal shame, we have regularly taken the title all too literally and used this one to chill out after a session at the screen. This is very close to late-nite-and-lite, exquisitely done as you would expect, given the personnel, but curiously lacking in bite and chew. 'Woody'N'You' is a great group performance, a real meeting of minds. Nothing that follows comes close to its elegant pace. Flanagan is in magisterial form, leading a rhythm section that is recorded with gentle authority, a Concord strength.

*** Late Night Christmas Eve

Concord CCD 4922 *Hamilton; Alan Broadbent (p); Dave Cliff (g); Dave Green (b); Allan Ganley (d); London String Ensemble; etc.* 4/97.

It's almost axiomatic that we'll pretend to hate Christmas albums. How many do you know that are really worth hearing?

Ella's, maybe, and this one. Hamilton is ironic enough to cut through the schmaltz, and Broadbent is an intelligent enough arranger to give these familiar tunes an extra level of interest. It would be redundant to list them all, since you know them anyway.

*****(*) Concord Jazz Heritage**
Concord CCD 4819-2 *As above.* 77–98.

A useful and attractive selection of the saxophonist's work for his home label. Anyone who's been on board from the start will find it a rather predictable trawl, but for anyone who's new to Hamilton it's going to be a delightful surprise.

***** Blues, Bop & Ballads**
Concord CCD 4866 *Hamilton; Greg Gisbert (t); Joel Helleny (tb); Norman Simmons (p); Duke Robillard (g); Dennis Irwin (b); Chuck Riggs (d).* 2/99.

As the title hints, this is an eclectic survey, too various to work entirely successfully as an album. As ever, Scott picks some fascinating material. He programmes Ike Quebec's 'Blue Harlem' alongside Eldridge's 'Fish Market', Hawk's 'Stuffy' and Dameron's 'Good Bait', but we really like 'Smile', the Charlie Chaplin song which has rarely sounded more joyous and more philosophically supple. The band isn't quite the unit you'd expect to hear round Scott. Gisbert is a leader himself and some of the others are all too obviously journeymen, leaving the album sound like a cobbled-together club or festival set. Not a classic and some way short of exceptional, but as ever a solidly executed jazz record.

***** Jazz Signatures**
Concord CCD 4939 *Hamilton; John Bunch (p); Dave Green (b); Steve Brown (d).* 5/00.

Another solid set from Hamilton, though no one but a solid fan could distinguish it from most of the others. The attempt on Denzil Best's 'Move' is interesting, given Hamilton's track record on bebop, but it's one track among ten. More in his natural vein are Don Byas's 'Byas A Drink' and Illinois Jacquet's 'You Left Me All Alone'. There's a lovely version of Dave Brubeck's 'In Your Own Sweet Way', but the highlight for us is a long 'Jitterbug Waltz'. It wouldn't stand in the front rank of Hamilton recordings, but it's mighty fine all the same.

*****(*) Live In London**
Concord CCD 2172 *Hamilton; John Pearce (p); Dave Green (b); Steve Brown (d).* 6/02.

England has become a second home to Hamilton and he has nothing but praise for British players. Here he is at the Pizza Express, playing a typically venturesome set of swing and jazz pieces, ranging from the familiar ('When I Fall In Love', 'When You Wish Upon A Star') to the more challenging (Dameron's 'The Squirrel', Al Cohn's 'The Goof and I'). Hamilton always likes to flatter a crowd with things they *won't* immediately recognize, though the musicians at the bar might and their nods somehow communicate a sense of occasion back to the dinner tables. It's a clever strategy and it's paid dividends. The backing group are all a saxophonist could want, attentive, assured and completely across the material. Green in particular sounds stately and wicked by turns.

***** Ballad Essentials**
Concord CCD 4885 *As for Concord dates above.*

But only essential if you haven't the original albums. Some of them may be disappearing in the next clear-out of the Concord stables, which might make this more desirable. As it stands, though, a fairly unremarkable selection of slower tunes, pitched at the easy listening end of the jazz market.

Tardo Hammer

PIANO

Something of a late developer in leadership terms, Hammer only began recording in the late '90s, having worked for two decades as a sideman and accompanist, including gigs with Junior Cook, Abbey Lincoln and with Art Farmer. His mature style betrays less than one might expect of his Tristano school training.

****(*) Hammer Time**
Sharp Nine 1014 *Hammer; Dennis Irwin (b); Leroy Williams (d).* 5/00.

***** Somethin' Special**
Sharp Nine 1020 *As above.* 01.

A long time in coming, Hammer's debut CD isn't so much disappointing as predictably professional and thus unlikely to light up the sky. Combining original material, all of which is solidly competent, with tunes by Monk, Duke Jordan and Bud Powell, he gives a good impression of his chops at a range of tempos. The standards – 'Moment To Moment', 'I Concentrate On You', 'You Leave Me Breathless' – are expressive enough but one looks for a little more drama than this.

The follow-up is rather better and the trio seems ready to tackle the same kind of material with more gusto and adventure. Hammer opens with a fierce display of technique on Powell's 'John's Abbey' and then loses the plot with his own 'Divertimento', which should have gone way down the programme. There are expressive interpretations of Rollins's 'Blues For Philly Joe' and the title-track is a Sonny Clark composition. Again the standards are the most expressive elements: 'Take Me Out To The Ballgame', 'You're My Thrill' and 'If I Loved You'.

Some claim to hear elements of Bill Evans's pianism in Hammer's recent work. Beyond a couple of technical flourishes which seem to come from that direction, we aren't picking up on it. Attractive modern piano jazz, but in an oversubscribed field where others are making the running.

Gunter Hampel (born 1937)

COMPOSER, VIBRAPHONE, PIANO, REEDS

Born in Göttingen, he studied music and architecture before firing up much of the German free scene of the early '60s. Formed his own Birth label in 1970, which has documented a broad span of work since; vibes and reeds vie for first place in his own playing.

****(*) The 8th July 1969**
Birth 001 *Hampel; Anthony Braxton (as, ss, sno, f, cbcl); Willem Breuker (ss, as, ts, b cl); Arjen Gorter (b); Steve McCall (d); Jeanne Lee (v).* 7/69.

Virtually all of Hampel's work since 1969 has appeared on the fissiparous Birth label (and virtually the whole Birth catalogue consists of Hampel's work, in small groups and in various versions of his improvisation collective, the Galaxie Dream Band; the only two exceptions are duos nominally led by singer Jeanne Lee, who is Mrs Hampel, and by the alto saxophonist, Marion Brown). Birth has transferred some of a substantial back-catalogue to CD, though collectors will still have to rely on vinyl bins and auctions. Completists can probably still find factory-condition LPs at specialist shops.

There are obvious and misleading parallels between Hampel's work and that of the similarly cosmically obsessed Sun Ra, but Hampel is typically saturnine rather than Saturnian and he lacks the ripping, swinging joy of Ra's various Intergalactic Arkestras. There is another obvious connection, another American one, which has the beauty of having a basis in this discography. However deeply absorbed he has appeared to be in Afro-American music, multi-instrumentalist composer Anthony Braxton learned a great deal from the European collective/free movement of the late '60s, and particularly from Hampel, who has written pieces with numbered and coded titles reminiscent of Braxton's own later practice.

8th July 1969 was the first Birth disc to become available on CD. It isn't quite as time-warped as some of his work of the time, but nor is it quite as individual. Lee's voice is one of the most significant in contemporary improvisation; only Linda Sharrock, Diamanda Galas and Joan La Barbara match her for sheer strength and adaptability. Willem Breuker is already an imaginative and powerful soloist. Braxton, who in 1969 had just completed the epochal solo *For Alto* (which then had to wait three years for commercial release), still sounds as if he's fishing for a music commensurate with his remarkable talent. It's not at all clear that he found it with Hampel.

*****(*) All The Things You Could Be If Charles Mingus Was Your Daddy**

Birth 031 *Hampel; Perry Robinson (cl); Thomas Keyserling, Mark Whitecage (as, f); Martin Bues (d, perc); Jeanne Lee (v).* 11/78, 7/80.

The reference, of course, is to Mingus's own elaborate contrafact on 'All The Things You Are'. Scored for just percussion and woodwinds (with Lee very much part of the horn section), it's a sprawling and contrary piece with moments when the ensemble perversely stretches taut as a hawser. Recording quality isn't the very best and some of the instruments are recessed or distorted. Robinson's clarinet is the main sufferer and there are a couple of moments on one of his main statements when there might also be tape problems.

This isn't music for hi-fi fiends. Its sheer energy and self-possession are what create the magic, and anyone who has yet to hear Hampel will find this an appealing place to start. The additional tracks, recorded two years earlier, were originally to be found on the Birth LP *All Is Real*.

***** Jubilation**

Birth 0038 *Hampel; Manfred Schoof (t); Albert Mangelsdorff (tb); Perry Robinson (cl); Marion Brown (as); Thomas Keyserling (as, f, af); Barre Phillips (b); Steve McCall (d); Jeanne Lee (v).* 11/83.

***** Fresh Heat – Live At Sweet Basil**

Birth CD 0039 *Hampel; Stephen Haynes, Vance R Provey (t); Curtis Fowlkes (tb); Bob Stewart (tba); Perry Robinson (cl); Thomas Keyserling, Mark Whitecage (as, f); Bob Hanlon (ts, f); Lucky Ennett (ts); Bill Frisell (g); Kyoto Fujiwara (b); Marvin 'Smitty' Smith (d); Arthur Jenkins, Jeanne Lee (v).* 2/85.

*****(*) Dialog – Live At The Eldena Jazz Festival, 1992**

Birth CD 041 *Hampel; Mathias Schubert (ts).* 7/92.

*****(*) Time Is Now – Live At The Eldena Jazz Festival, 1992**

Birth CD 042 *Hampel; Mike Dietz (g); Jurgen Attig (b); Heinrich Kobberling (d).* 7/92.

***** Celestial Glory – Live At The Knitting Factory**

Birth CD 040 *Hampel; Perry Robinson (cl); Mark Whitecage (as, ss); Thomas Keyserling (as, f); Jeanne Lee (v).* 9/91.

Promising signs that Hampel, now in his mid-50s, is branching out in new directions and at the same time attracting a wider following. *Jubilation* is an excellent album – 'Little Bird' is particularly strong – which lacks some of the instinctive empathy of the Galaxie Dream Band but also some of its increasingly hermetic inwardness. The live New York City set smacks of no one more forcibly than Charles Mingus, who was at the very least a conscious presence in Hampel's thinking as far back as 1980 and the double reference of *All The Things You Could Be* ... (Birth 0031). Mingus's legacy is still largely unexplored and Hampel, now that he has abandoned the more indulgent aspects of free music, may be the man to do it.

The Knitting Factory would seem on the face of it to be a potential home away from home for Hampel, the kind of place where his approach to improvisation meets with a ready acceptance and understanding. Unfortunately, the three pieces included on *Celestial Glory* are a bit drab and slabby. Robinson is always interesting, and his solo passages and duets with the leader provide much of the interest. Lee is recorded very close, which introduces some ugly pops and squawks, and there is an overall lack of good production which CD cruelly exposes.

The duos with Schubert at Eldena are very good indeed and 'After The Fact' is one of the best-documented performances by any of the Hampel 'family'. The other record, taped a day earlier at the same festival, has a less familiar line-up but is marked by 'Serenade For Marion Brown', a heartfelt tribute to a loyal ally who seems to have been ill with dental problems at the time. One wouldn't wish the same thing on Hampel but, at this stage in the game, it may be time for him to lay down the bass clarinet and concentrate his attention exclusively on vibes.

Collectors may be interested to note that there are also videos of some of Hampel's activities, also available from Birth, and that he has also published four books of music and interviews which offer important insights into one of Europe's most independent improvisers.

***** Next Generation**

Birth 0043 *Hampel; Christian Weidner (as, ts); Mike Dietz (g); Christoph Busse (p); Fritz Feger (b); Michael Verhovec (d); Barbara Studemann, Shaun Vargas, Rumi, Spax, One Soul (v).* 9/95.

Subtitled 'Concepts in Jazz-Rap-Hip-Hop', which rather makes the flesh crawl in anticipation, this turns out to be no more self-consciously fashionable than anything else this determined individualist has ever done. The rappers do a creditable job with some pretty cumbersome words, though things like 'Paradise Of The Haves And Hell Of The Have Nots' are so completely *sui generis* that no one is likely to compare them with similar syntheses Stateside. Hampel is unmistakably a European and, though he remains devoted to what he sees as the anarchic dimension in jazz, he is also a passionate believer in order.

As before, Weidner is the key instrumentalist, but the new rhythm section functions with ferocious intensity and drummer Verhovec deserves special mention for combining freedom and control. Hampel is still hard to pin down as an instrumentalist. His vibes work is incomparable – which is not to say that he is greater than Bags or Hamp or Hutcherson, simply that he can't be compared to anyone, living or dead. His bass clarinet playing has become more conventional over the years, perhaps as his technique has grown sounder, but it is still broodingly effective.

*** Solid Fun

Birth 044 *Hampel; Christian Weidner (as, ts).* 9/95, 1/96.

All but one of these eight tracks were recorded live at Auerbach Jazznight. 'Solid Fun' itself bears relation to pieces like 'Iron Fist In A Velvet Glove' and 'You Ever Saw Birds Gather And Lift Off?' but is freshly conceived and executed. Once again, Weidner is responsive and intelligent, but Hampel himself rarely rises to his usual level of imagination and some of his solo playing is pedestrian in the extreme.

***(*) Legendary

Birth 045 *Hampel; Manfred Schoof (t, flhn); Alexander von Schlippenbach (p); Arjen Gorter (b); Pierre Courbois (d).* 5/97.

A reunion for Hampel's late-'60s band, the same line-up which recorded *Heartplants.* It is now – seemingly – available as a Japanese CD issue. For the rest of us, this latter-day encounter will have to do. 'Legendary' is a flute solo by Hampel, as lateral and sardonic as ever, but with his usual romantic burnish. There is also a reprise of 'Spielplatz', a group composition with a rough-hewn architecture that is entirely Hampel's own. The album is bulked out with a new reading of 'All The Things You Could Be If Charles Mingus Was Your Daddy', a perverse, jolly idea that cements Hampel's open-form approach.

Schlippenbach's contribution is considerable. He is courtly and thoughtful but swings outrageously even when the metre is almost uncountable. Schoof is the Darth Vader of contemporary trumpet-playing, a sweet and accommodating talent who has turned to the dark side. His tone is expansive, but with an astringent, tobacco-y quality. Hampel's multi-instrumentalism is no longer a surprise, but his adaptability and ability to shift between idioms is consistently impressive.

*** Köln Concert: Part 1

Birth CD 047 *Hampel; Christian Weidner (as, ts); Smudo, Christian Vargas, Nuclear B, Sprite, Nore (v); other instrumentation not specified.* 5/97.

**(*) Köln Concert: Part 2

Birth CD 048 *As above.* 5/97.

Recorded just a day after *Legendary* and at the same festival. It was a good wheeze, naming these records after one of the best-selling jazz records of all time. Unfortunately, instead of Keith Jarrett's tortured intensity and virtuosic handling of technical problems and instead of the thoughtful penetration of the *Legendary* quintet, the Next Generation band indulge themselves mercilessly. It's no accident that the most impressive music here is instrumental, the beautiful 'Jazz Life' on Volume One, and the equally touching 'Sun Down' on the sequel. Jeanne Lee's role seems restricted these days to writing. She has a hand in 'You Ever Saw Birds Gather And Lift Off?' which opens the set, but one misses that rising, potent voice and the sense of danger she always brings. There is nothing on either of these discs that doesn't sound processed, pre-formed and entirely formulaic. Hampel fans will treasure them for the jazz playing but will be put off by some nonsensical trend-chasing. What a contrast to *Next Generation.*

Lionel Hampton (born 1908)

VIBES, PIANO, DRUMS, VOCAL

Born in Louisville, Kentucky, Hampton went to Chicago as a boy and learned drums in a boys' band. He went on to work with various bands – including Les Hite's, backing Louis Armstrong – before switching to vibes and leading his own group in Los Angeles, where Benny Goodman heard him and invited him to join his band. RCA Victor let him lead pick-up dates in New York, 1936–40, and he ran his own big band from 1941, dominated by his own showmanship on vibes, piano and drums alike. That show-stopping style anticipated R&B and let the band survive even the lean rock'n'roll years, although he also recorded in many small-group situations. In the '80s and '90s he was also a major figure in education and publishing, and he assisted in housing programmes. At the end of the century, though suffering some poor health, Hamp continued to be one of jazz's grandest elder statesmen.

CORE COLLECTION

***(*) Lionel Hampton 1937–1938

Classics 524 *Hampton; Ziggy Elman, Cootie Williams, Jonah Jones (t); Lawrence Brown (tb); Vido Musso (cl, ts); Mezz Mezzrow, Eddie Barefield (cl); Johnny Hodges, Hymie Schertzer, George Koenig (as); Arthur Rollini (ts); Edgar Sampson (bs); Jess Stacy, Clyde Hart (p); Bobby Bennett, Allan Reuss (g); Harry Goodman, John Kirby, Mack Walker, Johnny Miller, Billy Taylor (b); Gene Krupa, Cozy Cole, Sonny Greer (d).* 2/37–1/38.

Lionel Hampton's Victor sessions of the '30s offer a glimpse of many of the finest big-band players of the day away from their usual chores: Hampton creamed off the pick of whichever band was in town at the time of the session and, although most of the tracks were hastily organized, the music is consistently entertaining. If one has a reservation, it's to do with Hampton himself: if you don't enjoy what he does, these discs won't live up to their reputation, since Hampton takes every lead offered. He'd already worked with Louis Armstrong in Les Hite's band as far back as the late '20s, and he came to New York in 1936, following an offer from Benny Goodman. The Victor dates began at the same time, and Hampton cut a total of 23 sessions between 1936 and 1941. The personnel varies substantially from date to date: some are like small-band sessions drawn from the Ellington or Goodman or Basie orchestras, others – such as the extraordinary 1939 date with Gillespie, Carter, Berry, Webster and Hawkins – are genuine all-star jams. Carter wrote the charts for one session, but mostly Hampton used head arrangements or sketchy frameworks. The bonding agent is his own enthusiasm: whether playing vibes – and incidentally establishing the dominant style on the instrument with his abrasive accents, percussive intensity and quickfire alternation of long and short lines – or piano or drums, or taking an amusing, Armstrong-influenced vocal, Hamp makes everything swing.

*****(*) Lionel Hampton 1938–1939**

Classics 534 *Hampton; Cootie Williams, Harry James, Walter Fuller, Irving Randolph, Ziggy Elman (t); Rex Stewart (c); Lawrence Brown (tb); Benny Carter, Omer Simeon (cl, as); Russell Procope (ss, as); Hymie Schertzer (as, bcl); Johnny Hodges, Dave Matthews, George Oldham (as); Herschel Evans, Babe Russin, Jerry Jerome, Chu Berry (ts); Edgar Sampson, Harry Carney (bs); Jess Stacy, Billy Kyle, Spencer Odun, Clyde Hart (p); Allan Reuss, Danny Barker (g); Billy Taylor, John Kirby, Jesse Simpkins, Milt Hinton (b); Sonny Greer, Jo Jones, Alvin Burroughs, Cozy Cole (d).* 1/38–6/39.

*****(*) Lionel Hampton 1939–1940**

Classics 562 *Hampton; Dizzy Gillespie, Henry 'Red' Allen, Ziggy Elman (t); Benny Carter (t, as); Rex Stewart (c); Lawrence Brown (tb); Edmond Hall (cl); Toots Mondello (cl, as); Earl Bostic, Buff Estes (as); Coleman Hawkins, Ben Webster, Chu Berry, Jerry Jerome, Budd Johnson (ts); Harry Carney (bs); Clyde Hart, Nat Cole, Joe Sullivan, Spencer Odun (p); Allan Reuss, Charlie Christian, Al Casey, Ernest Ashley, Oscar Moore (g); Billy Taylor, Milt Hinton, Artie Bernstein, Wesley Prince (b); Sonny Greer, Cozy Cole, Big Sid Catlett, Slick Jones, Zutty Singleton, Nick Fatool, Al Spieldock (d).* 6/39–5/40.

***** Lionel Hampton 1940–1941**

Classics 624 *Hampton; Karl George, Ernie Royal, Joe Newman (t); Fred Beckett, Sonny Craven, Harry Sloan (tb); Marshal Royal (cl, as); Ray Perry (as, vn); Dexter Gordon, Illinois Jacquet (ts); Jack McVea (bs); Nat Cole, Sir Charles Thompson, Marlowe Morris, Milt Buckner (p); Oscar Moore, Teddy Bunn, Irving Ashby (g); Douglas Daniels (v); Wesley Prince, Hayes Alvis, Vernon Alley (b); Al Spieldock, Kaiser Marshall, Shadow Wilson, George Jenkins (d); Rubel Blakey, Evelyn Myers (v).* 7/40–12/41.

Although we picked out the first volume for the Core Collection, it's in some ways a token choice. In the end, surprisingly few tracks stand out from these sessions: what one remembers are individual solos and the general climate of hot, hip good humour which prevails. One might mention Benny Carter on 'I'm In The Mood For Swing', Chu Berry on 'Shufflin' At The Hollywood', Dizzy Gillespie on 'Hot Mallets', J. C. Higginbotham on 'I'm On My Way From You' or Buster Bailey on 'Rhythm, Rhythm'; but there are few disappointments amid an air of democratic enterprise, despite the leader's showboating. Hamp's drum and piano features are less than enthralling after one has heard them once, but they don't occupy too much space.

The availability of this important music is still less than ideal. While the Classics CDs take a full chronological look up to December 1941 and the start of Hamp's own big band, the sound is inconsistent: some tracks field too much surface noise, others seem unnecessarily dull. Bluebird's series seems to have disappeared altogether: it is surely time for a comprehensive box of this music from that source. Classics 624 includes the final 13 tracks for Victor and, while these are a shade less interesting than the earlier dates, it's useful to have them in sequence. The European label, Memoria, has also issued four discs covering the same material.

***** Lionel Hampton 1942–1944**

Classics 803 *Hampton; Snooky Young, Wendell Culley, Joe Morris, Dave Page, Lamar Wright, Ernie Royal, Karl George, Joe Newman, Roy McCoy, Cat Anderson (t); Booty Wood, Vernon Porter, Andrew Penn, Fred Beckett, Sonny Craven, Allen Durham, Al Hayes, Harry Sloan (tb); Herbie Fields (cl, as); Gus Evans, George Dorsey, Ray Perry, Marshal Royal, Earl Bostic (as); Arnett Cobb, Fred Simon, Jay Peters, Dexter Gordon, Illinois Jacquet, Al Sears (ts); Charlie Fowlkes (bs); Milt Buckner (p); Billy Mackel, Irving Ashby, Eric Miller (g); Charles Harris, Ted Sinclair, Vernon King, Vernon Alley, Wendell Marshall (b); George Jenkins, Fred Radcliffe, Lee Young (d); Rubel Blakey (v).* 3/42–10/44.

***** Lionel Hampton 1945–46**

Classics 922 *As above, except add Joe Morris, Al Killian (t), Abdul Hamid, John Morris, Al Hayes (tb), Bobby Plater, Ben Kynard (as), Johnny Griffin (ts), Dardanelle Breckenridge, John Mehegan (p), Dinah Washington, Bing Crosby (v); omit Anderson, Newman, Dorsey, Royal, Bostic, Gordon, Jacquet, Miller, King, Alley, Marshall, Radcliffe, Young, Blakey.* 1/45–1/46.

****(*) Lionel Hampton 1946**

Classics 946 *Mostly as above, except add Jimmy Wormick (tb), Jack Kelso (cl), Joe Comfort (b), Curley Hamner (d).* 1–9/46.

***** Lionel Hampton 1947**

Classics 994 *Hampton; Wendell Culley, Duke Garrette, Jimmy Nottingham, Kenny Dorham, Leo Shepherd, Snooky Young, Teddy Buckner, Walter Williams, Benny Bailey (t); Britt Woodman, James Wormick, Sonny Craven, Andrew Penn, James Robinson (tb); Jackie Kelson (cl, as); Bobby Plater, Ben Kynard (as); Morris Lane, Johnny Sparrow (ts); Charlie Fowlkes (bs); Milt Buckner, Michael 'Dodo' Marmarosa (p); Billy Mackel (g); Charles Harris, Joe Comfort, Charles Mingus (b); Curley Hamner, Earl Walker (d); The Hamptonians, Wini Brown, Roland Burton (v).* 4–11/47.

*****(*) Swingsation**

GRP 059922-2 *As appropriate discs above.* 42–47.

Hampton's big bands of the '40s were relentlessly entertaining outfits, their live shows a feast of raving showstoppers which Hampton somehow found the energy to replenish time and again. He tended to rely on a repertoire – including 'Flying Home', 'Hamp's Boogie Woogie' and a few others – which he has stuck by to this day, but his ability to ignite both a band and an audience prevailed over any doubts concerning staleness. The studio sessions are inevitably a lot tamer than what happened on stage, but there's still some good, gritty playing, which opened the book on a blend of swing and R&B which other bandleaders followed with some interest. Classics 803 gets a bit stuck on some dull material – there are four different takes on 'Flying Home' in all, including a two-part V-Disc version – but there are also some strong charts by Clyde Hart and Milt Buckner. Classics 922 is another mixed bag, but there is a lovely Dinah Washington vocal on 'Blow Top Blues', two bits of fun with Bing Crosby, a couple of bacchanalian V-Disc sides and a thumping 'Rockin' In Rhythm'. The 1946 disc has fewer pickings and is really only for Hampton nuts, although Arnett Cobb gets off a couple of superheated solos. The 1947 set picks up a bit with the arrival of Dorham and Mingus, and some good set-pieces such as 'Three Minutes On 52nd Street', 'Red Top' and 'Mingus Fingers', ending on a vigorous sextet date. The *Swingsation* compilation usefully brings together the big hits of this era of Hamp and will do fine for anyone wanting to sample this period.

****(*) Lionel Hampton 1949–1950**

Classics 1161 *Hampton; Benny Bailey, Duke Garrette, Wendell Culley, Leo Shepherd, Walter Williams, Ed Mullen (t); Lester Bass, Al Grey, Benny Powell, Jimmy Wormick, Alfred 'Chippie' Outcalt, Paul Higakilee (tb); Johnny Board, Bobby Plater, Jerome Richardson (as); Gene Morris, Bobby Sparrow, Billy Williams, Curtis Lowe, Billy 'Smallwood' Williams (ts); Ben Kynard, Lonnie Shaw (bs); Albert Ammons (p); Doug Duke (p, org); Wes Montgomery (g); Roy Johnson (b); Earl Walker, Ellis Bartee (d); Sonny Parker, Rick Brown, Betty Carter, Jimmy Scott, The Hamptones, Irma Curry (v).* 1/49–1/50.

****(*) Lionel Hampton 1950**

Classics 1193 *Similar to above, except add Jimmy Cleveland (tb), Milt Buckner, Gus Domerette (p), Buddy Cole (org), Billy Mackel (g), Freddy Hamilton (v).* 1–9/50.

Never a man to deny popular tastes, Hamp's big band in these sessions sounds more like an R&B outfit, and with the ludicrous but effective 'Turkey Hop' (Classics 1193) he all but invents big-band rock'n'roll. The casualty is the jazz material, and even Hampton's own solos feel constrained by what he's left to work with. Classics 1161 is notable for the debuts of both Betty Carter (she gets a few sublime bars of scat to herself at the very end of 'The Hucklebuck') and Jimmy Scott. The second disc ends with two sextet dates, but coddled by Buddy Cole's organ these are more like easy-listening tracks. Remastering is fine on the big-band material, but there's a lot of hiss on the Scott feature, 'Please Give Me A Chance', and the sextet tracks sound foggy.

*****(*) Hamp: The Legendary Decca Recordings**

Decca GRD 2-652 2CD *As above discs, plus various other groupings, including Charlie Teagarden, Charlie Shavers (t), Willie Smith (as), Corky Corcoran (ts), Jerome Richardson (f), Buddy Cole (org), Barney Kessel (g), Slam Stewart (b), Betty Carter (v).* 5/42–3/63.

One could take issue with the 'legendary' description, but this is a very fair sifting-through of Hampton's years with Decca, starting with the May 1942 'Flying Home' and closing on two amusing small-group tracks from a Las Vegas club show of 1963 with, of all people, Charlie Teagarden. The main bonus of this set is the inclusion of Hamp's quite classic treatment of 'Star Dust' from a 1947 Gene Norman Just Jazz show: combative and lyrical in equal measure, this is a rare chance to hear Hamp at length in his prime and away from his big band. The second disc includes the swagger of 'Three Minutes On 52nd Street', Charles Mingus's dramatic composing debut with 'Mingus Fingers' and the lustrous treatment of 'Midnight Sun', as well as Betty Carter's improbably sexy vocal on 'The Hucklebuck' and another fine Hamp set-piece on 'Moonglow' – as well as a few less-than-immortal selections. After the respectable but uninvolving sound on the Classics discs, these tracks come over with tremendous punch, which is just as it should be.

***** The Complete Lionel Hampton Quartets And Quintets With Oscar Peterson On Verve**

Verve 559797-2 5CD *Hampton; Buddy DeFranco (cl); Oscar Peterson (p); Herb Ellis (g); Ray Brown (b); Buddy Rich (d).* 53–54.

*****(*) The Lionel Hampton Quintet**

Verve 589100-2 *As above.* 4/54.

***** Just One Of Those Things**

Verve 547437-2 *As above.* 54.

*****(*) Jazz Masters 26: Lionel Hampton With Oscar Peterson**

Verve 521853-2 *Hampton; Roy Eldridge, Dizzy Gillespie (t); Bill Harris (tb); Buddy DeFranco (cl); Flip Phillips, Ben Webster (ts); Oscar Peterson (p); Herb Ellis (g); Ray Brown (b); Buddy Rich (d).* 53–54.

Hampton's early sessions for Norman Granz were originally spread over some 15 LPs, so this comprehensive five-disc set from Verve clears up what was for many years something of a discographical muddle. Hampton and Peterson clearly enjoyed each other's company, and the generous solos, jocular interplay and general bonhomie which prevails is certainly uplifting from track to track. That said, we offer only a low rating since the music quickly starts to seem all the same, with very little variation in manner. There are great things to enjoy, such as a second classic treatment of 'Star Dust', but one wishes these discs had been made available separately in a more economical way. DeFranco arrives for one session and offers some useful contrast, but as a block of music this is one of those sets to dip into very sparingly. The ugly packaging is another minus.

The Jazz Masters package has been around for a while and is still a good place to hear Hampton with Verve. *Just One Of Those Things* fillets sundry 1954 tracks from the complete set. Best of the slimmer selections is the new *Quintet*, which brings together two full albums from these dates in a handsome Master Edition (with the original David Stone Martin artwork).

***** Mai 1956**

Emarcy 013880-2 *Hampton; Ed Mullens (t); Eddie Chamblee (ts); Robert Mosely, Jean-Claude Pelletier (p); Bill Mackel (g); Benoît Quersin, Paul Rovère (b); Albert 'June' Gardner (d).* 5/56.

A stopover on a mammoth European tour, this Paris date is good-natured if not terribly involving. Hampton completely dominates proceedings, with Mullens and Chamblee offered very little space, and if there are no flag-wavers here there's still some agreeable soloing on the likes of 'Jammin' On High Society'.

***** Olympia 1961/1966**

Laserlight 36181 2CD *Hampton; Dave Gonzales, Floyd Jones, Andrew Wood, Virgil Jones, Wallace Davenport (t); Vincente Prudente, Harlem Rasheed (tb); Bobby Plater (as, cl, f); John Neely (as, cl); Edward Pazant (as, ts, cl, f); Andrew McGhee (ts, cl); Edlin Terry (ts); Lonnie Shaw (bs, f); Harold Mabern, Zeke Mullins (p); Roland Faulkner, Billy Mackel (g); Lawrence Burgan (b); Wayne Robinson, Al Levitt (d); Bertice Reading, Pinocchio James (v).* 3/61–10/66.

***** Salle Pleyel 1971**

Laserlight 36133 2CD *Hampton; Roland Connors (t); Bob Snyder (cl); Tommy Gambino (ss, as); Illinois Jacquet, Chuck McClendon (ts); Milt Buckner, John Spruill (org, p); Billy Mackel (g); Eustis Guillemet (b); Kenny Bolds (d).* 3/71.

Previously released in RTE's series of French concert broadcasts, these are welcome retrievals from a Hampton period which is scarcely documented on CD at present. Both the 1961 and 1966 Olympia concerts are in excellent sound, and although there's the usual crowd-pleasing – via some of the hits, an over-excited Bertice Reading and Pinocchio James, a singer in the Joe Wiliams mould – there is some outstanding Hamp on 'Tenderly' (which he dedicates to Mezz Mezzrow), a boppish 'Glad Hamp', both versions of 'Midnight Sun' (especially the first) and a 'Stardust' which even allows a spot for Billy Mackel.

The 1971 concert gives plenty of space to Jacquet and Buckner, neither a shrinking violet, and something like the Sam Price blues 'Big Joe' works up an almost monumental head of steam. Hamp browses through a few standards that take his fancy – 'Summertime', 'Avalon', 'Who Can I Turn To' – and Jacquet gets beefy on 'Ghost Of A Chance'. Working with a smaller group, the set has more of an R&B-band feel, and although the second disc eventually runs aground on the flagging Hampton favourites, there's lots to listen to.

****(*) You Better Know It!!!**

Impulse GRP 11042 *Hampton; Clark Terry (t); Ben Webster (ts); Hank Jones (p); Milt Hinton (b); Osie Johnson (d).* 10/64.

This turned out to be a disappointment. Bob Thiele seems to have had everyone on their best behaviour and very little happens on a broad range of material from different stages of Hamp's career. Terry and Webster play a few juicy bars here and there, yet everything is strangely subdued.

***** Ring Dem Vibes**

Emarcy 159825-2 *Hampton; Claude Gousset (tb); Michel Attenoux (as); Gérard Badini (ts); Raymond Fol, Reynold Mullins (p); Danny Doriz (vib); Billy Mackel (g); Michel Gaudry (b); Sam Woodyard (d).* 5/76.

Cut during a low point in Hampton's recording regimen, he still sounds irrepressible, and if this is basically a routine mainstream jam with another gang of Parisian players (plus old faithful, Billy Mackel) he's enthusiastically up for it. Oddity: a long version of Horace Silver's 'Psychedelic Sally'.

**** Live At The Blue Note**

Telarc Jazz CD-83308 *Hampton; Clark Terry (t, flhn); Harry 'Sweets' Edison (t); Al Grey (tb); James Moody, Buddy Tate (ts); Hank Jones (p); Milt Hinton (b); Grady Tate (d).* 6/91.

**** Just Jazz**

Telarc Jazz CD-83313 *As above.* 6/91.

Hampton's final period of recording was, with the best will in the world, a mere echo of a major talent. Since he isn't the kind of artist to indulge in autumnal reflections, one has to use his earlier records as a yardstick, and these sessions inevitably fall short in energy and invention. No one can blame Hamp for taking things steady at this stage in what's virtually a 70-year career. The session recorded at New York's Blue Note is an expansive all-star session by musicians whose best work is, frankly, some way behind them: only the seemingly ageless Terry and the exuberant Grey defy the circumstances and muster a sense of commitment. Everyone else, including Hampton, falls back on simple ideas and tempos which give no cause for alarm. The second volume, *Just Jazz*, is more of the same.

Slide Hampton (born 1932)

TROMBONE

Locksley Hampton played with Lionel Hampton before joining Maynard Ferguson as an arranger in 1957. Freelanced in the '60s before a spell with Woody Herman and a long stint in Europe, though he returned to the USA in 1977. His arranging has often taken precedence over his playing, but he remains a quick and skilful trombonist.

***** Sister Salvation**

Collectables 6173 *Hampton; Freddie Hubbard, Ernie Royal, Richard Williams, Bob Zottola (t); Bernard McKinney (tb, euph); Billy Barber (tba); George Coleman (ts); Jay Cameron (bs); Nabil Totah (b); Pete LaRoca (d).* 2/60.

Slide often thought in quite large-scale musical terms, and he had a more distinctive personality as a member of ensembles than he does as a soloist. This is a crisply funky and often very intelligent octet session, packed with musical ideas, and nicely balanced between original material like his own title-tune, 'Asseveration' and 'A Little Night Music', and imaginative re-arrangements of pieces like Weston's 'Hi-Fli' and Ellington's rarely covered 'Just Squeeze Me (But Don't Tease Me)', which was written for and with Will Gaines.

***** Slide!**

Fresh Sound FSR-CD 206 *Hampton; Freddie Hubbard, Booker Little, Hobart Dotson, Willie Thomas, Burt Collins (t); Bernard McKinney (euph); George Coleman (ts, cl); Jay Cameron (bs, bcl); Eddie Kahn, George Tucker (b); Pete LaRoca, Lex Humphries, Charli Persip, Kenny Dennis (d).* 59–61.

The personnel, with Hubbard, Little and Coleman, looks mouth-watering, but the horns have an ensemble role; Hampton gives himself most of the solos, which is fair enough: they were his dates, now usefully combined on to a single CD. The earlier date has a fine 'Newport', among some smart originals; the second mixes five tunes from *Porgy And Bess* with a dance suite called 'The Cloister'. Hampton depends mainly on brass sound, the reeds used for low tone colours, and the absence of piano gives unusual weight to the front lines. An interesting survival.

***** Exodus**

Emarcy 013033-2 *Hampton; Nat Pavone, Richard Williams (t); George Coleman (ts); Butch Warren (b); Kenny Clarke (d).* 11/62.

Recently reissued as part of Emarcy's celebration of jazz in Paris, this is a thoughtful and well-balanced set that once again demonstrates Slide's skill as an arranger and bandleader. None of the tunes are originals, but the versions of 'I Remember Clifford', 'Straight, No Chaser' and Parker's 'Confirmation' are sufficiently unusual to merit a second and subsequent hearing. Slide himself restricts his own solo space to those tunes where the material lends itself to his particular voice. Hence he's not especially prominent on his own record. Coleman, though, is a very powerful voice and the group voicings lend the set a strong coherence. A valuable reissue.

***** Mellow-Dy**

Delta 17115 *Hampton; Nathan Davis (ts); Hampton Hawes, Martial Solal (p); Dave Pike (vib); Henri Texier (b); Daniel Humair (d).* 67, 68.

Slide comes somewhat to the fore as a soloist on this long-forgotten release, which has also appeared on LRC. Beginning with J. J. Johnson's 'Lament' is a deliberate nod to one of the masters of modern trombone, but Slide has a more old-fashioned approach to the instrument, and this comes through on original material like 'Impossible Waltz', 'Chop Suey' and the title-track. There is nothing terribly sophisticated about either writing or playing on this occasion, just a chance to blow against a nicely configured band. Excellent contributions from Davis, Pike and Hawes (whose 'Us Six' closes out the record). Slide was spending much of his time in France during this period. Texier and Humair join French genius Martial Solal for a couple of numbers, on which Slide blows hard but listens up to the pianist with obvious care.

**** Roots

Criss Cross 1015 *Hampton; Clifford Jordan (ts); Cedar Walton (p); David Williams (b); Billy Higgins (d).* 4/85.

A session in which everything worked out right. Hampton and Jordan are perfectly paired, the trombonist fleet yet punchy, Jordan putting a hint of dishevelment into otherwise finely tailored improvisations; and Walton has seldom played with so much vitality, yet without surrendering his customary aristocratic touch. Williams and Higgins are asked to play hard throughout the four long titles, and they oblige without flagging. Although a very fast 'Solar' is arguably the highlight, it's a fine record altogether.

***(*) Dedicated To Diz

Telarc 83323 *Hampton; Jon Faddis, Roy Hargrove, Claudio Roditi (t, flhn); Steve Turre (tb, shells); Douglas Purviance (btb); Antonio Hart (as, ss); Jimmy Heath (ts); David Sanchez (ts, ss, f); Danilo Perez (p); George Mraz (b); Lewis Nash (d).* 2/93.

Having Faddis in a Gillespie tribute guarantees a certain authenticity of sound. The idea of founding the Jazz Masters, as this group is known, was to record larger-scale arrangements of work associated with the greats. A great charts man as well as player, Hampton handles this one with entirely characteristic discretion and charm. Our only quibble is that it might have sounded better done in a studio than live at the Village Vanguard. There are moments when the sound is imperfect, and one or two of the ensembles could – and probably should – have been touched up. The high points are 'Lover Man' and (surprise, surprise) 'A Night In Tunisia'. Faddis is quite properly the star, but Hargrove, Roditi and Turre, Heath and Sanchez also have their moments in the sun on this thoroughly sun-warmed date.

*** Spirit Of The Horn

MCGJazz MCGJ1011 *Hampton; Jay Ashby, Bill Watrous, Michael Boschen, Steve Davis, Hugh Fraser, David Gibson, Andre Hayward, Tim Newman, Benny Powell, Douglas Purviance, Max Siegal, Issac Smith, David Taylor (tb); Martin Ashby (g); Larry Willis (p); John Lee (b); Victor Jones (d).* 5/02.

This is great fun, although a 14-strong band of trombonists does make one fear the worst. In the end, Slide deploys his huge team very deftly, making 'A Flower is A Lovesome Thing' sing (and reminding one how much Ellington liked his trombone section) and having them breeze through 'Dolphin Dance'. Watrous, who might be the greatest trombone technician jazz has ever seen, is sensibly used as a lead solo voice, and everybody gets their turn in 'Blues For Eric'. It can't quite escape the novelty-record tag, but you can't fault Slide for trying.

Herbie Hancock (born 1940)

PIANO, KEYBOARDS

One of the most significant composers in modern jazz, the creator of 'Watermelon Man' and 'Dolphin Dance' as well as the unforgettable 'Rockit'. Chicago-born Hancock was something of a child prodigy, playing Mozart as a youngster. He has embraced bebop, funk and elements of classical form and, though his work of recent years has lacked the sheer, unselfconscious brilliance of his early records, he is still a formidable technician.

***(*) Takin' Off

Blue Note 37643 *Hancock; Freddie Hubbard (t, flhn); Dexter Gordon (ts); Butch Warren (b); Billy Higgins (d).* 5/62.

Takin' Off was a remarkable debut. He had made his professional debut, following master's work at the Manhattan School of Music, just two years earlier with Coleman Hawkins, before signing up with trumpeter Donald Byrd and coming to the attention of Alfred Lion of Blue Note, who agreed to allow the 22-year-old to record with a horn-led group rather than as a trio. The result is astonishingly mature and poised. 'Watermelon Man' digs back into memories of Chicago's South Side, a gospelly roller which prompts a full-hearted solo from Hubbard; not the obvious choice for the gig, perhaps, with Byrd a more likely candidate, but he fits right in. As does Gordon, who was only getting back to serious work after his tribulations; he sounds earthy and intense, and much more focused than on the alternative take, which has been added to the CD. The collaboration was to firm up a friendship that would last till the end of Gordon's life; in the Tavernier movie *Round Midnight*, Hancock would accompany 'Dale Turner' in his pomp. 'Three Bags Full' is a curious piece, almost Eastern in harmony and apparently intended to underline the stylistic differences between the three soloists. This might almost be something by the '50s Miles Davis group, with Gordon emulating Coltrane. 'The Maze' is a puzzle-piece, and 'Driftin'' is a relaxed blowing tune featuring Hubbard's flugelhorn. Perhaps the most effective track of all is the ballad, 'Alone Am I', moody and philosophical, with a superb solo from Hancock. Can there ever have been a more auspicious debut?

*** My Point Of View

Blue Note 21226 *Hancock; Donald Byrd (t); Grachan Moncur III (tb); Grant Green (g); Chuck Israels (b); Tony Williams (d).* 3/63.

My Point Of View was the second of Hancock's records for Blue Note. It's never been the most celebrated, despite including the wonderful 'Blind Man, Blind Man', which is now represented in an extra take. Herbie's relationship with Tony Williams is often regarded as the key to this fine record, and revisiting it in this special Rudy Van Gelder edition merely reinforces that view. 'King Cobra' is a brilliant synthesis of Williams's rhythmic genius and Hancock's structural gifts. Herbie's passing interest in R&B surfaces on 'And What If I Don't', which most blindfold testees would be hard pressed to identify. Second albums are notoriously tricky, but Hancock made the best of his opportunity by casting his net wider still. It wasn't a format that he was to return to in later years, so *My Point Of View* remains one of a kind.

*** Inventions And Dimensions

Blue Note 84147 *Hancock; Paul Chambers (b); Willie Bobo (d); Chihuahua Martinez (perc).* 8/63.

The forgotten album. Hancock wanted to experiment and, short of going entirely free and outside, he pushed his personal concept as far as it would go. It seems that the leader gave his musicians nothing more than a time-signature and some general idea about the shape of the piece, and the session went from there. 'Succotash', named after the sound of Willie Bobo's brushes rather than the beans-and-corn mix, is in double waltz-time. 'Triangle' falls into three distinct sections, with the feel of the blues but no obvious blues content. 'For Jack Rabbit' and 'A Jump Ahead' were effectively co-written by Paul Chambers, who determined much of the content; on the former track he drives the improvisation along with a repeat figure, while the title of the latter derives from his four-note pedal at the start. Few Blue Note sessions of the time were created with such freedom, and *Inventions And Dimensions* does stand somewhat apart from the mainstream of Hancock's work. However, it remains to this day testimony to his restless, exploratory nature and it certainly shouldn't be overlooked.

♛ **** Maiden Voyage

Blue Note 95331 *Hancock; Freddie Hubbard (t); George Coleman (ts); Ron Carter (b); Tony Williams (d).* 64.

**** Empyrean Isles

Blue Note 98796 *As above, except omit Coleman.* 6/64.

***(*) Cantaloupe Island

Blue Note 29331 *As above, except add Donald Byrd (t), Grachan Moncur III (tb), George Coleman, Dexter Gordon (ts), Butch Warren (b), Billy Higgins (d).* 5/62, 3/63, 6/64, 3/65.

Maiden Voyage has been tussled over more than once. Revisionists will argue that it is glib and superficial, not at all the masterpiece it has been claimed to be. We disagree and have no hesitation in placing it in our premier league. Particularly when, considered as a pair with *Empyrean Isles*, it represents a colossal achievement from a man still just 24 years old. Both are quiet records, likened by Joachim Berendt to Debussy's *La Mer*. Coleman plays with delicate understatement and Hancock never puts a foot wrong. No great surprise that the chemistry was so good for, with the obvious exception of Hubbard, this was Miles's group.

Empyrean Isles is almost as good. 'Cantaloupe Island' is a glorious piece of quartet jazz, and 'Dolphin Dance' has seldom been out of the repertoire in the last 30 years. The absence of Coleman puts ever greater emphasis on piano and, though one misses his slightly breathy delivery, there's an amazing clarity to the other record from 1964.

Cantaloupe Island is a compilation of material from *Takin' Off*, *Empyrean Isles* and, from *My Point Of View*, a single track called 'Blind Man, Blind Man' which highlights Hancock's not yet fully developed skills as an arranger for larger ensembles.

**** The Complete Blue Note Sixties Sessions

Blue Note 4 95569 2 6CD *As above, except add Melvin Lastie (c), Johnny Coles, Thad Jones (flhn), Garnett Brown (tb), Jack Jeffers, Tony Studd (btb), Jackie McLean (as), Jerry Dodgion (as, f), Jerome Richardson (bcl, f), Romeo Penque (bcl), Hubert Laws (f), Stanley Turrentine (ts), Eric Gale, Billy Butler (g), Bob Cranshaw (b), Albert 'Tootie' Heath, Bernard Purdie, Mickey Roker (d).* 12/61–4/69.

Immaculately and expensively packaged, this is a set to die for and it is denied the coveted crown only on cost grounds. As well as the Blue Notes issued above, the set includes the whole of *Speak Like A Child* and Herbie's last album for the label, *The Prisoner*. Though little known now in comparison to the rest, this was much more than a contract filler. Herbie had been poached by Warner Bros, but he and Alfred Lion took the opportunity to create a unique sound for the last LP, augmenting the sextet with horns and allowing Herbie to experiment with a Fender Rhodes instrument during the ensembles. 'He Who Lives In Fear' and the title-piece are outstanding Hancock conceptions and the sound is awesome, yet the album has an air of hurry and unfinish as well, which is evident in some of the alternatives.

Blue Note have included some interesting filler material as well to round out the profile of Herbie's time with the label. There are early tracks recorded under the leadership of Donald Byrd and Jackie McLean, some material with Bobby Hutcherson from *Blow-Up* (see below), and 'The Collector' from Wayne Shorter's *Adam's Apple* date, issued only in Japan. At the very end of the set, a rarity: Herbie's one and only serious dabbling in R&B, in a band fronted by Melvin Lastie and Stanley Turrentine. That was a road not taken. This magnificent set compresses the real journey, its by-ways and stumbles; what a trip it was.

*** Blow-Up

Soundtracks 852280 *Hancock; other personnel not specified.* 66.

Hancock's brilliant soundtrack is a near-perfect correlative to the funky, ambiguous world of Michelangelo Antonioni's film. It could hardly be improved upon, and it's a wonder – though perhaps a blessing – that it didn't lead to more and yet more offers from directors. The album includes a song by The Yardbirds, who actually appeared in the film, and also the two songs commissioned from the band Tomorrow but not used. These are curiosities. It is unmistakably Hancock's album, and as transitional a work as Miles's moody score for *L'Ascenseur pour l'échafaud*.

*** Speak Like A Child

Blue Note 746136 *Hancock; Thad Jones (flhn); Peter Phillips (btb); Jerry Dodgion (af); Ron Carter (b); Mickey Roker (d).* 3/68.

An experiment in sound-texture, this was the first of Hancock's records to suggest that he might welcome a swing towards electronics. The sound is slithery and quite abstract, certainly not dance-orientated but full of intimations of what was to come in the '70s. Jones was an unexpected recruitment, but he plays with delicate beauty and some muscle throughout. An easy record to overlook; well worth hearing.

*** The Prisoner

Blue Note 25649 *Hancock; Johnny Coles (t, flhn); Garnett Brown (tb); Jack Jeffers, Tony Studd (btb); Romeo Penque (bcl); Jerome Richardson (bcl, f); Joe Henderson (ts); Buster Williams (b); Albert 'Tootie' Heath (d); Oren Waters (v).* 4/69.

Dedicated to the spirit of Martin Luther King Jr, this is one of Hancock's most ambitious projects. It's also significant in being his last record for Blue Note and his first since leaving the Miles Davis group. It's a notably thoughtful record, and the opening sequence of 'I Have A Dream', 'The Prisoner' and a version of Charles Williams's 'Firewater' (there are alternate take of the latter two on the reissue) is one of the most powerful in the whole range of Hancock's work. So why, then, is this album so little known, relative to the earlier Blue Notes and Columbias? The short answer is that it has been only sporadically available and, more pressingly, that it is a markedly inward and even solipsistic work, ironic given the subject. Henderson is magnificent, as is the underachieving Johnny Coles, and Hancock himself plays with a calm authority that was increasingly rare in his subsequent work.

***** Fat Albert Rotunda**

Warner 47540 *Hancock; Johnny Coles (t); Garnett Brown (tb); Joe Henderson (ts, af); Buster Williams (b); Albert 'Tootie' Heath (d).* 10 & 12/69.

Working with Miles Davis suggested the possibilities of an electric band. When he moved on, Hancock immediately experimented with his own version. The three albums for Warner Bros were *Fat Albert Rotunda*, *Mwandishi* (the Swahili name he had adopted for himself) and *Crossings*.

Written for Bill Cosby's *Fat Albert* cartoon, the music began to take on a life of its own and started Hancock's personal exploration of fusion. It also marks a first use on his own date of the Fender Rhodes which was to become something of a Hancock trademark over the next few years. With the criminally under-recorded Johnny Coles on trumpet and Joe Henderson on tenor and alto flute, the session has a surging, almost breathless power that takes it far beyond its origins.

***** Mwandishi**

Warner Brothers 1898 2CD *Hancock; Eddie Henderson (t); Julian Priester (tb); Bennie Maupin (sax, bcl, af); Jose Areas (g, perc); Ronnie Montrose (g); Buster Williams (b); Billy Hart (d); Leon Ndugu Chancler (d, perc).* 12/70.

Mwandishi is altogether more thoughtful and personal. On tunes like 'Wandering Spirit Song', Hancock experiments for the first time with sheer duration, and it's hard to believe that this album did not exert some sort of reciprocal influence on Miles Davis, notably the saturnine *Agharta* and *Pangaea*. Maupin's multi-instrumentalism has already become a key element, but the other Henderson's melancholic trumpet (like Miles without the strut and swagger) is the dramatic focus of a lot of the music. 'You'll Know When You Get There' is a long journey across the Kalahari, punctuated by harmonic mirages and sudden changes of pace.

The set was recorded in a single session over New Year's Eve 1970 and the long opening 'Ostinato (Suite For Angela)' has signs of being approached in the same way that Miles's sessions were taped, though with a greater sense of predetermined structure. Priester's 'Wandering Spirit Song' has the hazy, ethereal quality that came into jazz with *In A Silent Way* and is almost as beautiful.

***** Crossings**

Warner 475423 *As above, except add Patrick Gleeson (syn), Victor Pantoja (perc), Victoria Domagalski, Della Horne, Candy Love, Sandra Stevens (v).* 12/71.

The final episode of Hancock's Warner's period takes the electric group even further out into the avant garde. The electronic gadgetry is now almost the main focus of the sound, with everything pumped through echoplexes and wah-wah pedals, distorted and run through tape machines in any number of different ways. The long 'Sleeping Giant' is a wonderfully atmospheric piece – though, interestingly, Herbie cedes composition duties to Maupin for the remainder of the record, on 'Quasar' and 'Water Torture'. Where Hancock's own work differs markedly from Miles's superficially similar conception is in the level of structure and organization. 'Sleeping Giant' is almost symphonic in form, and has a wonderful sense of completion where Miles's pieces of the time felt as if they might rumble and clatter on indefinitely. Patrick Gleeson's Moog is an integral element of the sound here, spooky, tortured and sometimes giving off an eldritch beauty.

*****(*) Mwandishi: The Complete Warner Bros Recordings**

Warner 245732 2CD *Hancock; Johnny Coles, Eddie Henderson, Joe Newman, Ernie Royal (t); Garnett Brown, Bennie Powell, Julian Priester (tb); Ray Alonge (frhn); Bennie Maupin (ss, bcl, picc, af, perc); Joe Farrell (as, ts); Joe Henderson (ts, af); Arthur Clarke (bs); Patrick Gleeson (syn); Billy Butler, Eric Gale, Ron Montrose (g); Jerry Jermott, Buster Williams (b); Billy Hart, Albert 'Tootie' Heath, Bernard Purdie (d); Ndugu Leon Chancler (d, perc); Jose Areas, George Devens, Victor Pantoja (perc); Candy Love, Sandra Stevens, Della Horne, Victoria Domagalski, Scott Beach (v).* 10/69–2/72.

The three Warner recordings are still available on this compilation set but, given the rate of change that this music represents, it is still preferable to hear the albums individually. However, the box will appeal to those who are not troubled by not having the original packaging.

***** Sextant**

Columbia CK 64983 *Hancock; Eddie Henderson, Julian Priester (tb, atb, btb, perc); Bennie Maupin (ss, bcl, picc, perc); Jaco Pastorius, Buster Williams (b); Billy Hart (d, perc); Buck Clarke (perc); Scott Beach, Della Horne, Candy Love, Sandra Stevens (v).* 72.

The joyous dancing figures on the cover of Hancock's Columbia debut convey some of its lasting charm and appeal. In retrospect, it's hard to think of *Sextant* as anything other than a transitional phase in Hancock's career, and a shift towards the electronic funk of mid-decade, but it has an infectious freshness and lack of elaboration which is typical of the composer, if not of the label he had just signed to. 'Rain Dance' is one of his most delightful themes, shifting between metres and harmonically agile as well. 'Hidden Shadows' and 'Hornets' are more like long-form jams, though the basic architecture of the second track particularly is very impressive. Obviously influenced by Miles, it points in very different directions; where the trumpeter was interested in abstraction and pure sound, Hancock was devoted to melody. The doubling of lines, often by Priester and Maupin in conjunction with the bassist, was also a key element of Hancock's approach, and it's deployed to great effect here. In future, his groups would be much more obviously electrified. This carries over personnel from one phase to another, but it leaves behind a very definite period and ushers us on to the next. Out of circulation or available only as an import for some time, it fills in an important part of the Hancock story.

CORE COLLECTION

★★★★ Head Hunters

Columbia CK 65123 *Hancock; Bennie Maupin (ts, ss, saxello, bcl, af); Paul Jackson (b); Harvey Mason (d); Bill Summers (perc).* 73.

Miles legitimized a view of black musical history that made room for Sly Stone and James Brown, as well as Charlie Parker and John Coltrane. *Head Hunters* – and yes, it is two words at this stage – was the direct result, an infectiously funky and thoroughly joyous record; only the closing 'Vein Melter' hints at melancholy. Hancock includes 'Watermelon Man', not because he is short of ideas, but because he wants to demonstrate the essential continuity of his music. Earlier albums may have seemed a 'departure', as critics like to say. This one was confidently on the main line. For the simplest point of comparison, listen to Butch Warren's line on *Takin' Off* and then compare the toppling, dotted rhythm Paul Jackson brings to it on *Head Hunters*. A later generation, weaned on stuff like this and disillusioned with the designer gloss of the '80s, would disagree, but Hancock's electric keyboards sound pretty one-dimensional here and there; the Hohner Clavinet is very much an acquired taste. The latest remastering, coupled to budget release and including a new essay by Hancock, gives the biggest-selling jazz record of all time a new gloss and impetus, and once again 'Chameleon' and 'Sly' are thudding club walls up and down the country and coast to coast. Maupin performs a role much like Wayne Shorter in Weather Report, not soloing at length or necessarily carrying the line but placing brushstrokes and punctuating moods much as Miles did. 'Vein Melter', which is perhaps his best moment on the record, is to some extent a throwback to the more introverted music of the very early '70s, but it is no less effective in this context, a much-needed counterbalance. Hancock provides most of the colours, but he is also improvising with genius. Some of his very finest keyboard work can be heard during the quarter-hour span of 'Chameleon'.

★★★(★) Thrust

Columbia CK 64984 *As above, except Mike Clark (d) replaces Mason.* 74.

★★★ Man-Child

Columbia 471235-2 *Hancock; Wilbur Brisbois, Jay DaVersa (t); Garnett Brown (tb); Dick Hyde (btb, tba); Jim Horn, Ernie Watts (sax, f); Wayne Shorter (ss); Bennie Maupin (ts, ss, saxello, bcl, af); Stevie Wonder (hca); Blackbird McKnight, David T Walker (g); Henry Davis, Paul Jackson (b); Mike Clark, James Gadson (d); Bill Summers (perc).* 1/76.

★★(★) Secrets

Columbia CK 34280 *Hancock; Bennie Maupin (ts, ss, bcl, lyricon, perc); Wah Wah Watson (g, syn, v); Ray Parker (g); Paul Jackson (b); James Levi (d); Kenneth Nash (perc).* 76.

Thrust was conceived as a near-exact replica, but this time the bank of Arps – Odyssey, Soloist, 2600 synth and string synth – lack creative personality. 'Palm Grease' is unmistakable Hancock, oozing with class and a politely ironic menace. Jackson's bass is a little like a truncheon round the head and ribcage, not quite in earnest, but not quite easy to listen to either. Mike Clark is your basic Rock Skool drummer, but quite effective in this context and capable of some delicacy, as on 'Butterfly'.

Vividly textured and awash with new ideas of instrumental colour, *Man-Child* now sounds like Hancock's shade-card for the bands of the mid-'70s. He wasn't to use quite such a broad spectrum again, and on occasion he trades in drive and energy for surface tone. The work of the early '70s was influenced by Indian and African idioms and makes much use of doubled instruments, out-of-synch transitions and rhythmic overlaps that seem to happen in phase rather than at once. The horns are uniformly good, if a little too uniform in focus. The fast, semiquaver patterns were to become a little irritating later. Here they are modulated more carefully. Veering close to the 'space music' that was to be his commercial, if certainly not his critical, nadir, *Man-Child* isn't the easiest album to locate in the continuum. Even so, it remains eminently listenable.

Secrets dispensed with the sci-fi covers in favour of a more outdoor, sunlit look. The appearance of 'Cantaloupe Island' was further sign that Hancock wanted to accommodate his own back-catalogue to the new instrumentation, and yet what emerges is barely the same tune, pumped up and oddly aggressive. Despite a general simplification of texture over its predecessors, this is the mood of the album. 'Doin' It' (co-written with Ray Parker and Wah Wah Watson, who was shortly to join the Headhunters crew) is a slice of rather crude funk and, before long, guitars were to dominate the band. This is the first album on which Hancock ceded compositional control. It's no better for it.

★★(★) Death Wish

Sony International 491981 *As above; orchestra conducted by Jerry Peters.* 74.

The rating is purely for the album. As film music, it worked superbly well, albeit for a deeply unpleasant film whose moral ambiguities have been extensively discussed. Hancock dips into his bag for a range of styles, ranging from his recent fusion and funk experiments to older stuff, mixed with some generic movie music devices. Like most film soundtracks, it's not the easiest of listens and apart from the main title sequence, which deserves to be as well known as the *Shaft* theme, it's a pretty dull listen.

★★★ Flood

Sony International 35439 *Hancock; Bennie Maupin (ss, ts, bcl, f); Blackbird McKnight (g); Paul Jackson (b); Mike Clark (d); Bill Summers (perc).* 6–7/75.

Somewhat like Miles Davis's dark epics of the time, this was originally only released in Japan. Like them, it's a live recording, and a good representation of what the Headhunters sounded like out of the studio. 'Chameleon' sounds almost freely improvised or like a demonstration of electronic keyboards, depending on how you look at it. 'Watermelon Man' is more straightforward, and the long closing 'Hang Up Your Hang Ups' is rousing jazz-funk. The most illuminating section, though, comes right at the beginning, where Herbie plays a long acoustic introduction to 'Maiden Voyage' that reminds us he was still a jazz musician at heart and still not averse to playing a regular piano. Not the greatest item in the Hancock catalogue, this nevertheless has its place in any representative collection of Herbie's work.

★★(★) V.S.O.P.

Sony 34688 *Hancock; Freddie Hubbard (t); Eddie Henderson (t, flhn); Julian Priester (tb); Wayne Shorter (ss, ts); Bennie Maupin (af); Ray Parker Jr, Wah Wah Watson (g); Ron*

Carter, Paul Jackson, Buster Williams (b); James Levi, Tony Williams (d); Kenneth Nash (perc). 7/76.

****(*) V.S.O.P.: The Quintet**

Sony 65462 *Hancock; Freddie Hubbard (t); Wayne Shorter (ss, ts); Ron Carter (b); Tony Williams (d).* 7/77.

A pre-Internet grapevine buzzed with rumour before Hancock's retrospective at the 1976 Newport Jazz Festival. Could it really be that the great Miles Davis Quintet would take the stage with the great man himself (by then famously mired in his own dark agenda) playing trumpet *sans* pedals, fuzzes, wah-wahs and all the rest of his post-1969 paraphernalia? In the event, it was left to Freddie Hubbard, and probably it had been planned that way all along, but the gig had a disproportionate impact on modern jazz, inspiring younger-generation players who were tiring of electro-funk to revisit the classic Prestiges and Blue Notes.

'Maiden Voyage' and 'Nefertiti' are performed without much dynamism, and the complex line of the latter tune almost unfurls onstage. Hancock is playing an electric instrument, albeit the closest thing yet devised to a genuine Steinway, and, partly as a result, the sound of the band is hard and brittle. Hubbard is, as ever, unwilling to play himself in and blasts away; in comparison to the more reflective Eddie Henderson, who crops up later, he sounds almost vulgar and brusque. Almost perversely, the concert and album also reflect the changes that had overtaken jazz, with a final performance by the recent Hancock sextet (which included Henderson) and some post-*Head Hunters* funk from the new unit. The sextet is represented by just two tracks – but this, equally perversely, given that it was a farewell gig, is where the real musical action is. 'Toys' is a splendid piece of post-Miles jazz, and Henderson's part indicates the direction Miles might have gone in had he not opted for the dark, turbid landscapes of *Agharta* and *Pangaea*. The Headhunters stuff at the end is engaging enough but overlong and excessively indulgent. The abiding impression is of an immensely gifted player who had perhaps peaked too soon and who found himself desperately pursuing change to seem ahead of – or at least up with – a game that was already changing rules again. Much came of this moment, and it's the moment that's important rather than the rather patchy record.

Inevitably, it was too good and too money-spinning an idea to leave as a one-off so, in the summer of 1977, the quintet went on the road. Many bootlegs of these concerts have been circulated and those we have heard – which are of wildly variable quality – suggest that the band was no less consistent in delivery. This is one of the middling sets, recorded at two Californian venues. Unlike the retrospective event, this was a project of leaders, and so there are compositions by Hubbard ('One Of A Kind'), Shorter ('Dolores'), Williams ('Lawra') and Carter ('Third Plane') in a shapeless set. The band was clearly pulling in too many directions at once and, given the number of powerful egos on the stand, it's a wonder they got it together at all.

****(*) An Evening With Herbie Hancock & Chick Corea**

Columbia C2K 65551 2CD *Hancock; Chick Corea (p).* 2/78.

The most alarming thing here is what has gone wrong with 'Maiden Voyage', that exquisite tune turned into a sequence of rolls and fakes as Hancock tries to wrest something new out of it. This was a public shaking of hands as much with Mr Steinway as with Mr Corea. Hancock had certainly not given up playing acoustic piano in favour of Fenders, Hohners, Moogs, Mellotrons and Arps, but one might be forgiven for thinking so. Corea wipes the floor with him, and there is a further, rather better selection of material from the same night issued on Polydor, on which Chick majors.

It should be noted that Hancock endeavoured to keep his jazz playing going in parallel with his other interests. There was a solo piano album, recorded for Columbia in Japan. There were the duos with Corea, and there was the ongoing V.S.O.P. project. However, they were doomed to take second place in discographical terms, for the moment at least.

**** Magic Windows**

Columbia 486572 *Hancock; Michael Brecker (ts); Adrian Belew, George Johnson, Al McKay, Ray Parker Jr, Wah Wah Watson (g); Louis Johnson, Freddie Washington, Eddie Watkins (b); James Gadson, Alphonse Mouzon, John Robinson (d); Paulinho Da Costa, Kwasi Dzidzornu, Juan Escovedo, Pete Escovedo, Sheila Escovedo, Kwazu Ladzekpo, Moody Perry III (perc); Gavin Christopher, Dede Dickerson, Vicki Randle, Ngoh Spencer, Sylvester, Jeanie Tracy (v).* 81.

**** Lite Me Up**

Columbia 486573 *Hancock; Jay Graydon, Steve Lukather, David Williams (g); Randy Jackson, Louis Johnson, Abe Laboriel (b); Jeff Porcaro, John Robinson, Narada Michael Walden (d); Wayne Anthony, Patrice Rushen (v).* 82.

By the turn of the '80s there were signs that Hancock had almost exhausted the funk/disco seam and was turning his attention back towards jazz forms and instrumentations. Far be it from us to suggest that these two records represent rock bottom. It's almost inevitable that a great artist will produce something interesting in whatsoever form he chooses to work, and there isn't a moment on either disc that falls below that threshold. However, these are likely to be dispiriting moments for Hancock fans. A cameo from Brecker on 'Help Yourself' points a way forward.

*****(*) Mr Hands**

Columbia 471240 *Hancock; Bennie Maupin (ts); Wah Wah Watson (g); Ron Carter, Paul Jackson, Byron Miller, Jaco Pastorius (b); Leon Ndugu Chancler, Harvey Mason, Tony Williams (d); Sheila Escovedo, Bill Summers (perc).* 82.

A similar line-up to *Sunlight*, but behind it a strong recognition on Hancock's part that the funk experiment is over, both creatively and commercially. The first sign of change is that once again the leader is credited with all the material. 'Calypso' isn't 'Cantaloupe Island', but it is Hancock's strongest jazz writing for some years, and the attack is strong and pianistic. Other tracks, notably 'Just Around The Corner' and the gloriously danceable 'Shiftless Shuffle', are still at the fusion end of things, but with a less one-dimensional beat and a growing harmonic flexibility grafted on. And doesn't Maupin sound like the George Coleman and Dexter Gordon of the early Blue Notes? A conscious homage, no doubt, but not so slavish that his own slightly formal style doesn't emerge.

***** Quartet**

Columbia CK 38275 *Hancock; Wynton Marsalis (t); Ron Carter (b); Tony Williams (d).* 82.

As his interest in rock and pop receded, Hancock made carefully selected forays back into the world of straight jazz. Only his enduring enthusiasm for the Yamaha Electric Grand struck an unlikely chord. Perversely, the chops don't sound nearly as good as they did on *Head Hunters*, and the standard and repertory material, like 'I Fall In Love Too Easily' and a couple of Monk tunes, don't afford him much respite. Fortunately for the album, Marsalis is feeling his oats, dispatching his solos with testy arrogance, and of course the other two rhythm players are in superb shape. Only on 'Round Midnight', which was to become a career leitmotif from the moment Hancock got involved in the Tavernier project, does he sound much like his old self.

★★★ Future Shock

Columbia CK 65962 *Hancock; Michael Beinhorn (ky); Pete Cosey (g); Bill Laswell (b); Grandmixer DST (turntables); Sly Dunbar (d, perc); Daniel Ponce (perc); Bernard Fowler, Dwight Jackson, Lamar Wright (v).* 83.

★★(★) Sound-System

Columbia CK 39478 *Hancock; Wayne Shorter (lyricon); Henry Kaiser, Nicky Skopelitis (g); Bill Laswell (b, syn, elec); Johnny St Cyr (turntables); Will Alexander, Bob Stevens (elec); Anton Fier (d, perc); Aiyb Dieng, Hamid Drake, Daniel Ponce (perc); Jali Foday Musa Suso (doussn'gouni, balafon); Bernard Fowler, Toshinori Kondo (v).* 84.

A decade on from *Head Hunters*, Hancock was to have one last throw of chart success with 'Rockit', a number-one single that propelled *Future Shock* up the album charts as well. Working with Bill Laswell put him in touch with elements of the New Wave, a more brooding sound that once again kindled memories of Miles's organ bands (and the presence of Pete Cosey brought the connection into even sharper focus).

Sound-System is equally unmistakably of its moment, the new supporting cast again in evidence, and Shorter, the only familiar jazz face in the line-up, involved in his own rock'n'roll transformation and restricted to the characterless lyricon. Compared to *Future Shock*, it's a lumbering, ungainly affair – but, as always, it has its moments, and it provides further evidence of Hancock's restless shape-shifting in pursuit of the new commercial *Zeitgeist*.

★★★ Live

Jazz Door 1206 *Hancock; Greg Osby (as); Michael Brecker (ts); Buster Williams (b); Al Foster (d); Bobby McFerrin (v).* 88, 92.

★★★ Live In New York

Jazz Door 1210 *Hancock; Jeff Littleton (b); Gene Jackson (d).* 93.

We're not sure of the legitimacy of these releases, but Hancock collectors will certainly want to have them. *Live* was taped in Belgrade and New York in 1988 and 1992 respectively and shows Hancock once again working in a straight jazz context live even while his studio work was dabbling with hip-hop, funk and film music.

★★(★) Perfect Machine

Sony International 65960 *Hancock; Bill Laswell (ky); Micro Wave (b, syn, vocoder); Bootsy Collins (b, vocoder); Nicky Skopelitis (d, syn); D St (turntables, effects); Sugarfoot (v).* 10/88.

Again, one of the dullest bits of product Herbie has ever put his name to. The version of 'Maiden Voyage' is dire, which is enough to damn the rest of it for all eternity. Bill Laswell's hand is all over it, to the extent that it hardly seems like a Hancock project at all. Sugarfoot of the Ohio Players contributes vocals, or rather lends them out with little conviction or generosity. The presence of Bootsy Collins gives the album some credibility with the funk mafia, but to be honest his contribution is perfunctory. The funk is mechanical; the jazz component minimal. Hancock wasn't to make another studio album for some time and if this isn't sufficient proof of creative exhaustion, we've not heard a clearer one.

★★★ A Tribute To Miles

Qwest/Reprise 45059 *Hancock; Wallace Roney (t); Wayne Shorter (ts); Ron Carter (b); Tony Williams (d).* 9/92.

Hancock founded the jazz quintet V.S.O.P. in 1976, mainly as a festival outfit; the name stood for 'Very Special One-time-only Performance', but of course it was a one-off idea that was going to be in considerable demand. The tantalizing prospect that one night Miles would square the circle and complete the reunion kept the group going almost until his death, and there was always speculation who – when the inevitable happened – would take his place. Roney makes a creditable job of it, pungent, agile and a good deal more acerbic on 'So What' and 'All Blues' than the onlie begetter had ever been. Both are recorded live and seem a touch lifeless. The rest of the material was taped in studio, and it would be fascinating to hear the out-takes of something like 'Pinocchio', which is executed so smoothly it's hard to believe that it wasn't fully written out beforehand. Hancock seems increasingly in charge, not just of his own acoustic technique but of the overall shape of the music. The process of re-mainstreaming himself hasn't really stopped since.

★★★ Dis Is Da Drum

Mercury 528 185 *Hancock; Wallace Roney (t); Bennie Maupin (ts); Mars Lasar, Darrell Smith (ky); Darrell Bob Dog Robertson, Wah Wah Watson (g); Armand Sebal Leco, Frank Thibeaux (b); Guy Eckstine, Will Kennedy, Bob Strong (d); Will Roc Griffin (samples); Niayi Asiedu, Skip Bunny, Bill Summers (perc); Lazaro Galarraga, Marina Bambino, Yvette Summers, Lynn Lyndsey, Louis Verdeaux, Felicidad Ector, Huey Jackson (v); Chil Factor (rap); The Real Richie Rich (scratches).* 95.

What were we saying about the mainstream? Just when it seemed that Hancock had realigned himself with jazz, along came this odd mish-mash. The only conclusion is that Herbie really does still want to be a pop star. 'Butterfly' reappears from *Thrust*, albeit with a pungent '90s beat, and the other material is a catch-all synthesis of bebop and the gentler end of hip-hop. Even the raps sound polite. This is the first time, alarmingly, that he has seemed out of his depth with a new trend, all the more ironic in that Hancock is a father figure to a new cohort of youngsters who regard *Head Hunters* and *Thrust* as Holy Writ and the Mini Moog as the Ark of the Covenant. Always a gracefully purposeful player, he certainly doesn't relate to the almost nihilistic drive of the new generation, and he has little success getting even seasoned hands like Maupin, Watson and Summers to come along with him. Call us old-fashioned, but a record that needs a 'sound designer' is in trouble.

★★★(★) The New Standard

Verve 527715-2 *Hancock; Michael Brecker (ts, ss); John Scofield (g, sitar); Dave Holland (b); Jack DeJohnette (d); Don Alias (perc); woodwinds, brass.* 96.

Moving away from Columbia prompted a further re-examination of repertoire and market range from an artist who by this stage was certainly not scuffling for gigs. The notion of what constituted a 'standard' seemed to ossify in the aftermath of bebop: Broadway tunes, a few torchy ballads, a few novelty items, but a pretty consensual playlist of material. It was John Coltrane and, as ever, Miles who blew that away, deconstructing tunes like 'My Favorite Things', 'Chim Chim Cheree' and 'The Inch Worm' almost with savagery, and then in Miles's case digging into chart pop for 'Time After Time' (the Cyndi Lauper version) and Michael Jackson's 'Human Nature'. Hancock takes a very similar line on *The New Standard*, programming tunes like British soul diva Sade's 'Love Is Stronger Than Pride' (a lush, big-band interpretation) and Kurt Cobain's 'All Apologies', T.A.F.K.A. Prince's irrepressibly funky 'Thieves In The Temple' and Peter Gabriel's 'Mercy Street'. The essential approach is no different from any other standards recording, except that Hancock is obviously aware that some of these songs will not stand too much harmonic deconstruction at this stage in their public histories. They are not as yet true contrafacts, except for the more familiar 'Scarborough Fair', and the limitations of the record, excellently performed as it is, lie in the reliance on melodic variation of songs that in some cases are fairly cut-and-dried and not really susceptible to this treatment. One suspects that Brecker probably has a pop and rock collection at home; he revels in the challenge and turns in some fresh-voiced and unhackneyed solos. Holland and Scofield (who switches to electric sitar for 'Norwegian Wood') are masterful, and only DeJohnette, normally the most adaptable of players, seems to strain at the leash.

***** 1 + 1**

Verve 537564-2 *Hancock; Wayne Shorter (ss).* 96.

'The artists call upon the full palette of their musical resources to paint life's stories with all the texture of emotion and intensity of color – a process demanding the performance equivalent of a leap into the unknown.' Tosh. For a start, the palette is all too limited. Shorter's tenor remained in its case and there is a limit to how much of his eccentric soprano voice one wants to hear at a sitting. And there is no sense whatsoever that this is an exploratory, existential encounter. What one hears is two now-middle-aged players of huge ability and scope conversing idly, eliding much of the middle ground, elevating slight ideas to spurious grandeur. Nothing wrong with that, but a mistake surely to make extravagant claims for such a lightweight session. 'The evanescent made eternal'? Don't think so.

*****(*) Gershwin's World**

Verve 557797-2 *Hancock; Eddie Henderson (t, flhn); James Carter, Wayne Shorter (ss, ts); Kenny Garrett (as); Marlon Graves (g); Stevie Wonder (hca, v); Ron Carter, Stanley Clarke, Ira Coleman (b); Terri Lyne Carrington, Gene Jackson (d); Cyro Baptista, Massamba Diop (perc); Kathleen Battle, Joni Mitchell (v); Orpheus Chamber Orchestra.* 98.

Hancock has not generally been thought of an interpreter of other composers' music, but the centenary of George Gershwin was too significant an occasion to miss. Herbie delivers one of the most elegant and thoughtful records of his career, some of it on the fringes of jazz proper, but all of it marked by a profound musicianship and a genuine empathy with Gershwin's world and music. There are some additional, non-Gershwin items: a revival of the old duo with Chick Corea for James P. Johnson's 'Blueberry Rhyme', Duke's 'Cottontail', Ravel's Piano Concerto and W. C. Handy's 'St Louis Blues'. It features the unmistakable voice of Stevie Wonder, whose equally unmissable harmonica accompanies Joni Mitchell on 'Summertime'; Shorter's soprano solo on the same track completely transforms the song into something delicate and otherworldly. From a younger generation, James Carter makes his presence felt in a style derived from Shorter's Blue Note period, but with a distinctly contemporary edge. Kenny Garrett and Eddie Henderson keep the blues very squarely on the agenda and block any risk of drifting off into 'classics lite' mode. By blending together Gershwin originals and related material, Hancock has created a mini-musical that links the great man back and forward in time, and across the divide between 'popular' and 'classical' music. It is a bold and by no means obvious programme, and this album shouldn't be missed on any account.

****(*) Future 2 Future**

Transparent Music 50011 *Hancock; Wayne Shorter (ss, ts); Bill Laswell (b); Jack DeJohnette, Tony Ruption Williams (d); Karsh Kale (d, programming); Carl Craig, A Guy Called Gerald, Rob Swift (programming); Dana Bryant, Chaka Khan, Imani Uzuri (v).* 01.

Hancock has always looked forward and here he tries to engage with a whole new generation of music makers. Whether his style and philosophy are compatible with the likes of drum'n'bass producer A Guy Called Gerald or electronics wizard Carl Craig is always going to be open to question, but the fact is that Hancock keeps himself open to such influences. Most of these tracks are collaborations and there is an air of polite compromise about the proceedings. Almost all of these younger players are capable of delivering much stronger statements; on his own, Hancock is too, but the trade-off between the two is such that only a rather bland middle ground is ever occupied. Laswell's thunderous presence is dominant throughout and, as with his reworkings of Miles Davis material, one feels that his curatorial genius and sound philosophy are the dominant factors, leaving Hancock to bask in a thoroughly earned but now rather passive reputation. As the Zawinul tune has it: 'Doctor Honoris Causa', but how positive a contributor?

***** Directions In Music: Live At Massey Hall**

Verve 589654 *Hancock; Roy Hargrove (t); Michael Brecker (ts); John Patitucci (b); Brian Blade (d).* 11/01.

To mark the 75th anniversaries of both Miles Davis and John Coltrane, Hancock reconvened a latter-day version of his V.S.O.P. band. This date was recorded in the richly associative atmosphere of Massey Hall in Toronto, where, nearly 50 years before, Charlie Parker and Dizzy Gillespie had led another 'Quintet of the Year'. This time out, the repertoire was chosen to honour both. The best pieces are associated with Coltrane, though. 'Impressions' is given a radical overhaul, its blues idiom thoroughly investigated and updated. Brecker plays 'Naima' unaccompanied, a magnificent *tour de force* that confirms his status as the most influential Coltrane disciple and arguably the most influential saxophone player since Coltrane himself. Hancock's role is secondary to both the front-men (Hargrove has 'done' Miles Davis before), but he demonstrates anew that this kind of post-bop jazz is still in his blood.

****** The Herbie Hancock Box**

Columbia Legacy AC4K 64978 4CD *As for Columbia releases, above.* 73–87.

This is a supremely polished package and an ideal complement to the Blue Note retrospective. With 34 tracks spread over a nearly 15-year period, it's a no more than spotty coverage of Hancock's Columbia years, but it does the job. Disc one and disc two begin and end respectively with the V.S.O.P. band, Herbie introducing 'Maiden Voyage' followed by a long, long version of the track itself. The later V.S.O.P. plays Freddie Hubbard's 'Red Clay', the only previously unreleased track on the set, though there are some pieces which haven't had American release before this.

Side one also has fine piano-playing on 'Harvest Time' and 'The Sorcerer' as well as 'Finger Painting', 'Round Midnight' and 'Eye Of The Hurricane'. Disc two is equally eclectic, with a long version of 'Dolphin Dance', 'Milestones', 'On Green Dolphin Street' and then that Hubbard tune. This is where so-called purists might usefully stop, because the third disc takes Hancock into the heart of his electric period, touching on 'Watermelon Man' and the main title sequence from *Death Wish*. Apart from the long opening 'Chameleon', one of his most protean compositions and most gadget-heavy performances, disc four is a disappointment. One can't say that the whole set is, because this is a lot of music for your money. Collectors will wish there was more unreleased material. Newcomers to Hancock may find that one or more of the discs stays in the fancy box, which one or two depending very much on tastes and prejudices about the 'acoustic' or 'electric' Hancock. A fine buy by any calculation, though.

Captain John Handy (1900–71)

ALTO SAXOPHONE, CLARINET

A New Orleans musician working in the city from the '30s, Handy started on clarinet but preferred alto; when he became internationally known as a touring hired-gun in the '60s, his broad-based style suggested a synthesis of revivalism and a down-home R&B.

****(*) The Very First Recordings**
American Music AMCD-51 *Handy; Jimmy Clayton (t); Dave Williams, Louis Gallaud (p); George Guesnon (g, bj); Sylvester Handy, McNeal Breaux (b); Alfred Williams, Josiah Frazier (d).* 7/60.

*****(*) Capt. John Handy & His New Orleans Stompers Vol. 1**
GHB BCD-41 *Handy; Kid Thomas Valentine (t); Jim Robinson (tb); Sammy Rimington (cl); Bill Sinclair (p); Dick Griffith (bj); Dick McCarthy (b); Sammy Penn (d).* 12/65.

***** Capt. John Handy & His New Orleans Stompers Vol. 2**
GHB BCD-42. *As above.* 12/65.

***** Very Handy!**
GHB BCD-325 *Handy; Clive Wilson (t); Big Bill Bissonnette (tb); Sammy Rimington (cl, g); Bill Sinclair (p); Dick Griffith (bj); Dick McCarthy (b); Art Pulver (d).* 5/66.

***** John Handy With Barry Martyn's Band**
GHB BCD-377 *Handy; Teddy Fullick (t); Pete Dyer (tb); Sammy Rimington (cl, ts); Graham Paterson (p); Brian Turnock (b); Barry Martyn (d).* 3/68.

***** Television Airshots 1968–1970**
Jazz Crusade JCCD-3008 *Handy; Punch Miller, George 'Kid Sheik' Cola (t, v); Homer Eugene, Louis Nelson (tb); Andrew Morgan (cl, ts); Dick Wellstood, Bill Sinclair (p); Dave Duquette (bj); Sylvester Handy, Chester Zardis (b); Lester Alexis, Sammy Penn (d).* 3/68–6/70.

It still seems strange that John Handy should have had so much flak from New Orleans purists for so long. He seldom worked very far from the city and had been a fixture in local bands since 1919. But because he preferred to play alto over clarinet – there is just a single track of the smaller horn on the American Music CD – and his style anticipated such R&B players as Earl Bostic, he was almost ostracized for many years. Yet he is always the most interesting player on all these records, and the bounce and wit of his playing can sometimes be phenomenal in the strict channels of New Orleans playing.

Actually, many listeners will be reminded of the alto playing of Earl Fouche with Sam Morgan. One can't hear Handy that well on the *First Recordings* disc since he seems to be at the back of the band, but when he breaks through – as on the animated 'Panama' – he makes the music bristle. Most of the disc consists of previously unreleased music, but the band is clumsy and the final three tracks, where Handy works with a different rhythm section, slightly disappointing. The two live shows from 1965 are much more like it and a strong document of the New Orleans movement at its most spirited. Valentine's jabbing trumpet spars with Handy's almost pirouetting lines, with Rimington the elegant voice in the middle. This is great stuff and, though raggedness sometimes takes over – more often on the second volume – these are records to play if one wants to sample how vibrant this kind of jazz can be. *Very Handy!* has the Captain on board with Bill Bissonnette's band, and though the leader wasn't very happy with the results, as detailed in his curmudgeonly sleeve-note, the music has plenty of fizz. Handy plays with quite herculean abandon on such as 'Give Me Your Telephone Number', and the tempos seem to quicken towards helter-skelter as a result. The sound is a bit thin and strangled but it's not hopeless, and five previously unissued tracks take the CD over 60 minutes.

Recorded on tour with the Barry Martyn group, Handy seems in good spirits. The cover photo of six young Englishmen and the weatherbeaten New Orleans veteran seems redolent of an era of pre-history, but the music, driven along by Kid Martyn's unquenchable enthusiasm from the kit, has a gutsy excitement. Fullick, who was a new recruit to the group, has a tone that's even shakier than Kid Thomas Valentine on an off-day, but Rimington and Handy make a good team. The TV recordings are from two shows with different groups, though there's little between them in terms of either playing or sound, which is decent if flat. Miller and Kid Sheik divide honours about even and, though the presence of Wellstood on the first date is a surprise, neither pianist has much to do. Handy weathers all storms with soldierly fortitude and gets in some good blows on the way.

John Handy (born 1933)

ALTO SAXOPHONE, FLUTE, OTHER REEDS

Born in Dallas, Texas, 30 years before John F. Kennedy's fateful, fatal visit, Handy moved to New York in his mid-20s and found work with Charles Mingus and others. The 1965 Monterey Jazz Festival was his coming-out, and perhaps a premature climax.

*****(*) Live At The Monterey Jazz Festival**
Koch KOC 3-7820-2 *Handy; Mike White (vn); Jerry Hahn (g); Don Thompson (b); Terry Clarke (d).* 9/65.

***** The Second John Handy Album**

Koch CD 7812-2 *As above.* 7/66.

Not to be confused with the much older alto saxophonist, 'Captain' John Handy, the Texan is one of the few contemporary players who sounds as though he had listened carefully to Eric Dolphy, an enthusiasm that must have been encouraged during his association with Charles Mingus.

The 1965 Monterey Jazz Festival appearance was a roaring success and should have created more critical momentum than the work of later years suggests. The CD reissue has put the two long tracks back in the original order of performance, with 'If Only We Knew' placed ahead of 'Spanish Lady'. Handy's intriguing harmonics and ravelling lines are supplemented by White and Hahn, but it's the leader who really commands attention.

The studio follow-up has its dead spots, not least in the overlong 'Scheme #1', but there is no mistaking Handy's originality and desire to plough his own furrow. The CD adds three splendid tracks, an alternative version of 'Blues For A Highstrung Guitar' and two unissued items, 'A Bad Stroke Of Luck' and 'Debonair'. Once again, White is a key performer, used in ways that recall the violin parts in Albert Ayler's bands, only rather gentler. Hahn is more audible in the studio and seems more relaxed than at Monterey.

****** New View!**

Koch CD 7811-2 *Handy; Bobby Hutcherson (vib); Pat Martino (g); Albert Stinson (b); Doug Sides (d).* 6/67.

Handy's masterpiece, caught at the Village Gate in New York. The opening 'Naima', performed in the last month of composer John Coltrane's life, has a particular synchronicity, and a flavour that the unusual instrumentation hammers home. The real plus, though, is the restoration to full length of 'Tears Of Ole Miss (Anatomy Of A Riot)', which now comes in at a full half-hour. Also on the album, 'A Little Quiet', which also shows John Hammond's gifts as a producer, the live mix balanced with genuine taste.

***** Projections**

Koch KOC CD 7865 *Handy; Michael White (vn); Mike Nock (p); Bruce Cale (b); Larry Hancock (d, perc).* 4/68.

Ambitious, but deeply flawed, *Projections* was the work of Handy's pretentiously named Concert Ensemble, a group that was required to generate a bigger and fuller sound. Nock and White contribute compositions, and this perhaps allows Handy to concentrate on his playing. He doubles on flute and the rarely heard saxello, and he seems to be experimenting with a spectrum of sound-sources, something Dolphy did. The flute playing, rather like Dolphy's, is more enthusiastic than accomplished, but on saxello Handy finds a fascinating tonality that he doesn't reach on alto. 'Dance To The Lady' is glorious, but far in advance expressively of anything else on the disc.

Jake Hanna (1932–2002)

DRUMS

The good-natured Bostonian worked with Woody Herman, Toshiko Akiyoshi and Maynard Ferguson before striking out as a leader, though without making waves.

****(*) The Joint Is Jumpin'**

Arbors 19148 *Hanna; Jack Sheldon (t); John Allred (tb); Tommy Newsom (ts); Russ Tompkins (p); David Stone (b).* 98.

Jake's five albums for Concord didn't survive into the CD era and this is slim pickings for such a long and busy career. Unfortunately, like most of his recorded output as leader, it lacks drama or any sense of surprise and danger and while the playing by these veteran West Coasters is competent enough (Jack Sheldon is the surprise package, while non-WCer Allred has a few good moments), there isn't much to entice anyone new to Hanna's work.

'Exactly Like You' and the title-track are probably the best bets for a quick sample, but this isn't one to break the bank for.

Roland Hanna (1932–2003)

PIANO

Sir Roland was knighted by the President of Liberia in 1970. Bud Powell was the single most important influence on Hanna's playing style, but the Detroit man also took careful note of Tommy Flanagan and Teddy Wilson.

***** Easy To Love**

Koch 33121 *Hanna; Ben Tucker (b); Roy Burness (d).* 9/59.

Recently reissued, this early set finds the 27-year-old Hanna poised midway between bop orthodoxy (audible on 'A Night In Tunisia') and something closer to Ellington's capacious vision. Interestingly, the set does not represent the pianist's compositions at all but does include three tracks by bassist Tucker, who seems to have some pretensions as a writer. The recording is nicely balanced and well remastered; the title-track, a Cole Porter song, is the cut of choice. It is some time before we hear Hanna on record as leader again.

***** Bird Tracks**

Progressive 7031 *Hanna (p solo).* 2–3/78.

The Parker material fizzes and bounces in a convincing pianistic impersonation of the album's inspiration. Hanna's ability to capture the cadence of horn lines is something that again he shares with Tommy Flanagan, but he does it with his own distinctive spin.

***** Impressions: The Definitive Black & Blue Sessions**

Black & Blue 880 *Hanna; George Duvivier, Major Holley (b); Alan Dawson, Oliver Jackson (d).* 7/78.

Reissued in 2002 with two bonus tracks. Apart from 'The Lonely Ones' and 'Drinkin' Wine Slowly', the tunes are all standards or repertory pieces, but it's Hanna's flowing interpretation of John Coltrane's blues theme 'Impressions' that grabs the attention here. How much Trane's expansion of harmony affected him in this period is difficult to say, but here he shows an instinctive understanding of the saxophonist's respectful subversion of traditional harmony. Never an 'outside' player, Hanna tames the idiom somewhat, but it nonetheless affects the other performances here, notably the bonus inclusion of Miles's 'All Blues'. Two different trios were involved. Hard to make a qualitative distinction between them.

***** Swing Me No Waltzes**

Storyville 8309 *Hanna (p solo).* 73, 5/79.

Reissued in 2000, this unaccompanied set from the end of the '70s helps to fill in a blank in the Hanna discography; the new version also includes seven earlier cuts, which represent a very welcome bonus. A folkish element pervades many of the tracks, but the emphasis is on originals and things like 'A Little

Sweet'nin' for Sweden' and 'Free Spirit – Free Style' are testimony to Sir Roland's ability to mix up traditional and quite advanced idioms. The sound is not perfect but by the standards of the time pretty reasonable, and this is a worthwhile addition to the catalogue.

★★(★) Glove
Storyville STCD 4148 *Hanna; George Mraz (b); Motohiko Hino (d).* 87.

★★★(★) Round Midnight
Town Crier 513 *Hanna (p solo).* 3/87.

★★(★) This Time It's Real
Storyville STCD 4145 *Hanna; Jesper Thilo (ts); Mads Vinding (b); Aage Tanggaard (d).* 6/87.

★★★ Persia My Dear
DIW 8015 *Hanna; Richard Davis (b); Freddie Waits (d).* 8/87.

The solo album is the highpoint of a vintage year for Sir Roland. Mostly original material, and including 'Prelude' (originally written for solo cello) and 'Century Rag', it's a sepia-hued session recorded close up and very warmly.

Hanna sounds most obviously like Flanagan when duetting with the excellent Mraz. Formerly listed on Black Hawk, *Glove* is a set of tunes with 'love' in the title, a thematic approach more associated with another pianist, Dave McKenna. The sound is nothing like as exact as that on the DIW, also from Japan, and the drummer is all over the music, like a cheap suit. Surprisingly, perhaps, with Richard Davis, normally the most classically inclined of bassists, Hanna opts to groove. 'Persia My Dear' has a Monkish quality, but the stand-out tracks are 'Summer In Central Park' and 'Manhattan Safari', tributes to the city that has been the Detroit-born Hanna's working home for many years and focus of his long-standing New York Jazz Quartet.

Saxophonist Thilo gets equal billing on the Storyville and takes his full ration of solo space. It's a safe programme for the Tivoli Gardens punters – 'Stella', 'Cherokee', 'Body And Soul', 'Star Eyes' – and the only really startling bit is Hanna's segue between the title-track and the last of these, a glimmer of pure invention on an otherwise rather overcast night.

★★★ Plays Gershwin
Laserlight 17123 *Hanna; Bill Easley (ss, ts, f); Jon Burr (b); Ronnie Burrage (d).* 93.

Budget price and very familiar material, but as such a very decent introduction to Hanna's music, if you haven't sampled him before. This was a working quartet and they sound very comfortable with the keys and metres Hanna establishes, all of them slightly away from what you'd expect from the song. 'Summertime' almost sounds like one of the treatments Hanna favoured in his electric piano days and Easley responds with a scorching soprano solo. 'Oh Lady Be Good' follows and is more of a feature for the piano, an effortlessly clever and witty treatment. 'Bess, You Is My Woman Now' is pure emotion, Hanna touching in some heartbreaking harmonies, Easley floating above on flute. 'Embrace You' isn't a drastic reworking but exactly the song you thought it was. One misprint doesn't devalue the set, though.

★★★ Everything I Love
Ipo 1002 *Hanna (p solo).* 02.

★★★ Tributaries: Reflections On Tommy Flanagan
Ipo 1004 *As above.* 6/02.

These were among the last recordings of Hanna's life and both are very solid solo outings. Not for the first time, Miles's 'All Blues' is a signature cut on *Everything I Love*, with some clever modulation in the solo choruses. Hanna also includes 'Send In The Clowns', almost the only Sondheim song to achieve any kind of jazz presence, but here given a dramatic and almost operatic quality. The other delight is a tribute to the late Milt Jackson, who had gone on ahead. Nicely recorded with a rich and faithful piano sound.

The Flanagan tribute opens with one of Tommy's own tunes, 'Sea Changes', establishing a mood of thoughtful intensity that continues with 'A Child Is Born' and 'Body And Soul'. Flanagan aficionados may be able to pick up references to some of Tommy's classic performances here. The pace slackens, or rather quickens as the emotional temperature settles, and the latter half of the album has a slightly formulaic quality not typical of Hanna. More reissues and concert tapes are in the pipeline. For the moment, though, these give Sir Roland a very nice send-off.

Happy Apple

GROUP

Minneapolis trio, led by drummer David King from The Bad Plus.

★★★(★) Youth Oriented
Nato 066126-2 *Michael Lewis (ss, as, ts, b); Erik Fratzke (b, g); David King (d, ky).* 02.

A fiercely democratic trio, which shares around compositional credits as much as positions in the mix and musical priorities. King's drums – given a beautiful sound by Jason Orris, particularly his booming floor tom – are as polyrhythmical as Shannon Jackson's, but more pointed, more delicate – even as he hits them hard. Lewis seems like a multi-instrumentalist of some calibre: he sounds lucid and voluble on soprano, alto and tenor alike, and when he moves over to the double bass – when Fratzke picks up the guitar for 'The Landfall Planetarium' – that doesn't seem to give him any trouble either. Fratzke's bass guitar works in resonant waves, as if he were trying to be both Prime Time bassists in one set of fingers, but he's melodious with it. The result, unrolled across eight fertile compositions, is music which nods knowledgeably at various fields of jazz, rock and funk endeavour, and makes its own space in the middle. *Just* occasionally, fusion threatens to take over. But what an electrifying sound!

Alex Harding (born 1967)

BARITONE SAXOPHONE

A Detroit-born exponent of the big horn, who seems uninterested in playing it as a double but prefers to see what else there is in hard-bop-based forms for the baritone.

★★(★) Freeflow
CIMP 246 *Harding; Chris Dahlgren (b); Jimmy Weinstein (d).* 5/01.

***** Invocation For Pepper**

CIMP 270 *Harding; Dominic Duval (b); Jay Rosen (d).* 6/02.

Harding's boisterous post-bop baritone is a pleasure to hear, but he fails to stamp enough authority on this setting: as with many CIMP sessions, the hands-off approach allows most of the tracks to ramble on for too long, and the material doesn't focus the players. Nice to hear a strong baritone/bass/drums trio, but they need a firm hand on the tiller.

The follow-up is rather better, especially when they get into the meat of such themes as Cedar Walton's 'Bolivia' and Jay Jay's 'Lament'. It's a pity that several of the pieces start out with 'avant-garde' bits of rambling, since Harding sounds like a player who's best when he works to a structured vocabulary. He for sure gets a big sound here.

Bill Hardman (1933–90)

TRUMPET

Born in Cleveland, Hardman had several major associations in his career, playing with both Charles Mingus and Art Blakey in the '50s, '60s and '70s. Co-led a small group with Lou Donaldson in the early '60s and latterly one with Junior Cook.

***** Jackie's Pal**

Original Jazz Classics OJC 1714 *Hardman; Jackie McLean (as); Mal Waldron (p); Paul Chambers (b); Philly Joe Jones (d).* 8/56.

***** What's Up**

Steeplechase SCCD 1254 *Hardman; Robin Eubanks (tb); Junior Cook (ts); Mickey Tucker (p); Paul Brown (b); Leroy Williams (d).* 7/89.

Bill Hardman was a Jazz Messenger, a staunch sideman, and the long-time front-line partner of Junior Cook. A tough, no-nonsense hard-bopper of the second division, he usually raised the temperature of whatever date he was on. *Jackie's Pal* has lately returned: though often listed under Jackie McLean's name, it was really Hardman's coming-out, and is something of a hard-bop collector's-piece. Though he has a raw tone and some of the playing has a jittery quality, he's moving away from bop cliché and into the more individual delivery that he later put to good use with Blakey and Mingus.

From there, the current listing leaps forward, almost to the end of his life. *What's Up* was his final album and it was made not long before his sudden death. It's a typically likeable statement. Eubanks, who can play in almost any kind of modern setting, fits in comfortably alongside Hardman's regular colleagues and, as well as the customary hard bop and blues, there are a couple of sober ballads in 'I Should Care' and 'Like Someone In Love' which, in the circumstances, enact a poignant farewell to the trumpeter's art. Exceptionally well recorded by the Steeplechase team: Hardman's sound was probably never captured better.

Roy Hargrove (born 1970)

TRUMPET, FLUGELHORN

Raised in Dallas, Hargrove emerged as something of a Wunderkind at the end of the '80s, making a string of albums for BMG and subsequently signing to Verve. He leads his own touring band and has guested on many recent albums.

*****(*) With The Tenors Of Our Time**

Verve 523019-2 *Hargrove; Ron Blake (ss, ts); Johnny Griffin, Joe Henderson, Branford Marsalis, Joshua Redman, Stanley Turrentine (ts); Cyrus Chestnut (p); Rodney Whitaker (b); Gregory Hutchinson (d).* 1/94.

While much of the new jazz of the '90s attracted criticism for excessive orthodoxy or mere executive showmanship, it's less often remarked that many of today's younger players exhibit a rhythmic bravado and harmonic lucidity which are a natural step forward from (and within) the tradition. After the sideways evolutionary paths of fusion, the so-called neo-classicism which players like Hargrove represent offers a dramatic refocusing, if not any particular radicalism. Hargrove is a highly gifted trumpeter whose facility and bright, sweet tone bring a sense of dancing fun to his music. But on his early records he was steadily working towards a gravitas that might place him in the trumpet lineage as surely as Marsalis or Faddis. Antonio Hart, a friend and college colleague, is equally impressive on his early records, his searingly pure tone placed at the service of a canny understanding of bebop alto.

After five records for Novus there was still no classic on the shelves, and Hargrove departed for Verve. (Some of his Novus albums may still be available in some territories, but basically they're gone.) *With The Tenors Of Our Time* is no masterwork, but the trumpeter rises to the challenge of having five grandmasters sit in on the different tunes – although Blake holds his own with real class on 'Once Forgotten' and with Redman on 'Mental Phrasing'. Branford gets off a good one on 'Valse Hot', and Hargrove and Turrentine enjoy themselves on 'Soppin' The Biscuit'. The trumpeter plays with fresh resolve throughout, and his flugelhorn solo on 'Never Let Me Go' is a quiet showstopper.

***** Family**

Verve 527630-2 *Hargrove; Wynton Marsalis (t); Jesse Davis (as); David 'Fathead' Newman (ts, f); Ron Blake (ts); Stephen Scott, John Hicks, Ronnie Mathews (p); Rodney Whitaker, Walter Booker, Christian McBride (b); Gregory Hutchinson, Lewis Nash, Karriem Riggins (d).* 1/95.

*****(*) Parker's Mood**

Verve 527907-2 *Hargrove; Stephen Scott (p); Christian McBride (b).* 4/95.

Family is a sequence of dedications to personal and spiritual kin that opens out into an interesting meditation on Hargrove's possible future course. Fats Navarro's 'Nostalgia', delivered as a duet with Marsalis, sounds like two parallel reflections on bebop tradition, and the ruminative pieces which open the disc include some of the trumpeter's most skilful and personalized playing. His regular band provides decisive support, but the line-up of guest stars rocks the record at some moments where it ought to be steady, and in the end this still feels like a transitional disc.

Recorded in Parker's 75th anniversary year, *Parker's Mood* is a delightful meeting of three young masters, improvising on 16 themes from Bird's repertoire. Hargrove's luminous treatment of 'Laura' provides further evidence that he may be turning into one of the music's pre-eminent ballad-players, but it's the inventive interplay between the three men that takes the session to its high level. Scott, sometimes burdened by the weight of his conceptions on his own records, plays as freely as he ever has, and McBride is simply terrific.

***** Habana**

Verve 537563-2 *Hargrove; Frank Lacy (tb); Gary Bartz (as, ss); David Sanchez (ts, ss); Chucho Valdes (p); Russell Malone (g); John Benitez (b); Horacio Hernandez (d); Jose Luis Quintana, Miguel Diaz (perc).* 1/97.

Although the packaging seems to suggest that this was cut on a long weekend in Cuba, Hargrove's Latin project emanates from an Italian concert, even if the idea was conceived by his visiting and playing with Cuban musicians. Jostling with rhythms, plangent in its solos, this is a fun, lightweight record which isn't so much a departure for the trumpeter as a sunny vacation. There's little to suggest any profound commitment to the local style or indeed anything beyond a good-natured piece of opportunism, and some of the elements (particularly Lacy's awry trombone parts) just sound wrong; but it remains an enjoyable piece of hokum, whatever the subtext. As he approached 30, wasn't it right for Hargrove to take time out to make a masterpiece, though?

****(*) Moment To Moment**

Verve 543540-2 *Hargrove; Sherman Irby (as); Larry Willis (p); Gerald Cannon (b); Willie Jones III (d); strings.* 99.

Nothing doing here, either. A strings album is something that Hargrove might well aspire to in the fullness of time; at this point, it suggests a career that's lacking purpose and direction. His current working band is terrific, and much of it plays here, but they're swamped by arrangements which at best are serviceable and merely anodyne for much of the album.

Only a major label could afford to make an album like this, but with an agenda which involves taking a safety-first route so as not to frighten radio programmers, the results are dismayingly tame.

***** Hard Groove**

Verve 065192-2 *Hargrove; Steve Coleman (as); Keith Anderson, Jacques Schwarz-Bart (ts); Karl Denson (f); Marc Cary, James Poyser, Bobby Sparks, Bernard Palladino (ky); Chalmers Alford, Cornell Dupree (g); Pino Palladino, Reggie Washington, M'shell Ndegocello (b); Willie Jones III, Jason Thomas, Gene Lake (d); Erykah Badu, Common, Q Tip, D'Angelo, Anthony Hamilton, Rene Neufville, Stephanie McKay, Shelby Johnson (v).* 1–2/02.

Roy's difficulty is that he's always playing catch-up. If he'd made this move five years earlier, it might have seemed a lot sharper. As it is, he just seems like one of several near-stars searching for an elusive hit. As it turns out, the record's not bad at all. Funk and hip-hop rub up against Hargrove's tougher inclinations: he's still a trumpeter, not a soul singer, and of course he's going to make sure he gets good space and delivers on it. The record shifts back and forth between various popular bases and nothing on it sounds like either plastic soul or artificial fusion. 'Pastor T' might be one of Hargrove's best performances on record. In the end, though, the record's like almost everything else of the type: not wholly committed to any one position, and at the mercy of its own eclecticism, it feels too transitory to have a lasting impact – or convince whatever new audience Hargrove's in search of.

Cathy Harley

PIANO

Contemporary Australian pianist.

*****(*) Tuesday's Tune**

Rufus RF028 *Harley; Warwick Alder (t); Bernie McGann (as); Craig Scott (b); Alan Turnbull (d).* 2/95.

Entirely without frills or pretension, Harley's record is typical of the kind of modern hard bop that develops away from any obvious jazz limelight and exists on its own hard-won virtues and modest inspirations. The band are a group of (if they'll excuse us) veteran Australian modernists, with McGann the name that will be most familiar to those of us listening from afar: as ever, he's a wild card, solos full of unexpected incident and strange light and dark. Everybody else keeps up, though, and Harley herself writes tunes that are both functionally effective and naggingly memorable. Particularly gratifying: the ballad 'Old Heart'.

Billy Harper (born 1943)

TENOR SAXOPHONE, ALTO SAXOPHONE

Born in Houston, he studied at North Texas State before moving to New York in 1965. A regular sideman with Art Blakey, Jones–Lewis and Gil Evans and sometimes a leader, he is a conservative radical with a formidable command of most aspects of post-bop.

*****(*) Black Saint**

Black Saint 120001 *Harper; Virgil Jones (t); Joe Bonner (p); David Friesen (b); Malcolm Pinson (d).* 7/75.

***** In Europe**

Soul Note 121001 *Harper; Everett Hollins (t); Fred Hersch (p); Louis Spears (b); Horace Arnold (d).* 1/79.

Initially influenced by Sonny Rollins, Harper got his chops playing in church before going on to work with Art Blakey, Max Roach and Gil Evans, for whom he wrote 'Priestess' and 'Thoroughbred', two of the best modern-jazz compositions in the book. Coupled to his gifts as a writer, Harper's big, gospelly solo style should have made him a star, but he has never quite achieved the breakthrough his talents deserve, and the absence of major-label interest in his work remains a serious disgrace, even during a period when many of his contemporaries were being 'rediscovered'.

Like many of his countrymen, Harper had to look to Europe for recognition, and to the Black Saint/Soul Note stable (good trivia question: which artist kicked off both imprints?) for the beginnings of a discography. *Black Saint* is still the album people associate with Harper, a strong, eclectic blend of blues, hard-edged rock patterns and the by-now-familiar preaching style. Jones and Bonner are greatly admired in Europe, too, and the pianist makes his mark on the record from the very start with his tersely romantic approach and elastic chord-patterns which add fuel to the perfervid intensity of the leader.

The Soul Note is faintly disappointing, albeit full of potential and marked by pretty much the same strengths as Harper's other work. Hersch still hadn't quite come into his own at this point and he sounds a little acid here and there, but it's a good night's work for Everett Hollins, who had also recorded with Archie Shepp and who makes a strong case for himself here. 'Calvary' is superb. Launching two important contemporary labels is no mean feat. Both albums are well worth having.

***** Destiny Is Yours**

Steeplechase SCCD 31260 *Harper; Eddie Henderson (t); Francesca Tanksley (p); Clarence Seay (b); Newman Baker (d).* 12/89.

There is a bit of a hole in the discography at this point, almost a decade in which Harper was mainly involved in other projects, and other people's projects. This, though, unveils what was to be a working band. Henderson very nearly steals it, but it is the solid, melodic playing of Chessie Tanksley that holds the date together. The other two members of the group are somewhat mechanical – but, oddly, this contributes to our abiding feeling that this date is reminiscent of the Ayler brothers' association.

*****(*) Live On Tour In The Far East**

Steeplechase SCCD 31311 *Harper; Eddie Henderson (t); Francesca Tanksley (p); Louis Spears (b); Newman Baker (d).* 4/91.

****** Live On Tour In The Far East: Volume 2**

Steeplechase SCCD 31321 *As above.* 4/91.

***** Live On Tour In The Far East: Volume 3**

Steeplechase SCCD 31331 *As above.* 4/91.

This documents a poised and confident band. Having Henderson and Tanksley on the strength must have made an enormous difference, and both horns and piano are playing at full stretch for most of the first two volumes. It's a set which palls when less compelling material is brought in, and only then because the rhythm section is far from inspiring. The version of 'Priestess' on *Volume Two* is definitive, for now and all time, and there is a wonderful cover of 'My Funny Valentine'.

****** Soul Of An Angel**

Metropolitan 1120 *Harper; Eddie Henderson (t); Francesca Tanksley (p); Clarence Seay (b); Newman Baker (d).* 01.

Sterling modern jazz from a long established band. Henderson's mournful intro to 'Thine Is The Glory' is breathtakingly powerful and tees up one of Harper's best solos for years, thoughtful, well-structured and not a note too long. Chessy Tanksley has grown steadily in stature and her comping and soloing confirm the boss's confidence in her. 'Was It Here ... Is It There?' is relatively orthodox hard bop, but the title-track, with John Clark drafted in on french horn, is much more ambitious. Reminiscent of the classic 'Priestess', it weaves a waltz feel into something rather more complex, with each of the players hinting at a different time frame. One wonders if this was a miraculous first take, or if the band worked hard to get an effect so subtle, mysterious and beautiful.

Winard Harper (born 1962)

DRUMS

Born in Baltimore, Harper was already playing drums by the time of his teens and was with Dexter Gordon in 1982. He spent four years with Betty Carter, then worked with his brother Philip in the Harper Brothers Band, before leading his own dates.

****(*) Trap Dancer**

Savant SCD 2013 *Harper; Patrick Rickman (t); J. D. Allen (ts); George Cables (p); Eric Revis (b); Cecil Brooks (d).* 12/97.

***** Winard**

Savant SCD 2021 *As above, except add Abdou Mboup (perc).* 12/98.

Harper is a strong and capable drummer, recognized early by some top-flight players, but it may be that his emergence as a leader was premature, the success of the Harper Bros notwithstanding. Both of these discs are filled with brief, taster-like pieces which hint at directions without fulfilling them. Each has a quota of hard-bop hits such as 'Work Song', along with originals from band members that never receive any kind of development (possibly with radio play in mind). The second disc is ahead of the first, but that's not saying a great deal. Of the participants, Allen, who gets some clear space to work in on some tracks, is easily the standout performer.

Some aspects of what became a recognizable percussion style are already evident, not least a gift for bright, talkative work on cymbals, which are Winard's speciality.

***** Faith**

Savant 2030 *Harper; Patrick Rickman (t); Wycliffe Gordon (tb); Brian Horton (ts); George Cables (p); Brandon Owens (b); Alioune Faye (djembe); Abdou Mboup (perc); Carrie Smith (v).* 99.

***** A Time For The Soul**

Savant SCD 2048 *Harper; Patrick Rickman (t); Brian Horton (ss, ts); Jeb Patton (p); Ameen Saleem (b); Kevin Jones, Scott Harper (perc).* 1/03.

Faith is already much more promising and this time the inclusion of George Cables, somewhat lost on the earlier records, makes sense. Billed as a collaboration with singer Carrie Smith, the record looks at faith in all its many dimensions, and there is a real sense of uplift on tracks like 'Lift Every Voice And Sing'. Smith delivers the line with conviction but without mawkishness and fellow-guest Gordon confirms the trombone's standing as God's own instrument.

Big George is also effective on 'The Things We Did Last Summer' and trumpeter Patrick 'The Face' Rickman is given plenty of room to manoeuvre on his own feature 'Face Man'. Patrick also has a starring role on the later *A Time For The Soul*, on which the inspirational element is more in the intensity of the playing than in any lyrical content; the deity is even given a measure of anonymity on 'All Praise To G-d'. 'About Face' is Rickman's spot here and he tackles it with gusto. 'Dat Dere' is perfectly pitched and a nice vehicle for the ever-developing Horton. There are fewer 'ethnic' touches this time round, though there are important percussion parts for Jones and brother Scott Harper. 'Alone Together' is an odd inclusion and doesn't really work but as a whole the album is a success and suggests that Harper is going to be around for some time.

Tom Harrell (born 1946)

TRUMPET, FLUGELHORN, PIANO

Born in Urbana, Illinois, he was influenced by Clifford Brown and, later, John Coltrane. After service with Woody Herman and Stan Kenton, he started playing bop with Horace Silver, an association which added Blue Mitchell to his roster of influences. Despite often disabling illness, Harrell has created a substantial career as sideman and leader. His limpid tone in ballads is balanced by a ferocious attack on up-tempo numbers, with a round, full and very brassy timbre. Harrell is also a fine composer.

***** Moon Alley**

Criss Cross 1018 *Harrell; Kenny Garrett (as, f); Kenny Barron (p); Ray Drummond (b); Ralph Peterson (d).* 12/85.

*****(*) Open Air**

Steeplechase SCCD 31220 *Harrell; Bob Rockwell (ts); Hal Galper (p); Steve Gilmore (b); Bill Goodwin (d).* 5/86.

Anyone who has seen Tom Harrell perform live will understand the transformative power of music. When not playing, he stands slumped and bowed, stock-still in what looks like mute agony. When it comes time to take a solo, it is as if an electric charge has passed through him. Harrell is one of the finest harmonic improvisers in jazz today, a player with a fierce tone who is also capable of playing the most delicate ballad with almost unbearable feeling.

We have been criticized for pointing out that he has battled with psychiatric illness for many years. It does not define him, either personally or creatively, but schizophrenia has been a shaping influence for much of his adult life. Schizophrenics never make any bones about it, and Harrell has even been known to joke about his condition, once commenting as he entered a hotel suite that there was a room for each of his personalities. There are two playing personalities. They are not yet dramatically separated on the two early records as leader. *Moon Alley* has its slightly morose side, but this has as much to do with the recording as with Harrell's temperament. He is hugely secure in technique, already a veteran, evoking everyone from Kenny Dorham when at full tilt, to Freddie Hubbard when doubling on flugelhorn, to Miles inevitably. Teamed with Kenny Garrett, one of Miles's last saxophone players, he sounds bred in the bone, slightly out of synch with the rapid progressions of 'Scrapple From The Apple'. *Open Air* is a little flat. Galper is too lush and fulsome, and the rest of the rhythm section hangs back. Rockwell is a liability in the ensembles, though a fresh and often provocative soloist.

*****(*) Stories**

Contemporary C 14043 *Harrell; Bob Berg (ts); Niels Lan Doky (p); John Scofield (g); Ray Drummond (b); Billy Hart (d).* 1/88.

*****(*) Sail Away**

Original Jazz Classics OJCCD 1095 *Harrell; Joe Lovano (ss, ts); David Liebman (ss); Cheryl Pyle (f); James Williams (p); John Abercrombie (g, g syn); Ray Drummond (b); Adam Nussbaum (d).* 89.

*****(*) Form**

Contemporary C 14059 *Harrell; Joe Lovano (ts); Danilo Perez (p); Charlie Haden (b); Paul Motian (d).* 4/90.

****** Visions**

Contemporary C 14063 *Harrell; George Robert (as); Joe Lovano (ts, ss); Bob Berg, David Liebman (ss); Cheryl Pyle (f); Niels Lan Doky (p); John Abercrombie (g, g syn); Ray Drummond, Charlie Haden, Reggie Johnson (b); Bill Goodwin, Billy Hart, Paul Motian, Adam Nussbaum (d).* 4/87–4/90.

The records for Contemporary were something of a purple patch. *Visions* is actually a compilation of material recorded over a span of time during which Harrell recovered some of the snap and pointed delivery people noted during his sojourn with Horace Silver. Every now and then, as on 'Visions Of Gaudi' with Liebman and Abercrombie, he delivers something that is as hard-edged and as finely detailed as mosaic. He spends most of the album on flugelhorn, but 'Suspended View', with Berg on soprano, is a trumpet performance of magical skill, fleeting, ambiguous and endlessly replayable. Only 'April Mist' seems conventional.

Sail Away reappeared as an Original Jazz Classic in 2003 and certainly deserves that appellation. Harrell's writing – 'Eons', 'Dream In June', 'Visions Of Gaudi' (included as a bonus track) – is the sharpest it had yet been and a thoroughly sympathetic band help deliver a pointedly challenging statement that still sounds fresh and engaging 15 years later.

****** Passages**

Chesky JD 64 *Harrell; Joe Lovano (as, ts, ss); Danilo Perez (p); Peter Washington (b); Paul Motian (d); Cafe (perc).* 10/91.

*****(*) Upswing**

Chesky JD 103 *As above, except add Phil Woods (as), Bill Goodwin (d); omit Cafe, Motian.* 6/93.

Who knows what personal agony lies behind a title like *Upswing*, however wry and ironic it is? These are marvellous records, polished, forceful, beautifully recorded and absolutely fresh. Harrell's ability to shift up through the changes without losing the momentum of a song is uncanny and seems to be done with ideas to spare. On the second outing Motian is missed for the sheer subtlety with which he colours a phrase and the almost miraculous way that he can appear to be playing free while sustaining an absolutely metronomic line underneath the horns. Harrell and Lovano have struck up one of the great jazz partnerships and seem genuinely to enjoy teasing out each other's idiosyncrasies. Perez might quibble about the sound (and possibly the piano) he has been given, but he too has become an integral part of the trumpeter's concept. Woods is there to return a compliment, another former employer who has publicly acknowledged Harrell's gifts. And they are manifest; first-rate modern jazz.

CORE COLLECTION

****** Labyrinth**

RCA Victor 09026 68512 *Harrell; Steve Turre (tb); Don Braden, Joe Lovano (ts); Gary Smulyan (bcl); Rob Botti (ob); Kenny Werner (p); Larry Grenadier (b); Billy Hart (d); Leon Parker (perc).* 1/96.

Fine as the two Cheskys were, *Labyrinth* was Harrell's real coming out as a major figure. Just turning 50, he came to it with renewed fire. In a sense, the album takes him full circle, teaming him with players who were part of the Criss Cross operation almost a decade earlier. Braden and Smulyan have gone on to their own projects, and Turre is now an established star. Harrell writes all the tunes, with the exception of 'Darn That Dream', which is an overdubbed duet with himself on piano – and a piano formerly used by Bill Evans at that. The larger-scale arrangements with horns, like 'Majesty', 'Sun Cycle' and 'Blue In One', take him to a new phase of musical organization, a sequence of shifting themes which often defy

major/minor distinction and which resolve in the most unexpected ways, though individual parts sound perfectly logical. Harrell sticks mainly to trumpet, reserving flugelhorn for 'Marimba Song', with the basic group of Braden, Werner, Grenadier and Hart, and for 'Darn That Dream'. An essential modern record: the superlatives have pretty much been exhausted.

***(*) The Art Of Rhythm

RCA Victor 09026 68924 *Harrell; Dewey Redman (ts); David Sanchez (ts, ss); Gregory Tardy (cl, ts); Gary Smulyan (bs, bcl); David Kassoff (ob); Romero Lubambo, Mike Stern (g); Danilo Perez (p, harmonium); Regina Carter (vn); Ron Lawrence (vla); Akua Dixon (clo); Bryan Carrott (mar); David Finck, Ugonna Okegwo (b); Duduka Fonseca, Leon Parker (d); Waltinho Anastacio, Milton Cardona, Adam Cruz, Natalie Cushman (perc).* 5–7/97.

What has become increasingly obvious over time is how ebullient and rhythmic a player Harrell is. Listening back to some of the darker and more subdued tracks on previous albums, having heard this pungent set, one understands that he has learnt a good deal from Dizzy's Afro-Hispanic experiments. *The Art Of Rhythm* isn't, though, a soaraway south-of-the-border set. It might equally be subtitled 'the art of colour' or 'the art of arrangement'. Never before has Harrell, who is the composer of all ten tunes, experimented more freely with instrumental combinations. The string and guitar writing, for both Lubambo and Stern, is exquisite. He opens in gentle mode with clarinet, acoustic guitar and string trio on 'Petals Danse', builds in woodwinds elsewhere, but also allows himself a hefty dose of jazz horns on 'Oasis' (sharing solo space with Dewey Redman), 'Doo Bop' (a feature for Tardy's tenor) and 'Madrid'. He leans heavily on flugelhorn, perhaps too much so, though Harrell has always been able to give the bigger horn the bite and attack of trumpet when so required. A wonderful, accomplished record from an important player. The success of *Labyrinth* has given him considerable artistic leverage; here, he has used it to maximum effect.

*** Time's Mirror

RCA Victor 09026 63524-2 *Harrell; Joe Magnarelli, Chris Rogers, David Weiss, James Zollar (t, flhn); Earl Gardner (t); Conrad Herwig, Mike Fagan, Curtis Hasselbring (tb); Douglas Purviance (btb); Craig Bailey, Mark Gross, Alex Foster, Don Braden, David Schumacher (reeds); Xavier Davis (p); Kenny Davis (b); Carl Allen (d).* 3/99.

Our rather miserly rating shouldn't deter Harrell admirers from investigating this big-band set, but it does feel a little careful and even antiseptic here and there. It's a selection of Harrell charts which in some cases go back a long way ('Autumn Leaves' is dated to 1964) and, as thoughtful and accomplished as the writing is, it's sometimes too thoughtful and accomplished: some of the music looks inwards at the point where it should surely sound welcoming. 'Time's Mirror' itself is a handsome piece, which acts as a gorgeous setting for Tom's flugelhorn playing, yet only occasionally does that lustre spread through the rest of the music.

*** Paradise

RCA 63738 *Harrell; Jimmy Greene (ts); Xavier Davis (p); Freddie Bryant (g); Louis Colin (hp); Cenovia Cummins, Belinda Whitney (vn); Juliet Haffner (vla); Daniel Miller, Jeffrey Szabo (clo); Ugonna Okegwo (b); Adam Cruz, Leon Parker (d).* 01.

An intriguing project that is very different from the usual formulaic with-strings format. Harrell seems interested in incorporating some elements of classical practice into a bop-influenced jazz setting. 'Baroque Steps', the long 'Nightime', 'Wind Chant' and 'Paradise Spring', as well as the two-part 'Morning Prayer' all utilize a small string section not so much for sound colour as to create a different rhythmic and harmonic dynamic to the usual jazz group. The nine pieces seem organized according to some deep-seated thematic principle, very subtle and aware without being forbidding. Tom plays with his usual blend of fire and expression, utilizing Latin rhythms here and there. The strings are handled deftly, without mush and with impressive definition.

***(*) Live At The Village Vanguard

Bluebird 63910 *Harrell; Jimmy Greene (ts); Xavier Davis (p); Ugonna Okegwo (b); Quincy Davis (d).* 11/01.

This is Harrell's first official live record and it was worth the wait. He kicks off the set with the tough 'Asia Minor', which gets the band working up a sweat. What follows is more unorthodox. 'Manhattan 3 a.m.' has a misterioso feel that dramatically changes the temperature of the set. 'Blues In Una Sea' is one of his most original conceptions and a curiously estranging experience played at this length. 'A Child's Dream' and the closing 'Party Song' are lighter and more joyous. 'Where The Rain Begins', co-written with Angela Harrell, is appropriately divided in mood, with an off-kilter bounce to the main section and a softly mournful quality to the quieter intermezzo.

Of the other players, Okegwo surprisingly turns out to be the most effective. His solo on 'Manhattan 3 a.m.' is among the most memorable on the disc. Inevitably, though, the set is dominated by Harrell himself, punching out notes or slurring together long patterns of tones in a way that is unique in modern jazz but rooted in the masters.

*** Wise Children

RCA 53016 *Harrell; Kuamu Adilifu, Mondre Moffett (t); Luis Bonilla (tb); Douglas Purviance (btb); Vincent Chancey, John Clark (frhn); Howard Johnson (tba); Myron Walden (as); Milton Greene (ts, f); David Schumacher (bs); Xavier Davis (p, org, ky, kalimba); Marvin Sewell (g); Ugonna Okegwo, Reuben Rodgers (b); Quincy Davis (d); Milton Cardona, Joe Gonzalez (perc); Jane Monheit, Dianne Reeves, Cassandra Wilson (v); strings.* 02.

As on *Paradise*, Harrell has a markedly original approach to orchestral setting. Even so, the spirit of Gil Evans hangs over this lovely disc and especially on tracks like the opening 'Paz' and the long 'Kalimba', which allows another Davis to explore his repertory of instruments. The leader's horn never has any trouble breaking through sometimes dense textures, but the mix is subtle enough to give the arrangements a fluidity and speed of response one would expect from a smaller group. A couple of tracks – 'Radiant Moon' and 'Snow' – misfire slightly, mainly because Harrell's soloing is less emphatic than usual, and the vocalists aren't really integral to the whole, though Harrell's touch round singers is as good as ever.

Joe Harriott (1928–73)

ALTO SAXOPHONE

A Jamaican who came to London in 1951, Harriott played bebop alto but formulated a method of free jazz somewhat independent of Coleman's music. Recorded with his own quintet, and later in a collaboration with Indian violinist John Mayer, but he was marginalized by his times and eventually was killed by cancer.

***** Indo Jazz-Fusions I & II**

Redial 538 048-2 *Harriott; Shake Keane, Kenny Wheeler (t, flhn); Chris Taylor (f); Pat Smythe (p); John Mayer (vn, hpd); Diwan Motihar (sitar); Coleridge Goode (b); Bobby Orr, Jackie Dougan, Allan Ganley (d); Chandrahas Paigankar (tambura); Keshav Sathe (tabla).* 67, 68.

***** Indo-Jazz Suite**

Koch KOC CD 8512 *As above.* n.d.

Believers in the theory of simultaneous evolution always mention Joe Harriott, who seems to have worked out free jazz for himself, just as controversial Americans like Ornette Coleman were making similar noises. Unlike Coleman, Harriott played with a transparent emotion, like a blues man. Apart from Kippie Moeketsi, Dudu Pukwana and Jackie McLean on his day, no one has ever blown an alto saxophone with such obvious pain *and* joy.

Harriott suffered ill-health, and tuberculosis compromised his recording career substantially. Nevertheless, he has left at least these astonishing memorials to his genius. *Indo-Jazz Fusions* was a project more often cited and discussed than actually heard. Its reappearance on CD and Polygram's generous repackaging of Harriott's classic Jazzland sessions push past the mythology of the brilliant West Indian as a doomed tragedian. Like Charlie Parker, Harriott at his most typical is an effortless melodist. Look past the more forbiddingly abstract titles on now-deleted records such as *Free Form* and *Abstract* – 'Subject', 'Parallel', 'Straight Lines', 'Idioms' – and hear something altogether different. 'Calypso' on the 1960 session is the most obvious pointer, but almost everywhere Harriott blends freedom and abstraction with blues-inflected changes jazz in a way that has become almost definitive of British improvisation.

Indo-Jazz Fusions is more properly a John Mayer record, but Harriott is its defining presence. Much discussed, it remains a slightly unsatisfactory experience, not so much a synthesis as an awkward juxtaposition. It is performed by a double quintet of jazz and subcontinental players, somewhat on the model of Ornette's *Free Jazz* group. But whereas there the logic of the thing was the individual personality of the soloists, here the problems are more deep-rooted. Rhythms and tonalities lie alongside one another but fail to gel. After 30 years the original excitement of hearing these unexpected sounds has faded somewhat, but partly because the scalar experiments Mayer was making, building jazz improvisations on raga forms and on unfamiliar nine- and ten-beat patterns, have since 1968 become part of an extended jazz syntax. Once again, British-based musicians seemed to be moving in parallel to their American colleagues and in some cases ahead of them; the highly sophisticated rhythmic patterns John Coltrane and Rashied Ali were using as foundation blocks on some of Trane's last recordings are deployed here with great ease. By the same token, Harriott and Mayer sound untroubled about abandoning conventional changes.

The reissue includes original liner-notes by Max Harrison and Ian Carr and a retrospective essay after 30 years by Professor John Mayer. Taken together with the music, they establish a context for a historically significant record. New listeners simply shouldn't expect too much from it.

Barry Harris (born 1929)

PIANO

One of the leading Detroit pianists, Harris subsequently arrived in New York in the late '50s and has remained there ever since. The preferred accompanist of both Coleman Hawkins and Sonny Stitt, Harris's bebop methodology owes much to both Powell and Monk, while mining his own gentler persuasions. In the '80s and '90s he became revered as one of the great teachers in the music, although this has largely kept him away from recording.

***** At The Jazz Workshop**

Original Jazz Classics OJC 208 *Harris; Sam Jones (b); Louis Hayes (d).* 5/60.

***** Preminado**

Original Jazz Classics OJC 486 *Harris; Joe Benjamin (b); Elvin Jones (d).* 12/60–1/61.

*****(*) Listen To Barry Harris**

Original Jazz Classics OJC 999 *Harris (p solo).* 7/61.

****(*) Newer Than New**

Original Jazz Classics 1062 *Harris; Lonnie Hillyer (t); Charles McPherson (as); Ernie Farrow (b); Clifford Jarvis (d).* 9/61.

*****(*) Chasin' The Bird**

Original Jazz Classics OJC 872 *Harris; Bob Cranshaw (b); Clifford Jarvis (d).* 5/62.

*****(*) Luminescence!**

Original Jazz Classics OJC 924 *Harris; Slide Hampton (tb); Junior Cook (ts); Pepper Adams (bs); Bob Cranshaw (b); Lennie McBrowne (d).* 4/67.

The career of Barry Harris suggests a self-effacing man for, although he is among the most accomplished and authentic of second-generation bebop pianists, his name has never excited much more than quiet respect among followers of the music. Musicians and students – Harris is a noted teacher – hold him in higher esteem. One of the Detroit school of pianists which includes Tommy Flanagan and Hank Jones, Harris's style suggests Bud Powell as an original mentor, yet a slowed-down, considered version of Powell's tumultuous manner. Despite the tempos, Harris gets the same dark timbres from the keyboard.

His records are perhaps unjustly little known. There is no singleton masterpiece among them, just a sequence of graceful, satisfying sessions which suggest that Harris has been less interested in posterity via recordings and more in what he can give to jazz by example and study. Nevertheless, he cut several records for Prestige and Riverside in the '60s, and most are now back in the catalogue. The live date from 1960 finds him with the ebullient rhythm section of Cannonball Adderley, and the music is swinging if not especially absorbing. Rather better is the date with Elvin Jones, which features some fiery interplay between piano and drums, although the highlight is probably an uncommonly thoughtful solo reading of 'I Should Care'. *Listen To Barry Harris* is that rarity, a bebop pianist by himself, and while one sometimes misses the buzz of the rhythm section this is a thoughtful and focused example of Harris's music, from standards such as 'I Didn't Know What Time It Was' to characteristic excursions like 'Teenie'. *Chasin' The Bird* is a smart exercise in bebop piano: unfussy, unpretentious, but carried off with a distilled intensity that keeps the attention. *Luminescence!* brings together a fine group. We were rather cool about this in our last edition, but further acquaintance has revealed a thoroughgoing commitment which transcends the regulation professionalism of these players. Adams, Cook and Hampton solo with a taut assertiveness that makes a 1967 bebop date seem entirely relevant, despite its time and place. The only duffer is *Newer Than New*, which certainly isn't: a rote hard-bop date made on a day when, perhaps, nobody felt like saying very much.

CORE COLLECTION

****** Magnificent!**

Original Jazz Classics OJC 1026 *Harris; Ron Carter (b); Leroy Williams (d).* 11/69.

Hard to argue with the title on this immaculate recital. Turning 40, Harris is musing on his uncluttered bebop roots in 'Bean And The Boys' and seeing how far he can push the envelope in the ingenious fresh voicings of 'Ah-Leu-Cha', in which Carter is a willing partner. 'Just Open Your Heart' is a Monkian original that Harris subjects to a playful twist. 'Dexterity' takes us back to first-generation bebop, but again Harris casts it in a darker, more evasive setting. A neglected classic of its day.

***** For The Moment**

Uptown UPCD 2747 *Harris; Rufus Reid (b); Leroy Williams (d).* 3/84.

An enjoyable souvenir of one of Harris's '80s gigs, at the Jazz Cultural Theatre in New York. The JCT was organized by the pianist around his educational activities (it has since, alas, closed) and as a listening room it specialized in this kind of informal gig. As ever, the set's full of Monk, bebop and Harris originals in the classic manner, and while the date has its sloppy side – sound is only functional, and the music's ragged sometimes – it's in the spirit. Harris has made several later records, but at present it's only his earlier music which is in print – a rather poor showing for one of the great players of bebop piano.

Bill Harris (1916–73)

TROMBONE

Born in Philadelphia, Harris had an anonymous time of it until joining Woody Herman in 1944, with whom he stayed on and off until 1959. He disappeared into Las Vegas bands in the '60s and eventually retired from music.

***** Live At Birdland 1952**

Baldwin Street Music BJG-501 *Harris; Pete Candoli (t); John LaPorta, Salvatore Delegge (cl); Ted Wheeler (f); Mickey Folus (bcl); Eddie 'Lockjaw' Davis, Ray Abrams, Flip Phillips (ts); Don Abney, Horace Silver, Ralph Burns (p); Billy Bauer, George Burnes (g); Gene Ramey, Connie Henry, Chubby Jackson (b); Ed Shaughnessy, Alvin Burroughs, Barrett Deems (d).* 4/45–5/52.

****** Bill Harris And Friends**

Original Jazz Classics OJC 083 *Harris; Ben Webster (ts); Jimmy Rowles (p); Red Mitchell (b); Stan Levey (d).* 9/57.

Harris was always among the most distinctive and sometimes among the greatest of jazz trombonists. His style was based firmly on swing-era principles, yet he seemed to look both forward and back. His slurred notes and shouting phrases recalled a primitive jazz period, yet his knowing juxtapositions and almost macabre sense of humour were entirely modern. But he made few appearances on record away from Woody Herman's orchestra and is now a largely forgotten figure. *Bill Harris And Friends* should be known far more widely. Both Harris and Webster are in admirable form and make a surprisingly effective partnership. Ben is at his ripest on 'I Surrender, Dear' and 'Where Are You', and Harris stops the show in solo after solo, whether playing short, bemused phrases or barking out high notes. An amusing reading of 'Just One More Chance' caps everything. The remastering favours the horns, but the sound is warmly effective.

Baldwin Street Music's reissue brings three jam sessions from Birdland back to life, some of which have previously been on obscure vinyl in poorer sound (though the sound here still asks for patience). Harris shines throughout, peppering his fast solos with an armoury of techniques and making an extravagant essay out of 'You're Blasé'. However, his surroundings are dull, and Davis goes tiresomely over the top on his appearance. To fill out the disc, though, they've added Harris's two Keynote sessions of 1945–6. The first is crackling swing-to-bop by a fine septet (with Candoli, Phillips, Bauer and Burns), plus ballads for Harris and Phillips; the second puts the trombonist in front of a Burns-led aggregation of woodwinds. This is a patchy collection, but it's still essential for Harris acolytes.

Craig Harris (born 1954)

TROMBONE

Harris has played with Sun Ra, Abdullah Ibrahim, Henry Threadgill and David Murray, and has led bands which have bridged post-bop with funk. None of his own discs have really broken through to an audience, though, and he seems somewhat in shadow at present.

*****(*) Black Bone**

Soul Note 121055 *Harris; George Adams (ts); Donald Smith (p); Fred Hopkins (b); Charli Persip (d).* 1/83.

Harris plays in a strong, highly vocalized style which draws directly on the innovations of former Mingus sideman, Jimmy Knepper, and on players like Grachan Moncur III and Roswell Rudd who, in reaction to the trombone's recent desuetude, have gone back to the New Orleans and Dixieland traditions in an attempt to restore and revise the instrument's 'natural' idiom. This early set finds him in genial post-bop company. Adams was the perfect partner in any modern/traditional synthesis, and the rhythm section (Smith occasionally excepted) is rock-solid on such pieces as 'Conjure Man' and 'Song For Psychedelic Souls', which could almost have been by Roland Kirk. Excellent.

***** Shelter**

Winter & Winter 834408 *Harris; Eddie Allen (t); Don Byron (cl, bcl, bs); Rod Williams (p); Anthony Cox (b); Pheeroan akLaff (d).* 11–12/86.

****(*) Blackout In The Square Root Of Soul**
Winter & Winter 919015 *As above, except omit Williams; add Clyde Criner (syn); Jean-Paul Bourelly (g); Ralph Peterson (d).* 87.

Originally released on JMT and only rescued from oblivion in 2002, these are both Tailgaters Tales projects. Though they strive for a certain coherence of sound and theme, each succeeds only in parts. The earlier record is dominated by the large-scale 'Shelter Suite', an ambitious idea that is scrappy and self-conscious in delivery creating a fatal slackening of pace after the energy of the opening 'Africans Unite'. How much of this music is seriously agit-prop and to what extent Harris is tailgating a fashion for streetwise political pop isn't clear, but it jars.

Don Byron was emerging as a new star when these discs were made and he's certainly an important presence on both of them. On *Shelter*, he picks up on the leader's tendency to hector and most of his solo statements would have been improved by a bit of toning down. Harris himself is a formidable technician who now and again seems short of ideas and resorts to sheer dynamics. 'Cootie' catches him at his best, though he also does some interesting work on 'Sound Sketches', right at the end of the album. By then, though, it's too late.

On the second record, the fusion-influenced backgrounds from Criner and Bourelly impart a certain energy, but it seems at odds with the rest of the group, and particularly Harris's own sound. The title-track comes first and at ten minutes is the most substantial piece on the record, a strange amalgam of funk, free jazz and classic styles. Byron provides some of its best moments, though elsewhere on the album he seems out of place. Harris himself is wonderful on 'Love Joy', but it might have been more effective if he'd stuck with a trimmed down acoustic setting.

Blackout ... appeared immediately after we went to press with our last edition, so it has been with us for some time. Even repeated hearings fail to deliver. A disappointment.

*****(*) F-Stops**
Soul Note 121255 *Harris; John Stubblefield (ts); Hamiet Bluiett (bs); Bill White (g); Darrell Grant (p, ky); Calvin Jones (b); Tony Lewis (d).* 6/93.

A fascinating interconnected suite of themes and observations, realized by the best band Harris has had in a decade, if one leaves aside the more mainstream/crossover Tailgaters Tales. Using trombone and didjeridu, he conjures up dark, roiling shapes that confirm his growing interest in John Coltrane's music. Bluiett is the ideal partner in this enterprise and Stubblefield, having done some similar things as a dep with the World Saxophone Quartet and on his own account, seems absolutely across the music. Nothing new from him in several years, though.

Eddie Harris (1934–96)

TENOR SAXOPHONE, KEYBOARDS, TRUMPET, VOCAL

A Chicagoan, Harris learned several instruments in his youth and finally settled on sax as the main one. Scored a million-selling hit with a version of 'Exodus' in 1960, then made many records and experimented with electronic sax, a reed trumpet and other stylistic quirks. A great crowd-pleaser, but often at odds with critical acceptance, Harris remained a master technician, and in his final years, touring as a solo, he proved his enduring toughness as an improviser.

***** Exodus To Jazz + Mighty Like A Rose**
Vee Jay VJ-019 *Harris; Willie Pickens (p); Joe Diorio (g); William Yancey (b); Harold Jones (d).* 1–4/61.

***** A Study In Jazz + Breakfast At Tiffany's**
Vee Jay VJ-020 *As above, except add John Avant (tb), Charles Stepney (vib), Roland Faulkner (g), Donald Garrett, Richard Evans (b), Marshall Thompson, Earl Thomas (d).* 61–62.

Harris got off to a tremendous start with his first album, *Exodus To Jazz*, with the title-theme selling a million in single form. It rather knocked his jazz credibility, but Harris was a complex talent anyway and his range of ideas was a peculiar mix of the ingenious and the bizarre. His tenor sound was high – so high that he once received votes in a 'Best Alto' poll – and his tonalities suggested a kinship with the avant-garde which he actually had nothing to do with, preferring soft hard-bop or boogaloo situations that drew on the blues and gospel strains of his native Chicago. The first four Vee Jay albums have been reissued in these two-in-one discs, and they're a pleasing, likeable lot, if hardly immortal documents. 'Down' (*A Study In Jazz*) shows how useful a blues player he was, but the amusing 'Olifant Gesang' from the same album shows his wild side: blowing through the neckpiece, blowing without the neckpiece, using a trombone mouthpiece on the body of the sax. The earlier set is slightly preferred, since the *Tiffany's* disc is one of those jazz-at-the-movies albums that were fashionable at the time and is nothing special at all.

***** Here Comes The Judge**
Columbia 492533-2 *Harris; others unlisted, but may include Kenny Burrell (g), Bob Cranshaw (b), Billy Brooks (d), unknown organist.* 64–65.

A mild-mannered set of standards and current pop themes ('Goldfinger', 'People') cut during Harris's brief stay with Columbia. The one track he gets to stretch out on is 'That's Tough' at the end, a good one. Shoddily packaged with no information about the date.

***** The In Sound / Mean Greens**
Rhino / Atlantic 8122-71515-2 *Harris; Ray Codrington (t, perc); Cedar Walton (p); Sonny Phillips (org); Ron Carter (b); Billy Higgins, Bucky Taylor (d); Ray Barretto (perc).* 3–6/66.

***** The Electrifying Eddie Harris / Plug Me In**
Rhino/Atlantic R2 71516 *Harris; Melvin Lastie, Jimmy Owens, Joe Newman, James Bossy (t); Garnett Brown, Tom McIntosh (tb); King Curtis, David 'Fathead' Newman (ts); Haywood Henry (bs); Jodie Christian (p); Chuck Rainey, Ron Carter, Melvin Jackson (b); Richard Smith, Grady Tate (d); Ray Barretto, Joe Wohletz (perc).* 4/67–3/68.

*****(*) Artist's Choice: The Eddie Harris Anthology**
Rhino/Atlantic R2 71514 2CD *As above, except add Ray Codrington, Don Ellis, Benny Bailey (t), Willie Pickens, Cedar Walton, Muhal Richard Abrams, Milcho Leviev, Les McCann (p), Ronald Muldrow, Joe Diorio (g), Leroy Vinnegar, Rufus Reid, Bradley Bobo (b), Billy Higgins, Billy James, Billy Hart, Harold Jones, Donald Dean, Paul Humphrey (d), Felix Henry, Marshall Thompson (perc).* 1/61–2/76.

When he moved to Atlantic, Harris continued experimenting with electric saxes, trumpets played with sax mouthpieces and other gimmicks, with varying levels of success. The *Artist's Choice* compilation picks tracks from 16 albums, the best of them making a good case for Harris's eminence: he's no genius improviser, and many a solo seems to get too pooped to continue, but he had a knack for making simple licks and phrases fit on shuffling rhythms and have it all sound great. There's the extravagant range which became his trademark: the straight-ahead post-bop of 'Freedom Jazz Dance'; pretty pop-jazz with 'The Shadow Of Your Smile', a growling big-band chart in '1974 Blues', the knockout funk of 'Is It In' and the ragbag electric sax treatment of 'Giant Steps'. Much of it sounds hopelessly dated in the age of digital keyboards, but that only adds to the charm of Harris's futurism. The individual albums from the period are a patchy lot, evidenced by the pair of two-in-one reissues. Whatever easy-listening niche Harris, Nesuhi Ertegun (first album) and Arif Mardin (the next two) may have been thinking about, the saxophonist's strange sound and compulsive drive keep turning it inside out. He plays 'Shadow Of Your Smile' almost entirely straight, then plugs his way through whistling high notes which might have defeated even David Murray. His sentimental streak lets him get away with the likes of 'It Was A Very Good Year', but nothing of the time gave up the funk better than 'Freedom Jazz Dance'; and the first version of 'Listen Here', which pairs Harris on electric piano with Sonny Phillips on organ, makes a neat match with the second, where Harris is literally plugged in – to his Varitone sax, which has the same pre-digital quaintness as the oldest Moog synthesizers. It helps, for sure, that the first two albums had Walton, Carter and Higgins as the principal rhythm section, and Ray Codrington makes up the numbers without disgracing himself. The tracks from *The Electrifying Eddie Harris* have some hot stuff too, especially the choogling 'Sham Time', but there are almost bizarre moments such as 'Theme In Search Of A Movie' (baroque slush) and even a farewell waltz, 'I Don't Want No One But You'. Those from *Plug Me In* are more like a downright mess, the sax hollering against the brass to little purpose.

★★(★) Live At Newport / Instant Death
Collectables CD 6402 *Harris; Muhal Richard Abrams, Jodie Christian (p); Louie Spears, Rufus Reid (b); Bob Crowder, Billy James (d); Henry Gibson (perc).* 70–72.

A couple more of the Atlantic sessions reissued here. Eddie's set at Newport begins with what sound like spirit voices talking, before going into funky fun of the order of 'Carry On Brother' and the erroneous prophecy 'Don't You Know The Future's In Space?'. A dated-sounding set. *Instant Death* is a bit more cheerful than its title but in the end is similarly lightweight: too scrappy to boil water as a convincing record.

★★(★) I Need Some Money
Atlantic 7567-80781-2 *Harris; Ronald Muldrow (g, guitorgan); Bradley Bobo (g); Rufus Reid (b); Calvin Barnes (d); Frederick Walker (perc).* 75.

One of the later Atlantics and an uninspiring selection for the label's 50th anniversary release. Eddie's gimmicks – which include singing through the electric sax and playing his reed trumpet – overwhelm the musical content here, and the thin production makes the keyboards and rhythm sections sound even weedier than they were. The final 'That's It' gets a nice groove going, but it's too late. Either *Excursions* or *Is It In* would have been a better choice. This one is also available coupled with David Newman's *Bigger & Better* on Collectables CD 6408.

★(★) Yeah You Right
Eastside EURCD 801 *Harris; Dieter Ammann (t, b); Ronald Muldrow (g, b); Norman Fearrington, Franco Da Rozze (d).* 92.

Cut on a visit to Switzerland, this 'chilled jazz funk fusion' feels like Harris-by-the-numbers. He overdubs the piano parts, decorates in his customary saxophone manner, and as mixed in post-production it feels unpardonably lightweight. Not the kind of Harris record we want to remember.

★★(★) For You, For Me, For Evermore
Steeplechase SCCD 31322 *Harris (ts, p).* 10/92.

The idea was to do a duo session with another pianist but, when the second musician never turned up, Harris volunteered to set down his own piano parts first. While he's scarcely a dunce at the keyboard, having played professional piano in the past, the impromptu nature of the date forbade much preparation; too many of the pieces sound hesitant and the 'dialogue' is clumsily realized. There are some beguiling passages, and Harris's tenor tone was taking on a querulous, affecting frailty, but this is no solo masterwork.

★★★(★) Vexatious Progressions
Flying Heart FH-343D *Harris; Thara Memory (t); Peter Boe, Janice Scroggins (p); Phil Baker (b); Ron Steen (d).* 4/94.

This tough and uncompromising record is the last great Eddie Harris album. Jan Celt asked Harris to make a no-frills straight-ahead record (in Wilsonville, Oregon!), with mainly local players and few familiar names (Boe is recognizable from his work with Robert Cray). Harris came up with ten originals, and the band play the hell out of them. Whatever it may lack in finesse ('Memory' won't be challenging anyone's recollections of their favourite trumpet-playing), the music has a gutsiness which most of Harris's later records have had brushed away. It's a classic 'local' jazz record, of a sort which hardly ever comes to any prominence now, but which has a far more natural feel than most major-label dates.

★★ The Last Concert
ACT 9249 *Harris; Nils Landgren, Andy Haderer, Bob Bruynen, Klaus Osterloh, Rudiger Baldauf, John Marshall (t); Dave Horler, Henning Berg, Bernd Laukamp, Roy Deuvall (tb); Heiner Wiberny, Harald Rosenstein, Olivier Peters, Rolf Römer, Jens Neufang (reeds); Frank Chastenier, Gil Goldstein (p); John Goldsby (b); Bernard Purdie (d); Haywood J Gregory (v).* 3/96.

Harris's farewell date, live, makes moving listening, not for his weaknesses but for his strengths. It's not Harris's fault that the WDR Big Band only clump along in support, and for some reason there's a three-song coda featuring the self-regarding vocals of Haywood Gregory, a glaringly inappropriate touch. A shame, since the saxophonist himself sounds very game and his solos are definitively Eddie Harris, the odd, vocalized tone and strange flurries of notes still entirely his own.

Gene Harris (1933–99)

PIANO

Played in army bands in the early '50s, then formed a trio with Andy Simpkins and Bill Dowdy, The Three Sounds, which made many albums and was very successful. Lasted till 1974, then after a quiet spell Harris reappeared as a small-group and big-band-featured performer, making many records for Concord in a style that mixed simple bop, blues and gospel styles.

★(★) Nexus

Blue Note 581679-2 *Harris; various horns, strings and backing vocalists.* 5–6/75.

This is best left to oblivion, but Blue Note have reissued Harris's worst album when it could have been more kindly forgotten. Gene noodles away on synthesizers while a studio aggregation play funky licks and back-up singers prattle on about nothing in particular. There's a sober version of The Spinners' great 'Love Don't Love Nobody' and a strange one of Waller's 'Jitterbug Waltz' (not a tune much played in early '70s discotheques). A pretty shameless survival from the period of Blue Note where nothing went right.

★★★ Gene Harris Trio Plus One

Concord CCD 4303 *Harris; Stanley Turrentine (ts); Ray Brown (b); Mickey Roker (d).* 11–12/85.

★★★ Listen Here!

Concord CCD 4385 *Harris; Ron Eschete (g); Ray Brown (b); Jeff Hamilton (d).* 3/89.

Gene Harris finally assumed an 'own-name' reputation in the '80s and '90s via his work for Concord, specifically with big bands, but latterly with small groups as well. These small-band dates are good in their way – simply resolved light blues on the second record, a handful of standards on the first with Turrentine sitting in – but polish and good manners tend to stand in for genuine excitement. Brown, Roker and Hamilton can certainly cover their tasks here without having to try very hard. But it's agreeable enough to service those moments when the last thing one wants on the sound-system is some monumental masterwork. Turrentine sounds like his then sensible, middle-aged self on *Trio Plus One*.

★★★ Tribute To Count Basie

Concord CCD 4337 *Harris; Jon Faddis, Snooky Young, Conte Candoli, Frank Szabo, Bobby Bryant (t); Charles Loper, Bill Watrous, Thurman Green, Garnett Brown (tb); Bill Reichenbach (btb); Marshal Royal, Bill Green, Jackie Kelso (as); Bob Cooper, Plas Johnson (ts); Jack Nimitz (bs); Herb Ellis (g); James Leary III, Ray Brown (b); Jeff Hamilton (d).* 3–6/87.

★★★ Live At Town Hall, N.Y.C.

Concord CCD 4397 *Harris; Joe Mosello, Harry 'Sweets' Edison, Michael Philip Mossman, Johnny Coles (t); Eddie Bert, Urbie Green, James Morrison (tb); Paul Faulise (btb); Jerry Dodgion, Frank Wess (as, f); James Moody (ts, cl, f); Ralph Moore (ts); Herb Ellis (g); Ray Brown (b); Jeff Hamilton (d); Ernestine Anderson, Ernie Andrews (v).* 9/89.

★★★ World Tour 1990

Concord CCD 4443 *Harris; Johnny Morrison (t, flhn); Harry 'Sweets' Edison, Joe Mosello, Glenn Drewes (t); Urbie Green, George Bohannon, Robin Eubanks (tb); Paul Faulise (btb); Jeff Clayton, Jerry Dodgion (as, f); Plas Johnson (ts, f); Ralph Moore (ts); Gary Smulyan (bs); Kenny Burrell (g); Ray Brown (b); Harold Jones (d).* 10/90.

Like the latter-day records of such bandleaders as Basie and Herman, these discs tend to be enjoyable more for their gold-plated class and precision than for any special inventiveness. The first session, credited to Gene Harris and The All Star Big Band, is, in those circumstances, a very truthful kind of tribute to Basie's band, the eight charts offering a fair approximation of the familiar sound. The two discs by the later bands – now known as The Philip Morris Superband – are, we find, rather more entertaining. The *Town Hall* set boasts a vast digital presence, the brass particularly bright and all the soloists well catered for, but some may find its showbiz atmosphere less than ingratiating. Andrews and Anderson have some enjoyable vehicles and there are appropriately outgoing solos from Edison, Ellis, Dodgion and others. *World Tour 1990* reprises the situation, with a somewhat different cast but much the same atmosphere.

★★★ At Last

Concord CCD 4434 *Harris; Scott Hamilton (ts); Herb Ellis (g); Ray Brown (b); Harold Jones (d).* 5/90.

★★★ Black & Blue

Concord CCD 4482 *Harris; Ron Eschete (g); Luther Hughes (b); Harold Jones (d).* 6/91.

★★(★) Like A Lover

Concord CCD 4526 *As above.* 1/92.

★★★ At Maybeck Recital Hall

Concord CCD 4536 *Harris (p solo).* 8/92.

★★★ A Little Piece Of Heaven

Concord CCD 4578 *Harris; Ron Eschete (g); Luther Hughes (b); Paul Humphrey (d).* 7/93.

★★★ Funky Gene's

Concord CCD 4609 *As above.* 5/94.

★★★ Brotherhood

Concord CCD 4640 *As above.* 8/92.

Scott Hamilton's unwavering consistency is somewhat akin to Harris's own, but the tenorman has a slightly greater capacity to surprise and, while the material could have stood a couple of less familiar inclusions, the quintet plays with great gusto on *At Last*. Even 'You Are My Sunshine' is listenable. *Black & Blue* introduces a new Harris group: Eschete returns on guitar, but Hughes and Jones are first-timers, and they dig into the programme – dependent on traditional blues of the order of 'C C Rider' – with the same infectious enthusiasm as Harris. *Like A Lover* continues along the same path, but the ballads sound almost soppy in comparison with the upbeat tunes – Harris wasn't made to be tenderized. *A Little Piece Of Heaven* restores order by dropping the group into a live situation. This must be one of the most rollicking treatments of 'Take The "A" Train' on record, and there are somewhat bacchanalian treatments of 'Old Dog Blues' and 'Blues For Sainte Chapelle' (appropriately, since this is one of Concord's live-at-the-winery dates). Harris is always going to end up making the same record, but so far it still sounds pretty good.

His entry in the Maybeck Recital Hall series is typically straightahead and without frills. There are four more blues in the programme, but this time the ballads don't seem quite so ponderously tender, and he is assuredly enjoying himself throughout.

The next two Concords (*Brotherhood* apparently dates from 1992 but didn't get a release until 1995) continue a solid if scarcely arresting run. *Funky Gene's* is comfortably in the usual pocket and, although 'Children Of Sanchez' is a mistaken choice, most of the tunes fit Harris like his favourite tuxedo. *Brotherhood* is pretty much the same. Eschete's solo on 'I Remember You' makes one sit up and wish that perhaps he had more space than he usually gets; Harris, on the other hand, has never sounded more swinging than he does on Frank Loesser's 'The Brotherhood Of Man'. If you have some Gene Harris albums already, you probably won't need this one, but it's still a very good place to start.

****(*) It's The Real Soul**
Concord CCD-4692 *Harris; Frank Wess (ts, f); Ron Eschete (g); Luther Hughes (b); Paul Humphrey (d).* 3/95.

****(*) In His Hands**
Concord CCD 4758 *As above, except add Jack McDuff (org), Gregg Field, Steve Hockel (perc), Nikki Harris, Ralph E Beechum, Cherie Buckner, Curtis Stigers (v); omit Wess.* 12/96.

***** Down Home Blues**
Concord CCD-4785 *As above, except omit Field, Hockel, Beechum, Buckner.* 12/96.

Concord seemed ready to let Harris record whenever he wanted. It was scarcely worth the effort on *It's The Real Soul*, which simply re-runs one of his concert sets. The band are as usual, but guest Wess coasts through a couple of blues and a couple of flute features to negligible effect. Docked a notch for pointlessness.

Gospel and blues take up the next two, recorded at the same sessions. *In His Hands* partakes of the spirit well enough, even if Stigers and Nikki Harris are more Hallelujah-Hollywood than anything, but the material is groaningly obvious. The most interesting presence is McDuff, and he shares the billing with Harris on the next one, which is nearly all blues. Nikki Harris and Stigers again have cameos, but the meat of it is in the interplay between piano and organ. A bit airbrushed in the Concord style, but enjoyable.

***** All-Stars Live**
Concord CCD 4808-2 *Harris; Harry 'Sweets' Edison (t); Stanley Turrentine (ts); Kenny Burrell (g); George Mraz (b); Lewis Nash (d); Ernie Andrews (v).* 4/95.

***** Alley Cats**
Concord CCD-4859-2 *Harris; Ernie Watts (ts, as); Red Holloway (ts); Jack McDuff (org); Frank Potenza (g); Luther Hughes (b); Paul Kreibich (d); Nikki Harris (v).* 12/98.

The concert recording is a sweet-natured reunion of old-timers. Everybody does their usual, but the one who puts in a little more elbow-grease is Turrentine, continuing his good late run with a fine 'Time After Time'. *Alley Cats* is yet another live one, and the hero this time is the failsafe Watts, who burns up the changes on 'Bird's Idea' and completely outclasses the razzle of Holloway. Gene himself does his usual yet again, though nobody could begrudge him: 'If you leave here with a smile on your face, remember that Gene Harris put it there'.

Stefon Harris (born 1973)

VIBRAPHONE

Young vibes player at the forefront of new New York music, and already much in demand as a star sideman.

*****(*) A Cloud Of Red Dust**
Blue Note 23487 2 *Harris; Steve Turre (tb); Greg Osby (as); Steve Wilson (ss, as); Kaoru Watanabe (f); Mulgrew Miller, Jason Moran (p); Dwayne Burno (b); Alvester Garnett (d); Kimati Dinizulu (perc, 1-string hp); June Gardner (v).* 10/97.

****** BlackActionFigure**
Blue Note 99546 2 *Harris; Steve Turre (tb); Greg Osby (as); Gary Thomas (ts, af); Jason Moran (p); Tarus Mateen (b); Eric Harland (d).* 2/99.

Our Penguin colleague Jonny King, writing in his book, *What Jazz Is*, very perceptively notes how often the vibraphone attracts the most talented and versatile musicians. This is perhaps because the instrument, whether played with two mallets or four, demands such a perfect balance of melodic, harmonic and rhythmic awareness. It has long been our view that players as diverse as Lionel Hampton, Milt Jackson and Bobby Hutcherson (to say nothing of Joe Locke, Khan Jamal and Walt Dickerson) would be regarded far more highly if they were playing almost any other instrument.

It's a great pleasure to encounter a young player just about to join those august ranks. Harris has worked with an array of leaders, including Buster Williams and Steve Turre, but he is already a highly developed musical personality. His debut album is interestingly structured. Rather than a sequence of discrete tracks, Harris has woven them together with short interludes to create an almost continuous suite. It grips the attention from the very start and flags only very briefly, with June Gardner's vocal feature on 'In The Garden Of Thought', which seems to come from a different session altogether. Some of the shorter pieces, like 'One String Blues', co-written with Kimati Dinizulu, are quirky and playful, but Harris's most characteristic sound is a flowing lyricism, grafted on to a swinging shuffle beat, a combination of metres that is always threatening to fall apart but never quite does. There is something of Hutcherson's tightrope daring in his solo on 'Of Things To Come' on the second album.

The sequel builds on the strengths of its predecessor. As before, the writing is strong and archetypal, vindicating Harris's idealist belief that all music is pre-ordained, that it can't be composed, merely transcribed. 'The Alchemist' and the stately 'Chorale' which follows are perfect illustrations of this: timeless-sounding compositions that seem to exist in the mind before they're heard. This has the odd effect of making the album's two standards, 'There Is No Greater Love' and 'You Stepped Out Of A Dream', sound as if they might be brand-new conceptions. The only other repertory piece is a version of Onaje Allan Gumbs's 'Collage'.

A Cloud Of Red Dust established Harris as one of the most exciting prospects for years. It was slightly marred by inconsistent production – Greg Osby took over from Billy Banks for the follow-up and delivered a much more graceful product – but it put a new name on the distinguished Blue Note roster. Even so, there's a worry that three years later the career may already have stalled.

***** Kindred**
Blue Note 31868 *Harris; Jacky Terrasson (p); Tarus Mateen (b); Terreon Gully, Idris Muhammad (d).* n.d.

Co-led with Terrasson, and cynics might suggest that was an attempt to rekindle the pianist's shaky market stock by identifying him with the latest Young Turk. As it is, Harris pretty much dominates the record, playing some of his most incisive work on marimba, which is more easily differentiated from the piano. A suspicious number of tracks are standards, presumably in the interests of guaranteeing common ground. 'Summertime' is a curiosity, with a rewritten coda, but 'My Foolish

Heart' and 'What Is This Thing Called Love?', the latter a duet, are both excellent. Harris's 'Shane' stands out among the originals, while Terrasson has his best moments right at the end on 'Body And Soul', which is a very idiosyncratic version.

*** The Grand Unification Theory

Blue Note 32498 *Harris; Derrick Gardner (t); Steve Turre (tb, shells); Douglas Purviance (btb); Tim Warfield (ts); Mark Vinci (cl); Anne Drummond (f, af); Xavier Davis (p); Tarus Mateen (b, v); Terreon Gully (d); Khalil Kwame Bell, Myles Weinstein (perc).* 11/02.

Dare we say: the concept album. It worked for Mingus on *Pithecanthropus Erectus* and both Wayne Shorter and Grachan Moncur III had their shot at histories of the world in 11 musical chapters. Harris's, though, is so clotted by his desire to put a spin on every dimension of human experience that the music is all over the place stylistically and overpacked with detail. 'The Birth Of Time' must be one of the most way-out tracks to appear under a Blue Note title in many a year. It doesn't quite happen, but it certainly intrigues. 'The Velvet Couch' is more straightforward, though the bout of therapy only softens the listener up for more craziness in the middle section of 'Corridor Of Elusive Dreams', 'Escape To Quiet Desperation' and 'Song Of The Whispering Banshee', the last of which is very odd indeed.

Harris has rarely opened up the vibes so completely. His palette is very broad and his range of effects, from sharply struck chimes and runs to passages where it sounds as if the motors have been switched off, is impressive. Or would be if the listener weren't trying to negotiate a blandly pretentious programme which has no real correlative in the music being played.

Donald Harrison (born 1960)

ALTO AND SOPRANO SAXOPHONES, BASS CLARINET

Born in New Orleans, he studied with Ellis Marsalis and joined Art Blakey in 1982. Co-led a quintet with Terence Blanchard and has subsequently freelanced.

*** For Art's Sake

Candid CCD 79501 *Harrison; Marlon Jordan (t); Cyrus Chestnut (p); Christian McBride (b); Carl Allen (d).* 11/90.

Perhaps the key story in the jazz of the '90s has been the revival of New Orleans, the legendary cradle of the music, as a vital, thrusting, experimental location. Much of the credit goes to the Marsalis family and in particular to the patriarch, Ellis, who was one of Donald 'Duck' Harrison's teachers at NOCA. Like many of the younger generation, Harrison has tried to fuse traditional idiom with a thoroughly contemporary style, and this early album ('early' isn't quite right for a player already 30) reflects the instincts that pushed the Messengers as far as Art Blakey ever allowed the group to go. Harrison had been active for a good few years before this record was released and had worked out a strong, uncompromising voice.

For Art's Sake is a classic instance of a leader upstaged by his sidemen. Harrison has assembled a powerful young band (McBride was only 18) who know the tradition inside out and are brimming with their own ideas. The opening 'So What' helps settle the players and establish credentials. Chestnut's semi-autobiographical 'Nut' is the pianist's feature, elegantly sculpted, formal and unaffected. Harrison gives most of the opening statements to the 19-year-old Jordan, who emerges as a rawer version of Wynton Marsalis. The trumpeter comes into his own on a superb reading of 'In A Sentimental Mood', which he gradually cranks up from a melancholy ballad into a funky swinger. Offered as 'proof' that 'hard bop is the basis of '90s jazz', the record does no more than confirm that there are still lots of youngsters around who are willing to take it on. Not the same thing at all.

*** Indian Blues

Candid CCD 79514 *Harrison; Cyrus Chestnut, Mac Rebennack (Dr John) (p, v); Phil Bowler (b, v); Carl Allen (d, v); Bruce Cox, Howard Smiley Ricks (perc, v); Donald Harrison (v).* 5/91.

Hard bop is still the basic language here, but Harrison has also tried to combine the sound of the Messengers with that of a more literal father-figure. Donald Harrison Sr has been leader of the Guardians of the Flame, who also feature on the album. 'Hiko Hiko' and 'Two-Way-Pocky-Way' are traditional (the former is credited to the legendary Black Johnny); 'Ja-Ki-Mo-Fi-Na-Hay' and the opening 'Hu-Tan-nay' are credited to the Harrisons. Dr John sings and plays piano on the two originals, sings on Professor Longhair's 'Big Chief' and plays piano on 'Walkin' Home' and Big Chief Jolly's 'Shave 'Em Dry'.

If it's part of Harrison's intention to reflect the continuity of the black music tradition, he does so very convincingly, and there's no sense of a break between the densely rhythmic New Orleans numbers with their chattering percussion and the more orthodox jazz tracks. He plays 'Indian Red' pretty much as a straight alto feature, but then adds a rhythmic line to the prototypical standard 'Cherokee' that gives it an entirely new dimension. His own 'Indian Blues' and 'Uptown Ruler' reflect a decision in 1989 to 'mask Indian' again and join the feathered throngs that march on Mardi Gras. In touching his roots, he's brought them right up to date.

Paul Harrison

PIANO

Rising talent, voted Young Scottish Jazz Musician of the Year for 1998 and 1999.

*** Nemesis

Caber 013 *Harrison; Mario Caribé (b); Paddy Flaherty (d).* 12/99.

Rooted in the pianism of Chick Corea and the attractively splintered aesthetic of Bud Powell, Harrison is an exciting player who seems certain to go places. His debut is confident and packed with original ideas, of which 'Six Down', the insistent 'Foot In The Door' and the lovely 'Valse' are the most memorable. Sterling support from Caribé and Flaherty as well, and the kind of empathy that only comes from an established working line-up.

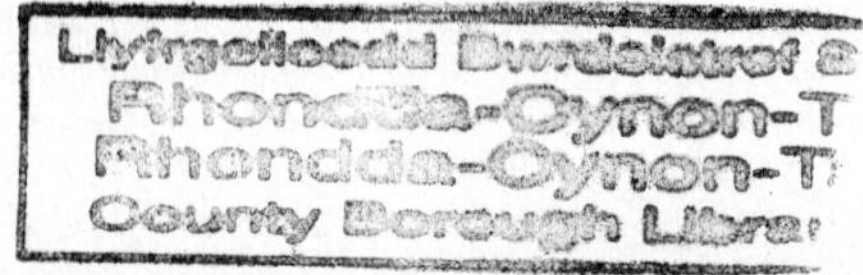

Nancy Harrow (born 1930)

VOCAL

Harrow's Candid album from 1960 seemed the only token from a modest career in New York and Paris until she returned to recording in the '80s and '90s, often working from literary texts and drawing from theatrical performance.

***** Wild Women Don't Have The Blues**

Candid CCD 9008 *Harrow; Buck Clayton (t); Dicky Wells (tb); Tom Gwaltney (cl, as); Buddy Tate (ts); Danny Bank (bs); Dick Wellstood (p); Kenny Burrell (g); Milt Hinton (b); Oliver Jackson (d).* 11/60.

***** You're Nearer**

Baldwin Street Music BJC-203 *Harrow; Bob Brookmeyer (vtb); Sir Roland Hanna (p); Ray Drummond (b); Terri Lyne Carrington (d).* 3/86.

***** Secrets**

Soul Note 121233-2 *Harrow; Clark Terry (t, flhn, v); Dick Katz (p); Ray Drummond (b); Ben Riley (d).* 11/90–1/91.

***** Lost Lady**

Soul Note 121263-2 *As above, except Phil Woods (cl, as) replaces Terry; add Vernel Bagnaris (v).* 6–11/93.

***** The Marble Faun**

Harbinger HCD 1707 *Harrow; John Mosca (tb); John Clark (frhn); Frank Wess (ss, ts, f); Sir Roland Hanna (p); George Caldwell (syn); Sanford Allen, Dale Stuckenbruck (vn); Richard Brice (vla); Frederick Zlotkin (clo); Jack Wilkins (g); Paul West (b); Akira Tana (d); Grady Tate, Amy London, Anton Kurkowski (v).* 3–4/97.

Harrow's 1960 debut record has worn rather better than we expected, and though the rowdy mainstream accompaniments are entirely inappropriate to her style, she doesn't do too badly at all on several of the songs, especially 'I Don't Know What Kind Of Blues I've Got'. Buck gets off a beautiful solo on the final 'Blues For Yesterday', but otherwise the playing is often close to shambolic.

While her recent records are something of an acquired taste, there are some delightful moments scattered through them. The voice has grown thinner and has a society-singer drawl to it, but on the right song it can be surprisingly affecting. *You're Nearer* reissues an album done for Ted Ono's Tono label. The ballads are charmingly done, with Hanna empathizing very well and Brookmeyer playing a few cameo solos, but there are some strange choices of tune – Lionel Richie's 'Hello', 'Hallelujah I Love Him So', 'You're Not The Only Oyster In The Stew'. She wrote five of the songs on *Secrets*, and has a good eye for a romantic irony. Terry is in good form and they do a pretty hilarious duet on 'Hit The Road Jack', and if you sample the duet between the singer and Ray Drummond on 'So Why Am I Surprised?' you may find yourself hooked.

Lost Lady initiates the direction she has since gone in: building a record around the literary text, in this case a novella by Willa Cather, with Bagneris taking the male vocal role. The songs don't make much impact by themselves, and Bagneris is no great personality, but the musicians are a sympathetic prop and Harrow treats her own work with gentle persuasion. Much more ambitious is *The Marble Faun*, based around Hawthorne's novel. It's a formidable cast of players and, indeed, voices. If the feel is of a kind of small-scale jazz musical, the performers approach the material with quiet dedication which carries it off, even if musical-theatre specialists may find it unremarkable. A record which really has few comparison points elsewhere in this book.

**** Winter Dreams: The Life And Passions Of F. Scott Fitzgerald**

Artists House AH0001 *Harrow; Michael Mossman (t, flhn); John Mosca (tb); Bill Easley (ss, as, f, cl); Frank Wess (ts, f); Roland Hanna (p); Jack Wilkins (g); Rufus Reid (b); Akira Tana (d, perc); Grady Tate (v).* 02.

Despite some beautiful themes and some lovely arrangements by Sir Roland Hanna, the songs in this cycle deliver nothing but bathos. Grady Tate shares vocal duties but for once sounds like a non-singing actor who's been roped in at the last minute. The only real consolation is the playing of trumpeter Michael Mossman and the multi-talented Bill Easley and Frank Wess, who rise to the challenge with some elegantly crafted solos. Otherwise, a non-starter.

Antonio Hart (born 1969)

ALTO SAXOPHONE

Based in New York from 1991, notably as a Roy Hargrove sideman, Hart made a string of albums for Novus, but has not since managed to settle with a sympathetic label.

***** Ama Tu Sonrisa**

Enja 9404 *Hart; Yosvany Terry (ts); Kevin Hays (p); Steve Nelson (vib); Richie Goods (b); Camille Gainer, Nasheet Waits (d); Rolando Morales, Renato Thoms (perc); Claudia Acuña, Khalil Kwame Bell, Lenora Zenzalai Helm (v).* 01.

Seemingly disillusioned with the music business, Hart took a four-year sabbatical and spent his time travelling and absorbing other musical traditions. The result is this unexpected album, which has a strong African feel. Apart from 'Have You Met Miss Jones?' and Bernstein's 'Somewhere', all the tunes are originals and find Hart trying to forge a new personal style out of a spectrum of fresh influences. It isn't always successful. Right from the opening 'For Amadou' one suspects he is trying too much and too hard, but the disc settles down with the lovely title-track, 'Distant Cousins' and 'Wayne's Lament'. After that, it starts to peter out again, though the standards give him some much needed purchase. Though the vocalists are reserved for the closing 'El Professor', there is a lot of percussion on the album and this requires a delicate touch at the controls, not always in evidence. One feels that Antonio is still searching, but the rich promise of the Novus years is still there, waiting for its moment.

Billy Hart (born 1940)

DRUMS

Originally active on his native Washington scene, where he played with Wes Montgomery and his brothers, Hart turned into one of the busiest drummers on the scene, recording with Miles Davis, Stan Getz, Jimmy Smith and McCoy Tyner. Despite a vast discography, he has rarely recorded as a leader.

***** Oceans Of Time**

Arabesque 129 *Hart; Chris Potter (ss, ts, bcl); John Stubblefield (ss, ts); David Kikoski (p); David Fiuczynski (g); Mark Feldman (vn); Santi Debriano (b).* 97.

A beautiful and unusual album that affords a rare glimpse of Hart the composer; 'Teule's Redemption' is a Coltrane-inspired epic that provides the drummer with a springboard for some lovely, imaginative playing. For the most part, the writing is done by his colleagues, who convened four years earlier for the now-deleted *Amethyst* disc. In our view, this one is better. Stubblefield's 'One For Carter' (Jefferson) is a great opener and Kikoski's 'Shadow' is testimony to his skills. Debriano kicks in with 'Mind Reader' and the closing 'Offering' which gives Billy a chance to show his mettle in unorthodox counts. A fine set, though you will have to look elsewhere for the (as the compilers like to say) 'very best of Billy Hart'.

Alfred Harth

SAXOPHONES, CLARINETS

Formerly known as Alfred 23 Harth because that was how many horns he owned. Now somewhat eclipsed in reputation.

***** Popending Eye**

Freeflow 0493 *Harth; Simon Nabatov (p); Mark Dresser, Vitold Rek (b); Vladimir Tarasov (d).* 92–93.

Harth's best known album, *This Earth* for ECM, has yet to make it into the CD catalogue, which leaves his catalogue rather depleted. This is a slice of mildly interesting retro-jazz from the saxophonist's Quasar Quartet, somewhat reminiscent of Keshavan Maslak, but without the wacky humour.

Johnny Hartman (1923–83)

VOCALS

Hartman's rich, lustrous baritone was really suited to only one tempo, slow enough for every syllable to be enunciated with loving attention. Oddly, having worked with Earl Hines, Errol Garner and Dizzy Gillespie, he is nowadays best remembered for a somewhat unlikely Impulse! pairing with the giant of modernism, John Coltrane.

*****(*) All Of Me**

Rhino 79849 *Hartman; Howard McGhee, Ernie Royal (t); Frank Rehak (tb); Anthony Ortega (as); Jerome Richardson (ts, f); Lucky Thompson (ts); Danny Bank (bs); Hank Jones (p); Milt Hinton (b); Osie Johnson (d).* 11/56.

Until recently, Hartman owed his small corner in the awareness of modern-jazz fans to his role in Bob Thiele's attempt to prettify John Coltrane by having him work with a singer. It was a relatively successful experiment on its own terms, but it did tend to obscure Hartman's own achievement. Possessed of a rich, full baritone, somewhere between Nat Cole and Al Hibbler, Hartman had the ability to caress even a banal lyric into shape, infusing it not so much with emotion as with a sort of intelligence. This is the quality most evident on *All Of Me*, reissued with four alternative takes which show how carefully, but also how instinctively, Hartman improvised on a melody. On this occasion, too, he had at his disposal a band of bop craftsmen who give him some challenging backgrounds to work against. The arrangements on 'I'll Follow You' and the much-reworked 'Blue Skies' (included as a bonus is take 13) allow him to do a good deal vocally, and he rises to the challenge every time. On the other hand, he gives take one of 'Birth Of The Blues' a resonant responsiveness which isn't quite there on the more polished issue take.

*****(*) And I Thought About You**

Blue Note 57456 *Hartman; unknown personnel.* 60.

For some reason, Hartman recorded only once between the Bethlehem sessions and his contract with Impulse!. There are scant pickings on this unaugmented reissue which weighs in at just over the half-hour. The voice is as rich as ever and the arrangements by Rudy Traylor are highly professional but there is too little to bite on, and not even the delicious cadences of the title-track right at the end are enough to make this a compelling addition to the Hartman discography.

*****(*) I Just Stopped By To Say Hello**

Impulse! 051176-2 *Hartman; Illinois Jacquet (ts); Hank Jones (p); Kenny Burrell, Jim Hall (g); Milt Hinton (b); Elvin Jones (d).* 10/63.

***** Unforgettable**

Impulse! 051152-2 *Hartman; Bud Brisbois, Conte Candoli, Jules Chaikin, Freddie Hill, Ollie Mitchell, Melvin Moore, Al Porcino (t); Mike Barone, Billy Byers, John Ewing, Lester Robertson, Ernie Tack (tb); Gabe Baltazar, Anthony Ortega (as); Curtis Amy, Teddy Edwards, Bill Green, Plas Johnson, Harold Land (ts); Jack Nimitz (bs); Mike Melvoin (p); Dennis Budimir, Herb Ellis, John Gray, Howard Roberts (g); Jimmy Bond, Ray Brown, Joe Mondragon (b); Stan Levey, Shelly Manne (d); James Lockert (perc); strings.* 2 & 9/66.

Hartman was a graceful interpreter of ballads particularly, and the later Impulse! albums succeed in direct ratio to the success of the slower songs. The earliest is enhanced by the musicians, while on the second they fulfil a pretty workmanlike function. Listen to Jones's accompaniment on 'Stairway To The Stars' and the Sinatra-associated 'Wee Small Hours Of The Morning', both on *I Just Stopped By* ... for a sense of how invaluable he could be to a singer. He'd shown a similar touch on the Bethlehem set, but it's here that he really comes into his own as an accompanist.

Unforgettable is a more recent reissue, consisting of 12 songs from the ABC Paramount release, *Unforgettable Songs By Johnny Hartman*, and a further five from a set called *I Love Everybody*, which was taped in a studio but with a substantial audience of invited guests who help give it its live ambience. It includes 'Girl Talk', one of Hartman's increasingly self-indulgent spoken monologues and certainly a little overcooked in this case. However, it's good to hear him work a room, even a room as acoustically unresponsive as the LA studio. Technically, the better stuff comes from the three-day February session. Presumably, as throughout his career there were a lot of abandoned or rejected takes, Hartman seems to have been something of a perfectionist, and once or twice even on issued material one hears him wandering slightly off the pitch. No evidence (unless it's been done very well indeed) of any internal splicing. Everything sounds like a complete and integral performance. All the songs are short and emphatic, with no room for instrumental embellishment or for vocal gymnastics. That isn't what Hartman was about. He liked to let the song do the work, and mostly that's what happens. A remarkable vocal talent, only now beginning to be recognized for his own achievement, rather than for that one-off association with one of the giants of modernism.

***** For Trane**

Blue Note 35346 *Hartman; Terumasa Hino (t); Masabuma Kikuchi, Mikio Masuda (p); Yoshio Ikeda, Yoshio Suzuki (b); Motohiko Hino, Hiroshi Murakami (d).* 11–12/72.

Recorded in Tokyo and very misleadingly titled, since most of the album consists of material with no Coltrane association at all but comes from a separate session. 'Violets For Your Furs', 'Nature Boy' and 'My Favorite Things' betray not the slightest hint that the singer is aware of Trane's versions, but the singing is good, and Hartman's voice still has a melting intensity on ballads. One for collectors, but don't be misled by the spurious Coltrane connection.

**** Today / I've Been There**

Collectables 5619 *Hartman; George Coleman (ts); Herman Foster (p); Roland Prince (g); Earl May (b); Billy Higgins (d).* 72–75.

Despite the sterling line-up, these two LPs for Perception were pretty forgettable affairs, an attempt to put Johnny across a pop repertoire that in no way suited his voice. 'By The Time I Get To Phoenix' might be by any one of half a dozen lounge singers of the time, and even the indestructible 'The First Time Ever I Saw Your Face' shows signs of abuse. Best avoided unless you are absolutely addicted to Johnny's voice.

***** Thank You For Everything**

Audiophile 165 *Hartman; Loomis McGlohon (p); Terry Lassiter (b); James Lackey (d).* 78.

****(*) This One's For Tedi**

Audiophile 181 *Hartman; Tony Monte (p); Lorne Lofsky (g); Chris Conner (b); Buff Allen (d).* 8/80.

Thank You consists of live performances from Alec Wilder's regular radio programme, and they find an older-sounding Hartman in very good form indeed. The band is nothing special, but they have little to do except nudge the singer through the melody and changes of 'Lush Life' and a couple of other Ellington–Strayhorn numbers. The title-track is a version of Strayhorn's 'Lotus Blossom' set for voice and it is very effective, though it would have been interesting to hear Hartman shadowed by a horn; his vocal line is a touch one-dimensional for such a glorious tune.

Hartman's final recording came three years before his death. It's an attractive but low-key set and there is nothing on it which suggests it should be part of anyone's vocal collection. 'Send In The Clowns' always seems to go best when the singer is a bit world-bitten and off the money. As farewells go, this isn't too bad, but this certainly isn't the Hartman who was to become such a posthumous hero in the wake of his association with Trane.

Michael Hashim (born 1956)

ALTO AND SOPRANO SAXOPHONES

Made his reputation when he joined – and later became leader of – the Widespread Depression/Jazz Orchestra, working out of Rhode Island. His New York experience in the '80s found him working with many senior figures, and he is a modern 'repertory' player of great skill.

****** Keep A Song In Your Soul**

Hep 2068 *Hashim; Claudio Roditi (t); Richard Wyands (p); Dennis Irwin (b); Kenny Washington (d).* 5/96.

Doing a Fats Waller repertory record in a contemporary idiom is about as tough a conceptual undertaking as one can imagine. Hashim's astonishing achievement is all the more praiseworthy in that he even gets new life out of the normally intractable 'Jitterbug Waltz' and the roasted 'Honeysuckle Rose'. This is the best band he's ever fronted in a studio; Roditi is his usual cavalier self, and he's a splendid foil for the leader. 'Get Some Cash For Your Trash' is improbably thoughtful and elegant, 'E Flat Blues' never stops cooking, and 'Two Sleepy People' is mildly gorgeous. The pinnacle comes on an extraordinarily dark and baleful 'Black And Blue', which Hashim does on soprano. The further back he looks for material, the more modern he seems to sound: and there are bits and pieces on the record that, say, Oliver Lake might have used. One of Hep's best-ever productions and catnip for Hashim's admirers.

*****(*) Multicoloured Blue**

Hep CD 2075 *Hashim; Joe Temperley (bs); Mike LeDonne (p); Peter Washington, John Webber (b); Kenny Washington (d).* 7–10/98.

Hashim continues to set a fine standard, the only quibble here being that he's done Strayhorn before, and with a similar personnel. But there are rarities of the order of 'Triple Play', 'Suite For The Duo' and 'Strange Feeling', alongside 'Chelsea Bridge', which may be getting a bit tired as everyone's piece of Strayhorn impressionism. Temperley trades phrases on the title-piece.

*****(*) Green Up Time**

Hep 2079 *Hashim; Wayne Barker (toy p); Will Holshouser (acc); Eddy Davis (bj, mandola); Dennis Irwin (b); Kenny Washington (d); Axis String Quartet.* 7–8/01.

An album of Kurt Weill music. Hashim manages to avoid most of the kitsch which is perhaps inherent in the idea, if not the material, through the sheer vigour of his playing. Some of the melodies have a slurping quality that Hashim actually turns to his advantage. If he can make 'Jitterbug Waltz' into something plausible, then 'Tango Ballad' and 'Love Song' are easy. The strings are on half of the tracks, and are infected with Hashim's own energy, but more important are the bedrock roles of Irwin and Washington. No piano: Holshouser's accordion, sometimes the only awkward note, is the substitute. Best taken a few tracks at a time, perhaps, but it's a worthy addition to Hashim's canon. What's next? Nothing new for us to consider this time.

George Haslam (born 1939)

BARITONE SAXOPHONE, TAROGATO, CLARINET

Emerged in the '80s as a can-do organizer, group leader and own-label boss, recording many venturesome players. His own work on baritone has taken him round the world in search of fellow spirits.

***** 1989 – And All That**

Slam CD 301 *Haslam; Paul Rutherford (tb).* 4/89.

***** Level Two**

Slam CD 303 *Haslam; Paul Rutherford (tb); Howard Riley (p); Marcio Mattos (b); Tony Marsh (d); Liz Hodgson (v).* 6/92.

A relatively late starter on the saxophone, Haslam was quick to see the potential of free or spontaneous music. The solos and duos on the record with Rutherford are, with the exception of a surprisingly subtle solo baritone version of Ellington's 'Come Sunday', improvised without predetermined structure. The record launched Haslam's own label, an operation which broadly reflects the range of his musical interests.

He has continued to play in a more conventional jazz context, concentrating largely on West Coast material, and, like other British free players, has shown a strong awareness of folk forms. The name of his regular improvising group, Level Two, reflects an interest in performance that falls between the realization of scored compositions – level one – and complete abstraction – level three. If Riley introduces a strong compositional element, Rutherford is again on hand to prevent the music drifting into a settled groove or fixed direction. Mattos and Marsh impart a constantly unpredictable swing, while Haslam himself and (on two tracks only) singer Hodgson provide a vigorous melodic focus that cements the interplay of otherwise disparate elements.

Haslam's baritone has the husky uncertainty of pitch one expects of a folk instrument, and in some respects the tarogato (a Hungarian instrument of parallel antiquity to the saxophone) is the horn that provides his definitive voice. Its graininess is ideally suited to the open-ended songs and quasi-pastoral themes on *Level Two*.

***(*) Argentine Adventures

Slam CD 304 *Haslam; Enrique Norris (t); Sergio Paulucci (as, v); Daniel Harari (ts, ss); Ruben Ferrero (p); Quique Sinesi (g); Pablo Blasich, Mono Hurtado (b); Horacio López, Sergio Urtubei (d); Fernando Barragan, Tim Short, Horacio Straijer (perc); Mirta Insaurralde (v).* 3/91–8/93.

**** Duos East West

Slam CD 309 *Haslam; Ruben Ferrero, Vladimir Solyanik (p); Mono Hurtado (b).* 6–8/97.

Haslam's enterprise and creative initiative are remarkable. He was the first British jazz musician to play in Argentina (and, earlier, in Cuba) and he has kept up contacts and a working association with musicians there. When plans to take his regular quintet in 1991 fell through, Haslam went as a single. The first track is an unaccompanied tarogato solo. Thereafter, *Adventures* consists of collaborations with Argentinian players, tracing Haslam's exploration of forms like the elegiac *vidala* – sung by Insaurralde – and rhythms like the *malambo* and *carnavalito*. The session ends with a remarkable trio performance of John Coltrane's 'Affirmation', for saxophones and bass, with Paulucci also adding a vocal component. Highly recommended.

The association has continued and *Duos East West* finds him back in Buenos Aires, playing three numbers with pianist Ruben Ferrero and one trio with double-bassist Mono Hurtado. Recorded on the night Diana, Princess of Wales died, against the stormy background of the Santa Rosa, heavy humidity, lightning and apocalyptic rain, they sound appropriately fiery and intense, in marked contrast to the folksier sound of Vladimir Solyanik. Recorded some weeks earlier on Haslam's second visit to the Ukraine, these improvised performances include a gloriously busked version of the English folksong 'Barbara Allen'. 'Bi-Bop' is a slightly breathless workout, apparently recorded at the very end of the session, but programmed first on the disc. Intriguing as these tracks are, it's the Latin American vector which seems to work best for George. His baritone is full-voiced on 'Rio De La Plata', a broad, weighty sound that seems to have no less buoyancy than Ferrero's. The pianist is a real discovery, capable of shifts from quite abstract sonic gestures, often inside the piano, to the most elemental swing. Solyanik's common-time playing has a touch of the metronome about it – notably on 'Waltzes With Wolves' – but Ferrero has the loose-limbed grace required of the tango dancer. Another intriguing record from Haslam and his now solidly established label.

*** Harmonance

Slam CD 310 *Haslam; Laszlo Gardonyi (p).* 2/91, 1/99.

Recorded eight years apart, but in the same wonderful acoustic of the Holywell Room in Oxford, these improvisations have an impressive consistency of tone. Gardonyi comes across as a romantic with a bit of steel, while Haslam, switching as ever between tarogato and baritone, espouses a gruff lyricism which is instantly attractive and doesn't cloy. Coltrane's 'Lonnie's Lament' kicks off the earlier set, which for some reason comes second on the CD, followed by a tiny 'Misty' and an only slightly longer curtain-piece. One wonders why more from each gig wasn't considered usable; perhaps it's waiting its moment.

***(*) Tredavoe Blue

Slam CD 312 *Haslam; Richard Leigh Harris (p, windchimes).* 11/98, 12/99.

This one is full of surprises. Harris's delicate touch is a masterly foil to Haslam's machine-tooled sound, but it's George who turns out to be the tear-jerker, with a stunningly beautiful baritone version of 'Goodbye Pork Pie Hat', which deserves to be up with the iconic interpretations of that great tune. There are tiny quotes from Lester Young buried in his short solo, just to pay homage to both composer and dedicatee. The originals are atmospheric, sometimes lacking in focus, but high on texture. Haslam doubles or trebles on clarinet this time out, another variation that adds to his considerable palette.

*** Argentine Adventures, Part 3

Slam CD 311 *Haslam; Pablo Ledesma (ss); Ruben Ferrero (p); Marcello Jeremiahs (p, ky); Mono Hurtado (b); Luis de la Torre (d); Fabian Tejada (udu d); Monito Vieira (perc).* 12/98.

Another fruitful trip to Buenos Aires and some wonderful duo and small group encounters. It doesn't get much better than the opening track, a tarogato/bass duet with the wonderful Hurtado; but there are good things, too, on the collectively improvised 'Five Go Free In Buenos Aires' with Ledesma, Ferrero, Hurtado and de la Torre, and just to prove the vintage, a lovely closing piece with the bassist. A great record, that whatever else proves Haslam's conviction that improvisation is a powerful *lingua franca*, but one that requires a bit of preparatory phrase-book work if it is to yield the highest dividends. All credit to him for shaping his accent and idiom to that of his collaborators and hosts.

*** Meltdown

Slam CD 243 *Haslam; Lloyd Payne, Steve Waterman (t); Andrew Claxton (tba); Julia Middleton (ss); Tim Hill, Pablo Ledesma (as); Ewen Baird, Geoff Hawkins (ts); Matthew F. Morris (bs); Richard Leigh Harris (p); Jez Cooke (g); Steve*

Kershaw, Jerry Soffe (b); Steve Harris (d); Adam Riley (d, perc); Robin Jones, Tim Turan (perc); Alison Bentley (v). 4 & 6/00, 1 & 3/01.

A fascinating large-scale project for different groups and composers, reflecting a rarely seen side of Haslam's musical practice. Indeed, this is only partly a Haslam album, featuring as it does compositions by the senior Graham Collier and by trumpeter Steve Waterman from a younger generation. Collier's piece 'Eggshell Summer' is a slice of fragile nostalgia, an evocation of something evanescent and on the point of vanishing, his characteristic harmonic subtlety put to quietly dramatic use. Waterman's 'Concerto for Congas' is a wonderful idea, pitched somewhere between Machito and Gunther Schuller. Pianist Harris's 'Our Days Were A Joy, And Our Paths Through Flowers' has the same fugitive pastoralism as the Collier piece, but with a strong spine. Haslam himself directs the opening 'Variations – Bop to Blues' and the brief, closing 'Automateric', which most blindfold listeners would guess was a Collier piece, though differently voiced from most of Graham's recent work. The focus here isn't on soloing *per se* but on the relation between individual parts and the overall ensemble. To that extent it marks an important step forward for Haslam, but also a re-engagement with composed structures and notated ideas. More is promised in the same vein and it should be fascinating.

*****(*) Anglo-Argentine Jazz Quartet Live At The Red Rose**

SLAM 313 *Haslam; Lol Coxhill (ss); Pablo Ledesma (ss, as); Elton Dean (as, saxello); Mono Hurtado, John Edwards (b); Paul Hession (d); Lukax Santana (perc).* 3/01.

The A-A foursome meet up in Finsbury Park for a series of quartet tracks, where Haslam and Ledesma get into some delightful dialogue, motored along by Hession's unstinting energy. Then there's a half-hour finale where the other listed guests climb aboard, starting with a bass duet by Hurtado and Edwards and leading to the saxophones in mighty if good-natured confrontation. World music of a kind that won't win cultural-establishment commissions but which sounds fine on its own terms.

*****(*) Pendle Hawk Carapace**

Slam CD 315 *Haslam; Paul Hession (perc).* 2/02.

Haslam and Hession seemed destined to work together. Their approaches are ruggedly complementary and united by the same awareness of how jazz language fits into a free idiom. Some of this came out on their trio collaboration with American piano titan Borah Bergman on *The Mahout* (also Slam), and it energizes this fine duo recording, made at Pendle Hawk studio in Colne. The architectural terms used for track titles – 'Corbels', 'Scantlings', 'Noggings', 'Jack Rafters' – make perfect sense of music so robust and artisanal, full of light and laughter and yet with a poignancy every now and then as well. Haslam's use of the tarogato is ever more sophisticated, and it has almost turned into his main voice, as his baritone playing becomes plainer-toned and less abrasive. There are moments on the big horn when Haslam sounds close to the West Coast figures – Chaloff and Mulligan – who originally inspired him. A strong and delightful record.

Gary Hassay

ALTO SAXOPHONE

Hassay is an improvising saxophonist active since the late '70s, with a wide-ranging CV of sideman appearances.

***** Blackwater Bridge**

Drimala 02-347-02 *Hassay; Anne LeBaron (hp, perc).* 12/01.

Hassay's dry sound and careful, at times almost pointillistic phrasing are an interesting pairing with LeBaron's almost limitless tonal palette. It's somewhat to his disadvantage to have such a partner, since her unfamiliar and disarmingly fresh vocabulary draws the ear almost continuously, while his more dour course of action seems to offer much less appeal. It's a rather strange match overall, the altoist resolutely avoiding extended techniques while the harpist seems to have such a wide range of resource at her disposal, from conventionally sonorous lines to grating 'prepared' sounds and guitar-like counterpoint. A comparatively hectic piece such as 'Never Told Tales' finds the duo at its most effective. Sampled in small doses, effective.

Ake 'Stan' Hasselgård (1922–48)

CLARINET

Despite his modest legacy of recordings, Hasselgård is widely recognized as a major player and one of the very few to make a convincing case for the clarinet as a bop instrument. After his apprentice years in his native Sweden, he went to New York in the '40s and worked for a time with his original idol, Benny Goodman. The evidence is that he was able to outplay the master when it came to bebop. But his life ended in a road accident while driving to California.

***** At Click 1948**

Dragon DRCD 183 *Hasselgård; Benny Goodman (cl); Wardell Gray (ts); Teddy Wilson (p); Billy Bauer (g); Arnold Fishkind (b); Mel Zelnick (d).* 5–6/48.

*****(*) The Permanent Hasselgård**

Phontastic NCD 8802 *As above, except add Tyree Glenn (tb), Red Norvo, Allan Johansson (vib), Thore Swanerud (p, vib), Hasse Eriksson, Lyman Gandee (p), Sten Carlberg (g), Rollo Garberg, Jud DeNaut (b), Uffe Baadh, Nick Fatool (d), Louis Tobin (v).* 10/45–11/48.

***** Cottontop 1946–1948**

Dragon DRCD 332 *Similar to above discs, except add Mary Lou Williams, Per-Erik Sperrings, Barbara Carroll (p), Chuck Wayne (g), Simon Brehm, Clyde Lombardi (b), Bertil Frylmark (d), Jackie Searle (v).* 1/46–11/48.

Stan Hasselgård left only a handful of legitimate recordings at the time of his death, but the diligence of Lars Westin of Dragon Records in Sweden has ensured that his legacy has been enriched by many airshots and private records. There is something like five CDs' worth of material to be issued. Dragon originally issued four LPs, and the *At Click* CD begins a programme of CD transfers, while the Phontastic release covers the broad spectrum of the clarinettist's work.

His precocious talent and early death have made Hasselgård something of a folk hero in Swedish jazz circles, and the evidence of the surviving tracks is that he was an outstanding player. He worshipped Goodman and never tried to evade comparisons with his guru, but the traces of bebop in his playing hint at a stylistic truce which he never had the opportunity to develop further. The Goodman septet, which featured Hasselgård, is comprehensively covered on *At Click*, where the Swede worked with his idol in a two-week engagement. The contrast between the two players isn't as interesting as the similarity: often it's quite hard to tell them apart, and whatever Hasselgård is reputed to have taught Goodman about bop isn't clear from this music. In fact, Hasselgård often gets short shrift in these tracks, with Goodman getting the lion's share of the solos, and Gray and Wilson taking their share. But it's surprising to hear Goodman playing on the likes of 'Mary's Idea' and even 'Donna Lee'. The sound varies, but the meticulous remastering has done the best possible job.

Anyone wanting a one-disc primer on Hasselgård, though, is directed to the Phontastic compilation, which includes many of the tracks on the earlier Dragon releases as well as four fine quintet tracks led by the clarinettist (in excellent sound), a feature for Tyree Glenn and a sextet track with Red Norvo. A generously filled and respectful memorial to a fine player.

Cottontop, the most recent retrieval work by Dragon (Lars Westin is clearly a concerned guardian of Hasselgård's spirit), is something of a hotch-potch. Some rare private recordings and acetates are in poor shape aurally, and on some tracks there's no more than a glimpse of Hasselgård. Yet the solos on two takes of 'Patsy's Idea', taken down only weeks before his death, and a few other passages, all point to his mastery.

Hampton Hawes (1928–77)

PIANO

Born in Los Angeles, where he stayed, Hawes was a major player in West Coast '50s jazz, his career foundering when he was imprisoned for narcotics offences but quickly reviving on his release in 1963. Combined blues and bebop forms with rare energy and acumen and, though he toyed with fusion-lite towards the end, he remained a prodigious player.

****(*) Piano: East/West**
Original Jazz Classics OJCCD 1705 *Hawes; Larry Bunker (vib); Clarence Jones (b); Larance Marable (d). 12/52.*

Hampton Hawes is still something of a well-guarded secret, a name known to jazz piano fans but still to break through to a wider audience. Given the sheer exhilaration and lyrical intensity of his music, it is strange that he is not better known. All the more so, given the spectacularly self-destructive mythology he sketched out in his autobiography, *Raise Up Off Me*, one of the most moving memoirs ever written by a musician, and a classic of jazz writing.

An Angelean, Hawes worked with Charlie Parker on the West Coast and learned a huge amount from him. This set, shared with Freddie Redd, who represents the opposite seaboard, is a reasonable representation of the 24-year-old at work, still not quite settled into a personal idiom, still drawing more than he would later from a saxophone sound. He gets off a good solo on 'Hamp's Paws' and on 'I'll Remember April', but he never quite blends convincingly with vibraharpist Bunker, and Jones is too understated a player to give the group sound much presence.

****** The Trio**
Original Jazz Classics OJCCD 316 *Hawes; Red Mitchell (b); Chuck Thompson (d). 6/55.*

****** The Trio**
Original Jazz Classics OJCCD 318 *As above. 12/55.*

*****(*) Everybody Likes Hampton Hawes**
Original Jazz Classics OJCCD 421 *As above. 1/56.*

These were really Hawes's first serious statements as leader and they are still hugely impressive, combining long, demanding passages of locked-hands chording and fast, unpredictable melody lines. The bebop idiom is still firmly in place but already Hawes is demonstrating an ability to construct elaborate out-of-tempo solo statements which seem almost detached from the theme being approached but which are drawn entirely from its chord structure.

Mitchell is a wonderful accompanist, already experimenting with his trademark tuning and getting a huge sound out of the bass. Thompson is a resolute and often sophisticated player, who has been quite extensively recorded and always manages to catch the ear.

*****(*) All Night Session: Volume 1**
Original Jazz Classics OJCCD 638 *Hawes; Jim Hall (g); Red Mitchell (b); Bruz Freeman (d). 1/56.*

*****(*) All Night Session: Volume 2**
Original Jazz Classics OJCCD 639 *As above. 11/56.*

***** All Night Session: Volume 3**
Original Jazz Classics OJCCD 640 *As above. 11/56.*

Hawes's recording of the night of 12/13 November 1956 remains one of his very best. The material was mainly familiar bop fare – 'Groovin' High', 'I'll Remember April', 'Woody'N'You' – but cuts like 'Hampton's Pulpit' are a reminder of the pianist's church background and the curious underswell of gospel, Bach and Rachmaninov that keeps refreshing the topwaters of his harmony. Hall is magnificent, picking out clear, uncluttered lines against the leader's brisk chords.

The pace has certainly slackened and the quality fallen away by Volume Three, but this is a hugely enjoyable set which one day will doubtless be compiled and perhaps edited down in an affordable double-CD set. Roll on.

*****(*) Four!**
Original Jazz Classics OJCCD 165 *Hawes; Barney Kessel (g); Red Mitchell (b); Shelly Manne (d). 1/58.*

Kessel's rather conventional approach has always put us off *Four!* Renewed acquaintance suggests that it's a transitional record. Hawes was responsive enough to hear the first whispers of a new style coming in off the air and he tries to toughen up his delivery, sounding more like the great swing pianists (Teddy Wilson, especially) than boppers like Bud and Monk. If that seems ironic, it also makes sense, for Hampton was always trying to broker a style which combined the strengths of old and new, and this was one of the places where the synthesis worked *and* showed the joins.

****** For Real**
Original Jazz Classics OJCCD 713 *Hawes; Harold Land (ts); Scott LaFaro (b); Frank Butler (d). 3/58.*

A strong album from an exceptional band. LaFaro's short career had many spectacular moments, but few as sheerly joyous as this one. 'Wrap Your Troubles In Dreams' and 'Crazeology' use altered chords and passing notes to create a subtle harmonic environment in which piano and bass are equal front-line partners with the saxophone. Land is in cracking form and feeds exuberantly on cues in the leader's own solos. The closing

'I Love You' is one of Hawes's most completely satisfying recorded performances, every element balanced and communicative.

***(*) The Sermon

Original Jazz Classics OJC 1067 *Hawes; Leroy Vinnegar (b); Stan Levey (d).* 11/58.

This was on Contemporary's shelf for many years before its original release. A group of spirituals given a hefty injection of the blues, and at the end Hawes drops the prayer book altogether and plays nine minutes of 'Blues N/C'. If it feels of a lighter weight than some of Hawes's albums from this time, there's still a lot of great piano from one of the masters of this period – and listen to Stan Levey's delicious work on that closing blues.

***(*) The Green Leaves Of Summer

Original Jazz Classics OJCCD 476 *Hawes; Monk Montgomery (b); Steve Ellington (d).* 2/64.

Hawes spent the early '60s in jail, a tough woodshed for anyone; but, as he explains in the autobiography, one that gave him a new philosophy which couldn't help but come out in the playing. From here on, he seems devoted to a robust beauty and to an approach to ballad-playing that would almost become a mannerism towards the end but which is still new at this stage: opening a tune with a long rubato introduction, unaccompanied, and as yet uninvolved with the melody. Later it could seem a little contrived, but at this stage it has all the resonance and the chastened passion of a man who has not had his liberty or his voice for some time.

Monk Montgomery is the elder brother of guitarist Wes, a solid, dependable player without much sparkle or brio but constant in his task and capable of surprise here and there.

*** Here And Now

Original Jazz Classics OJCCD 178 *Hawes; Chuck Israels (b); Donald Bailey (d).* 5/65.

*** I'm All Smiles

Original Jazz Classics OJCCD 796 *Hawes; Red Mitchell (b); Donald Bailey (d).* 4–5/66.

*** The Seance

Original Jazz Classics OJCCD 455 *As above.* 5/66.

The later of these, recorded in performance at Mitchell's Studio Club in Hampton's native LA, marked his last recordings with the other Mitchell. 'The Shadow Of Your Smile' is quite exceptional, an elegantly crafted and intelligent response to the theme from *The Sandpiper*, which has often tempted even otherwise tasteful players into schmaltz. *Here And Now*, with the underrated Israels, still betrays some shades of the prison-house, a slight stiffness and irresolution, but it's difficult to make an absolute distinction between these records, which are pretty much form-guide performances from Hawes.

His touch is as good as it was ever to be, with variations in that familiar locked-hands approach that allowed him to roll chords and arpeggiate some of the more significant of them. He is also audibly listening to his bass player much more, drawing and feeding ideas, back and forth. Exhilarating music, marred only here and there by slightly tired formulae, like anecdotes told once too often.

*** Live At Memory Lane

Fresh Sound FSRCD 406 *Hawes; Harry 'Sweets' Edison (t); Sonny Criss (as); Teddy Edwards (ts); Leroy Vinnegar (b); Bobby Thompson (d); Joe Turner (v).* 70.

**(*) Live In Montreux 71

Fresh Sound FSRCD 133 *Hawes; Henry Franklin (b); Michael Carvin (d).* 6/71.

Live, Hawes was maddeningly inconsistent, but he usually managed to produce some diamonds out of the silt. The second of these is pretty much definitive of what the Hawes trio was about in the last decade of his life: funky, lyrical jazz, with a mixture of bop and pre-bop elements. The Montreux set has a verbose, grandstanding quality that might be explained by the glitzy setting; Hawes often sounded portentous away from what he regarded as his natural turf, as if compensating for his own insecurity.

The other Fresh Sound is interesting in teaming him with some of the other stalwarts of the Los Angeles scene. Good, too, to hear him with horns. Jazz has never been well served by television on either side of the Atlantic, but this record stands as a reminder of what could be done. Hawes and his group were captured at a beat-up club in LA as part of a series of short films made by Jack Lewerke. The combination of Criss and Hawes is irresistible and their blues interpretations are impeccable. The entry of Joe Turner dilutes the musical content a little, but the audience love it and the sound of cheering must have attracted Teddy Edwards, who sits in for a final extended blues jam on which Edison is rather disappointing. Good, clubby sound, though.

**(*) Plays Movie Musicals

Fresh Sound FSR CD 65 *Hawes; Bobby West (b); Larry Bunker (d); strings.* 8/68.

The strings kill it, reducing Hawes's crisp lines to mush. There is plenty of attractive music on the record and the sound is above average for the vintage, but it's lost in the background. By this, given how short time was, anything and everything was precious, and Hawes was spending much of his time in a slew of electronic instruments which brought him much-needed work and cash but reduced him to a middle-order funkster.

*** High In The Sky

Fresh Sound FSR 59 *Hawes; Leroy Vinnegar (b); Donald Bailey (d).* 70.

The final few years of Hawes's life saw a simultaneous resurgence and retreat from experiment. Heard out of context, this 1970 session is almost anonymous. As often as not, it is Vinnegar's distinctive walking style which catches the attention and only on 'Evening Trane' – an interesting exercise in altered changes – and 'High In The Sky' itself does the leader sound as if he is wholly engaged.

Fresh Sound releases are never the most glittering of recordings, and this one has a rather flat and unresonant ambience; not unattractive, but far from flattering.

**(*) Northern Windows Plus

Prestige 24278 *Hawes; Alan DiRienzo, Snooky Young (t); George Bohannon (tb); William Green, Jackie Kelso, Jay Migliori (sax, f); Bob Cranshaw, Carol Kaye (b); Kenny Clarke, Spider Webb (d).* 73, 74.

Very disappointing. This brings together two albums from the early '70s. The first and better is a live trio set from the

Montreux Jazz Festival with Bob Cranshaw and Kenny Clarke. Originally released as *Playin' In The Yard*, it opens with a fine version of the Rollins tune, followed by three so-so originals and a pleasantly emotive 'Stella By Starlight'. If only it had stopped there. Unfortunately, the second half of the set is the whole unedifying span of *Northern Windows*, with orchestral arrangements by David Axelrod. Anyone lucky enough to have the original *Playin' In The Yard* will continue to play it. We guarantee you won't give the rest a second go.

*** Something Special

Contemporary CCD 14072 *Hawes; Denny Diaz (g); Leroy Vinnegar (b); Al Williams (d).* 6/76.

Hawes kept super-busy right to the end. There is certainly no deterioration and no sense of fated hurry about his work during the summer of 1976. This is a particularly relaxed session, recorded almost on the beach at a club in Half Moon Bay, California. He had been working in commercial settings for some time and it was only on occasions like this that he could afford to slip back into straight jazz, though 'Fly Me To The Moon' has a quasi-pop feel to it. Also on the date was Denny Diaz, who had been working with Steely Dan and Al Williams, an undersubscribed player who eventually gave up performance to manage Birdland West (now sadly defunct). Vinnegar, as ever, is poised and resourceful, and it is often he who provides the musical stimulus to the leader, prodding him on rhythmically (Williams is too accommodating) and throwing in fresh melodic ideas. Great time-keeper, too; set your watch by him. Not a classic, but a valuable document and meat and drink to Hawes fans.

*** At The Piano

Original Jazz Classics OJCCD 877 *Hawes; Ray Brown (b); Shelly Manne (d).* 8/76.

Indian summer. Hawes seemed to find a measure of calm and contentment in the last year of his life, at least when there was a decent piano on offer. This is as good a place as any to take our leave of him. The second round of duos with Charlie Haden was still ahead, with its promise of more inventive improvisation, but this is in effect the last session as leader and as generous a send-off as he could have organized. As so often over the last few years, Hampton relied on a powerful bass player to reinforce the architecture of his changes playing. There are moments here, even on the relatively straight reading of 'Killing Me Softly With His Song', when the harmonic floor seems to drop out of the music. It's Brown who comes to the rescue every time.

'Blue In Green' and 'When I Grow Too Old To Dream' are sterling performances and the sound is balanced to perfection there and throughout.

*** Blues The Most

Prestige 11015 *Hawes; Harold Land (ts); Jim Hall, Barney Kessel (g); Ray Brown, Scott LaFaro, Red Mitchell (b); Frank Butler, Bruz Freeman, Shelly Manne, Chuck Thompson (d).* 58–76.

The emphasis falls entirely on the blues for this useful but one-dimensional selection from Hampton's career. There is nothing new to entice the collector and the packaging doesn't yield up any fresh insights either. Wisely, the emphasis falls on earlier material, with just one track from 1976, when the fires were almost out. A good buy only if you have no Hawes in the collection and even then we'd recommend you start elsewhere.

Coleman Hawkins (1901–69)

TENOR SAXOPHONE, VOCAL

Born in St Joseph, Missouri, Hawkins played in Chicago as a teenager and joined singer Mamie Smith's band in 1921. His reputation took off after joining Fletcher Henderson in 1924, and he stayed for ten years, before a European sojourn which lasted until 1939. That same year he recorded one of the biggest of all jazz hits, 'Body And Soul'. Ran small groups (with a nod towards bop) in the '40s and also played with Jazz At The Philharmonic. Worked as a solo artist in the '50s and '60s, often with compadres like Roy Eldridge, and maintained an elder-statesman aplomb, although he finally succumbed to a poor diet and a taste for brandy in 1969, having done everything he could in jazz. Hawkins modelled the saxophone for everyone who came after him, and he remained its most statesmanlike exponent.

**** Coleman Hawkins 1929–1934

Classics 587 *Hawkins; Henry 'Red' Allen, Jack Purvis (t, v); Russell Smith, Bobby Stark (t); Muggsy Spanier (c); Glenn Miller, J. C. Higginbotham, Claude Jones, Dicky Wells (tb); Russell Procope, Hilton Jefferson, Jimmy Dorsey (cl, as); Pee Wee Russell (cl); Adrian Rollini (bsx); Red McKenzie (comb, v); Frank Froeba, Jack Russin, Horace Henderson, Buck Washington (p); Bernard Addison, Jack Bland, Will Johnson (g); George 'Pops' Foster, Al Morgan, John Kirby (b); Gene Krupa, Charles Kegley, Josh Billings, Walter Johnson (d).* 11/29–3/34.

The first great role-model for all saxophonists began recording in 1922, but compilations of his earlier work usually start with his European sojourn in 1934. This valuable cross-section of the preceding five years shows Hawkins reaching an almost sudden maturity. He was taking solos with Fletcher Henderson in 1923 and was already recognizably Hawkins, but the big sound and freewheeling rhythmic command weren't really evident until later. By 1929 he was one of the star soloists in the Henderson band – which he remained faithful to for over ten years – and the blazing improvisation on the first track here, 'Hello Lola' by Red McKenzie's Mound City Blue Blowers, indicates the extent of his confidence. But he still sounds a little tied to the underlying beat, and it isn't until the octet session of September 1933 that Hawkins establishes the gliding but muscular manner of his '30s music. The ensuing Horace Henderson date of October 1933 has a feast of great Hawkins, culminating in the astonishing extended solo on 'I've Got To Sing A Torch Song', with its baleful low honks and daring manipulation of the time. Three final duets with Buck Washington round out the disc, but an earlier session under the leadership of the trumpeter Jack Purvis must also be mentioned: in a curious line-up including Adrian Rollini and J. C. Higginbotham, Hawkins plays a dark, serious role. Fine transfers throughout.

*** The Hawk In Europe

ASV AJA 5054 *Hawkins; Arthur Briggs, Noel Chiboust, Pierre Allier, Jack Bulterman, George Van Helvoirt (t); Benny Carter (t, as); Guy Paquinet, Marcel Thielemans, George Chisholm (tb); André Ekyan, Charles Lisée, Alix Combelle, Wim Poppink, Sal Doof, Andre Van der Ouderaa, Jimmy Williams (saxes); Stanley Black, Stéphane Grappelli, Nico De Rooy, Freddy Johnson (p); Albert Harris, Django Reinhardt, Jack Pet, Fritz Reinders, Ray Webb (g); Tiny Winters, Len*

Harrison, Eugene D'Hellemmes, Toon Diepenbroek (b); Maurice Chaillou, Kees Kranenburg, Tommy Benford, Robert Montmarche (d). 11/34–5/37.

*****(*) Coleman Hawkins 1934–1937**

Classics 602 *As above, except add Henk Hinrichs (t), Ernst Hoellerhagen (cl, as), Omer De Cock, Hugo Peritz (ts), Ernest Berner, Theo Uden Masman (p), Billy Toffel (g), James Gobalet (b), Benny Peritz (d), Annie De Reuver (v); omit Carter, Williams, Johnson and Webb.* 11/34–37.

Hawkins arrived in England in March 1934 and stayed in the old world for five years. Most of his records from the period have him as featured soloist with otherwise strictly directed orchestras, and while this might have been occasionally discomforting – the routines on such as 'What Harlem Is To Me' with the Dutch group The Ramblers aren't much better than a suave variation on Armstrong's contemporary struggles – Hawkins was polishing a sophisticated, rhapsodic style into something as powerful as his more aggressive, earlier manner. Two sessions with Benny Carter, including the four tumultuous titles made by the All Star Jam Band, are included on the ASV set, while the Classics sticks to the chronology; but the ASV sound is much more mixed. Classics begin with four titles made in London with Stanley Black at the piano, continue with dates in The Hague, Paris and Laren, and add the little-known Zurich session which finds Hawkins singing on the fairly awful 'Love Cries'! A spirited 'Tiger Rag' makes amends, and there's a curiosity in an unidentified acetate (in very poor sound) to close the disc. 'I Wish I Were Twins', 'What A Difference A Day Made' and 'Netcha's Dream' are three examples of the lush but shrewdly handled and often risky solos which Hawkins creates on an instrument which had still only recently come of age.

****** Coleman Hawkins 1937–1939**

Classics 613 *Hawkins; Jack Bulterman, George Van Helvoirt (t); Benny Carter (t, as); Maurice Thielemans (tb); Wim Poppink (cl, as); Alix Combelle, Andre Van der Ouderaa (cl, ts); Sal Doof (as); Nico De Rooy, Stéphane Grappelli, Freddy Johnson (p); Fritz Reinders, Django Reinhardt (g); Jack Pet, Eugene D'Hellemmes (b); Tommy Benford, Kees Kranenburg, Maurice Van Cleef (d).* 4/37–6/38.

****** Coleman Hawkins In Europe**

Timeless CBC 1-006 *As above discs.* 11/34–5/39.

The last of Hawk's European recordings. The All Star Jam Band titles turn up here again, as well as a further session with The Ramblers, but otherwise the main interest is in ten titles with just Freddy Johnson (and Maurice van Cleef on the final six). 'Lamentation', 'Devotion' and 'Star Dust' are masterclasses in horn technique, Hawkins exploring the registers and feeling through the harmonies with complete control. The sound is good, although the engineers aren't bothered about surface hiss.

The Timeless CD cherrypicks some of the best Hawkins of the '30s: the London quartet session of 1934, four tracks with The Berries, one with Reinhardt, five with The Ramblers, and a London pair with Jack Hylton from 1939. The very fine remastering is by John R. T. Davies: enough said.

*****(*) Coleman Hawkins 1939–1940**

Classics 634 *Hawkins; Tommy Lindsay, Joe Guy, Tommy Stevenson, Nelson Bryant (t); Benny Carter (t, as); Earl Hardy, J. C. Higginbotham, William Cato, Sandy Williams, Claude Jones (tb); Danny Polo (cl); Eustis Moore, Jackie Fields, Ernie Powell (as); Kermit Scott (ts); Gene Rodgers, Joe Sullivan (p); Ulysses Livingston (g, v); Lawrence Lucie, Bernard Addison, Gene Fields (g); William Oscar Smith, Artie Shapiro, Johnny Williams, Billy Taylor (b); Arthur Herbert, George Wettling, Walter Johnson, Big Sid Catlett, J. C. Heard (d); Thelma Carpenter, Jeanne Burns, Joe Turner, Gladys Madden (v).* 10/39–8/40.

Hawkins didn't exactly return to the USA in triumph, but his eminence was almost immediately re-established with the astounding 'Body And Soul', which still sounds like the most spontaneously perfect of all jazz records. Fitted into the session as an afterthought (they had already cut 12 previous takes of 'Fine Dinner' and eight of 'Meet Doctor Foo'), this one-take, two-chorus improvisation is so completely realized, every note meaningful, the tempo ideal, the rhapsodic swing irresistible, and the sense of rising drama sustained to the final coda, that it still has the capacity to amaze new listeners, just like Armstrong's 'West End Blues' or Parker's 'Bird Gets The Worm'. A later track on the Classics CD, the little-known 'Dedication', revisits the same setting; although masterful in its way, it points up how genuinely immediate the greatest jazz is: it can't finally compare to the original. If the same holds good for the many later versions of the tune which Hawkins set down, his enduring variations on the structure (and it's intriguing to note that he only refers to the original melody in the opening bars of the 1939 reading – which didn't stop it from becoming a huge hit) say something about his own powers of renewal.

The Classics CD is let down by dubbing from some very surfacey originals, even though it includes some strong material – two Varsity Seven sessions with Carter and Polo, the aforementioned 'Dedication' and a 1940 date for OKeh which features some excellent tenor on 'Rocky Comfort' and 'Passin' It Around.

***** The Radio Days 1940**

Jazz Unlimited 201 2075 *Hawkins; Tommy Stevenson, Joe Guy, Tommy Lindsay (t); Nelson Bryant (t, v); Sandy Williams, Claude Jones, William Cato (tb); Eustis Moore, Jackie Fields, (as); Ernie Powell (cl, as); Kermit Scott (ts); Gene Rodgers (p); Billy Taylor (b); J. C. Heard (d); Gladys Madden (v).* 8/41.

Airshots by Hawkins's short-lived big band. There were some strong soloists in the band, but they're not heard to much advantage in what is really a vehicle for the leader and little else. Some of the ensemble playing is as rough as the recording, but Hawkins didn't seem bothered and, in arguably his greatest period, this is a valuable survival.

****** The Complete Coleman Hawkins**

Mercury 830960-2 4CD *Hawkins; Roy Eldridge, Joe Thomas, Buck Clayton, Charlie Shavers (t); Jack Teagarden, Trummy Young (tb); Hank D'Amico (cl); Tab Smith (as); Don Byas (ts); Harry Carney (bs); Teddy Wilson, Earl Hines, Johnny Guarnieri, Herman Chittison (p); Teddy Walters (g); Israel Crosby, Billy Taylor, John Kirby, Al Lucas, Slam Stewart (b); Cozy Cole, Denzil Best, Big Sid Catlett, George Wettling (d).* 1–12/44.

*****(*) Rainbow Mist**

Delmark DD-459 *Hawkins; Dizzy Gillespie, Vic Coulson, Ed Vandever (t); Leo Parker, Leonard Lowry (as); Georgie Auld, Ben Webster, Don Byas, Ray Abrams (ts); Budd Johnson (ts, bs); Clyde Hart, Bill Rowland (p); Hy White (g); Oscar Pettiford, Israel Crosby (b); Max Roach, Specs Powell (d).* 2–5/44.

*****(*) Coleman Hawkins 1943–1944**

Classics 807 *As above, except add Cootie Williams, Roy Eldridge (t), Edmond Hall, Andy Fitzgerald (cl), Art Tatum, Ellis Larkins, Eddie Heywood (p), Al Casey, Jimmy Shirley (g), Shelly Manne, Max Roach (d).* 12/43–2/44.

***** Coleman Hawkins 1944**

Classics 842 *Similar to above discs.* 2–5/44.

1944 was a busy year for Hawkins in the studios. His Keynote recordings have been reissued in various editions over the years, but the Mercury set includes the whole series and has no fewer than 27 alternative takes. The eight sessions have a number of all-star line-ups; particularly outstanding are two quartet dates with Wilson, the Sax Ensemble session with Smith, Carney and Byas and a Cozy Cole group with Earl Hines. Hawkins plays on a consistently high level and there is treasure on all four discs. Delmark's *Rainbow Mist* includes three sessions for Apollo. The first includes what's thought of as the first bop recording, 'Woody'N'You', which also features Gillespie's first modern solo, and 'Rainbow Mist' itself is a little-known but superb variation on the 'Body And Soul' chords. A sextet with Auld and Webster is the makeweight. Sound is quite good, though these weren't the liveliest of recordings.

The Classics discs cover similar territory, but Classics 807 includes some other excellent material: an Esquire All Stars date with Tatum in imperious form, and three sessions for Signature, with Hawk outstanding on 'The Man I Love', 'Sweet Lorraine' and 'Lover Come Back To Me'.

*****(*) Coleman Hawkins 1944–1945**

Classics 863 *Hawkins; Charlie Shavers, Jonah Jones, Buck Clayton, Howard McGhee (t); Eddie Barefield (cl, as); Edmond Hall (cl); Hilton Jefferson (as); Walter Foots Thomas (ts); Clyde Hart, Thelonious Monk, Teddy Wilson, Sir Charles Thompson (p); Tiny Grimes (g); Billy Taylor, Edward Bass Robinson, Oscar Pettiford, Milt Hinton, Slam Stewart (b); Denzil Best, Cozy Cole (d).* 7/44–1/45.

****** Coleman Hawkins 1945**

Classics 926 *Hawkins; Howard McGhee, Dick Vance (t); Vic Dickenson, Tyree Glenn (tb); Hilton Jefferson (as); Sir Charles Thompson, Billy Taylor, Art Tatum (p); Allan Reuss, Al Casey (g); Oscar Pettiford, John Simmons (b); Denzil Best, Big Sid Catlett (d); Matthew Meredith (v).* 1/44–10/45.

The merit of the Classics discs is the way they catch sessions that have been missed off other Hawkins collections. Classics 863 includes some of the final dates for Keynote, but adds four tracks where Hawkins guested with a Walter Thomas group, a septet date with Shavers and Hall (lovely rhapsodizing on 'All The Things You Are'), four quartet tracks with Monk (though the pianist is disappointingly unexceptional) and a final date where Howard McGhee begins the fruitful association that would blossom on the Capitol sessions.

These form the bulk of Classics 926 and make it essential. The dozen titles were made on a recording trip to Los Angeles, with McGhee an ebullient and *simpatico* partner: 'Rifftide' and 'Stuffy' show the older man relishing the challenge of McGhee's almost-bop pyrotechnics, although the sly intrusions of Vic Dickenson on four other titles are just as effective, and Pettiford and Best are a crackling rhythm section. Excellent sound on these sessions. Four titles with a Sid Catlett group are less valuable, but there are two intriguing bonuses: a two-part *a cappella* solo for the Selmer label, comprising some themeless variations (though 'Body And Soul' never seems far away), and a glimpse of Hawkins with Art Tatum on a V-Disc of 'My Ideal'.

*****(*) Coleman Hawkins 1946–1947**

Classics 984 *Hawkins; Charlie Shavers, Buck Clayton, Miles Davis (t); J. J. Johnson, Kai Winding (tb); Pete Brown, Porter Kilbert (as); Allen Eager (ts); Harry Carney (bs); Hank Jones, Jimmy Jones, Teddy Wilson (p); Milt Jackson (vib); Mary Osborne, John Collins, Chuck Wayne (g); Al McKibbon, Chubby Jackson, Curley Russell, Jack Lesberg (b); Shelly Manne, Shadow Wilson, Max Roach (d); Delores Martin, Leslie Scott (v).* 2/46–10/47.

*****(*) Coleman Hawkins 1947–1950**

Classics 1162 *Hawkins; Fats Navarro, Erik 'Skippy' Hansen (t); J. J. Johnson, Benny Green, Nat Peck (tb); Budd Johnson, Hubert Fol (as); Frank Jensen (ts); Marion Di Veta (bs); Hank Jones, Al Haig, Jean-Paul Mangeon Leo Mathisen, Billy Taylor (p); Chuck Wayne, John Collins (g); Jack Lesberg, Nelson Boyd, Pierre Michelot, Erik Kirschner, Percy Heath (b); Max Roach, Shadow Wilson, Kenny Clarke, Gorm Lertoft, Art Blakey (d).* 12/47–8/50.

Again, the Classics sequence mixes up well-known material with interesting obscurities, making both of these musts for Hawkins specialists. Classics 984 starts with two fine sessions for Victor, one a boppish foray with Allen Eager spelling Hawk on two titles, the other an Esquire Award Winners group where Hawkins, Johnson and Clayton are terrific across four titles. Then a classic date with Navarro and Johnson featuring the debut of Monk's 'I Mean You', two obscure tracks with Delores Martin singing, four for Aladdin with Miles Davis and Kai Winding (Hawk superb on 'Isn't It Romantic') and four ballads by Leslie Scott, with the tenorman taking some beatific solos. Classics 1162 is almost as appealing a mix: it starts with the other top-notch date with Navarro and Johnson ('Half Step Down, Please' especially), then goes to the celebrated tenor solo on 'Picasso', a variation on his 'Body And Soul' matrix. Four almost R&B-ish titles for Mercury follow, before some dates in Paris, two tracks from a stopover in Copenhagen and four big-toned ballads cut for the Royal Roost label on his return to New York. No matter what the context, Hawkins plays with authority: the most striking thing to take away from all these various dates is the huge sound he made, even alongside the likes of Navarro.

***** The Alternative Takes Vol. 1 1935–1943**

Neatwork RP 2007 *As appropriate discs above.* 2/35–12/43.

***** The Alternative Takes Vol. 2 1943–1944**

Neatwork RP 2011 *As appropriate discs above.* 5/40–5/44.

***** The Alternative Takes Vol. 3 1944–1949**

Neatwork RP 2014 *As appropriate discs above.* 10/44–12/49.

The first volume of Neatwork's trawl through the alternate Hawkins is in the main devoted to his European recordings, all but four of the tracks emanating from various Dutch sessions. A nice addendum to the Classics sequence, mostly in good sound. Volume 2 is of somewhat less appeal since it offers alternatives to the Keynote and Emarcy sessions which are comprehensively included on the multidisc set listed above; there are, though, three alternates from Commodore sessions. The third volume has a lot more from Keynote, but it also has no fewer than 12 alternates from the Walter Thomas session for Joe Davis, as well as a couple of 1949 tracks for Vogue. As usual, specialists may welcome these issues more than will less hard-core Hawk devotees, but taken on their own merits each includes a lot of fine music.

CORE COLLECTION

***(*) Body And Soul

Dreyfus FDM 36721-2 *Hawkins; as various discs above.* 10/39–8/49.

Though it starts with the inevitable track, this actually takes a thoughtful and well-chosen journey through some of the best of Hawkins's '40s work, heavy on the ballads but with the occasional flag-waver to up the pace.

*** 1949 Lausanne

TCB 02132 *Hawkins; Nat Peck (t); Hubert Fol (as); James Moody (ts); Jean-Paul Mangeon (p); Pierre Michelot (b); Kenny Clarke (d).* 12/49.

Alive and well in Switzerland. Hawkins strolls on stage for 'Rifftide' and quickly establishes his authority. The band were alive to the new music and give him genial support, even if they are a bit overawed at the presence of the master, and Moody's showing off is a bit of an annoyance. Musty sound but a fine period-piece.

***(*) Body And Soul Revisited

GRP 051627-2 *Hawkins; Benny Harris, Idrees Sulieman, Joe Wilder (t); Rex Stewart (c); Tyree Glenn, Matthew Gee, Jimmy Knepper (tb); Tony Scott (cl); Cecil Payne (bs); Duke Jordan, Hank Jones, Sanford Gold, Tommy Flanagan, Claude Hopkins (p); Bill Doggett, Danny Mendelsohn (ky); Al Casimenti, Billy Bauer, George Barnes (g); Wendell Marshall, Gene Casey, Conrad Henry, Arvell Shaw, Trigger Alpert (b); Art Taylor, Bunny Shawker, Jimmy Crawford, Cozy Cole, Shadow Wilson, Walter Bolden (d).* 10/51–10/58.

This sweeps up miscellaneous Decca sessions of the '50s. Hawk is here with strings, with small groups, at a live date, with an odd group featuring Cozy Cole, Rex Stewart and Tyree Glenn, playing a two-minute unaccompanied solo and delivering a final (previously unreleased) blues with Tony Scott. Some tracks are little more than filler, but much excellent Hawkins too.

**(*) Bean And The Boys

High Note HCD 7075 *Hawkins; Charlie Shavers (t); J. C. Higginbotham, Bennie Green (tb); Pee Wee Russell (cl); Johnny Acea, Willie 'The Lion' Smith (p); Harry Sheppard (vib); Dicky Thompson (g); Tommy Potter, Al Lucas, Vinnie Burke (b); Osie Johnson, Art Taylor, Sonny Greer (d).* 5/50–9/58.

A ragged collection of bits and pieces from the '50s: three tracks with rhythm from 1954, where Hawkins sounds a bit breathless; three very rough-sounding pieces with Green, Potter and Taylor; a rather good 'Rifftide' from a 1950 Apollo broadcast; and a slapdash Dixieland jam on 'Avalon', in which Hawkins finally emerges over a ludicrously fast tempo. Specialists only.

***(*) The Hawk In Hi-Fi

Bluebird 63842-2 *Hawkins; Billy Byers orchestra including Charlie Shavers (t); Zoot Sims, Al Cohn (ts); Hank Jones (p).* 56.

A scrupulous reissue of a superficially slight Hawkins session, the excellent remastered sound brings the occasion vividly back to life (complete with a long string of discarded takes, although for once some of these are worth keeping). Byers's charts on a dozen tunes – mostly standards, but also a couple of blues and a reworking of 'Bean And The Boys' – are slightly more interesting than those for the easy-listening audience the album was doubtless aimed at, and from the fresh take on 'Body And Soul' onwards, Hawkins sounds keen and interested. A fine sleeve-note by Jeff Sultanof sets the contemporary scene very nicely.

***(*) The Genius Of Coleman Hawkins

Verve 539065-2 *Hawkins; Oscar Peterson (p); Herb Ellis (g); Ray Brown (b); Alvin Stoller (d).* 57.

**** Coleman Hawkins Encounters Ben Webster

Verve 521427-2 *As above, except add Ben Webster (ts).* 3/59.

*** Coleman Hawkins & Confreres

Verve 835255-2 *As above, except add Roy Eldridge (t), Hank Jones (p), George Duvivier (b), Mickey Sheen (d).* 10/57–2/58.

*** At The Opera House

Verve 521641-2 *Hawkins; Roy Eldridge (t); J. J. Johnson (tb); Stan Getz, Lester Young (ts); John Lewis, Oscar Peterson (p); Percy Heath (b); Connie Kay (d).* 9–10/57.

***(*) Coleman Hawkins: Verve Jazz Masters 34

Verve 521586-2 *As above Verve discs, except add Cecil Payne (bs), Al Haig, Tommy Flanagan, Teddy Wilson (p), John Collins (g), Major Locke, John Kirby, Israel Crosby, Nelson Boyd (b), Big Sid Catlett, Buddy Rich, Eddie Locke, Shadow Wilson, Cozy Cole (d).* 44–62.

Hawkins and Webster are incomparable together. On some of *Encounters* they seem to be vying to see who could sound, first, more nasty and, second, more charming. But there's an undercurrent of mutual feeling that makes 'It Never Entered My Mind' as moving as anything in Hawkins's discography. Ben is alternately respectful and keen to make his own points, and the rhythm section play up to their names. The new Master Edition of this session sounds very handsome. *The Genius Of* is only marginally less appealing: too many ballads, perhaps, when a couple of stompers would have put some more beef in the session, but the playing is very fine and, with a raft of extra material – three previously unissued tracks and various mono versions – that makes this Master Edition in Verve's series particularly attractive. *And Confreres* takes a couple of tracks off those sessions and puts them with a studio date with Eldridge: not a classic encounter, and Hawkins's tone sounds like solid granite on 'Hanid', but some agreeable music. Their Opera House meeting was actually recorded at two shows, one in stereo and one in mono, and the horns are in jousting mood, with the imperturbable MJQ rhythm section as a bonus. A 15-minute jam on 'Stuffy', with Getz and Young, comes from another JATP show.

The *Jazz Masters* disc rounds up Hawkins from various Verve and Keynote dates, with an especially valuable addition in the 'Picasso' *a cappella* solo from 1947.

**** The Hawk Flies High

Original Jazz Classics OJC 027 *Hawkins; Idrees Sulieman (t); J. J. Johnson (tb); Hank Jones (p); Barry Galbraith (g); Oscar Pettiford (b); Jo Jones (d).* 3/57.

*****(*) Soul**
Original Jazz Classics OJC 096 *Hawkins; Ray Bryant (p); Kenny Burrell (g); Wendell Marshall (b); Osie Johnson (d).* 1/58.

***** Hawk Eyes**
Original Jazz Classics OJC 294 *Hawkins; Charlie Shavers (t); Ray Bryant (p); Tiny Grimes (g); George Duvivier (b); Osie Johnson (d).* 4/59.

*****(*) Coleman Hawkins With The Red Garland Trio**
Original Jazz Classics OJC 418 *Hawkins; Red Garland (p); Doug Watkins (b); Specs Wright (d).* n.d.

*****(*) At Ease With Coleman Hawkins**
Original Jazz Classics OJC 181 *Hawkins; Tommy Flanagan (p); Wendell Marshall (b); Osie Johnson (d).* 1/60.

***** Night Hawk**
Original Jazz Classics OJC 420 *Hawkins; Eddie 'Lockjaw' Davis (ts); Tommy Flanagan (p); Ron Carter (b); Gus Johnson (d).* 12/60.

***** The Hawk Relaxes**
Original Jazz Classics OJC 709 *Hawkins; Ronnell Bright (p); Kenny Burrell (g); Ron Carter (b); Andrew Cyrille (d).* 2/61.

***** Jam Session In Swingville**
Prestige 24051 *Hawkins; Joe Newman (t); Vic Dickenson, J. C. Higginbotham (tb); Jimmy Hamilton, Pee Wee Russell (cl); Hilton Jefferson (as); Al Sears, Buddy Tate (ts); Claude Hopkins, Cliff Jackson (p); Danny Barker, Tiny Grimes (g); Joe Benjamin, Wendell Marshall (b); Bill English, J. C. Heard (d).* 4–5/61.

****(*) In A Mellow Tone**
Original Jazz Classics OJC 6001 *Variously as above.* 58–61.

***** Blues Wail**
Prestige 11006 *Variously as above.* 57–61.

Hawkins's records for Riverside and Prestige revived a career that was in decline and reasserted his authority at a time when many of the older tenor voices – Lester Young, Don Byas – were dying out or in eclipse. Hawkins could still feel at home with his immediate contemporaries – the same year he made *The Hawk Flies High*, he cut tracks with Henry 'Red' Allen and a Fletcher Henderson reunion band – but the younger players represented by J. J. Johnson and Idrees Sulieman on *Flies High* were a greater challenge; the tenorman responds, not by updating his style, but by shaping it to fit the context. The rhythm sections on these records are crucial, particularly the drummers: Jo Jones, Osie Johnson and Gus Johnson were men after Hawk's own heart when it came to the beat, and their bass-drum accents underscore the saxophonist's own rhythmical language.

Hawkins keeps abreast of the times, but he doesn't really change to suit them. *The Hawk Flies High* was an astonishingly intense beginning, almost a comeback record and one in which Hawkins plays with ferocious spirit. The notes claim that he picked all his companions on the date, and Sulieman and Johnson were intriguing choices: it brings out the bluesman in each of them rather than the bopper, and both seldom played with this kind of bite. 'Laura' is a peerless ballad, but it's the blues on 'Juicy Fruit' and 'Blue Light' which really dig in. *Soul*, though sometimes rattling uneasily over prototypical soul-jazz grooves courtesy of Burrell and Bryant, isn't much less intense, and 'Soul Blues' and the bewilderingly harsh 'I Hadn't Anyone Till You' are classic set-pieces. Unfortunately, the similar *Blues Groove* with Tiny Grimes is currently deleted, but *Hawk Eyes* brings in Grimes and Charlie Shavers, though to sometimes hysterical effect: Hawkins's opening solo on 'C'mon In' seems to be carved out of solid rock, but Shavers's preposterous bawling soon takes the pith out of the music. Still an exciting session overall, though.

The trio sessions with Garland and Flanagan are hot and cool respectively, and they prove that Hawkins could fill all the front-line space a producer could give him. The force he puts into his phrasing in this period sometimes undoes the flawless grip he once had over vibrato and line, but these are living sessions of improvised jazz. *Night Hawk* is a good-natured five-round contest with Lockjaw Davis, who was virtually suckled on the sound of Hawkins's tenor, and there's plenty of fun if no great revelations and little of the intuitive empathy with Webster (see above). *The Hawk Relaxes* puts him back with Kenny Burrell on a more peaceable programme, and there are no problems here. As a sequence of tenor albums, there aren't many this strong, in whatever jazz school one can name. *Jam Session In Swingville* is more lightweight and finds Hawkins in a situation – a studio jam – which he had more or less given up. The two bands involved (Hawkins is the only man common to both) each have their share of mavericks and straight men and, if the results are inevitably patchy, Hawkins, Russell and Dickenson in particular all have moments worth savouring.

The best-of, *In A Mellow Tone*, gets only moderate marks for an imbalance of ballads: there are already two fine ballad records listed above. Another compilation, *Blues Wail*, concentrates on Hawk handling the blues and is very enjoyable if a little one-noted.

***** At Art Ford's Jazz Party**
J&M 8001 *Hawkins; Charlie Shavers, Cootie Williams, Nat Adderley, Henry Allen (t); J. C. Higginbotham, Kai Winding (tb); Pee Wee Russell, Rolf Kuhn (cl); Lester Young (ts); Harry Sheppard (vib); Willie 'The Lion' Smith, Billy Taylor (p); Dick Thompson, Roy Gaines (g); Vinnie Burke, Earl May (b); Sonny Greer, Ed Thigpen (d); Lil Greenwood (v).* 9–10/58.

A selection of jams and party-pieces from a regular radio and television broadcast series, here featuring Hawk getting together with various chums, old and new – Allen, Shavers, Higginbotham and Russell make an agreeable line-up on the first date, but the second stirs in Kai Winding, the Adderleys and even Rolf Kuhn! An ailing Lester Young totters through 'Mean To Me' and Hawk shows him up with a blustery 'Indian Summer'. There is more music from the second session, which has the odd double of Cootie Williams and Nat Adderley sharing trumpet duties. An inevitable 'Body And Soul' is despatched with conscientious intensity, while 'Fine And Dandy', 'Airmail Special' and 'Bugle Call Rag' are shared round in united good spirits. Sound is respectably clean.

****(*) The Hawk Swings Vol. 1**
Fresh Sound FSR-CD 14 *Hawkins; Thad Jones (t); Eddie Costa (p, vib); Nat Pierce (p); George Duvivier (b); Osie Johnson (d).* 60.

****(*) The Hawk Swings Vol. 2**
Fresh Sound FSR-CD 15 *As above, except omit Pierce.* 60.

***** Coleman Hawkins & His All Stars**
Fresh Sound FSR-CD 88 *Hawkins; Emmett Berry (t); Eddie Bert (tb); Billy Taylor (p); Milt Hinton (b); Jo Jones (d). n.d.*

The two 1960 discs have been out on various labels in the past: Fresh Sound are docked a notch for spreading this 60-odd-minute session over two CDs, though. The band sound unfamiliar with the material but there is some fine playing, with Jones a compatible front-line partner for Hawkins and the mercurial Costa sounding good. The *All Stars* date comes in aircraft-hangar sound but, for all that, this is a swinging session, powered by Taylor, Hinton and Jones to terrific effect and with the undervalued Berry taking some strong solos. Hawkins is his consistent self.

***** Perdido**

Uptown UPCD 2745 *Hawkins; Ted Donnelly (tb); Norman Lester (p); Leon Spann (b); Jerry Potter (d).* 4/58.

***** Bean Stalkin'**

Pablo 2310-933 *Hawkins; Roy Eldridge (t); Benny Carter (as); Don Byas (ts); Lou Levy, Lalo Schifrin (p); Herb Ellis (g); Max Bennett, Art Davis (b); Gus Johnson, Jo Jones (d).* 10–11/60.

***** Masters Of Jazz Vol. 12: Coleman Hawkins**

Storyville SL4112 *Hawkins; Billy Taylor, Bud Powell, Kenny Drew (p); Oscar Pettiford, Niels-Henning Orsted Pedersen (b); Kenny Clarke, Albert 'Tootie' Heath, Jo Jones (d).* 11/54–2/68.

Live recordings from this period find Hawkins in variable but usually imposing form. His tone had hardened and much of his old fluency had been traded for a hard-bitten, irascible delivery which placed force over finesse. But he was still Hawkins, and still a great improviser, weatherbeaten but defiant. The meeting with Bud Powell found him in flag-waving form (the rest of the Storyville album is made up of odds and ends), and the two European sets on *Bean Stalkin'* are strong sessions.

The most remarkable of all these sets is the Uptown disc, *Perdido*. The music itself is relatively unremarkable, Hawkins playing with an out-of-town group at a students' ball in Jamestown. But the documentation is absolutely fascinating. The producers have transcribed the (often barely audible) onstage talk between the musicians and run it in the booklet, almost as a stage play; as an insight into the working musician's lot it must get a priority mark (Hawkins was clearly unhappy about the six-hour drive to the gig, the band and the circumstances, but his kingly demeanour ensured that he still gave a great performance and refused to undersell his own work). Donnelly died only weeks after the gig and the rest of the band are obscure but, for its presentation, it is nevertheless a remarkable disc.

***** At The Golden Circle 1963**

Dragon DRCD 265 *Hawkins; Goran Lindberg, Stig Holm, Adrian Acea (p); Kurt Lindgren, Hasse Tellemar, Al Lucas (b); Rune Carlsson, Bertil Frylmark, Osie Johnson (d); Thore Ehrling Orchestra.* 1/50–2/63.

Not just 1963: there are tracks from as far back as 1950 too. The material is mostly Hawkins favourites, played to varying degrees of interest: two 'Body And Soul's and quite a fierce 'It's The Talk Of The Town'. The tone gets gruffer and less tactile as he gets older, but that is the case for most of us. The various rhythm sections do appropriately respectful business. Sound isn't too bad, but some of it is rough.

**** Hawk Talk**

Fresh Sound FSR-CD 130 *Hawkins; Hank Jones, Dick Hyman (p); Milt Hinton, George Duvivier (b); Jimmie Crawford, Osie Johnson (d); Frank Hunter Orchestra.* 3/63.

****** Today And Now**

Impulse! 051184-2 *Hawkins; Tommy Flanagan (p); Major Holley (b); Eddie Locke (d).* 9/62.

***** Desafinado**

Impulse! 051227-2 *Hawkins; Tommy Flanagan (p); Barry Galbraith, Howard Collins (g); Major Holley (b); Eddie Locke (d); Willie Rodriguez (perc).* 10/62.

The great record in this batch is *Today And Now*. Despite the unpromising material, Hawkins is at his most engaging throughout. He seems to love 'Put On Your Old Grey Bonnet' and sounds as if he could play all night on it. 'Love Song From Apache' is distinguished by the loveliest of introductions by Tommy Flanagan, and Hawkins only has to breathe through the melody to make it work. There is little of the quaver in his tone that makes some of his later records bothersome, and nobody's coasting.

There was probably a great Hawkins-with-strings album to be made, but *Hawk Talk* wasn't really it. The pieces are trimmed too short to give the tenorman much space to rhapsodize, and too many of them sound foreshortened. Nor are Hunter's strings particularly well handled. *Desafinado* is disappointing in its way. Hawkins gets a sympathetic setting and a sense of time passing at just the pace he wants; still, like most such records of the period, it's finally little more than an easy-listening set with the saxophonist adding a few characteristic doodles of his own.

***** Supreme**

Enja 9009-2 *Hawkins; Barry Harris (p); Gene Taylor (b); Roy Brooks (d).* 9/66.

****(*) Sirius**

Original Jazz Classics OJC 861 *Hawkins; Barry Harris (p); Bob Cranshaw (b); Eddie Locke (d).* 12/66.

There's no need to be sentimental about Hawkins's later recordings: it's not as if his life was a tragic spiral, the way Young's or Holiday's was, and if his playing was audibly impaired in his final years he was doing his best not to reveal it. *Supreme*, a live session released for the first time, finds him in Baltimore, still playing chorus after chorus on 'Lover Come Back To Me' to open with. If this 'Body And Soul' has only a halting majesty about it, the phrasing broken into pieces, majesty there still is. Harris comps with the utmost sensitivity and, by the time of the playful treatment of 'Ow!' at the close, it sounds as though the players have enjoyed it. *Sirius* is more hesitant still, and perhaps this isn't the way to wind up a Hawkins discography; but that is what it currently does.

Erskine Hawkins (1914–93)

TRUMPET

Alabama-born, Hawkins made his start as an Armstrong disciple, and he began fronting his own group from the mid-'30s onwards. They were good enough and successful enough to outlast the decline of the swing era, and Hawkins switched to a small-group format only in the middle of the '50s. He worked the 'society' end of big-band music until the '70s and made occasional guest appearances as a soloist at festivals.

***** Erskine Hawkins 1936–1938**

Classics 653 *Collective personnel for first five discs: Hawkins; Sammy Lowe, Wilbur Bascomb, Marcellus Green, James Harris, Charles Jones, Willie Moore, Robert Johnson (t);*

Edward Sims, Robert Range, Richard Harris, Norman Greene, David James, Donald Cole (tb); William Johnson, Jimmy Mitchelle, Bobby Smith (cl, as); Julian Dash, Paul Bascomb, Aaron Maxwell (ts); Haywood Henry (cl, bs); Avery Parrish, Ace Harris (p); William McLemore, Leroy Kirkland (g); Leemie Stanfield (b); James Morrison, Edward McConney, Kelly Martin (d). 7/36–9/38.

***** Erskine Hawkins 1938–1939**
Classics 667 *Similar to above.* 9/38–10/39.

***** Erskine Hawkins 1939–1940**
Classics 678 *Similar to above.* 10/39–11/40.

***** Erskine Hawkins 1940–1941**
Classics 701 *Similar to above.* 11/40–12/41.

***** Erskine Hawkins 1941–1945**
Classics 868 *Similar to above.* 12/41–11/45.

***** Erskine Hawkins 1946–1947**
Classics 1008 *Similar to above, except add Bill Flood, Reunald Jones (t), Matthew Gee, Bob Range, Ray Hogan (tb), Frank Derrick (as), Aaron Maxwell (bs, ts), Ace Harris, Don Michael (p), Joe Murphy (d), Ruth Christian, Laura Washington (v).* 4/46–12/47.

***** Erskine Hawkins 1947–1949**
Classics 1148 *Hawkins; Sammy Lowe, Willie Moore, Robert Johnson, Charles Jones, James Harris Idrees Sulieman (t); Matthew Gee, Bob Range, David James, Edward Sims, Ray Hogan, Michael Wood, Renee Hall (tb); Frank Derrick, Bobby Smith (as); Jimmy Mitchelle (as, v); Julian Dash, Stretch Ridley (ts); Haywood Henry (bs, tsm, cl); Aaron Maxwell (bs, ts); Don Michael, Jimmy Phipps (p); Leroy Kirkland (g); Lennie Stanfield (b); Joe Murphy, Edward McConney (d); Laura Washington (v).* 12/47–11/49.

They called him the 'Twentieth-century Gabriel' and, although Erskine Hawkins was at heart only a Louis Armstrong disciple, his big band's records stand up remarkably well, considering their comparative neglect since the orchestra's heyday. They were certainly very popular with black audiences in the '30s and '40s, staying in residence at Harlem's Savoy Ballroom for close to ten years and delivering a smooth and gently swinging music that was ideal for dancing. Hawkins's rhapsodic high-note style has been criticized for excess, but his was a strain of black romanticism which, interestingly, predates the work of later Romeos such as Billy Eckstine, even if he did sing with his trumpet. Besides, the band had a number of good soloists, including Julian Dash, Paul Bascomb and Avery Parrish, who, with Sam Lowe, arranged most of the material.

The Bluebird compilation listed in previous editions has now gone, so swing specialists may want to invest in the chronological series on Classics. If the character of the music is comparatively bland, it was absolutely reliable, and playing through even this many tracks is a painless experience. The first CD documents Hawkins's sometimes uncertain but still swinging early sessions for Vocalion (as 'Erskine Hawkins And His 'Bama State Collegians') and goes up to his first session for Bluebird in 1938. Given the limited number of tracks on the Bluebird set, and the real consistency of Hawkins's individual records, there are many fine tracks to discover, including 'Hot Platter' (Classics 667), 'Baltimore Bounce' and 'Uptown Shuffle' (Classics 678) and 'No Use Squawkin'' (Classics 701); but it's the high professionalism of the section playing and the crisp, no-waste arrangements that make one wonder why Hawkins has been neglected in favour of Jimmie Lunceford or even Basie. Admittedly, his vocalists were never up to much. Classics 868 takes the sequence up to November 1945 and, although that includes the 30-month gap of the recording ban, Hawkins's style scarcely bothers to change. The outstanding tracks here are, as usual, the instrumentals: Sammy Lowe's excellent chart for 'Bear Mash Blues', one of the great Hawkins records, 'Tippin' In' and 'Drifting Along'. The certitude which is supposed to be a virtue of Basie's records is certainly here in abundance. Classics 1008 shows that, even though its era was slipping away, the Hawkins band was far from finished. 'Sneakin' Out' and 'Feelin' Low' are Ellingtonian in their execution, Bobby Smith's alto adopting the Hodges style to his own ends, and though there are plenty of the inevitable vocal features, a couple of pleasing charts such as 'Coast To Coast' and 'Sammy's Nightmare' sneak by. Classics 1148 takes Hawkins up to the end of the '40s: R&B set-pieces such as 'Corn Bread' are starting to creep into the band book, and there are still notably hot instrumentals in 'Gabriel's Heater' and 'Fish Tail' with a ripe solo from old faithful, Haywood Henry. Laura Washington is very appealing on 'I'd Love To Make Love To You'. Throughout this sequence, the transfers are the usual mixture from Classics: mostly solid enough, some from less than perfect sources. Overall, we must confess to a considerable fondness for this seldom-remembered band even if, record for record, there are few truly memorable tracks.

Edgar Hayes (1904–79)

PIANO

Hayes studied music at college and led his own bands in the south during the '20s, eventually joining the Mills Blue Rhythm band in 1932. He led his own orchestra again, 1937–41. His final years were spent in California, where he continued to play in clubs into the '70s.

***** Edgar Hayes 1937–1938**
Classics 730 *Hayes; Bernie Flood (t, v); Henry Goodwin, Shelton Hemphill, Leonard Davis (t); Robert Horton, Clyde Bernhardt, John 'Shorty' Haughton, David 'Jelly' James, Joe Britton (tb); Rudy Powell (cl, as); Roger Boyd, Stanley Palmer, Alfred Skerritt (as); Joe Garland (ts, bs); Crawford Wethington, William Mitchner (ts); Andy Jackson, Eddie Gibbs (g); Elmer James, Frank 'Coco' Darling (b); Kenny Clarke (d, vib); Orlando Roberson, Earlene Howell, Bill Darnell, Ruth Ellington (v).* 3/37–1/38.

***** Edgar Hayes 1938–1948**
Classics 1053 *Hayes; Bernard Flood, Henry Goodwin, Leonard Davis (t); Robert Horton, David James, Clyde Bernhardt (tb); Rudy Powell (cl, as); Roger Boyd (as); William 'Happy' Mitchner (ts); Joe Garland (bs, ts); Eddie Gibbs, Teddy Bunn (g); Frank 'Coco' Darling, Willie Price (b); Kenny Clarke (d, vib); Bryant Allen (d); James Clay Anderson (v).* 2/38–48.

Hayes led a very good orchestra, following his stint with the Mills Blue Rhythm Band. They had a big hit with 'Star Dust' – ironically, not one of their best records – which is on Classics 1053. There were good soloists: trombonist Robert Horton was exemplary on both muted and open horn, Joe Garland could play tenor, baritone and bass sax with equal facility, and Henry Goodwin's trumpet shines here and there. Garland was also a very capable arranger, and the rhythm section could boast the young Kenny Clarke, already restlessly trying to swing his way out of conventional big-band drumming: all of the band's records benefit from his presence. There are too many indifferent vocals, and some of the material is glum, but many of the 24 tracks on the first volume stand up to a close listen. The second disc picks up the story with their final Decca session from February 1938, but that was more or less the end of the Hayes story as far as big-band records were concerned. There are four titles made in Stockholm a month later under Kenny Clarke's nominal leadership, a sextet date where Clarke plays only vibes and Goodwin and Powell sound fine – but Anderson's unfortunate vocals take up too much time. The rest are tracks by Hayes and rhythm section alone, for V-Disc, Exclusive and Modern, obscure pieces that depend heavily on the blues and are features for Teddy Bunn as much as Hayes, though that's no bad thing. An intriguing rediscovery.

Louis Hayes (born 1937)

DRUMS

Born in Detroit, Hayes spent long periods as drummer with several of the key hard-bop leaders: Yusef Lateef, Horace Silver and especially Cannonball Adderley, with whom he stayed for six years. In the '80s he also emerged as a leader of considerable if relatively unassuming stature, and his seniority in the style makes him one of the grandmasters of this kind of drumming.

***** Light And Lively**
Steeplechase SCCD 31245 *Hayes; Charles Tolliver (t); Bobby Watson (as); Kenny Barron (p); Clint Houston (b).* 4/89.

*****(*) Una Max**
Steeplechase SCCD 31263 *Hayes; Charles Tolliver (t); Gerald Hayes (as); John Stubblefield (ts); Kenny Barron (p); Clint Houston (b).* 12/89.

***** The Crawl**
Candid CCD 79045 *Hayes; Charles Tolliver (t); Gary Bartz (as); John Stubblefield (ss, ts); Mickey Tucker (p); Clint Houston (b).* 10/89.

*****(*) Nightfall**
Steeplechase SCCD 31285 *Hayes; Eddie E. J. Allen (t); Gerald Hayes (as); Larry Willis (p); Clint Houston (b).* 1/91.

*****(*) Blue Lou**
Steeplechase SCCD 31340 *Hayes; Eddie E. J. Allen (t); Gerald Hayes (as); Javon Jackson (ts); Ronnie Mathews (p); Clint Houston (b).* 4/93.

Louis Hayes remains one of the master drummers in the hard-bop idiom, a key figure in the Detroit-based community and a player whose undemonstrative virtue of playing for the band has perhaps told against his wider reputation. The fine sequence for Steeplechase finds him making a serious mark as leader for the first time. Besides Hayes's own playing – and he is probably the star performer overall – the first point of interest is the return of Tolliver to active duty after a number of years away. He sounds in need of some further woodshedding on *Light And Lively*, but the two later records are better showcases for him. Watson sounds a shade too slick for the company on the first record, but *Una Max* is a record that grows in stature on repeated hearings: Stubblefield is in the mood for some grand oratory, Tolliver's spacious solos accumulate strength as they go forward, and the rougher, unpredictable alto of the younger Hayes is an interesting wild card. The Candid set, recorded live, could use some editing, but it's an atmospheric occasion and, although Bartz sounds a little sour at some moments, there is still some fiery hard bop in the programme. Going back into the studio for *Nightfall*, Hayes assembles a fresh front line: Allen's trumpet is less immediately distinctive than Tolliver's, but he has a very impressive solo on 'I Waited For You', and Hayes and Willis are in buoyant form. Besides that, the drummer's evolving command of the leader's role seems to be inspiring his own playing to new heights.

Blue Lou continues the exceptional run at Steeplechase. Still not quite in the absolute top bracket, but all three horns have some fine contributions to make, and what registers most strongly is the bustle and impetus of Hayes's group – a Blakey trademark which Louis seems intent on following through. 'Quiet Fire' is a classic example of what Hayes's bands can do, the soloists brimming with fire and excitement without surrendering the improviser's control. The distinguished Mathews is a valuable recruit to the team, too.

*****(*) Louis At Large**
Sharp Nine 1003-2 *Hayes; Riley Mullins (t); Javon Jackson (ts); David Hazeltine (p); Santi Debriano (b).* 4/96.

***** Quintessential Lou**
TCB 99652 *As above, except Abraham Burton (ts) replaces Jackson.* 3/99.

Louis At Large was Hayes's first American set as leader for many years. Mullins and Jackson are keen to please in the front line, but perhaps the most interesting performer here is Hazeltine, who builds on the good impression of his own records. The tunes offer some surprisingly strong originals from various hands – no simple hard-bop blues lines but genuine themes – and Hayes is clearly delighted at the shape the band's in.

Quintessential Lou is a shade less involving, though it's hard to say why – Burton is a characterful substitute for Jackson and the combo is on its mettle as standard-bearers of a hard-bop tradition. But there's a rote feel to some of this. Only two originals from within the ranks of the band and, although they choose such genre rarities as Sonny Rollins's 'Decision', the playing has settled into a measure of routine for the moment.

***** The Candy Man**
TCB 20972 *Hayes; Riley Mullins (t); Abraham Burton (ts); David Hazeltine (p); Santi Debriano (b).* 11/99.

*****(*) Dreamin' Of Cannonball**
TCB 21222 *Hayes; Jeremy Pelt (t); Vincent Herring (as); Rick Germanson (p); Vincent Archer (b).* 5/01.

The Candy Man follows its predecessor in suggesting a good but workmanlike performance. Nothing amiss with the playing, its intensity or thoughtfulness, but it can't quite find the spark of surprise which would take it out of itself. With this possibly in his mind, Hayes has since formed an all-new outfit, though this also goes out under the name The Cannonball Legacy Band. Nobody's better equipped than Hayes to boss such a concept, but he's helped no end by the horns. Herring is a natural for the Cannonball role, tonally close to the great man and as easily adept with the licks, but he's been himself for long enough to make sure that this isn't just copycat playing. The real impact, though, is made by Pelt, a very hot discovery and a soloist who pushes for the limit seemingly from bar one. His explosive attack on Victor Feldman's 'The Chant' really lifts the music up a notch, and that excitement percolates through the record. It's still repertory, and no fresh ground is broken – but Pelt must be heard.

Tubby Hayes (1935–73)

TENOR, BARITONE AND ALTO SAXOPHONES, FLUTE, VIBES, PIANO

Born in London, Hayes was a prodigy who took up saxophone at 11 and made his recording debut at 16 with Kenny Baker. The most forceful of soloists, he was completely at home in the virtuosity of bebop, and he also became an adept vibes player. He co-led the Jazz Couriers with Ronnie Scott in the '50s and visited New York in 1961 to play and record. His eminence on the British scene in the '60s was insufficiently recognized, partly through the eclipse of modern jazz by pop, and his final years were troubled by illness.

***** The Swinging Giant Volume 1**
Jasmine JASCD 610 *Hayes; Jimmy Deuchar, Dickie Hawdon, Dave Usdon (t); Mike Senn (as, bs); Jackie Sharpe (ts, bs); Harry South (p); Pete Blannin (b); Lennie Breslow, Bill Eyden (d).* 3–7/55.

*****(*) The Swinging Giant Volume 2**
Jasmine JASCD 617 *Hayes; Dickie Hawdon (t); Ronnie Scott (ts); Harry South, Terry Shannon (p); Pete Elderfield, Phil Bates (b); Bill Eyden (d).* 7/56–8/57.

*****(*) The First And Last Words**
Jasmine JASCD 626 *As above, except add Jimmy Deuchar (t), Kenny Napper (b), Phil Seamen (d); omit Hawdon, South, Elderfield.* 8/57–7/59.

****** The Eighth Wonder**
Jasmine JASCD 611 *Hayes; Terry Shannon (p); Phil Bates, Jeff Clyne (b); Bill Eyden, Phil Seamen (d).* 3–12/59.

Tubby Hayes has often been lionized as the greatest saxophonist Britain ever produced. He is a fascinating but problematical player. Having put together a big, rumbustious tone and a delivery that features sixteenth notes spilling impetuously out of the horn, Hayes often left a solo full of brilliant loose ends and ingenious runs that led nowhere in particular. Most of his recordings, while highly entertaining as exhibitions of sustained energy, tend to wobble on the axis of Hayes's creative impasse: having got this facility together, he never seemed sure of what to do with it in the studio, which may be why his studio records ultimately fall short of the masterpiece he never came to make.

His '50s sessions for Tony Hall's Tempo label have at last made their way to CD via the Jasmine imprint, though remastering is mostly no more than fair and the cheap-looking designs aren't very encouraging. The music crackles down the years. Besides Hayes himself, there are glimpses of a whole school of players whose music, especially in this period, was scarcely documented at all away from mere studio work. But it's Hayes himself that most will want to hear. The first, *Swinging Giant*, is made up of tracks from five (very rare) EPs, and spotlights the 20-year-old Tubbs already going majestically through the gears on the likes of 'Peace Pipe', a whirling amalgam of Zoot Sims and some of the more individual hard-bop tenors. Following his paciest lines is particularly interesting, since though they're never quite 'resolved' they're outside mere pattern-playing too.

The second volume couples the quintet date, *After Lights Out*, with the first half of a Jazz Couriers album, the band Hayes co-led with Ronnie Scott. Dickie Hawdon sounds almost excessively brassy on the quintet session, though that may be down to the original recording; but Hayes loves the setting and he is wonderful to hear on 'Message To The Messengers' and 'Hall Hears The Blues'. The Jazz Couriers were based around the tenor one-two of Scott and Hayes, which was often agreeably complementary, although Scott's bluesier sound and (at times) more circumspect phrasing could occasionally show up his younger cohort. *The First And Last Words* is often great fun in the manner of some of the Sims–Cohn sessions, although Hayes also picks up flute and vibes for contrast (he was an irrepressible multi-instrumentalist). Two bonus tracks, including Tubby's original 'Monk Was Here', are taken from an almost mythically rare cardboard seven-inch record.

The Eighth Wonder gets top rating: most of it comes from the sessions for *Tubby's Groove*, perhaps Hayes's most ebullient showcase. It's true that the virtuosity of 'Tin Tin Deo' comes out of his horn all too easily, almost as if it were a routine he'd mastered without thinking, but it's hard not to enjoy the spectacle; and there is much tough-minded improvising on the date too, especially in the magnificent feast he makes out of 'Blue Hayes'. The other figure to listen to here is Terry Shannon, hardly recalled these days but one of Britain's most capable small-group pianists.

****** Late Spot At Scott's**
Redial 558183-2 *Hayes; Jimmy Deuchar (t); Gordon Beck (p); Freddie Logan (b); Allan Ganley (d).* 5/62.

****** Down In The Village**
Redial 558184-2 *As above.* 5/62.

***** Night And Day**
Jazz House JHAS 602 *As above, except add Terry Shannon, Mike Pyne (p), Jeff Clyne, Bruce Cale (b), Benny Goodman, Phil Seamen (d).* 12/63–8/66.

***** Jazz Tête A Tête**
Progressive PCD-7079 *Hayes; Les Condon (t); John Picard (tb); Tony Coe (ts); Mike Pyne, Colin Purbrook (p); Frank Evans (g); Ron Mathewson, Peter Ind (b); Jackie Dougan, Tony Levin (d).* 11/66.

*****(*) For Members Only**
Miles Music MMCD 086 *Hayes; Mick Pyne (p); Ron Mathewson (b); Tony Levin (d).* 1–10/67.

***** Live 1969**
Harlequin HQ CD 05 *As above, except Spike Wells (d) replaces Levin.* 8–12/69.

At their best, Tubby's live albums are still breathtaking in their impact and excitement. The most famous are the two Fontana discs now reissued on Redial, dating from a pair of nights at the Ronnie Scott Club. On vibes, as in the title-track to *Down In The Village*, he is coolly melodic, but on tenor his playing is a rollercoaster of power and excitement. There is little to choose between the two records; perhaps we slightly prefer *Down In The Village*. But there is also some exemplary support from Deuchar, Beck, Logan and Ganley in what was one of the strongest groups of its era. *Night And Day* offers material from five dates at Ronnie's over a period of three years: the tenor playing on 'Night And Day', to choose one, is unquenchably vivid, even electrifying. But the issue offers little more than bootleg sound, and one is sometimes reminded of some of the old tapes of Coltrane that used to circulate among collectors.

Jazz Tête A Tête will be nostalgic for many British readers as a souvenir of one of the concerts promoter Peter Burman organized in the '60s, this one at Bristol University, with groups led by Les Condon (with Tubby sitting in), Tony Coe and Frank Evans. Hayes followers will welcome his rhapsodic ballad, 'When My Baby Gets Mad'; the rest is more routine, but Coe's playing is a reminder that there was more than one great tenorman at work in Britain then. The recording quality – the original album was issued on Doug Dobell's 77 Records – is of documentary standard, but isn't too bad, and there is a previously unheard version of 'Tenderly' by Coe.

For Members Only has some 70 minutes of music drawn from three broadcasts, with a couple of rare excursions on flute and plenty of rousing tenor, as well as a nice glimpse of Hayes the composer. The CD suffers from some occasional blinks and drop-outs, but nothing too distracting. *Live 1969* sounds pretty dusty, drawn from a couple of London gigs, and Hayes is too generous with everybody else's solo space. But the second date, with a tumbling reading of 'Where Am I Going' and a couple of Hayes originals, is a degree more intense.

***** Live In London**

Harkit HRKCD 8072 *Hayes; Jimmy Deuchar (t); Terry Shannon, Gordon Beck (p); Johnny Fourie (g); Freddie Logan, Kenny Napper, Jeff Clyne (b); Allan Ganley, Benny Goodman, Johnny Butts (d).* 1/64–12/65.

Vintage Tubbs from four different gigs at Ronnie's during 1964–65. The tapes come from Les Tomkins's collection and the final track is an interview between Les and Tubby, dating from 1963. The emphasis here is on Hayes the virtuoso saxophonist: 'Opus Ocean' is done at a tempo so quick that even Jimmy Deuchar has problems, while Hayes simply sails through it, taking an unaccompanied passage which beggars belief. He's just as formidable on 'On Green Dolphin Street' and the 20-minute 'By Myself', yet what one often thinks of is the remark about his playing – 'as easy as turning a tap on and off' – which suggests that for all his facility, Hayes had a glibness about his playing which may have told against him in the end. As with *Night And Day* above, the sound is often unkind to other members of the band, although Tubby comes through loud and fairly clear.

***** A Tribute: Tubbs**

Spotlite SPJ-CD 902 *Hayes; Jimmy Deuchar (t, mel); Terry Shannon (p); Freddy Logan (b); Allan Ganley (d).* 12/63.

***** Quartet In Scandinavia**

Storyville STCD 8251 *Hayes; Staffan Abeleen (p); Niels-Henning Orsted Pedersen (b); Alex Riel (d).* 2/72.

A couple of memories to add to the legacy of Tubbs on record. He is in his prime on the Spotlite set and, although the music isn't up to the electrifying standard of the two Redial albums, it's a valuable glimpse of the man in exuberant form. The sheer ebullience of his solo on 'Don't Fall Off The Bridge' is breathtaking. Deuchar doesn't have quite such a good night, but there is also little enough around of him in his pomp to make this a keeper.

The Storyville disc comes from a Swedish broadcast. This is typical visiting-soloist stuff with the local rhythm section, and Hayes – who had already suffered more than one serious illness – probably approaches this as just another gig. As a quartet, though, this is a class act and, if there are too many long solos shared around the band, the music has spirit as well as polish.

Phil Haynes (born 1961)

DRUMS

Born in Oregon, Haynes (no relation to the great Roy) came to New York as a promising youngster and has fronted or co-fronted a series of enterprising bands, including a powerful unit with trumpeter Herb Robertson.

*****(*) Live Insurgency: Set 1**

Soul Note 121302 *Haynes; Paul Smoker (t); Jeff Palmer (org).* 98.

***** Free Country**

Premonition 90744 *Haynes; Jim Yanda (steel g); Hank Roberts (clo, jazzophone fiddle); Drew Gress (b).* 00.

*****(*) Brooklyn–Berlin**

CIMP 2138 *Haynes; Herb Robertson (co, t); Marty Ehrlich, Vinny Golia (cl, bcl); Ken Filiano (b).* 2/00.

Haynes made his recording debut as leader as far back as 1991 with the intriguing *Four Horns & What* on Open Minds, which we think is now deleted or unavailable. It established the 30-year-old, previously known only as an enterprising sideman, as a writer of some promise. *Live Insurgency* consolidated that impression, but what an unusual 'organ trio'! Smoker was an important component of the first record and he comes back to bring his tight splintery sound to a set of mostly originals. The opening 'Where's The Door?' will lead you to think you're in for a pretty funky workout, but it's a deceptive overture to a quite advanced and thoughtful set. 'Saeta' and 'So Miles' suggest one line of influence, but one listens in vain for explicit echoes of *Kind Of Blue* and *Sketches Of Spain*, largely because Smoker's debt to Miles Davis is so idiosyncratically deployed.

Palmer is closer to Larry Young than Jimmy Smith but he doesn't really resemble any of the great Hammond players. It's to his credit that he sounds like no one but himself. On tunes like 'Premonition', the above pair and the single standard, 'My Funny Valentine', he develops a distinctive harmonic mood and develops some enterprising lines of attack on the material. The closing 'Blues For Israel' is a sucker punch, superbly paced and distilled.

One quality Haynes has taken from Miles is an instinct for stylistic shapeshifting. At first hearing, *Free Country* might almost be one of Bill Frisell's Americana projects, except that the steel guitar isn't part of Bill's usual armoury. Mostly Steven Foster tunes and traditional material, but as the project title suggests, country music radically reinterpreted. It kicks off with a Bible Belt favourite, 'How Great Thou Art', and a delightfully paced interpretation of 'Oh Susannah'. 'Danny Boy' (strictly the 'Londonderry Air') might have been hideous, but Haynes and his colleagues handle it beautifully and Roberts's cello gives this and other melodies a tough-tender masculine quality. Hank also has his jazzophone fiddle on set, delightfully scratchy and unapologetically inauthentic. Haynes's own role is quieter than on the freer projects, but he doesn't stick to strict timekeeping. Again, the final sequence of 'Shenandoah' (almost ten minutes) and a brief 'Mairi's Wedding' suggests he has a gift for shaping albums.

The final set reunites the drummer with another fine trumpet player. Herb Robertson is the star of the CIMP set, which is recorded with the label's typical lack of fuss and embellishment. In other ways, too, this goes back to the dense structure and carefully controlled freedom of the first record. Only three horns, but what a range of registers and timbres they conjure up. The clarinets consolidate the folkier side of Haynes's idiom while Robertson can do everything from circus barker to Angel Gabriel. Another wonderful record from a genuinely interesting talent.

Roy Haynes (born 1926)

DRUMS

Roy Haynes worked with Charlie Parker, Miles Davis, Bud Powell, Sarah Vaughan, Thelonious Monk and Eric Dolphy, and was dep for the classic John Coltrane Quartet. If power and swing were measured relative to physical size, the little man from Roxbury, Massachusetts, would be one of the major figures of the music. Recent years have seen him establish himself ever more confidently as a leader, with what is a consistently inventive discography.

***** We Three**
Original Jazz Classics OJC 196 *Haynes; Phineas Newborn Jr (p); Paul Chambers (b).* 11/58.

*****(*) Out Of The Afternoon**
Impulse! 051180-2 *Haynes; Roland Rahsaan Kirk (ts, manzello, stritch, f); Tommy Flanagan (p); Henry Grimes (b).* 5/62.

***** Cracklin'**
Original Jazz Classics OJC 818 *Haynes; Booker Ervin (ts); Ronnie Mathews (p); Larry Ridley (b).* 4/63.

Few contemporary drummers have been so precise in execution, and what Haynes lacks in sheer power – he is a small man and has generally worked with a scaled-down kit – he gains in clarity, playing long, open lines that are deceptively relaxed but full of small rhythmic tensions. In 1958 his work still clearly bears the mark of stints with Thelonious Monk and Miles Davis. Bar lines shift confidently or else are dispensed with altogether, without violence to the underlying pulse. Phineas Newborn's recent association with Charles Mingus had helped pare down his slightly extravagant style; he plays very differently against Haynes's slightly staccato delivery than with, say, Elvin Jones much later in his career or Philly Joe Jones in 1961, where Chambers again provided the harmonic substructure. Haynes himself sounds wonderful on 'Sugar Ray' and the romping 'Our Delight', where he is almost tuneful.

The Impulse! record is a splendid one-off. After a big, dramatic opening on cymbals, Kirk blasts off on the Artie Shaw theme, 'Moon Ray', using both manzello and tenor (beautifully in tune), doubling his lines against a big reverb that makes him sound like a whole section. Haynes's solo is low, slow and dramatic, halving the basic tempo at one point. That is not Kirk's bent. On 'If I Should Lose You', he squalls his way through a magnificent stritch solo which pulls the standard apart. (The original liner-note by Stanley Dance was slightly misleading about Kirk's two non-canonical horns; any misconceptions are corrected on this otherwise intact reissue by Michel Cuscuna.) 'Snap Crackle' was an expression coined by bassist Al McKibbon to describe Haynes's sound. The drummer adopts it here as a song title and, coupled to Kirk's weird vocalized flute and nose-flute solo, it rather stands out from the rest of the album.

Cracklin' is more mainstream but the fizz and pop are still very much there, and Haynes's polyrhythms are all the more evident for not being eclipsed by such an idiosyncratic front man. Which isn't to say that Ervin is less than exemplary. His solo on 'Under Paris Skies' is first rate and Mathews's accompaniment pushes a rather slight vehicle to the limit.

***** Cymbalism**
Original Jazz Classics OJCCD 1079 213030 *Haynes; Frank Strozier (as, f); Ronnie Mathews (p); Larry Ridley (b).* 9/63.

It hardly narrows the gap that has opened up in the Haynes discography, but the re-release of this 1963 session does help to fill out the picture. Roy's distinctive approach is best sampled on a brisk 'I'm Getting Sentimental Over You'. It follows the Frank Strozier-composed 'Modette', which also features the saxophonist on flute. Strozier has always been a marginal figure, seen as a Jackie McLean disciple and so perhaps twice removed from the well-spring of bebop, but when he plays well, as he does on the final medley, and when he resists the temptation to play flute, he is an arresting if rather cursory soloist.

Haynes drives things along from the drum chair with great musicality and wit. Good to have this early session back in circulation, but time now for some of his '70s work, like *Hip Ensemble* and *Equipoise*, to come in from the cold.

*****(*) Te Vou!**
Dreyfus FDM 36569 *Haynes; Donald Harrison (as); Pat Metheny (g); David Kikoski (p); Christian McBride (b).* 94.

Te Vou! is absolutely consistent with past form. Haynes dares to play quietly and delicately, and his solo on 'Trigonometry' is exquisite. He has some interesting companions here, not least Metheny, who quite clearly revels more in this setting than in the bombast of Denardo Coleman on *Song X*. The guitarist features strongly on 'John McKee', a beautiful thing made out of perfectly balanced parts. The recording is flatteringly balanced and very true, with no artificial heightening of the soloists.

***** My Shining Hour**
Storyville 4199 *Haynes; Tomas Franck (ts); Thomas Clausen (p); Niels-Henning Orsted Pedersen (b).* 3/94.

Recorded with Clausen's Jazz Participants, *My Shining Hour* is a Jazzpar project and a disappointing one by comparison with other records from the prestigious event. Haynes is in a showboating mood and there's too little of interest coming from the horn of Tomas Franck to balance up the drama. The saxophonist does contribute one lively composition to the set, but otherwise it might as well have been a trio session. Clausen and NHOP are fascinating in themselves and some of the best exchanges on the record are quite simply for piano and bass. 'Bessie's Blues' isn't the most covered of Coltrane compositions and it's good to hear it handled with such imagination. Otherwise, though, a borderline item.

****** Praise**
Dreyfus 36598 *Haynes; Graham Haynes (c, flhn); Kenny Garrett (ss, as); David Sanchez (ts); David Kikoski (p); Dwayne Burno (b).* 98.

Haynes plays one of his most persuasive recorded solos on the closing 'Shades Of Senegal', a performance that is as expressive as it is rhythmically astute. The album covers every possible permutation, from solo percussion to septet, and at every level it is Roy who dominates. Son Graham and the two saxophone players each have interesting things to say, but it is the rhythm section, with Kikoski very much in the foreground, that makes things happen. Some of the selections, like John Carisi's 'Israel', are less than ideally suited to this personnel but 'My Little Suede Shoes', the Charlie Parker classic, and the traditional 'Morning Has Broken' are both sterling performances, and Roy has rarely sounded more gleefully in charge.

***** The Roy Haynes Trio**
Verve 543534-2 *Haynes; Danilo Perez (p); John Patitucci (b).* 9–11/99.

The full title is *Featuring Danilo Perez And John Patitucci.* Strong as both guys are, it remains very much Roy's band. The little wizard uses the occasion to make reference to various stages in his career. Two sets – studio and live – include compositions by Thelonious Monk ('Bright Mississippi' and 'Green Chimneys'), Miles Davis ('Sippin' At The Bells') and Bud Powell (a rugged 'Wail'). There's also a nod to Sarah Vaughan on 'Shulie Bop'; Haynes worked with Sassie for almost five years.

The live sound is more convincingly three-dimensional – and by contrast the studio tracks sound anonymous. However, most of the numbers are generously extended, allowing Perez and Patitucci to earn their 'featured' ranking. Danilo clearly knows the pianists' material inside out and only sounds short of ideas on Pat Metheny's curiously old-fashioned 'Question And Answer'.

***** Birds Of A Feather**
Dreyfus 36625 *Haynes; Roy Hargrove (t); Kenny Garrett (as); David Kikoski (p); Dave Holland (b).* 01.

The market is glutted with tribute albums but here's a rare example (one to put alongside McCoy's or Rashied's Trane memorials) where the acolyte has gone on to make a substantial name for himself and forge a distinguished recording career of his own. Looking back at Charlie Parker, with whom he worked in later years, Haynes makes it clear that he comes neither to praise nor to bury, but to rework. The arrangements are often very subtle. 'Ah-Leu-Cha' is taken slower than usual and with unusual changes. 'My Heart Belongs To Daddy' is modernized with a scale that wouldn't have featured even in late bop, and 'Now's The Time' takes on a funky groove that makes it seem both more up-to-date and curiously dated.

There are a couple of unexpected inclusions, notably Gerry Mulligan's 'Rocker' and Billy Reid's 'The Gypsy', but for the most part this is an orthodox Bird programme. The quintet has an authentic balance of forces, but Hargrove and Garrett are such identifiable stylists that one wonders why, for some of the time at least, they seem content to play in the tradition, not slavishly, but not stretchingly either. Kikoski is a very responsive accompanist and, since no one knows what Tommy Potter or Curley Russell sounded like anyway, Holland can relax into his role and play with his usual calm authority. He does some of the best playing on a record that will appeal pretty broadly: Parker fans will lap up any sort of association; more studied listeners can enjoy unpicking the harmonic and rhythmic variations; everyone else can get high on the sheer energy. Yet there is some vital component lacking, an album that perhaps doesn't add up to more than the sum of its very fine components.

***** Love Letters**
Columbia 87197 *Haynes; Joshua Redman (ts); Kenny Barron, David Kikoski (p); John Scofield (g); Dave Holland, Christian McBride (b).* 5/02.

Originally released only in Japan on Yasohachi '88' Itoh's own label, this is a very run-of-the-mill set of standards enlivened by some lovely moments on Horace Silver's 'Que Pasa' and a Coltrane-influenced version of Mongo Santamaria's 'Afro-Blue'. Haynes is in great form as ever, but the record seems to lack a context, occasion or any real rationale and everyone coasts through it. Fans of the drummer's work will hear its merits immediately; others will take more convincing.

Kevin Hays (born 1968)

PIANO

Born in New York, Hays listened to Oscar Peterson and George Shearing as a teenager and was soon playing in clubs. He has been a frequent sideman in the Tri-State area.

*****(*) Sweet Ear**
Steeplechase SCCD 31282 *Hays; Eddie Henderson (t); Vincent Herring (ss, as); James Genus (b); Joe Chambers (d).* 1/91.

***** Ugly Beauty**
Steeplechase SCCD 31297 *Hays; Larry Grenadier (b); Jeff Williams (d).* 8/91.

*****(*) Crossroad**
Steeplechase SCCD 31324 *Hays; Scott Wendholt (t, flhn); Freddie Bryant (g); Dwayne Burno (b); Carl Allen (d).* 11/92.

Hays is a gifted young American pianist whose three Steeplechase albums include a lot of satisfying jazz: they're arguably still his best calling-card. The leader is sometimes a rather demure performer: his touch, if not exactly diffident, is a little reticent in making an impact on the keys, and rhythmically he tends to organize solos around certain patterns – halving the tempo or working a sequence of arpeggios – which crop up often enough to hint at routine. But his writing offers some interesting situations and on, say, the trio reading of 'You And The Night And The Music' on the first album he manages to create a logical and inventive development far away from the melody.

The first album is arguably the best by dint of some excellent teamwork: Henderson takes some very fine solos, Herring manages to step out of his Adderley impersonation for most of the date, and Chambers is as eccentrically inventive as ever (sample his solo on 'Neptune'). The quintet with Wendholt is notable for the trumpeter's beautiful solos, expertly paced and tonally exquisite, as well as fine covers of Ray Bryant's 'P.S. The Blues' and Duke Pearson's 'Gaslight'. The trio record is inevitably less absorbing, given Hays's light grip, but is still worth hearing. Hays subsequently signed to Blue Note and recorded three albums, but they have since been deleted.

David Hazeltine (born 1958)

PIANO

Born in Milwaukee and based there for many years, Hazeltine is a 'local' hard-bop pianist who has been making more frequent and prominent appearances on record of late.

***** After Hours**
Go Jazz 6032 *Hazeltine; Billy Peterson (b); Kenny Horst (d).* 9/88–5/91.

***** 4 Flights Up**
Sharp Nine 1002-2 *Hazeltine; Slide Hampton (tb); Peter Washington (b); Ray Appleton (d). 7/95.*

*****(*) The Classic Trio**
Sharp Nine 1005-2 *Hazeltine; Peter Washington (b); Louis Hayes (d). 8/96.*

***** How It Is**
Criss Cross 1142 *Hazeltine; Jim Rotondi (t, flhn); Steve Wilson (as); Peter Washington (b); Joe Farnsworth (d). 10/97.*

Hazeltine's comments draw a list of influences which are a key to his style, and to an interesting take on modern jazz piano: Oscar Peterson, Barry Harris, Buddy Montgomery, Cedar Walton. He's a communicator in the Peterson manner, voicing melodies in a recognizable yet inventive way, adding just enough rhythmic nuance to take an interpretation out of the ordinary, and placing absolute trust in his rhythm-section sidemen – Washington in particular, common to all three later records. *4 Flights Up* has Hampton as the sole horn but, though he performs likeably enough, his solos add a note of blandness and sometimes get in Hazeltine's way. *The Classic Trio*, with lovely, grooving work from Washington and Hayes, is a peach of a trio date. Though Hazeltine says he prefers to work with more modern material ('Betcha By Golly Wow', from the songbook of The Stylistics, is on the previous disc) he still does very well out of standards such as 'Sweet And Lovely' and 'These Foolish Things', an unerring sense of tempo helping to swing the melodies and set the pace for constructions that are intricate without seeming fussy or deliberately complex. 'My Stuff's On The Street' is a witty blues, Bud Powell's 'The Fruit' is bebop cooled off in a delightful setting, and 'One For Peter' is an adroit feature for Washington.

The Criss Cross date is disappointingly prosaic in comparison. Rotondi and Wilson play well enough, but they add little aside from extra weight to some of the tunes. The pianist's 'Nuit Noire' is a fine set-piece and his treatment of 'Pannonica' comes off with an expert flourish, but it's all a little ordinary. The retrospective release in the Go Jazz *After Hours* series is attractive: too long, and a few of the pieces sound a bit shapeless; but in such as the prototype version of '4 Flights Up' Hazeltine is already commanding.

***** Blues Quarters Vol. 1**
Criss Cross 1188 *Hazeltine; Eric Alexander (ts); Dwayne Burno (b); Joe Farnsworth (d). 12/98.*

*****(*) The Classic Trio Vol. 2**
Sharp Nine 1019 *Hazeltine; Peter Washington (b); Louis Hayes (d). 1/00.*

***** Good-Hearted People**
Criss Cross 1210 *Hazeltine; Steve Davis (tb); Jim Snidero (as, f); Jesse Van Ruller (g); Nat Reeves (b); Tony Reedus (d). 1/01.*

For some reason, Hazeltine can't quite muster the same intensity at Criss Cross that he does at Sharp Nine. The second volume of trio music with Washington and Hayes is another winner, driving and swinging through quick tempos and ranging back in a positive way at a more amenable pace. Originals and standards alike receive an absorbing reading.

Nothing wrong with the Criss Cross sessions, just nothing exceptional. The quartet date with Alexander has the saxophonist burning a few barns along the way, though the music seems not too far from well-practised formulae. *Good-Hearted People* benefits from the extra horn, although a standard such as 'Imagination' is voiced so mildly that it sounds sleepy, and the expected bop blow-out of 'Barbados' is as tame as a mouse.

*****(*) Close To You**
Criss Cross 1247 *Hazeltine; Peter Washington (b); Joe Farnsworth (d). 11/03.*

Hazeltine's best Criss Cross so far is energized by his going back to a trio format: he might be a capable accompanist, but he's better as a trio-leader, and this set is up there with the *Classic Trio* albums. One of his particular strengths is his ease in, seemingly, any kind of time: the opening tilt at Burt Bacharach's 'Close To You' (a terrific choice) works smoothly between four, 6/8 and Latin time, and they glide into three for the immediately following 'Waltzing At Suite One'. Washington and Farnsworth work their admirable line between failsafe and adventurous, and really there's hardly a moment that doesn't offer pleasure. The only drawback might be the easeful consistency of Hazeltine's music: without any hint of a jagged edge, it asks for real attention to stop it slipping into the background.

Jon Hazilla

DRUMS

Contemporary drummer moving from bop to freer forms.

***** The Bitten Moon**
Cadence CJR 1058 *Hazilla; James Williams (p); Ray Drummond (b). 3/94.*

Hazilla's ingenuity sets the tone for this session. He likes to dominate but realizes that a domineering drummer can be a bore, so he plays intrusively rather than giving himself lots of solos. Williams and Drummond are personalities in their own right, and they hold their own, but it must have been Hazilla's decision to do a snappy, up-tempo version of 'Naima', for one. There are two short but interesting solo pieces – one, 'Pancakes From Meductiv', is actually a cymbal solo – and the overall result is a sharp, out-of-the-ordinary rhythm-section record with some bite to it.

****** Form And Function**
CIMP 142 *Hazilla; John Pierce (tb); Jim Odgren (as); Greg Badolato (ts); Tim Mayer (bs). 3/97.*

This is the band Hazilla calls Saxabone – for obvious reasons – and their resonant, freshly peeled sound comes across wonderfully via CIMP's no-frills recording. The record is a sequence of eight drum solos interspersed with four hard-bop chestnuts performed by the band ('Eternal Triangle' appears in two takes). The result is a compelling and wholly original meditation on hard-bop form and, indeed, function, with the drummer's set-pieces pointedly breaking down aspects of the group player's art while the horns create a superbly expressive argument for the 'modern' possibilities in 'Our Man Higgins', 'Crepuscule With Nellie', 'A Little Brazil' and the aforementioned Stitt tune. Played end to end, it's a fascinating document and a notable essay on jazz tradition. Bravo!

***** Tiny Capers**
Double-Time DTRCD-180 *Hazilla; Bruce Barth (p); John Lockwood (b). 11/00.*

At once more conventional and more diverse than *The Bitten Moon* was, this second trio date is fashioned out of a familiar block, but gets by on the exceptionally smart playing by all three men. Some of the cover choices receive the sort of tampering which can feel too clever – 'Hello Young Lovers' doesn't really work as a samba, for instance. But even though it's by no means a regular line-up, they read each other's moves particularly well, and Hazilla himself affirms that he has a remarkable feel for lifting a small group while asserting himself.

The Headhunters

GROUP

Originally Herbie Hancock's paradigm-shifting backing group, responsible for the bestselling jazz album of its time. After Herbie's departure enjoyed mixed creative and commercial fortunes.

*****(*) Survival Of The Fittest**
RCA Victor 7432 140952 2 *Bennie Maupin (ts, bcl, p, v); Joyce Jackson (f, af); Blackbird McKnight (g, v); Paul Jackson Jr (b, v); Mike Clark (d, v); Bill Summers (d, perc); Harvey Mason Sr, Baba Duru Oshun (perc); Zak Diouf (djembe); The Pointer Sisters (v).* 75.

After Herbie Hancock's departure, the Headhunters attempted to carry on, buoyed up by the former boss's generous reference which yielded an RCA contract. The first of these albums is almost as good as anything they recorded with Herbie. 'God Made Me Funky' became a second Headhunters album and was to surface again in later years. 'Mugic', 'Here and Now' and 'If You've Got It, You'll Get It' are almost as good and the whole package is marked out with a joyous funk swing.

***** Return Of The Headhunters**
Verve Forecast 683148 2 *Bennie Maupin (ss, ts, bcl, f); Billy Childs, Mark Goodman, Herbie Hancock, Darrell Smith (ky); JK (g); Paul Jackson (b); Mike Clark (d); Bruce Gypsy Millstein, Bill Summers (perc); N'Dea Davenport, Tre Hardson (v).* 98.

***** Evolution Revolution**
Basin Street 0601 *Irvin Mayfield, Nicholas Payton (t); Bennie Maupin (ss, ts, bcl, f); Donald Harrison (as, ts); Aaron Fletcher (as); Victor Atkins (p); Ronald Markham, Harvey Mason Jr (ky); Samba Ngo, Shinji Shiotsugu, Bill Solley, Wah Wah Watson, June Yamagioshi (g); Edwin Livingston (b); Harvey Mason Sr (d); Bill Summers (perc); George Porter Jr (v).* 03.

That might have been the conclusion had these discs not appeared to prove us wrong. By the later '90s, a further market sea-change had elevated jazz-funk to a new prominence and there was a ready constituency for the band's infectious groove. Maupin is still the lead solo voice on *Return Of The Headhunters*, unveiling a battery of special effects that still couldn't be bought on any digital sampler. As if to underline the superiority of earlier technology, Hancock sounds drab and uninvolved on his four tracks. It was generous of him to make a return appearance, but his absence elsewhere isn't that important.

Both this and *Evolution Revolution* breathe new life into what seemed a moribund form. The second of the pair is a more various and in some respects a more consistent album, though it relies more heavily on guest spots from the likes of Patrice Rushen, Donald Harrison and the evergreen Wah Wah Watson. A retread of 'God Made Me Funky' is almost inevitably the highpoint, but there are great things on almost every track. A delightful return to form.

Jimmy Heath (born 1926)

TENOR, ALTO AND SOPRANO SAXOPHONES

Born in Philadelphia, the middle Heath brother led big bands and bebop groups in the original bebop era but did more writing than playing in the '50s. Since then, much more active as player-leader and a renowned teacher. A major contributor to the hard-bop book and a great patrician influence.

****** The Thumper**
Original Jazz Classics OJC 1828 *Heath; Nat Adderley (cl); Curtis Fuller (tb); Wynton Kelly (p); Paul Chambers (b); Albert 'Tootie' Heath (d).* 9/59.

***** Blue Soul**
Original Jazz Classics OJC 765 *As above.* 9/59.

***** The Riverside Collection: Nice People**
Original Jazz Classics OJC 6006 *Heath; Donald Byrd, Freddie Hubbard, Clark Terry (t); Nat Adderley (c); Curtis Fuller, Tom McIntosh (tb); Dick Berg, Jimmy Buffington, Don Butterfield (tba); Julius Watkins (frhn); Julian 'Cannonball' Adderley (as); Pat Patrick (bs); Herbie Hancock, Wynton Kelly, Cedar Walton (p); Kenny Burrell (g); Paul Chambers, Percy Heath (b); Albert 'Tootie' Heath, Connie Kay (d).* 12/59-64.

*****(*) Really Big!**
Original Jazz Classics OJC 1799 *Heath; Clark Terry, Nat Adderley (t); Tom McIntosh, Dick Berg (tb); Julian 'Cannonball' Adderley, Pat Patrick (sax); Tommy Flanagan, Cedar Walton (p); Percy Heath (b); Albert 'Tootie' Heath (d).* 60.

The middle of the three Heath brothers is perhaps and quite undeservedly now the least known. Jimmy Heath's reputation as a player has been partly overshadowed by his gifts as a composer ('CTA', 'Gemini', 'Gingerbread Boy') and arranger. *The Thumper* was his debut recording. Unlike most of his peers, Heath had not hurried into the studio. He was already in his 30s and writing with great maturity; the session kicks off with 'For Minors Only', the first of his tunes to achieve near-classic standing. He also includes 'Nice People'. The Riverside compilation which bears that name was until recently the ideal introduction to the man who was once known as 'Little Bird' but who later largely abandoned alto saxophone and its associated Parkerisms in favour of a bold, confident tenor style that is immediately distinctive. Now that *The Thumper* is around again, the compilation album is a little less appealing.

Also well worth looking out for is the big-band set from 1960. Built around the three Heath and the two Adderley brothers, it's a unit with a great deal of personality and presence. Sun Ra's favourite baritonist, Pat Patrick, is in the line-up and contributes fulsomely to the ensembles. Bobby Timmons's 'Dat Dere', 'On Green Dolphin Street' and 'Picture Of Heath' are the outstanding tracks, and Orrin Keepnews's original sound is faithfully preserved in Phil De Lancie's conservative remastering.

Heath's arrangements often favour deep brass pedestals for the higher horns, which explains his emphasis on trombone and french horn parts. The earliest of these sessions, though, is a relatively stripped-down blowing session ('Nice People' and 'Who Needs It') for Nat Adderley, Curtis Fuller and a rhythm section anchored on youngest brother, Albert, who reappears with Percy Heath, the eldest of the three, on the ambitious 1960 'Picture Of Heath'. Like Connie Kay, who was to join Percy in the Modern Jazz Quartet, Albert is an unassuming player, combining Kay's subtlety with the drive of Kenny Clarke (original drummer for the MJQ).

More than once in these sessions (and most noticeably on the 1964 'All The Things You Are' with Kenny Burrell and the brilliant Wynton Kelly) it's Albert who fuels his brother's better solos. This is a fine set, though chronological balance occasionally dictates a less than ideal selection of material. Well worth investigating.

*****(*) The Quota**
Original Jazz Classics OJCCD 1871 *Heath; Freddie Hubbard (t); Julius Watkins (frhn); Cedar Walton (p); Percy Heath (b); Albert 'Tootie' Heath (d).* 4/61.

***** On The Trail**
Original Jazz Classics OJCCD 1854 *Heath; Wynton Kelly (p); Kenny Burrell (g); Paul Chambers (b); Albert 'Tootie' Heath (d).* 64.

The Quota perfectly underlines Jimmy's ability to make three contrasting horns sound like a big band, or very nearly. This is a cleverly arranged session, and an agreeably fraternal one, with Percy and Tootie on hand as well. Hubbard was a killer at 23, soloing with fire and conviction, but it is Jimmy's own work, on his own title-track and on 'When Sonny Gets Blue', that stands out, arguably some of his best tenor-playing on record.

On The Trail is less arresting; more of a straight blowing session, it doesn't play to Jimmy's real strengths and the production seems oddly underpowered, as if everything has been taken down a notch to accommodate Burrell's soft and understated guitar lines. 'All The Things You Are' has some moments of spectacular beauty, as when Jimmy floats across Wynton Kelly's line with a soft restatement of the melody and a tiny fragment of the 'Bird Of Paradise' contrafact patented by Charlie Parker. Good, straightforward jazz, but not a great Jimmy Heath album.

*****(*) Triple Threat**
Original Jazz Classics OJCCD 1909-2 *Heath; Freddie Hubbard (t); Julius Watkins (frhn); Cedar Walton (p); Percy Heath (b); Albert 'Tootie' Heath (d).* 1/62.

A dry run for the Heath Brothers project and another object lesson in how to give a relatively small unit an expansive sound. Jimmy takes a couple of numbers with just rhythm and even there manages to suggest a massive structure behind his elegantly linear melody lines. Watkins has an enhanced role and demonstrates once again what an exciting player he can be on an instrument usually consigned to a supportive role.

Jimmy's blues waltz, 'Gemini', is probably better known in the version recorded by Cannonball Adderley, but the little man's own solo statement confirms ownership rights. Hubbard is in quiet form, but already gives notice of what he was capable of.

*****(*) Swamp Seed**
Original Jazz Classics OJCCD 1904-2 *Heath; Donald Byrd (t); Jimmy Buffington, Julius Watkins (frhn); Don Butterfield (tba); Herbie Hancock, Harold Mabern (p); Percy Heath (b); Albert 'Tootie' Heath, Connie Kay (d).* 63.

Jimmy's genius as an arranger is evident here, where he manages to make three brass sound like a whole orchestra. With no supplemental reeds to support his own muscular lines, Jimmy is the most prominent voice. On 'Six Steps', 'Nutty' and 'D Waltz', he creates solo statements of genuine originality, relying on the subtle voicings given to Butterfield, Buffington and Watkins to support his more adventurous harmonic shifts. As 'D Waltz' demonstrates, Jimmy learned a lot from listening to Charlie Parker, but also to the older bandleaders like Lunceford and Eckstine, who understood how to give relatively simple ideas maximum mileage.

***** You've Changed**
Steeplechase SCCD 31292 *Heath; Tony Purrone (g); Ben Brown (b); Albert 'Tootie' Heath (d).* 8/91.

In the early '90s he was still playing with great character. The opening solo on *You've Changed* delivers 'Soul Eyes' at an easy lope that scarcely varies for the remainder of the set. Heath can now say more in half a dozen notes than most young players can in three choruses. He places accents so carefully that even straightforward theme statements become objects of considerable interest. The group – even Tootie on this occasion – is rather dull and sluggish, but Jimmy sails on regardless, often quite blatantly ignoring key shifts and rhythmic downshifts to follow an interesting thought to its destination.

****** You Or Me**
Steeplechase SCCD 31370 *Heath; Tony Purrone (g); Kiyoshi Kitagawa (b); Albert 'Tootie' Heath (d).* 4/95.

A session tinged with real sadness, after Jimmy learned of his elder sister's death just as they were about to record. Whether Elizabeth was on his mind when he set out to re-create the Ben Webster solo on Ellington's 'All Too Soon' isn't certain, but it's a performance of great gentleness and soft regret, one of his more open-hearted ballads. Hearing him in this, albeit rather exceptional, context is a reminder of how cool and detached he has often sounded in the studio.

Not here, though. There is a real bounce and bluster to the closing 'Hot House' and the work-out on Blue Mitchell's 'Fungi Mama' is anything but diffident. The album begins with three Heath originals, including 'The Quota', and thereafter sticks to repertory material, including the Ellington and Mitchell tunes, and Duke Pearson's seldom covered 'Is That So?', which was probably recorded at least once in the old Steeplechase studio. The digital set-up is flattering to Jimmy's sound, highlighting its glacial harmonics and filling out its bass register. As before, the understanding with Tootie is sensitive and subtle and some of their exchanges are wickedly clever.

Percy Heath (born 1923)

BASS, CELLO

The eldest of the Heath brothers is a major figure in any bass-playing dynasty, and has been both witness to and participant in many of the major staging posts in jazz since the '40s. At last, he gets to lead a session of his own, in his 80th year.

***** A Love Song**
Daddy Jazz, no number *Heath; Jeb Patton (p); Peter Washington (b); Tootie Heath (d).* 5/02.

Percy Heath's record isn't so much overdue – he's already taken a major part in an awful lot of great jazz records – as a friendly reminder of his eminence. His sound on both bass and cello is recorded in a burstingly lifelike timbre, and on such pieces as his old MJQ favourite 'Watergate Blues', John Lewis's 'Django' and the dedication to his father, 'Suite For Pop', the music feels wonderfully alive and immediate. Peter Washington backs up where necessary and brother Albert is happy to join in the fun, while young piano-man Patton plays some ringing lines too.

The Heath Brothers

GROUP

Among the first families of jazz, only the Joneses can have racked up anything like the list of credits put together in the Heaths' 150 collective years in the business. Older brothers Percy and Jimmy left Philadelphia in 1949 to join Howard McGhee's band; Albert is almost a decade younger but quickly became one of the ablest and busiest drummers on the circuit.

***** Expressions Of Life / In Motion**
Collectables 6896 *Jimmy Heath (ts, ss); Percy Heath (b, clo); Stanley Cowell (p); Tony Purrone (g); Keith Copeland, Akira Tana (d); plus brass: Irwin Markowitz (t); Wayne Andre (tb); Paul Faulise (btb); Joseph DeAngelis (frhn); Howard Johnson (tba).* 1–2/79, 80.

*****(*) As We Were Saying ...**
Concord CCD 4777-2 *As above; omit brass section, Copeland, Tana; add Albert 'Tootie' Heath (d); Jon Faddis (t, flhn); Slide Hampton (tb); Stanley Cowell, Sir Roland Hanna (p); Mark Elf (g); James Mtume (perc).* 97.

****** Jazz Family**
Concord CCD 4846-2 *Jimmy Heath (ts, ss); Percy Heath (b, clo); Albert 'Tootie' Heath (d); Earl Gardner, Joe Wilder, Tom Wiliams (t, flhn); Benny Powell (tb); John Clark (frhn); Bob Stewart (tba); Jeb Patton (p); Tony Purrone (g).* 98.

Albert Heath had left the family group before the first of these recordings were made, though he was to return later. That put the emphasis fairly squarely on Jimmy's compositions and one of the main pieces on the Collectables set (actually from the 1979 *In Motion* date) is 'Voice Of The Saxophone' from Jimmy's 'Afro-American Suite Of Evolution'. There are other good tracks, notably Cowell's 'Equipoise' on the second album, but there are no more than thin pickings on these dates, which have understandably been out of circulation for some time.

The Heath Brothers recorded several albums in the '80s, but *As We Were Saying* ... and *Jazz Family* are the first fraternal offerings since then. It would be nice to report that there are strong family traits in their playing. The fact is that all three brothers have very different styles and approaches, *except* when they play together, and then the Heaths seem to draw on a shared background and experience from the heyday of bebop. Jimmy's writing and playing have developed in many different directions since then, but as 'Bop Again' on *As We Were Saying* ... suggests, this is where their hearts lie. The title is obviously meant to suggest that the boys have just picked up where they left off, as brothers do, and there is nothing in the set to indicate that this was a historic reunion rather than a new album from a working band. In Sir Roland Hanna and Stanley Cowell, Percy and Albert have two perfect rhythm section partners, players who mix the almost classical precision of Percy's bass and cello work with Tootie's African-tinged rhythms. Just to make the family gathering complete, Jimmy's son, James Mtume, adds percussion on 'South Filthy'. The presence of Jon Faddis might lead you to think you were listening to some otherwise undocumented Dizzy project, an effect that seems to encourage Jimmy's now unabashed Parkerisms. They used to call him Little Bird; he switched to tenor but now he manages to sound like Parker's happy shade.

The follow-up album is better still, but it's hard to think of it as anything other than a Jimmy Heath project. Percy contributes one tune, 'Move To The Groove' (actually the weakest thing on the roster), but the rest is dominated by the middle brother. His writing and arrangements are endlessly inventive. '13th House' is one of the best things he has written, not a classic on a par with 'C.T.A.' or 'Gingerbread Boy', but a richly constructed tune nonetheless. 'A Harmonic Future' and 'Wind Print' are a little more schematic, the former an intriguing but slightly dry exercise in neo-bop, the latter more impressionistic. Yet, wedged as they are in between 'Easy Living', Otis René's 'I'm Lost' and Kenny Dorham's lovely 'None Shall Wander', they add to the texture of a wonderfully well-crafted album.

Duke Heitger (born 1968)

TRUMPET, VOCAL

Originally from Toledo, Heitger has worked on the New Orleans scene since the early '90s, with Jacques Gauthé and others, and was on the hit album by the Squirrel Nut Zippers.

***** Rhythm Is Our Business**
Fantasy 9684-2 *Heitger; Dan Barrett (tb); Brian Ogilvie, Tom Fischer (reeds); David Boeddinghaus (p); Rebecca Kilgore (g, v); Hank Mackie (g); Kerry Lewis (b); Chris Tyle (d).* 10/98–1/99.

*****(*) Prince Of Wails**
Stomp Off CD 1367 *Heitger; Evan Christopher (cl, as); John Gill (bj, g, v); Tom Saunders (tba, b).* 2/01.

It looks like *Rhythm Is Our Business* was made to cash in on the brief fad for swing-styled groups in America, and since it was largely made by experienced pros in the style, it's a lot more convincing than the discs made by various pretenders. That said, it feels a little more affected than if it had been made under Stomp Off's jurisdiction, and Heitger shouldn't have even thought about singing when Becky Kilgore was also on hand.

The trumpeter is very much a Louis Armstrong man, and he gets a much better showing on *Prince Of Wails*. He has iron chops (possibly from a seven-day-a-week gig on the Steamer Natchez) and he really does swing into some of these pieces like the young Armstrong. Gill and Saunders are old hands at this kind of gig and Christopher is nimble and bluesy, with a very ripe tone. Up to Stomp Off's best standard.

Mark Helias (born 1950)

DOUBLE BASS, ELECTRIC BASS

New Jersey-born and Yale-educated, Helias combines a street-wise toughness with real musical intelligence. Recent years have seen him as busy as ever, but somewhat diverted towards production and a consequent hiccup in his own recording career.

****** Loopin' The Cool**
Enja 9049 *Helias; Ellery Eskelin (ts); Regina Carter (vn); Tom Rainey (d, perc); Epizo Bangoura (djembe, perc).* 12/94.

***** Fictionary**
GMR 3037 *Helias; Ellery Eskelin (ts); Tom Rainey, Michael Sarin (d).* 98.

***** Come Ahead Back**
Koch 7861 *As above, except omit Sarin.* 98.

*****(*) New School**
Enja 9413 *As above, except omit Eskelin; add Tony Malaby (ts).* 01.

***** Verbs of Will**
Radio Legs 11 *As above.* 11/02.

Loopin' The Cool finds Helias refining his own sound quite considerably and putting ever greater emphasis on highly dissonant ideas and unsettling rhythms. 'Loop The Cool' is a long line that sets Eskelin's wonderfully relaxed tenor against Regina Carter's violin; it's a compelling combination, and Carter is first to the punch again on the following 'One Time Only', which is the most rhythmically challenging thing on the session. Some of the ideas have resurfaced from other contexts, like the Ed Blackwell Project, but here they seem to have found their ideal expression. Up into the top league.

In the later '90s, Helias was working with a group known as Open Loose. *Come Ahead Back, Verbs of Will* and *New School* are credited to what is very much a collaborative group. Though Helias is the featured composer, his dependence on Rainey's rhythmic prowess is evident in every track and the interest in drum/bass combinations is evident from the unusual line-up on the live *Fictionary*. Malaby will be new to some, but he is a player worthy of serious attention.

As always the writing is of a very high order. Difficult to single out individual performances from any of these albums. All require a measure of close attention and all repay it handsomely. We'd recommend you start with *New School* and scroll to the long, elaborate 'Mapa' and the lovely 'Gentle Ben' first. Helias's attention to structure is always going to be exposed in such a raw and unforgiving setting. These tracks, and most of the others, stand up strongly and point the way forward. Expect to hear some of these pieces in a more developed and elaborate setting in the near future.

Joel Helleny (born 1956)

TROMBONE

Talented New Yorker, yet to realize his full potential.

***** Lip Service**
Arbors 19161 *Helleny; Dan Barrett (tb); Richard Wyands (p); Ray Macchiarola (g); Murray Wall (b); Leroy Williams (d).* 12/95.

Helleny is an able mainstream player. His debut CD contains few surprises but will appeal to those who like the sound of old-fashioned trombone-playing of a resolutely lyrical and conservative sort. The choice of material is interestingly varied, with a fun version of 'The Andy Griffith Theme' (starring guest horn man Dan Barrett), a rare Manny Albam tune 'Lullaby Of Jazzland' and a Ronell Bright tune which we've not often heard on a jazz record (Hal Galper likes it). Though the leader is the main solo voice, Wyands makes as significant a contribution as one would expect. The guitarist is somewhat superfluous, but takes some nice passages.

Bob Helm (born 1914)

CLARINET, ALTO CLARINET, ALTO SAXOPHONE, VOCALS

A veteran of the Californian revivalist scene for more than 50 years, Helm began playing with Lu Watters in 1940 and with Turk Murphy from the mid-'40s until 1980.

*****(*) Hotter Than That**
Stomp Off CD1310 *Helm; Leon Oakley (c, v); Charlie Sonnanstine (tb); Ted Des Plantes (p, v); Vince Saunders (bj, g); Bill Carroll (tba); Marty Eggers (b); Bob Raggio (wbd).* 10/94–1/95.

***** Ma 'N' Bessie's Greater Tent Show Act 1**
Stomp Off CD1331 *As above, except add Ray Skjelbred (p), John Gill (bj, g, d, tb, v), Craig Ventresco (bj, g), Mike Walbridge (tba), Pete Devine (wbd, jug), Carol Leigh (v).* 10/94–9/97.

***** Ma 'N' Bessie's Greater Tent Show Act 2**
Stomp Off CD1332 *As above.* 10/94–9/97.

Bob Helm's matchless knowledge of traditional styles serves these records well, the first under his leadership since a Riverside session in 1954. *Hotter Than That* rounds up some of the best of the Stomp Off repertory company for a marathon 20-song session that almost bursts the CD's boundaries. Although here and there the band take things easy so as not to overwhelm the leader, some of the slower tempos suit the material better: 'Everybody Loves My Baby' is taken at an almost menacing slow jog, and Natty Dominique's 'Too Tight' sounds less clockwork at this pace. In any case, the likes of 'Hotter Than That' itself steam along.

The other two records are culled from sessions meant to re-create the style and feel of the sort of tent shows which Ma Rainey and the young Bessie Smith would have toured with, with the various aggregations listed as The Rabbit Foot Hoppers, The Barbary Coasters, The Banjo Papas and so on. Excellent fun, although Carol Leigh's singing may not be to all tastes and not all the pieces succeed as well as they might.

Gerry Hemingway (born 1955)

DRUMS, PERCUSSION

An important collaborator – with Anthony Braxton, Marilyn Crispell and others – and lately a considerable leader, as well as a solo-percussion performer, Hemingway has been a significant part of the mainstream avant-garde in the USA since the late '70s.

***** Acoustic Solo Works**
Random Acoustics RA 016 *Hemingway (perc solo).* 12/83–8/93.

***** Electro-Acoustic Solo Works**
Random Acoustics RA 017 *Hemingway (perc, elec solo).* 6/84–4/95.

Gerry Hemingway is still a little weighed down in critical terms by his part in what for a significant number of listeners remains *the* Anthony Braxton group, the 1985 quartet with Marilyn Crispell and Mark Dresser. A lot of water, as Sam Goldwyn used to say, has been passed since then. Hemingway has gone on to assert himself as a fine individual talent with a strong sense of tradition, incidentally revealing in the process, one suspects, that his attunement to Braxton's vibrational philosophy was an act of will rather than of instinct and conviction.

These solo records are a good representation of a drummer and composer whose earliest musical encounters were with rock music, but who quickly saw beyond backbeats and basic fours to a more adventurous rhythm. However, the sheer force and energy of rock remains embedded in all these performances, even when they seem quite rarefied. There is a tremendous consistency of sound material both within and between these discs. Hemingway has always explored restlessly, re-examining aspects of his work in contexts which emphasize time and ritual components, pure sonics and, on occasion, expressive and programmatic elements. 'Dance Of The Sphygmoids' (on the acoustic disc) was included on his debut solo disc, *Tibworks*, and is substantially reworked here, more obviously dance-based, but also more abstract in contour. The two 'Trance Tracks' are intriguing in the light of later developments in breakbeats and drum'n'bass, and Hemingway shows himself to be well ahead of the game on both counts. 'For Buhaina' is a straightforward tribute to Art Blakey, an example of Hemingway the less-is-more kinsman of the great novelist, while on 'Tyrolienne', he uses glockenspiel bars to create an almost vocalized sound, extending the range of the kit enormously.

This is clearly the purpose of the electro-acoustic compositions as well. The earliest of these, 'Waterways', is a fairly conventional piece for tape and percussion. It is only with the work of the '90s, perhaps influenced by Braxton, that the drummer begins to demonstrate an idiomatic understanding of the power and range of electronic processes. 'Polar' from 1990 and for two simultaneous tapes, is chill and acerbic, but the later 'Chatterlings', which combines live percussion and a Midi-triggered sampler, is much more responsive.

***(*) Slamadam

Random Acoustics RA 012 *Hemingway; Wolter Wierbos (tb); Michael Moore (as, cl, bcl); Ernst Reijseger (clo); Mark Dresser (b).* 11/91–2/94.

**** Perfect World

Random Acoustics RA 019 *As above.* 3/95.

The spanking *Slamadam*, which appears on Georg Graewe's ambitious small label, brings together material over quite some time, but the bulk of the recording was done within days of the now unavailable studio set, *The Marmalade King*, and it's interesting to hear how different the group (with the addition of Ernst Reijseger) sounds in concert, a lot fresher and more immediate and with a fire that the studio discipline seems to bank down and even extinguish. The closing 'Pumbum' was a quartet performance because Reijseger was in hospital with a slipped disc, and if you ever saw the way he waves a cello around …

He was available for duty again for the quintet's European tour of spring 1995, a vintage spell for Hemingway. The deal with hat ART now seems to be over, but this more casually assembled set (which was fraught with packaging problems) is perhaps the best thing currently available under Hemingway's name. The long 'Little Suite' and 'Perfect World' itself, recorded in England by the BBC, are the key to the record, occupying more than half its length and again suggesting how strong a grasp of large-scale structures Hemingway can call on. The only non-original item is Ellington's 'Village Of The Virgins', a startling inclusion but one that fits the group like a glove.

**** Waltzes, Two-Steps And Other Matters Of The Heart

GM Recordings Inc GM 3043 *Hemingway; Robin Eubanks (tb); Ellery Eskelin (ts); Mark Dresser (b)* 11/96.

The Hemingway Quartet toured tirelessly during 1996, at one point playing 27 concerts in a 28-day period. Two of those dates are sampled here. Hemingway had recently taken charge of his own management and distribution, an overload which might have been disastrous had one happenstance not lightened his load. The electronic samples which were to have accompanied the tour were lost when a computer crashed. The mishap threw Hemingway back on the band's internal resources, and *Waltzes* is a superb representation of its improvisational versatility. There are duos and trios, solo spots and areas of near silence as all five ponder decays in the markedly different acoustics of the Berlin Jazz Festival and Fasching in Sweden.

Hemingway had been writing a lot of material in waltz time, though in practice the count is often 7/4 or 9/4 rather than a strict three-quarter. That is acknowledged on the opening 'Waltz In Seven', with its mournful *rubato* opening. The first of the long tracks is the slow, stately 'Gitar', which opens with Hemingway on harmonica, albeit an instrument so oddly pitched that he sounds like a consort of Tibetan Buddhists playing shawms. The main melody could almost be Aaron Copland in a melancholic mood, with Wierbos playing in the lower reaches of his register.

By contrast to the open-form pieces, 'Gospel Waltz' is a relatively straightahead blowing piece, though each of the group approaches its changes and melodic form in a quite different way. 'XI' is an arrangement of a madrigal by Gesualdo, further evidence of how tirelessly Hemingway ranges for new inspiration. 'Ari' is a traditional German waltz and an ideal curtain-piece.

***(*) Johnny's Corner Song

Auricle 4 *As above.* 11/97.

There are two stunning performances on this hard-to-find CD: Mark Helias's lyrical 'Gentle Ben', which features a truly remarkable solo from Eubanks; and the long closing track, 'Toombow', which attempts a whole complex synthesis of styles and manages to pull them all together into a superbly coherent 20-minute piece. 'On It' is proof that Hemingway has never left orthodox bop-based jazz behind. It's an astonishing work, reminiscent of some of Dexter Gordon's more outré workouts, and only the rather distinctive instrumentation, with drums mixed well forward, will give away the provenance. A fine record, well worth searching out.

*** Chamber Works

Tzadik 7052 *Hemingway; Cuong Vu (t); Marty Ehrlich (cl); Sara Parkins (vn); Liuh-Wen Ting (vla); Mark Dresser (b); James Baker (perc).* 99.

This doesn't fall strictly within our purview, but fans of Gerry's work will find it consistently intriguing and hugely satisfying. Gerry's melodism comes through even when the language is fairly sparse and modernistic. Hemingway contributes only rather briefly as a player, working a sampler on 'The Visiting Tank'. Several of the performers are known from the jazz field, but here they play with accuracy and great attention to detail; no JAMFs were allowed, clearly.

*****(*) Devil's Paradise**

Clean Feed 10 *Hemingway; Ray Anderson (tb); Ellery Eskelin (ts); Mark Dresser (b). 2/99.*

This is much more like the thing, an intriguingly retrospective reworking of pieces Hemingway has had in his bag for some years. 'Back Again Some Time' was on 1991's *Down to the Wire*, 'Johnny's Corner Song' anchored a 1998 album of that name, and 'Toombow' has been on two previous discs. No matter. This is as strong a showing from the drummer as there is in the current catalogue. The group is a familiar one and well-versed in the compositions. The tightness of arrangements is a big plus, especially on material like 'Devil's Paradise', which gets the album off to a roaring start. Anderson is at his clever, subversive best and Dresser is the perfect partner in the rhythm section, drawing on a long association to carve some superbly understated and inventive playing.

***** Songs**

Between The Lines btl 024 *Hemingway; Herb Robertson (t); Wolter Wierbos (tb); John Butcher, Ellery Eskelin (ts); Thomas Lehn (syn); James Emery (g); Kermit Driscoll (b); Lisa Sokolov (v). 3–12/01.*

A surprise package and a considerable departure for Hemingway. His approach to pop still has a worthwhile improvisational component, largely down to the wonderful Wierbos, but for the most part these vocal pieces are outside our strict remit. We'd suggest, however, that Lisa Sokolov's voice is the wrong one for songs like 'Succotash' (which may contain an allusion to one of Robert Ashley's television operas), 'Hall of Mirrors' and 'Thump'.

Julius Hemphill (1940–95)

ALTO AND SOPRANO SAXOPHONES

No one talks about 'Texas alto' but Hemphill's most obvious kinship is with Ornette Coleman, and yet he is a very different style of composer and the resemblance is somewhat superficial. The complex polyphony of the World Saxophone Quartet, of which he was a founding member, leaches into all his work, which is urgent and throughtful. Hemphill's early death was a grievous loss.

*****(*) Live In New York**

Red RR 123138 *Hemphill; Abdul Wadud (clo). 5/76.*

*****(*) Roi Boye & The Gotham Minstrels**

Sackville SK2CD 3014/15 *Hemphill (ss, as, f, v). 3/77.*

***** Blue Boyé**

Screwgun 70008 2CD *Hemphill (sax solo). 77.*

Hemphill was the chief composer for the World Saxophone Quartet, and his signature style was lean – some said 'raw' when his Texas roots were showing – and often quite drastically pared-down. Seemingly inspired by Dolphy's collaborations with Ron Carter, he favoured cello as an alternative harmony instrument, enjoying a fruitful relationship with Wadud. Like Dolphy, his alto sound was piercing and intensely vocalized, and always locked into very clear musical logics. Hemphill exerted a major influence on the following generation of American musicans – people like Tim Berne especially – and his premature death was a significant loss.

It was Berne who reissued *Blue Boyé* on his own Screwgun label. Not the most successful or satisfying of Hemphill's records, it first appeared on Mbari and doesn't sound any better recorded on transfer to CD. Some of the saxophonist's most idiomatic compositions are included, though: 'Hotend', the Ornettish 'C.M.E.' and 'Homeboy Tootin' At The Dog'. By contrast, the vast 'audiorama' of *Roi Boye & The Gotham Minstrels* is enough in itself to guarantee Hemphill a place among the major figures of the last 50 years. Carefully multi-tracked, with Julius playing all the parts, it is an aural evocation of New York City and more abstractly a brilliant exercise in the integration of reed voices. For some it is the precursor of his work for and with the World Saxophone Quartet, which was an attempt to realize some of the ideas encapsulated here in real time. Hemphill's three voices, the bird-like flute, wavering, sinuous soprano and solidly vocalized alto weave together into a single musical personality. A classic.

The duos are not so well recorded, a little too loud and indistinct (certainly not as faithfully rendered, even in the studio, as the 1992 concerts on *Oakland Duets*, covered below), but the long 'Echo 2 (Evening)' offers a clear sense of how Hemphill's ears worked, harmonically speaking. There are moments when his stark lines seem to be light years away from Wadud's chocolatey chords and faster, more rhythmic devices. Then suddenly the whole improvisation clicks into focus as a whole. Ironically, it is these four pieces which, despite the limited personnel, offer the best introduction to Hemphill the composer, even in the context of the most basic personnel. Virtually all the later things, including his 'saxophone opera', *Long Tongues*, and his larger ensemble and big-band projects stem from this.

CORE COLLECTION

****** Flat-Out Jump Suite**

Black Saint 120040 *Hemphill; Olu Dara (t); Abdul Wadud (clo); Warren Smith (perc). 6/80.*

Initially a more abstract session than Hemphill's later output, the *Flat-Out Jump Suite* builds to a rousing funk climax on 'Body'. Hemphill intones the title to each part as it begins, starting with the soft, percussion-led figures of 'Ear', plunging into the complexities of 'Mind' (which is dominated by Wadud) and then picking up a more continuous rhythm with 'Heart', on which Hemphill begins to string together his light, slightly floating textures into a more continuous, jazz-based improvisation. On the original LP, 'Mind, Part 2' opened the second side with a brief coda to the long central piece. It makes more sense as an integral drum solo, typically understated. It is, until the very end, a remarkably quiet album that requires some concentration. Dara uses his mute a good deal and otherwise plays quite softly. Hemphill seems to play a wooden flute and gives his saxophone a soft-edged quality that is very attractive. An excellent record, easily overlooked.

***** Chile New York**

Black Saint 120146-2 *Hemphill; Warren Smith (vib, mar, perc). 5/80.*

Chile New York was devised as a sound environment for a sculpture and poetry installation by Jeff Schlanger (whose ceramics were to be used for later Hemphill album covers) and James Scully. The inspiration was the overthrow of the democratic Marxist government in Santiago and the subsequent killing of President Salvador Allende and singer Victor Jara. After 20 years, the music stands somewhat apart from its occasion, and one doesn't need to know much about the programme or its setting to appreciate Hemphill's slow, meditative themes which are gathered into three long pieces and three very short ones. Smith is a veteran of the Chicago free scene and he provides the scampering backgrounds, redolent of rat alleys and paper-strewn streets, through which Julius walks, alone and troubled. It's a powerful record, and its posthumous release fills in another corner of the Hemphill story.

*****(*) Fat Man And The Hard Blues**
Black Saint 120115 *Hemphill; Marty Ehrlich (as, ss, f); Carl Grubbs (as, ss); James Carter, Andrew White (ts); Sam Furnace (bs, f).* 7/91.

***** Live From The New Music Café**
Music & Arts CD 731 *Hemphill; Abdul Wadud (clo); Joe Bonadio (d, perc).* 9/91.

***** Oakland Duets**
Music & Arts CD 791 *As above, except omit Bonadio.* 11/92.

****** Five Chord Stud**
Black Saint 120140 *Tim Berne, James Carter (as, ts); Marty Ehrlich, Andrew White (ss, as, ts); Fred Ho, Sam Furnace (ss, as, bs).* 11/93.

'The Hard Blues', the last and longest track on Hemphill's first post-WSQ recording, is an old tune which seemed finally to have found its appropriate setting in Hemphill's all-horn groups of the early '90s. The sextets were an obvious extension of his work with the Quartet, with the emphasis on Hemphill's composition and arranging, and on a distinctive variation on conventional theme-and-solo jazz; often the group will improvise round a theme stated quite simply and directly by the 'soloist'.

The same process can even be heard in the duos with Wadud, still going strong after more than a decade. What's different this time around, perhaps reflecting the wider change in Hemphill's self-definition, is that the pieces are shorter and more self-contained, and they obey a more obvious structural logic. Good to have a live version of one of the 'Dogon' pieces. The longest single item, significantly, is Wadud's dull 'Sigure'; Hemphill palpably loses interest, and blares his impatience. Bonadio isn't the most virtuosic drummer, but he's right for this music precisely because he doesn't want to plug every hole, fill every silence with sound.

This has a bearing on the music for the larger, horn groups, which do tend to become rather heavy round the middle. Hemphill avoids extremes of pitch, often building long passages on minor seconds and quasi-microtonal ideas, scoring in such a way that small variations of register and timbre take on considerable significance. That stands out on the sinuous 'Tendrils', one of the more linear themes and written chiefly for the two flautists. The piece actually seems to unravel, in contrast to the melting, blurry quality of most of the other tracks. Unwise to review an album by recourse to its sleeve, but the deceptively liquescent lines of ceramic artist Jeff Schlanger's blue stoneware saxophone suggest something of Hemphill's hard centre. *Fat Man And The Hard Blues* was both an intelligent continuation of the last decade's work and a challenging new departure.

Unfortunately, Hemphill's health subsequently deteriorated to the extent that he was no longer able to perform. There is no error in the personnel detailed for *Five Chord Stud*. Even in his absence as a player – he was recovering from open heart surgery (alas, not successful in the long term) – this is unmistakably Hemphill's group and Hemphill's music. The title-piece is fascinating not least for an apparent lack of interest in textural and timbral variation: two tenor solos, three alto solos, sopranos and baritones reserved for ensembles. There is strong evidence that Hemphill has been listening to Ornette on harmolodics; 'Mr Critical' is a tribute and there are frequent allusions to Ornette themes throughout the session. It isn't absolutely clear whether the composer/conductor is directing the two collective improvisations (in which Ehrlich for one cuts loose) but he certainly puts his stamp very firmly on the rest. As with *Fat Man*, the back cover illustration is a ceramic figure: a saxophone player, languid but compact, dark, atavistic, and absolutely concentrated on his music.

Eddie Henderson (born 1940)

TRUMPET, FLUGELHORN

Henderson studied trumpet at the San Francisco Conservatory before embarking on medical studies; he has combined the two disciplines ever since. His sound is typically soft-edged, with a certain emotional rawness and a resistance to cut-and-dried resolutions.

***** Inside Out/Realisation**
Soul Brother CD SBPJ 11 *Henderson; Bennie Maupin (f, af, stritch, ts, bcl); Herbie Hancock (p, ky); Pat Gleeson (syn); Buster Williams (b); Billy Hart, Eric Gravatt, Lenny White III (d).* 2/73.

Nearly 30 years ago, Eddie Henderson had a pop hit with the disco-influenced 'Comin' Through'. It was just the latest twist in a career which had started with every ambitious parent's nightmare moment, when Henderson – having completed his medical studies – listened to Miles Davis and went off to become a professional musician instead. Actually, Miles was a Henderson house-guest during a residency at the Blackhawk and, while obviously impressed by young Eddie's ability to play through *Sketches Of Spain* without a fluff, pointed out that that was *him*; Eddie was going to have to work out his own approach and voice. That he has certainly done; though his tone and phrasing irresistibly recall Woody Shaw, Henderson is a highly distinctive stylist.

Despite gigs with Miles, Herbie Hancock and Joe Henderson and with his own group, he has remained essentially a part-time player, a fiercely difficult discipline to maintain. After working with Hancock, who is perhaps the most significant single influence after Miles on his general musical conception, Henderson made two records for the Capricorn label now reissued on single CD. The musicians are familiar from Herbie Hancock's group and the sound-world here is a modest version of Herbie's *Sextant*.

This was a relatively turbulent period in Henderson's musical life. The ensembles are busy, chaotic in places and packed with an excess of detail that if anything is more noticeable after CD mastering. The elements are familiar enough to seasoned listeners to this period in jazz: Williams's buoyant bass, Hancock's brief commitment to abstraction, Maupin's multi-instrumentalism and here and there the ferocious drumming of Eric Gravatt, who made a brief name with Weather Report. None of the compositions are memorable enough to merit separate mention; the overall effect is of hyperactive soundscape, against which Henderson's horn sounds out bright and very clear. Good to have these tracks back in circulation again, even if just as period-pieces.

*** Phantoms

SteepleChase SCCD 31250 *Henderson; Joe Locke (vib); Kenny Barron (p); Wayne Dockery (b); Victor Lewis (d).* 4/89.

*** Think On Me

SteepleChase SCCD 31264 *As above, except replace Lewis with Billy Hart (d).* 12/89.

The association with SteepleChase has been a very fruitful one, not least in throwing Henderson up against another of the label's unsung heroes, Joe Locke. The vibist dominates *Think On Me* with the extraordinary 'Seven Beauties' and with the long opening piece; as so often on his own records, Henderson seems perfectly content to remain in the background, listening, not judging or forcing a conclusion, the disinterest required of the practising psychiatrist. One is always impressed by Henderson's equanimity, which sits well beside Locke's often quite fulsome expressions. Henderson is perhaps a little too detached here and there on *Phantoms*, perhaps because the thrust of the rhythm section is more assertive than seems to suit him.

***(*) Flight Of Mind

SteepleChase SSCD 31284 *Henderson; Larry Willis (p); Ed Howard (b); Victor Lewis (d).* 1/91.

Equanimity and emotional balance of an almost superhuman sort must have been required to record *Flight Of Mind*, which followed very soon after the death of Henderson's son. Whatever else, it brings a fragile grace and philosophical calm to a set which includes a performance of Freddie Hubbard's 'Lament For Booker' (covered later on *Dark Shadows*) and a magnificent interpretation of 'Un bel dì vedremo' from *Madama Butterfly*, a solo worthy of Miles himself. There is no overblown emotion, no grandstanding, just simple and direct statement. Locke would have been wrong for this particular session; fine as he always is, this needed something different.

*** Inspiration

Milestone MCD 9240 *Henderson; Grover Washington Jr (ss); Joe Locke (vib); Kevin Hays (p); Ed Howard (b); Lewis Nash (d).* 7/94.

Vivid, emotive playing apart, Locke's other contribution to this slightly patchy but thoroughly accomplished session was to bring in the Bobby Hutcherson composition, 'Little B's Poem', which, though treated somewhat briefly, is one of the high points of the record. Otherwise the choice of material is fairly routine, even rather conventional, with 'On Green Dolphin Street', 'Surrey With The Fringe On Top' and 'When You Wish Upon A Star' all played in a rather perfunctory way. Henderson's seeming preference for putting the main piece at the centre of the album on this occasion dictates a pairing of another Hancock masterpiece, 'Oliloqui Valley' (a guest slot for Washington), with a re-run of Kenny Barron's 'Phantoms'. Washington also figures, rather less successfully, on 'I Remember Clifford', a tune that doesn't seem quite tailor-made for Henderson, but to which he brings quiet counsels of his own.

***(*) Dark Shadows

Milestone MCD 9254 *Henderson; Joe Locke (vib); George Colligan, Kevin Hays (p); Ed Howard (b); Billy Hart, Lewis Nash (d); Steve Berrios (perc); Lee Menzies (v).* 9/95.

Another Henderson family connection – and a happier one this time – attaches to this album. During the making of the record, Henderson's daughter Lee Menzies turned up unexpectedly after not seeing her old man for 15 years. It was decided on the spot that they would record the spiritual 'The Water Is Wide', which she knew from her vocal arts course. The result is a thing of delicate, almost glassy beauty, bringing to a close an album that manages to combine pain with a redemptive purity of expression.

Henderson has never sounded more like Woody Shaw, and the interplay of trumpet and vibes here unshakeably recalls Shaw's work with Bobby Hutcherson. The centrepieces of the disc are Gordon Jenkins's relatively little-known 'Goodbye' (which had also featured so poignantly on *Flight Of Mind*), followed by Locke's glorious 'Cerulean Blue', on which Hays switches to Fender Rhodes, and then the big Henderson statement. 'Dark Shadows' is one of the finest things he has ever written, rhythmically and thematically complex, and calling on a second drummer in the shape of Billy Hart. Its juxtaposition with namesake Joe Henderson's 'Punjab' is a brilliant piece of programming. Hugely satisfying and creating a sense of closure that has been present only sporadically in Henderson's work since *Flight Of Mind*.

**** Reemergence

Sharp Nine Records CD 1012-2 *Henderson; Kevin Hays (p); Joe Locke (vib); Ed Howard (b); Billy Drummond (d).* 3/98.

Dominated by the long and graceful 'Gershwin Suite', this is a triumphant record, a near-perfect articulation of Henderson's skills not just as a trumpet player but also as a bandleader. One of his great gifts is to allow his players to complete the process of creation by leaving themes, notably his own composition 'Dreams', open-ended and only loosely arranged, so that performance actually completes the process of composition and arrangement.

This time around, there are only a couple of Henderson originals in the set, which ends with the brief 'Natsuko-san', played straight and without solos, a simple message of love to his wife. Joe Locke is, as ever, a key element and he brings the epic sweep of 'Saturn's Child' to the date, a wonderful theme that would work for anything from solo piano to full symphony.

The Gershwin material is pitched just right for Henderson: clever, warm, life-aware and sardonic without a hint of cynicism. 'Summertime' needs something a bit special these days, and the trumpeter gives it a soaring presence that blows the clichés away. 'Embraceable You' is equally good at the end of the sequence, expressive but highly disciplined, not quite a politically correct hug, perhaps more a fraternal one. Everything on the album, from the opening 'This Is For Albert' (a Wayne Shorter theme) to the close, seems to be in exactly the right place and pitched dead on. A great place to make the acquaintance of Eddie Henderson if you haven't already.

★★(★) Encontro Em Lisboa

Groove Jazz 104/105 *Henderson; Perico Sambeat (as); Pedro Moreira (ts); Bernardo Sassetti (p); Bernardo Moreira (b); Sylvia Cuenca (d).* 01.

An oddity, Henderson guesting with a Portuguese group, of whom only Bernardo Sassetti and Sylvia Cuenca may be widely known. Almost all the material is by saxophonist Perico Sambeat, who is a decent player, though hardly an inspiring writer. We don't know what circulation this record has. Fans of Henderson will want to have it, but it isn't a priority purchase by any means.

★★★ Oasis

Sirocco Jazz 1015 *As for Reemergence.* 3/01.

An interesting themed project, with most of the tracks bearing dry and dusty titles. In contrast to the desert iconography, the music is warm and approachable and Eddie is playing with calm authority. At the heart of the set, which kicks off with Drummond's original 'Dubai', are Wayne Shorter's 'Lost', Lee Morgan's 'Melancholee' (a slightly surprising choice for Henderson) and, breaking the desert theme, a lovely reinterpretation of Herbie Hancock's 'Cantaloupe Island'. This is now a well-seasoned group and all participants sound comfortable with the material and the generous, open-textured arrangements. Eddie isn't as well recorded as we have heard him, sometimes faintly remote, sometimes hovering on the verge of distortion.

★★★ So What

Columbia 87172 *Henderson; Bob Berg (ts); David Kikoski (p); Ed Howard (b); Billy Hart, Victor Lewis (d).* 3/02.

One of the last recordings by the late Bob Berg, who was killed on the road later that year, *So What* is yet another Miles Davis tribute, redeemed by some fine playing and by an unslavish approach to the material. 'Prince Of Darkness' and 'Someday My Prince Will Come' might have made a strange medley; as it is, they are kept apart and neither is exceptionally strong. The best things on the record are a remarkably uncluttered reading of 'On Green Dolphin Street' which makes explicit reference to Miles and a wonderful version of Wayne Shorter's 'Footprints'. The title-piece is done with an airy insouciance, but with no shortage of new ideas.

Fletcher Henderson (1897–1952)

PIANO, BANDLEADER

Born in Georgia, Henderson arrived in New York in 1920, seeking scientific work but ending up as an A&R man in the fledgling black record industry. He played piano behind many blues singers and began leading an orchestra at the Roseland Ballroom, filling it with the best players he could find, including Louis Armstrong and Coleman Hawkins. It was the top band of its day, but a car crash in 1928 seemed to dissipate Henderson's interest and thereafter the orchestra went into a slow decline. He was a good arranger whose scores for Benny Goodman in the '30s helped the clarinettist establish his eminence. He still ran bands and small groups in the '40s, but a stroke in 1950 effectively finished him.

★★(★) Fletcher Henderson 1921–1923

Classics 794 *Henderson; Elmer Chambers, Russell Smith, Joe Smith (c); George Brashear (tb); William Grant Still, Edgar Campbell, Ernest Elliott, Don Redman, Billy Fowler (reeds); Leroy Vanderveer, Charlie Dixon (bj); plus various unknowns.* 6/21–6/23.

★★★ Fletcher Henderson 1923

Classics 697 *Henderson; Elmer Chambers, Howard Scott (c); Teddy Nixon (tb); Don Redman (cl, as); Coleman Hawkins (ts, bsx, cl); Billy Fowler (bsx); Allie Ross (vn); Charlie Dixon (bj); Ralph Escudero (bb); Kaiser Marshall (d).* 6/23–4/24.

★★★ Fletcher Henderson 1923–1924

Classics 683 *As above, except omit Ross.* 12/23–2/24.

★★★ Fletcher Henderson 1924

Classics 673 *As above.* 2–5/24.

★★(★) Fletcher Henderson 1924 Vol. 2

Classics 657 *As above, except add Charlie Green (tb), Lonnie Brown (as), Rosa Henderson (v).* 5–8/24.

★★★ Fletcher Henderson 1924 Vol. 3

Classics 647 *As above, except add Louis Armstrong (c, v), Buster Bailey (cl, as); omit Nixon, Brown, Rosa Henderson.* 9–11/24.

★★★ Fletcher Henderson 1924–1925

Classics 633 *Henderson; Louis Armstrong, Elmer Chambers, Howard Scott, Joe Smith, Russell Smith (t, c); Charlie Green (tb); Don Redman (cl, as, v); Buster Bailey (cl, as); Coleman Hawkins (cl, Cmel, ts, bsx); Charlie Dixon (bj); Ralph Escudero (bb); Kaiser Marshall (d); Billy Jones (v).* 11/24–11/25.

Henderson drifted into both music and bandleading after casually working for the Black Swan record label, and his first records as a leader are frequently no more than routine dance music. The arrival of Louis Armstrong – whom Henderson first heard in New Orleans at the turn of the decade – apparently galvanized everyone in the band and, eventually, every musician in New York. But it's hard to make assumptions about Henderson's band. He already had Don Redman and Coleman Hawkins working for him prior to Armstrong's arrival, and there are too many good records before Louis's first session of October 1924 to dismiss the group as jazz ignoramuses. The sequence of Classics CDs has now been expanded into a complete run of Henderson's recordings (though there remain a number of blues accompaniments yet to find their way to CD). These were skilful, if not particularly outward-looking musicians, and even as early as 1923 – on 'Shake Your Feet' or '31st Street Blues' – there are fragments of solos which work out. The first disc in the sequence is of no more than historical interest; only at the end does the band begin to stir into life beyond the most ordinary dance music, though there are three interesting early solos by Henderson himself. Classics 697 includes Coleman Hawkins's first session, where he played an extraordinary solo for 1923 on the Vocalion version of 'Dirty Blues'. The next three CDs are inevitably mixed affairs. Henderson cut some songs in a completely straight manner, barely allowing the musicians any leeway, and let them have their head on others. From session to session, though, there is usually something of interest. The weakest disc is probably Classics 657, which includes a preponderance of dull tracks; although even here there is Redman's interesting chart for 'The Gouge Of Armour Avenue', which features Green's rasping trombone, and two good versions of 'Hard Hearted Hannah'. Classics 647 goes up several gears with Armstrong's arrival, and though he doesn't exactly dominate, the music always catches fire when he takes a solo, even on an early piece like the Pathé version of

'Shanghai Shuffle'. He is present on most of Classics 633 and, luckily, gets a solo on most of the tracks. His cornet improvisations – often set against Marshall hitting the off-beat to heighten the dramatic effect – are breathtaking, especially on what would otherwise be dreary tunes, such as 'I'll See You In My Dreams' or 'I Miss My Swiss', where his amazing performance electrifies the whole band. But some of the other musicians were getting into their stride, too: Redman delivers some strong early arrangements, Hawkins and Bailey sneak through some breaks. The best of the material – 'TNT', 'Money Blues', 'Carolina Stomp' and, above all, their hit version of 'Sugar Foot Stomp' – lets the finest black band in New York play to their strengths.

Transfer quality is unfortunately often indifferent. Classics appears to have opted for a variety of sources and, while the original 78s differ strikingly in terms of their sound from label to label, the remastering is often less than ideal. The Vocalion originals sound a touch too heavy in the bass, and a comparison between the Classics Pathé tracks and those on Fountain's *The Henderson Pathés* (listed in our first edition but now out of print) shows a cleaner, lighter sound on the LP version. Classics, though, offers the only edition of many of the earlier tracks, which scholars should welcome.

CORE COLLECTION

**** The Complete Louis Armstrong With Fletcher Henderson

Forte F38001/2/3 3CD *As above.* 24–5.

For Henderson with Armstrong, the clear winner is the Forte three-disc collection. The 65 tracks include all known original and alternative takes, and the remastering by John R. T. Davies is of the very best.

*** Fletcher Henderson 1925–1926

Classics 610 *As above, except Rex Stewart (c) replaces Armstrong, Scott and Chambers.* 11/25–4/26.

***(*) Fletcher Henderson 1926–1927

Classics 597 *As above, except add Tommy Ladnier (t), Jimmy Harrison (tb), Fats Waller (p, org), June Cole (bb, v), Evelyn Thompson (v).* 4/26–1/27.

***(*) Fletcher Henderson 1927

Classics 580 *As above, except add Jerome Pasquall (cl, as); omit Escudero, Thompson.* 1–5/27.

***(*) Fletcher Henderson 1927–1931

Classics 572 *Henderson; Bobby Stark, Tommy Ladnier, Russell Smith, Rex Stewart, Cootie Williams (t, c); Jimmy Harrison (tb, v); Charlie Green, Claude Jones, Benny Morton (tb); Jerome Pasquall, Benny Carter, Harvey Boone (cl, as); Coleman Hawkins (cl, ts); Charlie Dixon, Clarence Holiday (bj, g); John Kirby, June Cole (bb, b); Kaiser Marshall, Walter Thompson (d); Lois Deppe, Andy Razaf (v).* 11/27–2/31.

***(*) The Harmony & Vocalion Sessions Vol. 1

Timeless CBC 1-064 *As appropriate discs above.*

***(*) The Harmony & Vocalion Sessions Vol. 2

Timeless CBC 1-069 *As appropriate discs above.* 12/26–9/28.

By the mid-'20s Henderson was leading the most consistently interesting big band on record. That doesn't mean all the records are of equal calibre, and the title of a famous earlier retrospective of Henderson's work – 'A Study In Frustration' – gives some idea of the inconsistencies and problems of a band that failed to secure any hit records and never sounded on record the way it could in person (at least, according to many witnesses). But Henderson's best records are classics of the period. Don Redman was coming into his own, and his scores assumed a quality which no other orchestral arranger was matching in 1926–7 (though it is tantalizing to ponder what Jelly Roll Morton could have done with the same band). 'The Stampede', 'The Chant', 'Henderson Stomp', the remarkable 'Tozo' and, above all, the truly astonishing 'Whiteman Stomp' find him using the colours of reeds and brass to complex, yet swinging ends. Luckily Henderson had the players who could make the scores happen. Though Armstrong had departed, Hawkins, Ladnier, Joe Smith, Jimmy Harrison and Buster Bailey all had the stature of major soloists as well as good section-players. The brass sections were, indeed, the best any band in New York could boast – the softer focus of Smith contrasting with the bluesy attack of Ladnier, the rasp of Rex Stewart, the lithe lines of Harrison – and the group had Hawkins (who was loyal enough to stay for ten years), the man who created jazz saxophone. Henderson's own playing was capable rather than outstanding, and the rhythm section lumbered a bit, though string bass and guitar lightened up the feel from 1928 onwards. It took Henderson many records to attain a real consistency; in 1925 he was still making sides like 'Pensacola' (for Columbia), which starts with a duet between Hawkins and Redman on bass sax and goofus! But there weren't many vocals, and this let the band drive through their three-minute allocation without interruption. If Henderson never figured out the best use of that time-span (unlike Ellington, who became his most serious rival among New York's black bands), his team of players made sure that something interesting happened on almost every record.

The Classics CDs offer chronological surveys which Henderson specialists will welcome, although no alternative takes are included (there are actually relatively few in existence). We would single out the 1926–7 and 1927 discs as the most important, but there are so many fine moments scattered through even second-rate pieces that any who sample the series may well find that they want them all. Remastering is again variable; the tracks made under the name 'The Dixie Stompers' were made for Harmony, which continued to use acoustic recording even after most other companies had switched over to the electric process in 1925, and some may find these a little archaic in timbre. However, we find that most of the transfers are acceptable, though they don't measure up to the relentlessly high standards of John R. T. Davies. The 1927–31 disc marks the departure of Redman and, the first steps by Henderson himself as arranger. Guest appearances by Fats Waller – who reportedly gave Henderson a dozen tunes in trade for a plate of hamburgers at a Harlem eaterie – and Benny Carter accompany the arrival of the fine and undervalued trumpeter, Bobby Stark, whose solos on 'Blazin'' and 'Sweet And Hot' find a lyrical streak somewhere between Joe Smith and Rex Stewart. But the band was already in decline, especially following Henderson's car accident in 1928, after which he was never the same man. They cut only three record dates in 1929 and three in 1930, compared with 17 in 1927.

The two Timeless compilations complicate matters somewhat, since they focus on Henderson's output for two companies alone. (He also had records issued on Columbia, Paramount, Gennett, Banner and other labels during the period.) Sprucer packaging and probably superior remastering – the Harmony sessions are always going to sound indifferent –

give these two strong claims, though at this point few other than specialists are likely to want such detailed coverage of even a major band of this period.

***** Fletcher Henderson 1931**
Classics 555 *As above, except add Sandy Williams (tb), Russell Procope (cl, as), Edgar Sampson (cl, as, vn), Horace Henderson (p); George Bias, Dick Robertson (v); omit Ladnier, Green, Pasquall, Dixon, Cole, Marshall, Deppe, Razaf.* 2–7/31.

****(*) Fletcher Henderson 1931–1932**
Classics 546 *Henderson; Russell Smith, Bobby Stark (t); Rex Stewart (c); Sandy Williams, J. C. Higginbotham (tb); Russell Procope (cl, ss, as); Edgar Sampson (cl, as, vn); Coleman Hawkins (cl, ts); Clarence Holiday, Ikey Robinson (bj, g); John Kirby (bb, b); Walter Johnson (d); John Dickens, Harlan Lattimore, Baby Rose Marie, Les Reis, Dick Robertson (v).* 7/31–3/32.

*****(*) Fletcher Henderson 1932–1934**
Classics 535 *As above, except add Henry 'Red' Allen, Joe Thomas, Irving Randolph (t), Keg Johnson, Claude Jones, Dicky Wells (tb), Buster Bailey (cl), Hilton Jefferson (cl, as), Ben Webster (ts), Horace Henderson (p), Bernard Addison, Lawrence Lucie (g), Elmer James (b), Vic Engle (d), Charles Holland (v); omit Robinson, Holiday, Lattimore, Marie, Reis and Robertson.* 12/32–9/34.

***** Fletcher Henderson 1934–1937**
Classics 527 *Henderson; Russell Smith, Irving Randolph, Henry 'Red' Allen, Dick Vance, Roy Eldridge, Joe Thomas, Emmett Berry (t); Ed Cuffee (tb, v); Keg Johnson, Claude Jones, Fernando Arbello, George Washington, J. C. Higginbotham (tb); Omer Simeon (cl, as, bs); Jerry Blake (cl, as, v); Buster Bailey, Hilton Jefferson, Russell Procope, Jerome Pasquall (cl, as); Benny Carter, Scoops Carey (as); Ben Webster, Elmer Williams, Chu Berry (ts); Horace Henderson (p); Bob Lessey, Lawrence Lucie (g); Elmer James, John Kirby, Israel Crosby (b); Walter Johnson, Big Sid Catlett (d); Teddy Lewis, Georgia Boy Simpkins, Dorothy Derrick (v).* 9/34–3/37.

****(*) Under The Harlem Moon**
ASV 5067 *As above two discs.* 12/32–6/37.

**** Fletcher Henderson 1937–1938**
Classics 519 *Henderson; Russell Smith, Emmett Berry, Dick Vance (t); George Washington, Ed Cuffee, Milt Robinson, George Hunt, J. C. Higginbotham, Albert Wynn, John McConnell (tb); Jerry Blake (cl, as, v); Eddie Barefield (cl, as); Hilton Jefferson (as); Chu Berry, Elmer Williams, Ben Webster (ts); Lawrence Lucie (g); Israel Crosby (b); Walter Johnson, Cozy Cole, Pete Suggs (d); Chuck Richards (v).* 3/37–5/38.

Henderson's music was already in decline when the '30s began, and by the end of the decade the orchestra was a shadow of what it had been in its glory days, as illustrated on the rather sad final disc in the Classics sequence. Ironically, it was Henderson's own work as an arranger in this period which set off the swing era, via the charts he did for Benny Goodman. The 1931 and 1931–2 discs offer sometimes bewildering juxtapositions of corn (Henderson employed some excruciating singers at this time) and real jazz. The extraordinary 'Strangers', on Classics 546, includes an amazing Coleman Hawkins solo in the middle of an otherwise feeble record, while some of the tunes which the Hendersonians might have been expected to handle well – 'Casa Loma Stomp' (Classics 546) and 'Radio Rhythm' (Classics 555) – turn out poorly. Yet the band was still full of fine ensemble players and soloists alike, and some of the Horace Henderson arrangements from this time – especially 'Queer Notions', 'Yeah Man' and 'Wrappin' It Up' (all on Classics 535) – are as well managed as any band of the period could do. Besides, while players of the calibre of Hawkins, Allen and (subsequently) Webster, Berry and Eldridge were on hand, there can't help but be fine moments on many of the records. Classics 535 is certainly the pick of these later discs, with a dozen excellent tracks included. Classics 527 and 519, which were recorded mainly after Henderson temporarily disbanded in 1934 and worked with Goodman, show the vitality of the band sagging the final dozen sides might have been played by any competent dance orchestra. (As a postscript, there are four nondescript 1941 tracks which wind up the Horace Henderson disc listed below.) Transfers are usually reasonably good and clear, although as usual it's the later discs that sound cleaner and less prone to track-to-track fluctuations in quality. The ASV disc compiles 23 of the better tracks from the 1932–7 period, but the sound appears muddier than on the Classics issues.

***** The Alternative Takes Vol. 1 1923–1925**
Neatwork RP2006 *As appropriate discs above.* 5/23–11/25.

***** The Alternative Takes Vol. 2 1926–1936**
Neatwork RP2016 *As appropriate discs above.* 1/26–8/36.

Neatwork's pair of discs are designed for hardcore collectors who want alternative takes which are otherwise missing from the Classics sequence of CDs. Lovers of minutiae will welcome these, also for the scrupulous way it has corrected some of the recording documentation in several of the Classics issues. Since these are designed entirely as gap-fillers, aesthetic considerations take something of a back seat, and it's doubtful if many will want all three alternates of the 1925 'I'll See You In My Dreams', for instance. But there is still plenty of good Hendersonia here. As with the Classics series, though, transfers seem to be a bit of a mixed bag.

Horace Henderson (1904–88)

PIANO

Fletcher's brother never had a career of the same stature but he was a gifted pianist and a fine arranger. He was still working as a musician in Denver in the late '60s.

****** Horace Henderson 1940**
Classics 648 *Henderson; Emmett Berry, Harry 'Pee Wee' Jackson, Gail Brockman, Nat Bates (t); Harold 'Money' Johnson (t, v); Ray Nance (t, vn); Edward Fant, Nat Atkins, Joe McLewis, Leo Williams, Archie Brown (tb); Delbert Bright (cl, as); Willie Randall, Howard Johnson, Charles Q. Price (as); Elmer Williams, Dave Young, Mosey Gant, Bob Dorsey, Lee Pope (ts); Leonard Talley (bs); Hurley Ramey, Leroy Harris (g); Jesse Simpkins, Israel Crosby (b); Oliver Coleman, Debo Williams (d); Viola Jefferson (v).* 2–10/40.

'One of the most talented yet most neglected and enigmatic figures in all of jazz' – Gunther Schuller's verdict on Horace Henderson sounds over-enthusiastic, but the 1940 tracks collected on this important CD go a long way towards bearing out his verdict. Fletcher's brother was a fine, Hines-like pianist, but it was his arranging that was outstanding: the 16 themes collected here include charts by both brothers, and the contrasts between Fletcher's stylized call-and-response figures and the fluid, overlapping ideas of Horace are remarkable. Horace's band was full of fine soloists who received sometimes unprecedented space: Nance has two full choruses of violin on the engaging 'Kitty On Toast' and Berry is generously featured throughout: his 'Ain't Misbehavin'' melody is beautifully sustained. But it's the section-work, the saxes full and rich, the brass outstandingly punchy, which brings complex charts to life: 'Shufflin' Joe', the very first track here, is a little masterpiece of varied dynamics and interwoven tone-colours. The rhythm players – including the young Israel Crosby on some of the later sides – are as good as their colleagues. This Classics CD displaces the Tax LP listed in our last edition, and though the sound is, as so often with discs from this source, a little inconsistent, the CD remains a very good buy. There are four tracks by the 1941 Fletcher Henderson band tagged on at the end, but these are a somewhat doubtful bonus.

Joe Henderson (1937–2001)

TENOR AND SOPRANO SAXOPHONES

Born in Lima, Ohio, Henderson arrived in New York in 1962 a fully formed stylist. He had stints with Horace Silver, Freddie Hubbard and Herbie Hancock before a brief but high-profile stay with Blood, Sweat And Tears. He moved to San Francisco in the '70s and made a string of albums for Milestone, before re-emerging in the mid-'80s, first on Blue Note and then with a sequence of acclaimed and best-selling albums for Verve. He was acknowledged as one of the last great tenormen to emerge from the original hard-bop generation.

****** Page One**

Blue Note 98795 *Henderson; Kenny Dorham (t); McCoy Tyner (p); Butch Warren (b); Pete LaRoca (d).* 6/63.

Joe Henderson became a magisterial jazz icon in the '90s, and as a consequence his back pages – long neglected by reissues – were extensively released on CD. He's a thematic musician, working his way round the structure of a composition with methodical intensity, but he's also a masterful licks player, with a seemingly limitless stock of phrases that he can turn to the advantage of any post-bop setting; this gives his best improvisations a balance of surprise, immediacy and coherence few other saxophonists can match. His lovely tone, which combines softness and a harsh plangency in a similar way, is another pleasing aspect of his music. *Page One* was his first date as a leader, and it still stands as one of the most popular Blue Notes of the early '60s. Henderson had not long since arrived in New York after being discharged from the army, and this six-theme set is very much the work of a new star on the scene. 'Recorda-Me', whose Latinate lilt has made it a staple blowing-vehicle for hard-bop bands, had its debut here, and the very fine tenor solo on Dorham's 'Blue Bossa' explains much of why Henderson was creating excitement. But everything here, even the throwaway blues, 'Homestretch', is impressively handled. Tyner, Warren and LaRoca are a rhythm section who seldom played together but they do very well here, as does the erratic Dorham. The new Rudy van Gelder Edition brings even more weight and power to the music.

****** Our Thing**

Blue Note 25647-2 *Henderson; Kenny Dorham (t); Andrew Hill (p); Eddie Khan (b); Pete LaRoca (d).* 9/63.

*****(*) In 'N Out**

Blue Note 29156 *Henderson; Kenny Dorham (t); McCoy Tyner (p); Richard Davis (b); Elvin Jones (d).* 4/64.

****** Inner Urge**

Blue Note 84189 *Henderson; McCoy Tyner (p); Bob Cranshaw (b); Elvin Jones (d).* 11/64.

*****(*) Mode For Joe**

Blue Note 91894 *Henderson; Lee Morgan (t); Curtis Fuller (tb); Bobby Hutcherson (vib, mar); Cedar Walton (p); Ron Carter (b); Louis Hayes, Joe Chambers (d).* 1/66.

Our Thing has long been a Blue Note fans' favourite and is the centrepiece in the tryptich of albums with Dorham which were issued under Henderson's nominal leadership. Dorham brought in three tunes, Henderson two, and, with no filler blues jam of any kind, this is an unusually consistent Blue Note date, with Hill's cryptic commentaries and superb work from Khan and LaRoca. While a serious collector wouldn't want to be without any of these sessions, the less committed could make do with this one on the shelf. The new RVG edition has a bonus alternative take of the opener, 'Teeter Totter'.

Inner Urge, which features Henderson as sole horn, is dark and intense music. The title-tune, commemorating Henderson's experiences of trying to make a living in New York, is a blistering effort at a medium tempo, and it's interesting to compare Tyner and Jones as they are with Henderson rather than with Coltrane. While the atmosphere isn't as teeth-grittingly intense, it's scarcely less visceral music. Even the sunny reading of 'Night And Day' musters a terrific urgency via Jones's continuously glittering cymbals.

Mode For Joe plants Henderson in a bigger environment, and at times he sounds to be forcing his way out: the solos on the title-track and 'A Shade Of Jade' make a baroque contrast with the otherwise tempered surroundings. Chambers drums with pile-driving intensity in places and, though the large number of players tends to constrict the soloists at a time when Henderson could handle all the stretching out he was given, it's still a fine record. The latest RVG edition includes an alternative take of Cedar Walton's tune 'Black'.

The earlier *In 'N Out* is more of Henderson and Dorham together. Henderson's three tunes are the standout pieces, the quizzical title-track, the haunting theme of 'Punjab', the charming 'Serenity'. Dorham seems to be thinking through his solos rather than punching them out and, while in general the temperature seems rather lower than on Henderson's other Blue Notes, it's fascinating, profound music.

***** Four!**

Verve 523657-2 *Henderson; Wynton Kelly (p); Paul Chambers (b); Jimmy Cobb (d).* 4/68.

***** Straight No Chaser**

Verve 531561-2 *As above.* 4/68.

A historical curiosity, brought to life courtesy of Henderson himself. He played these sets with the old Miles Davis rhythm section at an unrehearsed show at Baltimore's Left Bank. The sound is sometimes muddy, without much top end, but listenable. The quartet work through six themes on *Four!* with a mix of intensity and doggedness which leaves the music a bit colourless at times, yet the feeling of three old masters in conversation with a younger one comes through, and it's interesting to hear Henderson on standard material which he otherwise never plays. *Straight No Chaser* is a second helping from the same source, and with similar results.

*** The Milestone Years

Milestone 4413-2 8CD *Henderson; Mike Lawrence, Woody Shaw, Oscar Brashear (t); Grachan Moncur III, Julian Priester, Curtis Fuller (tb); Jeremy Steig, Ernie Watts (f); Haldey Caliman (ts, f); Lee Konitz (as); Kenny Barron, Don Friedman, Joe Zawinul, Mark Levine, Joachim Kühn, Herbie Hancock, George Cables, Hideo Ichikawa, George Duke, Alice Coltrane, Patrick Gleason (ky); Michael White (vn); George Wadenius, James Blood Ulmer, Lee Ritenour (g); Ron Carter, Victor Gaskin, Stanley Clarke, Kunimitsu Inaba, Dave Holland, Charlie Haden, Jean-François Jenny-Clark, David Friesen, Alphonso Johnson (b); Louis Hayes, Jack DeJohnette, Roy McCurdy, Lenny White, Motohiko Hino, Leon Ndugu Chancler, Daniel Humair, Harvey Mason (d); Airto Moreira, Carmelo Garcia, Bill Summers (perc); Flora Purim (v).* 67–76.

While there are many rewarding things in this exhaustive collection of Henderson's work for the Milestone operation, it's finally let down by the indifferent calibre of the early '70s sessions which he made for the label. Sessions such as *If You're Not Part Of The Solution, Live At The Lighthouse* and *In Japan* find him in sharp, creative form, adapting to rhythm sections that remained rooted in hard bop but which fed in the kind of groove playing that would lead to jazz-rock. Later sets like *Canyon Lady* find Joe fighting a losing battle with his backings, and the final set, *Black Miracle*, is close to disaster. Henderson fanatics will want this, and the packaging and annotation are exemplary, but there is too much driftwood to elicit a general recommendation. The discs listed below will be useful samplers of this period for most.

**(*) The Kicker

Original Jazz Classics OJC 465 *Henderson; Mike Lawrence (t); Grachan Moncur III (tb); Kenny Barron (p); Ron Carter (b); Louis Hayes (d).* 8/67.

***(*) Tetragon / In Pursuit Of Blackness

BGP CDBGPD 084 *Henderson; Woody Shaw (t, flhn); Curtis Fuller (tb); Pete Yellin (as, f, bcl); Kenny Barron, Don Friedman, George Cables (p); Ron Carter, Ron McClure, Stanley Clarke (b); Louis Hayes, Jack DeJohnette, Lenny White (d).* 9/67–5/71.

***(*) Joe Henderson In Japan

Original Jazz Classics OJC 1040 *Henderson; Hideo Ichikawa (p); Kunimitsu Inaba (b); Motohiko Hino (d).* 8/71.

*** Multiple

Original Jazz Classics OJC 776 *Henderson; Larry Willis (ky); James Blood Ulmer, John Thomas (g); Dave Holland (b); Jack DeJohnette (d); Arthur Jenkins (perc).* 1/73.

**(*) The Elements

Original Jazz Classics OJC 913 *Henderson; Alice Coltrane (p, hp, harmonium, tamboura); Michael White (vn); Charlie Haden (b); Leon Ndugu Chancler (d); Baba Duru Oshun (perc); Kenneth Nash (perc, v).* 10/73.

**(*) Canyon Lady

Original Jazz Classics OJC 949 *Henderson; Oscar Brashear, John Hunt, Lou Gasca (t); Julian Priester, Nicholas Ten Broeck (tb); Hadley Caliman (ts, f); Ray Pizzi, Vincent Dengham (f); George Duke, Mark Levine (p); John Levine (b); Eric Gravatt (d); Carmelo Garcia, Victor Pantoja, Francisco Aguabella (perc).* 10/73.

A disheartening step after the Blue Note albums, *The Kicker*, Henderson's debut for Milestone, is respectable but prosaic stuff, with Lawrence and Moncur adding little of interest and the tracks sounding short and 'produced'. BGP's coupling of two later albums on a single CD is a much better choice: the sessions for *Tetragon* offer some very hard-edged playing by the leader, with a riveting dissection of 'Invitation', and the four Henderson originals from the *Blackness* date are blown open over polyrhythmic bases that the horns meet head-on. The sound and feel are sometimes a little more dated than the straight tenor-and-rhythm tracks – Cables uses a tinkly electric piano, and there are elements of fashionable freak-out in some of the ensembles – but it's a valuable CD. *Multiple* is another that has worn less well: Henderson doubles on soprano, flute and percussion (and even does some chanting), Willis plays electric keyboards, and the guitarists strum to no great purpose; yet the saxophonist still earns the stars for the surprising tenor solos. *Tetragon* is also now available by itself on Original Jazz Classics OJC 844.

The Elements presses Henderson into the kind of role John Coltrane might have taken up, had he lived, with a world-music feel swirling around Alice Coltrane's exotic settings. *Canyon Lady* is more Latinized, with Henderson asked to be the soloist on some light, sweet arrangements in the idiom. The problem with both situations is that, as gamely as he responds, this was hardly useful employment for one of the premier jazz improvisers in what should have been one of his greatest periods.

At least we can give an unequivocal welcome to the reissue of *In Japan*, an old favourite from the vinyl era. Never mind that the in-concert sound (recorded at Tokyo's Junk Club!) is no better than documentary quality – this is hard, vital Henderson. He opens 'Round Midnight' with a typically severe cadenza, and the three longish tracks which follow have as much of the band as they do of him. This was a difficult period for players of Henderson's gifts, but he clearly received hosannas when he went to Japan, and the trio play above themselves in splendid support.

***(*) Relaxin' At Camarillo

Original Jazz Classics OJC 776 *Henderson; Chick Corea (p); Tony Dumas, Richard Davis (b); Peter Erskine, Tony Williams (d).* 8–12/79.

***(*) Mirror, Mirror

MPS 519092-2 *Henderson; Chick Corea (p); Ron Carter (b); Billy Higgins (d).* 1/80.

Henderson and Corea made an improbable but productive team: Joe's doggedly unpredictable lines asked the pianist to concentrate, and a fundamentally lyrical bent is something they both share, even if Corea usually oversweetens his playing. The OJC reissue just has the edge for a long, firmly sustained treatment of 'Y Todavia La Quiero', one of the best of Henderson's Latin tunes – but there is excellent jazz on both discs.

CORE COLLECTION

**** The State Of The Tenor Volumes One And Two

Blue Note 828779-2 2CD *Henderson; Ron Carter (b); Al Foster (d).* 11/85.

Although they had a mixed reception on their release, these records now sound as authoritative as their titles suggest. Henderson hadn't recorded as a leader for some time, and this was his return to the label where he commenced his career, but there is nothing hesitant or routine about the playing here. Carter and Foster provide detailed support –

the dates were carefully prepared, the themes meticulously chosen and rehearsed, before the recordings were made at New York's Village Vanguard – and the bassist in particular is as inventive as the nominal leader. Henderson takes an occasional wrong turning, noted perhaps in a recourse to a favourite lick or two, but he functions mainly at the highest level. The intelligent choice of themes – from Silver, Monk, Mingus, Parker and others, none of them over-familiar – prises a rare multiplicity of phrase-shapes and rhythmical variations out of the tenorman: as a single instance, listen to his manipulations of the beat on Mingus's 'Portrait' (on *Volume Two*), with their accompanying subtleties of tone and attack. Both discs have now been coupled as a mid-price two-disc set.

*** An Evening With Joe Henderson

Red 123215-2 *Henderson; Charlie Haden (b); Al Foster (d).* 7/87.

More of the same, with Haden substituting for Carter and the four longish tracks opening out a little further. The music isn't as comprehensively prepared, and Haden's flatter sound and less flexible rhythms make him no match for Carter; but Henderson himself plays with majestic power. Decent concert recording, from the Genoa Jazz Festival of 1987.

***(*) The Standard Joe

Red RR 123248-2 *Henderson; Rufus Reid (b); Al Foster (d).* 3/91.

***(*) Lush Life

Verve 511779-2 *Henderson; Wynton Marsalis (t); Stephen Scott (p); Christian McBride (b); Gregory Hutchinson (d).*

There is very little to choose between the two 1991 recordings, though they're very different from each other. The trio session for Red is an off-the-cuff blowing date, but it's obvious from the first measures of 'Blue Bossa' that all three players are in peak form, and the matching sonorities of Reid and Henderson create a startlingly close level of empathy. There is almost 70 minutes of music, including two long but quite different takes of 'Body And Soul', and the invention never flags. *Lush Life* is a programme of Billy Strayhorn compositions done as one solo ('Lush Life'), three duos (one with each member of the rhythm section), a lovely quartet reading of 'Blood Count' and three pieces with Marsalis joining the front line, of which 'Johnny Come Lately' is especially spirited. If Henderson's delivery sounds a fraction less assured than he does at his best, the quality of his thinking is as outstanding as always and, though there is the odd tiny blemish – Scott's treatment of 'Lotus Blossom' seems too irritatingly clever – it's a splendid record, which won wide acclaim – and sales – and brought Joe back to the forefront of jazz attention.

**** So Near, So Far (Musings For Miles)

Verve 517674-2 *Henderson; John Scofield (g); Dave Holland (b); Al Foster (d).* 10/92.

Great music. Henderson's virtual rebirth continued with a tribute to Miles Davis from four former sidemen (Henderson played with Davis briefly in the mid-'60s) that stands as a masterclass of top-flight improvising. Impeccably prepared charts for the likes of 'Miles Ahead', boiled down from the original Gil Evans arrangement to a setting for four-piece, directed the players to a particularly acute yet heartfelt memorial. Many of the tunes associated with Davis as composer have scarcely been covered by other players, which adds a note of unusual freshness, but the scope and calibre of the improvising by all four men is what one remembers. Scofield's runs of melody are a match for Henderson's own, and Holland and Foster – the latter in some of his finest playing – are a dream team.

*** Double Rainbow

Verve 527222-2 *Henderson; Eliane Elias, Herbie Hancock (p); Oscar Castro-Nueves (g); Christian McBride, Nico Assumpção (b); Paul Braga, Jack DeJohnette (d).* 95.

Though conceived as a collaboration with Antonio Carlos Jobim, this turned out to be a memorial to the composer after his death, a dozen tunes shared between one Brazilian and one all-American rhythm section. Everybody plays well and Henderson sounds supremely relaxed, but sometimes one longs for a really outstanding solo or for something to intrude on the general sunniness of the music: lush, charming, this is essentially high-calibre light-jazz.

***(*) Shade Of Jade: Joe Henderson Big Band

Verve 533451-2 *Henderson; Lew Soloff, Marcus Belgrave, Freddie Hubbard, Idrees Sulieman, Jimmy Owens, Jon Faddis, Virgil Jones, Nicholas Payton, Byron Stirling (t); Robin Eubanks, Jimmy Knepper, Kiane Zawadi, Douglas Purviance, Conrad Herwig, Keith O'Quinn, Dave Taylor, Larry Farrell (tb); Craig Handy, Joe Temperley, Bob Porcelli, Pete Yellin, Dick Oatts, Steve Wilson, Tim Ries, Gary Smulyan (reeds); Chick Corea, Ronnie Mathews (p); Christian McBride (b); Louis Nash (d); Bob Belden (cond).* 92–96.

A half-finished project in 1992, this was completed in 1996 and is almost Henderson's forgotten album. Yet it's one of his best. He did much of the scoring himself, in association with Belden, and his own solos have much of his old *brio* allied with the gravitas he has latterly assumed. The various orchestras involved offer a generational mix that doesn't seem to confound the continuity of the album, and in 'Shade Of Jade' and 'Without A Song' they frame the saxophonist with a sophistication that makes one wish that these expensive projects were less of a rarity.

*** Porgy And Bess

Verve 539048-2 *Henderson; Conrad Herwig (tb); Stefon Harris (vib); Tommy Flanagan (p); John Scofield (g); Dave Holland (b); Jack DeJohnette (d); Sting, Chaka Khan (v).* 5/97.

Gimcracked around Henderson as soloist (and chorus?), here is yet another jazz *Porgy And Bess*. Line by line there is much to enjoy, but the guest vocalists reek of bought-in stardom, the playing has a somewhat elephantine grace, and there is nothing here that Henderson didn't do better in other circumstances. A pity, really, that this was his final bow: 'The Phantom', as his fellow musicians often called him, slipped quietly away in 2001.

Jon Hendricks (born 1921)

VOCALS

Born in Newark, Ohio, Hendricks was spotted by Charlie Parker and advised to make music his career. With Dave Lambert and Annie Ross, he founded a stylish vocal trio devoted to vocalese, setting jazz arrangements to words. After its final break-up, he spent some time in England and as a music critic, but has continued to record into his seventies.

***** In Person At The Trident**

Verve 010601-2 *Hendricks; Noel Jewkes (ts); Flip Nunez (p); Fred Marshall (b); Jerry Granelli (d).* 64.

Reissued from the original Smash recording, this catches Hendricks near his best, scatting and singing with great authority. Jon's take on Herbie Hancock's 'Watermelon Man' is virtuosic, and most of the tracks feature at least some input from the singer himself, though in most cases he's credited as composer. The band swing pretty nimbly behind him; though Noel Jewkes could hardly be described as the most exciting soloist of all time, he gets in some interesting ideas.

***** Boppin' At The Blue Note**

Telarc 83320 *Hendricks; Wynton Marsalis (t, v); Al Grey (tb); Red Holloway (as); Benny Golson (ts); Mark Elf (g); Ugonna Okegwa (b); Andy Watson (d); Kevin Fitzgerald Burke, Judith Hendricks (v).* 12/93.

Nothing ever quite added up to the sheer *esprit* of Lambert, Hendricks & Ross, but there are flashes on the later records that allow one to gauge the size and scope of Hendricks's remarkable talent. It is a full, forceful voice, with near-perfect control right through its range and with a speed of articulation only matched by Ross in her heyday. Nonsensical too to suggest that he lacked either accuracy or expressiveness (these are common enough quibbles) when he bends notes with the same freedom as any saxophone player or trumpeter who would receive immoderate praise for what in Hendricks is considered to be uncertain technique.

The Blue Note disc offers an unexpected chance to hear Wynton Marsalis scatting like Dizzy Gillespie, which he does with great humour and some dexterity. Hendricks himself is in powerful and affecting voice on originals like 'Contemporary Blues' and the classic 'Roll 'Em Pete'. He hasn't quite the agility of yore, but the depth of expression is unmistakable, and the reprise of Basie-inspired Lambert, Hendricks & Ross material with the family and Kevin Burke is delightful. The instrumental support is also impressive, with a lovely contribution from Al Grey and sweet-toned choruses from Red Holloway.

Ernie Henry (1926–57)

ALTO SAXOPHONE

A Brooklynite, Henry was on the periphery of a major career in bebop, having worked with Tadd Dameron as far back as 1947, and also with Gillespie, Monk and Mingus. But his early death cut him off from a wider reputation.

***** Presenting Ernie Henry**

Original Jazz Classics OJC 1920 *Henry; Kenny Dorham (t); Kenny Drew (p); Wilbur Ware (b); Art Taylor (d).* 8/56.

***** Seven Standards And A Blues**

Original Jazz Classics OJC 1722 *Henry; Kenny Dorham (t); Wynton Kelly (p); Wilbur Ware (b); Philly Joe Jones (d).* 9/57.

***** Last Chorus**

Original Jazz Classics OJC 1906 *As above discs, plus Lee Morgan (t), Melba Liston (tb), Benny Golson (ts), Cecil Payne (bs), Thelonious Monk (p), Oscar Pettiford, Paul Chambers (b), Max Roach (d).* 8/56–9/57.

Henry left few records in a very brief career, but those he did make reveal a limited but vividly creative post-Parker altoist. His intense tone points towards Jackie McLean, even as his phrasing mixes the wistfulness of Tadd Dameron (with whom he made some of his early records) and Parker's high drama. *Presenting Ernie Henry* is sloppy in its execution, with Dorham sounding unsure of himself and the rhythm section seemingly unfamiliar with Henry's originals: the lingering power is in the leader's assertive and slightly off-centre improvising. *Seven Standards And A Blues* is arguably his best record: not quite fast enough to stand next to the best boppers, Henry instead makes a mark through the plangency of his phrases. On these showtunes (and the Dameron-like blues, 'Specific Gravity') he leaves a telling impression. *Last Chorus* was cobbled together from a four-tune session featuring Henry's 'All Stars' (Morgan, Liston, Golson and Payne in the front line), plus an alternative version of 'Cleo's Chant' from the debut and a track from Monk's *Brilliant Corners* session. Interesting bits and pieces.

Peter Herbert (born 1960)

DOUBLE BASS

Fine instrumentalist and composer, from whom much is expected.

*****(*) B-A-C-H A Chromatic Universe**

Between the Lines btl 013 *Herbert; Ingrid Jensen (t, flhn); Carol Robinson (bcl); Marc Copland (p); Kenny Wollesen (d).* 9/00.

In German notation, the letters of Bach's name yield the musical sequence B flat – A – C – B natural. It was a device known to the master himself, but in more recent times Schumann, Liszt and Webern have all exploited it, and Dmitri Shostakovich is remembered by a similar code: D-S-C-H. Few jazz musicians have ventured into this territory, but Peter Herbert has created an album of delicate beauty out of these materials. Most of these tracks are either instrumental exercises based on the B-A-C-H motif or else compositions inspired by moments in the composer's life: his father's role as '*Stadtpfeifer*', the Divi Blasii church where Johann Sebastian served, and so on.

Herbert's stroke of genius was in seeing that the ground bass of Baroque music – also an obsession of label boss Franz Koglmann – was similar to the chordal progression of jazz. Jensen, Copland and Robinson contribute delightfully improvised sections to the set, but the basic conception is Herbert's and the closing section consisting of 'Actus Tragicus' and 'Heavy Snow' will melt the hardest heart.

Woody Herman (1913–87)

CLARINET, ALTO AND SOPRANO SAXOPHONES, VOCAL

A child performer in vaudeville, Herman took over the Isham Jones band in 1936 and kept it afloat until the mid-'40s. His Second (1947–9) and Third (1952–4) Herds were star-studded big bands which he led with indomitable showmanship, his singing and playing a diehard element in all of his groups. He constantly updated his repertoire while never neglecting his library of swing-era hits and was still leading small groups and larger bands into his seventies, although his last years were troubled by desperate tax problems as a result of financial mismanagement.

*** At The Woodchoppers' Ball

ASV AJA 5143 *Herman; Clarence Willard, Kermit Simmons, Steady Nelson, Mac MacQuordale, Bob Price, John Owens, Ray Linn, Cappy Lewis, George Seaberg, Billy Rogers, Charles Peterson (t); Joe Bishop (flhn); Neal Reid, Toby Tyler, Buddy Smith, Vic Hamann, Tommy Farr, Walter Nimms (tb); Murray Williams, Don Watt, Joe Estrin, Ray Hopfner, Herb Tompkins, Joe Denton, Eddie Scalzi, Jimmy Horvath, Sam Rubinowich (as); Saxie Mansfield, Bruce Wilkins, Pete Johns, Ronnie Perry, Nick Caiazza, Sammy Armato, Mickey Folus, Herbie Haymer, Pete Mondello (ts); Skippy DeSair (bs); Horace Diaz, Tommy Linehan (p); Nick Hupfer (vn); Chick Reeves, Hy White (g); Walter Yoder (b); Frank Carlson (d).* 3/36–1/42.

*** Woody Herman 1936–1937

Classics 1042 *Similar to above.* 2/36–8/37.

*** Woody Herman 1937–1938

Classics 1090 *Similar to above.* 10/37–12/38.

Woody Herman didn't secure his principal fame until after these early tracks were made, but as an instrumentalist and vocalist he was already a characterful performer, and the pre-war sides – by a band that came together out of the Isham Jones Orchestra in 1936 – were centred mainly on him. There was some light pop fodder in among them and, while the band is short on strong soloists – trombonist Reid and flugelhorn player Bishop, who also contributed several of the charts, are about the best of them – the arrangements make the most of simple blues resources, one reason why the orchestra was called 'The Band That Plays The Blues'. By the '40s, though, Herman was seeking out superior material and hiring sharper musicians. Woody himself was a clarinettist whose easy-going playing lacked the brilliance of Goodman or Shaw but who made up in affable, on-the-beat timing. A few tracks on the ASV set are by the small band of The Four Chips and the immortal 'Woodchoppers' Ball' is here in its original version, a Joe Bishop head arrangement. ASV's reproduction isn't ideal but it will have to do as the sole compilation of the period.

Classics have begun their usual chronological survey with two volumes that start with some of the Isham Jones tracks and get as far as the small-group 'River Bed Blues' on Classics 1090. Herman sounds undecided at times whether to go for a Crosby-like Dixieland feel or choose the smooth Dorsey route. Either way, at this time he was still short on star soloists and took a lot of the weight himself. He sings on most of the early tracks, too, revealing an appealing mid-range voice that had to deal with songs such as 'I Wanna Be In Winchell's Column' and 'Broadway's Gone Hawaii'. Decent sound, although some of the very early tracks have a lot of surface noise.

***(*) Woody Herman 1939

Classics 1128 *Herman; Clarence Willard, Jerry Neary, Steady Nelson, Mac MacQuordale, Bob Price (t); Neal Reid, Toby Tyler (tb); Joe Bishop (flhn); Joe Estrin, Ray Hopfner, Joe Denton (as); Saxie Mansfield, Pete Johns (ts); Tommy Linehan (p); Hy White (g); Walter Yoder (b); Frank Carlson (d); Mary Martin, Mary Ann McCall, The Andrews Sisters (v).* 1–8/39.

*** Woody Herman 1939–1940

Classics 1163 *As above, except add Cappy Lewis (t), Nick Caiazza (ts), Carol Kay (v); omit Neary, Martin.* 1/39–9/40.

The key session on Classics 1128 took place on 4 April 1939, when the band cut five titles, including 'At The Woodchopper's Ball', 'Big Wig In The Wigwam', 'Blues Upstairs' and 'Blues Downstairs'. Although 'Woodchopper's Ball' was no more than Joe Bishop's head arrangement on the blues, it eventually became a huge hit, selling in the millions, and is the Herman side everyone remembers. Some of the later sessions on the disc feature music of similar quality, including 'Casbah Blues' and 'Midnight Echoes'; but Herman still lacked a major arranging presence, and Classics 1163 in some ways returns to the sweeter material of before, with novelties like 'Peace, Brother!' and 'The Rhumba Jumps' taking up too much of the band's studio time. Reasonable transfers of these sides, though every so often an inexplicably poor-sounding track turns up.

*** Woody Herman 1940

Classics 1243 *Herman; Steady Nelson (t, v); Bob Price, Cappy Lewis, Clarence Willard (t); Neal Reid, Toby Tyler, Buddy Smith (tb); Joe Bishop (fr hn); Herb Tompkins, Ray Hopfner, Bill Vitale, Joe Denton (as); Saxie Mansfield, Nick Caiazza, Sammy Armato, Ronnie Perry (ts); Tommy Linehan (p); Hy White (g); Walter Yoder (b); Frank Carlson (d); Dillagene (v).* 11/39–9/40.

*** Woody Herman 1940–1941

Classics 1304 *As above, except add John Owens (t), Vic Hamann (tb), Eddie Scalzi (as), Mickey Folus (ts), Muriel Lane (v); omit Willard, Tyler, Hopfner, Denton, Perry.* 9/40–1/41.

Herman's Decca sessions continue on this pair of discs. Classics 1243 has three sessions which are mostly instrumental, and played with typical Herman punch, before – as if the label suddenly realized what was going on – they're back to average material and vocal features. Woody sings on no less than 17 tracks on Classics 1304, though it also includes the hit arrangement of 'Golden Wedding', the successful coupling of 'Chips' Boogie Woogie' and 'Chips' Blues' and four V-Disc titles, including Muriel Lane going wild on 'There'll Be Some Changes Made'. Both a mixed bag, although sound is generally decent enough.

**(*) At The Hollywood Palladium 1942–1944

RST 91536-2 *Herman; Cappy Lewis, George Seaberg, Chuck Peterson, Neal Hefti, Chuck Frankhauser, Ray Wetzel, Pete Candoli, Carl Warwick (t); Neal Reid, Tommy Farr, Walter Nimms, Bill Harris, Ralph Pfeffner, Ed Kiefer (tb); Sam Rubinowich, James Horvath, Mickey Folus, Pete Mondello, Skippy DeSair, Sam Marowitz, John LaPorta, Flip Phillips (reeds); Tommy Linehan, Ralph Burns (p); Marjorie Hyams (vib); Hy White, Billy Bauer (g); Chubby Jackson, Walter Yoder (b); Dave Tough, Frank Carlson (d); Carolyn Grey, Frances Wayne (v).* 8/42–11/44.

A couple of broadcast shows, the first in quite good sound, the second very scrappy; and the pity is that the latter features the really interesting band. '125th Street Prophet' is a glimmer of what the band could do. Too many vocals, but the playing remains swinging.

CORE COLLECTION

**** Blowin' Up A Storm!

Columbia 503280-2 2CD *Similar to that of next item.* 2/45–12/47.

A brilliant rhythm section, a brass team that could top any big-band section on either coast and arrangements that crackled with spontaneity and wit: Herman's 1945 band was both a commercial and an artistic triumph. With Burns, Bauer, Tough and Jackson spurring the horns on, the band handled head arrangements and slicker charts such as Neal Hefti's 'Wild Root' with the same mixture of innate enthusiasm and craft. There was a modern edge to the group that suggested something of the transition from swing to bop, even though it was the Second Herd that threw in its lot with bop spirit if not letter.

Columbia have at last done their Herman recordings some justice in a full CD reissue of their best music from the period. Besides all the familiar material, there's the studio version of Stravinsky's 'Ebony Concerto' and a series of alternative takes of some of the best-known numbers – though even Ralph Burns, in his entertaining sleeve-note, says that most of these are clearly inferior to the masters. The remastering has been scrupulously done and, with 40 tracks at mid-price, this should rank as one of the great bargains in the area of big-band music on CD, with the likes of 'Northwest Passage', 'Your Father's Mustache', 'The Good Earth', 'Apple Honey' and 'Bijou' all sounding terrific.

**** The V-Disc Years Vols 1 & 2

Hep CD2/3435 2CD *Herman; Sonny Berman, Shorty Rogers, Cappy Lewis, Billy Rogers, Pete Candoli, Conte Candoli, Chuck Frankhauser, Carl Warwick, Ray Wetzel, Neal Hefti, Irv Lewis, Ray Linn, Marky Markowitz (t); Bill Harris, Ed Kiefer, Ralph Pfeffner, Neal Reid, Bob Swift, Rodney Ogle, Tommy Pederson (tb); Sam Marowitz, John LaPorta, Les Robinson, Jimmy Horvath (as); Mickey Folus, Flip Phillips, Pete Mondello, Vido Musso, Ben Webster (ts); Sam Rubinowich, Skippy DeSair (bs); Ralph Burns, Fred Otis, Tony Aless (p); Margie Hyams, Red Norvo (vib); Chuck Wayne, Billy Bauer, (g); Joe Mondragon, Chubby Jackson, Walt Yoder (b); Dave Tough, Don Lamond, Johnny Blowers (d); Martha Raye, Frances Wayne, Carolyn Grey (v).* 2/45–12/47.

The V-Disc collection now stands as a pendant to the Columbia set, while still essential in its own right for Herman fans. Impeccably restored by Jack Towers and John R. T. Davies, the music comes flag-waving through with most of its original punch intact. Showstoppers such as 'Red Top' and 'Apple Honey' still impress and, if the soloists don't always have the finesse of some of Woody's later section stars, there is still some superb playing from most hands, with rare glimpses of Berman, Burns, Bauer and others.

***(*) The Woody Herman Shows 1940–1946

Jazz Unlimited 201 2085 *Herman; Ray Wetzel, Pete Candoli, Conte Candoli, Neal Hefti, Billy Robbins, Shorty Rogers, Charlie Frankhauser, Sonny Berman, Carl Warwick (t); Bill Harris, Ralph Pfeffner, Ed Kiefer (tb); Sam Marowitz, Bill Shine, John LaPorta (as); Flip Phillips, Pete Mondello, Mickey Folus (ts); Skippy DeSair (bs); Ralph Burns, Tony Aless, Jimmy Rowles (p); Marjorie Hyams, Red Norvo (vib); Billy Bauer (g); Chubby Jackson (b); Dave Tough, Don Lamond (d); Mildred Bailey, Frances Wayne, Jo Stafford, The Four Blue Flames (v).* 8/44–6/46.

The First Herd sound terrific on these airshots, too. The tunes have been cherrypicked from numerous surviving shows and the inane chatter has been mostly eliminated (although Mildred Bailey chaffs Woody prior to one tune). There are 25 tracks and they balance a lot of swingers with the occasional vocal feature, for Woody or one of his guest stars. Sound is mostly excellent for the period.

*** At Carnegie Hall, 1946

Verve 559833-2 2CD *Herman; Sonny Berman, Pete Candoli, Conrad Gozzo, Marky Markowitz, Shorty Rogers (t); Bill Harris, Ed Kiefer, Ralph Pfeffner (tb); John Barrows (frhn); John LaPorta, Sam Marowitz (as); Mickey Folus, Flip Phillips (ts); Sam Rubinowich (bs, bcl); Red Norvo (vib); Tony Aless (p); Abe Rosen (hp); Billy Bauer (g); Chubby Jackson (b); Don Lamond (d).* 3/46.

Not much jazz had been played at Carnegie Hall up to this point, and Herman's band were recorded on acetate transcriptions. There's a fair amount of scratch or distortion, but the sound isn't too bad. 'Ebony Concerto' appears only as a fragment, as does 'Summer Sequence', but there is some new music which differs from the various truncated LP issues of this material in the past. Don Lamond's bomb-dropping on 'Four Men On A Horse' still shakes the speakers after nearly 60 years and all the Herman favourites are played with great spirit.

***(*) Keeper Of The Flame

Capitol 984532-2 *Herman; Ernie Royal, Bernie Glow, Stan Fishelson, Red Rodney, Shorty Rogers, Charlie Walp, Al Porcino (t); Earl Swope, Bill Harris, Ollie Wilson, Bob Swift, Bart Varsalona (tb); Sam Marowitz (as); Al Cohn, Zoot Sims, Stan Getz, Herman Marowitz, Gene Ammons, Buddy Savitt, Jimmy Giuffre (ts); Serge Chaloff (bs); Lou Levy (p); Terry Gibbs (vib); Chubby Jackson, Joe Mondragon, Oscar Pettiford (b); Don Lamond, Shelly Manne (d); Mary Anne McCall (v).* 12/48–7/49.

**** Four Brothers

Dreyfus FDM 36722-2 *As various discs above.* 2/45–7/49.

***(*) The Woody Herman Story

Proper PROPERBOX 15 4CD *As various discs above.* 4/39–7/49.

Finally a CD reissue for some of the best tracks by Herman's Second Herd. A look through the personnel reveals a formidable roll-call, and the obvious stand-out is the famous reading of 'Early Autumn' with Getz's immortal tenor solo. Chaloff is memorable in his outings, especially 'Lollipop', and 'That's Right' and 'Lemon Drop' are minor Herman classics; but there is some commercial chaff too, which reminds that this was a band that was looking for an audience as well as trying to swing.

Hard to quarrel with any of the selections in *Four Brothers*, a classy choice of nuggets by both the First and Second Herds. Sixteen tracks (including the full 'Summer Sequence') and nothing wasted.

The Woody Herman Story covers the entire period to date, bar the pre-1939 sessions. Again, few arguments about any of the music or the documentation, although docked a notch for remastering which gives no clue as to sources.

***(*) At Palladium Hollywood / Commodore Hotel New York 1948

Storyville STCD 8240 *Similar to above.* 3–5/48.

Herman's Second Herd in full flow in two broadcasts from early in its existence – actually before the arrival of Bill Harris and Lou Levy. To that extent the band is not quite as strong as it would be, but these are still performances full of interest and, with soloists like Getz, Cohn and Chaloff on some inventive charts, the music has genuine class. Also more than noteworthy is the overlooked but splendid Mary Ann McCall, one of the most gracious vocalists of the late swing era. Broadcast-quality sound but not at all bad.

*** The Great Soloists 1945–1958

Blue Flame BFCD-1003 *Personnels unlisted.* 45–58.

A scattering of mostly heated big-band workouts covering a 15-year period, this has scrappy documentation but is full of great music. There are starring moments for Getz, Sims, Berman, Chaloff and many more, with the extraordinary workout on Shorty Rogers's chart, 'More Moon', hitting a pinnacle of big-band energy. Sound varies widely – several bright and clean tracks, but a lot suffer from hiss, surface noise or general wear and tear.

*** The Third Herd

Storyville STCD 8241 *Herman; Don Fagerquist, Doug Mettome, Roy Caton, Shorty Rogers (t); Herb Randel, Urbie Green, Jerry Dorn (tb); Phil Urso, Bill Perkins, Jack Dulong, Kenny Pinson (ts); Sam Staff (bs); Dave McKenna (p); Red Wooten (b); Sonny Igoe (d); Dolly Houston (v).* 5–6/51.

Herd number three still mustered a string of great names in the personnel and there were fine charts in the book by Al Cohn, Ralph Burns, Neal Hefti and more. These three broadcasts from the Palladium in Hollywood have their share of features for Dolly Houston and some dull pieces, but there are good spots for Perkins and Urso and young Dave McKenna gets a piece of the action on 'Leo The Lion'. In reasonable sound.

*** Scene & Heard In 1952

Jazz Band 2125-2 *Herman; Don Fagerquist, John Howell, Lee Fortier, Roy Caton, Stu Williamson, Phil Cook (t); Carl Fontana, Urbie Green, Jack Green (tb); Arno Marsh, Dick Hafer, Bill Perkins (ts); Sam Staff (bs, f); Nat Pierce (p); Frank Gallagher, Chubby Jackson (b); Sonny Igoe, Art Madigan (d).* 7–10/52.

Two sessions here: a dance date in Washington and a Los Angeles TV show, the latter in the superior sound. The TV material is more ordinary and there's an awful routine on 'Holiday For Strings', as well as a surprise version (if somewhat cut-down) of Artie Shaw's 'Concerto For Clarinet' starring Woody. The dance date has its share of easy-going tunes, but there's a terrific 'Moten Swing' and some good work from Stu Williamson and Urbie Green.

*** Jantzen Beach Oregon 1954

Status DSTS 1020 *Herman; Dick Collins, John Howell, Al Porcino, Reuben McFall, Bill Castagnino, Charlie Walp (t); Cy Touff (bt); Dick Kenney, Keith Moon (tb); Bill Perkins, Dick Hafer, Jerry Coker, Dave Madden (ts); Jack Nimitz (bs); Nat Pierce (p); Red Kelly (b); Chuck Flores, Joe McDonald (d); Dolly Houston (v).* 1–8/54.

*** 1954 & 1959

Status DSTS 1021 *As above, except add Bill Chase, Larry Mosher, Paul Fontaine, Sam Scavone, Tony Phillatoni (t), Freddy Wood, Joe Clarvadone, Ray Winslow (tb), B. Boyd, Al Puccin, Don Lanphere (ts), Marv Holladay (bs) Jack Six (b) Jimmy Campbell (d); omit McFall, Coker, McDonald, Houston.* 8/54–6/59.

More dance dates rescued by the indefatigable Status label, a tribute to the work of the late Dave Kay. The Jantzen Beach sets (there are three leftover tracks on the second disc) show that while the Herman band may have lost some of its starrier soloists, it was still one of the best American bands of its day. The section playing offers some of the greatest pleasure: in the crisp delivery of the likes of Al Cohn's 'Cohn's Alley' and Nat Pierce's 'Mulligantawny', the Hermanites are at their best, and these certainly come across better than the bleary extended version of 'One O'Clock Jump'. Pierce in particular had come to be Herman's right-hand man (Woody calls him 'Basie's other brother, Nathaniel Pierce' at one point), and 'Like Some Blues Man, Like' from the 1959 date might also be a Basie homage. The earlier date is in decent mono, the later one in respectable stereo. Both have their share of dance-floor fillers (this was the band on its regulation work, after all) but each should please Herman followers.

*** Woody Herman And His Orchestra 1956

Storyville STCD 8247/48 2CD *Herman; John Coppola, Dick Collins, Burt Collins, Dud Harvey, Bill Castagnino (t); Wayne Andre, Bill Harris, Bob Lamb (tb); Richie Kamuca, Bob Hardaway, Arno Marsh (ts); Jay Cameron (bs); Vince Guaraldi (p); Victor Feldman (vib, perc); Ray Biondi (g); Monty Budwig (b); Gus Gustafson (d).* 7/56.

Live at The Lagoon in Salt Lake City, here's almost two and a half hours of music by The Third Herd. The balance is far from perfect, with some soloists sounding as if they're on another stage, the trombones sometimes louder than the trumpets. But there are still good moments for Harris and Kamuca among the soloists.

***(*) Songs For Hip Lovers

Verve 559872-2 *Herman; Harry 'Sweets' Edison, Charlie Shavers (t); Bill Harris (tb); Hal McKusick (as); Jerry Cook, Bob Newman, Ben Webster (ts); Jack Nimitz, Sol Schlinger (bs); Jimmy Rowles, Lou Stein (p); Billy Bauer, Barney Kessel (g); Milt Hinton, Joe Mondragon (b); Larry Bunker, Jo Jones (d).* 1–3/57.

This vocal album for Woody might seem a strange choice for Verve to reissue first, given that they have plenty of excellent big-band material which has yet to reappear. But it's a delightful set. Herman's singing was enduring and unpretentious, and he made a lyric line swing without manhandling it. Marty Paich wrote some decent charts and it's a great band, with handsome work from Webster, Edison, Kessel and the rest.

***(*) Woody Herman – 1963

Philips 589490-2 *Herman; Bill Chase, Paul Fontaine, Dave Gale, Ziggy Harrell, Gerry Lamy (t); Phil Wilson, Eddie Morgan, Jack Gale (tb); Sal Nistico, Larry Cavelli, Gordon Brisker (ts); Gene Allen (bs); Nat Pierce (p); Chuck Andrus (b); Jake Hanna (d).* 10/62.

*** 1963 Summer Tour

Jazz Hour JH-1006 *Herman; Bill Hunt, Dave Gale, Bill Chase, Gerry Lamy, Paul Fontaine (t); Bob Rudolph, Phil*

Wilson, Henry Southall (tb); Sal Nistico, Carmen Leggio, Bobby Jones, Jack Stevens (ts); Frank Hittner (bs); Nat Pierce (p); Chuck Andrus (b); Jake Hanna (d). 63.

The Fourth Herd in action. The Philips album has a bold sound-mix which lets the Herman punch land on the button, and there are classic fast ones including Sal Nistico's 'Sister Sadie' feature and 'Mo-Lasses' and 'Camel Walk'. A welcome return for an album making its first CD appearance.

On the Jazz Hour set, the swinging delivery of 'The Preacher' sets a notable tone from the start and, though sound is indifferently mixed and the programme is still reliant on some Herman warhorses, this confirms that this is a tough and hard-hitting edition of the band.

*****(*) The Jazz Swinger / Music For Tired Lovers**

Colllectables 6679 *Herman; Bill Chase, Marv Stamm, Alex Rodriguez, Paul Fontaine, Bill Byrne, Dave Gale, Linn Biviano (t); Carl Fontana, Jerry Collins, Henry Southall (tb); Frank Vicari, Bob Pierson, Andy McGhee, Sal Nistico, Tom Anastas (saxes); Nat Pierce, Erroll Garner (p); Mike Moore, Wyatt Ruther (b); Ronnie Zito, Eugene 'Fats' Heard (d).* 7/54–6/66.

♛ ** Woody's Winners / Jazz Hoot**

Collectables 6678 *Herman; Gerry Lamy, Bill Chase, Dusko Goykovich, Bobby Shew, Don Rader, Lloyd Michaels, Linn Biviano (t); Henry Southall, Frank Tesinsky, Donald Doane, Jim Foy, Mel Wanzo, Bill Watrous (tb); Al Gibbons, Steve Marcus, Bob Pierson, Gary Klein, Sal Nistico, Andy McGhee (ts); Tom Anastas (bs); Nat Pierce, Mike Alterman (p); Charlie Byrd (g); Tony Leonard, Bob Daughery (b); Ronnie Zito (d).* 6/65–3/67.

***** Live East And West**

Koch 8592 *As above, except add Lloyd Michaels, Dick Ruedebusch, Billy Byrne, John Crews (t).* 6/65–3/67.

The first of the Collectables sets focuses on Herman the vocalist. The 1954 meeting with Erroll Garner is delightful, if somewhat off the cuff, with both men coming up with material on the spot. *The Jazz Swinger* put up the bizarre notion of Woody-sings-Jolson, although there are actually so many moments to relish that the album is far from an A&R man's bad idea: 'Sonny Boy' especially has long been a favourite of ours, and the band play the charts (Holman, Burns and Pierce) with real gusto.

Woody's Winners is one of the best big-band records of its time, and it still sounds terrific. For sheer excitement, none of Herman's contemporaries could have outgunned the team he had here. Live at San Francisco's Basin Street West, the band roar through the likes of '23 Red', Sal Nistico's burn-up of 'Northwest Passage', Woody's serene 'Poor Butterfly' and the climactic demolition of Horace Silver's 'Opus De Funk'. Here it's been coupled with *Jazz Hoot*, a vinyl set which was made up of out-takes from both *Woody's Winners* and the subsequent *Live East And West*. It might seem baffling that all this music is available only through the work of smaller labels licensing it from its owners, Columbia, but at least it's out there.

Live East And West couples more from San Francisco and music from a 1967 engagement at New York's Riverboat Lounge. Not quite as hot, and 'Make Someone Happy' is a waste of space, but still a band anyone would like to hear.

*****(*) Wild Root**

TKO Magnum Collectors Edition CECD 018 *Herman; various groups and personnel, sometimes unlisted.* 53–67.

Sixteen live or broadcast performances, culled from all over the place, and it makes for something of a dog's breakfast, with wild variations in audio quality and style. Some exuberant playing as usual, but it's a string of tracks that makes little sense as an album. For hardcore Hermanites only.

***** Brand New**

Original Jazz Classics OJC 1044 *Herman; Tom Harrell, Tony Klatzka, Buddy Powers, Bill Byrne, Forrest Buchtel (t); Bob Burgess, Ira Nepus, Don Switzer (tb); Sal Nistico, Frank Tiberi, Steve Lederer (ts); Gene Smookler (bs); Alan Broadbent (p); Michael Bloomfield (g); Alan Read (b); Ed Soph (d).* 3/71.

****(*) The Raven Speaks**

Original Jazz Classics OJC 663 *Herman; Al Porcino, Charles Davis, John Thomas, Bill Stapleton (t); Bill Byrne, Bob Burgess, Rick Stepton, Harold Garrett (tb); Frank Tiberi, Greg Herbert, Steve Lederer, Tom Anastas (reeds); Harold Danko (p); Pat Martino (g); Alphonso Johnson (b); Joe LaBarbera (d); John Pacheco (perc).* 8/72.

****(*) Woody Herman & The Thundering Herd**

Jazz Band EBCD 2146-2 *Similar to above, except add Al Cohn, Zoot Sims, Stan Getz, Flip Phillips (ts), Chubby Jackson (b).* 4–7/72.

***** Feelin' So Blue**

Original Jazz Classics OJC 953 *Herman; Dave Stahl, Nelson Hatt, Buddy Powers, Dennis Dotson, Bill Byrne, Larry Pyatt, Gil Rathel, Walt Blanton, Bill Stapleton, Tony Klatka (t, flhn); Jim Pugh, Steve Kohlbacher, Harold Garrett, Geoff Sharp, Dale Kirkland, Vaughn Webster (tb); Greg Herbert, Frank Tiberi, Steve Lederer, Harry Kleintank, Gary Anderson, Jan Konopasek (reeds); Andy LaVerne (p); Joe Beck (g); Chip Jackson, John Paley, Wayne Darling (b); Jeff Brillinger, Ron Davis, Ed Soph (d); John Rae, Ray Barretto, Kenneth Nash (perc).* 4/73–1/75.

***** King Cobra**

Original Jazz Classics OJC 1068 *Herman; Tom Porrello, Dave Stahl, Nelson Hatt, Bill Byrne, Buddy Powers, Dennis Dotson (t, flhn); Jim Pugh, Dale Kirkland (tb); Vaughn Webster (btb); Greg Herbert (ts, f, picc); Gary Anderson (ts, f); John Oslawski (bs); Andy LaVerne (p); Ron Paley (b); Jeff Brillinger (d); Kenneth Nash (perc).* 1/75.

Herman's '70s bands were still impressive outfits, but their studio records tended towards a fashionable and ultimately pretty indifferent eclecticism. *The Raven Speaks* has a top-notch cast largely wasted on some dreary tunes and so-so charts which just occasionally flicker or burst into life. *Feelin' So Blue* has some deeply unpromising material – 'Killing Me Softly With His Song', James Taylor's 'Don't Let Me Be Lonely Tonight' – yet turns out surprisingly well. The rock rhythms and modish figures don't completely undercut the strength of the band, which breaks through on 'Brotherhood Of Man', 'Evergreen' and 'Echano' to surprising effect, considering that the original album was patched together from three sessions over a two-year period. *King Cobra* is also more than listenable. They manage to make a plausible fist out of Stevie Wonder's 'Don't You Worry 'Bout A Thing', and Chick Corea's perky 'Spain' was the sort of chart that the latter-day Herds liked to flex their muscles on. *Brand New*, the earliest of these, is less appealing: guitarist Bloomfield is a pointless guest on four tracks. Even so, Alan Broadbent's charts have something to say, and Herman has an old-fashioned twist on 'Since I Fell For You'.

The Jazz Band set brings together a 1972 Newport appearance with the old Brothers team guesting, and three tracks from a Roseland Ballroom broadcast. The Newport tracks are, alas, in very poor sound; the Roseland material is better, though this is for specialist Hermanites only.

****(*) Live In Warsaw**

Storyville STCD 8207 *Herman; Jeffrey Davis, Nelson Hatt, John Hoffman, Dennis Dotson, William Byrne (t); Jim Pugh, Dale Kirkland (tb); Vaughan Wiester (btb); Frank Tiberi, Gary Anderson, Salvatore Spicola, John Oslawski (reeds); David Mays (p); Wilbur Stewart (b); Stephen Houghton (d).* 2/76.

A typical late-period Herman concert, cut in Poland in 1976. The programme relies heavily on the Herman hits with an overblown 'MacArthur Park' there to test the stamina of some. Amazing, really, that the band could attack what were very old charts and tunes with such spirit.

****(*) From East To West**

Concord CCD2-2155-2 *Herman; Brian O'Flaherty, Bill Byrne, Scott Wagstaff, Mark Lewis, George Rabbai, Bill Stapleton (t, flhn); Gene Smith, John Fedchock, Randy Hawes, Larry Shunk (tb); Bill Ross (ts, f, af, picc); Paul McGinley (ts, f); Randy Russell (ts, f); Al Cohn, Zoot Sims, Sal Nistico, Jim Carroll, Med Flory, Flip Phillips, Frank Tiberi (ts); Nick Brignola (bs, bcl); John Oddo (p); Mike Hall, Dave Shapiro (b); Dave Ratajczak, Jeff Hamilton (d).* 8/81–9/82

Herman's final years were capably documented by Concord and, although there are no truly outstanding records in this stint, there are sound standards of big-band playing on the orchestral records and plenty of characteristic Herman dudgeon on the small-group discs. Though his final years were tragically marred by problems with the IRS, he somehow found the spirit to play jazz with much of his old fire. What had changed – as it did for Ellington, Basie and Goodman, his fellow survivors from a bygone era – was the traditional big band's place in the music. As a repertory orchestra, filled with good, idiomatic players but few real characters, Herman's last Herd had no more going for it than precision and automatic punch. The sole surviving entry at present is this two-disc reissue of *Live A The Concord Jazz Festival* and *World Class*, neither of which amount to much more than reruns of Herman's golden years.

Vincent Herring (born 1964)

ALTO AND SOPRANO SAXOPHONES

One of the best of the younger generation of post-boppers, Herring's similarity to Cannonball Adderley was reinforced by a long and happy stay in brother Nat's band. His own work as leader has tended to be less blues-driven and more lyrical, but the influence is still there.

***** Sterling Place All-Stars**

Metropolitan 1117 *Herring; Ronnie Mathews (p); Richie Goods (b); Carl Allen (d).* 8/99.

Vince and Ronnie hit it off instinctively, and though the record is somewhat formulaic in formal terms, sticking to theme–solos–recapitulation almost all the way through, the sheer drive and quality of playing lift tracks like 'Salima's Dance', one of the pianist's best compositions, and Carl Allen's tricky 'Alternative Thoughts'. Vince takes it on soprano, which he otherwise seems to be resting. 'Summer Night' and 'In A Sentimental Mood' are both quality performances. This is a group that rates a long residency somewhere; when the music catches fire, it's as exhilarating as anything currently going the rounds, but it's too apt to drift off into conventional forms.

*****(*) Simple Pleasure**

High Note HCD 7084 *Herring; Wallace Roney (t); Mulgrew Miller (p); Richie Goods (b); E. J. Strickland (d).* 3/01.

Vincent seems to want to get back to basics on this rollicking set. 'The Loop' gets things off to a fiery and freewheeling start, but the saxophonist then wisely takes the pace down and cranks the emotion up for 'Once In A Lifetime', a glorious ballad tune of Mal Waldron's. The title-track is by another great modern pianist, Cedar Walton, and here and elsewhere Miller demonstrates his thorough grounding in the lore and language of modern pianism. Strickland is the revelation, a brisk and effortlesly competent player who combines swing with power. 'Straight Street' is a homage to Coltrane, played with the same headlong strength as Trane's.

Herring shifts to soprano here and there, but it's the alto horn that cements his descent from Cannonball, and in combination with Wallace Roney on a couple of tracks he sounds absolutely in that company and of that distinguished ilk. The closing reading of 'There Is No Greater Love' would bring tears to a glass eye.

***** All Too Real**

High Note HCD 7106 *Herring; Jeremy Pelt (t); Anthony Wonsey (p); Richie Goods (b); E. J. Strickland (d); Jill Seifers (v).* 12/02.

Very much a retread of the earlier High Note album, and if that sounds like faint praise, it isn't intended to. Herring has hit a groove and found a formula that he likes and that suits his quick-witted, soulful approach. Again, the trumpeter is used only sparingly, putting the main emphasis on the leader's horn. 'Love For Sale' is unalloyed delight, probably the most effective single solo he has so far committed to record. The originals – credits, too, for Pelt, the rock-solid Wonsey and bassist Goods – are strong ideas that offer a deceptive whiff of familiarity without the over-ripe odour of clichéd rep. The sound is mostly good, though the rhythm section is rather too prominent here and there. Jill Seifers makes her sole appearance on 'I'll Sing You A Lullaby', with Herring on very much his second horn; his soprano playing is decidedly second-string. If he was hoping for the same kind of pay-off as the previous album, it doesn't quite come off.

Fred Hersch (born 1955)

PIANO

Born in Cincinnati, Hersch worked in his local scene as a young man, went to the New England Conservatory, and subsequently gained a wide range of experience under different small-group leaders, including Stan Getz and Joe Henderson. He has recorded for numerous labels as both leader and sideman.

***** Horizons**

Concord CCD 4267 *Hersch; Marc Johnson (b); Joey Baron (d).* 10/84.

***** Sarabande**

Sunnyside SSC 1024 *Hersch; Charlie Haden (b); Joey Baron (d).* 12/86.

*****(*) Etc**

Red 123233-2 *Hersch; Steve LaSpina (b); Jeff Hirshfield (d).* 5/88.

***** Heartsongs**

Sunnyside SSC 1047 *Hersch; Michael Formanek (b); Jeff Hirshfield (d).* 12/89.

In the past we routinely characterized Fred Hersch as a Bill Evans follower, but as his discography has grown it's clear that there's much more to him than that. He's actually a profoundly attentive scholar of many styles of jazz piano and a lucid and perceptive analyst of the forms that solo, trio and group playing can take for a pianist. His writing, which may be less important to him than his powers of interpretation, has something of Evans about it, as in originals such as 'Lullabye' (*Heartsongs*) and 'Child's Song' (*Sarabande*). But Hersch has an energy of his own, and all these records have something to commend them.

His first album, *Horizons*, has only recently made it to CD. It's a confident and typically catholic programme, with standards, Ellington, Shorter and one tune of his own, the stormy 'Cloudless Sky'. *Heartsongs* is one of the best integrated, since it's by a regular trio: Haden is a little too stodgy to make *Sarabande*'s liveliest tunes break out. *Heartsongs* also has the most individual approach to the material, and Hersch chooses good covers: Wayne Shorter's 'Fall' is done in *passacaglia* form, and Ornette Coleman's 'The Sphinx' casts the composer in an impish light. But a few of the freer pieces sound more effortful than they should: Hersch may be an impressive conservative, but at this stage he's a conservative all the same. *Etc* is a more straight-ahead date, and this time the music works out beautifully: a fine programme of jazz themes, with LaSpina and Hirshfield both constructive and challenging in support, the bassist in particular coming up with some quick ideas and agile lines.

*****(*) At Maybeck Vol. 31**

Concord CCD 4596 *Hersch (p solo).* 10/93.

Hersch's turn at Maybeck might not be his finest hour, but it sets up a near-perfect balance of his meditative and argumentative sides. The percussive, almost stabbing treatment of Coleman's 'Ramblin'' and the breezy lyricism of his own 'Heartsong' are set beside a glowing 'If I Loved You' and a very ambitious approach to 'Haunted Heart' which opens the song out into a long *fantaisie*. As usual, impeccable sound.

*****(*) Passion Flower: Fred Hersch Plays Billy Strayhorn**

Nonesuch 9395-2 *Hersch; Nurit Tilles (p); Drew Gress (b); Tom Rainey (d); Chief Bey (v); strings.* 7–8/95.

****** Fred Hersch Plays Rodgers And Hammerstein**

Nonesuch 79414-2 *Hersch (p solo).* 1/96.

****** Thelonious: Fred Hersch Plays Monk**

Nonesuch 79456-2 *Hersch (p solo).* 2/97.

The Strayhorn collection is limpidly beautiful and, while these are marginally less impressive features for the leader's piano than the discs listed below, it's difficult to carp at the lustre of Fred's string charts, even if 'Day Dream' and 'Lush Life' flirt with mush. The programme is a blend of solos, trios and three settings for the strings; Bey adds a lubricious vocal to 'Something To Live For', with the almost unknown verse an extra pleasure; Tilles joins Hersch for a duet on 'Tonk', which comes out sounding almost like ragtime.

Hersch's approach to Rodgers and Hammerstein is that of a recitalist. He doesn't try to 'swing' the tunes – and in any case many of them are vehicles which jazz musicians have seldom turned to. As familiar as they are, few improvisers have looked at 'A Cock-Eyed Optimist', 'Shall We Dance?', 'Getting To Know You' or 'I Have Dreamed'. The pianist plays them in a musing, respectful manner, rarely letting the melody drift too far from sight, and parading the structure of the song as he goes: one can almost see the choruses unfolding as he walks through them. Where he makes his mark is in the voicings and harmonies: with his immaculate touch and exacting delivery, the songs are recast as rich, graceful arias, parlour songs made modern by their fresh clothes. Fred's note tells of how he learned many of the tunes through Broadway cast albums played on the family gramophone, and that domestic memory is honoured by these wonderful treatments.

His Monk recital is more of the same, yet quite different. These are tunes which pianists have mulled over and covered until there's very little of the original flesh left. Hersch starts with 'Round Midnight', done first as a raindrop dance in the highest register, before the music thickens and grows dark. And then it's over – Hersch leaves no waste in these interpretations, and his judgement rarely fails him. The five choruses he takes on 'Misterioso', each a pristine investigation of that curious melody line, are a unique insight; but so is what happens to 'Let's Cool One' or 'Ask Me Now'. Rather than relying on Monk's rhythmic staggering for flavour, as so many pianists do, Hersch evens out the pulse and places the emphasis on the substance and colour of his chords. It's a fascinating essay on the master, and further proof that Hersch himself must now be counted among the contemporary giants of the instrument.

***** Songs We Know**

Nonesuch 79468-2 *Hersch; Bill Frisell (g).* 98.

It's possible to find Frisell's eclecticism a little tiresome, and these 11 standards and jazz tunes might have been overpowered by his signature methods. But Hersch keeps him on planet Earth. The pianist's incisive parts curb the guitarist's taste for outrageous harmonics and there's some terrific interplay. But the record doesn't sustain its running-time. As with all of Frisell's records, there's a novelty element which turns either cute or folksy at points, and the shameless romanticism which Hersch is partial to is something that the guitarist can't commit to without a lick of irony.

*****(*) Let Yourself Go**

Nonesuch 79558-2 *Hersch (p solo).* 10/98.

A concert recording from Jordan Hall, Boston. Hersch enjoyed this gig and he is in fine form. As ever, it's his ballads which highlight the best of his style: 'Black Is The Colour/Love Theme From Spartacus' is an almost transcendant treatment of the two melodies, and when he gets to an encore of 'The Nearness Of You' his reading scarcely ruffles the feathers of the tune. One or two pieces seem a bit overly calculated, such as the awkward gait chosen for 'Speak Low', but Hersch's admirers shouldn't be disappointed.

*****(*) Songs Without Words**

Nonesuch 79612 3CD *Hersch; Ralph Alessi (t); Rich Perry (ts); Reid Anderson, Drew Gress (b); Tom Rainey, Nasheet Waits (d).* 00.

Everything you always wanted to know about Fred Hersch, but were ... well, it can seem a little like that in this fairly massive three-disc set. While in the main it is still about Hersch as solo pianist, his trio with Gress and Rainey appears on one track, there are duets with Alessi and Rainey, and the other horns join in for a few quintet pieces. Show us a triple-CD and we'll show you a lot of filler, but it's hard to win any case on that point here: as ever, Hersch's pianism is rich, full and persistently pushing to expand his own horizons. Disc two, which features exclusively jazz material, includes a version of 'Caravan' in which he builds an imposing interpretation out of what sounds like an ongoing argument between each hand, and a 'Con Alma' where the endlessly recurring theme would be annoying but for his fastidious variations. The first disc presents originals, the third a Cole Porter songbook. It's a veritable feast, yet the sheer bulk of it (a smidgin over three hours) is finally a little wearing. Listeners have the option to sample at will, naturally, but some of the best moments get hidden in the grand design; and we felt that the Porter tunes weren't quite of the formidable standard which Fred had set with some of the previous recitals. All that said, he's some piano player.

*****(*) Live At The Village Vanguard**
Palmetto PM 2088 *Hersch; Drew Gress (b); Nasheet Waits (d).* 5/02.

A new label for Fred, though the trio carries over from his last Nonesuch session. Something of a test for him to do the Vanguard live record, given at least one illustrious predecessor in these shoes, but there's nothing self-conscious or restrained about the music. Nasheet Waits is a fine drummer for him (listen to Waits handle the rhythms of 'Phantom Of The Bopera') and he and Gress are pushily supportive, the kind of set-up that Hersch thrives on. Something like 'At The Close Of The Day' keeps the meditative side of the pianist's music intact, but uncommitted listeners are likely to respond positively to what is a vigorous session.

Conrad Herwig (born 1959)

TROMBONE

Born in Fort Sill, Oklahoma, Herwig was a fast learner who was already in New York at the beginning of the '80s. Like all trombonists, he is a prolific sideman, but he has also recorded relatively extensively as a leader.

***** New York Breed**
Double-Time DTRCD-108 *Herwig; David Liebman (ss, ts); Richie Beirach (p); Rufus Reid (b); Adam Nussbaum (d).* 1/96.

***** Heart Of Darkness**
Criss Cross 1155 *Herwig; Walt Weiskopf (ss, ts); Stefon Harris (vib); Bill Charlap (p); Peter Washington (b); Billy Drummond (d).* 12/97.

***** Osteology**
Criss Cross 1176 *Herwig; Steve Davis (tb); David Kikoski (p); James Genus (b); Jeff 'Tain' Watts (d).* 12/98.

*****(*) Unseen Universe**
Criss Cross 1194 *Herwig; Alex Sipiagin (t, flhn); Seamus Blake (ss, ts); David Kikoski (p); James Genus (b); Jeff 'Tain' Watts (d).* 12/99.

***** Hieroglyphica**
Criss Cross 1207 *Herwig; Bill Charlap (p); James Genus (b); Gene Jackson (d).* 1/01.

Herwig is an exemplar of trombone technique. He often talks about Coltrane in his sleevenote quotes, and he often covers Trane too: 'Syeeda's Song Flute', 'Cousin Mary' and a rip-off of 'Giant Steps' called 'Watch Your Steps'. He's fast, he likes the higher register, he ducks out of expressionism, he only rarely sounds like Jay Jay, and he's so sure-footed that you can't imagine him knocking one over. Sounds like a recipe for clean, boring records, but that's not being fair: Herwig wants a result. *New York Breed* is all but set up as a masterclass, and for all its classy playing it has a macho quality which stops the record really hitting any high spots. *Heart Of Darkness* is, in light of its intriguing line-up, disappointing: Weiskopf makes no impact, Harris tends to doodle in the margins, and while Herwig's opening two originals strike some interesting sparks, the record resolves into a routine blow from there.

Osteology is a rare example of the two-trombone record. While Herwig and Davis might be seen as close kin, they're further apart than some may expect: Davis goes low, Herwig high, and both follow a closely-argued, linear vocabulary which bypasses the sing-song Jay Jay and Kai model. Yet the record never really does anything to grab a listener who's not fascinated by trombones. It's fast and smart.

We are no more enthusiastic about *Hieroglyphica*, a code which the uncommitted will simply feel unenthusiastic about cracking. Herwig does nothing to challenge the avant garde masters of the trombone, but he's clearly keen about asserting the slide horn as a front-line instrument. Yet the impresson here is, again, a great executant in search of a context.

The one disc to break out of this good-but-not-great mould is *Unseen Universe*, which is the most democratic and most densely-voiced of the five discs. Sipiagin is a comparatively rough front-line partner, Blake can go inside or outside at will, and Kikoski knows how to play for everybody in the band. The result is as smart as the others, but with a few bumpier edges, which help no end.

Fred Hess (born 1944)

TENOR SAXOPHONE

Working in and around the Rocky Mountains, Hess runs the Boulder Creative Music Ensemble and has associations with many improvisers and post-bop players in the region.

***** Faith**
Cadence CJR 1112 *Hess; Ron Miles (t); Glenn Nitta (ss, as); Mark Harris (as, bs); Kent McLagen (b); Tim Sullivan (d).* 1/99.

*****(*) Exposed**
CIMP 249 *Hess; Paul Smoker (t); Ken Filiano (b); Damon Short (d).* 6/01.

The Boulder Creative Music Ensemble are responsible for the first disc. Hess seems most interested in the horns here, and he has them perform both trickily contrapuntal parts and conservative free playing, solos not really registering above the babble of brass and reed voices. It works best when there's a strong theme to start with, as in 'Lou-Bop' or (a nice choice) the Gary McFarland cover, 'Why Are You Blue'.

Exposed is a particularly effective use of the CIMP natural sound, which suits assertive players who prefer to keep within temperate boundaries of expression. Both Hess and Smoker fit that situation, and the music is a boisterous kind of free bop. The quartet work through Hess's material with fine gusto, and every man gets in some satisfying blows – Filiano, for instance, contributes a beautiful solo to 'JHM'. A splendid set.

*****(*) Extended Family**
Tapestry 76004-2 *As above.* 7/02.

***** Right At Home**
Tapestry 76005-2 *Hess; Marc Sabatella (p).* 8/02.

*****(*) The Long And Short Of It**
Tapestry 76006-2 *Hess; Ron Miles (t); Ken Filiano (b); Matt Wilson (d).* 8/03.

These records continue in the lively but amiable groove of *Exposed.* The more conventional studio sound of *Extended Family* may lend greater appeal than its predecessor (it was recorded on an awayday to Rochester, New York, which is actually Fred's home town). Short's swinging and unfussy time helps settle down the group, and Hess and Smoker clearly enjoy each other's company: they sound like a couple of Ellingtonians on 'High Street'.

Right At Home fields several of the same compositions, scaled back to the duo format. It's interesting to read the names Hess cites as his current heroes: Berg, Brecker, Lovano, Margitza, Potter, all relatively inside players. Sabatella makes rather heavy weather of some of the tunes, and even though Hess remains a pleasure to hear, he does sound more relaxed with a full rhythm section behind him.

A change in the quartet personnel for *The Long And Short Of It.* Good as Short was on the other discs, Wilson can dig into a groove with superb elan, and he and Filiano get excitingly funky straight away on the opening 'Norman Says'. Miles is a more outgoing trumpeter than Smoker, expressive in a different way, and he clearly has a fine rapport with Hess. This is literate, subtly modulated jazz, perhaps just a shade too self-effacing under Hess's shy leadership, but really very satisfying.

Eddie Heywood (1915–89)

PIANO

Born in Atlanta, Heywood arrived in New York in the '30s and worked under various leaders, before forming his own band. Despite spells of ill health, which eventually obliged him to retire until the '60s, he found much popularity as a small-group leader in the Teddy Wilson manner, and he worked up until his death.

***** Eddie Heywood 1944**
Classics 947 *Heywood; Ray Nance (t, vn); Doc Cheatham (t); Vic Dickenson (tb); Aaron Sachs (cl); Lem Davis, Johnny Hodges (as); Don Byas (ts); Al Lucas, John Simmons (b); Jack Parker, Shelly Manne (d).* 2–5/44.

***** Eddie Heywood 1944–1946**
Classics 1038 *Heywood; Dick Vance, Parr Jones (t); Vic Dickenson, Henry Coker, Britt Woodman (tb); Lem Davis, Marshall Royal (as); Ernie Shepard, Al Lucas (b); Keg Purnell, Charlie Blackwell (d); Bing Crosby (v).* 11/44–2/46.

****(*) Eddie Heywood 1946–1947**
Classics 1219 *Heywood; Parr Jones, Leonard Hawkins (t); Vic Dickenson, Henry Coker, Ed Momate (tb); Marshall Royal, Jimmie Powell (as); Roy Ross (org); Ernie Shepard, Billy Taylor (b); Keg Purnell (d); The Andrews Sisters, Peggy Mann, Bob Eberly (v).* 4/46–12/47.

Heywood sounds like Teddy Wilson's conservative brother on most of his records. He hired some fine jazzmen for his dates – Vic Dickenson is on many of these sides, and Doc Cheatham gets some space for himself early on – but there is precious little music of any other than a sedate disposition, and Heywood made sure that his own adept but uniformly uneventful solos took centre stage throughout most of these records. Classics 947 is something of an exception, since there are some beautiful moments for the Ellingtonians: two sessions for Signature brought in Nance, Hodges, Sachs and Byas, all of whom make their mark. By the time of the second disc, though, Heywood's formula had taken over: but even here there's music to enioy. Dick Vance gets off some fine solos on the first sessions, there are five vocals by Bing Crosby – who sounds like he's relishing the rare opportunity to play with a black small group rather than John Scott Trotter behind him – and only towards the end does the music start to really stiffen up. Classics 1219 is much less appealing, and by the end (when Heywood had signed to Victor) the horns have disappeared, and the Heywood trio might as well be competing for Frankie Carle's audience. Transfers are mostly decent.

John Hicks (born 1941)

PIANO

The elegant Georgian studied music at Lincoln University across the state line in Missouri, and has retained an urbane intelligence in his approach to form and structure. His time with Art Blakey and with Betty Carter significantly enhanced his public profile and in the '70s allowed him to explore the fringes of avant-garde jazz, while retaining his own essentially lyrical and melodic approach. Recent years have seen him work with Arthur Blythe, Oliver Lake and Bobby Watson. His composition, 'Naima's Love Song', is a modern classic.

***** After the Morning**
West 54 WW 8004 *Hicks (p solo).* 1/79.

Hicks was rising 40 when this solo recital was recorded, live at the Montreal Jazz Festival. It's very much a showcase performance, blending together a long meditation on Strayhorn's 'A Flower Is A Lovesome Thing', a medley of Monk tunes, faithfully played but without pastiche, and a gently swinging bossa nova. Some of the highlights, however, are the shorter pieces, often little more than a theme statement and a brief, cadenza-like solo. Coltrane's 'Moment's Notice' is a good example, but there is also a fine, accelerated version of Bud Powell's 'Oblivion'. The piano sound is respectable for the time, but a bit cavernous.

*****(*) Beyond Expectations**
Reservoir RSR CD 130 *Hicks; Ray Drummond (b); Marvin 'Smitty' Smith (d).* 9/93.

Drummond's introduction to 'There Is No Greater Love' on the Reservoir disc captures in just a few bars what a valuable player he is. His statement of the Isham Jones theme tees Hicks up for a firmly unsentimental set of variations that gains in stature (despite an uncertain beginning) with virtually every bar. The piano is recorded with a lot of presence, and the recording as a whole has Rudy van Gelder stamped all over it: lively, resonant, utterly musical. By this point in his career, Hicks records come with all sorts of expectations attached (the actual reference is to a composition with Elise Wood) and this one confounds none of them, an utterly professional performance from a seasoned performer.

***** Single Petal Of A Rose**
Mapleshade 02532 *Hicks; Jack Walrath (t); Elise Wood (f); Curtis Lundy (b).* 94.

Wood is still an acquired taste, but she makes some pretty sounds here and there, and it might be that there's a bit more stuff to her playing by this point. She's strongly featured on the Mapleshade session (Walrath has a guest role only) and there is considerable lyric invention in her statement on the title-piece. Working without percussion gives it all a very light, chamber-jazz feel, but there is enough substance to keep the level of interest high. For further examples of Hicks in peak form, turn to the Keystone Trio entry.

***** Trio & Strings**
Mapleshade 5532 *Hicks; Elise Wood (f); Steve Novosel (b); Ronnie Burrage, Steve Williams (d); string quartet.* 98.

Apart from Strayhorn's 'Passion Flower', a set of Hicks originals. 'Naima's Love Song' receives a rather bloodless reading, but 'West Side Winds' and 'Minor Collaboration' are both delicately and richly articulated and Pierre Sprey gets a lovely sound from trio and strings. Not our favourite Hicks record by any means, but an accomplished and pleasing record.

*****(*) Impressions Of Mary Lou**
High Note 7046 *Hicks; Dwayne Dolphin (b); Cecil Brooks III (d).* 6/98.

***** Something To Live For: A Billy Strayhorn Songbook**
High Note 7019 *As above.* 10/98.

*****(*) Music In The Key Of Clark**
High Note 7083 *As above.* 01.

***** Fatha's Day**
High Note 7110 *As above.* 5/03.

Towards the end of the '90s, Hicks embarked on a set of piano trio tributes to fellow-players from the Pittsburgh area. The Strayhorn set is totally *simpatico*, a genuinely understanding reading of some classic jazz themes that avoids any temptation to crank up the romanticism. Instead, Hicks emphasizes the structure of each song, articulating 'A Flower Is A Lovesome Thing' with admirable simplicity and grace. To accuse the pianist of being unchallenging is beside the point. These are not radical reinterpretations, nor are they sycophantic homages, just delicately nuanced restatements.

Imagine doing an Ellington tribute album and including material only from the Sacred Concerts. That's roughly what Hicks has done on *Impressions*, another of his homages to great predecessors. Interspersed with five originals, he treats half a dozen Mary Lou Williams themes to robust inspection; the result isn't quite as laid back and spiritual as the material might suggest, and both 'O. W.' (Williams) and 'Not Too Straight' (Hicks) are unexpectedly spiky and iconoclastic, the latter curiously redolent of Jaki Byard's work.

Dolphin creates a huge wrap-around sound and anchors the compositions admirably, allowing Hicks to play more freely than he's usually to be heard. The opening 'Lord Have Mercy' is firebrand preaching rather than gentle benediction, and there's a pretty stout injunction in the closing 'The Lord Says' as well. It couldn't be any other pianist than Hicks, but it does sound as though he's namechecking musicians other than the one explicitly honoured: hints of Bud Powell, Monk and Basie as well, and nods to swing and bop throughout. An intriguing record.

The Hines set is the most disappointing of the bunch, consisting largely of originals and lacking anything of the spirit of their intended subject. 'Monday Date' and 'Rosetta' have some nice moments, but the tone of the session is mystifying, perilously close to pastiche. By contrast, and unexpectedly, the Sonny Clark tribute is absolutely spot on. Hicks knew his long overlooked predecessor very well and obviously remembers him with great fondness. 'Angel With a Briefcase' – a reference to Clark's habit of rushing round with a stuffed portfolio of scores – is a tender and completely idiomatic musical portrait, kicking off a short sequence of originals inspired by Clark. The reworked material, though, is the best of the set. 'Minor Meeting' and 'My Conception' (the latter preceded by a beautiful solo cadenza) are given unexpected rhythmic treatments, while 'Sonny's Crib' drives along powerfully, marked by a strong gospel feel. A wonderful record.

****(*) Beautiful Friendship**
HiWood 46212 *Hicks; Elise Wood (f).* 2–11/00.

We're still mystified by this partnership. This time Wood's broad vibrato is heard front and centre in a set of sentimental ballads that rarely rises above easy listening. 'April in Paris', 'But Beautiful', an admittedly lovely 'Corcovado' and a good version of John Lewis's 'Afternoon in Paris'. Beyond that, we fear, nothing much for the jazz listener.

Eddie Higgins (born 1932)

PIANO

Higgins was born in Cambridge, Massachusetts, but spent 20 years working in Chicago, recording with Lee Morgan and Wayne Shorter. He now bases himself in Fort Lauderdale, plays in a swing-to-bop mainstream, and has a particular interest in Brazilian music.

***** Eddie Higgins**
Collectables COL-CD-7173 *Higgins; Paul Serrano (t); Frank Foster (ts); Jimh Atlas, Richard Evans (b); Marshall Thompson (d).* 61.

***** By Request**
Solo Art SACD-104 *Higgins; Milt Hinton (b); Bobby Rosengarden (d).* 8/86.

*****(*) Those Quiet Days**
Sunnyside SSC 1052D *Higgins; Kevin Eubanks (g); Rufus Reid (b).* 12/90.

*****(*) Zoot's Hymns**
Sunnyside SSC 1064D *Higgins; John Doughten (ts); Phil Flanigan (b); Danny Burger (d).* 2/94.

Higgins has been making occasional visits to the studio since the '50s. The Vee-Jay album, now reissued by Collectables, was his name debut in 1961 (bar an extremely obscure date made for the local Replica label in 1958). Split between three quintet numbers and four trio pieces, the music follows a bluesy-boppish path very much in the idiom of that moment, although the playing has infectious enthusiasm, and there's a glimpse of another Chicagoan less often sighted on record, Paul Serrano. Even 'You Leave Me Breathless' goes off at a jaunty step.

By Request sticks to well-trodden paths, so far as material is concerned, though the pianist's approach has a verve that takes it out of routine: he has some of the rocking ebullience of the great Chicago pianists, and touches of stride and boogie are integrated into a wide-ranging taste. Hinton and Rosengarden provide flexible support, and a couple of original Higgins rags round out the picture. The irreproachable *Those Quiet Days* is a more recent record and surely one of his best. The interplay of piano, guitar and bass has a natural litheness and melodic and harmonic tang and, with Eubanks and Reid sounding both attentive and inventive throughout, the ideas have a seamless momentum. Higgins is no great original, with a style much indebted to the deceptively easy swing of Hank Jones, but he has a calm authority perfectly suited to this kind of date. Eubanks continues his double life as a traditional modernist and a fusioneer with another distinguished turn in the former category, and Reid hunkers down on all the bass lines.

Zoot's Hymns – the dedication is obvious – is another unassuming beauty. Doughten can't quite live up to the Sims and Getz comparisons that come in the sleeve-notes, but he's still darn good: easy swing, good head for melody and proto-typical big tone. Higgins sounds more relaxed than ever, but he can't help coming up with ingenious turns in solos that never quite resolve into any of the clichés one expects in this setting. He also picks great tunes: three uncommon A. C. Jobim pieces are highlights to go with his pair of originals.

***(*) Haunted Heart

Sunnyside SSC 1080D *Higgins; Ray Drummond (b); Ben Riley (d).* 6/97.

A meeting of masters, and the fact that the material is so well-worn – the only remotely unusual choice is a medley of 'Stolen Moments' and 'Israel' – is the only hindrance to unqualified enjoyment. Measured but never outstaying their welcome, these nine interpretations are about as classic as a piano trio can be. Higgins exposes nothing new in these tunes: he simply reminds us why the likes of 'My Funny Valentine' and 'Isn't it Romantic?' have endured in the jazz canon, and why playing of this unassuming excellence will always be worth listening to.

*** Speaking Of Jobim

Sunnyside SSC 1092D *Higgins; Jay Leonhart (b); Terry Clarke (d).* 10/98.

*** Time On My Hands

Arbors ARCD 19236 *Higgins (p solo).* 12/99.

The Jobim interpretations on *Zoot's Hymns* paved the way for a full collection of that composer's work, and in the notes Higgins tells how he became infatuated with this music as far back as 1963. Perhaps he's come to know it a little too well, since the record has nothing surprising about it, and the trio play the music gracefully but without much particularity. Higgins's usual muscular style is an advantage, since the tendency to treat Jobim as a source for weepy or perfumed meditation is averted, but the record's no more than average. Ditto, unfortunately, for the solo record. As with many another well-mannered recital, this one is full of good things, short of great ones. Higgins has recently been busy in the studio making several sets for the Japanese Venus label.

Andrew Hill (born 1937)

PIANO

Born in Chicago and not Haiti as is sometimes reported, Hill draws on his Caribbean ancestry and always sounds torn between cultures – on the one hand analytical, on the other powerfully visceral. Influenced by Bud Powell and Thelonious Monk, but also thoroughly individual, Hill is both an avant-gardist and a loyal traditionalist whose basic language remains close to bebop.

CORE COLLECTION

♛ **** Point Of Departure

Blue Note 9364 *Hill; Kenny Dorham (t); Eric Dolphy (as, f, bcl); Joe Henderson (ts); Richard Davis (b); Tony Williams (d).* 3/64.

Hill's whole career has been marked by the silences that punctuate his compositions. Of the important bop and post-bop pianists – Bud Powell, Horace Silver, Mal Waldron, Paul Bley, Cecil Taylor – he is the least known and most erratically documented; even Herbie Nichols enjoys a certain posthumous cachet.

Point Of Departure **is one of the very great jazz albums of the '60s and is now available with bonus takes of three of its five compositions. Hill's Blue Note debut, *Black Fire*, was available briefly on CD but seems to be out of circulation at the moment. It is an altogether more conservative record than this magnificent statement. Hill's writing and arranging skills matured dramatically with *Point Of Departure*. Nowhere is his determination to build on the example of Monk clearer than on the punningly titled 'New Monastery'. Hill's solo, like that on the long previous track, 'Refuge', is constructed out of literally dozens of subtle shifts in the time-signature, most of them too subliminal to be strictly counted. Typically, Hill is prepared to hold the basic beat himself and to allow Williams to range very freely. The rejected take is less secure rhythmically and while Hill's solo is full of interesting material, the 'bonus' take adds little to the album's impact. Only the alternate take of 'Flight 19' contains much of moment.**

Of the issued tracks, 'Spectrum' is the one disappointment, too self-conscious an attempt to run a gamut of emotions and instrumental colours; an extraordinary 5/4 passage for the horns almost saves the day. Henderson at first glance doesn't quite fit, but his solos on 'Spectrum' and 'Refuge' are exemplary and in the first case superior to Dolphy's rather insubstantial delivery. The mood of the session switches dramatically on the final 'Dedication', a dirge with a beautiful structure that represents the sharpest contrast to the rattling progress of the previous 'Flight 19' and brings the set full circle. Unfortunately, Hill was offered few opportunities to record with similar forces in years to come and suffered long neglect, pigeon-holed with the awkward squad.

★★★ Passing Ships

Blue Note 90417 *Hill; Dizzy Reece, Woody Shaw (t); Julian Priester (tb); Bob Northern (frhn); Howard Johnson (tba, bcl); Joe Farrell (ss, ts, bcl, af, eng hn); Ron Carter (b); Lenny White (d).* 11/69.

These unissued tracks even fell outside Mosaic's compendious, 50-plus-track release of Hill's 1963–66 Blue Notes. *Dance With Death*, recorded in 1968, had to wait a dozen years to appear on disc. This one has had to wait longer still. The job of rescuing a stereo tape (actually a rough mix) that sounded like a 'train wreck' fell to Michael Cuscuna, who retrieved the session from the Blue Note vaults at Hill's repeated urging. It's fascinating to listen to it in the context of 2002's *A Beautiful Day* (reviewed below), since the sound-world – trombone, tuba, low woodwinds – is almost identical. Reece and Shaw complement one another perfectly at the top end, the one bright and funky, the other darker and more brooding. It wasn't quite Lenny White's recording debut; he'd been involved in the *Bitches Brew* sessions earlier on in the year, but he comes across as a dazzlingly confident debutant, capable of fire, precision and often a surprisingly delicate beauty.

The opening 'Sideways' is typical Hill, harmonically complex, rhythmically unpredictable, a curious mix of Afro-Cuban and avant-garde. The title-piece is more stately as the title implies, but there is something unexpected and subversive going on in the bass arrangements. Joe Farrell sounds the opening theme on cor anglais, an unexpected sound colour, but a perfectly appropriate one here. Farrell and Johnson add exponentially to the range of textures at Hill's disposal, and the latter tracks on the album, 'The Brown Queen', 'Cascade' and 'Yesterday's Tomorrow', are less structurally interesting than they are as essays in voicing. 'Plantation Bag', though, is a lost masterpiece, a brilliant funk figure held together by Howard Johnson's bass clarinet, over which trumpets and Farrell's soprano; Joe reaches for his tenor to solo, and delivers one of his strongest statements on record. 'Noontide' is a brisk, double-time Latin feature, which Cuscuna perceptively likens to Hill's earlier 'Catta', written for Bobby Hutcherson's *Dialogue*. It's a reminder just how fertile a composer he was in these years.

This is a fine record, one of the best Blue Note recoveries of recent times. A subjective point, but see what you think: aren't these tracks distantly reminiscent of what Joe Zawinul was doing in Weather Report just a little later?

★★★★ Lift Every Voice

Blue Note 27546 *Hill; Lee Morgan, Woody Shaw (t); Carlos Garnett (ts); Bennie Maupin (ss, ts, bcl, f); Ron Carter, Richard Davis (b); Ben Riley, Freddie Waits (d).* 69.

Long out of print, *Lift Every Voice* was a unique synthesis of jazz group and voices and one of the most ambitious records of Hill's career. The group was fiercely individual, with Woody Shaw and Carlos Garnett creating a unique front line, a million miles from the kind of conventional hard bop that was still coming out on Blue Note; Davis and Waits are equally unpredictable in the engine room of the band. There is now an internal comparison as well, because the 2001 reissue includes an unreleased session featuring Lee Morgan and Bennie Maupin. While it has some strong features and benefits immeasurably from Maupin's multi-instrumentalism, it is more of a sketch at what Hill was about than a properly achieved album. Hence, perhaps, its non-appearance at the time, though we suspect it may simply have been too far out of the ordinary run.

The vocalists are carefully integrated into the overall sound on *Lift Every Voice*, but it's Woody's wonderful singing tone on 'Ghetto Lights' and 'Lullaby Love Chant' that communicates most strongly. Garnett is a greatly underrated player, very much part of the fusion movement of the next few years but here already showing both a strong funk drive and a gift for harmonic unpredictability. To repeat: as a combination they are breathtaking.

The reappearance of this important record is perhaps the most significant breakthrough in the Hill discography. If Blue Note can now be persuaded to release some of the dozen Hill recordings that still languish in the vaults, justice will eventually be served.

★★★ Invitation

Steeplechase SCCD 31026 *Hill; Chris White (b); Art Lewis (d).* 10/74.

Like many of his contemporaries, Hill enjoyed greater visibility in Europe than in the USA during the '70s. This was one of his consistently good performances for the Danish label, a studio session rather than one of Steeplechase's notoriously unselective club recordings. Hill is playing well, albeit with a rather stiff and foot-soldierish rhythm section who don't seem altogether easy with the material.

Apart from the title-track, all the tunes are originals and Hill's gift as a composer-performer is well attested on the long, flowing 'Morning Flower', as well as the funkier 'Catfish' which starts the record. An alternate take of this tune comes at the end of the record, where it properly belongs. Presumably Nils Winther thought it made a more arresting opening than the more brooding 'Lost No More'. White and Lewis do their work with concentration but lack flexibility and tend to fudge some of Hill's more adventurous metres.

★★(★) Faces Of Hope

Soul Note 121010 *Hill (p, solo).* 6/80.

Marked by a forceful dissonance, unusual and unsettling harmonic intervals, Hill's dark, incantatory manner as a solo performer sometimes obscures a lighter, folksy side. Like Monk's, his gammy melodic patterns work better either solo or with horns; conventional trio-playing represents only a surprisingly small proportion of his output. There is an introverted and brooding quality that will not win over uncommitted listeners.

★★★ Divine Revelation

Steeplechase SCCD 31044 *Hill; Jimmy Vass (ss, as, f); Chris White (b); Leroy Williams (d).* 75.

The title-track of *Divine Revelation* is almost half an hour of concentrated Hill, a densely flowing, complex idea that doesn't quite pull off the transcendence it aims for, largely because the group doesn't seem quite to understand the rhythmic needs of music as open-form as this. Almost by way of compensation, Hill programmes a rare standard in 'Here's That Rainy Day', but the Van Heusen classic is delivered with a curiously sardonic touch, almost as if Andrew is dissociating himself from the material; or it may simply be that we're unused to hearing familiar themes delivered with his characteristically sombre attack.

***(*) **Strange Serenade**

Soul Note 121013 *Hill; Alan Silva (b); Freddie Waits (d).* 80.

This is as dour and dark as anything Hill has committed to record. Silva and Waits are ideal partners in music that isn't so much minor-key as surpassingly ambiguous in its harmonic language. Hill seems on occasion to be exploring ideas that can be traced back to Bud Powell – not the straight bebop language so much as the more impressionistic things. There are curious little broken triplets and wide-interval phrases which seem to come straight from Bud's last recordings, and it would be interesting to know if Hill had been studying these at the time *Strange Serenade* was recorded.

***(*) **Verona Rag**

Soul Note 121110 *Hill (p solo).* 7/86.

The mid-'80s saw something of a revival in Hill's critical fortunes and 1986 was one of his busiest years in two decades. Of the available solo albums, by far the best is *Verona Rag*, a gloriously joyous set full of romping vamps, gentle ballad interludes and Hill's characteristic harmonic ambiguities. Not recognized as a standards-player, he invests 'Darn That Dream' with an almost troubling subtext in the bass and stops just short of reinventing the tune wholesale. The whole album has the sound of a man who is enjoying his music and who is no longer troubled by the idea of experimentation.

**** **Shades**

Soul Note 121113 *Hill; Clifford Jordan (ts); Rufus Reid (b); Ben Riley (d).* 7/86.

Far from settling back into a comfortable accommodation with a 'personal style', Hill's work of the later '80s was as adventurous as anything he had done since *Point Of Departure.* Reid and Riley create exactly the right background for him, taut but undogmatic, elastic around the end of phrases, constantly propulsive without becoming predictable. His kinship with Monk (whom Riley had accompanied) was always obvious, but it was increasingly clear that the differences were more important (some have suggested Herbie Nichols and Ellington as more fruitful sources) and that Hill was nobody's follower. *Shades* is one of the very best jazz albums of the decade. The two trio tracks – that is, with the pungent Jordan absent – are probably the finest since his debut on *Black Fire*, one of the missing Blue Notes. Hill has been inclined to avoid the conventional trio format. Like Monk, he operates better either solo or with horns, but on 'Tripping' and 'Ball Square' he is absolutely on top of things, trading bass lines with Reid and constantly stabbing in alternative accents. 'Monk's Glimpse' pays not altogether submissive homage to Hill's spiritual ancestor. The one slight misgiving about the album is its sound, which is a trifle dark, even on CD.

*** **Les Trinitaires**

Jazz Friends 2 *Hill (p solo).* 98.

*** **Dusk**

Palmetto 2057 *Hill; Ron Horton (t); Marty Ehrlich, Gregory Tardy (reeds); Scott Colley (b); Billy Drummond (d).* 10/99.

*** **A Beautiful Day**

Palmetto 2085 *As above, except add Dave Ballou (t); Mike Fahn, Joe Fielder, Charlie Gordon (tb); José Antonio Dávila (tba); John Savage (as, f); Aaron Stewart (ts); J. D. Parran (bs, bcl); Nasheet Waits (d); omit Drummond.* 1/02.

Dusk was warmly, even rapturously received on its release, less for its content than because a major African-American composer seemed at last able to come out of the shadows. We confess to finding it something of a disappointment. Hill's recording career was very sporadic indeed in the '90s. He sounds ring-rusty and a touch formulaic, even diffident in places. Some of the material had been worked out well in advance and on the live solo album, recorded in France at a small club and, we fear, hard to track down, he showcases a couple of pieces that would feature on the later ensemble session.

There's some solo material on *Dusk* as well. 'Tough Love' and 'Formulaic' feature the pianist on his own; both are quirky and idiosyncratic, but after repeated hearings one begins to wonder if that is all they are. 'Sept' and '15/8' (the latter worked through at Les Trinitaires) sound like exercises in metre; there's not much that is emotionally involving in either of them. The long opening 'Dusk' is about the best thing on the record, and there are two takes of it on the live CD as well, so detailed comparison is possible. There is also a heartfelt tribute to the late Thomas Chapin, 'T.C.', which features Ehrlich and Tardy on what sound like bass clarinets, though none are listed on the sleeve.

The apparent programme to the record is Jean Toomer's Harlem Renaissance classic, *Cane*, but its enigmatic lyricism is replaced by something drier and more abstract here. That said, any new record by Hill is a cause for rejoicing.

The follow-up on Palmetto was always going to be the key disc and *A Beautiful Day* probably deserves two cheers. It's a live recording, made at Birdland. The arrangements by trumpeter Horton are precise and idiomatic, but again Hill doesn't seem to be playing with much fire and his thunder is stolen by the two tenors on a reorchestrated 'Divine Revelation' and by Savage (on flute) and Ehrlich (bass clarinet) on the long 'Faded Beauty'. The pianist is more central to the shorter tracks and one almost wishes some of these charts had been restricted to a small group. For some odd reason, there is not much action for the trombonists, who are the anchor of the ensemble passages and it's Davila's tuba which stands out, though it collides in some passages with the relatively inflexible rhythm patterns of Colley and Waits. Parran brings his own style of dry excitement to 'J Di', a baritone solo that must rank as one of the veteran multi-instrumentalist's best performances on record.

Unmistakably an Andrew Hill record, but not (yet, at least) the performance to confirm his major standing.

Teddy Hill (1909–78)

TENOR SAXOPHONE, BANDLEADER

A competent saxophonist, but Hill was better as a bandleader, and his New York outfit of the mid-'30s was a fine one. It broke up in 1940 and Hill took over Minton's Playhouse, the bebop crucible.

*** **Uptown Rhapsody**

Hep CD 1033 *Hill; Bill Dillard, Bill Coleman, Shad Collins, Roy Eldridge, Dizzy Gillespie, Frankie Newton (t); Dicky Wells (tb); Russell Procope (cl, as); Howard Johnson (as); Chu Berry, Robert Carroll (ts); Cecil Scott (ts, bs); Sam Allen (p); John Smith (g); Richard Fulbright (b); Bill Beason (d); Beatrice Douglas (v).* 2/35–5/37.

★★(★) Teddy Hill 1935–1937
Classics 645 *As above.* 2/35–5/37.

Nowadays Hill is guaranteed his slight fingerhold on lasting celebrity for his custodianship of Minton's Playhouse in New York City, the most pungent crucible of the bebop movement. By that point, his own musical career was pretty much over, but he had led a short-lived but quite significant big band which numbered among its most illustrious alumni Chu Berry, Bill Coleman, Roy Eldridge and Dizzy Gillespie. These two items are in pretty direct competition, and it behoves us to say that the Hep, intelligently and very faithfully remastered by John R. T. Davies, is the only one to consider. The 26 tracks in question, from 'Lookie, Lookie, Lookie, Here Comes Cookie' in February 1926 to 'Blue Rhythm Fantasy' a decade and a few months later, are the entire output of the orchestra. The first track is dominated by a blistering Eldridge solo; the last session marks Diz's first recorded solo, on 'King Porter Stomp'. This may seem a by-way in the history of the music, but it is one worth exploring.

Earl Hines (1905–89)

PIANO, VOCAL

Raised in Pittsburgh, Hines began leading groups in Chicago and soon teamed with Louis Armstrong in the later Hot Five. From 1929 he ran the band at the Grand Terrace Ballroom for 12 years. Ran another big band (with many prototype boppers in the ranks), then joined the Armstrong All Stars but left in 1951. More club work followed, but Hines was at a low ebb when a series of New York concerts made him a star all over again in 1964. Thereafter he worked constantly until his death. Along with Tatum, the greatest piano innovator and stylist of the pre-bop era, who outlived most of his contemporaries.

★★★(★) Earl Hines 1928–1932
Classics 545 *Hines; Shirley Clay, George Mitchell, Charlie Allen, George Dixon, Walter Fuller (t); William Franklin (tb, v); Lester Boone, Omer Simeon (cl, as, bs); Darnell Howard (cl, as, vn); Toby Turner (cl, as); Cecil Irwin (cl, ts); Claude Roberts (bj, g); Lawrence Dixon (g); Quinn Wilson (bb, b); Hayes Alvis (bb); Wallace Bishop (d).* 12/28–6/32.

★★★(★) Earl Hines 1932–1934
Classics 514 *As above, except add Louis Taylor, Trummy Young, Kenneth Stuart (tb), Jimmy Mundy (cl, ts), Herb Jeffries (v); omit Clay, Mitchell, Boone, Turner, Roberts and Alvis.* 7/32–3/34.

★★★(★) Earl Hines 1934–1937
Classics 528 *As above, except add Milton Fletcher (t), Budd Johnson (ts), The Palmer Brothers, Ida Mae James (v); omit Franklin.* 9/34–2/37.

★★★★ Earl Hines Collection: Piano Solos 1928–1940
Collector's Classics COCD 11 *Hines (p solo).* 12/28–2/40.

★★★(★) Swingin' Down
Hep CD 1003 *As appropriate discs above.* 6/32–3/34.

Earl Hines had already played on some of the greatest of all jazz records – with Louis Armstrong's Hot Five – before he made any sessions under his own name. The piano solos he made in Long Island and Chicago, one day apart in December 1928, are collected on the first Classics CD – a youthful display of brilliance that has seldom been surpassed. His ambidexterity, enabling him to finger runs and break up and supplant rhythms at will, is still breathtaking, and his range of pianistic devices is equalled only by Tatum and Taylor. But these dozen pieces were a preamble to a career which, in the '30s, was concerned primarily with bandleading. The remainder of the first Classics disc is filled with the first recordings by the orchestra which Hines led at Chicago's Grand Terrace Club for ten years, from December 1928. Their 1929 sessions struggle to find an identity, and only the leader cuts any impressive figures.

The 1932–4 sessions on the second record are better played, better organized and full of brilliant Hines. The surprising thing may be Hines's relatively subordinate role within the band: he had few aspirations to compose or arrange, entrusting those duties to several other hands (including Fuller, Mundy, Johnson, Crowder and Wilson); he revelled instead in the role of star soloist within what were increasingly inventive frameworks. By 1934 the band was at its first peak, with fine Mundy arrangements like 'Cavernism' (including a startling violin solo by Darnell Howard) and 'Fat Babes' and Wilson's vigorous revisions of older material such as 'Maple Leaf Rag' and 'Wolverine Blues'. It's a pity that the chronology has split the 1934 sessions between the second and third Classics volumes. Hines is a wonder throughout, both in solo and in the commentaries with which he counters the arrangements. The other principal soloist is Walter Fuller, a spare, cool-to-hot stylist whose occasional vocals are agreeable copies of Armstrong. The 1934–7 disc shows an unfortunate decline in the consistency of the material, and their move to Vocalion to record coincided with a dissipation of the band's energy.

All three records feature transfers which are respectable rather than notably effervescent, which is disappointing – the sound of the original recordings is excellent, as John R. T. Davies had shown on some earlier LP transfers for Hep, and these have finally appeared on *Swingin' Down*, which would be our first choice for a Hines band disc from this period. However, Davies has also done the remastering for the piano solos collection on Collector's Classics, which covers all the 1928 pieces, five takes of two solos from 1932/3, and a pair of titles from 1940. Excellent sound and strongly recommended.

★★★ Earl Hines 1937–1939
Classics 538 *Hines; Walter Fuller (t, v); Milton Fletcher, Charlie Allen, Freddy Webster, George Dixon, Edward Sims (t); Louis Taylor, Trummy Young, Kenneth Stuart, Joe McLewis, Ed Burke, John Ewing (tb); Omer Simeon (cl, as, bs); Leroy Harris (cl, as, v); Darnell Howard (cl, as); Budd Johnson (cl, as, ts); William Randall, Leon Washington (cl, ts); Robert Crowder (ts); Lawrence Dixon, Claude Roberts (g); Quinn Wilson (b); Wallace Bishop, Alvin Burroughs, Oliver Coleman (d); Ida Mae James (v).* 37–39.

★★★ Earl Hines 1939–1940
Classics 567 *As above, except add Shirley Clay, Harry Jackson, Rostelle Reese, Leroy White (t), Edward Fant (tb), Scoops Carey (as), Franz Jackson, Jimmy Mundy (ts), Hurley Ramey (g), Truck Parham (b), Billy Eckstine, Laura Rucker, Madeline Green (v); omit Allen, Taylor, Young, Stuart, Howard, Randall, Washington, Dixon, Bishop and James.* 10/39–12/40.

★★★ Earl Hines 1941
Classics 621 *Hines; Harry Jackson, Tommy Enoch, Benny Harris, Freddy Webster, Jesse Miller (t); Joe McLewis, George Hunt, Edward Fant, John Ewing, Nat Atkinson, Gerald Valentine (tb); Leroy Harris (cl, as, v); Scoops Carey (cl, as);*

William Randall, Budd Johnson, Robert Crowder, Franz Jackson (ts); Hurley Ramey (g); Truck Parham (b); Rudolph Taylor (d); Billy Eckstine, Madeline Greene, The Three Varieties (v). 4–11/41.

*** Piano Man!

ASV AJA 5131 *Similar to above.* 28–40.

It wasn't until the emergence of Budd Johnson as an arranging force that the Hines band recovered some of its flair and spirit. The most renowned of the later pieces – 'Grand Terrace Shuffle' and 'G.T. Stomp' – are both on the 1937–9 CD, which follows the band as it tries to recapture its earlier zip. Johnson himself is a significant soloist, and Hines softens into a more amiable version of his daredevil self. The important thing about the 1940 tracks, on Classics 567, is the arrival of Billy Eckstine, who would influence the band's move towards modernism and first provide it with a couple of major hits, starting with the 1940 'Jelly, Jelly'. He is featured further on the final Classics CD in the sequence, which also features arrangements from several hands – Johnson, Benny Harris, Jackson – and which includes a couple of imposing Hines features in 'The Father Jumps' and 'The Earl'. These tracks haven't been reissued very often, and they deserve to be better known.

Piano Man! sounds good for the most part, though some of the later Bluebird sides are inexplicably gritty, and the choice of tracks – including Armstrong Hot Fives and Bechet's 'Blues In Thirds' concentrates more on Hines the soloist than on Hines the bandleader.

**(*) Earl Hines 1942–1945

Classics 876 *Hines; George Dixon (t, as); Pee Wee Jackson, Maurice McConnell, Jesse Miller, Charlie Shavers, Palmer Davis, Billy Douglas, Willie Cook (t); Ray Nance (t, vn); George Hunt, Joe McLewis, Gerald Valentine (tb); Druie Bess, Walter Harris, Gus Chappell (tb); Rene Hall (tb, g); George Carry, Tab Smith, Johnny Hodges, Lloyd Smith, Leroy Harris, Scoops Carey (as); William Randall, Budd Johnson, Flip Phillips, Robert Crowder, Kermit Scott, Wardell Gray (ts); John Williams (bs); Skeeter Best, Tommy Kay, Al Casey (g); Red Norvo (vib); Truck Parham, Al Lucas, Oscar Pettiford, Gene Thomas, Al Hall (b); Rudy Traylor, Jo Jones, Big Sid Catlett, Chick Booth, Specs Powell (d); Billy Eckstine, Betty Roche, Madeline Green, The Three Varieties (v).* 3/42–1/45.

*** Earl Hines And The Duke's Men

Delmark DD-470 *Hines; Rex Stewart (c); Cat Anderson, Lee Brown, Don Devilla, Archie Johnson, Joe Strand (t); Lawrence Brown, Joe Britton, Floyd Brady, LeRoy Hardison, George Stevenson (tb); Curby Alexander, Vince Royal, Johnny Hodges (as); Jimmy Hamilton (cl, ts); John Hartzfield, Vincent McCleary, Flip Phillips (ts); Harry Carney (bs); Marlowe Morris, Horatio Duran (p); Al Casey, Teddy Walters (g); Oscar Pettiford, Bob Paige (b); Sonny Greer, Big Sid Catlett, Bobby Donaldson (d); Betty Roche (v).* 4/44–5/47.

The *1942–1945* Classics set is a motley set of tracks where Hines seems more sideman than leader. A final and fairly undistinguished big-band date for Bluebird is followed by a trio date for Signature with Al Casey and Oscar Pettiford, Hines uncharacteristically quiet; a brash quintet session led by Charlie Shavers for Keynote; and the more interesting sextet date for Apollo, which is also on the Delmark disc. Hines then returns to big bands for two tracks for Bluebird from 1945.

The Delmark disc is more interesting. Besides the sextet tracks with Hodges and Nance, the other groups are led by either Sonny Greer or Cat Anderson (Anderson's mysterious line-up of unknowns may actually be pseudonymously hiding more famous names). Some of these are minor mixtures of swing and jump-band R&B, but there are many nice touches – from Hodges, Stewart, Nance and Hines himself, though Anderson's usual top notes are a bore – and it's a useful sweep through an otherwise obscure period for many of these players. Good transfers.

*** Earl Hines 1945-1947

Classics 1041 *Hines; Arthur Walker, Vernon Smith, Willie Cook, Palmer Davis, Geechie Smith, Charlie Anderson (t); Bennie Harris, Joe McLewis, Clifton Small, Druie Bess, Walter Harris, Gordon Alston (tb); Scoops Carry, Lloyd Smith, Thomas Crump (as); Wardell Gray, Kermit Scott, Ernie Wilkins, Budd Johnson (ts); John Williams, Wallace Brodis (bs); Bill Thompson (vib); Bill Dougherty (vn); Skeeter Best (g); Gene Thomas, Oscar Pettiford (b); Calvin Ponder (b); Chick Booth, Rudy Traylor, Gus Johnson (d); Lord Essex, Johnny Hartman, Dolores Parker, Arthur Walker, Melrose Colbert (v).* 9/45–47.

Hines's 1947 big band isn't well known for its records, and this is an interesting sweep through the surviving recordings. Wardell Gray gets some solos as well as the leader, but there's nothing very forward-looking in the arrangements, and the performances aren't so much lacking in spirit as directionless. Vocal admirers will enjoy the four handsome contributions from Johnny Hartman, very much in the Eckstine mould, and Hines himself remains inimitable. Hard to say how good the transfers are from what are probably indifferent original recordings, but don't expect hi-fi: some of them are distinctly rough.

*** Earl Hines 1947–1949

Classics 1120 *Hines; Duke Garrett (t, v); Buck Clayton (t); Bobby Plater (cl, as); Barney Bigard (cl); Morris Lane (ts); Charlie Fowlkes (bs); Eddie South (vn); Skeeter Best, Billy Mackel, Floyd Smith (g); Calvin Ponder, Charles Mingus, Arvell Shaw (b); Gus Johnson, Curley Hamner, Big Sid Catlett, Wallace Bishop (d); Wini Brown (v).* 12/47–11/49.

Rather a thin period for Hines on record, since at the time he was in Louis Armstrong's All Stars. There's a strange session featuring, of all people, Eddie South, and another where Hines plays and sings on 'The Sheik Of Araby'. Four tracks with a quartet featuring Floyd Smith include the intriguing 'Bop Omlette'; but rather more substantial is the 1949 Paris date with Buck Clayton, Barney Bigard, Arvell Shaw and Wallace Bishop: though poorly recorded, the principals strut their stuff in some style. A scrappy sequence altogether but not without some rewards.

**(*) Earl Hines 1949-1952

Classics 1288 *Hines; Jonah Jones (t); Bennie Green (tb); Aaron Sachs (cl, ts); Arvell Shaw, Al McKibbon, Tommy Potter (b); Wallace Bishop, J. C. Heard, Osie Johnson (d); Helen Merrill, Etta Jones, Lonnie Satin (v).* 11/49–12/52.

Some scarce tracks here. One of the first appearances of the notorious 'Boogie Woogie On The St Louis Blues', with its endless right-hand tremolo (here kept within an acceptable three minutes) and Fatha giving us his command of the lingo in 'Singing For My French Brothers'. Thereafter it's back to New York for eight trio titles and a very obscure 1952 session for the D'Oro label, with vocals by Helen Merrill (making her debut),

Etta Jones and Lonnie Satin. The trio titles (made for Columbia, for their new series of ten-inch LP albums) are good, brisk fun. The D'Oro pieces, with Jones, Green and Sachs, are a very odd lot – considering that the label was supposedly set up by a Hines fan, why did he give the singers so much space and the piano so little? A fascinating listen, although the overall musical rewards are decidedly modest.

***** The Chicago Dates**

Storyville STCD 6037 *Hines; Muggsy Spanier (t, c); Jimmy Archey (tb); Darnell Howard (cl); Pops Foster (b); Earl Watkins (d).* 54.

The pairing of Hines and Spanier seems surprising on the face of it, but Muggsy was an amiable soul, content to work in a congenial situation, and the set-list here at least includes tunes which were a little different to Earl's usual list of familiars. In the end this is just a businesslike, traditional date from a good professional group, with nobody particularly dominating. The live recording is fair enough.

*****(*) Another Monday Date**

Prestige 24043-2 *Hines; Eddie Duran (g); Dean Riley (b); Earl Watkins (d).* 55–56.

Hines entered the LP era rather cautiously, and the '50s weren't his greatest decade on record. After several years with the Louis Armstrong All Stars, he found himself somewhat adrift as hard bop took over the jazz mainstream; but the mainstream itself was beginning a revival as swing-era musicians found their feet in the microgroove era, and in 1956 the pianist cut a pair of sessions for Fantasy which showed his old powers intact and unfettered by time constraints. One set of Waller interpretations is coupled with a collection of originals and, though the sidemen are almost a distraction from his own mercurial way with time, Hines sweeps through the music.

****(*) Earl Hines' Dixieland All-Stars**

Storyville STCD 6036 *Hines; Marty Marsala (t); Jimmy Archey (tb); Darnel Howard (cl); Red Garland (b); Joe Watkins (d).* 9/55.

Three broadcasts from The Hangover Club in San Francisco. This isn't the place to hear Hines, who seems very low in the balance, but there's some effusive if inelegant playing from Marsala and Archey.

***** Paris One Night Stand**

Emarcy 548207-2 *Hines; Guy Pedersen (b); Gus Wallez (d).* 11/57.

A studio set, not a concert, and there was controversy at the time that producer Boris Vian had forced this bass and drums pairing on Hines. In the event it's a rather strange, stop-start sort of session: some tunes are characteristic, full-flow Hines, such as 'Hallelujah', and others find him seemingly listless and bored.

***** Grand Reunion**

Verve 528137-2 *Hines; Roy Eldridge (t); Coleman Hawkins (ts); George Tucker (b); Oliver Jackson (d).* 3/65.

****(*) Live! Aalborg, Denmark, 1965**

Storyville STCD 8222 *Hines; Morten Hansen (b); Jorgen Kureer (d).* 4/65.

***** At Home**

Delmark DD-212 *Hines (p solo).* 69.

Hines really came back into his own in the '60s. He was able to unleash all the rococo elements in his methods at whatever length he chose, and the so-called 'trumpet style' – using tremolo to suggest a horn player's vibrato and taking a linear path even when playing an ensemble role – began to sound modern by dint of its individuality. Nobody played like Hines, influential though he had been. He was more or less rediscovered in 1964, following New York concerts that were greeted as a sensation, and thereafter embarked on regular tours and records. *Grand Reunion* effectively replaces an earlier issue on Xanadu. Eldridge and Hawkins were guests with Hines and they play on 8 of the 11 tracks, while Hines elaborates on a stack of tunes via three medleys. Recording is less than ideal, with Jackson's cymbals sounding all too loudly in the mix, but it isn't too bad. There is better playing by all three masters on other records, but the meeting has plenty of charisma and some genuinely inspired playing in patches.

It's hard to go wrong with Hines on record, but one should be a cautious in approaching some of his live recordings: the fondness for medleys and a weakness for an over-extended right-hand tremolo betray a hankering for applause which, merited though it may be, occasionally tips his style into excess. The Danish concert is insubstantial and is compromised by the noisy recording. Medleys take up much of the set, and Hines's closing party piece of 'St Louis Blues' is best heard only once.

At Home is a mild disappointment. There are too many slow tunes and too much meditation, perhaps brought on by the relaxed surroundings (he was recorded on his own piano, at home), and only when he gets to the marvellous finale of 'The Cannery Walk' does the best of Hines break through.

***** Once Upon A Time**

Impulse! 654492-2 *Hines; Cat Anderson, Billy Berry, Ray Nance, Clark Terry (t); Lawrence Brown, Buster Cooper (tb); Pee Wee Russell (cl); Johnny Hodges, Russell Procope (as); Jimmy Hamilton (ts, cl); Paul Gonsalves, Harold Ashby (ts); Richard Davis, Aaron Bell (b); Elvin Jones, Sonny Greer (d).* 1/66.

If you ever wondered what the Ellington band would sound like with Hines at the piano – and Elvin Jones at the drums! – this unlikely session provided something like the answer. They don't shirk the comparison, since there are four Ellington or Hodges tunes, including 'Black And Tan Fantasy'. In the event, however, it's all rather unremarkable. Hines takes a relatively quiescent role as band pianist, perhaps being respectful for the absent Duke, and Elvin (who shares duties with Greer) behaves himself. The horns take the major honours, including Pee Wee on 'Blues In My Flat'.

***** At The Party**

Delmark DE-535 *Hines; Johnny Rae (vib); Jack Crowley (g); Larry Richardson (b); Kahlil Mahdee (d); Escovedo (perc).* 5/70.

A San Francisco concert from the start of a new decade. The band isn't anything special and it's an odd instrumentation for a Hines group, but Earl's the perfect pro and the audience has plenty to enjoy.

*****(*) Four Jazz Giants**

Solo Art SACD 111/2 2CD *Hines (p solo).* 7/71.

Not quite on the exalted level of the Ellington set listed below, but this was still an unusually well-prepared and handsome set of sessions, one each in dedication to W. C. Handy, Hoagy

Carmichael and Louis Armstrong – the latter recorded only days after Pops's death. Hines chooses his favourite rocking mid-tempo for many of the tunes, but when he goes up a gear, as in the labyrinthine 'Struttin' With Some Barbecue', he's miraculous. There's a huge exploration of 'Star Dust', many of the Handy themes contain some of his most detailed examinations of the blues, and the Armstrong tunes find him at his most lyrical. In full and lifelike sound (though with a degree of tape hiss), this fine package is top-notch Hines.

***** Live At The New School**
Chiaroscuro CRD 157 *Hines (p solo).* 3/73.

*****(*) Masters Of Jazz Vol. 2**
Storyville STCD 4102 *Hines (p solo).* 3/74.

*****(*) Plays Cole Porter**
New World 80501-2 *Hines (p solo).* 4/74.

A spate of solo recording meant that, in his old age, Hines was being comprehensively documented at last, and he rose to the challenge with consistent inspirational force. The Storyville disc strings together six standards, and the playing is extravagantly strong and elaborate, with a couple of tunes that Hines seldom recorded ('As Long As I Live' and 'My Shining Hour') adding some spice. The 16-minute Fats Waller medley on *New School* and other flag-wavers let down the superior aspects of the set, but it has a share of Hines in regal form: he liked to play for people, and some of the pyrotechnics are *echt*-Hines.

CORE COLLECTION

****** Earl Hines Plays Duke Ellington**
New World NW 361/2 2CD *Hines (p solo).* 12/71–4/75.

*****(*) Earl Hines Plays Duke Ellington Vol. 2**
New World 80532 *Hines (p solo).* 12/71–3/74.

Made over a period of four years, these are much more than casual one-giant-nods-to-another records. Hines was cajoled by Stanley Dance into looking into many unfamiliar Ellington tunes and creating a memorial (Ellington died around the time of the final sessions) which is surely among the best tributes to the composer on record. Since Hines's more aristocratic touches are close in feeling to Ellington's own, there is an immediate affinity in such pieces as 'Love You Madly' and 'Black And Tan Fantasy'. But Hines finds a wealth of new incident in warhorses such as 'Mood Indigo' and 'Sophisticated Lady' and he turns 'The Shepherd' and 'Black Butterfly' into extravagant fantasies which go far beyond any of Ellington's own revisionist approaches. Even a simple piece such as 'C Jam Blues' receives a fascinating, rhythmic treatment, and the voicings conjured up for 'I'm Beginning To See The Light' upset conventional wisdom about Ellingtonian interpretation. In his variety of resource, Hines also points up all the devices he passed on to Powell, Monk and virtually every other post-swing pianist. A memorable lesson, and a fine tribute to two great piano players, spread over two hours of music. New World have now released a second volume, which covers the remainder of the sessions. This is just slightly less interesting as far as tune titles and interpretations go, but Hines collectors will surely want both.

*****(*) Hot Sonatas**
Chiaroscuro CR(D) 145 *Hines; Joe Venuti (vn).* 10/75.

***** In New Orleans**
Chiaroscuro CR(D) 200 *Hines (p solo).* 11/77.

Hines's final years offered fewer recording opportunities. *In New Orleans* would not be our first choice for one of his solo dates, but there are still felicities to savour, such as the almost demure warmth of 'I'm A Little Brown Bird'. *Hot Sonatas,* though, is an invigorating display by two inveterate swingers. With no previous meetings and no rehearsals, the results are just occasionally scatty, but more often each man is swept along on the jubilation of the other's playing. 'C Jam Blues' becomes almost Byzantine in its ramifications. Bravo, Joe and Earl! Five extra rehearsals and alternatives are taken from a TV video track which was made at the sessions.

Milt Hinton (1910–2000)

BASS

A great witness to most eras of the music, Hinton was playing with Tiny Parham in Chicago in the '20s. He went on to play and record with thousands of others, from Eddie South to Branford Marsalis, and since he was a dedicated photographer there is a picture of most of the occasions too.

***** East Coast Jazz/5**
Rhino 74235 *Hinton; Tony Scott (cl); Dick Katz (p); Osie Johnson (d).* 55.

***** Here Swings The Judge**
Progressive 7120 *Hinton; John Faddis (t); Budd Johnson (ts, bs); Frank Wess (ts); Ben Webster (ts, p); John Bunch (p); Jo Jones (d).* 64.

Hinton was a great entertainer, playing, singing and rapping about the good old days with undiminished vigour into his eighties. He was quite at ease working with players almost two generations below him. He had such an accumulated head of experience that he could pick – or, failing that, talk – his way out of almost any situation. The reappearance of the early East Coast set is a bonus. It's valuable for a glimpse of Tony Scott (who is listed under his original name of Anthony Sciacca on the sleeve) and for a bonus version of 'Milt To The Hilt'. The sound is a bit flat and boxy; even bassist-leaders didn't get the best of service in those days.

Here Swings The Judge was originally released on Harry Lim's Jazz Door label. It's one of Milt's earliest sessions as a leader, with an all-star cast and some fine soloing opportunities all round. A duo performance of 'Sophisticated Lady' with Ben Webster adds new dimensions to the song. A bonus take of 'Blues For The Judge' offers a further sample of Budd Johnson's baritone saxophone, but what we wouldn't give for extra takes of Ben and Milt together. Faddis does his Gillespie routine with typical conviction, sounding bright and breezy on 'Blue Skies' and more reserved on 'It Had To Be You' (two takes). The disappearance of Jazz Door was a pity but the catalogue's partial return in new livery is very welcome.

***** Bassically With Blue**
Black & Blue 890 *Hinton; Cliff Smalls (p); Sam Woodyard (d).* 74.

Arguably the best of Milt's few available small-group sets, this French-recorded set covers some favourite themes (including 'Joshua Fit De Battle Of Jericho', a staple of Milt's) and some original themes like 'Me And You', 'Mona Is Feeling Lonely', the cleverly paced 'Walking Through The Woodyard' and Small's 'Toneing Down'. As always, there's a lot of prominent bass playing, with Milt working at both extremes of his register, plucking high, fine notes one minute and going for low slapped rumbles the next. A bit of brightness has been lost in the mastering or remastering, but the sound is fairly good otherwise.

***** Back To Bass-ics**

Progressive 7084 *Hinton; Jane Jarvis (p); Louie Bellson (d).* 9/84.

A delightfully swinging trio set which gives Milt as much solo space as he's ever had on one of his own dates. Jarvis is a revelation, full of quirky and resonant ideas and their interplay (Bellson is relatively reserved throughout) on 'Fascinatin' Rhythm', 'Satin Doll', 'Prelude To A Kiss' and 'Joshua Fit De Battle Of Jericho' is varied and stylist. The sound isn't perfect by any means and some of Milt's solo spots are prone to rumble and distortion. Generally good, though, and the playing makes up for any minor technical insufficiencies.

***** Old Man Time**

Chiaroscuro CRD 310 2CD *Hinton; Doc Cheatham (t); Eddie Barefield (as, ts); Buddy Tate (ts); Red Richards (p); Al Casey (g); Gus Johnson (d); Cab Calloway, Dizzy Gillespie, Joe Williams (v).* 3/89–3/90.

Like a great many rhythm players, the discography is huge, but very little is credited to him, so the slightly overcooked two-volume *Old Man Time* has to be seen as a kind of *This Is Your Life* accolade, complete with all-star walk-on cast. The band, arranged and conducted by Buck Clayton, gives him plenty of room for his party pieces on the big bull fiddle, while the Mississippi voice spins its yarns; a special feature of the set is two long monologues, or 'Jazzspeaks'. Milt switches to bass guitar for a couple of numbers with Danny Barker. Joe Williams, Dizzy Gillespie and Cab Calloway all provide guest vocals and there is the intriguing (and as far as we know, rare) sound of Flip Phillips on clarinet behind Joe on 'Four Or Five Times'. One of the highlights of the set is the work of a band known as The Survivors, average age somewhat over 80; if they'd known they were going to live so long, they'd probably have taken better care of themselves. It's a fun set, entertaining but lightweight and with little enough of the solid bass-playing that has made Milt such an important figure in the business.

***** The Basement Tapes**

Chiaroscuro 222 *Hinton; Warren Vache (t); Frank Wess (ts, f); Kenny Davern (cl); Janice Friedman, James Williams (p); Howard Alden (g); Kenny Washington (b); Jackie Williams (d); Sylvia Sims (v).* 89–90.

Another 'and friends' set compiled over a couple of years and with another big, albeit less stellar, cast. This time round, 'Old Man Time' is a feature for Kenny Davern backed by Howard Alden. It's a lovely, wry piece. The first three titles are played with Warren Vache and the excellent Janice Friedman, another of the female players Milt backed; 'Raincheck' and 'Johnny Come Lately' are taken at unfamiliar metres, but both highly effective. 'Fascinating Rhythm' is a two-bass reading with one of the leading lights of the next generation, Kenny Washington, and a bit of a *tour de force*. The songs with Sylvia Sims are quite nice and there is some typically good saxophone and flute from Frank Wess.

For all the something-for-everyone good value, as a memorial to Milt, the set was possibly less effective than it might have been, particularly with good compilations to come; on the other hand, as an addition to a still small solo discography it marks a very welcome release.

****(*) The Trio: 1994**

Chiaroscuro 322 *Hinton; Derek Smith (p); Bobby Rosengarden (d).* 1/94.

This time, Milt's attempts to jolly things along fall flat. A very bland and one-dimensional set by the great man's usual high standard, and little for any but the most devoted collector. The following year saw his major label debut (aged 85!) with Sony's now deleted *Laughing At Life*. A shame it's not still around.

*****(*) The Judge At His Best**

Chiaroscuro 219 *Hinton; Ruby Braff (c); Flip Phillips, Zoot Sims (ts); Kenny Davern, Bob Wilber (cl); Lionel Hampton (vib); John Bunch, Dick Hyman, Jay McShann, Derek Smith, Ralph Sutton (p); Bucky Pizzarelli (g); Danny Barker (g, v); Joe Venuti (vn); Dottie Dodgion, Gus Johnson, Cliff Leeman, Ray Mosca, Bobby Rosengarden (d).* 73–79, 89–95.

Milt died in his ninetieth year and pretty soon the tributes started appearing. The most valid of all is the Chiaroscuro compilation, which brings together 18 tracks from his two periods at the label. Given that there was a decade break in his involvement with Chiaroscuro, there is some discontinuity of tone and material, but Milt's approach scarcely changed over the years and as a showcase *The Judge At His Best* is excellent. 'Milt's Rap' is an ideal introduction to the man himself, and joyous themes like 'Jumpin' At The Woodside' and 'Shine' (with fellow string man Joe Venuti) are classic performances. Cameos from Flip Phillips and Jay McShann are a bonus.

Al Hirt (1922–1999)

TRUMPET

Born in New Orleans, Hirt played trumpet in undistinguished surroundings before landing a contract with the Audio Fidelity label, which pushed him through hi-fi magazines and turned him into a star. During the '60s, he and Herb Alpert were the most popular trumpeters in America. He ran his own club in New Orleans for many years and played an uncomplicated, noisy but entertaining style of Dixieland.

****(*) The Best Of Dixieland: Al Hirt**

Verve 549362-2 *Hirt; Bob Havens (tb); Pete Fountain (cl, ts); Roy Zimmerman (p); Bob Coquille (b); Paul Edwards (d).* 56.

This session actually pre-dates Hirt's huge commercial success at Audio Fidelity, and is prehistoric for him and his great sidekick Pete Fountain. They play a suitably rowdy bunch of chestnuts from the idiom. Hirt sold millions of records but, as with Liberace and Mantovani, it's now hard to recall what any of them were called. He was a very American, homegrown phenomenon: although he was perhaps his country's most popular trumpeter during the '60s, he made relatively little impact elsewhere. This is actually not a particularly flattering memorial to him: the music has a raw, almost furious momentum, but it's very different in spirit to the great black New Orleans groups and the sneering notion that this was 'Dixieland for tourists' seems not far from the truth, at least here. If someone compiles a strong best-of from the Audio Fidelity records, there will be a worthy record under his name.

Fred Ho (born 1957)

BARITONE SAXOPHONE, CHINESE INSTRUMENTS, BANDLEADER

Ho's brand of engaged and ebullient big-band jazz has obvious ties to Charles Mingus, but there are many other influences at work as well, not least a desire to synthesize modern jazz and Eastern influences. This is most effective when it is least self-consciously signalled and when music is given priority over protest and ideology. Ho's baritone isn't a virtuosic voice; drawing somewhat on Carney, it's intended as the sheet anchor of the ensemble, holding the middle together and giving shape to ambitious structures.

***** Tomorrow Is Now**
Soul Note 121117 *Ho; Sam Furnace (as, ts); Sayyd Abdul Al-Khabyyr, Al Givens (ss, ts, f); Richard Clements (p); Jon Jang (p); Kyoto Fujiwara (b); Taru Alexander (d); Carleen Robinson (v).* 85.

****(*) We Refuse To Be Used And Abused**
Soul Note 1211167 *Ho; Sam Furnace (as, ss, f); Hafez Modir (ts, f); Jon Jang (p); Kyoto Fujiwara (b); Royal Hartigan (perc).* 11/87.

*****(*) The Underground Railway To My Heart**
Soul Note 121267 *Ho; Martin Wehner (tb); Sam Furnace, James Norton (as, ss); David Bindman, Hafez Modirzadeh, Allen Won (ts); Francis Wong (ts, f, picc); Peter Madsen (p); Kyoto Fujiwara, John Shifflet (b); Royal Hartigan (d, perc); Pei Sheng Shen (sona, ob); You Qun Fu (erhu); Pauline Hong (san shuen); Cindy Zuoxin Wang (v).* 90–93.

This is powerfully advocated music from a 'rainbow coalition' of fine young players, Afro- and Asian-Americans in the main. Houn, who has more recently phoneticized his name to Ho, has a big, powerful sound reminiscent of Harry Carney, and this sets the tone for ensembles with a strongly Ellingtonian cast. The title of the first album sets up all sorts of different expectations – from Ornette Coleman's *Tomorrow Is The Question* to Max Roach's *Freedom Now* suite – which are not so much confounded as skirted. There would seem to be little place for prettiness in music as aggressively programmatic as this, but the band plays with surprising delicacy and unfailing taste. CD transfer flatters Ho's skills as an orchestrator.

The second album is more bitty and has a much less coherent sound. There is also an unwonted and mostly unwelcome stridency. Unlike Charlie Haden and his Liberation Music Orchestra, Ho still hadn't quite found a way of synthesizing political urgency with lyricism. That's largely addressed in the excellent *Underground Railway*. It starts unpromisingly with a noodling ethnic jam featuring the double-reed *sona* over bass and drums. What follows is the title-piece: a long, elegantly communicated suite which Ho describes as 'anti-bourgeois boogie-woogie'. Here the Ellington (and Carney) influence is unmistakable and in character. Too much of the remainder is bland *chinoiserie*: full, unfamiliar sonorities used for their own sake. There is, though, an interesting 'revisit' to Billie Holiday's 'Strange Fruit' and a glorious reading of Tizol's 'Caravan'. They make it possible to forgive the multilingual 'Auld Lang Syne' (oh, go on, it's not that bad), or the two closing selections from an 'epic' score called *Journey Beyond The West: The New Adventures Of Monkey*. Nuts to that. Otherwise excellent.

***** Yes Means Yes, No Means No, Whatever She Wears, Wherever She Goes**
Koch 7897 *Ho; Robert Levin (tb, perc); Sam Furnace (as); David Bindman (ts, perc); Diana Herold (vib, perc); Kiyoto Fujiwara (b); Royal Hartigan (d, perc).* 98.

***** Warrior Sisters: A New American Opera**
Koch 7899 *Ho; Sam Furnace (as, f); Andy Laster (bs); Richard Harper (p); Diana Herold (vib, perc); Santi Debriano (b); Royal Hartigan (d, perc); Anthony Alioto, Lynn Randolph, Peter Stewart, Kenneth Williams, Shan Min Yu (v); additional personnel as above.* 99.

The title-piece of the first of these is a 22½-minute suite on a fairly rugged feminist theme. The political agenda of the Afro-Asian Music Ensemble moves in and out of focus, but here the music seems paramount and the playing is both committedly passionate and also admirably orderly. There is a reworking of John Coltrane's love theme 'Naima' at the centre of the set, sounding as if Ellington might have had a hand in the writing. Fine cover art of a nude Ho toting his baritone and looking as if he might be auditioning for Fishbone.

Warrior Sisters is billed as an opera but is really not much more than a loose suite of thematically linked songs with a strong political message. The best parallel for pieces like 'The Political Condition Of Amerikkka' is probably Ornette Coleman's *Skies Of America* but the vocal component constantly drags the album back to a literal and polemic vein that blunts some quite radical music-making.

*****(*) Once Upon A Time In Chinese America ...**
Innova 550 *Ho; Sam Furnace (as); David Bindman (ts); Diana Herold (marim, vib, perc); Aayodele Maakheru (b); uncredited (d, perc); Shyaporn Theerakulstit (narrator).* 12/99.

Ho's more recent records haven't easily found their way to us, but this score for 'a martial arts ballet' is great fun. The musicians are rather upstaged by a marvellous performance by Shyaporn Theerakulstit as the fiery narrator of the story, and clearly without the visual element of the dancers there's a pretty huge gulf between CD and in-person performance. Cutting it in a single day in the studio, the musicians presumably felt that they'd performed the piece often enough to allow for limited recording time, although there are still points which might have used some tidying-up. Still, a disc of enormous character – and, in passing, the latest Afro-Asian Ensemble, here no bigger than a sextet (though the drum and percussion roles mysteriously are uncredited), make a powerful sound.

***** All Power To The People: The Black Panther Suite**
Innova 585 DVD *Ho; Sam Furnace (as); David Bindman (ts, perc); Diana Herold (vib, mar, perc); Michele Navazio (g); Wesley Brown (b, perc); Royal Hartigan (d, perc); Jayne Cortez, Andrea Lockett (v).* 02.

Again, the reception of this ambitious work, presented as a complete audio-visual experience, is conditioned by the political agenda. The Black Panthers are presented as fallen American heros, dancers in a world of locksteps and prison marches. Ho's music is, as ever, powerful and evocative, and more than ever reminiscent of past models, though Mingus's chanted agit-prop pieces are probably a better analogy than Ellington or Coleman or even Sun Ra. The leader plays some of his best solos for some time on the disc, aided by Furnace and guitarist Navazio, who between them crank up the energy level considerably.

Radical poet Jayne Cortez's texts are an important aspect of the whole, and impressively well integrated. The visual element, derived from what was intended as a ballet suite, uses old propaganda and information materials to create a parallel collage. Impressive and, given a measure of sympathy with the subjects, very powerful.

Steve Hobbs

VIBRAPHONE

The talented North Carolinan studied at Berklee and elsewhere before forging a career as valued sideman to the likes of Tom Harrell and Joe Bonner. His solo career flourishes quietly.

***** On The Lower East Side**
Candid CCD 79704 *Hobbs; Kenny Barron (p); Peter Washington (b); Victor Lewis (d).* 93.

***** Second Encounter**
Candid CCD *As above.* 7/94.

We've said it before, in other contexts, but if Hobbs were a horn player and not a vibist, he'd be significantly better known. Like many recent players on his instrument, he plays what often sound like horn lines but is also capable of giving a line like 'Au Privave', one of the highlights on the second of these records, a distinct and idiomatic touch.

Barron almost steals the show on the first record. His delightful touch is a feature of almost every track, both the standards and the originals, but it is the strength of the writing that appeals most insistently here. Kicking off with a fast version of 'Amazing Grace' was a bold stroke, but Hobbs really hits home with his threnody to Chet Baker and with his intriguingly titled '18–35 (Together Again)', which seems to borrow a structure from 'Alone Together'. One or two of his originals sound like bebop contrefacts, but always with a sharply individual cast.

The same group reconvened in 1994 for a second, equally polished set which didn't see the light of day for another six years. Hobbs presumably still isn't a sufficiently bankable name to be a release priority. A shame, because the follow-up record is every bit as good. Possibly a bit same-ish in places with less dynamic variation than *On The Lower East Side*, but with tracks like 'The Amazing Spider Man' and 'Blues For A Way Of Life' Hobbs is establishing himself as a bold and original composer. Again, he kicks off with a familiar theme, this time 'La Vie En Rose'. It's a nice touch, but we think one of his own things deserves to be up there.

Art Hodes (1904–93)

PIANO

Hodes was brought to Chicago from his native Ukraine when he was only a few months old. As player, writer and broadcaster, he was a lifelong devotee and exponent of classic jazz, blues, stride and ragtime. Better known in later years as a solo performer, he began his career in groups run by Wingy Manone, Joe Marsala and Sidney Bechet. For a time Hodes ran his own label and magazine, both called Jazz Record. In origins, temperament and longevity, he was the Irving Berlin of jazz.

***** Vintage Art Hodes**
Solo Art Records SACD 20 *Hodes; Benny Moylan (v).* 30–50.

***** Art For Art's Sake**
Jazzology JCD 46 *Hodes; Freddie Greenleaf (t); Dave Remington (tb); Bill Reinhardt (cl); Truck Parham (b); Freddy Moore (d, v).* 8/39, 8/40, 6/57.

*****(*) The Jazz Record Story**
Jazzology JCD 82 *Hodes; Duke DuVal (t); George Brunies (tb); Rod Cless, Cecil Scott (cl); George 'Pops' Foster (b); Joe Grauso, Baby Dodds (d).* 43–46.

Until recently it was believed that, apart from a couple of cuts with Wingy Manone, Art didn't record on his own account before the summer of 1939, though it was known that he had used a Victor Home Recording machine to make half a dozen discs at a gig in Racine, Wisconsin. These were thought to be unplayable and incapable of being dubbed, but Barry Martyn has managed to reconstruct four of them here. 'Ain't Misbehavin'' and 'I Ain't Got Nobody' are indeed vintage Hodes, and no one will particularly mind the scrappy recordings of 'Tin Roof Blues' and 'Cherry', which is a vocal feature for saxophonist Benny Moylan. There is then a wonderful recording of Johnson's 'Snowy Morning Blues', recorded some time in the very early '40s, and a further array of solo sides cut in or around 1944, with two tracks at the end – 'Slow Boogie', 'Fast Boogie' – from 1949 or 1950. All dates are pretty uncertain, but there is no mistaking the importance of these tracks historically. They help to fill in the early history of a player whose awareness and understanding of jazz history were unequalled and priceless.

There are more early solo performances on *Art For Art's Sake*, though by far the best of the material comes later in the span of the compilation. There is a notably good version of Duke Ellington's 'The Mooche' from 1957, and there are group tracks from the same date. Freddy Moore sings on 'None Of My Jelly Roll' and 'Blues And Booze' (a title that chimed very strongly with Art) and Freddy also adds a touch of washboard to 'Tiger Rag'. Art's solo playing, though, is as ever the key element. His ballad touch is as sure as on faster tempos, and 'Someone To Watch Over Me' is a delight.

The Jazz Record material restores to circulation many of the sides Art cut and released with his own label. The very first tracks, '103rd Street Boogie' and 'Royal Garden Blues', appeared at the end of 1943, credited to the Columbia Quintet, which had played a residency at Childs' Restaurant in New Haven. The wonderful trio with Pops Foster and Baby Dodds is a little later, and there are further group recordings made by the band co-led by Art and three horns, including big Cecil Scott (who had 13 children, eating in shifts and sleeping in tiers). The performances are peppy and joyous, an unalloyed delight for anyone who loves traditional jazz.

***** Parlor Social**
Solo Art Records SACD 50 *Hodes; Fred Higginson (p); Russel Roth (d); Buddy Smith (perc).* 51.

The first six numbers, with Art and percussionist Buddy Smith, were recorded during a supper party at Chadwick Hansen's house in Minneapolis. While playing some Jelly Roll Morton records, Smith, who was Art's drummer at the time, revealed that he was the nephew of Andrew Hilaire, who had drummed for Morton. Using a beer case with newspaper taped over the top and a pair of whisk brooms, he improvised a drum kit and sat down to jam with the pianist. Naturally, they began with Morton and 'Granpa's Spells'. There were also versions of Johnson's 'Carolina Shout', Art's 'Stuff And Nonsense' and

'Plain Old Blues', and a wonderful theme called 'Blues Keep Calling', which reaffirms Art's decision to give up alcohol; he was to be a member of Alcoholics Anonymous in the second half of his life. The assembled guests add handclaps and there are sounds of drinking – except, touchingly, on 'Blues Keep Calling' – and train and street sounds from outside. As a document of musicians relaxing and playing for their own enjoyment and edification it is priceless, reminiscent of Bud Powell's recordings in François Paudras's Paris flat. The remaining cuts are by Fred Higginson, a literature scholar and college professor who was an admirer and disciple of Art's. Most of the tunes he tackles are Hodes arrangements, though his own 'Sapient Sutlers' Stomp' (we said he was a college professor) bespeaks an intelligent composer in his own right.

*** All Star Stompers

Jazzology JCD 20 *Hodes; Larry Conger (t); Charlie Bornemann (tb); Tony Parenti (cl); Johnny Baynes (b); Cliff Leeman (d).* 66.

A session recorded at Dreher High School in Columbia, South Carolina, and a relatively unknown band. Bornemann is the strongest of the sidemen; though not a strong soloist, his ensemble work is sparky and brisk, with a lovely tone. 'Willie The Weeper' merits comparison with the Louis Armstrong original, not because it is up to that galactic standard, but because it shows how much Art rethinks and colonizes a familiar theme. The set includes four previously unissued takes and an alternative ending to 'Shake That Thing'. Together with the eight main tracks, they represent an important contribution to a major body of work.

*** Recollections From The Past

Solo Art SACD 41/42 2CD *Hodes (p, v).* 7/71.

Unlike Jelly Roll Morton, Art never claimed to have invented jazz, or to have imported the music from his native Ukraine, but here he does something very similar to Ferdy's Library of Congress recordings. Taking the part of Alan Lomas is Dr Van Velser of Wilmington, North Carolina. Art narrates the story of his engagement with jazz and some of its leading personalities: Sidney Bechet, Bunk Johnson, Eddie Condon and others. There are reminiscences aplenty: of being picked up for speeding, of meeting Hollywood stars, and of drinking with Condon. The playing is illustrative rather than central this time out, but the playing is very good indeed and, though this isn't a set you'll play straight through that often, it's an irresistible self-portrait.

*** Up In Volly's Room

Delmark DE 217 *Hodes; Nappy Trottier (t); George Brunies (tb); Volly DeFaut (cl); Truck Parham (b); Barrett Deems (d).* 3–4/72.

When this was recorded, back in 1972, the clarinet *was* pretty much in abeyance as a jazz instrument and traditional jazz was at its lowest ebb commercially. A great deal has happened since then, of course. There is far greater respect for the tradition, and the emergence of a whole generation of young traditionalists has reduced the impact of this record's special pleading. On its own terms, as relaxed and matey old buzzards meet, it sounds pretty good. DeFaut is a decent player of the Dodds school, with traces of Jimmie Noone and even of Goodman thrown in. He actually appears on only four tracks; the rest are duets with Parham, and the whole thing is topped off like a rather wobbly sundae with two pieces featuring the splendidly monikered Trottier and George Brunies. Poorly recorded, but well worth a listen.

***(*) Tribute To The Greats

Delmark DE-238 *Hodes (p solo).* 76–78.

*** Indianapolis Concert

Solo Art SACD 20 *Hodes; Herb Guy (b).* 8/77.

At seventy-plus, Art was in his pomp, utterly confident and articulate and capable of navigating an imaginative course through the repertoire. The Delmark album sets him to work on plenty of old warhorses, and every one is made distinctive by his timing, left-hand variation (blues, boogie, stride, whatever) and courtly sense of melodic propriety. The highlights in Indianapolis are 'C Jam Blues', 'I Can't Get Started' (unusually modernist in conception), 'Mood Indigo' and – an old favourite – Morton's 'Granpa's Spells'. The sound is of intermittent quality, but the playing is good enough to overcome all but the most obsessive quibbles.

*** Echoes Of Chicago

Jazzology JCD 79 *Hodes; Ernie Carson (t); Charlie Bornemann (tb); Herman Foretich (cl); Spencer Clark (bsx); Jerry Rousseau (b); Spider Ridgeway (d); Maxine Sullivan (v).* 2/78.

Haunted by the Windy City, but recorded in the softer chill of Atlanta in February, this is a valuable addition to the roster of Hodes albums with full ensemble. The pairing of string bass and bass saxophone is unusual and stretches the tonality to the limit, with cornet and clarinet at the top end of the range. Maxine Sullivan contributes a vocal to 'It's The Talk Of The Town'. There are two alternatives to 'Sunday', which add little of substance but represent more than a footnote to Art's art.

***(*) Pagin' Mr Jelly

Candid CCD 79037 *Hodes; Nappy Trottier (t); George Brunies (tb); Volly DeFaut (cl); Truck Parham (b); Barrett Deems (d).* 11/88.

**** Keepin' Out Of Mischief Now

Candid CACD 79717 *As above.* 11/88.

If consistency and regularity are the keys to longevity, Hodes seems to have survived by *not* bending to the winds of fashion. His records – solos in particular – tend to be comfortably interchangeable, and only real enthusiasts for his rather throwaway style or for the South Side pianists in general will want shelf-loads. *Real* enthusiasts will already have the Mosaic box, *The Complete Art Hodes Blue Notes*, which remains the most important single item in his catalogue. Though over-represented as a solo performer in comparison with his group work, Hodes conjures some interesting variations on Jelly Roll Morton, his greatest single influence, on *Pagin' Mr Jelly*, and this, or the remaining material from that session on *Mischief*, is perhaps the place for fans of either to start. Hodes's only originals, the title-tune and the related 'Mr Jelly Blues', are virtually impossible to pick out from a session that sticks to only the most sanctified of early jazz tunes: the march 'High Society', 'Wolverine Blues', 'Mr Jelly Lord', 'Winin' Boy Blues', 'Buddy Bolden's Blues' and 'The Pearls'. What's wonderful about Hodes's approach to this material, the Morton stuff in particular, is how *natural* he sounds. There's no pressure or effort, no hint of pastiche, just straightforward playing of magnificent music. For a change, he's playing on a really decent piano, and that is perversely disconcerting.

***** Art Hodes Jazz Trio**
Jazzology JCD 307 *Hodes; Reimer Von Essen (cl, as); Trevor Richards (d).* 86.

****(*) Art Hodes Trio**
Jazzology JCD 237 *Hodes; Trevor Whiting (reeds); John Petters (d); Dave Bennett (v).* 9/87.

***** Art Hodes Blue Five And Six**
Jazzology JCD 172 *Hodes; Al Fairweather, Pat Halcox (t); Wally Fawkes (cl); Fapy Lapertin (g); Andy Brown (b); Dave Evans, Stan Greig (d); Johnny Mars (v).* 9–10/87.

Hodes's trip to Britain in 1987 was as a laying-on of hands, a chance to make contact with someone who belonged to an apostolic line going back to the origins of jazz. Traditional jazz players of all sorts made their way to listen to and sit in with the great man. The results are pretty uniform, with most of the best music coming in solo performances by Hodes himself. There is no apparent stylistic distinction between the Trio and the Jazz Trio; the latter is simply better. The larger groups called on more seasoned and experienced musicians and the playing is better in proportion, with some excellent moments from that Chris Barber stalwart, Pat Halcox. Fawkes is still underrated and Greig is as good in this style as one could hope to find.

Frederick Hodges

PIANO

A specialist in period performance of '20s piano styles, Hodges is a regular with Don Neely's Royal Society Jazz Orchestra.

***** Turn On the Heat**
Stomp Off CD 1333 *Hodges (p solo).* 7/97.

Hodges finds a middle ground between the formal, glittery novelty-piano styles of the '20s and the more freely played jazz delivery of the same period. His sleeve-notes display a remarkable understanding of the genre, and doubtless this is about as authentic as this idiom gets. That said, the music lacks the last spark of excitement which it may once have possessed, and Hodges' mastery of it may be all too perfect. Twenty-two solos in this style make for a less than compelling CD.

Johnny Hodges (1907–70)

ALTO SAXOPHONE, SOPRANO SAXOPHONE

Born in Massachusetts, Hodges studied with Sidney Bechet and took his place in Willie 'The Lion' Smith's group. In 1928 he joined the Ellington orchestra and remained with Duke for the next four decades, despite occasional forays into leadership himself. Rabbit's intense, bluesy tone is one of the most distinctive instrumental voices in jazz. Though he started out essentially as a soprano specialist, it is his alto playing, ever more pared down as the years went by, that is remembered.

***** Classic Solos: 1928–1942**
Topaz TPZ 1008 *Hodges; Bunny Berigan, Freddy Jenkins, Bubber Miley, Ray Nance, Arthur Whetsol, Cootie Williams (t); Rex Stewart (c); Lawrence Brown, Joe 'Tricky Sam' Nanton, Juan Tizol (tb); Barney Bigard (cl, ts); Harry Carney (bs, as, cl); Otto Hardwick (as, bsx); Ben Webster (ts); Duke Ellington, Teddy Wilson (p); Fred Guy (bj); Lawrence Lucie, Allan Reuss (g); Hayes Alvis, Jimmy Blanton, Wellman Braud, John Kirby, Grachan Moncur, Billy Taylor (b); Cozy Cole, Sonny Greer (d); Mildred Bailey (v).* 10/28–7/41.

***** Jeep's Blues: His Greatest Recordings: 1928–1941**
ASV CD AJA 5180 *As above, except add Buck Clayton, Louis Metcalf (t), Buster Bailey (cl), Lester Young (ts), Edgar Sampson (bs), Jess Stacy (p), Lionel Hampton (vib), Artie Bernstein, Harry Goodman (b), Gene Krupa (d), Billie Holiday (v).* 6/28–6/41.

There are probably no voices in jazz more purely sensuous than that of John Cornelius Hodge (the extra 's' was added later). Subtract Hodges's solos from Duke Ellington's recorded output and it shrinks disproportionately. He was a stalwart presence right from the Cotton Club Orchestra through the Webster–Blanton years and beyond. Sadly, perhaps, for all his pricklish dislike of sideman status in the Ellington orchestra (he frequently mimed counting bills in the Duke's direction when receiving his usual ovation for yet another perfectly crafted solo), Hodges was a rather unassertive leader, and his own recordings under-represent his extraordinary qualities, which began to dim only with the onset of the '60s.

The ASV and the Topaz do a fairly good job of compiling a representative profile and doing so with very little overlap. Probably the best guide to these is not personnel but session dates. Topaz ignore things like the 1940 'Good Queen Bess' and the slightly earlier 'Warm Valley', but material from the 1929 Cotton Club Orchestra *is* included, filling in an important gap in the transition from blues and jump to the lyrical majesty of later years. Hodges's alto (and occasionally soprano) stand out strongly wherever featured. He switches to soprano again for 'Rent Party Blues' (Topaz) and 'Tired Socks' (ASV).

***** Johnny Hodges 1945–1950**
Classics 1189 *Hodges; Joe Thomas, Taft Jordan, Harold Baker (t); Sandy Williams, Lawrence Brown, Quentin Jackson (tb); Al Sears, Don Byas (ts); Harry Carney (bs); Jimmy Jones, Raymond Fol, Billy Strayhorn (p); Brick Fleagle (g); Sid Weiss, Billy Taylor, Oscar Pettiford, Wendell Marshall (b); Shelly Manne, Wilbur De Paris, Butch Ballard, Sonny Greer (d).* 11/45–2/50.

Hodges had yet to undertake his ultimately brief sabbatical from the Ellington orchestra when these tracks were made, and Classics have basically put together a collection of bits and pieces here. Four titles for HRS under Sandy Williams's leadership are followed by four for the very obscure Wax label, then two sessions for Mercer (Ellington), one for Sunrise and one for Swing, cut in Paris in 1950. Reproduction is a mixed bag but the music's interesting enough. Hodges is cast as the major soloist on every track, and though the music's mostly variations on the blues, Rabbit does his usual supremely professional job, and there are occasional cameos from the likes of Quentin Jackson and Shorty Baker to enjoy.

*****(*) Caravan**
Prestige PRCD 24103 *Hodges; Taft Jordan, Cat Anderson, Harold 'Shorty' Baker (t); Lawrence Brown, Juan Tizol (tb); Willie Smith (as); Paul Gonsalves, Al Sears (ts); Jimmy Hamilton (ts, cl); Harry Carney (bs); Duke Ellington (p); Billy*

Strayhorn (p, org); Wendell Marshall, Oscar Pettiford (b); Wilbur De Paris, Louie Bellson, Sonny Greer (d). 6/47–6/51.

The sessions on *Caravan* were originally recorded for the short-lived Mercer label. Long unavailable, they include some classics, like 'Charlotte Russe' (aka 'Lotus Blossom'), for which Hodges, Duke and Strayhorn all claimed some credit at varying times. Recorded in 1947, it is one of the most graceful of Hodges's solos. 'Caravan' itself is performed by a band that includes Duke Ellington and the composer, Juan Tizol, himself. Hodges isn't featured on the later stages of what was originally a double LP, lest anyone mistake Willie Smith for him.

*****(*) Jazz Masters 35: Johnny Hodges**
Verve 521857-2 *Hodges; Cat Anderson, Harold 'Shorty' Baker, Emmett Berry, Willie Cook, Roy Eldridge, Dizzy Gillespie, Eddie Mullens, Ernie Royal, Charlie Shavers, Clark Terry, Snooky Young (t); Ray Nance (t, v); Lawrence Brown, Chuck Connors, Vic Dickenson, Quentin Jackson, John Saunders, Britt Woodman (tb); Tony Studd (btb); Russell Procope, Jerome Richardson, Frank Wess (cl, as); Jimmy Hamilton (cl, ts); Danny Bank (cl, bs); Benny Carter, Charlie Parker (as); Paul Gonsalves, Flip Phillips, Al Sears, Ben Webster (ts); Harry Carney, Gerry Mulligan (bs); Earl Hines, Jimmy Jones, Hank Jones, Leroy Lovett, Junior Mance, Oscar Peterson, Billy Strayhorn, Claude Williamson (p); Everett Barksdale, Kenny Burrell, Barney Kessel, Les Spann (g); Aaron Bell, Ray Brown, Buddy Clark, Richard Davis, Milt Hinton, Sam Jones, Lloyd Trottman, Jimmy Woode (b); Sonny Greer, J. C. Heard, Lex Humphries, Mel Lewis, Joe Marshall, Grady Tate, Sam Woodyard (d).* 2/51–8/67.

*****(*) Johnny Hodges With Billy Strayhorn And The Orchestra**
Verve 557543-2 *Hodges; Cat Anderson, Harold 'Shorty' Baker, Bill Berry, Howard McGhee, Ed Mullens (t); Lawrence Brown, Quentin Jackson, Chuck Connors (tb); Russell Procope (cl, as); Jimmy Hamilton (cl, ts); Paul Gonsalves (ts); Harry Carney (bs, cl); Jimmy Jones (p); Aaron Bell (b); Sam Woodyard (d).* 11/61.

Only Verve and Bluebird have done anything to bring Hodges into the CD era. At least the Verve Jazz Masters compilation is an ideal representation of later Hodges, at his most magisterial. Usually working with Ellingtonians, there is little to distinguish most of these settings from Ducal ones, except for the fact that Rabbit is even more generously featured than usual. It is wonderful to hear him in the company of a baritonist other than Carney on the 1959 session with Mulligan, and the compilation reprises the July 1952 Norman Granz jam which saw Hodges on stage with Benny Carter, Ben Webster and Charlie Parker.

A more recent arrival is the set arranged by Strayhorn and rather coyly credited to 'The Orchestra', in other words, Ellington with the Duke on holiday. Rabbit could hardly have been in more familiar company for a concerto-like situation and, if he doesn't exactly put himself out to make the most of the opportunities, that isn't what such a hardened pro would have done anyway.

*****(*) Johnny Hodges At Sportpalast, Berlin**
Pablo 2620 102 2CD *Hodges; Ray Nance (t); Lawrence Brown (tb); Harry Carney (bs); Al Williams (p); Aaron Bell (b); Sam Woodyard (d).* 61.

Still associating largely with Ellingtonians, Hodges entered his final decade possessed of a magisterial voice which was like no other in jazz and which increasingly seemed the ancestor of everyone from John Coltrane to Bobby Watson. A surprising dearth of live material makes the return of the 1961 Sportpalast recording doubly welcome. Hodges was in magnificent voice on this occasion, playing with the moody grace that was his stock-in-trade. A few moments into 'Satin Doll' one realizes how wonderful it would have been to have seen this complex, rather difficult man perform as he does on these discs. Considering Hodges's popularity with mainstream followers, it is hard to understand why so many of the 30-odd albums under his own name have yet to reach CD reissue, and that picture has scarcely changed across all six of our editions.

Amos Hoffman

GUITAR

Israeli-American guitarist, straight-ahead in essence.

***** The Dreamer**
Fresh Sound New Talent FSNT 060 *Hoffman; Duane Eubanks (t); Avishai Cohen (b); Jorge Rossy (d).* 2/99.

Hoffman's clear, clean style abjures effects and mannerisms and relies of streams of melody. That makes this a likeable record, though it won't exactly collar the attention. Rossy and Cohen are an excellent team for this kind of thing, propulsive without getting bossy about it, and Eubanks, though he's not on every track, is an interesting man to have on hand. The nine originals don't outstay their welcome, like the disc as a whole, which at 42 minutes is just the right length.

Jay Hoggard (born 1954)

VIBRAPHONE

On the fringes of the New Haven new-music scene in the '70s, then moved to New York and played in more straight-ahead, post-bop surroundings. Some profile as a leader in the '80s, but has rather slipped from sight of late.

***** Solo Vibraphone**
India Navigation IN 1040 *Hoggard (vib solo).* 11/78.

****(*) Rain Forest**
Original Jazz Classics OJC 800 *Hoggard; Chico Freeman (ts); Kenny Kirkland (ky); John Koenig (clo, g); Roland Bautista (g); Francisco Centeno (b); Harvey Mason (d); Paulinho Da Costa, Jose Guico (perc); Maxayn Lewis, Patryce Banks, Sybil Thomas (v).* 11/80.

There's a fierceness about Hoggard – 'the little tiger', the name of one of his albums, seems a perfect description – that communicates itself through almost everything he does, not just the more avant-garde aspects. His exposure is currently thin due to the disappearance of all his Muse albums, and this pair are merely worthwhile. The solo India Navigation set, now reissued with extra tracks, is one side of Hoggard's musical personality. Titles like 'May Those Who Love Apartheid Rot In Hell' give a sense of the burning intensity that fuels his work, but even here it's worth noting that such pieces sit alongside

'Toe Dance For A Baby' and a markedly jovial reading of 'Air Mail Special'. Recorded live, the disc doesn't give the best representation of Hoggard's clean, exact delivery. Technically, he sounds closer to Hamp than to Milt Jackson or Bobby Hutcherson. *Rain Forest*, a Contemporary date now reissued in the OJC series, is muddled by the Latin percussion and misguided vocals, and often seems inappropriately lightweight for such a dignified performer; but the sparkle of Hoggard's best playing glints through what looks suspiciously like a session he was talked into leading. Currently he seems disappointingly out of favour as a recording artist.

John Högman (born 1953)

TENOR AND BARITONE SAXOPHONES, SYNTHESIZER

Based in Uppsala, Högman was turned on to jazz by hearing an Edmond Hall record. He got to know Thomas Arnesen, Ulf Johansson and others as a youth and developed as a swing-to-bop player through the '70s and '80s.

*****(*) Good Night Sister**
Sittel SITCD 9202 *Högman; Ulf Johansson (tb); Knud Jorgensen (p); Thomas Arnesen (g); Nils-Erik Sparf (vn, vla); Bengt Hansson (b); Johan Dielemans (d).* 10/92.

***** 203 Park Drive**
Sittel SITCD 9229 *Högman; Bosse Broberg (t); Jens Lindgren (tb); Gösta Rundqvist (p); Bengt Hansson (b); Martin Lofgren (d); Omnibus Wind Ensemble.* 9/95.

Good Night Sister is hugely enjoyable. Högman's opening tune, 'Theodore', is a Sonny Rollins dedication that makes clear his primary influence, but it's Rollins without the soul-searching and the inner demons: what one hears is a confident unfurling of fine melodic ideas, etched in a big, shapely sound. He plays baritone on two cuts, and that sounds just as impressive. 'Look For The Silver Lining' is another Theodore-like performance, but the exquisite ballad-work on the title-piece and the wry, ambivalent bounce of 'Hiccup' prove his range. Johansson and Arnesen take cameo roles; more important is Jorgensen, who plays very well but who sadly died only weeks after the session.

203 Park Drive doesn't quite match up. Maybe Högman is just being too self-effacing here: he doesn't even start playing until three minutes into the first track, and guest spots for Broberg, Lindgren and the Omnibus Wind group take the focus off him when what we want to hear is his own playing, which remains full of charm and light. Unhurried at any tempo and gently smouldering on the ballads, Högman earns the stars by himself. But the disc is a bit too long, and the space offered to everyone else takes some of the appeal off what is still a good record. Disappointing that, again, we have nothing new for Högman to contribute to this edition.

Billie Holiday (1915–59)

VOCAL

Born in Baltimore, Holiday had a wretched childhood, but she was singing early and made her first records in 1933. Her pre-war sessions with Teddy Wilson established her reputation, followed by stints with Basie and Artie Shaw, before choosing to work as a soloist. Drink and narcotics problems, which attended the rest of her life, held her back, but she worked through the '40s, despite a spell in prison, and began recording for Decca in 1944. She tried but largely failed to make a career in films, and eventually signed to Norman Granz's operation in 1952. Her voice declined to a croak, but her musicianship stayed intact.

***** The Quintessential Billie Holiday Vol. 1 1933–35**
Columbia 450987-2 *Holiday; Charlie Teagarden, Shirley Clay, Roy Eldridge, Dick Clark (t); Benny Morton, Jack Teagarden (tb); Cecil Scott, Benny Goodman, Tom Macey (cl); Johnny Hodges (as); Art Karle, Ben Webster, Chu Berry (ts); Joe Sullivan, Teddy Wilson (p); Dick McDonough, Lawrence Lucie, John Trueheart, Dave Barbour (g); Artie Bernstein, Grachan Moncur, John Kirby (b); Cozy Cole, Gene Krupa (d).* 11/33–12/35.

*****(*) The Quintessential Billie Holiday Vol. 2 1936**
Columbia 460060-2 *Holiday; Chris Griffin, Jonah Jones, Bunny Berigan, Irving Randolph (t); Rudy Powell, Artie Shaw, Irving Fazola, Vido Musso (cl); Harry Carney (cl, bs); Johnny Hodges (as); Ted McCrae, Ben Webster (ts); Teddy Wilson (p); John Trueheart, Allan Reuss, Dick McDonough (g); Grachan Moncur, John Kirby, Pete Peterson, Artie Bernstein, Milt Hinton (b); Cozy Cole, Gene Krupa (d).* 1–10/36.

****** The Quintessential Billie Holiday Vol. 3 1936–37**
Columbia 460820-2 *Holiday; Irving Randolph, Jonah Jones, Buck Clayton, Henry 'Red' Allen (t); Vido Musso, Benny Goodman (cl); Cecil Scott (cl, as, ts); Edgar Sampson (cl, as); Ben Webster, Lester Young, Prince Robinson (ts); Teddy Wilson (p); Allan Reuss, Jimmy McLin (g); Milt Hinton, John Kirby, Walter Page (b); Gene Krupa, Cozy Cole, Jo Jones (d).* 10/36–2/37.

***** Billie Holiday 1933–37**
Classics 582 *As above three discs.* 33–37.

****** The Quintessential Billie Holiday Vol. 4 1937**
Columbia 463333-2 *Holiday; Cootie Williams, Eddie Tompkins, Buck Clayton (t); Buster Bailey, Edmond Hall (cl); Johnny Hodges (as); Joe Thomas, Lester Young (ts); Harry Carney (bs); Teddy Wilson, James Sherman (p); Carmen Mastren, Freddie Green, Allan Reuss (g); Artie Bernstein, Walter Page, John Kirby (b); Cozy Cole, Alphonse Steele, Jo Jones (d).* 2–6/37.

*****(*) The Quintessential Billie Holiday Vol. 5 1937–38**
Columbia 465190-2 *Holiday; Buck Clayton (t); Benny Morton (tb); Buster Bailey (cl); Prince Robinson, Vido Musso (cl, ts); Lester Young (ts); Claude Thornhill, Teddy Wilson (p); Allan Reuss, Freddie Green (g); Walter Page (b); Jo Jones (d).* 6/37–1/38.

*****(*) The Quintessential Billie Holiday Vol. 6 1938**
Columbia 466313-2 *Holiday; Bernard Anderson, Buck Clayton, Harry James (t); Dicky Wells, Benny Morton (tb); Buster Bailey (cl); Edgar Sampson, Benny Carter (as); Lester Young (cl, ts); Babe Russin, Herschel Evans (ts); Claude Thornhill, Margaret 'Queenie' Johnson, Teddy Wilson (p); Al Casey, Freddie Green (g); John Kirby, Walter Page (b); Cozy Cole, Jo Jones (d).* 5–11/38.

****(*) The Quintessential Billie Holiday Vol. 7 1938–39**
Columbia 466966-2 *Holiday; Charlie Shavers, Roy Eldridge, Hot Lips Page, Frankie Newton (t); Bobby Hackett (c); Trummy Young, Tyree Glenn (tb); Tab Smith (ss, as); Benny Carter, Toots Mondello (cl, as); Teddy Buckner (as); Kenneth Hollon, Ernie Powell, Bud Freeman, Chu Berry, Stanley Payne (ts); Teddy Wilson, Sonny Payne, Kenny Kersey (p); Danny*

Barker, Al Casey, Jimmy McLin, Bernard Addison (g); Milt Hinton, John Williams (b); Cozy Cole, Eddie Dougherty (d). 11/38–7/39.

*** **Billie Holiday 1937–1939**

Classics 592 *As above four discs.* 37–39.

*** **The Quintessential Billie Holiday Vol. 8 1939–1940**

Columbia 467914-2 *Holiday; Charlie Shavers, Buck Clayton, Roy Eldridge, Harry 'Sweets' Edison (t); Tab Smith, Earl Warren, Jimmy Powell, Carl Frye, Don Redman, Georgie Auld (as); Kenneth Hollon, Stanley Payne, Lester Young, Kermit Scott, Jimmy Hamilton, Don Byas (ts); Jack Washington (bs); Sonny White, Teddy Wilson, Joe Sullivan (p); Bernard Addison, Freddie Green, John Collins, Lawrence Lucie (g); John Williams, Walter Page, Al Hall (b); Eddie Dougherty, Jo Jones, Harold 'Doc' West, Kenny Clarke (d).* 7/39–9/40.

*** **Billie Holiday 1939–1940**

Classics 601 *As above two Columbia discs.* 39–40.

*** **The Quintessential Billie Holiday Vol. 9 1940–42**

Columbia 467915-2 *Holiday; Bill Coleman, Shad Collins, Emmett Berry, Roy Eldridge (t); Benny Morton (tb); Jimmy Hamilton (cl); Benny Carter (cl, as); Leslie Johnakins, Hymie Schertzer, Eddie Barefield, Ernie Powell, Lester Boone, Jimmy Powell (as); Lester Young, Georgie Auld, Babe Russin (ts); Sonny White, Teddy Wilson, Eddie Heywood (p); Ulysses Livingston, John Collins, Paul Chapman, Gene Fields, Al Casey (g); Wilson Meyers, Grachan Moncur, John Williams, Ted Sturgis (b); Yank Porter, Kenny Clarke, J. C. Heard, Herbert Cowens (d).* 10/40–2/42.

**** **Lady Day: The Complete Billie Holiday On Columbia 1933–1944**

CXK 85470 10CD *As all above discs.* 33–44.

***(*) **Lady Day: The Best Of Billie Holiday**

Columbia 504722-2 2CD *As above.* 36–42.

**** **The Billie Holiday Collection 1**

Columbia 510721-2 *As appropriate discs above.* 7/35-11/36.

**** **The Billie Holiday Collection 2**

Columbia 510722-2 *As appropriate discs above.* 11/36-9/37.

**** **The Billie Holiday Collection 3**

Columbia 510723-2 *As appropriate discs above.* 9/37-12/39.

***(*) **The Billie Holiday Collection 4**

Columbia 510724-2 *As appropriate discs above.* 12/39-1/44.

Billie Holiday remains among the most difficult of jazz artists to understand or study. Surrounded by a disturbing legend, it is very difficult to hear her clearly. The legendary suffering and mythopoeic pain which countless admirers have actively sought out in her work make it difficult for the merely curious to warm to a singer who was a sometimes baffling performer. Those records that she made in her later years often demand an almost voyeuristic role of any listener determined to enjoy her interpretations. Nevertheless, Holiday was a singular and unrepeatable talent whose finest hours are remarkably revealing and often surprisingly – given her generally morose reputation as an artist – joyful. New listeners may find the accumulated weight of the Holiday myth discouraging, and they may be equally surprised at how much fun many of the earlier records are.

Virtually all of her music is now available on CD. Columbia have taken their time about it, since their Holiday archive hadn't been remastered since the days of LPs, but the wait was worth it: their massive *Lady Day* edition offers the entire catalogue, 230 tracks including alternatives, airshots and a few V-Discs. The basic sequence starts with 6½ discs of the studio sessions in chronological order, then meanders through numerous alternative takes, and a small amount of broadcast material for the remainder. There are also numerous essays, photos, track-by-track analysis and all the paraphernalia we've come to expect in this age of whopping boxed sets. The standard of these records – particularly considering how many tracks were made – is finally very high, and the best of them are as poised and finely crafted as any small-group jazz of the period. One of Holiday's innovations was to suggest a role for the singer which blended in with the rest of the musicians, improvising a line and taking a 'solo' which was as integrated as anything else on the record. On her earlier sides with Wilson as leader, she was still credited as responsible for the 'vocal refrain', but the later titles feature 'Billie Holiday And Her Orchestra'. She starts some records and slips into the middle of others, but always there's a feeling of a musician at ease with the rest of the band and aware of the importance of fitting into the performance as a whole.

Her tone, on the earliest sides, is still a little raw and unformed, and the trademark rasp at the edge of her voice – which she uses to canny effect on the later titles – is used less pointedly; but the unaffected styling is already present, and there are indications of her mastery of time even at the very beginning. While the most obvious characteristic of her singing is the lagging behind the beat, she seldom sounds tired or slow to respond, and the deeper impression is of a vocalist who knows exactly how much time she can take. She never scats, rarely drifts far from the melody, and respects structure and lyrical nuance, even where – as has often been remarked – the material is less than blue-chip. But her best singing invests the words with shades of meaning which vocalists until that point had barely looked at: she creates an ambiguity between what the words say and what she might be thinking which is very hard to distil. And that is the core of Holiday's mystique. Coupled with the foggy, baleful, sombre quality of her tone, it creates a vocal jazz which is as absorbing as it is enduring.

Whatever one may think about the later albums, these sessions surrender nothing in gravitas and communicate a good humour which is all their own. The session producers – John Hammond or Bernie Hanighen – encouraged an atmosphere of mutual creativity which the singer seldom fails to respond to, and even on the less than immortal songs Holiday makes something of the situation: there is no sense of her fighting against the material, as there often is with Armstrong or Waller in the same period. On the many upbeat songs, in tempo or complexion, she's often irresistible. The informality starts to fade across the duration of these sessions, and she becomes more like a singer with accompanists, but the blitheness of her youthful voice persists. On an airshot with the Basie orchestra, she does 'Swing, Brother, Swing', which is much more the sort of thing you'd expect to hear from Ella Fitzgerald in this period, and every phrase has light and lift in it, all the jive language made into something almost spiritual.

As a trove of songs, this is also enormously valuable. The chestnuts produce predictably fine performances, but it's on the lesser, and lesser-known, material that Billie really works wonders. 'Romance In The Dark', 'Back In Your Own Backyard', 'They Say', 'I'm Gonna Lock My Heart', 'Says My Heart' and even a trifle such as 'Under A Blue Jungle Moon' come up like splendid tunes even when they're not. It's not so much that she transforms or transcends these songs, more that at this point she seemed to breeze through lines with a delight in her own talent that, in an odd way, makes the matter of the lyrics almost irrelevant. Not so much in love with her own voice, but in love with what it could do.

The musicianship is, inevitably, hard to criticize. Although Lester Young's presence on many of these dates is usually the one that's singled out, the greater achievement lies with Teddy Wilson: his blend of elegance and vitality has out-faced 65 years, and will continue to do so. Luckily, we can also hear everything that was going on: the transfers are at last just as they should be. The original Vocalion masters weren't always wonderful, but the engineers haven't been shy about leaving some surface noise in if it meant getting the music to sound as it should, and this is as close to hi-fi as we'll ever hear them. The many alternative takes don't tell us much that's new, agreeable though it is to have them, and the handful of airshot titles are maybe not much more than a pleasing bonus; but no need to complain about that.

If you don't want to spring for the full set, the two-disc Columbia best-of is a fine alternative. Their earlier sequence of Quintessential reissues appears to remain available, although if they continue the sequence which is now called *The Billie Holiday Collection*, drawn from the complete edition, they will presumably disappear soon enough. These four *Collection* discs certainly do the job well.

The Classics CDs cover all the material which isn't also included on their Teddy Wilson series: a useful way to fill gaps if the other discs are already in the collection, but splitting the music between Wilson and Holiday separates much of the best material. The transfer quality is mixed.

Other compilations from the period include: *The Early Classics 1935–40* (Flapper CD-9756), a decent cross-section in bright if sometimes thin sound; *Greatest Hits* (Columbia CK 65757), a recent and enjoyable pick of this period; *16 Most Requested Songs* (Columbia 474401-2), an excellent choice; and *Lady Day's 25 Greatest Hits* (ASV AJA5181), an ambitious title but a sound choice, which underlines that it's difficult to go wrong in choosing the tracks for early Holiday compilations.

CORE COLLECTION

**** Lady Day Swings!

Columbia 508608-2 *As various discs above.* 7/35–7/39.

One could say that she swung whatever the tempo was, but this absolutely delightful collection focuses in on the most skipping and beautifully upbeat of her '30s performances. There's tenderness, too, in the likes of 'Easy To Love' and 'Romance In The Dark'. It's possible to complain that it's a one-sided look at Holiday's art. We prefer to see it as her most consistently enjoyable collection, and definitely one for the library.

*** The Complete Commodore Recordings

Commodore CMD 24012 2CD *Holiday; Frankie Newton, Doc Cheatham, Freddy Webster (t); Vic Dickenson (tb); Lem Davis, Tab Smith (as); Stan Payne, Kenneth Hollon (ts); Eddie Heywood, Sonny White (p); Jimmy McLin, Teddy Walters (g); John Williams, John Simmons (b); Eddie Dougherty, Big Sid Catlett (d).* 4/39–8/44.

Holiday's Commodore sessions account for only 17 titles all told, but the numerous multiple takes make up enough music for a two-disc set, and this is the definitive edition. It opens on her signature set-piece, 'Strange Fruit', which sets a sombre tone for the first session, and though there's then a jump of some five years the rest of the tracks tend to follow the pattern of subdued tempos and rather severe interpretations. The ultra-slow speed of 'How Am I To Know' is startling in itself, and so in its way is the gently entreating 'Lover Come Back To Me'. The accompaniments include some excellent players, but Eddie Heywood's charts give them precious little chance to shine. This is one of the least well-known periods in the Holiday discography, and with the overabundance of rejected takes it's very much a set for hardcore collectors only. The remastering is good enough, even if the original recording left something to be desired.

***(*) The Complete Original American Decca Recordings

GRP 052601-2 2CD *Holiday; Russ Case, Joe Guy, Gordon Griffin, Rostelle Reese, Billy Butterfield, Jimmy Nottingham, Emmett Berry, Buck Clayton, Bernie Privin, Tony Faso, Dick Vance, Shad Collins, Bobby Williams, Bobby Hackett (t); Dicky Wells, George Matthews, Henderson Chambers, Mort Bullman, George Stevenson (tb); Milt Yaner, Bill Stegmeyer (cl, as); Hymie Schertzer, Jack Cressey, Lem Davis, Toots Mondello, Al Klink, Rudy Powell, George Dorsey, Johnny Mince, Pete Clark, Sid Cooper (as); John Fulton (ts, cl, f); Dick Eckles (ts, f); Larry Binyon, Paul Ricci, Dave Harris, Hank Ross, Armand Camgros, Bob Dorsey, Art Drelinger, Lester Young, Joe Thomas, Budd Johnson, Freddie Williams, Pat Nizza (ts); Eddie Barefield (bs, cl); Stan Webb, Sol Moore, Dave McRae (bs); Dave Bowman, Sammy Benskin, Joe Springer, Charles LaVere, Bobby Tucker, Billy Kyle, Horace Henderson, Bernie Leighton (p); Carl Kress, Tony Mottola, Everett Barksdale, Bob Bain, Mundell Lowe, Tiny Grimes, Jimmy Shirley, Dan Perry (g); Haig Stephens, Bob Haggart, Billy Taylor, John Simmons, Thomas Barney, George Duvivier, Joe Benjamin, Jack Lesberg, Lou Butterman (b); Johnny Blowers, George Wettling, Specs Powell, Big Sid Catlett, Kelly Martin, Denzil Best, Kenny Clarke, Norris 'Bunny' Shawker, Shadow Wilson, Cozy Cole, Wallace Bishop, Jimmy Crawford, Nick Fatool (d); Louis Armstrong (v); strings and choir.* 10/44–3/50.

*** Billie Holiday 1944

Classics 806 *Similar to above, except add Roy Eldridge, Doc Cheatham, Freddy Webster (t), Vic Dickenson (tb), Barney Bigard (cl), Lem Davis (as), Al Casey, Teddy Walters (g), Oscar Pettiford (b).* 3–11/44.

Holiday's Decca sessions have been impeccably presented here, in a double-CD set which has been remastered to make the music sound as big and clear as possible. Some may prefer a warmer and less boomy sound, but the timbre of the records is impressively full and strong. These sessions were made when Holiday had established a wider reputation, and their feel is very different from the Columbia records: carefully orchestrated by a multitude of hands, including Sy Oliver and Gordon Jenkins, the best of them are as good as anything Holiday did. Many listeners may, indeed, find this the single most entertaining set of Holiday reissues on the market, for the polish and class of the singing and playing – while less spontaneously improvisational in feel – are hard to deny. Her own songs, 'Don't Explain' and 'God Bless The Child', are obvious highlights, even if they mark the beginning of Holiday's 'victim' image, and here is the original reading of the subsequently famous 'That Ole Devil Called Love', two duets with Louis

Armstrong, slow and emotionally draining readings of 'Porgy' and 'My Man' (from the one session with the sole accompaniment of a rhythm section), and a lot of pleasing, brightly paced readings of superior standards. Few players stand out the way Young and Wilson do on the pre-war sides, but these aren't the same kind of records.

The Classics sequence continues with various 1944 tracks. It starts with three numbers from a Metropolitan Opera House show, with Eldridge and Tatum in the band, then goes through material with Eddie Heywood's Orchestra and finally reaches the first of the sessions on the MCA set. A useful in-between compilation.

***** Billie Holiday 1945–1948**

Classics 1040 *Holiday; Louis Armstrong (t, v); Joe Guy, Rostelle Reese, Billy Butterfield (t); Henderson Chambers (tb); Bill Stegmeyer (cl, as); Edmond Hall (cl); Toots Mondello, Al Klink, Lem Davis (as); Hank Ross, Armand Camgros, Bob Dorsey, Art Drellinger, Bernie Kaufman (ts); Stan Webb (bs); Sammy Benskin, Joe Springer, Billy Kyle, Bobby Tucker, Charlie Bateman (p); Mundell Lowe, Tiny Grimes, Jimmy Shirley, Dan Perri (g); John Simmons, Bob Haggart, Billy Taylor, Thomas Barney, Johnny Williams, John Levy (b); Specs Powell, Kelly Martin, Kenny Clarke, Big Sid Catlett, Denzil Best, Jimmy Crawford, Bunny Shawker (d); The Stardusters (v); strings.* 8/45–12/48.

An unhappy period, during which Holiday served time for narcotics possession, but there were nevertheless some fine records. 'Don't Explain' and 'Good Morning Heartache' appear in their definitive versions. 'The Blues Are Brewin'' is a beauty. The comeback date of December 1948 is saddled with the cooing Stardusters singing on two tracks, but 'Porgy' and 'My Man' are vintage Billie. Two V-Discs with Louis Armstrong fill out the disc. Excellent sound.

*****(*) Solitude**

Verve 519810-2 *Holiday; Charlie Shavers (t); Flip Phillips (ts); Oscar Peterson (p); Barney Kessel (g); Ray Brown (b); Alvin Stoller (d).* 52.

***** Recital By Billie Holiday**

Verve 521868-2 *Holiday; Harry 'Sweets' Edison, Joe Newman, Charlie Shavers (t); Willie Smith (as); Paul Quinichette (ts); Oscar Peterson (p, org); Bobby Tucker (p); Herb Ellis, Freddie Green, Barney Kessel (g); Ray Brown, Red Callender (b); Chico Hamilton, Gus Johnson, Ed Shaughnessy (d).* 7/52–9/54.

***** Lady Sings The Blues**

Verve 521429-2 *Holiday; Charlie Shavers (t); Tony Scott (cl, p); Budd Johnson, Paul Quinichette (ts); Wynton Kelly, Billy Taylor (p); Billy Bauer, Kenny Burrell (g); Aaron Bell, Leonard Gaskin (b); Cozy Cole, Lennie McBrowne (d).* 2/55–6/56.

*****(*) Music For Torching**

Verve 527455-2 *Holiday; similar to above.* 8/56.

****** All Or Nothing At All**

Verve 529226-2 2CD *Holiday; Harry 'Sweets' Edison (t); Ben Webster (ts); Jimmy Rowles (p); Barney Kessel (g); Joe Mondragon (b); Alvin Stoller (d).* 8/56–1/57.

****** Songs For Distingué Lovers**

Verve 539056-2 *As above, except add Larry Bunker (d).* 7/56.

*****(*) The Billie Holiday Songbook**

Verve 823246-2 *Holiday; Joe Newman, Charlie Shavers, Roy Eldridge, Buck Clayton, Harry 'Sweets' Edison (t); Tony Scott (cl); Willie Smith (as); Paul Quinichette, Al Cohn, Coleman Hawkins (ts); Wynton Kelly, Carl Drinkard, Mal Waldron, Oscar Peterson, Bobby Tucker (p); Kenny Burrell, Herb Ellis, Freddie Green, Barney Kessel (g); Aaron Bell, Ray Brown, Carson Smith, Milt Hinton, Red Callender (b); Gus Johnson, Chico Hamilton, Ed Shaughnessy, Don Lamond, Lennie McBrowne (d).* 7/52–9/58.

*****(*) Verve Jazz Masters: Billie Holiday**

Verve 519825-2 *Holiday; various groups.* 52–8/56.

***** Jazz Masters 47: Sings Standards**

Verve 527650-2 *As above.* 2/45–3/59.

*****(*) Lady In Autumn**

Verve 849434-2 2CD *Holiday; Buck Clayton, Joe Guy, Charlie Shavers, Joe Newman, Harry 'Sweets' Edison, Roy Eldridge (t); Tommy Turk (tb); Tony Scott (cl); Romeo Penque (as, bcl); Willie Smith, Gene Quill, Benny Carter (as); Ben Webster, Lester Young, Coleman Hawkins, Al Cohn, Paul Quinichette, Budd Johnson (ts); Oscar Peterson (p, org); Milt Raskin, Bobby Tucker, Mal Waldron, Carl Drinkard, Jimmy Rowles, Hank Jones, Wynton Kelly (p); Irving Ashby, Barney Kessel, Kenny Burrell, Barry Galbraith, Freddie Green (g); Janet Putnam (hp); Milt Hinton, Carson Smith, Joe Mondragon, Red Mitchell, Red Callender, Aaron Bell, Leonard Gaskin, John Simmons, Ray Brown (b); Dave Coleman, Alvin Stoller, J. C. Heard, Ed Shaughnessy, Chico Hamilton, Larry Bunker, Lennie McBrowne, Osie Johnson (d); strings.* 4/46–3/59.

****** First Issue: The Great American Songbook**

Verve 523003-2 2CD *Similar to above.* 52–59.

Holiday's last significant period in the studios was with Verve in the '50s, and this is the best-known and most problematical music she made. Her voice has already lost most of its youthful shine and ebullience – even a genuine up-tempo piece like 'What A Little Moonlight Can Do', where Oscar Peterson does his best to rouse the singer, is something she only has the energy to glide over. Whether this makes her music more revealing or affecting or profound is something listeners will have to decide for themselves. There are songs where the pace and the timbre of her voice are so funereal as to induce little but acute depression; others have a persuasive inner lilt which insists that her greatness has endured. And the best of the interpretations, scattered as they are through all these records, show how compelling Holiday could be, even when apparently enfeebled by her own circumstances.

Although there is a complete edition available (see below), Verve have now released Holiday's output in seven separate sets (the last, *All Or Nothing At All*, is a two-disc set, while the live records are listed below). Preference among the discs depends mainly on song selection and accompanists: whatever her own physical well-being, Norman Granz always made sure there were top-flight bands behind her. *Solitude* has some lovely things: a classic 'These Foolish Things', a marvellous 'Moonglow'. *Recital* has some happy work, including 'What A Little Moonlight Can Do' and 'Too Marvellous For Words', but there are some sloppy pieces too. *Lady Sings The Blues* (which basically replaces the previous disc under that title) has three or four of her best-known heartache songs and includes the rehearsal tape with Tony Scott where they work up 'God Bless The Child' – intriguing, but probably for scholars only. *Music For Torching* is small-hours music of a high, troubling calibre. *All Or Nothing At All* rounds up seven long sessions across two discs and includes some magnificent work from Edison and Webster (there is even a warm-up instrumental cut while they were waiting for her to arrive at the studio on one date) as well as what is probably Holiday's most regal, instinctual late work. It all seems to come to a peak on the very last track on disc two, the definitive version of 'Gee Baby, Ain't I Good To You?'.

Songs For Distingué Lovers has now been made available by Verve in their Master Edition series and, with the original programme expanded to 12 tracks, putting the entire session in one place, this is another front-rank recommendation, the music in its latest remastering sounding particularly handsome. In comparison, the compilations seem superfluous, except for those who prefer just the odd Holiday record in their collection. Both discs in the Jazz Masters series would do fine for that, though the *Standards* selection rather inevitably comes off second best. The *First Issue* two-disc set is, though, a beautifully chosen retrospective which eschews Holiday's tortured epics and lines up the choicest examples of Tin Pan Alley instead. Remastering has been done to a very high and meticulous standard.

★★(★) Masters Of Jazz Vol. 3: Billie Holiday
Storyville 4103 *Holiday; Hot Lips Page, Roy Eldridge, Neal Hefti (t); Herbie Harper, Jack Teagarden (tb); Barney Bigard (cl); Herbie Steward (cl, ts); Coleman Hawkins (ts); Teddy Wilson, Jimmy Rowles, Art Tatum (p); Al Casey (g); Iggy Shevack, Oscar Pettiford (b); Blinkie Garner, Big Sid Catlett (d).* 44/49.

★★★ Billie's Blues
Blue Note 748786-2 *Holiday; Monty Kelly, Larry Neill, Don Waddilove (t); Skip Layton, Murray McEachern (tb); Buddy DeFranco (cl); Alvy West, Dan D'Andrea, Lennie Hartman (reeds); Haywood Henry (ts, bs); Carl Drinkard, Bobby Tucker, Buddy Weed, Sonny Clark, Beryl Booker (p); Jimmy Raney, Mike Pingitore, Tiny Grimes (g); Red Mitchell, Artie Shapiro (b); Elaine Leighton, Willie Rodriguez (d).* 42–54.

★★★ Jazz At The Philharmonic
Verve 521642-2 *Holiday; Buck Clayton, Roy Eldridge, Howard McGhee (t); Tony Scott (cl); Illinois Jacquet, Wardell Gray, Al Cohn, Coleman Hawkins, Lester Young (ts); Carl Drinkard (p); Kenny Burrell (g); Charles Mingus, Carson Smith (b); Dave Coleman, J. C. Heard, Chico Hamilton (d).* 2/45–11/56.

★★★ 1949–52 Radio and TV Broadcasts
ESP 3002 *Holiday; other personnel uncertain, but includes Mal Waldron (p), Milt Hinton (b), Osie Johnson (d).* 49–52.

★★★ 1953–56 Radio and TV Broadcasts
ESP 3003 *As above.* 53–56.

★★★ At Carnegie Hall
Verve 527777-2 *Holiday; Buck Clayton, Roy Eldridge (t); Al Cohn, Coleman Hawkins (ts); Tony Scott (cl, p); Carl Drinkard (p); Kenny Burrell (g); Carson Smith (b); Chico Hamilton (d).* 11/56.

Holiday left a fair number of live recordings, most of them unauthorized at the time, and they can make a rather depressing lot to sort through. Unlike, say, Charlie Parker's live music, this presents a less than fascinating portrait, often of a musician in adversity. Club recordings find her in wildly varying voice, almost from song to song: truly affecting performances may sit next to ragged, throwaway ones. The 'Masters Of Jazz' series disc includes some good material from the '40s. *Billie's Blues* is an interesting cross-section of tracks: several from a European tour which was a mixed success, including three with Buddy DeFranco's group that feature some fine clarinet by the leader, and four from an obscure session for Aladdin with a group that puts the singer into a jump-band blues situation. She handles it unexpectedly well.

The ESP discs make an interesting pair, but we are still waiting for the new issue of what was the third volume in this series, which includes the famous 'Fine And Mellow' from the 1957 *Sound Of Jazz* telecast, as well as an excellent 'Porgy' from 1956. Look for ESP 3005 when it reappears. Her JATP appearances are collected on the Verve album, plus material from other (somewhat less inspiring) appearances from the '50s. *At Carnegie Hall* is the record of one of her last great live performances. The notes reveal she was scarcely in any fit state to perform and, with the music interspersed with readings from her book, there is a macabre quality which her artistry somehow rises above.

★★★★ The Complete Billie Holiday On Verve 1945–1959
Verve 517658-2 10CD *Holiday; various groups as above.* 45–59.

★★★(★) Billie's Best
Verve 513943-2 *As above.*

★★★(★) The Very Best Of Billie Holiday
Verve 547494-2 2CD *As above.*

With the appearance of this set, the circle is closed on Holiday's career: the various multi-disc packages impose an order which allows anyone to follow her from the beginning to the end. There are rarities in this major collection, which includes what are often wryly funny rehearsal tapes with Jimmy Rowles (it seems strange to hear this famously tormented woman laugh and tell jokes), but its main purpose is to provide first-to-last coverage of her major studio years. There is splendid documentation to go with the records. *Billie's Best* is a useful pocket edition that samples the big box. *The Very Best Of Billie Holiday* is a UK release and is a generous and splendid representation of her Verve years, although the necessary absence of any Columbia material means that it inevitably can't match up to the title.

(★★★) Lady In Satin
Columbia CK 65144 *Holiday; strings.* 58.

(★★★) Last Recordings
Verve 835370-2 *Holiday; Harry 'Sweets' Edison, Joe Wilder (t); Jimmy Cleveland, Billy Byers (tb); Romeo Penque (as, ts, bcl); Gene Quill (as); Al Cohn (ts); Danny Bank (bs); Hank Jones (p); Kenny Burrell, Barry Galbraith (g); Milt Hinton, Joe Benjamin (b); Osie Johnson (d); strings.* 3/59.

A troubling farewell which for some has a certain grim fascination. The croaking voice which barely gets through *Lady In Satin* has its admirers, and there is arguably some of the tormented revelation which distinguishes such earlier works as Parker's 'Lover Man', but we suggest that it be approached with care. Columbia have prepared a new edition that includes a fresh remastering, but frankly we see little reason to revise our earlier opinion; it's hard to find any artistic triumphs here, more a voyeuristic look at a beaten woman. *Last Recordings* emerges in much the same way, if it is in sum rather less harrowing.

Dave Holland (born 1946)

DOUBLE BASS, CELLO

Studied in London in the '60s, then joined Miles Davis, 1968–70. Has been constantly in demand ever since and has built a huge discography. Teaches and leads his own quintet when other demands allow. Occasional work on cello or electric bass, but basically a stand-up man with a peerless sound.

CORE COLLECTION

★★★★ Conference Of The Birds

ECM 829373-2 *Holland; Anthony Braxton, Sam Rivers (reeds, f); Barry Altschul (d, perc).* 11/72.

In 1968, the 22-year-old Holland recorded *Karyobin* with the Spontaneous Music Ensemble and *Filles De Kilimanjaro* with Miles Davis. Even allowing for Miles's left-field enthusiasms and seeming Anglophilia, and given that most bassists have a wide and varied CV, this is a pretty broad musical spectrum to pack into a few months. Holland has been spoken of in the same breath as the legendary Scott LaFaro; he shares the American's bright, exact intonation, incredible hand-speed and utter musicality.

If he had never made another record as leader, *Conference Of The Birds* would still stand out as a classic and as one of the finest things in the nascent ECM catalogue. The title-piece, marked out by Altschul's marimba figures and the two reedmen interweaving basket-tight, was inspired by the morning chorus outside Holland's London flat and not, as is sometimes suggested, by Attar's great mystical poem. But mystical much of the music is; indivisible and remarkably hard to render verbally.

On flutes, Rivers and Braxton are hard to separate; on saxophones, the differences are salutary. Altschul is at his very best. Perhaps the responsiblities of leading and writing weighed subtly on Holland himself. Though he is never less than audible, his contributions are more muted and reticent than usual. A quiet masterpiece nevertheless.

★★★ Emerald Tears

ECM 529087-2 *Holland (b solo).* 8/77.

★★★ Life Cycle

ECM 829200-2 *Holland (clo solo).* 11/82.

Though solo bass (and cello) performances were to become something of an ECM staple, with work by David Darling, Barre Phillips and Miroslav Vitous, Holland's two early solo discs stand out. *Emerald Tears* is a quiet and meditative album. Though it sustains interest for a full three-quarters of an hour (and after 20 years), it does on occasion begin to seem like a series of exercises. The eight tracks are more or less the same length, even when some, like the opening 'Spheres' or the beautiful 'Under Redwoods', seem to call out for further development, while others – the *arco* 'Combination' and 'Flurries' – seem to linger unnecessarily. One Miles Davis tune is included; 'Solar' sits comfortably for a bass player and it brings out Holland's singing tone. There is also a piece by Anthony Braxton, with whom the bassist worked in Circle.

The cello record is not quite such a tough listen, perhaps because it has an internal consistency *Emerald Tears* largely lacks. It is difficult to separate real echoes from simple association of ideas, but much of the language seems to be classical rather than jazz-based; some moments will suggest Bach, others Kodály, though there are also parallels with Oscar Pettiford and Ron Carter. For sheer musicianship, these records probably merit higher ratings; for most listeners, they demand a pretty substantial loyalty.

★★★(★) Jumpin' In

ECM 817437-2 *Holland; Kenny Wheeler (t, pkt-t, c, flhn); Robin Eubanks, Julian Priester (tb); Steve Coleman (as); Steve Ellington (d).* 10/83.

★★★ Seeds Of Time

ECM 825322-2 *As above, except replace Ellington with Marvin 'Smitty' Smith (d).* 11/84.

★★★ The Razor's Edge

ECM 833048-2 *As above, except omit Priester.* 2/87.

Holland's '80s bands were the antithesis of what he had been doing 15 years before, whether with the SME or with Miles. Tightly arranged, with much of the drama enacted between bass and brass, they manage to steer a path between freedom and the fixity of detail that, say, Braxton's music demanded. Holland also seemed to be much concerned with texture, and Kenny Wheeler's range of horns on *Jumpin' In* suggests a desire for subtle coloration that was to be developed, albeit less obviously, over the next couple of albums.

One obvious influence at this time was the Mingus Jazz Worskhop. 'Blues For C.M.' on *Razor's Edge* is the only fully explicit reference and, while it's difficult to reconcile the quiet and unassuming Holland with the volcanic American, the voicings and the interplay of structure and freedom come from the same root. The sound has paled a little by 1987, but these are all strong statements by a highly accomplished player and composer.

★★★ Triplicate

ECM 837113-2 *Holland; Steve Coleman (as); Jack DeJohnette (d).* 3/88.

★★(★) Extensions

ECM 941778-2 *Holland; Steve Coleman (as); Kevin Eubanks (g); Marvin 'Smitty' Smith (d).* 9/89.

There may be no such thing as an 'ECM sound', but there are certainly reference-points, career-wise, and one of the most obvious – it's also happened to Ralph Towner, to Jan Garbarek, even to the seemingly untouchable Keith Jarrett – seems to be a desire at some point to get back to jazz basics. At the end of the '80s, Holland – or Manfred Eicher – seemed to want a more mainstream approach. In prospect, *Triplicate* promised to be a stripped-down swinger, a deliberate increase in temperature. In reality, it appeared rather tame, even when Coleman bit down hard and vied with his namesakes. Passing time suggests it was a stronger and more durable exercise than it initially seemed. The follow-up was pretty duff, though. Eubanks is untameable and Smith can be ruthlessly self-indulgent. Poor old Holland found himself out of things at his own party.

★★★(★) Dream Of The Elders

ECM 529084-2 *Holland; Eric Person (as, ss); Steve Nelson (vib, mar); Gene Jackson (d); Cassandra Wilson (v).* 95.

This was Holland's first ECM record as leader for eight years. Our initial reaction was disappointment, but it wears better than expected. Despite the personnel, it has a strongly European feel, settled into a slightly dated folkish idiom. Person sounds very much like Coleman, albeit sharper and less groove-orientated, and he fits very comfortably into Holland's concept. As he was to do on the following record as well, Nelson is the one who pulls the sound closer to what Holland was doing a decade before: creating open-ended harmonies and a softly percussive pulse. Individual compositions are less clearly differentiated than they might have been, but perhaps because Holland was looking for something that had more of a unified feel.

Cassandra Wilson plays the wild card, and a rather effective one, bringing a delicate touch and a steely strength to the Maya Angelou lyric, 'Equality'. On this form, it's a performing relationship one would like to see developed. Holland has a sure, delicate touch around singers, strongly reminiscent of Ray Brown, whose example was to be honoured on *Points Of View* a couple of years later.

Our hesitant valuation first time round now seems too grudging. *Dream Of The Elders* may not belong in the front rank of Holland records, but it is a very impressive statement nevertheless.

****** Points Of View**
ECM 557020-2 *Holland; Robin Eubanks (tb); Steve Wilson (ss, as); Steven Nelson (vib, mar); Billy Kilson (d).* 9/97.

*****(*) Not For Nothin'**
ECM 1758 *As above, except omit Wilson; add Chris Potter (ss, as, ts).* 9/00.

From the faintly mournful opening of 'The Balance' to the soaring delight of 'Herbaceous', a dedication to Herbie Hancock, *Points Of View* is an altogether more even and generous record than its predecessor. Once again, Holland floats comfortably on top of the implicit pulse established by Nelson and secured by the new drummer. Kilson won't be to every taste and his solo on the Ray Brown tribute, 'Mr B', is lacking in substance, but he has a very secure time-feel, even when everything around seems to be drifting off-line. Reminiscent of a more mainstream Paul Motian, his has been a valuable recruitment.

Ironically, the strongest compositions on the album are by Eubanks and Wilson. The trombonist's 'Metamorphos' stands as a dark, ambiguous tailpiece to Holland's own 'Bedouin Trail'. Wilson creates his own mysteries on 'The Benevolent One', an idea which seems to draw on the same harmonic language as Coltrane's 'Alabama' and 'Wise One'. Nelson's feature comes right at the end, his own *faux*-Latin 'Serenade', which relegates the horns in favour of a gently swinging trio that cues up Holland's most relaxed playing of the set; unwary listeners might think they'd stumbled across one of Charlie Haden's romantic song projects. That good.

The quintet continued to evolve and to democratize with the arrival of Chris Potter, who is also a strong composer and contributes the excellent 'Lost And Found'. All five men have writing credits and Eubanks catches the attention immediately with the opening 'Global Citizen', a long, modulated suite of themes which triggers fine solos from Nelson, Holland and Eubanks himself. Dave long ago found in James Farber an engineer who gives him the rounded ensemble sound he favours and here the balance of voices is just about spot on. The loping title-track, led off by Nelson, is one of Holland's most good-natured compositions, with a gruff maturity that characterizes the whole of another strong record.

*****(*) What Goes Around**
ECM 014002 *Holland; Earl Gardner, Alex Sipiagin (t, flhn); Robin Eubanks, Andre Hayward, Josh Roseman (tb); Mark Gross (as); Antonio Hart (as, f); Chris Potter (ts); Steve Nelson (vib); Billy Kilson (d).* 1/01.

Apart from 'Upswing', these are all fairly familiar charts, giving a certain impression of scaled-up small group work. This isn't entirely fair because Holland has clearly thought through the implications of big band performance very carefully indeed. He has some very strong soloists in his line-up, but more importantly he has devised a powerful ensemble sound that carries tunes like 'Temple Dance', 'The Razor's Edge' and the title track into a new dimension.

Red Holloway (born 1927)

ALTO AND TENOR SAXOPHONE, VOCAL

Originally from Arkansas, James Holloway got his start in the blues and R&B bands which were all over Chicago in the late '40s and early '50s. He later worked in the sax–organ-combo format and has lately turned up in big-band and mainstream situations.

***** Brother Red**
Prestige 24141-2 *Holloway; Alvin Red Tyler (ts); Brother Jack McDuff (org); George Benson (g); Wilfred Middlebrooks (b); Joe Dukes (d).* 2/64.

***** Legends Of Acid Jazz**
Prestige 24199-2 *Holloway; John Patton, Lonnie Liston Smith (org); Norman Simmons (p); Eric Gale, George Benson (g); Leonard Gaskin, Charles Rainey, Paul Breslin (b); Herbie Lovelle, Ray Lucas, Frank Severino (d).* 10/63–12/65.

***** Nica's Dream**
Steeplechase SCCD 31192 *Holloway; Horace Parlan (p); Jesper Lundgaard (b); Aage Tanggaard (d).* 7/84.

***** Live At the 1995 Floating Jazz Festival**
Chiaroscuro CR(D) 348 *Holloway; Harry 'Sweets' Edison (t); Dwight Dickerson (p); Richard Reid (b); Paul Humphrey (d).* 11/95.

This Chicago alto and tenor veteran now has a better showing of his early work in the racks. *Brother Red* is basically the *Cookin' Together* collaboration with Jack McDuff, and a sturdy if unexceptional example of the sax/organ genre of the time. *Legends Of Acid Jazz* doubles up the original sets, *The Burner* (with Patton and Gale) and *Red Soul* (with Smith and Benson). Nothing ambitious, just sound, beefy playing by all hands.

More recent records have been somewhat mixed. The Steeplechase session reissues a mid-'80s date, and here Holloway hits a swinging groove that hardly lets up for 40-odd minutes: since he likes the high parts of the tenor and the middle range of the alto, it often sounds like he's playing a hybrid of the two horns, lean, many-noted and decidedly cheerful – he plays blues as if they were fun, and ballads tend to be amiable rather than deeply felt. Parlan and the Scandinavians do well for him.

Red's stint on board the S.S. *Norway* is captured on the Chiaroscuro CD. Sweets Edison sits in on three leisurely standards, and Red is in good enough spirits to sing one somewhat dubious love song.

***** Keep That Groove Going!**
Milestone 9319-2 *Holloway; Plas Johnson (ts); Gene Ludwig (org); Melvin Sparks (b); Kenny Washington (d).* 4/01.

More of a tenor skirmish than a battle, since both veterans are taking it rather easier these days, even if 'Go Red Go' gets things hot and bothered. Red probably edges ahead of Plas, given that he paces himself rather better, and it's the mutual joshing on the likes of the title-piece and 'Jammin' For Mr Lee', along with the blues balladry of 'Serenade In Blue', that works best.

Bill Holman (born 1927)

TENOR SAXOPHONE, ARRANGER

One of the most gifted of big-band arrangers, Holman studied music in California and then scored music for Stan Kenton in the early '50s. Though much of his work from the '60s onwards was in TV and session situations, he kept his hand in as a jazz writer and formed an 'occasional' big band to play his own charts beginning in 1975. His records in the '90s were few but memorable.

***** Jive For Five**

VSOP 19 *Holman; Lee Katzman (t); Jimmy Rowles (p); Wilfred Middlebrooks (b); Mel Lewis (d).* 6/58.

Holman is known these days as a grandmaster arranger. He has also been a more than useful saxophonist, tonally similar to the red-wine sound of Al Cohn, and this relic from a West Coast vintage has some particularly sinewy playing from the co-leader. Rowles is his customary splendid self and the almost forgotten Katzman holds his place without turning a hair, in the manner of the California movement. Lewis, who co-led the group, is discreet.

*****(*) Bill Holman Meets The Norwegian Radio Big Band**

Taurus TRCD 826 *Holman; Christian Beck, Atle Hammer, Bernt Anker Steen, Finn Eriksen, Gunnar Andersen (t, flhn); Jens Wendelboe, Tore Nilsen, Harald Halvorsen, Steffan Stokland, Frode Thingnaes (tb); Oivind Westby (btb); Harald Bergersen, Helge Hurum, Knut Riisnaes, Vidar Johansen, Nils Jansen, Johan Bergli (reeds); Erling Aksdal (ky); Steinar Larsen (g); Bjorn Kjellemyr (b); Svein Christiansen (d).* 6/87.

****** A View From The Side**

JVC 2050-2 *Holman; Carl Saunders, Frank Szabo, Ron Stout, Bob Summers (t, flhn); Andy Martin, Jack Redmond (tb); Bob Enevoldsen (vtb); Kenny Shroyer (btb); Lanny Morgan (as, f); Bill Perkins (as, ss, f); Pete Christlieb (ts, f); Ray Herrmann (ts, ss); Bob Efford (bs, bcl); Rich Eames (p); Doug Macdonald (g); Dave Carpenter (b); Bob Leatherbarrow (d).* 4/95.

****** Brilliant Corners**

JVC 9018-2 *As above.* 2/97.

Seldom in receipt of the kind of plaudits some other arrangers seem swamped in, Holman has quietly put together an awesome body of work, and recent records find him in peerless form. The Norwegian record was cut over a week's stay in Oslo: six new pieces plus a typically ingenious revision of 'All The Way'. The group rise to a challenge difficult enough to defeat many an ensemble, and on a piece such as 'A Separate Walking' the colours of brass, reeds and rhythm spin in perfect accord.

If the Norwegians did a fine job, they don't quite compare to Holman's own regular band, responsible for the two stunning JVC discs which testify not only to his undimmed creativity but to the ageless zest of West Coast jazz as a whole. Players such as Enevoldsen and Perkins are among the more notable survivors from the era's golden age, but this is a band almost indecently weighted with experience and they eat up whatever Holman can throw at them. *A View From The Side* is replete with frighteningly elaborate scores dispatched with the utmost elegance: to cite a mere two examples, sample the almost fantastical interplay of the sections on 'I Didn't Ask' or the rich, sobering treatment of 'The Peacocks', a concerto for Bob Efford's bass clarinet. *Brilliant Corners* is no less of an achievement and, considering the difficulty of arranging Monk tunes for big band, these ten charts seem like the work of a magician: has anyone dared score the title-piece in such a way? Here is one of the genuine masters doing his greatest work. These JVC CDs are now rather difficult to get, but there are 'audiophile' editions available, although collectors should be advised that they are expensive.

Richard 'Groove' Holmes (1931–91)

ORGAN

Discovered in Pittsburgh by Les McCann, who plays on his first records, Groove Holmes played organ in an old-fashioned swing style that was accommodating enough to any kind of soloist who happened to be out front. He stuck with his tested horn-plus-rhythm format and continued to work until his death, a few weeks after his sixtieth birthday.

***** After Hours**

Pacific Jazz 37986-2 *Holmes; Joe Pass, Gene Edwards (g); Leroy Henderson, Larance Marable (d).* 61–62.

***** Soul Message**

Original Jazz Classics OJC 329 *Holmes; Gene Edwards (g); Jimmie Smith (d).* 10/66.

**** Misty**

Original Jazz Classics OJC 724 *Holmes; Gene Edwards (g); Jimmie Smith, George Randle (d).* 4–7/66.

***** On Basie's Bandstand**

Prestige PRCD-11028-2 *Holmes; Gene Edwards (g); George Randall (d).* 4/66.

*****(*) Blues Groove**

Prestige PRCD-24133-2 *Holmes; Blue Mitchell (t); Harold Vick, Teddy Edwards (ts); Pat Martino, Gene Edwards (g); Paul Chambers (b); George Randle, Freddie Waits, Billy Higgins (d).* 3/66–5/67.

***** Legends Of Acid Jazz**

Prestige PRCD 24188-2 *Holmes; Rusty Bryant (as, ts); Earl Maddox, Billy Butler (g); Billy Jackson, Herbie Lovelle (d).* 2–8/68.

Holmes was one of the most big-sounding organists. A sometime bassist, he liked earthy, elemental bass-lines, and he decorated melodies with something like reluctance: he made the organ sound massive and implacable. He recorded most prolifically in the '60s, and he now has a fair showing on CD – though British readers will have to ask their importer for most of what's listed above. The Pacific Jazz discs were his earliest and are rather a mixed bag. Most of them have now been deleted again, but *After Hours* is still around. Holmes only has guitar and drums to contend with and it's a cogent show of what he did.

Soul Message is a fat, funky album which opens on the blues workout 'Groove's Groove', seven minutes that just about sum up Holmes's entire style. *Misty* is a ballad-orientated collection and the kind of thing that organists were obliged to make as songs for sedentary lovers: purely on those terms, it's rather good, but the formula is still boring over the long haul. A better choice is *Blues Groove*, which doubles up two Prestige albums,

Get Up And Get It! and *Soul Mist!* The first offers Edwards a guest role which he makes the most of: there's a long, expansive treatment of the tenorman's set-piece, 'Body And Soul'. Mitchell and the unimpressive Vick sit in on two tracks of the second set, but this is Groove's show, and he's at his best on the light touch of 'Up Jumped Spring'. *Legends Of Acid Jazz* is a modish disguise for two Prestige dates from 1968, *The Groover* and *That Healin' Feelin'*. Rusty Bryant livens up the latter session and Holmes rumbles and stomps his way around the likes of 'See See Rider' and some standards.

The new arrival in this batch is *On Basie's Bandstand*, a previously unissued set from Count Basie's Lounge, a Harlem club which lasted through most of the '60s and offered work to combos like Holmes's. It's rollicking, high-energy stuff almost all the way. On his studio albums Groove liked to settle back and roll out a ballad in his own time, but everything here is cooked at a tempo which is as close to frantic as the big man ever got. The nine-minute charge through 'Indiana' which opens the disc lays out almost everything the group has to say, even though there are six further tracks, and as a CD it's pretty exhausting, although there's an almost poignant ending with three minutes of 'Night Train' – a tune which reminds us that so many urban jazz clubs would be turned into strip joints in the '70s. A little bit of history.

Yuri Honing (born 1965)

TENOR SAXOPHONE

Dutch saxman, trying out unusual material in a post-bop vernacular.

★★★ **Gagarin**
A Records AL 73025 *Honing; Tony Overwater (b); Jost Lijbaart (d).* 9/95.
★★★ **Star Tracks**
Jazz In Motion 992102 *As above.* 7/96.
★★(★) **Playing**
Jazz In Motion JIM 75044 *Honing; Misha Mengelberg (p).* 3/98.
★★★(★) **Sequel**
Jazz In Motion JIM 75045 *Honing; Tony Overwater (b); Joost Lybaart (d).* 3/99.

Just don't mention Candy Dulfer ... The Netherlands' second-most-famous saxophonist could equally and quite legitimately trade on his looks; spaghetti-thin, cheekbones you could shave parmesan on (please insert the appropriate Dutch equivalent, if you know it), a wonderful beauty spot on his cheek, and a look of Harry Connick Jr. In addition, Honing is immensely talented, as both player and composer.

The earliest of these records consists entirely of moody, exploratory originals. Honing favours the lower end of the tenor range, and he works largely outside the chords, in the sort of free-but-controlled language Eric Dolphy may have bequeathed to Holland in his final days. The slower-tempo pieces, like 'Nuku'Alofa' and 'The Beauty Of Reason', almost suggest Warne Marsh at his most subtly seductive, while 'Gagarin' itself and the intriguingly titled 'Nelson's Victory' (Lord? Oliver? Louis? Steve?) are upbeat boppers.

On both albums, Lijbaart and the gifted Overwater (who has toured with David Murray) are equal and active partners, powering along the faster material, supporting and augmenting the gentler things. They are perhaps less prominent on *Star Tracks*, a fascinating attempt to generate a canon of new standards, 'West European pop music from the period 1974–1995', which explains Björk's 'Isobel', Abba's 'Waterloo' and the Police's 'Walking On The Moon', but not 'Body And Soul'. As on *Gagarin*, Overwater contributes an edgy composition, but the later record's emphasis is on stripping away all the production values of contemporary pop, exposing the basic theme and then examining its potential. As such, it succeeds very well indeed.

Playing is a bit of a misfire. Mengelberg tends to go his own sweet way, and Honing's self-confidence suddenly seems to ebb away. A few nice moments but a lot of wreckage.

Sequel puts things back together. Some strange choices of material in the end work out very well: closing on Gilbert O'Sullivan's 'Nothing Rhymed' – here in the best version since Martin Carthy's – was a masterstroke. Honing plays with steely confidence, and so, in their somewhat more deferential way, do the other two.

★★★★ **Seven**
Challenge 75086 *Honing; Paul Bley (p); Gary Peacock (b); Paul Motian (d).* 01.

This one just builds and builds, and by the time you reach the two closing numbers – 'Once Is Twice' and 'Vertical' – you're a more than willing convert. Honing still doesn't yet have the sly and wise maturity of his playing partners, but he stands up to the challenge well and plays some fine solos on the shorter opening tracks, reaffirming his ability to compress a lot of ideas into a short span. The senior players may not have had long to familiarize themselves with some of the material, for there is a faint impression that Bley in particular is following his own agenda, irrespective of the written theme, but the quality of musicianship on things like 'Yasutani' and 'Bley Away' is so considerable that such quibbles seem meaningless. Another very impressive showing from the Dutchman, who seems to have mainstreamed – or mainstream-moderned – himself on this one.

Tristan Honsinger

CELLO

After a classical education at the Peabody Institute in Baltimore, the New Englander moved to Amsterdam and founded the Instant Composers Pool (ICP) with Han Bennink. He has been a steady presence on the European free scene.

★★★(★) **Double Indemnity / Imitation Of Life: 1980–1981**
Atavistic Unheard Music 224 *Honsinger; Toshinori Kondo (t, perc, v); Steve Beresford (p, org, syn, b, flhn, euph, vn, perc); David Toop (f, af, g, b, perc).* 80, 81.

This reissue brings together two important albums originally issued on the Y label. The CD interestingly begins with two out-takes from the duo record with Beresford *Double Indemnity* and affords additional insight into how imaginatively the multi-instrumentalist/composer/producer melds with his playing colleagues, often to the detriment of his own celebrity. Beresford is one of the unsung geniuses of modern European music, a constant presence whose contribution is usually unremarked. These duos are among the best of his recorded efforts, witty, shrewd and often touching. The group tracks are less successful, largely because the two sides of *The Imitation of Life* seem to outstay their welcome at the same time as being artificially truncated for LP length. Great, though, to have these records back in circulation.

***** Map Of Moods**

FMP 76 *Honsinger; Alex Kolkowski, Stephano Lunardi (vn); Ernst Glerum (b); Louis Moholo (d).* 96.

On this set Honsinger and his group manipulate a predetermined sequence of themes within what he describes as 'areas'. This seems similar to Anthony Braxton's practice of overlaid and superimposed compositions within a single performance, except that here the players seem to be required to keep pretty much to the original conception of the piece unless they genuinely feel they can improve it. Moholo appears to direct proceedings by changing metre and by providing trig points and map references for the other players. Honsinger's love of string instruments is well evidenced and the sound of the group is lusciously 'classical', even when the attacks are quite extreme. A very fine record by an important innovator.

****** A Camel's Kiss**

ICO 036 *Honsinger (clo, v solo).* 98.

This superb solo recording sees Honsinger negotiate the entire range of his musical heritage, from Bach-like solo sonatas to Berliner Ensemble cabaret songs to free-form improvisations which camouflage a strong inner structure. It's a completely exhilarating 50-odd minutes of music, with not a dull spot or a sign that the performer is merely marking time, and it would be fascinating to know how much and what was left on the studio floor at the end of the session. Unlike a good deal of improvised music, this is beautifully recorded, bringing out the resonant woodiness of the cello, but also its percussive potential and its ability to set off ringing harmonics in the space around the performer. Strongly recommended to anyone interested in this branch of improvisation.

Bertha Hope (born 1936)

PIANO

Wife of the pianist Elmo Hope, Bertha is no mean talent herself at the keyboard, and she once cut an album of duets with her husband before these late-flowering examples of her work.

****(*) In Search Of ... Hope**

Steeplechase SCCD 31276 *Hope; Walter Booker (b); Billy Higgins (d).* 10/90.

***** Elmo's Fire**

Steeplechase SCCD 31289 *Hope; Eddie Henderson (t); Junior Cook, Dave Riekenberg (ts); Walter Booker (b); Leroy Williams (d).* 1/91.

***** Nothin' But Love**

Reservoir RSR CD 161 *Hope; Walter Booker (b); Jimmy Cobb (d).* 10/99.

Elmo Hope's widow makes no attempt to disguise her fealty to his music: there are two of his tunes on the first album, four on the second, and Bertha's own style is a gentle extrapolation of Elmo's off-centre lyricism. She is no great executant, happiest at a steady mid-tempo and unwilling to risk any flourishes in a solo, but her improvisations have a patient and rather beguiling beauty about them, a bebop vocabulary fragmented into very small pieces which she seems to turn over and over in her phrases. *In Search Of ... Hope* is a little too tasteful and laid-back, Higgins as solid as ever, Booker quiescent, and it bows before the superior quintet date (Riekenberg appears on only one tune). Eddie Henderson walks a measured line between elegance and real fire, with a remarkable improvisation on the blues 'Bai Tai'. Junior Cook is patchy, but Hope herself sounds convincing, and her treatment of Sonny Fortune's wistful 'For Duke And Cannon' is splendid.

Her album for Reservoir is also her first American record. No standards and nothing remotely hackneyed in the tune selection and, with Booker and Cobb offering sympathetic time, this is another charming session. Celia Reggiani's 'Mia' features in a long, musing treatment. The boppish feel of George Braith's 'Leslie' suits her less well than Elmo's 'Stars Over Marrakesh' or her own 'Gone To See T', a reflection on Monk. Thin on virtuosity, but better than many a flashier record.

Elmo Hope (1923–67)

PIANO

Elmo's finest moment was probably as a sideman on Harold Land's 1959 album, The Fox. Drug problems and a certain lack of self-assurance hampered his own career, but nevertheless there is a substantial body of work.

****** Trio And Quintet**

Blue Note 784438 2 *Hope; Freeman Lee, Stu Williamson (t); Frank Foster, Harold Land (ts); Percy Heath, Leroy Vinnegar (b); Frank Butler, Philly Joe Jones (d).* 6/53–10/57.

*****(*) Meditations**

Original Jazz Classics OJC 1751 *Hope; John Ore (b); Willie Jones (d).* 6/55.

Hope managed to sound sufficiently different from both his main influences, Bud Powell (with whom he went to school) and Thelonious Monk, to retain a highly individual sound. His reputation as a composer is now surprisingly slight, but he had a strong gift for melody, enunciating themes very clearly, and was comfortable enough with classical and modern concert music to introduce elements of fugue and canon, though always with a firm blues underpinning. Like a good many pianists of his generation, he seems to have been uneasy about solo performance (though he duetted regularly with his wife Bertha) and is heard to greatest effect in trio settings. The early *Meditations* sounds remarkably Monk-like in places and John Ore's slightly limping lines confirm the resemblance (Ore was a long-standing member of the Thelonious Monk quartet and Jones was one of Monk's favourite drummers, a rating passed on to Charles Mingus). 'Elmo's Fire' and 'Blue Mo' are deft originals.

The Blue Note sessions are taut and well disciplined, though the trio tracks are very much better than the quintets, where the sequence of solos begins to seem rather mechanical and Hope progressively loses interest in varying his accompaniments of others. Originals like 'Freffie' and 'Hot Sauce' come across well, and the sound stands up down the years.

***** Hope Meets Foster**

Original Jazz Classics OJC 1703 *Hope; Freeman Lee (t); Frank Foster (ts); John Ore (b); Art Taylor (d).* 10/55.

***** The All Star Sessions**
Milestone M 47037 *Hope; Donald Byrd, Blue Mitchell (t); John Coltrane, Jimmy Heath, Hank Mobley, Frank Wess (ts); Paul Chambers, Percy Heath (b); Philly Joe Jones (d).* 5/56–6/61.

Hope responded well to the challenge of Coltrane's developing harmonic language and the Milestone sessions contain some provocative indications of Trane's early willingness to deconstruct standard material, in this case a bold reading of 'Polka Dots And Moonbeams'. The sessions with Foster are rather more conventional, but 'Georgia On My Mind' demonstrates Hope's original and uncompromising approach to standard ballad material, and Foster is only able to embellish a very strong conception.

***** So Nice**
Fresh Sound FSRCD 194 *Hope; Rolf Ericson, Stu Williamson (t); Harold Land (ts); Curtis Counce, Leroy Vinnegar (b); Frank Butler (d).* 10/57, 4/58.

If ever an artist stoked the East/West controversy in jazz it was Elmo Hope. He was openly contemptuous of the jiveass Westerners who seemed too lazy to bother coping with his fast time signatures and complex harmonics. He might have overstated the case, for these 1957 and 1958 sessions from LA find him teamed with players who don't seem to be having any difficulty with his charts. The earliest dates, from October 1957, are quintet cuts with Williamson, Land, Vinnegar and Butler; Counce and Ericson are in for the later dates, though two of the best tracks from April are trio cuts. These are actually one and the same theme though given on the masters as 'Headgear' and 'The Countdown' and so attributed here. This was presumably an idea run down in the studio over a long, loping groove from Counce, who always offered more bounce. The April tracks were more developed: the sweetly swinging title-track, the eponymous 'St Elmo's Fire' (Hope's given name was actually St Elmo) and 'Vaun Ex', which is a forgotten masterpiece of bebop.

The later session reprises 'So Nice' with the more pungent Ericson in the line-up, but here much of the material is repertory bop and ballad swing: Denzil Best's 'Move', 'Angel Eyes', 'Someone To Watch Over Me' and Harold Land's nicely conceived 'Exploring The Future'. Full marks to Fresh Sound for keeping so much valuable Hope material in view (see also *Sounds From Rikers Island*, below).

***** Elmo Hope Trio**
Original Jazz Classics OJC 477 *Hope; Jimmy Bond (b); Frank Butler (d).* 2/59.

*****(*) Plays His Original Compositions**
Fresh Sound FSR CD 181 *Hope; Paul Chambers, Butch Warren (b); Granville Hogan, Philly Joe Jones (d).* 61.

***** Beacon And Celebrity Trio Recordings**
Prevue 15 *As above.* 61, 62.

*****(*) Homecoming**
Original Jazz Classics OJC 1810 *Hope; Blue Mitchell (t); Jimmy Heath, Frank Foster (ts); Percy Heath (b); Philly Joe Jones (d).* 6/61.

***** Hope-Full**
Original Jazz Classics OJC 1872 *Hope; Bertha Hope (p).* 11/61.

The 1959 trio, which was for Contemporary, is rather disappointing, but Hope had by this stage moved to the West Coast (which he found professionally conducive – i.e. more gigs – but artistically a little sterile) and had become further involved in drugs, for which he was eventually jailed. His fortunes were on a roller-coaster from then until his untimely death, aged only 43. The Fresh Sound is an excellent way of getting Hope's most interesting compositions on one disc, though the Blue Note *Trio And Quintet* album remains the item of first choice.

However, the very fine *Homecoming* is still available, restoring material from the trio and sextet dates in June 1961 and unveiling another batch of intelligent arrangements. Much of the same material is included on the Prevue compilation, though the sound is not exceptional, even by the disappointing standards of the original masters. Another return is the hitherto very rare *Hope-Full*, which includes three duets with Bertha and five solos. It would have been more interesting to hear the pianist improvising alone on some of his own themes: these are mainly standards, with the odd choice of 'When Johnny Comes Marching Home' the only real surprise; Hope sounds interesting but lacking the confidence to really assert himself on this material.

****** Sound From Rikers Island**
Fresh Sound FSRCD 338 *Hope; Lawrence Jackson (t); Fred Douglas (ss, as); John Gilmore (ts); Ronnie Boykins (b); Philly Joe Jones (d); Earl Coleman, Marcelle Daniels (v).* 8/63.

There's a certain irony, but also a fittingness, in finding Hope at the heart of a project warning of the dangers of narcotics. These sessions were put together by Elmo, composer Sid Frey and vibraharpist Walt Dickerson, who does not figure on the album. The anti-drug message – Rikers Island is the jail where many addicts ended up – is actually quite thin and what comes across is some stunning music. 'Ecstasy' and 'Trippin'' are as vivid an account of the drug experience as there is in modern jazz; the latter is a staccato, uneasy line with lots of harmonic variation and testimony to the creative chemistry between Hope and Frey. The set also includes versions of bop classics 'Groovin' High' (a fine scat from Marcelle Daniels) and 'A Night In Tunisia'. The real plus of the session is the extraordinary line-up Hope and his colleagues assembled. The brilliant John Gilmore is so thinly documented away from the Arkestra that any examples of his other work are fallen on like manna. He sounds full-toned and pungent here, but with a mournfulness appropriate to the project theme. Philly Joe, who had his own perspective on the album's theme, is also in great heart, driving the time on 'Trippin'' and the fierce opening 'Ode For Joe'. Earl Coleman's vocals are surprisingly affecting. A wonderful find.

*****(*) The Final Sessions**
Evidence ECD 22147-2 2CD *Hope; John Ore (b); Clifford Jarvis, Philly Joe Jones (d).* 3–5/66.

The Final Sessions, released in 1966 shortly before his death, help to fill in another corner of the picture. It was thought that he had made his last recordings as far back as 1963, but these tapes see him back in the company of Philly Joe, with whom he had worked in Joe Morris's R&B band, and with Ore. Jarvis was also a sensitive collaborator, and he is the drummer on two-thirds of these cuts.

At the end, Hope sounds thoughtful and technically sound, recording long takes (which are now issued unedited) that are jam-packed with ideas. His ability to reshape a standard like 'I Love You' and the bebop classic, 'A Night In Tunisia', is undiminished by time; but the real meat of the two discs comes in originals: a long version of 'Elmo's Blues', with altered changes and a curious long-form structure, the terse 'Vi-Ann', and the excellent 'Toothsome Threesome' and 'Punch'. The recordings are somewhat rough and ready. Though a certain degree of electronic sweetening has taken place, much of the texture of the original has been preserved, which is appropriate to music of historical importance. However frustrating the Elmo Hope discography still seems, it is in better shape than for years.

Stan Hope

PIANO

Self-taught and hugely experienced, with nearly 50 years in the business. Sadly, he's recorded little on his own account.

*** Pastels

Savant 2020 *Hope; Houston Person (ts); Ray Drummond (b); Kenny Washington (d).* 99.

Apparently, Stan Hope was inspired to play jazz by an aunt's gift of a record of Errol Garner playing 'Be Anything' and his own 'Pastels'. Both of those songs are included on what is, remarkably, only Stan's third album as leader. Given the range of experience with most of the major figures of jazz, it's a slim haul, but though we mourn the disappearance of his self-titled 1972 debut on Mainstream, this is a very desirable set. Person is a guest performer on what is essentially a trio set, but his solo on '(Back Home In) Indiana' sets the album alight. Stan's touch is not so much Garnerish as garnished Basie and sometimes you hope for a little more detail in the solo spots, but his sense of timing is impeccable and his humour obvious. The high point is 'A Flower Is A Lovesome thing', built into a nicely crafted medley.

Chris Hopkins (born 1972)

PIANO

Though born in New Jersey, Hopkins grew up in Germany, where he has been leading bands since his teens. His style is in debt to the pre-war American masters.

***(*) Daybreak

Arbors ARCD 19235 *Hopkins (p solo).* 2/00.

Recorded (with beautiful sound) in Switzerland, this exceptionally playable disc is a delightful surprise. Hopkins was still in his 20s when it was made, but his affections lie with the piano jazz of the early Harlem stride masters and their elegant successors in the '30s. The material goes back to Willie 'The Lion' Smith and creeps as far forward as the Ellington of 'Dancers In Love'. It's far from antiquarian in feel. Hopkins manages to make it sound lively and well-informed without getting too knowing or resorting to a pasticheur's suit. His take on Earl Hines's 'Caution Blues', for instance, hints at Fatha's 'West End Blues' appearance, as well as the 1928 solo. Teddy Wilson's 'Sunny Morning' may never have been touched by another pianist, and Hopkins makes you wonder why. If stride is his favourite rhythmic language, it's often present more by implication than in the figures themselves. He gets a crisp but not clattery touch out of the keyboard. Including only two originals of his own was unbecoming modesty, since they're both excellent.

Claude Hopkins (1903–84)

PIANO

Hopkins was bandleading by the early '20s. He had much success in New York from 1930 onwards and as a touring attraction from 1937. Hopkins did staff-arranging for CBS and switched to small-band work from 1947 when the big bands died. He carried on into old age, but his principal legacy is his '30s material.

*** Claude Hopkins 1932–1934

Classics 699 *Hopkins; Ovie Alston (t, v); Albert Snaer, Sylvester Lewis (t); Fred Norman (tb, v); Fernando Arbello, Henry Wells (tb); Edmond Hall (cl, as, bs); Gene Johnson (as); Bobby Sands (ts); Walter Jones (bj, g); Henry Turner (b); Pete Jacobs (d); Orlando Roberson (v).* 5/32–12/34.

*** Claude Hopkins 1934–1935

Classics 716 *As above, except add Snub Mosley (tb), Hilton Jefferson (cl, as); omit Wells.* 1/34–2/35.

***(*) Claude Hopkins 1937–1940

Classics 733 *Hopkins; Shirley Clay, Jabbo Smith, Lincoln Mills, Sylvester Lewis, Robert Cheek, Albert Snaer, Russell Jones, Herman Autrey (t); Floyd Brady, Fred Norman, Vic Dickenson, Ray Hogan, Norman Greene, Bernard Archer (tb); Gene Johnson, Chauncey Haughton, Ben Smith, Floyd Blakemore, Ben Richardson, Howard Johnson, Norman Thornton (as); Bobby Sands, Cliff Glover, Benny Waters (ts); Walter Jones, Rudolph Williams (g); Abe Bolar, Elmer James (b); Pete Jacobs, George 'Pops' Foster, Walter Johnson (d); Beverley White, Froshine Stewart, Orlando Roberson (v).* 2/37–3/40.

**(*) The Transcription Performances 1935

Hep 1049 *Hopkins; Albert Snaer, Sylvester Lewis (t); Ovie Alston (t, v); Henry Wells, Fred Norman (tb); Edmond Hall (cl, as, bs); Hilton Jefferson (cl, as); Gene Johnson (as); Bobby Sands (ts); Walter Jones (g); Henry Turner (b); Pete Jacobs (d).* 35.

Hopkins was a skilful pianist and he liked to get a lot of solos with his band – so much so that the demands of arranging around him may have told against the ambitions of the group. It certainly never worked as well as the Earl Hines orchestra and, though Hopkins had fewer imposing soloists – the brief stays by Smith and Dickenson in 1937 were wasted – the group's ensemble sound lacked character and the arrangements were often second rate. These chronological CDs tell the story in decent if unexceptional transfers. Some of the music on the early disc promises more than is eventually delivered: 'Mad Moments', 'Shake Your Ashes', 'Hopkins Scream' and especially Jimmy Mundy's arrangement of 'Mush Mouth' are exciting and surprising pieces. But the two later discs, while interesting, never break very far out of swing-era clichés. There is also a serviceable compilation of the earlier material on *Monkey Business* (Hep CD1031). Hep's set of transcription performances is nicely presented, but the music is very slight and the blackface-style vocals on tracks such as 'The Preacher And The Bear' show how quickly Hopkins and his band were outdated.

Glenn Horiuchi (1955–2000)

PIANO, SHAMISEN

Influenced to some degree by Cecil Taylor, this West Coast pianist attempted to synthesize jazz, Oriental and classical forms.

***** Oxnard Beet**
Soul Note 121228 2 *Horiuchi; Francis Wong (ts, f); Taiji Miyagawa (b); Leon Alexander (d, vib).* 88.

***** Calling Is It And Now**
Soul Note 121268 *Horiuchi; Francis Wong (ts); Anders Swanson (b); Jeanette Wrate (d).* 95.

Horiuchi's interest in the common ground between his various musical traditions is evident on *Oxnard Beet* where hints of Asian ritual and rice-pounding rhythms are interwoven with jazz. It's not always a successful amalgam, both traditions demanding a more totalizing philosophy that makes it difficult to abstract elements without destroying the whole. Nonetheless, here and on the later Soul Note, Horiuchi makes a convincing case for the attempt at least.

He's a fiery and pugnacious player who is sometimes inclined to soft pedal too self-consciously when exploring softer dynamics. The upshot is that his quieter passages can sound under-powered and a bit lightweight. Wong was a long-term collaborator and is integral to *Calling Is It And Now* as well. His tenor playing is agile and harmonically complex, sometimes oddly reminiscent of the late Joe Farrell, but it is as a flutist that he most completely fits into the Horiuchi aesthetic and the flute passages on the earlier album are among Wong's best on record.

There are earlier sets on Asian Improv, including the very good *Issei Spirit*, but these may not be currently available. Anyone wanting to sample Horiuchi's distinctive vision, snuffed out tragically early, would do well to start with these.

*****(*) Dewdrop**
AsianImprov 31 *Horiuchi; William Roper (tba, v); Francis Wong (ts, cl, f, v); Joseph Mitchell (perc).* 94, 95.

*****(*) Elegy For Sarajevo**
AsianImprov 35 *As above.* 95.

The programme of the title-piece is self-explanatory, the mood of *Elegy For Sarajevo* more wistful than tragic, but with a deep sense of lost connections and sundered relationships in the harmonies. Here, the quiet dynamic works perfectly and the balance of Western instruments with the quiet vocalizations and mournful whispers of the Japanese instruments seems to come from a different sonic dimension, almost as if ghosts were speaking. If one were told this was a threnody for the victims of Hiroshima (of which there are many, of course), it would be no surprise, but there are fragments of European classical melody dotted through the mix that help to concentrate the expressive focus. 'Watercolours #1' is more impressionistic and less successful and it seems perverse to start such a powerful album with its weakest track.

Dewdrop makes a similar mistake, but here the title piece doesn't have quite the same emotional resonance and works perfectly well at the end. Also, listeners can reprogramme their CD players to maximum effect. Wong's playing and narration is very powerful here and Roper continues to amaze with a technique all his own.

***** Hilltop View**
Music & Arts 935 *Horiuchi; William Roper (tba, v); Francis Wong (vn); Roberto Miguel Miranda (b); Jeanette Wrate (d).* 8–9/95.

***** Mercy**
Music & Arts 062. *As above, except Wong (ts, f, erhu, perc, v); omit Roper; add Joseph Jarman (as, f, shakuhachi, perc, v); Elliott Humberto Kavee (clo, perc).* 5–9/96.

For all its promise of an open vista, *Hilltop View* is a tough listen, but ultimately a rewarding one. Horiuchi has never played in such a concentrated way, drawing more heavily than usual on his classical bag and offering no quarter as far as dynamics are concerned. The set is basically two groups: an orthodox trio with Miranda and Wrate and the augmented Unit(a) which includes the multi-talented Wong and the truly remarkable Roper, whose tuba improvisations are again one of the album's genuine talking points. Playing sometimes with the fleetness of a valve trombonist, at other times in registers so dark they almost blot out other sounds, he is the star of the session. A word, though, for Wrate who has been a loyal collaborator of Horiuchi's for some years, a strong drummer with lots of lateral ideas. Check out her playing on 'Quick Cut' and 'Wide Beat'. Glenn plays shamisen on some selections.

If 'Mercy' is what some listeners might cry out after listening to the first Music & Arts set, the second, which bears that name, is more accommodating. In place of one remarkable soloist, another. Jarman is on splendid form on a whole range of instruments, complementing Wong who's back in his normal place. Apart from 'Earthworks', which has a suitably massy feel, most of the early tracks are quite short, in some cases too short to make much impact. At the end of the album, though, Horiuchi unveils two large-scale ideas with the keening title track and 'Another Space (A)'. These both require some digestion, and it's as well to track what Robert Miranda is doing on bass; otherwise the structures can seem slightly impenetrable.

*****(*) Fair Play**
Soul Note 121328 *Horiuchi; William Roper (tba, v); Francis Wong (ts, f, v); Jeanette Wrate (d, v).* 99.

Horiuchi's final recording before his untimely death is also one of his best. The Unit(a) group is now so well settled that they speak with an absolutely common language and an absolute unity of purpose. Some of the forced classicism has gone from Horiuchi's own playing and his long lines are now much more symmetrical and evenly paced. All four pieces are long, but it's 'Angel Tears' that stands out, a gloriously evocative and harmonically complex piece, equal with Glenn's best. The others don't quite come up to that level, but the closing 'Manzanar Voices Part II', which recalls the 1989 AsianImprov album, rounds out the career well and poignantly.

Johan Horlen (born 1967)

ALTO AND SOPRANO SAXOPHONES, BASS CLARINET, ALTO FLUTE

Swedish saxophonist with a couple of dates in a post-bop style.

***** Dance Of Resistance**
Dragon DRCD 260 *Horlen; Torbjorn Gulz (p); Christian Spering (b); Jukkis Uotila (d).* 6/94.

***** Chills**

Dragon DRCD 5/00. *Horlen; Peter Nylander (g); Christian Spering (b); Bengt Stark (d).* 5/00.

Playing alto on all but one of the seven themes on the debut, the Swede is equal parts lyricism and passion here. The title-piece exemplifies this tightrope walk: continually skirling up towards a false note, he keeps pulling himself back in line before matters get out of hand. That reserve makes the still waters of 'To Miss', a lovely duet for soprano and piano, and the contrary position of 'The Best Things In Life Are Free', an argument for alto and drums, the more effective. But some of his ideas go nowhere, and the closing blow-out on 'Everything I Love' is perhaps a step too far. Another horn shouldering some responsibility might have balanced out the session better.

Chills introduces bass clarinet and alto flute to his range and, with Nylander in on only four of eight tracks, he's got much more space to work in. That said, this feels like little more than an easy-going continuation of the previous set: rounded and harmonious playing, the odd touch of tartness, but more inclined to pacify than make war.

John Horler (born 1947)

PIANO

British pianist and composer, a regular with John Dankworth and Cleo Laine, and an occasional leader.

****(*) Gentle Piece**

Spotlite SPJ-CD 542 *Horler; Phil Lee (g); Dave Green (b); Spike Wells (d).* 93.

***** Unity**

Hi Hat 004 *Horler; Phil Lee (g).* 97.

Horler's amiable playing owes much to his acknowledged mentor, Bill Evans, though encouragingly it's Evans's tougher side that he comes closest to, and while some of this music is a bit wispy, as on Kenny Wheeler's title-track, there's an underlying assertiveness ever present. This comes out most effectively in the surprising *fast* version of 'My Funny Valentine', done as a hard-bitten duet for piano and guitar. Not much else makes a terrific impression, though, and the date is let down by Spike Wells's splashy drumming and a particularly ungracious studio sound. Lee is a sympathetic and engaging player, both on the group set and on the duos. He deserves a wider reputation.

Shirley Horn (born 1934)

PIANO, VOCAL

A native of Washington, DC, Horn studied piano at college and was leading her own small groups from 1954. She remained a well-kept Washington secret until the '80s, when she began touring Europe, and a contract with Verve marked her belated coming-out.

***** Loads Of Love / Shirley Horn With Horns**

Mercury 843454-2 *Horn; Jimmy Cleveland (tb); Hank Jones, Bobby Scott (p); Kenny Burrell (g); Milt Hinton (b); Osie Johnson (d); rest unknown.* 63.

A reissue of the two albums Horn made for Mercury in 1963. They're modest, pleasing records, much like many another light-jazz vocal record of the period, and, while Horn's voice is transparently clear and warm, she was used to accompanying herself; placed in the studios with a stellar but unfamiliar band, she occasionally sounds stilted. Nor was she allowed to work at her favourite dead-slow tempos on ballads. Fine remastering.

*****(*) A Lazy Afternoon**

Steeplechase SCCD 1111 *Horn; Buster Williams (b); Billy Hart (d).* 7/78.

***** At Northsea**

Steeplechase SCCD 37015/16 2CD *Horn; Charles Ables (b); Billy Hart (d).* 7/81.

***** The Garden Of The Blues**

Steeplechase SCCD 1203 *Horn; Charles Ables (b); Steve Williams (d).* 11/84.

Horn's first Steeplechase set broke a long silence; if anything, it was effectively a debut album. The manner here, and throughout these three fine and under-recognized records, is reflective and sparsely evocative. Horn establishes her liking for intensely slow tempos with a compelling treatment of 'There's No You', but she feels able to contrast that immediately with the hipsterish reading of 'New York's My Home', and the long trio instrumental on 'Gentle Rain' displays a piano method that works with the simplest materials and makes something distinctive. Williams and Hart – the latter an old friend who might understand Horn's music better than anyone – play with complete empathy. If anything, the remaining discs are a slight letdown after *A Lazy Afternoon*, since Horn had already made a nearly definitive statement in this context; but *At Northsea*, which catches the best from several sets at the 1981 Northsea Jazz Festival, is an attractive souvenir of Horn on stage and blends together many of her favourite set-pieces.

***** Softly**

Audiophile 224 *Horn; Charles Ables (b); Steve Williams (d).* 10/87.

***** I Thought About You**

Verve 833235-2 *As above.* 87.

*****(*) Close Enough For Love**

Verve 837933-2 *Horn; Buck Hill (ts); Charles Ables (b); Steve Williams (d).* 11/88.

*****(*) You Won't Forget Me**

Verve 847482-2 *Horn; Miles Davis, Wynton Marsalis (t); Buck Hill, Branford Marsalis (ts); Toots Thielemans (hca, g); Charles Ables (b, g); Buster Williams (b); Billy Hart, Steve Williams (d).* 6–8/90.

***** Here's To Life**

Verve 511879-2 *Horn; Wynton Marsalis (t); Steve Kujala, James Walker (f); Alan Broadbent (p); John Chiodini (g); Charles Ables, Chuck Domanico (b); Steve Williams, Harvey Mason (d); strings.* 91.

*****(*) Light Out Of Darkness**

Verve 519703-2 *Horn; Gary Bartz (as); Charles Ables (g, b); Tyler Mitchell (b); Steve Williams (d).* 4–5/93.

***** I Love You, Paris**

Verve 523486-2 *As above, except omit Bartz and Mitchell.* 3/92.

*****(*) The Main Ingredient**

Verve 529555-2 *As above, except add Roy Hargrove (flhn), Joe Henderson, Buck Hill (ts), Steve Novosel (b), Elvin Jones (d).* 5–9/95.

What amounts to Horn's second comeback has been distinguished by a perfect touch and luxury-class production values.

Actually, in terms of her own performances or those of her trio – Ables and Williams have been faithful and diligent disciples – there's no special advance on her Steeplechase albums, or on the single Audiophile set, which is an especially slow and thoughtful disc. The first two Verves continue to work at favourite standards, and Hill's presence adds a useful touch of salt to proceedings that may sound a little too sweetly sensuous for some listeners. But *You Won't Forget Me* is a step forward in its pristine attention to detail, awesome array of guest-star soloists – Davis was a great Horn admirer, and he sounds like himself, if well below his best – and the faithfulness with which Horn's voice is recorded. Marsalis turns up again on two tracks on *Here's To Life*, which is otherwise dedicated to arrangements by Johnny Mandel, and again there's a hint of overdoing the sentiment: some may find the title-track far too wobbly in its emotional appeal. But the particular qualities of Horn's singing – the eschewal of vibrato, the even dynamic weight – are given full rein. *Light Out Of Darkness* is pitched as a tribute to Ray Charles, and after the heavyweight emoting of the previous record Horn sounds almost carefree on the likes of 'Hit The Road Jack' and 'I Got A Man'. Bartz lends a few swinging obbligatos, but the emphasis here is on Horn's understanding of the beat, her dry, almost elemental phrasing, and the intuitive touch of her regular group.

I Love You, Paris comes from a French concert. Shirley makes no concessions to the occasion in terms of turning up her tempos, and 'It's Easy To Remember' is about as slow as it will ever get. But she has the art of making the time move, even at this kind of tempo: 'Wouldn't It Be Luvverly' is luvverly indeed. The disc is perhaps overlong at almost 75 minutes, but the best of it is top-flight Horn. Same applies to *The Main Ingredient*, cut mainly at her home, with famous names sitting in to add variety to what's now a long string of similarly inclined dates. Buck Hill outdoes Joe Henderson, and Hargrove is untypically laid back on his flugelhorn feature. Yet the highlight is surely her gorgeous version of 'The Look Of Love', done alone with her regular team of Ables and Williams, which suggests that Shirley can probably play this way for ever and still make it sound good.

★★★(★) Loving You

Verve 537022-2 *Horn; George Mesterhazy (ky, g); Steve Novosel (b); Steve Williams (d); Alex Acuña (perc).* 11/96.

★★★(★) I Remember Miles

Verve 557199-2 *Horn; Roy Hargrove (t); Toots Thielemans (hca); Charles Ables, Ron Carter (b); Al Foster, Steve Williams (d).* 97.

The inevitable complaint is that Horn goes on making the same record and, nine albums into her Verve contract, little seemed ready to change. Yet nobody grumbled much about the sameness of Ella, Billie or Sarah in their various careers. Shirley's difficulty is that her preference for achingly slow tempos and sung-spoken lyrics doesn't chime very easily with the modern attention-span. *Loving You* may be no masterpiece but it's probably as good as any record she's made: the tunes impeccably chosen, the delivery perfectly judged. Of course Lil Green never meant 'In The Dark' to sound like this; but it's just as sexy, maybe more so. The title-tune is bathos made bearable by the refinement of her methods, and 'It Amazes Me' might even amaze you.

Miles Davis was always a Shirley Horn fan, and the singer repays the compliment with a homage album that sounds a lot more genuine than most of the rash of tribute discs. Whether doing Gershwin, other standards or 'Blue In Green', this is a smoke-filled reminiscence that has the feel and weight of something real, and the spare charts (Hargrove plays the obvious role on four tracks and Thielemans is inspiring on 'Summertime') replicate something of the skeletal intensity of Davis in his golden age.

★★★ Ultimate

Verve 547162-2 *Horn; as various Verve and Impulse! albums above.* 62–97.

Chosen by Diana Krall, the tracks on Horn's entry in the Verve *Ultimate* series make up a sensible cross-section of her records in this series, although none of our particular favourites are here. But that is always the way with somebody else's compilations.

★★★(★) You're My Thrill

Verve 549417-2 *Horn; Carl Saunders (t); Alan Broadbent (p); Dori Caymmi, Russell Malone (g); Charles Ables, Brian Bromberg, Chuck Domanico (b); Steve Williams (d); strings.* 00.

A return match for Shirley and strings. Johnny Mandel provides some more unspeakably gorgeous backgrounds, while Shirley and trio (discreetly embellished here and there by an extra pair of hands) do their usual thing. 'You're My Thrill' and 'I Got Lost In His Arms' go at the patented Horn gallop (which, if you're new to her, is a whisker above dead slow), and when Mandel's violins creep into the picture, it always provokes a shiver of pleasure. Nobody else makes records like this, and it's hard to see anyone else getting away with it: yet the voice, the piano and the Ables–Williams support remain inimitable.

★★★★ May The Music Never End

Verve 7602829 *Horn; Roy Hargrove (flhn); George Mesterhazy, Ahmad Jamal (p); Ed Howard (b); Steve Williams (d).* 2/03.

Finally, a change in Shirley's recording regimen, although it's poignant on two counts: the absence of the late Charles Ables, and her decision to turn over piano duties to other hands. Mesterhazy sets up an improbably fast groove on the opening 'Forget Me', but once into the heartbreaking reading of Jacques Brel's 'If You Go Away', it's obvious that not that much has changed - if it had, it wouldn't be Shirley Horn. Jamal sits in on two tunes, Hargrove is on two others, but the mistress of slow-slow-slow is otherwise in command without too many distractions. Close to perfect are 'Yesterday', 'Never Let Me Go' and 'This Is All I Ask'. She's more frail than before, but if anything it only adds to the record's capacity to move, and by the closing, teasingly valedictory title track, any strong man or woman will be close to shattered. Even if most of Diana Krall's audience isn't even aware that she exists, she's utterly incomparable.

Wayne Horvitz (born 1955)

PIANO, KEYBOARDS

Horvitz was one of the leading personalities of the New York downtown circle and is now based in Seattle. He is a strong, even idiosyncratic player and composer who has roved back and forth between situationist improvisation and more generic grooves, as in his organ group, Zony Mash.

***** Some Order, Long Understood**

Black Saint 121159 *Horvitz; Butch Morris (c); William Parker (b).* 2/82.

*****(*) Miracle Mile**

Elektra Nonesuch 7559 79278 2 *Horvitz; J. A. Deane (tb, elec); Denny Goodhew (sax); Doug Wieselman (ts, cl); Stew Cutler, Bill Frisell, Elliott Sharp (g); Ben Steele (g syn); Kermit Driscoll (b); Bobby Previte (d).* 91.

Horvitz got off to a brisk start with a clattery sound that wasn't too proud to make use of user-friendly electronics and pop-punk dynamics. *Some Order, Long Understood* consists of just two long tracks, spun out of seemingly nothing by a surprisingly lyrical trio. Morris is revelatory in his use of classic-jazz shapes and modernist accents, and Parker's *arco* work is superb. It's possible to hear in this session embryonic intimation of everything that was to follow.

Miracle Mile offers moody and slightly threatening music from Horvitz's band, The President. Horvitz is an impressive melodist, but tunes are constantly set in front of rather sinister guitar and synth backgrounds as if to suggest that the 'kinder, gentler America' of George Bush, apostrophized in an interesting 'Open Letter', merely caps the kind of violence implied by the dramatic smoke-pall on the cover. The horns don't do much of interest, but Previte is absolutely superb, giving one of his best performances on record.

***** Pigpen: V As In Victim**

Avant AVAN 027 *Horvitz; Briggan Krauss (as); Fred Chalenor (b); Mike Stone (d).* 5/93.

Pigpen is an extra-curricular project of Horvitz's, a band which tries to make associations between jazz, advanced rock and country music, often in near-unrecognizable forms. The 'Portrait Of Hank Williams Jr' and the long title-piece are the heart of a session which bears the A&R stamp of label guru John Zorn, who also has a hand in production. Not much to say about the other players, beyond the obvious point that they execute Horvitz's wishes competently and with an authentic lack of feeling.

***** Cold Spell**

Knitting Factory KFW 201 *Horvitz; Timothy Young (g); Fred Chalenor (b); Andy Roth (d).* 97.

*****(*) Brand Spankin' New**

Knitting Factory KFW 223 *As above.* 98.

Horvitz's organ group specializes in moody cyber-funk. The later album drifts between genres like the soundtrack to some ironic comedy show about creatives in an unspecified city. It's not all atmosphere and SFX, though. As ever, Horvitz's line is rich in associations and as driving as any hard-bop master of the '50s. Even on Hammond B3, he always sounds like a piano player, and both records reveal a linear development very far removed from the average organ/guitar group.

Young is a fine player, reminiscent of Bill Frisell only in the loosest sense, because he lacks Bill's interest in great washes of sound and in competing lines and countermelodies. Roth has probably listened to his fair share of Tony Williams records down the years and has profited by them. He has much of Horvitz's own ability to combine power and propulsion with a real delicacy of touch.

****** 4 + 1 Ensemble**

Intuition INT 3224-2 *Horvitz; Julian Priester (tb); Eyvind Kang (vn); Tucker Martine (processing).* 98.

Martine has been Horvitz's *éminence grise* for some time, co-producing and adding effects to previous albums. Here, though, he really does seem to be part of a group project, transforming a remarkably well-balanced instrumentation into something surreal and delightful. Priester is, as ever, a thoughtful and atmospheric presence, playing low and slow in a tonality that often recalls french horn. The revelation is Kang, shadowing and bridging trombone and piano and often repeating the same melody higher in register, as he does on the mournful, penultimate 'Take Me Home'. Horvitz sticks to steam piano throughout, revealing himself again as a player of slightly limited dexterity but nimbler in thought than he is at the keyboard. This is a quietly powerful record from a group of genuine originality.

*****(*) Upper Egypt**

Knitting Factory KFR-259 *Horvitz; Timothy Young (g); Keith Lowe (b); Andy Roth (d).* 7/99.

***** American Bandstand**

Songlines SGL 1528-2 *As above.* 7/99.

***** Sweeter Than The Day**

Songlines SGL SA1536-2 *As above.* 1/01

Thinning down his range all the time, these revisit the same group's earlier music, ever more moody, ever more 'cool', and by the time of *Sweeter Than The Day* they could almost be studio guys reading the dots, even if just once or twice – notably in a groove piece perhaps ironically called 'In The Lounge' – they nearly get up and go. *Upper Egypt* sounds like it owes as much to instrumental beat groups as anything else, the tunes naggingly memorable, and with Horvitz getting out some nice old analogue keyboards the music feels warm and comfortable. *American Bandstand* is like an acoustic rerun. *Sweeter Than The Day* is managed in a trim and focused manner, and the music's dependably smart, but it does feel as if Horvitz at the moment is hung up on textures, and they're getting him into a rather small corner.

François Houle (born 1961)

CLARINET, SOPRANO SAXOPHONE

Vancouver-based, Houle studied the classics and is a thoroughgoing clarinet technician, looking to explore improvisatory worlds.

***** Hacienda**

Songlines 1501-2 *Houle; Brad Muirhead (btb, euph); Saul Berson (as, cl, f); Tony Wilson (g); Ian McIntosh (tba, didjeridu); Joe Williamson (b); Dylan Van der Schyff (d).* 3/92.

*****(*) Schizosphere**

Red Toucan RT 9203 *Houle; Tony Wilson (g, khaen, aktira); Dylan Van der Schyff (perc).* 8/94.

***** Any Terrain Tumultuous**

Red Toucan RT 9305 *Houle; Marilyn Crispell (p).* 9/95.

Houle is a classically trained Canadian who has been turned on to improvised music by the likes of Evan Parker and Steve Lacy. In sound, he is immediately reminiscent of another latter-day clarinet master, Michael Moore, but Houle is perhaps less interested in structures and navigable harmonies. *Hacienda* was recorded live at Vancouver's The Glass Slipper and was an early release on the enterprising Songlines label. Houle leads an energetic and enthusiastic septet through a barnstorming set. There's a rickety quality to some of the ensembles and the favoured low brass (an odd touch) lend a marching-band feel to some of the tunes, particularly 'Gospells'. Splashy recording and the sense that this is just a night at the club caught by chance mean that it's no masterpiece, but an interesting find.

The trio on *Schizosphere* is beautifully balanced; Houle's richly grained sound blending perfectly with Wilson's sudden electrical storms and Van der Schyff's Bennink-inspired drumming. There is a lot of gestural playing, passages of simul-instrumentalism *à la* Roland Kirk, and abstract effects from Wilson as he rubs the strings with his forearms while playing a Khmer mouth-organ.

The record with Crispell is inevitably very different, and the pianist does tend to dominate. However, she shows her partner considerable respect, and as time goes by it is Houle's voice which commands attention. His sheer quality of sound, clean, unfailingly accurate at the register break (though, as often as not, played chalumeau in the Giuffre style), is highly attractive, but it is the quiet urgency of the ideas which increasingly comes across.

***** Nancali**

Songlines SGL 1519-2 *Houle; Benoit Delbecq (p).* 4/96–5/97.

Having gone down the duo route with Crispell, Houle takes another trip with another pianist. Delbecq covers more abstract, unclaimed ground than his illustrious predecessor, with the rattle and twang of 'Early Dance' one example of using the piano's innards, and the contrary music-box rhyme of 'Late Dance' cast as a rejoinder to his own experiments. But the duo wire in strands from other disciplines too, such as the title-piece, where Delbecq turns his instrument into a simple thumb-piano, and the result feels like a Bedouin dance. Houle is sometimes outshone by his partner but, when he does assert, his beautiful tone keeps taking the ear, no matter how much he disfigures it in the line of duty.

*****(*) In The Vernacular**

Songlines SGL 1522-2 *Houle; Dave Douglas (t); Peggy Lee (clo); Mark Dresser (b); Dylan Van der Schyff (d).* 10/97.

Two brief interludes apart, this is a set of interpretations of John Carter's music – including, in 'Three Dances In The Vernacular', a debut recording. But Carter's music without Carter proves at times to be a surprisingly dour and difficult undertaking. Deprived of the composer's own gravitas, the more taxing pieces cry out for something more inspiring than this quintet provides. Yet they compensate with the fleet rush of 'Sticks And Stones', a marvellous collective throw of the dice, and the 'Juba's Run' section of 'Fields Medley'.

***** Au Coeur Du Litige**

Spool Field 2 2CD *Houle; John Korsud (t); Sheila McDonald (vn); Ron Samworth (g, elec); Tony Wilson (g); Chris Tarry (b, elec, v); Dylan Van der Schyff (perc, elec); Dan Gagnon (turntables, sampling); Thérèse Champagne, Robert Zatjmann, Paul Shatto, Catriona Strang, Nancy Shaw, Nicole Brossard (v).* 10/98–3/00.

Canada's inclement weather of 1998 provides the text for Houle's ambitious project. The first disc blends his clarinet improvising with media sound-bites, recitations and chilling sound-effects, although 'blends' isn't really the right word: in a treacherous environment, the musician has to pick his way through a frightening setting, with little in the way of a helpful grappling-hook. The second disc features his quartet working on pieces that seem like a reflective aftermath of the storms depicted in the first half, although here too there are samples and readings which intervene. An unsettling experience, and one finished with great skill: a return visit left us chilled, not quite stirred.

***** Cryptology**

Between The Lines BTL 012/EFA 10182-2 *Houle; Brad Turner (t, p); Sheila McDonald (vn); Peggy Lee (clo); Dylan Van der Schyff (perc).* 10/00.

Houle's exasperating sleeve-note reveals that the music here came out of his new interest in cryptology, but 'rather than launching into an elaborate explanation of the various processes used in writing this music, I have created a list of essential words', which he has then encrypted – very helpful. The music itself, aurally at least, offers no striking departure from Houle's other work, working a line between grave, chamberish pieces and more agitated ensemble music. McDonald appears on only one track, but there's an uncredited guitarist.

****(*) Dice Thrown**

Songlines SGL SA 1538-2 *Houle; Benoit Delbecq (p).* 5/01.

A return match for this duo. Recorded in sumptuous SACD sound, the music has less rhythmical life and – whether they're improvising, or playing through one of the compositions by either man – is more a game of small gestures following equally small gestures. For all the refinement, much of this sounds like posturing against an empty canvas.

Avery 'Kid' Howard (1908–66)

TRUMPET, VOCAL

He began as a drummer but switched to trumpet in the '30s, joining the George Lewis group in the following decade. In the last ten years of his life he was a much-loved regular at Preservation Hall.

(***) Prelude To The Revival Vol. 1

American Music AMCD-40 *Howard; Andrew Anderson, Punch Miller (t, v); Duke Derbigny (t); Joe 'Brother Cornbread' Thomas (cl, v); Martin Cole (ts); ? Harris (p, v); Joe Robertson (p); Leonard Mitchell (g, bj, v); Frank Murray (g); Chester Zardis (b); Charles Sylvester, Junious Wilson, Clifford 'Snag' Jones (d); Matie Murray (v).* 37–41.

So little jazz was recorded in New Orleans during the '30s that any archive material from the period is valuable. Sam Charters, perhaps not the most reliable judge, reckoned that Kid Howard would have been the next King of New Orleans trumpet after Joe Oliver. He is only on the first four tracks here, in barely passable sound, but they show a mature, hard-hitting musician displaying the inevitable debt to Armstrong but resolutely going his own way. Anderson and Derbigny are less individual but they bridge the older and younger New Orleans traditions unselfconsciously enough. The sleeve-notes detail the detective work that went into finding and restoring the original acetates, and ears unused to prehistoric sound must beware. The five tracks by Miller are discussed under his name.

****(*) Kid Howard's La Vida Band**

American Music AMCD-54 *Howard; Eddie Sommers (tb); Israel Gorman (cl); Homer Eugene (bj); Louis James (b); Josiah Frazier (d).* 8–9/61.

Recorded on the cusp of the oncoming revival of the '60s, this date went some way to re-establishing Howard's standing. It's a pity, though, that there's some rustiness, not only in his playing but with most of the band too: fluffs and sloppiness are a distraction, even in the name of authenticity. But there are great moments, such as the tribute to Chris Kelly, Howard's early idol, in 'The Three Sixes', or the opening ensemble of 'Nelly Gray', and New Orleans scholars will welcome an important record on CD. The sound has attracted some haziness in the digital remastering. Howard can also be heard on several records with George Lewis.

****(*) Kid Howard's Olympia Band & Sam Morgan Revisited**

American Music AMCD-58 *Howard; George 'Kid Sheik' Cola (t); Jim Robinson (tb); Albert Burbank (cl); John Handy (as); Andrew Morgan (ts, cl, v); George Guesnon (bj, v); Eddie Dawson, John Joseph (b); Alex Bigard, Alfred Williams (d).* 8/62.

If this were better recorded, it would probably be the great Kid Howard record. Cut over two consecutive days by two bands (Howard, Robinson and Guesnon are common to both), one set is typical New Orleans, the other a tribute to the Sam Morgan band – Guesnon's vocal on 'Everybody's Talkin' 'Bout Sammy' is curiously poignant. The groups play with something like complete abandon, verging on the uproarious. But for once, the 'authentic' recording doesn't help, the location sounding like an aircraft hangar, and enjoyment is often spoiled.

Noah Howard (born 1943)

ALTO SAXOPHONE

Howard grew up in New Orleans and had his first experience of music as a chorister. Moving to California in his late teens exposed him to the avant-garde in the shape of Dewey Redman and Sonny Simmons, but he never quite shook away his soulful, churchy quality.

***** Noah Howard Quartet**

ESP 1031 *Howard; Ric Colbeck (t); Scotty Holt (b); Dave Grant (d).* 66.

*****(*) At Judson Hall**

ESP 1064 *Howard; Ric Colbeck (t); Dave Burrell (p); Catherine Norris (clo); Sirone (b); Bobby Kapp (d).* 66.

Howard's dry, brushfire sound has never quite caught on. The avant-garde of the '60s was over-populated with saxophonists, and Noah seems to parade his influences somewhat like his Biblical namesake, two-by-two. There's a hint of Dolphy-and-Ornette, then Trane tempered with Marion Brown's wavery pitching: all of it adding up to something different and idiosyncratic, but not yet fully realized. Working without harmony back-up lends the music a certain nervous energy, mostly obviously on the boppish 'Henry's Street'. The Coleman/Cherry axis is obviously the influence on 'Apotheosis' and the unrelated 'Apotheosis: Extension I', but it's the gentler 'And About Love' which catches the attention on the studio record.

One of the iconic recordings of its period, the Judson Hall concert showcased Howard in the company of British trumpeter Colbeck and the polystylistic Burrell, who is under-recorded but still a dominant presence. The saxophonist plays with fire and attitude on a long tribute to John Coltrane, here and there verging on bitterness and spleen. The other track, 'This Place Called Earth', is lighter, more sanguine and almost folksy in places, an effect very much influenced by the interplay of piano and cello. Colbeck's soaring lines could also be better registered but, apart from his solitary LP as leader (*The Sun Is Coming Up* with Mike Osborne), this is the best place to sample his rich but fleeting talent.

***** Red Star**

Boxholder BXH 014 *Howard; Bobby Few (p); Guy Pederson (b); Kenny Clarke (d).* 5/77.

A fascinating meeting of styles as the saxophonist hooks up with bebop pioneer Kenny Clarke. The sound is excellent, despite the tapes having lain unissued for many years, and the empathy within the group is deeply impressive. Few is a much underrated player, better known for his association with Steve Lacy, but well adjusted to Howard's more incendiary approach. The long title-track is one of the saxophonist's best recorded performances and the record, issued only in 2001, is a valuable addition to the discography.

*****(*) Patterns / Message To South Africa**

Eremite MTE 019 *Howard; Chris McGregor, Misha Mengelberg (p); Jaap Schoonhoven (g); Earl Freeman, Johnny Mbizo Dyani (b); Noel McGee (d); Han Bennink (d, perc, Tibetan hn); Steve Boston (perc); Zusaan Kali Fasteau (v, sheng).* 10/71, 79.

Message To South Africa was written in the week that Steven Biko was killed and it features two of the Cape's most powerful and evocative exiles. It's a stunning performance, laden with passionate vocals from Howard, the magnificent Dyani and Zusaan Kali Fasteau. Howard is always sensitive to the *yin* aspects of the music, its feminine side, and even in the midst of violence and despair it sings.

The earlier material was originally released on Howard's own AltSax label. It was commissioned by Dutch Radio, just as that country nurtured the last wisdom of Eric Dolphy. As with Eric back in 1964, Bennink is magnificent: swinging, dark and funny. Mengelberg is more uncomfortable in the context, and at moments he treats the African material almost dismissively.

McGregor quotes the African National Congress anthem, 'Nkosi Sikeleli Afrika', once explicitly and once in inverted form on *Message To South Africa*. It's a tiny reminder of the political context against which this music is created. At this point, almost anything of Howard's is welcome. These, though, are genuinely important points in the story.

***** At Documenta IX**

Boxholder BXH 025 *Howard; Michael Joseph Smith (p); Jack Gregg (b); Chris Henderson (d).* 91.

A fine, if flawed, example of Howard's small group work in the early '90s, this disc was briefly available as a small-label LP before Boxholder reissued it in 2002. Some parts are heavily edited, notably 'Karma', which fades out straight after the initial statement, suggesting source problems, but there is enough to satisfy any Howard fan. The ballad 'Joy' is a delight and 'Bush Talk' (we assume bush as in undergrowth rather than George Sr) is a fiery, full-on post-bopper. The set was recorded not in a club called Documenta IX as some sources have suggested, but at the arts festival of that name in Kassel, Germany. A strong showing from the saxophonist and his responsive group.

***(*) In Concert

Cadence CJR 1084 *Howard; Bobby Few (p); James Lewis (b); Calyer Duncan (d).* 9/97.

The two FMP LPs of 1975 and 1977 have yet to reappear, leaving a ridiculous gap in the still underweight Howard discography which even the reissue of the '70s material above doesn't quite put right. 'Schizophrenic Blues' puts in an appearance on this 1997 live recording from Amsterdam. The saxophonist likes to introduce himself with the words 'I'm Noah Howard – of the world', and much of his travelling is compressed into this performance, with European and African elements blended into the mix. Mongo Santamaria might be surprised to see 'Afro-Blue' credited to John Coltrane, but he'd certainly be gratified by what has been done with his most famous theme. 'We Remember John' is presumably also for Coltrane, a long, clattering performance that throws into focus how good a drummer Duncan is. Bobby Few always responds well to gigs like this, his natural bluesiness mediating his rather dry attack.

**(*) Between Two Eternities

Cadence Jazz 1114 *Howard; Bobby Kapp (d).* 10/99.

Howard and Kapp hadn't worked together for many years and there are hints of ring-rust in this reunion duo. The opening title-track promises rather more than the set as a whole delivers. There are definite longueurs and Kapp isn't always as crisp and emphatic as the pace demands. The other long tracks, 'The Other Side', 'In Flight' and 'Space Probe', languish a bit round the middle and resist Noah's best efforts to get them back on course. An interesting record, but scarcely an essential purchase.

*** Live At Unity Temple

Ayler 001 *Howard; Bobby Few (p); Wilber Morris (b); Calyer Duncan (d).* 9/97.

Recorded in Chicago, this is a strong set of mostly familiar material, including 'The Blessing' and 'Schizophrenic Blues'. Few and the leader have a strong and empathic relationship and 'Lightning Rod: Part 1' sees them get out into some adventurous territory, reminiscent of Howard's with Dave Burrell back in the '60s. A welcome addition to a slowly consolidating body of recorded work.

Freddie Hubbard (born 1938)

TRUMPET, FLUGELHORN

Born in Indianapolis, Hubbard first worked with the Montgomery brothers and arrived in New York in 1959. He joined the Jazz Messengers in 1961 and was involved in important recordings with Ornette Coleman and Oliver Nelson, as well as leading his own dates for Blue Note and Impulse!, and later Atlantic. In the '70s he moved in a lite-fusion direction at CTI and sold many records but by the end of the decade he was out of fashion, and he spent much of the next two decades trying to decide what situation to play in. Recently, lip trouble has kept him away from playing at all.

CORE COLLECTION

**** Open Sesame

Blue Note 95341-2 *Hubbard; Tina Brooks (ts); McCoy Tyner (p); Sam Jones (b); Clifford Jarvis (d).* 6/60.

Freddie Hubbard was one of the liveliest of the young hard-bop lions of the late '50s and early '60s. As a Jazz Messenger, and with his own early albums for Blue Note, he set down so many great solos that trumpeters have made studies of him to this day, the burnished tone, bravura phrasing and rhythmical subtleties still enduringly modern. He never quite had the quickfire genius of Lee Morgan, but he had a greater all-round strength, and he is an essential player in the theatre of hard bop. His several Blue Note dates seem to come and go in the catalogue, but we are listing *Open Sesame* and the new Rudy van Gelder edition of *Hub-Tones*, each a vintage example of Blue Note hard bop. *Open Sesame* and *Goin' Up* were his first two records for the label and their youthful ebullience is still exhilarating, the trumpeter throwing off dazzling phrases almost for the sheer fun of it. The brio of the debut is paired with the sense that this was the important coming-out of a major talent, and Hubbard's solo on the title-track is a remarkable piece of brinkmanship: in the bonus alternative take, he's a shade cooler, but that more tempered effort is less exciting, too. This was an early appearance for Tyner, and a valuable glimpse of Tina Brooks, who contributes two tunes and plays with his particular mix of elegance and fractious temper. A great Blue Note set.

**** Hub-Tones

Blue Note 99008 *Hubbard; James Spaulding (as, f); Herbie Hancock (p); Reggie Workman (b); Clifford Jarvis (d).* 10/62.

Hub-Tones includes one of Hubbard's most affecting performances in the tribute to Booker Little, as well as his first jousting with James Spaulding (repeated in *Breaking Point*, listed below). Both of these number among Hubbard's choicest albums.

*** The Body And The Soul

Impulse! 051183-2 *Hubbard; Clark Terry, Ed Armour, Richard Williams (t); Melba Liston, Curtis Fuller (tb); Bob Northern, Julius Watkins (frhn); Eric Dolphy (as, f); Seldon Powell, Wayne Shorter (ts); Jerome Richardson (ts, bs); Charles Davis (bs); Cedar Walton (p); Reggie Workman (b); Philly Joe Jones, Louis Hayes (d); strings.* 3–5/63.

Hubbard made two appearances as a leader for Impulse!. *The Body And The Soul* is the quirkier offering of the two, thanks mostly to Wayne Shorter's sometimes peculiar arrangements, for septet, big band and strings. Hubbard plays with beautiful alacrity, his quicker solos dancing over the charts, his slower ones underscoring what melody he can find; but Shorter's arrangements have their problems: audible fluffs betray a lack of rehearsal, some of the tunes seem cut off before they're properly developed, and moments like Eric Dolphy's alto squiggle on 'Clarence's Place' seem to have strayed in from another situation altogether.

★★★(★) Breaking Point

Blue Note 84172 *Hubbard; James Spaulding (as); Ronnie Mathews (p); Eddie Khan (b); Joe Chambers (d). 5/64.*

One of the most 'out' of Hubbard's Blue Notes, but not so far out that it gives the trumpeter any real problems as regards sounding convincing when improvising on the material. 'Far Way', for instance, is a complex piece but not so difficult that it undercuts his natural virtuosity. 'D Minor Mint' is the kind of bebop swinger which he eats up. Spaulding is exemplary, and the unusual rhythm section do nothing amiss.

★★(★) Backlash

Atlantic 7567-90466-2 *Hubbard; James Spaulding (as, f); Albert Dailey (p); Bob Cunningham (b); Ray Appleton (d); Ray Barretto (perc). 10/66.*

A good enough session, but the emphasis on backbeats, riff tunes and squared-off solos is a broad hint at the lighter direction Hubbard was already looking towards, as jazz faced its slump in popularity. Perhaps he can't be blamed. A likeable 'Up Jumped Spring', the most enduring of the trumpeter's compositions, adds a little extra weight.

★★ A Soul Experiment

Atlantic 75679 3067-2 *Hubbard; Carlos Garnett (ts); Kenny Barron (p); Keith Illingworth (org); Eric Gale, Billy Butler (g); Gerry Jemott (b); Bernard Purdie, Grady Tate (d). 69.*

★★(★) The Black Angel

Atlantic 7567-80782-2 *Hubbard; James Spaulding (as, f); Kenny Barron (p); Reggie Workman (b); Louis Hayes (d); Carlos Patato Valdes (perc). 5/69.*

Hubbard's Atlantics are a rum lot, and these two are the nadir. 'The only difference between jazz and modern rock is the drum patterns and moving bass lines,' Freddie opined at the time, which suggested that certain marbles had already gone astray. What he had going for him in playing pop tunes was his lovely tone, and it's very pretty on the likes of 'Wichita Lineman' or the one half-decent original, 'Lonely Soul'. Anyone who wants to hear this kind of music, though, would do far better investing in a Willie Mitchell album.

The Black Angel goes to the other extreme, with the interminable ramble of 'Spacetrack' finishing off the set almost before it's started. More encouraging is the attractive 'Eclipse' and Walter Bishop's 'Coral Keys', but again it's Freddie's tone more than his improvising which carries him through, and the weedy studio sound given to what looks on paper like a heavyweight group is discouraging.

★★★(★) Red Clay

CTI/Epic 5051722 *Hubbard; Joe Henderson, Stanley Turrentine (ts); Herbie Hancock (p); Johnny 'Hammond' Smith (org, p); George Benson (g); Ron Carter (b); Lenny White, Billy Cobham (d); Airto Moreira (perc). 1/70.*

★★★ Straight Life

CTI EPC ZK 65125 *Hubbard; Joe Henderson (ts, f); Herbie Hancock (p); George Benson (g); Ron Carter (b); Jack DeJohnette (d); Weldon Irvine, Richie Landrum (perc). 11/70.*

Hubbard's CTI catalogue helped establish him as a commercial force, after the Atlantic sets had largely failed. It was an erratic period for him, and for many of his generation, trying to come to terms with jazz's commercial eclipse, and though these albums owe something to the contemporary work of Miles Davis, this is really a simpler, far less formidable equation the band is working on, and more a response to a prevailing wind of 'funkiness' which suddenly – rightly or wrongly – seemed a lot cooler than hard bop's 4/4. *Red Clay* has always been held in high esteem for the simple reason that it has a lot of great playing: rather than whatever contemporary trappings Hubbard and producer Creed Taylor were trying to graft on to the situation, it was exactly those verities that saw Freddie through the first half of the '60s which made the record work. There's a bonus live version of 'Red Clay' itself by a different septet (including Turrentine and Benson, and with Cobham whacking the back beats), not very eventful but fun. This is certainly the disc to have if you want Hubbard in this vein and this period.

On *Straight Life*, the title-piece and 'Mr Clean' are almost themeless blow-outs for the players, and in most hands this would be a complete mess, especially with DeJohnette crashing around the mix and the two percussionists adding little but further noise. But the soloists are Hubbard, Henderson, Hancock and Benson, not a bad band in anybody's book, and they take vociferous but plausible routes to some kind of catharsis. The disc is completed with a sweetly handled 'Here's That Rainy Day' on flugelhorn. What may dismay listeners used to hearing Hubbard in a Van Gelder mix is Creed Taylor's signature softcore production, which eventually bleeds a lot of the life out of the playing, and sounds no better in the new remastering.

★★★ Sing Me A Song Of Songmy

Atlantic 81227 3669-2 *Hubbard; Junior Cook (ts); Kenny Barron (p); Arif Mardin (org); Art Booth (b); Louis Hayes (d); The Barnard-Columbia Chorus (v); strings. 1/71.*

It seems odd that Hubbard went back to Atlantic to make this mildly notorious set, in the middle of his CTI run, and how he became involved with the project isn't clear. Written, composed and produced by Ilhan Mimaroglu, the result is an unsettling mix of pop-culture protest, doomy, deadpan poetry, synthesized sound and the incongruously straight-ahead playing of Hubbard's quintet. 'Threnody For Sharon Tate' and 'What A Good Time For A Kent State' lock the project inside a very specific timeframe, and the juxtapositions of music, noise and recitation are sometimes shocking, sometimes merely silly (and sometimes remind one of the old Third Rail hit 'Run Run Run'!). Although this is hardly the place to hear Hubbard's group doing what they did best, there are some fine moments for them, in amongst everything else. A very definite one-off in Freddie's discography – as it would be in anybody's!

★★★ Outpost

Enja 3095-2 *Hubbard; Kenny Barron (p); Buster Williams (b); Al Foster (d). 2–3/81.*

★★ Born To Be Blue

Original Jazz Classics OJC 734 *Hubbard; Harold Land (ts); Billy Childs (ky); Larry Klein (b); Steve Houghton (d); Buck Clark (perc). 12/81.*

★★(★) Face To Face

Original Jazz Classics OJC 937 *Hubbard; Oscar Peterson (p); Joe Pass (g); Niels-Henning Orsted Pedersen (b); Martin Drew (d). 5/82.*

Most of Hubbard's later '70s albums are still out of print. These records for Pablo are a disappointing lot. *Born To Be Blue* was recorded live on a European tour and, while the leader plays with much of his old energy, the group musters little distinction: Land sounds largely uninterested and Childs adds nothing special of his own. While there is the usual quota of virtuoso fireworks on the meeting with Peterson, the session is, like so many involving Peterson's group, built on technical bravura rather than specific communication. Interesting to hear Hubbard tackling 'All Blues', but this version is about a hundred degrees hotter than any Milesian treatment and the tune wilts in the furnace. The quartet session for Enja, though, is much more worthwhile. Hubbard sometimes sounds bland and, talented though the rhythm section is, they don't ask him to be demonstrative; but there are some glowingly executed solos and a particularly rapt flugelhorn treatment of 'You Don't Know What Love Is'. Excellent recording.

***** Keystone Bop: Sunday Night**
Prestige 24146-2 *Hubbard; Joe Henderson (ts); Bobby Hutcherson (vib); Billy Childs (p); Larry Klein (b); Steve Houghton (d).* 11/81.

***** Keystone Bop, Vol. 2: Friday And Saturday**
Prestige 24163-2 *As above.* 11/81.

A smoking live date, now spread across two discs. Hubbard sets a cracking pace on the Sunday show with his own blues, 'Birdlike', which leads to inspired solos from Henderson and Hutcherson too. Thereafter the pressure drops a little and the rest is merely very good, but it's a pleasure to hear three great improvisers, all on resolute form, and this time Hubbard's intensity actually counts for something. The second volume has a less-than-immortal 'Round Midnight', but there's enough headstrong blowing to keep the spirits up.

*****(*) The Freddie Hubbard And Woody Shaw Sessions**
Blue Note 32747-2 2CD *Hubbard; Woody Shaw (t); Kenny Garrett (as); Mulgrew Miller (p); Cecil McBee, Ray Drummond (b); Carl Allen (d).* 85–87.

In a way, these were comeback dates for both men: Shaw had to endure personal fallibilities which always stood in the way of his career, and Hubbard was still trying to shake off the aftermath of years of nonsense. They cut two albums for the 'new' Blue Note which found each man, if not at his best – Hubbard has never recaptured his youthful sparkle, and Shaw's inconsistencies are palpable – at least in keen and lucid voice. There is some merriment in the various jousts they put together, and with Garrett kibitzing very effectively there is enough here to overcome any awkwardness of delivery. Hubbard also reminds of his talents as a balladeer in 'Lament For Booker'.

***** Topsy**
Enja 7025-2 *Hubbard; Kenny Garrett (as); Benny Green (p); Rufus Reid (b); Carl Allen (d).* 12/89.

****(*) New Colors**
Hip Bop 8026 *Hubbard; David Weiss (t); Steve Davis, Luis Bonilla (tb); Myron Walden, Kenny Garrett, Ted Nash (as); Craig Handy (ss, ts); Javon Jackson (ts); Chris Karlic (bs); Xavier Davis (p); Dwayne Burno (b); Joe Chambers, Idris Muhammad (perc).* 10/00.

Hubbard sessions dating from the last 15 years or so have been hit-and-miss, but there's often something interesting going on, even when the leader isn't at his peak. *Topsy* is a batch of standards, beautifully recorded: Kenny Garrett comes in for three tracks, there is a 'Cherokee' which must be one of the fastest on record, and Hubbard keeps the mute in for the whole session, often a sign that he's a bit unsure about his tone that day.

Most of his '90s albums have been deleted, and recurring difficulties have kept him away from bandstands, but *New Colors* may be a comeback of sorts. Buttressed by a formidable list of sidemen, he works through a few of his greatest hits. Trumpeter Weiss comes up with arrangements that keep the other players busy and ensure that Freddie isn't too exposed, but it's sad to hear Hubbard struggling through even the brief solos that he takes. His music would these days, alas, be better celebrated by others playing it.

Diane Hubka

VOCALS

Though born in Maryland and now based in Washington, DC, Hubka's style points to West Coast cool. A fine technician with a deceptively laid-back approach, she is easily overlooked.

***** Haven't We Met?**
Challenge / A 73128 *Hubka; Lee Konitz (as); Frank Kimbrough (p); John Hart (g); Harvie Swartz (b); Ron Vincent (d).* 8/98.

*****(*) Look No Further**
Challenge / A 73182 *Hubka; Scott Whitfield (tb); Frank Kimbrough (p); John Hart (g); Dean Johnson (b); Tony Moreno (d).* 5/99.

*****(*) You Inspire Me**
VSOJazz Records 5173 *Hubka; Gene Bertoncini, Paul Bollenback, John Hart, Bucky Pizzarelli, Romero Lubambo, Frank Vignola, Jack Wilkins (g); John Hebert, Nilson Matta (b); Duduka Da Fonseca, Jeff Hirshfield (d).* 12/00–3/01.

Sometimes likened to Sheila Jordan, but with a clear, slightly dry diction that is all her own, Hubka isn't a singer one looks to for drama or great emotional insight. She is, however, greatly underrated and these sets are well worth investigating. Her scatting is controlled and logical, with a clear line of development, and none of the aimless warbling that passes for improvisation among lesser singers.

The first of the Challenges is strongly original in conception. 'It's Your Dance' is a version of John Carisi's 'Israel' with new lyrics by Ray Passman and a striking reworking of the Cool School masterpiece. Harold Danko's 'New Clichés' is also unexpected but not so much as a superb reading of 'Everybody Wants To Be A Cat' from *The Aristocats*, which suggests that Hubka's demeanour isn't so reticent as to rule out a tinge of humour. Konitz guests and does his usual trim and thoughtful job. Kimbrough and Swartz (Jordan's favourite bass player) are ideal accompanists. Bob Dorough, another neglected master of song, contributes an insightful liner note.

For the follow-up Hubka chooses if anything a more challenging roster of songs. The Dorough/Landesman collaboration 'Small Day Tomorrow' is a highlight, but so, too, are her versions of Herbie Hancock's 'Dolphin Dance' and Malachi Thompson's tribute to Coltrane 'In Walked John'. The Hoagy Carmichael song 'Baltimore Oriole' is further evidence that she can sing the blues with the best of them. Kimbrough again offers solid support and there is some vividly vocalized trombone playing from Whitfield as well.

A word, too, for the elegant comping of John Hart. Hubka's obvious pleasure in working with guitar players comes across strongly on the third disc, which is full of them. Hart is back for a beautiful rendition of 'Winter Moon' and 'Nothing Like You', but he is unfortunate in having to share the roster with the superb Romero Lubambo partnering Nilson Matta and Duduka Da Fonseca (aka Trio da Paz), and with the increasingly impressive Paul Bollenback who accompanies the singer on the title track. Bucky Pizzarelli and Frank Vignola shine on 'Nuages' with a clever lyric by Frank Forte, and Jack Wilkins is superb on his own 'Romance'. There's also another Bob Dorough/Fran Landesman tune 'Nothing Like You' and a brilliant original by Michael Moore, 'The Old New Waltz'. Through it all, Hubka sings with clarity, verve, an occasional whiff of risk and well-marshalled emotion. As a set, it has balance and authority, with just enough humour to leaven the more sombre items. A thoroughly delightful vocal record.

Spike Hughes (1908–87)

BASS, PIANO, CELESTE, REED ORGAN

A Londoner by birth, Hughes taught himself bass and worked as an arranger and composer in the British dance music field of the late '20s and early '30s. He visited New York in 1933 and organized recording sessions featuring some of the best black players on the scene. But he quit jazz altogether for classical music in 1934.

****** Spike Hughes & Benny Carter 1933**

Retrieval RTR 79005 *Hughes; Henry 'Red' Allen; Leonard Davis; Shad Collins; Bill Dillard; Howard Scott (t); Dicky Wells; Wilbur De Paris; George Washington (tb); Benny Carter (as, ss, cl); Howard Johnson (as, cl); Wayman Carver (as, cl, f); Coleman Hawkins (ts); Chu Berry (ts); Luis Russell, Nicholas Rodriguez (p); Lawrence Lucie (g); Ernest 'Bass' Hill (b); Big Sid Catlett; Kaiser Marshall (d).* 11/31–5/33.

Spike Hughes had a brief affair with jazz: 'I left jazz behind me at the moment when I was enjoying it most, the moment when all true love-affairs should end.' It was just after the sessions with the all-star American line-up which features on Retrieval. But he had already made an extraordinary mark on the music in Britain. His early 78s are intensely sought after and contain some of the best British music of the period. However, the two double-disc sets which collected these sides are now out of print, which leaves the Retrieval disc, containing all the American recordings that Hughes made on a visit to New York. It's still indispensable. Though the band was really the Benny Carter orchestra, Hughes did the writing and arranging, and in pieces such as 'Donegal Cradle Song', a luminous feature for Hawkins, and 'Sweet Sorrow Blues', with superb Henry Allen, Hughes closed his jazz career on an amazing high note.

Daniel Humair (born 1938)

DRUMS

Though often assumed to be a Frenchman, the big drummer was born in Geneva and moved to Paris only when he was twenty. His most important association was with pianist Martial Solal, but Humair also became a respected sideman for a roster of visiting Americans. He also became the regular drummer of the George Gruntz band.

*****(*) Humair–Louiss–Ponty: Volume 1**

Dreyfus 191018-2 *Humair; Eddy Louiss (org); Jean-Luc Ponty (vn).* 67.

***** Humair–Louiss–Ponty: Volume 2**

Dreyfus 191028-2 *As above.* 67.

Fascinating as much as anything for a glimpse of the 25-year-old Ponty, who takes the lead on a good few of these picturesque but undeniably swinging sessions. Louiss has an emphatic touch, with a lot of dissonance thrown in for sheer colour. Humair keeps things pretty neat, except on 'Bag's Groove' (*Volume 2*), which is a bit of a mess. The outstanding performances are all on the first set, with 'You've Changed', a shameless 'Summertime' and 'Round About Midnight', and a chipper 'So What' that manages to hang on to a thread of pure romance.

***** Pépites**

CELP C3 *Humair; André Jaume (reeds).* 4/87.

Like all duo records, this could just as easily have been listed under the other partner, except that here Humair does seem to be the driving force, increasing the energy levels on what might otherwise have been a rather stiffly filigreed session and adding his own wry awareness to pseudo-classical skits like 'Les Oiseaux Sont Marteaux', which has nothing whatever to do with either Messiaen or Boulez. Jaume turns in a splendid solo version of Coltrane's 'Naima'. All the other tunes are originals, with both men putting up pieces.

****** 9–11 p.m. Town Hall**

Label Bleu LBLC 6517 *Humair; Michel Portal (sax, bcl, bandoneon); Joachim Kühn, Martial Solal (p); Jean-François Jenny-Clark (b).* 6/88.

Humair's own records have the same thoroughgoing musicality that he brings to work with artists as different as Anthony Braxton, Stéphane Grappelli and Lee Konitz. *Town Hall* is a superb introduction to all the participants, and if the veteran Solal's part isn't as large as one might wish for, it's none the less significant as an exercise in the genealogy of the 'new' French jazz, whose roots actually strike a lot deeper than first appears. That is nowhere more evident than here and on ...

***** Up Date 3.3**

Label Bleu LBLC 6530 *Humair; François Jeanneau (as, ss, ts, f); Henri Texier (b).* 2/90.

... where Humair teams up with Texier (a bassist with a more folkish and structured approach than the more freely orientated Jenny-Clark) in an album of looser compositions and improvisations. Jeanneau more than makes up for any slight technical shortcomings by an intelligent disposition of his four horns, but the real foundation of the music is the interaction in the bass and drums. Both come highly recommended.

*****(*) Edges**

Label Bleu LBLC 6545 *Humair; Jerry Bergonzi (saxes); Aydin Esen (p); Miroslav Vitous (b).* 5/91.

Much of the interest here settles again on the interplay between Humair and another great European bassist. Vitous's own 'Monitor' is a strange stop-start theme that downplays Esen's rippling accompaniments and Bergonzi's full-ahead Coltranism in order to explore the complex times and sonorities that are meat and drink to both 'rhythm' players. Something of the same goes on throughout the very long 'Genevamalgame' (co-written by Joachim Kühn and the drummer, his only compositional credit on the album). The title suggests a much more exploratory, risk-taking endeavour. Humair's out-of-tempo sequences and dramatic *rallentando* passages must be extremely challenging to his players. There may be a hint of compromise to the market in Bergonzi's and Esen's dramatic soloing, but they are both capable of abstraction, too, and the net effect of their more obvious strategies is to concentrate attention on the drummer and bassist. The mix is nicely horizontal, though Vitous could have done with a slight lift, particularly on the early tracks.

★★★(★) Quatre Fois Trois

Label Bleu LBLC 6619/20 *Humair; Hal Crook (tb); George Garzone (ts); David Liebman (ss); Michel Portal (bcl); Joachim Kühn (p); Marc Ducret (g); Bruno Chevillon, Jean-François Jenny-Clark (b).* 4/96–3/97.

★★★ Humair Urtreger Michelot

Sketch 333006 *Humair; René Urtreger (p); Pierre Michelot (b).* 99.

After experimenting with larger-scale units for some time, Humair came to believe that the trio, with its balance of responsibilities and forces, was still the most satisfying equation for his music. The title is then explained easily enough: four very different triumvirates of improvising musicians, playing a repertoire very much dominated by Humair material. The best of the groups is the one with Dave Liebman and Jean-François Jenny-Clark. They open with a segue from Humair's 'Casseroles' to the Joachim Kühn tune, 'More Tuna', and pick up the story later with Daniel's 'Bas de Lou'. Then there is a string-based group with Bruno Chevillon and Marc Ducret, an intriguing association between Kühn and Michel Portal, and last – and, in some respects, least satisfactory – the enigmatic George Garzone and Hal Crook. The drummer plays very differently in each of these contexts, though it is always clear who the percussionist is and that he is very much the fulcrum of performance. Humair's fertile and eclectic imagination can be gauged from his arrangement of the famous Massenet 'Méditation' from *Thaïs*, deeply felt and well thought out. Garzone might have been more comfortable with his own material. He sounds ill at ease on the almost folksy theme of 'La Galinette', though he turns in a brisk and powerful performance on Franco Ambrosetti's 'For Flying Out Proud', which makes the most of the unusual instrumentation. A fine record and, like all good projects of this sort, one that might have yielded four different albums.

The trio with Michelot and Urtreger is mostly devoted to standards and repertoire material. 'Airegin' is brief, terse and absolutely to the point. 'Bye Bye Blackbird' is more developed and whistles by exuberantly. 'Hum Calshum' is a tribute to the great Egyptian singer (who we know as Om Kholsoum, though spellings do vary) and has some of the great lady's charismatic presence.

Urtreger has a nice touch and Michelot is a giant on his instrument, worthy of much more solo space than he gets here. Nice sound throughout, though the dynamic is a bit skew-whiff on some of the more upbeat numbers, with too much tizz on the cymbals.

★★★(★) Liberté Surveillée

Sketch 333018/19 *Humair; Ellery Eskelin (ts); Marc Ducret (g); Bruno Chevillon (b).* 1/02.

This is one of the toughest-minded sets the drummer has ever put his name to. Some of the credit has to go to Eskelin – always a fiery and even antagonistic player – and to Ducret – who manages to make his guitar sound like an entire orchestra – but it is Humair who leads from the back throughout. We heard this one only very close to press time, and more frequent auditions might yield an even more positive reaction, but rely on a first impression: this is European jazz at its very best.

★★★ Baby Boom

Sketch 333034 *Humair; Christophe Monniot (sno); Matthieu Donarier (ss, ts); Manu Codjia (g); Sebastian Boisseau (b).* 5/02.

Less incendiary than its predecessor, and with a simpler guitar line throughout, but very much the same concept and a really powerful record. Monniot's sopranino adds a fascinating colour and tonality but all praise, too, to bassist Boisseau, a regular member of Martial Solal's band, who understands texture as well as line and harmonics. Try *Liberté Surveillée* first, but give this one a whirl.

★★★★ Ear Mix

Sketch SKE 333031 *Humair; Marvin Stamm (t, flhn); David Friedman (vib); Sebastian Boisseau (b).* 1/03.

The bassist is back in excellent form for this superlative record. The two Americans, Stamm and Friedman, have a huge range of experience between them, the former from the Jones–Lewis band and other jazz orchestras, Friedman from a remarkable range of rock and jazz recordings. They combine wonderfully to complete this unusual instrumentation. As with previous Sketch discs, there's no danger anyone will mistake this for a club recording. It's very cleanly recorded with a lot of detail from the drums and vibraphone. Listening to the stunning 'Huchedu' and 'I Never Had My Second Breakfast', one longs for a live version, or even a glimpse of rehearsals. Slightly too pat on the release versions, but unmistakably powerful modern jazz.

Helen Humes (1913–81)

VOCAL

Sang in Chicago while still a teenager and worked with various bands in the '30s before joining Count Basie in 1938. Stayed until 1941, then sang as soloist and in package tours. Moved to Australia in 1964 but returned home three years later after her mother became ill. Began singing again and was a grand dame of the scene in the '70s.

★★★ Helen Humes 1927–1945

Classics 892 *Humes; Dizzy Gillespie, Bobby Stark, Ross Butler (t); Jimmy Hamilton (cl); Herbie Fields (cl, as); Pete Brown, John Brown (as); Prince Robinson, Wild Bill Moore (ts); J. C. Johnson, De Loise Searcy, Sam Price, Leonard Feather, Bill Doggett (p); Lonnie Johnson, Sylvester Weaver, Walyer Beasley, Chuck Wayne, Elmer Warner (g); Charlie Drayton, Oscar Pettiford, Alfred Moore (b); Ray Nathan, Denzil Best, Charles Harris (d).* 4/27–45.

Remarkably, Helen Humes made her first records in the 'classic' blues idiom when she was only 13. That OKeh coupling, and the results of two sessions a few months later, open this fascinating CD of her early work. She sounds amazingly confident for her age, and tracks such as 'Garlic Blues' and 'Alligator Blues' are handled with assurance and a degree of adventure. A 15-year jump leads to a fine session with a Pete Brown band (including Gillespie, who unfortunately gets little space), before a rather extraordinary date with a Leonard Feather group, pairing old-timers Stark and Robinson with what is almost a bebop rhythm section! Five titles with a chunkily swinging Bill Doggett jump band round off the disc. Helen sounds a bit prosaic here and there, but the sweetness of her voice and her gift for swing enliven what would otherwise be mostly ordinary sides. Transfers are surprisingly clear and clean; only the first 1927 coupling sounds really rough.

*****(*) Helen Humes 1945–1947**

Classics 1036 *Humes; Snooky Young, Buck Clayton (t); George Matthews (tb); Scoville Brown (cl); Edward Hale, Willie Smith (as); Wild Bill Moore, Maxwell Davis, Lester Young, William Woodman, John Hardee, Rudy Williams (ts); Arnold Ross, Jimmy Bunn, Meade Lux Lewis, Eddie Beal, Roger 'Ram' Ramirez, Teddy Wilson (p); Allen Reuss, Dave Barbour, Irving Ashby, Mundell Lowe (g); Red Callender, Jimmy Rudd, Walter Page, Jimmy Butts (b); Henry Tucker Green, Chico Hamilton, Jo Jones, Denzil Best (d).* 45–12/47.

Some excellent line-ups behind Helen on this scattering of Los Angeles and New York dates for Philo, Black & White and Mercury. The material is mostly a workable mix of blues, jump tunes and the odd novelty piece, with only the dreary 'Please Let Me Forget' coming out of the ballad bag. Snooky Young gets some great moments, Lester Young ambles slowly through a solo, and Buck Clayton is in charge of the last three dates. The trumpeter on 'Married Man Blues' is unidentified but he's useful. Helen is mistress of all this material, and she sounds terrific on the Mercury dates in particular. A few tracks are surfacey, but it's mostly clear and very listenable.

*****(*) Helen Humes 1948–1950**

Classics 1333 *Humes; John Anderson, Pete Candoli, Jack Trainor, Charles Gillum, Geechie Smith (t); Britt Woodman (tb); Marshall Royal, Jackie Kelso (as); Henry Bridges, Maxwell Davis, Jimmy Jackson, Dexter Gordon (ts); Jack McVea, Freddie Simon (bs); Eddie Beal, Camille Howard, Ernie Freeman (p); Johnny Rogers (g); Leonard Bibb, Lawrence Kato, Dallas Bartley, Red Callender (b); Oscar Bradley, Roy Milton, J. C. Heard (d).* 5/48–11/50.

Opening with six more titles for Mercury, including the superb 'Married Man Blues', there is more excellent Humes on this collection of 24 tracks.She is in fine voice for four titles made for Discovery in May 1950, but the real highlights here are the several belting blues numbers she made at a Gene Norman concert later that year, issued as singles and featuring an uproarious 'Million Dollar Secret', which became a best-seller on 78 (the later studio remake is also here).The last two sessions place her squarely in the new R&B idiom (complete with reverb on the vocals!), although the last four sides feature a fine sextet including Dexter Gordon – although they're out to misbehave, and the closing 'Airplane Blues' is pure hot sauce. Great stuff. Transfers are, as so often, inconsistent, but there's not too much to hinder enjoyment.

****** 'Tain't Nobody's Biz-ness If I Do**

Original Jazz Classics OJC 453 *Humes; Benny Carter (t); Frank Rosolino (tb); Teddy Edwards (ts); André Previn (p); Leroy Vinnegar (b); Shelly Manne, Mel Lewis (d).* 1–2/59.

****** Songs I Like To Sing**

Original Jazz Classics OJC 171 *Humes; Al Porcino, Ray Triscari, Stu Williamson, Jack Sheldon (t); Harry Betts, Bob Fitzpatrick (tb); Art Pepper (cl, as); Ben Webster, Teddy Edwards (ts); Bill Hood (bs); André Previn (p); Barney Kessel (g); Leroy Vinnegar (b); Shelly Manne (d).* 9/60.

*****(*) Swingin' With Helen**

Original Jazz Classics OJC 608 *Humes; Joe Gordon (t); Teddy Edwards (ts); Wynton Kelly (p); Al Viola (g); Leroy Vinnegar (b); Frank Butler (d).* 7/61.

Helen's sessions with Count Basie in the '30s established her career, but she never lost her way. Her three albums for Contemporary have luckily all been reissued in the OJC series, and they make a powerful argument for her standing as one of the finest (and most overlooked) jazz vocalists of the swing era and after. Recorded in stereo for the first time, her voice's natural mix of light, girlish timbre and hard-hitting attack creates a curiously exhilarating impact. She's like a less matronly Ella Fitzgerald, yet she can phrase and change dynamics with more inventiveness than Ella. The 1959 session, organized almost as a jam session by Benny Carter, has a rare grip and immediacy; although almost everything on it is fine, special mention should be made of a superbly structured 'Stardust' and 'I Got It Bad And That Ain't Good' and a perfectly paced 'You Can Depend On Me'. The band, a strange mix of players, work unexpectedly well together, with the rhythm section's modern grooving offsetting terrific solos by Carter, Rosolino and Edwards.

Swingin' With Helen is a shade less impressive, but the 12 standards here are all delivered with great charm and aplomb. The pick of the three is *Songs I Like To Sing*, which arranger Marty Paich built specifically around Humes's talents. The singer has no problem dealing with scores which would have taxed such a modernist as Mel Torme, and these eight tracks define a modern approach to swing singing. But the other four, with Humes set against a rhythm section and the sole horn of Ben Webster, are equally beautiful, particularly a glorious reading of 'Imagination'. Although Humes's voice isn't as forward in the sound balance as it might be, the remastering of all three records is crisp and strong.

*****(*) Sneakin' Around**

Black & Blue 950.2 *Humes; Gérard Badini (ts); Gerald Wiggins (p); Major Holley (b); Ed Thigpen (d).* 2/74.

***** 'Deed I Do**

Contemporary 14071-2 *Humes; Don Abney (p); Dean Reilly (b); Benny Barth (d).* 4/76.

A couple of late entries for Helen, cut during her '70s comeback. *'Deed I Do* has a plain old rhythm section for company and the material is too familiar, but the intimacy is nice and she sounds like she enjoyed it. The newly reissued *Sneakin' Around* is a better bet all round. The singer in fine voice, the band is swinging (and includes local lad Badini), and though she'd already sung these tunes many times, it doesn't hurt. 'Tribute To Jimmy Rushing' is a sweet medley of her old pal's hits. Five alternative takes fill up space, if you really think less than an hour is short measure.

Percy Humphrey (1905–95)

TRUMPET

The middle one of the Humphrey brothers started out as a drummer before switching to trumpet. He worked with George Lewis in the '50s and led the Eureka Brass Band for many years, as well as the Preservation Hall Jazz Band and the New Orleans Joymakers. He seldom played outside the city and also had a day job selling insurance for many years.

***** Percy Humphrey's Sympathy Five**
American Music AMCD-88 *Humphrey; Waldron Joseph, Jack Delany (tb); Willie Humphrey, Raymond Burke (cl); Stanley Mendelson, Lester Santiago (p); Johnny St Cyr (g, bj, v); Blind Gilbert (g, v); Richard McLean, Sherwood Mangiapane (b); Paul Barbarin (d).* 1/51–6/54.

****(*) Sounds Of New Orleans Vol. 1: Paul Barbarin & His Band / Percy Humphrey's Jam Session**
Storyville STCD 6008 *Humphrey; Joe Avery (tb); Ray Burke (cl); Sweet Emma Barrett (p); Billy Huntington (bj); Ricard Alexis (b); Cie Frazier (d).* 5/54.

***** New Orleans The Living Legends: Percy Humphrey's Crescent City Joymakers**
Original Jazz Classics OJC 1834-2 *Humphrey; Louis Nelson (tb); Albert Burbank (cl); Emanuel Sayles (g, bj); Louis James (b); Josiah Frazier (d).* 1/61.

***** Climax Rag**
Delmark DE-233 *Humphrey; Jim Robinson (tb); Albert Burbank (cl); George Guesnon (bj); Alcide 'Slow Drag' Pavageau (b); Cie Frazier (d).* 2/65.

***** Percy Humphrey's Hot Six**
GHB BCD-85 *Humphrey; Louis Nelson (tb); Albert Burbank (cl); Lars Edegran (p); Chester Zardis (b); Barry Martyn (d).* 11/66.

The middle one of the three Humphrey brothers was a substantial figure in New Orleans jazz. His most significant playing was usually done with the city's brass bands, and he became leader of the Eureka Brass Band in the early '50s until its disbandment some 20 years later. The 1954 jam session, one-half of a disc shared with a Paul Barbarin set, is relatively slight music, but Humphrey plays with the characteristically short-breathed phrasing of the New Orleans brassman and makes all his notes count: his solo on 'Everybody Loves My Baby', decorated with the familiar wobble which is the New Orleans vibrato, sums up his style, a mixture of abrasiveness and raw melody. The sound is quite good, although Sweet Emma Barrett, a minor legend who wore bells on her hat and round her ankles, is almost inaudible at the piano.

The Sympathy Five (the name derives solely from the handwritten title on a discovered reel of tape) offer six 1954 titles on the American Music CD. Humphrey sounds in good spirits and his solos have a lean, almost wiry quality; but he is if anything outshone by Burke and the splendid Delany. The remainder of the disc is filled out with four strong titles by a Paul Barbarin group (with both Humphrey brothers) and three odd pieces by a trio with Burke, Mangiapane and the mysterious Blind Gilbert, who sings and strums a guitar in questionable tune. The Sympathy Five tracks aren't exactly hi-fi but they sound a lot better than some American Music discoveries.

Most of Humphrey's later records are hard to locate, but this 1961 date in Riverside's Living Legends series is worth remembering, recorded in far superior sound to that often granted this kind of jazz. Humphrey himself is rather overpowered by Albert Burbank, whose clarinet predominates with an eagerness that recalls Boyd Senter, and Frazier's drumming is crashingly resonant; but the band live up to their name at many points.

Climax Rag is a good if somewhat uneventful session for Delmark, recorded at San Jacinto Hall on the day after Cie Frazier's birthday (they play a brief 'Happy Birthday' for him). Tight, rigorous playing, and for once Burbank is somewhat recessed in the sound. No fewer than eight alternative takes beef up the CD reissue, although if anything this dilutes the impact of the original LP.

The 1966 date captured on the GHB CD is a memento of one of Barry Martyn's trips to New Orleans – though Humphrey is the nominal leader, the date was organized by the drummer. The front line may have been a little tired (Jim Asman's notes record that they'd been playing the previous night till 7 a.m.) and the playing is ragged, though ably policed by Martyn's beat. The rough, open-hall ambience reeks of vintage New Orleans music and it's a charismatic disc.

Willie Humphrey (1900–1994)

CLARINET

A New Orleans forefather, he took up clarinet at fourteen and five years later was playing in Chicago with Joe Oliver and Freddie Keppard. He drifted around through the '20s and '30s but returned to his home town after the war and became a mainstay of the revivalist movement thereafter.

****(*) In New Orleans**
GHB BCD-248 *Humphrey; Norbert Susemihl (t, v); Mari Watanabe (p); Emile Martyn (d).* 4/88.

***** Two Clarinets On The Porch**
GHB BCD-308 *Humphrey; Brian O'Connell (cl); Les Muscutt (g, bj); Frank Fields (b); Ernie Elly (d).* 8/91.

**** A Kiss To Build A Dream On**
GHB BCD-428 *Humphrey; Joruis De Cock (t, v); Gerhard 'Doggy' Hund (tb); Klaus-Dieter George (cl); Rowan Smith (p); Büli Schöning (bj, g); Peter Wechlin (d).* 10/92.

Only a few months younger than George Lewis, Willie Humphrey harked back to an ancient New Orleans tradition. He didn't start recording until 1926, but these records come from over six decades later. *In New Orleans* puts him up with a German trumpeter, a Japanese-American pianist and a British drummer, and the youngsters play with an affectionate energy that Willie seems to enjoy being involved with. It's let down, though, by a sense that these are keen amateurs keeping the old man company, and there are some errors of judgement (such as Susemihl's four vocal performances) which tarnish the occasion.

Three years later, Humphrey palled up with another clarinet man 60 years his junior. His phrasing and gargled tone persuade the other players to walk a little gingerly round him: the seven trio pieces, which Willie and Ernie Elly sit out, probably account for the best music, deftly sprung round Muscutt's deferential banjo and O'Connell's sweet-toned clarinet. But 'I Want To Be Happy' or 'China Boy' feature some amusing interplay, and it's pleasant to hear an unalloyed New Orleans legend raising his voice in the '90s on what turned out to be a sprightly farewell.

Except it wasn't quite his last recording. That distinction goes to *A Kiss To Build A Dream On*, released by GHB in 2000, one hundred years after Willie was born. It features him guesting with the Maryland Jazz Band of Cologne. Willie sounds like he's having fun, but one has to make allowances for the occasion, and on its own terms this is pretty ramshackle music.

Charlie Hunter (born 1968)

8-STRING GUITAR

Part of a community of jamming musicians who emerged from the Bay Area in the early '90s, Hunter is a virtuoso guitarist playing an eight-string model, with bass and lead lines combined.

***** Bing ... Bing ... Bing**

Blue Note 31809-2 *Hunter; Jeff Cressman (tb); Dave Ellis (ts); Bing Goldberg (cl); David Phillips (pedal steel g); Jay Lane (d); Scott Roberts (perc).* 95.

***** Ready ... Set ... Shango!**

Blue Note 37101-2 *Hunter; Calder Spanier (as); Dave Ellis (ts); Scott Amendola (d).* 96.

****(*) Natty Dread**

Blue Note 52420-2 *As above, except replace Ellis with Kenny Brooks (ts).* 97.

It's always worth pointing out to anyone who laments the populist derelictions of the 'new' Blue Note that since the mid-'80s renaissance the label has done nothing more than go back some way towards its own rhythm-and-blues roots. Hunter's ability to make his 8-string guitar sound like – and occasionally *remarkably* like – a Hammond B-3 reinforces the historical link. The earliest of the group is probably the most guitaristic, if we may be forgiven the term, a brisk, bright session with more external input than the latter pair. Hunter sounds good with brass, and it's a shame that Cressman's contribution (and Goldberg's, for that matter) is so limited. Some of Hunter's own best songs are on the debut: 'Greasy Granny' and 'Scrabbling For Purchase' are excellent, but the outstanding track is a wholly unexpected cover of Nirvana's 'Come As You Are'.

The middle album sounds great, a thick, swampy performance which ironically is diluted only by the crispness and clarity of Lee Townsend's production. Inevitably, the two saxophone players occupy much of the foreground, interestingly trading their differences of approach, Ellis's dark, raw-edged tone and Spanier's lighter, bop-orientated delivery most effectively juxtaposed on 'Let's Get Medieval', less so on the not-quite-urgent '911'.

Natty Dread is an oddity, a track-by-track gloss on Bob Marley and the Wailers' classic reggae record, issued as part of Blue Note executive Bruce Lundvall's 'Cover Series'. Leaving aside the slightly uneasy relationship between jazz and reggae, Hunter's approach seldom adds much to the original. On what might be thought the most pristine and untouchable of the Marley compositions, 'No Woman No Cry', he does, however, import an opening section and some of the harmonic material from 'The Tennessee Waltz', which was a clever stroke. Here, the pristine sound makes more sense, a gentle, sometimes buoyant listen, but seldom as moving or inflammatory as the original. Be grateful that Hunter decided against Carole King's *Tapestry* or the Beach Boys' *Pet Sounds*, which – for entirely different reasons – would have made less sense.

*****(*) Return Of The Candyman**

Blue Note 23108-2 *Hunter; Stefon Harris (vib); Scott Amendola (d); John Santos (perc).* 98.

The big bonus here is Harris, the most exciting vibraharpist to appear on the scene since Hutcherson. His tight, ringing sound and long, pattering runs give the line-up – now going out as Pound For Pound – a heavily percussive emphasis which provides the perfect launch-pad for Hunter's increasingly idiosyncratic 8-string work.

Punctuated by five short interludes which serve no very obvious purpose beyond punctuation, the tunes are tough, funky and hit the mark every time. The title-track, 'Pound For Pound' and 'Enter The Dragon' are the ones to sample if you happen across it on a listening post.

*****(*) Duo**

Blue Note 99187-2 *Hunter; Leon Parker (d, perc).* 99.

Our earlier comments about the Beach Boys have come back to haunt us because Hunter includes a Brian Wilson song here. Most of the material is self-written, though, including the swinging 'Belief' by Parker, and the guitarist has never sounded jazzier, using his thick low strings to generate simple bass lines against those now familiar 'organ' chords and single-note lines, so that this almost sounds like a trio recording.

Wilson's 'Don't Talk (Put Your Head On My Shoulder)' is a lovely thing, laden with shimmering reverb and every bit as tender as the original. The pair also tackle one standard, 'You Don't Know What Love Is'. Parker's roots are more firmly in classic jazz than Hunter's, but he has a solid rock backbeat at his disposal as well. Nothing here to set the heather on fire, but an intriguing, low-key album.

***** Charlie Hunter**

Blue Note 25450 2 *Hunter; Josh Roseman (tb); Peter Apfelbaum (ts); Stefan Chopek, Leon Parker, Robert Perkins (d, perc).* 00.

The plainest of plain album titles for a record maybe intended to reposition Hunter in the jazz market. Despite the name, though, it only features one solo track, the closing 'Someday We'll All Be Free'. Elsewhere, he reprises the duos with Parker, on 'Al Green', 'Dersu (A Slight Return)' and a very effective 'Epistrophy'. For the rest, Charlie seems to be showcasing a new, jazz-orientated sound, drafting in Roseman and Apfelbaum to beef up the front line and allow him to develop his organ-influenced sound still further. 'Cloud Splitter' has a faintly sleazy atmosphere, with the horns murmuring in the middle distance over a descending figure on stopped strings that fades away like a slice of incidental music from a cop movie.

*****(*) Songs From The Analog Playground**

Blue Note 33550 2 *Hunter; John Ellis (sax); Stephen Chopek (d); Chris Lovejoy (perc); Mos Def, Theryl de Clouet, Kurt Elling, Norah Jones (v).* n.d.

There are some sublime moments here. The band sounds seasoned and strong, and has the flexibility to push these songs – stray memories from Charlie's youth – out into new territory. That's nowhere more evident than on things like 'Mighty Mighty', the old Earth, Wind & Fire tune, reworked by de Clouet, who also does a chillingly beautiful version of Willie Dixon's 'Spoonful'. Elling is more obviously a jazz singer. His vocal line on 'Desert Way' and 'Close Your Eyes' is exemplary. Mos Def is streetier but less convincing, and the real heartbreaker is Norah Jones's delightful alto on the Roxy Music swoon, 'More Than This', which becomes quite majestic, with Charlie strumming like a string section underneath. She tops that with Nick Drake's 'Day Is Done', which is near perfect. A gorgeous record.

★★★(★) **Right Now Move**
Rope A Dope 93137 *Hunter; Curtis Fowlkes (tb); John Ellis (ts); Grégoire Maret (hca); Derrek Phillips (d).* 03.

The move away from Blue Note after seven albums and some apparent uncertainty as to where he sits in the market has done Hunter some good already. It uses the same trombone/tenor front line as some of the tracks on that record, but the addition of Grégoire Maret's chromatic harmonica is a stroke of genius. He is the key to tracks like 'Mali' and the equally beautiful 'Try', which is the most substantial track of the set. Fowlkes is an agreeably eclectic player, with a considerable track record; Ellis isn't so well known, but together they create a vivid funk.

Hunter's own role is interesting. Increasingly, he shapes the music from behind the horns, rather than playing strong lead lines himself. He's still the dominant voice, but in a supportive and structural role. Only on the closing track, 'Le Bateau Ivre', does he engage in swapping lines and licks. It's an effective strategy and produces a thoroughly attractive album.

Bobby Hutcherson (born 1941)

VIBRAPHONE, MARIMBA, PERCUSSION

If Hutcherson were a saxophonist, trumpeter or pianist, he would be regarded as a major figure in modern jazz, but the vibes still have a slightly eccentric standing, a prejudice which has kept Bobby on the margins. Born in California, he was inspired by another undervalued genius, Milt Jackson, and took up vibraphone in preference to piano. Hutcherson's distinctive style is intensely rhythmic and harmonically subtle. Though extensively recorded, until recently his back-catalogue was very patchy indeed.

★★★(★) **Dialogue**
Blue Note 35586 *Hutcherson; Freddie Hubbard (t); Sam Rivers (ss, ts, f); Andrew Hill (p); Richard Davis (b); Joe Chambers (d).* 4/65.

Few have developed such a consistently challenging language for the instrument as Hutcherson. In the '60s he made a series of superb albums for Blue Note, the equal of any of the classic dates from that label. Their availability has been very intermittent, although some have recently returned fleetingly as limited editions. His debut as a leader, *Dialogue*, returned to the catalogue in early 2002. It is arguably the most adventurous thing Bobby ever did, though he had not yet found his confidence as a composer as well as soloist. Three of the group assembled – Hutcherson, Hubbard and Davis – had been involved in Dolphy's epochal *Out To Lunch!* sessions, and they carry over some of the energy and excitement of that great record.

Virtually all the writing is by Hill, though there are two tracks by the shrewd and very effective Chambers, who whirls his way through a rhythmically challenging set. Andrew's 'Ghetto Lights' was to become a staple of his own sets in the next couple of years, but the really astonishing piece here is 'Les Noirs Marchant', an ungrammatical but evocative title for a somewhat surreal composition. Bobby's articulation is bright, fast and supremely confident, and his ability to move in the spaces between Chambers and Hill is consistently impressive.

The drummer's two pieces are very different one from the other. The title-track is a long, open-formed idea which sees Bobby switch to the softer-sounding marimba, while 'Idle While' is almost a lullaby, weirdly pitched but unexpectedly elegant. For a debut disc, *Dialogue* is impressively disciplined and reined-in. There is very little grandstanding from a leader who in future occasionally indulged himself in high-wire escapades, and his colleagues seem right behind him. In the final analysis, though, this could also have been released as an Andrew Hill record. Whatever the attribution, good to have it back.

★★★(★) **Components**
Blue Note 29027 *Hutcherson; Freddie Hubbard (t); James Spaulding (as, f); Herbie Hancock (p, org); Ron Carter (b); Joe Chambers (d).* 6/65.

★★★★ **Stick Up!**
Blue Note 59378 *Hutcherson; Joe Henderson (ts); McCoy Tyner (p); Herbie Lewis (b); Billy Higgins (d).* 7/66.

★★★(★) **The Kicker**
Blue Note 21437 *Hutcherson; Joe Henderson (ts); Grant Green (g); Bob Cranshaw (b); Al Harewood (d).*

Components continues the purple patch with a set of short lyrical themes. The title-track is a cracker, and 'Little B's Poem' was to become a modern classic, a softly articulated but totally convincing modern ballad. Anyone who hasn't encountered Hutcherson before might do well to start with this one, but just to get into training for the glories of *Dialogue*. *Stick Up!* opens with Ornette's 'Una Muy Bonita', demonstrating how much of Bobby's conception came from that source. The remainder of the set is closer to the harmonic experimentation that was shortly to become an orthodoxy. 'Verse' is masterly and 'Summer Nights' a lusciously coloured and textured tone-poem, shaded (as Hutcherson compositions almost always are) with obliquely related tonalities.

The Kicker wasn't made available until 1999, an astonishing oversight on Blue Note's part. Even if Hutcherson's standing were thought to be marginal, the presence of Joe Henderson should have been enough to see this fine, imaginative session into the light of day. The saxophonist is the main composer and Bobby is represented only by the rather slight 'For Duke P.', a tribute to Blue Note's musical director. Joe's 'Kicker' and 'Step Lightly' are cracking tunes and blistering performances from all concerned. Hutcherson's fleet, ringing lines have rarely sounded more buoyant and persuasive, and it remains a mystery that this record should have been considered so marginal that it lay in the vault for 30 years.

★★★(★) **Montara**
Blue Note 84190 *Hutcherson; Oscar Brashear, Blue Mitchell (t); Fred Jackson Jr, Plas Johnson, Ernie Watts (ts, f); Larry Naxh (p); Eddie Cano (p, ky); Denis Budimir (g); Chuck Domanico, Dave Troncoso (b); Harvey Mason (d); Willie Bobo, Rudy Calzado, Ralph MacDonald, Bobby Matos, Johnny Paloma, Victor Pantoja (perc).* 4/75.

This is a delightful record, a sign that funky fusion jazz was possible without artistic compromise. Recording back home in LA and with a clutch of fine Latin players, the leader sounds easy and in high spirits. Hutcherson's chiming vibes blend well with the electric keyboards and basses and his ability to weave densely dancing figures over quite simple backbeat themes is a joy to observe. Apart from 'Montara' itself, a gentle funk groove, and 'Yuyo', Hutcherson isn't much featured as a composer. George Cables takes two credits, including the magnificent 'Camel Rise' which opens the set, and there is a fine version of

'Oye Como Va', a song forever associated with Carlos Santana. The cast of players pretty much speaks for itself but Watts and Mitchell are both outstanding. A forgotten treasure from the Blue Note vaults, reissued in 2003.

*** Un Poco Loco

Koch 7868 *Hutcherson; George Cables (p); John Abercrombie (g); Chuck Domanico (b); Peter Erskine (d, perc).* 79.

Restored to circulation after 20 years, this is uncomfortably time-locked and awkwardly registered relative to Bobby's earlier records. The rock rhythms, bass guitar, and electric piano shimmers are only superficially distracting, though. The recording doesn't help, but Hutcherson's angle on the Bud Powell title-track is utterly captivating, and his solos are as convincing as ever throughout.

*** Solos / Quartet

Original Jazz Classics OJC 425 *Hutcherson solo and with McCoy Tyner (p); Herbie Lewis (b); Billy Higgins (d); John Koenig (bells).* 9–10/81, 3/82.

The '80s saw something of a revival in Hutcherson's fortunes: uncompromised recording opportunities, sympathetic collaborators and, one suspects, a consequently renewed faith in his own abilities.

The quartet sessions, which include a sparkling 'Old Devil Moon' and 'My Foolish Heart', simply underline Tyner's astonishing eclecticism and adaptability. Those with longer memories will automatically track back to Hampton's interplay with Teddy Wilson in the classic Benny Goodman Quartets of 1936 and 1937. That good.

Ken Hyder (born 1946)

DRUMS, VOCALS, OTHER INSTRUMENTS

The Scottish-born percussionist formerly led the pioneering folk-jazz group Talisker. In recent years he has been a member of the Bardo State Orchestra and has explored shamanistic music in Siberia.

***(*) Bear Bones

Slam CD 247 *Hyder; Tim Hodgkinson (lap steel, as, elec); Gendos Chamzyryn (v, p, perc, doshpulur).* 96–00.

This is the project Hyder calls K-Space, a bold confrontation between his own remarkable spiritual improvisation and the Tuvan throat-singing of Chamzyryn. This is now a long-standing association and these amazing tracks are the result of what are effectively field recordings in a number of locations over a nearly five-year period. 'Nine-Eyed Horse-Alcohol' is a long improvisation, though most of the pieces are somewhat shorter and more precisely focused. They do not derive so much from harmonic or rhythmic ideas as from moods and feelings which are more particular than abstract. Hodgkinson's range of sounds and effects is an important component here, though one feels Hyder's controlling hand throughout. This music is completely *sui generis.* It requires time and patience and a state of evenly suspended attention to do it justice. Who knows but that here we may be catching glimpses of a whole new direction – not just cultural but philosophical – for improvisation?

Dick Hyman (born 1927)

PIANO, ORGAN, VOCAL

He studied with Teddy Wilson but became a staff player at NBC in the '50s and an organizer of concerts dedicated to the jazz repertory – a rarity at the time. He was playing synthesizers early on and, with the growing interest in jazz repertory, has assumed a central role in propagating a wider understanding of the music's history. In the '80s and '90s he recorded in a broad range of situations, on several kinds of keyboard.

*** Plays Fats Waller

Reference RR-33 *Hyman (p solo).* 8/89.

*** Stride Piano Summit

Milestone 9189 *Hyman; Harry 'Sweets' Edison (t); Ralph Sutton, Jay McShann, Mike Lipskin (p); Red Callender (b); Harold Jones (d).* 6/90.

*** Plays Duke Ellington

Reference RR-50 *Hyman (p solo).* 90.

Dick Hyman has had a pretty paradoxical career in many ways. In the '40s he was playing with both Charlie Parker and Benny Goodman. Working as a studio musician through much of the '50s and '60s, he also recorded novelty tunes under various pseudonyms, as well as Scott Joplin's complete works. He loves early jazz, is an expert on the jazz-piano tradition, can re-create pit-band orchestrations or ragtime arrangements to order – yet he was also one of the first to record an album of tunes played on prototype synthesizers. For a long time there was very little 'strict' jazz in the catalogue under Hyman's name, but recent times have found him busy on repertory albums of one sort or another. Most of these discs validate his findings with their exuberance as well as their attention to detail. The four-man *Stride Piano Summit* sets Hyman against two other masters (Lipskin is rather less of a giant) in a multi-combination show: he does his Fats Waller pipe-organ bit on 'Persian Rug' and roisters through 'Sunday' with McShann and Edison. Lightweight but entertaining.

His composer-dedicated records are unfailingly entertaining, if mixed in their profundities. Unfortunately, several have recently been lost to the deletions office. The Waller set wasn't one of his best: Hyman loves this music, but sometimes even he must feel that it sounds a little dated and, since he has little of Waller's genial uproar in his bones, he can't always bring it to life. Ellington also eludes him to some extent, since Duke's intimacies are just as personal to himself; but both records still have a degree of sophistication and elegance that set them some way above everybody's routine tribute record.

***(*) Elegies, Mostly

Gemini GMCD 90 *Hyman; Niels-Henning Orsted Pedersen (b).* 8/95.

***(*) Cheek To Cheek

Arbors ARCD 19155 *Hyman; Howard Alden (g); Bob Haggart (b).* 6/95.

Hyman is not in the business of making grand statements and, for all his virtuosity and insuperable accomplishment, his records are cast as almost modest affairs – conversations with good friends or with like-minded masters. That is the case on both of these discs and, while one regrets that a man of this eminence has made no single masterpiece album, perhaps this is the more appropriate way. *Cheek To Cheek* is an enchanting mix of material: Thelonious Monk, John Lewis, Irving Berlin, Flip Phillips and more. The triologue with Alden and Haggart is delightfully underplayed, so a test piece like 'Misterioso' (and who would ever have thought they'd hear Bob Haggart playing on this?) becomes charmingly restrained – it seems to glow, putting a new shine on Monk. Sometimes the bass parts aren't so helpful to the splendid guitar–piano interplay, but there's really nothing here to dislike. *Elegies, Mostly* may be a bit quiescent for some tastes, and perhaps they could have added a couple more tunes with the same pep as 'We're In The Money', the closer. But it's hard to argue with a duo this strong, and imaginative, and lyrically inventive. As a single sample, hear the gorgeous treatment of 'Some Other Time'.

***** Dick & Derek At The Movies**
Arbors ARCD 19197 *Hyman; Derek Smith (p).* 4/98.

Hyman has recorded duets with Smith before. Two-piano records are an odd breed and, since both men have a virtuosic streak, showmanship is frequently the order of the day. There are flashes of stride, ragtime, parlour-piano and more, and what grabs the attention are the set-piece quick tempos and superfast fingering. Fifteen tracks of this kind of thing are probably a few too many for most listeners, although from moment to moment the music is certainly joyful.

***** The Piano Giants At Bob Haggart's 80th Birthday Party**
Arbors ARCD 19266 *Hyman; Derek Smith, Ralph Sutton (p); Bob Haggart (b); Bobby Rosengarden (d).* 3/94.

The title says it all, and the three pianists play solo, in duo, and with rhythm. It's a joyful jumble, as it probably should be. Hyman introduces a note of old-fashioned elegance with a debonair treatment of 'In A Mist', though some of the harmonies are anything but old-fashioned. He and Smith are delightful together on 'I'm Through With Love'. Sound is slightly less than ideal, and Rosengarden is too loud on the tracks he plays on.

CORE COLLECTION

****** Forgotten Dreams**
Arbors ARCD 19248 *Hyman; John Sheridan (p).* 1/01.

At last, the Hyman album the world's been waiting for – Dick and John Sheridan tackle the buried legacy of novelty piano, one of the last undiscovered corners of the jazz tradition. Now that everyone from Reginald Robinson to Morten Gunnar Larsen has worked over the ragtime tradition, where next but the vast and almost untapped resources of the likes of Zez Confrey, Rube Bloom, Billy Mayerl and Willie Eckstein? Those last two don't figure here, but surely this one's crying out for a sequel already. Instead, they focus on Willie 'The Lion' Smith, Confrey, Bloom and Bob Zurke, with Bix's 'In A Mist' and W. C. Polla's 'Dancing Tambourine' to fill the gaps.

This set works better than Hyman's other two-piano dates because it's less about improvising (which scarcely plays a role here) and more about the graceful juxtaposition of complementary parts. These are, rhythmically, carefully honed essays on very early swing and syncopation; harmonically, they're dense with detail; but the melodies are so direct and wholesome, naïve in a pre-modern way, that some ideal balance is created which makes the results neither too knowing nor too gauche. Handsomely recorded, these forgotten dreams are, in their way, a daring revival.

Susie Ibarra (born 1970)

DRUMS

This gifted young percussionist really came to notice on saxophonist David S. Ware's contemporary classic, Godspellized, and since then has started to carve out a voice and place of her own.

*****(*) Home Cookin'**
Hopscotch HOP 1 *Ibarra; Assif Tsahar (ts).* 2 & 7/98.

****** Radiance**
Hopscotch HOP 2 *Ibarra; Charles Burnham (vn); Cooper-Moore (p, hp).* 7/99.

***** Flower After Flower**
Tzadik 7057 *Ibarra; Wadada Leo Smith (t); Chris Speed (cl) Assif Tsahar (bcl); Cooper-Moore (p, f); Charles Burnham (vn): Pauline Oliveros (acc); John Lindberg (b).* 99.

***** Songbird Suite**
Tzadik 7702 *Ibarra; Craig Taborn (p, elec); Ikue Mori (elec).* 01.

Are they destined to be the Geri and Wallace of the new decade? Ibarra and husband Assif Tsahar have arrived on the scene with the uncomplicated confidence of a shared mission. Ibarra will inevitably be compared to other female percussionists, earlier on the scene, players like Cindy Blackman and Marilyn Mazur, but she has moved the game along considerably. Her roots would seem to be in the avant-garde of the '60s, in the work of Rashied Ali and Andrew Cyrille, but she already plays with a highly distinctive voice: a light, pattering articulation which often disguises its punch; a musicianly ability to play or imply melody on the kit; and an unerring ear for pulses which go deeper than conventional metre.

The duos with Assif are perhaps closer to Archie Shepp's work with Max Roach than the more obvious example of Trane's *Interstellar Space* duets with Ali. They're interleaved with eight 'Dream Songs', played at home on a recently acquired array of Afro-Asian 'little instruments'. Nine times out of ten, such pieces would be an annoying distraction, but these work very well, and in intriguing ways they anticipate the language of *Radiance*.

An unusually constituted trio, it offers an even richer harmonic background for Ibarra's complex percussion. Burnham has long been an undervalued talent, and in tandem with the less familiar Cooper-Moore (no other name) he creates an intriguing dialogue which – if further analogy isn't redundant – recalls Billy Bang's duos with Dennis Charles. The inclusion of alternative versions of 'Dreams' and 'Laughter', two sections of the opening suite, 'Radiance', suggests how inventive and responsive a player Ibarra is.

The two more recent albums unveil a quieter and more lyrical side of Susie's personality. *Flower After Flower* consists of four substantial compositions, interspersed with short solo 'fractals' from Ibarra. The ensemble works best on 'Illuminations', dedicated to the charismatic Leo Smith, who dominates proceedings with his extraordinary tone and presence. 'The Ancients' pits the two clarinettists against one another, with Tsahar's brooding, melancholic sound steadily rising against Speed's more characteristic 'jazz clarinet'. *Songbird Suite* makes imaginative use of electronics; a difficult record to characterize or pigeonhole, it points to intriguing new directions for the young percussionist.

Abdullah Ibrahim (born 1934)

PIANO, SOPRANO SAXOPHONE, CELLO, VOICE

Ibrahim left his native South Africa in the aftermath of the Sharpeville massacre, settling first in Europe, latterly in the United States. He converted to Islam in 1968, but his given name, Dollar Brand, still has considerable currency and, however improperly, is apt to be used interchangeably. Along with Hugh Masekela and Kippie Moeketsi, Brand was a member of the epochal Jazz Epistles, the first black South African jazz group and a legendary catalyst on the scene there. Though influenced by Ellington and Thelonious Monk, he has a distinctive keyboard style, rocking bass tone ostinati punctuated by stabbing or more lyrical right-hand figures and melodies.

*** Duke Ellington Presents The Dollar Brand Trio

Warners/Reprise 6111 *Ibrahim; Johnny Gertze (b); Makaya Ntoshko (d).* 2/63.

It would be hard at first hearing to identify this as a Dollar Brand/Abdullah Ibrahim recording. There is not yet any clear evidence of his African roots and the abiding impression is of a forceful Monk disciple, edging towards a personal style. The clinching performance of 'Brilliant Corners' puts Brand in that camp rather than the Ellington one. Duke went to hear him play at the insistence of Sathima Bea Benjamin, who was Brand's wife at the time. He was impressed enough to recommend him to Reprise. The set begins with 'Dollar's Dance', a richly textured idea over a rather thick rhythmic base. 'The Stride' and 'Jumping Rope' are the most Monkian tracks, while 'Kippie' and 'Uku Suku' point somewhat in the direction of future developments, with repeated patterns built over a firm bass vamp. The sound quality is excellent and the piano is very much better than some Brand/Ibrahim has had to contend with over the years.

***(*) Ancient Africa

Sackville SKCD 3049 *Ibrahim (p solo).* 2/73.

*** Fats, Duke & The Monk

Sackville SKCD 3048 *As above.* 2/73.

These albums, recorded in one long session, were originally released as *Sangoma* and *African Portraits.* There's no obvious reason for the reordering of tracks on this reissue, though renaming one of the discs after Ibrahim's suite of pieces devoted to his piano mentors does make a certain sense. 'Fats, Duke & The Monk' is useful in that it shows how far he's moved away from their sphere and into his own language. 'Bra Joe From Kilimanjaro', something of a showpiece at this time, reappears on *Ancient Africa*, as does the beautiful 'Aloe And The Wild Rose', which exposes a more songlike side of his composing. The other album includes yet another recording of 'Kippie' and one of many contemporary versions of 'Xamba Khale', a traditional theme that became a signature of Ibrahim's later Afro-jazz approach. The sound is good on these reissues, with a lot of close detail.

*** The Journey

Downtown 1002 *Ibrahim; Don Cherry (t); Carlos Ward (as); Talib Rhynie (as, ob); Hamiet Bluiett (bs, cl); Johnny Mbizo Dyani (b); Ed Blackwell, Roy Brooks (d); John Betsch, Claude Jones (perc).* 9/77.

This is a very valuable reissue of a record originally on Chiaroscuro and unusual in that it teams Ibrahim (still known as Dollar Brand at the time; see the Alice Tully Hall poster on the cover) with forward-looking Americans. Good luck or empathy put him across the path of Don Cherry and Hamiet Bluiett, both of whom moved in the direction of world jazz later as their careers advanced. It's striking how much the top end of Bluiett's baritone, a register he's often favoured, sounds like Ibrahim's own work on soprano. It's also striking how much like the younger Keith Jarrett the pianist is on this date; nothing to do with occasional forays on the straight saxophone but in the rolling vamps and swaying rhythms that were part of Jarrett's vocabulary with his American group of the time. Brand's long-form improvisations work in a very different way, relying more on repetition than Jarrett's, but the cross-fertilization would be interesting to trace back to its source. The set is valuable, too, for Ibrahim's work with Johnny Dyani and Carlos Ward, both of whom played an important role in his duos and groups.

The opening 'Sister Rosie' (Ibrahim on soprano) is rollicking good fun and one of the highpoints of a slightly inconsistent set. 'Hajj' is Afro-misterioso, with the little-known Rhynie's oboe very prominent. The middle piece, 'Jabulani', had been better done before; this is a very muddy and congested piece. Indeed, the whole set reflects why Ibrahim has generally preferred to work alone or with a trio, at best a small group. Here, too many different musical personalities seem to clash. A riveting document, none the less.

***(*) Autobiography

Elephant 1267 *Ibrahim (p solo, f).* 6/78.

It isn't quite true that Ibrahim cut himself free of his Monk and Ellington roots as soon as he came into his own voice. This live set from 1978, recently reissued, finds him revisiting 'Take The "A" Train' and 'Coming On The Hudson' and performing both of them unexpectedly straight. There are newer pieces on the set as well, and at one point Ibrahim switches to flute, which he plays with a quavery poignancy. We heard an earlier release of this set which seemed to have problems with variable tape speed. Those seem to have been rectified.

**** Echoes From Africa

Enja 3047 *Ibrahim; Johnny Mbizo Dyani (b, bells, v).* 9/79.

Dyani towers on these fascinating and often moving duos, which move between a dark, almost tragic pessimism to a shouting, joyous climax. 'Saud' is a dedication to McCoy Tyner (the title reflects the other pianist's more briefly adopted Islamic name) and interestingly suggests how some of Ellington's modal explorations of the '60s filtered into the vernacular via younger piano players. The two voices entwine in celebration of the homeland. *Echoes* was originally released as an audiophile direct-to-disc recording. CD makes the music even more immediate and penetrative.

*** Africa Tears And Laughter

Enja ENJ 3039 *Ibrahim; Talib Qadr (ts, ss); Greg Brown (b); John Betsch (d).* 3/79.

There were signs that at this point in his career Ibrahim wanted to take stock of his progress so far. The Enja date examines its Africanness almost clinically, holding itself up to the light in a way that he either couldn't or wouldn't do in the company of Johnny Dyani later that same year. This – along with the Shepp encounter – is one of the only points in Ibrahim's career when the relentlessness of his approach begins to sound like self-parody, or at least self-pastiche.

*** Duke's Memories: The Definitive Black & Blue Sessions

Black & Blue 945 *Ibrahim; Carlos Ward (as, f); Rachim Ausur Sahu (b); Andre Strobert (d).* 6–7/81.

Recorded live and in studios in Berlin and Stuttgart, this tour saw Ibrahim dive back into the Ducal catalogue for some fine performances of 'Star-Crossed Lovers', 'In A Sentimental Mood', 'Virgin Jungle' and 'Angelica' and 'Purple Gazelle', the latter pair beautifully medleyed. The working band of the time fitted Ibrahim's conception very well indeed, though it's questionable how well bassist and drummer knew Duke's charts. They seem more familiar with Abdullah's 'The Wedding' (the first and best of the live tracks), 'For Coltrane' and the Ellingtonian 'Black And Brown Cherries'. As often, Ibrahim doesn't prominently feature himself but steers the whole, much as his mentor did. Good stuff, though, and a welcome return.

*** Zimbabwe

Enja ENJ 79632 *Ibrahim; Carlos Ward (as); Essiet Okun Essiet (b); Don Mumford (d).* 5/83.

*** South Africa

Enja ENJ 79618 *As above, except add Johnny Classens (v).* 7/85.

Zimbabwe is a curious set, unusually low-key and laid-back. The originals, 'Kramat', 'Bombella', the title-tune, and a tribute to John Coltrane, are much less fiery than one expects of Ibrahim, even at this period, and his attack at the keyboard is notably less vociferous than usual. The programme is interspersed with standard tunes, the best of which is 'Don't Blame Me'. Carlos Ward's appeal to very strong-minded piano-players – he has also worked extensively with Cecil Taylor, who had seemed to rely utterly on Jimmy Lyons – is still mysterious, but he blends well with Ibrahim's black-and-white approach to the keyboard, edging his way through some deceptively complex harmonies. On 'It Never Entered My Mind', Ibrahim and Ward seem to reference Miles Davis's version of the tune, reinforcing a feeling that on this disc he's putting to rest yet more parts of his musical background.

The live Montreux set on *South Africa* is inevitably more upbeat, but this also sounds a markedly disciplined band, constantly aware of the leader's changes of pace and mood. Ward's place in the sound has been widely discussed, but Essiet and the little-known Mumford both play important roles as well. This is the album that should have been titled *Autobiography*, since it offers an aural landscape of Ibrahim's childhood and growing up, his encounter with jazz ('African Dawn – For Monk') and a reprise of 'Zimbabwe' that is far better than the studio version. These sets sit nicely as a pair but the live disc is probably the better option if you can only stretch to one of them. An earlier Montreux appearance with Ward and a funkier electric band that also featured Craig Harris on trombone was released in 1981 on Inner City, but doesn't seem to have made it over on to CD.

**** Water From An Ancient Well

Tiptoe 88812 *Ibrahim; Dick Griffin (tb); Carlos Ward (as, f); Ricky Ford (ts); Charles Davis (bs); David Williams (b); Ben Riley (d).* 10/85.

The association with Carlos Ward has been the most productive and sympathetic of Ibrahim's career. The saxophonist has a high, exotic tone (superficially reminiscent of Sonny Fortune's, but much less raucous) that is ideally suited to his leader's conception. Working with Ward has reinforced Ibrahim's preference for song-like forms built over harmonically unvarying *ostinati* but has allowed him to develop a more abstract, improvisational feel, which reaches its peak on *Water From An Ancient Well*. This was made by Ibrahim's band, Ekaya (the word means 'home'); an earlier, eponymous disc on Black Hawk has disappeared. *Water* is a carefully structured album with something of the feel of Ellington's *Far East Suite*, and most of the drama comes from the interplay between Ibrahim and the horns. It includes another heartfelt tribute to Sathima Bea Benjamin, 'Daughter Of Cape Town'.

*** Desert Flowers

Enja 7011 *Ibrahim (p, ky solo).* 12/91.

This was meant to express a sort of homecoming to what was, even then, being hailed as the 'new' South Africa; Ibrahim had spent much of his creative life in exile. *Desert Flowers* is a very personal programme of music and there are moments when emotion (and the synthesizer) blur the focus badly. Ibrahim actually uses synth only on the first and last tracks, an uneasy welcome and farewell that completely belies the warmth radiating from the heart of the set. Significantly, middle position is occupied by Duke's 'Come Sunday', a gorgeous performance preceded by a breath of the past in 'Ancient Cape', followed by 'District Six', 'Sweet Devotion', and a passionate vocal tribute to John Coltrane. Though far from a classic Ibrahim album, it contains enough of real merit to lift it to the fringes of the first division.

***(*) Knysna Blue

Tiptoe 888816 *Ibrahim (p solo).* 9 & 10/93.

Frankly celebratory, and intended as a mystical reconsecration of post-apartheid South Africa as a country at the world's apex, between two great oceans and focusing the cultural energies of four continents. All this is probably too much freight for one piano album, and sometimes one feels Ibrahim is trying too hard to express the inexpressible, to catch the ineffable in a combination of heavy chords and floating melody lines. There is, though, no mistaking the joy with which it comes and the total identification in Ibrahim's mind of personal and political/cultural liberation. It is, very simply, an extended love song, and the closing Monk cover, 'Ask Me Now', is as nakedly personal and unguarded as Ibrahim has ever been.

CORE COLLECTION

**** Yarona

Tiptoe 888820 *Ibrahim; Marcus McLaurine (b); George Johnson (d).* 1/95.

A truly magisterial performance by the 60-year-old, bringing the house down at Sweet Basil in New York City. Ibrahim was on record around this time, reinforcing his conviction that the piano-trio format permitted the most fundamental representation of the African source; and it is very hard to argue with that on the basis of these performances. He still hits the piano very hard, using the bass almost as a drone, alternating narrow intervals and often allowing the drummer considerable licence to range outside the metre. The left hand is relentless and, in the other sense, timeless, the melody lines stripped down and ritualized. 'Duke 88' once again acknowledges a personal debt. 'Nisa' is an exclamatory hymn to another, the womenfolk of South Africa. There is a reworking

of 'African Marketplace' and a concert outing for 'Stardance', one of the lovelier themes from the *Chocolat* soundtrack. The love song, 'Cherry' (not, as one critic assumed, a tribute to the trumpeter), shows his more lyrical side.

★★★(★) Cape Town Flowers

Tiptoe 888 826 *Ibrahim; Marcus McLaurine (b); George Gray (d).* 97.

As Hans-Hurgen Schaal perceptively points out in his liner-note, Ibrahim is above all a great storyteller. These 11 narratives in jazz take the story on a step in time and in the context of a free country. Few artists have been as relentlessly consistent in style as Ibrahim and yet as endlessly changing. What's obvious here is that some of the anger and some of the sense of loss have already faded from his music. This, on something like 'Joan – Cape Town Flower' in particular, is the work of a man reconciled to his world, not complacent, still questioning, but certainly not in the throes of alienation. It is arguably Ibrahim's most peaceful album to date. Newcomers should still explore the earlier work, but this makes a delightful place to begin.

★★★(★) African Suite

Enja/Tiptoe TIP 888 832 2 *Ibrahim; Belden Bullock (b); George Gray (d); strings.* 11/97.

★★ African Symphony

Enja ENJ 9410 *Ibrahim; orchestra.* 98–01.

Beautifully arranged by Daniel Schnyder, *African Suite* opens out the orchestral dimension of Ibrahim's rich and multi-textured compositions and does so without swamping the music. The young players from the Youth Orchestra of the European Community (a Claudio Abbado brainchild) have obviously all come through as part of a generation that no longer makes hard and fast distinctions between 'classical', 'jazz' and 'world' styles. Their playing is accurate but not stiff and the ensembles are relaxed enough not to sound like a paid-by-the-hour session orchestra. Long-established favourites like the funky 'Tintinyanna' mean there are familiar reference-points, and Ibrahim takes a delightful piano solo on 'Aspen'. A very lovely record.

African Symphony reprises much of the same material but with a new prelude, 'Ritus', written by Schnyder and with markedly little input from Ibrahim whose vision survives only imperfectly in these settings. The playing is still wonderful but there is nothing convincingly symphonic about the work, so it's torpedoed by its own pretentious premise.

★★★(★) Cape Town Revisited

Enja/Tiptoe TIP 888 836 2 *Ibrahim; Feya Faku (t); Marcus McLaurine (b); George Gray (d).* 12/97.

Dominated by stunning performances of 'Tintinyanna', 'Water From An Ancient Well' and by the jazz suite, 'Cape Town To Congo Square', this is a summation of much of Ibrahim's musical experience and exploration over the last 20 years. Playing at Spier Estate in Cape Town and with Feya Faku on three tracks echoing the sound of Hugh Masekela all those years before, it is both the most backward-looking and one of the most sanguinely optimistic and exploratory of Ibrahim's recent discs. The sound is very good for a live recording, very present and alert, and the southern hemisphere summer warms and colours every track.

★★★(★) Ekapa Lodumo

Tiptoe 888840 *Ibrahim; Lennart Axelsson, Ingolf Burkhardt, Claus Stotter, Reiner Winterschladen (t, flhn); Mike Danner, Joe Gallardo (tb); Peter Bolte (ss, as, f); Fiete Felsch (as, f); Frank Delle (ts); Lucas Lindholm (b); Alex Riel (d); Jose Cortijo (perc).* 6/00.

The NDR Big Band are in cracking form on this set of inventive arrangements of Ibrahim themes. The pianist treats the occasion almost like a piece of theatre or *son et lumière*, intoning introductions to each impressionistic section, like 'African Market' and 'Black And Brown Cherries'. The German soloists are well up to the challenge of the music and Stotter in particular plays out of his skin on the tribute to Duke Ellington. Ibrahim himself isn't featured as extensively as he might once have been, and he comes across as slightly circumspect in these arrangements by Steve Gray and Fritz Pauer; but the music speaks for itself and as a concert experience it is magnificently presented and produced.

★★★★ Best Of Abdullah Ibrahim

Masingita 5839 *Ibrahim; Blue Mitchell (t); Buster Cooper, Dick Griffin (tb); Jimmy Adams, Morris Goldberg, Robbie Jensen, Kippie Moeketsi, Carlos Ward (as); Harold Land, Ricky Ford, Duke Makasi, Basil Manningberg Coetzee (ts); Charles Davis (bs); Sipho Gunede, Victor Ntori, Marcus McLaurine, Spencer Mbadu, Cecil McBee, David Williams (b); George Gray, George V. Johnson, Gilbert Matthews, Ben Riley, Doug Sides, Monty Weber (d).* 76–90.

This excellent career sampler puts the emphasis on early and, some would say, classic work. Traditional pieces like 'Lam Bayi' and 'Chisa' are given forceful interpretations and Ibrahim material like 'Bra Timing From Phomolong' and 'Blues For A Hip King' underline how strong a writer he is in an Africanized Ellington tradition. Like Duke, he delegates brilliantly to sidemen like Moeketsi and Ward who, in different generations, are perhaps his most effective interpreters. Fine as they are, the rest are also well up to the mark, and, though the sound-quality isn't always pristine, there isn't a dud track on this very valuable compilation.

★★★ Cape Town Songs: The Very Best Of Abdullah Ibrahim

Nascente 414 *As for Enja albums above.* 63–91.

As with so many 'best of' collections, this merely trawls one label's output. It's fair to say, though, that much of Ibrahim's best work has been for the German label and this is a very respectable sample of his work: 'African Marketplace', 'For Monk', 'Zimbabwe' and a seeming emphasis elsewhere on his most folkish compositions.

ICP Orchestra

GROUP

Named after the pioneer LP label which recorded many of the Dutch free players of the '60s and '70s, the orchestra offers a cross-section of American and European performers for this collection.

★★★ Herbie Nichols/Thelonious Monk

Bvhaast 026 *Toon De Gouw (t); Wolter Wierbos, George E. Lewis (tb); Steve Lacy (ss); Michael Moore (cl, as); Paul Termos (as); Ab Baars (ts, ss, cl); Sean Bergin (ts); Misha*

Mengelberg (p); Ernst Reijseger (clo); Maurice Horsthuis (vla); Larry Fishkind (tba); Han Bennink (d). 84–87.

A larger-scale version of the tributes which Mengelberg, Lacy and others recorded for Soul Note at much the same time, this highly coloured and generous programme makes light of the difficulties in both composers' work. Monk tributes have become commonplace, but Baars, Moore and Wierbos are soloists with an idiosyncratic accent, and Lewis appears on a few tracks for an extra brassiness. Mengelberg and Bennink, the most practised of in-to-out rhythm sections, make Monk's rhythmic eccentricities their own property, too. But the Nichols tracks are more interesting, since his tunes are less familiar, and the larger group – which includes Termos, Horsthuis, Bergin and Lacy – lends a firmer substance to music which is difficult to characterize.

*** Jubilee Varia

hatOLOGY 528 *Thomas Heberer (t); Wolter Wierbos (tb); Ab Baars (cl, ts); Michael Moore (cl, as); Misha Mengelberg (p); Ernst Reijseger, Tristan Honsinger (clo); Ernst Glerum (b); Han Bennink (d).* 11/97.

**** Oh, My Dog!

ICP 040 *As above, except add Mary Oliver (vn, vla); omit Reijseger.* 6/01.

Not quite a 'new generation' of the orchestra, but a few new faces, and plenty of new ideas to go with them. The hatOLOGY record suffers a bit from the first half, comprising the title-suite: while the Mengelberg–Bennink duo which opens it is a delight, the rest seems a bit strained and ordinary. Mengelberg's 'Jealousy' suite is much more engaging. Everything this group does is going to be fragmented, and here it works slightly against them overall.

No such problem with the subsequent *Oh, My Dog!*. The opening four-minute improvisation, 'Write Down Exactly', is a little miracle of nine people making a seemly racket without getting in each other's way. Baars pays peculiar homage to Charles Ives with 'A Close Encounter With Charles's Country Band', while Mengelberg's 'A La Russe' starts as a stately Russian folk-tune before gradually curdling into the mildest of dissonance. Michael Moore, whose piped, astringent delivery is a neat counter to Baars, brings in 'Ham On Air', which pirouettes between horn-lines of trenchant melancholy and string- and drum-parts that savagely undermine the equilibrium of the music. The string-players are, indeed, crucial to the Orchestra's sound, scurrying around the edges or howling antiphonal responses to the horns. For once, Bennink is given superb studio sound, which affirms what a master he is – in complete control, even as he tinkers at the edge of chaos.

***(*) Aan & Uit

ICP 042 *As above.* 11–12/03.

Nearly all Mengelberg pieces this time. 'Picnic', in six parts, is a day out in the country which works his customary magic, alternating between what sound like random acts of chaos and detailed chamber music without a perceptible stagger. 'Tijd Voor De Quadrille' is a solemn dance. Hoagy Carmichael's 'Barbaric' (how did they think of doing this?) is the Orchestra's take on the end of the first Jazz Age, and it's brusque and melancholy. Heberer's 'Let's Climb A Hill' is in the spirit.

Klaus Ignatzek (born 1954)

PIANO

German pianist in a conventional post-bop idiom, with a wide range of recordings and compositions to his credit.

**(*) The Klaus Ignatzek Trio

yvp 3020 *Ignatzek; Jean-Louis Rassinfosse (b); John Engels (d).* 7/89.

***(*) The Answer!

Candid CCD 79534 *Ignatzek; Claudio Roditi, Gustavo Bergalli (t); Jean-Louis Rassinfosse (b); Jorge Rossy (d).* 12/92.

Ignatzek has immersed himself so completely in the idioms of Horace Silver, Bill Evans, Sonny Clark and Wynton Kelly as to claim almost apostolic understanding of the roots of hard bop. Like some clairvoyant transcriber of 'posthumous' Mozart symphonies, he has produced a steady stream of rather unconvincing pastiche that may sound good in a club setting but which seems a thoroughly dull option when set against a random sample of late-'50s Blue Notes.

The most recent of the above records, *The Answer!*, is probably the best of all. A tight, well-disciplined set with a minimum of fuss, it has some sharp arrangements that make maximum use of the two horns and exploit the more percussive side of this saxophoneless band.

*** Silent Horns

Candid CCD 79729 *Ignatzek; Claudio Roditi, Gustavo Bergalli (t); Jean-Louis Rassinfosse (b); Jorge Rossy (d).* 94.

Ignatzek seems to like this curious instrumentation, and there's certainly some élan about this homage to deceased bebop trumpeters. If only Bergalli and Roditi were more individual than proficient, the music might be genuinely challenging, but what tends to emerge is a series of skilful set-pieces rather than an absorbing record.

*** Reunion

Acoustic Music 319.1084.2 *Ignatzek; Florian Poser (vib, mar).* 8/95.

*** Live

Acoustic Music 319.1097.21 *Ignatzek; Claudio Roditi, Gustavo Bergalli (t); Jean-Louis Rassinfosse (b); Chip White (d).* 10/95.

**(*) Obrigado

Acoustic Music 319.1113.2 *Ignatzek; Martin Wind (b).* 6/96.

*** Springdale

Acoustic Music 319.1166.2 *Ignatzek; Florian Poser (vib, mar).* 6–7/98.

Now on a new label, Ignatzek continues to work prolifically. The live album by the quintet goes off at a furious pace with 'Quasi-Modal' and, though it rarely stirs the blood beyond the expected muscle-flexing, it's a group which here makes the most of its collective chops, although the material offered by the leader isn't very inspiring. The duo album with Martin Wind benefits from the bassist's sonorous tone. Together they make a lovely, big, rich sound, and although the record is far too long at over 70 minutes, much of it (taken a track at a time) is appealing in a lightweight way. The same goes for the two discs which pair Ignatzek with vibist Poser. There's very little to say about this music except to note its neat, dovetailed interplay and *simpatico* nature. Everything falls where one expects, and the pleasure in it comes not from any kind of surprise but from professional inevitability.

★★(★) **Primal Sound**

Acoustic Music 319.1209.2 *Ignatzek; Jean-Louis Rassinfosse (b); Anca Parghel (v).* 4/99.

Parghel puts a bit of blood into Ignatzek's often mechanical situations, although she's not the most immediately appealing of singers, and some of the wordless vocalizing will try any listener's patience. When it works, as in the suitably luscious 'Desire', the results are more sensuous than most of Ignatzek's offerings.

Nikki Iles (born 1963)

PIANO

Iles studied at RAM and has been involved in the south-eastern scene since the later '90s.

★★★ **Veils**

Symbol SR 2002020201 *Iles; Stan Sulzmann (ss, ts); Mike Outram (g); Mick Hutton (b); Anthony Michelli (d).* 2/02.

★★★(★) **Everything I Love**

Basho SRCD 5-2 *Iles; Duncan Hopkins (b); Anthony Michelli (d).* 1/02.

The quintet record is a strong if at times slightly diffident showcase for Iles's writing. All bar one are her originals, and they're marked by episodic melodies, chord sequences which suggest the term 'writerly' and structures which set specific if not exactly insurmountable challenges for the players. Sulzmann is a regular duet partner with the pianist and he can get inside her ideas without sullying his essentially soft tone. Outram sounds as if he's going to get nasty on the opening 'Beauteous Beast', but it never really happens. That may be the weakness of the record – everyone behaves a little too politely.

The trio record is the more recent issue, although it was actually recorded a month earlier, in Montreal. It's a piano fan's programme, with compositions by John Taylor, Bill Evans and Enrico Pieranunzi in the set-list, and Nikki modestly offering only two of her own tunes, right in the middle of the disc and both despatched quickly. Michelli plays a lot more aggressively, oddly enough, than he does on the quintet date, at times too much so, though it does put a useful kick into the music. Iles likes to play good melodies, but they do sometimes come out in paragraphs and she has more of a problem with continuous flow. That said, it's an otherwise very agreeable set.

Implicate Order

GROUP

American free trio take on various guests.

★★★(★) **Sound Quest**

Cadence CJR 1140 *Steve Swell (tb); Martin Speicher (as); Ursel Schlicht (p); Ken Filiano (b); Lou Grassi (d).* 3/01.

★★★ **At Seixal**

Clean Feed CF001 *As above, except add Paulo Cuarado (as, ss), Rodrigo Amado (bs); omit Schlicht, Speicher.* 3/01.

Swell says that 'the whole point of naming this group after physicist David Bohm's theory of the same name was to ...' – but if you want to know the rest, you'll have to get the Clean Feed CD and read the notes. Less conceptually minded souls should know that the music on both discs is a typically unfettered, leaderless, ego-free (yes, of course) improvised blow-out. Since both discs are built up into a quintet by 'local' guests, circumstances tend to dictate how they're going to sound from place to place. The Cadence set (recorded in Germany) is slightly taken over by Schlicht, since she had the temerity to require the group to play one of her compositions, although it does open with a five-minute bass solo. Nevertheless, the two Germans are the most impressive performers on the disc, bringing a rigour (and, in Speicher's case, a fury) which the Americans aren't quite privy to.

The Portuguese session is mostly by the trio, although Amado and Cuarado arrive for the final two pieces. It sounds like a characteristic festival set, plenty of free showmanship, lots of bravado, though missing a degree of restraint which might have taken matters a step further than they go.

Peter Ind (born 1928)

BASS

Born in Middlesex, Ind began studying bass in the '40s and was a Tristano pupil in New York before moving to California. A clubowner in London in the '80s and early '90s, his Wave label documents much of his work.

★★★ **Looking Out / Jazz Bass Baroque**

Wave 111 *Ind; Ronnie Ball, Sal Mosca (p); Joe Puma, Al Schackman, Martin Taylor, Tony Bernard (g); Dick Scott, John Richardson (d); Sheila Jordan (v).* 4/58–8/98.

★★★ **Alone Together**

Wave 36 *Ind; Rufus Reid (b).* 11/98.

The earlier disc is a curious hybrid of home-made New York recordings and much later pieces with British players. It has a scrapbook element which feels like something important to its maker but is difficult for outsiders to get involved with; that said, there are a few exceptional performances, such as Mosca's take on 'Love Me Or Leave Me', and an outstanding Sheila Jordan vocal on 'Yesterdays'.

The bass-duet album will also be of greater interest to bassists than to anyone else, but in its way it is beautifully done. In what was designed as a nod of affection to Milt Hinton, the two men take a conservative but sonorous path through standards, bebop tunes and – in an acknowledgement of Ind's own roots – '317 East 32nd Street'.

Independence Hall Jazz Band

GROUP

Repertory traditional band under the leadership of trombonist Doug Finke, dedicated to classic material from the '20s.

★★★ **Chicago Rhythm**

Stomp Off CD 1371 *Jon-Erik Kellso, Duke Heitger (t); Doug Finke, Jim Beebe (tb); Paul Reichlin (tba); Orange Kellin (cl); Paul Asaro (p); Paul Scavarda (bj, g, uke, v); Vince Giordano (b, tba); Rob Garcia (d).* 11/00–1/01.

*****(*) Louis: The Oliver Years**
Stomp Off CD 1384 *As above except Bob Sundstrum (bj) and Mike DeMonte (d) replace Scavarda and Garcia, omit Giordano and Beebe.* 8/02.

***** Favorites**
Stomp Off CD 1386 *Dan Barrett (c); Jon-Erik Kellso (t); Doug Finke (tb); Pete Reichlin (tba); Dan Levinson (cl, Cmel, v); Paul Asaro (p); Scott Anthony (bj, g); Chris Tyle (d, c, cl, v).* 11/02.

Another repertory band from the Stomp Off label, and this time perhaps not one of our favourites. The pick of the three is the middle set, dedicated to the kind of material which Louis Armstrong played during his King Oliver years, with particularly fine versions of 'Chattanooga Stomp' and others. The other two are very well done, but so many of these kind of sessions have been undertaken – involving many of the same musicians, too – that, good as they are, the music is starting to sound like routine, to the listeners if not to the players.

Keith Ingham (born 1942)

PIANO

Born in London, Ingham was a familiar face in British mainstream in the '60s and early '70s; then he moved to New York in 1978, originally as an accompanist to Susannah McCorkle. He is a prime mover in the field of reviving hot jazz and dance from the '20s and '30s, often with Marty Grosz.

***** The Music Of Victor Young**
Jump JCD12-16 *Ingham; Bob Reitmeier (p); Frank Tate (b); Vernell Fournier (d).* 3/89.

***** Out Of The Past**
Sackville SKCD 2-3047 *Ingham (p solo).* 11–12/90.

*****(*) Donaldson Redux**
Stomp Off CD 1237 *Ingham; Peter Ecklund (c); Dan Barrett (tb); Bobby Gordon, Billy Novick (cl); Loren Schoenberg (ts); Vince Giordano (bsx, tba, b); Marty Grosz (g, bj, v); Greg Cohen (b); Hall Smith, Arnie Kinsella (d).* 6–11/91.

Ingham is the archetypal Englishman in New York (though the solo album was cut mainly in Toronto). He plays a history of jazz piano with unflinching finesse, taste and skill, and unearths tunes that few would think of trying. The 18 tracks on *Out Of The Past* cover composers from Richard M. Jones to Barry Harris, and resuscitate such cadavers as 'Just Like A Butterfly' and Rube Bloom's 'Truckin''. It is all beautifully played, the variations improvised with rag-like precision, but the unobtrusive nature of Ingham's talent is eventually frustrating. After a dozen tracks one wonders if there ought to be greater difference between such diverse sources than Ingham allows, and his version of, say, Jimmy Yancey's 'At The Window' is very pale next to the composer's own. The Jump CD is also all *politesse*, one of a series of composer-dedicated sessions: everyone sticks very closely to the melodies and it seldom seems like more than mood music. Very gracefully done, though, and musicians may like to hear some neglected melodies ('Golden Earrings', 'A Love Like This', 'Got The South In My Soul') played straight.

The Stomp Off album is another matter, since it documents the further adventures of Marty Grosz in hot-dance music. The songs are all by Walter Donaldson, and some of this archaeology is almost preposterously rarefied. Grosz does his usual update of Ukulele Ike at the microphone, and the band play a lilting approximation of old-time hot music with a few knowing modern licks. Ingham is co-credited as leader and no doubt approves of all the fun.

***** My Little Brown Book**
Progressive PCD 7101 *Ingham; Harry Allen (ts); Chris Flory (g); Dennis Irwin (b); Chuck Riggs (d).* 3/93.

*****(*) The Intimacy Of The Blues**
Progressive PCD 7102 *As above.* 3/93.

***** Music From The Mauve Decades**
Sackville SKCD2-2033 *Ingham; Bobby Gordon (cl); Hal Smith (d).* 4/93.

***** Just Imagine ...**
Stomp Off CD1285 *Ingham; Peter Ecklund (c, t); Dan Barrett (tb); Dan Levinson (cl, Cmel); Scott Robinson (cl, ts, bs, bsx); Marty Grosz (g, v); Greg Cohen (b); Joe Hanchrow (tba); Arnie Kinsella (d).* 4/94.

***** New York Nine Vol. 1**
Jump JCD12-18 *Ingham; Randy Reinhart (c, tb); Dan Barrett (t, tb); Phil Bodner (cl, as); Scott Robinson (ss, ts, bs); James Chirillo (g); Vince Giordano (bsx, b); Murray Wall (b); Arnie Kinsella (d).* 5/94.

***** New York Nine Vol. 2**
Jump JCD12-19 *As above.* 5/94.

*****(*) The Back Room Romp**
Sackville SKCD2-3059 *Ingham; Peter Ecklund (t); Scott Robinson (cl, ss, bs); Harry Allen (ts); James Chirillo (g); Murray Wall (b); Jackie Williams (d).* 1/95.

Ingham has been busy in the '90s. The two albums of Billy Strayhorn tunes on Progressive are a light, floating collaboration with the classically styled tenor of Harry Allen. This is Strayhorn done straight, the melodies softly enunciated, the improvisations taken only a few feline steps away from the melodies. Ingham varies the arrangements between groupings of musicians and plays a few tracks solo. Scarcely an adventurous approach to repertory, but very satisfyingly done: the second disc just edges ahead since it has the less frequently encountered material.

Music From The Mauve Decades covers 1900–20 in terms of material. Some of it is a little too musty, and the normally reliable Smith doesn't always sound appropriate in some of the tunes: a simple duet between Gordon and Ingham might have worked better. But there are still some exquisite moments, such as the lulling 'Just A-Wearyin' For You'. The remaining discs are all by bigger ensembles, and they whistle in several of the top repertory players in the field. *Just Imagine ...* is mostly infectious fun, though a shade below the Walter Donaldson set listed above. The two New York Nine albums slip between the '20s and '30s without any pain and, though the band could still use a little more heat on the fiercer tunes, the playing is impeccably crafted. Best of them is perhaps *The Back Room Romp*, which concentrates on the small-band swing repertory of the '30s. They rescue a couple of Rex Stewart rarities in the title-piece and 'San Juan Hill', and Allen continues his progress from Ben Webster and Paul Gonsalves to something approaching an individual style. Ecklund is irreproachable as usual. Ingham is often content to stay in the shadows on these records, but his calm hand on the arranging tiller seems rock-solid.

*****(*) Going Hollywood**
Stomp Off CD1323 *Ingham; Peter Ecklund (c, t); Joel Helleny (tb); Vince Giordano (tba); Scott Robinson (cl, ss, as,*

ts, bs, bsx); Dan Block (cl, ss); Andy Stein (vn); Marty Grosz (g, bj, v); Brian Nalepka, Greg Cohen (b); Arnie Kinsella (d). 5–9/96.

***** A Star Dust Melody**
Sackville SKCD 2-2051 *Ingham; Randy Reinhart (t); Bobby Gordon (cl); Scott Robinson (reeds); James Chirillo (g); Greg Cohen (b); Arnie Kinsella (d).* 8–11/97.

Going Hollywood sees Ingham and Grosz pal up with their 'Hot Cosmopolites' to excellent, if by now familiar, effect. Grosz digs up spectacular forget-me-nots such as 'The Wedding Of The Painted Doll' and 'The Woman In The Shoe', and the ensemble hit the right note of reverent irreverence.

The Sackville album is a more respectful saunter through the Hoagy Carmichael songbook. Gordon gets a starring role and, although some of it is rather plain-spoken, the quality of the melodies endures.

***** We're In The Money**
Sackville SKCD2-2055 *Ingham; Peter Ecklund (t); Bobby Gordon (cl); Chris Flory (g); Murray Wall (b); Steve Little (d).* 10/99.

Ingham says in his note that he 'wanted to get away from the contemporary stereotype where jazz is promoted either as "mood music" or "raw authenticity"', although that pretty much sums up his approach to every record listed under his name. So it's a lightly swinging rhythm section, a couple of horns that are good at old-fashioned melodies, and material that mixes the slightly familiar with the obscure. Difficult to envisage an Ingham project ever being less than enjoyable and this one doesn't fail but, aside from 'Lulu's Back In Town' and one or two others, it's a little sedate.

***** Music Music Everywhere**
Spotlite SPJ 577 *Ingham; Jim Richardson (b); Bobby Worth (d).* 5/03.

Some solos, mostly trio. The concept is, again, anti-concept, and that gives Ingham free rein on the tunes: Quincy Jones's 'For Lena And Lenny', 'Moon And Sand', 'Monk's Mood'. In its way, impeccable.

Yoron Israel

DRUMS

Chicago-born, Israel has long been an in-demand percussionist. His own groups are inventive outfits with a strong emphasis on imaginative funk and hard bop.

***** Chicago**
Double Time 145 *Israel; Joe Lovano (ss, ts); Larry Goldings (org); Marvin Sewell (g).* 99.

***** Live At The Blue Note**
Half Note 4901 *Israel; Steve Turre (tb); Eric Alexander (ts); Ed Cherry (g); Bryan Carrott (vib); Sean Conly (b).* 99.

These records are marked by strong playing from all concerned, but almost more intriguing is Israel's eclectic choice of material which includes compositions by, among others, Julian Priester, Jack DeJohnette, Jimmy Heath and Earth, Wind and Fire. His own writing is strong but not yet characterized by a definite personality.

The organ trio format suits Israel's playing style very well. He is happy to work off a backbeat, but also gets down to some powerful bop-derived drumming as well. Johnny Griffin's 'Nice And Easy' demonstrates how well he plays even at a gentler metre, while Clifford Jordan's 'Down Through The Years', one of Lovano's guest spots, is a deceptive burner that gets the whole group into a combustive vein. Joe also turns up, on soprano this time, on EWF's 'That's The Way Of The World', a clever reworking of a funk classic. For us, though, Priester's 'Battery Blues' is the standout track – a nice example of Chicagoans sticking together and speaking the same tough-tender language.

The live date is full of good things as well, though the sound is often quite disappointing. Carrott and Cherry tend to trip over one another in the ensembles and Bryan isn't always as audible as he ought to be. Again, the horns stand out. Alexander (who we understand was a dep in this band) plays an absolute blinder, reminiscent of Cliff Jordan, and Turre's briefer appearance adds a whole new dimension to the band. Again, Yoron has chosen unusual material that taxes his own chops and the solo skills of his band members, but without scaring off the paying guests, who must have warmed immediately even to lesser-known material like Jimmy Heath's too rarely covered 'Mellowdrama' and Mulgrew Miller's beautiful 'The Eleventh Hour'. A very attractive record from a fine musician.

Italian Instabile Orchestra

ENSEMBLE

Founded in 1990 by trumpeter Pino Minafra and the poet Vittorino Curci, but functioning as a co-operative, the Orchestra was an attempt to create an Italian ensemble with the eclectic range of the Vienna Art Orchestra, the Willem Breuker Kollektief or one of the more theatrical of the Russian free-jazz groups.

*****(*) Italian Instabile Orchestra**
Leo CD LR 182 *Pino Minafra (t, flhn, didjeridu); Guido Mazzon (t, flhn); Alberto Mandarini (t); Giancarlo Schiaffini (tb, tba); Sebi Tramontana (tb, v); Lauro Rossi (tb); Martin Mayes (frhn); Mario Schiano (as, v); Eugenio Colombo (as, ss, f); Carlo Actis Dato (ts, bs, bcl); Daniele Cavallanti (ts, bs); Gianluigi Trovesi (as, cl in A, bcl); Renato Geremia (vn); Paolo Damiani (clo, b, v); Bruno Tommaso (b); Giorgio Gaslini (p); Vincenzo Mazzone, Tiziano Tononi (d, perc).* 6/91, 1/92.

****** Skies Of Europe**
ECM 1543 *As above.* 5/94.

*****(*) European Concerts '94–'97**
NEL Jazz 0968 *As above.* 10/94, 9 & 11/96, 1/97.

***** Festival: Pisa Teatro Verdi December 1997**
Leo CDLR 292/293 2CD *As above, except add Luca Calabrese (t).* 12/97.

****** Litania Sibilante**
Enja 9405 *As above, except; add Enrico Rava (t); Antonella Salis (acc).* 99.

The Italian Instabile Orchestra is uncategorizable, not so much because it goes in for promiscuous genre-bending, but because it is a genuine convocation of equals, and because individual members and sub-groups are likely to go off in whatever direction takes their fancy. Like ARFI in France (of which Louis Sclavis is an adherent), the Orchestra seeks to articulate an 'imaginary folklore', an improbable common ground between popular forms, formal composition and free improvisation. There shouldn't be a strong enough gravitational field to hold it all together but, miraculously, there is. All but one of the pieces were recorded at Radio France's international jazz festival at Rive-de-Gier. The exception is perhaps the key to the whole enterprise. Giorgio Gaslini's 'Pierrot Solaire' proposes a sunshine cure for the moonstruck icon of musical modernism. Relaxed, funny, joyous, you're meant to think it's a long way from Schoenberg, except, of course, he's in there too.

Eugenio Colombo's 'Ippopotami' is a typically amphibian theme; satirically cumbersome ashore, it shows considerable if improbable grace once in the freer element of improvisation. There's also an element of that in Giancarlo Schiaffini's 'La Czarda Dell'Aborigeno', which manages to graft a didjeridu introduction on to a Hungarian dance and which features fine soloing from Carlo Actis Dato on baritone and transplanted Scot, Martin Mayes, on horn.

Pachyderms reappear in Minafra's 'Noci ... Strani Frutti', a title that contains one of the Orchestra's carefully veiled allusions to jazz. This has less to do with Billie Holiday's 'Strange Fruit' than with the improbable pickings of surrealist art. Divided into 'African' and 'Indian' sections, it sets Afro-American jazz off against the other major improvisational tradition with a flute raga by Colombo. Dato (wearing rubber elephant ears, allegedly) rants a tale of Latin intrigue and passion.

The set opens with cellist Paolo Damiani's 'Detriti', a Noah's ark of musical and textual specimens rescued from the latter-day flood of genres and styles. It ends with 'I Virtuosi De Noci', a free-jazz piece reminiscent of Globe Unity or the Berlin Jazz Orchestra, and a powerful statement of belief in the stabilizing and cohesive power of improvisation.

The orchestra benefits more than a little from the ministrations of ECM, and Steve Lake's meticulous production opens up dimensions and strata which simply aren't accessible on the Leo. The CD is divided into two long suits, 'Il Maestro Muratore', by Tomasso, which is inspired by the great Sard sculptor, Constantino Nivola, who took his genius and his passionate defence of Sardinia's place at the international table to the United States. The opening portrait features a powerful solo statement from Minafra and Dato, and a superb string duet between the composer and Damiani. Most of the other movements are short ensembles, but 'Meru Lo Snob' is another free-blowing track, with Gaslini bracketed by Schiano and Cavallanti.

The pianist is also the composer of 'Skies Of Europe', an extended meditation on some of the great outsiders of European culture – Duchamp, Satie, Antonioni and Fellini – and is also intended to echo the orchestral ambitions of Ornette Coleman's *Skies Of America*. As ever, Gaslini's ideas are simultaneously rooted in jazz and orthodox composition, and the texture of his orchestrations is very detailed. He structures the opening 'Du Du Duchamp' (a pun on the old Dubonnet advert) round a sequence of duets, which gives a first airing of the set to Martin Mayes's fruitily-toned horn. Mayes reappears on 'Il Suono Giallo' to equally strong effect. The brasses tend to dominate elsewhere as well, with Minafra and Mazzon trading ideas on the Antonioni tribute and trombonist Schiaffini catching the ear on 'Quand Duchamp Joue Du Marteau', which also has Gaslini moving back and forth from piano to anvil.

Like the VAO, the orchestra have never found their eclecticism a problem, putting them between the anvil of classicism and the hammer of jazz. The touring material on the NEL Jazz disc is quite various in style, sound and quality, but it offers a decent representation of the band in what has been a period of quite intense activity. Mazzon's 'Fall In Jazz', recorded in Rome in 1994, is the earliest of the pieces included, and certainly the closest to jazz proper. Later items, and particularly Tononi's 'La Leggenda Del Lupo Azzurro', have their premises elsewhere. As before, the soloing is virtuosic and cheerfully idiosyncratic. The Italian Instabile Orchestra has established a place and a very distinctive sound-palette.

Later discs attempted to make festival records sound like anything but festival records. The usual running order – small groups and solo spots first, then the full orchestra – makes logistic sense on the ground but none on disc, so the material is generously redistributed. Equally, unless a particularly wonderful solo was likely to be lost, technically suspect recordings were excluded. It isn't as pristine as the ECM disc, but it suffices. We just wonder whether a touch more judicious editing of excerpts and the quiet disappearance of a couple of less-than-riveting tracks might not have yielded just one powerful CD rather than dissipating the attention across two. Even committed listeners will dwell longer on CD one. Schiaffini and Tramontana's trombone duet with electronics is fascinating, and Dato's concluding 'AEIO' is powerful enough for many spins, but the second half definitely loses pace.

The trombonists are eclipsed by Rava and Minafra on 'Dialogo Instabile' and by the formal vigour of the Moers Brass Quintet. Trovesi's opening 'Scarlattina' (which refers to the composer and not the juvenile ailment) is rousing enough for any festival. Even so, we remain only partially convinced. This is a disc to dip in and out of.

Litania Sibilante makes it all good again. 'Scarlattina' is a wonderfully powerful theme, and the soloing throughout the album, from regular members and from guests Salis and Rava, are out of this world. For a change, the set also includes a standard, a brief, intense reading of 'Lover Man' that will rend your heart. A further fine disc from an astonishing ensemble.

Einar Iversen (born 1930)

PIANO

The leading Norwegian pianist of the bop and mainstream era, 'The Parson' (his dad was a clergyman) played in dance and pit bands as well as clubs, and after some quiet years began to be active again in the '90s. A deft stylist and a thoughtful soloist.

***** Portrait Of A Norwegian Jazz Artist**

Gemini GMOJCD 9503 *Iversen; Ragnar Robertson (cl); Erik Amundsen, Hakon Nilsen, Knut Ljungh, Terje Venaas (b); Egil Johanesen, Arnulfe Neste, Jon Christensen, Svein Christiansen, Tom Olstad (d).* 9/60–12/94.

A decent cross-section of the work of this fine player, hardly known outside his native Norway but a resourceful and thinking musician who seems able to work as easily in the midstream clarinet-quartet tracks (which recall something of the Buddy DeFranco–Sonny Clark sessions) as in the 'purer' bebop tracks: there's a very good workout on 'Our Delight', part of a 1963 session which also featured two charming pieces by composer Finn Ludt. The final session comes from 1994, where a beautiful treatment of 'Nardis' lines up alongside a poignant reading of

Phil Woods's ballad line 'Randi'. Some of the earlier tracks come in less than pristine sound, but it doesn't hurt.

Ethan Iverson

PIANO

New York-based pianist, born in Wisconsin – 'like my great compatriot, Liberace'. An original thinker and likely to be a very considerable force.

***(*) **Construction Zone (Originals)**
Fresh Sound FSNT 046 *Iverson; Reid Anderson (b); Jorge Rossy (d).* 4/98.

**** **Deconstruction Zone (Standards)**
Fresh Sound FSNT 047 *As above.* 4/98.

**** **The Minor Passions**
Fresh Sound FSNT 064 *As above, except Billy Hart (d) replaces Rossy.* 5/99.

Iverson seems implacably opposed to anything predictable, conventional or otherwise previously-done in the area of the piano trio, which is a pretty ambitious stance for someone working in this area of the literature. He has swinging rhythm sections but doesn't want them to swing in the expected ways, if at all. His own material seems cryptic, even baffling, but what he does to standards can be even more unsettling. He plays melodically, uses harmonies that are rarely outlandish, yet is always pushing a new, untried sound in the listener's direction. The first two records were made at the same sessions but they have been deliberately divided between the pianist's own compositions and a group of very familiar standards. If the latter set gets the nod as the more striking portrayal of Iverson's methods, it's only because, with a familiar framework to start from, the originality of the trio's playing is all the more apparent. There are so many ingenuities in the revision of the seven pieces on *Deconstruction Zone* that one is at a loss to catalogue them all. 'The Song Is You' is cast as a furious swinger, but Iverson teasingly holds back from stating the melody until he's turned the opening phrase into a tattoo. 'This Nearly Was Mine' is reharmonized and refashioned as a sepulchral waltz. 'All Of Me' hovers mischievously between metres. 'I'll Remember April' is anointed with a stunningly virtuosic intro before a deceptively constrained treatment that gets darker and more oblique as it progresses. Rossy is superb, but the key dialogue in all these pieces is between piano and bass: Iverson and Anderson have worked together for a long time, and it shows. The 'originals' record needs more time and more study, but much of it repeats the prestidigitation of the other disc, with all sorts of fascinating twists on perceived piano-trio routines in the likes of 'New Chimes Blues' and 'The Inevitable Wall'.

The Minor Passions is a snapshot of 'the state of our art, 28 and 29 May 1999' (the recordings are drawn from a couple of gigs at Greenwich House Music School in New York). Iverson's notes here are useful. He likens his intro on an enigmatic version of 'Milestones' to Herbie Nichols, and that is one shade who does seem to be manifest in an otherwise unclassifiable bag of influences. Iverson also cites the incomparable blues master, Jimmy Yancey, 'my hero', with 'Blues For The Groundskeeper'. One can go through these records track by track and pick out extraordinary things, but that would be an unnecessarily piecemeal analysis of a performer who needs to be heard at length and in the luxury of repeated listening to let his merits break through fully. Anderson is once again an admirable assist on *The Minor Passions*, but Hart, even more than Rossy on the previous sets, brings his best attention and all the skills of both swinging drummer and soundscaping percussionist to bear on this music. These are outstanding records which Fresh Sound deserve the strongest praise for sponsoring.

*** **Live At Smalls**
Fresh Sound FSNT 091 *Iverson; Bill McHenry (ts); Reid Anderson (b); Jeff Williams (d).* 2/00.

Six standards, the Mr Bean theme, Ornette's 'Chronology' and a blues to finish: just another night or two's work at Smalls' in New York, and a mere stop-gap live album, really. But there's still enough going on in all of this to make this gig a priority visit – and there's McHenry, a tenorman who, like Iverson and Anderson, is looking for something else. For the later adventures of Iverson, turn to the entry for The Bad Plus.

Vijay Iyer (born 1973)

PIANO, KEYBOARDS

An Asian-American with musical experience on both West and East Coasts, Iyer has made a considerable impact with a few records.

***(*) **Architextures**
Asian Improv AIR 0034 *Iyer; Rudresh Mahanthappa (as); Aaron Stewart (ts); Eric Crystal (ss, ts); Liberty Ellman (g); Jeff Brock, Kevin Ellington Mingus (b); Brad Hargreaves (d).* 8–9/96.

**** **Panoptic Modes**
Red Giant RGO11 *Iyer; Rudresh Mahanthappa (as); Stephan Crump (b); Derek Phillips (d).* 6/00.

***(*) **Your Life Flashes**
PI 05 *Iyer; Aaron Stewart (ts); Elliot Humberto Kaves (d).* n.d.

**** **Blood Sutra**
Artists House AH 09 *Iyer; Rudresh Mahanthappa (as); Stephan Crump (b); Tyshawn Storey (d).* 2/03.

**** **In What Language?**
PI 109 *Iyer; Ambrose Akinmusire (t); Rudresh Mahanthappa (as); Dana Leong (clo, tb); Liberty Ellman (g); Stephan Crump (b); Trevor Holder (d), Mike Ladd, Latasha N. Nevada Diggs (v, elec); Allison Easter, Ajay Naidu (v).* 5/03.

Iyer is a fascinating new emergence on the American scene. He's already been recording for several years, but the Asian Improv disc, good though it is, made little impact on its release. Divided between solo, trio and octet tracks, the music's strikingly individual. Iyer uses repetition and cyclical themes very effectively, with both the trio and the bigger groups, and a noted influence, Andrew Hill, often looms through these vigorous settings.

Panoptic Modes introduces his regular quartet and points up his close musical relationship with Mahanthappa. Iyer's Indian heritage comes though more strongly here than on the Asian Improv disc: the opening 'Invocation', a 'ritual for Rishi Maharaj', uses the echo of a Vedic chant; 'Configurations' includes South Indian rhythmic techniques ('but I found myself learning how to negotiate them from Bud Powell'). But these are comprehensively integrated into American jazz and other musical dialects which create a stunningly vivid synthesis.

'Invocation' is a quite electrifying start to the record, and from there the quartet power through a matrix of rhythms and melodic cells which create a tinglingly powerful whole. As tumultuously as the players improvise at various points, the record really impresses as a rigorous, whole entity.

Your Life Flashes is by his 'other' trio, Fieldwork. Minus a bass-player – and perhaps the bassist's role is one component which Iyer has yet to fully figure out in his music – this is still all about rhythm, even as Stewart spins dizzyingly long lines over piano and drums. One difference between this and the kind of unfettered free playing offered by, say, the axis of groups which CIMP record, is a complexity of tone displacing conventional ideas of 'freedom' in jazz. Transcribing this music would reveal clear, patterned, nuanced structures which titles such as 'Accumulated Gestures' and 'Mosaic' hint at. Yet its spirited performance, purged of obvious cliché, seems more profoundly in keeping with free-jazz doctrine than many a supposedly improvised situation.

Blood Sutra reconvenes the quartet with the astonishing young drummer Tyshawn Storey arriving at the kit. Mahanthappa plays ever tougher, harsher lines, while Storey has jazz and funk rhythms conjoined so intricately that it scarcely seems credible he could be feeling his way through this stuff so quickly and expertly. Iyer's own playing gets a brilliant solo set-piece in 'That Much Music', but he's master of what he surveys here, letting his tunes absorb an unsentimental impressionism which doesn't get vague or blandly emotional. That may be the crucial advance from the M-Base school which Iyer has clearly learned much from: he resists the neutral melodic feel which has often seemed to ice over Steve Coleman's groove. A brilliant record.

Political art doesn't come much more direct or shattering than *In What Language?* The title is drawn from the complaint of Iranian film-maker Jafer Panahi, detained for hours at JFK airport while passing through New York – 'I am just an Iranian, a film-maker. But how could I tell this, in what language?' The deeper irony is that this incident took place prior to 9/11. Speech and rap is integrated into music which, in fact, sounds much closer to the M-Base system than Iyer's other music. But this is clearly a different situation. It is uncomfortable listening, whatever your origins or sympathies, and as a piece of sonic collage it's been created with formidable skill and clarity. Another part of a musical progression which anyone interested in where jazz is heading must listen to without further delay.

Chubby Jackson (1918–2003)

DOUBLE BASS

The first musician to use an amplifier on his bass, Chubby had a long career, and became a minor star. Worked with the Woody Herman band, also had his own kids' show on television and worked in music projects for senior citizens.

***** The Happy Monster**

Blue Moon CB 109 *Jackson; Conte Candoli, Neal Hefti (t); Bill Harris (tb); Tony Aless (frhn); Frank Socolow (as, ts); Flip Phillips (ts); Woody Herman (cl); Lou Levy (p); Terry Gibbs (vib); Shelly Manne, Dave Tough (d); some other personnel.* 44–47.

***** Chubby Takes Over**

Fresh Sound FSRCD 324 *Jackson; Nick Travis, Ernie Royal (t); Bob Brookmeyer, Frank Rehak (tb); Sam Marowitz (as); Sam Most (as, cl, f); Al Cohn (ts); Danny Bank (bs); Marty Napoleon (p); Don Lamond (d).* 58.

***** Live At The Swiss Chalet**

Jazz Band 2141 *Jackson; Nat Adderley (c); Pete Minger, Vinnie Tanno (t); Frank Rosolino (tb); Danny Turner (as); Arnett Cobb, Jay Corre (ts); Duffy Jackson (d).* 62.

Chubby never stopped working and never stopped thinking about music. He was never the most virtuosic of players and when he worked opposite Oscar Pettiford it was only his sunnier personality that got him noticed. However, he did lead bands for much of his life and these survivals are enough to leave a mark now that he is no longer around. The small-group dates gathered on the Blue Moon compilation are mostly entertaining. Herman returns the compliment as do other players and leaders who'd possibly asked Chubby to turn down his bass in years gone by. The big-band date, formerly on Everest, is entertaining enough, and there are some fine solos from the sections, but it's on the live disc that his real strength comes through, an undentable enthusiasm that overcomes any technical flaws and a ragged approach to ensembles.

D. D. Jackson (born 1967)

PIANO, ORGAN

At the end of jazz's first century, there was an understandable search for figures who combined tradition and innovation, the heartland of the music and its new, global diaspora. Jackson seemed a better contender than most and his steady output of crafted, intelligent jazz confirmed all the hype and promise.

*****(*) Peace-Song**

Justin Time JUST 72-2 *Jackson; David Murray (ts); John Geggie (b); Jean Martin (d).* 11/94.

****** Rhythm Dance**

Justin Time JUST 89-2 *Jackson; John Geggie (b); Jean Martin (d).* 95.

Jackson is a Canadian of mixed race and unadulterated gifts, one of the most sheerly exciting piano-players to emerge in a decade. A regular associate of violinist Billy Bang, saxophonist David Murray and jazz *auteur* Kip Hanrahan, he brings a performing style which is both classically aware and uninterruptably swinging, and a writing concept which is similarly eclectic and unforced. Influences are easy enough to spot: Monk, Don Pullen, Jaki Byard. Where they give way to a more original conception is harder to specify.

Peace-Song is an impressive debut. Murray's presence is obviously advantageous, but not definitive. It's the sheer confidence of Jackson's writing and playing that commands attention. 'Waltz For A New Life', 'Seasons' and the title-piece are all strong statements, very much group efforts; only on 'Canon' and the closing 'Funerale' does Jackson seem a touch self-indulgent, too self-consciously eclectic.

The second album was a resounding coming-of-age, with Jackson responsible for all the compositions and for a startling range of expressive formats, from the roistering swinger 'No Boundaries' to a gentle ballad like 'For Mama'. His ease and poise are breathtaking, and even at speed his articulation and phrasing are inch-perfect, though never too precise to be unmusical.

★★★(★) Paired Down: Volume 1

Justin Time JUST 99-2 *Jackson; Hugh Ragin (t); James Carter (ts, Cmel); David Murray (ts); Hamiet Bluiett (bs); Billy Bang (vn); Santi Debriano (b).* 11 & 12/96.

★★★(★) Paired Down: Volume 2

Justin Time JUST 104-2 *Jackson; Ray Anderson (tb); David Murray (ts); Don Byron (cl); Jane Bunnett (f); Santi Debriano (b).* 97.

There are moments on the first volume of *Paired Down* when Jackson seems at some risk of disappearing into a private conversation with former employers, not so much over-respectful as too eager to please. Highlights are a pair of tunes with Hamiet Bluiett (including a wonderful tribute to the late Don Pullen), a trio of tracks with trumpeter Hugh Ragin (high skittering figures pitched against the busy action of the piano) and two with James Carter, who opens the disc on C melody saxophone, a harmonically awkward sound that nevertheless works. As ever, Jackson sounds aware and responsive to his playing partners, a fast, very melodic technique that seems unembarrassed by harmonic theory.

A second volume of duets reprises the association with Murray and also puts Jackson in the company of another former leader saxophonist (and here flautist) Jane Bunnett. Perhaps the best track of all, though, is a duet with bassist Debriano which recalls some of the late Red Mitchell's encounters with piano-players.

★★★(★) ... So Far

RCA Victor 09026 63549 2 *Jackson (p solo).* 5/99.

Jackson's first solo album is somewhat well-behaved, an exercise in form rather than virtuosic grandstanding. Debts to fellow-pianists – Don Pullen, Michel Camilo, Jackie Byard, Duke Ellington, Bud Powell and John Hicks – are uppermost in his mind, though Jackson makes it clear from the outset that he wishes to pay respects in his own voice and terms and not in a pastiche of 'influences'. Nods of respect to Debussy and Horowitz are less convincing, not because Jackson lacks the chops but rather because his classical mannerisms are worn too self-consciously.

Generally, though, one simply marvels at the fluency and sophistication of his playing. 'Suite New York' suggests the influence of fellow-Canadian Paul Bley, the only obvious ancestor not namechecked on the record, which may or may not be significant. It's a flowing, shapely composition, unreadable by anyone less comfortably two-handed than Jackson, whose bass chords are as featherlight as his melody lines are resonant and massive.

The piano (a modern Yamaha?) is in impeccable shape, accurate and without undue idiosyncrasy but with genuine character. The record flows easily from idea to idea, almost as if the whole session were a continuous performance. Jackson has already staked his place at the high table. The next few years are going to be very exciting indeed.

★★★(★) Anthem

RCA 63606 *Jackson; James Carter (ss, ts); Christian Howes (vn, g); Richard Bona (g); Jack DeJohnette (d); Mino Cinelu (perc).* 8/99.

A warm and rousing record from the young Canadian, *Anthem* underlines how many different directions Jackson can take in the coming years. The opening 'Spring Song' is a warm Latin groove that is infectious and powerful. 'Showcase Blues' is an outing on organ and is strongly reminiscent of the late Don Pullen's very pianistic take on that instrument. 'Water Dance' dabbles with asymmetric rhythms and makes them swing like crazy. Carter is only featured here and there, which throws the piano into high relief. Jackson is rapidly becoming a significant figure on the scene, perhaps the natural heir to Pullen.

★★★(★) Sigame

Justin Time 177 *Jackson; Christian Howes (vn); Ukonna Okegwo (b).* 6–7/01.

Again, there is some wonderfully funky and varied stuff on this homegrown set. The title-track, 'Sigame (Follow Me)', is a winner and Jackson takes two ears and a tail for the way he teases, lures and draws the listener on before delivering the *coup de grâce* of the oddly positioned 'Prologue'. The relationship with Howes is developing nicely and much can be expected of that in future.

★★★ Suite For New York

Justin Time 188 *Jackson; Brad Turner (t); Tom Walsh (tb); James Spaulding (as, f); David Mott (bs); Christian Howes (vn); Ugonna Okegwa (b); Dafnis Prieto (d, perc).* 12/02.

Shadowed inevitably by WTC attacks, but in no way an explicit response, this is more of a celebration of a city which has fulfilled the melting-pot dream and created a culture in which ethnic diversity and unified spirit really do coexist. Jackson's writing, from the opening 'Invocation' to the closing 'Towers Of Light', is uniformly strong. His playing is less virtuosic than, say, Craig Taborn or Matthew Shipp, closer perhaps to Dave Burrell's poly-cultural approach. No denying its power and authority on any front and his marshalling of this large group suggests that Jackson's musical ambitions may finally be taking wing. The veteran Spaulding, often a Cinderella figure, shines here, but no one has a bad day.

Franz Jackson (born 1912)

CLARINET

A veteran reed-player on the Chicago scene from the '30s onwards, Jackson played in countless groups until forming his Original Jass All-Stars in 1957, a very successful group which toured and worked residencies for many years. He was still touring Europe in the '80s.

★★★ Franz Jackson's Original Jass All-Stars

OJC 1824-2 *Jackson; Bob Shoffner (t); John Thomas (tb); Rozelle Claxton (p); Lawrence Dixon (bj); Bill Oldham (tba); Bill Curry (d).* 9/61.

One of the best in this series of revivals from the Riverside catalogue's 'Chicago Living Legends' sequence. Jackson was something of a modernist compared to the others – he worked with Earl Hines in the '40s, playing mainly tenor sax – and he approaches the ten warhorses in this programme with gusto, thick-toned and hard-hitting. Shoffner and Thomas, much older hands, play with comparative reserve but, while Jackson is right up in the front of the mix, they seem to be at the back of the room. Nevertheless Shoffner, who was already in his 60s, sounds well, and Thomas plays better than he ever did with Louis Armstrong. The steady-rolling rhythm is maintained throughout by the other four, and they all kick their feet up on a spiffing 'King Porter Stomp'.

Javon Jackson (born 1965)

TENOR SAXOPHONE

A later member of the Jazz Messengers, Jackson has since graduated to a position in New York's hierarchy of hired-gun tenormen, with a string of (mostly deleted) Blue Notes to his name. Recent years have seen him explore a funkier line of enquiry than his original, Joe Henderson-influenced style.

*** Me And Mr Jones

Criss Cross CRISS 1053 *Jackson; James Williams (p); Christian McBride (b); Elvin Jones (d).* 12/91.

*** Burnin'

Criss Cross CRISS 1139 *Jackson; Billie Pierce (ts); Kirk Lightsey (p); Christian McBride (b); Louis Hayes (d).* 12/91.

Mr Jones is, of course, drummer Elvin, with whom Jackson worked a productive internship after his stint in the Messengers. Whatever else he learnt from these luminaries, he has emerged as a leader of tremendous resourcefulness and self-confidence. Even if his soloing still doesn't sound completely mature, his sense of purpose is unmistakable. The first disc leans heavily on a restricted range of ideas and tempos and could sound a little formulaic compared to the later Blue Notes. Here Jackson benefits from more thoughtful production and a more relaxed approach to the material. His writing is quite blunt and unambiguous, sometimes a little too assertive, but that too will sort itself out when the time is right.

Burnin' is officially co-led by fellow tenorist Pierce, but it is Jackson who commands attention, opening and closing the record with two strong originals, 'So The Story Goes' and 'Not Yet'. The rhythm section is impeccable and, though the sound is rather dry and studio-based, Jackson has a warmth and fullness of sound, as well as his trademark responsiveness, which put Pierce in the shade. What the session really lacks is a sharp, acidulous brass voice to counter the tenor.

*** Easy Does It

Palmetto 2093 *Jackson; Fred Wesley (tb, v); Lonnie Liston Smith (org); Mark Whitefield (g); Eve Cornelious (v).* 10/02.

After nearly four years out of the recording spotlight, Jackson returned with a record that bore out our suggestion that he was moving in a funkier direction. The leader's thunder is very nearly stolen by Fred Wesley, who mugs irritatingly on 'House Party', but otherwise delivers his usual spot-on trombone. Plenty of soul on tracks like 'Right On', 'Wake Up Everybody' and Smith's 'If You See Kay' (which doesn't require sophisticated cryptographic skills to decipher), but the Jackson originals are very much in the same line. Javon's writing in this vein has come on in leaps and bounds with 'Kiss' and 'J Soul' outstanding examples. His tone is rawer and more abrasive than of yore, but he can still string together a sophisticated harmonic solo amid the barwalking stuff.

Milt Jackson (1923–99)

VIBES, PIANO, VOCAL

Born in Detroit, Jackson moved to New York after his studies and joined Dizzy Gillespie at the start of recorded bebop in 1945. He was with various leaders before rejoining Gillespie in 1950, then with his own quartet, which became the MJQ in 1954. Played with that group throughout its career but also made many records of his own. The master vibesman of jazz after the swing era, Jackson established the instrument in a competitive bop environment. At the same time he introduced a new elegance into its sound via his ballad-playing and reached back to basic jazz elements by remaining a peerless improviser on the simplest blues forms. His work inside and outside the MJQ is a model of consistency, without settling into a rut.

**(*) In The Beginning

Original Jazz Classics OJC-1771 *Jackson; Russell Jacquet (t); J. J. Johnson (tb); Sonny Stitt (as); Leo Parker (bs); Sir Charles Thompson, John Lewis (p); Al Jackson (b); Kenny Clarke (d); Chano Pozo (perc).* 47–48.

Obscure beginnings, though Jackson had already made a remarkable debut with Dizzy Gillespie on the sextet session for Victor which produced the astonishing 'Anthropology'. But there is nothing primitive about the playing on the four quartet tracks with three-quarters of the MJQ, from 1948, where Jackson's ballad-playing on 'In A Beautiful Mood' matches the title. An earlier sextet date is more conventional bebop.

**** Wizard Of The Vibes

Blue Note 32140-2 *Jackson; Lou Donaldson (as); Thelonious Monk, John Lewis (p); Percy Heath, John Simmons, Al McKibbon (b); Shadow Wilson, Kenny Clarke (d), Kenny Hagood (v).* 7/48–4/52.

Eight of these tracks can also be found on records under Monk's name, while a quintet date with Donaldson and what was to become the MJQ was first issued as a ten-inch LP. The tracks with Monk are flawless classics, rising to their greatest height with the riveting version of 'I Mean You'. The other date, though at a less exalted level, finds Jackson quite at home with Donaldson's uncomplicated, bluesy bop, and 'Lillie' is a handsome ballad feature for the vibesman. Blue Note's new RVG edition of this material adds five alternative takes, bringing the track total to 17.

*** MJQ

Original Jazz Classics OJC 125 *Jackson; Henry Boozier (t); Horace Silver (p); Percy Heath (b); Kenny Clarke (d).* 6/54.

*** Milt Jackson

Original Jazz Classics OJC 001 *Jackson; Horace Silver (p); Percy Heath (b); Connie Kay (d).* 5/55.

MJQ features four titles by the personnel listed (the remainder are by a first-generation MJQ). Though no more than a pick-up date, all concerned play well. *Milt Jackson* is more substantial, but the preponderance of slow tempos lends a rather sleepy air to the date. The exception is 'Stonewall', a blues with a 13-chorus vibes solo that effectively defines the principles of Jackson's art. Remastering up to the strong OJC standard.

***(*) Ballads And Blues / Bags And Flutes

Collectables COL-CD-6257 *Jackson; Lucky Thompson (ts); Frank Wess, Bobby Jaspar (f); John Lewis, Hank Jones, Tommy*

Flanagan (p); Skeeter Best, Kenny Burrell, Barry Galbraith (g); Oscar Pettiford, Percy Heath (b); Kenny Clarke, Lawrance Marable, Art Taylor (d); woodwinds. 1/56–5/57.

A pair of Atlantic albums which sound as clean as a whistle in these remasterings. *Ballads And Blues* is near-perfect Jackson fare. The others mostly keep out of his way and let him blow, although Lucky Thompson is on the final three tracks and in excellent fettle. The *Flutes* date shares duties between Wess and Jaspar and is slighter stuff, even though it ends on the textbook slow blues of 'Connie's Blues'.

*****(*) Bags Meets Trane**
Atlantic 81227-3685-2 *Jackson; John Coltrane (ts); Hank Jones (p); Paul Chambers (b); Connie Kay (d).* 1/59.

A newly remastered survivor from his Atlantic sessions of the late '50s. It's a genial if relatively unambitious meeting of giants. Always the most unprejudiced of collaborators, Milt simply goes ahead and blows, and though Coltrane is on the verge of his first great breakthroughs he responds to the less fearsome blues situations with his usual majestic command. A neglected record in the career of both men, and in this new mastering the music comes up uncommonly fresh and vibrant.

***** The Ballad Artistry Of Milt Jackson / Vibrations**
Collectables COL-CD-6258 *Jackson; Henry Boozier (t); Tommy McIntosh (tb); Jimmy Heath (ts); Tate Houston (bs); Romeo Penque (reeds); Don Hammond (f); Jimmy Jones, Tommy Flanagan (p); Kenny Burrell, Chuck Wayne, Barry Galbraith (g); Milt Hinton, Bill Crow, George Duvivier (b); Connie Kay (d); strings.* 5/59–2/60.

Two more Atlantics, although neither is really among the best of Bags. Quincy Jones swathes him in strings on the first; the second has him encumbered by a curious set of R&B-like charts from Tommy McIntosh. That said, Jackson steams past everything else and still gets off some great playing.

****** Bags Meets Wes**
Original Jazz Classics OJC 240 *Jackson; Wynton Kelly (p); Wes Montgomery (g); Sam Jones (b); Philly Joe Jones (d).* 12/61.

****(*) Invitation**
Original Jazz Classics OJC 260 *Jackson; Kenny Dorham, Virgil Jones (t); Jimmy Heath (ts); Tommy Flanagan (p); Ron Carter (b); Connie Kay (d).* 8–11/62.

***** Big Bags**
Original Jazz Classics OJC 366 *Jackson; Clark Terry (t, flhn); Bernie Glow, Ernie Royal, Snooky Young, Doc Severinsen, Dave Burns (t); Jimmy Cleveland, Melba Liston, Paul Faulise, Tom McIntosh (tb); Willie Ruff (frhn); James Moody (as, ts, f); Earl Warren, George Dorsey, Jerome Richardson (as); Jimmy Heath (ts); Tate Houston, Arthur Clarke (bs); Hank Jones (p); Ron Carter (b); Connie Kay, Philly Joe Jones (d).* 6–7/62.

***** At The Village Gate**
Original Jazz Classics OJC 309 *Jackson; Jimmy Heath (ts); Hank Jones (p); Bob Cranshaw (b); Albert 'Tootie' Heath (d).* 12/63.

***** For Someone I Love**
Original Jazz Classics OJC 404 *Jackson; Clark Terry, Thad Jones, Dave Burns, Snooky Young, Bill Berry, Elmon Wright (t); Quentin Jackson, Jimmy Cleveland, Jack Rains, Tom McIntosh (tb); Bob Northern, Julius Watkins, Ray Alonge, Willie Ruff, Paul Ingraham (frhn); Hank Jones, Jimmy Jones (p); Major Holley (tba); Richard Davis (b); Connie Kay, Charli Persip (d).* 3–8/63.

Jackson was firmly ensconced in the MJQ by this time, but occasional blowing dates were something he obviously enjoyed, and his association with Riverside led to some more challenging situations. *Invitation* is somewhat disappointing, given the personnel. Some of the tunes are cut off short, and Dorham and Heath never quite get into it as they might. Heath fares better on the live date from the Village Gate, which works mostly from a blues base. *Big Bags* puts Jackson to work in some Ernie Wilkins arrangements for orchestra, and there is a puissant 'Round Midnight' among the charts (an alternative take is also included on the CD reissue), although the vibraphonist's impassive assurance isn't ideal for this situation. *For Someone I Love* is another try at the same sort of thing, though here the front lines are all brass, working from charts by Melba Liston. Jackson approaches it in just the same way, digging in hard on 'Extraordinary Blues', rhapsodic on 'Days Of Wine And Roses'. The best of this group is the meeting with Wes Montgomery. This time the tunes seem just the right length, even on a miniature like the ballad, 'Stairway To The Stars', and the quintet locks into an irresistible groove on the up-tempo themes. The CD includes three alternative takes, all worth having, and there's now a 20-bit edition, issued as Riverside 9407.

***** In A New Setting**
Verve 538620-2 *Jackson; Jimmy Heath (ts, f); McCoy Tyner (p); Bob Cranshaw (b); Connie Kay (d).* 12/64.

'Hard-hitting and concise jazz statements' was the aim of the Limelight label, for which this set was originally recorded. It wasn't much interested in the open-ended jamming of hard bop, and most of its jazz output was like this – crisp, restricted tracks with just a chorus or two per man on the blues (most of the originals here) and a few standards. It suited Jackson well enough, and he has an excellent team on hand, with Tyner enjoying himself on 'Slow Death', and Heath big and bold throughout. Still, there's little here that one could call memorable jazz.

***** The Big Three**
Original Jazz Classics OJC 805 *Jackson; Joe Pass (g); Ray Brown (b).* 8/75.

*****(*) Centerpiece/At The Kosei Nenkin**
Pablo 2620-120-2 *Jackson; Teddy Edwards (ts); Cedar Walton (p); Ray Brown (b); Billy Higgins (d).* 3/76.

**** Feelings**
Original Jazz Classics OJC 448 *Jackson; Hubert Laws, Jerome Richardson (f); Tommy Flanagan (p); Dennis Budimir (g); Ray Brown (b); Jimmie Smith (d); strings.* 4/76.

***** Soul Fusion**
Original Jazz Classics OJC 731 *Jackson; Monty Alexander (p); John Clayton (b); Jeff Hamilton (d).* 6/77.

***** Montreux '77**
Original Jazz Classics OJC 375 *Jackson; Clark Terry (t); Eddie 'Lockjaw' Davis (ts); Monty Alexander (p); Ray Brown (b); Jimmie Smith (d).* 7/77.

****(*) Bags' Bag**
Original Jazz Classics OJC 935 *Jackson; Cedar Walton (p); Vaughan Andre, John Collins (g); Ray Brown (b); Billy Higgins, Frank Severino (d).* 12/77.

★★★(★) Milt Jackson + Count Basie + The Big Band Vol. 1
Original Jazz Classics OJC 740 *Jackson; Waymon Reed, Lyn Biviano, Sonny Cohn, Pete Minger (t); Bill Hughes, Mel Wanzo, Fred Wesley, Dennis Wilson (tb); Danny Turner, Bobby Plater (as); Eric Dixon (ts, f); Kenny Hing (ts); Charlie Fowlkes (bs); Count Basie (p); Freddie Green (g); John Clayton (b); Butch Miller (d).* 1/78.

★★★(★) Milt Jackson + Count Basie + The Big Band Vol. 2
Original Jazz Classics OJC 741 *As above.* 1/78.

★(★) Soul Believer
Original Jazz Classics OJC 686 *Jackson; Plas Johnson (ts); Cedar Walton (p); Dennis Budimir (g); Ray Brown (b); Billy Higgins (d).* 9/78.

★★★ All Too Soon
Original Jazz Classics OJC 450 *Jackson; Joe Pass (g); Ray Brown (b); Mickey Roker (d).* 1/80.

★★★ Night Mist
Original Jazz Classics OJC 827 *Jackson; Harry 'Sweets' Edison (t); Eddie 'Cleanhead' Vinson (as); Eddie 'Lockjaw' Davis (ts); Art Hillery (p); Ray Brown (b); Larance Marable (d).* 4/80.

★★★(★) Ain't But A Few Of Us Left
Original Jazz Classics OJC 785 *Jackson; Oscar Peterson (p); Ray Brown (b); Grady Tate (d).* 11/81.

★★★ A London Bridge
Pablo 2310-932 *Jackson; Monty Alexander (p); Ray Brown (b); Mickey Roker (d).* 4/82.

★★★ Mostly Duke
Original Jazz Classics OJC 968 *As above.* 4/82.

★★★ Memories Of Thelonious Sphere Monk
Original Jazz Classics OJC 851 *As above.* 4/82.

★★★ The Best Of Milt Jackson
Pablo 2405-405 *Compilation from the above.* 77–82.

★★★ Jackson, Johnson, Brown And Company
Original Jazz Classics OJC 907 *Jackson; J. J. Johnson (tb); Tom Rainier (p); John Collins (g); Ray Brown (b); Roy McCurdy (d).* 5/83.

★★★ Soul Route
Original Jazz Classics OJC 1059 *Jackson; Gene Harris (p); Ray Brown (b); Mickey Roker (d).* 11–12/83.

★★★(★) It Don't Mean A Thing If You Can't Tap Your Foot To It
Original Jazz Classics OJC 601 *Jackson; Cedar Walton (p); Ray Brown (b); Mickey Roker (d).* 7/84.

Jackson's signing to Pablo – which also snared the MJQ for a time – brought forth a flood of albums, nearly all of which are now available on CD. Just as he did with Count Basie, Granz basically set Milt up in the studio and let him go, which means that all these records are solidly entertaining without ever quite going the extra distance and becoming a classic.

However, one of the most obvious mix-and-match situations, the two albums cut with Count Basie, at a single session in 1978, proved to be a winner. Here are two kindred spirits, both in love with playing the blues, giving it their best shot, and with the orchestra in towering form behind them. There are a few small-group tracks, but it's mainly the big band with Jackson taking most of the solos, Basie restricting himself to the occasional rejoinder. The only disappointment must be that the material is nearly all Basie warhorses; nevertheless it gives Jackson the unshakeable platform which his previous records with a big band never finally secured. On 'Lil' Darlin'' he sounds gorgeous, and on a stomper like Ernie Wilkins's 'Basie' the studio nearly goes up in smoke, even if it's always a controlled explosion with this band.

Most of the other records keep to a high standard. *The Big Three*, a typical Granz set-up of masters, works pretty well – there is a lovely 'Nuages', and Pass digs in unusually strongly on a fast 'Blue Bossa' – without making a very deep impression. *Soul Believer*, where Jackson sings, is eminently avoidable, and the strings album, *Feelings*, is pretty but disposable. Gene Harris was a natural sideman for Bags, and *Soul Route* finds all hands in very good spirits. The Montreux jam session is slightly above par for this kind of course. Of the remainder, another standout is the quartet date on *It Don't Mean A Thing*. Cedar Walton and Jackson inspire each other to their best form, and an intensely swinging 'If I Were A Bell' and the Ellington near-title-track, taken at a daringly relaxed tempo, are marvels. *Ain't But A Few Of Us Left* is as swinging as the best Peterson records can be, and Jackson seems to have enjoyed his meeting with the great man; 'Body And Soul', set off with a bossa feel, is impressive, and they take luxurious time over 'If I Should Lose You'. *All Too Soon* is a little too laid-back as an Ellington tribute. *Jackson, Johnson, Brown And Company* has some lovely moments between Milt and J.J., although the record feels a bit stilted at points where they might have really stretched out. The rest of the band sometimes get in Jackson's way on *Night Mist*, an all-blues programme, but – pro that he is – Bags settles into the situation and takes some typically collected solos. *A London Bridge* and *Mostly Duke* were cut at the same engagement at Ronnie Scott's in London, and Alexander's carousing piano parts are an interesting foil for Jackson's imperturbable solos. *Memories Of Thelonious Sphere Monk*, from the same occasion, is also good, but in a sense a wasted opportunity. A full-scale meditation on Monk by Jackson, one of the pianist's canniest interpreters, should have been set down before now; here, though, three of the four themes are tossed to the other members of the quartet as features, and Bags tackles only the comparatively straightforward 'In Walked Bud'.

The newly-issued *Centerpiece* deserves a special commendation. Edwards was moving through a very quiet phase of a generally neglected career, and the stock of this kind of jazz was at a very low ebb in 1976. That didn't stop a superb band from turning in a superb performance, before a very appreciative crowd. Jackson sounds as good as at any point in his career here.

★★(★) Reverence And Compassion
Qwest/Reprise 945204-2 *Jackson; Oscar Brashear (t); George Bohannon (tb); Jeff Clayton (as); Gary Foster (ts, f); Ronald Brown (ts); Jack Nimitz (bs, bcl); Cedar Walton (p); John Clayton (b); Billy Higgins (d); strings.* 92.

Hugely overproduced, with thunderous orchestral arrangements draped over and round the music, but Jackson and his rhythm section still manage to make worthwhile music when the smoke clears. 'Young And Foolish' and the dreaded 'How Do You Keep The Music Playing' may sound like high-class mood music, but when the quartet digs into 'Bullet Bag' and 'Reverence' it sounds like the real thing.

★★★ Burnin' In The Woodhouse
Qwest/Reprise 945918-2 *Jackson; Nicholas Payton (t); Jesse Davis (as); Joshua Redman (ts); Benny Green (p); Christian McBride (b); Kenny Washington (d).* 94.

Milt's tenure with Qwest/Reprise offered him some nice opportunities to play, but the albums were largely unremarkable. The horns play on only three tracks of *Burnin' In The Woodhouse*, which is more like a slow simmer than anything with flames in it. Jackson's vibes sound different on all three of his records for this company, and they're notably muffled on the last two.

*****(*) Explosive!**

Qwest/Warners 9362-47286-2 *Jackson; Byron Stripling, Snooky Young, Oscar Brashear, Clay Jenkins, Bobby Rodriguez (t); Ira Nepus, George Bohannon, Isaac Smith (tb); Maurice Spears (btb); Jeff Clayton, Keith Fiddmont (as, cl, f); Rickey Woodard, Charles Owens (ts, cl); Lee Callet (bs, bcl); Bill Cunliffe (p); Jim Hershman (g); John Clayton Jr, Christoph Luty (b); Jeff Hamilton (d).* 6/99.

'Bags' Groove' – one more time. It's a splendid farewell for the old man, teaming up with a band, the Clayton–Hamilton Jazz Orchestra, full of old friends, still swinging with an absolutely indomitable assertion on tunes that he loved to blow on, such as 'Since I Fell For You', 'Indiana' and 'Along Came Betty'. Good, functional charts by John Clayton, and engineer Joel Moss gives everybody a big and illustrious sound, with Milton fashioning solos of such elegance that they celebrate a magnificent life of music.

Oliver Jackson (1933–94)

DRUMS

Born in Detroit, he worked in his local bebop scene in the '40s and '50s and also in a drums-and-dance variety duo with Eddie Locke, Bop And Locke. Made many sessions for Black & Blue in the '70s and '80s and a regular on European tours until his sudden death.

***** The Last Great Concert**

Nagel Heyer CD 063 *Jackson; Randy Sandke (t); Jerry Tilitz (tb); Antti Sarpila (cl, ts); Harry Allen, Danny Moss (ts); Brian Dee (p); Len Skeat (b); Jeanie Lambe (v).* 11/93.

A pleasing gesture by the Nagel Heyer operation to dedicate this set to Oliver Jackson, giving this doughty and much-liked musician at least one CD under his own name. It's really nothing more or less than another unpretentious and good-value concert set by the familiar Nagel Heyer gang. Honours evenly shared around the front line, though Randy Sandke is at his most ebullient. Oliver plays it straight and swinging, as he always did.

Ronald Shannon Jackson (born 1940)

DRUMS, PERCUSSION, OTHER INSTRUMENTS

Born in Fort Worth, Texas, Jackson studied history before receiving a music scholarship to New York. Played drums for Ayler, Mingus and Betty Carter; then, after a sabbatical, played with Ornette Coleman and Cecil Taylor in the late '70s and formed the Decoding Society in 1981. Also toured with Last Exit.

*****(*) Montreux Jazz Festival**

Knitting Factory 3031 *Jackson; Henry Scott (t); Zane Massey (ss, as); Vernon Reid (g, steel g, bj); Bruce Johnson (b).* 83.

****(*) Beast In The Spider Bush: Live At The Caravan Of Dreams**

Knitting Factory 3029 *Jackson; Eric Person (ss, as); Cary de Nigris (g); Akbar Ali (vn); Reggie Washington (b); Twins Seven Seven (perc, v).* 85.

****(*) Live At Greenwich House**

Knitting Factory 3030 *As above, except add Henry Scott (t), Vernon Reid (g), Melvin Gibbs (b).* 1/86.

The Greenwich House date was a New Year's Day gig by the reconvened Decoding Society; Reid and Gibbs had been doing their own thing for a while, but they are present here and seem to enjoy trading lines with their playing partners, de Nigris and Washington. The tracks are mostly long and rhythmically involved, reflecting Jackson's growing interest in African musics. Though Ornette Coleman is the presumptive ancestor, this set is perhaps closest to Miles Davis's experimental electronic groups, especially on tracks like 'Erri Moments' (where Henry Scott echoes the master on muted trumpet) and 'Chocolate Envy'. The main difference is that Miles always seemed blessed with responsive engineers who could deliver him a decent sound. The tape quality is pretty shocking and the set merits release only on historical grounds.

The previous record is if anything worse in quality, with some hideous distortion and a sound that would embarrass the average bootlegger. The set was originally released on the Caravan of Dreams label and should perhaps have been allowed to slide into history as a talked-about rarity that might have been lent a faint gloss by fond memory. The singers and drummers are amazing and one could listen to them all night, but the rest is pretty drab.

To continue working backwards in time, the Montreux set is almost the best of the bunch and certainly one of the best performances by the Decoding Society. 'Alice In The Congo' clocks in at a quarter of an hour and touches on virtually all the trademark Jackson devices: harmolodic complexity, straight blues, funk and bebop. Reid takes a number of passages on banjo, an instrument that has rather narrow and old-fashioned associations in jazz, but which works wonderfully here, spiky and raw.

***** When Colors Play**

Knitting Factory 2037 *Jackson; Zane Massey (ss, ts); Eric Person (ss, as); Masujaa, Cary DeNigris (g); John Moody (b).* 86.

Free-form funk of a high order, with saxophones and guitars running rings round one another in Jackson's idiosyncratic version of harmolodics. 'Sweet Orange' and the somewhat more reflective 'Listening To A Mirror' are the most extended and also the most interesting performances. Again, the sound is rather unforgiving, but Jackson is better balanced than on some of his records and this is a good representation of his group dynamic.

****(*) Red Warrior**

Knitting Factory 3032 *Jackson; Jef Lee Johnson, Stevie Salas, Jack DeSalvo (g); Conrad Matthieu, Ramon Pooser (b).* 91.

Originally a Mango LP and subsequently released on Axiom, this is one of Knitting Factory's less successful trawls, a mostly drab and unsophisticated set heavy on guitars and light on almost everything else. The titanic 'Elders' has some interesting moments and there is a smile at the end with 'Harmolodic Christmas'. For the most part, though, a forgettable item in a well-stocked discography.

***** Raven Roc**

DIW 862 *Jackson; Jef Lee Johnson, David Fiuczynski (g); Dom Richards (b).* 2/92.

***** What Spirit Say**

DIW 895 *Jackson; James Carter (ts, ss); Martin Atangana, Jef Lee Johnson (g); Ngolle Pokossi (d).* 12/94.

***** Live In Warsaw**

Knitting Factory 3035 *As above, except omit Atangana.* 94.

The sound of Shannon Jackson's Decoding Society is characteristically an unsettling amalgam of dark, swampy vamps, huge, distorted chorales and sudden outbursts of urban noise. Decoded, it yields up a grand range of putative influences, from Albert Ayler's increasingly abstract and fissile music (Shannon played with the saxophonist in the early '60s), to Mingus's open-ended compositional style, to Ornette Coleman's harmolodics, to black and white thrash-metal music; it was James Blood Ulmer's brutal funk *Are You Glad To Be In America?* that helped establish the drummer's reputation in Europe. He in turn has had a powerful impact on such once-fashionable outfits as Decoding Society guitarist Vernon Reid's Living Colour and the Black Rock Coalition, while his work with the heavyweight Last Exit spawned a shoal of imitators.

The early albums – for Antilles and About Time – are still not around at present, so some of his work in the '80s has been rather unfairly overlooked by the CD era. Jackson had spent much of the '70s in obscurity and has had to suffer oversights and unimaginative marketing throughout his career. *The* drummer of the late '80s looked like making only a slow and uneasy accommodation to the new decade, but *Raven Roc* found him in pleasingly murky and bad-tempered form, battering out themes of authentic unpleasantness like 'Sexual Drum Dance' and 'Hatched Spirit Blues'. The upgraded Decoding Society lacks some of its predecessors' metallic blare, but Jackson makes it clear that he doesn't need horns, and the guitarists demonstrate that they don't need optional extras like technique.

What Spirit Say is more from the same dark place, though the addition of saxophone in place of a second guitar gives the music a more vocalized and thus more humane sound. There is always a twinkle about Jackson, a slimmed-down, pawky version of the fat boy who 'wants to make yer flesh creep'. There's more sheer fun and soul food in his 'Sorcerer's Kitchen' than he'd like to pretend.

The Polish gig is pretty much a heavy R&B session, though it's worth the price of admission for a – possibly Prince-inspired – version of Parker's 'Now's The Time'. The opening 'Christmas Woman' romps along wonderfully, and is reprised at the end of the set, but much of the album is spoiled by long, inexplicable fades and a couple of poor edits. Carter is a star and is clearly enjoying himself, blaring away like a storefront preacher.

***** Talkeye**

Knitting Factory 3028 *Jackson; Zane Massey (ss, ts); Eric Person (ss, as, f); Masujaa, Cary de Nigris (g); John Moody (b).*

Bill Laswell-produced and every bit as thunderous and compelling as Bill's work usually is. The two saxophonists seem a little flummoxed by Jackson's concept, but it is good to hear Ronald in a more obviously jazz-based line-up again. 'Starhawk' and 'Gandhi' are outstanding tracks, but for sheer, effusive delight sample 'Jax's Dance' and 'Psychic Greeting'; they bring the set to a climax which is firmly capped by the closing 'Sheep In Wolf's Clothing'. Good stuff.

***** Puttin' On Dog**

Knitting Factory 3033 *Jackson; Onaje Allan Gumbs (p); Michael Harper (v).* 11/00.

Reissued in 2000, having previously been available as *Pulse*, this is effectively a drum and vocal work, with just a minimal contribution from Gumbs, heard solo on 'Lullaby For The Mothers'. Poet Harper also contributes an unaccompanied piece on 'Those Winter Sundays' and duets with Jackson on 'Bessie's Last Affair'. Jackson talks and sings across several of the tracks, struggling to be audible above his own thrashing percussion. The set opens well with the title-track (given as 'Puttin' On *The* Dog') and there is lots of excellent drumming to savour, especially on 'The Raven' which draws heavily on Edgar Allan Poe.

Willis Jackson (1928–87)

TENOR SAXOPHONE

Born in Miami, Jackson made his name with the Cootie Williams small group of the early '50s and thereafter toured and recorded mostly in small-combo R&B-styled settings.

**** Call Of The Gators**

Delmark DD-460 *Jackson; Andrew Fats Ford, Bobby Johnson (t); Booty Wood, Bobby Range (tb); Haywood Henry, Ben Kynard, Reuben Phillips (bs); Bill Doggett, Arnold Jarvis, Duke Anderson (p); Leonard Swain, Leemie Stanfield (b); Joe Murphy, Panama Francis (d).* 1–5/50.

***** Please Mr Jackson**

Original Jazz Classics OJC 321 *Jackson; Jack McDuff (org); Bill Jennings (g); Tommy Potter (b); Alvin Johnson (d).* 5/59.

***** Legends Of Acid Jazz**

Prestige 24198-2 *Jackson; Jack McDuff (org); Bill Jennings (g); Wendell Marshall, Tommy Potter, Milt Hinton (b); Alvin Johnson, Bill Elliot (d); Buck Clarke (perc).* 5/59–8/60.

***** Legends Of Acid Jazz – Keep On A Blowin'**

Prestige 24218-2 *Jackson; Jack McDuff, Freddie Roach (org); Bill Jennings (g); Tommy Potter, Wendell Marshall, Milt Hinton (b); Alvin Johnson, Frank Shea (d); Buck Clarke, Ray Barretto (perc).* 5/59–3/62.

****(*) Gentle Gator**

Prestige 24158-2 *Jackson; Jimmy Neely, Richard Wyands, Gildo Mahones, Tommy Flanagan (p); Kenny Burrell, Bucky Pizzarelli, Jose Paulo (g); Wendell Marshall, Peck Morrison, George Tucker, Eddie Calhoun (b); Roy Haynes, Bobby Morrison, Gus Johnson, Mickey Roker (d); Juan Amalbert, Montego Joe (perc).* 1/61–12/62.

***** Gravy**

Prestige 24254 *Jackson; Frank Robinson (t); Carl Wilson (org); Pat Martino (g); Leonard Gaskin (b); Joe Hadrick (d).* 5/63.

***** Nuther'n Like Thuther'n**

Prestige 24265-2 *As above, except Sam Jones, George Tucker (b) replace Gaskin.* 10/63–1/64.

***** Willis Jackson With Pat Martino**

Prestige 24161-2 *Jackson; Frank Robinson (p); Pat Martino (g); Carl Wilson (b); Joe Hadrick (d).* 3/64.

***** Soul Night Live!**

Prestige 24273-2 *As above.* 3/64.

Willis 'Gator' Jackson made a lot of records for Prestige and Muse, most of them in the tenor-and-organ format, and they've trickled back into circulation. Delmark have reminded us of where he began, with a compilation of ancient R&B sides: leathery, honking solos coughed out over sloppy-joe rhythms, good fun provided you don't have to hear more than a couple of tracks at a time. His long stint as a soul-sax man at Prestige has been rewarded with a bunch of reissues: reliably gritty playing by all hands, and – again – taken a few minutes at a time, this stuff can sound great. But don't expect a CD to have staying power. *Gentle Gator* has him turning the juice on with the ballad format, and this is frankly even slighter: no need to put this record on when there's a Lockjaw Davis, let alone a Ben Webster, album to hand.

His first entry in the *Acid Jazz* series couples the Prestige originals *Blue Gator* and *Cookin' Sherry*, and the second gathers in *Keep On A Blowin'* and *Thunderbird*. The 1963 sets on *Gravy* were first issued as *Grease 'N' Gravy* and *The Good Life*, while *Nuther'n Like Thuther'n* couples *More Gravy* and *Boss Shoutin'*. The personnels don't change very much and the music certainly doesn't, even over a four-year period. Old favourites like McDuff and Jennings do their duty, and Willis blows hard. Difficult to pick a winner, but track for track we still slightly prefer the first *Acid Jazz* set as the record to get if you want a single Jackson in your house: too bad about the silly psychedelic cover-art, though.

The latest retrieval is *Soul Night Live!*, which couples the set of that name with *Tell It ...*, although both of them were actually recorded on the same night at the Allegro in New York. The main point of interest here may be the chance to hear the 19-year-old Pat Martino, who burns through his solos like a young man in a big hurry, and it's always the guitarist you wait to hear. Jackson's penchant for throwing dopey quotes into his solos is tiresome after two tracks, and Robinson really isn't much of a trumpeter, but as with the other discs here, it's not music that asks to be examined too closely anyway.

C. W. Jacobi's Bottomland Orchestra

GROUP

A tribute band dedicated to the music of Clarence Williams, led by German arranger-saxophonist Jacobi.

***** A Tribute To Clarence Williams**

Stomp Off CD1266 *Roland Pilz (c, v); René Hagmann (tb); Matthias Seuffert (cl, as); Claus Jacobi (cl, as, ts); Rurik Van Heys (p); Gunter Russel (bj); Dietrich Kleine-Horst (tba); Gunter Andernach (wbd, perc); Gaby 'Ottilie' Schulz (v).* 3/93.

***** A Tribute To Clarence Williams Vol. 2**

Stomp Off CD1336 *As above, except Norbert Kemper (p) replaces Van Heys; omit Schulz.* 11/97.

Despite Williams's widespread influence on early jazz, only three of the 18 tunes on the first disc – 'Baby Won't You Please Come Home', 'I Wish I Could Shimmy Like My Sister Kate' and 'Old Folks' Shuffle' – could be called standards. Yet the entire programme is played with easy panache and fluency by this splendid outfit of German connoisseurs. The remarkable Hagmann is on loan from The Dry Throat Fellows, playing trombone this time, and the reed-players get very close to the warbling style of their '20s counterparts; Pilz, too, makes a good fist of the Ed Allen cornet parts. The result is a bright, happy session which flirts with the novelty flavour that Williams himself traded on without succumbing to it: symbolic in this regard is the ferocious trashing of 'Anywhere Sweetie Goes (I'll Be There)', but almost anything here would have sounded just fine on an original Vocalion of 65 years earlier. *Volume 2* continues where they left off four years earlier and, with a superior studio sound and a confident band, this one may edge out the earlier disc, though Williams fans may find this a less gratifying set of tunes. Unencumbered by any American affiliation – they never sound as if they're following the Murphy/Watters line, which many an American traditionalist does – they make this stuff sound very fresh. Perfection: the loco feel of 'Railroad Rhythm'.

Illinois Jacquet (born 1922)

TENOR SAXOPHONE, BASSOON, VOCALS

Jacquet made his reputation with a solo on Lionel Hampton's 'Flying Home' and condemned himself to playing it for the next 40 years. The quintessential Texas tenor, Jacquet was a stalwart of the Basie orchestra and later of Norman Granz's Jazz At The Philharmonic, sometimes generating more heat than light, but always playing inventive, full-toned jazz.

***** Illinois Jacquet, 1945–1946**

Classics 948 *Jacquet; Emmett Berry, Russell Jacquet (t); Henry Coker (tb); John Brown (as); Tom Archia (ts); Arthur Dennis (bs); Bill Doggett, Sir Charles Thompson (p); Freddie Green, Ulysses Livingston (g); Billy Hadnott, Charles Mingus, John Simmons (b); Johnny Otis, Shadow Wilson (d).* 7/45–1/46.

****** Illinois Jacquet, 1946–1947**

Classics 1019 *Jacquet; Miles Davis, Marion Hazel, Russell Jacquet, Fats Navarro, Joe Newman (t); Gus Chappell, J. J. Johnson, Ted Kelly, Fred Robinson, Trummy Young, Dicky Wells (tb); Porter Kilbert, Ray Perry (as); Leo Parker (bs); Bill Doggett, Leonard Feather, Sir Charles Thompson (p); John Collins, Freddie Green (g); Al Lucas, John Simmons (b); Denzil Best, Shadow Wilson (d).* 8/46–11/47.

***** Flying Home**

RCA 61123 *Jacquet; Russell Jacquet (t, v); Joe Newman (t); J. J. Johnson (tb); Ray Perry (as); Leo Parker, Maurice Simon (bs); Milt Buckner, Cedric Haywood, Sir Charles Thompson (p); Lionel Hampton (vib); John Collins (g); George Duvivier, Al Lucas (b); Alan Dawson, Jo Jones, Shadow Wilson (d).* 12/47–7/67.

***** Illinois Jacquet, 1947–1951**

Classics 1254 *As above; add Henry Coker (tb); Red Callender (b); Lee Abrams, J. C. Heard (d).* 12/47–1/51.

***** Jacquet A La Carte**

Ocium 25 *Similar to above; some additional personnel.*

*****(*) The Illinois Jacquet Story**

Properbox 49 4CD *Similar to above; some additional personnel.*

Born in Broussard, Louisiana, and raised in Houston, Texas – you somehow just know how Illinois Jacquet is going to sound. It's a big, blues tone, edged with a kind of desperate loneliness that somehow underlines Jacquet's status as a permanent guest star, an unbreakable mustang of a player who was never really given either the right amount of room or genuinely sympathetic sidemen. He learned his showmanship in the Lionel Hampton band of the early '40s, trading on his remarkable facility in the 'false' upper register and on sheer energy.

Jacquet seems permanently saddled with the largely meaningless 'Texas tenor' tag. In fact, his playing can show remarkable sensitivity and he is one of the fastest thinkers in the business. His ability to take care of his own business was obvious from the shrewd self-management that kept him in the forefront of Norman Granz's Jazz At The Philharmonic, a story that has yet to be told in revealing detail. Just a few days after his triumphant debut with JATP, Jacquet cut the first of the sides included on the Classics compilation. Inevitably, given the huge success he'd had with the Good–Hampton–Robin tune which propelled him to early fame, he includes another version of 'Flying Home', accompanied this time by brother Russell (who takes the vocal on 'Throw It Out Of Your Mind, Baby'), trombonist Henry Coker and Sir Charles Thompson. The four July sides for Philo are pretty forgettable, and there isn't a chance to hear what Jacquet is really made of until he starts recording for Apollo in August. 'Jacquet Mood' and 'Bottoms Up' are both impressive up-tempo numbers, and there is an early sighting of Jacquet the balladeer, an exquisite performance of 'Ghost Of A Chance'. He's back in the same mood early the following year, recording for Savoy in a band with Emmett Berry, who was credited as leader on half the releases. This time, it's 'Don't Blame Me' that reveals the romantic in him. The only other items on this first Classics compilation are a couple of obscurities recorded by the August 1945 band for ARA. The sharp-eyed will have noted a credit for the 23-year-old Charles Mingus, playing bass on the Apollo sessions.

Classics move in their typically dogged way, hoovering up everything that has been done under the artist's name, month by month, session by session. Jacquet was still with Basie in the summer of 1946, and used many of his day-job colleagues for his recordings for Apollo. These and what followed make the next Classics volume a near-essential buy for Jacquet fans and a highly recommended one for swing enthusiasts. A measure of the excitement generated by his newly configured big band of January 1947 (which doesn't seem to have performed live, simply as a studio line-up) can be judged by the quickest scan of the personnel. Four outstanding cuts, with Leonard Feather sitting in as pianist on 'Big Dog'. Illinois with big-toned, confident solos and the ensembles, on 'For Europeans Only' in particular, can't be faulted, all the more so if this really wasn't a regular working band.

The spring of 1947 saw the saxophonist back working with a smaller group, but no less impressive a personnel, with Russell Jacquet, Newman, J.J., Leo Parker, Sir Charles Thompson *and* Freddie Green on board to record just one rather scanty idea; the other cut, from April Fool's Day, is for saxophone and rhythm only. As so often, Jacquet is the only lead woodwind, with Parker used largely to fill out the mid-end of the ensembles when he is present. Larger and smaller versions of the All Stars line-up were to be Jacquet's working group for the rest of the year, and there are excellent things from May ('Robbins' Nest' and 'Jumpin' At The Woodside'), September (another sax-and-rhythm track, 'It's Wild', with one of his most intense solos on disc) and November (for some reason, 'I Surrender Dear' was issued only in France). A cracking vintage for the saxophonist and, despite the usual technical quibbles, a fine compilation.

The 1947 to 1951 Classics volume begins with the outrageous 'Jet Propulsion', famous for its obsessively repeated one-note finale. 'King Jacquet' goes off at rocket speed, with J. J. Johnson's fleet, saxophone-like counter-phrase shadowing the leader on the introduction. Illinois's power and raw, slightly out-of-tune delivery are insistently attractive. Most of these sides were cut for Victor, though there are some Clef and Mercury recordings made in California in January 1951, where the story will resume next time out.

The Ocium set has some excellent features, not least the enhanced CD format, but given the range of options for this material, it's hard to see why anyone would want this rather flat transfer even over the Classics option, or the Proper box, which does the usual cheap-and-cheerful job and offers 79 honking tracks for less than the price of a good bottle of wine. The packaging and documentation are quite decent, and for the majority of listeners this will be the most attractive option.

***(*) Illinois Jacquet

Columbia CK 64654 *Jacquet; Roy Eldridge, Ernie Royal (t); Matthew Gee (tb); Charlie Davies, Leo Parker, Cecil Payne (bs); Sir Charles Thompson (p); Kenny Burrell (g); George Duvivier, Jimmy Rowser (b); Jimmy Crawford, Jo Jones (d).* 2–5/62.

Recording for Epic, Jacquet called together the players who had stood him in good stead since the mid-'40s, and created perhaps the best music of his career. It was a period not unmarked by tragedy, because the session of 5 February 1962 was the last before the death of Leo Parker, who'd been a kingpin of the group. From the opening 'Frantic Fanny', which isn't quite as wild and woolly as the title suggests, to the superb 'Stella By Starlight', which is played by saxophone and rhythm, Jacquet doesn't put a foot wrong. A large-scale arrangement by Ernie Wilkins of 'Satin Doll' puts the saxophonist in the midst of the fuller, brassier sound he had grown to distrust a little. It's very close to the original Ellington version, but both Jacquet and Eldridge rework significant elements of it. Throughout these sessions, Thompson is masterful, playing deadly choruses and fills, and always swooping in right underneath the soloist, the best possible accompanist. One intriguing element of the work for Epic is Jacquet's return to the alto saxophone. He roars through an upbeat 'Indiana' on the smaller horn and returns to it for an exquisite arrangement of Debussy's 'Reverie', which draws out his romantic strain again.

*** Bottoms Up

Original Jazz Classics OJC 417 *Jacquet; Barry Harris (p); Ben Tucker (b); Alan Dawson (d).* 68.

*** The King!

Original Jazz Classics OJC 849 *Jacquet; Joe Newman, Ernie Royal (t); Milt Buckner (org); Billy Butler (g); Al Lucas (b); Jo Jones (d); Montego Joe (perc).* 68–69.

*** The Soul Explosion

Original Jazz Classics OJC 674 *Jacquet; Russell Jacquet, Joe Newman, Ernie Royal (t); Matthew Gee (tb); Frank Foster (ts); Cecil Payne (bs); Milt Buckner (org); Wally Richardson (g); Al Lucas (b); Al Foster (d).* 3/69.

***** The Blues, That's Me!**

Original Jazz Classics OJC 614 *Jacquet; Wynton Kelly (p); Tiny Grimes (g); Buster Williams (b); Oliver Jackson (d).* 9/69.

Jacquet seldom played the blues better than on these good sets, which were originally released on Prestige. As so often on that label, a period of concentrated activity with sympathetic colleagues gave a slightly directionless career a significant boost. Not much to be said about the music, except that the large-group material on *The Soul Explosion* is more sophisticated than might be supposed. There are fine versions of 'Still King' and 'Round About Midnight' on *The Blues, That's Me!*, both of which demonstrate, in markedly different ways, the delicacy of Jacquet's touch. *The King!* is a bit of a rag-bag, but it has some strong work from Newman and Royal and the doubled-up CD bonuses, extra takes of 'A Haunting Melody' and 'Blue And Sentimental', are well worth having.

***** Birthday Party**

Groove Note 1003 *Jacquet; Joe Newman (t); Art Farmer (flhn); James Moody (ts, f); Gerry Mulligan (bs); Jimmy Smith (p); Kenny Burrell (g); Jack Six (b); Roy Haynes (d).* 72.

Given a little simple arithmetic, the title becomes self-explanatory: an all-star cast get together to celebrate the saxophonist's 50th in style. To borrow a title from trumpeter Joe Newman, it was a grand night for swingin', but as ever Jacquet marshals the band with all the discipline and rigour that characterized his large ensembles. He is out on his own for 'Polka Dots And Moonbeams' and his solo on 'The "Sandpiper" Theme' is all schmaltz, with a strong blues pulse beating through it. The other soloists are well presented, too. Moody has his moment on flute with 'Ebb Tide' and elsewhere complements the leader's gruffer excursions with his own strangely feminine tonality. Burrell is outstanding from start to finish and Newman shines. There must surely be more material from this great event still awaiting release. What's on offer is wonderful but rather scant for the money.

***** The Man I Love**

Black & Blue 865 *Jacquet; Wild Bill Davis (org); Albert Bartee (d).* 73.

***** Jacquet's Street**

Black & Blue 972 *Jacquet; Francis Williams (t); Al Cobbs (tb); Milt Buckner (p); George Duvivier (b); Oliver Jackson (d).* 7/76.

***** God Bless My Solo**

Black & Blue 941 *Jacquet; Hank Jones (p); George Duvivier (b); J. C. Heard (d).* 3/78.

***** Live At Schaffhausen**

Storyville 8357 *As above.* 3/78.

Jacquet never sounded quite as effective in a small group and without the massive lift-off imparted by a big band behind him. Nevertheless these sessions from a French label that provided welcome work for veteran American players at a time the home market was very restrictive indeed are vigorously appealing. Buckner was a pretty steady presence in the B&B studio and his rather crude piano style, arguably more effective on Hammond, was ideal for Jacquet's approach. Check them both out on two takes of 'Don't Blame Me' and a fine 'Taps Miller'. Jones is a naturally bluesy player and his occasional solos – God bless them – are always effective. By contrast, Davis tries to drown him in sound and the result is a clotted, messy mix. The live album is an interesting point of comparison. Jacquet dominates from the start and explores his upper register as often as he gets the chance, though there is also a quieter strain to his playing on a very brief 'In A Sentimental Mood'. A nice find for IJ fans.

***** The JSP Jazz Sessions: Volume 1 – New York**

JSP 402 *Jacquet; Vic Dickenson (tb); Barry Harris (p); Slam Stewart (b); Grady Tate (d).* 6/80.

A must for Jacquet collectors, if only for the alternate takes of 'Bow Jest' and 'Limehouse Blues'. This is actually shared with some cuts by the Junior Mance trio. The Jacquet material is well up to snuff and Dickenson and Harris are in particularly fine form on the opener. The sound is good but falsely bright in the manner of jazz recording at this time and most listeners will want to fiddle with the dials a bit to get it down from a tooth-grating pitch.

Russell Jacquet (1917–90)

TRUMPET, VOCAL

Illinois Jacquet's older brother had a modest career, mostly in and around California. He led a number of sessions in the '40s but thereafter worked for other leaders, although he had his own label, Town Hall, for a period in the '70s.

***** Russell Jacquet 1945–1949**

Classics 1145 *Jacquet; Snooky Young, Harry 'Sweets' Edison, Gerald Wilson, Harry Parr Jones, Joe Newman, John Anderson, Calvin Boze (t); Eli Robinson, Ted Donelly, J. J. Johnson, Henry Coker (tb); Teddy Edwards, Preston Love, Willie Smith, Sonny Stitt, Gis Evans (as); Maurice Simon, Dexter Gordon, Illinois Jacquet, Lucky Thompson, Bumps Myers (ts); Arthur Dennis, Rudy Rutherford, Leo Parker (bs); Bill Davis, Jimmy Bunn, Bill Doggett, Sir Charles Thompson, Gerald Wiggins (p); Freddie Greene, Leo Blevins (g); Charles Mingus, Billy Hadnott, Herman Washington, Al Lucas, Charlie Drayton (b); Chico Hamilton, Albert Wichard, Shadow Wilson (d); Numa Lee Davis (v).* 45–3/49.

Russell Jacquet turned out to be a footnote in jazz history, but a glance through the personnels here shows that he could call on some impressive sidemen for the only 20 sides which ever appeared under his own name. The groups range from eight to 17 in size and were made for Globe, Modern Music, Jewel, Sensation and King. The earlier pieces are in a swing–R&B mould, but the final dozen are more boppish (and include Stitt and J. J. Johnson in the line-ups), even if they keep an eye on the jump-band jukebox music of the day. Jacquet's own style is cast in a pleasingly unpretentious sound which outshines several of the other soloists here, although brother Illinois gets a notably impressive turn on a track simply called 'Blues'. An enjoyable backwater of '40s jazz.

Ahmad Jamal (born 1930)

PIANO

Originally Fritz Jones of Pittsburgh, Jamal may well have adopted a more exotic name, but stylistically he went in the opposite direction, carving out a spare, spacious piano style, characterized by a subtle use of silence and much admired by

Miles Davis. His recordings from the Pershing Lounge are among the most commercially successful in modern jazz, despite which he remains something of a coterie enthusiasm.

****** At The Pershing**
Chess MCD 09108 *Jamal; Israel Crosby (b); Vernell Fournier (d).* 1/58.

***** Ahmad's Blues**
Chess 051803-2 *As above.* 9/58.

But for his enormous influence on Miles, Ahmad Jamal might by now have fallen into the pit dug for him by tin-eared critics, dismissed as an inventive cocktail pianist or (still more invidiously) as an entertainer rather than an artist. As Brian Priestley has pointed out, pianists who achieve a modicum of commercial success tend to move closer to the entertainment mainstream than any other musicians, except possibly singers, who are often thought to belong there anyway. For many years, Jamal gave much of his attention to running a chi-chi club, the Alhambra, rather than to playing.

He is certainly not a studio-friendly pianist and almost always sounds better caught live. The earlier of these records is something of an industry phenomenon, climbing to number three on the *Billboard* 'Hot 100' on its release and staying in the chart for more than two years. Now impeccably remastered, though unfortunately not supplemented with additional material (which leaves it at a measly 32 minutes), it demonstrates how and why Jamal was able to negotiate mainstream success. The former Fritz Jones had launched his career seven years earlier as part of The Three Strings and had caught the ear of the intuitive John Hammond with the subtlety and sophistication of his work.

His technique has scarcely changed over the years and remains closer to Erroll Garner than to anyone else, concentrating on fragile textures and calligraphic melodic statements, rather than the propulsive logic of bebop piano. His reinterpretations of 'Woody'N'You' and 'No Greater Love' were the kind of thing that brought him to Miles Davis's attention, cool and subtle, and a long way from the scrabble of bop. *Ahmad's Blues* is a lesser record all round, but it is still enjoyable unless one is looking for starburst virtuosity and a hint of romantic agony.

CORE COLLECTION

****** Cross Country Tour: 1958–1961**
Chess GRP 18132 2CD *Jamal; Israel Crosby (b); Vernel Fournier (d).* 1/58, 9/58, 6/61.

The contents of four Argo LPs on a double-CD set, filling out the picture of this hugely successful trio considerably. Volume 1 covers material from the Pershing in Chicago in January and September 1958, previously issued as *Ahmad Jamal At The Pershing* and *Jamal At The Pershing: Volume 2*. Other material comes from the Spotlite in Washington, DC (*Portfolio*), his own Alhambra back in Chicago (*All Of Me*) and at the Black Hawk in San Francisco (and so titled), though here the exact date of recording is unclear and, *pace* the subtitle of the set, might be 1962.

The outstanding performance on Volume 1, improbably, is 'Music! Music! Music!', to which Jamal gives the kind of spin that intrigued Miles Davis and influenced him in his approach to popular material. It is both faithful and deeply subversive. He does the same with 'Cherokee' and the traditional 'Billy Boy' on Volume 2. The remaining cuts are more conventionally provenanced, show-tunes in the main but with the usual deep understanding of melody and harmony in active interplay. Performances are rarely very long, often sticking to the dimensions of the original song; but here and there, as on 'Broadway' at the Alhambra, Jamal will cut loose and venture out into uncharted territory. It's perhaps his most searching performance of the period and, oddly, the least idiomatic, or at least the only one that couldn't immediately be identified as his work.

As ever, Crosby and Fournier are utterly sympathetic and responsive, bringing real feeling to the songs and sticking tight to the leader at every turn, so that the group really does function as a three-in-one rather than a loose coalition.

*****(*) The Awakening**
Impulse! 051226-2 *Jamal; Jamil Nasser (b); Frank Gant (d).* 2/70.

This more or less rounds out the picture of Jamal as a polished stylist, highly pianistic but disinclined to emote. What is once again clear, though, is how integrated and even-handed a Jamal group is; Nasser and Gant are no mere accompanists but significant performers in their own right, and the drummer brings a depth of focus to the music, a touch of darkness and danger even to a joyous theme like 'Dolphin Dance'. Apart from the title-track, with its dramatic four-note cell, and the more abstract 'Patterns', everything else is by other hands. Oliver Nelson's 'Stolen Moments' is the outstanding item.

***** Encore – Live At Bubba's**
Magnum 2104 *Jamal; Sabu Adeyola (b); Payton Crossley (d).* 80.

***** Live At Midem**
Magnum 2106 *As above; add Gary Burton (vib).* 81.

Two strong live sets from an otherwise poorly documented period in Jamal's career. Though unfavoured by the major labels at this time, he was still a considerable draw on the club and concert circuit and there are probably a couple of dozen equally good tapes lying in vaults and desk drawers, waiting for release. The association with Burton was a happy one and the Midem gig is probably the better of the pair by a whisker, largely because there is an element of dialogue missing on the other release.

***** Live In Paris, 1992**
Dreyfus 37019 2 *Jamal; James Cammack, Todd Coolman (b); David Bowler, Gordon Lane (d).* 4/92.

Jamal still plays with an easy grace that might be thought facile if there weren't so much going on harmonically. His medley of 'Alone Together', 'Laura' and 'Wild Is The Wind' is magnificently structured and quite theatrical. As always, he's very drawn to film soundtrack music. 'Caravan', 'Easy Living' and Erroll Garner's 'Dreamy' are also vintage performances. These were taped over two nights with two different trios, but it's Jamal who keeps the quality consistent.

****** Chicago Revisited**
Telarc CD 83327 *Jamal; John Heard (b); Yoron Israel (d).* 11/92.

***** The Essence: Part 1**
Dreyfus 37007 2 *Jamal; George Coleman, James Cammack, Jamil Nasser (b); Idris Muhammad (d); Manolo Badrena (perc).* 94–95.

***** Big Byrd: The Essence: Part 2**

Dreyfus 37008 2 *As above, except omit Coleman; add Donald Byrd (t); Joe Kennedy Jr (vn).* 10/94, 2/95.

The '90s saw a startling renaissance. Jazz piano became fashionable again, and Jamal started to play with something like the poise and brilliance of the '50s.

Chicago Revisited could hardly be bettered as an example of contemporary jazz piano. The elegance of his line on 'All The Things You Are', with which the set opens, is such that it could be balanced on a pin. Clifford Brown's 'Daahoud' recalls a whole era in just a few bars. The remainder of the set is typically eclectic, tunes by Irving Ashby, Harold Adamson and Jimmy McHugh, Nick Brodszky and Sammy Cahn, and John Handy, closing with a 'Lullaby Of Birdland' that is concentrated songfulness.

These days, he has the wise, thoughtful look of an African parliamentarian, and a measured, slightly unrevealing delivery, well represented on *The Essence*. Difficult to pick between the two volumes, though our suspicion is that one really cracking album might have been distilled from the sessions. In present form, they don't quite happen. Coleman's contribution is as substantial and thoughtful as always, but it's the appearance of the back-to-form (and, let's face it, back-to-jazz) Byrd which makes the second set swing. He's the featured soloist on the title-track. All three albums, now available in new editions, run counter to the prevailing expectation Jamal can still easily be dismissed as shallow and clinical, unemotional and even unexpressive. Nonsense; there are more things to be expressed than anguish and despair, or roaring delight. Jamal has chosen to refract a misunderstood band of the jazz spectrum, and the music would be poorer without him. Hard to make a clear distinction between them. This is wise and measured music, that requires a certain effort of attention, not because it is hypersubtle or 'difficult' but because it makes its points quietly and without histrionics.

*****(*) I Remember Duke, Hoagy & Strayhorn**

Telarc 83339 *Jamal; Ephraim Wolfolk (b); Arti Dixson (d).* 6/94.

A slow and stately performance, though Jamal often experiments in double-time improvisations over very stately rhythm tracks. The mood is almost bizarrely even and elegiac. This works less well, perversely, on material like 'Prelude To A Kiss', which sounds enervated rather than swooningly passionate, than on 'Skylark' and 'I Got It Bad ...' The Carmichael material is the scantest, though 'I Remember Hoagy', derived from the changes to 'Stardust', is a delightful conceit and a perfect showcase for Jamal's cool and playful approach. We know little about Wolfolk or Dixson, but they sound like competent and uncomplicatedly expressive players; and the trio sound, with Jamal pitched well to the forefront, is nicely recorded.

****(*) And The Assai Quartet**

Roesch 42 *Jamal; Jaroslaw Lis (vn); Claude Giron (clo); Ephraim Wolfolk (b); Arti Dixson (d).* 1/98.

This is pleasant enough, but so mild and modulated as to be almost subliminal in impact. Four live pieces, plus a short suite entitled 'Pots En Verre', which has no obvious rationale and is best heard as distinct pieces. Collectors only.

*****(*) Nature: The Essence, Part 3**

Dreyfus 37018 2 *Jamal; Stanley Turrentine (ts); James Cammack (b); Idris Muhammad (d); Othello Molineaux (perc).* 6/98.

For us the best of the *Essence* sequence, this shifts between dense, rhetorical piano solos – 'Chaperon', 'And We Were Lovers' – and quartet tracks like 'Devil's In My Den', which features a walk-on from the rejuvenated Stanley Turrentine. 'If I Find You Again', the opening track of *Nature*, is definitive, but there's also a wonderful version of the theme from *The Sand Pebbles*, testimony to Jamal's interest in unusual repertoire. He also does a delightful 'Cabin In The Sky'.

There is also an intriguing role for the steel drum player, Othello Molineaux. The rhythm section is well up to form and Cammack, as the junior partner, seems to have come on in leaps and bounds. Strongly recommended. Until a compilation of all the *Essence* sessions is issued, this is the one to go for.

***** Live in Paris 1996**

Dreyfus 37020 *Jamal; George Coleman (ts); Calvin Keys (g); Joe Kennedy Jr (vn); Jeff Chambers (b); Yoron Israel (d); Manolo Badrena (perc).* 96.

****** A L'Olympia**

Dreyfus FDM 36629 2 *Jamal; George Coleman (ts); James Cammack (b); Idris Muhammad (d).* 11/00.

Jamal was an honoured figure in Europe through the '90s, playing a sophisticated jazz that went down particularly well in France. The first of these is elegance itself and Coleman's harmonic wisdom comes through in every phrase. Check out the original 'Bellows' and the closing 'There's A Lull In My Life'. Sheer class.

The second one is also an absolutely cracking record. Marking his 70th birthday with another concert in Paris, Jamal doesn't seem content to lie back and enjoy the occasion. He has a point to prove, and seems bent on delivering a performance to rival the celebrated *At The Pershing*. That he does so – and royally – is, we're afraid, largely down to the magisterial presence of big George Coleman, whose solo on 'How Deep Is The Ocean' is one of the finest of his distinguished career, solidly engineered and delicately crafted. Jamal responds with one of several toughly lyrical solos.

The set gives early notice of intent with a long, pungent performance of 'The Night Has A Thousand Eyes' and Jamal astonishes – no other word for it – with a brilliantly inventive up-tempo introduction to 'Autumn Leaves'; a classic reinvented. Coleman creeps in slyly from off-mike and together they no more than tag the familiar melody before taking it off in new directions. Muhammad's drumming, which elsewhere is business-like and orderly, makes a substantial contribution. 'My Foolish Heart' is more straightforwardly melodic, but Coleman brings a gentle stridency to his solo, popping his pads softly here and there, which gives the tune a new poignancy.

'Appreciation' and the encore 'Aftermath' are showpieces for piano and rhythm. The latter, unusually, is the only Jamal composition on the set, though recent years have seen him concentrate ever more fixedly on reinvented standards and less on original fare. It would have been good to get George back on for one last hurrah but it was Jamal's night and it would be hard to better *A L'Olympia*.

***** Picture Perfect**

Birdology 85268 *Jamal; Marc Cargill (vn); James Cammack, Jamil Nasser (b); Idris Muhammad (d).* 4/01.

Instantly recognizable as a Jamal set, partly because the instrumentation has become quite familiar, but also because the writing and playing are so utterly idiomatic. That's not to say blandly repetitive – these are still inventive and often quite searching charts – but there's a lack of drama which some listeners may find off-putting.

***** In Search Of ... Momentum (1–10)**
Birdology FDM 36644 2 *Jamal; James Cammack (b); Idris Muhammad (d).* 8/02.

There is every indication that Jamal is moving into one of the busiest phases of his writing career. These are mainly new tunes, none of them instant standards but all thoughtful and well-balanced. He mentions a desire to be moving on to the next project which might well be a full recording of a piece called 'I'll Take The 20', which is briefly excerpted here, enough to suggest that it might be an interesting experience. Cammack and Muhammad give him everything he needs in support and the chops are still very fleet and elegant.

Khan Jamal (born 1946)

VIBRAPHONE, MARIMBA

Began playing vibes in the middle '60s and since then his various associations – with Byard Lancaster, Sunny Murray, Charles Tyler and others – suggest a restless but accommodating spirit.

*****(*) Dark Warrior**
Steeplechase SCCD 31196 *Jamal; Charles Tyler (as, bs); Johnny Mbizo Dyani (b); Leroy Lowe (d).* 9/84.

***** Three**
Steeplechase SCCD 31201 *Jamal; Pierre Dørge (g); Johnny Mbizo Dyani (d).* 10/84.

***** The Traveller**
Steeplechase SCCD 31217 *Jamal; Johnny Mbizo Dyani (b); Leroy Lowe (d).* 10/85.

The dedication to Cal Tjader on *Three* suggests one (outwardly unlikely) source for Jamal's firmly rhythmic but freely pulsed vibraphone style. Almost all of his albums, which have now returned to circulation on CD, have a dark freedom and surge which is curiously Europeanized, the kind of thing one hears when passing an African tea-house or café in the Paris Zone in Hamburg or Copenhagen. The partnership with Dyani was an immensely fruitful one, and on *Dark Warrior* the additional presence of Tyler's sour-sweet alto and bossy baritone delivers some fascinating music, which isn't quite matched on the two later Steeplechases. There is just a hint of Tjader's pattering approach, and vibes fans may hear echoes of just about everyone from Bobby Hutcherson to Steeplechase stablemate Walt Dickerson, to Karl Berger, and it may be that the lack of a settled identity and idiolect is the main problem with Jamal's work. Though his approach to a standard, like the usually saxophonic 'Body And Soul' on *The Traveller*, is reminiscent of Hutcherson's free counterpoint, in terms of diction it is even less horn-like, closer to Dickerson's abstract theme formulations.

*****(*) Speak Easy**
Gazell 4001 *Jamal; Dave Burrell (p); William Parker (b); Sunny Murray (d).* 88.

Strong and sympathetic company on this fine recording, which must be one of Jamal's best recorded moments. The vibes sing and resonate on track after track and the level of interactivity is at a high. Murray's intense patterns and Parker's deep-toned phrasing allow the leader to roam in as much space as he requires, as on 'Jennifer's Poem', or to pile on the notes, as he does on the delicate 'Rain Colors'. The session also sees him digging deeper into the tradition than formerly. Burrell is a master at this kind of polystylistic trawl and does his shape-shifting thing with masterly ease. 'Blues For An Endangered Species' is a highpoint of the set.

*****(*) Percussion And Strings**
CIMP 143 *Jamal; Dylan Taylor (clo); Ed Crockett (b); Craig McIver (d, mar); Pete Vinson (d, perc).* 3/97.

This is probably the sound Jamal has heard in his head for years but only now been able to evoke in real time, when he found a set-up willing to give him his head. The combination of instruments is very powerful, with strings acting as rhythmic accompaniment to the percussion-players. Vinson is involved on only a couple of tracks, playing cowbell on 'Return From Exile' and switching to drums for 'Round About Midnight', allowing Craig McIver to switch to marimba. Monk and Johnny Dyani are the presiding presences, with 'Blue Monk' and 'Witch Doctor's Son' the outstanding tracks. The sound, as always from CIMP, is raw and unvarnished, but very faithful to the performances.

***** Cubano Chant**
Jambrio 1002 *Jamal; Byard Lancaster (as, f); Omar Hill, Kino Speller (perc).* 01.

***** Cool**
Jambrio 1008 *Jamal; John F. Rodgers (clo); Dwight James (d).* 02.

More than a touch of Afro-Cuban about this pair. The first album is dominated by African percussion and has a slightly scattershot effectiveness. Tjader is invoked again, but in a new context. Lancaster's raw, bluesy alto is the other key voice, but it is very much the leader's set. *Cool* is a somewhat different kettle of fish. The cello proves to be an ideal accompaniment to the leader's vibes and percussion, offering a lighter and more singing version of what William Parker delivered on *Speak Easy*. The tunes are easier-paced and less taxing but, the title notwithstanding, Jamal finds the heat in most of them.

***** Balafon Dance**
CIMP 267 *Jamal; Roy Campbell (t); Jemeel Moondoc (as); Dylan Taylor (b); Dwight James (d).* 3/02.

The hurt, raw sound of Moondoc and Campbell in consort with the leader gives this fine session its distinctive cast. As with previous albums, Jamal explores elements of African rhythm and James proves to be an able collaborator. The title-piece is probably the best example so far of the vibist's rhythmic concerns to make it onto a record, but 'African Rhythm Tongues' is a clearer exposition of the same ideas. There is a lot of mutual experience lying behind these improvisations and the group sound is tight and coherent. The sound is pretty unforgiving, though, and some listeners will be reaching for the controls to tweak off some of the distortions.

Harry James (1916–83)

TRUMPET

Born into a family of musicians who played in a circus band, James joined Ben Pollack in 1935 and quickly became a hot property, switching to Benny Goodman as star soloist in 1937, then leading his own band from 1939, with Sinatra as vocalist. His taste for show-off virtuosity brought him million-selling records but the derision of many jazz followers. He moved into small-group work as the swing era declined and remained popular on the West Coast and in Las Vegas, having sold more records than most other jazz musicians. Eventually he moved back into big-band work.

*****(*) Harry James 1937–1939**

Classics 903 *James; Jack Palmer (t, v); Tom Gonsoulin, Claude Bowen, Buck Clayton (t); Eddie Durham, Vernon Brown, Russell Brown, Truett Jones (tb); Earl Warren, Dave Matthews, Claude Lakey (as); Jack Washington (as, bs); Herschel Evans, Arthur Rollini, Drew Page, Bill Luther (ts); Harry Carney (bs); Jess Stacy, Pete Johnson, Albert Ammons, Jack Gardner (p); Bryan Kent (g); Walter Page, Thurman Teague, Johnny Williams (b); Jo Jones, Dave Tough, Eddie Dougherty, Ralph Hawkins (d); Helen Humes, Bernice Byers (v).* 12/37–3/39.

***** Harry James 1939**

Classics 936 *James; Jack Schaeffer, Tom Gonsoulin, Claude Bowen, Jack Palmer (t); Russell Brown, Truett Jones (tb); Dave Matthews, Claude Lakey (as); Drew Page, Al Sears, Bill Luther (ts); Jack Gardner (p); Bryan Kent (g); Thurman Teague (b); Ralph Hawkins (d); Frank Sinatra, Fran Haines, Bernice Byers (v).* 4–10/39.

***** Harry James 1939–1940**

Classics 970 *As above, except add Dalton Rizzotto (tb), Mickey Scrima (d), Dick Haymes (v); omit Gonsoulin, Palmer, Sears, Hawkins, Byers.* 11/39–4/40.

*****(*) Harry James 1940–1941**

Classics 1014 *James; Claude Bowen, Nick Buono, Jack Palmer, Al Stearns (t); Truett Jones, Dalton Rizzotto, Bruce Squires, Hoyt Bohannon, Harry Rodgers (tb); Dave Matthews, Claude Lakey, Johnny Mezey (as); Vido Musso (ts); Chuck Gentry (bs); Jack Gardner, Al Lerner (p); Ben Heller (g); Thurman Teague (b); Mickey Scrima (d); Fran Haines, Dick Haymes (v).* 5/40–1/41.

***** Harry James 1941**

Classics 1052 *Similar to above, except add Sam Rosenblum, Stan Stanchfield, William Schumann, George Koch (vn).* 1–4/41.

****(*) Harry James 1941 Vol. 2**

Classics 1092 *James; Claude Bowen, Al Stearns (t); Dalton Rizzotto, Hoyt Bohannon, Harry Rodgers (tb); Claude Lakey, Sam Marozwitz (as); Vido Musso, Johnny Fresco (ts); Chuck Gentry, Clint Davis (bs); Al Lerner (p); Sam Rosenblum, Glenn Herzer, Leo Zorn, Alex Pevsner, Al Friede, Paul Lowenkron, Lou Horvarth, Bill Spears (vn); Ben Heller (g); Thurman Teague (b); Mickey Scrima (d); Helen Ward, Dick Haymes, Lynn Richards (v).* 5–8/41.

***** Harry James And His Orchestra Featuring Frank Sinatra**

Columbia CK 66377-2 *James; Jack Schaeffer, Claude Bowen, Tom Gonsoulin, Jack Palmer, Claude Lakey (t); Russell Brown, Truett Jones, Dalton Rizzotto, Bruce Squires (tb); Dave Matthews, Claude Lakey, Bill Luther, Drew Page (saxes); Jack Gardner (p); Brian Kent (g); Thurman Teague (b); Ralph Hawkins, Mickey Scrima (d); Frank Sinatra (v).* 7–10/39.

James's early period is now well represented on CD (at the time of our first edition he had almost nothing available in the medium) and there is plenty for admirers to choose from. The Classics discs start him off with three terrific sessions, two in which he fronts a small group drawn from the Basie band, one where he repeats the trick using Goodman sidemen (plus Harry Carney!). Unabashed by the heavy company, James often blows the roof off. Four tracks with Albert Ammons and Pete Johnson spotlight his tersest, hottest playing before the sessions with his proper big band close the disc, opening on his theme-tune, 'Ciribiribin', which exemplifies what James was about: no better trumpet technician, a great capacity to swing, but with a penchant for schmaltz mixed with bravado which has been his critical undoing. Classics 936 follows the band through six sessions in six months. Sinatra arrives for eight vocals and, though the band sound quite impressive on the likes of 'King Porter Stomp', James is the only soloist of any consequence and the arrangements are workmanlike. One is reminded of the Bunny Berigan big band, except that James has all of Berigan's technique and little of his judgement. The remastering on both discs is all right, if a little grey. *Featuring Frank Sinatra* is a good set of the young crooner's vocals with James and, though jazz followers will be disappointed at the low temperature, it remains a classy edition of smooth playing and singing. Transfers are mostly good, though one or two masters sound inexplicably rough.

Classics have continued their sequence, but those searching for hot music will be disappointed by these discs. Vocals by Sinatra and subsequently Haymes tend to dominate the band's output (James was reported as saying that he saw singers as 'a necessary evil', but he certainly wasn't shy about featuring them) and Classics 903 introduces such infamous showpiece hits as 'Concerto For Trumpet' and 'Carnival Of Venice', the sort of material which ruined James's reputation with many jazz followers. With hindsight, these are actually entertaining enough, but it's disappointing that the leader didn't see fit to balance such music out with some decent flag-wavers that could show off the chops of the band. Classics 1014 starts with 'Flight Of The Bumble Bee' and, unless one enjoys the Haymes features, pickings here are pretty slim. Classics 1052 at least has the likes of 'Duke's Mixture' and 'Jeffries' Blues', but the addition of a violin section allowed little but extra schmaltz and James recut new versions of 'Carnival Of Venice' and 'Trumpet Rhapsody'. Classics 1092 again has little to offer beyond the vocal features. Transfers are all right, but they're mysteriously inconsistent, on the last volume in particular.

***** Harry James 1941–1942**

Classics 1132 *James; Claude Bowen, Nick Buono, Al Stearns, Al Cuozzo (t); Dalton Rizzotto (tb, v); Hoyt Bohannon, Harry Rodgers (tb); Claude Lakey, Sam Marowitz (as); Dave Matthews (as, ts); Corky Corcoran (ts); Clint Davis (bs); Al Lerner (p); Ben Heller (g); Thurman Teague (b); Mickey Scrima (d); Dick Haymes, Helen Forrest, Jimmy Saunders (v); strings.* 10/41–1/42.

***** Harry James 1942**

Classics 1178 *As above, except add Willard Culley (frhn), George Davis (bs), Johnny McAfee (bs, as, v).* 2–7/42.

*****(*) Record Session '39–'42**

Hep 1068 *As various discs above.* 2/39–7/42.

An interesting period for James. As usual, there's a sprinkling of schmaltz, along with some genuinely effective, sweet performances and superior instrumentals. The sequential Classics approach means that one has to take the interestingly rough with the very smooth, but both of these discs have some fine sides: 'The Mole', 'The Clipper' and 'I Remember You' (Classics

1132) and 'James Session', 'Let Me Up' and 'Jump Town' (Classics 1178). The strings were being integrated into the orchestra's sound with increasing effectiveness, and with Helen Forrest (joining from Benny Goodman) James could boast a top-line singer, even though Sinatra (and subsequently Haymes) had departed. As is depressingly usual, the Classics discs are annoyingly erratic in their remastering quality, and a very rough-sounding track can be followed by a good one.

Hep's set picks out some of the plums from the period and is, naturally, in excellent sound. An ideal introduction to James in this era.

***** Harry James 1945–1946**

Classics 1313 *James; Red Berkin, Jimmy Campbell, Al Ramsey, Leonard Corris, Jimmy Salko, James Troutman, James Grimes (t); Vic Haymann, Chuck Preble, Ray Heath, Dick Noel, Dick Bellerose, Dalton Rizzotto (tb); Juan Tizol (vtb); Eddie Rosa (cl, f, as); Willie Smith (cl, as, v); Murray Williams (as); Corky Corcoran (ts); Stuart Bruner (ts, bs); George Davis (bs); Arnold Ross, Hayden Causey (g); Ed Milhelich (b); Ray Toland, Nick Fatool, Lou Fromm (d); Buddy DeVito, Kitty Kallen, Ginny Powell (v); strings.* 7/45–5/46.

At a time when big bands were in decline, James still had more than 30 men on his payroll on these dates. Kitty Kallen takes some very appealing vocals, but mostly this is the dance-band side of James, handsome as much of the playing is.

***** James With Haymes – 1941**

Circle CCD-5 *James; Claude Bowen, Al Stearns (t); Hoyt Bohannon, Dalton Rizzotto, Harry Rogers (tb); Claude Lakey, Vido Musso, Sam Marowitz, Chuck Gentry (saxes); Al Lerner (p); Ben Heller (g); Thurman Teague (b); Mickey Scrima (d); Dick Haymes (v); strings.* 41.

****(*) Spotlight Bands Broadcast 1946**

Jazz Hour JH-1046 *Personnel unlisted, but includes Willie Smith (as), Helen Forrest (v).* 43–46.

***** Feet Draggin' Blues**

Hep CD 62 *James; Jimmy Campbell, Al Ramsey, Uan Rasey, Red Berken, Jim Troutman, Jimmy Grimes, Lenny Corris, Hal Moe, Darl Berken, Zeke Zarchy, Paul Geil, Mannie Klein, Pinky Savitt, Nick Buono, Gene Komer, Ralph Osborn (t); Vic Hamann, Charlie Preble, Ray Heath, Dalton Rizzotto, Ed Kusby, Ziggy Elmer (tb); Juan Tizol (vtb); Willie Smith (cl, as, v); Eddie Rosa (cl, as); Claude Lakey, Les Robinson (as); Polly Polifroni (cl, ts); Corky Corcoran, Clint Davis, Herbie Haymer, Babe Russin, Sam Sachelle (ts); Stuart Bruner, Bob Poland (bs); Arnold Ross, Stan Wrightsmann, Bruce MacDonald (p); Allan Reuss, Hayden Causey, Tiny Timbrell (g); Ed Mihelich, Artie Bernstein (b); Carl Maus, Nick Fatool, Buddy Combine, Lou Fromm (d); Ginnie Powell (v); strings.* 11/44–11/47.

***** There They Go**

Fresh Sound FSRCD 2014 *James; Nick Buono, Pinky Savitt, Ralph Osbourne, Gene Komer, Everett Macdonald, Neal Hefti (t); Juan Tizol, Ziggy Elmer, Charlie Preble, Dave Robbins (tb); Eddie Rosa, Al Pellegrini, Willie Smith, Bob Walters (c, as); Jimmy Cook, Sam Sachelle, Corky Corcoran (ts); Bob Poland (bs); Bruce McDonald (p); Tiny Timbrell (g); Joe Mondragon (b); Don Lamond, Frank Bode, Louie Bellson (d).* 48.

***** Big John Special '49**

Hep CD 24 *Similar to above, except add Phil Cook (t), Tommy Greco (tb), Musky Ruffo (as), Bob Bain (g), Norman Seelig (b).* 6/49–11/50.

***** Trumpet Blues**

Sounds Of Yesteryear DSOY 617 *Basically as above.* 49–50.

*****(*) Bandstand Memories 1938–1948**

Hindsight HBCD503 3CD As all discs above, probably with numerous others! 38–48.

The easiest way to get a feel for James's better music at present is to listen to some of these numerous aircheck recordings. James seemed to remain popular on radio throughout the '40s, and plenty of material has survived in pro-am recordings. The disc with Dick Haymes luxuriates in the singer's impeccable vocals – extraordinarily deep and resonant for a man of 21. Not much jazz here, but a beguiling disc. The 1946 Spotlight Bands disc is rougher and, though the band take a good romp through 'King Porter Stomp' and generally give the impression that they're waking up rather more often, the sound tells against it – even more so on six pretty horrible-sounding transcriptions from 1943, here as a dubious bonus. *There They Go* is a better bet. James seemed to get more rather than less adventurous as the big-band era wore down, and there are some fine charts here from Neal Hefti in particular. The programme is rather exhaustingly fast and sometimes it seems the other soloists have caught James's showstopping infection to their detriment, but the music's exciting. Quite clean sound from airshot sources.

First choice must go to the handsomely boxed, three-disc set on Hindsight. This covers ten years of material and is as good a summary of James as we're likely to get for now. The first disc, with the earliest material, has many rough spots, but the next two range from good to excellent, and the third in particular is a strong manifesto for the band. James himself remained the main soloist, his style an idiosyncratic blend of schmaltz, practised routine and surprising twists. Some part of the young firebrand who started with Goodman remains, but the broad tone and sometimes broader taste of his later work is in there too.

It has some stiff competition now from the two Hep discs which are in excellent sound and which between them cover most of James's stylings from 1944 onwards. *Big John Special* duplicates much of what is on *There They Go*, but this is a superior edition. Track for track, there is nothing to get really excited about on any of these discs: James's modernism was always going to be cautious, and he valued precision as much as heat in his players. But they will confound listeners who expect the dreary routines of his hit records. *Trumpet Blues* is more of the same, a group of good charts, mostly in more than acceptable sound.

*****(*) Trumpet Blues**

Capitol 521224-2 *James; full personnel unlisted, but soloists include Willie Smith (as), Corky Corcoran (ts), Jack Perciful (p), Buddy Rich (d), Helen Forrest (v).* 7/55–7/58.

A compilation from the Capitol originals, *Harry James In Hi-Fi* and *More Harry James In Hi-Fi*, part of the label's initiative in asking swing-era bandleaders to redo their hits for LP. The warmest pieces have been chosen and they make a good fist of re-creating James's work, with a few nods to his more contemporary direction, the new Ernie Wilkins charts in particular. The Capitol engineers got a very grand sound out of the sessions and the sections play with fine panache.

*****(*) Jazz Masters 55: Harry James**

Verve 529902-2 *James; John Audino, Ollie Mitchell, Nick Buono, Bob Rolfe, Rob Turk, Larry Maguire, Vince Guertin, Jack Bohannon, Dick Cathcart, Sam Conte, Mike Conn, Bill*

Mattison, Fred Koyen (t); Ray Sims, Bob Edmondson, Ernie Tack, Vince Diaz, Joe Hambrick, Dick Leith, Joe Cadena, Dick McQuary (tb); Matty Matlock (cl); Willie Smith, Herb Lorden, Pa Cahrttrand, Joe Riggs, Larry Stoffel (as); Corky Corcoran, Sam Firmature, Bob Poland, Jay Corre, Modesto Brisenio, Dave Madden (ts); Ernie Small, Bob Achilles (bs); Jack Perciful (p); Dave Koonse, Terry Rosen, Guy Scalise, Dempsey Wright (g); Joe Comfort, Russ Phillips, Red Kelly (b); Charli Persip, Jackie Mills, Buddy Rich, Tony DeNicola, Jake Hanna (d). 59–3/64.

***** Harry's Delight**

Sounds Of Yesteryear DSOY 607 *James; personnel drawn from above listing.* 4/61–8/62.

***** 1964 Live! Holiday Ballroom, Chicago**

Jazz Hour JH-1001 *James; Buddy Rich (d); rest unlisted.* 64.

**** The Golden Trumpet Of Harry James**

London 820178-2 *James; rest unknown.* 68.

The Verve *Jazz Masters* compilation of some of the best of James's MGM tracks will be a revelation to any who thought the bandleader a swing-era relic. This was some of the best music of his career: excellent charts by Thad Jones, Ralph Burns (including two previously unheard ones) and Ernie Wilkins; an impeccable band enjoying a catholic choice of material, from 'Walkin'' to 'Cornet Chop Suey'; and James himself still without peer as a trumpet executant. His solos on 'I Surrender Dear' would be enough to defeat most rivals, and his delivery is tempered by a certain thoughtfulness.

A pair of shows from 1961–2 take up *Harry's Delight.* Most of these are familiar pieces from James's book of the day and they're played with great heart. The 1964 show was obviously a happy occasion too, with the band playing with real fire on some excellent charts and Rich firing everyone up from the drums. But the sound is very trebly, with a lot of top end that lends a shrillness to everything from the hi-hat downwards. Tune that out and anyone will enjoy.

The Golden Trumpet is pure Las Vegas. James reprises some of his old hits in front of a suitably faceless orchestra.

Jon Jang (born 1954)

PIANO

Originally Jang Jian Liang, Jang is a young Chinese-American who was first recognized when a member of Fred Ho's Afro-Asian Ensemble. He took up piano rather late and still has a fairly limited range as an instrumentalist – but in any case his main strength lies elsewhere, in composition and cultural activism. In 1987 he co-founded Asian Improv Records, devoted to what might realistically be called frontier music

*****(*) Self Defense!**

Soul Note 121203 *Jang; John Worley Jr (t, flhn); Jeff Cressman (tb, perc); Melecio Magdaluyo (as, ss, f, perc); Jim Norton (bcl, ss, f, dizi); Mark Izu (b, sheng); Anthony Brown (d, perc); Susan Hayase, James Frank Holder (perc).* 6/91.

*****(*) Tiananmen!**

Soul Note 121223 *Jang; Liu Qi-Chao (suona, erhu, sheng, v); Zhang Yan (guzheng); John Worley Jr (t, flhn); Jeff Cressman (tb); James Newton (f); Melecio Magdaluyo (as, ss, f); Francis Wong (ts, f); Jim Norton (cl, bcl, af); Mark Izu (b); Anthony Brown (perc).* 2/93.

It was widely assumed that the title of Jang's Arkestra was a reference to Sun Ra's intergalactic academy of musicians. In fact, it relates to the Pan African People's Arkestra, led by radical Californian composer Horace Tapscott. Like Tapscott, Jang is an activist. The pieces on *Self Defense!* relate to issues such as anti-Japanese violence in America, the demand for reparations for Japanese-Americans interned during the war, Jesse Jackson's pan-ethnic Rainbow Coalition. Even 'A Night In Tunisia' has a political resonance; Dizzy Gillespie was once put forward as a write-in candidate for the presidency. Jang gives it a huge programme that links it to 'The Butterfly Lovers Song' and Jang's own 'Never Give Up!'. The original pieces may depend too heavily on exclamation marks, but 'Concerto For Jazz Ensemble And Taiko' demonstrates Jang's ability to give large-scale structures a quietly appealing directness that doesn't depend on either volume or a ready-to-wear outfit of worthy slogans. Even in live performance (and this is a recording of a festival appearance in Seattle), there is no tendency to hector. There are fewer actual references to Asian music on *Self Defense!* than on *Tiananmen!*, a magnificent suite of pieces dedicated to the activists and martyrs of the Chinese democracy movement. Jang repeats the 'Butterfly Lovers Song' and calls repeatedly on Chinese folk-tunes, but the main influences are Charles Mingus (for his integration of polemical ideas with jazz) and Duke Ellington (particularly the later 'world music' suites); 'Come Sunday, June 4, 1989' contains an explicit homage, when Ellington's tune is played in counterpoint to Jang's theme by James Newton, a long-time supporter of the Asian jazz movement.

Jang's use of Asian instruments like the taiko drums on 'Concerto', the guzheng zither, the double-reeded suona, the two-stringed erhu and harmonica-like sheng is never purely for local effect. Frequently, as in 'Come Sunday', he exploits them to highlight a dramatic contrast between East and West, or to effect an integration between jazz and non-Western styles and concerns. The effect is less shambolic, more carefully marshalled than Ho's collective, and ultimately more satisfying.

*****(*) Two Flowers On A Stem**

Soul Note 121253 *Jang; James Newton (f); David Murray (ts, bcl); Chen Jiebing (erhu); Santi Debriano (b, Chinese gong); Billy Hart (d).* 6/95.

At last a group that is commensurate with Jang's gifts and which allows him to probe deeper into contemporary jazz while preserving his passionate interest in synthesizing Eastern and Western styles. The presence of Murray and Newton gives the music both gravity and a wonderful lightness of spirit, and there can rarely have been such a sanguine interpretation of Mingus's 'Meditation On Integration'. Most of the material is Jang's own, a suite of pieces dedicated to family members and friends, but there is also a closing reprise of the 'Butterfly Lovers Song', which is as exquisitely beautiful as the title-piece, dedicated to his mother.

***** Immigrant Suite No. 1**

Soul Note 121303 *Jang; Francis Wong (ts, f); Jim Norton (ss, af eng hn); Min Xiao-Fen (pipa); Wang Hong (erhu, guanzi, zhongu); Royal Hartigan (perc); Elliot Humberto Kavee (perc, clo); Genny Lim (v, perc).* 97.

Jang's passionate historical sense comes through strongly in this suite of pieces inspired by the life histories of Chinese immigrants to America. The overall tone of the piece is stoical rather than fiery, though there is an anger under the surface, expressed in free-form dissonant piano as much as in the texts read and sung by Genny Lim. Western and traditional Chinese instruments coexist reasonably easily. Recording quality is somewhat indifferent and there are distortions and fudged passages here and there which suggest that the whole set was done to a rather hasty timetable. And yet the music has a raw, unfinished power which is further testimony to Jang's ability to harness emotion very effectively.

***** Beijing Trio**

Asian Improv 0044 *Jang; Jiebing Chen (erhu); Max Roach (d).* 98.

The idea of mixing American jazz with oriental sounds wasn't new when the Beijing Trio was founded. Coltrane had done it, and Asian-Americans like Toshiko Akiyoshi had imported new sonorities and rhythms into bebop. Jang's instrument guarantees that he remains solidly allied to Western harmony, and the inclusion of Chen's erhu – basically a two-stringed fiddle – in place of contrabass adds no more than an unusual sound-colour to what is essentially a conventional piano trio. The key player is Roach, who always manages to sound multi-cultural, even when playing in a familiar jazz setting. Rhythmically, these tunes – 'Moon Over The Great Wall', 'Fallen Petals' and 'The Flowing Stream' – aren't so very far from what he might be doing anyway, but he bends to meet the context, as ever.

***** Self-Portrait**

Asian Improv 0050 *Jang (p solo).* 99.

Jang and producer Francis Wong founded Asian Improv as an outlet for some of the bright Asian-American talent that was surfacing in the '80s. This solo recording by the pianist (overseen by Wong) is a surprisingly modest statement, entirely devoid of apparent agenda and mostly couched in a conventional jazz idiom. Jang takes the opportunity to reprise his own 'Two Flowers On A Stem', touch base with Duke Ellington on 'Come Sunday' and show an individual touch on standard fare as romantic as 'Amazing Grace' and 'You'll Never Walk Alone'. Even a piece as seemingly coded as 'Chinese Sorrow Song For Paul Robeson' comes across as a gentle, bluesy threnody, by no means desolate or bereft. A gentle piano record with a few unusual touches; otherwise unsurprising.

***** River Of Life**

Asian Improv 0062 *Jang; David Murray (ts, bcl).* 9/98–2/01.

A fascinating East–West encounter that immediately reveals how much of each other's sensibility Jang and Murray share. The saxophonist is most convincing when he explores the lower reaches of his main horn and when he switches to bass clarinet. Jang's declamatory style alternates with a more delicate and impressionistic sound. There are two versions of 'Eleanor Bumpurs' (one of them live), passionate portraits of the late Johnny Dyani and Julius Hemphill and a two-part meditation on capital punishment, a matter of profound concern to Jang.

Guus Janssen (born 1951)

PIANO, HARPSICHORD

Dutch pianist who's investigated the spectrum of the keyboard repertoire and how it can be adapted to playing entirely free.

***** Pok**

Geestgronden 3 *Janssen; Paul Termos (as); Wim Janssen (d).* 1/88–7/89.

***** Harpsichord**

Geestgronden 7 *Janssen (hpd solo).* 90.

*****(*) Klankast**

Geestgronden 9 *Janssen (p solo).* 6/87–8/91.

*****(*) Lighter**

Geestgronden 11 *Janssen; Ernst Glerum (b); Wim Janssen (d).* 11/92–4/95.

****** Zwik**

Geestgronden 19 *As above.* 3/96–9/97.

Janssen's music is funny and accomplished. *Pok*, which starts with a dedication to Sandy Nelson and moves on through nods to boogie-woogie and swing time, tends to crash around various points, suggesting free jazz but always tied to a quite strict, formal aesthetic. The pianist's playing incorporates many styles, and Wim Janssen's drums are similarly diverse, but Termos's rather spindly alto parts could use an ounce more determination. The recording is rather distant. *Harpsichord* is a possibly unique example of solo free music on a keyboard that scarcely ever enters into the field. As with the previous disc, Janssen's taste runs to odd, wide-ranging ideas within a distinct formal grasp, and there are perhaps unsurprising echoes of the baroque repertory within an otherwise unpredictable record.

Klankast does much the same for the piano, though in a piece like 'Hi-Hat' Janssen seems to be back to guying the swing tradition. Some of the tunes run out of steam before they're done, and this set is perhaps not the one to try first. *Lighter*, on the other hand, is consistently good. Though pieced together from sessions over a three-year period, this is a more thorough-going exploration of jazz and free playing and how the two might work together. Janssen's use of silences, long form and satire makes the most of these sketched (not sketchy) frameworks and, when they get to a version of 'Lennie's Pennies', the connection between this kind of free playing and the Tristanoite school suddenly seems clear. Glerum and the other Janssen add a merry accompaniment.

This trio is surely his best set-up, because *Zwik* is a tremendous continuation. Janssen does nothing less than reinvent the piano-trio record with this one. The first piece, 'I Mean', sounds like Thelonious Monk having a go at 'The Song Is You' and not getting beyond the first few bars. After that, the pianist lights on bebop, swing, various classical traditions and whatever else he can find to make the music new. Every one of the 12 pieces is quite different from every other one – listen to 'Pollux' and follow that with 'Azuur' and you'll wonder if it's the same group playing. Glerum and Wim Janssen seem completely in tune with the pianist's cliffhanger choices, so nothing sounds wayward or merely cute. Brilliant. Guus has a new small-group CD which arrived just as we went to press – next time.

Lars Jansson (born 1951)

PIANO, KEYBOARDS

A frequent visitor to the studios from the late '70s onwards, Jansson is a charter member of the contemporary Swedish movement, though currently he spends much of his time teaching.

*****(*) Trio 84 / The Eternal Now**

Dragon DRCD 301 *Jansson; Lars Danielsson (b, clo); Anders Jormin (b); Anders Kjellberg (d).* 84–87.

***** A Window Towards Being**
Imogena IGCD 019 *Jansson; Brynjar Hoff (ob); Lars Danielsson (b); Anders Kjellberg (d).* 2/91.

***** Invisible Friends**
Imogena IGCD 055 *As above, except omit Hoff.* 1/95.

Jansson is an excellent post-bop pianist whose affection for Bill Evans's manner is wedded to an attractive way with melody in his writing: it means that his music comes out with a little more brightness than that of the typical Evans disciple. The fine *Trio 84* on Dragon is now back in print, coupled with the subsequent *The Eternal Now* in an attractive package. Far from the willowy impressionism one might expect, this was a vital and attacking trio (Danielsson subs for Jormin on the second set), lighting up all the instinctive lyricism of the leader by playing with unaffected brio on the likes of 'Längtans Berg' and 'Yanina'. 'To Bill Evans' is a muscular workout, not a weepy requiem, with Jansson carrying the improvisation on a Moog synthesizer. At the same time, Jansson isn't afraid to darken the harmonic substance of pieces such as 'At Once Always' and 'After The Storm'.

A Window Towards Being picks up where the earlier set left off. Hoff is used for instrumental colour on three atypically lightweight tracks; but the main interest is in the piano improvisations on Jansson's own originals. *Invisible Friends* is four years on and in the same impeccable vein. Here and there Jansson drifts off a little, but his playing partners pilot a firm rhythmic course that admits of no rambling. The portentousness of some of the titles seems to be nicely deflated by the penultimate one: 'I Have Nothing To Say And I Am Saying It'.

*****(*) The Time We Have**
Imogena IGCD 069 *Jansson; Lars Danielsson (b); Anders Kjellberg (d).* 3/96.

Jansson's note muses on the human lifespan, before getting on to the facts about the recording: as he dryly notes, it refers to 'the short amount of time we had to complete the recording', a studio booked only three hours before a flight to the next gig. Most of this is improvised from the germ of an idea. The trio is a long-standing unit at this point and can read each other's moves with no little skill. The result is a surprisingly focused session, relaxed yet free of time-wasting or noodling. Two standards are useful signposts. Danielsson comes to the fore in some lyric sketches where the bass is predominant.

*****(*) Ballads**
Imogena IGCD 092 *Jansson; Paolo Fresu (t); Johan Borgström (ts, f); Paul McCandless (cor); Brynjar Hoff (ob); Lars Danielsson, Christian Spering (b); Anders Kjellberg, Morten Lund (d).* 91–97.

This compilation of lyric pieces, culled from Jansson's various sessions for Imogena, is surely the best place to make his initial acquaintance. It points up his firm touch and fastidious manner and gathers in some of his most memorable tunes: 'More Human', 'Why Was I Left Under The Sky' and 'To The Mothers In Brazil' among them. With horn-players guesting on six out of 18 tracks, there's an attractive variation in delivery too.

*****(*) The Blue Pearl**
Phono Suecia PSCD 97 *Jansson; Lars Lindgren, Lennart Grahn, Hildegunn Öiseth, Jan Eliasson, Fredrik Norén (t); Bengt Ake Andersson, Christer Olofsson, Ralph Soovik (tb); Niclas Rydh (btb); Claes Lindqvist (ss, as); Niklas Robertsson (as); Ove Ingmarsson (ts, ss); Mikael Karlsson (ts, f); Erik Norström (ts); Jan Forslund (bs); Ulf Wakenius (g); Yasuhito Mori (b); Anders Kjellberg (d); Jacob Andersen (perc).* 6/96.

*****(*) One Poem, One Painting**
Imogena IGCD 074 *As above except add Steen Raahauge (perc), omit Lindqvist, Wakenius, Andersen.* 6/98.

Beautifully played by the Bohuslän Big Band, western Sweden's premier jazz orchestra, these scores by Jansson smoothly translate his trio style to the bigger context. Good tunes, lively voicings, crisp rhythms: Jansson is one writer at least who goes against what has become something of a cliché of Scandinavian brooding and gloom. If anything, the composer's pieces have the heft and swing of American big-band writing, and a piece such as 'A Cup Of Mintzer-Tea', on the first record, is a clever take on Bob Mintzer's methods in the idiom. Naturally, he has a crack team of soloists on hand, many familiar from their own records. The second set is a collection of pieces in dedication to the 500th aniversary of Uddevalla, which is home town to both Jansson and the Big Band, but either disc will give much pleasure.

Joseph Jarman (born 1937)

SAXOPHONES, OTHER REEDS, FLUTE

He grew up in Pine Bluff, Arkansas, but found himself serendipitously in Chicago at a moment when the very foundations of jazz were being rethought. He worked with Muhal Richard Abrams and made the acquaintance of Roscoe Mitchell, playing Eric Dolphy-influenced saxophone in Mitchell's jazz group. He is best known, though, for his work with the Art Ensemble Of Chicago, for which his needle-sharp tone and vivid alternation of free and melodic ideas were a key element.

***** Song For**
Delmark DE-410 *Jarman; Bill Brimfield (t); Fred Anderson (ts); Christopher Gaddy (p, mar); Charles Clark (b); Thurman Barker, Steve McCall (d).* 10 & 12/66.

***** As If It Were The Seasons**
Delmark DE-417 *Jarman; John Jackson (t); Fred Anderson, John Stubblefield (ts); Lester Lashley, Joel Brandon (f); Richard Abram (p, ob); Charles Clark (b, clo, koto); Thurman Barker (perc); Sherri Scott (v).* 68.

Jarman is, depending on your viewpoint, either the quintessential voice of the AEOC or else its squarest peg. He was the first to leave the Ensemble in the '90s and his solo work has assumed more significance, even if many of the records feel locked-in as documents of their time. *Song For* is relatively standard AACM fare, intercut with neo-Dada recitations and characterized by a lack of formal shape. The supporting performers, with the exception of the two drummers, are not always up to scratch, though Clark produces some wonderfully sonorous bass on 'Adam's Rib', which certainly benefits considerably from CD transfer. The long tracks – 'Non-Cognitive Aspects Of The City', 'Song For' and a second and longer unissued take of Fred Anderson's 'Little Fox Run' with its skittering marimba patterns – pall slightly on repeated hearings. Of great documentary and historical significance, though unlikely to effect any dramatic conversions.

As If It Were The Seasons was made some 18 months later: involving many of the same musicians, it feels like a direct continuation, and the title-piece exemplifies Jarman's particular blending of lyricism, free space, drifting time and occasional bursts of intensity. At this distance, the records feel like inadequate episodes from what should have been a comprehensive setting-down of this ensemble's work, but on their own terms they retain an elusive, somewhat mysterious attraction.

***** Together Alone**

Delmark DE 428 *Jarman; Anthony Braxton (as, cbcl, f, perc, v).* 12/71.

A rather disappointing showing from two reed masters. Braxton's compositions seem mysterious to Jarman, who noodles frenziedly whenever he loses his place, while Braxton seems unwilling to listen to what his partner is doing. There are some fine moments on the opening title-track (which recalls the standard 'Alone Together', a favourite duo vehicle) and on the tiny 'Morning', which is the best track, redeemed by its freshness and immediacy of language. Otherwise, though, a less than successful encounter.

***** Egwu-Anwu**

India Navigation 1033 2CD *Jarman; Famoudou Don Moye (d).* 1/77.

Generously spread across two CDs, this duet between two musicians who already knew each other's work and methods very well has little surprise but is enjoyable as a mobile, colourful, sometimes joyful encounter. Jarman plays three saxophones, two flutes, conch and vibes along the way, and the favourite theme, 'Ohnedaruth', offers some of his most intense tenor-playing. Like so much AACM work, this feels as if it belongs to another time and place, but at least it's history as entertainment.

Keith Jarrett (born 1945)

PIANO, ORGAN, SOPRANO SAXOPHONE, OTHER INSTRUMENTS

It's often forgotten by those who wish to do down Keith Jarrett's jazz credentials that he was a member of the unimpeachable Messengers before he joined Charles Lloyd's crossover quartet and long before he began to experiment with long-form piano improvisation. The young Pennsylvanian was, like Chick Corea, something of a child prodigy. He learned his craft in the Boston area. Jarrett is a restless experimenter whose more extravagant flights seem to have won uncritical acclaim while his more straightforward work is overlooked. His standards trio of the '80s and '90s has rewritten the American songbook every bit as thoroughly as Jarrett has reworked the idiom of jazz piano.

***** Life Between The Exit Signs / El Juicio**

Collectables COL CD 6254 *Jarrett; Dewey Redman (ts); Charlie Haden (b); Paul Motian (d).* 5/67, 7/71.

***** Restoration Ruin**

Collectables COL CD 6274 *Jarrett (all instruments); string quartet.* 3/68.

****(*) Somewhere Before**

Atlantic 7567 81455 *Jarrett; Charlie Haden (b); Paul Motian (d).* 8/68.

****** El Juicio (The Judgement)**

Atlantic 7567 80783-3 *Jarrett; Dewey Redman (ts); Charlie Haden (b); Paul Motian (d).* 7/71.

***** The Mourning Of A Star**

Atlantic 8122 75355-2 *Jarrett; Charlie Haden (b); Paul Motian (d).* 71.

****** Foundations: The Keith Jarrett Anthology**

Rhino R2 71593 *Jarrett; Chuck Mangione (t); Joe Farrell, Hubert Laws, Charles Lloyd (f); Frank Mitchell, Jim Pepper, Dewey Redman (ts); George Benson, Sam Brown (g); Gary Burton (vib); Ron Carter, Charlie Haden, Reggie Johnson, Cecil McBee, Steve Swallow (b); Art Blakey, Bill Goodwin, Bob Moses, Paul Motian (d); Airto Moreira (perc).* 66–75.

Now nearly 60, Jarrett is a senior figure, and some kind of revised perspective seems in order. Inevitably, for an artist of his range and ambition, he divides critical opinion wildly and is himself, as every great artist must be, wildly inconsistent. The sheer momentum of early success has allowed him to experiment freely, but it has also allowed an unusual and not always desirable licence to experiment in public. (Many artists might have attempted the material documented on *Spirits*, below; few would have expected to see it make the shops.)

It's tempting to suggest that the essential Jarrett is to be found in the solo performances and that these are the place to begin. He has now, though, reached the position where there is more than one essential Jarrett, and it is worthwhile backtracking a little. The appearance of *Foundations* and now the re-emergence of Jarrett's original Atlantic recordings make this possible. The compilation is a remarkably modest selection, just two discs to cover the seven years from his tough New York apprenticeship to the much-underrated and very ambitious Atlantic session, *El Juicio*, with the Redman/Haden/Motian quartet. It remains one of the high points of his career. The joyous countrified swing of 'Gypsy Moth' and 'Toll Road' could hardly be more infectious, at the opposite remove to the dour atmosphere of 'El Juicio' itself, a strange, brooding tone-poem, or indeed to the experimental melodism of 'Piece For Ornette'. It exists in two forms, one at nine and a quarter minutes, the other at 12 seconds! A sly nudge from Jarrett: this is all it's about, this little idea, but see what we do with it!

Collectables have put out a strange but appealing array of material over the years. Pairing Jarrett's early *Restoration Ruin* with the Art Ensemble Of Chicago's *Bap-Tizum* is a little strange, but it is good to have this early example of multi-instrumentalism back in the catalogue. The pieces are all very short, sometimes almost perfunctory, but there is no mistaking Jarrett's gifts and, as an exercise in instrumental eclecticism, it is a much more appealing and convincing performance than the later *Spirits*.

The other Collectables set brings together *El Juicio* and the fine early trio, *Life Between The Exit Signs*. Interesting to compare this unit with the later 'Standards Trio'. It is immediately apparent how much more straightforwardly rhythmic Jarrett sounds in 1967, but as yet how uncomfortably co-ordinated he is with the group. 'Lisbon Stomp' is a cracking opener. The two tunes called 'Love No. 1 and No. 2' are extremely individual and 'Life ...' itself has the distinctive jazz/pop/country feel one associates with Jarrett. What is as yet unformed is his ability to shape a group as if it were a single instrument compounded of different personalities, rather than a contending alliance bent on similar ends.

The early *Somewhere Before* is for trio, reuniting the line-up that made *Life Between The Exit Signs*. Heavily rock-influenced and still reminiscent of the methodology of the Charles Lloyd Quartet, of which Jarrett had been a member, it includes a version of Bob Dylan's 'My Back Pages' and two delightfully cadenced rags. Recorded live and slightly rough in texture, it has a freshness of approach that Jarrett quickly lost and was slow to regain.

The Mourning Of A Star is an odd, offbeat record that never quite fixes itself in the mind. Returning to it is both a surprise and a slight disappointment. Its main problem is a bittiness that was presumably supposed to cohere into something larger and grander. Good though it is to have the Atlantics back in catalogue again, for many purchasers the compilation set will be enough. What is immediately striking, listening to Jarrett play a standard, 'Smoke Gets In Your Eyes', in Bob Moses's group behind the gruff, squally tenor of Jim Pepper, is how fully formed he already sounds. 'Love No. 3', nominally a Charles Lloyd Quartet cut, is actually a Jarrett solo, played in front of a first-house crowd at the Fillmore West; again, it's the same voice, not even in embryo, but already working out its own priorities. Go back a further year (the tracks aren't in strict chronological order on the disc, either) and listen to the 21-year-old hold his own with Art Blakey, albeit in a non-vintage Messengers. It all reinforces the impression of a young man who came of age with his artistic and creative agenda already in place and who has spent the last 30 years or so working through all of its ramifications and by-ways.

He is perhaps the most sophisticated technician working today outside the 'straight' repertoire (and he has, of course, crossed that boundary, too). The early piano style – the Lloyd group apart – is less obviously influenced by rock and country music than by the jazz mainstream, but then he was playing for other leaders at this stage and was required to do so in the idiom, a discipline that has paid colossal dividends in the recent 'Standards Trio'. Lloyd's influence and tolerance shouldn't be underestimated; that extraordinary group was clearly the catalyst. From 'Love No. 3' to the closing selection on disc two, the improvised 'Pardon My Rags', there is plentiful evidence of Jarrett's gifts as an 'instant composer', an instinctive melodist who seems able to find a match and a harmonic logic for almost any musical given. As his premisses become more searching, then with almost Wagnerian logic the improvisations grow proportionately longer and more intense. He's still capable, even at his most intense, of throwing in cheesy little songs or marking time with big, time-killing exercises straight out of h&c class at the conservatory. There is also a slightly fluffy track under Airto's leadership and some sub-standard material with Gary Burton, a partnership that might have been better represented.

There is an unavoidable problem with an output of this bulk – a cash problem if nothing else. ECM have arguably released too much material, more than 50 hours' worth in the present catalogue, of which perhaps only one-third has the stamp of greatness. It's a fascinating story all the same and, for newcomers or seasoned enthusiasts alike, *Foundations* is an excellent way of getting up to speed.

★★★★ Expectations

Columbia/Legacy C2K 65900 2CD *Jarrett; Dewey Redman (ts, perc); Sam Brown (g); Charlie Haden (b); Paul Motian (d); Airto Moreira (perc); brass; strings.* 9 & 10/71.

Not for the first time, Columbia hesitated about how to deal with a major and challenging artist, and Jarrett was dropped less than a month after this record was released, even though they are now claiming it as his breakthrough disc. Perhaps inevitable on both counts, given corporate expectations at the time and recent rewrites of the label's own history, but a dismal miscall, given the quality of this record, which is now restored to its full length over two CDs and with accurate track-listing.

There are few better places to sample Jarrett's uncanny ability to make disparate musical ideas work together. It's possible to argue for *Expectations*' breakthrough status rather more disinterestedly by pointing to the pianist's increasingly confident synthesis of jazz ('Circular Letter'), rock ('Sundance'), gospel ('There Is A Road') and Latin ('Common Mama') themes into a passionate, occasionally ecstatic mix. Some of the more extravagant freedoms relate closely to his work with a man who stayed with Columbia a while longer. Jarrett learned – or allowed himself – to play free on Miles Davis's *Live–Evil* and there is ample evidence of that here. Redman plays on only half the tracks, Brown on six; Jarrett plays soprano saxophone in addition to piano, but also (and despite Columbia's silence on the matter) organ and percussion. The new issue restores the strings piece, 'Visions', and revises the running order to its original form, ending on 'There Is A Road (God's River)'. Much as we liked the revised order, this makes better sense. Everything else now leads up to it. The logic of the session is impeccable, with seemingly abstract tonalities deployed chorally, much like the raw and unvarnished singing of the Black Church, and yet always anchored in something much more formal and familiar. 'Nomads' is the only really long track and it – appropriately, perhaps – meanders quite a bit, its climaxes a little hollow relative to what now follows. The best of the session lies in well-crafted tunes and textures. The addition of guitar changes the feel more than a little. Brown wasn't yet or wasn't here doing the single-note sustains that he made an integral part of Paul Motian's group sound but, even when playing the distorted chords typical of fusion music at the time, he sounds wholly convincing. It's taken a while to establish this record at the heart of Jarrett's output. This issue, with its generous documentation, surely does that.

★★★ Rutya And Daitya

ECM 513776-2 *Jarrett; Jack DeJohnette (d).* 5/71.

It will sound like a slice of bland promotional puff to say that here DeJohnette plays like the piano man he also is and that Jarrett plays with a percussive edge which is not always heard in his work. This isn't so much a matter of timbre and attack as of general approach. Jack is one of the most musical drummers ever, and his phrasing constantly recalls his other instrument. Jarrett varies his playing accordingly, and the result is a very happy collaboration, much stronger with every hearing.

CORE COLLECTION

★★★★ The Köln Concert

ECM 810067-2 2CD *As above.* 1/75.

This is perhaps Jarrett's best and certainly his most popular record. ECM has been dining out or, to be fairer, recording others on the proceeds for two decades. Made in conditions of exceptional difficulty – not least an audibly unsatisfactory piano – Jarrett not for the first time makes a virtue of adversity, carving out huge slabs of music with a rare intensity. His instrument does sound off-puttingly bad-tempered, but his concentration on the middle register throughout the performance has been a characteristic of his work throughout his career.

★★★(★) Facing You
ECM 827132-2 *Jarrett (p solo).* 11/71.
★★★(★) Solo Concerts
ECM 827747-2 2CD *As above.* 3 & 7/73.
★★★ Spheres
ECM 827463-2 *Jarrett (org solo).* 9/76.
★★(★) Staircase
ECM 827337-2 2CD *Jarrett (p solo).* 11/76.
★★ Sacred Hymns Of G. I. Gurdjieff
ECM 1174 *As above.* 11/79.
★★★ Sun Bear Concerts
ECM 843028-2 6CD *As above.* 3/80.
★★ Invocations
ECM 1201/2 2CD *Jarrett (p, pipe org, ss solo).* 7–10/80.
★★★ Concerts
ECM 827286-2 *Jarrett (p solo).* 5 & 6/81.
★★ Book Of Ways
ECM 931396-2 2CD *Jarrett (clavichord solo).* 7/86.
★★(★) Spirits
ECM 829467-2 2CD *Jarrett (assorted instruments).* 4/87.
★★ Dark Intervals
ECM 847342-2 *Jarrett (p solo).* 10/88.
★★ Paris Concert
ECM 839173-2 *As above.* 10/88.
★★★(★) Vienna Concert
ECM 513437-2 *As above.* 7/91.

There was an uneasy giantism in Jarrett's work of the later '70s, culminating in the release of the infamous *Sun Bear Concerts*, hours of densely personal piano improvisations in a 10-LP box, and only slightly less cumbersome on CD. It's clear that these episodically remarkable performances occupied a very significant, slightly chastened place in Jarrett's rather lonely and dogged self-exploration, but that doesn't automatically make for good music. Without being excessively Dr Johnsonish ('It is not done well; but you are surprised to find it done at all') about music so naked and questing, one wonders how much of the critical excitement it garnered was simply a response to its size and to Jarrett's brass neck in releasing product on a scale usually only accorded the great and the dead.

The jury needn't stay out quite so long on the preposterous *Spirits*, a double (of course) album of overdubs on a bizarre variety of ethnic instruments. To be fair, the album has its serious proponents (including Jarrett's biographer, Ian Carr) but, for all its healing and restorative intent and putative impact on the music that followed, it occupies only a marginal place in Jarrett's output. Other offences to be taken briefly into consideration are the thin *Gurdjieff* essays, the jangly clavichord improvisations on *Book Of Ways* (which is also burdened by the fact that the clavichord is an inherently unpleasant instrument to listen to at any length) and the dismal *Invocations*, executed in part on the same organ as *Spheres* but lacking that album's extraordinary experimental intensity and concentration. *Spheres* derives from the double-LP set, *Hymns Spheres*. It is by no stretch of the imagination a jazz record, but it does belong to another great improvisatory tradition, and it may be significant that, in contrast to the critical spanking it received in the United States, the album was favourably reviewed in Europe, though without quite enough leverage to see it transferred in full to compact disc. A great shame. Jarrett's approach to the unfamiliar keyboards and their associated pedals and stops is quite remarkable and generates one of his finest ever performances, easily the equal in conception and intelligence of the best-selling *Köln Concert*.

The Bremen and Lausanne sets on *Solo Concerts* are almost as good. Jarrett's first multi-volume set was extraordinarily well received on its release and stands up particularly well now (by contrast, *Facing You* seems slightly time-locked for some reason). These are friendlier, less intense performances than the *Köln* sides, but no less inventive for that, exploring Jarrett's characteristic blend of popular and 'high' forms. The 1981 *Concerts* was also recorded in Germany and in slightly easier circumstances (Jarrett suffered agonizing back pain throughout the Bremen *Solo Concert*) and perhaps as a consequence there's far less tension in the music; this is the surviving half of a two-LP release from Germany, of which the Munich half was probably better. That same quality of tension is noticeable on both *Facing You*, the earliest of the solo recordings and the best place to get a feel of Jarrett's characteristic method before tackling the multi-volume sets, and *Staircase*, where he seems to range across a multiplicity of idioms (many of them identifiably classical rather than popular) with no apparent urgency.

Much has been made of the cohesion and unity of Jarrett's solo performances. They are often likened to multi-movement suites rather than collections of discontinuous tunes or numbers. This is certainly true of *Facing You*, which shares with the *Köln Concert* a satisfying roundness; it certainly isn't true of *Staircase* or of the recent *Dark Intervals* and *Paris Concert*. The former is a moody, sonorous affair, recorded live in Tokyo and interspersed with thunderously disciplined applause. Apart from 'Fire Dance' – track titles are rare or *ex post facto* in the improvised performances – the music has a very formal, concertizing solemnity. The *Paris Concert*, by contrast, is lively at least but is also disturbingly predictable. The idiomatic shifts have become mannered almost to the point of self-parody, and there's a slightly cynical quality to Jarrett's apparent manipulation of audience expectations. The notorious grunting and moaning, with which he signals ecstasy and effort, have never been more intrusive.

By the turn of the '90s Jarrett's solo concerts had their own terms of reference; it is hard to imagine where one might find a critical language larger than the music itself. The *Vienna Concert* is at once more formal and more coherent than the disappointing *Paris Concert*. If there is a dominant influence it is Bach, who is explicitly (though possibly unconsciously) quoted at a number of points, as is Shostakovich, whom Jarrett has also been recording. It opens with a quiet, almost hymnic theme which develops very slowly over sombre pedals for just over 20 minutes, before opening out into a broken-tempo country theme that still preserves the original material in inverted form. The second and third pieces seem to develop material from the first, but in such a way that one wonders if they have been released in the order of the original concert. Long-standing Jarrett fans will find all the required elements in place; newcomers may find this more approachable than *Köln* or *Sun Bear*, but only if they're not put off by the classical resonances of the opening movement.

★★★ Fort Yawuh
Impulse! 547 966-2 *Jarrett; Dewey Redman (ts, perc); Charlie Haden (b); Paul Motian (d); Danny Johnson (perc).* 2/73.

★★★(★) **The Survivor's Suite**
ECM 827131-2 *Jarrett; Dewey Redman (ts, perc); Charlie Haden (b); Paul Motian (d).* 4/76.

★(★) **Eyes Of The Heart**
ECM 825476-2 *As above.* 5/76.

Jarrett's American quartet probably never reached the heights or achieved the almost telepathic understanding of the European group responsible for the classic *Belonging*, below. The addition of Dewey Redman to the basic trio on *Fort Yawuh* gives that album a dark power; the CD includes unedited performances of all tracks and the addition of one more from the session, the long 'Roads Travelled, Roads Veiled', which previously appeared on *Impulse! Artists On Tour*.

Survivor's Suite, two years further down the road, is a masterpiece, with the quartet pulling together on an ambitiously large-scale piece, each member contributing whole-heartedly and passionately. By the sharpest of contrasts, *Eyes Of The Heart*, a live exploration of much the same material, is a near-disaster. The original release was as a double LP with one blank side. What it documents – and the format is in every way symbolic – is the final break-up of a rather fissile band; Dewey Redman contributes scarcely anything, and the album ends with Jarrett playing alone.

★★★(★) **The Impulse Years: 1973–1974**
Impulse! 237 5CD *Jarrett; Dewey Redman (ts, musette, perc); Sam Brown (g); Charlie Haden (b); Paul Motian (d); Danny Johnson, Guilherme Franco (perc).* 73, 74.

★★★(★) **Mysteries: The Impulse Years 1975–1976**
Impulse! IMPD 4 149 4CD *As above, omit Brown, Johnson.* 12/75, 10/76.

Jarrett is too big a commodity to lose and having seen him go on to world-shaking demographics at ECM, Impulse! were anxious to milk their investment. The five-CD set brings together an augmented *Fort Yawuh, Treasure Island, Death and the Flower* and the little-known *Backhand*. The alternate takes are often illuminating, but it's the unedited version of 'Roads Travelled, Roads Veiled', originally from the *Fort Yawuh* session, that is most interesting. Alternates of 'De Drums', 'Death and the Flower' and '(If The) Misfits (Wear It)' are primarily of interest to collectors.

Superseding the earlier *Silence* compilation, which put together most of *Bop-Be* and *Byablue*, the handsome *Mysteries* also includes two slightly earlier and better albums, *Shades* and the title-disc, and a significant amount of previously unissued material from the sessions. The albums were recorded in pairs, in December 1975 and October 1976, and it's quite clear that by the later date the group, always more volatile than the 'European quartet' reviewed below, was now in a pretty terminal state, which Jarrett has likened to an attempt to save a rocky marriage. It's always a mistake to personalize or psychologize music, but the contrast between Jarrett's joyous, sometimes bumptious, and still country-tinged vamps and improvisations and Redman's sour-toned and often rather grouchy solos on the later sessions is very striking. The more important difference, though, is that for the October 1976 studios Jarrett very largely ceded writing credits to Haden, Redman, Margot Jarrett and, in particular, Motian. Though he and the drummer clearly hold a good deal of musical territory in common, Jarrett doesn't sound much at ease on 'Yallah' or 'Byablue', and his soloing is schematic and at times unwontedly laboured.

The big plus on these transfers is being able to hear Haden in full voice and in a sensible stereo position, unexpectedly foregrounded and bridging saxophone and piano with great dexterity. The 11 unreleased tracks are of mixed interest. The unissued version of 'Everything That Lives Laments' (*Mysteries*) stretches to more than a quarter of an hour without adding anything of substance, but there is much to ponder in three versions of 'Rose Petals' from *Shades*, flawed but subtly modulated performances in each case.

★★★★ **Belonging**
ECM 829115-2 *Jarrett; Jan Garbarek (ts, ss); Palle Danielsson (b); Jon Christensen (d).* 4/74.

★★★(★) **My Song**
ECM 821406-2 *As above.* 1/77.

★★★ **Personal Mountains**
ECM 837361-2 *As above.* 4/79.

★★★ **Nude Ants**
ECM 829119-2 2CD *As above.* 5/79.

Both *Belonging* and *My Song* have also been covered in the entry on Jan Garbarek, because the saxophonist's contribution to both albums seems particularly significant. The 'European Quartet' was probably the most sympathetic grouping Jarrett ever assembled and *Belonging* in particular is a superb album, characterized by some of the pianist's most open and joyous playing on record; his double-time solo on 'The Windup' is almost Tatum-like in its exuberance and fluency. The country-blues feel of 'Long As You Know You're Living Yours' is a confident reflection of his music roots. The ballads 'Blossom', 'Solstice' and the title-piece – the first two powerfully extended, the last uncharacteristically brief – are remarkable by any standards; Garbarek's slightly out-of-tune opening statement on 'Solstice' and Danielsson's subsequent solo are masterful, while Jarrett's own split chords accentuate the mystery and ambiguity of the piece.

Nude Ants is a live set from New York City (the title is a metathesis of the bouncing 'New Dance'). It's a valuable documentation of the European Quartet outside the studio, but the performances are somewhat below par and Garbarek (who admits dissatisfaction with the performances) sounds alternately forced and diffident. Recording quality is also disappointing and well below ECM's usual standard. *Personal Mountains* sounds very much better, but the playing has a sleepy, jet-lagged quality (it was taped in Tokyo) that blurs the impact of the title-piece and the momentarily beautiful 'Prism', 'Oasis' and 'Innocence'.

★★(★) **In The Light**
ECM 835011-2 2CD *Jarrett; Ralph Towner (g); string quartet; brass quintet; strings.* 73.

★★(★) **Luminessence**
ECM 839307-2 *Jarrett; Jan Garbarek (ts, ss); strings.* 4/74.

★★(★) **Arbour Zena**
ECM 825592-2 *Jarrett; Jan Garbarek (ts, ss); Charlie Haden (b); strings.* 10/75.

★(★) **The Celestial Hawk**
ECM 829370-2 *Jarrett; symphony orchestra.* 3/80.

If it's every jazzer's dream (it was certainly Charlie Parker's) to play with strings, then it seems hard to deny Jarrett his moment. Hard, but not impossible. These mostly sound like the indulgences of a star figure unchecked by sensible aesthetic criteria and doubtless encouraged by sheer bankability. And why not? The *Köln Concert* is still shifting units like a life-jacket sale before the Flood.

Jarrett would doubtless argue that critical sniffiness about these albums is the result of sheer prejudice, the jazz community's snotty, elbows-out attitude to anything scored or on the grand scale and, on the other hand, the sheer exclusivism of the 'straight' music cartel. *Arbour Zena* and *Luminessence* contain some beautiful moments, but what an opportunity missed for a stripped-down duo with Garbarek. The overall mood of *Arbour Zena* is elegiac and slightly lorn, and the strings melt like marshmallows over some of the sharper flavours; the later album has simply been left cooking too long.

The earlier *In The Light* was a composer's showcase and, as such, a forerunner of ECM's much-admired New Series. The individual works struggle to stay in focus, but as a whole the album has surprising consistency. *The Celestial Hawk* is pure tosh ... with some nice bits.

★★★(★) **Standards: Volume 1**
ECM 811966-2 *Jarrett; Gary Peacock (b); Jack DeJohnette (d).* 1/83.

★★★ **Changes**
ECM 817436-2 *As above.* 1/83.

★★★★ **Standards: Volume 2**
ECM 825015-2 *As above.* 7/85.

★★★ **Standards Live**
ECM 827827-2 *As above.* 7/86.

★★★(★) **Still Live**
ECM 835008-2 2CD *As above.* 10/86.

★★★(★) **Standards In Norway**
ECM 521717-2 *As above.* 10/89.

★★(★) **Tribute**
ECM 847135-2 2CD *As above.* 10/89.

★★★(★) **Changeless**
ECM 839618-2 *As above.* 4/90.

★★★★ **The Cure**
ECM 849650-2 *As above.* 4/90.

One of the less fair subtexts to the widespread critical acclaim for Jarrett's 'Standards Trio' is the implication that he is at last toeing the line, conforming to an established repertoire, finally renouncing the extravagances of the *Köln Concert* and the other multi-volume sets.

In practice, nothing could be much further from the truth. Jarrett's approach to standards is nothing if not individual; for all his obvious respect and affection for the material, he consistently goes his own way. The main difference from the solo performances is the obvious one: Peacock's firmly harmonic bass and DeJohnette's astonishingly imaginative drumming adjust his improvisatory instincts to the degree that they simplify his articulation and attack and redirect his attention to the chords and the figuration of melody.

It doesn't always come off. There are moments on *Standards: Volume 1* which are simply flat and uninspired, as on 'God Bless The Child'. *Volume 2* immediately feels more confident. The themes, which are less familiar anyway, are no longer an embarrassment; Jarrett clearly feels able to leave them implicit a little longer. That is even more obvious on the fine *Standards Live* and *Still Live*, though it's a pity – from the point of view of comparison – that Jarrett hasn't repeated any of the studio titles. The only occasion where this is possible is on the strangely patchy *Tribute*, which repeats 'All The Things You Are' from *Standards: Volume 1*. The later version is more oblique, but also simpler. Like the rest of the tracks, it is intended as a *hommage*, in this case to Sonny Rollins, which is pretty typical of the curious but doubtless very conscious matching of standards and dedicatees. Typically, perhaps, Jarrett adds two of his own compositions to an already rather overblown and diffuse set, as if to inscribe himself more legibly into the tradition he is exploring and rediscovering.

In that same vein, the 'Standards Trio' hasn't limited itself to existing repertoire. *Changes* and *Changeless* contain original material which is deeply subversive (though also respectfully aware) of the whole tradition of jazz as a system of improvisation on 'the changes'. Typically, Jarrett invests the term with quite new aesthetic and philosophical considerations. On *Changeless*, there are no chord progressions at all; the trio improvises each section in a single key, somewhat in the manner of an Indian raga. The results are impressive and thought-provoking, like everything Jarrett has attempted.

★★★(★) **Bye Bye Blackbird**
ECM 513074-2 *Jarrett; Gary Peacock (b); Jack DeJohnette (d).* 10/91.

★★★(★) **At The Deer Head Inn**
ECM 517720-2 *Jarrett; Gary Peacock (b); Paul Motian (d).* 9/92.

Bye Bye Blackbird is Jarrett's tribute to the late Miles Davis, with whom he worked in the '60s and about whom in later years he had made some decidedly snitty comments. It is certainly startling to hear him talk in a rare ECM liner-note about Miles's 'purity of desire' (the phrase, or a version of it, is repeated) when the burden of on- and off-stage comments in the '80s had been that Miles had seriously compromised the music – to electricity, to mere fashion, and so on.

Taken on its own merits, *Bye Bye Blackbird* is a wonderful record. The choice of material is refreshingly unobvious (how often is Oliver Nelson's 'Butch And Butch' covered?) and immaculately played, as this group always plays. The two originals, 'For Miles' and a coda 'Blackbird, Bye Bye', are as intensely felt as anything Jarrett has done in recent years, and the level of abstraction that has crept back into the music is well judged and unobtrusive. DeJohnette performs wonders, changing metre subtly with almost every bar on 'Straight No Chaser'. An excellent record, beautifully packaged. What one wouldn't have given for an LP-sized print of Catherine Pichonnier's magnificent silhouette cover-photo.

It's a recurrent craving of superstars that they should turn their backs on the big halls and all the paraphernalia of stardom and play small venues again. The Dear Head Inn in Allentown, Pennsylvania, was the scene of Keith Jarrett's first serious gig on piano. It has now sustained a jazz policy for more than 40 years, a dedication passed on by the original owners to their daughter and son-in-law. In order to relaunch the club in 1992, Jarrett agreed to play a gig there, taking along Paul Motian, with whom he had not worked since the time of *Silence*. Motian brings a lighter and more flowing pulse to the music than DeJohnette. The obvious point of comparison is 'Bye Bye Blackbird', which glides along without wires or other obvious support for more than ten minutes, a beautiful, airborne performance. This might almost be a second tribute to Miles. It opens with a superb reading of 'Solar', but then follows with skilful readings of 'Basin Street Blues' and Jaki Byard's

'Chandra', two pieces that belong to an entirely different musical realm, but which take on a similar coloration to the Miles tune. As so often, Peacock is more forceful and less complex out of the studio. He drives 'You And The Night And The Music', giving it a pugnacious edge one doesn't normally hear. It seems unlikely that Jarrett will ever need to go back to bar-room gigs, but here he's demonstrated his ability to work a small audience with powerful, unpretentious jazz. Anyone who has never heard him could hardly be better advised than to start with one of these.

****** At The Blue Note: The Complete Recordings**
ECM 527638-2 6CD *As above.* 6/94.

This is an extraordinary piece of documentation, two sets from each of three consecutive nights at the New York club. It might be considered warts-and-all but for the fact that there are no warts. Nor is there any repetition or aimless noodling. It's fascinating, given sufficient time and attention, to hear Jarrett import ideas – harmonic resolutions, phrases, improbable interval jumps like elevenths and thirteenths – from one piece to another on different nights. As an insight into how spontaneously creative he can be, it is unparalleled even in this extraordinary discography.

It was played, one suspects, with the recording very much in mind. One might almost prefer more repetition of tunes, but he goes his own individual way, leaning a little more than previously on top-ten standards – 'Autumn Leaves', 'Alone Together', 'On Green Dolphin Street' – and on jazz repertory pieces like Rollins's 'Oleo'. There may ultimately be a scaled-down compilation from this, but if you can afford the cash and patience to get the full set, don't hesitate for a moment.

*****(*) La Scala**
ECM 537268-2 *Jarrett (p solo).* 2/95.

There were already rumours of ill-health at this stage, over and beyond Jarrett's chronic lower-back problems. A certain weary simplicity creeps into this immaculately recorded solo set, which is certainly the best for some time. Jarrett's improvisations are as long and as densely textured as ever, but there is a modesty and philosophical calm about the music which seems new. The second part of 'La Scala', the generic title for the two main pieces, has outbreaks of quiet violence, but nothing that doesn't have its own resolution. The instrument is immaculate, warm and full-voiced. As so often, Jarrett encores with 'Over The Rainbow', a touchingly uncomplicated performance that will stand comparison with anyone's cherished private C90.

***** Tokyo '96**
ECM 539955-2 *Jarrett; Gary Peacock (b); Jack DeJohnette (d).* 3/96.

The story continues, unstaunchable, maddeningly indulgent and selflessly brilliant by turns. There are moments of pure genius here, like the tiny treble figures on 'Autumn Leaves' or the bass vamp that underpins 'My Funny Valentine', but the overall impression is of low-key predictability. Jarrett has always exposed his own creative facility to new challenges, but this group now sounds too comfortable with its language. Interesting to compare it with the Haden/Motian line-up of years gone by, where beauty of form never precluded enterprise and a hint of danger.

****** The Melody At Night, With You**
ECM 547949-2 *Jarrett (p solo).* 98.

And just when you thought the story would simply run '... and so on', Jarrett pops up with a record of fragile magnificence, a sequence of filigreed songs from a common musical past. Hearing him do 'My Wild Irish Rose' and 'Someone To Watch Over Me' back to back is to hear a musician who recognizes no tension between improvisation and 'tradition', between the recalled and the intuitive. It is a quite simply magnificent record, swinging in a way that Jarrett has rarely before been swinging ('I Got It Bad And That Ain't Good'), and sweetly melodic ('Shenandoah'). The totality of his work for ECM now amounts to one of the most significant in the whole literature of piano jazz, however uneasily some of it sits in that particular bin.

***** Whisper Not**
ECM 543816 *Jarrett; Gary Peacock (b); Jack DeJohnette (d).* 7/99.

The trio was about to take a fresh turning (see items below), but this was a celebratory occasion, taped live in Paris and one of the first times when Jarrett seemed clear of the chronic fatigue that had afflicted him over the previous two years, a condition that might have ended his playing career. Listening to him on 'Bouncing With Bud', the title-track and 'Groovin' High', one is struck more by the renewed interest in bebop than concerned that there seems to be a slight, almost subliminal dulling of his articulation and phrasing. The notes don't seem to run along as cleanly now, though perhaps this is down to the piano.

Peacock and DeJohnette are both in magisterial form, though again one suspects they are required to do more than on previous tours, and Peacock himself was to suffer major ill-health which would level more question marks at the group's continuance. The body of work is now enormous. Doubtless it will be excerpted and archived many times over in years to come. Our nominations for immortality from this set would be 'What Is This Thing Called Love?' and a magnificent 'Poinciana'.

***** Inside Out**
ECM 1780 *Jarrett; Gary Peacock (b); Jack DeJohnette (d).* 7/00.

*****(*) Always Let Me Go**
ECM 1800/01 2CD *As above.* 4/01.

He may have borrowed the *Inside Out* title from his biographer, Ian Carr, who wrote about the British free scene under this rubric. Jarrett's interest in free playing has always been evident but has rarely been registered as explicitly as on this set, which takes a further step on from the *Changeless* project.

Drummer and bassist don't sound entirely convinced at the start of 'From The Body'. This surely wasn't sprung on them without notice? The blues is the basic idiom, but Peacock seems to toy with edgy melodic shapes which don't come from that tradition until the whole thing unfurls in ever longer lines that suggest there is a rubbed-out architectural drawing behind the piece. 'Inside Out' and 'Free Fade 341' are less immediately satisfying, but then the trio hits stride with 'Riot' and another major statement is complete. Irritatingly, ECM saw fit to include an encore of 'When I Fall In Love', a favourite of these guys, but an intruder in this context. Jarrett's explorations continue to fascinate.

Always Let Me Go was recorded live in Japan, where Jarrett has played to rapt attention throughout his career. The philosophy is the same as on *Inside Out*, a free programme without standards or predetermined structures. The opening 'Hearts In Space' is a full half-hour of intense trio improvisation, ranging from taut blues and boogie passages to more abstract shapes. 'Waves' is longer still and yet more eclectic in terms of its stylistic references. Jarrett even seems to impersonate Bud Powell at one point. Interspersed are much shorter tracks, like the roistering 'Paradox', which touches on similar areas, and the tiny 'The River', which Jarrett plays solo. 'Facing East', 'Tsunami' and 'Relay' round out the set, but one wonders if this were any other artist and any other group whether these tracks would have been first-choice inclusions. As a document of Jarrett's almost 150th performance in Japan, it's impeccable, but there are unevennesses towards the end and only very dedicated Jarrett fans will be along for the complete ride more than once.

***** Up For It: Live In Juans Les Pins**

ECM 004602 *Jarrett; Gary Peacock (b); Jack DeJohnette (d).* 5/03.

The title is cheerfully defiant, the album cover as sunstruck blue as the Mediterranean, the material all somehow associated with Miles Davis and his formidable appearances in the south of France with a classic quintet forty years earlier. Having momentarily set aside their free playing, the trio reverts to standard material, or rather to material from the Miles songbook: 'If I Were A Bell', wonderfully conceived and played, the bopper 'Scrapple From The Apple', 'My Funny Valentine', 'Autumn Leaves' and 'Someday My Prince Will Come' in gentle swing tempo. There's also a surprising inclusion, Oliver Nelson's funky 'Butch And Butch', not a theme you'd ever expect to hear Keith Jarrett play. His touch is immaculate and if anything it's Peacock and DeJohnette who wilt a bit as the set progresses. Even if he hadn't suffered debilitating illness, Jarrett's energy and concentration here would be remarkable.

**** :rarum – Selected Recordings: Volume 1**

ECM 014168 2CD *As for ECM discs above.*

The rationale for the handsomely packaged :rarum imprint is that the artist rather than the label selects the material from his back catalogue. Jarrett seems wilfully perverse here, opening the first disc with clavichord pieces from *The Book Of Ways*, and then as if to compound the mischief, five selections from the multi-instrumental *Spirits* and a movement from the pipe organ *Spheres* (which isn't available on CD). He even includes a highly percussive section from the Munich concert, which out of context makes little sense. There is a background to these choices. Jarrett is keenly aware of the problems of instrumentalism, of having one's creative voice identified or over-identified with a particular horn, keyboard or set of strings. Even given that this is the first of a two-volume selection, that there is already a *Works* anthology in the ECM catalogue, and that much of the rest of the material, by the great quartet and the so-called 'Standards Trio', is first-rate, it's a very odd selection and virtually useless for a newcomer, unless Jarrett wishes for new listeners who won't think of him as 'the pianist', but as a musician of some rather more undifferentiated stamp.

Robert Jarvis

TROMBONE

Formerly a member of the Hugh Hopper band, Jarvis extends the boundaries of free jazz with extended techniques and creative use of electronics and samples.

***** Carving Up Time**

Slam CD 242 *Jarvis; Frank van der Kooij (sax); Henk de Laat, Alan Niblock (b); Jean-Victor de Boer, Oscar Schultz (d).* 00.

Jarvis makes the trombone sound delightfully forlorn rather than declamatory, and his use of effects and field recordings adds a dimension to this debut record that might not be there were it down to the group – or rather groups – alone. 'Global Village' is a suite of pieces which doesn't seem to reflect the programme implicit in the title, but emphasizes isolation and individuality rather than community; in fact, it was written for a festival of that name in Northern Ireland. Jarvis's technique is finely tuned, and allows him to range from strong and emphatic blowing to softer dynamics that hover on the verge of tonelessness and silence.

Bobby Jaspar (1926–63)

TENOR SAXOPHONE, FLUTE

Born in Liège, Jaspar made his name in Paris in the '50s, and he moved to the USA when he marrried Blossom Dearie. His most famous association was a brief spell with Miles Davis in 1957. He died in 1963 following heart surgery.

***** Modern Jazz Au Club St-Germain**

Emarcy 159941-2 *Jaspar; René Urtreger (p); Sacha Distel (g); Benoît Quersin (b); Jean-Louis Viale (d).* 55.

***** Bobby Jaspar With George Wallington, Idrees Sulieman**

Original Jazz Classics OJC 1788 *Jaspar; Idrees Sulieman (t); George Wallington (p); Wilbur Little (b); Elvin Jones (d).* 5/57.

***** Bobby Jaspar With Friends**

Fresh Sound FSRCD-166 *Jaspar; Mundell Lowe, René Thomas (g); George Duvivier, Monty Budwig, Jean Marie Ingrand (b); Ed Shaughnessy, Jean-Louis Viale (d).* 58–62.

Jaspar sounded like Lester Young might have done if Lester had been Belgian. Bobby's pale tone and amorphous phrasing on tenor were matched with an agile and exceptionally pointed flute style, abjuring the mere prettiness which normally attends that instrument. He has two flute features on the agreeable if unexceptional 1957 session: Sulieman sits out on four of the seven numbers, but Jaspar is quite confident enough to handle the front line by himself. Rather better is the new arrival in Emarcy's excellent Jazz In Paris series: Jasper and Urtreger work through a programme which is set up as obvious cool-bebop copy, but Jaspar puts in enough to individualize the likes of 'You Stepped Out Of A Dream'. The rhythm section are very plain.

With Friends is a motley but absorbing collection of mainly live tracks, most with a small group under Mundell Lowe's leadership, but two were cut in Paris with René Thomas – excellent, sinuous bebop workouts. The tracks with Lowe are a mixed lot: Jaspar has a gorgeous flute feature on 'It Could Happen To You' and generally uses this horn over the tenor.

Lowe's own work shouldn't be discounted: he has a fine improvisation on 'Gal In Calico'. Still not much Jaspar around at present: he is becoming very much a forgotten figure.

André Jaume (born 1940)

TENOR SAXOPHONE, FLUTE, CLARINET, BASS CLARINET

After beginning with Dixieland groups, Jaume sought out more modern company in the '60s, and since then his work on record has been rather unpredictable, with solo and duo recordings (with Joe McPhee, a long-time associate) sequenced with more large-scale efforts. He is also much interested in gamelan music and is a close associate of Jimmy Giuffre.

*****(*) Pour Django**
CELP C1 *Jaume; Raymond Boni (g).* 6/85.

***** Songs And Dances**
CELP C4 *As above, except add Joe McPhee (t, ss).* 5/87.

****** Cinoche**
CELP C7 *Jaume; Rémi Charmasson (g); François Mechali, Claude Tchamitchian (b); Daniel Humair (d).* 1/84–3/88.

*****(*) Piazza Di Luna**
CELP 10 *Jaume; Rémi Charmasson (g); Jean-Marc Montera (g-syn); Claude Tchamitchian (b); Fredy Studer (d); Jackie Micaelli, Jean-Pierre Lanfranchini, Jean-Claude Albertini, Jean-Etienne Langianni, Francis Marcantei (v).* 8–9/89.

***** Standards**
CELP 12 *Jaume; Jean-Sebastien Simonoviez (p); François Mechali (b); Olivier Clerc (d).* 4/89.

****(*) Something ...**
CELP 15 *Jaume; Joe McPhee (ss, vtb); Clyde Criner (p); Anthony Cox (b); Bill Stewart (d).* 4/90.

*****(*) Peace/Pace/Paix**
CELP 19 *Jaume; Charlie Haden (b); Olivier Clerc (d).* 5/90.

*****(*) Abbaye De L'Epau**
CELP 20 *Jaume; Charlie Mariano (as, f).* 3/91.

****** Giacobazzi, Autour De La Rade**
CELP 25 *Jaume; Barre Phillips (b); Barry Altschul (d).* 6/92.

Jaume's sequence of records for the French CELP company is a superb body of work, as well as his only representation in the catalogue, since his old hatART albums have now gone. His own playing has acquired tremendous stature: the tenor is still his primary instrument, and he gets a granitic, almost Gothic tone out of it when he wishes, though he's as likely to play quietly, almost deferentially. The alto he picks up only occasionally, but his bass clarinet and flute work are also distinctive: lyrical, but with a dark, sometimes misshapen side to them. His tribute to Django casts only a sidelong look at Reinhardt's material: he and Boni play 'Mélodie Pour Julie' relatively straight, but there are also abstract originals here that honour the guitarist's spirit as well as the letter of his music. Boni's effects colour much of the festival set recorded on *Songs And Dances*, where they play Coleman's 'Blues Connotation' as well as Otis Redding's 'Dock Of The Bay' and do three solos in tribute to Jimmy Lyons. *Cinoche* is a masterful record, music for '*un film policier qui n'existe pas*': split between one group with Humair and Mechali and another with Charmasson and Tchamitchian, Jaume's playing has a Rollins-like authority on tenor, with the superb 'Ballade A Perdre Le Temps' outstanding. *Piazza Di Luna* documents a project with Tavagna, a group of Corsican polyphonic singers. An unlikely collaboration, with two of the vocalists reciting the words of Andrée Canavaggio as well as singing; but Jaume makes it work by choosing to create two contrasting vistas rather than a fusion.

The *Standards* collection seems to set Jaume off on a new midstream course. Aside from a single original, 'Escapade', the programme offers nine familiar songs to work with, and Jaume's querulous tone and slightly tortuous phrasing make deliberately unsettled work of the music. He takes out the bass clarinet as often as the tenor and soprano, and it lends a mooching air to 'Nancy'. Jaume's first recording with an American rhythm section is a little disappointing. Criner, Cox and Stewart play as if this were just another post-bop date, and that's how it ends up sounding: with compositions by Jackie McLean and Grachan Moncur in the programme, as well as four Jaume originals, the feel is reminiscent of Blue Note's experimental mid-'60s period. But Jaume and McPhee give the impression of being tranquillized by the setting. An austere reworking of Moncur's 'Love And Hate' is rather effective, and Jaume's terseness works well with the splashier playing of McPhee, but the record is slack overall.

On the next two records Jaume sounds as if he's growing ever more quiet and introspective. He seldom raises his saxophone voice on either one, yet both make a firmer impression than some of the earlier discs. The trio session establishes a line of descent from Ornette Coleman, which 'Peace' and 'Blue Connotation' make manifest, but Jaume's playing has little of Coleman in it: he's too quirkily himself, and the steady-rolling pulses devised by Haden and Clerc support what's now a very personal kind of melodic improvisation. *Abbaye De L'Epau* is more soberly reflective, and the very even pacing of the music makes this sequence all-of-a-piece, with Mariano turning his own light down a little to remain in keeping with the occasion. Both discs are well recorded (the second is from a concert session) and gently absorbing.

Any fear that Jaume might be heading towards silence is dispelled by the most recent trio session, a series of dedications to painter Jean-Pierre Giacobazzi, performed in collaboration with the sombre, earth-solid bass of Phillips and the magnificent Altschul, whose exacting, intensely detailed playing is remarkable by itself. Jaume makes the most of all his horns, with the soprano and bass clarinet finding new depth; but his tenor continues to impress the most, and the best music here is as absorbing as Coleman's great Golden Circle sessions.

*****(*) Team Games**
CELP 31 *Jaume; John Medeski (p).* 5/94.

A very improbable meeting, with the keyboardist of Medeski, Martin And Wood producing some inspired playing. Steve Lacy's 'Blues For Aida' is a favourite of Jaume's (it appears on *Borobodur Suite*, listed below) and the alternately harsh and gentle treatment it gets here is memorably invigorating. Otherwise it's Monk and Coltrane on the set-list, and unhackneyed choices at that, with a beautifully irreverent 'Ba-Lue Bolivar Ba-Lues Are' to highlight what they can do.

***** Borobodur Suite**
CELP 30 *Jaume; Septo Raharjo, Setyaji Dewanto, Gatot Djuwito, Poernomo Nugruho, Sonny Suprapto (gamelan orchestra).* 2/95.

★★★ Merapi

CELP 34 *As above, except add Rémi Charmasson (g); S. P. Joko and Azied Dewa replace Dewanto and Djuwito.* 4/96.

There's no gainsaying Jaume's inquisitive spirit, and these two collaborative meetings with Septo Raharjo's gamelan orchestra are handled with great confidence by all the players. Jaume is the central figure throughout the first disc; he shares improvising duties with Charmasson – low-key but very sympathetic – on the second. Raharjo and his men play to the letter of their music, creating a rustling, river-like flow of sound that complements what the jazz-players are doing without subsuming them. In the end, though, one finds it all rather interesting and very seldom fascinating. As graciously as the players share their space, there seems to be very little genuine interaction, and saxophones and clarinets don't sit all that well with gamelan instruments (Charmasson does rather better in that respect).

★★★(★) Clarinet Sessions

CELP 40 *Jaume; Rémi Charmasson (g); Bruno Chevillon, Alain Soler (b); Randy Kaye, Barry Altschul (d).* 1–6/96.

★★★(★) A Portrait Of Jimmy Giuffre

CELP 39 *Jaume; Jean-François Canape (t, bugle); Rémi Charmasson (g); Bob Harrsion (b); Randy Kaye (d).* 6/98.

Jaume's fascination with the clarinet and with Jimmy Giuffre gets full rein on these two. *Clarinet Sessions* has its misfires, such as the misjudged duets with Altschul which open the disc, but there are also some sublime moments: 'Mountain By The Sea', a fine mood piece, and the three duets with Chevillon. The conventionally swinging 'Bonne Course' and the feathery duet with Kaye, 'West Stockbridge Impression', round out a quietly provocative set.

The set in dedication to Giuffre finds a ground common both to its dedicatee and to Jaume's more abstract side. 'Apes', for instance, is taken further out than the composer himself would probably sanction, but Harrison and Kaye (himself a former Giuffre sideman) know just how far to push their roles without surrendering the chamberish feel of the group, and the three principal soloists make any journeys from inside to out entirely logical within what is a carefully designed group framework. Cut live at two Avignon concerts, this was a splendid event.

★★★(★) Jaisalmer

CELP 43 *Jaume; Bernard Santacruz (b); Marc Mazzillo (d).* 2/00.

★★★(★) Pour Théo...

CELP 44 *Jaume; Alain Soler (g).* 6/00.

Working in seeming isolation from the main European currents, Jaume continues to make very good records. The trio record starts out with Rollinsian authority on 'Lenox Avenue', walks through a spirited mood piece with 'Ratuboko', wrangles past the abstractions of 'Errance'; and so on. As an introduction to Jaume's colourful kind of post-bop, it works superbly. The duo record is, surprisingly, a lot tougher than the instrumentation might suggest. The record was inspired by the playfulness of a friend's infant son, and instead of pastoral musings there's an argumentative, almost a barking quality to the dialogue, with both men in high spirits.

The Java Quartet

GROUP

Formed by bassist Galeazzi in 1994, the Australian group model their variation on post-bop via original compositions.

★★★ Passages

Rufus RF043 *Richard Maegraith (ts); Greg Coffin (p); Michael Galeazzi (b); Mike Quigley (d).* 6/98.

★★★ Dark Garden

ABC/EMI 531607-2 *As above.* 1/00.

Quigley and Galeazzi are the main writers, leaving Maegraith's Coltrane-inspired tenor to go aloft over Coffin's funky piano licks. That puts it simply, but it's a formula which they vary and occasionally depart from to engaging effect across the two CDs. Several of the tunes on *Passages* revolve around a single idea, such as the bass figure of 'Big Sky Mind', and the group skilfully knows when to quit on each track (aside, maybe, from the lengthy 'Lifetime Dreaming' and 'Una-Med' – Coffin and Maegraith are more likely to hit bullseye on brief solos). *Dark Garden* takes a more leisurely course, although the tracks number only five and the record is commendably fat-free. The disc is meant as a meditation on memory and its effects, and perhaps it's appropriate that it has the quality of sketchwork, even if there are some bold strokes along the way. It could use a big tune.

Stefan Jaworzyn

GUITAR

British noise-guitar specialist who bars no holds.

★★★ In A Sentimental Mood

Incus CD 25 *Jaworzyn; Alan Wilkinson (as, bs).* 96.

It would be delightful to think that a few extra punters picked this up expecting a set of gentle Ellington covers only to be confronted with 'My Psychotic Valentine' instead. What's not clear about Jaworzyn and his partner is whether their sense of humour stretches past the album- and track-titles, which sound like the titles to Dadaist exhibits and are too long to reproduce here. On balance, it probably does, even though parts of these five extended improvs, none of them under 11 minutes in length, sound grimly serious rather than light-hearted. Jaworzyn explores the whole gamut of effects on his guitar, but beneath it all, there is still the jazz player's emphasis on line and structure. Wilkinson, likewise, sounds free but with ties to something undefined. It's exhilarating, slightly wearying music that maybe works better still when you can see the guys at work.

Jazz At The Philharmonic

SUPERGROUP

Instigated by Norman Granz, this took its name from a single concert at the Philharmonic Theater in Los Angeles in 1944, but became a generic title for multi-artist package shows or tours, promoted by Granz and featuring an evolving repertory cast of players. It was a phenomenon which lasted into the '80s.

****** The Complete Jazz At The Philharmonic On Verve 1944–1949**

Verve 523893-2 10CD *Shorty Sherock, Al Killian, Neal Hefti, Charlie Shavers, Buck Clayton, Ray Linn, Dizzy Gillespie, Howard McGhee, Roy Eldridge, Joe Guy (t); J. J. Johnson, Bill Harris, Tommy Turk (tb); Charlie Parker, Willie Smith, Georgie Auld, Pete Brown (as); Illinois Jacquet, Lester Young, Flip Phillips, Coleman Hawkins, Bumps Meyers, Babe Russin, Corky Corcoran, Charlie Ventura, Joe Thomas, Jack McVea (ts); Meade Lux Lewis, Garland Finney, Buddy Cole, Nat Cole, Milt Raskin, Arnold Ross, Hank Jones, Bobby Tucker, Kenny Kersey, Ralph Burns, Oscar Peterson, Teddy Napoleon, Mel Powell (p); Slim Gaillard (g, p, v, d); Tiny 'Bam' Brown (g, p, v); Les Paul, Irving Ashby, Barney Kessel, Dave Barbour, Bill De Arango, Ulysses Livingston, Tiny Grimes (g); Johnny Miller, Red Callender, Curley Russell, Ray Brown, Charles Mingus, Billy Hadnott, Al McKibbon, Rodney Richardson, Charlie Drayton, Benny Fonville (b); Lee Young, Joe Marshall, Dave Coleman, Gene Krupa, J. C. Heard, Jo Jones, Alvin Stoller, Dave Tough, Big Sid Catlett, Jackie Mills (d); Carolyn Richards, Billie Holiday, Ella Fitzgerald (v).* 44–49.

***** The First Concert**

Verve 521646-2 *Shorty Sherock (t); J. J. Johnson (tb); Illinois Jacquet, Jack McVea (ts); Nat Cole (p); Les Paul (g); Lee Young (d).* 7/44.

****** Carnegie Hall 1949**

Pablo 5311-2 *Fats Navarro (t); Tommy Turk (tb); Charlie Parker, Sonny Criss (as); Flip Phillips, Coleman Hawkins (ts); Hank Jones (p); Ray Brown (b); Shelly Manne (d).* 11/49.

***** Norman Granz's Jazz At The Philharmonic, Hartford, 1953**

Pablo 2308240 *Charlie Shavers, Roy Eldridge (t); Bill Harris (tb); Benny Carter, Willie Smith (as); Flip Phillips, Ben Webster (ts); Oscar Peterson (p); Herb Ellis (g); Ray Brown (b); Gene Krupa (d).* 5/53.

*****(*) JATP In Tokyo**

Pablo PACD 2620 104 2CD *As above, except add Raymond Tunia (p), J. C. Heard (d), Ella Fitzgerald (v).* 11/53.

***** The Exciting Battle: JATP, Stockholm '55**

Pablo 2310713 *Roy Eldridge, Dizzy Gillespie (t); Bill Harris (tb); Flip Phillips (ts); Oscar Peterson (p); Herb Ellis (g); Ray Brown (b); Louie Bellson (d).* 2/55.

***** The Greatest Jazz Concert In The World**

Pablo 2625-704-2 3CD *Clark Terry, Cat Anderson, Mercer Ellington, Herbie Jones, Cootie Williams (t); Buster Cooper, Chuck Connors, Lawrence Brown (tb); Benny Carter, Johnny Hodges, Russell Procope (as); Jimmy Hamilton (cl, ts); Coleman Hawkins, Zoot Sims, Paul Gonsalves (ts); Harry Carney (bs); Duke Ellington, Oscar Peterson, Jimmy Jones (p); T-Bone Walker (g, v); Sam Jones, Bob Cranshaw, John Lamb (b); Louis Hayes, Bobby Durham, Rufus Jones, Sam Woodyard (d); Ella Fitzgerald (v).* 6–7/67.

*****(*) JATP In London, 1969**

Pablo 2620119 *Dizzy Gillespie, Clark Terry (t); Benny Carter (as); Coleman Hawkins, Zoot Sims (ts); James Moody (ts, f); Teddy Wilson (p); T-Bone Walker (g); Bob Cranshaw (b); Louie Bellson (d).* 3/69.

*****(*) JATP At The Montreux Festival, 1975**

Pablo 2310748 *Clark Terry (t, flhn); Benny Carter (as); Zoot Sims (ts); Joe Pass (g); Tommy Flanagan (p); Keter Betts (b); Bobby Durham (d).* 7/75.

***** Return To Happiness: JATP At Yoyogi National Stadium, Tokyo**

Pablo 2620117 *Harry 'Sweets' Edison, Clark Terry (t); J. J. Johnson, Al Grey (tb); Zoot Sims, Eddie 'Lockjaw' Davis (ts); Joe Pass (g); Oscar Peterson, Paul Smith (p); Keter Betts, Niels-Henning Orsted Pedersen (b); Louie Bellson, Bobby Durham (d); Ella Fitzgerald (v).* 10/83.

Jazz At The Philharmonic dates from 2 July 1944 at the Philharmonic Auditorium in Los Angeles, when Norman Granz mounted a concert headlined by Nat Cole, Illinois Jacquet, Meade Lux Lewis and others who will probably sound slightly unfamiliar in this context at least. A decade later, when JATP had reached the peak of its international celebrity, there was a relatively fixed roster of stars, all from within Granz's recording empire, who took part in these events – part concerts, part public jams – which gained him such success and which lasted, virtually uninterrupted, over the span of these records and beyond.

Granz was a passionate believer in the racial integration of jazz. He was also shrewd enough to recognize that more very definitely meant more so far as marketing big jazz names was concerned. There is often a sense of 'never mind the quality, count the names' on a JATP record, and finesse and expressive sophistication were very often lost in polite cutting sessions which put high-note-playing and amicably fiery exchanges at a premium. The JATP discography has always been something of a shambles, the records issued and reissued in all manner of combinations, and very little of the kosher Verve material has even made it to CD – until, that is, the long-awaited and much-delayed set of all the '40s material, displayed in an elaborate construction which includes ten CDs and a huge booklet. Considering that so many of these dates are little more than institutionalized jam sessions or platforms for showmanship, listening through the discs is unexpectedly easy and rewarding. As the JATP package was formulating itself, it still accommodated a great variety: there is Slim Gaillard and Bam Brown (doing their pretty hilarious schtick on 'Opera In Vout'), solos by Meade Lux Lewis, Nat Cole groups, a trio of Gene Krupa, Charlie Ventura and Teddy Napoleon, Ella and Billie in their own sets, Coleman Hawkins with Hank Jones, Buddy Rich and Ray Brown (here with three previously unheard numbers), features for Bill Harris and Charlie Shavers ... the range of jazz on offer is in the end pretty extraordinary. Every so often someone such as Roy Eldridge goes too far, but that is also part of the atmosphere. There's a lot of newly discovered material and, although the sound is basically rather thin, everything comes through clearly. As a feat of reorganization alone, the set has merit, but it's hard to see anyone being disappointed with a glorious set of performances too.

That high standard persisted through the later JATP survivals, the rest of which are currently available through Pablo (Verve will presumably tackle their remaining material in due course, but since it took them many years to get the first set out, we advise readers against holding their breath – and there has been no hint of any progress since our last edition). It's difficult to identify highs and lows or to make qualitative judgements about the playing. There are no bad or even disappointing records. The earlier Japanese session recommends itself on grounds of sheer length and also because there is a winning freshness to everybody's playing; but that might also be said of the 1969 London concert or the triumphant return to Japan (and 'to happiness') which neatly rounds off the 40-year span of these particular discs.

Of the two most recent arrivals on CD: the 1949 session is quite exceptional, and something which goes beyond the JATP legacy and into the realm of important jazz recordings. There are three long jams featuring a front line of Navarro, Parker, Criss, Turk and Phillips, with the Jones–Brown–Manne rhythm section: though there's a degree of showing off, the solos remain remarkably cogent and exciting in a tough, unforgiving way, with Parker and Criss striking memorable sparks off each other, Phillips keeping matters under surprising control, and Navarro – only months away from his death – simply riveting. Then Coleman Hawkins comes on, and shares the front line with Navarro and the rhythm section for an exceptional set. This is the first official release of this music (Granz's announcements induce apprehension because they're so poorly recorded, but the music itself comes across firmly and clearly), and it's a marvellous rediscovery.

Anything calling itself *The Greatest Jazz Concert In The World* is asking for trouble, although the title is merely a flag of convenience: it's drawn from concerts in three different locations, involving everyone from Oscar's trio to Duke's orchestra. Zoot and Benny Carter sit in with the Ellington band, T-Bone Walker plays the blues, and Ella and Duke wind things up with 'Cotton Tail'. Plenty of fun.

An astonishing feat of organization, JATP also made great marketing sense, and Granz has to be admired for keeping the music going during a period when in market terms it was more than embattled. Mainstream fans will love any of these.

Jazz Composers Alliance Orchestra

ENSEMBLE

Adventurous big band working on the Boston scene since 1985.

*** Flux

Northeastern NR 5010 *John Carlson, Bob Levy, Mike Peipman, Walter Platt (t); David Harris, Russell Jewell, Bob Pilkington (tb); W. Marshall Sealy, Mark Taylor (frhn); Jim O'Dell (tba); Sam Rivers (ss); Ron Scheps (ss, ts); Julius Hemphill (as); Jay Brandford, Doug Yates (as, cl); Joel Springer (ts); Kathy Halvorsen (bs, ob); Susan Calkins (f); John Medeski (p, syn); Duane Johnson (syn); John Dirac, Andrew Hurlbut, James Kelly (g); Diana Herold (vib); Howard Britz (b); Grisha Alexiev (d); Jerry Leake (perc).* 92.

*** In, Thru And Out

Cadence CJR 1153 *Mike Peipman, Keiichi Hashimoto (t); David Harris, Bob Pilkington (tb); Jim Mosher (frhn); Jim Gray (tba); Jim Hobbs, Jeff Hudgins (as); Phil Scarff (ts); Hans Indogo (bs); Hiro Honshuku (f); Art Bailey (p); Norm Zocher (g); Rick McLaughlin (b); Rich Greenblatt (vib); Harvey Wirht (d); Taki Masuko (perc); Rebecca Shrimpton (v).* 5/01.

One feels an immediate, if sometimes fatalistic, admiration for outfits like the JCAO. First, for the sheer moxie required to put together an operation like this; and second, because they're bound to be confused, for good or ill, with Michael Mantler's Jazz Composers Orchestra, who pioneered this kind of thing in the late '60s.

The first album is attractive largely because of the presence of John Medeski of Medeski, Martin And Wood (albeit on piano rather than trademark organ) and guest stars Sam Rivers and Julius Hemphill, who each contribute a significant composition to the set. In addition, there are compositions – one each – by Calkins, Schaphorst, Hurlbut and Johnson, who sound like a team of uptown lawyers. These are competent and interesting enough, but one feels that the performances are constrained by the rigours of the material, especially on Schaphorst's 'Loggerhead Blues', which could have been a lot looser in execution. It also suffers from following Katz's fine 'Variations On A Theme By Jimi Hendrix' (guess which one), which is distinguished by some unexpected sonorities, not least Kathy Halvorsen's delightful oboe part. It's a piece that firmly underscores JCAO's lineage from the Gil Evans orchestra of the previous decade.

Hemphill's 'Hard Blues' was an important component of his live set for a while and it is distinguished here by a tense, mournful solo from the composer. His impact on JCAO is acknowledged in a tribute piece on the second album. The Rivers piece, 'Flux', is typical of his later interest in *concerto grosso* structures in a jazz context, with the main ensemble broken down into small and often unexpected sections. All in all, an impressive album.

The later, live date for Cadence is a more sober beast and less immediately likeable, though to go out without guest support speaks volumes for JCAO's confidence. Nearly a decade on, the personnel is almost entirely different. The featured composers include Warren Senders, a professor at the New England Conservatory, the Argentinian Laura Andel, trombonist David Harris, and JCAO founder Darrell Katz, who contributes the four-part Hemphill suite, which is properly grounded in the blues.

The soloing is committed, intelligent and inventive, even when the basic structures are masochistically demanding. Andel's 'El Tiempo – To My Mother' and 'Caruara' are the standout tracks, along with 'Hemphill' – Katz's heartfelt memorial to a great teacher and collaborator. Fine work.

Jazz Composers Alliance Saxophone Quartet

ENSEMBLE

Spin-off from the JCA Orchestra founded by Darrell Katz.

*** I'm Me And You're Not

Brownstone 9906 *Jeff Hudgins (ss, as); Phil Scarff (ss, ts); Eric Rasmussen (as); Dan Bosshardt (bs).* 11/99.

Katz's devotion to the example of Gil Evans and to the music of Jimi Hendrix and Julius Hemphill is clearly reflected here. The skilful quartet kicks off with a version of 'Belly Button Window', from the posthumous *Cry Of Love*, one of the rarer tunes in Jimi's legacy, and climaxes with a slice of anguished Hemphill R&B. There's even room for an outrageous version of Jimmy Giuffre's 'The Train And The River'. The other pieces are by Katz, interesting enough in their way but saxophone quartets are temperamental creatures and this one doesn't have the character to match its competence.

Jazz Composers Orchestra (founded 1967)

GROUP

An American ensemble formed by Michael Mantler, part of an initiative to commission and perform new large-scale jazz compositions. It gradually became, effectively, a Carla Bley–Mantler orchestra.

*****(*) Communications**

JCOA 841124-2 *Michael Mantler (dir); Don Cherry (c); Randy Brecker, Stephen Furtado, Lloyd Michels (flhn); Bob Northern, Julius Watkins (frhn); Jimmy Knepper, Roswell Rudd (tb); Jack Jeffers (btb); Howard Johnson (tba); Al Gibbons, Steve Lacy, Steve Marcus (ss); Bob Donovan, Gene Hull, Frank Wess (as); Gato Barbieri, George Barrow, Pharoah Sanders, Lew Tabackin (ts); Charles Davis (bs); Carla Bley, Cecil Taylor (p); Larry Coryell (g); Kent Carter, Ron Carter, Bob Cunningham, Richard Davis, Eddie Gomez, Charlie Haden, Reggie Johnson, Alan Silva, Steve Swallow, Reggie Workman (b); Andrew Cyrille, Beaver Harris (d).* 1–6/68.

The JCO was formed to give improvising musicians an opportunity to play extended structures in larger formations than were normally considered either economic or artistically viable. Its best-known product is still the massive opera – or 'chronotransduction' – *Escalator Over The Hill.* From the same period came *Communications,* if anything a more ambitious work. It consists of four enormous slabs of orchestrated sound and a brief 'Preview' (which comes fourth of five), each with a featured soloist. Or, in the case of the opening 'Communications No. 8', two soloists: Don Cherry and Gato Barbieri. Mantler's scoring is interesting in itself. Cherry's squeaky cornet is the only high-pitched brass instrument; the sections are weighted towards french horns and trombones, with flugelhorn accents generally located in the middle register and the higher-pitched parts assigned to soprano saxophones. In addition, Mantler scores for five double basses on each track (perm from the list above), which gives each piece a complex tonal rootedness for the soloists' (mostly) unrestrained excursions. Restraining Gato Barbieri would be pointless. He tends to begin a solo where most saxophonists climax. It's redundant to say he sounds strained on 'Communications No. 8' but, tone apart, he seems to be straining for ideas. By contrast, Pharoah Sanders has to squeeze everything into a brief three and a half minutes on 'Preview' and nearly achieves meltdown in the process. On 'Communications No. 9' Larry Coryell is used as a sound-effects department. If Barbieri seems slightly short of ideas, Coryell is a *tabula rasa.* Fortunately, the best is still to come. Roswell Rudd's playing on the longer 'No. 10' is some of the best he has committed to record; Steve Swallow's bass introduction establishes its parameters with great exactness, and again the dark scoring works superbly. The final two-part section fully justifies Cecil Taylor's top billing. His solo part is full of huge, keyboard-long runs and pounded chords and arpeggios that leave Andrew Cyrille sounding winded and concussed. Very much of its time, and betraying occasional signs of a dialogue of the deaf, *Communications* is still an important historical document. However demanding its headlong progress may be on the intellect and the emotions, Mantler – like Barry Guy, who followed his example in the United Kingdom – has a considerable musical intelligence and shapes performances that have logic, form and a sort of chastening beauty.

The Jazz Five

GROUP

A band of London-based modernists, circa 1960, whose few surviving recordings are these days collectors' pieces.

***** The Five Of Us**

Jasmine JASCD 623 *Vic Ash (ts, cl); Harry Klein (bs); Brian Dee (p); Malcolm Cecil (b); Bill Eyden (d).* 10–11/60.

Another album from the Tempo series of sessions masterminded by Tony Hall, *The Five Of Us* catches a hot quintet in enthusiastic form. The main point at this distance is to hear the playing of Ash and Klein, accomplished saxophonists who rarely enjoyed much time in the limelight. Ash's mobile, heavy-toned tenor (and, for a nice change, the clarinet as an alternative) is the punchy lead voice, but Klein's gruffly assertive playing is perhaps even more listenable. The music is in the Messengers/Couriers mould, with a more easy-going feel to it, and though the originals are nothing special they are, at least, originals rather than mere hard-bop covers. Dee gets as much solo space as the horns but at this stage at least was rather less interesting in that role. A welcome reissue of a very rare LP.

Jazzhearts

GROUP

Afro-modernists led by Australian flautist/saxophonist Louise Elliott.

***** The Way It Feels**

Ronnie Scott's Jazz House RSJH CD 060 *Claude Deppa (t); Annie Whitehead (tb); Louise Elliott (ts, f); Mervyn Africa (p); Chris Thorn (g); Steve Lamb (b); Greg Leppard (d); Richard Ajileye (perc).* 5/99.

Louise Elliott is still seriously unrecognized. Her bright, pungent saxophone style and brisk flute cut to the chase on almost every track. With Deppa and Whitehead alongside, she sounds unstoppable on the title-track, 'Tierra Rioja' and 'Flute In Eleven', while Annie pays a fond farewell to Dudu Pukwana. There is a tune each by Africa and Duke Makasi, but the set belongs to the Australian.

Jazz Jamaica

GROUP

The impact of Caribbean music – ska, calypso, reggae, mento – on British jazz has been considerable. Figures like Shake Keane, Harry Beckett and guitarist Ernest Ranglin have left a substantial legacy; Gary Crosby, the former Jazz Warrior and de facto leader of Jazz Jamaica, is Ernest's nephew.

***** Skaravan**

Skazz Records SKACD 001 *Eddie Thornton (t); Rico Rodriguez (tb); Michael Rose (ts, f); Cedric Brooks (ts); Clifton Morrison (ky, hca); Alan Weekes (g); Gary Crosby (b); Kenrick Rowe (d).* 93.

***** Double Barrel**
Hannibal 1421 *Eddie Thornton (t); Dennis Rollins (tb); Brian Edwards (as); Michael Rose (ts, f); Clifton Morrison (p, org, ky); Alan Weekes (g); Gary Crosby (b); Kenrick Rowe (d); Tony Uter (perc).* 98.

***** Massive**
Dune Records 06 *Kevin Robinson, Guy Barker, Edward Thornton, Claude Deppa, Sean Corby, Colin Graham (t); Harry Brown, Ashley Slater, Annie Whitehead, Barnaby Dickinson, Fayyaz Virji, Winston Rollins, Dennis Rollins (tb); Andy Grappy (tba); Denys Baptiste, Andy Sheppard, Michael Rose, Patrick Clahar, Adam Bishop, Jason Yarde, Soweto Kinch, Tony Kofi; Ray Carless (saxes); Alex Wilson (p); Orphy Robinson (vib); Alan Weekes (g); Gary Crosby (b); Kenrick Rowe (d); Tony Uter (perc); Juliet Roberts (v).* 01.

A unique and infectious fusion of musical styles, Jazz Jamaica's brand of 'skazz' sounds as if it's been around for ever. The best testimony to its naturalness is the title-arrangement of the Juan Tizol/Duke Ellington tune, which joins Charlie Parker's 'Barbados' and a couple of Skatalites songs in a joyous programme of blowing tunes. The rhythms may be a little unvaried and the solos lacking somewhat in subtlety, but the impact of players like Rico Rodriguez, the legendary trombonist of the Skatalites, and of Clifton 'Bigga' Morrison is unmistakable, and Crosby and Rowe hold the rhythm section together with great poise. Rico's solo on his own 'Ramblin'' is definitive. Hard to dislike, any of it, but possibly a bit one-dimensional for repeated hearings; almost inevitably, Jazz Jamaica are considerably more impressive as a live outfit.

Nevertheless, the second album suggests the group's staying power and an ambition to push into new musical territory. The inclusion of Bird's 'Dewey Square' alongside the Bacharach/David 'Walk On By', 'I Heard It Through The Grapevine', the theme from *Exodus* and Wayne Shorter's 'Night Dreamer' suggests a group prepared to cast its net wide. Crosby is still the driving force, though it is Rollins who does the excellent horn arrangements, and his big blatting sound is consistently attractive. Well worth a listen.

The All Stars big band on *Massive* brings together a remarkable array of British musicians from two generations, from young cats in their mid-20s to seniors of 70-plus. The sound is joyous and strong and bids fair to keep this strain of music going for another few years yet.

The Jazz Passengers

GROUP

The name was supposed to sound like the Jazz Messengers, but with a much lighter slant on life and music. They toured with Deborah Harry, for which the greatest respect.

*****(*) Implement Yourself**
New World 80398 *Curtis Fowlkes (tb); Roy Nathanson (as, ts, cl); Marc Ribot (g, hn); Bill Ware (vib); Jim Nolet (vn); Brad Jones (b); E. J. Rodriguez (d, perc); Waldwick High School Marching Band.* 3/90.

***** Live At The Knitting Factory**
KFWCD 107 *As above; omit Ribot, band; add Marcus Roja (tba); Dave Fiuczinski (g); Dougie Bourne (d); Yuka Honda (samples).* 1/91.

***** Plain Old Joe**
Knitting Factory KFWCD 139 *As above; omit Fiuczinski, Roja, Bourne, Honda; add Michael Dorf (hca); Helen Wood (v).* 92.

The original idea was a trombone/saxophone duo, consisting of Fowlkes and Nathanson, but it has steadily expanded into a flexible ensemble that does what can only be described as jazz cabaret. Many of the vocal arrangements are reminiscent, weirdly, of Carla Bley's *Escalator Over The Hill*, or one of Frank Zappa's jazzier projects, which may or may not be enticing news. If one could imagine an avant-garde or post-modern Crusaders, that might be even nearer the mark. The drill is not to expect anything too much like the last track or album. Fortunately, it's all done with too much wit and intelligence to risk the charge of mere perversity, and the playing, from Fowlkes and Nathanson especially, is so good that one seldom pauses to wonder why? or even what?

With impeccable illogic, the Passengers' first album appeared on the Crepuscule label, which hails from Belgium and enjoys a somewhat twilit reputation elsewhere. Since the turn of the '90s, the group has had a fairly regular berth at the Knitting Factory in New York City and their live album was cut there. It's by far the weakest of the available records and the only one to which the charge of self-indulgence sticks. Though they seem on the surface to be the quintessential live act, the Passengers are brilliant exponents of studio performance and *Implement Yourself* manages to combine a relaxed live feel with astonishing discipline and exactness. As befits a group that has grown organically, there is no obviously dominating voice, though the two founders are clearly the guiding personalities, somewhat like Zawinul and Shorter in Weather Report.

Even so, Jones, the remarkable Ware and Rodriguez add their two cents and it is difficult to think of the group (unlike WR) as anything other than a unit. That being so, guests are absorbed quite seamlessly, rarely sticking out or intruding. *Implement Yourself* has less vocal material than usual, but Ribot's vocalized guitar line intercutting with the vibes on the Dolphyish 'Peace In The Valley' takes the place of a conventional lyric. As a whole, it's a bruising but constantly fascinating listen.

Plain Old Joe is somewhat close to the group's music-theatre vein and doesn't come across so well on disc.

Eddie Jefferson (1918–79)

VOCALS

Along with King Pleasure, and Lambert, Hendricks and Ross, Eddie Jefferson was the big star of jazz vocalese, a style which involved putting lyrics to famous jazz solos; in Jefferson's case, the starting point was Coleman Hawkins's classic 'Body And Soul'. Originally a dancer, Eddie sang with a gruff grace and sustained a career as a member of James Moody's and then Richie Cole's groups right through to the end of his life.

*****(*) The Jazz Singer**
Evidence ECD 22062 *Jefferson; Frank Galbreath, John McFarland, Howard McGhee (t); Matthew Gee, Tom McIntosh (tb); Sahib Shihab (as); James Moody (ts); Musa Kaleem (ts, bs); Bill Graham (bs); Johnny Acea, Gene Kee, Tommy Tucker (p); Louisiana Red (g); John Latham, Peck Morrison (b); Clarence Johnson, Osie Johnson (d); Babs Gonzales, Honi Gordon, Ned Gravely (v).* 64–68.

***** Letter From Home**

Original Jazz Classics OJC 307 *Jefferson; Ernie Royal, Clark Terry (t); Jimmy Cleveland (tb); James Moody (as, f); Johnny Griffin (ts); Arthur Clarke (bs); Junior Mance, Joe Zawinul (p); Barry Galbraith (b); Louis Hayes, Osie Johnson, Sam Jones (d).* 12/61.

*****(*) Body And Soul**

Original Jazz Classics OJC 396 *Jefferson; Dave Burns (t); James Moody (ts, f); Barry Harris (p); Steve Davis (b); Bill English (d).* 9/68.

*****(*) Come Along With Me**

Original Jazz Classics OJC 613 *Jefferson; Bill Hardman (t); Charles McPherson (as); Barry Harris (p); Gene Taylor (b); Bill English (d).* 8/69.

A death sentence is a pretty harsh review, as Ralph Ellison wrote of Salman Rushdie. In 1979, the 60-year-old Jefferson was shot dead outside the Detroit club in which he'd been appearing. Like most of the bebop vocalists – and despite a brief recent revival in the critical fortunes of King Pleasure, who successfully co-opted Jefferson's style – he is little known among younger jazz fans, and various attempts at revival in recent years have fallen rather flat. A Muse disc, currently out of circulation with the rest of that label, dubbed him 'The Godfather Of Vocalese', and there is some justice in this. There is a widespread belief that Pleasure wrote the lyrics to 'Moody's Mood For Love', a vocalized transcription of James Moody's alto saxophone solo on 'I'm In The Mood For Love'; Pleasure certainly made it a monster hit, but the song was Jefferson's.

The early material on *The Jazz Singer* is taken from an Inner City LP, augmented by six rare tracks, some of which have not been available before. There are interesting duets from 1964 and 1965 with pianist Tommy Tucker ('Silly Little Cynthia') and guitarist Louisiana Red ('Red's New Dream'), but the key material is the well-known stuff: Parker's 'Now's The Time', Jimmy Forrest's 'Night Train' and, of course, 'Moody's Mood For Love' and the intelligent and inventive 'Body And Soul' (later revived by Manhattan Transfer as a tribute to Jefferson), which are also included on the fine 1968 session, also featuring Moody and a brilliant version of 'Filthy McNasty'.

Letter boasts a heavyweight line-up and some sure-footed – Jefferson was also a dancer – vocal arrangements. Four of the tracks are for sextet, but the better pieces use the full breadth of the band, with Jefferson high-wiring it over the 29-year-old Joe Zawinul's spry comping; check out Jefferson's version of the pianist's 'Mercy, Mercy, Mercy' on the 1968 *Body And Soul*. The singer's longest-standing partnership, with saxophonist Moody, is reflected in a dozen cuts, one of the best of which is a lively 'So What' (again on *Body And Soul*). Their relationship had rekindled in the '60s when Jefferson, who had been eclipsed by smoother talents like Jon Hendricks, staged something of a comeback; the later sessions (*Come Along With Me*) with Bill Hardman and Charles McPherson on staples like 'Yardbird Suite' and 'Dexter Digs In' are well worth catching, though the voice has lost some of its elasticity and bounce. Like King Pleasure, Jefferson improvised and wrote lyrics to some of the classic bop solos; precisely because they worked such similar turf, there was a constant risk of copyright wrangles, which explains why 'Body And Soul' is sometimes retitled 'I Feel So Good', 'Parker's Mood' and 'Bless My Soul'.

Vocalese has never recaptured the success it enjoyed when these sides were recorded. In recent years, though, it has shaken off something of the stigma it had acquired and is again being taken seriously. Eddie Jefferson commands a place – albeit a small one – in any comprehensive collection.

Billy Jenkins (born 1956)

GUITAR, PIANO, VOICE

Basing himself in Bromley, Kent, Jenkins has progressed from his pub-rock roots into a visionary figure whose embrace of jazz, rock and other musics is intensely personal and creative, even if it is constantly undercut by his satiric bent and bravura eccentricity. He recorded constantly in the '80s and '90s, mainly on his own labels, and has employed most of the best of the younger British jazz musicians to play on them at some point.

****** Scratches Of Spain**

Babel BDV 9404 *Jenkins; Chris Batchelor, John Eacott, Skid Solo (t); Dave Jago (tb); Ashley Slater (btb, tba, v); Iain Ballamy, Steve Buckley (sax); Dai Pritchard (sax, cl); Dave Cooke (g); Django Bates (ky); Jimmy Haycraft (vib); Jo Westcott (clo); Tim Matthewman, Simon Edwards (b); Steve Arguëlles, Roy Dodds (d, perc); Dawson (perc).* 87.

***** Entertainment USA**

Babel BDV 9401 *Jenkins; John Eacott (t); John Harborne (tb); Mark Lockheart (ts); Martin Speake (as); Django Bates (ky); Maria Lamburn (vla); Huw Warren (acc, clo); Steve Watts (b); Roy Dodds (d); Dawson, Martin France (perc); Lol Graves, Suzy M, Lindy Lou, Tina G, Tony Messenger (v).* 94.

***** Mayfest '94**

Babel BDV 9502 *Jenkins; Rainer Brennecke (t); Jorg Huke (tb); Thomas Klemm (ts, f); Huw Warren (p, acc, glockenspiel); Steve Watts (b); Martin France (d).* 5/94.

****** First Aural Art Exhibition**

VOTP VOCD 921 *Jenkins; John Eacott, Skid Solo (t); John Harborne, Dave Jago (tb); Ashley Slater (btb, tba); Iain Ballamy, Mark Ramsden, Martin Speake (as); Steve Buckley, Mark Lockheart (ts); Dai Pritchard (bs, bcl); Stuart Hall, Andy McFarlane (vn); Jo Westcott (clo); Dave Cooke, Robin Aspland (g); Jim Haycraft (vib); Steve Berry, Winston Blissett, Tim Matthewman, Steve Watts (b); Roy Dodds, Martin France (d); Dawson (perc).* 84–91.

*****(*) Still ... Sounds Like Bromley**

Babel BDV 9717 *Jenkins; Claude Deppa (t); Roland Bates (tb); Iain Ballamy (as, ts); Dai Pritchard (bcl); Django Bates (ky); James Taylor (org); Davey Williams (g); Steve Watts, Mike Mondesir (b); Martin France (d); David Vine (perc); strings.* 95.

Billy Jenkins is a musical anarchist. Notably resistant to ideology, he espouses a version of the kitchen-sink Situationism which lay behind the British punk movement. If music has become business (an equation he rejects), then the only refuge is a kind of unself-conscious anti-technique Jenkins has christened 'Spazz', which encourages the retention of 'wrong' notes and false starts, and the propagation of lo-fi recordings on the least sophisticated of formats. Jenkins is uniquely concerned with the packaging of music, not just in the cardboard-and-laminate sense but in terms of its perceived contours and limits. His 'Big Fights' encounters restrict duo improvisation to 12 three-minute 'rounds', the antithesis of the open-ended approach of most 'free' improvisers, but which also levels pertinent comment at their tacit belief that sheer duration is an end in itself. More satirically, Jenkins has presented 'uncommercial' samples of his work in chocolate wrappers, a neat comment on music's consumable nature, and has mimicked ECM and Windham Hill colophons and the ubiquitous 'Nice Price' cover to Miles Davis's *Sketches Of Spain*. *Scratches Of Spain* is, rightly, Jenkins's most celebrated single record, a frantic, un-Cool exposition of 'Spazz' technique and his deployment of a ragged army of co-religionists known as the Voice Of God Collective. *Scratches*' arrival on CD doesn't for a moment diminish its brutal simplicity or its deceptive sophistication as a piece of 'product'. Jenkins's transfer to CD is not yet total, and a good deal of his work, including the 'Big Fights', may still be found on Voice Of The People cassettes, but we have not listed these this time round. Jenkins has been around on the British scene long enough now for pieces like 'Benidorm Motorway Services' and 'Cooking Oil' to have become minor classics, albeit harder to hum than the adagio from *Concierto De Aranjuez*. In place of the 'Spanish tinge', a pervasive greasy taste. In place of Gil Evans's limpid orchestration, the 'ensemble' sound of a dozen lager louts going home at 2 a.m., like the discoboats that used to compromise Jenkins's rest in his studio home at Greenwich.

His gift for pastiche and even meta-pastiche is more evident still on the brilliant *Entertainment USA*, a collection of bilious and affectionate tributes to great American entertainers like Ronald Reagan, Oliver North, daffy-haired boxing promoter and philanthropist Don King, and Charles Manson, to say nothing of weightier individuals like Doris Day, Elvis Presley and Johnny Cash. Both the excellent *First Aural Art Exhibition* and the live Glasgow gig with the Fun Horns offer a chance to hear earlier Jenkins opus numbers on CD, in advance of some of the earlier vinyl and cassettes being reissued entire. The former includes 'Brilliant', 'Expensive Equipment', 'Fat People', 'The Blues', 'Sade's Lips', 'Discoboats At Two O'Clock', 'Cooking Oil', 'Donkey Droppings', and 'Elvis Presley', which – initiates will confirm – is a pretty fair representation. The Glasgow session has, *inter alia*, 'Arrival Of The Tourists', 'Greenwich One Way System' and 'Fat People', delivered in a rough-and-ready taping straight off the mixing desk at the old Renfrew Ferry. *Still ... Sounds Like Bromley* is a definitive Jenkins band line-up and seems to some extent like a dry run for the conceptual masterpiece which is listed below, although this is more specifically prepared for jazz band: David Vine's steel pan solo on 'High Street/Part Pedestrianized' virtually invents a jazz vocabulary for that instrument, and throughout there are marvellously vivid moments of Jenkinsization. As always, genres and the whole idea of 'genre' are turned upside down. It may be that Frank Zappa is the nearest measurable equivalent to Jenkins, but it seems unlikely that he would be flattered by the comparison and it may yet be that he is a more significant figure.

★★★ East/West

Babel 9601 *Jenkins; Rainer Brenneke (t); Jorg Huke (tb); Iain Ballamy (ss, ts); Thomas Klemm (ts, f); Volker Schlott (ss, as); Huw Warren (acc, glock, synclavier); Steve Watts (b); Roy Dodds, Steve Noble, Dave Ramm (perc); Hannah Heisenbuttel, VOGC Junior League (v).* 97.

More inspired insanity from Jenkins to mark the moment in history where London became a more divided city than Berlin. Here he's teamed with the effortlessly virtuosic Fun Horns in a set that asserts such universal truths as 'We All Eat Food' and 'We All Wear Socks' (tell that to Thelonious Monk), and celebrates the demolition of the Wall. 'The Unquestioned Answer' is a rebuttal to Charles Ives and 'Commercialism Is A Cancer' is a closing word from our (non-)sponsor. Great fun and more thoughtful than you might suspect.

★★★★ Suburbia

Babel BDV 9926 *Jenkins; Rainer Brennecke (t); Jorg Huke (tb); Mark Lockheart (saxes); Volker Schlott (as); Thomas Klemm (ts); Kit Packham (bs); Dave Ramm (ky); Huw Warren (p); David Le Page, Matt Sharp (vn); Neil Catchpole (vla); Chris Allen (clo); Steve Watts (b); Martin France, Roy Dodds, Steve Noble (d); Nicky Kemp, Gem Howard, Cassidy Howard-Kemp, Alice Jenkins, Harriet Jenkins, Daisy Lockheart, Rita Lockheart, Grace Messenger, Roxanne Messenger, Kati Tighe, Sophie Tighe (v); Suzy M (chorus mistress).* 99.

Jenkins has been busy, as usual, and while some may cavil at even including him in the book, it would be an outrage to omit this Home Counties masterpiece, a concept album about Bromley as a home of the blues, with all its attendant irritations and virtues alike. The titles of some of these pieces – 'The Unknown Car Across Your Drive', 'Corner Shop With Security Grills' and so on – make manifest the subtext of the record, but the music is vintage Jenkins, bits and pieces from all over the place, fused by great playing and sheer determination. American readers will be baffled by him; but he is, along with the Princess Royal and Walthamstow dog stadium, one of our national treasures.

★★★(★) Life

VOCD 023 *Jenkins; Perry White (p); Dave Ramm (org); Dylan Bates (vn); Richard Bolton (g): Gerry Tighe (hca); Thad Kelly (b); Roy Dodds, Mike Pickering (d); VOGC Junior League Choir.* 8/01.

A big title for this set of fierce and gentle blues impressions, but by this stage in his career, Jenkins seems well qualified to muse on life. The star of the session, apart of course from the leader, who spills glorious runs of sound, is Dylan Bates. Brother of the gifted Django, he plays electric violin with an intensity that will have music critics reaching for comparisons with Billy Bang and Leroy Jenkins, except that Bates has a folksier approach, by no means uncomplicated or gentle, but nothing like as biting as the Americans.

Billy's blues are, of course, as much celebratory as mournful, as much salacious as dignified. He's not the world's finest singer, but then neither were any of the very greatest bluesmen, and neither – bizarre comparison, perhaps – was Jimi Hendrix. This is Billy's Band Of Gypsies; not quite the classic outfit we remember fondly of yore, but a good line-up with great chops and complete musical understanding.

Great muttonchops on the cover of *S.A.D.* (not listed here for reasons which will become obvious). It is credited to Billy Jenkins and the Blues Collective and it begins with the song 'Ain't Gonna Play Jazz No More'. If he means it, it'll be a loss to this book and to jazz in Britain; if he doesn't, we'll wait the next move. Suffice it to say, though, that *S.A.D.* and *Blues Zero Two* and the other BC sets are worth getting for anyone who wants to hear how life in the Deep South (of London) can give you the down'n'dirty blues, too.

Clay Jenkins

TRUMPET

Jenkins writes thoughtful and often challenging modern jazz that builds on tradition.

***** Yellow Flowers After**

Chase Music 8051 *Jenkins; Reggie Thomas (p); Tom Warrington (b); Steve Houghton (d).* 99.

***** Azure Eyes**

Jazz Compass JC1003 *As above, except omit Houghton; add Larry Koonse (g); Joe LaBarbera (d).* 11/99.

Jenkins seems interested in the more highly structured and orchestrated end of bebop. Tadd Dameron tunes appear on both these records – 'Soultrane' on *Yellow Flowers After* and 'Hot House' on its rather better successor – and his own impressive writing is thirled to harmonic ideas that have their origins in Tadd's still under-exploited charts. As a horn-player, Jenkins has a clear, rather bleak sound that is not the most attractive you'll hear. Nevertheless, it is the quality of his thought that impresses and his colleagues on both albums are clearly responsive to his idiom. On the first record – not his debut, but the first to come our way – he mixes up originals with challenging repertory pieces: 'Brilliant Corners', an unaccompanied 'Don't Get Around Much Any More' and an unexpectedly beautiful 'Let's Fall In Love'. The original melodies are not that memorable and most newcomers will find it easier to have familiar material as a peg.

The integration is more accomplished on the second album, though – swings and roundabouts – it seems to have lost some of the freshness and spontaneity. LaBarbera is a fine, powerful drummer and brings a robust architecture to the original songs, anchoring them more securely than Houghton did on the earlier record. 'It Never Entered My Mind' is a showcase for Jenkins and he uses the opportunity to the full, with a lovely, developed solo.

Jazz Compass is an artist-run label, co-founded by the musicians involved here.

Leroy Jenkins (born 1932)

VIOLIN, VIOLA

Jenkins spent some time away from his native Chicago, teaching in the south, before returning to Chicago and becoming part of the influential AACM. His extended approach embraces classical violin of the Heifetz era with contemporary free jazz. Jenkins has been a member of the Revolutionary Ensemble and was leader of the advanced group, Sting.

***** Lifelong Ambitions**

Black Saint 120033 *Jenkins; Muhal Richard Abrams (p).* 3/77.

***** The Legend Of Ai Glatson**

Black Saint 120022 *Jenkins; Anthony Davis (p); Andrew Cyrille (d, perc).* 7/78.

*****(*) Mixed Quintet**

Black Saint 120060 *Jenkins; John Clark (frhn); James Newton (f); J. D. Parran (cl); Marty Ehrlich (bcl).* 3/79.

****(*) Urban Blues**

Black Saint 120083 *Jenkins; Terry Jenoure (vn, v); James Emery, Brandon Ross (g); Alonzo Gardner (b); Kamal Sabir (d).* 1/84.

*****(*) Live!**

Black Saint 120122 *Jenkins; Brandon Ross (g); Eric Johnson (syn); Hill Greene (b); Reggie Nicholson (d).* 3/92.

Leroy Jenkins and George Lewis share one often-forgotten characteristic that makes them ideal improvising partners. Though both are given to very forceful and even violent gestures, they are also capable of great lyricism; the same has to be said of Andrew Cyrille. In a period when Billy Bang is, rightly or wrongly, perhaps the benchmark jazz violinist, critics have often missed the fact that Jenkins's percussive, rasping delivery rarely departs from an identifiable tonal centre or melodic logic. His preference is for looping statements, punctuated by abrupt rhythmic snaps; the most obvious influence is Stuff Smith, but there are also parallels with the way saxophonist Anthony Braxton used to deliver improvised lines. Like pianist Anthony Davis, Jenkins has an almost 'legitimate' technique and a tone that one can imagine negotiating with Bartók or Stravinsky.

Davis is present on *The Legend Of Ai Glatson*, which was recorded shortly after the Revolutionary Ensemble disbanded. It is one of the few places in contemporary jazz where the direct and unassimilated influence of Cecil Taylor can be detected, and it remains strongly reminiscent of Cecil's Café Montmartre sessions. Jenkins is in stunningly good form, and his solo play on tributes to two modern saxophone-players, 'Brax Stone' and 'Albert Ayler (His Life Was Too Short)' is as good as anything in his catalogue. *Legend* isn't the prettiest of recordings, but it has all the intensity Jenkins brings to live performance.

The *Mixed Quintet* session is a foretaste of the classical configurations that were to follow. Some of the titles might sound restrainedly formal – 'Quintet #3', 'Shapes, Textures, Rhythms, Moods' – but none of these is a merely abstract étude or exercise, and all of them have Jenkins's trademark blend of intense expression and admirable control. The four wind-players who join him are all, of course, masters in their own right, and Ehrlich is revelatory, a player as strongly rooted in classic jazz as he is in European art music.

Jenkins released no commercial recordings between 1984 and 1992, and his back-catalogue is in a rather threadbare state. Jenkins's working band, Sting, were capable of great things in a live setting, but they're nothing compared to the later Computer Minds. The live session completely merits the exclamation mark. It's a fierce, urgent session, recorded in a New York public school, and sounds appropriately in contact with what's going on in the streets. To an extent, Jenkins is a traditionalist rather than a radical. His interests, though, have always reached well beyond jazz, and his band tackles a whole range of black musics.

The duos with Abrams are also both traditionally minded and innovative. All the compositions are from the violinist, even the closing 'The Father, The Son, The Holy Ghost', which clearly isn't the same as the Albert Ayler piece. Like their titles – 'The Blues', 'Meditation', 'Happiness' – the pieces are kept pretty abstract (and are all almost exactly the same length). There's a patient, almost schoolmasterly side to Abrams's playing. Jenkins moves off into pan-tonality a few times, but he stays firmly anchored in an identifiable key for most of the set, even when his partner has dissolved the normal ties of melody and accompaniment. It's difficult to tell when they're improvising and when reading, and the abiding impression is of formality rather than freedom.

Urban Blues is a less-than-representative account of a band that on its night could be wildly exciting. Recorded live in Sweet Basil in New York City (on 2 January, which might explain the liverish playing), it comes across as muddled rather than waspy. Terry Jenoure's vocals were a luxury that Sting could have dispensed with, and the twinned guitars (great players when on their own turf) are often repetitive and unilluminating. The CD brightens up the sound considerably, but doubts remain.

****** Solo**

Lovely Music 134 *Jenkins (vn solo).* 98.

There is a grizzled majesty to this unaccompanied set, a confident conflation of traditions. Tackling 'Giant Steps' and Dizzy's 'Wouldn't You' on solo fiddle and viola bespeaks some courage, but Jenkins skates across those familiar harmonics with breathtaking ease. The recording is up-close and very personal, and anyone who has not encountered his work previously will be captivated.

Jack Jenney (1910–45)

TROMBONE

An impeccable technician, Jenney was in demand on the New York scene during the '30s and led his own band at the end of the decade, but it was a financial disaster. Some of his best work was with the Artie Shaw band. He died very young from complications from alcoholism.

***** Stardust**

Hep CD 1045 *Jenney; Charlie Spivak, Red Solomon, Charlie Zimerman, Don Sprague, Oliver Suderman, Nick Galetta, Tom Gonsoulin, Rudy Novak, Joe DePaul, Don Stevens (t); Bob Jenney, Jack Bigelow, Henry Singer, Ray Noonan (tb); Eddie Brown (cl); Toots Mondello, Frank Myers, Hugo Winterhalter, Larry Gordon, Steve Madrick, Victor Garber (as); Johnny Pepper, Art Drelinger, Peanuts Hucko, Buddy Bardach, Edwin Keeghan, Maurice Kogan, Babe Russin (ts); Claude Thornhill, Frank Cohen, Arnold Ross, Gill Bowers (p); Chick Reeves, Al Costi, Morris Crossin (g); Fred Whiting, Lou Shoobe, Iggy Shevak (b); Johnny Williams, Gene Krupa, Sid Jacobs, Paul Richter, Frank Bond (d); Adelaide Moffat, Louise Tobin, Meredith Blake, Frank Bond, Kirby Walker (v).* 6/37–1/40.

Jenney's entire jazz legacy is bound up in Hoagy Carmichael's tune. His eight bars on Artie Shaw's 1940 record of 'Stardust' remain indelible, and the version he recorded with his own band – where he takes a musing journey through the tune, hardly referring to the original melody as he goes, almost in a manner akin to Coleman Hawkins on 'Body And Soul' – is extraordinary. He played as smoothly as Dorsey, as sonorously as Teagarden – but he was a disaster as a bandleader, going broke in the process, and ruining himself with alcohol, as Campbell Burnap's sleeve-note dolefully recounts.

The 18 surviving titles by Jenney's various big-band line-ups are collected here. Lacking in outstanding soloists or compelling arrangements, it's easy to see why the outfit made no significant impact, and this set is really for big-band specialists only. Jenney's own playing, though, remains haunting in its unblemished beauty, and the two takes of 'Stardust' included here should really rank among the great examples of trombone-playing on record. As usual with Hep, excellent transfers.

Ingrid Jensen (born 1969)

TRUMPET, FLUGELHORN

Jensen's musical progress has been astonishing. At 25, she became the youngest faculty member at the Bruckner Conservatory in Linz, adding academic honours to a growing list of performing and recording credits with the likes of Kenny Barron, the Mingus Big Band and the Maria Schneider Orchestra. Her trumpet tone is highly distinctive, like oiled silk.

***** Vernal Fields**

Enja ENJ 9013-2 *Jensen; Steve Wilson (as, ss); George Garzone (ts); Bruce Barth (p); Larry Grenadier (b); Lenny White (d).* 10/94.

*****(*) Here On Earth**

Enja ENJ 9313-2 *Jensen; Gary Bartz (as, ss); George Colligan (p); Dwayne Burno (b); Bill Stewart (d); Jill Seifers (v).* 9/96.

*****(*) Higher Grounds**

Enja ENJ 9353-2 *Jensen; Gary Thomas (ts, f); Dave Kikoski (p, el p); Ed Howard (b); Victor Lewis (d).* 98.

Jensen is a young Canadian propelled on to an international stage by the growing confidence and adventurousness of the scene back home. It's perhaps significant, though, that she should have been picked up by a European label, fruit of a period of study in Vienna with pianist Hal Galper. Purely in terms of sound, she resembles a cross between Woody Shaw (an acknowledged hero) and Art Farmer, with whom she has also taken classes. The latter debt is predictably most evident when she switches to flugelhorn; when she does so on the title-track of *Here On Earth*, it is immediately evident that she intends to do things her own way, as she did on the debut album, where 'Every Time We Say Goodbye' sounds like a Farmer pastiche only until Jensen is ready to make her own statement. Though 'Here On Earth' is pianist George Colligan's composition and though Jensen is sharing the front line with the veteran Gary Bartz (who has rarely sounded better, incidentally), she stamps her personality even on this rather slight, Latinized waltz. On 'Woodcarvings', the other debt is made explicit, a dense but curiously floating theme that one might imagine Woody playing himself. This time Bartz is on soprano, masterfully negotiating a theme that sits awkwardly for the horns but which is made to sound as natural as breathing. Stewart is a calm and steady presence throughout, less showy than White in the way that Bartz is less emphatically expressive than Wilson, but unfailingly musical all the same.

What sets the second album apart more than anything isn't the playing – which is superlative – so much as the choice of material. It's a beautifully judged set: just the one original, and this time one by sister Christine Jensen (who wrote four of the tunes on *Vernal Fields*); alongside this, themes by Cole Porter, Hank Mobley, Kenny Wheeler, Miles Davis and Gil Evans's 'The Time Of The Barracudas', and Mercedes Rossi's 'Ninety-One', the latter an unexpectedly lyrical gem. Jill Seifers's two vocals are somewhat dispensable, but they do contribute an intelligent change of pace and add a new range of colours to a beautifully modulated set. One simply basks in Gary Bartz's warm-hearted wisdom, and in Jensen's own poise and confidence.

The third album simply builds on its predecessors, but there are signs that Jensen is increasingly thinking of the band as a unit, a collective instrument, rather than as an aggregate of individuals. The arrangements, especially on 'Litha' and the closing 'Land Of Me' are very tight and highly organized, though not so excessively programmed that they lose the feeling of improvisational looseness which is also a characteristic of her work. The rhythm section is utterly sympathetic, and in Gary Thomas she has found a second horn who challenges her in the most positive way. *Higher Grounds* includes some of his best work of recent times. Jensen continues to impress.

***** Now As Then**

Justin Time 8499 *Jensen; Seamus Blake (ts); Christine Jensen, Steve Wilson (as, f); Gary Versace (org); Jon Wikan (d).* 02.

Officially, this is credited to Project O, a thoughtful organ trio in which Jensen takes equal credit with Versace and the powerful Wikan. She is still the dominant voice, though the addition of guest reeds changes the nature of the group quite substantially and possibly to its detriment. One wants to hear more of the interplay between Ingrid's ripe-sounding trumpet and Versace's rolling B3 sound, which is reminiscent of Larry Young, if closer in articulation to Dan Wall's work. The opening 'Night Has A Thousand Eyes' is a highpoint that the rest of the album fails to reach again. A good, thoughtful listen none the less.

Jerry Jerome (1912–2001)

TENOR SAXOPHONE, CLARINET

Busy since the '30s, Jerome had a long jazz life, working as a section-player with Miller, Goodman and Shaw, and as a studio regular thereafter.

*****(*) Something Old, Something New**

Arbors ARCD 19168 2CD *Jerome; Yank Lawson, Chris Griffin, Bobby Hackett, Dale McMickle, Mel Davis, Randy Sandke (t); Henry 'Red' Allen (t, v); George Masso, John Messner, Frank Sirocco, Vernon Brown, Ray Coniff (tb); Tyree Glenn (tb, vib); Bill Stegmeyer (cl); Toots Mondello, Paul Rickey, Wolfie Tannenbaum (as); Arthur Rollini, Hymie Schertzer (ts); Joe Grim (bs); Teddy Wilson, John Potoker, Dick Hyman, Johnny Guarnieri, Frankie Hines, Dick Cary, Bill Clifton (p); Phil Kraus (vib); Charlie Christian, Johnny Smith, Allen Hanlon (g); Oscar Pettiford, Bob Haggart, Sid Weiss, George Roumanis, Tommy Abruzzo (b); George Wettling, Joe Ascione, Mousie Alexander, Dave Tough, Specs Powell (d).* 9/39–3/96.

***** Something Borrowed Something Blue**

Arbors ASRCD 19213 2CD *Similar to above, except add Charlie Shavers (t), Lou Colombo (t, flhn), Lawrence Brown, John Allred (tb), Tommy Newsom (ts), Hank Jones (p), Bob Leary (g), Frank Tate (b), Ed Metz (d), Lynn Roberts (v).* 9/39–3/01.

This was Jerome's first jazz album for 40 years. The first disc is almost a 'bonus' album, since it consists of Jerry reminiscing on his career – with Glenn Miller, Goodman and Shaw, and as a studio regular. There are some fascinating fragments from many years of work – a 1939 jam with Charlie Christian, small groups with Charlie Shavers and Teddy Wilson, commercials featuring Bobby Hackett and Henry Allen and plenty more besides. Not a record to hear often, but an engaging audio-documentary. The 'New' section is a delight. Jerome was almost 84 when he made the date, but his tenor sound is still big and unfaltering, and none of the tempos troubled him. Arbors assembled one of their repertory casts for the session and, with Sandke and Masso at their best, it's a fine hour or so of blue-chip mainstream, and a beguiling tribute to a likeable old pro.

Amazingly, they did it all again five years later. As before, the first disc has Jerome reminiscing about some of his old recordings before we hear them; the second, cut only weeks before his 89th birthday, is his farewell to jazz (he died the following November). The old stuff is interesting if rather tame, though it ends with a 1964 jam on 'I Found A New Baby' from a birthday-party gig with Shavers, Lawrence Brown and Hank Jones. The new music is solid mainstream, and Jerry holds his own.

Jet All Star Quartet

GROUP

Four guys, all stars, playing like rockets, not jets.

****** Live At Jazz En Tete 1994**

Blue Geodesics 9704 *Gary Bartz (as); Kenny Barron (p); Billy Drummond (b); Ben Riley (d).* 94.

A line-up to die for and a performance to match. Whoever called for Hank Mobley's 'This I Think Of You' as an opener knew what he was about. It gives the group lots to chew on and provides Bartz with one of his trickily pitched solos. Barron isn't normally thought of as a Monk interpreter, so it may have been Riley who nominated 'Blue Monk' and 'Ask Me Now'. The quartet chews them both up and adds some interesting flourishes to the chestnut. Freddie Hubbard's 'Up Jumped Spring' (a l-o-n-g version) and Miles's 'The Theme' provide the rest of the meat and there's a nice version of Perez Prado's rarely jazzed-up 'Time Was' as filler. The rhythm section is sometimes a bit muffled but by and large the sound is good; the music is better than good.

Pucci Amanda Jhones

VOCAL

New York-based singer, in standards territory but with some freer stylings mixed in.

*****(*) Sweet Dreams**

Cadence CJR 1088 *Jhones; Kenyatta Beasley (t); Casey Benjamin (as); Karl-Martin Almqvist (ts); Kenny Barron (p); Morten Faerestrand (g); Hilliard Greene (b); Dwayne Broadnax (d).* 2/97.

****(*) Wild Is The Wind**

CIMP 170 *Jhones; Casey Benjamin (ss, as); Rory Stuart (g); Hilliard Greene (b); Wade Barnes (d).* 3/98.

Jhones takes an agreeably individual line on the modern jazz singer's position. While she makes the slow pace of 'A Sunday Kind Of Love' into something properly sensual, it's never submissive, and the sardonic follow-up of 'Trouble In Paradise' is played out with cool detachment. These are on the first album, which has a largely unfamiliar instrumental line-up, though Barron is brought on as a failsafe paterfamilias. Jhones has a timbre which is dark without being heavy, and though her position in the mix sounds curiously artificial at times, she has no difficulty in standing as the strongest presence on the date. Even the brief blues of 'Red Top' is handled intensely.

Wild Is The Wind was the first attempt by CIMP to record a vocal project. Their unglamorous sound really doesn't fit the situation. With no piano, and with Benjamin too exposed as sole horn, the band sound clumsy on a piece such as 'Porgy', which undermines the singer's treatment. It's frustrating, since she's otherwise in excellent voice on what resembles a demo more than a finished album.

Jan Johansson (1931–68)

PIANO, ORGAN, VIBES

Born in Söderhamn, Johansson studied piano from the age of eleven. He moved to Copenhagen in the late '50s and then to Stockholm in 1962. He became a prolific composer and performer in the Swedish modern scene of the '60s and wrote music for film, radio and TV, as well as recording his own albums, but a meteoric career was cut short by his death in a car accident en route to a concert.

****(*) En Resa I Jazz Och Folkton**

Heptagon HECD-0101 *Johansson; Bernt Rosengren (ts); Rune Gustafsson (g); Sture Akerberg, Roman Dylag (b); Egil Johansen (d); Rupert Clemendore (perc).* 2/61–8/66.

****** 8 Bitar Johansson / Innertrio**

Heptagon HECD-005 *Johansson; Gunnar Johnson, Georg Riedel (b); Ingvar Callmer, Egil Johansen (d).* 2/61–7/62.

****** Folkvisor**

Heptagon HECD-000 *As above, except add Bosse Broberg (t), Arne Domnérus (cl), Lennart Aberg (ts); omit Johnson and Callmer.* 2/62–9/67.

***** Spelar Musik Pa Sitt Eget Vis**

Heptagon HECD-012 *Johansson; Andreas Skjold (tb); Arne Domnérus (as, cl); Claes Rosendahl (cl, f); Rune Gustafsson (g); Sture Nordin (b); Egil Johansen (d); Rupert Clemendore (perc).* 10/64–11/66.

*****(*) Jazz Pa Ungerska / In Pleno**

Heptagon HECD-014 *Johansson; Svend Asmussen (vn); Rune Gustafsson (g); Palle Danielsson, Georg Riedel (b); Egil Johansen (d); Rupert Clemendore (perc).* 64.

*****(*) Live In Tallinn**

Heptagon HECD-007 *Johannson; Rune Gustafsson (g); Georg Riedel (b).* 6/66.

***** Spelar Musik Pa Sitt Eget Vis**

Megafon MFCD-2021 2CD *Johansson; Andreas Skjold (tb); Arne Domnérus (cl, as); Claes Rosendahl (cl); Bjarne Nerem (ts); Rune Gustafsson (g); Georg Riedel, Sture Nordin, Sture Akerberg (b); Egil Johansen, Rupert Clemendore (d).* 9/64–11/66.

****** Den Korta Fristen**

Heptagon HECD-001 *Johansson; Bertil Lövgren, Rolf Ericson, Jan Allan, Bosse Broberg, Lars Samuelsson (t); Runo Ericksson (btb); Arne Domnérus, Claes Rosendahl, Lennart Aberg, Erik Nilsson, Rune Falk (reeds); Rune Gustafsson (g); Georg Riedel (b); Egil Johansen (d).* 67–68.

***** 300,000**

Heptagon HECD-006 *Johansson; Lennart Aberg (ts); Georg Riedel (b); Egil Johansen, Rupert Clemendore (d); Gote Nilsson (elec).* 8/67–7/68.

***** Musik Genom Fyra Sekler**

Heptagon HECD-002 2CD *Johansson; Claes Rosendahl (cl, f); Sven Berger (f, ob, bsn); Rune Gustafsson (g); Georg Riedel (b); Arne Wilhelmsson, Sture Akerberg (b).* 9–10/68.

Johansson seems destined to remain a local legend, rarely mentioned outside his native Sweden, despite several contemporary masters from the region acknowledging his importance. The wider jazz audience should certainly be aware of this pioneering composer-pianist whose inquiring mind was extraordinary enough to demand a place for him among the modern masters of the music. Heptagon's initiative has done much to bring back several of Johansson's major albums. Though most of his recording was compressed into an eight-year period, he was prolific enough to have cut some 20 LPs, and several of the best are now back in circulation. Many may know him for his work with Stan Getz on some of the saxophonist's recordings in Scandinavia, but that seems like mere 'prentice-work compared with the two marvellous discs reissued on *8 Bitar Johansson / Innertrio*. Beautifully shaded between differing jazz styles, the music seems entirely fresh and unjaded, even after almost 40 years. The standards include a lovely 'She's Funny That Way' and a remarkable revision of Morton's 'The Chant', while the originals drift placidly between bebop and swing tempo, improvisations falling out of the set patterns, tamed by the lucidity of Johansson's touch and the variety of his voicings. *Folkvisor* is, if anything, even more impressive, bringing together the original albums, *Jazz Pa Svenska* and *Jazz Pa Ryska*. The 12 variations on Swedish folksong, with only the solid Riedel for company, make up a heartfelt meditation that equals any fusion of jazz and folk music so far committed to disc and, if the Russian themes that make up the rest of the disc are less affecting, they're a delightful makeweight. Johansson's insights are uniquely valuable and it's fitting that his own notes mention Jimmy Giuffre, since one is reminded of the American folklore which Giuffre inculcated into his own masterpiece, *The Jimmy Giuffre Clarinet*.

A recent reissue couples *Jazz Pa Ungerska*, where Johansson's usual team are joined by Svend Asmussen for another investigation of local themes, this time from Hungary, and the almost experimental *In Pleno*, where strange pieces such as 'Musik' and 'Mitt Piano' mingle with Coleman's 'Una Muy Bonita' and a tremendous fast blues, 'Pleno'. With the Asmussen tracks a fine legacy, this is another strong issue. Less successful is the patched-together *En Resa I Jazz Och Folkton*, which includes some early mischief-making – 'Tea For Two' is double-tracked with a backwards-tape solo, and 'Tico Tico' is ludicrously fast – as well as an unexpected appearance by Rosengren on one track, a waltz, a couple of polkas and some unfunky Hammond organ. For Johansson collectors only.

The live album suffers from indifferent sound but gains from the intense communication among the three men, Gustafsson sounding especially involved: sample the interplay on 'Blues For Lange', or the jaunty treatment given to Oscar Pettiford's 'Laverne Walk'. *Spelar Musik Pa Sitt Eget Vis* is comparatively disappointing, a hotch-potch of bits and pieces from various radio sessions: there's a fine 'Django' with strings and some other telling fragments, but some of the experiments take on an unappealing cast – a strange 'Camptown Races', for instance. Half of this set is also available on the one-disc *Spelar Musik Pa Sitt Eget Vis*, now also available on Heptagon. This is completely outdone by the compelling scores for Radiojazz Gruppen on *Den Korta Fristen*, music of real power and originality that makes one realize why his fellow-musicians held Johansson in such high regard. The almost shocking revision of 'A Night In Tunisia', set up as a feature for Nilsson's superb baritone, is a revelation – but so is 'Hej Blues', a haunting feature for Domnérus, the sparse setting for Gustafsson on 'Samba Triste' and several of Johansson's own scores, crowded with ideas.

Another live album, *300,000*, is less essential: Johansson had a taste for flirting with the edges of the avant-garde, and the two pieces which involve electronics and radio static sound as dated as most such adventures of the period. *Musik Genom Fyra Sekler* is a curious coda to the rest, a double-CD covering further explorations into Swedish traditional music. Johansson handles his group like a chamber ensemble, the reed-players switching between instruments from track to track, melodies given a poker-faced treatment or just slightly subverted by the leader's variations. 'Ack Varmeland Du Skona', which every Swedish jazzman has played at some point, is given a soberly attractive reading, but some of the other tunes run dangerously close to kitsch. An odd if intriguing end: Johansson's death was only weeks away.

Sven-Ake Johansson (born 1943)

DRUMS, VOCAL

Although Swedish, Johansson was in at the start of the free-music scene in Germany, working with Brötzmann and Schoof in the '60s. He formed a regular pairing with Alex von Schlippenbach, eventually performing with him as a singer, and began composing operettas.

***** Schlingerland**
Atavistic *Johansson (d solo).* 10/72.

*****(*) Six Little Pieces For Quintet**
hatOLOGY 538 *Johansson; Axel Dörner (t); Rudi Mahall (bcl); Sten Sandell (p); Matthias Bauer (b).* 1/99.

***** Barcelona Series**
hatOLOGY 559 *Johansson; Axel Dörner (t); Andrea Neumann (pianoharp).* 99.

Johansson's *Six Little Pieces* were conceived as a retrospective look at the '60s free jazz he came up with – 'early free jazz on period instruments' (and, suitably enough, he uses his old Slingerland kit for the job). The music has a nostalgic *fin de siècle* feel, but lacks nothing in vitality. The pieces are pitched mostly at a steadily rolling lope, the drummer directing in Sunny Murray-like style from the kit, and it's all done with sufficient restraint – no Brötzmannesque brawling here – so that the solos and ensembles have an almost painterly feel to them. Dörner and Mahall play with fine lyrical feeling for the settings, although if anyone stands out it's Sandell, who finds a way into what was often thought of as pianoless music with great insight. If you want to hear what Johansson was doing three decades earlier, Atavistic have reissued his old solo album for SAJ, *Schlingerland*, where the drummer simply rambles around the kit for what were originally two side-long pieces. Not, perhaps, the most interesting rediscovery in this series, but since we're nostalgics ourselves, we found it an entertaining glance back.

Johansson is not really a sentimentalist about music. For one 1996 festival set, as recounted in the notes to *Barcelona Series*, he conducted an ensemble of 12 vintage tractors. He's also pin-sharp on what his groups are about: for this trio, he offers the description: 'a mechanistic, almost non-expressive playing stance, with the aesthetics of renouncement or of leaving out instead of filling in'. As with the other group record, the music has a reposeful quality: purposeful rather than busy, and steadily accruing detail rather than teeming with activity. As a record, though, it does ask for the right moment: of the 11 pieces, some are interesting, some aren't.

Budd Johnson (1910–84)

TENOR, SOPRANO AND ALTO SAXOPHONES, CLARINET

Born in Dallas, Johnson was on the road as a drummer at 14 and then switched to saxophone. Worked in a Kansas City band in the late '20s and then co-led a band with Teddy Wilson in Chicago. Joined Louis Armstrong, 1933, then Earl Hines, 1935, for whom he wrote many arrangements. Stayed until 1942, then was with Dizzy Gillespie, Boyd Raeburn and Billy Eckstine. In the '50s he toured with Benny Goodman and Quincy Jones. Then often in a small band with Earl Hines. A classic stylist in the Hawkins mould and an outstanding arranger, Johnson is often overlooked, but he was a figure of real stature. He continued playing until his death in 1984.

***** Budd Johnson 1944–1952**
Classics 1307 *Johnson; Little Benny Harris, Al Killian, George Treadwell, Howard McGhee, Joe Newman (t); Trummy Young, Dickie Harris, Dicky Wells, J. J. Johnson (tb); Aaron Sachs (cl, as); Herbie Fields, George Dorsey, Hilton Jefferson (as); Charlie Singleton (ts, v); Harry Carney, Cecil Scott, Cecil Payne (bs); Clyde Hart, Marty Napoleon, Jimmy Jones, Luther Henderson, Kenny Drew, Billy Taylor (p); Chuck Wayne, Herman Mitchell (g); Oscar Pettiford, Joe Shulman, Al McKibbon, Trigger Alpert, Oscar Pettiford, Milt Hinton (b); Denzil Best, George Jones, Jimmy Crawford, Kansas Fields, Kelly Martin (d); Joe Gregory, Mary Stafford, Leslie Scott, Freddie Jackson, Johnny King (v).* 12/44–3/52.

***** Budd Johnson And The Four Brass Giants**
Original Jazz Classics OJC 1921 *Johnson; Nat Adderley (c); Ray Nance (t, vn); Clark Terry (t, flhn); Harry 'Sweets' Edison (t); Jimmy Jones, Tommy Flanagan (p); Joe Benjamin (b); Herbie Lovelle (d).* 8–9/60.

*****(*) Let's Swing**
Original Jazz Classics OJC 1720 *Johnson; Keg Johnson (tb); Tommy Flanagan (p); George Duvivier (b); Charli Persip (d).* 12/60.

***** The JPJ Quartet**
Storyville STCD 8235 *Johnson; Dill Jones (p); Bill Pemberton (b); Oliver Jackson (d).* 69–6/71.

Budd Johnson was a jazz giant for over five decades, yet he made comparatively few recordings under his own leadership, and it's sad that fewer still are currently in circulation.

Classics have entered the fray with a disc that musters a typical hotchpotch of sessions that cross between bop, swing and the early stirrings of mainstream. Four tracks by Clyde Hart's Hot Seven, for Savoy, are as close as Budd got to playing straight bebop (and there is the bonus of hearing Benny Harris, otherwise hardly recorded, in close-up). Otherwise there are one-off dates for labels such as Manor and Continental, under the nominal leadership of Al Killian, J. C. Heard and Dicky Wells, where Budd sails serenely through solo duties. Of the eight titles he cut for Cyclone in 1947, only a single coupling could be turned up. There are two soupy Leslie Scott vocals from 1947, then a jump to an All Stars date from 1951, which is a bit ordinary, though there's a fine Johnson ballad feature on 'It's The Talk Of The Town'. A journeyman's diary, interesting if hardly essential.

The OJC reissues are a thin representation, but at least a couple of good records are restored to the catalogue. Johnson was already a veteran when he made these, the tone settled in a classic Hawkins mould: big, broad, soaked in blues feeling. 'Blues By Budd', on *Let's Swing*, is an inimitable example of Johnson at his best. There is a certain dry humour in his playing which never spills over into parody or flippancy: listen to the way he opens his solo on 'Uptown Manhattan' on the quintet album, and hear how he intensifies his playing from that point. His brother Keg plays some cheerful solos, but it's Budd's record – try the lovely reading of 'Someone To Watch Over Me', in which the saxophonist composed a unison passage for himself and Duvivier.

Four Brass Giants was a session instigated by Cannonball Adderley, who'd been listening to some of Johnson's scores for the Hines band. Johnson swings almost blandly through this one and the brassmen aren't given the most compelling of duties to perform, but it has its moments.

The later quartet was recorded in the studio (exact date not reliably known) and at the Montreux Jazz Festival in 1971. Of the two, the live performances are immeasurably superior, and one wonders whether there wasn't more material from the same event to make the record a concert set without recourse to what could justifiably be dismissed as rehearsal material. The group has a seasoned, familiar sound, as if used to working together, and Johnson obviously thrives on a conducive harmonic environment.

Bunk Johnson (1889–1949)

TRUMPET

Though he originally claimed a birthdate of 1879, Johnson was born in New Orleans ten years later. He was a frequent second-trumpet man in the city's pioneer ragtime-to-jazz groups, but left in 1915 to tour the South, and in the '30s more or less quit music. Rediscovered in 1942, he became emblematic of the New Orleans revival, cantankerous and difficult, but playing in a style which many found moving and mystically primeval.

***** Bunk Johnson And His Superior Jazz Band**
Good Time Jazz 12048 *Johnson; Jim Robinson (tb); George Lewis (cl); Walter Decou (p); Lawrence Marrero (bj); Austin Young (b); Ernest Rogers (d).* 6/42.

****(*) Bunk Johnson 1942/1945**
Document DOCD-1010 *Johnson; Louis Armstrong (t); Jim Robinson, Albert Warner, J. C. Higginbotham (tb); Sidney Bechet (cl, ss); George Lewis (cl); Walter Decou, James P. Johnson (p); Lawrence Marrero (bj); Austin Young, Alcide 'Slow Drag' Pavageau, Ricard Alexis (b); Ernest Rogers, Edgar Mosely, Paul Barbarin, Abbie Williams (d).* 6/42–2/45.

***** Bunk And Lou**
Good Time Jazz 12024 *Johnson; Lu Watters, Bob Scobey (c); Turk Murphy (tb); Ellis Horne (cl); Wally Rose, Burt Bales (p); Clancy Hayes, Russ Bennett, Pat Patton (bj); Dick Lammi (bb); Squire Girsback (b); Bill Dart (d).* 2/44.

A difficult and contentious man, Bunk Johnson remains mysterious and fascinating, still the figurehead of 'revivalist' jazz even though his records remain relatively difficult to find, on small labels, and have been marginalized where those by, say, George Lewis have kept their reputation. Deceitful about his age – he was long thought to have been born in 1879, which would have made him even older than Buddy Bolden – Johnson was rediscovered in 1942 and, after being fitted out with new teeth, began making records. He had never recorded before, even though he'd played in Bolden's band, had moved on from New Orleans at some time in his mid-teens and had gone on to play all over the South. But many records came out of the next five years. Those for Good Time Jazz were among the earliest. *Bunk Johnson And His Superior Jazz Band* establishes the best-remembered Johnson line-up, with fellow veterans Robinson, Lewis and Marrero, and the material is mostly New Orleans staples such as 'Down By The Riverside'. *Bunk And Lou* pits him against the Lu Watters band, who mix 'modern' items such as 'Ory's Creole Trombone' with a number of truly ancient ragtime pieces like 'Smokey Mokes' although, frustratingly, Johnson plays on only the more recent material. While neither is a really satisfactory record – Watters and company sound too slickly amateur to suit an original like Johnson, and the other record lacks the awareness which Johnson would quickly develop – both establish the tenets of his own trumpet style: a polished, almost courtly sort of phrasing, the elimination of 'hot' tricks such as growls or shakes or needless vibrato, a bright and optimistic open tone and a way of swinging which sounds like a development out of ragtime and older brass traditions than jazz. Something, perhaps, between swing and syncopation.

The Document CD fills an important gap, bringing together the 14 sides Johnson made following his initial Jazz Man dates. Unfortunately, the band isn't as good as the first line-up, with the very poor Albert Warner a dull substitute for Robinson. Lewis fares much better, but isn't as audible as he might be in what's a very average recording. Johnson chose some arcane material for the date and a lot of it goes straight back to ragtime. Four titles from 1945 with Robinson and Lewis fare much better, although the sound-quality is even worse. Finally, a single piece from a poll-winners' concert which is the only example of Johnson playing alongside Louis Armstrong, and it's only a fragment.

*****(*) Bunk Johnson In San Francisco**
American Music AMCD-16 *Johnson; Thomas 'Mutt' Carey (t); Jim Robinson, Kid Ory, Turk Murphy (tb); Wade Whaley, Ellis Horne (cl); George Lewis (cl); Buster Wilson, Burt Bales, Bertha Gonsoulin (p); Frank Pasley (g); Lawrence Marrero, Pat Patton (bj); Sidney Brown (bb); Ed Garland, Squire Gersback (b); Everett Walsh, Clancy Hayes, Edgar Moseley (d).* 9/43–1/44.

***** The King Of The Blues**
American Music AMCD-1 *Johnson; Jim Robinson (tb); George Lewis (cl); Lawrence Marrero (bj); Sidney Brown (b, bb); Alcide 'Slow Drag' Pavageau (b); Baby Dodds (d).* 44–45.

****** Bunk Johnson 1944**
American Music AMCD-3 *Johnson; Jim Robinson (tb); George Lewis (cl); Sidney Brown (bb); Lawrence Marrero (bj); Alcide 'Slow Drag' Pavageau (b); Baby Dodds (d).* 8/44.

★★★★ Bunk Johnson 1944 (2nd Masters)
American Music AMCD-8 *As above.* 8/44.

Johnson's American Music recordings are his most substantial legacy, even if there is occasionally indifferent sound-quality and various incompatibilities with sidemen and material. Robinson and Lewis may have been New Orleans's finest, but Johnson didn't seem to like them all that much, and he frequently plays much better than Lewis on these sessions. Nevertheless *The King Of The Blues* and *1944* – as well as its subsequent CD of alternative takes on AMCD-8 – feature much fine music, the first all on blues themes, the second a mix of the obvious ('Panama' and so forth) and tunes which show Johnson's weakness for popular novelties, such as 'There's Yes Yes In Your Eyes'. It is mostly an ensemble music, leads being passed around the front line and small inflexions making each performance unique to itself; but there is a freshness and intensity here (Johnson had, after all, been waiting a long time to make serious records) which give the music a real cumulative power that grows with each listening. Any raggedness in the playing or flaw in the sound is made to seem insignificant by the surpassing rigour of Johnson's men and their fierce craftsmanship, especially on the 1944 discs (recorded on a hot day: a photo of the session shows everyone in their undershirts). Bill Russell's session-notes make fascinating reading in the booklet with AMCD-8.

The other disc is at least as interesting. *In San Francisco* includes a *This Is Jazz* broadcast with an all-star band including, intriguingly, Johnson's trumpet contemporary Mutt Carey, and though Johnson sounds unhappy on 'Dipper Mouth Blues' it's absorbing music. Even better, though, are the six trumpet/piano duets with Bertha Gonsoulin. Nowhere else can one hear Johnson's silvery tone and proper phrasing so clearly.

CORE COLLECTION

★★★★ Bunk's Brass Band And Dance Band 1945
American Music AMCD-6 *Johnson; Louis 'Kid Shots' Madison (t); Jim Robinson (tb); George Lewis (cl); Isidore Barbarin (ahn); Adolphe Alexander (bhn); Joe Clark (bass hn); Lawrence Marrero (bj, d); Alcide 'Slow Drag' Pavageau (b); Baby Dodds (d).* 5/45.

***Bunk's Brass Band And Dance Band* is a fine introduction to Johnson's music, since it features what would have been a regular parade band line-up on 11 tracks and a further nine by a typical Johnson dance group (recorded at George Lewis's home). Lewis sounds a little shrill on the *Brass Band* tracks, which makes one wonder about the pitching, though there is a credit for 'pitch rectification' on the CD. It is a pioneering record nevertheless, as the first authentic, New Orleans brass-band session. The 'dance' tracks are very sprightly and feature some fine Lewis, as well as some of Johnson's firmest lead and even some respectable solos. The sound is quite clean as these sessions go, though some of the *Brass Band* acetates are in less than perfect shape.**

★★★(★) Bunk Johnson And His New Orleans Band 1945–1946
Document DOCD-1001 *Johnson; Jim Robinson (tb); George Lewis (cl); Alton Purnell (p); Lawrence Marrero (bj); Alcide 'Slow Drag' Pavageau (b); Baby Dodds, Red Jones (d).* 11/45–1/46.

Four Decca titles, eight for Victor and two V-Discs, plus eight alternative takes. Compared to the original American Music sessions, these are less heavy with authenticity, and some may prefer them for that. Even so, the band still stumbles along at times (listen to the opening ensemble on 'Maryland, My Maryland') and one can sometimes understand Johnson's own frustrations, even if he is as frequently to blame as everyone else. The Victor dates have a chugging intensity which the rather close recording tends to accentuate. The two V-Disc tracks are surprisingly expansive and relaxed. Fascinating music.

★★★ Bunk & Leadbelly At New York Town Hall 1947
American Music AMCD-46 *Johnson; Jimmy Archey (tb); Omer Simeon, Edmond Hall (cl); Ralph Sutton (p); Huddie 'Leadbelly' Ledbetter (g, v); Danny Barker (g, bj); Cyrus St Clair (bb); Freddie Moore (d, v); Mama Price (v).* 9/47.

★★★ Bunk Johnson & Mutt Carey In New York 1947
American Music AMCD-45 *Johnson; Thomas 'Mutt' Carey (t); Jerry Blumberg (c); Jimmy Archey, Bob Mielke (tb); Albert Nicholas, Jack Sohmer (cl); James P. Johnson, Dick Wellstood (p); George 'Pops' Foster, Charles Treager (b); Baby Dodds, Irv Kratka (d).* 10/47.

Two souvenirs from Johnson's stay in New York during 1947. The *Town Hall* concert with an all-star group is sound, spirited Dixieland: Johnson isn't on his best form but he plays decently enough. Leadbelly's billing is a bit misleading since he sings for only four minutes on the entire record. The sound, drawn from previously bootlegged acetates, has been cleaned up very respectably.

The other disc finds Bunk at the Caravan Ballroom, once with a team of old hands, the other time with a very young group of white Dixielanders, including the 20-year-old Wellstood. Mutt Carey replaces Bunk on four tracks, rather than sitting in with him. None of this counts as 'authentic' Johnson, but it shows that he was more adaptable than his roots following might wish to think, since there's nothing that disgraces him.

★★★(★) Last Testament
Delmark DD 225 *Johnson; Ed Cuffee (tb); Garvin Bushell (cl); Don Kirkpatrick (p); Danny Barker (g); Wellman Braud (b); Alphonse Steele (d).* 12/47.

Johnson's farewell was reportedly the only session in which he really got his own way, choosing both sidemen and material; and New Orleans purists must have been surprised on both counts: he lined up a team of players quite different from the American Music cronies, and he chose rags and pop tunes to perform. 'The Entertainer', 'Kinklets' and 'The Minstrel Man' have a rather wistful animation about them, while a tune such as 'Till We Meet Again' has a (perhaps inevitable) air of valediction about it. Cuffee and Bushell play with more fluency and zip than Robinson and Lewis ever did, but their slightly anonymous quality stops them from overwhelming Johnson himself, who sounds far from finished. He plays a firm lead and takes simple, bittersweet solos. The sound is a drawback: though recorded in the Carnegie Recital Hall, the quality is indifferent, often boxy and without much definition, and Jack Towers and Bob Koester haven't been able to do much with it in the remastering.

Gunnar Johnson (born 1924)

Born in Gothenburg, Johnson was a key presence in the modern jazz which was heard in Sweden's major cities in the '50s.

Though he later worked as a semi-pro, he never lost touch with the music and in the '90s he was still working, frequently with Jack Lidström's traditional group.

***** Gunnar Johnson Quintet 1957–1959**
Dragon DRCD 335 *Johnson; Erik Norström (as); Curth Severö (bs); Jan Johansson (p); Ingvar Callmer, Rolf Svensson, Björn Ageryd (d); Sonya Hedenbratt (v).* 57–59.

A valuable reissue which documents what remains of the music of Johnson's quintet, which buzzed Swedish jazzgoers for a brief period in the mid- to late-'50s. The main point of these mostly dusty broadcasts is to hear the quicksilver tenor of Eric Norström, a Getzian stylist who turns in one terrific solo after another. But there is also the star-crossed Johansson, who is constantly turning bebop clichés on their heads and reaching towards the amazing albums he would go on to make in the '60s. The group supported Hedenbratt on many occasions, and she sings agreeably enough on six tracks. Lars Westin's outstanding sleeve essay tells you all you may be curious about regarding the group's history. The less than ideal audio-quality will probably deter the uncommitted, but this is in its way a precious survival in the story of European jazz.

J. J. Johnson (1924–2001)

TROMBONE

The dominant bebop trombonist, Johnson's saxophone-influenced sound has been criticized as unidiomatic and insufficiently 'brassy' – whatever that means – but there is no mistaking his pre-eminence in the recent history of jazz. Born in Indianapolis, Johnson emerged in Benny Carter's orchestra and as part of Jazz at the Philharmonic, but he left an indelible mark as half of Jay and Kai with fellow-trombonist Winding.

***** J. J. Johnson's Jazz Quintets**
Savoy 78813 *Johnson; Cecil Payne (as); Leo Parker (bs); Hank Jones, John Lewis, Bud Powell (p); Leonard Gaskin, Al Lucas, Gene Ramey (b); Max Roach, Shadow Wilson (d).* 6/46–11/49.

***** Jay & Kai**
Savoy 17220 *Johnson; Kai Winding (tb); Wally Cirillo, Lou Stein (p); Billy Bauer (g); Al Lucas, Charles Mingus (b); Kenny Clarke, Tiny Kahn (d); Al Young (perc).* 10/49.

***** Origins: The Savoy Sessions**
Savoy 17127 *As above.* 46–49.

*****(*) Savoy, Prestige & Sensation: Complete Early Master Takes**
Definitive 11161 *As above.* 46–49.

***** J. J. Johnson, 1946–1949**
Classics 1176 *As above; add Kenny Dorham (t); Sonny Stitt (ts).* 46–49.

*****(*) Trombone By Three**
Original Jazz Classics OJC 091 *Johnson; Kenny Dorham (t); Sonny Rollins (ts); John Lewis (p); Leonard Gaskin (b); Max Roach (d).* 5/49.

J. J. Johnson is one of the most important figures in modern jazz. Once voguish, the trombone, like the clarinet, largely fell from favour with younger players with the faster articulations of bebop. Johnson's unworthily low standing nowadays (his partnership with Kai Winding, as 'Jay and Kai', was once resonantly popular) is largely due to a perceived absence of trombone players with whom to compare him. In fact, Johnson turned an occasionally unwieldy instrument into an agile and pure-toned bop voice; so good was his articulation that single-note runs in the higher register often sounded like trumpet. He frequently hung an old beret over the bell of his horn to soften his tone and bring it into line with the sound of the saxophones around him.

The Savoys were recorded when J.J. was in his early 20s. They're already the work of a mature and confident talent. The playing is brisk, full-toned and never short of an idea, though Johnson's writing ('Jay Bird', 'Boneology', 'Riffette', 'Bee Jay', 'Jay Jay') is as generic as the titles suggest. The Savoy compilation and the Definitive set overlap the same fine additional material, including the lovely 'Audubon' and a rake of other elegant bebop tunes that help to round out the picture of J.J. in this early period. 'Blue For Trombones', 'What Is This Thing Called Love?', 'Lament' and 'The Major' on *Origins* offer a first glimpse of the legendary Johnson–Winding partnership, but no sooner was this set available than *Jay & Kai* reappeared with bonus tracks. The Definitive set skips all of that material but includes three cuts of J.J. with the Russell Jacquet group. The Classics set as usual sticks to stuff under his leadership, though there are a couple of other things thrown in to make up the duration. Any of these will do as an introduction to young Johnson. All, though, have their gaps and absences and only rare original LPs will fill them for the moment.

CORE COLLECTION

♛ ** The Eminent Jay Jay Johnson: Volume 1**
Blue Note 32143-2 *Johnson; Clifford Brown (t); Hank Mobley (ts); Jimmy Heath (ts, bs); Wynton Kelly, John Lewis, Horace Silver (p); Paul Chambers, Percy Heath, Charles Mingus (b); Kenny Clarke (d); Sabu Martinez (perc).* 6/53–6/55.

****** The Eminent Jay Jay Johnson: Volume 2**
Blue Note 32144-2 *As above.* 6/53–6/55.

The first volume of the Blue Note set is one of the central documents of post-war jazz and should on no account be missed. Johnson – who was working as a blueprint checker at the time of the earliest sessions recorded, apparently dissatisfied with his output to date – sounds fleet and confident, and he has a marvellous band round him, including a young Clifford Brown. 'Turnpike' and 'Capri' exist in two versions each and show Johnson's ability to rethink his phraseology, adjusting his attack on the original-release versions to accommodate Clarke's powerful but unemphatic swing (which is rather swamped on the sessions of September 1954 by Mingus's chiming bass and the slap-happy Martinez); even on the slow-tempo 'Turnpike', Clarke provides an irresistible moving force underneath the melody. 'Get Happy' is appropriately up-beat and joyous, with notes picked off like clay pipes at a shooting gallery. In contrast, 'Lover Man' is given a mournful, drawn-out statement that squeezes out every drop of emotion the melody has to offer. The 1954 session yields some fine exchanges between Johnson and Kelly, notably on 'It's You Or No One' and 'Too Marvellous For Words', where the leader's tone and attack are almost as perfect as on 'Turnpike'. Volume 2 is filled out with a less than inspiring 1955 date featuring Hank Mobley and Horace Silver, neither of whom seems attuned to Johnson's taxing idiom. In their new RVG remastering, the records have come up as fresh as paint.

*** The Birdlanders

Fresh Sound FSCD 186 *Johnson; Al Cohn, Gigi Gryce (as); Milt Jackson (vib); Henri Renaud (p); Percy Heath, Charlie Smith (b); Walter Bolden, Jerry Lloyd (d).* 5/54.

*** Live At Café Bohemia

Fresh Sound FSCD 165 *Johnson; Bobby Jaspar (ts, f); Tommy Flanagan (p); Wilbur Little (b); Elvin Jones (d).* 2/57.

As ever, Fresh Sound rescue lost and forgotten tapes from the dusty back of the cupboard. The first of these, which we remember fondly for a wonderful version of 'Indian' and a totally unexpected Milt Jackson vocal on 'The More I See You', was formerly issued on Inner City, but has long been out of catalogue. Given how little live J.J. there is in the official catalogues, these are hugely welcome releases. The mixed personnels and boppish repertoire on *The Birdlanders* are highly effective in their different ways and there is some astonishingly good playing on the Bohemia date; also a chance to hear the pale but interesting sound of Bobby Jaspar, who often sounds anaemic alongside more rambunctious horn-players, but spot on with Johnson. J.J. takes the opening shot in the broadcast, roaring away on 'Bernie's Tune'. Jaspar comes in after that for 'In A Little Provincial Town' and showcases his lyrical flute behind the leader's muted solo. An all too short 'Angel Eyes' and 'Old Devil Moon' are the other outstanding tracks. On neither album is the sound particularly good, but the historical importance of these sets outweighs any such reservation.

***(*) Jay and Kai + 6 / J J In Person

Collectables 5677 *Johnson; Nat Adderley (c); Kai Winding (tb, trombonium); Urbie Green, Bob Alexander, Eddie Bert, Jimmy Cleveland (tb); Bart Varsalona, Tom Mitchell (btb); Hank Jones, Tommy Flanagan (p); Milt Hinton, Ray Brown, Wilbur Little (b); Osie Johnson, Albert 'Tootie' Heath (d); Candido Camero (perc).* 4/56–2/58.

*** Trombone Master

Columbia CK 44443 *Johnson; Victor Feldman (p, vib); Tommy Flanagan (p); Paul Chambers, Wilbur Little, Sam Jones (b); Albert 'Tootie' Heath, Max Roach (d).* 57–60.

***(*) The Great Kai And J.J.

Impulse! 051225-2 *Johnson; Kai Winding (tb); Bill Evans (p); Paul Chambers, Tommy Williams (b); Roy Haynes, Art Taylor (d).* 60.

The Impulse! recording was a commercially motivated reunion, some time after the partnership had been amicably dissolved. Perhaps because the band behind them was so good, J.J. and Kai very quickly rediscovered their old groove. The two horns are exactly in balance, and the vibrato, which in Winding's case was apt to get wider as he aged, is exactly co-ordinated. There is much good-natured four-bar swapping which might pall after a while, were it not so sweetly and tunefully done. There is nothing like Bill Evans's brief but elegantly articulated solos on the first record, and he makes an enormous difference to the overall feel of the Impulse!, which sounds like a proper group project rather than a trombone feature with accompaniment. The best point of comparison, before-and-after, is 'Going, Going, Gong', which refers back to the lively 'Gong Rock' on a 1955 Bethlehem session. If this is qualitatively representative, and we tend to feel it is, then the later sessions have gained considerably in sophistication and sheer class and, though dedicated J.J. and Kai fans will think the suggestion heretical, the Impulse! is the one to go for, though trombone nuts will find themselves drawn to the earlier Columbia, which features eight – count 'em – of the sliding fellows, often in jubilant unison. The two frontmen vary the sound a bit on the self-explanatory 'Piece For Two Tromboniums', which is interesting enough to suggest that these admittedly less limber valved horns could have been developed a step further. The arrangements are very good indeed and the material (with the exception of 'Surrey With The Fringe On Top') highly original and exciting. The Columbia edition has now been displaced by the Collectables disc, which has a more than agreeable bonus in the shape of the *J.J. In Person* date, a quintet session from 1958 with Nat Adderley and Tommy Flanagan: a very good buy. *Trombone Master* corrals material from four different albums, so it isn't much more than a sampling compilation from a relatively quiet period in J.J.'s career. There are some fine moments, notably his solo on 'Misterioso' and the almost eponymous 'Blue Trombone', but it isn't a particularly coherent or satisfying album.

*** Four Trombones: The Debut Recordings

Prestige PCD 24097 *Johnson; Willie Dennis, Bennie Green, Kai Winding (tb); John Lewis (p); Charles Mingus (b); Art Taylor (d).*

Originally recorded for the short-lived independent label co-run by Mingus and Max Roach, this suffers slightly from its own ungainly format, which buries Johnson a little. There are, though, fine and fresh performances all round, including a stirring account of 'Now's The Time'. Mingus takes charge more than once. The sound is a shade too bright on the transfer and the top notes are inclined to be a bit vinegary.

***(*) Live At The Café Bohemia

Fresh Sound FSRCD 143 *Johnson; Bobby Jaspar (ts, f); Tommy Flanagan (p); Wilbur Little (b); Elvin Jones (d).* 2/57.

Despite Jaspar's shortcomings as a soloist and a degree of unease in the ensembles, the Café Bohemia sessions provide an ideal blowing context for Johnson; he lets go joyously on 'Angel Eyes', 'Old Devil Moon' (see also *Eminent*, Volume 1) and, a favourite, 'Solar'. Flanagan's chording and fills are as near perfect as they could be. A constant delight.

*** At The Opera House

Verve 847340-2 *Johnson; Stan Getz (ts); Oscar Peterson (p); Herb Ellis (g); Ray Brown (b); Connie Kay (d).* 9–10/57.

Later the same year as the Café Bohemia session, Johnson and Stan Getz co-led a band at the Civic Opera in Chicago, and then again at the Shrine in LA. Someone had the nous to get the first one down in stereo, but the West Coast tracks, which are probably the better musically, are in very four-square mono. It's fascinating to be able to compare versions of 'Billie's Bounce' (which Getz doesn't really treat as a bebop tune either time), 'Crazy Rhythm', 'Blues In The Closet' and 'My Funny Valentine', though of course the variance in recording means that some of the apparent stylistic differences are artefacts. One great beauty of the session is the opportunity to hear both front men playing songs not normally associated with them. As such, it has to be considered a footnote rather than a centrally important record. Even so, it's well worth the investment.

***(*) J. J. Inc

Columbia Legacy CK 65296 *Johnson; Freddie Hubbard (t); Clifford Jordan (ts); Cedar Walton (p); Arthur Harper (b); Albert 'Tootie' Heath (d).* 8/60.

'Aquarius' is the best evidence yet of J.J.'s great skills as a composer-arranger. As fellow-trombonist Steve Turre points out in a thoughtful liner-note to this augmented reissue, it's a work that is almost orchestral in conception, making full use of the three-horn front line, and also Walton's elegant accompaniment. Brasses are pitched against saxophone and piano in a wonderful contrapuntal development, and Tootie Heath gets a rich sound out of the kit. Apart from this piece and 'Minor Mist', most of the material is deeply rooted in the blues. The reissue includes a longer version of 'Fatback', which shows just how funky J.J. could be when he let go. 'Blue 'N' Boogie', another of the extra tracks, is no less down-home and basic, and the leader's ease in a minor blues is evident from the off on 'Mohawk'. The sound has been considerably enhanced on this 20-bit digital remastering. The rhythm section, who sounded a bit remote on LP, are now absolutely central to the music, and the horns are much better balanced than previously. A valuable addition to the story.

*** J. J.'s Broadway

Verve 000060402 *Johnson; Urbie Green, Lou McGarity, Tommy Mitchell (tb); Paul Faulise (btb); Hank Jones (p); Richard Davis, Chuck Israels (b); Walter Perkins (d).* 3 & 4/63.

The sound of five trombones working the theme of 'My Favorite Things' takes a bit of getting used to if your benchmark is Coltrane's eldritch soprano, but it works surprisingly well. The first tracks on this recent reissue are all for the larger, multi-trombone format, which palls quite quickly for all its sophistication. The remaining tracks are with the quartet, with material again from Broadway shows. Johnson is crisp, boppish and clever when he's heard in isolation. The saxophone-like articulation works well in this context and Jones's accompaniment is spot on for the repertoire and for the leader's voice. A valuable addition to the Johnson catalogue.

*** Live In London

Harkit 108 *Johnson; Stan Tracey (p); Malcolm Cecil (b); Tony Crombie (d).* 64.

J.J. obviously enjoyed working with the house band at Ronnie Scott's and this recent issue helps to fill in another blank in the trombonist's discography. The harmonic action between Johnson and Tracey is cheerfully strained in places, with the pianist's Monkish mannerisms prompting J.J. to make some unusually abrasive statements in some of his solos, always with tongue in cheek and a smile on his face. The sound-quality isn't terrific and there are some distortions on the busier passages and when the dynamics get exciting. Mostly, though, it's a middle-register gig and perfectly well documented.

***(*) The Total

RCA 74321 47791 2 *Johnson; Bert Collins, Art Farmer, Ernie Royal, Danny Stiles, Snooky Young (t); Paul Faulise, Benny Powell (tb); Ray Alonge, Jimmy Buffington (frhn); Jerome Richardson (as, cl, f); Phil Bodner (ts, cl, f, ob); Tom Newsom (bs, bcl, f); Hank Jones (p); Ron Carter (b); Grady Tate (d); Bobby Rosengarden (perc).* 12/66.

Recorded over the course of an intense week in New York City and a showcase for some thoughtful and adventurous new material, including sections from J.J.'s *Euro Suite*, which was written for Friedrich Gulda's Eurojazz Orchestra earlier the same year. The opening 'Say When' sets a tough tempo and puts a well-coached band through its paces. J.J. solos strongly on 'Blue' and is then upstaged by the consistently undervalued Jerome Richardson. 'Short Cake' and 'Space Walk' suggest how advanced the trombonist's harmonic thinking was at the time, two really strong ideas done full justice, while 'Ballade', originally for Art Farmer, probably needs a more intimate setting and a closer recording to pull it off. Otherwise, though, a most welcome reissue from a time when Johnson was still experimenting with hybrids of jazz.

***(*) Yokohama Concert

Pablo 262019 *Johnson; Nat Adderley (c); Billy Childs (ky); Tony Dumas (b); Kevin Johnson (d).* 4/77.

*** Chain Reaction: Yokohama Concert – Volume 2

Pablo 2121 *As above.* 4/77.

J.J. had spent most of the preceding decade working as a full-time arranger, and this was his first recording for the better part of a decade. Since he had also been writing extensively over that period, it's less surprising than it might have been that he should have opted to go mainly for originals, though the gig also includes a version of Nat's 'Work Song', Tony Dumas's clever 'It Happens' and the standard 'Walkin''. Despite too much emphasis on wishy-washy electric keyboards, and the naivety of Johnson Jr's drumming, the live sound is very good indeed and J.J.'s solos are strong enough to suggest that he'd never really been away.

Volume 2, released only after J.J.'s death, adds in another eight tracks. There's nothing revelatory, though the opening 'Blue 'N' Boogie' is quite good. Not so 'Suicide Is Painless', the theme from *M*A*S*H*, a rare instance of Johnson's taste slipping.

*** Pinnacles

Original Jazz Classics OJCCD 1006 2 *Johnson; Oscar Brashear (t); Joe Henderson (ts); Tommy Flanagan (p, ky); Ron Carter (b); Billy Higgins (d); Kenneth Nash (perc).* 9/79.

Dated to a degree by the sound of Tommy Flanagan on Fender Rhodes and clavinet, and by J.J.'s use of pitch-shifters on a couple of tracks, *Pinnacles* is nevertheless a very fine record that has been out of circulation for too long. His solo on the opening 'Night Flight' is fleet and eloquent, and his arrangement of the traditional 'See See Rider' suggests how hard he was working to keep up with a prevailing taste for blues and rock. Flanagan switches to synth on the cheesy 'Mr Clean', which doesn't benefit from being cluttered with additional percussion. It also lacks the sterling presence of Joe Henderson, who's probably the most effective soloist on the set, playing with calm authority and a sharper than usual edge to his tone for this period. J.J. has a reasonably quiet time of it but makes his choruses count.

*** Concepts In Blue

Original Jazz Classics OJC 735 *Johnson; Clark Terry (t, flhn); Ernie Watts (ts, as); Pete Jolly (ky); Victor Feldman (vib, ky); Ray Brown (b); Tony Dumas, Kevin Johnson (d).* 9/80.

What's obvious again, even before a note is played, is Johnson's ability to put together great bands. Despite a few '70s giveaways (like electric keyboards) and a rather busy mix, it's a terrific disc. A sameness starts to creep in before the end, particularly from Watts, who seems to have only a handful of ideas in his bag, but Terry's clear upper-register notes and broad smears are an ideal complement to Johnson, and it might even have been possible to dispense with a saxophonist altogether. Recommended.

*****(*) We'll Be Together Again**
Pablo 2310911 *Johnson; Joe Pass (g).* 10/83.

***** Things Are Getting Better All The Time**
Pablo Today 2312141 *Johnson; Al Grey (tb); Kenny Barron (p, ky); Ray Brown (b); Mickey Roker (d).* 11/83.

Johnson kept out of sight for most of the '70s, composing and arranging for the movies and television. Within five weeks in 1983, however, he made two sterling albums that belied the full stop some critics had put after his name. The sanguinely titled *Things* looks suspiciously like another attempt to reduplicate the Jay and Kai sound, but it comes across much more individually. Grey, a year younger than Johnson, is a more traditional stylist; a genius with the plunger mute, he has a big, belting tone that goes well with Johnson's increasingly delicate fills and recapitulations. 'Soft Winds', 'Paper Moon' and 'Softly, As In A Morning Sunrise' are particularly good. Pianist Barron is contained and exact, but Brown and Roker are uncharacteristically listless, perhaps recognizing that the two principals (who shared the billing) play to their own inner metre. Good stuff.

Like Johnson, Joe Pass represents an extraordinary cross-section of modern jazz idiom, all carefully assimilated and absorbed. His constant lower-string pulse makes him particularly adaptable to solo and duo performance, and *Together Again* has the fullness of texture that might be expected of a larger group. The performances – 'Nature Boy', 'Bud's Blues', 'Solar', 'When Lights Are Low' and six others – have a fresh-minted sparkle and immediate currency. Strongly recommended.

*****(*) Quintergy – Live At The Village Vanguard**
Emarcy 842814 *Johnson; Ralph Moore (ts); Stanley Cowell (p); Rufus Reid (b); Victor Lewis (d).* 7/88.

***** Standards – Live At The Village Vanguard**
Emarcy 510059 *As above.* 7/88.

Even nearing retirement age, Johnson sounds as full of controlled energy as ever on this fine pair of sets from a New York residency. The first record is perhaps the most grabbing, with a wonderful opening arrangement of 'When The Saints Go Marching In' and a brief but beautiful unaccompanied version of 'It's All Right With Me'. J.J.'s tone and phrasing are faultless on the faster numbers, Kenny Dorham's 'Blue Bossa', Wayne Shorter's exacting 'Nefertiti' and his own title-track.

The standards set is probably shrewd economics but makes for a duller listen. There are some lovely moments, particularly when J.J. hits pungent, single-note lines over Lewis's vivid cymbalism, but these tunes really ought to be out in a field somewhere, grazing.

James P. Johnson (1894–1955)

PIANO, COMPOSER

An enormously versatile and subtle player who played jazz and composed classical music, Johnson is the inventor of stride piano, a mixture of ragtime and other styles. He came to New York as a youngster and was exposed to a huge range of music in the ghetto region known as 'the Jungles', where rent parties and shebeen provided regular work for talented players. His interest shifted to formal composition during the '30s and '40s, but he left a body of more than 250 small-scale compositions and his influence on jazz piano is inestimable.

***** Carolina Shout**
Biograph BCD 105 *Johnson (p rolls).* 5/17–6/25.

***** Hot Piano**
Topaz 1048 *Johnson; Henry 'Red' Allen, Max Kaminsky, Frankie Newton, Cootie Williams (t); J. C. Higginbotham, Dicky Wells (tb); Mezz Mezzrow, Pee Wee Russell, Omer Simeon (cl); Pete Brown (as); Al Gold, Gene Sedric (ts); Fats Waller (p); Al Casey, Eugene Fields, Freddie Green (g); Wellman Braud, George 'Pops' Foster, John Kirby, Joe Watts (b); Big Sid Catlett, Cozy Cole, Zutty Singleton (d); Perry Bradford (v).* 21–44.

*****(*) Harlem Stride Piano, 1921–1929**
Hot'N'Sweet 151032 *Johnson; Louis Metcalf (c); Joe 'King' Oliver, David Nelson, Cootie Williams (t); James Archey, Geechie Fields (tb); Ernest Elliott (cl); Bobby Holmes (cl, as); Charles Frazier (ts); Fats Waller (p); Teddy Bunn, Bernard Addison (bj, g); Harry Hull, Joe Watts (b); Edmund Jones, Fred Moore (d); Perry Bradford (d, v); other personnel unidentified.* 8/21–11/29.

*****(*) James P. Johnson, 1921–1928**
Classics 658 *As above, except omit Oliver, Archey, Fields, Elliott, Frazier, Addison, Hull, Jones, Moore.* 8/21–6/28.

***** James P. Johnson, 1928–1938**
Classics 671 *Johnson; Louis Metcalf (c); Joe 'King' Oliver (t); James Archey, Geechie Fields, Joe 'Tricky Sam' Nanton (tb); Ernest Elliott (cl); Barney Bigard (cl, ts); Johnny Hodges (as, ss); Charles Frazier (ts); Clarence Williams (p, v); Bernard Addison (bj, g); Harry Hull (b); Sonny Greer, Edmund Jones, Fred Moore (d); Perry Bradford, Gus Horsley, Andy Razaf (v).* 10/28–3/38.

Too little is known now about James P. Johnson's orchestral music (of which much has been lost) to make any settled judgement about his significance as a 'straight' composer. Ironically, though, his enormous importance as a synthesizer of many strands of black music – ragtime, blues, popular and sacred song – with his own stride style has been rather eclipsed by the tendency to see him first and only as Fats Waller's teacher. Johnson was in almost every respect a better musician than Waller, and perhaps the main reason for his relative invisibility has been the dearth of reliable recorded material. The early Biograph brings together Johnson's rather staccato and lumpy piano rolls, an acquired taste but of unmistakable significance for the history and development of jazz in the period. 'Charleston' is a rarity, and 'Carolina Shout' had a profound impact on Duke Ellington.

As so often, the French Classics label has made up a considerable deficit. The early material overlaps at around the dates indicated with the Hot'N'Sweet compilation and the Topaz. This is as close as anyone is going to get to the sound of Harlem rent parties – if there were an additional quarter-star for quality of sound, *Harlem Stride Piano* might just nip it – and it's a pity that some of these sessions are not more fully documented. The group that recorded the autumn 1921 'Carolina Shout' (there is a solo version from the same period, different label) goes unidentified. Johnson is unmistakable from the first moments of 'Harlem Strut', a subtle, propulsive player with bags of ideas.

The Topaz compilation offers an excellent introduction to the pianist's work, covering a generous sweep of material from the middle of his career. Most of the tracks that a seasoned Johnson listener would expect to find are present – 'Snowy Morning Blues', 'Harlem Strut', 'Worried And Lonesome Blues', 'Mule Walk' – but with two dozen tracks on the disc, well mastered and clearly documented, there is something for everyone at a budget price.

Classics omit a piano-roll 'Charleston (South Carolina)' from June 1925 but fill in with four Original Jazz Hounds numbers from March 1927 and March 1928. The second volume takes the story on a full decade, opening with a couple of numbers by the Gulf Coast Seven (an uncertain personnel but possibly including Ellingtonians Nanton and Hodges) before covering the overlap with Hot'N'Sweet. Among the highlights here are two duets and chirpy *kvelling* with Clarence Williams, together with three songs from 1931 with Andy Razaf (co-author of 'Honeysuckle Rose') as vocalist. As on Classics 658, Johnson tends to get buried in the group recordings. Ultimately it is the solo tracks, including little gems like 'You've Got To Be Modernistic' and the earlier 'Riffs', that are most significant. The disc ends with a session by Pee Wee Russell's Rhythmakers; Johnson solos on a second take of 'There'll Be Some Changes Made'.

One to avoid is Columbia's *Father Of The Stride Piano* (501652-2), a shoddy reissue of a hotchpotch compilation album from the '60s – poor sound and cheap presentation.

*****(*) James P. Johnson, 1938–1942**

Classics 711 *Johnson; Henry 'Red' Allen (t); J. C. Higginbotham (tb); Pee Wee Russell (cl); Gene Sedric (ts); Al Casey, Eugene Fields (g); George 'Pops' Foster, Johnny Williams (b); Big Sid Catlett, Zutty Singleton (d); Anna Robinson, Ruby Smith (v).* 8/38–7/42.

*****(*) The Original James P. Johnson, 1942–1945**

Smithsonian Folkways 40812 *Johnson (p solo).* 42–45.

***** James P. Johnson, 1943–1944**

Classics 824 *Johnson; Sidney De Paris (t); Vic Dickenson (tb); Ben Webster (ts); Jimmy Shirley (g); John Simmons (b); Big Sid Catlett (d).* 7/43–4/44.

***** James P. Johnson, 1944**

Classics 835 *Johnson; Frankie Newton, Sidney De Paris (t); Vic Dickenson (tb); Al Casey, Jimmy Shirley (g); George 'Pops' Foster, John Simmons (b); Big Sid Catlett, Eddie Dougherty (d).* 4–6/44.

***** James P. Johnson, 1944 – Volume 2**

Classics 856 *Johnson; Sterling Bose, Max Kaminsky (t); Frank Orchard (vtb); Rod Cless (cl); Eddie Condon (g); Bob Casey, George 'Pops' Foster (b); Eddie Dougherty, George Wettling (d).* 44.

***** James P. Johnson, 1944–1945**

Classics 1027 *Similar to Classics above.* 44–45.

The picture is getting steadily more patchy as the decade advances. Classics 711 is significant because it contains a lot of band material which scarcely saw the light of day during the LP era and which is now heard for the first time since its first release. One of these features vocals by Ruby Smith, a niece of the great Bessie. The disc overlaps with Classics 671 in the shape of a trio with Pee Wee Russell and Zutty Singleton, apparently recorded at the end of the August 1938 date. There are excellent solo performances from the following spring, made for Columbia.

The Smithsonian Folkways release is of excellent quality. The remastering, by Malcolm Addey and Alan Yoshida, is clean and unfussy, and classics like 'Yamekraw', 'Snowy Morning Blues' (two versions), and 'Daintiness Rag' come through clear and unwavering alongside tunes by Handy, Joplin and Pickett.

The later Classics anthologies have filled in much of the rest of the picture, inevitably with some further overlap with earlier releases. Some of the 1944 and later cuts already betray signs of the ill-health that, as a series of mild but progressively debilitating cerebral haemorrhages, was to overtake Johnson later in the decade, finally incapacitating him in 1951. The basic elements of the style are still in place, though, and on the most recent Classics volume there is an opportunity to hear several versions of themes like 'Blue Moods' and 'Yamekraw', as well as a session devoted to Handy material. The subtly varied bass figures and the forward motion of his sophisticated melodic variations place him closer to later jazz than to the increasingly basic syncopations and repetitions of ragtime. For that reason alone, and for his incorporation of jazz and blues tonalities, Johnson sounds much more 'modern' than many of his contemporaries, and a far more compelling musician than the overrated Waller. As so often with the Classics reissues, the transfers are seldom as meticulous as they might be and they are from unlisted sources, although for the most part the music comes through clearly enough.

****(*) James P. Johnson, 1945–1947**

Classics 1059 *Johnson; Albert Nicholas (cl); Danny Barker (g, v); George 'Pops' Foster (b).* 6/44–6/47.

These few cuts round out Classics' documentation of Johnson. Only serious collectors will be troubled by these rather lame performances, recorded for Folkways, Riverside and Circle, with a couple of tracks rejected by Moses Asch, including the recently rediscovered 'Woman Blues' and the two-part 'Jazz-amine Concerto'. Though only just turned 50, Johnson sounds tired and slightly disorientated. His recovery from a stroke sustained while working with Eddie Condon (which couldn't have been anyone's idea of a rest cure) was temporary and this compilation marks a sad conclusion to such a distinguished and influential career.

***** Feelin' Blue**

Halcyon 107 *As above.* 28–44.

*****(*) Carolina Shout**

ASV/Living Era 5355 *Johnson; Sidney De Paris, Max Kaminsky, Frankie Newton, Albert Snaer, Cootie Williams (t); George Brunies, Vic Dickenson, J. C. Higginbotham, Dicky Wells (tb); Muggsy Spanier (co); Sidney Bechet (ss, cl); Charlie Holmes (ss, as, cl); Al Gold, Gene Sedric, Ben Webster (ts); Buster Bailey, Albert Nicholas, Pee Wee Russell, Omer Simeon (cl); Fats Waller, Clarence Williams (p); Danny Barker, Eugene Fields, Freddie Green, Jimmy Shirley (g); Wellman Braud, Israel Crosby, Pops Foster, Walter Page, John Simmons, Joe Watts (b); Baby Dodds, Eddie Dougherty, George Wettling, Zutty Singleton (d) Perry Bradford, Bessie Smith, Ethel Waters (v).* 28–45.

At one point, Johnson compilations were falling as thick as the flakes on a snowy morning. Only a couple of new ones since our last edition. The Halcyon set is quite respectable and decently mastered: 'You've Got To Be Modernistic', 'Rifs', the 1930 'What Is This Thing Called Love' and, of course, 'Snowy Morning Blues' – so a decent introduction for the uninitiated. We much prefer the generous and eclectic selection on the ASV disc. A glance at the personnel here will show how much

Johnson's development criss-crossed with the pioneering moments in classic jazz and anyone who hadn't heard a note of this great music would find *Carolina Shout* a useful entrée, not just to Johnson, but to jazz itself.

Marc Johnson (born 1953)

DOUBLE BASS, ELECTRIC BASS

Made his first mark with the final Bill Evans trio, 1978–80, then with various leaders and fronting his own Bass Desires band. In the '90s he was among the most sought-after of bassists and proved adaptable to most jazz situations.

***** Bass Desires**
ECM 827743-2 *Johnson; Bill Frisell (g, g syn); John Scofield (g); Peter Erskine (d).* 5/85.

****(*) Second Sight**
ECM 833038-2 *As above.* 3/87.

Johnson is a magnificent bass stylist, with all the limitations such a description suggests. Everything he does has an inbuilt grandeur and seriousness; even a tune like the well-worked 'Samurai Hee-Haw', which has immense potential, is treated with undue seriousness. The original *Bass Desires* was a record of immense potential which failed to deliver a real punch. Frisell's disciplined surrealism was an interesting foil to Scofield's more logically organized play. The John Jacob Niles song, 'Black Is The Colour Of My True Love's Hair', is freshly reworked, but Johnson the stylist is never far from centre stage and constantly rumbles front and centre. No reason whatever why a bass-player shouldn't occupy the foreground, but on both these records it's underlined so heavily that one's only just finished getting to one's feet in respectful attention when the idea is over.

Second Sight lacks the freshness and the occasional flash of wry humour. In their place, a slightly wishy-washy sound, replete with high-note twiddles and drab rock effects that would have had the late Sonny Sharrock hiding his head in shame. While its predecessor wears well, this palls steadily.

****** The Sound Of Summer Running**
Verve 539299-2 *Johnson; Bill Frisell, Pat Metheny (g); Joey Baron (d, perc).* 97.

Exquisite. A set of delicate responses to Americana, reminiscent of Frisell's *Have A Little Faith* and Metheny's set of duets with Charlie Haden, *Missouri Skies.* Johnson has finally found an idiom and a group of collaborators who give his lovely sound a proper context. Every one of these ten tracks opens up on an inscape: childhood, unsentimental innocence, a forgotten and abandoned America. Frisell's and Metheny's folksy lines have very little to do with jazz harmony, but the ease and freedom of their playing are the real thing.

***** If Trees Could Fly**
Intuition INT 3228 2 *Johnson; Eric Longsworth (clo).* 11/96, 6/97.

Though Johnson's name is listed first, most of the material is by the young cellist. It sounds a very comfortable collaboration – Johnson describes it as 'effortless', which is slightly worrying – obviously aimed at overturning preconceptions about both instruments. Longsworth plays an electric cello, which allows him to articulate more quietly and softly than on a conventional instrument. His strums and double stops resemble baritone guitar, while Johnson favours single lines and interwoven counter-melodies. His only compositional credit comes with 'Ton Sur Ton' which is reprised right at the very end, almost as if to remind us which of the pair is the ranking star. Johnson can be forgiven everything for the delicate, bowed melody on 'Lullaby'. This is the kind of music Jaco Pastorius might have played if he had managed to find some peace and tranquillity in his life. As a place to be, that sounds fine. As a listening experience, this lacks a certain edge.

Pete Johnson (1904–67)

PIANO

Born in Kansas City, Johnson became prominent during the boogie-woogie craze of the late '30s, with Albert Ammons and Meade Lux Lewis. He faded rather quickly from sight in the '40s, but was still playing until his death.

****** Pete Johnson 1938–1939**
Classics 656 *Johnson; Harry James, Hot Lips Page (t); Buster Smith (as); Albert Ammons, Meade Lux Lewis (p); Lawrence Lucie, Ulysses Livingston (g); Abe Bolar, Johnny Williams (b); Eddie Dougherty (d); Joe Turner (v).* 12/38–12/39.

*****(*) Pete Johnson 1939–1941**
Classics 665 *Johnson; Hot Lips Page (t); Eddie Barefield (cl, as); Don Stovall (as); Don Byas (ts); Albert Ammons (p); John Collins, Ulysses Livingston (g); Abe Bolar, Al Hall (b); A. G. Godley, Jimmy Hoskins (d).* 12/39–6/41.

*****(*) Pete Johnson 1944–1946**
Classics 933 *Johnson; Hot Lips Page (t); Clyde Bernhardt, J. C. Higginbotham (tb); Albert Nicholas (cl); Don Stovall (as); Budd Johnson, Ben Webster (ts); Jimmy Shirley (g); Abe Bolar, Al Hall (b); Jack Parker, J. C. Heard (d); Etta Jones (v).* 2/44–1/46.

***** Central Avenue Boogie**
Delmark DD-656 *Johnson; Arnold Wiley (p, v); Charles Norris, Carl Lynch (g); Bill Davis, Al McKibbon (b); J. C. Heard, Jesse Price (d).* 4–11/47.

***** Pete Johnson 1947–1949**
Classics 1110 *As above except add Jewel Grant (as); Maxwell Davis (ts); Johnny Rogers, Herman Mitchell (g); Johnny Parker, Ralph Hamilton, Bill Cooper (b); Al Wichard, Roy Milton, Jesse Sailes (d); omit Wiley.* 4/47–4/49.

Johnson's mastery of boogie-woogie and blues piano is given a near-definitive airing on these CDs. The chronological survey on Classics begins with the Kansas City pianist accompanying Joe Turner on the singer's first studio date, before two quartet tracks with Harry James: 'Boo-Woo' is an outright classic. His complete 1939 date for Solo Art is another memorable occasion, nine solos that go from the Tatum-like elaborations on Leroy Carr's 'How Long, How Long Blues' to the furious 'Climbin' And Screamin'' and 'Shuffle Boogie'. The sound here is rather thin, but Johnson's energy and invention shine through. There are four more tracks with a small band including Page and Turner, a solo 'Boogie Woogie', two trio pieces and the first trio with Albert Ammons and Meade Lux Lewis on 'Café Society Rag'. There are shortcomings in the remastering, but this is a marvellous disc.

His 1939 session for Blue Note is, unfortunately, split across the end of Classics 656 and the beginning of Classics 665, which opens on the stunning 'Holler Stomp', the most audacious of boogie showcases. 'You Don't Know My Mind', from the same date, is contrastingly dreamy and may remind blues aficionados of pianists such as Walter Davis and Lane Smith. Aside from another track with Joe Turner's Fly Cats and a small group with Page and others, the rest of the disc is made up of duets with Ammons; as elegant as these sometimes are, they also fall prey to routine from track to track.

The 1944–6 collection starts with eight superb solos made for Brunswick: 'Answer To The Boogie' and the breathtaking 'Dive Bomber' are Johnson at his most powerful. Then follow three band dates made for National, with various swing veterans helping out in the front line (and with two vocals by the young Etta Jones). The later two both feature variations in line-up, with the players entering one at a time on the first and Webster, Page and Higginbotham taking turns out front on the second. It all ends on the rent-party stomping of 'Pete's Housewarming'. Another fine Johnson CD.

Delmark's compilation sets Johnson back in front of guitar, bass and drums, and includes several previously unheard takes. He still sounds best by himself, but there is some virtuoso stuff on 'Margie' and the several takes of 'Hollywood Boogie'.

The original master-takes from that session are all on the final CD in the Classics sequence, which goes on to take in the final studio sessions under Pete's leadership: three trio pieces for Modern, four live pieces from a Gene Norman concert (he goes down a storm) and six sextet tracks made in Los Angeles in 1949. The saxophonists play mooing R&B licks and would be better out of the way, but when Johnson's at the front on a mighty two-part 'Rocket 88 Boogie' he still sounds in fine form. Decent sound on all these tracks.

Philip Johnston (born 1955)

ALTO AND SOPRANO SAXOPHONES

During the '80s, Johnston was leader of the Microscopic Sextet, a medium-sized band with big ideas. No less a personage than John Zorn was a charter member. The group combined modern ideas with the sound and feel of a swing band and a cinematic vividness in the colours. Johnston declared a self-imposed 'recording ban' between 1988 and 1992, but returned with Big Trouble and an impressive bag of unrecorded tunes.

*****(*) Philip Johnston's Big Trouble**
Black Saint 120152-2 *Johnston; Bob DeBellis (ss, bs, bcl); Jim Leff (tb); Marcus Rojas (tba); Joe Ruddick (ky, as); Adam Rogers, David Tronzo (g); David Hofstra (b, tba); Kevin Norton (d, perc, mar); Richard Dworkin (perc).* 6 & 7/92.

***** Flood At The Ant Farm**
Black Saint 120182-2 *Johnston; Bob Henke, Ron Horton (t); Steve Swell (tb); Bob DeBellis (f, af, bcl, bs); Joe Ruddick (p, syn); David Hofstra (b); Kevin Norton (d, perc, vib).* 95.

*****(*) Normalology**
Koch 7884 *Johnston; Allan Chase (as); Paul Shapiro (ts); Bob DeBellis (bs); Joe Ruddick (p, org); Stew Cutler (g); David Hofstra (b); Richard Dworkin (d).* 5/96.

Big Trouble was formed following the demise of the Microscopic Sextet, one of the more original of the saxophone-based '80s bands, which drew much of its inspiration from the tight arrangements of the swing era but added a beat that was often coloured by contemporary rock and pop. In the new band, Johnston has pushed even further his offbeat arranging skills. 'Chillbone' on the later Black Saint album is scored for soprano saxophone, tuba and marimba, set over a stark wind *ostinato*. The set also includes notably complex compositions by Steve Lacy (the brief but awkwardly structured 'Hemline') and by Herbie Nichols, who's credited with both 'Step Tempest' and 'Twelve Bars'. The addition of slide guitar gives the last of these and the closing 'Powerhouse' an entirely unexpected dimension.

Johnston uses space brilliantly, often leaving yawning gaps precisely where one expects to hear fills or returns to a head theme. But *Flood At The Ant Farm* was a slight disappointment. In a rush to get some of the band's better material recorded – an opportunity denied to the Microscopic Sextet – this set feels surprisingly flat and prosaic. Opening and (almost) closing with a Steve Lacy tune (including another version of 'Hemline') underlines again this crucial influence on Johnston's writing, but his own tunes receive an often studied treatment: 'Pontius Pilate Polka' should have been a scabrous knees-up, surely, instead of this perfunctory reading. That said, there's still some strong playing (from Swell especially) which keeps the ears involved.

Normalology gets up to date with a lot of material written some years ago but left unrecorded. As ever, the tunes flirt confidently with dissonance. There are moments when one might almost be listening to an out-of-whack Grover Washington gig. Johnston's soprano is very much in that territory, and the arrangements are expansive and generously proportioned. All four horn-players have an individual touch, and the rhythm section (augmented by guitar on three numbers) is as elastic and flowing as the original band. Johnston's touch as a film composer comes out on things like the tiny 'My Grey Heaven', a melancholy celebration of everyday heroism. Our favourite tracks are 'Spilled Perfume' (which seem to come from an unperformed musical), 'Lobster Leaps In' and the closing blues 'No Mistakes In Hell'.

***** Music For Films**
Tzadik 7510 *Johnston; Steven Bernstein, Dave Douglas, Ray Vega (t); Don Davis (as); Bob DeBellis (ts, cl, f, af); Allan Chase (as); Paul Shapiro (ts); Mike Sim (bs, cl); Joel Forrester, Joe Ruddick (p, org); Guy Klucevesek (acc); Stew Cutler, Jody Harris, Adam Rogers, Kevin Trainor (g); David Tronzo (dobro); Cenovia Cummins, Mark Feldman, Sue Pray, Laura Seaton (vn); Juliet Haffner (vla); Erik Friedlander, Beverley Lauridsen (clo); Elizabeth Panzer (hp); Richard Dworkin (d).* 98.

*****(*) The Merry Frolics Of Satan: The George Méliès Project**
Koch 7885 *Johnston; Joe Ruddick (bs, p); Mark Josefsberg (vib); Dave Hofstra (b, tba).* 99.

In some regards, Johnston is the perfect Tzadik artist: intellectual, playful, perverse and generically undefinable. His music for Doris Dorrie's *Geld*, Philip Haas's *Money Man* and *Music Of Chance*, and the collaborative *Umbrellas* touches on a wide variety of styles and approaches. Individual soundtracks are not programmed consecutively, so the album is best heard as a sequence of essentially unrelated ideas. Heard this way, 'Atonal Hillbilly Music' (and it sounds just like that) and the opening

'Hymn Of The Souls Who Are Passing' demand special attention, but few other tracks last long enough to impinge more than subliminally and as abstract ambience. The ensemble is quite large and Johnston places a lot of emphasis on sound colour, to the extent that some tracks come across as brief, intense sketches, core ideas for pieces that don't require orchestration so much as development. We have not had the opportunity to hear this music in context; as a purely aural experience, it is clever, committed and often enjoyable.

The Méliès project, credited to the drummerless Transparent Quartet, is a much more substantial piece of work and can be recommended wholeheartedly as an album. The famous cover-image of the space rocket bunged in a weeping Man in the Moon's eye is reflected in 'Trip To The Moon', a rackety, surreal conception that gives the leader plenty of opportunity to shine. 'The Damnation Of Faust' and 'Hydrotherapie Fantastique' are equally strong, but it's the concluding pair of 'The Merry Frolics Of Satan' and 'Journey Across The Impossible' that gives the album its coherence. Both are immaculately structured and played with real fire and intelligence. Lovely stuff, and great playing from the supporting cast.

Randy Johnston (born 1956)

GUITAR

Accomplished guitarist in the Grant Green mould, with a track record covering Etta Jones records and latter-day tours with soul-jazz man Lou Donaldson.

*****(*) Somewhere In The Night**
High Note 7007 *Johnston; Uri Caine (p); Nat Reeves (b); Mickey Roker (d).* 7/97.

Johnston's spare and uncomplicated delivery was noted during his time with Muse. These later sessions are no less appealing and no less deceptive. Two brilliant takes of 'Secret Love' on *Somewhere In The Night* confirm the initial impression of intelligence. 'Dat Dere' gets the set off to a good start. The guitarist has an ability to make small gestures read large on tunes that are normally piano vehicles but strong enough to last a less full-bodied reading. 'Sack O' Woe' and Hank Mobley's 'Third Time Around' keep Johnston's funkier side in view, but it's the closing run of 'In The Wee Small Hours Of The Morning' and that second 'Secret Love' that represent Johnston's more effective side. The band is top-flight, with the infinitely subtle Caine taking a relatively boisterous course through the charts and Roker pushing them along like a drill sergeant. Houston Person runs the joint and presides.

*****(*) Riding The Curve**
J Curve 898 *Johnston; Johnny Griffin (ts); Joey DeFrancesco (org); Idris Muhammad (d).* 9/98.

***** Homage**
J Curve 7010 *Johnston; Jim Rotondi (t); Wayne Coniglio (btb); Eric Alexander (ts); Nick Brignola (bs); Xavier Davis (p); Nat Reeves (b); Kenny Washington (d).* 4/00.

Johnston has a genius for getting top-flight players on to the strength. Muhammad was the ideal choice for the Grant Green-ish *Riding The Curve*, an old-fashioned organ/guitar trio (with fine guest spots from Griff on 'All Through The Night' and his own 'You've Never Been There!'). Johnston springs his first surprise after the first of those Griffin features with a stallingly slow version of 'I Get Along Without You Very Well', a most unexpected tempo that takes the song into new and unfamiliar territory. The two originals are a floating Latin idea set in 'The Park', and a nostalgic evocation of the late Thomas Chapin, who roomed with Johnston at college.

The other J Curve disc is a homage to ten artists who've made a substantial impact on Johnston. No nod for Grant Green, surprisingly, given the last record, though Kenny Burrell and 'Pat and Wes' are acknowledged. The other names dropped are perhaps more surprising: Cedar Walton on 'Cedar's Place', Jimi Hendrix with 'Angel', Warne Marsh, Dexter Gordon and, on 'All Or Nothing At All', Frank Sinatra. Johnston plays with his usual easy swing and sophistication, but it's a low-key performance in comparison to his recent form.

*****(*) Detour Ahead**
High Note 7027 *Johnston; David 'Fathead' Newman, Houston Person (ts); Joey DeFrancesco (org); Byron Landham (d).* 4/01.

Producer Houston Person gets out of his booth for a tenor solo on the very first track, but isn't heard from again. He does his stuff, though, in shaping a notably full-voiced set that goes back to the organ/guitar/saxophone/drums format of *Riding The Curve*. 'Blues for Edward G.' (a hymn to the charismatic Robinson) is again one of only two originals by the guitarist, who seems uneager to push himself forward as a writer. The other new one here, 'The Triangle Pose', is his best yet, written as if for a forgotten Blue Note of the early '60s and featuring the initially unplaceable and then utterly distinctive tenor voice of David Newman.

*****(*) Hit & Run**
High Note 7098 *Johnston; Bruce Barth (p); Joe Locke (vib); Nat Reeves (b); Grady Tate (d).* 10/02.

The writing gets more confident by the album, and here Johnston ends with 'For The King', a delightful tune for his girlfriend which ought to sprout lyrics one of these days. No organ this time round, but a clever use of Joe Locke, either doubling Barth on three of his four appearances or standing in for him on 'The Best Thing For You'. One of the originals, 'Down Time', seems to be based on the 'Autumn Leaves' line, while 'Hit & Run' itself is an old-fashioned hard bopper that gets the group roaring along like a runaway car.

Pete Jolly (born 1932)

PIANO, ACCORDION

A veteran West Coast man of the '50s and '60s, Jolly made countless sideman dates, but his own work as a leader is rather infrequent and mostly of little account. He has also made a go of jazz on the accordion.

****(*) Jolly Jumps In**
RCA Victor 74321 592632 *Jolly; Shorty Rogers (t); Jimmy Giuffre (ts, bs); Howard Roberts (g); Curtis Counce (b); Shelly Manne (d).* 3/55.

**** Pete Jolly And Friends**
VSOP 78 *Jolly; Howard Roberts (g); Chuck Berghofer (b); Larry Bunker, Nick Martinis (d); strings and brass.* 11/62–8/64.

***** Timeless**
VSOP 105 *Jolly; Chuck Berghofer (b); Nick Ceroli (d).* 7/69.

★★(★) Yeah!
VSOP 98 *Jolly; Chuck Berghofer (b); Nick Martinis (d). 10/95.*

A definitive West Coast man, Jolly has spent most of his professional life in studios and on soundtracks. He likes to use his right hand at the very top of the keyboard and the insistently dinky phrasing which results gets a bit tiresome over CD length. The RCA album is a relic of vintage West Coast days, and not one of the better ones: the three sextet tracks put Pete to work on the accordion, and the trio pieces seem oddly melodramatic. Manne, though, plays as superbly as ever. *And Friends* pulls together tracks from three rather obscure early-'60s dates, and they're an indifferent lot with hack orchestral arrangements on seven tracks and a thin sound on all of them. *Timeless* is rather better. Drawn from a few sessions at Donte's, the playing has an expansive feel which softens Jolly's insistently trebly style and, though 'Stars And Stripes Forever' and 'Hey Jude' weren't ideal choices, the music has the feel of jazz guys on holiday from studio chores and having fun – a glimpse of Californian cool from a time when it was going out of business.

A generation later, he is still playing with Berghofer and Martinis, and *Yeah!* isn't bad – some nice choices of tune, and the trio are as comfortable as an old pullover. But it's a potboiler.

★★★ Collaboration
Fresh Sound FSR 5038 *Jolly; Jan Lundgren (p); Chuck Berghofer (b); Joe LaBarbera (d). 9/01.*

Button-bright and twinkling, these duets-with-rhythm are entertainingly delivered, although it's really one of those discs which is best handled a few tracks at a time. Jolly and Lundgren get a solo apiece, but otherwise it's interlocking improvs worked out with seemingly military precision (as the detailed session-notes make clear). It's fun hearing one man start a phrase and the next finish it, although, as suggested, the format does grow a little wearying across CD length.

Chris Jonas

SOPRANO SAXOPHONE

New York-based, Jonas has worked with Anthony Braxton and with young Turks Assif Tsahar and Susie Ibarra. Superficially reminiscent of Steve Lacy at his freest, he has perhaps also learnt from Braxton and Julius Hemphill.

★★★ Ensembles Unsynchronized
Newsonic 18 *Jonas; Cuong Vu (t); Joe Fiedler (tb); James Fei (ss, as); Kevin Norton (perc). 12/98.*

★★★(★) The Sun Spits Cherries
Hopscotch HOP 4 *Jonas; Joe Fiedler (tb); Chris Washburne (btb); Andrew Barker (d). 9/99.*

★★★ The Vermilion
Hopscotch HOP 8 *Jonas; Joe Fiedler (tb); Chris Washburne (btb); Myra Melford (p); Andrew Barker (d). 2/00.*

Jonas's sleeve-note to *Ensembles Unsynchronized* offers a rebuke to sentimentalists: 'Don't look for overt meaning in my music. For me a piece of music does not tell a specific story.' That and the functional title may lead to expectations of a dreary experience but, for all its abstractions, the music – open, but much of it based around canonic principles – has plenty to, er, 'say'. A few sections flag rather badly as the process goes forward.

The poetic title of *The Sun Spits Cherries* (now used as a group name by Jonas) refers to the fact that four and a half pounds of sunlight strike the earth every second, and there is a juicy warmth to be extracted from these spare and uncomplicated sounds. Jonas exploits the interesting textures available from saxophone and trombones, with no harmony instrument. Some of it is little more than old-fashioned musical pointillism, but it is clear that the leader's imagination is more capacious and more structured than that. Heard as a continuous suite, *The Sun Spits Cherries* has a compelling logic that repays many hearings.

The Vermilion is by the same group, with Melford guesting. Jonas does sometimes get hung up on his processes, although the clear organization of the music is one of its strengths – there's the feeling that anything aimless has been rigorously cut out. It's a peculiar instrumentation and sometimes (as in 'Portico') it generates a feeling of some sort of novelty music. We await his masterpiece.

Carmell Jones (1936–96)

TRUMPET

Born in Kansas City, Jones worked locally until he tried his luck in California in the '60s. He did sterling sideman work with Gerald Wilson and Horace Silver, but never made much impact as a leader, and eventually returned to his hometown after spending some years in Europe. Although affectionately remembered, he was always a nearly man on his horn.

★★★ Jay Hawk Talk
Original Jazz Classics OJC 1938 *Jones; Jimmy Heath (ts); Barry Harris (p); George Tucker (b); Roger Humphries (d). 8/65.*

Jones had a lovely take-my-time way about his trumpet-playing, even though he could play in an almost old-fashioned hot style when he chose – a legacy of his KayCee roots – and he was a more than capable member of a Horace Silver front line. His few albums as a leader have never attracted much attention and in the CD era they have been entirely neglected. This likeable date is no great shakes, but Jones, Heath and Harris each plays himself rather than any more fashionable model, and the session has an honest, men-at-work feel to it which has held its integrity. Carmell's sweet-and-sour treatment of 'Willow Weep For Me' is a capsule summary of his thoughtful skills. Five of his sessions for Pacific Jazz have been released by Mosaic in one of their limited-edition sets: while it would be good to see these in more general circulation, admirers are advised to try and locate one of these while they're still around.

Elvin Jones (1927–2004)

DRUMS, GUITAR

The kid brother of the Jones family, and almost a decade younger than Hank, Elvin started his career in Detroit, before moving to New York City, and established himself as an intense bebop drummer, adding a new and complex dimension to the rhythmic language of bop. His key musical encounter was with John Coltrane, with whom he worked for five intense years, before Trane's desire to introduce a second percussionist severed the relationship. Elvin continued to tend the flame, but also to develop his own fiery brand of jazz.

*** Elvin!

Original Jazz Classics OJCCD 259 *Jones; Thad Jones (c); Frank Wess (f); Frank Foster (ts); Hank Jones (p); Art Davis (b).* 7/61–1/62.

Elvin remains an enigma; a shy but affable man whose exterior masks a turbulent and often self-destructive nature, he transformed modern jazz drumming like no one else since the early heyday of Max Roach. Jones's introduction of African 'polyrhythms' became a key feature of the John Coltrane quartet, of which he was arguably the key member, and it has fed into a long recording history as a leader.

Elvin! is noisy, heated bop, with some good interplay between Jones and a front line that refuses to play by the rules. The trio tracks with elder brother Hank and Art Davis are particularly good, at once fiery and lyrical, stretched out rhythmically and yet sounding quite accommodating. Wess and Foster are perhaps too strait-laced for this session, but both are adventurous enough to go along for the ride, and Wess in particular turns in some lovely ideas.

***(*) Live At The Village Vanguard

Enja 2036 *Jones; Hannibal Marvin Peterson (t); George Coleman (ts); Wilbur Little (b).* 68.

This was a tough gig in terms of its abrasive, compellingly forceful soundscapes, but also more technically, since what we are hearing for most of the time is a pianoless trio, a form Jones was to experiment with for some years. Working without a harmony instrument, and leaning very heavily on big George's very sophisticated and often lateral harmonic sense, Jones, as ever, plays as if he's conducting an entire orchestra – but also on occasion as if he has a personal grudge against each and every member. Little is something of a passenger in this setting and spends most of his time laying down steady, patient figures with just the odd embellishment to keep himself interested. Peterson gatecrashes on 'Mr Jones', taking the shine off another perfectly good trumpet.

** Heavy Sounds

Impulse! 547959-2 *Jones; Frank Foster (ts); Billy Green (p); Richard Davis (b).* 6/67.

Billed as a collaboration between Jones and Davis, this breaks down into a series of feature spots, stitched together with some suspect ensemble play which suggests that this wasn't a regular working band. Foster is responsible for two compositions, 'Raunchy Rita', on which Davis indulges a curious out-of-tempo excursion, and the classic 'Shiny Stockings', and these are actually rather good, if it weren't for bassist and drummer constantly vying for attention like overgrown schoolkids. Green is a very decent accompanist, not someone who will be widely recognized but a creditable player. Jones's one composition credit is the dismal 'Elvin's Guitar Blues' on which he strums the opening choruses like a teenager who's just learnt about Bert Weedon. 'Summertime' is spoiled by rain, and not until 'Here's That Rainy Day' does the sun come out. Too late by then.

*** New Agenda

Universe 15 *Jones; Steve Grossman, Azar Lawrence (ss, ts); Joe Farrell, Frank Foster (ts, f); Kenny Barron, Gene Perla (p); Roland Prince (g); Dave Williams (b).* 75.

*** The Main Force

Universe 24 *Jones; Frank Foster, Steve Grossman, Pat LaBarbera, Dave Liebman (sax); Albert Dailey (p); Ryo Kawasaki (g); Dave Williams (b); Angel Allende (perc).* 76.

*** Time Capsule

Universe 38 *Jones; Bunky Green (as); George Coleman (ts); Frank Wess (f); Kenny Barron (p); Ryo Kawasaki (g); Junie Booth, Milt Hinton (b); Angel Allende (perc).* 77.

Three sessions originally made for Vanguard and only recently reissued. The earliest is a fairly routine set that again sticks mostly to straightahead material, leavened by Jones's patented polyrhythms and a fairly high energy level. 'Naima' is bland (which is saying something, given the beauty of the basic theme) and the most exciting performance is Frank Foster's opening 'Someone's Rocking My Jazzboat', which is good, unpretentious swing-bop.

The Main Force dabbles with fusion and only really comes alive when Liebman is at the microphone. Kawasaki's guitar seems to have been bought at the family motorcycle factory and is wildly out of place here, even given the high-energy approach Jones always favours. It's a set that belongs more appropriately in a time capsule, even more so than the record of that name. As before, Jones relies on sidemen for charts and it's the little-known Bunky Green who emerges as the most prominent voice. Coleman is in good shape as well, but Barron's electric piano, normally an effective option for him, sounds slushy and ill-defined. A nice cameo from Milt Hinton, expressive flute from Wess, but a scrappy session that brought the Vanguard period to a close.

*** Very R.A.R.E.

Evidence ECD 22053 2 *Jones; Art Pepper (as); Frank Foster, Pat LaBarbera (ss, ts); Roland Hanna (p); Roland Prince (g); Richard Davis, Andy McCloud III (b).* 78.

*** Love & Peace

Evidence ECD 22065 2 *As above, except omit Pepper, Hanna; add Pharoah Sanders (ts); McCoy Tyner (p); Jean-Paul Bourelly (g).* 78, 79.

The first of these brings together material by a wonderful quartet fronted by Art Pepper with some other stuff recorded in the far East, of which more in a moment. Pepper's salty alto works well, though sometimes you feel he is floundering with the count, especially on 'Tin Tin Deo'. Richard Davis's dark-toned bass is, as ever, a delight. The bonus material consists of a 26-minute run through of 'A Love Supreme' and begs the unavoidable question: was Jones by this staging capitalizing too cynically on his association with Coltrane? It's a dud performance, not worth padding the original CD with.

Love & Peace also includes one dispensable track from the group with Foster, Prince, LaBarbera and McCloud which adds nothing to the importance of this record, Jones's first reunion with McCoy Tyner since Coltrane days. It's not the meeting of minds it might have been. Tyner's agenda is very different, harmonically and rhythmically, and the two spend more time duelling than communicating. Pharoah Sanders's presence is ironic, since it was his addition to the classic Coltrane Quartet line-up that sparked the split. He's in mildly antagonistic form, but the whole thing is muddied and sometimes drowned by

Bourelly's squalling guitar. If you have the original LPs, hang on to them; the bonus tracks are a liability.

***** Earth Jones**

Quicksilver 4015 *Jones; Terumaso Hino (t); Dave Liebman (ss, ts, f); Kenny Kirkland (p); George Mraz (b).* 82.

****(*) Brother John**

Quicksilver 4001 *Jones; Pat LaBarbera (ss, ts); Kenny Kirkland (p); Reggie Workman (b).* 83.

'Three Card Molly' underlines the feeling that composition was never Jones's strong suit. 'Day And Night', based on a very familiar tune indeed, underlines 'composer' Dave Liebman's brilliance as a harmonic improviser. Between those two poles this album just about succeeds and very nearly fails. The interplay between trumpet and saxophone never quite takes off and Jones's typically hyperactive drumming seems to drive Kenny Kirkland into the buffers. Mraz is masterful.

Jones's affection for LaBarbera is evident on *Brother John*, where he is called on to take up the mantle and, to his credit, doesn't overreach himself in the attempt. The most interesting tune here is Tadd Dameron's 'Whatever Possessed Me', but for the most part the album is taken up with either obvious or over-elaborate blues changes. Disappointing.

Etta Jones (1928–2001)

VOCAL

Touring with Buddy Johnson at 16, later with Earl Hines, and eventually making a solo success with her Don't Go To Strangers album. A big, bluesy voice and an in-my-own-time relationship to the beat.

***** Etta Jones 1944–1947**

Classics 1065 *Jones; Joe Thomas, Hot Lips Page, Jessie Drakes, George Treadwell, Joe Newman (t); Clyde Bernhardt, Dickie Harris (tb); Barney Bigard (cl); Joe Evans, Floyd Williams, Don Stovall, Pete Clarke (as); Georgie Auld, Budd Johnson, Big Nick Nicholas (ts); Leonard Feather, Duke Jordan, Pete Johnson, Jimmy Jones, Luther Henderson (p); Chuck Wayne, Jimmy Shirley, John Collins, Herman Mitchell (g); Billy Taylor, Eugene Ramey, Abe Bolar, Al McKibbon, Trigger Alpert (b); Stan Levey, J. C. Heard, Jack Parker, Denzil Best (d).* 12/44–10/47.

*****(*) Don't Go To Strangers**

Original Jazz Classics OJC 298 *Jones; Frank Wess (ts, f); Richard Wyands (p); Skeeter Best (g); George Duvivier (b); Roy Haynes (d).* 6/60.

***** Something Nice**

Original Jazz Classics OJC 221 *Jones; Lem Winchester (vib); Richard Wyands, Jimmy Neeley (p); George Duvivier, Michael Mulia (b); Roy Haynes, Rudy Lawless (d).* 9/60–3/61.

*****(*) Lonely And Blue**

Original Jazz Classics OJC 702 *Jones; Gene Ammons, Budd Johnson (ts); Patti Bown (p); Wally Richardson (g); George Duvivier (b); Ed Shaughnessy (d).* 4–5/62.

***** So Warm**

Original Jazz Classics OJC 874 *Jones; Ray Alonge (frhn); Eric Dixon, Jerome Richardson, Phil Bodner, Arthur Clarke (reeds); Mal Waldron (p); George Duvivier (b); Charli Persip, Bill English (d); strings.* 61.

***** Hollar!**

Original Jazz Classics OJC 1061 *Jones; Oliver Nelson, Jerome Richardson (ts); Jimmy Neeley, Richard Wyands, Sam Bruno (p); Lem Winchester (vib); Wally Richardson, Kenny Burrell, Bucky Pizzarelli (g); Michael Mulia, George Duvivier, Ernest Hayes (b); Rudy Lawless, Roy Haynes, Bobby Donaldson (d).* 9/60–11/62.

***** Love Shout**

Original Jazz Classics OJC 941 *Jones; Jerome Richardson (ts, f); Kenny Cox (p); Sam Bruno (p, org); Larry Young (org); Kenny Burrell, Bucky Pizzarelli (g); Peck Morrison, Ernest Hayes, George Tucker (b); Oliver Jackson, Bobby Donaldson, Jimmie Smith (d).* 11/62–2/63.

Jones began recording as a teenager in the '40s, and her earliest sides have been collected on the Classics compilation. She was singing lightweight blues at this point, even if one of the tracks is called 'Blues To End All Blues' (other titles include 'Osculate Me Daddy' and 'Misery Is A Thing Called Moe'!). Some pretty useful groups backed her up on these sessions, for Black & White, Chicago, Savoy and Victor, with Budd Johnson in several of the bands and Pete Johnson leading a group with Lips Page. A rediscovery of some largely forgotten tracks.

By the time she came to make *Don't Go To Strangers*, Jones was already a veteran. But the title-song from the LP became a gold record, and she subsequently made several albums for Prestige. In its modest way the album remains a fine achievement, with Jones's heavy, blues-directed voice piling extra substance on to fluff such as 'Yes Sir, That's My Baby', with rolling support from an excellent band. The subsequent *Something Nice* is more quiescent, the 11 songs dispatched matter-of-factly, although Jones's regal delivery makes such as 'Through A Long And Sleepless Night' into sometimes heady stuff. *Lonely And Blue* was a prescient suggestion of the kind of albums she would make for Muse, a generation later: small-hours, lonesome music which is barely a step away from outright blues. Johnson handles most of the tenor chores (as Houston Person would later do) and his wry rejonders on 'Gee Baby Ain't I Good To You' are delightful. *So Warm* tips the scales towards MOR, but Etta's natural warmth heats up the string charts, and it's a beguiling result. *Love Shout* goes back to a small-band setting: Jerome Richardson turns in a great solo on the fine 'The Gal From Joe's', and the twin guitars of Burrell and Pizzarelli are a bonus on 'Hi-Lilli, Hi-Lo'. Some of the rest is fluff. *Hollar!* lifts tracks from three different sessions (some of them leftovers from dates heard on the other discs) but it's by no means a bin-end selection. There's a very fine 'I Got It Bad (And That Ain't Good)', a seemingly impromptu 'Our Love Is Here To Stay' and a musing 'Looking Back' among the highlights. Taken together, this is an undeservedly lesser-known sequence of vocal records which are very satisfying.

*****(*) The Best Of Etta Jones: The Prestige Singles**

Prestige 11021-2 *Jones; various line-ups as in above OJC discs.* 7/60–11/62.

Given that Etta's Prestige catalogue contains no single defining album, a top-notch best-of would surely have been an essential purchase, but by making up an album from singles released off the various sets, the chance was just slightly fudged. Still, not too many quarrels with most of these tracks, and it would certainly make a nice introduction for someone who hadn't heard her before.

***** The Melody Lingers On**
Highnote HCD 7005 *Jones; Houston Person (ts); Tom Aalf (vn); Dick Morgan (p); Keter Betts (b); Frankie Jones (d).* 11/96.

*****(*) Easy Living**
High Note HDCD 7059 *Jones; Houston Person (ts); Richard Wyands (p); Ray Drummond (b); Chip White (d).* 2/00.

****** Sings Lady Day**
High Note HCD 7078 *As above, except add Peter Bernstein (g), John Weber (b) omit Drummond.* 6/01.

Etta recorded steadily through the '80s and '90s. She seems comfortable back with a band on *The Melody Lingers On*, a sequence of tribute songs to departed singers, and with Person returned to her side it's a pleasing if unexceptional occasion. Like Shirley Horn, Jones prefers a slow-to-ambling tempo that she can take her own time with, and though some of the songs are a bit obvious, on a less frequently encountered tune like 'For Sentimental Reasons' she's very good.

It would be almost an impertinence to say that Etta got better, the older she grew. But her final pair of records are at least as fine as, and often superior to, anything she'd done earlier. The great, heavy voice is the most characterful kind of instrument, and her way with time and the way a phrase can be pulled into just the shape she wants became imperious. *Easy Living* is a delightful mix of standards with the most basic of bands: Houston, old master Wyands, and the attentive Drummond and White. But even this bows to the quite magisterial *Sings Lady Day*. Recorded, sadly, only months before her death, she takes on the Holiday repertoire and never once bows to Billie's dreaded pathos. 'But Beautiful' is an incomparable version of the song; but nothing here is less than wonderful.

Hank Jones (born 1918)

PIANO

The eldest of the three brothers, Hank Jones is as quiet and unassuming as drummer Elvin is extrovert, but he shares something of the late Thad Jones's deceptive sophistication. After working in territory bands, Hank became part of the first bebop generation and has retained much of that complex idiom in his recent solo and small-group recordings.

***** Urbanity**
Verve 537749-2 *Jones; Johnny Smith (g); Ray Brown (b).* 47, 53.

The early material on *Urbanity* reappears on CD, over 50 years after the original solo tracks were recorded. Six light-footed standards, dispatched with Hank's usual grace and lack of fuss. Some find him lacking in substance, but there is such ease in the playing that it is hard to criticize it on those grounds. Unfortunately, the CD is padded out with an inordinate amount of unissued material from a 1953 trio session, unusual for being drummerless. There are no fewer than five takes of 'Things Are So Pretty In The Spring' (none of them revelatory) and four of 'Thad's Pad'. It requires a certain commitment to listen to these in sequence, and only the subtlest and most highly attuned listener will find much essential difference between them.

****** The Talented Touch / Songs From Porgy And Bess**
Okra-Tone 4972 *Jones; Kenny Burrell, Barry Galbraith (g); Milt Hinton (b); Osie Johnson, Elvin Jones (d).* 58, 60.

The best news for Jones for some time is the reissue of these two LPs from 1958 and 1960. *The Talented Touch* brought together four good friends for a relaxed album of music that was a common currency for all of them. Their rapport on 'My One And Only Love', 'Star Eyes' and even Gigi Gryce's seldom played 'Blue Lights' is little less than miraculous. Hinton sounds as if he wrote every tune, Hank is effortless and Barry Galbraith and Osie Johnson contribute to a wonderfully confident and well-rounded record. Helping to fill out the picture on a very thin time in the Jones discography is the *Porgy And Bess* material with Kenny Burrell, Hinton again and brother Elvin Jones – a lovely opportunity to hear the siblings working together at a time when Elvin's health was good and his stint with the Coltrane quartet was just around the corner. Hank plays these familiar themes as if they were still rooted in the opera: dramatic, passionate and poignant by turns.

**** Happenings**
Impulse! 9071 *Jones; Joe Newman, Ernie Royal, Snooky Young (t); Clark Terry (t, v); J. J. Johnson, Britt Woodman (tb); Bob Ashton, Danny Bank, Jerry Dodgion, Romeo Penque, Jerome Richardson, Phil Woods (reeds); Ron Carter, George Duvivier (b); Ed Shaughnessy, Grady Tate (d); Joe Venuto (perc).* 10/66.

Hank's most disappointing record. Despite some fine Oliver Nelson arrangements, this is a woolly and inconsequential session, marred further by Jones's bizarre decision to play an electric harpsichord on seven of the tracks; Stanley Dance reckoned it might be the next big thing in jazz instrumentation, but it's a grating and unattractive sound that does Hank no favours. The pop material is also not Hank's bag and he sounds uncomfortable with 'Winchester Cathedral' (Clark Terry sings it) and 'Spy With A Cold Nose'.

***** Arigato**
Progressive 7004 *Jones; Ray Rivera (g); Richard Davis, Jay Leonhart (b); Ronnie Bedford (d).* 10/76.

***** The Trio**
Chiaroscuro 188 *Jones; Milt Hinton (b); Bobby Rosengarden (d).* 77.

***** I Remember You**
Black & Blue 947 *Jones; George Duvivier (b); Oliver Jackson (d).* 7/77, 7/78.

***** Tiptoe Tapdance**
Original Jazz Classics OJC 719 *As above.* 6/77, 1/78.

****(*) Just For Fun**
Original Jazz Classics OJC 471 *Jones; Howard Roberts (g); Ray Brown (b); Shelly Manne (d).* 6/77.

Like everyone else, Jones had a quiet time of it in the '60s, but he re-emerges with a bang in the following decade, which really marks the beginning of his now substantial output of high-quality solo and trio jazz. Never much of a composer, a fact often adduced to downplay his significance, Jones is not given to wholesale reassessment of standard progressions but prefers to concentrate on the *sound* of a tune. His delicacy and balance, that tiptoeing, tap-dancing feel, are among the qualities which have enhanced and prolonged his reputation as a great accompanist, but (unfairly) only a rather lightweight soloist.

The Trio, not to be confused with an earlier disc of the same unrevealing name, is a great set, largely because the rapport with Hinton is so good and so unflappable. Sadly the reissue comes without additional tracks and the CD was remastered from the original LP. Given how revealing some of the alternates on Hank's Black & Blues of this period can be, it would have been good to hear more of this fine group. What there is, however, is excellent. ''S Wonderful' and 'Right Here, Right Now' are first rate and 'Lullaby Of The Leaves', so hackneyed it almost gets a cab licence, works like a dream off Hinton's resonant accompaniment.

Jones recorded in France every July from 1977 to 1979 and turned in some respectable dates for Black & Blue. *Bluesette* (below) is a more solid session, despite the variation of personnel, but Jones fans will enjoy the relaxed bluesy swing of *I Remember You* as well. Some good bonus tracks on the reissue. *Arigato* is a splendid date, a basic trio (either Davis or Leonhart on bass) augmented for a couple of easy Latin swingers by Rivera, who is composer of 'Night Flight To Puerto Rico' and 'Majorca'. Jones's vigour is evident on 'Allen's Alley' and his own 'Recapitulation'. There's more south of the border atmosphere on Gary McFarland's 'Notte Triste'. Nicely recorded, with a full, round sound in the bass and lots of unintrusive presence from the drums.

Just For Fun is a grower, a record that initially comes across as rather superficial, but gradually yields up subtleties not audible first time around. Despite the presence of Manne (the players actually split into two – drummerless and guitarless respectively – trios) the results are slightly uncertain. Jones is too straightforward an executant to be able to rely on irony, and pieces like 'A Very Hip Rock And Roll Tune' and 'Kids Are Pretty People' fall flat on that account. Though they perhaps lack the inventive fire of the Savoys (currently waiting to be repackaged), the '70s sets are to be preferred for their almost magisterial calm and command.

*** Ain't Misbehavin'

Original Jazz Classics OJCCD 1027 *Jones; Teddy Edwards (ts, cl); Kenny Burrell (g); Richard Davis (b); Roy Haynes (d). 8/78.*

Hank pays his dues to the spirit of Fats Waller on six elegantly crafted themes. The title-piece gets the record off to a rollicking start, but it's only with 'Joint Is Jumpin'' and 'Honeysuckle Rose' that it hits top form. Edwards is also in very good form and Burrell's guitar-playing is both elegant and propulsive, and Roy Haynes is masterful at the kit. Arranged by Bill Holman and produced by Ed Michel, the set lacks nothing but a touch of fire and passion.

*** Bluesette

Black & Blue 907 *Jones; Rob Franken (ky); George Duvivier, Niels-Henning Orsted Pedersen (b); Alan Dawson, Alex Riel (d). 7/78, 7/79.*

Blues dominated European sessions, marked by good, strong playing but no particular originality. NHOP shines as he did with Oscar Peterson and Riel underlines why he was considered the best drummer in Europe at this time. The reissue has some fine bonus tracks, including a superb version of Thielemans's title-tune.

** Darji's Groove

Prevue 22 *Jones; Darwin Gross (vib); Rodney Jones (g); Victor Gaskin (b); Mickey Roker (d). 82.*

This is an oddly disappointing record, largely because the bulk of the material is so flat and uninspired. Though Jones is listed as leader, most of the material (all except 'Happy Blue' and a couple of standards) is credited to vibist Gross, who is a decent enough performer but certainly not a composer of any substance. Jones's generosity is well known, but here he seems to have backed the wrong horse. 'My Romance' provides some attractive moments, with Rodney Jones playing Spanish guitar. Roker is as polished and involving as ever, and Hank himself plays some lovely things on 'A Time For Love', but not enough to rescue an extremely dull set.

**** Lazy Afternoon

Concord CCD 4391 *Jones; Ken Peplowski (as, cl); Dave Holland (b); Keith Copeland (d). 7/89.*

*** The Touch

Concord CCD 2157 2CD *As above, except add Ray Brown (b); Jimmie Smith (d). 77, 89.*

Lazy Afternoon is a peach: warm, vibrant jazz with the modulation and pace of a good club date. Jones is generous with solo space for his sidemen, though his unusual approach to Kurt Weill's 'Speak Low', a striking choice for openers, is marred by an intrusive Copeland solo. Holland and Copeland had acted as the pianist's performing trio, with an evident empathy; quite properly, the bassist is featured strongly, with particularly fine excursions on the J. J. Johnson composition, 'Lament', and the succeeding 'Comin' Home Baby'. Jones's fine touch as a colourist is evident on the title-track, where a hint of Ellingtonish celeste under Ken Peplowski's smooth clarinet spices a slightly bland approach.

Lazy Afternoon and the 1977 *Rockin' In Rhythm* are now available as a two-header called *The Touch*. Warmly recommended to anyone who admires Hank's piano-playing.

***(*) Live At Maybeck Recital Hall: Volume 16

Concord CCD 4502 *Jones (p solo). 90.*

***(*) Jazzpar 91 Project

Storyville STCD 3091 *Jones; Mads Vinding (b); Al Foster (d). 3/91.*

**** Upon Reflection

Verve 514898-2 *Jones; George Mraz (b); Elvin Jones (d). 2/93.*

Jones entered the '90s one of the music's elder statesmen. His Maybeck recital was, predictably, one of the high points of the series, and his recent recording has all been of a tremendously high standard. There are inconsistencies in the disc from the Danish Jazzpar project (signal moment of recognition). There is, however, a second masterwork to sit alongside the Maybeck. *Upon Reflection* is devoted to the music of his brother, Thad, who died in 1986. Quite properly, the drummer's job went to Elvin rather than to Foster or Higgins, who might have been more suitable musically. It's a tender, but by no means sentimental, record. However, if you can listen to 'A Child Is Born' without a tear, tear up your donor card; they can't transplant hearts of stone.

*** Sarala

Verve 528783-2 *Jones; Cheick-Tidiane Seck (org, perc, v); The Mandinkas. 4/95.*

The result of Jones's desire to record an album of traditional African music, *Sarala* tends to marginalize him slightly, so powerful and compelling is the playing and sheer presence of

Cheick-Tidiane Seck and his Mandinkas. Mixing flutes, guitars, other native instruments and intense vocalization, they generate textures of close, grainy detail that frequently capture the foreground from Jones. If one is looking for jazz 'roots' in the contemporary world, this is as close and as deep as it gets.

Jo Jones (1911–85)

DRUMS

Known as Chicago Jo Jones to distinguish him from Philly Joe, he changed the sound of the drums in jazz by switching the emphasis from bass to hi-hat. His fleet sound was a mainstay of big-band jazz during the late '30s and '40s.

***** The Essential Jo Jones**
Vanguard 101/2 *Jones; Emmett Berry (t); Lawrence Brown, Freddie Green (tb); Lucky Thompson (ts); Rudy Powell (cl); Count Basie, Ray Bryant, Nat Pierce (p); Tommy Bryant, Walter Page (b).* 8/55, 4/58.

Jones was the subtle driving force of the Basie band between 1934 and 1948 and the Count repaid the compliment with a guest spot on Jo's solo disc, giving 'Shoe Shine Boy' a touch of the old magic. The other participants are familiar enough as well, with Berry, Green and Thompson all prominent. Inevitably, a lot of emphasis falls on the drums, which may not be to every taste, but Jones is such a nimble, light player that he is always estimably listenable. The 1958 session with Ray and Tommy Bryant (originally an album called *Plus Two*) is mostly the pianist's work but Jo revels in those bluesy themes and produces some of his best small-group work on record. A good compilation of the drummer's work for John Hammond and a thoroughly enjoyable CD.

***** The Main Man**
Pablo/Original Jazz Classics OJCCD 869 *Jones; Harry 'Sweets' Edison, Roy Eldridge (t); Vic Dickenson (tb); Eddie 'Lockjaw' Davis (ts); Tommy Flanagan (p); Freddie Green (g); Sam Jones (b).* 11/76.

Jo didn't lose any of his fire when retirement age came round. When he made this, he still had nearly a decade left to him, a time he spent cheerfully running down each and every symptom of milquetoast modernity. Jones's spoken word sessions for Jazz Odyssey were a mixture of percussion masterclass and settling of scores. Here, he simply gets down to the business of playing classic swing jazz.

Jonah Jones (1908–2000)

TRUMPET

Born in Louisville, apprenticed in various territory bands, then worked with Lunceford, Stuff Smith and, through most of the '40s, Cab Calloway. Eventually scored a huge hit with the album Jonah Jones At The Embers, and became a cabaret star. Worked through the '60s, '70s and '80s and, though basically retired, he could still play useful trumpet even at the end of his life.

****(*) Jonah Jones 1936–1945**
Classics 972 *Jones; Tyree Glenn (tb, vib); Joe Marsala, Buster Bailey, Al Gibson (cl); Edgar Sampson, Hilton Jefferson (as); Ike Quebec (ts); Dick Porter (p, v); Clyde Hart, Buster Harding, Dave Rivera (p); Eddie Condon, Bobby Bennett, Danny Barker (g); Wilson Myers, John Kirby, Milt Hinton (b); George Wettling, Cozy Cole, J. C. Heard (d).* 10/36–7/45.

Jones began as a minor Armstrong disciple. His big, blowsy style tends to dominate the groups he's in, and these rather motley sessions are more like swing-era footnotes than anything. Six tracks with the Fats Waller copyist, Dick Porter, are scarcely worth remembering, and two sessions for Keynote and one for Commodore form the meat of this CD. They have their moments, but the slow tunes are dreary and the most interesting player is Tyree Glenn, whose sleepy-sounding solos have the odd quirk in them. The Porter tracks have very indifferent sound; the later ones are all right.

Oliver Jones (born 1934)

PIANO

Born in Montreal, Jones was playing in local clubs when he was still in high school. He formed a showband which played in Puerto Rico, where he stayed for some years, before returning to Canada in 1980 and releasing a steady stream of records, mostly in the trio format. He retired from full-time playing in 1995.

****(*) The Many Moods Of Oliver Jones**
Justin Time JUST 3 *Jones (p solo).* 2–3/84.

****(*) Lights Of Burgundy**
Justin Time JUST 6 *Jones; Fraser McPherson (ts); Reg Schwager (g); Michel Donato (b); Jim Hillman (d).* 4/85.

***** Requestfully Yours**
Justin Time JUST 11 *Jones; Skip Beckwith (b); Anil Sharma (d).* 11/85.

***** Speak Low Swing Hard**
Justin Time JUST 17 *Jones; Skip Beckwith (b); Jim Hillman (d).* 7–9/85.

***** A Class Act**
Justin Time JUST 41 *Jones; Steve Wallace (b); Ed Thigpen (d).* 4–5/91.

Oliver Jones is destined to be no more than the second most famous piano export from Canada, after Oscar Peterson. Although he actually studied with Daisy Peterson and grew up in Montreal, he didn't get serious about a jazz career until after he'd spent 20 years directing music in Puerto Rican tourist shows. Maybe his showmanship derives from that experience; either way, he clearly aspires to being a communicator the way Peterson himself does, and his closeness to the master's methods extends to his composing. Original tunes such as 'Blues For Helene' (*Just Friends*) or 'Fulford Street Maul' (*Lights Of Burgundy*) are exactly the kind of up-tempo blues which Peterson himself writes.

Jones is an engaging enough soloist, filling his records with good-hearted, swinging music, but they seldom add up to a very convincing whole and there always seem to be stretches of sheer professionalism in place of genuine feeling. His ballads are glossy rather than introspective, but perhaps one listens to Jones for his generous virtuosity, not his tenderness. He worked away from any limelight until the '80s, but since then he has recorded regularly for Justin Time.

Since his playing scarcely varies in intensity or prowess from record to record, preferred sessions are more a matter of the setting. The solo set is slightly less interesting since, like Peterson, Jones thrives on a propulsive rhythm section. *Speak Low Swing Hard* finds everyone playing with huge enthusiasm, and the session is distinguished by some interesting material, including Ferdie Grofé's 'On The Trail' and a reading of 'I'm An Old Cowhand' that sounds as if it was played on tiptoes. *Lights Of Burgundy* is let down by the unattractive studio-sound and rote performances. *A Class Act*, though, might be the best of these discs, with two of his best originals in 'Mark My Time' and 'Peaceful Time', and a couple of mature embellishments on Kenny Wheeler's 'Everybody's Song But My Own' and Bill Evans's 'Very Early'. Thigpen and Wallace offer seamless support.

***** Have Fingers, Will Travel**

Justin Time JUST 102-2 *Jones; Ray Brown (b); Jeff Hamilton (d).* 5/97.

Here's a recent set by Oliver to set beside the others. The essential sameness and predictability of his output suggests, in its way, something about jazz's commercial dilemma: it's often those qualities which have brought his audience to him. The difference with this disc is the rhythm section, the best he has ever recorded with: Brown has more gravitas than any bassman alive, Milt Hinton excepted, and Hamilton is a drummer whose merits far outweigh his wider recognition. On a medium-tempo groove, they're close to peerless, and Jones revels in the situation. There's surely nothing here that the pianist hasn't played for us before, somewhere or other, but it's as smiling and warm-blooded as he's ever been, and it feels fine.

****(*) Yuletide Swing**

Justin Time 71 *Jones; Richard Ring (g); Dave Young (b); Wali Muhammad (d).* 94.

Bah! And indeed Humbug! Try as we might, though, we can't fault this for seasonal appeal. As Christmas albums go – and most of ours went to the second-hand shop years back – this is pretty decent.

*****(*) Just In Time**

Justin Time JUST 120/1-2 2CD *Jones; Dave Young (b); Norman Marshall Villeneuve (d).* 11/97.

Jones may have gone into semi-retirement but he's still enjoying his jazz. He's always fun to hear in person, so this concert set, replete with the usual dazzle, is a nice place to make his acquaintance. Two and a quarter hours is far too much, but there's nothing that's less than enjoyable and swinging and, since our grades have been rather harsh with Jones in the past, he deserves the extra point.

****(*) From Lush To Lively**

Justin Time 73 *Jones; Guido Basso, Arnie Chycoski, Steve MacDaid, John MacLeod (t); Al Kay, Rob McConnell, Ernie Pattison (tb); Alex Dean, John Johnson, Bob Leonard, P. J. Perry (sax); Jim Vivian (b); Ted Warren (d); strings.* 02.

Smooth orchestral sounds of limited appeal to anyone who likes a bit of fibre and muscle in their jazz. Jones's approach to things like 'The Way You Look Tonight' and 'Our Love Is Here To Stay' is resolutely old-fashioned and literal, to the extent you listen to these tracks wondering if the singer has been edited off for karaoke purposes. Nice for background, but a frustrating listen.

***** Then & Now**

Justin Time 180 *Jones; Skip Bey (b).* 86, 01.

Our favourite Jones record. No themes, no orchestra; just a simple duo and a hatful of well-seasoned themes. Hokey as it is, 'Over The Rainbow' is magnificent, with some of the childish simplicity of the original still in there. 'Perdido' and 'I Remember Clifford' have a touch more muscle, and Bey's strong, resourceful presence is a huge plus on both. Half of the album was recorded as early as 1986, the remainder as a retirement package in 2001. All we can say is enjoy your time off, Oliver, and thanks for the music.

Philly Joe Jones (1923–85)

DRUMS

So called to distinguish him from 'Chicago' Joe Jones, he became one of the key modern-jazz drummers, despite succumbing to heroin abuse at intervals. Originally influenced by Sid Catlett, he had a ferociously powerful delivery which blended with modernist cross-rhythms to dazzling effect, though his jazz-rock group, Le Grand Prix, turned into self-parody. Philly Joe's work with Miles Davis in the mid-'50s was definitive of an era and a style.

***** Blues For Dracula**

Original Jazz Classics OJC 230 *Jones; Nat Adderley (c); Julian Priester (tb); Johnny Griffin (ts); Tommy Flanagan (p); Jimmy Garrison (b).* 9/58.

***** Drums Around The World**

Original Jazz Classics OJCCD 1792 2 *Jones; Blue Mitchell, Lee Morgan (t); Curtis Fuller (tb); Julian 'Cannonball' Adderley (as); Benny Golson (ts); Sahib Shihab (bs); Herbie Mann (f, picc); Wynton Kelly (p); Jimmy Garrison, Sam Jones (b).* 5/59.

***** Philly Joe's Beat / Philly Joe & Elvin Jones Together!**

Collectables 6264 *Jones; Michael Downs (co); Blue Mitchell (t); Curtis Fuller (tb); Bill Barron, Hank Mobley (ts); Walter Davis Jr, Wynton Kelly (p); Paul Chambers (b); Elvin Jones (d).* 5/50–64.

***** Showcase**

Original Jazz Classics OJCCD 484 2 *Jones; Blue Mitchell (t); Julian Priester (tb); Bill Barron (ts); Pepper Adams (bs); Charles Coker (p); Jimmy Garrison (b).* 11/59.

These bracket a torrid decade in Philly Joe's personal life, but his most productive as a musician. *Blues For Dracula* was recorded towards the end of the drummer's main association with Miles Davis's touring band, a period in which he was much in demand musically, but also making absurd demands on himself by means of a well-developed habit. There are some signs of strain on a mainly good-natured blowing album, with Jones well up in the mix and his characteristic rimshots slightly overloud; 'Two Bass Hit', which inspired some of Philly Joe's best moments on Davis's *Milestones*, is particularly strong. The three horns were well chosen but sound ragged in some of the less frenetic ensembles. The 'European' sessions sound altogether less certain, though Wheeler and King in particular produce an acceptable synthesis of their own slightly abstract idiom with Jones's whacking verve and oblique intelligence. *Showcase* is notable for a multi-tracked trio, 'Gwen', on which Philly Joe plays piano, bass and drums and does so very swingingly. The other tracks are strongly coloured by the horn-players, Mitchell's raw earth colours, Priester's slightly surreal tinge, Garrison's magnificently centred bass playing. By contrast, the drummer is something of a bit-player.

The 1959 large-ensemble record was intended to show off rhythm styles from around the world and it reflected Philly Joe's fascination with the multi-culturalism of another of his great influences, Max Roach. It isn't entirely successful, but the playing is uniformly good – as well it might be, given such a dream band. Two versions of Benny Golson's 'Stablemates' stand out strongly, as does the long, Dameron-composed 'Philly J. J.', but quite how 'Cherokee' fits into the global perspective isn't clear.

The Collectables pairing brings together two Atlantic records which have long been out of circulation. Both feature strong bands, as will be seen from the personnels. Downs is little known but he plays his part on the first disc, which includes some bebop staples ('Salt Peanuts') and 'Dear Old Stockholm', which is oddly attributed to Jimmy Garrison. The second date is a fascinating pairing with non-sibling Elvin, who's a very different kind of drummer, though partly inspired by Jo. The percussion work is as busy as you'd expect, but these are immaculately recorded and there's lots of detail. None of these can be said to be absolutely essential to a good modern collection; nevertheless, Philly Joe was a significant presence for three decades, and his influence can be heard today in the likes of Andrew Cyrille.

*** Philly Mignon

Original Jazz Classics OJC 1935 *Jones; Nat Adderley (c); Ira Sullivan (ss, ts); Dexter Gordon (ts); George Cables (p); Ron Carter (b).* 11–12/77.

Jones didn't live quite long enough to enjoy the elder-statesman status which the '80s and '90s conferred on many of his generation, and this 1977 comeback was more like business as usual, with a strong-looking line-up. Gordon was in a comeback mode himself, recently returned to the USA, but he makes heavy weather out of both 'Neptunis' and 'Polka Dots And Moonbeams'. Better are three pieces with Adderley and the restless-sounding Sullivan, although the star performer is probably Cables – why he sat out both 'Jim's Jewel' and 'United Blues' is a mystery. Philly Joe plays well enough, although in the end this is scarcely anybody's finest hour.

Quincy Jones (born 1933)

ARRANGER, BANDLEADER, TRUMPET

Jones played trumpet with Lionel Hampton in 1951–3, then did freelance arranging, including a stint in Europe. Toured with his own big band, 1959–61; arranged for Basie and several singers; then took an industry job at Mercury Records. He has since scored many film soundtracks, run his own record label, Qwest, and overseen numerous high-profile projects at the very top end of the music business. All of his projects include at least a nod to his jazz roots, no matter how remote they may become.

*** Free And Easy

Ancha ANC 9500-2 *Jones; Lennie Johnson, Benny Bailey, Floyd Standifer, Clark Terry (t, flhn); Ake Persson, Melba Liston, Quentin Jackson, Jimmy Cleveland (tb); Julius Watkins (frhn); Porter Kilbert, Phil Woods, Jerome Richardson, Budd Johnson, Sahib Shihab (reeds); Patti Bown (p); Les Spann (g, f); Buddy Catlett (b); Joe Harris (d).* 2/60.

*** Q Live In Paris Circa 1960

Qwest 946190-2 *As above.* 2/60.

*** Swiss Radio Days Jazz Series Vol. 1

TCB 02012 *As above, except Roger Guerin, Clyde Reasinger (t), Harold McNair (as) replace Terry, Lennie Johnson and Budd Johnson.* 6/60.

*** The Quintessence

Impulse! 051222 *Jones; Jerry Kail, Clyde Reasinger, Clark Terry, Joe Newman, Thad Jones, Freddie Hubbard, Al De Risi, Snooky Young, Ernie Royal (t); Billy Byers, Melba Liston, Paul Faulise, Rod Levitt, Curtis Fuller, Tony Mitchell (tb); Julius Watkins, Jimmy Buffington, Earl Chapin, Ray Alonge (frhn); Phil Woods, Jerome Richardson, Eric Dixon, Oliver Nelson, Frank Wess (reeds); Gloria Agostini (hp); Bobby Scott, Patti Brown (p); Milt Hinton (b); Harvey Phillips (tba); Buddy Catlett, Stu Martin, Osie Johnson (d).* 11–12/61.

*** Strike Up The Band

Mercury 830774-2 *Joe Newman, Clark Terry, Ernie Royal, Snooky Young, Jimmy Nottingham, Al Perisi, Jimmy Maxwell, John Bello, Benny Bailey (t); Curtis Fuller, Urbie Green, Richard Hixson, Billy Byers, Quentin Jackson, Tony Studd, Paul Faulise, Jimmy Cleveland, Kai Winding, Thomas Mitchell, Santo Russo, Melba Liston (tb); Zoot Sims, Roland Rahsaan Kirk, Walter Levinsky, James Moody, Phil Woods, Frank Wess, Al Cohn, Jerome Richardson, Seldon Powell, Romeo Penque, Walter Kane, Sahib Shihab, Eric Dixon, Stanley Webb, Budd Johnson, Seldon Powell (reeds); Jimmy Buffington, Tony Miranda, Bob Northern, Ray Alonge, Julius Watkins, Earl Chapin, Bob Ingraham, Fred Klein, Willie Ruff (frhn); Charles McCoy (hca, perc); Toots Thielemans (hca); Lalo Schifrin, Bobby Scott, Patti Bown (org, p); Gary Burton (vib); Wayne Wright, Sam Herman, Kenny Burrell, Jim Hall, Vincent Bell, Mundell Lowe, Don Arnone (g); Bill Stanley, James McAllister (tba); Milt Hinton, Art Davis, George Duvivier, Major Holley, Ben Tucker, Chris White (b); Rudy Collins, Osie Johnson, Ed Shaughnessy, Stu Martin, Jimmy Crawford (d); Tito Puente, Carlos Patato Valdes, Mike Olatunji, Martin Grupp, Philip Kraus, James Johnson, Carlos Gomez, Jack Del Rio, Jose Paula, Bill Costa, George Devins (perc).* 1/61–2/64.

*** Big Band Bossa Nova

Verve 557913-2 *Jones; Clark Terry (t); Roland Rahsaan Kirk, Jerome Richardson (f); Phil Woods, Paul Gonsalves (as); Lalo Schifrin (p); Jim Hall (g); Chris White (b); Rudy Collins (d); Jack Del Rio, Carlos Gomez, Jose Paula (perc).* 62.

Jones has been among the most charismatic figures in black music in the past 40 years. His specific jazz records have been few, since he's chosen to make his mark as a producer/Svengali to countless other artists, involving himself in some of the most successful recording projects of recent years with Michael Jackson and others. But his best music assuredly deserves a place in a comprehensive jazz collection.

Disastrously, his best CD, *This Is How I Feel About Jazz*, which combined the original album of that name with most of *Go West, Man* has been consigned, temporarily we hope, to jazz limbo. Currently, his story on record starts with the three releases from his 1960 sojourn in Europe with a big band. The

Ancha disc, recorded for Swedish Radio in Goteborg, is marginally more hi-fi, though the performances here sound more buttoned-up; the similar (and slightly longer) programme in Lausanne swings with greater abandon, though ensembles are paradoxically more secure. Interesting to compare solo spots between the two shows: Clark Terry and Benny Bailey each take a crack at 'I Remember Clifford' (Terry wins), while Melba Liston and Quentin Jackson go through 'The Phantom's Blues' (honours even). The Qwest album is another one from Europe and is another spirited set of performances from what was often a less-than-happy tour; sound is not much better than on the other discs, though.

The Quintessence is something of a disappointment after *This Is How I Feel About Jazz*. The tracks are concise and undeveloped, the charts considerably less imaginative and, though the players (all top studio pros) don't stint of themselves, there's little to turn the head other than a few breezy passages of section-work. With hindsight, *Bossa Nova* now looks like a typical piece of Jones opportunism, arranging pop hits and 'genuine' bossa nova pieces in a light, pleasing froth, although the excellent band can't help but do a good job on what is high-class fluff. *Strike Up The Band* is culled from various Mercury albums of a commercial bent, though Jones again assembles several remarkable orchestras and persuades them to make the most of 'Baby Elephant Walk' and 'Cast Your Fate To The Wind'.

**(*) Gula Matari

A&M 393030-2 *Jones; Freddie Hubbard, Danny Moore, Ernie Royal, Marvin Stamm, Gene Young (t, flhn); Wayne Andre, Al Grey, Benny Powell, Tony Studd (tb); Jerome Richardson (ts, f); Danny Bank (bs, bcl); Pepper Adams (bs); Herbie Hancock, Bob James, Bobby Scott (ky); Milt Jackson (vib); Eric Gale (g); Ron Carter, Ray Brown, Richard Davis, Major Holley (b); Grady Tate (d); Don Eliott, Jimmy Johnson, Warren Smith (perc).* 3–5/70.

**(*) Smackwater Jack

A&M 393037-2 *Similar to above.* 71.

*** Straight No Chaser: The Many Faces Of Quincy Jones

Universal 541542-2 2CD *Jones; as all discs above, plus other unlisted personnel.* 61–81.

By the late '60s, Jones was leaving jazz to other hands, though he usually found room for soloists in his prolific film and TV scoring. *Gula Matari* has a simpering treatment of 'Bridge Over Troubled Water', but it also has 'Walkin'' and, although Jones was clearly already in hock to the pop market, at least he was giving well-paid studio gigs to quality jazz musicians. *Smackwater Jack* walks a similar line, but it has a certain metropolitan flash to it which Jones liked to keep hold of.

Universal's two-disc compilation concentrates on his pop/lounge-music side, and within that brief it's very entertaining, getting as far as '80s hits such as 'Ai No Corrida' and 'Razzamatazz'. But since it ignores all of his most interesting early material – it includes two and a half minutes of 'Straight No Chaser' and then calls the album after it, thus raising false hopes among those hoping for more of Jones's best jazz scores – it seems disappointingly likely that we now won't get a compilation that genuinely explores the breadth of Jones's work.

Richard M. Jones (1889–1945)

PIANO, VOCAL

Jones worked in New Orleans as a teenager and was an important A&R man for Okeh in Chicago, often doubling as pianist and session-leader. He was still working in a similar capacity for Mercury in the '40s.

*** Richard M. Jones 1923–1927

Classics 826 *Jones; Shirley Clay, Eddie Mallory, Don Nelson, Willie Hightower (c); Preston Jackson, Henry Clark, John Lindsay (tb); Albert Nicholas (cl); Artie Starks, Fred Parham (cl, as); Warner Seals (ts); Johnny St Cyr, Ikey Robinson, Bud Scott, Leslie Corley (bj); Rudy Richardson (d); Lillie Delk Christian (v).* 6/23–7/27.

*** Richard M. Jones 1927–1944

Classics 853 *As above, except add Jimmy Cobb, Elisha Herbert (c), Jimmy McLeary, Eddie McLaughlin, Milton Fletcher, Thomas Gray, Lee Collins, Bob Shoffner (t), William Franklin, Roy Palmer, Edward Fant, Albert Wynn (tb), Darnell Howard (cl), Omer Simeon (cl, as), John Davis, John McCullin (as), Otha Dixon, Herschel Evans (ts), Dave Peyton, Gideon Honore, George Reynolds (p), Huey Long, Hurley Ramey (g), Quinn Wilson (tba), John Lindsay, Bob Frazier, Oliver Bibb (b), Wallace Bishop, Eddie Green, Roy Slaughter, Baby Dodds (d); George Washington (v); omit Nicholas, St Cyr, Corley, Seals, Nelson, Hightower, Scott, Parham and Richardson.* 11/27–3/44.

Composer, talent scout and studio A&R man, Jones did much for jazz in the Chicago scene of the '20s. As a performer, though, he is all but forgotten. He might have helped bring about the Armstrong Hot Five sessions in the Okeh studios, but his own records are relatively mild and undistinguished. The best tracks are on the first disc listed above. After a couple of doughty 1923 piano solos there are six good tracks by a trio of Jones, St Cyr and the young Albert Nicholas. Various tracks by Jones's Jazz Wizards, with the indifferent lead cornet of Shirley Clay, don't amount to much, although a stray 1927 trio date for Paramount – of cornet, clarinet and piano! – is surprisingly hot and furious. Scholars of the period will nevertheless want this CD for the presence of just two tracks: the incredibly rare sides by Hightower's Night Hawks featuring the somewhat legendary Willie Hightower, whose cornet lead is for once becoming that of a legend.

The second disc features some very obscure music. After four sessions at the far end of the '20s there's a leap forward to 1935, and the remaining dozen tracks offer an anachronistic survival of old-style Chicago hot music in a swing era that had gone light-years ahead. The final session, made some 18 months before Jones's death, is a competent if pointless attempt at recalling what had been happening 20 years before. 'Jazzin' Babies Blues', which Jones had cut solo at his first date in 1923, appears again in what with hindsight seems a poignant farewell.

Sam Jones (1924–81)

BASS, CELLO

His most important association was with Cannonball Adderley, working with him during 1956–7 and 1959–66. He then led occasional groups (including a 12-piece band), worked often with Cedar Walton, and mostly as an unassuming but rock-solid hard-bop rhythm player. Sometimes doubled on cello.

***** The Riverside Collection: Sam Jones – Right Down Front**

Original Jazz Classics OJC 6008 *Jones; Nat Adderley (c); Blue Mitchell, Clark Terry, Snooky Young (t); Melba Liston, Jimmy Cleveland (tb); Julian 'Cannonball' Adderley, Frank Strozier (as); Jimmy Heath, Jimmy Smith (ts); Charles Davis, Tate Houston, Pat Patrick (bs); Bobby Timmons, Victor Feldman, Joe Zawinul, Wynton Kelly (p); Les Spann (g, f); Keter Betts, Ron Carter, Israel Crosby (b); Louis Hayes, Ben Riley, Vernell Fournier (d).* 3/60–6/62.

***** The Soul Society**

Original Jazz Classics OJC 1789 *Jones; Nat Adderley (c); Blue Mitchell (t); Jimmy Heath (ts); Charles Davis (bs); Bobby Timmons (p); Keter Betts (b); Louis Hayes (d).* 3/60.

***** The Chant**

Original Jazz Classics OJC 1839 *As above, except add Melba Liston (tb), Julian 'Cannonball' Adderley (as), Tate Houston (bs), Wynton Kelly (p), Victor Feldman (p, vib), Les Spann (g); omit Davis, Timmons.* 1/61.

***** Down Home**

Original Jazz Classics OJC 1864 *Jones; Blue Mitchell, Snooky Young, Clark Terry (t); Jimmy Cleveland (tb); Frank Strozier (as, f); Jimmy Heath (ts); Pat Patrick (bs, f); Les Spann (f); Joe Zawinul, Wynton Kelly (p); Israel Crosby, Ron Carter (b); Ben Riley, Vernel Fournier (d).* 6–8/62.

Sam Jones had a beautiful sound on bass – fat, resonant, and fluid without any loss of body – and he was among the first to make the cello a plausible instrument in post-bop jazz. The compilation is chosen from five sessions he made during his time with Cannonball Adderley. Although the settings are mostly rather ordinary, two tracks by a big band with Melba Liston charts are more challenging, and Jones's quiet good humour gives as much buoyancy to the music as his bass. A quintet reading of 'Round Midnight' with Jones on cello is a little fluffy, and 'Some Kinda Mean' gives a better idea of his powers on that instrument; the latter track is drawn from the Soul Society sessions, which has also been reissued as a single album. The fast cello tracks, in which Keter Betts takes over bass duties, are a little gimmicky in the fashion of the day, but the band is a rousing one. The other session, with Mitchell in for Adderley, boils water on 'All Members' and 'The Old Country'.

The Chant is another good record. Cannonball takes a back-seat role, but most of the other horns get in a blow, and the studio sound gets a nice burnish on the section-work. Jones himself has a number of features, but what one remembers is his drive in the ensembles and alongside his old partner Louis Hayes.

Down Home repeated the formula of biggish-band tracks and small groups, with Sam taking up cello in the latter setting. Ernie Wilkins's charts are unemphatic and unsurprising, but there are some nice moments for Strozier, and Jones himself improvises against the grain of the orchestra to telling effect. The small-group pieces are more about the neatness of his cello playing than anything, though the instrumentation retains an appealing freshness.

****(*) Visitation**

Steeplechase SCCD 31097 *Jones; Terumasa Hino (c); Bob Berg (ts); Ronnie Mathews (p); Al Foster (d).* 3/78.

Sam's few sessions as a leader in the '70s found him pursuing a lyrical kind of hard bop. *Visitation* is dependable rather than especially exciting, although Hino's peculiar mix of rhapsody and restlessness is as engaging as usual.

Thad Jones (1923–86)

TRUMPET, CORNET, FLUGELHORN, VALVE TROMBONE

Joined Count Basie in 1954 and stayed for some ten years, while also cutting some small-group records. Began arranging and composing and formed an orchestra with drummer Mel Lewis in 1965, which lasted until Jones left for Denmark in 1978. Ran the Basie band after its leader's death for a spell but himself died not long afterwards.

*****(*) The Fabulous Thad Jones**

Original Jazz Classics OJC 625 *Jones; Frank Wess (ts, f); John Dennis, Hank Jones (p); Charles Mingus (b); Kenny Clarke, Max Roach (d).* 54.

***** After Hours**

Original Jazz Classics OJC 1782 *Jones; Frank Wess (ts, f); Kenny Burrell (g); Mal Waldron (p); Paul Chambers (b); Art Taylor (d).* 6/57.

*****(*) Mad Thad**

Fresh Sound FSR CD 117 *Jones; Henry Coker (tb); Frank Foster (ts); Frank Wess (ts, f); Tommy Flanagan, Jimmy Jones (p); Eddie Jones, Doug Watkins (b); Elvin Jones, Jo Jones (d).* 12/56.

***** Mean What You Say**

Original Jazz Classics OJC 464 *Jones; Pepper Adams (bs); Duke Pearson (p); Ron Carter (b); Mel Lewis (d).* 4–5/66.

***** Three And One**

Steeplechase SCS 1197 *Jones; Ole Kock Hansen (p); Jesper Lundgaard (b); Ed Thigpen (d).* 10/84.

Though better known than the quiet Hank, the middle Jones brother was consistently underrated as a soloist, recognized mainly as an arranger for the band he co-led with drummer Mel Lewis (see below). Not usually considered a small-group player, or even a soloist of any unusual interest, Jones's recorded output on this scale is disappointingly slight, relative to his significance as a composer. His early sessions for Blue Note never seem to come to the fore in their reissue plans. On the measure of the late *Three And One* alone, this is a pity. He's a subtle and vibrant player with a cornet tone similar to Nat Adderley but able to sustain big transitions of pitch with absolute confidence, much as he demands of his big bands. 'But Not For Me' is marred by a slightly tentative accompaniment, but Thigpen splashes in sensuous slo-mo, almost tuneful.

Mad Thad is even better. The trumpeter was signed to Basie for most of the late '50s and early '60s, a period that firmed up his reputation as an arranger but afforded regrettably few solo flights. He'd recorded on Mingus's demanding *Jazz Experiment* and won the bassist's heart for ever with his bustling, opportunistic runs and confident entanglements in and around the theme. On *Mad Thad*, playing trumpet only, he sounds full-throated and sure of himself; there are what appear to be very minor articulation problems on a couple of tracks, but these are incidental stammers in some beautifully crafted ('Whisper Not' especially) solos.

The sessions done for Mingus's and Roach's Debut label are very good indeed; these are also to be found in the 12-CD Debut compilation. Mingus admired the trumpeter inordinately and Jones was the only artist to record twice under his own name for Debut. Their duo on 'I Can't Get Started' is interesting first of all for Mingus's restructuring of the harmony, but Jones's response to this bare-boned setting and to the quasi-modal 'Get Out Of Town' is full confirmation of his ability to improvise at the highest level. Wess's flute makes a fine contrast on 'Sombre Intrusion'. The slighter *After Hours* has nothing quite so daring, but it's a solidly inventive session nevertheless, and the CD sound on both is very good.

Mean What You Say comes just after the formation of the Jones–Lewis big band. Though it casts the trumpeter in what should be completely sympathetic company, it's a rather uncertain affair, with most of the honours going to baritonist Pepper Adams, named as co-leader on the session. The sound is exemplary, though, with a representation of bass and percussion that was better than average for the time.

*****(*) Greetings And Salutations**

Four Leaf Clover FLC CD 125 *Jones; Jon Faddis, Americo Bellotto, Bertil Lövgren, Jan Allan, Al Porcino (t); Torgny Nilsson, Lars Olofsson, Bengt Edwardssont, Sven Larsson (tb); Lennart Aberg, Claes Rosendahl, Wage Finer, Rune Falk, Erik Nilsson, Arne Domnérus, Bernt Rosengren (reeds); Håkan Nyqvist, Sven-Ake Landström, Kurt Puke, Bengt Olsson (frhn); Bengt Hallberg (p); Rune Gustafsson (g); Georg Riedel, Stefan Brolund (b); Mel Lewis, Egil Johansen (d).* 6/75–1/77.

Jones wasn't the kind of writer-arranger to blow down barriers, but in his steady way he influenced a generation of arranger-composers, and his way with brass had few peers. These sessions with the Swedish Radio Jazz group – five titles from 1975, three from 1977 – have a startling crispness and panache, even when the structures seem comparatively straightforward and unfussy. The french horn section on the earlier date adds a glistening extra layer of brass muscle, and in '61st And Rich'It' and 'Forever Lasting' the music reaches an almost ecstatic precision and punch. The title-track might be the intended masterpiece at 13 minutes, but it actually feels a little overlong. The three later scores (two on Rhoda Scott compositions) sound less monumental. A little-known record which deserves a revival.

****** Live At Montmartre**

Storyville STCD 4172 *Jones; Benny Rosenfeld, Palle Bolvig, Idrees Sulieman, Allan Botschinsky, Perry Knudsen (t); Vincent Nilsson (tb); Erling Kroner, Richard Boone (tb); Ole Kurt Jensen (btb); Axel Windfeld (btb, tba); Jesper Thilo (ss, as, cl, f); Per Carsten Petersen (ss, as, f); Bent Jaedig (ts, f); Uffe Karskov (ts, as, f, cl); Flemming Madsen (bs, cl, bcl); Ole Kock Hansen (p); Bo Sylven (g); Niels-Henning Orsted Pedersen (b); Bjarne Rostvold (d); Ethan Weisgard (perc).* 3/78.

One of the authors was present at the concert recorded here and can confirm that this is an authentic documentation of one of the very finest concerts of Jones's later career, made on the eve of his departure from the long-standing Jones–Lewis band, and the trumpeter (or, rather, cornetist) played his socks off. His tone on the ballad, 'Old Folks', on his own 'Tip Toe' and 'A Good Time Was Had By All' is pure and bell-like and the solos are relaxed enough to allow digressions into other themes and harmonic displacements without losing the thread.The sound is considerably better than in the rather cramped acoustic of the Jazzhus Montmartre. Bass trombonist Jensen co-produced and gets the brasses sounding as shiny as Gabriel's. Completely enjoyable, and one of the best big-band records of that period.

***** Eclipse**

Storyville STCD 4089 *Jones; Jan Glasesel, Tim Hagans, Egon Petersen, Lars Togeby, Erik Tschentscher (t); Richard Boone, Ture Larsen, Niels Neergaard, Bjarne Thanning, Axel Windfeld (tb); Michael Hove, Bent Jaedig, Ole Thoger Nielsen, Jorgen Nilsson, Sahib Shihab (sax); Horace Parlan (p); Jesper Lundgaard (b); Ed Thigpen (d).* 9/79.

After leaving Mel Lewis in 1978, Jones spent most of his remaining years in Scandinavia, where he formed and led the Eclipse big band, an outfit which reflected some of the old partnership's combination of power and complexity. For all his virtues, Thigpen is no Lewis, but the band sounds well drilled and the charts are razor-sharp. In the late '70s, Jones took up valve trombone as an alternative horn. It sounds fleet and subtle, and it lends him a breadth of tone he could not have achieved with trumpet. The sound doesn't hold up to current digital standards, but it's big and warm and preserves enough of the grain in the ensembles to afford a hint of what this band was like in concert.

Clifford Jordan (1931–93)

TENOR SAXOPHONE

Jordan went to school in Chicago with Johnny Griffin and John Gilmore, a detail that bears out the pointlessness of talking in terms of 'Chicago tenor'. His characteristic sound was warm and breathy, with something of both Ben Webster and Lester Young in it, and only rather later a hint of the harmonic innovation of John Coltrane.

***** Blowin' In From Chicago**

Blue Note 42306 *Jordan; John Gilmore (ts); Horace Silver (p); Curley Russell (b); Art Blakey (d).* 3/57.

***** Cliff Craft**

Blue Note 81582 *Jordan; Art Farmer (t); Sonny Clark (p); George Tucker (b); Louis Hayes (d).* 11/57.

****** Spellbound**

Original Jazz Classics OJC 766 *Jordan; Cedar Walton (p); Spanky DeBrest (b); Albert 'Tootie' Heath (d).* 8/60.

***** Mosaic**

Milestone 47092 *Jordan; Kenny Dorham (t); Sonny Red (as); Tommy Flanagan, Ronnie Mathews, Cedar Walton (p); Art Davis, Wilbur Ware (b); Albert 'Tootie' Heath, Elvin Jones (d).* 61.

*****(*) Bearcat**

Original Jazz Classics OJC 494 *Jordan; Cedar Walton (p); Teddy Smith (b); J. C. Moses (d).* 10/61, 62.

At first blush, Jordan is 'just' another Chicago tenor. That was very much the way he was perceived and marketed. His Blue Note debut, *Blowin' In From Chicago*, was reissued in 2002. It's a raw-sounding jam with old friend Gilmore, offering more heat than light, but still enjoyable as a two-tenor jam. There's one alternate on the CD issue, a workmanlike 'Let It Stand', but the consensus is that the best of this first album is to be found on 'Billie's Bounce' and on the Gigi Gryce tune 'Blue Lights', which was a favourite with saxophonists for a time. Unfortunately, the contemporary eponymous Blue Note is still not available and nor is the OJC *Startin' Time*. The earlier reissue of *Cliff Craft* was a step in the right direction but the picture is still patchy for these early years.

For some reason, Jordan didn't seem to find much favour at Blue Note, perhaps because his style in these years did seem to reflect an interest in the swing era. Forty years ago, his style was much closer to the tempestuous approach associated with such natives of the Windy City as Johnny Griffin and – in timbre particularly – Von Freeman. And yet *Cliff Craft* is a markedly laid-back session, almost taken at a stroll. Never a true bebopper, Jordan takes his own route through 'Confirmation' and 'Anthropology', pulling the teeth of both somewhat but managing to make the results sound logical and engaging. Art Farmer is the co-star, playing with all the grace and sensitivity that was to be his stock in trade in later years.

Two groups are involved in *Mosaic*, a quintet with Dorham and another with a second saxophone in the form of the underrated Sonny Red, who blows a forceful blues chorus when he gets the space. Almost all of the material is original, though Walton and Jordan vie for priority, with the pianist winning out on 'Mosaic' itself and the splendid 'One Flight Down'. Cliff's big, bruising sound is ideally suited to this context and producer Orrin Keepnews keeps him solidly in the front line.

Bearcat is the perfect characterization of Jordan's sound, sometimes growling, sometimes purring. This old Jazzland set isn't particularly well recorded and the bassist is prone to sudden surges towards the mike, but the music is fine and Jordan is in good voice on 'How Deep Is The Ocean?' and the original 'Middle Of The Block'. The old home town is eulogized in 'Dear Old Chicago', a performance that name-checks one or two distinguished ancestors. A word of praise is in order for Walton and Moses, both of whom play exceptionally well.

Spellbound contains one of Jordan's very finest recorded performances, on 'Lush Life'. His understanding with Walton was only to grow and deepen with the years, but their level of communication here is most impressive and they hurtle through 'Au Privave' with almost cavalier abandon. The sound – originally a Riverside – is very full and authentic. A recommended purchase.

***** These Are My Roots: Clifford Jordan Plays Leadbelly**
Koch 8522 *Jordan; Roy Burrowes (t); Julian Priester (tb); Cedar Walton (p); Chuck Wayne (g, bjo); Richard Davis (b); Albert 'Tootie' Heath (d); Sandra Douglass (v).* 1/65.

Clifford Jordan and Huddie Ledbetter aren't the most obvious bunkmates, but this '60s album of interpretations of classic blues songs works better than it has any right to. Recorded for Atlantic, it was very much part of an ongoing rediscovery of American folklore, though it was mainly rock musicians who explored this strand of black American music. Jordan assembled a very fine band and got a big, brash sound from engineer Phil Lehle and producer Donald Elfman. Intriguingly, the saxophonist includes his own signature-piece, 'Highest Mountain', in the middle of the set as if to indicate Leadbelly's influence on it. The connection isn't entirely clear, but each of the ten performances – which include 'Yellow Gal', 'Silver City Bound' and the classic 'Goodnight Irene' – is beautifully handled and, though almost all the tracks are very short, nothing longer than four and a half minutes, the solos are compressed and effective. Of the supporting cast, Priester is excellent and fans of the trombonist will welcome a chance to hear this little-known selection. Bassist Richard Davis, another schoolmate of Jordan's, simplifies his playing markedly for the occasion and doesn't seem hampered by the idiom. We've heard little of singer Sandra Douglass, but she makes a very decent shift of 'Black Girl' and 'Take This Hammer'.

***** Half Note**
Steeplechase 31198 *Jordan; Cedar Walton (p); Sam Jones (b); Albert Heath (d).* 3/74.

Recorded live at the New York club of that name, *Half Note* is actually a very good introduction to Cliff's music, with 'Highest Mountain' and 'The Glass Bead Game' (the latter the title-track of a 1973 Charly disc) both given definitive readings. There is also a fine interpretation of Monk's 'Rhythm-A-Ning' which points up the differences between Jordan and Charlie Rouse, who played that tune hundreds of times in his association with Monk without plumbing some of the blues connotations Cliff finds in it. Walton is superb and his solos are always triggered by ideas from the tenor, so there is continuity and logic to these cuts. Jones (albeit poorly recorded) and Heath are excellent, too.

***** On Stage: Volume 1**
Steeplechase SCCD 31071 *Jordan; Cedar Walton (p); Teddy Smith (b); Billy Higgins (d).* 3/75.

***** On Stage: Volume 2**
Steeplechase SCCD 31092 *As above.* 3/75.

***** On Stage: Volume 3**
Steeplechase SCCD 31104 *As above.* 3/75.

***** The Highest Mountain**
Steeplechase SCCD 31047 *Jordan; Cedar Walton (p); Sam Jones (b); Billy Higgins (d).* 3/75.

***** Firm Roots**
Steeplechase SCCD 31033 *As above.* 4/75.

***** Magic In Munich**
Steeplechase SCCD 37013/14 *As above.* 3 & 4/75.

***** Night Of The Mark VII**
Savoy Jazz 17299 *As above.* 4/75.

It was having such firm roots that allowed Jordan to drift through a theme as cavalierly as he often did. Throughout the highly productive mid-'70s, he was probably playing more 'legitimately' than at any other time in his career, but there are constant reminders of his Mingus-influenced tendency to regard the note as a dartboard (which, of course, you don't always want to hit dead centre) and a progression as a series of mentally totted-up scores that always come out right in the end. Though he had a fair change of pace, he was definitely more successful at a medium-to-slow clip. He was a consummate ballad-player (see 'Stella By Starlight' on *On Stage: Volume 2*), with the kind of articulation and presence that suggest unused gears. Throughout these sets, it is the romantic ballads that consistently score high points. Compared to, say, Griffin, he never quite convinces at a gallop.

The mid-'70s were a very good time for Clifford Jordan. He was playing regularly with Cedar Walton, Sam Jones and Billy Higgins under the name The Magic Triangle, gigging pretty steadily and recording a substantial amount. *Night Of The Mark VII* was on Muse, then 32 Jazz, and has just reappeared on

Savoy, restoring another part of our picture of that hyperactive year and another splendid outing by Cliff's working band of the time.

Much has been said about Jordan's supposed John Coltrane influence – some find it dominant by this stage; some profess not to hear it at all – so Bill Lee's 'John Coltrane' seems a reasonable place to test the hypothesis. Unlike Trane, Jordan strays over bar lines and stretches theme statements out, without seeming to elaborate unnecessarily. His solos on 'Highest Mountain' and on 'Blue Monk' suggest influences from an earlier generation, combined with a phraseology that is entirely his own. Excellent news that this fine album is back in the catalogue. It further fills out documentation of what was to be a busy year.

Firm Roots was more prosaic, but the evocative title captures something like the equidistance and responsiveness that Jordan, a great arranger, achieved with his colleagues. They work hard for one another, creating spaces and textures, laying off chords that lead whoever is soloing out into new territory, then gently pulling on the strings. *Magic In Munich* doesn't contain any new material, but simply pulls together *Highest Mountain* and *Firm Roots*, delivering pretty exceptional value at budget price.

***** Repetition**
Soul Note 121084 *Jordan; Barry Harris (p); Walter Booker (b); Vernell Fournier (d).* 2/84.

***** Two Tenor Winner**
Criss Cross Criss 1011 *Jordan; Junior Cook (ts); Kirk Lightsey (p); Cecil McBee (b); Eddie Gladden (d).* 10/84.

*****(*) Royal Ballads**
Criss Cross Criss 1025 *Jordan; Kevin O'Connell (p); Ed Howard (b); Vernell Fournier (d).* 12/86.

In later years Jordan perfected a ballad style that was strikingly reminiscent of Wardell Gray's. *Royal Ballads* is a lovely record; if it steers close to easy listening on occasion, a more attentive hearing uncovers all manner of subtleties and harmonic shifts. The opening 'Lush Life' is almost lost in Fournier's constant cymbal-spray, but the drummer – who has worked to great effect with Ahmad Jamal – is a great ballad-player and every bit as adept as Jordan at varying an apparently sleepy beat with odd, out-of-synch metres and quiet paradiddles. As Jordan quotes 'Goodbye Pork Pie Hat' on the original 'Royal Blues', Fournier squeezes the tempo almost subliminally, so that the reference evades identification as the mind subconsciously readjusts to the beat. Subtle and intelligent jazz, and a sure sign that ballads albums are not just the preserve of MOR acts.

The slightly earlier *Repetition* and *Two Tenor Winner* have more variation of pace (though no less inventive a trawl of material). Fournier doesn't seem quite so much at ease, but Harris is a much subtler player than O'Connell. Cook plays with a loose-limbed ease, but he lacks the chops to go head to head with Jordan in this way. Once again, nothing to choose between them. Late-nighters might prefer the ballads.

****** Down Through The Years**
Milestone MCD 9197 *Jordan; Dizzy Reece, Stephen Furtado, Dean Pratt, Don Sickler (t); Brad Shigeta (tb); Kiane Zawadi (euph); Jerome Richardson, Sue Terry (as); Lou Orenstein, Willie Williams (ts); Charles Davis (bs); Ronnie Mathews (p); David Williams (b); Vernell Fournier (d).* 10/91.

The hand-picked orchestra on *Down Through The Years* was the fulfilment of considerable planning and thorough rehearsal. Recorded at Condon's in New York City, the disc captures the sound of an excellent ensemble playing at full stretch. The programme includes such long-standing favourites as 'Highest Mountain', on which the saxophonist is, appropriately, the only soloist, singing away on his solitary eminence, 'Japanese Dream', which provides an outlet for Dizzy Reece, and the strangely moving 'Charlie Parker's Last Supper', which brings the set to a close. Jordan played better many times, but rarely in such a completely sympathetic setting. His phrasing is almost always right on the beat, but he manages to avoid sounding mechanical.

Duke Jordan (born 1922)

PIANO

Jordan was recruited from the Three Deuces by Charlie Parker and became a bit player in the bebop movement. His style is an amalgam of Art Tatum and Bud Powell, the parts not always cohering with absolute authority. A player of great facility, he may have recorded too much to be absolutely distinctive.

****(*) Flight To Denmark**
Steeplechase SCCD 31011 *Jordan; Mads Vinding (b); Ed Thigpen (d).* 11/73.

***** Two Loves**
Steeplechase SCCD 31024 *As above.* 12/73.

Duke Jordan's career has an odd trajectory. At 25, with an apprenticeship under Coleman Hawkins behind him, he was thrust into the limelight with Charlie Parker and proved himself an able and frequently imaginative accompanist. Thereafter, though, his progress has been curiously elided, with long disappearances from the scene. Perhaps as a consequence, he is by far the least well-known of the bebop pianists, surprisingly diffident in performing manner and little given to solo performance. Though he is a fine standards player, he has from time to time preferred to rework a sizeable but tightly organized body of original compositions. These have been documented by the Danish Steeplechase label with a thoroughness bordering on redundancy and seemingly quite inconsistent with the pianist's rather marginal reputation. There are very many recorded versions of some of the pianist's most successful themes. 'Jordu', in particular, has become a popular repertoire piece. A Jordan theme tends to be brief, tightly melodic rather than just a launching-pad of chords, and disconcertingly unmemorable, in the positive sense that they resist being hummed.

Unlike his later work for Steeplechase, these are essentially albums of standards, and in some sense an attempt to come to terms with the legacy of bebop. There are finely judged readings of 'Here's That Rainy Day', 'On Green Dolphin Street' and 'How Deep Is The Ocean?' on *Flight*, 'I'll Remember April' and 'Embraceable You', 'Blue Monk' and 'My Old Flame' on *Two Loves*, which also includes the ubiquitous 'Jordu' and 'Lady Dingbat', an unaccountably popular original. Jordan's career had been rather stop-start since the mid-'50s and there are occasional rust-spots on his faster runs and a slight stiffness in his octaves. The CD transfers aren't perfect. There are alternative takes of several tracks; newcomers might find *Two Loves* preferable.

★★(★) Misty Thursday
Steeplechase SCCD 31053 *Jordan; Chuck Wayne (g); Sam Jones (b); Roy Haynes (d).* 6/75.

★★★ Lover Man
Steeplechase SCCD 31127 *Jordan; Sam Jones (b); Al Foster (d).* 11/75.

★★★(★) Duke's Delight
Steeplechase SCCD 31046 *Jordan; Richard Williams (t); Charlie Rouse (ts); Sam Jones (b); Al Foster (d).* 11/75.

★★★ In Concert From Japan
Steeplechase SCCD 37005/6 2CD *Jordan; Wilbur Little (b); Roy Haynes (d).* 9/76.

★★(★) Flight To Japan
Steeplechase SCCD 31088 *As above.* 9/76.

★★★ Duke's Artistry
Steeplechase SCCD 31103 *Jordan; Art Farmer (flhn); David Friesen (b); Philly Joe Jones (d).* 6/78.

★★★ The Great Session
Steeplechase SCCD 31150 *As above, except omit Farmer; add Paul Jeffrey (bells).* 6/78.

★★(★) Tivoli One
Steeplechase SCCD 31189 *Jordan; Wilbur Little (b); Dannie Richmond (d).* 11/78.

★★(★) Wait And See
Steeplechase SCCD 31211 *As above.*

★★(★) Duke Jordan Solo Masterpieces Vol. One
Steeplechase SCCD 31299 *Jordan (p solo).* 1 & 2/79.

★★(★) Duke Jordan Solo Masterpieces Vol. Two
Steeplechase SCCD 31300 *Jordan (p solo).* 2–11/79.

★★★ Double Duke
Steeplechase SCCD 37039/40 *Jordan; Niels-Henning Orsted Pedersen (b); Billy Hart (d).* 10/79.

★★(★) Midnight Moonlight
Steeplechase SCCD 31143 *Jordan (p solo).* 79.

★★★(★) When You're Smiling
Steeplechase SCCD 37023/24 2CD *Jordan; Jesper Lundgaard (b); Billy Hart (d).* 79–7/85.

The late '70s were a remarkably productive time for Jordan. In Billy Hart and Dannie Richmond he found drummers with the kind of rhythmic tension he required on which to sound his taut melodic figures. The mix of material is much as usual, but some mention should be made of 'Light Foot' and 'The Queen Is Home To Stay' on *Double Duke*, which brings together two single albums – *Thinking Of You* and *Change A Pace* – and makes an attractive package out of them, though one wonders sometimes at the logic of this recent bout of rationalization at the Danish label.

Compare the studio version of 'Night Train To Snekkersten', one of his best compositions, on *Misty Thursday* with the live versions recorded in Osaka 15 months later. Sam Jones has a more contained approach and lacks Little's strength, but he is absolutely right for the lovely 'Hymn To Peace'. The sound is a little flat.

The *Tivoli* sessions with Richmond are again standards-based, with an accent on bebop-associated themes. Jordan adds vocals to *When You're Smiling* (which brings together two single albums, *Time On My Hands* and *As Ditto Goes By*) but in all conscience we can't recommend him as a singer. Much as Ahmad Jamal is popularly supposed to, Jordan occasionally skirts a Vegas-style 'entertainment' approach that obscures his more interesting ideas to all but the most attentive listeners. *Duke's Delight* has long been one of our favourites among the Steeplechases, an inventive set by an interesting band.

Jordan was warmly received in Japan. As with much of the catalogue, Steeplechase have rationalized scattered material on a double-CD set. Since favourites like 'Misty Thursday', 'Jordu' and 'Flight To Jordan' are all included, it might make a sensible introduction to the pianist's work, although as a stand-alone disc it's not all that strong. The recording quality is very good, if a bit cavernous in places.

'Lady Bird' on *The Great Session* helpfully points to Tadd Dameron as a further factor in the development of Jordan's approach (Lennie Tristano, at the opposite pole from bebop, is another). These are unexceptionable sessions; Philly Joe plays with his incomparable verve and exactness, and Friesen sounds confident and aware.

What all this amounts to is very difficult to judge. Though there are later recordings from the mid-'80s on *When You're Smiling* and the playing sounds as solid and untroubled as ever, Jordan's *annus mirabilis* had been and gone. Nils Winther of Steeplechase was a sympathetic and attentive patron, but it must be said that few collectors will want more than two or three of these discs at best, and none of them makes a genuinely pressing demand on the casual listener. This is a vast body of work, with only the most obvious reference-points in the shape of oft-repeated themes and compositions. Doubtless there are aficionados who can speak with authority on the question of their respective merits. However, since we are dealing with records and not tracks, only a rather impressionistic valuation is feasible. Perhaps the two *Masterpieces* discs offer the best music.

★★★ One For The Library
Storyville STCD 4194 *Jordan (p solo).* 10/93.

What an odd, even cynical title for a record. One does begin to wonder how much of the Jordan discography has been merely 'for the library', documentation for the sake of it. The galling thing is that this is a perfectly respectable record, swinging in the rather restrictive mode of solo-piano records, packed with melody and invention (18 tracks in 65 minutes) and beautifully recorded in the studio on a responsive, big-hearted piano. But ask us to differentiate it blindfold from half a dozen others of Duke's records and we'd have to bow out.

Louis Jordan (1908–75)

ALTO AND BARITONE SAXOPHONES, CLARINET, VOCAL

Jordan, who came from Arkansas and had a father in vaudeville, quit playing in big bands in the early '40s to form his Tympany Five, one of the most successful small bands in jazz history. The Five lasted until 1951, and thereafter Jordan toured and often guested with local bands, such as Chris Barber in Britain. He helped to father R&B with his mix of jive, jump music and small-band swing.

★★★ Louis Jordan 1934–1940
Classics 636 *Jordan; Mario Bauza, Bobby Stark, Taft Jordan, Courtney Williams, Charlie Gaines (t); Ed Allen (c); Claude Jones, Sandy Williams, Nat Story (tb); Pete Clark (cl, as, bs); Cecil Scott (cl, as); Lem Johnson (cl, ts); Ted McRae, Stafford Simon (ts); Wayman Carver (ts, f); Stafford Simon (ts);*

Tommy Fulford, Clarence Johnson, James P. Johnson (p); John Trueheart (g); Cyrus St Clair (tba); Beverley Peer, Charlie Drayton (b); Chick Webb, Walter Martin (d); Floyd Casey (wbd); Rodney Sturgis, Clarence Williams (v). 3/34–1/40.

***** Louis Jordan 1940–1941**
Classics 663 *Jordan; Courtney Williams, Freddy Webster, Eddie Roane (t); Stafford Simon (cl, ts); Kenneth Hollon (ts); Arnold Thomas (p); Charlie Drayton, Henry Turner, Dallas Bartley (b); Walter Martin (d); Mabel Robinson, Daisy Winchester (v).* 3/40–11/41.

*****(*) Louis Jordan 1941–1943**
Classics 741 *Jordan; Eddie Roane (t); Arnold Thomas (p); Dallas Bartley, Jesse Simpkins (b); Walter Martin, Shadow Wilson (d).* 11/41–11/43.

***** Louis Jordan 1943–1945**
Classics 866 *As above, except add Idrees Sulieman, Aaron Izenhall (t), Freddie Simon, Josh Jackson (ts), William Austin, Wild Bill Davis (p), Carl Hogan (g), Al Morgan (b), Slick Jones, Razz Mitchell, Eddie Byrd (d), Bing Crosby (v); omit Bartley.* 11/43–7/45.

***** Louis Jordan 1945–1946**
Classics 921 *As above, except add James Wright (ts), Joe Morris (d), Harry Dial, Vic Lourie (perc), Ella Fitzgerald (v); omit Roane, Thomas, Sulieman, Simon, Martin, Wilson, Jones, Mitchell, Crosby.*

*****(*) Louis Jordan 1946–1947**
Classics 1010 *Jordan; Aaron Izenhall (t); James Wright, Eddie Johnson (ts); Wild Bill Davis (p); Carl Hogan (g); Jesse Simpkins, Dallas Bartley (b); Joe Morris (d); The Calypso Boys (perc).* 10/46–12/47.

*****(*) Louis Jordan 1947–1949**
Classics 1134 *Jordan; Aaron Izenhall, Bob Mitchell, Harold Mitchell (t); Eddie Johnson, Josh Jackson (ts); Wild Bill Davis, Bill Doggett (p); Carl Hogan, Bill Jennings, James Jackson (g); Dallas Bartley, Bob Bushnell, Billy Hadnott (b); Joe Morris (d); Martha Davis, Ella Fitzgerald (v).* 12/47–8/49.

***** Louis Jordan 1950–1951**
Classics 1238 *Jordan; Louis Armstrong (t, v); Aaron Izenhall (t); Josh Jackson (ts); Wild Bill Davis (p, org); Bill Doggett (p); Bill Jennings (g); Bob Bushnell (b); Joe Morris (d); Ella Fitzgerald (v).* 6/50–3/51.

****** Swingsation**
GRP 059951-2 *As above discs.* 39–53.

Jordan was an incomparable funster as well as being a distinctive altoman and smart vocalist. His hit records, 'Five Guys Named Moe', 'Choo Choo Ch'Boogie', 'Caldonia' and many more, established the idea of the jump band as a jiving, irrepressible outfit which persists to this day. Rightly so: Jordan was a pro's pro, tirelessly seeking out fresh songs and constantly touring. But, surprisingly, the music seldom suffered, which is why his best sides still sound fresh. Most of the hits – which mixed comic lyrics with spirited swing-style playing and paved the way for R&B – are collected on the GRP record, an irresistible platter to warm up a room. The Classics series tells much of the story. Classics 636 starts with an obscure 1934 Clarence Williams date where Jordan croons 'I Can't Dance, I Got Ants In My Pants'. The usual approach of chronological order is then followed through to the end of the 1945–6 disc and, though some of the material is just a tad strained – try 'Sam Jones Done Snagged His Britches' – there is some unbeatable jive here too. Classics 741 is probably the first choice, given that there are the first versions of some of Jordan's most enduring hits: 'Five Guys Named Moe' (also present in a V-Disc version), 'The Chicks I Pick Are Slender, Tender And Tall' and so on. But Classics 921 has 'Choo Choo Ch'Boogie' and 'That Chick's Too Young To Fry' plus a couple of duets with Ella Fitzgerald. Classics 866 includes eight tracks made for V-Disc, a radio ad for Oldsmobile and the sublime duet with Bing Crosby on 'Your Socks Don't Match'. Classics 1010 has a sublime put-down in 'You're Much Too Fat And That's That', as well as Jordan's first two versions of 'Open The Door Richard!'. These and a few other favourites of ours, such as 'Boogie Woogie Blue Plate' and the straight blues, 'Roamin' Blues' and 'Inflation Blues', persuade us to award an extra point. Excellent sound on these later tracks, although by and large most of these discs are in decent fidelity. Classics 1134 picks up the story with one last session before the 1948 recording ban, including two especially appealing duets for Louis and wife Martha Davis, before dashing through five eventful sessions in the first half of 1949. Besides the ridiculous Jamaican skit, 'Push-Ka Pee She Pie', there is a sequence of duets with Ella, including at least two immortals in 'Baby It's Cold Outside' and 'Saturday Night Fish Fry'. Jordan carries on through the sessions on Classics 1238, including two more duets with Ella and a pair with Pops, as well as 'Blue Light Boogie', which offers Bill Doggett the chance to start working on the kinds of thing that would make him a success in the later '50s. But Jordan's jive is starting to wear thin, all the same.

CORE COLLECTION

****** Louis Jordan & His Tympany Five**
JSP CD 905 4CD *As above discs.* 38–50.

Compared to the above discs, this four-decker is an unrivalled bargain: four CDs remastered from original copies, creaming off the best of Jordan from all through the '40s, and delivered at a bargain price. Yes, please!

***** Rock 'N' Roll**
Mercury 838219–2 *Jordan; Ernie Royal (t); Jimmy Cleveland (tb); Budd Johnson (ts, bs); Sam 'The Man' Taylor (ts); Ernie Hayes (p); Jackie Davis (org); Mickey Baker, Irving Ashby (g); Wendell Marshall, Billy Hadnott (b); Charli Persip, Marvin Oliver (d); Francisco Pozo (perc); Dorothy Smith (v).* 10/56–8/57.

***** No Moe!**
Verve 512523-2 *As above.* 10/56–8/57.

Jordan's later recordings were remakes of his old ones. On the Mercury sessions it worked out well, since Quincy Jones's arrangements brought in some sterling instrumentalists and updated Jordan's sound just enough without prettifying it too much. As a result, the likes of 'Is You Is Or Is You Ain't My Baby' become rejuvenated, and Louis never sounded wilder than he did on 'Salt Pork, West Virginia'. The Verve disc is almost the same: five fewer tracks, but three from a later small-group session which *Rock 'N' Roll* misses.

Sheila Jordan (born 1928)

VOICE

Born in Detroit, Jordan was turned on to modern jazz by hearing Charlie Parker, and her first work was with vocalese groups, singing lyrics to Bird material. She was married to pianist Duke Jordan for a decade, studied under Lennie Tristano and worked with George Russell, Roswell Rudd and others. Her style covers an enormous range, from scat and ballads to art song.

CORE COLLECTION

****** Portrait Of Sheila**

Blue Note 789902-2 *Jordan; Barry Galbraith (g); Steve Swallow (b); Denzil Best (d).* 9 & 10/62.

Sheila Jordan shows much of her former husband's concentration on the melodic progress of a song and much of his intelligent, unhistrionic and almost diffident delivery. Like the truly great instrumentalists, Sheila Jordan is content to explore all the potential of the middle register, where words are more likely to remain intact (with lesser talent, prosaically so), rather than over-reach a range which is nevertheless greater than sometimes appears. At the end of phrases, she deploys a superbly controlled vibrato.

On *Portrait*, her most complete artistic statement, she ranges between the rapid and slightly alienating 'Let's Face The Music And Dance', which anticipates the surrealism of her contributions to Roswell Rudd's remarkable *Flexible Flyer* (Affinity), and the fragile beauty of 'I'm A Fool To Want You' and 'When The World Was Young' with its extraordinary, ambiguous ending. The instrumentation is highly subtle. Bobby Timmons's 'Dat Dere' is given just to voice and bass (and Swallow is superb), 'Who Can I Turn To?' to voice and guitar, while 'Hum Drum Blues' and 'Baltimore Oriole' are set against rhythm only, as if she were a horn.

***** Sheila**

Steeplechase SCCD 31081 *Jordan; Arild Andersen (b).* 8/77.

If one is looking for an exact instrumental analogy for Sheila Jordan's voice, it's probably the round, precariously controlled wobble of the flugelhorn. Tom Harrell was an ideal foil on *The Crossing*, a fine Black Hawk record from 1984, since deleted but worth looking out for. The sparser landscape of *Sheila*, where she is accompanied only by double bass, suits her much better, and this has been her preferred format for many years.

*****(*) Jazz Child**

High Note 7029 *Jordan; Steve Kuhn (p); Theo Bleckmann (v).* 97.

Bracketed by Sheila's autobiographical 'Jazz Child', this is another astonishingly eclectic and various set, taking in Don Cherry ('Art Deco'), Jimmy Webb ('The Moon's A Harsh Mistress') and a lovely medley for Miles Davis, it features the singer in the kind of adventurous setting that shows off her bebop background and her straighter and more narrative approach to a song. Kuhn is not the most obvious accompanist, but he is a magnificent player and provides sterling support throughout this session.

***** Sheila's Back In Town**

Splasc(h) 804 *Jordan; Robert Cipelli (p); Attilo Zanchi (b); Gianni Cazzola (d); Modern Ensemble.* 99.

A fine encounter with the top-drawer E.S.P. Trio (not to be confused with Esbjörn Svensson's EST), who deliver the kind of deceptively relaxed swing and harmonic sophistication that Jordan enjoys. She's in great form on a long ambitious version of Don Cherry's 'Art Deco', scatting like a horn-player, more straightforwardly on 'Inchworm' and 'Someone To Watch Over Me'. Cipelli's string arrangements for the Modern Ensemble couldn't be bettered and Sheila's moving version of 'The Water Is Wide', with that rich accompaniment, is one of her most powerful recorded statements, though less adventurous than we are used to hearing from her.

***** I've Grown Accustomed To The Bass**

High Note 7042 *Jordan; Cameron Brown (b).* 11/97.

This is the kind of set Jordan previously made with Harvie Swartz. Brown is a more percussive and also more flowing player and their interchanges, also touched on in interview, are revealing, as they unpick 'Dat Dere', 'Pork Pie Hat', Charlie Parker licks and original blues. Sheila more than ever sounds as if she's possessed by the spirits of great jazzmen who've gone before. She's not an impressionist so much as a medium, channelling the jazz of the past through an imagination that constantly reinvents its own material.

****** Little Song**

High Note 9076 *Jordan; Tom Harrell (t, flhn); Steve Kuhn (p); David Finck (b); Billy Drummond (d).* 6/02.

Quite wonderful. When she sings 'When I Grow Too Old To Dream', you know it's never going to happen. There is a dreamlike quality to much of this set, noticeable whenever Tom Harrell's otherworldly trumpet breaks through, but also evident in old friend Steve Kuhn's thoughtful and tasteful accompaniments. The title-track is segued with the Beatles' 'Blackbird'. Bassist Finck gets a credit with 'The Way He Captured Me' but it's a pity there's nothing from the pianist's pen. Kenny Dorham's 'Fairweather' is a fascinating inclusion, underlining how much of Jordan's musical language is still rooted in bebop, even though she nowadays sounds easier with the slower transitions of show tunes and occasionally art song.

Kristian Jørgensen (born 1968)

VIOLIN

Danish violinist with a modern mainstream approach that touches several bases.

****(*) Quartet**

Stunt STUCD 19402 *Jørgensen; Kim Sjøgren (vn); Jacob Fischer (g); Thomas Ovesen (b); Michael Axen (d).* 10/93.

***** Secret Love**

Stunt STUCD 19804 *Jørgensen; Jacob Fischer (g); Jesper Lundgaard (b).* 9/97.

***** Meeting Monty**

Stunt 121 *Jørgensen; Monty Alexander (p); Jacob Fischer (g); Thomas Fonnesbaek (b); Kresten Osgood (d); Caterina Zapponi (v).* 4/02.

Jørgensen is a cheerful player with a considerable bag of tricks. He's fond of the tango, of romantic tunes, of a kitsch kind of humour. His duet with Sjøgren on the first record, 'Orangu Tango', is pretty remarkable, but it's only a beat away from a cabaret act, and much of this set feels slight – the rhythm section sounds as if it'd be happier playing jazz-rock licks. The more compact and serious feel of *Secret Love* suits him better. Lundgaard centres the trio's music with no-nonsense authority, and Jørgensen gets a more dour, less whimsical sound in this setting. The material is probably too eclectic – Peterson's 'Night

Train', 'Mack The Knife' and 'Wee' all among ten tracks – but the closing 'Flight Of The Foo Birds', surely its first cover since *The Atomic Mr Basie*, is a neat surprise.

The opening of *Meeting Monty* is similarly unexpected, almost a rock'n'roll feel to 'The Mill', but thereafter the eclecticism is more measured and Fischer gives place to guest star Alexander, who does his usual style-switching thing with great delight. The highlight is probably his duo with Jørgensen on 'Willow Weep For Me', which closes out the set, but he's excellent throughout and Mrs Alexander, Caterina Zapponi, adds a lovely touch to 'Estate'. As far as the violinist's own work is concerned, 'Jespers Vuggevise' is the best showing, a delicate ballad with a considerable measure of thought behind it.

Theo Jörgensmann (born 1948)

CLARINET

Though he has always been a clarinet man, Jörgensmann started out in hard bop and in the '70s made a string of albums for independent German labels in a modal free-bop style (they are all out of print). He later led a clarinet quartet, CL-4, and in the '90s worked with chamber groups and string-players.

***** Ta Eko Mo**

Z.O.O. 29-1 *Jörgensmann; Christopher Dell (vib); Christian Ramond (b); Klaus Kugel (d).* 97.

*****(*) Snijbloeman**

hatOLOGY 539 *As above.* 1–4/99.

He might have stuck by the clarinet, but Jörgensmann followed few of his forebears on the instrument, preferring Coltrane as an influence. He is, nevertheless, a performer of classical rigour; he likes shapely, well-modelled lines, rarely resorts to tonal distortion, and projects a clean, full-bodied sound. Rarely sighted in the CD era, these recent records mark a return to action with a new quartet of young German players. The key combination is with Dell, and much of the music feels like a dialogue for vibes and clarinet, with Ramond and Kugel working sometimes as a means of propulsion, sometimes as colourists. Both records are rather short and compact (the hatOLOGY disc is longer with two alternative takes), and they offer up their ideas sparingly. This doesn't stop the likes of 'Kospi' (with an extraordinary solo by Dell) and 'Wiesengrund' from emerging as eventful and dense pieces, packed with ideas. A welcome return for a singular voice.

****** Pagine Gialle**

hatOLOGY 553 *Jörgensmann; Eckard Koltermann (bcl).* 2/95.

Recorded in 1995, but not released until 2001, this is 51 minutes of beautiful interplay. A rare combination, despite the fact that woodwind duets have become relatively commonplace in improvised music, and both players only rarely push the tonal envelope. Distortion or caricature is eschewed in favour of streams of melody and precise conversational interplay, although the writing and improvisation work together at a temperature which feels hot rather than cool. Any question over Jörgensmann's mastery will be comprehensively answered by the solo which constitutes the opening of part two of the concert. This music can stand in John Carter's noble tradition.

***** Miniatures**

Not Two MW 748-23 *Jörgensmann; Marcin Oles (b); Bartlomiej Brat Oles (d).* 3/03.

Strictly speaking, this is a record where Jörgensmann is a guest of the (Polish) Oles brothers. The clarinettist moves from inside to out on these tracks, which aren't terribly taxing in terms of structure and give him quite a free rein to improvise on. They're not the most inventive partners he's ever had, but it doesn't stop the trio from making some lively and vivid music, and some of the pieces find Jörgensmann constructing some very elaborate flights.

Anders Jormin (born 1957)

BASS

Though still relatively young, Jormin is a long-standing leader and catalyst in Swedish post-bop. Raised in Jönköping, he came to prominence with the important '70s group, Rena Rama. Although he has a number of sideman credits, he has worked extensively as a leader and has several large-scale commissions to his credit as composer.

*****(*) Nordic Light**

Dragon DRCD 305 *Jormin; Thomas Gustafson (ss, ts); Bobo Stenson (p); Christian Jormin (d).* 5/84.

***** Eight Pieces**

Dragon DRCD 306 *Jormin; Staffan Svensson (t); Dave Wilczewski, Thomas Gustafson (ss, ts); Thomas Jäderlund (as, f); Bobo Stenson (p); Harald Svensson (ky); Göran Klinghagen (g); Audun Klieve (d).* 2/88.

These entries from Dragon's LP era have recently made it to CD. *Nordic Light* has certainly worn the better of the two. The quartet plays seven pieces based around Scandinavian compositions of the past, from Grieg, Peterson-Berger, Sjöberg, Nielsen and Ekström. Stenson is his usual powerful self and the quartet has much in common with the Garbarek–Stenson group. The original themes are elaborated on thoughtfully, rather than bowdlerized or turned into something else, and if this sounds conservative next to other such projects, the musicians clearly have the spirit of these pieces in their bones.

Next to this, *Eight Pieces* actually sounds more dated: Harald Svensson's keyboards, as so often with synthesizers, now sound timelocked to their period, and the blending of styles seems more effortful. But the writing still has many points of interest, and it's a good band.

***** Alone**

Dragon DRCD 207 *Jormin (b solo).* 91.

***** Jord**

Dragon DRCD 243 *Jormin; Per Jorgensen (t, perc, v); Harald Svensson (ky); Severi Pyysalo (vib); Lisbeth Diers (perc, v).* 10/94.

***** Opus Apus**

LJ 5212 *Jormin; Mats Gustafsson (ts, bs, f); Christian Jormin (d).* 5/96.

Jormin's entries purvey a catholic sense of adventure keyed in to a fundamental restraint. On the solo album he says he aimed for something 'naked, pure and lyrical', cutting the 40-odd minutes of music in a single evening with a DAT machine, and the unaffected qualities of the playing lend the music much charm – where most bass albums are deliberately cumbersome and sombre in texture, this one is songful and optimistic. Jormin plays only three brief tunes of his own: the rest is dominated by three burnished melodies by Silvio Rodriguez and the unforgettable melody of A. Ramirez's 'Alfonsina'. Those hoping for the kind of sumptuous bass-sound which hallmarks studio bass albums may be disappointed in the relatively light and 'live' atmosphere here, but it emphasizes the calibre of the playing over any mere hi-fi experience.

Jord is a live-in-the-studio group record, carefully balanced between the four musicians. Svensson's keyboards provide melting electronic textures which Pyysalo's vibes dance gently over; Jorgensen comes on as principal soloist, and Diers and Jormin create elliptical rhythms. A bit shapeless, but some exquisite passages.

The trio record with Gustafsson and brother Christian is typically refined, detailed improvisation. There are a handful of climactic moments but otherwise this is nearly *pointilliste* in feel, the percussionist working almost in microtones and even the normally boisterous Gustafsson apparently reined in. Most of the pieces are dedicated to birds, with 'Lagopus Lagopus' (a willow grouse, ornithologists will note) pecking and scratching out a plausible miniature. As with all of Jormin's music, there is a dedication to beauty which seems to shine through even in abstraction.

*****(*) Once**

Dragon DRCD 308 *Jormin; Thomas Gustafson (ss, ts); Jarle Vespestad (d); Jeanette Lindström (v).* 8/96.

Beautifully pitched between something formal and something quite abstract, this quartet's music is complex without being demanding of anything more than a sympathetic ear. Vespestad is crucial to the freeness of the playing, frequently doing anything but playing straight time and using the kit in its most percussive form, often getting a tympani-like sound out of the bass and floor toms. Gustafson is alternately dramatic and respectful, and Jormin brings in some good themes as well as choosing works by Ornette Coleman, Evert Taube and Kurt Weill. But it's Lindström's singing, in English, Swedish or wordless, which mollifies any danger of stepping too far into formlessness. She is at least as good here as she is on her Caprice albums.

***** Silvae**

Dragon DRCD 338 *Jormin; Arve Henriksen (t); Fredrik Ljungkvist (cl, ss, ts); Severi Pyysalo (vib, marim); Marc Ducret (g); Christian Jormin (d, p).* 1/98.

Drawn from a commission for two hours of music, *Silvae* (forests) is typically imaginative music, but the success of the record may depend on your response to Ducret. For us, he unbalances the rest of the group, his rockier solos too splashy to fit in with Jormin's concept. For once, a Jormin record seems stitched together out of disparate pieces, with his usual impeccable flow suffering too many changes of mood; but much of it, such as the cod-Japanese 'Koto', with lovely trumpet from the under-exposed Henriksen, is still more than worthwhile. Had Henriksen and Pyysalo (the latter employed largely as a colourist) been made more use of, this might have been a classic.

*****(*) Xieyi**

ECM 1762 *Jormin; Robin Rydqvist (t, flhn); Krister Petersson (frhn); Lars-Gorean Carlsson (tb); Niclas Rydh (btb).* 12/99.

Where else to go to make a solo bass record, interspersed with gravely beautiful pieces for a brass quartet, than ECM? Jormin's light, melodious approach to the bass violin is refreshing after the instrument's often portentous history as a solo instrument, and, as he did on *Alone,* he finds sweetness and uncluttered delicacy in several of the meditations presented here. If the brass pieces are modest enough to suggest that they wouldn't seem like anything much on their own, here they function as an engaging sequence of interludes.

Vic Juris (born 1953)

GUITAR

Juris took up the guitar in 1963 and started playing in fusion situations in the '70s. He began to record as a leader in the '90s.

***** Night Tripper**

Steeplechase SCCD 31353 *Juris; Phil Markowitz (p); Steve LaSpina (b); Jeff Hirshfield (d).* 4/94.

***** Pastels**

Steeplechase SCCD 31384 *Juris; Phil Markowitz (p); Jay Anderson (b); Matt Wilson (d).* 11/95.

***** Moonscape**

Steeplechase SCCD 31402 *Juris; Dick Oatts (as, ts, f); Jay Anderson (b); Jeff Hirshfield (d).* 10/96.

*****(*) Music Of Alec Wilder**

Double-Time DTRCD 118 *Juris; Tim Hagans (t, flhn); David Liebman (ss, ts); Steve LaSpina (b); Jeff Hirshfield (d).* 9/96.

Having worked extensively with Larry Coryell and Bireli Lagrene as duet partners and with fusion bands in the '70s, Juris has rather belatedly begun to acquire a leadership profile. He's a keen technician and likes to vary the pace on all his own albums: one tune done on open electric might be followed by another on nylon acoustic, before the guitar-synth comes out for the next. All the Steeplechases are nicely rounded and there's little to choose between them – though one could complain that there's not much that stands out either. *Night Tripper* has a lovely take on 'Estate', and Markowitz's 'Dekooning' is a clever and challenging piece; *Pastels* pulls out another charmer in 'Berlin', and Anderson and Wilson, if less ambitious than the other rhythm sections, do great service to the soloists. Oatts is a welcome addition to *Moonscape* and they open with the terrific 'Vampicide', but some of the other tunes seem a touch routine in the delivery. On balance, *Pastels* is our favourite of the three.

The Double-Time release is better still, though mostly for the superb horn-players. Liebman and Hagans could have had a more gracious sound in the studio, but they steal this date from Juris, who sounds more like the good and true sideman that he is here. The material, all Alec Wilder tunes and plenty of interesting obscurities among them (such as his extraordinary valedictory song for Sinatra, 'A Long Night'), is a bonus and the treatments are consistently imaginative.

*****(*) Remembering Eric Dolphy**

Steeplechase SCCD 31453 *Juris; Dick Oatts (as, ts, f); Jay Anderson (b); Jeff Hirshfield (d).* 4/98.

A provocative concept for a guitarist to essay, and this set of four Dolphy tunes and five in-the-spirit originals by Juris doesn't shirk any comparisons. Oatts gets a lean, almost rubbery sound, not much like the dedicatee but observant of the master's abstracted bebop roots, and the accuracy of the playing on the likes of 'Miss Ann' and 'Out There' – not to mention Oatts's own original 'Emphasizing Eric', which Juris admits is the hardest thing he's ever tried to play on the guitar – is a pleasure in itself. Anderson and Hirshfield create a free-flowing and open-minded pulse which is very suitable for the occasion. An excellent record.

****** Songbook**

Steeplechase SCCD 31483 *Juris; Jay Anderson (b); Jeff Hirshfield (d).* 11/99.

*****(*) Songbook 2**

Steeplechase SCCD 31516 *Juris; Michael Formanek (b); Jeff Hirshfield (d).* 3/01.

Juris is a favourite among guitarists, in part because his exceptional technique is all but masked by his dedication to playing interesting things. A plain old trio date which features the likes of 'Soul Eyes', 'Billie's Bounce' and 'All The Things You Are' hardly sounds like a candidate for major honours, but the first *Songbook* has claims to be his best record. Instead of playing Bill Evans's 'Time Remembered' as a sweet piece of fluff, he plays it solo with a focus and calm intensity which turn it into a thoroughgoing transformation, almost a scored improvisation. 'I Won't Dance' has the jocularity taken out, displaced by a beautifully lyrical feel. 'Milestones' and 'Billie's Bounce' are tough and direct. 'Nuages' is a set-piece that has always tempted technicians, but Juris breezes through it, completely secure. Anderson and Hirshfield are excellent, too.

If the second edition is only a shade behind, it's still as good a guitar record as will turn up in the straightahead racks. As before, Juris goes just slightly outside expectations: 'Django' is given a bluesy twang in the mid-section, 'Giant Steps' is almost serene. Because he now prefers a softly articulated tone, Juris won't necessarily take the ear straight away, but every solo seems to ripple with melodic bounty in these top-drawer sessions.

***** While My Guitar Gently Weeps**

Steeplechase SCCD 31553 *Juris; Jess Chandler (org); Tim Horner (d).* 11/02.

Naming your album after a Beatles tune isn't a traditional way to the jazz audience's heart, even if times are changing. It is, in any case, misleading, since the programme is actually based around compositions by guitarists, everyone from Raney and Montgomery to McLaughlin and Stryker (and, of course, the late George Harrison). The organ-combo setting is another surprise, moving away from the bass–drums duo of the last two records, which might have been the very setting which Juris could have chosen for the project. And that's the drawback: given that Juris uses a sound which is very soft in its articulation, the edges of every note furred over, it blends so completely in with the equally cosy organ timbre to the extent that there are times when the two deliveries seem interchangeable. The playing's thoughtful and smart, but it's disappointingly homogeneous too.

Richie Kamuca (1930–77)

TENOR SAXOPHONE

Born in Philadelphia, where he was spotted by Roy Eldridge, Kamuca worked with Stan Kenton and Woody Herman and with smaller West Coast groups, notably Shelly Manne's. Despite a late flurry of discs for Concord, he recorded very little as leader despite an appealing freshness and a tender ballad style.

***** Richie Kamuca Quartet**

VSOP 17 *Kamuca; Carl Perkins (p); Leroy Vinnegar (b); Stan Levey (d).* 6/57.

***** Jazz Erotica**

Fresh Sound FSR 500 *Kamuca; Conte Candoli, Ed Leddy (t); Frank Rosolino (tb); Bill Holman (bs); Vince Guaraldi (p); Monty Budwig (b); Stan Levey (d).* 58.

***** West Coast Jazz In Hi-Fi**

Original Jazz Classics OJC 1760 *As above.* 58

Apart from his late recordings for Concord, which were packed into the final year of Richie's life, this is pretty much the sum of his work as leader. The 1957 session, unfortunately without additional takes, offers a better measure of his quality than the two slightly later discs. The tracks are mostly very short and to the point, with just one original in a nicely judged set. 'Rain Drain' is closer to the quirky modernism of his big-band work, but it's an appealing enough tune. Perkins puts up two ideas of his own, 'Early Bird' and 'Fire One', and here and there steals the show with his terse, unshowy phrasing and offbeat ideas.

The title of the Fresh Sound (not the 'Jazz' part) is perhaps a shade misleading, though Kamuca favoured an intimate, close-to-the-ear murmur which comes direct from Lester Young, seductive with little hint of Pres's native ambivalence. The 'Jazz' part in the title is important because there isn't much sign either of the gimmicky Kenton approach in which much of the band was schooled. Kamuca's approach to standards – 'Star Eyes', 'Angel Eyes', 'Stella By Starlight' – is direct and unsentimental, and for combined impact and sophistication there's little to choose between the four quartet tracks and Holman's arrangements for the larger group. There are one or two minor technical quibbles about the transfer, and the identical OJC sounds a little brighter and cleaner, but, in the continued absence of three excellent Concords, *Drop Me Off In Harlem*, *Richie* and *Richie Kamuca's Charlie* (where he explores the Parker legacy), this makes for a highly desirable introduction to the saxophonist's work.

Michael Kanan

PIANO

Bostonian pianist with a liking for the Tristano school.

*****(*) Convergence**

Fresh Sound FSNT 055 *Kanan; Ben Street (b); Tim Pleasant (d).* 1/99.

*****(*) The Gentleman Is A Dope**

Fresh Sound FSNT 147 *As above.* 5/02.

Kanan takes on the Tristano approach and makes it sound warm and approachable – more so, perhaps, than sceptical listeners imagined it could be. He studied with Sal Mosca for a year before becoming disenchanted with the style, but these two discs show him trying it on for size again, mollified a little by influences such as Monk and jamal. The result is two swinging, delicate, sinewy recitals of standards and jazz tunes. He does Lennie and Lee favourites such as 'Ablution' and 'Tautology', and manages to heat them up and soften their astringencies without losing the essential flavour of the compositions. Hard-core Tristano-ites might consider this a cop-out, but to us it sounds like a beautiful synthesis of complementary approaches. He has a very graceful pianistic touch, and Street and Pleasant create light, skipping rhythms behind him. These discs should be as well-known as those of many a more fashionable piano name.

Seppo Kantonen

PIANO, KEYBOARDS

Finnish pianist, working in free-form, post-bop, mostly whatever takes his fancy.

*****(*) Klang**

Impala 001 *Kantonen; Uffe Krokfors (b); Markku Ounaskari (d).* n.d.

Kantonen isn't well known, but some may be familiar with his CD of duets with Jarmo Savolainen, *Phases* (Love BECD 4020), as well as sideman work with Eero Koivistoinen and Rinneradio. This excellent record shows how much mileage there still is in the piano trio. The writing is consistently intriguing, always looking to vary the dynamics of the group, the way the players move between form and freedom, the tonal colours available. Krokfors must take a big share of the credit, since he wrote four of the nine themes. 'Good Things', one of them, bounces off the simplest of bass riffs into a sizzling workout for the trio. Ounaskari can work up a terrific amount of noise, as he does on the climax of 'Lammen Haltija', without toppling the group over, but at least some of the time he's working in tiny strokes, or playing the kit – as on 'The Way In' – as if he's got a set of tuned tympani. Kantonen is quick and thoughtful and he uses what sounds like an old-fashioned analogue synth on a couple of pieces. Some of this music calls to mind a certain old-fashioned European elegance, as in some of the early ECM sessions. The impression is of a group that's thought long and hard about their music, without desiccating the essential spontaneity of their interaction.

Ori Kaplan (born 1969)

ALTO SAXOPHONE

Born in Tel Aviv, Kaplan studied in New York in the early '90s and has since worked on that scene with his Trio Plus band, recorded here.

***** Realms**

CIMP 190 *Kaplan; Tom Abbs (b, tba); Geoff Mann (d, t).* 1/99.

***** Delirium**

CIMP 223 *As above, except add Steve Swell (tb).* 5/00.

The music of *Realms* takes some cues from Ornette Coleman (though Kaplan himself sounds nothing like the master) and the tunes touch on the folky feel of Coleman's trio music, but there are interesting envelopes opened here and there: especially when Abbs switches to tuba and Mann picks up the trumpet, as they do in the haunting later stages of the title-track. Kaplan writes some neat melodies, and he does best when he's playing melodically, too: when the group gets too intense and the saxophonist starts overblowing, cliché beckons. An agreeable date – as is the follow-up, with frequent CIMP guest Swell sitting in. This one is a little more groove-oriented, especially in 'Air' and 'Hazy Dazy On Mars', although a particularly peppy jam on Carla Bley's 'Ictus' works well. Nothing seems to linger long in the mind once it's over, though.

Egil Kapstad (born 1940)

PIANO

Kapstad learned piano as a child and was working in the Oslo jazz scene by 1960. He performed with Karin Krog and in a long association with Bjørn Johansen, as well as writing choral and orchestral music and pieces for TV and theatre.

*****(*) Cherokee**

Gemini GMCD 61 *Kapstad; Terje Venaas (b); Egil Johansen (d).* 11/88.

A beautiful and typically individual record by a modern master of Norwegian jazz. Kapstad's thoroughgoing absorption of the requisite piano influences lets him put a personal spin on what is actually his first-ever trio date: the nine standards all have a novel point of view, such as the piano–bass duet on 'Autumn Leaves' or the dreamily slow treatment of 'Cherokee' itself. His solo reading of 'Darn That Dream' is modelled out of a simple but detailed look at the harmonies, and the opening run through 'When You're Smiling' freshens even that tune. Venaas and the redoubtable Johansen are perfectly in step, and the only disappointment is that there isn't more of Kapstad's own writing. He restricts himself to a blues and the brief, charming 'Our Autumn Waltz'.

****** Remembrance**

Gemini GMCD 82 *As above.* 10/93.

Even more remarkable. Kapstad's record is, in effect, a celebration of Norwegian jazz, since it draws from the work of eight native composers (including the members of the trio). The abiding factor is his meticulous technique: even in the middle of a fast piece such as 'Big Red', he displays a refinement of touch that elevates the composer without relinquishing his own stamp on the piece. If the overall feel of the session is romantic, even a trifle forlorn, the exacting lyricism which he gets out of most of the tunes is intensely satisfying. Venaas and Johansen take honours, too.

***** Storytellers**

Hot Club Records HRCD 110 *Kapstad; Roy Nicolaisen (t, flhn); Bernt Rosengren (ts, f); Nisse Sandström (ts); Einar Iversen (p); Jacob Young (g); Terje Gewelt (b); Ole Jacob Hansen (d); Jan Erik Vold (v).* 5/98.

If you don't know any Norwegian, this one's likely to cause some difficulties. Jan Erik Vold (who once worked with the Stenson–Garbarek Quartet) reads texts from writers as diverse as Robert Creeley, D. H. Lawrence and Kristofer Uppdal, while Kapstad and his team follow it with music of similar range: Creeley's piece is matched with 'St Thomas', Lawrence's with

'How Deep Is The Ocean', and a Claes Gill text goes with Eric Dolphy's '245'. Vold (he contributes one poem himself) is defiantly upfront in the mix, which may exasperate listeners wanting to hear what's a splendid group; but the effect, once you're accustomed to the reader's intense delivery, is imposing.

Pandelis Karayorgis

PIANO

Raised in Greece, he studied at the New England Conservatory and under Paul Bley and plays a ruggedly abstract style of piano. Has worked with viol(in)ist Mat Maneri.

***** Lift & Poise**
Leo Lab 041 *Karayorgis; Joe Maneri (cl); Mat Maneri (vn); John Lockwood (b).* 12/96, 1/97.

****** Heart & Sack**
Leo Lab 048 *Karayorgis; Nate McBride (b); Randy Peterson (d).* 4/98.

****(*) Let It**
Cadence 1115 *As above; omit Peterson.* 2–5/99.

*****(*) Blood Ballad**
Leo LRCD 325 *As above; add Peterson (d).* 8/01.

***** No Such Thing**
Boxholder BXH 104 *As above; omit Peterson; add Ken Vandermark (reeds).* 01.

***** Disambiguation**
Leo LR CD 334 *Karayorgis; Tony Malaby (ts); Mat Maneri (vn); Michael Formanek (b); Randy Peterson (d).* 1/02

Karayorgis has made several albums on Leo Records with Maneri. *Lift & Poise* is probably the best of them, with the bonus of Joe M. (clarinet on two tracks) and John Lockwood on the strength. There are 12 tracks, divided into solo, duo and trio pieces, exploring a range of sonorities and improvising languages, ranging from the quasi-classical to the free-form and brutalist.

Heart & Sack is much more obviously a jazz album and Pandelis's Monk influence comes across strongly. He does a wonderful cover of Dolphy's bluesy 'Miss Ann', Ellington's 'Frustration' and Ken McIntyre's rarely (if ever) covered 'Lautir'. That's enough to lend it interest, but the playing is richly evocative and never predictable, even if McBride and Peterson occasionally lapse into free-jazz argot during some of Karayorgis's more abstract passages.

The duo date with McBride is actually rather dull, though there are moments of genuine illumination as well, and it's the reconvened trio that captures the attention on *Blood Ballad.* It's a tighter and more organized album than the first, and there are no reference points apart from the closing version of Coltrane's 'One Up, One Down', which might be taken from a Marilyn Crispell session were it not so punchy and Monkian. The opening sequence of 'In The Cracks Of Four' and 'Blood Ballad' probably represents Pandelis's best moments on record and a very good place to start exploring his music.

The trio with Vandermark will appeal mostly to fans of the reedman, though Karayorgis's suppressed Cecil Taylor influence moves to the fore briefly. Best to move straight on to *Disambiguation,* which reunites the pianist with Maneri in a scratch line-up that brings out the best in both of them. Again, Pandelis's Monk influence is very evident, and he swings more easily and relaxedly than on most of his previous records. The long 'Three Plus Three' (which might be a lost Monk score) and the title-piece are the most effective cuts.

Jan Kaspersen (born 1948)

PIANO

A contemporary Danish pianist, composer and bandleader, with a distinguished record of work since 1970 and a penchant for leopardskin hats and Thelonious Monk.

***** Memories Of Monk**
Olufsen DOCD 5208 *Kaspersen; Peter Danstrup (b); Ole Romer (d).* 11/86.

****** Live In Sofie's Cellar**
Olufsen DOCD 5136 *Kaspersen; Anders Bergcrantz (t); Bob Rockwell (ts); Peter Danstrup (b); Ole Romer (d).* 8/91.

*****(*) Heavy Smoke**
Olufsen DOCD 5188 *As above.* 12/92.

Marvellous records from a Dane whose music is a beautifully personal, inventive and humorous response to the particular influence of Thelonious Monk. This is made crystal-clear by the Monk tribute album (DOCD 5208) which distils a nice blend of homage, celebration and evolution from the model. Kaspersen has done better since and perhaps he can be a shade too slavish in some of his tribute, but the sense of enjoyment shines through. The great disc here is the glorious live session: Bergcrantz reveals himself as a major (and so far shamefully under-recognized) soloist, Rockwell is only a beat behind, and Kaspersen directs with great exuberance from the piano. There is the third version of his favourite 'I Mean Monk' and this is surely the best. *Heavy Smoke* returns the band to the studio and, while the music is unimpeachably inventive, we slightly prefer the dash of the live session.

***** Joinin' Forces**
Olufsen DOCD 5184 *Kaspersen; Horace Parlan (p).* 4/94.

*****(*) Special Occasion Band Live In Copenhagen Jazzhouse**
Olufsen DOCD 5303/4 2CD *Kaspersen; Lars Vissing (t); Erling Kroner, Lis Wessberg (tb); Simon Cato Spang-Hanssen (as); Bob Rockwell, Fredrik Lundin (ss, ts); Henrik Sveidahl-Hansen (ts, bs); Aske Jacoby (g); Peter Danstrup (b); Ole Romer (d); Jacob Andersen (perc).* 9/94.

The duo with Parlan is an enjoyable if lightweight meeting in which the two keyboards bump and jostle over some familiar ground. The big-band set is much more exciting. With seven horns in the front line, Kaspersen marshals a serious force to get the most out of his writing and, in what's almost a greatest-hits set of his own tunes, the band play with unquenchable enthusiasm and flair. Sound is just a little rough, but the ambience of the occasion – recorded when the band were flying at the end of a tour – communicates a tremendous amount of fun.

***** Portrait In Space And Rhythm**
Olufsen DOCD 5356 *As above discs.* 11/86–6/95.

A useful best-of, culled mostly from the above sessions, although there is a track apiece from Kaspersen's two solo sets of Satie piano music. Fans will also welcome two out-takes from the live record at Sofie's Cellar, not quite up to the rest of the programme but still splendid. A pocket portrait of a man who loves his jazz.

*****(*) Live At Copenhagen Jazzhouse**
Olufsen DOCD 5355 *Kaspersen; Jan Kohlin, Benny Rosenfeld, Palle Bolvig, Henrik Bolberg Pedersen, Lars Togeby (t); Vincent Nilsson, Steen Hansen, Kjeld Ipsen (tb); Axel Windfeld (btb, tba); Giordano Bellincampi (btb); Michael Hove (ss, as, cl); Christina Von Bülow (ss, as); Uffe Markussen, Tomas Franck (ts); Flemming Madsen (bs, bcl); Anders Lindvall (g); Thomas Ovesen (b); Jonas Johansen (d); Ole Kock Hansen (cond).* 10/95.

Kaspersen meets the Danish Radio Jazz Orchestra and together they give eight of his tunes a good going-over. 'Roll Jelly Roll' is a clever slant on Morton's music; 'Duke Directions' is an exuberant boogaloo for the rhythm team and is not as Ellingtonian as 'Naja's Dream', which features Hove as Hodges. This is colourful, easy-going music, inventive without feeling the need to be too incessantly clever, and the DRJO, stacked with talent as it is, brings it all to vivid life. Kaspersen gets plenty of solos, but it's his scores which are the thing. Very good location sound, too.

***** Den Blå Munk**
Scanbox/Music Mecca 2072-2 *Kaspersen (p solo).* 11/97.

Kaspersen was the obvious choice to do this music for a film soundtrack concerning his beloved idol, Thelonious. He starts and finishes with a slow 'Blue Monk', plays a livelier version as track two, then ruminates through six of his own themes. A brief, not especially heavyweight record, but Kaspersen's admirers will surely enjoy.

*****(*) Katuaq Concert**
Olufsen DOCD 5384 *Kaspersen (p solo).* 3/97.

Jan has a group of new records on Olufsen, but the elusiveness of the label has conspired to allow us to hear only one of them. Here he is in Greenland, playing the first jazz gig at Katuaq Arts Centre. As ever, his dedication to Monk is steadfast, with 'Round Midnight', 'Ugly Beauty' and 'Light Blue', along with his own 'Red Monk' and 'I Mean Monk': yet the deeper he goes, the more he seems to find. A sober occasion, illuminated by the sparest flashes of Kaspersen wit.

Four new records by Jan arrived just as we went to press – we'll report on them next time!

Bruce Katz (born 1952)

PIANO, ORGAN

Energetic post-bop keyboardist, now with substantial track record as a leader.

***** Crescent Crawl**
Audioquest AQ CD 102 *Katz; Bob Malach (ts); Marty Ballou (b); Lorne Entress (d).* 92.

*****(*) Transformation**
Audioquest AQ CD 1026 *Katz; Tom Hall (ts); Kevin Barry (g); David Clark (b); Lorne Entress (d).* 11/93.

***** Mississippi Moan**
Audioquest AQ CD 1047 *Katz; Tom Hall (ts, bs); Mike Costello (hca); Julian Kasper (g); Mark Poniatowski (b); Ralph Rosen (d); Mighty Sam McClain (v).* 10/97.

***** Three Feet Off The Ground**
Audioquest AQ CD 1056 *Katz; Julien Kasper, Duke Robillard (g); Blake Newman (b); Ralph Rosen (d).* 8/00.

Katz's piano and organ sound had been heard in and around Boston for a while (including recordings with Ronnie Earl and the Broadcasters) before he took the plunge with a recording date of his own. Strictly the first couple are co-led with drummer Entress, who's also a fine composer. The first album comes right out of the box, an eclectic mix of styles from blues to near-folk things. 'Contrition', played on the Hammond, was originally co-written with the drummer for the Earl band; 'BK's Broiler' is another B3 groove, but Katz has the ability to change pace entirely, as he does with an astonishing piano version of 'Just A Closer Walk With Thee'.

The favoured groove is a medium funk shuffle, but with lots of unexpected elements – weird bent notes, busy little percussion interludes, top line/bass line swaps – that lift it out of the ordinary. Again on *Transformation*, the organ tracks are a bit more energetic and forceful, but it is Katz's piano-playing that is the key to his sound. He's an active, multi-directional player, often building solo ideas out of fast, narrow-interval arpeggios, with occasional excursions out into free time, almost like the young Cecil Taylor. Sensibly, he seldom dwells on an idea past its due time, preferring to spin off in a new direction. Like Malach, Tom Hall is more than just a bar-room honker and he turns in some very nifty solo work, as do bassist and guitarist on the second album.

It's tempting to start a new section for the third album, since the sound has changed substantially since Katz and Entress went their separate ways. The emphasis is much more on blues than on jazz strictly conceived and the addition of vocalist Mighty Sam McClain on 'Hanging On The Cross' and 'I'm Gonna Love You' puts the whole set in a rather different bag from past discs. Our instinct about Katz's piano-playing appears on the money, for while the organ would seem perfectly appropriate to this repertoire Bruce sticks largely to the piano.

But then the old B3 reasserts itself on *Three Feet Off The Ground*, a fast and funky set that seems to have gone up a notch in energy terms over the first albums. 'Wrecking Ball' is fantastic, but so, too, is the soul-jazz opener 'Beef Jerky' and the moving 'Walk With Me'. Katz has gone his own course and has created a vibrant body of work which deserves attention.

Roger Kellaway (born 1939)

PIANO

He studied at New England Conservatory in the late '50s, spent the early '60s in New York, then moved to California in 1966, playing in jazz and rock session situations. Most of his subsequent work has been as composer, arranger and producer, often in TV and film, and straightahead jazz appearances have unfortunately been rare.

****** A Portrait Of Roger Kellaway**
Fresh Sound FSR-CD 147 *Kellaway; Jim Hall (g); Steve Swallow, Ben Tucker (b); Dave Bailey, Tony Inzalaco (d).* 63.

*****(*) The Roger Kellaway Trio**
Original Jazz Classics OJC 1897 *Kellaway; Russell George (b); Dave Bailey (d).* 5/65.

Kellaway's early records are buried treasure. He has a scholar's approach to jazz history, bundling together stride, boogie and swing devices into a manner which was and is otherwise entirely modern. *Portrait* is a forgotten classic. 'Double Fault' calls to mind such contemporaries as Andrew Hill, yet the off-centre lyricism and abstracting of melody mark Kellaway as very much his own man. Tucker and Bailey offer prime, swinging support on four tracks, which keeps the composer's ideas in accessible domain, while the trio of Hall, Swallow and Inzalaco create a contrapuntal music of sometimes bemusing intricacy to go with the pianist's work. Two solos are equally rich and detailed, and there is a brilliant transformation of 'Crazy She Calls Me'. Slightly brittle sound doesn't mar a very fine record.

If it is not quite as fine as *Portrait*, there is still some outstanding music on the the trio record for Prestige. His treatment of the then-contemporary Lennon and McCartney tune, 'I'll Follow The Sun', is a rare example of successfully jazzing the Beatles. The blues waltz, 'Signa: O.N.', is indecently rich and 'Ballad Of The Sad Young Men' is as sober as Kellaway is playful elsewhere – especially on the prepared-piano knockabout 'Brats'. A pity that the remastering couldn't get a better sound out of the piano.

***** Cello Quartet**

A&M SP 3034 *Kellaway; Joe Pass (g); Ed Lustgarten (clo); Chuck Domanico (b); strings.* 70.

A surprise reissue from the Verve Group, this is a nice light-music excursion. The name is a misnomer, since the pieces were written for cello/piano/bass/drums, were performed live by the same group with marimba in for the drums – yet there's neither drums nor marimba on the record. Instead, strings and Joe Pass on two tracks. It's coolly pleasant and entirely forgettable music, with the cello a less than inspiring lead voice, since it does tend to drone in this context. 'On Your Mark Get Set; Blues' is a brief drop of the hard stuff.

***** Alone Together**

Dragon DRCD 168 *Kellaway; Red Mitchell (b).* 7/88.

Kellaway has been sighted on and off, away from studio and film-score work, and his records are always welcome. This duo with Red Mitchell is very like the ideal of eavesdropping on a couple of old friends after hours. The album sounds better all the time, though Mitchell's whimsical search for the lowest note a bass can produce may still irritate some listeners, and sometimes they ramble, as after-hours sessions will. But there are some beautiful deconstructions of choice standards.

***** That Was That**

Dragon DRCD 201 *Kellaway; Jan Allan (t); Red Mitchell (b).* 1/91.

While this is something of a rerun of the earlier session with Mitchell, the presence of Jan Allan seems to focus the music much more and, though most of the tracks run to seven or eight minutes in length, there's no sense of excessive meandering. Mitchell's amusing vocals on 'Leavin' Blues' and the title-track add to the fun and there are some very pleasing solos by Allan, whose unassuming and rather frail playing suits this context very well.

*****(*) Roger Kellaway Meets Gene Bertoncini And Michael Moore**

Chiaroscuro CR(D) 315 *Kellaway; Gene Bertoncini (g); Michael Moore (b).* 2/92.

The trio session is a densely packed series of performances that can seem a bit much over CD length, given the high, concentrated interplay among the three men. On 'All The Things You Are' their contrapuntal thinking is astonishing, yet their simple, songful treatment of Moore's sweet-natured 'Old New Waltz' is as charming as it is naggingly memorable. Kellaway continues to surprise, improvising on the melody or the chords just when one expects the opposite, turning the device of 'locked hands' into something ingenious. Bertoncini's acoustic guitar never sounds altogether right in the context, and Rudy Van Gelder's somewhat eccentric studio sound might be the cause.

Greg Kelley

TRUMPET

Studied at the Peabody before moving to Boston and beginning to work on the free scene. Founded his oddly named group nmperign in 1998 and has recorded with them and others since. Also associated with Anthony Braxton.

***(*) Trumpet**

Meniscus 009 *Kelley (t solo).* 00.

We only have his word for it that a trumpet was actually used. Some of these sounds could probably be duplicated using some old plumbing pipe and a couple of tuned thermostats. No one denies Kelley's sincerity or indeed his musical gifts, but they're hard to find on this raw and unlovely set of free sounds.

***** Forlorn Green**

Erstwhile 019 *Kelley; Jason Lescalleet (computers, samples).* 11/01.

This is a very different proposition, an album of bizarre atmospheres and contexts that is reminiscent of some of Braxton's more dramatic concert pieces. Found sound combines with eerie trumpet blasts that might be shouts of delight or fear or the cries of someone in pain. 'Conquest Of The Earth' is a desolate and initially forbidding soundscape that gradually acquires an aura of human tenderness; one can imagine this soundtracking the story of people who live in harsh places. 'Man On The Outside' is more specifically dramatic, a sound poem about estrangement and lack of contact. The techniques are very similar to those heard on *Trumpet*, but here they seem to have a *raison d'être* and aren't just deployed because they can be. We'd rate the album higher if it weren't such demanding music.

*****(*) If I Never Meet You In This Life, Let Me Feel The Lack**

Rossbin RS006 *Kelley (t solo).* 8/02.

And the same goes for this one. It's also quite a short record, though it's unlikely that any but the most committed listener would be up for more of it. It opens with dramatic clangour, sounds from inside the bell of a mic'ed trumpet and continues for a time as a collage of loud processed sounds, some instrumental, some electronic artefacts. Then, bizarrely and wonderfully, the surface detail disappears and all one hears for the rest of the set is a low roar, through which tiny details emerge almost subliminally. This may be what it sounds like in the womb, but for the absence of a countable heartbeat, or it may be the submarine wash heard by the drowned. For music so spare and abstract, it's remarkably humane and if you find the title pretentious as you approach the disc, you may have changed your mind 36 minutes later.

Brian Kellock (born 1962)

PIANO

Born in Edinburgh and still based there, Kellock is beginning to carve out an international reputation. Technically secure, he has the ability to create great emotion with his playing, whether on fast, bop-based numbers or on romantic ballads. Influences are hard to pin down, but Kellock has clearly listened carefully to everyone from Bud Powell to Chick Corea, and can bring off a version of Monk's percussive drive at will.

***** Something's Got To Give**
Caber Music 003 *Kellock; Kenny Ellis (b); John Rae (d).* 98.

****** Live At Henry's**
Caber Music 020 *As above.* 11/00.

Kellock's debut CD on Caber is a tribute to Fred Astaire. What is immediately impressive, apart from the obvious empathy of the trio, is how comfortably the pianist manages to blend standard material with a thoroughly contemporary sound. Rae's drumming calls on everything from Elvin Jones-inspired polyrhythms to a steady, folkish backbeat; above all, it swings. 'The Continental' (which can be sampled on the label website) is an obvious choice and by far the best single track on the album. Nothing to fault elsewhere, though.

The appearance of *Live At Henry's* cemented his emergence as a major player. The decision to catch the pianist in his natural habitat – a popular jazz cellar in his native city – was a wise one and has yielded an extraordinary set. One surprise is the inclusion of two Tristano tunes, including the demanding contrefact on 'Pennies From Heaven' ('Lennie's Pennies'). It's an interpretation which calls for impressive hand-speed and inch-perfect co-ordination throughout the trio. 'TP In NYC' is written by saxophonist Phil Bancroft, an abrasive tune that establishes the tenor of a mostly upbeat set. There is less than might be expected of Kellock's more meditative ballad style, though his interpretation of Jimmy Rowles's 'The Peacocks' is pretty definitive. It's not (yet) *The Village Vanguard Sessions*, but it has the same unity of purpose, the same intelligence and equilibrium and the same ability to yield new dimensions with each hearing.

Wynton Kelly (1931–71)

PIANO

Born in Jamaica, Kelly also ended his life outside the United States, perhaps symbolically, because he has also seemed strangely marginal to the main thrust of bebop. And yet it was he more than anyone other than Charlie Parker who sustained its origins in the blues. Some of Kelly's finest work was for Miles Davis, but he also left behind a substantial body of work as leader.

***** Wynton Kelly – Piano**
Original Jazz Classics OJC 401 *Kelly; Kenny Burrell (g); Paul Chambers (b); Philly Joe Jones (d).* 1/58.

On the face of it, Kelly didn't seem the most obvious replacement for Bill Evans and Red Garland in the Miles Davis group, but he had a lyrical simplicity and uncomplicated touch that appealed enormously to the trumpeter, who hired him in 1959; Kelly played on only one track on the classic *Kind Of Blue*, but 'Freddie Freeloader' is enough to show what distinguished him from Evans's more earnestly romantic style and to establish his quality. *Piano* is a full-voiced quartet that makes full use of Burrell's boppish grace.

****** Kelly Blue**
Original Jazz Classics OJC 033 *Kelly; Nat Adderley (c); Bobby Jaspar (f); Benny Golson (ts); Paul Chambers (b); Jimmy Cobb (d).* 2 & 3/59.

The gentle but dynamic bounce to his chording comes to the fore on the marvellous *Kelly Blue* (which also reunites the *Kind Of Blue* rhythm section). On the title-track and 'Keep It Moving', the addition of Adderley and Jaspar makes perfect sense, but Benny Golson's robust contributions tend to unbalance the delicate strength of Kelly's arrangements. The trio cuts are far superior.

***** Kelly Great**
Vee Jay 003 *Kelly; Lee Morgan (t); Wayne Shorter (ts); Paul Chambers (b); Philly Joe Jones (d).* 60.

*****(*) Kelly At Midnite**
Vee Jay 006 *As above, except omit Morgan and Shorter.* 60.

***** Wynton Kelly**
Vee Jay 011 *Kelly; Paul Chambers, Sam Jones (b); Jimmy Cobb (d).* 61.

***** Someday My Prince Will Come**
Collectables 714 *As for the above.* 10/61.

Something of a Bill Evans influence (unless the route is in the opposite direction) creeps into Kelly's playing at this time, and it is possible also to hear echoes from the market dominance of Ahmad Jamal, who was being talked up by Miles Davis at every available opportunity. The three Vee Jays are good, strong albums, though the hard-bop horns on the first of the trios sit uneasily with the leader's conception. The 1961 session with Jones, Cobb and Chambers is now available as a Collectables disc and very good it is, too, with 'Wrinkles' featuring the two horn men and some five bonus tracks to fill out the original session.

***** It's All Right!**
Verve 557750-2 *Kelly; Kenny Burrell (g); Paul Chambers (b); Jimmy Cobb (d); Candido Camero (perc); Tommy Rey Caribe Street Band.* 3/64.

*****(*) Full View**
Original Jazz Classics OJCCD 912 *Kelly; Ron McClure (b); Jimmy Cobb (d).* 66.

Leaving in some studio noise on *It's All Right* adds a touch of atmosphere but doesn't add much to the musical presence. The musicianship is beyond question and will probably appeal to some far more than the rougher sound of the earlier date, but for us it is a dilution of an important and still unregarded artist.

Ron McClure replaced Paul Chambers in 1966 and brought an immediate change of dimension to the music. *Full View* is an excellent record, an eclectic mix of styles and genres, with a much more balanced feel to the trio, not just piano and rhythm. Cobb is an asset, too, with a relaxed, springy pulse and the ability to cut in behind the melody line with near-instantaneous response figures.

★★★(★) Live At The Left Bank Jazz Society 1967
Fresh Sound 1031 2CD *Kelly; Hank Mobley (ts); Cecil McBee (b); Jimmy Cobb (d).* 11/67.

★★★ Interpretations
Vee Jay 30039 *Same as above.* 11/67.

★★★(★) Live At The Left Bank Jazz Society 1968
Fresh Sound 1032 2CD *Kelly; George Coleman (ts); Ron McClure (b); Jimmy Cobb (d).* 9/68.

★★★ In Concert
Collectables 7141 *As above.* 9/68.

Rather scruffily recorded, with sudden and unexpected changes of balance, these are nevertheless valuable glimpses of Kelly at work with two distinguished guests. While hardcore hard-boppers will be eager to hear both Mobley and Coleman – rare instances of live sessions by both men in this period – the music's at least as interesting for Kelly himself. Obliged to solo at much greater length than on his studio dates, he never does anything to startle a listener, but even over many choruses the merits of his bright, swinging, communicative style refuse to fade, and concentrated listening reveals much – remarkable for a man who once said, 'I'd just like to get a groove going and never solo.' Mobley is more unbuttoned than he is on many of his studio dates, while Big George simply piles through his solos – their set starts with marathon versions of 'Unit 7' and 'Surrey With The Fringe On Top'.

The Collectables issue – just two long tracks: Grofe's 'On The Train' and a superb 'On A Clear Day' – were released on Vee Jay before disappearing again. They fill out the picture nicely and the disc should be easy enough to find.

★★★ Last Trio Session
Delmark 441 *Kelly; Paul Chambers (b); Jimmy Cobb (d).* 8/68.

This had been a long-standing unit since leaving Miles Davis and spending a further tenure as Wes Montgomery's rhythm section. As a curtain-call, it's deeply disappointing and is rendered all the more poignant by the early death of Paul Chambers (just five months after these cuts were made) and then of Kelly. The choice of material is suspect. The Doors' 'Light My Fire' isn't a comfortable theme for a trio of this sensitivity, though the version of Aretha's 'Say A Little Prayer For Me' is very affecting. Chambers is in good, if slightly detached form, and Jimmy Cobb rarely slipped below standard.

Kelly's death, still on the wrong side of 40, robbed jazz of one of its most inventive and hard-working figures. A British reviewer recently referred to him as simultaneously underrated and overrated. It sounds perverse, but it makes the point. Kelly has for too long been admired by those who haven't troubled to listen to him carefully. The dividends for those who do are considerable.

The Ken Colyer Trust Band

GROUP

Formed in honour of 'The Guvnor', the group has a fluid personnel which plays in the spirit of Colyer's kind of diehard trad.

★★★ It's All Down To You
P.E.K. Sound PKCD-220 *Allen Beechey (c, v); Len Baldwin (tb); Alan Robinson (cl); Pete Morcom (bj); Mickey Ashman (b); Malc Murphy (d, v).* 3/03.

The KCTB have made a number of records in the past, but this one was compiled from the wish-lists of various fans and features youth and experience, with young hothead Beechey lining up alongside veterans Ashman, Murphy and the rest. Colyer's mordant shadow is never far away, though, and the group get close to the signature trudge of a kosher Colyer group. Beechey even sounds a little like the old man when he takes a vocal on 'Postman's Lament'. 'Nobody Knows The Trouble I've Seen' is very slow and generously done. There is an almost shocking departure, though, in 'Sim', which comes from the Portuguese fado tradition(!). Recorded with plenty of atmosphere at The Bull's Head in Barnes, though not with an audience present.

Stacey Kent (born 1968)

VOCAL

Kent is a New Yorker who came to London and studied at the Guildhall School. She is an unapologetic mainstreamer in terms of material and approach.

★★★ Close Your Eyes
Candid CCD 79737 *Kent; Jim Tomlinson (ts); David Newton (p); Colin Oxley (g); Andy Cleyndert (b); Steve Brown (d).* 11/96.

★★★(★) The Tender Trap
Candid CCD 79751 *As above, except Dave Green (b), Jeff Hamilton (d) replace Cleyndert and Brown.* 2/98.

★★★(★) Let Yourself Go
Candid CCD 79764 *As above, except Simon Thorpe (b), Steve Brown (d) replace Green and Hamilton.* 7/99.

Kent's curiously lean voice and unmannered phrasing have become very addictive to British audiences, and these neatly tailored records are a fine calling-card for her work. There's hardly a song on any of these records which is less than familiar from the American songbook – and this may discourage collectors familiar with the classic vocalists – but at least she makes no self-conscious attempt at crossing over into pop material. The band, directed largely by saxophonist Tomlinson, is absolutely assured and glances off and around the singer's vocals. The third record is dedicated to music associated with Fred Astaire and is arguably the pick of the three, although both *Close Your Eyes*, with its sexy-samba title-track, and *The Tender Trap*, a graceful smooch record of a high order, have had a profusion of admirers. Where she takes it from here is hard to say, but there ought to be another dozen or so records in this mould before she runs low on material.

★★★ Dreamsville
Candid CCD 79775 *Kent; Jim Tomlinson (ts); David Newton (p); Colin Oxley (g); Simon Thorpe (b); Jesper Kviberg (d).* 6/00.

★★★ In Love Again
Candid CCD 797786 *As above.* 7–9/01.

One record of dreamy ballads, one of Richard Rodgers music and, since Kent is not a singer to offer any kind of surprise, the results should be entirely satisfactory to her followers. For anyone less committed, either would be a plausible place to sample what she does, but if you already have one or two on the shelf, these will seem less than essential. As skilful as her accompanists are, the music has started to feel practised and almost anodyne, and she doesn't have the force of character to make that unimportant. One track at a time, this is still sweetly appealing.

***** The Boy Next Door**

Candid CCD 70797 *Kent; Jim Tomlinson (sax, v); David Newton (ky, v); Colin Oxley (g); Dave Chamberlain (b); Matt Home (d); Curtis Schwarz (v).* 2/03.

Not much change to talk about here, but this one really only just scrapes its three stars: some of these song-choices, supposedly by Kent's musical heroes, will make the uncommitted wince, such as 'What The World Needs Now' and James Taylor's unlistenable 'You've Got A Friend'.

Stan Kenton (1911–79)

PIANO, VOCAL, BANDLEADER

Born in Wichita but raised in California, Kenton learned piano early and was touring with bands as a teenager. Formed his own band in 1940 and through tours and broadcasts became widely known, yet had a yen to experiment and tried to create a 'progressive jazz'. Ran a 40-strong innovations orchestra in the early '50s, with strings, but gradually reverted to more conventional big-band music, though he later tried a Neophonic Orchestra and the so-called Mellophonium Orchestra (early '60s). Many of the principal West Coast soloists passed through his band, and many leading arrangers did their early work for Kenton. Often dismissed as pretentious, but his orchestra and their records still have a huge following.

***** Stan Kenton 1941–1944**

Classics 828 *Kenton; Franck Beach, Chico Alvarez, Earl Collier, Ray Borden, John Carroll, Buddy Childers, Karl George, Dick Morse, Mel Green, Gene Roland (t); Harry Forbes, Dick Cole, George Faye, Bart Varsalona, Bill Atkinson, Freddie Zito, Milt Kabak, Lory Aaron (tb); Jack Ordean, Ted Romersea, Eddie Meyers, Art Pepper, Boots Mussulli, Al Harding, Bill Lahey, Chester Ball (as); Red Dorris (ts, v); Maurice Beeson, Dave Matthews, Stan Getz, Emmett Carls (ts); Bob Gioga (bs); Bob Ahern, Ralph Leslie (g); Buddy Hayes, Clyde Singleton, Gene Englund, Bob Kesterson (b); Chauncey Farre, Jesse Price, John S. Bock, Joe Vernon (d); Anita O'Day, Gene Howard (v).* 11/40–12/44.

****(*) The Formative Years**

Verve 589489-2 *Similar to above.* 9/41–2/42.

***** Balboa Bash**

Naxos Jazz Legends 8.120517 *Kenton; Frank Beach, Chico Alvarez, Earl Collier (t); Dick Cole, Harry Forbes (tb); Jack Ordean, Bill Lahey (as, cl); Red Dorris (ts, cl, v); Ted Romersea (ts, cl); Bob Gioga (bs, cl); Al Costi (g); Howard Rumsey (b); Marvin George (d).* 41–42.

***** Etude For Saxophones**

Naxos Jazz Legends 8.120518 *As above.* 41–42.

The further away the Kenton era gets, the more prodigious the outpourings of Kenton material. Yet while the number of airshot and semi-official concert CDs seems to increase all the time, there are still a lot of latter-day vinyl discs which are unavailable, particularly from his own Creative World enterprise. As a source of controversy, Kenton has been at last passed by. He often had the biggest of big bands and, with his penchant for symphonic uproar, grandiose conception and a demanding menu, his discography is a curious achievement. Given the 'modernist' tag which stuck to him, it's odd how at this point a lot of his music can seem almost quaint in its methods and matter. Kenton seemed to believe in principles which often had little to do with musical substance: volume, power, weight, noise. Much of the orchestra's output seems to derive from half-assimilated ideas of 20th-century orchestral composition, and it always sat uneasily next to more familiar notions of jazz scoring. Later editions of the band pilfered from rock and soul idioms, with another batch of mixed results, even if Kenton seemed more at home in that milieu than Woody Herman ever did. His best music still swung mightily, was brilliantly played, and went to exhilarating extremes of both musicianship and showmanship.

The very early sessions for Decca and Capitol are collected on the Classics disc. 'Artistry In Rhythm', Kenton's theme, turns up in the fourth session, but otherwise these are often run-of-the-mill swing arrangements, and the main point of interest is the early vocal features for Anita O'Day. Similar ground is covered by the Verve disc (actually all Decca material), although this offers only a miserly 28 minutes (!) of music. The Naxos discs gather together the band's series of McGregor broadcast transcriptions: very early days for the band, two years before even their first date for Capitol, and at this point still a comparatively raw mix of dance orchestra, swing band and 'new design in modern music'. No outstanding soloists yet, but these tracks still have their moments. Classics have fair if erratic sound, from unlisted sources. The Naxos discs sound their age but are clear enough.

***** On AFRS 1944–1945**

Status DSTS 1019 *Kenton; Buddy Childers, Ray Wetzel, John Anderson, Russ Burgher, Bob Lymperis, John Carroll, Karl George, Gene Roland, Mel Green, Dick Morse (t); Harry Forbes, Freddie Zito, Milt Kabak, Jimmy Simms (tb); Bart Varsalona (btb); Bob Lively, Boots Mussulli, Al Anthony, Eddie Meyers, Chet Ball (as); Stan Getz, Dave Matthews, Emmett Carls, Vido Musso, Bob Cooper (ts); Bob Gioga (bs); Bob Ahern (g); Eddie Safranski, Bob Kesterson, Gene Englund (b); Jesse Price, Ralph Collier, Jim Falzone (d); June Christy, Gene Howard, Anita O'Day (v).* 5/44–11/45.

***** The Transcription Performances 1945–1946**

Hep 47 *Kenton; Buddy Childers, Ray Wetzel, John Anderson, Russ Burgher, Bob Lymperis, Chico Alvarez, Ken Hanna (t); Freddie Zito, Jimmy Simms, Ray Klein, Milt Kabak, Kai Winding, Miff Sines (tb); Bart Varsalona (btb); Al Anthony, Boots Mussulli (as); Vido Musso, Bob Cooper (ts); Bob Gioga (bs); Bob Ahern (g); Eddie Safranski (b); Ralph Collier, Shelly Manne (d); June Christy (v).* 11/45–7/46.

***** Live At The Café Rouge & Hollywood Palladium 1945**

Jazz Unlimited JUCD 2055 *Similar to above.* 9–11/45.

Not so different from the studio dates, although here and there on these transcriptions the band stretch out a little. Musso's tenor treatment of 'Body And Soul', for instance, features an extended coda on the version on Status, whereas it's briefer and sharper on the Hep disc – though both times he ends it with the Hawkins tag. The earlier tracks on Status mean that O'Day is still present for a couple of features and there's a couple of interesting rarities – 'Conversin' With The Brain', for one. Sound on the Hep disc is superior; the Status transfers tend to sound their age rather more. Jazz Unlimited jump in with a generous 70 minutes of material from three September 1945 broadcasts. The programmes aren't terribly interesting but the sound is more than fair for the period.

***** Stan Kenton 1945**
Classics 898 *Basically similar to above discs.* 12/44–5/45.

*****(*) Stan Kenton 1946**
Classics 949 *As above.* 1–8/46.

Anita O'Day left the band at the beginning of 1945 (her last two features open the *1945* disc) and the introduction of June Christy brought a sweeter, brighter sound to Kenton's palette. The other key import was arranger Pete Rugolo, who charted several staples and hits for Kenton's book. Classics 898 has its share of novelties, which Kenton himself probably detested, such as 'Shoo Fly Pie And Apple Pan Dowdy', and Christy's big hit, 'Just A-Sittin' And A-Rockin''. More typical is the protoype of 'Opus In Pastels' (rejected from a May 1945 date and not cut again until August 1946) and six titles from a hard-hitting V-Disc session. Classics 949 sees Rugolo flexing his muscles and the debut of several Kenton classics: 'Intermission Riff', 'Artistry In Boogie', 'Artistry In Bolero' and the brooding 'Concerto To End All Concertos', a good deal more reflective in its original incarnation than in some subsequent versions. It ends on the accepted version of 'Opus In Pastels'. Remastering is mostly good, if a little harsh on some tracks.

*****(*) Stan Kenton 1947**
Classics 1011 *Kenton; Buddy Childers, Ray Wetzel, Chico Alvarez, John Anderson, Ken Hanna, Al Porcino (t); Kai Winding, Skip Layton, Milt Bernhart, Harry Forbes, Bart Varsalona, Eddie Bert (tb); Eddie Meyers, Boots Mussulli, George Weidler, Frank Pappalardo (as); Red Doris, Bob Cooper, Vido Musso, Warner Weidler (ts); Bob Gioga (bs); Bob Ahern, Laurindo Almeida (g); Eddie Safranski (b); Shelly Manne (d); Jack Costanzo (perc); June Christy, Don McLeod, The Pastels (v).* 2–9/47.

***** Stan Kenton 1947 Vol. 2**
Classics 1039 *As above, except add Dizzy Gillespie (t), Bill Harris (tb), Buddy DeFranco (cl), Art Pepper (as), Flip Phillips (ts), Nat Cole (p), Billy Bauer (g), Buddy Rich (d), Carlos Vidal, Machito (perc); omit Winding, Layton, Meyers, Mussulli, Doris, Musso, Ahern, Mcleod, The Pastels.* 9–12/47.

Kenton was busy in the studios in 1947 and there are 13 sessions for Capitol spread across these two discs. There are many surprising things in what was an adventurous period for the band. Rugolo's 'Machito' is an astonishing explosion. 'Collaboration' (here in both the rejected and issued versions), the two-part 'Rhythm Incorporated', George Weidler's virtuoso turn on 'Elegy For Alto', Kenton's own curiously effective playing on 'How Am I To Know' and a couple of gorgeous Christy vocals make Classics 1011 a priority for Kentonians. Classics 1039 includes the issued version of Rugolo's 'Monotony' (Charlie Parker: 'Very weird, marvellous idea!'), a fine Pepper solo in 'Unison Riff', Christy at her best in 'I Told Ya I Love Ya, Now Get Out' and 'Lonely Woman', several more full-on Rugolo scores and the kitsch masterpiece that is 'The Peanut Vendor'. Pretty good sound throughout. The Metronome All Stars sit in on one track, which accounts for the presence of the starry names listed in the personnel.

****** The Innovations Orchestra**
Capitol 59965-2 2CD *Kenton; Buddy Childers, Maynard Ferguson, Shorty Rogers, Chico Alvarez, Don Paladino, Al Porcino, John Howell, Conte Candoli, Stu Williamson, John Coppola (t); Milt Bernhart, Harry Betts, Bob Fitzpatrick, Bill Russo, Eddie Bert, Dick Kenney (tb); Bart Varsalona, Clyde Brown, George Roberts (btb); John Graas, Lloyd Otto, George Price (frhn); Gene Englund (tba); Bud Shank, Art Pepper, Bob Cooper, Bart Caldarell, Bob Gioga, Bud Shank (reeds); Laurindo Almeida, Ralph Blaze (g); Don Bagley, Abe Luboff (b); Shelly Manne (d); Carlos Vidal, Ivan Lopez, Stenio Orozo, Jose Oliveira, Jack Costanzo (perc); strings.* 2/50–10/51.

***** Carnegie Hall – October '51**
Hep CD 68 *Similar to above.* 10/51.

***** Stan Kenton 1950**
Classics 1185 *Similar to above discs.* 2/50.

This is all of the LPs *Innovations In Modern Music* and *Stan Kenton Presents*, along with 14 extra tracks, offering a detailed look at Kenton's 1950–51 orchestra – one of his finest. With the swing era gone, and with the harsher propensities of bebop acclimatizing jazz to more oblique areas of expression, there was no need for Kenton to be shy about the kind of scores he offered here; 'Mirage', 'Conflict', 'Solitaire' and 'Soliloquy', where the orchestra was carefully sifted with strings, are intriguing little tone-poems which, for all their occasionally arch details and overreaching style, work well enough to survive the years. There is one of Christy's finest vocals in 'Lonesome Road'; smart scores by Shorty Rogers like 'Jolly Rogers' and 'Round Robin'; Bob Graettinger's eerie 'House Of Strings'; skilful features for Manne, Pepper, Rogers and Ferguson; Bill Russo's lovely 'Ennui', one of four live tracks used to round off the second disc; and the feel of a very considerable orchestra entering its most challenging period, with soloists befitting an important band. Along with *City Of Glass*, this is surely Kenton's most valuable CD entry. Classics 1185 covers the first half of the same material and, while this may appeal to those following the label's sequential offerings, it obviously takes second place to the parent-label edition.

The Hep transcription of a couple of Carnegie Hall concerts emerges as an interesting pendant to the studio sessions. There are the inevitable sonic shortcomings compared to the Capitol dates, and much of it is no more than secondary versions of the studio sides, but there's a movement from 'City Of Glass' and the soloists – Pepper, Candoli, Cooper, Betts – make their mark.

*****(*) Stan Kenton 1950–1951**
Classics 1255 *Kenton; Buddy Childers, Maynard Ferguson, Shorty Rogers, Chico Alvarez, Don Paladino, Jimmy Salko, Al Porcino, John Howell, Ray Wetzel (t); Milt Bernhart, Harry Betts, Bob Fitzpatrick, Bill Russo, Herbie Harper, Eddie Bert, Dick Kenney (tb); Clyde Crown, John Halliburton, Bart Varsalona (btb); John Graas, Lloyd Otto (frhn); Bud Shank (as, f); Art Pepper (as, cl); Bob Cooper (ts, ob, cor); Bart Calderell (ts, bsn); Vido Musso (ts); Bob Gioga (bs, bcl); Nat Cole (p, v); Laurindo Almeida, Ralph Blaze (g); Gene Englund (tba); Don Bagley (b); Shelly Manne (d); June Christy (v); strings.* 5/50–3/51.

*****(*) Stan Kenton 1951**
Classics 1292 *As above except add Conte Candoli, Stu Williamson, John Coppola (t), George Roberts (tb), Paul Wiegand (btb), Stan Fletcher (tba), Abe Luboff (b), Jay Johnson (v), omit Paladino, Porcino, Salko, Wetzel, Harper, Bert, Crown, Varsalona, Musso, Cole, Almeida, Englund.* 3–10/51.

Some measure of Kenton's range can be gleaned from the first tracks on Classics 1255, which start with the Innovations In Modern Music Orchestra tackling five fairly extraordinary charts – before Nat Cole sits in with a version of 'Orange Coloured Sky'. They carry on through most of the rest of the 'Innovations In Modern Music' material. Classics 1292 is entirely different, again, and starts with the hokum of 'Tortillas And Beans', before such vintage pieces as Bob Cooper's feature 'Coop's Solo', three splendid settings for June Christy, solid Capitol singles such as 'Dynaflow' and 'Night Watch', and finally four tracks from a live session by the Innovations In Modern Music Orchestra, convened again. A formidable cross-section of Kenton's work.

**(*) On The Air

Status DSTS 1022 *Kenton; Buddy Childers, Clyde Reasinger, Conte Candoli, Don Dennis, Ruben McFall, Maynard Ferguson, Ray Wetzel, John Howell, Shorty Rogers, Chico Alvarez (t); Bob Burgess, Frank Rosolino, Keith Moon, Bill Russo, Milt Bernhart, Harry Betts, Bob Fitzpatrick, Dick Kenney (tb); George Roberts, Bart Varsalona (btb); Dick Meldonian, Vinnie Dean, Bud Shank, Art Pepper (as); Bill Hilman, Lee Elliot, Bob Cooper, Bart Caldarell (ts); Bob Gioga (bs); Sal Salvador, Ralph Blaze (g); Don Bagley (b); Stan Levey, Shelly Manne (d); Tommy Brown (v).* 3/51–7/52.

*** One Night Stand

Candid Choice CHCD 71051 *Similar to above.* 3/51.

Some good music in these airshots from three different shows – in Hollywood, Catalina Island and Bristol, Connecticut – but the sound, particularly in the second half, is very crackly and thin, spoiling the likes of Art Pepper in 'Pepper Pot'. Bill Russo's score for 'Moonlight In Vermont' and Gerry Mulligan's chart for 'Too Marvellous For Words' are among the saving graces. *One Night Stand* also comes from the Hollywood Palladium and is in rather cleaner sound overall. A decent set of the day.

***(*) New Concepts Of Artistry In Rhythm

Capitol 92865-2 *Kenton; Conte Candoli, Buddy Childers, Maynard Ferguson, Don Dennis, Ruben McFall (t); Bob Fitzpatrick, Keith Moon, Frank Rosolino, Bill Russo (tb); George Roberts (btb); Lee Konitz, Vinnie Dean (as); Richie Kamuca, Bill Holman (ts); Bob Gioga (bs); Sal Salvador (g); Don Bagley (b); Stan Levey (d); Derek Walton (perc); Kay Brown (v).* 9/52.

Laden with top-flight musicians, this was another of Kenton's best bands. There is one arrangement by Bill Holman – the intriguing 'Invention For Guitar And Trumpet' – but most of the scores were penned by Bill Russo, including the glorious kitsch of the opening 'Prologue: This Is An Orchestra!', a kind of Young Person's Guide with Kenton himself narrating and characterizing each member of the band (considering the personalities he's describing, it's both funny and oddly moving at this distance, especially when he calls Frank Rosolino – who would later take his own life – 'this fellow who has few if any moody moments'). The brass section is top-heavy and blows all else before it, but the rhythm section swings hard, and there are some wonderful interjections on almost every piece by the major soloists, especially Salvador on 'Invention', Konitz on 'Young Blood' and 'My Lady', and Rosolino on 'Swing House'. The remastering is bright and just a little harsh in places, but it makes the band sound grandly impressive, which is as it should be.

**** Easy Go

Capitol 24553-2 *As appropriate discs above.* 8/50–3/52.

A smartly compiled set which covers 20 instrumentals, all set down between the first Innovations In Modern Music tour and the New Concepts band of 1952, with the orchestra in its most swinging, straightahead mode. There are charts from Shorty Rogers, Pete Rugolo, Gene Roland, Johnny Richards and Bill Russo, and Stan's own hand is immediately apparent in the relaxed swing of the opening 'Easy Go'. As compiler Michael Sparke suggests, it's 'the perfect CD to play for anyone who says the Kenton band never swings'.

CORE COLLECTION

**** City Of Glass

Capitol 832084-2 *Similar to above discs.* 12/47–5/53.

The 16 pieces arranged by Bob Graettinger which make up this CD number among the most exacting works Kenton was ever responsible for. Graettinger's two major pieces, 'City Of Glass' and 'This Modern World', are extraordinary works – Ellingtonian in their concentration on individuals within the band, yet using the bigger resources of the orchestra to create its own sound-world. All of his 14 originals (there are two arrangements on standards) create their own kind of jazz, and its suitability to Kenton's orchestra might almost be likened to Strayhorn's music for Ellington – except Graettinger was by far the more original thinker. Splendidly remastered, this is an important memorial to a man often forgotten in the annals of jazz composition, and Max Harrison's typically elegant sleeve-note supplies the fine context.

***(*) 'Live' In Munich 1953

Sounds Of Yesteryear DSOIY 608 2CD *Kenton; Buddy Childers, Conte Candoli, Don Dennis, Don Smith, Ziggy Minichiello (t); Bob Burgess, Frank Rosolino, Bill Russo, Keith Moon (tb); Bill Smiley (btb); Lee Konitz, Davey Schildkraut (as); Bill Holman, Zoot Sims (ts); Tony Ferina (bs); Barry Galbraith (g); Don Bagley (b); Stan Levey (d); June Christy (v).* 9/53.

Kenton's European tour of 1953 was a sensation: British fans still talk about making the trip to Dublin to hear him (the MU ban prevented them from playing in London), and the band and their leader were all but mobbed everywhere they went. This concert from the Kongress-Saal Deutsches Museum gets a tumultuous reception and almost every piece is cheered to the echo. Packed with some of the best soloists he could ever boast, this was certainly a vintage edition of Kenton's orchestra, and there are great moments for Konitz ('Lover Man'), Sims ('Zoot') and a sequence of features for Christy, by then working as a solo but persuaded back to join for this tour. Though the sound is clearly from an amateur tape it's survived in pretty good shape, and though the rhythm section has one of those 'stadium' sounds, the soloists and sections come through clearly.

**(*) Let's Go To Town

Magic DAWE 108 *As above except Sal Salvador (g) and June Valli (v) replace Galbraith and Christy.* 9/53.

Four sets for the radio show which was intended to attract recruits to the National Guard, so the announcements by 'Corporal Eddie Carter' (actually an actor, Mason Adams) are here too. June Valli sings on numerous tunes (to the arrangements which she brought) and the Kenton band handle everything like pros. For collectors only.

*** Live At Palo Alto

Status DSTS 1036 *Kenton; Al Porcino, Ed Leddy, Sam Noto, Stu Williamson, Bob Clark (t); Bob Fitzpatrick, Gus Chappell, Kent Larsen, Ted Dechter (tb); Don Kelly (btb); Lennie Niehaus, Charlie Mariano (as); Bill Perkins, Dave Van Kriedt (ts); Don Davidson (bs); Ralph Blaze (g); Max Bennett (b); Mel Lewis (d); Ann Richards (v).* 5/55.

A completely new line-up. Bill Holman's charts are driving the book at this point, although there's still the odd piece from Mulligan and Russo – and Kenton, whose 'Street Of Dreams' score is a highlight. The band sound in very good form at this dance at The Surf Club, Stanford University, and the sound is very clear, although some soloists seem to be badly off-mic at times. Among the soloists, a perhaps surprise stand-out is Lennie Niehaus.

*** At Ernst-Merck-Halle, Hamburg, Germany

Sounds Of Yesteryear DSOD622 2CD *Kenton; Sam Noto, Vinnie Tanno, Lee KatzmanL, Phil Gilbert (t); Bob Fitzpatrick, Kent Larsen, Carl Fontana (tb); Don Kelly (btb); Irving Rosenthal, Fred Fox (frhn); Lennie Niehaus (as); Bill Perkins, Don Rendell (ts); Harry Klein (bs); Ralph Blaze (g); Jay McAllister (tba); Curtis Counce (b); Mel Lewis (d).* 4/56.

A fascinating memento of Kenton's second European tour, given that Britishers Klein and Rendell are in the band, depping for two reed-players who had had to go home. Niehaus and Perkins take solo honours, although Holman's feature for Fontana, 'Carl', is a peach. Not the best sound in this series: Mel Lewis's bass drum sometimes overpowers every section.

***(*) Kenton In Hi-Fi

Capitol 84451-2 *Kenton; Ed Leddy, Dennis Grillo, Lee Katzman, Phil Gilbert, Tom Slaney (t); Archie LeCocque, Kent Larsen, Jim Amlotte (tb); Ken Shroyer (btb); Irving Rosenthal, Joe Mariani (frhn); Lennie Niehaus (as); Bill Perkins, Richie Kamuca (ts); Pepper Adams (bs); Ralph Blaze (g); Jay McAllister (tba); Don Bagley (b); Mel Lewis (d).* 2/56–7/58.

***(*) Live At The Macumba Club Vol. 1

Magic DAWE 48 *As above.* 11/56.

***(*) Live At The Macumba Club Vol. 2

Magic DAWE 49 *As above.* 11/56.

*** Rendezvous Of Standards And Classics

Music For Pleasure 833620-2 2CD *Similar to above discs.* 43–57.

*** Cuban Fire

Capitol 96260-2 *Kenton; Ed Leddy, Sam Noto, Phil Gilbert, Al Mattaliano, Bud Brisbois, Dalton Smith, Bob Rolfe, John Audino, Steve Hofsteter (t); Bob Fitzpatrick, Carl Fontana, Kent Larsen, Don Kelly, Dick Hyde, Ray Sikora (tb); Jim Amlotte, Bob Knight (btb); Dwight Carver, Joe Burnett, Bill Horan, Tom Wirtel, Gene Roland (mel); Gabe Baltazar, Lennie Niehaus (as); Bill Perkins, Lucky Thompson, Sam Donahue, Paul Renzi (ts); Wayne Dunstan (bs, bsx); Billy Root, Marvin Holladay (bs); Ralph Blaze (g); Jay McAllister, Albert Pollan (tba); Curtis Counce, Pete Chivily (b); Mel Lewis, Art Anton (d); Sol Gubin, George Gaber, Tommy Lopez, George Laguna, Roger Mozian, Maro Alvarez, George Acevedo (perc).* 5/56–9/60.

The mid-'50s found Kenton somewhat in transition, from the more stylized West Coast touches of the early-'50s band to another kind of progressive-orchestral music which he had tried in the '40s with mixed results. Live sessions were customarily a blend of straightahead swing variations on standards, the Afro-Cuban element, and Kenton's penchant for orchestral bombast.

The 1956 albums are a patchy group. The two discs from the Macumba Club are a rather motley lot in no more than respectable sound. The two original studio albums are the most important. *Kenton In Hi-Fi* was a hit album for the bandleader and offered a reworking (almost Ellingtonian in intent) of many of his early successes, seeking the crisper definition of LP-era sound. If hardly a dramatic improvement or a startling revision (Kenton kept many of the patterns intact), it reasserts the orchestra's clout on its staple themes. The CD is beefed up with three 1958 tracks. *Cuban Fire* chronicles the arrival of arranger Johnny Richards, who had been studying Latin rhythms and came up with a series of charts which incorporated a six-man percussion team. The results catch much of the undertow of explosive kitsch which Latin bands love, although how 'authentic' it is in other ways is harder to judge. The six later tracks, from 1960, document one of Kenton's so-called 'mellophonium' bands, with five men playing that instrument among what is incredibly a band with 16 brass. Much of it sounds like mood or movie music, taken at tempos which tend towards trudging. The remastering is strong on the brass, but the bass frequencies are less well handled and the percussion section is mixed well off-mic on the earlier session.

Rendezvous Of Standards And Classics is a two-disc set (at bargain price) which collects no fewer than five Capitol albums: *Milestones, Sketches On Standards, Kenton Classics, Portraits On Standards* and *Rendezvous With Kenton.* Familar material and some of the hits dominate the first disc, but most of the rest offers often relatively subdued arrangements of songbook tunes. A nice package for fans, though one slight caveat on the remastering: very shrill on some tracks, with the brass deafening, and misty on others – the power of the band comes through, but not very subtly.

*** Stompin' At Newport

Pablo 5312-2 *Kenton; Ed Leddy, Sam Noto, Billy Catalano, Lee Katzman, Phil Gilbert (t); Kent Larsen, Archie LeCocque, Don Reed, Jim Amlotte (tb); Kenny Shroyer (btb); Lennie Niehaus, Bill Perkins, Bill Robinson, Wayne Dunstan, Steve Perlow (reeds); Red Kelly (b); Jerry McKenzie (d).* 7/57.

*** Live At The Patio Gardens Ballroom Vol. 1

Magic DAWE 56 *As above.* 8/57.

**(*) Live At The Patio Gardens Ballroom Vol. 2

Magic DAWE 57 *As above.* 8/57.

**(*) Live At The Patio Gardens Ballroom Vol. 3

Magic DAWE 58 *As above.* 8/57.

The Newport set comes from a year in which Norman Granz ran the event and insisted on handling all the recording, which meant that sets by people who weren't his artists never got released. Its belated appearance is welcome, though the sleeve-note suggestion that it's in much superior sound to the likes of the Status material simply isn't true. In the end, it's no more than a typical Kenton festival set. The Magic discs cover music from a two-night engagement in Salt Lake City. These are typical Kenton sets for a dancing audience, which means less ambitious programmes, many standards, brief interpretations, careful solos. Given all that, the playing is still pointed and skilful, and Niehaus, Perkins and Noto have many good moments. Sound isn't as good as on some of the Status CDs, but isn't bad. *Volume 1* has the best material.

***** Back To Balboa**
Capitol 96591-2 *Kenton; Jules Chaikin, Bill Catalano, Lee Katzman, Phil Gilbert (t); Kent Larsen, Archie LeCocque, Jim Amlotte, Don Reed (tb); Kenny Shroyer (btb); Lennie Niehaus (as); Bill Perkins, Richie Kamuca (ts); Bill Robinson, Steve Perlow (bs); Red Kelly (b); Jerry McKenzie (d).* 5–6/58.

***** The Ballad Style Of Stan Kenton**
Capitol 56688-2 *As above except add Ed Leddy, Don Fagerquist (t); Bob Fitzpatrick (tb); Mel Lewis (d).* 5–6/58.

Recorded during a disastrous residency at Balboa's Rendezvous Ballroom, when Elvis was decimating the audience for big-band jazz, *Back To Balboa* is an attractive Kenton album, with Johnny Richards setting the band some fearsome tasks in his charts. 'Royal Blue' is a Holman tune where Kenton asked simply for something very fast. The sound is spectacular, perhaps too much so: the surroundings of the Rendezvous seem to turn the brass into something that tires the ears.

Ballad Style is 'Kenton Plays Pretty'. In a way this isn't so different from the kind of easy-listening records that were going under Jackie Gleason's name for Capitol, with the leader the principal soloist and most of the melodies only slightly Kentonized. But it *is* a very pretty record of big-band ballads.

***** Live From The Las Vegas Tropicana**
Capitol 35245-2 *Kenton; Frank Huggins, Bud Brisbois, Jack Sheldon, Joe Burnett, Roger Middleton (t); Archie LeCocque, Kent Larsen, Jim Amlotte (tb); Bob Olsen, Bill Smiley (btb); Lennie Niehaus (as); Richie Kamuca, Bill Trujillo (ts); Billy Root, Sture Swenson (bs); Red Kelly (b); Jerry McKenzie (d).* 2/59.

Stan opens with a self-deprecating announcement to the effect that they're going to try and make a record that sells. Admittedly, there's little from his obviously progressive side to the programme: mostly standards, a few Gene Roland originals, and the band are relatively quiescent, but the playing is up to scratch and a few nice routines, like the piano/bass embellishments on 'Bernie's Tune', give it plenty of appeal.

*****(*) Standards In Silhouette**
Capitol 94503-2 *Kenton; Bud Brisbois, Clyde Reasinger, Dalton Smith, Bill Chase, Rolf Ericson, Roger Middleton (t); Archie LeCocque, Don Sebesky, Kent Larson (tb); Jim Amlotte, Bob Knight (btb); Charlie Mariano (as); Bill Trujillo, John Bonnie (ts); Jack Nimitz, Marvin Holladay (bs); Pete Chivily (b); Jimmy Campbell (d); Mike Pacheco (perc).* 9/59.

***** Adventures In Blues**
Capitol 20089-2 *Kenton; Dalton Smith, Marvin Stamm, Bud Brisbois, Bob Rolfe, Bob Behrendt, Sam Noto, Steve Huffsteter, Norman Baltazar (t); Bob Fitzpatrick, Dee Barton, Bud Parker, Jack Spurlock, Dick Hyde, Ray Sikora (tb); Jim Amlotte, Ray Knight, Dave Wheeler (btb); Gene Roland (mel, ss); Dwight Carver, Joe Burnett, Bill Horan, Tom Wirtel, Keith La Motte, Carl Saunders, Ray Starling (mel); Gabe Baltazar (as); Buddy Arnold, Paul Renzi, Sam Donahue (ts); Marvin Holladay, Allan Beutler (bs); Wayne Dunstan (bsx); Albert Pollan (tba); Pat Senatore, Red Mitchell, Pete Chivily (b); Jerry McKenzie, Art Anton (d).* 9/60–12/61.

***** Adventures In Jazz**
Capitol 21222-2 *As above, except add Joel Kay (bsx); omit Noto, Huffsteter, Hyde, Sikora, Knight, Burnett, Horan, Wirtel, Pollan, Chivily, Anton.* 7–12/61.

Standards In Silhouette is a modest gem in this period of Kenton. The charts were by the 22-year-old Bill Mathieu, and they fashion 'concert' settings for nine ballads, from 'Little Girl Blue' (which is barely recognizable) to John Lewis's 'Django', which survives Kentonization mainly through a beautiful contribution from Charlie Mariano. There are some other good soloists – LeCocque in 'Ill Wind', Roger Middleton on 'The Thrill Is Gone'. It still makes a long haul over CD length, but track by track this is an accomplished and handsome big-band record.

The two *Adventures* records have their moments. The *Blues* set was arranged by Gene Roland, who seldom bothers to tax the resources of this over-resourced band, although he does what he can to vary the sonorities coming out of this brass-heavy orchestra. There were fewer interesting soloists in the band at this point, though, and both this and *Jazz* could use a maverick spirit to cut loose here and there.

****(*) Live In Biloxi**
Magic DAWE 30 *Kenton; Frank Huggins, Bud Brisbois, Jack Sheldon, Billy Catalano, Bob Ojeda (t); Archie LeCocque, Kent Larsen, Jim Amlotte (tb); Bob Olsen, Bill Smiley (btb); Lennie Niehaus (as); Bill Perkins, Bill Trujillo (ts); Bill Robinson, Steve Perlow (bs); Red Kelly (b); Jerry McKenzie (d). c.* 60.

****(*) Return To Biloxi**
Magic DAWE 35 *As above. c.* 60.

***** Live At Barstow 1960**
Status DSTS1001 *Kenton; Bud Brisbois, Dalton Smith, Bill Chase, Rolf Ericson, Danny Nolan (t); Bob Fitzpatrick, Kent Larsen, Bill Smiley (tb); Jim Amlotte, Bob Knight (btb); Lennie Niehaus (as); Bill Trujillo, Ronnie Rubin (ts); Jack Nimitz, Marvin Holladay (bs); Pete Chivily (b); Jimmy Campbell (d); Mike Pacheco (perc).* 1/60.

There is a rash of live material by the Kenton band from this period but several of the better Status CDs seem to have been deleted. The two Biloxi sets – the first is the more progressive material, the second a more standards-orientated session – are recorded mistily and the orchestra comes over rather waywardly. *Live At Barstow* is nearly all standards, with many nice solo spots for Niehaus, Ericson and Trujillo, and the band sound strong on what must have been a dance date for the marine corps.

***** Together**
Sounds Of Yesteryear DSOY 601 *Kenton; Marvin Stamm, Steve Huffsteter, Bob Rolfe, Bud Brisbois, Dalton Smith (t); Gene Roland (mel); Dick Hyde, Jack Redmond, Ray Sikora (tb); Jim Amlotte, Bob Knight (btb); Gabe Baltazar (as); Sam Donahue, Sam Renzi (ts); Marvin Holladay, Wayne Dunstan (bs); Pete Chivily (b); Jerry Mackenzie (d); George Acevedo (perc); June Christy (v).*

A reunion of Stan and June, the occasion being another four National Guard transcription programmes. Not too many surprises in the programme – 'Opus In Chartreuse' is about the only unusual score – but June sounds fine and the sound is good enough.

*****(*) Mellophonium Moods**

Status STCD 106 *Kenton; Dalton Smith, Marvin Stamm, Bob Behrendt, Keith La Motte, Bob Rolfe (t); Gene Roland, Dave Wheeler (btb, tba); Ray Starling, Dwight Carver, Carl Saunders (mel); Bob Fitzpatrick, Dee Barton, Bud Parker (tb); Jim Amlotte (btb); Gabe Baltazar (as); Charlie Mariano, Ray Florian (ts); Allan Beutler (bs); Joel Kaye (bsx); Val Kolar (b); Jerry McKenzie (d).* 3/62.

****(*) 1962**

Sounds Of Yesteryear DSOY 603 *As above except add Jean Turner (v).* 5/62.

****(*) One Night Stand**

Magic DAWE 66 *Similar to above.* 9/61–7/62.

***** More Mellophonium Moods**

Status DSTS1010 *As above, except add Bill Briggs (t), Lou Gasca (mel), Tom Ringo (tb), Bucky Calabrese (b), Bill Blakkested (d), Jean Turner (v); omit Rolfe, Roland, Kolar, McKenzie.* 8/62.

****(*) At The Holiday Ballroom, Northbrook, Chicago**

Status DSTS1018 *As above.* 5/62.

Kenton's 'Mellophonium' band took his fascination with brass to new lengths: there are 15 brass players in both of these bands. The leader's verdict was that the band represented 'the New Era in Modern American Music', but it actually sounds like a beefier, more metallic edition of the old Kentonian machine. By this time Kenton had become entirely *sui generis*, and the prevailing winds of jazz fashion had little effect on the orchestra's direction. But he was still usually on the dinner-dance circuit, and all of these discs contain somewhat rueful admissions from the leader that they'll play something people can dance to, but he wouldn't mind if some people also wanted to listen. No false pride: this was a great, swinging band and, if Kenton had lost most of his best soloists, the features for Baltazar, Mariano and some of the brassmen are handled with great aplomb. The *Mellophonium Moods* set is the best one in terms of fidelity – the sound is quite superb for a supposedly private recording – and, with a higher degree of original material, including a number of Kenton rarities, it's marginally the most interesting musically, too. The two concerts on *One Night Stand* are from AFRS broadcasts from New Jersey, something of a throwback; while the band still sound well, the sound is far below that achieved on the Status CDs. *1962* is from Chicago's Holiday Inn: Jean Turner sings a couple of sexy vocals, and Stan, in a state of complete exasperation, plays a Twist in answer to several requests. *More Mellophonium Moods* doesn't quite have the hi-fi of the other one, but it still sounds pretty good, and there is some lovely playing: Ray Starling takes a perfectly poised solo on 'Misty', and 'Maria' is a resplendent treatment of Johnny Richards's arrangement. The comedy version of 'Tea For Two' is a drawback, though. The same band took to the boards at Northbrook, Chicago, and this time the sound is muzzier and the programme a little lacking in lift. Nevertheless, Status should be congratulated for unearthing so much by this edition of the band.

***** Adventures In Time**

Capitol 55454-2 *Kenton; Dalton Smith, Bob Behrendt, Marvin Stamm, Keith La Motte, Gary Slavo (t); Bob Fitzpatrick, Bud Parker, Tom Ringo (tb); Jim Amlotte (btb); Ray Starling, Dwight Carver, Lou Gasca, Joe Burnett (mel); Dave Wheeler (btb, tba); Gabe Baltazar (as); Don Menza, Ray Florian (ts); Allan Beutler (bs); Joel Kaye (bs, bsx); Bucky Calabrese (b); Dee Barton (d); Steve Dweck (perc).* 9/62.

One of the studio entries by the mellophonium band. The charts are all by Johnny Richards, neither the best nor the worst of Kenton's arranging clique, and their particular trait is a hankering to use as much of this 24-strong band as possible, as much of the time as possible. There's an awful lot of *fff* in the scoring and some of the crescendoes are apocalyptic, even by Kenton's standards. Soloists make their mark – Gabe Baltazar's alto in particular – but this isn't about the jazz improviser, it's about Kentonian hosannas. On those terms, a great one.

***** At Brant Inn 1963**

Sounds Of Yesteryear DSOY 6018 *Kenton; Gary Slkavo, Ronny Ossa, Ron Keller, Bob Behrendt, John Ecqart (t); Jiggs Whigham, Bob Curnow, (tb); Chris Swanson (vtb); Jim Amlotte, Dave Wheeler (btb); Tony Scodwell, Dick Martinez, Bob Faust, Bob Crull (mel); Gabe Baltazar (as); Steve Marcus, Ray Florian (ts); Archie Wheeler (bs); Joel Kaye (bsx, picc); John Worster (b); Dee Barton (d).* 6/63.

Modern times are starting to creep into Stan's music here. Steve Marcus is the first tenorman who sounds as if he's a Coltrane follower, and even Jiggs Whigham is clearly not looking back to the '40s. Less than 40 minutes of music, the brass and reeds sound fine, but the piano sounds like an old upright. For fans only, but in its way, intriguing.

***** A Merry Christmas**

Capitol 92601-2 *As various sessions above.* 10/60–4/63.

Perhaps the strangest jazz Christmas album ever made. Kenton was prevailed upon by Capitol to do it, and he agreed – as long as it was only carols and serious stuff. Surprisingly, it works pretty well, Kenton's baroque leanings coming out to the music's advantage. 'What Is Santa Claus?' is a lighter moment, and it ends on Maynard Ferguson's 'Christmas For Moderns' spectacular. Gorgeous studio sound.

***** Stan Kenton Conducts The Los Angeles Neophonic Orchestra**

Capitol 94502-2 *Kenton; Dalton Smith, Frank Higgins, Gary Barone, Ronnie Ossa, Olie Mitchell (t); Bob Fitzpatrick, Vern Friley, Gil Falco (tb); Jim Amlotte (btb); Vince DeRosa, Bill Hinshaw, John Cave, Richard Perissi, Arthur Maebe (frhn); Bud Shank, Bill Perkins, Bob Cooper, Don Lodice, John Lowe (reeds); Claude Williamson (p); Emil Richards (vib); Dennis Budimir (g); John Worster (b); Nick Ceroli (d); Frank Carlson (perc).* 9/65.

The Neophonic Orchestra was to be permanently based in Los Angeles and would use some of the mass of former Kentonians who'd gone on to regular studio work there. As it happened, this session was a mix of the regular men with old hands such as Shank, Cooper and Perkins. The music came from various hands, including Hugo Montenegro, Jimmy Knight and John Williams, but the only really interesting piece is the bonus track which wasn't even on the original album, Clare Fischer's 'Piece For Soft Brass, Woodwinds And Percussion'. The rest is standard if accomplished Kentonian grandiloquence. Excellent sound.

***** Stan Kenton With The Danish Radio Big Band**

Storyville 101 8340 *Kenton; Palle Mikkelborg, Idrees Sulieman, Allan Botschinsky, Palle Bolvig, Svend Ludvig (t); Torolf Molgaard, John Lind, Ole Kurt Jensen, Poul*

Kjaeldgaard, Steen Engelholt, Helmuth Hansen (tb); Preben Garnov, David Sternbach, Knud Sorenson, Per Larsen (frhn); Uffe Karsov (as, ts); Rolf Billberg, Erling Christensen (as); Bent Jaedig (ts); Bent Nielsen (bs); Ole Molin (g); Niels-Henning Orsted Pedersen (b); Bjarne Rostvold (d); John Steffensen, Per Nielsen (perc). 3/66.

It's interesting to hear how the doughty men of the DRBB coped with some vintage Kenton scores with their distinguished guest leader at this 1966 Copenhagen concert. The music doesn't seem to have given them any real trouble and they even get through all of Johnny Richards's 'Cuban Fire Suite', but the brassy spark which an American orchestra would have brought to these charts is lacking to some extent.

**** At Fountain Street Church Part One**

Status DSTS 1014 *Kenton; Mike Price, Jim Kartchner, Jay Daversa, Carl Leach, John Madrid (t); Dick Shearer, Tom Whittaker, Shelley Denny (tb); Joe Randazzo (btb); Bob Goodwin (btb, tba); Ray Reed (as, f); Mike Altschul, Bob Crosby (ts); Earle Dumler (bs); Bill Fritz (bs, bsx); John Worster (b); Dee Barton (d); Efrain Logreira (perc). 3/68.*

**** At Fountain Street Church Part Two**

Status DSTS 1015 *As above.*

There are some good things here, particularly among the more shaded sections of the arrangements, which catch the band midway between its subtler middle period and the supposed populism of the '70s. But for once Dave Kay's source material let him down: the sound isn't much better than an average bootleg, with balances off and the drums booming like an artillery range.

****(*) At The Pavilion, Hemel Hempstead**

Status DTS1017 *Kenton; Dennis Noday, Paul Adamson, Frank Minear, Mike Snustead, Robert Winiker (t); Dick Shearer, Harvey Coonin, Lloyd Spoon (tb); John Park (as); Chris Galuman (ts, f); Richard Torres, Willie Maiden (ts); Roy Reynolds (bs); John Worster (b); Peter Erskine (d); Ramon Lopez (perc). 2/73.*

***** Live At London Hilton 1973 Vol. I**

Status DSTS1005 *As above. 2/73.*

***** Live At London Hilton Vol. II**

Status DSTS1006 *As above. 2/73.*

***** Live At Carthage College Vol. 1**

Magic DAWE 69 *Kenton; Mike Barrowman, Kevin Jordan, Glenn Stuart, John Harner, Mike Snustead (t); Dick Shearer, Lloyd Spoon, Brett Stamps (tb); Bill Hartman (btb); Mike Wallace (btb, tba); Terry Cooke (as); Richard Torres, Dick Wilkie (ts); Roy Reynolds, Rich Condit (bs); Kirby Stewart (b); Peter Erskine (d); Ramon Lopez (perc). 2/74.*

****(*) Live At Carthage College Vol. 2**

Magic DAWE 70 *As above. 2/74.*

****(*) Plays Chicago**

Creative World STD 1072 *Kenton; John Harner, Dave Zeagler, Mike Barrowman, Mike Snustead, Kevin Jordan (t); Dick Shearer, Lloyd Spoon, Brett Stamps, Bill Hartman (tb); Tony Campise, Greg Smith, Rich Condit, Dick Wilkie, Roy Reynolds (reeds); Mike Wallace (tba); Mike Ross (b); Peter Erskine (d); Ramon Lopez (perc). 6/74.*

****(*) At The Arcadia Theatre 1974**

Magic DAWD 94 2CD *Kenton; John Harner, Dave Zeagler, Mike Barrowman, Kevin Jordan, Tim Hagans (t); Dick Shearer, Lloyd Spoon, Dave Keim, Greg Sorcsek, Mike Suter (tb); Tony Campise, Greg Smith, Rich Condit, Dan Salmasian, Roy Reynolds (reeds); Mike Wallace (tba); Mike Ross (b); Peter Erskine (d); Ramon Lopez (perc). 10/74.*

Like any bandleader working through this period, Kenton had to change and compromise to survive, and the orchestra he worked with through the '70s became as modish and subject to fads as any big-band survivor. But at least Kenton had always stood by his 'progressiveness' and, subject to trashy material and clockwork charts though many of the later records are, the orchestra is no less predictable or bombastic than, say, the Basie band in the same period. Kenton had no charmed team of soloists by now but, as with the Buddy Rich band, he valued precision and overall effect, and all the surviving records (on CD – presumably there is much more that could be reissued) have virtues of their own.

Kenton's own Creative World label seems to have gone into abeyance for now, which leaves out a lot of his later recordings – not that there is exactly a shortfall in his current showing! More live material has appeared on Status and Magic. The British concerts from February 1973 appear in good sound on their respective discs, but since the programme at Hemel Hempstead is largely duplicated on the Hilton show, which is spread across two discs (with a lot of chat, banter and introductions), only fanatics would consider getting both. Each is a decent set, though, with some of Kenton's most jazz-directed charts and Park, Winiker and Torres all taking good turns – Park's feature on 'Street Of Dreams' at the Hilton is a gem. The Carthage College date also sounds full and vivid, with occasional bass-heaviness. The programme is a typically catholic mixture, with 'Peanut Vendor' sitting next to 'MacArthur Park'. Probably for hardcore fans only, well though the band play. At the Arcadia Theatre (in St Charles, Illinois) the programme is very mixed: 'Speak Softly Love' is a cheesy treatment which is suddenly woken up by startling solos from Tony Campise and Kevin Jordan, and set-pieces such as the boring Lopez feature, 'Bogota', mingle with some better music. Overall, though, not a great one.

***** Live At Sunset Ridge Country Club, Chicago**

Magic DAWE 59 *Kenton; Jay Sollenberger, Dave Kennedy, Steve Campos, Tim Hagans, Joe Casano (t); Dick Shearer, Dave Keim, Mike Egan (tb); Allan Morrisey (btb); Doug Purviance (btb, tba); Terry Layne (as); Roy Reynolds, Dan Salmasian (ts); Greg Smith, Alan Yankee (bs); John Worster (b); Gary Hobbs (d); Ramon Lopez (perc). 5/76.*

****(*) Live In Cologne 1976 Vol. 1**

Magic DAWE 64 *As above, except Jeff Uusitalo (tb), Teddy Andersen (ts), Greg Metcalf (bs) replace Keim, Salmasian and Smith. 9/76.*

***** Live In Cologne 1976 Vol. 2**

Magic DAWE 65 *As above. 9/76.*

Two concerts from towards the end of the band's life. Kenton is still reprising his remarks about music for dancing versus music for listening at the start of the Chicago dance date, but he's humorous enough about it, and the band sound very full and strong (though the sound-mix shoves Worster to the very front). Terry Layne sounds good on alto and, though the tempos are easy-going, they don't get slack. The Cologne date is more ambitious, though not necessarily more enjoyable: sound is a bit less palatable, and 'Intermission Riff' on the first disc is a bit of a never-ending story, but the band sound fit and Kenton enjoys it, even though his own health was in serious decline.

***** Live At Newport 1959 – 1963 – 1971**
Jasmine JASBOX 1 3CD *As various discs above.* 7/59–7/71.

Three editions of the Kenton band at three different Newport Festivals. Stan was too ill to attend his own set at the ill-fated 1971 festival, and it does seem to be lacking in sparkle – or, at least, the old man's authority. The earlier sets are decent enough representations. As a bargain-box of live Kenton, a fair enough deal.

*****(*) Live Hits And Rarities**
Status DSTS 1041 *As various Status discs above.* 52–76.

It seems fitting to end this entry with a compilation of what the title says, a track each from the numerous live releases on Dave Kay's Status label, which did much to keep Kenton's music out there in the '80s and '90s. Doubtless dedicated Kentonites will have it all, but it makes for one of the very few long sweeps through the bandleader's career, and there is a bonus version of the previously unreleased 1976 version of 'Mack The Knife'.

A few words to close on the availability or otherwise of some of these discs. Kenton fans are a dedicated lot, and the existence of so many airshot and similar packages should come as no surprise: there are even more which we have not discussed (or, in some cases, heard). The Magic and Status CDs in particular have an in-and-out existence, pressed in limited numbers and, possibly, re-pressed as the occasion demands. For those who really want this material, you may sometimes have to be patient.

Freddie Keppard (1890–1933)

CORNET

A bandleader in New Orleans at 16, Keppard was touring by 1910, his massive sound shaking up the pre-jazz scene. Secretive about his own playing, he missed the chance to record early and in the '20s was overtaken by Armstrong and others, alcoholism adding to his decline. He died of TB in Chicago.

*****(*) The Complete Set 1923–1926**
Retrieval RTR 79017 *Keppard; Elwood Graham, James Tate (c); Fred Garland, Eddie Vincent, Fayette Williams, Eddie Ellis (tb); Jimmie Noone (cl, as, v); Clifford King (cl, as); Johnny Dodds, Angelo Fernandez (cl); Joe Poston (as); Jerome Pasquall, Norval Mortroin (ts); Arthur Campbell, Antonia Spaulding, Adrian Robinson, Jimmy Blythe (p); Jimmy Bell (vn); Stan Wilson, Erskine Tate (bj); Bill Newton (tba); Bert Greene, Jasper Taylor, Jimmy Bertrand (d); Papa Charlie Jackson (v).* 6/23–1/27.

One of the great unanswerable questions in jazz is how good Freddie Keppard really was. The second 'King' of New Orleans cornet, after Buddy Bolden and before Joe Oliver, his handful of records offer ambiguous evidence for his stature and suggest a musician who cottoned on to ragtime but never quite got a grip on jazz, or at least on where it was going. He has a big, jabbing sound, when you can hear him – more often than not he's hidden in several of these groups – and cut loose from his surroundings he can work up some genuine excitement. That happens only a few times on the 24 tracks which are his entire legacy, and even then his presence on a few of them is doubtful. The bigger-band sides with Doc Cook and Erskine Tate are often a disappointing lot, and one has to turn to the small-group performances with Jimmy Blythe, Jasper Taylor and Keppard's own Jazz Cardinals to hear him working at something like optimum level, in the rough-and-ready Chicago jazz of the day.

The Retrieval edition is so well remastered that it made us reconsider our verdict on Keppard. The Doc Cook band numbers have never sounded finer, and even the Erskine Tate tracks from 1923 stand up much better than before. One still needs ears sympathetic to the music of that day, but more than any other previous issue this brings Keppard back to life.

Barney Kessel (1923–2004)

GUITAR

Born in Muskogee, Oklahoma, Kessel was playing in big bands in Los Angeles in the mid-'40s. He spent much of the next two decades doing studio work but also led many sessions of his own, and he formed The Pollwinners Trio with Ray Brown and Shelly Manne. He continued touring until 1992, when he suffered a stroke.

***** Easy Like**
Original Jazz Classics OJC 153 *Kessel; Bud Shank, Buddy Collette (as, f); Harold Ross, Claude Williamson (p); Harry Babasin (b); Shelly Manne (d).* 11/53–2/56.

***** Plays Standards**
Original Jazz Classics OJC 238 *Kessel; Bob Cooper (ts, ob); Claude Williamson, Hampton Hawes (p); Monty Budwig, Red Mitchell (b); Shelly Manne, Chuck Thompson (d).* 6–7/54.

*****(*) To Swing Or Not To Swing**
Original Jazz Classics OJC 317 *Kessel; Harry 'Sweets' Edison (t); Georgie Auld, Bill Perkins (ts); Jimmy Rowles (p); Al Hendrickson (g); Red Mitchell (b); Irv Cottler (d).* 6/55.

***** Music To Listen To Barney Kessel By**
Original Jazz Classics OJC 746 *Kessel; Buddy Collette, Jules Jacob, George Smith, Howard Terry, Justin Gordon, Ted Nash (reeds); André Previn, Jimmy Rowles, Claude Williamson (p); Buddy Clark, Red Mitchell (b); Shelly Manne (d).* 8–12/56.

'The blues he heard as a boy in Oklahoma, the swing he learned on his first band job and the modern sounds of the West Coast school': Nesuhi Ertegun's summary of Kessel, written in 1954, still holds as good as any description. Kessel has often been undervalued as a soloist down the years: the smoothness and accuracy of his playing tend to disguise the underlying weight of the blues which informs his improvising, and his albums from the '50s endure with surprising consistency. *Easy Like*, with flute by Shank and Collette, is a little too feathery, but the guitarist's clean lines spare little in attack and the terrific 'Vicky's Dream' emerges as furious bop. The two subsequent albums suggest a firm truce between Basie-like small-band swing – hardly surprising with Edison on hand – and the classic West Coast appraisal of bop. The inclusion of such ancient themes as 'Louisiana', 'Twelfth Street Rag' and 'Indiana' suggests the breadth of Kessel's interests and, although most of the tracks are short, nothing seems particularly rushed. Lester Koenig's superb production has been faithfully maintained for the reissues: Manne, especially, is well served by the engineering. *Music To Listen To Barney Kessel By* sweetens the mix by sticking to cute woodwind and reed arrangements of familiar tunes while Kessel swings smilingly through it; nothing demanding, but it's done so breezily that it cuts most of the so-called easy-listening jazz of recent years.

★★★(★) The Poll Winners
Original Jazz Classics OJC 156 *Kessel; Ray Brown (b); Shelly Manne (d). 3/57.*

★★★ The Poll Winners Ride Again
Original Jazz Classics OJC 607 *As above. 8/58.*

★★★(★) Poll Winners Three
Original Jazz Classics OJC 692 *As above. 11/59.*

Since Kessel, Brown and Manne regularly scored high in jazz fans' polls of the day, Contemporary's decision to record them as a trio was commercially impeccable. But they were a committed musical group too. *The Poll Winners* includes jamming on 'Satin Doll' and 'Mean To Me' which is sophisticated enough to imply a telepathy between Kessel and Manne. But the group push harder on the remaining records, although *Ride Again* includes some weak material. The superb studio sound highlights inner detail.

★★★ Let's Cook!
Original Jazz Classics OJC 970 *Kessel; Frank Rosolino (tb); Ben Webster (ts); Victor Feldman (vib); Jimmy Rowles, Hampton Hawes (p); Leroy Vinnegar (b); Shelly Manne (d). 8–11/57.*

★★ Plays Carmen
Original Jazz Classics OJC 269 *Kessel; Ray Linn (t); Harry Betts (tb); Buddy Collette (cl, f); Bill Smith (cl, bcl); Jules Jacobs (cl, ob); Pete Terry (bcl, bsn); Herb Geller (as); Justin Gordon (ts, f); Chuck Gentry (bs); André Previn (p); Victor Feldman (vib); Joe Mondragon (b); Shelly Manne (d). 12/58.*

★★★ Some Like It Hot
Original Jazz Classics OJC 168 *Kessel; Joe Gordon (t); Art Pepper (cl, as, ts); Jimmy Rowles (p); Jack Marshall (g); Monty Budwig (b); Shelly Manne (d). 3–4/59.*

★★★ Swingin' Party!
Original Jazz Classics OJC 1066 *Kessel; Marvin Jenkins (p, f); Gary Peacock (b); Ron Lundberg (d). 7/60.*

★★★ Workin' Out!
Original Jazz Classics OJC 1061. *Kessel; Marvin Jenkins (p, f); Jerry Good (b); Stan Pepper (d). 1/61.*

★★★ The Artistry Of Barney Kessel
Contemporary 60-021 *As OJC albums listed above.*

Let's Cook! Offers a couple of tracks where Barney jams with a band including Rosolino, Webster and Rowles: an unusual line-up (playing 'Tiger Rag'!) which has its moments. The rest is a more conventional quintet with Feldman and Hawes. Enjoyable if largely unexciting. The *Carmen* album was a cute idea that might best have stayed as no more than that, although Kessel gives it enough dedication to create some typical swinging blues out of the likes of 'Carmen's Cool'. *Some Like It Hot* works much better, since this set of tunes from the then-hit film offered the kind of new-lamps-for-old which Kessel had already been trying on earlier records. Pepper shines on all three horns, Gordon contributes some acrid solos on one of his rare appearances on record, and Kessel experiments with three different guitars and a couple of duo-only tunes. 'Runnin' Wild', taken at a blistering pace, is a tiny gem.

Swingin' Party! has a studio audience to applaud, and works up a fine head of steam on Milt Jackson's 'Bluesology' and Brownie's 'Joy Spring', with the young Peacock sounding very good; but Jenkins is no great shakes at the piano and his flute feature is querulous. *Workin' Out!* finds Kessel starring in front of a very workmanlike quartet. *The Artistry Of* is a user-friendly selection from the OJC albums and is an effective sampler of the period.

★★(★) Breakfast At Tiffany's / Bossa Nova / Contemporary Latin Rhythms
Collectables COL-CD-2857 2CD *Kessel; Conte Candoli (t); Bud Shank (as, f); Paul Horn (saxes, picc); Ray Johnson (org); Emil Richards (marim); Victor Feldman (vib, marim); Al Hendrickson, Bill Pitman (g); Chuck Berghofer, Red Mitchell (b); Earl Palmer, Stan Levey (d); Frank Capp, Edward Talamantes, Francisco Aguabella (perc). 1/62–63.*

Three albums which Kessel made for Reprise, here collected into a two-CD package. They're very much period pieces. *Tiffany's* is a typical jazz-version-of-a-hit-soundtrack. The *Bossa Nova* date is a bit of a misnomer, since Kessel is asked to play rock'n'roll licks over a big-band beat which has a vague hint of the bossa rhythm about it. Despite the snootily academic title, the *Latin Rhythms* set is a pop-goes-Latin affair where the likes of 'Blues In The Night' and 'The Peanut Vendor' get a nattily groovy update for bachelor hipsters to play in their pads. Kessel gets in a few decent passages here and there, but this is strictly kitschville.

★★★(★) Feeling Free
Original Jazz Classics OJC 1043 *Kessel; Bobby Hutcherson (vib); Chuck Domanico (b); Elvin Jones (d). 2/69.*

★★★ The Poll Winners / Straight Ahead
Original Jazz Classics OJC 409 *Kessel; Ray Brown (b); Shelly Manne (d). 7/75.*

Kessel spent most of the '60s as a studio session guitarist. *The Poll Winners* reunion is as good as their earlier records, yet looser, less drilled. 'Caravan' and 'Laura' become springboards for playing as freely as they ever could together.

The odd one out is *Feeling Free*, as unbuttoned a record as Kessel ever made. As ever, Jones makes a huge amount of noise which the guitarist does his best to ride over, and with Hutcherson also in volatile mood (though less well served by the recording) this is excitingly spontaneous. The material is rather drab – a couple of blues, 'This Guy's In Love With You' and 'The Sounds Of Silence' – but the group plays with real involvement, as if to see what they could make out of a situation which in other hands would have been just another pop-jazz date.

★★★ Solo
Concord CCD 4221 *Kessel (g solo). 4/81.*

Kessel's only solo album isolates the virtues and the vulnerabilities of his art. In an age of superfast guitarists and everyday eclectics, Kessel's simplicity and trust in his touch seem almost elemental. On a ballad like 'What Are You Doing The Rest Of Your Life?' he treats the melody like a recitalist, brushing through it, the soul of discretion. His finger technique makes you feel the physicality of the guitar, and the strumming on the up-tempo section of 'Manha De Carnaval' reminds one that he helped establish the grammar for rock'n'roll guitar, playing on some of the Coasters' classic sides. He touches on bebop almost as an aside, and one can hear him thinking back to Charlie Christian some of the time. This is the most unpretentious of solo records and, while nothing like a masterpiece, it affords much pleasure.

★★★(★) **Red Hot And Blues**
Contemporary 14044 *Kessel; Kenny Barron (p); Bobby Hutcherson (vib); Rufus Reid (b); Ben Riley (d). 88.*

Poor health curtailed Kessel's playing, and this was his farewell. *Red Hot And Blues* puts him in front of a superb band and, with Hutcherson and Barron in aristocratic form, the music teases Barney out of his shell a little on the likes of 'Barniana', while the blues themes get a timeless treatment. A great one to close on.

Keystone Trio

GROUP

Top-of-the-line piano trio, living up to its on-paper promise.

★★★★ **Heart Beats**
Milestone MCD 9256 *John Hicks (p); George Mraz (b); Idris Muhammad (d); Freddy Cole (v). 12/95.*

★★★★ **Newklear Music**
Milestone MCD 9270 *As above, except omit Cole. 2/97.*

The odd, electric-motor sound is the authors purring. This is piano-trio jazz of the very highest quality, two records which just beg to be played again and again. Hicks has his critics, some of whom condemn him for insubstantiality. This, we think, is missing the point. Almost always, he is more concerned to work within the dimensions of a song than to go off into the stratosphere. On *Heart Beats* he is admirably disciplined, relying on the exquisitely toned Mraz for counter-lines and embellishment. The opening 'Speak Low' is a *tour de force* and 'How Deep Is The Ocean?' wrings more feeling out of that rather tired song than any group we have heard in years.

As the awkwardly punning title suggests, the later record is a tribute to the music of Sonny Rollins, and a highly adventurous sampling of Newk's workbook at that: 'O.T.Y.O.G.', 'Times Slimes', 'Wynton', the inevitable 'Airegin', and others. The initial idea for the project came from session producer Todd Barkan, who is responsible for a pristine sound, and it comes to mark the great man's 25 years with the label. If people think of him as a saxophonist first and foremost and a composer only in a somewhat pragmatic sense, this is the record which may reshape that consensus. What is immediately clear is that Newk writes *songs*, not chord shapes. Hicks and Mraz intuit that and build on them gracefully. Muhammad provides the appropriate rhythmic impulse, and the results could hardly be better. The pianist signs off with 'Love Not For Sonny', a piece that bears more than a passing resemblance to his own classic 'Naima's Love Song', and none the worse for that.

Steve Khan (born 1947)

GUITAR

Born in Los Angeles, Khan arrived in New York in 1970 and did session-man chores on both pop and jazz records. Made several fusion records in the '80s, but subsequently returned to straight-ahead guitar styles.

★★★(★) **Tightrope**
Columbia 496852-2 *Khan; Randy Brecker (t); David Sanborn (as); Michael Brecker (ts); David Spinozza, Jeff Mironov (g); Bob James, Don Grolnick (ky); Will Lee (b); Steve Gadd (d); Ralph McDonald (perc). 77.*

★★★ **The Blue Man**
Columbia 496853-2 *As above, except add Rick Marotta (perc). 78.*

★★★★ **Got My Mental**
Evidence ECD 22197-2 *Khan; John Patitucci (b); Jack DeJohnette (d); Cafe (perc, v); Don Alias, Bobby Allende, Marc Quinones (perc). 9/96.*

Khan's occasional adventures in fusionland are far behind him by now, but his progress through the '80s and '90s is now hard to follow since many of his records have been deleted. However, Columbia have unexpectedly restored two of his earliest efforts to the catalogue (although they are already becoming difficult to find – collectors beware). These were heady days for this kind of fusion, and the music holds up surprisingly well, particularly on *Tightrope*. Khan rounded up the princes of the New York studio gang for these sessions and, with Sanborn and both Breckers at their (comparatively) youthful best, the music has a tough urban edge to go with the top-of-the-line chopsmanship. Maybe the subsequent *The Blue Man* is a little more standardized (how quickly fusion tumbled into clichédom!) but both discs are frequently electrifying in all senses.

Khan's Verve albums have been given the axe, but his newer label brought off his best record for years in *Got My Mental*. The nucleus of Khan, Patitucci and DeJohnette play with stunning authority. Ornette Coleman's 'R.P.D.D.' is beautifully stretched out, light yet intense. 'The Last Dance' and 'I Have Dreamed' are gorgeous ballads, the latter glimpsed through a pollen drift of percussion that seems unlikely yet works superbly. 'Paraphernalia' and 'Cunning Lee' are full-blooded jazz performances that are perfectly weighted. DeJohnette, who can often be overpowering in the studio, is at his most subtle and searching throughout and Patitucci seems twinned with the guitarist's lines. A very fine disc. We're waiting for something new from Steve.

David Kikoski (born 1961)

PIANO

After studying at Berklee, Kikoski worked for a while on the Boston scene before moving to New York, where he worked with Roy Haynes and David Sanchez. Now an in-demand sideman in the city.

★★★(★) **Inner Trust**
Criss Cross 1148 *Kikoski; Ed Howard (b); Leon Parker (d). 12/97.*

★★★ **The Maze**
Criss Cross 1168 *Kikoski; Seamus Blake (ts); Scott Colley (b); Jeff 'Tain' Watts (d). 6/98.*

★★★★ **Almost Twilight**
Criss Cross 1190 *Kikoski; John Patitucci (b); Jeff 'Tain' Watts (d). 12/99.*

★★★(★) **Surf's Up**
Criss Cross 1208 *As above, except James Genus (b) replaces Patitucci. 1/01.*

Kikoski's sole album for a major label (*David Kikoski*, made for Columbia/Epic in 1993) took him precisely nowhere, and typically it's been left to a European-owned label to document the leadership records of a considerable American player. *Inner Trust* documents a superb but one-off trio: Howard and Kikoski worked together in the Roy Haynes band for many years, and Parker was with the pianist in the Sanchez band. It's a handsome repertory record where all the music seems to flow freely under the fingers of the musicians: Monk's 'We See' is as sprightly as 'You Don't Know What Love Is' is flowingly lyrical, the melody voiced in a way that offsets the normally dolorous feel of the song. Parker plays some remarkable things, not least on Kikoski's original title-track.

Writing is, indeed, a strength of the pianist, and he even gets away with an all-original programme for both *The Maze* and *Almost Twilight*. The former is slightly undone by Blake's rather faceless offerings as the sole horn, although the material has much food for thought, especially the opening 11-bar blues 'revival' and the ensuing 'Puddles Of Memory'. *Almost Twilight* is, by contrast, almost overpowering in its assurance. Watts and Patitucci are fail-safe pros who need something out of the ordinary to make them sit up and play above themselves, and they get it with the leader's material as well as his own playing. Clever, musicianly stuff like the oddly timed 'Water' is part of the story, but Kikoski is good at making this kind of music speak for itself in a clear voice, and he refuses to obfuscate what could be merely inscrutable jazz. 'Blues In The Face' is a classic essay, and the closing 'Immediacy', fast enough to make the unwary giddy, is showing off at a sublime level.

Surf's Up is perhaps not quite so good, but it might be the best place to start for listeners looking for a few signposts, since Kikoski picks some smart pieces to cover. Brian Wilson's title-tune is a pretty daring choice, even if the pianist doesn't finally convince of its jazz-worthiness, but Frank Zappa's 'Oh No' comes over as a melody just waiting for this treatment, and Jackie McLean's 'Little Melonae' is turned into something surprisingly spare, even desolate. Another powerful entry from a musician who's surely in his prime.

Rebecca Kilgore (born 1949)

VOCAL

Previously a computer programmer, Kilgore took up singing part-time in 1980 and worked in and around Portland, Oregon. She now sings full-time and specializes in vintage repertory.

***** I Saw Stars**
Arbors ARCD 19136 *Kilgore; Dan Barrett (t, tb); Scott Robinson (cl, ts, bsx); Chuck Wilson (as); David Frishberg (p); Bucky Pizzarelli (g); Michael Moore (b).* 4/94.

*****(*) Not A Care In The World**
Arbors ARCD 19169 *Kilgore; David Frishberg (p); Dan Faehnle (g).* 11/95.

****** Rebecca Kilgore**
Jump JCD 12-22 *Kilgore; Dan Barrett (c, tb); Bob Reitmeier (cl, ts); Keith Ingham (p).* 10/98.

Becky Kilgore isn't a profound singer, at least not in the way we understand Billie Holiday and Sarah Vaughan to be, but she has enormous charm and a sweet control over her material that make these entries unfailingly enjoyable. The first finds her matched with one of Dan Barrett's swing groups, and they sparkle on his canny arrangements of standards and obscurities. If it all sounds a fraction precise and calculated, it must be because this kind of repertory date has become a commonplace in its craft and sunny expertise; labels like Arbors, Concord and Nagel-Heyer have done so many similar projects of late.

We prefer the duets with Frishberg (Faehnle sits in on about half of the record). The pianist and singer work regularly together and there is a free-flowing empathy between them that makes the music almost sing itself. Out of 22 songs, several of them medleyed, more than half are rarely encountered nuggets from long ago, and Kilgore's fresh voice renews their acquaintance with perfect *brio*. When she gets to a wistful one, 'Talkin' To Myself About You', it's surprisingly affecting. Frishberg proves himself again to have no peers as an accompanist.

Appropriate that the Jump CD was recorded at the Manchester Craftsmen's Guild. The music is sheer unpretentious class, as close to perfect as a repertory CD can be. Barrett and Ingham confect little arrangements for 18 songs, of which only 'Just You, Just Me' could be called even close to hackneyed, and Becky's clear, melodious voice sings through the lyrics without any trace of routine. She finds a poignancy in 'Very Good Advice' which makes one wonder why this song is so obscure, and even the cutesy 'Ain't We Got Fun' has a dignity about it. And the instrumentalists are in superb fettle.

*****(*) The Starlit Hour**
Arbors ARCD 19255 *Kilgore; David Frishberg (p).* 2/97.

*****(*) Harlem Butterfly**
Audiophile ACD-308 *Kilgore; Bobby Gordon (cl); Chris Dawson (p); Hal Smith (d).* 4/00.

*****(*) Rebecca Kilgore With The Keith Ingham Sextet**
Jump JCD 12-24 *Kilgore; Joe Wilder (t); Ken Peplowski (cl, ts); Keith Ingham (p); Gene Bertoncini (g); Frank Tate (b); Steve Little (d).* 2/01.

Recorded on the final night of the duo's residency at Portland's Heathman Hotel, *The Starlit Hour* is delightful. Francis Davis makes the point in his sleeve-notes that Kilgore never resorts to any kind of melodrama, so even the likes of 'It's The Talk Of The Town' are swinging and upbeat, almost in defiance of the lyrics. Yet she never does anything but put herself at the service of the song. Her control of pitch and way with time are unfussily exact, and though Frishberg can sometimes challenge an unwary performer, there's never anything less than ideal communication between the two, even on comparatively rare songs such as 'Not Mine' and 'I Hear The Music Now'. The perfunctory audience noise and applause is a distraction, though; it feels almost tacked on to such agreeable performances.

Four years on, the Jump session continues the good work of the earlier disc with Ingham, although a few of the arrangements work a little too cleverly, as if the pianist were trying too hard to gild some of these lilies; and three instrumental interludes weren't needed – they only make you impatient for Becky to return. She's at her most persuasive on 'For You, For Me, For Evermore', and again there are some entrancing finds in the songlist: 'Make With The Kisses' and 'You Say The Sweetest Things, Baby' are two.

In between, Kilgore paid gentle homage to that gentlest of singers, Maxine Sullivan. The feel of *Harlem Butterfly* is so smilingly laid-back that the music sometimes approximates the horizontal, but it lets Becky get into her sultriest threads for 'When A Woman Loves A Man', and 'Enjoy Yourself' seems to be sprung off a calypso beat. Gordon sounds like a dozing Pee

Wee Russell and Dawson and Smith get up to some interesting business when they get the chance. But it's the singer's show, and quite right too.

Soweto Kinch

ALTO SAXOPHONE, VOCAL

Working until recently out of Birmingham, this young British saxman mixes straightahead and hip-hop influences into a personal synthesis which has excited much attention in the UK.

***** Conversations With The Unseen**

Dune CD08 *Kinch; Abram Wilson (t, v); Femi Temowo (g); Michael Olatuja (b); Troy Miller (d); Eska Mtungwazi (v).* 12/02–1/03.

A fresh, smart debut by this talented saxophonist. A lot of what he plays still has the feel of sessions of practice in it, but he's already thinking his way into more original settings, and the deftly inserted flavours of hip hop which bubble through every so often are more striking given that basically he's a hardcore alto man with nods to cool-school players as much as anything more modish. The band are somewhat less impressive, and they're asked to provide a sometimes unambitious support, with Miller not exactly the most swinging drummer on record. The most interesting partnership here is with Temowo. The record attracted a great deal of attention more for who he is than the content, and he'll surely make stronger and more durable music than this.

Niki King

VOCAL

Vocalist at work on the contemporary Scottish scene, here making her debut on record.

*****(*) Azure Caber**

Vocl 002 *King; Ryan Quigley (t); Chris Greive (tb); Marcus Ford (g); Ed Kelly (b); David Robertson (perc).* 03.

King's impressive debut works some absorbing variations on the singer-standards record. Although standards dominate the record, they do so in a curiously sidelong way: her own 'Winter Blues' and an unfamiliar song called 'Ordinary Fool' make some of the strongest impact, Ellington's 'Azure' (rarely done by singers) is a beautiful touch, and 'Estate', done slowly and at a level barely above a whisper – King is especially good at singing quietly – is really exquisite. She handles the opening measures of 'The Very Thought Of You' entirely alone, and her trace of an accent adds to the individuality. Ford's guitar is the key instrument in the accompaniments (trumpet and trombone are used very sparingly) and the overall sparseness of both music and interpretation sets the disc apart from the abundant tide of new jazz vocal sets. A fine beginning.

Peter King (born 1940)

ALTO AND SOPRANO SAXOPHONES, CLARINET

Born in Kingston, Surrey, King was still a teenager when he opened at the Ronnie Scott Club in 1959. For many years a straightforward bebopper, playing in countless bands and situations as a sideman, King has gradually taken on more recent influences and has begun to assemble a body of recorded work under his own leadership.

*****(*) East 34th Street**

Spotlite SPJ-CD 24 *King; John Horler (p); Dave Green (b); Spike Wells (d).* 1/83.

***** Brother Bernard**

Miles Music MM CD 076 *King; Guy Barker (t); Alan Skidmore (ts); John Horler (p); Dave Green (b); Martin Drew, Tony Levin (d).* 88–89.

***** Tamburello**

Miles Music MM CD 083 *King; Steve Melling (p, ky); James Hellawell (ky); Alec Dankworth (b); Stephen Keogh (d, perc).* 10/94.

King remains Britain's most eminent keeper of the bebop alto flame. Although his recent work has sought wider fields and a way out of perceived restrictions, the best and most convincing music on most of the available records under his own name remains broadly in the bebop idiom.

It's good to have the Spotlite LP back in circulation. This presented King's working group of the period and is the best of four Spotlite records. If it seemed comparatively plain in its time, the resounding impact of King's playing seems more impressive at this distance. There are six originals, each just individual enough to take the context out of the ordinary, and the saxophonist's brimming virtuosity goes in tandem with an inner calm that gives the music a satisfying depth.

Brother Bernard includes extended solos on 'Overjoyed' and 'But Beautiful' which offer intensely lucid thinking on fertile melodies, but the rhythm section contribute facelessly admirable support and the guest spots by Barker and Skidmore add little except extra weight. *Tamburello* is a deal more ambitious yet doesn't hang together very well as an album. Fine improvisations on Wayne Shorter's 'Yes And No' and McCoy Tyner's 'You Taught My Heart To Sing' sit alongside a couple of diffident King originals and arrangements on Bartók and Purcell, with the final four tracks standing as a linked meditation on the death of Ayrton Senna. Touchingly effective in parts, but too much of the music is compromised by the electric keyboards. It's not that their presence is disagreeably 'modern', but that they're just not recorded or mixed with any subtlety. When King gets clear space and plays, he still sounds terrific.

***** Speed Trap**

Jazz House 41 *King; Gerard Presencer (t); Steve Melling (p); Alec Dankworth (b); Steven Keogh (d).* 96.

Recorded at Ronnie Scott's (where another unrelated Pete King is manager), this is a fine set by an established group. Mixing originals like the fiery title-piece with standards ('My Man's Gone Now') and modern jazz repertoire (Coltrane's love theme 'Naima') King puts the group through their paces. Presencer is superb in the ensembles though possibly a little reserved in his solo spots, while Melling and Dankworth keep things tight but not restricted at the back. The only slight question mark is Keogh's drumming, but this is the fault of the recording rather than the player. There is some distortion around his cymbal work that makes his contribution harder to assess. Otherwise, the sound is pretty faithful and captures a hot and even stormy night at the famous club.

★★★ Lush Life

Miles Music MM CD085 *King; Gerard Presencer (t); Steve Melling, Gordon Beck (p); Steve Hamilton (ky); Jeremy Brown (b); Stephen Keogh (d); Lyric String Quartet.* 7/98.

King's own playing remains a marvellous burst of saxophone sound. But he is still searching for something which suggests a more meaningful context as far as records are concerned, and we are unconvinced by some of these settings. For a bebop disciple, it's noticeable how much King is taking on later influences: Coltrane looms large over the intense soprano improvisation on 'Ronnie's Sorrow', and the solo treatment of 'Lush Life', if a bit rehearsed in feel, is something new in his work on record. Yet it's still the straightahead burners such as 'Flying Scotsman' which carry the most pleasure. Perhaps Peter's version of 'Nefertiti', a clever paraphrase of the composer's ideas, is the track which best suggests how he might make the recorded masterpiece which he must have in him.

John Kirby (1908–52)

BASS

Joined Fletcher Henderson in 1930 and then in various bands until scoring a big hit with a small group at the Onyx Club in 1937, with Charlie Shavers and latterly vocals by Maxine Sullivan. Very successful until the '40s, then drifted into a decline which ended with his death from diabetes in California.

★★★(★) John Kirby, 1938–39

Classics 750 *Kirby; Charlie Shavers (t); Buster Bailey (cl); Russell Procope (as); Billy Kyle (p); O'Neil Spencer (d, v).* 10/38–10/39.

★★★(★) John Kirby 1939–41

Classics 770 *As above.* 10/39–1/41.

★★★ John Kirby, 1941–43

Classics 792 *Kirby; Charlie Shavers (t); Buster Bailey (cl); George Johnson, Russell Procope (as); Clyde Hart, Billy Kyle (p); Bill Beason, Specs Powell, O'Neil Spencer (d, v).* 7/41–12/43.

They played in white ties and tails – and they often sounded that way – but the Kirby Sextet has exerted a small and subtle influence on the jazz of the '80s and '90s, a cool, sometimes almost chill sound that was utterly unfashionable for the better part of 40 years. The original septet, led by Buster Bailey, shed a member and Kirby (a better organizer and front man, despite his instrument) was appointed leader. Many of the early arrangements are, surprisingly, credited to Charlie Shavers, and it's fascinating to hear him sound so well-mannered, both with horn and with pencil. Titles like 'Opus 5', 'Impromptu' and 'Nocturne' on Classics 750 point to classical sources and ambitions for some of the material; the earlier 'Anitra's Dance' sounds like Grieg, and there are borrowings from Schubert, Chopin ('The Minute Waltz', alas) and Dvořák elsewhere. There's a simple reason for this: an ASCAP ban meant that groups could only perform out-of-copyright material.

★★★(★) John Kirby, 1945–46

Classics 964 *Kirby; Emmett Berry, Clarence Brereton, George Taitt (t); Buster Bailey (cl); Hilton Jefferson, George Johnson (as); Budd Johnson (ts); Billy Kyle, Roger 'Ram' Ramirez, Hank Jones (p); Bill Beason (d); Shirley Moore, Sarah Vaughan (v).* 4/45–9/46.

At the end of the war the Kirby band reinvented itself, with a new, fuller sound that combined some of the strengths of the old line-up, but also with a richer and darker palette. Budd Johnson's tenor is oily and intensely coloured, perfectly suited to 'Mop Mop' and 'K. C. Caboose' on the solitary 1945 session, less so to 'Passipied'. Kirby had made some V-Discs during the war, but he found his activities a little restricted at war's end. The following year began with a session backing Sarah Vaughan on four sides for Crown. She is very much the focus, and the arrangements are unusually formulaic in response; they're a little off the money on 'It Might As Well Be Spring', but Sassy more than makes up the deficit. Working from a lower league, Shirley Moore is included on two tracks from the April session, and there is also a single track ('Freedom Blues', which was done for Danish Baronet) on which the nominal leadership reverts to Buster Bailey. The final session – indeed the final date under Kirby's name – is an oddity, reworked versions of Sextet staples like 'Schubert's Serenade' and 'Sextet From Lucia', as well as the Jones/Kirby 'Ripples'. The main point of interest is the participation of Hank Jones, sounding very different indeed from his mature self.

★★★ Complete Associated Transcriptions: Volume 1 – 1941

Storyville 2047 *As for the above.* 41.

★★★ Complete Associated Transcriptions: Volume 2 1941–1943

Storyville 2052 *As above.* 41–43.

★★★ Complete Associated Transcriptions: Volume 3 1943–1944

Storyville/Jazz Unlimited 2058 *As above.* 43–44.

★★★ John Kirby And His Orchestra, 1941–1942

Circle 14 *As above.* 41–42.

There wasn't much to choose between the Kirby Sextet in the studio and on the stand, so these radio transcriptions are somewhat beside the point, especially when so exhaustively documented. It's hard to imagine that anyone could be passionate enough about Kirby's brand of chamber jazz to want everything he ever did, but if you are, here you go. There are a few things not covered in the studios, but they're presented in very much the same way, without undue drama and the exigencies of broadcasting being even more exacting than the duration of 78s, they're all pretty brief.

★★★ Biggest Little Band In The Land

ASV/Living Era 5304 *As above.* 39–46.

A nice budget selection of tunes from Kirby's brief heyday. The remastering is certainly brighter than on the notorious Classics, but maybe a little artificial in places. It's an undemanding listen and apart from a few solos there's nothing much here to stir the loins.

Roy Kirby (born 1942)

BANJO

Loyal keeper of the British trad flame, based in Stroud, Gloucestershire, and leader of the Paragon Jazz Band.

★★★ Way Down Yonder In New Orleans

P.E.K. Sound PKCD-152 *Kirby; Gwyn Lewis (c, v); Mike Owen (tb); Chris Rogers (c, as); Bob Pearce (b); Colin Bushell (d).* 3/00.

A superior example of the British trad style, as it stood at the beginning of the new century, recorded live at Wycliffe College, Stonehouse. Kirby and his Paragon Jazz Band model themselves on a classic New Orleans sound, the ensemble taking honest precedence over solo showboating, although the group can actually boast some decent soloists; Lewis plays a strong lead when he's not singing in a lusty baritone, Owen is impressive with the plunger mute, and Rogers makes with the old-fashioned vibrato when he's on alto. They come up with plenty of interesting tunes to go with the familiars, and Peter Kings gives them an excellent sound, with Roy's strumming coming through loud and clear. Good value!

Steven Kirby

GUITAR

Works on the Boston scene. A light, contemporary sound not unlike Pat Metheny but with a hint of Kenny Burrell.

***** Point Of Balance**
Challenge 73124 *Kirby; Carl Clements (ss); Bevan Manson, Bennett Paster (p); Harvie Swartz, Gerald Wilfong (b); John Mettam, George Schuller (d).* 98.

*****(*) North Light**
A Records 73193 *Kirby; Tony D'Aveny (t, flhn); Chris Potter (ts); Bill Vint (ss, ts); Bruce Barth, Laszlo Gardonyi (p); Mark Shilansky (p, org); Scott Colley, Keala Kaumeweiha, Gerald Wilfong (b); Matt Wilson (d).* 01.

The young Bostonian's touch and ideas are by no means as featherlight as they might seem on first exposure. The debut album, which uses a range of players, is cleverly programmed and well executed. Soprano saxophonist Clements is only in for a couple of numbers, which leavens the sound but also keeps the emphasis squarely on the leader's delicately spun themes. The central sequence of 'An Ever Fixed Mark', 'High Place' and 'Nima's Way' contains most of the session's substance, and even here there are some longueurs, but Kirby has set out his stall convincingly.

The second album also uses a range of players but this time Kirby's own range is greater, from softer ballad themes where he very definitely sounds like Pat Metheny to more upbeat rock-tinged essays. All but two of the tunes are originals, and the closing version of 'When You Wish Upon A Star' is brief enough to seem a throwaway or maybe it's just there to prove he can do it. 'North Lights' is strongly constructed around two simple melodic cells but it has a lot of harmonic subtlety. The organ-driven pieces don't always come off, largely because Kirby doesn't rev up quite enough, but he's getting there and the next couple of albums should be fascinating.

Andy Kirk (1898–1992)

BANDLEADER, BASS SAXOPHONE, TUBA

Kirk took over Terrence Holder's Dark Clouds Of Joy in 1929 and turned the band into a successful touring and recording unit, very largely dependent on the magnificent writing and arranging of Mary Lou Williams. His biggest success was with 'Until The Real Thing Comes Along' in 1936, after which the band did little more than consolidate and deliver more of the same material.

***** Andy Kirk 1929–1931**
Classics 655 *Kirk; Clouds of Joy (various personnel).* 29–31.

****** Andy Kirk 1936–1937**
Classics 573 *Kirk; Paul King, Harry Lawson, Earl Thomson, Clarence Trice (t); Ted Donnelly, Henry Wells (tb); John Harrington (cl, as, bs); John Williams (as, bs); Earl Miller (as); Dick Wilson (ts); Claude Williams (vn); Mary Lou Williams (p); Ted Brinson, Ted Robinson (g); Booker Collins (b); Ben Thigpen (d); O'Neil Spencer, Pha Terrell (v).* 3–12/36.

*****(*) Andy Kirk 1937**
Classics 581 *As above.* 2–12/37.

*****(*) Andy Kirk 1937–1938**
Classics 598 *As above.* 2–12/38.

****** Andy Kirk, 1929–1940**
ASV 14321 2 *As above.* 29–40.

***** Andy Kirk 1939–1940**
Classics 640 *As above, except add Harold 'Shorty' Baker (t); Fred Robinson (tb); Edward Inge (cl, ts); Rudy Powell (as); Don Byas (ts); Floyd Smith (g); June Richmond (v).* 11/39–7/40.

***** Andy Kirk 1940–1942**
Classics 681 *Similar to above.* 40–42.

***** Andy Kirk 1943–1949**
Classics 1075 *Kirk; Art Capehart, Talib Daawood, Claude Dunson, Harry Lawson, John Lynch, Howard McGhee, Fats Navarro, Fip Ricard, Clarence Trice (t); Joe Baird, Bob Murray, Wayman Richardson, Milton Robinson, Henry Wells (tb); Reuben Phillips, Ben Smith (as); Eddie 'Lockjaw' Davis, Jimmy Forrest, John Harrington, J. D. King, John Taylor (ts); Ed Loving, John Porter (bs); Hank Jones, Johnny Young (p); Floyd Smith (g); Lavern Baker, Booker Collins, Al Hall (b); Ben Thigpen (d); Jimmy Anderson, Bea Booze, Billy Daniels, June Richmond, Beverley White, Kenny White, Joe Williams, The Four Knights, The Jubalaires (v).* 12/43–5/49.

Though he was often out front for photo opportunities, Andy Kirk ran the Clouds Of Joy strictly from the back row. The limelight was usually left to singer June Richmond or vocalist/conductor Pha Terrell; the best of the arrangements were done by Mary Lou Williams, who left the band in 1942; as a bass saxophonist, Kirk wasn't called on to take a solo. All the same, he turned the Clouds Of Joy into one of the most inventive swing bands. His disposition was sunny and practical and he was a competent organizer (who in later life ran a Harlem hotel, the legendary Theresa, and organized a Musicians' Union local in New York City).

Inevitably, given Kirk's low musical profile, critical attention is more usually directed to other members of the band. The classic Clouds Of Joy cuts are those that feature Mary Lou Williams's arrangements and performances, and for these the three earliest Classics compilations are essential, though many of the best tracks can be found on compilations under Williams's own name. The earlier material is still the best, with 'Moten Swing', 'Until The Real Thing Comes Along' and the hit 'Froggy Bottom' prominent. There are, though, fine performances from 1937 and 1938, most notably 'Mary's Idea' from December 1938. Sound is reasonable if not startling.

As the lengthening chronology suggests, opportunities to record were fewer and further between in the mid- to late-'40s, though Kirk successfully negotiated the band through the draft and a recording ban. As ever, the outfit sounds like a proving ground for artists who were to make the grade on their own account in future years. Players like Fats Navarro, Howard McGhee and Jimmy Forrest enjoyed a valuable apprenticeship with Kirk. But the writing was already on the wall and gigs were becoming more sporadic. By the end of the war, the musical and commercial impetus was elsewhere and Kirk's later band-leading career was very much *ad hoc*.

The ASV sampler is a serviceable compilation, and with significantly better sound than the notoriously muddy and hissy Classics.

Rahsaan Roland Kirk (1936–77)

TENOR SAXOPHONE, MANZELLO, STRITCH, FLUTE, ASSORTED INSTRUMENTS

Lost his sight as an infant, and learned clarinet and sax at a blind school. Learned to play three saxophones at once, and tinkered with hybrid instruments; began recording under his own name at 20, and worked with Charles Mingus but otherwise as a soloist-leader. Records and performances alike were extravagant carnivals of sound, often only intermittently successful, but always full of indomitable spirit. Fought back from a debilitating stroke in 1975, but a second one killed this much-loved maverick at 41.

***** Introducing Roland Kirk**

Chess 051821-2 *Kirk; Ira Sullivan (t, ts); W. E. Burton (p, org); Don Garrett (b); Sonny Brown (d).* 6/60.

This is perhaps the first time the real Kirk can be heard on disc, the first time that his astonishing range is put to real use. With the remarkable Sullivan on hand, and with Burton providing big, raw organ chords on some tracks, the harmonic spectrum sounds far bigger than a quintet date would normally offer. The opening track is 'The Call', and it immediately identifies itself as Kirk's work, a haunting blues-derived theme with weird polytonal appendages as all three of the leader's horns are called into play. As ever, though, he varies the texture and timbre by modulating from tenor to tenor-plus-manzello to manzello alone during his solo. 'Soul Station' follows, a more straightforward blowing theme that demonstrates his credentials as a mainstream jazz musician. On 'Our Love Is Here To Stay' he opts for the manzello alone, a forlorn, emotional sound that is unlike anything or anyone else. Sullivan's trumpet feature on 'Spirit Grill' is backed by two of Kirk's horns, presumably tenor and stritch, but sounding like a whole section. The rhythm section is fairly run-of-the-mill and Burton's closing tune, 'Jack The Ripper', really isn't up to the quality of the rest of the session, a refugee from an R&B date.

*****(*) Kirk's Work**

Original Jazz Classics OJC 459 *Kirk; Jack McDuff (org); Joe Benjamin (b); Art Taylor (d).* 7/61.

'Skater's Waltz' is one of Kirk's best bits of surreal kitsch, combined with his familiar inventive ambiguity. He clearly enjoys the big, bruising sound of McDuff's electric organ and boots furiously on all three saxophones and flute. On 'Three For Dizzy' he executes difficult tempos with quite astonishing dexterity. A largely forgotten Kirk album, but one which generally deserves the classic reissue billing.

*****(*) We Free Kings**

Mercury 826455 *Kirk; Richard Wyands, Hank Jones (p); Art Davis, Wendell Marshall (b); Charli Persip (d).* 61.

This is the first major Kirk record, and the opening 'Three For The Festival', a raucous blues, is the best evidence there is on record of his importance, even greatness. Kirk's playing is all over the place. He appears out of nowhere and stops just where you least expect him to. On 'You Did It, You Did It', he creates rhythmic patterns which defeat even Persip and moves across the chords with a bizarre crabwise motion. A wonderful record that every Kirk fan should have.

****** Rahsaan**

Mercury 846630 10CD + bonus *Kirk; Nat Adderley, Al Derisi, Freddie Hubbard, Virgil Jones, Jimmie Maxwell, Joe Newman, Jimmy Nottingham, Ernie Royal, Clark Terry, Richard Williams, Snooky Young (t); Martin Banks (flhn); Garnett Brown, Billy Byers, Jimmy Cleveland, Paul Faulise, Curtis Fuller, Charles Greenlee, Dick Hixon, Quentin Jackson, J. J. Johnson, Melba Liston, Tom McIntosh, Tom Mitchell, Santo Russo, Tony Studd, Kai Winding (tb); Ray Alonge, Jimmy Buffington, Earl Chapin, Paul Ingraham, Fred Klein, Tony Miranda, Bob Northern, Willie Ruff, Julius Watkins (frhn); Don Butterfield, Jay McAllister, Henry Phillips, Bill Stanley (tba); Benny Golson, Lucky Thompson (ts); Tubby Hayes (ts, vib); James Moody (ts, f; as 'Jimmy Gloomy'); Pepper Adams (bs); Al Cohn, Jerry Dodgion, Budd Johnson, Walt Levinsky, Romeo Penque, Seldon Powell, Jerome Richardson, Zoot Sims, Stan Webb, Frank Wess, Phil Woods (reeds); Walter Bishop Jr, Jaki Byard, Hank Jones, Wynton Kelly, Harold Mabern, Tete Montoliu, Bobby Scott, Horace Parlan, Richard Wyands (p); Andrew Hill (p, cel); Patti Brown, Lalo Schifrin, Bobby Scott (p, org); Eddie Baccus (org); Gary Burton, Milt Jackson, Bob Moses (vib); Vincent Bell, Kenny Burrell, Mose Fowler, Jim Hall, Wayne Wright (g); Sonny Boy Williamson (hca; as 'Big Skol'); Charles McCoy (hca); Bob Cranshaw, Art Davis, Richard Davis, George Duvivier, Michael Fleming, Milt Hinton, Sam Jones, Wendell Marshall, Vernon Martin, Eddie Mathias, Don Moore, Niels-Henning Orsted Pedersen, Major Holley, Abdullah Rafik, Ben Tucker, Chris White (b); Art Blakey, Sonny Brown, George Cook, Rudy Collins, Charles Crosby, Henry Duncan, Steve Ellington, Louis Hayes, Roy Haynes, Albert 'Tootie' Heath, Osie Johnson, Elvin Jones, J. C. Moses, Walter Perkins, Charli Persip, Ed Shaughnessy (d); Bill Costa, Jack Del Rio, George Devens, Charles Gomez, Phil Kraus, Montego Joe, Jose Paula, Manuel Ramos (perc); Crystal Joy Albert (v); others unidentified.* 61–64.

***** Roland Kirk's Finest Hour**

Verve 549676 *Similar to above.* 61–64.

*****(*) Verve Jazz Masters 27**

Verve 523489-2 *As above.* 61–64.

*****(*) Domino**

Verve 543833-2 *Kirk; Herbie Hancock, Andrew Hill, Wynton Kelly (p); Vernon Martin (b); Henry Duncan, Roy Haynes (d).* 4–9/62.

***** Does Your House Have Lions?**

Rhino R2 71406 2CD *Kirk; Ron Burton, Jaki Byard, Hank Jones, Charles Mingus, Trudy Pitts, Lonnie Liston Smith, Sonelius Smith, Richard Tee (p); Ron Carter, Major Holley,*

Vernon Martin, Steve Novosel, Henry Pearson, Henry Metathias Pearson, Bill Salter, Doug Watkins (b); Sonny Brown, Charles Crosby, Jimmy Hopps, Oliver Jackson, James Madison, Khalil Mhridri, Bernard Purdie, Robert Shy, Harold White (d); woodwinds, strings. 61–76.

Potential purchasers shouldn't be misled into thinking that *Rahsaan* is a 'Complete' or 'Collected' Kirk. It represents only the – admittedly marvellous – recordings he made for the Mercury label during five of his most productive years. Serious collectors will also want to have later material like *The Inflated Tear*, and something from the group of unpredictable Atlantics. Anyone just passing through should opt for the *Finest Hour* compilation, which includes 'Blue Rol', 'Serenade To A Cuckoo', a wonderful version of Mingus's 'Ecclusiastics' and plenty more meaty Kirk.

Disc 1 of the Mercury set is a repackaging of the popular *We Free Kings* with a good alternative take of Parker's 'Blues For Alice' and an unissued 'Spring Will Be A Little Late This Year'. This is roughly the pattern observed throughout the set: alternatives have been included on merit, not (as with some Parker compilations) merely for the sake of checking matrix numbers. The other original releases are *Domino* (disc 2), *Reeds And Deeds* (discs 3–4), *The Roland Kirk Quartet Meets The Benny Golson Orchestra* (disc 4) where Kirk sounds quite at home in Golson's rich, Gil Evans-like arrangements; there is the live *Kirk In Copenhagen* (discs 5–6, with nine unissued tracks) featuring Sonny Boy Williamson, *Gifts And Messages* (disc 7), *I Talk With The Spirits* (disc 8), *Rip, Rig And Panic* (disc 9 – but see below), and *Slightly Latin* (also disc 9). In addition to an uncredited and mostly unissued 1964 session on disc 7, there are also cuts made under the leadership of Tubby Hayes, organist Eddie Baccus (one track only) and Quincy Jones.

The Jones tracks bear much the same relation to the better material as the Bird-with-strings sessions to the classic Verve small groups. Jones's advocacy – like Ramsey Lewis's – was critical to the hornman's career and helped overcome a deadweight of industry suspicion, but the mid-market pitch was unfortunate. Eminently professional, the arrangements smooth out Kirk's eldritch sound in a way that Golson's imaginative charts don't.

Of the small groups, the *We Free Kings* session is still as fresh as paint; Kirk's mildly irreverent reworking of the Christmas carol sounds hokey at first hearing but makes increasing sense on repeated exposure, much like Thelonious Monk's 'straight' 'Abide With Me'. 'Three For The Festival' became one of his most frequently performed compositions. There are marvellous things, too, on the 1962 and 1963 sessions with Andrew Hill (his first working group) and Harold Mabern slip-anchoring sympathetic rhythm sections. *Domino* has now been issued separately as a Verve Master Edition, with no fewer than ten alternative takes – a bit much even for Kirkophiles. Some of the real surprises come in the one-off collaboration with Tubby Hayes. Also featuring James Moody (under the contractual *nom de studio* 'Jimmy Gloomy'), the pairing of flutes over Hayes's vibes on 'Lady "E"' is masterful. The tenor-chase effects recall 'Three For The Festival'. Elsewhere, Kirk and Moody play off against the visitor's less abstract bop style. During a superb ballad medley, Kirk attacks 'For Heaven's Sake' without a reed in his tenor saxophone; the sound is both startling and beautiful.

The live Copenhagen sessions with bluesman Williamson are credited with two bassists, Don Moore and the ubiquitous NHOP. They don't seem to play together, but it isn't always easy to pick detail out of a raucous, clubby recording which has Montoliu optimistically bashing an out-of-tune and tinny piano much as his model, Bud Powell, had to do in later years. Needless to say, Kirk remains triumphantly unfazed.

Inevitably expensive but beautifully packaged, and with an intelligently detailed booklet by critic Dan Morgenstern, *Rahsaan* nevertheless affords unparalleled detail on perhaps the most significant single phase of Kirk's career. Newcomers should certainly start elsewhere, ideally with the well-selected but inevitably very selective *Jazz Masters* set; but enthusiasts will find these ten discs (and the brief bonus 'Stritch In Time' from the 1962 Newport Festival) essential acquisitions.

The smaller *Does Your House Have Lions?* covers his recording for Atlantic and is both more selective and less richly funded in the first place. The label deliberately encouraged his more maverick side on the assumption that Kirk unfettered was the only Kirk anyone really wanted, when in fact he was an artist who, more than most, needed a sympathetic but steadying hand. As a result, these discs are patchy and sometimes downright disappointing. But Kirk is Kirk, and it would be a mistake to expect smoothly crafted mainstream jazz.

***** I Talk With The Spirits**

Verve 558076-2 *Kirk; Bob Moses (vib); Horace Parlan (p); Michael Fleming (b); Walter Perkins (d); Crystal Joy Albert (v).* 9/64.

The flute album. As Edith Kirk attests, Roland had a heavy, sometimes massive sound, often vocalized and multiphonic, that contrasted sharply with the thin, skittery voicings of players who were saxophonists first and foremost and who used the flute solely for colour. The title-track and the opening 'Serenade For A Cuckoo' are essential Kirk. The rest is fine, but rather wearisome, even over the scant 40 minutes the CD offers. Whether any more from these sessions – if indeed the tapes exist – would be welcome is very much a matter of taste.

I Talk is a fascinating exercise, as perverse and quirky as anything he ever put on tape. As a concept album, it's right up there. As a listening experience, it's a little unrelieved and shrill, but let's be clear: listening to Rahsaan playing a kettle for 40 minutes was always going to be more interesting than listening to the average jazz player on a Selmer Mark V.

***** Gifts And Messages**

Ronnie Scott's Jazz House JHAS 606 *Kirk; Stan Tracey (p); Rick Laird (b); Allan Ganley (d).* 10 & 11/64.

On the opening tune, 'Bags' Groove', Kirk shouts at Stan Tracey to 'Play them blues', something the Englishman has always done with absolute authenticity. This band was something of a gift for an American musician 'going single' through Europe. Poor Eric Dolphy, who had died in Berlin in the summer of 1964, had had to make do with much less. The understanding between group and leader was cemented by Tracey's familiarity with material like Tadd Dameron's 'On A Misty Night' and Duke's 'Come Sunday', which receives a rather short performance.

There's more emphasis on vocal devices than was usual for the time, perhaps because Kirk's lip doesn't seem to be in tip-top working order. He does a good deal of singing through the flute and on 'It Might As Well Be Spring' he pioneers the 'saxophonium', a sax without mouthpiece. The whole set is peppered with quotes, allusions and tags from other songs, sometimes punning, sometimes surreal, always absolutely musical. Not the best recording (the first in the Jazz House to use the same machine the original tapes were made on), but the music more than makes up for any technical deficiencies.

CORE COLLECTION

***(*) Rip, Rig And Panic / Now Please Don't You Cry, Beautiful Edith

Emarcy 832164 *Kirk; Lonnie Liston Smith, Jaki Byard (p); Ronnie Boykins, Richard Davis (b); Elvin Jones, Grady Tate (d).* 1/65, 4/67.

Now included on the Emarcy CD twofer, *Now Please Don't You Cry, Beautiful Edith* revives one of Kirk's unaccountably least-known recordings; it was his only record for Verve, made between contracts. Kirk's usual approach to schmaltz was to pepper it furiously. Brief as it is, 'Alfie' is given a half-ironic, half-respectful reading that is genuinely moving, with a typically ambiguous coda. Elsewhere, Kirk ranges from big Ellingtonian themes to out-and-out rock'n'roll.

***Rip, Rig And Panic* justifies single-CD release in this packaging (it's also to be found in the *Rahsaan* compilation, above) by its sheer energy and popularity (a British-based funk band named themselves after the album). The opening 'No Tonic Pres' is a tribute to Lester Young developed without definite key resolution. Like the succeeding 'From Bechet, Fats And Byas', it underlines Kirk's allusive invention and ability to make music with the most attenuated materials. Both 'Slippery, Hippery, Flippery' and the furious title-track develop Kirk's interest in 'found' or chance effects; Byard's piano playing switches between Bud Powell, the rhythmic fractures of Monk and the uncentred tonality of Cecil Taylor. Elvin Jones's drum solo on 'Rip, Rig And Panic' is one of his very best on record. On the final 'Mystical Dream', Kirk plays stritch, tenor and, incredibly, oboe at the same time, posing articulation and harmonic problems that would have sunk a less complete musician.**

*** Talkin' Verve: Roots Of Acid Jazz

Verve 533101-2 *Personnel as for Verve, Mercury and Emarcy items above.* 61–67.

A shrewd piece of marketing, aimed at a younger audience whose experience of this music is filtered through the club scene and an on-again/off-vogue for acid jazz and rare groove. The selection is pretty uncontroversial, including favourites like 'A Sack Full Of Soul', 'Theme From Peter Gunn' and the ridiculously groovey 'Dyna-Soar'. Again, anyone who owns the box set or who has a run of Polygram material won't be bothered, but a decent compilation and a fairly representative sample of what the great man is all about. Was he cool? Does it snow in Greenland?

*** Here Comes The Whistleman

Atlantic 7567 80785-2 *Kirk; Jaki Byard, Lonnie Liston Smith (p); Major Holley (b); Charles Crosby (d).* 66.

The Inflated Tear was Roland Kirk's first studio album for Atlantic. This, though, was the result of determined coat-tugging by Kirk fans. Recorded live, it has a raw immediacy which is instantaneously beguiling. Kirk's tenor solo on 'I Wished On The Moon', which he introduces as something he used to busk with washboard players and phonebook drum at house parties, has an almost unbearable simplicity of feeling. The title-track is a more virtuoso performance, doubled on tenor and nose flute, and 'Making Love After Hours' sees him run the whole range of his horns; but by and large *Here Comes The Whistleman* gives the lie to any impression of Kirk as a gimmicky showman. Most of the horn-playing is straight and unadorned, almost deliberately minimal. Of particular interest is his alto work on the closing 'Step Right Up'. At first hearing he might almost be Eddie Cleanhead Vinson: the same bop-pish, bluesy phrasing, but behind it a dark and almost tearful intensity of feeling. Not a classic album, but a most enjoyable representation of Kirk in a club setting, and working with a player of Byard's roots-aware sophistication.

***(*) The Inflated Tear

Rhino R2 75207 *Kirk; Ron Burton (p); Steve Novosel (b); Jimmy Hopps (d).* 5/68.

One of the finest of all Kirk's albums, his first studio cut is also one of the most contained and straightforward, establishing his gifts as an improviser beyond all contradiction. It's also now available in an enhanced digital version. The title-track relates to his blindness and conveys the dreamlike oddity and human passion of his music to perfection. The band are by no means top-drawer, but Kirk had a happy knack not just of getting the best out of players but also of subtly adapting his own delivery to the men round him. An ideal place to begin if you've never heard a note of Kirk; but prepare for surprises elsewhere. The CD sound is pretty good.

** The Case Of The Three-Sided Dream In Audio Color

Atlantic 1674 *Kirk; Pat Patrick (bs); Cornell Dupree, Keith Loving, Hugh McCracken (g); Arthur Jenkins, Hilton Ruiz, Richard Tee (ky); Francisco Centeno, Henry Metathias Pearson, Bill Salter (b); Sonny Brown, Steve Gadd, John Goldsmith (d); Lawrence Killian; Ralph McDonald (perc).*

This later album is disappointing. The much-hyped *Three-Sided Dream* was a self-conscious bid to bring Kirk to the attention of rock audiences. The cover-art was a good match for his surrealist approach, but the arrangements are too flabby for the imaginative suite-like approach, and the performance as a whole tumbles between two stools. Given that Kirk could almost always levitate in exactly that position, its failure is all the more galling.

***(*) Volunteered Slavery

Rhino R2 71407 *Kirk; Charles McGhee (t); Dick Griffin (tb); Ron Burton (p); Vernon Martin (b); Charles Crosby, Sonny Brown, Jimmy Hopps (d); Joe Habao Texidor (perc); Roland Kirk Spirit Choir (v).* 7/69.

**(*) Rahsaan Rahsaan

Collectables 6341 *Kirk; Dick Griffin (tb); Howard Johnson (tba); Ron Burton (p); Sonelius Smith (p, cel); Leroy Jenkins (vn); Vernon Martin (b); Alven Bunn, Joe Habad Texidor (perc).* 12/69.

***(*) Blacknuss

Rhino R2 71408 *Kirk; Charles McGhee (t); Dick Griffin (tb); Richard Tee, Sonelius Smith (p); Mickey Tucker (org); Cornell Dupree, Billy Butler, Keith Loving (g); Henry Metathias Pearson, Bill Salter (b); Bernard Purdie, Khalil Mhridri (d); Richard Landrum, Joe Habao Texidor, Arthur Jenkins (perc); Cissy Houston, Princess Patience Burton (v).* 8 & 9/71.

*** (I, Eye, Aye)

Rhino R2 72453 *Kirk; Ron Burton (p); Henry Pete Pearson (b); Robert Shy (d); Joe Habao Texidor (perc).* 6/72.

*** Bright Moments

Rhino R2 71409 2CD *As above, except add Todd Barkan (syn, perc). 6/73.*

Blacknuss, Volunteered Slavery and *Bright Moments* are the records which brought Kirk to a wider audience in the '70s but which maintained a degree of creative integrity that was lost on nonsense like *The Case Of The Three-Sided Dream*. There were signs of failing powers even before the debilitating stroke of 1975. *Bright Moments* is disconcertingly bland (and overlong, scarcely justifying two CDs'-worth) and for the first time Kirk's multi-instrumentalism began to seem a mere gimmick. Ironically, the most obvious effect of the stroke was to throw him back into much straighter playing.

He is at his best on *Volunteered Slavery*: five powerful studio tracks, followed by a set from the 1968 Newport Festival, at which Kirk played a deeply felt and touching 'Tribute To John Coltrane' before finishing with his own 'Three For The Festival'. There is nothing quite so powerful on *Blacknuss*, but it holds up triumphantly as a record. Kirk was playing a lot of pop tunes at this point. On *Blacknuss* he includes Marvin Gaye's 'What's Goin' On' and 'Mercy Mercy Me'; on *Slavery*, Burt Bacharach's 'I Say A Little Prayer' and Stevie Wonder's 'My Cherie Amour'. Though doubtless under a certain amount of pressure from the label to do so, he sounds completely comfortable with the slight change of emphasis, and throws in old spirituals and hymn tunes as well. What it essentially does is reassert the continuity of Afro-American music; to give just one example, the Cissy Houston who sings on 'Never Can Say Goodbye' and 'Blacknuss' itself is the mother of present-day pop star Whitney Houston. Some of the arrangements are a little guitar-heavy and the backbeats are decidedly uncouth, but Kirk can transcend difficulties of that sort. These are by no means peripheral to his main output.

Rahsaan Rahsaan, credited to Kirk and the Vibration Society, is plain odd and a most unsatisfying listen. 'The Seeker', a long, through-composed suite, is unbearably dull, even when punctuated by Kirkian idiosyncrasies. If you can survive that, there are tiny takes of 'Satin Doll', the original 'Sweet Fire' and 'Lover', before Roland goes for broke and for seemingly certain dental damage on 'Baby, Let Me Shake Your Tree', which is the purest hokum.

(I, Eye, Aye) – another reference to sight and self – was recorded at the 1972 Montreux Jazz Festival, an occasion which has also been documented and released on commercial video. At this point Kirk had a young band who were responsive to his every need and forbearing enough to allow him the full glare of the spotlight. If this was jazz showmanship, the straight men were there as well. The passage from 'Balm In Gilead' to a rousing version of 'Volunteered Slavery' is one of the best of this period, and this is a record rich in period feel. For some the video version will be more entertaining, but there is more than enough strong musicianship to sustain interest on CD alone.

The remaining years were to be marked by illness and failing powers, but in the early '70s Kirk worked tirelessly to propagate his version of 'black classical music'. This is it at its rawest and most immediate.

♛ **** A Meeting Of The Times

Warner Brothers 81227-3689-2 *Kirk; Hank Jones, Lonnie Liston Smith (p); Ron Carter, Major Holley (b); Oliver Jackson, Charles Crosby (d); Al Hibbler, Leon Thomas (v). 9/66–3/72.*

A small masterpiece, all the better for Kirk's decision to set aside his usual multi-instrumentalism and concentrate on single horns for this deeply felt but by no means pious tribute to Ellington. Al Hibbler, also blind, had been a member of Duke's band in the '40s. By 1972, he was almost forgotten, but here his rich baritone and bizarre diction are the perfect complement. Just as nobody every sounded quite like Kirk, nobody sang a lyric quite like Al. He slides into 'Do Nothing Till You Hear From Me' as if giving dictation, and never quite lets go the speech-song until he starts to syncopate phrases in the middle. On 'Don't Get Around Much Any More', he stretches weird triphthongs on phrases like '*moy moy-und*'s never at ease'. Not since Dick Van Dyke has English diction been put through the mincer quite so thoroughly. Al also turns Hal Sanicola, Sol Parker and Frank Sinatra's peerless 'This Love Of Mine' into a thing of almost operatic splendour, before Kirk picks up and doubles the time on his beautifully simple solo. 'Daybreak' features Kirk on clarinet before he switches to flute for a tremulous out passage. On 'Lover Come Back To Me', the harmonization of horns is so bizarre that it sounds as though the saxophonist is playing fiddle. Roland takes 'Carney and Bigard Place' as an instrumental, which is a welcome respite from the surrealism. The other Ellington tunes are 'Something 'Bout Believing' and 'I Didn't Know About You' and there's a wonderful version of the Hammerstein/Romberg classic 'Lover, Come Back To Me', which manages to sound deeply threatening underneath the romance. There's also a stray track from another session, with Leon Thomas reprising Kirk's autobiographical 'Dream', but it's very much Hibbler's moment back in the spotlight. The accompaniments are simple, funky and straightforwardly loyal to the song at hand. The set, reissued by Warners in 2004, is also available on a Collectables twofer, bizarrely paired with *Ornette!* However you get it, get it. It's wonderful.

**(*) The Man Who Cried Fire

Hyena 9302 *Kirk; Steve Turre (tb); Hilton Ruiz (p); Henry Pearson, Sonny Brown, John Goldsmith (d); other personnel. 70s.*

*** Prepare Thyself To Deal With A Miracle

Hyena *Similar to above. 73.*

***(*) Compliments Of The Mysterious Phantom

Hyena 9311 *Kirk; Hilton Ruiz (p); Henry Pearson (b); John Goldsmith (d); Samson Verge (perc). 11/74.*

Hyena is an unfortunate name for a record label, suggesting a skulk round the carcase in hope of scraps. In Kirk's case, reissue producer Joel Dorn hasn't the best track record, having made a monkey (if that isn't mixing the zoological metaphor) of *The Man Who Cried Fire*, a shoddy mix of '70s live material, now augmented with yet another off-cut. No such problem, though, with *Compliments*, which catches Kirk live in San Diego towards the end of 1974, his last year of full health.

It's a vivid and enterprising set. The earlier set includes some unexpected material: Coltrane's 'Mr PC', a rollicking 'Night Train' and an entertaining spoof on Miles's approach to 'Bye Bye Blackbird'. The later issue has some much better material for Kirk to get his teeth into, and it really sounds as if he's biting down hard on the reed. It's an amazing performance, punctuated by three monologues or 'Rahspeaks' in which Roland talks about life, music and, with disturbing prescience, death as well: 'Bring it on.' He starts in top gear on McCoy Tyner's 'Passion Dance', which Hilton Ruiz takes on like he wrote it himself.

There's a superb version of 'Volunteered Slavery' and another moment's meditation at the foot of that 'Old Rugged Cross'. The highlight, though, is the bizarre 'Freaks For The Festival' and the, er, 'Fly Town Nose Blues', though fans of a more traditional bent will either love or hate Kirk's studiously unromantic take on 'My One And Only Love'. Kirk solos unaccompanied, a *tour de force* of real harmonic ingenuity but quite hard to listen to. None the less, this is a great record and a wonderful souvenir of an American original.

Prepare Thyself is another important survival. Dominated by the three-part 'Saxophone Concerto' (really no such thing), it's a brazenly innovative trawl through his ever-growing array of drones, multiphonic lines and ever more extreme sonorities, including sopranino saxophone. The shorter tracks are generally better. Originally released on Atlantic, this has been out of circulation for some time before Collectables dug it out in 2002.

***** Other Folks' Music**

Collectables 6343 *Kirk; Richard Williams (t); Trudy Pitts, Hilton Ruiz (p); Gloria Agostini (hp); Leroy Jenkins (vn); Kermit Moore (clo); Sonny Brown, Roy Haynes (d); Arthur Jenkins, Joe Habao Texidor (perc). 76.*

Kirk survived his stroke and continued to make music despite the physical limitations it imposed. This is a curiously poignant set, with an elegiac mood established right from the off with a moving sample of Paul Robeson singing. 'Water For Robeson And Williams' is the only original, hence the title; elsewhere, Kirk tackles Parker's 'Donna Lee', Hilton Ruiz's spooky 'Arrival' and electric pianist Trudy Pitts's 'Anysha'. It's by no means an essential Kirk set, but there is plenty of good music on it, and the orchestral approach that attracted him in later years is well represented.

***** Simmer, Reduce, Garnish & Serve**

Warner Brothers 45811 *Kirk; Steve Turre (tb); Howard Johnson (tba); Romeo Penque (bs, ob); Hank Jones, Sammy Price (p); Hilton Ruiz (p, ky); Trudy Pitts (org); William Butler (g); Percy Heath (clo); Milt Hinton, Arvell Shaw, Buster Williams (b); Sonny Brown, Bill Carney, Charli Persip (d); Todd Barkan, Joe Habao Texidor (perc); Fred Moore (wbd); William Eaton (whistler); Adrienne Albert, Francine Carroll, Milt Grayson, Hilda Harris, Roland Peyton Quartet, Arthur Williams, Betty Neals (v). 76–77.*

This is a valuable compilation from Kirk's three final – and painfully heroic – albums for Warners: *The Case Of The 5000 lb Man, Kirkatron* and *Boogie Woogie String Along For Real.* No one will ever claim this is classic work; the miracle is that it happened at all, but even with restricted mobility Kirk was still able to play and by dint of some Rube Goldberg attachments to his horns, still able to sustain a measure of his multi-instrumentalism. Quibble as we might about the choice of tracks, this is a better option than the original records, which were notably patchy. The best of the tracks are 'J Griff's Blues', a likeable tribute to one of Kirk's acknowledged forebears on the tenor saxophone, a tiny 'Summertime', a lovely 'Sweet Georgia Brown', and 'Dorthaan's Blues' and 'Watergate Blues', the two tracks that closed out his last record. The humour is still irrepressible and the interspersed archive and closing montage help to fill out the portrait of a man who died too soon, but not without changing for ever what was possible in jazz.

Yoshiko Kishino (born 1960)

PIANO, KEYBOARDS

Japanese contemporary pianist recording in America with the local talent.

**** Tenderness**

GRP 014120-2 *Kishino; Sal Marquez (t); Ernie Watts (ts); Tommy Morgan (hca); Tom Kennedy (b); Dave Weckl (d); strings and woodwinds. 00.*

After two agreeable small-group dates, which presumably did little business for GRP, Kishino has been importuned into making this softcore fudge of a record. Prettily done, from the opening meander through 'Danny Boy' onwards, but with Sal Marquez hired to make Miles Davis-like noises, and strings and woodwinds hired to sweeten what's already sugar, it's a waste of a talented pianist.

***** Siesta**

GRP 450737-2 *Kishino; Romero Lubambo (g); Marc Johnson, Nilson Matta (b); Danny Gottlieb (d); Bashiri Johnson (perc); Emiko Shiratori (v). 7/02.*

'I hope listeners would enjoy a siesta of their own, on a quiet afternoon, with this album', is Yoshiko's rather unfortunate suggestion in the sleeve-note. This is a bit more substantial than the last one, though. The originals are still pretty and some imported Brazilian tunes sit nicely with a band that makes a fine job of playing ersatz-bossa grooves, with Gottlieb and Johnson or Matta apparently enjoying themselves.

Ryan Kisor (born 1973)

TRUMPET

Already a veteran of New York's contemporary jazz scene, Kisor made albums for Columbia before he'd turned 21. A much-in-demand player for big-band and small-group gigs alike.

*****(*) Battle Cry**

Criss Cross 1145 *Kisor; Sam Yahel (org); Peter Bernstein (g); Brian Blade (d). 10/97.*

***** Point Of Arrival**

Criss Cross 1180 *Kisor; Justin Kisor (t); Peter Zak (p); John Webber (b); Willie Jones III (d). 12/98.*

Kisor has some of the ebullience of the young trumpet masters of hard-bop yore. He doesn't have that measure of originality or capacity to surprise, but there's a kindred energy in his playing, and he has quite a personal, immediate sound. His two Columbia albums put him in more heavyweight company, but none of these guys is exactly a slouch either, and if both dates are quickly organized blowing sessions, they're cultured with it. He's a schooled player, so he treats a melody such as 'Falling In Love With Love' or 'I'm Old Fashioned' with a kind of old-fashioned respect. Those are both on *Battle Cry*, which isn't quite the stormy affair suggested by the title, based around several long ballad features, but it has a lot of beguiling trumpet, and Bernstein and Yahel are excellent.

Point Of Arrival seems that bit more ordinary, a rather plain trumpet-and-rhythm outing. Kisor is always worth hearing, even on a prosaic blues such as 'Smoke Signal', but the date needs an extra spark from somewhere. Brother Justin arrives for one duet, his own 'Sir Lancelot'.

★★★★ Power Source

Criss Cross 1196 *Kisor; Chris Potter (ts); James Genus (b); Gene Jackson (d).* 6/99.

★★★ The Dream

Criss Cross 1215 *Kisor; Eric Alexander (ts); Peter Zak (p); John Webber (b); Willie Jones III (d); Renato Thoms (perc).* 5/01.

With no keyboard on *Power Source*, Kisor takes a risk which he is fully up to facing and, with the invincible Potter standing at his shoulder, the music has a feel of synthesis which takes in all manner of post-bop jazz directions. As he gets older, the tone's losing some of its brassy snap, taking on a faintly cloudier edge and, with the saxophonist if anything moving in the other tonal direction, it makes for an attractive contrast. The covers are a superb lot, with Jimmy Heath's 'New Picture' outstanding. We're not so keen on 'Boogie Stop Shuffle', which doesn't really scale down, but the closing 'Bird Food' was an audacious choice that the players peck off in the hungriest manner. Surely Kisor's best to date.

For some reason he sounds much less involved in the strangely disappointing follow-up, *The Dream*. This has a much more conventional, even quiescent feel (Alexander arrives only for the closing 'Fiesta Mojo'), the rhythm section do nothing special and, though Kisor still gets off some sharp ideas (check his 'Minor Ordeal' solo), the record never really gets started.

★★★ Awakening

Criss Cross 1239 *Kisor (t); Grant Stewart (ts); Peter Bernstein (g); Sam Yahel (org); Willie Jones III (d).* 12/02.

Again, a touch disappointing – good skills on show, interesting tunes, but both Kisor and Stewart feel underprepared, and they don't articulate the themes with the precision which would create a springboard for the solos to work effectively. Perhaps the trumpeter needs to settle back and think carefully about the next one.

John Klemmer (born 1946)

TENOR AND SOPRANO SAXOPHONES, FLUTE, PIANO, VOCAL

Born in Chicago, Klemmer's conservative beginnings – working in dance bands and big bands – provide few clues to his big success with a hybrid of jazz, electronics and a prototype world music in the early '70s. He drifted off the scene in the '80s, and little has been heard of him since.

★★★ Involvement

Verve 076139-2 *Klemmer; Jodie Christian (p); Sam Thomas (g); Melvin Jackson (b); Wilbur Campbell (d).* 5/67.

★★(★) Priceless Jazz Collection

GRP 059946-2 *Klemmer; Dave Grusin, Mike Nock, Mike Lang (p); Larry Carlton (g); Phil Upchurch (b); Shelly Manne, Jim Keltner (d); Victor Feldman (perc).* 67–72.

★★ The Best Of John Klemmer Vol. One

GRP 059838-2 *As above, except add Jorge D'Alto, Milcho Leviev (p), Richard Thompson (org), Oscar Castro-Nueves (g), Abe Laboriel, Chuck Domanico, Bernie Fleischer (b), John Guerin, Lenny White, Harvey Mason, Morris Jenning (d), Joe Porcaro, Emil Richards, Airto Moreira, Alex Acuña, Chino Valdez (perc); omit Nock, Lang, Manne, Keltner and Feldman.* 75–78.

This pioneer of the kind of smooth-sax meandering which has become a commonplace in American radio in the '90s has some CD representation, although these are now US-only releases, leaving his European following bereft. Klemmer made a stack of records in that style in the '70s, and they – along with a few sessions of even earlier vintage – have been filleted for the two GRP compilations. Vaguely exotic (hence the large number of percussionists getting credits) but laden with cornball romanticism, Klemmer comes on like Gato Barbieri's soft country cousin. He blows quite fiercely at times, and *Priceless Jazz Collection* has its moments, especially on the earlier tracks where he hadn't yet patented the successful formula. But the later stuff is more like sucking on cotton wool, and the quaint echoplex and electric-sax effects do little now except date the music. Titles such as 'My Love Has Butterfly Wings' and 'Poem Painter' tell their own story.

Verve have gone through their Cadet archives to reissue *Involvement*, which may surprise both Klemmer's fans and sceptics. He plays in an attractively steely and forceful style, much more a characteristic Chicago sound, and a ferocious improvisation on 'How Deep Is The Ocean' is a real head-turner, stoked by Campbell's vigorous rhythms. The music has a somewhat stonefaced quality to it, though it's a lot more involving than Klemmer's later work, as conventional as the basic setting is. For some reason the CD has been mastered back to front, with the tracks from side two of the LP preceding the original side one.

Goran Klinghagen (born 1955)

GUITAR

A stalwart guitarist on the modern Swedish scene, Klinghagen worked with Lars Danielsson in the early-'80s group, Time Again, and has since played with numerous different groups and soloists.

★★★ Time Again

Dragon DRCD 247 *Klinghagen; David Wilczewski (ss, ts); Lars Jansson (p); Bruno Raberg (b); Magnus Gran (d).* 6/93.

The opening track, 'Include', is one of those set-pieces that linger long in the mind. After a rambling introduction, the music settles into a shifting groove in which Wilczewski's soprano picks out a melody against Klinghagen's lonesome guitar arpeggios. The record is never quite as haunting as this again, though it's an interesting showcase for the guitarist's range, which extends from Hendrix licks to the kind of wind-swept impressionism that Terje Rypdal made his own. Jansson guests on one track only.

★★★ Trometric

Dragon DRCD 325 *Klinghagen; Christian Spering (b); Leroy Lowe (d); Lina Nyberg (v).* 12/97.

Klinghagen's second Dragon CD is much more of a group record, closely argued between himself and the superbly talented Spering in particular. Their lengthy investigation of 'Hello Young Lovers', where the bassist contributes a roving, virtuosic line, repays many listens. Lowe seems content to take a more quiescent role, but his more reserved style is just what's needed. Tonally, though, the record becomes a bit monochromatic after a while, the soft articulations a little too lulling. Nyberg comes in right at the end for a duet on 'Prelude To A Kiss'.

***** Diimst**

Dragon DRCD 371 *Klinghagen; Ylva Nilsson (clo); Terje Sundby (d).* 01.

No fewer than 17 tracks on this interesting three-way encounter. Klinghagen is by no means the dominant voice; Terje Sundby has more composer credits, and several shorter pieces are group improvisations. A lot of it is soundscaping in the tradition of Rypdal, Frisell and Tibbetts, but there's a close-up, resinous quality which Nilsson's cello – apparently unadorned by electronics – brings to the music. It's a pity, actually, that some of the improvisations weren't allowed to reach their natural conclusion; the brevity of 'Bollnäs', which has a lot more energy than some of the meandering pieces, is frustrating. Next time they may do better by throwing caution to the winds.

Eric Kloss (born 1949)

ALTO AND TENOR SAXOPHONES

Born blind, Kloss was something of a prodigy who was working as a teenager in Pittsburgh and cut his first album at 16. A flurry of albums in a similar flurry of styles followed, but he has not been heard from much in recent years.

****(*) About Time**

Prestige 24268 *Kloss; Richard 'Groove' Holmes, Don Patterson (org); Pat Martino, Vinnie Corrao, Gene Edwards (g); Billy James, Grady Tate (d).* 1/65–4/66.

***** Sky Shadows In The Land Of Giants**

Prestige 24217 *Kloss; Booker Ervin (ts); Jaki Byard (p); Pat Martino (g); Richard Davis, Bob Cranshaw (b); Jack DeJohnette, Alan Dawson (d).* 8/68–2/69.

*****(*) Eric Kloss And The Rhythm Section**

Prestige PRCD-24125-2 *Kloss; Chick Corea (ky); Pat Martino (g); Dave Holland (b); Jack DeJohnette (d).* 7/69–1/70.

Kloss caused ripples of excitement when he arrived on the American scene in the late '60s. His Prestige dates have started to reappear in a two-on-one series. The first CD brings together *Introducing Eric Kloss* and *Love And All That Jazz*, neither of which stands up too well: Kloss is dumped straight down into the land of clichés which was the organ–sax–guitar combo, and he can't do much with the situation. *Sky Shadows* and *In The Land Of The Giants* are (surprise!) coupled on the next one. The latter featured Booker Ervin as second horn and they have some engaging fisticuffs on 'So What' and 'Things Ain't What They Used To Be'. The previous one is more ordinary, but these were typical Prestige rush jobs: at 19, Kloss already had eight albums behind him.

The next one doubles up two more, *To Hear Is To See!* (a discreet reference to Kloss's blindness) and *Consciousness!*, both faintly reminiscent of the beatific aspirations of the day but filled with hard-edged blowing that teeters on a line between bop and the oncoming explorations of Miles Davis's electric music. Given the rhythm-section personnel, this was hardly a surprise: Holland and DeJohnette lay down some of their funkiest parts (and they're recorded rather better than they were by Teo Macero with Miles), and Corea's almost minimalist electric piano cushions the harshness of Kloss's solos. Martino arrives for the second session, which opens on the bizarre choice of Donovan's 'Sunshine Superman'. No problem, though, since the quintet pile into it, Kloss lets go with some of his greasiest licks and they almost succeed in turning it into a blues. Most of the music bumps along on this path, and perhaps the souped-up tightness palls a little in the way that some of Gene Ammons's records do, but it's a superior example of the style. Kloss hasn't been heard from on record for a long time, but he's heavily involved in education these days.

Jimmy Knepper (1927–2003)

TROMBONE

Born in Los Angeles, he spent time in various big bands before going to New York and joining Charles Mingus in 1957. Injured in a contretemps with Mingus, he then worked in pit bands from 1962, returning to various jazz situations in the '60s and '70s. A considerable technician but an unassuming figure, he has a small and rather scarce discography as a leader.

***** Cunningbird**

Steeplechase SCCD 31060 *Knepper; Al Cohn (ts); Roland Hanna (p); George Mraz (b); Dannie Richmond (d).* 11/76.

***** Special Relationship**

Hep CD2012 *Knepper; Bobby Wellins (ts); Joe Temperley (bs, ts); Pete Jacobsen, Derek Smith (p); Dave Green, Michael Moore (b); Billy Hart, Ron Parry (d).* 10/78–11/80.

***** Tell Me**

Challenge 75048 *Knepper; Eddie Engels (flhn); Dick Vennik (ts); Nico Bunink (p); John Engels (d).* 8/79.

*****(*) I Dream Too Much**

Soul Note 121092 *Knepper; John Eckert (t); John Clark (frhn); Roland Hanna (p); George Mraz (b); Billy Hart (d).* 2–3/84.

***** Dream Dancing**

Criss Cross Jazz 1024 *Knepper; Ralph Moore (ts); Dick Katz (p); George Mraz (b); Mel Lewis (d).* 4/86.

Long associated with Charles Mingus, Knepper has an astonishingly agile technique (based on altered slide positions) which allows him to play extremely fast lines with considerable legato, more like a saxophonist than a brass player. Doing so has allowed him to avoid the dominant J. J. Johnson style and to develop the swing idiom in a direction that is thoroughly modern and contemporary, with a bright, punchy tone. A dramatic contretemps with Mingus drove him out of active jazz performance for some time, and much of the next decade was spent in the relative obscurity of recording sections and theatre work. *Cunningbird* effectively marked his renaissance as a soloist and leader. It's a strong enough album, though Knepper's tone isn't quite as assured here as it became in the '80s, and Al Cohn is below par. Mraz's firm melodic sense makes him the ideal accompanist, but Knepper has also been shrewd or lucky in his choice of drummers. Hart has the right kind of swing and Richmond is endlessly adaptable; an initial question mark about Lewis's big sound on *Dream Dancing* resolves into an ignorable quirk of the mix. It's not quite the best of the bunch, but it's still a fine album. Ralph Moore still had some growing to do, but he didn't make the mistake of doing it in the studio, concentrating on playing within his perfectly respectable limits.

The beautifully arranged brass tonalities of *I Dream Too Much* make it Knepper's most ambitious and fulfilling album. Hanna's comping is first-rate throughout.

Tell Me kicks off strongly and then just gets better. There is a fine version of former employer and sparring partner Mingus's gospel-tinged 'Ecclusiastics' and two lovely takes of 'I Thought About You', taken as a trombone–piano duo. Brief as it is, it's probably the highlight of the album and well worth the inclusion of the alternate. Not a group laden with personalities, though Bunink is an interesting footnote in modern jazz.

Special Relationship, as the name and personnel imply, is a transatlantic project, two quintets of respectively Americans and Brits, though Joe Temperley really falls into both categories. Bobby Wellins (strictly speaking, a Scot) is the star turn here. His tone is as airy as ever and his soloing on 'Round About Midnight' and 'Latterday Saint' underlines once again what a loss his absences from the scene always were. Knepper plays against him with great delicacy and control, reserving his more expansive gestures for the sessions with an engagingly gruff and even impatient-sounding Temperley.

Hans Koch (born 1948)

SAXOPHONES, CLARINETS

Similar in configuration to the Clusone 3, but very different in conception, the Swiss reedman's long-standing trio with cellist Schutz and percussionist Studer generates a rich amalgam of jazz, classical and folk forms. Koch's saxophone sound is slightly raw and unfinished, but always profoundly evocative.

**** Acceleration**
ECM 833473-2 *Koch; Martin Schutz (b, clo); Marco Käppeli (d).* 6/87.

****** Uluru**
Intakt CD 014 *Koch (solo).* 1/89.

One of the most significant and certainly one of the most adventurous improvisers on the European scene. Until the appearance of the utterly marvellous *Uluru*, Koch was heard to best advantage on the FMP record, *Duets, Dithyrambisch*, with Evan Parker and Louis Sclavis. On the 1989 record he creates a bewildering variety of voices with his three horns. 'Whirly Bird' and 'Tongue Salad' are both virtuosic, but there are more accessible things as well. There is some harsh, interesting music on the well-named *Acceleration*. Schutz and Käppeli play a subsidiary but highly interactive role: against some ponderous improvising by Koch on a variety of horns, they work up a vivid rhythm partnership. But the programming of the album, with dreary interludes such as the clarinet solo on 'Loisada', lets it down.

***** Chockshut**
Intakt CD 031 *Koch; Andreas Marti (tb); Martin Schutz (clo); Jacques Demierre (p); Stephan Wittwer (g); Fredy Studer (d, perc).* 12/91.

*****(*) Hardcore Chambermusic**
Intakt CD 042 *As above, except omit Marti, Demierre, Wittwer.* 10/94.

****** Heavy Cairo Traffic**
Intuition INT 3175-2 *As above, except add El Nil Troop.* 95.

***** Fidel**
Intakt CD 056 *As above, except add Musicos Cubanos.* 3 & 4/97.

*****(*) With DJ M. Singe and DJ I. Sound**
Intakt CD 062 *As above, except add DJ M. Singe, DJ I. Sound (turntables).* 99.

Koch, Schutz and Studer take on all-comers; they are among the most fearless and welcoming collaborators in European jazz. The boldest association is the encounter with El Nil Troop on *Heavy Cairo Traffic*, a haunting musical soundtrack that draws inspirations from Sun Ra to Grace Jones and which is invested with the passionate improvisational spirit of the great Omm Kholsoum. 'Belly Button Rave' and the Sun Ra-dedicated title-track are great jazz, and there are moments on 'Vice Versa' which recall Herbie Hancock at his most extreme ... in the days when Herbie flirted with extremes. The mix is heavy with found sounds and overlaid vocal and horn lines from the members of El Nil Troop. Live, this must be an awesome conjunction, and it's almost as powerful on record.

The Cuban album is a disappointment by comparison, a messy, sprawling postcard from another culture that never quite rises above its own limited premisses. Episodically, it sounds gorgeous, but there's little cohesion and it's a hard album to absorb other than in fragments. Perhaps the best place to start, and before plunging into the dense sound-world of *Heavy Cairo Traffic*, is the trio performance on *Hardcore Chambermusic*, on which the individual contributions of the three members are most straightforwardly evident. Koch's squalling, fervid saxophone harks back to an early age in European free jazz, but he is also aware of how and what that idiom took from other disciplines and he makes an entirely convincing synthesis. He is responsible for all compositions except the closing 'Airglow' and 'Megalith', which seem to be spontaneously created, and his use of samplers and sequencers generates much of the background ambience.

Chockshut is more straightforwardly instrumental, but Koch uses the harmonic range of the 'shadow' trio to create a spacious background of effects which is more open-textured than the electronics-laden vistas of *Hardcore* and *Heavy Cairo Traffic* but no less effective. Something of its energy is carried over into the recent trio set with DJs, a logical step for Koch and the trio and a highly effective one. 'Thai Speed Parade' is a nervy, twittering thing, built round an insistent pulse which seems to be the dominant metre for the album as a whole. Other tracks are less compelling and mostly a touch overlong, but the eight tracks are packed with musical ideas.

Franz Koglmann (born 1946)

TRUMPET, FLUGELHORN

The Austrian trumpeter believes that jazz, as an active and developing genre, is dead. This doesn't rule out – indeed, the example of Bach and the Baroque suggests the opposite – that great jazz may still be created, but that it now requires to move in new directions. Koglmann's own work is a quiet, understated hybrid of classic jazz and classical modernism.

*****(*) We Thought About Duke**
hatOLOGY 543 *Koglmann; Rudolf Ruschel (tb); Raoul Herget (tba); Lee Konitz (as); Tony Coe (cl, ts); Burkhard Stangl (g); Klaus Koch (b).* 6/94.

***** O Moon My Pin Up**

hatOLOGY 566 *Koglmann; Rudolf Ruschel (tb); Raoul Herget (tba); Mario Arcari (ob, ob d'amore, eng hn); Tony Coe (cl, ts); Angelika Riedl (bsn); Michael Hintersteininger (g); Barre Phillips (b); Phil Minton, Wiener Vokalisten (v).* 3/97.

Until the end of the '90s and the formation of his own label, Between The Lines, Koglmann's recorded output was exclusively on the hat ART label. With the deletion of its 6000 series, almost all of the trumpeter's records have disappeared. The most appealing survivor is the Ellington tribute, which has Konitz as co-leader, now available in the new and elegantly packaged hatOLOGY imprint. The saxophonist has worked in very similar territory – cool to abstract – over recent years and he sounds like a soulmate, albeit better adjusted, to the so-called Monoblue Quartet of Koglmann, Coe, Stangl and Koch than to the stripped-down Pipe Trio who are credited with the other five tracks. Koglmann contributes three original compositions under the generic heading 'Thoughts About Duke', and otherwise explores the less familiar reaches of the Ducal canon. 'Dirge' and 'Zweet Zurzday' bear the countersignature of Billy Strayhorn and 'Pyramid' is a Tizol tune; otherwise, it's 'Lament For Javanette', 'Ko-Ko', 'Love In My Heart' and 'The Mooche'. All are beautifully played and atmospheric, as you'd expect by now.

A recent return to the catalogue, *O Moon My Pin Up* is one of the more ambitious and formally structured of Koglmann's projects for hat HUT. Like *Cantos*, it reflects his long-standing obsession with Ezra Pound, the most controversial but also the most musical of the literary Modernists. Deriving its texts from the *Pisan Cantos*, written while Pound was held by the American army at the end of the Second World War, accused of making pro-Fascist and anti-Semitic broadcasts (he was eventually declared insane and incarcerated in the US), the poems are a curious mixture of floating lyricism and the most bilious polemic against the modern world and its works. As he would later on *Fear Death By Water* Koglmann worked to a libretto by Christian Baier. The choice of Phil Minton as the voice of EP is a stroke of genius and the choral accompaniment by the Wiener Vokalisten is superbly conducted by Alois Glassner and conductor Gustav Bauer.

***** Make Believe**

Between The Lines btl 001 *Koglmann; Tom Varner (frhn); Tony Coe (ts, cl, v); Brad Shepik (g); Peter Herbert (b).* 11/98–99.

*****(*) An Affair With Strauss**

Between The Lines btl 006 *As above.* 6/99.

****** Venus In Transit**

Between The Lines btl 016 *Koglmann; Chris Speed (ts, cl); Michael Rabinowitz(bsn); David Fiuczynski (g); Mat Maneri (vn, vla); Peter Herbert (b); John Mettam (d).* 2/01.

***** Don't Play, Just Be**

Between The Lines btl 021 *Koglmann; Tony Coe (ts, cl); James Emery (g); Ulli Fussenberger, Peter Herbert (b).* 02.

The first releases on Koglmann's new label continue the project of recent years and the work with hat ART. *Make Believe* is a quiet and thoughtful set, not easily assimilated at first hearing. Koglmann has cited writer and film-maker Jean Cocteau before, but *Make Believe* is a series of meditations on the Frenchman's classic *Les Enfants Terribles.* It represents an attempt to demonstrate by musical means 'the hidden world of dreams, the intoxication of fantasy and the artificial reality of life in closed spaces'. As such, it succeeds pretty well. Koglmann, Coe and Varner evoke a world of claustrophobic intimacy. As ever, it is a world governed by rules and forms, but also prey to irruptions from elsewhere, slashed across by the opium nightmares and sudden estrangements of Shepik's effects-laden guitar. An instrumental 'Interlude', led by Coe in his Pink Panther mode, seems to lead out into a more brightly lit world, but then 'Rue Montmartre' (home to Elisabeth, Agathe, Paul and Gérard) re-establishes the mood of threat and existential danger. Set as *faux*-rock, it bears just one instruction to the players, the simple, devastating 'Stupid'. Rarely has he allowed players even the freedom to be dumb. This is certainly the least predetermined and written-out project Koglmann has released. In addition to the material based on *Les Enfants Terribles*, there is a new appearance of an old Koglmann composition, 'Der Vogel', and, as a final tag, a flugelhorn interpretation of a rare Cocteau poem written in German, 'Blut', a dark, suave lullaby with a hint of menace under the midnight blue. *An Affair With Strauss* again imaginatively hybridizes classical procedures and standards jazz in a way that sparks new ideas. Coe is, as ever, such a brilliant technician with such a remarkably poised and focused tone that he dominates proceedings; and yet Koglmann, always a slightly diffident player, asserts himself more completely on 'A Metropolitan Affair' and 'Out Of Strauss' than he ever has before. The remaining members of the group are also highly responsive to Koglmann's needs and the whole project is sophisticated and very aware.

The two later releases consolidate Koglmann's project with ever greater confidence. *Don't Play, Just Be* is a clever and playful set, marked by the trumpeter's usual gift for delicate instrumentation. But it is *Venus In Transit* which really stands out. The first sequence of tracks is dedicated to Marilyn Monroe and was apparently first written for a theatre piece. The remainder touches on ideas in architecture and continues Koglmann's attempt to harness the harmonic energies of early jazz to the abstraction of early-20th-century classical music. Some of the tracks are as tiny and jewel-like as any by Webern and are written in a version of the great Austrian *Klangfarbenmelodie* approach, with each instrument taking different tones in a line. Consummately brilliant music.

*****(*) Fear Death By Water**

Between The Lines btl 034 *Koglmann; Tony Coe (cl, ts); Martin Siewert (g, elec); Peter Herbert (b); Wolfgang Reisinger (d); Birgit Doll, Morenike Fadayomi, Walter Raffeiner, Alexander Waechter (v); members of Ensemble XX Jahrhundert.* 3/03.

Koglmann's long-standing interest in the literary modernists emerges again in this jazz opera to a libretto by Christian Baier. As the title suggests, *Fear Death By Water* is inspired by *The Waste Land*, not such an unlikely source since T. S. Eliot's poem is full of jazz and jazz rhythms, juxtaposed with images of human frailty and death. Koglmann's core unit, the Monoblue Quartet, is both the protagonist – the piece's Tiresias, you might say – and an ironic commentary on a society that has lost its ability to feel even as it catalogues ever worse disasters. At the première, where this recording was taped, the audience were shown images of war casualties as the music unfolded.

The basic group is augmented by drummer Wolfgang Reisinger, and the main parts, named after Tarot characters, are performed by a group of very able and flexible vocalists who manage to balance the Grand Guignol elements of the libretto with the studied cool of the score. The orchestra is drawn from members of the Ensemble XX Jahrhundert, a very capable and adventurous new-music outfit.

It's difficult to separate out the elements that make up a piece divided into 17 short, songlike passages. The quartet's uninflected tonality is defined by Koglmann's Chet-like flugelhorn, Coe's weeping clarinet and Siewert's Hawaiian guitar; it's reminiscent of the most laid-back West Coast jazz, transcribed and played back mechanically, and offers a disturbing perspective on the disasters that lurk on the horizon. No coincidence that the piece was performed as the world slid towards the second Gulf War.

Eero Koivistoinen (born 1941)

TENOR, SOPRANO AND SOPRANINO SAXOPHONES

One of a richly talented generation of Finnish horn-players, Koivistoinen was a member of the rock group Blues Section before diversifying into funk and jazz. He studied at Berklee in the early '70s when already an accomplished and distinctive player.

***** Wahoo!**

Warner Music Finland 8573 83580-2 *Koivistoinen; Kaj Backlund (t); Juhani Aalto (tb); Juhani Aaltonen (as, f); Umto Haapa-Aho (bs, bcl); Olli Ahvenlahti, Esa Helsvuo, Esko Linnavalli (p); Matti Kurkinen, Ilja Saastamoinen (g); Ilkka Willman, Heikki Virtainen (b); Reino Laine, Esko Rosnell (d); Edward Vesala, Sabu Martinez (perc).* 12/72.

****(*) The Front Is Breaking**

Love Records LRCD 188 *Koivistoinen; Olli Ahvenlahti (p); Wlodek Gulkowski (syn, ky); Jukka Tolonen, George Wadenius (g); Pekka Pohjola (b); Esko Rosnelli (d).* 5/76.

***** Labyrinth**

Love Records LRCD 232 *Koivistoinen; Vladimir Shafranov (p); Pekka Sarmanto (b); Reino Laine (d).* 5/77.

Koivistoinen has a pungent, spicy tone that is deceptively 'American' in accent. His kinship with the dominant Garbarek approach is only incidental, and he veers towards a free style that dispenses with orthodox changes. The earlier of these reissued records now sound a little dated. *Wahoo!* is somewhat overburdened with generic electric-piano ripples and guitar chords, but the level of musicianship is such that there is always enough incident to keep the attention focused. At this point Koivistoinen hadn't yet found the delivery that later made him such a compelling soloist, but his tone is superb and on long tunes like 'Suite 19', 'Hot C', '7 Up' and '6 Down' he has genuine presence.

The Front Is Breaking is even more time-stamped with 'funky' electronics, pastiche *Shaft* wah-wah accompaniments and soft-edged production. Gulkowski's synth solo on 'Safari', though, is testimony to the high level of musicianship in Finland at the time and the kind of quality accompaniment that has made Koivistoinen such an enterprising player. The saxophonist is relatively unemphatic on this occasion, blending with the ensemble as often as not.

Labyrinth is much more securely Koivistoinen's album and a more idiomatic session. It also marks the end – for the time being at least – of the saxophonist's electronic groups. Koivistoinen again demonstrates his skill on the treacherously pitched sopranino, playing the tiny horn in the middle section of the title-suite and on the delicious 'Arabeski'. The reissue includes a second take of the latter and a further unreleased take of 'Spring Song', which he performs soprano. The former composition student is as deeply aware as his ex-teacher, the distinguished Aulis Sallinen, of the richness of Finnish folk music and includes an arrangement of 'Yksi Ruusu On Kasnavut Laaksossa', on which he plays his tenor with an almost vocal inflection.

***** Altered Things**

Timeless 367 *Koivistoinen; Randy Brecker (t); Conrad Herwig (tb); David Kikoski (p); John Scofield (g); Bugge Wesseltoft (syn); Ron McClure (b); Jack DeJohnette (d).* 92.

Koivistoinen's American debut was reissued in 2000. He holds his own in quite distinguished company, sounding for all the world like Randy Brecker's younger brother. Themes like 'Everblue' confirm the leader's liking for strong grooves, though he adopts a more mysterious mien on 'Magreb' and 'Clear Dream', the latter a duo spot for piano and soprano saxophone. Wesseltoft's synthesizer role is sensibly limited and most of the electricity comes from Scofield's four appearances, which find him still very much in jazz mode and not yet the fusioneer of later years. The Finn's chops are good but what he does best is create atmosphere and the slower ideas suit him best. 'Van Gogh' is like a mini-concerto for tenor saxophone with a ripe horn backing. What relation it has to the painter is a matter for individual listeners. DeJohnette and McClure hold the session together with their customary class.

***** Sometime Ago**

A Records AL 73139 *Koivistoinen; Seppo Kantonen (p); Severi Pyysalo (mar); Jesper Lundgaard, Ron McClure (b); Jeff Hirshfield (d).* 10/92–10/94.

Koivistoinen has always been an attractive ballad-player, but this is the first time he has made a whole album of slower and mainly standard tunes. The sessions involved three separate units, all of them anchored on Kantonen. Trio X is completed by Severi Pyysalo on marimba, a warm and responsive sound that works wonderfully on the title-piece and on the only original, 'Relation'. Koivistoinen concentrates on soprano for both these tunes, spreading the sound as broadly as possible. The quartet with McClure and Hirshfield revives an association that goes all the way back to Berklee days. 'Where Are You' begins the album with an authoritative tenor solo, very clean-lined and uncomplicated. 'Every Time We Say Goodbye' is masterly, with some detailed interplay between saxophone and bass. The third group is a drummerless trio with Lundgaard, similar in conception to Trio X but more boppish in conception. They do a version of Duke Pearson's 'You Know I Care' and Kurt Weill's 'My Ship'. Rounding out the album, two Monk compositions, 'Monk's Mood' and 'Crepuscule With Nellie', the latter played as a straight melody without soloing, bringing to an end an impressively varied and textured album.

****(*) Eero Koivistoinen and Senegalese Drums**

PROCD 009 *Koivistoinen; Seppo Kantonen (p, ky); Yama Thiam, Papa Sarr, Labasse Sall, Ousseynou Mbeye (perc, v).* 00.

What must have been a vivid live experience fails to come across on record. The percussion and vocal accompaniment is too dense to give the saxophonist much room for manoeuvre, and the writing is predictable in all the wrong ways and places.

But the Finn has always enjoyed experiment, and doubtless the lessons of this experience will filter through in later projects.

Krzysztof Komeda (1931–69)

PIANO

Komeda is the Lost Leader of Polish jazz. A brilliant composer rather than a virtuosic player, he remained better known in the West for film scores like Knife In The Water and Rosemary's Baby for his friend, Roman Polanski. Komeda's death remains mysterious but recent years have seen him emerge from an almost conspiratorial cult to wider and more intelligent appreciation.

***(*) **Volume 1: Ballet Etudes / Breakfast At Tiffany's**
Power Bros PB 00155 *Komeda; Tomasz Stańko (t); Eje Thelin (tb); Zbigniew Namyslowski (as); Michal Urbaniak (ts); Jerzy Lesicki (f); Janusz Sidorenko (g); Roman Dylag, Jacek Ostaszewski (b); Rune Carlsson, Adam Jedrzejowski (d); Wanda Warska (v).* 10/62, 1/63.

*** **Volume 2: Memory Of Bach**
Power Bros PB 00157 *Komeda; Tomasz Stańko (t); Zbigniew Namyslowski (as); Michal Urbaniak, Jan Ptaszyn Wroblewski (ts); Jerzy Milian (vib); Roman Dylag, Jozef Stolarz, Maciej Suzin (b); Czeslaw Bartkowski, Rune Carlsson, Jan Zybler (d).* 56–67.

*** **Volume 3: Nightime, Daytime Requiem**
Power Bros PB 0159 *Komeda; Tomasz Stańko (t); Zbigniew Namyslowski (as); Roman Dylag (b); Rune Carlsson (d).* 11/67.

*** **Volume 4: Moja Ballada**
Power Bros PB 0161 *Komeda; Tomasz Stańko (t); Michal Urbaniak (ts); Adam Skorupka, Maciej Suzin (b); Czeslaw Bartkowski, Adam Zielinski (d); other personnel.* 11/61, 67.

♛ **** **Volume 5: Astigmatic**
Power Bros PB 00163 *Komeda; Tomasz Stańko (t); Zbigniew Namyslowski (as); Günter Lenz (b); Rune Carlsson (d).* 12/65.

**** **Volume 6: Crazy Girl**
Power Bros PB 00165 *Komeda; Bernt Rosengren (ts); Roman Dylag (b); Leszek Dudziak, Adam Skorupka, A Zielinski (d).* 60, 61.

*** **Volume 7: Sophia's Tune**
Power Bros PB 00167 *Komeda; Tomasz Stańko (t); Michal Urbaniak (sax); Bo Stief (b); Simon Kopel (d).* 65.

*** **Volume 8: Roman Two**
Power Bros PB 00169 *As above.* 65.

*** **Volume 9: What's Up Mr Basie?**
Power Bros PB 00171 *As above, except omit Stief, Kopel; add Maciej Suzin (b), Czeslaw Bartkowski (d).* 63.

***(*) **Volume 10: Astigmatic In Concert**
Power Bros PB 0173 *Komeda; Tomasz Stańko (t); Michal Urbaniak (ts); Janusz Kizlowski, Bo Stief (b); Rune Carlsson, Simon Kopel (d).* 65.

***(*) **Knife In The Water**
Power Bros PB 00175 *Komeda; other musicians unidentified.* 57–62.

Komeda was born Trzcinski and trained as an ear, nose and throat specialist. He changed his name to avoid the attentions of both the political and medical authorities, neither of whom would have taken kindly to his extracurricular activities; later, in America, he was to anglicize his first name to Christopher. In 1956 he made his musical debut at a small, semi-official jazz festival at the coastal town of Sopot in Poland, the forerunner to the now annual Jazz Jamboree in Warsaw. In 1960 he recorded a standards album with Adam Skorupka and Andrzej Zielinski.

The following year Komeda wrote the music for *Knife In The Water*, using the gifted Swedish saxophonist, Bernt Rosengren, who reappears in wonderful form on *Crazy Girl*. The title-piece became a favourite concert-piece and is included in a rather rambling version on the Copenhagen live set. It also includes disappointingly lax interpretations of themes from his masterpiece, *Astigmatic*, which in our view (now reinforced by expert remastering) is not just one of the best Polish or European jazz records, but quite simply one of the best jazz records, full stop. Komeda was at the height of his powers when he made the disc in 1965 and he had with him a sympathetic and highly gifted group of young Poles, including trumpeter Stańko, then making his professional debut. 'Kattorna' and 'Svantetic' are both highly original, combining jazz tonality with folk and classical idioms; however, it is 'Astigmatic' itself, a swirling, multi-part suite with a skewed, elusive quality, that represents his masterpiece. There is not so very much solo space devoted to Komeda himself and it is one of the ironies of his career that his importance is less as a performer than as a composer and catalyst.

The second soloist, Zbigniew Namyslowski, was replaced on the Scandinavian tour by Michal Urbaniak, who was then still playing saxophone. The Danish tapes were released by Komeda's widow to mark the 25th anniversary of his death. In our last edition, all that was generally available of Komeda's work was the mighty *Astigmatic* and these very unsatisfactory live sessions. The initiative did, though, spark off a major reassessment and reissue of his work, a digitally remastered Komeda edition with excerpts from an extended interview with Zofia Komeda included on each handsomely packaged disc. The best of the music from the live Copenhagen set – a cracking reading of 'Svantetic' – is incorporated into other discs in the sequence – notably *Sophia's Tune* and *Roman Two* – and it demonstrates how Komeda's working band handled the *Astigmatic* material out on the road. Unfortunately the tape-quality is diabolical, with extraneous noise and unignorable dropouts. In addition, Urbaniak is playing poorly, leaving Stańko again to carry much of the weight of the music, which he does with characteristic fire. And yet there is no mistaking either the quality of the music or its jazz fire.

The series – which is not chronological – begins with a set of ballet studies Komeda made for an experimental troupe at Cracow Engineering College, together with a score for a theatre production of Truman Capote's *Breakfast At Tiffany's*. Both suggest a musician with a clear but idiosyncratic understanding of American jazz, and also a composer with a wonderful gift for suggestive musical drama. Some of that comes out again on Volume 11, where the famous score for *Knife In The Water*, a chillingly effective piece of writing, is paired with soundtracks for two avant-garde films, *Two Men And A Wardrobe* and *When Angels Fall*. These discs and *Memory Of Bach* bracket the series very effectively indeed, offering the clearest possible picture of Komeda as a composer whose early style was delineated by swing, the Baroque and silent movies.

Memory Of Bach includes material written for Komeda's Sopot debut and the title-track is the original version of an important piece for the composer, one that established him as an original, albeit respectful voice. In addition to the title-track, the record includes one of the Copenhagen tracks, a version of 'Crazy Girl', one of the tunes on *Knife In The Water*. For comparison, there is an earlier version from the Sopot Jazz Festival in 1961 (*Crazy Girl*, Volume 6); this is an important disc because it offers early and alternative readings of key pieces – 'Moja Ballada' is another – and because it also offers a glimpse of Komeda playing a standard, two very different versions a year apart, of 'Stella By Starlight'. 'Crazy Girl' was a dedication to Zofia, who emerges as the composer's muse. 'Sophia's Tune' appears in another slice of the Copenhagen concert on Volume 7. The remainder occupies the whole of *Roman Two*. The sound is still appalling, the quality of music unexceptionable.

'Nighttime, Daytime Requiem' on the album of that name is a good example of Komeda's otherworldly impressionism. This is unmistakably the composer of the film music, a musician with a keen but maverick sense of structure. Mood almost always dictates the dimensions and pace of a piece and subtly invests the harmonic language as well. For once it is easy to pick out his further debt to Polish Romanticism.

What's Up Mr Basie? is the Komeda set from the 1963 Warsaw Jazz Jamboree, the gathering which evolved out of Sopot and which is now the world's longest continuously running jazz festival. The group is by now a familiar one. Stańko, who later felt snubbed by the festival organizers, is in cracking form, and the only pity is that the piano is so far back in the mix, not at all true to the balance of the group.

Which leaves *Astigmatic*, in both studio and live forms. We cannot recommend this record highly enough and we envy anyone who can come to it fresh, ideally with no prior knowledge or expectations of Komeda. It is a record that never fails to repay close attention, but one that has an engrossing emotional physicality. Stańko's tone is lustrous and intense and the great Namyslowski projects his complex bop-derived lines in phrases that link together like pieces of DNA into living wholes. One misses him on the live version, where again the spotlight falls on Stańko. As ever, Komeda is a presence and a unifying element rather than a commanding soloist. The studio sound favours his rather unemphatic touch, and he certainly had a better piano in Warsaw than on the road – though, listening to it again, we wonder if the instrument wasn't perhaps tuned a little dark. Deliberately? There is no indication that tape speed is the problem, but it raises the interesting possibility that Komeda was already experimenting with the kind of detuning and pure sound that would resurface on *Rosemary's Baby*. The soundtrack album to that still-frightening film can probably be found in good film music sections and in specialist stores; it merits comparison with these records. It also hints at the tragic aura that seemed to hang round Polanski and his circle. Scarcely was Komeda established in Hollywood than he was brought home to Poland in an irreversible coma. The exact circumstances have never been clear, but even without conspiracy theories and a whiff of martyrdom his death was to be a symbolic moment in the assimilation of jazz in Eastern Europe. Whether he would have succumbed to the lure of Hollywood or whether the embryo of another *Astigmatic* perished with him can never be known. What is certain is that he created one permanent masterwork.

There is a good deal more work by Komeda on CD than we have listed above. Much of it is film or theatre music and, strictly speaking, beyond the scope of this book. There is also, however, the question of availability. One authority on Komeda points out that the discography he cites is hard to track down even in Poland itself. We have encountered similar problems; all we can say is that finding a Komeda record is almost always worth the effort.

Jan Erik Kongshaug

GUITAR

Internationally renowned as an engineer, mainly through his work for ECM, he also plays guitar, as here.

★★★ The Other World

ACT9267-2 *Kongshaug; Svein Olav Herstad (p); Harald Johnsen (b); Per Oddvar Johansen (d).* 4 & 6/98.

★★★ All These Years

Hot Club HCRCD 2027 *As above.* 1/03.

If the name seems familiar, but not quite familiar in this context, then let us tell you that *The Other World* was recorded at the Rainbow Studio and that guitarist, producer and engineer are all one and the same fellow. Responsible for working the faders on literally dozens of sessions for ECM and other labels at the Oslo studio, Kongshaug now steps briefly into the limelight himself.

Over the years he has continued to perform club dates and the occasional studio session, but this is the first time he has put together a group to record his own material. It's a set shrewdly sandwiched with standards, from the opening 'If I Should Lose You', which establishes his bouncy, clean-cut attack, to Rollins's 'Airegin', Brubeck's 'In Your Own Sweet Way' and a delicate reading of 'Like Someone In Love'. Jan Erik's own writing won't melt any glaciers, but 'Mina's Waltz', 'Going West', 'July First' and the title-track all bespeak a comfortable facility for melody, while the closing 'When I Met You' is genuinely affecting.

The follow-up – a mere five years later – goes round the same circuit with the same likeable results (and with the same team on hand, too). No real reason to have more than one of these, but either will afford pleasure.

Lee Konitz (born 1927)

ALTO, SOPRANO AND TENOR SAXOPHONES

The redoubtable Chicagoan worked with Miles Davis but came under the influence of Lennie Tristano quite early in his career, thereby avoiding the overdetermining sound of Charlie Parker on the alto saxophone. Along with tenorist Warne Marsh, Konitz created the definitive cool saxophone sound. He was out of active music-making for some years, but came back and increasingly – but entirely at his own pace – assimilated bebop to his personal style. He also flirted with the avant-garde and has dabbled in free improvisation as well as harmonic jazz. Konitz has been a prodigal recording artist, with a huge number of records to his name, many of them on very small labels.

★★★(★) Subconscious-Lee

Original Jazz Classics OJC 186 *Konitz; Warne Marsh (ts); Sal Mosca, Lennie Tristano (p); Billy Bauer (g); Arnold Fishkind (b); Denzil Best, Shelly Manne, Jeff Morton (d).* 1/49–4/50.

Most of the more casual generalizations about Lee Konitz – cool, abstract, passionless, untouched by bebop – were last relevant about 40 years ago. A stint in the Stan Kenton band, the musical equivalent of Marine Corps boot camp, toughened up his articulation and led him steadily away from the long, rather diffuse lines of his early years under the influence of Lennie Tristano, towards an altogether more pluralistic and emotionally cadenced approach. Astonishingly, Konitz spent a good many of what should have been his most productive years in relative limbo, teaching when he should have been playing, unrecognized by critics, unsigned by all but small European labels (on which he is, admittedly, prodigal). Despite (or because of) his isolation, Konitz has routinely exposed himself over the years in the most ruthlessly unpredictable musical settings, thriving on any challenge, constantly modifying his direction.

Subconscious-Lee brings together material made under Lennie Tristano's leadership in January 1949, with quartet and quintet tracks made a few months later, featuring the wonderful Warne Marsh on the anything but redundant 'Tautology' and four other numbers. The remaining group material with Mosca and Bauer is less compelling (and certainly not as good as the 1951 sessions with Miles Davis on the deleted *Ezz-thetic*), but there is a fine duo with the guitarist on 'Rebecca' which anticipates some of the saxophonist's later intimacies.

***(*) Konitz Meets Mulligan

Pacific 46847 *Konitz; Chet Baker (t); Gerry Mulligan (bs); Joe Mondragon, Carson Smith (b); Larry Bunker (d).* 1/53.

Konitz was to remember Chet Baker more fondly as the years went by and later dedicated an album to his memory. Here the relationship sounds creatively acerbic, even prickly as two of the coolest voices of the time vie for supremacy without seeming to lift a finger. Mulligan's light-toned baritone fits into the mix perfectly and there are moments on 'Lover Man', 'I'll Remember April' and 'All The Things You Are' when it sounds as if this must be a permanent line-up, so closely aware are the three front men of what the others are doing. Phrases and whole lines are traded back and forth; Konitz and then Mulligan modulates unexpectedly; the rhythm section – without piano – slips the rhythm here and there. The reissue has a short alternate take of 'Lady Be Good', but no one should need any extra inducement to buy this.

**(*) Complete 1953 The Haig Performances

Jazz Factory 22861 *Konitz; Chet Baker (t); Gerry Mulligan (bs); Carson Smith (b); Larry Bunker, Chico Hamilton (d).* 53.

A pretty exhaustive documentation of Konitz with Gerry Mulligan and Chet Baker at the Los Angeles club. The fare is very familiar and delivered with a typical cool that in places might almost pass for detachment. Chico Hamilton gingers things up a bit when he comes along to replace Larry Bunker, but there is little on the set that will appeal to any but a very committed purchaser. 'I'll Remember April', 'Five Brothers' and the inevitable 'MFV' stand out, but there are another 18 tracks, including a totally unnecessary 'alternate' of 'Lady Be Good'.

***(*) With Warne Marsh

Warner Bros 75356 *Konitz; Warne Marsh (ts); Ronnie Ball, Sal Mosca (p); Billy Bauer (g); Oscar Pettiford (b); Kenny Clarke (d).* 6/55.

It is one of the most famous saxophone partnerships in jazz, not quite the Four Brothers (though it derives something from that) and not yet John Coltrane-plus-acolyte (though it distantly anticipates some of Coltrane's wilder harmonic flights) but a cool and oblique approach to jazz material that still remains misunderstood and sometimes maligned. Heard again, there is nothing remotely chill or soulless about these tracks. To be sure, 'Donna Lee' is given a drier and less wild delivery than its composer Charlie Parker and his followers would have favoured, but it is no less true to the dictates of bebop and should confound forever the notion that neither Konitz or Marsh understood bop's essence; they did … and then stood aside from it, on their own turf. 'Don't Squawk' is the most developed piece here, a sinuous and deliberately awkward idea that moves with almost reptilian grace. 'Topsy', 'I Can't Get Started' and 'There Will Never Be Another You' aren't merely the best of the rest, but genuinely powerful tracks. While not always the most engaging and comfortable of records, this one should be in every modern jazz library.

*** Inside Hi-Fi

Atlantic Masters 81227 3615 2 *Konitz; Sal Mosca (p); Billy Bauer (g); Arnold Fishkind, Peter Ind (b); Dick Scott (d).* 9/56.

*** Peter Ind Presents Lee Konitz In Jazz From The 1950s

Wave 26 *As above, except omit Fishkind; add Don Ferrara (t).* 57.

Something curious happens immediately after the guitar solo on the opening 'Kary's Trance'. The only saxophonist on the date comes back in, but with a new and unfamiliar tonality. Kontitz had put down his alto and switched to tenor, the first time he used the bigger horn on record. He found it a liberating experience, and though he persists with alto on the first side of this 1957 LP, he switched to tenor for the second, with a different group.

The only common factor in the two groups is drummer Dick Scott, who'd caught Lee's ear with his fresh, flexible delivery and was an important collaborator for a time in the later '50s. The 'tenor group' was completed by pianist Sal Mosca and bassist Peter Ind. It's obvious that what the tenor gave Konitz was merely a confirmation that he had left behind the whispery, gossamer-light alto sound of his early days. Even on the smaller horn, on 'Sweet And Lovely', he is playing with more edge and attack. A fascinating insight into an evolving style.

*** Meets Jimmy Giuffre

Verve 527780 2CD *Konitz; Hal McKusick (as); Ted Brown, Warne Marsh (ts); Jimmy Giuffre (bs); Danny Bank (f); Bill Evans, Lou Stein (p); Billy Bauer (g); Ray Brown, Buddy Clark (b); Ronnie Free, Jo Jones (d); brass, strings.* 51–59.

A valuable two-CD reissue brings together a great deal of experimental Third Stream work from the '50s. In addition to the original *Meets Jimmy Giuffre* LP, there are selections from Ralph Burns's 1951 *Free Forms*, from *An Image*, written and arranged by Bill Russo as well as other Giuffre material including 'Mobiles', a suite of somewhat inconsequential miniatures for clarinet. This is probably a more interesting release for Giuffre fans than Konitz acolytes, but it's good to have a chance to listen to these largely forgotten sets. Konitz shines brightest on the standard tunes and on 'Music for Alto Saxophone and Strings' and there is an important role for Bill Evans which heightens the historical importance of the recording, but this is surely a case of more is less. These sets don't strictly belong together and no one is likely to listen to an album like this from start to finish. We struggled.

CORE COLLECTION

♛ ★★★★ Motion

Verve V6 8399 *Konitz; Sonny Dallas (b); Elvin Jones (d).* 8/61.

***Motion* is quite simply one of the great modern jazz records. Its unique chemistry is due in part to the seemingly unlikely pairing of the 'cool' Konitz with the hyperactive Jones, whose polyrhythms were helping to make the John Coltrane Quartet the epochal band they became. The sessions were recorded pretty much straight down and some of the additional material was issued on a Verve triple set some years back; a 1990 reissue increased the track listing of the original LP to eight tunes. Nothing, though, quite matches the impact of the issued LP, which is now available again in digipack with original liner-notes. It's an initiative we applaud.**

The trio, with Dallas playing strongly, start off with 'Foolin' Myself', and Konitz's fleet, agile alto sound immediately gels with the surprisingly soft playing of Jones. 'You'd Be So Nice To Come Home To' is superb. Again, Konitz floats round the melody more than he disappears on the back of the chords. Dallas is firm-footed and precise. 'I'll Remember April' is another of the highlights but anyone who has the three-CD set will know that 'I Remember You' caused the trio some grief and had to be retaken. The release take is quite brilliant, flowing and seamless and harmonically subtle. The set ends with 'All Of Me', Konitz rippling through the theme and embellishing the structure from beginning to end. Essential.

★★★(★) The Lee Konitz Duets

Original Jazz Classics OJC 466 *Konitz, with Marshall Brown (vtb, euph); Joe Henderson, Richie Kamuca (ts); Dick Katz (p); Karl Berger (vib); Jim Hall (g); Ray Nance (vn); Eddie Gomez (b); Elvin Jones (d).* 9/67.

★★★★ I Concentrate On You

Steeplechase SCCD 1018 *Konitz; Red Mitchell (b, p).* 6/74.

★★★(★) Windows

Steeplechase SCCD 31057 *Konitz; Hal Galper (p).* 77.

Improvising duets fall somewhere between the intimacies of a private dinner and the disciplines of the boxing ring. If there are minor embarrassments in being overheard with, so to speak, the emotional gloves off, that's nothing to being caught out by a sudden rhythmic jab or harmonic cross from your partner; there's no band waiting in the corner. In a very real sense, the duo is Konitz's natural constituency. Perhaps only fellow alto saxophonist Marion Brown gets near him for sheer quality in a demanding setting that perfectly suits Konitz's balancing of almost conversational affability with a gimlet sharpness of thought.

On the 1967 record, Konitz comes on like a cross between an all-comers' booth boxer and a taxi dancer: a lover, not a fighter. The album pivots on five versions of the classic duo piece, 'Alone Together'; the first is solo, the next three are duets with Karl Berger, Eddie Gomez and Elvin Jones (with whom he made the marvellous *Motion*), culminating in a fine quartet reading. The pairings with saxophonists Joe Henderson ('You Don't Know What Love Is') and Richie Kamuca ('Tickle Toe'), and with trombonist Marshall Brown are astonishing, as far as possible from the comforting horn-plus-rhythm options, most of them refused, of the tracks with Dick Katz, Jim Hall and even Ellingtonian Ray Nance (who plays his 'second' instrument). It all culminates in a fine, all-in nonet, an intriguing numerical anticipation of one of Konitz's best later bands.

Hal Galper's lush, velvety backgrounds inspire some of Konitz's most lapidary performances. There is very little harmonic tension in the pianist's approach, in contrast to Red Mitchell (on either double bass or piano), and the result is to focus Konitz very much on the tune rather than on its changes. That is particularly noticeable on 'Stella By Starlight'. Each man has one (improvised) solo slot; Konitz's 'Soliloquy' is a lean, un-self-indulgent exercise in low-fat improvisation and, as such, an illustration of the album's considerable strengths; Galper's 'Villainesque' is exactly the opposite, clotted like some multi-layered Viennese confection.

The Cole Porter readings with Red Mitchell explore equally familiar territory, but as if by night. Konitz clearly enjoys this kind of dead-reckoning performance and steers through the chords with finely tuned instinct. He also seems to like the extremes of pitch he gets opposite the notoriously straight-backed Mitchell, a man who prefers to play bass-as-bass, and it's a pity that the saxophonist wasn't currently toting a soprano instrument as well. Minor quibbles can't detract from the unfailing quality of the performances, which are absolutely top-notch. An essential Konitz album.

★★★(★) European Episode

Camjazz 214 *Konitz; Martial Solal (p); Daniel Humair (b); Henri Texier (d).* 10/68.

★★★(★) Impressive Rome

Camjazz 216 *As above.* 10/68.

The association with Solal, revived so memorably in duo in 1983, was important to Konitz during what was, recording-wise at least, the thinnest time in his career. These two discs belong as much to the pianist as to Lee, but the empathy is evident in every track and the level of music-making is superb throughout. Sound lets it down a bit, but only the excessively finicky will baulk.

★★★ Spirits

Milestone/Original Jazz Classics OJCCD 1024 *Konitz; Sal Mosca (p); Ron Carter (b); Mousie Alexander (d).* 2/71.

Most of these cuts are actually duos with Mosca, and so might better fit alongside the double-headers above, but Carter and Alexander are wheeled on for part of a set that consists largely of Tristano tunes, including a superlative 'Wow'. The Konitz originals are 'Hugo's Head', 'Kary's Trance' and 'Another 'Nother', the latter pair played at some length to round out the set. Also on the roster is Warne Marsh's 'Background Music'. Given how familiar all this material and its roots must seem, and how often Konitz and Mosca have trodden this ground, it's difficult to be over-excited about the music. It's solid fare, intelligent and well crafted but you'd be forgiven for feeling you'd come this way before. Carter and the little-known Alexander provide some diversion, but not enough to make it an essential purchase.

★★★(★) Jazz A Juan

Steeplechase SCCD 1072 *Konitz; Martial Solal (p); Niels-Henning Orsted Pedersen (b); Daniel Humair (d).* 7/74.

Top-of-the-range standards jazz by a marvellously Esperantist quartet. Solal is one of the great harmonists, with the ability to find anomalous areas of space within the most restrictively familiar themes; his statement and subsequent excursions on 'Round About Midnight' are typical of his innate resistance to cliché. NHOP is the Terry Waite of jazz: big and bearded; willing to go anywhere; able to communicate in almost any company; a reconciler of opposites, gentle, but with a hard centre. His low notes behind 'Autumn Leaves' merit at least one listen with the 125-Hz slide on the graphic equalizer up at +10 and the rest zeroed. Konitz sounds relaxed and easy, flurrying breathy top notes and leaving space round the brighter middle register.

***(*) Lone-Lee

Steeplechase SCCD 31035 *Konitz solo.* 8/74.

Even three years after the release of Anthony Braxton's groundbreaking *For Alto*, solo-saxophone performance was still considered a radical strategy. Konitz's unaccompanied treatment of just two standards – 'Cherokee' and 'The Song Is You' – contains some of his very best playing. Smooth *legato* passages are interspersed with harsher, almost percussive sections in which his pads snap down impatiently on the note. There are few if any hints of the free playing he essayed during a thoroughly unexpected collaboration with Derek Bailey's improvising collective, Company, in 1987; but there is a further dimension of freedom in his playing on the record that is rarely encountered elsewhere in his work. Even so, nowhere does he lose contact with the source material, which is transformed with a robust logic that never degenerates into pointless noodling. Recording quality is unexceptional and the CD sounds rather metallic.

**** Satori

Original Jazz Classics OJCCD 958 *Konitz; Dick Katz, Martial Solal (p); Dave Holland (b); Jack DeJohnette (d).* 9/74.

Long out of circulation, this was the last of four important albums Konitz made for the Milestone label. With a top-flight rhythm section who had seen service with Miles Davis, he dips a toe into rock-influenced free funk, adding producer Dick Katz on second (electric) piano on the long title-track. Solal also uses a Fender Rhodes on 'Sometime Ago', a rare chance to hear him flirt with technology, and a not entirely happy blend. The mix of material is determined by the instincts of the group, not just the leader. 'What's New' and the closing 'Free Blues' are geared to Holland in particular and he makes a sterling job of yoking together sometimes incompatible elements. DeJohnette strains at the leash, clearly wanting to inject more power and pace than the session calls for, but never for a moment breaking the bounds of taste. A most welcome reappearance in what is now an impressive output.

*** Figure & Spirit

Progressive 7003 *Konitz: Ted Brown (ts); Albert Dailey (p); Rufus Reid (b); Joe Chambers (d).* 10/76.

Konitz apparently wanted to do something in the spirit of Lennie Tristano and wanted Warne Marsh to play second saxophone. In the event, Ted Brown turns out to be an excellent second choice, with a warmer and less complex delivery. Tristano's 'April' is the key track, played at length and with considerable thought. Konitz's own song, 'Dream Stepper' and the title-track, are disappointingly generic and it's Brown who surprises with three very strong ideas, including the closing 'Feather Bed', which finishes the album very much on a high.

*** Tenorlee

Candid 71019 *Konitz; Jimmy Rowles (p); Michael Moore (b).* 1/77, 3/78.

As the title suggests, Konitz put down his alto for this one. On the bigger horn, he sounds much as Bird and Ornette sounded on tenor: very much like themselves. He favours a soft middle register that is often within alto range, but the lower sonority puts him in a different relation to both piano and bass, and on 'Skylark' and 'Autumn Nocturne' it's possible to hear him renegotiating his line as Moore moves too close. 'Tenorlee' is unaccompanied saxophone; it's not quite Coleman Hawkins, indeed much closer to Lester Young, which is why the segue into a trio 'Lady Be Good' is so effectively redolent of Pres's and Basie's version of the song. An experiment, and very much a sidebar, but an intriguing issue none the less and now augmented by two extra tunes.

*** Yes Yes Nonet

Steeplechase SCCD 31119 *Konitz; Tom Harrell (t, flhn); John Eckert (t, picc t, flhn); Jimmy Knepper (tb); Sam Burtis (btb, tba); Ronnie Cuber (bs, cl); Harold Danko (p); Buster Williams (b); Billy Hart (d).* 8/79.

**(*) Live At Laren

Soul Note 121069 *Konitz; Red Rodney (t, flhn); John Eckert (t, picc t, flhn); Jimmy Knepper (tb); Sam Burtis (btb, tba); Ronnie Cuber (bs, cl); Ben Aronov (p, electric p); Harold Danko (p); Ray Drummond (b); Billy Hart (d).* 8/79.

The Nonet was one of Konitz's more successful larger groups. The brass settings were well ventilated and open-textured and Konitz soloed confidently, often oblivious to the constraints of metre. The Steeplechase is the better of the two (though the title is unforgivable), largely because Harrell sounds more sympathetic to Konitz's own conception; Wayne Shorter's 'Footprints' is the outstanding cut. On *Live At Laren*, generally a good concert rendering, the saxophonist rather too generously accommodates Rodney's somewhat backward-looking bop manner with what occasionally sound – on 'April' and 'Moon Dreams' – like pastiches of himself.

*** Toot Sweet

Owl 013 432 2 *Konitz; Michel Petrucciani (p).* 5/82.

Recorded in the slightly cavernous acoustic of the Centre Musical Bosendorfer in Paris, with Petrucciani on a ripe-sounding house piano, this set has only recently been reissued, though with no additional material. From the beginning, the little Frenchman plays rather properly and without much in the way of swing, leading Konitz through the melody and chords of 'I Hear A Rhapsody', before taking things in a slightly more promising direction on his own 'To Erlinda', though without the saxophonist; the later 'Ode' is a solo from Lee. The two big performances are 'Lover Man' and 'Round About Midnight', both of them mined to exhaustion for fresh ideas but given new life here. The closing track is a worked-up theme for the date which suggests that some musical empathy emerged. For the most part, though, these two seem as politely remote as they sound on the mix.

*** Dovetail

Sunnyside 1003 *Konitz; Harold Danko (p); Jay Leonhart (b).* 2/83.

How a 'terzet' differs from a trio isn't clear, though we'd argue that the geometry of this set is very different from the average jazz threesome. Rhythm duties are distributed round the group and, particularly on tunes like 'Alone Together' (a Konitz favourite) and 'Cherokee', it is hard to differentiate between melodic, harmonic and time-keeping roles. Delightful stuff.

★★★(★) Dedicated To Lee

Dragon DRCD 250 *Konitz; Jan Allan (t); Gustavo Bergalli (t, flhn); Torgny Nilsson (tb); Hector Bingert (ts); Gunnar Bergsten (bs); Lars Sjøsten (p); Lars Lundstrom (b); Egil Johansen (d).* 11/83.

A decade before this session, Konitz had played on one of the last studio sessions by Lars Gullin. Though the great Swedish baritonist, who died in 1976, is widely acknowledged as one of the best European players of his day, his compositional output is still very little known. Hence the happy idea of putting Konitz together with Lars Sjøsten's octet and a group of Gullin pieces. Sjøsten was Gullin's regular accompanist during the last decade-and-a-half of his career, and he knows this material inside out. 'Dedicated To Lee' and 'Late Date' had actually been written for Konitz 30 years before, when the two saxophonists recorded in Stockholm; the originals are included on a Gullin composition issued by Dragon. The immediate reaction to these tracks is that Gullin was a deceptively simple melodist. Pieces like 'Fine Together' and 'Happy Again' may be generic, and might have been written by any one of a dozen American song-writers, but 'Peter Of April' (dedicated to his son) is a subtle and masterful conception that is very difficult to reduce to its essential parts. A couple of pieces have been reconstructed from piano scores, which partly explains the inclusion of Jan Allan, a guest spot in thanks for bringing in the chart for 'Peter Of April'. Anyone who hasn't made Lars Gullin's acquaintance would be well advised to start sampling the Dragon discs (see above), but this is a very worthwhile piece on its own account, and the combination of Gullin and Konitz is, as ever, irresistible.

★★★★ Star Eyes: Hamburg 1983

hatOLOGY 518 *Konitz; Martial Solal (p).* 11/83.

Of the quite literally dozens of duo recordings now credited to Konitz, this is one of the most remarkable, and much of the credit has to go to the French pianist who creates such challenging accompaniments on such familiar themes. Even 'Cherokee', tucked away at the end of the set, seems reinvented, but it's the duo's approach to 'Star Eyes', 'It's You' and even 'Subconscious-Lee' that startles. Solal stays well inside the tune in terms of chordal patterns and basic trajectory, but his harmonies are so rich and ambiguous that Konitz is initially obliged to work his way back to the source before taking the theme out as he would normally do. It's a hugely impressive performance from start to finish and one of maybe four or five Konitz albums that should be in every collection. (Given that hatOLOGY releases are limited editions that should create some competition.)

★★★★ Wild As Springtime

Candid CCD 79734 *Konitz; Harold Danko (p).* 3/84.

Recorded in Glasgow by Elliot Meadow, this pairs Konitz with his most responsive accompanist of the '80s. The big plus on this carefully mastered CD issue is an unreleased track, 'It's You', and two alternatives, Chick Corea's 'Hairy Canary' and George Russell's classic 'Ezz-thetic', his elaborate contrafact on the changes to 'Love For Sale'. This is the territory Konitz loves, and his own 'Hi, Beck', which is mined from 'Pennies From Heaven' takes on a startling new profile in this version. Meadow's liner-note makes it clear that the set wasn't just a tired souvenir of what had been a long tour but a patiently crafted and very thoughtful session. Including 'Hairy Canary' is certainly a sign that they weren't coasting; it's a very different Corea from the wistful composer of 'Duende', also represented here, and the release take is certainly a couple of degrees more accomplished and polished than the rejected one. Danko weighs in with a couple of typical themes, both dance-based: 'Silly Samba' is an invitation to Konitz to step and slide away on one of his fugitive lines, while 'Spinning Waltz', a Danko favourite, is delicately woven out of the lightest of materials. Perhaps the best place to judge the empathy between these two remarkable players is the spontaneously composed 'Ko', its title derived from the first two letters of the saxophonist's name and the last two of the pianist's. Hard to believe that no element of this exquisite performance was predetermined; Danko sweeps the open strings of the piano, creating a shimmering backdrop to one of Konitz's most formally perfect off-the-cuff statements. Utterly delightful from start to finish.

★★★ Ideal Scene

Soul Note 121119 *Konitz; Harold Danko (p); Rufus Reid (b); Al Harewood (d).* 7/86.

★★★ The New York Album

Soul Note 121169 *Konitz; Harold Danko (p); Marc Johnson (b); Adam Nussbaum (d).* 8/87.

Danko's exact chording and fine grasp of durations on *Ideal Scene* open up the challenging spaces of George Russell's 'Ezz-thetic' and the more familiar, but inexhaustible, 'Stella By Starlight'. He is more conventional but no less inventive on *The New York Album*. Constant duo performance tended to reinforce Konitz's early preference for very long, unpunctuated lines. Working with a band as closely attentive as both of these allows him to break up his development and give it an emotional directness which is reminiscent – in mood if not always in tonality – of the blues. Johnson's and Reid's moody delivery, and Nussbaum's almost casual two-fours on the later album, reinforce the slightly darker sound – 'Limehouse Blues' included! Hard to choose between them.

★★★ Medium Rare

Label Bleu LBLC 6501 *Konitz; Dominique Cravic (g); Francis Varis (acc); Hélène Labarrière (b); Jean-Claude Jouy (d).* 86.

Positively undercooked in places, but there's enough juicy substance from the mid-point 'Monk's Mood' onwards to keep eyes on the plate. 'Ezz-thetic' is marvellous again, one of the most imaginative covers the piece has ever received; 'Chick Came Round' also reappears from *Ideal Scene* (and is worth a brief comparison); and Dominique Cravic's three originals (notably the name-checking 'Blue Label', with its fine intro from Hélène Labarrière) are all excellent. The accordion functions very differently from a piano or even a vibraphone in the mix, keeping the harmonies from tightening up, laying on areas of colour, accentuating a softly shuffling rhythm. Konitz ranges between alto and soprano saxophones, with a tight clarinet sound in the higher registers which is exactly right for this company. Unusual and fine.

★★★(★) Zounds

Soul Note 121219 *Konitz; Kenny Werner (p, ky); Ron McClure (b); Bill Stewart (d).* 5/90.

Konitz continues to surprise with three remarkable free improvisations on which he abandons chord changes, conventional melody and straightforward rhythmic computations in favour of an exploration of pure sound. These tracks are interspersed with two staple items ('Prelude To A Kiss' and 'Taking A Chance On Love'), an original samba and the astonishing 14-minute 'All Things Considered', which sounds like a summation of what Konitz has been doing for the last 25 years. The whole set has a freewheeling, spontaneous feel that confirms the saxophonist's status as one of the most original players on the scene. As a free player, Konitz has well-attested credentials, having worked in unscripted formats with Lennie Tristano, four decades before his surprise inclusion in Derek Bailey's Company collective for 1987. 'Synthesthetics' is a set of duets over Werner's highly individual synthesizer lines (an individual player, he brings a doom-laden atmosphere even to the Ellington tune); Konitz vocalizes with surprising self-confidence. His soprano saxophone playing on 'Soft Lee' is probably the best he's yet committed to record. Werner and McClure are both magnificent, but there has to be a slight hesitation over Bill Stewart, who seems to fall in and out of synch with the music, overcompensating furiously when a more regular groove is re-established. Otherwise absolutely sterling.

★★★ Swiss Kiss

TCB 93072 *Konitz; Matthieu Michel (t); Emilio Soana (t, flhn); Vincent Lachat, Bernard Trinchan (tb); Yves Massy (tb); George Robert, Michel Weber (as); Christian Gavillet (ts); Dado Moroni (p); Isla Eckinger (b); Peter Schmidlin (d); Alain Guyonnet Big Band.* 90.

Konitz reacted warmly to the music of Swiss composer/bandleader Alain Guyonnet. In 1992 he recorded a duo set of Guyonnet pieces with pianist Kenny Werner (see below). Here, he's in more expansive company with the Guyonnet Tentet and Big Band. The full orchestra appears only on the last four selections, and these are the weakest part of an otherwise excellent record. Konitz always sounds better and his oblique harmonic approach always works better when the arrangements are left sparser, as with the mid-size group's echoes of the *Birth Of The Cool* ensemble. Guyonnet also absorbed George Robert's quartet into the proceedings, so there is a certain layers of the onion feel to this disc. At the heart of it is Konitz himself, playing calm and stately whatever the surroundings, and positively inspired on 'Mister Dream', which sees him switch to soprano, and the testing 'Friends', which was written by the saxophonist. The other soloists work at an impressively high level, notably trumpeter Matthieu Michel on 'Days Of Wine And Roses', but there's onlee one star on this date.

★★★(★) Lullaby Of Birdland

Candid CCD 79709 *Konitz; Barry Harris (p); Calvin Hill (b); Leroy Williams (d).* 9/91.

As with *Jazz Nocturne*, below, this is valuable for showing Konitz on home turf and with a front-rank *jazz* accompanist. Harris plays the changes immaculately, eschewing fancy modulations and non-canonical key-changes. If it sounds boringly conventional, it ain't. Both men are at the top of their craft, and the solos on a totally standards-based programme are packed with invention. Konitz's solo on 'Cherokee' even manages to squeeze in a couple of Ornette phrases, just as he inverts a Parker idea, stretching out its metre in the process, on 'Anthropology'. The only quibbles about *Lullaby Of Birdland* concern the rhythm section, who are either playing too loud or else have been badly balanced in Mark Morganelli's final mix. Otherwise, hard to fault.

★★★ Friends

Dragon DRCD 240 *Konitz; Gunnar Bergsten (bs); Lars Sjøsten (p); Peter Soderblom (b); Nils Danell (d).* 12/91.

The performances of two Lars Gullin compositions – 'Lars Meets Jeff' and 'Happy Again' – suggest that Konitz may have been studying the great Swede's records, since he quotes from original solos in a couple of places. This sort of gig is now pretty run-of-the-mill for him, but there's never a moment when the attention seems to flag or waver. Sjøsten's quartet is highly professional and very musical, and the permutation of alto/soprano with baritone saxophone works delightfully.

★★★ Lunasea

Soul Note 121249 *Konitz; Peggy Stern (p); Vic Juris (g); Harvie Swartz (b); Jeff Williams (d); Guilherme Franco (perc).* 1/92.

Stern's a gutsy, uncomplicated player with a very individual delivery that somehow recalls Tommy Flanagan. Konitz clearly enjoys the settings Stern and Juris lay out, for he plays with great freedom and relaxation, compressing ideas into short, slightly enigmatic, solo statements that frequently drift outside the confines of the song in question. Swartz and Williams keep things securely moored, but Franco is mixed up way too loud and his busy percussion intrudes more than once.

★★★(★) Unleemited

Owl 014 727 2 *Konitz; Kenny Werner (p, cel).* 1/92.

During a fantastically prolific spell for Konitz, he hooked up with yet another fine pianist to record this set of Alain Guyonnet compositions. The title-piece is a very fair approximation of the kind of sliding, angular blues-based tune that Konitz creates himself, but it is with pieces like 'Brazilian Fondue' and 'Baby, I'm A Legend' that the Swiss bandleader reveals his eclectic originality, switching from neo-bop harmonies to rich Latin structures to relatively abstract chord shapes, all within the space of a couple of songs. Werner is in excellent form and his celeste adds a hint of spice to the session.

★★★ Leewise

Storyville STCD 4181 *Konitz; Jeff Davis (t); Allan Botschinsky (t, flhn); Erling Kroner (tb); Niels Gerhardt (btb, tba); Jens Sondergaard (ss, as, bs); Peter Gullin (ts, bs); Butch Lacy, Peggy Stern (p); Jesper Lundgaard (b); Svend-Erik Norregaard (d); Brigitte Frieboe (v).* 3/92.

Konitz was the 1992 winner of the prestigious Jazzpar Prize, an accolade which brings with it the opportunity to record with a hand-picked Danish group. Only the first three tracks – 'Partout', 'Alone Together' and 'Body And Soul' – were recorded at the Jazzpar concert. The All-Star Nonet, directed by Jens Sondergaard, is exemplarily professional but lacks a little in relaxed expressiveness. As probably befits a celebratory event, the emphasis is on playing rather than on ground-breaking new material. There are a couple of more improvisatory duets, with saxophonist Sondergaard and with Botschinsky, but these are less focused than usual, even a little casual and bland.

***(*) Jazz Nocturne

Evidence ECD 22085 *Konitz; Kenny Barron (p); James Genus (b); Kenny Washington (d).* 10/92.

Great to hear Konitz in a straight jazz context and in such a good band. Though his younger European collaborators deserve every credit and respect for their musicianship, these are the saxophonist's peers – Barron at least – and this is the kind of music where his gifts are best deployed. It's entirely a standards session: 'Misty', 'Body And Soul', 'You'd Be So Nice To Come Home To', 'Everything Happens To Me', 'Alone Together', 'In A Sentimental Mood'. Impeccably played and engineered with taste and discretion by Peter Beckerman, who's managed to iron out some shaky moments with discreet edits (or so it sounds on a very careful listen). All of the material was laid down in a day, but it does sound as if the studio was rearranged at least once; Genus certainly moves in the mix.

*** Thingin

hatOLOGY 547 *Konitz; Don Friedman (p); Attila Zoller (g).* 3/95.

Art Lange's liner-notes present this set as a confluence of several different strands of musical history, although he seems to blunt his own argument by showing how Zoller (seemingly the odd man out) learned much of what he knows of 'Tristano school' harmony from Lars Gullin and Hans Koller. The reality of the session is three musicians of somewhat different sensibilities coming together on a body of readily agreed material. There's not much contention here, just a confident sweep across familiar turf. 'Thingin'' (which seems to have lost its ellipsing comma for the album title) is Konitz's familiar contrafact on 'All The Things You Are' and provides the group with a marvellous starting point in standards that surfaces again on 'Alone Together'. Zoller's original 'Joy For Joy' is more obviously rooted in his own CV, as is Don Friedman's 'Opus D'Amour', but these two share a past in Herbie Mann's group, so the light, Latinized swing is second nature. They also contribute 'Cloisterbells' and 'Images' respectively, two more impressionistic sketches that don't require much development. The real payoff, after the Dietz/Schwartz warhorse, is the pianist's 'Suite For 3' – a cleverly confected theme and variations that puts each voice in the forefront for a time. Nice stuff; not a classic album, but an enjoyable record of a live gig in Thalwil, Switzerland.

*** Meets Don Friedman

Camerata 10 *Konitz; Don Friedman (p).* 96.

Same chemistry as on the hatOLOGY date, but with just the duo, Friedman has more room for movement and seems keen to stretch himself. 'Alone Together' and 'Opus D'Amour' are again on the agenda, the former played with much more muscle than in the trio format, the latter every bit as lovely but possibly lacking a touch of bite. Nice record, though.

*** Body And Soul

Camerata 12 *Konitz; Gary Foster (as); Jimmie Smith (d).* 96.

Dedicated to the memory of Warne Marsh, this consists of nine fairly extended variants on familiar chord progressions, all of them except 'Body And Soul' itself given a present participle title on the lines of the now familiar 'Thingin'', which is one of the better cuts. Both saxophonists have a subtle grasp of vertical harmony and there are moments when one feels one's listening to a 'Prelude and Fugue' exercise which might work almost as well on paper. But Foster plays with some emotion and Konitz's attack is always sharper when around other saxophone-players, so there's lots to listen to.

*** It's You

Steeplechase 31398 *Konitz; Ron McClure (b); Billy Hart (d).* 3/96.

Without a piano again, Konitz almost recaptures the fleeting quality of his classic *Motion*. McClure and Hart are both well up to the job and McClure in particular seems to relish the job of filling in the missing chords with crisp double stops and slow arpeggios across the fingerboard. The title-piece is a long, somewhat enigmatic meditation and the best moment of the set comes on 'Angel Eyes', when Konitz rhapsodizes in the driest and most unromantic tone imaginable and still comes away with the girl.

*** Strings For Holiday

Enja 9304 *Konitz; Cenovia Cummins, Mark Feldman (vn); Jill Jaffe, Ron Lawrence (vla); Eric Friedlander, Daniel Pezzotti (clo); Michael Formanek (b); Matt Wilson (d).* 3/96.

Sometimes with Lee, you wonder if the album-title comes first and the concept follows on behind. Usually, he manages to confound any such cynicism and this is one such case. It's always an interesting challenge, recording with strings, and here Lee has assembled some very strong jazz-aware players who know how to swing but don't attempt to do it self-consciously. All the tunes are associated with Billie Holiday, though no 'Strange Fruit', thank God. 'God Bless The Child' is full of sliding, plangent string sounds, and 'Lover Man' has a yearning quality that tears at the heart. For a player who is utterly at ease in the sparsest settings, Konitz thrives in this context and *Strings For Holiday* contains some of his most elegantly shaped solos.

*** Subconscious-Lee

Summit 213 *Konitz; Peter Decker (ts); Dany Schwickerath (g); Johannes Schaedlich (b); Oliver Strauch (d).* 96.

Though otherwise dominated by Konitz themes, this live recording from a European tour kicks off with a rousing line on 'Yardbird Suite' that finds the nearly 70-year-old saxophonist faster on his feet than his German colleagues. By the time they get to the staple 'Thingin'' they've just about caught up. Decker occasionally forgets he's not Warne Marsh and slips into a dry, fluttery idiom that doesn't suit him or the band. Lee has played with guitarists since the Billy Bauer days and often seems to favour the open, even ambiguous tonality he gets when non-piano chords are about. That's true here; due praise to Schwickerath for his role on a very attractive session.

***(*) Dearly Beloved

Steeplechase SCCD 31406 *Konitz; Harold Danko (p); Jay Anderson (b); Billy Drummond (d).* 10/96.

**** Out Of Nowhere

Steeplechase SCCD 31427 *As above, except omit Danko; add Paul Bley (p).* 4/97.

In many respects, Paul Bley is a musician whose career trajectory has been broadly similar to Konitz's: a huge output, almost unfeasibly large, and yet with only a rather vague and insubstantial purchase on popular recognition. Listen to the two veterans negotiate 'Lover Man' and you realize how much of this business depends on experience, not just technical facility but the ability to distil sound from the brute business of getting by. The two other long numbers, 'Sweet And Lovely' and 'I Can't Get Started', are more abstract, but no less effective. Anderson and Drummond provide unflagging support, and Nils Winther's production skills are once again evident, as they are on the slightly earlier *Dearly Beloved*. Danko is more of a melodist than Bley, and on 'The Way You Look Tonight' and 'Bye Bye Blackbird' he sticks close to the basic code, only really breaking loose on the closing 'Night Has A Thousand Eyes'. By then, though, the spell has been cast; a less venturesome and cerebral album than *Out Of Nowhere*, but no less vibrantly exciting for all that.

***** Inside Cole Porter**
NEL JAZZ NH7 967 *Konitz; Franco D'Andrea (p). 96.*

***** Inside Rodgers**
Philology W 153 2 *Konitz; Franco D'Andrea (p). 96.*

****(*) Where's The Blues**
Giants Of Jazz 53303 *Konitz; Mario Rusca (p). 98.*

The Rodgers material is probably suited to Lee's drier personality and delivery. 'My Funny Valentine' has always figured prominently in his output and this is a very fine interpretation of it. We preferred 'Thou Swell' and the long closing take of 'The Lady Is A Tramp'.

The record with Rusca features a competent pianist with some distinctive touches. It includes what by our reckoning is the 28th recorded outing of 'Thingin'', which might make an interesting line of enquiry for the serious student but scarcely counts as a vital contribution to the canon. 'Anthropology', 'Summertime', 'Have You Met Miss Jones?', 'Autumn Leaves', 'On Green Dolphin Street': something new in all of them, but nothing that stretches the language by so much as the thickness of an alto reed. This is not an appeal for fewer records but a warning that unless you're a Konitz completist (in which case: good luck and a healthy credit card), these are not essential purchases.

****** Alone Together**
Blue Note 57150 *Konitz; Brad Mehldau (p); Charlie Haden (b). 12/96.*

*****(*) Another Shade Of Blue**
Blue Note 98222 *As above. 12/97.*

At this point, Konitz seemed to have his pick of the major labels and was issuing records with prodigal self-assurance. This live session is one of his best ever. Turning 70, he was playing with magisterial calm and an elder statesman's mischief, as when he turns more than one of these chestnuts inside out. 'Round Midnight' is the most thoroughly subverted, with every cliché going registered and passed over almost mockingly. 'Cherokee', 'The Song Is You', 'What Is This Thing Called Love' and the title-tune are the other standards covered but, lest this suggest a pedestrian run-through of familiar changes, nothing is taken for granted in any of these performances. Everything, from the basic harmony to the final detail of the tune, is open to question and to rearrangement. Mehldau and Haden are equal partners, the latter not unexpectedly so, given his immense experience; but the pianist too has things to say and is temperamentally resistant to easy options, creating a sense of space and relaxed time whenever he is featured, accompanying his seniors with a solid musical scaffolding.

The sequel certainly doesn't match up to the original record, but the long, thoughtful versions of 'Body And Soul' and 'What's New' are packed with musical detail and with some drama as well.

***** Self Portrait**
Philology W121 *Konitz (as solo and multitracked). 2/97.*

Not quite, as producer Paolo Piangarelli claims, Konitz's only solo recording since *Lone-Lee*, but an unexpectedly rare return to such a successful and technically uncomplicated formula. The difference here is that the saxophonist is heard in counterpoint with himself and in canonical groups of up to four lines. The effect is actually quite mechanical, and when one turns to the central 'Self Portrait In Blues', a wry, self-effacing diary entry in an idiom that hasn't always been Konitz's most comfortable, it's clear that much of the multitracked material relies too much on technical trickery and not quite enough on straightforward expression. Made to celebrate the saxophonist's 70th birthday, it lifts another corner on a fascinating career. The 'Self Portrait', a long 'Dearly Beloved' and parts of 'Subconscious-Lee' are worth having. The rest is for dedicated collectors only.

***** L'Age Mur**
Philology 123 *Konitz; Enrico Rava (t); Rosario Bonaccorso (b); Massimo Manzi (d). 98.*

A surprisingly unadventurous and straightahead album given Rava's appetite for experiment. On 'Cherokee', which is admittedly given a Latin groove, he sounds more like an orthodox swing trumpeter than at any point in his career. The title-track is his and is the dullest item on the set, seeming to start in mid-thought and neither travel backwards to a premise or forwards to a conclusion. Konitz is absolutely himself – which is to say, instantly recognizable but utterly unpredictable in delivery, messing round with the structure of 'What's New' and giving his signature 'Thingin'' (aka 'All The Things You Are') a new twist.

*****(*) Three Guys**
Enja ENJ 9351 2 *Konitz; Steve Swallow (b); Paul Motian (d). 5/98.*

A trio of radical individualists, doing their several and collective thing on a set of clever and challenging themes, most of them originals. 'Thingin'', Lee's version of 'All The Things You Are', is now a central component of his repertoire, and this is a fabulous performance of it, with the trio weaving and interlocking in the most imaginative way. The really interesting writing is Swallow's, 'Ladies' Wader' and 'Eiderdown', but Motian delivers two cracking themes on 'From Time To Time' and 'Johnny Broken Wing'. Beautifully recorded and mixed, a high-gloss showcase for three astounding players.

***** Dialogues**
Challenge 70053 *Konitz; Bert Van den Brink (p); Hein Van de Geyn (b); Hans Van Oosterhout (d). 4/98.*

Recorded almost in real time, this easily swinging session is further evidence of Konitz's ability to catalyse and transform a seemingly ordinary pick-up session. He and trio leader Van den Brink tackle 'Moonlight In Vermont' on their own, but one immediately misses the solid, evocative presence of Van de Geyn, who always adds interest to even the simplest bridge passage or intro. 'Thingin'' is Lee's long-standing contrafact on

'All The Things You Are' and here it receives a solid work-out, while 'Cherokee' is almost thrown away. Great work from all concerned.

***** Tender Lee (For Chet)**

Philology W.163 2 *Konitz; Stefano Bollani (p); Pietro Giangaglini (b); Fabrizio Sferra (dv).* 12/98.

Bollani is one of the emerging figures of Italian jazz and he's enormous on this live set, taken from two nights at La Palma in Rome and dedicated by Lee to the memory of Chet Baker who had died ten years earlier. The opening 'Blues For Chet' leads almost inevitably into 'My Funny Valentine', which is given as fulsome and openhearted a performance as you'll ever hear. The highlights of the set come over the final stretch with 'But Not For Me', 'What's New' and a lovely closing version of 'I'll Remember April'. The sound isn't perfect, but the playing is first rate and the set will conjure up memories of Chet's own association with fine Italian groups like this one.

****** Sound Of Surprise**

RCA Victor 69309 *Konitz; Ted Brown (ts); John Abercrombie (g); Marc Johnson (b); Joey Baron (d).* 99.

The key track here is the classic 'Subconscious-Lee', played by each of the players individually, then as an ensemble, then as a more orthodox theme-plus-solos. Brown has something of Warne Marsh's smooth, cool, thoughtful tone, and the echoes are confirmed time and again, on 'Blues Suite', 'Hi Beck' and 'Thingin''. Johnson and Baron are magnificent and Joey's pattering, rapid-fire percussion is the key to a thoroughly enjoyable and endlessly thought-provoking set.

****(*) At The Mississippi Jazz Club**

Philology W 503.2 *Konitz; Giovanni Ceccarelli (p); Mauro Battisti (b); Carlo Battisti (d).* 3/00.

This starts so shakily you wonder why it's on an issued record, but after a stumble through 'Yesterdays'/'The Song Is You', Konitz pulls the Italian band into line and coasts into a superb 'Body And Soul' that works new variations on a venerable theme. Ceccarelli's role is vital: crisp, intelligent comping and some flair as a soloist as well. The bassist and drummer (who are presumably brothers) show more sibling rivalry than affectionate understanding and several times to be trying to outdo each other and to drown out Konitz, who isn't specially well recorded. As just another night on the stand, it's perfectly decent, but we'd doubt that you'd want to listen to it over and over.

*****(*) Richlee**

Steeplechase SCCD 31440 *Konitz; Rich Perry (ts); Harold Danko (p); Jay Anderson (b); Billy Drummond (d).* 00.

A fairly straightforward blowing date in comparison to many of Konitz's projects of recent years. Perry is no Warne Marsh soundalike but Lee has the ability to modulate his own delivery to suit his partners, without compromising one millimetre on what he has to say. The set kicks off with 'You're A Weaver Of Dreams', and the two saxophones whirl away. Between them, 'Three Little Words' and a profound 'How Deep Is The Ocean' take up about half the set, but they are endlessly listenable performances, packed with detail and with ideas crossing the studio at a furious pace. Konitz slackens off only on a short 'Out Of Nowhere', a song that now has Warne Marsh (and Marsh's onstage demise) imprinted all over it.

***** Dig-It**

Steeplechase SCCD 31466 *Konitz; Ted Brown (ts); Ron McClure (b); Jeff Williams (d).* 00.

The association with Ted Brown goes back some time now and really bears fruit on this free-wheeling piano-less set. As one might expect, McClure makes the harmonic base sound as solid as anyone could want. At any point in any song, check what McClure is doing and he's always there, either anticipating the next direction or quietly tidying up the loose ends. There are some ragged spots on Brown's own 'Smog Eyes' and even on familiar stuff like 'Hi Beck' and 'Subconscious-Lee', perhaps explained by an odd air of haste that surrounds the whole session. Given the number of recordings Konitz was making at this period, he probably had another studio booked down the road.

*****(*) Live-Lee**

Milestone MCD 9329 2 *Konitz; Alan Broadbent (p).* 10/00.

If you want to sample just how extraordinary a session this is, scroll straight forward to track five, where Broadbent deconstructs 'Cherokee' from the headdress downwards, leaving Konitz to make a few cursory embellishments to the melody. The pianist is in absolutely titanic form throughout this wonderful live date from the Jazz Bakery in LA. Not since the 1983 duets with Martial Solal has Konitz sounded so thoroughly tested by his playing partner. Broadbent has a confidently percussive, ringing tone which combines precision of touch with a lot of power and authority. On the less familiar material – Konitz originals like 'Gundula' and 'Keepin' The News' – he's a touch more reticent and restricts himself to filling in the background, but whenever he does one finds oneself willing him to break loose again. A genuinely fine album from two remarkable musicians.

***** After Hours: Volume 7**

Go Jazz GO 6056 2 *Konitz; Billy Peterson (b); Kenny Horst (d).* 1/01.

Konitz was unaware that tapes were running on the final hour of this lock-in session at the St Paul, Minnesota club owned by the bassist and drummer. The saxophonist apparently told producer Ben Sidran that he'd liked the set and hoped the tapes preserved 'a looking around feeling'. They certainly do. This is the sound of three men playing unself-consciously, no longer for an audience or to a producer's signal, but simply thinking their way through 'It's You Or No One', 'Alone Together', 'Sweet And Lovely', another couple of standards and Lee's own 'Mr Green' (which he takes pretty much alone, Peterson and Horst touching in a bit of detail behind). It's a terrific set and a sign that Konitz had extended his activities into the new millennium which, strictly speaking, had only began days before.

***** Duas Contas**

Philology W 501.2 *Konitz; Irio De Paula (g).* 4/01.

***** Outra Vez**

Philology W 502.2 *Konitz; Sandro Gibellini (g); Barbara Cassini (v).* 4/01.

Philology seemed to go into overdrive with Konitz albums after 2000. These two guitar-backed sessions were taped in Italy in April 2001. They present Lee in a setting that harks back to the early days with the likes of Joe Puma and both De Paula and Gibellini are clearly hip to that whole school, even if both players are more individual and more romantic. *Duas Contas* is a lovely, undemanding set, opening on a moody 'Once I Loved' and touching on lots of Brazilian material before delivering a delightful sucker punch with 'On A Slow Boat To China', which is as fresh a Konitz performance as you'll hear.

The vocal album inevitably features less of Konitz at any length but he is there throughout, floating round Cassini with the same slightly dry and vibrato-free delivery she favours. It's an attractive combination and the kind of thing Philology obviously believe they can sell. For most tastes, though, this will seem lightweight fare.

*****(*) Some New Stuff**
DIW 939 *Konitz; Greg Cohen (b); Joey Baron (d).* 99.

This is delicious. Baron's witty, light percussion is a perfect foil for Lee on 'Lennie's Pennies' and the set opens with every promise of something special. It doesn't quite deliver on that promise, but there is enough here to convince anyone of Konitz's endless harmonic invention and rhythmic flexibility. 'Debussy' may be a reference to recent classical experiments; 'Tripletting' and 'Folk Tune' are meant to sound like diffident technical exercises and are, of course, much more; the 'new stuff' is no newer than he was putting about at any time previously but it comes across fresh and direct in this company. By now, Lee was making albums as if there was no tomorrow; the damnable thing is that they're nearly all wonderful.

***** Pride**
Steeplechase SCCD 31479 *Konitz; George Colligan (p); Doug Weiss (b); Darren Beckett (d).* 5/99.

The band here is patchier than most of Lee's recent line-ups. Individually, all three rhythm-section players are fine, but we'd question the chemistry – or non-chemistry – between Weiss and Beckett. As ever, Konitz is magisterially good and for much of the set he and Colligan just work away together; his own 'Stellar' and 'Once I Had A Secret Love' make the set.

(***) And The Axis String Quartet Play French Impressionist Music From The 20th Century
Palmetto 2064 *Konitz; Axis String Quartet.* 1/00.

And he does exactly what it says on the tin: compositions by Satie, Ravel, Fauré, Koechlin, Chausson and Debussy, delivered with very little attempt to jazz them up, but mercifully without the unctuous bleat of 'French classical saxophone' (we have a petition to hand if you share our toxic reaction). Arranger Ohad Talmor has taken substantial liberties with some of the pieces, adding elements that cosmetically enhance the modernism of some of them, but also suggesting allusions to other, unrelated works, which is slightly baffling. An adventurous project in its way and certainly far removed from either the usual 'with strings' gig or more banal attempts to jazz up classics.

***** Parallels**
Chesky 240 *Konitz; Mark Turner (ts): Peter Bernstein (g); Steve Gilmore (b); Bill Goodwin (d).* 12/00.

Released in Super Audio, this makes the most of a recording done in a downtown New York church, a lovely acoustic for a very relaxed but not uninventive session. The addition of guitar offers Konitz some interesting possibilities which he exploits to the full. The opening 'How Deep Is The Ocean?' has been partly restructured, 'For Hans' is beautifully constructed and deeply felt and the co-composition 'Eyes' with guest Mark Turner, who also sits in on '317 East 32nd St' (the gig address, presumably), is a worthy attempt to keep clear of Warne'n'Lee clichés.

****(*) Gong With Wind Suite**
Steeplechase SCCD 31528 *Konitz; Matt Wilson (d).* 3/02.

The title is slightly misleading. In no sense is this a suite, but rather a shapeless collection of mostly free improvisations. Konitz is in pretty acerbic form without songs to get his teeth into, and there is something unlovely about his attack. Wilson can't really be said to be a genuine collaborator, since his task is clearly that of accompanist; but he does it well and Lee is playing with great thought and concentration, so the results may appeal to some.

Olga Konkova

PIANO

Russian-born, she studied classical music in Moscow before coming to the US for a course at Berklee. Now based in Oslo and a fine composer/performer.

***** Her Point Of View**
Candid 79757 *Konkova; Adam Nussbaum (d).* 97, 98.

***** Northern Crossings**
Candid 79766 *Konkova; Ole Mathisen (ss, ts); Per Mathisen (b); Jojo Mayer (d).* 9/97.

***** Some Things From Home**
Candid 79777 *Konkova; Per Mathisen (b); Jon Christensen, Adam Nussbaum (d).* 5/97–3/01.

There aren't enough women in this book and there are very few living practitioners of Olga's class. She takes remarkable liberties with familiar material, recomposing rather than merely improvising on changes. Her very exact technique isn't any obstacle to swing and she lags behind or pushes ahead of the beat as the spirit moves her. On the first disc, she gives 'Round Midnight' one of the freshest readings it's had in years, as well as introducing new compositions like 'The Little Prince' and 'Adam's Checking In'.

The second record features all original material, by Olga and husband Per Mathisen. The drummer is Swiss, so the group has an international feel and certainly doesn't play like a New York outfit. The best of the writing is the pianist's, though Mathisen's 'Fifth Corner' and 'Northern Crossing', which bookend the set, are both very fine compositions and 'Olga's Dream' is delightful. As will be clear, most of this material was recorded within a very short space of time and doesn't seem to have been followed up. The last trio album is well up to scratch, and features two of the world's best drummers, but no sign as yet that Olga's reputation is any more firmly established.

Bernd Konrad

TENOR, SOPRANO AND BARITONE SAXOPHONES

German reedman with advanced ideas, but so far no wider reputation.

***** Phonolith**
hatOLOGY 520 *Konrad; Herbert Joos, Kenny Wheeler (t); Hans Koller (as); Paul Schwartz, Christoph Spendel (p);*

Didier Lockwood (vn); Thomas Heidepriem, Thomas Stabenow (b); Martin Bues, Pierre Favre, Michael Kersting (d). 80, 94.

As the recording dates suggest, Konrad has had to wait some time before breaking out. It seems a pity because his music is far from inaccessible. Harmonically adventurous and rhythmically tough it may be, but it has a graceful quality that comes out on the nonet recordings, with Wheeler and Joos very much to the fore. Lockwood is riveting on 'Phonolith 1', demonstrating a range that goes beyond the usual Jean-Luc Ponty style and hints at a familiarity with tough Americans Billy Bang and Leroy Jenkins. The other 'Phonolith' is distinguished by Hans Koller's tenor and sopranino solos, the difficult pitching of the small horn troubling him not in the least. Koller is another artist still to acquire the reputation he deserves; his solo on 'Lush Life' is richly inflected and logical, sticking closer to the tune than initially evident. Konrad himself occasionally recalls other European giants Bobby Jaspar and Lars Gullin, but though he has his own voice (and plays beautiful baritone on 'Phonolith 2', one suspects that his greatest talent lies in shaping large structures with relatively restricted means. It's to be hoped that more of his remarkable work will be brought forward, if not by hatOLOGY then perhaps by another label that can offer him equally sympathetic company.

Larry Koonse

GUITAR

Much in demand as an accompanist, Koonse has a substantial discography, but few titles as a leader. His smooth lyrical style is always engaging.

***** Secret Tea**

Sea Breeze 3048 *Koonse; Anders Swanson (b); Chris Wabich (d).* n.d.

***** Americana**

Jazz Compass 1001 *Koonse; Chris Roitstein (p); Scott Colley (b); Kendall Kay (d).* 2/97.

***** Dialogues Of The Heart**

Jazz Compass 1005 *Koonse; Dave Koonse (g).* 00.

The most recent set is a father–son collaboration that will immediately conjure up echoes of the Raneys. It's a not unhelpful guide to the kind of music Larry makes on his own. His is a quiet and unassuming talent, very correct in execution but endlessly adaptable. The *Americana* set is different in that he is less responsible for the chords and can concentrate more on flowing lead lines, all of them delivered like the lines of a song, legacy of his considerable experience working with singers. Colley is the main composer on that set, revealing a still unrecognized talent. The first record is in some ways the best, certainly the most adventurous of the three.

Kristin Korb

VOCALS

San Diego-based singer making her debut in impressive company.

***** Introducing Kristin Korb With The Ray Brown Trio**

Telarc 83386 *Korb; Conte Candoli (t); Plas Johnson (ts); Benny Green (p); Oscar Castro-Nueves (g); Ray Brown (b); Gregory Hutchinson (d).* 96.

The line-up alone should be enticing. The Count's trumpet-playing is always worth hearing, in any context, and Johnson (still best known for the saxophone line in Henry Mancini's 'Pink Panther Theme') is greatly under-recognized. And, of course, any chance to hear the late Ray Brown is to be welcomed. But this is the singer's gig and Kristin acquits herself very nicely on her first outing. It isn't a big or specially dramatic voice, but inherently musical and she is wise enough not to tackle material that doesn't suit her. 'Peel Me A Grape' is the first highlight, delivered with an innocence that probably isn't all it seems. 'Take the "A" Train' is done slow, almost funereally on first hearing, but with a good deal of expression. Johnson brightens up 'Yeh Yeh' considerably and guitarist Castro-Nueves is an asset on 'Black Orpheus'. Our favourite cut, though, is something of a rarity, Neal Hefti's 'Whirlybird', which lifts the pace and sets the listener up nicely for the more relaxed stuff.

Hakon Kornstad

TENOR SAXOPHONE

Saxophonist working out of the Norwegian axis which revolved around Universal's Jazzland imprint.

*****(*) Space Available**

Jazzland 014724-2 *Kornstad; Mats Eilertsen (b); Paal Nilssen-Love (d).* 00.

Kornstad's outsize sound and extravagant phrasing suggest a line back to the Rollins lineage rather than the ubiquitous Coltrane gene-pool, and with Nilssen-Love fanning the flames with his usual nonchalant tumult, the music's superbly brawny, ferocious, gristle-free. Eilertsen at first sounds like a potential casualty in this tough arena, but his solo passage on the opening 'Arched Shape' – as refined and solid as Wilbur Ware – shows that he often just bides his time and waits for the moment. Perhaps they're not saying anything especially new in this music, but they're definitely saying it their own individual way.

Peter Kowald (1944–2002)

DOUBLE BASS

One of the key figures in European free music – as leader, sideman and eminence grise.

***** Touch The Earth – Break The Shells**

FMP CD 67 *Kowald; Wadada Leo Smith (t); Gunter Sommer (d, perc).* 11/79, 1/81.

One of the most individual of the European free players, Kowald is more often adduced as an influence on other players than for his own work, which is a great pity. The catalogue is thin enough, but what is available is of consistently excellent quality, concentrated and intense, with an independence of spirit audible in the voice which recalls Pettiford and Mingus.

This trio was out of catalogue for some time. Smith's free-jazz credentials are beyond question, and he brings a great range of voices to the session, whether on the tiny 'Wind Song In A Dance Of Unity' or larger conceptions on which he has stamped his personal concerns like 'Rastafari In The Universe' and 'In Light', a trio of tracks in the middle of the album which are almost a Smith project in miniature – except that Kowald is so obviously the master of all one hears: guiding, directing, sometimes cajoling.

***(*) **Bass Duets**
FMP CD 102 *Kowald; Maarten van Regteren Altena, Barry Guy, Barre Phillips (b).* 3/79–3/82.

This reissues (slightly frustratingly) large parts of three FMP vinyl releases, *Die Jungen: Random Generators, Paintings* and *Two Making A Triangle.* Kowald's uncanny mastery of the duet form – and the duet-with-another-bassist form – ensures that even over a long CD duration the music keeps the attention. His three partners shirk nothing in terms of each engagement, and Kowald is as interested in the songful sonorities of Phillips as he is in the disjunctive leaps of Guy and Altena.

**** **Duos: Europa America Japan**
FMP CD 21 *Kowald; with Derek Bailey, Conrad Bauer, Han Bennink, Peter Brötzmann, Tom Cora, Andrew Cyrille, Danny Davis, Floris Floridis, Diamanda Galas, Junko Handa, Masahiko Kono, Jeanne Lee, Joelle Léandre, Seizan Matsuda, Keiki Midorikawa, Akira Sakata, Irène Schweizer, Tadao Sawai, Evan Parker.* 86–90.

Kowald's discography took a pasting with the demise of FMP's vinyl catalogue. Indeed, three geographically divided LPs containing material from the *Duos* were the last to be issued by the German label. This is not a compilation, but a sampling of material not included on the vinyl release. Serious collectors will want to have both formats. For everyone else, the CD issue is a respectable sampling of Kowald in various performing contexts, and it affords a clear view of his changing priorities, sometimes playing time, sometimes accentuating double-stopped chords, sometimes producing pure sound.

Nothing is more than seven minutes long – and most of the tracks are very much shorter than that. By no means all are the product of free improvisation; the pieces with Evan Parker, Conny Bauer, Andrew Cyrille, Akira Sakata, Peter Brötzmann and some others were developed on predetermined ideas. Nor is the usual convention of absolute democracy and equality among instruments strictly observed. In quite a number of cases, Kowald is content to take an accompanist's role, backing Diamanda Galas's fraught vocal with doomy pedals, and Andrew Cyrille's complex body-language with quite conventional octaves and a vocal drone. Always musical, though, and thoroughly responsive to the needs of the moment.

The instrumental combinations are of particular interest, and other bassists will learn enormously from Kowald's capacity to vary his attack according to context. He takes a more prominent role with the horn-players, building counter-melodies, right-angled lines and even little retrograde progressions which create an impression of harmonic resolution even where no such thing is actually happening. This works fine with the Westerners, but there are inevitable difficulties with the Japanese performances. The problems certainly aren't to do with sonorities (Bailey's guitar often sounds like a shamisen or a biwa) but of basic aesthetic philosophies. Though Sakata and Kono are well versed in jazz and formal harmony from the West (and they play familiar improvising instruments), most of the others espouse a kind of violent synthesis between great formality of diction and a transgressive abstraction. If this sounds unduly abstract, then so does the music, almost as if realistic images have been collaged on to painterly canvases. The LPs are stunning and should be considered prize finds if they turn up. The CD is more selective and, in some respects, haphazard. Well worth having, though.

***(*) **When The Sun Is Out You Don't See The Stars**
FMP CD 38 *Kowald; Lawrence Butch Morris (c); Werner Ludi (as, bs); Sainkho Namtchylak (v).* 11/90, 7/91.

The problem with Namtchylak is that the sheer strangeness of her vocal technique tends to overpower everything around it. In the context of this project she is the sun, scorchingly intense and tending to blot out her partners. Even Kowald seems slightly diffident. The presence of Morris points up a long-standing problem, the fundamental incomprehension that divides European and American improvisers. He seems prepared to trade off some cherished notions, but there isn't much leeway in return. Fortunately, individual performances are strong enough to sustain interest and attention, and Kowald himself has some magnificent moments.

♛ **** **Was Da Ist**
FMP CD 62 *Kowald (b solo).* 94.

It may seem difficult, if not impossibly perverse, to justify the highest ranking for a record of solo contrabass improvisations. We remain unrepentant. This is music of the very highest order, technically adroit, emotionally and intellectually concentrated, and beautifully recorded. Only Derek Bailey and Evan Parker have shown themselves capable of sustained solo performance at this level; what distinguishes Kowald is the light, dry humour he brings to these pieces, philosophical quiddities that seem perfectly content not to be answered. Without other instruments in attendance, Kowald goes for a stronger and more than usually resonant attack which mitigates a slightly dry sound. A record to savour and ponder; a record to return to, as often as time allows.

***(*) **Open Secrets**
Forward 01 *Kowald; Carlos Bechegas (f).* 10/99.

For sheer exhilaration, the duets with Bechegas take some beating. Whether going at top speed, all over their instruments, or inventing ballad-like counterpoint, the music has a joyful quality rare in this kind of improvising. While Bechegas clearly has extended techniques in abundance, he prefers to make his instrument sound like what it is: a flute. The recording itself doesn't always feel entirely truthful, but this is otherwise an encounter to rank with the best of Kowald's many duo situations.

(*) **Mirror – Broken But No Dust
Balance Point Acoustics BPA 001 *Kowald; Damon Smith (b).* 4/00.

*** **The Victoriaville Tape**
Victo 88 *Kowald; William Parker (b).* 5/02.

Peter Kowald died in New York in September 2002. This should make these duo recordings all the more precious; in practice, it makes them all the more disappointing. The inaugural release on starstruck bassist Smith's own label is well short of vintage. What interest there might have been in their long live performance is lost in a muddled and imprecise recording. The studio material is at least clearer, but one senses that Kowald is politely standing by while a young acolyte 'does' him, even imitating Kowald's occasional vocalizations.

Kowald's final appearance at Victoriaville teamed him with the finest bass-player of a younger generation. Neither is in impressive form and the shortish numbers that make up the set seem like conversation pieces rather than effective duet improvisations. There had been no intention to record the occasion but a tape was acquired from the mixing desk and Kowald's death made release inevitable. Fortunately, sufficient fine work from earlier in his career remains available to leave a lasting monument to a genuine pioneer.

Krakatau

GROUP

Much sound and fury from this Finnish blend of improvisation and dark rock-music, led by guitarist Björkenheim.

***** Ritual**
Cuneiform RUNE 86 *Raoul Björkenheim (g, shekere, talking d, rebab); Jorma Tapio (as, bcl, bf, perc); Tapani Rinne (ts, bs, wood f); Sampo Lassila (b); Michael Lambert, Heikki Lefty Lehto (d).* 88–90.

***** Volition**
ECM 511983-2 *Raoul Björkenheim (g, shekere); Jone Takamaki (ts, krakaphone, toppophone, whirlpipe); Uffe Krokfors (b); Alf Forsman (d).* 12/91.

***** Matinale**
ECM 523293-2 *As above, except Ippe Kätka (d) replaces Forsman.* 12/93.

Krakatau is essentially guitarist Björkenheim's band, hived off from percussionist Edward Vesala's Sound & Fury collective in the mid-'80s. Where Vesala mixed free playing with '60s psychedelia, tangos and straight composition, Björkenheim has a declared interest in Hendrix, Cream, Zappa, and a line of post-bop jazz that takes in Coltrane, Eric Dolphy, and the Miles of *Agharta*. The debut *Ritual* suggests a folkier edge to the music than will be familiar to those who first heard the group in a later incarnation, and the continuity with Vesala's workshop bands is more obvious. 'Ritual' and 'Relentless' perhaps too neatly sum up the overall impact. Björkenheim is a very concentrated musician, but he does occasionally leave his foot on the pedal too long, sometimes literally so.

Volition is a cheerfully noisy record with remarkably little of the big-biceps nonsense that often comes with guitar-fronted groups. In Sound & Fury, Vesala had used Björkenheim a little aside from the main thrust of a composition, often asking him for explosively abstract sound-shapes that encouraged non-standard techniques: bowed and scrabbled strings, electronic distortion, 10+ volume readings. A dedicated instrument-hunter, like Vesala, saxophonist Takamaki supplies his own fair share of unusual sonorities, most notably the 'krakaphone', a copper organ pipe two feet taller than the performer and fitted with a baritone saxophone mouthpiece and reed. It lends its bulk most effectively to 'Little Big Horn', a title that's also been used by Gerry Mulligan. It's a not entirely absurd parallel, for there is a softer and more lyrical side to Krakatau, most obviously heard on the soothingly oriental 'Changgo' and the folkish 'Nai', but clearly audible too on the closing ballad, 'Dalens Ande', which has a cool modality far removed from the all-out impact of the title-track.

Matinale is a second helping of the ECM-era band, the music again somewhat mediated by the studio but recorded with a handsome degree of clarity and body that helps punch up the impact. When they're going for the visceral, that is; pieces such as 'Unseen Sea Scene' and 'Rural' are more about brooding atmosphere than any sonic fisticuffs. 'Sarajevo' and 'Matinale' itself even echo some of Terje Rypdal's old work for the label. Attractive in a sluggish, world-weary way, the music finally doesn't seem to go anywhere much.

Diana Krall (born 1964)

VOCALS, PIANO

A Canadian from Nanaimo, Krall was a teenage prodigy who studied with Jimmy Rowles and began recording for the local label, Justin Time, in 1992. She has since signed to Impulse!/ Verve and has become a major crossover star, helped by shrewd marketing.

***** Stepping Out**
Justin Time 50-2 *Krall; John Clayton (b); Jeff Hamilton (d).* 93.

*****(*) Only Trust Your Heart**
GRP 059810-2 *Krall; Stanley Turrentine (ts); Ray Brown, Christian McBride (b); Lewis Nash (d).* 94.

***** All For You**
Impulse! 051164-2 *Krall; Benny Green (p); Russell Malone (g); Paul Keller (b); Steve Kroon (perc).* 10/95.

Vocally and stylistically, Krall sounds a generation older than her chronological age. She has a rich, resonant contralto and a preference for standard repertoire. The most obvious influences on her singing are Carmen McRae and Shirley Horn, who has also doubled vocals and piano. As 'Straighten Up And Fly Right' and 'Frim Fram Sauce' on the first of these suggest, Krall has also listened attentively to Nat Cole. Indeed the third album is intended as a tribute to his great trio, hence the basic instrumentation of piano, guitar and bass, with just a touch of percussion thrown in on 'Boulevard Of Broken Dreams'. What the third album lacks, inevitably, is musicianship of the sort guaranteed by Brown, McBride and Nash. Turrentine does more than just show up, contributing hugely on his three tracks. Our preference for *Only Trust Your Heart* is based solely on their roles; Krall's singing is impeccable throughout. The debut set has been remastered with an extra track, an ebullient 'Sunny Side Of The Street'; listening again, it's surprising to hear how much piano she was playing – compared with the recent records at least.

*****(*) Love Scenes**
Impulse! 051234-2 *Krall; Russell Malone (g); Christian McBride (b).* 97.

At this point, Krall had become the warmest commercial property in the music. It can be difficult to evaluate her music in light of the attention she has received, but at least (unlike Cassandra Wilson) she seems unencumbered by her status. Where Wilson already seems to have invested in the hype surrounding her, Krall has so far hardly let it invade her records. This one may be cannily pitched at an audience hungry for a sexy young jazz singer, but the performances are hard to fault, and Malone and McBride are more than willing partners in the affair. The obvious killer is Dave Frishberg's 'Peel Me A Grape', cheekily done; but more demurely effective are 'The Gentle Rain' and 'Garden In the Rain'. Krall's understatement is part of her strength, and she hasn't given up on it yet.

***** When I Look In Your Eyes**

Verve 050304-2 *Krall; Larry Bunker (vib); Russell Malone (g); Ben Wolfe, John Clayton (b); Lewis Nash (d); strings.* 98.

... although, on this evidence, she may eventually have little choice in the matter. This is still just about a jazz record, but it's pitched to make Krall a vocal star, and the accompaniments are almost peripheral. Johnny Mandel contributes some of his most weeping arrangements to seven tracks (the title-piece is almost glutinous), and although Krall is still at home with her small group, mannerism is clearly being encouraged to excess by her producer.

***** The Look Of Love**

Verve 549846-2 *Krall; Russell Malone, Dori Caymmi, John Pisano, Romero Lubambo (g); Christian McBride (b); Peter Erskine, Jeff Hamilton (d); Paulinho Da Costa, Luis Conte (perc).* 1–3/01.

Krall's progress as a commercial artist has been unstoppable, with this record quickly passing a million copies worldwide. The rush to invest in a sexy voice has never been more frantic. It's not a bad album, but aside from its million-dollar upholstery, supplied by two orchestras, Claus Ogerman's crawling arrangements and a band of players on a very tight rein, there's not much happening, which puts a lot of pressure on the singer. Her voice is what the people want to hear – it sure isn't the piano – and every husk on every syllable is lingered over in a mix which is borderline pornographic. 'Love Letters' is taken at a pace which would have even a funeral director drumming his fingers with impatience, and the only hint of tartness comes in a mildly aggressive 'Cry Me A River'. Somehow, we already feel nostalgic for the Krall of 'Straighten Up And Fly Right'.

*****(*) A Night In Paris**

Verve 065369-2 *Krall; Michael Brecker (ts); Rob Mounsey (ky); Anthony Wilson, John Pisano, Ron Eschete (g); John Clayton, Christian McBride (b); Jeff Hamilton, Lewis Nash (d); Paulinho da Costa (perc); strings.* 12/01.

Her best since *Love Scenes* makes its mark through a warmly effective concert performance, with a good band – mainly Wilson, Clayton, Hamilton and da Costa – and some of the affectation of her recent studio work set to one side. 'The Look Of Love' is the sexiest since Dusty Springfield's version, and 'East Of The Sun' is nicely languorous rather than horizontal. There's a lot more piano, too, though if anything it exposes a style that can't stand too much exposure. An orchestra heaves through three tracks, but it's not too overbearing. A studio treatment of 'Just The Way You Are', with a superstar band including Michael Brecker, is rather gratuitously stitched on to the end. Now that her crown has been handed to young pretender Norah Jones, though, what next for Krall in the studio?

***** The Girl In The Other Room**

Verve 9862063 *Krall (p, v); Anthony Wilson (g); Christian McBride, John Clayton (b); Peter Erskine, Jeff Hamilton, Terri Lyne Carrington (d).* 4/04.

Krall's husband Elvis Costello helped write much of an album which is generously stacked with originals. Whether Krall's audience will welcome this development or not so far remains to be seen. She sounds terrific on Mose Allison's 'Stop This World', which starts the record, but her version of Costello's 'Almost Blue', cut at a tempo which a tortoise would breeze past, is wincingly self-conscious, and the new songs often sound either weepy or sarcastic, the latter not a trait which Krall does well. There's more piano, and the band are very good.

Maj-Britt Kramer

PIANO

Danish pianist, much interested in her native music, leading a post-bop quartet.

***** Once**

Stunt STUCD 19701 *Kramer; Andy Sheppard (ss, ts); Jens Skou Olsen (b); Benita Haastrup (d).* 4–11/96.

*****(*) Something About Heroes**

Stunt STUCD 19903 *As above.* 9/98.

Kramer leads a capable group through two programmes of Danish music set to modern jazz manners. *Once* uses older material, from folk and composed sources, while the second disc has a more contemporary feel, with five originals from members of the quartet. British readers may welcome the chance to hear Sheppard in the kind of straightahead setting which he rarely inhabits these days, and he sounds strong. *Once* is handsomely turned, with the odd surprise, such as the curious, faintly chaotic finale to 'Ulandsvise' but tends towards pale meditation, and the unfamiliarity of the material may deter some listeners. *Something About Heroes* is an improvement, and has a bit more go in it, especially in the two-minute subversion of Benny Andersen's 'En Svante Vise' and the marching 'Take It Easy Boy, Boy'. Kramer herself seems reluctant to take too much of a lead, although her playing works a nice blend of poise and working for the band.

Wayne Krantz (born 1956)

GUITAR

Born in Oregon, Krantz came to New York in the mid-'80s and has been a regular on the scene there ever since.

***** Signals**

Enja 6048-2 *Krantz; Jim Beard (ky); Leni Stern (g); Hiram Bullock, Anthony Jackson (b); Dennis Chambers (d); Don Alias (perc).* 5–6/90.

*****(*) Long To Be Loose**

Enja 7099-2 *Krantz; Lincoln Goines (b); Zach Danziger (d).* 3/93.

*****(*) 2 Drink Minimum**

Enja 9043-2 *As above.* 2–4/95.

Krantz works an interesting furrow somewhere between Frisell's displaced ruralisms and a bluesier improvisation that sounds plausible as either jazz-rock or, well, rock-jazz. In other words, another good guitar-player who's hard to slot in. What he enjoys is the resonant sound of strong lead guitar: he's not much interested in FX, delay, fuzz, or whatever. The starry cast on the first record suggests a typical fusion slugging match, but the support team is used rather sparingly (drums and percussion on only five out of ten tracks) and, though the pieces are rather short and curtailed, they're an entertaining bunch. The trio-orientated records put Krantz in a setting that plays tight or loose as he pleases and has a lot of fine, unassumingly accomplished guitar. The studio set is structured piece by piece, even though the titles tell a story if you read them end to end; but to get a handle on what this group is about, the live *2 Drink Minimum* is an even better choice. Though spliced together from various shows at New York's 55 Bar, the disc plays like a single, well-paced, explosive concert set: the cumulative intensity of 'Whippersnapper' and the lyricism of 'Isabelle' work despite (or because of) their rough edges, the occasion adding a pinch of seasoning to music that a studio might have dried out a little. The fine, interlocking work of Goines and Danziger comes over with the same power as Krantz's.

*****(*) Separate Cages**

Alchemy ALCD 1007 *Krantz; Leni Stern (g, v).* 96.

Although this is more in tune with Stern's aesthetic than Krantz's, it's a charming and very playable series of duets, performed with a two-way sympathy that is very fetching. 'King's Cross', in dedication to Emily Remler, and Stern's softly effective vocal on 'Something Is Wrong In Spanish Harlem' are but two highlights in a programme that goes quietly and thoughtfully without meandering.

*****(*) Greenwich Mean**

Wayne Krantz Records no number *Krantz; Timothy Lefebvre, Will Lee (b); Keith Carlock (d).* 7–8/99.

A return visit to New York's 55 Bar for Wayne's regular gig, although this set is a distillation of many hours of gigs into what's effectively a single piece. The new trio is playing harder, faster and louder, but Krantz still surrenders nothing in sophistication or harmonic elegance, making only sparing use of effects such as wah-wah and relying on his own imagination to meld his rock and country interests into what's an unequivocally modern approach to jazz guitar. As fine a soloist as he is, it's also very much a group music. The slightly unkempt sound (recorded on portable DAT machines) may trouble some, but the music's terrific. However, the record is available only directly from Wayne himself. Contact him at www.waynekrantz.com. He may have more stuff available by now, too.

Ernie Krivda (born 1945)

TENOR SAXOPHONE, VOCAL

His father was a swing-era reedsman, and he followed in those steps in the '70s with an individual approach to hard-bop orthodoxy.

***** Ernie Krivda Jazz**

Cadence CJR 1049 *Krivda; Dennis Reynolds, Mike Hazlett (t); Pat Hallaran (tb); Joe Hunter (p); Pete Selvaggio (acc); Jeff Halsey, Gary Aprile, Roger Hines, Chris Berger (b); Paul Samuels, Scott Davis (d).* 1–8/91.

***** So Nice To Meet You**

Cadence CJR 1056 *Krivda; Joe Hunter (p); Bill Plavan, Chris Berger (b); Val Kent, Mark Gondor (d); Paula Owen (v).* 6/93–1/94.

***** Sarah's Theme**

CIMP 102 *Krivda; Bob Fraser (g); Jeff Halsey (b).* 9/95.

Krivda has a markedly individual approach to the tenor: wildly elongated lines with barely a pause for breath, a hiccupy kind of rhythm that abjures conventional hard-bop phrasing, and a tone that evades obvious comparison, though he sometimes gets a scuffling sound that is rather like Warne Marsh. The ingredients tend to make his music exciting but unresolved. On *Ernie Krivda Jazz*, the three duets with bassist Halsey are the most interesting things: two pieces with accordionist Selvaggio are unusual but not terribly involving, 'The Bozo' is a more complicated chart involving the two trumpeters, and the final quartet/quintet tracks are lively but let down slightly by the modest support. The album is further compromised by the scrawny, indifferent production. The pairing with singer Paula Owen is even stranger: Owen's basically straightforward style is embellished by Krivda's jaw-breaking solos, everything pitched in double-time, each solo a blitz on its surroundings. It's oddly exhilarating stuff, but over a CD's duration a little exhausting. One could say the same about *Sarah's Theme*: the title-track runs just over 20 minutes and, aside from the three subsequent interludes, each of the tracks seems obsessively long. Halsey and Fraser play a shadowy role, but Krivda himself is actually in comparatively restrained mood on this set. CIMP's two-track digital sound, designed for 'realism', tends to sound rather dry and unappealing, but in some ways it suits Krivda's tough and uncompromising approach.

*****(*) The Art Of The Ballad**

Koch 7806 *Krivda; Bill Dobbins (p).* 6/93.

*****(*) Golden Moments**

Koch 37310 *Krivda; Dan Wall (p).* 6/95.

Krivda doesn't mind the most exposed situations, but on the face of it he seems an unlikely choice for two duo albums of ballads for horn and piano. The dryness of his sound, the oddball phrasing and the refusal to colour a melody with any of the horn's bell notes are scarcely food for Ben Webster addicts. Both Dobbins and Wall – the latter especially, with a flourish and a readiness to quicken the pace – push and prod him all the way, but each of these belongs to Krivda as a self-challenging performer. 'Darn That Dream' on the first disc and 'Angel Eyes' on the second are model instances of making a new song out of an old one, which for some is what jazz is meant to be about. These absorbing (and swinging, it should be added) records will be a tonic for anyone bored with hushabye tenor recitals.

*****(*) The Band That Swings**

Koch 7880 *Krivda; Keith Powell, Joe Miller, Steve Enos, Brad Goode (t); Garney Hicks, George Carr, Chris Anderson (tb); Paul Abel (btb); Dave Sterner (as); George Shernit (as, cl, f); Chris Burge, Tom First (ts); Dick Ingersoll (bs); Joe Hunter (p); Lee Bush (g); Sherry Luchetti (b); Rick Porello (d).* 11/98.

Krivda as frontman for a '40s-style big band, sometimes playing sweet (listen to the Lawrence Welk chords in 'I Should Care', actually a Billy May chart) as well as hot? We didn't believe it either. But the record is great fun, and Krivda is clearly having a ball with this group (the Fat Tuesday Big Band, here recorded in Cleveland). There's nothing modern in the sound, but it doesn't feel especially retro either and, with Krivda's tenor taking on a new swagger in his features, this baker's dozen of tunes will raise spirits wherever they're played.

*****(*) The Music Of Ernie Krivda**

Cadence CJR 1154 *Krivda; Dominic Farinacci (t); Steve Richko (p); Bob Fraser (g); Demetrius Steinmetz (b); Carmen Intorre (d).* 8/01.

****** Plays Ernie Krivda**

CIMP 293 *As above except Kurt Kotheimer (b) replaces Steinmetz, omit Richko. 7/03.*

Krivda goes back to basics. As the titles suggest, these are two albums of his own originals with working line-ups. If these are among his most conventional records, they're also satisfyingly rounded and accomplished – excellent players stretching out on decent material, with no hang-ups about concepts or experimentalism. Krivda suggests that the earlier set is part blowing date, part 'composed', while the second is more like a straightforward blow, yet neither really falls back on routine. Farinacci, still in his teens at the time of the earlier session, is a real find, with a singing tone and a beautifully clean attack. Even when asked to carry a long solo, as on 'The Jerry Turn', he's unfazed. Fraser works in a classic electric sound, and handles his role with quiet skill: he's especially effective on the second disc, where Richko's absence doesn't seem to matter. As for the leader, his chops are in top shape: check 'The Bebop Interlude' for the evidence.

The sound of the CIMP session, in its usual bone-dry acoustic, is a bit of a shock after the lush feel of the Cadence record, although this is one time we find that it works better for this group. For all its set-up-and-go feel, it's arguably Krivda's best record.

Karin Krog (born 1937)

VOCALS

Karin Krog apparently dodged school one afternoon to see Billie Holiday perform in Oslo. What she learned or absorbed by osmosis that day has stood her in better stead than many hours of bokmal or civics. Krog is an expressive, technically astute singer with advanced musical ideas of her own. Her recordings, now largely on her own label, are thoughtful, utterly musical and desperately underrated.

*****(*) Some Other Spring**

Meantime MR10 *Krog; Dexter Gordon (ts); Kenny Drew (p); Niels-Henning Orsted Pedersen (b); Epsen Rud (d). 5/70.*

*****(*) Gershwin With Karin Krog**

Meantime MR4 *Krog; Egil Kapstad (p); Arild Andersen (b); Jon Christensen (d). 74, 89.*

***** You Must Believe In Spring**

Meantime MR5 *Krog; Palle Mikkelborg (t); Per Carsten (as, f); Bent Larsen (f, af, bf); Niels Peters (ob); Ole Koch-Hansen (p); Philip Catherine (g); Niels-Henning Orsted Pedersen (b); Alex Riel (d); Kasper Vinding (perc); strings. 5/74.*

Krog is one of Europe's most stylish and significant jazz singers. The early work (documented on the capacious but deleted Verve compilation, *Jubilee*) finds her working an idiosyncratic swing vein, with strong intimations of bebop, perhaps of Annie Ross's vocalese. Her first recordings are with Arild Wikstrom's group, professional, swinging and sufficiently offbeat to seem individual. Her work with Dexter Gordon, with the refiguring of bop that that entailed, is also documented on the set recently reissued on Meantime: blues and ballads, with Dexter in handsome form. The Gershwin set is one of her simplest and most straightforward dates, and the voice sounds at its most appealing in this classic material. Simplicity is at more of a premium in the Legrand session, *You Must Believe In Spring*, where the outstanding track is 'Once Upon A Summertime' (also on the Verve). She's a little swamped here by Mikkelborg's dense orchestration but manages to rise above the waves most of the time.

****** One On One**

Meantime MR7 *Krog; Nils Lindberg (org); Bengt Hallberg (p); Red Mitchell (b). 7 & 10/77, 2/80.*

Krog made a number of recordings in the late '70s for Frank Heman's Bluebell label. Three of those duo performances are compiled here. Mitchell's lyricism is immediately evident on 'Blues In My Heart' and his subtle sense of structure is the key to 'God Bless The Child', a beautifully plain and untheatrical reading by Krog. The set with Hallberg begins – unexpectedly – with Leon Russell's all too rarely covered 'A Song For You'. The pianist is discretion itself, touching in the harmonies without fuss or undue embellishment. The real treat of the set is the duets with Lindberg. One rarely hears organ in this context, and his accompaniments to 'Sometimes I Feel Like A Motherless Child' and 'Psalm' from Coltrane's *A Love Supreme* are striking in their rich simplicity. A wonderful collection of songs, accompanied by three master musicians.

***** Hi-Fly**

Meantime MR3 *Krog; Archie Shepp (ts); Charles Greenlee (tb); Jon Balke (p); Arild Andersen, Cameron Brown (b); Beaver Harris (d). 6/76.*

***** I Remember You**

Meantime MR 8 *Krog; Warne Marsh (ts); Red Mitchell (b). 4/80.*

***** Two Of A Kind**

Meantime MR1 *Krog; Bengt Hallberg (p). 4/82.*

*****(*) Freestyle**

Odin NJ 4017 *Krog; John Surman (ss, syn, perc); Brynjar Hoff (ob). 8/85, 4/86.*

***** Something Borrowed ... Something New**

Meantime MR2 *Krog; Kenny Drew (p); Niels-Henning Orsted Pedersen (b); Alex Riel (d). 6/89.*

A fine technician, Krog doesn't allow an impressive understanding of 'extended technique' to over-reach itself, keeping the words and their attendant emotions in view. Perhaps because of this, she sounds best in small-scale and rather intimate surroundings. The session with Surman is quite exotic in sonority, with overdubbing and electronic treatments on some tracks, unusual percussion and synth patterns on the original material. The repertoire is pretty ambitious, even including 'Raga Variations' by the composer Arne Nordheim, who writes brilliantly for voice. A Fran Landesman medley strongly recalls the work of the late Radka Toneff, a Norwegian compatriot of Krog's, but is even more musical in conception.

Something Borrowed is more straightforwardly jazz-orientated, as is the Gershwin record. A gap of 15 years between them (or the contrast between the 1974 and 1989 material on *Gershwin With Karin Krog*) demonstrates how completely the singer has absorbed the basic repertoire and made it her own. Krog's versions of well-tramped turf like 'Summertime' and 'Someone To Watch Over Me' (*Gershwin*, later sessions) or 'I Get A Kick Out Of You' and 'Every Time We Say Goodbye' (*Borrowed*) are entirely her own. Hallberg is a graceful accompanist who gives her a softly insistent beat as a springboard into her vocal, and there isn't a track that one wouldn't want to listen through again, so subtle is some of her phrasing and her awareness of harmony.

She's under a different sort of pressure on the session with Shepp, a player who turned himself from a screamer into a (relatively) sensitive balladeer rather late in the day. Krog adds lyrics to Carla Bley's 'Sing Me Softly Of The Blues' and makes an impressive job of Mal Waldron's 'Soul Eyes' (a singer's tune if there ever was one) and Randy Weston's affirmative 'Hi-Fly'. The horns are too dominant and Harris is slightly overpowering in places; Krog also sounds uncomfortable on Shepp's own 'Steam', though their duet, 'Solitude', suggests that there was more than enough common ground.

The cool stylings of *I Remember You* with Marsh and Mitchell are fascinating. The saxophonist's take on the title-track gives a good impression of how abstract a date this is going to be, and it progresses in very much that vein. Mitchell's singing lines and unusual tuning complements Karin's voice beautifully and she's rarely sounded so adventurous on a jazz date, giving 'Moody's Mood For Love' a fine run for its money. 'Lover Man' and 'Speak Low' come from more familiar territory, but even these are bold renditions.

The group on *Borrowed* is much better attuned to what Krog is doing. NHOP emerges as the dominant voice, easing aside a rather lacklustre and uncharacteristically heavy-handed Drew. The sound is far from ideal, pinching some of the top notes, but the vocal performances are generally of a very high standard.

**** Bluesand

Meantime MR9 *Krog; John Surman (ss, bs, bcl, cbcl, p, syn).* 99.

Immaculately recorded by Jan Erik Kongshaug at the legendary Rainbow Studio in Oslo, this fine duo set conjures up a huge range of timbres and tonalities, the product of now 20 years working as a duo. Krog's voice has rarely sounded better and Surman's finely developed accompaniments are deployed as effectively here as on his own solo records. The longer tracks are the most powerful, allowing both performers to stretch out, but the shorter pieces, like the mysterious 'Hidden Dreams', are equally effective. The title-track is equally enigmatic, a terse central theme strung out across a rich, almost orchestral backdrop. Even when the arrangements are stripped down to basics, there is so much grain and texture to Surman's playing that one senses much larger forces at work. An exceptional record.

***(*) Where You At?

Enja ENJ 9144-2 *Krog; Steve Kuhn (p); David Finck (b); Billy Drummond (d).* 02.

Kuhn and Krog recorded together back in 1974, an album called *We Could Be Flying* (still available in Japan) and she apparently has wanted to repeat the experience ever since. A still underrated pianist, Kuhn is also the ideal accompanist, neither intrusive nor self-consciously unobtrusive. He plays and listens, listens and plays, and his interplay with Krog is immaculate throughout. Add David Finck and Billy Drummond to the mix and you have a band poised between the drummer's rugged swing and a robustly underwired lyricism.

Krog heard and admired Kuhn on Pete LaRoca's fine *Basra* and it was agreed to reprise 'Lazy Afternoon' from that album. Karin's softly enunciated vocal, often near to speech in pace if not pitch, is perfect for the melody. She brings the same qualities to Kuhn originals like 'Speak Of Love' and the mysterious 'Saharan'. Other tracks are collaborations with partner and producer John Surman. 'Kaleidoscopic Vision' is one of their best wheezes yet and the mysterious intro to 'Canto Mai', spoken in a seemingly invented language, gives a shimmer of drama to a lovely song.

The real pay-off of the set is the swinging, Latinized 'Missing Calada' followed by a slow and mournful 'Gloomy Sunday'. The sound isn't ideal but it's another fine record.

*** Where Flamingoes Fly

Norway Music 5189 *Krog; Jacob Young (g).* 5/03.

Again produced by partner John Surman, this is a lovely, softly swinging set, which sticks to fairly predictable material – 'Cry Me A River', 'Prelude To A Kiss', 'Once I Loved', 'Caravan', 'Every Time We Say Goodbye' – but lavishes a lot of imagination on it. Young's playing is unspectacular but more than functional and his harmony is spot on, even on pacier things like 'K.C. Blues'. Krog's voice has acquired something of the depth of experience you hear from Sheila Jordan (the only workable comparison, but still not a helpful one) and makes every song seem as full of life and emotion as a movie.

Gene Krupa (1909–73)

DRUMS

Born in Chicago, Krupa joined Benny Goodman's orchestra and stayed for the better part of half a decade before striking out on his own. His sheer energy is infectious, and he remained a master drummer to the end of his life.

***(*) Gene Krupa, 1935–1938

Classics 754 *Krupa; Tom Di Carlo, Tom Gonsoulin, Dave Schultze, Roy Eldridge, Nate Kazebier (t); Chuck Evans, Joe Harris, Charles McCamish, Bruce Squires (tb); Murray Williams, George Siravo (as); Chu Berry, Dick Clark, Vido Musso, Carl Bleisacker (ts); Benny Goodman (cl); Milt Raskin, Jess Stacy (p); Ray Biondi, Allan Reuss (g); Israel Crosby, Horace Rollins (b); Helen Ward, Jerry Kruger (v).* 11/35–7/38.

*** Gene Krupa, 1938

Classics 767 *Krupa; Tom Di Carlo, Ray Cameron, Tom Gonsoulin, Nick Prospero, Dave Schultze (t); Charles McCamish, Bruce Squires, Toby Tyler, Chuck Evans (tb); Murray Williams, Mascagni Ruffo, George Siravo (as); Vido Musso, Carl Bleisacker, Sam Musiker, Sam Donahue (ts); Milt Raskin (p); Ray Biondi (g); Horace Rollins (b); Irene Daye, Leo Watson (v).* 7–12/38.

There is a memorable photograph of the young Gene Krupa at the kit, hair slick, tux sleeves and collar soaked with sweat, mouth and eyes wide and hungry, his brushes blurred to smoke with the pace of his playing. Received wisdom has Krupa down as a showman who traded in subtlety for histrionic power. George T. Simon, in the hopped-up prose that was almost *de rigueur* in the *Metronome* of the late '30s, referred to the drummer's 'quadruple "f" musical attacks'; it's interesting to speculate how many people read that as 4F (that is, unfit for military service) rather than as some battering dynamic above *molto fortissimo*, for there is no doubt that Krupa's film-star looks and superb technique also made him a target. During the war, which he spent as a very combative non-combatant, he was twice set up for police arrest and spent part of his 35th year waiting on remand until a witness contracted amnesia. The critics have taken much the same route, sniping, then forgetting. Even in neglect, Krupa's impact on the jazz rhythm section is incalculable. He himself said, 'I made the drummer a high-priced guy.' Though black percussionists who had worked for years in the shadow of the front men had some cause to be resentful, Krupa's respectful investigation of the African and Afro-American drumming tradition was of tremendous significance, opening the way for later figures as diverse as Max Roach, Elvin Jones, Andrew Cyrille and Milford Graves.

The documentation is in much better shape these days with the issue of Classics' typically detailed job. Krupa joined the Benny Goodman band in 1934 and stayed till 1938, when his boss finally decided there was room for only one of them on stage. The drummer recorded under his own name only twice during the Goodman years. The sessions of November 1935 (made for Parlophone UK) and February 1936 kick off the first Classics volume on a high. Being able to call on Goodman, Jess Stacy and the remarkable Israel Crosby offered some guarantee of quality, and 'Three Little Words' and Krupa's own 'Blues For Israel' are spanking performances, driven along by that dynamic drumming. The following session included Chu Berry and Roy Eldridge, an established double-act in the Fletcher Henderson outfit and always ready to try something new. Berry cheekily weaves in and out of Goodman's line, while Eldridge dive-bombs from above. Great stuff.

There is then a chronological hiatus until Krupa's break with Goodman and the chance to capitalize on his own rising stardom. The April 1938 Brunswicks also signalled a move to New York City, which seems to have put a slight brake on Krupa's invention for a while, unless it was the new burden of managing his own orchestra. Not yet the banked strings of the later band but a slightly cumbersome feel nevertheless, and the fourth item ('The Madam Swings It') of an uninspired session was eventually rejected. Singers Helen Ward, Jerry Kruger and Irene Daye fail to add very much, but vocals were commercially essential and these discs did big business right through 1938, with the band averaging a session a month. Leo Watson's scats were lively and often very musical, but Krupa must have felt partly inhibited by the formula and there's an audible sense of relaxation and renewed vigour about the sessions recorded back in Chicago in October, when he is able to lay down a couple of fine instrumentals, including the excellent 'Walkin' And Swingin''. November and December saw the band on the West Coast, where a new audience was conquered and three excellent recording sessions laid down. Watson's 'Do You Wanna Jump, Children?' brought the year to a happy close.

***** Gene Krupa, 1939**

Classics 799 *Krupa; Ray Cameron, Charles Frankhauser, Tom Gonsoulin (t); Toby Tyler, Bruce Squires, Dalton Rizzotto (tb); Bob Snyder, Mascagni Ruffo (as); Sam Musiker, Sam Donahue (ts); Milt Raskin (p); Ray Biondi (g); Horace Rollins (b); Irene Daye (v).* 2–7/39.

*****(*) Gene Krupa, 1939–1940**

Classics 834 *Krupa; Johnny Martel, Corky Cornelius, Torger Halten, Nate Kazebier, Johnny Napton, Shorty Sherock (t); Al Sherman, Floyd O'Brien, Red Ogle, Al Jordan, Sid Brantley (tb); Bob Snyder, Clint Neagley (as); Sam Donahue (ts); Sam Musiker (cl, ts); Tony D'Amore, Milt Raskin (p); Ray Biondi (g); Biddy Bastien (b); Irene Daye, Howard DuLany (v).* 7/39–2/40.

The following year was no less busy and there is a strong sense of consolidation in the band, which begins to sound like a more solidly integrated unit. Krupa's leadership is tight and very musical. A new version of 'The Madam Swings It' is cut and this time passes muster. Nate Kazebier returns to the fold and Floyd O'Brien signs up to stiffen the brasses. Apart from a couple of novelty instrumentals made for dancing ('Dracula' and 'Foo For Two') the standard is very high and Krupa can increasingly be heard to experiment with rhythmic embellishments, off-accent notes, single beats on the edge of his cymbals, and with the dynamics. Even with such a powerful group, he was always prepared on occasion to play quietly and to contrast *fff* and *pp* passages within a single song, relatively unusual at that time when up was up and a ballad was a ballad. Into 1940, it's pretty much a question of steady as she goes, even with the inevitable personnel changes. By this point Krupa can be heard to be shaping the band to his new requirements, which were much more musicianly and much less histrionic. The Benny Carter piece, 'Symphony In Riffs', recorded for Columbia in September 1939, and the majestic two-part 'Blue Rhythm Fantasy' (nearly seven minutes in total) stand out as representative masterpieces, making this, along with the first volume, essential buys.

***** Gene Krupa, 1940 – Volume 1**

Classics 859 *Krupa; Corky Cornelius, Torg Halten, Nate Kazebier, Rudy Novak, Shorty Sherock (t); Al Jordan, Jay Kelliher, Babe Wagner (tb); Clint Neagley, Bob Snyder (as); Walter Bates, Sam Donahue, Sam Musiker (ts); Tony D'Amore (p); Ray Biondi (g); Biddy Bastien (b); Irene Daye, Howard DuLany (v).* 3–5/40.

***** Gene Krupa, 1940 – Volume 2**

Classics 883 *As above.* 11/39, 1–9/40.

***** Gene Krupa, 1940 – Volume 3**

Classics 917 *As above, except omit Jordan and d'Amore; add Pat Virgadamo (tb), Bob Kitsis (p).* 9–11/40.

Annus mirabilis, or what? Krupa could hardly have been busier during 1940, churning out a series of slick, pop-orientated sides for OKeh, milking a market that could hardly have been more responsive. The element of showmanship is inevitably missing on record, and most of these extended solos drag their feet. The bands increasingly seem to be foils for the soloist, chugging away anonymously and with little of the personality that made the Goodman, Dorsey and James units so distinctive. Collectors of this sort of material will find much to enjoy, including two rarities on Volume 2 from November 1939 and January 1940, rejected takes of 'Time Out' and 'The Birth Of Passion' for Columbia. More of the material for the label is collected on the item below.

***** Drum Boogie**

Columbia Legacy 473659 *Krupa; Norman Murphy, Torg Halten, Rudy Novak, Shorty Sherock (t); Pat Virgadamo, Jay Kelliher, Babe Wagner (tb); Clint Neagley, Mascagni Ruffo (as); Walter Bates (ts); Sam Musiker (cl, ts); Bob Kitsis (p); Ray Biondi (g); Biddy Bastien (b); Irene Daye (v).* 40–41.

It would be hard to ignore the Columbia compilation, which affords a glimpse of the band in a somewhat more reflective mood. Jimmy Mundy's arrangements often cleave to a rather mechanical shuffle-beat that doesn't suit a group of this size or inclination, but the horns are nicely voiced and there is a lot more space round the music than in earlier days. Irene Daye is still the singer, still leaning on ballads rather than faster numbers. She was soon (in 1941) to be replaced by one of the great presences in the band. Anita O'Day refused to wear a spangly frock and turned out in a band jacket like the rest of them, emphasizing that she was part of things and not just a walk-on. (Re)joining with her was Eldridge, who helped transform the group yet again, into a less poppy, more jazz-based and improvisational unit.

*** Gene Krupa, 1941

Classics 960 *As above.* 41.

*** Gene Krupa, 1941 – Volume 2

Classics 1002 *Krupa; Roy Eldridge (t, v); Torg Halten, Norman Murphy, Graham Young (t); John Grassi, Jay Kelliher, Babe Wagner (tb); Sam Listengart, Jimmy Migliore, Clint Neagley, Mascagni Ruffo (as); Walter Bates, Sam Musiker (ts); Bob Kitsis, Milt Raskin (p); Ray Biondi (g); Biddy Bastien, Ed Mihelich (b); Johnny Desmond, Howard DuLany, Anita O'Day (v).* 6–10/41.

*** Gene Krupa, 1941–1942

Classics 1006 *As above, except add Al Beck, Mickey Mangano (t), Ben Feman, Rex Kittig (as), Don Brassfield (ts), Joe Springer (p).* 10/41–2/42.

This was the period of maximum productivity, with the band going into the studio virtually every month in the period before Pearl Harbor. The key recruitment during 1941 was singer Anita O'Day; her presence tends to distract attention from the band itself, which is steamingly powerful. Roy Eldridge is the featured soloist and singer elsewhere, and the vocals certainly can't be dismissed. Gene doesn't vary much from an alternation of 4/4 and 6/8, but his sheer presence is infectious and his attack unfailingly dramatic. The vocal contributions tend to predominate, but Gene's own playing is revelatory for anyone who thinks that polyrhythms began with Elvin Jones and the Coltrane quartet.

*** Gene Krupa, 1942–1945

Classics 1096 *Krupa; Tommy Allison, Al Beck, Bill Conrad, Don Fagerquist, Mickey Mangano, Norman Murphy, Tony Russo, Pinky Savitt, Al Stearns, Joe Triscari (t); Roy Eldridge (t, v); Leon Cox, Joe Conigliaro, John Grassi, Tommy Pedersen, Greg Phillips, Babe Wagner (tb); Francis Antonelli, Ben Feman, Rex Kittig, Harry Klee, Jimmy Migliore (as); Murray Williams (as, cl); Don Brassfield, Andy Pino, Charlie Ventura (ts); Sam Musiker (ts, cl); Buddy DeFranco (cl); Earl Hines, Dodo Marmarosa, Teddy Napoleon, Joe Springer, George Walters (p); Marty Olson (p, t); Ray Biondi, Teddy Walters, Ed Yance (g); Ed Mihelich, Clyde Newcombe, Sid Weiss (b); Joe Dale (d); Johnny Desmond, Dave Lambert, Lilian Lane, Anita O'Day, Buddy Stewart (v).* 42–45.

*** Gene Krupa, 1945

Classics 1143 *As above; add Johnny Bothwell, Bill Hitz (as); Stuart Olson (bs); Frank Worrell (g); Harry Babasin (b).* 45.

*** Gene Krupa, 1945–1946

Classics 1204 *Similar to above and to Hep sets below.* 9/45–12/46.

Things were changing, not so much for Krupa personally, as in the music industry. These sides include Gene's recordings with strings, not high points in his canon, but interesting in their way. The set also takes in some V-Discs made with Marmarosa and DeFranco, which are curiously evocative of their wartime provenance. Trio work was what lay ahead as the bands became increasingly unsustainable and the disc ends with three cuts made with guest soloist Ventura. They're less exuberant than one might expect, but there are signs of an incipient bop influence even here on 'Body And Soul', though the only overt bebop comes in the vocals of Lambert and Stewart on 'What's This'. Inevitably, other singers still figure strongly: Anita O'Day is still very much part of the operation at the tail end of 1942 and Roy Eldridge is on hand with a rambunctious spot on 'Knock Me A Kiss'. If there's a signature piece from the set, it's 'The Drummer's Band', which just about says it all.

Anita's back in 1945, as is the trio with Ventura, from whom there are a couple of previously unissued cuts. This was another hectic time for the Orchestra, and all the recordings on Classics 1143 were made over a four-month period. The highlights are O'Day's 'Opus No. 1' and some good band tracks, though there's a certain feeling that Krupa is marking time professionally at this stage. The next volume picks up the story, but some of this material is already available on a better-sounding option ...

*** Gene Krupa: 1946 – Volume 1

Hep CD 26 *Krupa; Ed Badgley, John Bello, Gordon Boswell, Richard Dale, Don Fagerquist, Vince Hughes, Jimmy Milazzo, Al Porcino, Red Rodney, Joe Triscari, (t); Bob Ascher, Nick Gaglio, Urbie Green, Tasso Harris, Cley Hervey, Emil Mazanec, Emil Melnic, Dick Taylor, Jack Zimmerman (tb); Charlie Kennedy, Tommy Lucas, Sam Marowitz, Harry Terrill (as); Mitch Melnic, Charlie Ventura, Buddy Wise (ts); Joe Koch, Larry Patton, Jack Schwartz (bs); Bob Lesher, Mike Triscari (g); William Baker, Buddy Neal, Teddy Napoleon (p); Irv Lang, Bob Strahl (b); Carolyn Grey, Dolores Hawkins, Buddy Hughes, Anita O'Day, Buddy Stewart (v).* 46.

*** Gene Krupa: 1946 – Volume 2

Hep CD 46 *Similar to above.* 46.

*** Gene Krupa: 1946–1947 – Volume 3

Hep CD 51 *Similar to above.* 46–47.

Krupa was almost forced out of the music business altogether in 1943 when he was charged with 'contributing to the delinquency of a minor'; in our view, this is what jazz music is all about, but marijuana was involved and musicians presented a soft target at the time. Typically, the drummer bounced back and the following year formed his second orchestra, an outfit which achieved a rare peak of popularity for the time, consistently outperforming its rivals not just by showmanship but by the sheer force and concentration of the ensembles. Krupa regulars like Sherock, Neagley, Bondi and Bastien became instinctive interpreters. Not much in the way of musical subtlety was required and only genuine devotees of this style and period will have much use for three volumes, albeit discmastered with a care that puts the Classics to shame. The presence of Anita O'Day made this a rather special band. Her replacement, Carolyn Grey, was a reasonable band singer, but she entirely lacked Anita's sense of drama and swing. There are a group of interesting trio tracks, Krupa with Teddy Napoleon and Charlie Ventura, recorded in February 1946, on which the crash and bash give way to something a little more spacious; these make Volume 3 perhaps the most worthwhile of the sequence. Not much in it, though.

*** Gene Krupa & His Orchestra, 1947–1949

Classics 1319 *Krupa; Ed Badgley, John Bello, Gordon Boswell, Buddy Colaneri, Dick Dale, Roy Eldridge, Don Fagerquist, Al Porcino, Ed Shedowski, Ray Triscari (t); Urbie Green, Clay Hervey, Allan Langstaff, Emil Mazaneo, Frank Rehak, Frank Rosolino, Dick Taylor, Walter Robertson, Jack Zimmermann (tb); Lennie Hambro, Charlie Kennedy, Tommy Lucas, Sam Marowitz, Harry Terrill (as); Carl Friend, Mitch Melnick,*

Buddy Wise (ts); Dale Keever, Bob Morton, Larry Patton, Jack Schwartz (bs); Bill Baker, Joe Cohen, Teddy Napoleon, Buddy Neal (p); Ralph Blaze, Bob Lesher (g); Pete Ruggiero, Don Simpson, Bob Strahl (b); Joe Dale (d); Hernando Bravo, Ramon Rivera (perc); Bill Black, Carolyn Grey, Delores Hawkins, Buddy Hughes (v). 1/47–1/49.

This is the fourteenth disc in Classics' Krupa series. The exuberant showboating isn't so much in evidence here. The first few tracks, from the early months of 1947, are dominated by Carolyn Grey's vocals. She's no Anita O'Day, but they're very decent performances.

The first glimpse we get of Gene as leader comes on the peerless 'Disc Jockey Jump', which originally went out backed with 'By The River St Marie', near enough the perfect party record. 'Jump' owes its place in musical history very largely to a crisp arrangement by the 19-year-old Gerry Mulligan, who'd already done the charts for 'How High The Moon' a year or so earlier. George Williams and Eddie Finckel do the honours elsewhere and herein lies the problem, for these were astute industry guys who knew what was going to sell. There's little here to reflect what the Krupa band was capable of as a live act.

There was, however, a new sound around and the fascination of this disc is hearing Gene tackling bebop. On 'Gene's Boogie', he declines Williams's invitation to give it a go, but also concedes that swing might not be the thing any more. But given that even at his most restrained Krupa could give the USAF lessons in 'dropping bombs', bop held no terrors for him and it was inevitable he'd at least flirt with it. Recorded in January, 'Bop Boogie' and the even crunchier 'Lemon Drop' are model big-band bop, the latter graced by a superb Frank Rosolino. That later group also features high-wire work by Roy Eldridge, though for the most part Krupa stuck to his familiar pool of quick-fingered swing players.

*** The Instrumental Mr Krupa

Jasmine 2572 *As above.* 38–49.

The Jasmine set will appeal to those who don't want their music mussed up by singers, though to our way of thinking this rather misses the point of Krupa's heyday. A relatively modest 21 tracks this time, but as long as you accept the premise, a good option.

*** Krupa And Rich

Verve 521643-2 *Krupa; Roy Eldridge, Dizzy Gillespie (t); Illinois Jacquet, Flip Phillips (ts); Oscar Peterson (p); Herb Ellis (g); Ray Brown (b); Buddy Rich (d).* 5 & 11/55.

*** The Drum Battle: Gene Krupa & Buddy Rich At JATP

Verve 559810 *Krupa; Roy Eldridge, Charlie Shavers (t); Benny Carter, Willie Smith (as); Flip Philips, Lester Young (ts); Oscar Peterson, Hank Jones (p); Barry Kessel (g); Ray Brown (b); Buddy Rich (d); Ella Fitzgerald (v).* 52.

Krupa And Rich shouldn't be confused with an earlier Compact Jazz compilation on Verve which included some of the material. This record documents a typical Norman Granz summit, bringing together the younger Rich and probably the only man who could properly be said to have influenced his own fiercely swinging style. Given the nature of the occasion, this wasn't nearly as arid and tiresome as the majority of contemporary 'drum battles'. Each takes a big solo spot – 'Gene's Blues', 'Buddy's Blues' – and, for the rest, it's a matter of trading fours and eights until the customers are satisfied. Fortunately the band is good enough to assert itself and nobody will feel percussed out of countenance when they hear Oscar Peterson's sweepingly elaborate accompaniments or Dizzy poking gentle fun at the vanities of drummers.

The 'drum battle' is something of an acquired taste, but there are enough interesting diversions along the way. Smith plays some masterly pre-bop ideas and Ella's scatting on 'Perdido', which emerges out of 'Drum Battle' itself, is wonderful. Jones is also in very solid form. The duel with Rich is entertaining enough but you feel the all clear should be sounded at the end.

*** Live From The Inn Club, Chicago, Illinois – January 11 1957

Soundcraft 5011 *Krupa; Eddie Shu (t, ts, cl, hca); Dave McKenna (p); Johnny Drew (b).* 1/57.

Most interesting, one suspects, for the early glimpse it affords of pianist McKenna, though to be honest it could be almost anyone at the piano. A long, closing version of 'Drum Boogie' is Gene's most prominent feature and for the most part he seems willing to let the band do the work. Shu's multi-instrumentalism is more impressive on paper than in fact, but he does some decent work on 'Stompin' At The Savoy' and on 'Harmonica Shu Boogie'. No one will mistake who's behind the kit, but even his most loyal fans will have to recognize that this isn't the Krupa of years gone by.

*** Live At The New School 1973

Chiaroscuro CR(D) 207 *Krupa; Eddie Shu (ts, cl, hca); John Bunch (p); Nabil Totah (b).* 4/73.

Only six months away from being claimed by leukaemia, Gene still played this gig with evident enthusiasm, and with some old friends – Eddie Shu had been a Krupa sideman since the '50s – he revisits some of the music which made his name, one final time. They go from 'Don't Be That Way' to a closing 'Sing Sing Sing', and that Krupa still sounds good (if inevitably diminished a little) makes it all the more poignant.

*** The Gene Krupa Story

Properbox 1001 4CD *As for the above.* '30s, '40s, '50s.

This ought to be the ultimate resource for collectors and fanatics, but actually it's a slightly tiresome procession of same-y material, 99 tracks delivered off an assembly line. The booklet is quite useful and as always the packaging is robust and colourful. One wonders, though, whether most Krupa-ites wouldn't prefer a single-disc option, even, God help us, the Classics discs with their ultra-functional approach and minimal documentation.

There are, needless to say, many more Krupa compilations out there. We have counted 21 more of more or less legitimate provenance currently available. These might be worth investigating, or they may meet your budget. For serious collectors, though, there's no need to go outside the above listing.

Tom Kubis

REEDS, ARRANGER

LA big-band leader and arranger with a Steve Allen fixation.

*** Slightly Off The Ground

Sea Breeze 109 *Kubis; Wayne Bergeron, George Graham, Stan Martin, Dan McGurn, Charlie Peterson (t); Rich Bullock, Andy Martin, Bill Watrous (tb); Gordon Goodwin, Dan Higgins, Greg Huckins, Bill Liston (sax); Matt Catingub (as, ky); Kevin Axt (b); Matt Johnson (d); Jack Sheldon (v).* 1/89.

***** At Last**

Cexton 21251 *Similar to above; add Jeff Bunnell, Darrel Gardiner (t); Alex Iles, Charlie Morillas (tb); Eric Messerschmidt (tba); Bob Reitmeier (cl); Sal Lozano, John Mitchell (sax); Doug Mattocks (bj); Jack Reidling (p); Kurt Rasmussen (perc).* 92.

*****(*) It's Not Just For Christmas Anymore**

Cexton 21333 *Similar to above; add Gary Halopoff (t); Jack Sheldon (t, v); Pete Christlieb, Mike Whitman, Brian Williams (sax); Trey Henry (b); Ray Brinker, Dick Weller (d); Pat McCormick, Jack Riley (v).* 95.

*****(*) Fast Cars And Fascinating Women: The Tom Kubis Big Band Plays Steve Allen**

Sea Breeze 2079 *Similar to above; add Steve Allen (v).* 96.

***** Keep Swingin': The Tom Kubis Big Band Plays Steve Allen**

Sea Breeze 2090 *Similar to above.* 97.

***** You Just Can't Have Enough Christmas**

Cexton 21444 *Similar to above.* 97.

Slightly off the ground seems the ideal location for a musician who goes to work with a smile on his face and since 1989 has produced a consistently high standard of big-band jazz. Jack Sheldon is a vital factor in the band's success, working a wonderful riff on *Casablanca* behind 'Play It Again Sam' and appearing on the Steve Allen sessions as well.

These are probably the best of the bunch, though we'd recommend the first album to any big-band fanatics. Allen's compositions are little known and less covered these days, but Kubis is a devoted disciple and even engineers an appearance from the great man on 'The Girl Can't Help It' (*Fast Cars*) and 'Livin' In LA' (*Keep Swingin'*). Sheldon almost upstages him on the second record with wonderful interpretations of 'Chittlins' and 'Tango Blues', the latter a clever vocal.

The first Christmas album is the best ever, a wonderful romp through some very familiar fare, but done with unpretentious flair and that engaging smile. 'Rudolf The Red Nosed Reindeer' should be played at high volume in all shopping malls when the tension starts to mount around 19 December. The follow-up Yuletide set is a bit more laboured but the musicianship is so tight that you stop worrying about the material and just enjoy it.

The personnel has shifted somewhat over the stretch but Kubis retains a very distinctive crisp sound inherited from his predecessors and perfectly attuned to the repertoire. He's a more than decent saxophonist himself and his soprano features are always particularly good.

Joachim Kühn (born 1944)

PIANO, KEYBOARDS

Born in Leipzig, Joachim is the brother of clarinettist Rolf Kühn. He studied and performed as a classical pianist through his teens and then worked with his brother. He is best known for virtuosic solo and duo performances in which he calls upon a wide range of advanced compositional ideas and a broad palette of sound derived from his interest in playing direct on the piano strings.

***** Easy To Read**

Owl 014 802 2 *Kühn; Jean-François Jenny-Clark (b); Daniel Humair (d).* 85.

Technically astute, often virtuosic, but ultimately rather dry and emotionless, Kühn seems here to be working through a huge range of pianistic influences (Evans, Jarrett, Tyner) without settling on anything he can distinctively claim as his own. 'Guylene' is a rousing opener but many listeners will feel that the pace slips away as the record progresses. Back once again in the Owl catalogue, it serves as a memorial to the late Jenny-Clark, one of Europe's finest-ever bass-players.

****(*) Famous Melodies**

Label Bleu 6564 *Kühn (p solo).* 95.

An interesting and eclectic mix of material, including some Weill interpretations that look forward to a very successful rendition of songs from *The Threepenny Opera*. But again one feels that Kühn has subordinated emotion to technique, and many of these performances (check 'Lili Marlene') fail to engage with the song in question.

***** The Diminished Augmented System**

Emarcy 542 320 2 *Kuhn (p solo).* 5 & 6/99.

For those who argued that Western harmony begins with J. S. Bach and ends with Ornette Coleman, this is the ideal record since the composers involved are Bach, Coleman and Kühn, recorded in three distinct blocks and in the reverse of that order. Kühn seemed to fall under Ornette's spell when they worked together and the experience has significantly reshaped his own harmonic (make that harmolodic) thinking. The original pieces are short, dissonant sketches in asymmetrical metres. The first of them sound very much like test-pieces, though 'Portrait Of My Mother' and 'Thought Of JF' (presumably the recently deceased Jenny-Clark) are more personal. After that, Kühn plays four Coleman pieces, 'Sex Is For Woman', 'Pointe Dancing', 'Researching Has No Limits' and 'Foodstamps On The Moon', followed by the sarabande, chaconne and allemande from Bach's *Partita II*, cleverly arranged by Kühn himself. It's a heady mix and very much a keyboardist's album, too technical to be comfortably approachable, too good to be overlooked.

Rolf Kühn (born 1929)

CLARINET, SYNTHESIZER

The elder Kühn brother played in '40s dance orchestras before going to America, where he depped for Benny Goodman and formed his own group. Latterly returned to Germany and has gone through swing, bop, cool, free and fusion styles without any apparent awkwardness, even on the awkward clarinet.

***** Rolf Kühn And His Sound Of Jazz**

Fresh Sound FSR-CD 326 *Kuhn; Jack Sheldon (t); John Bunch (p, org); Jim Hall, Chuck Wayne (g); Henry Grimes, George Duvivier (b); Don Lamond, Ray Mosca (d).* 60.

Rolf Kühn may not have made as many records as his brother, but there is still a paucity of his work available in the CD era. The dedicated may like to try to ferret out his work for the Blue Flame label, but the only widely circulated material at present is this reissue of some sessions he made in New York in 1960. At the time, he was very much in thrall to Buddy DeFranco (building on an earlier admiration for Benny Goodman), and the sound of these sessions isn't far from DeFranco's '50s dates for Verve. It's coolly pleasant jazz which Kühn and some sympathetic collaborators move fluently through without really striking any original sparks.

Steve Kuhn (born 1938)

PIANO, KEYBOARDS

A piano pupil of the celebrated teacher Margaret Chaloff (Serge's mother), Kuhn worked the New York jazz scene from the late '50s. He lived in Stockhom in the late '60s and frequently accompanied Sheila Jordan as well as leading his own groups.

*** The Country And Western Sound Of Jazz Pianos

Dauntless 4308 *Kuhn; Toshiko Akiyoshi (p); Barry Galbraith (g); David Izenzon, John Neves (b); Pete LaRoca Sims (d).* 63.

This is a strange one, long out of print as an LP, and until Dauntless put it out again recently seemingly destined for the obscuro racks at record fairs. The idea was to record a set of C&W and traditional tunes with jazz arrangements. It's not such a radical notion, but nobody had pushed it quite as far as this before. Kuhn and Akiyoshi have strikingly different styles, as do the two bassists, so it's left to Barry Galbraith to strike some kind of balance between her coltish bop and Kuhn's more deliberate delivery, which often sounds like a singer holding back the metre. In the same way, Neves plays fairly orthodox walking lines, while Izenzon plays cello-like lines with the bow. 'Nobody's Darling But Mine' and 'Along The Navajo Trail' are pretty orthodox country, but it's with the gospel songs that the sextet really starts to come together. Akiyoshi is on celesta for 'May The Lord Bless You And Keep You' and one suspects that just a few years later, this set would have been done on Fender Rhodes and other electric keyboards. A fascinating experiment and a welcome return from oblivion.

*** Three Waves

BMG 37272 *Kuhn; Steve Swallow (b); Pete LaRoca Sims (d).* 10/66.

A first chance to hear Kuhn as a composer. 'Today I Am A Man', 'Memory' and 'Bits And Pieces' all point to a classically alert and harmonically sophisticated player who uses the whole of the keyboard without much left-hand/right-hand split. It's left to Swallow to keep the metre flowing and this he does right from the opening 'Ida Lupino', the Carla Bley tune of four non-originals which include the title track. Sims is a great drummer and a seriously neglected figure now; both Kuhn and Swallow had worked on his Blue Note session for *Basra*. This is a tightly organized trio, reminiscent of some of the things Swallow would be doing with Paul Bley in later years.

*** Oceans In The Sky

Owl 013428-2 *Kuhn; Miroslav Vitous (b); Aldo Romano (d).* 9/89.

Even the label this time will spark off further associations with Paul Bley's trios, notably the one with Steve Swallow and Jimmy Giuffre. Vitous has a very different sound and philosophy from Steve, but the same intricate counterpoint is at work and Romano's drumming keeps the set light, open and intricate. This is one of the most interesting items Owl ever issued and it's good to have it available again as news spreads of Kuhn's neglected importance. The title-track, 'The Island' and 'In Your Own Sweet Way' are the outstanding cuts.

*** Remembering Tomorrow

ECM 529035-2 *Kuhn; David Finck (b); Joey Baron (d).* 3/95.

The most recent ECM is just a little lacking in spark and variety. The pianist sounds thoughtful and relaxed but, despite Baron's playfulness, it never quite catches light.

*** Dedication

Reservoir 154 *Kuhn; David Finck (b); Billy Drummond (d).* 98.

***(*) Countdown

Reservoir 157 *As above.* 99.

**** The Best Things

Reservoir 162 *As above, except add Luciana Souza (v).* 12/99.

Kuhn has struck a rich seam since moving to Reservoir, and these trios find him not just in the company of sympathetic collaborators, but also playing some of the best jazz of his career. The earliest of the three is the most easily overlooked but it is a more than competent and often very thoughtful session that paves the way for the achievement of *Countdown*. This is modern jazz pianism at its best. Opening with a Coltrane composition (the title-track) was a stroke of genius and the inclusion of Steve Swallow's 'Wrong Together' – the two Steves seem like creative soulmates – is the clincher. Miles Davis's 'Four' and Kurt Weill's 'Speak Low' are both titanic performances. Steve kicks off the most recent of the group with a chestnut, 'The Best Things In Life Are Free', but manages to transform it into something quite magnificent, as he does to Parker's 'Confirmation' and the following 'Poem For #15', which takes every second of its ten-plus minutes to unravel. The vocalist is used to add some wordless tone-colours to 'Adagio', but by then the set has been firmly clinched. An artist in his pomp, overdue some serious attention.

*** Love Walked In

Sunnyside 1109 *Kuhn; Buster Williams (b); Bill Stewart (d).* 9/98.

A relatively orthodox but consistently swinging set of bop and jazz tunes. Kuhn's liking for very expressive, even dominant, bass-players is amply served here. Buster Williams plays like a whole string-section behind him, laying down delicious lines on Sheila Jordan's 'No Problem' and transforming 'Prelude To A Kiss' into something almost classical. Bill Stewart is one of the best drummers of his generation and very much the third leader here, putting his considerable authority behind 'The Land Of The Living Dead' (as wry a thing as Kuhn will ever do) and a magisterial 'Autumn Leaves'. We didn't like the sound that much: too plush and soft-focused, hence just three stars.

Jonas Kullhammar

ALTO, TENOR AND BASS SAXOPHONES

Swedish saxophonist, pushing the modern envelope, with his own label to play with.

*** Salut

Moserobie MMP CD001 *Kullhammar; Torbjörn Gulz (p); Torbjörn Zetternberg (b); Jonas Holgersson (d).* 5/00.

*** The Soul Of Jonas Kullhammar

Moserobie MMP CD002 *As above.* 7/01.

★★★(★) **Plays Loud For The People**

Moserobie MMP CD009 *As above except add Per Johansson (as).* 12/02.

★★★(★) **Nacka Forum**

Moserobie MMP CD005 *Kullhammar; Goran Kafjes (t, flhn, pkt-t); Johan Berthling (b); Kjell Nordeson (d).* 8/02.

Kullhammar's blazing music is freebop with a crazy edge to it. The first two records are both live gigs from Stockholm's uncelebrated Glenn Miller Café (a tiny venue – how do they get all the people in there?) and the music is fast, exciting and sometimes funny, but it's also prone to dead spots which the musicians coast over yet never quite disguise. Kullhammar is an accomplished and power-packed soloist – he sticks to tenor on these discs – but he doesn't quite have the structural command of Petter Wettre, to choose an illustrious contemporary, and in the end both discs feel like rowdily entertaining but limited gig souvenirs. Gulz plays acoustic piano on the first, electric on the second.

Plays Loud For The People is a studio set although, oddly, the sound is if anything less clear. The opening 'Snake City East' is about as tumultuous as a sax-and-rhythm quartet piece is going to get, and though there's a certain amount of pressure drop after that, this is a more finely honed and satisfying set. Johansson comes in on one track only. Holgersson plays out of his skin.

The *Nacka Forum* record is arguably the best of the four. The excellent Kafjes provides a very useful foil to Kullhammar, who picks up (or, at least, sticks in his mouth) the bass sax for Sun Ra's 'We Travel The Spaceways'. If the music doesn't quite have the zany momentum of the other quartet records, it has a compensating assurance which is nicely sustained. Either way, Kullhammar is a man to follow.

Sergey Kuryokhin (1954–96)

PIANO, OTHER INSTRUMENTS

Born in Murmansk, Kuryokhin barnstormed his way through music, ejected from conservatories, playing in rock bands, forming vast and unwieldy 'pop mechanics' ensembles, creating musical-theatre events and playing a lot of piano along the way. Cancer killed this mercurial man at 42.

★★★ **Ways Of Freedom**

Leo Golden Years Of New Jazz 14 *Kuryokhin (p solo).* 81.

★★★(★) **Divine Madness**

Leo CD LR 813–816 4CD *Kuryokhin; Igor Butman (as, ss); Vladimir Chekasin (sax, v); Boris Grebenschikov, Yuri Kasparyan, Alexander Pumpyan, Victor Sologub, Igor Tikhomirov, Alexander Titov, Viktor Tzoi (g); Elvira Shylkova (acc, v); Seva Gakhil (clo); Sergey Panasenko (b, tba); Sergey Belischenko, Alexander Kondrashkin (d); Anatol Adasinsky, Gustav Gurianov, Leonid Leykin, Valentina Ponomareva (v).* 3/80–10/86.

★★★ **Some Combinations Of Fingers And Passion**

Leo LRCD 178 *Kuryokhin (p solo).* 91.

Classically trained and capable of playing quite legitimately in the midst of an otherwise chaotic performance, Kuryokhin was easily the most charismatic of the younger Russian players. He fronted his own pop mechanics performances, mixed-media pieces that ape Western forms in a deliberately exaggerated, 'Martian' fashion that is not so much satirical as clownishly respectful. His Leo LPs have been noted in previous editions of this *Guide*. The big plus this time out is the reissue of his first record *The Ways Of Freedom* which, rather remarkably, was first released on the official Soviet label Melodiya. The recording is no better than average, and there are moments when one suspects problems with tape speed, but the reissue offers a quick primer in Kuryokhin's dazzling range of voices, effects and keyboard attacks. He can sound as tightly disciplined as a classical player and as vividly intense and rapid-fingered as Tatum. 'Theory And Practice', 'Archipelago' and 'The Other Way' are the main statements, but other tracks call on extended technique to give the piano a percussive quality that makes it sound like a whole ensemble.

Since his death, though, the major source for Kuryokhin enthusiasts is *Divine Madness*, a multiple-CD set of mostly unreleased material which covers his solo-piano work and his pop mechanics projects in some detail.

Disc one includes two long piano-improvisations, a 15-minute track from 1980 with the Creative Ensemble, and a 12-minute 'Opera' with the Vladimir Chekasin Big Band. The saxophonist was already chafing against what he saw as the limitations of the Ganelin Trio and was looking for a more overtly theatrical formulation. Kuryokhin helped steer him in that direction. The second disc features solo-piano material formerly released on the Leo LP, *Popular Zoological Elements*, as well as *Pop Mechanics No. 17*, a key development in Kuryokhin's multi-genre theatre. The disc begins with a performance recorded in Novosibirsk with Valentina Ponomareva, Sergey Belischenko and Sergey Panasenko, who were the mainstays of Pop Mechanics.

There is a story attached to the late-night improvisations on disc three. Allegedly, Kuryokhin and guitarist Grebenschikov bribed their way into the Kirov Ballet and Opera Theatre in Leningrad with bottles of vodka, in order to record 'Subway Culture' on the theatre organ. The technical difficulties of taping pipe organ and guitar (which is played with a razor blade) were scarifying, but the result is grandly operatic. A middle section with the addition of saxophonist Igor Butman was recorded two years earlier. The final disc is the big-band *Introduction To Pop Mechanics*, which was released as Leo LP 146. Taped live in Leningrad, in a country on the brink of disintegration and political realignment, it has a quality compounded of optimism and nostalgia, a sense that things are never going to be quite the same again. And so it proved. Whether Kuryokhin was a dissident who used irony as a polemical weapon or one of the *yurodivye* – the holy fools – who work outside the bland logics of politics and establishment culture is never going to be clear, any more than Shostakovich's or Solzhenitsyn's exact aesthetic and political orientation can be decoded. What remains is an extraordinary legacy of recorded work and the memory of a man constantly on the move, burning oxygen faster than seemed possible, let alone advisable. *Divine Madness* is too concentrated and too personal a testament to unpick. Anyone who has fallen under his spell should experience it. Anyone who remains sceptical should perhaps start with his one current solo album on CD.

Kuryokhin was more likely to refer to Rachmaninov than to Art Tatum in his solo performances, and he seemed to make it a point of principle to avoid direct reference from the jazz tradition. 'Blue Rondo A La Russ – A Tribute To Dave Brubeck' on *Some Combinations* is an apparent exception; Brubeck is perceived in a very different way in Russia than in his native

United States and he enjoys honorific status as one of the first major jazzmen to appear there, but Kuryokhin's tribute is typically oblique.

Technically, his technique is interesting largely for its avoidance of the usual jazz-piano dichotomy between the left hand, with its rhythmic chording, and the right, which carries the melody and the subsequent improvisation. In addition, Kuryokhin was a virtuosic user of the pedals (a sharp contrast to Cecil Taylor, who uses them sparingly), creating some quite remarkable two-piano illusions. Rapidly pedalling also creates an occasional sense, as on the long 'Passion And Feelings' section of the later session, that tiny segments of music are being edited together at high speed, creating the studied artificiality of tone one hears throughout his earlier work, an apparent refutation of conventional pianistic 'passion', whether of the Horowitz or the Taylor variety.

Kuryokhin's is difficult music to characterize, because it consistently undermines its own premisses. These are quite alien to Western ears in any case. Kuryokhin believed that the end of state suppression of improvised music would be an aesthetic disaster on a par with the death of Satan. There is certainly a slackness of purpose to the later record which one does not associate with Kuryokhin and which dilutes its considerable technical achievements. In order to prevent him slipping further into the margins, perhaps Leo should compile something akin to a best-of.

Billy Kyle (1914–66)

PIANO

Philadelphia-born, Kyle worked with Tiny Bradshaw and Lucky Millinder before a four-year stint with John Kirby, ending only with his being drafted. He joined the Louis Armstrong All Stars in 1953 and stayed there until his unexpected death while on tour with the group.

***** Billy Kyle 1937–1938**

Classics 919 *Kyle; Charlie Shavers, Billy Hicks (t); Rex Stewart (c); Tyree Glenn (tb, vib); Buster Bailey (cl); Eddie Williams (cl, as); Tab Smith, Rudy Williams, Russell Procope (as); Harold Arnold, Don Byas, Ronald Haynes (ts); Danny Barker, Brick Fleagle (g); John Williams, Walter Page, John Kirby (b); O'Neil Spencer (d, v); Fran Marx, Jo Jones (d); The Palmer Brothers, Leon Lafell, Jack Sneed, Inez Cavanaugh (v).* 3/37–9/38.

***** Billy Kyle 1939–1946**

Classics 941 *Kyle; Nat Gonella (t, v); Dick Vance, Charlie Shavers (t); Trummy Young (tb); Buster Bailey (cl); Benny Carter, Lem Davis (as); John Hardee (ts); Milt Herth, Bob Hamilton (org); Teddy Bunn (g, v); Brick Fleagle, Dave Barbour, Jimmy Shirley (g); John Kirby, Marty Kaplan, John Simmons (b); O'Neil Spencer (d, v); Jack Maisel, Buddy Rich (d).* 1/39–9/46.

The Philadelphian was a great acolyte of Earl Hines, so much so that his best work sounds like Hines on a good day: for a blindfold-test teaser, try the solo on 'The Song Is Ended' on the first record. Eventually, Kyle replaced Hines in the Louis Armstrong All Stars. But he also had a touch of Teddy Wilson urbanity in his playing, and the two trio sides he made for Decca in 1939, on the second disc, are beautiful examples of how elegant he could be. Classics have gathered together a group of sometimes obscure small-group swing dates which have Kyle's presence as their common element and, while some of them are forgettable – the feeble tracks with Bob Hamilton and Milt Herth on the second set especially – most have some bright moments on even a routine chart. There is a very agreeable 1938 date for Victor with Rex Stewart and (making their debuts) Tyree Glenn and Don Byas, while four tracks find Kyle turning up in support of Nat Gonella with Benny Carter and Buster Bailey. There is an intriguing 'Afternoon In Africa', from a trio date with Bailey and O'Neil Spencer, and the closing 1946 session includes the idiosyncratic tenorman, John Hardee. A trio session from the same year includes some splendid music but is marred by poor-sounding masters. The backwaters of swing on some almost-forgotten recordings.

Charles Kynard (1933–79)

ORGAN

Los Angeles-based organist of the '60s who made a string of albums for Prestige during the period.

***** Reelin' With The Feelin' / Wa-Ta-Wa-Zui**

BGP CDBGPD 055 *Kynard; Virgil Jones (t); Wilton Felder, Rusty Bryant (ts); Joe Pass, Melvin Sparks (g); Carol Kaye, Jimmy Lewis (b); Paul Humphrey, Idris Muhammad, Bernard Purdie (d).* 8/69–71.

****(*) The Soul Brotherhood**

Prestige PRCD-24257-2 *Kynard; Blue Mitchell (t); Wilton Felder, David 'Fathead' Newman (ts); Grant Green, Joe Pass (g); Jimmy Lewis, Carol Kaye (b); Mickey Roker, Paul Humphrey (d).* 3–8/69.

Kynard, who was from Kansas City, was perhaps the last of the jazz organists to make his mark in the '60s. The BGP reissue doubles up two of his five Prestige albums. The first session is sagging with organ-combo clichés and Humphrey is a pedestrian drummer; the second adds electric piano to Kynard's instrument-list and is a bit brighter, thanks to the reliable Jones and Bryant, who can play the legs off a blues when they feel like it. Prestige's entry manages to couple *Reelin' With The Feelin'* with the slightly earlier *The Soul Brotherhood*, which has a cracking ensemble – Blue Mitchell, David Newman and Grant Green – yet quickly congeals into a series of glaringly obvious set-pieces. Docked a notch for raising expectations.

L.A.4

GROUP

One bossa nova pioneer, one cool West Coaster, one of the key bebop bass players, and a drummer who must have been a Time Lord; result: a genuine supergroup.

****(*) The L.A.4 Scores!**

Concord CCD 4018 *Bud Shank (as, f); Laurindo Almeida (g); Ray Brown (b); Shelly Manne (d).* 7/74.

***** Concord Jazz Heritage Series**

Concord CCD 4827 *As above except, add Jeff Hamilton (d).* 74–81.

This West Coast supergroup foundered only when bassist Ray Brown's career as a bandleader under his own name began to take off. The quartet's legacy of material is rather muted in hindsight. While it shares something of the Modern Jazz Quartet's intelligent conflation of jazz with classical forms, it hasn't had the same staying power. Even though the palette and dynamic range are greater, it's hard to recall an L.A.4 album in the way one remembers the classic MJQs.

The obvious difference was the hefty infusion of Latin-American themes and rhythms which came from Almeida. As well as a few residual Parkerisms, Shank has something of the tendency of his next model, Art Pepper, to float free of the rhythm section, which in this context permits some interesting counterpoint with Almeida. Shank's flute-playing is usually more challenging but tends to accentuate a vapidity which overtakes Almeida on slower ballads, as on his (mostly forgettable) Concord albums with Charlie Byrd. The rhythm section are unimpeachable and, though Manne was a more interesting drummer, Hamilton is a better blend with the overall sound.

As an introduction, or as an alternative to the group's eight discs on Concord (all bar one now deleted), the Jazz Heritage Compilation is a very attractive buy. It covers a fairly uneventful waterfront, but with a nice variation of pace and emotional temperature that is probably better than any of the individual albums.

Joe La Barbera (born 1948)

DRUMS

Worked with Woody Herman and Chuck Mangione before playing in Bill Evans's last trio. In-demand sideman who has made many records for others and recently a couple under his own name.

***** The Joe La Barbera Quintet Live**
Jazz Compass 1004 *La Barbera; Clay Jenkins (t); Bob Sheppard (ts); Bill Cunliffe (p); Tom Warrington (b).* 11/99.

*****(*) Mark Time**
Jazz Compass 1437 *As above.* 00.

'Kind of Bill' and 'Message for Art', the two closing numbers on the live record, pay tribute to Joe's most celebrated employer and to his greatest influence respectively. The Buhaina tinge is evident throughout this lively 1999 date with La Barbera's working group. They kick off with Freddie Hubbard's 'On The QT', a nice feature for Jenkins, continue with 'Speak Softly', Monk's 'Evidence' and Mal Waldron's peerless 'Soul Eyes'. By this stage, it's pretty clear that this is a robust but slightly unsubtle band, lacking the leader's ability to modulate mood without losing energy and momentum.

The second record is a good deal more sophisticated, as charts by Kenny Wheeler (the title-piece) and John Abercrombie ('Suite Sixteen') might suggest. There is also a feeling tribute to another West Coast great, the late Conte Candoli, who is dedicatee of 'Bella Luce'. La Barbera has got his band working with him now, rather than just blazing away on their own, and his arrangements are thoroughly impressive. Anyone interested in the Messenger's legacy as it emerges in a new decade would be well advised to give either of these a try.

Steve Lacy (1934–2004)

SOPRANO SAXOPHONE

The staggeringly prolific Lacy is almost unique in his dedication to the treacherously pitched soprano saxophone. Inspired by Sidney Bechet, he in turn inspired John Coltrane to turn to the small horn. Born Steven Lackritz in New York, he began his career playing Dixieland but was recruited by Cecil Taylor to the nascent avant-garde and subsequently became a Monk disciple, regularly returning to Monk compositions over the years. Lacy has performed in many contexts, from solo saxophone, small groups with his wife Irène Aëbi, to larger, almost classically configured ensembles. Sadly, he died as we were going to press.

***** Axieme**
Red RR 123120 *Lacy (ss solo).* 9/75.

***** Straws**
Cramps CRSCD 066 *As above.* 77.

*****(*) Only Monk**
Soul Note 121160 *As above.* 7/85.

****(*) Solo**
In Situ 590051 *As above.* 85.

****** More Monk**
Soul Note 121210 *As above.* 4/89.

The Lacy discography is huge, with a substantial proportion of those as leader or solo performer, although many are in vinyl limbo and several CDs have also slipped away. His prolific output anticipates that of Anthony Braxton, consisting as it does of group performances with a relatively conventional – if Thelonious Monk can ever be considered conventional – 'standards' repertoire, large-scale compositions for ensembles and mixed-media groups, right down to solo improvisation. In one significant respect, though, the two part company utterly. Where Braxton has been promiscuously eclectic in his multi-instrumentalism, tackling all the saxophones from sopranino to contrabass, and all the clarinets as well, Lacy has concentrated his considerable energies throughout his career on the soprano saxophone, which is why we have listed this group of solo performances first and out of chronological sequence. Drawing his initial inspiration from Sidney Bechet, he has combined a profound interest in Dixieland jazz with an occasionally extreme modernism. In a typical performance there may be short, almost abecedarian melodic episodes, repeated many times with minimal variation; there will be passages of free, abstract sound, often produced by sucking through the reed; there may even be strange, onomatopoeic effects, bird-calls and toneless shouts. The 1975 *Axieme* is probably the best available example of his more abstract style. *Straws*, recorded in Italy and available on CD only somewhat recently, is more eclectic in its inspiration, with pieces dedicated to Stravinsky (who had died some time before) and Janis Joplin, dedicatee of the moving 'Hemline'. Recorded in extreme close-up, it's one of the most revealing of the records in terms of the microstructure of Lacy's saxophone sound, exposing all the gritty little resonances, breath sounds and clicks.

Lacy favours tremendously long lines with no obvious developmental logic – which might be reminiscent of Lee Konitz's work, but for Lacy's insistence on long, sustained notes and modestly paced whole-note series. The weakness of *Solo*, caught live in the mid-'80s and perhaps best left in the vaults, is that such devices do untypically seem to be in default of anything larger. A melodist rather than an orthodox changes player – those unfamiliar with his music can find it deceptively simplistic, almost naïve, on first exposure – Lacy has been obsessed with the compositions of Thelonious Monk for more than 30 years and has become perhaps the foremost interpreter of Monk's music. The two solo Monk albums are among the finest of Lacy's multifarious and often interchangeable recordings. If the earlier of the pair is less immediately appealing, it is also more challenging and requires a closer acquaintance with the source material; with the exception of 'Pannonica' and 'Misterioso', the pieces are less well known than those established favourites on *More Monk*: 'Ruby My Dear', 'Straight No Chaser', 'Trinkle Tinkle', 'Crepuscule With Nellie'. Lacy has turned to Monk's music many times during his career. (There is more of it, alongside work by fellow-Monastics, on DIW's four-CD *Interpretations Of Monk*.) It represents a source of inexhaustible inspiration for him.

However, Lacy also draws on many other musics, both formal and popular. In his solo improvisations he often accelerates essentially simple 12-tone figures to the point of disintegration, allowing each piece to end unresolved. The antithesis of bebop expressionism or the huge inscapes of John Coltrane (whose use of soprano saxophone was directly inspired by Lacy's example), the solos are cold and impersonal but not without a certain broad humour that skirts burlesque. There are perhaps more completely achieved recordings than these, but there's no better place to make acquaintance with one – or perhaps two – of the music's great originals.

*** Soprano Sax

Original Jazz Classics OJC 130 *Lacy; Wynton Kelly (p); Buell Neidlinger (b); Dennis Charles (d).* 11/57.

**** Reflections

Original Jazz Classics OJC 063 *Lacy; Mal Waldron (p); Buell Neidlinger (b); Elvin Jones (d).* 10/58.

As with *The Straight Horn*, below, there was some attempt at the end of the '50s to market Lacy as the soprano saxophone specialist, trading on the instrument's relative unfamiliarity. *Soprano Sax* is somewhat atypical in that it consists of rather more developed harmonic improvisations on open-ended standards. Kelly's time-feel and exuberant chording aren't obviously suited to Lacy's method, and 'Rockin' In Rhythm' sounds much as if a lion were playing see-saw with a swan. There is, though, an excellent, slightly off-beat reading of 'Alone Together'. Some hints still of the problems recording engineers faced in miking Lacy's horn.

Reflections was the first of Lacy's all-Monk recordings. Waldron was one of the few piano-players who understood how such intractable material could be approached, and there are hints already of what he and Lacy were capable of in duo performance. Neidlinger has an attractively firm sound on both records, but Jones sounds slightly out of place, reinforcing Lacy's characteristic tendency to ignore the explicit metre. The sound is not altogether well balanced, and Neidlinger's lower-register fills are lost on the vinyl format. Lacy, on the other hand, sounds rather acid on the CD, but the performances more than make up for minor cosmetic defects.

*** The Straight Horn Of Steve Lacy

Candid 9007 *Lacy; Charles Davis (bs); John Ore (b); Roy Haynes (d).* 60.

One of the best-known and certainly most accessible of Lacy's records, *The Straight Horn* sounds rather muted and tentative after the passage of four decades. In conception it marks a bridge between bebop (which was never Lacy's natural constituency) and the New Thing, as represented by two Cecil Taylor compositions. Monk again provides the keystone, but whereas the saxophonist sounds in complete sympathy with this material – 'Introspection', 'Played Twice' and 'Criss Cross' – his approach to Charlie Parker's 'Donna Lee' sounds remarkably hesitant, all the more so given Roy Haynes's palpable delight in the accelerated metre. Nor is it certain that Lacy or his sidemen have got a firm purchase on Taylor's 'Louise' and 'Air'; compare Archie Shepp's handling of the latter on *The World Of Cecil Taylor*, also Candid. Nevertheless, this is a significant and not unattractive record. Davis's throaty baritone fulfils much the same timbral function as Roswell Rudd's or George Lewis's trombone on later recordings, and the pianoless rhythm section generates a more sympathetic context than Elvin Jones's wilder rush. Recommended, but with reservations.

***(*) Evidence

Original Jazz Classics OJC 1755 *Lacy; Don Cherry (t); Carl Brown (b); Billy Higgins (d).* 11/61.

Lacy's associations with Monk and Cecil Taylor are well known, and there was an intriguing attraction-of-opposites in his impact on John Coltrane. Rarely, though, is he ever mentioned in the same breath as the other great modernist, Ornette Coleman. In part, this is because they worked on parallel tracks, rarely intersecting but concentrating on a similar redistribution of melody and rhythm. *Evidence* is the closest Lacy comes to the sound if not the substance of Coleman's great quartets. On 'The Mystery Song' and 'Evidence', he achieves something like Ornette's lonely stillness. Cherry, on trumpet rather than one of his squeaky miniatures, provides a strong tonal contrast (but wouldn't it have been interesting to pair Lacy's soprano with cornet or pocket trumpet?) and the rhythm section, pianoless again and with the little-known Carl Brown standing as acceptable substitute for Charlie Haden, plays with good understanding.

*** Plays Monk

Fuel 2000 061830 *Lacy; Michael Graillier (p); Jean-François Jenny-Clark (b); Aldo Romano (d).* 69.

Made just after he moved to Paris and originally released on BYG, this is a surprisingly straight and un-idiosyncratic reading of seven Monk tunes, or six if you count the two parts of 'Epistrophy', which was the original title-track. Lacy's swinging approach still betrays his origins in Dixieland jazz, as does his articulation on the straight horn. It's surprising to hear him, too, in such resolutely straightahead company, though the rhythm section doesn't seem perturbed by the harmonics and staccato rhythm and keeps faith with Monk's originals all the way. 'Thelonious', 'Light Blue' and the closing 'Friday The Thirteenth' are the outstanding cuts. Reissued in 2003, this helps to fill in another part of the Lacy story.

**** Scratching The Seventies / Dreams

Saravah SHL 2082 3CD *Lacy; Enrico Rava (t); Lawrence Butch Morris (c); Italo Toni (tb); Steve Potts (as, ss); Claudio Volonte (cl); Takashi Kako (p); Michael Smith (p, org); Derek Bailey, Boulou Ferre, Jack Treese (g); Irène Aëbi (clo, v); Jean-Jacques Avenel (b, kora, cheng, autoharp); Kent Carter (b, clo); Kenneth Tyler (d, perc, f); Oliver Johnson, Carlo Tonaghi (d).* 6/69–77.

A rich garnering of material from a period and an association that yielded one of Lacy's classic records, *The Owl*, and also some of his least-known material. To deal with the latter first, there are two long parts to 'Roba', from the 1969 group featuring Enrico Rava and recorded by arch-modernist Alvin Curran. This includes a rare excursion by Lacy on sopranino saxophone, a dry, bat-squeak sound that floats outside the harmonic scale, and a 1971 solo performance, chronologically the next thing on the record, which makes inventive use of tape.

The material on the original LPs *Scraps* and *Dreams* (which features Derek Bailey) is more familiar in conception and execution, and the latter includes a wonderful version of what is still one of the saxophonist's most durable compositions, 'The Wane'. 'The Uh Uh Uh' is inspired by Monk and could almost pass for a composition of the master's except that it is so far removed from the blues.

The Owl is masterly, and the inclusion of these seven tracks is what makes this compilation indispensable. Morris is only present for part of the set, but his urgent, pungent tone makes a huge difference. Lacy has not worked much with trumpeters and, apart from Roswell Rudd, has not demonstrated much kinship with brass. Here, though, he feeds off Butch's delivery and flow of ideas, and weaves himself into a double helix with the cornetist.

*** Cinco Minutos de Jazz

Strauss ST 1087 *Lacy; Steve Potts (as); Irène Aëbi (clo, hca, radio); Kent Carter (b); Noel McGhie (d, perc).* 72.

Recorded in Lisbon to celebrate the sixth anniversary of a radio show which dedicated the same length of time to jazz that orthodox psychoanalysts give to their patients. And just to sustain that improbable analogy, Lacy digs deep into the collective unconscious (uh oh, that's Jungian) to create a network of allusions and references that tap back into the early history of jazz, something that Lacy was to do at moments of maximum confidence. He tags Hodges and Bechet, there is a brief nod to Johnny Dodds on 'No Baby', and lots of ironic pastiche elsewhere.

**** Weal & Woe

Emanem 4004 *Lacy; Steve Potts (as, ss); Irène Aëbi (v, vl, clo); Kent Carter (b); Oliver Johnson (d).* 72, 73.

Two important components to this very valuable reissue of Emanem and Quark LP material. The earlier recording is a document of Lacy's first-ever solo soprano saxophone concerts, made in Avignon. Just four years after Anthony Braxton's pioneering *For Alto*, it is fascinating to hear Lacy take a very different course, sinuously melodic, less antagonistic in attack than Braxton but no less percussive and definite, and no less willing to superimpose different rhythmic shapes over a pretty basic line. *The Woe* was Lacy's anti-war suite, a powerfully advocated protest that gave this classic group something to get their teeth into. The recording is a little unfriendly to Aëbi and to some of the quieter soprano saxophone parts, but there is so much meat and meaning to the performances that one hardly notices any such shortcomings.

*** Saxophone Special

Emanem 4024 *Lacy; Steve Potts; Trevor Watts (ss, as); Evan Parker (ss, ts, bs); Derek Bailey (g); Michel Waisvisz (syn); Kent Carter (b); John Stevens (d).* 7/73, 12/74.

These are tapes recorded in concert at the 100 Club in London's Oxford Street and the more up-market Wigmore Hall a year and a half later. At the time, Lacy was experimenting with saxophone harmonics based on seconds; Potts, who came to Britain with Lacy and Kent Carter, is supremely confident in the idiom. '38', performed at the 100 Club with Bailey and Stevens, is a tribute to Coleman Hawkins, and it's followed by 'Flakes' and 'Revolutionary Suicide', the latter derived from a damaged tape. The whole session was originally released in faulty stereo, but the reissue uses a single good mono channel. The 1974 session makes use of pure noise and found sounds, on LP on 'Dreams' and from Michel Waisvisz's crude but expressive synth effects. Essentially, though, it's a saxophone quartet spread out across the stereo picture, and dramatically different from the kind of work done by a conventional SATBar line-up. When all four players are on soprano, the overtone field is immensely complex, and one wishes for a chance to hear this same grouping recorded with more up-to-date technology.

**** Hooky

Emanem 4042 *Lacy (ss solo).* 3/76.

Set down in a capacious (church) acoustic, this can perhaps be seen as a characteristic solo set of its time. Some of the tracks are built on spoken phrases which yield intervals and a certain rhythmic foot on which Lacy builds elaborate improvisations in quite minimalist form; 'No Baby' (ambiguously spoken) and 'Hooky' work like this. The latter, 'The Tao' pieces, 'Pearl Street' and 'Revolutionary Suicide', for instance, all also feature on the New York recording listed below. But this one is faithfully transcribed, there is a particularly fine specimen of 'New Duck', and its focus on some of the composer's most significant texts make this one an important entry for Lacy followers.

*** Trickles

Black Saint 120008 *Lacy; Roswell Rudd (tb, chimes); Kent Carter (b); Beaver Harris (d).* 3/76.

With his brief, substantive titles, Lacy almost seems to be attempting a new generic definition with each succeeding album. There is certainly a sense in which *Trickles* works by the slowest accumulation, like the slow accretions of limestone. There is also, unfortunately, an obduracy and resistance in this music that one doesn't often find elsewhere. The fault is not with the band. Rudd plays wonderfully, carving big, abstract shapes that are shaded in by Carter and Harris, coaxing a more intense sound from the saxophonist. It's Lacy who seems unyielding. On sabbatical from his lifelong study of Monk, he seems at something of a loss, stating ideas without rationale or conviction, redeeming them only by the absolute consistency of his playing. Utterly fascinating, like all of Lacy's work, and perhaps all the more significant for being less entire and achieved, but certainly not his most successful recording.

*** Snips

Jazz Magnet JAM-2001 2CD *Lacy (ss solo).* 5/76.

Recorded on a return visit to New York, this was his first-ever solo concert there, right at the heart of the then-busy Loft Jazz scene. It's very shabbily recorded, unfortunately, but it's still intriguing to hear his then-current thoughts on staple Lacy texts such as 'The Tao', 'The 4 Edges' and 'Revolutionary Suicide'. Also a vintage 'New York Duck'.

***(*) Clinkers

hatOLOGY 546 *Lacy (ss solo).* 6/77.

A reissue of an early Hat Hut LP, this finds Lacy in Basel, delivering five solos. There is another (Swiss) 'Duck', and this and 'Micro Worlds' are explorations of soprano sound which

Roscoe Mitchell might have listened to enviously. 'Clinkers' itself is high-spirited. A very good one.

★★(★) Troubles

Black Saint 120035 *Lacy; Steve Potts (as, ss); Kent Carter (clo, b); Oliver Johnson (d); Irène Aëbi (v, vl, clo).* 5/79.

This was the period when Lacy characterized his music as 'poly-free', an attempt to categorize his still rather ramshackle combination of unfettered group improvisation with scored or predetermined passages. One of the problems with the album is that it sounds precisely like that: uneasy alternations with little coherence or flow other than the sidewinding motion of Lacy's own lines.

★★★ NY Capers & Quirks

hatOLOGY 532 *Lacy; Ronnie Boykins (b); Dennis Charles (d).* 12/79.

These are not players one immediately associates with Lacy, though his association with Charles went back more than 20 years when this lovely trio record was made. Boykins is strikingly similar in sound to Jean-Jacques Avenel, suggesting that this is the kind of bass tone Lacy hears as he negotiates his high-wire stuff on the soprano. The five cuts are all Lacy originals, and all beautifully crafted. 'Bud's Brother' and 'Kitty Malone' are long, nostalgic-sounding pieces with lots of action from both bass and percussion, but focusing on Steve's winding, at times almost microtonal lines.

★★★(★) The Flame

Soul Note 121035 *Lacy; Bobby Few (p); Dennis Charles (d).* 1/82.

Whenever he plays, Few emerges as the fulcrum of Lacy's groups. His composition, 'Wet Spot', is the briefest and the only non-Lacy number on the album, but it's a particularly clear example of how Lacy and his loyal group of collaborators have rationalized the stretched-out improvisations of Cecil Taylor and the tautness of Monk. In timbre and tonality these sessions strongly resemble Taylor's 'bass-less' trios, but with the emphasis switched unequivocally to the saxophone. Lacy's four compositions form part of an ongoing series of dedications to 'eminent source figures', or what Lacy calls his 'Luminaries'; 'The Match' is for the surrealist Man Ray, 'Gusts', 'Licks' and 'The Flame' for an assortment of instrumentalists from around the world whose music has inspired him. In the trio context, Lacy sounds much more rhythmic than usual and appears to adapt his line to the drummer's beat, punching his own little toneless accents at appropriate moments.

★★★(★) Clichés

hatOLOGY 536 *Lacy; George Lewis (tb); Steve Potts (ss, as); Bobby Few (p); Irène Aëbi (vn, clo, v); Jean-Jacques Avenel (b); Oliver Johnson (d); Cyrille Few, Sherry Margolin (perc).* 11/82.

This is edited from the original release of *Prospectus*, which is a different strategy from the usual one of piling in yet more material to fill out the CD. Whether *Clichés* benefits from the trimming we'd beg leave to doubt, but it's resolutely unclichéd music from the start (the opening 'Stamps', written in honour of Miles Davis according to Lacy) to the closing title-track, which was inspired by an African postcard from a friend. As ever, Lacy works from short lines which seem to come from spoken phrases, as on the solo *Hooky*, but then unravel into ever-subtler and more sophisticated scalar forms. The septet is ironically not as full-voiced as the more familiar sixsome. Lewis is a deconstructionist, even if he isn't pulling his instrument apart, and he treats each of these lines as minimal strategies that require little in the way of embellishment. Margolin, Cyrille Few and an unidentified 'friend' add some fun to the title-piece, but for the most part this is a taut and beautifully organized set. Established fans will regret the omission of a couple of tracks from *Prospectus*. For the majority of listeners, though, this is an ideal Lacy set.

★★★ The Condor

Soul Note 121135 *Lacy; Steve Potts (ss, as); Bobby Few (p); Irène Aëbi (vn, v); Jean-Jacques Avenel (b); Oliver Johnson (d).* 6/85.

★★★(★) The Window

Soul Note 121185 *Lacy; Jean-Jacques Avenel (b); Oliver Johnson (d).* 7/87.

'Morning Joy' kicks off the fine 1985 *The Condor*, where the balance of written-out passages and freer improvisation seems almost ideal; it also features some of the best interplay between the two saxophones, with Potts in exceptionally good form. If one of the great pleasures of investigating Lacy's mammoth output is the comparison of (sometimes drastically, sometimes only minimally) different versions of the same repertoire piece or 'instant standard' (his term), then these are critical performances for an understanding of how unconventionally he relates to a 'rhythm section'.

Stripped down to just saxophone, bass and drums on *The Window*, he reveals just how unconventional a player he actually is, refusing all the obvious rhythmic and chordal clues, playing lines so oblique as almost to belong to another piece altogether. 'Flakes' is another of those apparently self-descriptive compositions that resist all external reference. Again, very fine.

★★★★ Chirps

FMP CD 29 *Lacy; Evan Parker (ss).* 7/85.

By the turn of the '80s, Lacy appears to have regarded total improvisational abstraction as a way-station rather than a long-term direction in his work. Nevertheless, in *Chirps* he and fellow soprano saxophonist Evan Parker produced one of the best and most significant free albums of the decade. Concentrating on high, brief sounds that are more like insect-twitter than bird-song, the two players interleave minimalist episodes with a level of concentration that seems almost superhuman. Endlessly demanding – and a quarter of an hour longer on CD reissue – it's unlikely to appeal to anyone primed for hummable melody or more than usually susceptible to sounds at the dog-whistle end of the spectrum. It is, though, curiously involving and has considerably more accessible charm than the sere whisperings of the now-deleted duos with British guitarist Derek Bailey.

★★★★ Morning Joy

hatOLOGY 556 *Lacy; Steve Potts (ss, as); Jean-Jacques Avenel(b); Oliver Johnson (d).* 2/86.

One of our favourites, and a welcome return to the hatOLOGY catalogue. Though simply a recording of a Paris gig, where the sextet of the time was missing Few and Aëbi, the music comes across with rare intensity, Lacy and Potts working off each other even more strikingly than usual. With two outstanding

Monk covers and four Lacy themes where the spiked melodies are sharpened to pristine points, this is an ideal entry level for listeners new to his work.

****** Sempre Amore**

Soul Note 121170 *Lacy; Mal Waldron (p).* 2/86.

*****(*) Let's Call This ... Esteem**

Slam CD 501 *As above.* 5/93.

****** Communiqué**

Soul Note 121487 *As above.* 6/97.

The dedication to Waldron signals one of the most productive partnerships in Lacy's career. The pianist's name comes first on the wonderful *Sempre Amore*, but the honours are strictly shared. Waldron's big, dark left-hand chords and single-note statements take some of the acid out of Lacy's frail and thinly voiced takes on a bag of Ellington and Strayhorn themes. The opening 'Johnny Come Lately' is appealingly off-centre and 'Prelude To A Kiss' sounds at the edge of sleep. It's worth comparing 'A Flower Is A Lovesome Thing' to the version Waldron recorded with Marion Brown the previous year on *Songs Of Love And Regret*, where his accompaniment is little more than a sequence of moodily recessed pedals. With the undemonstrative Lacy, he's all over the place, arpeggiating and trilling furiously, like Wordsworth trying to explain to Newton what a flower really is.

Let's Call This ... Esteem shouldn't be confused with the hatART *Let's Call This*, which still hasn't made it to CD. The Slam disc was recorded during a concert at the Oxford Playhouse, compèred by another soprano specialist, Lol Coxhill. The sound is oddly cavernous but the performances are uniformly excellent. Another version of 'Johnny Come Lately' suggests how much they've grown into the partnership. The Monk tunes – 'Let's Call This', 'Monk's Dream', 'Evidence' and the inevitable 'Epistrophy' – are expertly co-ordinated and by no means soulless. Waldron's own 'Snake Out' sounds great without a larger band, and the pianist has his moment again on 'In A Sentimental Mood'. The other Soul Note disc catches the duo in one of their better latter-day encounters.

***** Spirit Of Mingus**

Freelance FRLCD016 *Lacy; Eric Watson (p).* 12/91.

Lacy got different things from Watson than from Waldron and their close proximity here helps point them up. Where Waldron is harmonically dark and brooding, albeit in a romantic vein, Watson likes to throw light into the structure of a composition and show off its scaffolding and struts. These nine Mingus compositions, including 'Goodbye Pork Pie Hat', 'Pithecanthropus Erectus', 'Peggy's Blue Skylight' and the extreme agitprop of 'Remember Rockefeller At Attica' have never been heard in quite this way and it's wonderfully effective. Lacy's horn implies whole areas of harmony that even the pianist seems unwilling to explore, while he also keeps the rhythm of each piece moving forward. A remarkable record.

***** We See: Thelonious Monk Songbook**

hatOLOGY 529 *Lacy; Hans Kennel (t, flhn); Steve Potts (ss, as); Sonhando Estwick (vib); Jean-Jacques Avenel (b); John Betsch (d).* 92.

Most of these pieces had been played by Lacy umpteen times before. The originality of this set, though, lay in the instrumentation he chose, adding a vibraphone player and trumpeter to his more familiar instrumentation. It all makes great sense of Monk, even though there are a couple of moments when it sounds as though one might have stumbled across a lost Dolphy session with Bobby Hutcherson and a ghostly Booker Little. The bonus track for the CD release is 'Thelonious', easily the least successful thing on a generally quite conventional set.

***** Dummy**

Splasc(h) 843 *Lacy; Riccardo Fassi (p); Gianluca Renzi (b); Ettore Fioravanti (d).* 92.

This is very much a collaborative effort, with some emphasis on Riccardo Fassi's writing as well as Lacy's. The pianist's 'Dark Water' was composed with Steve in mind and it's an ideal number with which to open the set, identifiably in his voice, but equally obviously from another hand. Fassi's grasp of complex harmonics and his advanced rhythmic sense are both obvious from his solo, which would seem alien to all but the most Europeanized of American players. Lacy has so rarely played with other groups in recent years, certainly on record, that it is strange to hear him in this context. 'Replicante' is another powerful outing, with some fine interaction between the trio and its fourth wheel, while the title-track, apparently originally written for Alan Shorter, is an astonishing variation on an atonal blues. The remainder of the set palls slightly, but only because it is difficult to absorb so much challenging music in real time that one starts to hear only surfaces. Best sampled slowly and thoughtfully.

*****(*) Revenue**

Soul Note 121234 *Lacy; Steve Potts (as, ss); Jean-Jacques Avenel (b); John Betsch (d).* 2/93.

****** Vespers**

Soul Note 121260 *As above, except add Ricky Ford (ts), Tom Varner (frhn), Bobby Few (p), Irène Aëbi (v).* 7/93.

Betsch's arrival on board gave the Lacy group a less raw, slightly more delicate rhythmic feel. Even so, as he proves on 'The Rent' and the title-track, the new drummer is no slouch when it comes to sticking his foot in the door and demanding a hearing. He powers these tracks along very crisply and, on 'Gospel', subtly stretches and compresses the time exactly in keeping with Lacy's own elastic pulse. Potts more than ever brings in ideas of his own and a range of contributions that might be likened to Don Cherry's in the classic Ornette quartet: responsive, aware of the leader's intentions and requirements, but still absolutely individual and effortlessly taking up point on 'The Uh Uh Uh'. Now in the middle of a long purple patch, Lacy seems incapable of making an indifferent album.

Vespers is focused on Blaga Dimitrova's lyrics for Aëbi; the songs are softly melancholy farewells and remembrances of departed friends and idols: Miles Davis, Corrado Costa, the artists Arshile Gorky (whose 1946 abstract graces the cover) and Keith Haring (whose bold, stark lines had something in common with Lacy's saxophone sound), clarinettist John Carter, John Coltrane, Charles Mingus and Stan Getz. This is perhaps the most personal music we've heard from Lacy, and it is all the more affecting in coming from a man normally so reticent about inward states. Aëbi is magnificent, as is Ricky Ford, who now notoriously plays better on other people's records than on his own.

CORE COLLECTION

★★★★ 5 × Monk 5 × Lacy

Silkheart SHCD 144 *Lacy (ss solo).* 3/94.

Having spent a good deal of time over the past few years working with the group and with larger-scale arrangements, Lacy shows every sign of wanting to return to unaccompanied performance. This one is exactly as described, five tunes by the master and five originals, including the familiar 'The Crust' and 'Deadline', both of them well-established Lacy repertory tunes. The Monk compositions are also things Lacy has covered in detail in the past, but this time his take on 'Pannonica' and 'Evidence' is notable for subtle shifts in the geometry of the tune, as if he is trying some virtual recomposition, changing internal relationships without changing the components, rather like one of those relativity diagrams in which time-space is presumed to be gridded on a sheet of rubber which can then be stretched and folded but not cut or torn. All the material was recorded during an improvisation festival in Stockholm. It isn't clear whether these ten tracks were the whole of Lacy's performance or an edited segment. At 45 minutes – and this is a hobby-horse of ours – it seems perfectly balanced as a CD. Any more material would simply blur the lines.

★★★★ Actuality

Cavity Search CSR 24 *Lacy (ss solo).* 4/95.

The liner-note begins with a useful comparison. It was Anthony Braxton who pioneered the solo saxophone record and, as we have noted elsewhere, Braxton is perhaps the only other performer on the planet to have had his career so thoroughly documented. However, Pierre Coussault of Cavity Search is more and rightly concerned to point up differences rather than similarities, and he is probably right in claiming priority for Lacy in developing the art of solo reed improvisation. 'Actuality' is an interesting word because – as this European exile understands – it doesn't mean 'real', the opposite of false or imaginary, but 'here and now', as in the French word for the present, *actuelles*. And what this live record documents is Lacy's commitment to the thought of the moment, to a kind of articulation in which a phrase or a note is not predetermined and then not analysed or debated, but simply articulated and allowed its moment in the air. As usual, Lacy draws on compositions from the span of his career. 'Revolutionary Suicide' is dedicated to the life of Black Panther Huey Newton, but was called back to mind by news of violent struggle elsewhere. 'Moms' is exactly what it says, a song of affection and thanks to Steve's and Irène Aëbi's mothers. 'The Door', with its knocking sounds, is devoted to Joseph Haydn, perhaps the most at-hand of all the classical composers; for Lacy, the knock at the door (something of a 20th-century bogey) is also the moment of maximum immediacy, a challenge. Challenging music this is. With the exception of the final club track, *Actuality* was recorded in a Portland, Oregon, church, an acoustic that throws a wrap round Lacy's chill tone. Congratulations to Cavity Search for having the foresight to tape and issue one of the best performances of recent years.

★★★ The Joan Miró Foundation Concert

New Contemporary Music NCM 10 *Lacy; Irène Aëbi (v).* 6/95.

This was never intended for release and there are flaws and inconsistencies of pitch on the source tape which haven't been successfully addressed, but the Lacys' Barcelona concert was one of those magical occasions where the yin–yang of Steve's dry, cerebral line and Irène's floating melodism mesh perfectly. The opening sequence is Monk material, the closing section settings of poetry by Robert Creeley and an excellent example of the couple's response to literary texts. There is also a fantastic arrangement of Herman Melville's literary credo, 'Art'.

★★★ Bye-Ya

Freelance 25 *Lacy; Jean-Jacques Avenel (b, kora); John Betsch (d); Irène Aëbi (v).* 3/96.

In addition to the title-tune, Lacy and the trio also play 'Trinkle Tinkle', underlining Monk's near presence whenever the saxophonist takes the stage or goes near a studio mic. Aëbi has only a walk-on role this time, so Steve, Jean-Jacques and John are left to their own thing, spinning out taut, well-structured songs and improvisations which always seem too short and yet like a sentence of Robert Louis Stevenson couldn't be improved by the addition of a single word. There's a similar sense of adventure, as if these three seasoned musicians were exploring something for the very first time. Check 'The Bath' and 'Prayer' for that. Avenel plays his kora on 'Pi-Pande' and with enough conviction to make you think a whole album of duets would be no bad thing.

★★★★ Five Facings

FMP CD 85 *Lacy; Marilyn Crispell, Ulrich Gumpert, Misha Mengelberg, Vladimir Miller, Fred Van Hove (p).* 4/96.

Five nights at the 1996 Workshop Freie Musik and five confrontations with piano-players of markedly different disposition. Four of the eight performances are Lacy compositions. Two rather short items with Crispell open the record and fail to catch light, mainly because she tends to think in great massy blocks of sound and doesn't seem prepared to follow the saxophonist's long, weaving lines. At the opposite end, Miller is perfectly content to act as accompanist on 'The Wane', making no attempt to stamp his personality on the music.

The real meat of the record lies in between, a magnificent duo improvisation with Van Hove, a long meditation on 'Art' with the classically inclined and suitably dry Gumpert (a collaborator on the 1985 *Deadline*), and three Monk tunes performed with the redoubtable Mengelberg. Of these, 'Ruby, My Dear' is a masterpiece that almost justifies the price on its own; 'Off Minor' and 'Evidence' are a little drier, but no less thoughtful and accomplished. A wonderful record, in what has become Lacy's favourite and most successful setting.

★★★ Solo: Live At Unity Temple

Wobbly Rail WOB 003 *Lacy (ss solo).* 11/97.

Unity Temple is an ecumenical religious building in Chicago, designed by Frank Lloyd Wright. As such, and given its humane acoustic, it's the perfect setting to run through an unusual, comfortable and familiar set of themes, including his now well-attested Monk medley and the delightfully wry 'Revenue'. 'Crust' and 'Art' are textbook Lacy, and this is the kind of record with which you might win round someone who's previously found his unaccompanied performances hard to follow.

★★★(★) The Rent

Cavity Search 44 *Lacy; Jean-Jacques Avenel (b); John Betsch (d).* 98.

A cracking trio record that retreads some of Lacy's most distinctive themes, 'Door', 'Flakes', 'Shuffle Boil (Monk)', and re-energizes them considerably. His playing has of late taken on a warmer and more expressive cast, a more vocalized tone than in the past, and it suits this context extremely well. Avenel and Betsch are entirely in tune with the approach and the recording is very plain and faithful.

***** Sands**

Tzadik 7124 *Lacy; Irène Aëbi (v).* 98.

Pages from Lacy's musical workbook, spun out at leisure and with admirable concentration at home. Steve's tone is warm, precise and refreshingly ambiguous. There are more exciting solo performances, but this is well up to scratch.

*****(*) Monk's Dream**

Verve 543090-2 *Lacy; Roswell Rudd(tb); Jean-Jacques Avenel (b); John Betsch (d); Irène Aëbi (v).* 6–8/99.

Response to this, a cherished project of veteran jazz producer Jean-Philippe Allard, may depend on how much one warms to Rudd's playing: not the force of yore, some of his expressionism can sound more like short-windedness, even if the musical intelligence remains keen. Lacy himself is magnificent on this quartet date, which is meant to rekindle his work with Rudd from four decades earlier. Two Monk tunes (only two?), 'Pannonica' being especially attractive, a nod to Duke with 'Koko' that starts in very remote places indeed, and a bunch of typical Lacy originals, two with texts sung by Irène. Beautifully recorded and a beguiling reflection on many years of patient work.

****** The Holy La**

Freelance 0201 *Lacy; Jean-Jacques Avenel (b); John Betsch (d); Irène Aëbi (v).* 01.

The title refers to the A-natural note that orchestral musicians tune to, which suggests a going back to basics. Here, Lacy revisits some of the music he and his companions have created over the previous 30 years. 'Flakes' is there, played with something approaching solemnity. 'The Door' is classically inspired and very moving. They kick off with Monk's 'Shuffle Boil', which helps to establish a language that grows in eloquence as the set advances. Aëbi sings Robert Creeley's lyrics to 'Inside My Head', but otherwise it is Lacy, Avenel and Betsch who command attention. A stunning record, whether or not you know some of this repertoire.

***** The Beat Suite**

Sunnyside 3012 *Lacy; George Lewis (tb); Jean-Jacques Avenel (b); John Betsch (d); Irène Aëbi (v).* 03.

An ambitious attempt to set some of the Beat Poets to a jazz score that goes far beyond their 'spontaneous bop prosody' and into something much more lasting and substantial. Aëbi's voice is the stumbling block here and what the project needs more than anything is a variety of vocalists to bring to life the very different registers required for Kerouac, Creeley, Burroughs, Ginsberg, Rexroth and Corso. The texts are included in the liner-note and make for interesting reading, but the real drama is in the accompaniment, which is subtle and carefully inflected by the two horns and the rest of the band. These guys have worked together for so long and with such intensity that there are moments when too much is elided, a conversation conducted in winks, nods and monosyllables. Fascinating, none the less.

Guy Lafitte (1927–98)

TENOR SAXOPHONE

Originally a clarinettist, Lafitte switched to tenor in the '40s and soon established himself as one of the leading French mainstreamers, working with many Americans, including Bill Coleman and Wild Bill Davis.

***** Blue And Sentimental**

Emarcy 159852-2 *Lafitte; Peanuts Holland (t); Raymond Fol, Jean-Claude Pelletier (p); Geo Daly (vib); Jean Bonal (g); Alix Bret, Charlie Blareau (b); Bernard Planchenault, Mac Kac Reilles (d).* 54.

***** Corps Et Ame**

Black & Blue 915-2 *Lafitte; Hank Jones (p); George Duvivier (b); J. C. Heard (d).* 3/78.

***** Three Men On A Beat**

Black & Blue 973-2 *Lafitte; Wild Bill Davis (org); Alvin Queen (d).* 1/83.

Lafitte was a much-liked figure whose relatively scarce recordings have marginalized him for many mainstream admirers. These two, made a quarter-century apart, are likeable testaments from a man with a big sound and a grand manner. The Emarcy set reissues some mild mainstream from a pretty obscure French issue, mostly standard ballads where Lafitte's Hawkins influence is given full rein. Geo Daly throws in a little vibes shimmer but otherwise the group is no more than quietly supportive.

The earlier Black & Blue date finds Guy in top company, and he obviously enjoyed it. Once past the feeble line, 'One For The Bean' (which at least makes his dedication clear), the quartet tuck into the material like hungry men, though Jones is as polished as usual. No classic, just a good mainstream blow. With Bill and Alvin, Guy comes on like Lockjaw Davis. The tracks are too samey, perhaps, but one or two at a time, they're a modest tonic.

Bireli Lagrene (born 1966)

GUITAR

Born to a Sinti gypsy family, Lagrene began playing guitar at four and quickly became a prodigy. He was touring as a teenager and showed a style that went back to Django as well as taking in the recent past and the present.

***** Routes To Django**

Jazzpoint JP 1003 *Lagrene; Jorg Reiter (p); Wolfgang Lackerschmidt (vib); Gaiti Lagrene, Tschirglo Loeffler (g); Scmitto Kling (vn); Jan Jankeje (b).* 5/80.

***** Bireli Swing '81**

Jazzpoint JP 1009 *As above, except omit Reiter, Lackerschmidt and Kling; add Bernd Rabe (ss), Allen Blairman (d).* 4/81.

If Django Reinhardt were to have a spiritual heir, it would surely be Lagrene, who emerged from a gypsy community in the '80s to stun European and American audiences with his virtuosity. Both of the above were recorded in concert, with Lagrene's electrifying improvisations (all done on acoustic guitar) conducted on a range of material which includes swing, blues, bop and original themes, all of it mastered with effortless aplomb, even when it sounds as if the guitarist isn't sure of his ground.

That hint of flying blind gives the greatest excitement to the debut album, *Routes To Django*, which includes a nerve-racking romp through the tune identified as 'Night And Day' (actually 'Don't Worry 'Bout Me'). The 1981 session is nearly as good, although Rabe is an irrelevance; but from this point Lagrene began to fall foul of seeming like a novelty act.

***** A Tribute To Django Reinhardt**

Jazzpoint JP 1061 2CD *Lagrene; Vic Juris, Diz Disley, Gaiti Lagrene (g); Jan Jankeje (b).* 7/81–6/85.

Probably the best and the worst of Lagrene in this rather confusingly presented two-disc package. It's not really a Reinhardt tribute, more a combination of two concerts (there is a stray track from 1981, for no apparent reason) from Carnegie Hall and the Freiburg Jazz Festival. Juris is co-featured on the second gig and takes a guest turn on the first. Bireli's blues ('Toulouse Blues') are little more than superfast clichés, and there is plenty of showboating but also some daredevil interplay which is genuinely exciting. Chick Corea's 'Spain' has a solo which will have most guitarists shaking their heads in disbelief. Sound on both discs is rather (excuse us) stringy and inconsistent.

****(*) Stuttgart Aria**

Jazzpoint JP 1019 *Lagrene; Vladislaw Sendecki (ky); Jaco Pastorius (b, p, v); Jan Jankeje (syn, v); Peter Lubke (d); Serge Bringolf (perc, v).* 3/86.

Lagrene meets Pastorius. This souvenir of a European tour is good-humoured but tends to go the way of all live fusion albums: a noisy dead-end. Salvaged by flashes of brilliance by both front-men, including a ferocious 'Donna Lee', it doesn't amount to very much. Lagrene's subsequent Blue Note albums all seem to be missing in action at present.

***** Blue Eyes**

Dreyfus Jazz FDM 36591-2 *Lagrene; Maurice Vander (p); Christian Minh Doky (b); André Ceccarelli (d).* 6/97.

This entry by Lagrene is a bit of a shock, a Sinatra tribute which features the guitarist turning in vocals on four tracks. Sensibly, he sings only on chucklesome tunes like 'Luck Be A Lady' and doesn't go for the heartbreakers, since he's scarcely the crooning type. The guitar-playing remains heroic in a dashed-off sort of way, but this is a relentlessly swinging rhythm section and they're pushing him pretty hard. Rather pin-bright a lot of the time; he could relax a little more on the ballads.

****(*) Front Page**

Emarcy 549045-2 *Lagrene; John McLaughlin (g); Dominique Di Piazza (b); Dennis Chambers (d).* 1/00.

Boy, can these guys play fast! Set up with the most rapid-fire drummer in fusion (outside of Dave Weckl), Lagrene isn't inclined to pace himself, and with Di Piazza playing electric lines of similar velocity, this is a muscle-bound showcase for the three talents which only rarely lets up. McLaughlin arrives for the final track, and even he has to get his skates on. We were soon bored – it feels old-fashioned already – but it will no doubt bang a few heads.

***** Duet**

Dreyfus FDM 36604-2 *Lagrene; Sylvain Luc (g).* 6/99.

***** Gipsy Project & Friends**

Dreyfus FDM 36638-2 *Lagrene; Holzmano Lagrene, Stocheo Rosenberg, Hono Winterstein, Thomas Dutronc (g); Florin Niculescu (vn); Diego Imbert (b); Henri Salvador (v).* 2/02.

As flush as it is with lightning picking, the duet record has a softness of timbre which is very appealing. Luc matches Lagrene line for line, strum for strum, and the tunes are a likeable mix of pop, jazz and the odd original. Hardly a matter of profundity, and maybe that isn't Bireli's style anyway.

The Gipsy Project set is inevitably more bombastic (with five pickers on hand that's hardly surprising), and in a post-Gypsy Kings world, maybe this music has settled into an idiom which takes its place in whichever aisle of the world-music supermarket, and just stays there. Not that Lagrene doesn't make it go molten every time he puts fingers to strings: some of the playing here really takes the breath away, whoever's playing it. As so often with this kind of thing, one feels awfully replete at the end of it all.

Oliver Lake (born 1944)

ALTO AND OTHER SAXOPHONES, FLUTE

One of the few alto saxophonists who has whole-heartedly taken up the challenge of Eric Dolphy, not in terms of multi-instrumentalism, but in striving to play 'inside' and 'outside' at the same time. Still best known as a member of the World Saxophone Quartet, Lake has created a substantial body of recordings as a leader, almost all of them reflecting that sometimes schizophrenic but profoundly adventurous ambition.

***** Prophet**

Black Saint 120044 *Lake; Baikida Carroll (t, flhn); Donald Smith (p); Jerry Harris (b); Pheeroan akLaff (d).* 8/80.

***** Clevont Fitzhubert**

Black Saint 120054 *As above, except omit Harris.* 4/81.

*****(*) Expandable Language**

Black Saint 120074 *Lake; Geri Allen (p); Kevin Eubanks (g); Fred Hopkins (b); Pheeroan akLaff (d).* 9/84.

Expandable Language sets Lake alongside Geri Allen and Kevin Eubanks for six provocative explorations, alternately fierce and lyrical, almost a mainstream situation for this powerful voice. *Prophet* is a less cohesive album but also a far bolder one, and it's interesting to track the path of Lake's engagement with free procedures over this (almost) five-year period. The tension between orthodox, changes-based jazz and abstraction has always been a creative one for him; in his interchanges with Carroll one can detect distant echos of Parker and Gillespie duelling at Massey Hall, and indeed Ornette and Cherry trading ever sharper phrases on the early Atlantics. The middle record with its enigmatic dedication to a 'good friend' is packed with intriguing themes and counter-themes, not least the title-track. 'November '80' is also finely judged, and there is a single composition by the fiery Carroll, who features on his own 'King'.

*****(*) Virtual Reality: Total Escapism**

Gazell 4004 *Lake; Anthony Michael Peterson (g); Santi Debriano (b); Pheeroan akLaff (d).* 10/91.

Not always the easiest label to track down, but still in print and well worth the hunt. This was Lake's working quartet and perhaps the most pungent band he'd had for a decade. Having dipped a toe into more formal, 'sheet-driven' composition, this marked a return to post-Dolphy jazz. Eric is represented by 'Prophet', which follows a version of Mingus's 'Fables Of Faubus' even more deeply rooted in Dolphy's style. Bobby Bradford's 'Shedetude' is also meat and drink to Lake, who is in great form, relaxed but poised and thinking fast on his feet. A fine album.

*** Edge-ing

Black Saint 120104 *Lake; Charles Eubanks (p); Reggie Workman (b); Andrew Cyrille (d).* 6/93.

*** Dedicated To Dolphy

Black Saint 120144 *Lake; Russell Gunn (t); Charles Eubanks (p); Belden Bullock (b); Cecil Brooks (d).* 11/94.

Lake has a powerful enthusiasm for the work of Eric Dolphy and, on *Prophet*, he included two of Dolphy's most vibrant compositions, 'Hat and Beard' and 'Something Sweet, Something Tender', both from the classic *Out to Lunch!*. They're imaginative re-readings, not just pastiches, and certainly a good deal more inventive than the straight versions of those same two tracks (plus 'Miss Ann', 'G. W.', '245' and Mal Waldron's 'Fire Waltz') on *Dedicated To Dolphy*, which is a disappointment. The one quantifiable plus is the trumpet-work of Russell Gunn from St Louis, sounding brisk and bright, just like the young Freddie Hubbard.

Lake veers towards lyricism again on *Edge-ing*, rejigging 'Zaki' for a fuller-voiced band and bringing in material like John Hicks's almost schmaltzy 'Peanut Butter' and Curtis Clark's unexpected 'Verve Nerve'. His bluesy tone is eloquent enough to sustain some rather bland arrangements, and the bass and drum interactions are consistently interesting. Which leaves the finger pointing at Eubanks, a rather dull accompanist who doesn't quite have the Hicks trick of playing spikily *and* lyrically off pat.

***(*) Movement, Turns & Switches

Passin' Thru 41210 *Lake; Kenyatta Beasley (t); Donal Fox (p); Sandra Billingslea, Ashley Horne, Regina Carter (vn); Maxine Roach (vla); Eileen Folson (clo); Belden Bullock (b).* 8/96.

*** Matador Of 1st & 1st

Passin' Thru 40709 *Lake (ss, as, f, bells, v).* 97.

These records signal a new label and a new phase in Lake's career. *Matador* is a strange montage of instrumental miniatures, some of them only a matter of seconds long, others shaped almost like scaled-down bebop tunes. It's not the easiest or most accommodating of listens, but it reveals a great deal about the micro-structure of Lake's playing and compositions. Increasingly he seems to cast himself in the latter role. The saxophonist doesn't play at all on the title-track of the earlier album, which is a duo for Carter and Fox. The remainder of the album is credited to his String Project, with additional instrumentalists added *ad hoc*. The album begins with stunning simplicity on 'Fan Fare Bop', a sharp, declamatory theme which is catchier than you'd imagine possible. The role of Kenyatta Beasley is all too brief. It might have been better to have included bassist Bullock on more of the tunes as well. He adds bottom to a sound that is a little shrill and unsupported. Otherwise, a fascinating record that constantly throws up new insights.

***(*) Talkin' Stick

Passin' Thru 41213 *Lake; Geri Allen (p); Jay Hoggard (vib); Belden Bullock (b); Cecil Brooks III (d).* 3/97.

Given the experimentation of recent years, it's quite surprising to find Lake playing in a relatively orthodox bebop format. The partnership of alto and vibes will inevitably make some listeners think of Dolphy's *Out to Lunch!*, and the connection is definitely there. Fortunately, the material is so strong and the group so well suited to the project that the results are high quality. Including the late Julius Hemphill's 'Hard Blues' was a powerful stroke, and Curtis Clark's 'Only If You Live There' will be an ear-opener for many, but it is the long 'Masaai Moves' which dominates the album, heard here in a much more direct version than the original.

Allen is as efficient an accompanist as one could wish for, and her straightforwardness is a huge asset on the closing 'Song for Jay' and 'Philly Blues', a pair of compositions which sum up the album perfectly. Strongly recommended, as long as you aren't looking for more left-field experimentation. This is as orthodox as it gets from Lake.

*** Kinda Up

Justin Time 1362 *Lake; Reggie Washington (b); Pheeroan akLaff (d); Lyndon Achee (steel d).* 99.

** Have Yourself A Merry ...

Passin' Thru 41216 *As above, except add Judy Bady (v).* n.d.

Lake has been closely involved with setting up Passin' Thru which under Gene Lake's supervision has diversified into rap as well as jazz. The earlier of these Steel Quartet projects was made for the Canadian label Justin Time and is one of the most infectious recordings Lake has ever been involved with. There is enough darkness for anyone in a long interpretation of Coltrane's 'Lonnie's Lament' but the upbeat calypso of 'Yes You Broke' (an unexpected Lake original) and a brilliant reading of Sonny Simmons's 'Land of the Freaks' fulfil the promise laid out in the title-track which opens the album. The set closes with a dispensible rap, but as dispensability goes it has nothing on the vocal contributions to the follow-up Steel Quartet disc. We are not snobbish about Christmas albums ... Yes, we are, but not unduly. It's just that this one seems to have no really effective rationale. Lake's alto is as nimble and expressive as ever, but he lacks things to say on this baker's dozen Yuletide themes.

*** Cloth

Passin Thru 41217 *Lake; Peck Allmond, Winston Byrd, Baikida Carroll, Duane Eubanks (t); Joseph Bowie, Aaron Johnson, Al Patterson, Josh Roseman (tb); Marty Ehrlich, Bruce Williams (as); Jimmy Steward (ts, f); Ron Blake (bs); Michael Cochrane (p); Mark Helias (b); Otis Brown (d).* 02.

A bold and mostly successful big-band project. Lake's charts are not so much complex as detailed and call for a lot of textural variation even within ensemble passages. The effect is perhaps less Ellingtonian and more reminiscent of a Mingus band, except that the melodic lines are much less straightforward. 'Cloth Two' is the opener and establishes the basic language of the set: oblique, rhythmically dense, and with action all over the warp and weft of probably the biggest unit Lake has ever assembled. His own soloing, especially on the inevitable 'Dedicated To Dolphy', is beautiful but somewhat constrained, and it's players like Carroll who snatch at the attention. Peter Karl's engineering and mastering make sense of what might have been quite a muddled sound. A strong effort all round.

Ralph Lalama (born 1951)

TENOR SAXOPHONE

The son of a drummer and a singer, Lalama began playing at 14. He studied at Youngstown State and moved to New York in 1975. Stints with Woody Herman, Buddy Rich and the Jones–Lewis band followed, and he is a regular on the city's scene.

*****(*) Feelin' And Dealin'**
Criss Cross 1046 *Lalama; Tom Harrell (t, flhn); Barry Harris (p); Peter Washington (b); Kenny Washington (d).* 11/90.

***** Momentum**
Criss Cross 1063 *Lalama; Kenny Barron (p); Dennis Irwin (b); Kenny Washington (d).* 12/91.

***** You Know What I Mean**
Criss Cross 1097 *Lalama; George Cables (p); Dennis Irwin (b); Leroy Williams (d).* 12/93.

A former section-player with the Jones–Lewis big band, Lalama plays with iron in his tone. His choice of composer credits gives his idols away – Rollins, Dexter, Mobley – and, though he sometimes falls prey to the habitual anonymity of the great section-man, his improvising has real class and substance from moment to moment. A very fine solo on Mobley's 'Third Time Around' on the first record shows what he can do: the way he masters the rhythmic suspensions in the tune, throws in a couple of unexpected, whistling high notes and takes in a timbral exploration along the way suggests both technical and conceptual mastery. The record isn't consistently good, and Harrell doesn't seem quite at his best, but there is a lot to enjoy. *Momentum* is a degree more ordinary: Lalama handles the casting as sole horn with aplomb, but the session ends up as merely decent hard bop. *You Know What I Mean* follows a similar pattern, although Lalama's playing continues to give much pleasure: his persuasive handling of 'This Love Of Mine', where his solo manages to get all over the horn without any apparent effort, is very beguiling, and nearly every track has its own satisfactions.

***** Circle Line**
Criss Cross 1132 *Lalama; Peter Bernstein (g); Peter Washington (b); Kenny Washington (d).* 12/95.

***** Music For Grown-Ups**
Criss Cross 1165 *As above, except Richard Wyands (p) replaces Bernstein.* 12/98.

Circle Line is something of a homage to *Bridge*-era Sonny Rollins: listen to the way Lalama swaggers into 'My Ideal'. 'Giant Steps' is ordinary and, while Lalama and the others are never less than assured, one waits in vain for some kind of surprise along the way. Despite the somewhat snobbish title, *Music For Grown-Ups* has a welcoming atmosphere, four pros flexing their collective muscle. Lalama has spent many years in sections and his tone has been buffed to a hard matt surface: he wouldn't do anything to unbalance either band or listener and, while his stability is unarguable, it means that his records will rarely collar the attention. Best shot: a gruff, feisty stroll through 'Lullaby Of The Leaves'.

Lambert, Hendricks & Ross

VOCAL GROUP

Along with Eddie Jefferson and King Pleasure, the original trio cemented a brief fashion for vocalese, a style in which instrumental jazz is replicated in sung lines and invented lyrics. The trio came together in 1957 with other singers to record an album of Basie tunes. The results were unsatisfactory and the material was re-recorded by just LH&R, using overdubs. Five years later, with Ross ailing, the group was reconvened with Bavan.

*****(*) Sing A Song Of Basie**
Verve 543827-2 *Lambert, Hendricks, Ross; Nat Pierce (p); Freddie Green (g); Eddie Jones (b); Sonny Payne (d).* 55.

****** The Hottest Group In Jazz**
Columbia C2K 64933 2CD *Lambert, Hendricks, Ross; Harry 'Sweets' Edison(t); Pony Poindexter (as); Gildo Mahones(p); Ike Isaacs, Ron Carter (b); Walter Bolden, Jimmy Wormsworth, Stu Martin (d).* 8/59–3/62.

***** Live At Basin Street East**
RCA 25756 *Lambert, Hendricks, Yolande Bavan (v); Pony Poindexter, Gildo Mahones (p); George Tucker (b); Jimmie Smith (d).* 9/62.

****(*) Havin' A Ball At The Village Gate**
RCA 22111 *As above, except add Thad Jones (c), Booker Ervin (ts).* 12/63.

Jazz vocalese may have begun with the Mills Brothers and their clever vocal mimicry of brass and saxophones, developed along very different lines when Jefferson and then King Pleasure and Annie Ross began to fit words to famous jazz solos. Jefferson's vocalization of James Moody's solo on 'I'm In The Mood For Love' was perhaps better known in the King Pleasure version. Ross's virtuoso interpretation of Wardell Gray's 'Twisted' was a huge hit. Perhaps the finest exponent of vocalese, though, was Jon Hendricks, who seemed to have an unfailing facility for words to fit instrumental effects and for glib rhymes to link lines together.

The Basie record is in a sense atypical: the group had sought to re-create the Basie band with a large vocal ensemble but ended up singing all the lines themselves via overdubbing, and the set became a kind of novelty hit. Hendricks's lyrics are often a hoot, and the record set a precedent for a style which many have followed, few bettered. The best bet is the Columbia set, which pulls together their three albums for the label and a few odds and ends. Forty years and more on, the likes of 'Twisted', 'Cookin' At The Continental' and 'Swingin' Till The Girls Come Home' are still cool enough to overcome the stigma of jazz showbiz.

The group continued for a little time with Bavan standing in for the indisposed Ross; and currently, ironically, there is more stuff from this line-up than from the wonderful original. We have always found it hard to put a value on these records. Bavan's accent always militated against convincing solo performance, and the group sounds more and more like Hendricks-plus-rhythm. Technically, Bavan is unexceptionable; expressively, she leaves a good deal to be desired.

Basin Street East includes a fine version of Coltrane's 'Cousin Mary', and a clever, debunking version of 'This Here'. The final disc is clever, bordering here and there on novelty vocal territory, as 'Three Blind Mice' and 'With 'Er 'Ead Tucked Underneath 'Er

Arm' suggest. A further version of 'Jumpin' At The Woodside' merely underlines how good the LH&R line-up had been.

Byard Lancaster (born 1942)

ALTO SAXOPHONE, FLUTE

Though he made his name working with Sunny Murray and Bill Dixon, Philadelphia-based Lancaster has also worked in soul and blues contexts, an influence that spills over into his jazz playing.

*** It's Not Up To Us

Water 115 *Lancaster; Sonny Sharrock (g); Jerome Hunter (b); Eric Gravatt (d).* 12/66.

Much of Lancaster's career has been spent in and around his native Philadelphia and most of his output is on small, Philly-based labels. This valuable reissue captures him in the same year as his storming emergence on Sunny Murray's eponymous ESP session. It captures the saxophonist in fine form, wailing and honking righteously but also veering towards abstraction, even on standard material like 'Misty' and 'Over The Rainbow'. The original material seems to be a mixture of Lancaster compositions – like the fine title-tune and 'Dog Town' – and collective improvisations/jams like 'Satan'.

The album is of special interest to fans of the late Sonny Sharrock, whose guitar-playing was steadily evolving in this period but cleaving to the same mix of free jazz and funk that Lancaster was pioneering. Sharrock is credited with one composition, 'John's Children' (nothing to do with the David Bowie project of that name), and provides ringing accompaniment throughout. The disc also lifts a corner of the curtain on the astonishing Eric Gravatt, best known for his work with Weather Report but no longer working in music; one report suggests he has made his living as a prison guard. All in all, an intriguing and worthwhile issue.

*** Documentation/The End of a Decade

Jambrio 1005 *Lancaster; Alfred Pollitt (p); David Eyges (clo); Bobby Byrd (b); Chucky Lee (d); Keno Speller (perc); Joan Hansom (v).* 2–12/79.

There is a 13-year gap in the Lancaster discography at this point. Compared to the 24-year-old who made *It's Not Up To Us*, the mature player sounds drier and more sober, less inclined to flights of gospelly euphoria. There is some excellent playing on this compilation of two locally recorded dates pairing Lancaster with the Broadway Local Dance Band. Cellist David Eyges plays an interesting role and contributes a fine composition, 'A Bird's Eye View Of The World', but mostly the music is crossover stuff, driven along tramline grooves by Pollitt's rinky-rink electric piano. Percussionist Keno Speller was to be a long-term associate of Lancaster's and his role here shouldn't be underestimated.

*** Philadelphia Spirit In New York

CIMP 239 *Lancaster; Odean Pope (ss, ts); Ed Crockett (b); J. R. Mitchell (d).* 01.

Lancaster had often favoured guitar over piano in his groups but here he dispenses with a harmony instrument altogether. It makes for a tough listen, with the two saxophonists weaving complex lines that sometimes appear to lean on a chordal structure and sometimes veer away from it altogether. The rhythm section is less than impressive, but there is an energy and obvious commitment to the session that beguiles for all its shortcomings. Worth a try.

Harold Land (1928–2001)

TENOR SAXOPHONE, FLUTE, OBOE

Born in Texas but raised in San Diego, Land worked with Max Roach before becoming a fixture on the West Coast scene of the late '50s and '60s. Later sightings in the Timeless All Stars and on the Postcards session suggest his durability.

*** Harold In The Land Of Jazz

Original Jazz Classics OJC 162 *Land; Rolf Ericson (t); Carl Perkins (p); Leroy Vinnegar (b); Frank Butler (d).* 1/58.

Made towards the end of his stint with bassist Curtis Counce's band, this is the first of a series of fine Land records. A still underrated player, hampered by a rather dour tone, Land favoured – or happened across – unusual piano players, giving more than one of his albums a harmonic unease that is more disconcerting than genuinely attractive. Perkins's crab-wise gait across the keyboard is mitigated by the vibrant rhythm-work of Vinnegar and Butler, and the best track on the album is the quartet, 'You Don't Know What Love Is', which the showy Ericson sits out (Land made some interesting brass appointments as well).

***(*) The Fox

Original Jazz Classics OJC 343 *Land; Dupree Bolton (t); Elmo Hope (p); Herbie Lewis (b); Frank Butler (d).* 8/59.

Jazz history has drawn something of a veil over the subsequent career of trumpeter Dupree Bolton. Though this is his solitary appearance in the current catalogue, he plays with confidence and some fire, seemingly at ease at the accelerated tempo of 'The Fox' and the easier flow of 'Mirror-Mind Rose'. If Carl Perkins recalls a crab, then Elmo Hope has to be, yes, a butterfly. His touch was as light as his ideas and colours were fleeting. One of the least dynamic of players (and singularly dependent on drummers of Butler's kidney), he was nevertheless able to keep track with a rhythm line he wasn't actually playing, laying out astonishing melody figures on 'One Down' in what is probably his best recorded performance, certainly a step ahead of *Harold In The Land Of Jazz*. Land is an underrated composer with a deep feeling for the blues, who never quite translated his most compelling ideas into practice. *The Fox*, tricky and fugitive as much of it is, must be thought his finest moment.

**(*) Eastward Ho!

Original Jazz Classics OJC 493 *Land; Kenny Dorham (t); Amos Trice (p); Joe Peters (d).* 7/60.

Pianist Trice was briefly known for his work with Wardell Gray and, heard blindfold, this rather unusual session might well suggest Gray's work. Land and Dorham are both in fine voice but rarely seem to be thinking along the same lines. 'Slowly' and 'On A Little Street In Singapore' (the latter well known to Glenn Miller fans) are both engagingly handled. Not one of Land's best records, though. He enjoyed a modest Indian summer in the studios but at the moment those records are missing in action.

Art Lande (born 1947)

PIANO, PERCUSSION

American pianist-composer whose brief tenure with ECM was responsible for the major part of his reputation. In the '80s he moved into full-time teaching.

****(*) Red Lanta**
ECM 829323 *Lande; Jan Garbarek (ss, ts).* 11/73.

***** Rubisa Patrol**
ECM 519875-2 *Lande; Mark Isham (t, flhn, ss); Bill Douglas (b, f); Glenn Cronkhite (d).* 5/76.

Lande's anagrammatic ECM debut doesn't stand up well to the test of time. It might look like a collaborative album, but the pianist is responsible for all the compositions and Garbarek is decidedly *sub fusc* for most of the record, which has a wan and pastel quality. Ironically, this is as close as one will find to what has been satirized as the 'ECM sound'.

Renewed acquaintance with *Rubisa Patrol* suggests that it is rather more durable than we had previously allowed. Isham, who has spent most of his time subsequently in film music, plays with a steely elegance and contributes two of the best themes, 'Many Chinas' (which opens the record after Douglas's remarkable bamboo flute solo) and 'For Nancy'. Although Lande's improvising is unremarkable, his own music displays a sense of nocturnal quiet that the group distil with great skill. The sound remains limpidly beautiful on CD.

***** Skylight**
ECM 531025-2 *Lande; Paul McCandless (ss, cor, ob, bcl, f); David Samuels (vib, mar, perc).* 5/81.

Another charming record, though more of a co-operative venture: Lande contributes two tunes, and one of them, 'Dance Of The Silver Skeezix', is pure floss. It's McCandless's pair of compositions that suit the trio best. But the music as a whole is unaffectedly sweet: a bright summer's day after the cool evening of *Rubisa Patrol.*

**** World Without Cars**
Synergy 5 *Lande; Mark Miller (ss, ts, f, v).* 99.

This looks like an attempt to recapture the sound of *Red Lanta.* Miller isn't quite a Garbarek copyist, but there are moments on these curious musical etudes that make the connection. Most of the original music is inoffensive Americana – pastoral themes that need an injection of energy to make them really sing. Here and there, one comes across harmonic oddities, which are just that, curios rather than original thinking. One is reminded of Lande's obscure Arch LP *The Eccentricities of Earl Dant* (another transparent anagram); it's hard not to wonder whether the eccentricity is a trifle too studied.

Nils Landgren (born 1956)

TROMBONE, TRUMPET, VOCAL

His father played cornet and his grandfather was a pastor: the music of both influenced him. Worked with Thad Jones, 1981–3, then theatrical work as singer and dancer. Wide experience as a sideman, then formed his own Funk Unit.

**** Follow Your Heart**
Caprice 21393 *Landgren; Leif Lindvall, Lars Lindgren (t); David Wilczewski (ts); Johan Stengard (as, bs); Stefan Blomqvist, Peter Ljung, Pal Svenre (ky); Staffan Astner, Johan Folke Norberg, Henrik Janson (g); Lars Danielsson (b); Per Lindvall, Andre Ferrari (d); Sharon Dyall (v).* 90.

***** Gotland**
ACT 9226-2 *Landgren; Tomasz Stańko (t); Anders Eljas, Claus Bantzer (org).* 96.

****(*) Paint It Blue**
ACT 9243-2 *Landgren; Till Bronner (t); Randy Brecker (t, flhn); Michael Brecker (ts); Per Johansson (saxes); Steffen Schorn (bcl); Esbjörn Svensson (ky); Henrik Janson (g); Lars Danielsson (b); Bernard Purdie (d); Airto Moreira, Marcia Doctor (perc).* 96.

The first and third records would barely even qualify Landgren for entry here. *Follow Your Heart* is an inoffensive but entirely unremarkable set of softcore pop tunes with the slightest lite-jazz flavour. Landgren actually sneaks in some good fills, but he's hardly a commanding vocalist. *Paint It Blue* sets his Funk Unit to work on a Cannonball Adderley tribute. There's some perfectly serviceable playing, although the samples of Cannonball's voice scarcely anoint the occasion with any distinction, and there's nothing that isn't done better on a Maceo Parker or Fred Wesley record.

Gotland could hardly be a greater contrast. Landgren soliloquizes on some beatific melodies – most of his own writing, though two are adapted from ancient Swedish folk-tunes – in churches in Stockholm and Hamburg; Stańko joins him on some pieces, and there are lowering commentaries from the organists. Spare and contemplative, there is some lovely music from the trombonist, even if the situation at times seems a touch too calculated.

***** Ballads**
ACT 9268-2 *Landgren; Joakim Milder (ts); Bobo Stenson, Esbjörn Svensson (p); Johan Norberg (g); Palle Danielsson, Dan Berglund (b); Anders Kjellberg, Magnus Oström (d).* 3/93–5/98.

*****(*) Swedish Folk**
ACT 9257-2 *Landgren; Esbjörn Svensson (p).* 8/97.

***** Live In Montreux**
ACT 9265-2 *Landgren; Per Johansen (ss, as); Esbjörn Svensson (p); Henrik Janson (g); Magnum Coltrane Price (b, v); Janne Robertson (d).* 7/98.

***** 5000 Miles**
ACT 9271-2 *As above, except add Till Brönner, Roy Hargrove (t, flhn), Tim Hagans (t), Fred Wesley (tb), Robert Ostlund (g, org), Johan Norberg (g), Dan Berglund (b), Ake Sundqvist, Magnus Oström (perc), Viktoria Tolstoy (v).* 3/98–7/99.

The appeal of all Landgren's records depends on how much one warms to each of the styles he works in. *Ballads,* a slightly augmented reissue of a 1993 CD, has him as a vocal stylist on a range of standards and pop tunes: the supporting cast play with typical acuity, and Svensson's trio do back-up on the bonus track, 'You Stole My Heart', but the singing is enough of an acquired taste to offer a reservation. The two records by the Funk Unit, one live at the 1998 Montreux Festival, the other a studio set with several star guests, have a problem shaking off the sense that the manner of the music is too old-fashioned – it holds back sophisticated players such as Landgren and Svensson, or at least encourages them to settle for easy routes to resolution. Which doesn't stop both men turning in some hard and exciting solos on the live material, jazz-funk licks toasted to a righteous frazzle. *5000 Miles* takes advantage of studio crispness, and Hargrove, Hagans and the others have fun on their sit-in assignments. It's not that material such as 'Da Fonk' and 'In A Fonky Mood' is beneath jazz musicians, more that they sit awkwardly beside their more demanding material (and a 'genuine' funk record would be produced differently too).

Next to these, *Swedish Folk* seems a bizarre alternative. Although there are a couple of pieces drawn from the classical Swedish repertoire, the material is otherwise all by Landgren and Svensson, a deeply felt meditation on their country's roots music. Played with the barest of detail, the musicianship is impeccable and often bewitchingly beautiful.

***** Fonk Da World**

ACT 9299-2 *Landgren; Per Johansson (as); Jesper Nordenstrom, Esbjörn Svensson (ky); Robert Ostlund (g); Magnum Coltrane Price (b, v); Niklas Gabrielsson (d); Magnus Oström (perc).* 6/01.

The title looks like trouble, but this is the Funk Unit, after all, and what they do – especially with Svensson writing five titles and playing on three – inevitably has some proper jazz spice. The studio sound is a plus and minus: you can hear the finesse in the playing more easily, but it inevitably downgrades the feel – this is a band which must surely be heard and felt live.

****(*) Sentimental Journey/Ballads 2**

ACT 9409-2 *Landgren; Karin Hammar, Mimi Hammar (tb); Andweers Widmark, Esbjörn Svensson (p); Robert Ostlund (g); Lars Danielsson, Chrille Olsson, Magnum Coltrane Price (b); Wolfgang Haffer, Janne Robertson (d); Rigmor Gustafsson, Viktoria Tolstoy (v); Flesh Quartet (strings).* 6/02.

Landgren as crooner again, with Rigmor and Viktoria arriving for a couple of duets, and his usual crew offering cogent back-up. It depends on how much eclecticism you want from this undeniably talented man. We could do with a little less.

Adam Lane

BASS

Brooklynite bassist-composer, dividing his time between East and West Coasts, and investigating both large-scale composition and miniature free dialogues. Also a big cat-lover.

***** Hollywood Wedding**

Cadence CJR 1102 *Lane; Paul Thompson, Wadada Leo Smith, Josef Leimberg, Todd Simon (t); Scott Ray (tb); Marty Walker (cl, bcl); Fawntice McCain, Tonya Ridgely, Chelsea Czuchra, Tracey Cladwell (f); Lynn Johnston, Eddie Felix, James King (reeds); Art Hirahara (p); Vicki Ray (p, org); Robin Lorentz, Mark Chung (vn); Lynn Angebrand (clo); Ryan Francesconi, Jeremy Keller (g); Art Jarvinen (b, v, elec); Kentaro Ebiko (b); Koki Kumagai (d); Dave Shaffer, Greg Diamond, Jason Roth, Amy Knowles (perc); Douglas Repetto, Steve Hise, Joel Fox, Randy Gloss (elec); Matt Akuff, Rebecca Bolum, Tiffany Meador, Caat Hay, Cozmo Segurson (v).* 3/95–8/98.

***** No(w) Music**

Cadence CJR 1133 *Lane; Darren Johnston (t); Aaron Bennett (ss, ts, cl); Jeff Chan (ts, f, bcl); John Finkbeiner, Myles Boisen (g); Vijay Anderson (d).* 10/99–3/01.

***** Fo(u)r Being(s)**

CIMP 263 *Lane; Paul Smoker (t); John Tchicai (ts, v); Barry Altschul (d).* 1/02.

*****(*) DOS**

CIMP 281 *Lane; John Tchicai (ts, bcl).* 10/02.

Lane offers a pretty wide spectrum of music-making on these four discs. The first, carpentered out of a mix of live and studio dates stretched over three years, is an engaging 'sonic representation of my soul', with a series of carousing large groups playing music somewhat in the tradition of groups such as Peter Apfelbaum's Hieroglyphics Ensemble. Structure gives way to noise-making on the likes of 'Fire Up The Pig' (which features Jason Roth on vacuum cleaner), and 'Peace', which features Leo Smith, is a curious brew of muted trumpets and cacophonous tenor sax. The closing 'New Mars', which features four vocalists, three flutes and three electronics handlers, is an impenetrable hunk of space debris. A mixed bag. *No(w) Music*, credited to Lane's Full Throttle Orchestra, is in more of a new noise-making tradition (Lane mentions The Ruins and Motorhead as points of reference), although it's not quite nasty enough to really shock or surprise, and when they turn off the fuzzboxes and play 'proper' solos and swing-band riffs and counterpoint, the group get grudgingly melodious. Good titles include 'Grape Ape Meets The Working Man' and 'Post-Industrial Folksong'. Probably more fun live than on record, but not bad.

The small-scale records might almost be the work of another man altogether. 'House Of Elegant', which is also on the Full Throttle Orchestra set, is denuded of instruments and might almost be a sketch of the bigger version. As with so many CIMP dates, too many of the tracks last too long and end up with the listener's attention tiring, but it's an interesting and sometimes beguiling mix of personalities. Smoker is in great fettle and he thoroughly outplays Tchicai here. As if in compensation, the saxophonist plays much more clearly and purposefully on the duo record, which is elegantly performed by both men. Lane's tunes here exhibit a soft lyricism, his own playing flows serenely, and Tchicai responds with some of his most spare and aristocratic playing of recent times.

Eddie Lang (1904–33)

GUITAR

Born Salvatore Massaro in Philadelphia, Lang began his partnership with violinist Joe Venuti at school. They worked the New York dance-band scene throughout the '20s. Lang visited London with the Mound City Blue Blowers, duetted with bluesman Lonnie Johnson, and became Bing Crosby's favourite accompanist. He also recorded with Louis Armstrong, King Oliver and the Ponce Sisters, though not at the same time. His bell-like tone is always audible on the records he plays on. He died as a result of complications following a tonsillectomy.

*****(*) A Handful Of Riffs**

ASV AJA 5061 *Lang; Joe 'King' Oliver (c); Leo McConville, Andy Secrest, Bill Margulis (t); Tommy Dorsey, Bill Rank (tb); Jimmy Dorsey (cl, as); Charles Strickfadden, Bernard Daly (as); Issy Friedman (cl, ts); J. C. Johnson, Frank Signorelli, Arthur Schutt (p); Hoagy Carmichael (p, cel); Henry*

Whiteman (vn); Lonnie Johnson (g); Joe Tarto, Mike Trafficante (b); George Marsh, Stan King (d); Justin Ring (perc). 4/27–10/29.

***** Jazz Guitar Virtuoso**

Yazoo 1059 *Lang; Frank Signorelli, Rube Bloom, Arthur Schutt (p); Lonnie Johnson, Carl Kress (g); Justin Ring (chimes).* 27–29.

****** The Quintessential Eddie Lang 1925–1932**

Timeless CBC 1-043 *As above discs, except add Bix Beiderbecke (c), Tommy Gott, Fuzzy Farrar, Ray Lodwig, Manny Klein, Bill Moore, Louis Armstrong, Harry Goldfield (t), Boyce Cullen, Miff Mole, Wilbur Hall, Loyd Turner (tb), Arnold Brilhart, Alfie Evans, Harold Sturr, Don Murray, Doc Ryker, Frankie Trumbauer, Andy Sannella, Tony Parenti, Happy Caldwell, Chester Hazlett, Red Mayer (reeds); Otto Landau, Matty Malneck (vn); Roy Bargy, Clarence Williams, Itzy Riskin, Joe Sullivan, Irving Brodsky (p); Cliff Edwards (uke, v); Harry Reser, Tony Colucci, Mike Pingitore (bj); Red McKenzie (comb); Dick Slevin (kz); Arthur Campbell, Min Leibrook (tba); Steve Brown, Ward Lay (b); Neil Marshall, Vic Berton, Kaiser Marshall (d); Bessie Smith, Noel Taylor, The Rhythm Boys, Bing Crosby (v).* 1/25–2/32.

*****(*) Pioneers Of Jazz Guitar 1927–1939**

Retrieval RTR 79015 *Lang; Arthur Schutt, Frank Signorelli, Rube Bloom (p); Carl Kress, Dick McDonough (g); Justin Ring (perc).* 4/27–8/39.

Eddie Lang was the first guitarist to make a major impact on jazz away from the blues, and even there he took a hand by recording many duets with the 'authentic' bluesman, Lonnie Johnson. Lang's polished, civilized but swinging art was worked out in dance bands and as an accompanist – after joining Paul Whiteman in the late '20s, the guitarist struck up a professional kinship with Bing Crosby, who hired him until his early death. He was an important member of the white New York school of the period and can be found on records by Beiderbecke, Joe Venuti and the Dorseys; but the sides made under his own name were also plentiful and, for all his restraint and good taste, he was a jazzman through and through. His most characteristic playing is as rhythmically driving as it is harmonically deft and inventive.

We are better served by Lang reissues now than we have been for some time, although there is annoying duplicaton between all of these. As a general cross-section, the Timeless disc sweeps the board for now: quite beautifully remastered by John R. T. Davies, and with a shrewd and wide-ranging set of tracks, it's a very strong introduction. Lang is immediately identifiable on the early piece by the Mound City Blue Blowers, from 1925, and he turns up elsewhere in dance bands led by Fred Rich, Jean Goldkette, Roger Wolf Kahn and Paul Whiteman, backing Ukulele Ike and Bessie Smith, partnering Lonnie Johnson, sitting in with Louis Armstrong and King Oliver, and taking a solo turn on Rachmaninov's Opus 3 Prelude. Could any other musician of the era claim such a CV? Twenty-four tracks and not a dud among them.

Eight of the Yazoo tracks are also included on the ASV set. Yazoo concentrate on Lang the soloist, including all eight of the sides he made in that context, plus two tracks with Carl Kress and three with Johnson. There isn't much jazz in 'April Kisses', but showpieces like 'Eddie's Twister' and the luxuriant duet with Johnson on 'Blue Guitars' show all of Lang's beauty of touch, harmonic shrewdness and rhythmical dexterity. A couple more spirited tracks wouldn't have come amiss here, and the ration of 14 tracks is somewhat short measure.

The ASV issue offers a wider choice of 21 pieces, including the famous session with King Oliver on cornet and the five tracks by an orchestra led nominally by Lang. Sound on both issues is generally very good: the Yazoo is a little livelier but has a higher level of surface hiss.

Retrieval's edition contains all of Lang's solo and guitar–piano pieces, the two duets with Carl Kress, and a further ten tracks featuring Kress, either by himself or with Dick McDonough. For those who want to hear the guitar away from any band situations, this is excellent, although over CD length it palls a bit unless you're a confirmed guitar-lover. Kress and McDonough are a shade more modernistic, but they had the benefit of Lang going before them.

Don Lanphere (1928–2003)

TENOR AND SOPRANO SAXOPHONES

Out of the business for nearly three decades following drug problems, Lanphere returned to recording in 1981 after running the family music shop in Washington state. His early days were spent with the bebop crowd; his mature style was more measured and chastened.

***** Stop**

Hep 2034 *Lanphere; Jon Pugh (co); Marc Seales (p); Chuck Deardorf (b); Dean Hodges (d).* 8/83, 1/86.

*****(*) Don Loves Midge**

Hep 2027 *As above, except add Camille Peterson (hp).* 10/84.

***** Don Lanphere/Larry Coryell**

Hep 2048 *As above, except add Marc Seales (ky); Larry Coryell (g).* 4/90.

***** Go ... Again**

Hep 2040 *As above, except add Jeff Hay (tb); Jay Clayton (v).* 12/95.

*****(*) Don Still Loves Midge**

Hep 2072 *Lanphere; Jon Pugh (co); Jeff Hay (tb); Dave Peterson (g); Doug Miller (b); Dean Hodges (d).* 6/97.

***** Where Do You Start?**

Origin 82410 *As above, except omit Hodges; add John Bishop (d).* 02.

Lanphere is still an underrated improviser, somewhat in the way that J. R. Monterose's dogged originality was marginalized. All credit to Alastair Robertson of Hep for picking up on him. The earliest of these is a fine quintet session, though Pugh sits out 'Body And Soul' (as trumpeters should in the presence of the tenor saxophone) and 'Laura' is done as a saxophone/bass duet. Don's soprano work is crisp and cool in comparison to his husky sincerity on tenor and the modulation from one to the other makes *Stop* a well-rounded and satisfying record.

Don Loves Midge is better still, a confident but always thoughtful run through an impressive array of standards and repertory pieces. 'I Remember Clifford' has a breezy intensity and a telling Benny Golson quote in the first chorus; 'God Bless The Child' is drier and wryer than usually played; and 'My Foolish Heart' is terse and resigned. The album coda 'There's A Sweet, Sweet Spirit In The Place' is completely unexpected, but reflects a musician whose beliefs run deep.

Coryell steals the third one, emerging at the time as a formidable bop player who'd pretty much put fusion behind him, but without regret and with all of its power-plays still available. 'Spring Can Really Hang You Up The Most' is just a guitar/keyboard duet, while Don and Larry duet on Horace Silver's 'Peace', an unexpected choice but a tune that obviously has a real importance for the saxophonist. The other compositions are fairly standard fare, but there is nothing routine about the playing, which is committed and utterly professional.

Midge, as you'll have guessed, is Mrs Lanphere, and the repeat Valentine is no less sincere than the first. One of the highlights of the set is a rarity. 'Early Autumn' was on Lanphere's music stand when he took over from Stan Getz in the Woody Herman band; he hung onto it and it gets a rare outing here. There's some other fairly obscure material in the line-up but part of the appeal of Lanphere's playing at this time was his desire to explore neglected corners of the repertoire, not because he felt uneasy about testing himself on the warhorses, but because he was first to last a musician whose faith was very much a questioning one.

The final album is still restless, still looking for answers beyond the obvious. Pugh's tight, ripe cornet sound is so much a part of these sessions that one almost overlooks it. He always seems to know when to come in and when to stay silent and his reactions to Lanphere are almost telepathic on 'The Scene Is Clean', the longest and best of the cuts on what turns out to be Lanphere's curtain appearance.

Steven Lantner

PIANO

An associate of saxophonist Joe Maneri, Lantner helped set up the Boston Microtonal Society. In addition to acoustic piano, he uses a digital electronic instrument which allows variation of pitch, thus getting round the fixity of conventional or even altered piano tuning.

***** Reaching**

Leo Lab 062 *Lantner; Mat Maneri (vn).* 8/97.

*****(*) Voices Lowered**

Leo LR 317 *Lantner; Joe Maneri (as, ts); Joe Morris(g).* 8/00.

Lantner has performed extensively with the younger Maneri, whose application of microtonality is highly sophisticated on both his conventional and extra-stringed violins. The best sample track from which to get an impression of their collective aims is 'In The River', a slow, dirge-like theme using pitch-shifting on the keyboard and changes of string tonality. There is something of a sameness to the dozen tracks, but anyone who has listened to Ornette Coleman will have some familiarity with the language; use of piano apart, this is very much the territory that Ornette mapped out in the '60s. As such, it is less radical than its admirers would suggest but is no less intriguing for that.

As Lantner says in his sleeve-note, the trio form 'suggests entering into a more complicated world' than the duo, and *Voices Lowered* is the fascinating result. If we've entered this world before, it probably had the sign 'Tristano' over the way in, since there's much which offers at least a misshapen echo of Tristano-ite doctrine. It's quiet but not monotonal music, often agitated in a contained way, and the sense of endlessly going forward, not up or down, makes the music seem to override any occasional dryness of inspiration.

Lou Lanza (born 1970)

VOCAL

Born in Philadelphia; his parents are professional classical musicians. This is his third CD as a vocalist-leader.

***** Corner Pocket**

J-Bird 80185-2 *Lanza; John Swana (t, flhn); Louis Taylor (as); Rob Roth (ts); Rich Budeas (p); Rob Budesa (g); Pete Colangelo (b); Ari Hoenig (d).* 97.

*****(*) Shadows And Echoes**

A Records AL 73131 *Lanza; Dick Sudhalter (t, flhn, c); Allen Farnham (p); Jimmy Bruno (g); Pete Colangelo (b); Ari Hoenig (d).* 5/98.

Lanza's earlier records are on independent labels and most have eluded us, although we have caught up with *Corner Pocket.* The later A set is a sweet-natured set of standards. Lanza has a smooth, clean-shaven sort of voice, moving easily up and down the scale and most gracious in a high tenor register. Excellent choice of songs, with only 'Get Happy' and 'Lover Come Back To Me' even approaching the obvious. Farnham is an old hand at arranging this kind of date, and there is a wonderful flugelhorn solo by Dick Sudhalter on Jerome Kern's 'Make Believe'. Lanza isn't a familiar styling of male jazz singer – 'I feel that I'm a bit of a wild card', he says in the notes – but he's fundamentally a conservative, and those who prefer something less idiosyncratic than Kurt Elling will go for this in a big way. The earlier disc is a bit greener and the production is rather flat, but Lanza makes a good play at the material – starting with Miles's 'Four' was no piece of coasting – and Swana has some good moments too.

John LaPorta (born 1920)

CLARINET, ALTO AND TENOR SAXOPHONES

Tristano-influenced and associated with Charles Mingus and Teo Macero, LaPorta left active playing behind to teach at the Manhattan School of Music. His legacy is small but consistently interesting.

***** Themes And Variations**

Fantasy 24776 *LaPorta; Louis Mucci (t); Sonny Russo (tb); Larry Wilcox (ts); George Barrow, Sol Schlinger (bs); Wally Cirillo (p); Wendell Marshall (b); Clem de Rosa (d).* 56, 57, 58.

LaPorta's most significant work can be found on Charles Mingus's Debut recordings, and sounds like an adventurous cross between Cool School noodling and Third Stream ambition. The set brings together LaPorta's *Conceptions* LP with some later unreleased material. It offers an intriguing insight into a player whose musical education was worn rather too prominently for comfort but who was always able to come up with an effective idea, even if he isn't the most interesting soloist to listen to, on either of his main horns, clarinet or alto. He does have the classic jazz virtues, though: an understanding of the blues, a distinctive solo voice (albeit a rather pale one) and an ability to swing even such an unpromising line as 'Blues Chorale', which sets off the sequence of variations. The supporting cast isn't any better known but is equally professional.

Ellis Larkins (1923–2003)

PIANO

Larkins was a child prodigy in his native Baltimore, graduating from Peabody and Juilliard before turning to a jazz career in the clubs of New York. He recorded most frequently as a favoured accompanist to singers, but he has occasional discs where he is in the spotlight himself.

***(*) A Smooth One

Black & Blue 591232 *Larkins; George Duvivier (b); J. C. Heard (d). 7/77.*

Larkins's mastery is so understated that his reputation lagged some way behind his abilities. Although he was active for 60 years, there are relatively few records under his own name. *A Smooth One* is Larkins's only available trio date. Several of the eight pieces remind one of his judgement that with some songs 'you just play them and get out'; but there are some bewitching moments hidden behind his professional excellence.

Mostly, Ellis has to be sought out in other situations – with singers, and with old pal Ruby Braff, with whom he recorded for Vanguard in the '50s and again in the '90s for Arbors.

Prince Lasha (born 1929)

FLUTE, ALTO FLUTE, ALTO AND BARITONE SAXOPHONES, CLARINET

Little-recorded Texan avant-gardist who worked with major figures but failed to make more than an idiosyncratic impact in his own right.

*** Firebirds

Contemporary OJCCD 1822-2 *Lasha; Sonny Simmons (as, eng hn); Bobby Hutcherson (vib); Buster Williams (b); Charles Moffett (d). 9/67.*

Born William B. Lawsha in Forth Worth, Lasha – pronounced 'la-shay' – was in the same high school band as King Curtis, Ornette Coleman and Charles Moffett. He shares qualities with both saxophonists, but his closest musical cousin is surely another multi-instrumentalist, Eric Dolphy, with whom he recorded on *Iron Man* and elsewhere.

Primarily a flautist, Lasha has a frail, slightly thin tone on alto saxophone, explained in part by his occasional choice of a plastic instrument; he often sounds as though he is playing some Middle Eastern wind instrument of unknown provenance. His flute technique is more orthodox, but still sufficiently original to make one wonder why he has not become better known.

Firebirds was his second collaboration with the like-minded Sonny Simmons, and the two lead voices engage in some intriguing exchanges on 'Psalms Of Solomon' and the title-tune. Moffett, Buster Williams and Hutcherson are powerful in support. 'Prelude To Bird' perhaps hints at a more orthodox bebop lineage, but the real inspiration here is Ornette. The flautist drifted out of the business in the later '70s and, despite a return to recording in 1983, has not – unlike Simmons – enjoyed a critical revival.

Steve LaSpina (born 1954)

BASS

Born in Texas but growing up in Chicago, LaSpina followed his father, also a bassist. He went to New York in 1979 and became a regular on the scene there, teaching and performing; subsequently moved to Milford, PA.

*** New Horizon

Steeplechase SCCD 31313 *LaSpina; Billy Drewes (ss, as, ts); Marc Copland (p); Jeff Hirshfield (d). 4/92.*

*** Eclipse

Steeplechase SCCD 31343 *As above. 4/93.*

*** When I'm Alone

Steeplechase SCCD 31376 *As above, except add Vic Juris (g). 95.*

***(*) The Road Ahead

RAM RMCD 4526 *As above, except Jim McNeely (p) replaces Copland. 12/95.*

***(*) Story Time

Steeplechase SCCD 31396 *As above, except omit McNeely; Drewes also plays cl. 3/96.*

*** When Children Smile

Steeplechase SCCD 31419 *As above, except add Dave Ballou (t). 10/96.*

A good run of records by the accomplished bassist-leader. He writes most of the material, which tends towards soft-focus harmonies and elliptical melodic lines, and the basic band is well attuned to the feel: Drewes especially gets the mood right with his rather light sound (he usually favours the upper reaches of the horn) and patient delivery. *New Horizon* and *Eclipse* are solidly inventive without being startling, and the originals on the latter pass dreamily by (Drewes plays alto for much of the record, contrary to the sleeve). Juris arrives for *When I'm Alone* and adds some piquant weight, although if there's a problem with these discs it's Copland, who's effective enough but tends to add a pretentious note with some of his solos. There's a noticeable upping of the ante with the arrival of McNeely on the RAM date: he's a superior player, and the trio version of 'Body And Soul' is just one instance of why this is the pick of the five discs. That said, *Story Time* is only just behind. With Juris handling what might have been the piano parts, the harmonic base expands further and some of LaSpina's originals are deliciously songful. There's also a rather surprising clarinet turn by Drewes on the curious 'Scott's Bop'.

When Children Smile continues the sequence and adds Ballou as a new voice in the group. Nothing wrong with it, but LaSpina's tunes here are so laid-back and uneventful that the music starts to seem tranquillizing. In this company, Coleman's 'Ramblin'' sounds almost raw, even in a relatively tame treatment.

*** The Bounce

Steeplechase SCCD 31502 *LaSpina; Dave Ballou (t, flhn); Billy Drewes (ss, ts); Vic Juris (g); Jeff Hirshfield (d). 12/00.*

A solid Steeplechase–LaSpina entry: material which asks something of the players, players who ask something of each other without being combative, and music which can sit agreeably in the background or provide at least some food for thought with hard listening. Ballou and Drewes are nobody's choice for an all-star front line, but without preening or fuss they go hard at this situation.

Andy Laster

ALTO AND BARITONE SAXOPHONES

Laster is a saxophonist at work in New York's current avant-garde, now extensively documented as a small-group leader.

***** Polyogue**
Songlines 1507–2 *Laster; Herb Robertson (t, c); Brad Shepik (g); Drew Gress (b); Tom Rainey (d).* 1/95.

***** Interpretations Of Lessness**
Songlines 1515–2 *Laster; Cuong Vu (t); Erik Friedlander (clo); Kenny Wolleson (d, marim, glock, perc).* 1/96.

*****(*) Soft Shell**
Knitting Factory KFW 281 *Laster; Herb Robertson (t, c); Drew Gress (b); Tom Rainey (d).* 5/98.

Laster's music has its quirks, as does his playing, but mostly it's a melodious kind of free-bop. He likes to mix up matters like time and counterpoint but wants every line clear and making a point. The first and third of these discs is by his band Hydra which has plenty to say. *Polyogue* is sometimes a bit cryptic, and the nine originals for all their smartness finally seem more about process than content, at least in these incarnations. The standout is the beautiful 'Chrysolite', which suggests that Laster is at his most appealing when he's looking to make his music as lyrical as possible. *Interpretations Of Lessness* is by a different band and has more of a chamberish feel. Vu makes only a modest impact, and the leader's baritone distortions are less impressive than his alto solos. Wolleson is also obliged to make more use of a tinkling arsenal of percussion and hammered instruments than his kit. Still, in the likes of 'Earth Sky Body' and 'Pale Blue' the music has much of interest.

Soft Shell slims Hydra down to four, and Laster plays alto throughout. This time the music sounds both more varied and more focused. It's a rare instance of this instrumentation owing little or nothing to the Coleman quartet, and in an attractive reading of the standard 'Here I'll Stay' (which is transformed into an original called 'Go') Laster explores his own kind of tradition. Rainey's ironic rock beat on 'South Shore Reform Experience Part II' is an amusing interlude, but in the main this is felt and powerful music-making by four accomplished performers.

Yusef Lateef (born 1921)

TENOR SAXOPHONE, OBOE, FLUTE, OTHER SAXOPHONES, COR ANGLAIS, OTHER INSTRUMENTS, VOCALS

Born Bill Evans in Chattanooga, Lateef was taught in Detroit and went to New York in 1946, later moving back to the Detroit area after a spell with Dizzy Gillespie. He then played with Mingus and with Cannonball Adderley for three years, before leading his own groups and teaching and studying philosophy as well as music. He taught in Nigeria during the '80s and now teaches at Amherst College, running his YAL label for his own music.

***** The Last Savoy Sessions**
Savoy 92881 2CD *Lateef; Wilbur Harden (flhn); Hugh Lawson, Terry Pollard (p); Bernard McKinney (euph); William Austin, Ernie Farrow (b); Frank Gant, Oliver Jackson (d).* 10/57–6/59.

***** Cry! – Tender**
Original Jazz Classics OJC 482 *Lateef; Lonnie Hillyer (t); Wilbur Harden (flhn); Hugh Lawson (p); Ernie Farrow, Herman Wright (b); Frank Gant, Oliver Jackson (d).* 10/59.

*****(*) The Centaur And The Phoenix**
Original Jazz Classics OJC 712 *Lateef; Clark Terry, Richard Williams (t); Curtis Fuller (tb); Tate Houston (bs); Josea Taylor (bsn); Barry Harris, Joe Zawinul (p); Ernie Farrow, Ben Tucker (b); Lex Humphries (d); Roger Sanders (perc).* 10/60, 6/61.

****(*) Lost In Sound**
Collectables 5792 *Lateef; Vincent Pitts (t); John Hormon (p); Ray McKinny (b); George Scott, Clifford Jarvis (d).* 8/61.

*****(*) Eastern Sounds**
Original Jazz Classics OJC 612 *Lateef; Barry Harris (p); Ernie Farrow (b); Lex Humphries (d).* 9/61.

*****(*) Live At Pep's Vol. 2**
Impulse! 547961-2 *Lateef; Richard Williams (t); Mike Nock (p); Ernie Farrow (b); James Black (d).* 6/64.

***** The Golden Flute**
Impulse! A-9125 *Lateef; Hugh Lawson (p); Herman Wright (b); Roy Brooks Jr (d).* 6/66.

***** The Blue Yusef Lateef**
Atlantic 82270 *Lateef; Blue Mitchell (t); Sonny Red (as); Buddy Lucas (hca); Hugh Lawson (p); Kenny Burrell (g); Cecil McBee, Bob Cranshaw (b); Roy Brooks (d); Selwart Clarke, James Tryon (vn); Alfred Brown (vla); Kermit Moore (clo); Sweet Inspirations (v).* 4/68.

****(*) The Diverse Yusef Lateef / Suite 16**
Rhino Atlantic R2 71552 *Lateef; Richard Tee, Joe Zawinul, Hugh Lawson, Barry Harris (p); Neil Boyar (vib); Eric Gale (g); Chuck Rainey, Bob Cunningham (b); Albert 'Tootie' Heath, Roy Brooks, Bernard Purdie, Jimmy Johnson, Ray Lucas (d); Ray Barretto (perc); strings, voices.* 5/69–4/70.

**** Hush 'N' Thunder**
Collectables COL-CD-6353 *Lateef; Jimmy Owens (flhn); Kenny Barron, Ray Bryant (p); Al White (org); David Spinozza, Cornell Dupree, Keith Loving (g); Kermit Moore (clo); Bob Cunningham, Gordine Edwards, Bill Salter (b); Tootie Heath (d); Bones Constantino, The J. C. White Singers (v).* 73.

Lateef avoided the confusion of yet another Evans in the catalogue by adopting a Muslim name in response to his growing and eventually life-long infatuation with the musics of the Levant and Asia. One of the few convincing oboists in jazz and an ancestor of East–West outfits like Oregon (whose Paul McCandless has, consciously or unconsciously, adopted some of Lateef's tonal devices), he has suffered something of Rahsaan Roland Kirk's fate in finding himself dismissed or marginalized as a 'speciality act', working apart from the central dramas of modern jazz. Like Kirk's, Lateef's music was cartoonized when he came under Atlantic's wing, making albums that were enthusiastically promoted and received, but which rarely represented the best of his work.

Savoy's stop-start reissue programme has so far come up with his final dates for the label (when the early ones will emerge is anyone's guess). They catch him blowing rough, burly tenor alongside two solid, hard-bop rhythm sections, together with the elegant Harden. Already, though, there are the exotic touches: 'A Night In Tunisia' gets off to a suitably authentic start with the muezzin-like wail of the *argol*. 'Gypsy Arab' and 'Prayer To The East' mix with 'Lover Man', and there is an 'Oboe Blues'. Rough-and-ready music, but worth reviving. *Lost In Sound* reissues a generic hard bop date from the short-lived Charlie Parker label: Lateef plays with customary vigour, but his playing companions are frankly undistinguished.

The OJC records are consistently interesting, with relatively unfussy arrangements leavened by unusual timbres and instrumental colours. *The Centaur And The Phoenix* isn't well known, despite the presence of critically OK names like Terry and Fuller. The vocal 'Jungle Fantasy' is dire, but the large-group pieces are as good as anything on the earlier *Cry! – Tender*, and 'Summer Song' is among the most straightforwardly lyrical things in Lateef's whole output. *Live At Pep's Vol. 2* has returned to the catalogue, and it stands up extremely well, substantiating Lateef's often queried jazz credentials. He plays with great spirit and an authentically bluesy drive that makes the exact choice of instrument (oboe, saxophone, shenai, flute) pretty much irrelevant. The other Impulse! set, *The Golden Flute*, is in comparison a bit on the thin side. Bob Thiele's production seems to be directed towards cutting off Lateef just as he's getting going, and the tracks feel too short, aside from the closing 'The Smart Set', which at least lets the band stretch. The studio mix catches his sound nicely, though.

Like Kirk, the tenor saxophone is Lateef's 'natural' horn, but in his best period he made jazz whatever he was playing. In approach, he is somewhat reminiscent of the pre-bop aspect of Sun Ra's long-time associate, John Gilmore, working in a strong, extended swing idiom rather than with the more complex figurations of bebop. Just occasionally this spilled over into something schmaltzier. The *Eastern Sounds* session also included film music from *The Robe* and *Spartacus*, on flute and oboe respectively, that borders on kitsch, but the tenor-led 'Snafu', a thoroughly occidental expression of fatalism, has a surging energy that has Lateef's very good band panting.

There are good things on *Blue*, with an orchestra fronted by Lateef, Mitchell and Lucas and anchored on two basses (upright and electric) and the power drumming of Brooks. However, the vocal tracks and the string arrangements on 'Like It Is' are pretty shallow, or only rather shallowly pretty in a *Summer Of Love*-ish way, and the album as a whole lacks focus. Matters worsen with the terribly mixed double-reissue of *The Diverse Yusef Lateef / Suite 16*: the first album is a strange blend of funk, a lot of Lateef flute, some pseudo-gospel singing and oddball string charts, ending on a blowsily exotic 'When A Man Loves A Woman'. *Suite 16* is an extended concerto for Lateef that veers wildly from passionate improvising to mere pretentiousness and exposes some of his wider ambitions as fatally dilettantish: there is much of interest in the writing which is sunk by the wrong-headed parts.

Lateef's vocal contributions on some of the earlier records merely anticipate the grosser insult of 'Hey, Jude' on the (deleted) *The Gentle Giant*. In turning Lateef into a marketable crossover performer, Atlantic took most of the bite out of his playing. *Hush 'N' Thunder* is a typically motley collection of pieces which Lateef does his best to master. Kenny Barron's boogaloo tune 'The Hump' is pretty lame, but Yusef dignifies it. Mysterious rumblings on the flute feature 'Sunset', wordless howls from Bones Constantino, gospel hollerings by The J. C. White Singers: it's very much a period piece.

****(*) Heart Vision**

YAL 900 *Lateef; Everett Haffner (syn); Christopher Newland (g); Adam Rudolph (perc); Nnenna Freelon, Tsidii Le Loka, Richard Ross, Mount Nebo Baptist Church Choir (v).* 1/92.

****** Tenors**

YAL 977 *Lateef; Archie Shepp (ts); Tom McLung (p); Avery Sharpe (b); Steve McCraven (d); Adam Rudolph, Mulazimuddin Razool, Tony Vacca (perc).* 1/92.

***** Plays Ballads**

YAL 333 *As above, except omit Razool and Vacca.* 12/92.

*****(*) Tenors**

YAL 911 *Lateef; Von Freeman (ts); John Young (p); John Whitfield (b); Terry Morrisette (d).* 7/92.

*****(*) Tenors**

YAL 019 *Lateef; René McLean (ts); Andrew Hollander (p); Avery Sharpe (b); Kamal Sabir (d).* 5/93.

*****(*) Metamorphosis**

YAL 100 *As above, except omit McLean and Hollander.* 12/93.

***** Woodwinds**

YAL 005 *Lateef; Ralph M. Jones (ts, ss, f, bf, hirchirki); Andrew Hollander (p); Avery Sharpe (b); Adam Rudolph (d).* 7/93.

***** Tenors**

YAL 105 *Lateef; Ricky Ford (ts); Avery Sharpe (b); Kamal Sabir (d).* 94.

****(*) Suite Life**

YAL 111 *Lateef; Andrew Hollander (p); Marcie Brown (clo).* 94.

***** In Nigeria**

YAL 707 *Lateef; Shittu Iskyaku (d); P. Adegboyega, Salisu I. Mashi, Awwalu Adamu (perc); voices.* 7/83.

In his 70s, Lateef's energy and commitment are astonishing. He has now formed his own label and released a stack of records in the '90s. They are a fascinating sequence. *Heart Vision* has the closest links with Lateef's recent work: the use of voices and choir, the shimmering electronics and Lateef's occasional bursts of tenor flirt with pretension but as often return to planet earth. The next four discs, though, are all about the tenor saxophone. *Ballads* is a slow, almost ritual unpeeling of the ballad form, with the rhythm players seemingly itching to get at the kernel but Lateef consistently holding them back: a tense, sometimes strange session, but the saxophonist has some imperious improvising on what are all original themes. The four meetings with other tenormen are all remarkable in their way. He challenges Shepp into his best form: there's little of the bleariness which has tarnished all of Archie's later music, just irascible, grouchy saxophone playing: Lateef with his eyes on higher things, Shepp always dragging matters back to worldly affairs. It's like a sour rerun of a Hawkins/Webster date, and it's splendid music. With McLean, all taut, biting lines, Lateef sounds sagacious; with Freeman, whose ragged phrasing and street-fighter tone crowd into the microphone like a swelling bruise, he ducks and weaves in what sometimes sounds like a punch-drunk cutting contest. But the extraordinary thing about all three encounters is that all the material is new, abstract, almost no more than a few sketchy lines: this is anchorless free playing much of the time, and the gutsy performances by all the rhythm players are compelling too. *Metamorphosis* is also much about rhythm: stripping the cast back to himself, Sharpe and Sabir, Lateef looks for a free kind of funk, the pulse staggered across an indeterminate time. Lateef rails away on tenor but adds a chorus of murmuring flutes as well: a workshop date, perhaps, but full of energy and surprise.

The *Tenors* meeting with Ricky Ford is another good blowout, cast as a sequence of tributes to other saxmen. *In Nigeria* is an archive piece from an African visit, a slowly simmering backdrop of percussion and voices framing the leader's improvisations, some simple, some deceptively complex. *Suite Life* is a sequence of chamberish pieces of no great weight or import, while *Woodwinds* is more about the hushed whisper of confiding flutes than reeds: only on the closing 'Brother Man' do Jones and Lateef get stuck into a tenor duel. An effective set. YAL has its share of indulgences, but overall this is an absorbing body of work from a man who clearly has a lot of music in him.

***** The World At Peace**

YAL 753 2CD *Lateef; Charles Moore (t, dumbek, kudu horn); Ralph Jones (ss, ts, f, bcl, musette); Jeff Gauthier (vn); Federico Ramos (g, kudu horn); Susan Allen (hp); David Johnson (vib, mar, perc); Bill Roper (tba, kudu horn); Eric Von Essen (b); Adam Rudolph, Jose Luis Perez (d).* 6/95.

****(*) Full Circle**

YAL 000 *Lateef; Tom McLung (p); Avery Sharpe (b); Steve McCraven (d).* 5/96.

**** Earth And Sky**

YAL 794 *As above, except add Sayyd Abdul Al-Khabyyr (ts, f), Kamal Sabir (d); omit McCraven.* 1/97.

**** CHNOPS, Gold And Soul**

YAL 497 *Lateef; Avery Sharpe, Mark Saltman (b); Adam Rudolph (d).* 97.

These are frankly disappointing and YAL is suddenly beginning to seem like another of Lateef's indulgences (though one could complain that if you have your own label, you can do anything you like with it – including giving the records apparently random catalogue-numbers). *Earth And Sky* finds the group mooching around some of Lateef's open-ended structures to no feasible purpose, while he sort of sing-raps over the top for quite a lot of the time. *CHNOPS, Gold And Soul* is a bit more listenable but wanders off to no avail, usually with Lateef noodling away on the keyboards: what are these tracks about, with so little melodic, textural or rhythmic interest? *Full Circle* is a bit more pointed, and one has to give Yusef some marks for choosing to sing 'When The Saints Go Marching In' as a dirge! The 12-strong group on *The World At Peace* were recorded in concert and, while it doesn't justify its two-disc status, it's interesting to hear Lateef and Rudolph (co-credited as leaders) trying to make a world-jazz concept work as a live performance. The ensembles tend to have a wheezing, chamberish feel to them, and more illuminating are the moments when a soloist (Lateef himself, in particular) takes off from the intricate patterns that Rudolph, Perez and Johnson weave through the whole event. Worth experiencing, by no means unmissable.

**** A Gift**

YAL 292 *Lateef; M. Abidh Waugh (g, syn); Kamal Sabir(d); Adam Rudolph (perc).* 99.

****(*) Beyond The Sky**

YAL 5 *Lateef; Charles Moore(t, flhn, conch); Joseph Bowie (tb, conch, perc); Ralph Jones (reeds); Alex Marcelo(p); M. Abidh Waugh (g, computer); Adam Rudolph (perc).* 2/00.

Lateef increasingly seems to be working to an agenda which cares little for anything other than various kinds of interstellar musing, with Rudolph helping out on a vast arsenal of percussion. These two are basically neither here nor there, but suspended somewhere in space. The doodlings of *A Gift* will make little appeal to earthbound souls. *Beyond The Sky* (which is where, exactly?) benefits from a tougher group syntax and some more directed playing, though it still suggests a polycultural grab-bag where anything may or may not go.

Mark Latimer

PIANO

Latimer is a British pianist who divides his time between classical repertory and jazz, although the former has occupied more of his recording time.

***** Take #1**

Spotlite SPJ CD 569 *Latimer; Andy Panayi (ts, f); Mick Hanson (g); Mick Hutton, Andy Cleyndert (b); Trevor Tomkins, Hal Fisher (d).* 6/98.

****(*) Unhinged Take #2**

Spotlite SPJ CD 573 *Latimer; Andy Panayi (cl, ts, bcl, f); John Etheridge (g); Mario Castronari (b); Asaf Sirkis (d).* 1/02.

Latimer's classical background doesn't, for once, impinge noticeably on his jazz playing. He has an agreeably cool and fluent way with his material. His only original on the first record is 'Pick 'N' Lix', a sort of bebop conundrum in 37 seconds, and he's chosen some rarely frequented jazz material, along with a few standards. The music comes from two different trios, with Hanson added for two tunes and Panayi for three more. Latimer is good behind soloists (listen to his cute fills behind Hanson on 'Gone With The Wind') and his own improvising has a smartness to it which is just this side of being overly clever. There's a vague sense of flippancy, as if Latimer were really too good for the whole situation, and the music might have made use of more bite in the rhythm sections.

The follow-up pursues similar ground, although there are more originals, and a somewhat exasperating sense that Latimer is clubbing listeners over the head with his musical acumen. Settings of Domenico Cimarosa and Gustav Mahler (the latter particularly irritating) tend to get in the way of the more interesting writing. Castronari's 'Peace Piece' gets an attractive treatment via Panayi's flute, but 'Giant Steps' is given an absurd deconstruction. Some of this would be better left in the rehearsal room.

Ingrid Laubrock (born 1970)

SOPRANO, ALTO AND TENOR SAXOPHONES

Grew up in Germany and came to London in 1989, where she studied with Jean Toussaint and became intrigued by Brazilian jazz, an influence reflected in these early releases.

***** Who Is It?**

Candid CCD 79745 *Laubrock; Kim Burton (p, acc); Ife Tolentino (g); Davide Mantovani (b); Helder Pack (d, perc); Chris Wells (perc).* 7/97.

★★★ Some Times

Candid CCD 79744 *Similar to above, except add Byron Wallen (t); Julien Segal (ts); Nikki Iles, Karim Merchant (p).* 98.

Laubrock is one of the most gifted young musicians in Britain today. Her saxophone style is distinctive on all three horns and her grasp of Brazilian jazz is reminiscent of Jane Bunnett's sympathetic absorption in Cuban music. The band is not well known but ideally suited to Laubrock's delivery, which is smart, evocative and, on 'Piracuama' and 'Brasitaleiro' (the debut album's two best tracks), completely idiomatic without sounding like pastiche.

The second album reinforces what some thought was a strong Tristano influence on Laubrock's alto-playing. 'Lennie's Pennies' seems to clinch it, but there are other factors at play as well; Bird's Latin tinge, Bunnett's liberating example and teacher Jean Toussaint's easy eclecticism. A fine talent who has yet to break through to a wider audience.

Christof Lauer (born 1953)

TENOR SAXOPHONE

Born in Melsungen, Germany, he studied piano and took up sax at 18. Played with Austrian bands of various stripes and has since freelanced, cut occasional leadership dates, and done big-band work, all in a tough post-Coltrane style.

★★★(★) Fragile Network

ACT 9266-2 *Lauer; Michel Godard (tba, serpent); Marc Ducret (g); Anthony Cox (b); Gene Jackson (d).* 9/98.

One of the younger generation of European players who have stepped beyond the overpowering influence of John Coltrane, Lauer has assimilated such a range of styles – from Stan Getz's smooth *legato* to Albert Ayler's all-out fury – that it is impossible to accuse him of being derivative of anyone. Engineer Walter Quintus is on hand on *Fragile Network* and creates a brooding but brightly registered canvas of sound for Lauer and tubist Godard, who emerges here in the Stewart role but with a much more developed solo part. His serpent feature on 'Ferma L'Ali' is breathtaking, and his virtuosity on tuba transforms 'Vernasio' and steals it from under the saxophonist's nose. Guitarist Ducret is sometimes a little overcooked, but on 'Human Voice' he shows what a delicate touch he also has at his disposal. This time out, Lauer is much more obviously part of a group rather than a horn-player-plus-rhythm. His placement of lines and phrases is exact and always telling and, though it is Godard who commands much of the foreground, the saxophonist continues to produce compelling jazz.

★★(★) Shadows In The Rain

ACT 94512 *Lauer; Jens Thomas (p); Sidsel Endresen (v); Cikada String Quartet.* 01.

A murky and disappointingly bland setting for Lauer. Despite Colin Towns's arrangements, the music never takes off and the saxophonist sounds flat and short of ideas, falling back on a few favourite devices whenever the impetus flags. Newcomers would be well advised to start with the earlier disc.

Cy Laurie (1926–2002)

CLARINET

A major figure on the London trad scene of the '50s, Laurie won admiration among hardcore revivalists since he refused to go mainstream. In 1960 he left to live in India until the end of the decade. Upon his return he decamped to Southend but continued to lead groups on the surviving trad circuit.

★★★(★) Blows Blue Hot

Lake LACD122 *Laurie; Al Fairweather, Alan Elsdon (t); John Picard, John R. T. Davies (tb); Alan Thomas, Dick Hughes (p); Johnny Potter, Brian Munday (bj); Dave Wood, Stan Leader (b); Ron McKay (d, wbd).* 7/54–1/55.

★★★ Chattanooga Stomp

Lake LACD61 *Laurie; Alan Elsdon, Sonny Morris, Ken Sims (t); Graham Stewart, Terry Pitts (tb); Tedd Ramm, Ian Armit, Anne Varley (p); Brian Munday, Diz Disley (bj); Stan Leader (b); Peter Mawford (d); Viv Carter (d, wbd).* 6/55–5/57.

★★(★) Jazz From The Roots

Lake LACD 156 *Laurie; Dennis Field, (c); Terry Pitts (tb); Allan Bradley (p); Nevil Skrimshire (g); Hugh Rainey (bj); Peter Corrigan, John Sirett (b); Colin Bowden, Steve Nice (d).* 3/89–5/92.

Laurie is in some ways the forgotten man of British trad clarinet, but he was as good a player as any of his peers. His style walked a rather awkward line between imitation and individuality: very much in thrall to Johnny Dodds, he led a band that, on the *Chattanooga Stomp* tracks, mostly taken from Esquire masters, could play with surprising heat. Dodds favourites like 'Goober Dance' and 'Perdido Street Blues' emerge unscathed, but rather more interesting is the way they recompose 'Twelfth Street Rag', a variation on the Armstrong Hot Five version. 'St Phillips Street Breakdown' has nothing of George Lewis in it, and two amusing bits of Mozart (including 'Minuet Wobble'!) are entertaining features for the leader. Morris is the pick of the three trumpeters and, although mastered from vinyl and shellac rather than the original tapes, the sound is bright and lively.

The earlier sessions on *Blows Blue Hot* have now also been reissued in another conscientious Lake release. The first eight tracks comprise the original Esquire ten-inch of the same title, with the balance made up of one 78 and three EP sessions. We slightly prefer these intense and full-blooded tracks, with the excellent Fairweather out front and Picard's blasting trombone just about manageable.

The later sessions (previously a cassette-only release) are a good simulation. There seems little point in a band such as this attempting 'West End Blues' or 'Potato Head Blues', and they do better by some of the less familiar items from the Oliver–Armstrong axis. But this is really more of a gig souvenir.

Andy LaVerne (born 1947)

KEYBOARDS

A pianist born in New York, LaVerne studied at Berklee for only weeks before turning professional and joining Woody Herman in 1973 and Stan Getz in 1977, the latter job lasting almost four years. He has since recorded extensively as a leader.

★★(★) Another World

Steeplechase SCCD 31086 *LaVerne; Mike Richmond (b); Billy Hart (d).* 9/77.

*****(*) Frozen Music**
Steeplechase SCCD 31244 *LaVerne; Rick Margitza (ss, ts); Marc Johnson (b); Danny Gottlieb (d).* 4/89.

**** Fountainhead**
Steeplechase SCCD 31261 *LaVerne; Dave Samuels (vib).* 6/89.

***** Standard Eyes**
Steeplechase SCCD 31280 *LaVerne; Steve LaSpina (b); Anton Fig (d).* 10/90.

LaVerne is a dedicated, accomplished player, but we've found difficulty getting excited about his records in the past. His considerable technique and prolific output as a composer are unarguable. The problem is finding any character at the heart of it all. Rhythmically he can be a little four-square, and he plays so many notes that his solos can get hung up on a rush to reharmonize. His earlier Steeplechase albums tend to be worthy rather than exciting sessions. *Frozen Music* offers a glimpse of the useful young Margitza, but the LaVerne originals are disappointingly unmemorable. The meeting with Samuels creates a lot of pretty music and not much more. *Standard Eyes*, though, is better, and benefits from LaSpina and Fig, who make an excellent team for LaVerne to work with.

***** Nosmo King**
Steeplechase SCCD 31301 *LaVerne; John Abercrombie (g).* 12/91.

**** Buy One Get One Free**
Steeplechase SCCD 31319 *LaVerne (p solo).* 4/92.

***** Plays Bud Powell**
Steeplechase SCCD 31342 *LaVerne (p solo).* 2/93.

LaVerne and Abercrombie work well together, and *Nosmo King* is sensibly varied in pace; but several of the pieces meander past their natural climax and LaVerne's heavy voicings make one wish for a lighter touch. The main highlight is the rarefied treatment of 'I Loves You, Porgy'.

The solo albums seem only to indulge the pianist's temptations to overdo things. *Buy One Get One Free* double-tracks him with piano parts recorded earlier on a Disklavier, and it all gets fulsome beyond words on the endless glisses of 'Fine Tune'. *Plays Bud Powell* is a smart idea, since Powell is still surprisingly neglected as a composer, and for once LaVerne says his piece on each of the tunes briskly and without undue ornamentation: probably the best of his solo sessions to this point.

*****(*) Severe Clear**
Steeplechase SCCD 31273 *LaVerne; Tim Hagans (t); Rick Margitza (ts); Steve LaSpina (b); Anton Fig (d).* 3/90.

A great band for sure, and this time LaVerne brought some of his best writing to the date, eight provoking if not exactly memorable originals that the musicians swarm all over. Fig's powerhouse display on 'No Guts, No Glory' or the flowing melodies of 'Plasma Pool' catch the ear, and Margitza and Hagans play up to their reputations.

***** Glass Ceiling**
Steeplechase SCCD 31352 *LaVerne; Steve LaSpina (b); Anton Fig (d).* 10/93.

What seems to be the final album with LaSpina and Fig benefits from a strong tune selection, with LaVerne finding new muscle in Corea's 'Litha' and 'Tones For Joan's Bones', and from the specific empathies which the group had developed: it really is an all-of-a-piece session.

****(*) Tadd's Delight**
Steeplechase SCCD 31375 *LaVerne (p solo).* 5/95.

A reader took us to task for saying in a previous edition that 'Tadd Dameron's legacy as a composer is ultimately slight'. What we should have said was that only a handful of his works figure much in repertory exercises, and this interesting idea for a homage includes most of the familiar pieces. Unfortunately this one's a disappointment. LaVerne seems to make heavy weather out of most of the melodies, as if deliberately stepping away from bebop velocity, and while some of the harmonizations are thought-provoking, one hardly feels that 'Hot House' or 'The Chase' really emerge in the spirit of the composer. Steeplechase also opt for a heavy 'classical' piano sound and it tends to add needless weight to an already hefty conception.

***** Serenade To Silver**
Steeplechase SCCD 31388 *LaVerne; Tim Hagans (t); Rick Margitza (ts); Steve LaSpina (b); Billy Drummond (d).* 11/95.

Not bad, but this is a bit thin when one remembers how tough and attacking *Severe Clear* was – and on a set of tunes that should have cued up a little vim and vigour. LaVerne's tribute to Horace Silver takes up the pretty rather than the funky side of the hard-bop master and, while it pays dividends on an interesting reworking of 'Song For My Father' and the sweet 'Peace', the other tunes sound merely polite.

***** Bud's Beautiful**
Steeplechase SCCD 31399 *LaVerne; Peter Washington (b); Billy Hart (d).* 3/96.

***** Stan Getz In Chappaqua**
Steeplechase SCCD 31418 *LaVerne; Don Braden (ts); Dave Stryker (g); Steve LaSpina (b); Danny Gottlieb (d).* 10/96.

LaVerne never seems short of a concept, and he has another go at Bud Powell with another new rhythm section on *Bud's Beautiful.* There are half a dozen rarities here and simply as a piece of scholarship this has its virtues. LaVerne, Washington and Hart swing through the programme with suitable energy and, if no surprises are sprung, it has a bopper's tautness about it, something LaVerne hasn't always found in this kind of material.

The Getz album is his inevitable nod to his former boss. The quartet (Stryker appears only on the 'Bossa Nova Medley') tackles a plausible set of tunes, from 'Early Autumn' to 'Windows'; but Braden, stylistically a useful alternative to the Getz sound, doesn't seem especially engaged with the material, and the session turns out as a potboiler.

***** Another World Another Time**
Steeplechase SCCD 31457 *LaVerne; Tim Hagans (t); Mike Richmond (b); Billy Hart (d).* 4/98.

The concept here says something about Nils Winther's loyalty to his artists: the same programme from LaVerne's 1977 debut, with the same band (plus Hagans), in new interpretations. We can't say that the date exactly had us rushing back to the original, but it's pleasant enough. LaVerne's composing was hardly 'outrageously modern' in 1977, as Winther opines, and now the material feels like typical contemporary repertory: helpful changes, open endings, but no really memorable melodies. Hagans at least applies himself with some force to tunes such as 'Tallboys'.

****(*) Between Earth And Mars**
Steeplechase SCCD 31478 *LaVerne; Dave Samuels (vib); Jay Anderson (b).* 11/98.

***** Pianissimo**
Steeplechase SCCD 31512 *LaVerne; Rich Perry (ts); Jay Anderson (b); Matt Wilson (d).* 12/00.

The coolly agreeable sound of vibes, piano and bass makes *Between Earth And Mars* into high-calibre mood music, but with players this deferential and sweetly cooperative there's very little spark. Docked a notch for complacency.

There aren't many players on the Steeplechase roster left for LaVerne to 'meet', and now Perry can also be ticked off the list. The programme is all contemplative balladry, which Perry is good at, even if a whole disc of it leaves the listener dry: LaVerne's customary equanimity makes it difficult to feel that the music has much to say, although there is the odd surprise – like a slow rock beat for 'Nineteen'.

John Law

PIANO

Law first emerged as a force to be reckoned with in 1989 as one-third of Atlas, a group that also featured percussionist Mark Sanders. The gifted Englishman straddles modern/free jazz and a lightly worn classical learning. He is capable of almost violently percussive rhythms alternated with a meditative lyricism.

****** Exploded On Impact**
Slam CD 204 *Law; Alan Wilkinson (as, bs); Roberto Bellatalla (b); Mark Sanders (d).* 2 & 7/92.

****(*) Talitha Cumi**
FMR CD06 081994 *Law (p solo).* 8/93.

Law is an improviser whose background in and understanding of classical piano language alternately fuels and haunts him. His harmonics and sense of structure are unexceptionable, but there are moments on *Talitha Cumi*, a set of meditations on the *Dies irae*, when he sounds much too correct and self-absorbed. Compared to the group and duo work, it is a disappointing appearance.

On *Exploded On Impact* Law's writing breathes intelligence through and through, and is distinguished by a firm architecture seldom encountered in free bop of this type. It's often difficult to discern what is predetermined and what is spontaneously improvised, particularly on the two main statements, 'Mothers' Lament' (a threnody for Yugoslavia) and the punning 'A Pissed-Off Tree', which nods in the direction of a 'felonious monk'. Bellatalla is a less percussive and somewhat less energetic player than some others, and much of the harder-edged stuff has been consigned to Wilkinson, one of the unsung heroes of new music in Britain. Sanders plays briskly and with humour, as he does with Jon Lloyd's similarly disposed group. Law himself develops relatively small harmonic areas with great intensity, building up climaxes that are as logical as they are explosive.

****** Giant Leaves (Autumn Steps)**
FMR CD 32 *Law; Tim Wells (b); Paul Clarvis (d, perc).* 12/95.

Giant Leaves (Autumn Steps) provides a welcome opportunity to hear Law in a conventional trio setting. The most obvious precedent is Howard Riley's elegantly freewheeling trio of the mid-'60s. What Law brings in addition is a quasi-classical expansiveness that has more in common with Keiths Jarrett and Tippett, great rolling figures and pure sound. The toy keyboard 'Rockaby' at the start of 'Playground ... So There!' kicks off an irritatingly memorable theme that flounces and taunts all the way to the finish. A beautiful 'Sarabande' is dedicated to the late John Stevens and is well worthy of reprise at the close. What relation 'Giant (Steps)' bears to the Coltrane theme and 'Autumn (Leaves)' to the standard isn't always clear. Both are meditations rather than strict covers, but the coda to 'Giant (Steps)', in which the theme is played absolutely straight, makes it perfectly clear how close to the original Law had been working. A splendid record, full of invention, wit, sadness and fire.

*****(*) Pentecost**
FMR CD27 0396 *Law (p solo).* 2/96.

***** The Hours**
FMR CD 41 V0697 *As above.* 9–10/96.

These two records complete Law's cycle of improvisations based on monastic plainchant. The earlier of the pair was recorded at a solo concert which happened to fall on the Feast of Pentecost, which suggested the thematic material to Law. In contrast to *The Hours*, it's a single large slab of music, relatively static and curiously reminiscent of similar – and similarly spiritual – performances by the South African Bheki Mseleku. In contrast to *Talitha Cuma*, whose success suggested the series, it's not a performance that wears its classical antecedents openly on its sleeve. It isn't strictly a jazz performance, either. Law develops ideas in an impressively logical way, building by accretion and occasionally indulging changes of direction which suggest a *coup de théâtre* rather than anything inherent to the music itself. His use of the 'Veni Creator Spiritus' is highly intelligent and highly spontaneous. There is very little outward evidence that much was predetermined. Perhaps oddly, *The Hours*, which is based on the eight hours of prayers observed in the monastic tradition, sounds more organized and deliberate, though Law himself concedes that he benefited from earlier performances of the piece in festival settings (including one in an abbey at Le Mans). Divided into two parts – 'The Exposition of the Chants' and 'The Hours' – it's a work with an unexpectedly grand internal architecture, which is somewhat mitigated by the rather clinical sound of the studio piano. Nevertheless, a substantial achievement and a piano sequence which invites the closest study and reflection.

***** The Onliest – Pictures From A Monk Exhibition**
FMR CD38 *Law; Tim Wells (b); Paul Clarvis (d, perc).* 98.

This was conceived as a musical correlative to artist Melanie Day's series of works inspired by Thelonious Monk. Law weaves in different versions of 'Thelonious', much like the 'Promenade' in Mussorgsky's 'Pictures At An Exhibition'. It's a clever idea and the most obvious representation of his jazz/classical crossover. Without the images, which are reproduced in full colour on the sleeve, it all sounds a bit flat and mechanical, but the musicianship is unquestionable and Law's vision is unique.

***** Abacus**
hatOLOGY567 *Law; Jon Lloyd(ss, as); Tim Wells (b); Gerry Hemingway (d).* 5/00.

If only it weren't delivered so humourlessly, Law's 'Partita For Piano, Saxophone, Bass and Drums' would have the bearings of a triumphant fusion of jazz dialect with baroque form. There's much talk of Bach in the sleeve-notes, but not much evidence of Western music's great genius in the delivery, which feels curiously desiccated and 'proper', as if the players were afraid to step outside the lines of something which seems completely preordained and in its place. That said, much of the playing musters a grave beauty, and Law's modelling has its own merits, even if its joints feel unwontedly stiff.

Claude Lawrence

ALTO SAXOPHONE

A sometime sideman with William Hooker, Lawrence has a long association with Morris and Charles.

★★★ Presenting

CIMP 147 *Lawrence; Wilber Morris (b); Dennis Charles (d).* 4/97.

Lawrence plays with the kind of wounded lyricism that used to belong to Jimmy Lyons; he nags at certain phrases and makes whole pieces out of them. Some of this feels like little more than a man running up and down the horn, but the music is redeemed by the wonderful team of Morris and Charles, who make even simple free rhythms fascinating. Although Lawrence apparently played with them many times in the '80s, this CIMP disc is his first as a leader. It's not unworthy.

Hubert Laws (born 1939)

FLUTE

A seemingly ubiquitous presence on '70s fusion records, Laws had considerable success with his own recordings. The Texan, an original member of the Jazz Crusaders, has a strong, very clear sound, classically trained. Brother Ronnie is an able tenor man.

★★★ The Laws Of Jazz

Rhino 71636 *Laws; Jimmy Owens (t); Garnett Brown, Tom McIntosh (tb); Benny Powell (tb, btb); Chick Corea, Rodgers Grant (p); Richard Davis, Israel Cachao Lopez, Chris White (b); Jimmy Cobb, Ray Lucas, Bobby Thomas (d); Bill Fitch, Carmelo Garcia, Raymond Orchart, Victor Pantoja (perc).* 4/64, 8/65, 2/66.

As was too often the case with Herbie Mann, critics and listeners tended to forget that Laws began his career as a pretty straight jazz player. He sounds very crisp and dynamic here on both flute and piccolo, making a surprisingly convincing solo voice of the latter instrument. His articulation is exact but the phrases still swing and there are enough blue notes and syncopated measures to justify the jazz standard waved in the title. Almost all the material is original and 'Baila Cinderella' is an idea that resurfaces later in the flautist's career. The Latin tinge is heightened by the inclusion of Armando 'Chick' Corea, but it's a pity that none of the pianist's compositions are included on the set.

The sound is quite resonant and a touch over-produced, but this is a very impressive album and anyone who thinks of Laws as a fusion colourist should sample this reissue of his Atlantic debut, packaged with his sophomore effort *Flute Bylaws* which was a more ambitious but ultimately less engaging disc. The brass arrangements tend to overpower the flute, which works better in the smaller line-up.

★★(★) The Rite Of Spring

Epic/Legacy 651827 *Laws; Walter Kane, Jane Taylor (bsn); Bob James (p, ky); Gene Bertoncini, Stuart Scharf (g); Ron Carter (b, clo); Jack DeJohnette (d); Airto Moreira (perc); Dave Friedman (perc, vib).* 6/71.

This was a really terrible idea which nearly worked, dammit. It wasn't the first and certainly won't be the last attempt to jazz up favourite classical themes. The problem is that Laws and his colleagues bleed the stately swing out of the two movements from the *Brandenburg Concerto No. 2* and manage to pull the sting out of the still shockingly subversive *Le Sacre du printemps.* The Stravinsky piece is one of the most nakedly pagan works ever penned by a Western composer. Here, it sounds merely lame and a bit salacious.

The better pieces are Fauré's *Pavane* and Debussy's *Syrinx*, where the flute is at least idiomatic, though not necessarily the way Hubert blows it. A lot of thought and some sensitive musical effort went into this record. Most classically versed listeners will find it irritating in the extreme, but if it leads anyone to the original, especially the *Rite*, well and good.

★★★(★) In The Beginning

Columbia 65127 *Laws; Ronnie Laws (ts); Clare Fischer, Bob James (p, ky); Rodgers Grant (p); Richard Tee (org); Gene Bertoncini (g); Ron Carter (b); Steve Gadd (d); Airto Moreira (perc); Dave Friedman (perc, vib); string ensemble.* 74.

Hubert's best album and a good, expansive representation of his flute-playing. There's also the plus of some very good spots by brother Ronnie who shines and shows an unsuspected Coltrane influence on a couple of tracks, notably Trane's own 'Moment's Notice'. By the time he began to record for Creed Taylor's CTI label (from which this is a reissue), Hubert had softened his tone somewhat, but his harmonic awareness and clarity of diction are impressive here on a very mixed programme that includes an interpretation of a Satie *Gymnopédie* (a better classical option than the *Rite Of Spring* stuff), the traditional 'Come Ye Disconsolate' and Sonny Rollins's 'Airegin', which falters a little on a rather too rigid tempo but is a creditable performance nonetheless. With-strings phobics should be reassured that the arrangements are impeccable and in no way intrusive. All in all, a fine record.

Some of the best of this disc, *The Rite Of Spring* and other CTI sets like *Chicago Theme, Morning Star,* and *Afro-Classic* can be found on a Columbia compilation *The Best Of Hubert Laws*, still in circulation in some territories.

★★(★) Baila Cinderella

Scepterstein 1238 *Laws; Otmaro Ruiz (p, ky); Hussain Jiffry, Carlos Puerto Jr (b); Joe Heredia (d); Kevin Ricard (perc); Eloise Laws (v).* 02.

The '80s were a lean time for Laws and the '90s revival was only very partial. This Latin set has an irritating narration and a programmatic feel that doesn't amount to anything of substance. 'Baila Cinderella' makes a fresh appearance, but good as it is it's not enough to sustain a whole album. Again, he feels compelled to add a classical dimension and finishes the disc with the big theme from *Swan Lake*. There are flashes of the old precision but no fire and not much funk.

Ronnie Laws (born 1950)

TENOR AND SOPRANO SAXOPHONES, FLUTE, VOCALS

Younger brother of Hubert, he's spent much of his career away from jazz proper, playing with the likes of Earth, Wind and Fire. Even so, he does have the ability to surprise and delight on occasion.

**** Pressure Sensitive**
Blue Note *Laws; Joe Sample (ky, g); Mike Kavanaugh, Jerry Peters (ky); Ronald Bautista, John Rowin (g); Wilton Felder (b); Steve Guittierrez, Mike Willars (d); Joe Clayton (perc).* 3–4/75.

****(*) Fever**
Blue Note 89541 *Laws; Michael Hepburn, Bobby Lyle (ky); Marlon the Magician (g); Wilton Felder, Clint Mosley (b); Bruce Carter, Steve Guittierrez (d); strings, backing vocals.* 1–3/76.

Ronnie has the right kind of saxophone voice for a certain strain of soul-jazz and his mid-'70s Blue Notes attracted some notice, even if that label was living largely off its past reputation. These are typical of the period – smoothed-out funk with a heavy production gloss and little in the way of imaginative improvisation. Listeners will be reminded of Grover Washington Jr on occasion, but none of these have Grover's soaring lyricism and sheer class. However, every now and then, Ronnie turns in a string of phrases, sometimes a whole chorus as on *Fever*'s terse closer 'From Ronnie With Love', that suggests he might have cut it in more challenging contexts.

**** Tribute To The Legendary Eddie Harris**
Blue Note 55330 *Laws; Oscar Brashear, Michael Stewart (t); Gary Bias (bs); Patrice Rushen (p); Craig Cooper (g); Vernell Brown (g, p); Larry Antonino, Mike Elizondo (b); Bubba Bryant, Jeffrey Suttles (d); Munyungo Jackson (perc); Andrea Coleman (v).* 10–11/96.

An unexpected attempt to play pretty much straight jazz, albeit of the funky, soulful sort associated with the cheerfully eccentric Harris who, for all his shortcomings, had an armoury of unusual instrumental devices at his disposal. The problem with this 'tribute' is that it is neither particularly funky nor filled with soul and the eight Harris themes (including the *de rigueur* 'Freedom Jazz Dance') are played with more efficiency than passion or humour. Some good players in the line-up, though, and Oscar Brashear in particular has some respectable moments. So not a complete write-off.

Some of the Harris material also appears in live form on a Scepterstein concert set which has had some circulation. There are other Laws sets around and there is a best-of the Blue Note sessions which might be worth tracking down. Sadly, though, Ronnie remains an underachiever whose commitment to jazz seems intermittent at best.

Yank Lawson (1911–95)

TRUMPET

Born John Rhea Lawson in Trenton, Missouri, he joined Ben Pollack's New York band in 1933, then spent a famous period (interrupted by an argument) with Bob Crosby. In the '50s and '60s he often worked with Crosby sideman Bob Haggart, and they formed the World's Greatest Jazz Band together in 1968. In the '80s, he and Haggart were still co-leading bands. He is somewhat taken for granted as a master of Dixieland trumpet.

****** Something Old, Something New, Something Borrowed, Something Blue**
Audiophile APCD-240 *Lawson; George Masso (tb); Johnny Mince (cl); Lou Stein (p); Bucky Pizzarelli (g); Bob Haggart (b); Nick Fatool (d).* 3/88.

***** Jazz At Its Best**
Jazzology JCD-183 *Lawson; George Masso (tb); Kenny Davern (cl); Al Klink (ts); John Bunch (p); Bucky Pizzarelli (g); Bob Haggart (b); Jake Hanna (d).* 2/89.

*****(*) Singin' The Blues**
Jazzology JCD-193 *As above, except Joe Muranyi (cl, ss) replaces Davern; omit Klink; add Barbara Lea (v).* 3/90.

***** With A Southern Accent**
Jazzology JCD-203 *As above, except add Kenny Davern (cl); omit Muranyi and Lea.* 3/91.

Yank Lawson and Bob Haggart played together for almost 60 years. Their Lawson–Haggart Jazz Band of the '50s was one of the best Dixieland outfits of its kind; their World's Greatest Jazz Band repeated the trick in the '60s and '70s. Their records for Audiophile and Jazzology maintained a formidable standard: Yank Lawson's tough, growling solos have a bite and pungency which he retained, even into his 80s, and Haggart's steady propulsion never faltered at all. This is a splendid group of discs and only the relatively tame repertoire on the latter three keep them out of the top bracket: the mostly recent material on the first disc is so fresh and is played so enjoyably that one wishes the group had stuck to originals over warhorses. A lovely 'Blues For Louise', a Spanish-sounding 'Bumps', played by a trio of Lawson, Stein and Fatool, and a swaggering 'Come Back, Sweet Papa' are only three highlights from a very fine set. The next three all rely for the most part on Dixieland and traditional staples and, though all are played with gusto and panache, there's a trace of weariness here and there in tunes that might be laid to a comfortable rest. *Jazz At Its Best* dispatches its tunes capably, with extended explorations of 'Willow Weep For Me' and 'Mandy Make Up Your Mind', as well as a memorial to Maxine Sullivan, 'Lonesome Yank'. *Singin' The Blues* finds Yank in tremendous form on the title-song, on a slow, sturdy 'Tin Roof Blues' and a fine 'Blue, Turning Grey Over You'. *With A Southern Accent* peaks on an intensely felt 'Creole Love Call'. This and *Jazz At Its Best* are somewhat pointlessly padded out with a couple of alternative takes.

Daunik Lazro (born 1945)

ALTO AND BARITONE SAXOPHONES

A free improviser who recorded rather more widely on the cusp of the '80s, Lazro has only recently got himself on to CD in any significant way.

*****(*) Hauts Plateaux**
Potlatch P 498 *Lazro; Carlos Zingaro (vn, elec).* 2/95.

*****(*) Dourou**
Bleu Regard CT 1954 *Lazro; Joe McPhee (pkt-t, ss, ts); Didier Levallet, Paul Rogers (b); Christian Rollet (d).* 11/96.

***** Zong Book**
Emouvance 1013 *Lazro (as, bs solo).* 1/97–11/99.

Lazro can't prevent himself from playing songful, temperate lines, even in the midst of an otherwise wild collective passage or a temptingly open canvas. He often shows a Lacy-like restraint on the alto (he plays baritone too, but it's clearly his secondary voice). The duets with Zingaro were recorded at a Marseilles concert and feature some interplay which has as much Gallic charm as ferocity. Zingaro dusts some of the sound with a ripple of electronics; but what you mostly hear is the melodious ache of the alto against the gymnastic tarantella of the violin.

Dourou is a good deal darker, with the yin and yang of Levallet and Rogers underscoring McPhee's characteristically tough tenor. But this is full of colour and energy. Lazro's 'Africa Lab', which derives in part from some traditional melody-lines, is a long piece that brilliantly shows off the individual and collective strengths of the band, the music changing from solo to duo to trio and quintet passages as it evolves through a full 20 minutes in which nothing feels overcharged or underpowered. The Levallet–Rogers combo proves to be the most inspired ingredient to this playing, from their delicious *arco* groaning under 'Catty' to the double-solo on 'Candide'. Lazro should take credit for a singular and original group record.

Lazro plays Ayler on the solo record – at least, for 'In Heart Only', which comes out as a nicely judged mix of melancholy homage and intense interpretation. The baritone work is for once rather more interesting than the alto. Some of the improvising feels a little dry, and maybe Lazro is simply better in group situations.

Nguyên Lê (born 1959)

GUITAR, DANH TRANH, GUITAR SYNTHESIZER

Vietnamese guitarist seeking a fusion of his musical roots with a more worldly jazz-rock synthesis.

***** Million Waves**

ACT 9221 *Lê; Dieter Ilg (b, v); Danny Gottlieb (d, perc).* 12/94.

Something about the overall packaging leads one to expect a hybrid of rock and world music from these records. The reality is quite otherwise. Lê favours soft, clean-picked lines and delicately arpeggiated chords, often using a nylon-strung electric guitar to get a rich 'acoustic' sound that is quite squarely in the jazz tradition. The synths are reserved for delicate background traceries or gently insistent ostinati.

Lê seemed to have gone as far as he could with this approach after two albums. *Million Waves* is both more of the same and very different. It isn't quite a conventional jazz trio, but the rudiments are definitely there and the long, spontaneously improvised 'Trilogy', the only track not recorded at Walter Quintus's state-of-the-art CMP studios, opens up sufficient files for a decade's-worth of experimentation; excellent stuff. The high gloss that Quintus brings occasionally diverts attention away from less than stirring material. 'Butterflies And Zebras' is a short gloss on Jimi Hendrix's 'Little Wing', which follows it without adding much to the original. Dominique Borker is co-credited again on the attractive 'Moonshine', confirming the fruitfulness of that relationship. Surprisingly, Lê plays out on James Brown's 'I Feel Good'; perhaps the jazz-funk album is just around the corner.

***** Tales From Viêt-Nam**

ACT 9225-2 *Lê; Paolo Fresu (t, flhn); Simon Cato Spang-Hanssen (sax, f); François Verly (p, ky, mar, perc); Michael Benita (b); Hao Nhien (danh tranh, dan bau, sao, perc); Thai An (dan nguyet); Joel Allouche, Steve Arguëlles (d); Trilok Gurtu (d, perc); Huong Thanh (v).* 10–11/95.

*****(*) Three Trios**

ACT 9245-2 *Lê; Renaud Garcia-Fons, Dieter Ilg, Marc Johnson (b); Peter Erskine, Danny Gottlieb (d); Mino Cinelu (d, perc).* 11/96.

***** Maghreb And Friends**

ACT 9261-2 *Lê; Paolo Fresu (t); Wolfgang Puschnig (as); Stefano Di Battista (as, ss); Alain Debiossat (ss); Hao Nhien (Vietnamese f); Aly Wagué (African f, v); Bojan Zulikarpasic (p); Cheb Mami (acc syn); Djemaï Abdenour (mandola, Algerian bj); Jean-Jacques Avenel (kora); Mejdoub Ftati (vn); Michel Alibo (b); Mokhtar Samba (d); Karim Ziad (d, perc, v); Mehdi Askeur, Gaëlle Hervé, Marielle Hervé, Aziz Sahmaoui, Huong Thanh (v); Zahra Bani, B'net Houariyat, Kadija Haliba, Saïda Madrani, Mohamed Menni, Malika Rhami, Halima Zaiter (v, perc).* 11/97–3/98.

Like Anouar Brahem and Rabih Abou-Khalil, Lê has already gone some considerable way towards broadening the constituency of 'world jazz'. No sign of the jazz-funk album we feared, but instead a steady consolidation of the different aspects of his work so far. *Maghreb And Friends* is an interesting attempt at synthesizing different traditions, probably too many and too different to pull off with absolute conviction. A hybrid like 'Funk Raï' is of questionable valuable, given that *raï* is a form with its own subtly propulsive dynamic, much of which is lost when rendered down into lumpy fours.

A lot of the material here comes from percussionist Karim Ziad, who acts as co-leader. His 'Louanges' – a near-untranslatable word for ecstatic praises favoured by composer Olivier Messiaen – is the most beautiful track on the album, an exquisite blending of Maghrebi, Vietnamese and Guinean voices. The horns are used sparingly throughout the album and really come into their own only on the closing 'Guinia' (Mahmoud Guinia is one of the greatest exponents of *gnawa* singing) and the closing love-chant, 'Nesraf'. An album of many elements, all of them fascinating and most of them rendered immaculately but without coherence.

Tales From Viêt-Nam was the album that allowed Lê to break through to a wider audience, partly because of the successful touring project that bore the same name. It is probably our least favourite of all so far, for most of the same reasons as *Maghreb And Friends.* Where its attempt to unite white and black Africa had a certain fresh logic, *Tales* sounds very much like an attempt to import new cuisine. Relying almost entirely on traditional material, it's a record that appears to struggle somewhere in the dead zone between 'authenticity' and the players' palpable desire to shake loose and pursue fascinating lines of inquiry. Arguëlles and Allouche share percussion responsibilities, and it's the Englishman (if he still considers himself such) who shows the more penetrating insight into the source material, playing brilliantly on an early trio of wistful narratives. The drummers alternate on the two-part 'Mangustao', the name of a strange, dual-natured fruit whose rugged exterior and delicate flesh seem to hold a symbolic importance for Lê. Trilok Gurtu adds chipper, slightly pointless cameo percussion to 'Hen Ho' and 'Ting Ning'.

By contrast to the others, *Three Trios* is coherent, expressively focused and brimming with extraordinary playing. The best of the three line-ups is, predictably, the reunion with Johnson and Erskine. It is also the most straightforwardly jazz-based. Lê characterizes the groups according to the titles of the first three tunes: 'Silk', 'Silver', 'Sand' – delicate but strong threads bind him to Marc and Peter; there is a shiny metallic edge to the group with Dieter Ilg and Danny Gottlieb; and a shifting, rhythmically looser quality to the performances with Garcia-Fons and Cinelu.

Some familiar themes are aired. 'Idoma' refers to an African tribe who wear white masks with slanting eyes, which strongly suggests Asian origin; the melody sounds Oriental but is actually a pygmy song. 'Woof' for Dieter and Danny and 'Foow' for Renaud and Mino are the same theme, a quick way of unpicking the differences in approach. The closing 'Straight, No Chaser', played *à l'argent*, is a complete surprise and a provocative close to a thoroughly unexpected and completely enjoyable jazz record.

***** Bakida**
ACT 9275-2 *Lê; Paolo Fresu (t); Chris Potter (ts); Kudsi Erguner (f); Jon Balke (p); Renaud Garcia-Fons (b); Ilya Amar (mar); Tino di Geraldo (d, perc); Karim Ziad (perc).* 5–10/99.

Lê spreads his net ever wider with a set of tunes that draw on an eclectic range of European and Asian influences. The basic trio instrumentation – Lê, Garcia-Fons and di Geraldo – is augmented by a range of effective guest stars, though Chris Potter seems a little out of place in this company. Fresu is once again a star turn, combining folksy themes with an element of welcome abstraction, but it is Lê's increasingly distinctive sound and strong compositional sense which dominate the album, all the way from the opening 'Dding Dek' through unexpectedly Hispanic ideas like 'Noche Y Luz' to the beautiful closing 'Romanichel'. As ever, Jan Erik Kongshaug and co-producer Siegfried Loch give the album a rich and detailed sound.

****(*) Purple: Celebrating Jimi Hendrix**
ACT 9410-2 *Lê; Bojan Zulfikarpasic (p); Michel Alibo, Meshell Ndegocello (b); Terri Lyne Carrington (d, perc); Tino di Geraldo, Karim Ziad (perc); Corin Curschellas, Aida Khann (v); B'net Houaryiat (perc, v).* 5/02.

All modern guitarists sooner or later turn to the Hendrix songbook for inspiration. It's not the most obvious spur to Lê's talents and the inclusion of spoken and sung vocals sounds a little like a failure of nerve, though co-leader Terri Lyne Carrington is obviously committed to the whole Hendrix oeuvre. She features on some of the better and simpler cuts, like 'Purple Haze', '1983 (A Merman I Should Turn To Be)' and the less familiar 'South Saturn Delta' and 'Up From the Skies'. Corin Curschellas is a more mannered singer, undoubtedly beautiful but not necessarily the right voice for this project. Bojan Zulfikarpasic adds some interesting piano and Fender Rhodes parts to a couple of tracks, but it's Lê's switch for much of the album to guitar synthesizer that defines the tone of the record and points to its shortcomings. One misses his usual subtle lines and rich, soft chords. Instead, the whole record is drenched in sound effects that neither quite recall Hendrix nor point to anything more innovative. An intriguing and one might argue inevitable project, but something of a disappointment.

The Leaders

GROUP

Conceived as a touring group trading on the starry nature of the line-up, this turned into a regular band for several years and went some way to developing an aesthetic of its own.

*****(*) Out Here Like This**
Black Saint 120119 *Lester Bowie (t); Arthur Blythe (as); Chico Freeman (ts, bcl); Kirk Lightsey (p); Cecil McBee (b); Famoudou Don Moye (d).* 6/86.

****(*) Unforeseen Blessings**
Black Saint 120129 *As above.* 12/88.

Occupying a mid-point between the now almost parodic anarchy of the Art Ensemble of Chicago and the more professional musical showmanship of Lester Bowie's Brass Fantasy, and offering a left-of-centre balance between Chico Freeman's freer style and the soul-funk of his Brainstorm band, The Leaders also helped redeem Arthur Blythe's skidding career. Never as impressive on record as they were live, *Out Here Like This* is nevertheless a powerful and varied sampling of contemporary styles. There's a better balance of sound between the front-row voices and a more prominent role for McBee, who shares some of Ron Carter's ability to style-shift while maintaining a basic consistency of tone. Bowie's theatrical approach manages to compress a huge acreage of jazz history, calling in references to Armstrong, Bix Beiderbecke and Miles Davis.

Unforeseen Blessings is a puzzle and a disappointment. At points it seems to be a Kirk Lightsey record, with occasional contributions from the horns. The pianist plays unaccompanied on the opening track and two others, and is often the most prominent soloist. Bowie only has one extensive feature, on 'Blueberry Hill', and there is precious little from Blythe and Freeman. If this were a rock supergroup, one might suspect dissent in the ranks, but perhaps all we're hearing is a change of direction that ultimately proved fruitless.

Joelle Léandre (born 1951)

DOUBLE BASS, VOICE

The French bassist and vocalist has produced a huge body of work, much of it with other leaders, in the anonymity of collectives and on small and hard-to-find labels. Consequently, her dramatic presence and stunning bass-work are less well known than they should be. She plays resonantly but with a great deal of detail.

*****(*) Blue Goo Park**
FMP CD 52 *Léandre; Rüdiger Carl (acc, cl).* 7/92.

A good proportion of Léandre's concert and recorded output consists of new music. She has either commissioned or received dedication of speciality pieces for double bass from composers such as Betsy Jolas, Jacob Druckman, Sylvano Bussotti and especially Giacinto Scelsi, and has adapted other materials, including John Cage's song, 'The Wonderful Widow Of Eighteen Springs', for bass and voice; all of these are on Adda 581043. This work apart, though, Léandre is a formidable improviser. She has appeared as part of Derek Bailey's Company project and has a number of improvisation-based recordings to her credit.

The FMP session might be her most concentrated to date. Consisting of 23 tracks, at just over an hour's tracking time, it emphasizes Léandre's interest in brief, almost song-like forms.

***(*) Contrabasses

Leo CD LR 261 *Léandre; William Parker (b).* 97.

***(*) E'Vero

Leo CD LR 275 *Léandre; Sebi Tramontano (p).* 97.

It would be hard to imagine a more compelling meeting between two contemporary improvisers than *Contrabasses.* Parker is a modern master and a musician of vast resource and intelligence. As on the duets with Tramontano which make up the slightly disappointing *E'Vero*, Léandre is comfortable enough to cede musical territory to her playing partners. With Parker, though, she is as forceful and full-voiced as we have ever heard her on disc. His sense of structure is without peer, and Léandre might seem a miniaturist by comparison, except that here she lengthens her line and adds weight to every stroke of the strings. A marvellous record; don't be put off by the rarefied instrumentation.

*** Incandescences

Jazz'halo TS 007 *Léandre; Giorgio Occhipinti (p).* 5/97.

***(*) Sapporo Duets

Jazz'halo TS 013 *Léandre; Ryoji Hojito(p).* 9/98.

Same again, but with two different partners. The duets with Occhipinti are all over the place, mercurial, manic, full of combative playing that is sometimes comic, sometimes merely inscrutable. Its appeal may depend on how much you take to Occhipinti's faintly exasperating tendency to stir in everything he's ever heard. An entertaining alternative to chamber music, but we also found that a CD's worth went further than we really wanted.

With Hojito, Léandre musters a more closely argued music. The Japanese pianist is another great borrower, but unlike Occhipinti he works an idea or a passage of technique to its logical conclusion, and several of these episodes have a finished, almost polished feel, to them. There's still some funny business at the end, though.

***(*) Joelle Léandre Project

Leo CD LR 287 *Léandre; Marilyn Crispell (p); Richard Teitelbaum (ky, elec); Carlos Zingaro (vn); Paul Lovens (d).* 1/99.

This is the group record that Léandre has threatened for a long time. Her past associations with all these players guarantee a strong empathy and, as with the Parker duets, she has a partner of equal force and expression in Marilyn Crispell. Using Zingaro and Teitelbaum allows her to create broad and complex soundscapes, but much of the music is unexpectedly spacious and detailed; there is no clutter anywhere on the nine numbered improvisations which made up the midwinter performance at Sons d'Hiver.

*** Tricotage

Ambiances Magnetiques 109 *Léandre; Danielle P. Roger (d).* 5/99.

*** Organic Mineral

In Situ 235 *Léandre; Kazue Sawai (b koto).* 6/99.

This wasn't the first time knitting had been used as an ironic – or maybe not – image for a female sensibility in improvised music. The image of the infamous *tricoteuses*, knitting one and purling one while the guillotines rumbled, was very much part of a feminist aesthetic in the '80s. Léandre and drummer Roger don't flog it to death but devote their energies instead to a set of sensitive and muscular improvisations (and a surprise version of Debussy's 'Clair De Lune'). It's bordering on the obvious to say that Leandre's bass is as percussive as Roger's drums are musical; check out 'Knit One, Purl Three', the best track on the album.

The set with Sawai is also a helpful introduction to another neglected female player, here playing a rarely heard instrument, the bass koto. The similarity of tone between the two is modified by the very different timbre and these are fascinating encounters, both structurally and tonally. Taken from a Radio Bremen broadcast, the sound is very good, clear and true.

**** C'Est Ça

Red Toucan 9315 *Léandre; François Houle (cl); Hasse Poulsen (g).* 3/00.

Recorded live in Paris, these ten free improvisations conjure the best out of both Léandre and Houle, who's something of a house artist at Red Toucan. Poulsen will be the unfamiliar name to most; he's a vigorous, angular player, closer to Bill Frisell in free mode than to Derek Bailey with a song in his heart. Often it's he who takes the 'bass' line, leaving Léandre to move freely with her bow work. The penultimate piece is one of the longest on the set, but also the best integration of the three voices. One of Léandre's best performances in years, also one of Houle's and a highlight of the Red Toucan catalogue, which had seemed to be in abeyance.

***(*) Signature (Two Duets)

Red Toucan 9321 2CD *Léandre; Masahiko Satoh, Yuji Takahashi (p).* 12/00.

Two concerts with Japanese pianists, recorded on consecutive days. Takahashi sounds the more classically inclined of the pair, and possibly more at ease playing Takemitsu than this sort of free music, but Satoh is superb, fast and light and with something of Marilyn Crispell's power. The self-titled tracks show no signs of advance preparation, though Léandre does increasingly draw on a large vocabulary of phrases and effects, many of them made with the bow, which familiarizes her approach even as she pushes out into unexplored territory. This was a purple patch for the bassist, who has rarely been so prominent. Slightly short measure on the album, which contains just over an hour of music on two CDs. One hopes they didn't edit the Satoh performance.

*** Evident

482 Music 1024 *Léandre; Mark Nauseef (perc).* 03.

Nauseef's use of frame drums and other percussion devices has opened up a rich seam of enquiry for him down the years. With Léandre, he sounds more expansive even than usual, but also very respectful of her authoritative voice. He's neither equal partner nor mere accompanist on this thoughtful set, almost a commentator or instantaneous translator of her thoughts. Fine stuff from a pairing who have lots more to say.

LeeAnn Ledgerwood

PIANO

Born in Ohio, Ledgerwood was taught classical piano but was won over by a Bill Evans LP. After studying at Berklee, she arrived in New York in 1982, where she plays and teaches.

*****(*) Now And Zen**

Steeplechase SCCD 31432 *Ledgerwood; Jon Gordon (ss, as); Matt Penman (b); Heinrich Köbberling (d).* 9/97.

***** Transition**

Steeplechase SCCD 31468 *Ledgerwood; Matt Penman (b); Jaz Sawyers (d).* 4/98.

LeeAnn Ledgerwood was first noticed by Marian McPartland and received enthusiastic acclaim for her role on McPartland's *Piano Jazz* radio series in 1990. Buoyed up by that success, Ledgerwood recorded her debut record with a degree more haste and enthusiasm than judgement, for a 1991 Triloka CD which is now deleted. These rather belated follow-ups to the debut are a lot more confident and settled. Gordon was an excellent choice for the horn on the quartet date, smoothly assertive in his solos but conservative enough not to bruise the reflexes of a rhythm section that had already worked together a lot. Ledgerwood doesn't write much – there are a meagre four originals spread over the two discs – and the focus here is on getting a group result. Even so, Ledgerwood's 'Now And Zen' sparks what's perhaps the best performance on that disc, the group gradually raising the intensity until Gordon's alto fireworks seem like a logical outburst. Some of the pieces, such as Wayne Shorter's 'Water Babies', are under-coloured, but it's an assured set.

The trio album isn't quite as convincing. Some of the tracks are too long, such as the smart but overbuilt revision of 'Night And Day'. She does better by the frantic but under-control scamper through McCoy Tyner's 'Four By Five'. Penman and the youthful Sawyers are more than keen in keeping up.

***** Compassions**

Steeplechase SCCD *Ledgerwood (p solo).* 10/98.

*****(*) Paradox**

Steeplechase SCCD 31497 *Ledgerwood; Ron McClure (b); Billy Hart (d).* 4/00.

Ledgerwood takes a chance which doesn't quite come off to her best advantage on her debut as an unaccompanied soloist. Addressing the Coltrane songbook may appeal to questing young minds and fingers, but it's a portentous task, and her conservatory training often gets the better of interpretations which ask for softness and guile as well as rigour. 'Naima' goes well.

She looks like she's had a k d lang makeover for the cover of *Paradox*, and this is a good group. 'Wise One', which meandered on the solo record, is buoyed up by Hart's dramatic percussion and McClure's stentorian lines, and when they move into time, the results are a surprising match of joy and bluesiness. 'India', which comes next, is similarly upbeat, and the good-natured swagger of McCoy Tyner's 'Blues On The Corner' is very likeable. Her best record, with one 'but'. Nils Winther has produced enough piano dates by now to make you think he'd have no problems with a sound-mix, but there's a lack of focus about the piano sound which is surely an engineering problem.

****(*) Walkin' Up**

Steeplechase SCCD 31541 *Ledgerwood; John Graham Davis (b); Brandon Lewis (d).* 9/02.

A disappointingly tepid continuation, and at this point it sounds dangerously like Ledgerwood has not much else to add to the earlier discs. Davis and Lewis are scarcely a match for McClure and Hart, and although the programme is an attractive set of themes from several (jazz) composers, Ledgerwood has very little to add to them which could be called her own.

Mike LeDonne (born 1956)

PIANO

He worked early on as the house pianist at Jimmy Ryan's in New York and played with many of the swing-to-mainstream masters there. Sideman duties include Benny Goodman, Art Farmer, James Moody and Sonny Rollins.

***** 'Bout Time**

Criss Cross 1033 *LeDonne; Tom Harrell (t, flhn); Gary Smulyan (bs); Dennis Irwin (b); Kenny Washington (d).* 1/88.

****(*) The Feeling Of Jazz**

Criss Cross 1041 *As above.* 1/90.

****(*) Common Ground**

Criss Cross 1058 *As above, except omit Harrell and Smulyan.* 12/90.

*****(*) Soulmates**

Criss Cross 1074 *LeDonne; Ryan Kisor (t); Joshua Redman (ts); Jon Gordon (as); Peter Washington (b); Lewis Nash (d).* 1/93.

*****(*) Waltz For An Urbanite**

Criss Cross 1111 *LeDonne; Steve Nelson (vib); Peter Bernstein (g); Peter Washington (b); Kenny Washington (d).* 6/95.

***** To Each His Own**

Double Time DTRCD 135 *LeDonne; Peter Washington (b); Mickey Roker (d).* 1/98.

LeDonne leads some very capable groups here. The first two discs are typical, consistent, slightly soft Criss Cross dates, despite the skilful team involved. Tunes, charts and solos all bespeak an unflagging but rather charmless dedication to hard-bop routine. Four of the themes on the second record are handled by the rhythm section alone, but otherwise there's little to tell the two records apart. *Common Ground* gives LeDonne the spotlight with only bass and drums in support; though the tunes are way out of the ordinary – Wes Montgomery, some rare Ellington – they sound as if they were meant to show off his ingenuity. *Soulmates* is a different matter. Kisor and Redman are an indecently talented front line and they finesse the material to a degree that takes this out of the usual neat-and-tidy session-man bag. Come to that, Gordon is quite up to their level. LeDonne himself doesn't do anything awesomely different from the other records, but it all sounds very accomplished.

Waltz For An Urbanite continues the good form. LeDonne is used to playing alongside vibes after many years with Milt Jackson, and he makes a seamless team with the typically elegant and quick-witted Nelson. His originals have a flavoursome touch – the title-piece is especially smart – and the music as a whole has a sexier, more lilting feel than some of the earlier records. One or two tunes take a longer route than they might have done, but the playing has real sass, and it sustains the disc.

Moving to Double Time, LeDonne turns in another genuine date. Wes Montgomery's 'Movin' Along', an inspired choice, shows how much he can get out of the basic material of the blues. He's never a filigree player, but he rarely wastes a note, and the almost spidery lines he extracts out of this one are compelling to follow as he unfolds them. Roker, less often sighted these days, is a fine choice for the drum role, and Peter Washington is his usual blameless self.

***** Then And Now**

Double-Time DTRCD-153 *LeDonne; Jim Rotondi (t); Eric Alexander (ts); Peter Washington(b); Joe Farnsworth (d).* 12/98.

***** Bags Groove: A Tribute To Milt Jackson**

Double-Time DTRCD-182 *LeDonne; Jim Rotondi (t); Steve Davis (tb); Steve Wilson (as); Jim Snidero (as, f); Steve Nelson (vib); Bob Cranshaw (b); Mickey Roker (d).* 2/01.

LeDonne's albums are becoming generic and predictable, although on their own terms they're pleasing enough. *Then And Now* risks trying Herbie Hancock's 'The Sorcerer', which has increasingly entered the recent jazz repertory, but there's very little magic in this one, and we could surely have done without yet another 'Round Midnight'. That said, the three principal soloists are fair value. The Jackson tribute is something LeDonne (who played with Bags for many years, as did Cranshaw and Roker) is entitled to, but Milton may have put on one of his famous furrowed brows if he listened to the overly complex arrangements. Average.

Jeanne Lee (1939–2000)

VOCALS, SYNTHESIZER

Powerful singer with strong avant-garde pedigree. Her associations cover the whole spectrum of modern improvisation and she's greatly missed.

***** The Newest Sound Around**

RCA 2500 *Lee; Ran Blake (p); George Duvivier (b).* 11–12/61.

This was the beginning of Lee's association with the like-minded Ran Blake, who's been a fellow-student at Bard College. They run a varied programme of material, from 'Summertime', 'Lover Man' and 'Laura' to Terry Jacks's 'Seasons in the Sun' and 'Blue Monk', all done with a cool and thoughtful sound that shouldn't be mistaken for passionless cerebralism. Jeanne's touch on the synthesizer is deft and sparing, and Duvivier makes the ideal third wheel on the date.

****** Natural Affinities**

Owl 3509 *Lee; Leo Smith (t); Mark Whitecage (as); Paul Broadnax, Amina Claudine Myers (p, v); Gunter Hampel (vib); Jerome Harris (g); Lisle Atkinson, Dave Holland (b); Newman Baker (d).* 92.

This is a wonderful set and the best place to sample Lee's strong, warm voice, especially if you've only ever heard her as a second or third horn on an avant-garde set. The opening 'Mingus Meditations' is a curious piece, with Lee reciting from *Beneath The Underdog*. Elsewhere she shifts from relatively abstract and free-form ideas to fairly straightahead standards. There's not much apparent swing to her singing, but listen closely and it has a low, slow pulse that is infectious and engaging. The personnel is extraordinary and fans of Smith, Holland and Myers will be pleased to hear them featured so strongly, even at times competing for attention with Lee herself. Hampel is an old collaborator and another who has chosen his own musical path.

***** After Hours**

Owl 013426-2 *Lee; Mal Waldron (p).* 5/94.

***** Travelling In Soul Time**

BvHaast 13214 *As above; add Toru Tenda (f).* 95.

Lee's horn-like delivery is ideally suited to sets like these, more abstract than Waldron liked to get in later years, but still very much in his deep-blue mode. *After Hours* is actually quite conventional, a standards session on which Lee does little more than sing the songs. Her only real improvisation is a wordless scat on 'Fire Waltz'. The other disc is more searching. Tenda makes some effective contributions, but it really is the interplay between voice and piano that makes it work.

Michel Legrand (born 1932)

PIANO, ORGAN, VOCAL

Studied at the Paris Conservatoire, then began composing for films in 1957 and has written numerous themes and songs which have entered the jazz repertory. A capable jazz pianist, he has been involved in several major recording projects involving jazz musicians and occasionally works in small-group situations.

****** Legrand Jazz**

Philips 830074-2 *Legrand; Miles Davis, Ernie Royal, Art Farmer, Donald Byrd, Joe Wilder (t); Frank Rehak, Billy Byers, Jimmy Cleveland, Eddie Bert (tb); Jimmy Buffington (frhn); Gene Quill, Phil Woods (as); Ben Webster, John Coltrane, Seldon Powell (ts); Jerome Richardson (bs, bcl); Teo Macero (bs); Herbie Mann (f); Bill Evans, Hank Jones, Nat Pierce (p); Eddie Costa, Don Elliott (vib); Betty Glamann (hp); Major Holley (b, tba); Paul Chambers, George Duvivier, Milt Hinton (b); Don Lamond, Kenny Dennis, Osie Johnson (d).* 6/58.

***** Paris Jazz Piano**

Emarcy 548148–2 *Legrand; Guy Pedersen (b); Gus Wallez (d).* 59.

*****(*) After The Rain**

Original Jazz Classics OJC 803-2 *Legrand; Joe Wilder (t, flhn); Phil Woods (as, cl); Zoot Sims (ts); Gene Bertoncini (g); Ron Carter (b); Grady Tate (d).* 5/82.

Legrand's name is so widely known as a pop composer that his jazz leanings are largely ignored. But this small discography is worth much more than a passing look. The sessions for the *Legrand Jazz* album are uniquely star-studded, and the quality of the writing matches up to the cast-list. Legrand chose many unexpected tunes – including ancient history such as 'Wild Man Blues', as well as the more predictable 'Nuages' and 'Django' – and recast each one in a challenging way. 'Night In Tunisia' is a controlled fiesta of trumpets, 'Round Midnight' a glittering set-piece for Davis, 'Nuages' a sensuous vehicle for Webster. The latter is placed alongside a trombone section in one of the three groupings devised by the arranger; another is dominated by a four-man trumpet group. The third has the remarkable situation of having Davis, Coltrane and Evans as sidemen, playing Fats Waller and Louis Armstrong tunes. Many of the arrangements are tellingly compact, seven not even breaking the four-minute barrier, and it ends on a *fast* treatment of Beiderbecke's 'In A Mist'.

Legrand the pianist was featured on the sessions which are here reissued as *Paris Jazz Piano*. The ten tunes are all with Paris in mind, hence such obvious blooms as 'La Vie En Rose' and 'The Last Time I Saw Paris'. Legrand tends to show off his Peterson stylings, and some of it is far too grandiose, but the music does seem to give off an authentic whiff of its locale, and it's *charmant*.

After The Rain, which dates from much later and long after Legrand had made his fortune, was done almost off the cuff and stands as a ballad album. The group works casually through six lesser-known Legrand tunes, yet the playing by the three front-liners is so exquisitely done that the music glows. 'Nobody Knows', in which Sims and Woods luxuriate through the lovely chords as if taking a bath in them, is an impromptu classic.

***(*) Legrand Grappelli

Verve 517028-2 *Legrand; Stéphane Grappelli (vn); Marc Michel (b); André Ceccarelli (d); strings.* 92.

*** L' Douce France

Verve 529850-2 *Legrand; Stéphane Grappelli (vn); Marc-Michel LeBevillon (b); Umberto Pagnini (d); strings.* 8–10/95.

Grappelli loved these records, which were among his last, and both he and Legrand had reason to be proud of the collaboration. Steph plays the jazz while Michel sets the most gorgeous, chocolate-box arrangements he can think of to swirl around the violin. Lots of sugar, spiced just a little by the wilier aspects of each man's art; when they do such Gallic heart-tuggers as 'La Vie En Rose' or 'Je Tire Ma Révérence', dry eyes are at a premium. The first set edges ahead for having the best of Legrand's own tunes.

*** Big Band

Verve 538937-2 *Legrand; Claude Egéa, Christian Martinez, Jean-Claude Verstraete, Stéphane Belmondo, Philippe Slominsky (t); Denis Leloup, Jacques Bolognesi, Christian Guizien, Maurice Cevrero (tb); Harvé Meschinet, François Théberge, Guillaume Naturel, Lionel Belmondo, Jean-Pierre Solves, Michel Goldberg, Claudio de Queiros (saxes); Marc-Michel LeBevillon (b); Umberto Pagnini (d).* 2/95.

Plenty of old pros in this band – followers of Claude Bolling's music will recognize many of his sidemen – and although there are two 'new' originals, mostly it's some of Michel's greatest hits that they're set to work on. Legrand didn't go for obvious retreads, though: 'I Will Wait For You' is peppered with funky trombones; 'You Must Believe In Spring' is a bass feature; 'Windmills Of Your Mind' is recast as the 'Warsaw Concerto'. Hard to tell, at times, if Legrand is merely kidding expectations or banging his composer's drum. In the end, entertaining but lightweight.

Peter Leitch (born 1944)

GUITAR

Drawing on every available aspect of the guitar tradition, Leitch is a smooth and accomplished performer whose very facility sometimes disguises the sophistication of what he is doing. Easy in the studio, he has created a substantial body of recorded work.

***(*) Red Zone

Reservoir RSR CD 103 *Leitch; Pepper Adams (bs); Kirk Lightsey (p); Ray Drummond (b); Marvin 'Smitty' Smith (d).* 11/84–7/88.

*** Exhilaration

Reservoir RSR CD 118 *Leitch; Pepper Adams (bs); John Hicks (p); Ray Drummond (b); Billy Hart (d).* 11/84–12/88.

*** On A Misty Night

Criss Cross Criss 1026 *Leitch; Neil Swainson (b); Mickey Roker (d).* 11/86.

***(*) Portraits And Dedications

Criss Cross Criss 1039 *Leitch; Bobby Watson (as); Jed Levy (afl); James Williams (p); Ray Drummond (b); Marvin 'Smitty' Smith (d).* 12/88–1/89.

A glance at the personnel on Leitch's records gives a quick summary of his standing in the jazz community. One moment the young guitarist was hacking a living in his native Canada, the next – or so it seemed – he was pumping out a steady flow of top-flight jazz albums. In a recording career stretching back to the mid-'80s, Leitch has evolved from an essentially horn-based style to a much more guitaristic (his own word) approach. The tracks with Pepper Adams on the November 1984 session worked because of the degree of separation between the baritone and Leitch's own lines. A couple of duos with Drummond explore a similar contrast. Hicks and Lightsey are both quite dominant, dark-toned piano players, and that contributed to the overall feel of these sessions.

When he came to Criss Cross, Gerry Teekens gave him the breadth and leeway he wanted to make swinging but intelligent records which refused to sit neatly in any currently agreed niche. *On A Misty Night* betrays some signs of having been his debut. Leitch tries to pack in too much and falls rather flat, caught between opposites rather than using them to fuel one another. Leitch has, though, always known what he wants. The change of emphasis on *Portraits And Dedications* was quite striking. It would be difficult to imagine a saxophonist who sounds less like Pepper Adams than Bobby Watson, and the switch to James Williams marked a clear recognition that Leitch was increasingly capable of sustaining a broader, self-accompanied sound, the very thing that seemed lacking on the first Reservoir's solo tracks. Jed Levy's alto flute is used very sparingly on *Portraits*, for the softly romantic 'Visage De Cathryn' and 'Portrait Of Sylvia'. His moment was to come later.

*** Duality

Reservoir RSRCD 134 *Leitch; John Hicks (p); Ray Drummond (b); Marvin 'Smitty' Smith (d).* 7/93.

*** A Special Rapport

Reservoir RSRCD 129 *Leitch; John Hicks (p).* 6/94.

Leitch gets on well with Hicks, and both these discs are full of appeal. The quartet date sometimes settles down too comfortably, though one can hardly blame Leitch for enjoying his surroundings, and in a medley of Strayhorn tunes the music reaches a peak of gentle but firm lyricism. In the pure duo situation, there's the same sageness of utterance and fertility of invention, although again there's a sense that the two men are basking in their abilities rather than going so far as to actually push each other. To that extent, the records don't compel the same attention. But they're equally hard to resist.

***(*) **Colours And Dimensions**

Reservoir Music RSRCD 140 *Leitch; Claudio Roditi (t); Gary Bartz (as); Jed Levy (ts); John Hicks (p); Rufus Reid (b); Marvin 'Smitty' Smith (d).*

Elegant and tasteful jazz from what sounds like a very settled group. Bartz is in excellent form, hot, intense and bluesy. 'Bluesview' is magnificent and 'Round Lake Burnt Hills' highlights the leader's smoothly elegant approach, with the big Zoller guitar ringing and singing in every chorus.

***(*) **Up Front**

Reservoir RSRCD 149 *Leitch; Sean Smith (b); Marvin 'Smitty' Smith (d).* 96.

***(*) **Blues On The Corner**

Reservoir RSRCD 160 *Leitch; Bobby Watson (ss, as); Renee Rosnes (p); Dwayne Burno (b); Billy Hart (d); Kendra Shank (v).* 97.

By this stage in the game, Leitch is such a reliable commodity that it is difficult to make meaningful distinctions between his records; they sound like an ongoing session with a steady procession of guests. Watson's plangent approach is even better suited to this material than is Bartz, and on 'The Hillary Step', 'Wendy's Shoes' and the title-piece he is magisterially good.

The trio album is an all-too-rare opportunity to hear Leitch out on his own, with just rhythm. 'You're My Everything' and 'Sea Change' are noteworthy for the interplay of guitar and percussion, underlining Leitch's strong rhythmic instincts. As a showcase for a quiet and understated talent, it comes highly recommended.

John/Jennifer Leitham (born 1953)

BASS

As album titles have tended to trumpet, Leitham is a left-handed bassist, based in California. The major gig in the '80s and '90s was in the trio backing Mel Torme. A straightahead player with a big sound.

*** **Live!**

CARS CP 0020 *Leitham; Pete Christlieb, Rickey Woodard (ts); Shelly Berg (p); Joe LaBarbera (d).* 3/97.

A gifted and exceptionally skilful player, Leitham is one of those mercurial session players who have been filling West Coast studios for the past 40 years. Earlier discs for USA seem to be in the dead-letter office for now. This live album is familiar stuff: Christlieb and Woodard have at it for an hour's worth of virile and often exciting blowing. There's little in it if you're looking for the winner out of the two horns; both play it big and hearty. Lots of bass features and Leitham gathers in a solo *arco* piece as well. Since this recording was made, John has become Jennifer Leitham.

Gary Le Mel

VOCALS

Originally a movie executive, responsible for the soundtracks for such various films as A Star is Born (the Streisand one), St Elmo's Fire and The Bodyguard, Le Mel has also recorded in his own right.

*** **The Best Of Times**

Concord CCD 2196 *Le Mel; Chris Botti, Lew Soloff (t); Jim Pugh (tb); Bob Sheppard (ss); Lawrence Feldman, Dave Tofani (af); Roger Rosenberg (bcl); Charles MacCracken (bsn); Roger Kellaway (p); Gregg Magniafico, Jon Werking (syn); Steve Carnelli, Steve Khan (g); John Beal, Lincoln Goines (b); Elvin Jones (d); Paulinho Da Costa, David Perullo (perc); Paula Cole (v); strings.* 03.

Le Mel is an able and expressive singer but there is nothing here to match the quality of his earlier work for Atlantic, discs like *Romancing The Screen* and *Moonlighting*. The programme is fairly predictable – 'I'm Old Fashioned', 'Skylark', 'Call Me Irresponsible' (with Paula Cole) and 'My Foolish Heart' – but the orchestrations by Roger Kellaway are good and Le Mel has enough clout to assemble a band that includes Elvin Jones.

Brian Lemon (born 1937)

PIANO

This stalwart of the British scene grew up in Nottingham and first came to prominence in the legendary group fronted by Sandy Brown and Al Fairweather. He has often worked as a jobbing sideman, often accompanying visiting Americans; with the advent of the Zephyr label he has also emerged – belatedly – as a regular recording star, often sharing billing with horn players.

*** **But Beautiful**

Zephyr ZE CD 1 *Lemon; Dave Cliff (g); Dave Green (b); Allan Ganley (d).* 1 & 3/95.

(*) **A Beautiful Friendship

Zephyr ZE CD 4 *Lemon; Warren Vaché (c); Roy Williams (tb); Dave Cliff (g); Dave Green (b); Martin Drew, Allan Ganley (d).* 2/95.

*** **How Long Has This Been Going On?**

Zephyr ZE CD 5 *As above, except omit Vaché, Drew; add Scott Hamilton (ts).* 8/95.

The answer to the third of these is: six decades now, or four at least as an active musician. Lemon is a stalwart of the British scene, a figure easily overlooked only because he seems always to have been there, turning out classy, unpretentious jazz with an effortless swing. Appearing on a 1993 Concord disc by American saxophonist Scott Hamilton (whose anglophile stance can be at least partly explained by his enthusiasm for working with Lemon) brought him to the notice of a bigger international audience, but it was the launch of John Bune's lemon-liveried Zephyr label (the only imprint around to give credits for 'benign gophery') that cemented Lemon's class and standing with record-buyers.

The first of the bunch is quality product. The title-track is a model of its kind, and the medley of 'Exactly Like You' and 'I Thought About You' is hard to fault. A version of Sonny Rollins's 'St Thomas' doesn't sit quite as obviously for Lemon's technique but, following as it does the one original on the set, 'Blues For Suzanna', it underlines his other gift, the pacing and direction of a set. The session with Vaché and Roy Williams is a little too polite and matey: 'After you, Claude', 'No, after you, Cecil', as they used to say in ITMA (apologies to non-British readers for a momentary descent into parochialism). However, the brass is nicely recorded and there are splendid readings of 'Moten Swing', 'Up With The Lark' and 'Skylark', further evidence of Lemon's skill in pacing a record. Hamilton makes a big contribution to *How Long?*, smooth, relaxed, but still challenging. The tracks are notably longer here, more stretched out and teasing, and 'Tenderly' is probably the best thing in the catalogue so far.

Other early titles in the Zephyr catalogue feature Lemon's group with star soloists and are listed under their names, trumpeter Derek Watkins, reed maestro Alan Barnes and Vaché again; *A Beautiful Friendship* really belongs in that category as well, but we've made an entirely arbitrary exception – that's the kind of people we are.

*****(*) Old Hands – Young Minds**

Zephyr ZECD 12 *Lemon; Alan Barnes, Gerard Presencer (t); Iain Dixon, Andy Panayi (reeds); Anthony Kerr (vib); Alec Dankworth, Dave Green (b); Clark Tracey (d).* 97.

Though most of the younger players on the roster are associated with a more contemporary approach to jazz, at least two of them – Tracey and Dankworth – have direct blood-ties to the older generation and grew up in the presence of this kind of music. Lemon and Barnes quite properly share the honours between them, but the excitement of the set comes when the two approaches rub up against each other, not aggressively, but with affectionate rivalry.

***** Lemon Looks Back – Just For Fun**

Zephyr ZE CD 14 *Lemon; Roy Williams (tb); Alan Barnes (as, cl); Ken Peplowski (ts, cl); Dave Cliff (g); Dave Green (b); Martin Drew (d).* 4/96.

A relaxed and utterly enjoyable programme of standards, distinguished by an elegant guest-slot from Peplowski, who has been going through a purple patch. Lemon lies back a bit more than usual and leaves much of the running to the horns. Again, though, the pacing of the set is immaculate, with 'When It's Sleepy Time Down South', 'When Your Lover Has Gone' and 'Cottontail' rounding out the album. Not a classic, but a gift for Lemonheads everywhere.

***** Brian Lemon And David Newton**

Zephyr ZECD 20 *Lemon; David Newton (p).* 98.

Once again, Lemon puts himself in the company of a younger player with a very definite stance on the tradition. Newton is an elegant melodist with a deceptively light left hand. However gentle and indefinite the chords might sound at first glance, there is no mistaking how surely Dave constructs a song. Hoagy Carmichael seems an ideal source for them both, and this songbook project will appeal to anyone who cherishes the originals or who simply likes piano jazz.

***** My Shining Hour**

Zephyr ZECD 30 *Lemon; Dave Green (b); Allan Ganley (d).* 12/99–3/00.

After setting him up in many different playing situations, Zephyr ask Lemon for a straightforward trio date. If the results are predictably enjoyable, they are also, of course, predictable. Brian knows all the tunes inside out and isn't shy about introducing wrinkles such as the eventful climax to 'It's Only A Paper Moon', but he's not the kind of player for wholesale revisions and the record does tend to play out in a nice, easygoing and unsurprising way. Sadly, arthritis has all but curtailed this great professional's playing in recent times.

Harlan Leonard (1905–83)

CLARINET, ALTO AND BARITONE SAXOPHONES, BANDLEADER

Leonard was born in Kansas City and took a job with the Bennie Moten band in 1923. He stayed until 1931, joined the Kansas City Sky Rockets, and took that band over in 1934. A new group, Harlan Leonard's Rockets, became the major Kansas City orchestra from 1938 until the mid-'40s, but it broke up in 1945 and Leonard left the music business.

*****(*) Harlan Leonard And His Rockets 1940**

Classics 670 *Leonard; James Ross (t); Edward Johnson, William H Smith (t); Fred Beckett, Walter Monroe, Richmond Henderson (tb); Darwin Jones (as, v); Henry Bridges (cl, ts); Jimmy Keith (ts); William Smith (p); Efferge Ware, Stan Morgan (g); Winston Williams, Billy Hadnott (b); Jesse Price (d); Myra Taylor, Ernie Williams (v).* 1–11/40.

The forgotten men of Kansas City jazz. When Basie left for New York, Leonard's orchestra took over many of the Count's local engagements. But he didn't make many records; all 23 surviving tracks are here, in quite good transfers. It was a good band rather than a great one, lacking something in individuality: some of the tracks are built round the kind of devices which Basie was personalizing to a much greater degree, the section work is occasionally suspect, and the KC rocking rhythm is something they fall back on time and again. But something good is to be found in nearly all these tracks, and some fine soloists, too – Henry Bridges is an outstanding tenorman, Fred Beckett (whom J. J. Johnson admired) a surprisingly agile trombonist, and the trumpets hit the spot whenever they have to. Scholars will prize the six early arrangements by the young Tadd Dameron, an intriguing hint of things to come, and one shouldn't miss the blues-inflected vocals of Ernie Williams, a lighter Jimmy Rushing.

Marilyn Lerner

PIANO

Born in Montreal, Lerner has been a presence on the Candian jazz scene since the early '80s, although few recordings have broken out of local appreciation.

****** Birds Are Returning**

Jazz Focus JFCD 022 *Lerner; Jane Bunnett (ss, f); Yosvanny Terry (as, ts); Javier Falbo (bs); Kieran Overs (b); Dafnis Prieto (d); Carlos Francisco Hernandez Mora, Ogduardo Diaz Anaya, Atonio Martinez Campos, Inor Sotolongo (perc).* 1/97.

Lerner's music demands a far wider hearing than it has so far received. This brilliant collection derives from a project to visit and record with local players in Havana. Unlike most such collaborations, Lerner's material refuses to simply lie back and get inundated with Cuban rhythm and the sunny (and, the less sympathetic might argue, sappy) sweetness of the country's music. While there is much that could be identified as Cuban – hardly avoidable, given the phalanx of local players that appear alongside visiting confederates Kieran Overs and Jane Bunnett – Lerner makes sure that what she wants comes first. The opening 'Runaround' may work off Latin polyrhythms, but the off-kilter melody and simple but dark harmonies are pure Lerner. 'I Loves You, Porgy' is set to a very stately bolero rhythm, fleshed out by thick, swelling chords. None of the original themes seems to fall in quite the place one expects: 'Imogene', set to a pulse that seems to snake alongside the melody, and 'Condensation', with its curious twinning of soprano and baritone, are striking in and of themselves, and the superb playing of the soloists – especially Bunnett and local man Terry – heightens their impact. For Lerner's own best moment, go to the tranquil but haunting 'Say Now Always'.

Elliott Levin (born 1953)

TENOR SAXOPHONE, FLUTE

Born in Philadelphia, his first pro New York gig was in at the deep end: Cecil Taylor at Carnegie Hall! Free jazz saxophone.

*****(*) The Motion Of Emotion**
CIMP #153 *Levin; Akira Ando (clo, b); Dominic Duval (b); Dennis Charles (d).* 6/97.

Levin's loud approach and busking vibrato don't obscure the point that he sometimes puts a humorous skin on his music. The opener is called 'The Psychopathology Of Everyday Life', and there's something a bit whimsical about this gathering of personalities: Charles, the most down-to-earth of free drummers, referees between the groaning sound of the two bassists (and lots of their detail is lost in the mix anyway) while Levin tries to soar above. It is chaotically busy for much of the way when the four of them play together; but two of the six tracks are trios and one is a duet for sax and drums. 'Lady Lord's Audacious Space' is a majestic parading of arpeggios. 'Burning Flames' is like a New Orleans march, gone sour in the heat. Entertaining.

Jed Levy (born 1958)

TENOR SAXOPHONE

Studied at New England Conservatory, then played with the Jaki Byard and Don Patterson groups. Now works in and around the New York City area.

*****(*) Sleight Of Hand**
Steeplechase SCCD 31383 *Levy; George Colligan (p); Ron McClure (b); Gerry Gibbs (d).* 11/95.

*****(*) Round And Round**
Steeplechase SCCD 31529 *Levy; Bill Gerhardt (p); Mike McGurk (b); Jeff Brillinger (d).* 3/02.

Very impressive and about as inventive a departure from the standard tenor-and-rhythm conventions as one can hope for. Levy's broad-shouldered tone and confident delivery give him the kind of full-on swing one associates with an earlier generation, but he's soaked in bebop and hard-bop practice. The superfast title-track and the closer, a recasting of the 'Cherokee' chords, show off his chops without just showing off. 'Three And Me' is an ingenious use of 3/4 and it's the setting for a quite extraordinary solo by Colligan, who takes the McCoy Tyner method to its limit here. Colligan is as imposing as Levy himself, with his playing on 'Nice And Easy' (a clever choice of standard) as humorous as it is inventive. McClure is his usual tower of strength and Gibbs is marvellously fluent and powerful. This is a great band and they change setting and pace throughout with no loss of interest: there's a bit of a dead spot in the middle with the long and uneventful 'Desert Church', but otherwise it's a first-class session.

The belated follow-up is just as good. The rhythm section aren't as well-known but they do just fine; the tunes are another largely familiar group (he even has another go at 'Cherokee'). Jed's playing, though, is again tremendous. He powers through themes and solos in a way which ought to seem bland, in terms of the steely confidence of the execution, yet it's nothing but full-throated enjoyment. The sort of record which empowers the jazz-repertory tradition without troubling to make any statements at all.

Lou Levy (1928–2001)

PIANO

Lou's credits would occupy many pages, but the Chicagoan's most important associations were as accompanist to Ella Fitzgerald, Peggy Lee and other singers.

***** Jazz In Hollywood**
Original Jazz Classics OJCCD 1890 *Levy; Harry Babasin (b); Larry Bunker (d).* 9/54.

***** Solo Scene**
RCA 1267 *Levy (p solo).* 2/56.

*****(*) Jazz In Four Colors**
RCA 1319 *Levy; Larry Bunker (vib); Leroy Vinnegar (b); Stan Levey (d).* 56.

***** A Most Musical Fella**
RCA 1491 *Levy; Max Bennett (b); Stan Levey (d).* 11/56, 1/57.

***** My Old Flame**
Fresh Sound FSRCD 154 *Levy; Fred Atwood (b); John Dentz (d).* 78.

Apart from 1952 to 1954, which he spent away from music, Lou's diary must have been stuffed. 'The kid's got ears' was the verdict of many a singer, and the title of one of his best-known albums, treasured by jazz piano fans. What was odd was that said ears were never quite aligned in the normal way. Levy was always looking for angles, tinkering with the changes. There's huge variety in these outwardly straightforward sets and it's difficult to offer more than a notional steer to those who want to sample Lou's art. Indeed, some of his best work can be found on his loyal mate Levey's *Stanley The Steamer*, which used to be on Affinity. In its absence, *Jazz In Four Colors* is the best bet, though it's as well to catch him in accompanist role as well. Influenced by Tatum and Bud Powell, with a fleet delivery and an oddly jangled approach to a solo, he was a most musical fella.

George Lewis (1900–68)

CLARINET

One of the great primitives of early and classic jazz, Lewis had a raw and untutored tone and an impassioned, technically unembellished approach to soloing. Lewis was very much part of the postwar revival in traditional jazz and in later years became an indefatigable touring artist, bringing his vision of New Orleans jazz to Europe and Japan.

*****(*) And His New Orleans Stompers: Volume 1**
American Music AMCD 100 *Lewis; Avery 'Kid' Howard (t); Jim Robinson (tb); Lawrence Marrero (bj); Sidney Brown (bb); Chester Zardis (b); Edgar Moseley (d).* 5/43.

****** And His New Orleans Stompers: Volume 2**
American Music AMCD 101 *As above, except omit Brown.* 5/43.

****** George Lewis With Kid Shots**
American Music AMCD 2 *Lewis; Bunk Johnson, Louis 'Kid Shots' Madison (t); Jim Robinson (tb); Lawrence Marrero (bj); Alcide 'Slow Drag' Pavageau (b); Baby Dodds (d).* 7 & 8/44.

****** Trios & Bands**
American Music AMCD 4 *Lewis; Avery 'Kid' Howard, Louis 'Kid Shots' Madison (t); Jim Robinson (tb); Lawrence Marrero (bj); Ricard Alexis, Alcide 'Slow Drag' Pavageau, Chester Zardis (b); Baby Dodds, Edgar Moseley (d).* 5/45.

***** At Herbert Otto's Party**
American Music AMCD 74 *Lewis; Herb Morand (t); Jim Robinson (tb); Albert Burbank (cl); Lawrence Marrero (bj); Alcide 'Slow Drag' Pavageau (b); Albert Jiles, Bob Matthews, Joe Watkins (d).* 11/49.

***** At Manny's Tavern, 1949**
American Music AMCD 85 *Lewis; Elmer Talbert, Johnny Wiggs (t); Lawrence Marrero (bj, g); Alcide 'Slow Drag' Pavageau (b); Joe Watkins (d).* 49.

Rarely has a traditional jazz musician been documented on record in so concentrated a way as clarinettist George Lewis was in the early '50s. American Music's patient documentation, which now extends beyond the capacity of this listing, even gives street numbers and times of day for the earliest material here. Having been coaxed out of a 'retirement' working as a dockhand at the start of the war, Lewis was by the mid-'50s the surviving pillar of 'serious' revivalism, which he'd helped kick off with Bunk Johnson, working what looked like a politician's itinerary across the United States; Johnson is featured on three tracks of the early *With Kid Shots* compilation.

The early material is absolutely pristine and comes across on CD with remarkable freshness. The first tracks on Volume 1 of the 1943 material were recorded in the drummer's house and, though they're more raggedy than the later sessions at the Gypsy Tea Room (high-point: two takes each of 'Climax Rag' and 'Careless Love'), they provide an excellent starting-point for serious examination of this remarkable musician. Lewis's solo breaks are oddly pitched (and there are a couple where this might be down to tape yaw) but the pitching remains consistent relative to other players so it has to be considered an idiosyncrasy rather than poor articulation. The *Trios & Bands* compilation includes some second takes from the group sessions with 'Shots' (including a marvellous second try on 'San Jacinto Blues' and the first, presumably rejected, take of 'High Society'). He was apparently unhappy about the quality of some of the performances and asked to make some more discs with just banjo and bass. These contain some of his best-ever improvisations, all delivered in that plaintive, singing style that is among the most imitated of jazz sounds. The bounce and economy of 'Ice Cream' and the brief, gentle optimism of 'Life Will Be Sweeter' contain in four minutes the essence of Lewis's music: clear melodic statement, rhythmic simplicity and straightforward emotion.

The live material from Manny's is all previously unissued. It's pretty raw fare, but interesting to hear Lewis on alto saxophone as well as his familiar clarinet and the versions of 'Weary Blues', 'Tishomingo Blues' and 'None Of My Jelly Roll', the last of which has an unfettered vocal by Talbert, are all worth having, and not just obscure collector's items.

***** Jazz Band Ball**
Good Time Jazz GTCD 12005 *Lewis; Elmer Talbert (t); Jim Robinson (tb); Alton Purnell (p); Lawrence Marrero (bj); Alcide 'Slow Drag' Pavageau (b); Joe Watkins (d).* 6/50.

Not strictly a Lewis record, and not, as sometimes hinted, documentation of a single evening. Nevertheless, this affords a valuable opportunity to hear Lewis in company with bands led by trombonists Turk Murphy and Kid Ory, and cornetist Pete Daily, thus providing a clear diagnostic section of what was going on in revivalist jazz between the end of the war and 1950, when the Lewis tracks were recorded. Talbert is a surprise, a little-recorded player with a fine individual tone and some interesting ideas to contribute on 'Willie The Weeper', where he keeps his main influence firmly in view.

*****(*) George Lewis With Red Allen**
American Music AMCD 71 *Lewis; Alvin Alcorn (t); Henry 'Red' Allen (t, v); Bill Matthews, Jim Robinson (tb); Lester Santiago (p); Lawrence Marrero (bj); Alcide 'Slow Drag' Pavageau (b); Paul Barbarin (d).* 8/51.

It's very rare that anyone catches American Music out in an error, but the Alcide Marrero playing bass on these tracks has to be old 'Slow Drag' Pavageau, who is listed for one session and garbled for the other. Nor would we accuse the label of short measure, but Allen fans should be aware that he appears on only five tracks, albeit five excellent ones. 'Hindustan' and the two versions of 'St James Infirmary' are up with the trumpeter's best recorded work and, if Lewis sounds a little shadowed, he makes up for it later (presumably) that same day with Alcorn. These are studio recordings, a little boxy but not unpleasantly so, and the quality of the music – other highlights include 'Bourbon Street Parade' and 'Who's Sorry Now', taped a fortnight later – more than makes up for any technical deficit.

CORE COLLECTION

*****(*) Jazz In The Classic New Orleans Tradition**
Original Jazz Classics OJC 1736 *Lewis; Alvin Alcorn (t); Bill Matthews (tb); Alton Purnell, Lester Santiago (p); Lawrence Marrero (bj); Alcide 'Slow Drag' Pavageau (b); Paul Barbarin (d).* 8/51–9/53.

This involves bandleader and drummer Paul Barbarin, a nearly exact New Orleans contemporary of Lewis, and one of the great originals in the music. The band is familiar enough by now, and the ability to extract the maximum expression from the most minimal of settings has rarely been better documented than here, coupled to an above-average standard

of recording. Heard side by side, Lewis and Barbarin underline many of the contradictions that underlay the revivalist movement. To a degree it was exploitative and naïve, as the blues boom of the '60s was to be, but it was also a living source, and few were as angrily in thrall to its political dimensions as Barbarin. Utterly obsessed, where Lewis was innocently untroubled (and thus manipulable), about the status of black musicians, Barbarin dropped dead on his first appearance at the hitherto segregated Proteus parade; Lewis beat him to the farm by a mere two months.

***** At The Municipal Auditorium, Congo Square**
American Music AMCD 47 *Lewis; Percy Humphrey, Albert Walters (t); Jim Robinson (tb); Alton Purnell (p); Lawrence Marrero (bj); Alcide 'Slow Drag' Pavageau (b); Louis Barbarin, Joe Watkins (d).* 9/51, 9/52.

The Congo Square material, recorded in New Orleans despite one recent critic's exuberant assumption that Lewis had taken the music 'back to Africa', is all pretty *comme il faut* for this period. The main interest here is that the personnel is slightly different, with Humphrey in for Kid Howard and Walters adding a second horn on the 1952 date. There are better recordings and there are certainly worse ones. These guys played together thousands of times and with pretty much the same repertoire. On some of them, we suspect boredom took over.

*****(*) The George Lewis Ragtime Band Of New Orleans: The Oxford Series – Volume 1**
American Music AMCD 21 *Lewis; Percy G. Humphrey (t); Jim Robinson (tb); Alton Purnell (p); Lawrence Marrero (bj); Alcide 'Slow Drag' Pavageau (b); Joe Watkins (d).* 52.

*****(*) The George Lewis Ragtime Band Of New Orleans: The Oxford Series – Volume 2 (Concert, First Half)**
American Music AMCD 22 *As above.* 52.

*****(*) The George Lewis Ragtime Band Of New Orleans: The Oxford Series – Volume 3 (Concert, Second Half)**
American Music AMCD 23 *As above.* 52.

***** The George Lewis Ragtime Band Of New Orleans: The Oxford Series – Volume 4 (Recording Session)**
American Music AMCD 24 *As above.* 3/53.

****(*) The George Lewis Ragtime Band Of New Orleans: The Oxford Series – Volume 5 (Concert, First Half)**
American Music AMCD 25 *As above.* 3/53.

***** The George Lewis Ragtime Band Of New Orleans: The Oxford Series – Volume 6 (Concert, Second Half)**
American Music AMCD 26 *As above.* 3/53.

***** The George Lewis Ragtime Band Of New Orleans: The Oxford Series – Volume 7 (Concert, First Half)**
American Music AMCD 27 *As above.* 3/53.

***** The George Lewis Ragtime Jazz Band Of New Orleans: The Oxford Series – Volume 8 (Concert, Second Half)**
American Music AMCD 28 *As above.* 3/53.

****(*) The George Lewis Ragtime Jazz Band Of New Orleans: The Oxford Series – Volume 9 (Church Service, Rehearsal And Party)**
American Music AMCD 29 *As above.* 3/53.

****(*) The George Lewis Ragtime Jazz Band Of New Orleans: The Oxford Series – Volume 10 (Party)**
American Music AMCD 30 *As above.* 3/53.

***** The George Lewis Ragtime Jazz Band Of New Orleans: The Oxford Series – Volume 11 (Concert – First Half)**
American Music AMCD 31 *As above.* 3/53.

****(*) The George Lewis Ragtime Jazz Band Of New Orleans: The Oxford Series – Volume 12 (Concert – Second Half)**
American Music AMCD 32 *As above.* 3/53.

***** Bands, Trios, & Quintets**
American Music AMCD 41 *As for the above; some other personnel.* 53, 54, 55.

In 1952, Lewis was recorded by the American Folklore Group of the English department at Miami University, an institution rather confusingly situated in Oxford, Ohio. The 'Oxford Series' CDs are well mastered and sound amazingly fresh for recordings five decades old. Lewis made a studio recording of seven quite extended pieces, including a long 'Tin Roof Blues' (on which Humphrey makes his presence felt) and a rousing 'Saint' to finish. The subsequent concert discs are better still, with excellent performances of Lewis staples like 'Over The Waves', 'Darktown Strutters' Ball' and 'Careless Love', closing with a vintage 'Sheikh Of Araby'. It seems unlikely that anyone other than stoneground experts will want to have the later rehearsal and party volumes, though these contain some of the most unfettered playing in the set. The concert of 21 March on Volumes 7 and 8 is superior to that of the day before only because the band now sounds played in and relaxed. Lewis is soloing well and Howard plays with great dexterity on 'Glad When You're Dead, You Rascal You'. The sound may also be a shade brighter in places, though that is probably a function of Lewis lifting his enunciation to compensate for a generally more buoyant ensemble. Purely as an experiment, it's fascinating to listen to this material continuously from start to finish. There are literally dozens of tiny changes of inflexion and emphasis (countless fluffs and missed cues, too, which might be overlooked on a more casual listen), but also a growing sense that the presumed spontaneity and freshness of this music are actually much less than its advocates might like to think. Lewis is prone to fall back on a set of stock phrases (though Howard is not) and there are very few real surprises. A double-CD of the very best performances would be welcome, particularly now that the series has been extended further, though discs 1–3 will already suffice for most tastes.

****** Jazz Funeral In New Orleans**
Tradition 1049 *Lewis; Avery 'Kid' Howard (t, v); Jim Robinson (tb); Alton Purnell (p, v); Lawrence Marrero (bj); Alvide Pavageau (b); Joe Watkins (d); Monette Moore (v).* 10/53.

**** Hello, Central, Give Me Doctor Jazz**
Delmark DE 201 *As above.* 53.

A classic New Orleans record and one of the best albums in Lewis's enormous catalogue, *Jazz Funeral* should be a building block in any decent jazz library. It's not entirely clear why the record bears this rather mournful title, since most of the music is decidedly upbeat and only the slow version of 'Just A Closer Walk With Thee' would be associated with a burial. What's exceptional about this album is that everyone seems to be in top form, with sparkling solos right through the band and tight, well-marshalled ensembles. The opening 'Ice Cream' sets things off in great style. 'Doctor Jazz' and 'When The Saints Go Marching In' are exemplary. George's clarinet is clearly pitched and in tune with everyone else, which isn't always the case at this vintage. We can't fault it. By way of contrast, the Delmark disc is a mess, and it's mystifying how knowledgeable label owners and critics should have been hypnotized by so much sub-standard Lewis. Indeed, the market is flooded with very indifferent and in some cases downright bad performances, many of them shambolic and out of tune. This is one of those: *caveat emptor.*

***** Second Bakersfield Concert 1954**

Storyville 6034 *Lewis; Avery 'Kid' Howard (t, v); Jim Robinson (tb); Alton Purnell (p, v); Alcide 'Slow Drag' Pavageau (b); Joe Watkins (d, v).* 2/54.

The repertoire is by now as familiar as the personnel. It remains unclear why some Lewis records are so fetishized, almost as if they were rare survivals from a bygone age. This, at least, captures a band in full flight and song, and George himself sounds in good shape. Highlights are 'Tin Roof Blues' and 'World Is Waiting For the Sunrise'.

***** The George Lewis Ragtime Jazz Band Of New Orleans: The Oxford Series – Volume 13 (Concert – First Part)**

American Music AMCD 33 *Lewis; Avery 'Kid' Howard, Johnny Lucas (t); Jim Robinson (tb); Alton Purnell (p); Alcide 'Slow Drag' Pavageau (b); Joe Watkins (d).* 2/55.

*****(*) The George Lewis Ragtime Jazz Band Of New Orleans: The Oxford Series – Volume 14 (Concert – Second Part)**

American Music AMCD 34 *As above, except add Jan Carroll (bj).* 2/55.

These were the last of Lewis's Ohio stopovers, which had acquired an almost hysterical following. There is certainly no sign of tiredness, either in the formula or in the playing, but larger projects beckoned and, over succeeding years, Lewis was to become an international superstar, albeit a modest and occasionally bewildered one. The later volume is the better of the pair, albeit dominated by Watkins's vocals. 'Loveless Love' is a singing feature for Johnny Lucas, whose lip doesn't seem to have been in the best of order. 'Closer Walk With Thee' and 'Walking With The King' are both magnificent, feeling performances, sacred and profane in near-perfect balance. As always, Barry Martyn gets the sound as good as this sort of thing can get. There are clinkers, mic noises, and assorted shuffles and bumps, but nothing that doesn't positively add to the atmospherics.

****** The Beverley Caverns Sessions**

Good Time Jazz GTCD 12058 *Lewis; Avery 'Kid' Howard (t, v); Jim Robinson (tb); Alton Purnell (p); Lawrence Marrero (bj); Alcide 'Slow Drag' Pavageau (b).* 5/53.

*****(*) Jazz At Vespers**

Original Jazz Classics OJC 1721 *As above.* 2/54.

*****(*) Jazz At Ohio Union**

Storyville STCD 6020/1 2CD *As above.* 3/54.

***** Sounds Of New Orleans: Volume 7**

Storyville SLP 6014 *Lewis; Avery 'Kid' Howard (t); Jim Robinson (tb); Alton Purnell (p); Lawrence Marrero (bj); Alcide 'Slow Drag' Pavageau (b); Joe Watkins (d); Lizzie Miles (v).* 12/53–1/54.

***** George Lewis Of New Orleans**

Original Jazz Classics OJC 1739 *Lewis; Avery 'Kid' Howard, Peter Bocage (t); Jim Robinson, Harrison Barnes, Joe Howard (tb); Alcide 'Slow Drag' Pavageau (b); Baby Dodds (d); Sister Berenice Phillips (v).* n.d.

***** The Fabulous George Lewis Band: Kentucky 1955**

American Music AMCD 39 *Lewis; Avery 'Kid' (t); Jim Robinson (tb); Alton Purnell (p); Lawrence Marrero (bj); Alcide 'Slow Drag' Pavageau (b); Joe Watkins (d).* 55.

***** Doctor Jazz**

Good Time Jazz GTCD 12062-2 *As above, except add Monette Moore (v).* 5 & 10/53.

***** George Lewis In Stockholm, 1959**

Dragon DRCD 221 *Lewis; Avery 'Kid' Howard (t); Jim Robinson (tb); Joe Robichaux (p); Alcide 'Slow Drag' Pavageau (b); Joe Watkins (d, v).* 2/59.

By contrast with the folksy, homely quality of most of his tours, including later ones to the United Kingdom, Lewis's appearances in Scandinavia and in Japan had all the appearance of an imperial progress. What this essentially quiet and modest man could have made of the adulation he received is anyone's guess. It certainly didn't always have a positive effect on his playing. Lewis seemed to strain for volume in larger halls, presumably largely unused to sophisticated amplification, and there are occasions on the otherwise excellent Stockholm disc, too, where he squeaks and overblows.

Lewis's almost studied primitivism and simplicity of tone beguiled even self-consciously sophisticated audiences, who often made the mistake of thinking that Lewis himself was a primitive. So many of these live discs, rough as they are, underline the extraordinary variety and depth of his playing, that disconcerting ability to invest almost subliminal changes of emphasis or diction with a disproportionate significance. The Beverley Caverns record, made in Hollywood, is a good case in point. A now familiar band, hardly a surprise in the set-list, and yet something to listen to and ponder in virtually every chorus. This is easily the most desirable of all the later sessions, and it should be a high priority for anyone who wants to get to grips with Lewis and his music.

The Kentucky set has pretty poor sound, but the playing is pretty much up to scratch and Lewis plays nice solos on 'Wabash Blues' and 'Linger Awhile'.

***** George Lewis And His New Orleans Stompers**

Blue Note 7243 8 21261 2 *Lewis; Avery 'Kid' Howard (t, v); Jim Robinson (tb); Alton Purnell (p); George Guesnon (bj); Alcide 'Slow Drag' Pavageau (b); Joe Watkins (d, v).* 4/55.

Richly textured and thoroughly authentic traditional jazz from a group who could and often did play this material in their sleep. Lewis himself is most impressive on 'Gettysburg March', 'See See Rider' and 'High Society', where the pace and pitching suit his still raw technique. A bywater in Lewis's recorded output, attractive enough in its way, but not a classic.

***** Famous Manchester Free Trade Hall Concert – 1957 – Rehearsal/First Half**

504 Records 50 *Lewis; Ken Colyer (c); Mac Duncan (tb); Ian Wheeler (cl); John Bastable (bj); Ron Ward (b); Colin Bowden (d, wbd).* 57.

***** Famous Manchester Free Trade Hall Concert – 1957 – Second Half**

504 Records 51 *As above.* 57.

***** 1959 – Live In Germany**
504 Records 56 *As above, except add Ray Foxley (p).* 3/59.

***** In Concert 1959 – Manchester Free Trade Hall – Opening House**
504 Records 58 *Lewis; Avery 'Kid' Howard (t, v); Jim Robinson (tb); Joseph Robichaux (p); Alcide 'Slow Drag' Pavageaux (b); Joe Watkins (d, v).* 1/59.

***** In Concert 1959 – Manchester Free Trade Hall – Second House**
504 Records 59 *As above, except add Pete Deuchar (bj).* 1/59.

Nothing cemented Ken Colyer's reputation as the most authentic of all the British revivalists than these stellar meetings with the great Lewis, who was an honoured figure in Europe, and particularly in England and Germany. The sound is somewhat cavernous despite CEDAR remastering and there are some shaky passages on the 1957 set, but the rehearsal tape is a great asset and the playing is fine throughout, though Lewis has articulation problems here and there.

The 1959 date with the Ragtimers was a triumphant return and from the beginning of 'Basin Street Blues' it's clear that the Americans are happy to rest on their laurels and soak up the applause, even for passages which are less than accurate, as during 'Bucket's Got A Hole In It'. These are treasured items for every British jazz collector old enough to remember the gigs or loyal enough to believe that British guys could cut it with the great Americans, but, hand on heart, they're not by any stretch the best representations of Lewis on record. He sounds out of tune more than once, as he was when he played with Papa Bue's band on the same tour.

****(*) With Papa Bue's Viking Jazz Band**
Storyville STCD 6018 *Lewis; Papa Bue Jensen (tb); Bjarne Svarre (cl); Bjarne Liller Petersen (bj); Mogens Seidelin (b); L. B. Linschouw (d).* 3/59.

Whether Lewis simply couldn't be bothered, was tired, or was having articulation problems, these are undistinguished sides and the American is continuously outplayed by the underrated Svarre. The reissue includes some alternates that suggest he wasn't too bothered about varying his approach to solos, either, though the first take of 'Mary Wore A Golden Chain' is lovely and the more musical of the two versions, despite some fluffs.

***** The Spirit Of New Orleans: Volume 1**
Music Mecca CD 1014 *Lewis; Avery 'Kid' Howard (t, v); Jim Robinson (tb); Charlie Hamilton (p); Emanuel Sayles (bj); Alcide 'Slow Drag' Pavageau (b); Joe Watkins (d, v).* 61.

****** Endless The Trek, Endless The Search**
American Music AMCD 59 *Lewis; Kid Thomas (t); Jim Robinson (tb); George Guesnon (bj); John Joseph (b); Cie Frazier (d).* 8–9/62.

*****(*) George Lewis In Japan: Volume 1**
GHB BCD 14 *Lewis; Punch Miller (t); Louis Nelson (tb); Joe Robichaux (p); Emanuel Sayles (bj); John Joseph (b); Joe Watkins (d).* 63.

***** George Lewis In Japan: Volume 2**
GHB BCD 15 *As above.* 63.

***** George Lewis And The Barry Martyn Band**
GHB BCD 37 *Lewis; Cuff Bilett (t); Pete Dyer (tb); Graham Paterson (p); John Coles (bj); Terry Knight (b); Barry Martyn (d).* 3/65.

***** Classic New Orleans Jazz: Volume 1**
Biograph BCD 127 *Lewis; George Blod (t); Jay Brackett (tb); J. R. Smith (tba); Ronnie Bill (bj); Alex Bigard (d).* 4/65.

***** George Lewis With Ken Colyer's Jazzmen**
Lake LACD 27 *Lewis; Ken Colyer (t, v); Geoff Cole (tb); Tony Pyke (cl); Johnny Bastable (bj); Bill Cole (b); Ryan Hetherington (d).* 9/66.

In later life, Lewis was a celebrity, a living link back to the prehistory of the music. As such he toured Japan and Europe, turning up in such unlikely places as the White Horse Inn, Willesden, and the Dancing Slipper, Nottingham, both occasions documented on the GHB set, above.

Endless The Trek, Endless The Search rounds out a session recorded by Ken Mills for Icon. The two new tracks, 'Tiger Rag' and 'Icon Blues', are quite properly given pride of place at the front of the CD, rather than tacked on at the end, and it's difficult to see why they were rejected first time out. This date saw Lewis working with banjoist Guesnon's 'authentic' New Orleans band, an outfit which only deserves the protective quotation marks because by this stage it was almost impossible to gauge what the word meant. The presence of Kid Thomas is a virtual guarantee of unvarnished realism, and Lewis himself plays with a raw and unpolished vigour. The legendary Josiah 'Cie' Frazier occupies the drum chair with his usual poise and confidence, and the sound is very good indeed.

In the autumn of 1963 the Lewis band played more than a hundred concerts during an extended tour of Japan, arriving to a rapturous welcome in August, and leaving on the same flight as the Japanese prime minister, who was travelling to the USA for the funeral of John F. Kennedy. Most of the concerts seem to have been in Osaka, a fanatical jazz centre. No exact date is given, but the big hall was obviously packed. Lewis sounds in excellent form, and only Punch Miller sounds jaded and slow-fingered, though his vocal on 'Sister Kate' (Volume 1) is characteristically vital. More material from the tour is in circulation and should be sampled as and when it becomes available. Lewis, who was in his early 60s by this stage, made little or no attempt to leave hotel rooms, preferring to nap and prepare for these long, carefully staged events. In contrast to the Oxford, Ohio, sessions, these are pure showbiz, but they are no less attractive for that.

His appearance with Ken Colyer's Jazzmen in Manchester over 30 years ago must have seemed a little like the Road to Emmaus for these very purist believers and their fans. It is perhaps ironic that clubs and concert halls in the British midlands and north should have become the last bastions of strict constructionism while players back in New Orleans were beginning to tinker with rock'n'roll. With that in mind, it's easy to see why Lewis became the icon and his work the sacred texts of the revivalist movement, susceptible as both are to myth-making and picayune analysis. Are occasional bent notes the result of carelessness or a gesture of experiment from a seemingly conservative man whose putative conservatism was what made him famous? Were rephrased licks the result of new ideas or, as appears to be the case on 'Walk Through The Streets Of The City' at Beverley Caverns, a combination of faulty memory and fast reflexes? The *Times-Picayune* in his native city became inclined to harshness about Lewis's technical shortcomings in succeeding years, and there is no doubt that constant performance of a severely limited repertoire seriously overstretched his abilities. The life, in a curious way, was always more interesting than the music. Lewis's residency at the Hangover Club in San Francisco was the high-water mark of revivalism, and the many recordings from this period have a joyous optimism which it is hard not to like; even so, it's equally hard to get over-excited about them. Lewis's fame largely depends on his willingness to be cast in a particular role.

***** Reunion With Don Ewell**
Delmark DE 220 *Lewis; Jim Robinson (tb); Don Ewell (p); Cie Frazier (d).* 6/66.

***** A Portrait Of George Lewis**
Lake LACD 50 *As above, except add Lars Edegran (p), Chester Zardis (b), Alex Bigard (d).* 3 & 5/66.

Both discs contain material from a June 1966 high-school gym in Salisbury, North Carolina. There's no overlap, so plenty of motivation to buy the Lake disc as well, which includes eight tracks recorded with Robinson at Preservation Hall in March of the same year. These are pretty standard fare for this vintage and may well be known from earlier Center and Biograph releases; these same labels also covered the Salisbury gig. The unacknowledged star of this late session is drummer Frazier, who died in 1985 and took with him at least some of the secrets of New Orleans drumming. At this age, he wasn't capable of the same flexibility as in his underdocumented youth, and he has cut back on some of the elements of sheer noise (untuned woodblocks, and so on) which were a part of his sound. Ewell is interesting in that he incorporated large elements of Harlem stride into the Morton-influenced New Orleans style that was his basic staple. The hybrid approach is most evident on tracks like 'Yes, Yes, In Your Eyes', one of four numbers here for which alternatives have been included on this CD reissue. Recorded in the high-school gym, it's further testimony to the sheer mileage Lewis put in over the decade, not just abroad, but within the United States as well. Something of a curiosity, this one, but meat and drink to more specialist collectors.

George E. Lewis (born 1952)

TROMBONES, SOUSAPHONE, TUBA, COMPUTER

The Chicagoan taught himself improvisation while still in his early teens by transcribing Lester Young solos for trombone. He later did formal study at Yale, but his real musical education was with the Association for the Advancement of Creative Musicians, whose ethos and aesthetics have remained with him. Lewis is technologically astute, but also profoundly subversive, making music on computer, but also dismantling his horn to get at its spectral sound-colours.

*****(*) Solo Trombone Album**
Sackville SKCD3-3012 *Lewis (tb solo).* 11/76.

****** Shadowgraph, 5 (Sextet)**
Black Saint 120016 *Lewis; Roscoe Mitchell (as, ss, bs, cassette recorder); Douglas Ewart (cl, bcl, sno, f, bsn, cassette recorder, perc); Muhal Richard Abrams, Anthony Davis (p); Leroy Jenkins (vn, vla); Abdul Wadud (clo).* 77.

***** Jila – Save! Mon – The Imaginary Suite**
Black Saint 120026 *Lewis; Douglas Ewart (as, f, perc).* 78.

♛ ** Homage To Charles Parker**
Black Saint 120029 *As above, except add Anthony Davis (p), Richard Teitelbaum (syn).* 79.

It is significant that, as a trombonist growing up in a period marked by the dominance of the saxophone, George E. Lewis should have taken saxophone players as his primary models. His rather emotional *legato* is reminiscent of both Lester Young and, depending on context, virtually all the evolutionary stages of John Coltrane's style. Context is of considerable importance, because Lewis has played in a bewildering variety of musical settings, from relatively conventional section-playing (a brief stint with the mid-'70s Basie band) to technically adventurous free playing. Lewis habitually plays either with intense and surprisingly gentle lyricism or with a deconstructive fury that has led him to dismantle his trombone in mid-performance, producing non-tempered and abstract tones on mouthpiece and slide. He has also taken a close interest in electronics, using computers with increasing technical assurance to provide backgrounds and to create a much-needed dialectical tension in improvised performances.

Lewis's discography as leader is scandalously thin, but the quality is very high indeed. The solo album is a fairly tough listen in places, but it establishes Lewis's deconstructionist approach with a vengeance and the long opening 'Toneburst (Pieces For Three Trombones Simultaneously)' already shows his willingness to embrace technology in the interests of music, something that came through ever more strongly with his use of computers later. *Shadowgraph* and the duos with Ewart are characteristic of the free abstract jazz that emerged out of AACM's explorations in the '60s and early '70s. Listening to them, one is aware how little of this music has been assimilated into the mainstream of either jazz or improvisation. 'Monads' is almost a philosophical primer for free players, an oblique and sometimes violent outburst of sound in which ideas fly around almost too fast to be absorbed. One wonders how it would ever have been possible to assimilate this music in live performance. 'Triple Slow Mix' is a more spacious and accommodating piece, with Abrams and Davis (in opposite channels) suggesting different points of focus for Lewis's gloriously flatulent sousaphone. 'Cycle' recalls the duos, but the real meat of the record is the title-track, part of a series of compositions written by Lewis under a grant from the National Endowment for the Arts. Though the sonic landscape is much more exotic, 'Shadowgraph' is identifiably in the line of one of Ellington's noise pieces. The main soloists are Mitchell and Abrams, with Lewis himself eschewing his synths in favour of an exotic selection of brasses, including Wagner tuba. The tension is almost palpable as potential grooves rise up and are systematically extinguished in a mass of sound that includes cassette players and (from Ewart) incidental percussion of the home-made variety favoured at the time. It's a wonderful record to have back in the lists, but it scarcely reaches the heights of what was to follow.

Ewart is Jamaican-born and 'Save! Mon' is his dedication to the poeple of his homeland. It features him on alto, which is more immediately appealing but less idiomatic and challenging than his work on flute and 'Ewart flutes'. 'Jila' is a more straightforward and expressive piece, indeed unexpectedly so, written as a posy for his daughter. Lewis is much more obviously in command on the two parts of *The Imaginary Suite* included on the record. These are inspired by figures or icons of ancient mythology and some of their modern counterparts; Anthony Braxton may or may not be pleased to learn that 'Charon' is dedicated to him. The addition of electronics greatly expands the available sound-palette and the playing is more expansive and sustained, rather than the staccato, pointillistic approach of the other two pieces. It is in this sense much closer to the blues-tinged world of Lewis's best work, *Homage To Charles Parker*.

The latter represents a further triumphant extension and synthesis of the same basic language premises, combining improvisation with predetermined structures – rather in the manner of Lawrence 'Butch' Morris or pianist-composer Anthony Davis, who plays on the date – and reintroducing a strong programmatic element to abstract music. As he shows in the fine duets with Ewart, using predetermined structures in indeterminate juxtapositions and dynamics can create a music of considerable resonance. 'Homage To Charles Parker' and 'Blues', the two long sides that made up the original LP, are among the most profound and beautiful performances of recent times and certainly rank in the top dozen or so jazz/improvised records made since 1960. Lewis's rather stilted liner-notes somewhat undersell the emotional impact of both pieces. 'Blues' consists of four independent diatonic 'choruses' of absolute simplicity which are played in shifting configurations by the four musicians. Despite the fact that there are no conventional resolutions and no predictable coincidence of material, the piece evokes order as much as freedom. Although none of the material conforms to the blues, its 'feel' is absolutely unmistakable and authentic. If 'Blues' is a triumphant extension of the black tradition in music, 'Homage To Charles Parker' concerns itself intimately with the saxophonist's putative afterlife and musical real-presence. There is a long opening section on electronics, synthesizers and cymbals which evokes Parker's 'reality'. Reminiscent of evocations of primeval Chaos by Marilyn Crispell on *Gaia* (Leo Records) and the electronic composer Bernard Parmegiani, it gradually yields place to a series of apparently discontinuous solos on saxophone, piano and finally with no ensemble backing beyond the synthesizer sounds, which recast and project Parker's life and language. There are no explicit bebop references and, indeed, the piece seems to serve as a healing response to the fractures that separated bop from the earlier history of black American music, of which it was also the apotheosis. The music is calm and almost stately, occasionally suggesting a chorale. Lewis's concluding statements are unbearably plangent but also forceful and intelligent. In their refusal of tragedy, they also have to be seen as political statements. This is an essential modern record.

***** Conversations**

Incus CD 32 *Lewis; Bertram Turetzky (b).* 11/97.

Bert Turetzky is less well known than one of his pupils, Mark Dresser, but much of his personality and artistic presence can be deduced from Dresser's intentness, humour and openness to experiment. *Conversations* is always a discouraging title for an improvised record, suggesting off-the-cuff musings and private dialogues. Nothing of the sort here. Lewis hasn't played such fine trombone – and indeed so much trombone – on record for a while. He deliberately remains in the upper register of his instrument for much of the time, leaving Turetzky to explore the depths. Though the tonality varies little, the pieces are quite different one from the other. 'After Dark' is the only item that wanders off course and, significantly, it's the longest item on a set composed largely of short forms and dedications – to Lester Bowie, more apologetically to Paul Desmond for 'Take One', and to 'The Ecumenical Blues'. A demanding listen, as these things often are, but the sheer musicianship of both participants and the openness of the musical language make it a delightful experience as well.

****** Endless Shout**

Tzadik TZ 7054 *Lewis; John Korsrud, Bill Clark (t); Ralph Eppel, Rod Murray (tb); Brad Muirhead (btb, tba); Mark Nodwell(ss); Saul Berson, Coat Cooke (as, f); Paul Cram, Graham Ord(ts); Vinny Golia (bs, picc); Paul Plimley, Sarah Cahill (p); Ron Samworth (g); Peggy Lee (clo); Paul Blaney, Clyde Reed (b); Dylan Van der Schyff (d); Steven Schick (perc); Quincy Troupe, Kate Hammett-Vaughan (v).* 9/95–11/97.

A beautifully diverse programme of Lewis's work, almost a sampler of his range of interests and achievements, from trombone–computer interactivity to a full-scale performance of one of the 'Shadowgraph' pieces.The title-piece is a four-part piano work, dedicated to Richard Abrams, and a homage to the stride and boogie masters – seeking to 'reinterpret blues utterance in the light of my own experience'. Sarah Cahill gives an eloquent performance. 'North Star Boogaloo' fragments and reshapes a Quincy Troupe poem around a notated percussion part – deft, humorous, vibrant. But the most imposing pieces are a 1997 revision of 'Shadowgraph 4', where Lewis conducts the NOW Orchestra and enables them to pack a tremendous amount into an 11-minute rendition; and a new version of 'Voyager', where the composer-trombonist and his technology explore 'one potential outcome between the improviser and the computer'. A memorable collection altogether.

*****(*) The Shadowgraph Series**

Spool 113 *As above, except add Rob Blakeslee (t), Bruce Freedman (ss); omit Clark, Nodwell, Cahill, Schick, Troupe.* 10/99.

Compared to his previous sightings, this counts as an unprecedented flurry of work by Lewis. Following the single example on the previous disc, here he conducts the NOW Orchestra in the other four 'Shadowgraph' pieces and two other works. As well as conducting, he takes a performing role – memorably so on the ferocious outburst in 'Shadowgraph 3'. While the NOW group is a Canadian ensemble, the sounds and shapes of much of this music are in an almost classic AACM mould, a sharp reconciliation of anarchistic sound, free-jazz extemporizing and sudden swerves into ensemble unity. The Orchestra rise famously to the challenge.

John Lewis (1920–2001)

PIANO

Born in Illinois, Lewis joined the Dizzy Gillespie band in 1946 and became an important figure in the bebop scene. He worked with numerous leaders until a stint with Milt Jackson in 1951 led to the formation of the MJQ, which he was associated with as the pianist and prime composer ever after. Away from the MJQ, he composed several film soundtracks, played Bach, and composed and scored pieces which are a unique blend of classical and jazz sympathies.

****** The John Lewis Piano / Jazz Piano International**

Collectables 6251 *Lewis; Dick Katz, Derek Smith, René Urtreger (p); Barry Galbraith, Jim Hall (g); Percy Heath, Ralph Pena (b); Connie Kay, Al Levitt (d).* 7/56–58.

*****(*) Improvised Meditations And Excursions / Eastern Exposure**

Collectables 6629 *Lewis; Fred Kaz(p); George Duvivier, Percy Heath, Victor Sproles (b); Connie Kay, Roger Wanderscheid (d).* 2/57–3/60.

****** Golden Striker / Jazz Abstractions**

Collectables 6252 *Lewis; Melvyn Broiles, Bernie Glow, Alan Kiger, Joe Wilder (t); Dick Hixson, David Baker (tb); Gunther Schuller, Albert Richman, Ray Alonge, John Barrows (frhn); Eric Dolphy (as, bcl, f); Ornette Coleman (as); Bill Evans(p); Eddie Costa (vib); Joe Hall (g); Harvey Phillips, Jay McAllister (tba); George Duvivier, Scott LaFaro, Alvin Brehm (b); Sticks Evans, Connie Kay (d); Contemporary String Quartet.* 2–12/60.

***** Original Sin / Essence**

Collectables 6605 *Lewis; Nick Travis, Louis Mucci, Freddie Hubbard, Herb Pomeroy (t); Mike Zwerin (tb); Bob SwisshelmBob Northern Gunther Schuller (frhn); Phil Woods (cl); Eric Dolphy (as, af); Harold Jones (f); Benny Golson (ts); William Arrowsmith (ob); Loren Glickman(bsn); Jimmy Giuffre, Gene Allen(bs); Jim Hall, Billy Bean (g); Richard Davis, George Duvivier (b); Connie Kay (d); orchestra.* 3/61–10/62.

***** A Milanese Story / Animal Dance**

Collectables 6253 *Lewis; Albert Mangelsdorff(tb); Bobby Jaspar (ts, f); Davor Kajfes (p); Bosko Petrovic (vib); René Thomas(g); Giovanni Tommaso, Miljenko Pohaska, Jozsef Paradi, Karl Theodor Geier(b); Buster Smith, Silvije Glojnaric (d); Quartetto di Milano.* 1–7/62.

*****(*) The Wonderful World Of Jazz**

Atlantic 90979-2 *Lewis; Herb Pomeroy (t); Gunther Schuller (frhn); Eric Dolphy (as, f); Benny Golson, Paul Gonsalves (ts); Jimmy Giuffre (bs); Jim Hall (g); George Duvivier (b); Connie Kay (d).* 7–9/60.

Lewis made occasional discs under his own name from the mid-'50s. Through the initiative of the American Collectables label, which licenses material from all of the major labels, many of the earlier sets have at last made their CD debut. *The John Lewis Piano* was his 'solo' debut and sets out all his primary concerns in impeccable detail: the blues ('D & E'), the intrigue with the *commedia dell'arte* ('Harlequin'), the refracting of standards through personal sensibility ('Little Girl Blue'), the almost film-score music ('The Bad And The Beautiful'). With a touch as individual as Basie's or Claude Thornhill's, and an ever more careful and considered phraseology, this is swing and bebop distilled down to their most lyrical and refined essences. The slightly later *Improvised Meditations And Excursions* is perhaps not quite as fine, a shade less personal, though even here Lewis makes some marvellous piano jazz out of 'Love Me' and 'Delauney's Dilemma'. The earlier set is coupled with *Jazz Piano International*, which features Dick Katz, Derek Smith and René Urtreger, the second with Fred Kaz's *Eastern Exposure*: minor albums, and in this context no more than nice bonuses to go with the Lewis sets.

Golden Striker indulges his baroque leanings with a set of Lewis tunes arranged for piano and a large brass ensemble: the tone colours are delightful, and 'Piazza Navona' and the reworked 'Odds Against Tomorrow' is gravely beautiful. But the point of this disc is the reissued *Jazz Abstractions*. Lewis doesn't play on this set (he is credited as 'presenter') but it does offer 'new music' by Jim Hall and Gunther Schuller – prime examples of what was once called third stream. Ornette Coleman is set to wail over the four minutes of 'Abstraction' for strings, and there are variations on Lewis's 'Django' and Monk's 'Criss Cross', as well as Hall's 'Piece For Guitar And Strings'. In the past the music received plenty of stick as merely pretentious fusion of a kind, but at this distance it now seems like precious examples of, for instance, Coleman, Dolphy and Scott LaFaro playing on the same sessions.

Original Sin is an orchestral ballet, composed and conducted by Lewis. Very brief, and scarcely sounding like a major work, but charming nevertheless. *Essence* was a showcase for Gary McFarland's charts and compositions, and while Lewis plays on it, it hardly feels like one of his projects. McFarland's music, an idiosyncratic mix of country-boy innocence and metropolitan manners, hasn't endured all that well, but the groups involved play the scores with skill and enthusiasm and there are some arresting moments.

A Milanese Story is a brief film score, where Lewis composes and plays with a Franco–Italian group. 'Winter Tale' and 'Monday In Milan' are typical Lewis European postcards, sweetly performed by a band that mixes strings with Bobby Jaspar. *Animal Dance* has the pianist encountering Albert Mangelsdorff, and this is one occasion where Lewis is definitely in a supporting role: Mangelsdorff plays like a man who's been bursting for the opportunity, and he's all over the likes of 'Autumn Leaves' and 'Set 'Em Up'. With his own catalogue currently in recession, this is one of the best places to hear the trombonist.

The Wonderful World Of Jazz, still separately available on Atlantic, is another great one. It opens with a superb Gonsalves solo on a 15-minute 'Body And Soul' and then works through a short programme of jazz standards, including a new '2 Degrees East, 3 Degrees West'. Newly available on the CD are 'The Stranger', precious for Eric Dolphy's solo, and a long quartet version of 'If You Could See Me Now'; but the whole disc is a thoughtful reflection on the jazz tradition as it was standing in 1960.

***** Mirjana**

Black & Blue 933-2 *Lewis; Christian Escoudé (g); George Duvivier (b); Oliver Jackson (d).* 7/78.

On a French visit, Lewis set down this session, where Escoudé joins in on a few tracks. Pick-up situations don't really suit the pianist and some of this feels either perfunctory or bullied by Duvivier and Jackson, though as always Lewis manages to make a few quieter spaces for himself. Escoudé turns in a great solo on 'La Ronde'.

*****(*) Afternoon In Paris**

Dreyfus 849234-2 *Lewis (p solo).* 11/79.

Lewis's solo albums are never alike. The 1979 session is a very short, almost clipped recital, his favourite themes skimmed through, a series of lightning sketches rather than the full oils of the Emarcy date. Yet there are fascinating revisions, the almost perky 'Django' for one, and a reverent take of Ellington's 'Come Sunday'.

****** Evolution**

Atlantic 7567-83211-2 *Lewis (p solo).* 1/99.

Lewis was one of the last senior survivors of the bebop era, and this marvellous solo album underscores what an extraordinary figure he was in jazz for over 50 years. As a composer, he is mysteriously neglected when it comes to source material for other players, but perhaps only Lewis's Lewis really hits the mark. He revisits five of his own favourites, and each is an affectionate new look at an old friend: 'Django', for instance, is elegantly recast around a left-hand bass that sounds almost like a tango. 'Sweet Georgia Brown' and 'Cherokee' are sketches that suggest a summing-up of both swing and bebop. 'Afternoon In Paris' muses on his lifelong affinity with the old world. Moving yet wonderfully fresh and unaffected, this is a consummate recital by the master.

★★★★ Evolution II

Atlantic 83313-2 *Lewis; Howard Alden, Howard Collins (g); Marc Johnson, George Mraz (b); Lewis Nash (d).* 00.

Hardly any less masterful, generous or absorbing, the second part of what sadly proved to be Lewis's farewell sessions is as fine as the first. Though he has support from other hands here, mostly this is all about what's going on at the piano – and that includes 'One! Of Parker's Moods', his final thoughts on the blues; 'That! Afternoon In Paris', a delightful revision of an old favourite; and another look at 'Django', the tango feel of the previous encounter here cleverly evolved into something else.

Meade Lux Lewis (1905–64)

PIANO, CELESTE, HARPSICHORD

A Chicagoan who made his name in the city, Lewis created a signature-piece in 'Honky Tonk Train Blues' and his teaming with Albert Ammons and Pete Johnson at the 1938 Spirituals To Swing concert at Carnegie Hall started a craze for boogie woogie. Although he worked on until his death, most of his few later recordings suggest a jaded spirit.

CORE COLLECTION

★★★★ Meade Lux Lewis 1927–1939

Classics 722 *Lewis; Albert Ammons, Pete Johnson (p).* 12/27–1/39.

Lewis encapsulated his contribution to jazz in his first three minutes as a soloist with his 1927 Paramount record of 'Honky Tonk Train Blues'. He recorded it again at his second session, and again at his fourth. All three are on this CD, along with 15 other variations on the blues and boogie woogie. His signature-piece remains a marvellous evocation of a locomotive rhythm, perfectly balanced through all its variations, and, if he became tired of it, his listeners never did. It's a pity, though, that it's about the only piece he's much remembered for, since there is plenty more excellent music among his various sessions and this recording brings together much of it.

★★★(★) Meade Lux Lewis 1939–1941

Classics 743 *Lewis; J. C. Higginbotham (tb); Albert Ammons (p); Teddy Bunn (g); Johnny Williams (b); Big Sid Catlett (d).* 1/39–9/41.

★★★ Meade Lux Lewis 1941–1944

Classics 841 *Lewis (p, cel, hpd solo).* 4/41–8/44.

★★(★) The Blues Piano Artistry Of Meade Lux Lewis

Original Jazz Classics OJC 1759 *Lewis (p solo).* 11/61.

His 1936 session for Decca includes two extraordinary pieces on celeste, 'I'm In The Mood For Love' and 'Celeste Blues', and his 1939 session for Blue Note – which supplied the first Blue Note issue, 'Melancholy' and 'Solitude' – opens with a five-part investigation of 'The Blues', all rejected at the time but a remarkable sequence, at least as personal and imaginative as his train pieces. The sound on the CD is frequently muffled, sloppily remastered or otherwise imperfect, but the music is marvellous. There's a modest decline on Classics 743: the 1940 version of 'Honky Tonk Train Blues' goes off at a faintly ludicrous tempo, and some of Lewis's boogie pieces end up as all the same. But three duets with Ammons and the rest of the Blue Note session tracks offer rewards, while the 1939 Solo Art session is mostly at a slow tempo and spotlights Lewis the bluesman to stunning effect. Sound here is far less than ideal once again, though the Blue Note tracks (from an unidentified source) are better, if brittle.

That disc ends on two rather nutty harpsichord solos, and the next one starts with the other two from the same session. A single V-Disc finds Lewis playing piano and celeste simultaneously on 'Doll House Boogie' before nine tracks cut at a date for the Asch label. Again, the fast pieces suggest a sinking into boogie clichés, but there are still some startling things, notably 'Denapas Parade' and above all the previously rejected 'Special No. One', with its melody carried in the left hand. There is yet another 'Honky Tonk Train', and this one is taken at a farcical pace. He must have been fed up with it.

His 1961 Riverside session, now reissued in the OJC series, wasn't a milestone or a major rediscovery. Lewis had clearly grown tired of his own work over the years, and this group of remakes is done professionally, without much joy. He died three years later, following a car accident.

Ramsey Lewis (born 1935)

PIANO, KEYBOARDS

Lewis is comparable to guitarist – later singer – George Benson, a musician whose genuine jazz gift has been at least partly eclipsed by enormous commercial success. The Chicagoan has a deft and understated touch at the keyboard, and echoes of past association with vibist Lem Winchester and master percussionist Max Roach might lie in his softly pattering, often consciously repetitive delivery.

★★★ Down To Earth

Verve 538329-2 *Lewis; Eldee Young (b); Red Holt (d).* 58.

★★(★) Sound Of Christmas

Universal 91566 *As above; add strings, conducted by Abe Meltzer.* 60-61.

★★★(★) In Person, 1960–1967

Chess 051 814 2 2CD *As above, except add Cleveland Eaton (b), Maurice White (d).* 60–67.

★★★(★) The In Crowd

Chess CHD 9185 *As above.* 5/65.

Failure to include Ramsey in some earlier editions has been interpreted as snobbery on the editors' part. Not a bit of it. We are as convinced as any of his greatness. His million-seller, *The In Crowd*, was a remarkable record and one that still repays listening. One suspects that Lewis had himself been listening to it when he decided to turn legit and return to acoustic piano in the '80s. Unfortunately, most of his latter-day material is drab, formulaic funk, sounding like a Herbie Hancock project gone disastrously wrong. These early records are now very curious to place when heard out of context. There is already more than a hint of the smoothed-out funk of later years, and a tendency to build in big show-stopping tunes, like the *Spartacus* theme, or else current pop ('Hang On Sloopy'), but at moments it's difficult to forget, apart from Lewis's characteristic attack, that the soloist isn't Ahmad Jamal. Lewis's happy-clappy soul-jazz is less harmonically resonant, but the connection is there. Though he doesn't seem to have been vocal about it, it would be good to know how many times Miles Davis – who adjudged Jamal a significant performer – had listened to these early records. 'The In Crowd' is still a crowd-pleaser (and also on the Chess compilation), and the trio's version of Duke's 'Come Sunday' should remove any doubts about his jazz credentials but Lewis has perhaps gone too far in the obvious A&R direction and built in too much chart pop, much of it unsuited to piano trio.

The Christmas album – *de rigueur* for successful recording artists at one time – is perfectly jolly. We'd have preferred more trio track and less of the syrupy strings. But there is no doubt that these old tunes come from somewhere deep in Lewis's musical unconscious. He doesn't play them as if they were novelty items but like viable standards.

His gospel roots are most clearly heard on the well-named *Down To Earth*. 'Sometimes I Feel Like A Motherless Child' is played with genuine feeling, and there are moments on the live discs when pomp and 'style' are put aside to permit some unalloyed improvisation. 'Django' is splendid and 'Come Sunday', with its unexpected harmonic shifts, could hardly be bettered.

**(*) Upendo Ni Pamoja

Collectables 6691 *Lewis; Cleveland Eaton (b); Morris Jennings (d).* 72.

Originally recorded for Columbia, and pretty much of its time, this is an attractive but ultimately rather bland trio set that never quite establishes itself. A version of Rodrigo's *Concierto de Aranjuez* and a long version of the title-track take up much of the space, and bassist Eaton's 'Trilogy' consumes much of the rest. Nicely engineered, with good registration of both Steinway and Fender Rhodes pianos, but hardly an important record.

** Funky Serenity

Collectables 6869 *As above, except add Ed Green (vn).* 73.

Produced by Teo Macero. This, we regret to announce, includes a cover of the Moody Blues' end-of-disco smoocher, 'Nights In White Satin', though fortunately it also features an upbeat 'Betcha By Golly Wow!' which almost redeems proceedings. There are lots of lines and riffs worthy of sampling, but as an album this is likely to appeal only to devoted collectors of '70s soul-jazz.

*** Classic Encounter

Columbia MK 42661 *Lewis; Bill Dickens (b); Frank Donaldson (d); Philharmonia Orchestra.* 88.

Easy to dismiss as mere mood music, this orchestral 'encounter' is slightly edgier and less formulaic than expected. James Mack's orchestral arrangements are full and unctuous, but interesting things start to happen when orchestra and trio get together. A version of the 17th-century William Byrd's 'Earl of Salisbury Pavan' is an astonishing *tour de force* and almost sounds like some lost rarity of Latin jazz. A version of Johnny Mandel's 'Time For Love' is very strong, as is 'Spiritual', on which Ramsey finally lets loose his cool, gospelly sound.

***(*) Priceless Jazz

GRP 059 898 2 *As for the above.* 58–95.

It could be that this excellent and thoroughly representative compilation contains all the Ramsey Lewis you'll ever need. 'The In Crowd' is included (of course), as are 'Django' and 'Since I Fell For You'. Of the later material, 'Sun Goddess 2000' from *Between The Keys* is by far the best, the sort of tune Grover Washington used to specialize in and which can warm up the drabbest urban day.

**(*) Appassionata

Narada 47996 *Lewis; Larry Gray (b); Ernie Adams (d).* 99.

A new label and something of a shot-in-the-arm artistically. As often recently, the material is drawn from classical music and opera as much as from jazz and pop. Some of this is cringingly overdone, like the *arco* bass intro to 'Nessun dorma', but some, like the opening version of Fauré's 'Pavane', is arresting, percussive jazz and shouldn't be too quickly dismissed. At 65 Lewis is still capable of surprise, and this retrospective of the tunes that helped shape his passion for music (hence the title) is very revealing.

*** Meant To Be

Narada 50774 *Lewis; Larry Gray (b); Ernie Adams (d); Nancy Wilson (v).* 01.

**(*) Simple Pleasures

Narada 80487 *Lewis; Orbert Davis (t); Kirk Tracy (tb); Steve Eisen (ts, f); Llew Matthews (ky); Henry Johnson (g); Larry Gray (b); Joyce Leon Jr (d); Alejo Poveda (perc); Nancy Wilson (v).* 7/03.

Ramsey and Nancy had recorded together back in the mid-'80s, an album called *Two Of Us*, and met again at the Ravinia Festival, which Lewis directs. These two sets pick up very much where that left off.

Apparently, the session for *Meant To Be* was to have been recorded on 11 September 2001. Whatever impact the events of that day had on the postponed session, it emerges as slick and as unproblematic as anything Ramsey does.

Van Morrison's 'Moondance' is a jazz favourite and in no way strains the credibility of the set. Blossom Dearie's 'Peel Me A Grape' is a more unexpected inclusion – though, coming as it does at the very start of the session, it doesn't intrude unduly. The Hague/Sherman 'Did I Ever Really Live' is a surprise, rarely covered and done here with a melting melancholy, but for the most part this is a rather forgettable set, lacking in substance and too dependent on unfamiliar material, including four of Lewis's own compositions; he may like to believe they are repertory pieces, but they fall some way short of that.

The second album isn't nearly as good. Wilson's approach to the pop idiom of Debarge's 'All This Love' shows her years. The slower tunes are more satisfactory: 'Give Me Something Real' and an unusual reading of 'God Bless The Child' are the tracks to savour. Llew Matthews's horn arrangements are intrusive and frankly dull.

*** Ramsey Lewis's Finest Hour

Verve 543763 *Lewis; various groups as above.* 56–67.

Part of a generously priced compilation series, this offers an introduction to Lewis's most familiar recordings – 'The In Crowd', 'Hi Heel Sneakers', 'Wade In The Water' – without breaking the bank.

Ted Lewis (1890–1971)

CLARINET, VOCAL, BANDLEADER

Born Theodore Leopold Friedman in Circleville, Ohio, Lewis was a vaudevillian who broke into jazz when he began playing clarinet with Earl Fuller's Famous Jazz Band in 1917, in the wake of the success of the ODJB. He ran a hugely popular and jazz-flavoured dance band throughout the '20s, with many important sidemen in its ranks. His own clarinet-playing and singing, though, remained in the realm of vaudeville. He continued to tour almost until his death in 1971.

*****(*) The Jazzworthy Ted Lewis**

Retrieval RTR 79014 *Lewis; Muggsy Spanier (c); Dave Klein, Manny Klein, Red Nichols (t); George Brunies (tb, kz); Harry Raderman, Sammy Blank (tb); Benny Goodman, Rod Cless (cl, as); Frank Teschemacher, Donald 'Slats' Long (cl, ts); Jimmy Dorsey (cl, as, bs); Hymie Wolfson (ts); Louis Martin (bs); Sol Klein, Sam Shapiro (vn); Fats Waller (p, v); Jack Aaronson (p); Tony Girardi (g); Jimmy Moore (b); Bob Escamilla, Harry Barth (tba); John Lucas, Rud Van Gelder (d); The Four Dusty Travellers, The Bachelors (v).* 8/29–7/33.

The defensive title will raise a smile among those who know Lewis's work; he is unfortunately remembered as much for Eddie Condon's remark – 'Lewis could make the clarinet talk, and usually it said "put me back in the case"'– as for his merits as bandleader. The hammiest of showmen, he nevertheless ran a very fine dance band throughout the '20s and early '30s, and there are numerous great spots for the heavyweight names listed in the personnel – particularly Spanier, who is magnificent on the likes of 'Lonesome Road' and 'Aunt Hagar's Blues'. This compilation cherrypicks the best of Lewis's later Columbia sessions, up until his final date for them in July 1933, the very rare (and surprisingly fine) 'Here You Come With Love'. The four tracks where Fats Waller sat in with the band are here; George Brunies lets rip on kazoo on 'San'; and Ted himself is, for all his egregious mannerisms, not too hard to take when there is a lot of good music surrounding him. Top-notch transfers, and with JSP's Lewis CD now out of circulation, what we need next are the best of the early Lewis tracks.

Vic Lewis (born 1919)

BANDLEADER, GUITAR
AND WEST COAST ALL STARS (FOUNDED 1963)

Played guitar in London clubs in the '30s, then he worked in the USA before RAF service. Formed a Kenton-styled big band in the '40s and ran it on and off into the '60s, while pursuing a career as manager of many major names. In the '90s he was recording with famous names once again.

***** New York Jazzmen and Jam Session**

Upbeat Jazz URCD192 *Lewis, Bobby Hackett (c, g); Billy Jones, Jake Koven (t); George Chisholm, Brad Gowans (tb); Bernie Billings, Joe Gudice (ts); Ernie Caceres (bs); Johnny Mince, Pee Wee Russell (cl); Dave Bowman, Dick Katz (p); Eddie Condon (g); Charlie Short (b); Jack Parnell (d); Zutty Singleton (d, v); Josie Carole (v)* 10/38, 2/44.

****(*) Singin' The Blues**

Upbeat URCD 163 *Lewis; Billy Riddick (t, mel); Laddie Busby (tb); Ronnie Chamberlain (ss, as); Derek Hawkins, Cliff Townsend (as, cl); Dick Katz (p); Charlie Short, Lou Nussbaum, Bert Howard (b); Jack Parnell (d).* 2/44–6/45.

Vic Lewis is one of the great fixers of modern music. In the '60s, having turned from playing to management, he was involved in the company out of which Brian Epstein managed the Beatles and Cilla Black, so it's no surprise to find him the prime mover in what seems to have been 'the first time a British jazzman recorded with American musicians in an informal setting'.

Spiking a chance to work in the family jewellery firm, Vic took the *Queen Mary* Stateside and immediately started sitting in on his favoured four-string guitar every chance he got. Taped privately at the Baldwin company's New York studio, the 5 October session is a showcase for the Chicagoans Vic so much admired. His idol Condon was to become a good friend, but the real star of the session is the lyrical trumpet of Bobby Hackett, whose opening statement on 'New York Blues' is as clear and open-hearted as anything he ever did. The next track is more of an oddity, with Bobby switching to Vic's guitar for 'Hackett Picking Blues', vocal by Zutty Singleton, whose cowbell accents are another delightful aspect of the date. Joe Marsala breezed in late, but makes his tentative mark on 'Sugar' and a more substantial contribution to 'Baby, Won't You Please Come Home' (sung by Vic) and 'Keep Smiling at Trouble'.

Vic seems to have been away in Texas for the next couple of weeks, but when he got back from his godmother's, he brokered another session, this time with saxophones and the peerless Pee Wee Russell on clarinet. His solo on 'Basin Street Blues' is a brilliant piece of harmonic sleight of hand. Hackett is in Bix mode throughout, sharper and more plangent than a fortnight before. Condon's laconic introduction – 'Tally ho!' – to a parody of the Original Dixieland Jazz Band's 'Tiger Rag' suggests that the hooch Vic brought along to the session might already have been sampled, and 'Leader's Headache Blues' implies it was just one of several in Vic's luggage.

The sessions have been available off and on down the years, but Dave Bennett's meticulous remastering has restored their freshness and spontaneity. 'Early Rising Blues' was badly degraded and is included only as a footnote, alongside a test recording of 'Hackett Picking Blues', which peters out after a minute, presumably to let Bobby do the six-strings-to-four conversion.

The 1944 dates were made by co-leaders Vic and Jack Parnell, who are also featured on Upbeat's *Singin' The Blues*. The special guests in wartime London were Johnny Mince and three fellow-Americans lured from the morale-boosting *This Is The Army* at the Palladium. The clarinettist's 'Johnny Idea' is a high-point of a delightful session, though Gudice's solo on 'Ain't Misbehavin'' is also wonderful. Slight as his contribution is by comparison, the date is also a reminder of just how great a player dear old George Chisholm was, lithe and mellow by turns. Cleaning the spit out of George's horn was, as I recall, one of the more printable 'worst jobs I ever had' in Derek and Clive's stage act. I can't think of a prouder avocation. The Scotsman's ensemble work is pitch-perfect and his solo fills full of meat and matter.

**** Play Bill Holman**

Candid CCD 79535 *Conte Candoli, Jack Sheldon (t); Andy Martin, Rob McConnell (tb); Ron Loofbourrow (frhn); Lanny Morgan, Lennie Niehaus, Bud Shank (as); Bob Cooper (ts, cl, f); Bill Perkins (bs, ss, f, as, bcl); Alan Broadbent, Mike Lang, Dudley Moore (p); John Clayton (b); Jeff Hamilton (d); Ruth Price (v).* 8/89, 3/93.

***** Shake Down The Stars**
Candid CCD79526 *Andy Martin (tb); Bob Cooper (ts); Bill Perkins (ts, bs, ss, cl, f); Mike Lang (p); Joe DiBartolo (b); Paul Kreibich (d).* 4/92.

***** Me & You!**
Candid CCD 79739 *Similar to above.* 93.

***** The Golden Years**
Candid CCD 79754 *Similar to above.* 94.

***** A Celebration Of West Coast Jazz**
Candid CCD 7971/2 *Steve Huffstetter (t, flhn); Andy Martin, Charlie Lopez, Alex Eyles, Bob McCheskie (tb); Don Shelton (as, cl, picc, f); Bill Perkins (f, cl, as, ts, bs); Bob Cooper (ts, cl, f); Bob Efford (bs, ob, ts, cl); Jack Nimitz (bs, bcl); Clare Fischer, Christian Jacob, Frank Strazzeri (p); John Leitham, Tom Worthington (b); Paul Kreibich, Bob Leatherbarrow (d); Sue Raney (v).* 4/93, 2/94.

***** With Love To Gerry**
Sea Breeze 3051 *Bob Summers (t); Andy Martin, Bob McChesney (tb); Christian Jacob (p); Trey Henry (b); Ray Brinker (d).* 95.

The most prominent of Vic's more recent projects has been the West Coast All Stars, who have recorded for Candid. As always, his role on this project – beyond having his picture taken standing alongside featured trombonist Martin – seems to have been purely fiscal. Even joint arranging (with Lang) and co-production credits with the reliably sharp-eared Perkins have to be regarded with some scepticism. He does, though, manage to persuade top-flight players to turn out and record for the same rates as session-men, which implies a gift of the gab if nothing else.

So what of the records themselves? *Shake Down The Stars* is attributed to Lewis's favourite songwriter, Jimmy Van Heusen. Among the tracks: 'But Beautiful', 'Here's That Rainy Day', the warhorse 'Polka Dots and Moonbeams', 'I Thought About You' and the title-track. Lewis had himself once turned to trombone, so featuring Martin on every track except 'I'll Only Miss Her' (a welcome outing for the stalwart Cooper, who is the only ever-present All-Star) smacks of surrogacy or wishful thinking. Martin has a nice old-fashioned sound and isn't troubled by too many fancy ideas, and there it really ends.

The Bill Holman set is pretty messy, padded out with an alternative version of 'Oleo' and a re-recorded vocal by Ruth Price. It sounds as if not one of them cares even remotely about what they're playing, and the solos, such as they are, fail to register. Dudley Moore played better solos off the cuff in the middle of comedy programmes, but at least he sounds as if he's enjoying himself.

The *Celebration* was also a fly way of marking Lewis's own 75th birthday. The box actually contains two sessions, recorded almost a year apart. Given that the band on the very first All Stars date included Shorty Rogers, Bud Shank, Laurindo Almeida, Victor Feldman and Shelly Manne, it might be thought that we have drifted into a Silver Age. The silvery quality of Perkins's flute playing only serves to underline that. Everything is bright and polished, very clean-edged and not very involving. Martin's solos are increasingly routine, and it is really only Perkins who continues to put some emotion into the playing; his 'Waltz For Coop' on disc two is lovely. But where are the trumpet-players of yesteryear?

Bob Summers may be one of them. He has a prominent feature on 'Go Home', one of the strongest tracks on the Mulligan tribute. He's in the unusual position of being partnered by two trombones and no saxophones on this record, which features arrangements by Bill Holman, Bob Brookmeyer and Manny Albam, and includes what seems to be the first recording of Jeru's 'I Heard The Shadows Dancing'. It's a lovely set and further tribute to Vic's curatorial skills.

Steuart Liebig

BASS

Bass guitarist based in California and recording in the Nine Winds community of West Coast improvisers and free-bop players.

***** Hommages Obliques**
Nine Winds NWCD 0158 *Liebig; John Fumo (t, flhn); Jeff Gauthier (vn); Jeff McCutchen (d).* 5/93.

*****(*) Lingua Obscura**
Nine Winds NWCD 0173 *As above, except Dan Morris (d) replaces McCutchen.* 5/95.

***** Pienso Oculto**
Nine Winds NWCD 0191 *As above.* 2/97.

*****(*) No Train**
Cadence CJR 1086 *Liebig; Vinny Golia (ss, bs); Billy Mintz (d).* 8/97.

*****(*) Antipodes**
Cadence CJR 1129 *As above.* 6/00.

Steuart Liebig plays what he calls ContraBassGuitars, getting a fluid, melodious sound that has plenty of air as well as boom in it. The three records by his Quartetto Stig are full of his own writing. Gauthier and Fumo are familiar from their own Nine Winds projects and, if this is a somewhat rarefied instrumentation, it presents many opportunities for the four men (McCutchen, who subsequently died, was replaced by Morris after the first disc) to play within structure while still getting good improvising space. Liebig's tunes aren't terrifically memorable, mixing brief pieces with what are in some cases hugely long tracks, such as 'Commedia' and 'Overcoming Goingunder', which seem to touch on all sorts of stylistic bases. *Lingua Obscura* might be our favourite of the three: 'Plums And Apricots Falling From The Sky' shows what they can do in a tiny episode, and the laments of 'Nef' and 'Coda', in dedication to McCutchen, are played with great feeling.

No Train is more of a free-jazz blowout, with long-time mainstays of the area Golia and Mintz digging in alongside. With Golia concentrating on baritone for much of the way, the music has a great rumbling feel that should blow away a few cobwebs as it goes. Fine and hard-headed virtuosity. There's a return match for the trio on *Antipodes*. The long track at the centre of the record is an outstanding blow for Golia at his most Trane-like on soprano (he brings the contra-alto clarinet along this time, too). Liebig adds some strange electronics, but it's a very good trio session altogether.

David Liebman (born 1946)

TENOR AND SOPRANO SAXOPHONES, FLUTES

Liebman studied with Lennie Tristano and saxophonist Charles Lloyd and founded his own group, Lookout Farm, while still working with Miles Davis. He was one of the few Coltrane-influenced saxophonists to go back to first principles and explore a parallel line of inquiry, attempting to synthesize jazz and Indian music. For a time, he abandoned tenor saxophone in favour of the soprano.

****** Drum Ode**

ECM 1046 *Liebman; Richie Beirach (p); John Abercrombie (g); Gene Perla (b); Bob Moses (d); Badal Roy, Collin Walcott (tabla); Steven Satten, Patato Valdez (perc); Elena Steinberg (v).* 5/74.

Liebman was still part of Miles Davis's band when he recorded this remarkable album, and the influence of Miles's extended percussion sections is evident in the personnel (no less than eight percussionists) as well as the free-form vamps and quasi-modal heads which make up the bulk of the music. There is also a discernible John Coltrane influence at work in Liebman's own playing. *Drum Ode* is one of the classics of the early ECM catalogue and, as such, it's surprising that it isn't better known and hasn't been available for some time until this reissue. Where many recordings of this kind are simply loose confederations of session players, Liebman was wise enough to recruit percussionists who were already or would be shortly stars in their own right: Moses, Walcott, Roy, Altschul would all be significant recording stars. The result is an album with an almost orchestral unity and complexity. One hears individual voices rising and falling in an impeccably choreographed mix. A great record that should be in every modern collection.

***** The Tree**

Soul Note 121195 *Liebman (ss solo).* 4/90.

It's one of the paradoxes of David Liebman's career that an improviser who has put such emphasis (in bands such as Lookout Farm and Quest) on collective improvisation and non-hierarchical musical tradition should so frequently evoke solitariness. *The Tree* is for unaugmented soprano saxophone. Liebman solemnly intones, 'Roots – take one,' gradually building up his image of jazz tradition as a vegetative organism with taproots and trunk representing origins and mainstays, giving way to branches and twigs of lesser structural or more individual significance, and finally the transitory leaves of fashion. Palindromic in structure, the second takes occur in mirror order, leading back to the roots. In its lonely oddity and *faux-naïf* simplicities, it's reminiscent of Joyce Kilmer's great-awful poem about trees. In sharp contrast to the creeping pretentiousness of the earlier sets, it's simple and direct, and the mimetic references – wind, mainly – are logical and unintrusive. Far removed from either Coltrane or Lacy, Liebman's sound is vocalized in a much more straightforwardly humane way, and one can easily reconstruct the impact it has had on the French saxophonist and clarinettist Louis Sclavis.

****** Double Edge**

Storyville STCD 4091 *Liebman; Richie Beirach (p).* 4/85.

***** Nine Again**

Red RR 123234 *Liebman; Franco D'Andrea (p).* 89.

At first glance, not at all the kind of set one would expect to find on the rather traditionalist Storyville. At second, Liebman's approach to an obvious-looking set of standards – 'Naima', 'Lover Man', 'Round Midnight', 'On Green Dolphin Street' – is even less likely to attract conservatives. It's the very lushness of Beirach's chording and the frequent but almost subliminal displacements of the rhythmic pattern that cue Liebman for his more adventurous explorations. On 'Naima', which became a pianist's tune in any case, he moves outside the chords; on 'Green Dolphin Street' he all but ignores them. Throughout, he sounds quizzical, as if reading from an early and much-revised manuscript of the tune. Liebman at his best.

D'Andrea is a less troubled romantic than Richie Beirach, but he's well up to Liebman's by now almost routine respraying of standards. 'Autumn Leaves', a tune that creaks with the weight of bad interpretations, sounds as if it was written yesterday. Repertoire pieces, like the once-fashionable 'Freedom Jazz Dance', are given a fresh gloss. The problem is that these brightened-up covers contain absolutely no suggestion of depth. With Beirach, Liebman seemed to reach down into a tune; with D'Andrea, it's all brushwork and no perspective or dimensionality. A lot more interesting than just watching paint dry, all the same.

**** The Energy Of The Chance**

Heads Up 3005 *Liebman; Dave Love (t, flhn); Royce Chambers (ts); Caris Visentin (ob); Tim Gilpin (syn); Kevin Brunckhorst, Adam Palma (g); Carl Hillman (b); Mike Dillon, Dennis Durick (perc).* 88.

Recorded at trumpeter Love's Heads Up studio in Texas, this is a curious piece of work, bordering on New Age soundscaping. Liebman's attraction to projects of this kind is mystifying. It's pleasant enough to listen to, though some will find the floating, synth-washed sound irritating after just a couple of tracks. One senses that more interesting things may be going on just offstage, but none of them declare themselves. Liebman is, inevitably, the best thing about the set, looping away on his soprano and taking some lines outside the atmosphere and into quite free territory. Sadly, no comeback from his colleagues, of whom Chambers sounds like a hopeful Sunday player.

*****(*) Classic Ballads**

Candid CCD 79512 *Liebman; Vic Juris (g); Steve Gilmore (b).* 12/90, 1/91.

****** Setting The Standard**

Red RR 123253 *Liebman; Mulgrew Miller (p); Rufus Reid (b); Victor Lewis (d).* 5/92.

The ballads album is dedicated to Liebman's mother-in-law, Natalie Visentin. She chose the material from the songs that she loved in her teens. Liebman plays them pretty straight but is still willing to introduce material from outside the basic sequence in a romantic version of bebop technique. It's a pity there isn't a track in common with the Red recording, which is more rhythmic and changes-based. Juris is used as a second lead as well as a harmony instrument, which means that Gilmore is also called into play as an accompanist. That's clearly the case on 'Angel Eyes' and 'If I Should Lose You', the two most developed tracks.

Setting The Standard is probably the straightest recording Liebman's made in years, and it suits him. Miller has the same rolling, harmonically dense quality that McCoy Tyner brought to the Coltrane quartet ('Grand Central Station' is a nod in that direction) and he pulls Liebman along more insistently than Beirach, say, or d'Andrea. Liebman's tendency to play in rather fixed metres is less evident with a rhythm section as probing as this, and on several of the tracks the pace changes quite dramatically, forcing the saxophonist to vary his phrasing and often his dynamics accordingly. The studio sound is full but not especially flattering.

***(*) Joy

Candid CCD 79531 *Liebman; Gregory Oaks, Donna Ott, Brian Garland, Christopher Breault, Kevin Lewis (t); Tom McKenzie, Michael Mosley, Kim Zitlau (tb); Steve Coonly (btb); Bill Schnepper, Mike Fansler (as, bcl); Jed Hackett, Kenny Flester (ts, bcl); Jim Wingo (bs); Kristi Blalock, Mary Kay Adams, Margaret Ross, Tracie Vies, Melinda Gryder, Kerry O'Connor, Jen Kuk, Dawn Rhinehart, Jennifer McQueen, Mandy Harris, Grace P. Manuel, Elisabeth L. Boivin, Susan L. Walker, Carrie Scattergood, Miranda Hopkins, Christine Fry (f); Butch Taylor (p); Michael Souders (ky); Jim Roller, Pete Spaar (b); Mike Nichols (d); R. J. Geger (perc).* 3/92.

In the later '80s, Liebman became much obsessed with the legacy of Coltrane. He'd already made one tribute album. *Joy* was recorded just after what would have been Coltrane's 65th birthday. It's an altogether more positive and coherent session, backed by a forward-looking and utterly competent campus jazz orchestra (from James Madison U. in Harrisonburg, Virginia) under the directorship of the impressive Mossblad, who solos himself on 'Alabama' and 'India'. On the latter, both he and Liebman switch to ethnic flutes, Mayan and Indian respectively. They collaborate on an astonishing arrangement of 'After The Rain' which uses the university flute choir, a strange but stirring sound. 'Alabama' is the only small-group track, and it exposes Spaar a little, though Taylor is an exceptional accompanist, capable of a thoughtful solo, as he proves on 'Naima', 'Untitled Original' and 'Joy/Selflessness'. Liebman more or less surrenders himself to the music, playing unaffectedly in a lower register than normal. The recording, made (catch this) by the Multitrack Recording Class, is first rate and puts a good many so-called professional efforts to shame.

*** The Seasons

Soul Note 121245 *Liebman; Cecil McBee (b); Billy Hart (d).* 12/92.

Big on the concepts, is Liebman. This interweaves some Vivaldi quotes, some pretty straightahead jazz and some free-form impressionism, with a few compositional ideas that have floated around for years in the Liebman canon. His dry, almost Lacy-like delivery suits this line-up very well indeed, though the fullness of accompaniment sometimes overpowers his lighter passages.

**(*) Besame Mucho

Red RR 123260 *Liebman; Danilo Perez (p); Tony Marino (b); Bill Goodwin (d); Mark Holen, Scott Cutshall (perc).* 3/93.

The Latin Album. Had to happen eventually, and of course Liebman handles it with consummate professionalism. It isn't the most inspiring group he's ever recruited, and there are *longueurs* when the focus is off the saxophone. Not much in the way of atmosphere, which may be the result of doing a south-of-the-border record in Saylorsburg, Pennsylvania. The rhythmic vigour of the leader's playing has never been more evident, but the overall sound is rather flat and uninflected.

*** Songs For My Daughter

Soul Note 121295 *Liebman; Phil Markowitz (p); Vic Juris (g); Tony Marino (b); Jamey Haddad (d); Scott Cutshall (perc).* 5/94.

Very much better, but still oddly focused and amazingly sloppy in execution here and there. Liebman's flute-playing is the main revelation, and there is some nice interplay between it and Juris's smoothly articulate guitar. A very enjoyable record, but still down the list of priorities for this artist.

**** Voyage

Evidence ECD 22157 *Liebman; Vic Juris (g); Phil Markowitz (p, ky); Tony Marino (b); Jamey Haddad (d); Café (perc).* 5/95.

This is the best of this group's records. It features a couple of superb Liebman originals, including 'The Gravel And The Bird' for soprano and piano, apparently written after Dave visited the site of Dachau, and the superb 'When To Love', which must count as one of his most impressive, and also most joyous compositions. There are also versions of Hancock's 'Maiden Voyage' and Coltrane's 'The Drum Thing', which he plays on wooden flute. A fine performance all round and certainly the best representative of this period.

*** John Coltrane's Meditations

Arkadia 71042 *Liebman; Tiger Okoshi (t); Caris Visentin (ob); Phil Markowitz (ky); Vic Juris (g); Cecil McBee, Tony Marino (b); Jamey Haddad, Billy Hart (d).* 12/95.

How brave it was to go back to Trane's classic album with a very different instrumentation, one that included brass, an extra woodwind, guitar and electric keys, as well as doubled-up bass and drums. The result is faithful to the spirit of the original tracks. 'The Father And The Son And The Holy Ghost', 'Compassion', 'Love' and the somewhat shorter but climactic 'Consequences' and 'Serenity' are integrated even more than on the original record, and Liebman, admittedly with the benefit of hindsight and long exposure to Coltrane's music, is able to import themes and ideas from one track to another, underlining the coherence of the project.

***(*) Return Of The Tenor / Standards

DoubleTime Records DTRCD 109 *Liebman; Phil Markowitz (p); Vic Juris (g); Tony Marino (b); Jamey Haddad (perc).* 1/96.

Liebman put away his tenor because he wasn't sure there was anywhere to go in the 'post-Coltrane' idiom he had been identified with. Returning to it brings a new simplicity and rawness to his sound, and a programme of familiar tunes – 'All The Things You Are', 'Summertime', 'Yesterdays', 'There Will Never Be Another You', and so on – encourages him to play with a minimum of embellishment and a refreshingly straightforward attack. The band is nothing exceptional. Markowitz is amiable and – for the most part – very appealing, leaving much of the straight rhythmic work to Juris. Bass and drums don't so much drive things along as punctuate and sustain the beat. It's left to Liebman himself to provide the surface interest and the deeper ideas, and for the most part that is exactly what he achieves.

***(*) Monk's Mood

Double Time 154 *Liebman; Eddie Gomez (b); Adam Nussbaum (d).* 98.

Wonderfully pared down and spacious, these 11 Thelonious Monk compositions are both entirely idiomatic and entirely recast in Liebman's own distinctive voice. The set is bracketed by two cleverly differentiated versions of 'Monk's Mood', but the outstanding performance is the leader's tenor solo on the relatively little-known 'Gallop's Gallop'. Eddie Gomez is in stunning form throughout, and the duet version of 'Monk's Mood' at the end of the record is hijacked by the great bassist. Among the other tracks included are 'Introspection', 'Nutty', 'Skippy' and a revelatory account of 'Ugly Beauty' which should become a standard study-piece for all Monk students.

***** Elements: Water**
Arkadia Jazz 71043 *Liebman; Pat Metheny (g, syn); Cecil McBee (b); Billy Hart (d).* 98.

Oddly concluded by a interview with Liebman on the theme of water, this opens a sequence of four records coming up on Arkadia celebrating the elements. Mercifully, *Water* isn't just a sequence of knocked-down Debussy, but a tough and surprisingly varied sequence of originals, which range from sparkly neo-bop on 'Storm Surge' to the more impressionistic 'Reflecting Pool' (which borders on mood music), to the surprising formal control of 'Ebb And Flow'. McBee and Metheny are both featured in solo interludes, which help to give the record a valuable change of pace. It will be interesting to hear how Dave tackles fire, air and earth.

***** The Unknown Jobim**
Global Music GMNJ 0501 *Liebman; Vic Juris (g); Tony Marino (b); Jamey Haddad (d, perc).* 11/99.

A debut release by the label, this really does work some intriguing changes on the usual Jobim clichés. We knew very few of these songs – 'Dindi' is the only one regularly covered – and were astonished by the beauty and mystery of items like 'O Morro Nao Tern Vaz' and 'Espelho Dos Aguas'. Dave, as ever, varies his approach from track to track, sometimes playing recognizable jazz lines, sometimes varying his attack so as to sound almost like a folk flute or other ethnic instrument. Juris and Marino also mix up their sound, experimenting with amplification and different strings, gut and steel. The overall effect is thoughtful, gently melancholic and somewhat lacking in conventional drama, but richly compelling nevertheless.

*****(*) Souls & Masters**
Cactus CAC 9901 *Liebman; Michael Gerber (p).* 99.

Dedicated to the music of a young composer called Rhoda Averbach, *Souls & Masters* is one of the most sheerly astonishing records of recent times, an enigmatic modern classic that depends for its impact on strange time-signatures, symmetrical scales on 'For Nanda' and an overdetermining concern with the spiritual and psychological power of music. However impressive Averbach's ideas might be (and we are convinced that they are), it is the playing of Gerber and Liebman which holds the attention here. A difficult album to describe, other than very technically, which somehow defeats the object.

***** Time Immemorial**
Enja 9389 *Liebman; Walter Quintus (treatments).* 5–11/97.

Divided into four sections, 'Before', 'Then', 'Now', 'After', this remarkable set allows Dave to improvise above and across acoustic environments created by virtuoso engineer Quintus. There is very little straight saxophone-playing, perhaps too little, but in a number of places Quintus takes saxophone lines and manipulates them to create an open-ended accompaniment. Liebman himself uses a variety of techniques, including playing just mouthpieces and creating toneless effects using just his keys and air pressure. The effect is very dense, very detailed but also very involving, a more compelling listen than the earlier *Loneliness Of The Long Distance Runner* project.

*****(*) Liebman Plays Puccini: A Walk In The Clouds**
Arkadia Jazz 71044 *Liebman; Phil Woods (as); Phil Markowitz(ky); Vic Juris (g); Tony Marino(b); Matt Wilson (d); Jamey Haddad, Sizao Machado, Dane Richeson (perc); Lenora Zenzelai-Helm (v).* 9/01.

A fascinating project by the eternally thoughtful Liebman. 'Un bel di, vedremo', the mournful aria from *Madama Butterfly*, has been used as a jazz standard before, but rarely has there been a more faithful or a more moving rendition than this one. The inclusion of Woods in the line-up is a masterstroke. His rather proper and 'legitimate' tone sits wonderfully well in this context, restoring alto saxophone to the woodwind section of the orchestra. We rather regret the inclusion of any vocal material, even of work by such a fine composer for voices, but Zenzelai-Helm has an undoubtedly beautiful voice and it blends gloriously with the ensembles. Something of an acquired taste, perhaps, certainly if your taste is for orthodox bebop-based jazz, but a rewarding and provocative set nevertheless.

***** Bookends**
hatOLOGY 587 *Liebman; Marc Copland (p).* 3/02.

This is a long set, mostly constructed out of familiar materials, unfamiliarly interpreted. Very often, the main theme is teased out rather than stated and then improvised. The blues basis of 'Impressions' and 'Blue In Green' is subjected to an almost forensic analysis. Not that the playing isn't passionately committed; Copland has rarely sounded better and Dave's soprano and tenor lines (he totes both at the moment) are as finely crafted and as craftily fine-tuned as ever. 'Lester Leaps In' is a revelation and you'll go far to find something as sheerly enjoyable as 'In Your Own Sweet Way'.

*****(*) Latin Genesis**
Whaling City Sound 013 *Liebman; Don Braden (ss, ts); Dan Moretti (ss, ts, bcl, f, af); Oscar Stagnaro (b); Mark Walker (d); Rick Andrade, Jorge Najarro, Pernell Saturnino (perc).* 01.

An interesting project, 30 years on, which takes material from Elvin Jones's *Genesis* album (now deleted) and gives it a Latin spin. Why this particular album was chosen isn't entirely clear, but the three-horn front line works some very interesting changes on a diverse range of material, from Lee Morgan's 'Calling Miss Khadija' to Frank Foster's 'Cecilia Is Love'. There is also a very good version of 'Have You Met Miss Jones?', the percussionists aren't too intrusive and bassist Oscar Stagnaro does some very fine things with his instrument. All in all, a highly successful and emotionally rewarding record.

****** Colors**
hatOLOGY 600 *Liebman (ts solo).* 02.

There are fulsome tributes from both Joe Lovano and Michael Brecker among the liner-notes to this remarkable solo project, further evidence of Liebman's standing with saxophone-players. This companion piece to his solo soprano work reveals a very different Liebman, muscular, full-voiced, playing to a sometimes dark inner rhythm. These are not virtuosic performances in the sense that they display extended or radical technique; they are, however, supremely complex in tonality and emotional timbre as Liebman explores the synaesthetic associations of colour. Hard, strong and irreducible music and one of the most impressive expositions of saxophone-playing you'll hear.

★★★(★) Conversation
Sunnyside 1112 *Liebman; Caris Visentin (ob, eng hn); Vic Juris (g); Tony Marino (b); Marko Marcinko (d).* 9/03.

Most of the tunes are relatively short, but when this band has a chance to stretch out, as it does on 'Anubis', it's obvious what a sympathetic and responsive group Dave has recruited. The presence of Visentin may evoke memories of Oregon, but so much the better if it does. The following 'Short Spoken' is almost as good, a clever idea played out at modest length as most of these compositions are; many another player would have spun out these pieces mercilessly. Liebman's soprano work has rarely been more precise and evocative. His phrasing on 'Snow Day' is delightful. A fine group performance and a great set.

★★★ Beyond The Line
Omnitone 2204 *Liebman; Pat Dorian, Laurie Frink, Bill Warfield (t); Dave Ballou (t, flhn); Sam Burtis, Jeff Nelson, Scott Reeves (tb); Gunnar Mossblad (ss, as); Dave Reikenberg (ss, as, cl, f); Jay Brandford (as, cl, f); Tim Ries (ts); Chris Karlic (bs, bcl, f); Jim Ridl (p, syn); Vic Juris (g); Tony Marino (b); Marko Marcinko (d, perc).* 9/03.

So much of Liebman's output has been either solo or in small groupings that it's hard to imagine – let alone hear – him working in a larger ensemble, even when he is the main soloist. The big band here is arranged by Gunnar Mossblad, and right from the start of 'Hiroshima Memorial' you know you're in the presence of something big and powerful, in terms of composition, arrangement and playing. 'Sing, Sing, Sing' and 'Done With Restraint' are equally good, and there are plenty of fine solo features from the other players: Juris, Ries and Ridl most effectively. The whole package works just fine, though it might take you a moment or two to recalibrate and work out who the front-man is. He sounds tougher and more free-blowing here than usual.

Lifetime

GROUP

A 'power trio' which presaged the fusion of the '70s and came to be used as the name for subsequent Tony Williams-led groups.

★★★(★) Emergency!
Verve 539117-2 *Tony Williams (d); John McLaughlin (g); Larry Young (org).* 5/69.

★★★(★) Turn It Over
Verve 539118-2 *As above, except add Jack Bruce (b, v).* 70.

★★★(★) Ego
Verve 559512-2 *Tony Williams (d); Ted Dunbar (g); Larry Young (org); Ron Carter (b, clo); Don Alias, Warren Smith (d, perc); Jack Bruce (v).* 2–3/71.

★★(★) The Collection
Columbia CK 47484 *Tony Williams (d); Allan Holdsworth (g); Tony Newton (b, v).* 7/75–6/76.

If all the people who claim to have seen Lifetime live during the band's relatively brief incarnation really had, they'd probably still be going. This was the power trio to end all trios, strictly known as the Tony Williams Lifetime, and it might be thought to be more appropriately discussed under the same heading as the late and much-lamented Williams's other work. On the other hand, whatever the official title, the original Lifetime was a collaborative group. John McLaughlin and Larry Young contributed substantially to its roiling, intense sound. Later additions didn't add much, and for most enthusiasts the only albums worth bothering about are *Emergency!* and *Turn It Over*. In the latter, Jack Bruce was brought in as bassist and vocalist. The first job had been done more than adequately by Young's pedals and, as 'Once I Loved' and 'This Night This Song' underlined on the second album, Williams himself could invest his light, almost toneless vocals with a curious poignancy which he traded on more forcefully later.

Acoustically, *Emergency!* was always a disgrace and it is scarcely improved on CD. By the time *Ego* was made, the band was explicitly 'The Tony Williams Lifetime' and there was a sharp move towards a more percussion-orientated sound. The addition of Alias and Smith took care of that. Dunbar's guitar playing was much more linear and blues-based than McLaughlin's, and Ron Carter's bass work provided a more solid spine than Bruce's blub-a-lib slurs. They had their place, but the new band was moving in different directions. Bruce returns for a solitary vocal on 'Two Worlds', but it is Williams's vocal on the storming 'Lonesome Wells' which haunts the mind. The record opens with a minute of virtuosic handclapping (presumably by the whole group) which would put the Steve Reich Ensemble to shame. It and the solo 'Some Hip Drum Shit' find their way on to *Ultimate Tony Williams*, a selection of Lifetime (and only Lifetime) material by the only drummer of the succeeding generation who can hold a candle to him, Jack DeJohnette. DeJohnette really was at the trio's first gig, at Count Basie's in Harlem, and immediately recognized that what was radical about it was that it was centred on the drumkit. Important to register that, whatever the title suggests, this isn't a career-best compilation but merely the Williams material held by Polygram. For a wider view of Williams, his work for Blue Note and elsewhere also need to be taken into account, and is reviewed under his name.

The bands after *Ego* frankly aren't worth a damn. Fans of Allan Holdsworth (and, to be fair, there are many) will value the 1975 and 1976 recordings on *The Collection*, though this must count as one of Williams's drabbest performances ever. These sessions were originally released as *Believe It* and *Million Dollar Legs* and promptly disappeared from sight. The real stuff comes right at the start of the group's life.

Young's swirling, piercing clusters on the organ are the key to the group's shifting polytonality. McLaughlin sounds almost linear by contrast, whipping out licks and lines almost like an illusionist pushing swords through a box. Williams, as ever, is both intensely driven and fierce, and romantically expressive. On 'Sangria For Three' (*Emergency!*) he sounds not unlike the great swing-era drummers, but hyped up to the maximum. Elsewhere, and notably on the more brooding and introspective *Turn It Over*, he doesn't seem to be keeping time at all, but pushing out beyond such considerations. We *did* catch them live. They *were* extraordinary, probably in ways that never could have been caught on record. Even given their technical limitations, the two first albums are soberingly powerful.

Chris Lightcap (born 1971)

DOUBLE BASS

The young Pennsylvanian was an experienced sideman before turning leader, with credits for an eclectic range of musicians, including Joe Morris, Anthony Braxton and Cecil Taylor.

***** Lay-Up**
Fresh Sound New Talent FSNT 74 *Lightcap; Tony Malaby, Bill McHenry (ts); Gerald Cleaver (d).* 99.

*****(*) Bigmouth**
Fresh Sound New Talent FSNT 148 *As above.* 4/02.

The most obvious model for Lightcap's group is the piano-less Ornette Coleman group, or maybe the later version with two saxophonists. As if to clinch the connection, Lightcap includes Ornette's 'I Heard It Over The Radio' on the debut album, a mournful and slightly eerie piece that sits well with this group. Other modern groups have experimented with two horns and no harmony instrument, but Lightcap has his own approach, laying down a heavy and very dependable ostinato and basically letting the horns get on with it.

Sometimes the philosophy is more abstract than others, but there is plenty of singing and dancing on these albums as well, and the slightly forbidding cast of the young bassist's CV shouldn't cause alarm. *Lay-Up* is a very enjoyable record, packed with good writing, some joyous playing and some very thoughtful experiments. *Bigmouth* is a very definite step forward. The opening 'Neptune 66' overturns any prejudiced notion you might have had about twin-tenor formations and tunes like 'Celebratorial' and the closing 'Music Minus One' are endlessly replayable. A cover of the Beatles' 'Dig A Pony' is less successful.

Lightcap is sure to become a significant presence and it's to be hoped that this band can stay together at least as long as Ornette's Atlantic group. They may not be revolutionaries on that scale of ambition, but they do have important things to say.

Terry Lightfoot (born 1935)

CLARINET, ALTO SAXOPHONE, VOCAL

Born in Potters Bar, Lightfoot was bandleading by the mid-'50s and became one of the big names during the ensuing trad boom. He weathered the leaner years of the late '60s and '70s, kept a pub, then went back to pro bandleading in the mid-'80s.

***** Strictly Traditional**
Lake LACD117 *Lightfoot; Paul Lacey, Alan Gresty (t); Ian Bateman (tb); Richard Simmons (p); Tony Pitt (g, bj); Andy Lawrence (b); Johnny Richardson (d).* 1–2/99.

****(*) Mainly Traditional**
Lake LACD 155 *As above, except omit Gresty and Simmons; add John Betts (p), Melinda Lightfoot (v).* 4/01.

Lightfoot might be seen as an also-ran in British trad, but he's served honourable time in the genre and when some of his Lansdowne albums are restored – as Lake will undoubtedly do in their new series – he should get a better representation than he does with these discs. Terry's best for years is a re-creative look at some of the favourites from his heyday, done by a band which mixes old hands (Richardson goes back to the original 1956 Lightfoot band!) with younger heads, and the results have an infectious good humour and chutzpah. It's just solid old British trad, but they're swinging. The *Mainly* follow-up is too tame: too many vocals (nice debut by chip-off-the-old-block Melinda, though), too much average Armstrong copy.

Kirk Lightsey (born 1937)

PIANO

Kirk Lightsey's career began with Ernestine Anderson and Melba Liston, and he made something of a speciality of working with singers. This may well have had some influence on his unfussily evocative improvisations, which always speak confidently but without excess. He has been a member of the Leaders and of the hornless Leaders Trio.

*****(*) Isotope**
Criss Cross Criss 1003 *Lightsey; Jesper Lundgaard (b); Eddie Gladden (d).* 2/83.

***** Kirk'N'Marcus**
Criss Cross 1030 *Lightsey; Marcus Belgrave (t); Jean Toussaint (ts); Santi Debriano (b); Eddie Gladden (d).* 12/86.

***** From Kirk To Nat**
Criss Cross Criss 1050 *Lightsey; Kevin Eubanks (g); Rufus Reid (b).* 11/90.

The excellent *Isotope* transferred predictably well to CD, gaining in resolution as a result; the performances are very good, with an unexpected 'Oleo', some more Monk stylings, and another fine version of Williams's 'Pee Wee' (the CD has 'I'll Never Stop Loving You' as a bonus track).

Kirk'N'Marcus was a fine idea, well executed. The Detroit trumpeter immediately registers a presence on the opening 'All My Love', his own composition, and proceeds to dominate proceedings from there. Toussaint has some gentle skirmishes with the leader on his own 'Lower Bridge Level', which has an attractive harmonic originality. Kenny Dorham's lyrical 'Windmill' and bassist Debriano's 'Fixed Wing' (a CD bonus, left off the original issue) help round out a strong set.

The immediate inspiration for *From Kirk To Nat* is Nat Cole's wartime piano–guitar–bass trio with Oscar Moore and Johnny Miller (see *The Early Forties*, Fresh Sound FSR CD 139). One of the most copied of piano and vocal stylists, Cole has rarely been imitated successfully, and Lightsey steers well clear of pastiche. His singing on 'Never Let Me Go' and 'Close Enough For Love' is growly and soft, almost spoken, and it draws something from late Chet Baker. On piano he is already individual enough not to risk unconscious echo, and his firm touch on the opening 'You And The Night And The Music' sets the tone for the whole album. Guitarist Eubanks, always more impressive on other people's albums, presents a useful latter-day version of Oscar Moore's single-note runs and softly strummed countermelodies; it's Rufus Reid who dominates the longest single track, a subtle 'Sophisticated Lady', with a resonant solo that is mixed too loud but which is as purposeful and strongly outlined as anything by Jimmy Blanton.

Abbey Lincoln (born 1930)

VOCALS

Worked as a singer in California under the name Anna Marie, then began recording for Prestige. Recorded with Max Roach (her husband, 1962–70), but her career faded in the '70s until a revival of interest in Europe in the '80s led to a new and successful contract with Verve. Now a matriarchal influence on a younger generation of female vocalists.

****(*) That's Him!**
Original Jazz Classics OJCCD 085 *Lincoln; Kenny Dorham (t); Sonny Rollins (ts); Wynton Kelly (p); Paul Chambers (b); Max Roach (d).* 10/57.

***** It's Magic**
Original Jazz Classics OJCCD 205 *Lincoln; Kenny Dorham, Art Farmer (t); Curtis Fuller (tb); Benny Golson (ts); Jerome Richardson, Sahib Shihab (bs, f); Wynton Kelly (p); Paul Chambers, Sam Jones (b); Philly Joe Jones (d).* 8/58.

*****(*) Abbey Is Blue**
Original Jazz Classics OJCCD 069 *Lincoln; Kenny Dorham, Tommy Turrentine (t); Julian Priester (tb); Stanley Turrentine (ts); Les Spann (g, f); Wynton Kelly, Cedar Walton, Les Wright (p); Bobby Boswell, Sam Jones (b); Philly Joe Jones, Max Roach (d).* 59.

Lincoln's own emancipation proclamation turned her from a conventional club singer into one of the most dramatic and distinctive voices of the day. To suggest that she owes her creative freedom to one-time husband Max Roach is to say no more than she has herself. Before working with Roach on the powerful *We Insist! Freedom Now Suite*, she had notched up a number of sessions under her own name.

She was never a conventional standards singer, indicating her individuality and occasionally her disaffection in subtle ironies, almost subliminal variations and, even more occasionally, hot blasts of fury. Like John Coltrane and Billie Holiday, she was both respectful of her material and inclined to manipulate it without mercy or apology. 'Afro Blue' with the Max Roach Sextet on *Abbey Is Blue* is one of her strongest performances at any period, though slightly hectoring in tone. The unaccompanied 'Tender As A Rose' on *That's Him!* is more than a little mannered but, like so many Lincoln performances, succeeds through sheer force of personality. Dorham is one of the most naturally vocal of the bop trumpeters and as such is an ideal partner, though it's the still underrated Kelly who carries the day, and it's a shame that there are not more voice–piano duets in the catalogue.

***** Straight Ahead**
Candid CCD 79015 *Lincoln; Booker Little (t); Julian Priester (tb); Eric Dolphy (as, bcl, f); Walter Benton, Coleman Hawkins (ts); Mal Waldron (p); Art Davis (b); Max Roach (d); Roger Sanders, Robert Whitley (perc).* 2/61.

Just look at the line-up. *Straight Ahead* brought together players from two distinct generations in jazz. If Hawkins was the sole representative of older cohorts, he was more than balanced by Little, Priester and Dolphy, who were just beginning to make waves at the turn of the '60s. Lincoln herself isn't quite on top of her game yet; 'expressive' flatting of notes has to be handled with great care if it isn't to sound like incompetence.

Three tracks stand out: 'When Malindy Sings', based on a Paul Laurence Dunbar poem, a vocalization of 'Blue Monk' (made with the composer's blessing), and the closing 'Retribution', co-written with Julian Priester. This is significantly placed. For the first time, Lincoln seems willing to confront her music rather than stand up-stage of it. 'Retribution' is raw, responsive and aware. It boded well for what was to come.

**** People In Me**
Verve 515246-2 *Lincoln; David Liebman (ts, ss, f); Hiromasa Suzuki (p); Kunimitsu Inaba (b); Al Foster (d); James Mtume Heath (perc).* 6/73.

The one moment where Lincoln's unflinching self-determination founders, rendered null by a ridiculously self-conscious *négritude*. The album finds herself possessed by the spirits of Bessie Smith, Billie Holiday, Betty Carter and even, God bless her, Diana Ross; and, while there is no reason to believe that all these styles can't be subsumed and synthesized, that isn't what's happening here.

Two tracks stand out: Max Roach's 'Living Room', a song that seems to be rooted in real experience, and 'You And Me Love', a Johnny Rotalla song to which Lincoln has written lyrics. The version of Coltrane's 'India' seems less awful with age, but a singer who depends so much on a meaningful lyric needs to be sure that it does mean something before launching off into territory like this.

****(*) Abbey Sings Billie: Volumes 1 and 2**
Enja ENJ 6012 2 CD *Lincoln; Harold Vick (ts); James Weidman (p); Tarik Shah (b); Mark Johnson (d).* 11/87.

It isn't clear what is intended here. Lincoln seems torn between paying tribute to her single most obvious influence and subverting it. There are moments, as in an overcooked 'Strange Fruit', when she almost sounds sarcastic, indulging in shifts of pitch and rhythm that in other contexts would require a major change of perspective. 'Lover Man', by contrast, sounds almost dismissive, though the singer's grasp of dynamics has never been more straightforwardly challenged.

The original Volume 2 was the better. 'God Bless The Child', something of a Holiday crux, is lovingly and creatively revisited, and there may even be a reference to Eric Dolphy's extraordinary solo bass clarinet deconstruction hidden in a few bars of low-register phrasing.

We felt previously that a solid single album might be edited from the two original CDs. In the event, Enja have gone down the not entirely satisfactory route of issuing both as a double album. We stand by our preference. This doesn't serve either Abbey or Billie particularly well.

***** The World Is Falling Down**
Verve 843476-2 *Lincoln; Clark Terry (t); Jerry Dodgion, Jackie McLean (as); Alain Jean-Marie (p); Charlie Haden (b); Billy Higgins (d).* 2/90.

A fine return to form. Lincoln came to the notice of a whole new audience when she guested on Steve Williamson's Verve debut, *A Waltz For Grace*, and everything she did from the turn of the decade seemed to be touched with that energy. The combination of Terry and McLean is irresistible and, with the session anchored by Haden and Higgins, it's hard to get the tunes back out of your head. As so often before and since, she manages to acidulate a ballad without making it sound either sardonic or cynical. 'How High The Moon' answers its own question astronomically, and 'African Lady' is perfectly judged.

*****(*) You Gotta Pay The Band**
Verve Gitanes 511110 *Lincoln; Stan Getz (ts); Hank Jones (p); Charlie Haden (b); Maxine Roach (vla); Marc Johnson (d).* 2/91.

Having once adopted the tough, survivalist persona, Lincoln found it hard to shrug off. This was the first indication that she was also willing to open the shutters a chink and let in a little sunlight and irony. With the sole exception of 'Bird Alone', which is dud, the material is excellent, and it's the sort of band singers will die for. After three previous albums, a word is due for drummer Johnson; not a fire-merchant like Roach or Higgins, but an elegant and subtle performer who knows where to place an accent and how to weight it. Getz was already ailing by this stage, but he still performs with consummate grace; 'A Time For Love' could hardly be improved upon.

*** Devil's Got Your Tongue

Verve 513574-2 *Lincoln; J. J. Johnson (tb); Stanley Turrentine (ts); Rodney Kendrick (p); Maxine Roach (vla); Marcus McLaurine (b); Yoron Israel, Grady Tate (d); Keninde O'Uhuru, Sole O'Uhuru, Babatunde Olatunji, Gordy Ryan (perc); The Noel Singers, The Staple Singers (v).* 2/92.

*** When There Is Love

Verve 519697-2 *Lincoln; Hank Jones (p).* 10/92.

Two albums within a year, but exhibiting the greatest possible contrast. *Devil's Got Your Tongue* goes in umpteen directions at once. It also begins to underline growing doubt about Lincoln's direction as a lyricist, never quite managing to combine a sophisticated and faintly surreal language with the urgently inflected repetitions of the blues. 'Story Of My Father' is ponderously rhymed and is marred by bathetic repetitions. Another family story, 'Evelina Coffey (The Legend Of)', fares better, perhaps because it doesn't have the Staple Singers wall-papering the arrangement. Vocally and musically, the material is too dense, almost as if she is trying to recapture the contours of the old Candid sessions, but not recognizing that modern recording and production will tend to swamp arrangements like this. 'People In Me' and 'Rainbow' had been heard before, but these too seem cloyingly sentimental. Only when Lincoln switches to Thad Jones's 'A Child Is Born' and Alex Wilder's lyric do we begin to hear her true voice.

The duets with Jones are not all they might have been. Hank is a superb accompanist, but this isn't one of his better dates. 'C'est Si Bon' is badly misjudged, but the main objection to the set is the mannered way it's been put together: showbizzy segues, big shouters followed by torchy ballads. Abbey tones down her more histrionic excesses, not having to compete with horns or percussion, but she overcompensates in other ways, on occasion enunciating the words as if she was reciting fire exits. A more satisfying set than many, all the same.

**** A Turtle's Dream

Verve Gitanes 527382 *Lincoln; Roy Hargrove (t); Julien Lourau (ts, ss); Kenny Barron, Rodney Kendrick (p); Pat Metheny, Lucky Peterson (g, v); Charlie Haden, Christian McBride (b); Victor Lewis (d); strings.* 5–11/94.

There has been a tension throughout Lincoln's years with Verve between letting her build a band of young, responsive players who can be moulded to her idiosyncratic vision, and surrounding her with established stars on the label's roster. The 1994 album is an almost perfect illustration of the point. One of the joys of the record, as with some of its predecessors, is flicking through and identifying one dream line-up after another – Metheny and house pianist Kendrick, or Metheny and Barron with Haden and Lewis – only to find that the saxophone solo you've just swooned to on 'A Turtle's Dream' or 'Not To Worry' is by the relatively unknown Lourau.

***(*) Who Used To Dance

Verve Gitanes 533559 *Lincoln; Graham Haynes (c); Riley T Bandy III, Steve Coleman, Oliver Lake, Frank Morgan, Justin Robinson (as); Julien Lourau (ts); Marc Cary, Rodney Kendrick (p); Michael Bowie, John Ormond (b); Taru Alexander, Alvester Garnett, Aaron Walker (d); Bazzi Bartholomew Gray, Arthur Green (v).* 4–5/96.

This very much picks up where the last album left off, except that it sounds an altogether better-integrated concept. The basic group is Cary, Bowie and Walker, teaming Lincoln with three of the brightest young instrumentalists around. The only track on which they don't appear at all is 'The River', a fantasia whose humour fails to overwhelm a certain melancholy. 'Love What You Doin'' is a big arrangement for three alto saxophones, and fine, terse solos from Coleman, Lake and the as-yet-unknown Bandy. Frank Morgan does alto duty on 'When Autumn Sings', one of two songs by R. B. Lynch. The only dud track is 'Mr Tambourine Man', a good enough idea but executed far too knowingly and redeemed only by Lourau's saxophone. The title-piece is intriguing in that it features tap-dancer Savion Glover, a young man in the great tradition of jazz hoofers, but with moves all his own; don't dismiss the concept out of hand – it works.

***(*) Wholly Earth

Verve Gitanes 559538 *Lincoln; Nicholas Payton (t, flhn); Marc Cary, James Hurt (p); Bobby Hutcherson (vib, mar); Michael Bowie, John Ormond (b); Alvester Garnett (d); Daniel Moreno (perc); Maggie Brown (v).* 6/98.

The pairing of Lincoln with vibist Hutcherson is irresistible, two entirely opposite rhythmic concepts working together more comfortably than they have a right to. Abbey's reworking of the Johnny Mercer–Lionel Hampton song 'Midnight Sun' is one of the truly great things in her catalogue. The title-track, which follows, is one of only a couple which don't include Bobby, but it illustrates her ability to invest a slightly banal, almost poppy idea with unmistakable conviction.

The voice is now so confidently intimate, so easily conversational, that it becomes difficult to think of Lincoln in terms of 'performance'. Her ability to make large harmonic shifts and reshuffle the tempo allows considerable leeway in the songs 'Conversation With A Baby' and 'Caged Bird', both of which sound considerably less artful than they actually are.

Cary continues to offer sympathetic support, and the pairing of Ormond and Garnett is tailor-made for Abbey's laid-back approach. The group interplay on 'If I Only Had A Brain' is a model for anyone attempting vocal jazz of this sort.

*** Over The Years

Verve 549101 *Lincoln; Jerry Gonzalez (t); Joe Lovano (ts); Brandon McCune (p); Kendra Shank (g); John Ormond (b); Jaz Sawyer (d).* 2/00.

*** It's Me

Verve 0126802 *Lincoln; James Spaulding (as, f); Julien Lourau (ss, ts); Kenny Barron (p); Ray Drummond (b); Jaz Sawyer (d); horns, strings.* 02.

The streak of fine form continues, though one increasingly feels that Lincoln has now settled into a reliably grand manner which will see her through. Some of these performances are excessively theatrical, especially the orchestral tracks on *It's Me*. Striking how much more convincing she sounds in the simpler setting of the title track, a duet with the redoubtable Barron based on a traditional theme, and on a brilliant working of Cedar Walton's 'The Maestro', where Kenny's genius shines out alongside Abbey's gift as a lyricist. She opens with 'Skylark' and then moves into a short suite of originals before delivering that double coup. By mid-point, though, the album has palled somewhat and the orchestral tracks, though nicely arranged by Alan Broadbent and Laurent Cugny, have grown tiresome.

The earlier record is distinguished by a superb solo spot from Lovano on 'Blackberry Blossoms' and a nice contribution from Shank as well. The working group sounds well-drilled and responsive, delivering the kind of taut, thoughtful and ever-alert accompaniment Betty Carter used to demand of her young sidemen. Lincoln fans will gobble up both records. Those less convinced may (rightly) feel that they're getting more of the same, tricked out with a few gimmicks. Why not a record of duos with Barron? Simple songs done simply and without decoration.

John Lindberg (born 1959)

DOUBLE BASS

As a 19-year-old, Lindberg was a member of the Human Arts Ensemble with Charles Bobo Shaw and Joe Bowie. Later associations included a demanding stint in Anthony Braxton's group and charter membership of the String Trio of New York. In recent years, he has become increasingly prominent as a composer.

****** Dimension 5**

Black Saint 120062 *Lindberg; Hugh Ragin (t, picc t); Marty Ehrlich (as, f); Billy Bang (vn); Thurman Barker (d).* 2/81.

Lindberg jumped to notice 20 years ago with a solo recording for the Leo label and since then has produced a steady sequence of thoughtful, intelligent records. This is not the sort of music you're going to hear in a club or bar; it repays attention and repeated hearings. Its very calm and orderliness may sometimes count against it, but Lindberg also knows how to harness musical chaos.

Dimension 5 is a live recording from New York City with a working group centred on two pairs of winds and strings. Bang and Lindberg do most of their head-to-head stuff on the opening 'Eleven Thrice', leaving the shorter middle numbers, 'Twixt C And D', as ensemble pieces. The sound is far from ideal, betwixt CD and some other carrier, very fuzzy at the lower end and decidedly peaky and percussive when Ragin and Ehrlich hit the upper registers.

Untypically for a bassist, Lindberg is a miniaturist, most successful when on a restricted canvas and dealing in tiny, almost calligraphic gestures. It's a style that was often lost on vinyl, not just the outer shadows, but some of the smaller motions as well.

*****(*) Trilogy Of Works For Eleven Instrumentalists**

Black Saint 120082 *Lindberg; Hugh Ragin (t); Mike Mossman (t, picc t); Ray Anderson (tb); Vincent Chancey (frhn); Marty Ehrlich (as, f, picc); J. D. Parran (ts, cl); Pablo Calogero (bs); Alan Jaffe (g); Eric Watson (p); Thurman Barker (d, perc, xyl).* 9/84.

Large-scale works of considerable sophistication that perhaps steer Lindberg away from jazz proper and towards the new music end of his bag. The closing 'Dresden Moods' is too long and episodic in this version, but it contains some beautiful voicings. The opening 'Holler' is more direct and again suggests a synthesis of classic jazz and new wave ideas. The whole band plays well and is beautifully caught by engineer Gennaro Garone, with the balance of brass and woodwinds exactly right and in perspective. It seems unlikely that Lindberg will have many opportunities to record on this scale, so the record is to be valued all the more.

****** Dodging Bullets**

Black Saint 120108 *Lindberg; Albert Mangelsdorff (tb); Eric Watson (p).* 6/92.

*****(*) Quartet Afterstorm**

Black Saint 120162 *As above, except add Ed Thigpen (d).* 94.

*****(*) Resurrection Of A Dormant Soul**

Black Saint 120172 *As above.* 2/95.

The deleted *Give And Take* with George Lewis is one of the best things in Lindberg's catalogue, suggesting that he relishes playing against the broad legato lines and the full, low-end timbre. Like the Lewis date, these are wonderfully open and uncluttered, and they suggest a fruitful synthesis between Lindberg's more avant-garde approach and a jazz tradition. Mangelsdorff is one of the true stars of European jazz, but there is nothing abstractly 'European' in his strong-toned playing or in writing like 'Dots, Ditches and Scratches' on *Resurrection* ... The addition of Thigpen on *Quartet Afterstorm* and the later record is as effective as it is unexpected. No sense that any of this is chamber jazz, but Ed's rootsy, funky approach slots in without a join. He solos joyously on 'X.1' and brings in his own 'E.T.P.' to the *Resurrection* date, and Lindberg turns into Ray Brown before your startled ears. A splendid group of records.

****** Bounce**

Black Saint 120192 *Lindberg; Dave Douglas (t); Larry Ochs (sax); Ed Thigpen (d).* 2/97.

The Lindberg Ensemble combined advanced ideas with sheer firepower. Thigpen's designation as 'Mr Taste' doesn't prevent him from cutting loose on occasion, but here he keeps the reins fairly tight, suggesting contained energy, but rarely breaking out into the open. Douglas's contribution is as distinctive and idiosyncratic as ever. His use of extended technique and non-standard timbres, some of them remarkably close to saxophone tonality, is a constant delight and his soloing on these taxing themes is perceptive to a degree not even suspected from his own recordings. 'Fortone On A Sphere' and 'The Terrace' are the two main pieces. Each negotiates a path between through-composition and improvisational freedom. Lindberg himself sounds roomy and relaxed and the recording gives due weight to each individual voice. A further step in a fascinating career.

***** The Catbird Sings**

Black Saint 120198 *Lindberg; Wadada Leo Smith (t); Larry Ochs (as); Andrew Cyrille (d).* 4/99.

*****(*) A Tree Frog Tonality**

Between The Lines BTL 008 *As above.* 3/00.

This group is one of Lindberg's best, and the two sessions already show a year's growth and a positive evolution. The Black Saint record is still the work of a band in the process of stabilizing itself, and much of the set is in a more or less conventional post-bop mode; Smith more attacking and incisive than on some of his own, moodier projects, Ochs booting himself clear of ROVA rigour. But the title-track at the end paves the way for the more ambitious and individual music of

A Tree Frog Tonality. The Ivesian leanings of 'Thanksgiving Suite' and the carefully considered mouldings of the other pieces bespeak a composer steeped in Americana – not the opportunistic borrowings of a Frisell, but a more deep-rooted blending of form and jazz language. If the quartet can build on this still further, they could emerge as a potent force indeed.

(★★★) Two By Five
Between The Lines btl019 *Lindberg; Rebecca Ansel, Gabriel Bolkovsky (vn); Wendy Richman (vn, vla); Miriam Bolkovsky (clo).* 6/01.

Not strictly a jazz record at all. The tunes are mostly through-composed, though there does seem to be some freedom to improvise here and there, particularly by the leader on the 'Basement Of Desires' suite, and there is certainly no attempt to swing. This is an important dimension of Lindberg's work, though, and anyone who has followed his career to date will want to hear it.

★★★★ Ruminations Upon Ives & Gottschalk
Between The Lines btl025 *Lindberg; Baikida Carroll (t); Steve Gorn (ss, cl, bansuri); Susie Ibarra (d).* 02.

The title is needlessly offputting, for this is an album of powerfully thoughtful modern jazz, executed by a group that thinks on its feet and remains alert at every turn to changes in texture and emotional temperature. For instance, the Gottschalk tribute is a piece called 'Spirit Great, Golden Shine', written in response to the classical composer's 'Holy Spirit, Light Divine' and in response to the September 11 attacks. The Ivesian element is less obvious and thus more effectively assimilated. The exotic timbre of 'Yatan-Na' could have been explored more thoroughly, but generally speaking the quartet is at its most effective when pitched in on challenging charts like the closing trio of 'Generations', 'Implications' and 'Upon Powerhouses'.

Nils Lindberg (born 1933)

PIANO

A giant of Swedish jazz through his composing and pianism, Lindberg has also worked as a composer in modern classical idioms, and his jazz recordings are comparatively few. He also pioneered the coupling of traditional Swedish music with jazz expression.

★★★★ Sax Appeal & Trisection
Dragon DRCD220 *Lindberg; Jan Allan, Idrees Sulieman, Lars Samuelsson (t); Sven-Olof Walldoff, Eje Thelin (tb); Rolf Billberg (as); Harry Bäcklund, Allan Lundstrom (ts); Lars Gullin (bs); Sture Nordin (b); Olle Holmqvist (tba); Sture Kallin, Conny Svensson (d).* 2/60–1/63.

★★★(★) Symphony No. 1 & Jazz From Studio A
Dragon DRCD 331 *Lindberg; Jan Allan, Benny Bailey (t); Ake Persson (tb); Rolf Billberg (as); Bjarne Nerem, Harry Bäcklund (ts); Lars Gullin, Erik Nilsson (bs); Sture Nordin, Georg Riedel (b); Sture Kallin, Egil Johansen (d); Swedish Radio Orchestra.* 6/61–8/63.

★★★(★) Saxes Galore / Brass Galore
Bluebell ABCD 3004 *Lindberg; Jan Allan, Allan Botschinsky, Markku Johansson (t, flhn); Torgny Nilsson (tb); Sven Larsson (btb, tba); Herb Geller (as, ss, f); Claes Rosendahl (ts, f); Bernt Rosengren (ts, as, f); Lennart Aberg, Erik Nilsson (bs, f); Mads Vinding, Red Mitchell (b); Rune Carlsson (d).* 5/79–5/81.

★★★(★) Melody In Blue
Dragon DRCD 245 *Lindberg; Anders Paulson (ss, ts); Johan Horlen (as); Joakim Milder, Krister Andersson (ts); Charlie Malmberg (bs); Jan Adefeldt (b); Bengt Stark (d).* 5/93.

★★★(★) Lindberg Mitchell Paulsson
LCM C-128 *Lindberg; Anders Paulsson (ss); Dan Almgren, Torbjorn Bernhardsson (vn); Hans Lindstrom (vla); Ulrika Edstrom (clo); Red Mitchell (b).* 92.

★★★ Alone With My Melodies
Dragon DRCD 277 *Lindberg (p solo).* 4/95.

Nils Lindberg plays piano, but what he loves to do is to write for horns, especially saxophones. His current CD listing has a rather unique distinction in that he has written saxophone records for three generations of Swedish reed players. The first, *Sax Appeal*, has been reissued in tandem with the slightly later *Trisection* on a single Dragon CD. In Jan Olsson's words, Lindberg's sound is 'the sound of Swedish summer nights and 52nd Street at the same time' – although, more accurately, it's the timbre of West Coast saxes that he gets here and on the later *Saxes Galore*. There are superb sequences not only for the whole section but also for Gullin and Billberg, and the subsequent *Trisection* brings in brass for a Gil Evans-like exploration of timbre.

The first track, 'Curbits', turns up again as the first on *Saxes Galore*, where Lindberg repeated his formula with another all-sax team, and this time inveigled a genuine West Coast man (Herb Geller) to participate. The sound he gets out of the section is a haunting drift that seems to float between traditions, with solos emerging from the ensemble like smoke drifting through clear, cold air. *Brass Galore* is coupled with this session on the Bluebell reissue: not quite as impressive, but there are still some inventive charts here, especially the 3/4 ballad, 'Waltz For Anne-Marie'.

The *Symphony No. 1* was a commission from Swedish television (those were the days). Lasse Sarri's very entertaining notes recall all the circumstances surrounding the preparation of the music (such as Lars Gullin's hospitalization, which meant he had to walk into the recording completely unprepared), yet they do not prepare one for the lovely freshness of the score and the uncomplicated melding of the soloists with the radio orchestra. Lindberg's writing might not always stand up to the most merciless scrutiny, but it is beautifully realized by the players, and at this distance is effortlessly nostalgic of a different time in European music-making. Making up the CD are five tracks from another all-but-impromptu session for Stockholm television, two years earlier, comprising five warm-natured tracks by a septet with Bailey, Billberg, Persson and Nerem in the front line. Hard to resist.

Melody In Blue puts together a third reed team, made up of the latest generation of Swedish saxophonists, and, if anything, this sounds like the best of the three, given a modern studio mix and vivid, energetic playing from all hands. One or two of the pieces sound comparatively ordinary, and Lindberg doesn't always set out to have the band swing; but 'Blue Bop' defies that judgement, and in the extraordinary miniature of 'Polska With All My Love' – once a student work of Lindberg's – the poise of the playing is breathtaking.

Lindberg Mitchell Paulsson is a typically beautiful session from this supreme melodist. Lindberg arranges parts for a string quartet, has old friend Mitchell (on one of his final dates) play a roving bass line, and adds embellishments by himself and the lyrical voice of saxophonist Paulsson. There are several pieces inspired by Swedish folksong, from the Dalarna district, plus reworkings of two pieces from his 'Seven Darlecarlian Pictures' and some new originals. Where other Scandinavian composers get an autumnal chill from their heritage, Lindberg seems to find only warmth and light. The charm and radiance of these settings is very hard to resist.

His solo piano album is a slow and reflective set, a bit ponderous in parts, and perhaps one of those records which means more to the maker than to his audience. Worth hearing, though, for his deeply felt 'In Memoriam', the piece he wrote on the untimely death of Rolf Billberg in 1966 – which brings this discography full circle for now.

Trevor Lines

DOUBLE BASS

British bassist and composer, with an interesting approach to traditional song material.

***** The Cats Hide Under The Bed When I Play My Gary Windo Records**

Wriggly Pig WPIG 002 *Lines; Duncan Mackay, Martin Shaw (t); Martin Dunsdon (ss, ts); Tom Porter, Liam Noble (p); Simon Pearson (d).* 99.

The title is, inevitably, one of our favourites ever, but the band Lines has put together is unexpectedly swinging and the material is never less than intriguing. His use of themes associated with the legendary Copper Family of folk singers (on 'Gentlemen Of High Renown') and the singer Triona Ni Dhombhnaill ('Coolmore') is inventive and not in the least arch or fey. 'The Pipe On The Hob' is taken from *O'Neill's Music Of Ireland* and 'Bonaparte's Retreat' is a folk tune well known in Britain and in Appalachia. The original material includes the powerful title-track which kicks off the record and a tribute to Spontaneous Music Ensemble pioneers Trevor Watts and John Stevens.

Anyone seeing any of these names on the cover might well expect an exercise in freebop or perhaps folk-free. Lines, though, is too intelligent a musician and too seasoned a player to let his influences show that clearly. He has created something genuinely original and consistently moving. Of the band, Simon Pearson is the most innovative, taking a strong feature on 'Howitt', while Mackay's high, declamatory trumpet is a true delight. Shaw and Noble appear only on the title-track and 'Weplaywattsandstevens'.

Worth hearing, and cat owners will be grateful for the behavioural observation; if the cover is to be believed, *His Master's Bones* is the Windo disc that will most disturb Fluffy.

Booker Little (1938–61)

TRUMPET

Born in Memphis and started as part of that community of players, though he went to Chicago in 1957 and subsequently joined Max Roach, then Eric Dolphy. A career of great promise was cut short by his death from uraemia.

***** Booker Little 4 And Max Roach**

Blue Note 84457 *Little; Louis Smith (t); Frank Strozier (as); George Coleman (ts); Tommy Flanagan, Phineas Newborn (p); Calvin Newborn (g); Art Davis, George Joyner (Jamil Nasser) (b); Charles Crosby, Max Roach (d).* 58.

***** Sounds Of The Inner City**

Collectables 6131 *Little; Booker Ervin (ts); Teddy Charles (vib); Mal Waldron (p); Addison Farmer (b); Ed Shaughnessy (d).* 60.

*****(*) Out Front**

Candid 9027 *Little; Julian Priester (tb); Eric Dolphy (as, bcl, f); Don Friedman (p); Ron Carter, Art Davis (b); Max Roach (d, timp, vib).* 3–4/61.

Some artists are simply in a hurry. It is probably pointless to mourn the waste and loss. With Booker Little, though, a scant 23 years really does seem like short change. More than Fats Navarro, more even than Clifford Brown, who put his stamp on the young man's bright, resonant sound and staunchless flow of ideas. What occasionally sounds like hesitancy, even inaccuracy in the harmonic language is probably something more positive, a rethinking of the syntax of bebop, parallel to what his friend and associate, Eric Dolphy, was doing. There was precious little chance to find out. When a creative life is as short as this one was, almost every survival is of value. The shapeless and technically flawed jams on 'Blue'N'Boogie' and 'Things Ain't What They Used To Be' on the Blue Note session would probably not be considered worth releasing if there had been more material around. (Even now, some good stuff on Time and the limited edition Jazz View is out of catalogue.) As it is, out-takes are required to fill out the picture to an undesirable degree, some of them falling short of the standard even the youthful trumpeter would have expected. The Blue Note reissue pairs him with fellow Memphisite George Coleman in a state-of-the-art '50s front line that on tracks like 'Dungeon Waltz' and 'Jewel's Tempo' – both Little compositions – suggests something like what Ornette Coleman and Don Cherry (and Bobby Bradford) were doing over over on the West Coast. The whole set is marred by technical problems, though, which blunt its impact. There are showers of static and Flanagan's piano is signficantly under-recorded.

Sounds Of The Inner City is a hugely welcome revival, pairing the two Bookers on a set of great originality. The saxophonist's opening 'Scroochie' is a strong idea that gets everyone's juices going. They do 'Stardust' almost as a dirge before settling into Little's remarkable 'The Confined Few', which you'd love to have heard him do with Dolphy. The closing 'Witch Fire' is also his, a tune of sinister complexion that has him valving tightly. Inadequately notated and blandly packaged, but well worth adding to a modern jazz collection.

Out Front is one of the best albums of the period, and not just because it also adds a brick to the Dolphy discography. The opening 'We Speak' is a relatively straightforward blowing theme, but the balance of tonalities and the use of abrasive dissonance evokes Ornette's *Free Jazz* experiment, which was recorded a bare four months before, and about which Dolphy would surely have talked and enthused. Little and Roach are once again the axis of the music. The drummer adds timps and vibes to his armoury, and this makes up somewhat for the shortcomings in Don Friedman's playing, but it blurs the bass lines to the extent that one wonders whether some of this material might not have been done just with horns and percussion, a radical notion for the time but perfectly feasible, given the architecture of the music. The shifting signature of 'Moods In Free Time' stretches Little's phrasing and 'Hazy Hues' explores his interest in tone-colour. The closing 'A New Day', with its hints of freedom and its fanfare-like acclamations, is an ironic end given how little time there was to go.

CORE COLLECTION

★★★★ **Booker Little And Friend**

Bethlehem/Avenue Jazz 79855 *Little; Julian Priester (tb); George Coleman (ts); Don Friedman (p); Reggie Workman (b); Pete LaRoca (d).* 8/61.

The wonderful *And Friend* contains some of Booker's best and loveliest playing. He's not thought of as a standards player, but his reading of 'If I Should Lose You' is a modern classic, superbly organized but unfailingly lyrical. 'Victory And Sorrow' is another classic (and, incidentally, the title of a still to be reissued Affinity set) and the new format has two takes of the very fine 'Matilde'. The band is superb, with Priester and Coleman in top form and Friedman earning his reputation as one of the most challenging accompanists on the scene. Booker died in October of this same year, joining the ranks of the unfulfilled as his friend Eric Dolphy was to do just three years later. It's a slim legacy, but a powerful one.

The Little Ramblers

GROUP

Basically a studio group which grew out of the parent band, the California Ramblers, originally organized by Ed Kirkeby, and involving some of the many session players in New York in the '20s.

★★★ **The Little Ramblers 1924–1927**

Timeless CBC 1-037 *Bill Moore, Red Nichols, Roy Johnston, Chelsea Quealey (t); Tommy Dorsey, Herb Winfield, Abe Lincoln (tb); Jimmy Dorsey (cl, as); Bobby Davis (cl, ss, as); Adrian Rollini (bsx, gfs); Irving Brodsky (p); Tommy Felline, Ray Kitchingman (bj); Stan King (d, kz, v); Herb Weil (d); Billy Jones, Arthur Fields, Ed Kirkeby (v).* 9/24–7/27.

The 'small' edition of the California Ramblers had the same pretensions as the principal orchestra – to play dance tunes of the day as warmly as possible – and because it was a leaner outfit their records were often hotter than those of the bigger Ramblers. This was the name they used, at any rate, on their Columbia sessions, capably collected and truthfully remastered here. Titles such as 'In Your Green Hat' and 'Those Panama Mamas' are these days recalled only by era connoisseurs, but a glance through the listing will tell anyone familiar with the field that these are all game and politely swinging performances that are liberally sprinkled with the kind of pertly inventive solos which the New Yorkers of the day could produce to order for eight or sixteen bars. Nichols and the Dorseys are the obvious names, but the true Ramblers stalwarts were Chelsea Quealey, Bobby Davis and Adrian Rollini, and they all turn in typically bright work. The first six tracks are acoustic, but the big sound of the electrical sessions is a nice reminder of how good the Columbia engineers were at that time.

Martin Litton (born 1957)

PIANO

Litton has worked in and around the established circle of British trad-to-mainstream for 20 years, with stints in the touring groups of Kenny Ball and Humphrey Lyttelton.

★★★(★) **Jazz Piano**

Solo Art SACD-114 *Litton; Terry Randall (tr); Peter Morgan, Harvey Weston (b); Allan Ganley, Eddie Taylor (d); Maxine Daniels (v).* 9/87–6/91.

★★★ **Falling Castle**

Asman Jazz 001 *Litton (p solo). n.d.*

Litton is a clever and accomplished practitioner of early jazz piano methods. The Solo Art set brings together the fruits of a group of dates made over a four-year period and is a sweetly pitched almanac of old-fashioned graces. 'Cherokee' has no bop in it but is in its way just as virtuosic. There are three features for Maxine Daniels (especially fine is 'Black And Blue'), a group of trio tracks and six solos, with a particular emphasis on Fats Waller material. A great deal to enjoy here.

Falling Castle is from rather later, and leaves Litton to his own devices. His stride playing is rather light and graceful, seldom resorting to the hammer-fisted approach, and in the original 'Litton On The Keys' he even suggests a link between the Harlem stride masters and the 'novelty' pianists of the same period. 'Limehouse Blues' is busy in a scurrying way. 'Alice Blue Gown' is amusingly knocked about. 'For Rebekah' is a fetching piece of impressionism which ends the record on a note that Litton might well explore at greater length. The record is sometimes a victim of its own unemphatic nature and slips into the background, but it's a pleasing recital.

Fredrik Ljungkvist

TENOR, ALTO, BARITONE AND SOPRANO SAXOPHONES, CLARINET

Contemporary Swedish post-bop saxophonist.

★★★ **Fallin' Papers**

Dragon DCD 267 *Ljungkvist; Torbjorn Gulz (p); Filip Augustson (b); Bo Soderberg (d).* 8/94.

A thoughtful set of originals, mostly by the leader and Gulz, although bassist Augustson sneaks in what might be the best tune in 'You Always Remember How'. Much of it is in the style of sombre lyricism which often characterizes music from this quarter, yet the unexpectedly spry 'Vilse I Fororten' is a smart change of pace. The title-track is an overwrought requiem, and Ljungkvist plays nothing that is strikingly individual, but there's much to enjoy in its cool way.

★★★(★) **Walk, Stop, Look And Walk**

Crazy Wisdom 013112-2 *Ljungkvist; Johan Berthling (b); Raymond Strid (d).* 6–9/00.

★★★(★) **Fungus**

Moserobie MMP CD014 *As above.* 6/03.

The two records by the trio LSB are a startling progression from the Dragon album. All the Nordic musings have been displaced by a bristling, argumentative jazz which at times moves beyond song form into a blasted kind of free playing. The huge title-track of *Walk, Stop, Look And Walk* is 22 minutes of flailing tenor–bass–drums, and they follow that with the even more impassioned 'Kurt', where Ljungkvist picks up the baritone, the horn which he uses for his slowest, loudest commentaries. Strid is a clattery drummer whose energies are thunderously dispersed across every part of his kit. Ljungkvist picks up the clarinet, too, and gets a sonorous sound which is more like the self he portrayed on the Dragon record.

This disc was recorded live at Glenn Miller Café and The Empty Bottle, but the Moserobie set was done in a studio. It's the same again, only more pointed. 'Fredriks Hörna' is a supremely ugly baritone blow, yet the clarinet treatment of Ornette Coleman's 'Mothers Of The Veil' has an almost pastoral feel to it. Two records that will make an open-eared listener sit up.

Charles Lloyd (born 1938)

TENOR SAXOPHONE, FLUTE, TIBETAN OBOE, TAROGATO

There has been a tendency to suggest that Charles Lloyd appeared on the stage of the Fillmore West fully formed, like any one of the pop performers who were breaking into the West Coast scene in and around the Summer of Love. The truth is that the almost 30-year-old Memphian had already had a rugged training and apprenticeship, with Gerald Wilson and Chico Hamilton and in the company of some of the most advanced musicians on the Coast. It's a strange-looking career now: pop adulation followed by silence and near-retirement followed by a latter-day re-emergence with a dark new sound.

***** Dream Weaver**
Collectables 6361 *Lloyd; Keith Jarrett (p); Cecil McBee (b); Jack DeJohnette (d).* 3/66.

***** In Europe**
Atlantic 80788 *As above.* 10/66.

*****(*) Journey Within / In Europe**
Collectables COL CD 6236 *As above, except add Ron McClure (b); Jack DeJohnette (d).* 66, 67.

*****(*) The Flowering Of The Original Charles Lloyd Quartet**
Collectables COL CD 6285. *As above, except omit McClure.* 7 & 10/66.

***** Forest Flower / Soundtrack**
Atlantic/Rhino 8122 71746 *As above, except add Ron McClure (b).* 2/67, 11/68.

***** Soundtrack / In The Soviet Union**
Collectables COL CD 6237 *As above.* 5/67, 11/68.

For a time Lloyd was so terminally uncool it was almost embarrassing to mention his name in mixed company. However, the leader who launched the careers of both Keith Jarrett and Jack DeJohnette, and who later was to propel Michel Petrucciani into a world-striding career, is worthy of a second look; most of the work which established his career and reputation has recently returned to the catalogue. All to the good, and an intriguing balance to his recent records.

At one time, Lloyd was, along with Miles Davis, considered the saviour of jazz, the only performer who could get young people weaned on the Dead and the Airplane to attend a jazz gig, and he did, at the Fillmores especially. If he was the token jazzer of Haight-Ashbury, he more than kept the lamp alight and the jazz was often of very high quality.

The first album slightly anticipates the group's legendary status as a live act. It's an easily overlooked project, marked by some bold writing – 'Dream Weaver', 'Sombrero Sam' – and fantastic interplay in the group, which already sounded seasoned and empathetic. DeJohnette is harder to hear clearly on the live records. In the studio, he's already a monster.

Lloyd also knew what a talent he had in Keith Jarrett and was generous with solo and unaccompanied spots; rich glimpses of future promise on 'Love No. 3', his feature on *Journey Within*. The album – also recorded in concert – also introduces Jarrett as a soprano saxophonist a year before his multi-instrumentalism was given its first full airing on his own *Restoration Ruin*. 'Lonesome Child' is a complex, multi-layered composition that requires concentration and flair from all four performers. 'Memphis Green' is a much more downhome idea, a nod back to the kind of stuff Lloyd grew up with in his home town.

In Europe was yet another live record, taped in Oslo in front of a crowd who were waking up fast to the new thing in both pop and jazz. 'Tagore' and 'Karma' underline how close Lloyd still was to the spiritualized voice of John Coltrane, but it's a looser and less assured performance than some. Perhaps the strain of touring – and by this stage the Quartet was mega – was taking its toll.

The opening 'Autumn Sequence' of *Dream Weaver* attests to Lloyd's interest in longer-form composition. On the strength of the material telescoped on *Forest Flower / Soundtrack*, he might well have made a decent living writing incidental music, film scores and dance suites – except that Lloyd thought of everything he wrote as a dance suite. Lloyd appeared, if not quite fully formed, then certainly already sounding like the light, uncertainly pitched but highly effective solo voice which was to re-emerge in the '80s.

Even without benefit of hindsight, the Lloyd quartet was pretty exceptional. In 1967 Jarrett and DeJohnette were bursting with promise. Neither of them quite lives up to potential on *Forest Flower*, which remains unmistakably the leader's gig with accompaniment, but there is enough on show to suggest important things to come. Jarrett's composer credit on 'Sorcery' is an early foretaste, and McBee is the only other band-member to get his name under the line. The two-part title-piece remained a favourite, almost a signature-tune, until the band broke up. It's much more robust and much less impressionistic than one remembers. Never thought of as much of a standards player, Lloyd does have a crack at 'East Of The Sun' and shows off something of the blues coloration that crept into his more idiomatic work.

Soundtrack is also available paired with *In The Soviet Union*, but this version unfortunately omits 'Voice In The Night', a tune and title that Lloyd was to return to in 1999, the year that saw his catalogue finally take on a more comprehensive shape. The Russian set is probably the poorest of the bunch, so we'd recommend the 1994 reissue with *Forest Flower*. Tallinn *was* still in the Soviet Union in those days, but in May 1967 it was rare for any but the real heavyweight jazz ambassadors to secure the necessary visas, and the trip attests again to Lloyd's enormous international pull.

The Flowering is another of Collectables' rather strange pairings: the Lloyd album shares the space with an eponymous Warne Marsh record. Again, most of the material (which includes 'Speak Low') is recorded in Norway, but there is a single track from the 1966 Antibes Jazz Festival, which segues

'Goin' To Memphis' with 'Island Blues', the latter tune's second appearance on the disc, for it also appears with 'Love-In'.

*** Fish Out Of Water

ECM 1398 *Lloyd; Bobo Stenson (p); Palle Danielsson, Jon Christensen (d).* 7/89.

Despite commercial success on a level rivalled only by pop musicians, Lloyd turned his back on jazz performance (more gradually than is sometimes supposed) after the end of the '60s. By the end of the following decade, the sabbatical was thought to be permanent and Lloyd was largely forgotten.

His return to performance has been much discussed. Whether it was at the behest of Michel Petrucciani or not is now a matter of question. The fact is that he came back, first at an event organized by Blue Note and then, somewhat later, as one of the most unexpected signings ECM ever made, though the presence of Jarrett and DeJohnette on the roster points to an obvious source for the suggestion. The comeback found him in much the same voice as before, more pastel and less rhythmically propulsive, but unmistakably himself. On *Fish Out Of Water* (a hugely unfortunate title for a new initiative) he takes six new but rather samey compositions at an easy pace, unhurried by the ECM house rhythm section, who can do most of this stuff with pyjamas on. Though there are flashes of increased intensity here and there, and an underlying urgency which impinges only rather gradually, it's mostly a rather enervated affair. Lloyd's tone, digitalized, has lost none of its soft burnish, but it is closer to the Coltrane of the 'sheets of sound' period and the great Atlantics than most people will remember. In the 1960s, he was something of a flute specialist, and that has not deserted him; the sound on 'Haghia Sophia' is deep and tremulous, almost as if he has switched to an alto instrument. Not a great album, but a very welcome return.

***(*) Notes From Big Sur

ECM 511999-2 *Lloyd; Bobo Stenson (p); Anders Jormin (b); Ralph Peterson (d).* 11/91.

This was a more varied and enterprising set, still dominated by the spirit of Coltrane but with a bedrock of invention underneath the rather melancholy delivery. It might have been preferable to start with the upbeat 'Monk In Paris'; it was certainly ill-advised to start with the rather melancholy 'Requiem', though this is the sort of programme that ECM have boldly essayed over the years, mostly succeeding, only sometimes miscueing. 'Sister', which comes second, is very similar in theme; and it's only really with Jormin's plangent introduction to 'Persevere', the first part of 'Pilgrimage To The Mountain', that interesting things start to happen. 'Sam Song' is a medium-tempo swinger underpinned by Peterson's gentle but unmistakably firm drumming and Stenson's impeccable accompaniment. After Christensen, it's a little hard to hear another drummer in this role, though Billy Hart was to come along later and make the gig his own.

The bassist introduces 'Takur' with horn-like harmonics down near the bridge, but the piece doesn't travel beyond its own opening bars. 'When Miss Jessye Sings', a tribute to opera singer Jessye Norman, begins disconcertingly close to Coltrane's most famous intro and, in the light of 'Pilgrimage To The Mountain: Persevere/Surrender', one almost wonders if Lloyd intends this album to be his *A Love Supreme*, a passionate personal statement in suite form rather than a collection of discontinuous pieces. If so, inevitably he falls short, but he has created something rather lovely in the attempt. Our favourite of the bunch.

*** The Call

ECM 517719-2 *Lloyd; Bobo Stenson (p); Anders Jormin (b); Billy Hart (d).* 7/93.

*** All My Relations

ECM 527344-2 *As above.* 7/94.

***(*) Canto

ECM 537345-2 *As above.* 12/96.

This is a group to match the line-up of the '60s, a perfectly balanced combination of power and delicacy, and fronted by a man who is once again at the top of his considerable powers. It took time for us to appreciate *The Call*, which occasionally seemed like a turn full circle to the rather bland and unfocused style Lloyd seemed to have left behind with the '60s. It's a record that grows with time and familiarity, particularly once one begins to hear the interchanges between saxophonist and drummer.

Hart is the key addition to the band, a fiery but endlessly inventive player with a seemingly inexhaustible supply of rhythmic ideas. His work on *All My Relations* is superb. The 'Cape To Cairo Suite' is a tribute to Nelson Mandela, overlong and fuzzy in conception but episodically very good. The shorter cuts – 'Thelonious Theonlyus', 'Little Peace' and 'Hymne To The Mother' – are very much group efforts, played with a snap and crispness one would not have expected of the Lloyd of old. One almost wonders if he handed Stenson a stack of Monk LPs before the sessions. He is the overdetermining influence and a very fruitful one.

The most recent of the batch is desperately slow to get going, but 'Tales Of Rumi' repays the effort, and the tracks that follow (many of them apparently influenced by northern landscapes) have a bleak and uneventful majesty that oddly recalls another ECM master, Jan Garbarek. He is certainly in the background on 'Desolation Sound' and the title-piece, and it would have been simply wonderful had he been around Rainbow Studio just before Christmas 1996 to sit in on one of the sessions.

**** Voice In The Night

ECM 559445-2 *Lloyd; John Abercrombie (g); Dave Holland (b); Billy Higgins (d).* 99.

As he passed his 60th birthday, Lloyd seemed to pause and take stock. Here, having seemed for many years to have turned his back on much of his past work, Lloyd revisits past glories like 'Voice In The Night' and the glorious 'Forest Flower', as well as covering Strayhorn's 'A Flower Is A Lovesome Thing' and Elvis Costello's and Burt Bacharach's 'God Give Me Strength'. Also, much as he once did with 'Memphis Green' and similar downhome numbers, he gives himself the space to blow righteously on 'Island Blues Suite'.

Much has been said about the differences between the 'European' and 'American' quartets led by Lloyd's one-time pianist, Keith Jarrett. A similar comparison emerges here for, with his recent ECM group parked for the time being, Lloyd makes his first recording with an all-American group (Holland long since went Stateside) for almost three decades. And what a band it is! Higgins does very much the kind of job that DeJohnette did in the first group, a driving beat that also contributes to the innate musicality of the band, while Abercrombie and Holland bring their own insights, compounded of rock, free music and the latter-day atmospherics associated with the label's core roster, European or American. 'Forest Flower' is a delightful re-creation, unfolding the song's rich colours in a series of time-lapse shifts. There is even a tiny hint of a reference forward to the Strayhorn tune, thematically linked of course, but also bearing an interesting harmonic kinship. Perhaps an insight into its genesis? The Costello/Bacharach tune is the wild card, but just as Lloyd, like Miles, understood that 'standards' repertoire had to evolve and keep up if it was to remain viable, he gives it an authentic jazz feel while preserving the song's curious emotional climate.

★★★(★) The Water Is Wide

ECM 549043-2 *Lloyd; Brad Mehldau (p); John Abercrombie (g); Larry Grenadier, Darek Oles (b); Billy Higgins (d).* 12/99.

★★★(★) Hyperion With Higgins

ECM 014000-2 *As above.* 12/99.

These sessions are overshadowed by the death at 65 of master drummer Higgins, just a year after the first record was released. It was originally to have been dedicated to Higgins's mother Ann. The most affecting moments are tributes to Billy himself, even when he doesn't actually play. 'Prayer' had been written for him by Lloyd during a previous bout of illness, but it's played here just on saxophone, guitar and, guesting on bass, the barely credited Darek Oles. Billy himself is the star of a duet version of 'There Is A Balm In Gilead', playing stark patterns behind Lloyd's Trane-like tenor.

Again, the backward glance; Lloyd includes 'Song Of Her', a Cecil McBee composition from the 1968 *Forest Flower*, and with it, two relatively unknown Ellington tunes, 'Black Butterfly' and 'Heaven', as well as Billy Strayhorn's 'Lotus Blossom'. Lloyd phrases almost like Hodges here and on the original ballad, 'Lady Day', and Mehldau proves to be an able and responsive accompanist.

The second album from the sessions is no filler and shows what a rich association this group has been for Lloyd. Tragically, its real heart no longer beats; Higgins's contribution to 'Secret Life Of The Hidden City' and the 'Darkness On The Delta Suite' is quite extraordinary, rhythmic but also profoundly melodic and with a gentleness of touch that demands the most exacting hand at the desk. Still unusually for an ECM disc, it was taped in Los Angeles and co-produced by Lloyd and Dorothy Darr. The sessions will be remembered, if for no other reason, for that duo, 'Gilead', with its bitter-sweet prescience.

★★★ Which Way Is East

ECM 1978/9 2CD *Lloyd; Billy Higgins (d, perc, g, v).* 1/01.

Lloyd's personal chemistry with Higgins was well-attested when, towards the end of the drummer's life, they spent a week together at Lloyd's house in Santa Barbara, talking and improvising. The resultant two-CD set, themed in loose groups of tracks or ideas, is intensely personal, episodically very beautiful, but in no wise a successful record. The range of instruments both men deploy turn part of it into a 'what was that?' game, which is distracting even on second and subsequent hearings. What they create is a species of world music or world jazz. Though Lloyd would certainly reject any notion that any of these sounds or processes are ethnically specific, it's their unresisted universality that makes them difficult to locate and ultimately difficult to enjoy. Some may find this record uplifting – and the circumstances of its making have a certain poignancy, since Billy died just four months later – but we find its charms unsustained.

★★★ Lift Every Voice

ECM 1832/3 2CD *Lloyd; Geri Allen (p); John Abercrombie (g); Larry Grenadier, Marc Johnson (b); Billy Hart (d).* 1–2/02.

This was Lloyd's response to 9/11, an emotional mix of Americana that embraces spirituals, Marvin Gaye's funky agitprop 'What's Going On', 'Amazing Grace', 'Lift Every Voice And Sing' and his own closing 'Prayer'. Never a cool or uninvolved player, here he comes across like a medicine man, a keening invoker of spirits who clearly sees music as something other than entertainment or 'product'. 'Hymn To The Mother' is a poem to Miss Liberty and to the idea of America as a nurturer rather than a denier. The problem with the set is that the intensity of Lloyd's own playing sometimes cancels out the sophistication of what he is trying to do harmonically and rhythmically, so in hearing the passion one misses the thought; more heat than light, in other words. The group is fantastic and completely in tune with what the leader is doing. The two bassists are particularly important this time out and one can hear why; Lloyd is exploring parts of his register that he has rarely touched in the past and a complex bass-line is part of what he is about. It's not completely new, of course; listen to what Cecil McBee and Ron McClure did for him 35 years ago and it all makes sense.

Geri Allen has had a quiet few years, but her gracefulness and quiet power are a huge asset here, as is Abercrombie's similarly understated breadth of vision. With Billy Higgins gone, Hart is the ideal drummer.

Jon Lloyd (born 1958)

ALTO AND SOPRANO SAXOPHONES

British improviser who emerged in the late '80s as a leader and London-based performer.

★★★ Syzygy

Leo CDLR 173 *Lloyd; John Law (p); Paul Rogers (b); Mark Sanders (d).* 1 & 5/90.

★★★(★) Head

Leo CDLR 186 *As above.* 1/93.

Lloyd stands somewhat apart from musical fashions. His is an unmistakably British sound, related to Trevor Watts and Peter King, to Ray Warleigh and the troubled shade of Mike Osborne; but it also touches on darker – which is also to say blacker – sources, reaching into the deep blue centre which defines this music. There is no straightforward way to categorize this music. It flows over and round some notably strong compositional ideas which manage to hint at antecedents, particularly on the deleted *By Confusion*, without ever making them explicit, though the 1996 album does conclude with a rare cover, Eric Dolphy's 'Straight Up And Down'.

The earlier records are more obviously angular and, though one tended to think that Paul Rogers was a driving force, it turns out, following his replacement by Tim Wells on *By Confusion*, that he actually stopped up some of the music's energy. *Syzygy* (splendid word) is cross-grained, even perverse. By the time of *Head*, which was recorded live during a major

Arts Council tour, Lloyd had not so much mellowed as allowed himself the time and space to let ideas breathe.

*****(*) Praxis**

FMR CD 47 V0198 *Lloyd; Marc Stutz-Boukouya (tb); Aleks Kolkowski (vn); Stanley Adler (clo); John Edwards (b); Mark Sanders (perc).* n.d.

A significant change of direction for Lloyd, a move to a more harmonically grounded music and, in some respects, a more classically formal sound. *Praxis* is through-composed, with plenty of space for solo, duo and trio improvisation. The combination of horns and strings – which may have suggested itself because of Paul Rogers's resonant contribution to the Quartet – offers up a huge range of textures, counterpoints and independent lines. Stutz-Boukouya is a startling presence, perhaps registered a little too forcefully here and there, though the acoustic of Colchester Arts Centre could have something to do with that.

****** Four And Five**

hatOLOGY 537 *Lloyd; Stanley Adler (clo); Marcio Mattos (b); Paul Clarvis (d, perc).* 12/98.

If *Praxis* had been the substantial recorded performance to date, *Four And Five* took Lloyd off on a new evolutionary direction, one in which even an implied pulse was very much central and the music behaved according to its own internal dictates rather than metrical and rhythmic road-signs. The title-tune works by a process of repetition and variation, as does the clever, classically inspired 'Zilch, Zero, Zed', which shuffles a parallel sequence of atonal ideas. 'Blues For' has no dedicatee and no underlying blues sequence either, while a version of Ellington's 'Take The Coltrane' underlines the technique involved more accurately than anything.

The new line-up maintains the sound and logic of earlier groups. As a cellist himself, Mattos understands the instrument's capacities and requirements and, though he doesn't play cello here, he slots into Adler's mood with precision. Clarvis is a less pungent player than Mark Sanders, more of an impressionist and certainly quite at ease where groove is at a discount. Lloyd himself sounds calm and thoughtful, feeding off the two string-players, spinning out intriguingly mathematical lines and commanding the sound with an air of patient authority.

Joe Locke (born 1959)

VIBRAPHONE

Journeyman vibes player whose versatility on an instrument which is difficult to pigeonhole has obliged him to make his own way: so far, he's been doing a fine job of it.

***** Present Tense**

Steeplechase SCCD 31257 *Locke; Larry Schneider (ts); Kenny Werner (p); Ron McClure (b); Ronnie Burrage (d).* 7/89.

*****(*) Longing**

Steeplechase SCCD 31281 *Locke; Mark Ledford (t, v); Johannes Enders (ss, ts); George Cables (p); Jeff Andrews (b); Ronnie Burrage (d).* 10/90.

****** But Beautiful**

Steeplechase SCCD 31295 *Locke; Kenny Barron (p).* 8/91.

****** Wire Walker**

Steeplechase SCCD 31332 *Locke; Danny Walsh (as, ts); David Kikoski (p); Ed Howard (b); Marvin 'Smitty' Smith (d).* 11/92.

While Joe Locke can easily assert the kind of virtuosity associated with Gary Burton, it's Bobby Hutcherson's asymmetrical lines and dark, eruptive solos to which he sounds most in debt. Tonally, he gets an idiosyncratic sound from the notoriously faceless instrument – he keeps the sparkle of the vibes but loses their glassiness. As an improviser, he weaves very long lines out of open harmonic situations, maintaining a momentum over short or long distances – he can send up resonant clouds of notes or pare a trail back to its sparsest origins. He can also make the most of slow tempos: the duo album with Barron strikes a meditative pose that is remarkably well sustained for the 70-plus minutes it lasts.

Present Tense is dominated by the interplay of Locke and the rhythm section (Schneider makes three somewhat cursory appearances), and Werner's probing accompaniments are particularly acute, although the sometimes inconclusive air of the music suggests that more preparation might have yielded a better result. *Longing* exchanges Werner for Cables, who's equally involved (Ledford and Enders are on only three tracks between them): 'The Double Up' and a profoundly felt 'A Child Is Born' offer very effective music. *But Beautiful*, as noted, is impeccably done, with Barron's felicities as telling as Locke's: this version of 'My Foolish Heart' is on a par with Hutcherson's classic set-piece. *Wire Walker* continues a memorable run: Smith stokes the fires on the burning title-track, Kikoski has seldom played with more point, and the leader's solos on 'A New Blue', 'A Time For Love' and the mesmerizingly complex introduction to 'Young And Foolish' figure among his best work. It scarcely matters that Walsh is little more than a bystander. A strongly recommended sequence.

****** Very Early**

Steeplechase SCCD 31364 *Locke; Ron McClure (b); Adam Nussbaum (d).* 10/94.

*****(*) Moment To Moment**

Milestone MCD 9243-2 *Locke; Billy Childs (p); Eddie Gomez (b); Gene Jackson (d).* 11/94.

Joe is still in great form here. The trio date with Nussbaum and McClure is another perfectly paced session, with the swinging tempo for 'You Don't Know What Love Is' giving way to a rapt 'I Loves You, Porgy', a dramatic 'Nature Boy' and on through eight tunes. McClure's bass lines are the ideal melodic/rhythmic counterweight, indecently rich but always on the right part of the chord, and Nussbaum is at his most subtle. *Moment To Moment* is really only a shade behind, starting with a terrific workout on 'Slow Hot Wind' and making the best of an ingenious choice of standards and connoisseur's pop. After McClure, Gomez can sound unnecessarily busy, and sometimes one wants to stop and revel in Locke's sound more, but this is basically another good 'un.

*****(*) Inner Space**

Steeplechase SCCD 31380 *Locke; Mark Soskin (p); Harvie Swartz (b); Tim Horner (d).* 4/95.

***** Sound Tracks**

Milestone 9271-2 *Locke; Olivier Ker Ourio (hca); Billy Childs (p); Rufus Reid (b); Gene Jackson (d).* 3/96.

Inner Space is no more or less than another report from a top-flight working band, even if it actually existed as such for no more than a year or so. Reunited in the studio, the group tackles chestnuts such as 'Django' and 'Skylark' alongside Andrew Hill's 'Tripping', Chick Corea's title-tune and Frank Kimbrough's 'Sanibel Island'. If Soskin seems less of an individual force than some of his predecessors, it doesn't stop Locke from delivering a typically eloquent and forceful performance on all the tunes.

Sound Tracks assembles nine Hollywood themes for Locke to investigate, going as far back as *Gone With The Wind* and as contemporary as *The English Patient*. Nothing wrong with the idea, and the leader seems as involved as usual, but Jackson's over-zealous drumming upsets the normally sensitive balance of Locke's music and some of the treatments seem a bit brash and overheated.

*****(*) Slander (And Other Love Songs)**
Milestone 9284-2 *Locke; Billy Childs (ky); Vic Juris (g); Rufus Reid (b); Gene Jackson (d).* 3/97.

With pop tunes in the programme and Childs switching on his synth here and there, fears that Locke may have sold out to smooth jazz need to be allayed. Mostly, this is as tough and uncompromised as any record in his discography. The original tunes are the usual blend of lyrical and challenging, and he plays both Lalo Schifrin's 'Mission Impossible' and Joni Mitchell's 'Blue' without making them seem either kitsch or cute. He is a hard-nosed player and he's assembled a band that follows his instincts. Strong, intelligent playing from all hands – Juris especially thrives in the environment.

***** Beauty Burning**
Sirocco SJL 1008 *Locke; Frank Kimbrough (p); Paul Bollenback (g); Ray Drummond (b); Jeff Tain Watts(d).* 12/99.

**** State Of Soul**
Sirocco SJL 1019 *Locke; Tim Garland (ts, bcl); Henry Hay (p, org); Paul Bollenback(g); Mike Pope (b); Billy Kilson (d); Mark Ledford (v).* 11/01.

There's some attractive music on *Beauty Burning*, but as soon as the rock beat (pounded out with sledgehammer subtlety by Watts) on 'Twilight' comes on, you sense that Locke's looking for a way out of the straightahead straitjacket. Things pick up from there, actually, but the originals (from within the group) are here a fairly tame lot and Locke and Kimbrough turn in merely good performances.

State Of Soul also has its moments, but this time the project is so obviously bound up in pop material – from Elton John to Steve Winwood, with Ledford's curiously asexual tenor taking all the vocals – that the record never gets going at all, and even Locke's originals sound pale and in need of nourishment.

***** 4 Walls Of Freedom**
Sirocco SJL 1021 *Locke; Gerard Presencer (flhn); Bob Berg (ts); James Genus (b); Gary Novak (d).* 9/02.

Here Locke's march towards some sort of pop fusion is arrested, although on its own terms the record is perhaps nothing that special. Berg (on one of his final appearances on record) is, as ever, prone to overdoing it, and the more temperate Presencer is a better voice in the ensemble, which tackles the six-part title suite with some aplomb. There is, though, some awkwardness in the match between the horns and the more introspective slant of Locke's writing, which seems to be chasing after autobiographical ambitions. Maybe an all-solo album should be next.

Didier Lockwood (born 1956)

VIOLIN, MANDOLIN, TRUMPET, ALTO SAXOPHONE

Born in Calais, Lockwood started with rock and blues and joined Magma in 1972, before trying mainstream jazz and then fusion. In the '80s and '90s he worked in numerous international post-bop settings.

***** 'Round About Silence**
Dreyfus FDM 36595-2 *Lockwood; Claude Egéa (t, flhn); Damien Verherve(tb); Eric Séva, (ss, ts); Marc Berthoumieux (acc); Benoît Sourisse (p); Bireli Lagrene(g); Marc-Michel Lebevillon(b); Carline Casadesus (v).* 3/98.

***** Tribute To Stéphane Grappelli**
Dreyfus FDM 36611-2 *Lockwood; Bireli Lagrene (g); Niels-Henning Orsted Pedersen (b).* 12/99.

Lockwood has recorded frequently enough, but there isn't too much of this talented musician around at present. *Round About Silence* is a curious set, pitched as a series of ballads or quiet moments, with 14 brief episodes that touch various light-music as well as jazz bases. Lockwood sometimes sounds so tired he can barely draw the strings over the bow, yet he also picks up the mandolin, trumpet and alto sax at different moments, and the result is a sometimes lovely but often insubstantial set of mood-music pieces.

The Grappelli tribute is strangely disappointing. Lockwood isn't much like Steff as a player, but with two other great virtuosos on hand there should surely have been more exciting music than this. One problem is the studio sound, which is particularly unflattering to the bassist. Of course there are moments to savour along the way, but it's all pretty average.

Giuseppi Logan (1935–9?)

ALTO AND TENOR SAXOPHONES, CLARINET, FLUTE, PAKISTANI OBOE

One of the more enigmatic figures on the free jazz scene of the '60s, Logan either played with radical technique or no technique. His professional associations included Earl Bostic, Patty Waters, Byard Lancaster; he also worked with Dave Burrell, Don Pullen and other emerging figures. Having recorded two records under his own name, Logan disappeared and is believed to have died.

***** The Giuseppi Logan Quartet**
ESP/Calibre 1007 *Logan; Don Pullen (p); Eddie Gomez (b); Milford Graves (d).* 5/64.

**** More**
ESP/Calibre 1013 *As above, except add Reggie Johnson (b).* 5/65.

It's never been entirely clear whether Logan was a radical genius, some kind of *idiot savant* or simply a fraud. At first glance, his playing seems artless and crude, but he manages to structure relatively complex solos on both of these records, and his multi-instrumentalism on 'Tabla Suite' and the long 'Bleecker Partita', both on the earlier ESP, suggest a certain sophistication of musical thought, even if the execution lacks polish. Pullen and Gomez are radicals of a somewhat less radical stamp and seem anxious to swing the music round to a more conventional principle of organization; Logan and Graves are out-and-out freedom exponents, though, and while such axes may have worked for the John Coltrane Quartet, they establish an unresolvable tension here. The other long track 'Taneous' has some effective moments that overcome the feeling of strain, but this is very much an acquired taste.

The second album is pretty dud, or at least Logan's contribution is. One gets the feeling that his sidemen (Johnson is a later draftee) have simply had enough and are getting on with their own thing. Logan tries to get his own back by playing piano himself on 'Curve Eleven' but to no avail. Interestingly again, the most effective work is on the longest track, here 'Wretched Saturday', as if Giuseppi has to work himself up to a certain pitch before he delivers. The jury is not so much out as bent on a not proven verdict. Logan remains one of the enigmas of the new jazz.

London Improvisers Orchestra

ENSEMBLE

Originally convened for a British visit by American 'conduction' specialist Butch Morris, the LIO aims to extend small-group improvisation into larger-scale ensembles and to draw in the process on the city's incredibly rich pool of improvising musicians.

***(*) Proceedings

Emanem 4201 2CD *Chris Burn (t, p); Matt Davis, Roland Ramanan (t); Ian Smith (t, flhn); Gail Brand, Alan Tomlinson (tb); Neil Metcalfe (f); Alex Ward (cl); Harrison Smith (bcl); Tom Chant, Lol Coxhill (ss); John Butcher, Evan Parker (ss, ts); Caroline Kraabel, Adrian Northover (as); Terry Day (pipes); Nigel Coombes, Mee, Joe Townsend, Philipp Wachsmann (vn); Nikos Veliotis (clo); John Edwards, Simon H. Fell (b); Steve Beresford (p); Rhodri Davies (hp); John Bissett (g); Ansuman Biswas (perc, toys); Steve Noble, Mark Sanders (perc); Adam Bohman (amplified objects); Kaffe Matthews (sampling).* 7/99.

***(*) The Hearing Continues ...

Emanem 4203 2CD *Harry Beckett (t); Ian Smith (t, flhn) Robert Jarvis (tb); Alan Tomlinson (btb); Neil Metcalfe (f); Terry Day (pipes, p); John Rangecroft, Alex Ward (cl); Jacques Foschia (cl, bcl); Harrison Smith (bcl); Hans Koch (bcl, cbcl) John Butcher, Evan Parker (ss, ts); Caroline Kraabel, Adrian Northover (as); Garry Todd (ts); Nigel Coombes, Philipp Wachsmann (vn); Charlotte Hug (vla); Marcio Mattos, Mark Wastell (clo); Dave Tucker (clo, bjo); John Edwards, Simon H. Fell (b); David Leahy (b, tb); Steve Beresford, Veryan Weston (p); Orphy Robinson (mar); Rhodri Davies (hp); John Bisset (g); Tony Marsh, Louis Moholo, Steve Noble, Mark Sanders (perc); Adam Bohman (amplified objects); Knut Aufermann (elec); Pat Thomas (elec, p).* 9/00, 2/01.

Benefiting from the discipline of a monthly session at the Red Rose in London, and from the flexibility and diversity of its membership, the LIO delivers at many different levels. Several of these pieces are composed or directed by the composer/conductor, but the emphasis is on freedom, and on the careful integration of individual expression within a collective. Steve Beresford's magnificent 'Concerto For Alan Tomlinson' actually has no pre-composed elements at all and Fell's 'Ellington 100 (Strayhorn 85)', also on *Proceedings*, is an excellent example of freedom within structure, a key Ellingtonian principle.

Many of the names involved will be familiar to habitués of the British free scene, but these long and richly varied discs also offer an opportunity to hear work by relative newcomers and hitherto undocumented improvisers. Caroline Kraabel's 'Virus' and 'Notes For Terry Day' are good examples, and the latter also provides a welcome return for percussionist Day, who has been sidelined by ill health and currently plays only bamboo pipes.

Both albums feature interpolated free improvisations, and the second disc very much picks up where its predecessor left off a year earlier. Kraabel is again prominent. Weston presents the astonishing 'Concerto For Soft-Loud Key Box' (Anglo-Saxon for piano), and the very experienced Wachsmann directs 'Fire In The Air'. 'Dingos Creep' is an intriguing sextet improvisation for saxophones only and the range of instrumental effects seems richer second time around. The other big plus is that vibist Robinson, not normally associated with free playing, and an unfortunate absentee on *Proceedings*, is featured on Parker's typically thoughtful 'Orphy:Us'.

London Jazz Composers' Orchestra

ENSEMBLE

Founded in 1970, a seminal ensemble of British free-music and modern-jazz figures, giving themselves a chance of working from a large-scale compositonal base. Barry Guy, the original founder, remains the central figure behind the LJCO.

♛ **** Ode

Intakt CD 041 *Barry Guy (b, leader); Harry Beckett, Dave Holdsworth (t); Marc Charig (c); Mike Gibbs, Paul Nieman, Paul Rutherford (tb); Dick Hart (tba); Trevor Watts (as, ss); Bernard Living, Mike Osborne (as); Evan Parker, Alan Wakeman (ts, ss); Bob Downes (ts, f); Karl Jenkins (bs, ob); Howard Riley (p); Derek Bailey (g); Jeff Clyne, Chris Laurence (b); Paul Lytton, Tony Oxley (d, perc); Buxton Orr (cond).* 4/72.

The London Jazz Composers' Orchestra was directly inspired by the example of the American trumpeter and composer Michael Mantler's Jazz Composers' Orchestra, which afforded improvising players a rare opportunity to work outside the small-group circuit and to experiment with enlarged structures. The points of departure are, thereafter, much more interesting than the similarities. Whereas Mantler's group still remains audibly rooted in blues-based jazz, however subtly mediated by 12-tone music and other avant-garde inflexions, the LJCO is much closer in spirit to a European strain of collective improvisation. It also depends very heavily on the vision and eclecticism – and never has that overworked term been more apposite – of founder and leader, Barry Guy, who, in an age of hyper-specialization and stylistic antagonism, has been able to combine a passionate commitment to free improvisation with an interest in large-scale composition (something which remains anathema to some of his more dogmatic brethren) and also in Baroque music, an area which for a time at least he regarded as being every bit as radical in potential as free improvisation.

Ode is a landmark work. Conceived as a 'social framework' for improvisers, it is a brilliant response to the difficulty of combining what were considered to be irreconcilable musical philosophies. Inspired by Olivier Messiaen's masterpiece of orchestral coloration, *Chronochromie*, Guy devised and disguised structures, a series of philosophical quiddities to which the orchestra – both as collective and as a sum of expressive individuals – were asked to respond. The result is, as John Corbett suggests, not dense in the way that orchestral *tutti* are dense. It is dense in that the level of musical communication is such that every statement implies more than it states, creates networks of interaction between players, between constituent instrumental groups, and between types of musical response. If the latter sounds unclear, it is possible to hear players interacting vertically, rhythmically, timbrally, but also in constituent sub-groups, much as Guy was to do more formally much later in *Portraits*. *Ode* proved to be a little hard-boiled for most of the critics, and for some of the players, and at the time probably represented a blind alley in Guy's attempt to maximize soloists' freedom while maintaining a very cohesive overall argument. Hearing it many years on, and in the context of later and – in some ways – even more ambitious projects, what comes across most of all is that integrity of purpose and unity of musical language. It stands as one of the masterpieces of European improvisation.

★★★(★) Zurich Concerts

Intakt CD 005/1995 2CD *Barry Guy (b, leader); Anthony Braxton (leader); Jon Corbett, Henry Lowther (t); Marc Charig (c); Radu Malfatti, Paul Rutherford, Alan Tomlinson (tb); Steve Wick (tba); Paul Dunmall, Peter McPhail, Evan Parker, Simon Picard, Trevor Watts (reeds); Philipp Wachsmann (vn); Howard Riley (p); Barre Phillips (b); Paul Lytton (d).* 11/87–3/88.

★★★★ Harmos

Intakt 013 *Barry Guy (b, leader); Jon Corbett, Henry Lowther (t); Marc Charig (c); Radu Malfatti, Paul Rutherford, Alan Tomlinson (tb); Steve Wick (tba); Paul Dunmall, Peter McPhail, Evan Parker, Simon Picard, Trevor Watts (reeds); Philipp Wachsmann (vn); Howard Riley (p); Barre Phillips (b); Paul Lytton (d).* 4/89.

★★★(★) Double Trouble

Intakt 019 *As above.* 4/89.

In the years that followed, the LJCO changed somewhat in ethos, opening up its repertoire to compositions other than those by Guy. These included challenging graphic scores by drummer Tony Oxley, looser structures from trombonist Paul Rutherford and, from outside the band, challenging works from 'straight' composers with an interest in improvisation, like Krzysztof Penderecki. Anthony Braxton was a thoroughly like-minded collaborator, and this is one of the few occasions when his contact with British and European improvisers has seemed to yield a genuinely communicative music. Whereas Guy likes to work with existing sub-groups of the orchestra, Braxton layers compositions – in this case 'Nos. 135 (+41, 63, 96)', 'No. 136 (+96)', 'No. 108B (+86, 96)' and 'No. 134 (+96)' – in dense palimpsests. There is a marked difference in the cast of sound during his pieces, a denser, less angular quality that doesn't always seem familiar from previous large-scale projects by the American. There is also a difference in ambience and acoustic which probably exaggerates the contrast.

Harmos and *Polyhymnia* (recorded at the earlier of the Swiss concerts) represent what Guy considers to be a third stage in the band's progress. The title alone aroused some anxiety before the fact that Guy was clambering on the bandwagon of neo-tonality. In fact, he interprets the Greek word in its original meaning of 'coming together'. It opens sharply enough with a broken fanfare from the trombones that is almost a station ident for British improvisation, a statement of jagged authority not unmixed with a tender joy. It's followed by a stately chorale which will inevitably bring to mind Guy's other musical enthusiasms, the Baroque filtered through a modern, radical consciousness. If the piece has a real centre, it is the long, winding saxophone melody played by Trevor Watts, a veteran of the band and in this composition its First Mate and co-pilot. Coming quite early (it's a long piece), Watts's solo nevertheless shapes the composition around itself, proposing some sort of rapprochement with harmony. No other player strays as far in this direction. Other individual contributions are, by comparison, harder-edged and more confrontational, but the piece does confirm what was to become a regular feature of Guy's LJCO work, a mutuality of effort between a single solo voice and the ensemble.

Double Trouble is a slightly tougher nut, originally conceived as a two-piano project for Howard Riley and Alex von Schlippenbach, whose Globe Unity Orchestra has trod similar territory. In the event, the recorded version is anchored on Riley alone, with a sequence of carefully marshalled instrumental groupings (notably two trios: Guy, Parker and Pytton, and Riley, Charig and Phillips) orbiting the centre. As a whole, the piece has a tremendous centrifugal coherence that balances the apparently anarchic but tightly organized behaviour of soloists and section players. If it's a less compelling record than *Harmos*, that's simply because it is also much less immediately accessible. On the other hand, it may pay a longer dividend.

★★★★ Theoria

Intakt CD 024 *As above, except omit Riley, Rutherford; add Conrad Bauer (tb), Irène Schweizer (p).* 2/91.

Theoria is effectively a piano concerto for Irène Schweizer, a player who had close contacts with the British avant-garde of the '60s and who has since been a stalwart of Intakt's output. The difficulty presented was that of balancing individual and ensemble elements in a work of this scale and complexity; neither Guy nor Schweizer would have welcomed anything as fixed and definitive as a classical or Romantic concerto, yet clearly it would be undesirable to have a soloist improvise freely for nearly an hour against a fixed orchestral score. The solution is to demarcate very precisely the starting and finishing point for individual soloists and for internal subdivisions of the orchestra, allowing the players a paradoxical degree of freedom within the basic structure. Guy attempts not to juxtapose blandly different styles of playing, but to overlap them creatively, creating diffraction patterns and points of maximum energy. In an orchestra of soloists, Schweizer stands out clearly but does not dominate; what happens is that her improvisations become the constituent elements of other musicians' activity, a process parallel to but obviously very different from jazz musicians' reliance on chord sequences or standard tunes. It is a formidable achievement.

**** Portraits

Intakt 035 2CD *As above, except omit Bauer; add Paul Rutherford (tb).* 3/93.

**** Double Trouble II

Intakt CD 048 *As above, except omit Malfatti, Wick; add Chris Bridges (tb); Marilyn Crispell (p).* 12/95.

***(*) Three Pieces For Orchestra

Intakt CD 045 *As above, except add Maggie Nicols (v).* 6/96.

Portraits continues the line that began with *Ode*. Guy subdivides the orchestra into pre-existing and (in some cases) concurrent groups – Paul Rutherford's Iskra 1903, Evan Parker's Trio, John Corbett's Doppler – and thus to serve as a confederation rather than a vertically organized 'orchestra'. This posed fascinating problems and possibilities – in equal measure – which relate directly to Guy's running concerns. It is very much of its time, most obviously in the decision to include some explicitly melodic material (which seems to have antagonized some of the more dogmatic performers), which certainly makes *Portraits*, though long, one of the most approachable of the records. In the fifth of the main sections, which are interspersed by portrait subsections, there is a ballad, written for Simon Picard, an exquisite creation which is one of Guy's finest moments, let alone the saxophonist's. Alan Tomlinson is given a blues (words by Paul Rutherford, recited by the players), and there are other identifiable generic outlines as well. However, because of the internal configuration of languages and of personnels, none of these insists on anything like generic autonomy. Along with Guy himself, Evan Parker is the player who sustains the networks making up the piece, communicating at one point with several of the players around him, maintaining associations that would seem to be dispersed in time. It is a remarkable achievement. *Ode* may have a greater historical resonance, but *Portraits* is a work of masterful control and profundity.

Three Pieces continues in very much the same vein, uniting the distinct components in a way analogous to tensile structure, but once again using the existence of intra-relationships as a positive structural device. 'Owed To JS' is both an explicit homage to the late John Stevens and also a pun on *Ode* itself. It is written largely for Amalgam (Watts, Rutherford, Guy), for the long-standing duo of Parker and Lytton, and for the Howard Riley Trio (which also involves Guy in a prominent role). Generically, the material is distributed similarly to the previous project, though it seems that, having consulted with Crispell, Guy abandoned the idea of writing another ballad for her in favour of three more fractured, *haiku*-like figures. The American brings her usual serene strength to the music. The closing 'Strange Loops' is written for the extraordinary improvising voice of Maggie Nicols and features Corbett, Charig, Phillips, McPhail, Hayward and Wachsmann. The textual dimension of *Portraits* is extended and developed, opening up new possibilities for the ensemble.

Double Trouble II is, naturally, a realization of the earlier work with something closer to the original conception of two pianists. They are, of course, very different pianists from those first intended, and the difference in texture and in harmonic sympathy is staggering. Crispell and Schweizer have collaborated in a number of contexts. This must be one of the most powerful. It is a culminating moment for the LJCO.

Eddy Louiss (born 1941)

ORGAN, PIANO

A Parisian, he played in his father's band in the '50s and studied at the conservatoire. Sang with Double Six, 1961–63, then backed horn players on piano and moved to organ in the late '60s. He later worked with his own big band, Multicolour Feeling.

**** Trio

Dreyfus FDM 36501-9 *Louiss; René Thomas (g); Kenny Clarke (d).* 68.

*** Bohemia After Dark

Emarcy 013140-2 *Louiss; Jimmy Gourley (g); Guy Pedersen (b); Kenny Clarke (d).* 72.

***(*) Conférence De Presse

Dreyfus FDM 36568-2 *Louiss; Michel Petrucciani (p).* 6/94.

***(*) Conférence De Presse Vol. 2

Dreyfus FDM 36573-2 *As above.* 6/94.

***(*) Sentimental Feeling

Dreyfus FDM 36600-2 *Louiss; Bernard Balestier, Georges Beckerich, Thierry Bienayme, Julien Buri, Pascal Epron, Michel Hamparsumyan, Eric Hupin, Jean-Yves Martyinez (t); Frédéric Cerny, Philippe Jacquiet, Christophe Jardin, Gueorgui Kornazov, Philippe Lapeyre, Anne Lété (tb); Daniel Huck, Jo Bennaroch, Jean-Marc Bouchez, Alain Brühl, Tina Charlon, Jean-Bernard Charlot, Christophe Dunglas, Bernard Hugonnet, Claude Montis, Alain Villanneau (as); Xavier Cobo (ts, f); Thierry Bellenger, Christophe Beuzer, Christian Bonnanfant, Guillaume Christophel, Jean-Christophe Cornier, Eric D'Enfert, Alexis Drossos, Sylvain Miller (ts); Armand Antonioli, Claude Georgel, Daniel Martinez, Georges Varenne (bs); Didier Havet, Philippe Laroza, Jean-Noël Rochut, Bastien Stil (tba); Julio Rakotonanahary (b); Paco Sery (d).* 11–12/98.

Louiss's records have been in and out of circulation, but Dreyfus have restored some of his past as well as more recent activity. The 1968 session by his trio is a tremendous rediscovery. The six themes mix bop staples like 'Hot House' and 'No Smoking' with Thomas's haunting 'Blue Tempo' and a line by Clarke, and the playing has enormous power and energy. Louiss swarms all over the organ, charming out sweet melodies as well as thrashing together blues-drenched solos; Thomas plays with what is for him a rare intensity; and Clarke, recorded in hot close-up, is magnificent. This takes most similar Jimmy Smith and Jack McDuff records to the cleaners. In comparison, *Bohemia After Dark* is a bit disappointing. Jimmy Gourley is always worth hearing, but the record seems cool to the point of perfunctory at times.

A big leap to 1994. Two sets of duets with the mercurial Petrucciani are full of interest. While there are the expected hard-swinging vehicles, each man thinks carefully about how best to accommodate the other, and the initiative is generously traded back and forth. Louiss comes up with lots of colouristic devices to underpin the pianist's lines – 'Naissance', on the second disc, is a fine instance – but the excitement here is in two masters of the keyboard swapping notes.

Sentimental Feeling is altogether more grand; three tracks are with a trio, but the others feature the enormous Fanfare band, 41-strong and not afraid to sound it. Louiss wrote all the music, and he tends to use the orchestra, perhaps unsurprisingly, in great blocks or washes of sound. On 'Le Destin', in dedication to

Michel Petrucciani, there's an effect where the big band seems to be stalking the organist, and the result is close to unforgettable. Sometimes the band seems too unwieldy to make sense: when the trio sets up the slinky pace of 'La Scorpionne', it's hard to see how it will accommodate the orchestra, and sure enough the mass of players tend to lumber alongside the action. But it's a courageous and unpredictable record and well worth trying.

****(*) Sang Melé**

Dreyfus FDM 36516-2 *Louiss; Dominique Pifarély (vn); Michel Albino, Sylvio Marie (b); Paco Sery (d).* 87, 92.

***** Récit Proche**

Dreyfus FDM 36609-2 *Louiss; Daniel Huck (as); Xavier Cobo (ts); Jean-Marie Ecay (g); Julio Rakotonanahary (b); Paco Sery (d).* 4/00.

Sang Melé actually combines the 1987 record of that title and 1992's *Wébé*. The earlier record does seem to have something of an '80s hangover to it, with Louiss's drum programming giving the music a tinkertoy feel which undermines even a tough workout like 'Blues For Kenny'. The sole duet with Pifarély is a solitary change of pace. The later set has a more live, organic feel to it, but again Louiss is ready to settle for 'lite' rather than anything to light up the listener.

Récit Proche updates this groove for the new century. It's bright, optimistic music. Louiss is still settling for situations that flirt with instrumental pop, but just when you're ready to give up on it a lick or a solo keeps things close to honest, and it's good to hear the odd turn from Cobo and Huck. 'Pour Toujours' at least has more blues in it than any slice of American smooth.

Julien Lourau (born 1970)

SAXOPHONES

The Parisian has developed from a Brecker acolyte into a player of broad-ranging tastes, with African, dance and electronic music taking their place alongside his jazz thinking. He led a band called the Groove Gang in the later '90s.

**** Gambit**

Warner Music 8573 83439–2 *Lourau; Malik Mezzadri (f, v); Stéphanus Vivens, Dondieu Divin (ky); Shalom (turntables); Sylvain Daniel, Noel Ekwabi (b); Maxime Zampieri (d); Minino Garay (perc).* n.d.

***** The Rise**

Label Bleu LBLC 6640 *Lourau; Malik Mezzadri (f); Bojan Zulfikarpasic, Gerardo Di Giusto (p); Krassen Lutzkanov (kaval); Fred Chiffoleau, Carlos Bushini (b); Ari Hoenig, Minino Garay, Maxime Zampieri (d); Gustavo Ovalles (perc); Elvita Delgado (v).* 6–9/01.

Lourau has made some head-turning appearances as a sideman (on Abbey Lincoln's *A Turtle's Dream*, for instance), and these dates as a leader might have promised much. *Gambit* is all over the place, with the saxophonist selling his sound to a gang of samplers, programmers and the like. Lourau's been working with this sort of thing for some time, and his interest seems genuine rather than merely faddish; yet he's no closer to making the fusion work than any other saxophonist. Live tracks, doctored or otherwise, blend with studio concoctions notable only for their abstraction. Recorded after an 'extraordinary' 1999 tour, this is entirely forgettable.

The frustrating thing is that when he gets space, Lourau is playing fresh things. The Label Bleu record sees him seemingly recanting on the previous effort, based around acoustic quartet music, with piano duties split between Di Giusto and the admirable Zulfirkarpasic. Lourau's sound hasn't suffered from his electric-band associations, and in this clearer air he gets a full, powerful tone, scuffed at the edges in a way which can suggest either aggression or poignancy. Much of the record carries reminiscences of his late father, and there's a sometimes drooping feel, but catchiness too. 'Bulkamer' lopes along over a songful chord sequence, and 'Contigo Distancia', with a charming vocal from Delgado, is as sweet as vintage Getz–Gilberto. A bit too long and dependent on the listener's empathy with the musing tone, but it's a keeper.

Joe Lovano (born 1952)

TENOR, ALTO, C-MELODY AND SOPRANO SAXOPHONES, ALTO AND BASS CLARINETS, PERCUSSION

Worked with Woody Herman in the late '70s, but it was not until the mid-'80s – and featured recordings with Paul Motian – that Lovano made a real mark. Since then, a sequence of acclaimed Blue Note albums and a fat book of star-guest engagements have made him a fans' favourite.

***** Tones, Shapes And Colors**

Soul Note 121132 *Lovano; Kenny Werner (p); Dennis Irwin (b); Mel Lewis (d).* 11/85.

***** Village Rhythm**

Soul Note 121182 *Lovano; Tom Harrell (t); Kenny Werner (p); Marc Johnson (b); Paul Motian (d).* 6/88.

Coming up for two decades into his recording career, Joe Lovano now stands at the heart of contemporary jazz, a figure who, solo by solo, album by album, demonstrates the continuing fertility of the genre, straddling innovation and tradition. He first came to wider prominence with the Lovano–Frisell–Motian trio, a unit which generated tile-melting excitement in a live setting but which on record revealed a few more subtleties, more opportunities for sophisticated interplay. Lovano started out a relatively straightforward technician, often relying on others to embellish his slightly throaty but plain-speaking lines. Long association with Motian has accustomed him to a very strong pulse embedded in a vibrant surface; he gets much the same thing from the late Mel Lewis, who is surprisingly reminiscent of Krupa in a small-group setting, and also from guitarist Frisell, whose chords and single-note figures are ever more clearly enunciated as his delay-and-distort effects become more dominant.

Experience, however, has turned Lovano into perhaps the most distinctive tenor-player at work today, and a hectic recording schedule has greatly added to his discography. It must be said that Lovano is one of the artists that Soul Note have handled with sympathetic intelligence in recent years, allowing him to work with an impressive cross-section of contemporary players. What's become obvious since the turn of the '90s is how much of Lovano's mature style was present in germ in his earlier work.

Village Rhythm is as impressive for the writing as for the playing, and reveals Lovano to be a surprisingly accomplished bop melodist. 'Sleepy Giant' is particularly memorable. On a couple of tracks the saxophonist overdubs his own rather World Music-al drumming. An indulgence? No more so than the ghastly poem to his father on ''Twas To Me'.

Bearish and slightly withdrawn of aspect, Lovano hadn't yet made a completely individual impact, but both of these are worthwhile efforts, steering clear of clichéd effects and overworked material.

*** Ten Tales

Owl 3507 *Lovano; Aldo Romano (d).* 89.

Back in catalogue along with much of the revived Owl label (it was also reissued on Sunnyside in the US), this set of live duos sounds like it comes from a larger group. Lovano's sheer diversity of tone and attack makes him sound like several players at once, and Romano has the ability and the sheer energy to create overlapping textures (particularly on the opening 'Remanence' and 'Koua 1') to make you forget you're listening to just two guys. 'Monologue For Two' is the only schematic track and even it merits the narrative label Joe and Aldo applied to the album. It swings furiously and never fails or falters even when the music goes free.

**** Landmarks

Blue Note 796108 *Lovano; John Abercrombie (g); Kenny Werner (p); Marc Johnson (b); Bill Stewart (d).* 8/90.

This is Lovano's breakthrough record, a wholly satisfying set that shouts for the repeat button before the last raucous notes of 'Dig This' (with its curious, Monkish interruptions) have died away. Stylistically it's poised midway between Monk and Coltrane, but with a pungent sauce of latter-day urban funk poured over the top, as on the mid-point 'Here And Now', with Abercrombie's uncharacteristically vocalized guitar well to the fore. The (impeccable) production is by John Scofield, who might have been a more obvious choice for the guitarist's role, but Abercrombie seems to take in Scofield's virtues as well as his own, absolutely howling through 'Dig This'. Lovano's ballad-playing, as on the tribute to Elvin Jones, is increasingly impressive, with a virile focus that belies the slightly tremulous delivery.

**** Sounds Of Joy

Enja CD 7013 2 *Lovano; Anthony Cox (b); Ed Blackwell (d).* 1/91.

Working without a harmony instrument still places considerable demands on a horn-player. The opening 'Sounds Of Joy' immediately recalls the stark, melodic approach of the classic Ornette Coleman Atlantics, a jolting, unpredictable saxophone sound that seems to select notes from all over the scale without reference to anything other than the simplest sequences of melody. There are clear signs that Lovano is anxious to broaden his sound as much as possible. In addition to tenor and soprano (the latter given its most thorough and demanding workout to date on the dedication 'This One's For Lacy'), he has also taken on the alto saxophone (giving it a sonority somewhere between Bird and Ornette) and the seldom-used alto clarinet, which he unveils on Judith Silverman's free-tonal 'Bass Space', an almost formal theme executed over a tense 7/8 beat from Blackwell (the actual count varies considerably) and huge, *arco* effects from the fine Cox, who solos magnificently on 'Strength And Courage'.

♛ **** From The Soul

Blue Note 798363 *Lovano; Michel Petrucciani (p); Dave Holland (b); Ed Blackwell (d).* 12/91.

Lovano's 'Body And Soul' wins him lifetime membership of the tenor club. Interestingly, though, he takes John Coltrane's rarely covered 'Central Park West' on alto, as if doing it on the bigger horn were unpardonable arrogance. What's wonderful about the record – aside from the playing, which is gilt-edged all round – is how beautifully modulated the tracks are. There's not a cliché in sight. Lovano's own writing – 'Evolution', 'Lines & Spaces', 'Modern Man', 'Fort Worth', and the closing waltz, 'His Dreams' – has a clean muscular edge and, from the opening fanfare of 'Evolution' onwards, it's clear that the album is going to be something special.

Petrucciani established such a presence as a recording artist in his own right that it's easy to forget how superb an accompanist he could be. The Frenchman's responses on 'Left Behind', unfamiliar territory for him, are startling. He sits 'Fort Worth' out, leaving Holland and Blackwell to steer a markedly abrasive theme. Though ailing and by no means as dynamic as in former years, the drummer still sounds completely masterful. His delicate mallet figures on 'Portrait Of Jenny' are one of the instrumental high-points of a thoroughly compelling record.

*** Universal Language

Blue Note 799830 *Lovano; Tim Hagans (t); Kenny Werner (p); Scott Lee, Steve Swallow, Charlie Haden (b); Jack DeJohnette (d); Judi Silvano (v).* 6/92.

Whereas *Sounds Of Joy* seemed like a genuine attempt on Lovano's part to push himself out into rather edgier territory, *Universal Language* is rather self-consciously eclectic, an attempt to broaden the sound by bringing in all sorts of World Music touchstones and shifting the emphasis over heavily to Lovano the composer, an individual still much less resourceful than Lovano the player. Even the latter is somewhat compromised by the shift to a multi-instrumental approach that lacks the logic it undoubtedly had on the Enja session. 'Lost Nations', in memory of the late Jim Pepper, features Lovano on both soprano and alto clarinet. 'Cleveland Circle' has him moving off into Coltrane harmonics; but, significantly, the most effective piece on the record is the ballad 'The Dawn Of Time', on which Jack DeJohnette is magnificent.

The rhythm section isn't quite as ambitiously constructed as might appear. Haden and Lee don't appear on the same tracks, and Swallow is used essentially as a guitarist, weaving lines round Werner's ramrod comping.

***(*) Tenor Legacy

Blue Note 827014 *Lovano; Joshua Redman (ts); Mulgrew Miller (p); Christian McBride (b); Lewis Nash (d); Don Alias (perc).* 6/93.

Even given the impossibility of topping *From The Soul*, this is a slightly muted set, with a tentative quality that hasn't been evident in Lovano's work before. Redman had been garnering a huge amount of press before this was recorded, and it may be that both men felt that reputations were at stake. Certainly Lovano sounds edgy and over-assertive, making a decidedly strange fist of 'Love Is A Many-Splendored Thing'.

The two-tenor front line gives the music a rather old-fashioned aspect that is accentuated by probably the straightest rhythm section Lovano's worked with in years. The centrepiece is a version of Monk's 'Introspection', delivered with few frills and patient development by all the soloists. Nothing else quite comes up to that standard, though, and the long ballad 'To Her Ladyship' has a cloyingly soft centre.

At this stage in his career, Lovano's entitled to lay a couple of eggs. This isn't one of them but, in the context of its predecessors, it's a bit of a disappointment.

***(*) Quartets

Blue Note 829125 2CD *Lovano; Tom Harrell (t, flhn); Mulgrew Miller (p); Anthony Cox, Christian McBride (b); Billy Hart, Lewis Nash (d).* 95.

A slightly worrying development, albeit a highly accomplished record. Why should either Blue Note or Lovano feel it was necessary at this juncture to confirm his bona fides in avant/progressive and mainstream jazz with these differently constituted quartets at the Village Vanguard? That he functions well in both realms has been beyond doubt for so long, who remained to be convinced?

**** Rush Hour

Blue Note 829269 *Lovano; Jack Walrath (t); James Pugh (tb); David Taylor (btb, tba); John Clark, Julie Landsman (frhn); Richard Oatts (f, ts); Charles Russo (cl, bcl, as, ts); Dennis Smillie (cbcl); Robert Botti (eng hn); Michael Rabinowitz (bsn, bcl); Gloria Agostini (hp); James Chirillo (g); Fred Sherry (clo); Mark Helias, Ed Schuller (b); George Schuller (d); Mark Belair (perc, vib); Judi Silvano (v); Gunther Schuller (cond).* 4–6/94.

Previously, we were inclined to worry that *Quartets* represented anxiety on Blue Note's part about what to do with Lovano long term. Fortunately, there has been no sign of anything since but a continued commitment to experiment and diversification. In a sense, *Rush Hour* emerges directly out of the stylistic shifting of the previous record. Certainly, the long 'Headin' Out, Movin' In' is very largely concerned with moving in and out of conventional harmony and grooves, a superb orchestration by the piece's composer, Gunther Schuller, who also contributes the atmospheric 'Rush Hour On 23rd Street'.

There could hardly have been a more sympathetic or understanding collaboration. Whether there has been any direct influence or not, Lovano's liking for overlaid voices, parallel melody lines floated over low-toned brass and woodwind, and for extremes of sonority is remarkably close to Schuller's conception. It works triumphantly not just on the original piece but also on 'Peggy's Blue Skylight', 'Prelude To A Kiss', and 'Crepuscule With Nellie', one of the most significant performances in Lovano's growing attachment to Monk. It works, too, in scaled-down form, on a version of Ornette's 'Katheline Gray', which features a small string and woodwind ensemble built on the Schuller rhythm section, Ed and George, and coasting Lovano's acerbic soprano; it might almost be some forgotten nugget from the Third Stream.

Lovano's multi-instrumentalism is well aired as well. 'Wildcat' is an overdubbed duet for tenor and drums; 'Juniper's Garden' is for soprano saxophone and Judi Silvano's voice; 'Chelsea Bridge' is a magnificent *a cappella* performance. A major restatement and consolidation rather than a substantial step forward, this is Lovano's best work since *From The Soul.*

***(*) Celebrating Sinatra

Blue Note 837718 *Lovano; John Clark (frhn); Billy Drewes (ss, bcl); Dick Oatts (ts, f); Ted Nash (ts, cl); Tom Christensen (ts, ob, eng hn); Michael Rabinowitz (bsn); Kenny Werner (p); Emily Mitchell (hp); Mark Feldman, Sara Perkins (vn); Lois Martin (vla); Erik Friedlander (clo); George Mraz (b); Al Foster (d); Judi Silvano (v).* 6/96.

Interest in the great singer's pedigree as a *jazz* artist grew during the last few years of his life, and there have been a number of tribute albums by improvisers. This is one of the very best, distinguished by fine arrangements from the veteran Manny Albam and by some extraordinary playing from Lovano. The formula is now pretty familiar: saxophone and soprano voice over a conventional rhythm section and imaginatively deployed horns and strings.

The selection of material is unexpected and persuasive. At the heart of the set, a seductive reading of Sinatra's own composition, 'This Love Of Mine', a favourite of Sonny Rollins. Wedged between 'I've Got You Under My Skin' and 'Someone To Watch Over Me', it's the best small-group performance Lovano has turned in for some time. On other tracks, though, the emphasis is on an ensemble feel, and Albam's great skill is to make these familiar tunes sound fresh-minted. Opening with 'I'll Never Smile Again' was a clever choice, giving the least familiar of the songs the most conventional setting of the set, before striking out into more obviously revisionist territory with 'Chicago' and 'I'm A Fool To Want You'.

For a change, Lovano plays tenor throughout, and it's good to hear him concentrate on the big horn. He sounds as if he's steeped himself in mid-period Rollins, the same loping pace, unpredictable changes of direction and constant fidelity to the melodic line. By now, though, Lovano is his own man and nothing here is anything less than fresh and unhackneyed. And no, he doesn't do 'My Way'.

***(*) Flying Colours

Blue Note 856092 *Lovano; Gonzalo Rubalcaba (p).* 97.

Speaking in interviews, Lovano was as enthusiastic about this encounter as about anything in his career to date. On the face of it, it sounds like a dream ticket for Blue Note, their most enterprising horn-player of recent times and the irrepressible Cuban. For all that, it could have been a rather flat and uninspiring encounter, and what really lifts it is the selection of material. Monk's 'Ugly Beauty' and Ornette's 'Bird Food' were inspired, left-field choices. There's a somewhat more conventional attack on 'How Deep Is The Ocean', an opportunity for both men to show off a more lyrical side, but the real payoff comes on a magnificent interpretation of 'Gloria's Step', on which Rubalcaba quotes Scott LaFaro's original bass line in the left hand, at which Lovano immediately counters with the response figure.

Lovano sometimes sounds recessed relative to the piano, and there are a couple of slightly erratic edits. Nothing, though, that dents the appeal of a wonderful album by two instinctive but highly intelligent players.

**** Trio Fascination (Edition One)

Blue Note 833114 *Lovano; Dave Holland (b); Elvin Jones (d).* 9/97.

Supergroup, ahoy. Lovano's early days in saxophone/organ trios and later dabbling in starker bass-and-drum settings are generously synthesized on this fine session. Lovano's ninth Blue Note session revived a happy association with Jones, who used the big man as a dep for Pat LaBarbera and Sonny Fortune on a European tour that must have been one of the steepest points on his learning curve.

'Cymbalism' is a tribute to another drummer – Paul Motian – but also to a raft of other percussionists from whom Lovano has learnt the supremacy of the drums in jazz. 'Impressionistic' is more obviously saxophone-orientated, a clever, wry history lesson that looks forward and back with relaxed self-confidence. The mood on 'Days Of Yore' is more sombre, a reminder that, beyond his recent multi-instrumentalism, Lovano is a formidable tenor stylist, able to conjure everyone from Chu to Trane. 'Villa Paradiso' and '4 On The Floor' are as uncompromisingly straightahead as anyone could ask for, broad blowing themes with generous detail right through the trio. 'Studio Rivbea' recalls the loft scene of New York City and the brave days of the late '60s. The only standard, 'Ghost Of A Chance', sounds like an emotional moment for Jones, who plays like a dream.

*** Friendly Fire

Blue Note 499125 *Lovano; Greg Osby (as, ss); Jason Moran (p); Cameron Brown (b); Idris Muhammad (d).* 12/98.

The idea came from label boss Bruce Lundvall: separate invitations to Lovano and Osby to put down something special for Blue Note's 60th anniversary. Each, it seemed, mentioned the other, and the result is a warm, uncompetitive jam that harks back to the kind of loosely congregated session the label issued by the shelfload in the '50s and '60s. Much as Lovano has lengthened his operational radius over the years, Osby has shown a growing interest in mainstream harmonic jazz. *Friendly Fire* is a genuine meeting of minds.

Compositions are shared between the two saxophonists. Osby's opening 'Geo J Lo' is a free-form idea that could have turned up in a Ben Webster–Chu Berry workout. The middle of the set is occupied by three repertory pieces, Eric Dolphy's maverick blues, 'Serene', Ornette Coleman's 'Broadway Blues' and Thelonious Monk's 'Monk's Mood', all three of them performed with respectful *brio*. 'Idris', Lovano's tribute to the date's endlessly inventive drummer, lags a touch over the stretch, as does the closing 'Alexander The Great'.

The young pianist, a member of Osby's current working band, is endlessly inventive, working in an idiom that recalls a roster of Blue Note greats from Bud Powell to Andrew Hill. Brown and Muhammad are superbly matched; but it's the saxophonists who command attention, two guys not quite speaking the same dialect but happy to trade. Happy stuff for an auspicious occasion.

*** Flights Of Fancy: Trio Fascination Edition Two

Blue Note 27618-2 *Lovano; Dave Douglas (t); Billy Drewes (ss, af, perc); Toots Thielemans (hca); Kenny Werner (p); Cameron Brown, Mark Dresser(b); Idris Muhammad, Joey Baron (d).* 6/00.

An indulgent project from this most idiosyncratic of modern 'stars', though it's the kind of thing that any number of post-mod stylists might have prized as an opportunity. There are four trios (Lovano with Brown–Muhammad, Drewes–Baron, Thielemans–Werner and Douglas–Dresser) and, for three of the pieces, a performance by each of two threesomes was spliced together. So, for example, Lovano, Thielemans and Werner start off a sweetly gliding 'Giant Steps' before Lovano, Brown and Muhammad confer a more grooving finish on the tune. Some of the pieces, whatever the intention, seem like either sketch-work or unfinished abstracts. Those with Thielemans and Werner are so melodious and resolved – like the gorgeous 'Infant Eyes' – that you wish they'd done the whole record. Oddly, though he's the one constant, Lovano himself sounds distracted some of the time, as if he was thinking more about his concept than his playing (it perhaps doesn't help that he spreads himself across six different horns as well as drums and percussion).

*** Viva Caruso

Blue Note 35986-2 *Lovano; Billy Drewes(cl); Gil Goldstein(acc); Ed Schuller, Scott Lee (b); Joey Baron, Carmen Castaldi (d); Judi Silvano(v); strings.* 01.

Lots of gurgling Neapolitan melodies, from 'O sole mio' to 'Vesti la giubba' and 'Pecche?' – Caruso's greatest hits, in fact, given a Lovano treatment. String charts and tango rhythms, Gil Goldstein's accordion and the saxophonist strolling through it. Lovely moments, inevitably, but it's hardly the stuff that *Landmarks* was made of.

***(*) On This Day ... At The Vanguard

Blue Note 43277 *Lovano; Barry Ries (t); Larry Farrell (tb); Steve Slagle (as); George Garzone, Ralph Lalama (ts); Scott Robinson (bs); John Hicks (p); Dennis Irwin (b); Lewis Nash (d).* 7/03.

It's been some time since the Lovano Nonet was heard from and it's been worth the wait. Right from the opening sequences of the Basie-inspired 'At The Vanguard', the band is in sympathetic motion. Hicks can be a dull soloist, but his feature on this, following Joe, Slagle and the still underrated Ries, is a model, particularly as it recasts the original theme quite substantially, ending the number in a different place from where it began. Nothing else on the set quite comes up to that level of excitement, though there is plenty to ponder on Dameron's 'Focus' and 'Good Bait', Coltrane's 'After The Rain' (Joe continuing his exploration of some of the themes which Trane left relatively unexplored in live settings), 'Laura', 'On This Day', another long original written for the occasion, and finally 'My Little Brown Book', from which Joe extracts every imaginable vestige of pathos and wistful longing.

Frank Lowe (1943–2003)

TENOR SAXOPHONE

Lowe comes from Memphis and has the same big, abrasive tone as fellow-Tennessean, George Coleman. What makes him interesting is that even back in the late '60s, when he was coming through as an individual stylist, he had no truck with the scorched-earth radicalism of most of his generation, constantly asserting an unfashionable (it was then) interest in classic swing players like Chu Berry and proto-boppers like Don Byas. He remains rather thinly documented before the mid-'90s.

**(*) Black Beings

ESP 3013 *Lowe; Joseph Jarman (ss, as); Leroy Jenkins (vn); William Parker (b); Rashied Sinan (d).* 73.

Lowe's second recording for ESP – the follow-up to *And his Friends* – hasn't worn too well and nowadays sounds like shapelessly generic free jazz. Typically, Jarman's composition 'Thulani' is the most emphatic and convincing of the original three tracks, and Joseph's alto and soprano work is often pointed and acute. By contrast, Lowe's long, long tribute to

John Coltrane bespeaks adulation rather than real understanding. The original release had Jenkins listed under a pseudonym, 'The Wizard', but nobody would have been fooled. He's indifferently recorded but plays with some intriguing ideas. Parker is not yet a completely distinctive voice, still perhaps as much in the shadow of Jimmy Garrison as Lowe was of Trane.

**** The Flam

Black Saint 120052 *Lowe; Wadada Leo Smith (t, flhn, wood f); Joe Bowie (tb); Alex Blake (b); Charles Bobo Shaw (d).* 10/75.

A wonderful band and a very fine record which was unavailable for far too long. Unlike the generation that took Trane as its model, Lowe has never seemed to regard the length of a solo as any measure of its importance, and here he is admirably concise and to the point, driving home ideas one after the other, like a country boy driving in spikes at a fair. 'Sun Voyage', 'Be Bobo Be' and 'Third Street Stomp' are all wonderful ideas, executed with such flair and confidence that one has to assume they were well worked out in advance. Smith and Bowie are both in good heart and voice, and the drummer reminds us yet again what an inventive player he can be in the right context. A good place to start if you haven't encountered Lowe before.

*** Don't Punk Out

Emanem 4043 *Lowe; Eugene Chadbourne (g).* 10/77, 79, 00.

Modelled on Derek Bailey's duo recordings with Anthony Braxton, this unlikely project was occasioned when Chadbourne sent his own newspaper review of that Emanem disc to Martin Davidson. The session took place in a New York apartment and is as determinedly lo-fi as Lowe's later discs for CIMP.

Predictably quirky, the material includes a mournful version of Albert Ayler's 'Ghosts' and a Rollins-influenced improvisation on the traditional 'Fire Down There'. Some of the duos are extremely short in duration but still manage to pack in theme statements, solos and reprises, on 'The Clam' all within 55 seconds. To flesh out the disc for reissue, Chadbourne supplied some 1979 tapes of himself running down some Lowe compositions (on a broken guitar), having just returned from a rehearsal with the saxophonist. The effects heard are acoustic and not electronic and seem to have been created by wedging a paintbush under the strings. Quirky, but oddly effective, and an illuminating contrast to Derek Bailey's approach. Lowe's later contribution consisted of three unaccompanied tunes, one by Oliver Nelson, one by Don Cherry and one original. The digital sound on these is very good indeed, despite some odd background noises, and a salutary reminder of how compelling a player Lowe can be.

**** Exotic Heartbreak

Soul Note 121103 *Lowe; Lawrence Butch Morris (c); Amina Claudine Myers (p); Wilber Morris (b); Tim Plesant (d).* 10/81.

Lowe's turn-of-the-decade band traded in a curiously raw finesse. There is nothing here, either live or from the studio, which swaps subtlety for power. And both should help dispel any notion of Lowe as an unsubtle roarer. Though both the horns are strong voices, neither ever goes for the obvious option, and Morris always seems a more interesting player on other people's projects (Lowe's, David Murray's) than on his own increasingly overcooked 'conductions'.

***(*) Decision In Paradise

Soul Note 121108 *Lowe; Don Cherry (t); Grachan Moncur III (tb); Geri Allen (p); Charnett Moffett (b); Charles Moffett (d).* 9/84.

Unlike most of his generation, there isn't much bebop residue in Lowe's thinking, and it's unusual to hear him turn to post-bop like 'Cherryco', an inclusion presumably suggested by the trumpeter present on this wonderful session. It doesn't suit Lowe's chops altogether well, though he slows it down a touch and smooths out a couple of the rougher harmonic shifts. A heavyweight rhythm section, led off by Allen's forcefully eclectic chords and runs, keeps the energy level high. Don is having one of his best outings for years, bright, warmly antagonistic and full of melody. Moncur plays as well as ever (why is he still so underexposed?), varying his slide positions and embouchure to stay just this side of multiphonics. Perhaps not the best introduction to Lowe, who has to make room for three very strong soloists and for the Moffetts, but a powerful group record and an approach that sits wide of most else that was going on in 1984.

**** Bodies & Souls

CIMP 104 *Lowe; Tim Flood (b); Charles Moffett (d).* 11/95.

***(*) Vision Blue

CIMP 138 *Lowe; Steve Neil (b, Guinea hp); Anders Griffen (d).* 2/97.

*** Lowe-down And Blue

CIMP 275 *Lowe; Bern Nix (g); Dominic Duval (b); Michael Carvin (d).* 00.

As spare and stern as the great Ornette Coleman Trio of the '60s, which Moffett also graced, the first of these is the Frank Lowe disc of choice. CIMP (Cadence Improvised Music Project) is dedicated to raw and unvarnished slice-of-life veritism, and there are no frills to any of these performances. A long set, with the usual intensity, *Bodies & Souls* mixes four originals with material by Pharoah Sanders, Don Cherry (who is also the dedicatee of two joyous, complex numbers by Lowe himself), Ornette ('Happy House') and, on the stirring 'Impressions' which opens the set, Coltrane himself. It stands first, one feels, because Lowe wants to demonstrate both his respect for and distance from Coltrane's and later Coleman's language. By placing 'Body And Soul' last, he demonstrates more clearly than ever before how much he sees himself standing on the shoulders of earlier giants. It's a delicate performance, unaccompanied, lighter-toned and more intimate than Lowe often is. Flood and Moffett combine well, and they represent the real difference between the first CIMP and *Vision Blue*. Again, there's a mix of original and repertory material. Rollins's theme from 'Alfie' is an unexpected choice, and Percy Mayfield's 'Please Send Me Someone To Love' doesn't often figure in this sort of setting. 'Softly As In A Morning Sunrise' contains a couple of references to Coltrane, just so that we know he knows, and the now-obligatory Coleman numbers ('Law Years' and 'The Blessing') have the usual mixture of respect and self-reliance. The final two numbers seem a bit throwaway, a duo performance of Lowe's 'Dream State' with the drummer, and the only other acoustic variation, Neil's Guinea harp on the last track, his own 'Bobbo's Face', a bit wasted in that position. Outstanding track? For us, a blistering run-through of Jackie McLean's 'Little Melonae', one of the best things Lowe has recorded.

The later '90s were a difficult time for the saxophonist and ill-health interfered with work. However, when he has recorded, he sounds as good as ever and the latest CIMP set is a cracker. Duval and Nix are in great form, despite not having worked with Lowe together previously, while Carvin – an old buddy – is his solid, inventive best. The material is well chosen; alongside originals there are things like 'Cherryco', Dewey Redman's 'Dewey's Tune' and former associate Grachan Moncur III's rarely covered 'Riff-Raff'. The now familiar unvarnished sound works well on a set like this and the graininess and physicality of Lowe's playing comes across in every track.

***** Short Tales**
Bleu Regard 1959 *Lowe; Bernard Santacruz (b).* 01.

Santacruz has become a close associate of Lowe's; there is also a trio album under the bassist's name on AA. These would-be narrative pieces have a gently enigmatic quality, like fragments from a worm-eaten story-book. Lowe's increasingly old-fashioned delivery is as beguiling as ever, and he has rarely sounded more like his lost mentor Chu Berry than on some of these delicately nuanced numbers. Santacruz more than keeps up and bears listening to on his own account. Worth searching for.

Mundell Lowe (born 1922)

GUITAR

A survivor of the late big-band era, Lowe worked with several major bands in the '40s as well as crossing over to bop territory with Navarro and Parker. Thereafter studio work took up much of his career, with TV duties from the '60s onwards, but he has become a touring soloist in the last two decades.

***** The Mundell Lowe Quartet**
Original Jazz Classics OJC 1773 *Lowe; Dick Hyman (p, org, cel); Trigger Alpert (b); Ed Shaughnessy (d).* 8–10/55.

***** A Grand Night For Swinging**
Original Jazz Classics OJC 1940 *Lowe; Gene Quill (as); Billy Taylor (p); Les Grinage (b); Ed Thigpen (d).* 3–4/57.

*****(*) Mundell's Moods**
Nagel-Heyer 065 *Lowe; Hendrik Meurkens (hca, vib); Larry Porter (p); Pat O'Leary (b); Chuck Redd (d).* 1/00.

Lowe's albums under his own leadership are modest in number, and few have so far seen CD release. The OJC entries make entertaining if lightweight fare. *Quartet* has some smart playing, and the opening 'Will You Still Be Mine?' spells out how ably Lowe was able to bridge the worlds of swing and bop; he makes subtle harmonic touches and rhythmic inflections, while setting down his roots in swing beats. But Hyman plays organ a lot of the way, bringing a rinky-dink sensibility to the occasion, and several tracks opt either for mood-music or a quick, early finish. *A Grand Night For Swinging* is more pointed. Quill adds some sharp alto to three tracks, and there's plenty of swinging, though somehow the set feels no more substantial than the earlier one. Each is just another Riverside quickie of its day.

These days Mundell plays for fun, and *Mundell's Moods* was cut in Hamburg on a day off from a tour. The guitarist defers to Meurkens much of the way, which doesn't hurt, and dividing his time between harmonica and vibes, Meurkens plays some excellent things. And when Lowe steps out – wistful on 'Darn That Dream', fast and nippy on 'Seven Steps To Heaven' – he's lost little of his old facility. With five originals from within the band as well as the expected string of standards, the date's not just a quota filler, and Redd in particular keeps the pots on. Very enjoyable.

Henry Lowther (born 1941)

TRUMPET, FLUGELHORN

Lowther has been a consistent presence on the British scene for 40 years, working with most of the major big bands of the time and diversifying into rock and classical contexts as well. His ubiquity, coupled with a dearth of recordings under his own name, has undeservedly muted his reputation.

***** Fungii Mama**
GWB 444 *Lowther; Simon Picard (ts); Jim Mullen (g); Dave Green (b); Stu Butterfield (d).* 4/02.

Lowther's bright, evocative tone is always a joy to hear. He has recorded as leader before – 1970's *Child Song* is still a treasured item in some LP collections – but not often enough. This live set, recorded at a London pub, is co-led with guitarist Mullen. The material is not as challenging as some of the work Henry has been associated with over the years, but it's an elegantly programmed set centred on 'I Fall In Love Too Easily', 'On Green Dolphin Street' and 'Nutty'.

The leader's solos are well-shaped, finely crafted and always have real substance. He and Mullen enjoy some good natured exchanges, notably on the closing title-piece, but Picard seems a little out of place in this band. The sound is good enough but one wishes for a smoother and more professional context. A rare spotlit glimpse of a quiet master.

Jimmie Lunceford (1902–47)

ALTO SAXOPHONE, BANDLEADER

Lunceford studied music in Denver and at Fisk University and then taught in Manassas, forming a band there. After four years of scuffling, it played at New York's Cotton Club and made a big name as a touring act. Much of its show was almost vaudevillian, with band members singing and performing routines, but the records were very fine too. Lunceford toured relentlessly and took up flying. Disgruntled bandsmen left in the early '40s after feeling cheated over their pay, and the band went into a slow decline. Lunceford died of a heart attack while signing autographs.

****** Jimmie Lunceford 1930–1934**
Classics 501 *Lunceford; Sy Oliver, Eddie Tompkins, Tommy Stevenson, William 'Sleepy' Tomlin (t); Henry Wells (tb, v); Russell Bowles (tb); Willie Smith, Earl Carruthers (cl, as, bs); LaForet Dent (as); Joe Thomas (cl, ts); Edwin Wilcox (p, cel); Al Norris (g); Moses Allen (bb, b); Jimmy Crawford (d, vib).* 6/30–11/34.

*****(*) Jimmie Lunceford 1934–1935**
Classics 505 *As above, except add Paul Webster (t), Elmer Crumbley, Eddie Durham (tb, g), Dan Grissom (cl, as, v); omit Tomlin.* 11/34–9/35.

***** Jimmie Lunceford 1935–1937**
Classics 510 *As above, except add Ed Brown (as); omit Stevenson, Wells.* 9/35–6/37.

★★★(★) Jimmie Lunceford 1937–1939
Classics 520 *As above, except add Trummy Young (tb, v), Ted Buckner (as).* 6/37–1/39.

★★★(★) Jimmie Lunceford 1939
Classics 532 *As above, except omit Durham; add Gerald Wilson (t).* 1–9/39.

★★★ Jimmie Lunceford 1939–1940
Classics 565 *As above, except add Snooky Young (t), Dandridge Sisters (v); omit Tompkins.* 12/39–6/40.

★★(★) Jimmie Lunceford 1940–1941
Classics 622 *As above, except omit Dandridge Sisters.* 7/40–12/41.

★★(★) Jimmy Lunceford 1941–1945
Classics 862 *Lunceford; Snooky Young, Gerald Wilson, Paul Webster, Freddy Webster, Bob Mitchell, Pee Wee Jackson, Melvin Moore, William 'Chiefie' Scott, Russell Green, Ralph Griffin, Chuck Stewart (t); Elmer Crumbley, Russell Bowles, Trummy Young, Fernando Arbello, Earl Hardy, John Ewing, James Williams (tb); Willie Smith, Earl Carruthers, Dan Grissom, Joe Thomas, Benny Waters, Ted Buckner, Dan Grissom, Omer Simeon, Ernest Purce, Chauncey Jarrett, Kirkland Bradford (reeds); Edwin Wilcox (p, cel); Al Norris, John Mitchell (g); Truck Parham, George Duvivier, Moses Allen (b); Jimmy Crawford, Joe Marshall (d); Delta Rhythm Boys, Claude Trenier, Bill Darnell (v).* 41–45.

★★★ Jimmie Lunceford 1945–1947
Classics 1082 *Lunceford; Melvin Moore, Ralph Griffin, William 'Chiefie' Scott, Russell Green, Chuck Stewart, Bob Mitchell, Reunald Jones, Joe Wilder (t); Trummy Young (tb, v); Fernando Arbello, Earl Hardy, John Ewing, James Williams, Russell Bowles, Willie Tompkins, Alfonso King, Al Grey, Al Cobbs (tb); Omer Simeon (cl, as); Kirkland Bradford (as); Joe Thomas (ts, v); Ernest Purce, William Horner, Lee Howard (ts); Earl Carruthers (bs, cl); Edwin Wilcox (p); John Mitchell, Al Norris (g); Truck Parham, George Duvivier (b); Joe Marshall (d); Nick Brooks (v).* 12/44–5/47.

★★★ Jimmie Lunceford 1948–1949
Classics 1151 *Lunceford; Willie Cook, Bob Mitchell, Paul Webster, Rostelle Reese, Tommy Sims (t); Elmer Crumbley, Russell Bowles, Al Cobbs, Arnette Sparrow (tb); Omer Simeon (cl, as); Otis Hicks, Curby Alexander (as); Joe Thomas (ts, v); Lee Howard, Todd Rhodes, Slim Henderson (ts); Earl Carruthers (bs); Edwin Wilcox (p); Al Norris (g); Ed Sneed (b); Joe Marshall, Danny Farrar (d); Freddy Bryant, Savannah Churchill (v).* 48–49.

Lunceford's orchestra is doomed always to be remembered behind Ellington and Basie as the great also-ran big band of its day. Part of the reason for that is its sheer class. There were no special idiosyncrasies which lifted the Lunceford orchestra away from the consistent excellence to which it aspired. Its principal arrangers – Sy Oliver in particular, but also Edwin Wilcox (in the earlier days) and Willie Smith – created superbly polished, interlocking sections which made their records exude a professional élan. Soloists stepped naturally out of and back into this precision machine, and there was never much danger of a Rex Stewart or a Lester Young breaking any rule. Lunceford's virtues were entirely different from those of the rough-and-ready (early) Basie band, or from Ellington's unique cast of characters. Still, the records endure well, even though the later sides show a dramatic falling-off, as so often with the big bands of the period .

The first volume of the Classics chronological survey shows the band coming together; there is a single 1930 session in the discography, followed by an incongruous jump to 1934. The important hit coupling of 'Jazznocracy' and 'White Heat' is here, as well as the remarkably nonconformist versions of 'Mood Indigo' and 'Sophisticated Lady'; once under way in earnest, Lunceford turned out some fine records. The first two CDs feature some of the best of Oliver and Wilcox – and the 1934–35 disc includes the rare instance of two Ellington compositions, 'Rhapsody Junior' and 'Bird Of Paradise', which were never recorded by Duke. The 1935–37 session includes one of Oliver's masterpieces, 'Organ Grinder's Swing'. But a certain staleness sets in to the band from about 1936 onwards, with the Lunceford precision taking on a formulaic feel that fast tempos and good soloists – Smith was a rival to Hodges and Carter as one of the great alto stylists of the day, and Joe Thomas and Eddie Tompkins were excellent half-chorus players – never quite overcame.

The band continued to develop in minor ways. New players such as Trummy Young and Snooky Young were given tasks that raise the overall game on several of the tracks. Trummy's extraordinary playing (and singing) on 'Annie Laurie' and 'Margie' (Classics 520) is enough to make one wonder whether this is the same man who was such a dullard with Louis Armstrong's All Stars. Nevertheless the band's records started to sound as if they were being churned out by the end of 1939, although considered track by track there is still much eloquent and occasionally surprising music here. The departure of Oliver and then Smith was a blow that Lunceford's orchestra never recovered from, though to its last records it still sounds like a skilful band, a tribute to Lunceford's meticulous preparations and his admiration for Paul Whiteman. There is some dreary material on the next two discs, particularly the 1940–41 set, but even here there are a couple of interesting arrangements by new arrival Gerald Wilson ('Hi Spook' and 'Yard Dog Mazurka'), and the closing two-part 'Blues In The Night', though laden with kitsch, is effective in its way. The 1941–45 set has little going for it. The band lost several of its key members during this period, notably Willie Smith and Snooky Young, and even with arrangements by Tadd Dameron and Horace Henderson (a tame 'Jeep Rhythm') there is little to set the orchestra apart from its rivals. Nothing embarrassing here, at least, but the music is very reserved. The set of 1945–47 performances are in some ways rather better and may surprise those who feel that Lunceford'a decline was irreversible. Though he had lost so many of his key personalities, this was still a strong and professional outfit. A V-Disc date from October 1945 offers four straight-ahead swing titles, and a final look at 'One O'Clock Jump' (with Joe Wilder and Al Grey as young recruits) closes the disc.

We recommend the first two discs as the essential Lunceford, with the next three still full of interesting music. Transfers are, as usual from this source, rather variable: some of the earliest sides sound scratchy, and some of the later ones have a reverberant feel which at times suggests dubbings from tape copies. For the most part, though, it's been cleanly done.

The last disc is an early example of a 'ghost' band at work. Joe Thomas and Eddie Wilcox took over after Lunceford's death and managed 18 more sides before calling it a day. While there's nothing startling here, the old Lunceford virtues of precision and rehearsal are present, and the band sounds as if it could compete with most swing-era survivors. 'One For The Book' shows what it could still do. A dubious bonus is a version of 'When The Swallows Come Back To Capistrano' made some years earlier by an unknown personnel.

Jesper Lundgaard (born 1954)

DOUBLE BASS

Denmark's other great bass-player studied at the University of Aarhus before starting a distinguished career as sideman to visiting Americans.

***** This Bass Was Made For Walking**
Music Mecca 10432 *Lundgaard; Bob Rockwell (ts); Jacob Fischer (g); Alex Riel (d).* 94.

***** Two Basses**
Touché Music TMcCD 020 *Lundgaard; Mads Vinding (b).* 6/02.

The Repertory Quartet was founded to play the music of Thad Jones. Later projects – and different personnels – were devoted to compositions by Ellington, Bill Evans, Charles Mingus and classic performers like Louis Armstrong and Fats Waller. We're not clear if those sets are still available, but this one certainly is, and it's a thoroughly enjoyable album of swinging modern jazz. Thad's 'A Child Is Born' also features on the duo album with the equally redoubtable Vinding. Even when one bassist plays *arco* underneath another's picked figures, such dates can be a difficult listen. This one, though, is so elegantly constructed and so thoroughly lyrical and expressive that one scarcely notices the absence of a more conventional line-up.

Jan Lundgren (born 1966)

PIANO

Danish pianist who has worked extensively in California as well as at home in the '80s and '90s.

***** Conclusion**
Four Leaf Clover FLCD 136 *Lundgren; Jesper Lundgaard (b); Alex Riel (d).* 5–6/94.

*****(*) Bird Of Passage**
Four Leaf Clover FLCD 145 *Lundgren; Anders Bergcrantz (t); Rich Perry (ts); Hans Andersson (b); P. A. Tollbom (d).* 7/95.

***** California Connection**
Four Leaf Clover FLCD 148 *Lundgren; Peter Asplund (t); Dave Carpenter (b); Paul Kreibich (d).* 1/96.

***** Cooking! At The Jazz Bakery**
Fresh Sound FSR 5019 2CD *Lundgren; Chuck Berghofer (b); Joe LaBarbera (d).* 9/96.

Lundgren knows his post-bop piano, and he takes his time over tempos and in filling up space. *Conclusion* has nothing green about it (Lundgren spent much of the '80s playing behind various giants) though nothing to make one gasp at the originality. His own tunes are cute enough, but the standout is a glowing 'I See Your Face Before Me', played with the utmost finesse. He also starts *Bird Of Passage* with a slow ballad, 'This Is All I Ask', before any of the horns come in. Perry is a reliable type for a date like this, and he even comes a little way out of his usually deferential shell on the title-track, where the hollowed-out honks he uses to climax his solo are a surprise. These are longer, more expansive performances, and the show is stolen by Bergcrantz, who comes in on only two tracks yet delivers two outstandingly fine improvisations on Lundgren's originals. Excellent record. After that, Asplund's perfectly agreeable playing is a slight anticlimax on the third record, cut on an American visit with a local rhythm section. Intelligently varied for pace and material, this peaks on a wistful trumpet–piano version of Thore Swanerud's 'Sodermalm'.

Lundgren is back for more with a couple of live sets from Los Angeles's Jazz Bakery. Spreading them over two CDs makes the set an expensive introduction on his methods, and all 20 tracks are prime cut of bebop, bar a farewell solo on 'Värmlandsvisan'. Still, the vigour of the playing is emphatically sustained across both discs, and Berghofer and LaBarbera play with enough vim themselves to suggest that they're giving the young man plenty of respect.

*****(*) Something To Live For**
Sittel 9258 *Lundgren; Matthias Hjorth (b); Rasmus Kihlberg (d); orchestra.* 10/98.

***** For Listeners Only**
Sittel 9271 *Lundgren; Mattias Svensson (b); Rasmus Kihlberg (d).* 12/00.

***** Plays The Music Of Victor Young**
Sittel 9269 *As above, except add Johnny Griffin (ts), Stacey Kent, Deborah Brown (v).* 8/00–1/01.

Something To Live For is an Ellington–Strayhorn homage. Abetted by orchestral arrangements by Bo Sylvén, which are thereabouts without becoming too intrusive, this works better than many a tribute record, thanks to the impish energy the trio inveigle into the setting. It's irreverent enough to find something fresh even in the likes of 'Caravan', but not so disrespectful that the source material sounds debased. There's also a 15-minute 'Reminiscences Of A Duke' by Magnus Linden, which cleverly works any number of Ducal quotes into a bright pastiche.

For Listeners Only is an attractive set of originals. Lundgren's writing doesn't cut very deep, but he likes perky, upbeat vehicles, a little in the vein of such contemporaries as Benny Green or the early Niels Lan Doky, and he ties each of them up smartly. The Victor Young collection is varied by the guests: Kent and Brown take three songs apiece, but the best shot comes when Griffin swaggers in to do 'A Weaver Of Dreams' – good enough to make you wish he'd stuck around for the whole set (though he sounds a bit bleary on 'When I Fall In Love').

Carmen Lundy (born 1954)

VOCALS

Began working in New York in 1979 and, in a career which has made modest progress, she sings in a style that blends the classic jazz vocal with soul influences, and has a penchant for writing songs herself.

***** Good Morning Kiss**
Justin Time 8495 *Lundy; Jon Faddis, Earl Gardner (t); Steve Turre (tb); Rene McLean, Bobby Watson (as); Jim Hartog (bs); Harry Whitaker (p, ky); Curtis Lundy (b); Victor Lewis (d); Myra Casales (perc).* 1 & 8/85.

***** Moment To Moment**

Arabesque 102 *Lundy; Cecil Bridgewater, Chico Freeman (ts); Onaje Allan Gumbs (ky); Kevin Eubanks (g); Ben Brown, Kenny Davis (b); Buddy Williams (d); Myra Casales (perc).* 4/91.

***** Self Portrait**

JVC 2047 *Lundy; Ernie Watts (ts); Gary Herbig (ss, f, af, bf, cl); Cedar Walton (p); John Clayton Jr, Nathan East (b); Ralph Penland (d); strings; woodwinds.* 11/94.

***** Old Devil Moon**

JVC 9016 *Lundy; Randy Brecker (t, flhn); Frank Foster, Bob Mintzer (ts); Billy Childs (p); Harry Whitaker (syn); Victor Bailey, Santi Debriano (b); Winston Clifford, Omar Hakim (d); Mayra Casales, Ralph Irizarry (perc); Tawatha Agee, Dennis Collins, Lani Groves, Gwen Guthrie (v).* 97.

A strong, instrumental singer rather than a great interpreter, Lundy has taken to heart Billie Holiday's overused line about 'playing a horn'. Clearly influenced by saxophone-players, Carmen often doesn't seem to be unduly concerned about the programme or the theme of a song, just by its chords and melody. If this makes her sound detached, she isn't, but technique has tended to come before expression, and this is only slowly righting itself.

The debut album was a good illustration. What you listen to is the impeccable harmonic understanding rather than the meaning of the words (true even on 'Love For Sale') and Carmen's ability to come off big resonant bottom notes and build elaborate, curving scales on the foundations of a song is most impressive. Bobby Watson's arrangements sit beautifully for her own rich alto. The first album was originally released on Black Hawk and it's good to have it back in circulation. What's more surprising than that doughty label's demise is that it took Carmen five years to record a follow-up.

Moment To Moment is also bold enough to combine original material with some relatively unexplored standards like 'Invitation'. No apparent temptation to go for more obviously crowd-pleasing songs. *Self Portrait* opens on a very strong reading of 'Spring Can Really Hang You Up The Most', continues with an excellent original – 'Better Days' – one of several in the set, and peaks with a truly special performance of Kurt Weill's 'My Ship'. Cedar Walton dominates the small group, a player who understands the dynamics of a song better than anyone around. The orchestrations are lusher than they strictly need to be and there are a couple of occasions when one wishes for a simpler, less fussy background, which is what she gets on 'I Don't Want To Love Without You', with Ernie Watts on tenor. The later record is very good, too, but the Billie-isms have become ever more noticeable and are hampering her approach. She opens with 'Star Eyes' this time, and gives it a big send-off. 'In A Sentimental Mood' is the killer-diller, pushed along by a tense, almost threatening rhythm section. Fewer originals this time out, perhaps because they don't sell, perhaps because Carmen has hipped to the unavoidable recognition that she's never going to outwrite Rodgers and Hart or Donny Hathaway.

***** This Is Carmen Lundy**

Justin Time 174-2 *Lundy; Kevin Louis (t, flhn); Bobby Watson (as); Mark Shim (ts); Onaje Allan Gumbs, Anthony Wonsey (ky); Curtis Lundy (b); Ralph Peterson, Victor Lewis (d); Mayra Casales (perc).* 6/01.

It's a great band, and sometimes they take the ears off Carmen, which is unfair: she's in fine voice throughout. But the material comprises nine of her own originals, and she tends to over-personalize them. The result is more like a manifesto than a vocal album, as well meant and involved as such pieces as 'One More River To Cross' may be. It's in the softer moments ('Is It Love') that she makes the most lasting impression.

Lunge

GROUP

A quartet of London-based improvisers who originally came together out of a 1997 tour by a Butch Morris-directed orchestra.

***** Braced & Framed**

ACTA 13 *Gail Brand (tb); Pat Thomas (ky, elec); Phil Durrant (vn, elec); Mark Sanders (d).* 2–7/99.

*****(*) Strong Language**

Emanem 4079 *As above.* 12/00–6/02.

Lunge's music can be dark and thickly layered, but they have an agreeably humorous side too, often itemized via Thomas's electronics. Brand's trombone lines aren't especially powerful in themselves but she ends up playing the 'voice' of the group and her comparative restraint assists in establishing the group's democratic nature. As a group of individual stylists they're an unlikely alliance and there's a palpable sense of the group feeling its way forward on *Braced & Framed.*

Strong Language is served by much more vivid recording (four pieces from an Amsterdam concert and two from a studio session) and is a brawnier, more aggressive set all round – which some may not count as an improvement, as some of the gaiety (if that doesn't seem too absurd a description) may have left the group. The hardest thing in all of this may be figuring out which sounds Durrant is making, since his violin rarely sounds like one and his electronics seem more of a subliminal rumble in comparison with Thomas's tweet and chatter. Sustained across 16 minutes, 'Planarchy', which goes through the quartet's dynamic range with seamless and intense activity, is an exemplary showing of what they can do.

Claude Luter (born 1923)

CLARINET, SOPRANO SAXOPHONE

A Parisian, Luter led the French revivalist movement in the late '40s and recorded first with Bechet and later with other clarinettists including Mezzrow, Nicholas and Bigard. Has stuck to his idea of jazz ever since.

***** Red Hot Reeds**

GHB BCD-219 *Luter; Jacques Gauthé (cl, ss); Steve Pistorius, David Boeddinghaus (p); Neil Unterseher (g, bj); Amy Sharpe (bj); Tom Saunders (tba, b); Rick Elmore (tba); Ernie Elly, Dicky Taylor (d).* 4/86.

Not much survives of Luter's discography at present, but he was one of the leading forces in French traditional jazz for decades and this 1986 date, co-led with Jacques Gauthe, is more like a postscript to a ubiquitous career. The horns play in a manner that offers an inevitable echo of Luter's records with Sidney Bechet in the '50s, and the set-list covers Morton, Handy, Bechet and Jimmy Blythe. Recorded on consecutive days in

New Orleans, with entirely different accompanists each day, and performed with much *brio* and enjoyment by the two front-line veterans.

Chick Lyall

PIANO

Scottish pianist making his debut after much activity through the '80s and '90s.

***** Tilting Ground**

Caber CAarch 001 *Lyall; Tore Brunborg (ss, ts).* 90.

***** Solitary Dance**

Caber 004 *Lyall (p solo).* 1/98.

Though until recently Scotland lacked a solid infrastructure for jazz, the country has continued to produce inventive players. Of the current generation of piano players – which also numbers Dave Newton and Brian Kellock – Chick Lyall is the most exploratory and adventurous. A charter member of improvising ensemble Green Room, he has the ability to switch from playing changes to quasi-classical contexts to free.

Solitary Dance is his belated solo debut. Its appearance on Caber is a sign that Scottish jazz is beginning to devise its own flotation system. It's hard to imagine any major label taking on a record as calmly unfashionable and cliché-free. The title-tune is a dedication to Sir Michael Tippett, a slow, understated essay in spatial relationships. Other titles have a more tentative quality. There are three pianistic 'Epigrams' and two 'Objects Of Contemplation', all of them beautifully executed and flawlessly tasteful, but very much academic studies. Elsewhere, as in the pairing of 'Flow River Flow' and 'Blow Wind Blow', the language is more obviously jazz-based, and Lyall's exceptional metrical sense becomes evident. On this showing Lyall is perhaps too reflective to captivate a wider audience.

Caber's first 'archive' release is the record of duets with Brunborg. Some interesting moments in a kind of impressionistic style – Lyall uses a sampler for percussive sounds and some vocal tones too – but this feels like notes towards a proper record rather than a finished piece of work, though Brunborg's keening tone makes its mark.

*****(*) Broken Poems**

Caber 031 *Lyall; Joakim Milder (ss, ts); Mike Dunning (b); Tom Bancroft (d).* 12/02.

Whatever the perceived meeting points between Scotland and Scandinavia may be, the Swedish sax master fits in with Lyall's group without a murmur of dissent. There's a meandering sense to much of the music, especially in the likes of 'White Horse In Distance' and the three-part 'Iliac Suite' which is spread through the record, but that setting is meat and drink to Milder and he makes the most of every timbral nuance and inflection. It somewhat overshadows the leader's own playing, though he takes the composing credits anyway.

Brian Lynch (born 1955)

TRUMPET, FLUGELHORN

Lynch has worked with Art Blakey and The Artist Formerly Known As Prince and has a well-deserved reputation for free-blowing swing in a whole range of genres and styles. His own records are largely an outlet for long-lined, complex themes influenced by bebop but often using Coltrane changes in imaginative ways.

*****(*) Peer Pressure**

Criss Cross Criss 1029 *Lynch; Ralph Moore (ts); Jim Snidero (as); Kirk Lightsey (p); Jay Anderson (b); Victor Lewis (d).* 12/86.

****(*) Back Room Blues**

Criss Cross Criss 1042 *Lynch; Javon Jackson (ts); David Hazeltine (p); Peter Washington (b); Lewis Nash (d).* 12/89.

***** At The Main Event**

Criss Cross Criss 1070 *Lynch; Ralph Moore (ts); Mel Rhyne (org); Peter Bernstein (g); Kenny Washington (d); Jose Alexis Diaz (perc).* 12/91.

Peer pressure, indeed. One of the occupational horrors of the jazz musician's life is 'going single', travelling from town to town, playing with local rhythm sections. Eric Dolphy suffered profoundly by it, Lee Konitz seems to thrive on it; *Back Room Blues* would seem to put Brian Lynch squarely with the Dolphys. There's nothing amiss about the leader's playing. His bright, brassy sound – particularly vivid on the often smudgy flugelhorn – is well up to scratch. But the band seems entirely devoid of ideas and the sound might just as well be live.

The line-up on *Peer Pressure* makes weight-for-weight comparison of the two albums as uneven as a Don King boxing bill. Where Jackson is sophomoric, the British-born, Berklee-graduated Ralph Moore is right on the case, responding to Lynch's unpretentious hard bop with a mixture of fire and intelligence. Jim Snidero has less to say but says it with unapologetic verve; his own *Mixed Bag* (Criss Cross Criss 1032 – the label's titles are always curiously self-revealing!) also features Lynch and is worth checking out. Tommy Turrentine's roistering 'Thomasville' gets everybody in and warmed up for the subtler cadence of Benny Golson's 'Park Avenue Petite'. Horace Silver's 'The Outlaw' gets a slightly camp reading but, apart from the low-key CD bonus, 'I Concentrate On You', the rest of the material is by the trumpeter and is generally very impressive, both in conception and in execution. Amazing what a bit of peer pressure can do.

The last of the Criss Crosses is a good-hearted, expansive, blowin'-in-from-Milwaukee date, which celebrates local club The Main Event. There's plenty of playing to enjoy, even if Lynch acts as not much more than the genial host, and the round-robin of solos on the seven tracks elicits nothing knockout from any of the musicians.

***** Keep Your Circle Small**

Sharp Nine CD 1001-2 *Lynch; David Hazeltine (p); Peter Washington (b); Louis Hayes (d).* 95.

*****(*) Spheres Of Influence**

Sharp Nine 1007-2 *Lynch; Tony Lujan, Pete Rodriguez (t); Luis Bonilla, Conrad Herwig (tb); Chris Washburne (tba); Donald Harrison (as); Kavid Kikoski (p); Essiet Okon Essiet (b); John Benitez, Adam Cruz, Jeff Tain Watts, Milton Cardona (perc).* 6/97.

A change of label and signs of growing confidence from Lynch, whose writing here is ever more ambitious and capacious. The earlier of the pair is relatively modest in scope and the quartet aren't unduly stretched by the charts. It's with *Spheres Of Influence* that Lynch signals a desire to move on to a new plane, debuting some of his larger-group compositions and arrangements. The opening track uses soulful jazz measures, set to a kind of relaxed reggae beat. Lynch's solo is punctuated with glorious blares and smears. 'Green Is Mean' seems to be a contrafact on 'On Green Dolphin Street', with adventurous changes that recall Coltrane. The Wayne Shorter-composed 'Oriental Folk Song' is an unexpected delight, tucked away at the end of the record but worth programming earlier now and again. The most ambitious performances of the set are the two with extra horns. 'Palmieri's Mood' is a delightful Latin swinger; but, for an insight into Lynch's skill as an arranger, a standard, 'I've Grown Accustomed To Her Face', is the point of reference. Subtly modulated and richly voiced, it makes no compromises, working through a sequence of subtle changes before triggering Lynch's typically elaborate solo. A fine, assured performance from an ever-better player. In support, Donald Harrison plays more freshly and with more bite than he has since the days with Terence Blanchard. Some tracks seem to dispense with bass altogether, which is an interesting tack; on the others, Essiet and Watts mesh as surely as ever.

*****(*) Tribute To The Trumpet Masters**
Sharp Nine 1017-2 *Lynch; Mulgrew Miller (p); Essiet Okon Essiet (b); Carl Allen (d).* 4/00.

The concept looks tired already, and a perilous one: nine trumpeters paid homage, either via an original – 'Tribute To Blue', 'Charles Tolliver' (!) – or a suitable cover. But it actually works out very well. Lynch didn't do himself many favours by picking tunes as tough as 'Search For The New Land' (Lee Morgan) or Booker Little's almost frightening 'Opening Statement', but he pulls them off with serene confidence, and throughout he manages to pay respects without actually sounding like anyone in particular – except, possibly, himself. Miller and crew are in excellent supportive fettle.

Jimmy Lyons (1932–86)

ALTO SAXOPHONE, FLUTE

Emerged in the early '60s as a free-thinking alto-player who became a key member of Cecil Taylor's group; he remained close with Taylor, besides teaching and playing in other groups, but was killed by lung cancer in 1986.

*****(*) Something In Return**
Black Saint 120125 *Lyons; Andrew Cyrille (perc).* 2/81.

*****(*) Burnt Offering**
Black Saint 120130 *Lyons; Andrew Cyrille (d).* 82.

***** Wee Sneezawee**
Black Saint 120067 *Lyons; Raphe Malik (t); Karen Borca (bsn); William Parker (b); Paul Murphy (d).* 9/83.

*****(*) Give It Up**
Black Saint 120087 *Lyons; Enrico Rava (t, flhn); Karen Borca (bsn); Jay Oliver (b); Paul Murphy (d).* 3/85.

If Charlie Parker had a true heir – in the sense of someone interested in getting interest on the inheritance, rather than merely preserving the principal – it was Jimmy Lyons. Compared to his light-fingered onrush, most of the bop *epigoni* sound deeply conservative. He didn't have the greatest tone in the world, though it seems rather odd to describe a saxophonist's tone as 'reedy' as if that were an insult. Lyons's delivery was always light and remarkably without ego. Years of playing beside Cecil Taylor, in addition to accelerating his hand-speed, probably encouraged a certain self-effacement as well.

On *Give It Up*, Lyons seems quite content to remain within the confines of the group. Significantly pianoless and with only a rather secondary role for the bassist and drummer, it resolves into a series of high, intermeshed lines from the saxophone and horn, with the bassoon tracing a sombre counterpoint. Karen Borca's role might have been clearer were she not so close in timbre to Jay Oliver's bass, but it's worth concentrating for a moment on what she is doing; the effect is broadly similar to what Dewey Redman used to do behind Ornette Coleman and Don Cherry. She also appears to great effect on the earlier *Wee Sneezawee*, perhaps the most conventional of these discs in free-bop terms but a similarly invigorating session. Only on the brief, uncharacteristic 'Ballada', with which the album ends, does Lyons occupy the foreground. It's immediately clear that his fey, slightly detached tone doesn't entail an absence of feeling; the closing track is a sad monument to an undervalued career that had little more than a year left to run.

Among the most fruitful encounters of Lyons's sadly under-documented career were his duos with Cyrille, a fellow-alumnus of Cecil Taylor Academy. Cyrille is a one-man orchestra, conjuring layered energies that make a sax-and-drums 'Take The "A" Train' seem anything but absurd. He can play at astonishing volume (at one point almost sounding as if he was trying to re-create a Cecil Taylor trio *à deux*), but also with considerable subtlety and a user-friendly reliability of beat. 'Exotique', on the later session, is a wonderfully structured and emotionally committed performance. Both this and the concert recording, *Burnt Offering*, are superb examples of two masters in full flight.

****** The Box Set**
Ayler 036 5CD *Lyons; Karen Borca (bsn); Hayes Burnett, William Parker (b); Andrew Cyrille, Henry Letcher, Paul Murphy, Syd Smart (d, perc).* 72–85.

Not the sumptuous repackaging of studio material that the title might imply, but an oddly moving compilation of live material from the early '70s, when Jimmy was a regular fixture on the New York loft scene (there are sets from Sam and Bea Rivers's Rivbea studio), to the year before his death, a slightly shaky recording of him working with bassist Parker, percussionist Paul Murphy and bassoonist Karen Borca, who was a loyal associate.

The sheer bulk of material is less impressive than the doggedness of Lyons's search for a sound that led the alto saxophone on from Charlie Parker's innovations (and the consolidations of his followers, like Jackie McLean and Sonny Stitt) and towards a new freedom of expression. A solo recording from 1981 in New York, documented on disc three, is almost painfully poignant in places. And yet it was precisely Lyons's sympathetic merging of personalities with others and especially with the strong leadership of Cecil Taylor that made him such a quietly compelling figure.

Long-term fans will recognize Lyons themes like 'Wee Sneezawee' and 'Jump Up' and value alternative performances of 'Shakin' Back'. There's also an interview with Jimmy where he talks about aspects of his career and feelings about music. This isn't a package for newcomers, who'd be better directed to one of the Black Saint records, but it is a hugely valuable record of a lost master of free jazz who might well still have been contributing today.

Johnny Lytle (1932–96)

VIBES

Played drums with Ray Charles in 1950 but switched to vibes and led his own groups from the late '50s onwards.

*** Nice And Easy

Original Jazz Classics OJC 1013 *Lytle; Johnny Griffin (ts); Bobby Timmons (p); Sam Jones (b); Louis Hayes (d).* 1/62.

*** Got That Feeling / Moon Child

Milestone MCD 47093-2 *Lytle; Milt Harris (org); Milt Hinton (b); Steve Cooper (d); William Peppy Hinnant (d); Ray Barretto (perc).* 62–63.

*** The Village Caller

Original Jazz Classics OJC 110 *Lytle; Milt Harris (org); Bob Cranshaw (b); Peppy Hinant (d); Willie Rodriguez (perc).* 64–65.

**(*) The Loop / New & Groovy

BGP CDBGPD 961 *Lytle; unknown p, b and d.* 65.

If there is a classic record by this Ohio-born vibesman, it's surely *The Village Caller*, where he lives out all the clichés of organ–vibes rhythm combos and delivers a perfectly cooked slice of soul-jazz in the title-tune. The rest of the album bumbles past inoffensively enough. The reappearance of *Nice And Easy* challenges our assertion, though, since this is simply an excellent band for Lytle to jam with. Griffin is in a good mood, tucking into the standards and blues with his customary speed and aplomb, and the leader plays some fine solos on 'But Not For Me' and '322–Wow!'. Still, in the end, this is really no more than a decent hard-bop workout, and for once Louis Hayes isn't as sharp as he could be (or, at least, he's messily recorded).

The Milestone set couples two of Lytle's four Jazzland albums. It might be an obvious call to describe a vibes player as percussive, but Lytle's drumming background seems to have directed his vibes playing, and both sessions are crisp and rhythmically tight. His companions have little of their own to offer, although Barretto's work on the *Moon Child* tracks adds to the sense that this band is all about rhythm.

The BGP CD couples two rare albums from the same period, originally issued on Tuba with no personnel details, and the music is slight; the titles include 'The Snapper' and 'Screamin' Loud'. The formula wears thin after a number of tracks but, taken a few at a time, they certainly stir the feet. The pianist sounds like Wynton Kelly here and there, and the remastering is good if a little bright. Lytle's subsequent Muse albums were a mostly disappointing lot and his passing left his status sadly unrealized.

Humphrey Lyttelton (born 1921)

TRUMPET, CORNET, CLARINET, VOCAL

The doyen of post-war British jazz, Lyttelton has been active for more than 50 years as a performer, broadcaster, writer, wit and general man-about-jazz, a tireless force whose early links with trad jazz soon blossomed into a shrewd pan-stylistic outlook. His toff's background (Eton and the Guards) might have instilled certain qualities of leadership, but he has never been shy about his work and he still leads a band and runs his own record label.

*** Delving Back With Humph 1948–1949

Lake LACD 72 *Lyttelton; Harry Brown, Ian Christie, Bobby Mickleburgh (tb); Wally Fawkes (cl); Ernie Mansfield (ts); George Webb, Dill Jones (p); Nevil Skrimshire, Bill Bramwell (g); Buddy Vallis (bj); Les Rawlings, John Wright, Bert Howard (b); Dave Carey (d, wbd); Bernard Saward, Carlo Krahmer (d).* 1/48–11/49.

This is almost prehistoric for Lyttelton, who is still on active duty both as musician and emcee for jazz on stage and in radio. A very fine discography attests to his command as a trumpeter (and clarinettist, though that side of his playing is less often remarked on). These early sessions are the prelude to the full-blown British trad movement of the early '50s: six tracks with a Carlo Krahmer group of 1948, followed by 15 from the following year, each led from the front by Lyttelton's tight, crisp trumpet and Fawkes's serpentine clarinet, at this stage almost entirely in Sidney Bechet's debt. The rhythm sections range from awkward to competent, and the material is mostly Oliver, ODJB and the like; but the peculiarly British fierceness of the music hasn't gone stale, and even in less than ideal sound the enthusiasm of the band cuts through.

CORE COLLECTION

**** The Parlophones Volumes One–Four

Calligraph CLG CD 035-1/2/3/4 *Lyttelton; Keith Christie, John Picard (tb); Wally Fawkes, Ian Christie (cl); Bruce Turner (ss, as, cl); Tony Coe (as, cl); Ade Monsborough (as); Jimmy Skidmore, Kathy Stobart (ts); Joe Temperley (bs); George Webb, Johnny Parker, Ian Armit (p); Freddy Legon (g, bj); Buddy Vallis (bj); Mickey Ashman, Brian Brocklehurst, Jim Bray (b); Bernard Saward, Stan Greig, Eddie Taylor, George Hopkinson (d); Iris Grimes, Neva Raphaello (v).* 11/49–8/59.

At last, the bulk of Lyttelton's Parlophone sessions make it to CD. One hundred titles are neatly spread across the four discs (available only separately, though Humph might do you a deal at one of his gigs) and, although in absolutist terms it isn't complete – there are no alternative takes, and titles by the collaborative bands with Graeme Bell and Freddy Grant are being saved for a possible follow-up – what remains is a comprehensive picture of ten years of work by the leading jazz force of his day and arguably the most influential jazzman Britain has ever produced.

Even the earliest tracks show how Lyttelton wasn't content to regard jazz as any kind of routine and, although the 1949–50 sessions are relatively formulaic, the playing – these were among the best players the country could muster, after all – is consistently creative and supple, with the rhythm sections never resorting to the trudge of regulation trad. Lyttelton's own playing is wasteless and controlled, without losing the terminal vibrato which was a feature of the '20s stylists he admired. Fawkes and Christie were important elements in this band, and so was Bruce Turner, a notorious recruit when he arrived in 1953 but a crucial aide in assisting Lyttelton's move from trad to mainstream. The progress through the '50s is marked by milestones such as 'The

Onions' and the great hit, 'Bad Penny Blues', before concluding with the 1957–59 sessions which suggest how far Lyttelton had progressed, from the sparky trad of 'Memphis Blues' to the sophisticated mainstream inflexions of the likes of 'Hand Me Down Love'. There are also glimpses of young tykes such as Tony Coe, Kathy Stobart, Jimmy Skidmore and Joe Temperley.

Throughout the four discs there are surprises, such as the extraordinary, haunting 'Jail Break' or Lyttelton's blues playing behind Neva Raphaello on 'Young Woman Blues'. As a record of a crucial chapter in British jazz, it's peerless stuff. Remastering, by Dave Bennett when tape masters haven't been used, is excellent, although some of the original engineering wasn't up to all that much.

***(*) The Best Of Humphrey Lyttelton

EMI Gold 583280-2 3CD *Lyttelton; John Picard, Keith Christie (tb); Wally Fawkes (cl, bcl, v); Ian Christie (cl); Bruce Turner (as, cl, v); Tony Coe (as, cl); Ade Monsborough (as); Jimmy Skidmore (ts); George Webb, Johnny Parker, Ian Armit (p); Freddy Legon (bj, g, v); Buddy Vallis (bj); John Wright, Jim Bray, Mickey Ashman, Brian Brocklehurst (b); George Hopkinson (d, wbd); Stan Greig, Eddie Taylor, Tommy Jones, Bernard Saward (d).* 11/49–6/57.

This sets something of a poser for Lyttelton fans, since it covers a lot of the same ground as the Calligraph set listed above but adds numerous other tracks. The key extra, which will probably sway most of the undecided, is the presence of all 14 tracks from two ten-inch Parlophone LPs, *Humph Swings Out* and *Here's Humph*, which effectively documented Humph's move from trad to mainstream. Good remastering, but we dock a notch because the documentation is very poor, with no personnels (we tentatively provide the above) and no reference to which tracks come from where. Still, at a bargain price, churlish not to recommend.

***(*) The Conway And Royal Festival Hall Concerts

Calligraph CLG CD 038 *Lyttelton; John Picard (tb); Wally Fawkes (cl); Bruce Turner (ss, as); Johnny Parker (p); Freddy Legon (g, bj); Mickey Ashman (b); George Hopkinson (d).* 8–11/54.

A valuable glimpse of Humph in a vintage year, 1954, this reissues the twelve-inch LP, *Humph At The Conway*, with the ten-inch *Jazz At The Royal Festival Hall* as a bonus. John Picard comes in for the second date. A strong element of blues material on the first session is balanced by a more populist choice of tunes on the second, but for both gigs the band were in good spirits and fine form. Sound is decent rather than outstanding, with some eccentricities of balance on the first date.

***(*) I Play As I Please

Lake LACD 189 *Lyttelton; Bert Courtley (t); Maurice Pratt, Rick Kennedy, Alec McGuinness (tb); Ronnie Ross, Tony Coe (as); Jimmy Skidmore, Don Rendell, Kathy Stobart (ts); Alex Leslie (bs); Stan Farnsworth, Larry Saunders (f); Phil Goody (bf); Ron Davey (vib); John Blanchard (mar); Ian Armit (p); Denny Wright (g); Brian Brocklehurst, Jack Fallon (b); Eddie Taylor (d); Jack McHardie, Sidney Rich (perc).* 8–12/57.

Tracks by the regular Lyttelton bunch mixed with some biggish-band sides and a pair by the revived Lyttelton Paseo Band. It ruffled a few traditional feathers at the time, but it's all vintage Humph. Jimmy Skidmore gets a tremendous blow into 'Skid Row'.

**** Triple Exposure

Calligraph CLG CD 041 2CD *Lyttelton; Bruce Turner, Tony Coe (as); Kathy Stobart, Jimmy Skidmore (ts); Joe Temperley (bs); John Picard, Eddie Harvey (tb); Johnny Parker, Ian Armit (p); Freddy Legon (g); Jim Bray, Brian Brocklehurst (b); Stan Greig, Eddie Taylor (d).* 8/56–8/59.

A set which fills in a lot of the picture of Humph's late '50s music, since it includes the four albums *Humph Swings Out* (1956 – mostly trad, short tracks), *Kath Meets Humph* (1957 – Stobart arrives for the then ailing Jimmy Skidmore, and plays some lovely solos), *Humph In Perspective* (1958 – Joe Temperley is the new man, and the session has an almost rowdily energetic feel to it) and *Triple Exposure* itself (1959 – one of the most varied of all Lyttelton's records, with Afro-Latin tunes, swing, blues and his by now inimitable mainstream take). A beautifully assembled set which gives consistent pleasure and will delight Lyttelton collectors with its availability.

***(*) BBC Jazz Club, Autumn 1958

Upbeat URCD 174 *Lyttelton; Bobby Pratt, Duncan Campbell, Eddie Blair, Bert Courtley (t); Keith Christie, John Picard, Eddie Harvey (tb); Tony Coe, Ronnie Ross (as); Jimmy Skidmore, Kathy Stobart (ts); Joe Temperley (bs); Ian Armit (p); Brian Brocklehurst (b); Eddie Taylor (d); Jimmy Rushing (v).* 58.

Cut at the end of a tour in which Jimmy Rushing guested with the eight-piece Lyttelton band, this broadcast session (where the audience was banned from applauding to save studio time!) is a memorable survival. Although it starts with the standard line-up, they're soon augmented by members of the Ted Heath orchestra, and under Eddie Harvey's direction the music swings as mightily as the vocalist, who is in prime form. Even if some of the material is a bit too familiar, nobody seems to be either coasting or less than lively. One of the best of Upbeat's archaeological series.

*** Scatterbrains

Lake LACD 180 *Lyttelton; Kenny Davern (cl); Stan Greig (p); Al Casey (g); Paul Seeley (bj); Paul Bridge (b); Adrian Macintosh (d).* 12/82.

A reissue of a set from Swindon Arts Centre. The instrumentation and the tunes are a deliberate recall of (of all things) the 1932 Billy Banks Rhythmakers sides. Kenny Davern is the star turn here and Humph has to play second biling to his virtuosity, but it makes an interesting premise and the music's not short of either fun or astute thinking.

***(*) ... It Seems Like Yesterday!

Upbeat URCD 168 *Lyttelton; Wally Fawkes (cl); Bruce Turner (as, cl); John Barnes (as, bs, cl); Mick Pyne (p); Paul Bridge (b); Adrian Macintosh (d).* 9/83–11/84.

The Calligraph album of the title, reissued with five tracks from *Humph At The Bull's Head* as a bonus. Fawkes was rejoining his old boss for the occasion and everyone has a high old time of it. In consequence, the live tracks feel like a reduction in temperature, although still very engaging.

*****(*) Beano Boogie**
Calligraph CLG 021 *Lyttelton; Pete Strange (tb); John Barnes (cl, ss, ts, bs); Alan Barnes (cl, ss, as); Stan Greig (p); Paul Bridge (b); Adrian Macintosh (d).* 3/89.

***** Rock Me Gently**
Calligraph CLG 026 *As above, except Kathy Stobart (cl, ss, ts, bs) replaces John Barnes; add Dave Cliff (g).* 7/91.

The formation of Calligraph, his own label, has produced a steady stream of new records from Humph, and they maintain a standard which many jazz musicians should envy. Some fine records from the early '80s, including *At The Bull's Head* and *Gigs*, have yet to acquire CD transfer, though there may still be some LP stocks in circulation. *Beano Boogie* is notable for the arrival of Alan Barnes, whose alto turns add fresh fizz to a well-established front line. Though the record gets off to a slow start, when it reaches 'Apple Honey', a nearly explosive reading of the Woody Herman tune, it lifts off. The elder Barnes departed with *Rock Me Gently*, but Kathy Stobart's return to the fold (35 years after they recorded 'Kath Meets Humph') means there is no drop in authority, and she delivers a grippingly unsentimental version of 'My Funny Valentine' on what's a generously filled CD.

*****(*) At Sundown**
Calligraph CLG 027 *Lyttelton; Acker Bilk (cl, v); Dave Cliff (g); Dave Green (b); Bobby Worth (d).* 1/92.

It seems little short of amazing that these two veterans had never recorded together before, but apparently not! The result is a warmly amiable meeting which holds up throughout CD length. Humph's own interest in the clarinet – there's at least one clarinet feature for him on most of the Calligraphs listed above – makes him a fine match for Bilk here on 'Just A Little While To Stay Here', but it's the easy give-and-take between trumpet and clarinet, over an almost lissom rhythm section, which gives the record its class; even Acker's vocals sound sunny enough, and his clarinet has become as idiosyncratic and engaging as Pee Wee Russell's.

***** Rent Party**
Stomp Off CD1238 *Lyttelton; Keith Nichols (tb, tba); John Beecham (tb); Wally Fawkes (cl); Stan Greig (p); Paul Sealey (bj, g); Jack Fallon, Annie Hawkins (b); Colin Bowden (d).* 8/91–1/92.

*****(*) Hear Me Talkin' To Ya**
Calligraph CLG CD 029 *Lyttelton; Pete Strange (tb); Jimmy Hastings (cl, as, f); Kathy Stobart (cl, ts, bs); Stan Greig (p); Paul Bridge (b); Adrian Macintosh (d).* 5/93.

These bulletins from Humph make a neatly contrasting illustration of the breadth of his interests. *Rent Party* is straight out of the traditional pocket, with ancient material such as 'Texas Moaner' and 'Viper Mad' given a lusty workout. Fawkes, who goes, as they say, way back with Lyttelton, gets as close to Bechet-like authority as he ever has, and the banjo-driven rhythm sections find the necessary feel without resorting to caricature. *Hear Me Talkin' To Ya* is a pleasing jazz-history lesson, with obscure Ellington (one of Humph's specialities), Carla Bley and Buck Clayton in the set-list as well as carefully revised treatments of 'Beale Street Blues' and 'St James Infirmary'. Jimmy Hastings comes on board for the first time and makes a keen addition to what is now a very commanding front line. The joints may creak a bit here and there, but this is still excellent jazz.

***** Three In The Morning**
Calligraph CLG 30 *Lyttelton; Acker Bilk (cl, v); John Barnes (cl, as, bs); Dave Cliff (g); Dave Green (b); Bobby Worth (d).* 9/93–4/94.

After-hours with Humph and Acker. The newly established old firm sound fine again here, though the session droops a little in places, possibly because of the absence of the late Bruce Turner, who fell ill before he could play the parts which ultimately fell to John Barnes. As usual, Lyttelton has done some inspired work in choosing material: 'I'd Climb The Highest Mountain', Al Fairweather's 'Ludo' and Ida Cox's 'Last Smile Blues' are among the nuggets that nobody else would have thought of.

***** ... Lay 'Em Straight!**
Calligraph CLG 33 *Lyttelton; Pete Strange (tb); Jimmy Hastings (as, f); Alan Barnes (as); Kathy Stobart (ts, bs); Joe Temperley (bs, ss); Ted Beament (p); Paul Bridge (b); Adrian Macintosh (d).* 2–10/96.

Frankly, a bit of a disappointment. Humph recalls Alan Barnes and Joe Temperley as guests on some tracks, and they certainly lend extra merit, especially Temperley's lovely baritone on 'Echoes Of The Duke'. There are the customary small ingenuities, too, in the likes of 'Zoltan's Dream', the old favourite 'Late Night Final' and more. But here and there the playing sounds fallible.

***** Between Friends**
Calligraph CLG CD 037 *As above, except Jim Tomlinson (ts), Stacey Kent (v) replace Barnes and Temperley.* 3/00.

Characteristic mix of ingredients: some Humph originals, plenty of Ellington (including 'Unbooted Character') and a few obvious standards made new by a few piquant twists. Tomlinson and Kent find a little space for themselves and the singer appears on five tracks. Humph says he found it one of his most enjoyable dates to make, and we wouldn't wish to take issue.

Paul Lytton (born 1947)

DRUMS, PERCUSSION, LIVE ELECTRONICS

British improvising percussionist, often at work with contemporaries Evan Parker and Paul Lovens; something of a pioneer in playing an amplified and electronically altered kit.

*****(*) The Balance Of Trade**
CIMP 114 *Lytton; Herb Robertson (c, t, vtb, tba, horn, flageolet etc.); Philipp Wachsmann (vn, vla, elec); Dominic Duval (b, elec).* 5/96.

Lytton's first disc as nominal leader for many years is, as usual in this area of music-making, both visionary in scope and piecemeal in its actuality. The individual items range from a couple of minutes to over 19 in length, but each seems to last as long as it ought to, or has to. Lytton, whose history stretches back to all the British and European free musics of the '60s and '70s, continues to be one of the drummer-percussionists least hidebound by the idea of time, rhythm or determined pulse. His enormous kit (which apparently took several hours to set up) is something he uses as sparsely as possible: it seems that a lot of it might be there for the purpose of perhaps one tiny gesture somewhere in the music. Nobody has ever used electronics in the way he does; in fact, it's hard to hear how his electronics even affect the music. Wachsmann is someone fully attuned to this situation, but Duval and Robertson are Americans who are remote from what is a very European style of free music – yet they both handle themselves extraordinarily well, idiomatic to a 't'. About as difficult as it gets.

Harold Mabern (born 1936)

PIANO

Allegedly influenced by Phineas Newborn, the big man from Memphis has a far more beguilingly melodic approach and more muscular delivery than Phineas. He worked with Art Farmer and Benny Golson and with Lionel Hampton, and spent many years as an accompanist. There are few early recordings still in circulation, but Mabern has released several sessions as leader in the '80s and '90s.

***** Wailin'**

Prestige PRCD 24134 *Mabern; Virgil Jones (t, flhn); Lee Morgan (t); George Coleman (ts); Hubert Laws (ts, f); Boogaloo Joe Jones (g); Buster Williams (b); Idris Muhammad (d).* 6/69, 1/70.

***** Philadelphia Bound**

Sackville SKCD 23051 *Mabern; Kieran Overs (b).* 4/91, 2/92.

There is something about Harold Mabern that just breathes Memphis. Few jazz pianists have come so close to the essence of the blues, yet there is nothing crude or revivalist about his playing, which also indicates a heavy debt to Ahmad Jamal and Phineas Newborn Jr, both pianists who made a distinctive use of space. This is never more obvious than on the most recent of these sets. He brings a special touch to Carl Perkins's seldom recorded 'Grooveyard' and invests 'Baubles, Bangles And Beads' with a weighty, masculine charm. Working with lighter-touched trio partners only accentuates the effect.

Even when Philadelphia bound, as on the duos with that marvellous accompanist, Kieran Overs, he sounds like a man happily locked into his own corner of the world. There is much that can be learnt about Mabern from this record, not least his awesome flexibility and awareness within his chosen stylistic field. Being in Philly (they were actually in Toronto, but the mood-setting number was Ray Bryant's 'Philadelphia Bound'), he touches on Coltrane ('Dear Lord' and 'Lazybird') and plays a solo version of 'The Cry Of My People', written by Trane's friend Cal Massey. There are also two Benny Golson numbers ('Are You Real' and 'Whisper Not') which take him back to the kind of material he was doing a couple of decades earlier.

Wailin' brings together two Prestige sessions from the late '60s. The electric piano dates it a little on 'Blues For Phineas'; however, like Kenny Barron, Mabern invests the instrument with a bit of character. *Wailin'* also traces his development as a composer of original themes, still largely blues-based but forward-looking and surprisingly memorable (surprising only in that they seem to be covered so rarely); 'Greasy Kid Stuff' and 'Waltzing Westward' sit up and ask to be played. Morgan is an essential component of the 1970 group and Mabern was to return the compliment in the trumpeter's last group before his untimely death. For more recent Mabern go to Eric Alexander's entry.

Laura Macdonald

SOPRANO AND ALTO SAXOPHONES

Scottish saxophonist in the modern idiom, here making her debut.

***** Laura**

Spartacus STS002 *Macdonald; David Budway (p); James Genus (b); Jeff 'Tain' Watts (d).* 9/00.

Macdonald has a notably personal alto tone which manages to make its way past even Tain Watts in full flow. This is a smart set of originals, a couple of standards and Mingus and Metheny tunes, made with a New York rhythm section. As with most debuts there's a hit-and-miss quality to some of the pieces, but on pieces which suit her best – Metheny's 'Always And Forever', where Watts gives us all some relief by sitting it out, and her own 'Last Confession' – she puts down her most individual playing. Stronger sets will inevitably follow, though.

****** Awakenings**

Spartacus STS 009 *Macdonald; Claus Stoetter (t, flhn); Donny McCaslin (ts, f); Steve Hamilton (p); Gildas Bocle (b); Antonio Sanchez (d).* 6/03.

Album two is a giant step forward. The great change here is in the writing, a programme of originals which seem mature, advanced and rich with interesting ideas. There are bits of what might be termed 'Scottish music' here, yet they're fully absorbed into a jazz idiom that requires Macdonald to know just what she wants from her band and how best to deploy them. 'Angles' and 'Fantasy And Function' are the two long pieces, the written parts sharp and combustible, allowing the solos to boil up out of a fertile simmer. 'Meaning' and 'Whispers' use a toned-down lyricism to get the best out of the group's lyrical side (and offer Laura her own best solo on the latter). Stoetter and McCaslin are mightily impressive but if one player is key to making Macdonald's music work, it's the admirable Hamilton. In the end, though, the set marks a coming-out of an important leadership talent.

Teo Macero (born 1925)

TENOR SAXOPHONE

Though guaranteed his place in the jazz pantheon for his pioneering production work on Miles Davis's Bitches Brew and other records, a process which made creative use of tape editing, Macero is little known as a saxophonist. He did, however, record several times as leader and, following the end of his working relationship with Miles in 1983, returned to recording and released a much-admired tribute to his former boss, Charles Mingus.

****(*) With The Prestige Jazz Quartet**

Original Jazz Classics OJCCD 1715 2 *Macero; Teddy Charles (vib); Mal Waldron (p); Addison Farmer (b); Jerry Segal (d).* 4/57.

Possessed of a tremendous technique – Teo can or could play the entire harmonic scale simply by adjusting his embouchure – he is not particularly individual as an improvising soloist and the strength of what little music there is under his own name is in the compositions themselves. As a soloist he is very limited and is reminiscent in tone and phrasing of the Belgian Bobby

Jaspar. Lester Young was the obvious model for both, and Teo also seems to have derived something from Warne Marsh. Minus the interest of his more challenging compositional side, the Prestige set is rather flat and conventional. Gently paced and consisting mainly of new ballads – 'Star Eyes' is the only standard – it moves at an even, thoughtful pace which allows Macero to unspool his solos.

Vanessa Mackness

VOCAL

British vocal improviser, working in and around the London free-music community.

★★★(★) Respiritus
Incus CD014 *Mackness; John Butcher (ss, ts).* 4–12/94.

A long-awaited debut from the British improvising vocalist, here with frequent partner Butcher, recorded at two concerts in 1994. This is funny, serious music, and the two musicians strike up a brilliant empathy at many moments. An operatic bark might come from Mackness in response to some entirely different gesture by Butcher, and yet the juxtaposition can sound exactly right. The singer's range is wide, if not quite as awesome as, say, Diamanda Galas's, and it's her acute grasp of dynamics which makes these ten duets sound vital and vivid. Mouth, glottal and dialect effects are used sparingly and effectively. Butcher, in many ways as vocal a performer himself, is sensitive but never submissive in the dialogues. A splendid encounter session, and a shame we have no follow-up.

Katrine Madsen (born 1971)

VOCAL

Danish singer working with the American songbook and some more contemporary material.

★★★ Dream Dancing
Music Mecca 2044-2 *Madsen; Thomas Fryland (t, flhn); Lars Jansson (p); Jesper Bodilsen (b); Morten Lund (d); Steen Raahauge (perc).* 9/97.

★★★ You Are So Beautiful
Music Mecca 2088-2 *Madsen; Carsten Dahl (p), Jesper Bodilsen (b); Ed Thigpen (d); Svante Thuresson (v).* 12/98.

It's a surprise when Madsen's voice – a heavy, low contralto that almost slouches through the lyrics – enters on the slow, tropical beat of Meredith D'Ambrosio's 'August Moon'. The lilting rhythms and Fryland's perky trumpet lighten the mood and make a peppery contrast with the singer's methods. The playing is, indeed, vital and expressive throughout, so much so that attention is often taken away from the singer. Much may depend on whether Madsen's diction – slightly wayward and slurred, as is often the case with Scandinavian voices singing in English – appeals. She does best on the slow to mid-tempo pieces, and the three D'Ambrosio lyrics all suit her well.

The second disc is a shade more inhabited by the singer. She's lucky with her pianists. After the excellent Jansson comes the admirable Dahl, whose solo on the opening 'Early In The Autumn' gives early notice that he's going to play a considerable part in the record. Thuresson comes in to sing a couple of duets but Madsen is not overshadowed, and her own writing appears in a few places. 'Speak Low' works from a slow pace which she handles in a way that's fatigued and sexy at the same moment. Recommended to the adventurous.

★★★ My Secret
Music Mecca 3020-2 *Madsen; Lars Møller (ts); Jan Lundgren (p); Bjarne Hansen (ky); Jesper Bodilsen (b); Morten Lund (d).* 1/00.

These are all originals by Madsen, bar 'I Hear A Rhapsody', and it's agreeable to find that she hasn't chosen to try and go pop with them. With Møller turning on the heat in moments such as his solo on the title-track, it's as uncompromised a jazz setting as she could look for. Her singing remains close to inimitable – heavy, sometimes graceless, but in the right moments and on the right lines she can bring a unique piquancy to the situation. The songs are a brave rather than a wholly convincing lot. The band is terrific.

Alex Maguire

PIANO

Brilliant British improviser, yet to receive due recognition.

★★★(★) Mt Olympus
Ramboy 13 *Maguire; Michael Moore (as, cl).* 9/99.

Maguire's enormous musical resource is well matched here. Moore's quiet, sometimes almost subliminal melody lines are a perfect foil for the pianist's patient exploration of harmonic ideas. One hears it most clearly on the opening two numbers, 'Mt Olympus' itself, on which Moore plays a composed clarinet line against a freely moving background of chords and Ellington's 'Azure', which seems to assemble itself as it goes along. Other delights are 'My Man's Gone Now', the quirky 'Twinkling Beaks' and 'Tufty', and the closing 'Viola', which at nearly ten minutes gives the album a solid send-off. Maguire always sounds powerful, even when he is playing *pianissimo*, a tactic that suits Moore's dynamically varied approach down to the ground. Great stuff.

Mahavishnu Orchestra

GROUP

After the death of Jimi Hendrix, the mantle fell on the shoulders of John McLaughlin. For a time, the known world seemed to be divided between his Mahavishnu Orchestra and Chick Corea's similarly Miles-influenced Return to Forever. Easy now to parody the Orchestra's uneasy shifts from gentle arpeggiation to flat-out screaming in un-jazzy metres. At the time, they really seemed like the last best hope.

★★★★ The Inner Mounting Flame
Columbia CK 31067 *John McLaughlin; Jan Hammer (p, syn); Jerry Goodman (vn); Rick Laird (b); Billy Cobham (d).* 71–72.

★★★(★) Birds Of Fire
Columbia CK 66081 *As above.* 72.

★★★ The Lost Trident Sessions
Columbia CK 65959 *As above.* 6/73.

★★★ Between Nothingness And Eternity
Columbia 468225 *As above.* 8/73.

**** Apocalypse**

Columbia CK 46111 *John McLaughlin; Jean-Luc Ponty (vn); Gayle Moran (ky, v); Carol Shive (vn, v); Marsha Westbrook (vla); Philip Hirschi (clo, v); Ralphe Armstrong (b, v); Narada Michael Walden (d); Michael Gibbs (arr); London Symphony Orchestra, Michael Tilson Thomas (cond).* 3/74.

**** Visions Of The Emerald Beyond**

Columbia CK 46867 *John McLaughlin; other personnel unidentified.* 75.

One of the few jazz-rock bands of the early '70s whose work seems certain to survive, the Mahavishnu Orchestra combined sophisticated time-signatures and chord structures with drum and guitar riffs of surpassing heaviness. Wielding a huge double-neck incorporating 6- and 12-string guitars, McLaughlin produced chains of blistering high notes, influenced by Hendrix and by earlier R&B, but still essentially in a jazz idiom. Less obviously dominant than on *Extrapolation*, McLaughlin works his group collectively, like an orchestra rather than a theme-and-solo outfit. Billy Cobham's whirlwind drumming was and remains the key to the group's success, underpinning and embellishing McLaughlin's and Hammer's often quite simple lines. His opening press-roll and subsequent accents on (the still incorrectly titled) 'One Word' (*Birds Of Fire*) clear the way for Rick Laird's finest moment on record. Even where he is poorly recorded on the live album, he is still dominant. Goodman came from the American 'progressive' band Flock and is used largely for embellishment, but his rather scratchy sound contributed a great deal to the overall impact of *Inner Mounting Flame*, still the group's best album, and he has no apparent difficulty playing in 13/8.

The first Mahavishnu album was one of the essential fusion records, largely because it was more generously promoted and more obviously rock-derived than *Extrapolation*. Ironically, just as he was pushing the iconic guitar solo to new heights of amplification and creative abandon, McLaughlin was also working against the dominance of electricity and setting a new standard for 'acoustic' performance. 'Thousand Island Park' and 'Open Country Joy' on *Birds Of Fire* recall the beautiful acoustic 'A Lotus On Irish Streams' from the first album. They ought to have done more in that vein, and McLaughlin's subsequent work with Shakti strongly suggested that it was far from exhausted.

One of the most intriguing musical rediscoveries of recent years has been a pair of quarter-inch tapes, unearthed by record producer Bob Belden. These contained the 'lost' sessions which would have been the Orchestra's fourth studio album. Personal and artistic differences had blocked progress with what would have been the follow-up to the successful *Birds Of Fire* and the last issued recording by the original Mahavishnu Orchestra. In the event, Columbia released the live recording, *Between Nothingness And Eternity*, which was taped in concert at Central Park. For Mahavishnu loyalists, it's quite difficult now to hear these tracks in any form other than the original issue. Word of bootleg copies of the studio session has circulated for some time, but we've never been offered a copy. Hearing it cold, it seems a little flat and unatmospheric, and whoever in the band it was who wanted a bit of sweetening and perhaps a few overdubbed strings has some justification. The opening 'Dream' lacks the drama – heralded by gongs and hissing cymbals – which made the start of *Nothingness/Eternity* so compelling.

There was clearly some conflict regarding composition credits on what was supposed to be a co-operative band rather than McLaughlin's band. The 'lost' session includes Hammer's 'Sister Andrea' – also on the live record – but also two short tunes by Rick Laird ('Steppings Tones') and Jerry Goodman ('I Wonder'), though it seems that Billy Cobham was inclined to keep his counsel and retain new tunes for his own projects. Interesting as the Trident tapes are, we remain resolutely underwhelmed.

Unfortunately Columbia have not drawn the Great Veil of Kindly Oblivion over the expanded Orchestra's subsequent recordings, *Apocalypse* and *Visions Of The Emerald Beyond*; apart from flashes of quality from replacement violinist Jean-Luc Ponty, these were as drearily directionless as the three quintet albums were forceful, developing the line McLaughlin had begun with *Extrapolation* and *Where Fortune Smiles.*

Jack Maheu (born 1930)

CLARINET

One-time veteran of The Dukes Of Dixieland and the Salt City Six, Maheu is a battle-hardened Dixieland pro who retired to New Orleans in 1990 – and decided to carry on.

***** In New Orleans**

Jazzology JCD-278 *Maheu; Kevin Clark, Duke Heitger (t); Charles Fardella (c); Al Barthlow (tb); Tom Fischer (ts); Tom Saunders (bsx); Tom McDermott, John Royen (p); Steve Blailock (g); Matt Perrine (b, sou); Richard Taylor (d); Big Al Carson (v).* 6/96.

Maheu is a dedicated traditionalist who has moved from his New York patch to New Orleans for this smart, entertaining set of updates on the classic repertoire. He assembled a local ensemble for the 13 tunes, and they perform with fine chops and good gusto, getting a sound somewhere between commercial Dixieland and the more respectful feel of the heartland style. An original like 'Bourbon Moon' fits snugly beside an uproarious 'Cakewalkin' Babies From Home' (with a terrific vocal by Carson) and a treatment of 'Just A Closer Walk With Thee' that chugs along to a dead-slow R&B shuffle. Plenty of good solos, and Maheu himself is in fine fettle, but docked a notch for a couple of fillers and a daft ending with a variation on 'Chopsticks'!

Adam Makowicz (born 1940)

PIANO

Originally Matyszkowicz. Born in Czechoslovakia and studied in Cracow before working with Tomasz Stańko on and off through the '60s and '70s; more familiar as a soloist and trio player in the '80s and '90s, with several American discs to his credit.

***** A Handful Of Stars**

Chiaroscuro *Makowicz; George Mraz (b); Jack DeJohnette (d).* 9/81.

It has become almost a cliché to characterize Adam Makowicz's style as a hybrid of Tatum and Chopin. Technically at least, it's pretty near the mark, and there is a persistent romantic (even tragic) tinge to even his most exuberant playing that makes the parallel with his (adoptive) compatriot a reasonable one. His first jazz partnership was with the trumpeter Tomasz Stanko. Together they explored modal forms and free jazz but, whereas Stanko was a wild, instinctual risk-taker, Makowicz approached the music in a more orderly and conceptual way. In the '70s he wrote perceptive music criticism while he was working with both Michal Urbaniak and his then wife, Urszula Dudziak, in a number of fusion projects.

The catalogue has been drastically foreshortened as a result of Concord's rationalization of its jazz list, but *A Handful Of Stars*, recorded as early as 1981 but not released until the end of the '90s, is a welcome reminder of Adam's gifts. 'Bye Bye Blues' is the most obviously Tatumesque item, but don't be so dazzled by the pianist's right-hand improvisations that you don't listen to DeJohnette and Mraz, who are the secret weapons on this date; both are technically astute and utterly musical in every note and gesture. The pianist's originals 'Satin Wood' and 'Opalescence' are typical of his gracious, Chopin-tinged approach. There's also a 'Jazzspeak' interview which provides some useful insight into his life and musical philosophy.

***** Reflections On Chopin**
Musicians Showcase Records MSR CD 1027 *Makowicz (p solo). 12/99.*

***** Plays Duke Ellington**
Musicians Showcase Records MSR CD 1028 *As above.* 12/99.

MSR is a classical label and these two sets are pitched to that end of Makowicz's range. The Ellington material is imaginatively varied, with more obvious things like 'Prelude To A Kiss', 'Come Sunday' and 'Don't Get Around Much Anymore' placed alongside rarities like 'To The Bitter', a theme that has otherwise been favoured only by Mal Waldron. The touch is precise but not unswinging and it sounds like a beautiful piano for both sessions. The Chopin material is even more deeply embedded in Makowicz's unconscious and these improvisations on the work of a master improviser are almost like new creations, certainly in the case of pieces like the Op. 28 *Preludes* and the Op. 48 *C minor Nocturne*. Beautiful records, both.

Llanfranco Malaguti

GUITAR

Contemporary Italian guitarist, performing in a conservative but creative idiom.

***** Inside Meaning**
Splasc(h) 403-2 *Malaguti; Stefano D'Anna (ss, ts); Enzo Pietropaoli (b, perc). 2/93.*

*****(*) Percorsi**
Splasc(h) 419-2 *Malaguti; Umberto Petrin (p). 5/93.*

****(*) New Land**
Splasc(h) 443-2 *Malaguti; Dario Volpi (g, g-syn). 1/95.*

***** Aforismi**
Splasc(h) 606-2 *Malaguti (g solo). 11/96.*

Malaguti shies away from effects and noise. He plays with a clean, slightly pinched open tone and prefers spareness to lots of notes. Some earlier vinyl for Splasc(h) suggested a conventional stylist, but these are wide-open records with plenty of space and air around the music. *Inside Meaning* seems to take off from a group of standard harmonic bases and into a series of triologues where the normally tempestuous D'Anna is unusually restrained. These are sometimes rather piecemeal, but there are some bewitching moments and the entirety is oddly satisfying in a modest way. *Percorsi* is a duo concert from Slovenia with the splendid Petrin. They feel their way through a group of standards – the way the opening improvisation turns into 'Solar' is quite magical, and there's a similar transformation of 'Just Friends' – before each man takes a few solos and they climax with 'Autumn Leaves'. Petrin's abstruse but acute methods are an ideal partner for the guitarist's own delivery and, though the location sound isn't ideal, it's pretty good.

New Land is comparatively tame, almost finicky in parts, with Volpi very much a second fiddle. Malaguti's tunes have their virtues, but this one is too becalmed to sustain the attention. *Aforismi* is a solo record in which the improviser uses echo effects with a memory expander to create real-time multi-tracking. With only two pieces breasting the five-minute barrier, the guitarist again impresses with his reserve, eliminating flab from the music, even if some of it lacks a distinctive flavour. Guitarists may enjoy this more than the uncommitted, but Malaguti has an interesting agenda.

***** Parole, Parole ...**
Splasc(h) 706-2 *Malaguti; Stefano D'Anna (ts); Enzo Pietropaoli (b); Roberto Gatto (d). 1/92.*

A recent release, despite the date. Malaguti takes on the Italian song heritage (anticipating a favourite tactic among many players of his generation of late) and the quartet tackle the likes of 'Estate' and 'Quando Quando' here. D'Anna sits out four of the 12 tracks and is subdued (or at least respectful of the material), while the leader patiently explores the melodies. Not bad, but unless you love these tunes it's hardly a priority listen.

Raphe Malik (born 1948)

TRUMPET

Often working around Boston or with San Francisco-based saxophonist Glenn Spearman, Malik is a free-form trumpeter and group leader who combines abstraction with a solid grounding in blues harmony and bop.

*****(*) 21st Century Texts**
FMP CD 43 *Malik; Brian King Nelson (Cmel); Glenn Spearman (ts); Larry Roland (b); Dennis Warren (d). 6/91.*

*****(*) Sirens Sweet And Slow**
Outsounds 01972 *As above, except add Jamyll Jones (b). 94.*

***** The Short Form**
Eremite MTE05 *As above, except omit Nelson, Jones, Roland; add George Langford (b). 7/96.*

***** Consequences**
Eremite MTE013 *Malik; Sabir Mateen (as); William Parker (b); Dennis Charles (d). 7/97.*

Malik is a sometime Cecil Taylor sideman who has managed to derive something from the pianist's style without being swamped by it. On *21st Century Texts* he marshals a tight little posse of like-minded improvisers (Spearman inevitably dominant, as he is wherever he plays) in the sort of session ESP Disk used to have a corner in. Nelson's C-melody sax has a strikingly unfamiliar tonality but, with no piano or guitar as a reference point, it's able to find its own territory, often coming in under Malik in a series of call-and-response passages that are both alien and highly traditional. *Sirens Sweet And Slow* breaks up the unit a little, with two long duets, trumpet with bass, and trumpet with drums. Malik manages to play big and loud without losing focus: he rarely goes for the buzzy, spluttery effects that avant-garde brassmen often rely on, and his note choices are boldly decisive. 'Companions' is an impressive group piece and there's a sort of stop-start blowout on 'Tenor', to which Spearman makes his usual full-blooded contribution. The unvarnished sound suits the band.

Energy-music followers will love *The Short Form*, a concert recording that pares the band back to a quartet and lets them explode. It's exhilarating enough, but the more specific restraint which Malik uses so effectively on the studio discs is missed. Similar state of affairs on the following year's *Consequences*, rather dustily recorded, and although this is a chance to hear Denis Charles in one of his final recordings, and Malik and Mateen play some vociferous solos, a strong live performance transfers rather uneasily to CD.

*****(*) Storyline**

Boxholder 5 *Malik; Cecil McBee (b); Cody Moffett (d).* 98.

Malik demonstrates his deep familiarity with blues and jazz traditions on 'Minimal Blue', which uses a basic 12-bar to generate a complex group improvisation. Other tunes, like 'First Valve Blues' and 'The Hard Way', follow a similar procedure with equal effect, but there is a law of diminishing returns on this fine record and it is probably best sampled a track or two at a time.

McBee is at his magisterial best, weaving in and out of Malik's tightly valved phrasing, but he is occasionally drowned by Moffett. A certain democracy of sound is a good thing, but this time it is perhaps taken too far and Cody needs reining in on occasion. There are moments here, though, when you might think it was his father playing, with David Izenzon and the trumpet-wielding Ornette at the Gyllenecirkelt.

***** Looking East: A Suite In Three Parts**

Boxholder 019/020 2CD *Malik; Sabir Mateen (reeds); Larry Roland (b); Cody Moffett (d).* 99.

Again, the problem here is an excess of musical information, with insufficient variation in performance to distinguish one piece or 'part' from the others. There is no real evidence that this is a continuous suite at all, and it is certainly not danceable. The main drama is contained in two long pieces, 'The Old Your Majesty' and 'The New Majesty', which in the old days would have made two sides of a very decent LP. As it is, they're bracketed by an awful lot of generic play. Malik is in top form, but Mateen tends to go off at half-cock, and very abrasive half-cock at that, which just encourages Moffett to go mad. Roland is an able player, but surely this isn't his natural territory?

***** Companions**

Eremite MTE 034 *Malik; Glenn Spearman (ts); William Parker (b); Paul Murphy (d).* 5/98.

Good to hear Malik back in company with the redoubtable Parker. He always sounds best with a strong bass-player. The other reason to treasure this disc is a further last glimpse of a lost master of modern free. Glenn Spearman was close to death when these tracks were recorded during a Jimmy Lyons tribute at the Orensanz Arts Centre in New York City. He looks desperately ill on the cover but is still in fierily good voice, burning through an impassioned if slightly shapeless solo on the opening 'Lyons's Jump'.

Malik's fate on this outing was to be upstaged by his colleagues. After Spearman's statement, Parker weighs in with a solo that conjures up recollections of every bull fiddler from Jimmy Blanton to Mingus. The trumpeter is rather quietly recorded and displaced in the stereo mix. There are echoes of Ornette's *Crisis*-period group with Dewey Redman, but also of Leo Smith especially in the slow processional which opens 'Emblematic'. The remaining tracks are shorter and probably surplus. A fine record, but not one of Malik's most commanding outings.

***** Speak Easy**

Le Systeme 004 *Malik (t solo).* 01.

Marred by technical problems, but a rare and welcome chance to hear the trumpeter unaccompanied and in the kind of recital favoured by Wadada Leo Smith. There is always a danger that such a set comes across as little more than a collection of technical exercises. Not surprisingly, Malik avoids this gracefully. There are blues-based compositions, boppish heads and the occasional completely free-form idea. 'Odds Out' and 'Cruise Control' are the stand-out tracks.

Malik recorded the disc in Toronto in early 2001. It's not clear whether a rehearsal tape has been over-recorded or whether print-through has occurred in storage. Whatever the reason, a 'ghost' trumpeter can be heard throughout the setting. Disconcerting, but only really evident on headphones and not enough to mar enjoyment.

Russell Malone (born 1963)

GUITAR, VOCAL

A conservative among modern guitarists, Malone matches deep knowledge of his instrument's history with a stance that suggests an investment in old values. He has worked extensively with many leading names as sideman and was previously listed for two albums on Columbia, Impulse! and Verve.

****(*) Heartstrings**

Verve 549786-2 *Malone; Kenny Barron (p); Christian McBride (b); Jeff 'Tain' Watts (d); strings arranged by Johnny Mandel, Alan Broadbent, Dori Caymmi.* 2–3/01.

*****(*) Playground**

Maxjazz MXJ601 *Malone; Gary Bartz (as); Joe Locke (vib); Martin Bejerano (p); Tassili Bond (b); E. J. Strickland (d).* 11/03.

Malone has had little luck in the way of his major-label ventures. Two albums for Columbia, one for Impulse! and the first for Verve have disappeared, which leaves this decidedly tame with-strings venture. *Heartstrings* is all marshmallow, ten ballads ('Tain' Watts keeps trying to sneak in some quicker licks, but it's no good) that can't get started. Sounds like Johnny Mandel all but phoned in his two charts, and even Alan Broadbent's three barely cause a ripple of interest. Malone lets his tone do the talking, and again it's sometimes enough. But not often enough.

A fresh start at Maxjazz, and Russell sounds like he's had all the cares lifted. This is an unpretentious set which bounces between the supercharged bop lickery of 'Sugar Buzz' and pop covers where even bland melodies come up shining in the guitarist's gorgeous tone (not bad for The Carpenters and James Taylor). Bartz gets to blow on only a single track but the band is otherwise in good shape. Malone can't quite escape getting a tad too sentimental here and there, but it's a very enjoyable record.

Stefano Maltese (born 1955)

SOPRANO, ALTO AND TENOR SAXOPHONES, BASS CLARINET, FLUTE, PAN PIPES, VIOLIN

The Sicilian is a versatile multi-instrumentalist, but his own-name albums are exercises more concerned with composing and arranging, especially for big ensembles.

***** Sombra Del Sur**

Splasc(h) 406-2 *Maltese; Roy Paci (t, pkt-t, flhn); Sebastiano Dell'Arte (t, flhn); Paolo Reale, Rino Caraco (tb); Claudio Giglio (f, bamboo f); Giuseppe Bonanno (f, picc); Paola Ammatuna, Jasmin Avitabile Leva, Andrea Cianci, Barbara Forzisi, Paola Milazzo (f); Salvatore Carnemolla (cl); Angelo Ragaglia (bsn); Ciccio Tiné (acc); Michele Conti (vn, mand); Salvo Amore (g); Michele Salerno (clo); Pino Guarrella (b); Antonio Moncada (d); Walter Di Mauro (perc); Gioconda Cilio (v).* 7/92.

***** Book Of Yesterday**

Splasc(h) 438-2 *Maltese; Ray Paci (t, pkt-t); Rosario Patania (tb); Alfio Sgalambro (cl); Giovanni Di Mauro (ob); Michele Conti (vn); Salvo Amore (g); Nello Toscano (clo); Giuseppe Guarella (b); Antonio Moncada (d); Gioconda Cilio (v, perc).* 2/95.

***** Seven Tracks For Tomorrow**

DDQ 128025-2 *Similar to above, except omit Sgalambro, Di Mauro, Amore, Toscano.* 3/97.

***** Living Alive**

Leo LR 265 *Maltese; Arkady Shilkloper (flhn, bugle, frhn); Sophia Domancich (p); Paul Rogers (b); Antonio Moncada (d); Gioconda Cilio (v, perc).* 9/98.

A sprawling, sometimes malevolent-sounding work, the big-scale suite which is *Sombra Del Sur* is about the slowness and heat-saturated quiet of the Italian 'South'. Slowness seems apt, since Maltese started it in 1986, and much of it is in turn based on an earlier piece dating back to 1978. His reluctance to use keyboards and his interest in woodwinds and strings introduces a variety of tone which is unusual: the massed flutes which are brought in for two tracks, the curious effect of free percussion and tenor over the fixed handclap of 'Hombre Lobo', the unearthly chorales of 'Estrellas'. It's an odd construction, sometimes very arresting, but often plain turgid. *Book Of Yesterday* is a retrospective of Maltese's writing over 25 years, going back to the lumbering 1974 'Trois Petits Chevaux Pour Erik Satie' and ending on a new (1994) piece. You can't say Maltese doesn't try hard: he creates an orchestra of 16 bass clarinets through overdubbing on 'Dans Les Nuits', and assembles such groups as a soprano/clarinet/oboe trio and various chamberish quintets. The sleeve-notes call him 'a poetic of estranged visionariness'. Much of this carefully arranged and cockeyed music seems deliberately eccentric, but there are shafts of humour to go with the many po-faced passages.

One of his key collaborators is Cilio, who takes a significant role as wordless vocalist on *Seven Tracks For Tomorrow*, a set which pursues Maltese's composing interests without reaching any clear indication of progress: he seems to flit from episode to episode, never quite settling into a style and passing the initiative round his players so restlessly that it's hard to focus on what each is doing. That issue is sidestepped by the more *ad hoc* Leo record, which was an opportunistic date following the players' appearance at the 1998 Labirinti Sonori Festival. Maltese is reluctant to present himself as a full-on free improviser and he leaves much of the main space to both Shilkloper and Cilio, with piano, bass and drums taking their own independent parts. Untypical, though arguably this has the greatest share of satisfying music of the four discs. Maltese will be an acquired taste, but more adventurous spirits may find him not a little intriguing.

****(*) Double Mirror**

Splasc(h) 469.2 *Maltese; Evan Parker (ss, ts); Keith Tippett (p); Antonio Moncada (d).* 8/95.

A mismatched quartet which nevertheless makes some striking music along the way. The very long 'Enter Alloy: Exit Rust' takes up most of the record and will take up a lot of listeners' patience too. The first half of the track develops in a chamberish way before Tippett starts making a tremendous racket and matters tend to fall apart. This doesn't feel like Maltese's forte.

Junior Mance (born 1928)

PIANO, HARPSICHORD

Junior Mance has been playing professionally for almost 60 years. His first lessons with Julian Mance Sr and his grounding in blues, stride and boogie woogie have stood him in good stead ever since. Though by no means widely documented or particularly well-known, Mance has concentrated very largely on his own groups and projects. A significant proportion of the existing recorded material is live.

***** Live At The Village Vanguard**

Original Jazz Classics OJC 204 *Mance; Larry Gales (b); Ben Riley (d).* 61.

****** Junior's Blues**

Original Jazz Classics OJCCD 1000 *Mance; Bob Cranshaw (b); Mickey Roker (d).* 2/62.

*****(*) Happy Time**

Original Jazz Classics OJCCD 1029 *Mance; Ron Carter (b); Mickey Roker (d).* 7/62.

Unmistakable from a random sample of half-a-dozen bars as a Chicago man, Mance can be a maddeningly predictable player on record, resorting to exactly the figure one expects him to play rather too often to leave any interest for his often adventurous variations and resolutions. That's certainly evident on the live OJC, a rare available example of pre-1980 Mance. It's a notably self-confident performance, and it will be clear to anyone who has hitherto heard only the recent stuff that Mance's expert chops and obvious awareness of the earlier literature did not appear magically on his 50th birthday. It's a fairly representative programme, with the favoured 'Smokey Blues' (see below) prominent, and a slot for Basie's '9.20 Special'.

Recorded on Valentine's Day 1962, *Junior's Blues* is a love letter to jazz itself, as direct and uncomplicated a declaration as you'll find in the whole history of the music. Junior covers themes by Monk (with a few embellishments of his own), Ellington ('Creole Love Call') and the Jay McShann/Charlie Parker swinger 'The Jumpin' Blues'. He kicks off with his own 'Down The Line', which is as orthodox and full-hearted a twelve-bar as you'll ever hear. Needless to say, highly recommended.

The switch around of bassists for the July session doesn't make a huge difference, but Carter is a more melodic player than Cranshaw and so the music is busier, somewhat to its detriment, but not fatally. The opening theme – the title-track – should be played to anyone suffering nervous prostration or depression: better than Prozac or hours with a strict Freudian. 'For Dancers Only' and 'Azure-Te' are the best of the rest, until you get to the final tune, Clark Terry's 'The Simple Waltz', which is worth the rest of the disc put together. Simply lovely.

*** Harlem Lullaby / I Believe To My Soul

Collectables 6606 *Mance; Mel Lastie, Joe Newman, Jimmy Owens (t); Hubert Laws (ts, picc, f); David 'Fathead' Newman, Frank Wess (ts); Bobby Capers, Haywood Henry (bs); Bob Cunningham, Richard Davis, Gene Taylor, James Tyrell (b); Alan Dawson, Ray Lucas, Bobby Thompson, Freddie Waits (d); Ray Barretto (perc); Sylvie Shemwell (v).* 9–11/66.

There was a brief fashion for non-electric keyboards other than the piano. Harpsichord, clavichord and even celeste dates weren't unknown in the later '60s, though history has drawn a discreet veil over most of them. Mance wasn't immune and the trio(s) album *Harlem Lullaby* features some harpsichord tracks that count among the weakest in his entire output. 'What Becomes Of The Broken Hearted' wins polls as the weakest track. The rest of the album is pretty good and there are some nice things on the horn-heavy *I Believe To My Soul,* which has a rich, gospelly swing throughout and shows that 1966 was by no means a negligible year for the pianist. Sylvie Shemwell turns up for a vocal on the title track.

*** With A Lotta Help From My Friends

Collectables 6166 *Mance; Eric Gale (g); Chuck Rainey (b); Billy Cobham (d).* 3/70.

Those nice people at Collectables love their piano jazz. In addition to Mance, they've made tracts of Ray Bryant available again. This is one of the less essential and might be thought to be not much more than a period piece. Junior kicks off with Sly Stone's 'Thank You (Falettinme Be Mice Elf Agin)' and takes in Curtis Mayfield ('Never Say Naw') and David Clayton-Thomas's 'Spinning Wheel' as well. Hey, people, it's 1970! There's also a co-written 'Don't Rush Us', written with Rainey and Cobham, with Billy's 'Well I'll Be White Black' as a centrepiece. The main interest of the record is in the drummer's pre-Mahavishnu groove, but Junior does some nice stuff with fairly unpromising material.

*** That Lovin' Feeling

Milestone 47097 *Mance; Aaron Bell, Bob Cranshaw, Bob Cunningham (b); Oliver Jackson, Jimmy Lovelace, Harold White (d); Ralph MacDonald (perc); Melba Liston (cond); orchestra.* 61–62, 9/73.

The trios again toy with pop repertoire, but this time Junior seems much more interested in their jazz potential than in playing recognizable versions of 'Blowin' In The Wind' or the Righteous Brothers hit that gives the album its title. The reissue pairs an averagely OK trio album (with various personnels) and a 1962 set of Hollywood themes arranged for orchestra which is so far from Junior's real strengths as to be laughable. 'Maria' is plaintively beautiful and 'One Eyed Jacks' has some pep and verve but the 'Exodus' theme and the 'Tara' melody from *Gone With The Wind* really don't suit Junior's beat. Melba Liston conducted, so the arrangements were professional at least, just a shade soulless.

*** Junior Mance Special

Sackville CD 3043 *Mance (p solo).* 9/86, 11/88.

***(*) Smokey Blues

JSP CD 219 *Mance; Marty Rivera (b); Walter Bolden (d).* 6/80.

**** For Dancers Only

Sackville 3031 *As above, except omit Bolden.* 7/83.

There's an immediate lift to the five live tracks on *Special,* recorded at Toronto's intimate and much-documented Café des Copains, which suggests that studio performance really isn't Mance's strong suit. Certainly the opening 'Yancey Special', done on a better-tempered studio piano, is remarkably flat and unvaried; the long interpretations of 'Careless Love', Billy Taylor's 'I Wish I Knew How It Would Feel To Be Free' (familiar to British fans as the theme to a well-known TV programme) and Ivory Joe Hunter's 'Since I Lost My Baby I Almost Lost My Mind' are characteristically bluesy but also rather tentative. It's only among the live tracks – which include 'Blue Monk', Golson's 'Whisper Not' and two Ellington numbers – that Mance really seems to let go, working towards those knotted climaxes for which he is rightly admired.

Rivera is a bassist who fits snugly into the pianist's conception of how the blues should be played: strongly, but with considerable harmonic subtlety. The trio album is perhaps the best of the recent recordings, despite a rather uncertain sound-mix. Mance's ability to suffuse relatively banal ballad material with genuine blues feeling (a characteristic noted by the late Charles Fox in a typically perceptive liner-note) is nowhere more obvious than on 'Georgia On My Mind', a melody that can sound footling and drab but which acquires something close to grandeur here. Bolden's 'Deep' is basically a feature for the rhythm players and doesn't add very much to the total impact, but the closing 'Ease On Down The Road' and 'Smokey Blues' are authentic Mance performances.

The duos with Rivera are lovely and the opening 'Harlem Lullaby' (a Mance tune), 'Prelude To A Kiss' and the long closing 'Summertime' (almost 12 minutes of it) are among the best things in the whole Mance catalogue.

*** Here 'Tis – Play The Music Of Dizzy Gillespie

Sackville 3050 *Mance; Bill McBirnie (f); Reg Schwager (g); Kieran Overs (b); Norman Marshall Villeneuve (d).* 92.

Junior is an admirer of Gillespie the composer and has previously tackled 'Salt Peanuts' and 'Tin Tin Deo'. Here he takes a more measured view of things like the latter, 'Blue'N'Boogie', 'Ow', 'Night In Tunisia', 'Con Alma' and 'Woody'N'You', often adding his own curlicues and embellishments to the familiar melodies. The band is nothing to write home about, and Villeneuve's drumming is very tame. Junior's great strengths are still in evidence, but this is a B-list project from the great pianist and not a priority item.

*** Milestones

Sackville SACD2-3065 *Mance; Don Thompson (b); Archie Alleyne (d).* n.d.

A typically rhythmic and well-paced set of standard and repertory tunes featuring Mance in his favourite playing context. Most of the tunes are quite long and developed, though nothing else on the set quite matches up to the expectations established by a thorough rethink of Nat Adderley's 'Work Song', a swingingly brisk opener that has more ideas per chorus than anything Junior has released for years.

*****(*) Blue Mance**
Chiaroscuro 331 *Mance; Keter Betts (b); Jackie Williams (d).* 5/95.

In the spring of 1995, Junior began what was to be a fruitful association with the Floating Jazz cruises – Caribbean weather, good food and drink and music thrown in (while some people have to work) – and the trio reconvened for a studio session shortly afterwards. 'Blue Mance' follows 'Blue Monk' in short order, perhaps as a sign that Thelonious's 'radicalism' isn't so very different from Junior's unaffected simplicity of approach. He starts the city with an easy, gracious 'Falling In Love With Love' and then throws in Betts's 'Head Start', a basic blowing theme that is more effective than its slim materials might suggest. After the Monk/Mance exchange, a surprise. Junior isn't known particularly as an Ellington interpreter (though he did devote a later Floating Jazz programme entirely to the great man), but how many of Duke's loyalest men include 'Shepherd Of The Night Flock' in their programmes? It's a beautiful thing, at once moving and impressively structured. At the end of the set there's a 'Jazzspeak' interview with Mance; no blinding revelations, but confirmation that he's a thoughtful exponent of the art, and a thoroughly good bloke.

*****(*) Jubilation**
Sackville 2046 *Mance (p solo).* 9/96.

There haven't been too many solo records from Mance and for this one he sticks (the title-track apart) to well-seasoned standards and jazz tunes, including wonderful versions of 'St Louis Blues', 'Old Folks', 'Autumn Leaves', one well-loved Ellington, 'Single Petal Of A Rose' and one Ducal obscurity, 'Just Squeeze Me (Don't Tease Me)' which is co-credited to Will Gaines. The piano sounds a good one, warm and case-hardened and Junior is in great form throughout. Cause for jubilation among his fans.

***** Floating Jazz Festival Trio**
Chiaruscuro 340 *Mance; Benny Golson (ts); Keter Betts (b); Jackie Williams (d).* 95.

*****(*) Live At The 1996 Floating Jazz Festival: The Music Of Duke Ellington**
Chiaroscuro 352 *As above, except omit Golson; add Joe Temperley (bs).* 96.

***** The Floating Jazz Festival Trio**
Chiaroscuro 359 *As above, except omit Temperley; add Red Holloway (ts), Henry Johnson (g).* 98.

***** Mance**
Chiaroscuro 0363 *As above, except add Arturo Sandoval (t); Lou Donaldson (as); Etta Jones (v).* 11/98.

Very much in the 'nice work if you can get it' mould, these annual appearances on a Caribbean jazz cruise have been central to Junior's gig diary for a while now and they always yield up joyous, entertaining jazz. Inevitably, it's the guest performers who provide much of the leaven. Golson's presence on his own 'Blues Alley' is a major plus on the first set, but it's Joe Temperley's reincarnation as Harry Carney that makes the 1996 cruise such a delight. Here the tunes stretch out generously, allowing Junior to do his familiar overhaul of the entire composition and giving plenty of solo space to the rest of the group. Temperamentally, the third volume is probably the most representative of Junior's style and the kind of company he likes. Johnson and Holloway are less celebrated names, but the tenorman has the blue-toned wail that suits Mance's playing to a 't', and the terser, more melodic tunes will suit those who don't go the whole bundle on the pianist's usual full-on approach.

In the early winter of 1998 (and what better way to escape northern fogs?) Mance and the trio were joined by Arturo Sandoval and the veteran soul-jazz master Lou Donaldson for what turns out to be a lively and unexpectedly boppish date. The horns are prominently featured on Bird's 'Now's The Time' and 'Confirmation', while the late Etta Jones brings her pure/impure tones to 'I Got A New Daddy' (which leaves no doubt as to what kind of daddy) and 'Falling In Love With Love'. Another great set from the SS *Norway*.

*****(*) Plays Monk**
Chiaroscuro 370 *Mance; Joe Temperley (ss, bs, bcl); Keter Betts, Peter Washington (b); Mickey Roker, Jackie Williams (d).* 96, 11/00.

The Floating Jazz cruises have subsequently moved to the *Queen Elizabeth II* and in 2000 Mance and Joe Temperley presented an all-Monk programme to passengers and fans. It's a strong set, probably the most challenging of the series. Temperley is a revelation on bass clarinet (the opening 'Blue Monk') and on soprano saxophone ('Straight, No Chaser') and the identity of the soloist would fox most blindfold listeners in both cases, though there are some distinctive low-toned phrases on the former tune that might give it away. The baritone is still the main horn and Joe is as fluid and graceful as ever with it. He drops out to allow Junior and the new rhythm section to take 'Ask Me Now' on their own, and there's a nice reminder of the old band with an out-take from the 1996 cruise: 'Hackensack' taken at respectable speed and with some distinctively Monkian flourishes from the pianist.

***** Blues, Ballads And 'A' Train**
Trio Records 101 *Mance; Andrew Cleyndert (b); Steve Brown (d).* 11/00.

***** On The Road**
Trio Records 102 *As above.* 2/02.

Junior Mance brings civilization to the north of England, and some much needed funk to the douce burghers of the south west. *On The Road* was recorded in Wakefield, Sheffield and Cheltenham. The sidemen aren't of the standard the pianist normally expects, but he breezes through some occasionally sticky rhythms and turns in two thoroughly enjoyable piano sets which cover exactly the ground implied in the first title. Not in the front rank of Mance records, but most enjoyable.

Augusto Mancinelli

GUITAR

Italian guitarist who takes a highly individual line between different improvising disciplines.

*****(*) Extreme**
Splasc(h) H 303-2 *Mancinelli; Roberto Rossi (tb, shells); Valerio Signetto (cl); Pietro Tonolo (ts); Mario Arcari (ob); Giulio Visibelli (f); Piero Leveratto (b); Tony Oxley (d).* 10/88–3/90.

A fascinating set which will appeal to anyone interested in improvisation. Mancinelli includes three very precise and hair-fine compositions, 'Poiesis' consisting of 23 sounds and a dodecaphonic series, written for oboe, flute and clarinet and designed to go with a display of electronic art. The other 29 tracks are all free improvisations, some lasting less than a minute, none more than five. Some are guitar solos – Mancinelli uses everything from wide, Frisell-like sweeps to hectic fingerpicking and strangled-tone twangs – while others involve Oxley, Leveratto, Rossi and Arcari (but not Tonolo or Signetto) in various combinations. As fragmented as it all is, the even dynamic of the music binds the various pieces together, and several of the improvisations sound so whole and finished that they might as well be compositions in any case.

*****(*) Jazz Work**

Splasc(h) 494-2 *Mancinelli; Paolo Ghetti (b); Massimo Manzi (d).* 12/95–6/96.

On the face of it this is a more prosaic set and, with bebop set-pieces like 'Cherokee' and 'All The Things You Are' in the programme, one could be forgiven for thinking Mancinelli has soft-pedalled this one. Yet he gets more inventive and original improvising out of a classic open-tone electric than most players do with a battery of effects, and the title – *Jazz Work* – suggests that this is his dissertation on modern history and how it works for him. The four standards (plus Monk's 'Evidence') are all handsomely delivered, but it's his originals that hang in the mind: 'Sassi Neri', 'When Love Is Over' and 'Aria' seem like rare blends of jazz exercise and Italian song-form. There are six solo 'Interludio' pieces interspersed throughout, and the guitarist saves some of his most startling work for these miniatures. Ghetti and Manzi are relatively workmanlike in support, and it would be fascinating to hear what Mancinelli can do with a 'heavyweight' rhythm section.

Joe Maneri (born 1927)

ALTO AND TENOR SAXOPHONES, CLARINET, PIANO

Like Hal Russell before him, Maneri was 'discovered' only rather late in his career, having influenced a whole generation of students with his theories on microtonality. He was born in New York City and he played clarinet with an eclectic procession of bands, embracing Irish, Middle Eastern and Greek music and bebop. After the war, he began studying twelve-tone music and to experiment with microtones. He was appointed to the faculty of the New England Conservatory of Music and published Preliminary Studies In The Virtual Pitch Continuum, now almost as celebrated – and probably almost as rarely read – as his colleague George Russell's magnum opus. Only in the '90s did he become widely known as a player and recording artist.

***** Paniots Nine**

Avant AVAN 067 *Maneri; Don Burns (p); John Beal (b); Pete Dolger (d).* 63.

These early demos, roughly recorded and unvarnished as they are, confirm to what extent Maneri is the natural ancestor of offbeat syncretists like John Zorn and klezmer fiend Don Byron. The album mixes free-jazz material with Levantine grooves. 'Shift Your Tail' is influenced by the *syrto*, a Greek dance Maneri must have played hundreds of times in wedding bands; 'Jewish Fantasy – At The Wedding' comes out of the same experience, an inauthentic but convincing blend of klezmer rhythms. 'After Myself' by the *kalamentiano* is in 7/8, which is broadly typical of the rhythms he favours. The title-piece is a Dolger composition, this time in 9/8 and already featuring the microtonal language that was to be a trademark in later years. Maneri's clarinet-playing blows just about everything else out of the water. He has a huge tone, at the opposite end of the instrumental galaxy from fellow-Bostonian Jimmy Giuffre. It's fierce, angular, often shawm-like in its drift between pitches. None of the other players registers with anything like the same intensity, but the playing is generally very good, with Dolger an important presence. Given what was to come, this is of historical interest rather than anything else; Maneri enthusiasts will want to know where the great man was coming from; newcomers now have the luxury of starting the story at the very beginning.

****** Get Ready To Receive Yourself**

Leo Lab CD 010 *Maneri; Mat Maneri (vn); John Lockwood (b); Randy Peterson (d).* 93.

*****(*) Let The Horse Go**

Leo CD LR 232 *As above.* 6/95.

Maneri's coming-out as a jazz star – 65 years to become an overnight success – was at the 1992 Montreal Jazz Festival, where he appeared alongside Paul Bley, an old associate from New York days. The buzz was immediate, and Ornette Coleman's name was dropped more than once by way of comparison. Ornette's eldritch, 'off-pitch' sound is certainly the closest parallel, but Maneri works very much further from the blues. In combination with son Mat Maneri's squalling fiddle and bassist John Lockwood, it generates a sound that is utterly unique and distinctive, and dismayingly hard to categorize. 'Let The Horse Go' on the second of the two Leo Lab releases (and how typical of Leo Feigin to be hip to what Maneri is doing) opens up more questions about jazz harmony in its near-quarter-of-an-hour span than anyone has since the early days of Cecil Taylor. The language is not so much atonal as polytonal. Almost anything might resolve; almost nothing does. It's hard, even at this distance, to recapture the sheer alienating wallop of the earlier record. 'Anton' is presumably a nod in the direction of Herr von Webern, but it's items like 'Skippin' Thru The Turnips', 'Evolve' and the title-track that signal something radically new, teeing up a truly outrageous cover of 'Body And Soul' which blows every saxophone solo cliché off the face of the earth. Inevitably the second album isn't quite so shocking. It's a consolidation rather than a radical departure. In both cases the sound is very direct and unadorned, something of a contrast with what was to come.

****** Coming Down The Mountain**

hatOLOGY 501 *Maneri; Mat Maneri (vn); Ed Schuller (b); Randy Peterson (d).* 10/93.

***** Tenderly**

hatOLOGY 525 *As above.* 99.

An earlier record for hatART, *Dahabenzapple*, is now unfortunately deleted, but the first of these is also a live performance, recorded in a Boston synagogue in the autumn of 1993. It's a bittier record in some ways, but the opening and closing tracks, 'Swing High' and 'To End Or Not To End', frame a record of quite extraordinary rhythmic concentration. Often very slow, but intensely focused, the interplay is little short of telepathic, with Schuller – who always sounds absolutely right in this context – contributing more than usual, perhaps making up for lost time. 'Joe's Alto' is a caprice, but it says more in under two minutes than most saxophonists squeeze out in a year.

The later disc is patchier, dotted with 'Vignettes' and 'Short Pieces' which seem rather inconsequential on subsequent hearings. The title-track, by contrast, is fantastic, but tucked away right at the end, by which time we suspect some listeners might have struck camp and moved on.

★★★★ Three Men Walking

ECM 531023-2 *Maneri; Joe Morris (g); Mat Maneri (vn).* 10–11/95.

As with Hal Russell, Maneri's belated apotheosis was signalled by a call from ECM. It was apparently Paul Bley, that tireless and selfless talent scout, who put the label in touch. The cathedral acoustic is all wrong, but Maneri sounds wonderful in this context. Excellent as Randy Peterson and John Lockwood were in the quartet setting, this is an exceptional line-up. The album title comes from a Giacometti sculpture of three attenuated figures, insecurely attached to the ground and heading off in different directions, yet for the moment bound to the same patch of earth. It's a lovely visual echo of music that is both airy and earthy, solid and insubstantial, jazz and something else. As with other ECM sessions of this vintage, the group breaks down into its constituents. Joe opens on unaccompanied clarinet, a sound harder and darker than Giuffre's, though superficially similar. The group improvisations, 'Bird's [*sic*] In The Belfry', 'Three Men Walking' and 'Arc And Point', are exceptional, but the features for Mat and Joe are equally impressive, underlining the different idioms and responses at work in this material. While Mat seems resolutely committed to his father's idiom, often using the lower end of his six-string electric violin as the bass and percussion voice, Morris often sounds detached and even remote – but companionably so, the most errant of those three bronze men. The one standard in the book at this point, 'What's New', was a revelation in performance and is again here, richly rethought and brightly played. 'For Josef Schmid' is a little bouquet to the man who taught Joe the 'Schoenberg method'. It brings a remarkable album to a satisfying close.

★★★(★) Out Right Now

hatOLOGY 561 *Maneri; Mat Maneri (vn, vla); Joe Morris (g).* 95.

How many musical outsiders does it take to change a light bulb? Three's a fair guess, because the lights go on almost at once on this beautifully constructed trio session, in which Maneri Sr floats over contending accompaniments from the lad and from the redoubtable Morris, who is incapable of playing a dull session. The best things are the long opening improvisation 'Some And Then Some', the compressed epic 'Roots Go Deep' and the title track, which could probably have been shorter, though we wouldn't wish it trimmed by a note. The only quibble this time regards the sound, which seems unduly lumpy and centred, with not enough separation between the players. Otherwise, a fine and endlessly replayable record.

★★★(★) In Full Cry

ECM 537048-2 *Maneri; Mat Maneri (vn); John Lockwood (b); Randy Peterson (d).* 6/96.

Good to hear the Maneri Quartet together again, but now that the first shock has passed, does this music still sound as startling as it once did? Does Ornette's? Does Cecil Taylor's? The answer ought to be 'yes' in all three cases. It's a function of music as wholeheartedly cross-grained as this that it will never enter a comfortable mainstream. The opening string sounds and the first entrance of Joe's tenor on 'Coarser And Finer' are enough to convince anyone that the old fellow is still the wildest player on the block, for all his professorial hats. As before, Joe's included some standard material: a long, haunted reading of 'Tenderly', 'Prelude To a Kiss' to close the set and two spirituals, 'Nobody Knows' and 'Motherless Child', which bring out the folkier side of his playing. He's never stuck closer to melody than on this album, but the estranging microtones are still in evidence from start to finish. A superb record, even if doesn't quite meet the standard of its predecessor.

★★★ Blessed

ECM 557365-2 *Maneri; Mat Maneri (vn, baritone vn, vla).* 10/97.

The immanence of blessing doesn't always keep at bay the imminence of boredom – or, perhaps fairer, a sense of exclusion. This is an intensely private dialogue between father and son, and only occasionally does the listener find much real purchase. Joe's piano work on the traditional 'Never Said A Mumblin' Word' and on the beautiful closing title-track are the high points, reinforcing the suspicion that this was really a set to showcase Mat, with the old man acting as accompanist and household god. Mat's string-playing on a deconstructed 'Body And Soul' is tremendous and this is perhaps the first time on record that he has put his full range of fiddles to such coherent and sheerly musical use. No sign that he is merely switching axes for the sake of change. The long 'Is Nothing Near?' is a key Maneris performance, tense, but throbbing with some promised revelation, though again very private in idiom. Not a record for a newcomer.

★★★ Tales of Rohnlief

ECM 559858-2 *Maneri; Mat Maneri (vn); Barre Phillips (b).* 98.

Punctuated with odd vocal performances and with Monkish outbreaks on the piano, notably on 'When The Ship Went Down', this is essentially a Maneri-and-strings session. Mat and Barre spend a good deal of time adding complex, squiggly accompaniments to Joe's increasingly elegant – or are we just getting used to them? – dances between the piano tones. The long title-track is an unvarnished delight and, though this isn't necessarily the best place to start with Maneri, it's varied enough and certainly beautiful enough to win over the uncommitted listener.

★★★★ The Trio Concerts

Leo 307/308 2CD *Maneri; Mat Maneri (vn, baritone vn, vla, g); Randy Peterson (d).* 10/97–11/98.

This is astonishingly good contemporary improvisation, delivered with freshness, a good deal of thought and considerable elegance. The Maneris' playing has got prettier over time and, though the sound-world here is still pretty rugged – especially on things like 'Balance & Pulse', the long opening track – the overall effect is a good deal less alienating than one might expect. Peterson is instinctively responsive to the demands of this music. His metre is wonderfully elastic and he is able to change the dynamic of his kit within a phrase or two. Mat has the most varied palette, given his range of instruments, but his father switches over to piano on the second CD, sounding a little like some of Anthony Braxton's keyboard forays. For anyone who hasn't experienced the Maneris' music, this is a very good place to start.

★★★★ Going To Church

Aum Fidelity 24 *Maneri; Roy Campbell (t); Mat Maneri (vla); Matthew Shipp (p); Barre Phillips (b); Randy Peterson (d).* 02.

A new line-up for the Maneri ensemble. Phillips is an even more distinguished performer than Ed Schuller and his authority is immediately evident on these three long improvisations (the middle 'Before The Sermon' is less than a third of the length of the powerful opening 'Blood And Body', which is one of the most intense things the Maneris have recorded to date). Campbell is another key recruitment, sounding like a cross between Leo Smith and the late Lester Bowie. The exact religious resonance of these pieces isn't immediately obvious, but this could be Joe's *A Love Supreme*, except that his faith isn't just a matter of acknowledgement, resolution and pursuance, but of conflict and doubt as well. This is very intense music and an album that should be a priority for everyone interested in the direction of modern jazz.

Mat Maneri (born 1969)

VIOLIN, VIOLA

The son of maverick saxophonist Joe Maneri, he is a distinctive and adventurous player on his own account with a sound that synthesizes the untutored genius of Ornette Coleman with the relentless swing of Stuff Smith.

★★★ In Time

Leo Lab CD 002 *Maneri; Pandelis Karayorgis (p).* 4/93.

★★★(★) Fever Bed

Leo Lab CD 022 *Maneri; Ed Schuller (b); Randy Peterson (d).* 12/94, 1/96.

Mat began working in his father's quartet at the age of fourteen and has remained refreshingly loyal to the old man's concept ever since, even when playing on his own projects. Unlike Denardo Coleman, who also helps negotiate sometimes difficult transactions between paternal genius and an uncomprehending outside world, Mat has a very distinctive approach of his own. The knowledge that he has taken lessons with both Miroslav Vitous and Dave Holland will help point listeners to the number of times he is cast as a bass-line player in the Joe Maneri Quartet. On these two albums he is freer to shape his own abstractly romantic lines, which recall nothing so much as the more lyrical side of Elliott Carter.

The group with Peterson and Schuller has a remote, slightly eerie quality. Lacking a horn or piano, the music is very difficult to pin down. 'Fever Bed' itself is restlessly dissonant, tossing and turning, finding no place of rest either harmonically or rhythmically. Peterson provides what little chordal information is made explicit and, though throughout the whole 11 minutes he seems constantly on the brink of breaking out into a climactic, convulsive statement, it is kept at bay, remaining tantalizingly unarticulated. After such an arresting opening, the remainder is less compelling. The long 'Iris' is more personal and expressive, and it may be (there are a couple of almost subliminal allusions) that 'Almost Pretty' is an oblique reference to Monk's 'Ugly Beauty', which features on the duo album with Karayorgis. Interesting that while the old man name-checks Webern on one of his albums, Mat's final word is for Gustav Mahler.

Apparently proposed by Paul Bley, who has a significant role in the Maneris' story, *In Time* is delicately beautiful and thoughtful, almost like a classical duo in timbre and dynamics, but dealing with a language that is far from classical. There are actually two versions of 'Ugly Beauty', framing a set of originals by both men. Karayorgis's 'Speaking' and 'Part III Of A Name', and Mat's 'Blue Seven' are exceptional. This, though, is a much milder project than the trio and it's probably advisable to catch up with Mat Maneri's work either via his dad's records or on *Fever Bed*.

★★★(★) Acceptance

hatOLOGY 512 *Maneri; Gary Valente (tb); Joe Maneri (as); John Dirac (g); Ed Schuller (b); Randy Peterson (d).* 8/96.

The new element here is the warmly textured viola, which sits in behind Valente's raucous trombone and blends exquisitely with Dirac's clean, crisp guitar. Maneri kicks off with the rhythmically offbeat 'Dolphy Dance', a funky 5/4 theme which puns on a Herbie Hancock composition. Boldly, he follows with 'My Funny Valentine', a version that will startle even those who felt inured by a thousand covers. In this reading it is neither sentimental nor sour, but plain-spoken, even blunt. The long 'Shroud' follows, before an even more startling version of Rollins's 'East Broadway Run Down'. 'Fever Bed' makes a reappearance, before the title-piece, written by the gifted Dirac and co-starring Joe Maneri with a distinctive statement of his own which generously refuses to step on the lad's toes.

★★★(★) Fifty One Sorrows

Leo LR CD 278 *Maneri; Ed Schuller (b); Randy Peterson (d).* 97.

The title-track is a set of meditations and variations on a poem by the violinist's wife Christine Coppola Maneri. It sets a certain agenda for the album, which can be summed up as a search for the moment of joy that exists in the heart of sadness, which in this context is taken to be the blues, but blues in the manner of Ornette Coleman. Mat plays his baritone violin throughout, and in his usual restrained microtonal style, which means it often sounds as if it were fitted with sympathetic drone strings, like a *hardfele*. It's a rich and beautiful noise and Schuller's string bass is the perfect accompaniment. This is a trio bound together by mutual liking and a great deal of common spirit, but there's also a striving character to the music that comes out best on Ornette's 'Tone Dialling', given here in two intriguingly different versions.

★★★★ So What?

hatOLOGY 529 *Maneri; Mathew Shipp (p); Randy Peterson (d).* 8/98.

As the title suggests, this is something of a homage to Miles Davis. There are four Miles compositions and five by Mat, sequenced in such a way as to suggest he has attempted to stretch the trumpeter's modal ideas into the 21st century. It's quite possible, listening to 'Solar' and 'No Blues', to imagine Maneri slipping into place in a never actually convened Miles group. Interestingly, the intuitive understanding between Shipp and Peterson is such that Maneri has to tread carefully to avoid breaking the spell. The result is a beautifully balanced trio performance, with no dominant personality.

***** Light Trigger**

No More 9 *Maneri; Randy Peterson (d).* 00.

Mat and Randy have considerable mileage together as members of father Joe Maneri's trio. The language that they speak on this fierce and confrontational record, which runs together individual themes and ideas into a long, loosely confederated suite, is very different from the closely detailed, microtonal language that Joe's group uses. Mat is such a powerful and impassioned player that he more than holds his own against Peterson's crackling percussion. The individual compositions are less significant than the totality of sound communicated in the performance as a whole. By no means easy listening, this will appeal to anyone who likes their music to offer a few challenges.

*****(*) Trinity**

ECM 543444 *Maneri (vn, vla solo).* 7/99.

Trinity is an astonishing performance, richly textured and deftly executed. A recent association with Matthew Shipp is reflected in the opening 'Mode', which is testimony to Mat's ability to give a complex line the kind of funky simplicity you'd expect of early jazz. He also attempts Dolphy's 'Iron Man' and brings something extra to it, cutting through the slightly fogged and murky dimensions of the song to expose its core. The set ends with father Joe's composition, 'Lady Day's Lament', a lovely thing that seems to transcend its source material and rises to a new level.

*****(*) Blue Decco**

Thirsty Ear 57092 *Maneri; Craig Taborn (p); William Parker (b); Gerald Cleaver(d).* 6/00.

This is a wonderful modern-jazz group. Any line-up that features the talented Parker is bound to offer something special, and this group is no exception. Four of the compositions are by Maneri himself, and he calls on his full range of sonorities on six-string electric violin, five-string viola and baritone violin. The sound is more carefully modulated here than on other sets, more responsive to the dynamics of the group; but it is an undoubtedly powerful voice and Maneri utilizes it to the maximum. Another fine and impressive recording.

****** Sustain**

Thirsty Ear 57122 *Maneri; Joe McPhee (ss); Craig Taborn (p, ky); William Parker (b); Gerald Cleaver (d).* 7/01.

If you wanted to pick just one record to give a complete tyro some insight into where jazz was heading at the start of a new century and/or millennium, this would be a strong contender. The group is a near-perfect match for Maneri's distinctive approach and McPhee, who restricts himself to soprano saxophone on this occasion, rather than his usual multi-instrumentalism, is in towering form. Five of the nine tracks are headed 'Alone', with 'Origin', 'Construct', 'Unravel', 'Cleanse' and 'Mourn' as subtitles. Interspersed are generally longer and more obviously composed pieces, of which 'Nerve' and the title track are the most substantial. Taborn's huge palette of sounds and McPhee's seemingly endless harmonic resource are woven into Maneri's now familiar viola-playing. The result is beguiling, fiercely intelligent and possibly the most coherent and impressive statement from the string man to date.

****** For Consequence**

Leo LR CD 360 *Maneri; Ed Schuller (b); Randy Peterson (d).* 5/01.

The best of the three trio albums on Leo and one of the best records of its year. The label describes the sequence as a 'trilogy', which implies more of a connection than we can discern. Each is robustly free-standing and *For Consequence* is a culminating success in Maneri's output, a richly textured and constantly evolving record that bears many, many listens. Maneri's parallel blues have never seemed more plangent and never more in search of some point of transcendence. His solos on 'Goodbye' and 'Abundance' are full of soul, and conspicuously in the line of John Coltrane's spiritual explorations via harmony. Using double-stops and other effects, he creates a bleakly evocative world that always seems poised just before the dawn. Essential.

Albert Mangelsdorff (born 1928)

TROMBONE

The younger Mangelsdorff brother is the virtual inventor of modern German jazz. Only with his post-war recordings is it possible to trace the emergence of a distinctive idiom, rather than a mere copy of British and American models.

*****(*) Shake, Shuttle And Blow**

Enja ENJ 9374-2 *Mangelsdorff; Bruno Spoerri (ss, as, elec); Christy Doran (g); Reto Weber (d, perc).* 1/99.

Mangelsdorff's most recent ensemble, Movin' On, began as far back as 1990, originally with cellist Ernst Reijseger in the line-up. He was replaced by the resourceful Doran. Himself is a one-man orchestra but he just about meets his match in Bruno Spoerri. The saxophonist is a crafty user of electronics, working in the same multiphonic territory Mangelsdorff has made his own.

This is the old master's most joyous and unfettered record for many years. 'Do You Like Pastrami?' and 'Bolghatty Dreams' get the disc off to a cracking start and, if the rest doesn't quite match up to the beginning, 'Saxobonia' is a hysterical, hilarious subversion of bop orthodoxy, a piece of satire that is more musical than the forms it tries to knock down. The sheer ease and delight of Mangelsdorff's playing are infectious, quite delightful, and this is a cracking modern-jazz record, pushing through to a new and fresh idiom that takes its inspiration from all over the shop.

Chuck Mangione (born 1940)

TRUMPET, FLUGELHORN

Co-led The Jazz Brothers with brother Gap, then joined the Jazz Messengers in 1965. Began playing a kind of easy-listening jazz in the '70s and scored several big-hit albums and singles. Much less active in the '80s and '90s.

****(*) The Jazz Brothers**

Original Jazz Classics OJC 997 *Mangione; Larry Combs (as); Sal Nistico (ts); Gap Mangione (p); Bill Saunders (b); Roy McCurdy (d).* 8/60.

***** Hey Baby!**

Original Jazz Classics OJC 668 *Mangione; Sal Nistico (ts); Gap Mangione (p); Steve Davis (b); Roy McCurdy (d).* 3/61.

***** Spring Fever**

Original Jazz Classics OJC 767 *As above, except Frank Pullara (b); Vinnie Ruggieri (d); replace Davis and McCurdy.* 11/61.

****(*) Recuerdo**

Original Jazz Classics OJC 495 *Mangione; Joe Romano (ts); Wynton Kelly (p); Sam Jones (b); Louis Hayes (d).* 7/62.

Mangione worked his way out of small-time hard bop to big-band section-playing before settling for easy-listening jazz with a series of hugely successful albums in the '70s (*Feels So Good* sold in the millions). None of this later music is worth listing here, although it's no more offensive than a typical lite-fusion date of today; life's too short, though, to bother with even the compilation, *Finest Hour* (Verve 490670-2). Back at the beginning are some serviceable (and sometimes excitable) sessions for Riverside, now in the racks as OJC reissues. The three albums with brother Gap offer a genial reworking of some of the boppish trends of the day, but in each case the album is stolen from under the brothers' noses by Sal Nistico, whose tenor tear-ups are just the kind of thing he would do with Woody Herman on some of the best of Herman's '60s dates. The debut, *The Jazz Brothers*, sounds very green, and Larry Combs is no bonus. A similar situation occurs on the pick-up date, *Recuerdo*, where Joe Romano's irascible solos undercut Mangione's efforts at fronting the action. The leader has a rather thin tone on trumpet, which hints at why he later switched to flugelhorn as his sole instrument; but his best solos are bright enough.

***(*) The Feeling's Back**

Chesky JD 184 *Mangione; Gerry Niewood (f); Cliff Korman (ky); Jay Azzolina (g); Sarah Carter (clo); David Finck, Kip Reid (b); Paulo Braga (d); Cafe (perc); Maúcha Adnét, Jacki Presti, Annette Sanders (v).* 10/98.

It is? The feeling we have is a faint queasiness (nothing so strong as revulsion). Mangione spells out melodies which present as much challenge as a nursery rhyme, and the use of a largely acoustic, real-time band is a mere pretence: it's as contrived as the sappiest smooth jazz. Feeble.

Herbie Mann (1930–2003)

FLUTE, ALTO FLUTE, PICCOLO SAXOPHONE, BASS CLARINET

Extensive tours abroad – to Europe, Africa and Brazil – helped to hone Mann's style and open him to a sometimes bizarrely eclectic range of influences, everything from bebop and bossa nova to rock and Japanese classical music. He is a brilliant flautist with a light, skipping attack and an unfailing rhythmic sureness.

*****(*) Just Wailin'**

Original Jazz Classics OJCCD 900 *Mann; Charlie Rouse (ts); Kenny Burrell (g); Mal Waldron (p); George Joyner (b); Art Taylor (d).* 2/58.

Mann occupies a similar position to Charles Lloyd's in recent jazz history. Influential, but cursed by commercial success and an unfashionable choice of instrument, both have been subject to knee-jerk critical put-down. Where Lloyd's flute was his 'double', Mann's concentration slowly evolved a powerful and adaptable technique which gave him access to virtually every mood, from a breathy etherealism, down through a smooth, semi-vocalized tone that sounded remarkably like clarinet (his first instrument), to a tough, metallic ring that ideally suited the funk contexts he explored in the late '60s.

Originally issued on New Jazz, this is Mann at his best. The rhythm section and the choice of front-line partners gave him exactly the balance between rhythmic toughness and melodic delicacy that he needed, enough instrumental chiaroscuro and a bag of blowing tunes ('Minor Groove', 'Jumpin' With Symphony Sid', 'Gospel Truth' among them) to stave off any risk of pale whimsy. Arthur Taylor is the key man on this session, throwing out ringing accents and dark bass figures, pattering away at the melody and conjuring up a whole chain of islands on the lovely 'Trinidad'. The CD sound is very good indeed, with plenty of definition in the rhythm section (which had been a problem on vinyl) and with no hint of distortion on Mann's horn.

***** Flute Soufflé**

Original Jazz Classics OJC 760 *Mann; Bobby Jaspar (f, ts); Tommy Flanagan (p); Joe Puma (g); Wendell Marshall (b); Bobby Donaldson (d).* 3/57.

*****(*) Sultry Serenade**

Original Jazz Classics OJCCD 927 *Mann; Urbie Green (tb); Jack Nimitz (bs, bcl); Joe Puma (g); Oscar Pettiford (b); Charlie Smith (d).* 4/57.

***** Flute Fraternity**

VSOP 38 *Mann; Buddy Collette (as, ts, cl, f, afl); Jimmy Rowles (p, cel); Buddy Clark (b); Mel Lewis (d).* 7/57.

Flute Soufflé is unusual in not having a vibes player on the strength. Mann found that soft metallic chime an ideal complement to the flute and, for the most part, one would have to agree with him. Flanagan does a similar job on the early disc, moving out into pentatonic scales on 'Tel Aviv', pattering through 'Let's March' and controlling the tempo on 'Chasing The Bird', obliging his colleagues to bring the beat back a notch in the last chorus.

Sultry Serenade is a delicately modulated and totally jazz-centred set which makes use of attractive and unfamiliar sonorities and sees Mann make a rare switch to bass clarinet on 'Lazy Bones', one of two Hoagy Carmichael tunes in the programme. Nimitz and Puma are both in revelatory form; the guitarist is terse and sharp, while the saxophonist reveals a depth of expression which is out of all proportion to Jack's rather lowly reputation.

Flute Fraternity pitched Mann up against that oddly underachieving multi-instrumentalist, Buddy Collette. Endlessly varied in tonality and timbre, it's also a low-key and undramatic set which will appeal mainly to those who like their jazz abstract and unflustered. There are a couple of good things by Jimmy Rowles on the set but too much of it is devoted to showing off the number of possible instrumental permutations. Most of this material along with another co-led session fronted by Machito is available on the Fuel 2000 compilation *Afro-Jazziac Bop*.

***** Jazz Masters 56**

Verve 529901-2 *Mann; Leo Ball, Jerry Kail, Ziggy Schatz (t); Jimmy Rowles (p); Laurindo Almeida, Tony Rizzi, Howard Roberts (g); Johnny Rae (vib, perc); Buddy Clark, Tony Reyes, Knobby Totah (b); Rudy Collins, Mel Lewis, Santo Miranda (d); Ray Barretto, Ray Mantilla, Babatunde Olatunji, Chico Guerrero, Milt Holland, Jose Mangual, Carlos Patato Valdes (perc); strings.* 8/57–7/60.

Before signing for Atlantic, Mann signed to Verve for three years and three records, a move that had important repercussions on his future career, for it pushed him away from straight jazz and in the direction of the crossover artist of the '60s. *The Magic Flute Of Herbie Mann, Flautista!* and *Herbie Mann's Cuban Band* opened up a new constituency to him, but also helped him rethink his own playing by adding Latin jazz elements to the rhythmic mix and foregrounding the flute as a light singing voice with a soft metallic rasp rather than the saxophone-emulating sound he had become stuck with up to that point. 'Evolution Of Mann', included on *The Magic Flute*, was perhaps the single item which broke his new career. It was taken by Symphony Sid Torin and given considerable airplay in the New York region, establishing Mann as a figure on the nascent Afro-Cuban scene. Most of the material on these sides was standards-based – 'You Stepped Out Of A Dream' and 'Strike Up The Band' being the obvious examples – or else Latin-tinged jazz like Ellington and Tizol's 'Caravan'; but there are also signs that Mann is working his way towards a new hybrid idiom, on such pieces as 'A Ritual', 'Todos Locos' and 'Come On, Mule' (a rare glimpse of the leader's bass clarinet). These were transitional albums, with all that that overworked expression suggests.

****(*) Flautista!**
Verve 557448-2 *Mann; Johnny Rae (vib, mar); Knobby Totah (b, perc); Carlos Patato Valdes (perc).* 59.

Mann goes Afro-Cuban and with some conviction, though for us this is a bland and formulaic set that doesn't show off Mann to the best advantage. Production values seem to take precedence over creative performance and, apart from Juan Tizol's 'Caravan', the charts chosen are relatively undemanding and somewhat one-dimensional, as is the production, which has the blurry indistinctness which was starting to become the norm for popular music. The band is just Mann plus rhythm and one feels there is nothing for him to play off, leaving the flautist to process rather routine gestures.

***** Monday Night At The Village Gate**
Wounded Bird 1462 *Mann; John Hitchcock, Mark Weinstein (tb); Chick Corea(p); Earl May (b); Dave Pike (vib); Bruno Carr (d); Carlos Patato Valdes (perc).* 5/61.

*****(*) At The Village Gate**
Atlantic 7567 81350 *Mann; Hagood Hardy (vib); Ahmed Abdul-Malik (b); Rudy Collins (d); Chief Bey, Ray Mantilla (perc).* 11/61.

***** Herbie Mann Returns To The Village Gate**
Wounded Bird 1407 *As above.* 4 & 11/61.

***** Nirvana**
Koch 51400 *Mann; Bill Evans (p); Chuck Israels (b); Paul Motian (d).* 12/61, 5/62.

***** Live At Newport**
Wounded Bird 1413 *Mann; Don Friedman (p); Dave Pike (vib); Attila Zoller (g); Ben Tucker (b); Bobby Thomas(d); Willie Bobo(perc).* 63.

***** Standing Ovation At Newport**
Wounded Bird 1455 *Mann; John Hitchcock (tb); Dave Pike (vib); Chick Corea (p); Earl May Ben Tucker (b); Bruno Carr (d); Carlos Patato Valdes (perc).* 65.

***** Memphis Underground**
Atlantic 7567 81364 *Mann; Roy Ayers (vib, perc); Bobby Emmons (org); Larry Coryell, Sonny Sharrock, Reggie Young (g); Bobby Wood (p, electric p); Tommy Coghill, Mike Leach, Miroslav Vitous (b); Gene Christman (d).* 68.

***** The Best Of Herbie Mann**
Atlantic 7567 81369 *Mann; Marky Markowitz, Joe Newman (t); Jack Hitchcock, Mark Weinstein (tb); Quentin Jackson (tb, btb); King Curtis (ts); Pepper Adams (bs); Chick Corea, Charlie Palmieri, Bobby Wood (p); Bobby Emmons (org); Larry Coryell, Al Gorgoni, Charlie Macey, Sonny Sharrock (g); Roy Ayers, Hagood Hardy, Dave Pike (vib); Tommy Coghill, Juan Garcia, Mike Leach, Joe Macko, Ahmed Abdul-Malik, Knobby Totah, Ben Tucker (b); Bruno Carr, Gene Christman, Rudy Collins, Bernard Purdie (d); Chief Bey, Ray Mantilla, Warren Smith, Carlos Patato Valdes (perc); Tamiko Jones (v).* 4/61–8/68.

Though most of the Atlantics remain out of catalogue, the perennial *Memphis Underground*, one of the founding documents of the fusion movement, has made a successful transfer to CD. Though the recording quality would scarcely pass current muster, the music has survived unexpectedly well. The interplay of three guitarists, notably the Cain and Abel opposition of Sonny Sharrock and Larry Coryell, gives it a flavour that from moment to moment gives off a whiff of Ornette Coleman's *Prime Time*; the addition of Roy Ayers's vibes and Bobby Emmons's organ gives the background a seething quality that adds depth to Mann's slightly unemotional virtuosity. The presence of one-time Weather Report bassist, Miroslav Vitous, on a single track, the excellent 'Hold On, I'm Comin'', may also attract notice. Head and shoulders with Lloyd above most of the crossover experimenters of the time, Mann deserves to be heard, and it's a pity there isn't more around. The live performances are much more what we've come to expect of the flautist and, all prejudice aside, they're jolly good. His reading of 'Summertime' echoes some of Coltrane's trills and grace notes, and there are some telling moments on 'It Ain't Necessarily So'.

The Village Gate set overlaps with *Returns* to some degree, which is slightly puzzling, but the later set, which was reissued in 2001, also includes tracks recorded several months earlier and includes some of the same sessions as released on *Monday Night At The Village Gate.* It's still a good, strong set, but hardly as significant as the original release. *Monday* is interesting for the insight it offers into the young Chick Corea's playing at the time. He fits into Oliver Nelson's arrangements with effortless ease and plays some intriguing breaks and figures that are already distinctively his own. For the most part, though, it's very much the leader's record.The set with the Bill Evans Trio – which was only just recovering from the recent death of Scott LaFaro – has been out of circulation for some time and appeared on CD only in 2002. It's an unexpected association, but Herbie's original material, 'Nirvana' and 'Cashmere', sits very well indeed for the pianist, who lays off some highly elegant solos. A tiny version of Satie's 'Gymnopédie' shows how legitimate a sound Herbie's flute could have when called upon. Also putting in a belated appearance on CD is the 1963 Newport set. Herbie tackles a couple of Jobim themes but plays them almost as if they were regular pop songs, which makes 'Desafinado' in particular sound very unfamiliar. Herbie also manages to anticipate the hit vocal version of 'The Girl from Ipanema' by a couple of seasons, further sign of how ahead of the game he could be in those years.The later Newport sets aren't quite as compelling or original, but they are still quality performances and it seems odd that they haven't been available on CD till now. No additional material over the LP version, but the long curtain-piece, 'Comin' Home Baby', and an interpretation of Oliver Nelson's 'Stolen Moments' are the highlights of 1965, while Wayne Henderson's 'Scratch' stands out strongly on the later disc. As will be seen, the chronology of these records is somewhat confused, with earlier or later material being used to fill out space. But however frustrating they may be to discographers, they are very welcome returns for Mann fans, and they may well help to build a new audience for the flautist.

****(*) London Underground**

Wounded Bird 1648 *Mann; Ian McDonald (as); Pat Rebillot (p, ky); Albert Lee, Mick Taylor (g); Stéphane Grappelli (vn); Alan Gorrie, Fuzzy Samuels (b); Bruno Carr, Aynsley Dunbar, Robbie McIntosh (d).* 12/73.

**** Reggae**

Wounded Bird 1655 *As above, except omit Grappelli, Gorrie, Samuels, Dunbar; add Bobby Ellis (t), Tommy McCook (ts), Gladstone Anderson (p), Winston Wright (org), Hux Brown, Radcliff Bryan (g), Jackie Jackson (b), Michael Richard (d).* 74.

Towards the end of 1973, Mann recorded the pop tracks on *London Underground* with a group of British rock musicians. It's an attractive enough record, and there is a certain curiosity value in hearing Mann tackle themes like Clapton's 'Layla' and Traffic's 'Paper Sun', or indeed the Stones' 'Bitch', on which Mick Taylor plays lead; but there is little scope for extended improvisation and most of the material really doesn't fit the concept. The real stand-out is a guest spot for the tireless Stéphane Grappelli on Donovan's 'Mellow Yellow'. A sidebar on Herbie's career, but considerably less impressive even than his R&B and soul epics of previous years.

It isn't clear why *Reggae* is so named. There isn't more than a hint of it on the record, which is mostly pop- and-rock influenced material. 'Rivers Of Babylon' is the only track that strikes one as Jamaican in provenance or influence, and it is very brief indeed. 'My Girl' is a great club recording, but most home listeners will find it a bit over the top at 18 minutes.

***** Caminho De Casa**

Chesky JD 40 *Mann; Eduardo Simon, Mark Soskin (p); Romero LuBambo (g); Paul Socolow (b); Ricky Sebastian (d); Cafe (perc).* 3/90.

Mann calls his bossa-influenced band Jasil Brazz; fortunately the synthesis is slightly more elegant than the nomenclature. Like Gato Barbieri's more obviously Latin 'Chapters', this is pan-American music with a vigorous improvisational component, not just a collection of exotic 'stylings'. Guitarist LuBambo is particularly impressive, but it's the drummer who keeps the music rooted in jazz tradition, leaving most of the colour work to percussionist Cafe. Mann himself is in fine voice, particularly on the beautifully toned alto flute. Only one of the nine tracks – the rather weak 'Yesterday's Kisses' – is credited to him; the rest are substantial enough. Recommended.

***** Peace Pieces**

Lightyear 54193 *Mann; Randy Brecker (flhn); Bruce Dunlap (g); Paul Socolow (b); Lewis Nash, Ricky Sebastian (d); Sammy Figueroa (perc).* 3/95.

Mann had something of a purple patch in 1995, recording this entirely jazz-based record and then going to mark a significant birthday with a residency that was also a career retrospective; see below. This record, which explores the compositions of Bill Evans, is something of a backward glance as well. Mann had recorded with the pianist as long ago as 1961. Working without piano, though with additional solos from Randy Brecker and with some elements of overdubbing (which, of course, had been an Evans device as well), Mann sounds as if he's turned back the clock and traced a path he moved off with his switch of Latin fusion in the '60s. The themes will be familiar to Evans admirers, though it's the relatively little-known 'Peri's Scope' and 'Interplay' which immediately catch the ear, rather than the more evenly trod 'Waltz For Debbie' and 'Blue In Green' (which is still the subject of a freehold dispute with Miles Davis). Mann's ability to play complex figures and sustain difficult harmonics will surprise those who know only his mid-period work.

*****(*) Celebration**

Lightyear 54185 *Mann; Randy Brecker, Claudio Roditi, Terell Stafford (t); Jim Pugh (tb); Paquito D'Rivera, Bobby Watson (as); David 'Fathead' Newman (ts); Dave Valentin (f); David Leonhardt, Edward Simon, Mark Soskin (p); Bruce Dunlap, Romero Lubambo, Lou Volpe (g); Sergio Brandao, Ron Carter, Eddie Gomez, Frank Gravis, Larry Grenadier, Nilson Matta (b); Adam Cruz, Duduka Fonseca, Winard Harper, Victor Lewis, Ricky Sebastian, Buddy Williams (d); Cyro Baptista, Cafe, Milton Cardona, Ray Mantilla, Tito Puente (perc).* 4/95.

***** America/Brasil**

Lightyear 54233 *As above.* 4/95.

Mann turned 65 and celebrated with a residency at the Blue Note in New York, a week that seemed to revivify his career and sharpen up his appetite for playing. The intention clearly was to take in as much of his career – varied and eclectic as it has been – as humanly possible, touching on hits like 'Memphis Underground' along the way. With that in mind, the personnel was as adaptable as possible, there were a number of rhythm permutations on offer, and the guest spots were judiciously placed so as to complement the leader rather than steal his thunder. Mann's origins in bebop are acknowledged in a very good version of 'Au Privave', and his even deeper roots in jump and swing in a very good interpretation of 'Jeep's Blues', in the arrangement of which Bobby Watson may very well have had a hand. 'Memphis Underground' is played with wry affection and a more tailored approach than in the old days, but the really outstanding performance is 'Give And Take'. Mann obviously had the time of his life and sings on his flute. Strongly recommended.

The second album is also drawn from the same week of concerts, but the selection doesn't have the same impact. Mann is playing every bit as well, but the accompaniments seem more routine and the material, with the exception of 'All Blues' and another Lins/Martins composition, 'America/Brasil' (they also composed 'Give And Take'), is lacklustre.

***** Eastern European Roots**

Lightyear 84488 *Mann; Mihaly Borbely (ss, fujara); Gil Goldstein (acc); Bruce Dunlap (g); Alexander Fedoriouk (cimbalom); Paul Socolow, Matyas Szandai (b); Geoff Mann (d, perc, mand).* 00.

After a lifetime playing bossa nova and jazz, it might seem strange to come across a Herbie Mann album with a title like this, but, as he explains, his roots are Jewish and Eastern European and it's a heritage that, this late in life, started to interest him again. Geoff Mann was responsible for much of the arranging and adds percussion and other instruments. Working with Sona Terra, Mann attempts to recover some of the more life-affirming and joyous aspects of that great tradition, steering his programme away from the Holocaust-darkened tonality of most *shtetl* projects. Despite the occasional exotic sound, it comes across pretty much like any other Herbie Mann record, though without the obvious Latin tinge. It's clearly a very personal project and deeply felt, but set against his finest work, it seems like a belated self-discovery.

Shelly Manne (1920–84)

DRUMS

One of the finest – and shrewdest – musicians in modern jazz, Manne is also one of the most fully documented, playing with everyone from Charlie Parker and Coleman Hawkins to modernists. He grew up in New York but became definitive of the West Coast sound, playing drums with a cool melodism and restrained dynamics. For a time, he ran his own club, the Manne Hole, and bred horses, but he was never anything other than a whole-hearted musician.

*****(*) The Three And The Two**

Original Jazz Classics OJC 172 *Manne; Shorty Rogers (t); Jimmy Giuffre (cl, ts, bs); Russ Freeman (d).* 9/54.

***** The West Coast Sound**

Original Jazz Classics OJC 152 *Manne; Bob Enevoldsen (vtb); Joe Maini, Art Pepper (as); Bob Cooper (ts); Jimmy Giuffre (bs); Russ Freeman, Marty Paich (p); Curtis Counce, Joe Mondragon, Ralph Pena (b).* 4 & 8/53, 9/55.

A useful wrong-footer for a jazz Trivial Pursuit: who played drums on Ornette Coleman's *Tomorrow Is The Question*? Shelly combined the classic qualities of reliability and adaptable time with a much more inventive side that has more to do with the *sound* of the drums, an ability to play melodically, than with self-conscious fractures and complications of the basic four-in-a-bar. In the same way, Manne's solos could hardly have been more different from those of important predecessors like Gene Krupa. Where Krupa made the drummer a 'high-price guy', giving him a prominence from which Manne benefited, Manne draws attention to himself not by showmanship but by the sophistication of his playing.

The early Contemporary set includes sessions made with a septet in spring 1953, together with later material for smaller groups. The arrangements, by Giuffre, Enevoldsen, Holman and Shorty Rogers among others, are too full of meat and matter for the durations. Tracks are over almost before one's had a chance to absorb what's going on. Repeated hearings reveal their sophistication but also heighten the sense of frustration.

The trios with Rogers and Giuffre find the players working in parallel, not in a horns-and-rhythm hierarchy. On 'Flip', Manne plays in counterpoint with his colleagues. On 'Autumn In New York', the horns diverge almost entirely, giving the standard the same rather abstract feel that pianist Freeman brings to a notably unsentimental duo reading of 'With A Song In My Heart'. 'Three In A Row' is an experiment in serial jazz, giving a tone-row the same status as a 'head' or standard. Cool and almost disengaged it may be, but it's also compellingly inventive. The duos with Freeman have survived rather less well, but broadly the same instincts are at work. On 'The Sound Effects Manne', Freeman plays a sharply percussive line alongside Manne's 'theme statement'. 'Billie's Bounce' is compact, bluesy and very intense. Strongly recommended.

The mid-'50s saw Manne turning his back slightly on the experimentalism still evident on *The West Coast Sound* in favour of a more direct idiom which nevertheless incorporated quietly subversive harmonic devices and a much-enhanced role for the drummer. The material may be interesting, but there's that almost academic quality to the delivery which one associates with some of Giuffre's work of the time. 'Grasshopper' and 'Spring Is Here' are worth the money on their own, though.

*****(*) Swinging Sounds**

Original Jazz Classics OJC 267 *Manne; Stu Williamson (t, vtb); Charlie Mariano (as); Russ Freeman (p); Leroy Vinnegar (b).* 1–2/56.

***** More Swinging Sounds**

Original Jazz Classics OJC 320 *As above.* 7–8/56.

Manne was a prolific releaser of records, most obviously with the Blackhawk sessions, but also including this excellent early material from a notably light and vibrant band, fronted by the underrated Stu Williamson and the always inventive Mariano, who contributes 'Dart Game' and 'Slan', two of the most interesting pieces on an album notably free of familiar standards. Shelly plays as softly as he ever did, and with great control on the mallets.

'More' just about covers it. The later album has the slightly anonymous, kit-built feel of a hundred contemporary West Coast discs. The playing is fine, of course, and Williamson's valve trombone mixes richly with Mariano's more acid saxophone tonality to create an attractive sweet-and-sour front line on 'Quartet'. The remaining material is less distinctive. Like Rogers, Williamson isn't an agile and virtuosic player so much as a tasteful colourman with a good sense of the broader structure. Manne shows no signs of wanting to go further in the direction of polyrhythms than he had previously, but he is unmistakably calling the shots, and the shots are by no means routine.

*****(*) Shelly Manne And His Friends Vol. 1**

Original Jazz Classics OJC 240 *Manne; André Previn (p); Leroy Vinnegar (b).* 2/56.

*****(*) My Fair Lady**

Original Jazz Classics OJC 336 *As above.* 8/56.

*****(*) My Fair Lady / West Side Story**

Contemporary CDCOPCD 942 *As above.* 8/56.

The first and probably the best of these Contemporary reissues (now on OJC) establishes firmly what a fine trio this was. The two-piano *Double Play*, co-led by André Previn and Russ Freeman, with Manne on drums, and also on OJC, is well worth catching, as are Previn's *West Side Story* covers, now reissued as a twofer with Manne's outwardly less promising *My Fair Lady*. It has taken on a life of its own. The bonus of the Previn tracks could outweigh the slightly less vivid sound on the (British) Contemporary double-set. Manne's handling of 'Get Me To The Church On Time' and the surprisingly swinging 'I Could Have Danced All Night' comes as no surprise, but he works a kind of magic on 'Ascot Gavotte', and the reading of the standard 'I've Grown Accustomed To Her Face' is exemplary. *My Fair Lady* is now also available as a 20-bit remastering (Contemporary 7527–2).

***(*) The Gambit

Original Jazz Classics OJCCD 1007 *Manne; Stu Williamson (t, vtb); Charlie Mariano (as); Russ Freeman (p); Monty Budwig (b).* 1/57.

Dominated by Mariano's chess-inspired suite, this is one of the more unusual items in Contemporary's detailed documentation of Manne and the Men. It really is such a good record that it's surprising we haven't seen it transferred before now. The saxophonist is in cracking form, working several moves ahead like a good chess player and, though the main section suffers from a slight loss of spontaneity, the musical ideas are interesting enough to hold the attention. The remainder is looser but still packed with intelligent jazz. Mariano's 'Blue Gnu' is a clever reworking of a basic blues, transposed into unfamiliar keys, and Russ Freeman's 'Hugo Hurwhey' underlines his great contribution to the band and to the library of strong West Coast themes.

*** Li'l Abner

Original Jazz Classics OJCCD 1087 *Manne; André Previn (p); Leroy Vinnegar (b).* 2/57.

My Fair Lady yielded up no end of repertory hits. Johhny Mercer and Gene DePaul's *Li'l Abner* yielded up precisely none, but was obviously considered current enough in 1957 for this songbook treatment. If you've never heard of it or of songs as memorable as 'Jubilation T. Cornpone', 'If I Had My Druthers' or 'Progress Is The Root Of All Evil', don't worry; neither had we. Predictably, though, the trio swings manfully and there's an air of chipper confidence to the set which makes this reissue unexpectedly welcome.

*** Bells Are Ringing

Original Jazz Classics OJC 910 *Manne; André Previn (p); Red Mitchell (b).* 7/58.

*** Play Peter Gunn

Original Jazz Classics OJC 946 *Manne; Conte Candoli (t); Herb Geller (as); Victor Feldman (vib); Russ Freeman (p); Monty Budwig (b).* 1/59.

Manne on Broadway, and TV. These jazz versions of show tunes and television-via-Hollywood soundtracks were always a popular schedule-filler, and after the success of *My Fair Lady* there was bound to be a formula to follow. Manne's men do the *Peter Gunn* music with a kind of cartoon tough-guy expression, but this was a great combo anyway and Candoli and Geller seldom knew how to be boring. *Bells Are Ringing* is a lovely score, too, and the trio make the best of it.

CORE COLLECTION

♛ **** At The Black Hawk

Original Jazz Classics OJC 656–660 5CD (separately available) *Manne; Joe Gordon (t); Richie Kamuca (ts); Victor Feldman (p); Monty Budwig (b).* 9/59.

One of the finest and swingingest mainstream recordings ever made, *At The Black Hawk* benefits immeasurably from CD transfer. Feldman's slightly dark piano-sound is lightened, Gordon and Kamuca lose a little of the crackle round the edges, and Budwig reappears out of the vinyl gloom. From the opening 'Our Delight' to the previously unissued material on Volume Five, and taking in a definitive performance of Golson's 'Whisper Not' along the way, this is club jazz at its very best. 'A Gem From Tiffany', heard on *Swinging Sounds*, above, had become Manne's signature-theme and it is rather indifferently played and repeated. Otherwise, everything sounds as fresh as paint, even the previously rejected 'Wonder Why' and 'Eclipse In Spain'. Utterly enjoyable ... nay, essential.

*** Yesterdays

Pablo 5318 *Manne; Joe Gordon (t); Richie Kamuca (ts); Russ Freeman (p); Monty Budwig (b).* 60.

These tapes lay in the vaults for more than 40 years unreleased. Their appearance will only be a major event for Manne specialists but as ever the standard of musicianship is more than just professional and there are some fine things in the five live cuts taped on a Jazz at the Philharmonic tour through Europe. Manne wasn't usually associated with Norman Granz's roadshow and generally preferred more intimate settings, but whatever the context he always delivered. A 13-minute 'Bags' Groove' is probably the highlight, showing off the boppish trumpet of Joe Gordon and the restless tenor of Richie Kamuca. Other highlights are a medium tempo 'Straight, No Chaser' and a fine rendition of the title-piece. The sound is good, but not up to the exemplary standard of the Black Hawk discs.

**** Live At The Manne Hole: Volume 1

Original Jazz Classics OJC 714 *Manne; Conte Candoli (t); Richie Kamuca (ts); Russ Freeman (p); Chuck Berghofer (b).* 5/61.

***(*) Live At The Manne Hole: Volume 2

Original Jazz Classics OJC 715 *As above.* 5/61.

Nothing matches up to the Black Hawk sessions, but these come pretty close, confirming beyond doubt Manne's quality and staying power in the toughest gig of all, regular club work. This was his home turf, the joint he opened a year earlier as a hedge against failing chops and capricious bookers. That may be why he sounds more relaxed, even a little lazy, breaking out of a pleasant reverie only for one or two rather contrived solos. Again, though, as with the similar band on *Peter Gunn*, it's the quality of the group as a whole that registers. Even on warhorses like 'Softly As In A Morning Sunrise' (Volume 1) and 'Green Dolphin Street' (the sequel), they have original and incisive points to make. Both discs have a place on the shelf alongside the Black Hawk stuff.

*** Checkmate

Original Jazz Classics OJCCD 1083 *Manne; Conte Candoli (t); Richie Kamuca (ts); Russ Freeman (p); Chuck Berghofer (b).* 10/61.

Li'l Abner may have sunk into obscurity, but there will be readers who do remember the television series *Checkmate*. This is another of Manne's successful reworkings of film, stage and TV music. The composer this time is John Williams and all the themes have a chess reference: titles include 'The Isolated Pawn', 'En Passant' and 'The Black Knight'. Arranging them for quintet rather than the trio was a good idea since there isn't much action in Williams's writing (no Lalo Schifrin, he) and the fuller sound of the working band makes quite a difference. Like the aforementioned *Li'l Abner*, nothing too memorable; just a very competent and thoroughly enjoyable jazz disc.

***** The Navy Swings!**
Studio West 109 *Manne; Gary Barone, Conte Candoli (t); Frank Strozier (as); John Gross, Richie Kamuca (ts); Russ Freeman, Mike Wofford (p); Chuck Berghofer, Monty Budwig (b).* 61–70.

This is very definitely for Manne completists only. These 22 tracks were all taken from the radio show *The Navy Swings!* and feature a number of different versions of the Manne group. Candoli is just about the common factor, but there are four rare tracks from a group featuring trumpeter Gary Barone (somewhat in the same mould as the Count, but with more of a Dizzy influence) and tenor man John Gross. There are also a couple of tracks, including a fine 'The Man I Love', with the underrated Strozier, and a beautiful 'Love For Sale' with Kamuca. Given its provenance, though, the songs are all very short and there is little feature space from the leader.

***** Boss Sounds**
Koch International 8539 *Manne; Conte Candoli (t); Russ Freeman (p); Monty Budwig (b).* 6/66.

A cool and eloquent set with lots of expressive detail: despite the comparatively late date, this was an affirmation that the West Coast language formulated a decade earlier still represented a valid part of jazz's way of talking. 'Frank's Tune' and 'Breeze And I' are well worth having.

*****(*) Alive In London**
Original Jazz Classics OJC 773 *Manne; Gary Barone (t, flhn); John Gross (ts); Mike Wofford (p); John Morrell (g); Roland Haynes (b).* 7/70.

Recorded during a fondly remembered residency at Ronnie Scott's club, this saw Manne experimenting in a slightly freer idiom, relaxing the usually watertight rhythms, exploring areas of pure sound. With the exception of Wofford (who plays an electric instrument throughout), the band are not particularly well known, but they play with great vigour and application, and Manne's original production job gives them all a decent representation. A branch line, perhaps, in view of what went before and what ensued, but an interesting and thoroughly enjoyable set nevertheless.

Wingy Manone (1900–82)

TRUMPET, CORNET, VOCAL

Born in New Orleans, Joseph Manone based himself in Chicago around 1930 and developed a reputation for showmanship. Led his own groups in New York from 1934 and made many records. Worked in Hollywood and on radio in the '40s and '50s, in Las Vegas in the '60s, making occasional touring appearances. His nickname came from losing an arm in a streetcar accident.

***** The Wingy Manone Collection Vol. 1 1927–1930**
Collector's Classics COCD-3 *Manone; Bob Price, Ed Camden (t); Orville Haynes (tb); Hal Jordy (cl, as); Wade Foster, Benny Goodman, Frank Teschemacher, George Walters (cl); Bob Sacks, Bud Freeman, George Snurpus, Joe Dunn (ts); Frank Melrose (p, acc); Johnny Miller, Jack Gardner, Art Hodes, Joe Sullivan, Maynard Spencer (p); Steve Brou, Ray Biondi (g); Miff Frink (bj, tb); Herman Foster (bj); Arnold Loyacano, Orville Haynes (b); John Ryan, Gene Krupa, Augie Schellange, Bob Conselman, Dash Burkis, George Wettling (d); Earl Warner (v).* 4/27–9/30.

*****(*) The Wingy Manone Collection Vol. 2 1934**
Collector's Classics COCD-4 *Manone; George Brunies, Santo Pecora, Dicky Wells (tb); Matty Matlock, Sidney Arodin (cl); Eddie Miller, Bud Freeman (ts); Gil Bowers, Jelly Roll Morton, Teddy Wilson, Terry Shand (p); Nappy Lamare (g, v); Frank Victor (g); Harry Goodman, John Kirby, Benny Pottle (b); Ray Bauduc, Bob White, Kaiser Marshall (d).* 5–9/34.

***** The Wingy Manone Collection Vol. 3 1934–1935**
Collector's Classics COCD-5 *Manone; Russ Case, Phil Capicotta, Harry Gluck (t); Santo Pecora, Will Bradley, Charlie Butterfield (tb); Toots Mondello, Sid Trucker (cl, as); Matty Matlock, Sidney Arodin (cl); Eddie Miller (cl, ts); Arthur Rollini, Paul Ricci (ts); Terry Shand, Gil Blowers, Claude Thornhill (p); Joe Venuti, Nick Pisani, Tony Alongi (vn); Nappy Lamare (g, v); Jimmy Lewis (g); Benny Pottle, Harry Goodman, Charlie Barber (b); Bob White, Ray Bauduc, Chauncey Morehouse (d).* 10/34–5/35.

Wingy Manone was a New Orleans man, much in thrall to Louis Armstrong as both trumpeter and vocalist, and the leader of a great stack of records made in the '30s. The first disc is very rough-and-ready, with the small groups offering glimpses of precocious youngsters such as Bud Freeman, Benny Goodman and Gene Krupa, yet stumbling on the scrappy recording quality, off-the-peg arrangements and other, second-rate sidemen. For those whose taste runs to the offbeat music of the day, this is worthwhile – it also features the famous first appearance of the 'In The Mood' riff on 'Tar Paper Stomp' – but non-specialists should start with the fine second record. Manone's derivative playing has grown in stature, his singing has a hip, fast-talking swagger about it, and the bands – with Miller, Matlock, Brunies and the excellent Arodin extensively featured – set a useful standard of small-group playing in the immediate pre-swing era. One remarkable session even has Teddy Wilson and Jelly Roll Morton sharing keyboard duties.

Volume Three has three more sessions in the same mode before the one that produced 'The Isle Of Capri', Wingy's big hit. By this time the run of material was shifting away from jazz and into novelty pop, and it's ironic that Manone's 'Capri' vocal sent up the genre, only to secure a hit (a previously unissued non-vocal version is also included). Even so, the group often mustered a surprisingly hard-bitten treatment on a tune such as 'March Winds And April Showers'. The transfers throughout are lifelike and vivid: some scratch, and some of the early records (from Champion and Gennett masters) will always sound harsh, but otherwise entirely listenable. True to form, the Classics label has commenced its own survey of Manone material (Classics 774, 798 and 828) which more or less follows the same sequence as these discs. Transfers, from unlisted sources, are certainly no improvement on these, and there seems little reason for this sequence to be displaced.

***** The Wingy Manone Collection Vol. 4 1935–36**
Collector's Classics COCD-6 *Manone; Jack Teagarden (tb, v); George Brunies, Ward Silloway (tb); Matty Matlock, Joe Marsala (cl); Bud Freeman, Tony Zimmers, Eddie Miller (ts); Horace Diaz, Gil Bowers (p); Carmen Mastren, Nappy Lamare (g); Sid Weiss, Artie Shapiro (b); Sam Weiss, Ray Bauduc (d); Johnny Mercer (v).* 7/35–3/36.

***** Wingy Manone 1936**
Classics 849 *Manone; Ward Silloway (tb); Joe Marsala, Mike Viggiano (cl); Matty Matlock, James Lamare (cl, ts); Tommy Mace (as); Eddie Miller (ts); Gil Bowers, Conrad Lanoue (p);*

Nappy Lamare, Carmen Mastren, Jack LeMaire (g); Artie Shapiro (b); Ray Bauduc, Sam Weiss, Abby Fisher (d). 3–7/36.

***** Wingy Manone 1936–1937**

Classics 887 *As above, except add Al Mastren, George Brunies (tb), Babe Russin (ts), George Wettling, Danny Alvin (d), Sally Sharon (v); omit Mace, Silloway, Bowers, Mastren, Lamare, Bauduc, Fisher.* 8/36–5/37.

***** Wingy Manone 1937–1938**

Classics 952 *Manone; Al Mastren (tb); Brad Gowans (vtb); Joe Marsala, Al Kavich (cl, as); Doc Rando (as); Babe Russin, Chu Berry (ts); Conrad Lanoue, Wilder Chase (p); Jack LeMaire, Bobby Bennett (g); Artie Shapiro, Sid Jacobs (b); Danny Alvin (d).* 5/37–5/38.

***** Wingy Manone 1939–1940**

Classics 1023 *Manone; Buck Scott (tb, v); Buster Bailey, Gus Fetterer, Phil Olivella (cl); Chu Berry (ts); Conrad Lanoue, Ernie Hughes (p); Zeb Julian, Danny Barker (g); Jules Cassard, Sid Jacobs (b); Cozy Cole, Danny Alvin (d).* 4/39–1/40.

***** Wingy Manone 1940–1944**

Classics 1091 *Manone; Marty Marsala (t); Babe Bowman, George Brunies, Pete Beilman, Jack Flores, King Jackson, Floyd O'Brien, Abe Lincoln (tb); Bill Cobey (cl, as); Joe Marsala, Archie Rosati, Matty Matlock (cl); Stan Wrightsman, Mel Powell (p); Russell Soule, Carmen Mastren, Nappy Lamare (g); Bill Jones, Al Morgan, Jim Lynch, Artie Shapiro, Phil Stevens (b); Dick Cornell, Zutty Singleton (d); Johnny Mercer (v).* 8/40–3/44.

As the '30s progressed, Manone began to seem like Fats Waller, also on Bluebird, for most of these sessions: he didn't send up his material the way Waller did but he seemed to get stuck with a lot of cornball tunes, and the records soon become formulaic. That said, his exuberance and the contributions of the better players enliven many of the tracks and it's hard not to enjoy most of these sessions. Collector's Classics go up to the start of the Bluebird era with their fourth disc, which includes a session with Jack Teagarden and Wingy's version of 'The Music Goes 'Round And Around'. From here we pick up the Classics sequence, which starts with the final Vocalion date – and a very good one, with four very swinging tracks – before shifting into the first Bluebird sessions. Marsala and Miller are the principal interest besides the leader, and some of the other players seem a bit stiff but, when they get to either a rare instrumental ('Panama') or a superior jazz piece like 'Basin Street Blues' or 'Jazz Me Blues', the band noticeably perk up. Manone's singing is inventive in its way, and on an unlikely piece such as 'Formal Night In Harlem' he's genuinely creative.

Classics 952 offers a session with Chu Berry (though the material is disappointing here) and paves the way for the two 1939 dates which commence Classics 1023. The 'In The Mood' riff turns up again, this time as 'Jumpy Nerves', and although Bailey and Berry are somewhat subdued they do increase the musical interest in these titles. Much better material and more of a focus and playing small-group jazz makes this arguably the best of these later discs. Classics 1091 has two final dates for Bluebird with a reversion to less promising tunes: the very last title is 'Stop The War (The Cats Are Killin' Themselves)'! A single date for Decca produced the six-part(!) 'Jam And Jive', with a lot of chaff between Wingy and straight man Eddie Marr. After the record ban, he returned with a single date for Brunswick and then four Capitol titles, with a band that included three trombonists and Johnny Mercer guesting on 'The Tailgate Ramble'. An entertaining miscellany. Transfers on these later discs seem consistent enough.

**** Trumpet Jive!**

Prestige PCD-24119-2 *Manone; Ward Silloway, Frank Orchard (tb); Joe Marsala, Hank D'Amico (cl); Nick Ciazza (ts); Conrad Lanoue, Dave Bowman (p); Chuck Wayne (g); Irv Lang, Bob Haggart (b); George Wettling (d).* 12/44–7/45.

Wingy shares this record with a couple of Rex Stewart sessions. His eight titles aren't up to much: feeble novelty material ('Where Can I Find A Cherry?' is pretty lamentable) and scruffy recording. But when the band starts to swing, they manage to squeeze some life out of the situation, and Joe Marsala especially is always worth hearing.

Michael Mantler (born 1943)

TRUMPET, COMPOSER

Born in Vienna and educated at the Akademie there, Mantler brought a species of bleak European modernism to America, where he settled at the age of 19. He married Carla Bley and founded the Jazz Composers Orchestra Association. His works are slow, dark and intense, an acquired taste but often a rewarding one.

****** No Answer / Silence**

Watt 2 / 5 2CD *Mantler; Don Cherry (t); Carla Bley (p, org, v); Chris Spedding (g); Clare Maher (clo); Ron McClure (b); Jack Bruce (b, v); Robert Wyatt (perc, v); Kevin Coyne (v).* 2/73–6/76.

***** The Hapless Child**

Watt 4 *Mantler; Terje Rypdal (g); Carla Bley (ky); Steve Swallow (b); Jack DeJohnette (d); Alfreda Benge, Albert Caulder, Nick Mason, Robert Wyatt (v).* 7/75–1/76.

Mantler's music inhabits a world of dark whimsy stretched somewhere between Edward Gorey (whose writings provide the text to *The Hapless Child*) and Samuel Beckett. Beckett's shorn morality pops up throughout the Mantler *œuvre*, almost all of which is released on a label named after the Irishman's jolliest character. There are moments when Mantler seems almost perversely bleak and unrelieved. Jack Bruce's tortured enunciation of texts from Beckett's *How It Is* on *No Answer* still makes for difficult listening after nearly 20 years, but it is undoubtedly compelling and the spare, almost static accompaniment provided by bass, keyboards and Don Cherry's tiny voiced trumpet conveys a cosmic loneliness. *Silence*, also reissued in the same package, is a reworking of Harold Pinter's Beckett-inspired play, with Robert Wyatt, Carla Bley and Kevin Coyne in the parts of Bates, Ellen and Rumsey respectively. As music drama it is absolutely compelling; whether it qualifies as jazz is not a question we're inclined to engage; but certainly one misses the terse, bleached sound of the composer's trumpet on both these discs. Looking forward, it's possible to see Mantler as a harbinger of the death-of-jazz scenarios of his fellow-Austrian, Franz Koglmann.

****** Movies / More Movies**

Watt 7/10 *Mantler; Gary Windo (ts); Carla Bley (p, org, syn, ts); Philip Catherine, Larry Coryell (g); Steve Swallow (b); D. Sharpe, Tony Williams (d).* 3/77–3/80.

Time and distance have been kind to Mantler, and CD remastering has brightened up the sound on these two albums. They fall into the genre of imaginary soundtracks and are perhaps best heard individually rather than one after the other. As ever, there is more sheer musicality in a three-minute Mantler composition than in half a dozen jazz themes, but they require time and patience. 'Movie Four' from the first album is the place to set the cueing button, though the final pair of eight are equally compelling, hybrids of jazz harmony and the Second Viennese School.

Tony Williams is the drummer on the first set, but we aren't clear whose illustrious identity the (presumed) pseudonym of 'D. Sharpe' disguises on *More Movies*. The two bands are pretty much identical in configuration, except that Carla's ABC tenor saxophone part is handed to Gary Windo and the fiery Coryell is replaced by the much more lyrical Philip Catherine.

It's been some time since we listened to these albums and the reunion has been a happy one, confirming Mantler's standing as one of the most adventurous composers of recent times and a player who every now and then reaches in and tugs the heart strings.

***(*) Something There

Watt 13 *Mantler; Carla Bley (p); Mike Stern (g); Steve Swallow (b); Nick Mason (d).* 83.

*** Alien

Watt 15 *Mantler; Don Preston (syn).* 3–7/85.

Presumably scaled down from writing for full ensemble, the dark meditations that make up *Alien* are – hard as it is to write this without suspicion of overstating the case – the bleakest and most nihilistic pieces in Mantler's canon. Compared even to the numerically coded group and orchestra works on *Something There* they seem almost unbearably sunless and yet, as on the earlier album, there are glints and gleams of sardonic humour and an engaging humanity which doesn't come through often or readily in Mantler's work. To that extent, he is not the true heir of Beckett and Pinter, and still less of Gorey, but it is best to be alert to those moments, as on *Alien* part three, and on 'Something There' itself, where he allows a gentler and more accommodating side to emerge. As ever, Michael Gibbs's string arrangements are immaculate, sophisticatedly simple but full of depth and texture.

***(*) Live

Watt 18 *Mantler; Don Preston (syn); Rick Fenn (g); John Greaves (b, p); Nick Mason (d); Jack Bruce (v).* 2/87.

The live record is certainly the best place to sample Mantler's music if you haven't come across it before. Though not intended as a career retrospective, it does range across the work of the previous decade, touching on some of the material from *The Hapless Child*, to which Bruce brings his usual querulous strength and jazzy unfixity of pitch. While Bley's touch is missed, Preston has his own strengths and Fenn is very much in the line of previous guitar players.

***(*) Many Have No Speech

Watt 19 *Mantler; Rick Fenn (g); Jack Bruce, Marianne Faithfull, Robert Wyatt (v); orchestra.* 5–12/87.

*** Folly Seeing All This

ECM 1485 *Mantler; Wolfgang Puschnig (af); Rick Fenn (g); Karen Mantler (p, v); Dave Adams (vib); Balanescu Quartet; Jack Bruce (v).* 6/92.

Compared to *How It Is*, the more recent Beckett settings on *Folly Seeing All This* are positively humane and accommodating. Bruce still likes to skin a lyric until it shows the nerves and sinews beneath, but of late his voice has acquired a mellower timbre, and the strings here and on *Many Have No Speech* raise the temperature above the glacial. The Balanescu Quartet are able crossover performers, bringing a hint of swing to these rather dry scores. Puschnig has been appearing in all sorts of eclectic settings in recent times. He's also an asset here.

Many Have No Speech adds Philippe Soupault and Ernst Meister to the lyricists' roster and Marianne Faithfull to the singers'. Wyatt, for so many years a standby, is used disappointingly little. He has exactly the right level of sheer artlessness to make Mantler's ideas come convincingly alive. Faithfull's gravel larynx is certainly authentic; her French diction is emphatically not, and she's guilty of some nightclub histrionics which don't fit this particular bill.

**** Cerco Un Paese Innocente

ECM 1556 *Mantler; Bjarne Roupe (g); Marianne Sørensen (vn); Gunary Lychou, Mette Winther (vla); Helle Sørensen (clo); Kim Kristensen (p); Mona Larsen (v); Danish Radio Big Band.* 1/94.

A moody inscape, very much in the slow and dimensionless idiom of earlier orchestral writing. Mantler follows Luciano Berio in setting a group of poems by Giuseppe Ungaretti, and he makes a very convincing job of rendering these curious lyrics transparent. As with most of his projects in this vein, it depends wholly on the quality of the singer. Mona Larsen does a wonderful job, huskily beautiful and totally unaffected, delivering the words like a folk singer and not a diva. An unexpected classic.

*** The School Of Understanding

ECM 1648/49 2CD *Mantler; Roger Jannotta (cl, bcl, f, ob); Bjarne Roupe (g); Mette Brandt, Marianne Sørensen (vn); Mette Winther (vla); Helle Sørensen (clo); Tineke Noordhoek (vib, mar); Kim Kristensen (p, syn); Don Preston (syn, v); Jack Bruce, John Greaves, Susi Hyldgaard, Per Jorgensen, Mona Larsen, Karen Mantler, Robert Wyatt (v).* 8–12/96.

At least he had the decency not to call it a 'chronotransduction', as his former wife did *Escalator Over The Hill*. 'Sort-of-an-opera' serves very well. This is a piece of ambitious music-theatre on the slippages and breaks that afflict meaning – a previous version was called 'The School of Languages' – and so almost inevitably the presiding spirit is that of Samuel Beckett, whose text, 'What Is The Word', ends the work.

Mantler is least comfortable when he is writing *récit* and basic dialogue. Some of the set-pieces, notably those involving Larsen as a refugee and Bruce as the far from omniscient 'Observer', are very good indeed, and the small ensemble plays with admirable delicacy and control. Like *Escalator*, the piece is probably best heard as a series of episodes, rather than as a continuous work. It might well gain from staging (and has been produced in Denmark), but it is hard to penetrate the rather stiff exterior off a record. One for confirmed Mantlerians only.

***(*) Songs And One Symphony

ECM 1721 *Mantler; Kim Kristensen (p, syn); Bjarne Roupé (g); Marianne Sørensen (vn); Gunnar Lychou, Mette Winther (vla); Helle Sørensen (clo); Mona Larsen (v); Radio Symphony Orchestra Frankfurt; Peter Rundel (cond).* 10/93, 11/98.

Intriguing to hear a composer so utterly in thrall to the musical languages of the 20th century square up to the 21st with a record so true to his own origins and yet so replete with new possibility. This time, for *Songs*, Mantler has taken his inspiration from the poems of Ernest Meister, texts that deal with the difficulties of 'relationships', not just in the bland, agony-column sense, but in a much more philosophical context. They are still uneasy and to a degree unrelieved, but there is a sanguine beauty that has not been heard overtly in Mantler's work before now. Mona Larsen's voice is very beautiful and her feel for space is in keeping with previous Mantler vocalists, except that here there is a hint of lyricism he would not have admitted previously.

We were tempted to suggest that *Alien* was his first symphony. This one – which is *One Symphony* rather than Symphony No. 1, note – is surprisingly orthodox in its modernism and played rather flatly by the Frankfurt orchestra. Jazz purists will run a mile, but they should listen up to Mantler's intuitive voicings, which still have the resonance of jazz in their root notes and a slowed-down after-echo of swing in every measure.

★★★★ Hide And Seek

ECM 549612 *Mantler; Vincent Nilsson (tb); Roger Janotta (cl, f, ob); Bjarne Roup (g); Susi Hyldgaard (acc, v); Robert Wyatt (v); strings.* 01.

A collaboration between Mantler and American novelist Paul Auster makes sense even on paper. Auster's chill and thoughtful city stories have exactly the right trajectory for Mantler's music, and the result is a coherent and completely satisfying set of pieces.

Hyldgaard is an able accordionist and her tango-like themes provide an element of continuity between the various set-piece sections, which also feature her and Robert Wyatt's voices. Bob is in stunningly good form, tough and tender by turns, and at moments not quite human, so graceful is his delivery. The echoes of Beckett are overt and meaningful, especially when Wyatt laments the emptiness of 'words'. The narrative is as clouded and ambiguous as one might expect (occasional echoes of *Escalator Over The Hill*) and the orchestrations are perfectly weighted. This is, of course, a long way from jazz, even generously defined, but the music is of such a richness and strength that only the most niggardly listeners will quibble over demarcations.

Frank Mantooth (1947–2003)

KEYBOARDS, ARRANGER

Californian arranger-pianist who led a big band for these Sea Breeze recordings.

★★★ Suite Tooth

Sea Breeze SB 2055 *Mantooth; Bobby Shew, Danny Barber, Art Davis, Mike Steinel (t); Art Farmer (flhn); Scott Bentall, Tom Garling, Mark Bettcher, Mike Young (tb); Howie Smith (as, ss); Bill Sears (as, f); Ed Petersen, Jim Massoth (ts); Scott Robinson (bs, f); Sam LiPuma (g); Kelly Sill, Curt Bley (b); Louie Bellson, Steve Houghton (d); Tim Kitsos (perc).* 11/87.

★★★ Persevere

Sea Breeze SB 2062 *As above, except add Clark Terry (t, flhn, v), Steve Wiest (tb), Pete Christlieb (ts), Jerry DiMuzio (bs, f, cl), Steve Erquiaga (g), Bob Bowman (b), Alejo Poveda (perc); omit Farmer, Massoth, Robinson, LiPuma, Sill, Bellson, Kitsos.* 10/89.

★★★ Dangerous Precedent

Sea Breeze SB 2046 *As above, except add Jeff Jarvis (t), Paul McKee, Leland Gause (tb), Kim Park, Scott Robinson (reeds), Matt Harris, Ramsey Lewis (ky), Danny Embrey (g), Kelly Sill (b), Kevin Mahogany (v); omit Christlieb, Bentall, Sears.* 12/91.

★★★ Sophisticated Lady

Sea Breeze SB 2074 *As above, except add Roger Ingram, Marvin Stamm, Randy Brecker (t), Tom Matta (tb), Pat LaBarbera, Pete Christlieb, Nick Brignola (reeds), Jon McLean (g); omit Terry, Jarvis, Steinel, Gause, Petersen, Robinson, Lewis, Embrey, Sill, DiMuzio, Erquiaga.* 94.

More mighty big-band music from the West Coast, charted by the genial Mantooth, whose arrangements bristle with energy and sometimes hit a note of invention that carries them past the often rote nature of this kind of jazz. The first three albums all trade in fusion-based licks to some extent, though Mantooth finds a surprisingly provocative balance between that kind of jazz-lite and a more demanding arranger's taste. The three-part title-piece on *Suite Tooth* has some terrific playing and writing alike, especially in the mini-concerto for Shew which opens the disc, and the vim and vigour of 'Scam And Eggs' goes well enough with the mood-jazz feel of 'Lauralisa'. *Persevere* goes much the same way: Terry has a bumptious 'Mean To Me' mainly to himself, but four other standards are shrewdly arranged and there are good spots for Shew, Christlieb and Steinel. Terry and Shew have some more good moments on *Dangerous Precedent*, and Mahogany comes on like a young Joe Williams on his two appearances; but again it's the crackle of the band that overcomes any sense of muzak which could have overtaken relatively conventional scores such as 'Imagination'. *Sophisticated Lady* is in some ways the most traditional of the four discs, with Mantooth sticking to piano, the bassist staying acoustic and the charts hewing close to, say, the Jones–Lewis style of delivery. Excitements nevertheless exist in the knockout tribute to Woody Shaw, 'The Messenger', three more very able vocals by Mahogany and Brignola's authoritative solo on the title-piece. Little to choose among the discs, though we might pick *Dangerous Precedent* as the best sampler, if pressed.

★★★ A Miracle

Sea Breeze SB-2094 *Mantooth; Danny Barber, Kirk Garrison, Rob Parton, Art Davis, Bobby Shew, Peter Olstad (t); Tom Garling, Mark Bettcher, Mike Young, Tom Matta, David Steinmeyer, Paul McKee (tb); Mike Smith, Jim Massoth, Howie Smith, Kim Park (as); Pete Christlieb, Pat LaBarbera, Steve Eisen, Mark Colby (ts); Jerry DiMuzio, Scott Robinson (bs); Larry Harris (ky); John Mclean, Danny Embrey (g); Larry Kohut, Lou Fischer (b); Phil Gratteau, Ray Brinker (d); Alejo Poveda (perc); Kevin Mahogany, Diane Schuur (v); strings.* 99.

Smooth without turning into smooth jazz, pop material but proper big-band delivery, Mantooth walked the line with complete assurance. None of his records is likely to convince anyone that there's anything new to say with big bands, and there are plenty of generic things in his arrangements. What he was about was the continued well-being of a distinctive American music, the big-sounding, hard-hitting orchestra that adapts within a changing climate while preserving its old values. The ten arrangements here (eight by Mantooth) are all comfortably within that idiomatic reach and sit squarely inside the leader's own modest tradition. That he makes something like Jimmy Webb's 'Wichita Lineman' plausible and effective is justification enough. As ever, a strong team of soloists, strings on one track, and no bum notes. Mantooth's early death at the end of 2003 was a bad blow to his musical community.

Guido Manusardi (born 1935)

PIANO

Somewhat nomadic Italian pianist who has spent time in several European locations but is known as a distinguished player in the Italian post-bop scene of the '60s onwards.

****(*) Downtown**

Soul Note 121131-2 *Manusardi; Isla Eckinger (b); Ed Thigpen (d).* 5–6/85.

***** Outstanding!**

Splasc(h) 512-2 *Manusardi; Piero Leveratto (b); Luigi Bonafede (d).* 3/86–6/90.

Guido Manusardi is well known in many parts of Europe and scarcely even recognized in many others: a perhaps typical fate for a journeyman (he spent long periods in both Sweden, where he made his first album in 1967, and Romania) whose often lovely music touches many bases. He revels in the kind of unabashed lyricism that one day will be acknowledged as the premier bequest of the post-bop Italian jazzmen, but his up-tempo playing has a lot of Oscar Peterson in it too, and he likes to swing hard on the blues and on favourite standards. Rather disappointing was *Downtown*: four originals, two good standards, a fine rhythm section and good Soul Note recording, but 'Alexandria' is a merely doleful ballad, and only the Red Garland-like manoeuvres of 'Downtown' find the pianist at his most resourceful. *Outstanding!* reissues a strong live trio session, with a few solo tracks as a bonus.

***** Together Again**

Soul Note 121181-2 *Manusardi; Red Mitchell (b).* 11/88.

***** So That**

Splasc(h) H 328-2 *Manusardi; Eddie Gomez (b); Gianni Cazzola (d).* 10/90.

Manusardi liked working with Red Mitchell and their duo session is very *simpatico*, though the bassist is as wilful as ever – eccentrically dawdling over figures but doing so in such a charming way that the music picks up an idiosyncratic lilt which the pianist also takes note of. 'But Not For Me' is a delightful game of cat-and-mouse. *So That* is more obviously open-handed, the trio barrelling through most of the tunes at a rapid-fire tempo; but Gomez crowds out Manusardi at times and it's the sly interjections of Cazzola (listen to his fours on 'There Is No Greater Love') which referee the playing. Gomez's singalong bass is irritatingly picked up by the microphones, but recording is otherwise excellent.

***** Concerto**

Splasc(h) 437 *Manusardi (p solo).* 6/90–6/92.

Concerto offers excerpts from some recent solo concerts. Manusardi isn't one for doodling to himself in solo recitals: he plays for the audience, and there is some very energetic variation on his favourite standards here, though the prettiest moments come on originals like 'Velvet Sunset' and 'The Ruins Of Piuro'. Warm and good-natured piano.

***** Within**

Soul Note 121281-2 *Manusardi; Jerry Bergonzi (ts); Dave Santoro (b); Victor Lewis (d).* 8/95.

This is a forceful chunk of post-bop and it's wrapped up with few problems by the quartet but, despite the pianist bringing a couple of attractive themes to the studio, the results lack much individuality. Only when piano and tenor have 'Laura' to themselves does the music get personal.

****** The Village Fair**

Soul Note 121331-2 *Manusardi; Paolo Fresu (t, flhn); Roberto Rossi (tb); Gianluigi Trovesi (cl, bcl, as); Furio Di Castri (b); Roberto Gatto (d).* 10/96.

Not exactly a departure and not quite typical, this is a triumph for Manusardi and a magical example of European jazz at its most unaffectedly 'authentic'. Manusardi made a record based around Romanian folk music many years before. This time he's assembled the cream of Italy's front rank to deliver a brilliantly coloured suite of inspired-by pieces, with dance rhythms and folkish melodies made transcendent by the vibrant playing and his own impressionistic (though not vague) arrangements. He knows his materials and what he wants to evoke – this is hardly the travelogue of some tourist, after all – and, with Fresu, Rossi and Trovesi at their most persuasive, the results are joyously convincing. On-the-ball support from Dalla Porta and Pillot.

*****(*) Doina**

Soul Note 121381-2 *Manusardi; Fabrizio Bosso (t, flhn); Roberto Rossi (tb); Giulio Visibelli (as, ss); Guido Bombardini (cl, bcl, as); Lucio Terzano (b); Mauro Beggio (d).* 3/00.

***** The Woodpecker**

Splasc(h) 815-2 *Manusardi; Lucio Terzano (b); Gianni Cazzola(d).* 4/00.

***** Live At The Jazz Spot**

Splasc(h) 821-2 *Manusardi; Trevor Ware (b); Billy Higgins (d).* 7/00.

Doina revisits the style of the previous set, with ten Romanian melodies given a bright and sweet-natured reading. Manusardi's signifying trait is that he approaches all this with jazz uppermost in his mind: there's no third-stream posturing, nothing folky beyond the melodies, and the players work to a post-bop agenda. The result sounds entirely in keeping with the rest of his output. Excellent playing from a talented band.

The two trios build on an already substantial body of work in the idiom. *The Woodpecker* tends to run on the spot as far as creativity is concerned, but anyone coming to the pianist's music for the first time would find plenty to listen to: the penetrating bop of 'Ramble' or a songful 'The Peacocks' would be good places to start. The live session has some unintended poignancy in that it may well be Billy Higgins's final recording. It would be using hindsight to suggest that the drummer sounds underpowered here, since Manusardi isn't the sort of pianist who wants or expects overplaying from the kit; in any case, Higgins sounds fine, and the perkiness of this version of 'The Woodpecker' sets a nicely upbeat tone from the off.

Marc O'Connor's Hot Swing Trio

GROUP

Not to be confused with the saxophone-playing Mark O'Connor, this one does convincing Hot Club stylings. In the Stéphane Grappelli role.

*** In Full Swing

Sony 87880 *Mark O'Connor (vn); Wynton Marsalis (t); Frank Vignola (g); Jon Burr (b); Jane Monheit (v).* 1/03.

So many sessions of this kind turn out to be little more than nostalgia exercises, the musical equivalent of reproduction antique furniture, that it's quite a thrill to find a group that really understands the Hot Club idiom and is musically sussed enough to take it on to the next level. The very presence of Wynton Marsalis – superb in conjunction with O'Connor on 'Tiger Rag' – lends the session a valuable imprimatur and a relaxed second solo voice. Burr and Vignola (the latter in particular) bring a completely authentic sound to the date, without trying to sound like 'authentic' Hot Club stylists. And even dear Jane Monheit's vocals are in keeping on 'Misty' and 'Fascinating Rhythm'. O'Connor has one unbeatable trump: we'll never know how the dedicatees might have sounded on his 'Stéphane and Django'.

Michael Marcus (born 1952)

SOPRANO AND SOPRANINO SAXOPHONES, MANZELLO, STRITCH, CONN-O-SAX, BASS CLARINET

Marcus began his apprenticeship out on the 'chitlin'' circuit, working with the likes of Bobby 'Blue' Bland and Albert King, and has always insisted that behind even free jazz, which he imbibed from Frank Lowe and Sonny Simmons and which he plays with fundamentalist zeal, there is always the blues.

***(*) Here At!

Soul Note 121243 *Marcus; Ted Daniel (t); Steve Swell (tb); Fred Hopkins, William Parker (b); Dennis Charles, Sadiq Abdu Shahid (d).* 9/93.

Marcus didn't get the idea of manzello and stritch directly from Roland Kirk, but from a musician called George Braith, a Rahsaan follower who figured briefly in the Blue Note and Prestige catalogues in the '60s. Michael's microtonal approach is a near equal hybrid of R&B and modernist polytonality. And though he's basically an incendiarist, he's happy to set firestarting aside now and again and indulge the odd weird ballad, like 'Hidden Springs' on *Here At!*, where he uses an even greater oddity, the conn-o-sax, a saxophonic version of the cor anglais, pitched in F. The title-piece is a highly organized workout for double trio; Marcus doubles up stritch and manzello to counterbalance Swell's portamento effects, Hopkins and Parker (a recorded first, it seems), Shahid and Charles creating a shifting *moiré* effect. In the absence of a harmony instrument, the trombonist or – more often – Hopkins is called on to touch in the chords, often quite implicitly. It's a shame that Parker doesn't feature in a trio context; 'This Happening' and 'Hurdles', perhaps the best things on the record, are both played by Hopkins and Charles, though the two bassists appear again on 'Ithem'. The final track, 'In The Center Of It All', is an eye-of-the-hurricane roarer for reeds and bass, a brief, astonishing epilogue to a fine record.

*** Reachin'

Justin Time 87 *Marcus; Steve Neil (b); Cindy Blackman (d).* 96.

Always difficult to pull off this kind of gig with no harmony instrument, but Marcus keeps up the flow of musical ideas and arresting sonorities, and there's barely a dull moment. Only the long title-track flags a little, a touch optimistic at over ten minutes. Michael uses bass clarinet in addition to his more familiar stritch and saxello, but it's the sheer range of sound commanded by drummer Blackman that impresses. Her co-composition credit on 'Into Nowheresville' perhaps suggests how much she brought to the group.

**** This Happening

Justin Time JUST 98 *Marcus; Jaki Byard (p).* 12/96.

*** Involution

Justin Time JUST 104 *As above.* 97.

These will either set your teeth on edge or warm your heart; no middle course seems likely. Justin Time has acquired an impressive knack of putting together intriguing duos – Paul Bley and Kenny Wheeler being a more obviously homegrown promotion for the Montreal label – and on this one it has excelled itself. Byard's slightly weird barrelhouse-meets-free-jazz-style suits Marcus perfectly. On *This Happening* he sticks largely to the stritch (a straightened-out alto, also in E flat) but on this occasion doubles on the saxello, an instrument most closely associated with Elton Dean. On just one track he reverts to bass clarinet, a medley of Coltrane's 'Giant Steps' and 'Naima' that will unfailingly suggest the influence of Eric Dolphy. The only other familiar tune is 'Darn That Dream', an eccentrically romantic end to a wonderful, offbeat record. Jaki's death in 1999 robbed Marcus of his most responsive playing partner to date, a musician who instinctively understood his balance of traditionalism and experiment. Given how brief the association was, and still occasionally tentative – the second record is less sure-footed – these recordings are all the more valuable. The title of *Involution* was given incorrectly in our last edition; for which, apologies.

*** In The Center Of It All

Justin Time JUST 130 2 *Marcus; Gary Strauss (t); Clark Gayton (tb); Rahn Burton (org); Nasheet Waits (d).* 4/99.

With this trio set – the horns play on only two tracks – Marcus digs back into the catalogue and to early Prestige and Blue Note work by saxophonists Eric Kloss and, once again, George Braith. He also draws explicitly on Larry Young and evokes Roland Kirk more overtly than ever before. The result is an intoxicating brew that moves from the heat and dust of Death Valley on 'Badwater' to the church aisle on 'In The Center Of It All'. Burton is a key element, supplying the same rich ambiguities as Jaki Byard, but with his own amiable spin. Young Waits is equally well suited to the project – a terse, unflappable player who sounds remarkably mature and seasoned on a glorious version of Monk's 'Pannonica' and behind the horns on the two augmented tracks. Marcus includes the trickily pitched sopranino this time out and manages to give the midget horn an uncommonly generous tone and bright attack. The waifs and strays of the saxophone family have never been so well appreciated.

*** Live In NY

Soul Note 121343 *Marcus; Chris Sullivan (b); Cody Moffett (d).* 00.

The ghost of Eric Dolphy and the living spirit of Ornette Coleman hang over this pungent club date. Marcus is typically adventurous in what has become relatively familiar territory, the pianoless group. Some of the material, like the long 'Thematic Collisions', sounds a little like rehearsal material, but the opening 'Blue Halo' is as arresting and as beautiful a thing as you'll hear in this idiom. There is a tricky, wilful reading of 'Round Midnight' and a rare cover of Dolphy's lovely blues 'Serene'. Moffett contributes powerfully as ever, though Sullivan is sometimes a bit difficult to hear.

*****(*) Sunwheels**

Justin Time 156 *Marcus; Rahn Burton (org); Nasheet Waits (d); Carlos Patato Valdes (perc).* 9/00.

The billing for this emphasizes the collaboration with Cuban percussionist Valdes. He and Marcus briefly duet on 'Moonvoices', but the album really is the reedman's. He opens with what sounds like a Coltrane pastiche on 'Eternal All' and elsewhere makes deep obeisances to some of the other master saxophonists, including a trick out of Roland Kirk's book with two horns on 'Psychic Circles'. 'Pinball', though, is the outstanding take – fiery freebop with a highly individual spin. For a change, he has big rolling chords to play off, courtesy of Rahn Burton's organ, and this allows him to play more sparely than usual instinct dictates. All the compositions are credited to Marcus, and for all his apparent deference to the tradition, he seems at last to be recognizing his own idiosyncratic authority. Another impressive record.

****** Blue Reality**

Soul Note 121383 2 *Marcus; Tarus Mateen (b); Jay Rosen (d).* 10/01.

This is the ideal vehicle for Marcus's ideas, a tightly marshalled trio in which the individuals speak very much in their own voices, but in a common language. The key element is Rosen, who takes up the challenge laid down by Cody Moffett and Nasheet Waits and takes it on a stage further. His feature on the opening track is a welcome acknowledgement of his importance to the concept, a solo full of whiplash accents, sudden time-shifts and a superb grasp of dynamics. He's there again in the very next track, splashing exuberantly in the wake of Marcus's wailing testimony.

Mateen is easily overlooked, but he comes into his own on the long and beautifully constructed 'Metopia' and on the curiously formal 'Flight Of The Monarch' (which we take to mean the migrating butterfly rather than a deposed king). Mateen is also heard to great effect at the start of the title track, picking out a low, soft line on bass guitar and opening the way for Marcus's mournful but pragmatic blues. Rosen is again on hand with big gong splashes and tight little fills.

Rick Margitza (born 1963)

TENOR AND SOPRANO SAXOPHONES

Margitza first made waves as the saxophonist in the Miles Davis group of 1987–89. He signed to Blue Note as a solo artist but left after three records, and is now based at independent labels.

****** Work It**

Steeplechase SCCD 31358 *Margitza; James Williams (p); George Mraz (b); Billy Hart (d).* 4/94.

*****(*) Hands Of Time**

Challenge 70021 *Margitza; Kevin Hays (p); George Mraz (b); Al Foster (d).* 12/94.

Margitza's recordings have rarely secured the attention they deserve. These two are filled with such exemplary work that one wonders at his apparent neglect. On the other hand, he's hardly a fashionable player: he takes a long, thoughtful time over his solos, resists any excess of double-time or scalar exhibitionism, and presents a sonorous yet rather oblique tone which puts an ambivalent edge on his improvising. The long, Rollinsish cadenza on 'My Foolish Heart', the compelling circles cast through 'Widows Walk', the neo-blues shapes of 'Steppin' Out' and the unexpectedly jaunty revision of 'It Could Happen To You' are four highlights of the Steeplechase disc; but there really isn't a bad passage on it and, with Williams in top form and Mraz and Hart perfectly comfortable, this is leagues ahead of the typical tenor-plus-rhythm date. If the Challenge album is just a shade behind, it's still very fine: more emphasis on his own writing here, with six out of the seven tunes, and an unpredictable set they make – 'Hip Bop' turns organ-band clichés inside out and 'Forty Five Pound Hound' does the same for the blues. 'Embraceable You' gets one of its bleakest treatments since Coleman's famous rendition. These are very strong entries from an outstanding saxophonist.

*****(*) Game Of Chance**

Challenge CHR 70044 *Margitza; Jeff Gardner (p); Lars Danielsson (b); John Vidacovich (d).* 10/96.

Less obviously centred around Margitza and often unassumingly reticent to make its mark, this compilation of tracks from two nights of live work in Amsterdam is nevertheless a fine and detailed set that needs a few plays to sink in. Gardner shares composing credits with the leader, and with intriguing pieces like 'Jazz Prelude #9' and 'Blades Run' he sets a high standard for Margitza himself to aim at. Danielsson and New Orleans drummer Vidacovich make a fascinating team and the balance of the quartet is beautifully poised, swinging but always suggesting a sense of reserve. Margitza himself is reluctant to dominate in the way he does on some of his earlier records but the music has its own, slightly abstruse character which only rarely has the attention wandering.

*****(*) Heart Of Hearts**

Palmetto PM 2058 *Margitza; Joey Calderazzo (p); Scott Colley (b); Ian Froman (d).* 11/99.

A balance of originals and standards. Margitza presents his music very plainly, a this-is-all-there-is manner which perhaps makes it hard for his records to stand out from the countless sax-and-rhythm dates which still constitute much of the jazz release schedules. '14 Bar Blues' has a soprano solo which, for controlled rigour at a fast tempo, takes some beating, but it's as unshowy as it is accomplished. The middleweight feel he gives to his tone on tenor makes it easy to miss the subtlety of the playing on the title-track. Calderazzo is a much more voluble performer and Froman is at least as busily propulsive as his predecessors on Margitza dates. Nothing to win new admirers here, but it should please those who've been following this gracious musician.

***** Memento**

Palmetto PM 2076 *Margitza; Mulgrew Miller (p); Scott Colley (b); Brian Blade (d).* 4/01.

Most of the way this is well up to par – useful originals, accomplished playing, pretty much the accustomed Margitza verities. But it does run out of steam, and in particular the last couple of tracks sound like a quartet looking to fill up space. If you haven't sampled Margitza's work before, better to start earlier in the listing.

Charlie Mariano (born 1923)

ALTO AND SOPRANO SAXOPHONES, FLUTE, NAGASWARAM

Mariano grew up in Boston, worked with Shorty Sherock and Stan Kenton, and then formed a small group with his then wife Toshiko Akiyoshi. He has long had an interest in Indian music and brought the nagaswaram into jazz. His reedy, slightly plaintive alto sound has deepened in intensity down the years, but there is a clear continuity from Mariano's cool, boppish early records to his more eclectic recent work.

***** Boston All Stars / New Sound From Boston**

Original Jazz Classics OJC 1745 *Mariano; Joe Gordon, Herb Pomeroy (t); Sonny Truitt (tb); Jim Clark (ts); George Myers (bs); Roy Frazee, Richard Twardzik (p); Bernie Griggs, Jack Lawlor (b); Gene Glennon, Carl Goodwin, Jimmy Weiner (d); Ira Gitler (bells).* 12/51, 1/53.

***** Boston Days**

Fresh Sound FSRCD 207 *Mariano; Herb Pomeroy (t); Jaki Byard (p); Jack Carter (b); Peter Littman (d).* 11/53.

****(*) Charlie Mariano Plays**

Fresh Sound FSR CD 115 *As above, except add John Williams (p).* 7/54.

Critics were quick to locate the much-underrated Mariano in the gaggle of post-Bird alto-players. It's true as far as it goes. Mariano was born only three years after Parker, and his first and greatest influence remains Johnny Hodges. His studies in Indian music, and on the wooden, oboe-like *nagaswaram*, have helped emphasize the exotic overtones he absorbed from Hodges and which are already evident in the early, bop-inspired sessions on OJC. The wrenching intensity of later years is not yet apparent, though Mariano invests 'Stella By Starlight' on *New Sound From Boston* with entirely convincing and personal feeling. It's interesting to compare this performance with that on the Fresh Sound *It's Standard Time* (below), made after a long break from standards repertoire. In the '50s, Mariano was still playing in a very linear way, without the three-dimensional solidity and textural variation that he developed later; he was also still more or less rooted in conventional bop harmony, an attachment that weakened as he came to understand Indian music. *New Sound From Boston* is excellent, if a little raw. *Boston Days* is good, too, though many will find it more useful for its insights into the under-recorded Pomeroy; he very nearly steals the show, and his solo on 'Sweet And Lovely' is definitive. Byard, who reappears on a later Mariano session, is in highly inventive form as well.

***** A Jazz Portrait Of Charlie Mariano**

Fresh Sound FSRCD 176 *Mariano; Bernie Glow, Himmy Sedlar, Jimmy Nottingham, Marvin Stamm (t); Wayne Andre, Bob Brookmeyer, Joe Ciarvadone, Paul Faulise (tb); Bob Abernathy, Dick Berg, Dave Clevenger, Aubrey Facenda (frhn); Don Butterfield (tba); Phil Bodner (reeds); Roger Kellaway (p); Bob Phillips (p, cel, vib); Jim Hall (g); Art Davis, Richard Davis (b); Albert 'Tootie' Heath, Mel Lewis (d); Ed Shaughnessy (perc).* 7/63.

This helps to fill the yawning gap in the Mariano discography a little. One doesn't usually think of him as a big-band player, though he had worked with Pomeroy's outfit and, of course, he had the closest association with Toshiko Akiyoshi, one of the best arrangers and band composers in America at the time. This was recorded after the couple had flitted to Japan. The saxophonist was back in America to teach at campus jazz clinics, and these sessions were put together over two days during a slack spell in the summer. 'To Taoho' shows the most obvious Oriental influence. A modal theme, like much of the stuff he was doing at this time, it uses some unexpected intervals, and again Mariano is slightly upstaged by one of his playing partners. Marvin Stamm's contributions are consistently excellent; this was billed as his coming-out gig and he certainly made best use of the opportunity. Don Sebesky's writing for the larger group is limited to 'Portrait Of An Artist', which sits for Charlie the way Mingus's 'Portrait Of Jackie' sat for McLean, a perfect opportunity to be at their best. The other stuff is nicely balanced, though the three tracks with Jim Hall, strings, harp and celeste err on the side of mush. Leaving Mariano as the only woodwind against trumpets and an array of french horns was a slightly risky strategy but it works, and the small-group material nicely modulates the session as a whole.

****(*) Reflections**

Warner 0927 40165 2 *Mariano; Eero Koivistoinen (ss, ts); Olli Ahvenlahti, Penti Hietanen, Esko Linnavalli (p); Jukka Tolonen (g); Pekki Sarmanto, Heikki Virtanen (b); Reino Laine, Esko Rosnell (d); Sabu Martinez (perc).* 3/74.

Recorded in Finland, this pitched Mariano in with some of the very fine young fusion-oriented players that country seemed to throw up in profusion. The sound is fairly heavily amplified, as on the opening swinger 'Glenford Crescent', but it's toned down for a shimmering version of Trane's 'Naima', on which Mariano sounds attractively quavery. It's marred only by bomb-dropping percussion under the solo. His own 'Brother Muthaiah' and 'Thiruvarankulam' are placed either side of Miles's 'Blue In Green' and Eero Koivistoinen's 'Spanish Dance No. 2', neither of which offer Mariano much in the way of blowing material.

Somewhat time-locked now, this is how northern European jazz sounded for the better part of a decade. As an exercise in nostalgia, it's just about OK.

***** Jyothi**

ECM 811548-2 *Mariano; Karnataka College of Percussion: R. A. Ramamani (v, tamboura, konakkol); T. A. S. Mani (mridamgam); R. A. Rajagopal (ghantam, morsing, konakkol); T. N. Shashikumar (kanjira, konakkol).* 2/83.

Only fans of a certain age remember Joe Harriott's and John Mayer's *Indo-Jazz Fusions*, released by Columbia in 1966 and 1967, hailed as the Next Big Thing, and then consigned to collector status. With a tonal approach not unlike Harriott's and with a similar awareness of the boundaries of tonality and abstraction, Mariano's album with the Karnataka College of Percussion makes a perfectly valid comparison. The saxophone is paired with R. A. Ramamani's expressive voice, and it's unfortunately easy to ignore the intricate rhythmic canvas being stretched behind them by the other players; in *Jyothi* (with the close-mic'ed and lapidary sound typical of ECM), most of the emphasis is on Mariano's fervid upper-register playing.

*** It's Standard Time: Volume 1

Fresh Sound FSR 97 *Mariano; Tete Montoliu (p); Horacio Fumero (b); Peer Wyboris (d).* 4/89.

***(*) It's Standard Time: Volume 2

Fresh Sound FSR 98 *As above.* 4/89.

Mariano has not been closely associated with standards jazz in recent years. Like Miles Davis (and only those who haven't heard the saxophonist play would consider the analogy absurd), he believes in confronting the 'music of today' rather than endlessly reworking changes. However, on the basis of a performance at the Kenton Festival in Oldham, Lancashire, where Mariano had played 'Stella By Starlight', producer Jordi Pujol persuaded him to cut a standards album in Barcelona with Catalan pianist Tete Montoliu and two other local players. Mariano is in perfect voice. On Volume 1, 'Stella' is wonderful, given a harmonically 'flatter' but more resonant reading than Lee Konitz tends to. He misfires briefly on 'Billie's Bounce' and makes a bit of a nonsense of 'Poor Butterfly', but it's a highly appealing album nevertheless, ideal for anyone who hasn't previously made contact with the saxophonist's work or who has a constitutional aversion to the *konakkol* or the *kanjira*.

Unusually, the follow-up volume, drawn from the same two nights, is even better. The songs are no more demanding, though 'I Thought About You' and a second take of 'Billie's Bounce' include some stretching harmonic notions. Perhaps it's taken a CD's worth to get used to the idea of Mariano back playing this kind of material; neither volume will disappoint.

***(*) Mariano & Friends

Intuition 2149 *Mariano; Kenny Wheeler (flhn); Jasper Van't Hof, John Taylor (p); Mike Herting (ky); Dino Saluzzi (acc); Rabih Abou-Khalil (oud); Nicolas Fiszman, Jean-François Jenny-Clark (b); Jerry Granelli, Aldo Romano (d); Ramesh Shotham (perc).* 93.

If there is a generic ECM sound, this comes close to it, though producer Vera Brandes has to work with a less resonant timbre and still comes up with something that transcends the limitations of the source tapes. To celebrate his 70th birthday, Charlie invited along as many pals as he could muster for a programme of long and fascinating musical explorations. Only two of the tunes bear his signature, and one of them is a variant on the traditional 'Deep River', but the saxophonist is the dominant solo voice throughout and he sounds in sparkling form.

With the exception of Aldo Romano's 'Il Piacere', everything is over the ten-minute mark, allowing for maximum interplay and some extended soloing. Mariano is magnificently poised on Kenny Wheeler's 'Everybody's Song', but it is the composer who steals the show with a delicately weighted and unusually sardonic performance on flugelhorn. Saluzzi is as open-hearted and eclectic as ever, and 'Seva La Murga' comes across as the classic it unquestionably is. A marvellous record that should win Charlie some new friends as well.

*** An American In Italy

Timeless 443 *Mariano; Andrea Pozza (p); Ares Tavolazzi (b); Fabio Grandi (d).* 98.

Charlie on the road and as usual sampling the local fare. The themes are mostly from the group and mostly fairly impressionistic, but he sounds in good shape and the interaction is sometimes at an impressively high level. There is another outbreak of classicism with a segment from Mahler's Symphony No. 5. It's a mystifying obsession of Charlie's and, given imaginative recent work in this vein by Uri Caine and others, not a particularly fruitful direction. But it's an enjoyable album and worth looking out for.

***(*) Savannah Samurai

Jazzline JL 1153 2 *Mariano; Vic Juris (g); Dieter Ilg (b); Jeff Hirshfield (d).* 98.

A fresh and uncomplicated session with a very bright band, co-fronted by Vic Juris's guitar. The simplicity of the opening 'Children Steps' doesn't quite prepare the way for the detailed exposition on saxophone and guitar, and it isn't until 'Dark Alley', the atmospheric third tune, that one starts to penetrate the emotional thickets. There is a reprise of the Juris tune at the end of the record and anyone interested in comparative science might usefully put this performance against the notorious Ornette/Metheny encounter on *Song X*. We know where our preferences lie. Whether on acoustic or electric instrument, the guitarist is a fine collaborator; Ilg, always an interesting writer, contributes the title-tune and the delightful 'Waltz For Dani', which tips its hat in the direction of Bill Evans. Charlie's high, plaintive tone is so pure one might almost be listening to an oboe or cor, perhaps the pay-off from his own dabbling with double-reeded horns. The final four tracks constitute a 'Climate Suite' – a 'Four Seasons' to you and me – and are collectively composed. Here again, Mariano combines an elemental straightforwardness of outline with real musical thought and expressiveness. The album is consistently delightful from start to finish, and it was cunning of Mariano to present so much adventurous music in such an accessible format.

*** Bangalore

Intuition INT 3246 2 *Mariano; V. K. Raman (f); Louis Banks (ky); Amit Heri (g); T. A. S. Mani (mridangam); Dr K. Raghavendra (veena); Jacob Williams (b); R. A. Rajagopal (ghatam, konakkol); B. N. Chandramouli (kanjira, konakkol); T. N. Shashikumar (tavil); G. Omkar (morsing, konakkol); S. Sudashan (dholak); R. A. Ramamani (v).* 98.

A fascinating multicultural montage, but not necessarily an album that Mariano fans will take on board wholeheartedly. The music comes accompanied by a booklet of sketches by Dorothée Mariano, and it is pretty thoroughly pictorial and impressionistic, with a heavy emphasis on instruments from the subcontinent. The other key dimension, apart from Charlie's alto, is the vocal style of R. A. Ramamani, a singer of considerable standing and great power. She tends to predominate wherever she appears, and the fact that her vocal line is always more limber than any conventionally keyed horn gives her a signal advantage. Listening to her wavering trills and scats, it's easy to hear what John Coltrane was drawn to in Indian classical music.

***(*) Tango Para Charlie

Enja 9128-2 *Mariano; Quique Sinesi (g).* 10/00.

Inquisitive as ever, Mariano risks exposure but turns it into near-triumph in this collaboration. Sinesi has tango rhythms under his fingers, but also superbly nimble classical fingerwork and even jazz to go with it: as an accompanist, he's both swarming all over everything and doing it with sensitivity. Mariano loves the setting, and plays some wonderful things, especially in the four-part 'Berliner Tanguismos' and his own 'The Lady'. Here and there imagination and stamina run short, but only here and there.

★★(★) Deep In A Dream
Enja 9423-2 *Mariano; Bob Degen (p); Isla Eckinger (b); Jarrod Cagwin (d).* 11/01.

Approaching 80, Mariano showed no signs of slowing down. This is a polished and articulate performance but possibly lacks a bit of fire. Charlie has never been the hottest player around, but here the lack of passion leaves the standards sounding like press circulars. Degen's original 'Etosha' is an interesting addition and a useful sign that he might be worth watching. Otherwise, a forgettable set.

René Marie (born 1956)

VOCAL

From Roanoke, Virginia, Marie sang in clubs as a teenager but didn't return to any kind of career until 1996.

★★★(★) How Can I Keep From Singing?
MaxJazz MXJ 109 *Marie; Sam Newsome (ss); Mulgrew Miller (p); Marvin Sewell (g); Ugonna Okegwo (b); Gerald Cleaver (d); Jeffrey Haynes (perc).* 1/00.

♛ ★★★★ Vertigo
MaxJazz MXJ 114 *Marie; Jeremy Pelt (t); Chris Potter (ts); Mulgrew Miller (p); John Hart (g); Robert Hurst (b); Jeff 'Tain' Watts (d); Jeffrey Haynes (perc).* 2/01.

★★★(★) Live At Jazz Standard
MaxJazz MXJ 116 *Marie; John Toomey (p); Elias Bailey (b); T. Howard Curtis III (d).* 11–12/02.

It might seem unlikely for a 40-something mother of two to suddenly re-ignite a dormant jazz-singing career in such astonishing style, but that's what these three records do. Marie's smooth, clear, powerful voice seems to do everything she bids of it, with a luscious middle range, big low notes that can startle and a thrilling high reach too. She does the expected number of standards, but she also tries out unusual material – Nina Simone's 'Four Women', a striking moment on the debut disc – and she writes originals too. *How Can I Keep From Singing?* has very little wrong with it: 'Afro Blue', 'A Sleepin' Blue' and 'The Very Thought Of You' are each shaped in an individual way, 'Four Women' is a virtuoso performance quite different to Simone's ritualized anger, and 'I Like You' and 'Hurry Sundown' are strong originals. Maybe she overdoes 'Tennessee Waltz', and there are a few moments of oversinging.

Vertigo is simply sensational, the most compelling singer's record outside of Kurt Elling in recent times. Bruce Barth's production is wonderfully sympathetic and gets the best out of a crack band. There can't be better versions of 'Surrey With The Fringe On Top', 'Them There Eyes' or 'I Only Have Eyes For You'. The title-track is a risky piece, delivered with rare assurance. Combining 'Dixie' with 'Strange Fruit' was chillingly effective. 'Blackbird' is a memorable coda to the rest. As an enlightened repertory record, this walks all over Cassandra Wilson's recent music.

How to follow a masterpiece? For her third MaxJazz release, she's gone for the live performance souvenir. She's not a singer to impress you with her range, and there's a degree of showing off, as there is on every live record, but for Marie it's more down to the bull's-eye way she hits a note, extends a phrase, or improvises a new song, as she does on 'Where Or When': this is the Betty Carter method made palatable to non-believers, a whole new melody imposed on the lyric, but not in such a way that you feel she's taken a liberty too far. 'I Loves You Porgy' is a brilliant new take on a song which Nina Simone once turned into a kind of cold bathos. Maybe we could have done with one more of her originals – or a better one than 'Shelter In Your Arms', which is the only place where American sentimentality intrudes. The one which might divide the house, though, is her melding of Ravel's 'Bolero' with Leonard Cohen's 'Suzanne'. As a live set piece it must be little short of spellbinding, and even on record it's pretty extraordinary.

Michael 'Dodo' Marmarosa (1925–2002)

PIANO

Born in Pittsburgh, Marmarosa worked with Krupa and Barnet while still a teenager, then moved to California and recorded on several important bebop sessions. He returned to Pittsburgh in the '50s and, despite a brief reappearance in the early '60s, was seldom heard from thereafter.

★★★ On Dial: The Complete Sessions
Spotlite SPJ-128 *Marmarosa; Howard McGhee, Miles Davis (t); Teddy Edwards, Lucky Thompson (ts); Arvin Garrison (g); Harry Babasin (clo); Bob Kesterson (b); Roy Porter, Jackie Mills (d).* 46–12/47.

★★★ Dodo's Bounce
Fresh Sound FSCD-1019 *As above, except add Barney Kessel (g), Gene Englund, Red Callender (b); omit Davis, McGhee, Edwards, Garrison, Kesterson, Porter.* 46–47.

★★★ Dodo Lives
Topaz TPZ 1058 *Marmarosa; Al Killian, Peanuts Holland, Jimmy Pupa, Art House, Roy Eldridge, Lyman Vunk, Paul Cohen, Bernie Glow, George Schwartz, Carl Green, Ray Linn, Dale Pierce, Nelson Shalladay, Howard McGhee, Miles Davis (t); Eddie Bert, Ed Fromm, Spud Murphy, Bob Swift, Porky Cohen, Tommy Pedersen, Ben Pickering, George Dikson, Harry Rogers, Ollie Wilson, Britt Woodman (tb); Charlie Barnet, Buddy DeFranco, Artie Shaw, Lou Prisby, Rudolph Tanza, Ralph Roseland, John Walton, Ray De Geer, Milt Bloom, Mike Goldberg, Danny Bank, Chuck Gentry, Andy Pinbo, Harry Klee, Lucky Thompson, Charlie Parker, Ralph Lee, Gus McReynolds, Hy Mandel, Boyd Raeburn, Hal McKusick (reeds); Turk Van Lake, Barney Kessel, Slim Gaillard, Dave Barbour, Arvin Garrison (g); Russ Wagner, Morris Rayman, Sam Brown, Ray Brown, Vic McMillan, Andy Ricardi, Red Callender, Harry Babasin (b); Harold Hahn, Lou Fromm, Zutty Singleton, Jackie Mills, Roy Porter (d).* 10/43–46.

A bebop enigma. Marmarosa played an important minor role in bop's hothouse days, recording with Parker in Los Angeles; but less than two years later he was back in his native Pittsburgh and heading for an obscurity and silence that was seldom broken thereafter. He had a foot in swing as well as the modern camp, and his precise articulation and sweeping lines make one think of Tatum as much as any of his immediate contemporaries: a pair of solos from 1946, 'Deep Purple' and

'Tea For Two', are strikingly akin to the older man's conception. But he had a gentle, even rhapsodic side which colours the trio tracks on both of these discs and, while he flirts with an even more audacious conception – hinted at on the two 'Tone Paintings' solos from 1947 – one feels he never satisfactorily resolved the different strands of his playing. Much of his best playing is to be found on Parker's Dials (a solitary example, 'Bird Lore', is on the Spotlite CD), but the solo, trio and sextet (with Howard McGhee) tracks on *On Dial* include much absorbing piano-jazz. The Fresh Sounds CD duplicates 14 of the 22 tracks on the Spotlite disc, but also includes ten tracks cut for the Atomic label prior to the Dials, plus six quartet sides with Lucky Thompson. Neither disc solves the problem of the indifferent sound of the originals, and both feature an atrocious speed wobble on the two 'Tone Paintings' solos (which originally were privately recorded in any case).

The Topaz disc is fine on its own terms but features Marmarosa mainly as a sideman – with Artie Shaw, Charlie Barnet ('The Moose'), Slim Gaillard and Boyd Raeburn, plus the six titles with Lucky Thompson, 'Mellow Mood', 'Deep Purple', 'Tea For Two' and a stray track with a Lyle Griffin group. So it's not quite an addendum to the other discs, and anyone who has a smattering of '40s swing will probably have the Barnet and Shaw tracks already.

★★★(★) Dodo Marmarosa, Pittsburgh 1958

Uptown UPCD 27.44 *Marmarosa; Danny Conn (t); Buzzy Renn (as); Carlo Galluzzo (ts); Danny Mastri, Jimmy DeJulio, Johnny Vance (b); Henry Sciullo, Chuck Spatafore (d).* 3/56–62.

An amazing discovery and enough to warrant a fresh look at this remarkable jazzman. The lion's share of the disc is a tape recorded by Danny Conn of Marmarosa playing at the Midway Lounge in Pittsburgh in 1958. Indifferent sound, but the piano comes through clearly, and Marmarosa's powers seem undiminished on a mix of bebop and standards. Even more interesting are three tracks from a 1962 TV broadcast with a quintet led by Conn: 'Horoscope, Vigo Movement' and 'Dodo's Blues' are intriguing glimpses of how Marmarosa might have developed after bop's heyday. There is also an after-hours tape from a few years earlier by a similar band, including a starkly effective 'You're My Thrill'. Robert Sunenblick's documentation is superb, with revealing notes on all the musicians and a 1995 interview with Mike Marmarosa (as he preferred to call himself). While this is basically a memoir of bits and pieces, reading through the notes and hearing the music evokes a deeply moving portrait of a community of jazzmen whose efforts will hardly be remembered by posterity, sustained mainly by the rewards of the music itself.

Chuck Marohnic

PIANO, SYNTHESIZER

Inspired by Red Garland and a sometime associate of Chet Baker, Marohnic is probably better known as an educator. His body of work is well worth investigating.

★★★ Copenhagen Suite

Steeplechase SCCD 31408 *Marohnic; Bennie Wallace (ts); Steve Gilmore (b); Bill Goodwin (d).* 9/78.

★★★ Permutations

Steeplechase SCCD 31155 *Marohnic (p solo).* 5/81.

The touch is reminiscent of Hal Galper's, particularly on a tune like Corea's 'Windows' on the solo album, and there are times on *Copenhagen Suite* when the delivery seems a little overripe. Basically, though, Marohnic is a clear-sighted and swinging pianist with an excellent ear for a melody. 'Maverick' and 'Julie's Waltz' open the earlier album on a high that isn't quite sustained. The playing career wasn't either, and it was to be a decade before he went into the studios again. A pity, we think.

★★★(★) Many Mansions

Challenge 73127 *Marohnic; David Friesen (b); Joe LaBarbera, Alan Jones (d).* 98.

Like Paul Bley, whom he also occasionally resembles, Marohnic dabbled in electronics for a time. There are moments here which suggest he might have taken the experiment further, but what strikes is not so much the confidence of technique as a deft touch for selecting material. Putting Hancock's 'Speak Like A Child' up against 'All The Things You Are', John Abercrombie's 'Ralph's Piano Waltz' alongside a rolling version of 'How Deep Is The Ocean?' and his own title track beside 'Autumn Leaves' and Friesen's lovely 'Goal In Mind' suggests a jazz musician who is also a fan and a fan who understands what makes a great record. This isn't quite great, but it has an extra something nudging around it. Friesen is himself guilty of over-ripeness, but LaBarbera has a pungency that keeps the trio to the matter at hand. The occasional synth warble was forgivable, even this late in the day, if it was deployed as effectively and sensitively as here.

★★(★) White Men Can't Monk

Summit 291 *Marohnic; John Stowell (g); Don Mio (d).* 02.

The best measure of our disappointment is to compare the versions of 'Nardis' here and on *Copenhagen Suite*. One can accept that performance and recording have had to take second and sometimes third place to other imperatives in Marohnic's life, but that isn't to say that we should willingly pay hard cash to listen to a Sunday musician indulge his hobby. Marohnic is obviously much more than that, but the lightweight execution of this set – which incidentally doesn't include a single Monk tune – is very far from his best. He once had a tune called 'Melodious Thunk', which might have been revived for this, and might have reminded Chuck that a bit of melodic energy and rhythmic verve does no harm, even in a late night club setting. Marohnic has also issued a nonet album somewhat in *Birth Of The Cool* mode but we have not had an opportunity to hear it.

Hank Marr (born 1927)

ORGAN

Neglected Hammond master.

★★★ It's 'Bout Time

Double Time 102 *Marr; Gene Walker (ts); Kevin Turner (g); Jim Rupp (d).* 5/95.

★★★ Groovin' It

Double Time 112 *Marr; Wilbert Longmire (g); Bill Stewart (d).* 5/96.

★★★(★) Hank & Frank

Double Time 134 *Marr; Frank Foster (ts); Cal Collins (g); Jim Rupp (d).* 4/98.

When the wheel of fashion turned again and organ samples became a mainstay of the acid jazz vogue, Hank Marr must have been looking the other way. Unlike most of the Hammond specialists of his generation – Groove Holmes, Jack McDuff, even Larry Young – Hank was rarely cited as an influence by the young Turks and only occasionally sought out by the DJs.

A pity. He's a classic B3 man, funky and greasy, with a rich danceable throb running through the best of his work. The early stuff on Charly and King is long gone, but the revival of Hammond jazz did at least allow Marr to start recording under his own name again. *It's 'Bout Time* might have been made at any time in the mid-'60s. It's lifted out of the ordinary by a remarkably touching version of Mal Waldron's 'Soul Eyes', though for the most part Hank sticks to basic grooves, lapsing only with a pointless assassination of 'Amazing Grace'. It was, indeed, about time he made an impression. Unfortunately, the follow-up was slightly disappointing, though Bill Stewart's funky drumming is worth getting *Groovin' It* for, even if you aren't enamoured of Hank's two takes of 'Misty' (ballad and swing) or his strange version of 'Battle Hymn Of The Republic'. The themes are more adventurous, but Marr goes over the top way too often and could have been reined in a bit by producer Jamey Aebersold.

The naval cap propped on the piano lid on the cover of *Hank & Frank* gives the game away. It's a tribute to Bill Basie and the recruitment of Frank Foster (in great shape) gives a ring of authenticity to a set-list that has only rather remote connections to the Count. Which is a good thing, because there's more thoughtful playing on this disc than on any of Hank's previous outings. 'Paris In April' is a cleverly conceived variation and the originals 'Rhythmesque' and 'Basie-cally Speaking' are deceptive in structure and range. Marr will never be cited as one of the masters of organ jazz, but he's been neglected too long.

Joe Marsala (1907–78)

CLARINET, VOCALS

A Chicagoan, Marsala already had ten years in clubs and circus bands before taking a group which featured a mixed-race line-up into New York's Hickory House in 1937. Worked there for some ten years but retired in 1948 and went mainly into music publishing, though he played again in the '60s. A versatile swing stylist on reeds.

★★★ Joe Marsala 1936–42

Classics 763 *Marsala; Pee Wee Erwin, Max Kaminsky, Marty Marsala (t); Bill Coleman (t, v); George Brunies (tb); Pete Brown, Ben Glassman (as); John Smith (ts); Dave Bowman, Joe Bushkin, Dick Cary, Frank Signorelli (p); Ray Biondi (vn); Adele Girard (hp); Eddie Condon, Carmen Mastren (g); Jack LeMaire (g, v); Jack Kelleher, Artie Shapiro, Haig Stephens, Gene Traxler (b); Danny Alvin, Stan King, Shelly Manne, Buddy Rich, Zutty Singleton (d); Dell St John (v).* 1/36–7/42.

★★★(★) Joe Marsala 1944–46

Classics 902 *Marsala; Dizzy Gillespie, Bobby Hackett, Joe Thomas (t); Frank W Orchard (tb); Gene DiNovi, Leonard Feather, Cliff Jackson, Charlie Queener, Gene Schroeder (p); Eddie Condon, Chuck Wayne (g); Adele Girard (hp); Bob Casey, Irving Lang, Clyde Lombardi, Sid Weiss (b); Buddy Christian, Rollo Laylan (d); Linda Keene (v).* 3/44–11/45.

Armed with Wagnerian good looks (that's Robert rather than Richard Wagner) and a dark, winey tone, Marsala also claims an honourable place in jazz history for his efforts to break down the race divide. It was an endeavour that won the respect of Leonard Feather, a poacher rather than a gamekeeper in those days and composer of all the material on the April 1940 session. Though Marsala had the projection and the sense of structure to perform effectively in big bands, he functioned best in small groups, notably the band which maintained a residency at the Hickory House on 52nd Street. These sides represent most of his recorded output. A couple of early tracks were made for Decca under the name The Six Blue Chips; Pee Wee Erwin was the main attraction. In 1937 Marsala married harpist Adele Girard, who had brought an attractive balance and sense of space to a front line of clarinet, trumpet and violin. In later years, and particularly on the sessions of May and November 1945, she was given ever more prominent status, perhaps as a result of market pressure, and on the late pair made for Musicraft ('East Of The Sun' and 'Slightly Dizzy') she is pushed well forward.

The second volume is distinguished by some fine playing from trumpeter Joe Thomas and a brief glimpse of Dizzy Gillespie in 1945, doing 'My Melancholy Baby' and 'Cherokee'. Another reason for Marsala's appearance in the history books is his prescience in recruiting young players like Buddy Rich and Shelly Manne, who made their debuts as jazz players under Marsala's leadership in March 1938 and April 1941 respectively. These associations aside, there is no mistaking the quality of the jazz Marsala played. The Chicagoan's band, featuring brother Marty on trumpet and Eddie Condon on guitar, swings like fury, as does the later All Timers set-up which opens Volume Two, with Bobby Hackett sounding harder-toned than usual (to a degree which might puzzle Hackett buffs) but unmistakably himself on 'Clarinet Marmalade' and 'Tiger Rag'. Linda Keene's vocals add nothing much to the November 1944 date, and for the most part Marsala steered clear of singers; Dell St John has a bit part on the earlier set and Joe himself takes a brief turn at the mic on 'Gotta Be This Or That'. Otherwise, straight, driving small-group jazz.

Branford Marsalis (born 1960)

TENOR AND SOPRANO SAXOPHONES

The eldest of the Marsalis brothers started on alto saxophone and joined Art Blakey's Jazz Messengers in 1981. After a period in brother Wynton's group, he has been his own man in various situations ever since: sideman with Sting, leader of the Tonight Show band, guest with the Grateful Dead, movie actor, leader of the hip-hop jazz band Buckshot Le Fonque, teacher at Michigan University and A&R consultant for Columbia Records. All this besides touring and making albums with his own quartet.

★★★ Scenes In The City

Columbia 468458-2 *Marsalis; John Longo (t); Robin Eubanks (tb); Mulgrew Miller (p); Ray Drummond, Ron Carter, Charnett Moffett, Phil Bowler (b); Marvin 'Smitty' Smith, Jeff 'Tain' Watts (d).* 4–11/83.

*****(*) Royal Garden Blues**
Columbia 468704-2 *Marsalis; Ellis Marsalis, Kenny Kirkland, Herbie Hancock, Larry Willis (p); Ron Carter, Charnett Moffett, Ira Coleman (b); Ralph Peterson, Marvin 'Smitty' Smith, Al Foster, Jeff 'Tain' Watts (d).* 3–7/86.

***** Renaissance**
Columbia 40711 *Marsalis; Kenny Kirkland (p); Charnett Moffett (b); Jeff 'Tain' Watts (d).* n.d.

*****(*) Random Abstract**
Columbia 468707-2 *Marsalis; Kenny Kirkland (p); Delbert Felix (b); Lewis Nash (d).* 8/87.

Articulate, hip, funny, the eldest of the Marsalis brothers was almost as ubiquitous a figure as his trumpeter–sibling in the '80s and '90s. His tenor playing is stonily powerful in the Rollins tradition, and he has stuck by the bigger horn on most of his solo records, with soprano – granted a sometimes reedy but usually impressive full tone – as second instrument. *Scenes In The City* was an entertaining debut, with a wry version of the Mingus title-tune (complete with dialogue), and the storming manifesto of 'No Backstage Pass' to show what he could do; but it's a bit of a jumble. *Royal Garden Blues* is a step down, the playing messy and subdivided among a bewildering variety of rhythm sections. *Renaissance* and *Random Abstract* emerge as accomplished but undecided sessions. On *Random Abstract* Marsalis seems to explore the mannerisms of a number of preceding tenor influences: Coltrane, Shorter, Coleman, even Ben Webster, whose celebration in a bathetic reading of 'I Thought About You' seems more of a parody than a tribute. The chief problem with all these sessions, though, is that Marsalis promises more than he delivers, both conceptually and in the heft and weight of his playing. While still sounding imaginative and technically top-line, he can't seem to focus an eloquent battery of remarks into a proper speech. Delfeayo Marsalis's production is idiosyncratic. His interest in 'more bass wood' tends to make the lower frequencies sound woolly and unclear.

***** Trio Jeepy**
Columbia 465134-2 2CD *Marsalis; Milt Hinton, Delbert Felix (b); Jeff 'Tain' Watts (d).* 1/88.

A rambling jam session, illuminated by some brilliant moments. 'The Nearness Of You' is a mature ballad reading, 'Doxy' a convincing nod to Rollins, and 'Random Abstract' features the Marsalis–Felix–Watts trio in full, exhilarating flight; the amazingly durable Hinton plays on most of the other tracks. While hailed (mystifyingly) as a breakthrough masterpiece in some quarters, it's actually a lightweight, fun record.

***** Crazy People Music**
Columbia 466870-2 *Marsalis; Kenny Kirkland (p); Robert Hurst (b); Jeff 'Tain' Watts (d).* 1–3/90.

***** The Beautyful Ones Are Not Yet Born**
Columbia 468896-2 *Marsalis; Wynton Marsalis (t); Robert Hurst (b); Jeff 'Tain' Watts (d).* 5/91.

Hurst and Watts are musicians of resolute power and high craft, and they provide Marsalis with the bedrock he needs to contextualize his playing. *Crazy People Music* is a solidly realized tenor-and-rhythm date, full of elegant playing, but the music on *The Beautyful Ones Are Not Yet Born* is better still. The recording sounds warmer and more specifically focused, and the long, stretched-out improvisations insist that Marsalis has his perfect, singular setting in the trio with Hurst and Watts (brother Wynton makes a brief cameo appearance on one track). 'Citizen Tain' – which has some of the wit of Sonny Rollins working against Philly Joe Jones on *Newk's Time* – 'Gilligan's Isle' and the steeply driven title-tune are aristocratic improvisations in which the leader finds a path away from merely discursive blowing. His soprano sounds pretty good, too.

***** I Heard You Twice The First Time**
Columbia 472169-2 *Marsalis; Wynton Marsalis, Earl Gardner (t); Delfeayo Marsalis, David Sager (tb); Wessell Anderson (as); Kenny Kirkland (p); B. B. King, John Lee Hooker (g, v); Russell Malone, Joe Louis Walker (g); Reginald Veal, Robert Hurst (b); Jeff 'Tain' Watts, Herlin Riley, Bernard Purdie (d); Thomas Hollis, Roscoe Carroll, Carl Gordon, Charles Dutton, Linda Hopkins (v). n.d.*

*****(*) Bloomington**
Columbia 473771-2 *Marsalis; Robert Hurst (b); Jeff 'Tain' Watts (d).* 9/91.

Branford's blues album is somewhat lighter than Wynton's three-volume dissertation, but there's still a tendency to ramble. The crackling 'Rib Tip Johnson', with superb guitar by Russell Malone, would have been better at five minutes rather than nine, and B. B. King's feature also runs into flab. 'Sidney In Da Haus' is an impeccably arranged small-group piece, 'Mabel' hires John Lee Hooker for one of his show-stealing cameos, and the rest is good Branford, swinging hard, often connecting. *Bloomington*, though, is his least adorned, maybe his best record. A snapshot of a live date from Indiana with his regular partners, the music makes a virtue of its open-ended situation; away from studio microphones, one can hear the terrific heat and tumbling spontaneity that this group can put out in a live situation. There is a treatment of 'Everything Happens To Me' that wipes out the song itself, all stark corners and cold stares; a bumping 'Friday The Thirteenth'; a vast 'Xavier's Lair'. Dead spots, too, and Delfeayo Marsalis's sound is as questionable as usual, but a fine record.

***** Buckshot Le Fonque**
Columbia 476352-2 *Marsalis; Roy Hargrove, Chuck Findley (t); Matt Finders (tb); Delfeayo Marsalis (tb, p); Greg Phillinganes (ky); Kenny Kirkland (p); David Barry, Kevin Eubanks, Ray Fuller, Nils Lofgren, Albert Collins (g); Robert Hurst, Darryl Jones, Larry Kimpel (b); Jeff 'Tain' Watts, Chuck Morris (d); Mino Cinelu, Vicki Randle (perc).* 94.

Branford's hip-hop album. Wacky, ironic, full of in-jokes, sardonic, embracing the idiom and rising over it at the same time, these are fragments from a busy man's workbook and chips off an old block: black music from the streets, clubs and concert halls. Marsalis doesn't suggest that he has any real faith or interest in hip-hop, but he likes the style and he's interested in a piece of it. There is some inventive use of sampling, cut-ups, whatever, and some great playing. But it never seems like anything more than an ingenious bag of filed-down pieces. It is also starting to sound very dated.

*****(*) The Dark Keys**
Columbia CK 67876 *Marsalis; Kenny Garrett (as); Joe Lovano (ts); Reginald Veal (b); Jeff 'Tain' Watts (d).* 96.

Where Wynton's records become more precise, more finished, Branford's get looser, even wilder – or so it seems on the surface. Marsalis never quite surrenders himself to the music, even when, as in the tornado title-track, he gets as close as he ever has to Coltrane-ish outpourings. As free-flowing as this date is, the man's sense of control is ironclad. On gentler terrain ('A Thousand Autumns', 'Blutain') he plays with a kind of impassive stoicism. When challenged by Lovano or Garrett, as he is in one track apiece, he digs in and plants his feet. As usual, a record to admire, a tough one to warm to, but prolonged acquaintance has increased our admiration.

***(*) Requiem

Columbia 069655-2 *Marsalis; Kenny Kirkland (p); Eric Revis (b); Jeff 'Tain' Watts (d).* 8–11/98.

Recorded shortly before the death of Kenny Kirkland. The pianist's demise came while the group was planning a third session to complete the album, and its 'unfinished' state is how it has been left. Marsalis has had a distinctly unfocused career on record, certainly compared with his trumpet-playing brother, and as ever this is an imperfect statement from a perfectionist musician. But its merits are powerful indeed. The sting of Kirkland's death is made more unhappy by the excellence of his playing here, from the forcefulness of 'Doctone' to the bittersweetness of 'A Thousand Autumns'; and in 'Lykief' he and Marsalis seem to be running virtuoso rings around each other. But there remains the sense that these are brilliant men playing for themselves, and these overlong tracks could use editing which a more detached producer might have encouraged. No gainsaying the often scathing virtuosity of the saxophonist in this situation. Whether the listener responds to it is more than ever a matter of individual taste.

*** Contemporary Jazz

Columbia CK 63850 *Marsalis; Joey Calderazzo (p); Eric Revis (b); Jeff 'Tain' Watts (d).* 12/99.

His farewell to Columbia is striking, more for its pointlessness than anything else. The music is replete with the usual muscle – Watts shows off (but what a show-off!), Calderazzo fills up space and most of the tracks are too long. 'Cheek To Cheek' has a sense of humour, sort of. Took four days in the studio. At Criss Cross, they'd have nailed it in one.

***(*) The Steep Anthology

Columbia 512913-2 *As various albums above.* 4/83–8/98.

This best-of draws on nine albums and adds one previously unreleased live track (Monk's 'Evidence') from the Village Vanguard in 1989 – which is good enough to make one hanker to hear the rest of that set. We've grumbled and generally given Branford a bit of a hard time in this entry, but when boiled down to the ten great tracks in this collection, the man's mastery of the saxophone and his love of just playing jazz do shine through. Away from conceptual agendas, he sounds in a great lineage of tenor players – Hawkins, Rollins, Coltrane, why not? – and able to add something of his own to that distinguished roll-call.

**(*) Footseps Of Our Fathers

Marsalis Music MARCD 3301 *Marsalis; Joey Calderazzo (p); Eric Revis (b); Jeff 'Tain' Watts (d).* 12/01.

Hubris, surely, for anyone to essay an album of cover versions of 'The Freedom Suite' and 'A Love Supreme', and top and tail it with Ornette's 'Giggin" and John Lewis's 'Concorde' – especially when it's the first offering on your own, new label. Marsalis succeeds mainly in reducing the stature of those titanic obelisks to mere repertory – in other hands, perhaps a legitimate debunking, but that was not his intention. The problem was that the album actually had very little impact, which diminished the statement.

*** A Jazz Celebration

Marsalis Music MARCD 3302 *Marsalis; Wynton Marsalis (t); Delfeayo Marsalis, Lucien Barbarin (tb); Ellis Marsalis, Harry Connick Jr (p); Roland Guerin (b); Jason Marsalis (d).* 4/01.

Which suggests that not all Marsalises are created equal. Delfeayo and Jason may be all in the family, but as players they're in another country to Wynton and Branford, neither of whom are really trying all that hard here. It's the trumpet and tenor interplay which counts, and it's good enough to make one wish that the old quintet of 20 years earlier could still be around and striking the kind of sparks they do on the glittering 'Cain And Abel'. Otherwise, this family show of strength, in celebration of their pop's retirement from education, is good-natured and democratically entertaining. Harry Connick sits in and has a couple of funny lines. It's fine.

***(*) Romare Beardon Revealed

Marsalis Music 11661-3306-2 *Marsalis; Wynton Marsalis (t); Delfeayo Marsalis (tb); Ellis Marsalis, Joey Calderazzo, Harry Connick Jr (p); Doug Wamble (g); Eric Revis, Reginald Veal (b); Jason Marsalis, Jeff 'Tain' Watts (d).* 7/03.

A bit of a strange one, in dedication/homage to painter Romare Beardon. The music includes pieces by Lovie Austin, James P. Johnson, Ellington and Morton, which makes it sound more like a Wynton than a Branford project. There's also 'J Mood', revived for the first time since the '80s, and a reminder that the Marsalis family have their own dynastic heritage. It's a vivid record, more likeable than many a Marsalis project, and maybe it'll have more durability too.

Ellis Marsalis (born 1934)

PIANO

Marsalis played and taught for many years in his native New Orleans with no recognition whatsoever beyond his playing circles. But he also sired a family of musicians who have gone on to become the most famous jazz dynasty of their day. Their success has also afforded him some wider exposure.

*** The Classic Ellis Marsalis

Boplicity CDBOP 016 *Marsalis; Nat Perrilliat (ts); Marshall Smith (b); James Black (d).* 1–3/63.

*** Piano In E

Rounder 2100 *Marsalis (p solo).* 84.

*** Heart Of Gold

Columbia CK 47509 *Marsalis; Ray Brown, Reginald Veal (b); Billy Higgins, Herlin Riley, Jason Marsalis (d).* 2–6/91.

*** Whistle Stop

Columbia CK53177 *Marsalis; Branford Marsalis (ss, ts); Robert Hurst (b); Jeff 'Tain' Watts, Jason Marsalis (d).* 3–6/93.

The founder of the Marsalis dynasty is no mean player himself. One can hear where Wynton got his even-handed delineation of melody from and where Branford's aristocratic elegance of line is rooted. Marsalis *père* isn't beyond tossing in the occasional surprise, but mostly he favours careful interpretations of standards, sparsely harmonized and delicately spelt out, with a few simple but cleverly hooked originals to lend a little extra personality. *The Classic Marsalis* is a surprising rarity, a quartet date from the early '60s in which the pianist leads a group featuring the Coltrane follower, Nat Perrilliat, and the jittery, post-Elvin Jones drums of James Black, whose unsettling beats keep the group teetering on the brink of a chaos that the others carefully navigate. The recording is monochromatic, but it's an interesting period-piece.

Of the contemporary sessions, *Whistle Stop* is one of the Marsalis family affairs, and this is impressive playing – perhaps a degree too impressive. The sleeve-notes belabour the point that the group are actually playing in 5 on some tunes, even though this is hardly the revolution the author suggests, and the quartet's resolve to make it all sound so easy gives the music a steeliness that detracts from the writing, much of which comes from former Marsalis sidemen, Black and Perrilliat: five of the tunes were previously covered on *The Classic Marsalis.*

***(*) A Night At Snug Harbor, New Orleans

Evidence ECD 22129-2 *Marsalis; Nicholas Payton (t); Tony Dagradi, Rick Margitza, Donald Harrison (ts); Bill Huntington (b); Art Blakey, David Lee Jr (d).* 4/89.

This is the best album Marsalis has put his name to, a wonderfully disciplined jam session of sorts that has amazingly few *longueurs* (even at over 70 minutes). Payton's only appearance is with Blakey sitting in on one track, and the trumpeter (then only 15!) does nothing special. It's the keen interplay of the three tenormen with a splendid rhythm section that makes the music happen. Dagradi is all muscle and intensity, Harrison (present on only three tracks) is the epitome of refinement, and Margitza finds himself somewhere between the two. The blend works beautifully, and Marsalis himself seems to quietly call the various changes of dynamic via his own playing. Harrison's ballad feature on 'I Can't Get Started' is gorgeous; Ellis has a notably graceful 'The Very Thought Of You' to himself; and the expected blowout on the closing 'A Night In Tunisia' actually has power in reserve all through. Engineer David Farrell also got a very handsome location sound.

** Loved Ones

Columbia CK 67369 *Marsalis; Branford Marsalis (ss, ts).* 8–9/95.

Ellis has five solos to himself, which are fair enough. But the nine duets with his son are about as rambling and self-indulgent as detractors always think jazz is. This is a low point for both men.

*** Duke In Blue

Columbia CK 63631 *Marsalis (p solo).* 3/99.

A sequence of Ellington interpretations, with a blues coda in the form of the title-track. Marsalis is at his most thoughtful and wide-ranging: stride, boogie and even Latin-styled piano forms are on show at various points. Appearing in Duke's centenary year, this was a worthy homage, but it doesn't stand out from many others. Ellis's catalogue (still) remains intact at present, but whether Columbia will keep it so now that the rest of the family have left the label remains to be seen.

Jason Marsalis (born 1977)

DRUMS

The youngest Marsalis to make records, Jason has so far kept closer to his New Orleans background than his brothers.

*** The Year Of The Drummer

Basin Street BSR 0301-2 *Marsalis; Antonio Gambrell (t); Derek Douget (ss, as); Jonathan Lefcoski (p); Jason Stewart (b).* 98.

*** Music In Motion

Basin Street BSR 0302-1 *As above, except John Ellis (ts) and Peter Harris (b) replace Gambrell and Stewart.* 12/99.

Marsalis sets up his New Orleans necessities from the start of the first disc, with the overdubbed drum prelude 'In The Tradition'. The city's second-line rhythm dominates both discs one way or the other, with sidebars on march, montuno, maracatu and more. They're drummers' discs, and the other players are at times almost locked into whatever rhythmical essay their leader wants to deliver. Not that the music is exactly intimidating. 'Death March Of Our Time' is meant to use the funeral-march groove of old marching bands, 'modern harmonies and Elvin Jones-influenced swing', but it sounds like an ordinary slow blues to us.

Still, Marsalis is out to enjoy his music, and the records have a sense of fun. Only here and there, as on 'Discipline Strikes Again' from *Music In Motion*, does the family earnestness overtake matters. If there's a problem, it's that the other players in each edition of the band say nothing to make them individuals.

Wynton Marsalis (born 1961)

TRUMPET

One of six brothers, he learned trumpet as a child in New Orleans, was already playing concertos in his teens – and in funk bands on the side – then studied at Juilliard. Joined Art Blakey in 1980, then formed his own band with brother Branford in 1982 and began recording as a leader for Columbia. Since then he has followed a meteoric course of recording, teaching, touring, composing, acting as Artistic Director of Jazz at Lincoln Center (since 1992), speaking out, accepting awards, attracting controversy and playing the trumpet. The most powerful jazz musician in America today.

***(*) Wynton Marsalis

Columbia CK 37574 *Marsalis; Branford Marsalis (ts, ss); Herbie Hancock, Kenny Kirkland (p); Ron Carter, Charles Fambrough, Clarence Seay (b); Jeff 'Tain' Watts, Tony Williams (d).* 81.

What a weight of expectation and responsibility fell on Wynton Marsalis's shoulders. At 20, not quite overnight, though it perhaps seemed like that away from New Orleans, he became the nominate leader and mouthpiece of a new traditionalism in jazz. Easy to parody his platform as 'Forward to the '20s!', but for the first time in many years a young man stood up and declared a commitment to the tradition and, as a corollary, a measure of hostility to the compromises (as he saw it) of fusion and the anarchic bloodletting of the avant-garde. In the passionately articulate Stanley Crouch he had his *éminence noire*, an able polemicist and spokesman with a voice as ringingly clear as Marsalis's trumpet.

A front-line role in the Jazz Messengers obviously doesn't constitute obscurity, but there was a dramatic turn from gifted apprentice to star-in-waiting. The earliest recordings, made at Bubba's in Fort Lauderdale, came a year after his recruitment to the Messengers and, though available only on small labels, they bespoke a great talent and – already – a great purity of vision. In 1981, he parted company from Art Blakey, with the boss's blessing, and went on the road with a quartet that immediately and controversially cemented his claim to the then discarded mantle of Miles Davis, who later spurned the young pretender at a bizarre showdown in Canada.

Record companies have often miscued by putting promising talent in the company of grizzled veterans, but Marsalis shows total class in the company of Hancock, Carter and Williams. It's clear, though, that he is also building his own cohort of like-minded players. The opening 'Father Time', which features elder brother Branford and the lyrical Kirkland, is an astonishing major-label debut, a beautifully structured piece which uncovers a slew of improvisational ideas in a short span. Marsalis himself never sounds as if he's up on a soapbox, as happened from time to time later on. He's always got something to say and he does so with a simplicity that is as refreshing as rain.

Perhaps inevitably, perhaps rightly, much of the critical attention was directed towards the tracks with the senior players. Carter's 'RJ' and Williams's melancholic 'Sister Cheryl' bracket a furious stop-action Marsalis composition called 'Hesitation', which is actually a neo-bop variation on 'I Got Rhythm' and was presumably got up for the Messengers. A near-perfectly weighted programme closes with 'Twilight', one of the loveliest things he has ever done.

*** Think Of One

Columbia CK 38641 *Marsalis; Branford Marsalis (ts, ss); Kenny Kirkland (p); Phil Bowler (b); Jeff 'Tain' Watts (d).* 83.

*** Hothouse Flowers

Columbia CK 39530 *Marsalis; Branford Marsalis (ts, ss); Kent Jordan (af); Kenny Kirkland (p); Ron Carter (b); Jeff 'Tain' Watts (d).* 5/84.

The younger players must indeed have felt like hothouse flowers, brought on unseasonally in a rich mulch of label enthusiasm and under a glare of media attention. Marsalis's tone, forged in the Messengers, is hard and unflawed, producing patterns of sound like petals made of some hard but malleable metal. On 'Later', one of the better tracks on the 1983 album, he manages to find an idiom that contrives to evoke connections from Bubber Miley all the way to Butch Morris.

A year on, he sounds curiously detached, even a little remote. *Hothouse Flowers* sounds like a man under a bell-jar; the colours are intense, the ideas as rich and exotic as one would wish, but there is no real emotional engagement with the music, just a series of brilliantly executed ideas. 'Stardust' is a *tour de force* and, like 'When You Wish Upon A Star', seems confected out of next to nothing, just the melody and a gently oscillating chord-pattern. Even by this stage, Branford seems to be on board as a result of sibling loyalty rather than anything else, increasingly pushed into the background, as Jordan is. Watts is a key element, bright and crisp, often echoing Kirkland's chordal patterns on his toms and cymbals. If he resembles anyone of an earlier generation, it must be Max Roach: the same devotion to threes, the same urgency, the same melodic facility.

**** Black Codes (From The Underground)

Columbia CK 40009 *Marsalis; Branford Marsalis (ss, ts); Kenny Kirkland (p); Ron Carter, Charnett Moffett (b); Jeff 'Tain' Watts (d).* 1/85.

As jazz vintages go, this twelvemonth has to be considered pretty special. Within a year, two of Marsalis's very best showings on record, neither of which he has ever bettered. Watts is again absolutely central to the sound, particularly given the not unexpected decision to dispense with a second horn. *Black Codes* is a highly committed record, not just in its referencing of 19th-century slave law, but also in the sheer commitment of Marsalis's playing. The title-piece is his strongest single performance since 'Father Time', sorrowful and full of unaffected wisdom. 'Phryzzinian Man' has him playing stately modes, almost classical in conception. 'Chambers Of Tain' is a Kirkland composition, a caustically intense feature for the drummer.

CORE COLLECTION

**** J Mood

Columbia CK 40308 *Marsalis; Marcus Roberts (p); Robert Leslie Hurst III (b); Jeff 'Tain' Watts (d).* 12/85.

***J Mood* was perceived at the time as a key recording for Marsalis. It is the first time he sounds completely relaxed and in possession of his own language and, though it was a record that intensified the debate about neo-traditionalism against experiment and contemporaneity, the actual music gives no sense of having a part in that. 'Much Later' might just be a reference to Miles Davis's favourite exit-line; there are certainly a couple of moments when Marsalis appears to allude to the classic Davis performances of the '50s. 'Skain's Domain' and the beautiful 'Presence That Lament Brings' touch the opposite boundaries of the trumpeter's range, suggesting that his great quality is not after all virtuosic flash and fire but a deep-rooted expressiveness which maintains its integrity all the way across the spectrum, from fiery individualism to elegiac regret.**

***(*) Marsalis Standard Time: Volume 1

Columbia 468713 *Marsalis; Marcus Roberts (p); Robert Leslie Hurst III (b); Jeff 'Tain' Watts (d).* 5–9/86.

*** Standard Time: Volume 2 – Intimacy Calling

Columbia 468273 *Marsalis; Wessell Anderson (as); Todd Williams (ts); Marcus Roberts (p); Robert Leslie Hurst III, Reginald Veal (b); Herlin Riley, Jeff 'Tain' Watts (d).* 9/87–8/90.

***(*) Standard Time: Volume 3 – The Resolution Of Romance

Columbia CK 46143 *Marsalis; Ellis Marsalis (p); Reginald Veal (b); Herlin Riley (d).* 90.

The first of these albums was wonderfully judged, a programme of pieces that distanced him from the modernists without ever consigning him to the ranks of the Old Believers. Even after more than a decade, *Marsalis Standard Time* retains its burnish and class. As ever, there is a faint suspicion that the trumpeter is thinking through his solos several choruses ahead, trading in spontaneity and fire for control, but nevertheless the ideas are always vivid. Two versions of 'Cherokee', the first with mute and one of his most uncomplicatedly inventive essays, the second more orderly and discursive, but left curiously unresolved. Roberts has an unaccompanied feature on 'Memories Of You', a fitting recognition of his part in the music and an obvious showcase for his developing solo career.

Marsalis has always shown tremendous loyalty and respect to his sidemen, qualities that significantly dent charges of arrogance and remoteness. He also sits out 'East Of The Sun (West Of The Moon)' on *Intimacy Calling*, the less effective of the two later *Standard Times*. The extra horns bring nothing of any great substance, and Roberts seems to have difficulty making his presence felt. The quartet with Marsalis Sr, Veal and Riley offers a different, quieter sound from that of the groups with Roberts and Watts, and this is the one of the three which most consistently surprises now. Marsalis himself is in reflective mood throughout, relying on soft, almost *sotto voce* harmony effects and a wonderfully lachrymose wah-wah on 'The Seductress'.

A remarkable group of records, which put paid to one cavil and pointed the way towards a new and more broad-based approach to the repertoire.

*****(*) Live At Blues Alley**
Columbia CK 40675 2CD *Marsalis; Marcus Roberts (p); Robert Leslie Hurst III (b); Jeff 'Tain' Watts (d).* 12/86.

Exactly a year on from the breakthrough *J Mood*, Marsalis answered the other question and proved that black-tie gigs, classical concertos and the almost ingratiating attention of Columbia hadn't compromised the terse, fiery performer who'd appeared with the Messengers. Recorded in Washington, DC, these club cuts establish him as the heir of Fats Navarro, Lee Morgan, Freddie Hubbard and even the uptight little cat who'd just frosted him off a stage in Vancouver and who had just quit Columbia for Warners, leaving the field clear for the youngster.

As before, the actual sound of Marsalis's trumpet (as opposed to the idiom in which he was playing) seems to come from an even earlier age, from 'Sweets' Edison, Roy Eldridge and from Armstrong again, and yet everything about these rollicking performances is as contemporary as the morning newspapers. In particular, Marsalis seems to be enjoying a flirtation with dissonance, bending notes at the edges, teasingly suggesting that he is going to go outside and then punching the orthodox changes with dead-centre accuracy.

Virtually all the material is familiar from earlier records. 'Knozz-Moe-King' from *Think Of One* gets the set off to a ripping start and is reiterated as a band theme throughout. An excoriating 'Skain's Domain' gives that well-worked theme its definitive rendition, while 'Delfeayo's Dilemma' and 'Chambers Of Tain' are both strongly argued versions. 'Do You Know What It Means To Miss New Orleans' is puzzling, but it squares with Marsalis's admirable refusal to overcook classic material of this sort.

Only a sound-balance which does scant justice to our main-man Watts denies this one a fourth star. In performance terms, it's a key moment for Marsalis.

***** The Majesty Of The Blues**
Columbia CK 45091 *Marsalis; Teddy Riley (t); Freddie Lonzo (tb); Michael White (cl); Wessell Anderson (as); Todd Williams (ts, ss); Marcus Roberts (p); Reginald Veal (b); Herlin Riley (d); Rev. Jeremiah Wright (v).* 10/88.

A first glimpse of a new phenomenon: Marsalis the self-appointed guardian of the flame. It is inaccurate to call *Majesty* a revivalist album. As before, Wynton manages to combine a classical sound with a thoroughly modern diction, but this concept-piece, a celebration of the music and culture of New Orleans, is hog-tied by worthy ambitions. Dr Michael White, who is perhaps more convincing as a scholar than as a player, appears on 'New Orleans Function', a suite of authentic-sounding ideas which consigns Marsalis to second place behind Teddy Riley. White is a curious performer, consistently sharp in tone and not too agile, but somehow always able to make a significant contribution and here without any doubt adding something to a group sound that has moved on a step from the 'classic' quartet. Roberts's use of bebop harmonies on the title-track, also known as 'The Puheeman Strut', and 'Hickory Dickory Dock' helps draw attention to Marsalis's restorative concern for the continuity of jazz music, which he believes was betrayed by the scorched-earth aesthetics of the '60s and by pop.

The long suite is essentially a funeral procession for 'The Death Of Jazz' and is dominated by a 17-minute sermon, 'Premature Autopsies', written by Stanley Crouch and delivered by the Rev. Wright. The sonorous text – a good deal more convincing than Crouch's usual one-note spiel – draws attention away from the instrumental backing, but this deserves attention, too, an excellent example of the way Marsalis's music retains its connections with impassioned speech. Crouch's tribute to the nobility of jazz, and in particular the example of Duke Ellington, is surprisingly moving. A little breathless and unargued, it reads pretty poorly but, as performed, has an undoubted majesty, even if it cleaves closer to William Bradford Huie than to Martin Luther King.

*****(*) Crescent City Christmas Card**
Columbia CK 45287 *Marsalis; Wycliffe Gordon (tb); Wessell Anderson (as); Todd Williams (ts, ss, cl); Alvin Batiste (cl); Joe Temperley (bs, bcl); Marcus Roberts (p); Reginald Veal (b); Herlin Riley (d); Kathleen Battle, Jon Hendricks (v).* 89.

Any disposition to cynicism at 'Wynton's Christmas Album' is dispelled by even the most sceptical hearing. Interestingly, this is much more authentic New Orleans jazz than the previous record, and there are moments of real beauty. Marsalis's attempt to combine the awe and sheer fun of Christmas works very well indeed, and the arrangements are inventive from first to last. 'Hark! The Herald Angels Sing' is conceived as a dialogue between European harmony and a jazz groove, but it's 'The Little Drummer Boy' that takes the breath away; hear this and still claim that Wynton Marsalis is a dry technician without a sentimental corner of his soul. Vocal features for Jon Hendricks (wonderful on 'Sleigh Ride') and Kathleen Battle, though even this wonderful soprano is upstaged by Wynton's muted solo on 'Silent Night'. The supporting cast is excellent, and Roberts's feature this time out is 'O Come All Ye Faithful', to which he brings a characteristic spin and invention, characteristic both of himself and of the boss.

*****(*) Thick In The South**
Columbia CK 47977 *Marsalis; Joe Henderson (ts); Marcus Roberts (p); Robert Leslie Hurst III (b); Elvin Jones, Jeff 'Tain' Watts (d). n.d.*

***** Uptown Ruler**
Columbia CK 47976 *Marsalis; Todd Williams (ts); Marcus Roberts (p); Reginald Veal (b); Herlin Riley (d). n.d.*

★★★(★) Levee Low Moan

Columbia CK 47975 *Marsalis; Wessell Anderson (as); Todd Williams (ts); Marcus Roberts (p); Reginald Veal (b); Herlin Riley (d). n.d.*

Three simultaneous issues from Columbia's capacious vault, issued under the more or less meaningless rubric, 'Soul Gestures in Southern Blue'. Clearly it was felt that the market would support a blanket release of this kind. *Thick In The South* stands up best a few years further on, though mostly for Joe Henderson's wonderfully wise and unruffled performances. Marsalis himself sounds like a man casting about for things to say; that he manages to find and utter them can't be questioned, but there is an air of contrivance which isn't particularly attractive. Jones is the other senior guest, but he's over-emphatic and rather dull in comparison to Watts's muscular groove. Roberts seems ill-at-ease this time around – whether suffering from creative depletion or champing at the bit of his own ambitions isn't clear. As Sun Ra used to say of himself, the Marsalis jail was the best jail built, but it could still have been seen as a jail to a progressive young stylist with ideas of his own.

Uptown Ruler is one of the least attractive-sounding Marsalis albums in the catalogue, reasons unknown and obscure. The accompaniments seem very recessed and almost cloudy, perhaps to throw into high contrast the leader's strongly etched blues ideas. 'Down Home With Homey' seemed an interesting attempt to combine an old-fashioned idiom with the rhythmic and colouristic values of the M-Base generation. The third of the group is interesting largely for pointing the way forward to Marsalis's new mid-size band and a new, more obviously arranged sound. The saxophones are beautifully voiced and Roberts regains something of his accustomed vigour. 'Jig's Jig' is extraordinary.

★★★(★) Blue Interlude

Columbia CK 48729 *Marsalis; Wycliffe Gordon (tb); Wessell Anderson (as); Todd Williams (ts, ss, cl); Marcus Roberts (p); Reginald Veal (b); Herlin Riley (d). 92.*

At the turn of the '90s, Marsalis's sights were fixed on bigger game; one senses that a gigging quartet no longer interested him much and that he had largely exhausted the possibilities of 'guest' horns. The new septet was a breath of fresh air, a big, spacious sound, with plenty of incident, varied textures and a remarkable even-handedness when it came to handing out solo space.

Increasingly, Marsalis was being seen as the heir apparent to Duke Ellington, a composer/performer with the totalizing gift of absolute organization and a parallel ability to give his colleagues enough freedom to express themselves. Todd Williams's 'Jubilee Suite' is a good case in point, or not a *good* case in point since it emerges as a flabby and shapeless sequence of unrelated ideas. The trombonist's 'And The Band Played On' is infinitely more interesting, a tune that other bandleaders must surely have looked at with envy. Marsalis is playing astutely and with infinite assurance. His long monologue on 'Sugar Cane And Sweetie Pie' sets up the title-piece's very Ellingtonian opposition of motifs, moods and harmonic atmospheres, out of which develops one of the trumpeter's most flowing improvisations, a graceful, swirling thing which could not have been conceived by anyone else on the planet at this time.

As an album, *Blue Interlude* is most interesting for what it promised. The septet's subsequent live appearances were to be among the finest moments in an already remarkable career.

★★★★ Citi Movement (Griot New York)

Columbia C2K 53324 2CD *As above, except replace Roberts with Eric Reed (p). n.d.*

It says something about Marsalis's redefinition of himself as teacher, *griot* and *auteur* that the record which very nearly achieves greatness should have been made for a collaborative project with a strong extra-musical component. As the '90s advanced, it was clear that he required dramatic and programmatic triggers to give the music the definition he demanded. *Citi Movement* was written for the brilliant choreographer Garth Fagan, whose approach to the dance balances traditional and contemporary values in much the same way as Marsalis's music.

By this point, the septet is playing with a greased precision of movement which makes it communicate like a single entity. The first section, 'Cityscape', has an energy and drive that are reminiscent of Charles Mingus's Jazz Workshop projects, and surely Stanley Crouch's invocation of Mingus is no coincidence. It's a deeply stratified and textured piece, with an enormous inner propulsion. A further dimension of the score is Marsalis's new interest in the African components of Afro-American culture. 'Transatlantic Echoes' is searching and thoughtful and it resolutely refuses to lean on bland musicological borrowings. Instead, Marsalis has created his own sense of Africanism, one that is entirely conditioned by his personal circumstances and ideas, rather than being adopted like fancy dress. The final movement, 'Some Present Moments Of The Future', sketches out in ever more lifelike outline his vision of a viable jazz tradition.

★★★ In This House, On This Morning

Columbia C2K 53220 2CD *As above, except add Marion Williams (v). 5/92.*

Given that, by this stage, Ellingtonian parallels were almost *de rigueur*, this was mentioned as the first Sacred Concert. In fact, it's not so very different from what Marsalis was doing on *Majesty Of The Blues*, plunging back into church music and the homely liturgy of the Afro-American communion to give an expressive impulse to the highly sophisticated sound of the septet.

Why this was released as a double CD is mystifying, since there simply isn't enough high-quality material to justify release on this scale. The ritual slowness of 'Call To Prayer' and 'Recessional' is doubtless deliberate, but it suggests creative uncertainty and, for the first time in his career, Marsalis sounds as if he may be relying on stock phrases. The band as a whole creaks through the sermon which begins the second disc, and it's only when the Sunday business is over and the 'Uptempo Postlude' and 'Pot Blessed Dinner' re-establish secular communion that the music regains something of its impetus.

There have, of course, been many earlier attempts to marry jazz and church ritual, Ellington's being only the grandest of them. One suspects that here, exceptionally, Marsalis isn't sufficiently engaged in the belief-system and that the rituals he observes survive in him only as abstract 'pieties'. This may sound incidental, even irrelevant, but – given the claims made for *In This House, On This Morning* when it was first performed – its credibility has to be questioned.

*****(*) Joe Cool's Blues**

Columbia CK 66880 *Marsalis; Chuck Findley (t); Wycliffe Gordon, Delfeayo Marsalis (tb); Wessell Anderson (as); Branford Marsalis (ts); Victor Goines (ts, cl); Tom Peterson (bs); Ellis Marsalis, Eric Reed (p); Reginald Veal, Benjamin Wolfe (b); Martin Butler, Herlin Riley (d); Germaine Bazzle (v).* 4–8/94.

Marsalis has said that the only jazz heard on television when he was a boy was in Charlie Brown cartoon themes, written by Vince Guaraldi. Guaraldi was a friend of Ellis Marsalis, and the latter performs with his trio – Reginald Veal and Martin Butler are his partners – four of the 13 numbers, with a fifth, 'Little Birdie', arranged for a larger group with vocalist. For the rest, this was a joyously nostalgic curtain-call for the septet. If Schulz seems an unlikely source for the blues, then consider how finely his world balances hope and pain, disappointment, frustration, sheer delight.

'On Peanuts Playground' is a wonderful piece, delightful and brooding by turns. With perverse inevitability, Marsalis's own themes sound more like the real thing than Guaraldi's familiar signatures. 'Little Birdie' should probably have ended proceedings, with just a return of 'Joe Cool's Blues' to round things out, but the weakest of the originals, 'Why, Charlie Brown', comes in at that point to blunt the impact just a touch. A shame, for this is one of Marsalis's most unaffected and affecting records.

*****(*) Blood On The Fields**

Columbia C3K 57694 3CD *Marsalis; Russell Gunn, Roger Ingram, Marcus Printup (t); Wayne Goodman, Ron Westray (tb); Wycliffe Gordon (tb, tba); Wessell Anderson (as); Victor Goines (ts, ss, cl, bcl); Robert Stewart (ts); Walter Blanding (ss); James Carter (bs, bcl, cl); Michael Ward (vn); Eric Reed (p); Reginald Veal (b); Herlin Riley (d, perc); Miles Griffith, Jon Hendricks, Cassandra Wilson (v).* 94.

Written almost half a century after Ellington's *Black, Brown And Beige*, this is a work which sets out to rival that great Afro-American masterpiece. A huge achievement, inevitably patchy and in places overcooked, but filled with superb jazz writing. Indeed, one can imagine – and may yet hear – a magnificent instrumental or orchestral suite derived from the music in *Blood On The Fields*. As a meditation on Southern slavery, its human and cultural impact, it is most wholly convincing when it delivers its points simply and plainly. Some of the texts, though sung well by Wilson, Griffith and the veteran Hendricks, are a little too pointedly earnest, but the emotion and the depth of thought behind them cannot be questioned.

It starts on a slave ship on the notorious 'middle passage', and puts together two characters, Jesse and Leona, divided by birth but united by the shared circumstance of the 'peculiar institution' of slavery. The music digs deep back into the traditions, and is marked by dancing syncopations, deep blues and African songs, powerful chants and testimonies. The dramatic thread is simple enough to sustain conviction and not to overpower the more purely musical elements of the work. If *Blood On The Fields* is an 'opera', it is within a very American subdivision of the genre. It is tragic and joyous, a numbers piece with a powerful unifying thread.

Marsalis's soloing is central to the drama, but he has wisely chosen to treat this is as an ensemble piece, spreading the emphasis over a number of players, allowing them to underline the vocal line with sometimes literal, sometimes ironic motifs. As a recorded experience, it is too long and difficult to absorb comfortably. Anyone who saw either the Lincoln Center première on All Fools' Day 1994 or subsequent European performances will understand its sheer impact. Others may well have to navigate their own most effective course through three densely packed CDs, selecting tracks, passing over others, dwelling where the emotional and dramatic impact seems most concentrated.

*****(*) Standard Time, Volume 4 – Marsalis Plays Monk**

Columbia CK 67503 *Marsalis; Wycliffe Gordon (tb); Wessell Anderson (as); Walter Blanding, Victor Goines (ts); Eric Reed (p); Reginald Veal, Ben Wolfe (b); Herlin Riley (d).* 9/93–10/94.

Fascinating that Wynton's stated intention for this near-inevitable but long-deferred encounter should be to recast Monk's music in the form of the ensemble jazz of Louis Armstrong's jazz orchestras of 1927 and 1928. A double homage, or a deliberate act of subversion of the great modernist? Marsalis's own characterization sums up the unexpected sound of the fourth *Standard Time* project: '... [T]extural changes. Thick ensembles, then a duet, or just a few people playing. Breaks. Surprises. Long solos. Very short ones. Strange tags on the end of tunes.'

Marsalis uses himself quite sparingly as a soloist, placing the emphasis very much on ensemble values. The problem is perhaps that he has not stamped an individuality and authority firmly enough on music that will always have the last laugh on any revisionist. The jaggy urgency of 'Evidence' and the almost skittish playfulness of 'We See' which follows point to the extremes the album skirts and hint at some of its oddity of mood, though this oddity is of a different sort from Monk's.

Perhaps predictably, Marsalis has chosen to include amid the 14 tracks some less well-known items: 'Worry Later', 'Brake's Sake' and 'Let's Cool One' may take some moments to provenance. The standard of playing is as high and as disciplined as ever. The melting unisons of 'Monk's Mood' are glorious, and Marsalis and Anderson weave some absolute magic on 'Hackensack', but it's as hard as ever to approach this with affection rather than admiration.

***** Standard Time, Volume 5: The Midnight Blues**

Columbia CK 68921 *Marsalis; Eric Reed (p); Reginald Veal (b); Lewis Nash (d); strings.* 9/98.

Interestingly, this time out, Stanley Crouch's liner-note steers sharply away from rhetorical underpinning of Marsalis's traditionalism. Instead, it's a miniature film treatment about a woman called Ardella Jefferson, who divides her time between reading Derek Walcott's Nobel Lecture, 'The Antilles: Fragments Of Epic Memory', and musing on the sound of trumpet and strings.

Compare these dozen immaculately executed tracks with, say, Chet Baker's final concerts and it immediately becomes clear that Ardella's likening of the sound to 'a brass cherry' on top of orchestral cream is all too accurate. Even with busted chops and no great appetite for the struggle, Chet sounded lived-in, wearily passionate, precariously alive. Marsalis plays with total authority, but the effect is still hard and oddly virginal. 'Glad To Be Unhappy' touches neither end of the spectrum convincingly, and yet as an exercise in controlled articulation it is genuinely awe-inspiring. Only Frank Sinatra was ever able to pull off a whole album of such uniform melancholy, because Frank was able to invest loss and absence with a complex freight of experience. Marsalis can't quite avoid referencing Miles's classic 'It Never Entered My Mind' and thereby throwing up another unflattering point of comparison.

The muted solo on 'Baby, Won't You Please Come Home' is thin and weakly recorded, the only time that Steve Epstein and Todd Whitelock's open and unscreened 'live' recording at the Masonic Grande Lodge in New York City sounded underpowered. The emotional charge picks up almost at the end with a superb reading of 'My Man's Gone Now', four and a half minutes that are almost worth all the rest put together, but then Marsalis throws away the moment with the long and indulgent title-track, a mini-opera without conflict and without a convincing protagonist.

****** Mr Jelly Lord: Standard Time – Volume Six**

Columbia CK 69872 *Marsalis; Lucien Barbarin (tb); Wycliffe Gordon (tb, tba, t); Wessell Anderson (as); Victor Goines (ss, ts, cl); Michael White (cl); Harry Connick Jr, Eric Lewis, Danilo Perez, Eric Reed (p); Donald Vappie (bjo, g); Reginald Veal (b); Herlin Riley (d).* 1/99 (12/93).

At first hearing this is a hard record to date and a hard record to place instantly as Marsalis's work. We have listed it out of strict chronological sequence because these sessions lay in the vault for nearly six years before release and they do, to some extent, need to be heard in a different context because of that.

Sometimes even Wynton must wish Stanley Crouch would keep his mouth shut. Likening these modern – but unmodernized – versions of Jelly Roll Morton tunes to actor/director Kenneth Branagh's Shakespearean films isn't necessarily the most helpful imprimatur. As it turns out, Wynton's performance needs no Mortonesque hyperbole. There is no attempt to lend these astonishing compositions any false grandeur; they have quite enough as it is.

Wynton's playing has rarely sounded so relaxed and so raw. Even his cover-picture, looking tired, slumped astride a packing crate and resting an elbow on his instrument, suggests a measure of artisanly relaxation, like a man just coming off shift rather than a man waiting backstage at Carnegie Hall. 'The Pearls' and 'Dead Man Blues' see him reach levels of expression that will astonish even admirers.

Perez and Connick have cameo parts only, but the basic line-up is by now a familiar one. We have never been persuaded by the clarinet-playing of Dr Michael White, which almost sounds a quarter-note sharp, but the two trombone players are majestically idiomatic (as at least one of them should be, bearing a name like Barbarin) and the saxophonists never sound as if they are on day-release from Bebop Academy. Our only faint quibble would be the drumming of Herlin Riley, which occasionally seems anachronistic.

A must for blindfold tests of the future is track 15. On 6 December 1993, Wynton and pianist Eric Reed went to the Edison National Historic Site at West Orange, New Jersey, and recorded 'Tom Cat Blues' direct to a wax cylinder. The result is still unmistakably Marsalis, but the old technology helps provide a ghostly coda to a remarkable record.

****** Live At The Village Vanguard**

Columbia CK 69876/ACK 61408/14 7CD (US)/8CD (Europe) *Marsalis; Wycliffe Gordon (tb); Wessell Anderson (as); Victor Goines, Todd Williams (ts); Marcus Roberts, Eric Reed (p); Reginald Veal, Ben Wolfe (b); Herlin Riley (d).* 3/90–12/94.

Priced as a bargain deal and presented as a parade of great sets at jazz's most celebrated venue, here's Wynton and his men across a four-year span, with some eight hours of music (European collectors have a bonus CD in their edition, although that runs to only some 25 extra minutes of music). The discs are programmed to represent a week's work, with each having a different character, of sorts. Besides new versions of some choice pieces from his own canon, there are standards, blues, plenty of Monk, 40 minutes of 'Citi Movement', and 55 minutes of 'In The Sweet Embrace Of Life'. Wynton chaffs with the audience, welcomes celebrities – Sweets Edison, Lionel Hampton – and generally sets out to make sure that everyone has a good time. It's a fun set to play through: the music always seems lively and on its toes, the band precise but flying on the flair of the leader and his appetite for work. Besides the leader's playing, perhaps the greatest pleasure comes in the efforts of Veal, Wolfe and Riley, an engine-room of superb polish and palpable swing.

There are some inevitable historical parallels – with Rollins at the Vanguard, or, more specifically, with the comprehensiveness of the Miles Davis *Plugged Nickel* set. Yet this is a more calculated scripture than those on-the-hoof documents, and it suits the moment of the Marsalis doctrine. What one hears is elegance and poise; there is little in the way of risk, even less in the way of danger. But that is Wynton's way, and for the duration of this set – and kudos to him for releasing a lot of music for a modest price – it sounds terrific.

*****(*) The Marciac Suite**

Columbia CK 69877 *Marsalis; Wycliffe Gordon (tb); Wessell Anderson (as); Victor Goines (ts, ss bcl); Eric Lewis, Farid Barron, Cyrus Chestnut, Marcus Roberts(p); Rodney Whitaker (b); Herlin Riley (d); Roland Guerrero (perc).* 2/99.

One of Wynton's happiest and most sheerly enjoyable sets, made as a love letter to the Marciac Festival where he has taught and performed for a number of years. Lovely playing from all hands, the leader at his sunniest, the writing more than welcoming, and in the final 'Sunflowers' one of his catchiest pieces.

***** Popular Songs – The Best Of Wynton Marsalis**

Columbia 502298-2 *Marsalis; various line-ups as above.* 85–99.

Wynton's farewell to Columbia is scarcely an ideal best-of: how could such an ambitious and dedicated man be well represented by filleting the huge body of work listed above? There is the classic, perhaps defining solo from 'Black Codes', the million-dollar balladry of 'Where Or When', the signature Marsalis step of 'Down Home With Homey' ... as a collection of tracks, it's fine.

****(*) All Rise**

Sony Classical 89817 *Marsalis; Lincoln Centre Jazz Orchestra; Los Angeles Philharmonic.* 9/01.

Contrary to its reputation as a memorial to the events of 11 September 2001, this was originally conceived as a millennium project for the New York Phil. A subsequent performance with these groupings was scheduled for the Hollywood Bowl immediately before the World Trade Center attacks and so the piece has acquired a retrospective significance. It's a titanic work, far grander than any of Duke Ellington's sacred concerts and with a far less subtle emotional dynamic.

Constructed in 12 movements, almost as if it were a massive 12-bar blues, *All Rise* is crippled by its own ambition and by

Wynton's seeming desire to pack in everything he knew about music into a duration rather less than the epic *Blood On The Fields*. It's an awkward mix of freedom and structured complexity and the climaxes are delivered like hammer blows, nullifying their impact. A scaled-down version might perversely work better, allowing the lines of 'Save Us, O Lord' (a seemingly anti-war passage which gained additional gravitas after 9/11) to come through more simply. The coda is a brilliant second-line conception, expressing delight in resurrection or just in continued existence.

*** The Magic Hour

Blue Note 91717 *Marsalis; Eric Lewis (p); Carlos Henriquez (b); Ali Muhammad Jackson (d); Bobby McFerrin, Dianne Reeves (v).* 8/03.

The big industry story of the last few years has been who might have the courage and the cash to sign up an out-of-contract Wynton Marsalis. He had known Bruce Lundvall at Columbia and it seemed very probable that Blue Note would be the favourites to get his John Hancock.

On paper, it sounds a wonderful association. In practice, certainly on this early showing, it's been something of a disappointment. Marsalis sounds as if he's gone back several years in developmental terms, or perhaps he's pitching his thing to what he thinks is a less sophisticated audience. Either way, it's a mistake and *The Magic Hour* doesn't even sit with the middle order of his Columbia albums. The title-track almost sounds like an audition performance: here's everything I can do, packed into 13 minutes. The opener is much better and 'Free To Be' and 'Big Fat Hen' are clever, accomplished tracks which mix subtlety and boisterous humour. 'Stardust' is the trumpeter's signature theme, played here with hints of melancholy and a stoical defiance. Who knows what is going on in Marsalis's head? Who knows what will follow? We ended our entry last time with speculation about the future. It hasn't yet been resolved.

Warne Marsh (1927–87)

TENOR SAXOPHONE

Marsh's death onstage, playing 'Out Of Nowhere' at Donte's club in Hollywood, was a strangely fitting end to a life that seemed to have been spent mid-solo, unweaving one of his long, harmonically subtle improvisations set against a deceptively simple and unembellished beat. Born in Los Angeles, he came under the influence of Lennie Tristano and, along with Lee Konitz, was Lennie's most prominent disciple. His association with the altoist was close but not as long-standing as is often thought. Marsh's slightly dry, almost papery tone is instantly recognizable.

*** Jazz Of Two Cities

Fresh Sound FSR CD 196 *Marsh; Art Pepper (as); Ted Brown (ts); Ronnie Ball (p); Ben Tucker (b); Ben Morton (d).* 56, 57.

*** Music For Prancing

VSOP 8 *Marsh; Ronnie Ball (p); Red Mitchell (b); Stan Levey (d).* 9/57.

By far the most loyal and literal of the Tristano disciples, Warne Marsh sedulously avoided the 'jazz life', cleaving to an improvisatory philosophy that was almost chilling in its purity. Anthony Braxton called him the 'greatest vertical improviser' in the music, and a typical Marsh solo was discursive and rhythmically subtle, full of coded tonalities and oblique resolutions. He cultivated a glacial tone (somewhat derived from Lester Young) that splintered awkwardly in the higher register and which can be off-putting for listeners conditioned by Bird and Coltrane.

The early quartets are witty and smooth-toned, though Marsh sounds much closer to Stan Getz than he was to in later years. The Fresh Sound dates are bright and impeccably delivered, but it's the consistently overlooked Brown who takes both ears and tail with his 'Free Wheeling'. On the later date, the warmth is leavened by a rhythm section led by the remarkable Mitchell, whose unusual tunings and almost offhand ability to turn out terse countermelodies are a key element of a fine record. The association with Mitchell would prove to be one of the most successful in later years as well.

***(*) Release Record – Send Tape

Wave CD 6 *Marsh; Ronnie Ball (p); Peter Ind (b); Dick Scott (d).* 12/59–8/60.

*** More Jazz From The East Village

Wave CD 9 *As above, except omit Scott; add Eddie De Haas (b); Bob Minnicucci (d).* 60.

Recorded largely at Peter Ind's home studio and consisting almost entirely of improvised solos played without the original melody, *Release Record – Send Tape* was considered commercial suicide on first release in 1967, but Marsh's growing reputation since then and certainly posthumously has justified Ind's confidence. The lightness of the saxophonist's touch and the agility of his playing are reminiscent of his fellow Tristano pupil, Lee Konitz, but with more substance on open-ended tunes like 'Sweet Georgia Brown' and 'Alone Together', where the chords are susceptible to almost infinite variation. Konitz has always tended to favour tighter structures. What shines through here is a capacious musical intelligence which turns each of these brief performances – only the improvised 'Marshlight' is longer than five minutes – into something much more substantial. The other record is less compelling but fills in more of the picture of Marsh's activities at this time. He seems tirelessly inventive and unfailingly thoughtful but there is something slightly unnerving about the sound of him weaving those lines and stacked up chords in front of such abecedarian accompaniments.

*** Live In Las Vegas 1962

Naked City 7 *Marsh; Don Overberg (g); Carson Smith (b); Frank Severino (d).* 62.

Marsh never seemed a Las Vegas kind of guy, but it should be remembered that almost all of his career was spent playing changes-based small-group jazz in clubs and joints. He was not of a type or of a generation that dreamed of big-band projects or ambitious compositional ploys. This set, released in 2000, is archetypal Marsh. There's a wanly romantic cast to a date marked by fine, long versions of 'People Will Say We're In Love' and 'Hello, Young Lovers', the last tinged by some of Lester Young's latter-day melancholy and a hint of Pres's blurred pitch and breathy timbre. The band is a good one, with Smith in prominent place and mercifully audible; bassists were always vitally important to Marsh and on 'Joy Spring' you can hear him plot his course by reference to Carson's accurate accompaniment. A valuable discovery that starts to fill in a long blank in the Marsh discography.

*****(*) Warne Marsh/Lee Konitz: Volume 1**
Storyville STCD 4094 *Marsh; Lee Konitz (as); Ole Kock Hansen (p); Niels-Henning Orsted Pedersen (b); Svend Erik Norregaard (d).* 12/75.

***** Warne Marsh/Lee Konitz: Volume 2**
Storyville STCD 4095 *As above.* 12/75.

***** Warne Marsh/Lee Konitz: Volume 3**
Storyville STCD 4096 *As above.* 12/75.

***** Live At The Montmartre Club: Volume 1**
Storyville STCD 8201 *As above, except add Alex Riel (d).* 12/75.

***** Live At The Montmartre Club: Volume 2**
Storyville STCD 8202 *As above.* 12/75.

***** Live At The Montmartre Club: Volume 3**
Storyville STCD 8203 *As above.* 12/75.

Marsh's reputation still falls far short of that of his exact contemporary, Lee Konitz, with whom he interlocks gracefully like dancing master and pupil on the live sessions from Fasching in Stockholm and the parallel sets from the Jazzhus Montmartre in Copenhagen. Where Konitz changed down the years, Marsh remained a dogged strict-constructionist, perhaps the last major exponent of Tristano's 'Cool School'. By the time of this much-heralded tour, Lee had moved somewhat to the left in musical terms and was playing a personalized bebop, as is evident on 'Au Privave' and 'Chi Chi' (*Montmartre: Volume 3*). Marsh isn't left behind on the Parker tunes but they aren't quite his meat, and he attempts to spin the short, segmented themes out into longer, much more discursive and angular forms; by no means unattractive, but slightly alien to the concept.

***** Unissued 1975 Studio Recordings**
Storyville 8259 *Marsh; Dave Cliff (g); Niels-Henning Orsted Pedersen (b); Alan Levitt (d).* 12/75.

*****(*) Unissued Copenhagen Studio Recordings**
Storyville 8278 *As above, except omit Cliff.* 12/75.

Marsh rarely played standards as straightforwardly as this, and these discs, released only in the late '90s, are a revelation for anyone who has tried to trace Marsh's course on record. The earlier disc, with Cliff providing harmonic accompaniment, is the less interesting, but there is no denying its attractiveness, and on 'God Bless The Child' the saxophonist touches areas of emotion rarely associated with him. The second album, recorded during the same sessions, comprises a dozen familiar tunes, from Parker's 'Confirmation' (already a contrafact) to 'When You're Smiling' and 'Every Time We Say Goodbye'. Supported by NHOP and the inventive Alan Levitt, he turns in a series of performances that confirm his brilliance as a melodic improviser. This is the kind of music that was to influence later avant-gardists like Anthony Braxton, who instinctively responded to Marsh's flow of ideas.

***** I Got A Good One For You**
Storyville STCD 8277 *Marsh; Kenny Drew (p); Jesper Lundgaard (b); Alex Riel (d).* 4/80.

For some reason, Marsh seems haunted by the spirit of Charlie Parker on this fine quartet session, which comprises 11 tersely performed bebop and standard themes. His solos on 'Sippin' At Bell's', 'Ornithology' and 'Star Eyes' are bursting with melodic ideas. Drew's accompaniment is only slightly marred by what sounds like a rather dull piano.

***** Sweet Basil 1980**
Fresh Sound FSR CD 187 *Marsh; Red Mitchell (b).* 9/80.

This was one of the happiest associations of Marsh's career. Mitchell's distinctive singing bass offers a fuller accompaniment than he often looked for and there are times on these beautiful live cuts when it's the bassist who takes the initiative, forging along his own solitary harmonic pathways. Mostly, though, they're right there together. An object lesson in duo improvisation and a thoroughly enjoyable jazz record into the bargain.

*****(*) Star Highs**
Criss Cross 1002 *Marsh; Hank Jones (p); George Mraz (b); Mel Lewis (d).* 8/82.

***** A Ballad Album**
Criss Cross 1007 *Marsh; Lou Levy (p); Jesper Lundgaard (b); James Martin (d).* 4/83.

***** Newly Warne**
Storyville STCD 4162 *Marsh; Susan Chen (p); George Mraz (b); Akira Tana (d).* 3/85.

***** Back Home**
Criss Cross 1023 *Marsh; Jimmy Halperin (ts); Barry Harris (p); David Williams (b); Albert 'Tootie' Heath (d).* 3/86.

The Criss Crosses are a strong sequence, with *Star Highs* definitely the one to plump for. Listen to the straightened-out 'Moose The Mooche', on which Marsh does his patented elongation and simplification of the melody and its rhythmic accompaniment. So entire is it that theme and solos almost sound through-composed. Barry Harris and Albert 'Tootie' Heath are highly responsive on *Back Home*, with the pianist playing in a boppish blues idiom similar to that of Hawes 30 years before. Jimmy Halperin is a superfluous presence on *Back Home*, taking a second tenor part on 'Two, Not One', but adding nothing of substance to Warne's edgy solo.

***** Two Days In The Life Of ...**
Storyville STCD 4165 *Marsh; Ron Eschete (g); Jim Hughart (b); Sherman Ferguson (d).* 87.

Just before Christmas 1987, Marsh collapsed and died at Donte's; he was playing 'Out Of Nowhere'. *Two Days* was recorded late in the day and with no warning that the end was already in view. Marsh plays superbly to a very routine accompaniment, and only flashes of invention from the drummer relieve the one-dimensional nature of the group. Marsh, as ever, needs to be listened to patiently and carefully. The discography is in better shape than it used to be but someone needs to do some serious reconstruction work, and we still await CD reissue of important albums on Atlantic, Revelation and Wave.

*****(*) An Unsung Cat: The Life And Music Of Warne Marsh**
Storyville 8314 *Marsh; Ollie Mitchell, Chris Price (t); Robert Butler, Billy Byers, David Carbonara, Clint Sandusky, Fred Simmons (tb); Gary Foster, Lee Konitz, Art Pepper (as); Robert Drasnin, Ronnie Lang (as, cl, f); Ted Brown (ts); Toshiko Akiyoshi, Joe Albany, Ronnie Ball, Kenny Barron, Kenny Drew, Sal Mosca, André Previn(p); Dave Cliff, Larry Koonse (g); Frank Canino, Ron Carter, Arnold Fishkin, John Heard, Red Mitchell, Niels-Henning Orsted Pedersen, Bo Stief, Dean Taba, Ben Tucker (b); Denzil Best, Larry Bunker, Stan Levey, Al Levitt, Jeff Morton, Ben Riley, Skip Scott, Aage Tanggaard (d); Ralph Garretson (perc).* 44–85.

This was released in parallel with an excellent book about Warne and offers a splendid soundtrack to the narrative. The real interest of the compilation for devoted Marshians is the inclusion of early material like Herman's 'Apple Honey', played with the Teenagers, and a very rare rehearsal tape of Warne playing along to 'How High The Moon' from a Jamey Aebersold disc, from which Kenny Barron's piano part has been edited out. The range of material is as impressive as the personnel will suggest. There is some fine early material with Lee Konitz, including a contrafact of 'Cherokee' which has been renamed 'Marshmallow'. Two versions of 'Body And Soul' are absolutely archetypal Marsh, and they have sensibly been put back to back for purposes of comparison. A truly comprehensive and well thought-out anthology.

*****(*) Marshlands**

Storyville 1018366 *As for Storyville discs, above.* 75–87.

If *An Unsung Cat* is primarily of interest to Marsh and Cool School students, with its bits of historiography and its rarities, this is an ideal introduction to Marsh for anyone who hasn't previously encountered him. Unlike the earlier compilation, this is limited to material from the Storyville catalogue, so it inevitably only tells part of the story, albeit a very fruitful period. With anthologies, there are either no quibbles or endless quibbles. This falls somewhere in between: a good selection but perhaps erring on the side of the unobvious. Why, apart from the duplication with *Unsung Cat*, no version of 'Body And Soul'? Why 'Little Willie Leaps' and not the better 'Confirmation'? And so on.

John Marshall

TRUMPET

Formed Bopera House group with pianist Tardo Hammer.

***** Bopera House**

VSOP #72 *Marshall; Ralph Lalama (ts); Tardo Hammer (p); John Weber (b); Tom Melito (d).* 6/88.

***** Keep On Keepin' On**

Mons 10652 *Marshall; Jesse Davis (as); Tardo Hammer (p); John Goldsby (b); Leroy Williams (d).* 96.

Hard bop of a curiously unreconstructed sort, recorded under the tutelage of Rudy Van Gelder, who virtually wrote the book. On the first record 'Sippin' At Bells' could almost be from a lost Blue Note of the late '50s. The second disc is slightly more appealing, but no more responsive to current trends. If that appeals, this is very much the album for you, crisply recorded and nicely packaged; if you want a little more contemporary challenge in your music, Bopera House aren't your guys. The only hint of controversy seems to have come when the Met objected to the band name and called their lawyers ...

Andy Martin

TROMBONE

West Coast slide player in the Frank Rosolino mould.

***** Andy Martin Quartet With Dave Pell**

Woofy 113 *Martin; Dave Pell (ts); Larry Koonse (g); Trey Henry (b); Ray Brinker (d).* 01.

***** It's Fine ... It's Andy!**

Fresh Sound FSRCD 5037 *Martin; Jan Lundgren (p); Tom Warrington (b); Paul Kreibich (d).* 8/02.

Martin paid his dues with Les Brown's band and still sounds as if he were working in a big section rather than at the front. There is not much drama and not much unexpected harmonic action on either disc. Martin hits his notes cleanly and strongly, creates competently engineered solos and has a nice ringing tone. Beyond that, it's hard to get excited. The first record features some nice duet work with Koonse which stretches him a bit. The second, with its 'Fine And Dandy'-punning title, is conceived as a tribute to Rosolino and incidentally also to Carl Fontana, who is dedicatee of the opening track. From there, though, it wends its predictable way. Pell is another competent player, but you feel he has a dangerous side that's being kept in check here. Trombone tutors will probably put this on to encourage their sloppier students, who'll then go off to slur and snarl their way through a Roswell Rudd record just out of spite.

Claire Martin (born 1967)

VOCAL

Relaxed, technically sound and able to invest a lyric with genuine drama, Martin was the most exciting female jazz singer to emerge in the '90s. As well as original and standard material, she has shown how contemporary rock and pop material is adaptable to her unfussy and emotionally nuanced approach.

***** The Waiting Game**

Linn AKD 018 *Martin; Jim Mullen (g); Jonathan Gee (p); Arnie Somogyi (b); Clark Tracey (d).* 12/91.

*****(*) Devil May Care**

Linn AKD 021 *As above, except add Rick Taylor (tb, perc), Nigel Hitchcock (as), Iain Ballamy (ts, ss).* 2/93.

*****(*) Old Boyfriends**

Linn AKD 028 *As for The Waiting Game, except replace Gee with Steve Melling (p).* 5/94.

Martin was an inspired signing for Linn, but one wonders how she would have developed if she'd been picked up by Blue Note or Concord. She has always surrounded herself with sympathetic players, but one does wonder to what extent they push her hard enough. The voice matures considerably between *The Waiting Game* and *Devil May Care*, not so much in range or articulation as in sheer expressiveness. Martin never overdramatizes or dwells indulgently on a lyric, but delivers it with commendable conviction. She brings a playful poise to Bob Dorough's 'Devil May Care', a song that can sound more arch than Broxburn Viaduct, and she gives Noël Coward's 'If Love Were All' just the right mixture of sentiment and stiff upper lip. The other significant factor about the second album was Martin's songwriting skill. She has absorbed enough from the masters to handle the idiom with some confidence, and 'On Thin Ice' is a superb creation. Puzzlingly, and with the exception of the boppish 'Chased Out', co-written with Arnie Somogyi, the songs on *Old Boyfriends* are all covers. A later reference to writer's block may explain the hiatus. They are, though, covers which are picked with taste and imagination. Harold Arlen's 'When The Sun Comes Out' is a relatively conventional warm-up, but it's followed by an emotionally eclectic range of material, including Rupert Holmes's tough 'Partners In Crime', Artie Shaw's 'Moon Ray' and Jonathan

Blair's oddly affecting 'I've Got News', which is as moving an account of the end of an affair as anyone's ever put to music. The Tom Waits-composed title-song is one that was written for Coppola's *One From The Heart*, and Martin delivers it straight from Breast Central. Not quite a concept album, but one that has a satisfyingly melancholy coherence, capped by Jule Styne and the late, great Carolyn Leigh's 'Gentleman Friend'.

It should have been much harder to replace Jonathan Gee, but Steve Melling does an impressive job, paving the way for a more intimate, less hectic approach on subsequent outings with Gareth Williams, who may yet turn out – with producer Joel E. Siegel and enthusiastic patron Richard Rodney Bennett – to be Claire Martin's most significant collaborator.

***** Offbeat: Live At Ronnie Scott's Club**

Linn AKD 049 *Martin; Mark Nightingale (tb); Gareth Williams (p); Martin Taylor (g); Anthony Kerr (vib); Arnie Somogyi (b); Clark Tracey (d).* 8/95.

****** Make This City Ours**

Linn AKD 066 *Martin; Gerard Presencer (t, flhn); Antonio Hart (as); Gareth Williams (p, v); Peter Washington (b); Gregory Hutchinson (d).* 10/96.

Martin approached her 30th birthday with a solid reputation on both sides of the Atlantic, but not yet with a statement on record that matched up to her live presence. *Offbeat* was recorded at Ronnie Scott's with a working group, but not even guest spots like label-mate Martin Taylor's superb cameo on 'Some Other Time', a delightful encore duo, lift what seems with hindsight a rather pedestrian album compared to what preceded it and what was to follow. 'Wishful Thinking', co-written by David Newton (who also scored 'Victim Of Circumstance' on *Devil May Care*), is perhaps the high-spot, and there are some vivid exchanges between Williams and Tracey.

If one album deserves to establish Martin as a singer with real star potential, then it's *Make This City Ours*. Even the title sounds like a confident declaration of intent. Recorded in New York, with Washington, Hart and Hutchinson guesting, it has a more international sound, a more cosmopolitan feel than any of its predecessors. Presencer's trumpet-playing conveys a nice mixture of innocence and faintly weary maturity, and Hart always sounds good around singers. There is a new Martin composition, 'Empty Bed', which bodes well for more from that source. There are still occasional lapses into formula: 'Another Night' doesn't sound entirely assured, and an arrangement of Bruno Martino's 'Estate' with words by Joel Siegel doesn't quite come off. For the most part, though, this is an ideal showcase. (A word, too, for William Claxton: at last, a photographer who can make Claire look as beautiful on her album covers as she is in person.)

***** The Linn Box: 3 – Claire Martin**

Linn 123 3CD *As for The Waiting Game; Devil May Care; Offbeat.* 91, 93, 95.

Released in 2000, this straight repackaging of three early Martin CDs may well have been intended to recognize her shift from jazz to pop. Claire's later work has rarely had the swing and improvisational freedom of these records. No new material included, so this option will appeal only to those who haven't previously owned Martin's discs.

*****(*) Perfect Alibi**

Linn AKD 122 *Martin; Duncan McKay (t); Nichol Thomson (tb); Mornington Lockett (ts, cl); Charlotte Glasson (bs, f); Jo Richards (f); Jason Rebello (p); Robin Aspland (ky); Paul Stacey (ky, g); Andy Wallace (org); Anthony Kerr (vib); Arnie Somogyi (b); Andrew Newmark, Mathew Skeaping, Jeremy Stacey (d); Luis Jardim (perc); John Martyn (v).* 11/99, 1–2/00.

A range of material from Hendrix and Todd Rundgren to Laura Nyro and Julia Fordham, and an astonishing duet with John Martyn on his 'Man In The Station' make this Claire's most inventively adventurous album to date. It also takes her a half-step away from a conventional jazz repertoire, but so thoroughly is her style invested in the jazz tradition that the feel is consistent, improvisational and un-trendy. Phoebe Snow's 'Inspired Insanity' is the closest it gets to pure pop, a tendency nicely balanced by Al Kooper's 'More Than You'll Ever Know' and Hendrix's 'Up From The Skies'. The instrumentation and arrangements (largely by Paul Stacey and Charlotte Glasson) are varied from track to track and *Perfect Alibi* once again has the feel of a well-planned and modulated jazz set.

***** Take My Heart**

Linn AKD 093 *Martin; Mornington Lockett (sax, cl); Gareth Williams(p); Jason Rebello (ky); Paul Stacey(ky, g); Noel Gallagher (g); Arnie Somogyi (b); Jeremy Stacey (d).* 00.

The appearance of Noel Gallagher (of Oasis, jazz people!) in a cameo role is even stronger proof of Martin's pop ambitions than her choice of material here. Kicking off with Nick Drake's haunting 'Riverman' sets the agenda, and the mood is clinched by a lovely version of Elvis Costello's ballad of betrayal, 'Baby Plays Around', which closes the record. In between, some bright and effective singing and some strong playing from a now pretty settled and regular line-up.

***** Every Now And Then: The Very Best Of Claire Martin**

Linn AKD 177 *As for the above.* 91–00.

A decade's worth of recording, and a pretty useful introduction to Martin's work. It kicks off with 'When The Sun Comes Out' from *Old Boyfriends* and takes in Nick Drake's 'Riverman' from the recent *Take My Heart*, so as a compilation it can't be accused of not covering the waterfront.

*****(*) Too Darn Hot**

Linn AKD 198 *Martin; Nigel Hitchcock (ts); Geoff Keezer, Gareth Williams (p); Richard Cottle (ky, org); Phil Robson (b); Geoff Gascoyne, Laurence Cottle (b); Clark Tracey (d).* 01.

She's in great form, singing with passion and ambition. Richard Rodney Bennett's arrangement of 'Raining In My Heart' is a gem and the opener 'Something's Coming' from *West Side Story* gives the set something of the drama of a stage show. Claire still likes to dabble in pop repertoire and there's a Joni Mitchell song here again, but for the most part, this is a jazz gig, delivered with sass and sophistication. Other highlights include 'The Gentleman Is A Dope' and of course the title-track. Able support from the band.

Joe Martin

DOUBLE BASS

Able young player who hasn't yet developed a convincing voice.

**** Algorythm**
Orchard 3694 *Martin (all instruments).* 00.

**** Passage**
Fresh Sound New Talent FSNT 139 CD *Martin; Mark Turner (ts); Kevin Hays (p); Jorge Rossy (d).* 12/01.

Joe plays everything on the first record but without having much to say on any of his instruments. It's a slightly odd idea, but no odder than his notion that giving clever titles – 'Particle Accelerator', and others of that ilk – to pretty lame themes will win him fans. It seemed that only a switch to a more professional set-up and a proper group setting would do the trick, but laudable as Fresh Sound's showcase imprint is, *Passage* isn't the kind of set that will do the label or the artist any favours. Martin emerges as a mild and unemphatic player and writer, with no strong agenda. Saxophonist Turner is the only soloist of any note on the record and the originals 'Poppy's Song', 'Closure', 'Five On You' and the ballad 'Overwhelmed' are pretty generic. A cover of Bob Dorough's little-played 'Nothing Like You' looked like a promising idea but fails to deliver. Martin's rite of passage is still to come.

Rebecca Martin

VOCAL

Singer making her mark with crack New York band.

*****(*) Middlehope**
Fresh Sound FSNT 118 *Martin; Bill McHenry (g, v); Steve Cardenas, Kurt Rosenwinkel (g); Larry Grenadier (b); Jorge Rossy (d).* 1/01.

Martin used to front a group named Once Blue and made an earlier solo set called *Thoroughfare*, but this is effectively a debut in a jazz context. She's more an exponent of an Americana style than a jazz singer as such, with these settings inhabiting an interesting rural–urban mix which the use of sax, two guitars, bass and drums makes notably haunting. She offers little in the way of ornamentation or rhythmic licence and the songs take on an appealingly plain-spoken feel, whether it's 'The Sweetest Sounds', 'Midnight Sun', 'Dindi' or some much lesser-known pieces. With McHenry and the guitarists playing some superb things – the saxophonist's lines in particular often seem to wrap themselves around the vocals – there's as much instrumental interest as there is in the singing.

Pat Martino (born 1944)

GUITAR

Born In Philadelphia, Martino was working as a teenager in combos led by Jack McDuff, Willis Jackson, Don Patterson, Groove Holmes and others. His career was interrupted by illness in 1980, following which he had to completely re-learn his playing technique, and it was not until 1984 that he began working again. Although seldom recognized as an influence, he has been a distinctive and resourceful figure in jazz guitar for many years, and his fine technique and determination have inspired many players.

****(*) El Hombre**
Original Jazz Classics OJC 195 *Martino; Danny Turner (f); Trudy Pitts (org); Mitch Fine (d); Abdu Johnson, Vance Anderson (perc).* 5/67.

***** Strings!**
Original Jazz Classics OJC 223 *Martino; Joe Farrell (ts, f); Cedar Walton (p); Ben Tucker (b); Walter Perkins (d); Ray Appleton, Dave Levine (perc).* 10/67.

***** East!**
Original Jazz Classics OJC 248 *Martino; Eddie Green (p); Tyrone Brown, Ben Tucker (b); Lennie McBrowne (d).* 1/68.

**** Baiyina (The Clear Evidence)**
Original Jazz Classics OJC 355 *Martino; Gregory Herbert (as, f); Bobby Rose (g); Richard Davis (b); Charli Persip (d); Reggie Ferguson (perc); Balakrishna (tamboura).* 6/68.

***** Desperado**
Original Jazz Classics OJC 397 *Martino; Eric Kloss (ss); Eddie Green (p); Tyrone Brown (b); Sherman Ferguson (d).* 3/70.

After graduating from soul-jazz organ combos and the John Handy group, Martino led his own bands on a series of records for Prestige, all of which have now been reissued in the OJC series. Both *El Hombre* and *Strings!* depend on blues-based formulas and are typical of the genre; but Martino's maturing style – heavily indebted to Grant Green and Wes Montgomery, but built for greater speed than either of those masters – is good enough to transcend the settings. *Strings!* is noteworthy for a long, burning treatment of Gigi Gryce's 'Minority', where Farrell's thunderous tenor solo is matched by equally flying statements by Martino and Walton. Aside from the prophetically 'mystical' title-track, *East* offers some of Martino's clearest and most articulate soloing against a straightforward rhythm section. *Baiyina* nodded towards incense and peppermints with its noodling rhythm parts, but Martino's own playing remained tough underneath, and the rambling themes sometimes dissolved in the face of his improvising. *Desperado* is a little-known stab at fusion: Martino plays electric 12-string against rumbling electric piano and bass, and the results are akin to a tighter, less violent Lifetime. 'Express' and 'Desperado' hit a particularly compelling movement, although Green isn't a very stimulating partner (Kloss plays on only one track, 'Blackjack'). All the OJC remastering is good, although *Desperado*'s original production betrays how engineers didn't really know how to deal with that sort of music at the time.

***** All Sides Now**
Blue Note 837627-2 *Martino; Charlie Hunter, Kevin Eubanks, Les Paul, Joe Satriani, Mike Stern, Tuck Andress, Lou Pollo (g); Paul Nowinski, Scott Colley (b); Ben Perowsky, Michael Hedges, Jeff Hirshfield (d); Cassandra Wilson (v).* 6/96–1/97.

Martino arrives at Blue Note for a typical example of the jazz concept album. An improbably eclectic team of guitarists line up for a series of duets, with the perhaps inevitable result that the album stops and starts, and ends up a bit of a mess. There are some genuinely compelling episodes: the sparring with Charlie Hunter on 'Too High', the tough virtuosity of the meeting with Eubanks on 'Progression', the purling lyricism of

'Two Of A Kind', with Tuck Andress. On the debit side are the ponderous 'Both Sides Now' with Cassandra Wilson, two fairly meaningless chunks of interplay with Joe Satriani and the OK-but-effortful tracks with Mike Stern. Martino himself can largely be exempted from criticism: he brings dedication and inventiveness to all the tracks and earns the stars on his own. But this isn't a great deal of fun as a whole album.

***** Stone Blue**
Blue Note 853082-2 *Martino; Eric Alexander (ts); Delmar Brown (ky); James Genus (b); Kenwood Dennard (d).* 2/98.

Concentrated around the band which Martino calls Joyous Lake, this is an energetic and spirited album which has a lot of fine Martino guitar on it, as well as lusty blowing from Alexander. But its merits are compromised by the vague nods towards modishness provided by Brown's keyboards, sound effects and so forth. Martino is a player's player, like, say, Jim Hall: whatever his roots in the soul-jazz of the '60s onwards, he doesn't really need trappings which are going to date the record more quickly than it deserves. If you can filter out the smooth-jazz inflexions that surround him, you'll find Pat in gregarious mood here.

*****(*) Live At Yoshi's**
Blue Note 499749-2 *Martino; Joey DeFrancesco (org); Billy Hart (d).* 12/00.

****(*) Think Tank**
Blue Note 92009-2 *Martino; Joe Lovano (ts); Gonzalo Rubalcaba (p); Christian McBride (b); Lewis Nash (d).* 1/03.

And this one is a roots exercise again, even though the idiom is by now classic enough to transcend such considerations. The tough thing for Martino is to find a way for his qualities to reach an audience without leaning back on show-off situations. This set is arguably no different to anything he's done in the past in its frame of reference: all he can do is prove the state of his chops, and what he can achieve with material that all but says to its exponent: show me what you can do. 'Oleo' is just like that, and the clarity of line and power of invention is set up at once. It helps that the trio is nicely balanced, between DeFrancesco's natural exuberance and Hart's sage rhythm-master. But the guitar's the thing.

Think Tank presents a band which is likely more loaded with perceived talent than any group Martino's worked with. Problem is, it feels like bought-in class. Ingenious tunes and heavyweight solos, but it's not exactly soulful music. Lovano's done several gigs too many in this idiom, and Rubalcaba simply isn't the pianist for Pat.

Barry Martyn (born 1941)

DRUMS, VOCAL

Formed his own band in London at 16 and visited New Orleans in 1961, where he became a tremendous force for organizing tours and recordings for the local players and visitors, also bringing them back to Europe. In Los Angeles from 1972 and resident in New Orleans from 1984. A tireless promoter of original New Orleans jazz, with a special interest in the brass band medium.

***** Vintage Barry Martyn**
GHB BCD-75 *Martyn; Clive Blackmore, Dennis Jones, Cuff Billett (t); Mike Pointon, Pete Dyer, Freddy John (tb); John Defferary (cl, as); Sammy Rimington, Dick Douthwaite (cl); Bill Greenow (as); Ken Saunders (ts); Graham Paterson, John Marks (p); John Coles, Bill Stagg (bj); John Renshaw, Bill Cole, Terry Knight, Brian Turnock (b).* 11/59–70.

**** On Tour 1969**
GHB BCD-255 *Martyn; Clive Wilson (t); Frank Naundorf (tb); Dick Douthwaite (cl, as); Jon Marks (p); Brian Turnock (b).* 68.

****(*) Legends Of Jazz & Barney Bigard**
GHB BCD-338 *Martyn; Andrew Blakeney (t, v); Louis Nelson (tb); Barney Bigard, Joe Darensbourg (cl); Alton Purnell (p, v); Ed Garland (b).* 5/74.

***** Barry Martyn's Down Home Boys**
Sackville KCD2-3056 *Martyn; Wendell Eugene (tb); Chris Burke (cl); Ron Simpson (g).* 10/93.

This cigar-chomping Londoner went to New Orleans in 1961 and became an unlikely champion of the city's traditional jazz. Basing his own style around that of the New Orleans masters, he not only sought out his heroes but played with them, recorded them and conducted interviews that have become integral to the archives on the music. At the moment there are still only a few of his many records available on CD, and this handful is rather unrepresentative. *Vintage Barry Martyn* collars four different British sessions – from Southall, New Bond Street and Basingstoke! – starting with Kid Martyn's early group (including Rimington, and Clive Blackmore lying on the floor to sing the vocal on 'Robert E. Lee') and getting as far as 1970. Some of it is little more than amateur enthusiasm, but the music gets stronger as it goes on and Martyn himself is unfailingly swinging in the New Orleans style. His own memories in the sleeve-note are a priceless record in themselves.

The 1968 set features a band of Brits whose ardour doesn't wholly make up for the lack of finesse on ancient history such as 'Dardanella'; the recording sounds rusty, too. Martyn formed his Legends Of Jazz with a crew of venerable old-timers in 1973, and they became something of a festival attraction. This is quite a spirited recording, with guest Bigard sounding much stronger than he does on the *Pelican Trio* sessions (listed under Bigard's name). Some of the pieces shake along rather than swing, and Purnell's two vocals sound like pure sandpaper, but somehow Martyn (who was some 40 years junior to all the others) makes the whole thing work. His playing is strong enough to lift the band but never rough enough to knock the players about.

The recent Sackville CD is a good-natured jazz beano and, though the interesting instrumentation is never used to any surprising ends, the way that the players seem to blend agility with amiable sloppiness is rather beguiling. Bonus marks for playing 'Blue Hawaii', 'Sail Along Silvery Moon' and 'Dolores' instead of the usual old scrolls.

***** On The Sophisticated Side**
Jazzology JCD-282 *Martyn; Freddy John, Mike Owen (tb); Chris Burke (cl); Jan Engebretsen (p); Les Muscutt (bj); Bill Evans (b).* 4/97.

Martyn having fun with this pair of 'bones (Burke and Muscutt make a single appearance only). The material stretches from 'Tuxedo Junction' to 'Sleepy Lagoon' and much of it is borderline novelty music, but the Kid's drumming swings as famously as ever and Engebretsen is a strong two-fisted pianist.

★★(★) Reunion Band In Italy

GHB BCD-413 *Martyn; Joseph 'Beppi' Zancan (t, v); Fabrizio Cattaneo (t); Luciano Invernizzi (tb); Rudy Balliu (cl); Guido Cairo (p); Pierre-Luc Puig (b). 3/00.*

Well, he gets around. Here he is in Milan with a gang of Italian New Orleanians and Rudy Balliu. For once, Barry sounds a bit subdued – or at least, he's not all that prominent in the mix. Definitely a second-string date.

★★(★) Let's Go England

GHB BCD-443 *Martyn; Mike Owen (tb); James Evans (as, ts, cl); Jonny Boston (ts); Tom Kincaid (p); Ben Martyn (b). 3/01.*

Nothing subdued about this one, with Martyn taking a spirited vocal on 'Caledonia' and his band of new English recruits romping through this gig at Gresham's, Cambridge. The material is scandalously non-purist – 'Buona Sera'? 'Moonlight Becomes You'? 'Help Me Make It Through The Night'?? – and while the sense of exuberant fun is obvious, it does sound like a strange night.

Steve Masakowski (born 1954)

GUITAR

Masakowski is a veteran of the modern New Orleans scene, having gone back there after studying at Berklee. He has flirted with wider recognition – notably via a couple of albums for Blue Note – but has remained on home turf. He usually plays a seven-string guitar.

★★★ For Joe

Compass 7 4289 2 *Masakowski; Bill Huntington (b); Johnny Vidacovich (d). 1/00.*

Some of Masakowski's work has been in a rockier (or at least more fusionoid) vein, but this is deep in the straightahead bag. Conceived as a tribute to Joe Pass, a stylist whom Masakowski doesn't much resemble, the set is nicely satisfying by dint of its plain speaking. There are a few tunes associated with Pass, although the guitarist contributes five originals of his own, and instead of the gentler idiom which Joe rendered so well, the music works off the kind of rocking New Orleans swing which these guys have entirely mastered: Brubeck's 'In Your Own Sweet Way', for one, is beautifully paced in this style. There's nothing flashy on show, and maybe the even-tempered delivery may strike some as a bit ordinary, but it helps that Huntington and the admirable Vidacovich swing so deeply, even in a comparatively laid-back setting for them.

Masaoka Orchestra

ENSEMBLE

Creative big band player-led by koto virtuoso Miya Masaoka.

★★★ What Is The Difference Between Stripping And Playing The Violin?

Victo 58 *Masaoka; George Lewis (tb); Hafiz Modirzadeh (ss, ts, ney, other instruments); Francis Wong (ts); Lee Yen (ts, hichiriki); Jim Norton (cl, bsn); Glenn Horiuchi (shamisen); Vijay Iyer (p, vn); India Cooke, Kei Yamashita (vn); Elliott Humberto Kavee (clo, perc); Mark Izu (b, sho, other instruments); Trevor Dunn (b); Anthony Brown (perc); Robbie Kauker (elec); Jeff Song (tape). 7/98.*

The title isn't a joke waiting for a punchline. Masaoka was moved to anger by public indifference at the murder of five prostitutes in her home district in San Francisco where the piece was first performed with the aid of local lap and pole dancers. So the question is sarcastically rhetorical. Apart from the first piece on the album, the violins aren't particularly prominent and the composition moves between spare classical lines and hard-edged rock and funk. Mr Bungle bassist Trevor Dunn is an important factor in this aspect of the sound. The evocation of a noisy cityscape, bustling with desires and promises, indifference and explosive anger, is very powerful indeed, if a little disjointed. Far more effective is the other composition on the set, '24,000 Years Is Forever', written to commemorate the 50th anniversary of the destruction of Hiroshima and Nagasaki and referring in the title to the half-life of enriched plutonium. It's a beautifully constructed piece, more elegiac than angry but tempered with the awful sadness of lost promise as the voices of schoolchildren are interwoven with the violin lines. Masaoka doesn't play koto on this record, concentrating on her role as conductor, but it breathes with her passionately engaged musical personality. The orchestra members could scarcely be more varied, with prominent parts for the veteran Lewis and an early appearance of pianist/violinist Vijay Iyer, soon to become the most exciting new name in jazz. It all adds up to a challenging listen (and a startling cover for a jazz record).

Hugh Masekela (born 1939)

TRUMPET, FLUGELHORN, VOCAL

Though a minor figure on his own terms as an instrumentalist, Masekela is significant as a South African jazzman who worked in both the US and British scenes, before returning to Africa and rooting his playing in its home soil.

★★★(★) The Lasting Impressions Of Ooga Booga

Verve 531630 *Masekela; Larry Willis (p); Harold Dotson (b); Henry Jenkins (d). 65.*

★★★ Grrr

Verve 0602 49860 3093 *Masekela; other personnel unknown. 4–5/66.*

★★★ Stimela

Connoisseur Collection 200 *Masekela; other personnel unknown. '60s–'70s.*

Masekela is one of the key figures in South African music, a passionate voice whose sound has the throaty urgency of a street-corner preacher and the delicacy of emotion associated with Miles Davis and Chet Baker. At 20, Masekela was a founder member, with Dollar Brand and Kippie Moeketsi, of the Jazz Epistles, South Africa's first significant jazz group. Masekela then married singer Miriam Makeba and left South Africa for the United States, recording classic songs like 'Grazin' In The Grass' (which sold four million copies and climbed to the top of the pop charts) and becoming a spokesman and icon of the anti-apartheid movement. *The Lasting Impressions Of Ooga Booga* is a compilation of two records taped live at the Village Gate in the winter of 1965. The original LP release, *The Americanization Of Ooga Booga*, was not initially followed, and it was only after the success of Masekela's blend of township *mbaqanga* and what he himself dubbed 'township bop' that the remaining tracks were released as *The Lasting Impression Of Hugh Masekela*, one track of which has been omitted on this reissue for reasons of space. Masekela's plangent, vocalized tone is unmistakable and these tunes, written by himself, Makeba, Willis and Caiphus Semenya, are among the strongest he ever recorded. Herbie Hancock's 'Canteloupe Island' is a reminder of how different he was from American jazz musicians of the same generation; the familiar changes are utterly transformed, pushed out into new harmonic and rhythmic territory. A marvellous record, both of its time and timeless, two great continents in fruitful collision.

The slightly later *Grrr* is more obviously packaged for an American audience; full-tilt Afro-boogie of an infectiously accessible sort. 'Zulu And The Mexican' sees Masekela trying to sound like a mariachi player, but managing only to sound like himself. The opening 'U-Dwi' and pieces like 'Sharpeville' and Miriam Makeba's 'Ntjilo Ntjilo', both very moving, are more successful and more obviously idiomatic. It's not clear who his playing partners were on this session. Jonas Gwangwa was the arranger on 'Kwa Blaney', but for the most part Masekela was in charge of proceedings and personnel can probably be inferred from that.

The Connoisseur compilation brings together some of Hugh's finest and most celebrated work, including 'Grazing In The Grass' and 'Stimela'. A valuable introduction to his work.

****(*) Live At The BBC**
Fuel 2000 061197 *Masekela; various personnel.* 85.

Recorded at the Glastonbury Festival and at the Nelson Mandela concert, this finds Masekela at a moment when his personal protest and vision of a free South Africa had entered the mainstream. As such it seems both extra-relevant and sadly also superseded by other voices. The best of the music, perversely, is celebratory rather than protest-led, and the opening 'Zulu Wedding' is worth the rest of the album on its own.

***** Hope**
Razor & Tie 85215 *Masekela; Ngenekhaya Mahlanghu (ts, f, v); Themba Mkhize (ky, v); Lawrence Matshiza (g, v); Bakithi Kumalo (b, v); Damon Duewhite (d); Remi Kabaka (perc, v).* 7–8/93.

After the fall of apartheid, Masekela returned to South Africa. This concert from Washington, D.C. finds him exploring and reattaching roots, telling his story to the country which had given him shelter and support during the years of oppression. Inevitably, 'Grazing In The Grass', his big American hit, has pride of place in the set, but Hugh also goes back to songs by Miriam Makeba (opening with 'Abangoma') and by Caiphus Semenya, to 'Bring Him Back Home', which had lost its political impact by 1993, if not its emotional resonance, and also to the very first songs he remembers hearing, like the township chant 'Languta'. Gentle as it all is, there's a sting in the tail and a recognition that all is still not well in modern South Africa. The closing 'Stimela' is a mineworkers' lament and protest that has a very bitter flavour indeed, proof that Masekela can still say *grrr* when he needs to, even if that trumpet has lost much of its fire.

***** Black To The Future**
Shanachie 5056 *Masekela; Jasper Cook (tb); Khaya Mahlangu (ts, f); Bushy Seatlholo (p); Don Laka (ky); Kenny Mathaba, John Selolwane (g); Tuli Masoka (b); Jethro Shasha (d); Godfrey Mgcina (perc); Family Factory, Children of Mathaba Centre (v).* 97.

Masekela's best record, the Chisa recording *Home Is Where The Music Is*, remains to be reissued, but recent years have seen a resurgence of activity, both in the back-catalogue and in new recording. Returning to a changed South Africa was inevitably a charged and emotional experience, but for Masekela it also seemed to blunt the edge of his playing. Never before had he sounded so unfocused and prettified. *Black To The Future* is stronger than some of his later records not because the writing is better, but simply because there is more convincing playing. The album brings together some of the best musicians in present-day South Africa and, while there is no Mongezi Feza or Kippie Moeketsi coming through, Khaya Mahlangu is a forceful and exciting player, and there is no mistaking the professionalism of the ensembles. The kids' choir sounds fantastic on 'Strawberries', one of the best tracks on *Black To The Future.* Still, the feeling persists that this talented musician has only rarely been served well by his recordings.

***** Sixty**
Shanachie 5070 *Masekela; Don Laka (p); Kenny Mathaba (g); Victor Ntoni (b); Dave Reynolds (d); Innocent Modiba, Stephen Molakeng, Fana Zulu, Sibongile Makgathi, Thabo Mdluli, Margaret Motsage, Nonhlanhla Radebe, Vicky Vilakazi (v).* 99.

****(*) Time**
Sony 508295 2 *Masekela; Prince Lengoasa, Sydney Mavundla, Sam Nako (t); John Davies, Jasper Cook, Mokone Senkhane (tb); McCoy Mrubata, Barney Rachabane (as); Khaya Mahlangu, Sydney Mnisi (ts); Karabao Mohlala (bs); H. K. Moilwa, Arthur Tshabalala (ky); Lawrence Matshiza, John Blackie Selolwane (g); Mandla Zikalala (b); Dumisani R. Hiela, Sello Montwedi (d); Swazi Dlamini, Vicky Vilakazi, Margaret Motsage, Letoya Makhene, Andrew Maloisane, Lesley More, Lucky Ramodibe, Siphiwo Sibeko, Thabo Tsotetsi (v).* 02.

As he turned 60, Hugh looked back once again across a career that embraced marriage to Miriam Makeba, political dissidence, some measure of commercial success and, with the fall of apartheid, the restoration of his country to some measure of freedom and democracy. A shame that such a dramatic story should take on such a bland and unexciting form. Musically, Masekela is no longer strictly a jazz player, and it's all the more frustrating when brief glimpses of his former genius shine through. Despite revisiting early themes like Caiphus Semenya's 'Part Of A Whole' (originally on *Home Is Where The Music Is* in 1971 with Dudu Pukwana), *Time* is a further disappointment, punctuating overproduced Afro-soul-jazz with a few echo-y trumpet features from Hugh and a wearisome overemphasis on vocals. Nevertheless, it won him a BBC Radio International Artist Award.

***** Grazing In The Grass: The Best Of Hugh Masekela**
Columbia 85759 *Masekela; various personnels and dates.*

A useful roundup of Masekela's work for Columbia, it includes such oddities as 'Vasco Da Gama, The Sailor Man' alongside the inevitable title-track, the equally unavoidable 'Bring Him Back Home' and the bitter 'Stimela', which always seems to be found at the end of Masekela albums to remind us that underneath the warmth there's still a chill of anger.

Keshavan Maslak

ALTO SAXOPHONE, BASS CLARINET, SYNTHESIZERS, OTHER INSTRUMENTS

Born in New York but claiming Ukrainian ancestry, Maslak is a mercurial performer in a somewhat wild variety of styles and on a wide range of instruments, acoustic and otherwise. Known as Kenny Millions.

***** Loved By Millions**
Leo CD LR 105 *Maslak; John Lindberg (b); Sunny Murray (d).* 10/80.

***** Not To Be A Star**
Black Saint 120149 *Maslak; Paul Bley (p).* 10/92.

A talented but enigmatic figure, Maslak cultivates a broadly satirical tone, as in the rock-influenced fantasies of another disc called *Loved By Millions* (formerly on ITM, but not to be confused with the fierce free-bop session listed above).

The duos with Bley on *Not To Be A Star* are extraordinary, if beset by Maslak's gimmickry. All freely improvised – sometimes over lyrics written by Maslak in his Kenny Millions guise – they are some of the most intense and abstract performances the pianist has ever recorded, surprisingly so at a time when he seemed to have rediscovered the jazz heartland. Access to a 24-track studio allowed the saxophonist to multi-track himself on clarinet at a couple of points. Reissue of the 1980 record shows how little Maslak's basic approach has changed in the interim. Murray pushes him further than usual in the direction of abstraction, but the saxophonist tends to stick to a fairly linear programme nevertheless, creating an impression throughout that he is accompanying his own rhythm section. The music remains difficult to categorize: 'everyday magic/very deep/almost impossible to understand'.

Public service announcement (reprise): Maslak has established his own label, Humha, and under his *alter ego* of Kenny Millions has released more than 20 CD-Rs of his music, dating back to the '70s and covering very recent work too. Unfortunately we haven't managed to audition any of them, as yet.

Eugene Maslov

PIANO, SYNTHESIZER

An expatriate Russian pianist with classical training, here working in New York with various American teams.

***** When I Need To Smile**
Mack Avenue MAC 1001 *Maslov; Eddie Gomez (b); Omar Hakim (d).* 99.

****(*) The Face Of Love**
Mack Avenue MAC 1002 *Maslov; Toots Thielemans (hca); Eddie Gomez (b); Willie Jones, George Schuller, Steve Williams (d); Shirley Horn (v).* 99.

***** The Fuse Is Lit**
Mack Avenue MAC 1006 *Maslov; Pete Christlieb (ts); Hubert Laws (f); Boris Kozlov (b); Vinnie Colaiuta, Joe LaBarbera (d).* 02.

Maslov is a bold player, his classical background perhaps impinging on the jazz content of his playing: rather than offering any kind of swing, he delivers his music at the bruising level of fusion, and Stix Hooper (who produced all three sessions for his Mack Avenue imprint) gives him the kind of mix which underlines that sort of momentum. It doesn't work at all on the first date: the piano's too far behind the drums, which are handled by Hakim at his insensitive worst, and with Gomez blandly pottering along it's heartless music, even when they're tackling the likes of 'The Man I Love' and 'Dindi'.

The Face Of Love is much better, if only because it has some much gentler music, and there are good spots for Shirley Horn and Toots Thielemans (although why he was asked to do 'Bluesette' yet again mystifies us). Maslov takes an interesting path through 'The Peacocks' and a cover of Jerome Richardson's 'Groove Merchant' offers solid chopsmanship. The third set (recorded on the West Coast, unlike the first two) is back to licks-based music and doesn't do so well. Laws and Christlieb cheer up the ears with a few bright solos, but session-man ennui breaks down the impact and that seems a disappointing verdict on someone who's only up to his third record.

George Masso (born 1926)

TROMBONE, PIANO

Son of a local trumpet player, Masso grew up in Rhode Island and mainly taught music before beginning full-time playing in the '70s. He has since built a considerable reputation in mainstream circles.

***** The Wonderful World Of George Gershwin**
Nagel-Heyer 001 *Masso; Randy Sandke (t); Kenny Davern (cl); Danny Moss (ts); Eddie Higgins (p); Len Skeat (b); Jake Hanna (d).* 9/92.

***** Just Friends**
Nagel-Heyer 5001 *Masso; Ken Peplowski (cl, ts); Brian Dee (p); Len Skeat (b); Jake Hanna (d).* 8/94.

*****(*) That Old Gang Of Mine**
Arbors ARCD 19173 *Masso; Lou Colombo (t, c); Dick Johnson (as, cl); Dave McKenna (p); Marshall Wood (b); Artie Cabral (d).* 11/96.

***** Shakin' The Blues Away**
Zephyr ZECD6 *Masso; Roy Williams (tb); Brian Lemon (p); Dave Cliff (g); Dave Green (b); Allan Ganley, Martin Drew (d).* 11/95–11/96.

More examples of quality repertory jazz by men who know the style so well that they have to come up with something new – they'd be bored themselves otherwise. Masso, who started out with Jimmy Dorsey 50 years ago, has a generous, peppery, surprising sound on the trombone, some notes turning into an abrupt bark, others crooning across bar lines, and his solos are nearly always a pleasurable education. The two Nagel-Heyer CDs are both live sessions from the label's Hamburg base, and perhaps not quite out of the potboiler class. The *Gershwin* disc assembles a list of chestnuts for the band to blow on, which they do with gusto and without leaving much that's memorable behind them. The quintet date, *Just Friends* (a 24-bit reissue of *Trombone* Artistry, listed in the previous edition), benefits from Peplowski's cunning playing, though when they get to 'Blue Monk' it seems like the band think they're just blowing on the blues. The Arbors CD is by a band in which all the hands come from southern New England, Rhode Island to Massachusetts, and it's genial regional jazz at its best, ten good tunes given an affectionate going-over. *Shakin' The Blues Away* transplants him to the other side of the Atlantic for some good-natured duelling with Williams over the Zephyr house rhythm section. Not quite as strong, perhaps, even though the solos are mostly great fun.

***** C'est Magnifique!**

Nagel-Heyer 060 *Masso; Lou Colombo (t, flhn); Harry Allen (ts); Johnny Varro (p); Phil Flanigan (b); Jake Hanna (d).* 3/99.

***** At Long Last Love**

Arbors ARCD 19249 *Masso; Lou Colombo (t); Artie Mentanarao, Dick Whaley, David Masso (tb); Dick Johnson (cl, ts); Mark Phaneuf (bs, f, cl); Jon Wheatley (g); Marshall Wood (b); Artie Cabral (d).* 8/99.

C'est Magnifique! is another in the seemingly endless run of live recordings from a team of Nagel-Heyer all-stars. Never less than full value from a gang like this, and the concept is Cole Porter, composer of all seven tunes. Masso does 'Why Shouldn't I' and Allen gets 'I Love You Samantha'. If you have several of these on your shelf already, there's no pressing need to add this one.

At Long Last Love features a tentet, with a trombone trio plus baritone at its core, and the arrangements have class and skill; but the record feels a little lacking in some basic spirit, and a few of the tempos feel fatigued. Johnson adds a little vigour with a few hectic tenor solos.

Sabir Mateen

ALTO AND TENOR SAXOPHONES, CLARINET, FLUTE

Fiery reedman who polished his technique as a subway busker before working with Horace Tapscott and occasionally with Sun Ra.

****(*) Divine Mad Love**

Eremite 11 *Mateen; John Voigt (b); Laurence Cook (d).* 97.

Very much a group effort, with solo spots for both bassist and drummer, this seems too consciously designed to show off Mateen's not yet developed multi-instrumentalism. He's no Dolphy yet and his flute and clarinet playing seem to lag behind the fiery entrances he makes on saxophone. He plays relatively conventionally, with not much in the way of multiphonics or other extended technique and you find yourself checking the date on this from time to time, lest it prove to be a lost tape from a late '60s loft session. Somewhat dated, and a less than convincing introduction to a player who'd made a splash on other leaders' dates.

*****(*) Secrets Of When**

Bleu Regard 1961 *Mateen; Raphe Malik (t); Naoko Ono (p); Jane Wang (clo, b, v); Ravish Momin (d).* 5/01.

A huge step forward musically. Malik is the ideal front line partner, and together the group carve out lines that are as empathetic and as fiercely logical as those Coleman and Cherry were making in the '50s. Most of the tracks here are long-form, with relatively simple ground structures providing a platform for high-level improvisation. The interest is always greatest when the two horns are locked together, leaving the other instruments very much as accompaniment. This is not to denigrate their role, however. Wang in particular is a remarkable musician who deserves to be heard more widely.

Mat Mathews (born 1924)

ACCORDION

Born Matthieu Schwartz in the Netherlands and grew up during the Nazi occupation, when jazz was officially proscribed if not effectively banned, and he's been fighting different sorts of censorship ever since. A rare exponent of jazz accordion.

***** The Gentle Art Of Love**

Dawn DP 1101 *Mathews; Art Farmer (flhn); David Amram (frhn); Chasie Dean (as, ts, ob); Herbie Mann (f); Barry Galbraith, Joe Puma (g); Harry Lookofsky (vn); Oscar Pettiford (b).* 2/56.

***** The Modern Art Of Jazz**

Dawn DP 1104 *As above, except omit Lookofsky, Galbraith; add Julius Watkins (frhn); Gigi Gryce (as); Dick Katz (p); Kenny Clarke (d).* 2/56.

***** Swingin' Pretty And All That Jazz**

Design 1036 *Mathews; Bucky Pizzarelli (g); Gene Bianco (hp); Gunnar Hansen (vn); Vinnie Burke (b); Ted Sommer (perc).* 59.

Any concern about the marginality of Mathews' effort will be dispelled by the personnels here if by nothing else. The accordion is still in some respects an awkward jazz instrument, relatively slow in articulation and with that slightly creaky, emphysemic sound that some find beguiling, others intensely irritating. Lookofsky is another little known player on a (relatively) unfashionable instrument, but he is a formidable soloist and his 1960 Atlantic *Stringsville* is worth searching out. Similarly, Amram is best known as a classical composer, with an interest in Latin jazz, and for his association with the Beat writers, but he adds an interesting dimension and some harmonic depth to the sound on these neglected sides, as does Watkins on the other date. And had it not been for Mathews, Herbie Mann might have remained in obscurity for longer. Mat was one of the flautist's first employers.

Mathews returned to Holland shortly after making *Swingin' Pretty*, apparently disillusioned with the business. Again, though, he'd produced some challenging music with another unconventional group. This time, he spoke out for jazz harpists by including Gene Bianco and cigars for anyone who can claim familiarity with his oeuvre; he was an associate of Paul Desmond and Harry Chapin and has shown up on rock and soul records. Like the Dawn discs, these All-Stars sides aren't jazz classics and may be of more interest as sidelights on famous and less well-known musicians, but anyone interested in the music's by-ways and branch lines should certainly sample Mathews's work. A few moments will suffice to let you know whether you've fallen for it or not.

Bennie Maupin (born 1946)

SAXOPHONES, BASS CLARINET, OTHER INSTRUMENTS

Studied in Detroit until 1962, then with many leaders – Roy Haynes, Horace Silver, Herbie Hancock. A failsafe sideman.

***** Driving While Black ...**

Intuition INT 3242 2 *Maupin; Dr Patrick Gleeson (ky, perc).* n.d.

A defiant restatement of jazz-rock by one of the most talented multi-instrumentalists on the scene. Always more than a spear-carrier in the movement, Maupin has never had the critical attention he is due. He exemplifies better than anyone the continuities between hard bop and fusion, having worked in one of trumpeter Lee Morgan's later groups, before helping to hybridize jazz and rock with Miles Davis and, crucially, with Herbie Hancock's Headhunters.

Even so, this is an odd record. It sounds old-fashioned, but at the same time suggests the retro-jazz styling of many contemporary drum'n'bass and jungle projects. Reiterating Miles's desire to make Stockhausen dance with Sly Stone, it runs some risk of reinventing the wheel but succeeds almost despite itself. The title-track is the drabbest thing on the set, a slice of processed funk with none of the anger the title implies and none of the boiling fury Miles brought to similar ideas.

Gleeson's rhythms are more than wallpaper for Maupin's plangent saxophone. Synth technology was in its infancy at the end of the '60s and Gleeson has embraced high-spec keyboards and sampling equipment with great confidence, even though the sound is still close to what one might have heard in 1970. Maupin doesn't so much improvise solos as throw shapes and make expressive gestures, but he does so with great beauty. Try *Driving While Black ...* on someone and see if they can guess who – and, crucially, when – it was.

Tina May (born 1961)

VOCAL

Born in Gloucester, May trained as both an actress and a singer, and she has become one of the principal British jazz singers, at home in both repertory situations and with a broader choice of material.

*****(*) Jazz Piquant – N'Oublie Jamais**
33 Jazz 042 *May; Tony Coe (cl, ss, ts); Brian Dee (p); Alec Coburn (g); John Francis (vn); Julie Walkington (b); Vince Clarke (d).* 1/98.

****** One Fine Day**
33 Jazz 050 *May; Alan Barnes (cl, ss, ts, bs); Nikki Iles (p); Mick Hutton (b); Simon Morton (d).* 7/99.

***** Live In Paris**
33 Jazz 055 *May; Patrick Villanueva (p); Pierre Maingourd (b); Daniel Garcia (d).* 12/99.

May's approach is both classic and completely individual. She has some of the lean, light quality of the bop singers of Buddy Stewart's generation, yet her deep, English voice is strikingly apart from American influences; and she has a worldly, been-around-the-block quality which doesn't prevent her from instilling wonder into lyrics which might otherwise be familiar. *Jazz Piquant* shows off her complete mastery of the French language in a set of the native songs, and with Coe on top form this is an irresistible confection. But it has to bow to the quite superb *One Fine Day*, a repertory record so finely achieved it should make most singers nod in appreciation at least. Starting with a gorgeous version of Anthony Newley's 'Pure Imagination' and ending on the heartbreaking folk-piece 'Waley Waley', May works through every style and, abetted by wonderful work from Barnes and Iles, creates an intimate, intense atmosphere which asks for a listener's finest attention.

Live In Paris is something of a stopgap live album: recorded in a dry and unflattering acoustic and with one or two choices which don't stand up to an album's repetitions, this is a comparatively middleweight set. It does ask the question what this accomplished singer could do on a big budget and with decent studio-time.

*****(*) I'll Take Romance**
Linn AKD 202 *May; Scott Hamilton (ts); Nikki Iles, Robin Aspland (p); Alec Dankworth (b); Tristan Mailliot (d).* 4/02.

With Scott Hamilton along as co-producer and soloist, this is Tina at her happiest and most sheerly entertaining. The set-list might look a bit tired but the record hardly stops swinging from 'I'll Take Romance' inwards, and band and vocalist cruise through the 11 songs (Iles and Aspland split piano duties between them). Ellington's 'Tonight I Shall Sleep' was one inspired choice, the almost unheard-of verse included, and 'Trust In Me' should delight *Jungle Book* fans. One might have wished for a single heartbreaker among the ballads; otherwise, light of heart and light on its feet.

Bill Mays (born 1944)

PIANO

Born in Sacramento, Mays studied in San Diego and played in small groups, as an accompanist, and with his own outfit. Settled in New York in the mid-'80s.

***** Out In PA**
No Blooze 01 *Mays; Martin Wind (b); Matt Wilson (d).* 11/99.

****** Summer Sketches**
Palmetto 2070 *As above.* 10/00.

*****(*) Going Home**
Palmetto 2090 *As above.* 02.

The title-piece is a moody, fugitive thing, but it offers generous scope for each member of the trio, particularly its composer Wind, and like every other piece on the set one hardly notices its length. There aren't many Mays compositions here, though 'Kaleidoscope' is one his best and has been part of his set for thirty years. A reading of Jobim's 'Zingaro' is the only questionable item on *Out In PA*, not because it's no good or badly executed, but because it seems to belong to a different set. You'll see from the numbering that No Blooze wasn't around to bid for the Hot Fives and Sevens. How easy it will be to find this, we don't know; but persist, anyway.

Like so many other senior players, Mays has been taken up by the highly professional Palmetto outfit, who seem determined to make musical quality rather than musical fashion their byword. Bill's 'Fireflies' on the summer-themed album is a token of his brilliance as a composer but he's in strong company. 'Estate' is the obvious repertory tune but Wind's mellow 'Late August' and Wilson's wry '(Gotta Go To) Summer School' are vividly complementary. There's a fantastic bass/piano duet on 'The Things We Did Last Summer' and, would you have guessed it, they get through the whole set without doing a certain Gershwin tune, though both Bill and Martin allude to it more than once. Deceptive as heat haze, this is a lovely, thoughtful album.

The follow-up album is also themed. This is the kind of project Dave McKenna used to like, and the challenge is to make as varied and inventive a job as possible of tunes that are linked by title rather than key or tempo. 'You'd Be So Nice To Come Home To' is the obvious first call, but how often do you hear Red Mitchell's 'I'm A Homebody'? There are, as usual, some vivid originals, each very much in keeping with the temperament of the trio members. Guess who wrote 'Nosey Neighbours'? Too many rhetorical questions; this is a wonderful record by an artist at the top of his powers and blessed with a truly sympathetic group.

Marilyn Mazur (born 1955)

PERCUSSION, VOCAL

Born in New York but growing up in Denmark, Mazur has become a rare star among percussion players. She led her own Primi Band in the '80s before high-profile stints with Miles Davis, Wayne Shorter and Jan Garbarek, but for much of the past decade she has been working local Danish turf, and was recognized when she won the 2001 JAZZPAR prize.

*****(*) All The Birds**

Stunt STUCD 02072 2CD *Mazur; Palle Mikkelborg (t); Hans Ulrik (saxes, cl, bcl, f); Fredrik Lundin (ts, f, bf, elec); Elvira Plenar (ky); Eivind Aarset (g); Anders Jormin, Klaus Hovman (b); Audun Klieve (d); Benita Haastrup, Birgit Lokke, Lisbeth Diers (perc, v); Aina Kemanis, Josefine Cronholm (v).* 4/01.

Certainly among the best of the recording projects which have come out of the annual Danish JAZZPAR events, this double-disc offers more than two hours of music by Mazur's groups Future Song and Percussion Paradise, with Mikkelborg and Lundin among the guest soloists. Jazz survives in the improvising from trumpet, saxes, guitar and bass, but the music is essentially a personal take on the kind of global fusion which Mazur has spent much of her playing career investigating: lots of airy textures and polyrhythmical this-and-that, yet done with a sparse and feelingful, tactile grace which is quite unlike the bland and unyielding style of most fusion. Some tolerance is called for in some of the wordless vocalizing, admittedly, although the record has been cannily sequenced out of material from four different concerts and the impeccable sound is a pleasure – it's almost startling when applause breaks in. A worthy souvenir of Mazur's prizewinning year.

Robert Mazurek

TRUMPET, CORNET

Chicago-based trumpeter who spent a period in Scotland before returning to the USA. Has moved from a basic hard-bop stance to more freely focused music with the Chicago Underground Trio and others.

***** Man Facing East**

Hep CD 2059 *Mazurek; Randolph Tressler (p); Tom Allen, John Webber (b); George Fludas (d).* 12/93.

***** Badlands**

Hep CD 2065 *As above, except omit Allen; add Eric Alexander (ts).* 9/94, 7/95.

***** Green & Blue**

Hep CD 2067 *As above.* 9/94, 7/95.

Musically, at this point Mazurek comes straight out of late-'50s Blue Note hard bop, direct and unadorned, sounding not unlike drummer Tommy Chase's groups of the early '80s in London, but with a more brittle, less abrasive sound. Tressler, who hails from Detroit, provides a solid harmonic anchor, over which the trumpet skates and bounces with absolute conviction and authenticity. To say that this is a band that isn't going to 'develop' is a description rather than a criticism; Mazurek delivers, then delivers again: a fast up-tempo blues, a ballad, a mid-paced groove with a minor feel; and then the same again. No frills.

The debut album is unmistakably capable but somewhat one-dimensional. 'Flora's House' and the title-track stand out. The addition of saxophonist Eric Alexander on the two subsequent discs cements the Blue Note lineage and adds a richness of texture which is welcome indeed. *Badlands* kicks off with a tribute to 'Arthur's Seat', the volcanic lump which dominates the city he adopted, and it immediately suggests a musical personality that has matured in less than a calendar year. The inclusion of standards – 'Deep Purple', 'Every Time We Say Goodbye', 'Stranger In Paradise' and 'I Fall In Love Too Easily' – was a wise decision; though not the most melodic of players, Mazurek is absolutely across the chords, and Alexander trails him every inch of the way.

Green & Blue is interesting not least because Mazurek, whose sound can be one-dimensional, decides to double not on flugelhorn but on cornet, a tight, fat sound that suits him very well. Non-Scottish listeners will probably not understand the implications of a title like 'Streets Of Raith', the long opener. A football commentator, reporting on a Cup victory, declared that 'they'll be dancing in the streets of Raith tonight'. There is actually no such town. Raith Rovers play in Kirkcaldy, once the world capital of linoleum. However, all this work now seems like an apprenticeship for Mazurek's subsequent adventures with the much more profiled Chicago Underground Trio – find him under that entry.

***** Silver Spines**

Delmark DG-540 *Mazurek (c, ky, bells).* 3/02.

Playing this straight after any of the above makes little sense unless one has auditioned some of the discs by the Chicago Underground Trio in the interim. The opening seconds will, indeed, have you checking to see if the disc is dysfunctional. Actually, the skipping and sundry bursts of offstage noise fit in with the modus operandi of a set which is more of an ambient pantechnicon seasoned with the odd dash of improvisation. When he wants to, Mazurek can still play stark, Cherry-flavoured lines, as he does (superbly) on track two here, although that is scarcely the point of this record – which also has little in common with, to pick a perhaps inevitable point of comparison, any of Jon Hassell's ethnomusicological adventures. It's more about pointillist sketches on empty air, or perhaps a patterning of frost on a window pane.

Christian McBride (born 1972)

DOUBLE BASS

Emerged in the '90s as the young giant of the bass on the New York session scene. Influenced by Paul Chambers and Ray

Brown, McBride has already built a sideman discography that vies with his two mentors. Leadership duties were inevitable but so far inconsistent.

***** Gettin' To It**
Verve 523 989 2 *McBride; Roy Hargrove (t); Steve Turre (tb); Joshua Redman (ts); Cyrus Chestnut (p); Ray Brown, Milt Hinton (b); Lewis Nash (d).* 8–9/94.

***** Number Two Express**
Verve 529 585 2 *McBride; Gary Bartz, Kenny Garrett (as); Kenny Barron, Chick Corea (p); Steve Nelson (vib); Jack DeJohnette (d); Mino Cinelu (perc).* 11/95.

*****(*) Fingerpainting**
Verve 537 856 2 *McBride; Nicholas Payton (t, flhn); Mark Whitfield (d).* 4/97.

Only just past 30, McBride has the potential to become one of the giants of his instrument, up with the likes of Ray Brown and Milt Hinton. By the time he signed with Verve, he was already a first-call sideman for a huge variety of sessions and to date has appeared on something like a hundred records. The young man has a big, woody sound and a fluent delivery. He is one of the few mainstream players who is always interesting to listen to and who always has things to say.

Brown and Hinton join him on the first record for a remarkable three-bass version of Neal Hefti's 'Splanky', but for the most part the date is unreconstructed and unapologetic hard bop. *Gettin' To It* might almost be a Blue Note disc of a previous generation. McBride has perhaps been stalked by too many ancestors; add Paul Chambers and Oscar Pettiford to the list. There is something of O.P. to 'In A Hurry', with Josh Redman and Steve Turre, but the sound is also fresh and new.

Christian works a number of variations on the basic quintet, and for 'Sitting On A Cloud' and 'Stars Fell On Alabama' he dispenses with horns altogether in favour of a basic piano trio. The final track is an unaccompanied trip on Jimmy Forrest's 'Night Train', with a magnificent bowed passage.

The second album suffers only from the fact that McBride's quality is now so well attested that it is no longer a surprise. Again, he varies the line-ups, duetting with Barron on the Wayne Shorter tune 'Mikayo', and with Cinelu on the closing 'Little Sunflower'. Barron and Corea share piano duties, notably on Chick's 'Tones For Joan's Bones'. Kenny has always been a very useful exponent of the Fender Rhodes and 'A Morning Story' is written for amplified instruments. As far as the horns are concerned, Bartz is well up to his fine recent form and Garrett's uncluttered, bluesy lines are most attractive. Production by Richard Seidel and Don Sickler is absolutely top-drawer, with McBride placed centre and left and the others ranged around him very naturally.

Fingerpainting is devoted to the music of Herbie Hancock and performed by three of the brightest stars in Verve's latter-day firmament. Divided into two loosely organized sections, 'Suite Herbie I/II', the album covers much of the pianist's recording career, including such classics as 'Dolphin Dance' (a magnificent cup mute solo from Payton) and 'Driftin'', on which McBride is out of this world. 'The Sorcerer' and 'Sly' recall Herbie's association with Miles Davis. 'Speak Like A Child' is performed on flugelhorn, electric guitar and bass and there are delightful tracks from Hancock's *Blow Up* sessions. A delightful record all round.

***** A Family Affair**
Verve 314 557 554 *McBride; Tim Warfield (ts); Charles Craig (p, ky); Russell Malone (g); Gregory Hutchinson (d); Munyungo Jackson (perc); Will Downing, Vesta (v).* 1/98.

***** Sci-Fi**
Verve 314 543 915 *McBride; Ron Blake (ss, ts); James Carter (bcl); Toots Thielemans (hca); Herbie Hancock, Shedrick Mitchell (p); David Gilmore (g); Rodney Green (d); Dianne Reeves (v).* 9/00.

A Family Affair was the sort of album Miles was making two decades earlier, streetwise jazz-funk that was meant to appeal to head, hips and heart all at the same time. It just about comes off, largely because McBride and his fellow players are all such formidable technicians. Gregory Hutchinson is a drummer of the sort Miles searched after for years and Charles Craig has the ability to combine straightforward grooves with some thoughtful harmonic information. Kool and the Gang's 'Open Sesame' and Sly's 'Family Affair' are high-points, but there is some lovely bass work on Stevie Wonder's quiet 'Summer Soft'. A lovely record, but not for anyone who found *Big Fun* hard going.

Sci-Fi picks up where the earlier Verve records left off and sees McBride exploring something like Miles and Herbie's interest in pop music as a source of new standards. The album kicks off with Steely Dan's already pretty jazzy 'Aja' and includes a brilliant version of Sting's 'Walking On The Moon'. There are also tunes by Jaco Pastorius and Stanley Clarke. Great guest spots from Toots Thielemans and James Carter on bass clarinet (a great duet with McBride on the Sting tune) make this a memorable record though perhaps a little anxious to hit a bigger demographic.

***** Vertical Vision**
Warner Bros 9362 48278 2 *McBride; Ron Blake (ss, ts, f); Geoffrey Keezer (p); Terreon Gully (d).* 6/02.

Depending on how you looked at it, Miles's career either got a shot in the arm or ended when he switched from Columbia to Warners. There is no such dilemma with McBride, who delivered his new label an album of great charm, considerable intelligence and a promising return to straightforward jazz chops. The inclusion of Joe Zawinul's 'Boogie Woogie Waltz' right at the end was a great stroke, but for the most part these are originals by the group, with Keezer well represented by two strong, dancing themes and Ron Blake checking in with the lovely 'Song For Maya'.

The group sounds like a regular working outfit. The members are easy with each other and solos are distributed democratically and with due feeling for individual talents. Check out 'Technicolor Nightmare' for a taste of a group on top of its form. All the tracks sound as if they might be good played out at length and the only criticism of the album as a whole is (unusually for us) that it isn't quite long or developed enough. With the exception of the Weather Report warhorse and 'Nightmare', most of these are delivered at pop song length. A live set from this group would be worth hearing.

Les McCann (born 1935)

PIANO, VOCAL

Born in Lexington, Kentucky, McCann had an undistinguished career until the mid-'60s, when he wrote some crossover hits and became popular on the nascent jazz festival circuit. He later worked extensively with Eddie Harris, and their Swiss Movement album became a great success in its day.

***** Talkin' Verve: Les McCann**
Verve 557351-2 *McCann; Lee Katzman (t); Plas Johnson, Seldon Powell, Jerome Richardson (ts); Warren Chiasson, Lyn Blessing (vib); Jimmy Georgantones, Vinnie Bell, Carl Lynch (g); Leroy Vinnegar, Victor Gaskin (b); Paul Humphrey, Frank Severino, Booker T. Robinson (d); Ron Rich, Joseph Torries, Ric DeSilva, Aki Aleong (perc).* 12/64–9/67.

***** Much Les**
Rhino/Atlantic R2 71281 *McCann; Leroy Vinnegar (b); Donald Dean (d); Willie Bobo, Victor Pantoja (perc); strings.* 7/68.

****(*) Swiss Movement**
Atlantic 781 365-2 *McCann; Benny Bailey (t); Eddie Harris (ts); Leroy Vinnegar (b); Donald Dean (d).* 6/69.

***(*) Layers**
Rhino/Atlantic R2 71280 *McCann; Jimmy Rowser (b); Donald Dean (d); Ralph MacDonald, Buck Clarke (perc).* 11/72.

****(*) Talk To The People / River High, River Low**
Collectables COL-CD-6255 *McCann; John Mayer (p); Keith Loving, Miroslaw Kudykowski (g); Jimmy Rowser (b); Donald Dean, Harold Davis, Paul Humphrey (d); Buck Clarke (perc); The Persuasions, Eugene McDaniels, Susan McDaniels, Sister Charlotte, Billy Barnes, Joel Dorn (v).* 72–76.

**** Another Beginning / Hustle To Survive**
Collectables COL-CD-6608 2CD *McCann; Herbie Hancock (p); Roy Gaines, Miroslaw Kudykowski (g); Chuck Rainey, Jimmy Rowser (b); Paul Humphrey, Harold Davis (d); Buck Clarke (perc); strings, horns, choir.* 74–75.

Les McCann has made dozens of albums, although there is still not that much in print – somewhat fortunately for his reputation, since far too much of his production has been disfigured by faddish vocals and arrangements and by feeble material. At least the *Talkin' Verve* compilation sifts together some of the livelier material from a generally undistinguished run of LPs made for Limelight in the mid-'60s. There are some fun moments in the percussion-heavy 'Watermelon Man', an overcooked but entertaining 'Sunny' and an early version of what's practically his signature piece, 'Compared To What?' – even if, like much of his stuff, it was actually written by somebody else.

Perhaps we've been a bit harsh on him, since McCann's background is more about good-time, low-light entertainment than anything out of the 'serious' hard-bop book (even if, apparently, Miles Davis once recommended him for the piano chair in the Cannonball Adderley band). Even so, the albums are a bit thin on persistently strong music. *Much Les* isn't bad. There are some fairly unobtrusive strings on some tracks, but McCann sets up some grooving tempos that Vinnegar and Dean help him to keep moving, and some of it is as good as any soul-jazz of the decade. There's also a pleasing version of his charming ballad 'With These Hands'. A hit album in its time, the appeal of *Swiss Movement* has faded fairly drastically. Cut live at Montreux, it's a ragged set of soul-jazz vamps, with a probably definitive version of 'Compared To What?', but the excitement is mitigated by what remains atrocious sound, even for a live session. Bailey's solo on 'You Got It In Your Soulness' offers the best moment, but overall the revival of interest in soul-jazz has uncovered many better records than this. *Layers* is a trashy relic of thin, early-'70s soul-jazz, barely worth reviving.

The two Collectables sets pick up some more of McCann's '70s dates. Les was shamelessly chasing after the soul audience and opening (*Talk To The People*) with a full-blown cover of Marvin Gaye's 'What's Going On' was typical of what he was up to. The vocal tracks are a bit frowsy, but elsewhere he and the band manage to hit some nice grooves: 'Shamading' is a steaming three minutes, and the nine-minute clavinet opus 'North Carolina' , while not exactly bursting with great improvising, is good period fun. Too bad that this one's been coupled with a real dud in *River High, River Low*, a grim set of songs which reaches rock bottom with 'I'm A Liberated Woman'. Three other songs from this set have been left off the reissue to squeeze it on to one CD, and they're no loss.

Another Beginning and *Hustle To Survive* continued Les's attempts at turning full-time soul crooner. While he's a decent enough singer, much of the material is woeful, and the studio jam 'Us' which opens the second disc is easily the best thing on it. Herbie Hancock tinkles away on one track and 'Got To Hustle To Survive' is one of McCann's attempts at rewriting 'Compared To What'. But anyone who wants music like this would be far better off with something like a Teddy Pendergrass album. *Hustle To Survive* is also available as a single disc in the Atlantic Masters series (81227-3688-2).

**** Pump It Up**
ESC 03678-2 *McCann; Bill Churchville (t); Maceo Parker, Tom Saviano (as); Keith Anderson (ts, as); Ricky Peterson, Billy Preston (ky); Paul Jackson Jr, Adam Kirk, Tony Maiden, Paul Peterson, Dean Brown (g); Abraham Laboriel, Marcus Miller, Herbie Lewis (b); John Robinson, Ron Jefferson (d); Paulinho Da Costa (perc); Bonnie Raitt, Dianne Reeves, Margaret Fowler, Jim Gilstrap, Maxayn Lewis (v).* 10–12/01.

Les is back – but only as a vocalist, and in front of a very expensive crew of session-men. He sounds like a mating of Barry White and Dr John and, with Dianne Reeves and Bonnie Raitt cooing alongside on a couple of tracks, the pipes tend to have their shortcomings exposed. But it's the material which hurts, a useless collection of bought-in funk tunes, with only McCann's own 'The Truth' (revamped over his 1963 Pacific Jazz original track, complete with surface noise) cutting mustard. Misguided.

Ron McClure (born 1941)

DOUBLE BASS

A follower of Paul Chambers – whom he replaced in Wynton Kelly's group – McClure has also been a prolific recording artist in his own right. He worked in big bands for a time, before joining Charles Lloyd's highly successful group, after which he began to emerge as a significant composer and leader.

***** Yesterday's Tomorrow**
EPC 884 *McClure; John Abercrombie (g); Aldo Romano (d).* 7/89.

*****(*) McJolt**
Steeplechase SCCD 31262 *McClure; John Abercrombie (g); Richie Beirach (p); Adam Nussbaum (d).* 12/89.

McClure's fusion group, Fourth Way, extended the jazz-rock idiom he had helped create with Blood, Sweat and Tears and the Charles Lloyd Quartet into more adventurous compositional territory. A fine bassist, with an excellent *arco* technique (see 'Tainted Rose' on *Yesterday's Tomorrow*), he is also an exceptional composer who draws on non-jazz tonalities with great confidence. One of his most characteristic devices is a percussive, almost marimba-like thrum achieved by striking the strings against the fingerboard. McClure's preference for players with a similar sound is obvious from the trio session with Romano and Abercrombie (whose guitar synthesizer takes the place of an electric piano). This is more abstract, impressionistic music, and very different from the standards approach of *McJolt*, where McClure develops the LaFaro sound very impressively on tracks like 'Nardis', 'Stella By Starlight' and 'Once I Had A Secret Love'. The trio set, released on the Montpellier-based EPC, is slightly short on conventional jazz virtues but features some of McClure's best writing and some of his best *arco* work since 'Line' on *Descendants*. 'Midi Evil' presumably refers to the south of France rather than to MIDI technology. The set *is* rather dominated in places (on 'Panchito' to a great extent) by Abercrombie's effects, sometimes at the expense of McClure's and Romano's more delicate interchanges. The sound is also a bit overcooked.

***** Strikezone**
Steeplechase SCCD 31277 *McClure; Marc Copland (p); Dave Stryker (d).* 90.

***** Never Forget**
Steeplechase SCCD 31279 *McClure; Eddie Henderson (t); Vincent Herring (as); Kevin Hayes (p); Bill Stewart (d).* 10/90.

***** For Tonite Only**
Steeplechase SCCD 31288 *McClure; Randy Brecker (t, flhn); John Abercrombie (g); Adam Nussbaum (d).* 3/91.

*****(*) Sunburst**
Steeplechase SCCD 31306 *McClure; Tim Hagans (t); Conrad Herwig (tb); Joe Gordon (as, ss); LeeAnn Ledgerwood (p); Jeff Hirshfield (d).* 12/91.

*****(*) Inner Account**
Steeplechase SCCD 31329 *McClure; Rich Perry (ts); Kenny Drew Jr (p); Vic Juris (g); Sylvia Cuenca (d).* 11/92.

The bassist sounds less persuasive in a conventional horn-led quintet and Herring has an uneasy time of it on the later of the 1990 sessions. We have only been able to sample *Strikezone*, recorded around the same period. McClure's preferred instrumentation is one that trickily pairs guitar and piano, usually allowing the keyboard player long, developed lines, while the guitarist plays 'free' over the top. That's essentially what Abercrombie does on *For Tonite Only*, and what Juris attempts to do, less confidently but in some regards more successfully, on the impressive *Inner Account*.

That's two reasons why *Sunburst* registers so strongly. The recording is very bright and detailed, without too much rumble from the bass, and the playing is straightforward and to the point. McClure has rarely sounded better, but this was only the beginning of a streak that was to continue through the '90s.

*****(*) Never Always**
Steeplechase SCCD 31355 *McClure; Don Friedman (p); Billy Hart (d).* 94.

Friedman's classically influenced approach is the key to this slightly deliberate set. Despite the presence of Hart, who seemed to be getting better by the session through the mid-'90s, it never achieves the sheer verve and excitement of McClure's other discs. Yet it is an album which grows with every hearing, and we recommend it to your patient attention.

*****(*) Concrete Canyon**
Steeplechase SCCD 31391 *McClure; Tim Hagans (t); Marc Copland (p); Billy Hart (d).* 3/96.

****** Closer To Your Tears**
Steeplechase SCCD 31413 *McClure; Jay Azzolina (g); Marc Copland (p); Billy Hart (d); Manolo Badrena (perc).* 9/96.

***** Pink Cloud**
Naxos Jazz 86002 *McClure; Rick Margitza (ts, ss); Jon Davis (p); Jeff Williams (d).* 9/96.

A busy year, with a surprise switch of label in the autumn, doubtless a one-off. Hagans's Miles-influenced (but *early* Miles-influenced) trumpet makes an attractive and unexpected contribution to *Concrete Canyon*. With the exception of the opening 'All That's Left', which was written by Copland, everything else on the set is a McClure original and, though there's not much variety in the thematic material, it's open-ended enough to be lifted in performance, as is emphatically the case on the long 'Lock', originally written for vibist Joe Locke, *before* Ron learned to spell his name. Much of the material has a minor-key feel, even when it appears to be in the major, and there is a constant drift towards polytonality on things like 'Deception', 'Ears' (a more than usually reflective idea), and the title-piece, which is a poem to McClure's beloved New York. Fine as Copland and Hagans are, one finds oneself listening out for the bass and drums most of the time. Hart is at the top of his powers and this is one of his best guest appearances for years.

He's back, and in form, on the lovely *Closer To Your Tears*, which has confusingly similar, indeed almost identical cover art to the other Steeplechase. The title-piece is the most movingly personal McClure has ever allowed himself to be on record. All of his writing and playing comes from the heart – he is an instinctive player above all – but this one seems to come from some inner recess he hasn't tapped before. If there is a drawback to the set, it's probably too deliberate a swing from bright, up-tempo tunes to more expressive themes, like the delightful 'Eli's Wine', inspired by the Jewish tradition of Elijah's Cup, and the closing 'He, Who Cares', which seems to include a string of subliminal references to Miles Davis. The album isn't quite solidly balanced but, unlike that extra cup of wine, it's one that will be tasted and refilled many times.

The Naxos disc maybe should have been left to stand and breathe a little longer. Whereas Azzolina and Copland seemed absolutely in tune with the session, the players on *Pink Cloud* sound a little awkward with the settings, which are even more varied, and perhaps a little mannered, this time out. 'Where's Manuel?' is a strange, almost militaristic evocation of the pursuit of the Panamanian dictator Noriega (famously driven out of hiding by high-volume David Bowie tapes, pumped into the Vatican consular compound by the CIA and US army). 'Milk And Cookies', on the other hand, is a tribute to the wholesome values of Pat Metheny, another of McClure's kind-words-in-a-troubled-world pieces. 'Little Big One' is a gently complex waltz. Margitza only really shows his mettle on the Coltrane-tinged 'Street Smart', but he shows a much more traditional turn of phrase on 'Day By Day', the only standard in the set. Williams and Davis combine well, but are absolutely straightahead and uncomplicated, lacking the subtlety Copland and Hart brought to the Steeplechases. The Naxos set was something of a homecoming and a reunion for the bassist. Almost his first act after the break-up of the Charles Lloyd group was to phone his friend Mike Nock who was forming Fourth Way; he promptly hired McClure and, 27 years later, he's on hand again as executive producer.

★★★(★) Dream Team

Steeplechase SCCD 31435 *McClure; Rich Perry (ts); Marc Copland (p); Billy Hart (d).* 98.

A fascinating set that gets off to a wonderful start with 'Denial's Goat', a double-waltz-time groove which has Perry snaking off into a strange, shawm-like solo. The title-track comes next, a floating minor feel with a hint of song form. Copland brings 'Darius Dance' to the set, but otherwise all the tunes are McClure's, united by his characteristic attention to voicings that work right through the band, including the drummer. Hart seems to get better every time he records, and his delicacy of touch here is a key element of the overall sound. A dream team it may very well have turned out to be.

★★★(★) Double Triangle

Naxos 86044 *McClure; Tim Hagans(t); Conrad Herwig (tb); Rich Perry (ts); Marc Copland(p); Billy Hart (d).* 99.

The concept here is that the horns and rhythm section represent two interlocking triangles, a musical geometry that yields some fascinating rhythmic and harmonic variations. Herwig is an astonishingly powerful presence. His lead line on 'We'll Be Together Again' is perfectly echoed by the bass, while master-drummer Hart weaves in and out of the mix. Perry is not such a commanding presence this time around and there are moments when he seems to lose his place and simply mark time with chromatic figures that do little more than unpick the theme.

McClure's writing is as strong and as idiosyncratic as ever. Like the early beboppers, he likes to develop new ideas out of existing material. 'Night Bird' is an imaginative reworking of the line of Herbie Hancock's 'Speak Like A Child', while Joe Henderson's 'Gazelle' is said to be the source material for 'Thunder'. Ron's playing by this point is utterly confident and articulate. His theme statements are brisk and uncomplicated and his solos have a calm authority. Don't miss this one.

★★★(★) Match Point

Steeplechase SCCD 31517 *McClure; Jed Levy (ts); Bob DeVos (g); Jeff Brillinger (d).* 02.

Amazingly, this is Ron's tenth album for the Danish label, but instead of celebrating a decade's association with an upbeat set, he plays one of the most introspective and searching programmes of his career. Most of the material is written by Levy and DeVos, two competent players but uninspiring writers. The real climax comes with Ron's own 'The Day After Christmas', which in nine minutes sums up why the bassist is such a treasure; a mournful but lyrical theme, it conjures some superb double-stopped passages and some lovely rhythmic variation. The other delight is a rare interpretation of Artie Shaw's 'Moonray'. No doubting it, McClure has more fine music in him.

Rob McConnell (born 1935)

TROMBONE, VALVE TROMBONE

Born in London, Ontario, McConnell began by working in the Canadian dance-band scene of the '50s and '60s, before forming his first Boss Brass group in 1968 and writing in a style which involved the brass sections working in particularly close harmony, often in unaccompanied stretches. The group abides to this day.

★★(★) The Brass Is Back

Concord CCD 4458 *McConnell; Arnie Chycoski, Steve McDade, John MacLeod, Guido Basso, Dave Woods (t, flhn); Ian McDougall, Bob Livingston, Jerry Johnson (tb); Ernie Pattison (btb); Gary Pattison, Jim McDonald (frhn); Moe Koffman, John Johnson (ss, as, f, cl); Eugene Amaro (ts, cl, f); Rick Wilkins (ts, cl); Bob Leonard (bs, bcl, cl, f); Don Thompson (p); Ed Bickert (g); Steve Wallace (b); Terry Clarke (d); Brian Leonard (perc).* 1/91.

McConnell has kept his Boss Brass together on and off for more than 30 years. Initially, they did without any kind of sax section, but by the time of these records the band had grown bigger. McConnell's charts suggest expansiveness as the band's signifying element: although the leader worked with Maynard Ferguson for a spell, the brassiness of the BB is exploited for sonority rather than clout, and there's a kind of reluctance to even their toughest arrangements. The music is skilfully handled, but the various editions of the orchestra never seem really to set light to the charts. Even where McConnell seeks to evade cliché, he can't altogether shrug off the MOR atmosphere that hangs round most of their records. The 'return' album by the Boss Brass is as accomplished as before, but there's too much lingering over detail and texture for a band in which details tend to disperse its impact. Most of the scores unfold at far too languorous a pace, each track clocking in between 7 and 11 minutes. Moe Koffman's vigorous (in Boss Brass terms, splenetic) alto feature on 'All The Things You Are' is the most interesting event.

★★★ Our 25th Year

Concord CCD 4559 *As above, except Alistair Kay (tb) replaces McDougall.* 93.

★★(★) Don't Get Around Much Any More

Concord CCD 4661 *As above, except Judy Kay (frhn), Alex Dean (cl, f, ts), David Restivo (p), Lorne Lofsky (g), Jim Vivian (b), Ted Warren (d) replace Pattison, Amaro, Thompson, Bickert, Wallace, Clarke and Brian Leonard.* 4/95.

★★(★) Even Canadians Get The Blues

Concord CCD 4722 *McConnell; John Mcleod, Guido Basso, Arnie Chycoski, Steve McDade (t); Alastair Kay, Bob Livingston, Jerry Johnston (tb); Ernie Pattison (btb); Gary Pattison, James McDonald (frhn); Moe Koffman, John Johnson, Alex Dean, Rick Wilkins, Bob Leonard (reeds); David Restivo (p); Ed Bickert (g); Jim Vivian (b); Ted Warren (d).* 4/96.

In and of themselves these are all plausible entries in McConnell's chosen genre. *Our 25th Year* is more businesslike than celebratory, and by the time of *Don't Get Around Much Any More*, which really starts to roll out the clichés, one feels that the band might be ready for its collective pension. It probably wasn't a great inspiration for the band to do a programme of blues, since the limitations on thematic material scarcely bring out the best in McConnell's charts. Perfectly adequate, but few will find this in any sense necessary.

*****(*) Thank You, Ted**
Justin Time 173-2 *McConnell; Steve McDade (t); Guido Basso (flhn); Terry Promane (tb); P. J. Perry (as); Alex Dean, Mike Murley (ts); David Restivo (p); Steve Wallace (b); Terry Clarke (d).* 4/02.

***** Music Of The Twenties**
Justin Time 196-2 *As above.* 4/03.

Pared back to a tentet, McConnell's music strips a lot fitter on these outings. The music's less about a band punching over its weight than a mobile and lively ensemble with a good gang of soloists for spice. Guido Basso, for instance, is quite superb on 'If I Were A Bell' on *Thank You, Ted*, which track for track is surely the best disc under McConnell's name. The title is an homage to veteran jazz-jock Ted O'Reilly.

Music Of The Twenties isn't quite so good, although McConnell picked durable tunes from the era in question rather than trying to do the Charleston. Still, it's only a shade behind, and it's nice to be complimentary about a leader who clearly loves his jazz.

Susannah McCorkle (1946–2001)

VOCAL

A Californian by birth, McCorkle moved to Europe in 1971 and began working as a jazz vocalist in London. She returned to the USA in 1977 and, after a spell with The Jazz Alliance, she made many records for Concord, crossing between mainstream, blues and Brazilian material. Afflicted with depression, she tragically took her own life in 2001.

***** The Beginning 1975**
A AL 73233 *McCorkle; Keith Ingham (p).* 75.

****** The Quality Of Mercer**
The Jazz Alliance TJA-10031 *McCorkle; Digby Fairweather (t, c); Danny Moss (ts); Keith Ingham (p); Ron Rubin (b); Derek Hogg (d).* 9/77.

*****(*) The People That You Never Get To Love**
The Jazz Alliance TJA-10034-2 *McCorkle; Keith Ingham (p); Al Gafa (g); Steve LaSpina (b); Joe Cocuzzo (d).* 11/81.

***** How Do You Keep The Music Playing?**
The Jazz Alliance TJA-10036-2 *McCorkle; Al Cohn (ts); Ben Aronov (p); Gene Bertoncini (g); Steve LaSpina (b); Joe Cocuzzo (d).* 6/85.

***** Dream**
Concord TJA-10037-2 *McCorkle; Frank Wess (ts); Ben Aronov (ky); Gene Bertoncini (g); Steve LaSpina (b); Joe Cocuzzo (d).* 12/86.

*****(*) No More Blues**
Concord CCD 4370 *McCorkle; Ken Peplowski (cl, ts); David Frishberg (p); Emily Remler (g); John Goldsby (b); Terry Clarke (d).* 11/88.

*****(*) Sabia**
Concord CCD 4418 *McCorkle; Scott Hamilton (ts); Lee Musiker (p); Emily Remler (g); Dennis Irwin (b); Duduka Fonseca (d); Cafe (perc).* 2/90.

***** I'll Take Romance**
Concord CCD 4491 *McCorkle; Frank Wess (ts, f); Allen Farnham (p); Howard Alden (g); Dennis Irwin (b); Keith Copeland (d).* 9/91.

The Beginning is not a reissue but a first release for some demos which Susannah made with Keith Ingham, for a putative EMI contract. The 22 songs are a strange mix of jazz, blues, cabaret tunes and characteristic Ingham rediscoveries, but the singer approaches everything with a fresh enthusiasm which overcomes the sense that this is someone finding her way – even if 71 minutes of this is too much. McCorkle's records in the '70s, now returning via the Jazz Alliance imprint, established her as a major songbook interpreter, uncovering rarities and seldom-heard verses from some of the best American composers. But they did her few commercial favours. *The Quality Of Mercer* has made it back to CD, and it's an absolute gem: 14 choice Johnny Mercer songs done with wit, feeling and guile in perfect balance, the charm of 'Love's Got Me In A Lazy Mood' matched to the wistfulness of 'Skylark'. A peerless session, with deft support from Ingham, Fairweather and the rhapsodic Moss. *The People That You Never Get To Love* is nearly as good. This is a more modern set of songs, with Blossom Dearie, Dave Frishberg, Neil Sedaka and A. C. Jobim represented, and McCorkle handles all of the lyrics in a hip, intelligent way, the pose just slightly world-weary, but with a clear streak of emotion below the surface cool. The somewhat later *How Do You Keep The Music Playing?* is the weakest of these three. Although there are a couple of sublime glimpses of Al Cohn in one of his last dates, some of the songs seem mishandled: a slow 'There's No Business Like Show Business' starts well but ends up far too overwrought, 'By The Time I Get To Phoenix' was a poor choice, and she overplays 'Blizzard Of Lies'.

Her tenure with Concord provided her with what became a wide variety of settings. *Dream* is a recent reissue, and has two great ones – 'Bewitched' and 'At Long Last Love' – mixed in with doubtful song choices such as Paul Simon's 'Train In The Distance'. *No More Blues* benefits from a superbly integrated band, with Peplowski and Remler chiming in with pithy solos and Frishberg adding the most alert and gracious of accompaniments: McCorkle's big, courageous voice is huskily entreating on the ballads and assuredly swinging on the faster tunes. She's an interpreter rather than an improviser, which sees her through the Brazilian songs on *Sabia*: the task here is to drift through the coolly appealing melodies rather than swinging them to pieces, and McCorkle does it with perfect aplomb. A couple of the ballads sound too stretched, but her take on Astrud Gilberto on 'So Danço Samba' is wholly beguiling, and Hamilton (in the Stan Getz role) and Remler (in her final studio date) are marvellous.

I'll Take Romance is perhaps a shade disappointing as a follow-up. Nothing wrong with the arrangements or the players, with Wess defining his role as strong-but-tender tenorman. But the material – all of it very well known, and excessively so in the case of 'Lover Man' and 'That Old Feeling' – seems like a deliberate attempt to play down McCorkle's knack for discovering forgotten gems, and some of her interpretations sound like false trails towards 'new' transformations. 'My Foolish Heart' and 'I Concentrate On You' are studied enough to suggest caricature, although occasionally – as on a wonderfully sustained 'It Never Entered My Mind' – it works out, and the faster pieces are magical. All three discs are recorded with fine lustre.

*****(*) From Bessie To Brazil**
Concord CCD 4547 *McCorkle; Randy Sandke (t, flhn); Robert Trowers (tb); Dick Oatts (as, f); Ken Peplowski (ts, cl); Allen Farnham (p); Howard Alden (g); Kiyoshi Kitagawa (b); Chuck Redd (d).* 2/93.

Almost a classic – what holds it back, as often seemed to happen with this tremendously gifted singer, is the odd, strange lapse of judgement as to the kind of song she can get away with. The flaws this time are an embarrassing 'My Sweetie Went Away', done as a misplaced tribute to Bessie Smith, and a wincingly cavalier 'Still Crazy After All These Years'. On the plus side are a dozen gorgeous interpretations. Her second attempt at 'The People That You Never Get To Love', Rupert Holmes's only memorable song, is as wryly affecting as Jobim's 'The Waters Of March' is coolly hypnotic, and she does Dave Frishberg ('Quality Time') and Mercer and Arlen as well as anyone today. Sound backing from one of the Concord repertory teams, with Allen Farnham directing.

***** From Broadway To Bebop**
Concord CCD 4615 *As above, except add Frank Vignola (g), Richard De Rosa (d); omit Alden and Redd.* 4/94.

It will take tolerance to get through the aged kitsch of 'Chica Chica Boom Chic', and if she could do Broadway then bebop wasn't really her thing. But there are some great ones here: a Nancy Wilson-type drama called 'One Of The Good Girls', a fine 'Guys And Dolls'. And the husk in her voice became the more attractive, the older she got. Farnham's group offer gold-plated support.

***** Easy To Love – The Songs Of Cole Porter**
Concord CCD 4696 *McCorkle; Randy Sandke (t); Robert Trowers (tb); Chris Potter (as); Ken Peplowski (ts); Allen Farnham (p); Howard Alden (g); Steve Gilmore (b); Richard De Rosa (d).* 9/95.

She's in good voice, and the songs are impeccable, if sometimes worn smooth: one wonders whether there's really anything more a singer can elicit from 'Night And Day' and 'Just One Of Those Things'. So she does the latter at an unsuitably slow tempo, while 'From This Moment On' sounds too fast, and the choice of tempos generally seems like her Achilles' heel. The lesser-known songs, such as 'Goodbye Little Dream, Goodbye', are the ones that turn out for the best, although 'Weren't We Fools?' is overdone. Farnham's arrangements are fair enough, if blandly Concordian at times.

***** Let's Face The Music**
Concord CCD-4759-2 *McCorkle; Greg Gisbert (t, flhn); Conrad Herwig (tb); Jerry Dodgion (as, f); Chris Potter (ts, cl, f); Allen Farnham (p); Al Gafa (g); Steve Gilmore (b); Richard De Rosa (d, ky).* 10/96.

***** Someone To Watch Over Me**
Concord CCD-4798-2 *McCorkle; Randy Sandke (t, flhn); Conrad Herwig (tb); Jerry Dodgion (as, af); Chris Potter (ts, af); Allen Farnham (ky); Howard Alden (g); Steve Gilmore, Dick Sarpola (b); Richard De Rosa (d).* 10/97.

*****(*) From Broken Hearts To Blue Skies**
Concord CCD-4857-2 *McCorkle; Greg Gisbert (t, flhn); John Fedchock (tb); Jon Gordon(as, f); Dick Oatts (ts, ss, f); Allen Farnham (p); Al Gafa(g); Steve Gilmore (b); Richard De Rosa (d).* 10/98.

The first is an Irving Berlin tribute, and the rarities are what emerge best: 'Love And The Weather', a beautifully spare 'Better Luck Next Time' and a languorous 'Supper Time'. She has another go at 'There's No Business Like Show Business' and again overdoes it, although Farnham's arrangement also leans towards bombast. Excellent band, all the same.

Allen Farnham handles the charts again for the Gershwin album. These are among the most-sung and most-recorded songs of their century and, while the singer doesn't do anything to hurt them, it's asking a lot for anyone to make something fresh out of them at this stage (only the closing pairing of 'Will You Remember Me' and 'Drifting Along With The Tide' could be called unusual). Susannah does best by the slowest pieces, especially 'How Long Has This Been Going On'.

The subsequent *From Broken Hearts To Blue Skies* was her best for years. The only false note is 'I Ain't Gonna Play No Second Fiddle': McCorkle may harbour a great affection for the Bessie Smith style but it really doesn't suit her. 'Nuages' and a lovely 'Caminhos Cruzados' are impeccable, 'Laughing At Life' is wistful, 'A Phone Call To The Past' is a Henry Mancini nocturne that she handles supremely well, and even 'I Wish I Were In Love Again' isn't overdone.

*****(*) Hearts And Minds**
Concord CCD-4897-2 *McCorkle; Dick Oatts (ts); Allen Farnham (p); Paul Meyers (g); Steve Gilmore, Dennis Irwin (b); Tim Horner, Vanderlei Pereira (d); Thiago DeMello (perc).* 3/00.

She ought to be remembered as an important building-block in Diana Krall's style, a smart and wilful interpreter herself, and a stylist who did better than most in handling old standards with new manners, as well as trying to combine writers of different generations. She was getting that right more than ever: she does Dave Frishberg with the right measure of flipness, and the Simon Wallace–Fran Landesman tunes are a surprise, with 'Scars' a poignant climax. If she never made her masterpiece, she came close.

Jack McDuff (1926–2001)

ORGAN

'Brother' Jack McDuff – the familial prefix predated its fashionable use – was born in Champaign, Illinois, and made his name on the Chicago club circuit, subsequently touring with his own small combo. He touched on soul music and latterly called his band The Heating System, but it all remains based around his own style of bluesy organ jazz.

***** Brother Jack – Legends Of Acid Jazz**
Prestige 24220-2 *McDuff; Harold Vick (ts); Bill Jennings, Grant Green (g); Wendell Marshall (b); Alvin Johnson, Joe Dukes (d).* 1/60–61.

***** Tough 'Duff**
Original Jazz Classics OJC 324 *McDuff; Jimmy Forrest (ts); Lem Winchester (vib); Bill Elliot (d).* 7/60.

***** The Honeydripper**
Original Jazz Classics OJC 222 *McDuff; Jimmy Forrest (ts); Grant Green (g); Ben Dixon (d).* 2/61.

***** Brother Jack Meets The Boss**
Original Jazz Classics OJC 326 *McDuff; Harold Vick, Gene Ammons (ts); Eddie Diehl (g); Joe Dukes (d).* 1/62.

***** Screamin'**

Original Jazz Classics OJC 875 *McDuff; Leo Wright (as); Kenny Burrell (g); Joe Dukes (d).* 62.

***** Crash!**

Prestige 24131-2 *McDuff; Harold Vick, Eric Dixon (ts); Kenny Burrell (g); Joe Dukes (d); Ray Barretto (perc).* 1–2/63.

***** Live!**

Prestige 24147-2 *McDuff; Red Holloway, Harold Vick (ts); George Benson (g); Joe Dukes (d).* 6–10/63.

'Brother' Jack McDuff managed to shake loose from a basic Jimmy Smith influence to explore a subtler and less heavy-handed approach to organ jazz. The earlier stuff picked up by OJC now has a considerable CD showing and any of these discs will be welcomed into the library of any collector who feels they have sufficient Smith albums by now. Little to choose between the studio dates, though Harold Vick is rather unfairly made to play second fiddle to Ammons on *Brother Jack Meets The Boss*: his feature on 'Strollin'' is as good as anything the other tenorman comes up with. *Brother Jack* is in Prestige's 'Legends Of Acid Jazz' series and couples McDuff's first albums, *Brother Jack* and *Goodnight, It's Time To Go*. These are among his freshest records, the tightness of the earlier date blending with the excitement of the new band with Vick and Green, although Joe Dukes's messy drumming lets the second set down. 'McDuff Speaking' is a definitive rocker by the man. *Crash!* brings together the LPs *Somethin' Slick*, Kenny Burrell's *Crash!*, and a stray track from *Steppin' Out*. A generous selection, and the doubled-up punch of Vick and Dixon, who unite on the first two tracks, is a different twist. *Live!* gets the nod for an extra ounce of excitement, with the likes of 'Rock Candy' and 'Sanctified Samba' digging deep without losing sight of McDuff's inventiveness and willingness to pace himself through both a solo and a set. There are also interesting glimpses of the young George Benson at work.

***** Tobacco Road**

Atlantic 81227 3583 *McDuff; Fred Berry, King Kolax(t); John Watson (tb); Danny Turner(ts, f); Red Holloway (ts); Lonnie Simmons (bs); Roland Faulkner, Calvin Green (g); Loyal Gresham (b); Robert Guthrie, Joe Dukes (d); Bobby Christian (perc, vib).* 8/66.

Jack goes pop – though the track-listing is a bizarre one on that score. Only on a '60s crossover jazz record would you find 'Blowin' In The Wind' and 'Alexander's Ragtime Band' side by side. Amazingly, McDuff takes it all in good part and turns in some excellent playing.

****(*) Color Me Blue**

Concord CCD 4516 *McDuff; Red Holloway (as, ts); George Benson, Phil Upchurch, Ron Eschete (g); Kevin Axt (b); Joe Dukes (d); Denise Perrier (v).* 5/91.

***** Write On, Cap'n**

Concord CCD 4568 *McDuff; Byron Stripling, Joe Magnarelli (t); Herb Besson (tb); Andrew Beals (as); Jerry Weldon (ts); John Hart (g); Winston Roye (b); Van Romaine, Rudy Petschauer (d); Johnnie Lambert (v).* 6/93.

*****(*) It's About Time**

Concord CCD 45705 *McDuff; Andrew Beals (as); Jerry Weldon (ts); Joey DeFrancesco(org); Paul Bollenback, John Hart(g); Rudy Petschauer, Byron Landham (d).* 12/95.

***** That's The Way I Feel About It**

Concord CCD 4760 *As above, except add Chris Potter (f, af), Kip Reed (b); omit DeFrancesco, Bollenback, Landham.* 12/96–1/97.

*****(*) Bringin' It Home**

Concord CCD 4855-2 *McDuff; Andrew Beals (as); Red Holloway, Jerry Weldon (ts); John Hart, George Benson, Mark Whitfield (g); Frank Gravis (b); Rudy Petschauer, Grady Tate (d).* 8/98.

*****(*) Brotherly Love**

Concord CCD 4893 *McDuff; Red Holloway (ts, as); Andrew Beals (as); Jerry Weldon(ts); Joey DeFrancesco (org); John Hart, Pat Martino (g); Frank Gravis (b); Grady Tate, Rudy Petschauer (d).* 9/96–3/00.

McDuff's career – or mission – revived in the '80s and '90s, and there are several latter-day sets to savour. The musical equivalent of soul food, they're undemanding and curiously effective, and as the Cap'n settled in at the label they grew in calibre. *It's About Time* sets him up with Joey DeFrancesco, and all sorts of sparks and feathers fly along the way: their opening romp through 'Pork Chops And Pasta' is definitive. *Bringin' It Home* is also very much one to get. Graduates from the McDuff school like Benson and Holloway are here for the reunion, along with younger hands Whitfield, Hart and Beals, and the whole show is a thick, rich stew of bluesy small-combo sound that feels intensely satisfying. His final session, *Brotherly Love*, brings in Pat Martino and Red Holloway and again the whole thing feels as satisfying as ham hocks and gravy. 'Pork Chops And Pasta' does, indeed, make a return appearance in the shape of two live tracks in which the Cap'n and Joey renewed their friendly rivalry. Great fun and a lovely farewell for the old master.

***** The Best Of The Concord Years**

Concord CCD2-2171-2 2CD *As Concord albums above.* 91–00.

Concord's homage to one of the most reliable of their later signings has lots of fine stuff spread across the two discs, but surprisingly the music works better in its original album-length incarnations, where McDuff seemed to settle a band down across the course of a session and make it work for him. Retooled as a highlights package, the music seems somehow less effective. Still, not a bad buy.

Gary McFarland (1933–71)

VIBES, ARRANGER

McFarland began working as an arranger on the New York scene of the early '60s and quickly made a substantial name for himself with scores for Mulligan's Concert Jazz Band and others. After a series of albums for Verve and Impulse!, though, he retreated into a kind of small-group mood-music which has done his posthumous reputation no favours. He died suddenly of a heart attack, aged 38.

***** The October Suite**

Verve 654413-2 *Steve Kuhn (p); Ron Carter (b); Marty Morell (d); strings and woodwinds.* 10–11/66.

Although Kuhn's name is at the top of the marquee, this is more properly McFarland's album: he wrote and arranged all six pieces, and at present it's the only survivor of his 11 albums for Verve and Impulse! which is widely available. It's a strange record. Kuhn's playing dances inside and outside the underlying harmonies, resolutely avoids conventional areas of swing, and at times sounds like a rather bitter parody of Bill Evans's delivery (no coincidence, perhaps, that Evans had already recorded a comparable collaboration with McFarland). The composer scores a string quartet around the first three tracks, and a woodwind and harp group for the second: on 'Traffic Patterns', they seem to approximate the random interventions of car horns. The overall result is a mix of romanticism and atonality which is both very much of its period and queerly experimental. The piano sound is rather unglamorous in this remastering.

Rod McGaha

TRUMPET

Raised in Chicago by a jazz-buff father, McGaha has moved from an interest in soul and funk towards more straightahead playing.

***** Preacherman**
Compass 4273-2 *McGaha; Lori Meecham (p); Marc Harris (org); Roger Spencer (b); Chris Brown (d). 2/99.*

McGaha's debut eluded us but it was apparently an exercise in jazz hip-hop. This is much more straight down the line. Clark Terry is one of his mentors and there's a lot of Clark in his playing, which is full of squeezed notes, growls and brassy shouts ('Splip, Bam, Boom' is almost a Terry homage). The record seems designed more for airplay than anything and the tracks tend to come out as a series of routines, but within that framework it's enjoyably done, even if by the end one feels that McGaha has been set up as a kind of pasticheur. Another horn might help him to balance the books a little better.

Bernie McGann (born 1937)

ALTO SAXOPHONE

One of the major figures in contemporary Australian jazz, McGann has accrued an international reputation only slowly, but his intense playing is a classic example of 'deserving wider recognition'.

***** Ugly Beauty**
Rufus RF038 *McGann; Lloyd Swanton (b); John Pochee (d). 1/91.*

***** McGann McGann**
Rufus RF011 *As above, except add James Greening (tb). 8/94.*

*****(*) Playground**
Rufus RF023 *As above, except Sandy Evans (ts) replaces Greening.* n.d.

McGann's base in Sydney isolates him from a wider awareness, but he's a powerful, surprising, individual player whose work deserves wider currency. By working without a piano he opens these sessions up harmonically, yet he's a rather chameleonic player, as much in debt to the hard-bop masters as to Dolphy or Coleman. The weight and heft of his playing sometimes make him sound like a tenor player who's picked up the alto almost by chance, and when he locks horns with Pochee, especially on the extended rumpus created out of 'Without A Song' on *Ugly Beauty*, the music attains a terrific intensity. For all its heat and light, though, the trio session could use a centre of gravity: here and there the music seems to be grinding forward, and there's a lot of weight on McGann's shoulders.

Some of that is solved by *McGann McGann* and the recruitment of Greening, who actually takes the first solo on the record. With a Brookmeyer-like sense of humour and a big, vocal (rather than vocalized) sound, he's an apposite foil to the altoman. Some of the tunes have a bucolic charm about them, such as 'Brownsville' and 'June Bug', which makes one think of some of Jimmy Giuffre's more spirited music. But the whimsicality doesn't always work to the music's advantage.

Playground, though, solves that problem by introducing the tenor of Evans. She's not in the same league as McGann when it comes to putting together a convincing solo, relying too heavily on licks here and there, but for all that she's a tough and clear-headed performer whose contributions throw McGann's own solos into a fresh light. He's seldom sounded better than here, as fierce as ever when he wants to be, but as often turning to a slippery kind of phrasing which – given that he refuses to trade in clichés – is intriguingly personal and in hock to nobody else's jazz history. Swanton and Pochee play up to their best and Evans brings some fine tunes to the date, especially 'Snap' and the unsentimental 'Eulogy To A Friend'.

***** Kindred Spirits**
Rufus RF049 *McGann; Bobby Gebert (p); Jonathan Zwartz (b); John Pochée (d). 6-7/87.*

*****(*) Bundeena**
Rufus RF053 *McGann; Lloyd Swanton (b); John Pochée (d). 2/00.*

The reissue of *Kindred Spirits*, originally available as an Emanem LP in 1987, and the arrival of *Bundeena* allow McGann some stocktaking. There are drawbacks to the older session: Gebert isn't very helpful and the sound is often ragged, but it does pin down much of McGann's intensity, a drive to get the music out which his records don't always capture. *Bundeena* is, for McGann, almost tranquil. This is a long-established and harmonious trio by now, and for this session at least they sound like they feel like cooling off. So the likes of 'Big Moon', 'Maianbar' and 'The Last Postman' feature a hard-won lyricism that's all the more convincing for its relative scarcity in McGann's fierce output. Pochée especially plays with beautiful hands.

Howard McGhee (1918–87)

TRUMPET

The iconic young man with a horn, brooding, intense and self-destructive, McGhee was born in Tulsa, Oklahoma, grew up in Detroit and won his spurs in territory bands. Less of an innovator than either Fats Navarro or Dizzy Gillespie, his rather light tone and legato phrasing reflect an apprenticeship on clarinet. Maggie's recreational habits were to cost him dear but he was also a survivor, still gigging until late in life.

***** Howard McGhee On Dial – The Complete Sessions: 1945–47**
Spotlite SPJ CD 131 *McGhee; Teddy Edwards, James D. King, James Moody (ts); Vernon Biddle, Jimmy Bunn, Hank Jones,*

Michael 'Dodo' Marmarosa (p); Milt Jackson (vib); Ray Brown, Bob Kesterson (b); J. C. Heard, Roy Porter(d). 9/45–12/47.

*** Howard McGhee 1945–1946

Classics 1125 *As above, except add Karl George, Snooky Young (t); Vic Dickenson, Gene Roland (tb); Jimmy Bunn (p); Stan Morgan (g); Charles Mingus (b); Nat McFay (d); Pearl Taylor, Estelle Edison (v).* 45–46.

*** Howard McGhee 1946–1948

Classics 1089 *Similar to above, except add James Moody (ts); Hank Jones (p); Milt Jackson (p, vib); Percy Heath (b).* 46–48.

Howard was a prime mover in bebop on the West Coast. He came with Coleman Hawkins' group and stayed on, to the detriment of his health. The 1945–1946 Classics covers a range of material, including a big-band date and a few vocal sessions with Pearl Taylor and Estelle Edison. There's also an early glimpse of Charles Mingus. The most famous of his recordings of this time, however, are those made with Charlie Parker.

Bird's infamous 'Lover Man' sessions were originally issued under McGhee's name, but the four sides recorded in Los Angeles in 1945 for the Philo Aladdin label (and subsequently taken up by Dial) were his first as leader. They feature the twin tenors of Teddy Edwards and James D. King, the latter a friend from the Andy Kirk band. These and the jam band cuts from July 1946 are raw and rather shapeless. McGhee shows early signs of the bruised lyricism that became his signature in later years, but his phrasing is often indistinct and the line isn't always entirely convincing.

The Hollywood sextet of October 1946, which again uses Dingbod Kesterson and Roy Porter, but with the perennially undervalued Dodo Marmarosa on piano, is the first time one can really hear how fruitful an association the McGhee/Edwards front line was going to be. 'Dialated Pupils' (*sic*) and 'Up In Dodo's Room' (of which two versions survive) are strong bebop performances, and these were the cuts that began to reinforce McGhee's reputation, which was also being fostered by appearances with Jazz at the Philharmonic.

The New York tracks from December 1947 are oddly unsatisfactory, and 'Sleepwalker Boogie' may be the most telling title of the bunch, for McGhee seems to be running on autopilot. 'Night Mist' is magnificent (and also in two versions), but much of the interest comes from tenor saxophonist Moody and from the interplay between Milt Jackson and Hank Jones.

There are signs even this early that McGhee was turning into not just a powerful soloist but a useful composer as well. 'Thermodynamics' from 1946, the delightful 'McGhee Special' and earlier cuts like 'Intersection' and 'Life Stream' bespeak a thoughtful talent who threw off his earliest influences quite quickly. It does sometimes happen that Classics sets come out unchronologically. Whether the decision to release 1946–1948 and its successor before the 1945–1946 disc was enforced or deliberate isn't clear, but it certainly represents the trumpeter at the peak of his powers, having thrown off not just a borrowed style but also the shakiness that overtook some of his playing on the notorious Parker date. In these cuts from right across the country, he sounds in fine fettle, blowing strong and free in a variety of contexts and for a number of prominent and less prominent labels. The disc following is better still and completes the story of a wonderful year.

*** Howard McGhee 1948

Classics 1058 *McGhee; Fats Navarro (t); Billy Eckstine (vtb); Kenny Mann, Jesse Powell (ts); Jimmy Heath (as, bs); Milt Jackson (vib); Will Davis, Hank Jones (p); Ray Brown, Percy Heath (b); Joe Harris, J. C. Heard (d).* 2/48.

*** Maggie: The Savoy Sessions

Savoy 269 *As above, except add J. J. Johnson (tb); Rudy Williams (ts); Skeeter Best (g); Charlie Rice (d).* 2/48–52.

*** Howard McGhee 1949–1952

Classics 1294 *As above, except add Brew Moore (ts); Kenny Drew (p); Clifton Best (g).* 49–52.

Until very recently, McGhee wasn't well represented on CD, but Classics have now moved forward into the bebop era and the early picture is now a lot clearer. These sides from 1948 catch the trumpeter at a particularly tempestuous time, when music was taking a back seat to other imperatives. As ever, McGhee seems to alternate between intense, intuitive playing and banal passage-work, but the partnership with Milt Jackson is unexpectedly calm and centred, and there are half a dozen breathtaking moments from the trumpeter. 'I'm In The Mood For Love' is one of the finest things in Maggie's entire catalogue, but it is Jackson who shines on the opening 'Sweet And Lovely'.

The Classics compilation also includes material recorded in Paris for Vogue and Blue Star, working with Jimmy Heath, who was still on alto and not yet ready to shake off his 'Little Bird' tag. By the same analogy, Jesse Powell finds himself in the Lucky Thompson role, helping to anchor the top line but creating unexpected little paths of his own through the changes.

The set ends with one of the classic bebop encounters, the October 1948 one with the trumpeter who'd made the biggest impact on his developing style. These four sides are included on *The Fabulous Fats Navarro*, which anyone committed either to bebop or to the golden years of Blue Note will already have. As usual, the mastering does the music no favours, but hearing these numbers – 'The Skunk', 'Boperation' and two parts of 'Double Talk' – under McGhee's nominal leadership perhaps slants the emphasis away from Fats for a moment. Maggie's phrasing on the first track is intriguing, because again he seems to be imitating clarinet lines, a habit he shrugs off later on in the session in favour of a much crisper attack. Interesting as it is to approach these familiar tracks from an unfamiliar direction, the only real way to hear them is on the original Blue Note issue, which is reviewed under Fats Navarro's name.

One thinks of Charlie Parker's career as punctuated by the Savoy and Dial sessions, and the same is true of McGhee who made these dates for Savoy between February 1948 and 1952. There are some excellent things on the Savoy reissue from a jammed session with Jimmy Heath, Billy Eckstine on valve trombone and others; also later recordings made in the Pacific with a pianoless group that included J. J. Johnson and the little known Rudy Williams. The Classics set brings the story up to date, but the would-be buyer needs to do some judicious cross-checking of personnels and dates to get the best value out of this selection. We'd probably recommend the cheap and cheerful Classics route.

*** Maggie's Back In Town!

Original Jazz Classics OJC 693 *McGhee; Phineas Newborn (p); Leroy Vinnegar (b); Shelly Manne (d).* 6/61.

★★(★) Just Be There
Steeplechase SCCD 31204 *McGhee; Per Goldschmidt (t); Horace Parlan (p); Mads Vinding (b); Kenny Clarke (d).* 12/76.

McGhee was out of circulation for much of the '50s. On *Maggie's Back In Town!* he sounds straightened-out and clear-headed, tackling 'Softly As In A Morning Sunrise' and 'Summertime' at a hurtling pace that sounds good in the ensembles but flags a little when he is soloing. The opening 'Demon Chase', dedicated to Teddy Edwards's son, is similarly hectic, but is good-natured enough. 'Brownie Speaks', included in homage to Clifford Brown, stretches him a little more convincingly, but by then the set is over. There is really only one ballad, and 'Willow Weep For Me' takes a slightly hysterical edge (as do one or two of the other tracks) from Newborn's very tensed-up accompaniment.

★★★ Home Run
Storyville STCD 8273 *McGhee; Benny Bailey (t); Teddy Edwards, Sonny Redd (ts); Barry Harris, Art Hillery (p); Lisle Atkinson, Leroy Vinnegar (b); Bobby Durham, Billy Higgins (d).* 10/78–10/79.

★★★(★) Wise In Time
Storyville STCD 8272 *As above, except omit Redd, Harris, Durham.* 10/79.

McGhee was still holding his act together at the end of the '70s. The tone was still light and almost fragile, but there was an obduracy and determination in the logic of the playing which is still very appealing. Thirty years on from his debut, McGhee is once again happy to work in a more or less straight bebop form on occasions, programming Parker tunes like 'Moose The Mooche', 'Yardbird Suite' and 'Relaxin' At Camarillo'.

These albums are slightly confusing in that both also include material from the related Storyville set, *Young At Heart*, which was reviewed on LP in our first edition. The 1978 tracks with Benny Bailey sound like an attempt to recapture something of the sabres-at-dawn excitement of the McGhee–Navarro records. And yet it is the lyricism the two men share which comes across, rather than a simulacrum of the heady days of bop. The quintet with Edwards is by this stage rather like a comfortable old shoe, still capable of tramping out the miles without a pinch, and still capable of putting in a burst of speed on something like 'Moose The Mooche'. Autumnal jazz, but very beautiful.

Jimmy McGriff (born 1936)

ORGAN

Philadelphia-born, he learned a variety of instruments before studying organ at Juilliard. Had some single hits in the early '60s and has worked steadily as a club attraction since.

★★★ I've Got A Woman
Collectables 5752 *McGriff; Walter Miller (g); Richard Easley (d).* 62.

★★(★) One Of Mine
Collectables 5715 *McGriff; Morris Down (g, hca); Larry Frazier (g); Willie Jenkins (d).* 63.

With 'I Got A Woman' and 'All About My Girl', Jimmy became something of a jukebox star. They're both on this first record, which was originally released on Sue and is excerpted on the Blue Note compilation below. McGriff has more in common with Booker T. Jones than with the Jimmy Smith school, which is neither praise nor blame, but a description of what you'll hear: funky, unsubtle jazz-blues, played with maximum power and a minimum of introspection. Fans of this kind of music regard this first album as a sacred text.

The follow-up isn't anything like as exciting, as if Jimmy recognized even this early that he could make twice as many records by expending half as much energy. There's still more vim and vigour than you get later on, but it's all pretty haphazard stuff.

★★★ Jimmy McGriff At The Organ
Collectables 5716 *McGriff; Rudolph Johnson (ss, ts); Larry Frazier (g); Jimmie Smith (d).* 63.

★★★ Christmas With Jimmy McGriff
Collectables 5747 *As above.* 63.

★★(★) At The Apollo
Collectables 5316 *As above, except omit Smith; add Willie Jenkins (d).* 63.

In the wake of 'I Got A Woman', McGriff recorded prolifically. Less than a year after hitting the charts, he'd been back to the studio several times. *At The Organ* landed him another hit with 'Kiko', but there's some more jazz stuff here, with 'Jumpin' At The Woodside' and 'Shiney Stockings'. There's not much sophistication to the live set. Johnson (who doubles on soprano on the studio record) plays tenor the way Rocky Balboa speaks English; you get the emotion without necessarily understanding all of the vocabulary. Jimmy grinds and wheezes manfully and everyone presumably gets up and dances. The sound's pretty one-dimensional on the Apollo date, with the mics trained on Jimmy and no one else. The Christmas album is exactly how you imagine it, right down to the girl half-wearing a Santa Claus costume on the cover.

★★ Topkapi
Collectables 5717 *McGriff; rhythm section; orchestra.* 64–65.

A bunch of film and TV themes done the McGriff way. 'The Man With The Golden Arm' has a certain menace, but it's slim pickings apart from that.

★★★ Blues For Mister Jimmy
Collectables 5147 *McGriff; Larry Frazier (g); Jimmie Smith (d).* 65.

McGriff's last recording for Sue yielded another minor hit in 'Turn Blue' but the sound is increasingly formulaic and Frazier could almost be replaced with a guitar machine, so mechanical he sounds.

★★★ Pullin' Out The Stops! The Best Of Jimmy McGriff
Blue Note 830724-2 *McGriff; various unlisted groups.* 64–71.

★★★ The Worm
Blue Note 38699 *McGriff; Blue Mitchell (t); Danny Turner (as); Fats Theus (ts); Bob Ashton (bs); Thornel Schwartz (g); Bob Bushnell (b); Mel Lewis, Grady Tate (d).* 8/68.

★★ Electric Funk
Blue Note 84350 *McGriff; big band including Horace Ott (p).* 9/69.

His name will for ever be associated with his hits, 'I Got A Woman' and 'All About My Girl', chunks of organ funk that set a tone for instrumental soul in the same way (and at a similar moment) as the MGs were cooking up their stuff at Atlantic and Stax.

Both of those are on the *Pullin' Out The Stops!* compilation, which adds a further 15 tracks of steadily diminishing virtue. By the time of the awful 'Fat Cakes', from 1970, McGriff's groove sounds pooped. *The Worm* has some good moments, and some fine, excitable trumpeting from Mitchell, who revelled in this kind of thing. 'The Worm' itself was supposed to deliver a hit of 'Sidewinder' proportions, but didn't. Check out the nutty version of 'Take The "A" Train' at the other end of the disc. *Electric Funk* is a whole album of sad-sack funk from 1969 and it's hardly anything to get excited about, on or off a dance floor.

****(*) Countdown**
Milestone 9116 *McGriff; Clifford Adams Jr (tb); Marshall Keys (as); Arnold Sterling (ts, as); Melvin Sparks (g); Vance James (d).* 4/83.

***** The Starting Five**
Milestone 9148 *McGriff; Rusty Bryant (as); David 'Fathead' Newman (ts); Mel Brown, Wayne Boyd (g); Bernard 'Pretty' Purdie (d).* 86.

***** Blue To The 'Bone**
Milestone 9163 *McGriff; Al Grey (tb); Bill Easley (as, ts); Melvin Sparks (g); Bernard 'Pretty' Purdie (d).* 7/88.

****(*) Right Turn On Blues**
Telarc CD-83366 *McGriff; Hank Crawford (as); Rodney Jones (g); Jesse Hameen (d).* 1/94.

***** Blues Groove**
Telarc CD-83381 *McGriff; Hank Crawford (as); Wayne Boyd (g); Vance James (d).* 7/95.

***** The Dream Team**
Milestone 9268 *McGriff; David 'Fathead' Newman (ts); Red Holloway (ts, as); Mel Brown (g); Bernard 'Pretty' Purdie (d).* 8/96.

There seems little merit in differentiating between these records, since they're all basically the same. McGriff, these days playing Hammond's XB-3, which offers the old sound plus various MIDI tricks, pumps away at the blues in his filigree manner, rarely working up a head of steam and instead settling for a leaner line that carries the music on a slow simmer. He gets some of his favourite hornmen to keep him company, has either Vance James or Pretty Purdie thump out the beat, and that's it. Oh, and there's some guitar, too – Sparks, Boyd or Brown, what's the difference? Even Bob Porter, who produced *The Dream Team*, says that 'the best thing is to stay the hell out of the way and let them do their thing'. Well, yes and no. It wouldn't have hurt to have most of these records tuned up a bit. The studio sound is so polite that when the band hits a groove it sounds no different from when they're laying back and floating on the chords. Both the Telarcs (actually co-credited with old chum Crawford) and the Milestones are smooth enough to spread on toast, and if they'd piled everything right to the front of the mix it might actually sound exciting. But that isn't the way jazz records are made these days.

***** Straight Up**
Milestone MCD 9285 *McGriff; David 'Fathead' Newman (ts); Frank Wess (ts, f); Wayne Boyd, Rodney Jones (g); Bernard 'Pretty' Purdie (d).* 8/97.

Not half bad, as recent McGriff albums go. This was something of a renaissance for the organ man, though to be strictly honest, it's the supporting cast who make it the record it is. The cover image of a aerobatics team – smoke on – in vertical climb is less honestly descriptive than a World War II bomber in a slow dive would have been, but at least there's some energy to the playing here, even if each track drops its bombs in an entirely predictable pattern. The Isley Brothers' 'It's Your Thing' is the best thing of all – a long, steadily developing tune, with lots to do for the soloists.

***** McGriff's House Party**
Milestone MCD 9300 *McGriff; Kenny Rampton (t); Eric Alexander, Bill Easley (ts); Rodney Jones (g); Lonnie Liston Smith (org); Bernard 'Pretty' Purdie (d).* 00.

And wisely he invited along the impressively turbaned Dr Lonnie Smith and young turk saxophonist Eric Alexander, who blows his socks off. The party mood isn't always obvious on the record, which at moments sounds quite sober and studied, but when Smith and McGriff get their thing together, the walls shake. As on the earlier record, Purdie adds some fire and despatch to the rhythm, and shakes the dust off of McGriff's rather mechanical bass lines.

***** Feelin' It**
Milestone MCD 9313-2 *McGriff; Bill Easley (as, ts); David 'Fathead' Newman (ts); Ronnie Cuber (bs); Melvin Sparks, Wayne Boyd (g); Don Williams, Kenny Washington (d).* 10/00.

Still pretty smooth, but this one does have a bit more go in it. Getting in David Newman and doing remakes of 'Hard Times' and the like hardly strikes a blow for originality, and even when Fathead digs in, he's not exactly going in deep. If anything, Bill Easley outblows him. But the record has a nice, homecooked feel.

***** McGriff Avenue**
Milestone MCD 9325 *McGriff; Gordon Beadle, Bill Easley (ts); Ronnie Cuber (bs); Melvin Hassan, Rodney Jones (g); Wilbur Bascomb Jr (b); Bernard 'Pretty' Purdie, Don Williams (d).* 10/01.

One of a host of dates apparently booked into the studio on 11 September 2001 and brought to a premature halt. There's no obvious sign of shock or trauma about the reconvened session, but there is something dismayingly predictable about a version of 'America The Beautiful' on an album like this. Jimmy does also reprise 'The Worm' and 'All About My Girl' – two favourites of years gone by given fresh, if rather thin-voiced makeovers. Easley is still in top form and Ronnie Cuber makes his presence felt with some weighty baritone.

Bill McHenry

TENOR SAXOPHONE

New York tenorman with an insinuating style, part of a nexus of musicians recently recorded by Fresh Sound.

***** Jazz Is Where You Find It**
Fresh Sound FSNT 021 *McHenry; Ben Waltzer (p); Alexis Cuadrado (b); Jo Krause (d).* 3/97.

*****(*) Rest Stop**
Fresh Sound FSNT 033 *McHenry; Ben Monder (g); Chris Higgins (b); Dan Rieser (d).* 9/97.

***** Graphic**
Fresh Sound FSNT 056 *McHenry; Ben Monder (g); Reid Anderson (b); Gerald Cleaver (d).* 9/98.

***** Quartet Featuring Paul Motian**
Fresh Sound FSNT 160 *McHenry; Ben Monder (g); Reid Anderson (b); Paul Motian (d).* 5/02.

McHenry's limber sound and delivery lacks little in muscularity, but it's of a different order to the more brawny delivery of a traditional manner on the instrument. He has a thoughtful and somewhat introverted style which shouldn't be mistaken for diffidence. The first record was cut while he and Waltzer were spending time in Barcelona, and even in an ordinary live club set (in excellent sound) the musicians take pains to avoid the obvious. The tunes include Elisabeth Raspall's haunting 'Eix', John McNeil's 'Greenwich' and John Lewis's blues 'Two Degrees East, Three Degrees West'. Waltzer has a simple, supportive approach which is very appealing. The piano itself, though, seems pretty average.

The next three are in a sense all of a piece, Monder and McHenry making their way through music (mostly originals by Bill) which sounds like rather more abstruse variations on the Ornette Coleman style. Long melodic lines are twinned between tenor and guitar, or aphoristic little phrases are shaped into the basis of a theme. *Rest Stop* is our favourite because it seems like the most natural and least self-conscious, happy to play a 'Blues' which might have been a Lee Konitz–Billy Bauer set-piece, yet full of fresh and idiomatic improvising. Monder uses more effects on the subsequent *Graphic* and somehow the music feels a shade less appealing. The problem with the third album is the gentleman in the title. If you're a Motian fan, you'll likely find this the best record of all, but to us the drummer is simply too loud and strong for music which suits a quieter, defter touch. But McHenry's own playing, individual and hardly ever routine, is a consistent pleasure.

Kalaparusha Maurice McIntyre (born 1936)

TENOR SAXOPHONE, BASS CLARINET, PERCUSSION

One of the less well-known adherents of AACM in Chicago, McIntyre absorbed more from New York-based players like Coltrane and Ayler and still sounds very much in thrall to their intensely spiritual approach but with his own open tone and texture.

***** Humility In The Light Of The Creator**
Delmark 419 *Mcintyre; Leo Smith (t, flhn); John Stubblefield (ss); Malachi Favors (b); Thurman Barker (d); George Hines (v).* 2/69.

At first blush, McIntyre is a fairly orthodox New Thing modernist, exploiting Coltrane's extended harmony and the hands-on, little-instrument approach which was the AACM aesthetic. He also prefers open-textured music, with an emphasis on space, to the multi-note, broad-brush approach of some of his saxophone peers. The first album is very much in that more web-like sound-world and in an exploratory mould, though McIntyre always sounds more focused and organized than most of his contemporaries; compare him to a figure like Giuseppi Logan and he seems almost formal in organization. The opening sequence is a suite of short tracks under the general title 'Ensemble Love' followed by the far longer, almost 20-minute 'Ensemble Fate' and on this reissue by an alternate of 'Humility ...' which helps to show how organized McIntyre's concept of freedom was. Hines sings wordlessly, almost like another horn, and Smith helps to give the date its pan-cultural resonance.

***** Forces And Blessings**
Delmark DE 425 *McIntyre; Sarnie Garrett (g); Fred Hopkins (b); Wesley Tyus (d); Rita Omolokun Worford (v).* 11/70.

*****(*) Peace And Blessings**
Black Saint 120037-2 *McIntyre; Longineu Parsons (t, flhn, f, recorders); Leonard Jones (b); King I. Mock (d).* 6/79.

As time goes by, though, McIntyre seems a more individual figure, interested in African musics – most notably on *Forces And Blessings* – and in non-Western rhythms. The reissue of the 1970 album includes unissued alternatives of 'Behold! God's Sunshine' and 'Ananda', but neither is particularly revelatory.

Much more interesting is the Black Saint album, which is somewhat dominated by Parsons, a neglected figure. He is credited with probably the best number, 'Anyway You Want It', a tough, hard-edged piece with less improvisational hinterland than McIntyre's pieces. The album as a whole has the looseness and immediacy of a live set, but is crisply recorded.

***** Dream Of**
CIMP 174 *McIntyre; Michael Logan (b); Pheeroan akLaff (d).* 6/98.

The CIMP session is, as ever, taped with maximum veracity and no frills. McIntyre's first album in almost 20 years sounds like a throwback to an earlier age in jazz. Still a commanding voice, he has a hard and unforgiving sound which probably needs a gentler acoustic environment. 'Kalaparusha's Blues Changes' and 'Denise's Song' suggest he has veered closer to the mainstream over the years, but the overall impression is oddly forbidding.

**** South Eastern**
CIMP 247 *McIntyre; Jesse Dulman(tba); Ravish Momin (d).* 5/01.

***** The Moment**
Entropy Stereo 012 *As above.* 11/01.

****** Morning Song**
Delmark 553 *As above.* 9/02.

South Eastern needs a very sympathetic ear to extract much pleasure. As with the previous CIMP date, the sound doesn't suit the saxophonist, and it exposes the other two (both more than a generation younger than the leader) as near-charlatans. Dulman's daft tuba parts are a nonsense and Momin does a lot of clattering to no special effect. The later album, recorded live in front of a studio audience, is considerably better. Dulman's intros and accompaniments have the benefit of plainness, and Momin seems to have reined in his 'freedom' a bit in order to play some music. Henry Threadgill and John Coltrane are both given respect, and the spiritual agenda of 'I Don't Have An Answer Unless It's God' is clearly felt without being cloying or pretentious.

And then, back with Delmark after all those years, Kalaparusha And The Light (as he calls the trio) turn in an album that really has been worth waiting for. Despite the silliness of titles like 'Symphony No. 1', he turns in a set in which blues, bebop, raw field shouts and more abstract classical forms all seem to have contributed to an extraordinary musical alloy. There is a further and better version of 'I Don't Have An Answer ...', which suggests how much the group has evolved. Take our advice and treat the CIMPs as rehearsal tapes, interesting to listen to later, but certainly not a patch on this marvellous disc.

Ken McIntyre (1931–2001)

ALTO SAXOPHONE, FLUTE, OBOE, BASSOON

Studied in his native Boston and made some striking early records with Eric Dolphy, but moved into education after that and, aside from some Steeplechase sets from the '70s, that is largely where his energies have been directed since.

****(*) Stone Blues**

Original Jazz Classics OJCCD 1818 *McIntyre; John Mancebo Lewis (tb); Dizzy Sal (p); Paul Morrison (b); Bobby Ward (d).* 5/60.

*****(*) Looking Ahead**

Original Jazz Classics OJCCD 252 *McIntyre; Eric Dolphy (as, f, bcl); Walter Bishop Jr (p); Sam Jones (b); Art Taylor (d).* 6/60.

It remains McIntyre's misfortune to be remembered chiefly for his brief association with Eric Dolphy and to have been almost entirely overlooked for his work since, except in Scandinavia, where his stock remains high, partly due to the sponsorship of the Steeplechase label, who kept him from obscurity in the '70s. *Stone Blues*, with its obscure line-up, is a pretty undistinguished record, and only someone already securely interested in McIntyre's work will find much in it. It reveals a musician deeply influenced by Parker, but sounding like his own man in the search for a language beyond the orthodoxies of bebop. With the like-minded Eric Dolphy in tow, McIntyre made a more promising excursion on the well-named *Looking Ahead*, which is one of the most progressive recordings of its time, though Bishop, Jones and Taylor are still obviously thinking in the older idiom. Dolphy is, of course, superb, if still raw, and McIntyre almost inevitably plays second fiddle, but the younger man has his own things to say and he makes significant contributions to 'Lautir', 'Geo's Tune' and 'Dianna', not quite putting Dolphy in the shade but certainly making him wait in the shadows for a moment or two. The two saxophonists shared a joyous quality that was not much in evidence in the jazz of the time and there is an infectious exuberance to their side-by-side playing.

*****(*) The Complete United Artists Sessions**

Blue Note 57200 2CD *McIntyre; John Mancebo Lewis (tb); Jaki Byard, Ed Stoute (p); Ahmed Abdul-Malik, Ron Carter, Bob Cunningham (b); Edgar Bateman, Louis Hayes, Ben Riley, Warren Smith (d); Selwart Clarke (vn, cond).* 6/62–5/63.

For a period after recording his two discs for New Jazz, McIntyre had to go into teaching to make a living; he finally retired in 1996, with the promise that he would thenceforward concentrate on music again. In 1961 and 1962, though, gigs and recording opportunities were in perilously short supply. Of the few things that did emerge, *The Year Of The Iron Sheep* grabbed the attention, if only for its strange title and for the listing of a trombone player (John Mancebo Lewis) who didn't actually figure on the released disc. Michael Cuscuna, a McIntyre enthusiast, figured that there must be more material in the can and squirrelled away until he uncovered another half-dozen tracks from June 1962 which had not seen the light of day. They are included here on the second disc of this compilation of material produced by Alan Douglas and George Wein. The *Iron Sheep* session and the slightly earlier *Way, Way Out* should have established McIntyre as a significant player, but neither seems to have attracted more than sporadic attention, mainly from fellow musicians. *Way, Way Out* had come at the height of the enthusiasm for Third Stream crossovers; it features a largish string section under the direction of Selwart Clarke. 'Miss Ann', identified here as a McIntyre composition, makes some effort to swing, but the problem with the strings format is that the pace and sheer angularity of the material run counter to the players' ability to articulate it. It is, however, an intriguing experiment, and mostly successful. The group which made *Iron Sheep* was one that might well have served Dolphy, and the abiding impression of these sides is that they might well come from the older saxophonist, who at the time was just about to head off to his uncertain future in Europe. The previously unreleased material contains no great revelations, though 'Bootsie' and the long 'Turbospacey' are tracks that historians of the New Thing and believers in the continuum of African-American music should certainly look at with interest.

****(*) Hindsight**

Steeplechase SCCD 31014 *McIntyre; Kenny Drew (p); Bo Stief (b); Alex Riel (d).* 1/74.

***** Home**

Steeplechase SCCD 31039 *McIntyre; Jaki Byard (p); Reggie Workman (b); Andre Strobert (d).* 6/75.

***** Open Horizon**

Steeplechase SCCD 31049 *McIntyre; Kenny Drew (p); Buster Williams (b); Andre Strobert (d).* 11/75.

McIntyre recorded nothing for a decade, but came back when Steeplechase began to show an enthusiastic interest in progressive American jazz. These records have been out of circulation for some time but, as with much of the label's catalogue, are now reappearing on CD with vastly improved sound. Technical qualities apart, *Hindsight* still seems rather dull, and McIntyre's treatment of repertory material – 'Naima', 'Sonnymoon For Two', 'Body And Soul' and 'Lush Life' – is eccentric rather than creative. *Home* ranges from bouncy, Caribbean impressions to funkier 'portraits' and dark-toned essays which bring together Byard and Workman in tight, adventurous arrangements. *Open Horizon* covers a similar range of material (no standards) but with a wider improvisational purview, and McIntyre appears to use his alternative horns structurally rather than to cosmetic effect. One of the few jazz players to make convincing use of the bassoon (Illinois Jacquet is another), he generally keeps to the centre of its range, much as he does with the bass clarinet, eschewing Dolphy's furious overblowing.

***** Introducing The Vibrations**

Steeplechase SCCD 31065 *McIntyre; Terumasa Hino (t); Richard Harper (p); Alonzo Gardner (b); Andre Strobert (d).* 10/76.

*****(*) Chasing The Sun**

Steeplechase SCCD 31114 *McIntyre; Hakim Jamil (b); Beaver Harris (d).* 7/78.

The two later Steeplechases, which come just before McIntyre's effective retirement from recording, are interesting in comparison of scale. The larger group with second horn and piano sounds rather drab now, partly because the cast of players doesn't throw up a natural front-man to stand alongside the saxophonist. The trio with Jamil and Harris is perhaps the best thing McIntyre ever did, a rather delicate, spacious sound which uses Jamil to generate a bit of harmonic width as well as keeping time, and allows Harris, always a busy player, to state melodies as well as sustain the count. All the tunes are McIntyre originals and are uniformly of a length, nicely structured and contained.

***** A New Beginning**
Passin Thru 41215 *McIntyre; JoAnne Brackeen (p); Wilber Morris (b); Charli Persip (d).* 01.

It's hard not to trip over the ironies surrounding a record of this title, released in the final year of McIntyre's life on the Passin Thru label. Having devoted most of his energy to other pursuits, mostly jazz education, the multi-instrumentalist teamed up with this fine quartet and released a strong, forthright disc that suggested he was far from finished with jazz music. The tracks are mostly fairly short, song-based and atmospheric: 'Witch's Brew', 'Monk And Trane' and 'Breadfruit' are among the best of a dozen vivid originals that helped to restore Ken's reputation just as he left us. Fortunately, the discography is now in pretty good shape, with only the 1991 *Tribute* unaccounted for.

Dave McKenna (born 1930)

PIANO

Born in Rhode Island, McKenna spent much of the '50s in quiet sideman roles and much of the '60s with Bobby Hackett. He was still relatively unknown before signing with Concord in the '70s, where he has blossomed into an international name, one of the most reliable and hard-swinging of mainstream piano stylists with an encyclopedic knowledge of songs.

***** By Myself**
Shiah CD1 *McKenna (p solo).* 78.

***** Double Play: No Bass Hit / Major League**
Concord CCD 2123 *McKenna; Scott Hamilton (ts); Jake Hanna (d).* 3/79, 86.

***** Giant Strides**
Concord CCD 4099 *McKenna (p solo).* 5/79.

Dave McKenna hulks over the keyboard; *Giant Strides* it is. He is one of the most dominant mainstream players on the scene, with an immense reach and an extraordinary two-handed style which distributes theme statements across the width of the piano. It's a quality that's already evident on the early *By Myself*, now reissued by Shiah. Not the most impressive moment in the canon, but a good early sighting of a pianist who these days is recognizable at a hundred paces. The pace is mostly gentle and ballady, but there is a good version of Dave's original 'No More Ouzo For Puzo', which will intrigue those who remember later outings.

With the beginning of his Concord contract, Dave starts to punch his impressive weight. He doesn't threaten, he just plays, and on the earliest of these he plays up a storm. Long a 'players' player', he has grown in popularity and stature in recent years, not least through his association with the young Scott Hamilton, who plays a forceful but unquestionably secondary role on *No Bass Hit* and the follow-up *Major League*, which are now available as a twofer in line with Concord's policy of doubling up back catalogue items. The bass-less trio gives Dave some extra work to do, but it sounds like meat and drink to him.

***** No Holds Barred**
Progressive 7135 *McKenna; Warren Vaché (t); Al Cohn, Scott Hamilton (ts); Milt Hinton (b); Butch Miles (d).* 86.

Credited to the Dave McKenna Swing Six, this generational summit is now available with alternate takes of most of the songs. The reissue suggests a fairly relaxed and untroubled session with much of the attention diverted away from the nominal leader. Cohn is in great form and Hinton plays as if nobody else was around. The one original – 'Dave's Blues' – is despatched by the other guys with scant regard for its subtleties. An intriguing association, but by no means an essential McKenna record.

***** A Celebration Of Hoagy Carmichael**
Concord CCD 4223 *McKenna (p solo).* 5/83.

*****(*) Dancing In The Dark**
Concord CCD 4292 *As above.* 8/85.

*****(*) Live At Maybeck Recital Hall: Volume 2**
Concord CCD 4410 *As above.* 11/89.

*****(*) Shadows And Dreams**
Concord CCD 4467 *McKenna (p solo).* 3/90.

*****(*) A Handful Of Stars**
Concord CCD 4580 *As above.* 6/92.

McKenna is that rare phenomenon, a pianist who actually sounds better on his own. Though he is sensitive and responsive in group playing, and the association with Hamilton proves that, he has quite enough to say on his own account not to need anyone else to hold his jacket. The Hoagy tribute, recorded at the Second Story Club and the Tubaranch in Bloomington, Indiana, demonstrates his ability both to tame an audience and illuminate some turgid material in the process. No such problems (the former, at any rate) at Maybeck Hall, where the audiences are famously well behaved and attentive. McKenna's first Berkeley recital – *Handful Of Stars* was also played on that warm-hearted piano – is among the best of his solo performances. He medleys – a frequently tiresome practice – with considerable ingenuity and absolute logic, switching hands, reversing the direction of the new theme and carefully disguising the welds. The 'Knowledge Medley' sounds odd and contrived on paper ('Apple For The Teacher', 'I Didn't Know What Time It Was', 'I Wish I Knew', 'You'll Never Know' – you get the idea?) but works superbly in performance. The final 'Limehouse Blues' is archetypal.

Jazz players owe Arthur Schwartz an enormous debt. There are well over 50 versions of 'Alone Together' in the current catalogue, a record that approaches old warhorses like 'Body And Soul' and 'All The Things You Are'. McKenna treats the tunes on *Dancing In The Dark* with considerable respect, preserving their shape rather than just winkling out the meat of the chords. 'A Gal In Calico' and 'I See Your Face Before Me', both routinely sentimentalized, are played with exemplary taste, and the title-track has almost as much innate energy as a much later composition of the same name by a Bruce Springbok or Springstream, something like that. The 1990 solo disc is a 'Dreams' and 'Shadows' medley, but McKenna is as distinct and wide-awake as ever. One of his best.

***** You Must Believe In Swing**
Concord CCD 4756 *McKenna; Buddy DeFranco (cl).* 97.

As if to confound our insistence that McKenna is best heard solo, Concord started to pair him off with interesting horn men.

The ten duets with Buddy DeFranco offer a few more highs, though also some rather pedestrian stuff. 'The Song Is You' is stunning and there is a bit of clever bebop on 'Anthropology', with DeFranco hardening his tone slightly to cope with the more frantic pace. It's Buddy who comes off best here. Though Dave plays some very effective solos, he's not the main focus of the record and his fans might be disappointed.

*****(*) An Intimate Evening With Dave McKenna**
Arbors ARCD 19264 *McKenna (p solo).* 11/99.

On the eve of his 70th, the saloon pianist turns in a typical solo recital. Nicely recorded on a decent piano, this is as fine a place as any to hear him, now that his Concord run has apparently finished. His encyclopaedic knowledge of songs comes out in three characteristic medleys; 'Fidgety Feet' takes in ragtime and stride.

Carlos McKinney

PIANO

Gifted sideman, now making a mark as leader.

***** Up-Front**
Sirocco 1002 *McKinney; Antoine Roney (ss, ts, bcl); Buster Williams (b); Ralph Penland (d).* 00.

Carlos starts his solo debut with a standard, 'You And The Night And The Music', and introduces his muscular romanticism that way. It comes out again on the short, self-written 'Mademoiselle Gregoire' and on the following 'Black Beauty'. He claims most of the writing credits, and it's interesting that Buster Williams, also a fine writer, isn't given a track to himself. He's quieter here, and more workmanlike and subdued than on most of his recent outings; indeed, it's not until later in the set that you'd be able to say definitively that Buster is the bass-player. Roney brings a range of timbres and tonalities with his three horns and Penland goes to work with his usual lack of fuss.

McKinney's Cotton Pickers

GROUP

Originally led by drummer Bill McKinney, they were hired by Jean Goldkette for a residency at his Detroit Graystone Ballroom in 1927. Hugely popular, they eventually recorded several sessions in New York, but the band declined when several key players left in the early '30s, and it disbanded in 1934.

*****(*) McKinney's Cotton Pickers 1928–29**
Classics 609 *John Nesbitt, Langston Curl, Joe Smith, Leonard Davis, Sidney De Paris, George 'Buddy' Lee (t); Rex Stewart (c); Claude Jones, Ed Cuffee (tb); Don Redman, George Thomas (reeds, v); Milton Senior, Prince Robinson, Jimmy Dudley, Benny Carter, Coleman Hawkins, Ted McCord (reeds); Todd Rhodes, LeRoy Tibbs, Fats Waller (p); Dave Wilborn (bj, g, v); Ralph Escudero, Billy Taylor (tba); Cuba Austin, Kaiser Marshall (d); Jean Napier (v).* 7/28–11/29.

****** Put It There Vol. 1**
Frog DGF25 *As above.* 7/28–11/29.

*****(*) McKinney's Cotton Pickers 1929–1930**
Classics 623 *As above, except add James P. Johnson (p).* 11/29–11/30.

****** Cotton Picker's Scat Vol. 2**
Frog DGF 26 *As above.* 1–12/30.

***** Shag Nasty Vol. 3 – The Alternate Masters**
Frog DGF 27 *As above.* 7/28–9/31.

It was primarily John Nesbitt who built McKinney's Cotton Pickers (although Jean Goldkette, who booked the band into his Graystone Ballroom in 1927, gave them their name). Redman's arrival in 1928 brought his distinctive touch as arranger to the band's book, but Nesbitt's driving and almost seamless charts were as impressive, and they remain so, more than 60 years later. McKinney's Cotton Pickers were among the most forward-looking of the large bands of their era: while the section-work retains all the timbral qualities of the '20s, and the rhythm section still depends on brass bass and banjo, the drive and measure of the arrangements and the gleaming momentum of their best records both suggest the direction that big bands would take in the next decade.

On the later, New York sides, guest soloists include Coleman Hawkins, Rex Stewart and Fats Waller, and Benny Carter has one of his sharpest early outings on 'I'd Love It'. But Nesbitt, Robinson and Redman himself are significant players on the earlier sides, and the precision and verve of the band *in toto* is the main point of most of these tracks. Some of the vocals are banal, but that's the price on many such discs of the period. The recent reissues on Frog are easily the first choice in this important music, top-notch remastering by John R. T. Davies from fine original copies, and the great power and swing of the band come through better than ever. Whatever sources Classics used, they weren't as good, and in any case these discs came out some years earlier. *Shag Nasty* completes the story by rounding up various alternative takes: for specialists only, perhaps, but in itself still a fine CD.

Mike McKoy

VOCAL, GUITAR

Son of a Jamaican father and German mother, he grew up in England, with Italian neighbours. A cinch for the bossa nova.

***** Swings To The Bossa Nova**
Zephyr ZECD 35 *McKoy; Bobby Wellins (ts); Anthony Kerr (vib); Pete LeTanka (p); Simon Woolf (b); Simon Morton (d).* 7/02.

In his liner-note, Dave Gelly points to McKoy's instinct for languages as a key to his success with this repertoire. Certainly, it's difficult to hear these as anything other than authentic performances, and the decision to tape the sessions live (at London's Pizza on the Park) was an inspired one. Jobim dominates the set-list and 'Chega De Saudade', 'Retrato Em Branco E Preito', as well as a certain girl from Ipanema, are wonderfully graceful performances. That said, the stand-out track is Pat Martino's 'Estate', given a wonderfully fluent and evocative reading. Wellins is as light-toned and wistfully romantic as ever and the rhythm section is solid but relaxed, with Kerr in spanking form.

Hal McKusick (born 1924)

ALTO SAXOPHONE, CLARINET, BASS CLARINET

Work with Claude Thornhill and Boyd Raeburn was followed by small-group recordings in the '50s, some of which McKusick led himself. A cool stylist on alto and quite an adventurous thinker, but much of his best work is currently out of print.

*** Triple Exposure

Original Jazz Classics OJCCD 1811 *McKusick; Billy Byers (tb); Eddie Costa (p); Paul Chambers (b); Charli Persip (d).* 12/57.

It was meeting George Russell in the mid-'50s that set McKusick on a course which might have seemed deliberately perverse to other players, exploring the outer edges of harmony, a complex approach to counterpoint, unusual and sometimes awkward time-signatures, and instrumentations that are not normally associated with jazz.

McKusick always took a thoughtful, melodic approach to soloing, keeping the tune in view at all times, rarely straying far into vertical fantasies. He's still perhaps best known for his clarinet work with Charlie Parker, and for the fine *Cross Section Saxes*, where he mixes ballad standards, 'Now's The Time', and 'Stratusphunk' by George Russell, a composer with whom he had a close relationship. *Triple Exposure* is probably the most straightforward representation of his playing style. The two horns blend particularly well on 'Con Alma', which is the archetypal McKusick performance. With *Quintet* and *Cross Section Saxes* still both in limbo, he's rather marginalized at present.

John McLaughlin (born 1942)

GUITARS, GUITAR SYNTHESIZER

The story of the Yorkshire-born guitarist's recruitment by Miles Davis is a modern musical legend. McLaughlin was very much part of the reinvention of jazz and its accommodation to rock in groups like Miles's, Lifetime and his own Mahavishnu Orchestra. An intense electric player, he has also been influenced by Indian philosophies and by the flamenco tradition.

♛ **** Extrapolation

Polydor 841598 *McLaughlin; John Surman (bs, ss); Brian Odges (b); Tony Oxley (d).* 1/69.

*** My Goal's Beyond

Rykodisc 10051 *McLaughlin; David Liebman (ss); Jerry Goodman (vn); Billy Cobham (d); Mahalakshmi, Airto Moreira, Badal Roy (perc).* 6/70.

*** Devotion

Movie Play 74058 *McLaughlin; Larry Young (org); Billy Rich (b); Buddy Miles (d).* 9/70.

**** Where Fortune Smiles

BGO 1006 *McLaughlin; John Surman (bs, ss); Karl Berger (vib); Dave Holland (b); Stu Martin (d).* 71.

Extrapolation is one of the finest jazz records ever made in Europe. Ranging between gently meditative runs, as on 'Peace Piece', and furious 13/8 scrabbles, it combines all of McLaughlin's virtues (accuracy, power, vision) on a single disc. It has transferred to CD reasonably well, though Odges and some of McLaughlin's lower runs sound slightly artificial. The band was state-of-the-art for 1969. Oxley's drumming has the firmness of a rock beat, even when the count is extremely irregular, and Surman's playing is cast midway between folksy melodizing and complete abstraction. Tie to a chair any British jazz fan who came of age between 1967 and 1972, and a substantial number will confess that 'Binky's Beam' is their favourite track of all time. Those who attempt to deny McLaughlin's *bona fides* as a jazzman or more generally as an improviser almost always refer to *Shakti*, pseudo-classical pieces like the *Mediterranean Concerto* or one of the duff Mahavishnu Orchestra records like *Visions Of The Emerald Beyond*. They generally keep stumm about *Extrapolation*. This is essential and timeless. The record's availability is vexingly erratic, but we are listing it anyway

My Goal's Beyond is by no means as wet as the album's design and image might suggest, and it is also a great deal more securely lodged in a jazz tradition. The original side one is a series of brief blowing themes, most of them dispatched very crisply, with McLaughlin's acoustic lines almost abrasively focused. The remainder of the album is devoted to two longer pieces 'Peace One' and 'Peace Two'. The objection to these is not so much that they are 'Indian' rather than 'jazz' as that they are so slackly conceived. The punning titles strongly suggest that these were worked up quickly and without much in the way of expressive focus and they make rather sorry listening 30 years on.

We've always been very drawn to *Devotion*, which is about as close as McLaughlin gets to straightforward rock'n'roll. Much in the vein of McLaughlin's power trio, Lifetime, it again features the churning organ of Larry Young, as well as members of Jimi Hendrix's controversial and underrated Band of Gypsies line-up. 'Dragon Song' was popularized by British organist Brian Auger and the Trinity, but this is an equally invigorating performance. 'Don't Let The Dragon Eat Your Mother' and 'Devotion' are very similar to the Mahavishnu Orchestra's extended rock but grittier than the later band was to be, more's the pity.

If anyone wants to trace back the lineage of the Orchestra, then the reissued *Where Fortune Smiles* is the place to look. Anticipations of Jan Hammer's rippling arpeggiations and electronic soars can be heard in Berger's vibes and Surman's deceptively plain-spoken saxophone lines. It would be stretching it a bit to suggest that Dave Holland fulfilled the violin part, except that he does play genuine counter-melodies and does so in a rich, stringy tone that was so different from the amplified bass playing of the time. When this record came along, a new idiom seemed securely in place. Later, as we've said, it became fashionable to deride it, but even after 30 years the musicianship is immediately impressive and the overall conception still valid. *Extrapolation* is still the masterwork, but its successor repays attention as well. Catch it while it's still around.

*** Shakti

Columbia CK 46868 *McLaughlin; L. Shankar (vn); R. Raghavan (mridangam); T. H. Vinayakaram (perc); Zakir Hussain (tabla).* 75.

Sweetly complex acoustic music that was initially hard to absorb after the fantastic energy of the original Mahavishnu Orchestra, but which was infinitely more impressive than the OTT gestures and uneasy syntheses of Mk II. Shankar quickly went on to personal stardom, but the real drama of this set (which is much superior to the later *Handful Of Beauty*) is the interplay between McLaughlin and the tabla and clay pot percussion. Though it appeared to many fans that McLaughlin had simply gone native, it's easier in hindsight to see the continuity of all his work, in bop-influenced advanced rock, fusion, flamenco and Eastern forms, rather than its apparent breaks and changes of direction.

***** Electric Dreams**

Columbia CK 48892 *McLaughlin; David Sanborn (as); Stu Goldberg (p, org, syn); L. Shankar (vn); Fernando Sanders (b); Tony Smith (d, v); Alyrio Lima (perc).* 11–12/78.

The One Truth Band was the successor to Mahavishnu. It conspicuously lacked both the spiritual intensity and the sheer musicianship of the earlier band, though there was no longer any doubt as to who was in charge. This is much more obviously a lead instrument and rhythm, without much in the way of group improvisation. Echoes of John's first dabblings in electric jazz are reinforced by a piece dedicated to and named after 'Miles Davis', returning the trumpeter's *Bitches Brew* compliment. 'Dark Prince' is in similar vein. Stu Goldberg is revelatory on keyboards, and Sanborn as ever creates some emotional excitement, but by and large the group never rises above competent anonymity and a kind of pumped-up energy.

***** Friday Night In San Francisco**

Columbia CK 65168 *McLaughlin; Paco DeLucia, Al DiMeola (g).* 80.

*****(*) Passion, Grace & Fire**

Columbia 38645 *As above.* 10–11/82.

Though honours are very deliberately closed at even and the illusion of joint leadership scrupulously maintained throughout, we have always found these sets to be rather pointlessly adversarial. Separating the component voices is easier on the later session, where the separate strands of interaction can be teased out. All three contribute characteristic themes: McLaughlin with 'Aspen' and 'David', which come from the milder end even of his recent output. *Friday Night* has been a successful and very popular album, but it never rises above its occasion or the simple fact of having this distinguished trio on a single stage together. Appealing as they are, we've found that these sets pall even after a couple of visits to the CD player.

****(*) Adventures In Radioland**

Verve 519397-2 *McLaughlin; Bill Evans (sax, ky); Mitchel Forman (ky); Abraham Wechter (g); Jonas Hellborg (b); Danny Gottlieb (d, perc).* 1–2/86.

Confusingly, McLaughlin revived the Mahavishnu name for this project which bears no discernible relation to the early-'70s group. Dropping the 'Orchestra' tag was a little ironic, because all the synclavier digital equipment and Sycologic PSP drum interfaces and synths give the band a b-i-g expensive sound that conjures up adjectives like 'orchestral' willy nilly, but not without some irony. It seems that these recordings lay in the vault for some time before release. If so, one can easily relate to the marketing problem. Having done the stratospheric electric god bit, McLaughlin had recolonized a corner of the acoustic empire, and it must have been difficult to know how this testosterone-dripping sound would take. The problem lies not so much with the playing as with the writing, which is uniformly drab and unconvincingly macho. Evans's squawking solos flap through chicken-coop effects from Forman's keyboards, while Hellborg and Evans plug away humourlessly in the background. There are flashes of the old McLaughlin on 'Reincarnation' (not just the title) and 'Florianapolis', but generally this is bankrupt stock, and the much-heralded return to electricity goes nowhere fast.

****** Qué Alegría**

Verve 837280-2 *McLaughlin; Kai Eckhardt, Dominique De Piazza (b); Trilok Gurtu (d).* 11–12/91.

Designer stubble on the liner-photo and the most robust set from McLaughlin in a long time. Gurtu has always been a pulse-driven percussionist, rarely content merely to provide exotic colours round the edges of the music, and he and the bassists (Eckhardt appears on 'Reincarnation' and '1 Nite Stand', the two most forceful tracks) push McLaughlin's acoustic but subtly MIDI'd lines almost to the limits. Very little sign of the rather soft-centred flamenco approach and Indo-fusions that have dominated his work for many years. Excellent.

****(*) Time Remembered**

Verve 519861-2 *McLaughlin; Aighetta Guitar Quartet: François Szonyi, Pascal Rabatti, Alexandre Del Fa, Philippe Loli (g); Yan Maresz (b).* 3/93.

McLaughlin's equation of Bill Evans = romanticism = guitars is the first and most serious thing wrong with this record. The Aighetta Quartet have performed many of the finest works for guitar ensemble, including, trivia collectors, one by the late British novelist and composer *manqué*, Anthony Burgess. Though there is nothing inherently wrong with having an essentially classical group play Evans's music (after all, the Kronos Quartet had done it), this is just not the group. In a brief personal memoir of Evans, McLaughlin remembers the pianist performing at the Village Vanguard and going into what he, very perceptively, describes as a 'state of grace'. The point was that Evans's trances were hard-won, the result of a profound dialectical approach to his material, not just an on/off mysticism. *Time Remembered* drifts all too readily into such a state. The music (familiar and beautiful themes like 'Turn Out The Stars' and, of course, 'Waltz For Debby') has no tension. Lacking drama, it ultimately lacks interest, and a rather short set is beset with longueurs which eventually torpedo it.

***** Tokyo Live**

Verve 521870-2 *McLaughlin; Joey DeFrancesco (org, t); Dennis Chambers (d).* 12/93.

*****(*) After The Rain**

Verve 527467-2 *As above, except replace Chambers with Elvin Jones (d).* 10/94.

McLaughlin calls this new group the Free Spirits. The organ/guitar/drums line-up has become modestly fashionable again; John Abercrombie has experimented with it, and McLaughlin really sounds as if he's having *fun* for the first time in a long while. He extends the big, chunky sound he was exploring again in the mid-'80s, throwing in Wes Montgomery octave-runs and some of his own old wobbly chords. 'JuJu At The Crossroads' is terrific, though it has to be said that some tracks, notoriously the closing 'Mattinale', drag their feet unconscionably in a way they couldn't have been allowed to do in a studio. Positive sign, though: wanting to play as long as that.

Still Free Spirited, but darker and more serious in tone and with one significant change of personnel, *After The Rain* is a set of Coltrane and Coltrane-associated pieces, with a couple of McLaughlin originals thrown in. The immediate reaction on hearing those organ bass-lines and every-which-way cymbal patterns is that this is some forgotten item from the McLaughlin–Larry Young–Tony Williams terror trio, Lifetime. Too cleanly recorded, though, and McLaughlin's guitar has a plainer, quasi-acoustic ring, not the full-choke distortion of earlier years. Like his predecessor, but with less competition, Jones is almost too much in this context. The opening workout on 'Take The Coltrane' very nearly damps enthusiasm for what's to come, except that 'My Favorite Things' and 'Sing Me Softly Of The Blues' and then 'Naima' (in which Jones dramatically switches to big palpitating tattoos on his skins) are so damn beautiful that you'd forgive him anything.

The mood is more sombre in the second half, and the drummer is less dominant, as if satisfied by his spot on McLaughlin's 'Tones For Elvin Jones'. On the face of it, 'Crescent' and 'After The Rain' aren't the likeliest items for this treatment, but they are exquisitely re-imagined, and demand to be heard again and again. A lovely record; shame about the rock album fades, though.

***** The Promise**

Verve 529828-2 *McLaughlin; David Sanborn (as); Michael Brecker (ts); Jeff Beck, Philippe Loli, Paco DeLucia, Al DiMeola (g); Joey DeFrancesco (org, t); Jim Beard, Tony Hymas (ky); Nishat Khan (sitar, v); Pino Palladino, James Genus, Yan Maresz, Sting (b); Dennis Chambers, Vinnie Colaiuta, Mark Mondesir (d); Don Alias, Trilok Gurtu (perc); Zakir Hussain (tabla); Susana Beatrix, Stephania Bimbi, Mariko Takahashi (v).* 95.

What is 'the promise'? The notion perhaps that, just as there are always new fields to explore, so too the past is never quite shut off, that there are always places to go, forward or back. McLaughlin has always been a restless explorer of his own past, unusually conscious of his own back-catalogue. In a sense, this record is a re-run of *Electric Guitarist*, a sampling of tracks by half-a-dozen different line-ups, collaged with readings from Dante, Lorca and haiku. The effect is bitty and slightly bewildering, but there are treasures to be found. The Free Spirits trio is convened for 'Thelonious Melodius'. It immediately follows a guitar workout on John Lewis's 'Django', with Jeff Beck – of all people – as second guitar. An even less likely personnel credit is Sting, who joins McLaughlin and Vinnie Colaiuta for one minute and twelve seconds of head-down jamming; wonder if he kept the cab waiting. Another long-standing trio, with DeLucia and DiMeola, reappears for 'El Ciego', a slightly routine dip into their emotive contrapuntal bag. The really substantial stuff (and the bulk of the album) is contained in two saxophone-led tracks: 'Shin Jin Rui' with the guest performer *par excellence*, David Sanborn; and the long, long 'Jazz Jungle', with the even more ubiquitous Michael Brecker up front. The latter degenerates into a bit of a jam but, with saxophone and guitar swapping ideas at ever higher altitudes, it's sustained by sheer excitement and pace, even over 14 minutes. One fascinating oddity is 'No Return' (which is presumably not McLaughlin's philosophy). Here he swaps places with DeFrancesco, who gets out his trumpet while the boss doubles on keyboards. Most of the ideas have been heard before, but never in this configuration, and it might have been more effective to leave it to the end of the record, which concludes on an ultra-mellow acoustic reading of Jimmie Rowles's 'The Peacocks'. Though this is a minor miscall, what comes across throughout the album is the extent of McLaughlin's fascination with the studio and its potentialities. He clearly wants to create an integrated and emotionally supple product that cancels out the item-by-item approach. He hasn't quite succeeded, but with continued major-label backing he has the opportunity to experiment further. A valid experiment by a major artist.

***** The Guitar Trio**

Verve 533215-2 *McLaughlin; Paco DeLucia, Al DiMeola (g).* 5–7/96.

Divided by a common instrument, common language, or by a gentle ambition to make the strongest impact on this collaborative set? Composition, solo and production credits are divided with almost schoolboyish even-handedness, and the disc gives every indication of having been A&R'd by committee. Not that the playing isn't superlative. McLaughlin's two solos on 'Le Monastère Dans Les Montagnes' and his introduction on 'Midsummer Night', both his own compositions, are magisterial and quite beautiful. His partners contribute their share and more, with DeLucia sounding relaxed and unemphatic, but totally focused. DiMeola is the wild card, but for once he resists a long-standing tendency to grandstand and overstate; his composition, 'Azzura', is perhaps the best thing on the whole album, a rich soundscape that inspires a wonderful opening solo from McLaughlin as well. Despite a slightly contrived summit conference feel, this is a marvellous album and one that will appeal to jazz guitar fans of every persuasion.

*****(*) The Heart Of Things**

Verve 539153-2 *McLaughlin; Gary Thomas (ts, ss, f); Jim Beard (p, syn); Jean-Paul Celea, Matthew Garrison (b); Dennis Chambers (d); Victor Williams (perc).* 97.

****** Live In Paris**

Verve 543536-2 *As above, except omit Beard, Celea; add Romario Ruiz (ky).* 11/98.

Old question: What would Charlie Parker, Eric Dolphy, Jimi Hendrix, Jaco Pastorius, Emily Remler, whoever, be doing if he, she, it were alive in the late '90s? In all but name, this is a Mahavishnu Orchestra for the end of the century, stripped of much of the Eastern philosophy, hooked into a more contemporary sound, but identifiable from the same balance of ensemble and individual playing, the same flyaway soloing, and the easily missed glint of steel amid the gentleness. Compared to previous horn players – Liebman, Evans – Gary Thomas is a tough customer, and he prompts a more abrasive and confrontational sound from McLaughlin who, as in recent years, alternates electric and acoustic with MIDI guitars. The last of these performs much the same function as Jan Hammer's Moog had in the Ork, leaving Beard and Thomas to round out the front line in the same top-heavy way. The best of the music is concentrated in three long tracks: 'Acid Jazz' (which ain't), 'Seven Sisters' and a beautiful idea called 'Fallen Angels', which does as the album-title suggests and cuts to the essential. These days, McLaughlin doesn't sound so chilled as to be uninvolving, but he has managed to broker a philosophical position which allows him to play relatively free without lapsing into free-jazz cliché, and to revisit aspects of his own past without succumbing to nostalgia or self-regard.

The live album may well be compared in future to Miles's classic set in the same city and it focuses the energies of what has become McLaughlin's repertory band to an impressive degree. If this is what they can reproduce on tour, the prospects are scarily good. 'Fallen Angels' and 'Acid Jazz' are again the standout tracks and there is a beautiful tribute to the late Tony

Williams, who would have enjoyed music of this intensity and rhythmic complexity. With a Ruiz, a Garrison, a Chambers and a Williams in the line-up, to say nothing of the redoubtable Thomas, it's hard to see how John McLaughlin can go wrong.

***** Remember Shakti**

Verve 559945-2 2CD *McLaughlin; Hariprasad Chaurasia (bansuri); Zakir Hussein (tabla); T. H. Vinayakram (ghatam).* 97.

Reconvened for a tour that included these British dates, Shakti is still a compelling unit, though lacking the sheer percussive impact of the original group. Split over two discs, the set is dominated by an hour-plus performance of Chaurasia's 'Mukti', and there are also long versions of the flautist's 'Chandrakauns' and McLaughlin's 'Wish'. The pace is inevitably rather slacker and more meditative than of yore, but there is plenty of virtuosic playing and a joyous abandon which fans of the original group will value.

***** Remember Shakti – The Believer**

Verve 549044-2 *McLaughlin; Zakir Hussain (tabla); U. Shrinivas, V. Selvaganesh (perc).* 99.

***** Remember Shakti – Saturday Night In Bombay**

Verve 014164-2 *As above, except add Debashish Bhattacharya (g); Sivamani Bhavani Shankar (perc); Shankar Mahadevan (v).* 00.

Stopgap live albums while he figures out what to do next. The Shakti reunion clearly has festival mileage in it, but there's little pressing reason for these sets to exist in merely musical terms, and certainly no hint of fresh ground. Two more for fans to put on the shelf.

****** Montreux Concerts**

Warner Music Switzerland 50-50466-9701-21 17CD *McLaughlin; Bill Evans (ss, ts); Gary Thomas (ts, f); Bob Knapp (f, perc); Steve Frankovitch (horns); Chick Corea (p); Gayle Moran (org, v); Joey DeFrancesco (org, t); Jim Beard, Mitchell Forman, Stu Goldberg, Chester Thompson (ky); Paco DeLucia, Carlos Santana (g); Uppalapu Shrinivas (mand); Jean-Luc Ponty, L. Shankar, Carol Shive (vn); Marsha Westbrook (vla); Philip Hirschi (clo); Ralphe Armstrong, Myron Dove, Matthew Garrison Jonas Hellborg, Tom Stevens (b); Dennis Chambers, Danny Gottlieb, Walfredo Reyes, W. Sonship Theus, Michael Walden (d, perc); T. H. Vinayakram (ghatam, mridangam); Zakir Hussain (tabla); Armando Peraza, Raul Rekow, Karl Perrazzo, V. Selvaganesh (perc); Alex Ligertwood (v).* 74–99.

A kind of extended love story. Twenty-five years' worth of visits to the Montreux jazz festival with a variety of bands that effectively retell the story of McLaughlin's career from the mid-'70s on. It's a pricey set and perhaps only really of interest to collectors.

The basic insufficiency of the Mahavishnu Orchestra was that it wasn't one. When the original quintet split, John set about recruiting other strings, flutes and horns, drafted in Jean-Luc Ponty to fill Jerry Goodman's shoes, and that's where the Montreux story begins. In all, McLaughlin has performed 15 times at the Swiss festival, with 44 different musicians and in four different halls. Latterly, he's done his thing in auditoria dedicated to Stravinsky and Miles Davis. On 7 July 1974, the new Mahavishnu Orchestra were in the old Convention Centre.

The set was a virtual run-through of the dismal *Apocalypse*, with just a clumsy version of 'Sanctuary' from *Birds Of Fire* to recall the old band. It wasn't until 1978, in the Casino, that John and the One Truth Band revisited 'Meeting Of The Spirits' from the very first album and 'Hope' from the second. As in earlier days, the Orchestra was a more impressive consideration live than in the studio. Sometimes it's hard to judge where the strings, Ponty apart, actually are, so dominated is the mix by McLaughlin's guitar. The vocals, from organist Gayle Moran, are pretty weedy and it still takes a bit of a gulp to document titles like 'Hymn To Him', 'Vision Is A Naked Sword' and 'Smile Of The Beyond', especially when 'Squatty Roo' or 'Ugly Beauty' may be lurking on the facing page. The real find was Michael Walden, as powerful a drummer as McLaughlin ever recruited.

John was back in 1976 with Shakti, a new Anglo-Indian outfit, but actually not so new when you recognized that L. Shankar was in to do the same job as Goodman and Ponty and that the Karnatic rhythms and faux-ragas weren't so very different from the stuff John had been doing in 1970 on the lovely, quietly complex and still overlooked *My Goal's Beyond.* Once again, though, Shakti came into their own on stage and while some of the compositions are played at inordinate length – 'Nata' on disc four comes in at 36 minutes – it's clear that something genuinely inventive is taking place, as solidly driven by Zakir Hussain's tabla as it ever was by Cobham or Walden.

After two visits (1976 and 1977) with Shakti, which he and Shankar revived with different percussionists in the '90s, McLaughlin moved into a superstar, 'with friends' phase at Montreux. The One Truth Band was, as suggested above, an attempt to get back something of the energy of the first Mahavishnu Orchestra with a more limber rhythm. By and large it works – 'Friendship' and 'Two Sisters', which celebrates something else going on in McLaughlin's life – but it was to be another dead end.

John wasn't back in Montreux until 1981, at the end of a fallow period that yielded only the backward-looking *Electric Guitarist* (everything from Lifetime power trips to 'My Foolish Heart') and the beginnings of an interest in flamenco and other Mediterranean musics. Not until 1987 did the duo with Paco de Lucia grace a Montreux stage, not so much a meeting of minds as a creative submersion of differences. 'My Foolish Heart' is a key moment on disc ten, but so too is the two-guitar version of 'Florianopolis', which McLaughlin had co-written a couple of years before with Mitchell Forman, anchor of yet another Mahavishnu Orchestra.

That skips ahead a bit and jumps over a superb duo with Chick Corea, one of the outstanding events of the 1981 festival. This was a period when McLaughlin became more used to playing other musicians' material. His phrasing on Chick's 'Romance', 'Waltz', 'Sketches' and 'Turn Around' is exquisite, power and delicacy combined, and with none of the abstract noodling that was a besetting vice of earlier years. Something of the same combination of qualities emerges on Chick's 'Spain', played in 1987 with DeLucia.

Forman was one star of the 1984 Orchestra. The other was Jonas Hellborg. We've always been slightly mystified as to why Jaco Pastorius was regarded with such unqualified respect and adulation (other than as a big-band arranger, at which he has no peer) while Hellborg has been relatively marginalized. His bass-playing is stunning here, albeit in an idiom that veers closer to funk than any previous McLaughlin group. Put 'East Side West Side' or 'Pacific Express' alongside anything from the '70s Mahavishnu and the differences in rhythm and tonality are immediately evident.

The Free Spirits with Joey DeFrancesco and Dennis Chambers was an attempt at an old-fashioned guitar-organ trio. McLaughlin had road-tested 'Thelonious Melodius' with Chick a few years before, but in 1993 it has a burning pungency. 'When Love Is Far Away', which sees DeFrancesco double on trumpet, is ample proof that the old delicacy and filigree precision hasn't been lost, even in as free-swinging a format as this. The Free Spirits were back two years later, still doing 'Mother Tongues' and 'Matinale', but with some of the fire taken out. The next line-up was The Heart of Things, with Gary Thomas, Jim Beard, Matthew Garrison and Chambers, and marked an unexpected turn to bop-based jazz, with tinges of M-Base.

And apart from the Shakti reunion of 1999 and a bonus disc of guest spots with Carlos Santana and with Paco DeLucia, that's it – as many hours of live John McLaughlin as any fan could possibly want and in every mood from wistful to as close to antagonistic as John ever gets. The packaging is wonderful, though the bilingual liner-notes are mostly vapid nonsense. He's repaid Miles's confidence many times over and when he took the stage in 1999 in the Miles Davis Hall, he must have remembered how it all started.

Jackie McLean (born 1932)

ALTO SAXOPHONE

McLean's father worked with Tiny Bradshaw, and young John grew up surrounded by music, a discipline that he later passed on to his son René. During a spell in the finishing school known as the Jazz Messengers, Jackie struck out on his own, recording prodigally with his own quartet and patenting a sound that was compounded equally of bebop and the new, free style. Raw and urgent – no one else sounds quite like him.

*****(*) Lights Out**
Original Jazz Classics OJC 426 *McLean; Donald Byrd (t); Elmo Hope (p); Doug Watkins (b); Art Taylor (d).* 1/56.

***** 4, 5 And 6**
Original Jazz Classics OJC 056 *McLean; Donald Byrd (t); Hank Mobley (ts); Mal Waldron (p); Doug Watkins (b); Art Taylor (d).* 7/56.

***** McLean's Scene**
Original Jazz Classics OJC 098 *McLean; Bill Hardman (t); Red Garland, Mal Waldron (p); Paul Chambers, Arthur Phipps (b); Art Taylor (d).* 12/56, 2/57.

***** Makin' The Changes**
Original Jazz Classics OJC 197 *McLean; Webster Young (t); Curtis Fuller (tb); Gil Coggins, Mal Waldron (p); Paul Chambers, Arthur Phipps (b); Louis Hayes, Art Taylor (d).* 2/57.

***** Alto Madness**
Original Jazz Classics OJC 1733 *McLean; John Jenkins (as); Wade Legge (p); Doug Watkins (b); Art Taylor (d).* 5/57.

***** A Long Drink Of The Blues**
Original Jazz Classics OJC 253 *As above.* 8/57.

****(*) Jackie McLean & Co.**
Original Jazz Classics OJC 074 *McLean; Bill Hardman (t); Ray Draper (tba); Mal Waldron (p); Doug Watkins (b); Art Taylor (d).* 2/57.

***** Strange Blues**
Original Jazz Classics OJC 354 *McLean; Webster Young (t); Ray Draper (tba); Gil Coggins, John Meyers, Mal Waldron (p); Arthur Phipps, Bill Salter (b); Louis Hayes, Larry Ritchie, Art Taylor (d).* 2 & 8/57.

***** Fat Jazz**
Fresh Sound FSR CD 18 *McLean; Webster Young (t); Ray Draper (tba) Gil Coggins (p); George Tucker (b); Larry Richie (d).* 12/57.

Charlie Parker once invited Jackie McLean to kick him in the ass as pay-off for some typically selfish transgression. There were those who felt that McLean in turn could have used similarly robust encouragement in the '50s, when his life and career teetered towards the edge.

These come from a turbulent but productive period in McLean's career. The OJCs mine almost to exhaustion the mid-1956 and early-1957 sessions with Waldron, filling in with other Prestige and New Jazz materials. McLean's pure, emotive blues tone, characteristically taking off with a wail at the break, has already become a manner, but there is a searching, troubled quality to his work on 'Abstraction' (*4, 5 And 6*), 'Flickers' and 'Help' (*& Co.*), and the two takes of 'Long Drink Of The Blues' (OJC 253, which also includes desirable versions of 'I Cover The Waterfront', 'Embraceable You' and 'These Foolish Things'). Given the range and familiarity of material, this might seem a good place to start, but *Scene* ('Mean To Me' and 'Old Folks') and *Changes* ('I Hear A Rhapsody' and 'Chasin' The Bird') are more challenging, pointing a way out of the still-dominant Parker influence.

Perhaps the best of the group is the earliest. *Lights Out* has a directness and simplicity of diction that are not so evident elsewhere; where McLean does attempt something more adventurous, as in the 'bagpipe' introduction and carefully harmonized final chorus of 'A Foggy Day', he does so with taste and precision. As on *4, 5 And 6*, Byrd is a fine collaborator, soloing in a sweet, Dorham-influenced tone on the ballad 'Lorraine' and on 'Kerplunk', both of which were written by the trumpeter.

The Fresh Sound is desirable for freshly minted charts, and the inventive brass interplay of Young and Draper (who led his own session with John Coltrane a year later – *A Tuba Jazz*, Fresh Sound CD 20). 'Tune Up' is one of McLean's leanest and most daring performances of the period.

***** Jackie's Bag**
Blue Note 42303 *McLean; Donald Byrd, Blue Mitchell (t); Tina Brooks (ts); Sonny Clark, Kenny Drew (p); Philly Joe Jones (d).* 1/59, 9/60.

McLean's debut for Blue Note is split across two sessions more than a year apart. The September 1960 date is effectively co-led by Tina Brooks, a more experienced player whose reputation set with his short life. Some of that material was issued in Japan under Brooks's name and the title *Street Singer* and it's by far the best of the stuff here, quite exotic in tonality and ambitious in scope. 'Medina', 'Isle Of Java' and 'Street Singer' are all excellent themes, too rarely covered. Jackie's alto acquires a quavery, almost shawm-like quality in places that is clearly deliberate and very attractive. 'Appointment In Ghana' is similar in conception to the Brooks things. The stuff issued under his own name isn't as sophisticated, and only three cuts were considered good enough for release, which is why the Brooks materials filled out the original release. Even on the strength of those tracks, it's still a respectable debut. McLean seemed a natural signing for Blue Note, a prolific, hyperactive player with a deep grounding in the blues, able to turn his hand to any repertoire even remotely connected to a 12-bar theme and already turning out his own material. There was better to come, but there's no better place to start making the acquaintance of Mclean's work for the label.

****** New Soil**

Blue Note 784013 *McLean; Donald Byrd (t); Walter Davis Jr (p); Paul Chambers (b); Pete LaRoca (d).* 5/59.

***** Vertigo**

Blue Note 22669 *As above, except add Kenny Dorham (t), Herbie Hancock (p), Butch Warren (b), Billy Higgins, Tony Williams (d).* 5/59, 2/63.

***** Swing, Swang, Swingin'**

Blue Note 56582 *McLean; Walter Bishop Jr (p); Jimmy Garrison (b); Art Taylor (d).* 10/59.

Transitional and challenging, *New Soil* seems reasonably tame by present-day standards. McLean had passed through difficult times and was visibly reassessing his career and direction. The extended 'Hip Strut' is perhaps the most conventional thing on the album, but the saxophonist is straining a little at the boundaries of the blues, still pushing from the inside, but definitely looking for a new synthesis. 'Minor Apprehension' has elements of freedom which are slightly startling for the period and wholly untypical of McLean's previous work. Davis contributes a number of compositions, including the previously unreleased 'Formidable' (which isn't). Byrd is still a more than viable player. The transfer isn't as good as usual, with a lot of mess on the drummer's tracks, but the music is important enough to be labelled historic.

Vertigo has more material from the May date, together with further tracks from a 1963 session which marked the recorded debut of Tony Williams. Historically, this makes the album more important than the quality of performance might suggest. As ever, McLean seems poised between innovation and conservatism, and it's often hard to pin down where the music is coming from, less fruitfully so than on other discs.

The October session is less immediately compelling, partly because Jackie sticks to standards, but more because he so obviously remains within his comfort zone. The record was presumably an attempt to recapture commercial success, for it is palpably less compelling than its predecessors and some of the sessions that followed. Only the closing '116th And Lenox' has any of the saxophonist's ability to meld new and old in a single blues-based theme.

***** Capuchin Swing**

Blue Note 84038 *McLean; Blue Mitchell (t); Walter Bishop Jr (p); Paul Chambers (b); Art Taylor (d).* 4/60.

McLean is still relatively orthodox here, but there are signs of the more avant-garde (and Ornette Coleman-influenced) approach that was looming. The sidemen are all hard-boppers with a strong grounding in the blues and while the tonality does tilt in unexpected directions on the opening 'Francisco', 'Condition Blue' and the title-cut, there's nothing yet to frighten the horses. This is one of the lumpier bands McLean worked with at this time. Only Chambers stands out, though even he seems diffident and tired in places, lagging awkwardly on a couple of cuts for no discernible musical reason.

*****(*) Bluesnik**

Blue Note 84067 *McLean; Freddie Hubbard (t); Kenny Drew (p); Doug Watkins (b); Pete LaRoca (d).* 1/61.

Tough, unreconstructed modern blues that reveal considerable depths on subsequent hearings. That's particularly noticeable on the outwardly conventional title-track, on which McLean's solo has a formidably unexpected logic. The other soloists tend to take up space that one might prefer to have seen left to the on-form leader, but Hubbard is dashing and Drew affectingly lyrical. A word, too, for the seldom-discussed Watkins, who gives his lines a lazy-sounding drag that nevertheless holds the beat solidly together. An excellent record that should be a high priority for anyone interested in McLean's music.

***** A Fickle Sonance**

Blue Note 24544 *McLean; Tommy Turrentine (t); Sonny Clark (p); Butch Warren (b); Billy Higgins (d).* 10/61.

Now available in the Rudy Van Gelder Edition, *A Fickle Sonance* finds Jackie still firmly locked into hard bop and still sounding like a blues man, even when the harmonies are slightly unorthodox. The title-piece is his, though most of the rest of the date is by other hands, including Clark's boisterous 'Five Will Get You Ten' and 'Sundu'. Turrentine's 'Enitnerrut' is pretty generic, but the surprise is Butch Warren's closing 'Lost', the final cut of the set, the shortest, but one of the best. It's never been Jackie's best-known or best-loved record, but it has its own strengths.

CORE COLLECTION

****** Let Freedom Ring**

Blue Note 46527 *McLean; Walter Davis Jr (p); Herbie Lewis (b); Billy Higgins (d).* 3/62.

A classic. Influenced by Ornette Coleman – with whom he was to record for Blue Note on *Old And New Gospel* – McLean shrugged off the last fetter of bop harmony and pushed through to a more ruggedly individual post-bop that in important regards anticipated the avant-garde of the later '60s. McLean's phenomenally beautiful tone rings out on 'Melody For Melonae', 'I'll Keep Loving You', 'Rene' and 'Omega'. Higgins's bright, cross-grained drumming is exemplary and the band is generously recorded, with plenty of bass.

*****(*) Destination ... Out!**

Blue Note 32087 *McLean; Grachan Moncur III (tb); Bobby Hutcherson (vib); Larry Ridley (b); Roy Haynes (d).* 9/63.

Though he emerged as a relatively orthodox bebopper, McLean was deeply influenced by the free-jazz movement, as his collaboration with Ornette Coleman underlined. Its title was significant, though, because McLean was unwilling to throw over entirely a more traditional idiom. *Destination ... Out!* is a great album for the way it combines both idioms. Moncur has the bulk of the composing credits, with just 'Kahlil The Prophet' from the leader. Complex, tricky and thoroughly engaging, this is one of the forgotten records of the period but it is well worth a visit now. (It's a limited edition, so hurry!)

*****(*) Dr Jackle**

Steeplechase SCCD 36005 *McLean; Lamont Johnson (p); Scott Holt (b); Billy Higgins (d).* 12/66.

***** Tune Up**

Steeplechase SCCD 36023 *As above.* 12/66.

The later '60s were a somewhat dead time for McLean, and it looked as though the huge strides he had taken at the beginning of the decade led nowhere. He acted in Jack Gelber's *The Connection* and played some of the script for real. His playing of the time has a slightly tired edge and a hesitancy that comes not from lack of confidence but from a seeming lack of motivation to develop ideas. *Dr Jackle* includes a take of 'Melody For Melonae' which is quite discouraging in its diffidence and defensive show; McLean clearly isn't helped by the rhythm section, but Higgins alone should have been enough to spur him to better things. *Tune Up* has an air of afterthought; an attractive enough session, it can safely be left to completists, though Higgins is a revelation throughout, a mischievous, endlessly inventive performance.

*** Jacknife

Blue Note 40572 *McLean; Lee Morgan, Charles Tolliver (t); Larry Willis (p); Don Moore, Larry Ridley (b); Jack DeJohnette (d). 75*

Only released in 1975 as a double LP, this fine set seems an odd one to have left mouldering in the vaults. There are two basic groups involved, a quintet/sextet with either Morgan or Tolliver (both of them on 'Soft Blue'), Willis, Ridley and DeJohnette and a later quartet group with Moore replacing Ridley. Fine as the brass-players are, and Tolliver in particular, the quartet date is the better part of this session and McLean's playing on 'Moonscape', 'Combined Effort' and the frantic 'High Frequency' is as good as any of the period. It isn't entirely wishful thinking to imagine that he sounds not unlike Ornette Coleman here and there, particularly when he lets tones slide into dissonance over Willis's already open-ended chords. The assumption has to be that this was considered too avant-garde and challenging a set for mid-'60s release. It certainly fits comfortably into Jackie's bag now.

**** Live At Montmartre

Steeplechase SCCD 31001 *McLean; Kenny Drew (p); Bo Stief (b); Alex Riel (d). 8/72.*

*** A Ghetto Lullaby

Steeplechase SCCD 31013 *As above, except replace Stief with Niels-Henning Orsted Pedersen (b). 7/73.*

For sheer *joie de vivre*, albeit with a chastened edge, *Live At Montmartre* is hard to beat. Full-voiced and endlessly inventive, McLean romps through 'Smile', adding the 'shave-and-a-haircut-*bay-rum*' cadence to the end of his first statement with an almost arrogant flourish. 'Parker's Mood' is perhaps the best of his later bebop essays, shifting out of synch with Drew's excellent chording for a couple of measures. *Lullaby* is less immediately appealing, though NHOP adds a significant element to the group's harmonic output, and he is a much more solid player than Stief. 'Mode For Jay Mac' is interesting, and the title-track calls up some of McLean's most purely emotive playing.

**(*) Ode To Super

Steeplechase SCCD 31009 *McLean; Gary Bartz (as); Thomas Clausen (p); Bo Stief (b); Alex Riel (d). 7/73.*

A disappointing confrontation that recalls the *Alto Madness* session with John Jenkins from 1957. Bartz already sounds as if he has set his sights on a rock/fusion future and McLean battles against Clausen's apparent insistence on closing up the harmonies. 'Monk's Dance' makes a promising but unfulfilled opening, and 'Great Rainstreet Blues' bogs down rather too quickly.

*** The Meeting

Steeplechase SCCD 31006 *McLean; Dexter Gordon (ts); Kenny Drew (p); Niels-Henning Orsted Pedersen (b); Alex Riel (d). 7/73.*

*** The Source

Steeplechase SCCD 31020 *As above. 7/73.*

For once, Steeplechase's obsessive over-documentation makes sense. Recorded over two nights, this isn't a good album and a makeweight but a 'double' of genuine quality. Gordon and McLean were poles apart stylistically, but temperament and geography suggested such a meeting was inevitable. The first volume is darker and more sensitive, and the opening 'All Clean' hits close to home. McLean is usually quicker to the punch, but Gordon spins out his ideas (particularly on the standards) with confidence and some in reserve. 'Half Nelson' and 'I Can't Get Started' (*The Source*) depend to a large extent on Drew's teasing out of the chords. The sound isn't spectacularly good, with a tendency to fragment round the edges; no better on the CD unfortunately, but the playing makes up for it.

*** New York Calling

Steeplechase SCCD 31023 *McLean; Billy Skinner (t); René McLean (ts, ss); Billy Gault (p); James Benjamin (b); Michael Carvin (d). 10/74.*

New York Calling is a respectable performance from a band capable of better. The Cosmic Brotherhood featured McLean's talented and indoctrinated-from-the-cradle son, René. Far from sounding like a chip, he shows considerable individuality on both his horns, carving out intriguing counter-melodies and straightforward responses, neither over-respectful nor wilfully defiant. The charts are impressively varied, but *New York Calling* isn't a first choice for CD transfer; the sound is unaccountably flat. McLean *père* takes his best solo early, on the title-track, and finds little to add to it. Skinner sounds as if he could do with a bottle of valve oil and has intonation problems throughout (unless he intends some of his middle-register notes to be flatted). Once again, it's the drummer who attracts positive attention.

*** Antiquity

Steeplechase SCCD 31028 *McLean; Michael Carvin (d, perc, v). 8/74.*

The duo with Carvin is as far out as anything McLean has attempted. The core of the session is an impressionistic account of slave days, with the drummer's passionate vocals helping to fill out the story. McLean's own passions seem a little muted by contrast, but there are moments when the two spiral up on a single motif and the music starts to fire up. Then there's no mistaking McLean's mastery.

*** Rhythm Of The Earth

Birdology FDM 37009-2 *McLean; Roy Hargrove (t); Steve Davis (tb); Alan Jay Palmer (p); Steve Nelson (vib); Nat Reeves (b); Eric McPherson (d). 3/92.*

*** Fire And Love

Blue Note 93254-2 *McLean; Raymond Williams, (t); Steve Davis (tb); René Mclean(ts, perc); Alan Jay Palmer (p); Phil Bowler (b); Eric McPherson (d). 97.*

** Nature Boy

Blue Note 523273-2 *McLean; Cedar Walton (p); David Williams(b); Billy Higgins (d). 6/99.*

McLean's handful of '90s records are basically a disappointing lot. If his chops aren't in the finest order, he doesn't have a compensating group-sound vision to make up the difference, and too often these stumble over structures and situations that feel misconceived. *Rhythm Of The Earth*, recently back on CD, has some excellent playing in the cracks – Hargrove is very good, for instance – but the themes and settings get in the way. *Fire And Love*, made for Blue Note's Japanese Somethin' Else imprint, again has its moments which get tangled in various undercarriages. This time McLean leaves the writing (bar the opening 'Mr E') to other hands; but they're either tricksy bits of hard bop or dubiously worldly episodes, and his signature sourness of tone sounds odd next to such a groomed sound as that of Davis's trombone.

Worst of the lot is the quartet session. Despite the promising line-up and programme of standards, this sounds sadly like a man with nothing left to say in his idiom.

Paul McNamara

PIANO

Contemporary Australian pianist.

***** Point Of No Return**
Rufus RF008 *McNamara; Craig Walters (ss, ts); Ashley Turner (b); Martin Highland (d).* 8/93.

***** Conversations**
Rufus RF046 *McNamara (p solo).* 1–2/99.

****(*) Duo Logic**
Rufus RF051 *McNamara; Sandy Evans (ss, ts); Craig Scott (b); Jim Piesse, Alan Turnbull (d).* 1–6/99.

McNamara confesses to a Bill Evans influence, which comes through intermittently on the solo record, but he's less lush and more honestly thoughtful than many an Evans disciple. *Conversations* is introspective much of the way, until the brisk complexities of 'Salsa Sally', and the rather clever 'A Tribute To Mr Kenny Barron', which toys with the harmonies in a Barron arrangement and makes something naggingly memorable out of them. The pianist displays no special subtleties of touch, but that makes his scrupulous note choices all the more effective.

The Rufus debut, a quartet session that runs close to 80 minutes, has some of the spacious and patient feel of a vintage ECM. Eleven McNamara originals of varying length and intensity are bridged by the centrepiece of the record, a long and steady reading of 'The Peacocks'. Some of the music feels inscrutable, and as enthusiastically as the others play – 'Thirty Wells' is a good instance of the group at its best – the record feels a bit adrift from the listener.

Duo Logic is claimed as a 40-minute free improvisation, and seems to be designed around pairs of instruments, although the two drummers apparently count as one, and by halfway through the rules seem to have broken down. A departure from the other records, and a slightly baffling one.

Jim McNeely (born 1949)

PIANO, KEYBOARDS

Born in Chicago, he studied piano and saxophone, then from a New York base spent substantial periods with the Jones–Lewis Orchestra, Stan Getz and Phil Woods. Holds a conducting position with Danish Radio Big Band and is now composer-in-residence for Vanguard Jazz Orchestra.

***** Rain's Dance**
Steeplechase SCCD 31412 *McNeely; Larry Schneider (ss, ts); Mike Richmond (b); Bob Merigliano (d); Sam Jacobs (perc).* 10/76.

***** Winds Of Change**
Steeplechase SCCD 31256 *McNeely; Mike Richmond (b); Kenny Washington (d).* 7/89.

Having worked with Mel Lewis, Stan Getz and Joe Henderson, McNeely has long since acquired a substantial reputation which these albums confirm in their unfussy way. A clever writer and a mercurial though restrained soloist, McNeely likes a lot of space to develop ideas in. *Rain's Dance* was his first date as a leader and it has recently made its bow on CD with an alternative take of the long title-track as a bonus. There are elements of 'prentice work about it and some of the tracks overrun their welcome, but it's hard to fault the commitment of the playing (Schneider could burn along modal lines as capably as any tenorman of that moment) and McNeely was already flexing a composer's muscles.

Currently it's a long gap to *Winds Of Change*. Each of the five originals has a specific turn of phrase, while 'Bye-Ya' is a particularly fluent reading of a Monk piece that not many tackle. Richmond, whose voluble yet lightly weighted lines are entirely apt, is certainly his ideal bass partner.

****** Group Therapy**
Omnitone 15101 *McNeely; Tony Kadleck, Greg Gisbert, Scott Wendholt (t, flhn); Ed Neumeister (tb); Tom Varner (frhn); Billy Drewes (ss, as, ts, cl, f); Dick Oatts (ss, as, f); Scott Robinson (bs, bcl); Cameron Brown (b); John Hollenbeck (d).* 6/00.

McNeely's writing is completely contemporary, yet there are numberless echoes of and nods towards craftsmen of the jazz past: Shorty Rogers, Bill Holman and Pete Rugolo are three which come easily to mind, although that suggests that he's merely updating the book of West Coast ingenuity, and *Group Therapy* doesn't really sound like that. Where he resembles those masters is in his deftness, his concern to keep everybody busy, to make all the pieces full of incident without overcrowding the score or the ear. The treatment of Bud Powell's 'The Fruit', which opens the set, delivers a bebop scramble turned into something flawlessly trim and elegant, 11 soloists accommodated without a stagger. 'Lost' solves the dilemma of what to do behind a soloist in fascinating style. Ten minutes is about the average length of these pieces, but as he says, Tennessee Williams had two hours to say what he wanted in a play, and nothing here feels either overlong or too stuffy with detail; and a picked gang of New York's finest respond with their best and most attentive playing.

Marian McPartland (born 1920)

PIANO

Born in Windsor, Marian Turner went to the USA when she married her husband, Jimmy McPartland, in 1945. She worked as a soloist in Chicago and had a long trio residency at New York's Hickory House in the '50s. A low period in the '60s was succeeded by three decades of prolific and successful work: as pianist, composer, pioneer jazz educator, writer, and – most effectively of all – as broadcaster, her Piano Jazz interviews with fellow pianists running for many years on American public service radio.

***** On 52nd Street**

Savoy 92880 *McPartland; Vinnie Burke, Bob Carter (b); Joe Morello(d).* 4–10/53.

A few studio tracks, but most of this was cut live at one of McPartland's regular Hickory House sets. The playing has a bright, chipper quality to go with the pianist's deft takes on standard material – not quite as fully orchestrated as her playing would later become, but a pleasure to hear. Rudy van Gelder did the location recording.

****** Contrasts**

The Jazz Alliance TJA2-12044-2 2CD *McPartland; Jimmy McPartland (c, v); Vic Dickenson, Hank Berger (tb); Jack Maheu (cl); Buddy Tate (ts, bs); Michael Moore, Rusty Gilder (b); Gus Johnson, Larry Bell, Mike Berger, Joe Corsello, (d).* 11/72–6/73.

Forward to 1973. This new edition couples the discs we have previously listed as *A Sentimental Journey* and *Music Of Alec Wilder.* The former offers a lovely memento of two engagements by bands led by Jimmy, with Marian on piano and two entertaining front lines. Jack Maheu blends a spiralling virtuosity with Pee Wee-type licks, Tate is reliable (and picks up the baritone here and there), Dickenson is absolutely himself (his 'When You Wish Upon A Star' is priceless) and Jimmy leads with typical aplomb. The piano sounds a bit difficult in places, but the pianist is obviously enjoying herself, and she contributes a delightful sleeve-note.

The Wilder programme is one of the great single-composer recitals and it should be far better known than it is. McPartland has been intensely involved in Alec Wilder's difficult, bittersweet music for decades and she gets closer to the heart of it than any jazz player ever has. 'Jazz Waltz For A Friend', the first track, was written for her, and several of the other pieces have scarcely been touched by other improvisers. The five pieces with the lone support of Michael Moore are wonderfully lyrical and searching and, though the remaining five with Gilder and Corsello are a shade less involving, it is a memorable occasion. The only regret must be that she didn't play Wilder's unforgettable 'Where Do You Go?' at the date.

***** From This Moment On**

Concord CCD 4086 *McPartland; Brian Torff (b); Jake Hanna (d).* 12/78.

****** Windows**

Concord CCD2-2233-2 *As above, except add Jerry Dodgion (as, f), Mary Fettig (as).* 5–8/79.

***** Willow Creek And Other Ballads**

Concord CCD 4272 *McPartland (p solo).* 1/85.

McPartland's playing and composing have remained amazingly fresh and interested. Besides performing, she has hosted a long-running American radio series which features her with a different jazz pianist on every edition; and, perhaps as a result, her own playing seems sensitive to all the possible directions in contemporary jazz piano. Even though this would be classed by most as ostensibly 'mainstream jazz', there are inflexions in it which would be unknown to most of McPartland's immediate contemporaries. *From This Moment On* offers a clear-headed examination of some standards. *Windows* is a new edition of the albums *Portrait* and *At The Festival*, the latter a live set made a few months after the studio session. Dodgion's bristling alto and beautifully articulated flute is a bonus on the studio tunes. An incisive version of Herbie Hancock's 'Tell Me A Bedtime Story', a tart Dodgion blues called 'No Trumps' and an ideal treatment of the pianist's gorgeous 'Time And Time Again' are the highlights. The live music finds Marian in high-voltage form herself, sparkling on Chick Corea's 'Windows' and thinking through a rhapsodic version of her own 'In The Days Of Our Love'. Mary Fettig sits in on the last three tunes, which slackens things somewhat. If the solo set is a shade behind the others, it's only because McPartland uses the resources of a trio so intelligently that she seems relatively quiescent by herself. While her treatments of the likes of 'Someday I'll Find You' are typically original, it would be agreeable to hear her tackle an entire set of her own compositions.

***** Plays The Music Of Billy Strayhorn**

Concord CCD 4326 *McPartland; Jerry Dodgion (as); Steve LaSpina (b); Joey Baron (d).* 3/87.

*****(*) Plays The Benny Carter Songbook**

Concord CCD 4412 *McPartland; Benny Carter (as); John Clayton (b); Harold Jones (d).* 1/90.

Two fine excursions into repertory by McPartland. Strayhorn's suave impressionism is hard to evoke, let alone sustain for an entire album, but this is at least as convincing as any similar homage. Despite a couple of less successful entries – 'A Flower Is A Lovesome Thing', for instance, is a little too doleful – the quartet have the measure of this deceptive music. There is a witty, unpredictable revision of 'Take The "A" Train', a springy 'Intimacy Of The Blues' and a purposefully crafted 'Lush Life' by the trio without Dodgion. The meeting with Carter, who plays on 6 of the 11 tunes chosen from his book, is flawlessly paced. Though his technique is still astonishing for a man in his 80s, Carter's sound and delivery are rather old-world compared to McPartland's astute command. Trio versions of 'When Lights Are Low', the beautiful 'Key Largo' and 'Summer Serenade' are probably the most distinguished moments on the record. Both sessions are recorded excellently.

*****(*) Live At Maybeck Recital Hall Vol. 9**

Concord CCD 4460 *McPartland (p solo).* 1/91.

This solo recital finds the pianist in characteristically adventurous mood. The composers represented here include Alec Wilder, Ornette Coleman, Mercer Ellington and Dave Brubeck; there are her latest reflections on the tune she startled Ellington himself with, 'Clothed Woman', and one of the most affecting of her own themes, 'Twilight World'. Each interpretation contains nothing unnecessary in the way of embellishment, yet they all seem ideally paced, properly finished. She makes it sound very easy. Ripe, in-concert recording, typical of this series from Concord.

CORE COLLECTION

****** In My Life**

Concord CCD 4561 *McPartland; Chris Potter (as, ts); Gary Mazzaroppi (b); Glenn Davis (d).* 1/93.

A marvellous record. This time Marian sets Coltrane and Ornette alongside Lennon and McCartney, quietly introduces

a couple of her own tunes, and invites one of the sharpest new saxophonists on the scene to sit in. The result is as catholic and accomplished a jazz record as one can find among modern releases. Chris Potter's unfussy virtuosity is a serenely appropriate match for the pianist's diverse tastes, and he is as purposeful and convincing on 'Close Your Eyes' as he is on 'Naima'. To close, there is a deeply affecting solo treatment of 'Singin' The Blues', done as a memorial to Marian's late husband, Jimmy. Essential.

★★★(★) **Plays The Music Of Mary Lou Williams**
Concord CCD 4605 *McPartland; Bill Douglass (b); Omar Clay (d).* 1/94.

This must have been a project close to Marian's heart, and she does this still-little-known songbook fine justice. One of the striking things about the playing is how Marian has an unerring instinct for the right tempo on a particular piece: 'Easy Blues' and 'It's A Grand Night For Swinging' hit an ideal pace from the start, and 'Cloudy', probably the most famous of Williams's tunes, is a beauty. If the disc has a weakness, it's that Marian doesn't always convince the listener that Williams's themes are as strong as they might be: her own composition, 'Threnody', a delightful tune in three, actually outclasses several of the pieces here.

★★★ **Live At Yoshi's Nitespot**
Concord CCD 4712 *McPartland; Bill Douglass (b); Glenn Davis (d).* 11/95.

★★★(★) **Silent Pool**
Concord CCD 4745 *McPartland; Andy Simpkins (b); Harold Jones (d); strings, arr. Alan Broadbent.* 2/97.

The live album might not quite rank among Marian's best, but this is still a hugely enjoyable date. 'Pretty Women', 'Chasing Shadows' and her own 'Silent Pool' are beautiful rarities in the repertory, and her version of Ellington's 'Warm Valley' is exquisite enough to remind any who have forgotten that she is one of our great ballad interpreters. A couple of the standards are comparatively routine, though, and newcomers should perhaps start with one of the earlier discs.

Her strings album is handsomely arranged by Alan Broadbent and at last offers a showcase of 12 McPartland originals in one place, with 'Twilight World', 'Time And Time Again' and 'There'll Be Other Times' among the most beautiful pieces. The only quibble might be that the languorous tempos and Broadbent's luxury-class scores are just a shade too relaxed at times. But this should still be filed alongside her other classics in what is now a superlative discography.

★★★(★) **Just Friends**
Concord CCD 4805-2 *McPartland; Tommy Flanagan, Renee Rosnes, George Shearing, Geri Allen, Dave Brubeck, Gene Harris (p).* 9/97–1/98.

★★★(★) **Reprise**
Concord CCD 4853-2 *McPartland; Bill Crow (b); Joe Morello (d).* 9/98.

Marian's 80th birthday was greeted with the warmest of affection throughout the jazz world, with several special concerts to mark the occasion, and a reunion of her trio from the Hickory House days at New York's new Birdland. *Reprise* is the delightful result, the old firm still in joyful form, and the pianist still picking the most pleasing tunes, here including Hoagy Carmichael's 'New Orleans', the same arrangement of 'I Hear Music' which once started one of their Capitol dates, Henry Mancini's 'Two For The Road', and a piano–drums dialogue on 'Cymbalism'.

Just Friends is an album of duets, of the sort which she has been spontaneously performing on her *Piano Jazz* broadcasts for many years. Though one or two don't really come off – such as, surprisingly, a rather doom-laden 'Twilight World' with George Shearing – there are many more good ones: stomping along with Rosnes on 'It's You Or No One', playing tag with Brubeck on 'Gone With The Wind'. She closes it with a simple, lovely solo on 'When The Saints', dedicated to Jimmy.

★★★ **The Single Petal Of A Rose**
Concord CCD 4895-2 *McPartland; Bill Douglass (b).* 4/00.

★★★(★) **Ain't Misbehavin'**
Concord CCD 4968-2 *McPartland; Willie Pickens (p).* 12/00.

Recorded at the venerable Maybeck Hall, *The Single Petal Of A Rose* is a programme of Ellington tunes, either solos or duets with Bill Douglass. This isn't one of our favourites by Marian: the playing is as impeccable as ever, with some handsomely orchestrated versions ('Mood Indigo' taken at a very slow pace which still works); the problem is that the material by now is all too familiar. Her sole original, 'Creulescence', is the most enjoyable moment.

At this point, nobody has played as many piano duets, with as many different pianists, as Marian. Cut over three nights at Joe Segal's in Chicago, the First Lady of jazz piano meets the ebullient bounce of Willie Pickens – solos, duets, a fine old time, with their contrasting styles meeting co-operatively head on.

There are currently only four releases on The Jazz Alliance, drawn from editions of Marian's Piano Jazz series for NPR, featuring meetings with Oscar Peterson (TJA-12033-2), Bill Evans (TJA-12038-2), Carmen McRae (TJA-12039-2) and Chick Corea (TJA-12040-2). Each is a mixture of chat, reminiscence and piano playing.

Joe McPhee (born 1939)

TENOR AND SOPRANO SAXOPHONES, POCKET-CORNET, FLUGELHORN, VALVE TROMBONE, ELECTRONICS

McPhee is that rare doubler, a musician equally at ease on brass and woodwind. Only Benny Carter has sounded as comfortable and idiomatic, but Joe's fierce anger and political engagement provide an important additional element.

★★★ **Underground Railroad**
Atavistic Unheard Music 226 2CD *McPhee; Otis Greene (as, hmca); Reggie Marks (ts, ss, f, org); Joe Virgillio (ts, ss); Tyne Crabb (b); Ernest Bostic (d).* 10/68–4/69.

★★★ **Nation Time**
Atavistic Unheard Music 201 *As above, except omit Virgilio; add Mike Kull (p, ky); Dave Jones (g); Bruce Thompson (perc).* 12/70.

A rare document in American free music, the first of these features McPhee's semi-legendary *Underground Railroad* (pressed up only as 450 vinyl copies at the time) coupled with a previously unreleased set by the Contemporary Improvisational Ensemble, live at Holy Cross Monastery six months earlier. While both sets are a fascinating document of a little-known enclave of free players, they're not exactly lost masterpieces, with McPhee still finding his way towards the quality of his '70s performances and the others ranging from incoherent to awkwardly passionate. The LP session has some beautiful moments nevertheless, the long title-piece taking a natural trajectory through tension and release, while the rambunctious free-funk of 'Windy City Head Stompin' Blues' on the Ensemble session is exhilarating. Both are dustily recorded, though the remastering makes the most of what there is.

The second disc comes from a little later in McPhee's effort to meld free jazz and the kind of raw electric funk that was creeping into jazz in the wake of Miles Davis's experiments. Mike Kull's electric piano, rather than the leader's playing, confirms the connection. 'Nation Time' is credited to McPhee and played by his quintet of the time but the other two pieces, again recorded live, are group improvisations by an expanded group with an extra saxophone, guitar and organ. Though quite easily dateable – and therefore somewhat dated in sound – it would be hard for even a relatively well-versed listener to guess who was playing. Fascinating stuff from an important reissue programme. Like the earlier record, this originally appeared only on a tiny, limited-edition label.

*** Trinity

Atavistic Unheard Music 214 *McPhee; Mike Kull (p); Harold E. Smith (d).* 71.

Also first released on CJR in a very limited run, this trio saw McPhee continue his reduced group. The long 'Ionization' begins with trumpet, then tenor and drums, and it's some time before Kull enters very softly to pick up what turns into a long and possibly Coltrane-influenced improvisation. The second track is only a third of the length, with McPhee's assertive, almost preachy tenor playing over electric piano chords. Smith is hyperactive, sometimes too busy for the health of the music, which is much simpler in outline and more blues-driven than at first appears. 'Delta' is reminiscent of both Albert Ayler and Leo Smith, a threatening, deceptively low-key theme that builds to an enormous climax, ending a short but powerful CD reissue.

*** Survival Unit II: At WBAI's Free Music Store

hatART 6197 *McPhee; Clifford Thornton (co, bhn); Byron Morris (ss, as); Mike Kull (p); Harold E. Smith (d, perc).* 10/71.

Taken from a radio broadcast, this live set has McPhee on trumpet and tenor, with Morris doubling on soprano and alto and Thornton alternating a sharp, Olu Dara-like cornet tone with some meaty baritone horn, which helps to fill in the lower end of the register. No bassist – Tyrone Crabb had left the group to go into local activism – but no obvious need for one. A long version of 'Nation Time' is more coherent and also somehow edgier than the earlier released version, while 'Message From Denmark' suggests the way McPhee was going at the turn of the '70s. Typically, this set wasn't issued on record until 1996, offering belated understanding of McPhee's earlier career.

*** Tenor & Fallen Angels

hatOLOGY 544 *McPhee (ts solo).* 10/77.

There are few more demanding disciplines in music than unaccompanied wind-playing. Typically, McPhee goes at it with abandon and shrewdness combined. His phrasing – disconcertingly like Lucky Thompson's on a couple of occasions here – is dazzlingly agile and he is never short of an idea. The long title-track is a *tour de force*, more than 20 minutes of concentrated musical thought which also allows Joe to explore the further reaches of his horn. Added to the CD reissue is the quarter-hour 'Fallen Angels', which is so powerful one is surprised it didn't see the light of day much sooner.

*** Visitation

Boxholder 34 *McPhee; Bill Smith (ss, as); David Prentice (vn); David Lee (b); Richard Bannard (d).* 11/83.

This is not the Bill – or William O. – Smith who played clarinet with Dave Brubeck, but an avant-garde player whose ensemble provide a new context for McPhee. Bill and Joe contribute two pieces each, of which Smith's 'Home At Last' and McPhee's 'Eleuthera' are the most impressive; Prentice, who is a revelation on violin, is the composer of 'If I Don't Fall' and there is also a rugged reading of Albert Ayler's 'Ghosts', which shows how much Joe took from the late saxophonist's misunderstood effort to marry free jazz with R&B and other black forms. This is an unusual record in the McPhee canon, in that it was not strictly his group at all; but it's a good one.

***(*) Impressions Of Jimmy Giuffre

Celp C 21 *McPhee; André Jaume (ts, bcl); Raymond Boni (g).* 4/91.

McPhee's discography is currently diminished by the disappearance of his substantial hatART catalogue, at least some of which we hope to see resurrected. This disc stands a little apart from his normal line of work, but there is no mistaking how much pleasure he took in making it. The trio kicks off with a glorious version of 'The Train And The River', with McPhee in the Brookmeyer role, and carries on with a mixture of Giuffre originals and specially written pieces which might have been laid down by the clarinettist's slightly wacky brother. There's even a posy for Juanita Giuffre, who has been a substantial influence on her husband's recent career. A sundae to balance the meatier side of McPhee's output.

**** As Serious As Your Life

hatOLOGY 514 *McPhee (solo).* 5/96.

Twenty years after McPhee's first solo record, *Tenor*, this marks a return to unaccompanied performance, an aspect of his career which he regards as being of paramount importance, but which is almost unknown. McPhee has identified 1996 as an important transitional year in his career, a point at which he looks back and forward, with the oneiric logic that dominates 'Project Dream Keeper', his latest sequence of work. Working alone and with ambient sound welcomed rather than edited out, he creates a body of work which is as evocative and expressive as anything he has ever made. 'Tok' is a Coltrane-influenced tenor piece which harks back to the earlier solo performance. 'Conlon In The Land Of Ra' documents an imaginary meeting between Sun Ra and the radical composer Conlon Nancarrow, who spent much of his life writing for player piano. Dedicated to Marilyn Crispell, who has made the tune something of a speciality piece, Coltrane's 'After The Rain' is a piano solo played on the house piano of the Village Gate jazz club and played with the sustain pedal depressed throughout, giving it a floating, fugitive quality. On 'The Man I Love'

McPhee brings a highly personal focus to the Gershwin standard, a similar tonality and language to the two parts of 'As Serious As Your Life', named after an important book by British jazz writer and photographer Val Wilmer. As well as these, there is the opening 'Death Of Miles Davis', a heartfelt tribute, and 'Haiku Study #1', a sketch for work included on the duets with violinst David Prentice, below.

**** Legend Street One

CIMP 115 *McPhee; Frank Lowe (ts); David Prentice (vn); Charles Moffett (d).* 6/96.

*** Legend Street Two

CIMP 132 *As above.* 6/96.

***(*) Inside Out

CIMP 120 *As above, except omit Lowe and Prentice.* 6/96.

McPhee's openness to all sound, natural and instrumental, recommends him to the unvarnished, non-hierarchical aesthetic espoused by CIMP. These two sessions are very much in keeping with the 'Dream Keeper' project, broodingly surreal and expressive encounters which refuse to obey the jazz rulebook. Like Henry Threadgill, McPhee now seems to have evaded bebop altogether and to be playing in an idiom that is entirely his own and almost beyond critical analysis. The bald session details are slightly misleading because on *Legend Street One* there are actually only two quartet tracks. The rest are either duos, like the two-tenor encounter of 'Loweville', a couple of tracks with Prentice anticipating the head-to-head of *Inside Out*, and the extraordinary flugelhorn/drums confrontation of 'Not Yet'. 'For Panama' is a drum solo, Moffett's tribute to Panama Francis, and one of the drummer's very best recorded performances. Indeed, the album is notably selfless, with considerable time and space for the remaining members of the group to establish their own musical personalities. The long group-track, 'Up, Over And Out', is all the better for knowing more about how these remarkable men think and interact.

Volume two of *Legend Street* opens with a stunning version of Eric Dolphy's 'Something Sweet, Something Tender', with Lowe tracking the leader every inch. Again, Prentice is a significant presence, while the late Charles Moffett sustains a pulse that is at once clear and unambiguous but also elastic. 'Double Ten' and 'Dark Doings' are equally monumental performances, with great interplay between the saxophones and riveting detail from the violinist and drummer.

**** A Meeting In Chicago

Okkadisk OD 12016 *McPhee; Ken Vandermark (reeds); Kent Kessler (b).* 96.

Like Henry Threadgill, McPhee is hard to pin down critically because he belongs to no identifiable generic niche. This extraordinary set could almost be the work of some as yet unknown, conservatory-trained but sceptical modernist who has written his thesis on the wind groups of early modernism, those experimenters who took a perverse delight in trying combinations that had not been heard during the classical era. As a meeting of minds, this one is hard to improve on. Vandermark's NRGetic style is more cautiously modulated here and Kessler is, almost in compensation, much more pungent and confrontational than usual. McPhee, doubling as ever on trumpet and reeds, sounds in charge, signalling changes of direction and conducting the transitions from full-on collaborative batter to a more delicate choice of brush-strokes.

*** The Brass City

Okkadisk OD12025 *McPhee; Jeb Bishop (tb).* 10/97.

McPhee was to turn his back somewhat on brass after this astonishing *tour de force*. Brass duos are pretty rare in the canon, but this one sounds as straightforward and idiomatic as saxophone and piano or trumpet and organ, with Bishop providing much of the harmonic foundation. McPhee includes both soprano saxophone and valve trombone but concentrates for much of the time on pocket cornet, a tight, terse sound similar to Don Cherry's. Most of the record is taken up with a suite of dance exercises for two horns, but there are also tributes to Tom Guralnick, and a delightful nod to Roswell Rudd in the oddly spelt 'Rozwell Incident'. Touches of distortion here and there when the two horns are playing *forte*, but generally speaking the sound is very good.

*** The Watermelon Suite

CIMP 183 *McPhee; Dominic Duval (b, elec); Jay Rosen (d, perc).* 5/98.

*** Rapture

Cadence CJR 1106 *As above, except add Rosi Hertlein (vn, v).* 12/98.

The trio with Duval and Rosen has proved to be a fruitful one for McPhee, the relationship with Cadence even more so. The elements of 'The Watermelon Suite' itself – whole, rind, meat, seeds – are treated with a strangely analytical certainty, but the playing is as refreshing and raw as ever. McPhee these days restricts himself to saxophone, and mostly the soprano. It is most effective on the long 'Putter Piece', but his solo on the closing 'My Funny Valentine' is wry and touching. Rosen and Duval (who also uses a scaled-down Hutchins bass) take time out for a duet on 'Soundboard Safari'.

Rapture is hijacked by the astonishing violinist and singer Rosi Hertlein, who is destined for great things. With Duval's deployment of live electronics, the sound-world is greatly expanded and McPhee's prominence is scaled down somewhat. The opening fragment was inspired by composer and diarist Ned Rorem's eulogy on his partner of more than 30 years, but the main component of the album is a centenary reinterpretation of James Weldon Johnson's magnificent Negro anthem, 'Lift Every Voice And Sing', a performance that comes in at more than three-quarters of an hour.

***(*) In The Spirit

CIMP 199 *McPhee; Joe Giardullo (ss, bcl, f); Michael Bisio, Dominic Duval (b).* 3/99.

The 'Spirit' is, of course, the Spirit Room at Rossie, New York, where CIMP sessions are always recorded. But it also reflects the spiritual tradition that McPhee explores with his drummerless Bluette group. Almost all the material here – the only exceptions are McPhee's 'Astral Spirits' and his meditation on 'Come Sunday/Birmingham Sunday' – is from the church or its adherents. 'Deep River' and 'Just A Closer Walk With Thee' are performed alongside Curtis Mayfield's 'People Get Ready' and Billie Holiday and Arthur Herzog Jr's 'God Bless The Child'. In this context, and played with McPhee's usual fervour, they sound spiritually consistent one with another. Pairing off with a second horn has always had an interesting effect on McPhee's approach and here he often sits back out of the foreground, working on the deep melody while Giardullo embellishes and improvises in the foreground. Joe's gift for using an unmodified live acoustic to create very subtle effects, the kind of thing that would normally involve retakes, overdubbing and careful mixing, is as impressive as ever, as on 'Birmingham/Come Sunday', when he uses microphone positioning and altered articulation to suggest changes of instrument, creating his own horn section live and on the stand.

***** No Greater Love**
CIMP 209 *McPhee; Joe Giardullo (ss, nbcl); Michael Bisio, Dominic Duval (b).* 3/99.

Six of these nine pieces are duets in various combinations, although none of them is quite as effective as the mournful treatment of the spiritual 'Deep River' which opens the set. The rest run the gamut between playful, passionate and plain gloomy. An oddball mix 'n' match.

***** Specific Gravity**
Boxholder BXH 021 *McPhee; Joe Giardullo (ss, f, bcl, elec).* 9/97.

*****(*) Mr Peabody Goes To Baltimore**
Recorded 005 *McPhee; Michael Johnsen (ss, elec); Jack Wright (reeds); James Cleman (theremin); Jerry Lim (g); Ian Nagoski (elec); Sean Meehan (perc).* 9/00.

Both of these develop some interesting lines of inquiry involving electronics. The duets with Giardullo use delay effects and there is some odd clicking in 'A Priori', a very long piece which mixes organic horn-playing and analogue effects to create a curious old-new hybrid. But they do better yet by a drily lyrical soprano duet on 'After The Rain', and the introduction of valve trombone into the McPhee instrument-stand on the final 'Sienna'.

Mr Peabody Goes To Baltimore offers four pieces recorded at the 2000 High Zero Festival. 'Before The Fall' is a fascinating half-hour duet between McPhee (on pocket trumpet) and Wright, with a constant electronic rumble provided by Nagoski, a soundscape which has the ambience of an abandoned industrial temple. 'Night Of The Krell' is even more bizarre, and 'Klatu', a trio for tenor, guitar and theremin, evolves into a fierce three-cornered punch-up. Joe ends proceedings with a trumpet solo recorded on Howard Street Bridge as the traffic roars past! One of his strangest records, but we find it improbably effective.

***** On Tour ... Toronto/Rochester**
Cadence CJR 1134 *McPhee; Dominic Duval (b); Jay Rosen(d).* 3/01.

***** In Black And White – On Tour ... Ann Arbor/NYC**
Cadence CJR 1144 *As above.* 4/01.

Souvenirs from the road. A voyage around 'Blue Monk' opens, before a couple of distinctly dishevelled standards and a peculiar revision of 'Send In The Clowns', meant as a dedication to Jim Pepper. A new look at 'Old Eyes', a McPhee greatest hit, ends the show. Joe picks up the trumpet again for part of the way, but despite some vivid moments this feels like a scrappy document. The other set is more coherent, but still shapeless.

***** Let Paul Robeson Sing**
CIMP 257 *McPhee; Joe Giardullo (f, bcl); Michael Bisio, Dominic Duval (b).* 9/01.

As McPhee himself insists, not so much a jazz album as a sonic homage to the great American singer and activist, collaging snippets of songs associated with him into usually quite abstract contexts. 'Old Man River' is wisely tucked away right at the end. McPhee's re-creation of a genuine American hero is intense, sincere and genuinely moving, and his band are right behind him every step of the way, with Giardullo particularly effective.

***** Journey**
CIMP 283 *McPhee; Dominic Duval (b); Jay Rosen (d).* 2/03.

Trio X performing in real time in the Spirit Room at CIMP and extending a body of music that is one of the most interesting in contemporary improvisation. McPhee plays alto and tenor saxophones, with a greater emphasis than recently on long lines and sustained harmonic ideas. The episodic structure of the record is mildly distracting when it seems that most of these pieces run together like stages in a real journey.

Charles McPherson (born 1939)

ALTO SAXOPHONE

McPherson's training took place in a tough school called Mingus, with whom he worked for almost 15 years, transforming what had been the Jackie McLean sound into something rather more purely derived from Charlie Parker. An inventive soloist and a very effective writer, he remains oddly unappreciated, perhaps written off as a Bird copyist.

***** Be Bop Revisited**
Original Jazz Classics OJC 710 *McPherson; Carmell Jones (t); Barry Harris (p); Nelson Boyd (b); Albert 'Tootie' Heath (d).* 11/64.

*****(*) Con Alma!**
Original Jazz Classics OJCCD 1875 *McPherson; Clifford Jordan (ts); Barry Harris (p); George Tucker (b); Alan Dawson (d).* 8/65.

***** The Quintet Live!**
Original Jazz Classics OJC 1804 *McPherson; Lonnie Hillyer (t); Barry Harris (p); Ray McKinney (b); Billy Higgins (d).* 10/66.

***** Live At The Five Spot**
Prestige PRCD 24135 *As above.* 10/66.

McPherson credits the relatively unsung Barry Harris for his schooling in bebop, but it's clear that Parker has marked his saxophone playing so deeply that he will always be identified as a faithful disciple. *Con Alma!* was reissued in 1995, and it's immediately clear from 'In A Sentimental Mood' and the title-track that Johnny Hodges was also a strong influence on the youngster. The straightforward bop covers on *Revisited* and the slightly more individualized live material have an energy and clarity of tone that are completely missing from the later, overproduced sessions once reissued on Mainstream.

Of this early group, the Five Spot recording and *Con Alma!* are probably the most immediately approachable, but McPherson remains a performer who is hard to identify other than by his ancestral traits – which is a pity, because he has a lovely tone and seems constantly responsive to his colleagues. Some of the exchanges with Jordan, who takes a much more sceptical view of bop, are revelatory, though few of them are allowed to develop.

***** From This Moment On!**
Original Jazz Classics OJCCD 1899-2 *McPherson; Cedar Walton (p); Pat Martino (g); Peck Morrison (b); Lenny McBrowne (d).* 1/68.

***** Horizons**

Original Jazz Classics OJCCD 1912-2 *As above, except omit Morrison, McBrowne; add Nasir Hafiz (vib), Walter Booker (b), Billy Higgins (d).* 8/68.

*****(*) McPherson's Mood**

Original Jazz Classics OJC 1947 *McPherson; Barry Harris (p); Buster Williams (b); Roy Brooks (d).* 12/69.

McPherson's growing confidence was cemented by a new working relationship with the up-and-coming Cedar Walton and with Pat Martino, a guitarist of genuine originality. The alto/guitar duet on 'Lush Life' on the August 1968 session is a remarkable performance, mining new insights from the old song and turning it into something altogether more solid and durable than the average 'standards' reading. The later of the 1968 albums starts stronger than it finishes, as if the summer heat of New York City gets to the players halfway and they lose pace and commitment.

From This Moment On! is a much more even album. If it lacks the excitement and sheer imagination of its successor, it is probably a more successful entity. McPherson has rarely sounded as briskly swinging, and the sheer drive and energy of these seven relatively short numbers is infectious. Again, Martino is a key element in a line-up with just a single horn, and his playing veers between rich chording and strong, saxophone-influenced lines. The rhythm section of Morrison and McBrowne is less graceful and sophisticated than that of Booker and Higgins (even Booker and Higgins on a slightly off-day) but it gets down to business with a will. Two excellent records from a player now completely in command of his voice and idiom.

Reunited with Barry Harris for *McPherson's Mood*, he still sounds in prime voice and the music is a convincing marriage of on-the-edge bebop and a more personal, outward-looking music. The title blues, opening with a resplendent Williams solo, is sheer class, and even the modish choice of Stevie Wonder's 'My Cherie Amour' gets a songful treatment, though it does tame the more daring elements of the set. McPherson's delivery is full of little inflexions and subtleties which even in his favoured high gear make a telling difference.

*****(*) First Flight Out**

Arabesque AJ 0113 *McPherson; Tom Harrell (t, flhn); Michael Weiss (p); Peter Washington (b); Victor Lewis (d).* 1/94.

First Flight Out is a good example of McPherson's more recent style. He still does a lot of Mingus material, which he presumably knows like the back of his hand, and there is a version of Monk's 'Well You Needn't' which suggests he's spent a bit of time on that fruitful source as well. The playing is lighter in touch but fuller in tone than it used to be and here it sits perfectly with Harrell's lyrical flugelhorn, a rare example of McPherson deliberately pitching himself against another horn.

****** Come Play With Me**

Arabesque AJ0117 *McPherson; Mulgrew Miller (p); Santi Debriano (b); Lewis Nash (d).* 3/95.

A smashing record from a dream band. McPherson still likes to pay homage on occasion, and 'Bloomdido' allows him to show how much he still draws from Charlie Parker's complex legacy but also how well he's invested his inheritance in new ideas. Mulgrew has never sounded comfortable round orthodox bop (none of McCoy Tyner's progeny ever did), but here he slips easily into the idiom and creates a space for himself which is as fruitful as it is challenging. McPherson's originals are as inventive as ever. 'Lonely Little Chimes' might well sound banal in other hands, but he creates a touchingly poignant song that swings in its own individual way. Debriano and Nash are beautifully caught by engineers Malcolm Addey and John Reigart, who both deserve a bigger credit for the set. The romping conclusion, a run-in of three wonderful new songs, might have sounded muddy and confused with the four musicians so closely placed, but the separation is near-perfect and McPherson cuts through without sounding as if he's been recorded separately, which has occasionally happened in the past.

*****(*) Manhattan Nocturne**

Arabesque AJ 01189 *McPherson; Mulgrew Miller (p); Ray Drummond (b); Victor Lewis (d); Bobby Sanabria (perc).* 97.

Poised and quietly charismatic bop from a group which extends the new confidence that has suffused McPherson's recent work. 'Blue'N'Boogie' manages to sound both calm and hectic, and both 'How Deep Is The Ocean' and the title-track have a settled authority which even Bird never achieved. Lewis is in exceptional form and the only disappointment is the rather offhand playing of Mulgrew Miller.

****** Is That It? ... No But**

Vega ART 1005 *McPherson; Don Friedman (p); Earl May (b); Akira Tana (d).* 8/00.

Recorded in Tokyo, where McPherson's Parker apostleship is unquestioned, this is one of his best records in years: immaculately played with a top-drawer band and nicely recorded too. Friedman's intelligent approach to bop is always a delight and his accompaniment on 'But Beautiful' is heart-warming. Tana also has managed to combine power with a musical sophistication that keeps him in the top flight of contemporary drummers. The saxophonist steals the show completely, though; never better.

Carmen McRae (1920–94)

VOCAL

Born in New York, she played piano and wrote songs at an early age. Sang with Benny Carter, Basie and Mercer Ellington in the '40s, then began recording under her own name in 1953 and worked as a soloist from the late '50s. Retired in 1991, after a bad asthma attack.

*****(*) Torchy / Blue Moon**

MCA MCLD 19392 *McRae; orchestras led by Jack Pleis, Tadd Dameron and Jimmy Mundy.* 12/56–3/59.

***** Torchy**

Verve 543829-2 *As above, except omit Pleis.* 3/58–3/59.

***** Birds Of A Feather**

Verve 589515-2 *McRae; orchestra arranged by Ralph Burns.* 58.

****** I'll Be Seeing You**

GRP 050647-2 2CD *McRae; orchestras and groups led by Jack Pleis, Ralph Burns, Jimmy Mundy, Frank Hunter, Luther Henderson.* 55–59.

*****(*) Carmen McRae's Finest Hour**

Verve 543760-2 *As above.* 55–59.

An accomplished pianist, Carmen McRae was something of a late starter as a featured vocalist, not recording a vocal session under her own name until 1954. Her fame has always lagged behind that of her close contemporaries, Sarah Vaughan and Billie Holiday, but eventually she did achieve something like the honour she deserved, and her commitment to jazz singing was unflinching. The CD era has not been very kind to her. Universal's stewardship of her Decca catalogue has been insultingly negligent. It eventually took the British arm of MCA to double up *Torchy* and *Blue Moon*, although the latter has subsequently been released as a Verve Master Edition, albeit with a miserly playing time.

There's always a tigerish feel to her best vocals – no woman has ever sung in the jazz idiom with quite such beguiling surliness as McRae. *Torchy*, the earlier disc, sets her against smoochy Jack Pleis orchestrations, and this is Carmen at her most amenable. Pitched as a set of slowish ballads, she sings them very straight, with an accommodating sweetness. The later *Blue Moon* may make some collectors sit up at the sight of Tadd Dameron and Jimmy Mundy orchestrations, but they're nothing remarkable. The tunes are rather more interesting, though. 'Nowhere' is a wry set-piece which is perfect for McRae, and the final 'All This Could Lead To Love' is a rarity which she handles well. The Verve edition comes in a smarter package but is docked a notch for meanness.

Birds Of A Feather wouldn't have been our first choice for a McRae reissue: respectable Ralph Burns charts, but the decision to make the concept all 'bird' songs meant foisting the likes of 'When The Red Red Robin' and 'When The Swallows Come Back To Capistrano' on the singer. She does her best – and there is compensation in 'Baltimore Oriole' at least. *Finest Hour*, which includes a few scarce 45 sides as well as LP tracks, is a good buy; but this is at least the fourth McRae compilation which the label has done and at this point it's the original ten albums that should be back in print.

****** Sings Lover Man**

Columbia CK 65115 *McRae; Nat Adderley (c); Eddie 'Lockjaw' Davis (ts); Norman Simmons (p, cel); Mundell Lowe (g); Bob Cranshaw (b); Walter Perkins (d).* 6–7/61.

McRae's original tribute to Billie Holiday was something she had wanted to do during her Decca period. At Columbia, where she made only one other album, she got her chance. The deft arrangements are by the often undersung Norman Simmons, and Adderley and Lockjaw Davis take on the Harry Edison and Ben Webster roles. Though she follows Holiday's manner almost to the letter on some songs, notably 'Them There Eyes' and 'Trav'lin' Light', this is all Carmen McRae. She is quite imperious on 'Yesterdays', finds a deadly, almost sardonic note in 'Strange Fruit' and is ineffably tender on 'If The Moon Turns Green'. The musicians play superbly alongside her.

*****(*) The Sound Of Silence / Portrait Of Carmen**

Collectables COL-CD 6835 *McRae; with orchestras arranged by Shorty Rogers, Benny Carter, Jimmy Jones, Gene DiNovi, Oliver Nelson.* 68.

***** The Art Of Carmen McRae / For Once In My Life**

Collectables COL-CD 6836 2CD *As above, except add Jimmy Rowles (p), Johnny Keating Orchestra.* 67–70.

Carmen's love–hate relationship with pop songwriters gets a fascinating airing on the pair of albums which make up the first of the Collectables discs. At a time when the jazz singers of her generation were being importuned to cover everything from The Lovin' Spoonful to the New Vaudeville Band, McRae did it absolutely her way. The charts are in decent hands, and she does some extraordinary things to the material: 'The Sound Of Silence' is transformed into a ferocious anthem of dissent, 'Gloomy Sunday' is chilling, 'I Sold My Heart To The Junkman' oddly ambivalent, as she often was. She ditches the 'cake' half of the 'MacArthur Park' lyric and sings only the haunting verse. *Portrait Of Carmen* isn't quite as good, and the mastering on this session isn't kind to the vocals.

The second set is a bit strange, since it reissues what was originally a double-LP compilation of her various Atlantic dates (and therefore duplicates some of the tracks on the other set) along with what was her first Atlantic LP, *For Once In My Life*. On the latter, she barely conceals her disdain for 'Got To Get You Into My Life' and 'Our Song', but 'The Look Of Love' is superbly Carmenized. Track for track a perfectly playable edition.

*****(*) The Great American Songbook**

Atlantic 781323-2 *McRae; Jimmy Rowles (p); Joe Pass (g); Chuck Domanico (b); Chuck Flores (d).* 72.

A couple of the songs are only questionably 'great', and some of the treatments seem surprisingly hurried or perfunctory. Otherwise this is blue-chip material, a top band, and Carmen in excellent voice, cut live at Donte's in Los Angeles. There are too few such occasions in the McRae discography, so it's a welcome reissue.

****(*) Heat Wave**

Concord CCD 4189 *McRae; Al Bent, Mike Heathman (tb); Mark Levine, Marshall Otwell (p); Cal Tjader (vib); Rob Fisher (b); Vince Lateano (d); Poncho Sanchez, Ramon Banda (perc).* 1/82.

****(*) Fine And Mellow**

Concord CCD 4342 *McRae; Red Holloway (ts); Phil Upchurch (g); Jack McDuff (org); John Clayton Jr (b); Paul Humphrey (d).* 12/87.

*****(*) Ballad Essentials**

Concord CCD 4877-2 *As above Concord albums, except add George Shearing (p).* 82–7.

Her records for Concord were mostly rather disappointing, even if there is something good on all of them. The session with Tjader is blemished by the vibesman's usual flavourless Latin-jazz stylings which offer no backbone to the singer's efforts, and the Stevie Wonder tunes on the record scarcely suit a vocal personality which has a pronounced streak of cussedness when she warms up. Yet *Fine And Mellow* goes to the other extreme without much more conviction; McRae is too sophisticated a stylist to convince as an earthy R&B singer, which this programme and these accompanists are tailored for. However, the very shrewdly chosen compilation *Ballad Essentials* creams off all the best tracks from her three dates (including the deleted *You're Looking At Me*), plus three duets with George Shearing, and makes this definitely the one to get.

***** Carmen Sings Monk**

RCA Bluebird 09026-63841-2 *McRae; Charlie Rouse, Clifford Jordan (ts); Larry Willis, Eric Gunnison (p); George Mraz (b); Al Foster (d).* 1–4/88.

McRae's tribute to the bebop mentor hasn't worn all that well. Some of Jon Hendricks's lyrics, for all their ingenuity, make too much of an effort out of fitting the music, and Carmen's vocals sometimes sound overworked, even tired. Nevertheless the session finds passages of real beauty, such as the properly grand 'Ruby, My Dear', and the instrumentalists acquit themselves well. This new edition has three alternative takes.

Jay McShann (born 1916)

PIANO, VOCAL, BANDLEADER

It's often assumed that 'Hootie' hails from Kansas City, but he was born in Muskogee, Oklahoma, and attended the famous Tuskegee Institute. He worked with Don Byas as a 15-year-old and later moved to KC, where his famous big band became a recruiting centre for some soon-to-be-legendary names. McShann's unaffected playing and singing have remained durable through many comebacks.

***(*) Jay McShann, 1941–1943

Classics 740 *McShann; Harold Bruce, Orville Minor, Bernard Anderson, Bob Merrill, Willie Cook, Dave Mitchell, Jesse Jones (t); Joe Baird, Alonzo Pettiford, Alonso Fook, Rudy Morrison (tb); Charlie Parker, John Jackson, Rudolf Dennis (as); Bob Mabane, Harry Ferguson, Fred Culliver, Paul Quinichette, Bill Goodson (ts); Rae Brodely (bs); Leonard Enois (g); Gene Ramey (b); Gus Johnson, Harold 'Doc' West, Bob Merrill (d); Al Hibbler, Walter Brown (v).* 4/41–12/43.

Historically, McShann's swing band will always be remembered as the incubator for Charlie Parker's raw talent to start to blossom. The orchestra pack a Kansas City punch that stands squarely as second-generation Basie, and the blues performances on 'Hootie Blues', 'Swingmatism' and 'Dexter Blues' still have an authentic tang of KC *brio*. The Classics includes material from December 1943, three tracks of no special consequence, not least in not including Parker, who had already taken the next step in his career. McShann, who was considered a footnote in that story ever since, scarcely sounds it here, chugging away at his own thing without a shred of anxiety about what might be going on elsewhere in New York City.

*** Jay McShann, 1944–46

Classics 966 *McShann; Major Evans, Clarence Thornton, Oliver Todd (t); Tommy Douglas, Edmond Gregory, Theodore Smalls (as); Cleophus Curtis, Seeward Evans, Claiborne Graves (ts); Efferge Ware (g); Percy Gabriel, Walter Page, Raymond Taylor (b); Sam Lovett, Jesse Price, Albert Wichard (d); Numa Lee Davis, Julia Lee, Charles Waterford, Jimmy Witherspoon (v).* 11/44–11/46.

After his discharge from the army, McShann had to rethink his strategy more than a little, scaling down his working band to a small, workable combo. The group's return to Kansas City, his home town, in November 1944 yielded one of the best sessions of his career. Julia Lee's vocals were an integral part of the equation, but it is the quality of playing in this terse, taut small group that attracts the attention. Nothing else on this disc is as good. The vocal material with Witherspoon and others has its moments, but the verve and wit of 'Moten Swing' and 'On The Sunny Side Of The Street' aren't matched in the 1945 material for Philo and Premier, and the pace picks up again only after McShann signed for Mercury, using Witherspoon as front-man on material like 'Voodoo Woman Blues', 'Have You Ever Loved A Woman' and 'Gone With The Blues'.

*** Jumpin' The Blues

Proper Pairs 131 2CD *As for the above.* 41–46.

A good-value option for those who'd rather not go down the Classics route. This is a nicely produced and packaged set, with all the stuff one would want from this early period. It's arguable, though, whether Jay really hit his stride until later in life and we'd recommend you sample one of the later small-group discs first.

*** Confessin' The Blues

Black & Blue 867 *McShann; T-Bone Walker (g); Roland Lobligeois (b); Paul Gunther (d).* 3/69.

Unusual to find Walker in this role, but he contributes manfully to a fine set of blues-driven tunes that in this reissue marks a break in the long hiatus in McShann recordings. Black & Blue did sterling work in recording Americans at this time, many of them artists who'd spent little time in the studio in the previous decade. Hootie sounds strong and confident and isn't afraid to let a few raw edges put him off his stride.

**(*) Kansas City Memories

Black & Blue 965 *McShann; Arnett Cobb (ts); Milt Buckner (p, org); Clarence Gatemouth Brown, Al Casey (g); Roland Lobligeois (b); Paul Gunther (d).* 70, 7/73.

Co-led with Buckner, whose locked-hands approach was an insidiously imitable new style, this is a rather dull and muddled set. The two pianists don't strike sparks off one another and even when Milt switches to organ, the chemistry is wonky. Cobb is in as a guest soloist for a couple of tracks, but while they're amiable enough they lack the energy and the dignified power we expect of him. Jay's had better days, though he must have been grateful for the gig at the time. This was still a lean spell.

**(*) After Hours

Storyville 8279 *McShann; Thomas Muller (g); Ole Skipper Mosgard (b); Thorkild Moller (d).* 4/77.

The personnel is slightly misleading because, apart from two tracks, *After Hours* is entirely solo. McShann is in good if unexciting form, knocking out a solid, blues-based performance which includes hits like 'The Man From Muskogee' and 'Yardbird Waltz'. The group are buoyant and competent enough, but it's very much a question of McShann taking care of business in the old familiar way.

***(*) Last Of The Blue Devils

Koch Jazz 8525 *McShann; Joe Newman (t); Paul Quinichette, Buddy Tate (ts); John Scofield (g); Milt Hinton (b); Jack Williams (d).* 78.

A remarkable line-up and a wonderful set. One of the problems with the McShann discography is the relatively limited range of tunes and songs on offer, but even familiar things like 'Hootie Blues', which he famously co-wrote with young Charlie Parker, and 'Jumpin' At The Woodside' are as fresh-minted as if they'd just been written on the piano lid. The two tenors – a configuration which Jay has always loved – give even the lightest of tunes a resonance and warmth and both Tate and Quinichette get off some very fine solos. The surprise in the personnel is, of course, the young Scofield. Should you have cause to wonder, listening to his work of the '90s, where and how he acquired such astonishing chops, this may well be the answer. A recommended album.

***** Last Of The Whorehouse Piano Players**
Chiaroscuro 206 *McShann; Ralph Sutton (p); Milt Hinton (b); Gus Johnson (d).* 12/79.

***** Last Of The Whorehouse Piano Players**
Chiaroscuro 306 *As above.* 3/89.

A veteran's symposium aimed at raising consciousness of the social and aesthetic needs of keyboard artistes. Or: two of the craftiest old beggars ever to step on a sustain pedal, having a laugh. You decide. A decade apart, these are great sessions, full of rumbustious energy. Having Old Father Time on hand with the bull fiddle was an inspired decision. Milt has almost as much history as these two and still sounds as if he could run round the block if you dared him to. Entertaining, vigorous piano jazz. You'll probably find them listed under Sutton's name as well.

**** Best Of Friends**
JSP CD 224 *McShann; Al Casey (g); Kenny Baldock (b); Robin Jones (d).* 4/82.

***** Swingmatism**
Sackville 2-3046 *McShann; Don Thompson (b); Archie Alleyne (d).* 10/82.

***** Just A Lucky So And So**
Sackville 2- 3035 *McShann; Jim Galloway (ss, bs); Don Thompson (b); Terry Clarke (d).* 8/83.

****(*) Airmail Special**
Sackville 2-3040 *McShann; Neil Swainson (b); Terry Clarke (d).* 8/85.

***** At Café Des Copains**
Sackville 2-2024 *McShann (p solo).* 8/83–9/89.

McShann has recorded many albums for Sackville and they are starting to reappear on CD. At his best, he blends a wide variety of mannerisms into a personal kind of swing–stride–blues piano; at anything less than that, he can sound like a less-than-profound and overly eclectic performer. Most of these records feature moments when he's caught between those positions. The meeting with Al Casey is jolly, unprepossessing stuff, both men jogging along to no great end except to have a bit of fun. *Swingmatism* is rather better: focused by a decent rhythm section, McShann sets his mind to a programme that depends heavily on Ellington for source material, and 'The Jeep Is Jumpin'' and 'The Mooche' are good accounts of less frequently heard tunes. Jim Galloway is an engaging partner on *Lucky So And So*, which features some attractive playing from both men. McShann excels on 'Red Sails In The Sunset' and gives 'On A Clear Day You Can See Forever' an emotional impact that previously only Barbra Streisand has ever delivered. What a duet that would be.

Airmail Special is all right, if a bit uneventful, but the best disc is probably the solo set. McShann thinks through a wide spectrum of material – going as far back as Ferde Grofé's 'On The Trail' and ending up with Michel Legrand – and the good piano and live atmosphere elicit a sound series of interpretations, recorded during several visits over a period of six years.

***** Havin' Fun**
Sackville 2-2047 *McShann; Major Holley (b).* 91.

****(*) Some Blues**
Chiaroscuro CR(D) 320 *McShann; Clark Terry (t, v); Al Grey (tb); Major Holley (b, v); Milt Hinton (b); Ben Riley, Bobby Durham (d).* 2/90–9/92.

***** My Baby With The Black Dress On**
Chiaroscuro 345 *McShann (p, v).* 92.

***** The Missouri Connection**
Reservoir RSR CD 124 *McShann; John Hicks (p).* 9/92.

Now into his '80s, McShann remains amazingly spirited. His meeting with John Hicks is a discussion about the blues over two keyboards and, while it hardly says anything new about the form, it's a genial encounter, neither man having to compromise his ground to any extent.

In Major Holley he has a partner of the old school, a bassist who can 'walk' with the best of them, but who's also capable of playing strong melody lines. A completely engaging album. *Some Blues* is a hotchpotch that starts with more duos cut with Major Holley and two sessions with Terry, Grey and the others. The bass-and-piano tracks hit a characteristic McShann note of rough good humour, but the band titles are a bit thin. There's also a bonus track of the leader reminiscing for the microphone.

My Baby comes with a very racy cover and Hootie immediately whisks you back to a world of speakeasies, gin joints and women of easy virtue, a mini-musical of the old jazz world. The voice is in great shape, ever more intimate and confiding, and Jay plays the blues as brilliantly as ever.

***** Hootie!**
Chiaroscuro 357 *McShann; Phil Woods (as); Flip Phillips, David Newman (ts); Keter Betts (b); Jackie Williams (d).* 10/97.

Phil, Flip and Fathead line up to blow alongside the old master (on board the SS *Norway*, on one of their famous jazz cruises) and it's Mr Newman who comes off best. Must be something in the water. The whole show is good fun, though.

***** Hootie's Jumpin' Blues**
Stony Plain 1237 *McShann; Bob Tildesley (t); Gordon Beadle (ts); Dave Babcock (bs); Marty Ballou (b); Marty Richards (d).* 98.

***** Still Jumpin' The Blues**
Stony Plain 1254 *McShann; Dave Babcock (as, ts); Dennis Taylor (ts); Duke Robillard (g); Marty Richards (d); Maria Muldaur (v).* 99.

'Still' because Hootie is one of the elder statesmen of the music and a living link back to the days of classic jazz and blues. Which is why no one will begrudge him the final interview track on this excellent disc. He is almost as convincing a storyteller as he is a bluesman, but it's his playing, still vibrant and alert, that really recommends this album. The inclusion of Maria Muldaur will make some hearts beat faster and her slow, moody delivery is an exact foil to McShann. The best of the tracks are 'Goin' To Chicago' and 'Moten Swing', old stuff to be sure, but played with absolute conviction.

The slightly earlier release adds a touch of brass to the ensemble and puts a bit of punch into the old tunes. As ever, the material is straightforwardly generic, though 'Hootie Ignorant Oil' and 'Profoundly Blue' may surprise some listeners. The saxes are very good and the recording has a relaxed live feel. As McShann well knows and is shrewd enough to exploit, he's become a living monument. The life story is in the music, but it's good to have the old man tell it straight as well.

***** Goin' To Kansas City**
Stony Plain 1286 *McShann; Johnny Johnson (p, v); Duke Robillard (g); Maria Muldaur (v).* n.d.

This was McShann's first KC album for several decades, all appearances to the contrary. It wasn't made in a single session, hence a curious inconsistency of tone that creeps in at points. It's enlivened by the contributions of both Johnson on 'Some Kinda Crazy' and by Robillard, who does superb work on his tracks as accompanist, and also by Maria Muldaur, who joins the old boy for a version of 'Confessin' The Blues'. Leiber & Stoller's 'Kansas City' kicks off a fairly themed programme of tunes and he returns to it later in the set for a very different duo reading. There's an interview with Jay at the end, which makes this one additionally attractive to collectors, even if it isn't a top pick musically.

Medeski, Martin & Wood

GROUP

New York trio who built a nationwide audience in the '90s by back-of-the-bus touring, fashioning a Grateful Dead-style cult of followers. The music is organ, bass and drums, jazz, rock and whatever else they can stir in.

***** It's A Jungle In Here**

Gramavision R2 79495 CD *John Medeski (org, p); Billy Martin (d, perc); Chris Wood (b); Steven Bernstein (t, flhn); Josh Roseman (tb); Jay Rodrigues (ts, as); Dave Binney (as); Marc Ribot (g).* 8/93.

... and in that jungle called Noo Yawk strange cries and rhythms proliferate like orchids. Where else would anyone put Monk's 'Bemsha Swing' in on top of Bob Marley's 'Lively Up Yourself' and make it work? Or follow it with King Sunny Ade's 'Moti Mo', and make that seem like a perfectly sensible juxtaposition? The basic organ trio is steaming enough not to require the assistance of horns (though Ribot's guitar is a definite fillip, by turns abstract and funky).

***** Friday Afternoon In The Universe**

Gramavision GCD 79503 *As above, except omit Bernstein, Roseman, Rodrigues, Binney, Ribot.* 94.

***** Shack-man**

Gramavision GCD 79514 *As above.* 6/96.

We were initially disappointed by the second album, but it stands up well over time, and it's here that one can start to hear the subtle mix of jukebox R&B and modern jazz which would subsequently lead MMW into the arms of Blue Note. The trio also showed itself to be capable of adding a floaty impressionism to its armoury of styles. The absence of additional players oddly didn't seem to strip down the sound unduly. *Friday Afternoon* ... is every bit as richly textured as its predecessor.

The third in line was recorded at the Shack in Hawaii and has a sun-warmed ease deep down in the grooves. Less spiky than its two predecessors, *Shack-man* is firmly located in an acid-jazz bag, but John Medeski's wry grasp of sonics and Billy Martin's tight beat, loose-wristed but absolutely on the button, lift it right up there. The opening take on 'Is There Anybody Here That Love My Jesus' is simply glorious. Think Brian Auger Trinity. Think '90s, and you just about have it.

****** Combustication**

Blue Note 7243 4 93011-2 *As above, except add DJ Logic (turntables).* 98.

MMW were a gift to the new look Blue Note, and the trio paid back their advance with a subtle, swinging album which is not nearly as trendily accessorized as the presence of turntable whizz DJ Logic might suggest. Logic actually figures on only three numbers and is subtlety itself, creating fills and cross-grained beats round the trio.

The album gained extra currency by being sampled for a mobile phone company's television commercials, but there is a haunting *déjà-vu* quality to the album as a whole, a perseveration that hints at how thoroughly it is inscribed in the Blue Note idiom. All the same, it is a completely individual work, and tracks like 'Nocturne' and 'Whatever Happened To Gus' are haunting. The latter features a surreal, nostalgic narration by Steve Cannon, a Beat-inspired celebration of the great days of jazz. A pity it fades away so irresolutely.

More than ever the trio sound revolves round the polyrhythms and deceptive embellishments of Billy Martin, who has emerged as a drummer of real gifts. His introduction to 'Latin Shuffle' is virtuosic and John Medeski's piano solo just about tops it for sheer energy. Chris Wood holds the theme together with a sinewy ostinato.

***** Uninvisible**

Blue Note 35870-2 *John Medeski (ky); Billy Martin (d); Chris Wood (b) Jordan McLean, Todd Simon (t, flhn); Aaron Johnson (tb); Stuart D Bogie (ts, bcl); Michael Herbst(bs, bcl); Scotty Hard(g, elec, turntables); Danny Bloom (g); Eddie Bobe(perc); Brad Roberts, Col Bruce Hampton (v); DJ Olive, DJ P. Love (turntables).* n.d.

They won't thank us, but in a way MM&W are beginning to sound like a comedy group – not quite the Spike Jones of the organ-combo field, but it's hard not to laugh at tracks such as 'Your Name Is Snake Anthony', with Hampton's Amerikan-gothick text, and 'Where Have You Been', which features Brad Roberts. Vocals and sound effects are perhaps their Achilles heel, since they're distractions from their own kind of fusion – new and old-fashioned at the same time. They've become the influencing force on a whole school of new groups, or so some press statements claim, yet that can only be in some procedural sense: nothing else sounds much like this mix of mixes, horns, keyboards, drums, boogaloo rhythms, textures, grooves, blues, movie-music and mood-music. Like we said, it's a laugh. And since there's nothing new to add since, maybe the joke's over.

John Mehegan (1920–84)

PIANO

Better known as a jazz educator than as a player, Mehegan's recording career effectively ended before he was 40. He enjoyed brief prominence in partnership with Kenny Dorham and some notoriety after getting into difficulties with apartheid-era South African authorities for 'fraternizing' with black musicians.

***** Casual Affair**

Fresh Sound FSR 1612 *Mehegan; Kenny Dorham (t); Chuck Wayne (g); Ernie Furtado (b).* 5–6/59.

Mehegan's early work for Savoy is long out of print, including a fine duo set with fellow-pianist Eddie Costa which is worth picking out of a second-hand bin. It's Dorham who makes this unexpected reissue attractive, playing with his customary warmth and vivacity. A shame he isn't featured prominently on every track. Mehegan sounds very much like a man who plays jazz as a pastime rather than an avocation. That's not to undermine his technique, which is very solid, but there isn't much drama in these seven tracks.

Brad Mehldau (born 1970)

PIANO, VIBES

Born in Florida, Mehldau arrived in New York in 1989 and was soon getting plenty of sideman work, with Jimmy Cobb, Cecil Payne and Joshua Redman. Worked in Europe with Perico Sambeat and the Rossys, then signed to Warners as a solo artist.

*****(*) New York–Barcelona Crossing**
Fresh Sound FSNT 031 *Mehldau; Perico Sambeat (as); Mario Rossy (b); Jorge Rossy (d).* 5/93.

***** New York–Barcelona Crossing**
Fresh Sound FSNT 037 *As above.* 5/93.

*****(*) When I Fall In Love**
Fresh Sound FSNT 007 *As above, except omit Sambeat.* 10/93.

****** Introducing Brad Mehldau**
Warner Bros 945997-2 *Mehldau; Larry Grenadier, Christian McBride (b); Jorge Rossy, Brian Blade (d).* 3–4/95.

Mehldau continues to excite enormous interest. In our last edition we suggested that he was set fair to become one of the major voices in the music, and he's done little to disappoint that expectation, although a fair number of voices have been nay-sayers on the issue. His Warner records are a formidable lot, but the Fresh Sound releases, which he will probably look back on as mere student-work, are exceptional. Both of the *New York–Barcelona Crossing* discs were cut live in a Spanish club and, besides the exemplary alto of Sambeat (who was the real leader of the date) and fine work from both the Rossys, Mehldau plays some uncannily beautiful jazz. His introduction and improvisation on 'Old Folks' are quite breathtaking and it's clear that the pristine touch of the later discs was already in place. The second volume isn't quite so impressive, although 'It's Easy To Remember' is another gorgeous ballad performance, at a dangerously slow tempo.

The trio record is a good display of chops. 'Anthropology' goes off at a hurricane tempo. The title-ballad takes a very long, expansive time over itself, and it does ramble a bit. 'At A Loss' and 'Convalescent' are fascinating originals and, as much as he enjoys exploring standards, Mehldau does seem to save some of himself for his own writing. Recorded live, this doesn't have the polish of the later records, but it still cuts most piano trio sessions.

The first album for Warner was a flying start. Though Mehldau's playing is structured in a familiar post-bop mode, it's as if he were aware of jazz tradition but entirely unencumbered by it. That lends such freshness to, say, the opening 'It Might As Well Be Spring' that he seems to be uncovering a previously overlooked but brilliant piano interpretation. On Coltrane's 'Countdown' he creates a logical solo out of phrases and whole passages that seem superficially disparate from one another. His slow playing is distinguished by an exquisitely light touch – 'My Romance' is made to glow – and it's lightness that characterizes his manner. He shies away from dense voicings and will leave a daring amount of space in even a fast improvisation. His own writing fits in with the rest of his style: sample the unexpectedly jaunty 'Angst'.

CORE COLLECTION

****** The Art Of The Trio Vol. 1**
Warners 46260-2 *Mehldau; Larry Grenadier (b); Jorge Rossy (d).* 9/96.

The titles suggest some heavyweight expectations, and the records deliver on them all. The studio disc is a focusing of some of the flights he looked into on *Introducing*. An original like 'Lucid' is a beautiful, sculpted miniature which suggests that composing is something that comes easily to Mehldau – but also something which he may not actually be all that interested in, since his greatest energy seems to be reserved for his improvising on standards. 'Blame It On My Youth' sparkles at a slow-to-medium tempo, 'Blackbird' is shaped into a glittering new song, but it's his celestial treatment of 'I Fall In Love Too Easily' which is the heart of the record.

****** The Art Of The Trio Vol. 2: Live At The Village Vanguard**
Warners 46848-2 *As above.* 97.

At The Vanguard, he played another version of Coltrane's 'Countdown', which can act as a marker for his progress from the debut album on Warner. Where the earlier version was created out of disparate lines, this one is detailed and dense – he gets a long, long way into the piece, which his unaccompanied passage seems suddenly to illuminate, as if abruptly finding answers to a lot of questions. This is perhaps a more ambitious record, sparked by the live situation, and it's like a detailed addendum to the finished elegance of the first volume. Rossy and Grenadier are inevitably overshadowed, but to their credit they follow Mehldau without a stumble.

*****(*) Songs: The Art Of The Trio Vol. 3**
Warner Bros 9362-476051-2 *As above.* 5/98.

****** The Art Of The Trio Vol. 4: Back At the Vanguard**
Warner Bros 9362-47463-2 *As above.* 1/99.

Mehldau has been exciting a lot of conversation, both for and against him, and he seems keen to join in the fray if his sleeve-note to *Vol. 4* is anything to go by. In so far as every white pianist who does a good ballad gets compared to Bill Evans, he's right to complain about many of the comments (and he doesn't much sound like Evans at all). More germane may be the fact that he's on a major label: if all these records had come out on some worthy independent, they would most likely have received uniform approbation.

So to the music. The third volume sets his own songs alongside Rodgers and Hart, Nick Drake and Radiohead, the kind of juxtaposition – in a straightahead context – which a new generation of jazz players is making plausible. Mehldau takes what he wants from each of these songs and fashions it into a plausible improvisation, without entirely abstracting the original material. Admittedly, it works better with some pieces than with others – 'Bewitched' seems set in aspic – and his five originals, including new versions of 'At A Loss' and 'Convalescent', might sit better in an all-original programme. But the trio are growing more individual as a unit all the time, too. That's made even more clear by the return to the Village Vanguard for *Vol. 4*, another superbly effective session. The long 'Nice Pass' contains enough food for thought by itself, 17 minutes of steadily evolving trio music, with the pianist suddenly taking a solo part midway through that suggests a stride-piano fantasia, before the other players are cleverly reintegrated into the action. Marvellous, but there is also a superbly compact 'Solar', a brimming 'All The Things You Are' which is a genuinely enjoyable show-off piece, and a general sense that Mehldau and his companions are pushing themselves and their audience that bit harder to cast away any demons of excessive introversion.

***** Elegiac Cycle**

Warner Bros 9362-47357-2 *Mehldau (p solo).* 2/99.

No reason why Mehldau shouldn't be ready to do a solo record. But this one seems likes a severe disappointment after the bounty of the trio albums. As bullish (and entertaining) as his sleeve-notes are, he seems defensive about his right to play this way. He can play whatever and however he chooses, but the audience has the same option of listening or not. In the end, with its rather stiff truce between song form, jazz and classical piano, this seems like a recital in search of a context.

***** Places**

Warner Bros 9362-47693-2 *Mehldau; Larry Grenadier (b); Jorge Rossy (d).* 1–3/00.

***** Progression: The Art Of The Trio Vol. 5**

Warner Bros 9362-48005-2 2CD *As above.* 9/00.

One interesting matter about Mehldau's recordings is the way Warners have left him almost to his own devices: there've been no guest stars, no walk-on parts for singers, no remixes, no electricity, no one-composer concepts, no homages. After eight records, apart from the mild diversion of the solo record, it's been nothing but the trio, playing standards, jazz themes, a few originals and the odd piece of pop bricolage. At this point, we're so used to novelty in the way jazz players are handled at major labels that it almost seems perverse. Yet on they go. Maybe *Places* is a kind of concept-homage to various stopovers and watering holes in the lives of travelling musicians, all of it Mehldau-written, half-solo and half-group. It's sunny, even breezy, rather like a holiday record, although as with any vacation there are moments when one can feel suddenly tired, or homesick. 'Amsterdam' has a few dissonances that upset the carousel feel, and 'Paris' is under cloudy skies.

Back, yet again, at the Vanguard, the trio work though two-and-a-quarter hours of intense music. It's too much and there are pieces which emerge barely alive from the pianist's quite ruthless style of inquiry. Nick Drake's 'River Man' is exposed as a tune that can only be taken so far. But it's a set for ingesting slowly, and even in smaller pieces the music suggests a group and a pianist who are working at a very high level. Several pieces are made into vehicles for pianistic displays of a striking kind, where the improvising is like a self-contained passage of virtuosity, Mehldau looking for a result far removed from a mere development out of chords or melody. It may strike some as pretentious, but when it comes off it's a dizzying alternative to what comes out of most piano trio music.

*****(*) Largo**

Warner Jazz 9362-48114-2 *Mehldau; John Brion (g, syn); Larry Grenadier, Darek 'Oles' Oleszkiewicz, Justin Medal-Johnson (b); Matt Chamberlain, Jorge Rossy, Jim Keltner, Victor Indrizzo (d).* 4/02.

Since Mehldau was the first to cover Radiohead, he's entitled to have another go, this time on 'Paranoid Android'. It's perhaps the central text in what some may have seen as his rock record: originals mixed in with a significant measure of contemporary writing (if The Beatles can be called contemporary), some studio experimentation, a carefully-weighted degree of electronic injection. The trio is still the fulcrum, but Brion and the other players play their significant part, and horn sounds orchestrate a lush counterpoint on several pieces. There's little one could call experimental here, since it all sounds focused and finished, as if Mehldau knew just what he wanted from the idiom. And there's still a lot of piano.

****** Anything Goes**

Warner Jazz 9362-46082-2 *Mehldau; Larry Grenadier (b); Jorge Rossy (d).* 9/02.

If, on the face of it, this is another template for Mehldau's Accessible Album – standards, a bossa nova, a couple of rock tunes, a Monk – it's to his credit that he leaves the project unmarked by any hint of what might be called 'compromise'. 'Tres Palabras' – rarely covered since the Kenny Burrell–Coleman Hawkins version of 40 years earlier – is recognizable as what it is, but the pianist injects his own spin on the melody. 'Get Happy' gets one of Mehldau's almost patented diversions half-way through, the kind of thing his live sets delight in. And the Monk tune is 'Skippy', one of the toughest calls in the master's book, which is evolved via a thoroughgoing transformation into a trio orchestration, the kind of thing its composer shied well away from. He's a hard listen, for all the attention he's gathered, and for that very reason Mehldau is fascinating to follow.

Rajesh Mehta (born 1964)

TRUMPET, BASS TRUMPET

Calcutta born, of American nationality, trained in France and now living in Amsterdam, Mehta studied under Anthony Braxton and belongs to that 'school' of structured improvisation.

***** Innovative Music Meeting**

True Muze 0002 *Mehta; Rohan de Saram (clo); Trichy Sankaran (perc, v).* 11/97.

Rohan de Saram is one of the finest instrumentalists in Europe, an accomplished modern-classical player with the Arditti String Quartet and an occasional member of improvisers AMM. What he brings to this one-off encounter is a fabulous technique and a thoughtful approach to improvisation that pays dividends on the 'Bhava 3' duo with Mehta. One shouldn't lump the influences here simply as 'Indian'. Sankaran is from the South and de Saram is Sinhalese, which means that all three draw on very diverse backgrounds. Sankaran brings an array of Indian percussion, but also a wonderful vocal style, which spills over joyously on 'Trichy's Rap'. More interesting than Tricky, we'd dare to say. The 'Bhava' duos are often better than the trio cuts, where the players tend to get in each other's way, though that is also a function of a rather lumpen record and mix. Stimulating and unusual.

****(*) Orka**

hatOLOGY 524 *Mehta; Paul Lovens (d, perc).* 98.

Tough listening. Mehta has explored otherwise uncharted aspects of his instrument, utilising the rarely heard bass trumpet (Michael Zwerin is the only other familiar exponent), deconstructing his horn in performance *à la* George Lewis, and playing multiple trumpets using extensions and outer mouthpieces. As a technical experiment, much of this is fascinating, but *Orka*, with the exception of the opening solo 'Tu-Vas' and the title-piece, also unaccompanied, is not an easy or particularly rewarding experience. Paul Lovens could accompany the sound of a lawnmower and make it interesting, but even he doesn't lift the duo tracks, which are strangely desiccated and flat.

****** Window Shopping**

True Muze 9802 *Mehta; Felicity Provan (t, pkt-t, v); Tom Fryer (g); Paul Stouthamer (clo); Alan Purves (d).* 98.

After the lukewarm reception we gave the hatOLOGY disc, some readers will assume that the generous rating above is a conscience vote. No such thing. This is a stunningly good record, full of life, light and joy, with the exception of one track, 'Aarti', which is a kind of pan-tonal blues. Mehta's basic trio – with Provan in the Don Cherry role and Purves on percussion – is augmented by Australian Fryer on electric guitar (brilliant on the rocky 'Grublein') and Stouthamer giving Hank Roberts a run for his money on cello. Ethnic influences inspire some great writing and playing: everything from Karnatic rhythms to the sort of stuff you might pick up on shortwave from Cairo. Splendid record.

***** Reconfigurations**

Between the Lines btl 010 *Mehta; Vlatko Kucan (ss, ts, cl, bcl, hca); Alexander Kolkowski (vn, vla); Peter Niklas Wilson (b); Ray Kaczynski (d, perc).* 6/00.

The Mehta/meta puns lie in wait for this one. The trumpeter is very interested in the mystical significance of numbers and some of that thinking comes out here in this three-part suite of markedly abstract music by the Mehta-Metric ensemble. The instrumentation is as effective as it is unusual, with Mehta adding slide trumpet to his arsenal to allow him to play glissandi and long portamento effects which sit comfortably with the strings. It's still not easy music to absorb in a single sitting and there are definite longueurs, but it's worth rising to the challenge.

Myra Melford (born 1957)

PIANO, HARMONIUM

New York-based pianist and composer, working on the cusp of completely free playing and post-bop composition.

*****(*) Alive In The House Of Saints**

hatOLOGY 2-570 2CD *Melford; Lindsey Horner (b); Reggie Nicholson (d).* 2/93.

Melford's discography is a still missing a few good records, but hatOLOGY have reinstated this excellent set with 40 minutes of extra music, turning it into a double-disc package. The sheer brio and bustle of this trio still sound like a tonic. Caught live, the group rattle through some of Melford's premier compositions with apparent abandonment one moment (the tumultuous 'Now & Now 1') and an almost grandiose sense of dignity the next ('Between Now And Then'). Bluesy and swinging but encompassing a lot of complexity and outward-bound structural freedoms, this was an exceptional band. The live recording may lack the last ounce of finesse but there's nothing obscured, and even though there's almost two hours of music here there's very little in the way of spacefilling – even Nicholson's drum solos are worth waiting for.

*****(*) Eleven Ghosts**

hatOLOGY 507 *Melford; Han Bennink (d).* 2/94.

This was an unlikely match – although who *is* a likely partner for Bennink? Drummed up on a visit to Zurich, this meeting is terrific fun, from the funeral-march tempo for Leroy Carr's 'How Long Blues' to the farewell punchline of 'Maple Leaf Rag'.

***** Dance Beyond The Color**

Arabesque AJO147 *Melford; Stomu Takeishi (b); Kenny Wolleson (d, sampler).* n.d.

She calls this trio Crush, but it's not that violent – if anything, her early band with Lindsay Horner and Reggie Nicholson was a lot more indecently power-packed. Takeishi uses electric bass, which adds a rubbery feel to the bottom section, and when Melford moves over to the harmonium (!) and Wolleson sneaks in a few samples, the group develops into a colourful, pocket-size chamber band. It's graceful, rather cheery music – not all that terpsichorean but with vitality enough.

*****(*) Yet Can Spring**

Arabesque AJO154 *Melford; Marty Ehrlich (as, cl, bcl).* 3/00.

They've worked in this pairing often enough to make a record date not just a happenstance collaboration, and with a mere 52 minutes of music there's nothing wasted, from the noise and subsequent resolution of the opening title-track to the finish on an Otis Spann blues. There's a nice bite to the upscale music, but not so much that it makes the more reposeful pieces seem too harsh a contrast; and Ehrlich continues to be one of the most melodious reed players of his generation.

Gil Melle (born 1931)

BARITONE SAXOPHONE, KEYBOARDS

Melle's picaresque life is a fanciful subject too involved to list here: it takes in aviation, science and, for some of the time, jazz. Some of his '50s recordings are neglected classics.

****** Primitive Modern / Quadrama**

Original Jazz Classics OJC 1712 *Melle; Joe Cinderella (g); Bill Phillips (b); Ed Thigpen, Shadow Wilson (d).* 4–6/56.

****** Gil's Guests**

Original Jazz Classics OJC 1753 *Melle; Art Farmer, Kenny Dorham (t); Hal McKusick (as, f); Julius Watkins (frhn); Don Butterfield (tba); Joe Cinderella (g); Vinnie Burke (b); Ed Thigpen (d).* 8/56.

Melle's original sleeve-note for *Primitive Modern* suggests that 'modern jazz at its best is a wedding of the classics with the more modern developments native to jazz'; while that implies third-stream dogma, at least Melle put the notion to very striking use. Anyone who lists Bartók, Varèse and Herbie Nichols as major influences is going to do something more than hard bop, and the leader's attempts at shifting the parameters of standard jazz form remain surprising and invigorating. The fast-moving complexities of 'Ironworks', the mysterious dirge, 'Dominica', and the Russell-like 'Adventure Swing' mark out a path very different from most other developments of the time. Cinderella reveals himself as a fine soloist and perceptive interpreter of Melle's needs, and the rhythm section are also fine; while Melle himself is content to play an often reserved role, although his improvisations are melodically as strong as those of Lars Gullin, the baritone player he admits to admiring most. There are a couple of drawbacks – the original studio sound is rather flat, with the leader a little remote in the mix, and some of the structures are delivered a little stiffly by the quartet – but otherwise this is a significant and too little-known record. The CD edition is greatly welcomed, especially since it includes the entire *Quadrama* album as a bonus on the original programme, another remarkable quartet date with two exceptional Ellington transformations and the fine original 'Rush Hour In Hong Kong'.

If anything, *Gil's Guests* is even better, thanks to Rudy van Gelder's superior engineering and the opportunities that a bigger ensemble permits for Melle to create heightened colours, more vivid texture and counterpoint, and a smoother transition between his classically inspired ideas and a jazz execution. Even a conventional feature such as 'Sixpence', written for Kenny Dorham, has an ingenious arrangement for tuba and guitar at the beginning. 'Ghengis' is a direct borrowing from Bartók, and the shifting voicings of 'Block Island' merge brilliantly into a theme that works just as well as a blowing vehicle. An outstanding record, well remastered. Melle's first sessions for Blue Note have been briefly available as one of their Connoisseur Editions, *The Complete Blue Note Fifties Sessions* (Blue Note 495718-2, 2CD).

Steve Melling (born 1959)

PIANO

Born in Accrington, Melling has brought a touch of northern grit to London jazz for many years. Has played with numerous high-profile British bands covering a wide expanse of post-bop ground.

*****(*) Trio Duo Solo**

Jazz House JHCD 045 *Melling; Arnie Somogyi, Simon Woolf (b); Dave Ohm (d).* 4/95–1/96.

Cut at four different sessions, this is an impeccable set. Melling brings the sort of no-nonsense fluency and skill suggested by the title to the various tunes and situations. 'What Is This Thing Called Love' is an individual essay to start, the source used as a prop for a solo that goes entirely its own way. Similarly, in the trio version of 'Night And Day' he comes up with a take on Porter's melody which seems new yet inevitable. McCoy Tyner, perhaps the most pertinent influence on Melling's delivery, has a hand in this and in the original 'In A Monochrome', while on the extended look at Coltrane's 'Wise One' (one of three live tracks) the pianist cleverly blends the Tyner blockbusting with his own kind of lyricism. An unpretentious and fine record to which we have returned more often than many more touted items.

George Melly (born 1926)

VOCAL

Writer, art critic and singer, Melly is perhaps the greatest maverick in British jazz. He began singing in the trad movement of the '50s and has been at it ever since, first with Mick Mulligan, later with John Chilton, now with Digby Fairweather. His books are even funnier than his singing.

***** The Pye Jazz Anthology**

Castle CMDDD 483 *Melly; groups led by Mick Mulligan and John Chilton.* 60–88.

*****(*) Goodtime George**

Spectrum 544465-2 *Melly; other personnel unlisted.* 51–73.

*****(*) Nuts / Son Of Nuts**

Warner Jazz 8122-73747-2 2CD *Melly; John Chilton (t); Wally Fawkes (cl); Bruce Turner (as, cl); Colin Bates (p); Steve Fagg (b); Chuck Smith (d).* 72–73.

****(*) Singing And Swinging The Blues**

Robinwood RWP 0019 *Melly; Digby Fairweather (t, v); Chris Gower (tb); Julian Marc Stringle (cl, as, ts, v); Derek Nash (ts); Craig Milverton (ky, v); Dominic Ashworth (g, v); Julian Tear (vn); Len Skeat (b); Bobby Worth (d).* 4/03.

The current state of Melly's CD catalogue is suitably chaotic. He began as the singer with Mick Mulligan's Jazz Band, in the peak years of the trad boom (memorably recounted in his *Owning Up* memoir), and has ever since delighted in treading the boards as an entertainer and raconteur, displaying his various affections for hot jazz, Bessie Smith, Fats Waller and others. The *Pye Jazz* collection covers a thoroughly motley group of titles, none of them reliably documented, but covering some 25 years of work: some of it is all over the place, other pieces are relatively smart, and Melly's chesty baritone makes the best of whatever's put in front of him.

Goodtime George is an appropriately cheap and nasty compilation that goes as far back as 'Send Me To The 'Lectric Chair' (1951!), but it concentrates on his '50s tracks and on that basis is probably the best example of his recorded work in print. That said, *Nuts / Son Of Nuts* is a welcome revival of his early association with the Chilton group, who kept him company as far as the new century, and there are fine moments for John and Bruce Turner, as well as the singer.

The news that John Chilton was retiring might have led the more foolish among us to think that George was going to do the same. No such thing. Instead, he's simply embarked on a new lease of life with Digby Fairweather's gang. Going on 77, he might be gargling (or swallowing) more lines than he used to, but crisp enunciation was never Melly's thing, and it's not as if Charley Patton was ever marked down on his consonants. The Fairweather Half-Dozen are too slick at the moment. The slow pieces are much the best. 'Michigan Water Blues' has just the right kind of weary, reflective feel, and 'September Song' is, affected or not, a notably poignant climax, even if the string parts are overdoing it.

Misha Mengelberg (born 1935)

PIANO, COMPOSER

Mengelberg comes from a deeply musical family and has always straddled musical styles with ease. His place in jazz history was secured when he appeared on Eric Dolphy's last recording. Later, he co-founded the Instant Composers Pool and became a key figure in the Dutch avant-garde. Mengelberg has continued to combine improvisation with notated composition.

*****(*) Change Of Season**
Soul Note 101104 *Mengelberg; George E. Lewis (tb); Steve Lacy (ss); Arjen Gorter (b); Han Bennink (d).* 7/84.

****** Impromptus**
FMP 7 *Mengelberg (p solo).* 6/88.

****** Mix**
ICP 030 *As above.* 4 & 5/94.

****** Who's Bridge**
Avant AVAN 038 *Mengelberg; Brad Jones (b); Joey Baron (d).* 94.

Robert Frost once characterized free verse as 'playing tennis with the net down'. Improvisers like Dutchmen Mengelberg and Bennink have been very largely concerned with putting the net back, sometimes up to badminton height, searching for ways of combining the freedoms of improvisation with traditional jazz and even more formal structures. Mengelberg is also a 'legitimate' composer, albeit one in the Louis Andriessen mould, with a very strong jazz influence in his work. The collectivism that was so strong a component of the Dutch '60s avant-garde is evident in the autonomy granted to the performers (all of them expert players) on *Change Of Season*. Lewis seems most comfortable in the mixed idiom, though Lacy (a purist's purist) sounds a little glacial. Bennink whips up little rhythmic storms, but he plays with unwonted reserve and an often unrecognized sensitivity. Mengelberg plays with great assurance and a graceful disposition of apparently self-contained and discontinuous ideas that are more reminiscent of the Swiss Irène Schweizer than of his compatriots, Fred Van Hove and Leo Cuypers. Interesting, if for no other reason than that there are other directions for 'free' piano than the one taken and dominated by Cecil Taylor.

Impromptus makes a generic nod to a (minor) classical form. The 13 individual pieces aren't obviously linked by theme or as variations, but they follow a barely discernible logic that can be picked up via Mengelberg's untutored vocalese, which is of the Bud Powell/Keith Jarrett/Cecil Taylor persuasion. *Mix*, recorded at a couple of live solo concerts in Amsterdam and The Hague, is very much in the same territory: huge, quasi-tonal shapes and structures jumbled together in what at first glance seems disorder but which is suddenly pierced by light, a simple melodic line that pulls the whole 'mix' into symmetry; perhaps the effect of a magnet on iron filings would be a more effective analogy.

Who's Bridge is intriguing in that it takes Melgelberg much closer to jazz idiom than he normally attempts. He has two very adept sidemen, and Baron is, when one thinks of it, the only younger-generation American who might remind listeners of Bennink. There are even songs here: the Monkish 'Romantic Jump Of Hares', the skittish, Morton-influenced 'Rumbone' and the real surprise, 'Peer's Counting Song', which finds Mengelberg in unwontedly lyrical and expressive mood.

****** The Root Of The Problem**
hat OLOGY 504 *Mengelberg; Thomas Heberer (t); Michel Godard (tba, serpent); Steve Potts (sax); Achim Kramer (perc).* 96.

Recorded in Cologne, this fine set pits Mengelberg in duo and trio settings with a group of fine and highly eclectic players. The sound of Godard's serpent is still one of the most unusual in contemporary music; however, contrasting as it does with Potts's drily vivid saxophone and Heberer's hard-edged, throaty trumpet, it makes perfect textural sense. Above all, one senses that Mengelberg is enjoying himself here. His touch is relaxed and light, his ideas suitably skittish, and there is not a hint of strain in the flow of ideas.

*****(*) Two Days In Chicago**
hatOLOGY 2-535 2CD *Mengelberg; Fred Anderson (ts); Ab Baars (ts, cl); Ken Vandermark (ts); Fred Lonberg-Holm (clo); Wilbert De Joode, Kent Kessler (b); Hamid Drake, Martin Van Duynhoven (d).* 10/98.

In October 1998 Mengelberg and a group of Dutch musicians met and created some of the best music of his career. His encounter with the locals was at Fred Anderson's Velvet Lounge and the live material on disc two is indicative of the understanding that developed between them during their stay. Misha's long opening solo is typical of his approach: highly detailed, pan-tonal and sophisticated. His take on 'Body And Soul' and 'Round Midnight' is more constrained but highly effective. The first disc, actually recorded the next day finds the group in the studio. There are two Monk tracks, 'Eronel' and 'Off Minor', but the bulk of the session is taken up with improvised trios and quartets, American and Dutch, that negotiate some common ground between the two improvising cultures. It's an impressive set, smartly played, and it enhances Mengelberg's visibility considerably.

Ian Menzies & His Clyde Valley Stompers

GROUP

Scotland's most eminent trad outfit, the Clydes were formed in 1952 and Menzies took over leadership in 1954. They lasted till 1963, having been regulars at all the Scottish clubs and halls, but re-formed for a couple of albums in 1981.

****(*) Ian Menzies & His Clyde Valley Stompers**
Lake LACD79 *Malcolm Higgins (t); Ian Menzies (tb); Forrie Cairns (cl); John Cairns (p); Norrie Brown, (bj); Bob Bain, Andrew Bennie (b); Bobby Shannon (d); Fionna Duncan, Lonnie Donegan (v).* 4/59–5/60.

****(*) Traditional Jazz**
Lake LACD126 *As above, except add Pete Kerr (cl), Jim Douglas (bj), Robbie Winter (d).* 4/59–5/61.

The CVS did staunch duty for Scottish trad followers, and their surviving records are in some ways disappointing. Recorded for Pye, and issued mainly as singles and EPs (their single album is on LACD79), their output is mostly sub-three-minute tracks at sometimes unsuitably fast tempos, with the rhythm section thumping along. The standout player is Forrie Cairns, a clarinet player with a touch of Celtic fire about him. Fionna Duncan belts out several vocals, and Donegan, who produced the original sessions, sings on three tracks.

Helen Merrill (born 1930)

VOCAL

Born in New York, Merrill was associated with the first-generation boppers and began recording for Emarcy in 1954. She lived in Italy for some years, later in Japan, and returned to Chicago and New York in the '70s. Many of her recordings were for smaller labels, but her albums for Verve in the '80s and '90s restored her eminence, and a style based around slow, considered ballad singing. She is married to the arranger, Torrie Zito.

CORE COLLECTION

**** Helen Merrill With Clifford Brown And Gil Evans

Emarcy 838292-2 *Merrill; Clifford Brown, Art Farmer, Louis Mucci (t); Jimmy Cleveland, Joe Bennett (tb); John LaPorta (cl, as); Jerome Richardson (as, ts, f); Danny Bank (f); Hank Jones, Jimmy Jones (p); Barry Galbraith (g); Oscar Pettiford, Milt Hinton (b); Joe Morello, Osie Johnson, Bobby Donaldson (d); strings, horns.* 12/54–6/56.

Helen Merrill has never made a bad record and, while she scarcely conforms to the image of a swinging jazz singer, she's a stylist of unique poise and sensitivity. Her early work is as involving as her mature records. She sings at a consistently slow pace, unfolding melodies as if imparting a particularly difficult confidence, and she understands the harmonies of the songs as completely as she trusts her way with time. That gives these lingering performances a sensuality which is less of a come-hither come-on than the similarly inclined work of a singer such as Julie London. Merrill thinks about the words, but she improvises on the music too. Her treatment of 'Don't Explain' is cooler yet no less troubling than Billie Holiday's exaggerated pathos, and 'What's New' is a masterpiece. Brown's accompaniments on seven tracks make an absorbing contrast to his work with Sarah Vaughan, and Evans's arrangements on the other eight songs are some of his most lucid work in this area.

***(*) Helen Merrill In Italy

Liuto LRS 0063/5 *Merrill; Nino Culasso, Nino Rosso (t); Dino Piana (tb); Gianni Basso (ts); Gino Marinacci (f); Piero Umiliani, Renato Sellani (p); Enzo Grillini (g); Berto Pisano, Giorgio Azzolini (b); Sergio Conti, Ralph Ferraro, Franco Tonani (d); strings.* 59–62.

This is flawed by the sometimes unlovely sound, but it's otherwise a compelling collection of all the pieces Merrill recorded on various trips to Italy. Three songs by Umiliani for film scores have lyrics by the singer, and those for 'My Only Man' and 'Dreaming Of The Past' are original and hard to forget. Most of the others are standards, again treated to the most rarefied of ballad settings – 'The More I See You' is almost impossibly slow – but the four closing tracks, sung in Italian with an orchestra conducted by Ennio Morricone, have a *Lieder*-like quality that's disarmingly direct.

**** The Feeling Is Mutual

Emarcy 558849-2 *Merrill; Thad Jones (c); Dick Katz (p); Jim Hall (g); Ron Carter (b); Arnie Wise, Pete LaRoca (d).* 65.

**** A Shade Of Difference

Emarcy 5558851-2 *As above, except add Gary Bartz (as), Hubert Laws (f), Richard Davis (b), Elvin Jones (d); omit Wise and LaRoca.* 7/68.

These albums fill a huge gap in Helen's discography and their reissue is very welcome (although two slightly later ones have already been deleted). *The Feeling Is Mutual* and *A Shade Of Difference* are unique records in the jazz vocal canon. Co-credited to pianist-arranger Dick Katz, their extraordinary range of material, offbeat charts and intensely concentrated musicianship contribute to an atmosphere that would be hard to breathe if it weren't for Merrill's conviction. On the earlier disc, she makes 'It Don't Mean A Thing' swing at a tempo that would bemuse most singers, and her almost abstract 'Baltimore Oriole' challenges even Sheila Jordan's unforgettable version. 'The Winter Of My Disconent' is an Alec Wilder tune which suits her perfectly, and 'Deep In A Dream' is done as a motionless duet with Jim Hall. *A Shade Of Difference*, with its larger group, starts with an amazingly dark treatment of Coleman's 'Lonely Woman' with a baroque solo by Bartz, and proceeds through a pin-drop 'While We're Young', a boppish 'A Lady Must Live' and a coolly effective blues in 'I Want A Little Boy'. It ends with Wilder again and his numbing 'Where Do You Go?'. Besides Merrill herself, credit to the players – especially Jones and Hall – and to Katz, who clearly took great pains over the arrangements, which are tight-knit yet open and unconstricting.

***(*) No Tears ... No Goodbyes

Owl 013435-2 *Merrill; Gordon Beck (ky).* 11/84.

***(*) Music Makers

Owl 014729-2 *Merrill; Steve Lacy (ss); Gordon Beck (p); Stéphane Grappelli (vn).* 3/86.

Good to welcome these new CD editions of some of Helen's music from the '80s. We were ambivalent about the duos with Beck in the past, preferring the more upbeat demeanour of 'Bye Bye Blackbird' to 'The Thrill Is Gone', but both ends of the spectrum are personalized by the singer and Beck's slightly testy accompaniments work extremely well for most of the way. The second record is an unrepeatable collaboration which, in its strange way, also holds up well. Lacy plays on the first half, Grappelli on the second. The saxophonist's playing seems as private as Merrill's own path through the lyrics, whereas Grappelli offers an antidote by pouring on the Gallic charm in 'As Tiime Goes By'.

*** Just Friends

Emarcy 842007-2 *Merrill; Stan Getz (ts); Joachim Kühn, Torrie Zito (p); Jean-François Jenny-Clark (b); Daniel Humair (d).* 89.

Merrill's return to a small-group format brings forth some quietly resolute performances, their autumnal feel heightened by the appearance of Getz in his twilight phase. 'Cavatina' and 'It's Not Easy Being Green' were questionable choices of material, though.

***(*) Carousel

Finlandia 0630-14914-2 *Merrill; Juhani Aaltonen, Pentti Lahti (reeds); Heikki Sarmanto (ky); Laura Hynninen (hp); Juha Bjorninen (g); Pekka Sarmanto (b); Terry Clarke (d); Tapio Aaltonen (perc); Tapiola Sinfonietta.* 3/96.

Merrill's albums for Verve in the '90s have almost all disappeared from the catalogues. The Finlandia album is the realization of a cherished project for composer Heikki Sarmanto, to write a series of songs for Merrill. Torrie Zito arranges for the Tapiola Sinfonietta and, if the results seem lighter and sweeter than one expects from one of her records, there's a wistful gaiety in the music which is very appealing. Pleasing also to hear the great Juhani Aaltonen taking several featured solos.

*****(*) Jelena Ana Milcetic A.K.A. Helen Merrill**
Verve 543089-2 *Merrill; Dennis Anderson (ob, eng hn); Steve Lacy (ss); Sir Roland Hanna (p); Gil Goldstein (p, acc); Jeff Mironov (g); Gloria Agostini (hp); Jesse Levy (clo); George Mraz (b); Terry Clarke (d); Steve Kroon (perc); strings, choir.* 4–9/99.

A remarkable exercise in seeking out the past, with Merrill choosing songs like Judy Collins's 'My Father' and 'Among My Souvenirs' – even 'I'll Take You Home Again, Kathleen'. These intermingle with glimpses of an East European folk heritage in the opening 'Kirje' and 'Imagining Kirk'. The key instrumental voice is Steve Lacy's; his soprano dialogue moves in and out of view like a passing acquaintance. The bloom is gone from Merrill's voice, but any who've followed her career to this point will be untroubled by that in what is clearly a profoundly personal record.

Neil Metcalfe

FLUTE

Fine British improviser, yet to make much impression as a solo recording artist.

***** 2gether**
Slam CD 237 *Metcalfe; John Rangecroft (cl).* 99.

Metcalfe lent his quiet authority and questioning spirit to the later years of the Spontaneous Music Ensemble, never garnering more than an occasional respectful mention. These 29 untitled improvisations are about as far from ego-driven 'performance' as it's possible to get. They are not so much dry and abstract as purposefully objective, almost like stray pebbles of sound picked up on a beach. Rangecroft has the more varied range and the more emphatic presence but it's Metcalfe's dogged examination of his instrument that wins the day.

Pat Metheny (born 1954)

GUITAR

A Mid-Westerner from Missouri, Metheny was a quick learner, and by the time he was 19 he had already been teaching at Berklee and playing with the Gary Burton group, an important early association. He made a string of records for ECM and formed a hugely successful touring group, with keyboardist Lyle Mays the other key performer. His switch to Geffen, and subsequently to Warner Brothers, ensured that his records were given major exposure, and he has built an audience in both the jazz and rock camps. In the '90s he increasingly returned to playing in straight-ahead situations as a sideman, while still pursuing his own muse as he pleased.

***** Bright Size Life**
ECM 827133-2 *Metheny; Jaco Pastorius (b); Bob Moses (d).* 12/75.

***** Watercolours**
ECM 827409-2 *Metheny; Lyle Mays (p); Eberhard Weber (b); Danny Gottlieb (d).* 2/77.

****(*) Pat Metheny Group**
ECM 825593-2 *As above, except Mark Egan (b) replaces Weber.* 1/78.

***** New Chautauqua**
ECM 825471-2 *Metheny (g solo).* 8/78.

***** American Garage**
ECM 827134-2 *Metheny; Lyle Mays (ky); Mark Egan (b); Danny Gottlieb (d).* 6/79.

Metheny has become a key figure in the instrumental music of the past 20 years. His stature as a jazz musician is more open to debate, and it's interesting to muse on a career which has grown increasingly diverse and self-challenging, even as his global audience has grown. He sees nothing incompatible about his sometimes bewildering range of appearances on record, which now encompasses companions such as Ornette Coleman and Derek Bailey, yet he continues to create own-name group records which can sound as lightweight and undemanding as those of the leading smooth-jazz performers. Most would call this a double-life. Metheny sees it as doing whatever he wants.

When he first appeared, as a coolly melodic electric guitarist for the ECM label, originally discovered by Gary Burton (one of his best early appearances is with the Burton group on *Ring*), Metheny seemed content to drop his playing into whatever context it might find. The first two ECM albums are a little untypical – each depends more on its respective star bassist to give it some clout – but, like the ones that follow, they are pleasant, hummable records with a degree of fine playing which the high-grade production values and sometimes over-sensitive musicianship can occasionally block out with sheer amiability. At this time Metheny favoured a clean, open tone with just enough electronic damping to take the music out of 'classic' jazz-guitar feeling, but he clearly owed a great debt to such urban pastoralists as Jim Hall and Jimmy Raney, even if he seldom moved back to bebop licks.

The Metheny Group albums settled the guitarist's music into the niche from which he is still basically working: light, easily digested settings that let him play long, meticulous solos which can as often as not work up a surprising intensity. *Pat Metheny Group* and *American Garage* each have their ration of thoughtful improvising which the guitarist settles inside a gently propulsive rhythm, more ruralized than the beefy urban beats of the contemporary fusion bands. That strain also colours the playing and composing of Mays, who has been Metheny's principal collaborator for 20 years. Scarcely a major voice in his own right – his own solo records have been entirely inconsequential – Mays is the perfect second banana. He feeds Metheny all kinds of tasteful orchestration without getting too much in his way.

New Chautauqua is a rare all-solo album in the Metheny canon. A pleasant, sweet-toned diversion, it hints at the multifariousness; with various electric and acoustic settings, including a 15-string harp-guitar, with which which Metheny has grown fascinated in recent times.

***** 80/81**
ECM 843169-2 2CD *Metheny; Dewey Redman, Michael Brecker (ts); Charlie Haden (b); Jack DeJohnette (d).* 5/80.

At the time this sounded like an almost shocking departure, but Brecker and Redman adapt themselves to Metheny's aesthetic without undue compromise and Haden and DeJohnette play with great purpose. There's too much music here and some dreary spots, but some excellent moments too.

★★(★) As Falls Witchita, So Falls Witchita Falls
ECM 821416-2 *Metheny; Lyle Mays (ky); Nana Vasconcelos (perc).* 9/80.

★★(★) Offramp
ECM 817138-2 *As above, except add Steve Rodby (b), Danny Gottlieb (d).* 10/81.

★★★ Travels
ECM 810622-2 2CD *As above.* 7–11/82.

The Metheny band was by now an international concert institution. *As Falls Witchita* is basically a duo situation for Metheny and Mays, with guest Vasconcelos adding a little zest: lots of pastels. *Offramp* brings back the quartet for another mild-mannered sequence, although here Metheny's knack for the melodic hook starts to blossom. 'Are You Going With Me', over a gently percolating bass vamp, remains an enduring set-piece which he is still playing today. *Travels* effectively summed up the band's tenure with ECM with a studious and densely packed live set. There are the kind of longueurs that one associates more with the double-live-album in rock, rather than the creative stretch of the jazz concert disc, but Metheny's group had built up a charisma of its own by this time and this is a good souvenir.

★★★(★) Rejoicing
ECM 817795-2 *Metheny; Charlie Haden (b); Billy Higgins (d).* 11/83.

All right, it's all too obvious citing this capital-letter jazz album as Metheny's best up to this point, but he finds a loneliness in Horace Silver's 'Lonely Woman' and a happiness in Ornette Coleman's 'Rejoicing' for which more severe interpreters of those composers don't seem to have time or room. By itself the playing isn't so remarkable, but pairing him with Haden and Higgins, on a programme of mostly Coleman and Metheny originals, sheds new lustre both on himself and on music that's often somewhat neglected.

★★(★) First Circle
ECM 823342-2 *Metheny; Lyle Mays (ky); Steve Rodby (b); Paul Wertico (d); Pedro Aznar (perc, v).* 2/84.

The last ECM album is no kind of departure and even some fans were disappointed, but its larger sonic palette was a clear indication of where Metheny wanted to go next: expanding his group to a quintet, he staked a place in a much bigger sound. Unlike his ECM contemporary, Steve Tibbetts, who has never secured Metheny's audience yet whose works are an absorbing counterpart to his contemporary's, the guitarist seemed set on mediating his group's music through a fundamentally conservative synthesis of jazz, Latin and rock flavours; a catholic taste put through a blender to take all the harmful pieces out. And then he made …

★★★★ Song X
Geffen 924096 *Metheny; Ornette Coleman (as, vn); Charlie Haden (b); Jack DeJohnette, Denardo Coleman (d).* 12/85.

Metheny's great departure still seems like a bolt from the blue after playing through the previous half-dozen albums. There is still a sense that some of the best and most extreme material was left off the record (which Metheny has subsequently confirmed). Otherwise it's the most astonishing move ever made by any musician perceived as a middle-of-the-road jazz artist. Not only does the guitarist power his way through Coleman's itinerary with utter conviction, he sets up opportunities for the saxophonist to resolve and creates a fusion with which Coleman's often impenetrable Prime Time bands have failed to come to terms. Melody still has a place here, which suggests that Metheny's interest in the original Coleman legacy may be carrying forward in his own work more intently than it is in the composer's. Either way, on many of the more raving episodes here both men sound exultant with the possibilities. Highly recommended.

★★(★) Still Life (Talking)
Geffen GED 24145 *Metheny; Lyle Mays (ky); Steve Rodby (b); Paul Wertico (d); Armando Marcal (perc, v); David Blamires, Mark Ledford (v).* 3–4/87.

★★★ Question And Answer
Geffen GED 24293 *Metheny; Dave Holland (b); Roy Haynes (d).* 12/89.

★★ Secret Story
Geffen GED 24468 *Metheny; Gil Goldstein (p, acc); Lyle Mays (ky); Toots Thielemans (hca); Charlie Haden, Steve Rodby, Will Lee (b); Steve Ferrone, Paul Wertico, Sammy Merendino (d); Nana Vasconcelos, Armando Marcal (perc); Mark Ledford (v); strings and brass.* 91–2.

★★★ The Road To You
Geffen GED 24601 *Metheny; Pedro Aznar (sax, vib, mar, perc, g, v); Lyle Mays (ky); Steve Rodby (b); Paul Wertico (d); Armando Marcal (perc, v).* 92–3.

Metheny's albums for Geffen have followed an inexorable course towards (excuse these labels) light rock. *Still Life (Talking)* is an exemplar of the style, which peaks on the infectious 'Last Train Home'; but there's an awful lot of fluff that goes with it, often courtesy of Mays's noodling keyboards. The wordless vocals of Ledford and Blamires remove the final barrier to a crossover audience by getting the human voice in there somewhere, and, though the increased orchestration of the sound may have displeased some of Metheny's admirers, it waved in many more. *Question And Answer* – which seems to be the kind of periodic vacation that Metheny takes from his regular band, and may it continue – finds the guitarist, bassist and, especially, the drummer playing with great *brio* and suppleness. The tunes are another mix of standards, Coleman and Metheny originals; and if some of the charm of the ECM trio date is missing and a few pieces seem to end up nowhere, it's well worth hearing.

Secret Story is hopelessly overblown and would feel intolerably pompous were Metheny himself not so likeable: he usually salvages something interesting to play, even when the music's obese with strings, brass and whatever. But this remains his least tractable and most overworked record. *The Road To You*, a concert album, is much livelier and is one of the best records by the regular group since the last live set. They are a fun group to see live (even if some of their sets go on longer than the Grateful Dead used to), and this pared-down souvenir will find plenty of appeal.

★★★ We Live Here
Geffen GED 24729 *Metheny; Mark Ledford (t, flhn, v); Lyle Mays (ky); Steve Rodby (b); Paul Wertico (d); Luis Conte (perc); David Blamires (v).* 94.

Back on undeadly ground. A few tracks work off programmed drum beats, and Metheny gets to do a Bensonesque bit here and there, but by the middle of the disc he's returned to his favourite platform, the soft cadences of Brazilian beat. Once there, he actually sounds in very good form, confirming that, with the rotten *Secret Story* behind him, this is a good period for him.

***** Quartet**

Geffen GED 24978 *As above, except omit Ledford, Conte, Blamires.* 5/96.

Written and recorded quickly by the nucleus of the group, this is interesting if hardly substantial Metheny fare. The improvisation 'Badland' suggests that this is not an improvising group. They do far better by pristine miniatures such as 'Seven Days' and 'Oceania'. The feel is not so much acoustic, as intended, more softly electric in its resonance, and it's surely no coincidence that the title suggests a record of chamber music.

***** Imaginary Day**

Warner Bros 46791 *As above, except add Mark Ledford (t, vtb, flhn, v), David Blamires (mel, g, vn, melod, v), David Samuels (vib), Glen Velez, Mino Cinelu, Don Alias (perc).* 97.

Metheny plays at least ten different kinds of guitar on this one, the kind of arsenal one might once have associated with, say, Steve Howe, and perhaps it suits the kind of widescreen, almost symphonic music he seems to be increasingly in search of. If the jazz elements continue to filter away, he still manages to squeeze in solos of considerable moment. 'Follow Me' is a near-classic piece of instrumental pop with overtones of the jazz disciplines that he started out with. But too much of the rest runs stickily into the kind of bombastic terrain which he should have left behind after *Secret Story*. A perplexing artist.

***** A Map Of The World**

Warner Bros 9362-47366-2 *Metheny; orchestra. n.d.*

*****(*) Trio 99–00**

Warner Bros 9362-47632-2 *Metheny; Larry Grenadier (b); Bill Stewart (d).* 8/99.

A Map Of The World is a soundtrack album, and since it consists of 28 brief tracks, this is Metheny as miniaturist, playing acoustic against a full orchestra. It suits him rather well; big and sweeping motifs for a film set in Wisconsin, and the disciplines of the form result in some of his most precise and unrambling playing. But it is, in the end, a film soundtrack, and a backwater in his discography.

The trio record is his most straight-ahead situation since *Question And Answer*, although as a sideman he's been doing plenty of this sort of playing elsewhere. It would be interesting to poll Metheny's following on how they rate this kind of record next to his Group albums. For us – call us predictable if you have to – it rates ahead because it affirms what a graceful and quick-witted improviser the man is, away from his big-sound predilections. His version of 'Giant Steps' is light and airy but full of notes and intensely played. That said, there are many good guitar records like this out there, and it assists him enormously to have Grenadier and the admirable Stewart on hand, since they're integral to the record's success.

***** Speaking Of Now**

Warner Bros 9362-48025-2 *Metheny; Cuong Vu (t, v); Lyle Mays (ky); Steve Rodby (b); Antonio Sanchez (d); Richard Bona (v, perc).* 01.

Back to business as usual with the PM Group. The association with Mays now stretches back 25 years and in this setting it's perhaps foolish to expect any kind of departure from a writing team who, by this juncture, have honed their formula to a very fine point. There is a slight shaking-out of excess in the production, but Mays continues to layer quasi-symphonic backdrops for Pat to solo over, while the drummer decorates what is essentially a rock beat. The surprise new name in the line-up is Vu, who's displaced Ledford's funky injections with a more consciously lyrical flow; his solo on 'Proof', the longest track, might almost have come out of Kenny Wheeler's bag. Bona, who makes world-music records for Columbia, registers less forcefully. And while they may be speaking of now, the PMG has begun to take on a notably old-fashioned sense of musos at work.

**** One Quiet Night**

Warner Bros 9362-48473-2 *Metheny (g solo).* 02.

Quiet is about right. There is some vigorous strumming here and there, but mostly this is Metheny at his most subdued. It's all very pretty and drifts away nicely in the background, but the musical-incident count is depressingly low. Since he's playing only one acoustic guitar throughout, and puts every solo amidst the same politely reverberant wash, there's an unfortunate capacity for one track to sound precisely like another. A variety of composition might have helped, but the only thing that really perks up the ears is when the familiar tones of 'Ferry Cross The Mersey' crop up, and that isn't until track eight. Metheny sees this project as a line of inquiry, investigating a certain tuning on a certain guitar, but while that's fine for the artist, his audience might want a bit more to chew on. Docked a further notch for sheer self-indulgence.

Mezz Mezzrow (1899–1972)

CLARINET, SAXOPHONES

If ever there was a real-life version of Norman Mailer's 'White Negro', it has to be Mezzrow, who turned his back on a respectable and well-off white Jewish background to pass as black. Mezz's skills as a clarinettist were limited; his skills as a fixer, self-mythologizer and acquirer of lifestyle sundries were beyond question. The autobiography, Really The Blues, ghosted by Bertram Wolfe, can't be trusted as far as it can be thrown, but it remains a great read.

***** Mezz Mezzrow, 1928–1936**

Classics 713 *Mezzrow; Muggsy Spanier (c); Max Kaminsky, Frankie Newton, Freddy Goodman, Ben Gusick, Reunald Jones, Chelsea Quealey (t); Benny Carter (t, as, v); Floyd O'Brien (tb); Frank Teschemacher (cl, as); Rod Cless (as); Bud Freeman, Art Karle, Johnny Russell (ts); Joe Bushkin, Teddy Wilson, Willie 'The Lion' Smith, Joe Sullivan (p); Eddie Condon (bj); Al Casey, Clayton Sunshine Duerr, Ted Tonison (g); Wellman Braud, George 'Pops' Foster, John Kirby, Louis Thompson (b); Jim Lannigan (bb); Gene Krupa, Jack Maisel, George Stafford, Chick Webb (d); Chick Bullock, Elinor Charier, Red McKenzie, Lucille Stewart (v).* 4/28–3/36.

***** Mezz Mezzrow, 1936–1939**

Classics 694 *Similar to above.* 36–39.

Eddie Condon nicknamed him 'Southmouth' in ironic recognition of his obsessive self-identification with black musicians and self-consciously disenchanted and un-ironic pursuit of a 'Negro' lifestyle. He claims to have insisted on being put in the black cells of a segregated police block, on the grounds that he was only 'passing for white'. His nickname also carries an echo of Louis Armstrong's soubriquet, 'Satchelmouth'. Mezzrow idolized the trumpeter and once worked for him as factotum and grass distributor. His music was considerably more 'authentic' than his personal manners: sinuous if slightly repetitive lines, a dry, sharp tone (compare George Lewis's) and a flow of ideas which, if not endless, were always imaginatively permed and varied. For the time being, the best sources for Mezzrow are the Classics discs, which exclude material made under Sidney Bechet's leadership. These concentrate on various (often motley) small-group swing dates from the '30s in which Mezzrow took some kind of leading role. There's nothing here that requires a wholesale revision of Mezzrow's oddly unbalanced reputation.

***** Mezz Mezzrow, 1944-1945**
Classics 1074 *Mezzrow; Hot Lips Page (t); Sidney Bechet (ss); Art Hodes, Sammy Price, Fitz Weston (p); Danny Barker (g); George 'Pops' Foster (b); Danny Alvin, Big Sid Catlett, Kaiser Marshall (d); Douglas Daniels, Pleasant Joe (v).* 3/44–8/45.

Much of the Mezzrow discography was under the joint nominal leadership of Sidney Bechet, and the recordings of summer 1945, made for King Jazz and for Storyville, featured some of Sidney's best work of the period. 'Revolutionary Blues', 'Sheik Of Araby' and 'Perdido Stomp' (which also reappears on a later version, recorded in New York for the Royal Jazz label) are among the best of Bechet's performances of the period, and Mezz provides stalwart support, more enthusiastic than subtle.

***** Mezz Mezzrow, 1947**
Classics 1095 *Mezzrow; Sidney Bechet (ss, cl); Sammy Price (p); Sox Wilson (p, v); Wellman Braud (b); Baby Dodds, Kaiser Marshall (d); Coot Grant (v).* 9 & 12/47.

Rounding out the story of King Jazz, the sessions of September 1947 and those later sides for Royal and Storyville are pretty orthodox – but what fun they must all have had. The joyousness is tempered by the knowledge that drummer Kaiser Marshall was dead a matters of days after the sides were cut, which is why the final track is posthumously titled 'Kaiser's Last Break'. Many of those who praise Mezz's playing like the *idea* of him and would be dismayed if they were presented with a Mezzrow solo blindfold; by the same token, many of those who dismiss his playing out of hand do so because they have chosen to believe he is merely an ofay dabbler, indulging a species of *nostalgie de la boue*.

****(*) Mezz Mezzrow, 1947–1951**
Classics 1302 *Mezzrow; Guy Longnon, Lee Collins (t); Bernard Zacharias, Mowgli Jospin (tb); Claude Luter (cl); Sidney Bechet (ss); Guy Lafitte (cl, ts); Sammy Price, Christian Azzi, Andre Persiany (p); Pops Foster, Roger Bianchini (b); Kaiser Marshall, Francois 'Moustache' Galipedes, Zutty Singleton (d).* 12/47–11/51.

The fifth Classics set ties up the last of the Mezzrow–Bechet titles, four from December 1947, before three sessions from Paris in 1951, eight titles with Claude Luter and another eight with a band that has Lee Collins and Zutty Singleton alongside Guy Lafitte. As a display of Mezz's powers, this one is, frankly, a bit risible at times, and the closing 'Blues No One Dug' seems to be a painfully apposite title. Longnon and Lafitte take most of the playing honours here.

***** The Alternative Takes, Volume 1**
Neatwork RP 2046 *As appropriate discs above.* 11/38–8/45.

***** The Alternative Takes, Volume 2**
Neatwork RP 2047 *As appropriate discs above.* 9–12/47.

The majority of both discs are taken up with some of the many alternates from the King Jazz sessions with Bechet. The exceptions are six sides with Tonny Ladnier from their 1938 Victor sessions, although this was scarcely the finest hour for either man. Mezzrow is quite awful on 'Swingin' For Mezz', although he is in better order for the December titles, and the star here is arguably Teddy Bunn. Any who don't have one of the complete Mezzrow–Bechet editions previously on CD will find Neatwork's trawl through the other tracks attractive, and for Bechet alone there's plenty of interest in the alternates.

Nando Michelin (born 1965)

PIANO

A native of Uruguay, Michelin moved to Boston to attend Berklee in 1989. He continues to work in the city, in Brazilian groups and his own post-bop bands.

***** Art**
Double-Time DTRCD-144 *Michelin; Jerry Bergonzi (ts); Fernando Huergo (b); Steve Langone (d); Sergio Faluotico (perc).* 10/98.

****(*) Chants**
Double-Time DTRCD-169 *As above, except add Alex Alvear, Chiara Civello, Sharine Ganse, Katie Viqueira (v); omit Faluotico.* 12/99.

A series of dedications to Matisse, Miro and so forth, *Art* is suitably cultured post-bop. Bergonzi seems at home in Michelin's thoughtful compositions; 'Portrait', for instance, is a Wayne Shorterish ballad which suits him well. In return the pianist centres the saxophonist's occasional oddities. But the date lacks an individual note or two. If Michelin is bringing something of his background to what he does – in the notes he claims he uses the Uruguayan *candomb* rhythm 'constantly' – at this point it sounds as if it's been buried under his Berklee training.

Perhaps in response, *Chants* is a specific essay on his roots, subtitled 'A Candomblé Experience'. Each piece is named after a god of the Candomblé religion, and the vocalists set down the original chant while Michelin and company create music arising out of phrases from the vocal line. If it sounds integrated, in practice it isn't. The jazz and the voices hardly seem to meet in any useful way, except when the individual singers follow Michelin's own lines, which could be any bit of wordless vocalizing. Bergonzi, too, doesn't sound like the right man for the project at all.

Palle Mikkelborg (born 1941)

TRUMPET, FLUGELHORN, COMPOSER

Although he has been a professional since 1960, Mikkelborg's own playing has lately taken a secondary role to composing and conducting, often with big ensembles. Aura for Miles Davis is his best-known work. Unafraid of electronics, and he often uses them on his own instrument.

★★★(★) **Imagine**

Storyville STCD 4114 *Mikkelborg; Kenneth Knudsen (ky); Niels-Henning Orsted Pedersen (b).* 86.

A player of enormous technical capability and lyrical strength, Mikkelborg has always worn his influences on his sleeve. The 1984 composition, *Aura*, was a harmonically coded dedication to Miles Davis (on which Davis was to play a guest role). Much of Mikkelborg's most important work in the late '70s and '80s has been for large-scale conventional forces, much like his sometime collaborator, the guitarist–composer Terje Rypdal, but he remains more deeply rooted in jazz than the Norwegian, having served an impressively documented apprenticeship with the exiled Dexter Gordon. Mikkelborg is one of the few convincing exponents of electric trumpet, which he uses, unlike Don Ellis, to produce great sheets of harmonic colour against which he dabs acoustic notes of surprising purity. *Aura* underlined the Miles influence to the apparent exclusion of any other; but he is perhaps closer in conception to Chet Baker and, even on an impressionistic set like *Imagine*, formerly released as *Heart To Heart*, he can sound astonishingly like both Clifford Brown and Howard McGhee. The opening track is an unashamed Miles rip-off, though played with a clear, brassy resonance that is Mikkelborg's own. Fortunately, perhaps, it doesn't set a tone for the set, which is quite varied in temper, though mainly in a meditative mood. Knudsen's keyboard structures are always highly effective, and NHOP is far better recorded than usual.

★★★(★) **The Voice Of Silence**

Stunt 01042 *Mikkelborg; Anders Gustafsson, Benny Rosenfeld, Thomas Kjaergaard, Henrik Bolberg Pedersen, Thomas Fryland (t, flhn); Vincent Nilsson, Steen Hansen, Peter Jensen (tb); Alf Vestergaard (btb); Axel Windfeld (btb, tba); Michael Hove (ss, as, cl); Nicolai Schultz (as, cl, f, af); Tomas Franck (ss, ts, cl); Uffe Markussen (ss, ts, cl); Flemming Madsen (bs, cl, bcl); Helen Davies (hp); Nikolaj Bentzon (p, ky); Anders Chico Lindvall (g); Thomas Oversen (b); Soren Frost (d); Ethan Weisgard (perc).* 3–4/00.

This is Mikkelborg's first major composition for large jazz ensemble since *Aura*, his Sonning Prize 'concerto' for Miles Davis. Again, it reflects the intense spirituality of a trumpeter and composer whose music has always attempted to push out into new expressive dimensions. *The Voice Of Silence* is a wonderfully integrated and coherent work which nonetheless manages to preserve an aura (!) of mystery.

Lest there be any confusion the 'Louisiana' in question is the modern art gallery founded near Humlebaek, north of Copenahgen, by the wealthy Knud W. Jensen. *The Voice Of Silence* is a tribute to a visionary man and the artists he collected. The opening and closing sections are devoted to Jensen himself, the museum and to Pablo Picasso. Both 'Prologue' and 'Epilogue' are dominated by flute and harp, evoking the otherworldliness of Louisiana.

Perhaps curiously, the second section is the most substantial, with guitarist Lindvall evoking the self-consciously flimsy throwaway aesthetic of Pop Art. Mikkelborg's musical intuition has never been more clearly expressed than in this deceptive composition. Most of the other tracks are considerably shorter, and mostly built round pairs of solos. The architects and designers of the Bauhaus and the arts of Japan are celebrated in 'Those Who Build', with trombonist Nilsson and percussionist Weisgard taking the lead. Sculptor Albert Giacometti is the inspiration behind 'The Forest', a strangely bleak and anguished statement from trumpeter Pedersen which nonetheless manages to assert a profound humanity by its close. Another long composition, 'Authenticity' is the most overtly mystical and the most robustly structured, a typical Mikkelborg paradox. The title-track is dedicated to René Magritte and soprano saxophonist Franck manages to evoke both the quotidian plainness and the disturbing air of displacement that the great Surrealist always conveys. Take away the art reference and this is still a formidable work, the composer's finest for many years.

★★★(★) **Song – Tread Lightly**

Columbia 498202 *Mikkelborg; Oli Poulsen (multi-inst); Terje Rypdal (g); Helen Davies (hp); Per Lindvall (d, perc); Gert Sorensen (perc); Moussa Diablo (v). Bergen Chamber Orchestra; other personnel.* 2/00.

A delightful set, marked by Mikkelborg's glorious use of sound-colour – somewhere between Olivier Messiaen and Miles Davis – and brilliant integration of jazz and orchestral elements. The material includes John Lennon's 'Beautiful Boy' and Strayhorn's 'A Flower Is A Lovesome Thing' among others.

Joakim Milder (born 1965)

TENOR SAXOPHONE

Studied at Stockholm Conservatory, then worked with Fredrik Norén and in the Stockholm Jazz Orchestra. Several records as a leader and many collaborations with his Swedish contemporaries.

★★★(★) **Still In Motion**

Dragon DRCD 188 *Milder; Steve Dobrogosz (p); Christian Spering (b); Rune Carlsson (d).* 9/89.

★★★(★) **Consensus**

Opus 3 CD 9201 *Milder; Johan Hölén (as); Anders Persson (p); Christian Spering (b); Magnus Gran (d).* 2/92.

Milder sounded like one of the most adventurous and least conformist of players to emerge from the Swedish scene in the '80s. As an improviser he eschews both easy licks and long, heavily elaborate lines, preferring a scratchy tone to the open-voiced timbre of most tenor players and fragmenting his lines with silences, rushes and retards, anything he can think of that varies the attack. Yet there is Rollins-like logic to some of his melodic paths, and on some standards he keeps the sense of the song to hand even as he takes it crabbily apart. The all-original *Still In Motion* was a tiny disappointment after the memorable debut LP, *Life In Life*, which is still on vinyl only; a more unified but fractionally less compelling session, since nothing quite aspires to the interplay with Palle Danielsson and Carlsson on the earlier set. *Consensus* returns to standards – there are 12 of them here – and refuses to take any obvious routes. 'My Funny Valentine', for instance, hints only obliquely at its melody, 'Some Day My Prince Will Come' gets a notably sour treatment – the tune almost exploded by Gran's crackling toms – and the use of a second saxophone to counterpoint some of the tenor parts is always different from what might be expected.

***** Ways**

Dragon DRCD 231 *Milder; Lasse Lindgren (flhn); Håkan Nyqvist (frhn); Staffan Martensson (cl); Steve Dobrogosz (p); Henrik Frendin (vla); Bertil Strandberg (euph); Christian Spering (b); Rune Carlsson (d); Peter Ostlund (perc); string section.* 12/90–8/92.

Milder has been turning up on other records, but his own discography as leader is progressing slowly, carefully and with absorbing results. That said, this album of low-key, chamber-like music will be a distraction for those more interested in Milder's straight-ahead saxophone. The 11 originals are directed by their textural and tonal qualities rather than by anything rhythmic, and only 'Apart' and 'Where Do Pies Go When They Die' push Milder into his most effective improvising form. Otherwise it's the contrasting brass and string sections that drive the content; lyrical and desolate in the almost typecast manner of Scandinavian jazz, it's a meritorious record, but one for reflective tastes.

*****(*) Sister Majs Blouse**

Mirrors MICD 002 *Milder; Bobo Stenson (p); Palle Danielsson (b); Fredrik Norén (d).* 1/93.

***** Remains**

Dragon DRCD 285 *Milder; Steve Dobrogosz (p); Max Schultz (g); Henrik Frendin (vn, vla); Mats Rondin (clo); Christian Spering (b); Peter Ostlund (perc).* 10/94–3/95.

***** Ord Pa Golvet**

LJ LJCD 5210 *Milder; Tobias Sjogren (g); Johannes Lundberg (b); Gunnar Ekelof (v).* 1/95.

Three interesting records, but no masterpiece, and at this point Milder's work seemed to be slipping into a love of texture and sonic intricacy which may disappoint those who admire his saxophone playing. The *Sister Majs Blouse* project is dedicated to the music of the late Swedish saxman, Börje Fredriksson, with his original rhythm section standing in behind Milder. Fredriksson's tunes are a fascinating lot, from mood pieces to a wedding waltz, and the quartet characterize them with superb skill. Stenson, Danielsson and Norén have seldom sounded better, although ironically, Milder himself doesn't quite get hold of some of the tunes; but as a quartet disc this is very fine. *Remains* is distilled from woodwind, piano and strings; it is bountiful in terms of texture and variation, but not terribly vital to listen to. A theme like 'Simply Drift' shows how skilled Milder has become at fashioning themes out of fragments (and harmonic hooks), but his own playing here sounds relatively becalmed. Much the same could be said of the trio project, *Ord Pa Golvet*, but this is rather more mysterious, with pieces of *audio vérité* passing into the music via traffic sounds and the enigmatic spoken commentary of Gunnar Ekelof. The most striking player here is actually Sjogren, whose wide vocabulary of sounds and influences creates the palette from which most of the music is drawn.

*****(*) Epilogue**

Mirrors MICD 007 *Milder; Bobo Stenson (p); Palle Danielsson (b); Fredrik Norén (d).* 1/97–1/98.

*****(*) Associations**

Mirrors MICD 009 *Milder; Christian Spering (b); Fredrik Norén (d).* 8/00.

Back-to-basics projects which assert that Milder still has much to say as a straightahead modernist. *Epilogue* puts him at the head of a quartet of elders playing the music of Börje Fredriksson. There's the odd trace of impressionism (as on 'Epilogue II') but much of this is plainly cast and asks the players to work through gritty and deceptively demanding material. Hardly a false step.

He's never a player to collar the attention, and some may wonder if a gathering of nine standards and jazz themes, given an unfussy and at times introverted delivery, is really going to compel the interest. But *Associations* draws the listener in. It helps that Spering is a very alert and creative part of the music, almost constantly in dialogue with Milder on melodic as well as rhythmical levels, and that old pro Norén is in good heart. It's Milder's playing, though, which attracts the ear, as if he was asking us to help him puzzle out the route to the heart of material such as J. J. Johnson's 'Lament'.

***** Silent Room**

Apart APCD 001 *Milder; Mats Äleklint (tb); Nils Ölmedal (b); Jon Fält (d).* 11/02.

*****(*) Monolithic**

Apart APCD 002 *Milder; Staffan Svensson (t); Peter Dahlgren (tb); Mattias Ståhl (vib); Christian Spering (b); Peter Danemo (d).* 11/02–5/03.

Considering the tumult which often comes out of the Glenn Miller Café, the appositely titled *Silent Room*, recorded live there, seems like an anomaly. Bar one original, it's all Monk and Coleman tunes, sometimes played as ghostly laments: sample the very slow 'Sadness'. Given the lugubrious trombone–tenor tonality and the pianoless sound, it all has a skeletal, almost parched quality to it. Milder's admirers will warm to it anyway, but this probably isn't the place to start listening to him.

Monolithic is calm, detailed, but coiled too – the horns seem always about to burst into some unfettered sequence of blowing, but something in the 13-section structure holds them in. Again, Milder trades in sombre tonalities and pastel shadings, but there's much tension in the music. Ståhl appears on only a single track. It's a faintly unnerving but certainly absorbing listen.

Ron Miles (born 1963)

TRUMPET

Born in Indianapolis, he studied in Colorado before working with the Mercer-led Ellington orchestra. Associations with Bill Frisell and Ginger Baker began in 1995.

*****(*) Heaven**

Sterling Circle SCS 151 *Miles; Bill Frisell (g).* 01.

Recorded in a very dry acoustic, this sounds wonderful. Given that Miles's previous albums have quickly disappeared, with Gramavision turning into a twilight property, this seems like a curious set to have as his first entry; but the simple elegance of the playing, even if it has a once-removed quality – how simple can any Frisell collaboration be? – falls so sweetly on the ear that it's hard to resist. There's an almost busking plainness to the likes of 'Coward Of The County', but once they get to 'We See', Ellington's 'Heaven' and Morton's 'King Porter Stomp', the manners of jazz repertory impose a discipline which puts them on their mettle, sort of. It's still a superb simulation of a back-porch conversation, and we can worry about authenticity later.

★★★★ Laughing Barrel

Sterling Circle 5C1219 *Miles; Brandon Ross (g); Anthony Cox (b); Rudy Royston (d).* 9/02.

This is a wonderful record and recompense for the disappearance of *Women's Day* from the catalogue. Miles is working with a new group which seems ideally sensitive to his needs. Cox and Ross are Cox-and-Box from the opening phrases of 'Parade' and on 'Psychedelic Black Man' they push Miles out into brand new territory, a remarkable performance. 'Sunday Best' is very similar to the work Miles did with Bill Frisell, particularly since the guitar part has a jangle between banjo and National Steel.

It's a tricky name for a trumpeter to have. We don't see much prospect of it being shortened to a familiar Ron to avoid confusion. Davis, though, is only one of his more obvious influences on an album that seems to explore less familiar areas of the trumpet literature, anything from Joe Oliver (just a hint on 'Parade') to Dave Douglas; compare the Tiny Bell Trio to this and Miles isn't found wanting. Whether he's capable of effecting the same quiet musical revolution as Douglas – or the other Miles – remains to be seen. Unlike them, Ron Miles is seriously under-recorded.

Harry Miller (1941–83)

DOUBLE BASS

Much love and missed, Miller was the anchorman of the British free-jazz scene in the '70s. His big, vocalized tone worked in every context, from solo performance to big bands. Born in Johannesburg, he came to London at the age of twenty and joined drummer Don Brown's Sounds Five. Harry died in a car accident in the Netherlands, where he was living in his last months.

★★★★ The Collection

Ogun HMCD 1/2/3 3CD *Miller; Marc Charig (c, ahn); Malcolm Griffiths, Radu Malfatti, Wolter Wierbos (tb); Mike Osborne (as); Trevor Watts (ss, as); Willem Breuker (ts, bcl); Sean Bergin (ts); Keith Tippett (p); Louis Moholo (d); Julie Tippetts (v).* 74–3/83.

Harry Miller was an inspirational presence wherever he played, a musician who spoke entirely in his own voice, and with a quiet passion. The gentleness of his solo bass on *Children At Play* was perfectly at ease with the rhythmic intensity of his section-work on group albums like *Down South* or *Family Affair*, which he made with his group, Isipingo. Most of his records as leader were released on the label he helped found, and *The Collection* has been put together with loving care by Hazel Miller and John Jack, keepers of the flame. In addition to the three albums already mentioned, the set includes *Bracknell Breakdown*, a set of duets with trombonist Radu Malfatti, and *In Conference*, with the two-saxophone front line of Trevor Watts and Willem Breuker. The box also includes a booklet of photographs and the memories of friends and fellow-players.

The best measure of Harry's gifts can be had from the solo record, which has overdubbed flute and percussion parts, played over a rolling township beat that conveyed Harry's profound immersion in the musics of his native country. As with many of the South African exiles who came to Britain in the '60s, he found the transition from settled grooves to free music perfectly congenial, and his out-of-tempo work on *Bracknell Breakdown* and *Down South* (made during the last year of his life and the only record not released on Ogun) is suggestive of a player who worked to a deeper, inner rhythm. He always had a special understanding with trombonists, perhaps drawn to that low, vocalized tonality, and some of his best work was in the company of Malfatti, Wierbos and Griffiths.

Harry was often so busy that he had little time for his own projects; however, he did establish one extraordinary band. On its day, Isipingo was one of the most incendiary and compelling bands around and, caught live at Battersea Arts Centre, proved a compelling experience even on record. 'Aitchy' lives.

Marcus Miller (born 1959)

BASS, BASS CLARINET, KEYBOARDS, GUITAR, VOCAL

Born in Brooklyn, he studied clarinet and took up the electric bass in the '70s. Played bass with Miles Davis in the early '80s and was the producer and arranger on several of Davis's final records. Subsequently worked extensively as a rock and all-purpose black-music producer, occasionally getting the time to make his own records.

★★★ The Sun Don't Lie

Dreyfus FDM 36560-2 *Miller; Miles Davis, Michael Stewart, Sal Marquez (t); David Sanborn, Kenny Garrett (as); Everette Harp (ss, as); Kirk Whalum, Wayne Shorter (ts); Joe Sample (p); Christian Wicht, Philippe Saisse (ky); Jonathan Butler, Vernon Reid, Paul Jackson Jr, Dean Brown, Hiram Bullock (g); Poogie Bell, Michael White, Tony Williams, Andy Narell, Steve Ferrone, Omar Hakim, William Calhoun, Lenny White (d); Don Alias, Paulinho Da Costa, Steve Thornton (perc).* 90–92.

★★(★) Tales

Dreyfus FDM 36571-2 *Miller; Michael Stewart (t); Kenny Garrett (as); Joshua Redman (ts); Bernard Wright (ky); Hiram Bullock, Dean Brown (g); Poogie Bell, Lenny White (d); Lalah Hathaway, Me'Shell Ndege Ocello (v).* 94–95.

★★★ Live & More

Dreyfus FDM 36585-2 *Miller; Michael Stewart (t, flhn); Kenny Garrett (as, ss); Everette Harp, Roger Byam (ts); Bernard Wright, David Ward, Dave Delhomme (ky); Hiram Bullock, Drew Zingg, Dean Brown (g); Poogie Bell (d); Lalah Hathaway (v).* 7–10/96.

Miller has had a relatively quiet time of it in the last few years, but he's still much in demand as a musician-producer. Scientific and punctilious in the studio, as likely to get out his bass clarinet as his bass guitar, he masterminded most of the final Miles Davis studio records, and there are some notes from Miles on one track from *The Sun Don't Lie*, along with bits and pieces from some of the most famous session names in the business. Typically, it ends up being an album of brilliant fragments that, for all its skill, has a peculiarly unfinished feel to it, shards of jazz, rock, funk and film music flying in all directions. The ghost of Jaco Pastorius also haunts Miller's work – 'Mr Pastorius' is a simple solo tribute on bass, but so is the note-for-note re-creation of Weather Report's 'Teen Town'. If there's such a thing as post-modernist jazz-funk, it surely sounds like this. *Tales*, though strung around some sort of concept, works in much the same way: Garrett, Stewart and Redman toss in some jazz content, but some of the zing has also slipped away since the last record.

The live album has the aura of something that used to hang around many a live rock album, years ago: the necessary souvenir of a top live show that has little musical reason to exist. Certainly Miller's takes on his own 'Panther' and 'Tutu' add little to their various studio incarnations. But it's a formidable band behind him, and the leader is a chopsman of such strength that the music takes on a degree of character that the spotless studio work sometimes misses. His bass clarinet treatment of 'Strange Fruit' shows what a wide-ranging virtuoso he is. The vocals are relatively painless. And if you miss the elasticated funk of his homebound sound, there are two studio tracks to fill up the disc. Miller has subsequently recorded another disc for Dreyfus, *M2*, but his claims on our pages have started to slip away.

Mulgrew Miller (born 1955)

PIANO

Born in Greenwood, Minnesota, Miller emerged as a major pianist in the '80s, following stints with Woody Shaw, the Duke Ellington Orchestra and Art Blakey's Jazz Messengers. He has since worked mostly as a small-group leader himself.

***** The Sequel**

Max Jazz 204 *Miller; Duane Eubanks (t); Steve Wilson (ss, ts); Steve Nelson (vib); Richie Goods (b); Karriem Riggins (d).* 9/02.

Miller hadn't recorded under his own name since 1995, a self-imposed decision that saw him concentrate on sideman duties but in no way temper his hyperactive output. *The Sequel* reunites him with the Wingspan group. Rather than retread work from that session he has written a hatful of new pieces, all of which sound very much of a piece with the work of the '90s. 'Go East, Young Man' is a bright and breezy opening, based on familiar chords, but unfamiliarly deployed. 'The Sequel' is every bit as good, but it's 'Know Wonder', a vaguely Middle Eastern idea conceived as a feature for Steve Wilson, that stands out. It's nice to welcome the big man back, even though he hardly seems to have been away.

Punch Miller (1894–1971)

TRUMPET, VOCAL

Miller made an early name with Kid Ory in New Orleans, then worked in Chicago and New York in the '20s and '30s, before moving in revivalist circles and in show bands. He was still playing in his flashy, almost defiant style in the last year of his life, including a last appearance at the Newport Jazz Festival.

***** Prelude To The Revival Vol. 1**

American Music AMCD-40 *Miller; – Harris (p, v); Clifford 'Snag' Jones (d).* 1/41.

There are five tracks by this group on the CD (the rest are covered under Kid Howard's entry). It's a fascinating glimpse of a fine New Orleans hornman (Punch wasn't a native of the city, but he is closely associated with its music) in mid-life, following plenty of sideman appearances in the '20s. Miller's quick-fingered lines and excitable attack are unencumbered by other horns on these rough but quite listenable recordings, made at the H&T Tavern in Chicago. Harris and Jones offer knockabout support to what are really trumpet and vocal showcases, an idiosyncratic adaptation of the Armstrong method.

****(*) Punch Miller's New Orleans Band 1957**

504 CD 34 *Miller; Eddie Morris (tb); Simon Frazier (p); Ricard Alexis (b); Bill Bagley (d).* 3/57.

**** 1960**

American Music AMCD-52 *Miller; Eddie Morris (tb); Captain John Handy (cl); Louis Gallaud (p); Emanuel Sayles (bj); Sylvester Handy (b); Alex Bigard (d).* 7/60.

**** Punch Miller And Louis Gallaud**

American Music AMCD-68 *As above, except add Emanuel Paul (cl); omit Morris, Handy, Handy and Bigard.* 5–7/61.

It's hard to know how good a player Miller really was: he wasn't recorded very often in what should have been his prime, and by the time of these informal tracks he was clearly wavering. The 504 CD is part of their 'Larry Borenstein Collection' and is probably the best of these, though that's not saying all that much: cobwebby sound, Frazier mostly almost inaudible, and Morris, not much of a soloist, taking a lot of solos. But the rhythm players set a hearty pace and Miller's best solos have much of his showmanship in good order (his vocals are hopelessly off-mic).

The *1960* disc suffers from a somewhat chaotic personnel – John Handy was unused to playing clarinet, Miller struggles at the often too-fast tempos, and Morris drifts in and out of focus – and a pinched, dry sound. The second disc sounds better, but Gallaud's stentorian piano is a lumbering partner for Punch – he sounds better in the oddball duet with Sayles, 'I Never Had A Chance' – and the trumpeter veers between lovely singing notes and fumbling lines that are barely linked together. Approach with caution.

**** Punch Miller & John Handy In California**

GHB BCD-192 *Miller; Big Bill Bissonnette(tb); Captain John Handy (as); Sing Miller (p); Jim Tutunjian (b); Sammy Penn (d).* 8/69.

Live at Earthquake McGoon's. Punch does as much singing as trumpet playing, the piano's dire, Bissonnette does a lot of the soloing and Handy sounds thoroughly out of sorts. It's all pretty hopeless, but every so often a chorus will suddenly cohere and you almost feel like cheering.

Dave Milligan

PIANO

Fine Scottish player, recently eclipsed by Brian Kellock, but still a formidable presence.

***** Late Show**

Caber CD 030 *Milligan; Tom Lyne (b); Tom Bancroft (d).* 02.

Fine debut showing from a band who're as seasoned and case-hardened as Inspector Rebus. Milligan's influences are increasingly hard to separate out. His attack is vigorous and his solos – notably on 'Tom, Tom, Tom' and 'Boiler Man' – are pungent and accurately played. Nice group sound on the record and sterling work as ever from label boss Bancroft.

Lucky Millinder (1900–1966)

BANDLEADER, VOCAL

Grew up in Chicago and had all kinds of showbiz jobs – including a stint as a fortune-teller – before fronting bands, including the Mills Blue Rhythm Band before its demise. Made his own records, 1942–52, and later worked in the liquor business.

*** Lucky Millinder 1941–1942

Classics 712 *Millinder; William Scott, Archie Johnson, Nelson Bryant, Freddy Webster, Dizzy Gillespie (t); George Stevenson, Eli Robinson, Donald Cole, Floyd Brady, Edward Morant, Sandy Williams, Joe Britton (tb); Bill Bowen, George James, Ted Barnett, Tab Smith (as); Buster Bailey (cl, ts); Stafford Simon, Dave Young (ts); Ernest Purce (bs); Bill Doggett, Clyde Hart (p); Trevor Bacon, Sister Rosetta Tharpe (g, v); Sterling Marlowe (g); Abe Bolar, George Duvivier, Nick Fenton (b); Panama Francis (d).* 6/41–6/42.

*** Lucky Millinder 1943–1947

Classics 1026 *Millinder; Joe Guy, Frank Humphries, Joe Jordan, Chiefie Scott, Curtis Murphy, Leroy Elton Hill, Lamar Wright, Henry Glover, Thomas 'Sleepy' Grider, Archie Johnson, John Bello, Harold 'Money' Johnson, Leon Meriam (t); Joe Britton, Gene Simon, George Stevenson, Alfred Cobbs, Money Johnson, Frank Mazzoli (tb); Billy Bowen, Tab Smith, Preston Love, Bill Swindell, Burnie Peacock, John Harrington, Sam Hopkins, Big Nick Nicholas (as); Eddie 'Lockjaw' Davis, Michael Hadley, Sam 'The Man' Taylor, Bull Moose Jackson, Elmer Williams (ts); Ernest Purce (bs); Ray Tunia, Ellis Larkins, Bill Doggett, Sir Charles Thompson (p); Trevor Bacon (g, v); Lawrence Lucie, Bernard McKey (g); George Duvivier, Beverly Peer, Al McKibbon, Jerry Cox (b); Panama Francis (d); Sister Rosetta Tharpe, Wynonie Harris, Judy Carol, Leon Ketchum, The Lucky Seven, The Lucky Four, Annisteen Allen, Paul Breckenridge (v).* 8/43–4/47.

Millinder had been fronting bands for years before he finally got his own name on a record label in 1942. His sessions for Decca (there are a scant four titles for V-Disc on Classics 1026) are energetic but middleweight titles which the occasional bright solo brings to life. Much of it yearns to be slimmed-down to R&B small-band size, and Millinder's use of vocalists such as Rosetta Tharpe and Wynonie Harris – as well as instrumentalists like Sam Taylor, Bull Moose Jackson and Bill Doggett – tells its own story about the direction of the music. A solitary date right at the end of Classics 712 hints at a different direction: Dizzy Gillespie is in the band, and there's a spirited version of 'Little John Special' (alias 'Salt Peanuts'). But that was a moment of madness in the Millinder story. He sings here and there, but otherwise his great contribution – an almost maniacal energy in directing the band onstage – has been lost to posterity. These discs pall over the long haul, but in small doses they're a worthwhile reminder of a staple part of black music in the early '40s.

Mills Blue Rhythm Band

GROUP

One of the major Harlem orchestras of the '30s. The 'Mills' was impresario Irving Mills, who took over the original band in 1930, but it subsequently had several different leaders, including Harry White, Edgar Hayes, Baron Lee and Lucky Millinder.

*** Blue Rhythm

Hep CD 1008 *Wardell Jones, Shelton Hemphill, Ed Anderson (t); Harry White, Henry Hicks (tb); Crawford Wethington (cl, as, bs); Charlie Holmes (cl, as); Ted McCord, Castor McCord (cl, ts); Edgar Hayes (p); Benny James (bj, g); Hayes Alvis (bb, b); Willie Lynch (d); Dick Robertson, Chick Bullock, George Morton (v).* 1–6/31.

*** Mills Blue Rhythm Band 1931

Classics 660 *As above.* 1–6/31.

***(*) Rhythm Spasm

Hep CD 1015 *As above, except add George Washington (tb), Gene Mikell (cl, as), Joe Garland (cl, ts, bs), O'Neil Spencer (d), Billy Banks (v).* 8/31–8/32.

*** Mills Blue Rhythm Band 1931–1932

Classics 676 *As above.* 7/31–9/32.

**** Mills Blue Rhythm Band 1933–1934

Classics 686 *Wardell Jones, Shelton Hemphill, Ed Anderson, Eddie Mallory, Henry 'Red' Allen (t); George Washington, Henry Hicks, J. C. Higginbotham (tb); Crawford Wethington, Gene Mikell, Joe Garland, Buster Bailey (reeds); Edgar Hayes (p); Benny James (bj, g); Lawrence Lucie (g); Hayes Alvis, Elmer James (b); O'Neil Spencer (d); Lucky Millinder, Chuck Richards, Adelaide Hall (v).* 3/33–11/34.

***(*) Mills Blue Rhythm Band 1935–1936

Classics 710 *As above, except add Tab Smith (cl, as); omit Anderson, Mallory, Hicks, James and Alvis.* 1/35–8/36.

Although it lacked any solo stars in its early years, the Mills Blue Rhythm Band was a very hot outfit when the first of these records were made, even though it was originally used by its boss, Irving Mills, as a substitute band for either Ellington or Calloway. The lack of a regular front-man and a rag-tag sequence of arrangers prevented the band from ever establishing a very clear identity of its own, but it still mustered a kind of fighting collectivism which comes through clearly on its best records. These chronological CDs tell the band's story. Cover versions of Ellington ('Black And Tan Fantasy') and Calloway ('Minnie The Moocher') reveal what the band's purpose was to start with, and the most interesting thing about the earlier tracks is usually the soloists' role, particularly the impassioned and badly undervalued trumpeter, Ed Anderson. But by the time the music on *Rhythm Spasm* was made, the band was energizing itself in splendid charts such as 'The Growl' and the overwhelmingly swinging 'White Lightning', which reveals the dynamism of Hayes Alvis and O'Neil Spencer in the rhythm section. There are some cringingly awful vocals from such experts as Billy Banks and Chick Bullock, but those used to music of the period will know what to expect. John R.T. Davies remasters with his usual care and attentiveness to the music on the Hep discs; the Classics counterparts are, as usual, more mixed.

The 1933–6 material shows a steady if unspectacular growth in the band's abilities, the personnel remaining surprisingly stable over the period, although the arrival of Henry Allen,

Buster Bailey and J.C. Higginbotham, all from Fletcher Henderson's band, gave the orchestra a new team of star soloists. Classics 686 is one of the best of the series, with swinging scores in 'Kokey Joe', 'The Growl', the terrific 'The Stuff Is Here (And It's Mellow)' and Allen's debut with 'Swingin' In E Flat'. There is also Adelaide Hall's extraordinary treatment of Ellington's 'Drop Me Off In Harlem', although the Classics remastering seems to be faulty here. There are more vital pieces on the next disc – the superb 'Harlem Heat' is one of Will Hudson's best scores, and 'Cotton', 'Truckin'' and 'Congo Caravan' aren't far behind – but the occasional show of routine and Chuck Richards's consistently unappealing vocals let matters down. As a sequence of records, though, an important portrait of a great Harlem orchestra.

Pino Minafra (born 1951)

TRUMPET, BUGLE, DIDJERIDOO, OCARINA, PERCUSSION, VOCAL, ETC.

Italian brass player whose range spans post-bop, orchestral work and entirely free improvisation.

***** Noci ... Strani Frutti**

Leo LR 176 *Minafra; Ernst Reijseger (clo); Han Bennink (d).* 7/90.

****** Sudori**

Victo CD034 *Minafra; Lauro Rossi (tb, perc, v); Carlo Actis Dato (ts, bs, perc, v); Giorgio Occhipinti (ky, perc, v); Daniele Patumi (perc); Vincenzo Mazzone (d).* 1/95.

Look out: genius at work. Minafra's early LPs for Splasc(h) were enjoyable post-bop outings of a comparatively conventional bent, but these are something else. The Leo disc catches him on the hoof at a late-night festival set with Reijseger and Bennink: his confiding, sputtering sound reminds one at different moments of Miles Davis, Ted Curson and Donald Ayler; but it's a very personal manner, and it fits well over the tumbling dialogue of the other two. Forty-five minutes of strong improvisation.

Sudori is entirely different. Meticulously arranged yet spontaneously exciting, Minafra's Sud Ensemble must be among the smartest outfits in European jazz today. With daredevil spirits like Dato and Rossi on hand, matters could have descended into chaos, given Minafra's own taste for excitement. Yet everything is perfectly realized, from the mounting movie-score drama of 'Exorcism' to the astonishing blues fantasy of 'Au Fond Je Suis Un Africain Du Nord'. The ensemble playing is as impeccable as the solos are rich and detailed, and in meltingly beautiful pieces like the gorgeous 'Tango', dedicated to Federico Fellini, one can hardly credit that this is the same band responsible for the uproarious stuff. A major piece of work that deserves the widest attention.

***** Canto Libero**

Victo 077 *Minafra; Sandro Satta(as); Giorgio Occhipinti (p); Vincenzo Mazzone (d).* 3/00.

Minafra's Banlieues Blues Quartet, captured at that festival (in Paris) in 2000. Four of the six pieces are entirely free, and only the first and last have sketched-out melodies by Minafra. He describes it as a refreshing change in his notes, after the stricter environments he's been working in, but with so little of the Sud Ensemble on record it's a bit frustrating for us listeners. As a free-ish blow, not bad, though some of it seems like inappropriate showboating (especially the 'Night In Tunisia' episode). A stop-gap till we hear some of Minafra's more substantial music. And we're growing impatient!

Dom Minasi (born 1943)

GUITAR

A New Yorker whose appearances on record are rare, Minasi plays electric guitar with a semi-acoustic sound on this 'comeback' session.

****(*) Finishing Touches**

CIMP 196 *Minasi; Michael Bocchicchio (b); Jay Rosen (d).* 2/99.

A strange one. This is Minasi's return to recording after a hiatus of some 25 years: he cut a couple of lite-jazz albums in the twilight stages of Blue Note's Liberty period, but has done nothing visible since. He plays these open-ended pieces with dexterity and spirit, but his rather shapeless style suggests that fundamentally he wants to play pretty and is awkward with the wilder leanings which this setting encourages. His thin, light tone shies away from any effects and he sometimes sounds a bit intimidated by loud bass and drums. The record is far too long and is interesting as an unvarnished block of music, but it's scarcely a cogent statement.

Charles Mingus (1922–79)

DOUBLE BASS, PIANO, COMPOSER

The turbulent voice of Beneath the Underdog, Mingus's self-told story of life and hard times, is audible in every note of the music as well. He was born in Nogales, Arizona, and grew up in Los Angeles, in the combustible district of Watts. After learning cello and trombone, he took to double bass and almost at once started to write a workbook of compositions that was to continue developing through his life. Working with vibist Red Norvo was his first exposure to critical attention, and thereafter he became involved in the bebop scene, playing with Charlie Parker, Miles Davis and Bud Powell at the famous Massey Hall concert. In the '50s he devised a workshop approach to improvisation and started moving towards the ambitious large-scale work that yielded the classic Black Saint And The Sinner Lady. Mingus regularly fell foul of authority and fell out with colleagues, but he was a tireless activist for the music, founding Debut Records and starting the Jazz Artists Guild in opposition to the commercialization of jazz. This marginalized him, and in the later '60s Mingus more or less went into seclusion as Thelonious Monk had before him. Later years were happier, more productive and won him belated critical attention. Near the end of his life, disabled by illness, he was honoured by the White House, and by a president from the segregationist South. It was both a fitting and an ironic end to a fiery career.

***** West Coast: 1945–1949**

Uptown 2748 *Mingus; John Anderson, Buddy Childers, Hobart Dotson, John Coppola, Karl George, Eddie Preston (t); Henry Coker, Jimmy Knepper, Britt Woodman (tb); Jewell L. Grant, Art Pepper (as, cl); Willie Smith (as); Eric Dolphy (as, cl, f); Maxwell Davis, Don Smith, Lucky Thompson (ts);*

William Woodman Jr (ts, bs); Gene Porter (bs, cl); Wilbert Barranco, Jimmy Bunn, Russ Freeman, Don Trenner, Richard Wyands (p); Red Callender (b); Roy Porter, Chuck Thompson, Cal Tjader, Lee Young (d); Helen Carr, Claude Trenier (v). 45–49.

***** Complete 1945–1949 West Coast Recordings**
Jazz Factory 22825 *As above.* 45–49.

Credited to Charles 'Baron' Mingus, this compilation of early sides needs a bit of work before the bassist's personality shines through. There are some extraordinary bass breaks and introductions, notably on Helen Carr's 'Say It Isn't So', and there is a fantastic solo on 'Mingus Fingers'. There are early chances to hear Eric Dolphy (though not as a soloist) in the Roy Porter band and a precocious composition in 'The Story Of Love', a tiny big-band arrangement that encapsulates much of what was to come in future years. For the most part, though, this is a specialist's record and won't contain much that will appeal to the more casual listener. There are more wonders to come later in the story.

The Jazz Factory option is probably more widely available now and worth a look if you're interested in the man and his later work. 'Weird Nightmare' and 'Shuffle Bass Boogie' are both here and first signs of the important stuff that was to follow.

****** The Complete Debut Recordings**
Debut 12DCD 4402 12CD *Mingus; Miles Davis, Dizzy Gillespie, Louis Mucci, Thad Jones, Clarence Shaw (t); Eddie Bert, Willie Dennis, Bennie Green, J. J. Johnson, Jimmy Knepper, Kai Winding, Britt Woodman (tb); Julius Watkins (frhn); Charlie Parker, Lee Konitz, Joe Maini (as); Paige Brook, Eddie Caine (as, f); George Barrow, Phil Urso (ts); Frank Wess, Shafi Hadi, Teo Macero (ts, f); Danny Bank, Pepper Adams (bs); John LaPorta, Julius Baker (woodwinds); Spaulding Givens, Hank Jones, Wynton Kelly, Wade Legge, John Lewis, John Mehegan, Phyllis Pinkerton, Bill Triglia, Mal Waldron, Hazel Scott (p); Teddy Charles (vib); George Koutzen, Jackson Wiley (clo); Fred Zimmerman (b); Elvin Jones, Kenny Clarke, Al Levitt, Joe Morello, Dannie Richmond, Max Roach, Art Taylor (d); Phineas Newborn Jr, Horace Parlan (perc); Bob Benton, George Gordon, George Gordon Jr, Honey Gordon, Richard Gordon, Jackie Paris (v).* 4/51–9/57.

***** Debut Rarities: Volume 1**
Original Jazz Classics OJC 1807 *Mingus; Ernie Royal (t); Willie Dennis, Jimmy Knepper (tb); Joe Maini (as); Eddie Caine (as, f); Teo Macero (ts, f); John Lewis, Bill Triglia (p); Jackson Wiley (clo); Kenny Clarke, Dannie Richmond (d).* 10/53, 6/57.

*****(*) Debut Rarities: Volume 2**
Original Jazz Classics OJC 1808 *Mingus; Spaulding Givens (p); Max Roach (d).* 4/51, 4/53.

***** Debut Rarities: Volume 3**
Original Jazz Classics OJC 1821 *Mingus; Clarence Shaw (t); Shafi Hadi (as, f); Pepper Adams (bs); Wade Legge, Wynton Kelly (p); Henry Grimes (b); Dannie Richmond (d).* 9?/57.

****(*) Debut Rarities: Volume 4**
Original Jazz Classics OJC 1829 *Mingus; Lee Konitz (as); Paige Brook (as, f); John Mehegan, Hank Jones, Phyllis Pinkerton (p); George Koutzen, Jackson Wiley (clo); Al Levitt, Max Roach (d); Bob Benton, Jackie Paris, The Gordons (v).* 4/52, 4/53.

****(*) Jazzical Moods**
Original Jazz Classics OJCCD 1857 *Mingus; Thad Jones (t); John LaPorta (cl, as); Teo Macero (ts, bs); Jackson Wiley (clo); Clem De Rosa (d).* 12/54.

Mingus's true significance has taken a long time to be recognized, though most of his innovations have long since been absorbed by the modern/avant-garde movement. In that regard, he is very different from the broadly comparable Monk, whose work is still not fully assimilated and understood but who has been almost casually canonized. In addition to pioneering modern bass-playing, Mingus is responsible for some of the greatest large-scale compositions in modern 'jazz', beside which overblown efforts like Ornette Coleman's *Skies Of America* look positively sophomoric; Mingus also transformed the conception of collective improvisation, restoring the energies and occasionally the sound of early jazz to an identifiably modern idiom. He pioneered overdubbing and editing, thereby paving the way for Miles Davis and Teo Macero, who appears on these curiously lifeless, virtually identical compilations from two albums recorded for Period.

These can really only be mined for pointers to more impressive work later. 'Four Hands' experiments with overdubbed piano (not quite like Claude Williamson's two-piano essays on the same label), and there are out-of-tempo sections that anticipate later, more radical experiments. 'What Is This Thing Called Love' undergoes interesting transformations, in keeping with Mingus's palimpsest approach to standards and new composition, and the use of cello (one of Mingus's first instruments) is intriguing. The problem lies in the playing. Macero – later to achieve his apotheosis as producer/arranger for Miles Davis – is unpalatably dry, and the drummer tackles his part with no discernible enthusiasm. *Jazzical Moods* and overlapping *Jazz Experiments* (which was formerly issued under the name *Abstractions*) also contain Macero's Third Streamish 'Abstractions', but that's a fairly minor plus. For serious Mingus scholars only.

The inevitably pricey Debut set, which covers the period 1951 to 1957, is a completist's dream. The musician-owned Debut was started by Mingus and Max Roach as a way of getting their own adventurous music recorded, and it was briefly influential. With nearly 170 individual tracks under 19 nominal leaderships, and including many alternative takes, it's an exhaustive and occasionally exhausting compilation, well out of the range and probable requirements of the average fan, who may have some of the material elsewhere. One example might well be Mingus's own tape-recording of the famous Massey Hall, Toronto, 'Quintet of the Year' gig of 15 May 1953, and it's good to know that even some of the lesser material remains in circulation. The four *Rarities* abstracts may well be enough for most people, particularly those who have other, more accessible stuff on LP. The duos with Givens on *Volume 2* are well worth dusting down, as are the 1957 Workshop pieces on *Volume 4*, which point the way forward to Mingus's '60s masterpieces.

***** Mingus At The Bohemia**
Original Jazz Classics OJC 045 *Mingus; Eddie Bert (tb); George Barrow (ts); Mal Waldron (p); Willie Jones, Max Roach (d).* 12/55.

***** Plus Max Roach**
Original Jazz Classics OJC 440 *As above.* 12/55.

The Jazz Workshop in fine, searching form. Jones, who was to figure on the classic *Pithecanthropus Erectus* but who nowadays is little regarded, came to Mingus at Thelonious Monk's behest. The opening theme on *At The Bohemia* is a Monk dedication (with Waldron re-creating an authentic cadence) that underlines Mingus's increasing emphasis on the rhythm section as a pro-active element in improvisation. 'Septemberly' is a characteristic hybrid of 'Tenderly' and 'September In The Rain', and 'Percussion Discussion' a duet between Mingus, on bass and cello, and Max Roach, just one of a long line of challenging duos set up by or for the great drummer. The rest of the material from this session was issued on a Prestige album called simply *Charles Mingus* (HB 6042).

CORE COLLECTION

**** Pithecanthropus Erectus

Atlantic 81227 5357-2 *Mingus; Jackie McLean (as); J. R. Monterose (ts); Mal Waldron (p); Willie Jones (d).* 1/56.

One of the truly great modern jazz albums. Underrated at the time, *Pithecanthropus Erectus* is now recognized as an important step in the direction of a new, freer synthesis in jazz. To some extent, the basic thematic conception (the story of mankind's struggle out of chaos, up and down the Freytag's Triangle of hubris and destruction, back to chaos) was the watered-down Spenglerism which was still fashionable at the time. Technically, though, the all-in ensemble work on the violent C section, which is really B, a modified version of the harmonically static second section, was absolutely crucial to the development of free collective improvisation in the following decade. The brief 'Profile Of Jackie' is altogether different. Fronted by McLean's menthol-sharp alto, with Monterose (a late appointee who wasn't altogether happy with the music) and Mingus working on a shadowy countermelody, it's one of the most appealing tracks Mingus ever committed to record, and the most generous of his 'portraits'. McLean still carried a torch for orthodox bebop and soon came to (literal) blows with Mingus; the chemistry worked just long enough. 'Love Chant' is a more basic modal exploration, and 'A Foggy Day' – re-subtitled 'In San Francisco' – is an impressionistic reworking of the Gershwin standard, with Chandleresque sound-effects. Superficially jokey, it's no less significant an effort to expand the available range of jazz performance, and the fact that it's done via a standard rather than a long-form composition like 'Pithecanthropus' gives a sense of Mingus's Janus-faced approach to the music.

*** The Clown

Atlantic 8122-73749-2 *Mingus; Jimmy Knepper (tb); Shafi Hadi (as, ts); Wade Legge (p); Dannie Richmond (d); Jean Shepherd (v).* 2 & 3/57.

With the first appearance of 'Reincarnation Of A Lovebird' and the *mano a mano* simplicities of 'Haitian Fight Song' (which saw Mingus build a huge, swinging performance out of the simplest thematic material), this is not a negligible record. It has never, though, been a great favourite. 'Blue Cee' is a dedication to Mingus's wife and has an almost gloomy cast. Throughout the album, the bassist grunts and hollers encouragement to himself and his players; perhaps he was still thinking about Bud Powell, who was apt to vocalize over his solos, because he had planned a 'portrait' of Powell before these sessions. The title-track is a reminder of Mingus's obsession with words and texts; Jean Shepherd's narration is fine, but one quickly longs for the instrumental versions that Mingus included in club sets thereafter.

***(*) Tijuana Moods Complete

RCA Victor 74321 74999-2 *Mingus; Clarence Shaw (t); Jimmy Knepper (tb); Shafi Hadi (as); Bill Triglia (p); Dannie Richmond (d); Frankie Dunlop (perc); Ysabel Morel (castanets); Lonnie Elder (v).* 7 & 8/57.

*** A Modern Jazz Symposium Of Music And Poetry

Bethlehem 6015 *As above, except omit Triglin, Morel, Dunlop, Elder; add Bill Hardman (t), Bob Hammer, Horace Parlan (p), Melvin Stewart (v).* 10/57.

Tijuana Moods Complete combines the original release with the complete (that is, unedited) performances from which the label not always successfully spliced together LP-length tracks. 'Ysabel's Table Dance'/'Tijuana Table Dance' is the classic track, with Mingus's structures constantly erupting into group improvisations. Nothing else quite compares with that track, though 'Dizzy Mood' is also very fine, and 'Los Mariachos' is an impressive piece of writing. There is inevitably a bit more room on the longer versions for the soloists to stretch out; but, apart from that, most seasoned listeners will probably still want to cue the original releases on their CD players rather than the restored versions. What *Tijuana Moods* called for was better editing, not no editing.

The *Symposium* – and how extraordinary that title now seems – was an opportunity for Mingus to experiment with texts and with pure sound. 'Scenes In The City' reworks some of the ideas he had sketched in 'Foggy Day' on *Pithecanthropus Erectus*, but with a much greater degree of finish. The 'New York Sketchbook' is a parallel piece, finely drawn and performed, with Shaw rising above himself and playing some of the best trumpet heard on a Mingus album for some time before or since.

***(*) Jazz Portraits: Mingus In Wonderland

Blue Note 827325 *Mingus; John Handy (as); Booker Ervin (ts); Richard Wyands (p); Dannie Richmond (d).* 1/59.

Mingus's appearance as part of the Nonagon Art Gallery Composers' Showcase series in 1959 was a significant moment of recognition for a man whose life was passed in resistance to the 'jazz musician' tag. Previous composers showcased there had been Virgil Thomson, Aaron Copland and Carlos Chavez, and in addition there had been notable appearances by the MJQ and Cecil Taylor.

Working with something of a scratch band (the all-important Horace Parlan wasn't available), more emphasis than usual fell on Mingus's bass playing, which is consistently marvellous from the opening moody strains of 'Nostalgia In Times Square', written as part of the soundtrack to John Cassavetes's movie, *Shadows*, to the closing 'Alice's Wonderland', which gave the record its first release title. 'I Can't Get Started' had become one of his favourite standards, indeed the only non-original that seemed to fire him up to the heights of invention audible here, fiery double-stops and intense lyrical passages alternating with softer, almost guitar-like strums. Until recently, this has been one of the less well-known Mingus records (and on a label not normally associated with him). It's a welcome addition to the catalogue.

*****(*) Blues And Roots**

Rhino/Atlantic R2 75205 *Mingus; Willie Dennis, Jimmy Knepper (tb); John Handy, Jackie McLean (as); Booker Ervin (ts); Pepper Adams (bs); Horace Parlan, Mal Waldron (p); Dannie Richmond (d).* 2/59.

♛ ** Mingus Ah Um**

Columbia CK 65512 *As above, except omit Waldron, McLean; add Shafi Hadi (ts).* 5/59.

A classic period. This was the point where, rising forty in just a couple of years and aware of the encroachment of younger and perhaps more accommodating musicians, he began to show his absolute understanding of the African-American musical tradition. *Ah Um* is an extended tribute to ancestors, cemented by the gospellish 'Better Git It In Your Soul', a mood that is also present on *Blues And Roots* with the well-loved 'Wednesday Night Prayer Meeting' in its doubled-up 6/4 time. Everything here has its place. The shouts and yells, the magnificently harmonized *ostinati* which fuel 'Tensions' and the almost jolly swing of 'My Jelly Roll Soul' (*Blues And Roots*), the often obvious edits and obsessive recycling of his own previous output, all contribute to records which are entire unto themselves and hard to fault on any count. The latest (digipack) reissue of *Blues And Roots*, however, contains four alternative tracks, perfectly viable performances in their own right, albeit lacking the indefinable dramatic tension of the release versions.

***** Mingus Dynasty**

Columbia CK 65513 *Mingus; Don Ellis, Richard Williams (t); Jimmy Knepper (tb); Jerome Richardson (f, bs); John Handy (as); Booker Ervin, Benny Golson (ts); Teddy Charles (vib); Roland Hanna, Nico Bunink (p); Maurice Brown, Seymour Barab (clo); Dannie Richmond (d); Honey Gordon (v).* 11/59.

Often, mistakenly but understandably, thought to refer to a posthumous album, *Mingus Dynasty* is a pretty obvious pun when looked at twice. It wraps up a period of activity that seems to catch Mingus in mid-mood-swing between fired up and confident and way down low. 'Strollin'' is a version of 'Nostalgia On Times Square' and the music written for the (mostly improvised) John Cassavetes film, *Shadows*, in which jazz almost takes the place of orderly narrative dialogue. There is also a version of 'Gunslinging Bird', a take each of 'Song With Orange', 'Far Wells, Mill Valley', 'Slop' and, memorably, 'Mood Indigo'. As with so many other Mingus albums, this is somehow better and more coherent than it ought to be. Though not intended to be put together in this form, it works as an entity, and one wouldn't want the original sessions to be reconstructed in any other way.

*****(*) The Complete 1959 Columbia Recordings**

Columbia 65145 3CD *Mingus; Don Ellis (t); Willie Dennis, Jimmy Knepper (tb); John Handy (as, cl); Shafi Hadi (as, ts); Booker Ervin, Benny Golson (ts); Jerome Richardson (bs, f); Sir Roland Hanna, Horace Parlan (p); Teddy Charles (vib); Dannie Richmond (d); Honey Gordon (v).* 5 & 11/59.

***** Alternate Takes**

Columbia CK 65514 *As above.* 5 & 11/59.

Lifted from the sessions that went to the making of *Ah Um* and *Mingus Dynasty*, this elegant three-CD set includes a good deal of unreleased and alternative material previously available only on the exhaustive Mosaic box. It's obviously good to have it all back together again, though it isn't clear why Sony decided to release the alternatives separately as a single CD. Of largely specialist interest, this compilation of rejected takes includes 'Better Git It In Your Soul', 'Bird Calls', 'Jelly Roll', 'Song With Orange', 'Diane' and 'New Now Know How'. Though almost any Mingus performance of almost any period is likely to contain music of interest, and very little of it merely routine, there isn't much here that changes the existing picture. For trainspotters only. The boxed set is more appealing, but no amount of extra material adds any gloss to the magnificence of the original albums.

***** Pre-Bird**

Verve 538636-2 *Mingus; Marcus Belgrave, Ted Curson, Hobart Dotson, Clark Terry, Richard Williams (t); Eddie Bert, Charles Greenlee, Slide Hampton, Jimmy Knepper (tb); Don Butterfield (tba); Robert DiDomenica (f); Harry Schulman (ob); Eric Dolphy (as, bcl, f); John LaPorta (as, cl); Yusef Lateef (ts, f); Bill Barron, Booker Ervin (ts); Jake Hanna (p); Dannie Richmond (d).* 60.

***** Mingus Revisited**

Emarcy 826 496 *As above, except add Danny Bank, Charles Greenlee (tb), Don Butterfield (tba), Joe Farrell, Harold Shulman (woodwinds), Paul Bley, Sir Roland Hanna (p), Charles McCracken (clo), Sticks Evans, George Scott (d, perc), Lorraine Cousins (v).* 5/60.

Mingus Revisited was originally released as *Pre-Bird* in 1960, before being reissued by the Limelight label five years later with a liner-note by Leonard Feather. With the exception of 'Half-Mast Inhibition', a piece written by Mingus when he was just eighteen, conducted by Gunter Schuller, all the material is in short-song form, opening with a strikingly original sandwich of 'Take The "A" Train' and Dorothy Fields' 'Exactly Like You' and continuing later with another Ducal interpolation, 'I Let A Song Go Out Of My Heart' amidst 'Do Nothing Till You Hear From Me'; this is a record that puts all its emphasis on ensemble playing rather than extended soloing. Verve have now reissued the original session as it was intended to be heard, though it seems slightly odd that both albums should remain in catalogue. All that is extra on *Revisited* are two songs, albeit two of Mingus's most important, 'Eclipse' and 'Weird Nightmare', sung with estranged passion by Lorraine Cousins, one of the few Mingus interpreters to understand the balance between music and text.

****** Mingus At Antibes**

Atlantic 7567 90532-2 *Mingus; Ted Curson (t); Eric Dolphy (as, bcl); Booker Ervin (ts); Bud Powell (p); Dannie Richmond (d).* 7/60.

Charles Delaunay memorably likened Mingus's performance in the mellow warmth of Juan-les-Pins to a 'cold shower'. Certainly in comparison with the rest of the Antibes line-up, the '60s band was intellectually recherché and somewhat forceful. Unreleased until after Mingus's death – the tapes had lain, unexamined, in Atlantic's vault – the set contains a valuable preview of some of the material to be recorded that autumn for Candid, below, and for a thumping 'I'll Remember April' with the exiled Bud Powell guesting. Mingus himself gets behind the piano on a number of occasions, perhaps trying to give the slightly chaotic ensembles more shape. The essence of the performance lies in the solos. Ervin is fine on 'Better Git Hit In Your Soul', as is Dolphy, still sounding like a renegade Parker disciple, on a first version of the gospelly 'Folk Forms', which reappears on *Presents*, below. The bass/bass-clarinet sparring on 'What Love' isn't quite as over the top as the later, studio version, but it shows how far Dolphy was prepared to move in the direction of Ornette Coleman's new synthesis. Not just another 'previously unreleased' money-spinner, the *Antibes* set contains genuinely important material. The chance to hear a Mingus concert in its entirety offers valuable clues to his methods at the time.

CORE COLLECTION

**** Charles Mingus Presents Charles Mingus

Candid CCD 79005 *Mingus; Ted Curson (t); Eric Dolphy (as, bcl); Dannie Richmond (d).* 10/60.

Mingus's association with Candid was brief (though no briefer than the label's first existence) and highly successful. His long club residency in 1960 (interrupted only by festival appearances) gave him an unwontedly stable and played-in band to take into the studio (he recorded a fake – and uncommonly polite – night-club intro for the set), and the larger-scale arrangement of 'MDM' negatively reflects the solidity of the core band. *Presents* is for piano-less quartet and centres on the extraordinary vocalized interplay between Dolphy and Mingus; on 'What Love' they carry on a long conversation in near-comprehensible dialect. 'Folk Forms' is wonderfully pared down and features a superb Mingus solo. 'All The Things You Could Be By Now If Sigmund Freud's Wife Was Your Mother' has a wry fury (Mingus once said that it had been written in the psych ward at Bellevue) which is more than incidentally suggestive of 'harmolodic' and 'punk' procedures of the '80s. The 'Original Faubus Fables' was a further experiment in the use of texts, here a furious rant against what Mingus later called 'Nazi USA', and his later '60s brothers 'Amerika'. It's powerfully felt but less well integrated in its blend of polemic and music than Max Roach's *Freedom Now Suite* on the same label.

***(*) Charles Mingus

Candid CCD 79021 *As above, except add Lonnie Hillyer (t), Jimmy Knepper, Britt Woodman (tb), Booker Ervin (ts), Paul Bley, Nico Bunink (p).* 10/60.

*** Reincarnation Of A Love Bird

Candid CCD 79026 *As above, except omit Woodman, Bunink; add Roy Eldridge (t), Tommy Flanagan (p), Jo Jones (d).* 11/60.

**(*) Mysterious Blues

Candid CCD 79042 *As above.* 10 & 11/60.

If *Presents* is a classic, *Charles Mingus* falls slightly short. The augmented band on 'MDM' sounds uninspired, either unfamiliar or unhappy with the material (which isn't exceptionally demanding). 'Stormy Weather', also released on *Candid Dolphy*, below, features a monster introduction by the saxophonist. Like 'ATTYCBBNISFWWYM' above, 'Lock 'Em Up' makes some reference to Bellevue (or to Charlie Parker's 'holiday' in Camarillo), if only because it's taken at the same hare-brained pace, and Mingus bellows instruction to his troops in a voice that sounds on the brink. At producer Nat Hentoff's suggestion, he had attempted to vary the existing band and re-create the energy of the 'Newport rebels' anti-festival by bringing in past associates. The most notable of these was Roy Eldridge, who is featured (with Knepper, Flanagan and Jo Jones also guesting, as the Jazz Artists Guild) on the long 'R & R', a superb 'Body And Soul', and a previously unreleased 'Wrap Your Troubles In Dreams'. 'Reincarnation Of A Love Bird' and 'Bugs' are both Parker-inspired. The title-track features Hillyer, McPherson and Ervin over Dolphy's uncredited bass clarinet (Curson isn't listed either, and is mentioned only in Brian Priestley's characteristically detailed liner-note). By no means a classic Mingus album, it restores some fascinating performances and alternatives from a critical period in his career. Needless to say, worth having (and enthusiasts should take note of another 'Reincarnation' along with the Dolphy-led 'Stormy Weather' on the label compilation, *Candid Dolphy* (CCD 9033).

The descending order of stars gives a fair account of *Mysterious Blues*' place in this sequence. Not much more than a collection of bin-ends and alternatives, it's likely to appeal only to serious Mingus collectors. Taking up nine and a half minutes with a drum solo by Richmond (who was never an inspiring soloist) is the main symptom of padding. The rejected 'Body And Soul' has some nice Dolphy and Flanagan, but still isn't particularly compelling.

*** Oh Yeah

Rhino/Atlantic R2 75589 *Mingus; Jimmy Knepper (tb); Rahsaan Roland Kirk (ts, manzello, stritch, f, siren); Booker Ervin (ts); Doug Watkins (b); Dannie Richmond (d).* 11/61.

The addition of Rahsaan Roland Kirk gave the Mingus band the kind of surreality evident on the spaced-out blues, 'Ecclusiastics', which Mingus leads from the piano. Kirk is also the main attraction on 'Wham Bam, Thank You Ma'am', a typically de-romanticized standard. On the closing 'Passions Of A Man' Mingus overdubbed a bizarre, associative rap, which is rather more effective than the instrumental backing. Odd. Damned odd, even; but a significant instance of Mingus's often desperate conflation of music and words in the search for some higher synthesis.

**** Passions Of A Man

Rhino/Atlantic R2 72871 6CD *As for Atlantic albums.* 56–61.

As will have been seen from the above sequence, it doesn't make entire sense to talk about 'the Atlantic years', because the label was never an exclusive focus of attention, and there is a considerable amount of overlap with other imprints, often using identical line-ups. However, the albums the bassist made for the Erteguns are among the best in the canon: *Pithecanthropus Erectus, The Clown, Mingus At Antibes*, the little-known *Tonight At Noon, Mingus Oh Yeah!* and the user-friendly *Blues And Roots*. Some of the material from it turned up, reworked, on the earliest of Mingus's Columbia sessions, and *Ah Um* almost feels like a record from the same stable. This, though, was a period in which the creative and experimental fires were at their height; there is an astonishing level of creative interplay between projects. As throughout his career, it wasn't so much a case of plans going awry as of ideas becoming fragmented and being distributed across foreground and background of the discography. Rhino's compilation has restored *Tonight At Noon*, a two-part work, to its position amid the sessions that yielded *Oh Yeah!* and *The Clown*. The set contains about 30 minutes of previously unissued music, not much for a six-CD (or effectively five, since the last of the run is devoted to interview material, more than an hour of Mingus's blustery 'What, then, I contradict myself ...' observation of his life, music and milieu). Of the new material, the most important is alternative tracks from *Blues And Roots* which has itself recently been polished and reissued to the same crisp standard. Inevitably an expensive item, but one that every genuine Mingus fan will want to have, since so much of this music was, as another American poet put it, the 'cry of its occasion', less meaningful when heard out of context and out of chronology.

***** The Very Best of Charles Mingus**
Atlantic 79988 *As for Atlantic albums above.*

The real subtitle is, of course, 'the Atlantic years'. This set attempts the impossible and does it as well as can be expected. The opening sequence of 'Pitchecanthropus Erectus', 'Profile Of Jackie', 'Tonight At Noon' and 'Haitian Fight Song' is about as good a half-hour introduction to Mingus as you'll find, though the second track really was a showcase for Jackie McLean. The rest goes off the boil slightly and there are a couple of obvious and slightly puzzling omissions, though we can't really complain with one breath that compilers are predictable and then criticize them for omitting the obvious.

***** The Complete Town Hall Concert**
Blue Note 28353 *Mingus; Snooky Young, Ernie Royal, Richard Williams, Clark Terry, Lonnie Hillyer, Ed Armour, Rolf Ericson (t); Britt Woodman, Quentin Jackson, Willie Dennis, Eddie Bert, Jimmy Cleveland (tb); Don Butterfield (tba); Charles McPherson, Charlie Mariano (as); Buddy Collette (as, ts, f); Eric Dolphy (as, bcl, f); Booker Ervin, Zoot Sims (ts); Dick Hafer (ts, cl, f, ob); Pepper Adams (bs); Jerome Richardson (bs, ss, f); Teddy Charles (vib); Toshiko Akiyoshi, Jaki Byard (p); Les Spann (g); Milt Hinton (b); Dannie Richmond (d, tim).* 10/62.

An object case in the extraordinary performance history of Mingus's music. These ambitious charts, which were related to the huge *Epitaph* suite performed only after his death, were being prepared for a recording or concert-recording (the ambiguity was never quite settled) at New York's Town Hall. (This shouldn't be confused with the later occasion listed and discussed below.) Preparations were chaotic and there was no proper run-through on the night, leaving a body of material which was significantly flawed and in some cases considered unreleasable. The original LP lasted only 36 minutes. This reissue, digitally remixed from the original three-track tapes and produced by biographer Brian Priestley, restores the whole extraordinary occasion with one minor re-ordering of tracks. 'Clark In The Dark', a feature for trumpeter Terry, is marred by a completely skew-whiff mix; the engineer still apparently hadn't managed to effect a proper balance. The next piece, 'Osmotin', breaks off, much like some of the internal sections on *Blues And Roots* and *Ah Um*. The opening part of 'Epitaph' features a glorious solo from Dolphy, communicating with the leader on a level far beyond any of the other soloists. There are versions of 'Peggy's Blue Skylight', more from 'Epitaph' and a new contrafact, 'My Search', on 'I Can't Get Started'. With time marching on, and the audience – presumably unused to the disciplines of recording – becoming restless, Mingus was signalled to stop towards the end of 'Please Don't You Come Back From The Moon', one of the previously unissued tracks. At this point, with the leader heading offstage and many of the players winding up, Terry, who'd kicked the whole thing off, went into 'In A Mellotone', and brought the band together again.

It was, to be sure, something of a shambles, but a magnificent shambles. The reconstructed evening has its rough edges and unresolved parts, but it is an essential document in Mingus's progress, and who can say what might have happened had the record company been more accommodating and smart enough to realize that it was virtually impossible and also undesirable to tape so much brand-new music, some of it being (re)written on the spot in front of an audience. For all its frustrations and its rather shambolic feel, this is essential Mingus.

♛ ** The Black Saint And The Sinner Lady**
Impulse! 051174-2 *Mingus; Rolf Ericson, Richard Williams (t); Quentin Jackson, Don Butterfield (tba); Jerome Richardson (as, bs, f); Booker Ervin (ts); Dick Hafer (ts, f); Charlie Mariano (as); Jaki Byard (p); Dannie Richmond (d).* 1/63.

*****(*) Mingus Mingus Mingus Mingus Mingus**
Impulse! 051170-2 *As above, except add Britt Woodman (tb), Jay Berliner (g).* 1 & 9/63.

Almost everything about *Black Saint* is distinctive: the long form, the use of dubbing, the liner-note by Mingus's psychiatrist. On its release, they altered its usual slogan, 'The new wave of jazz is on Impulse!', to read 'folk', in line with Mingus's decision to call the group the Charles Mingus New Folk Band. Ellingtonian in ambition and scope, and in the disposition of horns, the piece has a majestic, dancing presence, and Charlie Mariano's alto solos and overdubs on 'Mode D/E/F' are unbelievably intense. There is evidence that Mingus's desire to make a single continuous performance (and it should be remembered that even Ellington's large-scale compositions were relatively brief) failed to meet favour with label executives; but there is an underlying logic even to the separate tracks which makes it difficult to separate them other than for the convenience of track listing. Absolutely essential.

Mingus etc. comes from the same and one later session. It includes 'Celia' and 'I X Love', both older pieces, both distinguished by great Mariano performances, with 'Theme For Lester Young', which is a variant on 'Goodbye, Pork Pie Hat', and 'Better Git Hit In Your Soul'. Nothing comes close to *Black Saint*, but the pair give an even better account of Mingus's thinking at the time. Whatever the compromises forced upon him in the past by musicians (or now by his label), he is creating music of classic scope and lasting value.

***** Mingus Plays Piano**
Impulse! 051217-2 *Mingus (p solo).* 7/63.

Mingus played something more than 'composer's piano' throughout his career. His touch and harmonic sense were so secure that, though hardly virtuosic, he more than passes muster on a very resonant and richly toned instrument with what sounds like a very brisk action. It's interesting to hear themes like 'Orange Was The Color Of Her Dress, Then Blue Silk' reduced to their essentials in this way, though the true highlights are 'When I Am Real' and a thoroughly unabashed 'Body And Soul'. Not in the front rank of Mingus albums, but certainly not just for collectors.

****** Town Hall Concert 1964**
Original Jazz Classics OJC 042 *Mingus; Johnny Coles (t); Eric Dolphy (as, f, bcl); Clifford Jordan (ts); Jaki Byard (p); Dannie Richmond (d).* 4/64.

***** Mingus In Europe: Volume 1**
Enja 3049 *As above.* 4/64.

***** Mingus In Europe: Volume 2**

Enja 3077 *As above.* 4/64.

*****(*) The Great Concert, Paris 1964**

Musidisc 500072 2CD *As above, except add Johnny Coles (t).* 4/64.

This is undoubtedly the most heavily documented period of Mingus's career. The Town Hall concert predated the European tour, and this set consists of two long tracks which strongly feature Dolphy (the dedicatee) on each of his three horns. The release shouldn't be confused with a 1962 Blue Note recording of the same name, which contains entirely different material.

There is a vast amount of bootleg material from the European tour of April 1964. We have omitted all but respectably licensed releases. Dedicated collectors may want to check dates and itinerary in our second edition and argue about the respective merits of individual performances, for the repertoire overlaps very considerably. 'Peggy's Blue Skylight' is ubiquitous, only omitted on *Great Concert*; other staples include 'Orange Was The Color Of Her Dress, Then Blue Silk' and 'Fables Of Faubus'. 'So Long, Eric' is sometimes described as a threnody or epitaph to the multi-instrumentalist, who died on 29 June of that year, but there he is playing it; the piece was actually supposed to be a reminder to Dolphy (who'd decided to try his luck in Europe for a while) not to stay 'over there' too long. Sadly, it was all too soon to become a memorial.

A bonus on the Enjas (which were recorded in Wuppertal at the opposite end of the month to the Amsterdam material, which was taped on the 10th) is a flute–bass duo credited to Dolphy as 'Started', but actually based on 'I Can't Get Started'. 'Fables' was awkwardly split on the LP format, and is very much better for being heard entire.

***** Right Now**

Original Jazz Classics OJC 237 *Mingus; John Handy (as); Clifford Jordan (ts); Jane Getz (p); Dannie Richmond (d).* 6/64.

Two long cuts – 'Meditation (On A Pair Of Wire Cutters)' and a revised 'Fables Of Faubus' – which were originally released on Fantasy, featuring Mingus's Californian band of that summer. Handy comes in only on 'New Fables' but sounds funky and a lot more abrasive than McPherson. Jane Getz is by no means well known, and is certainly less individual than the otherwise-engaged Byard, but she acquits her piano duties more than adequately.

*****(*) Live At Carnegie Hall**

Rhino/Atlantic R2 72285 *Mingus; Jon Faddis (t); Charles McPherson (t); John Handy (as, ts); George Adams (ts); Roland Rahsaan Kirk (ts, stritch); Hamiet Bluiett (bs); Don Pullen (p); Dannie Richmond (d).* 1/74.

What deep satisfaction he must have felt to see his name bracketed with that of America's toniest concert hall, a small step forward in his insistence that jazz was Afro-America's classical music. There is nothing classically calm about the music, which rumbles threateningly, then hints at a sunnier mood and then, just when the sky seems clear, delivers bolts of lightning. If it was Duke Ellington who cleared the way for Afro-Americans to be recognized as full partakers in the country's musical culture, then the concert's apparent dedication to Duke and his spirit seems entirely appropriate, with 'C Jam Blues' and 'Perdido' delivered with respect. To be frank, there are better Mingus albums and even the more chaotic live appearances delivered more compelling music than anything here, but it was an important step for him and for creative jazz in general. Sometimes the event is bigger than any single element it contains.

*****(*) Changes One**

Rhino/Atlantic R2 71403 *Mingus; Jack Walrath (t); George Adams (ts); Don Pullen (p); Dannie Richmond (d).* 12/74.

*****(*) Changes Two**

Rhino/Atlantic R2 71404 *As above, except add Jackie Paris (v), Marcus Belgrave (t).* 12/74.

Long out of print, these are among the best of Mingus's later works. Recorded in a single session, they represent definitive performances by a group that had played and gradually transformed this material – 'Orange Was The Color Of Her Dress', 'Devil Blues', two versions of 'Duke Ellington's Sound Of Love', one instrumental, one vocal – over a longer period than almost any previous Mingus unit. Some of the fire has definitely gone, and there is a hint of studio polish that was never evident on the band's live dates; but they are powerful records nevertheless, and essential documents for Mingus enthusiasts.

****** Thirteen Pictures: The Charles Mingus Anthology**

Rhino R2 71402 3CD *Mingus; Jack Walrath, Marcus Belgrave, Hobart Dotson, Clark Terry, Bobby Bryant, Lonnie Hillyer, Melvin Moore, Eddie Preston, Richard Williams (t); Lou Blackburn, Jimmy Knepper, Eddie Bert, Jimmy Greenlee, Slide Hampton, Britt Woodman (tb); Don Butterfield, Red Callender (tba); Mauricio Smith (as, ss, f, picc); John Handy (as, ts); Eric Dolphy (as, f, bcl); Lee Konitz, Jackie McLean, John LaPorta, Charles McPherson (as); Buddy Collette (as, f, picc); Booker Ervin, Dick Hafer, Shafi Hadi, Roland Rahsaan Kirk, J. R. Monterose, George Barrow, Bill Barron, Joe Farrell, Ricky Ford (ts); Paul Jeffrey (ts, ob); Yusef Lateef (ts, f); Danny Bank (bs); Bob Didomenica (f); Harry Schulman (ob); Jerome Richardson, Jack Nimitz (bs, bcl); Gary Anderson (bcl, cbcl); Gene Scholtes (bsn); Jaki Byard, Phyllis Pinkerton, Sir Roland Hanna, Wade Legge, Mal Waldron, Horace Parlan, Duke Ellington, Bob Neloms (p); George Koutzen, Charles McCracken (clo); Doug Watkins (b); Willie Jones, Al Levitt, Walter Perkins, Sticks Evans, Dannie Richmond, Max Roach (d); Candido Camero, Alfredo Ramirez, Bradley Cunningham (perc); Jackie Paris (v).* 52–77.

An excellent compilation of Mingus's work for Atlantic, beautifully packaged in a box with a booklet of photographs. It contains material from *Pre-Bird, Chazz!/At The Bohemia, Plays Piano, Cumbia And Jazz Fusion, The Clown*, the immortal *Ah Um, Oh Yeah* and *Mingus Mingus Mingus Mingus, Pithecanthropus Erectus, Money Jungle, At Monterey* and a rare Debut single from 1952 with Jackie Paris as vocalist. The packaging and accompanying documentation are immaculate; the music is, of course, brilliant. One can hardly imagine a nicer present for someone who hasn't got all this stuff already.

***** Three Or Four Shades Of Blues**

Atlantic 7567 81403 *Mingus; Jack Walrath (t); Sonny Fortune (as); George Coleman (ss, ts); Ricky Ford (ts); Bob Neloms, Jimmy Rowles (p); Philip Catherine, Larry Coryell, John Scofield (g); Ron Carter, George Mraz (b); Dannie Richmond (d).* 3/77.

Despite Mingus's deep and vocal reservations, this was one of his most successful albums commercially. The addition of guitarists clearly pitched it in the direction of the younger rock-buying audience that Atlantic had targeted, and the record also included staples like 'Goodbye, Pork Pie Hat' and 'Better Git Hit In Your Soul' (presumably with a view to initiating that younger audience). The title-track, though, is rather too broad in its catch-all approach and sounds almost self-parodic. Mingus's health was beginning to break down in 1977, and there are signs of querulousness throughout, not least on 'Nobody Knows The Trouble I've Seen'.

*****(*) Cumbia And Jazz Fusion**

Atlantic 8122 71785-2 *Mingus; Jack Walrath (t, perc); Dino Piana (tb); Jimmy Knepper (tb, btb); Mauricio Smith (f, picc, as, ss); Quarto Maltoni (as); George Adams (ts, f); Ricky Ford (ts, perc); Paul Jeffrey (ts, ob); Gary Anderson, Roberto Laneri (bcl); Anastasio Del Bono (ob, eng hn); Pasquale Sabatelli, Gene Scholtes (bsn); Bob Neloms (p); Danny Mixon (p, org); Dannie Richmond (d); Candido Camero, Daniel Gonzalez, Ray Mantilla, Alfredo Ramirez, Bradley Cunningham (perc).* 3/76–3/77.

'Cumbia And Jazz Fusion' is a slightly messy piece that levels some doubts at Mingus's remaining talents as arranger and instrumentator. The ensembles are all rather congested, which mars a fine and vibrant piece that ranks as one of his best late compositions. There is a regularity to the basic metre and a simplicity of conception which make the rather opaque surface all the more disappointing. The fault doesn't seem to lie with the recording, which is well transferred. 'Music for *Todo Modo*' was written (sight unseen) as soundtrack to the film by Elio Petri. The ten-piece Italo-American band works a typically volatile score, which includes a variant on 'Peggy's Blue Skylight' and some fine blues.

***** His Final Work**

Master Dance Tones 8471 *Mingus; Woody Shaw, Jack Walrath (t); Peter Matt (frhn); Ricky Ford (ts); Gerry Mulligan (bs); Lionel Hampton (vib); Bob Neloms (p); Dannie Richmond (d); additional personnel.* 11/77.

Arranged and led by Lionel Hampton, this was a last fling in the studio for the ailing Mingus, though he was to direct a couple more sessions from his wheelchair. To be frank, the music is rather routine. 'Fables Of Faubus' and 'Peggy's Blue Skylight' have lost their antagonism and eager passion respectively and now sound like well-structured charts, played with competence. The new things are a bit drab, almost pastiche Mingus. Arranger Paul Jeffrey has done a fine job, and even though the ever-mischievous Jack Walrath lobs a few well-aimed cherry bombs, the general impression is polite and unemphatic. Even so, it's remarkable that a player of Hampton's generation and persuasion should have chosen to be involved in this at all, even though he played a part in promoting Mingus's early career. The record has a rather complicated discographical history and there may be other versions of it in circulation. The version of 'So Long, Eric' certainly doesn't appear on them all.

Mingus Big Band

GROUP

A 'ghost' group playing the music of Charles Mingus, featuring ex-Mingusians and younger players in the spirit.

***** Nostalgia In Times Square**

Dreyfus FDM 36955 2 *Randy Brecker, Christopher Kase, Ryan Kisor, Lew Soloff, Jack Walrath (t); Art Baron, Sam Burtis, Frank Lacy (tb); Dave Taylor (btb, tba); Alex Foster, Steve Slagle (as); Chris Potter (as, ts); John Stubblefield, Craig Handy (ts); Ronnie Cuber, Roger Rosenberg (bs); Joe Locke (vib); Kenny Drew Jr (p); Michael Formanek, Andy McKee (b); Victor Jones, Marvin 'Smitty' Smith (d); Ray Mantilla (perc).* 3/93.

***** Gunslinging Birds**

Dreyfus FDM 36575 2 *As above, except omit Kase, Walrath, Baron, Burtis, Taylor, Cuber, Rosenberg, Formanek, Jones, Smith, Mantilla; add Philip Harper (t); Jamal Haynes, Earl McIntyre (tb); Gary Smulyan (bs); David Lee Jones (as); Adam Cruz (d).* 95.

****** Live In Time**

Dreyfus FDM 36583 2 2CD *Similar to above, except add Earl Gardner, Alex Sipiagin (t); Robin Eubanks, Conrad Herwig, Britt Woodman (tb); Gary Bartz (as); Seamus Blake, Mark Shim (ts).* 96.

***** Que Viva Mingus**

Dreyfus FDM 36593 2 *Similar to above, except add Ryan Kisor (t); Steve Turre (tb, shells); Earl McIntyre (btb, tba); Vincent Herring (as); David Sanchez (ts); Ronnie Cuber (bs); David Kikoski (p); Gene Jackson (d); Steve Berrios, Milton Cardona (perc); La Conja (v, perc).* 9/97.

*****(*) Blues And Politics**

Dreyfus FDM 36603 2 *Similar to above, except add Alex Sipiagin (t); Bobby Watson (as); John Hicks (p); Boris Kozlov (b); Jonathan Blake (d); Eric Mingus (v).* 1/99.

Of the projects dedicated to the great man's memory and legacy, this is perhaps the most important, and now the most durable as well, enjoying the active blessing of the composer's widow and access to tapes and manuscripts from the huge Mingus archive. The band began round a regular Thursday session at Fez under the Time Café in New York City. Mingus had shrewdly recognized that a band could rehearse at the public's expense if an event was labelled a 'workshop' rather than a concert, and so the Mingus Jazz Workshops were born. These days the task is perhaps less urgent, and less driven by constraint; the Big Band provides an opportunity to work through the scrolls, providing exegesis and commentary on a vast body of work, little of which received definitive performance during its creator's lifetime.

But what of the records themselves? The sleeve of *Gunslinging Birds* is misprinted Mingus Big Bang, which is just about right. Both the first records listed deliver with ferocious power and, when required, some delicacy as well. As usual, the material is taken from throughout the Mingus archive. *Nostalgia* is probably more interesting in terms of material – 'Don't Be Afraid, The Clown's Afraid, Too', 'Weird Nightmare', the title-piece – but the playing and the recording are sharper and more exact on the later album, which centres on a superb reading of 'Fables Of Faubus'.

Live In Time of course refers to the venue, but it also underscores the vital, ongoing nature of the project and the fact that all of this music is being worked out in real time, in the laboratories of the spirit rather than in the formaldehyde of musicological analysis. A huge slab of music spread over two discs, it comes the closest of the group to recapturing the spirit of Mingus himself. The opening is stunning; 'Number 29' was written by Mingus as a challenge to all the gunslinging trumpet players in town – and, as written, it was impossible. Arranger Sy Johnson has spread the part through the trumpet section and given it a hard, bi-tonal quality that is pure Mingus. Two early pieces, 'Baby, Take A Chance With Me' and 'This Subdues My Passion', are recorded here for only the second time since they were written in the '40s. Conrad Herwig solos on the second, Frank Lacy and Gary Bartz on the first. 'So Long Eric' is a *tour de force*, a solo feature for the entire horn section and one of the most sheerly exciting jazz performances we have heard for years.

Disc two is not quite as powerful as the first, though Johnson's long arrangement on 'The Shoes Of The Fisherman's Wife Are Some Jive-Ass Slippers' and the superb 'E's Flat, Ah's Flat Too' are impeccably conceived and performed. The night ends a day late with 'Wednesday Night Prayer Meeting', a stunning solo from Randy Brecker, ably supported by Mark Shim and Robin Eubanks. A great jazz record and a worthy homage to one of jazz's greatest composers.

Que Viva Mingus can't hope to reach the same heights, and for some reason the band this time out doesn't sit quite right, sounding rather tired and lacking in lustre. There are some superb moments, needless to say. Lacy, Stubblefield and Brecker make a wondrous thing of 'Love Chant' and Sy Johnson's arrangement of 'Cumbia And Jazz Fusion' could hardly have been bettered by the man himself. Many of the other arrangements are by Michael Mossman, and he directs 'Tijuana Gift Shop', teeing off fine solos from Ryan Kisor and Vince Herring. Ysabel – in the boisterous form of La Conja – does her table dance to end the session. Satisfying to Mingus buffs in unfolding further aspects of the oeuvre, but it will perhaps appeal less to the uncommitted.

As the title suggests, *Blues And Politics* foregrounds Mingus's fierce activism. It begins with the great man's voice, reciting 'It Was A Lonely Day In Selma, Alabama' at the Tyrone Guthrie Theater in Minneapolis, with interjections from the band of the time. That segues into a new recording of 'Freedom', arranged by Mike Mossman and bracketed by archive and new recordings of the narration by Charles and Eric Mingus. Boris Kozlov plays the opening cadenza of 'Haitian Fight Song' on Mingus's own lion-head bass, and the young Russian steals the apostolic thunder of Andy McKee, who is relegated to a single solo on 'Pussy Cat Dues'. The Russian surfaces again on 'Goodbye Pork Pie Hat', which shifts the emphasis from politics to blues, and 'Meditations For A Pair Of Wire Cutters'.

The lament for Lester Young opens with a magnificent Seamus Blake cadenza which confirms his rising status, but he is upstaged by Bobby Watson's searingly beautiful statement on 'Pussy Cat Dues', a high point on the album. No sign that the legacy is in anything but the safest and most committed hands, and certainly no sign that Mingus's turbulent output will not continue to inspire big-band performance of the highest quality and the strongest passion.

*****(*) Tonight At Noon: Three Or Four Shades Of Love**
Dreyfus 36633 *Randy Brecker, Earl Gardner, Jeremy Pelt, Kenny Rampton, Alex Sipiagin, Jack Walrath (t); Conrad Herwig(tb); Ku-umba Frank Lacy (tb, v); Vincent Herring (ss, as); Alex Foster (ss, as, cl, f); Wayne Escoffery, John Stubblefield (ts); Ronnie Cuber (bs); Doug Yates (bcl); Michael Rabinowitz (bsn); David Kikoski(p); Adam Rogers (g); Boris Kozlov, Andy McKee (b); Jeff Tain Watts(d); Jonathan Blake (d, perc); Elvis Costello (v); other instruments.* 11–12/01.

The latest of the ensemble's tributes to the master is perhaps the most beautiful yet, dedicated as it is to the theme of love which, in its most turbulent forms, was a dominant one for Charles Mingus. Four of the songs are orchestrated and feature a newly convened orchestra which is intended to complement the big band, but for the most part this is a regular MBB disc. 'Passions of a Woman Loved' is nearly ten minutes of rousing jazz; 'Tonight at Noon' is no less involving, and features a stunning solo from trumpeter Sipiagin.

On the vocal side, Elvis Costello brings a hurt passion to 'Invisible Lady', but it is Frank Lacy's vocal on the long, extraordinary 'Black Saint And The Sinner Lady' which clinches the set. Frank's singing has always taken second place to his horn work, but this is a man who is musical to his very toes and there is no one better qualified to take forward the Mingus legacy.

*****(*) The Essential Mingus Big Band**
Dreyfus 36628 *As above.* 93–99.

We'd still recommend that you explore the original CDs, but this compilation offers a very decent representation of the Big Band's output since 1993. The track listing includes 'Haitian Fight Song', 'Gunslinging Bird', 'Self Portrait In Three Colours', 'Boogie Stop Shuffle', 'Nostalgia In Times Square' and 'Goodbye Pork Pie Hat', so pretty much as you'd expect theme-wise.

Phil Minton (born 1940)

VOICE, TRUMPET

Worked with Mike Westbrook as singer and trumpeter in the '60s and '70s, but moved increasingly towards entirely free vocal music, often working with other singers in that context.

*****(*) A Doughnut In Both Hands**
Emanem 4025 *Minton (solo v).*

Minton's singing has virtually overtaken his trumpet playing. Associated with Mike Westbrook on a number of text-based projects, he is also a stunning vocal improviser, with a tonal and timbral range that seems quite uncanny. Most of the material on this remarkable record was released in America years ago as a Rift LP. Its concentration is extreme, both technically and emotionally. Seemingly inspired by the literature of the First World War, which (if Paul Fussell is to be believed) is definitive of many twentieth-century attitudes and obsessions, 'Cenotaph' and 'Wreath' are only three-quarters of a minute apiece, but overflowing with pain and pride, anger and redemption. A group of five 'Wood Songs' aren't quite so compelling, but a tiny dedication to German revolutionist Emma Goldman and the stunning 'Notes On Avarice' and 'Blasphemy' demand frequent recourse to the repeat button. 'Blasphemy' is one of half a dozen additional tracks not included on the original album.

***** Songs From A Prison Diary**
Leo CDLR 196 *Minton; Veryan Weston (p).* 10/91.

The duos with Weston seem much more formalized than Minton's improvised work with Peter Brötzmann and others on a deleted FMP album, and they lack the sheer power of the slightly earlier work with Roger Turner on *AMMO*, but they are compelling all the same. The Ho Chi Minh texts on *Songs From A Prison Diary* are intensely moving and Minton brings to them a natural actor's ability to deliver apparently banal lines with a weight of experience that far exceeds their ostensible meaning.

★★★(★) Two Concerts

FMP OWN 90006 *Minton; John Butcher (ts, ss); Erhard Hirt (g, elec).* 6 & 8/95.

★★★(★) Mouthfull Of Ecstasy

Victo CD 041 *Minton; John Butcher (ts); Veryan Weston (p); Roger Turner (perc, v).* 1/96.

The FMP record documents a long-standing group which has over time achieved an almost perfect balance and economy of means. Hirt is something of a miniaturist; he has been described as the Webern of improv guitar, and there is certainly something in that, splitting up a line into an array of different sounds, and then drifting in behind Minton's shredded semantics and Butcher's wonderfully elegant, almost courtly wooing of the saxophone. The surprising revelation about this music is how romantic it seems, how full of expressive meaning. There's an unevenness of quality between the two sets represented, one from Vandoeuvre in June, the other from the Antwerp Free Music Festival later in the summer. The five numbers from Musique Action are oddly scrappy and unformed, impressive in bulk but hard to come to terms with individually. The Antwerp set consists of a massive central movement, fiercely dramatic and delicately modulated by turns, surrounded by two shorter items, prologue and epilogue, introduction and peroration, fascinatingly discursive by the standards of this music and, as so often, hovering on the fringes of orthodox song form.

That side of Minton is always more obvious when Veryan Weston is in attendance, and the London recording on Victo is full of moments when some melodic revelation seems near. Butcher loves to toy with such shapes, but it is clear that – as with a performer like Lol Coxhill – familiar material is both intellectually present and very distant. What one is hearing is pre-standard material, shapes and anticipations of song. Minton himself does much the same thing, constantly reworking the timbral and dynamic envelope within which songs can exist, creating his own vast sound-bank, an archive which is not there to be exploited but simply to exist on its own magnificent terms.

★★★★ A Doughnut In One Hand

FMP CD 91 *Minton (v solo).* 1/96.

This category-stretching return to solo singing has no intrinsic relation to the earlier disc that (almost) shares its title. Now one doughnut short (which makes better sense on the cholesterol front), Minton also has a spare hand free to conduct himself through a disciplined and rigorous sequence of miniatures, 30 tracks in an hour of spectacular vocal acrobatics.

Relations between groups of pieces – 'Dough Songs', 'Para Songs', songs about 'drainage' and a Mr Wilkins, and 'Tip Head' – are never made entirely explicit, but by sequencing the CD differently one gets a strong impression of areas of concern approached and developed organically and then re-ordered to create a fractured narrative. The voice has seldom been better and Minton's use of space and microphone distance (the only kind of processing on the record) adds dimensions that are entirely unexpected. Don't expect an easy ride if this is your first experience of Phil Minton, but do expect your expectations and anticipations to be substantially re-ordered.

Bob Mintzer (born 1953)

TENOR SAXOPHONE, BASS CLARINET

Mintzer's experience is primarily with big bands, from Tito Puente and Buddy Rich in the '70s onwards. He has played, written and arranged for many orchestral situations since, although his most significant small-group experience may have been his association with the pop-jazz group, The Yellowjackets, beginning in 1991.

★★★ Latin From Manhattan

DMP CD-523 *Mintzer; Bob Millikan, Larry Lunetta, Scott Wendholt, Michael Mossman (t); Larry Farrell, Keith O'Quinn, Sam Burtsi, Dave Taylor (tb); Bob Malach, Lawrence Feldman, Pete Yellin, Roger Rosenberg (saxes); Phil Markowitz (p); Jay Anderson (b); John Riley (d); Louis Bauza (perc).* 1/98.

★★★ Quality Time

TVT Jazz TVT-3230-2 *Mintzer; Phil Markowitz (p); Russell Ferrante (ky); Jay Anderson, Jimmy Haslip (b); Peter Erskine, William Kennedy (d).* 3/98.

Mintzer is an accomplished soloist and arranger who's been recording big-band albums for a more than a decade. Earlier albums have been hit-and-miss affairs, with too much piling on of effects and a certain cuteness standing in for wit or ingenuity. Mintzer is, though, still making big-band records for DMP, and *Latin From Manhattan* is in an ongoing sequence. Tom Jung's sleeve-note captures the flavour of their accomplishments pretty well: top-flight technique and musicianship, meticulous studio sound. For people who want a drilled, hi-fi experience out of a big-band record, Minzter's albums are hard to top. A glance through the personnel shows what a formidable team he's got. This one has nine new tunes and an agreeable revamp of Tito Puente's 'Oye Como Va'. In its way, though, this music is for specialized tastes, just as much as, say, a Vinny Golia large-ensemble record. It seeks a perfection which many will find hard to warm to.

His small-group records have been less than compelling in the past, but *Quality Time* is a rather surprising success. The rhythm section of Markowitz, Anderson and Erskine (the others appear on only two rather annoying smooth-jazz tracks) play with such relaxed good humour that they soften all the rather clenched virtuosity which Mintzer is otherwise prone to fall into as a soloist (Erskine must be the best drummer in the world at making a complex groove seem beatifically simple). The result is one of Mintzer's most enjoyable dates – but docked a notch for including the electric tracks, obviously pitched for radio-play, which spoil the album's karma.

Giovanni Mirabassi

PIANO

Self-taught and resident in France since 1992, Mirabassi is one of the most interesting young pianists of his generation.

★★★ Architectures

Sketch SKE 333010 *Mirabassi; Daniele Mencarelli (p); Louis Moutin (d).* 98.

★★★ Avanti!

Sketch SKE 333015 *Mirabassi (p solo).* 5/00.

*** **Dal Vivo!**
Sketch SEK 333021

As for *Architectures.* 11/01

***(*) **(((air)))**
Sketch SEK 333036 *Mirabassi; Flavio Boltro (t); Glen Ferris (tb).* 3/03.

Strong, committed piano jazz from this pianist and his well-established trio. An early duo album with bassist Pierre Stéphane Michel, *En Bonne Et Due Forme*, is unfortunately not available at the moment, but the others are well worth exploring. *Avanti!* is an album of revolutionary chants and songs from around the world, transcribed and arranged for piano, something close to what Frederic Rzewski and Cornelius Cardew have done but with definite swing. The live version of 'The People United Will Never Be Divided' (it's also on the solo album) which closes *Dal Vivo!* is as rousing as anything you'll hear from this instrumentation, while other tracks, notably 'Requiem', could be by some faintly exotic version of the Bill Evans Trio. Other influences adduced here and on Mirabassi's other records include Keith Jarrett and Kenny Barron, as well as Europeans like Enrico Pieranunzi. His rippling, lyrical style is evident on the debut duo with Michel and is heard in a dramatic new context in the unusual new trio with Boltro and American Ferris; *(((air)))* is one of the most refreshing albums we've heard for some time and the arrangement of Georges Brassens's 'Birds Of Passage' is a delight.

Miss Lulu White's Red Hot Creole Jazzband

GROUP

A Dutch combo dedicated to ensemble playing in the early New Orleans tradition. They're named after one of the leading 'landladies' in the Storyville district during the teens of the last century.

*** **My Sweet Lovin' Man**
Stomp Off CD 1370 *Mart Mous, Tom Goosen (c); Bart Goosen (tb); Alain Marquet (cl); Matthias Seuffert (cl, as, ts); Daniel Huck (as); Wil Van Baarle (cl, bs); Mart Jacobs (p); Wouter Nowens (bj); Marcel Van De Winckel (tba).* 4/01.

Mart Mous and his men set out to re-create the sound of the Oliver Creole Jazz Band at its densest and most rumbustious: as he says in the notes, 'you have to make a thorough search for the individual musician', and in most of these pieces breaks and solos take a decided second place to the thick, rolling sound of a front line with either six or seven horns in it (Huck is present only on the final eight tracks), and no drums. Most of the tunes come from Oliver's repertoire and it's interesting to hear them done in modern sound, in faithful arrangements and by players who are dedicated to the original techniques. At its stomping best, in 'Alligator Hop' and 'Chattanooga Stomp', the band reach a pitch of rocking abandon which is mightily exhilarating. That said, a certain measure of listener fatigue sets in after half-way, and the difficulties in balancing the band sometimes defeat the engineers. If best heard a few tracks at a time, this should still intrigue scholars of the early idiom.

Billy Mitchell (1926–2001)

TENOR SAXOPHONE

A Kansas City native, Billy worked a journeyman path until joining – perhaps inevitably – Count Basie in 1958, though he was only rarely featured. He later appeared regularly with Al Grey and Frank Wess and enjoyed a residency at a Seaport club called Sonny's Place, which began in 1972 and lasted for some 25 years.

*** **This Is Billy Mitchell**
Verve 065507-2 *Mitchell; Dave Burns (t); Bill Wallace (p); Clarence 'Sleepy' Anderson (org); Bobby Hutcherson (vib); Herman Wright (b); Otis Finch (d).* 10/62.

Mitchell was out front for only a handful of albums in a 50-year career, and this was the earliest – originally for Smash, and now part of Verve's LPR reissue series. Although a typical two-day album of the time, there is plenty of interesting variety: Wallace does five tracks, Anderson the other three, Burns sits out the organ pieces and there's the surprise presence of Hutcherson, as well as an unpredictable programme of material, including Melba Liston's 'Just Waiting' and originals by Burns, Gene Kee and John Hines. Mitchell works through the date with an attractively cloudy sound which gets pushed aside by a rhythmic urgency just when you think he's coasting it. 'Sophisticated Lady' brings out an Ellingtonian rather than Basieish side to the leader, and Burns's 'Automation' displaces the swing feel with a smart hard bop line. No classic, but a worthwhile visit to an all but forgotten date.

Blue Mitchell (1930–79)

TRUMPET, CORNET

A fair proportion of the Miami-born trumpeter's career was spent away from jazz in R&B and blues outfits led by artists as various as Earl Bostic and John Mayall, and as a soloist with the likes of Ray Charles and Lena Horne. His soulful delivery was an asset wherever it was deployed and Blue, having inherited the Horace Silver band, made some fine recordings on his own account.

**** **Big Six**
Original Jazz Classics OJC 615 *Mitchell; Curtis Fuller (tb); Johnny Griffin (ts); Wynton Kelly (p); Wilbur Ware (b); Philly Joe Jones (d).* 7/58.

***(*) **Out Of The Blue**
Original Jazz Classics OJC 667 *Mitchell; Benny Golson (ts); Cedar Walton, Wynton Kelly (p); Paul Chambers, Sam Jones (b); Art Blakey (d).* 1/59.

***(*) **Blue Soul**
Original Jazz Classics OJC 765 *Mitchell; Curtis Fuller (tb); Jimmy Heath (ts); Wynton Kelly (p); Sam Jones (b); Philly Joe Jones (d).* 9/59.

***(*) **Blues On My Mind**
Original Jazz Classics OJC 6009 *Mitchell; Curtis Fuller (tb); Benny Golson, Johnny Griffin, Jimmy Heath (ts); Wynton Kelly (p); Paul Chambers, Sam Jones, Wilbur Ware (b); Art Blakey, Philly Joe Jones (d).* 7/58–9/59.

A stalwart of the Horace Silver band, Mitchell took it over in 1964, replacing the former leader with the young Chick Corea.

The debut recording isn't particularly memorable; though Corea has a fine grasp of the required idiom, which is blues- and gospel-drenched hard bop of the kind Silver pioneered, it never quite ignites. The heavy-duty line-up on the Riverside reissues on OJC is much more satisfactory and *Big Six* is unquestionably the trumpeter's finest achievement. It contains the first recorded version of Golson's classic 'Blues March', a punchy version of what was to become a chestnut. The *Blues On My Mind* compilation is, for most casual purchasers, a good buy, bringing together 'Brother Ball' and 'There Will Never Be Another You' from OJC 615 and 'It Could Happen To You' and a rousing 'Saints' from *Out Of The Blue*.

Blue Soul is also very good, though here Mitchell is occasionally outclassed by his band; Heath in particular sounds as if he's trying not to muscle in and one or two of his solos are curtailed rather suddenly, perhaps lest he outstay his welcome. Jimmy Heath resurfaces to equally good effect on *A Sure Thing* (below), especially on 'Gone With The Wind', which is arranged for just trumpet, saxophone and rhythm, a welcome variation on the big-band material but rather wastefully tucked away at the end. The two baritones and french horn provide a solid bottom for Heath's arrangements.

***** Blue's Moods**
Original Jazz Classics OJCCD 138 *Mitchell; Wynton Kelly (p); Sam Jones (b); Roy Brooks (d).* 4/60.

***** Smooth As The Wind**
Original Jazz Classics OJC 871 *Mitchell; Burt Collins, Bernie Glow, Clark Terry (t); Jimmy Cleveland, Urbie Green, Britt Woodman, Julian Priester (tb); Willie Ruff (frhn); Tommy Flanagan (p); Tommy Williams (b); Philly Joe Jones, Charli Persip (d); strings.* 12/60, 3/61.

*****(*) A Sure Thing**
Original Jazz Classics OJC 837 *Mitchell; Clark Terry (t); Julius Watkins (frhn); Jerome Richardson (as, f); Jimmy Heath (ts); Pepper Adams, Pat Patrick (bs); Wynton Kelly (p); Sam Jones (b); Albert 'Tootie' Heath (d).* 3/62.

***** The Cup Bearers**
Original Jazz Classics OJC 797 *Mitchell; Junior Cook (ts); Cedar Walton (p); Gene Taylor (b); Roy Brooks (d).* 4/63.

At the start of the '60s, Blue was still with Horace Silver but was already branching out on his own. Like many of his contemporaries, Mitchell long nursed a desire to work with strings. *Smooth As The Wind* is the result, an on-again, off-again mish-mash of terse big-band jazz arranged by Tadd Dameron and Benny Golson with oddly distanced orchestral washes that neither add nor significantly detract but which over the entire session pall rather badly.

The Cup Bearers is a bit of a disappointment. Unlike the urbane Henderson on the earlier record, Cook is forever in a tearing rush to get back and have a further say, not quite knowing how to get out of what he's set up for himself. What it palpably needs is someone of Heath's intelligence to tie up the loose ends.

Blue's Moods suggests some forgotten Lee Morgan session with the leader sounding unusually raw and unsettled. It's an oddly inelegant performance from Mitchell. 'Scrapple From The Apple' settles any doubt about who is playing, a definitive performance on material that doesn't obviously suit him, though towards the end of his life he was to form a bebop group with Harold Land. Kelly was a long-time collaborator and he brings his usual fresh-faced composure to all these tracks. *A Sure Thing* is another excellent record from Mitchell, an artist who needs to be experienced in depth before he starts to pay dividends.

***** Down With It**
Blue Note 54327 *Mitchell; Junior Cook (ts); Chick Corea (p); Gene Taylor (b); Al Foster (d).* 7/65.

Recently returned from soul-jazz limbo, *Down With It* is an undemanding and largely entertaining session that delivers on promise without scattering any pigeons. The soloists – Corea, Cook, Mitchell – are good enough to sustain attention over a rather scant 40 minutes, even though the material is fairly light and trite. 'Hi-Heel Sneakers' is pitched straight at the jukeboxes, while tunes like 'Perception' (credited to Blue and Chick) and 'March On Selma' are more demanding. The horns are beautifully separated and balanced, but the bass could be more emphatic, and Al Foster is wasted.

Red Mitchell (1927–92)

BASS, PIANO

Born Keith Moore Mitchell, he came from New York but did much of his most familiar work on the West Coast, from 1954. Left for Stockholm in the '60s and stayed there almost until his death. A humorous, energetic, clever musician with many important credits in his discography.

*****(*) Presenting Red Mitchell**
Original Jazz Classics OJC 158 *Mitchell; James Clay (ts, f); Lorraine Geller (p); Billy Higgins (d).* 3/57.

Mitchell was known for a fluent improvising style in which pulled-off (rather than plucked) notes in a typically low register (Mitchell used a retuned bass) suggest a baritone saxophone rather than a stringed instrument; Scott LaFaro was later sanctified for a broadly similar technique. Mitchell is also an accomplished pianist, with a hint of the romantic approach of his former colleague, Hampton Hawes. The early stuff on OJC with the short-lived Geller instead of Hawes is decent, boppish jazz consistently lifted by Mitchell's singing lines. 'Scrapple From The Apple' is a joy and a delight. The Sunnyside originals – with titles like 'I'm A Homeboy' and 'It's Time To Emulate The Japanese' – quash any notion that Mitchell is merely a standards hack, though he is more approachable in that territory.

****(*) Chocolate Cadillac**
Steeplechase SCCCD 1161 *Mitchell; Idrees Sulieman (t); Nisse Sandström (ts); Horace Parlan (p); Rune Carlsson (d).* 12/76.

On *Chocolate Cadillac* the writing is good and Mitchell is playing well (top form on a couple of tracks). Unfortunately, the band simply isn't behind him. Parlan, normally a stylistic chameleon, seems to have his mind on something else, and the two horns lock only infrequently. Disappointing.

***** Red Mitchell–Warne Marsh Big Two: Volume 1**
Storyville 8252 *Mitchell; Warne Marsh (ts).* 4/80.

*****(*) Red Mitchell–Warne Marsh Big Two: Volume 2**
Storyville 8257 *As above.* 4/80.

Recorded over two nights at the Fasching Club in Stockholm and released for the first time in the mid-'90s, this is a fascinating but relatively unvaried set of improvisations in Marsh's familiar abstract–harmonic style. The chemistry between the two is interesting enough, but there's very little action off the ball, as it were, in the absence of a pianist, or guitarist, and drummer. Rhythmically, Mitchell has no problems and Marsh sticks to his own patiently metronomic delivery, but one consistently feels the lack of an extra element. The second volume has some interesting bebop excursions, notably 'Hot House' (the highlight of the two discs), 'Ornithology', 'Lover Man' and 'Scrapple For the Apple'. It's a more ragged set of tunes than the first issue and thus perhaps preferable in that the joins show and Mitchell in particular is required to work very hard to keep up the harmonic momentum. Genuinely fascinating stuff, but probably for specialists only.

***** Simple Isn't Easy**
Sunnyside SSC 1016 *Mitchell (p solo).* 9/83.

Simple Isn't Easy is entirely for piano and voice, and to that extent isn't typical; even so, it suggests that most of the elements of Mitchell's shaping intelligence are at work: harmonically limber, melodically sophisticated and rhythmically just dynamic enough to be listenable.

***** The Red–Barron Duo**
Storyville STCD 4137 *Mitchell; Kenny Barron (p).* 8/86.

The Red–Barron Duo was the closest Mitchell came to duetting with himself until the overdubbed solo project below stretched his possibilities. The pianist shares Mitchell's harmonic and rhythmic preoccupations to a productive degree, and their exploration of quite basic themes ('Oleo', 'The Sunny Side Of The Street') is compellingly inventive. So, too, is the collaboration with Rowles, except that here there is an entirely surprising element of tension, most of it generated by Mitchell's taut ostinati and a fresh set-list, in which only 'There Is No Greater Love' sounds like a chestnut.

****(*) A Declaration Of Interdependence**
Four Leaf Clover FLC CD 105 *Mitchell (p, b, v solo).* 88.

The solo album allowed him (via the wonders of overdubbing) to pull off the trick and do the one-man duet. Given his quirky keyboard methods and the delicious bass sound, the passages for the two instruments together are rather good; but his singing is frankly pretty awful and his original numbers – culminating in the mildly notorious 'You Can Take Your Funny Money And Run Honey' – aren't candidates for the songwriting hall of fame.

***** Mitchell's Talking**
Capri 74016 *Mitchell; Kenny Barron (p); Ben Riley (d).* 1/89.

Towards the end of his life, Mitchell went back to the US to live in Oregon, where he died three years after this session was taped. In company with his most sympathetic piano-playing partner, Red sounds in good form, still low-toned and full-voiced on the title–piece, which is an original. He's even more prominent on 'I'm Old Fashioned', which he introduces almost like a singer. Barron's swinging 'El Sueno' is a highlight and the long 'Don't Explain' and 'She's Funny That Way' make this a top pick for Mitchell fans, and for Barron collectors as well.

***** Live At Salishan**
Capri 74033 *Mitchell; Joe Beck (g).* 3/92.

Fine, late duets with the often overlooked guitarist, who takes his share of front-line duties without ever overpowering Mitchell or reducing him to journeyman duties. The themes are fairly nondescript, but 'Tenderly', 'Body And Soul' and 'Like Someone In Love' are all benchmark performances in the bassist's later career.

Robert Mitchell

PIANO

Nominated Rising Star in the BBC Jazz Awards 2002, Mitchell draws on a classical training and an ear-opening journey to Africa and Asia.

***** Voyager**
Dune CD04 *Mitchell; Steve Williamson (ss); Barak Schmool (ss, as); Omar Puente (vn); Roberto Bellatalla, Nico Gomez (b); Victor Spaven (d); Volker Strater (perc); Eska Mtungwazi (v).* 02.

Mitchell has talent, passion and a generous spirit and they all come out on the debut album. Built around his Panacea sextet (and you suspect listening to him that he really does think of music as the key to all the world's problems), it's a rhythmic, densely layered set that recalls some of the African-tinged British groups of the '60s and '70s in the wake of the Brotherhood of Breath. It takes a certain style to programme both an Alec Wilder and a Keith Jarrett tune in a set of this kind, but the pianist pulls it off with aplomb and his arrangement of Jarrett's 'Days And Nights Waiting' is one of the best things on the album. His own writing is terse and loping by turns, with a revolving rhythm that horn–players enjoy. Williamson and Puente are the guest musicians; Jason Yarde and Gary Crosby produce and deliver a solid ensemble sound, perhaps a little overpowering for some of the soloists.

Roscoe Mitchell (born 1940)

REEDS, PERCUSSION

One of the key figures in the Chicagoan avant-garde, Mitchell is a native of the city and has been active as a musician and associated with the city's 'new music' for close to 40 years. His group was transmuted into the Art Ensemble Of Chicago; several of his records are among the significant documents of post-Coleman jazz. Some of his solo and small-group records have set the tone for both solo and ensemble-based improvisers in free jazz and beyond.

CORE COLLECTION

****** Sound**
Delmark DE 408 *Mitchell; Lester Bowie (t, flhn, hca); Lester Lashley (tb, clo); Maurice McIntyre (ts); Malachi Favors (b); Alvin Fielder (d).* 6/66.

What a vital, electrifying document this remains! Restored to an excellent CD edition (original Delmark vinyl was seldom very clean), with an alternative version of 'Ornette' and the title-track, originally a composite of two versions, heard as two separate takes, there is a lot more music and nothing to diminish the power of the occasion. The two key pieces, 'Sound' and 'The Little Suite', are a message of freedom quite different from that being communicated by the contemporaneous recordings of Albert Ayler and Peter Brötzmann. Mitchell organizes his group around the notion of sounds

entering into – and interrelating with – silence. So there are tiny gestures and startling emptinesses alongside long lines and soliloquies. Bowie, Lashley and McIntyre work in overtones and distortions more than they do in 'true' tones, and in 'The Little Suite' the sound of toys and bells and other found instruments carries as much sensitivity as the horns do elsewhere. Both a manifesto and an unrepeatable event, *Sound* remains a marvel.

***** Roscoe Mitchell**
Chief CD 4 *Mitchell; Wadada Leo Smith (t, pkt-t, flhn); George E. Lewis (tb, sou, tba); Thurman Barker, Anthony Braxton, Don Moye, Douglas Ewart, Joseph Jarman, Henry Threadgill, Malachi Favors (perc).* 7–8/78.

Several of Mitchell's crucial recordings have disappeared with the apparent demise of Chicago's Nessa label, but the above reissue of one of them returns some of his most significant '70s work to the catalogue. Away from the Art Ensemble Of Chicago, this dedicated reed theoretician and experimenter has sought out some very rarefied terrain. There are three long pieces here: a trio for woodwinds, high brass and low brass, with Smith and Lewis; a phantasmagoria for eight percussionists, 'The Maze'; and almost 18 minutes of Mitchell blowing as softly as he can through the soprano sax, 'S II Examples', drifting through a world of shadowy microtones. A remarkable programme, but there are drawbacks: the 'L-R-G' trio is full of fascinating juxtapositions and echoes of countless other composers, yet its deliberately piecemeal nature seems laboured next to the spontaneous structures conceived as a matter of course by European improvisers. 'The Maze' has a burnished, glistening quality, but the fact that only two 'genuine' drummers are among the percussionists makes one wonder what Mitchell could have achieved with the involvement of eight full-time drum exponents. As it stands, the piece is a matter of shifting textures, when it might have transcended that. 'S II Examples', too, is more of an intriguing idea than a valuable musical one – or, at least, one more important to Mitchell than to the listener. All that said, it's a rather bewitching set altogether, and a useful notebook on what Chicago's playing élite were looking into at the period. The equally significant *Nonaah* from the same period has yet to appear on CD.

***** 3×4 Eye**
Black Saint 120050-2 *Mitchell; Hugh Ragin (t, picc-t, flhn); Spencer Barefield (g); Jaribu Shahid (b); Tani Tabbal (d).* 2/81.

****** Roscoe Mitchell And The Sound And Space Ensembles**
Black Saint 120070-2 *Mitchell; Mike Mossman (t, flhn); Gerald Oshita (ts, bs, Conn-o-sax, cbsrspn); Spencer Barefield (g, v); Jaribu Shahid (b, v); Tani Tabbal (d, v); Tom Buckner (v).* 6/83.

**** The Flow Of Things**
Black Saint 120090-2 *Mitchell; Jodie Christian (p); Malachi Favors (b); Steve McCall (d).* 6–9/86.

***** Live At The Knitting Factory**
Black Saint 120120-2 *Mitchell; Hugh Ragin (t, picc-t, flhn); Spencer Barefield (g); Jaribu Shahid (b); Tani Tabbal (d).* 11/87.

Two of the best of Mitchell's Black Saint records are now available on CD. *3 × 4 Eye* features a picked team tiptoeing around a number of themes, including his tribute to Jarman, 'Jo Jar', and the ironic 'Variations On A Folk Song Written In The Sixties'. Improvisation becomes almost ritualized, yet the leader's idiosyncratic deployment of sound and space renders the sequence of events as something extraordinary. The subsequent *Sound And Space Ensembles* is completely *sui generis*. The trio of Mitchell, Oshita – on some of the oddest reed instruments ever made – and the classical tenor Tom Buckner perform an eerie mixture of Kurt Schwitters and Wilton Crawley, before a pseudo-funk rave-up by the whole ensemble, which features probably the only recorded solo on the contrabass sarrusophone. The two ensembles go on to blend again in two long, beautiful tracks, the needle-fine 'Linefine Lyons Seven' and the scuttling-drifting 'Variations On Sketches From Bamboo'.

In the latter part of the '80s, though, Mitchell seemed to lose his listeners. While a colleague such as Anthony Braxton worked out many directions through obsessive recording, Mitchell scarcely recorded at all. The only studio date, *The Flow Of Things*, is a static and tamely conventional reeds-and-rhythm date which yields little advance on his earlier experiments. *Live At The Knitting Factory* replaces the live album from 1988 on Cecma, which so far is not on CD. The group is in good shape, but Mitchell's notebook-like approach to recording tends to make for a fragmented listening experience: the short pieces and the two cut-out solos break up the impact of the powerful 'Almost Like Raindrops' and the blowout memorial, 'The Reverend Frank Wright'. Ragin's impassioned yet curiously selfless playing is as effective as Mitchell's own.

***** New Music For Woodwinds And Voice / An Interesting Breakfast Conversation**
Mutable 17501-2 2CD *Mitchell; Gerald Oshita (as, ts, bs, Conn-o-sax, srspn, cbsrspn); Thomas Buckner (v).* 1/81–84.

***** 8 O'Clock: Two Improvisations**
Mutable 17505-2 *Mitchell; Thomas Buckner (v).* 12/00.

The trio Space arguably had more to do with extended techniques in contemporary composition than with jazz, though one of their two 1750 Arch albums (now reissued as the two-disc Mutable set) was entirely improvised. If the group had a dominant member soundwise, it was Oshita rather than Mitchell, partly because of the extraordinary sonorities of the sarrusophones and straightened-out saxes which he employed. Their surviving recordings are exercises in sound and space which, however, are entirely in keeping with Mitchell's most specialized solo work.

Many years on, the Mitchell–Buckner duo continues to perform. Buckner's techniques are drawn from what often sounds like conventional counter-tenor vocabularies: he seldom explores the kind of range which Phil Minton pursues as a matter of course, and he works often quietly and carefully around Mitchell's equally sparing sound-making. Both sets will appeal to admirers of Mitchell's researches; the less committed listener may balk at what is, for all its deftness and intensity, difficult music.

**** Duets And Solos**
Black Saint 120133-2 *Mitchell; Muhal Richard Abrams (p).* 3/90.

****(*) This Dance Is For Steve McCall**
Black Saint 120150-2 *Mitchell; Matthew Shipp (p); William Parker (b, perc); Jaribu Shahid (b); Tani Tabbal, Vincent Davis (d).* 5/92.

The meeting with Abrams is a terrible disappointment. Each man's solo section rambles dutifully along to no great purpose, Abrams constructing a rolling but directionless panorama of piano styles, Mitchell practising some of his minimalist licks. Together they provide a few felicitous moments, but Abrams's decision to use a synthesizer for most of these passages pushes the music towards routine impressionism. *This Dance Is For Steve McCall* debuts a new group, The Note Factory, though not very auspiciously; aside from a thoughtful new treatment of Jarman's 'Ericka', several of the nine pieces sound half-realized or foreshortened, with the bass and percussion textures unclear. 'The Rodney King Affair', a stew of disquiet, is suitably blunt political art.

**(*) Hey Donald

Delmark DE-475 *Mitchell; Jodie Christian (p); Malachi Favors (b); Albert 'Tootie' Heath (d).* 5/94.

Another largely disappointing affair. When the rhythm section are playing straight time and setting up a groove underneath, Mitchell's honking and mordant saxophone often sounds frankly ludicrous. On the Tab Smith-styled smoocher, 'Walking In The Moonlight', it's close to absurd. Yet there are still felicitous moments – the simple, sweet flute piece, 'Jeremy' – and four duets with Favors evoke some of the mystery of the old days. But this is, in sum, not much of a record.

*** Sound Songs

Delmark 2DE-493 2CD *Mitchell (reeds solo).* 94–97.

No lack of energy here: in some of the longer pieces, such as the concert recordings, 'Full Frontal Saxophone', 'Near And Far' and 'Closer', Mitchell has never sounded more powerful and adroit. Elsewhere, particularly in the application of little instruments to a saxophone line, as in much of disc two, he harks back not only to his early soliloquies but also to some of Julius Hemphill's overdubbed solo music. But the record is simply too long. The more absorbing pieces sit next to what could be called sound-exercises, a useful notebook for the performer and a test for impatient listeners. Mitchell's music often seems to need a large-scale overview; as with Braxton, one tries to fathom out the big picture. As an individual component, this tends towards the inscrutable.

*** Nine To Get Ready

ECM 539725-2 *Mitchell; Hugh Ragin (t); George E. Lewis (tb); Matthew Shipp, Craig Taborn (p); Jaribu Shahid (b, v); William Parker (b); Tani Tabbal (d, v); Gerald Cleaver (d).* 5/97.

The grand, expansive sound which this nonet is granted by ECM may divide some listeners. It surely benefits the processional feel of 'Leola', but does the luxurious reverb of the production suit the testy interplay of the following 'Dream And Response'? Mitchell notes on the sleeve that he wished for many years to put together 'an ensemble of improvising musicians with an orchestral range', but only rarely does this album suggest a palette denied to the leader of the Nessa sessions of 20 years earlier. Tracks such as 'For Lester B' and 'Bessie Harris' suggest, indeed, a preference for a middleweight ensemble that blends a bigger sonority with the mobility of a medium-sized group. The most notable thing about the band – the double-rhythm section – is something that Mitchell seems reluctant to make much of. The results are in keeping with much of Mitchell's recent music: lots of interesting threads but none of them tied into a truly memorable result.

*** In Walked Buckner

Delmark DE-510 *Mitchell; Jodie Christian (p, bells); Reggie Workman (b, perc); Albert 'Tootie' Heath (d, f, didgeridoo).* 7/98.

A slight return to the terrain of the previous Delmark group-record, and this one is better. 'Off Shore' proposes the sort of elliptical, intuitive aesthetic which Mitchell has made something like his own, and when they shift from there into the bleary bop of the title-piece it seems like a discouraging retreat. But the record has more in common with Mitchell's taste for the baroque. He picks up the piccolo and the bass recorder as well as the saxophones and, if Christian and Heath couldn't help their orthodox tendencies on the previous album, they seem willing to chance their arm a little further here. It remains an awkward rapprochement, but it's working a little more easily.

*** Song For My Sister

PI 03 *Mitchell; Corey Wilkes (t); Anders Svanoe (cl, bcl); Willy Walter(bsn); Craig Taborn, Vijay Iyer (p); Spencer Barefield (g); Janse Vincent(vn); Nels Buttmann(vla); Jaribu Shahid, Leon Dorsey (b); Gerald Cleaver (d, xy); Vincent Davis (d).* 01.

As a record, this is another curious assemblage. Helter-skelter group improvising in 'Sagitta', 'When The Whistle Blows' and 'The Inside Of A Star' is balanced by the meticulous sound-and-space essay, 'This', the oddly gloomy title-piece and the large-scale group music of 'Wind Change'. Mitchell closes the set with one of his attempted funk tunes, 'Count-Off'. As an entity, the ensemble feels shapeless in the way it handles its various talents, and Mitchell himself never imposes enough of himself to unify it all. A probably logical continuation of what's now a perplexing discography.

*** Solo 3

Mutable 17515-2 3CD *Mitchell (sax, f, perc solo).* n.d.

A marathon which recalls some of Mitchell's Nessa recordings of a quarter-century earlier, these three discs include 38 separate solo performances. Most of the sax pieces are solo, though a few feature bits of overdubbing, and disc three is performed in Mitchell's 'percussion cage', a construction which holds scores (hundreds?) of percussion implements. We've had little time to absorb this music, but on early acquaintance it suggests a more musing, spacious approach - less agitated, less momentous. Not that Mitchell is growing peaceable in his old age – there's nothing especially lyrical or ballad-like here, either. If there's a sweetness, it comes out in the percussion passages on the third disc, which have a charm that the saxophone solos reject. For further study.

Hank Mobley (1930–86)

TENOR SAXOPHONE

Mobley was playing in R&B bands before joining Max Roach in 1951. Came to prominence in the Jazz Messengers in 1954 and then worked on numerous Blue Note record dates, many of which he led. With Miles Davis, 1961–2, then toured in other hard-bop situations, but eventually left music in the late '70s through ill health. Brief attempt at a comeback in 1986 but died of pneumonia shortly after.

*****(*) Peckin' Time**
Blue Note 81574-2 *Mobley; Lee Morgan (t); Wynton Kelly (p); Paul Chambers (b); Charli Persip (d).* 2/58.

****** Soul Station**
Blue Note 95343-2 *Mobley; Wynton Kelly (p); Paul Chambers (b); Art Blakey (d).* 2/60.

*****(*) Workout**
Blue Note 84080-2 *Mobley; Wynton Kelly (p); Grant Green (g); Paul Chambers (b); Philly Joe Jones (d).* 3/61.

***** The Turnaround**
Blue Note 24540-2 *Mobley; Freddie Hubbard, Donald Byrd (t); Herbie Hancock, Barry Harris (p); Paul Chambers, Butch Warren (b); Billy Higgins, Philly Joe Jones (d).* 3/63–2/65.

*****(*) No Room For Squares**
Blue Note 524539 *Mobley; Lee Morgan, Donald Byrd (t); Andrew Hill, Herbie Hancock (p); Butch Warren, John Ore (b); Philly Joe Jones (d).* 3–10/63.

***** Dippin'**
Blue Note 46511 *Mobley; Lee Morgan (t); Harold Mabern (p); Larry Ridley (b); Billy Higgins (d).* 6/65.

***** A Caddy For Daddy**
Blue Note 84230-2 *Mobley; Lee Morgan (t); Curtis Fuller (tb); McCoy Tyner (p); Bob Cranshaw (b); Billy Higgins (d).* 12/65.

***** Reach Out**
Blue Note 59964-2 *Mobley; Woody Shaw (t, flhn); Lamont Johnson (p); George Benson (g); Bob Cranshaw (b); Billy Higgins (d).* 1/68.

Mobley's music was documented to almost unreasonable lengths by Blue Note, with a whole raft of albums granted to him as a leader, and countless sideman appearances to go with them. A collectors' favourite, his assertive and swinging delivery was undercut by a seemingly reticent tone: next to his peers in the hard-bop tenor gang, he could sound almost pallid. But it shouldn't detract from appreciating a thinker and a solidly reliable player. Despite frequent personal problems, Mobley rarely gave less than his best in front of the microphones.

Peckin' Time is typical Blue Note hard bop, fired up by the ebullience of Morgan and the persuasiveness of Mobley's solos. He made many records with Morgan as his partner and they already knew each other's moves so well that there's a symmetry to go with the regulation fireworks. Mobley fans are divided as to whether *Soul Station* or the currently absent *Roll Call* is his masterpiece, but the Rudy Van Gelder Edition of the former is a welcome reminder of how creative a player Mobley was, here transcending his normal consistency and making a modest classic. Good as the other drummers on his records are, Blakey brings a degree more finesse, and their interplay on 'This I Dig Of You' is superb. Hank seldom took ballads at a crawl, preferring a kind of lazy mid-tempo, and 'If I Should Lose You' is one of his best. 'Dig Dis' is a top example of how tough he could sound without falling into bluster. A virtually perfect example of a routine date made immortal by master craftsmen.

Workout is really only a shade behind. Listen to how Mobley flirts with stomping-tenorman clichés on 'Uh Huh' and still turns in a decisively individual solo. Green is a splendid assist and Philly Joe's beat is unstoppable. *The Turnaround* is made up of two sessions, either side of a problem period for Mobley, and is a mixed bag: the title-piece is a 'Sidewinder' clone of the sort that Alfred Lion insisted on from numerous Blue Note dates of the time and some of the other material is routine, but the two ballad features are lucid examples of Mobley's exceptional way with a slow tempo and make one wish that he'd managed a full album in that vein.

No Room For Squares brings together the results of two 1963 sessions, one with Morgan and Hill, the other with Byrd and Hancock. The tenorman's solo on 'Three Way Split' is classic Mobley, cooked up at a very fast space but built without excessive hurry and good enough to spark Morgan into turning in a dramatic solo of his own. 'Carolyn' is a lovely ballad feature for Morgan. The date with Byrd isn't quite so strong, but this is still an excellent Mobley Blue Note.

Dippin' and *A Caddy For Daddy* are, by the high standards of his best Blue Notes, relatively ordinary sessions, but they will still satisfy any appetite for authentic and hard-won hard bop. Some of Hank's other Blue Notes remain in limbo and, of his late-'60s records, *Reach Out* is one which has been back of late; but what a peculiar session. They start with jazzed versions of 'Reach Out (I'll Be There)' and 'Goin' Out Of My Head', which are as soft as a marshmallow cushion. Thereafter it's down to Blue Note business with four hard-bop nuggets. Hardly Hank's best, but enough to keep the flame just about lit.

***** The Flip**
Blue Note 93872 *Mobley; Dizzy Reece (t); Slide Hampton (tb); Vince Benedetti (p); Alby Cullaz (b); Philly Joe Jones (d).* 7/69.

***** Thinking Of Home**
Blue Note 40531 *Mobley; Woody Shaw (t); Cedar Walton (p); Eddie Diehl (g); Mickey Bass (b); Leroy Williams (d).* 7/70.

Mobley was a faithful Blue Note man even when the label was beginning to die away in the face of jazz's late-'60s retreat. *The Flip*, recorded in Paris by what looks like a suspiciously *ad hoc* line-up, goes cheerily through the motions of what would have passed for cutting-edge hard bop a decade earlier and has a welcome guest in the form of the seldom-encountered Dizzy Reece. The record feels under-rehearsed and a good tune such as 'Feelin' Folksy' slips by without making the impression it might. Mobley followers will be glad to see its return, though, even in Blue Note's limited Connoisseur edition.

Thinking Of Home has a wistful feel to it which unfortunately flirts dangerously close to blandness. The long 'Suite' and the similarly multi-structured 'Justine' set a few interesting tasks for the players, and Shaw's finely turned playing is just about spot on for this music, but they could use a more decisive hand than Mobley offers and in the end the music feels undercooked. The three pieces which fill up the date are much more in the older Blue Note boogaloo bag, and Hank's exhausted-sounding solo on 'Gayle's Groove' suggests that he felt pretty tired of the style.

Modern Jazz Duo

GROUP

A pairing of veteran big-band trumpeter Don Rader and Australian pianist-composer-educator Roger Frampton.

**(*) Off The Beaten Track

Tall Poppies TP130 *Don Rader (t, flhn); Roger Frampton (sno, p, recorder).* 7/98.

Rader and Frampton struck up a partnership following the former's move to Australia in the '90s, and this duo session is one result. They do well by the jazz and other standards, including Horace Silver and Jimmy Heath tunes; the originals and improvs are less appealing. Rader's big sound is somewhat effaced by the overdressed mix, which sites them in what sounds like a huge concert hall: intimate is better. There's also far too much music here – 50 minutes of the best stuff would have been better than the 75 on offer. Frampton has also made three solo improv records for the same label, but from what we've heard of them, they're very hard work. Better to hear him with the larger group Ten Part Invention.

Modern Jazz Quartet

GROUP

The MJQ was originally the rhythm section of Dizzy Gillespie's post-war band, initially with Ray Brown on bass and Kenny Clarke on drums. After 1955, Connie Kay became a permanent member, joining pianist John Lewis, vibraphonist Milt Jackson and bassist Percy Heath in what was to become one of the most enduring jazz groups of all time. Often quietly understated and with a conservative image, the MJQ nevertheless created thoughtful and often innovative structures, a reminder that the rhythm section has always been the engine-room of innovation in jazz.

*** Beginnings

Savoy Jazz 17528 *Bill Massey (t); Julius Watkins (frhn); Frank Morgan (as); Walter Benton (ts); Walter Bishop Jr, John Lewis, Gerald Wiggins (p); Milt Jackson (vib); Nelson Boyd, Ray Brown, Percy Heath (b); Kenny Clarke, Roy Haynes (d); other personnel.* 49–54.

A glimpse of the MJQ when they were still the Milt Jackson Quartet and still not settled into their long-serving line-up. The 2003 reissue changes the original *Modern Jazz Quartet* title. There are extra tracks here from bigger groups, but the nub of the material is still recognizable, though Ray Brown, Kenny Clarke and, briefly, Al Johns all give the group a different rhythmic slant. 'D & E', 'Heart And Soul' and 'Movin' Nicely' all give a flavour of the highly rhythmic, blues-based group that was gradually taken over by John Lewis's classically tinged composition. There are a couple of extra tracks added to the original Savoy releases; 'Bluesology' has Milt Jackson in front of a biggish band, while 'Blue Mood' is credited to Kenny Clarke's All-Stars.

***(*) The Artistry Of The Modern Jazz Quartet

Prestige 60 016 *Sonny Rollins (ts); John Lewis (p); Milt Jackson (vib); Percy Heath (b); Kenny Clarke (d).* 12/52–7/55.

***(*) Django

Original Jazz Classics OJC 057 *As above, except omit Rollins.* 6/53–1/55.

***(*) MJQ

Original Jazz Classics OJC 125 *As above, except add Henry Boozier (t), Horace Silver (p).* 6/54, 12/56.

Frequently dismissed – as unexciting, pretentious, bland, Europeanized, pat – the MJQ remained hugely popular for much of the last 30 years, filling halls and consistently outselling most other jazz acts. The enigma lies in that epithet 'Modern' for, inasmuch as the MJQ shifted more product than anyone else, they were also radicals (or maybe that American hybrid, radical-conservatives) who have done more than most barnstorming revolutionaries to change the nature and form of jazz performance, to free it from its changes-based theme-and-solos clichés. Leader/composer John Lewis has a firm grounding in European classical music, particularly the Baroque, and was a leading light in both Third Stream music and the *Birth Of The Cool* sessions with Gerry Mulligan and Miles Davis. From the outset he attempted to infuse jazz performance with a consciousness of form, using elements of through-composition, counterpoint, melodic variation and, above all, fugue to multiply the trajectories of improvisation. And just as people still, even now, like stories with a beginning, middle and end, people have liked the well-made quality of MJQ performances which, on their night, don't lack for old-fashioned excitement.

The fact that they had been Dizzy's rhythm section led people to question the group's viability as an independent performing unit. The early recordings more than resolve that doubt. Lewis has never been an exciting performer (in contrast to Jackson, who is one of the great soloists in jazz), but his brilliant grasp of structure is evident from the beginning. Of the classic MJQ pieces – 'One Bass Hit', 'The Golden Striker', 'Bags' Groove' – none characterizes the group more completely than Lewis's 'Django', first recorded in the session of December 1954. The Prestige is a useful CD history of the early days of the band, but it's probably better to hear the constituent sessions in their entirety. Some of the material on the original two-disc vinyl format has been removed to make way for a Sonny Rollins/MJQ set ('No Moe', 'The Stopper', 'In A Sentimental Mood', 'Almost Like Being In Love'), which is a pity, for this material was long available elsewhere.

*** Third Stream Music

Wounded Bird 1345 *As above, except add Paul Ingraham (frhn); Jimmy Giuffre (cl, ts); Bill McColl (cl); Manuel Zegler (bsn); Jim Hall (g); Betty Glamann (hp); Gerald Tarack (vn); Joe Tekula (clo); Ralph Pena (b); Beaux Arts String Quartet.* 8/57–1/60.

Curious how old-fashioned the idea of Third Stream music now sounds, given that crossover projects of all sorts are now the norm rather than a bold exception. This interesting set pairs the MJQ with Jimmy Giuffre's trio on the opening two cuts, 'Da Capo' and the clarinettist's 'Fine', with additional contributions from the orchestral and chamber players on other tracks. It's all a bit dry and lifeless, though Max Harrison's typically perceptive liner–note makes sense of the music and, of course, John Lewis was one of the guiding lights of Third Stream.

*** Concorde

Original Jazz Classics OJC 002 *John Lewis (p); Milt Jackson (vib); Percy Heath (b); Connie Kay (d).* 7/55.

★★★ Live At Music Inn With Sonny Rollins
Atlantic 75687-80794-2 *As above, except add Sonny Rollins (ts).* 8/55.

★★★(★) Fontessa
Atlantic 81329 *As above, except omit Rollins.* 1 & 2/56.

★★★(★) Pyramid
Atlantic 81340 *As above.* 8 & 12/59, 1/60.

★★★★ Dedicated To Connie
Atlantic 82763 2CD *As above.* 5/60.

★★★(★) Lonely Woman
Atlantic 8122 75361-2 *As above.* 62.

★★★ The Comedy
Atlantic 81390 *As above, except add Diahann Carroll (v).* 10/60, 1/62.

Connie Kay slipped into the band without a ripple; sadly, his ill-health and death were the only circumstances in the next 40 years of activity necessitating a personnel change. His cooler approach, less overwhelming than Clarke's could be, was ideal, and he sounds right from the word 'go'. His debut was on the fine *Concorde*, which sees Lewis trying to blend jazz improvisation with European counterpoint. It combines some superb fugal writing with a swing that would have sounded brighter if recording quality had been better. Though the integration is by no means always complete, it's more appealing in its very roughness than the slick Bach-chat that turns up on some of the Atlantics.

The label didn't quite know what to do with the MJQ, but the Erteguns were always alert to the demographics and, to be fair, they knew good music when they heard it. One of the problems the group had in this, arguably their most consistent phase creatively, was that everything appeared to need conceptual packaging, even when the music suggested no such thing. Chance associations, like the celebrated version of Ornette's 'Lonely Woman', were doubtless encouraged by the fact that they shared a label, and this was all to the good; there are, though, signs that in later years, as rock began to swallow up a bigger and bigger market share, the group began to suffer from the inappropriate packaging. Though home-grown compositions reappear throughout the band's history (there's a particularly good 'Django' on *Pyramid*), there are also constant references to standard repertoire as well and some of these are among the group's greatest achievements.

By the same inverted snobbery that demands standards rather than 'pretentious classical rubbish', it's long been a useful cop-out to profess admiration only for those MJQ albums featuring right-on guests. The earlier Silver collaboration isn't as well known as a justly famous encounter with Sonny Rollins at Music Inn, reprising their encounters of 1951, 1952 and 1953, which were really the saxophonist's gigs. Restored in a fresh mastering, it's clear how much Sonny was an interloper in an already skilled, tight unit. Most of the record is by the MJQ alone, including one of their delicious standard medleys and a brilliant reading of Lewis's 'Midsömmer'. The two (live) tracks which Rollins appears on aren't entirely satisfactory, since he cannot make much impression on 'Bags' Groove', already a Jackson staple, and sounds merely discursive on 'A Night In Tunisia'. Overall, this set very much belongs to the MJQ.

Lewis's first exploration of characters from the *commedia dell'arte* came in *Fontessa*, an appropriately chill and stately record that can seem a little enigmatic, even off-putting. He develops these interests considerably in the simply titled *Comedy*, which largely consists of dulcet character-sketches with unexpected twists and quietly violent dissonances. The themes of *commedia* are remarkably appropriate to a group who have always presented themselves in sharply etched silhouette, playing a music that is deceptively smooth and untroubled but which harbours considerable jazz feeling and, as on both *Fontessa* and *Comedy*, considerable disruption to conventional harmonic progression.

Given Lewis's interests and accomplishments as an orchestrator, there have been surprisingly few jazz-group-with-orchestra experiments. More typical, perhaps, than the 1987 *Three Windows* is what Lewis does on *Lonely Woman*. One of the very finest of the group's albums, this opens with a breathtaking arrangement of Ornette Coleman's haunting dirge and then proceeds with small-group performances of three works – 'Animal Dance', 'Lamb, Leopard' and 'Fugato' – which were originally conceived for orchestral performance. Remarkably, Lewis's small-group arrangements still manage to give an impression of symphonic voicings.

Kay's ill-health finally overcame him in December 1994, and the following February the MJQ issued in his memory a concert from 1960, recorded in what was then Yugoslavia, a relatively innocuous destination on the international tour. Whatever its historical resonance, it inspired (as John Lewis discovered when he auditioned these old tapes) one of the truly great MJQ performances, certainly one of the very best available to us on disc. It knocks into a cocked hat even the new edition of the so-called *Last Concert*. Jackson's playing is almost transcendentally wonderful on 'Bags' Groove' and 'I Remember Clifford', and the conception of Lewis's opening *commedia* sequence could hardly be clearer or more satisfying. *Dedicated To Connie* is a very special record and has always been our favourite of the bunch, but renewed acquaintance suggests a few glossed-over cracks in the edifice, which is why, this time at least, it's denied the ultimate accolade of a crown.

★★★ The Sheriff
Atlantic 8122-73520-2 *As above.* 5/63.

A nod to prevailing winds in this set, which includes 'Bachianas Brasilieras' and 'Carnival', both with a bossa nova feel. But 'In A Crowd' and a classic standard reworking on 'Mean To Me' reassert MJQ verities.

★★★ Jazz Dialogue
Wounded Bird 1449 *As above; add Bernie Glow, Ernie Royal, Clark Terry, Snooky Young (t); Jimmy Cleveland, Tony Studd, Kai Winding (tb); Charlie Mariano, Phil Woods (as); Seldon Powell (ts); Wally Kane (bs); Howard Collins (g).* 5/65.

The MJQ members were all seasoned big-band players and it's less surprising that they should have wanted to do the occasional gig like this than it is that they did it so ineptly. The horns seem grafted on to the group's performances with little organic logic and with little regard for some fine individualists who don't get a chance to shine; in other words, no solos. The material is pretty familiar, with versions of 'Django' and 'The Golden Striker' prominent on the set-list, but it's not unreasonable to expect something a bit more imaginative than this.

★★★(★) Blues At Carnegie Hall
Collectables CD 6279 *As In A Crowd above.* 67.

Peculiarly, this is doubled up with the classic Art Blakey–Thelonious Monk Atlantic album – and annoyingly that's left no space for two tracks from the original MJQ LP, which have been omitted. Still, it was a great concert. All blues, as the title infers, a great shout for Milt Jackson and a warm crowd.

★★★(★) Blues On Bach

Atlantic 7831393 *As above.* 11/73.

Lewis was always suspended somewhere between Bach and the old blues, and this intriguing project alternates original blues tunes with adaptations of J. S. Bach which stop short of suggesting that he and not W. C. Handy was the father of jazz blues but which nevertheless point up the kinship between the styles. As a further tribute to the father of classical music, Lewis doubles on harpsichord and still manages to get a solid, flowing sound. Jackson is as masterful as ever and his own 'Blues in H (B)' even makes reference to the traditional B-A-C-H signature theme.

★★★ Plastic Dreams

Collectables 6185 *As above, except add Joe Newman, Snooky Young (t); Garnett Brown (tb); Jimmy Buffington (frhn); Don Butterfield (tba).* 5/71.

The garish cover image, a Pop Art rendition of a blow-up sex doll, seemed wildly out of place for the MJQ and has little relevance to the music inside. The title–track is a faux-tango into which Lewis sews some clever variations, but it's hardly bump-and-grind jazz. 'Walkin' Stomp' gets the set moving in brisk fashion, but nothing else comes up to this pace or quality and 'England's Carol', based on 'God Rest You Merry, Gentlemen', is a very curious selection in this context. 'Piazza Navona' is one of Lewis's tone-pictures, and as such very effective, but one comes away from *Plastic Dreams* feeling as if one's just sampled a disc of off-cuts rather than the attention-grabbing Atlantic wanted. The brass quintet make an interesting contribution on a couple of tracks, but again the integration of guests with the group isn't securely done.

CORE COLLECTION

★★★(★) The Complete Last Concert

Atlantic 81976 2CD *As In A Crowd above.* 11/74.

Given the closeness of the relationship and its prolific nature, it wasn't entirely surprising that the four should have decided after more than 20 years as a unit to give their individual careers a little space and air. What was billed as the last concert was very much considered to be just that, rather than a shrewd marketing ploy at the start of a short sabbatical. It would be wrong to say that the music was inspired or more intense than usual, but certainly these are all very fine performances. The short bebop section in the middle – 'Confirmation', 'Round Midnight', 'A Night In Tunisia' – gives the lie to any prejudice that the group were uneasy with those jaggy changes and rhythms; they had, after all, cut their professional teeth in such a context. But it's the other, more familiar MJQ material that is most impressive. There are several blues pieces carried over from *Blues On Bach*, versions of 'The Golden Striker' and 'Cylinder' and a few of Lewis's more impressionistic compositions, such as 'Skating In Central Park' and 'Jasmine Tree'. One additional outstanding performance was the arrangement of Rodrigo's Miles-blessed 'Concierto De Aranjuez'. Strongly recommended to anyone who values the group, and effortlessly representative of its ability to shift between styles and moods.

★★(★) Together Again

Pablo 2308244 *As above.* 7/82.

★★★ Together Again – Echoes

Pablo 2312142 *As above.* 3/84.

★★★ Topsy – This One's For Basie

Original Jazz Classics OJC 1073 *As above.* 6/85.

There is little question that the energy and inventiveness of the band were diluted by time. By the early '70s the MJQ had become stylists first and improvisers only then. They disbanded in 1974, after a final flourish; but after seven years in the wilderness, and they were notably uncreative years for each of the members, they got together again and continued to produce vital music, much of it written by Lewis and all of it, as before, technically and structurally challenging. *Together Again* was recorded at the Montreux Jazz Festival. After the hiatus, the group seems content to deliver a set of familiar material – 'Django', 'The Cylinder', 'Woody'N'You' and what is listed as 'Bags' New Groove', though how substantially it really differs from the old one isn't entirely obvious. It's a nice, light performance, typical festival fare. The 1985 disc isn't, as it has sometimes been advertised, a programme of Basie tunes, but a tribute to the Count written almost entirely by Lewis. The only exceptions are 'Topsy' itself, 'Nature Boy' (which is played, unaccompanied, by Jackson) and Milt's composition, 'Reunion Blues'. The playing is sharp and engaging and both Lewis and Jackson are in fine form.

★★★★ The Complete Prestige And Pablo Recordings

Prestige 4438 4CD *As above.* 52–85.

Music from *Django, Fontessa, Concorde,* the film soundtrack *No Sun In Venice, Reunion At Budokan, Together Again, Echoes* and *Topsy – This One's For Basie.* All of which most MJQ fans will already have. Should you not, this is a very attractive buy. What is striking is how tough and swinging the group is, belying the chamber jazz, Third Stream reputation that some purists found off-putting. The remastering is very clean and precise and the packaging is detailed enough without offering *War and Peace*-proportioned liner–notes.

★★★ Three Windows

Atlantic 8176 *As above, except add New York Chamber Symphony.* 87.

Almost a John Lewis album, this beautifully executed orchestral project included music which had been written for the Roger Vadim film, *No Sun in Venice*, almost 30 years earlier. There is also a wonderful tone poem, 'Day In Dubrovnik', and one of the best-recorded arrangements of the evergreen 'Django'. Not an essential purchase, but a deeply satisfying record.

★★★ A Celebration

Atlantic 782538 *As above, except omit Kay; add Wynton Marsalis, Harry 'Sweets' Edison (t), Freddie Hubbard (flhn), Phil Woods (as), Nino Tempo, Illinois Jacquet (ts), Branford Marsalis (ts, ss), Mickey Roker (d), Bobby McFerrin (v).* 6/92, 4/93.

The fortieth-anniversary celebrations had to continue without Connie Kay and with Mickey Roker standing in. The guest-star formula worked as well as ever, and the MJQ machine moved smoothly along, the Cadillac of jazz groups.

★★★★ MJQ 40

Atlantic 7 82330 2 4CD *John Lewis (p); Milt Jackson (vib); Percy Heath (b); Connie Kay (d); with Bernie Glow, Joe*

Newman, Ernie Royal, Clark Terry, Snooky Young (t); Paul Ingraham, Jimmy Buffington (frhn); Jimmy Cleveland, Garnett Brown, Tony Studd, Kai Winding (tb); Don Butterfield (tba); Jimmy Giuffre, Bill McColl (cl); Robert DiDomenica (f); Manny Ziegler (bsn); Paul Desmond, Charlie Mariano, Phil Woods (as); Sonny Rollins, Richie Kamuca, Seldon Powell (ts); Wally Kane (bs); Laurindo Almeida, Howard Collins (g);Joe Tekula (clo); Betty Glamann (hp); Diahann Carroll, The Swingle Singers (v). 52–88.

***** The Best Of The Modern Jazz Quartet**

Pablo 2405 423 *John Lewis (p); Milt Jackson (vib); Percy Heath (b); Connie Kay (d).* 80s.

The Atlantic is magnificently packaged ruby-anniversary celebration which draws on all stages and aspects of the group's career. Fifty-four tracks on four CDs taking in music from such records as *Plastic Dreams, Live At The Lighthouse, Third Stream Music*, and from the fine 1966 concert in Japan. As an introduction to the group's music, the accompanying booklet (which includes a complete discography) could hardly be bettered. The Pablo sampler does a pretty good job of boiling down and reducing the group's work since the reunion of 1981, but most fans will have the bulk of this material anyway and the selection doesn't have the logic and pace of an original album.

Paul Moer (born 1916)

PIANO

Briefly an associate of Charles Mingus, Moer has worked as a studio arranger for much of his career. These discs are virtually unknown to the wider jazz community.

***** The Contemporary Jazz Classics Of The Paul Moer Trio**

Del-Fi 71212 *Moer; Jimmy Bond (b); Frank Butler (d).* 61.

***** Plays The Music Of Elmo Hope**

Fresh Sound 1019 *Moer; John Heard (b); Larance Marable (d).* 91.

A solidly competent player with an easy if slightly rigid swing, Moer deserves to be somewhat better known. No one can claim he is a significant innovator, but these sets, recorded three decades apart, are worthy of attention for the sharp writing on the earlier set and for Moer's attempt to bring to light some of Elmo Hope's least known compositions.

The earlier record has languished in obscurity since its first release. The originals, like the generic 'Moer Or Less', don't take much time to absorb but the driving rhythm set up by Bond and Butler gives the set a certain energy that fans of piano jazz will enjoy. The Hope disc is full of good things – 'Minor Bertha', 'Carving the Rock', 'Low Tide', 'Moe's Bluff', 'Later For You' – but we suspect its main value will be to send you straight back to Elmo's still undervalued body of work. Which may be exactly what Paul Moer wants.

Louis Moholo (born 1940)

DRUMS, PERCUSSION

Born in Cape Town, Moholo led his own big band before joining the mixed-race Blue Notes in 1962. Left with them for Europe in 1964. Toured with Steve Lacy before returning to London in 1967, which has been his base since. In numerous groups, from Brotherhood Of Breath to his own Viva La Black, Moholo has been a powerhouse of versatility and strength.

***** Bush Fire**

Ogun OGCD 131 *Moholo; Evan Parker (ss, ts); Pule Pheto (p); Barry Guy (b); Gibe Pheto (d).* 75.

***** Tern**

Atavistic Unheard Music 176 *Moholo; Larry Stabbins (ts); Keith Tippett (p).* 82.

***** Exile**

Ogun OGCD 003 *Moholo; Sean Bergin, Steve Williamson (reeds); Paul Rogers (b).* 90.

***** Freedom Tour: Live In South Afrika, 1993**

Ogun OGCD 006 *Moholo; Claude Deppa (t, flhn, v); Sean Bergin (ts, f, concertina, v); Tobias Delius (ts, v); Jason Yarde (as, ss, v); Pule Pheto (p); Roberto Bellatalla (b); Thebe Lipere (perc).* 93.

***** Mpumi**

Ogun OGCD 132 *Moholo; Mervyn Africa, Keith Tippett (p).* 95.

In the '60s, radical American improvisers (with separatist agenda firmly in mind) renewed their interest in African percussion. What was quickly evident was that traditional African musics frequently anticipated the methodologies of free jazz and that the sometimes anarchic energies of contemporary African jazz were already more abstract than the prevailing American models. In Europe, for a variety of reasons, this was perceived much more readily, and there was a quicker and less ideological trade-off between African jazz and popular music on the one hand, and free music. Louis Moholo, more than most of the South African exiles active on the jazz scene in Britain (but much like the late Johnny Dyani and the late Dudu Pukwana), was able to make the transition without undue strain. His own bands – Spirits Rejoice, Viva La Black, the African Drum Ensemble – have always contained free or abstract elements, and Moholo has always been in demand as a more experimental improviser, where his drive and intensity are comparable to those of Americans Milford Graves and Andrew Cyrille.

The early quintet with Parker and Guy underlines Moholo's extraordinary ability to mix the hottest African grooves with entirely free playing. It's hugely impressive and moving, as is the live session captured on *Tern* where Moholo discovers the chemistry with Tippett that is evident again on the piano duo set *Mpumi*, where he is listed as Louis Moholo-Moholo. Pule Pheto is the connecting thread between those earlier and the more recent sets, a fine rhythmic player with his own idiosyncratic harmonic language.

Exile is a hot, dangerous session, with Bergin's ferocious statements in constant opposition to Williamson's much cooler delivery, and with Rogers and Moholo working independently of the horns most of the time. 'Wathinta Amododa' is the main piece, but most of its initial power is thrown away in an overlong development-cum-denouement.

Viva La Black's tour and roving workshop for young South African musicians was, inevitably, a powerfully moving experience for Moholo; much of that comes across on the live record, fighting through a not very good recording which resists even Steve Beresford's skill at the final mix. Many of the tracks are short song-forms, some of them traditional; only the opening 'Woza' is substantially longer than five minutes, but the whole thing has the feel of a long, continuous suite, mostly celebratory in nature but with a few, entirely expected, dark corners and ambiguities.

Miff Mole (1898–1961)

TROMBONE

Mole pioneered the development of the trombone as a viable jazz instrument, having mastered a fluency and mobility on the horn which was almost unprecedented at the time of his earliest recordings in 1921. He became one of the kingpin figures in the New York dance-band and session-scene of the '20s but moved into more anonymous studio work in the '30s. Later spells with the Condon gang and some '40s dates for Commodore have been largely forgotten, as was Mole himself, ill and up against it in the '50s. He died, in penury, in 1961.

CORE COLLECTION

**** Slippin' Around

Frog DGF19 *Mole; Red Nichols (c, t); Leo McConville, Phil Napoleon (t); Dudley Fosdick (mel); Jimmy Dorsey (cl, as); Fud Livingston, Pee Wee Russell (cl, ts); Frank Teschemacher (cl); Babe Russin (ts); Adrian Rollini (bsx); Arthur Schutt, Lennie Hayton, Ted Shapiro, Joe Sullivan (p); Eddie Lang, Carl Kress (g); Dick McDonough (bj, g); Eddie Condon (bj); Joe Tarto, Jack Hansen (tba); Vic Berton, Ray Bauduc, Chauncey Morehouse, Gene Krupa, Stan King (d).* 1/27–2/30.

Miff Mole was one of the master jazz musicians of the '20s. Though subsequently eclipsed by Teagarden, Dorsey and others, he was the first trombonist to make any significant impression as a soloist, sounding fluent and imaginative as far back as the early recordings of the Original Memphis Five and Ladd's Black Aces at the beginning of the decade. His partnership with Red Nichols was as interesting in its way as that of Armstrong and Hines or Beiderbecke and Trumbauer. Though sometimes seen as a kind of jazz chamber music, or at worst a white New York imitation of the real thing, their records were a smart, hard-bitten development out of their hot-dance environment and, with no vocals, little hokum and plenty of space for improvisation, the music has an uncompromising stance which may surprise those who've heard about it second-hand.

The first of these overdue compilations brings together most of the sessions by Miff's Molers for OKeh, along with four Victor titles by Red and Miff's Stompers and a further pair of tunes credited to the Red Nichols Orchestra. The earlier dates have no more than five or six musicians on them, and titles like 'Hurricane' and 'Delirium' are intense little set-pieces. The later sessions have more players and feel more orchestrated, less private, though no less intriguing: two versions of Fud Livingston's 'Feeling No Pain' are remarkable, and so is the furious charge through 'Original Dixieland One Step'. Nichols, Russell, Rollini and others all have their moments, but Mole himself, alert and quick-witted and always able to find a fruitful line, has no peers here. The final two sessions, with the much-praised 'Shim-Me-Sha-Wabble' among them, seem rowdier and less personal. John R. T. Davies has worked his usual magic with what sounds like a set of mint originals: these have never sounded better.

**** Slippin' Around – Again!

Frog DGF20 *Similar to above, except add Gordon Griffin (t), Paul Ricci (cl), Toots Mondello (as), Frank Signorelli (p), Sid Weiss (b), Sam Weiss (d), Chick Bullock (v).* 2/27–2/37.

This volume is handled to similar standards as the one above. There are six titles by Red & Miff's Stompers, 15 by the Molers, two interesting airshots from 1936 featuring Mole with an unidentified band, and most of the titles from a 1937 date for Vocalion by a 'new' set of Molers. It should be noted that Classics have issued two discs which cover almost identical ground, *Miff Mole 1927* (Classics 1269) and *Miff Mole 1928-1937* (Classics 1298). As Max Harrison once remarked, the later sessions by the Molers are less private and more public, which makes them neither better nor worse, only different. Mole's solo on 'Moanin' Low', delicate and nuanced next to the rowdiness of the closing chorus, underlines his originality, and it's a small sadness in jazz history that this talented man was largely left behind by the music as it progressed.

Nils Petter Molvaer (born 1963)

TRUMPET, ELECTRONICS

The gifted Norwegian dabbles in electronica as well as jazz, to sometimes devastating effect.

**** Khmer

ECM 1560 *Molvaer; Eivind Aarset, Roger Ludvigsen, Morten Molster (g, etc); Reidar Skar (ky, samples); Rune Arnesen (d); Ulk W. O. Holand (samples).* 96 & 97.

This was probably the first time that ECM released remixed singles of an artist's work. Herbalizer, Rockers HiFi and Mental Overdrive were the trendiest names ever to be associated with the imprint. Molvaer's appropriation of drum'n'bass, jungle and techno beats wasn't the most surprising thing about *Khmer*, nor was the label he chose to release it on. What startled was his ability to meld these sample-heavy contemporary sounds with what was unmistakably a jazz aesthetic, post-Miles, post-rock, post almost everything but still jazz. There have been more effective experiments in this same vein since, including Iain Ballamy's Anglo-Nordic group Food, but *Khmer* still enjoys priority in the field and is as startling five years on as it was on first release. Beautiful, nuanced music.

*** Solid Ether

ECM 1722 *Molvaer; Eivind Aarset (g, elec); Audun Erlien (b); Sidsel Endresen (v); DJ Strangefruit (v, samples, turntables); Rune Arnesen, Per Lindvall (d); Reidar Skar (vocoder).* 99.

After *Khmer*, the follow-up could not but be a disappointment. It is also just a step further away from jazz. By this point, Molvaer was not so susceptible to outside influences and the group was generating its own language and ideas. Surprisingly, he begins with solo trumpet, a strange quiet prologue on the piccolo horn with the fourth valve held down to create a strange out-of-tune effect. 'Dead Indeed' continues with Molvaer the only player beyond a few overdubbed effects from Aarset, who of course has explored this territory in his own way. Endresen's vocals are an important component on two acoustic tracks, reuniting the trumpeter with one of the musicians who helped shape his new and exploratory style. Elsewhere the DJ keeps the music closer to the new club culture.

★★(★) NP3

Emarcy 0177952 *Similar to above.* 9/02.

Stalled and self-duplicating, this could hardly be more disappointing. Technically, it's probably the best album of the bunch, but it has a chill remoteness that was not there before and which is immediately offputting. There is also a remix album on Emarcy called *Recoloured* which is episodically interesting in the way of such projects.

Antonio Moncada

DRUMS

Contemporary Italian drummer, working in both free improvisation and a more structured post-bop.

★★ The True Story Of Twelve Colours

Splasc(h) H394-2 *Moncada; Sebi Tramontana (tb, v); Stefano Maltese (ss, as, bcl, hca, p); Gioconda Cilio (v, p).* 8/91.

★★(★) Trois Éclats De Temps

Splasc(h) H740-2 *Moncada; Tony Cattano (tb); Stefano Maltese (ss, as, ts, f, bcl, p, perc); Michele Conti (vn); Fred Casadei (b).* 5/00.

Moncada and Maltese are regular workmates, but *The True Story* showed very little creative understanding among the four players across a dozen improvisations. Tramontana is painfully inept at times, Maltese rattles away at the piano (when he's not on reeds) and Cilio is the acquired taste which so many improvising vocalists turn out to be. A misfire.

The wait for the follow-up was nearly ten years. Though the group is working from more specific structures this time, there remains a sense that these are mere props (or cues) for rambling improvisations. Not hopeless, but there are many more worthwhile examples of the style – and this is not the place to hear Maltese for sure.

Jane Monheit (born 1978)

VOCAL

Prominent in the 1998 Monk vocal competition, Monheit was soon signed to a major deal and has been very successful since.

★★★ Never Never Land

N-Coded NC-4207-2 *Monheit; Hank Crawford (as); David 'Fathead' Newman (f); Kenny Barron (p); Bucky Pizzarelli (g); Ron Carter (b); Lewis Nash (d).* 1/00.

★★★ Come Dream With Me

N-Coded NC-4219-2 *Monheit; Tom Harrell (t); Michael Brecker (ts); Kenny Barron (p); Richard Bona (g, b); Christian McBride (b); Gregory Hutchinson (d).* 2/01.

★★★ In The Sun

N-Coded 509475-2 *Monheit; Joel Frahm (ts); Ivan Lins (p, v); Michael Kanan, Kenny Ascher, Alan Broadbent (p); Rene Toledo (g); Ron Carter (b); Kenny Washington, Rick Montalbano (d); Don Alias (perc); strings.* 3–6/02.

Monheit tends to be presented as all pout and glamour, but she's better than that. The heavyweight company on the first two records looks like bought-in credibility, but she's done her share of club gigs and dues-paying and the records have a classy feel to them which floats free of the photogenic trappings. She has quite a big, at times somewhat ungainly voice, and the first two records feel like a limbering-up: a track such as 'Over The Rainbow' is lit up for showbiz. But *In The Sun* is a degree more idiosyncratic. 'No More Blues' is a virtuoso duet with guitarist Toledo that swings, and 'Waters Of March' on the previous record was certainly a keeper which suggested a full Latin album would do her good. The disappointing thing is the way she seems to be packaged for a middle-aged and seniors market. There are too many maudlin songs on *In The Sun*, to the point where you wonder why a successful and happy young woman is investing so much in doleful lyrics.

T. S. Monk (born 1949)

DRUMS

Thelonious Jr made his public debut with his dad at the age of just ten and, after some time away from jazz, has devoted himself to the old man's memory and to a sound that is intended to recapture the melodic energy of '50s Blue Note hard bop. Influenced by Max Roach and Tony Williams, T.S. has become a strong, clear-voiced exponent and a fine writer.

★★★★ Monk On Monk

N2K Encoded Music N2KW 10017 *Monk; Laurie Frink, Virgil Jones, Wallace Roney, Arturo Sandoval, Don Sickler, Clark Terry (t); Roy Hargrove (flhn); Eddie Bert (tb); David Amram, John Clark (frhn); Bobby Porcelli, Bobby Watson (as); Wayne Shorter (ts, ss); Jimmy Heath, Roger Rosenberg, Grover Washington, Willie Williams (ts); Howard Johnson (bs, tba); Geri Allen, Herbie Hancock, Ronnie Mathews, Danilo Perez (p); Ron Carter, Dave Holland, Christian McBride, Dave Wang (b); Nnenna Freelon, Kevin Mahogany, Dianne Reeves (v).* 2/97.

By the time *Monk On Monk* appeared, one might have expected the rising-50-year-old to have pushed out into territory he could legitimately call his own, rather than continue playing dad's work. The dedication and the affection that go with it are hard to fault and some of the playing is very fine indeed. On this occasion, T.S. has assembled a superband which must have been the envy of the block. All the songs are by Monk, though 'Ruby My Dear' and 'In Walked Bud' have been transformed into vocal vehicles for Kevin Mahogany and Nnenna Freelon respectively. Herbie Hancock and Ron Carter solo on 'Two Timer', but the best double act of the evening bouquet goes to Bobby Watson and Wallace Roney for their spirited and lyrical attack on 'Jackie-ing'. A big, stellar cast and an album that entirely lives up to its billing. Fair do's; whatever our misgivings about earlier outings and however much we might question T.S.'s continued devotion to the flame, this is a spendid recording, multi-dimensional, richly textured, carefully thought out and thoroughly satisfying.

★★(★) Cross Talk

N2K 4202 *Monk; Don Sickler (t, flhn); Willie Williams (ss, ts, cl); John Gordon (as); Bobby Porcelli (as, cl, af); Ray Gallon (p, syn); Gary Wang (b); Patricia Barber (v).* 5/99.

A turn towards a new and funkier sound, or perhaps a partial return to R&B roots. T.S. uses electric drums and relies somewhat on synthesizers as well as conventional horns. Don Sickler's arrangements are generous and tough-minded and 'Heart' is testimony to his skills, reminiscent of the work he has done with Bobby Watson. 'A Chant For Bu' pays a debt to an ancestral influence, though *Cross Talk* as a whole is as far from the Messengers as could be imagined.

★★★(★) Higher Ground
Thelonious 9313 *Monk; Winston Byrd (t, flhn, v); Bobby Porcelli (as, f); Willie Williams (ts); Ray Gallon (p, syn, ky); David P. Jackson (b); Jeremy Berberian, Victor See-Yuen (perc); Miles Griffith (v).* 02.

Released on a home label devoted to his own work and to his father's legacy of live – and often bootlegged – concert tapes, this is T. S. Monk's most eclectic set yet, a mix of hard bop, funk and fusion styles. No Monk tunes at all this time, though Kenny Dorham's 'Philly Twist' is very much of that vintage. Saxophonist Willie Williams is in strikingly good form, certainly for a man whose promise seemed to have faded, and the flagrantly underrated Bobby Porcelli beefs up the front line and brings in the brilliant opening track, 'Haristocracy'. There's a guest appearance from Miles Griffith as well, adding a vocal line to Cedar Walton's 'Mosaic'. Despite the diversity of its parts, this is one of the most coherent and consistent albums from T.S. yet.

Thelonious Monk (1917–82)

PIANO

One of the giants of music, Monk conforms to no school or movement, and to no known law of development. Far from being unrecognized in his lifetime, he was a major star who retired early, recording nothing in the last few years of his life, presumably in order that the rest of the musical world could catch up. His angular, asymmetrical themes are rooted in the blues, but they accord to no logic other than their own. A Monk performance was always an adventure.

★★★ After Hours At Minton's
Definitive Classics 11197 *Monk; Roy Eldridge, Hot Lips Page (t); Herbie Fields, Al Sears (ts); Charlie Christian (g); Nick Fenton(b); Kenny Clarke (d).* 5/41.

★★★★ Genius Of Modern Music: Volume 1
Blue Note 32137 *Monk; Kenny Dorham, Idrees Sulieman, George Taitt (t); Lou Donaldson, Sahib Shihab, Danny Quebec West (as); Billy Smith, Lucky Thompson (ts); Milt Jackson (vib); Nelson Boyd, Al McKibbon, Bob Paige, Gene Ramey, John Simmons (b); Art Blakey, Max Roach, Shadow Wilson (d).* 10/47–7/48.

★★★★ Genius Of Modern Music: Volume 2
Blue Note 32138 *As above, except add John Coltrane (ts).* 10/47–5/52.

★★★★ The Best Of Thelonious Monk: The Blue Note Years
Blue Note 795636 *As above.* 47–51.

★★★ Thelonious Monk 1947–1948
Classics 1118 *As above.* 10/47–7/48.

Monk is one of the giants of modern American music whose output ranks with that of Morton and Ellington, as *composition* of the highest order. Though no one questions his skills as a pianist (they were compounded of stride, blues and a more romantic strain derived from Teddy Wilson and filtered through Monk's wonderfully lateral intelligence), it is as a composer that he has made the greatest impact on subsequent jazz music. Even so, it is vital to recognize that the music and the playing style are necessary to each other and precisely complementary. Though he has attracted more dedicated interpreters since his death than almost any musician (Ornette Coleman and John Coltrane perhaps approach his standing with other players, but from very different perspectives), Monk tunes played by anyone else always seem to lack a certain conclusive authenticity. Frequently misunderstood by critics and fans (and also by the less discerning of his fellow musicians), he received due public recognition only quite late in his career, by which time younger pianists originally encouraged by him and his example (Bud Powell is the foremost) had recorded and died and been canonized. It's now questioned whether Monk was ever, as he once appeared, a founding father of bop.

The *Minton's* material catches him in the crucible of bebop, and working through some of the innovations that were to make the new style so vital and very quickly so central to the jazz mainstream. The material is still very much what you'd expect from a swing set – 'I Got Rhythm', 'Sweet Georgia Brown', 'Body and Soul' – but one can hear Monk starting to think through the harmonic variations that would fuel the bop revolution. Whether he can claim priority in some of these, or whether the action was elsewhere remains unproven, but *Minton's* was certainly one of the places where the new style was worked out, and Monk was certainly one of the players who was thinking in new ways, so this is a more than valid document.

Though some of his work, like 'In Walked Bud' on *Genius Of Modern Music*, utilized a straightforward chord sequence, and though 'Eronel', one of the additional tracks from the critical July 1951 session with Milt Jackson, is relatively orthodox bop, Monk's interest in tough, pianistic melody, displaced rhythm and often extreme harmonic distortion (as in his treatment of 'Carolina Moon') rather sets him apart from the bop mainstream.

Monk recorded only intermittently over the next ten years, which makes them particularly valuable. Thwarted first by an American Federation of Musicians recording ban and later by a prison sentence and a blacklisting, Monk took time to regain the highs of these remarkable sides. The earliest of the sessions, with Sulieman, Danny Quebec West and Billy Smith, is not particularly inspired, though the pianist's contribution is instantly identifiable; his solo on 'Thelonious', built up out of minimal thematic potential, is emotionally powerful and restlessly allusive. A month later he was working with a more enterprising group (the difference in Blakey's response between the two sessions is remarkable) and producing his first classic recordings – of 'In Walked Bud' and 'Round About Midnight'.

The addition of Milt Jackson exactly a year later for the session that yielded 'Epistrophy' and 'Misterioso' was a turning point in his music, enormously extending its rhythmic potential and harmonic complexity. Jackson, who, because of his association with the Modern Jazz Quartet, is now rather apt to be dismissed as a player lacking in improvisational excitement, makes an incalculable contribution to the music, here and on the session of July 1951 which yielded the classic 'Straight, No Chaser'. The later recordings on the set are much more conventionally arranged and lack the excitement and sheer imaginative power of the earlier cuts, but they do help overturn the received image of Monk as a man who wrote one beautiful ballad and then so dedicated the rest of his career to intractable dissonance as to set himself apart entirely from the main currents of modern jazz. Between 1952 and 1955, when he contracted to Riverside Records, Monk's career was relatively in the doldrums. However, he had already recorded enough material to guarantee him a place in any significant canon. No jazz fan should be without these records. No self-respecting one will flaunt the Classics set rather than the original Blue Notes, but the French label is now squarely established in the bebop era, the music is the same, if muzzily transferred, and they're cheap.

CORE COLLECTION

♛ **** The Complete Blue Note Recordings

Blue Note 830363 4CD *As above, except add Ahmed Abdul-Malik (b), Kenny Hagood (v).* 47–58.

The Blue Notes are essential Monk recordings, no less achieved and magisterial for being his first as a leader. *The Complete Blue Note Recordings*, which takes in a rediscovered live recording with John Coltrane at the Five Spot in New York City (far from pristine but musical gold-dust), inevitably changes the picture slightly. It is tempting to say that all that the newcomer needs is here, expensive as it is. For those who can't quite stretch to it or who need convincing, the *Best Of* set is very acceptable indeed, with 'Epistrophy', 'Misterioso', 'Round About Midnight', 'Evidence', 'Ruby, My Dear' and 'Straight, No Chaser' all included from the classic performances.

*** Criss Cross

Proper 114 2CD *Monk; Joe Guy, Idries Suliemann, George Taitt (t); Sahib Shihab (as); Coleman Hawkins (ts); Milt Jackson (vib); Charlie Christian (g); Nick Fenton, Al McKibbon, Bob Paige, Gene Ramey, John Simmons (b); Denzil Best, Art Blakey, Kenny Clarke, Harold Doc West, Shadow Wilson (d); Kenny Hagood (v); other personnel, dates as above.*

*** Round Midnight

Definitive DRCD 11133 *Similar to above.*

The Proper set is a generous 31-track survey of Monk's music as it evolved in the transition from swing to bop (the title is of the Charlie Christian piece which opens the set) and towards the mature work of the Blue Notes and the Riversides. As will be seen from the personnel, *Criss Cross* finds Monk in a wide array of line-ups and the quality – both musical and aural – varies considerably. With that in mind, this is probably more effective as a reminder of roots, influences and roads not taken for the experienced listener rather than as an introduction for the uninitiated. The Definitive set is slightly shorter and with a different range of personnels but very nicely put together. Again, though, we'd not recommend it to a newcomer.

**** Thelonious Monk Trio / Blue Monk: Volume 2

Prestige CDJZD 009 *Monk; Ray Copeland (t); Frank Foster (ts); Percy Heath, Gary Mapp, Curley Russell (b); Art Blakey, Max Roach (d).* 10/52–9/54.

***(*) Thelonious Monk

Original Jazz Classics OJC 010 *Monk; Percy Heath, Gary Mapp (p); Art Blakey, Max Roach (d).* 10/52–9/54.

***(*) Thelonious Monk/Sonny Rollins

Original Jazz Classics OJC 059 *Monk; Sonny Rollins (ts); Julius Watkins (frhn); Percy Heath, Tommy Potter (b); Art Blakey, Willie Jones, Art Taylor (d).* 11/53–10/54.

***(*) MONK

Original Jazz Classics OJC 016 *Monk; Ray Copeland (t); Julius Watkins (frhn); Sonny Rollins, Frank Foster (ts); Percy Heath, Curley Russell (b); Art Blakey, Willie Jones (d).* 11/53–5/54.

The end of Monk's Prestige period included some remarkably inventive and adventurous music, which isn't always played as well as it deserves. The trios with Heath and Blakey remain among the best performances of his career, however, and should on no account be missed. The first of this group is a valuable twofer reissue of Prestige P7027 and 7848, with original liner-notes in each case; though it involves repetition with the OJCs, it's a useful way of getting the best of the material on a single CD. OJC 010 repeats all the material save for four quintet tracks from May 1954 featuring Copeland and Foster on 'We See', 'Smoke Gets In Your Eyes', 'Locomotive' and the too-little-played 'Hackensack', all of which are taken from *MONK*. The latter album also includes additional material from the November 1953 recordings with Sonny Rollins which yielded OJC 059. That date was marked by the astonishing 'Friday The 13th', a brilliant use of simultaneous thematic statements which doesn't quite come off in this performance but which sufficiently survives the group's uncertainty to mark it out as daring. The September 1954 session with Heath and Blakey was originally the basis of the Prestige *Monk's Moods*, and it's good to have it filled out with the additional 'Work' and 'Nutty', which are also on *Monk/Rollins*. Even with a repeat of 'Blue Monk' (the definitive version) and the solo slot, 'Just A Gigolo', the Prestige is unbeatable value, clocking in at nearly 78 minutes.

Monk's treatment of standards is remarkable. When he strips a tune down, he arranges the constituent parts by the numbers, like a rifleman at boot camp, with the overall shape and function always evident. On 'These Foolish Things' and 'Sweet And Lovely' he never for a moment loses sight of the melody and, as with the originals, builds a carefully crafted performance that is light-years away from the conventional theme–solo–theme format into which even relatively adventurous jazz performance seemed to be locked. A vital episode in modern jazz; the precise format chosen will depend on level of interest and budget, for it's almost impossible to go wrong.

**** The Complete Prestige Recordings

Prestige 4428 3CD *As above.* 52–54.

The Prestige years went by very quickly and there isn't a massive body of work to anthologize. There are half-a-dozen extra takes included in this three-CD set, but most listeners will have this material already.

**(*) Monkism

Laserlight 17179 *Monk (p solo).* 6/54.

In between contracts, Monk recorded these eight short tracks for Vogue while in Paris. There is another cut from the session, also previously released and it's unclear why it's not included here, even if only to pad out a very skimpy set. Not an essential purchase, though there's some fine playing on both originals and standards.

*** Plays Duke Ellington

Original Jazz Classics OJC 024 *Monk; Oscar Pettiford (b); Kenny Clarke (d).* 7/55.

***** The Unique Thelonious Monk**

Original Jazz Classics OJC 064 *Monk; Oscar Pettiford (b); Art Blakey (d).* 3–4/56.

A curious start at Riverside. Orrin Keepnews remembers that Monk spent an age simply picking out the Ellington tunes at the piano and trying to get them straight. It's a respectful nod from one master to another, but not much more. *The Unique* is a standards album which doesn't quite go to the extremes of demolition which Monk chose when dropping a standard into one of his otherwise original dates, and Pettiford doesn't seem like the best choice for bassist.

CORE COLLECTION

****** Brilliant Corners**

Original Jazz Classics OJC 026 *Monk; Clark Terry (t); Ernie Henry (as); Sonny Rollins (ts); Oscar Pettiford (b); Max Roach (d).* 12/56.

A staggering record, imperfect and patched together after the sessions, but one of the most vivid insights into Monk's music. The title-tune was so difficult that no single perfect take was finished (after 25 tries), and what we hear is a spliced-together piece of music. Full of tensions within the band, the record somehow delivers utterly compelling accounts of 'Pannonica', 'Bemsha Swing', 'Ba-Lue Bolivar Ba-lues Are' as well as the title-piece, and Monk ties it up with a one-take reading of 'I Surrender Dear'.

****** Thelonious Himself**

Original Jazz Classics OJC 254 *Monk; John Coltrane (ts); Wilbur Ware (b).* 4/57.

****** Thelonious Monk With John Coltrane**

Original Jazz Classics OJC 039 *Monk; Ray Copeland (t); Gigi Gryce (as); Coleman Hawkins, John Coltrane (ts); Wilbur Ware (b); Shadow Wilson, Art Blakey (d).* 4–6/57.

****** Monk's Music**

Original Jazz Classics OJC 084 *Monk; Ray Copeland (t); Gigi Gryce (as); Coleman Hawkins, John Coltrane (ts); Wilbur Ware (b); Art Blakey (d).* 6/57.

Thelonious Himself is a solo album, and one of his definitive statements up to this point. Alone at last, Monk's prevarications on his own pieces begin to sound definitive as each progresses: he unpicks them and lays them out again with almost scientific precision, but the immediacy of each interpretation is anything but detached. 'Functional' was probably never given a better reading than here, and his accompanying interpretations of standards are scarcely less compelling, melody and rhythm placed under new lights in each one. Capping it is the trio version of 'Monk's Mood' with Coltrane and Ware, and again, even with all the many versions of this tune which are extant, this one is unlike any other.

The sessions which made up *Thelonious Monk With John Coltrane* and *Monk's Music* are arguably the most compelling records with horns that he ever made. The first is actually by the quartet with Coltrane, Ware and Wilson on three tracks (frustratingly, the only ones the quartet made, despite working together for no less than six months at a New York residency), which include a lovely reading of 'Ruby, My Dear', and throughout Coltrane seems to play humbly, in almost complete deference to the leader. This contrasts pretty strikingly with Hawkins on the second session, of which two alternative takes are also on OJC 039. The sonorous qualities of the horns make this one of the most beautiful-sounding of Monk sessions, and his inspired idea to start the record with an *a cappella* arrangement of 'Abide With Me' sets an extraordinary atmosphere at the very start. There are still problems: the group play stiffly on these rhythms, Hawkins comes in wrongly a couple of times and, as fiercely as everyone is trying, it often sounds more like six men playing at Monk rather than with him. But the flavour of the session is fascinating, and Monk himself sounds wholly authoritative.

****** Live At The Five Spot: Discovery!**

Blue Note 799786 *Monk; John Coltrane (ts); Ahmed Abdul-Malik (b); Roy Haynes (d).* 57.

****(*) Immortal Concerts: At The Five Spot Café, New York, August 1958**

Giants of Jazz *Monk; Johnny Griffin (ts); Ahmed Abdul-Malik (b); Roy Haynes (d).* 8/58.

On atmosphere, *Live At The Five Spot* can't be faulted. The music's pretty amazing, too. These tapes were made by Juanita Coltrane (better known to posterity as Naima) during the band's residency at the Five Spot. The track order has been altered only slightly from the original performance, putting 'Crepuscule With Nellie' at the end of the disc in order to give the opening a rather more cosmetic quality. Predictably, the quality of sound is thoroughly archaeological. The tapes were made on a portable machine with a single mic. The wonder is that so much does actually register. From the prominence of Abdul-Malik's bass it has to be assumed that Mrs Coltrane was in front of him, to her husband's left and at some distance from the piano, which actually registers most poorly of all the instruments, sounding like an out-of-tune clavichord. Collectors of Coltrane solos will be transfixed by his opening statement on 'Trinkle Tinkle', where Monk drops out to let him play with just bass and drums, a practice that is repeated later. This is still in the 'sheets of sound' period and that much-misapplied concept may well become clearer after a listen to this record. There are many electrical and mechanical noises on the tape, a huge dropout during 'Epistrophy', where a portion was accidentally over-recorded (imagine having done that!) and an odd, dissociated feel to the whole thing, not unlike the effect of listening to a sold-out gig through a fire-escape door or side window. A discovery, indeed. However, a remastered version of the tape, with a speed correction, is now available on the complete Blue Note edition listed above.

The Giants of Jazz date from the following year is not much better in quality and Griffin's contributions feel like more heat than light. But there's an excitement to proceedings, 'In Walked Bud' and 'Misterioso' deliver 20-plus minutes of top-flight music, and it's a bargain purchase, so Monk fans should consider it.

*****(*) Thelonious In Action**

Original Jazz Classics OJC 103 *Monk; Johnny Griffin (ts); Ahmed Abdul-Malik (b); Roy Haynes (d).* 8/58.

*****(*) Misterioso**

Original Jazz Classics OJC 206 *As above.* 8/58.

It might, on the face of it, seem improbable that such a headstrong and unmysterious character as Johnny Griffin could be such a masterful interpreter of Monk. But their partnership was an inspiring one, the tenorman unperturbed by any idea that Monk's music was difficult, and the quartet is on blistering form on these dates, recorded live at New York's lamented Five Spot.

*****(*) At Town Hall**

Original Jazz Classics OJC 135 *Monk; Donald Byrd (t); Eddie Bert (tb); Bob Northern (frhn); Phil Woods (as); Charlie Rouse (ts); Pepper Adams (bs); Jay McAllister (tba); Sam Jones (b); Art Taylor (d).* 2/59.

Although Monk regarded this Town Hall concert as a triumph, the results seem rather mixed now. The long and suitably grand attempt at 'Monk's Mood' sounds rather lugubrious, and in general the ensemble catches only elements of Monk's intentions: his peculiar truce between a sober gaiety, bleak humour and thunderous intensity is a difficult thing for a big band to realize and, while there is some fine playing – by Woods and Rouse in particular – the band could probably have used a lot more time to figure out the composer's vision. Still, it's a valuable document of Monk's one personal involvement on a large-scale reading of his music.

***** 5 By Monk By 5**

Original Jazz Classics OJC 362 *Monk; Thad Jones (t); Charlie Rouse (ts); Sam Jones (b); Art Taylor (d).* 6/59.

A relatively little-known Monk session, but a very good one. Jones is another not much thought of as a Monk interpreter, but he carries himself very capably and commits a brilliant improvisation to 'Jackie-Ing', even though (as Orrin Keepnews remembers) he had to struggle with what was then a new piece that Monk attempted to teach everybody by humming it. The CD includes the first two (rejected) takes of 'Played Twice', another new tune.

****** Thelonious Alone In San Francisco**

Original Jazz Classics OJC 231 *Monk (p solo).* 10/59.

Another ruminative solo masterwork. Besides six originals, here is Monk elevating (or destroying, depending on one's point of view) 'There's Danger In Your Eyes, Cherie' and 'You Took The Words Right Out Of My Heart'. As a primer for understanding his piano-playing, there is probably no better introduction than this one.

***** The Art Of The Ballad**

Prestige 11012 *Monk; Ray Copeland (t); Gigi Gryce (as); John Coltrane, Frank Foster, Coleman Hawkins (ts); Gerry Mulligan (bs); Oscar Pettiford, Curley Russell, Wilbur Ware (b); Art Blakey, Kenny Clarke, Shadow Wilson (d).* 55–62.

The album begins and ends – inspired selection – with interpretations of 'Ruby, My Dear', featuring respectively Coleman Hawkins and John Coltrane. 'Monk's Mood' is for trio without percussion, and there is a generous smattering of solo tracks as well. 'Sweet And Lovely', as so often, is an occasion for extended performance, but 'Monk's Mood' and 'Ruby, My Dear' are also the object of notably tender readings. This being Monk, the interpretation of 'ballad' is somewhat idiosyncratic, but this is a delightful compilation from the Riverside and Prestige years.

***** At The Blackhawk**

Original Jazz Classics OJC 305 *Monk; Joe Gordon (t); Charlie Rouse, Harold Land (ts); John Ore (b); Billy Higgins (d).* 4/60.

Live in San Francisco. Land and Gordon were late additions to the band but both men play well. It's not a classic Monk date by any means but there seems to be a good spirit in the playing and the leader sounds at his most genial.

*****(*) San Francisco Holiday**

Milestone 9199 *Monk; Joe Gordon (t); Johnny Griffin, Harold Land, Charlie Rouse (ts); Sam Jones, Ahmed Abdul-Malik, John Ore (b); Art Blakey, Frankie Dunlop, Billy Higgins, Art Taylor (d).*

A generous compilation of sessions on which Monk finds himself briefly outclassed by an in-form Griffin and an unexpectedly powerful Land. Not much here for anyone but a devoted Monkian, but a good buy for all that.

*****(*) The Thelonious Monk Memorial Album**

Milestone 47064 *As for OJC discs above.* 55–62.

*****(*) Thelonious Monk And The Jazz Giants**

Riverside 60-018 *As above.*

♛ ** The Complete Riverside Recordings**

Riverside 022 15CD *As above.*

The two single-disc compilations are perfectly adequate snapshots of Monk's Riverside period, though casual listeners would be better off zeroing in on the four-star records listed above. *The Complete Riverside Recordings* is another monument for the shelves, but there is so little flab and so much music in this set that it defies criticism. Superbly annotated by producer Keepnews, and including many out-takes and extras absent from the original records (though many of those have now been restored to the CD reissues of the appropriate albums), this is enough for a lifetime's study. On that basis alone we award it our crown.

***** Monk In France**

Original Jazz Classics OJCCD 670 *Monk; Charlie Rouse (ts); John Ore (b); Frankie Dunlop (d).* 4/61.

****(*) Monk In Italy**

Original Jazz Classics OJCCD 488 *As above.* 4/61.

The last Riverside albums were recorded during a wide-ranging tour of Europe which has been pretty extensively documented. There are also recordings from the Scandinavian capitals (assessed below), and they are consistently better than the oddly dull and unresponsive effort from Italy which marked Monk's farewell to the label. These sound horribly like contract-fillers. The band don't seem to be getting along, with Dunlop in particular all over the place on 'Straight, No Chaser' and most of the work left to Monk and Rouse, who might have taken a couple of the tunes as an unaccompanied duet.

Three days earlier, the Paris date has much more light and shade. Riverside decided against any overlap of material, so there are no direct comparisons to be made; but the band as a whole seems to be well fed and harmonious, and firing on all cylinders. 'I'm Getting Sentimental Over You' was meant to strike a chord in the French audience, and the little right-hand Django figures in the second chorus are a delightful posy for the home crowd. It's not clear whether the date was intended as a recording session but, whatever the circumstances, the sound is fine – which perversely tends to point up the flat-line dynamic. Monk was on a creative and professional cusp when this session was taped, but it certainly shouldn't be used as a measure of where he was in the spring of that key year.

***** Monk In Copenhagen**

Storyville 8283 *As above.* 5/61.

★★★(★) Live In Stockholm

DIW 315/6 2CD *As above.* 5/61.

The 1961 European tour and the subsequent Columbia contract put the seal on Monk's critical reputation. It's arguable that the end of his great association with Riverside marked the watershed in his creativity and that nothing he did after 1962 had the inventiveness and authority of the Blue Note, Prestige and Riverside years. Certainly the concert recordings from the 1961 tour (and there have been others in circulation, from both sides of the contractual blanket) have a strange *fin de siècle* quality, with a more than usually repetitive carry-over of ideas and very little sign of the pianist's usual ability to reinvent songs night after night. And yet, comparing these two concerts, which were recorded a day apart, it's easier to hear how subtly Monk reinflects not so much his solos as his basic theme statement, adding notes to 'Well You Needn't' in Copenhagen and restructuring the second subject in 'Monk's Mood' with the help of the resourceful Ore. On balance, we favour the Swedish date (which was presumably also a radio broadcast) for its extra length and a rather sharper sound; but both give a flavour of the band on the road. It's ironic that he should have been so warmly received in Europe, for Monk's compositional sense and his playing style were largely overdetermined by American models, rarely (as was the case with Bud Powell) by direct or ironic reference to the European classical tradition. What may have appealed to European audiences, even to Swedes weaned on marathon blowing sessions by American exiles, was precisely his emphasis on *compositions*, rather than schematic chord progressions, as the basis of improvisation.

As so often, Rouse is the bellwether, uneasy and aggressive by turns in the presence of a rather diffident Monk on the first of the records (see 'Off Minor') but finding his feet with a vengeance in Stockholm. The DIW sound is very clear and pristine, but it lacks the warmth and sheer 'feel' of the Dragon, and those who already have that needn't feel they have to update urgently. The Swedish date offers welcome performances of 'Ba-Lue Bolivar Ba-Lues Are' from *Brilliant Corners* and a fine 'Body And Soul'. 'Just a Gigolo' is a solo performance, played in a self-consciously distracted manner, as if saying, It's a *hell* of a job, but someone has to do it.

★★★ Monk's Dream

Columbia CK 40786 *Monk; Charlie Rouse (ts); John Ore (b); Frankie Dunlop (d).* 10 & 11/62.

★★★ Criss Cross

Columbia Legacy 513356 2 *As above.* 11/62, 3/63.

Columbia shrewdly signed Monk just as he was making the transition from underground to mainstream, which is why there's a certain irony in the choice of *Underground* as the title of his last small-group album for the label. *Dream* was his first, and, as Peter Keepnews points out in the reissue notes, it established the pattern for those that followed. Each contained a mixture of originals – most of them now getting quite long in the tooth – and standards, and marked a slight softening of Monk's once rather alien attack. The standards performances – 'Body And Soul', 'Just A Gigolo', 'Sweet And Lovely' – are not always immediately identifiable with the brittle, lateral-thinking genius of the Blue Notes and Riversides and are increasingly dependent on rather formulaic solutions. 'Monk's Dream' and 'Bye-Ya' are slightly tame and the changes of title on 'Bolivar Blues' (weirdly phoneticized in its first version) and 'Five Spot Blues' (originally 'Blues Five Spot') suggest how much Monk was unconsciously and partially moving towards the mainstream. No one seems to have told Charlie Rouse, who really takes over on some of these tracks. The saxophonist sounds jagged and angular where the rhythm has been somewhat rationalized, intensely bluesy where the harmony begins to sound legitimate. Worthy of three stars for Rouse alone, despite the slighting column of Monk scholar Brian Priestley who questions that Thelonious ever took the saxophonist seriously.

Seriously enough to hang on to him through the Columbia years. Rouse is back on *Criss Cross*, which uses up the last of the material from November 1962, 'Hackensack', 'Rhythm-A-Ning' and a retaken 'Coming On The Hudson'. The last of these previously appeared only on the *Giants Of Jazz* anthology, so it's good to have it in circulation and in proper context. The reissue also includes variant takes of 'Eronel' and 'Tea For Two', and what riches they contain for Monk fans, dramatically rethought solos and altered chords in the accompaniment. The idea that Monk was used up by the time he got to Columbia is one that will take some shifting, but only ever appealed to those for whom a measure of commercial success necessarily entails creative decline. No longer the firebrand of earlier days, Monk has consolidated and steadily builds a body of new and rethought work. It's still full of surprises, but by the same token there was a lot of tradition in the early stuff.

★★★ 1963: In Japan

Prestige PRCD SP 202 *As above, except Butch Warren (b) replaces Ore.* 5/63.

★★★(★) Monk In Tokyo

Columbia C2K 63538 2CD *As above.* 5/63.

Monk's reputation in Japan was cemented much more quickly even than in Europe, and these document his first successful visit. The first of the pair was recorded at the TBS television studios. The group initially sound wary and uninspired, but almost every track catches light at some point. The standout performances on *Tokyo* are 'Pannonica' and a marvellous 'Hackensack'. By his own high standard, Rouse is rather anonymous and plays surprisingly little of consequence, but the set as a whole is well worth hearing, and the closing 'Epistrophy' is a virtual lesson in jazz piano history; have fun picking out all the quotes.

★★★(★) At Newport 1963 And 1965

Columbia 63905 *Monk; Pee Wee Russell (cl); Charlie Rouse (ts); Larry Gales, Butch Warren (b); Frankie Dunlop, Ben Riley (d).* 63, 65.

At Newport 1963 Monk proved he was still more subversively radical than the so-called Newport Rebels of an earlier year. In 1965, he was a major American star, sanctified by *Time* magazine. These tapes have been available in different forms down the years, but it is instructive to have them complete and together. The surprise package in the earlier set with Rouse, Warren and Dunlop is a guest appearance by clarinettist Pee Wee Russell, who might seem to belong to an earlier generation and an alien style, but who proves to be as lateral a thinker as the pianist, piling dissonances on one another until the chords almost seem irrelevant. It's possibly all too much of a surprise for Russell as well, because he gets lost here and there, notoriously in the middle of 'Nutty', when Monk pulls the carpet out from under his feet. His other appearance on 'Blue Monk' is more assured, but no less inventive.

It's not a vintage date for Monk, who always seems slightly reserved and in places either uneasy or diffident, and Rouse has to do some work on 'Epistrophy' and 'Criss Cross' (both quartet tracks) to keep the impetus going. He has less to do in 1965 with the later group, but these four performances, highlighted by a quirky 'Hackensack' and a monumental reading of 'Off Minor', are a hugely valuable addition to the canon.

*****(*) Monterey Jazz Festival '63**

Storyville 8255 2CD *As above, except John Ore (b) replaces Warren.* 9/63.

Try to imagine having been there. The quartet was perfectly attuned to Monk's conception and, apart from two long standards – 'I'm Getting Sentimental Over You' and 'Sweet And Lovely' – all the tunes are originals and are dispatched with a sardonic insouciance. Rouse is in exceptional form, carving out blunt, massy solos that are a near-exact corollary of the leader's. Unless the source tapes are compromised in some way, the piano is slightly off in the middle register, but Monk works round its limitations and dead spots.

***** Live At The Village Gate**

Prevue 9 *Monk; Charlie Rouse (ts); John Ore (b); Frankie Dunlop (d).* 11/63.

Previously issued on Xanadu, this helps fill in another corner of what was probably Monk's most densely documented year and the moment when he began to emerge as a major star, not quite a mainstream figure, but certainly a recognizable presence on the wider scene. The opening version of 'Rhythm-A-Ning' is reminiscent of those taped in Paris in the spring of 1965, but the highpoint(s) again are Monk's highly individual solo take on 'Body And Soul', then a regular component of his live set. Not bad sound, though everything sounds a bit boxy.

*****(*) Big Band / Quartet In Concert**

Columbia 476898 2CD *Monk; Thad Jones (c); Nick Travis (t); Eddie Bert (tb); Charlie Rouse (ts); Steve Lacy (ss); Phil Woods (as, cl); Gene Allen (bs, cl, bcl); Butch Warren (b); Frank Dunlop (d).* 12/63.

The original LP release trimmed this important document in an irritatingly Procrustean manner, lopping off two long orchestral numbers, 'Bye-Ya' and 'Light Blue', a tiny quartet version of 'Epistrophy' and a long, magisterial 'Misterioso', also by Monk, Rouse, Warren and Dunlop. The sound has also been tweaked into something like acceptable form, reducing the cavernous boom of the Philharmonic Hall at Lincoln Center, where the concert was recorded the day before New Year's Eve 1963. Monk himself sounds very relaxed, and one can't help comparing his almost Zen-like calm on occasions like this with Charles Mingus's torrential outpourings. The pianist's exchanges with Rouse on 'Misterioso' are some of his gentlest on record, and his reinvention of the obscure 'When It's Darkness On The Delta', a pop song from 1932, is redolent of great predecessors like Tatum, Waller and, at one point near the end, usually unnoticed, Earl Hines. The orchestra plays vigorously and well, seemingly well acquainted with Hall Overton's charts and able to handle some of the quicker turns on 'I Mean You' and 'Oska T', neither of them unchallenging charts, with great aplomb. Fascinating to see (and occasionally hear) that most resolute Monkian, Steve Lacy, in the ensemble; what this must have meant to him.

*****(*) It's Monk's Time**

Columbia Legacy 513557 2 *Monk; Charlie Rouse (ts); Butch Warren (b); Ben Riley (d).* 1–3/64.

It's Monk's Time is one of the best sessions of the period, recorded at the height of Monk's critical standing. In 1964 he was the subject of a cover story in *Time* magazine, one of only three jazz artists (all piano-players, but no more clues) to have been accorded that accolade. There's certainly nothing compromised or middle-market about this tough, abrasive set. Monk's sound had softened considerably over the past decade, partly as a result of playing on better instruments, partly because of more sensitive recording set-ups. He still sounds angular and oblique, but he does so without the percussive edge he was wont to bring to theme statements like 'Lulu's Back In Town', 'Stuffy Turkey' and 'Shuffle Boil', which stand out from the rest for the piquancy of the melodic invention. As with the other discs in the Legacy programme, this reappears with alternate takes, but also more significantly with unedited performances.

***** Solo Monk**

Columbia Legacy 513558 2 *Monk (p solo).* 10/64, 3/65.

His only solo record for Columbia, but full of gems. Compared to the unaccompanied performances of the mid-'50s, it's a relaxed set, though spiked with acid here and there. His attack on 'Dinah' and 'These Foolish Things' is impeccable, planting an idiosyncratic flag on both tunes. 'North Of The Sunset' reprises the stride references of 'Lulu's Back In Town' but makes them more integral to this rare and precious performance. There are no fewer than nine bonus tracks, including a variant on 'Dinah', a first, flawed take of 'Ruby, My Dear' and the unissued 'Introspection'. To what extent this finds Monk in more than usually introspective mode isn't clear. One suspects that he went his own sweet way whether surrounded by the quartet or entirely alone in the studio, and there is more outgoing bravura even in these relatively reined-in performances than most piano men manage in a year.

***** Monk**

Columbia Legacy 86564 *Monk; Charlie Rouse (ts); Larry Gales (b); Ben Riley (d).* 64.

A good set, often overlooked but now available with additional materials. Almost none of the material is Monk's own, just 'Pannonica' (two versions) and a curious reworking of the traditional 'Children's Song (That Old Man)'. There's also a second version of 'April In Paris' and a fine medley of show tunes that has had some limited release before. The standout is a solo reading of Irving Berlin's 'I Love You (Sweetheart Of All My Dreams)'. Deserves to be better known.

****** Live At The It Club – Complete**

Columbia C2K 65288 2CD *Monk; Charlie Rouse (ts); Larry Gales (b); Ben Riley (d).* 10/64.

***** Live At The Jazz Workshop**

Columbia C2K 65189 2CD *As above.* 11/64.

Established connoisseurs of live Monk material will value the latter of these for a fizzing performance of the challenging 'Hackensack' and for a rhythmically adroit 'Bright Mississippi', on which Monk calls the shots to his rhythm section. The earlier session is more convincing all round, though, with particularly fine readings of 'Misterioso', 'Blue Monk' and 'Ba-Lu Bolivar Ba-Lues Are'. As with several of these reissues, the sound reveals significantly more of the bass and drums than on earlier sessions. The It Club session, recorded live in San Francisco, is now available complete and as performed, with three tracks which were previously unreleased and another nine restored to their original length. What's restored isn't simply empty duration but the whole feel of a Monk gig, its texture and pace, and something of its enigmatic logic. The previously unavailable 'Teo', 'Bright Mississippi' and 'Just You, Just Me' aren't revelatory in themselves. What is, though, is the dynamic of the session as a whole and, with the sound also restored to present-day standards, this is as good as it gets for live jazz performance.

★★★★ Monk In Paris: Live At The Olympia
Thelonious TMF 9316 + DVD *Monk; Charlie Rouse (ts); Larry Gales (b); Ben Riley (d).* 3/65, 4/66.

★★★ Olympia, 6 Mars 1965, Part 1
Trema 710591 *As above.* 3/65.

★★★ Olympia, 6 Mars 1965, Part 2
Trema 710592 *As above.* 3/65.

★★★(★) Olympia, 7 Mars 1965
Trema 710590 *As above.* 3/65.

★★★ Paris At Midnight
Varese 061243 *As above, except add Ray Copeland, Clark Terry (t); Jimmy Cleveland (tb); Phil Woods (as); Johnny Griffin (ts).* 65.

Thelonious Records was set up by T. S. Monk Jr to release his own music and, perhaps more significantly, to legitimize the vast body of bootleg recordings that have circulated since Monk's death. *Live At The Olympia* covers material available elsewhere and in fuller form, even if it does give these rather shaky tapes a professional gloss. Just as we'd recommend the original Blue Notes over a Classics compilation, we'd have to recommend the Thelonious release, which includes a stunning 'Bright Mississippi' and a moody 'Body and Soul' on which Monk pays tribute to the harmonic genius of Coleman Hawkins, while saxophonist Rouse contents himself picking splinters out of the melody. However, there is a genuine fascination in tracing these performances over two nights. Monk came onstage on the night of March 7 in blistering form. He launches straight into 'Rhythm-A-Ning' as if the fire bells were about to go and doesn't put it down until he's wrung every conceivable variation and a few inconceivable ones out of it. The intensity of these performances is usefully compared to those of the night before, which are quieter, less flowing and much more deliberate.

Not to build up the suspense unnecessarily, the Thelonious tapes are of the second night and they are certainly the better ones, but anyone seriously interested in Monk will want to hear the March 6 date as well, if only to compare 'Rhythm-A-Ning', which was the climax, not the opening, of the earlier set. A fascinating insight into Monk's practice at the time. To sway your decision, the Thelonious disc has a DVD component, three tracks ('Lulu's Back In Town', 'Blue Monk', 'Round Midnight') filmed in Oslo the following year with the same personnel. If Eric Dolphy was right and you had to see Monk as well as hear him, this is a key purchase.

★★★ Straight, No Chaser
Columbia CK 64886 *Monk; Charlie Rouse (ts); Larry Gales (b); Frankie Dunlop (d).* 11/66–1/67.

Recently restored to its full recorded length by Orrin Keepnews, this is a complete version of the sessions of November 1966 and January 1967. This impeccably remastered issue includes a full version of the intriguing 'Japanese Folk Song' (which had been reduced by almost six minutes to conform to LP length) and a spanking version of 'We See', which had lost almost three minutes for the same reason. There are two unaccompanied piano solos, 'Between The Devil And The Deep Blue Sea' and the tiny 'This Is My Story, This Is My Song'. The two additional tracks are an alternative of 'I Didn't Know About You' and the original 'Green Chimneys', both of them well worth having. This is as late as Monk remains interesting. There are already *longueurs* and too many of the eccentricities seem carefully studied. Much of the material is derived from a film made about Monk that further raised his critical standing without contributing substantially to awareness of what truly made him distinctive.

★★★ The Nonet – Live!
Le Jazz 7 *Monk; Ray Copeland, Clark Terry (t); Jimmy Cleveland (tb); Phil Woods (as); Johnny Griffin, Charlie Rouse (ts); Larry Gales (b); Ben Riley (d).* 11/67.

A rare chance to hear Monk work with a larger group on this November 1967 recording from Paris, which seems to contain all the music from the concert. Strictly, it isn't a Nonet date, but the usual touring quartet with guest contributions on some tracks. Long versions of 'We See', 'Epistrophy' and 'Evidence' allow the solos to stretch out, though Clark Terry restricts himself to a rather cautious and perhaps even sceptical appearance on 'Blue Monk'. Woods is a revelation on this repertoire, his idiosyncratic tack on bop bringing something quite individual to the ensemble. The recording quality is unexceptional but mainly clear and certainly more faithful than the bootleg editions of the gig which circulated for some years.

★★★★ Underground
Columbia Legacy 513559 2 *Monk; Charlie Rouse (ts); Larry Gales (b); Ben Riley (d); Jon Hendricks (v).* 11/67, 2/68.

The Grammy-winning cover art was pitched at the new youth culture in a year of stillborn revolutions. It shows Monk at the piano in his bunker, machine pistol slung over his shoulder, grenades on the table and a Wehrmacht officer tied to a chair behind him, while a *fille de la Résistance* poses like a fashion model in the background.

It doesn't work quite so well at CD size, but there are a few musical grenades and rapid-fire tunes to enjoy as well. And there is that cameo appearance by Jon Hendricks on 'In Walked Bud'. On his last quartet date for Columbia, Monk introduced no fewer than four new tunes, unprecedented in this period and unrepeated after as his output slowed prior to the dramatic retirement/disappearance of 1978. One of the four, 'Ugly Beauty', is Monk's only documented composition in three-quarter time, an amazing detail only if you're unused to the devoted foursquare of his subversively traditional pianism. The other new tunes are 'Raise Four', yet another brilliant reinterpretation of blues form, and two less well-known items, 'Green Chimneys' and 'Boo Boo's Birthday'. Neither of these has found much favour with piano-players, though Kenny Drew Jr is a great exponent of 'Boo Boo'.

The real plus of the set isn't the addition of bonus tracks but that five of the seven original titles are in unedited form. The band is as tightly disciplined and single-minded as a Resistance cell, explosive outbursts from Riley, a strict cadence from Gales, bristling wires of melody from Rouse and strong revolutionary philosophy from Monk, still very much the master of surprise. The irony is that the most notorious Monk cover should conceal some of his least-known tunes, though it's hard to contradict producer Peter Keepnews's assertion that this would be a significant moment in the canon even if it came in plain brown wrappers.

*** Monk's Blues

Columbia CK 53581 *Monk; Robert Bryant, Frederick Hill, Conte Candoli, Bob Brookmeyer (t); Billy Byers, Michael Wimberley (tb); Ernie Small, Tom Scott, Gene Cipriano, Ernie Watts, Charlie Rouse (sax); Howard Roberts (g); Larry Gales (b); Ben Riley (d); John Guerin (perc).* 11/68.

For some reason, this one was credited to Thelonious Sphere Monk, his full name. Given the cost of this session, arranged and produced by Oliver Nelson, perhaps Columbia wanted it to sound as black-tie as possible. Monk came out to the Coast to do the session and to pick up a few side-gigs at the same time. It had apparently been impossible for Nelson, who was a busy television and film music writer and arranger, to get over to New York. What isn't clear is whether the pianist was attracted first and foremost by Nelson or by the chance to work in the sunshine for a while. Nelson certainly gives the complex tunes highly convincing arrangements. The horn players have some lip-busting parts to negotiate on 'Little Rootie Tootie' and 'Brilliant Corners', but they seem to manage. There was only one non-Monk tune on the list, Teo Macero's wryly titled 'Consecutive Seconds', and it stands out very prominently. The CD is filled out with about ten minutes of new material, including a rather slushy 'Round Midnight' which was quite properly omitted from the original release.

**** Monk Alone: The Complete Columbia Solo Studio Recordings, 1962–1968

Columbia 2K 65495 2CD *Monk (p solo).* 62–68.

Glorious. Unaccompanied performances pulled together from *Monk's Dream, Criss Cross, It's Monk's Time, Monk, Straight, No Chaser*, the less well-known *Always Know* and the whole of *Solo Monk*. In addition, there are 14 previously unreleased tracks, mostly alternatives, some of them clearly sub-standard, like the rejected 'Body And Soul' from 31 October–1 November 1962, but all of them absolutely packed with musical invention. Remastered to the highest quality, these brisk, bright sessions show how complete a musician Monk was, using his piano like a drum kit, horn and full orchestra. This is an essential purchase, uncategorizable and resistant to the adjectival attentions of critics; the work of an artist who was completely *sui generis*, it's the kind of record that needs to be lived with for a time.

*** Standards

Columbia CK 45148/465681-2 *Monk; Charlie Rouse (ts); Larry Gales, John Ore (b); Frankie Dunlop, Ben Riley (d).* 62–68.

But, almost needless to say, not predictable standards. Selected from the Columbia years, this is the obvious counterbalance to the assumption that Monk played just Monk. Apart from 'Tea For Two' and 'Nice Work If You Can Get It', these are songs from down the Broadway bill. Gershwin's 'Liza (All The Clouds'll Roll Away)' and Eubie Blake's 'Memories Of You' are stunning reinventions, but there isn't a dull track on the album. We'd still counsel turning to the original records but, as a sample of Monk as an interpreter, it's hard to fault.

**** The Columbia Years: 1962-1968

Columbia 64887 3CD *As above.* 62–8.

*** The Essential Thelonious Monk

Columbia 89175 *As above.* 62–8.

The great joy of *The Columbia Years*, which might otherwise seem another expensive box in an already oversubscribed market is the inclusion of three restored performances. These are 'Think Of One', a version of 'Blue Monk' and 'Don't Blame Me', none of which has been released before. Thanks to Orrin Keepnews, they come across crisply and pristinely, but they don't add anything too substantial to the picture. As a selection from the pianist's final pomp, these three discs are about as good as one might hope for. The performances are magnificent. The *Essential* plucks just 11 tracks from the Columbia years; good budget option but a tyro Monk-listener is going to need an earlier sampler to cover the Blue Note, Prestige and Riverside periods.

J. R. Monterose (1927–93)

TENOR AND SOPRANO SAXOPHONES

Hard-bop stylist, in thrall to few influences, rarely recorded and often forgotten now. His Blue Note album remains unreissued.

*** Jaywalkin'

Fresh Sound FSRCD 320 *Monterose; Phil Sunkel (t); Wade Legge, Ralph Sharon (p); Teddy Charles, Eddie Costa (vib); Joe Puma (g); Milt Hinton, Charles Mingus, Doug Watkins (b); Bill Bradley, Kenny Clarke, Jo Jones (d).* 55, 56.

Quite where J.R.'s public profile would be without the support of Jordi Pujol and Fresh Sound probably isn't worth thinking about. With no sign of the 1956 Blue Note *Quintet* in the offing, these '50s dates with mixed personnel are the best guide to what the saxophonist was doing at the time. Prominently featured is Charles Mingus – revelatory on 'Have You Met Miss Jones?' – with whom Monterose recorded the peerless *Pithecanthropus Erectus* the same year. This was J.R.'s purple patch, so much so that it's still mysterious why in later years he was so eclipsed. Other tracks see him working with the less-celebrated Wade Legge and Phil Sunkel, both of whom are worthy of further notice. Ralph Sharon, later associated with Tony Bennett, is an able and adroit accompanist and Teddy Charles, very much part of the Mingus circuit in those days produces some fine, swinging vibes on a number of cuts; Eddie Costa, more of a Latinist than a bebopper, does a similar job elsewhere.

***(*) The Message

Fresh Sound FSRCD 201 *Monterose; Tommy Flanagan (p); Jimmy Garrison (b); Pete LaRoca (d).* 11/59.

*** Live At The Tender Trap

Fresh Sound FSCD 1023 *Monterose; Dale Oehler (p); Dick Vanizel (b); Joe Abodeely (d); Al Jarreau (v).* 63.

Detroit-born Monterose fell into none of the familiar tenor-playing niches and so fell out of jazz history. If there was a single strong influence, it was probably John Coltrane; but Monterose was anything but a slavish Trane copyist and forged his own odd but inimitable style: a slightly tight, almost strangled tone, delivered before and behind the beat, often in successive measures, thin but curiously intense and highly focused. He was also a pioneer of electric sax, an interest that few others have followed. And yet, just half a dozen years after his largely unreported death, a significant European jazz label is capable of releasing a valuable late live session with J.R.'s surname consistently misspelt on cover, in personnel and in notes, all the while wagging an admonitory finger at those who confuse him with the slightly younger West Coaster, Jack Montrose.

Even neglected dogs have their day. Monterose made a considerable impression on Charles Mingus's *Pithecanthropus Erectus*, an understated foil to Jackie McLean's impassioned alto. Sadly, not even that remarkable session won him enough leverage to build a significant body of work as leader. On parts of *The Message* the resemblance to Warne Marsh is almost uncanny, even down to specific phrases on 'Violets For Your Furs' and 'I Remember Clifford', in which he uses simple arch shapes with altered harmonics to create a strange, slightly distanced quality. Garrison, as was his fate, remains poorly audible, but LaRoca is very good and totally musical.

The early-'60s session features J.R.'s regular band, an able if slightly colourless unit, based at The Tender Trap in Cedar Rapids, Iowa. The group (with minor variants) enjoyed a long residency at The Tender Trap. Occasional guest players were David Sanborn and the young Al Jarreau, who studied psychology at the University of Iowa. His vocals are a must for collectors, as an earnest of the subtle stylist he was to become in later years. Alas, no glimpse of the young Sanborn, who went on to make more money per record than J.R. did in his entire career.

*** A Little Pleasure

Reservoir RSR CD 109 *Monterose; Tommy Flanagan (p).* 4/81.

*** T. T. T.

Storyville STCD 8291 *Monterose; Hod O'Brien (p); Guffy Pallesen (b); Jesper Elen (d).* 7/88.

A Little Pleasure is Monterose's recording debut with soprano saxophone, and it casts him in mostly reflective mood. There are two good originals: the 3/4 'Pain And Suffering ... And A Little Pleasure' and the less satisfying 'Vinnie's Pad'. Monterose stays with the straight horn for 'A Nightingale Sang In Berkeley Square' (with Flanagan playing the verse) and on 'Central Park West', whose solo underlines just how little dependent on Coltrane Monterose has been down the years. It's very intimately miked, and Monterose's breathing is very audible.

We'd be much more enthusiastic about the Storyville disc if they had taken the trouble to spell J.R.'s surname correctly. Late in life, and rather flatly recorded for Danish Radio in live performance at the Jazzhus Slukefter, it catches him sounding rather strained but still generating ideas at an impressive rate. As ever, the programme is largely standards-based, with a movingly querulous 'You Don't Know What Love Is' and 'All The Things You Are'. He covers 'Central Park West' once again but also Sonny Rollins's 'Airegin', two themes coming from very different musical premises. The house band is sound enough, but by this point J.R. seemed fated to spend his career working with groups who chugged ahead almost despite him.

Buddy Montgomery (born 1930)

PIANO

The youngest of the Montgomery brothers, Charles began his career playing vibes with Monk in the Mastersounds and later with Wes as well. At the end of the '60s, he settled in Milwaukee and combined playing and teaching.

*** Here Again

Sharp Nine 1008 *Montgomery; Jeff Chambers (b); Ray Appleton (d).* 97.

*** A Love Affair In Paris

Spacetime 2116 *Montgomery; Donald Brown (p); Robert Hurst (b); Lenny White (d); Anga Diaz (perc).* 10/00.

The last surviving Montgomery brother, Buddy seems ever-quieter and more wistful as the years go by. There's not much drama in recent work, just a quiet application and a gentle expressiveness. So uniform is the material on *Here Again* that one appreciates it more as a rolling suite of themes, some familiar, some less so, than as individual tracks. Originals like '1,000 Blues' and 'Hob Nob For Brother Bob' are nicely crafted but unmemorable and one tends to pick up on the standards (including a lovely 'That Old Black Magic') just for reference points.

On *A Love Affair In Paris*, which mixes live and studio material, he returns to vibraphone for some tracks, using Donald Brown as accompanist. The surprise package on this French release is White, now better known as a fusioneer but still a compelling jazz drummer with a fine sense of time and a gentle snap to his snare work that he didn't learn in Return To Forever. The opening 'Night Has A Thousand Eyes' even manages to wring some fresh ideas out of the old warhorse, while the originals 'Waterfall' and 'Irregardless' are surprisingly fresh and unhackneyed for a 70-year-old whose career has never been about innovation and everything about simple devotion to melody and to the logical progress of chords.

Wes Montgomery (1925–68)

GUITAR, BASS GUITAR

The middle and most celebrated of the Montgomery brothers was born like the others in Indianapolis. He took to guitar late and only began his professional career – in Lionel Hampton's band – when he was 25. Influenced by Charlie Christian, he developed a style in which thumb-plucked single-note lines were backed with softly strummed octaves and chords. Wes worked with his brothers Monk and Buddy, and with groups of his own. Montgomery died unexpectedly, at the height of his commercial appeal if not of his creative powers.

*(*) Complete Recordings With Lionel Hampton

Definitive DRCD 11241 2CD *Montgomery; Lionel Hampton Orchestra.* 1/49 & 1/50.

***(*) Fingerpickin'

Pacific Jazz 8 37987 *Montgomery; Freddie Hubbard (t); Wayman Atkinson, Alonzo Johnson (ts); Buddy Montgomery (vib); Joe Bradley, Richie Crabtree (p); Monk Montgomery (b); Benny Barth, Paul Parker (d).* 12/57, 4/58.

Wes Montgomery gave off a sense of effortlessness that is always bad karma in jazz; a little *sweat* and preferably some pain are almost considered *de rigueur*. But Montgomery used to loose off solos as if he was sitting on his back porch talking to friends. He used a homely, thumb-picking technique, rather than a plectrum or the faster finger-picking approach. Stylistically, he copied Charlie Christian's Ur-bop and added elements of Django Reinhardt's harmonic conception. It's interesting and ironic that Montgomery's most prominent latter-day disciple, George Benson, should have made almost exactly the same career move, trading off a magnificent improvisational sense against commercial success.

The Hampton set is a swindle. If you enjoy Hamp's hyperactive jazz, there is lots to enjoy, but it would take an acoustic detective to find, let alone appreciate, the 24-year-old Wes's guitar playing amid these hefty arrangements. Our rating for this isn't so much for the music as for the barefaced cheek of passing off this hefty two-CD set as a Wes Montgmery record.

The story under his own name starts with Pacific Jazz. This is a strong, assured set which benefits from a string of horns. Hubbard is in good form on his four tracks, though Buddy Montgomery's themes don't give him a great deal to bite on. The remaining tracks from the Christmas 1957 session are too short to establish much of a presence, and one is left feeling slightly short-changed by something like 'All The Things You Are', which bounces by in little more than it would take to deliver the song, and with much less going on. The remaining three tracks were taped at the Forum Theater in Los Angeles the following spring, with Crabtree and Barth joining the brothers. 'Baubles, Bangles And Beads' is lovely, if a touch raggedy round the edges. The sound lets things down here and there, and there may be a couple of reconstructed dropouts on 'Not Since Nineveh'. Otherwise, though, a very collectable item.

***** Far Wes**

Pacific Jazz 94475 *Montgomery; Pony Poindexter (as); Harold Land (ts); Buddy Montgomery (p); Monk Montgomery (b); Tony Bazley, Louis Hayes (d); collective personnel.* 4/58–10/59.

A welcome reissue (of the better 1958 sessions particularly). Montgomery plays fluently if a trifle dispassionately but emerges here as a composer of some substance. The title-track is in relatively conventional bop idiom but has an attractive melodic contour (which Land largely ignores) and a well-judged 'turn' towards the end of the main statement. The later sessions are a trifle disappointing, though the great Louis Hayes weighs in at the drum kit with characteristic confidence. It's worth buying for the first half-dozen tracks alone.

***** A Dynamic New Jazz Sound**

Original Jazz Classics OJC 034 *Montgomery; Mel Rhyne (org); Paul Parker (d).* 10/59.

*****(*) Movin' Along**

Original Jazz Classics OJC 089 *Montgomery; James Clay (ts, f); Victor Feldman (p); Sam Jones (b); Louis Hayes (d).* 10/60.

*****(*) So Much Guitar**

Original Jazz Classics OJC 233 *Montgomery; Hank Jones (p); Ron Carter (b); Lex Humphries (d); Ray Barretto (perc).* 8/61.

*****(*) Full House**

Riverside 9434/Original Jazz Classics OJC 106 *Montgomery; Johnny Griffin (ts); Wynton Kelly (p); Paul Chambers (b); Jimmy Cobb (d).* 6/62.

****(*) Boss Guitar**

Riverside 9459/Original Jazz Classics OJC 261 *Montgomery; Mel Rhyne (org); Jimmy Cobb (d).* 4/63.

***** Portrait Of Wes**

Original Jazz Classics OJC 144 *Montgomery; Johnny Griffin (ts); Wynton Kelly (p); Paul Chambers (b); George Brown (d).* 10/63.

***** Fusion!**

Original Jazz Classics OJC 368 *Montgomery; Phil Bodner (sax, f); Dick Hyman (p, cel); Hank Jones (p); Kenny Burrell (g); Milt Hinton (b); Osie Johnson (d); strings.* 4/63.

***** Guitar On The Go**

Original Jazz Classics OJC 489 *Montgomery; Melvin Rhyne (org); George Brown, Jimmy Cobb, Paul Parker (d).* 10–11/63.

****** The Complete Riverside Recordings**

Riverside 12 RCD 4408 12CD *As for the above, except add Nat Adderley (c), Joe Gordon (t), Julian 'Cannonball' Adderley (as), Johnny Griffin, Harold Land (ts), Barry Harris, George Shearing, Bobby Timmons (p), Victor Feldman, Milt Jackson, Buddy Montgomery (vib), Ray Brown, Monk Montgomery (b), Walter Perkins (d); woodwinds; strings.* 59–63.

***** The Artistry Of Wes Montgomery**

Riverside FCD 60 919 *As above.* 59–63.

***** Dangerous**

Milestone 9298 *As above.* 59–63.

In career terms, Montgomery really did seem to prefer his back porch. During the '50s, which should have been his big decade, he hung around his native Indianapolis, playing part-time. When his recording career got going again, he was still capable of great things. The massive Riverside box, including everything he did under the auspices of the label, has turned this entry on its head. Though much of the best material was and still is available separately, access to it in this bulk, and with a huge range of material recorded for other leaders – the Adderleys, Shearing, Land – and with the Montgomery Brothers makes a substantial difference to our view of the guitarist, highlighting his awesome consistency, pointing a slightly accusing finger at his tendency to settle for the obvious and familiar on occasion, rarely pushing out into the more experimental mode that he had flirted with early on. The boxed set has a price-tag commensurate with its size, and many listeners will feel the need to pick one or more of the individual discs instead.

Guitar/organ trios take a little getting used to nowadays, but *New Sound* and *Boss Guitar* contain some of the guitarist's most vibrant recordings. While some of the best of the material – 'Round Midnight', 'Fried Pies' and so on – has been sampled on the Milestone sets, below, these are worth hearing and having in their entirety. For no readily discernible reason, *Boss Guitar* sounds flatter than the others.

On *So Much*, Montgomery's smooth and uncannily fluent lines and Jones's elegant two-handedness lift 'Cotton Tail' out of the ordinary. Never a blindingly fast player, Montgomery specialized in sweeping oppositions of register that lend an illusion of pace to relatively stately passages.

Guitar On The Go was Wes's last release on Riverside before the label went pear-shaped. The dating may seem odd, but there is just one track – 'Missile Blues' – from the 1959 album. It was a remarkable and powerful end to a very fruitful relationship and, as well as the extra track, there is a spankingly good alternative of 'The Way You Look Tonight' and an untitled solo-guitar improvisation which will intrigue established fans and make them wish there were more of Wes's rehearsal work and solitary musings available. *Dangerous* is a valuable compilation of alternatives and live tracks, issued at a price that is more approachable than the box set.

The title *Fusion!* is interesting because in a sense Wes was one of the figures who lay behind later attempts to integrate the rhythm and energy of rock with jazz harmonies. Ironically, there isn't much trace of that here. Jimmy Jones's arrangements are engagingly tight and spare – one has to admire the sheer workmanship of 'Baubles, Bangles And Beads' – but the one thing these sessions lack is energy. Wes sounds positively pipe-and-slippers and, but for 'God Bless The Child', rather detached and disengaged. As with all these later recordings, though, remastering significantly improves the overall balance of sound.

The live *Full House!* pitched Montgomery in with the Wynton Kelly Trio, an association that promised a lot and delivered more. The set is now available in an audiophile edition, beautifully remastered, and with extra cuts of some tracks.

CORE COLLECTION

**** Incredible Jazz Guitar

Original Jazz Classics OJC 036 *Montgomery; Tommy Flanagan (p); Percy Heath (b); Albert 'Tootie' Heath (d).* 1/60.

***Incredible Jazz Guitar* is probably the best Montgomery record currently available. His solo on 'West Coast Blues' is very nearly incredible, though there are hints of banality even there, in his trademark octave runs, which he borrowed from Django. Flanagan may have slipped the engineer a sawbuck, for he's caught beautifully, nicely forward in the mix. His lines on Sonny Rollins's buoyant 'Airegin' are exactly complementary to the guitarist's. There's a 'D-natural Blues' and covers of 'In Your Own Sweet Way' and 'Polka Dots And Moonbeams', which further hint at Montgomery's eventual artistic inertia, but for the moment he sounds like a master, and this is the one to go for if you aren't investing in the big box.**

*** Complete Live At Jorgies

Definitive DRCD 11247 *Montgomery; Buddy Montgomery (p, vib); Billy Taylor (p); Monk Montgomery, Ben Tucker (b); Billy Hart, Grady Tate (d); Joe Williams (v).* 8/61–11/63.

Live tapes of Wes have been turning up over the past few years, some as reissues and some previously unreleased. These have been available before, though not in complete form. The extras are somewhat beside the point because the sound quality is poor throughout. Wes sounds very far away and bass and drums are rackety. There's not much definition on Buddy's piano either and 'Summertime' sounds as though there's heat haze all over it. Four extra tracks from 1963; a different group consisting of Billy Taylor, Ben Tucker and Grady Tate, who always sounds good with Wes. Nice stuff, but a shaky bit of product that will only appeal to committed Wes fans and to those who don't already suffer from tinnitus.

*** The Alternative Wes Montgomery

Milestone M 47065 *Montgomery; Johnny Griffin (ts); James Clay (f); Victor Feldman, Wynton Kelly, Buddy Montgomery (p); Mel Rhyne (org); Milt Jackson (vib); Paul Chambers, Sam Jones, Monk Montgomery (b); George Brown, Jimmy Cobb, Louis Hayes, Philly Joe Jones, Bobby Thomas (d); orchestra.* 10/60–11/63.

A mass of material, and no maps. Some of Montgomery's better later performances were buried away on rather unselective, buffet-table Milestone LPs, but the cumulative impression is of incipient commercial *longueur*, certainly the extra takes on *Alternative* don't contain any real revelations. Montgomery himself claimed to have been at his best a full decade before, but he spent most of the '50s out of the limelight. It's hard to think that any but the most dogged of fans would want all the alternatives if the original releases were freely available on CD. For the time being, though, they represent a decent purchase.

*** Encores: Volume 1 – Body And Soul

Milestone 9252 *Montgomery; Milt Jackson (vib); Victor Feldman (vib, p); Wynton Kelly, Buddy Montgomery (p); Sam Jones, Monk Montgomery (b); Louis Hayes, Philly Joe Jones, Bobby Thomas (d).* 10/60–11/63.

***(*) Encores: Volume 2 – Blue'N'Boogie

Milestone 9261 *Montgomery; Johnny Griffin (ts); Wynton Kelly (p); Paul Chambers (b); Jimmy Cobb (d).* 6/62–11/63.

Two very different and inevitably rather patchy sets from the Milestone archive. The first album pulls together a disparate body of material and makes a certain sense of it. 'Body And Soul' is worthy of its title position, a smooth but not unsubtle reading. Volume 2 has rather more bite. Under normal circumstances Griff is too incendiary for a gig like this, but he and Wes struck up a strong relationship, and the fruits are very impressive indeed, with strong, punchy choruses from both on 'Born To Be Blue' and the inevitable 'Baubles, Bangles And Beads'.

***(*) The Incredible Jazz Guitar Of Wes Montgomery

Definitive 11224 *Montgomery; Johnny Griffin (ts); Martial Solal (p); Arthur Harper, Michel Gaudry (b); Jimmie Lovelace, Ronnie Stephenson (d).* 2 & 4/65.

**** Complete Live In Paris, 1965

Definitive 11244 *As above; omit Solal, Gaudry, Stephenson.* 65.

***(*) Quintessential Wes

Fuel 2000 061254 *Same as above.* 65.

Montgomery in Europe and a star in the spring of 1965. Johnny Griffin was the guest at the Paris and Hamburg dates, the latter comprising the second half of *Incredible Jazz Guitar.* That set begins with rare live tapes from the Half Note Clue in New York City, a try-out for Wes with Mabern, Harper and Lovelace. Though the sound isn't wonderful – Wes is fine but the excellent pianist sounds as if he's in the corridor – the playing is exquisite and this has to count as one of Wes's most sympathetic bands. Mabern is often overlooked in the roster of important piano-players of the time, but here he is a revelation, quick-fingered and dextrous and endlessly subtle in his choice of chords and passing notes. The Paris concert is one of the best things Wes ever did. His read of 'Impressions' is awesome in its simplicity and blues fire; it's done in an unusual time sequence, though, something like 11/8 in threes and a two and so delighted is Wes to have pulled it off that he laughs audibly during the final chorus. Griffin helps build up the drama, though apart from the Coltrane theme nothing here is quite as exciting as Griff's solo on 'Blue Monk' from the Hamburg date. That occasion saw Wes working with the exquisite Solal as well, an unexpected association that works better than anyone could have expected. These are all wonderful documents of Montgomery at his peak. The Paris concert should be in every jazz guitar fan's collection and *Quintessential* has basically the same material, different order, three tracks fewer; the New York/Hamburg date is a qualified success – fine music, less than fine sound.

*** Body And Soul

Ronnie Scott's Jazz House JHAS 604 *Montgomery; Stan Tracey (p); Rick Laird (b); Ronnie Stephenson (d).* 4 & 5/65.

Souvenirs from a fondly remembered British visit, on which the guitarist won round even an audience that was decamping by the score to rock'n'roll. His easy rapport, with listeners and fellow musicians alike, is evident long before the spoken-word coda. He perhaps finds Tracey slightly jagged and, on 'Wes' Easy Blues' and 'Body And Soul', he attempts to soften the attack a touch. There's just one unaccompanied track, the slightly inconsequential 'Solo Ballad In A Major', a familiar idea but not one we can peg down to a known source. Laird and Stephenson are, as ever, reliable in support, though neither is very well recorded on these tapes.

**** Impressions: The Verve Jazz Sides

Verve 521690-2 2CD *Montgomery; Donald Byrd, Mel Davis, Bernie Glow, Danny Moore, Joe Newman, Jimmy Nottingham, Ernie Royal, Clark Terry, Snooky Young (t); Wayne Andre, Jimmy Cleveland, Urbie Green, Quentin Jackson, Melba Liston, John Messner, Tony Studd, Bill Watrous, Chauncey Welsh (tb); Jimmy Buffington (frhn); Don Butterfield, Harvey Phillips (tba); Jerome Richardson (ts, ss, f); Stan Webb (as, bs, cl); Ray Beckenstein (as); Bob Ashton, Jerry Dodgion, Romeo Penque (reeds); Danny Bank (bs, af, f, bcl); Walter Kane (bs, cl); Herbie Hancock, Roger Kellaway, Wynton Kelly, Bobby Scott (p); Jimmy Smith (org); Jack Jennings (vib); Al Casamenti, Bucky Pizzarelli (g); Paul Chambers, Bob Cranshaw, George Duvivier (b); Jimmy Cobb, Sol Gubin, Grady Tate (d); Ray Barretto, Willie Bobo (perc).* 11/64–11/66.

*** Movin' Wes

Verve 521433-2 *Montgomery; Ernie Royal, Clark Terry, Snooky Young (t); Jimmy Cleveland, Urbie Green, Quentin Jackson, Chauncey Welsh (tb); Don Butterfield (tba); Jerome Richardson (sax, f); Bobby Scott (p); Bob Cranshaw (b); Grady Tate (d); Willie Bobo (perc).* 11/64.

*** Bumpin'

Verve 539062-2 *Montgomery; Roger Kellaway (p); Bob Cranshaw (b); Helcio Milito, Grady Tate (d); strings.* 5/65.

***(*) Smokin' At The Half Note

Verve 829578 2 *Montgomery; Wynton Kelly (p); Paul Chambers (b); Jimmy Cobb (d).* 5 & 9/65.

*** Willow Weep For Me

Verve 589486 2 *As above; unknown brass and woodwinds.* 6 & 10/65.

**(*) Tequila

Verve 547769-2 *Montgomery; George Devens (vib); Ron Carter (b); Grady Tate (d); Ray Barretto (perc); Bernard Eichem, Arnold Eidus, Paul Gershman, Emmanuel Green, Julius Held, Harry Lookofsky, Joe Malin, Gene Orloff (vn); Abe Kessler, Charles McCracken, George Ricci, Harvey Shapiro (clo).* 3 & 5/66.

***(*) California Dreaming

Verve 827842-2 *Montgomery; Mel Davis, Bernie Glow, Jimmy Nottingham (t); Wayne Andre, John Messner, Bill Watrous (tb); Jimmy Buffington (frhn); Don Butterfield (tba); Ray Beckenstein (as, picc, f); Stan Webb (as, bs, cl, eng hn); Herbie Hancock (p); Al Casamenti (g); Jack Jennings (vib); Richard Davis (b); Grady Tate (d); Ray Barretto (perc).* 66.

The 'jazz' in the title of the two-CD set is a careful hedge, in recognition of the unreconstructed commerciality of much that Wes was doing at the time. Just as the Riversides have realigned the pre-1963 material, this elegantly packaged compilation brings together the best of albums like *Willow Weep For Me, The Small Group Recordings, Just Walkin', Smokin' At The Half Note, California Dreaming, Goin' Out Of My Head* and *Movin' Wes.*

Bumpin' was the record that established a working relationship between Wes, Creed Taylor and arranger Don Sebesky, who is responsible for the strings. As with much of the guitarist's work, it has acquired a new currency through the acid-jazz movement. Without those loyalties it isn't so much revelatory as pleasantly irrelevant. Restored to pristine condition, it's technically flawless and expressively a bit dead, though 'Bumpin'' itself is as lovely as ever.

As an entity, *Movin'* has a lot more presence than the majority of the later discs; remastering brings guitar and band into better balance than on the original release. The only soloist on the date, Wes is playing very smoothly indeed. Tunes like 'The Phoenix Love Theme', 'Moca Flor' and 'Theodora' are little more than beefed-up elevator music. The title-tune (which comes in two parts, 'Born To Be Blue' and 'People') is a bit more focused, but there still isn't much excitement.

Willow Weep For Me isn't quite as soporific as it maybe sounds, but there isn't much drama there either; the later brass and woodwind overdubs, conducted by Claus Ogerman, swamp a perfectly good quartet date. As if to underline the missed potential, it's *Smokin' At The Half Note* that stands out. Pat Metheny is on record as saying this is the greatest guitar jazz album of all time, an extravagant claim and, without context, a misleading one. It's certainly Wes's most stimulating association. Kelly stokes the blues material and emerges as a subtle and dynamic soloist, to the extent that an equally enthused fan might claim this as the best piano trio with guitar album of all time. 'No Blues' and 'Unit 7' are extraordinary performances; Wes's solo on the latter is his time capsule piece, quintessential Montgomery played with taste and fire combined. Whatever its league position, *Smokin'* is well worth having.

Tequila is one of the sessions that Verve have plundered in order to reposition Wes as a founding father of both acid jazz and a smooth, ambient saloon funk. It finds Montgomery rather wearily putting in his time with the Claus Ogerman Orchestra. 'Bumpin' On Sunset' is of course a long-standing favourite (subsequently revived by Brian Auger's Oblivion Express in the jazz equivalent of minimalist trance music). Montgomery is still harmonically inventive, but the arrangements are too pre-packaged for very much in the way of surprises.

California Dreaming kicks off with another pop hit but the record contains some brief flashes of Montgomery the jazz master. They're not evident other than episodically but, heard over time, this is a more substantial record than first appears and we recommend it ahead of almost any of Wes's later records.

*****(*) Jazz Masters 14**

Verve 519826-2 *Montgomery; Wynton Kelly (p); Paul Chambers (b); Jimmy Cobb (d); Ray Barretto (perc); Oliver Nelson Orchestra; Don Sebesky Orchestra; Johnny Pate Orchestra.* 64–66.

***** Ultimate**

Verve 539787-2 *As above.* 64–66.

***** Talkin' Verve – Roots Of Acid Jazz**

Verve 529580-2 *As above, except add Jimmy Smith (org), Jack Jennings (vib), Kenny Davis (b), Claus Ogerman Orchestra.* 64–66.

Three strong compilations drawn from Verve's capacious catalogue of Montgomery material. Inevitably, there is some overlap of tracks: 'Bumpin' On Sunset' is on both *Jazz Masters* and the acid jazz genealogy; 'OGD (Road Song)' can be found on the latter and *Ultimate*, and so on. It seems unlikely, though, that anyone will be tempted by more than one of these, and our recommendation is the *Jazz Masters* disc. A crossover star of a later generation, George Benson, is responsible for curating the *Ultimate* collection, but he adds no real insight to what seems like a haphazard selection from Wes's Verve years.

****(*) A Day In The Life**

A&M 75021 0816 2 *Montgomery; Herbie Hancock (p); Ron Carter (b); Grady Tate (d); Ray Barreto (perc); woodwinds, strings.* 6/67.

**** Down Here On The Ground**

A&M 396994-2 *Montgomery; Hubert Laws, George Marge, Romeo Penque (f, ob); Mike Maineri (vib); Ron Carter (b); Grady Tate (d); Ray Barretto, Bobby Rosengarden (perc); strings.* 12/67, 1/68.

**** Road Song**

A&M 75021 0822 2 *Montgomery; Marvin Stamm (t); Wayne Andre, Paul Faulise (tb); Jimmy Buffington (frhn); Herbie Hancock, Hank Jones (p); Ron Carter, Richard Davis (b); Ed Shaughnessy, Grady Tate (d); Ray Barreto (perc); woodwinds, strings.* 5/68.

By the last year of his life, Montgomery was a pop star, and there is precious little jazz on these chart-orientated sessions for Herb Alpert's label. The familiar parallel octaves are there in plenty, but Montgomery does little more than register the melody, repeat it with some slight elaboration, negotiate a middle eight as straightforwardly as possible, and then on out to a faded ending.

A Day In The Life and the feeble *Road Song* are both larded with pop songs in unchallenging but often overbearing arrangements; 'Eleanor Rigby', 'A Day In The Life', 'Greensleeves' are all played straight. Wes's moments of genuine artistry are few and far between and one longs to hear some of the tracks done as small groups with more attention to Hancock and Carter in particular, but also with a more realistic mix for the lyrical Tate, who made the drums sing.

One can't begrudge Wes his moment of commercial success but given how little time he had to enjoy it – he succumbed to a heart attack just five weeks after *Road Song* was taped – these final records seem like an ironic curtain-call.

Montgomery Brothers

GROUP

The Montgomery 'family' group, which worked in San Francisco in 1960–61.

***** Groove Yard**

Original Jazz Classics OJC 139 *Buddy Montgomery (vib, p); Monk Montgomery (b); Bobby Thomas (d).* 1/61.

A little like the Jackson Five, it can be a bit difficult to maintain an even focus on all the members of this once rather successful group. Monk and Buddy doubtless gained considerably from their association with Wes, but he also gained a sympathetic, supportive group which never quite attained its full potential in the midst of Wes's Riverside period. This record (and another recorded in Canada, still not on CD) represent the group's best output. Buddy's vibes playing was not quite in the Milt Jackson class but it was more than workmanlike, and his piano playing, which developed in years to come, is bright and rhythmic, with a slightly melancholy quality which suits the group very well. Monk has always been overshadowed, but the CD transfer allows him to come through quite strongly and his passagework on 'If I Should Lose You' and 'Groove Yard' is quite impressive.

Tete Montoliu (1933–97)

PIANO

Born blind – and subsequently hearing-impaired too – Montoliu was born in Barcelona and played and recorded with visitors to his local scene in the '50s before being internationally discovered. He toured widely in the '70s and '80s but died from lung cancer in 1997.

***** That's All**

Steeplechase SCCD 31199 *Montoliu (p solo).* 9/71.

***** Lush Life**

Steeplechase SCCD 31216 *Montoliu (p solo).* 9/71.

*****(*) It's About Blues Time**

Fresh Sound FSR-CD 305 *Montoliu; Dusko Goykovich (t); Ferdinand Povel (ts); Robert Langereis (b); Joe Nay (d).* 11/71.

Montoliu was a European maverick whose ebullient music could be tender, memorably exciting, gracefully virtuosic. Dazzlingly fast in execution, his improvisations are mostly based on a standard bebop repertoire, yet at his best he seemed driven to making his music fresh and new from record to record. From moment to moment he might suggest Tatum, Powell or Garner, and his feeling for blues playing was particularly sharp. He began recording in 1958, but most of his '60s sessions as a leader are still hidden on obscure, out-of-print Spanish labels (for contemporaneous work as a sideman, see under Dexter Gordon's entry). Frustratingly, a live set for Impulse! at the Village Vanguard in 1967, with Richard Davis and Elvin Jones, has never been released.

Montoliu opened a prolific decade of recording with a single session in Munich, half of which was released at the time by Enja, the remainder turning up many years later on the Steeplechase albums. Little to choose among the three discs (the Enja will have to be sought in the second-hand bins now). The question of Montoliu's employment of his Catalan roots in a jazz environment is an interesting one: his oft-quoted remark, 'Basically, all Catalans are blacks', isn't very helpful, but there's little doubt that he is exceptionally responsive to using his native music in a post-bop setting.

It's About Blues Time brings back an enjoyable quintet session from the Barcelona scene of 1971. Joe Nay makes a tremendous noise at the drums and, with Povel coming on like he's just heard his first Coltrane record, the marathon blues which opens the set hits a formidable high. Goykovich is in spanking form throughout and his 'Bosnia Calling' is impressive. The one who suffers, ironically, is Montoliu: the fierce studio separation shunts him to one side, and he's well down in the mix anyway.

***** Temas Brasilenos**
Ensayo ENY-CD-3951 *Montoliu; Alberto Moraleda (b); Miguel Angel Lizandra (d).* 11/73.

***** Catalonian Fire**
Steeplechase SCCD 31017 *Montoliu; Niels-Henning Orsted Pedersen (b); Albert 'Tootie' Heath (d).* 5/74.

*****(*) Tete!**
Steeplechase SCCD 31029 *As above.* 5/74.

***** Music For Perla**
Steeplechase SCCD 31021 *Montoliu (p solo).* 5/74.

***** Boleros**
Ensayo ENY-CD-3473 *Montoliu; Manuel Elias (b); Peer Wyboris (d); Rogelio Juarez (perc).*

*****(*) Tete A Tete**
Steeplechase SCCD 31054 *Montoliu; Niels-Henning Orsted Pedersen (b); Albert 'Tootie' Heath (d).* 2/76.

*****(*) Tootie's Tempo**
Steeplechase SCCD 31108 *As above.* 2/76.

***** Words Of Love**
Steeplechase SCCD 31084 *Montoliu (p solo).* 3/76.

***** Blues For Myself**
Ensayo ENY-CD-3954 *Montoliu; Eric Peter (b); Peer Wyboris (d).* 1/77.

Montoliu seemed to release a lot of records in the '70s, but actually he had only a few concentrated bursts of recording. The four albums by the trio with NHOP and Heath remain among his most impressive offerings: played with both elegance and fire, his improvisations on favourite themes have a poise and dash that make one overlook the frequent appearance of many familiar runs and manipulations of the beat. Pedersen, who loves to play with a pianist of outsize technique, holds nothing back in his own playing, while Heath's rather gruff and unfussy drumming makes him a nearly ideal timekeeper for the situation. Of the Steeplechases, *Tootie's Tempo* and *Tete!* are particularly good, but any one is highly entertaining. The solo records are slightly less interesting.

The Ensayo albums, all recorded in Barcelona, feature Tete in congenial local company and offer some of his most relaxed playing. *Temas Brasilenos* is based around four long medleys of choice material by Jobim, Barroso and others, and there are unusual touches on well-worn tunes like 'La Chica De Ipanema' and 'Desafinado' to refresh jaded ears. *Boleros* is a set of Spanish compositions and as such is a rarity in Montoliu's discography. But the problem with both discs is the unimaginative rhythm section in each case, and neither is especially well recorded. *Blues For Myself*, a set of five blues and two standards, is marginally ahead, with Peter and Wyboris reading Montoliu's moves ably enough, though again the Steeplechase sets offer better work. *Words Of Love* is a sound if finally unremarkable solo session from the same period.

***** Boston Concert**
Steeplechase SCCD 31152 *Montoliu (p solo).* 3/80.

***** I Want To Talk About You**
Steeplechase SCCD 31137 *Montoliu; George Mraz (b); Al Foster (d).* 3/80.

***** Catalonian Nights: Volume 1**
Steeplechase SCCD 31148 *Montoliu; John Heard (b); Albert 'Tootie' Heath (d).* 5/80.

***** Catalonian Nights: Volume 2**
Steeplechase SCCD 31241 *As above.* 5/80.

***** Catalonian Nights: Volume 3**
Steeplechase SCCD 31433 *As above.* 5/80.

Another year that turned out to be a busy one. Mraz and Foster weren't Tete's ideal rhythm section but they don't get in his way too much, and the solo concert from Boston includes some of his most detailed and handsome playing. The concert session on the *Catalonian Nights* discs makes up an exciting meeting, but it's let down by an indifferent balance – Montoliu is almost drowned out by Heath at times – and a suspiciously battered piano. The second disc is worth having for the almost ecstatically driving 'I'll Remember April', but the music maintains a high standard throughout. New is the third volume, which has a further quota of his grandstand playing, as well as a pleasing original in 'Jo Vull Que M'Acariciis'.

***** Face To Face**
Steeplechase SCCD 31185 *Montoliu; Niels-Henning Orsted Pedersen (b).* 4/82.

***** The Music I Like To Play: Volume 1**
Soul Note 121180-2 *Montoliu (p solo).* 12/86.

***** The Music I Like To Play: Volume 2**
Soul Note 121200-2 *As above.* 12/86.

***** The Music I Like To Play: Volume 3**
Soul Note 121230-2 *As above.* 1/90.

***** The Music I Like To Play: Volume 4**
Soul Note 121250-2 *As above.* 1/90.

Face To Face suffers slightly from the abundance of virtuosity on show, and occasionally there's a sense of each man cancelling out the other. Otherwise, though, there's some music-making which at moments verges on the ecstatic.

The Soul Notes remind that Montoliu tended throughout his career to get maximum mileage from each session. It should be noted here, though, that the two later volumes are from a later date. The difference is immediately apparent, not so much qualitatively as in the nature of his playing, which is much more percussive and direct. The earlier Soul Notes number among the most finished of Montoliu's albums, with a superior studio sound and one or two unexpected choices: Bobby Hutcherson's 'Little B's Poem', for instance, on the first record. But some routine improvisations betray that the pianist can defer to familiar patterns on some tunes that he knew a little too well. There's a nice smattering of Monk tunes on the latter pair and some ballads that have not previously figured in the Catalan's discography. Though it might seem a hefty investment to spring for all four, these are better value than most.

***** Sweet 'N' Lovely: Volume 1**
Fresh Sound FSR-CD 161 *Montoliu; Mundell Lowe (g).* 9/89.

***** Sweet 'N' Lovely: Volume 2**

Fresh Sound FSR-CD 162 *As above.* 9/89.

The clean and persuasive interplay here suggests a friendly empathy that makes this unlikely combination work out very well: Lowe keeps to his unassumingly skilful, swing-based style, and the ease with which it slips alongside Montoliu's playing suggests that the pianist is more of a conservative than his more ferocious moments suggest. Both discs were recorded on the same day and, as pleasing as they are, one will be enough for most listeners.

***** Music For Anna**

Mas I Mas 002 *Montoliu; Hein van de Geyn (b); Idris Muhammad (d).* 10/92.

Montoliu surfaced only rarely in the '90s, but this club set suggests that his playing lost little of its flash or surprise. The dramatic deconstruction of 'I'll Remember April' is a single example, but it's something he does at some point on most of the tunes on offer. As with Solal, the pianist's uncommon syntax has become a commonplace with the wider currency of his work via recordings, yet the impact of his most vivid improvising remains startling, and it's good to have this recent reminder. Sound is decent – Van de Geyn comes through strongly – though the piano itself sounds like a sometimes unresponsive instrument.

James Moody (born 1925)

TENOR, ALTO AND SOPRANO SAXOPHONES, FLUTE, VOCALS

'I'm In The Mood For Love' was a big hit for Moody after the war, in its turn inspiring one of the highlights of vocalese. Moody – and he prefers to be called that – was initially influenced by Lester Young, but he has utilized a harder and more abrasive tone since the '60s, as he responded to the challenge of younger players. Flute has from time to time been his major horn. In his 70s, his career has enjoyed a further resurgence.

****(*) James Moody 1948–1949**

Classics 1116 *Moody; Dave Burns, Elmon Wright, Trummy Young, Leppe Sundwall (t); Frank Hooks, Nat Peck(tb); Arne Domnérus, Ernie Henry, Red Allen (as); Don Byas, Sandy Scott (ts); Cecil Payne, Per Arne Croona (bs); James Forman, Art Simmons, Bernard Peiffer, Gösta Theselius (p); Nelson Boyd, Alvin Banks, Lucien Simoëns, Yngve Akerberg (b); Teddy Stewart, Clarence Terry, Ritchie Frost, Art Blakey, Anders Burman (d); Chano Pozo (perc, v); Al Edwards (v).* 10/48–10/49.

'Moody, just call me Moody,' he says to anyone who dares to use either 'Mr' or first name. Moody's affability and slightly zany vocals have led some to dismiss him as a lightweight. Even on the song with which he is now inextricably associated he demonstrates fine if unorthodox improvisational skills. His debut 'I'm In The Mood For Love', recorded with a Scandinavian group in 1949, was a big hit, establishing him as a bopper with a quirky sensibility and a sombre, tense side. Moody's distinctive sinuousness became even more obvious when he added soprano saxophone to his kit a little later in his career.

The first Classics CD works through his earliest name sessions. Eight titles for Blue Note are no more than average bop (by 'James Moody And His Modernists') from a line-up which the leader has little trouble in dominating (something very peculiar happens to the sound on one of Payne's baritone solos). After the second date he left for Europe, and the remaining sessions were cut in Lausanne, Zurich, Paris and Stockholm. Two titles have him trading gentlemanly solos with Don Byas, and the final date offers a pair of tracks with a Swedish sextet. None of this music is exactly immortal and, while Moody outclasses most of his surroundings, even he sounds slipshod here and there.

***** James Moody 1949–1950**

Classics 1169 *Moody; Ernie Royal (t); Ted Kelly, Nat Peck (tb); Arne Domnérus, Russell Procope (as); Jacques Dieval, Raymond Fol, Thore Swanerus, Gosta Theselius (p); Rolf Berg (g); Yngve Akerberg, Pierre Michelot, Emmanuel Soudieux (b); Anders Burman, Kenny Clarke, Richard Frost, Jack Noren (d); Annie Ross (v).* 49–50.

***** Moody's Blues**

Prestige 24228 *As above.* 49–50.

***** James Moody 1950–1951**

Classics 1263 *Moody; Ernie Royal (t); Leppe Sundwall (bt); Ted Kelly, Nat Peck (tb); Marshall Allen, Arne Domnérus, Hubert Fol (as); Carl Henrik Norin (ts); Lars Gullin (bs) Raymond Fol (p, cel); Rolf Larsson, Rafe Schecroun (p); Gunnar Almstedt, Alvin Banks, Wendell Marshall, Pierre Michelot (b); George Ballard, Benny Bennett, Anders Burman, Kenny Clarke (d).* 4/50–1/51.

Moody was in Europe for most of this period, working in France and Sweden, where he achieved considerable celebrity. Some of these sides were cut under Ernie Royal's leadership, which makes their inclusion slightly suspect under Classics' usually restrictive ethos. However, it's the saxophonist's gossamer-light tenor lines that distinguish these cuts, which overlap the two volumes. Most of the other material on 1263 was made in Paris or Stockholm with a variety of competent but hardly eye-opening bands. Arne Domnérus provides some interest on the 1949/1950 compilation, as he did on the earlier disc. This material is also available – with rather cleaner sound – on a Prestige reissue from 1999. The sound of Leppe Sundwall's bass trumpet is of interest on the 23 January 1951 cuts, but there's not much else to listen to except Moody's relaxed and unchallenged soloing. 'I Can't Get Started', from 9 October 1950, is a gem and worth the set on its own.

*****(*) Moody's Moods For Blues**

Original Jazz Classics OJC 1837 *Moody; Dave Burns (t); William Shepherd (tb); Pee Wee Moore (bs); Sadik Hakim, Jimmy Boyd (p); John Latham (b); Joe Harris, Clarence Johnson (d); Eddie Jefferson, Iona Wade (v).* 1, 4 & 9/54, 1/55.

*****(*) Hi Fi Party**

Original Jazz Classics OJC 1780 *Moody; Dave Burns (t); Bill Shepherd (tb); Numa Moore (bs); Jimmy Boyd (p); John Latham (b); Clarence Johnson (d); Eddie Jefferson (v).* 9/54.

*****(*) Wail, Moody, Wail**

Original Jazz Classics OJC 1791 *As above, except omit Jefferson.* 1, 8 & 12/55.

He's joined on *Hi Fi Party* and on the extra 'I Got The Blues' on *Moods* by Eddie Jefferson, who reworked a vocal version of the hit, thereby (allegedly) giving King Pleasure the idea for adding his own lyrics to bebop tunes. Moody has a strongly vocalized tone and frequently appears to shape a solo to the lyric of a tune rather than simply to the chords or the written melody, and that vocalized sound is perhaps more evident on his alto-playing, though he even adapts it later in his career to flute, using a 'legitimate' version of Roland Kirk's vocalization. The saxophonist was off the scene for much of the '70s, certainly as far as significant recording was concerned, and his reputation went into something of a decline. Without star names, though, both *Hi Fi Party* and the rather less gimmicky and straightahead *Wail* establish a strong, individual sound that deserves to be more widely known and that certainly stands up very strongly alongside later works.

***** Moody's Mood For Love**

Chess 051 823 2 *Moody; Johnny Coles, Donald Cole (t); Tate Houston (bs); Jimmy Boyd, Benny Golson (p); Johnny Latham (b); Clarence Johnston (d); Eddie Jefferson (v).* 12/56, 1/57.

Eddie Jefferson's classic vocalese response to 'I'm In The Mood For Love' is the main attraction on this buoyant and well-crafted set from Chicago. Moody alternates tenor and flute and plays with jovial skill, belying the dark shadows that were supposed to be stalking him at this period. The band was picked and produced to flatter the leader and Moody is the chief soloist, though Golson (on piano!) and Coles both have effective moments of their own. Briefly available on Jewel, this marks a welcome return for one of the happiest Moody sets; check out his playing on 'Billie's Bounce'.

***** Don't Look Away Now!**

Original Jazz Classics OJCCD 925 *Moody; Barry Harris (p); Bob Cranshaw (b); Alan Dawson (d); Eddie Jefferson (v).* 2/69.

It was relatively unusual at this time for Moody to steer clear of flute, but the defining item of this session is the saxophonist's last-ever recording with Eddie Jefferson, who turns up on 'Hey Herb! Where's Alpert!', not the best thing they ever did together, but an effective enough use of Eddie's vocal skills. Moody plays alto on 'When I Fall In Love' and 'Don't Look Away Now' and gives a superb performance on tenor on the long 'Hear Me'. There's a retread of 'Last Train From Overbrook', which will appeal to anyone who loves the song or who's hipped to Moody's extraordinary story of survival and growth. At just 40 minutes, one looks to more material, even if just a miscued alternative, but none is forthcoming. We have no idea how much – if any – of this session still lies in the vaults.

****(*) Blues And Other Colors**

Original Jazz Classics OJCCD 954 *Moody; Johnny Coles (t, flhn); Tom McIntosh, Britt Woodman (tb); Jimmy Buffington (frhn); Cecil Payne (bs); Joe Farrell (as, ob); Kenny Barron, Dick Katz (p); Sam T. Brown (g); Alfred Brown (vla); Charles McCracken, Kermit Moore (clo); Ron Carter, Ben Tucker (b); Connie Kay, Freddie Waits (d); Linda November (v).* 69.

For some reason, Moody decided to restrict himself to soprano and flute for this odd session. The nonet format, arranged by trombonist Tom McIntosh, gives the soloist a lot of harmonic support, and the strings are imaginatively deployed; even the tracks with vocalist Linda November are interesting, and 'Gone Are The Days' is an unexpected gem. It's not altogether surprising that Moody should have returned to soprano so rarely in future. It's a thin sound and only Duke's 'Main Stem', coming right at the start of the record, has much emotional resonance. At the opposite end, 'Old Folks' merely sounds clichéd; compare Charlie Parker's version with the Dave Lambert Singers.

***** The Teachers**

Sanctuary 81222 *Moody; Richard Meisterman, Jay Silva, Bob Summers, Jay Thomas (t); Michael Gibson (tb); John Hutson (vtb); Adam Ippolito (tba); Joe Brazil (ts); Bill Chelf, Mike Longo (p); Howie Wyeth (p, org); Paul Dickler, Steve McCord (g); Billy Elmiger, Clint Houston, Sam Jones, Peter Petruccelli (b); Barry Lazarowitz (d, perc); Freddie Waits, Chip White (d); Otis Smith (perc); Eddie Jefferson (v).* 70.

***** Heritage Hum / The Teachers**

Collectables 5617 *As above.* 70.

Teachers, just one of two very different albums Moody released in 1970, is ostensibly an extended tribute to those figures – musical and non-musical who inspired him. An eclectic bunch to be sure, including JFK, Martin Luther King, Malcolm X and the Beatles. The two albums (*Heritage Hum* is also available in the same reissue package) could hardly be more different, the first thick with production by Howie Wyeth and others, the second a quartet date with a crisper attack from the leader and much simpler lines. The album's every bit as varied, featuring some deeply felt things like Bill Chelf's 'Rest Sweetly, Brother Dove' and 'Unchained', alongside more skittish things like the Lennon–McCartney 'Hello Goodbye' and 'Travel On' and 'Parker's Mood', which see the quartet augmented by singer Eddie Jefferson, a significant reunion for Moody. Neither is a great album, though the small-group tracks from *Heritage Hum* are streets ahead of the bigger arrangements. As a sample of Moody's range and ability to juggle tones and moods, it's pretty good. Also available on the Collectables format, though it has one track fewer; for some reason 'Soul Searching' is missing.

***** Feelin' It Together**

Savoy 17276 *Moody; Kenny Barron (p); Larry Ridley (b); Freddie Waits (d).* 73.

Formerly on Muse, then from 1998 on Joel Dorn's short-lived reissue label 32 Jazz, this quartet session from 1973 has defied oblivion again, offering a further glimpse into Moody's overlooked work from the '70s. Again, Barron is on electric piano, an instrument he invested with considerable expressive personality; we're not too sure about the harpsichord switch, though. The redoubtable Waits does his thing at the kit as he did on a number of Moody dates from this time. Long versions of 'Anthropology' and 'Autumn Leaves' will attract standards lovers, but there are also two strong originals from the pianist and a helping of Jobim just to alter the swing a bit. It would be good to see some more of Moody's Muse catalogue back in circulation: *Never Again* from the previous year was his promise to stick to tenor and abandon the alto for ever. As *Feelin' It Together*, with its alto and flute features, bears out, it was promise made to be broken.

***** Timeless Aura**

Universe 52 *Moody; Joe Newman (t); Kenny Barron (p); Bob Cranshaw (b); Eddie Gladden (d).* 76.

Less 'of its time' than most of what appeared in the '70s, this is a set of graceful Moody solos built round initially unpromising material by producer Ed Bland. Though the album is a studio confection and doesn't suggest much of Moody's undiminished power in a live setting, it's immaculately done and the leader is heard clearly throughout, bright, burnished and spotlit. Moody's 'A Statement' opens the set and establishes certain agenda that aren't fully carried through in what follows. Bland's tunes are mostly funky, blues-based things: 'Pot Licka', 'Keep It

Greasy', and the more delicate 'Stefanie'. 'Funky Jazz Walk' is a Barron/Moody collaboration and one of the best things on the set. Kenny's playing, right in the middle of his electric period, is restrained and lyrical, even when the grooves are at their dirtiest. Cranshaw similarly revelled in this kind of thing.

***** Moody's Party**

Telarc 83382 *Moody; Arturo Sandoval (t); Grover Washington Jr (ss); Mulgrew Miller (p); Todd Coolman (b); Terri Lyne Carrington (d); Roy Ayers (v).* 3/95.

The old dog turned 70 with a party at the Blue Note, compèred by the one and only Bill Cosby. The seven tunes selected for release are pretty familiar, but with an unexpected emphasis on bebop classics: 'Groovin' High', 'Parker's Mood', 'Bebop'. Moody is in sparkling form on all his horns and rises to the guest appearances of Washington and Sandoval with just the right mixture of challenge and graciousness. A lively, uncomplicated record to mark a significant anniversary.

*****(*) Young At Heart**

Warner Bros 9362 46227 *Moody; Alex Sipiagin (t); Slide Hampton, Avi Leibovitz, Jack Schatz (tb); Dave Bargeron (tb, tba); Alan Cox, Timothy Malosh (f); Jerry Dodgion (f, af); Frank Wess (af, bf); Larry Goldings, Mulgrew Miller (p); Gil Goldstein (p, cel); Sara Cutler (hp); Todd Coolman (b); Billy Drummond (d).* 2/96.

At 70-plus, Moody entered what was to be his pomp, playing with a grace and confidence which blew away everything that had happened before. This tribute to Sinatra is hugely entertaining, but it's also one of the most thoughtful records in the Moody canon. Working with horns or with orchestra, he sounds absolutely on the case, with a relaxed, insouciant swing and the gentlest delivery you ever heard. He had been playing for half a century by this stage, and only a performer with that pedigree and those dues could possibly have delivered the solo he creates on 'The Song Is You' or manage the wistful splendour of 'It Was A Very Good Year', without sounding flat or ironic. Gil Goldstein's arrangements are *comme il faut*, note-perfect but also relaxed enough to suggest a live session. There might be too much emphasis on the orchestra on a couple of tracks, acoustically speaking, a rather overdone mix that blunts the impact of the basic quartet, but for the most part the sound is flawless.

****** Mainly Mancini**

Warner Bros 9 46626 *Moody; Gil Goldstein (ky); Todd Coolman (b); Terri Lyne Carrington (d).* 97.

While attending a tribute dinner to Ella Fitzgerald, Moody talked to Henry Mancini about the possibility of a songbook album and thereafter received in the mail a collection of scores, with some marked as the composer's special preferences. In the event, this is a posthumous celebration of Hank's great music, but it is none the less a true celebration. Working with a small group allows Moody to follow the line of a song with a concentration he has not often been permitted in recent years. 'Silver Streak' and 'Charade' are small masterpieces of harmonic improvisation and should be required listening for all wind players. Moody takes the vocal on 'Moon River' and '(I Love You And) Don't You Forget It', dispensable but curiously touching. As on the previous Warner Bros release, Goldstein has a major impact on the overall sound. Here, though, he demonstrates a rare touch as an accompanist, caressing the themes with a sensuous understanding. It's Moody one hears, though, full-voiced, philosophical and full of sly wit.

*****(*) Homage**

Savoy Jazz 17200 *Moody; David Hazeltine (p); Todd Coolman (b); Anthony Pinciotti (d).* 03.

As he approaches his 80th birthday, Moody shows no sign of slowing up or, worse still, hanging up his saxophones. The closing track, 'Love Was The Cause For All Good Things', is a reworking of a Kid Next Door rap which might seem inappropriate for a man of Moody's age, except when you think that his role in the framing of vocalese put him at the epicentre of an earlier craze. Most of the material is for quartet, with Hazeltine very much in charge and contributing one fine original, 'We All Love Moody'. There is, though, the delightful experiment of an arrangement of James Newton Howard's main title-sequence to the film version of *Glengarry Glen Ross*, the David Mamet play. Moody is here augmented by a larger wind ensemble, but it's the leader's voice that carries the track, as he does everything else. Joe Zawinul and Herbie Hancock both contribute to a celebratory liner note, and both deliver a tune, 'A Message To Moody' and 'Into The Shadows' respectively. The best thing on a thoroughly entertaining set – that hip-hop nonsense apart – is a version of Kenny Barron's 'And Then Again', testimony to Kenny's great gifts but also the lasting affection in which Moody is held.

Jemeel Moondoc (born 1951)

ALTO AND SOPRANO SAXOPHONES

Comparisons between Moondoc's alto style and those of Ornette Coleman, Marion Brown and Jimmy Lyons are useful as navigation lines, but they don't do justice to Moondoc's originality. A fiery player, but with much of Ornette's fragile vulnerability ...

***** Konstanze's Delight**

Soul Note 121041 *Moondoc; Roy Campbell (t); Khan Jamal (vib); William Parker (b); Dennis Charles (d); Ellen Christi (v).* 10/81.

***** Judy's Bounce**

Soul Note 121051 *Moondoc; Fred Hopkins (b); Ed Blackwell (d).* 11/81.

***** We Don't**

Eremite 43 *Moondoc; Dennis Charles (d).* 81.

*****(*) Nostalgia In Times Square**

Soul Note 121141 *Moondoc; Bern Nix (g); Ron Burton (p); William Parker (b); Dennis Charles (d).* 11/85.

It was Cecil Taylor who turned the young Moondoc on to modern jazz, and he's remained a devoted disciple ever since. His early group, Ensemble Muntu, which also included the ubiquitous William Parker, was very much in the Taylor mould, but Moondoc remained open to other influences as well. 'One For Ornette' on *Judy's Bounce* accounts for only the most obvious; his playing style sits somewhere between Ornette's country wail and Jimmy Lyons's street-corner preaching.

Konstanze's Delight consists of just three long pieces, the first of them an opportunity for the whole band to show its stuff. As so often in this context, Parker is the cement, setting off on a dark, seductive chant that gradually reels in Moondoc, Campbell and the underrated Jamal, who conjures up storms on this record. The two horns seem to be engaged in a game of one-on-one ball, chasing, dodging, body-checking and setting up half a dozen false climaxes before the whole thing unwinds. At longer than half an hour, it palls pretty seriously before time's up, but it's part of a live set and is doubtless pretty typical of what Moondoc was doing at the time. 'Chasin' The Moon' is high-octane stuff, a starring vehicle for Jamal and Christi.

Judy's Bounce was recorded only a month later, but it's a very different sound, reminiscent more than anything of Ornette's trio with David Izenzon and Charles Moffett. The Coleman tribute is based on an authentically simple march-based riff, over which Moondoc declaims like a man possessed. 'Echo In Blue' might be one of Ornette's dirges, except that it stays much closer to bebop harmonies. The opening 'Judy's Bounce' is terser and tighter, almost joyous, with Hopkins pushing things along at a brisk walk. The set closes as far out as Moondoc has been. 'Nimus' is one of Jupiter's shattered moons, and Moondoc responds to the idea with a lonely, plangent sound that might well serve as an interplanetary lament, one of his strongest ideas and a perfect vehicle for this particular trio.

We Don't was finally issued in 2003 and offers a further fascinating glimpse of Jemeel's '80s work. Saxophone and drums is a tough discipline, sanctified by John Coltrane's duets with Rashied Ali. These are harsher and more abstract sessions, and the more realistic parallel might be Ornette Coleman and Ed Blackwell. 'Judy's Bounce' is there again and sounds all the more interesting for the stripped-down format.

The last album of the group is interesting for the addition of a guitar-player and the abandonment of vibes for piano. It's certainly a conservative step and there's nothing on the set that really grabs attention. Nix is most closely associated with Ornette's Prime Time experiments, but he gets little chance to play outside an Ulmer-ish R&B groove, with a few abstract flourishes.

***** Tri-P-Let**
Eremite MTE01 *Moondoc; John Voigt (b); Laurence Cook (d).* 6/96.

***** Fire In The Valley**
Eremite MTE08 *As above.* 7/96.

Moondoc's absence from the recording spotlight has done nothing to damp down the fires. During recent years he has worked with the Jus Grew Orchestra, reviewed below. The trio represented on these two discs has been Moondoc's bread-and-butter group. *Tri-P-Let* pretty much carries on from work he was doing on *Judy's Bounce* and other earlier records. Inspired in almost equal measure by Ornette and Albert Ayler, it trades in fierce harmonic runs, bursting rhythms and intense, free-form essays like 'Improv. #61696', which was seemingly prompted by hearing Johnny Mbizo Dyani on a Kalaparush Maurice McIntyre record.

Recorded live at the Fire In The Valley Festival in Amherst, the latter of the pair is a tough, often abrasive and, to be honest, slightly unrelieved set which doesn't benefit from a recording that makes no effort to buff up the blunter edges. A single continuous piece plus minuscule encore, it gives a reasonable account of Moondoc's current position, which is not so very far from where he was last sighted. Voigt and Cook are unfamiliar names, and one can only imagine them slogging away at this uncompromising and slightly unfriendly music. Anyone who's already converted will find much to savour, even if only episodically. For the most part, though, this is a specialist item.

****** New World Pygmies**
Eremite MTE020 *Moondoc; William Parker (b).* 7/98.

This is Moondoc's first recorded encounter with bassist Parker since *Nostalgia In Times Square*, and is a revelatory moment in the saxophonist's recorded output. People talk about the conversational quality of duo performance, but this is more like twin preachers in the mission hall, playing hard priest, soft priest alternately, the one threatening brimstone, the other promising redemption. Most of the writing is by Parker and includes the magnificent 'Huey Sees A Rainbow' and 'Theme For Pelikan', as well as the brief, intense 'Another Angel Goes Home', a dedication to drummer Dennis Charles, whose presence would have made this record near-perfect.

Moondoc's playing is most convincing on the opening title-track and the encore. It's Parker who holds the attention most securely, a master musician who continues to develop by the session.

***** Spirit House**
Eremite MTE 029 *Moondoc; Roy Campbell (t, flhn); Lewis 'Flip' Barnes (t); Tyrone Hill, Steve Swell (tb); Zane Massey (ts); Michael Marcus (bs); Bern Nix (g); John Voigt (b); Codaryl Moffett (d).* 3/00.

***** Revolt Of The Negro Lawn Jockeys**
Eremite MTE 028 *Moondoc; Nathan Breedlove (t); Khan Jamal (vib); John Voigt (b); Codaryl Moffett (d).* 5/00.

***** All-Stars Live In Paris**
Cadence CJR 1151 *Moondoc; Roy Campbell (t); Zane Massey (ts); William Parker (b); Cody Moffett (d).* 3/99.

Moondoc's mergings of various free-jazz and more traditionally inflected post-bop sounds have been difficult to catch right in front of microphones, and both of these live sets have moments to enthrall, others to dismay. The quintet record offers three longish pieces, two more declamatory themes sandwiching a ballad, and, while the more upbeat music draws succour from some fine improvising, the ballad seems merely drear. *Spirit House* gives the Jus' Grew Orchestra its first full outing. Unfortunately, the live sound is inadequate, which takes some of the sting out of the cacophonous blues, 'Quick Pick', and befuddles the details in a couple of intriguingly conducted improvisations. That said, this is a bustling, often teeming music, brought vividly to life and, given a full and flattering sound, the tremendous blow-out of 'Spirit House' itself would really shake the timbers.

The All-Stars gig is another slightly shambolic affair, a more pared-down sound than the Jus' Grew orchestra and therefore a sharper and less filled-in sound. Much of the emphasis falls on the leader, but Massey's rugged tenor and Campbell's yelping trumpet make their presence felt as well.

***** New World Pygmies Vol. 2**
Eremite MTE 030/1 2CD *Moondoc; William Parker (b, bombard, gralle); Hamid Drake (d).* 11/00.

A repeat match with Parker across two gigs on successive days: Drake enters the fray on the first, cut at Chicago's Velvet Lounge. Parker does some magnificent work – his *arco* intro to 'New World Pygmies 11/05/00' is mesmerizing – and there's a sense that he adapts better to this kind of exposed, long-form improvising than does Moondoc, who sometimes seems to noodle (though it's intense noodling, for sure). The session with Drake inevitably benefits from the drummer's mighty presence which carries them through all the eastern skirling of this day's version of 'Pygmies'. An intermittently powerful document which, as with so much in an obsessively documented area, sometimes feels like too much has been taken down.

***** Live At The Vision Festival**

Ayler ayl 047 *Moondoc; Roy Campbell, Nathan Breedlove (t); Steve Swell, Tyrone Hill (tb); Zane Massey (ts); Michael Marcus (bs); Bern Nix (g); John Voight (b); Gerald Cleaver (d).* 6/01.

It's not clear whether Moondoc's Tentet and the Jus' Grew Orchestra are one and the same or differently configured outfits. This live set is recorded pretty much as it happened and delivered raw and immediate, though with clunky edits here and there. The music is fine and fiery and the shorter tracks 'Opulent Continuum' and 'Cosmic Tabernacle' are more successful than the sprawling 'Variations on a Riff'. The sound isn't exceptional but gives a faithful representation of Moondoc's philosophy.

Brew Moore (1924–73)

TENOR SAXOPHONE

A faithful Lester Young disciple, Moore played in New York in the '40s, in San Francisco in the '50s and in Europe in the '60s. He made comparatively few records and his career was interrupted by drink problems.

***** I Should Care**

Steeplechase SCCD 36019 *Moore; Atli Bjorn (p); Benny Nielsen (b); William Schiopffe (d).* 4/65.

Moore was a terrific but star-crossed tenor player, at his best as good as Getz and Sims but never able to get a career together as they did. He left only a small number of records behind him. The Steeplechase album is a surviving memento from a stay in Copenhagen: solid, but not quite Brew at his best. The city turned out to be his nemesis: Moore died when he fell down some stairs in Copenhagen in 1973.

Michael Moore (born 1954)

CLARINET, BASS CLARINET, ALTO SAXOPHONE, ETC.

Moore is based in Europe, where he has found a more sympathetic outlet for his demanding music. A brilliant composer as well as instrumentalist, he mixes structural elements with passages of complete freedom and non-tempered sounds. He is a member of Gerry Hemingway's quintet and of the neo-traditionalist Clusone 3.

*****(*) Home Game**

Ramboy 02 *Moore; Herb Robertson (t, c); Fred Hersch (p); Mark Helias (b); Gerry Hemingway (d).* 10/88.

***** Négligé**

Ramboy 04 *Moore; Alex Maguire (p); Ernst Reijseger (clo); Michael Vatcher (perc).* 12/89, 5/92.

***** Klezmokum**

Ramboy 07 *Moore; Larry Fishkind (tba); Burton Greene (p, perc); Roberto Haliffi (d, perc).* 92.

****** Chicoutimi**

Ramboy 06 *Moore; Fred Hersch (p); Mark Helias (b).* 9/93.

****** Bering**

Ramboy 11 *As above.*

*****(*) Tunes For Horn Guys**

Ramboy 08 *Moore; Wolter Wierbos (tb); Frank Gratkowski (as, bcl); Ab Baars, Tobias Delius (ts, cl).* 4, 5 & 8/95.

*****(*) Mount Olympus**

Ramboy 13 *Moore; Alex Maguire (p).* 98.

Ramboy is Moore's own label, named for his son (apparently R. A. Moore or some such) and largely dedicated to disseminating his own music. *Home Game* was recorded in New York City with an intriguing quintet which embraces the avant-garde and mainstream jazz. As ever, Robertson is a dominant presence, squally and lyrical by turns, with a fierce attack and a gentle edge to temper it. On the long 'Suburban Housewives', he and Moore interact in an unexpectedly complex way, weaving together wind figures which might almost come from a more formal conservatory piece. Everything points to the record being an attempt to recapture early and family memories, but it's not just this that suggests a seemingly improbable similarity to some of Charlie Haden's Quartet West recordings. The relation of bass, piano and horns, together with old-fashioned, swing-influenced drumming from Hemingway, is very much the same, and Moore's clarinet has never again sounded so Goodman-like. Hersch is the surprise package, a notably eclectic player who moves freely between idioms and genres but who always maintains a consistency of presence and expression.

On *Négligé* Moore has assembled another like-minded group with a similar balance of sound. Maguire is completely at ease in environments like these, and his own 'Sparky' and 'Epigram' sit at the heart of the disc. There are 15 tracks, offering a good initial sample of Moore's music. *Chicoutimi* and *Bering* are the ones to have, exquisitely executed and thoughtfully expressed, poised between modernist and mainstream, wacky and sentimental by turns. The latter is intriguing for its choice of material, which ranges from Irving Berlin's 'The Best Thing For You' (probably worked up with the Clusone 3), Wayne Shorter's 'Albatross', John Lewis's '2 Degrees East, 3 Degrees West', Theodorakis's 'Vradiazi' and Jimmy Rowles's 'The Peacocks'. Either of these records will delight.

Klezmokum is superficially reminiscent of Don Byron's Mickey Katz project, but Moore is both a more serious and a more humorous musician, so the blend of moods is altogether more satisfactory. 'Oy Tate S'iz Gut' is spot on: emotive, wry and so totally ironic that it sounds entirely sincere. The presence of the legendary Burton Greene guarantees interest, and the two rhythm players yomp along with enthusiasm.

Moore's saxophone work on *Tunes For Horn Guys* is sterling, but the real meat of this still quite slim output (more may be found on Ramboy and on other small labels) is on the trio album with Hersch and Helias, where Moore is able to work in a free but strictly controlled environment, trading on that dry but not unexpressive tone.

The duos with Alex Maguire open up a new dimension again, drawing on free improvisation but also on formal composition. The Englishman is a stunningly good player, robust and muscular, who sounds as if he is climbing Olympus by some heroically self-reliant route. Moore is as quizzically lyrical as ever, popping question marks and inverted commas on top of even the simplest melodies. A beautiful album.

*****(*) Jewels And Binoculars**
Ramboy 15 *Moore; Lindsay Horner (b); Michael Vatcher (d, perc).* 11 & 12/00.

Recent years have seen several improvising projects that use the work of Bob Dylan as source material. None is more thorough-going and more effective than this one by Moore. He has managed to capture perfectly the precarious equilibrium of lyricism and fierce anger in songs like 'Visions Of Johanna', 'I Pity The Poor Immigrant', 'Boots Of Spanish Leather' and 'With God On Our Side'. Moore himself has never sounded more like a singer (his wife Jodi Gilbert is a particularly fine exponent and one suspects he has deferred to her on many occasions) and his tone is richly vocalized, alternately sardonic and celebratory.

Though Michael brings on his clarinets, saxophone, melodica and bells, the basic instrumentation is stripped down and there is an intriguing tension between the familiar themes and the basic freebop idiom of the trio. This is a bold and mostly very effective disc which we can heartily recommend, whether or not you are a Zimmerman disciple.

*****(*) White Widow**
Ramboy 16 *Moore; Alex Maguire (p); Mark Helias (b); Han Bennink (d).* 1/01.

Some of the numbers here, like the opening 'Moffat', seem to be spontaneously improvised. This was a London session, recorded in a very good studio acoustic and the album is faithfully and warmly produced with a fullness of sound that suits all four players very well indeed. The longest piece is a suite of pieces by Maguire, all of them named after some Parmigiano association – cheese, ham, violets. There is nothing cheesey, hammy or artificially perfumed about any of them. Like all of Alex's work, it flows logically, intelligently and with unexpected wit, and rounds out a very effective and desirable modern jazz record. A live set from this same group would be most desirable.

Ralph Moore (born 1956)

TENOR AND SOPRANO SAXOPHONES

British-born Moore returned to America in his teens to live with his father. He turned from trumpet to saxophone and nourished an already impressive talent with a diet of hard bop. Coltrane is the most evident influence, but assimilated with a lightness of touch and tone that has characterized an impressive array of discs.

***** Round Trip**
Reservoir RSR CD 104 *Moore; Brian Lynch (t, flhn); Kevin Eubanks (g); Benny Green (p); Rufus Reid (b); Kenny Washington (d).* 12/85.

***** 623 C Street**
Criss Cross 1028 *Moore; David Kikoski (p); Buster Williams (b); Billy Hart (d).* 2/87.

*****(*) Rejuvenate!**
Criss Cross 1035 *Moore; Steve Turre (tb, conch); Mulgrew Miller (p); Peter Washington (b); Marvin 'Smitty' Smith (d).* 2/88.

Moore has always known who he is and where he is going, even if in the early days his self-confidence was not yet accompanied by much profundity. A hard-bopper in the approved retro style, he has demonstrated that there is still plenty of good music to squeeze out of the idiom. Moore does nothing to ironize it or spice it up with contemporary references (other, perhaps, than Kevin Eubanks's soupy guitar on parts of *Round Trip*, for which he also wrote the final track).

Rudy van Gelder has been engineering this kind of material for longer than even he cares to remember, and all the records are technically flawless. The performances are equally unexceptionable but may prove a little cool. Though his writing skills have sharpened considerably ('Josephine', 'C.R.M.' and 'Song For Soweto' on *Rejuvenate!*), he draws much of his material from piano-centred late bop – Bud Powell's 'Un Poco Loco' on *623 C Street* – though rarely anything as ambitious as Elmo Hope's inventively Monkish 'One Second, Please', which appears on a later record.

His soprano playing, restricted to 'Cecilia' and 'Christina' on *623 C Street*, still needs thinking out, and he seems to have some intonation and breath-control problems, neither of which are remotely evident in his supremely confident tenor playing. Moore has not been lucky with records of late, and to have a 1988 date as your most recent available session suggests an unwonted neglect.

Tony Moore

CELLO

Since the days of Oscar Pettiford the cello has become a much more familiar voice in jazz and improvisation. Moore's practice has always been located at the free end of the spectrum, but with much of Pettiford's rapidity of attack and tonal sureness. Recently, Moore has been involved in a new improvising unit, Kiln, shortly to record.

*****(*) Observations**
Matchless MRCD 22 *Moore (clo solo).* 8/93.

*****(*) Assessments And Translations**
Matchless MRCD 28 *Moore; Josep Vallribera (gesto-grafia).* 5/95.

According to a liner-note, the apparently abstract cover art is a detail of a portrait of Moore by the Catalan artist, Josep Vallribera. Putting together these 16 improvised 'observations' is a little like doing a jigsaw without the lid, and doing a jigsaw of a late Jackson Pollock at that. There is a strongly marked personality in every gesture, but even the longest and most discursive sections (only two exceed five minutes, four are less than two minutes) manage to be both lucid and elusive. Moore's use of extended techniques is less overt than Marie-France Uitti's, closer perhaps to another classically literate improviser with ties to Matchless, Rohan de Saram. As label founder Eddie Prévost perceptively suggests in his introduction, Moore's main focus of observation is the cello itself, which is observed historically, dialectically, and sometimes even subversively. Set these pieces alongside any of David Darling's ECM albums and the difference will immediately be evident. The results may, however, be less readily palatable and, though the performances were in many cases continuous, some listeners will want a little space round individual tracks.

Vallribera's contribution to the second album requires a tiny gloss: 'gesto-grafia' appears to be a method of non-notational scoring in which graphic gestures (Pollock again) are assessed and then translated into the extra-temporal dimension that music demands. These are very much longer and more developed pieces, just four of them on the CD. It may be that some listeners will find it easier to get a purchase on this second disc. Not that there is any commercial compromise on either.

Jason Moran (born 1975)

PIANO

A youthful New Yorker, Moran has come to prominence as the pianist with Greg Osby's current group, and here debuts as a Blue Note leader.

★★★(★) Soundtrack To Human Motion
Blue Note 97431-2 *Moran; Greg Osby (as, ss); Stefon Harris (vib); Lonnie Plaxico (b); Eric Harland (d).* 8/98.

That's *motion*, rather than emotion, and as another of Blue Note's family of young stars takes his turn in the limelight it's a hint that what he's about – as with many of the most interesting young players in this precinct – is the momentum and the dynamic of his music as much as its body-weight of 'feeling'. Pieces such as 'Gangsterism On Canvas' and 'Snake Stance', the opening two here, are self-consciously hip and trickily built, as if Moran was concerned that he might be seen not to present strong enough meat for a top dog like Osby to work on. The pianist isn't given to preening, though. The trio piece which comes next, 'Le Tombeau De Couperin/States Of Art', is thoughtful and generously lyrical without falling back on any sort of navel-gazing.

He has a lively imagination, for sure. He says that 'Retrograde' was 'created from an Andrew Hill piece playing backwards on my record player'. The tracks with Osby and Harris tend to be stolen from under him, since those players are so strong; so it's the three trio pieces that offer the most exposure for a style that's unexpectedly dignified and even grandmasterly: listen to the beautifully voiced lines of 'Release From Suffering'. The brief solo, 'Kinesics', is three fascinating minutes by itself. A compelling start overall.

★★★(★) Facing Left
Blue Note 23884-2 *Moran; Tarus Mateen (b); Nasheet Waits(d).* 99.

★★★★ Black Stars
Blue Note 32922-2 *As above, except add Sam Rivers (ss, ts, f, p).* 01.

The trio has built itself into a group of quite breathtaking empathy and intensity, although for *Facing Left* they were still feeling their way: 'Another One', a rather extraordinary piece that keeps changing its pace, sounds like it's giving Mateen and Waits some trouble. But Moran asks all sorts of questions of the listener as well as his fellow players. 'Wig Wise' dupes us into thinking it might almost be a Blue Note boogaloo, but it gets turned every which way after that. Moran's complexities can be hard to fathom, but it's an exhilarating departure from the piano-trio norm, for sure.

Black Stars brings off the coup of enlisting paterfamilias Sam Rivers into the trio's fold. His presence is almost a bonus in what's otherwise a hard, detailed, highly achieved trio record. Moran goes back to an ancient piece of Ellington, 'Kinda Dukish', and mingles it with his own here-and-now, 'Draw The Light Out' and 'Gangsterism On A River'. Where some pianists impose themselves on their material by spinning out ever more fanciful embroidery, Moran already seems to be seeking essences and irreducible core matter. Nothing here goes on for very long; every piece seems brilliantly finished.

★★★(★) Modernistic
Blue Note 39838-2 *Moran (p solo).* 4/02.

★★★★ Presents The Bandwagon
Blue Note 91893-2 *Moran; Tarus Mateen (b); Nasheet Waits (d).* 11/02.

Solo, Moran is free to go wherever he pleases, so he starts with James P. Johnson's 'You've Got To Be Modernistic' and goes as far forward (into the past) as Afrika Bambaataa's 'Planet Rock' ('from my own era'). One curious piece is 'Moran Tonk Circa 1936', executed on what sounds like a toy honky-tonk keyboard. Two more 'Gangsterism' pieces rub shoulders with 'Body And Soul'. Live, he's developed these pieces far beyond their duration on the record, which feels a bit curtailed, as if it were a notebook of ideas in progress. Pretty interesting notebook, though.

The trio return for *Presents The Bandwagon*. Refracted through Ellington, Johnson, Byard, Monk and Hill, Moran's playing sounds ever more like himself, even as it is populous with spirits from every part of the jazz past. Anyone who's been mesmerized by his playing around samples in a club situation will be delighted to find three such instances here, and it would spoil it for the reader if we were to reveal what they consist of. More 'traditionally', there is his interplay with Mateen and Waits, which seems to be moving through ever-higher levels as the records progress: the abundant dialogue of 'Another One' is but a single instance. Vital and essential.

Herb Morand (1905–52)

TRUMPET, VOCAL

Born in New Orleans, Morand started there but did most of his playing in Chicago, especially with the Harlem Hamfats. Returned to New Orleans in the '40s, ran his own group and performed with George Lewis.

★★★ Herb Morand 1949
American Music AMCD-9 *Morand; Louis Nelson (tb); Andrew Morgan (ts, cl); Albert Burbank (cl, v); Johnny St Cyr, Raymond Glapion (g); Austin Young, Eddie Dawson (b); Albert Jiles, Andrew Jefferson (d).* 5–7/49.

★★★ Herb Morand 1950/Paul Barabarin 1951
American Music AMCD-106 *Morand; Eddie Pierson (tb); Albert Burbank (cl); Lester Santiango (p); Louis James (b); Morris Morand (d).* 2/50.

Morand wasn't a typical New Orleans brassman and he sounds a little out of place with these old-school players, but his firm lead and terse solos give the music an extra ounce of assertiveness. Most of it comes from a session recorded by Bill Russell, a large part of it too long for 78s and heretofore unreleased, but there are four rough and exciting tracks recorded at a dance at Mama Lou's Lounge two months earlier. The sound is a little muffled throughout but all the players come through clearly enough.

The second CD is shared with a session under Paul Barbarin's leadership. Morand's seven tracks were made for Oren Blackstone's New Orleans label. Routines such as 'If You're A Viper' and 'Have You Seen My Kitty' hark back to his Harlem

Hamfats days, which slightly contradicts Barry Martyn's description of the music as 'an important session of the "old-time" style'. Either way it's a tough, enjoyable date, with Burbank in particular stealing solo honours.

Frank Morgan (born 1933)

ALTO SAXOPHONE

Morgan grew up in Minneapolis but began his career in the nascent West Coast bebop scene. Drug problems interrupted his progress but also froze his Parker-indebted saxophone style at somewhere around the year Bird died. A passionate improviser, he organizes his solos in a songful, highly logical way.

***** Gene Norman Presents Frank Morgan**

Fresh Sound FSR CD 71 *Morgan; Conte Candoli (t); Wardell Gray (ts); Carl Perkins (p); Wild Bill Davis (org); Howard Roberts (g); Bobby Rodriguez, Leroy Vinnegar (b); Jose Mangual, Lawrence Marable (d); Ralph Miranda, Uba Nieto (perc).* 55.

Frank Morgan's story is not just about paid dues. Shortly after this record was made he was sentenced to a term in San Quentin for drug offences. He maintained his involvement in music while in jail, jamming with the likes of Art Pepper. Though he had worked locally following his release, he reappeared on a wider stage in the mid-'80s, purveying a brand of chastened bop, his initially bright and Bird-feathered style only slightly dulled by a spell in the cage.

In the mid-'50s, he was one of a group of saxophonists who hung on Charlie Parker's coat-tails. The currently deleted Savoy sessions aren't the best place to pick up on what Morgan was doing at the time, partly because the material is relatively unfamiliar and partly because the dominant figure on the session is Milt Jackson, who is already thinking in new directions. The Fresh Sound CD is a much better place to begin, though the septet tracks with Wild Bill Davis and three Latin percussionists are a touch crude; 'I'll Remember April' succumbs almost completely. Wardell Gray lends his easy swing to 'My Old Flame', 'The Nearness Of You' and four other tracks, and Carl Perkins's bouncy clatter at the piano keeps the textures attractively ruffled. These were also Wardell Gray's last recordings before his untimely death (which may not have been drug-related as originally thought).

***** Easy Living**

Original Jazz Classics OJC 833 *Morgan; Cedar Walton (p); Tony Dumas (b); Billy Higgins (d).* 6/85.

After so long off the scene, it seems extraordinary that Morgan should have returned with something as confidently shaped and expressive as this. It's still some way short of the work he was to do in the later '80s, but of all Morgan's records *Easy Living* is least in thrall to the ghost of Charlie Parker, despite a wonderful version of 'Now's The Time'. Frank also picks up on material that had been written while he was away, tunes by Jobim ('Easy Living'), Wayne Shorter ('Yes And No') and Cedar Walton ('Third Street Blues'). A remarkable comeback, tougher and more pointed than the records that followed.

***** Major Changes**

Contemporary 14039 *Morgan; McCoy Tyner (p); Avery Sharpe (b); Louis Hayes (d).* 4/87.

Modern recording makes his sound more intimate – grainier, anyway – so there's no reason to suppose that occasional huskiness is especially significant. What *is* noticeable, even with closely focused recording, is that he has grown quieter and more reflective. He seems rather hung up on favourite ballads. McCoy Tyner, himself a great romantic, provides the focus of *Major Changes* and looks after him well.

***** Yardbird Suite**

Original Jazz Classics OJC 1060 *Morgan; Mulgrew Miller (p); Ron Carter (b); Al Foster (d).* 11/88.

*****(*) Reflections**

Original Jazz Classics OJC 1046 *Morgan; Joe Henderson (ts); Bobby Hutcherson (vib); Mulgrew Miller (p); Ron Carter (b); Al Foster (d).* 89.

Probably the best of the comeback albums is the complex *Reflections*. The straight-shooting thing Morgan does with Joe Henderson nudges him into a different gear, sometimes reminiscent of Jackie McLean, sometimes – unexpectedly – of Lou Donaldson. Of all the pianists Morgan has worked with since his return, though, Miller is the least sympathetic, ironically because he is not forceful enough. He sounds much too respectful on *Yardbird Suite*; at this point in time, isn't it legitimate to interrogate that material a bit more vigorously?

Lee Morgan (1938–72)

TRUMPET

Like fellow-trumpeters Fats Navarro, Booker Little and Clifford Brown before him, Lee Morgan lived fast and died young. He is arguably the defining figure of hard bop. Born in Philadelphia, he played with the Messengers and, at first in parallel and later as a solo artist, embarked on a long series of tight, vociferous solo sessions on which his punchy, out-of-kilter phrasing is always the main component. Though he is scarcely underdocumented, Morgan's early death was a serious loss to jazz.

***** The Birth Of Hard Bop**

Savoy Jazz 17072 2CD *Morgan; Donald Byrd (t); John LaPorta (as); Hank Mobley (ts); Ronnie Ball, Barry Harris, Hank Jones, Horace Silver (p); Wendell Marshall, Doug Watkins (b); Kenny Clarke, Arthur Taylor (d).* 11/56.

***** Dizzy Atmosphere**

Original Jazz Classics OJCCD 1762 *Morgan; Al Grey (tb); Billy Mitchell (ts); Billy Root (bs); Wynton Kelly (p); Paul West (b); Charli Persip (d).* 2/57.

Though he gets the month wrong, David H. Rosenthal's history of *Hard Bop* gives central symbolic place to the death of Lee Morgan, victim not of overdose or car crash like so many of his peers, but murdered by a jealous girlfriend. If Morgan's passing in 1972 felt like the end of an era in jazz, it was an era he can certainly claim to have helped define. Masaya Matsumara's painstaking website discography lists 151 sessions at which Morgan was present. We would not presume to suggest there were more, but there were certainly umpteen undocumented live dates in that same 16-year period, a prodigious outpouring of music. In 'The Sidewinder' he created what may usefully stand as the representative hard-bop tune. If he was to repeat the formula to the point of redundancy in years to come, he had the justification of having shaped the formula in the first place.

The early material on Savoy was mostly recorded under Hank Mobley's leadership and Donald Byrd is featured on the first half of the reissue. However, there are enough examples of the 18-year-old Morgan on the set, including a superb 'Hank's Shout' and 'Bet' to make it worthy of inclusion in the discography. As an introduction to this corner of hard bop, it's a very attractive option.

Morgan was one of the very few top-flight players to adopt former boss Dizzy's trademark 'bent' trumpet. It's only the most obvious gesture of homage to the other player, who made a big impact on his playing style. This tribute band, which seems to have been called Dizzy Atmosphere, balances him on top of a substantial front line, skiting ideas around like a superball on string. The release of alternative takes on the CD gave a reasonable indication of how Morgan rethought his solo approach. 'Whisper Not' is a particularly good example, a subtle reworking which on the issued take 5 has a much sharper and more emphatic delivery. This is not a classic album by any stretch of the imagination. It gives a good indication of what the young man was capable of and where he came from stylistically. Beyond that, it is only intermittently engaging.

*** Candy

Blue Note 46508 *Morgan; Sonny Clark (p); Doug Watkins (b); Art Taylor (d).* 11/57, 2/58.

Recorded around the time the 20-year-old graduated from section duties with Dizzy Gillespie's group to featured soloist with the Jazz Messengers (with whom he was to record two classics, *Moanin'* and *A Night In Tunisia*), these quartet sessions have an attractive frosting of arrogance that doesn't quite disguise a callow romanticism on things like Buddy Johnson's 'Since I Fell For You' and 'Who Do You Love'.

*** Expoobident

Vee Jay VJ008 *Morgan; Eddie Higgins (p); Art Davis (b); Art Blakey (d).* 2/60.

*** Here's Lee Morgan

Vee Jay 30050 *Morgan; Clifford Jordan (ts); Wynton Kelly (p); Paul Chambers (b); Art Blakey (d).* 2/60.

A nice 21st present for the trumpeter: a session that most casual listeners will assume is a Messengers gig. Morgan's open, declamatory horn is always to the fore, at its best when the blues are the lingua franca, but equally at ease with the more lateral harmony of Shorter's 'Running Brook'. The original LP has been augmented with a number of alternative takes, notably of the opening 'Terrible T', and there is additional material from this and from an October 1960 date on *Here's Lee Morgan*. Buyers of another reissue on Le Jazz have a different combination of tracks. For Morgan enthusiasts and hard-bop scholars, this is doubtless a plus. For the majority of listeners, though, the additional material might well seem to blunt a tough, terse album, and they may choose to skip it. A useful reissue of the Vee Jay disc, all the same.

*** Lee-Way

Blue Note 40031 *Morgan; Jackie McLean (as); Bobby Timmons (p); Paul Chambers (b); Art Blakey (d).* 4/60.

One of the least known of Morgan albums even among his fans, this was a relatively late reissue. This is surprising given how good it is. Morgan sounds relaxed and soulful on four long tracks, ably supported by Jackie McLean, who contributes 'Midtown Blues'. There are also two Cal Massey numbers, further testimony to his once-high standing; of these, 'Nakatini Suite' at the end of the set is probably too rarefied for this context and company, though the other, 'These Are Soulful Days', is inch-perfect and brings out the best in Morgan. The trumpeter includes a blues of his own, dedicated to Blue Note bosses Alfred Lion and Francis Wolff. The gesture obviously stood him in good stead; the label was to be his regular berth for much of the rest of his life.

*** Take Twelve

Original Jazz Classics OJCCD 310 *Morgan; Clifford Jordan (ts); Barry Harris (p); Bob Cranshaw (b); Louis Hayes (d).* 1/62.

The years 1958 to 1961 were taken up mostly with Messengers duties, though Morgan also fitted in sessions for Ernie Henry, Curtis Fuller and fellow-Messenger Wayne Shorter. His own *Expoobident*, taped in October 1960, was a rare date as leader in this period. *Take Twelve* originally appeared on Jazzland, and it's one of the first places where one can assess Morgan the composer. It also offers evidence that he was developing as a performer as well, ironically by turning back to the work of older figures like Rex Stewart (who wrote the book on half-valving) and Roy Eldridge. 'Raggedy Ann', 'Lee-Sure Time' and 'A Waltz For Fran' all come pretty much from the basic lode: driven, blues-inflected themes with a brisk bounce. Hayes is a less dominant player than Blakey and he leaves more room for Morgan to develop his blues phrasing asymmetrically and with occasional unexpected nods in the direction of polytonality. Compositions like Elmo Hope's title-track suggest that Morgan was looking for something more than orthodox 'hard bop'. What was to follow the next year more or less guaranteed that he would never break the mould.

CORE COLLECTION

♛ **** The Sidewinder

Blue Note 95332 *Morgan; Joe Henderson (ts); Barry Harris (p); Bob Cranshaw (b); Billy Higgins (d).* 12/63.

The title-track was written in the heads towards the end of the session, a glorious 24-bar theme as sinuous and stinging as the beast of the title. It was both the best and the worst thing that was ever to happen to Morgan before the awful events of 19 February 1972. 'The Sidewinder' was an instant jazz hit, one of those themes, like 'So What', that insinuate themselves into the subconscious and remain there for ever. Unfortunately, it also established a more or less unbreakable pattern for future LPs, a bold, funky opener – often with a title intended to recall 'Sidewinder' – followed by half a dozen forgettable blowing themes, or, if you were lucky, another swinger to kick off the second side. The other pieces on the record have never been acknowledged to the same degree, but 'Totem Pole' and the superb 'Hocus Pocus' are the best available evidence for Morgan's gifts as a writer: vivid, often unexpectedly angled themes with every potential for extended blowing and not just off the back of a few algebraic chords. Of the other members of the group, Henderson stands out for his solo on the title-track and on 'Hocus Pocus'. Harris is rock solid from start to finish, and the bass-and-drums team can hardly be faulted.

★★★★ Search For The New Land

Blue Note 84169 *Morgan; Wayne Shorter (ts); Herbie Hancock (p); Grant Green (g); Reggie Workman (b); Billy Higgins (d).* 2/64.

This is the exception. Though much of Morgan's output for Blue Note after 1962 was pretty formulaic, *Search* was a musical exploration as much as a programmatic one. The presence of Shorter and Hancock guaranteed a measure of lyrical unpredictability, which is immediately registered on the title-piece. 'The Joker' might be thought to be the 'Sidewinder' piece this time around, except that it's a darkly playful, rather treacherous idea built on altered chords, and certainly not a theme that encourages a relaxed or lazy approach. Workman fits into this context particularly well, and the hyperactive Higgins drills away without a pause. 'Mr Kenyatta' may point towards one possible new inspiration for Morgan's music, though the two remaining numbers, albeit more than makeweights, are more off-the-peg: 'Melancholee' is a tight, bluesy ballad and 'Morgan the Pirate' another fairly orthodox improvising tune. A fine, questing record, and a pity that – *The Gigolo* apart – there weren't to be more like it. The latest release contains some bonus tracks, though nothing that prompts a wholesale reassessment of an already surprising set.

★★(★) Tom Cat

Blue Note 84446 *Morgan; Curtis Fuller (tb); Jackie McLean (as); McCoy Tyner (p); Bob Cranshaw (b); Art Blakey (d).* 8/64.

With complete absence of irony, the final track is 'Rigor Mortis', for this is the least distinguished of Morgan's Blue Notes, and one of the very few that doesn't manage to lift itself even for a couple of tracks. The three-horn front line sounds cluttered, despite some great episodic playing from Fuller and McLean. The fault lies not so much with the pristine Van Gelder recording as with the arrangements, which have no air in them.

★★★ The Rumproller

Blue Note 21229 *Morgan; Joe Henderson (ts); Ronnie Mathews (p); Victor Sproles (b); Billy Higgins (d).* 4/65.

A fairly transparent attempt to recapture the commercial success of *The Sidewinder*. The only obvious drawback is the lack of a theme with quite that sinuous memorability. This time, the composer is Andrew Hill, though 'The Rumproller' isn't quite the dark and brooding theme one associates with Hill. Either way, it didn't catch as the earlier album had and though it's been in catalogue pretty consistently, and is now available in a Rudy Van Gelder edition, it's hard to treat it with the same affection. Morgan was recording regularly at this point and playing with almost insulting ease. His solo on the bossa nova 'Eclipso' (an original) is as laid back as it's possible to be and still maintain an embouchure. Two Wayne Shorter tunes help fill out the package, and Joe Henderson rises to his fellow saxophonist's challenge on both of them.

★★★(★) The Gigolo

Blue Note 84212 *Morgan; Wayne Shorter (ts); Harold Mabern (p); Bob Cranshaw (b); Billy Higgins (d).* 6 & 7/65.

★★★ Cornbread

Blue Note 84222 *Morgan; Jackie McLean (as); Hank Mobley (ts); Herbie Hancock (p); Larry Ridley (b); Billy Higgins (d).* 9/65.

★★(★) Infinity

Blue Note 97504 *Morgan; Jackie McLean (as); Larry Willis (p); Reggie Workman (b); Billy Higgins (d).* 11/65.

The Gigolo is relatively unusual at this point for the inclusion of a standard – 'You Go To My Head' – but again Morgan seems to be trying to pull himself at least halfway free of the coils of *The Sidewinder*. Mabern is a strong, funky player, ably supported by Cranshaw, but Shorter keeps things broken up and unpredictable. 'Yes I Can, No You Can't' plays a brisk game of musical catch, while 'Speedball', which was to become a live favourite, pushes at the limits of orthodox hard bop. The title-piece is a slinky and seductive tune, one of the better compositions of recent years in this idiom.

Cornbread is production-line Morgan, no more inspired than that. With the exception of 'Ill Wind', all the tunes are the trumpeter's and, with the exception of 'Ceora', most of them pretty forgettable. Morgan still sounds brash, brassy and full-toned, but the urgency has gone out of his playing and he seems to rely more and more on predigested licks. They're still a lot more compelling than most of his peers', but they are too conventionalized to be involving.

Infinity is no less generic and formulaic, but by this point Morgan was so utterly confident that one tends to forget that most of these ideas are already well trodden. The title-track is overlong and a touch lumpy and it's only Jackie McLean's 'Portrait Of Doll' that changes the tonality by a degree or two.

★★★ Charisma

Blue Note 59961 *Morgan; Jackie McLean (as); Hank Mobley (ts); Cedar Walton (p); Paul Chambers (b); Billy Higgins (d).* 9/66.

By this point in his career, Morgan seemed to be on tramlines, writing and performing with an untroubled self-confidence that rarely deviated off course, and yet there are signs that he has sniffed the coming of fusion jazz grazing and taking on water just over the skyline. *Charisma* is the most formulaic of the Blue Notes, lifted by the delightful 'Rainy Night', a Cedar Walton composition, and including a bouncy version of Duke Pearson's 'Sweet Honey Bee'. The two saxophone-players are in excellent form. If Herb Wong's 'original liner-notes' are really that, then this set wasn't released until 1969, when Paul Chambers was no more. It may be that Blue Note were stockpiled with Morgan material and there wasn't slack in the market for any more.

★★★ Sonic Boom

Blue Note 90414 *Morgan; Julian Priester (tb); George Coleman, David Newman (ts); Harold Mabern, Cedar Walton (p); Walter Booker, Ron Carter (b); Billy Higgins, Mickey Roker (d).* 4/67, 10/69.

Because Blue Note had over-invested in falling stock where Morgan was concerned, *Sonic Boom* wasn't released until seven years after the trumpeter's sudden death. It's not altogether hard to see why. By any standard it's no better than workmanlike and most of Lee's solos are either cursory or slightly muddled. Also, Fathead Newman is something of an acquired taste, certainly when compared to other saxophonists of the period. For the later and ironically better session, most of it also unreleased, Morgan has the benefit of George Coleman's harmonic brilliance. His composition 'Free Flow' is one of the most advanced lines Morgan ever put his horn to and it almost comes off, certainly more interesting than the 'Untitled Boogaloo' that rounds the album out. The two groups – Newman, Walton, Carter, Higgins and Priester, Coleman, Mabern, Booker and Roker – could easily be divided and spliced to make one extraordinary line-up, with Walton, Carter and Higgins drafted in behind the 1969 horns who reappear on *The Procrastinator*, below. That would have been worth hearing. As it is, this is a slack and disappointing record, only for devoted Morganites.

*** The Procrastinator

Blue Note 33579 *Morgan; Julian Priester (tb); George Coleman, Wayne Shorter (ts); Herbie Hancock (p); Bobby Hutcherson (vib); Walter Booker (b); Billy Higgins, Mickey Roker (d).* 7/67.

*** The Sixth Sense

Blue Note 22467 *Morgan; Jackie McLean, Frank Mitchell (as); Harold Mabern, Cedar Walton (p); Victor Sproles (b); Billy Higgins (d).* 7/67.

The music on *The Procrastinator* isn't so very radical, and yet it was deemed sufficiently outside the market standard to justify holding it back for two years before release. Some of this material has found its way onto the augmented *Sonic Boom*. Morgan was never dully formulaic, but it would take a seasoned listener or a dedicated Morgan fan to distinguish this from any other album of the period. *The Sixth Sense* is virtually unknown, even by Morgan fans. Almost axiomatically of albums from this period, it sounds like the work of an artist who has heard the future and is anxious to make it work. On 'Psychedelic' and 'Leebop', and on the Cal Massey tune, 'City Of My People', Morgan is nudging at the frangible boundaries of hard bop, which was always one of those categories that were more useful than significant. The recorded sound has also got funkier and more rock-orientated, with extra weight on the bass and a hefty backbeat.

*** Taru

Blue Note 22670 *Morgan; Bennie Maupin (ts); John Hicks (p); George Benson (g); Reggie Workman (b); Billy Higgins (d).* 2/68.

*** Caramba

Blue Note 53358 *Morgan; Bennie Maupin (ts); Cedar Walton (p); Reggie Workman (b); Billy Higgins (d).* 5/68.

Taru is certainly only an inch away from the kind of stuff with which Miles Davis was to revolutionize jazz in the next couple of years. The presence of George Benson has something to do with it, and underneath his smooth and unguent approach there is a whiff of cold steel. The recruitment of Maupin to Morgan's group was to be a significant one. After Shorter, he was perhaps the most adventurous saxophonist Morgan was to work with. Often dismissed as a colourist with no real jazz centre, Maupin always sounds completely convincing in the trumpeter's company. Among the tracks on *Caramba*, on 'Suicide City', 'Helen's Ritual' and another Cal Massey song, 'A Baby's Smile', he brings a dark-toned eloquence which fits the bill exactly. Morgan himself is more reticent than in the past and, one suspects, short on new angles.

***(*) Standards

Blue Note 23213 *Morgan; James Spaulding (f, as); Wayne Shorter (ts); Pepper Adams (bs); Herbie Hancock (p); Ron Carter (b); Mickey Roker (d).* 1/67.

A lovely – in some regards unexpected – record from a vintage group. The combination of Morgan and Shorter was always an unlikely one, the driving, linear approach of the trumpeter pitched against the more lateral and enigmatic musings of the saxophonist. Spaulding and Adams glue it all together, and Hancock is absolutely on the case throughout. Marked out by its choice of material, which includes a glorious version of Tim Hardin's 'If I Were A Carpenter' and a yearning but tough-minded reading of the Sondheim–Bernstein 'Somewhere', this is playing of the highest order. It also serves as a reminder of what an excellent drummer Mickey Roker is. Like Grady Tate, one almost expects him to break into song at any moment. One to watch out for.

*** Blue Breakbeats

Blue Note 94704 *Morgan; Jackie McLean (as); Bennie Maupin, Hank Mobley (ts); Herbie Hancock, Barry Harris, McCoy Tyner, Cedar Walton (p); Bob Cranshaw, Reggie Workman (b); Billy Higgins (d).* 63–68.

Morgan was one of many artists whose work found a new audience with the rise of acid jazz and rare groove. These selections are very much with that market in mind, bringing together 'The Sidewinder', 'Cornbread', 'Caramba' and 'Nite Flight'. Superb party fare, but if you have the originals you can make your own party tape.

*** Live In Baltimore

Fresh Sound FSR CD 1037 *Morgan; Clifford Jordan (ts); John Hicks (p); Reggie Workman (b); Ed Blackwell (d).* 7/68.

Jordan claimed joint leadership and, in the event, dominates proceedings with his strong sound and bearish impact. For a change, there are no Morgan originals in the set. 'Straight, No Chaser' is the most compelling single performance, a vigorous reading from both the horns. 'Like Someone In Love' is a little lacking in definition and emotional resonance, and Miles's 'Solar' lacks sophistication. On the other hand, this must have been a great band to encounter live, and the patrons of the Royal Arms in Baltimore must have gone home happy.

***(*) Live At The Lighthouse

Fresh Sound FSRCD 140/141 2CD *Morgan; Bennie Maupin (ts); Harold Mabern (p); Jymie Merritt (b); Mickey Roker (d).* 6/70.

**** Live At The Lighthouse

Blue Note 35228 3CD *As above, except add Jack DeJohnette (d).* 7/70.

***(*) We Remember You

Fresh Sound FSR CD 1024 *Morgan; Jimmy Heath (ts); Billy Harper (ts, f); Barry Harris, Harold Mabern (p); Spanky DeBrest, Jymie Merritt (b); Albert 'Tootie' Heath, Freddie Waits (d).* 11/62, 1/72.

The Fresh Sound live set is misnamed. For a long time it was believed that it consisted of material excluded from Blue Note's *Live At The Lighthouse* release, when it fact it was recorded some time earlier at a club called the Both/And. Some of the material from the same session appeared on a disc called *Speedball* which was issued in Japan, but the Spanish issue is pretty decent, sharing a few technical shortcomings with the official Blue Note release from the Lighthouse, but bringing together a lot of good live stuff. At this stage in the game, Morgan was doubling on flugelhorn, perhaps looking for a richer, fatter sound. It isn't always possible to tell what horn he's on, which is some testimony to his razor-sharp accuracy and the hardness of his tone.

DeJohnette is the guest drummer on 'Speedball' on the official Blue Note release, and his brisk, contemporary sound points to some of the directions the trumpeter might have followed had he been allowed another few years of activity. Certainly Jack offers rhythmic possibilities which are not available elsewhere. Maupin's 'Peyote' and an extended version of 'The Sidewinder' are stand-outs. There seems to be some confusion between 'Meo Felia' (credited to Morgan) and 'Neophilia' (which is ostensibly a Maupin composition) and between 'Ujamma' on Fresh Sound and 'Meo Felia'. Both sets are compromised by technical shortcomings, with some drop-outs on the Blue Note, and one track on which the tape obviously ran out just before the finish. There are also some problems with the sound. The piano was pre-balanced and couldn't be altered, and there are some places where the bass seems to disappear. Blue Note seem to have been motivated by the existence – and the success – of bootleg sets from around this time to put the whole thing out, warts and all, and, given the quality of the music, who can blame them?

All the more reason to release it, when there was to be just one more session for the label, in September 1971. Thereafter, Morgan recorded with flautist Bobbi Humphrey and, a mere two days before his death, with Charles Earland's orchestra. In January 1972 he was playing with Billy Harper, Mabern, Merritt and Freddie Waits, a set that included a fine latter-day version of 'The Sidewinder'. Not enough material for a whole disc, so Fresh Sound, whose provenances aren't always immaculate, have added three items from almost a decade before, a band co-fronted by Jimmy Heath. It isn't quite the headstone Morgan deserves, but it does provide an insight into the changes in his playing style over ten years. Something mellower and more thoughtful has crept in, something almost vulnerable. Underneath the incendiary nature, a more reserved individual.

*****(*) The Last Session**

Blue Note 493401 *Morgan; Grachan Moncur III (tb); Billy Harper (ts, af); Bobbi Humphrey (f); Harold Mabern (p); Reggie Workman (b, perc); Freddie Waits (d, perc).* 9/71.

Originally released as a double album called simply *Lee Morgan*, this captured a young man trying to find a new direction, to push out beyond the borders of hard bop. It's a big and rangy group sound with the addition of Moncur and Humphrey and with the talented Harper, composer of 'Capra Black' (which occupied the original side one) and 'Croquet Ballet', coming on very powerfully. Though very similar to the band which played at the Lighthouse, this is much more modern in focus; the title 'In What Direction Are You Headed?', written by Mabern, is quite readily directed at both Morgan and the music, for at this point he seems determined to try out a harmonic direction which is close to what Coltrane was doing a few years before he died. Harper is less of a colour player than Bennie Maupin, but he is certainly not a one-dimensional bopper, and almost all his solo spots are engagingly lateral. Freddie Waits is also a great revelation, a freely swinging but never mechanical stylist whose composition, 'Inner Passions Out', is the most radical thing on the record, and one of the most 'out' pieces Morgan ever recorded under his own name.

On 19 February 1972, Lee Morgan was shot dead by Helen More as he relaxed between sets at Slugs Saloon in New York City. For some at least, a whole generation in jazz-playing was brought to an abrupt and tragic end.

Sam Morgan (1887–1936)

CORNET, VOCAL

Morgan led one of the classic New Orleans bands of the '20s, and their records are historically important as well as enduringly powerful. Illness forced him out of the busines in 1932.

♛ ** Papa Celestin & Sam Morgan**

Azure AZ-CD-12 *Morgan; Ike Morgan (c); Jim Robinson (tb); Earl Fouche (as); Andrew Morgan (cl, ts); Tink Baptiste, O. C. Blancher (p); Johnny Davis (bj); Sidney Brown (b); Nolan Williams, Roy Evans (d).* 4–10/27.

The eight titles by Morgan's band are among the classics of '20s jazz. They are a very rare example of a New Orleans group recorded in the city during this period, and it's been claimed that these are the most truthful recordings of how such a band sounded in its prime. Morgan's music is ensemble-based, solos and breaks threaded into the overall fabric, the playing driven by the gusty slap-bass of Sidney Brown. Fouche might be the outstanding player, with his mile-wide vibrato, but it's as a band that these players have endured. There are few more exhilarating records from the period than 'Steppin' On The Gas' or 'Mobile Stomp'. Together with the Celestin tracks, this makes up one of the most essential reissues of early jazz, in outstandingly fine sound.

Joe Morris (born 1955)

GUITAR

After a troubled childhood and adolescence, Morris found a means of self-expression. The Boston-based guitarist has a highly distinctive playing style, almost always in fast, single-note lines, with distinctive mid-phrase trills which may be influenced by saxophone-players. Morris rarely chords, unless one counts the rapid arpeggiations he builds into his more boppish ideas. His use of space is also characteristic, though his group improvisations rely heavily on dark accretions of sound.

***** Symbolic Gesture**

Soul Note 121204 *Morris; Nate McBride (b); Curt Newton (d).* 6/93.

***** Illuminate**

Leo Lab CD 008 *Morris; Rob Brown (as); William Parker (b); Jackson Krall (d).* 95.

****** No Vertigo**

Leo CD LR 226 *Morris (g, mand, banjouke solo).* 4/95.

A charter member of the Boston Improvisers' Group, Morris was an actively eclectic sideman and local star before he made it big as a recording artist. He has a facility for straight blues and fusion playing, but he works in a pumped-up free style that doesn't just put the emphasis on dynamics but also works in quite stark, abstract ways. The Soul Note is not a debut because Morris has put material out on his own Riti label for some time – though, alas, distribution is not exactly universal. As a first point of contact, it is slightly soft-centred, and it might be as well to move quickly on to *Illuminate* on Leo's radical Lab imprint, before coming to any settled conclusion. The quartet there is fresh and unclichéd, but comes off the back of saxophonist Brown's Riti session with Morris and other associations for different labels. A clangorous, unfussy record, it will appeal not just to guitar-trio fans (who may feel more comfortable with *Symbolic Gesture*) but also to those who don't like their free jazz too vegetarian and mild.

The best record of the three is the solo *No Vertigo*. Morris has obviously been influenced by British improviser Derek Bailey. His acoustic work is very reminiscent of Bailey's '70s work but with a hint of a jazz groove always hovering in the background, which Bailey seldom permits. He also includes tracks on an electric instrument (the long, very detailed 'For Adolphus Mica'), banjouke ('Long Carry') and even mandolin (a sequence called 'The Edges'). There is nothing slipshod about this music. Morris is a stern self-disciplinarian and the defining characteristic of the music on *Illuminate* is the responsiveness of the players to one another, a listening quality that extends not just to pitching but also to dynamics, rhythmic and para-rhythmic properties, even the use of space and (relative) silence.

★★★(★) Elsewhere

Homestead Records HMS233-2 *Morris; Matthew Shipp (p); William Parker (b); Whit Dickey (d).* 2/96.

The title-track was inspired by a sympathetic review of Morris's previous record and by the suggestion that music could take the listener to some super-real 'elsewhere'. Morris's dogged concentration on melody and his refusal to fall back on harmonic cushions and props is communicated to his three partners, all of whom also have a strong stake in this brand of rugged improvisation. Parker is, of course, already an established master and his contribution here is as calmly magisterial as always. Shipp occasionally sounds uneasy, but his great banging punctuations towards the end of 'Elsewhere' and his tremendous sense of structure are evident throughout, almost as if every phrase and every solo statement form the basis for some new, crystalline structure or architectural space; the pianist has often likened his own work to making buildings. Dickey is content to lay out here and there, perhaps with the sense that they are gravitating to his pulse. He doesn't so much keep time as generate new dimensions of it, within which the others can work. A still underrated talent, who will continue to make a mark.

★★★ You Be Me

Soul Note 121304 *Morris; Mat Maneri (vn); Nate McBride (b); Curt Newton (d).* 5/97.

We overlooked this in our last edition. In retrospect, it fits well into the development of Morris's musical language. Maneri's microtonal approach is an important component, though one feels that the bassist and drummer fulfil more conventional roles on this occasion. Four long themes, 'You Be Me', 'Adult Themes', 'The Object of Colour' and 'Real Reason', constitute the bulk of the set and one can hear in their construction something of Morris's long apprenticeship listening to open symphonic rehearsals and free performances in Boston.

★★★ Antennae

AUM Fidelity AUM 004 *Morris; Nate McBride (b); Jerome Dupree (d).* 7/97.

★★★(★) A Cloud Of Black Birds

AUM Fidelity AUM 009 *Morris; Mat Maneri (vn); Chris Lightcap (b); Jerome Dupree (d).* 6/98.

While Morris was attending a special school for troubled children in the Boston area, as he movingly relates, he spent a lot of time alone watching starlings flock and fly outside his bedroom window. Their movement – patterned, complex, only seemingly chaotic – made a great impression on Joe, and some of that experience comes out in the densely packed music on 'A Cloud Of Black Birds'. Reunion with Maneri sparks off a lot of shared experience, and their interaction, notably on the duo, 'Renascent', is close, intelligent and thoroughly sympathetic. The group tracks are inevitably denser in conception but no less powerful. The same language applies in the trio setting, except Morris is more obviously out front as a soloist. Here, Morris acknowledges a debt to the pianist and composer Lowell Davidson, whose advanced notational ideas involved colour imaging, use of light and extremes of concentration. The tracks on *Antennae* are among the most intense Morris has produced. He seems more inclined to dwell on notes and to explore the light and shade that gather between attack and delay. His use of upstrokes affects the sound significantly and he varies pressure on the strings to create subtle harmonic overtones which also emerge on the sessions with Maneri and are perhaps influenced by Mat's father Joe Maneri's theories on microtonality.

★★★ Like Rays

Knitting Factory 224 *Morris; Ken Vandermark (cl, bcl); Hans Poppel (p).* 98.

Hectic, clattering free improvisation with some interesting variations of texture. Morris's estranged vision has rarely been more intense and the presence of a second harmony instrument (albeit played rather unconventionally) allows him to range more widely than ever before. This time most of the pieces are quite short, which introduces an implication of structure even when there is none. Vandermark is a very impressive player, with a wide range of sonorities on his clarinets. Some of these pieces are dominated by him, to a degree that suggests the alphabetical listing of performers is no more than that and that this could usefully be reviewed as Ken's record.

★★★ Underthru

Omnitone 11904 *Morris; Mat Maneri (vn); Chris Lightcap (b); Gerald Cleaver (d).* 3/99.

★★★ Many Rings

Knitting Factory 243 *Morris; Rob Brown (as, f); Karen Borca (bsn); Andrea Parkins (acc).* 99.

Morris's brand of free-form composition/improvisation is well represented on these two contrasting sets. In some regards, *Underthru* is the more conventional, with front-line 'horns' supported by a relatively familiar rhythm section; but in actual practice, and for all its unconventional instrumentation, *Many Rings* feels more like a generic free-jazz date. As second leads, Brown and Maneri are very different and play instruments with sharply contrasting capabilities, but they both understand that with Morris most of the action takes place between the notes and across the bar lines; in other words, there isn't much about either set that is formulaic.

'Remarks' on *Underthru* is a remarkable performance, as is 'Two Busses And A Long Walk'. The title-piece of the Knitting Factory set is the most convincing representation of its unconventional sonority, and some care has been taken to register all the elements with something like democracy.

★★★(★) At The Old Office

Knitting Factory 272 *Morris; Mat Maneri (vla); Chris Lightcap (b); Gerald Cleaver (d).* 11/99.

*****(*) Soul Search**

Aum Fidelity 14 *Morris; Mat Maneri (vn).* 8/99.

Morris and Maneri are clearly soul-mates, and the relationship blossoms again on this powerful duo set, which takes forward many of the ideas represented on earlier Aum Fidelity recordings. The two stringed instruments frequently exchange roles, with Maneri producing big chords and Morris teasing out single-note lines at great speed.

The Knitting Factory set consists of two long improvisations and two composed tracks, though these sound almost as chaotically energetic as the free-form performances. Maneri's viola has a wonderfully rich quality that sits well with the guitar, probably more comfortably than the electric violin he characteristically uses, and on 'Matter Of Fact' the exchange of lead lines is virtuosic and completely convincing.

*****(*) Singularity**

Aum Fidelity 18 *Morris (g solo).* 5/00.

Morris hasn't previously been associated with acoustic guitar, but on *Singularity* he abandons amplification in favour of rapid picking and sonorous chords on a steel-strung acoustic. The themes are all quite abstract – 'Light', 'Gravity', 'Atmosphere', etc. – but the playing remains close to the blues and to jazz harmony and Morris's ability to keep several ideas in sight at once means that *Singularity* is almost inexhaustible as a listening experience.

***** Age Of Everything**

Riti 4 *Moris; Timo Shanko (b); Luther Gray (d).* 1/02.

Riti is Morris's own label, named after an African folk instrument. Its circulation is relatively restricted but records can always be tracked down on www.joe-morris.com. This trio set is pretty much of a piece with Joe's work over the last few years, though interestingly he has also turned to playing double bass and has been working as sideman for other leaders in that capacity. Again, just four large slabs of music, uncompromisingly played and with that deceptively linear approach which suggests that harmonic depth isn't the first thing that excites the guitarist.

Lawrence Butch Morris (born 1947)

CORNET, CONDUCTOR

Morris began as a cornetist in the Californian free scene of the early '70s and also played in Europe. He then moved to the loft scene of New York and worked frequently with David Murray. A prolific composer, he more recently largely gave up playing in order to pursue 'conduction', a system of conducted and improvised music.

*****(*) Burning Cloud**

FMP CD 77 *Morris; J. A. Deane (tb, f, elec); Le Quan Ninh (perc).* 10/93.

With Morris turning away from performing himself, at least as an instrumentalist, it is good to have this reminder of his powers in a small-group context, recorded at one of Berlin's Total Music Meetings. The key player here is arguably Deane; besides his trombone lines, his meticulous use of electronics creates much of the backdrop, while Ninh and Morris step in and out of view. Morris plays a jazzman's role, tightly muted, dappling the canvas with tiny, stringent melodies. As modest as the instrumentation is, this is a rich and exciting music.

***** Berlin Skyscraper '95**

FMP CD 92/93 2CD *Morris; Axel Dörner (t); Marc Stutz-Boukova (tb); Gregor Hotz (ss); Kirtsen Reese (f); Johanne Braun (ob); Wolfgang Fuchs (bcl); Elisabeth Böhm-Christl (bsn); Bernhard Arndt (p); Albrecht Riermeier (vib); Dietrich Petzold (vn, vla); Alex Kolkowski (vn); Nicholas Bussman (clo); Tatjana Schütz (hp); Olaf Rupp (g); Davide De Bernardi (b); Stephan Mathieu, Michael Griener (perc).* 11/95.

From the 1995 Total Music Meeting in Berlin, these are numbers 51, 52, 55 and 56 in the numbered sequence of Morris conductions. Although these events are difficult to evaluate from the cold evidence of a CD recording, this one seems like a considerable success, since it passes the litmus test of excellent sound, a team of skilful players and an ensemble willing to listen and be generous. Some truly fascinating and unpredictable textures arise from the instrumental combinations, often with a degree of refinement that makes it hard to believe that certain passages weren't composed.

****(*) Holy Sea**

Splasc(h) 802/3.2 2CD *Morris; J. A. Deane (tb, elec, sampling); Riccardo Fassi (p); Otomo Yoshihide (turntable, sampling, elec); Orchestra della Toscana.* 2/96.

This one points up two things: that Morris needs performers skilled in improvisation, and the recordings need a good mix and acoustics. The players of the Orchestra della Toscana don't really match up to the former requirement, and with Deane and Yoshihide playing too strong a role, the music often feels stiff and unappealing. Fassi, though, copes well. The three pieces also suffer from environments which damage the sensitivity the players are looking for. As ever, there are still moments to savour, but mostly this one's a miss.

Sonny Morris

TRUMPET, VOCAL

A founder-member of the Crane River Jazz Band, Morris led his own Delta Jazz Band for many years, and they play fundamentalist revivalism, British style.

***** The Spirit Lives On**

Lake LACD46 *Morris; Bob Ward (tb, v); Terry Giles (cl); Ben Marshall (bj); John Sirett (b); Colin Bowden (d).* 9/94.

****(*) For The Good Old Boys**

Lake LACD 63 *As above, except add John Clark (p), Eric Webster (bj, g); omit Marshall.* 3/96.

***** Sonny Meets Pat**

Lake LACD81 *As above, except add Pat Halcox (t, v).* 11/96.

*****(*) Silver Bell**

Lake LACD102 *As above, except Chris Satterly (p, v) replaces Clark; omit Halcox.* 3/98.

*****(*) Near The Cross**

Lake LACD125 *As above.* 6/99.

**** Sonny Morris And Friends In Germany**

Upbeat URCD 181 *Morris; Sven Küpper, Michael Schneider, Patrick Mader (tb); Ian Wheeler (cl); Mitch Kreilein (as); Ray Smith, Thomas Guthoff (p); Dickie Bishop (g, v); Sean Moyses, Sandra Mimstedt (bj); Gunter Barfuss, Franziska

Mouse (b); Lutz Eikelmann (d, tba); Colin Bowden (d); Benny Korn (wbd); Manfred Möhl (v). 4/99–7/00.

***** Sonny**

Lake LACD 152 *Morris; Roy Maskell (tb); Terry Giles (cl, as); Chris Satterly (p, v); Andy Maynard (g, bj); John Sirett (b); Colin Bowden (d).* 12/00.

The spirit in question is that of the Johnson/Lewis American Music groups of the '40s, and this congenial group of veterans pay a likeable homage on *The Spirit Lives On.* Morris and Marshall have their own authenticity in spades, both being founder-members of the Crane River Jazz Band alongside Ken Colyer, and the rest of the group hardly put a foot wrong. The anti-virtuosic solos are scarcely the point of this music. What counts is the steady beat, the *simpatico* ensembles and the irresistible sense of inevitability about it all. Crucially, the rhythm section are exactly right, with Bowden in particular outstanding in the Baby Dodds manner. Excellent choice of material, and docked a notch only for the occasional shakiness and the vocals, dispensable as usual. For some reason, *For The Good Old Boys* isn't quite so good: a few of the tracks lumber along, and the tunes aren't so appealing.

Recorded at Farnham Maltings, *Sonny Meets Pat* is very good fun, with guest Pat Halcox sitting in with Sonny's Delta Jazz Band. The horn players all hit the odd clinker here and there and nobody's that bothered. Morris and Halcox don't so much duel in the front line as nudge each other, and the crowd love it.

On the evidence of the next pair of discs, the band were getting better (except in the vocal department, so we'll gloss over what singing there is). Hard to say *how* it's better, since the playing isn't sharper or more accomplished as such: more that the ensembles gather momentum with an ounce more certainty, the tunes are carried with a shade more lightness. *Silver Bell* is the usual mixed bag but *Near The Cross* is all sacred material of some sort and, with many of the tempos extraordinarily slow, it's a tribute to the band that they muster so much conviction at that pace. Morris's little solo on 'Were You There?' is also a fine example of his perfectly appropriate improvising.

The German sessions are alright, and here and here work up a fine head of steam, but they also have a lot of very dispensable (to put it politely) vocals. Not a good example of Sonny's work. Sonny's passing in 2001 may have called time for the group. *Sonny* was recorded only weeks before his death, but shows no sign of the dimming of the day, and gathers a very pleasing range of rags, blues, old-time tunes and whatever else the band felt like doing.

Thomas Morris (1898–date unknown)

CORNET

A frequent visitor to recording studios in New York during the '20s, Morris thereafter joined a religious sect and gave up music during the '30s. Nothing is known of him after that.

****(*) When A 'Gator Hollers ...**

Frog DGF-1 *Morris; Rex Stewart, Jabbo Smith (c); Geechie Fields, Joe 'Tricky Sam' Nanton, Charlie Irvis (tb); Ernest Elliott (cl, ts, bs); Happy Cauldwell (cl, ts); Bob Fuller (cl, ss); Mike Jackson (p, v); Phil Worde (p); Buddy Christian (g, bj); Lee Blair (bj); Bill Benford (tba); Wellman Braud (b); Helen Baxter, Margaret Johnson (v).* 7–11/26.

Hardcore collectors will welcome this lovingly assembled set of early-jazz rarities; everybody else should be warned that this is second-rate music, for all its undoubted charm and savvy at this great distance. Morris – peculiarly little is known about his life – was a frequent accompanist to singers, but the sides made under his own leadership for Victor are more notable for the sidemen than for his own distinctly average playing. The best moment on the whole record is Rex Stewart's thrilling solo on 'Charleston Stampede', and that's even more thrilling on the Fletcher Henderson original. Elsewhere there are some interesting fragments from names usually consigned to the lumber-room of jazz history. Some typical hokum – 'Who's Dis Heah Stranger' or 'Jackass Blues', again not a patch on the Henderson version – mingles with the title-piece, sung by Margaret Johnson, and some later tracks that feature Joe Nanton just before he joined Henderson. The remastering is done superbly and every known take is here.

Jelly Roll Morton (1890–1941)

PIANO, VOCAL

Morton led a picaresque life in New Orleans in the earliest 1900s – as a pianist, pimp, billiards player, tailor, minstrel-show entertainer, hustler and more. Began recording in Chicago in 1923, then bandleading with his Red Hot Peppers, making some of the classic early jazz recordings. Arrived in New York in 1928 but found it hard to compete and gradually lost ground. Scuffled and fought over unpaid royalties during the '30s, then began recording his life story (and his history of jazz) for the Library of Congress in 1938. Various comebacks, 1939–41, but Morton died in Los Angeles, bitter and unrewarded. A great legend and perhaps the first great jazz composer.

*****(*) The Piano Rolls**

Nonesuch 79363-2 *Morton (p roll).* 20–2/97.

(***) Blues And Stomps From Rare Piano Rolls

Biograph BCD111 *Morton (p roll).* 24–26.

The Nonesuch disc is one of the most fascinating retrievals of recent years. Morton's twelve original piano rolls have been analysed in the light of his other recordings by Artis Wodehouse, who has subsequently converted the information to computer data and edited a previously missing interpretative element into the way the rolls are reproduced. The subsequently annotated rolls were then played back on a nine-foot Disklavier piano, in a concert hall, and recorded. The remarkable outcome may be the closest we can ever get to hearing what Morton might truly have sounded like at this early peak of his career. Or they may not. Sceptics will point to the issue that, however meticulous the homework, this is still only somebody's idea of how the rolls should sound. Yet the results are exhilarating enough to suggest that Jelly's ghost is indeed seated at the keyboard. If there is an inevitable sense of something mechanical in the delivery, it's offset by the rocking syncopations, rips and general *brio* which always seem to be among the hallmarks of a Morton performance. The odd combination of ferocity and gentility in 'Grandpa's Spells', the dizzying double-time break in 'Midnight Mama' and the unbridled virtuosity of 'Shreveport Stomps' have certainly never sounded more convincing. It is altogether a memorable event and indispensable to anyone intrigued by the early steps of the master. The

Biograph disc, unadorned renditions of the original rolls, is rendered somewhat redundant by the Nonesuch CD, but we list it anyway.

*** Jelly Roll Morton 1923–1924

Classics 584 *Morton; Tommy Ladnier, Natty Dominique (c); Zue Robertson (tb); Wilson Townes, Boyd Senter, Horace Eubanks (cl); Arville Harris (as); W. E. Burton (d, kz); Jasper Taylor (d).* 6/23–6/24.

**** Piano Solos

Retrieval RTR 79002 *Morton (p solo).* 7/23–4/26.

Although we are listing the piano-roll discs first, most assessments of the self-styled originator of jazz and stomps commence with these mainly solo sessions. Morton's all-embracing mastery of the keyboard makes these 19 solos a sublimation of everything jazz had done up to this point. He combines the formal precision of ragtime with a steady melodic flow and a portfolio of rhythms that are tirelessly varied: if Louis Armstrong finally liberated jazz rhythms, Morton had already set out the possibilities to do so. As a series of compositions, this was a storehouse of ideas which has yet to be exhausted: here are the first versions of two of jazz's most enduring masterworks, 'King Porter Stomp' and 'Wolverine Blues', as well as such definitive Morton portraits as 'The Pearls' and the brilliantly delivered 'Shreveport Stomps'. His timing is ambitious yet miraculously secure: listen to the poetic elegance of 'New Orleans (Blues) Joys' or the famous 'Spanish Tinge' in 'Tia Juana'. Considering the roughness of the original recordings, the fact that the music remains utterly compelling is testament to Morton's greatness. The piano-sound is still pretty awful to modern ears, and some of the (often very rare) originals are clearly in less than perfect shape, but this is essential music. The Classics CD scarcely improves on the earlier Fountain/Retrieval LP, now on CD, although the individual tracks have not been remastered from their 1972 incarnation. Admittedly, it adds what were really some false starts in Morton's career – two very cloudy 1923 tracks for Paramount, with a band that may or may not include Tommy Ladnier, a not much better session for OKeh with the feeble Dominique, Robertson and Eubanks, and a fairly disastrous 'Mr Jelly Lord', where he's buried behind Boyd Senter and some kazoo playing – but some may feel that it simply devalues the consistency of the solos. Retrieval's reissue now also includes the four solos for Vocalion from 1926, and this is certainly our first choice.

*** Jelly Roll Morton 1924–1926

Classics 599 *Morton; Lee Collins, Joe 'King' Oliver, George Mitchell (c); Roy Palmer, Kid Ory, Ray Bowling (tb); Omer Simeon (cl, bcl); Barney Bigard (cl, ts); Balls Ball, Volly DeFaut, Darnell Howard (cl); Alex Poole (as); W. E. Burton (kz); Clarence Black, J. Wright Smith (vn); Johnny St Cyr (bj, g); John Lindsay (b); Clay Jefferson, Andrew Hilaire (d); Edmonia Henderson (v).* 9/24–12/26.

**** Jelly Roll Morton 1926–1928

Classics 612 *Morton; Ward Pinkett (t); George Mitchell (c); Kid Ory, Gerald Reeves, Geechie Fields (tb); Omer Simeon, Johnny Dodds (cl); Stump Evans (as); Bud Scott, Johnny St Cyr (g); Lee Blair (bj); Bill Benford, Quinn Wilson (tba); John Lindsay (b); Andrew Hilaire, Tommy Benford, Baby Dodds (d).* 12/26–6/28.

**** Jelly Roll Morton 1928–1929

Classics 627 *Morton; Ed Anderson, Edwin Swayzee, Boyd 'Red' Rosser, Walter Briscoe, Henry 'Red' Allen, Freddy Jenkins (t); William Cato, Charlie Irvis, J. C. Higginbotham (tb); Russell Procope, Albert Nicholas, Wilton Crawley, George Baquet (cl); Paul 'Polo' Barnes (ss); Joe Thomas, Johnny Hodges (as); Joe Garland, Walter Thomas (ts); Luis Russell, Rod Rodriguez (p); Lee Blair, Will Johnson (g); Barney Alexander (bj); Bill Moore, Harry Prather (tba); George 'Pops' Foster (b); Manzie Johnson, William Laws, Paul Barbarin, Sonny Greer (d).* 12/28–12/29.

*** Jelly Roll Morton 1929–1930

Classics 642 *Morton; Ward Pinkett, Bubber Miley (t); Geechie Fields, Wilbur De Paris (tb); Albert Nicholas, Barney Bigard, Ernie Bullock (cl); Bernard Addison, Howard Hill (g); Lee Blair (bj); Billy Taylor, Bill Benford, Pete Biggs (tba); Zutty Singleton, Tommy Benford, Cozy Cole (d); Billie Young (v).* 12/29–7/30.

*** Jelly Roll Morton 1930–1939

Classics 654 *Morton; Ward Pinkett, Sidney De Paris (t); Geechie Fields, Claude Jones, Fred Robinson (tb); Sidney Bechet (ss); Albert Nicholas, Eddie Scarpa (cl); Happy Caldwell (ts); Bernard Addison, Lawrence Lucie (g); Billy Taylor (tba); Wellman Braud (b); Bill Beason, Zutty Singleton (d).* 10/30–12/39.

♛ **** Jelly Roll Morton Vols. 1–5

JSP JAZZBOX 903 5CD *As above discs.* 9/26–10/30.

Classics 599 starts with a 1924 date with Morton's (so-called) Kings Of Jazz, and horrible it sounds too, poorly transferred from grim originals and featuring diabolical clarinet from the suitably named 'Balls' Ball and even worse alto by Alex Poole. Trio versions of 'My Gal' and 'Wolverine Blues' with Volly DeFaut aren't much better, but a fine 1926 solo date for Vocalion *is* included, and these tracks (unavailable elsewhere) must make the disc attractive to Morton specialists. Two sides with (allegedly) King Oliver and Edmonia Henderson are a further bonus. They then go into the Victor sequence, which continues through Classics 612 and 627, although the latter adds an unremarkable session at the end under Wilton Crawley's leadership, with (somewhat mystifyingly) a number of Ellingtonians present.

Morton's recordings for Victor are a magnificent body of work which has been done splendid but frustratingly mixed justice by the various reissues now available. His Red Hot Peppers band sides, particularly those cut at the three incredible sessions of 1926, are masterpieces which have endured as well as anything by Armstrong, Parker or any comparable figure at the top end of the jazz pantheon. Morton seemed to know exactly what he wanted: having honed and orchestrated compositions like 'Grandpa's Spells' at the piano for many years, his realization of the music for a band was flawless and brimful of jubilation at his getting the music down on record. Mitchell, Simeon and the others all took crackling solos, but it was the way they were contextualized by the leader that makes the music so close to perfection. The 1926–7 dates were a summary of what jazz had achieved up to that time: as a development out of the New Orleans tradition, it eschewed the soloistic grandeur that Armstrong was establishing and preferred an almost classical poise and shapeliness. If a few other voices (Ellington, Redman) were already looking towards a more modern kind of group jazz, Morton was distilling what he considered to be the heart of hot music, 'sweet, soft, plenty rhythm', as he later put it.

While the earliest sessions are his greatest achievements, it's wrong to regard the later work as a decline. There are the two trio tracks with the Dodds brothers, with Morton tearing into 'Wolverine Blues'. The 1928 sessions feature his ten-piece touring band on the fine 'Deep Creek' and a small group handling the beautiful 'Mournful Serenade', while 1929 saw a memorable solo session which produced 'Pep', 'Fat Frances' and 'Freakish', and an exuberant band date that uncorked swinging performances in 'Burnin' The Iceberg' and 'New Orleans Bump'. But the sessions from 1930 onwards suffer from personnel problems and a vague feeling that Morton was already becoming a man out of time, with New York and territory bands moving into a smoother, less consciously hot music. His own playing remains jauntily commanding but sidemen become sloppy, and a piece like the complex 'Low Gravy', from July 1930, never reaches its potential on record. His last session for Victor until 1939 produced a final shaft of Mortonian genius in 'Fickle Fay Creep'; but a feeling was now deep-set that the pianist was a declining force, and he didn't record for Victor again until the end of the decade.

The 1939 tracks show the old master in good spirits, singing 'I Thought I Heard Buddy Bolden Say' and 'Winin' Boy Blues' with his old panache and directing an authentic New Orleans band with resilient aplomb. It is very old-time music for 1939 but it's still very different from the early Peppers sides, and none the worse for either. Classics 654 covers these sessions and also includes four titles from an excellent solo date from 1938.

Morton's music demands a place in any jazz collection. We are delighted to be able to welcome back the superlative set of five CDs from JSP. John R. T. Davies's remastering work is exemplary and does justice to music which has in the past been often brutally and shoddily presented, even by owning label RCA. At a modest price for the five-disc set, this is perhaps the greatest bargain in the jazz catalogue.

The Classics CDs have the field to themselves, in terms of single-disc sequences, and it's a pity that their remastering is often spotty and unpredictable. The stars are for the music rather than the presentation. To add to the glut of issues, there have also been sets available from Memoria (*The Complete Jelly Roll Morton, 1926–1930*, 2 CDs), EPM (*Creole Genius*, 3 CDs) and Fremaux (*The Quintessence*, 2 CDs) which go over the same ground. *Sweet And Hot* (Topaz TPZ 1003) is another good single-disc collection in the Topaz series of compilations.

****** Kansas City Stomp**

Rounder CD1091 *Morton (p, v).* 5–6/38.

*****(*) Anamule Dance**

Rounder CD1092 *Morton (p, v).* 5–6/38.

****** The Pearls**

Rounder CD1093 *Morton (p, v).* 5–6/38.

****** Winin' Boy Blues**

Rounder CD1094 *Morton (p, v).* 5–6/38.

In the summer of 1938, broke and almost finished, Morton was recorded – almost by chance at first – by Alan Lomax at the Library of Congress, and when Lomax realized the opportunity he had on his hands he got Morton to deliver a virtual history of the birth pangs of jazz as it happened in the New Orleans of the turn of the century. His memory was unimpaired, although he chose to tell things as he preferred to remember them, perhaps; and his hands were still in complete command of the keyboard. The results have the quality of a long, drifting dream, as if Morton were talking to himself. He demonstrates every kind of music which he heard or played in the city, recreates all his greatest compositions in long versions unhindered by 78 playing time, remembers other pianists who were never recorded, spins yarns, and generally sets down the most distinctive (if not necessarily the most truthful) document we have on the origins of the music. The sessions were made on an acetate recorder and, while the sound may be uncomfortably one-dimensional to modern ears, everything he says comes through clearly enough, and the best of the piano solos sound as invigorating as they have to be. The new remastering achieved by Rounder is the best attempt to date to reproduce the music in correct pitch and speed; while much talk has been omitted from the four CDs, it is a wonderfully illustrated lecture on Morton's music by the man who created it. Of the four discs, only Volume Two is slightly less than essential, with the final disc offering perhaps the best selection of solos, including his astonishing extended treatment of 'Creepy Feeling'. Indispensable records for anyone interested in jazz history. We are dismayed, however, that no further attempt has been made at restoring these important recordings in their 'original' form: many will want to hear the music unadorned, but minus Morton's anecdotage, the proper environment for the solos to emerge from, we are not hearing this music in its true form.

(***) Jelly Roll Morton 1939–1940

Classics 668 *Morton; Henry 'Red' Allen (t); Joe Britton, Claude Jones (tb); Albert Nicholas (cl); Eddie Williams (as); Wellman Braud (b); Zutty Singleton (d).* 12/39–1/40.

*****(*) Last Sessions: The Complete General Recordings**

Commodore CMD 14032 *As above.* 12/39–1/40.

Morton's final recordings are relatively little-known, cut originally for General and later appearing on Commodore. The tracks by the Morton Six and Seven find him back with several sons of New Orleans, but the music lacks the authority of his great days; a couple of solo sessions from 1939 do, though, reassert his enduring powers at the keyboard, with several favourites still sounding like pieces of jazz legend. When one tracks through his legacy, there is actually little enough (compare him with Ellington or Armstrong for prolificity!) to make any survivals rather precious. The new Commodore edition is in very decent sound and comes across much better than the Classics disc. It also has a far superior documentation.

***** The Alternative Takes Vol. 1 (1923–1929)**

Neatwork RP 2010 *As appropriate discs above.* 6/23–7/29.

***** The Alternative Takes Vol. 2 (1929–1940)**

Neatwork RP 2013 *As appropriate discs above.* 7/29–7/40.

Morton's out-takes offer little in the way of surprise – more an affirmation that the man's mastery was consistent. The various Red Hot Peppers alternates tend to sound like slightly imperfect variations on the master versions. The 1923 Paramount date by Jelly Roll Marton (sic) yields a quite atrocious-sounding alternate of 'Big Foot Ham'. But the second volume is slightly more interesting. The two Billie Young vocal titles (on Classics 642) proved to be originally-unissued alternates, and here are the master takes; there's a Wilton Crawley title from 1930, which has Morton as a sideman; and a fine 'Honky Tonk Music No. 2' solo from 1938, though it's in indifferent sound. As with so many in this series, for hardcore devotees only.

Sal Mosca (born 1927)

PIANO

A kindred spirit to Lennie Tristano, Mosca has carried on Tristano-ite trends by making himself scarce and recording only very sparingly. As a pianist, he displays the inevitable fealty to his mentor's methods.

*****(*) A Concert**
Jazz Records JR-8 *Mosca (p solo).* 6/79.

Belatedly released in 1990, this is a rare example of one of the leading followers of Lennie Tristano in a solo situation. Because Mosca has made so few recordings, his appearances always seem eventful and, despite the dour atmosphere of the CD – which settles for the grimmest monochrome packaging and presentation, a characteristic refusal to distract from the music's inner qualities – it is played electrically. Though most of the tunes are 'originals', they usually follow the standard Tristano-ite practice of an abstruse variation on a standard. Mosca's approach is formidably varied, both from piece to piece and within individual treatments. 'Co-Play', which starts as a relatively simple variation on 'Sweet And Lovely', becomes a labyrinthine investigation of the properties of the song, and 'That Time' turns 'That Old Feeling' into a fantasy on a number of kinds of jazz rhythm. Sometimes he plays it straight, but unexpectedly so: 'Prelude To A Kiss' has voicings more dense than in any authentic Ellington version. Always he is prodigiously inventive: while the music sometimes takes on a painstaking quality, Mosca's spontaneity is genuine enough to pack the programme with surprises. An important record, docked a notch only for the sound-quality: it's clear enough, but the piano's tone is scarcely ingratiating, and there's a lot of tape-hiss.

***** Sal Mosca / Warne Marsh Quartet Vol. 1**
Zinnia 103 *Mosca; Warne Marsh (ts); Frank Canino (b); Skip Scott (d).* 81.

***** Sal Mosca / Warne Marsh Quartet Vol. 2**
Zinnia 104 *As above.* 81.

More problems with sound-quality here. Mosca taped these Village Vanguard sessions himself and, for a recording dating from the '80s, it's pretty shabby, though Tristano-ites and other scholars will have their ears used to this sort of thing by now. Still, it does detract from music that is as refined and impeccable as chords-based improvising with no emotional agenda can get. Marsh's streaming elegance matches Mosca's slightly more fanciful playing to the expected 't'. As always, they are working on old staples such as '317 East 32nd' and the usual thinly disguised standards, and as always their inventiveness on material they'd mused on countless times already is enough to provoke disbelief. Canino and Scott are no more than functional, though that is presumably how the principals wanted it.

Danny Moss (born 1927)

TENOR SAXOPHONE

Made his name in dance and swing bands in the late '40s, and was then known as a sideman and occasional leader in British mainstream groups. Left for Australia in 1990, but currently enjoying an Indian summer via the patronage of the Nagel-Heyer operation.

****(*) The Good Life**
Progressive PCD 7018 *Moss; Ted Ambrose (t, v); Mike Collier (tb); Jack Jacobs (as); Terry Whitney (p); Alan Kennington (b); Derek Middleton (d).* 10/68.

***** At University College Oxford**
MacJazz MAC CD004 *Moss; Brian Lemon (p).* 2/85.

***** Weaver Of Dreams**
Nagel-Heyer 017 *Moss; Brian Lemon (p); Len Skeat (b); Butch Miles (d).* 11/94.

***** A Swingin' Affair**
Nagel-Heyer 034 *Moss; Heinz Buhler (t); Hans Meier (tb); Werner Keller (cl); Buddha Scheidegger (p); Peter Schmidli (g); Vinzenz Kummer (b); Carlo Capello (d).* 11/96.

***** Three Great Concerts**
Nagel-Heyer 019 *Moss; Tom Saunders (c); Bill Allred (tb); Chuck Hedges (cl); Brian Dee, Brian Lemon, Johnny Varro (p); Isla Eckinger, Len Skeat (b); Oliver Jackson, Butch Miles (d); Jeanie Lambe (v).* 11/3–9/95.

Moss has often been hidden by his surroundings on record, usually in sections or anonymous groups, and he's had only a few opportunities of clear space. These discs, almost a generation apart, give a decent idea of his powers. The Hawkins–Webster tradition is what he sticks to closest, and it comes out mainly on slow and medium tempos. The big, beefy tenderness on the two takes of 'The Good Life' itself, from the 1968 session, is enduringly impressive and affecting. Much of this date is taken up with time-wasting by the mixed British talents on hand: Ambrose insists on singing on some tracks, Jacobs's Willie Smith-styled alto falls into routine, and Moss simply doesn't get enough space, though he also has a Hawkins-like 'Star Dust' to himself.

With Lemon, the most fail-safe of accompanists, Danny lays back on the chords and relaxes. They hustle through some of the pieces, especially 'Struttin' With Some Barbecue', but the moments to savour come in the likes of 'You're Blasé'. Dave Bennett's sound catches the tone of both players nicely.

Weaver Of Dreams finds him in Hamburg, delivering a faithful set of tenorman's staples – '9.20 Special', 'Smoke Gets In Your Eyes', 'Blue Lou' – and a small number of choice ballads. Utterly reliable playing, though some of the old facility has been worn away, and one regrets that Moss wasn't featured more in his prime.

He seems to have made up a fruitful relationship with the Nagel-Heyer enterprise. *A Swingin' Affair* finds him guesting with the German mainstream group, Buddha's Gamblers, and while there's nothing remarkable the group takes great satisfaction in swinging through some fine old Basie, Goodman and Ellington staples. Moss is right at home here. *Three Great Concerts* works primarily as a feature for vocalist Lambe, whose big voice and buttonholing style may not be to all tastes, but he can certainly make the most out of a lyric like 'You Came A Long Way From St Louis'. The other horns turn up on only one track; Moss and the rhythm sections make most of the running. Sound enough, although, nudging the 80-minute barrier, there's too much music, and the CD could as easily have been judiciously pruned.

***** Keeper Of The Flame**

Nagel-Heyer CD 064 *Moss; John Pearce (p); Len Skeat (b); Charly Antolini (d).* 10/98.

Sampling any track from this baker's dozen will make one appreciate Hans Nagel–Heyer's appreciation for the tenorman, and why he wants to keep recording him – hefty sound, big swing, beefy imagination. But the record's too much of a good thing. Moss clobbers tunes at medium-up tempo, and he relies on the Websterian ballad method – do as little as possible, and let the sound and the melody carry it. Except Danny's not really Ben. The drummer often makes a difference in situations like this, and Charly Antolini is terrific, swinging all the time. Still, 76 minutes is a long haul for anyone.

***** At Bob Barnard's Jazz Party 1999**

Nif Nuf 43/004 *Moss; Peter Gaudion (t); Ed Wilson (tb); Kenn Jones (ts, bs); Ralph Sutton, Barry Bruce (p); Marty Grosz, Johnny Scurry (g); James Clark, Howard Cairns (b); Len Barnard, Andy Swann (d).* 4/99.

***** Returns To Bob Barnard's Jazz Party 2000**

Nif Nuf 43/07 *Moss; Peter Gaudion (t); Tom Baker (tb); Jo Stevenson (as, cl); Kenn Jones (ts, bs); Chris Hopkins, Bernd Lhotzky (p); George Washingmachine (vn); Johnny Scurry , Andy Baylor (g); James Clark, Howard Cairns, David Gardner (b); Len Barnard (d).* 5/00.

***** At Bob Barnard's Jazz Party 2001**

Nif Nuf 43/010 *Moss; Jon-Erik Kellso (t); Tom Baker (t, tb); Don Stewart (tb); Fred Parkes (cl); Paul Furniss (cl, ss); Jo Stevenson (ts); Chris Taperell, Ben Johnson (p); Andy Baylor (g); George Washingmachine (vn); James Clark, Leon Heale (b); Len Barnard, Andy Swann, Ron Sandilands (d).* 4/01.

Moss on what is now home territory, at St Kilda (1999) and Melbourne (the other two). Barnard's annual bashes are a typical mainstream jazz-party event, and the music's pretty much all of a piece across the three discs, various groupings settling into relaxed jamming on the expected standards. Ralph Sutton enlivens a few tracks on the first disc (although Barry Bruce is no slouch either). Moss is his usual big-sounding self on the ballads. Kellso shares top billing on the third disc and is in good heart. Some of his companions aren't all that special, and we have some doubts about the violinist's name...

Bennie Moten (1894–1935)

PIANO, BANDLEADER

Born in Kansas City, Moten was bandleading in the city by 1920, starting with a small group but expanding into a big band by the time of his first records. He built it into the best band in the region throughout the '20s and early '30s, but after visting Chicago in 1935 Moten died there, following a surgical accident.

****(*) Bennie Moten 1923–1927**

Classics 549 *Moten; Lamar Wright, Harry Cooper, Ed Lewis, Paul Webster (c); Thamon Hayes (tb, v); Harlan Leonard (cl, ss, as); Woody Walder (cl, ts); Jack Washington (cl, as, bs); LaForest Dent (as, bs, bj); Sam Tall, Leroy Berry (bj); Vernon Page (tba); Willie Hall, Willie McWashington (d).* 9/23–6/27.

***** The OKeh Sessions**

Cygnet CYG 1004 *As above; also personnel from* 1931 *sessions, listed below.* 9/23–4/31.

Moten's band was the most important group to record in the American south-west in the period, and luckily it made a large number of sides for OKeh and Victor; but the quality of the music is very inconsistent, and much of the earlier material is of historical rather than musical interest. This first CD in the complete edition on Classics couples the band's 14 sides for OKeh from 1923–5 with the first recordings for Victor. The OKeh tracks are a curious mixture: the very first two, 'Elephant's Wobble' and 'Crawdad Blues', are little more than strings of solos, while the subsequent 'South' and 'Goofy Dust' are driving, rag-orientated tunes which emphasize the ensemble. Wright is the only really interesting soloist from the period, and Walder, the apparent star, indulges in some idiotic antics on the clarinet; but, even so, the lumpy rhythms and clattery ensembles yield some strong, hard-hitting performances, sometimes redolent of Sam Morgan's New Orleans band of a few years later. The early Victors don't show a very great advance, despite electrical recording, and one must wait for the later sides for Moten's band to really shine.

Classics offer a fair remastering of what are very rare originals, although they are not superior to the old Parlophone LP which first collected the OKeh tracks. The Cygnet release, though, is in much better sound overall, and includes the bonus of four previously unissued takes from some of the final Victor sessions of 1931.

*****(*) Bennie Moten 1927–1929**

Classics 558 *As above, except omit Wright, Cooper, Tall and Hall; add Booker Washington (c), Buster Moten (p, acc), James Taylor, Bob Clemmons (v).* 6/27–6/2

***** Bennie Moten 1929–30**

Classics 578 *As above, except Count Basie (p) replaces Buster Moten; add Hot Lips Page (t), Eddie Durham (tb, g), Jimmy Rushing (v).* 7/29–10/30.

*****(*) Justrite**

Frog DGF29 *As discs above.* 26–7.

*****(*) Kansas City Breakdown**

Frog DGF 30 *As discs above.* 28–9.

Moten's band progressed rather slowly, handicapped by an absence of both truly outstanding soloists and an arranger of real talent. The surprisingly static personnel did the best they could with the material, but most of the tunes work from a heavy off-beat. Walder has barely improved, and the arrival of Bennie's brother, Buster, with his dreaded piano-accordion, was enough to root the band in novelty status. The second Classics CD still has some good moments – in such as 'The New Tulsa Blues' or 'Kansas City Breakdown' – but sugary saxes and pedestrian charts spoil many promising moments. Matters take an immediate upward turn with the joint arrival of Basie and Durham in 1929. 'Jones Law Blues', 'Band Box Shuffle' and 'Small Black' all show the band with fresh ideas under Basie's inspirational leadership (and soloing – here with his Earl Hines influence still intact). 'Sweetheart Of Yesterday' even softens the two-beat rhythm. The two Frog issues offer the music in splendid sound with excellent documentation and these are now a clear first choice over the Classics.

***** Bennie Moten 1930–1932**

Classics 591 *Moten; Ed Lewis, Booker Washington (c); Hot Lips Page, Joe Keyes, Dee Stewart (t); Thamon Hayes, Dan Minor (tb); Eddie Durham (tb, g); Harlan Leonard, Jack Washington, Woody Walder, Eddie Barefield, Ben Webster (reeds); Count Basie (p); Buster Moten (acc); Leroy Berry (bj, g); Vernon Page (tba); Walter Page (b); Willie McWashington (d); Jimmy Rushing (v).* 30–32.

Under Basie's effective leadership, the Moten orchestra finally took wing, and its final sessions were memorable. There were still problems, such as the presence of Buster Moten, the reliance on a tuba prior to the arrival of Page, and a general feeling of transition between old and new; but, by the magnificent session of December 1932, when the band created at least four masterpieces in 'Toby', 'Prince Of Wails', 'Milenberg Joys' and 'Moten Swing', it was a unit that could have taken on the best of American bands. Page, Rushing, Webster, Durham and especially Basie himself all have key solo and ensemble roles, and the sound of the band on 'Prince Of Wails' and 'Toby' is pile-driving. Ironically, this modernism cost Moten much of his local audience, which he was only recovering at the time of his death in 1935.

CORE COLLECTION

****** Band Box Shuffle 1929-1932**

Hep 1070/2 2CD *As discs above.* 29–32.

The Hep edition completely outclasses the Classics CDs, and with the Cygnet and Frog issues listed above this makes up the entire Moten story in fine and revealing detail.

Paul Motian (born 1931)

DRUMS, PERCUSSION

Born in Philadelphia, Motian is one of the most influential modern percussionists, having largely freed the drummer from strict time-keeping duties. He matured artistically as a member of pianist Bill Evans's trio. Later, he turned to composition as well; his work is atmospheric, unlinear and often complex under a deceptively calm exterior.

***** Conception Vessel**

ECM 519279-2 *Motian; Becky Friend (f); Sam Brown (g); Leroy Jenkins (vn); Keith Jarrett (p, f); Charlie Haden (b).* 11/72.

****** Tribute**

ECM 519281-2 *Motian; Carlos Ward (as); Sam Brown, Paul Metzke (g); Charlie Haden (b).* 5/74.

Time will tell how important Motian is ultimately considered to be in the development of jazz since the war; but if all revolutions in the music turn out to be upheavals in the rhythm section, then it seems likely that he will be seen as a quiet revolutionary, freeing the drummer from basic time-keeping service even more thoroughly than the radicals of the '60s – Murray, Cyrille, Graves – did. Motian's phrasing has less to do with the basic pulse of a piece than with its melody line. This has meant that he works best with very strong bass-players – Charlie Haden most obviously – and that in his own music the drums are pitched front and centre, not aggressively but as an emphatic structural component.

Both these early recordings for ECM illustrate the point perfectly. They were startling records when they first appeared, and they have retained their vigour and freshness. The single unaccompanied track on *Conception Vessel*, 'Ch'i Energy', provides a good representation of his basic sound-palette: sweeping cymbals, soft, delicately placed accents, a sense of flow and togetherness that is difficult to break down into components. Max Roach is the only other modern drummer who can sound anything like this, but Roach is a soapbox orator by comparison. Most of the first record is devoted to duo settings. The title-track and 'American Indian: Song Of Sitting Bull' are duos with Keith Jarrett (who plays flute on the latter). There are two trios with Haden and Brown, and the set closes with 'Inspiration From A Vietnamese Lullaby', which uses Friend and Jenkins, and points to the drummer's fascination with musical traditions outside the European/American orbit.

The 1974 album is a small classic. Ward is used sparingly, but the twinned guitars are a key component and, given the prominence of Bill Frisell in later years, it's interesting to note how Motian was using the instrument as early as this. The session consists of three Motian tunes, of which 'Sod House' and 'Victoria' are the best known; also on the session, wonderful readings of Ornette's 'War Orphans' and Haden's 'Song For Ché'. The leader is seldom far from the centre of things, but as ever he plays with grace and composure.

*****(*) Dance**

ECM 519282-2 *Motian; Charles Brackeen (ts); David Izenzon (b).* 9/77.

***** Le Voyage**

ECM 519283-2 *Motian; Charles Brackeen (ts, ss); Jean-François Jenny-Clark (b).* 3/79.

Timbrally, these trios are very different from the earlier ECMs. Motian plays in a more linear way, pushing the ideas along, and it is interesting to hear him in the company of such an emphatic horn-player as Brackeen, who seems to anticipate much of what Joe Lovano would bring to a Motian trio in later years. Izenzon and Jenny-Clark both carry deep, rich voices and an unorthodox approach to chords. Though neither will ever be mistaken for Haden, there is at least a consistency of sound. The earlier of the records is probably the more sheerly involving, largely because of Izenzon's immense power and throbbing, almost tragic voice. However, 'Folk Song For Rosie' and 'Le Voyage' itself are both delightful compositions, and Motian enthusiasts should certainly track down these fine discs.

***** Psalm**

ECM 847330-2 *Motian; Joe Lovano (ts); Billy Drewes (ts, as); Bill Frisell (g); Ed Schuller (b).* 12/81.

There was to be a later recording for ECM (we aren't quite sure how the contractual position worked itself out), but this already has a slightly intermediate feel. The bones of the great trio with Frisell and Lovano are there, but muddied by the second saxophone (we can't offer much information about Drewes, or much enthusiasm for his playing) and by the rather undefined bass-playing of Schuller. That having been said, this record contains some of Motian's darkest and most intriguing compositions: 'Mandeville' and 'Second Hand' are superb, and it's a pity that they aren't played with greater clarity. Here, the contours are blurred and imprecise.

***** The Story of Maryam**

Soul Note 121074 *Motian; Jim Pepper (ts, ss); Joe Lovano (ts); Bill Frisell (g); Ed Schuller (b).* 7/83.

***** Jack Of Clubs**

Soul Note 121124 *As above.* 3/84.

Unusually for a rhythm-section player, Motian has preferred to work with a very small group of like-minded interpreters, rather than constantly experimenting with line-ups. With the brilliant folksy Pepper replacing the anonymous Drewes, this was a settled band for some years in the '80s. *The Story Of Maryam* is probably the least well-known of Motian's recordings, and some might argue it's the least typical, driven by an edgy, boppish line. The addition of Pepper and the need to accommodate two horns made an impact, but one senses that Motian himself is rethinking aspects of his conception, perhaps trying to inject some gristle and fibre into the music. *Jack Of Clubs* seems self-consciously abrasive in places, though that may have something to do with production values at Soul Note. This is very different product from the ECM records.

***(*) It Should've Happened A Long Time Ago

ECM 823641-2 *Motian; Joe Lovano (ts); Bill Frisell (g).* 7/84.

What should? The end of the association with ECM coincided with the birth of a group that was to reshape Motian's thinking completely. A retake of 'Conception Vessel' gives some sense of how far the drummer had come in a decade. This a roller-coaster ride in comparison to what went before. Lovano and Frisell conjure up a storm of ideas, combative, stirring and to the point. The guitarist seldom sounds less dreamy than in this context.

**** Misterioso

Soul Note 121174 *Motian; Jim Pepper (ts, ss); Joe Lovano (ts); Bill Frisell (g); Ed Schuller (b).* 7/86.

Whereas in the past Motian had seemed anxious to match material to session without undue overlaps, he was increasingly tempted into reworking successful themes. 'Folk Song For Rosie' is the outstanding track here, a powerful, heart-filling version of one of his most unaffectedly beautiful ideas. He was also beginning to explore standards and repertory pieces with greater enthusiasm; Monk's 'Pannonica' glows with affection and imagination. The sound isn't pristine and some of the softer cymbal accents seem unduly hissy, but there is no mistaking the fact that Motian is playing with joy and enthusiasm.

*** One Time Out

Soul Note 121224 *Motian; Joe Lovano (ts); Bill Frisell (g).* 9/87.

Monk was the defining presence during this period, and he even stands behind some of the standard treatments on this disconcertingly mild and low-key recording. 'The Man I Love' is lent a jaggy, almost disillusioned quality that some will find troubling, while 'If I Should Lose You' and 'My Funny Valentine' are rethought almost from the bottom up. Lovano knows this material inside out, and one suspects that it's Frisell who's the sheet-anchor. The Monastic canon is explored direct via 'Monk's Mood', and you kind of suspect that an all-Monk set is only just around the corner.

***(*) On Broadway: Volume 2

Winter & Winter 919038 *Motian; Joe Lovano (ts); Bill Frisell (g); Charlie Haden (b).* 9/89.

Here, the material is so familiar as to seem almost hackneyed on paper. In performance, though, these songs are transformed. Not since Charlie Parker worked his magic on 'All The Things You Are' has the old love song vibrated with so much hidden significance. 'But Not For Me' is titanic, with Motian's rippling percussion providing a whole new scenario for Frisell's bent-out-of-shape solo and Haden's sweet, rocking bass. We heard this version of 'Moonlight Becomes You' the day Bob Hope died and the performance has captured something of his innocently cod romanticism.

CORE COLLECTION

**** Sound Of Love

Winter & Winter 910 008 *Motian; Joe Lovano (ts); Bill Frisell (g).* 6/95.

Just as JMT reached its tenth anniversary, with an enviable reputation for creative output (and a less enviable one for illegible design), it was decided to wind it up. Stefan F. Winter had begun the label as an independent before throwing in his lot with Polygram, and there are signs that he was already looking to secede even before the corporate wind turned chilly. No one looking at any of the first Winter & Winter releases would have doubted their parentage, though it seems clear that the brothers merely took back their own concept rather than stealing Polygram's. Fortunately, artistic and production values remain undimmed as well. This session clearly straddles the end of the affair. The first for the new label is a live session from the Village Vanguard, and it catches the trio in cracking form, opening with 'Misterioso' and Mingus's most yearning composition, 'Duke Ellington's Sound Of Love', before diving into two bright, effusive originals ('Once Around The Park' is menthol fresh) and closing on 'Good Morning Heartache'. There are some glorious moments of interaction between the three players. The obvious difference between now and 1984 is that in the interim Lovano and Frisell have become superstars in their own right. No sign of clashing egos. Every indication of complete creative understanding.

***(*) Flight Of The Blue Jay

Winter & Winter 910 009 *Motian; Chris Potter (as, ts); Chris Cheek (ts); Brad Schoeppach, Kurt Rosenwinkel (g); Steve Swallow (b).* 8/96.

The Electric Bebop Band, minus the irrelevant Alias this time (how *does* he get so much work?), in a strong, mixed programme. The two saxophonists have settled down and are more sympathetically separated in the stereo mix. Monk is once again the dominant presence; of three tunes, 'Light Blue' is the most unusually paced and inflected. The title-track is a Motian tune, and it's getting harder to find any more superlatives for him either as writer or as performer. The big plus this time out is that he's fronting a much more tightly integrated group, who're responsive to changes in mood and pace, and to subtleties of light and shade.

**** Monk & Powell

Winter & Winter 910045 2 *As above, except omit Schoeppach; add Steve Cardenas (g).* 11/98.

A Bill Evans programme would in some respects have been less surprising, but Paul brings tremendous insight and an instinctive musicality to five Monk compositions, of which 'Brilliant Corners' is the most compelling, and three by Bud. It is unusual to hear these familiar themes, and particularly something like 'Parisian Thoroughfare', arranged for horns and guitars, but the Electronic Bebop Band pulls off the transition with unnerving skill. Motian himself is somewhat in the background acoustically, and it's our growing impression that the subtler dimensions of his playing are lost in the mix.

*****(*) 2000 + One**

Winter & Winter 32 *Motian; Chris Potter (ts); Masabumi Kikuchi (p); Larry Grenadier, Steve Swallow (b).* 99.

Anticipating the millennium with a set of consolidated brilliance rather than millennial intensity, Motian springs no great surprises. The tracks are, familiarly enough, quite short and carefully paced; the drums sit well forward in the mix, but with just a single horn and with Swallow playing like a second lead there is plenty of action. 'One In Three' and 'Pas De Deux', sitting right at the centre of the album, provide some of the most stimulating action and there is a slight downturn after that point, partly because the sound seems less various than usual. But no quibbles; an excellent set.

*****(*) Europe**

Winter & Winter 63 *Motian; Pietro Tonolo(ss, ts); Chris Cheek (ts); Steve Cardenas, Ben Monder (g); Anders Christensen (b).* 7/00.

*****(*) Holiday With Strings**

Winter & Winter 69 *As above.* 11/01.

This is where the Electric Bebop idea really does pay off. Anders Christensen isn't the player that Steve Swallow is, but (much as Michael Henderson did for Miles) his occasional crudities are part of the message. On the first album, it's oddly disconcerting to hear Monk tunes, three of them, along with Parker's 'Bird Feathers', Herbie Nichols' '2300 Skidoo' and Tadd Dameron's 'If You Could See Me Now', played amplified and with an almost fusion twist. But right from the start, with Monk's rare 'Oska T', the idiom seems just right. Paul includes a couple of originals, 'Blue Midnight' and 'Fiasco', and demonstrates in each how much of his own thinking has grown out of – and now significantly out of – bebop. The time signatures wouldn't scare anyone of the founding generation, but the layering of harmonic ideas would certainly startle them. Motian never relies on preset licks; his own statements sound fresh and one can hear him cajoling and challenging the members of the band. Cheek is a doughty presence, but it's Tonolo who's a bit of a revelation, particularly on soprano.

Holiday With Strings conjures up certain expectations as a title. No orchestral accompaniment, however, just another rugged outing from an increasingly flexible outfit. Intriguing as the original material is, it's the standards that benefit from the closest attention. 'It Never Entered My Mind' has hints of Miles and Coltrane with slower and more spacious passages interspersed with harmonically busier sections. That same easy switch of registers and dynamics transforms 'Oh, What A Beautiful Morning' into a tiny epic. 'Arabesque', 'Endgame' and 'Look To The Black Wall' are all tightly constructed and crisply played. Tonolo again shines, though Cheek seems to be looking more to his laurels this time out and fires off some bursting solos.

***** :rarum – Selected Recordings**

ECM 000180102 *Motian; John Surman (ss); Billy Drewes (as); Charles Brackeen, Joe Lovano (ts); Paul Bley, Keith Jarrett (p); Bill Frisell (g); David Izenzon, Jean-François Jenny-Clark (b).* 72–85.

Artists make their own selections for the :rarum compilations and Motian has chosen to ignore everything for ECM after 1985. He begins with material from his debut *Conception Vessel*, takes in tracks from *Dance, Psalm* and *It Should Have Happened A Long Time Ago*, and also work for other leaders and in collaborative projects, like the album with Paul Bley, John Surman and Bill Frisell. Nothing from *Tribute*, which suggests either dissatisfaction or that it may be about to reappear.

Mound City Blue Blowers

GROUP

A group name used by the kazoo player and vocalist Red McKenzie (1899–1948) for many years, although at present only their swing-era records are available on CD.

*****(*) Mound City Blue Blowers 1935–37**

Timeless CBC-018 *Bunny Berigan, Yank Lawson (t); Al Philburn (tb); Red McKenzie (kz, v); Eddie Miller, Forrest Crawford (cl, ts); Gil Bowers, Frank Signorelli (p); Nappy Lamare (g, v); Dave Barbour, Carmen Mastren, Eddie Condon (g); Sid Weiss, Harry Goodman, Bob Haggart, Pete Peterson, Mort Stuhlmaker (b); Ray Bauduc, Stan King, Dave Tough (d); Billy Wilson, Spooky Dickenson (v).* 5/35–2/36.

Red McKenzie led this group through various incarnations from the early '20s onwards. Their Brunswick sessions with Eddie Lang, when the group was no more than a quartet, would still be welcome on CD, but in the meantime this third generation of the band gets a comprehensive airing on another fine John R.T. Davies mastering. By 1935 McKenzie's comb-and-paper solos and rather proper singing might have seemed anachronistic, but he was a surprisingly inventive performer and he sounds quite at home, even in the company of some illustrious sidemen. But the main point here is to catch glimpses of the superlative Berigan, frustratingly confined on some of the 15 tracks he appears on but a marvel nevertheless: sample the beautiful solo on 'You've Been Taking Lessons In Love'. There are eight tracks by what amounts to a prototype of the Bob Crosby Bob Cats, with Lawson and Miller in strong fettle, and the results overall are some of the most enjoyable examples of small-group swing of the time.

George Mraz (born 1944)

BASS

Mraz has a Czech background, but he has been a fixture in American rhythm sections for many years, a career reflected in the vast number of credits he receives in this book. He is based in and around New York.

***** Jazz**

Milestone MCD 9248-2 *Mraz; Rich Perry (ts); Richie Beirach, Larry Willis (p); Billy Hart (d).* 9–10/95.

***** My Foolish Heart**

Milestone MCD 9262-2 *As above, except omit Perry, Willis.* 6/95.

***** Bottom Lines**

Milestone MCD 9272-2 *Mraz; Rich Perry (ts); Cyrus Chestnut (p); Al Foster (d).* 4/97.

*****(*) Duke's Place**

Milestone MCD 9292-2 *Mraz; Cyrus Chestnut, Renee Rosnes (p); Billy Drummond (d).* 11/98.

After many years as the most dependable of rhythm men, Mraz suddenly accrued a small string of albums to his name. A bassist in the limelight is often not such good news, given the instrument's limitations as a solo force in the mainstream of the music, and Mraz seems aware of this – while still succumbing to temptation here and there. *Jazz* and *My Foolish Heart* are both basically trio dates (Willis and Perry have three guest appearances between them) with the bass given more prominence than usual. Beirach is a sympathetic confrère and Hart is appropriately discreet. There are some lovely things on both records: Beirach's almost motionless ballad, 'Sunday's Song', the steady investigation of 'Cinema Paradiso' and a surprisingly vivid *arco* reading of Strayhorn's 'Passion Flower'. But there's quite a lot of chaff, too. *Bottom Lines* introduces the concept of nine tunes all written by bassists. Perry is on hand throughout this time, and his rather gentle manner suits the occasion. 'Mr Pastorius', which Marcus Miller wrote for Miles Davis, has the original trumpet solo scored and played as a duo line by Mraz and Perry: handsomely done, if seemingly rather pointless. The best things come at the end, with a soft-centred 'Goodbye Porkpie Hat' and a very incisive reading of Steve Swallow's 'Falling Grace', surely the best thing on the record.

Duke's Place just shades the other records. Although it's yet another Ellington tribute, and at least half of it qualifies as over-familiar even by the standards of that songbook, the playing by Chestnut and Rosnes (they have five tracks each and share a mutual joust with 'Duke's Place' itself) affirms their individual eminence among today's pianists. Since they are featured on alternate tracks throughout the session, the record works nicely in terms of contrast, a fulsome Chestnut treatment of 'Come Sunday' followed by a quicksilver Rosnes version of 'Angelica', and so on. Mraz plays a somewhat more supportive role rather than a front-line one as on the other albums – and it doesn't hurt.

***(*) Morava

Milestone MCD 9309-2 *Mraz; Emil Viklicky (p); Zuzana Lapcíková (cymbalom, v); Billy Hart (d). 6/00.*

An extraordinarily beautiful record, of Moravian folk melodies and songs. Mraz himself is actually from Bohemia, but his father was a Moravian, and Viklicky also belongs to the region. When they play an almost straight jazz piece such as 'Myjavca' the record's not so strong, but in tandem with the simple, direct singing of Lapcíková, the haunting sound of the cymbalom, and melodies as heartbreaking as 'Aspen Leaf', the record mines a unique strain – as well as surrendering nothing in terms of the quality of the playing, completely integrated with the material. Though ignored in America, this is a personal triumph for the musicians.

Idris Muhammad (born 1939)

DRUMS, VOCALS

Born in New Orleans, he began his career in R&B before working with a number of leaders on the jazz scene, including Gene Ammons, Hank Crawford, Rusty Bryant, Houston Person, Pharoah Sanders and Grant Green. He was also a founding member of the Paris Reunion Band.

**(*) Black Rhythm Revolution

BGP 46 *Muhammad; Virgil Jones (t); Clarence Thomas (ss, ts, f); Kenny Barron, Harold Mabern (p); Alan Fontaine, Melvin Sparks (g); Ron Carter, Jimmy Lewis (b); Angel Allende, Buddy Caldwell (perc). 11/70.*

*** Legends Of Acid Jazz

Prestige 24170 *As above; add Willie Bivins (vib); Sakinah Muhammad (v). 11/70, 9/71.*

The dateline is a bit of a giveaway if the title is leading you to expect a slice of militant agit-prop. So is the personnel. By 1970, the fires had been banked down and Muhammad's debut as leader is a piece of remarkably soft-centred jazz fusion that is surprisingly unfocused in the rhythm department. Only the opening 'By The Red Sea' is an original and while it might have been an apocalyptic stormer – Children of Israel pursued by the wicked Pharaoh – it comes across as light as Egyptian cotton. The only time Muhammad's drumming becomes in any way interesting is on Jack McDuff's 'Soulful Drums', where he tinkers with the count. A cover of James Brown's 'Super Bad' makes you realize just how good and dirty the original was.

The first album is compiled with the second, *Peace And Rhythm*, on the *Legends* package, which is certainly better value. The follow-up disc is dominated by the 'Peace And Rhythm Suite', which is a little more rugged than it sounds. The rest is generic. So why have these obscure Prestige releases survived into the CD era? Quite simply because Muhammad has a certain reputation in acid jazz and rare groove circles. We've heard them both sampled more than once.

*** Power Of Soul

CTI 86149 *Muhammad; Randy Brecker (t, flhn); Grover Washington Jr (ss, ts); Bob James (p, ky); Joe Beck (g); Gary King (b); Ralph MacDonald (perc). 74.*

The title tune is by Jimi Hendrix, which means that Muhammad was in the vanguard as far as recognizing Jimi's jazz/fusion potential was concerned. It's a powerful piece and kicks off this soulful, groove-laden disc perfectly. Again, *Power Of Soul* owes its longevity to those DJs who've sampled and mixed Grover Washington's keening solos and Joe Beck's powerful riffing and top lines. Joe contributes 'The Saddest Thing', the most reflective of the four cuts; it isn't a long set and there's nothing extra on the CD. Arranger James is composer of 'Piece Of Mind', and Washington, on the cusp of major success himself, brings in the long and lovely 'Loran's Dance', which sees the album out on a high.

**(*) House Of The Rising Sun

CTI 8363 *Muhammad; Tom Harrell (t); Barry Rogers, Fred Wesley (tb); David Sanborn (as); Bob Berg, Michael Brecker (ts); Don Grolnick, Leon Pendarvis (p, ky); Sir Roland Hanna (p); Hugh McCracken (g); Wilbur Bascomb Jr, Will Lee (b); George Devens (perc); Patti Austin, Hilda Harris, Harmonica Frank Floyd (v); strings. 76.*

Much sought after in soul-jazz circles, but for us an overheated and overwrought piece of work that sees producer Creed Taylor's hand slip as he adds the seasoning. You'll have heard at least some of this record if you've spent any time in dance clubs. For jazz fans, the track that will be of most interest is 'Sudan', a collaboration with Tom Harrell and rhythmically the most interesting thing in the package. The Meters' 'Hey-Pocky-A-Way' is a fun cut, and Ashford and Simpson's 'Hard To Face The Music' will appeal to the same crossover audience. The traditional 'House' is given a fresh lick of paint and the Brazilian standard 'Bahia' is an excuse to let off some steam. A club staple it may be; it's not a record you'll spend a lot of time playing at home.

★★★ Kabsha

Evidence ECD 22096 *Muhammad; George Coleman, Pharoah Sanders (ts); Ray Drummond (b).* 80.

Somewhat surprisingly, after a string of albums for Fantasy in the later '70s, Muhammad turned back to a pretty straight jazz idiom, and an unexpectedly spare setting after the heavy production of previous discs. For this one, as if to prove the point, he hired Pharoah Sanders, though Pharoah in those days was heading in the other direction and becoming a club star. He spells the superb George Coleman, though the two tenors do go head to head on 'GCCG Blues', of which there are two fine takes on the reissue. Muhammad sounds pungent and tightly marshalled on his own 'Kabsha' (a second take is also included) and rides his kit delicately on 'Soulful Drums', which he'd made a bit of a signature piece on his very first record. Originally released on Teresa, this must have been a bit of a surprise to anyone who knew Idris's earlier work. It's still a refreshing surprise to us.

★★★(★) Right Now

Cannonball 27105 *Muhammad; Gary Bartz (as); George Coleman, Joe Lovano (ts); Curtis Lundy (b).* 98.

It should be obvious now what's happening. First a soul-jazz record (the deleted *My Turn*), then a hotter and more improvising project. Again, no harmony instrument, which puts a lot of pressure on the leader and Lundy to keep things swinging. The personnel on this is mouth-watering and some of the playing is first-rate. They kick off with 'Miles's Mode' and 'Straight Street', not part of the Coltrane oeuvre that is very often covered. There are a couple of strong Bartz originals, and some searing alto to go with them. Lundy, an underrated writer, contributes the title track, which grooves righteously from first to last and big George Coleman has his party piece on 'New Orleans Gumbo'. Muhammad's attack is sharper than ever, though it sounds as if he might be using a smaller kit than in the past. The only downside of this record is that you might struggle to find it in the store. But persist.

Jim Mullen (born 1945)

GUITAR

The Glaswegian began as a bass player, but guitar has been his calling, with stints in both rock and jazz situations. His partnership with Dick Morrissey was very successful in the '80s, but there's nothing left on CD. In the '90s, he became a leader and patrician-sideman of real stature and authority.

★★★(★) Rule Of Thumb

Jazzprint JPVP 104 *Mullen; Dave O'Higgins (ss, ts); Lawrence Cottle (b); Ian Thomas (d).* 8/94.

★★★ We Go Back

Jazzprint JPVP 105 *Mullen; Gareth Williams (p); Mick Hutton (b); Gary Husband (d).* 1/96.

★★★(★) Live In Glasgow

Jazzprint JPVP 103 *As above.*

Mullen is a redoubtable musician who's brought both an exciting style and a keen intelligence to playing situations which might have otherwise encouraged either noodling or showing off. He understands the attraction of rock as a crowd-pleaser, but what he plays is never diluted by mere showboating or self-indulgence. The Jazzprint releases document both his early-'90s band (with Cottle on electric bass) and the 'acoustic' quartet of more recent times. *Rule Of Thumb* is all snap and hustle, a lean group sound on which the soloists expand. O'Higgins goes a little too far here and there, but Mullen himself is quick to right any piece which sounds like it might have got out of hand. Crisp and smartly organized, with ten pieces despatched inside an hour, it works very well as a CD.

We Go Back lets Mullen nod acknowledgement to some of his favourite tunes, as well as a few originals such as the needle-fine 'Medication'. The quartet sound heavier and less mobile than the old unit, but there's nothing wrong with the playing. *Live In Glasgow* is a homecoming in front of old friends, and by now the quartet is well played-in. Horace Silver's 'Peace' gets things off to a powerful start, and Mullen is clearly in the mood to blow; it's a live set where you can feel the band flexing their muscles without losing their heads. 'My Ideal', with a particularly graceful cadenza, cools them off. Williams, like O'Higgins before him, occasionally overdoes it, but it does add to the excitement.

★★★(★) Burns

Black Box BBJ2016 *Mullen; Gareth Williams (p); Mick Hutton (b); Gary Husband (d).* 4/00.

Soft old sod. Here he is interpreting Rabbie Burns, from 'Banks And Braes' and 'Bonnie Wee Thing' to 'Comin' Through The Rye' and 'Red, Red Rose', and getting a hard man's tenderness out of them. Scottish folk music and jazz have rarely been comfy bedfellows, as the history of Ken Hyder's band Talisker has shown, but Jim makes these faded old blooms shine with new morning dew. It's a fearsomely lovely record. Williams and the others keep the music honest if it ever seems ready to fizzle into noodling, but Mullen's singing tone carries the day.

★★★(★) Somewhere In The Hills

Hep CD 2085 *As above.* 8/02.

The same band, but a couple of years on and sounding increasingly magisterial. 'Smile', 'The Night We Called It a Day' and Jobim's 'Somewhere In The Hills' are immaculate and thoughtful jazz performances with enough jazz-rock flavouring to add bite. There is a brief reprise of the Burnsian strain with 'The Craw That Killed The Pussy, O' (maybe more familiar as 'Green Grow The Rushes') but the emphasis this time is less eclectic. Williams is outstanding as usual and Husband always has interesting things to say without grandstanding. A fine, approachable record.

Gerry Mulligan (1927–96)

BARITONE SAXOPHONE, PIANO, SOPRANO SAXOPHONE

He took what looks like a cumbersome horn and made it sound fleet and natural. Mulligan began his career as an arranger with Gene Krupa and created the classic 'Disc Jockey Jump' as early as 1947. He was a key presence in the Birth Of The Cool project (usually attributed to Miles Davis) and co-led the famous pianoless group with Chet Baker. Later years saw him combine sophisticated arrangements with cool, often tender baritone on a host of small-group and big-band sessions.

★★★ Mullenium

Columbia CK 65678 *Mulligan; Ed Badgley, John Dee, Don Fagerquist, Don Ferrara, Jerry Lloyd, Al Porcino, Red Rodney,*

Phil Sunkel, Joe Techner, Ray Triscari (t); Sy Berger, Warren Covington, Jim Dahl, Chuck Harris, Frank Hunter, Frank Rehak, Jim Seaman, Dick Taylor, Jack Zimmerman (tb); Bob Brookmeyer (vtb); Louis Giamo, Charlie Kennedy, Lee Konitz, Hal McCusick, Joe Soldo, Harry Terrill (as); Charlie Rouse, Zoot Sims, Phil Urso, Charlie Ventura (ts); Gene Allen, Jack Schwartz (bs); Elliot Lawrence, Teddy Napoleon (p); Mike Triscari (g); Joe Benjamin, Bob Strahl (b); Dave Bailey, Gene Krupa (d). 46–57.

*** Young Mulligan

Proper PVCD 119 2CD *As above.* 46–52.

*** Legacy

N2K 10002 *Mulligan; Chet Baker, Pete Candoli, Miles Davis, Jon Eardley, Don Ferrara, Wallace Roney, Clark Terry, Nick Travis (t); Wayne Andre, Dave Bargeron, Kai Winding (tb); Bob Brookmeyer, Bob Enevoldsen (vtb); John Clark, Junior Collins, John Graas (frhn); Billy Barber, Ray Siegel (tba); Dick Meldonian, Bud Shank, Phil Woods (as); Gene Quill (as, cl); Zoot Sims (ts); Gene Allen, Don Davidson (bs); Al Haig (p); Dick Mathes, Greg Phillinganes (ky); Mike Renzi (syn); Joe Mondragon, Joe Shulman, Bobby Whitlock (b); Dave Bailey, Bernie Dresel, Mel Lewis, Max Roach (d); Patti Austin, Diva Gray, Darryl Tookes (v).* 49–96.

The most important baritone saxophonist in contemporary jazz, Mulligan took the turbulent Serge Chaloff as his model, but he blended his fast, slightly pugnacious delivery with the elegance of Johnny Hodges and Lester Young. This produced an agile, *legato* sound which became instinct with the cool West Coast style, the flipside of bebop. Mulligan's – and Claude Thornhill's – major role in what became known as Miles Davis's *Birth Of The Cool* is now increasingly acknowledged, as is his genius as a composer/arranger. On the model of the *Birth Of The Cool* nonet, his big bands have the intimacy and spaciousness of much smaller groups, preferring subtlety to blasting power. His small groups, conversely, work with a depth of harmonic focus that suggests a much larger outfit.

In his short story 'Entropy', the novelist Thomas Pynchon takes Mulligan's early-'50s pianoless quartets with Chet Baker as a crux of post-modernism, improvisation without the safety net of predictable chords. The revisionist argument was that Mulligan attempted the experiment simply because he had to work in a club with no piano. The true version is that there was a piano, albeit an inadequate one, but he was already experimenting with a much more arranged sound for small groups (to which the baritone saxophone was peculiarly adaptable) and the absence of a decent keyboard was merely an additional spur.

The material on *Mullenium* surfaced in the '70s on an LP called *The Arranger.* It comprises a lost big-band session from 1957 and a number of arrangements made for Gene Krupa ('Disc Jockey Jump' and 'How High The Moon') and for Elliot Lawrence. These do not feature Mulligan much or at all as a player, but they offer a valuable insight into his skill as an orchestrator, with a distinctive emphasis on the middle register and a relaxed and easy swing. There are valuable insights to be gleaned here, but it is probably best to leave this album till later in your exposure to Mulligan and his music, since any epiphanies are likely to be retrospective.

The material on *Legacy* covers a similar span of time. Mulligan is beginning to emerge as a soloist of some power and confidence, but even here the emphasis is still on arrangement. The selections are familiar enough – 'Jeru', 'Bernie's Tune', 'Mainstream', 'Boplicity' and 'Walking Shoes', as well as later stuff – but as a single-volume sampling of Mulligan's career this is hard to beat, scamped as the chronology is.

The Proper set is extremely good value and covers the waterfront with admirable thoroughness given the chronological span. We have some reservations about the mastering and sound quality, but there's nothing that will scare the horses.

*** Mulligan Plays Mulligan

Original Jazz Classics OJC 003 *Mulligan; Jerry Hurwitz, Nick Travis (t); Ollie Wilson (tb); Allen Eager (ts); Max McElroy (bs); George Wallington (p); Phil Leshin (b); Walter Bolden (d); Gail Madden (perc).* 8/51.

These early sessions already demonstrate what a fine composer and arranger the saxophonist was. In comparison to later work, they're slightly featureless and Mulligan's playing is very callow. It's perhaps best to come back to this stuff.

**(*) Nights At The Turntable, 1951–1952

Jasmine 2957 *Mulligan; Chet Baker, Jerry Lloyd, Nick Travis (t); Ollie Wilson (tb); Allen Eager (ts); Max McElroy (bs); George Wallington (p); Phil Leshin, Carson Smith (b); Chico Hamilton (d); Gail Madden (perc).* 51–52.

So-so compilation of material from the early West Coast days. There are things of interest here, not least a glimpse of the famously eccentric Allen Eager in one of his very collectable forays, but most of the songs – 'Walking Shoes', 'Line For Lyons', 'My Funny Valentine', 'Utter Chaos' and 'Bweebidda Bobbida' - are readily available elsewhere, often in better versions or in better aural shape.

CORE COLLECTION

**** The Original Quartet

Blue Note 94407-2 2CD *Mulligan; Chet Baker (t); Bob Whitlock, Carson Smith, Joe Mondragon (b); Chico Hamilton, Larry Bunker (d).* 8/52–6/53.

Mulligan's pianoless quartet is one of the epochal jazz groups, even if it had no such aspirations, formed for nothing more than a regular gig at The Haig (where some of the tracks were recorded) and even though many of its sessions were recorded quickly and with little preparation. In retrospect, it's the simplest pleasures which have made the music endure: the uncomplicated swing of the varying rhythm sections, the piquant contrast of amiably gruff baritone and shyly melodious trumpet, the coolly effective originals like 'Nights At The Turntable' and the irresistible 'Walkin' Shoes', and the subtle and feelingful treatments of standards such as 'Lullaby Of The Leaves'. Cool but hot, slick but never too clever, these are some of the most pleasurable records of their time. The two-disc set includes the basic library of 42 tracks and is an indispensable part of Mulligan's legacy.

***(*) The Best Of The Gerry Mulligan Quartet With Chet Baker

Pacific Jazz CDP 7 95481 2 *Mulligan; Chet Baker (t); Henry Grimes, Carson Smith, Bob Whitlock (b); Dave Bailey, Larry Bunker, Chico Hamilton (d).* 8/52–12/57.

This compilation CD, drawn from singles (including the classic 'Soft Shoe'/'Walkin' Shoes' combination) and subsequent 10-inch LPs, is an excellent sampling of Mulligan's 11-month association with Chet, with a single item, 'Festive Minor', from the same December 1957 sessions that yielded *Reunion.* It's fair (to Chet, at least) to record that it was Mulligan, not the famously unreliable trumpeter, who brought the line-up to an end. In June 1953, Mulligan was jailed for several months on a drugs offence. It is perhaps as well that the group was folded at its peak. Generously recorded in a warm close-up, the sessions convey all of Mulligan's skill as a writer and arranger, with the saxophone and a very foregrounded bass filling in the space normally occupied by piano.

*** With The Chubby Jackson Big Band

Original Jazz Classics OJCCD 711 *Mulligan; Chet Baker, Don Ferrara, Howard McGhee, Al Porcino (t); J. J. Johnson, Kai Winding (tb); Charlie Kennedy (as); Georgie Auld, Zoot Sims (ts); Tony Aless (p); Chubby Jackson, Carson Smith (b); Chico Hamilton, Don Lamond (d).* 5/53.

An odd, rather fudged release, pairing the classic quartet, with Mulligan as featured soloist, with the Chubby Jackson Big Band. Stellar as it was and magnificently organized, it seems to be in the wrong gear for Mulligan, who works through the dense, rather toppy arrangements like a man cheerfully walking through a rainstorm. Fascinating to hear so many remarkable soloists all pulling together, though they all sound as if they're protesting too much. Not an unqualified success, but a further interesting byway on Mulligan's recording career.

*** The Original Gerry Mulligan Tentet & Quartet

GNP Crescendo 56 *Mulligan; Chet Baker, Pete Candoli (t); Bob Enevoldsen (tb); John Grassi (frhn); Bud Shank (as); Joe Mondragon, Carson Smith (b); Larry Bunker, Chico Hamilton (d).* 53.

The presence of Tadd Dameron's 'Lady Bird' points to an obvious source for the mid-size arrangements of the tentet. The smaller group settings are more familiar territory for Mulligan fans, but these 1953 reissues of larger ensemble work are full of interest.

The mostly standards material of the latter half of the record is balanced by some superb Mulligan writing ('Simbah', 'Walking Shoes', 'Flash') on the first half. Nice sound as well, decently remastered.

*** California Concerts

Pacific Jazz 46860 *Mulligan; Jon Eardley (t); Red Mitchell (b); Chico Hamilton (d).* 11/54.

Post-Chet. As far as French fans and critics were concerned, this was how young America looked and sounded. Sunny, cooled-out, elaborated but determinedly un-profound, it smacks very strongly of a time and place. No less than the slightly epicene Baker, the crew-cut, square-jawed Mulligan became a kind of icon, in sharp counter-definition to the long-hair, goatee and beret image of jazz.

The California material showcases a bold and inventive group. Eardley sounds not a bit like Chet and shapes a solo entirely differently, and the whole rhythmic/harmonic cast of the group changes with the introduction of Mitchell and Hamilton, who mesh instantly on 'Blues Going Up' and turn in a remarkable rhythm performance on 'Yardbird Suite'. The inclusion of 'Darn That Dream' and 'Makin' Whoopee' only serves to highlight the originality of Mulligan's conception. Again one can hearing him working over chord variants which come out of bebop, but he may be influenced by classical precedents as well.

*** At Storyville

Pacific Jazz 94472 *Mulligan; Bob Brookmeyer (vtb); Bill Crow (b); Dave Bailey (d).* 12/56.

There is a romping self-confidence and camaraderie to this live date (from the Boston club rather than New Orleans). For all the buttoned-down sobriety of this group, it is also a fleet and powerful outfit, capable of generating a big, resonant sound. Mulligan takes the lion's share of solos, but Brookmeyer is often working softly just behind, his gentle attack and rhythmically relaxed delivery acting as counterpoise to the leader's unusually punchy articulation. It would have been interesting to hear an occasional switch to soprano at this stage; one can hear Mulligan striving for a tighter, more pinched tonality on occasion, though generally he favours a mid-range, playing a couple of solos which might just as easily have been done on tenor, but for a few tell-tale pedal points.

***(*) Mulligan Meets Monk

Riverside 1106 *Mulligan; Thelonious Monk (p); Wilbur Ware (b); Shadow Wilson (d).* 8/57.

Not an entirely probable encounter, but Mulligan more than keeps afloat on the Monk tunes, sounding least at ease on 'Rhythm-A-Ning', but absolutely confident on 'Straight, No Chaser' and, of course, 'Round About Midnight'. The dark, heavy sound of Wilbur Ware's bass is sufficiently 'below' Mulligan's horn and his intervals sufficiently broad to tempt the saxophonist to some unusual whole-note progressions. Monk darts in and out like a tailor's needle, cross-stitching counter-melodies and neatly abstract figures. The 2003 edition is 20-bit mastered but with no additional material, beyond the alternates included on earlier CD issues.

***(*) Gerry Mulligan–Paul Desmond Quartet

Verve 519850-2 *Mulligan; Paul Desmond (as); Joe Benjamin (b); Dave Bailey (d).* 8/57.

Another of Verve's summit conferences – and a felicitous one. There has probably never been a saxophone sound as finely blended as this, and our only quibble – 'Body And Soul' notwithstanding – is that the material is not really up to the playing. Some of the tunes are obscure enough to suggest that it wasn't just run down on the spot, but there is a lack of anything to get one's teeth into. The best moments are, as in 'Body And Soul', when Desmond moves to the front and Mulligan plays what are effectively piano chord-shapes behind him. Glorious.

***(*) Songbook

Blue Note 33575-2 *Mulligan; Lee Konitz (as); Allen Eager, Zoot Sims (as, ts); Al Cohn (ts, bs); Freddie Green, Paul Palmieri (g); Dick Wetmore (vn); Calo Scott (clo); Vinnie Burke, Henry Grimes (b); Dave Bailey (d).* 12/57.

The year 1957 was a busy one for Mulligan, which is perhaps why this largely forgotten session was arranged by Bill Holman. There is no discernible difference in the voicings, but of course the multi-saxophone line-up is already rather startling. Allen Eager was effectively lost to the music after this point, which seems all the greater pity given the strength and authority of his playing (like Zoot Sims, he also doubles unexpectedly on alto) and the calm, authoritative logic of his soloing. Mulligan is as ever the centre of attention, but only as the apex of a highly organized octet consisting of individualists. He reprises 'Disc Jockey Jump' in a new, more smoothly contoured form and he showcases 'Turnstile' and 'Venus De Milo', two of his best and most adaptable compositions. The CD also includes four bop-pish tunes recorded with bassist Vinnie Burke and what amounts to a non-classical string quartet: guitar, violin, cello, bass. Unusual and non-essential as far as a casual collector is concerned, but another aspect of Mulligan's eclectic brilliance.

***** Reunion With Chet Baker**

Pacific Jazz 46857 *Mulligan; Chet Baker (t); Henry Grimes (b); Dave Bailey (d).* 12/57.

For one reason and another, there weren't many opportunities to reconvene the classic group. After a gap of some years, there is a touch of reserve – and maybe suspicion – in this reunion recording. Chet's tone is reserved and his delivery rather wandery, and there is an oddly clenched quality to Mulligan's playing as well. There are still, though, wonderful moments to be had from the album. 'Ornithology' is unexpected in its freshness and vivacity, and the alternative takes of 'Trav'lin' Light' and 'Gee, Baby, Ain't I Good To You' are a measure of how intuitively these musicians responded to one another when given time and the right context. Also, the closing version of 'All The Things You Are' is very special and maybe stands as epigraph – if not epitaph – to Gerry's association with Chet.

*****(*) The Gerry Mulligan Quartets In Concert**

Pablo 5309-2 *Mulligan; Bob Brookmeyer (vtb, p); Joe Benjamin, Bill Crow (b); Dave Bailey, Gus Johnson (d).* 8/57–10/62.

New discoveries from the Granz archive (he introduces both gigs, the second in French), this couples quartet dates with Brookmeyer from the Hollwood Bowl (1957) and Paris (1962). The earlier set is over too soon, with Jeru and Brookmeyer dovetailing so beautifully you want it to go on and on. The 1962 session comes from a period when the Concert Jazz Band was taking up much of Mulligan's time. The originals here feel a little inscrutable. Brookmeyer goes over to the piano for 'Subterranean Blues'. A delightful survival.

****** What Is There To Say?**

Columbia CK 52978 *Mulligan; Art Farmer (t); Bill Crow (b); Dave Bailey (d).* 12/58, 1/59.

*****(*) News From Blueport**

Jazz Hour 73577 *As above.* 59.

Farmer doesn't quite have the lyrical poignancy of Chet Baker in this setting, but he has a full, deep-chested tone (soon to be transferred wholesale and exclusively to flugelhorn) which combines well with Mulligan's baritone. *What Is There To Say?* was Mulligan's first recording for Columbia. It's very direct, very unfussy, very focused on the leader, but with the same skills in evidence as on the earlier *The Arranger*, which was a dry run for the label. The first album proper is a small masterpiece of controlled invention. Mulligan's solos fit into the structure of 'As Catch Can' and 'Festive Minor' as if they were machine-tooled. Farmer responds in kind, with smooth *legato* solos and delicate fills.

The Newport tapes are technically flawed, with drop-outs and distortions on several tracks, but this was a wonderful performance from all concerned and Mulligan collectors will certainly want to hear it.

*****(*) The Complete Gerry Mulligan Meets Ben Webster Sessions**

Verve 539095-2 2CD *Mulligan; Ben Webster (ts); Jimmy Rowles (p); Leroy Vinnegar (b); Mel Lewis (d).* 11 & 12/59.

***** The Silver Collection: Gerry Mulligan Meets The Saxophonists**

Verve 827436-2 *Mulligan; Conte Candoli, Don Ferrara, Nick Travis (t); Bob Brookmeyer (vtb, p); Wayne Andre, Alan Ralph (tb); Paul Desmond, Johnny Hodges, Dick Meldonian, Gene Quill (as); Stan Getz, Zoot Sims, Ben Webster (ts); Gene Allen (bcl, bs); Lou Levy, Jimmy Rowles, Claude Williamson (p); Joe Benjamin, Ray Brown, Buddy Clark, Leroy Vinnegar (b); Dave Bailey, Stan Levey, Mel Lewis (d).* 57–60.

***** Verve Jazz Masters 36**

Verve 523342-2 *Mulligan; Conte Candoli, Don Ferrara, Doc Severinsen, Clark Terry, Nick Travis (t); Willie Dennis (tb); Bob Brookmeyer (vtb); Alan Ralph (btb); Gene Quill (as, cl); Bob Donovan, Dick Meldonian (as); Jim Reider, Zoot Sims (ts); Gene Allen (bs); Buddy Clark, Bill Crow (b); Gus Johnson, Mel Lewis (d).* 7/60–12/62.

In Mulligan's book, everyone (by which he presumably means soloists as well as punters) profits from the 'good bath of overtones' you get standing in front of a big band. The great saxophonists lined up on *The Silver Collection* sound mostly constrained rather than inspired by the small- to medium-scale arrangements, steered in the direction of Mulligan's recitalist's cool rather than towards any new improvisational heights. Webster is magisterial on the sessions of November and December 1959 ('Chelsea Bridge' and 'Tell Me When' are excerpted on *The Silver Collection*), and the two saxophones blend gloriously in the lower register. Any quibbles about some other aspects of the sound have been allayed by a new, digitally remastered edition which restores the whole of the session, complete with alternatives. There is probably a surplus of material for most tastes, but hearing these two remarkable figures, with their very different backgrounds and approaches, working in this proximity is a rare privilege. Of the other saxophonists sampled, Hodges probably sounds the happiest of the lot on the compilation, but then he was used to quite reasonable arrangements; these tracks were originally issued backed by the Paul Desmond sessions, which made perfect sense all round.

The *Jazz Masters* collection is an excellent buy but is relatively limited in scope. Drawn in the main from *The Concert Jazz Band* discs, *Gerry Mulligan '63* (albeit recorded a year earlier) and *A Concert In Jazz*, it nevertheless gives full measure from these and fills in an important stage in Jeru's progress.

***** Gerry Mulligan And The Concert Jazz Band**

RTE Europe 1 710382/83 2CD *As for Jazz Masters.* 60.

***** Live At Paris Olympia 1960**

Laserlight 14354 2CD *As above.* 60.

***** Live In Zurich, 1960**

TCB 02122 *As above.* 60.

***** Concert In The Rain**

Jazz Band 2129 *As above.* 62, 63.

The RTE set is one of a series of live airshots. The Concert Jazz Band was an extraordinary outfit, perhaps the best representation there was of Mulligan's music. Unfortunately, this recording is not especially good; it is muddy and indistinct in important areas, lacking in pep and definition at exactly the moment when one senses the music taking flight. The performances are mostly long and designed to give maximum exposure to the soloists, but there is enough tight ensemble work to confirm that, even in this environment, Mulligan was absolutely in the driving seat.

Concert in the Rain finds the Concert Jazz Band at a wet Newport, together with some later sextet material. Sound is again not great, but it's a valuable document for collectors. So, too, is the Laserlight set, also available on French Trema, and though not too clever a tape, a very enjoyable performance. The Zurich date is better recorded but the players sound rather distant, not so much sonically but in terms of ensemble and improvising.

*****(*) Live At The Village Vanguard**

Verve 589488 *Similar to above; add Clark Terry (t); Jim Reider (ts).* 60.

A limited reissue that will remain only on sale until 2005, this is at least a quality recording of the Concert Band in a club setting. Terry is the most obvious additional asset, but the long opening 'Blueport' has a nice solo by Jim Reider, who will be unknown to many fans. Mulligan himself is in excellent form throughout, as he tended to be on American soil and in terms of snap and tension, these are far more impressive performances than any of the European dates from the same year. 'Come Rain Or Come Shine' is Mulligan at his best, though Brookmeyer's reworking of 'Body And Soul' is worth having. Easily the best-buy live set from this period and further evidence of just how much live Mulligan has been languishing in label vaults and tape libraries.

**** Jazz Casual: Gerry Mulligan And Art Pepper**

Koch 8559 *Mulligan; Bob Brookmeyer (vtb); Wyatt Reuther (b); Gus Johnson (d).* 63.

Unfortunately, not Mulligan and Pepper together, but two broadcast sets taken from a public television series hosted by Ralph J. Gleason. The best thing on the album is Brookmeyer's own 'Open Country', but there are other points of interest, notably Gerry's switch to piano on 'Darn That Dream'. The liner-notes are inaccurate on personnels and the sound quality is inevitably a bit rough and grainy.

***** Night Lights**

Mercury 818 271-2 *Mulligan; Art Farmer (t, flhn); Bob Brookmeyer (vtb); Jim Hall (g); Bill Crow (b); Dave Bailey (d).* 63.

A somewhat overlooked Mulligan session, but marked out by some super playing from both Farmer and Brookmeyer. Mulligan himself is somewhat muted and concentrates as so often on filling out the middle of the orchestration. Hall is perhaps the key to the whole thing, an endlessly inventive and subtle player who takes great chances without fanfare.

***** Summit – Reunion Cumbre**

Orchard 802676 *Mulligan; Astor Piazzolla (acc); Bruno DeFilippi (g); Gianni Zilioli (mar); Tulio di Piscopo (d, perc).* 10/74.

A wonderful, one-off encounter between the saxophonist and the guiding spirit of *tango nueva,* recorded in Milan. Gerry instinctively understands the dark and shifting harmonies of Piazzolla's music and together they create a shifting fabric of softly understated sound that is unlike anything else in either man's canon. A delightful record that has had only intermittent circulation but which is well worth hunting down.

***** Carnegie Hall Concert**

Epic 450554 *Mulligan; Chet Baker (t); Ed Byrne (tb); Bob James (ky); John Scofield (g); Dave Samuels (vib, perc, v); Ron Carter (b); Harvey Mason (d).* 11/74.

This was only the second – and would be the last – reunion between Jeru and Chet, and it was by and large a happy one. If there were differences and ongoing problems, they were very largely kept off the stand and both frontmen respond to the gala occasion with impassioned and highly focused playing. The rhythm section was the obvious sign of the times, though it's discreet and under-amplified enough not to intrude. Anyone keen on tracing the early career and influences of John Scofield will be delighted to hear his clean, spacious lines. Needless to say, they did 'My Funny Valentine', but the tune which sounds most refreshed and urgent is 'Line For Lyons', one of the less celebrated products of their association. A strong album, and by no means an exhaustive document of the occasion.

***** Idol Gossip**

Chiaroscuro 155 *Mulligan; Hank Jones, Tom Fay, Bill Mays (p); Lionel Hampton, Dave Samuels (vib); Bucky Pizzarelli, Mike Santiago (g); George Duvivier (b); Bobby Rosengarden, Grady Tate (d); Candido Camero (perc).* 11/76.

Chiaroscuro seems exactly the right label, for this one has remained in the shadows for a quarter of a century. Mulligan's New Sextet, of which two contrasting versions are heard, was a showcase for new and reworked material (including a second version of 'Song For Strayhorn') and an unexpected cover of 'Waltzing Matilda'. Dave Samuels and Bucky Pizzarelli are key structural elements, though neither has much to say in solos. A lost curiosity, too accomplished to be set aside as 'transitional' and yet not entirely satisfactory as a finished album. Mulligan's soprano still sounds like an uneasy double, but it's kept to a sensible minimum.

***** Blues For Gerry: The Lionel Hampton Sessions**

Universe 65 *Mulligan; Hank Jones (p); Lionel Hampton (vib); Bucky Pizzarelli (g); George Duvivier (b); Grady Tate (d); Candido Camero (perc).* 10/77.

A delightful encounter that inspired some first-rate playing all round. Gerry sounds agile and quick-fingered round Hampton and there is more swing to his playing even than usual on 'Lion For Lyons' and 'Walking Shoes'. Hamp is pretty much the dominant partner, though Mulligan solos prominently on just about every track. Inevitably, there were a couple of themes got together to mark the occasion: the co-written 'Gerry Meets Hamp' is a breezy workout for baritone and vibes, while Hampton's 'Blues For Gerry' is more reflective and conceals a strain of sadness. Even more interesting is a first appearance of the new 'Song For Johnny Hodges'. Tate is masterful on these sessions, but there are good things from Pizzarrelli and Jones as well. These dates have been issued under half a dozen different imprints; this appears to be the latest and current one.

***** Midas Touch: Live In Berlin**

Concord CCD 2169 *Mulligan; Dave Brubeck, Ted Rosenthal (p); Dean Johnson (b); Ron Vincent (d).* 5/95.

Gerry Mulligan died in January 1996, so this really is a last throw. The set was recorded for German radio and it's impressive not so much for the quality of Jeru's playing as he battles with cancer as for the fine new writing he unveiled on what was to be his last European tour. 'Midas Lives', 'Sun On The Stairs' and (possibly an ironic title in the circumstances) 'Curtains' are all marked by the saxophonist's trademarks of firm, middle-register melody, solid harmonic grounding with some treacherous spots (notably on 'Midas Lives') and a subtle and unflurried approach to rhythm. He sounds in very good voice and his phrasing is anything but laid-back but often taut and propulsive. Rosenthal is a more than able accompanist, aware that Mulligan's ability to hold the chords in his head frees the pianist considerably. However, it's the final duet on 'These Foolish Things' with former employer and special guest Dave Brubeck which gives the set a special sense of occasion; deeply moving.

***** Walk On The Water**
DRG CDSL 5194 *Mulligan; Mike Davis, Laurie Frink, Tom Harrell, Danny Hayes, Alan Raph, Barry Ries (t); Dave Glenn, Keith O'Quinn (tb); Gerry Niewood, Kenneth Hitchcock (as); Seth Broedy, Gary Keller, Ralph Olsen, Eric Turker (ts); Joe Temperley (bs); Mitchel Forman (p); Mike Bocchicchio (b); Richard De Rosa (d).* 9/80.

Some years after the demise of the Concert Jazz Band, Mulligan reconvened a similar project with wonderful latter-day soloists of the quality of Tom Harrell and the long-overlooked Gerry Niewood. The set consists of four originals, among them the gorgeous 'Song For Strayhorn', a Mitchel Forman composition called 'Angelica' and Duke Ellington's 'Across The Track Blues'.

****(*) La Menace**
DRG 8475 *Mulligan; Tom Fay, Derek Smith (p); Dave Grusin (ky); Pete Levin (syn); Jay Leonhart, Jack Six (b); Michael DiPasqua, Bobby Rosengarden (d).* 82.

Soundtrack to a largely forgotten film and itself a fairly forgettable Mulligan set. The backgrounds are thick with synthesizers and whooshing percussion and Jeru's few solo moments are mostly over before they're properly under way. Some film scores do survive onto disc despite their fragmentary nature. This one doesn't.

***** Re-Birth Of The Cool**
GRP 059679-2 *Mulligan; Wallace Roney (t); Dave Bargeron (tb); John Clark (frhn); Bill Barber (tba); Phil Woods (as); John Lewis (p); Dean Johnson (b); Ron Vincent (d); Mel Torme (v).* 1/92.

There has been some rewriting of the history books on behalf of Mulligan and pianist/arranger John Lewis *vis-à-vis* the original *Birth Of The Cool.* Mulligan is on record as feeling that the project was subsequently hijacked in Miles Davis's name. Though Miles 'cracked the whip', it was Lewis, Gil Evans and Mulligan who gave the music its distinctive profile. In 1991, Mulligan approached Miles regarding a plan to re-record the famous numbers, which were originally released as 78s and only afterwards given their famous title. Unfortunately, Miles died before the plan could be taken any further, and the eventual session featured regular stand-in Roney in the trumpet part. With Phil Woods in for Lee Konitz, the latter-day sessions have a crispness and boppish force that the original cuts rather lacked. Dave Grusin's and Larry Rosen's production is ultra-sharp and perhaps too respectful of individual horns on 'Deception' and 'Budo', where a degree less separation might have been more effective (unless this is an impression based entirely on folk-memories of the original LP). The mix works rather better on the boppish 'Move' and 'Boplicity', and on the vocal, 'Darn That Dream'. An interesting retake on a still-misunderstood experiment, *Re-Birth* sounds perfectly valid on its own terms.

***** Paraiso: Jazz Brazil**
Telarc 83361 *Mulligan; Charlie Ernst, Cliff Korman (p); Emanuel Moreira (g); Rogerio Maio, Leonard D. Traversa (b); Duduka Fonseca, Peter Grant (d); Waltinho Anastacio, Norberto Goldberg (perc); Jane Duboc (v).* 7/93.

*****(*) Dream A Little Dream**
Telarc 83364 *Mulligan; Bill Mays, Ted Rosenthal (p); Dean Johnson (b); Ron Vincent (d).* 4/94.

***** Dragonfly**
Telarc 83377 *Mulligan; Warren Vaché (c); Ryan Kisor (t); Grover Washington Jr (ss, ts); Dave Grusin, Ted Rosenthal (p); Dave Samuels (vib); John Scofield (g); Dean Johnson (b); Ron Vincent (d); brass.* 3–6/95.

*****(*) Triple Play**
Telarc 84353 3CD *As above three discs.* 93–95.

***** The Art Of Gerry Mulligan: The Final Recordings**
Telarc 83517 *As above.* 93–95.

The final run of albums for Telarc have been boxed together, with no additional material, as *Triple Play.* Good value though it is, not every purchaser will be thrilled with *Paraiso* and might prefer to acquire the records individually, or to opt for the selections on *The Art*, which is a very respectable sampling of that last period. Mulligan towers head and shoulders above all the other musicians on the slightly cheesy Latin-American date. Jane Duboc's vocals are actually rather winning and grow with familiarity, but the arrangements lack the subtlety and depth of focus for which one always looked to Mulligan in the old days.

There had been rumours for some time about Mulligan's health, and most of them proved to be premature. Certainly there is no lapse in quality on the gloriously recorded *Dream A Little Dream.* Some of the best moments are the most intimate, a duo version with Rosenthal of Alec Wilder's 'I'll Be Around' and duet versions of 'My Funny Valentine' and 'As Close As Pages In A Book' with guest pianist Bill Mays, who had been a regular performer with the quartet. The closing 'Song For Strayhorn' pays tribute to one of the saxophonist's great friends and idols and the man who, perhaps more than any other – more than Ellington, arguably – influenced his approach to the jazz orchestra. But then, of course, Mulligan always thought of a small group, even a duo, as an orchestra in miniature, so the piece has the bigness of spirit and sound one would expect.

Mulligan's final studio recording was a compromise, boosted by overdubbed brass and redolent of nothing but failing powers. That said, Jeru remains very much the focus and is featured on most tracks, none of which is intrinsically arresting. We've returned to this record many times in the hope of catching some overlooked last wisdom, but in the final measure it's a competent and gently paced set, designed to flatter an ailing man.

Mick Mulligan (born 1928)

TRUMPET, VOCAL

A quixotic hero of the British trad boom, Mulligan was never much of a trumpet player, but his bandleading exploits have gone down in well-documented history. To non-British readers, his band's reputation will remain a mystery.

***** Ravers**
Lake LACD 150 *Mulligan; Dave Keir, Frank Parr (tb); Ian Christie, Wally Fawkes (cl); Ronnie Duff (p); Nevil Skrimshire*

(g); Tom Page, Terry Forster, Alan Duddington, Major Holley (b); Pete Appleby (d); George Melly (v). 1/56–6/57.

****(*) Live**

Lake LACD 176 *As above, except omit Fawkes, Keir, Page, Forster, Holley.* 56–57.

****(*) Meet Mick Mulligan And George Melly**

Lake LACD 66 *Mulligan; Frank Parr (tb); Ian Christie (cl); Ronnie Duff (p); Bill Bramwell (g, v); Gerry Salisbury (b, tb); Alan Duddington (b); Pete Appleby (d); George Melly (v).* 9/58–4/59.

Mulligan's band have gained a picaresque reputation via George Melly's memoirs; their records are frankly rather less interesting, although the earlier Lake records fare much better than the reissue of their Pye sessions. *Ravers* collects some tracks made for Tempo and presents the band at what was presumably their best: honest British trad, with Christie taking playing honours and George's vocals very spirited. *Live* finds them in a pub in Hampstead and at the Festival Hall (a certain dichotomy there), and they certainly sound more relaxed and outgoing in the hostelry, with Mulligan playing a decent lead. The 1958–59 sessions show them flagging. Nobody's useless, there are some worthwhile solos – especially Christie's somewhat crazed version of 'All Of Me' – and Melly contributes some entertaining vocals. But the band never sound like much of a unit, tending to play at the same time rather than together, and the dull material and thin sound tell against them.

Jimmy Mundy (1907–83)

ARRANGER, COMPOSER

Born in Cincinnati, he learned arranging while in Chicago and was soon writing for Earl Hines; then worked as a staff arranger for Benny Goodman. His great work was done for Goodman, Basie and others from the mid-'30s to the late '40s, but latterly much of his writing was for 'sweet' orchestras. Sessions under his own name are few.

***** Jimmy Mundy 1937–1947**

Classics 1200 *Mundy; Walter Fuller (t, v); Frank Galbreath, Bobby Moore, Elton Hill, Clyde Hurley, Ray Linn, Walter Williams, McClure Morris, Harry Parr Jones (t); Trummy Young, Eddie Johnson, Norman Greene, John Rocks McConnell, Juan Tizol, Britt Woodman, Henry Coker, Vernon Brown (tb); Omer Simeon (cl, as); Jimmy Hamilton (cl); Ted Barnett, Les Robinson, Willie Smith (as); Lucky Thompson, Skippy Williams, Babe Russin (ts); Alfred Gibson, Dick Clark (bs); Billy Kyle, Bill Doggett, Milt Raskin, Eddie Beal (p); Dick Palmer, Connie Wainwright, Irving Ashby (g); Quinn Wilson, Jack Jarvis, Artie Shapiro (b); Chick Webb, Shadow Wilson, Ray Hagen (d); Madeline Green, Jimmy Young, Ginger Snaps (v).* 3/37–47.

Mundy's story is largely tied up with the Goodman and Basie bands, but these surviving echoes of his own groups are interesting, sometimes terrific, and the disc neatly collects all his own 78-era material. Two 1937 tracks for Varsity include a group of Mundy's mates from the Earl Hines band and end up being features for the singing and playing of Walter Fuller. Then there's the only four sides made by Jimmy's 1939 big band (with Jimmy Hamilton making his debut); fair enough, although two are little more than settings for vocalist Madeline Green.

A session where Mundy arranges for the harmony group the Ginger Snaps was hardly worth reviving, but then we come to the meat in this sandwich – four excellent V-Disc tracks by Mundy's almost *ad hoc* Los Angeles big band of 1947. The trombone section alone was formidable – Tizol, Woodman, Henry Coker and Vernon Brown – and with presumably Mundy himself shouting on the soloists and the section-work, these versions of 'Fiesta In Brass', 'Hello, Goodbye, Forget It', 'Fiesta In Blue' and 'Airmail Special' have an infectious joy as well as real musical muscle. The Aladdin session of 1947 which rounds off the disc is more mysterious – the personnel largely a guess – but the boogie set-pieces and blues feature for Jimmy Young are attractive. Transfers are fair to excellent, although there's a terrible speed wobble at the end of one of the final tracks.

Tisziji Munoz (born 1946)

GUITAR, SYNTHESIZER

A key figure on the Toronto underground scene, New York-born Munoz overcame a crippling hand injury to learn percussion and then guitar. His music is intensely spiritual, in the manner of John Coltrane.

***** Divine Radiance**

Dreyfus FDM 36706 *Munoz; Ravi Coltrane, Pharoah Sanders (ts); Paul Shaffer (ky); Cecil McBee, Don Pate (b); Rashied Ali (d).* 02.

In the words of an early composition, Tisziji Munoz – you say it 'tee-see-ye moon-yos' – insists he is just visiting the planet. He studied music while in the military and made friends with associates of John Coltrane, who is still his main influence. Many recordings from the '80s and after have been issued on his own Anami Music label, but this is the only set that is generally available.

Like earlier albums, *Presence of Joy, Presence of Truth, Presence of Mystery* and *Death is a Friend of Mine*, the music is intensely mystical. The brief prologue, 'Moment of Truth', leads into a long and amorphous psychodrama. 'Initiation By Fire' is equally long but more impressionistic in concept. Munoz occasionally sounds like fusion-period Larry Coryell, but Carlos Santana's collaborations with both John McLaughlin and Alice Coltrane are possibly better points of reference. 'Fatherhood' is perhaps closest to a straight jazz number.

Sanders and Ravi Coltrane have both dabbled in funkier and more atmospheric projects and these backgrounds colour the music strongly, especially on the long title-track, where the drama unfurls and cools steadily, a besetting problem with earlier discs. The two bassists maintain a steady turbine of sound; Ali reproduces moments from *Interstellar Space*; and long-term associate Shaffer acts as fulcrum.

A genuinely original and beguiling character, Munoz is probably best considered a creative catalyst whose own productions are a shadow of his influence on others.

Mark Murphy (born 1932)

VOCAL

Worked in New York clubs in the '50s and made records for Capitol and Riverside. Lived in Europe for many years from the mid-'60s, then returned to the USA in 1975. Many albums for Muse, 1972–91. Originally perceived as a hipsterish stylist, Murphy's command increased and his chops allowed him to sing effectively in a wide range of settings.

*****(*) Crazy Rhythm: His Debut Recordings**
Decca/GRP 050670-2 *Murphy; orchestra including Ralph Burns (p); Don Lamond (d). 6/56–8.*

*****(*) Rah**
Original Jazz Classics OJC 141 *Murphy; Ernie Wilkins Orchestra. 9–10/61.*

***** That's How I Love The Blues**
Original Jazz Classics OJC 367 *Murphy; Nick Travis, Snooky Young, Clark Terry (t); Bernie Leighton, Dick Hyman (org); Roger Kellaway (p); Jim Hall (g); Ben Tucker (b); Dave Bailey (d); Willie Rodriguez (perc). 62.*

Mark Murphy's been hip all his professional life. His first sessions, released as *Meet Mark Murphy* and *Let Yourself Go*, are rarities which are welcome on CD for the first time. The sheer youthful ebullience of these dates comes as a tonic after the self-absorbed mooning of so many of today's would-be jazz crooners. Murphy hits the demanding tempo of 'Fascinating Rhythm' so quickly and confidently that it makes one gasp to think this was his first outing in a studio. Beautiful intonation, every word immaculately there, and with helpful charts from Ralph Burns, Murphy hardly takes a false step. On ballads he sometimes strains for a big *bel canto* sound, and just occasionally he tries too hard or attempts to do too much, but that is a young man's fancy, and it's kept the records alive (excellent remastering, too). This should be a welcome discovery for many Murphy fans.

His Capitol albums are still in limbo, but next come the Riverside sets. Five years of work made him a stronger and more capable performer. While his delivery is still sometimes self-consciously cool in its use of dynamics and bent notes, he's always an impassioned singer, sometimes too much so, such as on an overwrought 'Blues In My Heart' on the *Blues* collection. That record may annoy some with its showmanlike approach to a set of downbeat material, but Murphy is no more overbearing than Billy Eckstine or Al Hibbler. *Rah*, pitched as a college man's text of hipsterism, is marginally more enjoyable, but both records benefit from the singer's assurance – he's enough his own man never to shoot for black pronunciation – and canny arrangements by Ernie Wilkins and (on *Blues*) Al Cohn.

****(*) Night Mood**
Milestone MCD 9145 *Murphy; Claudio Roditi (t); Frank Morgan (as); Jose Bertrami (ky); Alex Malheiros (b); Ivan Conti (d). 86.*

***** September Ballads**
Milestone MCD 9154-2 *Murphy; Art Farmer (t); Larry Dunlap (ky); Oscar Castro-Nueves (g); David Belove, Jeff Carney (b); Donald Bailey (d); John Santos, Vince Lateano (perc). 87.*

With all of Murphy's 19 Muse albums wiped off the racks, a lot of important work is currently unavailable. The Milestone albums are so-so. *Night Mood* and *September Ballads* both set him up with a light fusion of jazz and Latin rhythms (the group Azymuth back him on the former), and although his singing is as accomplished as usual the thin material on *Night Mood* is discouraging; and nothing really stands out on the pleasing but muted *September Ballads.*

*****(*) Song For The Geese**
RCA Victor 74321 44865-2 *Murphy; Marc Seales (ky); Doug Miller (b); John Bishop (d); Full Voice (v). 97.*

You have to be a Murphy believer to agree with the rating, since this is the man at his most idiosyncratic and personal. Few singers would dare mix up 'Baltimore Oriole' and 'You're Blasé' with Steely Dan's 'Do It Again', and fewer still would take as many liberties with time, intonation and phrasing. The truth is that Murphy is now as singular and daring a singer as Betty Carter. The pipes may not be as flexible and smooth as they once were, but the intelligence and charismatic power in the singing are fascinating. The arrangements stick to a trusted small-group formula, dappled a little by synths and the surprisingly effective use of the vocal group Full Voice.

*****(*) Some Time Ago**
High Note HCD 7048 *Murphy; Dave Ballou (t); Allan Mezquida (as); Lee Musiker (p); Steve LaSpina, Sean Smith (b); Winard Harper (d). 12/99.*

*****(*) Links**
High Note HCD 7077 *As above, except add Cidinho Teixeira (p), Sergio Brandao (b); Tim Horner, Paulo Braga (d), Memo Acedivo (perc), Angela DeNiro (v). 12/00.*

Approaching 70 Murphy has all the command and serene eloquence of the great jazz instrumental seniors. Of course the voice isn't the limber trumpet of his youth, but listeners shouldn't expect some kind of old man's wisdom as the premier emotion – 'I'm A Fool To Want You', on the first record, is as torn and uncomprehending as any tyro in romance could express. At the same time, it takes enormous mastery to make such a convincing, beautiful matter out of 'The Peacocks' (with Norma Winstone's exceptional lyric). The second record, though it uses the same cast for much of the way, rings a few changes: DeNiro scats along on a few passages, the bossa nova sidles in with 'Breathing' (a Murphy original) and the Frishberg set-piece 'Wheelers And Dealers' is almost a touch of black humour. The instrumental line-ups are almost as hip as Murphy himself, and there's no fusion fudging anywhere along the line.

*****(*) Lucky To Be Me**
High Note HCD 7094 *Murphy; Scott Wendholt (t, flhn); Bobby Porcelli (as, f); Lee Musiker (p); Jay Leonhart, David Finck (b); Tim Horner (d); Memo Acevedo (perc). 12/01.*

*****(*) Memories Of You**
High Note HCD 7111 *Murphy; Bill Easley (ss, ts); Norman Simmons (p); Paul Bollenback (g); Darryl Hall (b); Grady Tate (d). 2/03.*

An Indian summer in the studios for Mark. As usual, one has to be a Murphy believer to accept these ratings: if you dislike scat, shy away from the melodic reconstructiion which he helplessly submits to, or otherwise prefer standards sung straight as a die, these records won't appeal. The first is a nicely-paced mixed bag of good songs, several relatively unexposed; the second is a Joe Williams tribute (with Joe's old pianist Norman Simmons on hand) which suits him splendidly, the rocking Williams swing and big, hearty emoting resting comfortably on Murphy's shoulders. The voice may have frayed a little, but the mastery is absolutely intact.

Paul Murphy

DRUMS

Free player with much experience behind him, including on New York turf; currently working in and around Washington, DC.

****(*) Red Snapper: Paul Murphy At CBS**
Cadence CJR 1167 *Murphy; Dewey Johnson (t); Jimmy Lyons (as); Karen Borca (bsn); Mary Anne Driscoll (p, v).* 6/82.

*****(*) Enarre**
Cadence CJR 1147 *Murphy; Joel Futterman (p); Kash Killion (clo).* 6/01.

The *Enarre* trio have worked together before and for this studio session they were clearly bursting to play: one piece, 'SFERICS', passes the 30-minute mark with no apparent loss of energy or – more surprisingly – invention. Murphy can stoke up some terrific bouts of noise at the kit, although for much of the way he's happy to play more sparsely – this is particularly effective in 'Desert Fire', a duet piece which Futterman sits out and where Killion keeps returning to the same figures in an abrasive show of repetition. Futterman is as fulsome as usual, but Killion is perhaps the most intereresting contributor, favouring the bow over the fingers and finding a powerful middle ground between cello and bass terrain.

The earlier record exhumes a session made at CBS studios but never previously released. Operating at an opposite extreme, here the tracks are all brief – 19 completed in just over an hour – and a lot of music gets started and stopped before it's done. Interestingly, Borca is one of the strongest voices here, but it's Lyons who gets the most space in what is actually a series of duos and trios rather than any full performances by the quintet. Johnson flails about all over the place and Driscoll does little of value, but even if everything else were filtered out, the dialogue between Murphy and Lyons yields some powerful episodes, although 'episodic' just about sums up the whole thing.

Turk Murphy (1915–87)

TROMBONE

Melvin 'Turk' Murphy is a sometimes exalted figure among followers of American jazz revivalism. He made his name while working alongside Lu Watters in the more celebrated Yerba Bunea Jazz Band and ran his Earthquake McGoon's Club in San Francisco for the rest of his playing life.

***** Turk Murphy's Jazz Band Favourites**
Good Time Jazz 60-011 *Murphy; Don Kinch, Bob Scobey (t); Bill Napier, Skippy Anderson, Bob Helm (cl); Burt Bales, Wally Rose (p); Bill Newman (g, bj); Pat Patton, Dick Lammi, Harry Mordecai (bj); Squire Gersback, George Bruns (b, tba); Stan Ward, Johnny Brent (d).* 49–51.

***** Turk Murphy's Jazz Band Favourites Vol. 2**
Good Time Jazz 60-026 *Similar to above, except add Claire Austin (v).* 49–51.

**** Turk Murphy And His San Francisco Jazz Band Vol. 1**
GHB 091 *Murphy; Leon Oakley (c); Jim Maichak (tb); Phil Howe (cl); Pete Clute (p); Carl Lunsford (bj).* 4/72.

**** Turk Murphy And His San Francisco Jazz Band Vol. 2**
GHB 092 *As above.* 4/72.

Murphy's music would be a little more credible if he hadn't gone on making it for so long. At the time of his earliest recordings, when he was a member of the Lu Watters circle, the Californian traditional jazz movement had some nous as revivalists of music which had lain, unjustly neglected, for many years. In that light, the two Good Time Jazz compilations, hammy though much of the playing is, and often painfully (as opposed to authentically) untutored, are both interesting and enjoyable. But after more than 20 years of this kind of thing, Murphy's one-track traditionalism sounds tiresome and soulless on the two GHB CDs, taken from a single 1972 session. It might be cheerful and boisterous enough, and Murphy's own playing has achieved a ready constituency, but there are many better arguments for revivalism than this music. Murphy's legacy is better handled by some of the superior outfits now recording for GHB and Stomp Off.

David Murray (born 1955)

TENOR SAXOPHONE, BASS CLARINET

The David Murray phenomenon seems less comet-like and fateful at the end of the decade than it did at the beginning, when Murray albums were coming in threes. He was born in Berkeley, where his mother was a gospel piano-player. Murray was alerted to modern jazz by Stanley Crouch and Arthur Blythe but became known to a wider public as a member of the World Saxophone Quartet. His signature style is a mixture of bebop, swing and free elements, alternated with boogie and funk. Even if the initial impact has faded somewhat, he remains the most formidable tenor soloist of his generation.

***** Interboogieology**
Black Saint 120018 *Murray; Lawrence Butch Morris (c); Johnny Mbizo Dyani (b); Oliver Johnson (d); Marta Contreras (v).* 2/78.

Over the last two decades David Murray would seem to have confirmed Ornette Coleman's famous claim that the soul of black Americans is best expressed through the tenor saxophone. A pivotal figure in contemporary jazz (and one of the most comprehensively documented), Murray has patiently created a synthesis of the radical experimentation of John Coltrane and (particularly) Albert Ayler with the classic jazz tradition.

Two compositions each by Murray and his most significant collaborator, Butch Morris. The opening 'Namthini's Song' is a stately procession, marked by Morris's typically unpredictable voicings. Marta Contreras sings wordlessly, somewhere up near the cornet's register; it's certainly a more convincing use of her voice than the Abbey Lincoln mannerisms of the title-track. 'Home' is a huge duet from Murray and Dyani, with the bassist's solid chant underpinning a free-flowing improvisation. 'Blues For David' is uncharacteristically direct for Morris, a fine blowing number with the leader's most shaped solo contributions of the set.

This album probably set the pattern for Murray's subsequent and now very substantial output. A tireless experimenter, he also has a strong and canny urge to communicate, and there is a thread of populism running through his music that belies the easy critical association with Ayler and makes a nonsense of many critics' professed surprise at his rejection of unmediated avant-gardism in favour of a 'back to the future' examination of the whole sequence of black musical tradition.

★★★(★) The London Concert

Cadillac SGCD 08/09 *Murray; Lawrence Butch Morris (c); Curtis Clark (p); Brian Smith (b); Clifford Jarvis (d).* 8/78.

Recorded in the Collegiate – now Bloomsbury – Theatre in London by John Jack, who was expecting to tape about an hour of good music and in the event managed to get down almost two and a half hours of Murray at his most joyously declamatory. Right from the opening 'JasVan', which sounds as if it might easily be reset for steelpans, the group is coasting with ease. Murray and Morris weave tight, high lines over Clark's Monkish comping, while Smith and Jarvis (both very prominent in the mix) fuel the engines. Some of these are titanic performances: 'Flowers For Albert' comes in at nearly half an hour and Smith's 'Spanish Love Song' isn't so very far behind. Murray deploys more extended technique here than in later years, and the main influence isn't Coltrane, surprisingly, but Eric Dolphy. The skittish, almost toneless yelps that start as accents and build into whole phrases, are reminiscent of the points and stops Eric would build into an otherwise conventional blues chorus. Even listening to this record is an exhausting experience, since it takes you by the scruff of the neck and doesn't let you go till the end, but it's worth every moment. An early highpoint in Murray's career and one that prompts the question why he has not released more live material.

★★★★ Sweet Lovely

Black Saint 120039 *Murray; Fred Hopkins (b); Steve McCall (d).* 12/79.

Stripped down to basics, this anticipates *The Hill.* The first version of 'Hope/Scope', which has a slightly odd subsequent history, is the clearest, pivoted on Hopkins's booming bass. 'Coney Island' and 'The Hill' are at opposite ends of Murray's repertoire, but the trio gives them an unexpected coherence.

CORE COLLECTION

★★★★ Ming

Black Saint 120045 *Murray; Olu Dara (t); Lawrence Butch Morris (c); George E. Lewis (tb); Henry Threadgill (as); Anthony Davis (p); Wilber Morris (b); Steve McCall (d, perc).* 7/80.

For many fans, *the* jazz album of the '80s was recorded before the decade was properly under way. *Ming* is an astonishing record, a virtual compression of three generations of improvised music into 40 minutes of entirely original jazz. The opening 'Fast Life' has a hectic quality reminiscent of another of Murray's household gods, Charles Mingus. 'Jasvan' is a swirling 'Boston' waltz that gives most of the band, led off by the marvellous Lewis, ample solo space. 'Ming' is a sweet ballad which follows on from the troubling, almost schizophrenic 'The Hill', a piece that occupies a central place in Murray's output, perhaps an image of the jazz *gradus ad Parnassum* that he is so studiously and passionately scaling.

★★★(★) Home

Black Saint 120055 *As above.* 11/81.

Recorded by the same octet as the earlier Black Saint recording – *Ming, Home* is very nearly the better album. The slow opening title-piece is a delicately layered ballad with gorgeous horn voicings. 'Last Of The Hipmen' is one of his best pieces, and the Anthony Davis vamp that leads out of Steve McCall's intelligent and exuberant solo is a reminder of how close to Ellington's bandleading philosophy Murray has come by instinct rather than design.

★★★ Murray's Steps

Black Saint 120065 *Murray; Bobby Bradford (t); Lawrence Butch Morris (c); Craig Harris (tb); Henry Threadgill (as, f); Curtis Clark (p); Wilber Morris (b); Steve McCall (d, perc).* 7/82.

This hasn't quite the sharpness of Murray's other octets and has to be considered (absurd as this will sound to anyone who has heard the disc) an off-day. The retake of 'Flowers For Albert' is an important index of how unwilling Murray has always been to leave his own output alone; there are more convincing versions; but, if the dedicatee represents some sort of magnetic north for Murray, then the piece is a good navigational aid.

★★★(★) Morning Song

Black Saint 120075 *Murray; John Hicks (p); Reggie Workman, Ray Drummond (b); Ed Blackwell (d).* 9/83.

Compare the version of 'Body And Soul' – the tenor saxophonist's shibboleth – here with the unaccompanied one on the first item, above. It is more assured, less willed and less concerned with deconstructing a piece that has been rendered virtually abstract by countless hundreds of improvisations. Note how Murray restores the tune in segments during his later statements of a freely-arrived-at counter-theme.

Hicks is a wonderfully supportive and sensitive partner, particularly on the standard (enthusiasts should check out their duo, *Sketches Of Tokyo*, DIW 8006 CD, which features a – then surprisingly rare, but now more frequent – take on Coltrane by the saxophonist), and Blackwell's drumming touches all the right bases. A pity they haven't done more together.

★★★ Live At Sweet Basil: Volume 1

Black Saint 120085 *Murray; Olu Dara (c); Baikida Carroll, Craig Harris (t); Bob Stewart (tba); Vincent Chancey (frhn); Steve Coleman (ss, as); John Purcell (as, cl); Rod Williams (p); Fred Hopkins (b); Billy Higgins (d); Lawrence Butch Morris (cond).* 8/84.

★★★ Live At Sweet Basil: Volume 2

Black Saint 120095 *As above.* 8/84.

Volume 2 kicks off with a version of the wonderfully cheesy 'Dewey's Circle' from *Ming*, one of those compositions of Murray's that many listeners swear they have heard somewhere before. It's not quite the best piece on the set, but it's the one where most of the constituent elements are coming together. 'Bechet's Bounce' and 'Silence' on the first volume redirect some of Murray's increasingly familiar obsessions in quite new ways. The final track is a brief dedication to Marvin Gaye; by this stage in his career Murray is namechecking at an impressive rate.

The live context, with a hefty band pushing from behind, makes for some inventive conjunctions, but Murray's tone is uncharacteristically acid. There's no obvious explanation for this; the production is well up to Black Saint's careful standard.

★★★ Children

Black Saint 120089 *Murray; Don Pullen (p); James Blood Ulmer (g); Lonnie Plaxico (b); Marvin 'Smitty' Smith (d).* 10 & 11/84.

Rededicated to his son, David Mingus Murray, this is one of the poorer '80s albums. Smith and Plaxico dominate unnecessarily, and Ulmer and Pullen make only cameo appearances. That's another two bankable modern names to tick off against Murray's list, with 'All The Things You Are' for anyone who's bird-watching the standards.

***(*) I Want To Talk About You

Black Saint 120105 *Murray; John Hicks (p); Ray Drummond (b); Ralph Peterson Jr (d).* 3/86.

Those who were disturbed by Murray's apparent abandonment of the avant-garde might have been reassured by his firm rejection of the backward-looking stance of Wynton Marsalis and others. It's clear from the live *I Want To Talk About You* that, while the saxophonist is looking increasingly to an earlier generation of saxophone players, Sonny Rollins pre-eminently, but also synthesizers like the fêted Ellingtonian Paul Gonsalves, he is doing so with instincts very explicitly conditioned by Coltrane and Ayler. His reading of 'I Want To Talk About You' has to be heard in the context of Coltrane's own version; as a ballad player, Murray is vibrant and expansive and 'Heart To Heart' (written by Hicks) is one of his most nakedly emotional recorded performances.

**** The Hill

Black Saint 120110 *Murray; Richard Davis (b); Joe Chambers (d).* 11/86.

One of the peaks of Murray's career. The title-piece, pared down from eight voices to three, doesn't fall apart but retains its rather mysterious and troubling presence. Murray has significantly toned down his delivery from the immediately previous sessions and sounds altogether more thoughtful. The material, by now, is quite self-consciously programmed, with 'Chelsea Bridge' and 'Take The Coltrane' mixed in with the originals. 'Herbie Miller' contains Murray's best-recorded bass clarinet solo; pitched against Richard Davis's rich *arco*, he develops an intense thematic discourse that takes enough time to vary its accents in keeping with the changing emotional climate of the piece. By contrast, 'Fling' is exactly as throwaway as it sounds. This is an essential modern album.

*** Hope Scope

Black Saint 120139 *Murray; Hugh Ragin, Rasul Siddik (t); Craig Harris (tb); James Spaulding (as); Dave Burrell (p); Wilber Morris (b); Ralph Peterson (d).* 5/87.

Released only in 1991 (by which time Murray was recording for DIW), this is a bright, exuberant album, full of the band's palpable delight in what they're doing. This version of 'Hope/ Scope' is much less convoluted than the one on *Special Quartet*, below, but it inspires some raggedly spirited ensemble improvisations. The tributes to Lester Young and Ben Webster are closer to pastiche than usual (see also DIW 851, below), reflecting a rather lightweight side to the album that is initially appealing but increasingly puzzling as the layers come off it.

*** The Healers

Black Saint 120118 *Murray; Randy Weston (p).* 9/87.

Though Weston's sense of structure is much like Murray's, which turns out to be inhibiting rather than particularly productive, he tends to conceive developments in discontinuous units rather than in Murray's uninterrupted flow. Several times the pianist falls back on set licks which make him sound a less sophisticated player than he is. 'Mbizo' is a further version of a dedication to Johnny Dyani, who died the previous year. A by-way on Murray's increasingly determined course, *The Healers* takes Murray down a road he has seemed disinclined to pursue. Which is a pity.

***(*) Tea For Two

Fresh Sound FSRCD 164 *Murray; George Arvanitas (p).* 5/90.

Headed 'George Arvanitas Presents: The ballad artistry of ... David Murray', there's a rabbit-out-of-hat quality to the ellipsis. Though no one's surprised any more to find Murray playing 'in the tradition', it's still rare to find him doing it quite this uncomplicatedly. The menu of standards doesn't really stretch him technically and there's a hint of a more mannered approach in his takes of past giants, almost as though he's over-anxious to inscribe himself into the history of jazz saxophone before the 40th birthday comes up. For the record (this is a relatively undiscovered Murray album), the track listing is 'Chelsea Bridge', 'Polka Dots And Moonbeams', 'Star Eyes', 'Body And Soul' again, 'Tea For Two', 'I'm In The Mood For Love', an original 'Blues For Two', and 'La Vie En Rose'.

*** The Jazzpar Prize

Enja CD 7031 *Murray; New Jungle Orchestra: Pierre Dørge (g); Per Jorgensen (t); Harry Beckett (t, flhn); Jörg Huke (tb); Jesper Zeuthen (as, bcl); Jacob Mygind (ts, ss); Horace Parlan (p); Irene Becker (ky); Jens Skou Olsen (b); Audun Kleive (d); Donald Murray (v).* 3/91.

In the spring of 1991 Murray was awarded the third annual Jazzpar Prize, perhaps the only major international jazz award in the world. It was a significant accolade for a man not yet 40. During the course of the prize project, Murray recorded with Pierre Dørge's New Jungle Orchestra. The two men share an interest in Ellingtonian composition and sounds, and Murray fitted into the band with his usual ease. The two opening pieces are by the guitarist; there follows a gospel medley, with vocals from Donald Murray, a beautifully constructed version of 'In A Sentimental Mood', finishing with full-throated performances of 'Shakill's Warrior' and 'Song For Doni'.

Murray's solo is more restrained than usual, and in this context his kinship with Paul Gonsalves becomes entirely unambiguous. Though he varies the melody of the Ellington tune to spark off his solo, ironically it's one of the straightest and most respectful repertoire performances to be found anywhere in his recorded output.

*** A Sanctuary Within

Black Saint 120145 *Murray; Tony Overwater (b); Sunny Murray (d); Kahil El'Zabar (perc, v).* 12/91.

This might almost have come from a decade previously, when Murray was firmly locked into his avant-garde phase. Yet he has become much more varied in his choice of sounds, plumbing not just the stoical moods of 'Ballad For The Blackman' but also the more buoyant and affirmative 'Waltz To Heaven', a theme that was to reappear over the succeeding couple of years in a number of playing contexts, not least the bass clarinet album, above.

El'Zabar, a founding member of the Ethnic Heritage Ensemble, creates a whirl of exotic tinges round the fringes of each piece, but he doesn't feel integral to the project and a couple of tracks would certainly be improved if he simply weren't there.

*****(*) Live '93 Acoustic Octfunk**

Sound Hills SSCD 8051 *Murray; Fred Hopkins (b); Andrew Cyrille (d).* 7/93.

This was a very successful tour for Murray, artistically if not always at the box office. Trio-playing encouraged him to play simply, in bold strokes and relatively unadorned. His solos, as here on 'Mr P.C.' and 'Flowers For Albert', are intense, but it is the interplay among the three members of the group that is so impressive, and it communicates itself even across a rather unforgiving recording that booms and thuds away awkwardly. Hopkins plays superbly, and Cyrille's fills and solo spots are packed with ideas.

****** Body And Soul**

Black Saint 120155 *Murray; Sonelius Smith (p); Wilber Morris (b); Rashied Ali (d); Taana Running (v).* 2/93.

By the end of the '80s, Murray's traditionalism was expressing itself in unambiguously literal form. Time and again, he plunged back into the history of the music, dredging up performances that fell somewhere between wholesale revision and an oddly uncertain faithfulness to the originals. Because it always sounded like Murray, nobody minded; but much of that was superficial, disguising how little he was prepared to disturb ancestral ghosts.

It was odds-on that Murray would one day record an album called *Body And Soul.* His understanding of Hawkins's classic solo is obvious from the outset of his own interpretation, which works a very specific, palindromic variation on the opening phrases. However, Murray's solo has only a rather artificial shape, not the almost organic unity of Hawkins, and the unity comes largely from Taana Running's vocal. The band on *Body And Soul* is superlative, always just poised to take the music one stage higher.

*****(*) Windward Passages**

Black Saint 120165 *Murray; Dave Burrell (p); Monika Larsson (v).* 12/93.

Not released for some time after recording, this basically duo session documents one of Murray's closest artistic partnerships. Burrell's range of influences, everything from calypso and reggae to the modernist avant-garde, fuels the saxophonist's own eclecticism. From the opening 'Sorrow Song', through two beautiful takes of Coltrane's 'Naima', to the vocal tracks, 'It Hurts So Much To See' and 'Cela Me Va', the partnership is flawlessly intuitive, a conversation in which ordinary niceties can be elided and both players get straight to the meat of a tune.

Murray has regularly expressed his desire to work with songs and singers. In Larsson he has found a lyricist who has just the right mixture of romanticism and sardonic bite. However, it might have been better to have saved her for another occasion. The chemistry with Burrell is strong enough to sustain a whole album and the vocal tracks here are more of a distraction than an asset.

*****(*) The Tip**

DIW 891 *Murray; Bobby Broom (g); Robert Irving III (org, syn); Darryl Jones (b); Toby Williams (d); Kahil El'Zabar (perc); G'Ra (poetry).* 5/94.

***** Jug-A-Lug**

DIW 894 *As above, except omit G'Ra; add Olu Dara (c); Daryl Thompson (g).* 5/94.

It keeps being said; it remains the case. Murray plays with magisterial calm and exactness, shows an intelligent awareness of the jazz tradition (*passim*), of the continuum of African-American music ('Sex Machine') and of his own back-catalogue ('Flowers For Albert'). This is an altogether funkier, more plugged-in project than he has previously seen fit to release, and it divided critical opinion somewhat: on the one hand, the 'sell-out' crowd bayed and barked in dismay; others found it a logical step along a long-established course.

It's not the best Murray album, of course; some of the Miles-derived electronic settings are pretty drab or drably pretty, but there is no mistaking the sheer intensity and individuality of Murray's own role. Like strong players before him – Parker, Coltrane, Miles – he simply breezes through uncertain accompaniments and contexts, transforming them in the process into something grander and more timeless. Quite a talent to have in this business.

The second of the pair is one of the least compelling items in the Murray canon and one of the few occasions when the multi-release approach isn't fully justified. The addition of Dara on 'Ornette' enlivens the opening section, but even he sounds a little tacked on and after the fact. (Do note that on both records it is Toby, not Tony, Williams at the kit; *caveat emptor.*)

*****(*) Dark Star**

Astor Place TCD 4002 *Murray; Omar Kabir, Hugh Ragin, James Zollar (t); Craig Harris (tb); Robert Irving III (p, org, syn); Bob Weir (g); Fred Hopkins (b); Renzell Merritt (d).* 1/96.

It was David Crosby who described the Grateful Dead's music as 'Electronic Dixieland'. Listening to this tribute, recorded not long after Jerry Garcia's death, it's not hard to see what he means, and the only surprise is that no one had thought of turning the Dead's long, floating lines and open-ended aesthetic to jazz use before. The material is far from predictable. It includes things like the traditional 'Samson And Delilah' and Bob Weir's 'One More Saturday Night' but saves the real joys for what was the vocal entry on 'Dark Star'; if anyone has heard anything as mysterious and joyous, anything more completely *right* over the last couple of years, then we'd be delighted to hear about it. In keeping with the Dead's own philosophy, there is more emphasis on group interplay than on soloing as such, though Murray does tend to dominate the foreground, as you might expect. Sometimes the brasses don't seem quite right, but that has more to do with their position in the mix than anything else. Bob Weir is on hand on 'Shoulda Had Been Me' to add a seal of approval to the project. Call us old hippies if you will ... oh, you already did?

***** Live At The Village Vanguard**

Luminescence LNCD 4002 *Murray; Hilton Ruiz (p); Kelly Roberty (b); Pheeroan akLaff (d).* 8/95.

Not issued until 2001, this is a curious release. One of the tracks listed – 'Obe' – doesn't appear on this album of uncertain provenance. One suspects that the tapes may have changed hands a few times before final editing. There are some fiery moments, notably on 'The Desegregation Of Our Children' and 'Hope/Scope', which see the saxophonist drifting into Albert Ayler's R&B idiom, somewhere between 'Ghosts' and the R&B period. AkLaff is very much in that mould and there are some tedious passages when the rhythm section lapses into production-line boogie – engine-like but boring. Ruiz is too gifted a performer to be swallowed up by anyone, but he comes close to losing the plot here on a number of occasions and falls back on clumpy vamps and chromatic runs when in doubt.

★★(★) Fo Deuk Revue

Justin Time JUST 94 *Murray; Hugh Ragin (t); Craig Harris (tb); Robert Irving III (p); El Hadji Bniancou Sembene (ky); Assane Diop (g); Abdou Karim Mane, Jamaaladeen Tacuma (b); Darryl Burgee, Ousseynou Diop (d); Omar Mboup (perc); Didier Awadi, Amiri Baraka, Amiri Baraka Jr, Amadou Barry, Tidiane Gaye, Hamat Mal, Doudou N'Diaye Rose, Moussa Sene, Junior Soul (v).* 6/96.

Canadian label, African recording: small wonder that there is an element of confusion here. The presence of Robert Irving III, who contributes a fair proportion of the music, suggests a parallel with Miles Davis's later albums and the possibility that Murray has simply swung in late in the day to add some personal twists and curlicues to an otherwise rather banal project. When Murray is actually playing, and there is less of that than anyone would like, things go pretty well; however, the disc is laden with leaden lyrics and drab Afro-urban beats and, while Murray has long expressed a desire to work in song form and with non-jazz partners, this was hardly the most flattering context in which to experiment.

The members of Senegalese bands Dieuf Dieul and Positive Black Soul in turn sound restrained in Murray's presence, and, instead of a genuine meeting of minds, what results is an overly polite exchange of cultural postcards. Murray fans will find enough of the saxophonist to win them over. For the rest, though, this is thin fare, unrepresentative and disturbingly low on jazz content, a lazy and unfocused record that relies heavily on predictable atmospherics.

★★★(★) Speaking In Tongues

Enja ENJ 9370-2 *Murray; Hugh Ragin (t); Jimane Nelson (org, p); Stanley Franks (g); Clarence Jenkins (b); Ranzell Merritt (d); Leopoldo Fleming (perc); Fontella Bass (v).* 98.

After trips to Senegal and Guadeloupe, this has Murray diving back into his own musical heritage in the most direct way yet. Murray's mother was a renowned gospel pianist and *Speaking In Tongues* mixes gospel-influenced originals with material that would have been deeply familiar to her, like 'Just A Closer Walk With Thee'. Musically, it is by far the most compelling of the recent trilogy of transcultural projects, perhaps because emotionally and expressively Murray has such a profound stake in it.

The idea came about when Hamiet Bluiett invited Fontella Bass to sing with the World Saxophone Project. Murray had himself been working with a gospel choir, and the ground seemed ready for a project of this sort. 'How I Got Over' establishes an atmosphere of passionate witness and has Murray make the first of his fiery, overblown solos. Ragin is another horn-player who can move with comfort from R&B grooves and shuffle rhythms to free-form playing, and his contribution here shouldn't be underestimated. The guitar/organ/electric bass section has an honourable ancestry in this music, and Jimane Nelson emerges as an authentic voice with very definite ideas of his own, as he reveals on 'Jimane's Creation'.

Bass is one of the great American voices, emotional and resonant but without the hysterical edge that overtakes some sanctified singers. Her 1965 hit, 'Rescue Me', would have been a delightful addition to this set but, even without it, *Speaking In Tongues* is a marvellous album.

★★★(★) Octet Plays Trane

Justin Time 131 *Murray; Ravi Best, Rasul Siddik (t); Craig Harris (tb); James Spaulding (as, f); D. D. Jackson (p); Jaribu Shahid(b); Mark Johnson (d).* 4–5/99.

Murray's own 'The Crossing' is dropped into the middle of this typically thoughtful and inventive tribute to John Coltrane. All five of the other cuts are Trane themes, played on tenor and bass clarinet with the octet boiling away behind. 'Giant Steps' is no merely academic work-out, but a radical rethinking of some aspects of the original harmonics. 'Lazy Bird' is a straightforward blowing vehicle which betrays some familiarity with the Tadd Dameron source material; Craig Harris is especially strong here, perhaps mindful of Curtis Fuller's role in the original. 'Naima' and 'India' change the pace markedly and coax some of Murray's most tender playing, set against a floating, almost Oriental accompaniment from the ensemble. The best is saved for last, a climactic version of 'A Love Supreme: Acknowledgement' which comes close to the original for sheer power, but yet manages to sound more light-hearted and less freighted.

★★★ Seasons

Pow Wow 7468 *Murray; Sir Roland Hanna (p); Richard Davis(b); Victor Lewis (d).* 98.

As close as it gets to David Murray Lite, this set of mostly ballad performances is testimony to the saxophonist's abiding interest in song. The seasonal theme is rather notional since the temperature remains pretty much the same throughout; a musical San Diego, then. Hanna and Davis play with magisterial calm and a rich, full sound, and Lewis is a subtle enough player to use the relaxed pace to make elaborate statements of his own without grandstanding. Murray, though, seems leashed and reserved, and with so few sharp edges to quicken the attention, *Seasons* is too readily consumable to be included among the saxophonist's more significant statements.

★★★ Like A Kiss That Never Ends

Justin Time 152-2 *Murray; John Hicks (p); Ray Drummond (b); Andrew Cyrille (d).* 6/00.

This is the group that Murray calls his Power Quartet, and yet the approach is less muscular, more lyrical than that might suggest. There are no spectacular stylistic revelations to be had from these seven originals (Drummond's 'Dedication' is the only non-Murray tune), but plenty of fiery playing that continues to reflect David's interest in extending the boundaries of song-form. The title-piece is confidently executed, and gracefully developed, but it's the following sequence of pieces, 'Suki, Suki Now', 'Ruben's Theme Song' and 'Mo' Bass' which most fully reflect Murray's inventive approach to the tradition. He is a less abrasive player than of yore, but his ability to shape a solo that is both well-structured and open-ended has been finely tuned over the years. The group delivers generously and enthusiasts will find much to admire.

★★★ Yonn-De

Justin Time 140 *Murray; Hugh Ragin (t); Craig Harris (tb); Santi Debriano (b); Pheeroan akLaff (d); Klod Kiavue, Francois Ledrezeau (d, v); Guy Konket (v).* 02.

Reminiscent of the West African experiments of *Fo Deuk Revue*, this sees Murray engaging with the musical culture of Guadeloupe and with three masters of *gwo-ka* music. It's a style that is reminiscent of voudou, full of whirling trances and ecstatic swoons. Konket is the composer of all the material, which imposes certain restrictions on Murray as soloist. To be truthful, he sounds reserved and almost marginalized on much of the set, however strong-voiced his statements, but it is clear that he is trying to align with the three guest stars as much as possible. The shorter cuts in the middle of the record are the easiest to sample, but it's only on the longer tracks that the integration of parts really makes sense; try 'On Jou Maten', which almost has the colouration and pace of a blues ballad.

★★★★ Now Is Another Time

Justin Time JUST 161 2 *Murray; Elpidio Chappotin Elpedo, Alexander Brown Cabrera, Crostobel Ferrer, Carmelo Andres, Hugh Ragin, Bacilio Bernardo Marquez, Rafael Gavilan (t); Amaury Perez Rodriguez, Craig Harris, Sergio Ricardo Luna Longchamp (tb); Cesar Lopez Martinez, Roman Felio O'Reilly, Ernesto Varona Rodriguez, Velasco Urdeliz, German Ferrin (as); Irvin Luichel Acao Sierra, Orlando Sanchez Soto (ts); Hamiet Bluiett, Moises Marquez Loyva (bs); Jose Luis Cortes, Kahil Ikshr-Smith (f); Miguel Angel de Armas, Tony Perez, Luis Manuel Guerra Crespo, Roberto Julio, Carcasses Colon (p); Feliciano Arango Noa, Narciso Jorge, Reyes Hernandez (b); Olivier Valdes Rey, Giraldo Piloto (d); Jose Luis Quentana Fuerte, Jorge Luis Guerra, Adel Gonzales Gomez, Tomas Ramos Ortiz, Evelio Ramos Delfin (perc).* 4/01–6/02.

Unlike most such sessions, and unlike most of Murray's earlier dabblings in other traditions, these Latin-inspired charts, almost all new material, sound absolutely authentic and absolutely David Murray. His orchestrations are chunky and massive, even when he is negotiating a detailed passage. In lesser hands, this could seem like ugly caricature, but Murray the arranger has the same deceptive delicacy as Murray the saxophonist, reminiscent of a brilliant neurosurgeon with huge stockman's hands.

In addition, he has peppered the Latin band – not such a big outfit as it first appears on paper, given all the triple handles – with familiar accomplices, of whom Bluiett and Harris give generously of themselves. 'Mambo Dominica' provides a vantage for both of them to soar, while Murray himself delivers an impassioned statement on 'Sad Kind Of Love' and the extraordinary 'Blue Muse', which sounds like *Africa/Brass*-vintage Coltrane rearranged by an Afro-Cuban outfit.

Murray continues to surprise and delight with fresh changes of direction. There has perhaps been a dearth in recent years of hard-driving small-group jazz, though it did seem that he had exhausted many of his signature themes. Few artists of recent times have more impressively worked their way out of the cul-de-sac of critical success.

Sunny Murray (born 1937)

DRUMS

Sunny Murray is the real inventor of free-jazz drumming. He had an early exposure to Cecil Taylor's atonality, but he heard something new in John Coltrane's rhythm and built his approach on that, using the kit as a colour palette rather than a metronome. Like all genuine innovators, as opposed to consolidators, he has been scandalously overlooked and is only thinly recorded as leader.

★★★ Sunny Murray Quintet

ESP Disk 1032 *Murray; Jacques Coursil (t); Jack Graham, Byard Lancaster (as); Alan Silva (b).* 66.

★★★ Sunshine & An Even Break (Never Give A Sucker)

Fuel 2000 061215 *Murray; Lester Bowie (t); Arthur Jones, Roscoe Mitchell (as); Byard Lancaster (ss, as, bcl, f); Archie Shepp (ts); Kenneth Terroade (ts, f); Dave Burrell (p); Malachi Favors (b).* 69.

All revolutions in jazz are fuelled and driven by the rhythm section. For every horn-player or pianist hailed as a 'revolutionary', you can assume that there is at least one bassist or drummer in the background, unacknowledged. The history of the '60s avant-garde is very largely the history of what Garrison and Jones, Haden and Blackwell or Higgins, Cyrille, Graves and Sunny Murray brought to it.

Despite his presence on some of the key recordings of the period, to wit Cecil Taylor's 1962 Café Montmartre sessions and Albert Ayler's *Spiritual Unity*, Murray has scandalously little under his own name. A trio of albums for BYG – including the wonderfully titled *An Even Break (Never Give A Sucker)* – and the remarkable *Apple Cores* for Philly Jazz were just about all there were until the '90s, except for the obligatory ESP Disk recording, more or less a rite-of-passage thing for players of this vintage and disposition

Murray had recorded a first disc some months before this, with Albert Ayler in the band, but the ESP set is his real coming-out as a leader. Like most of the label's output, it's pretty uncompromising fare. Murray isn't overly prominent on his own long composition, though his driving metres and fractured lines are the key to 'Phase 1, 2, 3, 4' and 'Hilariously'. Then a surprise. Alto saxophonist Jack Graham, otherwise subordinate to Lancaster and not at all widely known, contributes the Aylerish 'Angels And Devils', one of the strongest things on the set. Silva is majestic and much more audible on CD. Coursil seems a bit lost, though a few Don Aylerish flourishes allow him to make his presence felt.

An Even Break and *Sunshine*, both recorded for BYG, reappeared as a twofer in 2003. On *Sunshine* Murray again introduces an otherwise unknown horn man. Kenneth Terroade plays one trio track with Murray and Favors, while the rest of the set is played by two larger groups. There was never much coherence to the album and it's vastly improved, not least in duration, by being paired with the slightly later and rather better *Even Break*, which is Murray's finest hour of the fast-disappearing '60s. 'Giblets Part 12' and the rollicking 'Invisible Rules' are the equal of anything on the first disc, except perhaps 'Flower Trane', which is Sunny's only real repertory piece, occasionally covered since.

★★★(★) Illuminators

Audible Hiss 008 *Murray; Charles Gayle (p, ts).* 96.

★★★★ We Are Not At The Opera

Eremite MTE 014 *Murray; Sabir Mateen (as, ts, f).* 6/98.

The duo with Gayle was to provide some of the most ferociously beautiful live moments of the '90s. Inevitably, it transfers to record only with an overall loss of drive, but these five pieces, all but one by Murray himself, are as clear a representation of his art as one could hope for. Less Afrocentric than either Jones or Cyrille, less abstract than Milford Graves, Murray still cleaves to a dark, punchy groove, the percussion equivalent of what Cecil Taylor was doing, but with more song in it.

Much has been said in even more recent times about how happy and chilled Sunny is in Europe. Paris suits him and there has been a new tranquillity in his work. However, there are still occasional opportunities to visit the USA, and the June 1998 recital at the Amherst Unitarian Meetinghouse is a reflection of how different the 60-year-old is from his own younger self. Mateen is a much less incendiary partner than Gayle, and his almost boppish phrasing on 'Musically Correct' coaxes some inspired metrical drumming from Sunny. The opening 'Rejoicing New Dreams' is a much gentler piece, a duet for flute and the most delicately enunciated percussion. Apparently Sunny was so drawn to his kit that he started playing during an intended intermission, a sound which attracted Mateen out from the dressing-room to join him; 'Too Many Drummers, Not Enough Time'. We are most certainly not at the opera. The music is made in a spirit of sympathetic informality, unbuttoned and relaxed, and it includes some of Sunny's very best work on record. A gentle classic.

Music Improvisation Company

GROUP

An important group of improvisers from the iron age of British free music.

*****(*) The Music Improvisation Company 1968–1971**
Incus CD12 *Evan Parker (ss, autoharp); Hugh Davies (org, elec); Derek Bailey (g); Jamie Muir (perc).* 68–71.

British improvisers were already a determined if small and embattled community by the time these recordings were made. As documentary pieces, culled from years of occasional work, they are in some ways charming, with Davies's fiercely primitive electronics countering Bailey's resolutely un-guitar-like guitar playing, an ongoing dialogue that will seem nostalgic of a vanished era to some older listeners. Parker's soprano is years away from his major developments and discoveries, yet it still sounds startlingly original: like Bailey, he was set on searching out a new way to play. Muir's contributions are arguably the least impressive, at least when set beside what free percussionists have done both before and since, and he isn't so well served by the recording; yet the six pieces are in the main about a quartet thinking and speaking as freely with one another as they possibly could. CD transfer has brought up some of the detail lost in ageing vinyl pressings, and the chamber-like quality of much of the music is unsettled by harshness and strangeness. But it remains rather beautiful, too.

Michael Musillami

GUITAR

Moved from his Californian beginnings to the East Coast in the '80s and garnered much experience on the organ-combo circuit, before recording these more adventurous sessions.

***** Archives**
Playscape 20990 *Musillami; Thomas Chapin (as, f); Kent Hewitt (p); Nat Reeves (b); Steve Johns (d).* 12/90.

*****(*) Mar's Bars**
Playscape 20192 *Musillami; Randy Brecker (t, flhn); Thomas Chapin (as, f); Kent Hewitt (p); Ray Drummond (b); Steve Johns (d).* 12/92.

Musillami works with an interesting blend of tonal and harmonic orthodoxy while encouraging the music to extend itself. *Mar's Bars* is a reissue of an album which we had previously listed as *Glass Art* on Evidence, and *Archives* is a new edition of *The Young Child* from Stash. One interesting influence that the guitarist claims is Bill Barron, and his themes certainly manage to revise conventional forms in the way that Barron's compositions often would. The intricacies of 'Beijing' and 'Mohawk Mountain' on the first record typify his intentions. Both discs brim with strong improvisation and there's little to choose between them, with Chapin's generously featured flute another reason to listen; he plays with a sweetness that is turned around by the fierceness of his articulation. *Mar's Bars*, though, has a clear edge as a group performance, with Brecker and the rhythm section adding extra value.

***** Perception**
Playscape 40400 *Musillami; George Sovak (as, ts); Paul Arslanian (p); Dave Shapiro (b); Claire Arenius (d).* 4/00.

***** Those Times**
Playscape JO 12603 *Musillami; Ted Rosenthal (p); Dave Shapiro (b); George Schuller (d).* 1/03.

Strictly speaking, *Perception* should be credited as a group record to Playscape, but we are listing it under Musillami's name for convenience. The intention of the band is to work, evolve and record as a unit, going against the tide of *ad hoc* all-star combos which form the diet of contemporary jazz recording sessions. It's an honourable undertaking, and one which merits following, but the proviso should be that this initial report is work in progress. Musillami himself sounds like the outstanding player and Arslanian's suggestion that the music is 'like friendly, familiar and stimulating conversation' isn't too wide of the mark. But it doesn't necessarily make it a priority listen.

Those Times is back to heartland guitar-rhythm section music. Rosenthal plays some fine stuff, so does the leader, and in the end one looks for peaks in a record which is even-tempered enough to pass by pleasantly, and not linger.

Melton Mustafa

TRUMPET

Spent some time playing R&B but best known for his work with the Count Basie and Duke Ellington 'ghost' bands before setting out on his own.

***** Boiling Point**
Contemporary 14075 *Mustafa; John Bailey, Brian McDonald, Doug Michels (t); Jason Pyle, Tom Warfel (tb); Mike Balogh (tb, btb); Neil Bonsanti, David Fernandez, Scott Klarman, Ed Maina, Jose Vera (sax); Jesse Jones Jr (as, v); John McMinn (ts); Billy Ross (ts, f); Silvano Monasterios (p); Lonnie Smith (org); Jeff Grubbs (b); James Cotmon (d); Luis Roberto, Wiso Santiago (perc).* 95.

But the boiling point of what? Mustafa's big-band sound, honed by his years in the Basie outfit, could melt rock and he plays for heat rather than light for most of this session, which will appeal to big-band fans who enjoy the Maynard Ferguson end of the spectrum. Mustafa is a strong soloist who relies on his power rather than on any great sophistication of ideas. The ensembles are forceful to put it mildly; the more reflective solos not much more than oases. Saxophonist Jesse Jones Jr is Mustafa's brother and is strongly featured, though he's a less individual player than his sibling.

★★★(★) St Louis Blues

Contemporary 14085 *Mustafa; Kenneth Faulk, Pete Minger, Yamin B. Mustafa (t); Ira Sullivan (t, af); Milton Omar Dailey, Dante Luciani (tb); Joe Barati (btb); Jesse Jones Jr (ss, as, f, v); Elvis Paschal (as, f); Matais Oxidine (ts, f); John McMinn (p); Robert Grabowski (b); James Cotmon (d, perc, v); Rabecco Boyco (perc).* 97.

This is great big-band music, combining power and delicacy. Very much a family affair, as the other Mustafas on the liner details bear out. Jesse is back as a featured soloist, but so too is Pete Minger from the Basie band and the long-overlooked Ira Sullivan brings his oblique, hard-blowing lines as well. Ira's alto flute has a low, intense sound, perfect for the charts of 'Conquest'. The key performance, though, is Mustafa's own history of jazz trumpet on 'St Louis Blues Overture' in which the Handy tune (and the album is dedicated to W.C. and to the ailing Muhammad Ali) is portrayed as the catalyst for everyone and everything from Louis Armstrong to Miles Davis. There is also a tribute track to Miles. Of the Mustafa originals, 'Little Old Groove Maker', at the end of the set, is the least idiosyncratic and the most straightforwardly enjoyable. With this set, Melton proves his mettle not just as a player and arranger, but as a fine composer as well. Anyone interested in the afterlife of the big-band era should sample it.

Wolfgang Muthspiel (born 1965)

GUITAR

Thoughtful technician with ambitious ideas, sometimes cast as a European Scofield but far more individual than that.

★★★ Daily Mirror

Material 1 *Muthspiel; Chris Cheek (ts); Scott Colley (b); Brian Blade (d); Rebekka Bakken (v).* 2/00.

★★ Daily Mirror Reflected

Material 2 *As above.* 2/00.

★★★ Echos Of Techno

Material 3 *Muthspiel; Christian Muthspiel (tb, etc).* 00.

Muthspiel has been poorly served by the majors over the last few years and these discs are released on his own label. The duo set with brother Christian is full of interesting ideas, but as with so much of his work previously one suspects that an industry in a hurry rarely stops to ponder the potential of such ambitious work. The group set with Rebeka Bakken is a series of settings of lyrics by Bernd Hagg, entertaining in their way but a long way removed from the reflective jazz sets Muthspiel released on Amadeo a decade ago. The remix album is pretty dull, to be honest, but may be more to some tastes than the original.

★★★(★) Real Book Stories

Quinton Q0101 2 *Muthspiel; Marc Johnson (b); Bobby Battle (d).* 3/01.

And just when we thought all was lost, back comes Muthspiel with this delicately understated and beautifully crafted album of jazz standards ('All The Things You Are', 'I Hear A Rhapsody') and repertory pieces as challenging as 'Giant Steps' and 'Solar'. The guitarist's playing is exquisite and there are moments when the sophistication of harmony and integration of harmonic and rhythmic ideas equal the Bill Evans trio. Johnson, of course, cut his teeth there and must have been aware of the parallel, as he hints in some of his solo passages. A quiet but forthright record, that should be sampled by anyone interested in jazz guitar.

★★ Continental Call

Quinton Q0201 2 *Muthspiel; Concert Jazz Orchestra Vienna.* 1/02.

This is a kind of concerto for guitar, written for Muthspiel by Ed Partyka of the Vienna Art Orchestra. Written grudgingly, it would seem, since Ed claims to dislike the guitar and all who sail in her. His hostility is of the passive-aggressive sort, since he drowns Wolfgang in arrangements so sumptuous that they'd make Richard Strauss blush. The guitarist does his best to pick his way through it all, but it's an unequal challenge and we found ourselves unequal to listening to all of it.

Amina Claudine Myers (born 1943)

PIANO, ORGAN

Born in Arizona, Amina has forged her own hybrid of jazz, soul, gospel and blues, combined with a strong infusion of the avant-garde. Predictably, she has been largely ignored by the major labels and has recorded mainly in Europe.

★★★★ Salutes Bessie Smith

Leo CDLR 103 *Myers; Cecil McBee (b); Jimmie Lovelace (d).* 2/83.

★★★(★) The Circle Of Time

Black Saint 120078 *Myers; Don Pate (b); Thurman Barker (d).* 2/83.

Myers's discography is far skinnier than it ought to be, but natural selection has thinned the output to these two records. The Black Saint catches Amina in free-ish mode, but sounding remarkably like her great predecessor, Mary Lou Williams. Barker is a player of ferocious intensity and great concentration and occasionally sounds as if he has stopped listening to what's going on around him. Myers refuses to be browbeaten, though, and punches out chords and melody lines. Pate is largely surplus to requirements – no disrespect to him, but indicative of how much Myers likes to shape her own bass lines.

She had kicked off the soon-to-be-influential Leo label with an album called *Song For Mother E*, which had teamed her with percussionist Pheeroan akLaff but no bass player. McBee is always a strong presence and, freed from the normal requirement to keep time and anchor the chords, he creates some pungent figures. Without attempting to pastiche the great blues singer, Myers gets inside Bessie Smith's music completely. It's doubly unfortunate that later work should have been so blandly commercial.

Simon Nabatov (born 1959)

PIANO

An 'American of Russian origin', Nabatov is a contemporary of Pletnev and Pogorelich who turned from the classics to jazz. He works out of Cologne and is a structured player who pushes the frame as far as it will go.

***** Shall We Dance?**
2nd Floor 005 *Nabatov (p solo).* 5/94.

*****(*) Sneak Preview**
hatOLOGY 548 *Nabatov; Mark Helias (b); Tom Rainey (d).* 1/99.

Nabatov's classical studies and ongoing experimentation with metre are some of the trademarks of a complex, two-handed pianism. The best introduction to what he can do is the apparently deleted *Tough Customer* on Enja.

Reconvened in a studio after seven years, the trio picks up where it left off, on *Sneak Preview.* Nabatov's ideas are as extravagant as ever, in the elaborate dedication 'For Steve' (Lacy) no less than in the displaced accents and off-kilter harmonies of the otherwise almost dance-like 'Let's Go Baby'. Helias and Rainey are as reflexive and attentive as before. Just here and there Nabatov's ingenuities are almost too private to communicate, even to a sympathetic listener, but he's making exhilarating trio music for sure.

In between was the belatedly released solo session on the German label 2nd Floor. No dance music here, but a programme rooted in Nabatov's classical studies: derivations from Bach, Chopin, Brahms and Prokoviev, with his original 'Simple Simon' this time sounding like a compressed Jarrett hallelujah. Not much jazz here, either, but it will appeal to piano-music specialists.

***** The Master And Margarita**
Leo LR 322/3 2CD *Nabatov; Herb Robertson (t); Mark Feldman (vn); Mark Helias (b); Tom Rainey (d).* 2/99.

*****(*) Nature Morte**
Leo LR 310 *Nabatov; Nils Wogram (tb); Frank Gratkowski (cl, as, bcl, f); Phil Minton (v).* 4/99.

Nabatov set himself a couple of formidable tasks here: setting music for the phantasmagoric novel *The Master And Margarita* and creating a quartet piece to go with Joseph Brodsky's fierce poem *Nature Morte.* Mother Russia may be the environment, but the American group do an impressive enough job on the two hours of music in the former. Feldman, who these days seems to be asked to perform a bit of the old world to order, has some handsome moments, as does the similarly can-do Robertson; but if anything they get in Nabatov's way, and the writing is sometimes mixed – the Monk rip-off 'The Last Days' seems a poker-faced homage.

Nature Morte looks ready to challenge Michael Mantler's incomparable miserabilism, but this is an altogether juicier, darker, sometimes even funny piece – Wogram plays some sensational stuff, and the slimline group follow Nabatov's witty, scuttling score with great finesse. Minton, as so often in this kind of situation, has the gravitas and guts of a great Shakespearean. Where *The Master And Margarita* is the kind of piece you nod to respectfully, *Nature Morte* is one to return to.

***** Swing Kings**
ACT 9298-2 *Nabatov; Wolfgang Schlüter (vib); Charly Antolini (d).* 9/96.

***** Starting A Story**
ACT 9402-2 *Nabatov; Nils Wogram (tb).* 3/00.

***** Three Stories, One End**
ACT 9401-2 *Nabatov; Drew Gress (b); Tom Rainey (d).* 11/00.

Surveying the discography to date, one feels that Nabatov can play whatever he likes, however he likes, which endangers his individuality as much as enhances it. These three albums for ACT point up the problem. *Swing Kings* is a belated release of a club set where the pianist met up with the midstream swing duo of Schlüter and Antolini and they barnstormed their way through the likes of 'China Boy', with the pianist coming on like Art Tatum riding a rocket. It's frantically exciting at times, but there's also something disagreeable about it, as if Nabatov were simply laughing at the tradition and making himself too big for it. The other two do their stuff regardless.

With Wogram he's in dialogue with a similarly mercurial mind and temperament, and the wonder is that the trombonist is able to get his recalcitrant instrument to go at Nabatov's pace: try the lip-busting 'The Mistake' for evidence. There are plenty of beautiful passages, and concluding with the Herbie Nichols tune 'East 117th Street' centres the record nicely on a genuine jazz axis, but at 76 minutes it's far too long and several pieces do degenerate into merely showing off.

As for *Three Stories, One End*: doing a more-or-less standards piano-trio record is the sort of call which he might deem barely worth his while. Sometimes there's a sensitivity at work here which hardly seems a part of some of the sets above. 'Emily' is an object lesson in building a logical ballad-reading out of some abstracted beginnings. But Monk's 'Epistrophy' is taken too far out: he could be playing anything here, and maybe he is. 'I Wish I Knew' is bright and chipper, 'Giant Steps' is scaled down into a lush rhapsody, and 'St Thomas' is probably far too clever. A bemusing release.

*****(*) Chat Room**
Leo LR 378 *Nabatov; Han Bennink (d).* 9/01.

With Bennink, Nabatov is taking on the biggest show-off in the music, but since the drummer is also among the most diligent and shrewdest of improvisers, there's little here that could be called mere showmanship. Bennink's cunning means that he is as likely to go into straight time as treat the kit (and surroundings) as part of a demolition derby, and there's a fair amount of working off a groove here. Sometimes they linger on tiny, even annoying scraps of detail, at other times they're generously expansive. They're helped by an excellent studio-mix which is kind to both players.

Phil Napoleon (1901–90)

TRUMPET

A genuine pioneer, Filippo Napoli was one of the earliest white hot trumpeters, and his lead work in the Original Memphis Five, one of the key small groups of the '20s, was profoundly influential on men such as Red Nichols and Bix Beiderbecke. He remained active as a musician, making many latter-day Dixieland sessions into the late '50s.

*****(*) The Original Memphis Five / Napoleon's Emperors / The Cotton Pickers 1928–1929**
Timeless CBC 1-049 *Napoleon; Tommy Dorsey (tb, t); Glenn Miller (tb); Jimmy Dorsey (cl, as); Frank Signorelli, Arthur Schutt (p); Joe Venuti (vn); Eddie Lang (g, bj); Carl Kress (g); Perry Botkin (bj); Joe Tarto (b); Vic Berton, Stan King (d); Hoagy Carmichael, Marlin Hurt, Dick Robertson, Libby Holman, Scrappy Lambert (v).* 6/28–7/29.

***** Live At Nick's, NYC**
Jazzology JCD-39 *Napoleon; Andy Russo (tb); Phil Olivera (cl); Joe Rand (p); Jack Fay (b); Tony Spargo (d).* 49–50.

Napoleon is today virtually forgotten, yet he is among the most prolifically recorded of all jazz trumpeters, beginning with the Original Memphis Five in 1921 and still making tight, accomplished Dixieland for Capitol in the '50s. The Memphis Five sessions by themselves would be enough to fill a boxful of CDs, and the few so far reissued are listed under the group's name. The Timeless CD gathers in a couple of sessions where the name was used by Napoleon again, along with the five tracks by Napoleon's Emperors, and four dates featuring the Cotton Pickers, a name used on Brunswick for a slightly enlarged OMF. Whatever the names, the music's all of a piece: small-band white New York jazz at the close of the '20s, a degree hotter than the hot-dance situations for which these players were usually engaged. It's all built around Napoleon and the Dorseys, with the likes of Miller, Venuti and Lang going out front now and again. Not too many period vocals, but Hoagy Carmichael and Marlin Hurt (whoever that is) have some indecent fun on the two takes of 'St Louis Gal'. Track for track, this is one of the strongest representations of this school on CD, and the transfers are top notch.

The airshots on *Live at Nick's* were taken from radio sessions in New York and they find Napoleon in self-effacing mood. He gives almost all the solo space to Olivera and Rand and is content to play a firm, unshakeable lead horn himself. Besides the obvious staple tunes, strung together in medleys, there are some nice rarities such as 'In My Merry Oldsmobile', once recorded by Bix Beiderbecke with Jean Goldkette, and 'I Used To Love You'. There's nothing outstanding and the sound is about average for the source and period, but Napoleon's determined, unflashy leadership has its own rewards, and the sound the band makes (with the ODJB's drummer Spargo driving them along!) is appealing. We still await the advent of some of Napoleon's Capitol sessions on CD.

Derek Nash

SOPRANO, ALTO, TENOR AND BARITONE SAXOPHONES

Award-winning multi-horn player whose band Sax Appeal has won hearts in Britain. He also works as a sound engineer.

***** Setting New Standards**
Jazzizit JITCD 981 *Nash; Graham Harvey (p); Alec Dankworth (b); Clark Tracey, Ian Thomas (d).* 02.

Having cut his teeth with the late Spike Robinson on *Young Lions, Old Tigers*, Nash has moved forward with this bright, swinging set of mainstream originals. His rhythm section is about as good as there is in the country and though he tends to play all four of his saxophones with a similar intonation and phrasing, they give the set an attractive range of tonalities. Stand-out tracks are the opening 'Blue For You' and 'New York Walk'.

Ted Nash (born 1959)

TENOR SAXOPHONE

The nephew of Ted Nash who played tenor with the Les Brown band and briefly recorded for Columbia. Ted Jr is a modernist, who has veered between hard bop and the avant-garde. Has worked with Louie Bellson, with the Lincoln Center Jazz Orchestra and as part of the Herbie Nichols Project.

***** Rhyme & Reason**
Arabesque 196 *Nash; Wynton Marsalis (t); Frank Kimbrough (p); Erik Charlston (vib); Miri Ben-Ari, Joyce Hamman (vn); Ron Lawrence (vla); Tomas Ulrich (clo); Ben Allison (b); Tim Horner (d).* 96.

Billed as a Double Quartet record, which may conjure up memories of Ornette Coleman's *Free Jazz*, though a glance at the personnel should rule out any likelihood of that being an influence. Wynton Marsalis doesn't do Ornette. Basically, this is a small-scale with-strings project, though the quartet are not there for broad brush backgrounds but to add a different level of detail to some imaginative and unexpected charts. The presence of Allison, now a superb leader in his own right and leader of the Herbie Nichols Project, helps to integrate the two elements harmonically. 'Apollo 9' gets things off to a very promising start and immediately establishes the role the strings will play in what follows. 'Rhyme' features a brief vocal sample from the saxophonist's daughters, who are also the inspiration for 'Sisters', a delightful idea that conceals some hard-as-iron structure.

Nash's tone is quite rugged, forthright without being declamatory, and there are hints of both Wayne Shorter and Joe Henderson in his solos. Ted's Lincoln Center boss, Marsalis, is limited to two tracks, but his presence is intriguing, since this isn't his usual gig by any means. A nod to vibist Charlston as well for his sophisticated comping and splintery runs against the saxophone.

*****(*) Sidewalk Meeting**
Arabesque 156 *Nash; Wycliffe Gordon (tb, sousaphone); Miri Ben-Ari (vn); William Schwimmel (acc); Jeff Ballard, Matt Wilson (d).* 10/00.

This is the group Ted calls Odeon. The signature sound comes from trombone and sousaphone master Gordon, from Ben-Ari's violin, Schwimmel's accordion, and from Nash's own increasingly sophisticated solo presence. Just to wrong-foot the listener a tad more, he starts off with an unconventional arrangement of a Debussy rhapsody. Later material is less unexpected, a few sharp originals dotted round 'Bemsha Swing' and the relatively unknown Ellington/Strayhorn theme 'Amad'. Gordon, a further Marsalis connection, doubles on sousaphone and is used as the bass instrument, filling in broad intervallic leaps and swoops and keeping the music very much in a classic jazz idiom, despite the unfamiliar sonority of the other front-line players. 'Sidewalk Meeting' sees Ted switch to bass clarinet (he's also a fine flautist) for a delightful urban fantasy that has strong hints of Charles Ives.

The two drummers are terrific and their interwoven lines add the final lustre to a genuinely surprising and thoroughly delightful record.

***** Still Evolved**

Palmetto 2092 *Nash; Wynton Marsalis, Marcus Printup (t); Frank Kimbrough (p); Ben Allison (b); Matt Wilson (d).* 8/02.

Something of a disappointment after *Sidewalk Meeting*, but only because it lacks that album's lyrical originality and unique timbre. Marsalis is back again, in an unusual sideman's role and brings his taut, ripe tone to four Nash originals, the rest being co-fronted by the excellent Printup, who mixes Freddie Hubbard and early Donald Byrd in his sound. Kimbrough and Allison are back and all to the good, while Wilson stokes his growing reputation with a driving, subtly melodic accompaniment that suggests he's aware of some of the more inventive of the avant-garde percussionists: Andrew Cyrille, Milford Graves, Ed Blackwell. Nash concentrates on tenor and sounds ever more restlessly inventive, though here he focuses on line and harmony rather than the unusual orchestral effects of earlier records. There are earlier records, including a fine one on Mapleshade, but these three confirm Nash's emergence as a very singular and significant talent.

Fats Navarro (1923–50)

TRUMPET

The unfortunate but brilliant Navarro worked in Andy Kirk's band and in Billy Eckstine's legendary outfit, where he replaced the trumpeter whose style he had adopted and adapted. Fats was a more lyrical player than Dizzy Gillespie and sounded easier in the middle register of the instrument. His career was greatly foreshortened by a narcotic habit and tuberculosis, but he recorded some of the finest brass solos of the bebop era, many of them with bandleader Tadd Dameron.

CORE COLLECTION

**** The Complete Fats Navarro On Blue Note And Capitol

Blue Note 33373 2CD *Navarro; Howard McGhee (t); Ernie Henry (as); Allen Eager, Wardell Gray, Sonny Rollins, Charlie Rouse (ts); Tadd Dameron, Bud Powell (p); Milt Jackson (p, vib); Nelson Boyd, Tommy Potter, Curley Russell (b); Kenny Clarke, Roy Haynes, Shadow Wilson (d); Chano Pozo (perc).* 9/47–8/49.

These sessions are one of the peaks of the bebop movement and one of the essential modern-jazz records. Navarro's tone and solo approach were honed in big-band settings and he has the remarkable ability to maintain a graceful poise even when playing loudly and at speed. The contrast with McGhee (it seems extraordinary that some of their performances together have been misattributed) is very striking. Their duelling choruses on 'Double Talk' from a marvellous October 1948 session are some of the high-points of the record; there is, as with several other tracks, an alternative take which shows how thoughtful and self-critical an improviser the young trumpeter was, constantly refining, occasionally wholly rethinking his approach to a chord progression, but more frequently taking over whole segments of his solo and reordering them into a more satisfying outline. Navarro is rhythmically quite conservative, but he plays with great containment and manages to create an illusion, most obvious on 'Boperation', from the same session, that he is floating just above the beat; by contrast, McGhee sounds hasty and anxious. One hears the same effect rather more subtly on both takes of 'Symphonette' and on an alternative take of 'The Squirrel'.

***** Goin' To Minton's**

Savoy 92681 *Navarro; Sonny Stitt (as); Leo Parker (as, bs); Eddie 'Lockjaw' Davis, Charlie Rouse (ts); Tadd Dameron, Al Haig, Bud Powell (p); Nelson Boyd, Gene Ramey, Curley Russell (b); Denzil Best, Art Blakey, Kenny Clarke (d).* 9/46–12/47.

*****(*) Fats Navarro Featured With The Tadd Dameron Band**

Milestone M 47041 *Navarro; Tadd Dameron (p); Rudy Williams (as); Allen Eager (ts); Milt Jackson (vib); Curley Russell (b); Kenny Clarke (d).* 48.

***** His Best Recordings: 1946–1949**

Best of Jazz 4068 *As above; add Andy Kirk Orchestra, Coleman Hawkins Orchestra; Be Bop Boys, Tadd Dameron Sextet & Orchestra.* 46–49.

****** The Fats Navarro Story**

Proper 1011 4CD *As for the above.* 46–50.

*****(*) Fats Navarro, 1947–1949**

Classics 1108 *As above; add Earl Coleman (v).* 47–49.

***** Bird & Fats – Live At Birdland**

Cool & Blue C&B CD 103 *Navarro; Charlie Parker (as); Walter Bishop Jr, Bud Powell (p); Tommy Potter, Curley Russell (b); Art Blakey, Roy Haynes (d); Chubby Newsome (v).* 6/50.

Like Howard McGhee, Navarro came up through the Andy Kirk band, having already worked with Snookum Russell. Overweight, with a high, rather effeminate voice (and nicknamed either 'Fat Boy' or 'Fat Girl'), he had by 1945, when he replaced Dizzy Gillespie in the Billy Eckstine orchestra, developed a trumpet style which replaced Gillespie's burp-gun lines with a more elegantly shaped approach that emphasized a bright, burnished tone. The open texture of his solos was altogether better suited to the Tadd Dameron band, which became his most effective setting. Dameron is the accompanist on the best of the material, which provides an additional 20 minutes' top-flight Navarro, with four dispensable tracks from a drab December 1946 session alongside Lockjaw Davis and Al Haig. There's also a slice of pre-Dameron work on *Memorial*, credited to Gil Fuller's Modernists, together with later stuff by an equally good band (Henry, Dameron, Russell, Clarke) and marred only slightly by Kay Penton's inconsequential vocals.

Goin' To Minton's mops up some of the best of the material Fats recorded before his Blue Note apotheosis. Covering mainly tracks cut over five sessions round the autumn of 1946 and through the following year, they catch him developing into an ever more confident and moving soloist. His empathy with Bud Powell on 'Boppin' A Riff' and 'Fat Boy' is extraordinary and, generally speaking, he sounds better when unaccompanied by more than a single saxophone. Such was Fats's ability to blow resonant middle-register phrases that there is none of Dizzy's skyscraping which often sounded very far removed from the basic melody and key centre. Lennie Tristano may have been right in his valuation of the two trumpeters: Lennie thought Diz was a fine enough player, but he was no Fats Navarro.

There is an excellent version of 'Symphonette', from 1948, on the Milestone Navarro/Dameron compilation. Milt Jackson is present, but these performances, which also include 'The Squirrel', 'Dameronia' and two fine versions of 'Anthropology', are not up to the standard of the Blue Notes recordings above.

The tracks on *Live At Birdland*, one with his own quartet and 15 more with Bird's group, document his last public appearance. They find him still poised and lyrical, but lacking the dramatic edge of the classic sessions, and unmistakably weary.

The Classics set is, as always with this imprint, a respectably detailed but aurally unedifying option.There is some additional material on which Fats backs vocalist Earl Coleman, but the key recordings are there and if the budget is tight, this is a reasonable option. Also a generously proportioned career survey, *Story* includes all the material you would expect and does so at a very attractive budget price. The pioneering bebop material on the first disc is the freshest and the rawest. Fats would play better, but rarely with the same headlong urgency and *joie de vivre*. It traces his apprenticeship in the Billy Eckstine Orchestra and his emergence as a valid frontline soloist who might have rivalled the attainments of some of his now more celebrated colleagues had he lived. The second CD concentrates on Fats's work with two great tenors, Lockjaw Davis and Coleman Hawkins, though it also includes his forays with the Thin Men, his own first quartet as leader. The remaining two discs cover the Royal Roost sessions and Navarro's flurry of recording activity on a variety of larger and smaller labels in the period before his death. All the material has been available before but it is wonderful to have these sides in such accessible and affordable form. The Best of Jazz compilation also has the benefit of tracing Fats's development from his days with the Kirk band, with Coleman Hawkins, early stuff as leader with the Be Bop Boys and the Thin Men group and the best of the Dameron sides, but such was the concentration of Navarro's career that these sets are heavily overlapped and often pointlessly repetitive. Purchasers should be wary of buying umpteen versions of the same material, no matter how attractive the packaging or competitive the price.

Navarro died a week after the Birdland date of tuberculosis exacerbated by drug abuse. As an artist he was already astonishingly mature, and it's slightly ironic that many of the stylistic innovations and developments attributed to Clifford Brown were actually instigated by Navarro. Small as his legacy is, it is one of the finest in all of jazz.

'Big Eye' Louis Nelson (1885–1949)

CLARINET

Born in New Orleans, he played bass in the Buddy Bolden group in 1900 but switched to clarinet, later working with most of the major early groups in the city. Taught many up-and-coming talents and spent most of his life playing in cabaret and theatres, but was effectively rediscovered in the '40s and cut several tracks at the very end of his life.

***** Big Eye Louis Nelson Delisle**
American Music AMCD-7 *Nelson; Wooden Joe Nicholas (t, v); Charles Love (t); Louis Nelson (tb); Louis Gallaud (p); Johnny St Cyr, Louis Keppard (g); Austin Young, Albert Glenny (b); Ernest Rogers, Albert Jiles (d); William Tircuit (v).* 5–7/49.

The only record under the nominal leadership of a man who taught Bechet and was an acknowledged inspiration of Dodds and Noone. The CD consists of three informal studio or home sessions and seven tracks from a dance-hall date in New Orleans; ten tracks appear for the first time. Whatever the credentials outlined above, Nelson sounds like a man content to coast through his working life: the clarinet playing ambles along, mixing fluffs and good notes. The live tracks are a bit more animated, played over a very steady beat, and, though Love and Nicholas provide firm leads, the horns (the other Louis Nelson, on trombone, is no relation) play things very straight. Worth hearing by New Orleans scholars, but of limited appeal otherwise. The sound is able-bodied but muffled on most of the tracks.

Louis Nelson (1902–90)

TROMBONE

Born in New Orleans, although he grew up in nearby Napoleonville, Nelson played trombone with the Sidney Desvigne band for 15 years. After war service, he played extensively with the Kid Thomas band and was a regular at Preservation Hall with many leaders. A fundamentalist of New Orleans trombone, he had a long and prolific career, working until his death in 1990.

***** Louis Nelson's Creole Jazz Band**
GHB BCD-173 *Nelson; Cuff Billett (t, v); John Defferary (cl); Richard Simmons (p); Paul Sealey (g); Brian Turnock (b); Barry Martyn (d).* 66.

***** Jazz At The Palm Court Vol. 1**
GHB BCD-551 *Nelson; Wendell Brunious (t, v); Sammy Rimington (cl); Butch Thompson (p); Danny Barker (bj, v); Chester Zardis (b); Stanley Stephens (d).* 4/89.

This is the 'other' Louis Nelson, who came to prominence almost a generation after Big Eye Louis. Although most regularly appearing as a sideman, Nelson has a few records under his own name – although, strictly speaking, the first GHB date features him as a guest with the Barry Martyn Ragtime Band, a souvenir of a British visit. The record was made in an old hall attached to the White Horse pub in Willesden. Nelson contributes his unchanging, gruff trombone parts to the enthusiastic playing of these young Brits, and the session has a degree of charm as well as a bluff, good-humoured spirit, kept up to speed by Martyn's doughty and tireless drumming.

Louis was still determined to blow the horn, even at 86, and the Palm Court Jazz Band had plenty of fun on their regular gig. Brunious and Rimington will always seem like youngsters in this company, but they were pretty experienced themselves by this point, and the music has all the pungency it needs. Nelson himself is taking it easy, though his solos sound like a old man's defiance, even with Father Time knocking at the door.

Oliver Nelson (1932–75)

ALTO AND TENOR SAXOPHONES, CLARINET

Unremarkable sideman career until he began recording as a leader in 1959, then arranging for big-band settings, especially with Jimmy Smith and Wes Montgomery. His own playing featured less as he won commissions for film and TV work from the late '60s onwards. Died suddenly of a heart attack.

*** Meet Oliver Nelson: Featuring Kenny Dorham

Original Jazz Classics OJC 227 *Nelson; Kenny Dorham (t); Ray Bryant (p); Wendell Marshall (b); Art Taylor (d).* 10/59.

*** Taking Care Of Business

Original Jazz Classics OJC 1784 *Nelson; Lem Winchester (vib); Johnny Hammond Smith (org); George Tucker (b); Roy Haynes (d).* 3/60.

Nelson served his apprenticeship with Louis Jordan and the Erskine Hawkins and Quincy Jones big bands, and he probably learned most from working with Quincy, not least that ability to combine sophisticated intervals and expansive shapes with a raw blues feel. Sadly, Nelson was to spend his last few years in the same direction, writing TV themes like 'The Six Million Dollar Man', lucrative but an unsatisfactory legacy for a man with an impressive jazz discography.

These early records are nicely arranged, well textured, but ultimately a bit flat. Dorham's contributions to the earlier of the pair are exactly what you'd expect of him: fluid, punchy and lyrical in all the unexpected places. The second is much more of an arranger's record, and it's the interplay of timbres and textures that one remembers rather than anything in the themes.

***(*) Screamin' The Blues

Original Jazz Classics OJC 080 *Nelson; Richard Williams (t); Eric Dolphy (as, bcl, f); Richard Wyands (p); George Duvivier (b); Roy Haynes (d).* 5/60.

Nelson cottoned on to Dolphy before the latter began to make a mark as a solo artist, and he blatantly and quite forgivably used him as a colourist rather than a lateral improviser. Nelson's own solos weren't quite as pedestrian as they sometimes sounded (we suggested he played 'arranger's sax') but they were somewhat limited both in sound and ideas, so Dolphy was an ideal recruitment; Richard Williams, destined never to have much of a career under his own name, is excellent in this context, brighter and sharper than Dorham, though without the softer, lyrical quality. The rhythm section has an almost time-capsule quality. If one were played this in the dark, it would be possible to date it almost to the month. The bebop figures are less in evidence. There's a growing attraction to diminished and off-centre chords, and the drumming is beginning to sound multi-directional, free of the bomb-dropping aggression of a previous generation. Haynes is one of the key protagonists here in one of his best sessions of this vintage.

**(*) Soul Battle

Original Jazz Classics OJC 325 *Nelson; King Curtis, Jimmy Forrest (ts); Gene Casey (p); George Duvivier (b); Roy Haynes (d).* 9/60.

We've never much liked this record. It's slightly hard to work out what Nelson is doing on it. He's clearly not up to the earthy bravura of Curtis and Forrest, and without that there's not much point putting in an appearance. The rhythm section drive it along without a great deal of conviction, though Haynes is again wonderful, and Nelson's solos would (almost without exception) have best been left on the editing-room floor.

*** Nocturne

Original Jazz Classics OJC 1795 *Nelson; Richard Wyands (p); George Duvivier (b); Roy Haynes (d).* 60.

*** Straight Ahead

Original Jazz Classics OJC 099 *As above, except add Eric Dolphy (as, bcl, f).* 3/61.

The title of the second of the pair notwithstanding, these are both notably subtle records, perhaps too much so to catch the ear of most fans. Nelson thought out his arrangements with more care than instinct, and one sometimes finds oneself listening as if to tumblers falling into place. All items in the Dolphy catalogue are precious, but *Straight Ahead* has to be accounted one of the few disappointments, a rather unresolved and undifferentiated set with little of the brimstone and treacle one got on *Blues And The Abstract Truth* later.

**** Blues And The Abstract Truth

Impulse! 051154-2 *Nelson; Freddie Hubbard (t); Eric Dolphy (as, f); George Barrow (bs); Bill Evans (p); Paul Chambers (b); Roy Haynes (d).* 2/61.

Restored to its original cover artwork (a portrait of Nelson was substituted when the stereo version appeared), this is one of the classics of the period, and if there were one Nelson track to take away to a desert island it would have to be the one that starts the album, the haunting 'Stolen Moments' with its mournful Hubbard solo and a lovely statement from Dolphy on flute. The great man left his bass clarinet behind for this session, and it isn't missed. Nelson tended to arrange for higher voices, and for this record he didn't stray outside 12-bar blues and the chords of 'I Got Rhythm'. 'Stolen Moments' is a minor blues, opening in C minor, with some fascinating internal divisions. 'Hoe Down' is a 44-bar figure based on the opening two notes. 'Teenie's Blues' is dedicated to the composer's sister, a talented singer. It rests on just three intervals, with transpositions for the two altos to maintain a level of tension and release. The rhythm section is again very fine, with Haynes relishing this setting and Chambers producing some lovely countermelodies and stop-time figures under the basic changes. The sound is now as good as anyone could possibly want, close and sharp enough to hear Dolphy's breath across the embouchure of the flute.

*** Main Stem

Original Jazz Classics OJC 1803 *Nelson; Hank Jones (p); George Duvivier (b); Charli Persip (d); Ray Barretto (perc).* 61.

At the end of a hectically busy period for Nelson, he sounds tired and short of ideas. His own writing had become slightly formulaic and there was a dearth of real ideas in the playing. Jones has always been a player who is flattered by his companions, and here, though he sounds lovely, almost courtly, he is upstaged by everyone around him. Nelson is not playing well, falling back on licks and riffs that have been around for years. A word for Persip, who has been a constant presence on the scene for years but who is rarely given his due of recognition.

*** Afro / American Sketches

Original Jazz Classics OJC 1819 *Nelson; Billy Byers, Jerry Kail, Joe Newman, Ernie Royal (t); Paul Faulise, Urbie Green, Melba Liston, Britt Woodman (tb); Don Butterfield (tba); Ray Alonge, Jimmy Buffington, Julius Watkins (frhn); Bob Ashton, Eric Dixon, Jerry Dodgion, Charles McCracken (sax); Peter Makis (p); Art Davis (b); Ed Shaughnessy (d); Ray Barretto (perc).* 62.

Nelson prepared very carefully for this; indeed, he insisted that such a project was possible only with a lot of preparation. Perhaps that is the problem, for what this record desperately lacks is a measure of spontaneity, and this is a rather stiff and ungiving set. The story is that Nelson was originally unwilling to take on the project but eventually agreed to do so on his own terms. The themes are all very much in his normal range and there is more than enough space for the soloists, but something about the way the record is voiced leaves a rather flat impression. Nelson himself is not much interested in soloing and responds only perfunctorily when he does.

***** More Blues And The Abstract Truth**

Impulse! 051212-2 *Nelson; Thad Jones, Danny Moore (t); Phil Woods (as); Phil Bodner (ts, eng hn); Ben Webster (ts); Pepper Adams (bs); Roger Kellaway (p); Richard Davis (b); Grady Tate (d).* 9/64.

In this case, more means less. This lacks the impact and the punch of the original session, not because the players are lacking in fire (any session that boasts Thad Jones, Phil Woods *and* Ben Webster isn't struggling for charisma) but because the music is already drifting towards the formulaic television funk that was to occupy too much of Nelson's later life. 'Theme From Mr Broadway' and 'Blue For Mr Broadway' are the strongest things, both of them big, generous themes with more bottom end than is usual in a Nelson composition and arrangement.

*****(*) Jazz Masters 48**

Verve 527654 *Nelson; Nat Adderley (c); Burt Collins, Ray Copeland, Bernie Glow, Jimmy Maxwell, Joe Newman, Ernie Royal, Marvin Stamm, Joe Wilder, Snooky Young (t); Clark Terry (t, flhn); Wayne Andre, Jimmy Cleveland, Willie Dennis, Urbie Green, Quentin Jackson, Benny Powell (tb); Bob Brookmeyer (vtb); Tony Faulise, J. J. Johnson, Rod Levitt, Tony Studd (btb); Ray Alonge, Jimmy Buffington, Bob Northern (frhn); Don Butterfield (tba); Danny Bank, Phil Bodner, Al Cohn, Jerry Dodgion, Zoot Sims, Stan Webb, Phil Woods (reeds); Patti Bown, Albert Dailey, Hank Jones (p); Eric Gale, Jim Hall, Jimmy Raney (g); Harry Brewer (mar, cel); Ron Carter, George Duvivier, Milt Hinton (b); Ed Shaughnessy, Grady Tate (d); Phil Kraus, Bobby Rosengarden (perc).* 11/62–11/67.

A fine compilation of material spanning just five years but covering a huge amount of ground in stylistic terms. Nelson's skills as an arranger have never been in doubt, but this record brings them out triumphantly, a debt to Ellington and Bartók, and a swinging, uncomplicated approach which is at its best when faced with a full jazz orchestra. Pieces like the long 'Complex City' have a strong Ellingtonian strain and are nicely pitched between structure and freedom for the soloists (in this case Woods, Bown, Sims and Newman). Others, like the staple 'Hoe Down' and 'Full Nelson', are more straightforwardly conceived, less dependent on individual expression. Most tracks are short and to the point and Creed Taylor gets a very full and accurate sound from the band. A valuable compilation from a less than accessible period in Nelson's foreshortened career. Nelson made a lot of records for Impulse! and at present these have a rather scant showing in the catalogue.

***** Swiss Suite**

RCA Victor 74321 *Nelson; Charles Tolliver, Danny Moore, Bent Stean, Harry Beckett (t); Buddy Baker, Bertil Strandberg, Donald Beightol, C. J. Shiubly, Monte Holz, John Thomas (tb); Jim Nissen (btb); Jesper Thilo, Ozren Depolo (as); Michal Urbaniak, Bob Sydor (ts); Steve Stevenson (bs); Stanley Cowell (p); Victor Gaskin, Hugo Rasmussen (b); Bernard Purdie (d); Bosko Petrovic, Na Na, Sonny Morgan (perc).* 6/71.

A live set from Montreux in 1971. Nelson's star had waned a little but he was a favourite in central Europe and this kind of big-band commission was probably something that came easily to him. Besides the title-piece there are new versions of 'Stolen Moments', 'Black, Brown And Beautiful' and 'Blues And The Abstract Truth'. The players make up a Euro-American alliance of a sort which is rarely seen now, and it's nostalgic hearing the kind of uncomplicated but characterful writing and playing heard here.

Steve Nelson (born 1955)

VIBRAPHONE

Originally worked with Grant Green, but has diversified into modern settings and established a strong presence as leader with his Milt Jackson-influenced approach.

***** Communications**

Criss Cross 1034 *Nelson; Mulgrew Miller (p); Ray Drummond (b); Tony Reedus (d).* 12/87.

There are a handful of phrases on 'The Song Is You' and 'I Didn't Know What Time It Was' when it might have been Bags playing, except the phrasing is not so taut or rhythmically propulsive and the attack is sharper and more ringing. One of the most interesting vibists on the scene, Nelson has often been better recognized for his work with other leaders. The Criss Cross contract doesn't seem to have worked out, or at least wasn't continued, which is a great shame since this is the sort of context which suits Steve best and it would have been good to hear more in this vein and of this quality. The long work-outs, especially 'Dignity', are the best.

***** Live Session: Volume 1**

Red RR 123231 2 *Nelson; Bobby Watson (as); Donald Brown (p); Curtis Lundy (b); Victor Lewis (d).* 7/89.

***** Live Session: Volume 2**

Red RR 123232 2 *As above.* 7/89.

Watson and Nelson had struck up a good working relationship and Steve always plays well alongside Bobby's boppish, Rabbit-tinged alto. 'New Beginning' which opens Volume 1 is a terrific piece, packed with energy and marked by some agile, percussive playing from Nelson, who seems to strike his keys with power but maintains a warm, full tone, presumably something to do with the mallets. Brown is a bit lost in places, recessed in the live mix, and his contribution is hard to assess. Lundy is superb and Lewis can't be faulted, even though this might have been a better gig for Marvin Smitty Smith.

'Afro Blue' is the big piece on Volume 1, stretched out to more than twenty minutes; 'Quiet As It Is Kept' is a lovely ballad. On Volume 2, Watson is absent for 'I Can't Get Started', leaving Nelson to work his way through a thoroughly imaginative version of the standard that implies familiarity with the Mingus/Dolphy version. Most of the tunes are standards and though Watson isn't thought of as primarily a standards player, his tripping, graceful turn on 'Sweet And Lovely' and his passionate declamations on 'The Song Is You' make this a fine outing for the saxophonist as well as for Nelson.

*** **New Beginnings**
TCB 99302 *Nelson; Mulgrew Miller (p); Peter Washington (b); Kenny Washington (d). 99.*

The '90s were relatively quiet for Nelson in recording terms, though he became part of Dave Holland's regular band and poured much of his energies into that; he also worked with Kenny Barron, Jeanie Bryson and others. The chops are still very strong on this belated return to the studio. 'New Beginnings' is a powerful starting point, as it's intended to be, but working without a horn allows Steve to weave his own top line over Miller's open, Tynerish chords. After two more originals, Steve switches to standards fare, including an unexpectedly extended version of 'It's The Talk Of The Town' and beautiful closing meditation on Dmitri Tiomkin's 'Wild Is The Wind'. Lovely stuff.

Phineas Newborn Jr (1931–90)

PIANO

Technically, he was sometimes claimed to run a close second to Art Tatum. In reality, Newborn was a more effective player at slower tempos and with fewer notes; but he could be dazzling when he chose, even after illness and injury hampered his progress. A sensitive and troubled soul; even the lightest of his performances point to hidden depths of emotion.

*** **Here Is Phineas**
Koch International 8505 *Newborn; Oscar Pettiford (b); Kenny Clarke (d). 5/56.*

*** **Phineas' Rainbow**
RCA 74231421 2 *Newborn; Calvin Newborn (g); George Joyner (b); Philly Joe Jones (d). 10/56.*

(*) **While My Lady Sleeps
RCA 85157-2 *Newborn; George Joyner (b); Alvin Stoller (d); strings. 4/57.*

*** **Phineas' Rainbow / While My Lady Sleeps**
Collectables 2737 *As above two discs. 10/56–4/57.*

*** **Plays Jamaica / Fabulous Phineas**
Collectables 2740 *Newborn; Ernie Royal (t); Jimmy Cleveland (tb); Jerome Richardson (ts, f); Sahib Shihab (as, bs, bcl); Les Spann, Calvin Newborn (g); George Duvivier, George Joyner (b); Osie Johnson, Denzil Best (d); Francisco Pozo, Willie Rodriguez (perc). 9/57-4/58.*

***(*) **Fabulous Phineas**
RCA 74321257662 *Newborn; Calvin Newborn (g); George Joyner (b); Denzil Best (d). 3–4/58.*

***(*) **Stockholm Jam Session Vol. 1**
Steeplechase SCCD 36025 *Newborn; Benny Bailey (t); Oscar Pettiford (b); Rune Carlsson (d); unidentified (tb) and (bs). 9/58.*

*** **Stockholm Jam Session Vol. 2**
Steeplechase SCCD 36026 *As above. 9/58.*

A player of tremendous technical ability, often likened to Oscar Peterson (who had come on to the East Coast scene with similar suddenness and plaudits), the younger Newborn was flashy, hyped-up and explosive, eating up themes like Clifford Brown's 'Daahoud' and Rollins's 'Oleo' as if they were buttered toast. Underneath the super-confident exterior, though, there was a troubled young man who was acutely sensitive to criticism, particularly the charge that he was no more than a cold technician. Newborn suffered a serious nervous collapse from which he only partially recovered, and the remainder of his career was interspersed with periods of ill-health. His later recording output is spasmodic to say the least, marked by a chastened blues sound which contrasts sharply – in style and quality – with the early work.

The Koch reissue was originally made for Atlantic. A shameless display of technical virtuosity, it is almost too technically accomplished and is difficult to absorb at length. *Rainbow* is full of his patented dazzle, but *While My Lady Sleeps*, soaked in Robert Farnon's strings, is more like chrome-plated mood music. The *Plays Jamaica* session, now available on a twofer with *Fabulous*, is a curious set of calypso-ish themes ('Hooray For The Yankee Dollar' is one) with a full band; but *Fabulous* returns to a quartet and is a lot stronger, the material including the deathless 'Pamela'. And yet even here the tendency to elaboration won't be curbed. Absurdly fast octave runs follow one another in quick succession, and even in ballad performances Newborn seems compelled to scatter notes in every direction, when a degree of reticence would be far more effective. Piano-players will marvel, but most casual listeners may find the sum effect excessive.

Fortunately, it transpired in 1992 that tapes of Newborn's 1958 visit to Stockholm had survived, unheard, for 34 years. Expertly cleaned up by Nils Winther, they sound fresh and bright enough to counterbalance the vagaries of a single-mic recording and a ropy piano. The music is of an unexpectedly high quality for a spontaneous session. Some other instruments can be heard during the ensembles, but these did not play a major role and the individuals cannot be identified. Newborn's opening solo on the first session (Vol. 1) is patient and unhurried, growing in expressiveness as he moves outside the basic chords. It's perhaps his most complete statement of the evening. Elsewhere, he solos with great clarity and occasional glimpses of irony, as on Dizzy Gillespie's 'Woody'N'You', where, with Bailey sitting out, he mimics the punchy attack of the original trumpet-line. Though badly recorded, Oscar Pettiford nearly makes the session his own. The bass solos on 'Ladybird' (Vol. 1) and 'It's You Or No One' (Vol. 2) are equally valuable additions to the Pettiford canon, and Bailey's luminous account of 'Confirmation' (Vol. 2) deserves a star or two. Local man Carlsson does his thing politely and professionally.

***(*) **A World Of Piano!**
Original Jazz Classics OJC 175 *Newborn; Paul Chambers (b); Louis Hayes, Philly Joe Jones (d). 10-11/61.*

*** **The Great Jazz Piano Of Phineas Newborn Jr**
Original Jazz Classics OJC 388 *Newborn; Sam Jones, Milt Turner, Leroy Vinnegar (b); Louis Hayes (d). 11/61–9/62.*

***(*) **The Newborn Touch**
Original Jazz Classics OJC 270 *Newborn; Leroy Vinnegar (b); Frank Butler (d). 4/64.*

***(*) **Harlem Blues**
Original Jazz Classics OJC 662 *Newborn; Ray Brown (b); Elvin Jones (d). 2/69.*

*** **Please Send Me Someone To Love**
Original Jazz Classics OJCCSD 947 *As above. 2/69.*

Newborn made a string of records for Contemporary during the '60s, though he was also hampered by a hand injury that curtailed some of his more virtuosic effects. It might be argued that this, compounded by a growing self-doubt, made him a more expressive player. The best of these sides are genuinely moving, as when on 'Prelude To A Kiss' (*Great Jazz Piano*), he restates the theme in octaves and floats it away over his own restatement, like a ghost score. There are equally lovely moments on *Harlem Blues*, most obviously a version of 'Tenderly' that melts the heart.

Throughout this period, he benefited from superb rhythm players. Vinnegar and Butler weren't the right combination for him, but Jones's celebrated polyrhythms, coupled to Brown's resolute chording and fast runs, were an ideal match for his own omnidirectional approach. *Harlem Blues* remains our favourite of the bunch by just a whisker, though there isn't much in it. The remainder of the session was released as *Please Send Me Someone To Love*, and surely now there's a strong case for editing together a good single CD from this pair?

★★(★) Solo Piano
Collectables COL-CD-6372 *Newborn (p solo).* 75.

★★★ Back Home
Original Jazz Classics OJCCD 971 *Newborn; Ray Brown (b); Elvin Jones (d).* 76.

★★★ Look Out – Phineas Is Back!
Original Jazz Classics OJCCD 866 *Newborn; Ray Brown (b); Jimmie Smith (d).* 12/76.

Newborn enjoyed a brief resurgence in the '70s and was taken up by Pablo for a time. Interestingly, this was the closest he ever came to delivering a straight bebop record. Though his hand-speed would have suggested that the rapid-fire changes of bop would be meat and drink to him, he never seemed enamoured of the Monk/Powell axis, continuing to draw sustenance from Tatum and Peterson. On *Phineas Is Back!* he gives 'A Night In Tunisia' and 'Salt Peanuts' exuberant airings and adds the now familiar touch of pathos, even a hint of anger, to 'You Are The Sunshine Of My Life'. Brown and Smith are not well recorded, but both are audible and both play well.

Though there was a smattering of later records, for us these are the last on which Newborn plays like his old self. Stories were rife about his psychological frailty in these years and it is remarkable that he managed to sustain a career at all, let alone at this generally impressive level. The trio on *Back Home* was one that he had worked with in the late '60s and there is genuine enjoyment in each other's company. Brown is happy to fill when the pianist's thoughts wander or when inspiration deserts him, as it seemed to in latter days, but the closing four tracks – 'Back Home', 'On Green Dolphin Street', 'Pamela' and 'Love For Sale' – are almost back to classic form.

The Collectables edition restores his 1975 solo session, originally made for Atlantic. Despite credits for four different engineers and one producer, the piano sound is peculiarly thin and lacking in bottom end, and the interpretations are wilful and inconsistent. Moments of brilliance are often matched with misfingerings and alarming lapses of concentration. He twice mixes the Roberta Flack hit 'Where Is The Love' as part of a medley, and the second time he even tries out a bit of stride rhythm to underpin it. A very strange set.

★★(★) Tivoli Encounter
Storyville 8221 *Newborn; Jesper Lundgaard (b); Bjarne Rostvold (d).* 7/79.

Newborn recorded almost nothing in the final decade of his life, so this has to be regarded as some sort of farewell. Clearly frail and certainly not playing at anything like full stretch, Phineas battles manfully through old favourites like 'Daahoud' and 'Lady Be Good', as well as some classic bebop themes and a couple of clever medleys. The trio could hardly be more supportive, but the fires are almost out and some fans may prefer not to hear him this way.

New Departures Quartet

GROUP

Formed to accompany Michael Horovitz's New Departures poetry events.

★★★ New Departures Quartet
Hot House HH CD 010 *Bobby Wellins (ts); Stan Tracey (p); Jeff Clyne (b); Laurie Morgan (d).* 6 & 7/64.

In his liner-note, Victor Schonfield suggests that Bobby Wellins is the finest saxophonist to emerge outside America since the war. It's hard to argue on the strength of this and the Scotsman's work for the Stan Tracey Quartet on projects like the fabled *Under Milk Wood.* What Schonfield hears as a folkish strain is sometimes harder to detect, though the lightness and simplicity of the saxophonist's lines are strongly evident, as is that characteristically airy delivery. 'Culloden Moor' is a good example of the group's free-improvising sound, the kind of work they must have done at live New Departures events. 'McTaggart' is a more blues-based idea, meat and drink to both Wellins and Tracey. Bass and drums offer solid but unspectacular support (though Clyne's intro to 'McTaggart' is part of its success) and it's a pity that there isn't more material with just saxophone and piano. A reminder of how inventive British jazz was even in the early Beatles era.

New Jazz Composers Octet

GROUP

Founded by David Weiss and devoted to imaginative hard bop.

★★★ First Steps Into Reality
Fresh Sound New Talent FSNT 059 *David Weiss (t); Andrew Williams (tb); Myron Walden (as); Jimmy Greene, Greg Tardy (ts); James Farnsworth, David Reikenberg (bs); Xavier Davis (p); Dwayne Burno (b); Nasheet Waits (d).* 99.

★★★ Walkin' The Line
Fresh Sound New Talent FSNT 151 *As above; omit Reikenberg; add Steve Davis (tb); Craig Handy (ss, as, ts); Chris Karlic (bs); Joe Chambers (d).* 1/03.

The sharp-eyed will have noticed ten performers listed for the first CD. Greene and Reikenberg are in for their opposite numbers on three tracks, adding in the former case a very different flavour to the tenor solo on Freddie Hubbard's 'D Minor Mint'. Trombonist Williams is strongly featured on the same tune and one wishes there were more from him. Despite Weiss's nominal leadership, the two main composers are Davis and Walden; Myron's 'Untitled in A Flat Minor' isn't quite as schematic as it probably sounds and his touch with a big romantic theme is evident on 'I'll Always Love You' (*not* the Dolly Parton/Whitney Houston hit). Davis sets things in motion with the title-track and then delivers the sucker punch with the delightful three-quarter time 'When The Spirit Hits'. Burno gets his spot on 'I'm Comin' On Home'.

As music goes, it isn't quantum physics. There's a bright contemporary edge to the playing, but the basic idiom is 40 years old and none the worse for that, though it makes the 'new' ring with irony. The second album is lifted out of the ordinary by some fine guest appearances: Handy is always an exciting player and his 'Abdullah's Demeanour' is the longest and most ambitious track. This time the writing divides between Davis and Weiss, and the pianist's 'Dead Weight' and 'The Dove' are strong ideas which require nimble thinking. They also do Chick Corea's 'Inner Space' and do it more justice than most of the groups who've taken on the deceptively simple theme.

The New Jazz Wizards

GROUP

The traditionally inclined band, led by C. H. 'Pam' Pameijer, specializing in re-creative projects dedicated to (sometimes unsung) early jazz.

***** Good Stuff, Hot And Ready**

Stomp Off CD1244 *Peter Ecklund (c); Jim Snyder (tb); Reimer Von Essen (cl); Billy Novick (cl, as); Butch Thompson (p); Peter Bullis (bj); Vince Giordano (tba, bsx); Pam Pameijer (d).* 1/92.

***** Golden Lily**

Stomp Off CD1281 *As above, except John Otto (cl, as), Robin Verdier (p), Mike Walbridge (tba); replace Von Essen, Thompson, Giordano; add Dick Wetmore (vn).* 3/94.

Excellent repertory, arranged and recorded with much panache by Pam Pameijer's group of revivalists. The first disc is dedicated to the music of Richard M. Jones; the second, to that of Tiny Parham. It presents two different faces of classic jazz in the '20s – whereas Jones was a comparatively simple, blues-based, small-group man, Parham's more elaborate music hinted at an alternative to the arranged styles of Morton and Ellington. Oddly, the Wizards sound more formal and strait-laced on the Jones music, whereas the highly structured Parham tracks go off with a bang. Ted des Plantes (whose own disc of Parham interpretations has yet to make it to CD) describes the big man's music as 'stodgy and stompy rather than streamlined', yet the Wizards whistle it along. *Good Stuff, Hot And Ready* has much meticulously detailed hot playing but can't quite evade a certain stiffness. In their sincerity in dealing with both composers, the group makes no attempt at hiding the music's weakness as well as its strengths and, despite the fine solos by Ecklund and the others, their attention to the nuts-and-bolts of it holds a certain exuberance in check.

***** The Music Of Jelly Roll Morton Vol. 1**

Stomp Off CD1318 *Peter Ecklund (c); Jim Snyder (tb); Billy Novick (cl, as); John Otto (cl, ts); Ray Smith (p); Howard Alden (g, bj); Vince Giordano (tba, b); Pam Pameijer (d).* 2/97.

***** The Music Of Jelly Roll Morton Vol. 2**

Stomp Off CD1336 *As above.* 2/98.

This time, of course, they're dealing with a major jazz composer – and a notorious stickler for the correctness of the idiom at that. The 19 tunes on the first volume are (deliberately?) from the obscure end of Morton's repertoire, so, instead of the likes of 'Doctor Jazz', there are 'Try Me Out', 'Mushmouth Shuffle', 'Gambling Jack' and so on. Virtually all the pieces are extensions of Morton's originals, so they tend to last longer, and the various arrangers have fastened on rococo touches to Morton's music. It's played with great spirit, and there are fine players in the band: Alden and Giordano in particular make the rhythm section sound right and good. Novick and Otto, though, seem set on a style which tends to ape the old-time reed-players rather than pay homage to them, and while there is by necessity an element of vaudeville in this kind of jazz, it's an awkward thing to re-create.

The second instalment is done just as punctiliously and again draws from the less familiar aspects of Morton's book, although it seems to us that they've moved a little closer to the frameworks of the prototype recordings. To that extent, this disc feels a shade livelier than the other one, though there's little to choose. If you want to hear Morton's group music in contemporary sound, there's surely no more able re-creation than this.

***** The Music Of Louis Armstrong – Hot Five & Seven, Vol. 1**

Stomp Off 1350 *Bent Persson (t); Jim Snyder (tb); Matthias Seuffert (cl); Tom Roberts (p); John Gill (bj); Vince Giordano (tba); Pam Pameijer (d).* 5/99.

***** The Music Of Louis Armstrong - Hot Five & Seven, Vol. 2**

Stomp Off CD 1363 *As above except add David Sager (tb), Keith Nichols (p, v), omit Roberts.* 4/00.

This band never takes the easy option! After Parham, Jones and Morton, here come their translations of the Hot Five and Seven. Each treatment is stretched just sufficiently to allow an extra solo or chorus or elaboration which the Okehs didn't allow, and some of them are beautifully done – especially on titles such as 'I'm Gonna Gitcha' or 'You're Next', which are seldom remembered to start with. But Persson, for all his loyalty to the early Armstrong cornet sound, is really on a hiding to nothing: how can he compete with that original glorious explosion? To his credit, he doesn't try to; but the point of the originals is the grand exuberance of their leader: as group performances, many are relatively unremarkable. Still, this should interest any scholars, and modern ears will enjoy the excellent sound which the group has conferred on it. For the second volume, Keith Nichols, who knows more about this era than most, arrives on piano and David Sager shares trombone duties with Snyder. Comparison with an immortal such as 'Potato Head Blues' makes the same point: it's a perfectly enjoyable revision, and little more.

*****(*) Remember Johnny Dodds Vol. 1**

Stomp Off CD 1382 *Jon-Erik Kellso (c); Jim Snyder (tb); Matthias Seuffert (cl); David Boeddinghaus (p); Martin Wheatley (bj, g); Tom Saunders (b, tba); Pam Pameijer (d, wbd).* 5/02.

The rich and full-blooded studio sound reminds one again that one of the principal pleasures in this series of recordings is to hear period performance in state-of-the-art sound, which men like Dodds were never privy to in their lifetimes. Since material such as 'Frog Tongue Stomp' and 'Forty And Tight' is scarcely as familiar as the Armstrong music, there's a fresher feel to the script, and they really are playing with top commitment, with Seuffert right in the pocket and Persson switching from Armstrong to Natty Dominique.

David 'Fathead' Newman (born 1933)

TENOR, ALTO AND SOPRANO SAXOPHONES, FLUTE

Born in Dallas, Newman was recording with rhythm and blues bands in the early '50s and spent many years as the principal saxophonist in the Ray Charles group. A 40-year career as a leader on record has brought about a relatively sparing number of albums; not very many are in print.

***** Fathead**
Atlantic 8122-73708-2 *Newman; Marcus Belgrave (t); Bennie Crawford (bs); Ray Charles (p); Edgar Willis (b); Milton Turner (d).* 11/58.

***** Bigger And Better / The Many Facets Of David Newman**
Rhino/Atlantic R2 71453 *Newman; orchestra.* 3/68–2/69.

*****(*) House Of David**
Rhino/Atlantic R2 71452 2CD *Newman; various groups.* 52–89.

**** Back To Basics**
Milestone 9188 *Newman; Wilbur Bascomb, Jimmy Owens, Milt Ward (t); Earl McIntyre (tb); Babe Clark (ts); Clarence Thomas (bs); Kenneth Harris (f); Pat Rebillot, George Cables, Hilton Ruiz (ky); George Davis, Lee Ritenour, Jay Graydon (g); Abraham Laboriel (b); Idris Muhammad (d); Bill Summers (perc); strings.* 5–11/77.

In spite of his unfortunate nickname (which doesn't seem to bother him), Newman is an ornery, driving saxophonist whose R&B background – including 12 years with Ray Charles – has left him with a consummate knowledge in the use of riffs and licks in a soul-to-jazz context. He always swings and his unmistakable Texan sound is highly authoritative but, like so many musicians of a similar background, he's had trouble finding a fruitful context. His early Atlantic albums have been filleted to produce the excellent *House Of David* compilation, which starts with a date by Texas bluesman Zuzu Bollinand and goes through to the late '80s with Aretha Franklin, Dr John and others, taking in the years with Charles and the crossover albums of the '60s along the way. Newman plays it all with consummate heart, and there is a share of real classics: the irresistible theme of his own piece of jazz immortality, 'Hard Times'; the straightahead bop of 'Holy Land'; the suavity and grit of 'The Clincher'. But the miscellany does tend to prove Newman's second-fiddle status: he's a fine sideman, seldom a leader.

Fathead, newly reissued, was his name-debut on Atlantic, under the imprimatur of a Ray Charles 'presents' logo. The music is pitched a little awkwardly between jazz, R&B and proto-soul sax. Lightweight, yet heavy on the soul, the music retains a cheerfully bluesy appeal. The other Rhino disc is a double-header featuring Newman fronting a couple of albums of nice tunes and smoochy ballads, usually with a good rhythm section at bottom but with the whole always papered over with strings and brass. Newman's playing salvages the music time and again, but a little can go a long way.

The Milestone album is a waste of his time: puling backings, strings and horns sweeten up already saccharine material, and Newman's surviving solos are the only reason to listen.

****(*) Blue Head**
Candid CCD 79041 *Newman; Clifford Jordan (ss, ts); Buddy Montgomery (p); Ted Dunbar (g); Todd Coolman (b); Marvin 'Smitty' Smith (d).* 9/89.

Not much of a showing for Newman here. *Blue Head* has some decent stuff, thanks to Jordan's energetic solos, Montgomery's dextrous piano, and the tremendously shifting rhythms laid down by Coolman and Smith. But six very long jam tunes are probably at least one too many.

***** Chillin**
High Note HCD 7036 *Newman; Bryan Carrott (vib); John Hicks (p); Steve Novosel (b); Winard Harper (d); Cadino Newman (v).* 12/98.

*****(*) Keep The Spirits Singing**
High Note HCD 7057 *Newman; Steve Turre (tb); John Hicks (p); Steve Novosel (b); Winard Harper (d); Steve Kroon (perc).* 3/00.

The old warrior's taking things easy on *Chillin*, and, while not all the tempos are slow, none of them exactly canters out of the gate. Carrott takes rather more of the improvising honours, and son Cadino sings on two tracks, quite effectively too. A likeable reminder that Newman's still around.

It was a good idea to enlist the reliably forceful Turre for *Keep The Spirits Singing*, even if he's on only three of seven tracks. They get off on a terrific groove on the title-track, and things never look back from there. It's a textbook example of putting a veteran player in a setting which he can feel relaxed in without letting things settle down into too cosy a spot. Hicks (though he doesn't sound like he's on the best piano in the world) finds space for a few well-chosen words and Novosel and Harper get things swinging without trying to take over the show. Flute feature, tenor ballad, alto joust with 'Willow Weep For Me' – Fathead hasn't sounded this phat in years.

****(*) Song For The New Man**
High Note HCD 7120 *Newman; Curtis Fuller (tb); John Hicks (p); John Menegon (b); Jimmy Cobb (d).* 10/03.

Honourably done, but time is finally catching up with Newman and some of his cohorts here. There are fallibilities among the good moments which suggest that, for all the venerable wisdom on show, the players are no longer up to the demands of what is, after all, a taxing language.

Joe Newman (1922–92)

TRUMPET

A deep-thinking musician with a reflective sound in an age when lead trumpeters were supposed to sky-write in every solo, Newman was – mutatis mutandis – the Johnny Hodges of the Basie band. He also had stints with Illinois Jacquet and with Benny Goodman and continued to record under his own name until quite late in life. Newman was also a passionate jazz educator.

****** The Count's Men**
Fresh Sound FSR CD 135 *Newman; Benny Powell (tb); Frank Foster (ts); Frank Wess (f, ts); Sir Charles Thompson (p); Eddie Jones (b); Shadow Wilson (d).* 9/55.

****(*) I'm Still Swinging**

RCA 7432 160985 2 *Newman; Urbie Green (tb); Gene Quill (as); Al Cohn (ts); Dick Katz (p); Freddie Green (g); Eddie Jones (b); Shadow Wilson (d).* 10/55.

***** Byers' Guide**

Fresh Sound FSCD 2004 *Newman; Billy Byers (tb); Gene Quill (as, cl); Lou Stein (p); Milt Hinton (b); Osie Johnson (d).* 56.

Newman was never a whole-hearted modernist. His sharp attack and bright sound were derived almost entirely from Louis Armstrong and, though he was chief among the cadre of the 'Basie Moderns' in the '50s, he maintained allegiance to the Count's music over any other. That's perfectly obvious from the scaled-down arrangements on *I'm Still Swinging*, which sounds very much like what it is, a mid-size ensemble working at the sharp end of the Basie idiom. Though not, significantly enough, with Basie material. A broad-ranging and imaginative set includes Ellington and Cole Porter material, Irving Berlin's delightful 'Top Hat, White Tie And Tails' (one of three fine arrangements by Manny Albam) and Joe's own 'Slats!' and 'Daughter Of Miss Thing'. As always at this vintage, the solos are well developed, favouring the middle register, and rhythmically steady, though the trumpeter's ability to drift at will across the bar lines suggests a player of a later generation.

As a useful compare-and-contrast exercise, try 'A. M. Romp' on *The Count's Men* with the same tune on *Good'n'Groovy*, below. The later version is slightly wilder, but it's the tighter version with Sir Charles Thompson that really impresses, and newcomers to Newman's entertaining sound would do well to begin with the mid-'50s stuff.

The other Fresh Sound is co-led with Byers, who is an underrated figure and well worth sampling. Joe's Satchmo-influenced trumpet is still the dominant voice and it's a cracking set if you enjoy this brand of mild 'modernism'.

*****(*) Jive At Five**

Original Jazz Classics OJC 419 *Newman; Frank Wess (ts); Tommy Flanagan (p); Eddie Jones (b); Oliver Jackson (d).* 5/60.

***** Good'n'Groovy**

Original Jazz Classics OJC 185 *Newman; Frank Foster (ts); Tommy Flanagan (p); Eddie Jones (b); Bill English (d).* 3/61.

Good'n'Groovy was recorded at about the time of Newman's departure from the Basie band, though it's pretty clear that Joe retains a considerable loyalty to a sound and conception that he himself did so much to shape. *Jive At Five* has very much the same feel, but it's a more relaxed and poised performance. Newman always sounds good round Frank Foster, and the album bounces along with enough vigour to cut through a rather flat mix.

***** The Hot Trumpets Of Joe Newman And Henry Red Allen**

Prestige 24232 *Newman; Henry Red Allen (t); Tommy Flanagan, Lannie Scott (p); Wendell Marshall, Franklin Skeete (b); Billy English, Jerry Potter (d).* 61, 62.

Two different groups here, so a useful introduction for anyone who wants something of both the front men. Joe's in good form and Flanagan is an able and occasionally surprising accompanist.

***** I Love My Woman**

Black & Blue 970.2 *Newman; Hank Jones (p); George Duvivier (b); Alan Dawson (d).* 7/79.

Like a lot of Americans at the time, Newman found a place with the French Black & Blue imprint and in 1979 recorded a brisk, swinging jam set with what was effectively the house band. His plain-spoken trumpet is heard at its best on 'Softly, As In A Morning Sunrise', 'Prelude To A Kiss' and 'Summertime'. Jones for the most part keeps out of the way, but his solos are welcome when they come and he's in great form on the Gershwin tune. Duvivier could probably do these dates in his sleep and Dawson doesn't get over-exercised, though he's often a more interesting drummer than the other B&B regular J. C. Heard.

New Orchestra Workshop

GROUP

Canadian 'workshop' group, active in the early '90s, working in a free-form idiom and featuring some of the major players of the Canadian improvisation scene.

*****(*) The Future Is N.O.W.**

Nine Winds NWCD 0131 *Daniel Lapp, Bill Clark (t); Graham Ord, Coat Cooke, Bruce Freedman, Roy Stiffe (reeds); Paul Plimley (p); Clyde Reed, Paul Blaney, Ken Lister (b); Claude Ranger, Gregg Simpson, Roger Baird, Stan Taylor (d).* 90.

***** NOW You Hear It**

Nine Winds NWCD 0151 *Bruce Freedman (as); Graham Ord (ts, ss); Coat Cooke (ts); Joseph Danza (shakuhachi); Paul Plimley (p); Ron Samworth (g); Lisle Ellis, Clyde Reed, Paul Blaney (b); Gregg Simpson, Roger Baird, Buff Allen (d); Jack Duncan (perc); Kate Hammett-Vaughan (v).* 5–11/91.

Vancouver's New Orchestra Workshop is a co-operative venture inspired by Chicago's AACM. *The Future Is N.O.W.* offers the chance to sample the work of five different bands which have grown out of NOW. The outstanding piece is the opening track by Plimley's Octet, a swirling, compelling montage of rhythmic and melodic figures that is gripping throughout its nine-minute length; but there isn't a bad track among the six here. The harmolodically inspired quartet, Lunar Adventures, contribute two tracks; Chief Feature is a quartet that brews up a long, blustering workout reminiscent of early Archie Shepp; and Unity purvey a vivacious free improvisation, with excellent work by Lapp, Blaney, Ord and Baird. Only the muddled piece by Turnaround is in any way disappointing.

Their second report on *NOW You Hear It* is mildly disappointing: plenty of interest, but nothing that really stands out. The Plimley–Reed duo contribute three interactive duets, and MuseArt, a trio with Plimley, Ellis and Baird, offers a long abstraction of the blues. Lunar Adventures make brainy jazz-rock, Garbo's Hat are a chamberish trio featuring the singing of Kate Hammett-Vaughan; and the closing 'jam' by a group featuring Ord, Blaney and Baird, with Danza's shakuhachi hanging around the perimeter, isn't bad.

*****(*) WOWOW**

Spool SPL107 *John Korsrud, Bill Clark (t, flhn); Ralph Eppel, Rod Murray, George Lewis (tb); Vinny Golia (cl, f, saxes); Graham Ord (ss, as, ts, f, picc); Coat Cooke (as, ts, bs, f);*

Mark Nodwell (ss); Saul Berson (as); Paul Cram (bs, cl); Paul Plimley (p); Ron Samworth (g); Peggy Lee (clo); Paul Blaney, Clyde Reed (b); Dylan van der Schyff (d); Kate Hammett-Vaughan (v). 11/97.

Three long concert pieces from a celebration of NOW's 20th anniversary. Coat Cooke's title-piece is an arresting dedication to Ellington, with plenty of echoes of the master intermingled with a broad range of borrowings from 20th-century composition and sundry free passages. The orchestra play it with splendid commitment, and if it feels like fin de siècle pastiche to some extent, it's beautifully done. Samworth's 'The Yellow Sound', inspired by a text from Kandinsky, is on a similar scale, but darker, with more jarring switches of direction. Cram, one of three guest stars (the others are Golia and Lewis), offers 'The Tyranny Of Interest', which sounds like a Frank Zappa structure some of the way – charging brass and woodwind figures over rockish beats – and ends the disc in cacophonous exultation. A good show.

New Orleans Rhythm Kings

GROUP

Paul Mares put the band together to play in Chicago, and they were hugely popular at the Friars Inn, refusing all offers to play elsewhere. Split up in 1925 but there was a brief re-formation in the '30s. A big influence on the early Chicago white school.

****** The New Orleans Rhythm Kings And Jelly Roll Morton**

Milestone 47020-2 *Paul Mares (c); George Brunies, Santo Pecora (tb); Leon Roppolo (cl); Don Murray (cl, as); Charlie Cordella (cl, ts); Jack Pettis (Cmel, ts); Elmer Schoebel, Mel Stitzel, Jelly Roll Morton, Kyle Pierce, Red Long (p); Lou Black, Bob Gillett, Bill Eastwood (bj); Arnold Loyacano, Chink Martin (b); Frank Snyder, Ben Pollack, Leo Adde (d).* 8/22–3/25.

♛ ** New Orleans Rhythm Kings 1922–1925 The Complete Set**

Retrieval RTR 79031 2CD *As above except add Omer Simeon (cl), Boyce Brown (as), Jess Stacy (p), Marvin Saxbe (g), Pat Pattison (b); George Wettling (d).* 2/22–1/35.

One of the major groups of jazz records, from the first stirrings of the music in recording studios, the New Orleans Rhythm Kings' sessions still sound astonishingly lively and vital some 80 years later. The band recorded in Chicago but had come from New Orleans: Mares was already a disciple of King Oliver (who hadn't yet recorded at the time of the first session here), Roppolo played fluent, blue clarinet, and even Brunies made more of the trombone – at that time an irresponsibly comical instrument in jazz terms – than most players of the day. The rhythms tend towards the chunky, exacerbated by the acoustic recording, but the band's almost visionary drive is brought home to stunning effect on the likes of 'Bugle Call Blues' (from their very first session, in August 1922), the relentlessly swinging 'Tiger Rag' and the knockabout 'That's A Plenty'. On two later sessions they took the opportunity to have Jelly Roll Morton sit in, and his partnership with Roppolo on 'Clarinet Marmalade' and 'Mr Jelly Lord' – something of a sketch for Morton's own later version – invigorates the whole band. 'London Blues' and 'Milenberg Joys' find Morton more or less taking over the band in terms of conception. The final session they made, early in 1925, is slightly less impressive because of Brunies's absence, and there are moments of weakness elsewhere in the original records: the use of saxes sometimes swamps the initiative, Mares isn't always sure of himself, and the beats are occasionally unhelpfully overdriven. But this is still extraordinarily far-sighted and powerful music for its time, with a band of young white players building on black precepts the way that, say, Nick LaRocca of the ODJB refused to acknowledge.

It is a pleasure to welcome the superb Retrieval edition, which collects all of the original masters, twelve alternative takes, and the reunion session of 1935, where Mares convened a gang of contemporary Chicagoans to play alongside himself and Pecora, the results of which are surprisingly strong. In excellent sound from top-quality originals, this is the NORK as they should be heard, and a powerful case for placing them alongside King Oliver's early sessions in terms of stature.

Sam Newsome (born 1965)

TENOR AND SOPRANO SAXOPHONES

Began on alto, moved to tenor and finally, in the mid-'90s, chose to concentrate on soprano sax. Studied at Berklee and moved to New York in 1988. Settled on music after trying out as a stand-up comic!

*****(*) Sam I Am**

Criss Cross Jazz 1056 *Newsome; Marcus Miller (p); Steve Nelson (vib); James Genus (b); Billy Drummond (d).* 11/90.

***** The Tender Side Of Sammy Straighthorn**

Steeplechase SCCD 31452 *Newsome; Bruce Barth (p); Ugonna Okegwo (b); Matt Wilson (d); Elisabeth Kontomanou (v).* 4/98.

Newsome emerged as a tenorman of unpretentious authority with the Criss Cross album. He courts trouble by framing tributes to both Coltrane and Rollins here, but 'In The Vein Of Trane', basically a simple F minor vamp, manages to reflect on Coltrane without slavishly copying him, and 'Pent-up House' settles for the brazen confidence rather than the delivery of the young Sonny. Actually, Newsome takes his time in his improvising, building solos methodically, savouring his best phrases and going for tonal extremes only when he sees their logical point. A rich, dark tenor tone and a penchant for fitting in with the band rather than dominating them give this record much bonhomie as well as a lot of rigorous playing. Nelson is in his most attacking form, throwing off some dazzling solos in single lines rather than multiple-mallet chords, and the rhythm section is as impressive as always on Criss Cross dates.

By the time of the Steeplechase date, Newsome had decided to switch exclusively to soprano. He's recorded in a somewhat distant way on the session, and the music never quite takes a grip. The reaction of most will depend on how they respond to Kontomanou's singing, wordless but not resorting to scat, instead singing open-throated counterpoint to the leader's soprano lines. It's a curious combination, although she appears on only three of the seven tracks. A long fantasy on 'All The Things You Are' is intermittently impressive, and the Japanese 'Lullaby Of Takeda' is attractive.

****(*) Global Unity**

PalmettoPM-2074 *Newsome; Jean Michel Pilc (p); Jeff Berman (vib); Matt Balitsaris (g, mand); Marvin Sewell (g);*

Meg Okura (vn); Ugonna Okegwo, Mel Baker (b); Adam Cruz, Gilad, Satoshi Takeishi (perc); Elisabeth Kontomanou (v). 1–3/01.

Newsome had a brief dalliance with Columbia and released a similar set there to this one. Global unity may be the concept, but it needs more than this mild-mannered blending of pan-cultural tropes and affectations. Newsome hits on some nice melodic hooks and textures but nothing here digs below any kind of surface. Kontomanou's wordless vocalizing (much in the manner of Pat Metheny's singers) is a primary ingredient and, while it all passes very pleasantly, it needs the titanic self-assurance of a Zawinul to make the concept stand up by itself.

***** This Masquerade**

Steeplechase SCCD 31503 *Newsome; Bruce Barth (p); Ugonna Okegwo (b); Gene Jackson (d).* n.d.

Could be that this is a leftover from the previous Steeplechase session, since otherwise it looks like a retrenchment after the Palmetto album. The material is mostly straight from the jazz repertory – 'Pent-Up House', 'Footprints', 'Blue Monk' – with only a Japanese piece, 'Toryanse', hinting at the previous direction. There are unusual courses taken through some of the material, but so far Newsome hasn't really asserted an individualism on the soprano and it feels like good but unremarkable work.

Tommy Newsome (born 1929)

TENOR SAXOPHONE

Arranger and big-band sideman of long standing, Newsom spent many years in the Tonight Show band, and these albums are a belated coming-out for him.

***** The Feeling Of Jazz**

Arbors ARCD 19195 *Newsom; Ken Peplowski (ts); Ben Aronov (p); Mike Peters (g); Greg Cohen (b); Chuck Redd (d).* 11/97.

**** Friendly Fire**

Arbors ARCD 19251 *Newsom; Bob Enevoldsen (vtb); John F. Hammond (p); Bob Bain (g); Jim Hughart (b); Dave Hunt (d).* 10/00.

Newsom's style is all affable, amiable rambling. It works well enough on *The Feeling Of Jazz* because Peplowski is on hand to provide some real energy and the two tenors growl their way through an interesting programme, somewhat in the manner of a decent Zoot 'n' Al date. But *Friendly Fire* is very slack. Enevoldsen sounds past his best – what a pity this fine musician was never much use in the limelight – and while the music isn't exactly bad, it's awfully tame.

David Newton (born 1958)

PIANO

Born in Glasgow, Newton worked on the Edinburgh scene before a move to London helped establish him as one of the leading younger British pianists, much in demand as accompanist and sideman.

***** Eyewitness**

Linn AKD 015 *Newton; Dave Green (p); Allan Ganley (d).* 2/90.

****(*) Victim Of Circumstance**

Linn AKD 013 *As above, except add Alec Dankworth (b); Clark Tracey (d).* 1 & 5/90.

Like the young Americans of the same generation – from Geri Allen to Cyrus Chestnut – Newton served his apprenticeship as accompanist and musical director to a singer, in David's case stablemate Carol Kidd. His technique is briskly correct, sometimes a little too formal and orderly, though the rhythm section is so full-on that he's never allowed to sound stuffy. Newton worked with Dankworth and Ganley on a Buddy DeFranco record, and one can't quite escape the sensation that *Victim Of Circumstance* is a superior play-along disc, with a horn line constantly implicit. It certainly needs something. Hard to put air between them, but *Eyewitness* is perhaps more straightforwardly swinging. Green and Ganley appear only once on the second disc, and their absence is duly noted. *Victim* is one false climax after another, and only the unaccompanied 'It Never Entered My Mind' really stirs the blood.

*****(*) Return Journey**

Linn AKD 025 *Newton (p solo).* 2/92.

More like it. Newton will still be too self-dramatizing for some tastes, and the suite of pieces that makes up 'Return Journey' itself doesn't quite work. Even so, it's brave at this stage in a career to devote an entire solo disc to originals, and to work of such thoughtfulness. The technique is no less proper than before and, without the rough-hewn presence of Green and Ganley, something like the long 'While You're Away' does indeed become a protracted sojourn. Great sound; producer Elliot Meadow has great ears.

*****(*) In Good Company**

Candid CCD 79714 *Newton; Dave Green (b); Allan Ganley (d).* 9/94.

It was thought when Newton switched to Candid that he might go for broke and record with an American trio. No problems whatsoever with the line-up on this, as we've said before, but it does seem time to kick over the traces and take some chances on a wider stage. With almost any transatlantic pairing – and it would be invidious to throw names about – this would be a more compelling record. As played, it's chunky, cable-knit jazz which trades funk and attitude for a smooth sophistication that shortens its shelf-life considerably.

****** Twelfth Of The Twelfth: A Jazz Portrait Of Frank Sinatra**

Candid CCD 79728 *Newton (p solo).* 8/95.

The key track here is 'All The Way', just over half-way through the set. Newton reworks the tune and invests it with a sardonic quality that was never detectable in the original but which makes perfect sense, whether one takes the original as a jumping-off point or a sacred text. The pianist's long meditation on the Sinatra voice and legend, the title-track, is the most substantial single track. Everything else is at song length and absolutely faithful to the great man's own conception. It's easy to pick holes in this. Sinatra's own light legato and almost conversational phrasing are extraordinarily difficult to duplicate instrumentally, but it's hard to imagine them done better. Some will wish the choice of tracks were different – 'This Love Of Mine' in for 'It's Nice To Go Trav'lling', 'Fly Me To The

Moon' instead of 'This Is All I Ask' – except that one suspects Newton might well return to the territory, now that Sinatra is no longer around.

*****(*) D N A**

Candid CCD 79742 *Newton; Iain Dixon (ts); Matt Miles (b); Steve Brown (d).* 11/96.

The first time on record that Newton has worked with a horn-led quartet – and, by and large, a success. Dixon is a seasoned player, a little anonymous in tone and a little obvious in his range of ideas, but capable of giving even a relatively uncomplicated theme a mature lift and presence. His own 'The Scribe' was apparently worked out during the sessions.

Newton chips in with three originals, 'DNA', 'Julia' and 'Feet On The Ground', but the real substance of the record comes in Chick Corea's 'Highwire', an exuberant performance, and a long version of Tristano's and Konitz's 'Ablution'. The sound is impeccable, faithful to the physical reality and convincingly detailed.

***** Meets Brian Lemon To Play Hoagy**

Zephyr 20 *Newton; Brian Lemon (p).* 96.

The difficulty of this set was always going to be balancing the familiar and obvious ('Skylark', 'Stardust') with some more challenging themes. They pull it off magnificently with 'Two Sleepy People', which was made a hit by Shirley Ross and Bob Hope. It's the best thing on a set that could have done with more variation of approach, with perhaps some solo pieces, a couple with rhythm and even some a guest vocal or a ghostly sample of Carmichael to show how it was done. It's an engaging enough album, and as much of a coup for the veteran Lemon as for Newton, but it lacks surprises and changes of pace. 'Rockin' Chair' is fun, though.

***** Pacific Heights**

Bright New Day 001 *Newton; Dave Chamberlain (b); Colin Oxley (d).* 03.

*****(*) Bootleg Eric**

ASC ASCCD23 *Newton; Guy Barker (t); Mark Nightingale (tb); Iain Dixon (ts); Allan Curtis Barnes (as); Andrew Cleyndert (b); Clark Tracey (d).* 02.

Credited to Newton and Tracey, *Bootleg Eric* seems to fall somewhere between the two of them, an uneasy use of some fine players and fine charts. 'Faith In Alec' and the title-piece are the best tracks. Newton and Barker get off some good solos, though the trumpeter is oddly reined in and plays with an unusually clenched tone. The trio album launches a new jazz imprint, which is always good to see, except that what David Newton now needs more than anything is the patronage and reasoned support of a label able to invest in his talent and allow him the time and space to develop in challenging company.

Frankie Newton (1906–54)

TRUMPET

Played in several New York bands in the early-to-middle '30s, including Charlie Barnet's and John Kirby's, and led some record dates of his own, but he never made much of his career and recorded only rarely after 1940. After 1950 he more or less retired from music altogether.

*****(*) Frankie Newton 1937–1939**

Classics 643 *Newton; Cecil Scott (cl, ts); Edmond Hall (cl, bs); Mezz Mezzrow (cl); Pete Brown, Russell Procope, Tab Smith, Stanley Payne, Gene Johnson (as); Kenneth Hollon (ts); Don Frye, James P. Johnson, Kenny Kersey, Albert Ammons, Meade Lux Lewis (p); Frank Rice, Al Casey, Ulysses Livingston, Teddy Bunn (g); Richard Fulbright, John Kirby, Johnny Williams (b); Cozy Cole, O'Neil Spencer, Eddie Dougherty, Big Sid Catlett (d); Clarence Palmer, Slim Gaillard, Leon LaFell (v).* 3/37–8/39.

Newton was an intriguing, unguessable player whose small number of recordings represents the rare strain of swing-era small groups at their most interesting. In some ways he was an old-fashioned hot player, using a terminal vibrato borrowed directly from Armstrong and turning in oblique, poetic solos on otherwise slight material. He worked extensively at New York's Onyx Club in the late '30s, when these tracks were made. 'Who's Sorry Now' features a Newton solo which summarizes his style: the quirky lyricism and sudden bursts of heat make him exhilaratingly hard to predict. But it's his four choruses on 'The Blues My Baby Gave To Me' which are close to perfection, beautifully controlled and achingly lyrical reflections on the blues. There are other good solos from Brown and Hall scattered through these sides; Johnson is in fine form on the 1939 Bluebird session, and there are one or two strikingly unusual tunes, including 'Vamp' and the odd 'Parallel Fifths' from the final (1939) date. Classics take their material from unlisted sources and the sound is unfortunately very variable.

James Newton (born 1953)

FLUTE

Raised in California, Newton studied with Buddy Collette and dabbled in both funk and the avant-garde before devoting himself exclusively to flute. He characteristically projects a strong, very exact classical line, but he modifies it with various extended techniques, including multiphonics, flutter tonguing and toneless blowing.

****** Axum**

ECM 835019-2 *Newton (f solo).* 81.

***** Echo Canyon**

Celestial Harmonies 13102 *Newton (f solo).* 9/84.

One of the first contemporary players to foster a direct Eric Dolphy influence, Newton started out as a multi-instrumentalist but gave up alto saxophone and bass clarinet towards the end of the '70s. As a virtuoso flautist, he has worked in both formal and improvised contexts and has developed a wholly original means of vocalizing while he plays. This is by no means new (Roland Kirk was exceptionally proficient at it), but Newton has taken the technique far beyond unisons and harmonies to a point where he can sing contrapuntally against his own flute line. The results are frequently dazzling, as on the African-influenced *Axum*. Newton's vocalizations allow his pieces to develop with unprecedented depth, and his tone is quite remarkable. *Echo Canyon* sounds more classically inspired and there are a few places where Newton appears ready to drop into a concert hall manner and deliver subtle but unfunky tone poems. More often than not, though, he reverses and manages to create something deceptively raw and blues-soaked out of the most formal of materials.

New York All Stars

GROUP

Led by Randy Sandke, this varying group of mainstreamers is heard in mostly live albums of material associated with several jazz giants.

***** The Bix Beiderbecke Era**

Nagel-Heyer CD 002 *Randy Sandke (t, c); Dan Barrett (tb, t); Ken Peplowski (cl); Scott Robinson (Cmel, bsx, c); Mark Shane (p); Marty Grosz (g, v); Linc Milliman (b, tba); Dave Ratajczak (d).* 5/93.

***** Broadway**

Nagel-Heyer CD 003 *As above, except omit Peplowski.* 5/93.

***** We Love You, Louis!**

Nagel Heyer CD 029 *Randy Sandke (t); Byron Stripling (t, v); Joel Helleny (tb); Kenny Davern (cl); Mark Shane (p); David Ostwald (tba); Greg Cohen (b); Joe Ascione (d).* 11/95.

***** Count Basie Remembered Vol. 1**

Nagel Heyer CD 031 *Randy Sandke (t); Dan Barrett (tb); Brian Ogilvie (ts, as, cl); Billy Mitchell (ts); Mark Shane (p); James Chirillo (g); Bob Haggart (b); Joe Ascione (d).* 11/96.

***** Count Basie Remembered Vol. 2**

Nagel Heyer CD 041 *As above.* 11/96.

***** Oh, Yeah!**

Nagel Heyer CD 046 *Randy Sandke (t); Byron Stripling (t, v); Joel Helleny (tb); Allan Vaché (cl); Johnny Varro (p); Bob Haggart (b); Joe Ascione (d).* 2/98.

***** Hey Ba-Ba-Re-Bop!!**

Nagel Heyer CD 9047 *Randy Sandke (t); Roy Williams (tb); Antti Sarpila (cl, as, ts); Thilo Wagner (p); Lars Erstrand (vib); James Chirillo (g); Dave Green (b); Ed Metz Jr (d).* 10/98.

We previously listed a couple of these discs under Sandke's name but, since they have swelled in number, the group rates an entry on its own. Though they start with Beiderbecke and Armstrong and go as far as Basie and Hampton, the band approaches each situation with the same groomed, knowledgeable style: seven or eight pieces playing chestnuts associated with the faces shown on the CD sleeves. Since (with the exception of *Broadway*) these are all concert souvenirs, they don't emerge as particularly convincing records. The Armstrong discs in particular seldom catch fire, since Sandke is so respectful of the material. The Basie discs have too many obvious choices of tune: Mitchell is a good guy to have around, but he takes his place in the gang and never cuts loose. *The Bix Beiderbecke Era* was done on the occasion of Bix's ninetieth birthday and, though the sound isn't ideal, here at least Sandke's team punch through the Beiderbecke repertoire with plenty of fizz. *Broadway* is a studio date, cut the next day: it was hot, the group were tired, and the material is an unpromising set of warhorses. That it still sounds good is some tribute to a jazzman's professionalism and, though there are a couple of duds, the band play with an unexpected attack. The best of the live sessions, though, is probably *Hey-Ba-Ba-Re-Bop!!*, Lionel Hampton tunes performed by a slightly more mixed and interesting band, with Erstrand and Williams shining in their solos. These are records that have been widely welcomed, particularly by some British commentators, but we can't hear much difference between this type of jazz and the often-reviled trad which is still playing to keen audiences in Europe.

The New York Hard Bop Quintet

GROUP

Founded in 1990 as a quartet, the NYHBQ recruited saxophonist Eddie Weldon and replaced founding drummer Eddie Ornowski with Mickey Roker and later Clifford Barbaro. Unashamed revivalists, they play '50s Blue Note bop with a few modern flourishes.

***** The Clincher**

TCB 95202 *Joe Magnarelli (t); Jerry Weldon (ts); Keith Saunders (p); Bim Strasberg (b); Eddie Ornowski (d).* 94.

***** Rokermotion**

TCB 96352 *As above, except omit Ornowski; add Mickey Roker (d).* 96.

****(*) Whisper Away**

TCB 98702 *As above, except omit Roker; add Clifford Barbaro (d).* 99.

***** A Mere Bag of Shells**

TCB 20702 *As above.* 01.

Lee Morgan didn't die in vain! Or at least, not as long as the N.Y. Hardbop Quintet are around to carry the torch. To their credit, they've not been content to rehash old standards and bop warhorses but have built up their own repertoire of originals, leavened with just a couple of familiar cuts per album. The problem is that the musicianship is thoroughly derivative and unless one is particularly keen on apostolic re-creations of Morgan, early Trane and Horace Silver, there isn't much on offer here.

The earliest and most recent of the albums are probably the best of the bunch. *The Clincher* reflects a band already well played-in. Saunders is the dominant writer this time, with three carefully crafted tunes, of which the opening 'New Jazz World Order' is the best. Weldon shines on his own 'Leroy Street', sounding a little like Stanley Turrentine, and Magnarelli does his bit on 'Poor Little Birdie'.

The recruitment of Mickey Roker was a shrewd move. He brings a graceful authority to the second album and shows his moves to good effect on the waltz-time 'The Hip Naz' (written by Magnarelli) and an imaginatively reworked 'East Of The Sun, West Of The Moon'. Some of the originals this time are not much more than contrefacts on familiar tunes, but that never held back the first-generation boppers and the musical thinking is always intelligent.

Whisper Away is a disappointment; no less confident and accomplished than its predecessors, it lacks their drive and presence. The saving grace is a sense of humour – these guys know they're not the Messengers – which comes through again on *A Mere Bag Of Shells*, which was originally intended as a tribute to the Jackie Gleason television show *The Honeymooners*, a concept that perhaps mercifully survives only in the album title. New drummer Barbaro has his feet well under the table and swings righteously throughout. Bud Powell's 'Time Waits' is an interesting inclusion, again deftly reworked. It seems a bit sad that a band so American in philosophy should be dependent on a Swiss label, but hard bop is probably hipper in Zurich than in the Big Apple these days, and these guys keep time like watchmakers, with the occasional daft cuckoo just to remind us it's not meant to be high art.

New York Voices

GROUP

Founded in 1987 by Darmon Meader, who plays reeds as well as singing, the Voices were originally a college group who spotted a hole in the market.

***** New York Voices**
GRP 9589 *Darmon Meader (v, ts); Peter Eldridge (v, p); Caprice Fox, Sara Krieger, Kim Nazarian (v); with Bob Christianson (syn); Jon Werking (syn, ky); Tom Barney, Chuck Bergeron (b); Peter Grant, Tommy Igoe (d); Sammy Figueroa (perc).* 89.

***** Sing! Sing! Sing!**
Concord 4961 *NYV as above; omit Krieger; add Lauren Kinhan (v); with Barry Danielian, Greg Ruvolo (t, flhn); Marvin Stamm (flhn); Randy Andos, Jay Ashby, Larry Farrell (tb); Lawrence Feldman (ss, as, cl); Bobby Porcelli (as, f); Doug Lawrence (ts); Donny McCaslin (ts, f); Kenny Berger (bs); Roger Rosenberg (bs, bcl); Andy Ezrin (p); Bucky Pizzarelli (g); Paul Nowinski (b); Marcello Pelliteri, Ben Wittman (d).* 11/99.

The New York Voices seemed bizarrely out of place in the music world of the late '80s and '90s, but they managed to hook onto the tails of the Manhattan Transfer audience and turned in a series of decent, if unspectacular, albums. The first is unquestionably the best of the GRPs, all the rest of which are deleted, though it suffers from excessive production and from a jangling, synthesized quality where something sparer and more acoustic would have suited these voices better, even if it had left them somewhat more exposed. In fact, what one longs for is some straight singing, even if it is awkwardly pitched.

The most recent set is a surprise return to form. Having dabbled with other forms, notably a Paul Simon tribute, the group have returned to their core repertoire and should reclaim their core audience with bright arrangements of 'In A Mellow Tone', Nat Cole's 'Orange Coloured Sky' and the title-piece. The core group has survived one change of personnel without apparent difficulty and if anything the harmonies sound richer and more precise than in the earliest days. A well-drilled band produces a much happier noise than the synthed blandness of their earlier sets.

Albert Nicholas (1900–1971)

CLARINET

Bandleading in New Orleans in the early '20s, he then played with King Oliver before going to the Far East, then returning to work in the Luis Russell band. Spent the '30s in New York in various gigs, then re-emerged as a revivalist in the '40s. Moved to France in 1953 and became an honoured and much-travelled elder statesman.

*****(*) The New Orleans–Chicago Connection**
Delmark 207 *Nicholas; Art Hodes (p); Earl Murphy (b); Fred Kohlman (d).* 7/59.

***** Albert's Back In Town**
Delmark DE-209 *Nicholas; Nappy Trottier (c); Floyd O'Brien (tb); Art Hodes (p); Marty Grosz (g); Mike Walbridge (tba); Fred Kohlman (d).* 7/59.

***** Albert Nicholas With Alan Elsdon's Band Vol. One**
Jazzology JCD-259 *Nicholas; Alan Elsdon (t); Phil Rhodes (tb); Andy Cooper (cl, ts); Colin Bates (p); Johnny Barton (g, bj); Mick Gilligan (b); Billy Law (d).* 2/67.

***** Albert Nicholas With Alan Elsdon's Band Vol. Two**
Jazzology JCD-269 *As above.* 2/67.

*****(*) Baden 1969**
Sackville SKCD2-2045 *Nicholas; Henri Chaix (p); Alain Du Bois (b); Romano Cavicchiolo (d).* 9/69.

One of the least exposed of the New Orleans clarinet masters on record, Nicholas's surviving discs are mostly delightful. For a man who played with King Oliver and Jelly Roll Morton, he seemed quite at ease in the company of musicians generations younger than himself. Art Hodes at least was a contemporary, and their Delmark album is a spirited ramble through some of the old tunes, Hodes's Chicagoan blues meshing easily with Nick's pithy solos. He has an odd way of mixing a circumspect, behind-the-hand manner with a piercing attack: a diffident statement of the melody may suddenly blossom on a sudden high note with a fast vibrato, before the line drops back into the depths of his horn. 'He could always get you with that tone,' Barney Bigard remembered, and something of the young Bechet survives in Nicholas's most sprightly playing. The original Delmark album has been fleshed out with a stack of alternative takes, none of them especially meaningful, but the body of the music is fine. *Albert's Back In Town* was recorded around the same time with a larger group. More prosaic, less personal, but still plenty to enjoy, with Nicholas and Hodes again getting in some good moments for themselves.

Nicholas had fun with the Elsdon band, and these souvenirs of a gig in Manchester stand up respectably (although there seems to be hardly anyone in the audience to begin with). Not a very good piano, the trombonist is a bit of a lad, and even Elsdon himself has his shaky moments, but the New Orleans man hardly puts a foot wrong: listen to his lovely work on 'Blue Turning Grey Over You' on the second disc, which is perhaps marginally the better, though there's little in it. In Switzerland, with local man Chaix and his group, Albert played what was by this time a rather stock guest-star role, with most of his favourite pieces turning up in much the way he would always play them. But the music is very genuine. 'Rose Room' and 'Lover Come Back To Me' are swung off the stage and, though bass and drums aren't given a very pleasing sound, clarinet and piano come through strongly.

Wooden Joe Nicholas (1883–1957)

TRUMPET, CLARINET

Albert Nicholas's uncle played brass and clarinet, starting with the latter. Played with King Oliver in 1915 and modelled his style on Bolden, but missed out on recording in the golden age and left only a few documents of his sound during the revival of the '40s.

***** Wooden Joe Nicholas**
American Music AMCD-5 *Nicholas; Jim Robinson, Louis Nelson, Joe Petit (tb); Albert Burbank (cl); Johnny St Cyr (g);*

Lawrence Marrero (bj); Austin Young, Alcide 'Slow Drag' Pavageau (b); Josiah Frazier, Baby Dodds, Albert Jiles (d); Ann Cook (v). 5/45–7/49.

A legend calls down the years. Wooden Joe's main idol was Buddy Bolden, and hearing him play may offer us the best idea of what Bolden himself might have sounded like. Nicholas blew a very powerful open horn, and was famous for dominating a dance-hall sound. These were his only recordings, and they are clustered together from a session at the Artesian Hall and two later dates. A lot of New Orleans history is tied up here: the fearsome blues singer, Ann Cook, is on one track, the legendary trombonist, Joe Petit, on another. Nicholas and Burbank are the main voices on all the tracks (Wooden Joe also played clarinet, and does so on two numbers): compared with the clarinettist's weaving lines, Nicholas is reserved in his phrasing and takes only a few breaks and solos. But much of his power and stately delivery was intact. The music has been remastered from acetates and, though the fidelity isn't as good as in some of the American Music series, the history still comes alive.

Herbie Nichols (1919–63)

PIANO

Worked largely in swing, mainstream and R&B settings from the late '40s, mostly for other leaders; but his few own-name recordings show an original mind playing very different music. Since his death from leukaemia, enthusiasts such as Roswell Rudd have been determined to bring his music to wider attention.

****** The Complete Blue Note Recordings**

Blue Note 8 59355 2 3CD *Nichols; Teddy Kotick, Al McKibbon (b); Art Blakey, Max Roach (d).* 5/55–4/56.

'There is a kind of culpability in the discovery of dead artists', and in Herbie Nichols there is an almost perfect example of an artist who was (largely, and with one significant exception) ignored during his lifetime, only to be canonized as soon as he was gone. When Nichols died, he had been working professionally for a quarter of a century, ever since joining the Royal Baron Orchestra in 1937. Yet in all those 26 years, by A. B. Spellman's reckoning, there was not one during which he was able to earn a living making the music he loved. Nichols made his way 'playing grease', as he put it himself, in R&B bands like Horsecollar Williams's, backing singers (Sheila Jordan being the most creative) and even providing accompaniments for lesbian shows. Perhaps making the best of necessity, he claimed to prefer bar-room uprights, liking the percussive attack and the way the sound came back at him so quickly. One can certainly hear something of that in Nichols's compositions, which typically begin with a call-and-response between piano and percussion, before moving off into often quite unexpected harmonic and rhythmic territory. Nichols was rooted in the blues but regularly name-checked Bartók and Shostakovich among his influences, as well as Villa-Lobos, though the Latin inflexion in tunes like the delightful 'Terpsichore' probably came more directly from his West Indian ancestry; his parents had emigrated from Trinidad and St Kitts.

Nichols scuffled as a recording artist, doing R&B sides here and there, until Alfred Lion of Blue Note decided to sign him up. Two 10-inch LPs were issued from the May 1955 sessions, both called *The Prophetic Herbie Nichols*. How forward-looking he was as a composer may be judged by his use in 'The Third World', the opening item on *The Complete*, of a chord progression that would still sound radical when John Coltrane experimented with it more than a decade later (nearer two from the date of composition, since it seems to have been written as early as 1947). Typically, Lion gave him generous rehearsal time, and neither McKibbon nor Blakey sounds as though he is running down unfamiliar material. The playing is crisp and buoyant, and even alternative takes are worth hearing.

Nichols and McKibbon reconvened in August 1955 with Max Roach at the kit, and they recorded his best-known composition, 'Lady Sings The Blues', as well as the joyous 'The Gig'; but it is tunes like '23 Skiddoo' and 'Shuffle Montgomery' from the earlier sessions which have restored him to favour, largely through the advocacy of younger players like Geri Allen, a devoted Nichols fan. The three-CD *Complete* is his testament. No one interested in the development of bebop, or indeed of jazz piano, should be without it.

***** Love, Gloom, Cash, Love**

Rhino 76690 *Nichols; George Duvivier (b); Dannie Richmond (d).* 11/57.

The title sounds very much like Herman Melville's famous mantra, 'Oh, time, strength, cash and patience', which might equally well have applied to Herbie's career. These sessions for Bethlehem find him in quieter and less emphatic form than on the Blue Notes. Richmond and Duvivier seem relatively reined in as well. And yet 'S'crazy Blues', 'Infatuation Eyes' and the Bud Powell-influenced title-tune are among the best things Nichols did in his short career. He died just six years after this album was made, and fell into an obscurity which began to lift only in the '70s and '80s when a new generation recognized that here was another angle on bebop piano.

The Herbie Nichols Project

GROUP

A vivid, inventive tribute band, first convened in 1992, which goes way beyond the vague, wannabe gestures of less thoughtful projects.

***** Love Is Proximity**

Soul Note 121313 *Ron Horton (t, flhn); Ted Nash (ts, bcl, af); Michael Blake (ss, ts); Frank Kimbrough (p); Ben Allison (b); Jeff Ballard (d).* 5/95, 5/96.

*****(*) Dr Cyclops' Dream**

Soul Note 121333 *As above; omit Ballard; add Tim Horner (d).* 2/99.

*****(*) Strange City**

Palmetto PM 2077 *As above, except add Wycliffe Gordon (tb), Matt Wilson (d); omit Horner.* 5/01.

Gone are the days when it was possible to describe Herbie Nichols and Sonny Clark as 'neglected' relative to the giants of bebop piano, Thelonious Monk and Bud Powell. Pianist Kimbrough and his colleagues have gone as far into the Nichols *œuvre* as anyone, on the second album recording five tunes straight from manuscript, pieces that have not been put on record before. The debut disc is already arresting, with 'Love, Gloom, Cash, Love' particularly effective, and two versions of 'Wildflower', one for band at over ten minutes, one for solo piano at three and a half.

Some of the tracks on the second record are shorter still, almost vestigial: 'Cro-Mag At T's' weighs in at less than a minute, while 'Dreamtime' and 'I've Got Those Classic Blues' last only about two. Yet the remainder are pretty substantial further evidence for Nichols's overlooked genius. 'Riff Primitif', 'The Bebop Waltz' and the title-tune bear comparison with Monk's work. The use of blues and non-blues intervals is utterly distinctive and these players know exactly what they're dealing with.

Strange City builds on this start, though given the finite resources of the Nichols book it may not have too much further to go. As it is, of these pieces only one ('Shuffle Montgomery') was actually recorded by Nichols himself. Given that most of this is unfamiliar, the playing has a lot of confident sparkle, with Horton especially impressive. As a repertory project, its arcane starting-point is a plus: no need to pull and squeeze these materials out of shape in search of newness.

Keith Nichols (born 1945)

PIANO, VOCALS

Born in Ilford, Essex, Nichols has a versatile background in acting and entertaining, but is primarily a practising scholar of ragtime and early jazz repertory. Previous groups included, from the '70s on, the Ragtime Orchestra, Midnite Follies Orchestra and Paramount Theatre Orchestra. He records mainly on piano but also plays trombone, accordion and reeds.

*** I Like To Do Things For You

Stomp Off CD1242 *Nichols; Guy Barker (c); Gordon Blundy (tb); Mac White (cl, bcl, ss, as); Randy Colville (cl, as, ts); Mike Piggott (vn); Mike French (p); Martin Wheatley (g, bj); Graham Read (bsx, tba, sou, b); Barry Tyler (d); Janice Day, Johnny M, The Happidrome Trio (v).* 6–7/91.

*** Syncopated Jamboree

Stomp Off CD 1234 *Nichols; Bent Persson, Mike Henry (t); Alistair Allan (tb); Claus Jacobi, Mac White, Mark Allway, Randy Colville, Robert Fowler (reeds); Mike Piggott (vn); Martin Wheatley (g, bj); Graham Read (sou); Richard Pite (d); Janice Day, Johnny M, Tony Jacobs (v).* 9/91.

**** Henderson Stomp

Stomp Off CD 1275 *Nichols; René Hagmann (c, tb); Bent Persson, Guy Barker, Mike Henry, Rolf Koschorrok (t); Alistair Allan (tb); Claus Jacobi (ss, as, bsx, cl); Nicholas Payton (as, cl); Michel Bard (ts, cl); Martin Wheatley (bj); Graham Read (sou); Richard Pite (d).* 11/93.

Nichols is a British specialist in American repertory: ragtime, hot dance music, New York jazz of the '20s, Blake, Morton, Berlin, whatever. His piano-playing and Hoagy Carmichael-like singing are less important than the mastery of old form that he successfully displays on these records. *I Like To Do Things For You* is more of a chamber-jazz session: the instrumentation varies, but the largest group has eight players, while 'I'm Nobody's Baby' cuts the cast to three. Familiarity with any Nichols/Mole session or even the Bix and Trumbauer dates will give the idea. Janice Day's rather plummy contralto is much featured and may be an acquired taste. There are plenty of tunes among the 20 tracks that have probably been unrecorded since the '20s, and the irony of having a brilliant modernist like Barker on hand goes almost unnoticed (he is at least as good as Wynton Marsalis at this kind of thing). Recorded in a dry acoustic, but it has a very appropriate sound.

Syncopated Jamboree is by a bigger band and is more of a piece: Read, who moves between various bass instruments on the other record, plays strict brass bass here, and the section-work would surely have been good enough for Roger Wolfe Kahn. Another stack of obscurities, expertly reworked in a little over an hour of music. Sometimes it all seems like a pointless exercise – Nichols isn't trying to bring anything new to this music, he just loves to play it – but sympathetic ears will be rewarded.

Henderson Stomp, though, is surely his finest hour to this point and one of the most convincing pieces of authentic-performance jazz ever set down. Twenty-two of Fletcher Henderson's most effective pieces – from several hands, though many of Don Redman's somewhat familiar charts are bypassed in favour of other arrangements – are re-created by a picked team of some of the most talented repertory players and revivalists in Europe: the brass team alone is gold-plated, with the amazingly versatile Persson and Barker set alongside the brilliant Hagmann. The reed-section sounds totally schooled in the appropriate section-sound of the period, and each of the tunes emerges with the kind of rocking swing that sounds properly flavoursome of the era. With such a strong team of soloists, the various breaks and carefully fashioned improvisations have the nous needed to transcend any scripted mustiness. Dave Bennett engineers an ideal sound-mix. Result: a modern work of art wearing old-fashioned duds.

**** Harlem's Arabian Nights

Stomp Off CD1320 *As above, except add Bob Hunt (tb), Matthias Seuffert (cl, as, ts), Janice Day (v); omit Barker, Payton, Bard.* 9–10/96.

Outrageously good. This is the result of Nichols doing some digging for early manuscripts in the Library Of Congress – rarities by Ellington, James P. Johnson, Waller and others. So here are 'Yam Brown' and 'Rub A Dub-Lues' (Ellington), 'Mistuh Jim' and 'She's The Hottest Gal In Tennessee' (Johnson), 'Say It With Your Feet' (Waller) and 18 others, knocked out with stunning panache by Nichols's Cotton Club Orchestra, the finest assemblage of repertory players he could muster. As with the Henderson collection, they make it new by playing it old and, though some of the phrasing may suggest a vaudevillian bent, we prefer to hear it as old-fashioned virtuosity put to very specific ends. Dave Bennett once again gets an ideal sound in the 'ballroom' ambience of Pizza Express, Maidstone.

*** Rhythm Of The Day

PEK Sound PKCD-166 *Nichols; Norman Field (cl, as, Cmel, whistle, v); Colin Turner (bsx); Chris Howse (g, bj, v).* 5/01.

A live set from the 2001 Keswick Festival, by Keith's Blue Four. The music's great fun, a typical riffle through the archives, from 'Miss Hannah' to 'Mr Jelly Lord'. Field plays in a lively and notably authentic style, although his singing is a disaster (fortunately, one track only of that). Turner's occasional solos are a delight. Nichols croons and plays enough to overcome the home-made ambience of PEK and its usual bargain-basement presentation.

***(*) Kansas City Breakdown

Stomp Off CD 1387 *Nichols; Bent Persson, Enrico Tommaso, Mike Daniels (t); René Hagmann (tb); Claus Jacobi, Matthias*

Seuffert (cl, ss, as, ts); James Evans (cl, ss, as, bs); Martin Wheatley (bj, g); Malcolm Sked (sou); Richard Pite (d). 12/02.

The subject this time is the music of Bennie Moten. Good as it is, as a piece of repertory, we enjoyed Nichols's earlier adventures in this idiom slightly more: the material is variable, and the more studio-fied sound somehow loses an ounce of the liveliness of the earlier discs. No arguments about the calibre of the playing, though.

Red Nichols (1905–65)

CORNET, TRUMPET

Born Ernest Loring Nichols in Utah, he played in his father's brass band as a boy but soon turned to jazz. Arrived in New York in the early '20s and became one of the most recorded sessionmen as both bandleader and section-player. His 'Five Pennies' sessions resulted in scores of titles. Directed Broadway show bands and toured through the '30s, running his own big band. After a spell out of music, he returned with a small group in 1945. Worked on the West Coast through the '50s, the biopic The Five Pennies revitalizing his career, and was still successful when he died suddenly during a Las Vegas engagement.

***** Red Nichols On Edison 1924–27**

Jazz Oracle BDW 8007 *Nichols; Frank Cush, Leo McConville (t); Bill Trone (mel); Miff Mole, Tommy Dorsey (tb); Dick Johnson, Jimmy Dorsey, Arnold Brilhart, Phil Gleason, Fred Morrow (cl, as); Paul Cartwright (cl, ss, ts); Alfie Evans (as); Freddy Cusick (cl, ts); Jack Pettis (Cmel); Irving Brodsky, Arthur Schutt (p); Dick McDonough (g, bj); Tommy Felline (bj); Joe Tarto, Jack Hansen (bbs); Adrian Rollini (bsx); Stan King, Vic Berton (d).* 11/24–2/27.

*****(*) Red Nichols & Miff Mole 1925–1927**

Retrieval RTR 79010 *Nichols; Miff Mole (tb); Dick Johnson (cl, as); Jimmy Lytell, Alfie Evans, Jimmy Dorsey, Pee Wee Russell (cl); Rube Bloom, Frank Signorelli, Arthur Schutt (p); Tony Colucci (bj); Joe Tarto (tba); Vic Berton, Ray Bauduc (d); Irving Kaufman (v).* 11/25–9/27.

***** Red Nichols 1925–1927**

Classics 1212 *Similar to above.* 2/25–2/27.

*****(*) The Red Heads Complete 1925–1927**

Classics 1267 *Nichols; Brad Gowans, Wingy Manone; Leo McConville (t); Miff Mole (tb); Bobby Davis, Fred Morrow, Jimmy Dorsey (cl, as); Arthur Schutt, Bill Haid (p); Eddie Lang, Dick McDonough (g); Vic Berton (d).* 11/25–9/27.

***** Red Nichols 1927-1928**

Classics 1241 *Nichols; Leo McConville, Manny Klein, Bob Ashford (t); Miff Mole, Bill Rank (tb); Dudley Fosdick (mel); Jimmy Dorsey (cl, as); Pee Wee Russell, Fud Livingston (cl, ts); Mx Farley (as); Frankie Trumbauer (Cmel); Adrian Rollini (bsx, gfs); Arthur Schutt, Lennie Hayton (p, cel); Joe Venuti (vn); Eddie Lang, Dick McDonough (g); Joe Tarto, Jack Hanson (tba); Vic Berton, Chauncey Morehouse (d); Jim Miller, Charlie Farrell, Irving Kaufman (v).* 3/27-2/28.

***** Red Nichols 1928-1929**

Classics 1270 *As above except add Benny Goodman (cl, as), Murray Kellner (vn), Carl Kress (g), Art Miller (b), Harold Lambert (v); omit Ashford, Rank, Russell, Hayton, Venuti, McDonough, Tarto, Hanson, Miller, Farrell, Kaufman.* 3/28-2/29.

***** Red Nichols 1929**

Classics 1332 *Nichols; Manny Klein, Leo McConville, Tommy Thunen, John Egan (t); Jack Teagarden (tb, v); Miff Mole, Glenn Miller, Herb Taylor (tb); Dudley Fosdick (mel); Fud Livingston, Pee Wee Russell (cl); Alfie Evans, Pete Pumiglio, Jimmy Dorsey (cl, as); Jimmy Crossan (cl, ts, bsn, ob, f); Arnold Brilhart (cl, as, f, bsn, ob); Benny Goodman (cl, as, bs); Larry Binyon (ts, f, ob); Babe Russin (ts); Adrian Rollini (bsx, gfs); Arthur Schutt, Joe Sullivan, Irving Brodsky (p); Murray Kellner, Joe Raymond, Lou Raderman, Henry Whiteman, Maurice Goffin (vn); Lucien Schmidt (clo); Carl Kress (g); Tommy Felline (bj); Joe Tarto (tba); Art Miller, Jack Hansen (b); Vic Berton, George Beebe, Chick Condon (d). Harold Lambert, Red McKenzie, Dick Robertson (v).* 2-9/29.

****(*) Rhythm Of The Day**

ASV AJA 5025 *Nichols; Manny Klein, Leo McConville, Donald Lindley, James Kozak, Charlie Teagarden, Wingy Manone, Johnny Davis (t); Miff Mole, Glenn Miller, Will Bradley (tb); Dudley Fosdick (mel); Ross Gorman (cl, as, bs); Alfie Evans (cl, as, vn); Harold Noble (cl, as, ts); Jimmy Dorsey, Benny Goodman (cl, as); Billy McGill, Fud Livingston (cl, ts); Pee Wee Russell (cl); Babe Russin (ts); Adrian Rollini, Barney Acquelina (bsx); Nick Koupoukis (f, picc); Murray Kellner, Joe Venuti, Jack Harris, Saul Sharrow (vn); Milton Susskind, Arthur Schutt, Edgar Fairchild, Jack Russin, Fulton McGrath (p); Eddie Lang, Tony Colucci, Carl Kress (g); Tony Starr (bj); Artie Bernstein, Art Miller (b); Victor Engle, Chauncey Morehouse, Vic Berton, David Grupp (d).* 10/25–2/32.

These days it's a cliché to see Nichols as a maligned figure since the popular heyday of the white New York school of the '20s; but, with that era itself falling away into history, arguments about his stature *vis-à-vis* Beiderbecke or Armstrong (and for a long time he seems to have been more popular than either) seem even more academic. For a man who cut probably thousands of records in the '20s, under his name and in numberless dance orchestras, he still remains neglected in the CD era. His own precise, lightly dancing work on either cornet or trumpet might seem to glance off the best of Beiderbecke's playing, and the scrupulous ensembles and pallid timbre of the Five Pennies or whatever he chose to call a group on its day in the studios now seem less appealing. But it is unique jazz and, in its truce between cool expression and hot dance music, surprisingly enjoyable when taken a few tracks at a time.

The Retrieval disc brings together 23 titles by The (Six) Hottentots, The Original Memphis Five and The Arkansas Travellers, all basically co-led by Nichols and Mole and certainly dominated by their playing. The OM5 session is a cracker and, while some of the other titles are more like hot dance music (and the Travellers sessions are acoustic recordings, and less imposing), the playing has something to take the ear on every track. Top-notch transfers as always from this label.

Classics have finally entered the fray with their own Nichols edition. Classics 1212 starts with three sessions for Sam Lanin at Columbia, then goes to Vocalion for dates by The Hottentots, to Edison for a couple of Red And Miff's Stompers sessions, and finishes with the first three 'official' dates from Brunswick by The Five Pennies. So there is some duplication with several of the CDs here, though if you're a Classics collector you'll more than likely be satisfied with this as a choice: it imposes reasonable order on the slightly chaotic profligacy of Nichols's output, at least.

The Red Heads will make a strong appeal to specialists. This collects all of Nichols's sessions under this name for Pathé, and on titles such as 'Get A Load Of This', 'Plenty Off Centre' and 'Trumpet Sobs' the line-up is down to three or four players – chamber jazz of an unusually sparse sort, giving the young leader clear space to lead and improvise in. Pathé's thin recording wasn't helpful, but the music – lean, dancing and strikingly different from what was going on under either Armstrong or Beiderbecke in a similar period – exerts its own pale fascination. It's also as well to remember that when he made the earliest sides here, Nichols still hadn't even turned 21.

The ASV CD is something of a missed opportunity, since it purports to be a Five Pennies compilation yet includes two tracks by Mole's Molers and one by Ross Gorman's dance band, as well as including several of the later, lesser records. At least the 1925–7 selections – including 'Alabama Stomp', 'Buddy's Habits' and 'Cornfed' – are among the best of the Pennies. Sound is average, which is to say not good enough.

The Jazz Oracle disc collects some of the many sides Nichols cut for Edison: longer than the average 78, there are multiple takes of various sides from the Red And Miff's Stompers date of 1927, which forms the heart of the CD. Trim, elegant playing by Mole and Nichols, but Edison's comparatively thin sound isn't as good as the Brunswick sides, and there are more conventional hot-dance numbers by Don Voorhees, Golden Gate Orchestra and the Charleston Seven (on which Red's presence is anyway in doubt). A welcome set of some rare records, though.

Three further Classics discs take the story up to 1929. He was leaving the '20s with his best work already behind him, even though he wasn't yet 25 years old, and these sessions, studded with several future stars, are a little poignant because of that. The tracks on Classics 1241 and 1270 are still tilted towards jazz, especially the earliest sides: yet by the 1929 sessions the music has come to sound much more like dance music, with a string-section coming in. Even so, Nichols still sounds good when he emerges from what were good dance-band arrangements for a group larger than the early Pennies, and there isn't a track which can't boast a few good bars from somebody.

**** Red Nichols And His Orchestra 1936**
Circle CCD-110 *Nichols; rest unknown.* 11/36

***** Wail Of The Winds**
Hep CD 1057 *Nichols; Don Stevens, J. Douglas Wood, Hilton Brockman (t); Martin Croy, Robert Gebhart, Slim Wilbur, Al Mastren, Jack Knaus (tb); Harry Yolonsky, Ray Schultz, Conn Humphreys (as); Bobby Jones, Billy Shepherd, Heinie Beau (cl, ts); Billy Maxted (p); Tony Colucci, Mike Bryan, Merrit Lamb (g); Jack Fay, Frank Ray (b); Harry Jaeger (d, v); Victor Engle (d); Marion Redding, Bill Darnell (v).* 3/39–6/40.

The Circle CD offers some WBS transcriptions which are shared with a nondescript dance session by Will Bradley's orchestra. Not that Nichols's titles are much better: the music is so anonymous that this was long thought to be a session by the Ray Noble band. Red has a meagre number of solo spots, and the rest of the group are capable but unexceptional on routine arrangements. Good remastering, though, of what's a mere 28 minutes of music.

Hep's set plugs a big gap by bringing some of Red's big-band records on to CD for the first time. With all his experience behind him, Nichols was still only 33 when the first of these sessions was made. The band received good notices and was taking up a prestige engagement at New York's Famous Door, only to see the club abruptly close, whereupon Nichols broke up the band after losing some of his best men. These Victor sessions reveal a strong if not especially characterful outfit: Nichols and Jones take most of the solos, but at least the band gets the chance to dig into plenty of instrumental charts (mostly by Maxted), along with the expected vocal features. Excellent sound.

***** Red Nichols And His Five Pennies**
Jazzology JCD-90 *Nichols; Kingsley Jackson (tb); Reuel Lynch (cl); Joe Rushton (bsx); Bobby Hammack (p); Rollie Culver (d).* 3–10/49.

***** Red Nichols Vol. 2: Saints, Ramble And Sensation!**
Jazzology JCD-290 *As above.* 3–10/49.

None of Nichols's many records of Dixieland for Capitol have made it to CD so far (will they ever?). Jazzology's two sets of Lang–Worth transcriptions find Red and his team in good spirits, playing the kind of thing he did for the rest of his life. Those who see him as incontrovertibly wooden will be surprised to hear the soft-toned elegance of some of his playing and, though much of each disc is straight Dixieland, they play it with enough flexibility to give it freshness, and there's a nice chance to hear Joe Rushton's bass sax. Sound is clear, if a little metallic at times.

Michelle Nicolle

VOCAL, PIANO

Grew up in a small Australian country town and found out about jazz while studying at Adelaide. She now lives and works on the Melbourne jazz scene.

***** The Crying Game**
ABC Jazz 476123-2 *Nicolle; Nadje Nordhuis (t, flhn); Gianni Marinucci (c); Jex Saarelaht (p); Anthony Schulz (acc); Sam LeMann, Ed Bates, Geoff Hughes, Stephen Magnusson (g); Jordan Murray (euph); Phillip Rex (tba); Howard Cairns, Ben Robertson (b); Ronny Ferella (d); Ian Collard (v, hca).* 5/03.

Nicolle has a good voice – high, silvery, but with a strong middle range with a careful vibrato – and she likes to lay back on a steady slow-mid-tempo. This set of a dozen film-songs is well chosen. There are a few pieces we'd rather not hear, such as 'Everybody's Talkin'' and 'A Spoonful Of Sugar' – but she often uses a slowish pace to very striking effect, as on the sexy and languorous treatment of 'Hernando's Hideaway', and 'Pure Imagination' is done with a swing. Her quartet is the basic band but there are numerous guests, who don't intrude too much.

Maggie Nicols (born 1948)

VOCALS

Born in Edinburgh, she worked as a dancer before turning to jazz and to free music. Though her recorded output is quite small, her range of associations is enormous, touching almost everyone on the British and European free scene. She sings with power and humour, fuelled by a shrewd feminism.

***** Nicols'n'Nu**
Leo CD LR 127 *Nicols; Peter Nu (p).* 6/85.

Out of circulation for some time, this pairs Nicols's extraordinary voice, which seems capable of everything from pure abstraction and *Schrei* to the most delicate folk melody, with the little-known Nu's rich pianism. 'Kids' is one of the rawest and most open 'free music' performances you'll ever hear, breathtaking in its directness. There's nothing polished about the session, which sounds as if it happened pretty much as we're hearing it. If it's puzzling that we haven't got more of Maggie Nicols on record, it's just as mystifying why Nu isn't more widely documented. Apart from sessions with Kevin Coyne for John Peel's BBC radio programme, we know of nothing else currently bearing his name.

*****(*) Transitions**

Emanem 4068 *Nicols; Caroline Kraabel (as); Charlotte Hug (vla).* 6/01.

This trio first performed together as part of the Freedom Of The City festival documented elsewhere on the Emanem label. This reunion reflects the high level of creative empathy tapped on that occasion. Nicols is certainly the most powerful voice here, but she wears her seniority lightly and with the exception of the ferociously polemical anti-rape 'No Now' (a deeply uncomfortable listen) she is in remarkably lyrical form. The three long pieces, 'Lullaby For Clement', 'Hymn Indoors' and 'Coming Out', are the best of the set. Hug's viola is sometimes reduced to an accompanist's role on the first and last of them, but she finds a stance on the middle piece and is instrumental in turning it into a thing of real beauty. Kraabel has her own approach to the instrument, and though she is sometimes reminiscent of Trevor Watts, no one will claim a profound influence. A wonderful record, and a brave one.

Lennie Niehaus (born 1929)

ALTO SAXOPHONE

Much of the St Louis-born saxophonist's career has been spent as a studio musician and arranger and as a composer for film and television. He studied music in California and had two stints with Stan Kenton before becoming a fixture on the West Coast cool scene. Though more important as a composer than as a performer, Lennie has an engagingly conversational approach to phrasing and solo development.

*****(*) Zounds**

Original Jazz Classics OJCCD 1892 *Niehaus; Stu Williamson (t); Frank Rosolino (tb); Bob Enevoldsen (vtb); Vincent DeRosa (frhn); James McAllister (tba); Jack Montrose, Bill Perkins (ts); Pepper Adams, Bobby Gordon (bs); Lou Levy (p); Monty Budwig, Red Mitchell (b); Mel Lewis, Shelly Manne (d).* 8/54, 12/56.

****** The Octet No. 2: Volume 3**

Original Jazz Classics OJC 1767 *Niehaus; Bill Holman (t); Stu Williamson (t, vtb); Bob Enevoldsen (tb); Jimmy Giuffre (reeds); Pete Jolly (p); Monty Budwig (b); Shelly Manne (d).* 1–2/55.

***** The Quintets & Strings**

Original Jazz Classics OJCCD 1858 *Niehaus; Stu Williamson (t); Bill Perkins (ts); Bobby Gordon (bs); Hampton Hawes (p); Monty Budwig (b); Shelly Manne (d); strings.* 3–4/55.

***** Volume 5 – The Sextet**

Original Jazz Classics OJC 1944 *Niehaus; Stu Williamson (t, vtb); Bill Perkins(ts, f); Jimmy Giuffre(bs); Buddy Clark (b); Shelly Manne (d).* 1/56.

The smooth West Coast veneer belies a substantial portfolio of imaginative compositions and standards arrangements. He worked with Kenton before and after a period in the services and, though much of his recorded work is in the rather anonymous context of Stan's reed-sections, his own most distinctive work has tended to be for mid-size bands. The two contrasting octets on *Zounds* are both meticulously balanced, horns and woodwinds in opposition. Of the two groups, the December 1956 octet with Rosolino, Perkins and Adams is by far the more accomplished; its readings of Hampton Hawes's 'The Sermon', the first track on the disc, is also the most arresting, though a later reworking of Miles Davis's 'Four' by the same personnel is almost as good. *The Octet* is excellent, full of inventive and sophisticated arrangements that make up for a hint of blandness and propriety in the performances. Sadly, these fine sessions coincided with the beginning of a second stint with the Stan Kenton band. Niehaus also appears on a wilderness of Kenton albums (though there's little point looking for him there), after which he turned his music into a day job, writing and arranging for television and the movies. A loss and a lack. Only one of four quintet records is currently available, and it's not the best, though presumably the best-selling. It's almost entirely a standards session, and Perkins is again the star turn, though the West Coast rhythm section are hard to fault on any count. 'All The Things You Are' is a superb version and the brisk, breezy 'Star Eyes' would charm down the constellations. *The Sextet* is the latest arrival: it's smooth, it swings (Manne's the man to make sure of that) and it rarely stirs any embers, though Giuffre (on baritone here) is always worth his few featured bars and Williamson (these days, almost forgotten) is a pleasure to hear.

***** Patterns**

Fresh Sound FSR CD 100 *Niehaus; Bill Perkins (ts, bs, ss, bcl); Frank Strazzeri (p); Tom Warrington (b); Joe LaBarbera (d).* 8/89.

***** Seems Like Old Times**

Fresh Sound FSR CD 5016 *As above, except add Jack Nimitz (bs).* 89.

The Fresh Sound albums help to fill out a skimpy list, and they underline how thoroughly the saxophonist enjoyed playing in later years, having spent much of his career either behind the scenes or in the anonymity of big-band woodwind sections. As ever, Perkins does the work of ten men on these, but the revelation is Warrington, a huge-voiced bass player with an inexhaustible stock of ideas. The second album is weightier and more obviously arranged, with the three saxophones often functioning as a unit. Niehaus's compositions are quietly challenging, and on a piece like 'Yesterday's Gardenias' (which might contain a tiny Billie Holiday reference) he shows how well he can combine advanced harmonic ideas with straightforwardly beautiful melody.

***** Live At Capozzoli's**

Woofy 96 *Niehaus; Bill Perkins (ts, bs); Frank Strazzeri (p); Tom Warrington (b); Paul Kreibich (d).* 99.

Lennie's skills as an arranger are evident even on smaller group dates. The soloing here, from both the saxophonists (and, to a lesser extent, Strazzeri), is more than respectable, but what one remembers about the set, recorded in Las Vegas, is the crispness of the charts. Gerry Mulligan's 'Limelight' is the highlight, and highly appropriate to the setting, but there are also fine versions of 'If I Should Lose You' and 'I'm Old Fashioned'. A welcome issue that puts the Niehaus discography in ever better shape.

Lucas Niggli

PERCUSSION

The Swiss drummer and percussionist has made an impact with his Zoom trio and Big Zoom quintet.

****(*) Spawn Of Speed**

Intakt CD 067 *Niggli; Nils Wogrom (tb); Peter Schaufelberger (g).* 12/00.

***** Rough Ride**

Intakt CD 082 *As above.* 3–8/02.

***** Big Ball**

Intakt CD 083 *As above; add Claudio Pontin (cl); Peter Herbert (b).* 3–9/02.

The first of these now feels like a false start, though there are interesting aspects to it. The others are both taken from festival gigs and reflect the quiet excitement Niggli generates when he appears with these intriguingly configured groups. The trio version of Zoom is probably the clearest representation of the drummer's own work. He develops or picks up on what sound like melodic lines, spins them into a rhythmic figure and then makes them into the architecture of a piece that didn't exist before that stray phrase drifted across the stage, from either guitar, trombone or part of his own kit. It's harder to hear on the quintet recording, partly because the language of this group does seem closer to a horns-and-rhythm jazz combo. That's not to denigrate the music, which is intense and free-flowing. *Spawn Of Speed* may be interesting to revisit once one has absorbed the two later records; on its own, it still seems drab and unshaped to us.

Paal Nilssen-Love

DRUMS

Norwegian drummmer/percussionist whose powerful work has become a lynchpin for several leading groups in the contemporary European free scene.

***** Sticks And Stones**

SOFA 505 *Nilssen-Love (d solo).* 2/01.

****** I Love It When You Snore**

Smalltown Supersound STS 063 *Nilssen-Love; Mats Gustafsson (bs).* 11/01.

The solo record gives a good representative picture of this formidable drummer's skills. Recorded in a church acoustic and working from three different set-ups, his breathtaking dexterity – not fully appreciated unless you can see him in live performance, where he seems to get around a kit with effortless velocity – is captured in isolation. Like all solo drum records, though, it hardly demands the attention of a wide audience, and even Nilssen-Love can't escape a sense of ennui some of the time.

The duet with Gustafsson is devastating. Crucially, the two are recorded in a dry, intense close-up which has an almost shocking impact. As a dialogue, they get a maximal effect out of the precise technique each man favours, and it really does feel like a welding of hands and minds. Seven pieces explode off the record and the whole thing is done and dusted inside 35 minutes, a virtually perfect piece of documentation which works superbly as a record.

Vincent Nilsson

TROMBONE

Superb technician, especially adept with mutes, who also shows considerable imagination.

*****(*) Jazz Trombone Spirituals**

Storyville STCD 1014240 *Nilsson; Jan Lundgren (p); Bo Stief, Mads Vinding (b); Ed Thigpen (d).* 11/00.

Every track credit carries the simple word 'Traditional'. This set is exactly as described, except that the music is never predictable and far from traditional in approach. 'When The Saints Go Marching In' is taken at snail's pace, giving the most celebrated of all early jazz themes a thoroughly unexpected quality. 'Go Down, Moses', 'Were You There When My Lord Was Crucified?' and 'Sometimes I Feel Like A Motherless Child' are more conventional in pace and structure, but Nilsson exploits the trombone's closeness to human singing as thoroughly as anyone has done and at the same time exploits a range of techniques which include singing through the horn, multiphonics and almost toneless smears and rips that help give the set as a whole its curious flavour of both toughness and vulnerability. The piano-playing is the only weak link; otherwise, remarkable in every way.

Liam Noble

PIANO

Fine British pianist and composer.

***** Close Your Eyes**

FMR CD 25 *Noble (p solo).* 00.

***** In The Meantime**

Basho 108 *Nobel; Stan Sulzman (ss, as); Chris Biscoe (ss, ts, acl); Mick Hutton (b); Paul Clarvis (d).* 02.

Noble's clear sense of line and direction has yet to yield the work he is capable of, but one senses it coming, even in these two slightly tentative efforts. The FMR disc is not much more than a taster, but it bubbles with promise and with indications that Noble will not be content to play just jazz in the years ahead but intends to diversify. By contrast, on *In The Meantime* Noble is rather overshadowed by his playing partners and doesn't assert himself all that clearly. These are problems that will pass with time and growing confidence.

Steve Noble

PERCUSSION, TURNTABLES

A familiar figure in London's free-music scene since the mid-'80s, Noble has worked frequently in partnership with pianist Alex Maguire, as well as in numerous other configurations.

*****(*) Ya Boo, Reel And Rumble**
Incus CD06 *Noble; Alex Ward (cl, as).* 3/89, 7/90.

**** Flathead Reunion**
Ping Pong PPPCD001 *Noble; Davey Williams (g); Oren Marshall (tba).* 9/95.

Steve Noble came to wider notice during the 'Company Week' of 1987, when he joined one of Derek Bailey's most adventurous collectives for a week of improvisation. At the same time, Noble and his occasional partner, Alex Maguire, were winning a reputation in the London free-music community for improvised performances that combined intense, sometimes ferocious interplay with a rare infusion of wit. Another partner, reeds player Alex Ward, was only in his mid-teens when the first of the performances of *Ya Boo, Reel And Rumble* were recorded. A virtuosic player with a strong background in modernist formal repertoire, he plays with considerable authority, matched move for move by Noble's quick-witted percussion. Noble has plenty of fun playing turntables on *Flathead Reunion*, but since this takes him away from his kit and as there's not much else of musical interest going on – Williams has little useful to say on guitar, and Marshall just parps away on whatever 'electric tuba' is – the record's a disappointment.

Jimmie Noone (1895–1944)

CLARINET

Born near New Orleans, Noone studied with his contemporary Sidney Bechet before joining King Oliver in Chicago in 1918. He was one of the clarinet kings of the city during the '20s, and never had much impact in New York, continuing to work in Chicago until moving West in the early '40s. A fondness for eating did his health no good. His records never quite match his reputation, and these days he is all but forgotten.

***** Jimmie Noone, 1928–1929**
Classics 611 *Noone; George Mitchell (c); Fayette Williams (tb); Lawson Buford, Bill Newton (tba); Joe Poston (cl, as); Eddie Pollack (as, bs); Zinky Cohn, Alex Hill, Earl Hines (p); Junie Cobb, Wilbur Gorham, Bud Scott (bj, g); Johnny Wells (d).* 28–29.

***** Jimmie Noone, 1929–1930**
Classics 632 *Similar to above.* 29–30.

***** Jimmie Noone 1930–1934**
Classics 641 *Noone; Jimmy Cobb (t); Eddie Pollack (as, bs, v); Earl Hines, Zinky Cohn (p); Wilbur Gorham (g, bj); John Henley (g); Quinn Wilson, John Lindsay (b); Bill Newton (bb); Johnny Wells, Benny Washington (d); Georgia White, Elmo Tanner, Art Jarrett, Mildred Bailey (v).* 30–34.

***** Jimmie Noone 1934–1940**
Classics 651 *As above, except add Guy Kelly, Charlie Shavers (t); Natty Dominique (c), Preston Jackson (tb), Pete Brown (as); Richard M. Jones, Gideon Honore (p); Teddy Bunn (g); Henry Fort, Israel Crosby, Wellman Braud (b); O'Neil Spencer, Tubby Hall (d); Ed Thompson, Teddy Simmons (v); omit Hines, Newton, Bailey, White, Wells, Jarrett, Wilson.* 11/34–12/40.

***** The Alternative Takes 1923-1941**
Neatwork RP 2017 *As above discs except add Tommy Ladnier, Alex Calamese (c), Eddie Vincent (tb), Horace Diemer (as), Glover Compton, Frank Smith (p), John Basley (bj), William 'Bass' Moore (tba), John Frazier (b), Ollie Powers, Wallace Bishop (d).* 9/23-7/41.

Noone has long been reckoned to be one of the premier jazz clarinettists, but his records have fallen out of wide renown. Much of his output was spoiled by weak material, unsuitable arrangements, poor sidemen or a sentimental streak which eventually came to dominate the playing. These are all familiar characteristics of the period, but Noone seemed oblivious to the excessive sweetness which overpowered so many of the records with his Apex Club band, named after his resident gig in Chicago. He had a mellifluous, rather sad-sounding tone and preferred his solos to be insinuating rather than fierce. Where Johnny Dodds, the other great New Orleans player of the day, was comparatively harsh, Noone sought to caress melodies. But the plunking rhythm sections, still dominated by banjos even in 1928–9, and the unsuitable front-line partners failed to give Noone the kind of sympathetic settings which would have made his romantic approach more feasible. Poston tarnishes many of the tunes, and his replacement, Pollack, is even worse; even Earl Hines, who plays on 18 tracks on the first disc, can provide only flashes of inspiration. Mitchell arrives for a single session, and even that is ruined by some awful vocals, a final burden which afflicts far too many of these tracks.

What's needed here is a good sampler of Noone's earlier material. There are examples of the great musician Noone could be, but they're scattered. The ballad-playing on 'Sweet Lorraine' and 'Blues My Naughty Sweetie Gives To Me' is of a very high order and investigates a rare, cool vein in the Chicago jazz of the period. 'Oh, Sister! Ain't That Hot?', 'El Rado Scuffle', 'It's Tight Like That' and 'Chicago Rhythm' are further isolated successes, but the rest is rather discouraging.

Noone's questionable judgement pervades much of his remaining legacy. Classics 641 has some dreary material and vocals, and Hines's brief reappearance has little impact. But Noone had two great sessions left in him – the small-group swing tracks recorded in 1936–7 and featured on Classics 651. 'Blues Jumped A Rabbit' is the most memorable track, but all four from this session are impressive, and so are the tracks made with Charlie Shavers in New York the following year. The sound is mostly quite decent on the later Classics pieces, less so in the early sessions.

The set of alternative takes starts with no fewer than three different versions of the creaky Ollie Powers side 'Play That Thing', cut for Paramount in 1923, although Tommy Ladnier's solo remains invigorating (and two of them are in diabolical sound). The rest offer some alternates of some of Noone's better records, but the main interest is in the nine pieces from a Chicago airshot made in 1940 (and once issued on a Swaggie LP). With only a rhythm section in support - and fired up by Wallace Bishop's power-packed drumming – Jimmie sounds in fine heart, with the choruses on 'Blues' languorous but deeply felt and those on 'Honeysuckle Rose' an exercise in sonorous wailing. The sound is pretty awful to modern ears, but those used to swing-era broadcasts should be able to listen past it.

Caecilie Norby (born 1964)

VOCAL

After working with Danish rock groups, Norby moved into a jazz idiom with her debut album for Blue Note, although she still draws material from some rock composers.

****** Caecilie Norby**

Blue Note 832222-2 *Norby; Randy Brecker (t); Rick Margitza (ss); Scott Robinson (ts); Ben Besiakov (p, org); Lars Jansson, Niels Lan Doky (p); Jakob Foscher (g); Lennart Ginman (b); Billy Hart (d).* 9/94.

*****(*) My Corner Of The Sky**

Blue Note 8968-2 *Norby; Randy Brecker (flhn); Michael Brecker (ts); Scott Robinson (f); David Kikoski, Lars Jansson (p, org); Joey Calderazzo (p); Lennart Gunman, Lars Danielsson (b); Terri Lyne Carrington, Alex Riel (d).* 96.

The Danish singer's international debut was distinguished by a brilliant production by Niels Lan Doky. He chose an ingenious setting for almost every tune, deploying a crack team of players with spontaneous assurance, and the rich detail of the studio sound is a further embellishment. Inside all this, Norby isn't intimidated once. She has a big, rather awkward voice which she can use with great dramatic force, and on ballads she finds a low-key but steely power, with nothing downcast entering the interpretation. The songs are a fascinating lot, with initially unpromising things like Rod McKuen's 'I've Been Town' and Jimmy Webb's 'By The Time I Get To Phoenix' surprising successes, and a couple of oblique originals adding a further dimension.

The follow-up, *My Corner Of The Sky*, is more of a mixed success. This time the material is a shade too eclectic for the record's own good. She makes a fist of David Bowie's 'Life On Mars', for instance, but all it tends to display is how meaningless the lyric is; and Sting's 'Set Them Free' is no more than high-class jazz-pop. Yet there are again some impressive successes, such as her setting of Wayne Shorter's 'African Fairytale', the stark 'Suppertime' and 'The Right To Love', a beautiful lyric impeccably handled. And 'Snow' transfers her roots into a plausible New York framework.

***** Queen Of Bad Excuses**

Blue Note 522342-2 *Norby; Anders Bergcrantz (t, flhn); Hans Ulrik (ss, f); Lars Moller (ts); Lars Danielsson (ky, g, clo, b, d); Ben Besiakov, Lars Jansson (p); Aske Jacoby, John Scofield (g); Anders Kjellberg, Per Lindvall, Billy Hart (d); Xavier Desandre-Navarre (perc).* n.d.

A more personal record than its predecessors: Norby wrote all the material (partner and co-producer Danielsson assisting on three tracks) and adopts a more flexible, less interpretative approach. The result is nicely idiosyncratic and sometimes – as on the delightful 'Fly' – very appealing. But the material doesn't have enough outreach, and anyway the singer doesn't get it across so forcefully that you feel involved. In the end, it feels more like a quality singer-songwriter record, and the rock sections are full of those.

Fredrik Norén

DRUMS

The Swedish answer to Art Blakey's Jazz Messengers, the Fredrik Norén Band was formed in 1978 and carries the flame for the region's hard bop.

***** City Sounds**

Mirrors MICD 001 *Norén; Magnus Broo (t); Robert Nordermark (ts); Torbjörn Gulz (p); Dan Berglund (b).* 12/91.

***** One Day In May**

Mirrors MICD 004 *As above, except Fredrik Ljungkvist (ts), Filip Augustson (b) replace Nordermark and Berglund; add Lina Nyberg (v).* 5/95.

*****(*) T**

Mirrors MICD 008 *Norén; Anders Garstedt (t); Jonas Kullhammar (ts); Daniel Karlsson (p); Torbjörn Zetterberg (b).* 5/99.

Norén's band is something of an institution at this point and, with his ever-changing line-up and steady evolution – not to mention his own push and shove from the kit – he deserves the title of Sweden's Jazz Messenger. These three are in a long line of records, lately for the Mirrors label. *City Sounds* is live, and the most dependent on mere good blowing, but the band is hot and, though it smoulders rather than burns, the best of it – as on Gulz's 'I'm Ready' – is more than good enough. *One Day In May* benefits from the piquant contrast of Broo's rather careful trumpet with the bluster of Ljungkvist's tenor. Nyberg comes in for a rather strangely tempestuous 'Someone To Watch Over Me'.

The best of the three – and evidence that Norén is quite capable of revitalizing his old format – is surely the latest, *T*. The leader's own 'Trane Mode' calls up a fiercely individual sequence of solos and, as the record progresses, it's clear that Fredrik has found some fresh voices again – both Garstedt and Kullhammar refuse to conform to the obvious dialects on their horns. As just one instance, the trumpeter's snapping improvisation on his own 'No Choice' really grabs the lapels. Excellent variations on the grand old formula, and plangently recorded too.

Norrbotten Big Band

GROUP

Based in Lulea, this Swedish big band has been in existence for some years and has a policy of appointing guest MDs.

***** Animations**

Phono Suecia PSCD 75 *Bo Strandberg, Dan Johansson, Magnus Ekholm, Magnus Plumppu (t, flhn); P. O. Svanstrom, Magnus Puls, Tony Andersson, Anders Wiborg, Bjorn Hjangsel (tb); Håkan Broström, Christer Johnsson (ss, as); Jan Thelin (as, cl); Mats Garberg (ts, f); Bengt Ek (ts); Per Moberg (bs); Hans Andersson (ky); Hans-Ola Ericsson (org); Johan Granstrom (b); Christer Sjöström, Lennart Gruvstedt (d); Kjell Westerberg (perc); Orjan Dahlstrom (cond, arr, ky).* 9/92–2/93.

***** Norrbotten Big Band Featuring Nils Landgren**

Caprice CAP 21494 *As above, except add Tapio Maunuvaara (t, flhn), Nils Landgren (tb, v), Hans Delander (ky), Johan Norberg (g).* 2/93–2/95.

*** **Future North**

Double-Time DTRCD-140 *As above, except add Tim Hagans (t), Christian Spering (b), Jukkis Uotila (d); omit Plumppu, Andersson, Wiborg, Johnsson, Andersson, Ericsson, Sjöström, Gruvstedt, Westerberg, Dahlstrom, Norberg.* 6/97.

Demanding big-band charts played with panache and fastidious clarity by this typically impressive Swedish orchestra. Orjan Dahlstrom leads the first record and does most of the writing. *Animations* features two long works, a series of pieces to go with the silent film, *Witchcraft Through The Ages*, and the title-work, a full-scale concerto for pipe organ and big band. It's a little hard to see how the film scores really fit with Benjamin Christensen's startling old film, since they actually sound like an unlinked sequence of charts, but there's no denying the impact. 'Animations' is an impressive if finally improbable blending of the organ and the band: Klas Persson cleverly mixes the two factors, but the music is more a matter of competition than integration. The Caprice disc (which also includes a single left-over track from the previous sessions) is a sometimes unconvincing mixture, with a few rhythms straying towards rock. Landgren is the main soloist, but his singing on 'Stone Free' and 'Ticket To Ride' wasn't the smartest of ideas and the best music is on the more thoughtful scores: a big, punchy 'Impressions', a sonorous Philip Catherine tune, 'Twice A Week', and Landgren's mellifluous trip through 'The Midnight Sun Never Sets'.

Tim Hagans was an interesting choice as guest arranger/soloist, a post he held in 1996. The resulting record is an impressionistic programme of charts, suggesting his reaction to both the orchestra and its native environment in northern Europe. Some of it, such as 'Twist And Out' and 'Waking Iris', is almost too clever even for this expert band, but when Hagans settles things down a little – as in the impressive three-part title-piece – he does better.

Alex Norris

TRUMPET, FLUGELHORN

A Mid-Westerner, Norris played around the Baltimore/Washington precinct before arriving in New York in 1992. Highly regarded by many contemporaries, but this is his sole leadership credit so far.

***(*) **A New Beginning**

Fresh Sound New Talent FSNT 081 *Norris; Gregory Tardy (ts); George Colligan (p); Dwayne Burno (b); Joe Strasser (d); Claudia Acuña (v).* 02.

George Colligan's encomium in the sleevenotes isn't unfounded – Norris writes and plays with rare assurance and seldom walks on overly familiar paths. The music is typically brainy New York post-bop, though softened by the burnish of Norris's ideas. He's not an aggressive stylist and his penchant for thoughtful dynamics gives him the confidence to leave space and unexpected intervals in his solos. Paired with the altogether twistier and more impetuous phrasing of Tardy, it makes for an intriguing front line. The themes are a productive lot, especially 'Good Addiction', the rhythmically compelling 'Ontology' and the unusual blues fantasy 'Delta'. Colligan, as ever, is masterful as band pianist, and there are two appealing features for Acuna, who's less selfconscious than she is on her Verve records.

Kevin Norton

DRUMS, MARIMBA

A composer-drummer and sometime sideman in Anthony Braxton's groups, Norton leads a prodigious Ensemble of his own, responsible for two of the three discs below.

***(*) **Integrated Variables**

CIMP 121 *Norton; George Cartwright (ss, as, ts); Mark Dresser (b).* 7/96.

**** **Knots**

Music & Arts CD-1033 *Norton; Bob DeBellis (cl, bcl, as); David Krakauer (cl); David Bindman (cl, ts); Tomas Ulrich (clo); Joe Fonda (b).* 9–10/97.

*** **For Guy Debord**

Barking Hoop 001 *As above, except Anthony Braxton (as, cbcl) replaces Krakauer.* 9/98.

Norton is that rarity, a free drummer who's also a precision merchant. On *Integrated Variables* he gets a fireball momentum going on many of the tracks, but it's always ready to stop on a dime, switch gears or change direction. His rolls are pristine in their exactness and when he moves over to the marimba, which is often, he plays with the same attention to detail. This is one of the best of the CIMP albums: Norton is well matched with the imaginative Cartwright and the virtuosic Dresser, and their music is quick and funny as well as passionate. There's a lot of it, at over 70 minutes, but very few dead-ends. The unfiltered sound works well for this group – the music sounds raw and live without getting unduly messy.

Knots is by Norton's Ensemble, and presents a more considered sound – detailed and balanced compositions, though the players have sufficient space to let fly when they're asked to improvise. 'Hammer Or Anvil?' has the meticulous feel of composed chamber music, carefully weighted around the colours of the horns and the changing dynamics of Norton's own rhythms (including an overdubbed vibes solo). There are quite brilliant treatments of two Monk tunes – 'Epistrophy', its melody camouflaged by alternative lines drawn from one of Monk's own solos, then blown open by Bindman's blitzkrieg tenor solo, and 'Brilliant Corners', a tough challenge to start with but here evolved into a scintillating essay on the composer's rhythm-plan. 'Three Movements For Solo And Ensemble' is a setting for guest clarinettist Krakauer, who suggests klezmer-like ebullience, and the swing beats of 'Walking The Dogma' frame horn solos that eventually send the music somewhere else entirely. Very rich, and this is only half of a fine and thought-provoking record.

For Guy Debord is a nine-part piece in dedication to the French *provocateur* of that name, and it's a concert recording with a rare sighting of Braxton as sideman. A continuous 37-minute piece, it has many of the ingenuities of the studio date but a rougher ambience, and somehow Braxton's presence unbalances the group: his trademark timbres seem to sideline Bindman and DeBellis, and the multifarious threads of *Knots* seem less abundant (to be fair, it is but a single piece in what is clearly an ongoing and ambitious corpus of work in progress). Admirers of the first two discs will surely want to hear this, though – and whatever Norton comes up with next.

***(*) **In Context/Out Of Context**

Barking Hoop BKH-002 *Norton; David Bindman, Bob DeBellis (ss, ts, f).* 10/99.

***** Iron Monkey Trio**

CIMP 238 *Norton; Bob Celusak (ss, ts); Andy Eulau (b).* 1/01.

The five-minute drum solo which opens *In Context/Out Of Context* is impressive enough by itself, but it's merely the prelude to a sequence of pieces which the composer cites as the result of musing on Charlie Parker and the earlier work of Cecil Taylor. Historicity aside, the music does have a boppish lineage (the twin-tenor solos in 'Variations In B♭', for instance) while approximating some of the structural ideas suggested by *Unit Structures* (a notably unexplored tangent, it might be added). It's not a very long set, but it's packed with ideas; less good, alas, is the recording, which blunts some of the impact.

The trio of *Iron Monkey* is much more about freebop jamming. It's none the worse for that – Celusak has some good ideas, though his soprano tone isn't flattered one iota by the CIMP sound – but it's a good deal more lightweight.

*****(*) Change Dance**

Barking Hoop BKH-005 *Norton; Dave Ballou (t, c); Steve Lehmann (sno, as); Rachel Telesmanick (as, bs); Mark Dresser (b).* 6/01.

*****(*) Play Anthony Braxton**

Barking Hoop BKH-006 *Norton; Haewon Min (p).* 3/01.

The subtext of *Change Dance*, a dedication to the emotionally disturbed street-activist Kathleen Chang, who killed herself in the environment in which she worked, is troubling enough; but even away from this the music sounds like the most anguished work Norton has put down on record. The playing is often coruscatingly fierce, with Lehmann and Telesmanick in particular despatching some unflinchingly harsh solos. Dresser and Norton have to impose order without stifling expression, and they do it by blending tempo work with more abstract material. Nothing stays settled for long. The eerie coda regresses to a nursery rhyme jingle that eventually merely fades away. Strong stuff, compelling music.

Norton's immersion in Anthony Braxton's music leaves him well qualified for the concert recital on the next Barking Hoop. They tackle five Braxton works, from the signature 'Composition No. 60' to the finale of 'Composition No. 62'. Mostly, Norton is at the marimba and the vibraphone, and the unisons with Min have a glistening brilliance of sonority which makes one hear works that some may consider drear in dazzling new colours. More like a new-music chamber concert than anything, but in Min's virtuosity in particular one hears links with the Taylor continuum suggested in the earlier BH release – and the tradition goes forward, again.

***** Intuitive Structures**

Cadence CJR 1166 *Norton; Louie Belogenis (ss, ts); Tomas Ulrich (clo); John Lindberg (b).* 11/02.

***** The Dream Catcher**

CIMP 280 *Norton; Roy Campbell (t, flhn); Tomas Ulrich (clo); Hill Greene (b).* 1/03.

Intuitive Structures documents a Knitting Factory gig by Norton's Living Language group. His notes make the music sound, perhaps, a little more interesting than it actually is: they include two versions of the Norton staple 'Walking The Dogma', but in the end this piece sounds like a theme and a string of long solos, twice. Belogenis is an energetic if not especially individual saxophonist and Ulrich's solos are a long haul. *The Dream Catcher*, in dedication to Wilber Morris who was originally to have played on the date, is a bright sequence of freebop pieces, quite tightly structured and played, and not the sort of thing that the CIMP sound suits best: if Greene and Ulrich were in more particular focus, everything would sound stronger. As it is, it's a merely enjoyable Norton session.

Red Norvo (born 1908)

XYLOPHONE, VIBRAPHONE

Born Kenneth Norville in Beardstown, Illinois, Red started out playing marimba and graduated to vibes-playing without vibrato and with a light and almost delicate sound. He was married to singer Mildred Bailey and worked with her for some years. Attracted by bebop, he managed to synthesize swing with the new language of jazz.

*****(*) Dance Of The Octopus**

Hep CD 1044 *Norvo; Stewart Pletcher (t); Eddie Sauter, Jack Jenney (tb); Jimmy Dorsey, Donald McCook, Artie Shaw (cl); Benny Goodman (bcl); Charlie Barnet (ts); Bobby Johnson, Dick McDonough, George Van Eps (g); Fulton McGrath, Teddy Wilson (p); Artie Bernstein, Hank Hayland, Pete Peterson (b); Billy Gussak, Gene Krupa, Bob White, Maurice Purtill (d); Mae Questal (v).* 4/33–3/36.

***** Red Norvo 1933–1936**

Classics 1085 *Similar to above.* 4/33–2/36.

***** Jivin' The Jeep**

Hep CD 1019 *Norvo; Bill Hyland, Stewart Pletcher, Louis Mucci, George Wendt (t); Leo Moran, Eddie Sauter (tb); Frank Simeone (as); Slats Long, Hank D'Amico (cl, as); Len Goldstein (as); Charles Lanphere (as, ts); Herbie Haymer (ts); Joe Liss, Bill Miller (p); Dave Barbour, Red McGarvey (g); Pete Robinson (b); Mo Purtill (d); Mildred Bailey, Lew Hurst (v).* 36–37.

***** Red Norvo, 1936–1937**

Classics 1123 *Norvo; Bill Hyland Eddie Meyers, Louis Mucci, Stew Pletcher (t); Eddie Sauter (t, as); Al Mastern, Leo Moran (tb); Hank d'Amico (cl); Slats Long(as, cl); Lou Goldstein, Charlie Lanphere, Frank Simeone (as); Herbie Haymer (ts); Howard Smith (p); Dave Barbour (g); Pete Robinson (b); Moe Purtill (d); Mildred Bailey (v).* 36-37.

***** Red Norvo, 1937–1938**

Classics 1157 *Much as above, except add George Wendt (t), Maurice Kogan (ts), Allen Hanlon, Red McGarvey (g).* 37–8.

***** Red Norvo, 1938–1939**

Classics 1192 *Much as above, except add Al George, Charlie Shavers, Barney Zudecoff (t), Les Burness, Stuart Mckay (as), Buster Bailey (cl), Billy Kyle (p), John Kirby (b), Buddy Christian, O'Neill Spencer, George Wettling (d).* 38–9.

***** Nuances By Norvo**

Hep 1072 *Norvo; Steve Lipkins, Jack Owens, Bob Kennedy, Jack Palmer, Jimmy Salko, Barney Zudecoff (t); Eddie Bert, Al George, Wes Hein, Andy Russo (tb); Hank d'Amico (cl); Len Goldstein, George Koenig, Frank Simeone (as); Freddy Artzberger (as, cl); George Berg, Maurice Kogan, Stuart McKay (ts); Mickey Folus (ts, ob); Jimmy Gemus (bs); Les Burness, Bob Kitsis, Billy Kyle, Bill Miller (p); Allen Hanlon (g); Pete Peterson (b); Buddy Christian, George Wettling (d).* 9/38–3/42.

***** El Rojo: The Complete Keynote Recordings And More**

Definitive 11128 *Norvo; Bobby Sherwood (c); Manny Klein, Ray Linn (t); Vic Dickenson (tb); John Cave (frhn); Aaron Sachs (cl); Benny Carter (as); Jimmy Giuffre (as, ts); Dave Cavanaugh, Dexter Gordon, Eddie Miller (ts); Jules Kinsler, Bob Lawson (bcl); Art Fleming (bsn); Dodo Marmarosa, Arnold Ross, Jimmy Rowles, Teddy Wilson (p); Dave Barbour, Barney Kessel, Jack Marshall (g); Red Callender, Billy Hadnott, Slam Stewart (b); Irving Cottler, Eddie Dell, Jackie Mills, Specs Powell, Jesse Price, Jack Turner (d); Kay Starr (v).* 44–45.

*****(*) Red Norvo On Dial**

Spotlite SPJ 127 *Norvo; Dizzy Gillespie (t); Charlie Parker (as); Flip Phillips (ts); Teddy Wilson (p); Slam Stewart (b); J. C. Heard, Specs Powell (d).* 6/45.

***** The Modern Red Norvo**

Savoy 17113 2CD *Norvo; Dizzy Gillespie (t); Charlie Parker (as); Flip Phillips(ts); Teddy Wilson (p); Tal Farlow (g); Charles Mingus, Slam Stewart (b); J. C. Heard, Specs Powell (d).* 6/45–4/51.

*****(*) The Red Norvo Trios**

Prestige 24108 *Norvo; Jimmy Raney, Tal Farlow (g); Red Mitchell (b).* 53–54.

*****(*) Red Norvo Trio**

Original Jazz Classics OJC 641 *Norvo; Jimmy Raney (g); Red Mitchell (b).* 9/53–3/54.

*****(*) Music To Listen To Red Norvo By**

Original Jazz Classics OJC 1015 *Norvo; Buddy Collette (f); Bill Smith (cl); Barney Kessel (g); Red Mitchell (b); Shelly Manne (d).* 1–2/57.

***** Red Plays The Blues**

RCA 2113034 *Norvo; Harry 'Sweets' Edison, Don Fagerquist, Ed Leddy, Ray Linn, Don Paladino (t); Ray Sims (tb); Willie Smith (as); Harold Land, Ben Webster (ts); Chuck Gentry (bs); Jimmy Rowles (p); Jimmy Wyble (g); Bob Carter, Red Wooten (b); Bill Douglas, Mel Lewis (d); Helen Humes (v).* 1/57–1/58.

Norvo's early recorded work, before he made the switch from xylophone to vibraharp, illustrates the problem of placing so self-effacing an instrument in a conventional jazz line-up; it's sometimes difficult to separate technical limitations and compromises from conscious dynamic strategies in Norvo's recorded work. The material on the xylophonic Heps is generally pretty good, though inevitably much of the interest stems from the fantastic line-ups Norvo commanded as a youngster.

The Keynote sessions on *El Rojo* ('Mr Red', or something close to it) underline what a modernist Norvo was, for all his commitment to swing and to the harmonic bases of pre-bop jazz. The sound transfers on the Definitive collection are very good indeed and there is a sufficient range of source material and idiom to keep the level of interest high. Much of the earlier material is now available in a number of formats. Again, we would advise that the sound quality on Classics isn't tip-top, but these are a very affordable and reasonably well-documented option and shouldn't be overlooked. The last year of the war was a good one for Norvo. The super-session with the young Gillespie and Parker from 1945 is a significant moment in the development of bebop and the music that came after it. Though as ragged as any jam session, it is full of life and energy.

The Savoy compilation brings together a huge number of tracks and extra takes – to be exact 41 cuts – offering the best available insight into how Red shaped and changed his solos. Lest anyone think that these become formulaic and ready-made, it's worth looking more closely at how Charlie Parker shaped his seemingly effortless choruses; they, too, were built up out of phrases, licks and tiny melodic cells that become more familiar as his career advanced.

In those early, 'hands-off' days, Norvo frequently encountered engineers who would unilaterally boost the sound on quieter numbers or adjust the balances to accord with conventional expectations. Most of those were overturned in the 1950–51 trio in which Charles Mingus was the outwardly unlikely replacement for Red Kelly. Just as Norvo made a pioneering contribution to the use of vibraphone in jazz, so too did the early trios contribute enormously to the development of a style of 'cool' or 'chamber' jazz that became dominant much later in the decade. One of the more significant aspects of the early trio (it may also reflect the bassist's personality to some extent, particularly in the context of an otherwise white group) is the unprecedentedly prominent role assigned to Mingus.

The later trios with Raney and Mitchell are much less obviously adventurous, though again it's the bassist's singing lines that carry much of the interest. Sooner or later when dealing with so-called 'chamber jazz', the question of its supposed 'pretentiousness' is bound to come into play. Norvo's 1957 quintet with Buddy Collette on flute and Barney Kessel on guitar strongly recalls fellow-member Chico Hamilton's sophisticated chamber jazz, with its soft, 'classical' textures and non-blues material. Titles like 'Divertimento In Four Movements' on *Music To Listen To Red Norvo By* are apt to be seen as red rags by hard-nosed boppers. It's clear, though, from the album title if not immediately from the music itself that there is a hefty dose of humour in Norvo's work. Structurally, the 'Divertimento' is unexceptionable, with a beautiful division of parts, and is as lightweight as the genre demands. Other tracks, like 'Red Sails' and the boppish thematic puns of 'Rubricity', suggest a 'different' side to Norvo which is actually present throughout his work, even in his 60s.

***** Vibes A La Red**

Progressive PCD-7112 *Norvo; Hank Jones, Jimmy Rowles (p); Lloyd Ellis (g); Milt Hinton, Gene Cherico (b); Jo Jones, Donald Bailey (d).* 74–75.

***** The Second Time Around**

Progressive PCD-7121 *Norvo; Kenny Davern (ss); Dave McKenna (p); Milt Hinton (b); Mousey Alexander (d).* 6/75.

Reissues of some sessions for Famous Door. It's a pity that, of the two groups on the first disc, there are only four tracks by the group with Hank Jones, Milt Hinton and Jo Jones – the version of 'The One I Love Belongs To Somebody Else' is so swinging you want to shout out for more (and luckily, there's a decent alternative take too). The other band has Rowles, but it also includes the dull Lloyd Ellis and Donald Bailey's very noisy drumming. *The Second Time Around* has Davern on half the tracks and is padded out with four extra takes. Famous Door's cheesy production values tend to take some of the gilt off most of their records, but at least they were recording this kind of jazz at a moment when it had been largely sidelined by other companies: Red plays well here, and though Davern doesn't seem like his most suitable partner, there's some swinging stuff.

The Nu Band

GROUP

Quartet of contemporary American improvisers.

***** Live At The Bop Shop**

Clean Feed CF002 *Roy Campbell (t); Mark Whitecage (as); Joe Fonda (b); Lou Grassi (d).* 1/01.

A seasoned band of players, though this was only their third gig. The names will at this point be familiar to those who've followed the CIMP/Cadence axis of labels, but the main point of this set is to hear Campbell, whose playing – at times a ripsaw amalgam of Don Cherry and the hard-bop school, but mostly markedly individual – has asserted its own space in recent times. Four good blowouts, and beautifully packaged, although the sound is rather remote and we seem to be standing near the back of the venue.

Dick Oatts (born 1953)

ALTO AND TENOR SAXOPHONES

Raised in Iowa, Oatts is a latter-day bopper who saw service with Red Rodney in the trumpeter's late quintet, and in the Thad Jones–Mel Lewis Orchestra. He made some records with fellow Rodney sideman, pianist Garry Dial, but is now recording for Steeplechase as a leader, basing himself in the New England area.

*****(*) All Of Three**

Steeplechase SCCD 31422 *Oatts; Dave Santoro (b); James Oblon (d).* 4/96–1/97.

***** Standard Issue**

Steeplechase SCCD 31439 *As above, except add David Berkman (p).* 97.

*****(*) Simone's Dance**

Steeplechase SCCD 31458 *As above, except Bruce Barth (p) replaces Berkman.* 5/98.

Although Berkman and Barth play their parts on the two discs they appear on, this is really all about the trio of Oatts, Santoro and Oblon. Oatts has a classic bebop tone on alto (he picks up the tenor only occasionally) and his big, unwrinkled sound was born to fly across changes; but he builds a lot of what came after bop into his thinking, so there are often moments – as on the nearly free 'Single Line', on the trio disc – when he can sound very like the young Ornette Coleman, edging towards a free play of tonality. The three men work hard to find variations in their group sound throughout *All Of Three*, from a zydeco feel on one track to the stark march figures of 'In Love And Memory'. There's a lot of weight on Santoro, who gets a deal of solo space, but he acquits himself well enough. 'Alone Together' is sustained for over 11 minutes, and they aren't struggling.

Standard Issue is a live blowing date with six expansive workouts, five standards and a blues. Oblon really gives the quartet a push on the up-tempo tunes and it's hot and forthright music, if subject to the filler which seems unavoidable in such situations. Oatts plays the Keilworth straight alto on one track here, and he returns to it twice on the studio date, *Simone's Dance*. As he says in the sleeve-note, it gives him a funkier sound, the pitching reminiscent of a low soprano; on 'Reverse Locomotion', a mock-tribute to the Coltrane tune, only constructed backwards, his playing is superbly fired-up and inventive. Peter Kontrimas gives the quartet a big and convincing sound, and across the length of the date Oatts's playing is fierce and cultured in an even balance.

***** Standard Issue Vol. 2**

Steeplechase SCCD 31482 *Oatts; Harold Danko (p); Dave Santoro (b); James Oblon (d).* 97–99.

*****(*) South Paw**

Steeplechase SCCD 31511 *As above, except add Joe Magnarelli (t).* 3/01.

The second helping of *Standard Issue*, with Danko in for Berkman, offers more intensely played music, on the expected batch of standards: another very warm occasion, though no more essential than the other one. Much meatier all round is *South Paw*. This time Oatts wrote seven of the eight themes (the exception is 'What's New'), Danko plays on only three tracks, and the open harmonic book suits Oatts's airy, punctilious approach which seems to be cooling off some of his old boppish fire. There are some very satisfying results from unpretentious situations: a minor blues with an oddly familiar melody ('King Henry'), a deceptively individual gathering of chords ('Reconcile'). Magnarelli is a very able recruit to the front line.

Hod O'Brien (born 1936)

PIANO

A veteran bebop pianist, O'Brien has surfaced only intermittently on record but made a handful of leadership dates in the '90s.

***** Opalessence**

Criss Cross Criss 1012 *O'Brien; Tom Harrell (t, flhn); Pepper Adams (bs); Ray Drummond (b); Kenny Washington (d); Stephanie Nakasan (v).* 9/84.

****(*) Ridin' High**

Reservoir RSR CD 116 *O'Brien; Ray Drummond (b); Kenny Washington (d).* 8/90.

***** So That's How It Is**

Reservoir RSR CD 155 *As above.* 9/97.

Forty years ago, Hod O'Brien made an impressive contribution to Belgian guitarist René Thomas's *Guitar Groove*, playing alongside mavericks like J. R. Monterose and Albert 'Tootie' Heath. Later years saw him associated with Chet Baker (on the Criss Cross *Blues For A Reason*) and with saxophonist Ted Brown, strong bop credentials with a label not exactly short of respectable pianists.

Unfortunately his work as leader hasn't matched up to his sterling reliability and propulsive strength as a sideman. His solos seem studied to the point of predictability and he suffers from an irritating odd-handedness that sees him switching almost on cue from 'rhythm' to 'lead' like an electric guitarist. With players of Harrell's elegance and with Adams beefing up the arrangements, *Opalessence* is the more interesting of the first two albums but, like the semi-precious sheen of the title, it seems all surface and no durability. The trio album reintroduces standards material. 'You And The Night And The Music' reflects O'Brien's innate romanticism, but at opposite extremes 'Willow Weep For Me' and 'Yardbird Suite' simply expose his limitations.

The return match on *So That's How It Is* gets by on the generous good humour of the playing and the players. O'Brien still touches no great depths and his phrases all seem to end up exactly where one expects, but it's a shapely act, and Drummond and Washington are the kind of gregarious professionals who are always good for a groove worth hearing.

***** Have Piano ... Will Swing**
Fresh Sound FSR CD 187 *O'Brien; Tom Warrington (b); Paul Kreibich (d).* 99.

***** Fine And Dandy**
Fresh sound FSR CD 190 *As above.* 00.

O'Brien's working trio is a taut, well-organized unit, held together by mutual understanding, a certain competitive edge and a lot of laughter, one suspects. These aren't the greatest recordings, and in a market saturated with piano trios, it's hard to say that they stand out, but Hod is an inventive player and there isn't a moment on either set when it sounds as though he's marking time or simply playing for his cheque. So, to that degree, recommended.

Giorgio Occhipinti

PIANO

Italian pianist–composer with an amibitious agenda.

****** The Kaos Legend**
Leo LAB CD 012 *Occhipinti; Alberto Mandarini (t, flhn); Lauro Rossi (tb); Gianni Gebbia (as, ss); Eugenio Colombo (as, ss, f); Carlo Actis Dato (bcl, bs); Renato Geremia (vn); Giovanni Macioci (clo); Giuseppe Guarella (b); Vincenzo Mazzone (d, perc).* 10/93, 10/94.

Take our word for it, there is no need to be aware of or be distracted by the legend of primeval *kaos* to appreciate this remarkable record. It is, in any case, not a continuous performance, but two pieces from the studio and two from the Ibleo Festival. That two are live merely underlines what a thoroughly competent band this is and what excellent improvisers it includes. Of their number only Gebbia and Dato are otherwise discussed in these pages, and our enthusiasm for both speaks for itself. Occhipinti himself is not a dramatic soloist, though he does often generate considerable volume against the full ensemble. His style is difficult to pin down – which is probably a good thing. Do try *The Kaos Legend.* It is one of a kind.

***** Global Music & Circular Thought**
Jazz'halo TS 012 *Occhipinti; Luca Calabresi (t, flhn); Lauro Rossi (tb); Maurizio Maiorana (cl, v); Carlo Actis Dato (bcl); Tiziana Cavaleri, Vito Amatulli (clo); Paolo Botti (vla); Giuseppe Guarrella (b); Francesco Branciamore (d).* 3/00.

A suite for cellos (who have some sequences to themselves) and nonet, this is an instance of composition which touches lightly and distantly on jazz principles, but which attempts to prove itself in a different discipline. Dato can be heard, rather remotely in the mix, trying to inculcate something a little wilder into what are otherwise strict and unwelcoming structures. Possibly very good, of its kind.

Larry Ochs (born 1949)

SOPRANO AND TENOR SAXOPHONES

Born in New York City, Ochs was a founder member of ROVA and established the Metalanguage label for creative music.

***** The Secret Magritte**
Black Saint 120177 *Ochs; Steve Adams (sno, ss, as); Bruce Ackley (ss, ts); Jon Raskin (as, bs); Chris Brown, Marilyn Crispell (p); Lisle Ellis, Barry Guy (b); William Winant (mar, perc).* 6/95.

Understandably, Ochs's solo project is still very much a ROVA family affair. All his colleagues are present, but divided into smaller groupings as are the pianists and bassists. Each subgroup is given musical materials and a set of parameters as to when and where to play. Beyond that, the music is improvised. Ochs has been inspired by Magritte's surrealism, but it's difficult to hear that influence in these pieces and it's probably best to listen to the five parts (which aren't individually or poetically named) as if they were aspects of a process rather than expressive 'works'. That isn't to say this is unrealized or 'experimental' music, merely that its greatest impact is as an evolving form rather than a finished one.

****(*) The Neon Truth**
Black Saint 120217 *Ochs; Scott Amendola, Donald Robinson (d).* 8/00.

Similar procedures at work here. These aren't freely improvised pieces, but structured forms which allow the participants the maximum freedom within set parameters. The two percussionists, who work as Drumming Core, are superbly calibrated one to the other. Their patterns are seamless and often undifferentiable, which is impressive and troubling by turns. By the same token, Ochs manages to sound as if he is up to three players, not so much by switching horns – he carries just soprano and tenor – but by changing his attack, breathing, phrase length and tonal range so quickly it hardly sounds like the same player of the previous set of phrases. And the ideas keep pouring out. So why the lowly rating? Because it's actually a very dull listen, impressive rather than enjoyable or moving.

Mark O'Connor

TENOR SAXOPHONE

Confusingly, there are two Mark O'Connors in contemporary jazz. The saxophone guy is a Texan and much younger.

***** Mirage**
Rhombus 5002 *O'Connor; Ben Lewis (p); Dan DeLorenzo, Larry Kohut, Neil Kupersmith, Jonathan Paul (b); Joe Adamik, Tom Hipskind, Mike Schlick (d).* 7/03.

This is a bright and promising debut from the saxophonist, who now bases himself in Chicago. His opening number 'The Beast' has both excitement and authority, and the title track explores some interesting rhythmic possibilities. O'Connor has assembled a strong roster of players and uses them cleverly to maximize his possibilities on this first-shot record, where it's forgivable to take on too much and attempt to show off every wrinkle of your playing style. The ballads and standard tunes are less beguiling than the originals, though he gets off a fine version of 'It's Easy To Remember' and then rounds off a very pleasant set with a brisk read of Jackie McLean's 'Little Melonae'.

Anita O'Day (born 1919)

VOCALS

The legend of Billie Holiday and the huge, vocal presences of Ella Fitzgerald, Sarah Vaughan and Carmen McRae have tended to overshadow Anita's reputation. She remains, though, one of the toughest, most dramatic and most fiercely swinging of all jazz singers, with a personality like rough-cut diamond. A great survivor, she kept on past her real sell-by date, but energized by a sheer appetite for life and music.

*****(*) Anita O'Day: Volume 1**

Masters of Jazz 122 *O'Day; Al Beck, Don Fagerquist, Torg Halten, Vincent Hughes, Norman Murphy, Tony Russo, Shorty Sherock, Joe Triscari, Graham Young (t); Roy Eldridge (t, v); Leon Cox, Billy Cully, John Grassi, Jay Kelliher, Tommy Pedersen, Pat Virgadamo, Babe Wagner (tb); Ben Freeman, Rex Kittig, Sam Listengart, Clint Neagley, Mascagni Ruffo (as); Charlie Kennedy (as, ts); Adrian Tei (as, cl); Johnny Bothwell (as); Walter Bates, Don Brassfield, Jimmy Migliore Charlie Ventura (ts); Stewart Olson (sax); Sam Musiker (ts, cl); Bob Kitsis, Teddy Napoleon, Joe Springer (p); Ray Biondi, Edward Yance (g); Biddy Bastien, Irv Lang, Edward Mihelich (b); Joe Dale, Gene Krupa (d); Howard Dulany (v).* 3–6/41.

*****(*) Anita O'Day: Volume 2, 1941–1942**

Masters of Jazz 157 *As above, except add Joe Conigliaro (tb), Sam Musiker (as, cl), Walter Bates (ts), Johnny Desmond (v).* 8, 10 & 11/41, 2 & 4/42.

*****(*) Anita O'Day: 1941–1945**

L'Art Vocal 19 *As above, except add Jon Carroll, Buddy Childers, Karl George, Mel Green, Mickey Mangano, Pinky Savitt (t), Bill Atkinson, Harry Forbes, Nick Gaglio, Milt Kabak, Greg Phillips, Dick Taylor, Bart Varsalona, Freddie Zito (tb), Chet Ball, Bill Hitz, Bob Lively, Harry Terrill (as), Eddie Meyers (as, cl), Emmett Carls, Stan Getz, Dave Madden, David Matthews, Buddy Wise (ts), Sid Brown, Bob Gioga, Joe Koch (bs), Stan Kenton, Milt Raskin (p), Bob Ahern, Teddy Walters, Frank Worrell (g), Gene Englund (b), Jim Falzone, Jesse Price (d).* 41–45.

****** Let Me Off Uptown**

Columbia Legacy CK 65265 *As above.* 41–45.

****** The Big Band Years**

President 547 *As above.* 41–45.

***** And Her Tears Flowed Like Wine**

Past Perfect 4332 *Similar to above.* 41–45.

Anita O'Day lived the jazz life. She tells about it in *High Times, Hard Times* (1983). As a young woman she worked as a singing waitress and in punishing dance-marathons. And she shot horse until her heart began to give out in the '60s and she was forced to battle her demons cold. As is immediately obvious from her combative, sharply punctuated scatting and her line in stage patter, O'Day was a fighter. As a 'chirper' with the Gene Krupa band in 1941, she refused to turn out in ball-gown and gloves, and appeared instead in band jacket and short skirt, an unheard-of practice that underlined her instinctive feminism. With Stan Kenton, she gave a humane edge to a sometimes pretentiously modernist repertoire. O'Day's demanding style had few successful imitators, but she is the most immediate source for June Christy and Chris Connor, who followed her into the Kenton band.

These early cuts with the Kenton and Krupa bands are definitive of her desire (one more commonly and erroneously associated with Billie Holiday) to be one of the guys, not so much socially and chemically, as musically. She sings like a horn player, not only when scatting, but also when delivering a song-line straight. Her phrasing has a brassy snap and polish and, even through the acoustic fog that surrounds most of these transfers, her enunciation is exact and focused. The bands were among the most exciting of their day, or ever. Kenton's outfit called for more sheer strength, but the unvarnished vivacity and raw charm of the Krupa tracks are what recommends this material. 'Let Me Off Uptown' is the classic, of course, destined to become shopworn and hackneyed in later years, but right off the mint here and characterized by a warm and playful relationship with Roy Eldridge. 'Bolero At The Savoy' is a band original, presumably worked up during rehearsals. The Columbia set recaptures the sound with great fidelity and compresses the very best of the material from Anita's two stints with Krupa, though oddly this reissue breaks the chronology to no real purpose, starting with false logic on 'Opus One' from 1945.

The Masters of Jazz sets are pretty complete, not to say exhaustive, and if anyone wants a fuller documentation of Anita's early work in those two packed years before America entered the war, then these are the sets to go for, though we have found the sound rather flat and muffled. Containing more than two hours of music, they should be enough for the most devoted enthusiast.

Much of the material is duplicated on the French compilation, which fills in the years in between and is certainly fuller and more detailed than the Past Perfect set. The work with Kenton is typically more sophisticated in conception and abrasive in delivery. A pair of tunes in the middle of the set – 'I'm Going Mad For A Pad', 'And Her Tears Flowed Like Wine' – emphasize both the strengths and the drawbacks. A valuable and thoroughly enjoyable reissue.

The Big Band Years is a catch-up volume for newcomers or for those with only a limited appetite for swing of this sort. Recently remastered, the sound is very good indeed, with a lot of presence in the woodwinds and some of the tizz taken off the brass and drums. The duet with Eldridge on 'Let Me Off Uptown' has rarely sounded better.

***** Anita O'Day, 1945–1950**

Classics 1274 *O'Day; John Carroll, Chris Griffin, Charlie Griffith, Ray Linn, Jimmy Maxwell, Larry Neal, Carl Poole, Red Solomon (t); Will Bradley, Phil Giardina, Billy Pritchard, Al Philburn, Ray Sims, Jimmy Skyles (tb); Heinie Beau, Benny Carter, Manny Gersmann, Toots Mondello, Paul Ricci, Alvy West (as); Benny Lagasse (as, cl); Art Drellinger, Bob Dukoff, Herbie Haymer, Boyd Roland, Hank Ross (ts); Hank Freeman, Harry Suchman (bs); Dave Barbour, George Barnes, Danny Perri, Tony Rizzi (g); Ralph Burns, Stan Greeman, Paul Jordan, Milt Raskin (p); Hymie Fiddleman (p, b); Bob Gudina (acc); Bob Haggart, Mel Schmidt, Art Shapiro, Phil Stephens (b); Abbie Brown, Morey Feld, Milt Holland, Don Lamond, Frank Rullo, Zutty Singleton (d); other personnel unknown.* 1/45–1/50.

The bulk of O'Day's work, and many of her best performances, was made for other leaders, but after the end of the war she turned her back on the big-band scene and struck out on her own. Her personal and professional life were turbulent in this period, as she describes in *High Times, Hard Times* and recording opportunities were sparse. It's some measure of the low esteem her work was held in that the first four tracks on this compilation, made in January 1945 with Lowell Martin directing a fine band that included Zutty Singleton and Herbie Haymer doing his Pres-for-Billy thing, remained unissued. They're fine, swinging performances – 'Them There Eyes' and 'How Come?' particularly – that deserve wider circulation.

Later material is for Bob Thiele's Signature label but only after a fallow two years. There is an edge to Anita's voice that wasn't there before, a toughened diction but also a hint of melancholy. 'Sometimes I'm Happy' carries more drama than the slight vocal would suggest. Moving from LA to New York, she returned to the studio later in 1947, also for Signature, and cut three tracks, including the novelty 'Hi Ho Trailus Boot Whip', which allows her to cut loose a bit and have fun. A further session from LA later that same year is distinguished by a couple of Benny Carter arrangements, including the unwittingly poignant 'I Ain't Getting Any Younger'.

It's further testimony to the difficulties Anita was having that the next two sessions, just six cuts, were more than two years away, and there's an unfortunate significance to the moment on 'Your Eyes Are Bigger Than Your Heart', taped in Chicago in January 1950 and the end of this chapter of the O'Day story, when the microphone fails and the take proceeds as if nothing were wrong …

★★★ Incomparable!

Verve 314 589 516 2 *O'Day; Conte Candoli, Al Porcino, Ray Triscari, Stu Williamson (t); Bob Edmondson, Lew McCreary, Frank Rosolino (tb); Kenny Shroyer (btb); Charlie Kennedy, Joe Maini (as); Richie Kamuca, Bill Perkins (ts); Jack Nimitz (bs); Lou Levy (p); Al Hendrickson (g); Joe Mondragon (b); Mel Lewis (d).* 8/60.

O'Day's Verve output is now scattered across a bewildering array of compilations. This is one of the best of the single albums currently available, a smoothly swinging date under Bill Holman's expert direction. The highlight is an inventive scat on Richard Rodgers's 'Slaughter On 10th Avenue', one of her best recorded performances of this era. She also delivers an inch-perfect reading of 'Easy Living'.

★★★(★) Swings Cole Porter With Billy May

Verve 849266-2 *O'Day; main tracks with Billy May Orchestra, unknown personnel; other tracks include Conte Candoli, Roy Eldridge, Lee Katzman, Al Porcino, Jack Sheldon, Ray Triscari, Stu Williamson (t); Milt Bernhart, Bob Edmondson, Lloyd Elliot, Bill Harris, Joe Howard, Lou McCreary, Frank Rosolino, Si Zentner (tb); Kenny Shroyer (btb); Al Pollan (tba); Charlie Kennedy, Joe Maini (as); Budd Johnson, Richie Kamuca, Bill Perkins (ts); Jimmy Giuffre (reeds, arr); Jack Nimitz, Cecil Payne (bs); Ralph Burns, Lou Levy, Jimmy Rowles, Paul Smith (p); Tal Farlow, Al Hendrickson, Barney Kessel (g); Monty Budwig, Buddy Clark, Al McKibbon, Joe Mondragon, Leroy Vinnegar (b); Larry Bunker, Don Lamond, Mel Lewis, Lawrence Marable, Jackie Mills, Alvin Stoller (d); Buddy Bregman, Bill Holman (arr).* 1/52–4/59.

★★★(★) Verve Jazz Masters 49

Verve 517954-2 *O'Day; Conte Candoli, Lee Katzman, Jack Sheldon, Al Porcino, Ray Triscari, Stu Williamson, Roy Eldridge, Joe Ferrante, Bernie Glow, Herb Pomeroy, Doc Severinsen, Ernie Royal, Nick Travis (t); Milt Bernhart, Jimmy Cleveland, Bob Edmondson, Lew McCreary, Frank Rosolino, Billy Byers, Bill Harris, Joe Howard, Willie Dennis, J. J. Johnson, Fred Ohms, Kai Winding, Lloyd Ulyate, Si Zentner (tb); Bob Brookmeyer (vtb); Kenny Shroyer (btb); Al Pollan (tba); Richie Kamuca, Jerome Richardson, Zoot Sims, Bill Perkins, Budd Johnson, Eddie Shu (ts); Sam Marowitz, Hal McKusick, Charlie Kennedy, Joe Maini, Phil Woods (as); Walt Levinsky (as, cl); Aaron Sachs, Jimmy Giuffre (ts, cl); Bud Shank (as, f); Danny Bank, Jack Nimitz, Cecil Payne (bs); Dave McKenna, Joe Masters, Oscar Peterson, Bob Corwin, Lonnie Hewitt, Hank Jones, Arnold Ross, Jimmy Rowles, Paul Smith (p); Barry Galbraith, Herb Ellis, Barney Kessel (g); Morty Cobb, George Duvivier, John Drew, Ray Brown, Buddy Clark, Monty Budwig, Larry Woods, Al McKibbon, Joe Mondragon (b); Corky Hale (hp); Jo Jones, Gene Krupa, Mel Lewis, Don Lamond, Jackie Mills, Lawrence Marable, John Poole, Alvin Stoller (d); and as for Sings The Winners and Pick Yourself Up.* 4/54–2/62.

★★★(★) Pick Yourself Up

Verve 517329-2 *O'Day; Conte Candoli, Pete Candoli, Harry 'Sweets' Edison, Conrad Gozzo, Ray Linn (t); Milt Bernhart, Lloyd Elliot, Frank Rosolino, George Roberts (tb); Herb Geller (as); Georgie Auld, Bob Cooper (ts); Jimmy Giuffre (bs); Larry Bunker (vib); Paul Smith (p); Barney Kessel, Al Hendrickson (g); Joe Mondragon (b); Alvin Stoller (d); Buddy Bregman (cond); other personnels unknown.* 1–12/56.

★★★(★) All The Sad Young Men

Verve 517065-2 *O'Day; Bernie Glow, Herb Pomeroy, Doc Severinsen (t); Bob Brookmeyer (vtb); Billy Byers, Willie Dennis (tb); Walt Levinsky, Phil Woods (as, cl); Jerome Richardson, Zoot Sims (ts); Hank Jones (p); Barry Galbraith (g); George Duvivier (b); Mel Lewis (d); Gary McFarland (arr, cond).* 61.

★★★ Sings The Winners

Verve 837939-2 *As above, except add Bill Catalano, Jules Chaikin, Phil Gilbert, Lee Katzman, Sam Noto (t); Bob Enevoldsen, Jim Amlotte, Kent Larsen, Archie LeCocque, Ken Shroyer (tb); Lennie Niehaus, Bud Shank (as); Richie Kamuca, Bill Perkins (ts); Jack Dulong (bs); Gene Harris, Lonnie Hewitt, Joe Masters, Marty Paich (p); Cal Tjader (vib); Red Kelly, Freddie Schreiber, Andy Simpkins, Larry Woods (b); Bill Dowdy, Mel Lewis, John Poole, Johnny Rae (d).* 9/56–10/62.

★★★ Time For 2

Verve 559808-2 *O'Day; Cal Tjader (vib, d); Bob Corwin, Lonnie Hewitt (p); Freddy Schreiber (b); Johnny Rae (d, perc).* 62.

The most familiar image of O'Day is at the Newport Festival in 1958, a set preserved in the movie *Jazz On A Summer's Day*. In a spectacular black dress and a hat that must have accounted for half the egrets in Louisiana, she resembles one of those subtly ball-breaking heroines in a Truman Capote story. The voice even then is unreliably pitched, but there's no mistaking the inventiveness of 'Tea For Two' and 'Sweet Georgia Brown'. The woman who sang 'The *Boy* From Ipanema' with a sarcastic elision of the 'aahhs' was every bit as capable as Betty Carter of turning Tin Pan Alley tat into a feminist statement.

O'Day never sounds quite as effective with a full band, and May's beefy arrangements tend to overpower her subtler rhythmic skills. Fortunately, the reissue of the Cole Porter set includes six bonus tracks, including band arrangements by Buddy Bregman and Bill Holman, together with a magnificent small-group 'From This Moment On', a second, rather smoothed-out version of 'Love For Sale' to compare with May's, and Jimmy Giuffre's superb, throbbing arrangement of 'My Heart Belongs To Daddy'. The May tracks are virtually all at accelerated tempos (in contrast to the Rodgers and Hart sequel) but varied with Latin ('I Get A Kick Out Of You') or 'Eastern' ('Night And Day') settings. Even so, one would much prefer to hear O'Day swing Porter to the basic accompaniment of bass and drums. She sounds unusually husky at extremes of pitch, as if from the effort of projecting over the band, but these are still more than worthwhile performances, and a great deal wittier and more stimulating than most of the 'songbook' sessions that were rife at the time.

The 1956 sessions with Bregman's orchestra amount to a survivor's testament, a hard-assed, driving gesture of defiance that is still completely musical. The version of 'Sweet Georgia Brown', which she was to include in the Newport programme, is buoyant and lightfooted like all the Bregman arrangements, but the best of the record surely has to be among the small-group tracks with Sweets Edison. An alternative take of 'Let's Face The Music And Dance' is much broader than the released version; O'Day was nothing if not subtle and rarely attempted to nudge her audience. The 1958 performances are well above average and perfect examples of O'Day's wittily daring rhythmic sense. From the mid-'50s, her closest musical associate was drummer John Poole, who anchors the bonus 'Star Eyes' on *Winners*; she sticks close by him, leaving the pitched instruments to do their own thing, and, but for the words, she might almost be involved in a percussion duet. *Winners* is a useful compilation of material from the Verve catalogue and complementary to the excellent *Jazz Masters*, which is probably the best disc for an introduction to O'Day. It includes 'Sweet Georgia Brown' with Bregman's band, a duo 'God Bless The Child' with Barney Kessel from *Trav'lin' Light*, Giuffre's 'Four Brothers' chart from *Sings The Winners* and the marvellous 'I've Got The World On A String' from *Sings The Most*, one of her best records.

All The Sad Young Men is a delicious set, perhaps more distinguished for the instrumental arrangements than for Anita's singing, which is a bit flat. The material with Tjader on *Time For 2* is every bit as imaginative, but more sparsely arranged and all the better for it. 'Mr Sandman', 'Peel Me A Grape' and 'Spring Will Be A Little Late This Year' are all classic performances, and the 1962 Hollywood session, coming at a difficult time in Anita's progress, is worth hearing and having.

**** Anita O'Day's Finest Hour

Verve 543 600 2 *O'Day; Conte Candoli, Pete Candoli, Tommy Reeves, Jack Sheldon (t); Roy Eldridge (t, v); Milt Bernhart, Jimmy Cleveland, Gil Falco, Joe Howard, J. J. Johnson, Lester Robertson, Frank Rosolino, Lloyd Ulyate, Si Zentner (tb); Phil Woods (as); Bud Shank (as, f); Stan Getz, Jerome Richardson, Zoot Sims (ts); Jimmy Giuffre (bs); Bob Corwin, Hank Jones, Joe Masters, Oscar Peterson, Paul Smith (p); Herb Ellis, Barry Galbraith, Jim Hall, Barney Kessel, Howard Roberts (g); Cal Tjader (vib); Ray Brown, George Duvivier, Joe Mondragon, George Morrow, Freddy Schreiber, Eldee Young (b); Roy Haynes, Gene Krupa, Mel Lewis, John Poole, Johnny Rae, Alvin Stoller (d); Wilfrede Vicente (perc); Russell Garcia Orchestra, Gary McFarland Orchestra, Billy May Orchestra; Marty Paich Orchestra.* 55–62.

Released in 2000, this is the definitive Anita O'Day compilation, with classic material from right through her Verve career. The sheer excitement of O'Day as a big-band singer comes out strongly on cuts with Billy May's, Marty Paich's and Gary McFarland's orchestras. From the jovial banter of 'Let Me Off Uptown' with Eldridge, to the rapid scat of 'Tea For Two', recorded at Kelly's in Chicago, to the pathos of her almost operatic 'All The Sad Young Men' with McFarland and a duet version of 'God Bless The Child' with Kessel, there's not a dud track on the set. There is, however, something wrong with the sound balancing, which shifts dramatically from track to track and even allowing for differences in the source material, should have been rectified. Otherwise, unbeatable.

***(*) Rules Of The Road

Pablo 2310 950 *O'Day; Jack Sheldon, Wayne Bergeron, Ron King, Ron Stout, Stan Martin (t); Andy Martin, Bob McChesney, Bob Enevoldsen, Bob Sanders, Alex Iles (tb); Sal Lozano, Danny House (sax, f, cl); Pete Christlieb, Jerry Pinter, Brian Williams (sax, cl); Christian Jacob (p); Trey Henry (b); Ray Brinker (d).* 3/93.

She was in great shape for this 1993 one-off, and there's none of Billie's morose self-pity in this nicely structured and immaculately played saga of life on the road. The great thing about O'Day is the fact that she survived without turning hard. She sings gamily and with wit on material like 'Here's That Rainy Day', 'Soon It's Gonna Rain' and the title-song, still pumping out that beat like she's always done. The band is absolutely Rolls-Royce, two generations of players who combine verve and expertise in almost equal proportions. The only quibble: a rather flat and unresponsive sound and a positioning that sets O'Day way out in front, not where she needed to be and always used to be – in among the guys.

Arturo O'Farrill (born 1961)

PIANO, BANDLEADER

Son of Chico and guardian of the old man's flame. Responsibility for the music chest and an admirable involvement in educational programmes has limited Arturo Jr's time in the studio.

*** Bloodlines

Milestone 9294 *O'Farrill; Papa Vasquez (tb); Andy Gonzalez, George Mraz (b); Horacio Hernandez (d); Jerry Gonzalez (perc).* 7/99.

We now associate Arturo so completely with his father's legacy that we tend to forget he was part of the Carla Bley group for a time. Here, he remembers that association with 'Walking Batterie Woman', one of Carla's most finger-breaking ideas but played with a more stately gait on this occasion. O'Farrill begins this small group encounter with a fine 'Moment's Notice' and includes Panamanian bassist Santi Debriano's 'Brava' alongside other challenging fare like Randy Weston's 'Little Susan' and Rob Munsey's unusual 'Chinas Y Criollas'. His work with dad is best represented by the swinging 'Arturo's Closet'. Of the supporting players, George Mraz is magnificent and El Negro Hernandez is as vibrant as ever, a drummer whose reputation has still not made the jump from the Latin scene to the wider community of jazz; time it did. Arturo's dexterous style isn't idiosyncratic enough to be instantly identifiable. He occasionally sounds like McCoy Tyner but there's also a strong tinge of Armando 'Chick' Corea about him.

Chico O'Farrill (1921–2001)

COMPOSER, ARRANGER

Raised in Havana, he settled in New York around 1950 and did countless Latin-style arrangements for other bandleaders during the '50s and '60s, as well as leading his own Afro-Cuban Big Band. A seminal figure in the fusion of Cuban and American rhythms and the way they will work for an orchestra.

***(*) Cuban Blues: The Chico O'Farrill Sessions

Verve 533256-2 2CD *O'Farrill; Mario Bauza, Paquito Davilla, Harry 'Sweets' Edison, Roy Eldridge, Bernie Glow, Carlton McBeath, Doug Mettome, Jimmy Nottingham, Al Porcino, Dick Sherman, Al Stewart, Nick Travis, Bobby Woodlan (t); Eddie Bert, Carl Elmer, Vern Friley, Bill Harris, Bart Varsalona, Ollie Wilson, Fred Zito (tb); Vince De Rosa (frhn); Danny Bank, George Berg, Lenny Hambro, Ben Harrod, Leslie Johnakins, Gene Johnson, Charlie Kennedy, Jose Madera, Pete Mondello, Charlie Parker, Flip Phillips, Sol Rabinowitz, Wilbur Schwartz, Fred Skerritt, Howard Terry, Eddie Wasserman, Warren Webb, James Williamson (reeds); Ralph Burns, Gene DiNovi, Rene Hernandez, Fred Otis (p); Billy Bauer (g); Irma Clow (hp); Don Bagley, Ray Brown, Clyde Lombardi, Roberto Rodriguez (b); Jo Jones, Don Lamond, Buddy Rich (d); Candido Camero, Machito, Jose Mangual, Modesto Martinez, Luis Miranda, Ubaldo Nieto, Chano Pozo, Carlos Vidal (perc); Bobby Escoto (v).* 12/50–4/54.

The ideal background source for this attractive compilation is the atmospheric novel *The Mambo Kings Sing Songs of Love*, whose author, Oscar Hijuelos, provides the liner-note. O'Farrill studied composition in Havana before going to the USA in his later 20s, where he had considerable success writing charts for Benny Goodman, Stan Kenton, Charlie Parker and Dizzy Gillespie. On the strength of a powerful vogue for Afro-Cuban music, he built an orchestra of his own round Machito's rhythm section and recorded a series of 10-inch LPs for Norman Granz's Verve and Norgran labels. Technically the material stands up better than it does artistically. The recordings are wonderfully present and alive, and the remastering offers extra breadth without distorting the syrupy warmth of the originals. At more than 150 minutes, these two discs are a treat for the Latin-jazz enthusiast. All but the very committed, though, might find the diet a tad unrelieved and the pace a little relentless. The two *Afro-Cuban Jazz Suites*, one recorded under Machito's leadership in December 1950, the other under O'Farrill's own name two years later, are relatively ambitious in scope and content, but O'Farrill was not a man to overlook a successful formula, and the harmonic spectrum is otherwise kept comfortably narrow, with a substantial emphasis on danceable rhythms. One can readily imagine the brothers in *The Mambo Kings* moping through charts like 'Flamingo' while keeping an eye on the girls at the bar. This is music that requires some other sensory attraction.

*** Pure Emotion

Milestone 9239 *O'Farrill; Dan Collette, Michael Mossman, Tim Quimette, Victor Paz, Jim Seeley (t); Robin Eubanks, Earl McIntyre, Angel Papo Vasquez (tb); Sharon Moe (frhn); Bob Franceschini, Mario Rivera (ss, ts, cl, f); Rolando Napoleon Briceno (as, cl, f); Pablo Calogero (bs); Arturo O'Farrill (p); Andy Gonzalez (b); Elizabeth Monder (koro); Steve Berrios, Manny Oquendo (perc).* 2/95.

O'Farrill resisted all sorts of blandishments to get back into the recording studio until the right project came along. This was his first recording for nearly 30 years. The wait did no harm. The charts are strong and punchy and the band palpably can't wait to work for a legend. The shorter pieces are fine: 'Igor's Dream', 'Chico And The Men' and 'El Loco Blues' all have the authentic O'Farrill stamp; but the real delight of this session is what you might call his 'Enigma Variations' – except that 'Variations On A Well-Known Theme' is an elaborate (12-minute) excursion on the melody of 'La Cucaracha'. It's a stunning piece of writing/arranging, and the band eat it up like crickets in a field of corn. Of the soloists, Eubanks and Rivera are the most impressive; both come from musical families – Mario is the son of Tito Puente. Chico's own lad is in the line-up, which must have helped remind him how much time had passed since he'd done this kind of thing last.

***(*) Heart Of A Legend

Milestone 9299-2 *O'Farrill; Arturo Sandoval, Alfredo 'Chocolate' Armenteros, Jim Seeley, Matt Hilgenberg, Robert Ingram, Kenny Rampton, Peter Olstad, David 'Piro' Rodriguez (t); Gary Valente, Sam Burtis, Papo Vasquez, Juan Pablo Torres, Jack Jeffers (tb); Maurizio Smith (f); Mario Rivera (ss); Paquito D'Rivera (cl, as); Jimmy Cozier, Marshall McDonald, Bobby Porcelli (as); Mike Migliore, Peter Brainin, Gato Barbieri (ts); Pablo Calogero (bs); Arturo O'Farrill (p); David Orquendo (g); Ilmar Gavilan (vn); Andy Gonzalez, Joe Santiago (b); Horacio Hernandez, Willie Martinez (d); Joe Gonzalez, Eddie Bobo, Candido Camero, Orlando 'Puntilla' Rios, Carlos Patato Valdes (perc); Vivian Ara, Freddy Cole (v).* 12/98–7/99.

A smashing homage to the grand old man of Afro-Cuban music. With son Arturo at the piano and an all-star assembly of the great names in the genre, from Candido to Sandoval, it's a tumultuous affair. O'Farrill's tunes and arrangements won't win prizes for subtlety or restraint, but he has a very sure hand with the kind of massed forces on show here, and for sheer excitement a chart such as 'Locos De La Habana' is hard to beat. This is a tradition of show music, and it's more about larger-than-life virtuosity and entertainment than musical profundity. It might also sound best on the kind of hi-fi systems which few can afford (and which few neighbours will tolerate). But a hearty huzzah all the same.

***(*) Carambola

Milestone 9308-2 *O'Farrill; Michael Mossman, Jon Owens, Kenny Rampton, Jim Seeley (t); Gary Valente, Jack Jeffers, Papo Vasquez, Sam Burtis (tb); Jimmy Cozier, Marshall McDonald (as); Peter Brainin, Mike Migliore (ts); Vincent Chancey, Christopher Korner (frhn); Max Schweiger (bs); Arturo O'Farrill (p); Lewis Khan (vn); John Benitez, Andy Gonzalez (b); Steve Berrios, Horacio Hernandez, Victor Jones (d); Roland Guerrero, Joe Gonzalez (perc); Graciela, Yolanda Maldonado, Sandra Rodriguez (v).* 7/00.

Less overwhelming than the last one, but for some *Carambola* may be the better record: it brings back a couple of classics in 'The Aztec Suite' (written for Art Farmer) and the Machito–Parker showpiece, 'Afro-Cuban Jazz Suite'. While there's nobody to compare with Farmer or Parker here, both are mightily performed. 'Waller Exercise' is almost a novelty item and the only dud moment; the rest is hot and often lyrically sweet in the genre's most appealing manners.

***** In Memoriam**
Orpheon 16215 *O'Farrill; various orchestras.* 50–01.

This was put out shortly after Chico's death. There are no frills, but if smartly packaged boxed sets are in the offing there's no sign of them yet, and this has to be the best introduction to O'Farrill's jazz side (there's surprisingly little extended dance music) and his debt to the great composers. 'Frenesi' and 'Chico's Cha Cha Cha' (the latter a dancehall favourite) suggest his range. The transfers are a bit inconsistent and you'll find yourself reaching for the loudness dial as the dynamics shoot up and down between tracks. Distracting, but hardly a major problem.

Dave O'Higgins

SOPRANO AND TENOR SAXOPHONES

Originally influenced by Wilton Felder of The Crusaders, later by Charlie Parker

***** Fast Foot Shuffle**
Candid CCD 79772 *O'Higgins; Barnaby Dickinson (tb); Tom Cawley (p, org); Mike Outram (g); Sam Burgess (b); Simon Lea (d); Pete Eckford (perc).* 99.

***** Big Shake Up**
Candid/Big City BCCD 79208 *O'Higgins; Martin Shaw (t, flhn); Mark Nightingale (tb); Oren Marshall (tba); Alex Garnett (bs, f); Mike Outram (g); Jim Watson (p, org, syn); Sam Burgess (b); Winston Clifford (d, v); Pete Eckford (perc).* 12/00.

Fast Foot Shuffle was made in collaboration with the JazzCotech dancers, an inventive troupe based in London's Jazz Café. O'Higgins has never forgotten the dictum that jazz must always be directed to the body first. His easy, loping swing borrows a certain energy from rock without drifting even into view of fusion, and his inclusion of solid jazz charts here, notably a reading of Coltrane's 'Giant Steps' but also the opening 'Bebop', is a sign that he wants to inscribe himself clearly into a modern jazz tradition. The band is tight and funky, solidly anchored by Burgess's acoustic and electric bass and pumped up by Outram's energetic guitar. O'Higgins plays without too much of the insidious Trane influence of this generation. He phrases somewhat similarly to Rollins on Latin numbers, and like so many British players has a touch of George Coleman in his harmonic language. Bebop and jazz funk remain the key to his solo style, though.

Big Shake Up was a chance to write material that would reflect the history of jazz from New Orleans second lines to present-day funk and fusion and to do so without resorting to parody. How successful O'Higgins has been is to some degree contingent on his players here, who are gifted and sharp, but lack a certain depth of understanding of the history they are surfing. The results are good but not outstanding, and one longs to hear how the Biggish Band fared in live gigs round this time. Marshall is as illuminating as ever, and Winston Clifford's scat vocals are a bonus. The long 'Are You Mad?' is probably the best cut; no complaints here or elsewhere about O'Higgins's writing.

Old And New Dreams

GROUP

Founded by a quartet of sometime Ornette Coleman collaborators, the group devoted itself almost entirely to Ornette repertoire, a gesture of obvious and generous appreciation, but also a subtle reminder of the part each played in the formulation of one of the most challenging aesthetics of the last 50 years.

*****(*) Old And New Dreams**
ECM 829379-2 *Don Cherry (t, p); Dewey Redman (ts, musette); Charlie Haden (b); Ed Blackwell (d).* 8/79.

***** Playing**
ECM 829123-2 *As above.* 6/80.

*****(*) One For Blackwell**
Black Saint 120113 *As above.* 11/87.

One wonders if this is how the classic Ornette Coleman Quartet might have sounded with modern recording techniques and a more democratic sound-balance. Since Coleman started to concentrate largely on his electric Prime Time band and on large-scale projects, Old and New Dreams became the foremost interpreters of his acoustic small-group music. The dirges – 'Lonely Woman' on the first album and 'Broken Shadows' on *Playing* – are by no means as dark as the composer made them, and Redman adheres much more closely to a tonal centre on all the pieces, a role he performed in the Coleman quintet of the late '60s/early '70s. Cherry also seems to be using orthodox concert trumpet on at least the majority of the tracks, and its fuller tone sits more comfortably alongside Redman than the squeaky pocket cornet. Redman's eldritch musette, a two-reed oboe with a sound not unlike a shawm, gives 'Song Of La-Ba' (*O&ND*) a mysterious timbre.

Ed Blackwell was always prominently featured with the band; the tribute album, recorded live at a Blackwell festival in Atlanta, Georgia, is entirely appropriate, given his multifarious commitment to New Orleans music, modern free jazz and, of course, the work of Ornette Coleman, to which he often stood as *il miglior fabbro.* The live versions of Ornette's 'Happy House' (from *Playing*) and the Ghanaian theme, 'Togo' (from the first album), are slightly rawer and more extended but show no significant differences over the studio versions. Indeed, the main difference between the live album and the others is the extent to which the drummer solos. It's in his work that the 'old' and 'new' of the band title truly resonate. Drawn to the rough second-line drumming of the marching bands, he adds the sibilant accents familiar from bebop, and also a strong element of African talking drum. Altogether, these three albums are a worthy monument to a great innovator, and to the men (two of them now deceased) who walked the pioneer trail with him.

Joe 'King' Oliver (1885–1939)

CORNET, TRUMPET

A key figure in the first period of jazz history, Oliver's career was a mix of triumph and miscalculation. He was bandleading in New Orleans in the early years of the century, but it wasn't until the 1910s that he really rose above the other local groups. He went to Chicago in 1919 and created what became the Creole Jazz Band around 1921, which Louis Armstrong joined in 1922. They were a sensation, and made the first important group of records by black jazzmen. His later band, the Dixie Syncopators, was less successful, and turning down an offer from New York's Cotton Club may have been a crucial mistake (it went to Duke Ellington). Though he was still touring and recording, he was out of fashion by the early '30s and was often barely able to play, owing to poor teeth. He died in Savannah, Georgia, reduced to working as a pool-hall janitor.

****** King Oliver 1923**

Classics 650 *Oliver; Louis Armstrong (c); Honoré Dutrey, Kid Ory (tb); Johnny Dodds (cl); Jimmie Noone (cl, as); Charlie Jackson (bsx); Lil Hardin, Bud Scott, Bill Johnson (bj, v); Baby Dodds, (d).* 4–10/23.

*****(*) King Oliver 1923–1926**

Classics 639 *Similar to above, except add Buster Bailey (cl); Teddy Peters, Irene Scruggs (v).* 10/23–7/26.

The third King of New Orleans, after Buddy Bolden and Freddie Keppard, remains among the most stately and distinguished of jazz musicians, although newer listeners may wonder whether Oliver's records are really so important in the light of what his protégé, Louis Armstrong, would do in the years after the Oliver Jazz Band records of 1923. Joe Oliver was in at the inception of jazz and it's our misfortune that his group wasn't recorded until 1923, when its greatest years may have been behind it: accounts of the band in live performance paint spectacular images of creativity which the constricted records barely sustain. Yet they remain magnificent examples of black music at an early peak: the interplay between Oliver and Armstrong, the beautifully balanced ensembles, the development of polyphony. Oliver's tight-knit sound, fluid yet rigorously controlled, projects the feel of his New Orleans origins, vivified by the electricity of his Chicagoan success. There is the brightness of the young Armstrong, content to follow his master but already bursting with talent, and the magisterial work of both of the Dodds brothers (only the recording stops us from hearing Baby's work in its full intensity). Ragtime and brass-band music still guide much of what Oliver did, but the unsettled ambitions of jazz keep poking through too. If the music is caught somewhere between eras, its absolute assurance is riveting and presents a leader who knew exactly what he wanted. Oliver's subsequent band, the Dixie Syncopators, was far less successful, troubled by a feeble reed section and cluttered arrangements; but its best sides – such as the furiously paced 'Wa Wa Wa' – are as good as anything from their own period.

For those who want the 1923 sessions on a single disc, the Classics survey is good enough, though remastering seems only average next to the painstaking work of Davies. Classics 639 takes off from the end of the Creole Jazz Band sessions and includes both of the Oliver/Morton duets, seven titles by the Dixie Syncopators and three tracks in which the King accompanies blues singers Teddy Peters and Irene Scruggs.

CORE COLLECTION

♛ ** King Oliver's Creole Jazz Band – The Complete Set**

Retrieval RTR 79007 2CD *As above discs, except add Clarence Williams (p), Jodie Edwards, Susie Edwards (v); omit Shoffner, Dorsey, Nicholas, Paige, Howard, Russell, Schutt, Lang, Lonnie Johnson, Williams, Barbarin, King.* 4/23–12/24.

There are 37 surviving sides by the Oliver (Creole) Jazz Band, including a handful of alternative takes. This two-disc set is the first to include all of them in one place (one disc, the Gennett coupling of 'Zulu's Ball' and 'Working Man Blues', is so rare that only a single copy of the original 78 is known to exist) and, while Robert Parker's stunning remastering in his first Jazz Classics volume will sound better to some ears, we have transferred our number one choice to Retrieval, for whom John R. T. Davies has done his usual outstanding job. They also include a pair of 1924 titles by the vaudevillians, Butterbeans And Susie, with accompaniment by Oliver and Clarence Williams, and the famous pair of duets by Oliver and Jelly Roll Morton. Modern ears are still going to find this primitive in audio terms, but surely the excitement, panache and inventiveness of this incredible band will speak to anyone with even the slightest sympathy.

*****(*) Sugar Foot Stomp**

Frog DGF34 *Oliver; Bob Shoffner, Tick Gray (t); Kid Ory (tb); Johnny Dodds (cl); Omer Simeon, Albert Nicholas, Billy Page (cl, ss, as); Barney Bigard (cl, ss, ts); Stump Evans (ss); Darnell Howard (as); Luis Russell, Richard M. Jones (p); Bud Scott (bj); Bert Cobb (tba); Paul Barbarin (d); Teddy Peters, Irene Scruggs (v).* 3/26–4/27.

***** King Oliver 1926–1928**

Classics 618 *Similar to above.* 3/26–6/28.

*****(*) Farewell Blues**

Frog DGF35 *Oliver; Ed Anderson (c); Dave Nelson, Bill Dillard (t); Ward Pinkett (t, v); Jimmy Archey, Ed Cuffee, J. C. Higginbotham (tb); Buster Bailey (cl); Ernest Elliott (cl, as); Arville Harris, Omer Simeon, Barney Bigard (cl, as, ts); Henry L. Jones (as); Bingie Madison (ts, v); Fred Skerritt (bs, v); Clarence Williams (p, v); Leroy Tibbs, Gene Rodgers (p); Goldie Lucas (g, v); Leroy Harris, Will Johnson (bj); Cyrus St Clair, Richard Fulbright, Bass Moore (tba); Paul Barbarin, Bill Beason (d); Amy Pendleton, Willie Jackson (v).* 6/28–4/31.

***** King Oliver 1928–1930**

Classics 607 *Oliver; Dave Nelson, Henry 'Red' Allen (t); Jimmy Archey (tb); Bobby Holmes, Glyn Paque, Charles Frazier, Hilton Jefferson, Walter Wheeler (reeds); Don Frye, James P. Johnson, Hank Duncan, Eric Franker, Norman Lester (p); Roy Smeck (steel g, hca); Art Taylor (bj, g); Clinton Walker (bb); Fred Moore, Edmund Jones (d).* 6/28–3/30.

***** King Oliver And His Orchestra 1930–1931**

Classics 594 *As above, except omit Frye, Johnson, Smeck and Jones; add Ward Pinkett (t, v); Bill Dillard (t); Ferdinand Arbello (tb); Buster Bailey (cl); Henry L. Jones, Bingie Madison, Fred Skerritt (reeds); Gene Rodgers (p); Goldie Lucas (g, v); Richard Fulbright (bb); Bill Beason (d).* 4/30–4/31.

Oliver's later recordings are a muddle in several ways. Illness and problems with his teeth steadily cut down his instrumental powers, and some celebrated career errors – such as turning down a New York engagement which subsequently went to Duke Ellington – ruined his eminence. Oliver could still play very well: his phrasing is usually simple and unadorned, a very different tale from Armstrong's vaulting mastery, but the quality of his tone and the starkness of his ideas can be both affecting and exhilarating. The Classics series takes a chronological route from the first Dixie Syncopators sides to the final Vocalion session of 1931, while the recent Frog reissues cover all the Vocalion and Brunswick sessions (mostly by the Dixie Syncopators). Frog's pair of editions don't especially call for a re-evaluation of Oliver's work for these labels, but they're certainly in the best sound to date. The DS sessions are perhaps at least as disappointing – after Oliver's early work – as they are exciting, with some feeble music lining up against several outstanding pieces such as 'Snag It' and 'Wa Wa Wa'. *Sugar Foot Stomp* also offers the results of two dates where Oliver backed the blues singers Teddy Peters and Irene Scruggs. In excellent sound, with all known alternative takes to hand, these are important reissues which honour the King's music.

The Victor sessions were often plodding and routine orchestral jazz that ran aground on some inept material ('Everybody Does It In Hawaii' features a bizarre appearance by steel guitarist Roy Smeck), and Oliver's own contributions are in much doubt: it's very hard to know where and when he plays, for he may even have asked some of his trumpeters to play in his own style. Nevertheless there are still many records with interesting passages and a few genuinely progressive items, such as 'Freakish Light Blues' and 'Nelson Stomp'. On a piece such as 'New Orleans Shout', where the soloist does sound like Oliver, he shows he can still play with the kind of sombre authority which befits a King. For completists, the Classics series can be safely recommended, although reproduction is, as usual, varied.

***** The Alternative Takes**

Neatwork RP 2022 *As appropriate discs above plus J. C. Johnson (p), Eddie Lang, Lonnie Johnson (g), Hoagy Carmichael (perc, v).* 12/23–9/30.

Neatwork's gathering of 18 Oliver alternates goes as far back as the 1923 Jazz Band titles for Paramount and forward to the 1930 Victor date which produced 'Nelson Stomp'. Not much here which isn't accessible elsewhere, though it makes for quite an interesting cross-section of Oliver titles, and the pair of Blind Willie Dunn alternates (with Lang and Johnson, a celebrated coupling) may be new to some. There are four Luis Russell outtakes as a makeweight.

Sy Oliver (1910-1988)

TRUMPET, VOCAL, ARRANGER

One of the great arrangers of the swing era; Oliver's charts for Jimmie Lunceford and Tommy Dorsey dominated the book of both bands, and he subsequently enjoyed studio success in the '50s and '60s when writing for vocalists. He led bands briefly himself in the '40s and returned to that gig in his later years.

**** Sy Oliver 1945–1949**

Classics 1190 *Oliver; Jimmy Maxwell, Lamar Wright, Bill Coleman, Lyman Vunk, Skeets Reid, Paul Webster, Irving Randolph, Frank Galbraith, Wallec Wilson, Berbie Privin, Tony Faso, Buck Clayton, Shad Collins (t); Billy Pritchard, Dicky Wells, Henry Wells, Gus Chappell, Henderson Chambers, Mort Bullman, Sy Schaffer, Claude Jones, Bill Granzov (tb); Eddie Barefield, Hank D'Amico, George Dorsey, Dave McRae, Willard Brown, Fred Williams, Ernie Powell, Hymie Schertzer, Johnny Mince, Wolfie Tannenbaum, Wilford Holcombe, Sid Cooper, Eddie Brown, Art Drellinger, Budd Johnson, Charlie Ventura (reeds); Billy Rowland, Billy Kyle, Buddy Weed, Charles Bateman (p); Allen Hanlon, Aaron Smith, Earl Baker (g); George Duvivier, Al Hall, Joe Benjamin, Bill Pemberton (b); Specs Powell, Wallace Bishop, Bill Beason, Jimmy Crawford, Bob Rosengarden (d); Tommy Roberts, Charles McCormick, Joe Bailey, Bobby Marshall, The Aristokats (v).* 45–5/49.

Oliver's big band of the '40s was a commercial failure, and listening to this often dated and uneventful material it's not hard to see why it didn't have any hits of the sort he'd provided for Lunceford and Dorsey. There are a few better charts, and occasionally a decent soloist slips through, but quota tunes of the order of 'Forsaking All Others' and 'Dit Dot Dit' make the disc a long haul. By 1949 Oliver was directing studio orchestras, and the final two sessions for Decca are in this vein - although with songs like 'Gran'ma Plays The Numbers' Oliver wasn't exactly returning to form.

One For All

GROUP

A conglomerate of some of the regulars who record for Gerry Teekens's Criss Cross label in New York though their early records were made elsewhere.

****(*) Too Soon To Tell**

Sharp Nine 1006 *Jim Rotondi (t, flhn); Steve Davis (tb); Eric Alexander (ts); David Hazeltine (p); Peter Washington (b); Joe Farnsworth (d).* 97.

***** Optimism**

Sharp Nine 1010 *As above, except add Dwayne Burno (b).* 98.

The group's earliest incarnation was pitched as an Eric Alexander showcase. The rising tenor star is very much the featured artist on both these releases, and it was only with the move to Criss Cross that a measure of democracy prevailed. If, as we always insist, Criss Cross is the Blue Note of the '90s and '00s, this group is the confirmation. These are unblushing hard-bop sets. 'Alfie' gives Alexander a chance to do his Rollins impression, though of course he prefers to plough his own furrow. 'Betcha By Golly Wow' is a bit of a surprise; the original tunes aren't, for the most part these are rather formulaic blowing vehicles. The second album has more standards fare and is all the better for it. 'Spring Can Really Hang You Up The Most' gives everyone a chance to emote and they do it all with a wonderfully straight face, while laughing up their sleeves at how solemn it probably sounds. A sense of fun is vital to a band of this stamp, and One For All has a big one.

*****(*) Upward And Onward**

Criss Cross 1172 *As above.* 6/99.

***** The Long Haul**

Criss Cross 1193 *As above, except Ray Drummond (b) replaces Washington.* 5/00.

***** Live At Smoke Vol. 1**

Criss Cross 1211 *As above, except Peter Washington (b) replaces Drummond.* 5/01.

Three horns and a rhythm section, absolutely no fuss, and lots of choruses to solo on. Criss Cross have made a speciality subject out of this kind of music and most of these men have led their own dates for the label. If it stands as an almost identikit hard-bop repertory band, there's enough invention going on for the records to justify themselves, even if the group speaks with no real collective voice.

That's partly because it's a slightly less compatible mix of styles than at first seems obvious. The earliest of the three sets has, on a return visit, lost a little of the lustre we heard the first time round, partly because the records have multiplied and partly because the style's ubiquitousness seems to keep on growing. If neither of the studio dates really knocks the listener down, each repays careful attention, when details begin to poke through. The most interesting moments are, if anything, the theme statements and the little orchestrations for the three horns: in tracks such as 'The Long Haul' and 'A Cry For Understanding' the sober colourings of the front line have a curiously poignant impact.

As soloists, the manner stretches from Alexander's big, sweeping choruses to Davis's thoughtful if tonally bland statements. Rotondi tends to sit in the middle rather than on top – surprisingly for the trumpet man – yet he often gets off the most exciting solo. Hazeltine makes less of an impact than he does on his own records but here and there turns in a telling original or arrangement. The most notable of those comes with another reworking of 'Betcha By Golly Wow', on the live record. A rare outing from the studios for the label, this has a hot, blustery sound to the mix which benefits some members of the band more than others. All three sets are well worth hearing, though how often one wants to return to them is more contentious.

****(*) Wide Horizons**

Criss Cross 1234 *As above.* 12/02.

Criss Cross 1234 once again does it by the numbers. The cover is tricked out like an early '60s Blue Note, all blocky graphics, emphatic typefaces and the players' names presented in a blunt 'you know us and know what we do' format. Absolutely no surprises on this fourth record for the label, which means you will love it if you like your neo-hard bop with just a splash of water, and hate it if you expect jazz to keep moving. Steve Davis's title track and the beautiful Wayne Shorter theme 'Infant Eyes' come along in the middle of the record, and if it had stopped there, all would have been well, but it starts to flag thereafter. One For All are presumably great on the night, but they don't deliver quite enough new ideas for our money.

Oregon

GROUP

Ironic that Oregon should sit so close alphabetically to the Original Dixieland Jazz Band and Kid Ory, when the music the group played seemed so very far from classic jazz idiom. An offshoot of the Paul Winter Consort, Oregon was a hugely successful side-project that makes most 'crossover' music seem unbearably bland and unthoughtful.

***** Our First Record**

Universe 42 *Ralph Towner (g, 12-string g, p, syn, c, mel, frhn); Paul McCandless (ob, eng hn, ss, bcl, tin f, musette); Glen Moore (b, cl, vla, p, f); Collin Walcott (sitar, tabla, dulc, cl, v).* 70.

****** Music Of Another Present Era**

Vanguard VSD 79326 *As above.* 73.

****** Distant Hills**

Vanguard VSD 79341 *As above.* 73.

Hugely talented in terms of individual inputs and completely *sui generis* as an ensemble, Oregon has always managed to stay just a step ahead of critical prejudice. The band was formed at a point of low commercial ebb for jazz. By the time the music had come to seem viably marketable again, the group had evolved far enough beyond their filigree'd chamber-music origins and towards much more forcefully pulsed instrumental combinations to avoid the charge that they were 'merely' a Modern Jazz Quartet for the '70s. In much the same way, their assimilation of ethnic sources from Asian and Native American music was complete long before 'world music' became a marketing niche and a critical sneer.

The early records were largely, but not exclusively, devoted to Towner compositions and were characterized by delicate interplay between his 12-string guitar and Paul McCandless's equally 'classical' oboe. The debut is still rather tentative, but delicately lyrical. The music on *Music Of Another Present Era* and *Distant Hills* was widely perceived as ethereal and impressionistic, and there was a tendency (perhaps encouraged by intermittent sound-balance on the original vinyl releases) to underestimate the significance of Glen Moore's firm bass-lines (see 'Spring Is Really Coming' on *Present Era*) or the forcefulness of Collin Walcott's tablas. The music combined evocative thematic writing ('Aurora' on *Present Era*, re-recorded on *North West Passage*; the classic 'Silence Of A Candle' and McCandless's 'The Swan' on *Distant Hills*) with abstract, collectively improvised pieces (like the 'Mi Chirita Suite' on *Distant Hills*; a neglected aspect of the band's career) and forcefully rhythmic tunes like 'Sail' (*Present Era*) which should have confounded a lingering belief that the band were too professorial to rock.

*****(*) Winter Light**

Vanguard VSD 79350 *As above.* 74.

Winter Light was in some respects a transitional album. Simpler in outline and in its commitment to song forms, it is nevertheless curiously muted, lifted only by 'Deer Path' and by a version of Jim Pepper's 'Witchi-Tai-To', an item that has remained a staple of Oregon performances ever since. The album is also interesting for its (relative) avoidance of so-called ethnic elements in favour of Native American elements; Pepper is a North American Indian.

***** Oregon In Concert**

Universe 25 *As above.* 4/75.

The generous use of overdubbing and multi-tracking led some to doubt that Oregon were a viable live concern. This disc laid that to rest at once. The long version of 'Silence Of A Candle' is absolutely magisterial, and even more abstract pieces like 'Become, Seem, Appear' underline that what Oregon was best at was real-time improvisation, either over regular beats or to no beat at all. Walcott's influence on the group is even more obvious in a concert setting. There is rarely a moment when he is not shaping or reshaping the music.

*** Together

Universe 9 *As above, except add Elvin Jones (d).* 1/77.

At first glance, this seemed an improbable association, but Jones's polyrhythms held no fears for a group of such robust sensibilities and the great jazz-man throws them nothing that Collin Walcott would not have thought of already. Perhaps because Jones is there, the group sound is tougher and indefinably jazzier this time round. McCandless doubles on soprano saxophone, which has a harder edge than his trademark oboe and cor anglais. There are even moments when Towner might be pronounced Tyner, so rich are the modalities he explores on piano and guitar. A fine record, even if it sadly prophesied the group's need to find new percussionists in the years ahead. The best tracks are the opening 'Le Vin' and the joyous 'Three Step Dance'.

*** Violin

Universe 40 *As above, except add Zbigniew Seifert (vn).* 77.

Possibly the least known of the group's records, and for many only sampled via one of the compilation albums. The recruitment of the ill-fated Polish violinist was just another of the ironies that surrounded Oregon at this time. To an extent, he reduplicates what Walcott does on the sitar (and Collin sticks to percussion, tabla and piano this time round) and he occasionally seems to get in the way of the horn-guitar front line. And yet Seifert was such a charismatic performer – the Jaco Pastorius of the small fiddle – that his sheer presence carries the day.

***(*) The Essential Oregon

Vanguard VSD 109/110 *As above, except add Zbigniew Seifert (vn); David Earle Johnson (perc).* 78.

*** Moon And Mind

Vanguard VMD 79419 2 *As above, except omit Seifert and Johnson.* 79.

***(*) Jade Muse – The Best Of Oregon

Universe 58 *As above, except add Larry Coryell (g); Zbignew Seifert, Jerry Goodman (vn); Vasant Rai (g, f, p, perc); Bob Kindler (clo); Larry Karush (p); David Earle Johnson (perc).* 71–79.

The Essential Oregon compilation tends to highlight this side of the band's work, certainly at the expense of more abstract treatments, but offers a less balanced picture of the band's work than the original releases; the additional tracks featuring Johnson and Seifert are something of a distraction.

Moon And Mind is something of a footnote to the Vanguard years and it's an odd mix of material, ranging from the band's trademark hybrid of folk, classical and ethnic styles to a relatively straight version of a jazz tune, Scott LaFaro's 'Gloria's Step', a piece which entered jazz history through Bill Evans's classic Village Vanguard performances. It's also not strictly an Oregon album, but a sequence of duets in every possible combination and with a very stripped-down approach to instrumentation; with the exception of 'Elevator' (a Towner/Walcott collaboration), it makes little use of overdubs and studio sweetening. Depending on your point of view, either an imaginative new departure or a stalled moment in the band's stately progress.

Jade Muse is yet another compilation, but this time it does seem to cover all the bases. There is the long live version of 'Silence Of A Candle', one finds 'North Star' and 'Land Of Heart's Desire' from the early albums, and a nice mixture of other stuff. There is also a track, 'Song For Jim Webb', from Larry Coryell's *The Restful Mind* on which Towner played second guitar and Collin Walcott added delicately nuanced percussion. Other material from the Vanguard catalogue makes this a very attractive purchase.

*** In Performance

Wounded Bird 304 *As above.* 11/79.

Originally on Elektra and now available again, this was only the group's second live record. For us, Walcott is still the dominant force, though how much of this is wisdom of hindsight is difficult to judge. Some tracks – 'Deer Path', the peerless 'Waterwheel' and 'Icarus' – are very beautiful, but one senses that this may have been released just to get some product out under the Oregon name and not because the group had anything new to say at this stage. A switch to another label and another sound aesthetic was just around the corner.

*** Oregon

ECM 811711-2 *As above.* 2/83.

**(*) Crossing

ECM 825323-2 *As above.* 10/84.

Oregon represents a partial return to form in the new, upbeat manner. Clearly, too, the group-sound benefited enormously from ECM's state-of-the-art production. However, the writing seems remarkably tame and formulaic, a tendency reinforced on its successor. *Crossing* has acquired a slightly sentimental aura, since it is the last Oregon record on which Walcott appeared; between recording and release, he and the group's road manager were killed in an auto accident while on tour in Europe. It is, though, a very unsatisfactory record with few compelling themes and some of the group's most banal playing.

**(*) Ecotopia

ECM 833120-2 *As above, but Trilok Gurtu (tabla, perc) replaces the late Collin Walcott.*

It is, of course, idle to speculate what might have happened had Walcott survived. A hugely talented musician, with a recording career of his own, he was in some senses the most wayward of the group's members. To some extent, the range of his skills was at a premium in the 'new' Oregon. However, he was a vital component of the group's sound, and his death was a shattering blow which almost sundered the band permanently. Trilok Gurtu was recruited only after much heart-searching and because he combined many of Walcott's strengths with an individuality of voice and technique. His group debut on *Ecotopia* is uncertain, though the album's flaws can hardly be laid to his account. The group were still in personal and artistic shock, and there is a nostalgic rootlessness inscribed in every aspect of the album, from the title onwards.

***(*) Troika

Intuition 2078 *Ralph Towner (g, syn); Paul McCandless (ob, eng hn); Glen Moore (b).* 1–11/93.

The experiment with Gurtu seemed to founder despite successful tours. Whether this was as a result of artistic incompatibility or as a result of his own burgeoning solo career is difficult to judge. *Troika* would seem to find Oregon in their natural state again. The absence of a percussionist is partially compensated for by Towner's increasingly inventive touch on the Korg synth, and Moore seems to have devised ways of playing in a much more accented and forceful style. There are a couple of free pieces which hark back to the early days, but most of the tracks are short songs that concentrate on particular harmonic and textural areas. Only the longer 'Mariella' and 'Celeste' and, to a degree, 'Gekko' and 'Tower' show much emphasis on structure as a guiding principle. There is no mistaking Oregon's viability as a creative force. This isn't one of their classics, but it is a cracking good album.

***** Beyond Words**

Chesky 252 *As above.* 9/95.

This is a curious record, beautifully done and well worth having if just for the immaculately remastered sound on this 2003 reissue, but if ever the trio were seen to be marking time, this is it. They reprise 'Silence Of A Candle' and even 'Witchi-Tai-To', which might have seemed timely in 1970, but was a period piece 25 years on.

*****(*) North West Passage**

Intuition INT 3191 *As above, except add Arto Tuncboyaciyan, Mark Walker (d, perc).* 97.

In a revealing liner-note, Towner meditates on 27 years of the band's progress, the corners turned, the understated life-changes and shifts of direction; but, underlining them all, a basic faith and confidence in the kind of music Oregon makes, which is complex, eternally unfashionable and all too susceptible to charges of portentousness. One of the key factors he identifies is the constantly renewed desire to work with percussionists. Though Walcott's name is not mentioned, he is once again the unspoken presence behind this record. The recruitment of Tuncboyaciyan and the young, talented Walker (who has a specialist interest in hand drums) was a bold and imaginative one. Arto is a more appropriate player for the group than Trilok Gurtu ever would have been, and his drumming on the opening 'Take Heart' helps demonstrate what a jazzy group Oregon could be at their peak.

McCandless once again varies his horns, introducing sopranino saxophone on 'Nightfall', but sticking pretty much to soprano saxophone and oboe. Towner more or less abandons guitar in the middle of the record to concentrate on piano and keyboards. Somehow this makes sense of the shifting pace of compositions, but one still thinks of him as a guitarist first and foremost, and it is unfortunate that he feels unwilling to concentrate on guitar for at least one Oregon disc.

***** Oregon In Moscow**

Intuition 3303 2CD *As above, except add Moscow Tchaikovsky Symphony Orchestra.* 00.

This had to happen and it's both blessing and curse. Oregon's already orchestral palette both admirably fits and doesn't need an orchestral backing. What one gets here as often as not is a kind of *concerto grosso* with no obvious structural logic. The group setting of a song like 'Icarus' is already richly textured and doesn't need any more. Other pieces, such as 'Acis And Galatea' and 'Waterwheel', are more successful, but the 'Free Form Piece' for group and orchestra is a dud from the off. Oregon fans may lap this up, but it's an unrepresentative set.

**** Live At Yoshi's**

Intuition 3299 *As Troika, except add Mark Walker (d, perc).* 01.

The appearance of Walker here is the final confirmation that Oregon have become a kind of pop band for the college circuit. His drumming is maddeningly unsubtle, and Towner's synthesizer sounds are increasingly located in the area between abstract pink noise and the slow drip of the mellotron. It's also uncomfortable to hear a band once so creative do the 3,000th version of 'Witchi-Tai-To' as a curtain piece, and add nothing whatever new to it. Very disappointing.

Original Camellia Jazz Band Of New Orleans

GROUP

A mix of old-timers and younger spirits in this New Orleans group which was active in the early '80s.

***** Original Camellia Jazz Band**

GHB BCD-304 *Clive Wilson (t); Waldren 'Frog' Joseph (tb); Herb Hall, Norman Meyer (cl); Jeanette Kimball (p); Les Muscutt (bj, g); Emanuel Sayles (bj, v); Frank Fields (b); Freddie Kohlman, Trevor Richards (d).* 2/80–5/82.

This reissues the two LPs which the band made for New Orleans Records. It's a blend of old spirits – Hall (who was a guest on the first record), Joseph, Kimball, Sayles – and younger admirers of the style, such as leader Wilson and drummer Richards. The band's quite light on its feet and though the recording is a bit flat, it's clear enough to let even Muscutt's strumming come through on the earlier session. Some of the vim seems to have gone out of the group in the later date, though, and Meyer has less to say than Hall.

Original Dixieland Jazz Band

GROUP

A group of young white players from New Orleans who hung around many of the local leaders such as Joe Oliver and picked up ideas. Under LaRocca's leadership they began working in Chicago in 1916, then went to New York and created a sensation at Resenweber's restaurant the following year. Arrived in London in 1919 and played in Hammersmith for nine months. Returned to the USA and continued popularity, but went into abeyance when LaRocca became ill in 1925. Re-formed for a brief comeback in 1936. LaRocca retired to become a builder, back in New Orleans. The records they made are acknowledged as the first jazz sessions and remained enormously influential.

*****(*) Sensation!**

ASV AJA 5023R *Nick LaRocca (c); Emil Christian, Eddie Edwards (tb); Larry Shields (cl); Bennie Krueger (as); J. Russel Robinson, Billy Jones, Henry Ragas (p); Tony Sbarbaro (d).* 2/17–11/20.

(****) The 75th Anniversary

RCA Bluebird ND 90650 *As above.* 2/17–12/21.

*****(*) In London 1919–1920**

Retrieval RTR 79023 *As above except add Artie Seaberg (cl), Don Parker (as), Henry Vanicelli (p), omit Krueger and Ragas.* 4/19–4/23.

The ODJB, for all their anomalous position, remain the place to start in dealing with the history of jazz on record. Whatever effects time has had on this music, its historical importance is undeniable: the first jazz band to make records *may* have been less exciting than, say, the group that King Oliver was leading in the same year, but since no such records by Oliver or any comparable bandleader were made until much later, the ODJB assume a primal role. Harsh, full of tension, rattling with excitement, the best records by the band have weathered the years surprisingly well. Although the novelty effects of 'Barnyard Blues' may seem excessively quaint today, the ensemble patterns which the group created – traceable to any number of ragtime or march strains – have remained amazingly stable in determining the identity of 'traditional' jazz groups ever since. The blazing runs executed by Shields, the crashing, urgent rhythms of Sbarbaro and LaRocca's thin but commanding lead cornet cut through the ancient recordings. Although the band were at the mercy of their material, which subsequently declined into sentimental pap as their early excitement subsided, a high proportion of their legacy is of more than historical interest.

Fifty-four of their recordings between 1917 and 1923 have survived, but there is no comprehensive edition currently available. Their 1917 sessions for Aeolian Vocalion, very rare records, have yet to make it to CD. The ASV CD includes 18 tracks and offers a good cross-section of their work, although a couple of undistinguished later pieces might have been dropped in favour of the absent and excellent 'Mournin' Blues' or 'Skeleton Jangle'. One can hear the band grow in stature as performers as time goes on, but the excitement of their earliest dates remains crucial to the spread of the music.

Retrieval have gathered in the 17 sides which the group made for Columbia in London. These are tough records to find in good shape, and even the usually immaculate Retrieval have had to use one or two less than pristine originals, but sound is mostly fine. One problem with these tracks is that Shields is overpoweringly forward in the acoustic mix, leaving LaRocca almost in the shadows. The earlier performances, though, are up to the ODJB's best, including 'Satanic Blues' (recorded but never issued on Victor) and the first 'Tiger Rag' to be recorded in Britain. The 1920 sessions have poorer material, but there's a bonus in the four sides the group made for OKeh in 1922–3, with a different personnel. Although a full ODJB edition is still awaited, their legacy is close to complete on CD at last.

CORE COLLECTION

****** The Original Dixieland Jazz Band 1917–1921**
Timeless CBC 1-009 *As above.* 2/17–12/21.

This CD sweeps the board, since it covers all of their Victor sessions up to the end of 1921, a perfect duplication of the Bluebird CD – but in much livelier and more enjoyable sound, which gives the best idea of the sensation this remarkable group must have caused. The *75th Anniversary* CD (above) remains a decent alternative, but Timeless's remastering is clearly superior.

Original Indiana Five

GROUP

This was a very popular recording outfit which – despite its name – had little to do with Indiana, working and recording in New York during the '20s under the leadership of drummer Tom Morton.

***** The Original Indiana Five Vol. 1**
Jazz Oracle BDW 8019 *Johnny Sylvester (t); Vincent Grande, Charlie Panelli (tb); Nick Vitalo (cl, as); Johnny Costello (cl); Newman Fier, Harry Ford (p); Tony Colucci (bj); Tom Morton (d, v).* 5/23–5/25.

***** The Original Indiana Five Vol. 2**
Jazz Oracle BDW 8030 *Mickey Bloom, James Christie (t); Pete Pellizi (tb); Nick Vitalo (cl, as); Louis Measto (cl); Nick Moleri, Harry Ford (p); Christian Maesto, Tom Morton (d); Maggie Jones (v).* 4–12/25.

***** The Original Indiana Five Vol. 3**
Jazz Oracle BDW 8031 *James Christie, Tony Tortomas, Sammy Castin (t); Pete Pellizzi (tb); Nick Vitalo, Gus Fetterer (cl, as); Bill King (ts); Harry Ford (p); Tony Colucci (bj); Tom Morton (d); Johnny Ryan (v).* 1–10/26.

***** Everybody Stomp**
Frog DGF23 *Tony Tortomas (t); James Christie (c); Pete Pellizzi (tb); Nick Vitalo (cl); Harry Ford (p); Tony Colucci (bj); Tom Morton (d); Tony Pace, Irving Kaufman (v).* 10/25–5/29.

These are certainly pioneering reissues, as hardly anything by the OI5 has made it to either vinyl or CD in the past, despite their evident popularity (they made more than 100 titles during the '20s). The music is a closely argued example of the small-group jazz which several New York groups of the day pursued: perhaps not quite the equal of the Original Memphis Five, given that there were no soloists in the band the equal of Phil Napoleon and Miff Mole, but this is really ensemble music which picks up from the cues of the Original Dixieland Jazz Band. The Frog reissue is a decent sampler of some of their sessions, but it has been trumped by the comprehensive three-disc Jazz Oracle edition. Not only are the transfers excellent, but the documentation is superb, offering formidable research into the lives of all the leading players in the group, and there are a few ancillary sessions which are not strictly the work of the OI5 but which are closely related. Even though little of this has a pressing claim on the general listener, specialists will be impressed by the standard of these issues, and may be surprised at the heat which some sides generate.

Original Memphis Five

GROUP

Something of a generic group-name for white small groups of the '20s, it was first used by Phil Napoleon for his small band in New York, commencing in 1920, then in scores of sessions from 1922, although it was also used occasionally by Red Nichols and Miff Mole. Napoleon carried on using it, even into the '80s!

***** Columbias 1923–1931**
Retrieval RTR 79026 *Phil Napoleon (t); Miff Mole, Charles Panelli, Tommy Dorsey (tb); Jimmy Lytell (cl); Jimmy Dorsey*

(cl, as); Frank Signorelli (p); Ray Kitchingman (bj); Jack Roth, Ted Napoleon (d); Billy Jones, Joseph A. Griffith (v). 5/23–11/31.

At the moment we think this is the only disc dedicated to the earlier work of the group that came to be, usually, the Original Memphis Five, although even this one goes as far forward as 1931. Improvisation was often done more in breaks than in solos, but this is primarily an ensemble music, still edging away from the ODJB. It would be admirable to see this huge group of titles (more than 400 78-r.p.m. masters) given a proper reissue: so far, although there are some other tracks on a Timeless various-artists disc, not much progress. Excellent transfers of these 78s, all but eight of which were recorded acoustically. Phil Napoleon and Lytell remain the key players: Napoleon's little arpeggiated rip, which he uses to start a phrase, was how he decided to swing, and next to a sophisticate like Mole he can seem stolid, but at least he was a steadfast presence. Lytell is agile, but he never really progressed as a stylist – Jimmy Dorsey, who is on the 1931 'reunion', shows him up. An entertaining piece of history.

Niels-Henning Orsted Pedersen (born 1946)

DOUBLE BASS

The great Dane is one of the most prolific recording artists in the music. The number and diversity of his associations are enormous, though he is probably best known for his work with near-namesake Oscar Peterson; he also worked with a huge variety of visiting Americans when he was house bassist at the Jazzhus Montmartre in Copenhagen. Something of a prodigy, NHOP switched from piano to bass quite late and seemed to acquire his mature voice almost instantly, even receiving an offer to join the Basie orchestra.

***** Jaywalkin'**

Steeplechase SCCD 31041 *Orsted Pedersen; Philip Catherine (g); Ole Kock Hansen (p); Billy Higgins (d).* 9 & 12/75.

***** Double Bass**

Steeplechase SCCD 31055 *Orsted Pedersen; Sam Jones (b); Philip Catherine (g); Albert 'Tootie' Heath, Billy Higgins (d, perc).* 2/76.

***** Pictures**

Steeplechase SCCD 30168 *Orsted Pedersen; Kenneth Knudsen (p).* 12/76.

****** The Bassic Trio**

Steeplechase 37037/8 2CD *Orsted Pedersen; Philip Catherine (g); Billy Hart (d).* 10/77.

*****(*) Dancing On The Tables**

Steeplechase SCCD 31125 *Orsted Pedersen; David Liebman (ts, ss, af); John Scofield (g); Billy Hart (d).* 7 & 8/79.

Even though misspelt and mis-indexed (and we have been guilty of the odd inconsistency ourselves), NHOP's credits as a sideman almost defy belief. He plays on well over 100 currently available CDs, backing the likes of Chet Baker, Kenny Drew, Lee Konitz, Ben Webster and (crucially) Dexter Gordon and Oscar Peterson. He has recorded with younger-generation players as far apart in style as Niels Lan Doky and Anthony Braxton. If his playing on the two Steeplechases from the Club Montmartre in Copenhagen sounds particularly confident, that is because he spent much of his later 20s as house bassist there. His technique as a young man was staggering, combining forceful swing with great melodic and harmonic sense and a sure-fingeredness that gave his big, sonorous tone an almost horn-like quality.

Equally consistent as a leader, NHOP probably hasn't received his due of praise for his own records. They are all broadly of a piece, largely standards-based, with the group sessions placing greater emphasis on swing, and the duos on a more musing, intimate quality; the ratings above give a reasonable sense of their respective merits. A word, though, for the duo with Knudsen, omitted from our previous edition. This is a quality performance from both men, dominated by the pianist's compositions, but including two of NHOP's best pieces, 'Afternoon's Sentiment' and 'School Song'. Worth finding. The bassist has enjoyed a particularly fruitful relationship with guitarist Philip Catherine, who shares many of his virtues; the two in combination are responsible for some formidably beautiful music. The punning *Double Bass* is an interesting experiment that almost falters when a second drummer joins the group, doubling not just the bass lines but the whole rhythm section; Catherine is left with an unenviable continuity job, but 'Au Privave' (Oscar Peterson's favourite Charlie Parker theme) and Coltrane's 'Giant Steps' fare remarkably well. *The Bassic Trio* brings together two live sets from Café Montmartre onto a double CD. As with many of these budget-price sets, we're not sure there's enough material to justify the duration, but certainly they're value for money. *Dancing On The Tables* explores less familiar materials and tonalities. Liebman's saxophone playing is sufficiently light and spacious not to swamp the foreground, and NHOP produces some intriguing rapid-fire counterpoints to the guitarist.

****(*) The Eternal Traveller**

Original Jazz Classics OJCCD 966 *Orsted Pedersen; Ole Kock Hansen (p); Lennart Gruvstedt (d).* 6 & 11/84.

Apart from the opening 'Moto Perpetuo', where NHOP tackles a wrist-breaking Paganini solo, this is a fairly routine and conventional record as far as repertoire is concerned. However, the decision to mix the bass very far forward and keep accompaniments to a minimum doesn't yield the results Niels-Henning seems to have been looking for in his role as producer. The trio tracks often might just as well have been done as solos, for all the impact bass and drums actually make. It's an unfortunate irony that one of his most prominent recordings, issued by Pablo rather than a smaller European label, should be so poorly representative of his greatest skill, which is as a group player.

***** Catalonian Fire**

Steeplechase SCCD 31017 *Orsted Pedersen; Tete Montoliu (p); Albert Heath (d).* 9/94.

Montoliu is a remarkable pianist, fiery as the title suggests, but blessed with a graceful subtlety that comes across more often than not on this pungent trio session. NHOP's bass-playing always sounds more staccato and percussive when Tootie Heath is around. 'Falling In Love With Love' and 'Au Privave' are both outstanding, but there isn't a moment when the quality drops below VG.

*****(*) Friends Forever**

Milestone MCD 9269 *Orsted Pedersen; Renee Rosnes (p); Jonas Johansen (d).* 8/95.

Recorded as a tribute to the late Kenny Drew, with whom NHOP recorded over many years, *Friends Forever* is unmistakably in the spirit of the great pianist. Drew would have loved the straightforward and funky version of 'The Shadow Of Your Smile' and he could not have failed to be intrigued by the unison line of 'Kenny', the bassist's most explicit memorial. Rosnes was the perfect choice for the job; she obviously knows Drew's work pretty well, and she quotes more than once from *Dark Beauty*, his duo record with NHOP. Johansen is inevitably a quieter partner, but his brushwork on the closing 'Future Child – Friends Forever', a delicate bass feature with a glorious piano/*arco* middle section, is exemplary. The sound is very good indeed and Phil De Lancie's mastering is everything you would expect from this good friend of jazz music.

**** Those Who Were

Verve 533232-2 *Orsted Pedersen; Johnny Griffin (ts); Ulf Wakenius (g); Victor Lewis, Alex Riel (d); Lisa Nilsson (v).* 5/96.

***(*) This Is All I Ask

Verve 539695-2 *Orsted Pedersen; Phil Woods (as); Oscar Peterson (p); Ulf Wakenius (g); Jonas Johansen (d); Monique, Monica Zetterlund (v).* 7 & 9/97.

These two records are the work of a man entirely at peace with himself and his music. There is nothing to prove, no rival reputations to beat down. Niels Lan Doky's intuitive touch at the controls gives both a clarity and a warmth that make the music come alive. NHOP's opening on 'Our Love Is Here To Stay', first track on the faintly elegiac *Those Who Were*, demonstrates yet again what a master of harmony and time he is. As before, he programmes intelligently, including a Carl Nielsen theme, the title-song (a feature for the lovely Lisa Nilsson) and 'You And The Night And The Music', which is one of two guest spots for Griff, playing with his now familiar relaxed intensity. The other, 'The Puzzle', is marginally less successful. The second of the two albums is marked by a guest appearance from old boss Oscar Peterson, sounding fleet and unhampered on the traditional 'I Skovens Dybe Stille Ro', a tune that lends itself well to a jazz interpretation. As before, NHOP also includes a classical piece, this time a Bartók fantasia, played with completely idiomatic understanding as an unaccompanied solo. Elsewhere, Wakenius and Johansen are able companions and the guest saxophonist this time out is much more obviously in the bassist's bag. Woods sounds great on the title-piece, blowing with a warm, waxy quality. The vocals are attractive enough, but not particularly compelling. We remain Zetterlund sceptics, and her near-namesake Monique sounds ill at ease in a jazz context.

*** Hommage – Once Upon A Time

Emarcy 513 189 2 *Orsted Petersen; Palle Mikkelborg (t, flhn); Palle Bolvig, Jan Kohlin (t); Axel Windfeldt (tb); Flemming Madsen, Jan Zum Vorde (sax); Mogens Durholm (v); Ars Nova Choir; other personnel.* 97.

A lovely collaboration between NHOP and trumpeter Mikkelborg, who brings a characteristic richness of tone and density of texture to these delightful sessions. There is an almost autumnal maturity and poise to the bassist's recent solo work. While still very much rooted in bebop harmony and the need to drive the line forward, he is much more inclined than of yore to dwell on ideas for their sheer beauty, and the session is marked by some of his very best playing on record. The closing 'September Song (Epilogue)' is masterly.

Anthony Ortega (born 1928)

ALTO, TENOR, BARITONE AND SOPRANO SAXOPHONES, FLUTE, CLARINET, BASS CLARINET

A sideman with Lionel Hampton, then a leader in and around Los Angeles, Ortega incorporated some Ornette-like thinking into his basic bebop grammar. His early albums for Revelation were reissued by hatART in the '90s. Later records are scarce but worth seeking out.

*** A Man And His Horns

Blue Moon BMCD 1607 *Ortega; Hank Jones, Einar Iversen (p); Addison Farmer, Ivar Borsøm (b); Ed Thigpen, Karkl Otto Hoff (d).* 54–61.

This is an extraordinary collectors' piece, coupling up two exceptionally rare albums: a ten-inch LP for Vantage, made from a radio broadcast in Norway in 1954, and a 1961 set made for the Herald label with Jones, Farmer and Thigpen, in which Ortega overdubbed a section's worth of horns on to various tracks. The Norwegian set is in rough airshot sound but finds the young Ortega in urgent, Parkerish form: he embroiders 'Laura' with all sorts of detail. Unfortunately, the master seems to develop a seasick wobble towards the end. The American session is a typical curio of its time, but again the severe intensity of the saxophonist cuts through the procedural weight.

*** Earth Dance

Fresh Sound FSR CD 194 *Ortega; Art Farmer (t); Ray Starling (t, mel); Jimmy Cleveland (tb); Dick Hafer (ts, bcl); Jay Cameron (bs); Bobby Timmons (p); Dick Wetmore (vn); Earl May (b); Ed Thigpen (d).* 58, 59.

Originally released on Bethlehem with the title *Jazz For Young Moderns* (nobody ever noticed the subtitle *And Old Buzzards, Too*) this fine reissue still comes over strongly and with considerable invention. There are some unusual sonorities in the line-up: mellophone, bass clarinet, a fiddle; and there's a strong sense of restless invention in Ortega's solos on 'These Foolish Things' and the utterly original 'Cinderella's Curfew'. Worth tracking down, though it'll make you wonder why Ortega isn't better known.

*** New Dance

hatOLOGY 6065 *Ortega; Chuck Domanico, Bob West (b); Bill Goodwin (d).* 10/66, 1/67.

As well as reissuing key work from his own deleted back catalogue, Werner Uehlinger has also been picking up neglected obscurities on small labels. These saxophone-bass duets and trio recordings were originally released on Revelation, to no apocalyptic fanfare whatsoever. Listening casually, one can see why they caused no great stir. Ortega comes across as a rather more rasping version of Lee Konitz. And yet one can also hear what intrigued Uehlinger. These are clever, dancing pieces. The originals, 'Sentimentalize' and 'Conversation Piece' in particular, inspire a lot of intense playing, and there is wonderful extended version of the *Sandpiper* theme, 'The Shadow Of Your Smile'.

*****(*) Anthony Ortega On Evidence**

Evidence EVCD 213 *Ortega; Sylvain Kassap (bcl); Manuel Rocheman (p); Didier Levallet (b); Jacques Mahieux (d).* 4/92.

***** Scattered Clouds**

hatOLOGY 555 *Ortega; Mike Wofford (p); Joe Labarbera (d).* 7/00.

A huge gap, with some intriguing 'lost' sessions in between, which make the story frustratingly hard to follow. Ortega has lost none of his adventurousness. The 1992 session is a welcome return to the studios and finds him in ruminative rather than urgent mood: the tempos are often dreamily slow, the melodies (all originals by Ortega or his wife, bar Mal Waldron's 'Warm Canto') poignantly caressed, and his previously astringent tone has softened a little. But there are still improvisations of absorbing skill and cumulative power: he's again a trifle unconvincing on the 'out' moments of 'Gone Again', yet the spiralling trails of 'Avignon' or 'Norge' are bewitching in their quiet intensity, with a new interest in soprano offering a change of timbre. The rhythm section are fine, even if Rocheman is occasionally a shade too flowery in some of his solos, and Kassap appears only on the closing 'Warm Canto', a sparse, almost elemental treatment.

Scattered Clouds is akin, perhaps, to a latter-day date by a close contemporary of Ortega's, Lee Konitz. Standards such as 'Body And Soul' and 'Night And Day' are mined for jumping-off points where the saxophonist can spool out his improvisations. Wofford gives him plenty of feeds along the way. It's able, competitive improvising, but it does suggest Konitz on an average day: Ortega hasn't, in the end, established enough personal ground to make this music really grip or stand out.

Kid Ory (1886–1973)

TROMBONE, VOCALS

Composer of the immortal 'Muskrat Ramble' and an innovative player who made much use of mutes, slurs and other devices, Ory has a tutelary place in the history of recorded jazz. He also confounds Scott Fitzgerald's famous dictum about there being no second acts in American creative lives; having helped usher in the first jazz generation, the Kid was there to take part in its great revival.

****** Ory's Creole Trombone**

ASV CD AJA 5148 *Ory; Thomas 'Mutt' Carey, George Mitchell, Joe 'King' Oliver, Bob Shoffner (c); Louis Armstrong (c, v); Johnny Dodds, Dink Johnson, Omer Simeon (cl); Stump Evans, Albert Nicholas, Billy Paige (cl, as, ss); Darnell Howard (cl, as); Barney Bigard (cl, ts, ss); Joe Clarke (as); Lil Hardin Armstrong, Jelly Roll Morton, Luis Russell, Fred Washington (p); Bud Scott, Johnny St Cyr (bj); Ed Garland, John Lindsey (b); Bert Cobb (bb); Paul Barbarin, Ben Borders, Andrew Hilaire (d).* 6/22–4/44.

***** Kid Ory, 1922–1945**

Classics 1069 *Ory; Thomas 'Mutt' Carey (c); Darnell Howard, Dink Johnson, Omer Simeon (cl); Joe Darensbourg (cl, v); Fred Washington, Buster Wilson (p); Bud Scott (g); Ed Garland (p); Ben Borders, Minor Ram Hall, Alton Redd (d); Cecile Ory (v).* 22–45.

****** Kid Ory's Creole Jazz Band**

GHB BCD 10 *Ory; Thomas 'Mutt' Carey (t); Darnell Howard, Omer Simeon (cl); Buster Wilson (p); Bud Scott (bj, v); Ed Garland (b); Minor Ram Hall, Alton Redd (d).* 8/44–11/45.

*****(*) Kid Ory: '44–'46**

American Music AMCD 19 *Ory; Thomas 'Mutt' Carey (t); Barney Bigard, Albert Nicholas, Joe Darensbourg, Wade Whaley (cl); L. Z. Cooper, Buster Wilson (p); Huddie Leadbetter, Bud Scott (g, v); Edward Garland (b); Charlie Blackwell, Minor Ram Hall, Zutty Singleton (d).* 1/44–5/46.

***** Creole Classics**

Naxos 83421 *As above, and some below.* 44-47.

***** At The Green Room: Volume 1**

American Music AMCD 42 *As above, except omit Bigard, Nicholas, Whaley, Leadbetter, Singleton, Blackwell.* 2/47.

***** At The Green Room: Volume 2**

American Music AMCD 43 *As above.* 2/47.

***** At Crystal Pier, 1947**

American Music AMCD 90 *Ory; Andrew Blakeney (t); Joe Darensbourg, Archie Rosati (cl); Buster Wilson (p); Bud Scott (g); Ed Garland (b); Minor Ram Hall (d).* 8/47.

***** King Of The Tailgate Trombone**

American Music AMCD 20 *As above, except add Andrew Blakeney, Teddy Buckner (t).* 48–49.

Kid Ory's '40s albums (on Good Time Jazz) had Creole cooking tips printed on the sleeves. On his comeback, after nearly a decade out of music fattening up chickens, the trombonist's rhythmic tailgating style was still as salty as blackened kingfish and as spicy as good gumbo. Ironically, he spent much of his life away from Louisiana, going to California for his health just after the First World War, where he recorded the first ever sides by an all-black group, 'Ory's Creole Trombone' and 'Society Blues', in 1922. For some purists, these – collected on the ASV compilation, *Ory's Creole Trombone* – and not the Original Dixieland Jazz Band's earlier discs, mark the real start of jazz recording.

The Classics compilation contains only sessions recorded under Ory's name. Leadership switched to Mutt Carey in 1925, and it wasn't until 1944 that the trombonist tried to put together a revived version of the original group. Hence a large gap in the documentation which renders the chronology pretty redundant and enhances the desirability of the ASV set.

A man can learn a lot watching chickens forage, though. Ory's comeback coincided with the big Dixieland revival, and he turned an instinct for self-marketing to lucrative effect. Notoriously difficult to work for, he was particularly demanding of his trumpet players. When Mutt Carey died in 1948, Ory used the equally brilliant Teddy Buckner and later Alvin Alcorn in what was to be one of the best and most authentic of the revivalist bands. Kid Ory's Creole Jazz Band lasted until the '60s, by which time his exemplary stamina was failing and the big glissandi and slurs were sounding slightly breathless. Ory was a fine technician who cultivated a sloppy, 'rough' effect and a loud, forthright delivery that led some listeners to dub him a primitive. Like all the great Delta players, though, he thought of the whole group as a single instrument into which his own voice slotted perfectly.

The ASV also includes some important sides from 1926 with King Oliver and Louis Armstrong, and a group called the New Orleans Wanderers which was effectively the Hot Five without

Pops. There is also material from later that year with Jelly Roll Morton and a jump forward in time to the revivalist band of 1944. A very valuable collection indeed.

The first American Music disc is mostly airshot material from Standard Oil-sponsored broadcasts in the first half of 1946. There is a brief, fascinating encounter with Huddie Leadbetter, better known as Leadbelly, on 'Bye'N'Bye' and 'Swing Low, Sweet Chariot', but for the most part it's the group with Carey or Joe Darensbourg, with four studio tracks showing Albert Nicholas in particularly good lip. There is some excellent material from the Green Room in San Francisco; content-wise nothing out of the ordinary except for a rather moving version of the 'Rifle Rangers (1919 March)' which must have pleased any old soldiers in the room. *King Of The Tailgate Trombone* is less individual, Blakeney and Buckner (on this 1949 occasion) rather indistinct and waffly. Sound-quality varies on all these but isn't significantly better or worse than the norm for the period, and Ory himself always took care to come through at the front, loud and firm, just in case anyone forgot his name.

***** Portrait Of The Greatest Slideman Ever**

Upbeat 129 *Similar to above discs.* 44, 71.

Early and late Ory on one disc, which defies logic, but may appeal to those who only want to sample his long career.

***** Kid Ory, 1945-1950**

Classics 1183 *As various discs above.* 45–50.

Most of this material is available in various forms, as can be seen above, but the Classics format has a certain chronological simplicity and anyone who has the earlier volumes may well want to continue the series with this. Detail is as for previous entries and there is the usual *pro forma* statement: Classics sound isn't of the absolute best.

*****(*) Live At The Beverly Cavern – 1949**

504 CD85 A/B 2CD *Ory; Andrew Blakeney (t); Joe Darensbourg (cl); Buster Wilson (p); Ed Garland (b); Minor Ram Hall (d).* 49.

Transcription discs from 1949, covering Ory's residency at the Hollywood club immortalized in the title, this is a good way to audition the trombonist's music in this period: sound is generally clear (though the many subtleties in Hall's drumming are often obscured), the front line is in fine fettle and the set-list includes all of Ory's speciality numbers. By the middle of the second disc some of the same numbers are coming out again and, since 504 are promising a further three CDs from the same source, most may feel that this is enough, but it's a fine way to hear how this important group worked at length in a sympathetic setting.

***** Plays The Blues**

Storyville STCD 6035 *Ory; Alvin Alcorn, Teddy Buckner, Rico Valesti (t); Phil Gomez, Bob McCracken, George Probert (cl); Harvey Brooks, Don Ewell (p); Ed Garland (b); Minor Ram Hall (d).* 5/53–2/55.

*****(*) This Kid's The Greatest**

Good Time Jazz GTCD 12045 *Ory; Teddy Buckner (c); Pud Brown, Phil Gomez, Bob McCracken, George Probert (cl); Don Ewell, Cedric Haywood, Lloyd Glenn (p); Julian Davidson, Barney Kessel (g); Wellman Braud, Morty Cobb, Ed Garland (b); Minor Ram Hall (d).* 7/53–6/56.

*****(*) Kid Ory's Creole Jazz Band, 1954**

Good Time Jazz GTJ 12004 *Ory; Alvin Alcorn (t); George Probert (cl); Don Ewell (p); Bill Newman (g, bj); Ed Garland (b); Minor Ram Hall (d).* 8/54.

***** Sounds Of New Orleans: Volume 9**

Storyville STCD 6016 *Ory; Alvin Alcorn (t); Albert Burbank, Phil Gomez, George Probert (cl); Don Ewell (p); Ed Garland (b); Minor Ram Hall (d).* 5/54–2/55.

***** Kid Ory's Creole Jazz Band**

Good Time Jazz GTJ 12008 *Ory; Alvin Alcorn (t); George Probert (cl); Don Ewell (p); Barney Kessel (g); Ed Garland (b); Minor Ram Hall (d).* 12/55.

*****(*) The Legendary Kid**

Good Time Jazz 12016 *Ory; Alvin Alcorn (t); Phil Gomez (cl); Lionel Reason (p); Julian Davidson (g); Wellman Braud (b); Minor Ram Hall (d).* 11/55.

***** Favorites!**

Good Time Jazz 60-009 *Ory; Alvin Alcorn (t); Phil Gomez (cl); Cedric Haywood (p); Julian Davidson (g); Wellman Braud (b); Minor Ram Hall (d).* 55.

The Good Time Jazz catalogue is now pretty much up to date, and frankly there's very little to choose between individual items. The titles are confusingly unvaried and the Good Time Jazz discs have all the legendary Crescent recording sessions, excellent readings of 'Maple Leaf Rag', 'Ory's Creole Trombone', 'Careless Love Blues' and 'Oh, Didn't He Ramble', though not, unfortunately, Ory's own 'Muskrat Ramble', which was one of the revival hits of the mid-'50s. It's to be found on the good Storyville, with Alvin Alcorn's trumpet going sharp as a tack in and out of the melody, and also on *1954*.

Plays The Blues has been augmented with five tracks not included on the LP release. Of these, 'Blues For Jimmie Noone' and 'Wolverine Blues' are the most substantial, genuine additions to the Ory catalogue. Nothing else is as compelling and only serious collectors will feel the need for 'Wang Wang Blues' or 'Sugar Blues'.

***** In Denmark**

Storyville 6038 *Ory; Henry 'Red' Allen (t, v); Cedric Haywood (p); Wellman Braud (b); Minor Ram Hall (d).* 58.

This wasn't the easiest of associations, though very bankable at a time when New Orleans jazz was once again in vogue. Allen's was a restless and exploratory group, while by this stage Ory had pretty much decided that his style was set in stone. Red pushes the pace along and still sounds vital and alert, while the Ory group seems happy to dodge along at a consistent tempo. There are even moments when the trumpeter jumps a measure ahead. The programme of material is unsurprising, with 'St James Infirmary' a high point and bright, breezy renditions of 'Clarient Marmalade', 'Muskrat Ramble' and 'Indiana/Sheik Of Araby'. Ory's rewritten lyrics to 'I Wish I Could Shimmy Like My Sister Kate' suggest that Katherine has gone to the bad entirely. Entertaining stuff. We fear that there may be a long wait for the Allen–Ory studio dates on Verve, as well as the others which the Kid led for the same label, but they have all been put together in a super eight-disc set on Mosaic.

Mike Osborne (born 1941)

ALTO SAXOPHONE

Born in Hereford, Osborne became a major figure in the British contemporary scene of the '60s and '70s, although most of his recorded work is out of print and he has been inactive through illness since the early '80s.

****** Outback**

Future Music FMR CD 07 *Osborne; Harry Beckett (t, flhn); Chris McGregor (p); Harry Miller (b); Louis Moholo (d).* 70.

****** Shapes**

FMR CD 10 *Osborne; John Surman (ss, bs); Alan Skidmore (ts); Earl Freeman, Harry Miller (b); Louis Moholo (d).* 2/72.

For close to 20 years illness has silenced one of the most powerful and emotionally stirring voices in British jazz. A Mike Osborne gig, with whatever line-up, was a furious dance of disparate parts: simple hymnic tunes, wild staccato runs, sweet ballad formations and raw blues, all stitched together into a continuous fabric that left most listeners exhausted, and none unmoved. Osborne's early album, *Outback*, was rarely seen and highly collectable in its original LP issue on Turtle. With the Ogun catalogue, *All Night Long*, *Border Crossing*, *Tandem* and *Marcel's Muse* out of print, this is a more than worthwhile reissue. Readers of *The Wire* magazine voted *Outback* one of the records they would most like to see on CD, and one can immediately hear why. Ossie's wailing, turbulent voice fills up the room. He was probably always heard to greater advantage in the pianoless trio with Louis Moholo and the late Harry Miller, but before this session he invited friends Harry Beckett and Chris McGregor (who also has since passed away) to join in. Beckett lightens the sound with blinks of pure sunshine, but he's capable of a darker, freer tonality as well. There are just two long tracks, the title-piece and the more sanguine 'So It Is'. On the original LP they occupied opposite sides. Here, though, it's possible to hear them as two sides of a single musical personality, undoubtedly troubled, fiercely questing, but full of quiet humour as well.

Shapes is a somewhat different proposition, a much more turbulent and detailed record. The addition of two more saxophones and a second double bass creates possibilities that Osborne instantly knows how to exploit. Even given the rather one-dimensional recording techniques of 30 years ago, the horns are wonderfully separated, and this is testimony more to the players than to the engineers at Pye studios. The two-part title-track is an unusually abstract set of themes, certainly unusual by Osborne's expressive standards, but it is a formidably accomplished performance. The absence of piano throws a lot of weight on the two bass players, and Miller and Freeman lay down a richly suggestive matrix of sound for the front-line players. Moholo never sounds as if he's merely keeping time; every line and figure has its place in the whole. Ossie's finest moments come on the long 'Double It' and the shorter 'Straight Jack', which must be one of his best recorded solos. What's now impossible is to judge what Osborne might have gone on to do. All that's left is to hear his music and wish him well.

Greg Osby (born 1960)

ALTO AND SOPRANO SAXOPHONES

Born in St Louis, Osby studied in Washington, DC, and Berklee, then moved to New York. Worked with Ron Carter and Jack DeJohnette, then closely involved in the M-Base movement of musicians with Steve Coleman. Signed to Blue Note in 1990, pursued mix of rap, hip hop and jazz, but more recently reverted to acoustic music.

****(*) Greg Osby And Sound Theatre**

Winter & Winter 919011-2 *Osby; Michele Rosewoman (p); Fusako Yoshida (koto); Kevin McNeal (g); Lonnie Plaxico (b); Paul Samuels, Terri Lyne Carrington (d).* 6/87.

****(*) Mindgames**

Winter & Winter 9219021-2 *Osby; Geri Allen, Edward Simon (ky); Kevin McNeal (g); Lonnie Plaxico (b); Paul Samuels (d).* 5/88.

****(*) Season Of Renewal**

Winter & Winter 919034-2 *Osby; Edward Simon, Renee Rosnes (ky); Kevin Eubanks, Kevin McNeal (g); Lonnie Plaxico (b); Paul Samuels (d); Steve Thornton (perc); Cassandra Wilson, Amina Claudine Myers (v).* 7/89.

Osby's late-'80s albums for JMT have recently returned via the Winter & Winter imprint. None of them has worn especially well: the leader sounds like he's fishing around for a direction, switching between modal blowing, funk, fusion, song-based forms (the latter featuring especially strongly on *Season Of Renewal*), and the attempted moulding of a new dialect which the M-Base philosophy seemed dedicated to. For the pleasure of hearing him nailing an ambitious solo here and there, each of them is worth a listen, but there's little sense of a unified band present in any of them, and compared to the formidable achievements he was to set down at Blue Note, these seem like mere sketchpads. Likely to be of most future value to historians of a 'period of transition'.

*****(*) Zero**

Blue Note 493760-2 *Osby; Jason Moran (p, org); Kevin McNeal (g); Lonnie Plaxico, Dwayne Burno (b); Rodney Green (d).* 1/98.

****** New Directions**

Blue Note 522978-2 *Osby; Mark Shim (ts); Jason Moran (p); Stefon Harris (vib); Taurus Mateen (b); Nasheet Waits (d).* 5/99.

*****(*) The Invisible Hand**

Blue Note 520134-2 *Osby; Gary Thomas (ts, f, af); Andrew Hill (p); Jim Hall (g); Scott Colley (b); Terri Lyne Carrington (d).* 9/99.

Osby's M-Base period and the early records which came after it now seem like distractions from his mature work. It's somewhat surprising that, for an artist whom Blue Note clearly have a lot of faith in, even such recent records as *Art Forum* and *Further Ado* have been cut from the catalogue. Even so, Osby set a formidable pace with records of the calibre of those listed above. *Zero* establishes Moran and Green as key presences in his working group, musicians who can handle whatever tough tasks he can throw at them as ensemble players. Some of these themes still feel like holdovers from his earlier work, occasionally too hung up on effortful time-signatures or excessively knotted melody-lines; but relentless work has softened the edges of his writing and opened up what was previously too cryptic a content. The brilliant Moran finds all sorts of nourishment in these pieces – check his 'Minstrale' solo, blooming with Monkian quirks but less angular, more melodious – and Osby's own playing seems fuller, more singing, but no less intense.

New Directions is, strictly speaking, a co-operative effort, but it was picked and planned by Osby. The sextet examines nine pieces from the Blue Note past, along with three originals by the principals. Osby took care to confound expectations of a simple repertory project by creating dramatic revisions of each piece. 'The Sidewinder' is just slightly reharmonized, strung over a tauter pulse than it usually gets, and the result is something refined but unsettling. 'Song For My Father', originally jovially bluesy, is darkened and sprung off Nasheet Waits's ominous patterns. Mark Shim makes a piquant contrast to Osby's terse, metropolitan sound: his thick, foggy but mobile delivery gets a showcase in his tremendous tenor solo on Wayne Shorter's 'Tom Thumb'. A brilliant effort all round.

The Invisible Hand is slightly disappointing, given the mouth-watering line-up. Osby again creates some extraordinary new twists on such familiar material as 'Nature Boy', using Thomas mainly on flute for tonal colour in the ensembles. Hall, inquisitive as ever, does his best to negotiate the music, but he never really seems entirely at one with what he's asked to do, and Hill is at times apparently somewhere else altogether. On the trio performance of 'Indiana', where he counterpoints himself with some discreet clarinet lines, Osby remains magnificently creative. This is a musician at the peak of his endeavours, and he must be followed by anyone interested in where jazz is going.

CORE COLLECTION

★★★★ Banned In New York

Blue Note 496860-2 *As Zero, except Atsushi Ozada (b) replaces McNeal, Plaxico and Burno.* 98.

Banned In New York was sent out at mid-price and packaged like an official bootleg. It documents a single gig by the quartet, set down on a DAT player and rush-released as a report on work in progress. Osby's own '13th Floor' starts things off, but from there he brings in Rollins, Ellington, Parker and Monk tunes and uses the material to fashion an utterly compelling treatise on the tradition and how it can fuel the playing of contemporary spirits on the bandstand, here and now. Each of the musicians makes his individual mark, but it's the way the quartet develops and processes ideas, caught on the hoof, that makes the record so powerful and immediate. Osby has said that he wishes he could release several records a year, in the manner of the old Blue Note performers, and, if the results are like this, it's a sentiment we echo.

★★★(★) Symbols Of Light (A Solution)

Blue Note 31395-2 *Osby; Jason Moran (p); Christian Howes (vn); Judith Insell-Stack (vla); Nioka Workman (clo); Scott Colley (b); Marlon Browden (d).* 2/01.

Got up in fancy old European duds in the sleeve photo, is this Osby's charge into the neoclassic old world? Of course not – just because he's written for four strings doesn't mean that this has any air of the academy in its lungs. Besides his own originals (and Moran's keen melodrama 'Repay In Kind') there is one of Masabumi Kikuchi's translucent lines, 'M', and a reading of Dmitri Tiomkin's 'Wild Is The Wind' inspired not by the movie score but by a Johnny Mathis hit. The strings are used in a variety of approaches, sometimes as counterpoint, sometimes as a single extra horn or rhythmic bank, sometimes almost as a kind of sound effect. They have improvisational options without becoming soloists as such.

It's a fascinating encounter, but as a record it feels not quite there, possibly because – for all the care taken by engineer Joseph Marciano – when the quartet are in full flow, the sound of the strings is sometimes poorly integrated into the overall mix, confusing at just the point when we need clarity. In other passages – as in the beautiful soprano solo which the leader takes in 'M' – the music is both gripping and sonorously beautiful. Besides, even if you feel like tuning out the strings, there's always the ongoing dialogue between Osby and Moran, which is shaping up as one of the great creative conversations of this jazz period. Their final duet on 'Minstrale Again' (a revision of a track from *Zero*) makes one ache to hear an entire album, or three or four, of this pairing.

★★★(★) Inner Circle

Blue Note 99871 *Osby; Jason Moran (p); Stefon Harris (vib); Taurus Mateen (b); Eric Harland (d).* 4/99.

Actually recorded before *Symbols Of Light*, this adds Harris to the Osby group for a set of originals which make an explicit break with song form and blues form – based, instead, on 'several linear, intevallic and structurally based song constructs and forms, some of which have not been investigated to any great extent', a statement of intent which might as well apply to most of Osby's work in the past ten years or so. In pieces such as 'Stride Logic', where Osby eventually solos – or, at least, steps to the front – against a series of tolling chords which cycle around him, the strategy's merits are glowingly obvious. It's often a quiet and best-behaviour kind of record, pondering its options rather than exploding through them as the group did on *Banned In New York*, and it's among the warmest and most lyrical of Greg's recods, astringent though that lyricism may be.

★★★(★) St Louis Shoes

Blue Note 81699-2 *Osby; Nicholas Payton (t); Harold O'Neal (p); Robert Hurst (b); Rodney Green (d).* 1/03.

'I wanted to prove that you can play effectively on these tunes without being patronising or sounding like a repertory ensemble': Osby's justification, as if he needed one in this repertory-driven jazz world, for giving us Ellington, Gillespie-Parker, Monk, W. C. Handy, Gershwin, even 'Bernie's Tune'. Nothing, inevitably, is quite as it seems or might be expected, with the dizzy flight of 'Shaw Nuff' changed into a line obliged to run against a secondary melody spun off the same changes, and 'The Single Petal Of A Rose' sounding parched, its melody thinned to a bare-wires structure. Extra warmth is added by the deep swing of Hurst and Green and by the surprise presence of that hot-jazz specialist Nicholas Payton, who might be thought to be an emotional opposite to Osby but who eats up every opportunity given to him. O'Neal, at the time of the recording 21 years old, is exciting enough to diffuse disappointment that Moran has now gone his own way. And the leader is front and centre, leaping into his solos. The album's positioned as an homage to his hometown scene of some 25 years earlier, but it's tough, unsentimental, analytical too.

Roberto Ottaviano (born 1957)

SOPRANO AND ALTO SAXOPHONES, MANZANO

Italian saxophonist specializing in soprano. Has performed in several pan-European outfits, including Franz Koglmann's group, besides leading his own bands.

*****(*) Items From The Old Earth**

Splasc(h) H 332 *Ottaviano; Roberto Rossi (tb); Mario Arcari (ss, ob, eng hn); Martin Mayes (frhn); Sandro Cerino (cl, bcl, f, bf); Fiorenzo Gualandris (tba).* 12/90.

He has done significant work as a sideman with Ran Blake, Franz Koglmann and Tiziana Ghiglioni among others, but Ottaviano's albums as a leader offer some of the best indication of his powers. Although he occasionally picks up the alto, soprano is his favoured horn. He gets an unusually pure and unaffected sound, rarely going for a squawk or anything remotely expressionist, and it lends his improvisations a clear if somewhat terse intensity. *Items From The Old Earth* is by Ottaviano's all-horns group, Six Mobiles. The sonorities are hard to predict, brassy at some points, woody at others, and the compositions are crowded (perhaps excessively so at times) both with ideas and with techniques, some of which beg comparison with European composition rather than jazz. But Ottaviano's own solos add a sudden brightness at moments when the ensemble threatens to turn stiff and dry.

***** Above Us**

Splasc(h) H 330-2 *Ottaviano; Stefano Battaglia (p); Piero Leveratto (b); Ettore Fioravanti (d).* 11/90.

****(*) Otto**

Splasc(h) H 340-2 *Ottaviano (ss solo).* 1/91.

Ottaviano returns to more conventional ground on the quartet record, which matches him with the gifted Battaglia: loose modal blowing seems to be the mainstay of the date, and it's done with aplomb, although some of the music lacks anchor and compass. *Otto* takes a stab at a solo album but seems a mite too cleverly conceived: reverb and overdubs distract from the point of Ottaviano's improvising and some of the solos seem like mere technical points-winners. A pretty record, though, when the saxophonist locates an attractive line.

*****(*) Hybrid And Hot**

Splasc(h) H 453-2 *Ottaviano; Gianluca Petrella (tb); Tom Varner (frhn); Michel Godard (tba); Marcello Magliocchi (d).* 7/95.

This seems influenced at least in part by Ottaviano's work with Franz Koglmann, and the mordant humour of, say, 'The Lightwarrior' is something that the Austrian would surely appreciate. But Ottaviano has his own agenda here, with three Carla Bley themes and a solo treatment of Lacy's 'The Raps' alongside five of his own pieces; and his careful sifting of the four horns in front of Magliocchi's drums is fascinating and an absorbing study in light and shade. There are some wryly apposite solos from all four men, with the little-known Petrella at least as outstanding as his colleagues, yet it's the leader's meticulous playing which shines most particularly. Surely his best to date.

***** Black Spirits Are Here Again**

DIW 917 *Ottaviano; Mal Waldron (p).* 1/96.

A surprise meeting, even if Waldron was an old hand at this sort of thing with Steve Lacy. One feels that it isn't really Ottaviano's bag, impeccably though he plays, and standards like 'Come Sunday' are more like recitations than interactive dialogues. 'A Night In Tunisia', though, works splendidly, a very elegant dissertation from two cultured minds.

***** Live In Israel**

Soul Note 121332-2 *Ottaviano; Giorgio Vendola (b); Roberto Dani (d).* 11/01.

Recorded in the clattery acoustic of Tel Aviv's Museum Of Modern Art, Ottaviano and his cohorts are in good fettle here. The leader almost blurts out the opening motif of Steve Lacy's 'Bone' before scampering through a solo which shows how different a soprano man he is to the master. The rest is given over to Monk, Mingus, Miles and Carla Bley, including a notably hardnosed trawl through 'Evidence' and a fine meditation on 'Ida Lupino'. The main drawback is the sound, which does Dani no favours at all and at times reduces his kit to dustbin lids. Get past that and there's some fine music.

Harold Ousley (born 1929)

TENOR SAXOPHONE, FLUTE

Very much a Chicagoan, Ousley worked with Gene Ammons and later with Jack McDuff and George Benson. He gained valuable experience with both Billie Holiday and Dinah Washington and likes to work with songs rather than abstract chord changes. After a quiet spell, Harold returned to the studios in his 70s.

***** Grit-Grittin' Feeling**

Delmark 520 *Ousley; Arthur Hoyle (t); Jodie Christian (p); John Whitfield (b); Robert Shy (d).* 1/00.

Harold's earlier dates for Bethlehem and Muse are no longer available and there might have been nothing at all under his name had Delmark, devoted archivists of Chicago jazz, not offered the 71-year-old this session. It's for the most part pretty standard hard-bop, though there is a version of the Goffin–King song 'Go Away, Little Girl', famously covered by Donny Osmond. Ousley has a nice rounded tone and a vigorous attack, putting the stresses fairly squarely on the beat. None the less, he knows how to bend the metre to add pathos to a ballad and there are some affecting moments on an otherwise rather anonymous set.

Vardan Ovsepian

PIANO

Talented Armenian with rich vein of compositional ideas.

***** Abandoned Wheel**

Fresh Sound New Talent FSNT 108 *Ovsepian (p solo).* 9/01.

***** Sketch Book**

Fresh Sound New Talent FSNT 142 *Ovsepian; Mick Goodrick (g); Joshua Davis (b); Take Toriyama (d); Monica Yngvesson (v).* 9/02.

The debut record mixes longer form pieces with miniatures and fragments that don't seem ready for public consumption. The combined effect is of work still in progress, interesting enough in the detail, but not yet fully formed. A Keith Jarrett influence seems to weigh quite heavily. The follow-up has some equally interesting things, but working in company even as uneffusive as this, Ovsepian still sounds reserved and inchoate. Yngvesson often doubles his lines in wordless singing, while Goodrick plays his usual quiet and intense game, seemingly apart from the rest. The writing is very strong, though, and the pianist's future looks bright.

Tony Oxley (born 1938)

DRUMS, PERCUSSION

Oxley's importance to free music in Europe can scarcely be exaggerated, and yet he rarely plays in his native Britain, preferring exile and work in Germany. His apprenticeship ranges from a stint in the Black Watch band to the house section at Ronnie Scott's. He is a pioneer of metal and amplified percussion, and has retained a sense of swing and pulse even when playing free.

♛ ****** The Baptised Traveller**

Columbia 494438 2 *Oxley; Kenny Wheeler (t, flhn); Evan Parker (ts); Derek Bailey (g); Jeff Cline (b).* 1/69.

*****(*) Four Compositions For Sextet**

Columbia 494437 2 *As above, except add Paul Rutherford (tb).* 70.

Tony Oxley served an apprenticeship in pub bands and then learnt a more formal craft as a military conscript. He was a key player in the early days of the British free scene, notably the trio of Josef Holbrooke with Derek Bailey and Gavin Bryars. Later years saw another trio, sOH, with Alan Skidmore and Ali Haurand and the Celebration Orchestra, which reveals him to be a composer of some considerable sophistication. Most of his pieces move relatively slowly, even if there is a lot of surface detail. Large acoustic masses seem to operate in three dimensions, as if Oxley were rotating the musical material to examine its unconsidered aspects.

These albums have enjoyed legendary status for years, and if only *Ichnos*, an even more adventurous vehicle for Oxley's pin-sharp sound and ideas, had also been reissued, a whole generation of British free-ophiles would be celebrating. For us, *The Baptised Traveller* is the most representative and coherent expression of his gifts. Thirled to a quest for identity, its four themes are calmly questioning, the two horns restlessly ranging over Cline's and Oxley's unceasing shifts of direction. 'Crossing' and 'Arrival', which are segued into a single improvisation, wipe clean almost all formal expectations. The centerpiece of the album is, unusually, a theme by a jazz composer. Oxley's stately reading of Charlie Mariano's 'Stone Garden' is one of the masterworks of contemporary improvised music, a slow chorale rooted in Bailey's chiming guitar chords. Their almost orchestral quality provides a starting point for Parker's solemn quiddities and for virtuosic percussion from Oxley. The closing 'Preparation' isn't so much an anti-climax as an obvious afterthought.

Four Compositions was a title guaranteed to offend players and fans who wanted to set aside any implication of predetermined structures. In the event, Oxley's ideas are all geared to solo improvisation. The opening of 'Saturnalia' is a mordant fanfare that announces the arrival of Evan Parker (probably his best recorded solo to date), Kenny Wheeler and Derek Bailey. The long 'Amass' is constructed from a graphic score and gives Rutherford, the sole newcomer from the previous album, his most effective moments. The disc ends with the scratchy, slightly unattractive 'Megaera', an exercise in sonic conflict that doesn't entirely convince.

Even 30 years on, one marvels at Columbia/CBS investing in music like this. That it was a brief experiment is no surprise. That it was so commandingly creative is a source of renewed delight. Two albums to treasure from a long-gone age in British music, but one whose creative implications are still being worked out.

*****(*) The Tony Oxley/Alan Davie Duo**

a/1/1 005 *Oxley; Alan Davie (p, clo, sno, bcl, perc).* 74, 75.

Davie is a Scottish-born painter whose early work paralleled Jackson Pollock's much-mythologized discovery of archetypal shapes in otherwise abstract art. Davie is also a formidable musician and very much of a mind with Oxley. This reissue includes two extra tracks, but the heart of the session consists of relatively short improvisations based on pre-arranged instrumental combinations. So 'Cavern Of The Snail' is for cello and ring-modulated cymbals; 'Bird Trap' for cello again, but this time with Oxley dabbling in strings himself with some very odd violin-playing. It's at least consistent with his interest in the sustained tones that can be had from electronics, and the two extra tracks 'Fish Fascinator' and 'On The Seashore' (titles that sound very much like Davie canvases) are awash with crudely synthesized sounds. There's no outstanding track, just a record of a highly sympathetic musical encounter. Davie's reputation as a musician has never caught up with that as an artist, which seems a pity.

*****(*) The Tony Oxley Quartet**

Incus CD15 *Oxley; Pat Thomas (ky, elec); Derek Bailey (g); Matt Wand (drum machine, tape switchboard).* 4/92.

This quartet session (recorded by WDR, Cologne) is a memorable reunion with Bailey as well as a meeting with two talented younger members of British improv. There are three quartet pieces, one trio (minus Oxley) and a duet between each of the four players. The opening quartet is a mesmerizing feeling-the-way performance, the soundscape wide open, with every man vital, nobody overplaying, each sound of interest. Thomas varies between analogue-synth wheezes and crisp digital arpeggios, while Wand's bricolage of found sounds and drumbeats redefines notions of minimalism. Bailey remains imperturbably himself, and his duet with Oxley is a superb co-operative battle of wits. The leader, if such he be here, continues to make free rhythm and pulse out of crashings and bangings that in other hands would be, well, unmusical. A magnificent and important (as well as enjoyable) modern document.

*****(*) The Enchanted Messenger**

Soul Note 1231284 *Oxley; Bill Dixon (t, flhn); Johannes Bauer (tb); Ernst-Ludwig Petrowsky (sax, cl); Frank Gratkowski (sax, bcl); Philipp Wachsmann (vn, elec); Alex Kolkowski (vn); Marcio Mattos, Alfred Zimmerlin (clo); Pat Thomas (p, elec); Stefan Hölker, Tony Levin, Joe Thönes (d, perc); Matt Wand (elec); Phil Minton (v).* 11/94.

A superb large-scale composition for Oxley's Celebration Orchestra, performed at the 1994 JazzFest Berlin, *The Enchanted Messenger* consists of 19 interrelated parts or sections. The ensemble is very percussion-heavy, though Oxley doubles as drummer and conductor. The key soloists are trumpeter Bill Dixon, whose spirit suffuses the occasion almost as much as Oxley's, and violinist Philip Wachsmann, who always seems entirely at home in large ensembles like this.

Some of the material is atonal or pantonal but, as ever, Oxley gives a strong impression of pulse and swing. The balance of strings and winds isn't quite ideal and the sections fight in the mix, but it is possible to follow the course of this intriguing performance as it gradually dismantles its own initial premisses and pushes out into areas of freedom which only the London Jazz Composers' Orchestra and Globe Unity Orchestra have been able to explore with similar conviction. The use of electronics is what sets Oxley's ensemble apart from either of these. Wand, Thomas and Wachsmann create richly abstract textures, against which the acoustic instruments sound oddly alienated and strange. Not an easy record to absorb in just one or two sittings, but one that repays careful and prolonged attention.

****(*) Floating Phantoms**
a/1/1 001 *Oxley; Philipp Wachsmann (vn, elec); Pat Thomas (ky); Matt Wand (elec).* 99.

The inaugural release on FMP's spin-off label is something of a disappointment. When one thinks how comfortably Wachsmann has absorbed electronic processing into his work and how long Oxley has used electronics with his drum kit, this is a remarkably callow performance. Wand's contribution is exceedingly dull, and neither of the senior players finds much room to make a significant statement.

****(*) Triangular Screen**
Sofa 501 *Oxley; Ivar Grydeland (g); Tonny Klyften (b).* 3 & 5/00.

Tony here plays his acoustic set with tape backgrounds, which diminishes the flexibility of his response. Grydeland and Klyften seem content to play a relatively supportive role, as well they might given the drummer's seniority, but it also means that they tend to be distracting rather than integral. That said, Oxley is more than usually forthright, even aggressive in his playing, and there isn't much room for anyone else to muscle in, even briefly. It isn't the most impressive performance even of recent years.

Ivan Paduart

PIANO, KEYBOARDS

Belgian post-bopper with an interesting perspective on the old-fashioned piano-led combo.

***** White Knights**
Challenge 73061 *Paduart; Bob Malach (ts); Toots Thielemans (hca); Philip Catherine (g); Gwenael Micault (bandoneon); Phillipe Aerts (b); Hans Van Oosterhout (d); Michel Seba (perc).* 10/96.

***** Clair Obscur**
A 73061 *Paduart; Nic Thys (b); Hans Van Oosterhout (d).* 1/97.

It's difficult to pin down Paduart's main influences: Bill Evans, almost self-evidently, but also Chick Corea, Keith Jarrett and possibly Ahmad Jamal and Joe Zawinul as well. All of which may make him sound anonymously eclectic, which is not the case. The first of these is a beautifully crafted disc of mostly originals (Fred Hersch's 'Heartsong' is the only import), of which the opening 'Ecoline' is arresting and delightful, not in any way hampered by a Toots Thielemans solo. There's a smooth, poppy quality to some of the writing and playing, and 20 years ago Ivan might have been found hiding behind a bank of Fenders and Korgs. He plays old-fashioned piano here and plays it very well indeed, though his dynamics need stretching a touch.

On *Clair Obscur*, Ivan picks up a cue from the earlier album and plays a set dedicated entirely to the work of Fred Hersch, creator of some of the most exquisite jazz themes of recent times, and a natural successor to Bill Evans. 'Evanessence' is the key composition, though 'Rainwaltz' runs it a very close second.

***** Belgian Suites**
Challenge 73122 *Paduart; Bob Malach (ts); Hein van de Geyn (b); Hans Van Oosterhout (d).* 2/98.

The introduction of electronic keyboards accentuates Paduart's long-standing interest in a kind of jazz fusion which somehow manages to retain its jazz purity. The only other example we can think of is fellow-countryman Philip Catherine, so perhaps there is something in Belgian beer which does it. 'Precious Moments', dedicated to his son, is a wonderful piece, full of emotion but also tautly structured. 'Between Heaven And Earth' is almost as good and the closing tribute to his beloved is very touching, rounding out a very satisfying record. Malach is an able collaborator, sounding a bit like cut-price Brecker in places, but generally more individual than that.

***** Still**
A 73226 *Paduart; Rick Margitza (ts); Stefan Lievestro (b); Mimi Verderame (d).* 02.

****(*) Night At The Music Village**
Jazz 'N Pulz 395 *Paduart; Bert Joris (t, flhn); Toon Roos (ss, ts); Toots Thielemans (hca); Stefan Lievestro (b); Mimi Verderame (d); Fay Claasen (v).* 03.

An intriguing development from his previous records, this is at once jazzier and more rhythm-based and also the most abstract thing Paduart has done, though only in the sense that the emotional spectrum seems less clearly defined. Fred Hersch provides a generous liner-note, cementing what has been the most important artistic association of the Belgian's career. A lovely record, but enigmatic in places. *Night At The Music Village* is a first chance for most of us to catch Paduart live. He's not the most emphatic of performers, but there is plenty very individual music on the set and the band is first rate, with Thielemans making one of his now familiar guest appearances. Fay Claasen's vocals we could have lived without.

Hot Lips Page (1908–54)

TRUMPET, MELLOPHONE

Oran Thaddeus Page grew up in Texas and was bound for a medical career when his mother started him on music lessons. He worked at menial jobs in the oilfield before finding work as a trumpeter and being recruited by Bennie Moten to the Blue Devils, led by Walter Page (who, he sometimes claimed, was a kinsman). Page worked with Basie in his classic orchestra and was admired for his warm, full tone, hence his nickname. Despite his talent and popularity, he made few records under his own name.

*****(*) Pagin' Mr Page: His Greatest Recordings 1932–1946**
ASV CD AJA 5437 *Page; Bobby Hackett (c); Lee Castle, Buck Clayton, Shad Collins, Harry 'Sweets' Edison, Max Kaminsky,*

Joe Keyes, Ed Lewis, Steve Lipkins, Bobby Moore, Eddie Mullins, Dink Stewart (t); Ray Conniff, Vic Dickenson, Eddie Durham, J. C. Higginbotham, Jack Jenney, Lou McGarity, Dan Minor, Miff Mole, Benny Morton, Morey Samuel, George Stevenson, Jack Teagarden, Dicky Wells, Harry White, Sandy Williams (tb); Ernie Caceres, Edmond Hall, Pee Wee Russell (cl); Eddie Barefield, Ben Smith (cl, as); Earl Bostic, Charlie DiMaggio, George Johnson, Gene Kinsey, Les Robinson, Ulysses Scott, Don Stovall, Earl Warren, Floyd Horsecollar Williams (as); Jack Washington (as, bs); Georgie Auld, Don Byas, Nick Caiazza, Sam Davis, Herschel Evans, Mickey Folus, John Hartzfield, Ernie Powell, Ike Quebec, Sam Simmons, Benny Waters, Ben Webster, Lester Young (ts); Art Baker, Jack Washington (bs); Count Basie, Johnny Guarnieri, Clyde Hart, Cliff Jackson, Jimmy Reynolds, Rufus Webster (p); Danny Barker, Leroy Berry, Mike Bryan, Teddy Bunn, John Collins, Herb Ellis, Freddie Green, Tiny Grimes, Connie Wainwright (g); Abe Bolar, Wellman Braud, Bob Casey, Israel Crosby, George 'Pops' Foster, Al Hall, Bass Hill, Al Lucas, Eddie McKimmey, Al Morgan, Walter Page (b); Big Sid Catlett, A. G. Godley, Harry Jaeger, Jo Jones, Ed McConney, Willie McWashington, Buford Oliver, Jack Parker, Specs Powell, Alfred Taylor, Dave Tough, George Wettling (d). 12/32–46.

*** Hot Lips Page 1938–1940

Classics 561 *Page; Bobby Moore, Eddie Mullens (t); George Stevenson, Harry White (tb); Ben Smith, Buster Smith (cl, as); Jimmy Powell, Ulysses Scott, Don Stovall (as); Ben Williams (as, ts); Don Byas, Sam Davis, Ernie Powell, Sam Simmons, Benny Waters (ts); Pete Johnson, Jimmy Reynolds (p); John Collins, Connie Wainwright (g); Abe Bolar, Wellman Braud (b); A. G. Godley, Ed McConney, Alfred Taylor (d); Romayne Jackson, Bea Morton, Delores Payne, Ben Powers, The Harlem Highlanders (v).* 3/38–12/40.

***(*) Hot Lips Page 1940–1944

Classics 809 *Page; Jesse Brown, Joe Keyes (t); Vic Dickenson, Benny Morton (tb); Earl Bostic, Benjamin Hammond, George Johnson, Floyd Horsecollar Williams (as); Don Byas, Ike Quebec, Ben Webster, Lem Johnson, Lucky Thompson (ts); Ace Harris, Leonard Feather, Clyde Hart, Hank Jones (p); Sam Christopher Allen (g); Teddy Bunn (g, v); Al Lucas, John Simmons, Carl Flat Top Wilson (b); Ernest 'Bass' Hill (b, bb); Big Sid Catlett, Jack Parker, Jesse Price (d).* 12/40–11/44.

An Armstrong imitator who never quite made it out of that constricting sack, Page has always hovered just below the threshold of most fans' attention. Realistically, he is a much less accomplished player who wasted much of his considerable talent on pointless jamming and dismal but lucrative rhythm and blues. The material recorded for Bluebird in April 1938 features a band that might have gone places had Page not had to disband it. At the beginning of 1940 he was recording with the remarkable Buster Smith, a Texan out of Ellis County, who became a mainstay of the Kansas City sound during the war years and after. These are fine sides, not altogether improved by some very odd remastering wobbles, but they're surpassed by the four cuts made for Decca towards the end of the year with Pete Johnson and Don Byas, which (leaving aside an indifferent vocal by Bea Morton) are among the best of the period and unjustly neglected.

The title of the second Classics volume is slightly misleading. There is, to be sure, material from 1940 and from 1944, but nothing in between. Some of the interim period is covered in various bootlegged jam sessions which may be available. The drummerless 1940 group with Feather, Bunn and Hill is very good indeed, with Hill a considerable surprise for a bass player of his day. Page also shows off his touch on the now seldom-used mellophone. The real treat on this volume, though, is the later material featuring Byas. As Anatol Schenker's informative liner-notes suggest, 'These Foolish Things' is one of the high points of '40s saxophone jazz, worth playing to unsuspecting experts for a guess at the saxophonist involved. There are giveaway phrases here and there but, at these sessions for Commodore, Byas excelled himself. There is some Savoy material from June 1944, a bigger group in which Byas has to give ground to the great Ben Webster; but it is the two dates for Milt Gabler's label which stand out. Even the quasi-novelty items like 'The Blues Jumped A Rabbit' are excellent. It wouldn't be a Classics volume without an early appearance from a star of the future. On the last session, from November 1944, Hank Jones makes his recording debut backing Page, Dickenson and the very fine Thompson on 'The Lady In Bed' and 'Gee, Baby, Ain't I Good For You?'.

The ASV compilation is able to range more widely than Classics because it takes in material made for other leaders – Moten, Basie, Chu Berry, Artie Shaw, Albert Ammons and Eddie Condon – but does also sample the sessions of April 1938, January, November and December 1940, and June and September 1944. The sound is very good but, given how much of this material is available from other sources, it will be of limited value to anyone who isn't simply looking for a quick introduction to Page's work. For a quick comparison of sound, compare the Classics transfer of 'I Let A Song Go Out Of My Heart' with this. No comparison at all, really.

*** After Hours In Harlem

HighNote HCD 7031 *Page; Joe Guy (t); Rudy Williams (as); Herbie Fields (ts); Donald Lambert, Thelonious Monk (p); Tiny Grimes (g); other personnel unidentified.* 40, 41?

Originally released on Onyx in 1973, this fascinating set represents the work of jazz fan Jerry Newman who, like Dean Benedetti with Charlie Parker, staked out his favourite musicians and recorded them on a portable machine. Over the years, he accumulated an astonishing archive. Not the least remarkable of these recordings are the first documented performances of Thelonious Monk, heard with Page and Joe Guy on 'Sweet Georgia Brown' and 'Topsy'. The disc would be valuable for that alone but, coupled with its picture of Page at work away from the studio, it helps fill out some aspects of his playing style, not least how much more of an Armstrong imitator he seems on record than in front of a live audience when more of his wry, reckless nature comes through. The tones are bright enough to come off a shaky source-tape and Page's solo development has a nicely asymmetrical logic which is very different from Pops and from almost anyone else on the scene at the time. There is also a nice example of his singing, on 'Yazoo'; again very different from the master, but not without its charms.

*** Hot Lips Page 1944–1946

Classics 950 *Page; Billy Butterfield, Buck Clayton (t); Bobby Hackett (co); Vic Dickenson, Lou McGarity, Benny Morton, Jack Teagarden, Sandy Williams (tb); Earl Bostic, Earle Warren (as); Ernie Caceres (cl); Don Byas, Nick Caiazza, John Hartzfield, Lucky Thompson, Ben Webster (ts); Johnny Guarnieri, Hank Jones, Lannie Scott, Rufus Webster (p); Sam*

Allen, Danny Barker, Herb Ellis (g); Al Hall, Slam Stewart, Carl 'Flat Top' Wilson (b); Big Sid Catlett, Buford Oliver, Specs Powell, Jesse Price (d). 12/44–9/46.

Between 1944 and 1946, Lips recorded for Savoy, Commodore, Onyx, Foxy and Columbia and made a couple of V-Disc sessions as well with the All-Stars. That's just about where this chapter of the story begins, with an original tune Miss Martingale. There's a bit of a break in the story after that until the vocal 'Bloodhound' for Onyx in September 1945, when things started to look a touch brighter for the business with the end of hostilities. Page's best playing was possibly behind him at this point, but there are still some striking good solos and singing spots, notably on 'Love You Funny Thing' and 'They Raided The Joint', a collaboration with Roy Eldridge. It's all bright and unaffected stuff and the Page horn still rings loud when he gets the space to solo over a supportive foundation.

****(*) Hot Lips Page 1946–1950**

Classics 1199 *Page; Alfred 'Chippie' Outcalt, Jimmy Buxton (tb); Joe Evans (cl, as); Earl Bostic, Vincent Bair-Bey (as); John Hartzfield, Buddy Tate, Big Nick Nicholas, Ray Abrams, Tom Archia (ts); Lannie Scott, Bill Spooner, Skip Hall, Raymond Tunia, Joe Knight (p); Danny Barker, Tony Mottola, Al Caiola (g); Carl Wilson, Walter Page, Al Hall, Bob Haggart, Leonard Gaskin (b); George Jenkins, Sammie 'Sticks' Evans, Charles Smith, Specs Powell, Terry Snyder, Herbie Lovelle (d); Pearl Bailey, Janie Mickens, Sam Theard (v); strings; choir.* 10/46–2/50.

A stray final title for Apollo, then most of this consists of sessions for Harmony and, surprisingly, Columbia. Lips sings and mugs his way through material such as 'I Got An Uncle In Harlem' and 'Miss Larceny Blues' and there's an inevitable (in 1949, anyway) 'Hucklebuck'. A lot of this is generic, prototypical R&B but a few solos – from the likes of Big Nick Nicholas and the mysterious Tom Archia on the one standout track, 'Boodie Boodie' – collar the ear for a few seconds. As a collection, though, very average.

****(*) Dr Jazz: Volume 6 – 1951–1952**

Storyville STCD 6046 *Page; Wild Bill Davison (c); Lou McGarity, Sandy Williams (tb); Eddie Barefield, Peanuts Hucko, Pee Wee Russell, Cecil Scott, Bob Wilber (cl); Dick Cary, Charlie Queener, Red Richards, Joe Sullivan (p); Eddie Safranski, Jim Thorpe (b); George Wettling (d).* 12/51–3/52.

These late airshots were broadcast from Stuyvesant Casino at 2nd and 9th in New York City, under the auspices of drummer Wettling's group. There is one great session here, featuring Page with Wild Bill Davison and Lou McGarity on what occasionally sounds like an alto trombone, a sharp, puncturing sound that sits wonderfully with the two trumpets. Otherwise, it's fairly run-of-the-mill. To a large extent Page was yesterday's man; he can only occasionally, as on 'St Louis Blues' from February 1952, summon up the old fire. A valuable addition for dedicated collectors, but pretty marginal stuff compared to the above.

(***) Hot Lips Page – 1937–1949: The Alternative Takes In Chronological Order

Neatwork RP 2064 *As for Classics sets above.* 37–49.

A word of caution. The Neatwork discs complement the Classics series, which had previously maintained a policy of not including alternative takes. While all original masters are issued complete, these sessions are necessarily more selective, but do also include breakdowns and incomplete takes. More to the point, the discs have been made available in a strictly limited edition of 500 – that's five hundred – worldwide. We suspect this won't spark a rush on the record stores. These are specialist issues and won't be of much interest to casual buyers. The Page disc has some nice stuff: a breakdown on 'Miss Martingale' with the V-Disc All Stars and some on-mic comments from Fats Waller in a January 1942 recording of 'Blues In B flat' for Radiola. Otherwise, though, these are what alternatives usually are: inferior versions which can be mined for musicological detail but rarely of intrinsic appeal.

Pago Libre

GROUP

Named after the initial letters of original group members – who included Lars Lindvall and Steve Goodman – this long-standing unit works in a delicate and evocative avant-garde strain.

***** Pago Libre**

Leo CD LR 105 *Arkady Shilkloper (frhn, flhn, alphorn); Tscho Theissing (vn); John Wolf Brennan (p); Daniele Patumi (b).* 96.

*****(*) Wake Up Call: Live In Italy**

Leo CD LR 272 *As above.* 9/97.

***** Cinemagique**

TCB 01112 *As above.* 01.

We would not wish to suggest in our brief summation that Pago Libre is in any way a purveyor of avant-garde lite, but the group's unusual instrumentation and romantic sensibility give its work an appealing accessibility. Brennan is a master of this idiom, and his companions are absolutely like-minded.

The group's first recording, *Extempora*, released on Splasc(h) in 1990, is currently unavailable. *Pago Libre* was originally released on Bellophon and has since been reissued by Leo, a label that has long supported Brennan's work. The same disc has also been available on L&R as *Titles*. All four members contribute material, but Theissing's opening 'Rochade' is a stand-out track, cleverly pitched in a difficult, off-centre metre. 'J.P.S. (& Carla)' is marked by some curious Hot Club effects, and there is a four-part 'Stream Of Consciousness' suite by Patumi which suggests he is no slouch as a writer either.

The other key track is the vibrant 'Wake-Up Call', which became the title of a later Leo release. For much of its decade of operation, the group had gone undocumented in concert and at festivals, so a live album was an obvious and overdue decision. This was recorded to two-track at the Sol-Fest open-air festival in Sicily, which perhaps explains its bright and optimistic cast. Theissing's title-piece gets the set under way with a gentle urgency. Brennan is featured on his own 'Toccattacca', a brilliant sequence that includes Fibonacci series, palindromic inversions and a kind of sun-kissed serialism. Shilkloper switches to flugelhorn for both his own 'Folk Song' and Brennan's 'Kabak', the latter an unexpectedly funky theme that provides the record's main climax.

Cinemagique is, as it sounds, a collection of imaginary soundtracks, but unlike most such projects this is not an excuse for fragmentary writing and bland fade-outs. Brennan once studied under film-music maestro Ennio Morricone, and some of those lessons may well be surfacing here in these moody interiors and poised *mises-en-scène*. Many of the pieces seem closer to modern classical music than to jazz, but the varied sonority is endlessly beguiling, and in 'Synopsis' and 'Suonatina', Pago Libre has added a couple more evergreens to its repertoire, to put alongside 'Wake-Up Call' and 'Rochade'.

Palatino

GROUP

Unusual combination of instruments, played by thoroughly distinctive musicians. Result: intrigue and occasional delight.

***** Palatino**

Label Bleu *Paolo Fresu (t); Glenn Ferris (tb); Aldo Romano (d).* 95.

***** Tempo**

Label Bleu *As above, except add Michel Benita (b).* 97, 98.

***** Chap. 3**

Emarcy 013610 *As above.* 00.

Two brasses and drums might sound an unlikely combination for a jazz group, but it has history on its side as well as the sheer pedigree of these players. The subsequent addition of Benita on double bass lends a harmonic resonance that was not there before and was very occasionally missed, but it also makes Palatino sound more like a regular jazz group with horns and rhythm, and less a one-off. Most of the material is by the players themselves, though there is a telling interpretation of Tadd Dameron's 'On A Misty Night' on the third disc. These are hugely experienced musicians, with a body of work that embraces small-group improvisation and with complex big-band charts to call on. They're worth making time for.

Jeff Palmer (born 1951)

ORGAN

Born in New York state, Palmer is an organ specialist who doesn't double on piano. He actually started out as an accordionist and is self-taught.

*****(*) Abracadabra**

Soul Note 121201 *Palmer; Dave Liebman (ss); John Abercrombie (g syn); Adam Nussbaum (d).* 87.

Well-named. This top-flight group seems to coax magical sounds out of the air. Palmer has explored areas of the Hammond that are seldom heard in a jazz context. Some of it veers towards Sun Ra-style space-organ effects, but mostly it's fast and funky, as on the opening 'Hip Slick'. Liebman's plaintive but strong-willed soprano and Abercrombie's use of the guitar synth help create a sound-world that is now perhaps a little dated, though *Abracadabra* is more than a period piece. It wasn't Jeff's first record; however, its predecessor *Laser Wizard* is, we believe, long deleted.

****** Ease On**

Audioquest 1014 *Palmer; Arthur Blythe (as); John Abercrombie (g); Victor Lewis (d).* 92.

****** Island Universe**

Soul Note 121301 *As above, except omit Lewis; add Rashied Ali (d).* 3/94.

A carbon copy of the earlier band in some respects, except that Abercrombie seems to be playing more straight-ahead jazz lines and Blythe is a very different kind of saxophonist to Liebman, funkier and more obviously in a groove but still atmospheric enough to fit into Palmer's aesthetic. The tracks on *Ease On* are mostly long and, with the exception of McCoy Tyner's 'Blues On The Corner', Palmer originals. The only disappointment is 'Modal Scallopini', which sounds too similar to half a dozen other tunes you can't quite recall the name of. 'Ease On' is fine, and 'Gas Mask' is the sort of closing shot that guarantees you'll pay a return visit.

Island Universe confirms it's no fluke. Ali's recruitment in place of the excellent Lewis gives the session a different cachet and perhaps starts the listener wondering whether Alice Coltrane might be another place to start looking for influences; the Larry Young strain long since won out over Jimmy Smith. Blythe was returning to form in these years and he sounds stronger by the track, especially if the track is the off-kilter blues 'Amerigo'.

***** Shades Of The Pine**

Reservoir RSR 137 *Palmer; Billy Pierce (ts); John Abercrombie (g); Marvin Smitty Smith (d).* 9/94.

This is the first time that a Palmer project has sounded a bit like a sax-guitar-organ-drums project from the '60s. It's not just because the organist's hornmen have been wielding ever heavier horns over the spell and Pierce is very much in the strong tenor mould, nor that Smitty Smith wants to groove any harder than Nussbaum, Lewis or Ali; rather that Palmer seems to have run short, if not yet out, of original ideas. This is the most generic of his albums, still packed with interesting music, but lacking the sheer originality of the earlier sets. The best track, ironically, is Monk's 'Ba-Lue Bolivar Blues Are'; Jeff's own 'Hokus Pokus' is tame by comparison. Enthusiasts will want it anyway; newcomers would be better steered to *Island Universe* or *Ease On*.

***** Burnin' The Blues**

Consolidated Artists 949 *Palmer; Vincent Herring (ss, as); John Abercrombie (g); Bob Leto (d).* 4/99.

The Jimmy Smith influence rears again with this bluesy set, marking a return of the repressed rather than a fresh exploration of roots. The formula is a little tired by now, and while Palmer has the sheer chops and the musical integrity to make it work, *Burnin' The Blues* isn't a patch on past offerings. Herring is an interesting recruitment, a phenomenal player who has blown hot and cold on his own and other leaders' projects. Here, he's at his best for some time, playing fierce, funky lines one moment, sorrowful bleats of distress the next.

Papa Bue's Viking Jazz Band

GROUP

Led by trombonist Papa Bue Jensen, this is one of the most popular and durable trad-to-Dixie outfits in Europe, with more than 40 years of faithful service to their enthusiastic following.

***** Greatest Hits**

Storyville STCD 836 *Arne Bue Jensen (tb); Finn Otto Hansen (t); Jorgen Svare (cl); Jorn Jensen (p); Bjarne Liller (bj, v); Jens Solund (b); Knud Ryskov Madsen (d).* 58–70.

*****(*) Featuring George Lewis**

Storyville STCD 6018 *As above, except add George Lewis (cl).* 2/59.

***** Featuring Edmond Hall**
Storyville STCD 6022 *As above, except omit Lewis; add Edmond Hall (cl).* 66.

***** Original Studio Recordings: Volume 1**
Storyville STCD 5502 *As above.* 66–69.

***** Original Studio Recordings: Volume 2**
Storyville STCD 5503 *As above.* 66–69.

*****(*) In The Sixties: Volume 1**
Music Mecca CD 1088 *As above, except omit Hall.* 67–69.

***** In The Sixties: Volume 2**
Music Mecca CD 1089 *As above.* 67–69.

The Viking empire once stretched as far south as the Mediterranean, and considerable ingenuity has been expended in attempting to prove that a Norseman beat Christopher Columbus across the Atlantic. Arne Bue Jensen represents circumstantial evidence that the Vikings made it not just to a slippery rock off Newfoundland, but all the way down to New Orleans. Under the eponymous Jensen's leadership, the band became a tireless gigging unit, establishing a big reputation in Eastern Europe, as had Chris Barber. Like the Barber band, the Vikings sell a fair proportion of their CDs at gigs, and some of these items may be difficult to find in mainstream and multiple record stores. Specialists will be able to track them down without difficulty, however, and Music Mecca in Copenhagen, a sort of Valhalla for traditional jazz fans, can be contacted for mail order. Dare we say, though, that to savour these guys, it is really necessary to catch them live. Nonsense about 'authenticity' apart, Papa Bue's long-running band is one of the finest revival outfits ever to emerge north of the Mason–Dixon line. The emphasis, inevitably, is on ensemble-playing rather than soloing, and these are as confidently relaxed as anyone might wish for, with none of the stiffness that creeps into more studied revivalism. The rhythm-players have a particularly good feel, the giveaway with most such bands.

The band was founded in 1956, but was baptized and confirmed three years later when George Lewis paid a visit to Denmark. The encounter is preserved on the Storyville CD, which is well worth tracking down, not just to fill out the already generous Lewis discography. A similar encounter with Edmond Hall is more disappointing. Exactly a decade after entertaining (and startling) George, the Vikings played at the New Orleans Jazz and Heritage Festival and won the admiration of the unfoolable Ira Gitler, who pointed out that the band were more than revivalists with a cod gimmick, but serious players who could knock out Ellington charts as well as trad material. The material on the two '60s compilations comes from that period. Ellington staples 'Rent Party Blues' (a Johnny Hodges vehicle) and 'Misty Morning' are outstanding on Volume One, but the long version of 'St Louis Blues' is outstanding and could stand up against anything created on the other side of the Atlantic. Volume Two is less emphatic but, unless Music Mecca's claim that all these sides are 'previously unissued' is misleading, these are very important releases. They sound strikingly if implausibly modern, even if the sound-quality is boxy and unvaried.

*****(*) The Hit Singles: 1958–1969**
Storyville STCD 5533 *Arne Bue Jensen (tb); Finn Otto Hansen (t); Jorgen Svare (cl); Jorn Jensen (p); Bjarne 'Liller' Petersen (bj, v); Mogens Seidelin (b); Knud Ryskov Madsen (d).* 58–69.

A cheeky title concept, but an excellent introduction to the work of one of the hardest-wearing trad bands on the European circuit. The 23 tracks draw very heavily on traditional material, including hymn and folk tunes, while the playing is as direct and unadorned as ever. Like Chris Barber, Jensen keeps things together rather than pushing himself too much to the front as a soloist. Trumpet and clarinet tend to be the lead horns, but much emphasis is placed on the thumping solid accompaniment. Ideal for anyone who's still to encounter Papa Bue and his merry men.

***** Live In Dresden**
Storyville STCD 5530 *As above.* 71.

As with Chris Barber and Max Collie, Papa Bue's groups always proved to be big draws in the old Eastern bloc, where trad jazz was regarded with respect as the spontaneous expression of the pre-revolutionary proletariat. There's certainly plenty of horny-handed playing on 'Savoy Blues', 'Weary Blues' and Wingy Manone's 'Tar Paper Stomp'. There is room for a touch more sophistication, though, on an ambitious Ellington medley and in a cleverly extended version of 'Sweet Georgia Brown'. Issued in 2001, this live set helps fill in a gap in the Vikings' discography.

***** On Stage**
Timeless CD TTD 511 *Arne Bue Jensen (tb); Ole Stolle (t, v); Jorgen Svare (cl); Jorn Jensen (p); Jens Solund (b); Soren Houlind (d, v).* 4–9/84.

*****(*) In The Mood**
Timeless CD TTD 539 *As above.* 86.

***** Ice Cream**
Music Mecca CD 1000 *Arne Bue Jensen (tb); Ole Stolle (t, v); John Defferary (cl); Jorn Jensen (p); Ole Olsen, Jens Solund (b); Didier Geers (d, v); Soren Houlind (d).* 10/86–8/89.

***** Live In Slukefter Tivoli**
Music Mecca CD 1028 *As above.* 91.

*****(*) On Visit At Chlosterhof**
Music Mecca CD 1064 *As above.* 91–93.

*****(*) Everybody Loves Saturday Night**
Timeless CD TTD 580 *As above.* 12/92.

*****(*) Collection**
Music Mecca CD 2101 2CD *As above.* 86–93.

Personnel inevitably changed over the years. The key recruitment was of 'Englishman' (though we suspect Irish ancestry) John Defferary in 1985. He immediately became the key player, alongside the long-standing Jensen and Papa Bue himself, bringing a virile, Lewis-influenced sound to the group. *Ice Cream* is patchy because recorded over three years and several different sessions. The 1992 studio recording is a rather lacklustre introduction compared to what one knows the band can do at a regular gig. *In The Mood* is splendidly varied, our pick of the bunch, though some of the live recordings from the early '90s are almost as attractive. *On Stage* was recorded on the familiar turf of Copenhagen, and before a home crowd the Vikings play like they're all heading across the Rainbow Bridge, with a rousing 'Tiger Rag' and a genuinely affecting 'Just A Closer Walk With Thee'. *Collection* is a very fair summary of some of the high points of recent albums.

***** In The Mood**

Timeless CD TTD 539 *Arne Bue Jensen (tb); Ole Stolle (t); John Defferary (cl); Jorn Jensen (p); Jens Solund (b); Didier Geers (d).* 10/86.

Some unlikely inclusions in the set-list here, most obviously Kris Kristofferson's 'Help Me Make It Through The Night' and Brahms's famous Cradle Song. Of the rest, there is a characteristic mix of marches, rags and jazz tunes, of which Sidney Bechet's 'Coffee Grinder' is the most convincing. Not the best Papa Bue album, but a more than appealing one if you haven't yet made his acquaintance.

***** Canal Street Blues**

Music Mecca CD 1090 *Arne Bue Jensen (tb); Joe Errington (t); John Defferary (cl, v); Jorn Jensen (p); Ole Olsen (b); Didier Geers (d, v).* 95, 96.

Though a studio setting never gets the best out of the Vikings, it's good on occasion to hear the band in a pristine acoustic and professionally balanced. Errington isn't quite the ticket, but he fits in nicely with Defferary and Jensen, and 'Grandpa's Spells' is a miniature masterpiece of ensemble jazz.

***** 40 Years Jubilee Concert**

Music Mecca 2010 *Arne Bue Jensen (tb); Joe Errington, Finn Otto Hansen, Ole Stolle (t); Erik Andersen, John Defferary, Jorgen Svare (cl); Jorn Jensen (p); Ole Olsen, Mogens Seidelin, Jens Solund (b); Didier Geers, Soren Houlind, Ib Lindschouw, Knud Ryskov Madsen (d).* 7/96.

The Viking Jazz Band celebrated its 40th birthday in 1996 with a gala performance in the Tivoli. Jensen got together some of the players who had passed through the group and they turned in a bright, buoyant evening of music that must have been a delight to the crowd. On disc, it's a little muted and sounds as if it has been recorded through the desk, without much in the way of rebalancing or sweetening. 'The Old Rugged Cross' and 'Big Butter And Egg Man' are splendid. Much of the rest has an old-pals feel that doesn't draw in the listener.

***** German Concert Music**

Mecca CD 3040-2 *Joe Errington (t, v); Arne Bue Jensen (tb, v); Erik Andersen (cl, v); Jorn Jensen (p); Ole Olesen (b); Thomas Christensen (d).* 11/99.

The prosaic title hides what sounds like a happy occasion for the band. Errington has settled in nicely and he sounds grand on 'Basin Street Blues'. The set is absolutely unsurprising in terms of material, but the crowd love it. The sleeve now lists 44 Papa Bue CDs in print: we're getting there.

Paramount Jazz Band Of Boston

GROUP

Bostonian revivalists who started working together in 1980. They have since scattered to several locations so that, although the personnel remains constant, they get together less often than before.

****(*) Ain't Cha Glad?**

Stomp Off CD1205 *Jeff Hughes (c); Gary Rodberg (cl, ss, as); Steve Wright (cl, bcl, ss, as, ts, bs, c); Robin Verdier (p); Jimmy Mazzy (bj, v); Chuck Stewart (tba); Ray Smith (d).* 5–6/89.

***** ... And They Called It Dixieland**

Stomp Off CD1247 *As above.* 4/90–11/91.

***** March Of The Hoodlums**

Stomp Off CD1340 *As above.* 1–2/98.

Skilful if not very involving playing from another group of American revivalists. They avoid carbon-copying original arrangements on the first disc, preferring to try some new twists on Ellington, Dodds, Doc Cook and others; but the playing lacks much individuality and the ensemble work is too polite to muster any of the heat of hot dance. When they try a faded rose such as 'Yearning And Blue', it just sounds old. The second disc, recorded at two live shows, is a lot more energetic, if still a bit short on a style of their own, and the sound is a mixed bag – Mazzy's banjo often seems like the loudest instrument in the group.

The group returned after something of a hiatus with *March Of The Hoodlums.* Their go at 'Singin' The Blues' tells how much they love the music: this is the Bix and Tram version treated to an affectionate update, Trumbauer's solo played in unison by the reeds before stately cornet and piano improvisations and a return to the original last chorus. While the group still rarely rises above its collective (and entirely honourable) amateur status, this sounds like their best to date.

Tony Parenti (1900–1972)

CLARINET

A prodigy in his native New Orleans, Parenti was offered a job to go north by the Original Dixieland Jazz Band – he was too young to go, and he regretted it. He went to New York in the '20s and did a lot of non-jazz session-work for CBS in the '30s. From the mid-'40s onwards he worked in a sort of merger of Dixieland with more faithful New Orleans music, and he remained fascinated with the possibilities of ragtime.

****(*) Strut Yo' Stuff**

Frog DGF 4 *Parenti; Henry Knecht, Albert Brunies, Leon Prima, Johnny Wiggs (c); Russ Papalia, Charles Hartman (tb); Hal Jordy (ts, bs, b); Vic Lubowski, Buzzy Williams, Vic Breidis (p); Jack Brian (g, v); Mike Holloway (bj); Mario Finazzo (tba); Monk Hazel (d, v); George Triay (d).* 1/25–6/29.

****** Tony Parenti & His New Orleanians**

Jazzology JCD-1 *Parenti; Wild Bill Davison (c); Jimmy Archey (tb); Art Hodes (p); George 'Pops' Foster (b); Arthur Trappier (d).* 8/49.

***** Tony Parenti's New Orleans Shufflers**

Jazzology JCD-61 *Parenti; Jack Hine (c); Bob Thomas (tb); Hank Ross (p); Danny Barker (bj); Arnie Hyman (b); Arthur Trappier (d).* 54.

***** Parenti–Davison All Stars Vol. 1**

Jazzology JCD-91 *Parenti; Wild Bill Davison (c); Lou McGarity (tb); Eustis Tompkins, Ernie Carson (p); Jerry Rousseau (b); Bob Dean (d). n.d.*

***** Parenti–Davison All Stars Vol. 2**

Jazzology JCD-92 *As above. n.d.*

*****(*) Ragtime Jubilee**

Jazzology JCD-21 *Parenti; Wild Bill Davison (c); Larry Conger (t); Charlie Bornemann, Jimmy Archey (tb); Ralph Sutton, Kocky Parker (p); Edmond Souchon, Danny Barker (bj); Cyrus St Clair, Don Franz (tba); Baby Dodds, Pops Campbell (d).* 11/47–?

A New Orleans man who left the city in 1927, Parenti made many records but has frequently been overlooked. Never an original, he could still play with a ferocious intensity; though he approached the gaspipe manner at times, there was no little sophistication in an approach that seldom strayed far from Dixieland ideology. The Frog compilation gathers up rare early material and is a valuable if sometimes disappointing glimpse of New Orleans jazz recorded in its home city in the early years of the music: these were competent rather than capable players for the most part, and the acoustic tracks in particular have little distinction. Things improve on the electrical recordings, and the best session, from April 1928, features Parenti alongside the charmingly Bixian cornet of Johnny Wigg. The leader's own style progresses from merely tricksy playing to the showpiece 'Old Man Rhythm', a clarinet–piano duet (made after his arrival in New York) which closes the disc.

Jazzology JCD-1 was the one that started the Jazzology operation in 1949, and it still sounds hard-nosed and terrific: Davison was at his most vituperative-sounding, Parenti weaves his way round the front line with much invention, Hodes stomps through everything, and Foster slaps his strings harder than ever. Rough old recording, though that doesn't matter, and rather unnecessarily padded out with extra takes.

The All Stars session is of indeterminate date but was cut at a club in Atlanta. The balance is all off, the drums louder than everyone else; the other players are relatively undistinguished and Parenti himself sometimes sounds like he's playing on another stage. But the spirit comes through, and Wild Bill stops at nothing.

New Orleans Shufflers is from a 1954 session made in New York. Some of the names are unfamiliar but the music is a deft mix of the more hard-nosed traditionalism of New York and the sweeter feel of New Orleans music. Solos are generously shared out (and this exposes Thomas a bit) and, since he's very prominent in the mix, you can hear how hard Parenti really blew. Atmospheric and honest, and Trappier's excellent drumming is also worth paying attention to.

Ragtime Jubilee is an unusual example of two bands of traditionalists playing a pure ragtime repertoire, everything from 'Smokey Mokes' and 'Swipesy Cake Walk' to 'Grace And Beauty Rag' and '(That) Erratic Rag'. It starts with six tracks cut for Circle in 1947 by a group including Davison, Archey and Sutton and, if they found the music unfamiliar (Parenti had taken the trouble to write out a set of arrangements), the group bluster through it with rowdy excitement. The remaining tracks are from a much later (though undated) session, and again Parenti makes a dedicated effort at playing original rags without surrendering a Dixieland looseness. Good sound on these later tracks, and a very enjoyable reissue. This is a fine group of undeservedly little-known albums.

*****(*) Tony Parenti And His Downtown Boys**

Jazzology JCD-11 *Parenti; Dick Wellstood, Armand Hug (p); Chink Martin (b); Sam Ulano, Abbie Brunies (d).* 55–65.

Although the circumstances are difficult to decipher from the sleeve-notes, this disc is made up of three sessions. Two are with Wellstood and Hug, who cut seven titles in 1961 and added three more four (!) years later to complete the original LP. For the CD reissue, four titles from a 1955 Southland LP with Hug, Martin and Brunies have also been included. The trio sessions are boisterous and exciting music: all three musicians are right at the front of the mix, and when they dig in and start stomping it's hugely exciting music that comes out. Wellstood strong-arms the piano and Ulano seems to have a full percussion kit at his disposal: listen to the clatter he gets out of 'Chantez Las Bas'. Parenti sounds a bit off-key here and there, but clearly he's enjoying himself. The 1955 tracks are almost sedate by comparison but they swing along. Another terrific Parenti album.

***** The Final Bar**

Jazzology JCD-71 *Parenti; Max Kaminsky (t); Charlie Bornemann (tb); Bobby Pratt (p); Bill Payne (bj); Joe Tarto (tba); Buzzy Drootin (d).* 5/71.

Parenti's final session, made the year before he died, is another chunk of no-frills Dixieland. Veterans like Tarto and Kaminsky are welcome companions, and Parenti himself still sounds in hearty form. Rather noisily recorded and not exactly immortal, but as honestly delivered as the rest of this fine jazzman's music.

Tiny Parham (1900–1943)

PIANO

Born in Canada, the huge pianist (Tiny was his inevitable nickname: real name Hartzell Strathdene) was a busy man on the Chicago scene of the '20s, arranging for contemporaries such as King Oliver and leading his own groups, which made some idiosyncratic and intriguing records for Victor. He worked through the next decade too, but was playing in hotels and movie-houses at the time of his death.

*****(*) Tiny Parham 1926–1929**

Classics 661 *Parham; B. T. Wingfield, Punch Miller, Roy Hobson (c); Charles Lawson (tb); Junie Cobb (ss, as, cl); Charles Johnson (cl, as); Leroy Pickett, Elliott Washington (vn); Charlie Jackson (bj, v); Mike McKendrick (bj); Quinn Wilson (bb); Jimmy Bertrand, Ernie Marrero (d).* 12/26–7/29.

*****(*) Tiny Parham 1929–1940**

Classics 691 *As above, except add Dalbert Bright (cl, ss, as, ts); Ike Covington (tb); Darnell Howard (cl, as); Jimmy Hutchens (cl, ts); John Henley (g); Milt Hinton (bb); Bob Slaughter (d); Sam Theard, Tommy Brookins (v); omit Wingfield, Cobb, Pickett and Jackson.* 10/29–6/40.

***** The Alternative Takes**

Neatwork RP 2053 *Similar to above; add Freddy Keppard, James Tate, Tommy Ladnier (c); Sidney Desvignes, Amos White (t); Fayette Williams, Harvey Lankford (tb); Angelo Fernandez, Jimmy O'Bryant, Ernest Michall (cl); Buster Bailey, Norman Mason, Bert Bailey (cl, as); Norval Morton (ts); Walter Thomas (ts, bs); Adrian Robinson, Lovie Austin, Fate Marable (p); Narvin Kimball (bj, g); Erskine Tate, Ikey Robinson, Johnny St Cyr (bj); Henry Kimball (tba); Jimmy Bertrand, W. E. Burton, Zutty Singleton (d); Priscilla Stewart (v).* 6/23–11/30.

****** Tiny Parham 1928–1930**

Timeless CBC 1-022 2CD *Similar to above discs.* 7/28–11/30.

Parham's jazz was an idiosyncratic, almost eccentric brand of Chicago music: his queer, off-centre arrangements tread a line between hot music, novelty strains and schmaltz. The latter is supplied by the violinists and the occasional (and mercifully infrequent) singing – but not by the tuba, which is used with surprising shrewdness by the leader. Some of his arrangements are among the more striking things to come out of the city at that time – 'Cathedral Blues', 'Voodoo' and 'Pigs Feet And Slaw' don't sound like anybody else's group, except perhaps Morton's Red Hot Peppers, although Parham preferred a less flamboyant music to Jelly's. The 'exotic' elements, which led to titles such as 'The Head Hunter's Dream' or 'Jungle Crawl', always seem to be used for a purpose rather than merely for novelty effect and, with soloists like Miller, Hobson and the erratic Cobb, Parham had players who could play inside and out of his arrangements. The two-beat rhythms he leans on create a sort of continuous vamping effect that's oddly appropriate, and Tiny's own piano shows he was no slouch himself. There is a lot of surprising music on these discs, even when it doesn't work out for the best.

The Timeless two-CD edition sweeps past the Classics discs: consistently fine mastering, and with 12 alternative takes, this is an exemplary reissue. Diehards might want the obscure first coupling on Classics 661, which Timeless omit. The stray final tracks on Classics 691 date from 1940, by which time he was playing the electric organ; it was at a smart hotel engagement where he was the organist that this 300-lb. giant died of a heart attack in 1943.

Neatwork's round-up of alternates does have some claims on completists. Besides the 12 tracks on the Timeless set, there are a pair of 1930 alternates, as well as nine other tracks: the pair of 1923 sides by Erskine Tate which feature Freddy Keppard, the (frankly awful) 1924 session by Fate Marable, a single alternate by Lovie Austin from one of her Paramount dates, and four sides which do feature Parham, from exceedingly rare Paramount and Black Patti originals. 'Embarressement Blues' (sic!) and 'Lazybone Blues', by (King) Brady's Clarinet Band, are certainly interesting curios.

Paris Washboard

GROUP

Lively group of French traditionalists, well schooled in old hot music, who bag the occasional guest on their record dates.

***** ... Waiting For The Sunrise**
Stomp Off 1261 *Daniel Barda (tb); Alain Marquet (cl); Louis Mazetier (p); Gérard Bagot (wbd, perc); Michel Marcheteau (sou). 8/92.*

***** California Here We Come**
Stomp Off 1280 *As above, except Gérard Gervois (tba) replaces Marcheteau. 11/93.*

***** Truckin'**
Stomp Off CD1293 *As above, except add Peter Ecklund (t). 2/95.*

***** Love Nest**
Stomp Off CD1308 *As above, except add Olivier Lancelot (p); omit Ecklund. 4/96.*

*****(*) Love For Sale**
Stomp Off 1326 *As above, except omit Gervois and Lancelot. 12/96.*

Not since The Louisiana Five (in 1919!) has a group relied on a clarinet/trombone front line, and though the group is basically a quartet they tackle repertoire that's not dissimilar to The L5's output. There the comparisons stop. Mazetier is a play-anything stylist who can do Waller, James P., Morton or anybody, while Barda and Marquet are superbly lively on their horns, whether in ensemble, counterpoint or quickfire solos. Each of the discs is a smart mix of old-time classics and a sprinkle of rarities, with Mazetier helping himself to a couple of solos and originals. Yet the most important member may be Bagot: never has there been a washboard player this nimble and light with his fingers, working up a scurrying kind of rhythm that's light-years from the mistreatment this instrument received in skiffle bands or wherever. Some may find the general cheeriness an irritation; but if so, this kind of jazz won't appeal in the first place, and the group are actually at pains to differentiate their material.

Truckin' has Ecklund as guest on six tracks and he joins in the fun without blinking. *Love Nest* has Mazetier's occasional dep, Olivier Lancelot, on three tracks and he's awarded a solo version of 'Daintiness Rag'. As each of the discs has its own virtues, it's hard to make an individual choice, but we award a token extra notch to *Love For Sale*, which is their tenth-anniversary album and includes some of their best moments in 'Blue Because Of You', 'Grandpa's Spells' and the title-track – which they worry about sounding too modern.

*****(*) One More Time!**
Stomp Off 1338 *Daniel Barda (tb); Alain Marquet (cl, bcl); Louis Mazetier (p); Gérard Bagot (wbd). 2/98.*

Something of a celebration, this one, since it marks Daniel Barda's 100th record session (he started in 1964 with Les Haricots Rouges). It seems fanciful to hear them as getting better but this is at least as good as the best of their earlier work, the tempos brighter, the solos popping with jubilation. Marquet picks up the bass clarinet for a soulful 'When It's Sleepy Time Down South' and Mazetier gets a couple of tracks to himself: he plays a sensational solo on 'Runnin' Wild' too. A wonderful group at the height of their powers.

*****(*) Caravan**
Stomp Off 1347 *As above. 3/99.*

A tribute to Ellington in his centenary year. It's a good bet that none of the others paying homage came up with the notion of doing 'Frolic Sam' or 'Pelican Swing' from the master's book, although those are the only real rarities in a programme that plays up the Duke's most joyful music (and even they were by Cootie Williams and Harry Carney). A couple don't come off quite so well, but otherwise this is another delightful dose of Washboard.

*****(*) Wild Cat Blues**
Stomp Off 1359 *As above. 2–3/00.*

*****(*) 15 Years Fresh**
Stomp Off 1391 *As above. 3/03.*

There's no stopping them. No band that's 15 years into its career is going to turn out its best records. But these two scarcely hint at any sign of the arteries hardening or the reflexes slowing. As always, they enjoy a touch of kitsch, but it's not comedy jazz. It's humorous, but not silly. Every so often, they treat it gentle: Mazetier might get a solo to himself, as he does on 'Skylark' on *15 Years Fresh*, and everyone takes a breather. Marquet remains the great character of the band, Barda is lusty, Mazetier frolicsome, and Bagot plays a lot more than washboard, since he seems to have a whole set of cymbals too. It's all more great Washboard.

Charlie Parker (1920–55)

ALTO AND TENOR SAXOPHONES

For good or ill, Charlie Parker's now seems like the definitive jazz life, compounded of genius, drugs and early death. The reality is inevitably a lot more complex and mediated. That he was a genius there is no doubt, but the Kansan's genius was based on long, effortful study and some humiliation before coming into his true voice; similarly with drugs, they played a part, but not an overdetermining part, in his life and music and, while they certainly contributed to Bird's early demise, his addiction is too easily demonized. Though he had periods of disturbance, Parker's career, which began in local blues groups before he joined Jay McShann's orchestra, was one of steady and concentrated work. His role in the invention of bebop was critical, though he was certainly not the only begetter. The recorded legacy is very substantial indeed. Leaving aside airshots and other broadcast transcriptions, his recordings are among the key documents of modern music.

****** The Complete Dean Benedetti Recordings**

Mosaic MD7-129 7CD *Parker solos, with Miles Davis, Howard McGhee (t); Hampton Hawes, Duke Jordan, Thelonious Monk (p); Addison Farmer, Tommy Potter (b); Roy Porter, Max Roach (d); Earl Coleman, Kenny Hagood, Carmen McRae (v); other unknown personnel.* 3/47–7/48.

Parker's innovation – improvising a new melody line off the top, rather than from the middle, of the informing chord – was a logical extension of everything that had been happening in jazz over the previous decade. However, even though the simultaneous inscription of bebop by different hands – Dizzy Gillespie, Charlie Christian and Thelonious Monk all have their propagandists – suggests that it was an evolutionary inevitability, any artistic innovation requires quite specific and usually conscious interventions. With its emphasis on extreme harmonic virtuosity, bop has become the dominant idiom of modern jazz and Parker's genetic fingerprint is the clearest.

The British saxophone virtuoso, John Harle, has spoken of the remarkable *clarity* of Parker's music, and in particular his solo development. Even at his most dazzlingly virtuosic, Parker always sounds logical, making light of asymmetrical phrases, idiosyncratically translated bar-lines, surefooted alternation of whole-note passages and flurries of semiquavers, tampering with almost every other parameter of the music – dynamic, attack, timbre – with a kind of joyous arrogance. Dying at 35, he was spared the indignity of a middle age given over to formulaic repetition.

Because, in theory at least, he never repeated himself, there has been a degree of fetishization of many of Parker's solos, like 'The Famous Alto Break' from the Dial recordings (below) or some of the later Verve material, in which a solo is either preserved out of the fullest context on an incomplete take or executed with insouciant disregard for bland or faulty accompaniments. There is, though, an explanation that usefully combines mythology with sheer pragmatism. In his faulty biography of Parker, *Bird Lives!*, Ross Russell introduced a composite figure called Dean Benedetti (the Kerouac resonance was inescapable) who follows Bird throughout the United States capturing his solos (and the solos only) on a primitive wire-recorder. Though unreleased until 1990, the Dean Benedetti archive has enjoyed cult reputation with Parker fans, the Dead Sea Scrolls of bebop, fragmentary and patinated, inaccessible to all but adepts and insiders, but containing the Word in its purest and most unadulterated form.

The real Benedetti, routinely characterized by Russell as a saxophonist *manqué*, remained a practising player, and these remarkable recordings fall into place ever more clearly if one starts towards the end, with Benedetti's amateurishly dubbed attempts to play along with Parker records, and then accepts the absoluteness of his identification with his idol. Dean Benedetti died of *myasthenia gravis* (a progressive weakening of the musculature) two years after Bird. Benedetti was already fatally ill when he heard of Charlie Parker's death. He wrote: '*Povero C. P. Anche tu. Dove ci troveremmo?*' (Poor Bird. You too. Where will we meet again?) The answer is: here. Benedetti's archive was left in the care of his brother, Rick, who in turn died just too soon to witness the release of these astonishing records.

The Mosaic set, lovingly restored and annotated by Phil Schaap, consists of 278 tracks and a boggling 461 recordings of Charlie Parker, made between 1 March 1947 and 11 July 1948 in Los Angeles and New York (a much smaller span of time and geography than legend finds comfortable). The famous wire-recorder certainly existed but was not used for recording Bird. Benedetti worked with 78-r.p.m. acetate discs, and only later with paper-based recording tape. A good many of the recordings are vitiated or distorted by swarf from the cutting needle (which an assistant was supposed to brush away as a recording progressed) getting in the way; since the cutter moved from the outer edge of the disc towards the centre, there was also a problem with torque, and the inner grooves are often rather strained and indistinct. The sound-quality throughout is far from impressive. What is remarkable, though, is the utter dedication and concentration Benedetti brought to his task. Some of the tracks offer fully developed solos occupying several choruses; others, to take two examples only from a recording made in March 1947 at the Hi-De-Ho Club in Los Angeles, last as little as three ('Night And Day'!!) or seven (possibly 'I Surrender Dear') *seconds*.

As an insight into how Parker approached the same tune with the same group on successive nights (there are six separate solos from 'Big Noise'/'Wee' between 1 and 8 March 1947) or how he continued to tackle less familiar material associated with pre-bop figures like Coleman Hawkins (three helpings of 'Bean Soup' in the same period), it is an unparalleled resource. There is also valuable documentation of a rare meeting with Thelonious Monk, recorded on 52nd Street in July 1948. The density of background material (titles, durations, key-signatures, in some cases transcriptions) is awesome and, though some of the material has been available for some time as *Bird On 52nd Street* (Original Jazz Classics OJC 114 LP), the vast bulk of it has not been in the public domain. As such, *The Dean Benedetti Recordings* represent the last step in the consolidation of Parker's once inchoate and shambolic discography. Though there is a vast muddle of live material and airshots, there is a surprisingly small corpus of authorized studio material. Parker's recording career really lasts only a decade, from 1944 to 1953, and is enshrined in three main blocks of material, for Savoy (1944–8), for Dial (1946 to December 1947) and for Norman Granz's Verve (1948–53); throw in the significant Royal Roost live sessions and, but for the Benedetti archive, the main pillars of Parker's reputation are in place.

The painter, Barnett Newman, once said that aesthetics was for artists like ornithology was for the birds, and the unintended reference can usefully be appropriated in this context. Though essentially for specialists (and rather well-heeled experts at that) who are untroubled by the abruptly decontextualized nature of these performances, the Benedetti material represents a quite remarkable auditory experience. The initially exasperating sequence of sound-bites gives way to an illusion of almost telepathic insight, a key to the inner mystery of who and what Parker was.

***(*) Charlie Parker, 1947

Classics 1000 *Parker; Miles Davis (t); Duke Jordan (p); Tommy Potter (b); Max Roach (d).* 10, 11, 12/47.

Appropriate that Classics 1000 (phew!) should be devoted to Parker at the peak of his powers, recording his last three sessions for Dial in New York and, a mere five days after 'How Deep Is The Ocean', reconvening with Miles, Duke, Tommy and Max in Detroit to make his first four cuts for Savoy, of which more below. The usual quibbles apply to these reissues: poor sound and a too-literal chronology. There is – arguably – some merit in not dividing the oeuvre into discontinuous label blocks, Dial, Savoy, Verve, but to treat it as a continuous whole. It's hard to imagine much dramatic stylistic development between 17 December and 21 December. To that extent, this compilation is salutary, but we can't recommend it on aesthetic grounds.

♛ **** The Complete Savoy And Dial Studio Recordings

Savoy 92911-2 8CD *Parker; Miles Davis, Dizzy Gillespie, Howard McGhee (t); J. J. Johnson (tb); Flip Phillips, Lucky Thompson, Wardell Gray, Jack McVea (ts); Tiny Brown (bs); Slim Gaillard (p, g, v); Clyde Hart, Jimmy Bunn, Duke Jordan, Russ Freeman, Erroll Garner, George Handy, John Lewis, Sadik Hakim, Bud Powell, Michael 'Dodo' Marmarosa (p); Red Norvo (vib); Arvin Garrison, Barney Kessel, Tiny Grimes (g); Nelson Boyd, Ray Brown, Red Callender, Arnold Fishkind, Bob Kesterson, Vic McMillan, Jimmy Butts, Tommy Potter, Slam Stewart, Curley Russell (b); Max Roach, Harold 'Doc' West, Zutty Singleton, Don Lamond, Specs Powell, Jimmy Pratt, Stan Levey, Roy Porter (d); Earl Coleman (v).* 9/44–12/48.

*** Newly Discovered Sides

Savoy 17188 *As above.*

The sides Parker cut on 26 November 1945 were billed by Savoy on the later microgroove release as 'The greatest recording session made in modern jazz'. There's some merit in that. The kitchen-sink reproduction of fluffs, false starts and breakdowns gives a rather chaotic impression. Miles Davis, who never entirely came to terms with Parker's harmonic or rhythmic requirements, doesn't play particularly well (there is even a theory that some of the trumpet choruses – notably one on a third take of 'Billie's Bounce' – were played by Dizzy Gillespie in imitation of Miles's rather uncertain style), and some of the pianist's intros and solos are positively bizarre; step forward, pianist Argonne Thornton, who remembers (though he's the only one who does) being at the sessions. Despite all that, and Parker's continuing problems with a recalcitrant reed, the session includes 'Billie's Bounce', 'Now's The Time' and 'Ko-Ko'. The last of these is perhaps the high-water mark of Parker's improvisational genius.

Though this is undoubtedly the zenith of Parker's compositional skill as well (in later years he seems to have created fewer and fewer original themes), it is noticeable that virtually all of the material on these sessions draws either on a basic 12-bar blues or on the chord sequence of 'I Got Rhythm', the Ur-text of bebop. 'Ko-Ko' is based on the chords of 'Cherokee', as is the generic 'Warming Up A Riff', which was intended only as a run-through after Parker had carried out running repairs on his squeaking horn. The remainder of Parker's material was drawn, conventionally enough, from show tunes; 'Meandering', a one-off ballad performance on the November 1945 session, unaccountably elided after superb solos from Parker and Powell, bears some relationship to 'Embraceable You'. What is striking about Parker's playing, here and subsequently, is the emphasis on rhythmic invention, often at the expense of harmonic creativity (in that department, as he shows in miniature on 'Ko-Ko', Dizzy Gillespie was certainly his superior).

Availability on programmable CD means that listeners who find the staccato progression of incomplete takes disconcerting are able to ignore all but the final, released versions. Unfortunately, though these are usually the best *band* performances, they do not always reflect Bird's best solo playing. A good example comes on 'Now's The Time', a supposedly original theme, but one which may retain the outline of an old Kansas City blowing blues (or may have been composed – that is, played – by tenor saxophonist Rocky Boyd). There is no doubt that Parker's solo on the third take is superior in its slashing self-confidence to that on the fourth, which is slightly duller; Miles Davis plays without conviction on both.

None of the other constituent sessions match up to the erratic brilliance of 26 November 1945. There are nine other dates represented, notably intermittent in quality. The sessions with Slim Gaillard, creator of 'Vout', an irritating hipster argot, are pretty corny and time-bound; a bare month after 'Ko-Ko', Parker seems to have come down to earth. An early session with guitarist Tiny Grimes and an unusual August 1947 date (under Miles Davis's control) on which Bird played tenor saxophone, excluded from previous Savoy CD reissues, have been restored. Of the remaining dates, that of 8 May 1947, a rather uneasy affair, nevertheless yielded 'Donna Lee' and 'Chasing The Bird'; by contrast, on 21 December 1947, Parker seems utterly confident and lays down the ferocious 'Bird Gets The Worm' and 'Klaunstance'; the sessions of 18 and 24 September 1948 yielded the classic 'Parker's Mood' (original take 3 is suffused with incomparable blues feeling) and 'Marmaduke' respectively.

The other key figures on these recordings are Max Roach, barely out of his teens but already playing in the kind of advanced rhythmic count that Parker required, and Dizzy Gillespie. Miles Davis was demonstrably unhappy with some of the faster themes and lacked Parker's ability to think afresh take after take; by the time of the 'Parker's Mood' date, though, he had matured significantly (he was, after all, only 19 when 'Ko-Ko' and 'Now's The Time' were recorded). A word, too, for Curley Russell and Tommy Potter, whose contribution to this music has not yet been fully appreciated and who were rather sorely used on past releases, often muffled to the point of inaudibility.

A point of frustration for many in the past has been the scattered nature of these sessions, spread across numerous LP and CD editions. But with Tony Williams's agreement, the Savoys and the Dials are finally brought within a single set for the first time in this ring-bound eight-disc collection. The master tracks for each date are programmed first, followed by the various alternative takes. There is full documentation in a handsome booklet, and the harsh sound of the Savoys and Dials has been made as hi-fi as the originals will probably ever allow. We need hardly say, in short, that this is one of the most essential jazz CD sets in the marketplace. As the Dial sessions continue to be made available separately in their own Spotlite edition, we have discussed that music below.

The 'newly discovered sides' on the recent Savoy include an interesting enough 'Out Of Nowhere', 'Oop-Bop-Sh'bam', 'Jumpin' With Symphony Sid'/'Bebop' and a more unexpected 'East Of The Sun (And West Of The Moon)', which is not a number one associates with Parker. The rest of the tracks are familiar Savoys.

CORE COLLECTION

**** Charlie Parker On Dial: The Complete Sessions

Spotlite/Dial SPJ CD 4 4101 4CD *Parker; Miles Davis, Dizzy Gillespie, Howard McGhee (t); J. J. Johnson (tb); Flip Phillips, Lucky Thompson, Wardell Gray (ts); Jimmy Bunn, Duke Jordan, Russ Freeman, Erroll Garner, George Handy, Michael 'Dodo' Marmarosa (p); Red Norvo (vib); Arvin Garrison, Barney Kessel (g); Ray Brown, Red Callender, Arnold Fishkind, Bob Kesterson, Vic McMillan, Tommy Potter, Slam Stewart (b); Don Lamond, Specs Powell, Jimmy Pratt, Stan Levey, Roy Porter, Max Roach, Harold 'Doc' West (d); Teddy Wilson, Earl Coleman (v).* 6/45, 2, 3 & 7/46, 2, 10, 11, & 12/47.

On 26 February 1946, Parker signed what was intended to be an exclusive recording contract with Dial Records, an outgrowth of the Tempo Music Shop on Hollywood Boulevard in Los Angeles. The co-signatory was Tempo owner Ross Russell, subsequently author of *Bird Lives!* and disseminator of some of the more lasting myths about Parker. A contemporary headline declared rather enigmatically: 'West Coast Jazz Center Enters Shellac Derby With Be-Bop Biscuits'. Russell's original intention to specialize in classic jazz (largely ignoring swing, in other words) had been confounded by an unanticipated demand for bop 78s. With typical perspicacity, he lined up Parker, Gillespie and others, gave them unprecedented free rein in the studio and backed his commitment with the best engineers available. The investment predictably took some time to recoup. Parker's Dial period straddles a near-catastrophic personal crisis and a subsequent period of almost Buddhist calm, when his playing takes on a serene logic and untroubled simplicity which in later years was to give way to a blander sophistication and chastened professionalism.

On Volume 1 of the Spotlite Dial, a solitary February 1946 cut ('Diggin' Diz') under Gillespie's leadership pre-dates the remarkable session seven weeks later which yielded 'Moose The Mooche', 'Yardbird Suite', 'Ornithology' and 'A Night In Tunisia', four of his classic performances. Parker's solo on the third take of 'Ornithology' is completely masterful, by turns climbing fiercely and soaring effortlessly, always on the point of stalling but never for a moment losing momentum; close study reveals the daring placement of accents and a compelling alternation of chromatic runs (first refuge of beginners or those suffering temporary harmonic amnesia, but never handled with such grace) and dazzling intervallic leaps. Multiple takes of virtually every item (the six Spotlite volumes take in 39 tunes but 88 separate performances) demonstrate the extent to which Parker was prepared to re-take at constantly shifting tempi, never wrong-footing himself but often having to pull some of the rhythm players along in his wake. 'The Famous Alto Break', 46 seconds of pure invention on the saxophone, is all that remains of a first take of 'A Night In Tunisia'; before the Benedetti materials were made available, 'The Famous Alto Break' was Parker's best-known cameo solo.

In contrast to Curley Russell and Max Roach, Vic McMillan and Roy Porter can sound a little stiff, but Dodo Marmarosa (an undervalued player, now long since retired from active playing) has a bright, sharp-edged angularity which suits Parker perfectly and which is picked up generously by good digital remastering. On 29 July 1946, Parker was in the C. P. MacGregor Studios, Hollywood, with Howard McGhee, a fellow addict, in for Miles Davis or Dizzy Gillespie. Bird was practically comatose during the recording of 'Lover Man' (but nevertheless managed a brutal, convoluted solo that is a rare converse to his usual formal clarity) and collapsed shortly after the session, setting off a train of disasters that landed him in the State Hospital at Camarillo. Heroin addiction permits surprisingly extended activity at a high level, but usually at a high rate of interest. There has been a tendency again to fetishize work born out of appalling physical and psychological anguish at the expense of less troubled performances. In the summer of 1946 Parker was writing cheques that his body and normally indomitable spirit could no longer cash. 'Lover Man', like so many club and concert solos from the preceding years, was done on autopilot. Bird's headlong flight was briefly halted.

He emerged healthier than he had been for a decade. Rest (as in 'Relaxin' At Camarillo'), detoxification and the occasional salad had done him more good than any amount of largactil. A rehearsal session held at Chuck Kopely's house on 1 February 1947 is included, but the recording is very poor (Howard McGhee allegedly kept a hand-held mic pointing at Bird throughout). Parker's first post-release recording for Dial cast him in the unlikely company of Erroll Garner and the singer, Earl Coleman. Garner's intriguing two-handedness, offering apparent independence in the bass and melody lines, was a valuable prop for Parker, and he sounds remarkably composed. Coleman's singing on 'This Is Always' and 'Dark Shadows' is uncomplicated and rather appealing. The meat of the sessions comes with 'Bird's Nest' and the marvellous 'Cool Blues', again attempted at very different tempi. The fourth – or 'D' – take of 'Cool Blues' is positively lugubrious. The soloing is limpid and logical, and not much circumstantial knowledge is required to hear the difference between these tracks and the tortured 'Lover Man' of six months before.

A week later, Parker returned to the studio with McGhee and Marmarosa. 'Relaxin' At Camarillo' was allegedly written in the back of a cab *en route* to the date; it was cast in familiar blues form but with an intriguing tonality that suggested Bird was beginning to exercise greater inventiveness along the other, relatively neglected, axis of his work. Unfortunately, the 26 February performances are rather cluttered (Wardell Gray's tenor adds nothing very much; Barney Kessel sounds rather blocky) and the sound isn't up to previous standards.

The selections from 28 October and 4 November are some of the most lyrical in Parker's entire output. 'Bird Of Paradise' is based on the sequence of 'All The Things You Are', with an introduction (Bird and Miles) that was to become one of the thumbprints of bebop. Parker reinvents his solo from take to take, never exhausting his own resources, never losing contact with the basic material. 'Embraceable You' and the gentle 'Dewey Square', 'Out Of Nowhere' and single takes of 'My Old Flame' and 'Don't Blame Me' don't reach quite the same heights, but the third (unissued) take of 'Out Of Nowhere' is further demonstration of how much magnificent music had to be picked off the editing-room floor. The November session also included two of Parker's finest originals, 'Scrapple From The Apple' and the bizarrely entitled 'Klact-oveeseds-tene' (apparently a quasi-phonetic transcription of *Klage, Auf Wiedersehen* – some give it as 'Klact', meaning 'bad noise' – which could be taken to mean something like 'Farewell To The Blues'), which is a raw and slightly neurotic theme played entirely out of kilter.

Roach's grasp of Bird's requirements was by now completely intuitive. Only he seems to have been entirely in tune with the saxophonist's often weirdly dislocated entries, and there is a story that Roach had to shout to Duke Jordan not to elide or add beats or half-bars, knowing that Parker would navigate a course back to the basic metre before the end of his solo choruses. This intuitive brilliance is particularly easy to trace on the slower ballad numbers, where the saxophone's entry is often breathtakingly unexpected and dramatic, underlined by Miles Davis's increasingly confident ability to work across the beat, especially at lower tempi.

Bird's final recording session for Dial and with the great quintet was held in New York City on 17 December 1947, with the addition of trombonist J. J. Johnson. 'Crazeology' is fast and furious, and Parker's solos on both the 'C' and (released) 'D' takes are impeccable; he was allegedly playing with a new horn and his tone is more than usually full and precise. Johnson was certainly the first trombone player to understand bop completely enough to make a meaningful contribution to it. His solos on 'Crazeology' and 'Bird Feathers' are excellent, rhythmically much more daring than anyone had previously dared to be on slide trombone.

The Parker Dials, though perhaps of less concentrated brilliance than the Savoys, are among the greatest small-group jazz of all time; masters were cut in October 1949 and the album released shortly thereafter. They are also of considerable significance in that *Bird Blows The Blues*, formerly available as a separate LP, was the first long-playing record devoted to jazz performance. It was distinctive in two regards. In the first place, Russell favoured the 12-inch format, which maintained its hegemony (until the rise of tape cassette and the compact disc) over the more usual ten-inch format, which was the record dealers' preference. Dial later bowed to market pressure, but subsequent ten-inch releases were pressed on a poor-quality vinyl mix that created a great deal of background noise. In the second place, Russell began to include alternative takes of many tracks, setting in motion a discographical mania that has haunted Parker fans ever since. Solos are sipped like vintages and too often spat into a bucketful of matrix numbers rather than fully savoured and absorbed. For those who have problems on both counts, the availability of master performances on good-quality CD and without the distraction of multiple takes may well be a godsend. The fully documented Spotlite Dials are outstanding, for those who, for whatever reason, would rather have them separate from the Savoy material. There are, in the Dial documentation, a large number of alternatives, of which the following seem to be the most important and merit the closest attention: 'Yardbird Suite', 'The Famous Alto Break', 'Cool Blues', 'Relaxin' At Camarillo', 'Bird Of Paradise', 'Scrapple From The Apple', 'Out Of Nowhere', 'Drifting On A Reed' (another of Parker's themeless improvisations) and 'Bongo Beep' (a December 1947 track that shouldn't be confused with the slightly earlier 'Bongo Bop'). If listeners went no further down this entry, they could be assured of having the very best work that Parker did, the tracks that made him unequivocally great. They would, of course, also miss some wonderful music ...

***** Charlie Parker, 1945–1947**
Classics 980 *As for Savoy and Dial sessions above.* 11/45–5/47.

****(*) Volume 1 – 1945–1947: The Complete Alternative Takes In Chronological Order**
Neatwork 2008 *As above.* 45-47.

****(*) Volume 2 – 1947: The Complete Alternative Takes In Chronological Order**
Neatwork 2018 *As above.* 47.

****(*) Volume 3 – 1947–1948: The Complete Alternative Takes In Chronological Order**
Neatwork 2028 *As above.* 47–48.

Neatwork volumes are complementary to Classics' chronological approach. Though they may come into their own with some other artists, Parker alternatives are so well known and so readily available that it's unlikely there will be much of a market for these sets, which, as usual, suffer from indifferent sound. To be fair, this has been partially addressed, but we are still not dealing with aesthetically pleasing transfers.

****** Bird: The Complete Charlie Parker On Verve**
Verve 837141-2 10CD *Parker; Mario Bauza, Buck Clayton, Paquito Davilla, Kenny Dorham, Harry 'Sweets' Edison, Roy Eldridge, Dizzy Gillespie, Chris Griffin, Benny Harris, Al Killian, Howard McGhee, Jimmy Maxwell, Doug Mettome, Carl Poole, Al Porcino, Bernie Privin, Red Rodney, Charlie Shavers, Al Stewart, Ray Wetzel, Bobby Woodlan (t); Will Bradley, Bill Harris, Lou McGarity, Tommy Turk, Bart Varsalona (tb); Vinnie Jacobs (frhn); Hal McKusick, John LaPorta (cl); Benny Carter, Johnny Hodges, Gene Johnson, Toots Mondello, Sonny Salad, Fred Skerritt, Willie Smith, Harry Terrill, Murray Williams (as); Coleman Hawkins, Jose Madera, Pete Mondello, Flip Phillips, Hank Ross, Sol Rabinowitz, Ben Webster, Lester Young (ts); Manny Albam, Danny Bank, Leslie Johnakins, Stan Webb (bs); Artie Drelinger (reeds); Walter Bishop Jr, Al Haig, Rene Hernandez, Hank Jones, Ken Kersey, John Lewis, Thelonious Monk, Oscar Peterson, Mel Powell, Arnold Ross (p); Irving Ashby, Billy Bauer, Jerome Darr, Freddie Green, Barney Kessel (g); Ray Brown, Billy Hadnott, Percy Heath, Teddy Kotick, Charles Mingus, Tommy Potter, Roberto Rodriguez, Curley Russell (b); Kenny Clarke, Roy Haynes, J. C. Heard, Don Lamond, Shelly Manne, Buddy Rich, Max Roach, Art Taylor, Lee Young (d); Machito, Jose Mangual, Luis Miranda, Umberto Nieto, Chano Pozo, Carlos Vidal (perc); Ella Fitzgerald, Dave Lambert Singers (v); woodwinds; strings.* 1/46–12/54.

After the extraordinary Savoys and Dials, the sessions for Norman Granz's label mark an inevitable diminuendo. However, it must never be forgotten that Granz was a passionate and practical advocate of better treatment for black American musicians, and it was he who brought Parker to the attention of the wider audience he craved. For the saxophonist, to be allowed to record with strings was a final rubber-stamp of artistic legitimacy. Just as his association with Granz's Jazz At The Philharmonic jamborees are still thought to have turned him into a circus performer, the Parker With Strings sessions (fully documented here and on the special single CD noted below) have attracted a mixture of outright opprobrium and predictable insistence that Bird's solos be preserved and evaluated out of context; the point, though, would seem to be that Parker himself, out of naïvety, a wakening sense of self-advancement, or a genuine wish to break the mould of 'jazz' performance, was every bit as concerned with the context as he was with his own place in it. There is a fair amount of saccharin in the first strings performances, but Parker is superb on 'April In Paris' and 'I Didn't Know What Time It Was', and the release of the material in January 1950 propelled Parker on to a new, national stage. From February he toured with strings opposite Stan Getz. These experiments weren't always a perceived success. A vocal set to Gil Evans's arrangements foundered after 15 takes of just four numbers; there are major problems with balances (and Schaap has fulfilled Evans's wish by re-weighting the rhythm section), but the performances are by no means the disaster they're commonly thought to be.

Parker's signing with Verve almost coincided with a recording strike that was called by the AFM for 1 January 1948. Verve boss Norman Granz managed to fit in two hasty recordings before that time, both of which were for a compilation album called *The Jazz Scene*, but neither of them did Parker much justice. There is some controversy as to the exact circumstances of his recording 'Repetition' with Neal Hefti's orchestra. Some sources suggest that Bird is overdubbed; he sounds merely overpowered by a lush arrangement but manages to throw in a quote from *The Rite Of Spring* (Stravinsky was currently high on his playlist). 'The Bird' was recorded by a scratch quartet (Hank Jones, Ray Brown, Shelly Manne) and apparently done at speed. Parker fluffs a couple of times and the rhythm section accelerate and stutter like courtiers trying to keep an even ten paces behind the king.

The same group (with the unsuitable Buddy Rich in for the elegant Manne) sounded much better two and a half years later. On 'Star Eyes', 'I'm In The Mood For Love' and 'Blues (Fast)' Parker plays remarkably straight and with little of the jagged angularity of earlier recordings. The CD compilation adds no new material or alternatives, in sharp contrast to a session recorded two months later, in June 1950, for which Granz, ever on the lookout for eye-catching combinations, brought together Dizzy Gillespie, Thelonious Monk (their solitary studio encounter), Curley Russell (Bird's most sympathetic partner on bass) and, again, the wholly unsuitable Buddy Rich, who thrashes away to distraction. The new material consists of little more than tiny canapés of studio noise, false starts and run-downs, but there are previously undiscovered or unreleased takes of 'Leap Frog' and 'Relaxin' With Lee', tunes Parker is said to have composed spontaneously when it was discovered that he had forgotten to bring sheets with him. 'Ballade', apparently recorded for use in a film by Gjon Mili, partners Bird with Coleman Hawkins, their only known studio recordings together.

The most substantial single item uncovered by Phil Schaap in his painstaking trawl through the vaults is an acceptable master of Chico O'Farrill's 'Afro-Cuban Jazz Suite', recorded in December 1950 with Machito. Less adept at Latin rhythms than Dizzy Gillespie, Parker had nevertheless experimented with 'south of the border' sessions (there's a fine 1952 session with Benny Harris, co-composer of 'Ornithology') and he solos with great flourish on the 17-minute 'Suite'.

There are more Latin numbers on disc 6, which encapsulates Parker's finest studio performances for Granz. It covers three sessions recorded in January, March and August 1951. The earliest, with Miles, Walter Bishop Jr, Teddy Kotick and Max Roach, featured the classic original 'Au Privave', 'She Rote', 'K. C. Blues', and 'Star Eyes'. The 'Au Privave' solos (two takes) are rapid-fire, joyous Bird, deliberately contrasting with Miles's soft touch; on the alternative, Parker really pushes the boat out and Miles cheekily responds with mimicry of the last couple of bars. The tune is now an influential bebop staple, but it was originally issued as the B-side to 'Star Eyes' which, like the later 'My Little Suede Shoes', recorded in March with a Latin beat, enjoyed enormous success as a single. The August sessions featured a racially integrated line-up fronted by Parker and the young white trumpeter, Red Rodney, whose fiery playing reflected his nickname and hair coloration much more than it did his race, which presented a problem to some 'authenticity'-obsessed critics. The most poignant moment is a re-run, played at first with great correctness but with a bubbling eagerness coming up from underneath, of 'Lover Man', which had been the on-mic flashpoint of Parker's disastrous collapse in 1946. It is said that Bird was upset that the Dial performance was ever released; five years later, he gets his own back with an airy, problem-free reading (he even anticipates his own entry) and a snook-cocking 'Country Gardens' coda, a device Parker used frequently but which he intended here to be deflationary.

Swedish Schnapps (which covers the original LP of that name, the wonderful January 'Au Privave' sessions, and three alternatives from the May 1949 sessions with Kenny Dorham) is available as a separate CD and is an excellent buy for anyone not yet ready or not well enough funded for the kitchen-sink approach of the ten-CD set.

The small-group material thins after this point. There is a good December 1952/January 1953 quartet recording ('The Song Is You', 'Laird Baird', 'Cosmic Rays', 'Kim') with Jones, Kotick and Roach, and two late flourishes from an increasingly erratic Parker in July 1953 and March and December 1954. The latter sessions, which were to be the last studio recordings of his life, were devoted to Cole Porter themes. Parker plays much more within the beat than previously and, but for a near perfection of tone, some of these later performances could safely be relegated. Schaap has found a long alternative of 'Love For Sale', however, which suggests how thoroughly Parker could still rethink his own strategies. It also conveniently brings the whole extraordinary package full circle.

Bird will already have superseded the eight-volume vinyl *Definitive Charlie Parker* in most serious collections. The most important additional material, apart from a couple of genuinely valuable alternatives and the restored 'Afro-Cuban Jazz Suite', is a substantial amount of live performance recorded under the umbrella of Granz's JATP. The earliest item in the collection is a live jam from January 1946 at which Parker encountered (and, on 'Lady Be Good', totally wiped out) his great role-model, Lester Young, then already in his post war doldrums. The two men met once again at Carnegie Hall in 1949, but it's the earlier encounter that conveys the drama of Bird's precarious grasp on the highest perch. Absent at the beginning of the performance, he comes on stage to thunderous applause and tosses something on to Bud Powell's piano strings, creating a weird jangle. It may be his reed guard, but Phil Schaap suggests (rather improbably, one would have thought) that it was a hypodermic and spoon. The beauty of the 1946 concert lies in its spontaneity. The later, June 1952, 'alto summit' with Johnny Hodges and the veteran Benny Carter is by contrast rather stilted, with an 'after you' succession of solo appearances. (Oscar Peterson, being groomed for stardom by Granz, is also present.)

Pricey and perhaps a little overcooked for non-specialists, *Bird* is nevertheless a model of discographical punctiliousness. The sound is excellent, the notes detailed and fascinating (often backed by anecdotal material from interviews Schaap has conducted with surviving participants) and the packaging very attractive.

**(*) Charlie Parker, 1947–1949

Classics 1103 *As above.* 47–49.

Even those who have enjoyed collecting Classics in chronological and numerical order might baulk at these muzzy transfers of Bird's readily available Verve years. Doubtless a Neatwork set of alternates is in the offing, just to clog the market still further. Fine as the music is, we can't see a reason to recommend this.

*** The Complete JATP Concerts

Definitive 11146 *As above.* 46, 49.

Here are two of the jazz greats – Charlie Parker and Lester Young – in summit conference with some of the greatest players ever assembled in one place. The music is well enough known, see above, but it's always good to be reminded afresh of these extraordinary jams. An ideal present for a saxophone lover.

CORE COLLECTION

**** Charlie Parker

Verve 539757-2 *Parker; Kenny Dorham (t); Tommy Turk (tb); Coleman Hawkins (ts); Al Haig, Hank Jones (p); Ray Brown, Percy Heath, Teddy Kotick, Tommy Potter (b); Buddy Rich, Shelly Manne, Max Roach (d); Carlos Vidal (perc).* 12/47–7/53.

The first single-disc release of the quartet recordings since the monumental ten-CD set and an excellent buy for anyone who is unwilling to go that far. From the opening of 'Now's The Time' to the end of 'Visa', this is vintage Bird. We'd question the need, on a compilation of this sort, for five alternatives and false starts on 'Chi-Chi'. However, if you haven't experienced this kind of documentation before, it may well be beguiling and fascinating. Repackaged with Verve's usual understated care and attention to detail, this is a hugely attractive issue and one that may well help pull in new listeners to this extraordinary music. Listening to these familiar tracks again, we were struck by how magnificent even the occasionally dispraised later Bird could be.

**** A Studio Chronicle: 1940–1948

JSP 915 5CD *As above; and others.* 40–48.

A titanic project that brings together some of Parker's classic small-group recordings with early material recorded with Jay McShann and other sets under the (co-)leadership of Tiny Grimes, Slim Gaillard, Sir Charles Thompson and Machito. The material is as familiar as any in the jazz canon, the remasterings are professional and the packaging robust and informative. No one could ask for more.

*** Complete Onyx Recordings

Definitive DRCD 11229 *Parker; Miles Davis (t); Duke Jordan, Thelonious Monk (p); Tommy Potter (b); Max Roach (d); Earl Coleman, Carmen McRae (v).* 7/48.

We have discussed Dean Benedetti's heroic and often misunderstood attempt to document Charlie Parker's solos. Benedetti was neither a crazed fan – a stalker with recording equipment – nor a professional bootlegger. His first aim was to study Parker in the closest possible detail, as a means of improving his own musical development. The obvious problem with most of his recordings is that they are decontextualized, solos lifted out of the middle of a song with little sense of what went before or what Parker's associates were doing before and after him.

These sessions, recorded by Benedetti and band-mate trombonist Jimmy Knepper at the Onyx Club in New York City during a one-week residency in July 1948, have the benefit of giving complete recordings of many numbers. They also have the signal disadvantage of having been recorded from underneath the stage and via a microphone drilled through the platform near the rhythm section. Consequently, Bird often sounds as if playing in a different borough, while Roach and the usually inaudible Potter come across surprisingly clearly.

The value of these cuts, taken from public performances on July 7 and 11, with two cuts from a July 10 rehearsal, is largely historical. Among the rarities is an appearance by Thelonious Monk on his own 'Well, You Needn't', but the real value is precisely that set by Benedetti and Knepper. One can hear Bird change his tack on a standard like 'Out Of Nowhere', set by set and night by night; by contrast, Miles Davis, a much less uneasy bebopper than a weakening consensus insists, sticks pretty much to the same approach. In many respects, Davis comes out of these sessions better than his boss, not quite rehabilitated as a major player in the development of bop, but certainly a better technician than sometimes suggested. Carmen McRae and the now largely forgotten Earl Coleman turn up for guest vocals and suffer the same audibility problems as the horns.

Hard to judge how such discs could fit into the average record collection, since the effort of listening to them is considerable and only intermittently rewarding. They remain part of the Parker pseudepigrapha, damaged and enigmatic scrolls rather than orthodox gospels.

**** Confirmation

Verve 527815-2 2CD *As above.* 2/49–7/53.

**** Bird's Best Bop

Verve 527452-2 *Parker; Miles Davis, Kenny Dorham, Dizzy Gillespie, Red Rodney (t); Walter Bishop Jr, Al Haig, Hank Jones, John Lewis, Thelonious Monk (p); Ray Brown, Percy Heath, Teddy Kotick, Tommy Potter, Curley Russell (b); Kenny Clarke, Buddy Rich, Max Roach (d).* 5/49–7/53.

*** Jazz Masters 15: Charlie Parker

Verve 519827-2 *As above.* 47–53.

*** Jazz Masters 28: Charlie Parker Plays Standards

Verve 521854-2 *Parker; Buck Clayton, Roy Eldridge, Benny Harris, Jimmy Maxwell, Carl Poole, Al Porcino, Bernie Privin (t); Bill Harris, Lou McGarity, Tommy Turk, Bart Varsalona (tb); Willie Smith, Harry Terrill, Murray Williams (as); Coleman Hawkins, Flip Phillips, Hank Ross, Lester Young (ts); Danny Bank (bs); Walter Bishop Jr, Stan Freeman, Al Haig, Hank Jones, Oscar Peterson (p); Billy Bauer, Freddie Green (g); Ray Brown, Percy Heath, Teddy Kotick, Charles Mingus (b); Roy Haynes, Don Lamond, Buddy Rich, Max Roach, Art Taylor (d); Luis Miranda (perc); Butch Birdsall, Ella Fitzgerald, Dave Lambert, Jerry Parker, Annie Ross (v); woodwinds; strings.* 46–54.

****** Swedish Schnapps**

Verve 849393-2 *Parker; Miles Davis, Kenny Dorham, Red Rodney (t); John Lewis, Walter Bishop Jr, Al Haig (p); Ray Brown, Teddy Kotick, Tommy Potter (b); Kenny Clarke, Max Roach (d).* 49–51.

****** Bird: The Original Recordings Of Charlie Parker**

Verve 837176-2 *As above.* 2/49–7/53.

****** Now's The Time**

Verve 825671-2 *Parker; Hank Jones (p); Percy Heath, Teddy Kotick (b); Max Roach (d).* 12/52, 8/53.

*****(*) Gitanes Jazz – Round Midnight: Charlie Parker**

Verve 847911-2 *As above; various dates.*

***** Ultimate Charlie Parker**

Verve 559708-2 *Parker; Mario Bauza (t); Coleman Hawkins, Flip Phillips, Lester Young (ts); Hank Jones (p); Ray Brown, Curley Russell (b); Shelly Manne, Buddy Rich (d); Machito (perc); strings.* 46–52.

So humungous and expensive is the ten-CD set that all but the very well-heeled would be advised to pick and choose among these wallet-friendly repackagings of the Verve Parkers. Most of the titles are self-explanatory or have been glossed in some way above. *Confirmation* attempts a distillation of the whole shebang which is quixotic but admirable and done with excellent taste and sense of balance. The *Jazz Masters* series is irreproachably accurate and well documented, but the boxes are unattractive and the by-the-numbers approach to Verve's back-catalogue is a touch off-putting. More casual listeners might find it a helpful, if ultimately misleading way of building a library. *Swedish Schnapps* we have already commented on, and it should perhaps be a priority purchase. For the car stereo, mobile disc-player or the *pied-à-terre, Bird's Best Bop* would be a sensible investment, covering the strongest of the Verve tracks ('Now's The Time', 'Confirmation', 'Swedish Schnapps', 'She Rote' and the glorious 'Au Privave'); romantics will find the *Gitanes Jazz – Round Midnight* compilation a little more amenable.

The *Ultimate* series, each of them curated by a musician influenced by the artist concerned, offers no new insight. Jackie McLean's recollections of Parker are interesting in themselves, but most of his anecdotes have been told many times over, and his debt to Bird is so obvious as to require no restatement.

***** Talkin' Bird**

Verve 559859-2 *Parker; Miles Davis, Roy Eldridge, Dizzy Gillespie, Charlie Shavers (t); Tommy Turk (tb); Benny Carter, Johnny Hodges (as); Flip Phillips, Ben Webster, Lester Young (ts); Walter Bishop Jr, Al Haig, Hank Jones, Thelonious Monk, Oscar Peterson (p); Barney Kessel (g); Ray Brown, Percy Heath, Teddy Kotick, Curley Russell (b); Roy Haynes, J. C. Heard, Buddy Rich, Max Roach (d); Machito (perc).* 49–53.

*****(*) Hi-Fi**

Verve 539757-2 *Parker; Kenny Dorham (t); Tommy Turk (tb); Coleman Hawkins (ts); Al Haig, Hank Jones (p); Ray Brown, Percy Heath, Tommy Potter (b); Shelly Manne, Buddy Rich, Max Roach (d); Carlos Vidal (perc).* 47–53.

***** Bird & Diz**

Verve 521436-2 *Parker; Dizzy Gillespie (t); Thelonious Monk (p); Curley Russell (b); Buddy Rich (d).* 50.

Given the sheer creative density of Verve's holding of Parker material, it is hardly surprising that the label should have repackaged the work so insistently. What is more startling is that the later batches have often been better than the first pickings. That is certainly true of *Hi-Fi*, which is overstuffed with alternative takes of 'Chi Chi' but might otherwise serve as a very good introduction to Bird's work of the period. It is also true of *Bird & Diz*, which aims to document one central association within a limited time-frame and offers an opportunity to hear three of the giants of bebop in one session. Again, there are too many alternatives for the newcomer, though as always one of the best ways of studying Parker is to listen to how thoroughly he rethinks a solo from take to take, even if the broad melodic contour remains the same.

Talkin' Bird is a more expansive compilation but lacks any real logic and sense of progression. There are better introductions in the entry above, but we would direct your attention to *Hi-Fi* and *Bird & Diz* if you don't already have this material.

*****(*) The Cole Porter Songbook**

Verve 823250-2 *Parker; drawn from Bird: The Complete Charlie Parker On Verve.* 7/50–12/54.

Parker was very drawn to Cole Porter's music and was contemplating another all-Porter session at the time of his death. The slightly dry, pure melodism gave him the perfect springboard for some of his most unfettered solos. A lovely record and an ideal purchase for Parker or Porter addicts.

***** South Of The Border**

Verve 527779-2 *Parker; Machito Afro Cuban Orchestra; Roy Haynes, Buddy Rich, Max Roach (d).* 48–52.

****(*) Verve Latin Sides**

Definitive 11187 *As above; and others.*

***** Charlie Parker With Strings – The Master Takes**

Verve 523984-2 *Parker; Tony Aless, Al Haig, Bernie Leighton (p); Art Ryerson (g); Ray Brown, Bob Haggart, Tommy Potter, Curley Russell (b); Roy Haynes, Don Lamond, Shelly Manne, Buddy Rich (d).* 12/47–1/52.

***** Complete Verve Masters With Strings**

Definitive 11185 *As above.* 47–52.

There is still some pointless controversy as to the merits of Parker's With Strings projects. Pointless, because it is clear from a single chorus of 'Repetition' from 1947 (made for *The Jazz Scene*) or 'Stella By Starlight' in 1952 that here is a master at work. Bird's solo construction is poised and tasteful, and much of the talk about his 'impatience' with these smooth settings is a sort of wishful thinking. He basked in them and if on occasion he anticipates the beat, that's no more than he did with Al Haig or Thelonious Monk.

We find more to question among the Machito sessions on *South Of The Border*, but this aspect of Parker is hugely popular, too, and there is no mistaking his own pleasure in these rhythms, which challenged him to widen his phrasing and open up his tone a touch. Time, surely, to put paid to snobbery about these lovely records.

The Definitive set takes advantage of lapsed copyright. No reason to favour these over the Verves, but they're out there and relatively cheap.

***** The Quintets, 1945–1951 / Collaborations: Bird Meets The Jazz Giants**

Jasmine 630 2CD *As for many of the above.* 45–53.

In a flock of reissues, no real reason to pick out this one. As an introduction to Parker's small groups and high-profile JATP encounters, it's a very respectable set, and the sound mastering is more than acceptable. That, though, is as far as it goes, and most interested collectors would be better advised sticking to other formats.

***** Live Performances: Volume 1**

ESP Disk ESP 3000 *Parker; Kenny Dorham, Dizzy Gillespie (t); John LaPorta (cl); Billy Bauer (b); Al Haig, Lennie Tristano (p); Ray Brown, Tommy Potter (b); Max Roach (d).* 9/47, 12/48.

***** Broadcast Performances: Volume 2**

ESP Disk ESP 3001 *Parker; Miles Davis (t); Tadd Dameron, Al Haig (p); Tommy Potter, Curley Russell (b); Joe Harris, Max Roach (d).* 6 & 8/49.

Most of this material is already well known, though it's startling to find it on ESP Disk, a label more commonly associated with the '60s avant-garde. Like Blue Note, though, ESP were anxious to cash in – artistically, if not commercially – on the greatest figure of the preceding generation. The 1947 material on Volume 1 is prized for an opportunity to hear Bird playing with the pianist who seemingly represented the opposite tendency in modern jazz, Lennie Tristano. It is immediately obvious on 'Tiger Rag', the solitary cut, that the differences between them were not entirely irreconcilable. The Christmas night 1948 material is also well known from the LP era. 'White Christmas' is a piece of pure hokum but it shows how readily Bird could be triggered by the slightest piece of musical fluff. His solo is breathtaking. The Royal Roost recordings included on Volume 2 have had a rather chequered discographical history, but they are very well documented here, sounding clean and remarkably noise-free, particularly given that this is not a label normally much concerned with the niceties of hi-fi. Parker tackles his solo on 'Groovin' High' with ferocious application, trying out ideas that don't turn up elsewhere in the discography. He's more relaxed on 'East Of The Sun', which features a lovely statement from Dorham.

*****(*) 1949 Jazz At The Philharmonic**

Verve 519803-2 *Parker; Roy Eldridge (t); Tommy Turk (tb); Flip Phillips, Lester Young (ts); Hank Jones (p); Ray Brown (b); Buddy Rich (d); Ella Fitzgerald (v).* 9/49.

*****(*) Charlie Parker Jam Session**

Verve 833564-2 *Parker; Charlie Shavers (t); Benny Carter, Johnny Hodges (as); Flip Phillips, Ben Webster (ts); Oscar Peterson (p); Barney Kessel (g); Ray Brown (b); J. C. Heard (d).* 7/52.

The symbolic importance of these two jams was Parker's appearance on the same stage as fellow-saxophonists, Lester Young (in 1949) and Benny Carter, Johnny Hodges and Ben Webster on the later session. Prez and Bird nose round each other for a bit on 'The Opener', a routine B-flat blues, but things get a little tougher on 'Lester Leaps In', where the tenor master with the sound that made Bird's possible lets everybody know that he's still in charge and still able to cut it. Parker doesn't show as strongly again until 'How High The Moon'.

Norman Granz's *Jam Session* of July 1952 was more of a processional and, though there are some extremely fine moments, from Bird, Shavers (who has refined the Eldridge style) and the stalwart Phillips, the confrontation with Carter and Hodges is pretty anticlimactic, a dialogue of the deaf rather than a significant joust. Each plays completely in character, Hodges with the walk-on walk-off shrug he was prone to. The biggest summit since Yalta was every bit as much a diplomatic window-display. The future of the world – or of modern music – had been decided elsewhere.

*****(*) Charlie Parker In Sweden, 1950**

Storyville STCD 4031 *Parker; Rolf Ericson, Rowland Greenberg (t); Lennart Nilsson, Gosta Theselius (ts, p); Thore Jederby (b); Jack Noren (d).* 1/50.

Record of a hectic week during Parker's second visit to Europe. He had had great success at the Paris Jazz Festival the previous year and was revered in Scandinavia, where bebop took deep and lasting root. A measure of that is the quality of the local musicians, who more than hold their own (Rolf Ericson, of course, acquired a substantial American reputation later in his career). Though Parker also played in Stockholm and Gothenburg, the materials are taken from sets in the southern towns of Hälsingborg and Malmö, plus a remarkable restaurant jam session at an unknown location. This last yielded the most notable single track, a long version of 'Body And Soul', more usually a tenor saxophonist's shibboleth but given a reading of great composure. This item was previously known in an edited form (which dispensed with solos by Theselius, who plays piano on the other selections, and Greenberg); but the restored version is very much more impressive, again by virtue of relocating Parker's improvisation in the wider context of a group performance. The remaining material is pretty much a 'greatest hits' package, with two versions each of 'Anthropology' and 'Cool Blues'. Worthwhile, but not essential, and the sound, taken on a wire recorder by someone in the crowd, is pretty poor.

*****(*) Bird At St Nick's**

Original Jazz Classics OJC 041 *Parker; Red Rodney (t); Al Haig (p); Tommy Potter (b); Roy Haynes (d).* 2/50.

An attractively varied package of material (including 'Visa', 'What's New', 'Smoke Gets In Your Eyes' and other, more familiar themes) from a tight and very professional band who sound as if they've been together for some time. Haynes is no Max Roach, even at this period, but his count is increasingly subtle and deceptive, and he cues some of Rodney's better releases brilliantly. Worth watching out for.

****** Bird And Fats – Live At Birdland**

Cool & Blue C&B CD 103 *Parker; Fats Navarro (t); Walter Bishop Jr, Bud Powell (p); Tommy Potter, Curley Russell (b); Art Blakey, Roy Haynes (d); Chubby Newsome (v).* 6/50.

There are moments on this when Parker is very nearly eclipsed by Fats Navarro, whose death was not far away when they recorded the astounding 'Street Beat'. Somebody calls out, 'Blow, Girl!' (Navarro's nickname was Fat Girl) as he burns through an absolutely astonishing solo that combines fire and attack with near-perfect balance. On his day, there was no one to touch him. Unfortunately, there were very few days left.

Elsewhere, he is superb on 'Ornithology' and 'Cool Blues'. A marvellous moment, captured with lots of atmosphere and not too much extraneous noise.

*** Inglewood Jam

Fresh Sound FSRCD 17 *Parker; Chet Baker (t); Sonny Criss (as); Russ Freeman (p); Harry Babasin (b); Lawrence Marable (d).* 6/52.

A historic encounter, Parker playing with two hornmen who in dramatically different ways (but with equally tragic repercussions) would take his legacy forward into the next generation. Baker sounds a modestly accomplished bebopper, much like the young and hesitant Miles Davis, in fact; but Criss is much more individual and distinctive than all the Bird-and-water copy might suggest. There are moments of marvellous tension in this, as when Baker throws Gillespie phrases at Bird during 'Donna Lee'. Parker appears to ignore them, but during his final chorus stuffs them all together into a single hectic phrase and heaves them back. 15-all.

*** The Legendary Rockland Palace Concert: Volume 1

Jazz Classics JZCL 6010 *Parker; Walter Bishop (p); Mundell Lowe (g); Teddy Kotick (b); Max Roach (d); strings.* 9/52.

Not unknown, but previously available only on a home recording of execrable quality. This more professional taping restores a bit of definition, and some good interchanges between Bird and Mundell Lowe, and it makes available some tracks that didn't pass muster before. The occasion was a dance in honour of an American Communist Party official and *Daily Worker* staffer. Not too much should be read into Bird's involvement on such a gig, not because he was cynical enough to take anything on, but because even at this late date American attitudes to socialism were still (in advance of the McCarthyite freeze) fairly relaxed, and black musicians of less public stature than Paul Robeson were exempt from unwarranted attention. There are no classic tracks or performances, but the general standard is high and the string settings are not too egregious. Of the unissued material, a sequence of Cole Porter songs is perhaps the most compelling. What one wonders at, though, is Parker's ability to fire off solos of consummate grace on such an unpressured and, one would have thought, creatively stultifying occasion.

CORE COLLECTION

**** The Quintet – Jazz At Massey Hall

Original Jazz Classics OJC 044 *Parker; Dizzy Gillespie (t); Bud Powell (p); Charles Mingus (b); Max Roach (d).* 5/53.

Perhaps the most hyped jazz concert ever, to an extent that the actuality is almost inevitably something of a disappointment. Originally released on Debut (a musician-run label started by Mingus and Roach), the sound, taken from Mingus's own tape-recording, is rather poor and the bassist subsequently had to overdub his part. However, Parker (playing a plastic saxophone and billed on the Debut release as 'Charlie Chan' to avoid contractual problems with Mercury, Norman Granz's parent company) and Gillespie are both at the peak of their powers. They may even have fed off the conflict that had developed between them, for their interchanges on the opening 'Perdido' crackle with controlled aggression, like two middleweights checking each other out in the first round. There is a story that they didn't want to go on stage, preferring to sulk in front of a televised big game in the dressing-room. Parker's solo on 'Hot House', three-quarters of the way through the set, is a masterpiece of containment and release, like his work on 'A Night In Tunisia' (introduced by the saxophonist in rather weird French, in deference to the Canadian – but the wrong city, surely? – audience). Perhaps because the game was showing, or perhaps just because Toronto wasn't hip to bebop, the house was by no means full, but it's clear that those who were there sensed something exceptional was happening. Powell and Roach are the star turns on 'Wee'. The pianist builds a marvellous solo out of Dameron's chords and Roach holds the whole thing together with a performance that almost matches the melodic and rhythmic enterprise of the front men. The Massey Hall concert is a remarkable experience, not to be missed.

**** Charlie Parker At Storyville

Blue Note 785108 *Parker; Herb Pomeroy (t); Red Garland, Sir Charles Thompson (p); Bernie Griggs, Jimmy Woode (b); Kenny Clarke, Roy Haynes (d).* 3/53, 9/53.

First released in 1985, the tapes of these Boston club dates, made on a Rube Goldberg home-made system by John Fitch (aka John McLellan, the compère), have been magically reprocessed by Jack Towers and are among the most faithful live recordings of Parker from the period. Of the performances it is necessary only to say that Parker is magisterial. Pomeroy strives manfully but seems to be caught more than once in awkward whole-note progressions which start well but then lapse back into cliché. Local bassist Griggs (who appears again on Stash's compilation of rarities, below) chugs along manfully on the March sessions, but Roy Haynes is a heavy-handed disappointment. The September quintets are generally less enterprising, and there are even signs that Parker may be repeating himself. In an interview recorded in June of the same year, McLellan pointed to an increasingly noticeable tendency for Parker to play old and established compositions. By the turn of the '50s, the flow of new variations on the basic blues or on standards had virtually dried up. Despite that, Parker's ability to find new things to say on tunes as well worn as 'Moose The Mooche', 'Ornithology' and 'Out Of Nowhere' (March) or 'Now's The Time', 'Cool Blues' and 'Groovin' High' (September) is completely impressive. The addition of relatively unfamiliar pieces like 'I'll Walk Alone' and 'Dancing On The Ceiling' contributes to a highly attractive set. The McLellan interview concludes with one of Parker's most quoted articles of faith: 'You can never tell what you'll be thinking tomorrow. But I can definitely say that music won't stop. It will continue to go forward.'

*** The Washington Concerts

Blue Note 22626 *Parker; Bob Carey, Ed Leddy, Irvin Markowitz, Red Rodney, Charlie Walp (t); Earl Swope, Kai Winding (tb); Jim Riley (as); Zoots Sims, Angelo Tompros (ts); Jack Nimitz (bs); Charlie Byrd (g); Franklin Skeete (b); Don Lamond, Max Roach (d); other personnel.* 53.

Originally released on Elektra, the big-band sections of this are legendary for the way Bird turned up and joined in with a well-rehearsed big band without music and without any apparent preparation. He doesn't miss a cue all evening and indeed plays as if inspired in places, using the band voicings to trigger off some of his most inventive solos, though interestingly he almost always brings things back to familiar phrases and licks.

These, plus the quartet sides from the same time in Washington, are well worth making room for in even a modest Parker collection, because they hint at where he might have been going next, building on the energies of JATP appearances and thinking in terms of ever-larger instrumental structures.

***** The Street Beat**
Definitive 11107 *Various line-ups.* 45–49.

***** Ornithology: Rare Recordings**
Definitive 11108 *Parker; Miles Davis, Dizzy Gillespie (t); Trummy Young (tb, v); Don Byas, Jack McVea, Lucky Thompson (ts); Errol Garner, Clyde Hart, Dodo Marmarosa (p); Mike Bryan, Arv Garrison (g); Slim Gaillard, Tiny Grimes (g, v); Red Callender, Al Hall, Vic McMillan (b); Bam Brown, Jimmy Butts (b, v); Specs Powell, Zutty Singleton, Harold West (d); Earl Coleman, Rubberlegs Williams (v).*

The first of these is a respectable selection of Parker classics, with a curiously misleading title. The second is a further exercise in barrel scraping. Seasoned collectors will be able to identify most of these 'rare' cuts from the personnels. More casual listeners can be reassured that this is a rag-bag of minor Parkeriana, of little interest to any but the specialist, and indeed the student of early Miles Davis, whose career was taking off problematically at around the same time. Some interesting moments, but too much emphasis on vocals and not a vital investment.

***** Bird In Boston: Live At The Hi Hat, 1953/54**
Fresh Sound FSCD 1006 *Parker; Herb Pomeroy, Herbert J. Williams. (t); Dean Earle, Rollins Griffith (p); Bernie Griggs, Jimmy Woode (b); Marquis Foster, Billy Graham (d); Symphony Sid Torin (v).* 6/53, 1/54.

***** Bird At The High Hat**
Blue Note 799787 *As above, except omit Pomeroy, Earle, Graham.* 12/53, 1/54.

One gets so used to hearing Parker with Miles, Gillespie, Navarro or Dorham that the immediate reaction to this is to ask, 'Who the hell's that?' as Pomeroy starts to play on 'Cool Blues'. These were game professional bands who had spent hours listening to the classic Parker recordings. Griffith in particular cops riffs and runs from Bud Powell, and the two trumpeters have their own respective allegiances. The Blue Note corrals material from the same club on a different date, though there is doubt about precisely what dates are involved. Bird himself sounds tired but surprisingly focused, leaning into one or two choruses as if the clock had gone back half-a-dozen years. There is no mistaking the change in quality, though. There was a man called Billy Graham at the drumkit. Bird was already much nearer to God.

Evan Parker (born 1944)

SOPRANO AND TENOR SAXOPHONES

The saxophone can have had few more challenging exponents. The Englishman came through free jazz to the kind of radical improvisation associated with the Spontaneous Music Ensemble and other free-music groups flourishing in the '60s. Increasingly thereafter, he turned his attention to solo performance, very often on soprano saxophone, which he regards as his first instrument. His ability to create complex overtone series by overblowing is the source of music of formidable intellectual challenge, but there is also a gruff immediacy to much of his work which is closer to the sound-world of classic jazz. John Coltrane is perhaps the only audible influence, though more in spirit than in style.

***** Three Other Stories (1971–1974)**
Emanem 4002 *Parker; Paul Lytton (d, perc, harm, elec).* 6/71–7/74.

***** Two Octobers (1972–1975)**
Emanem 4009 *As above.* 10/72–10/75.

****** Saxophone Solos**
Chronoscope CPE 2002 *Parker (ss solo).* 6–9/75.

If genius is the sustained application of intelligence, then Evan Parker merits the epithet. Over 30 years he has laid down a body of work which is both virtuosic in terms of saxophone technique and profoundly resistant to 'instrumentalism'; it is both abstract and rooted, deeply tinged with the English philosophical and scientific tradition. Parker has made significant contributions to improvising collectives like the Spontaneous Music Ensemble and the London Jazz Composers' Orchestra; but he is perhaps best known as a solo improviser whose grasp of harmonics, derived initially from Coltrane, is entirely *sui generis.* An Italian enthusiast, Francesco Martinelli, has devoted considerable time and effort to documenting Parker's recorded and concert works over the years, much of it on small labels in out-of-the-way places; as will be seen here, the available discography is now very large indeed.

The unaccompanied material on the Chronoscope disc remains as fresh and urgent as it was 25 years ago. Parker named these pieces 'Aerobatics' and appended subtitles from Samuel Beckett, his favourite author. They take common cause with the playwright and novelist in addressing those moments when language cedes to silence, non-communication and sheer physicality; not for nothing was an earlier Parker LP called *The Topography Of The Lungs.* Parker can be heard experimenting with duration, changing the colour of sound even as pitches are sustained, but also using multiphonics to collapse the vertical organization of jazz – the province of ancestors like his namesake, Bird, and John Coltrane – in favour of sounds that have mass but no single obvious direction and destination.

The duets with Lytton are inevitably more directed. The material on *Three Other Stories* is a dense palimpsest of saxophone, percussion, other sound-sources and tapes of previous performances. The result is much denser and blockier than one normally expects from Parker, though recent electro-acoustic work suggests that there are elements here which he still considers valuable, perhaps as a dialectical response to unaccompanied saxophone. *Two Octobers* is sparser, autumnally stripped and surreal, taking its inspiration and titles ('Then Wept! Then Rose In Zeal And Awe', 'Two Horn'd Reasoning, Cloven Fiction', 'I Want! I Want!') from William Blake, the Blake of *An Island In The Moon* rather than the *Songs Of Innocence And Experience.* Parker's deployment of circular breathing still sounds a touch mannered and self-conscious, not yet integrated. Lytton responds with flawless intuition, stretching out his line and dropping blocks of sound in midstream. His own use of live electronics is more refined than the actual technology might be thought to allow. The sound on both records is above average for material of this vintage; albeit grainy and one-dimensional, it captures most of the detail.

*****(*) Collective Calls (Urban) (Two Microphones)**
PSI 02.05 *Parker; Paul Lytton (perc).* 4/72.

****** At The Unity Theatre**
PSI 03.01 *As above.* 1/75.

Or 'an improvised urban psychodrama in eight parts'. *Collective Calls* was recorded in the Standard Essence Co, a loft space near the Thames in London, which was loaned to Parker and Lytton to make this exciting disc. Parker admits that there was considerably more material taped during their two-day session, though its whereabouts is unknown. A pity, because these are riveting performances, intensely concentrated and very faithfully captured on tape. Two short tracks were edited to close the original LP sides, but the whole has a coherence and consistency that suggests a level of planning that presumably had no part in the duo's practice of the time. Lytton is a sound artist of genius, as the reissued Unity Theatre date also bears out, but he has perversely never sounded as close to jazz drumming, albeit of a free sort, as he does on this record. On the Unity set, that's less in evidence. The old left-wing theatre had long since fallen into disuse as a performance space and, as Parker concedes, was full of ghosts when the Musicians' Cooperative began using it for performances. Parker's usual armoury is extended on this occasion by the Lyttonophone, while Paul deploys an augmented kit and auxiliary sources. The LP is a classic, marked out by 'Mild Steel Rivets for P.H.', a tribute to poet Paul Haines, for whom the reissue is now a memorial. Two added tracks. Marvellous stuff and worth comparing with the earlier Emanem duos, though these stand triumphantly alone.

***** Monoceros**
Chronoscope CPE 2010 *Parker (ss solo).* 78.

These, along with the magnificent *The Snake Decides*, below, are the high-water mark of Parker's solo saxophone explorations. In an extended interrogation of the straight horn's notoriously difficult harmonic language, Parker uses multiphonics, circular breathing and various tongue-slapping techniques to create a unique and uniquely consistent language that makes even Anthony Braxton's *For Alto* seem conventional. As indeed it is, if one considers the American's jazz roots to be convention, however unbinding. Listening to this album in retrospect is a different experience, once one is aware how Parker has extended its real-time range by use of, first of all, overdubbing, and then full integration of the saxophone with live electronics.

***** 4,4,4**
Konnex KCD 5049 *Parker; Paul Rutherford (tb, euph); Barry Guy (b, elec); John Stevens (d, v).* 8/79.

An unsatisfactory record in a number of respects. Space is shared with a performance by the Spontaneous Music Ensemble from more than a decade later, but what gives the music its odd imbalance is that Parker still seems to be fighting with the remnants of a jazz aesthetic – Trane and Rollins, to name the names – which he seemed to have transcended a decade before. Why this should be isn't clear, but there is no avoiding the conclusion that it is Rutherford and Guy who hold the session together. Stevens rambles inconsequentially and often sounds detached and enervated; compare the absolute focus of his work on the SME track.

***** Six Of One**
PSI 02.08 *Parker (ss solo).* 80.

But not exactly half a dozen of 'the other'. These performances, recorded in St Judes on the Hill, London, continued Parker's heroic exploration of the saxophone. They are, as one might expect, intense, highly focused and extremely demanding, except that Parker has the ability to suspend normal time, musical or chronological, while he is playing, so that the impression is of densely packed musical singularities that unravel in what is no longer strictly 'real' time. There are better solo albums, in the sense that some are more accessible and some reach a higher level of harmonic and timbral sophistication, but this is well worth hearing, and if you are a student of Parker's, an essential point in the story.

****** From Saxophone And Trombone**
PSI 02.04 *Parker; George Lewis (tb).* 5/80.

'Too much has happened in the intervening decades to attempt a useful summary here': so Evan Parker in his brief liner-note to this reissue. Brief as it is, this '80s set from the Art Workers Guild in London is one of Parker's best recorded statements and one of the best documents of Lewis's radical deconstruction of the trombone. There is a hint of regular pulse to the opening improvisation, a long, slow, drone-based piece that has Lewis conjuring sounds of Aeolian simplicity from his tubes, while Parker moves around him more nervously and acutely. Later tracks are more antagonistic in effect, with sharper sounds from Lewis and more driven lines from the saxophonist, but much of the delight of the set lies in that exquisite opening track.

***** The Ayes Have It**
Emanem 4055 *Parker; Wolter Wierbos (tb); Paul Rogers (b); Jamie Muir (perc, toys).* 83, 91.

The long track here documents an astonishingly good group, but one that hitherto seems to have fallen into a bit of a black hole in Parker's discography. Evan seemed to like working with trombone players at this time and a couple of years after the first of these sessions he would convene a very similar group with Paul Rutherford, Hans Schneider and Paul Lytton (see below); however, we are increasingly persuaded that this is the line-up and these the recordings which clinched the format. The original trio sessions, made in 1983, yielded only just over half an hour of releasable material, quite acceptable in the LP era but not enough for a CD, which is why Martin Davidson waited until he had the 1991 recording with the powerful Wierbos. Even here, the problems didn't stop. Wierbos has to break off half way through the long title-piece when he experiences problems with a contact lens; it was apparently very hot and there are some signs of tiredness from Parker as well. This isn't one of his best performances and this is by no means an essential record.

***** Waterloo 1985**
Emanem 4030 *Parker; Paul Rutherford (tb); Hans Schneider (b); Paul Lytton (perc, elec).* 8/85.

This helps to plug an unexpected gap in the Parker discography and affords a glimpse of an otherwise undocumented group. Schneider is the unfamiliar element and, though he is a bassist very much in the Barry Guy mould, his approach is different enough to give the music a different impetus. The disc contains a continuous, unedited, one-hour improvisation. Sound-quality is not pristine and the horns distort at maximum dynamics, but most of the tape seems faithful to the music as played and there is a reasonable balance among the elements.

CORE COLLECTION

♛ ****** The Snake Decides**

PSI 02.09 *Parker (ss solo).* 86.

This is a great record. Or you might say, a great recording. In his liner-note to the reissue (it was originally on Incus), Parker pays tribute to recording engineer the late Michael Gerzon, possibly the only man in Britain whose ears were more finely tuned to the highest harmonic levels than Parker's own. His technical genius made the disc what it is, a hyper-subtle document of one of Parker's keynote performances, in which he takes the language experiments of the previous two decades and compresses them into one flowing and involving performance. The sonority is incredibly varied, and Parker's ability to sound 32nd harmonics and above demands a reciprocal talent on the technical side. The miracle of *The Snake Decides* is that everything is registered and everything is registered cleanly and faithfully. Listened to on headphones, it can create the impression that you are actually inside Parker's instrument, listening not just to produced sound but to all the artefacts and accidentals associated with the performance. We are aware that this is a demanding record and as far from Sidney Bechet playing 'Petite Fleur' or Rudy Van Gelder adjusting a couple of cardioid mics in front of the horns as it is possible to get. It remains, though, an essential document of modern music, and anyone interested in its progress should hear *The Snake Decides* at least once.

****** Atlanta**

Impetus IMP 18617 *Parker; Barry Guy (b); Paul Lytton (d, perc).* 12/86.

A glorious example of Parker in absolute sympathy with his fellow players. This comes three years after the group's first Incus recording, but a lot further down the path of association than that. Parker has spoken of offering up his solo style in 'sacrifice' when working in the trio context, and certainly it lacks something of the multi-dimensional complexity of the solo records. Newk's pianoless group may hover in the background, for here Parker has refined and simplified his small-group playing to the point where one can almost reconstruct the possibility – and no more than the possibility – of melody. This is one of the most accessible documents he has ever issued, the one most likely to appeal to listeners devoted to jazz and suspicious of anything that departs from chords. Guy and Lytton fulfil every expectation of a conventional bass-and-drums configuration without once touching fixed base.

***** Duets: Dithyrambisch**

FMP CD 19/20 2CD *Parker; Louis Sclavis (bcl, ss); Wolfgang Fuchs (bcl, cbcl); Hans Koch (ts, ss).* 7/89.

By the end of the '80s, Parker's unaccompanied soprano recitals were becoming a touch formulaic and repetitive. Indications were that Parker thrived better in a more responsive environment. The wind duos with Sclavis, Fuchs and Koch sometimes seem mismatched, even awkward, but they allow him to work on levels which are simply not possible in solo performance, evincing a simplicity of line and a directness of statement which were lost in the later solo performances. As ever, though, the technique is utterly assured and the tone is ironclad.

***** Hall Of Mirrors**

MM&T 01 *Parker; Walter Prati (elec).* 2/90.

***** Process And Reality**

FMP CD 37 *Parker (ts, ss solo, with multi-tracking).* 91.

These might almost have swapped titles. It's the solo multi-tracked album that suggests the *mise-en-abîme* of a mirror gallery, while Walter Prati's delicate acoustic environments constantly draw attention to their own processes, as against the hard-edged 'reality' of Parker's saxophone. Some of the backgrounds suggest that simple ring modulation would have sufficed. Others are as delicately imprecise as one of Morton Subotnick's subliminal 'ghost scores'. After *Atlanta*, 'Diary Of A Mnemonist' is among the most reachable things Parker has ever committed to record, by far the most interesting thing on *Process And Reality* and a fascinating anticipation of the electro-acoustic work he was to record for ECM some years later.

****** Imaginary Values**

Maya MCD 9401 *Parker; Barry Guy (b); Paul Lytton (d).* 3/93.

Named after the nine theorems of primary arithmetic in G. Spencer Brown's *Laws Of Form*, this supremely orderly set of improvisations is no less communicative, no less susceptible than the earlier trio disc. 'Variance' might almost be a written-out idea, so logically does it shape and reshape itself out of the stately processional sounded by Guy and Lytton. 'Distinction' is closer to the whirling intensity of the solo soprano records, but the bassist (who, as ever, doubles on chamber or piccolo bass) is almost playing *continuo*, strumming chords which seem to reach out and anchor the reed sounds. Lytton's mastery of cymbal overtones has never been documented better. Hard to attribute music as collective and mutual as this to any individual but, since we are concentrating on Parker here, we can say this is one of his finest hours on record. His tenor-playing on 'Invariance' is like seeing and hearing the instrument reinvented before the senses, from primal breaths and metal sounds to music of the highest organization.

***** Birmingham Concert**

Rare Music RM 026 *Parker; Paul Dunmall (ts, bs); Barry Guy (b); Tony Levin (d).* 3/93.

An unusually jazz-flavoured sound for Parker of this vintage, perhaps because Levin and Dunmall are so joyously devoted to a groove, however complex. The two-saxophone front-line is hugely powerful and perhaps at its best when both are playing tenor, though Dunmall's swoops down the range on his baritone provide some of the most dramatic moments on the whole set. Recorded and mastered by the indefatigable Dave Bernez in a somewhat soggy acoustic, it isn't the prettiest of products, but immensely listenable all the same.

****** Corner To Corner**

Ogun OGCD 005 *Parker; John Stevens (d, t).* 6/93.

In June 1977 Parker and John Stevens recorded an extraordinary two-LP set for the Ogun label called *The Longest Night*. It remains a benchmark performance in British free music, so much so that any attempt to reduplicate its fierce energies more than a decade later might be seen to be doomed to failure. *Corner To Corner* confounds any such expectation. Its titles – 'Angles', 'Incidence', 'Reflections', 'Acute' – gently mock the clichéd honorific of angularity, for there's also immense warmth and trust in these performances, two friends who can now comfortably elide at least some of the niceties, who can cross-talk and interrupt without offence, or simply hold the floor to the momentary exclusion of the other. Parker has rarely sounded as emotional as on the closing 'Each/Other'.

***** Synergetics – Phonomanie III**

Leo CD LR 239/240 2CD *Parker; George E. Lewis (tb, computer); Jin Hi Kim (komungo); Motoharo Yoshizawa (b, v); Carlo Mariani (launeddas); Thebe Lipere (imbumbu, perc); Walter Prati, Marco Vecchi (elec); Sainkho Namchylak (v).* 9/93.

***** Ghost-In-The-Machine Featuring Evan Parker**

Leo Lab CD 018 *Parker; Christer Irgens-Moller (p, ky, v); Peter Friis Nielsen (b); Pere Oliver Jorgens (d, perc); Martin Klapper (amplified object etc.).* 9/93.

*****(*) New Excursions**

Ninth World 19 *As above.* 98.

Like his early inspiration, Peter Kowald, Parker has become increasingly interested in the global dimensions of improvisation. At the same time he has developed a parallel involvement in electronics. The first work with what became the Electro-Acoustic Ensemble was done in 1992. The following year, the Phonomanie Festival in Ulrichsberg, Austria, provided an opportunity to put some of these aspects together. Parker's regular trio was not there, but Tuvan vocalist Sainkho Namchylak was, and so was another occasional collaborator, George Lewis, a pioneer of the interface between acoustic instrumentation and computers. Something of the same was involved in Parker's collaboration with the Danish improvising ensemble Ghost-In-The-Machine. The first record is a mixture of concert and studio material, the best of the former being the very intense and focused 'Intertuba/Extremii', the bulk of the remainder sounding rather abrupt and unachieved, and certainly no more than the sum of its parts. In a sense, the Danish project negatively illustrates what the other record was intended to represent. The follow-up performance, recorded at the Copenhagen International Experimental Festival, was much better, a more assured synthesis of ideas and practices and a more listenable artefact which is all that matters in this context.

The notion of synergy comes from Buckminster Fuller, another of the scientific thinkers who has made a substantial impression on Parker's creative processes. It is defined roughly as the residue or surplus of behaviour in systems which cannot be defined or predicted by the behaviours of the constituent elements, a notion which has an obvious application to improvising ensembles. The Ulrichsberg project made use of Lewis's Voyager software, a computer system which interacts with human agents, but, throughout the project, unpredictable and *ad hoc* groupings are required to interact with electronic resources. Different players are asked to define areas of interest and interaction, with Mariani, komungun player Jin Hi Kim, Parker, Lewis and Lipere defining the parameters on the first disc, Lipere, Yoshizawa, Namchylak, Lewis and Parker again establishing the defining relationships on the second. The music included represents two days of intensive activity and is, to be frank, very difficult to absorb in this form. For the vast majority of potential listeners who couldn't be at the Ulrichsberg event, it provides an opportunity to sample Parker in unfamiliar sonic contexts. One fears, though, that most will find it frustratingly enigmatic.

♛ ** 50th Birthday Concert**

Leo CD LR 212/213 2CD *Parker; Alexander von Schlippenbach (p); Barry Guy (b); Paul Lovens, Paul Lytton (d).* 4/94.

'The echoing border zones ...' Robert Graves's poetry seems the ideal source for titles for these performances, which again combine Parker's gritty involvement in ideas and history, this time his own. The two trios represented two of his most important long-term associations. Despite the essential Englishness of much of his aesthetic (not the Englishness of the pastoralists or the Georgians, but of those who built an empire on empiricism and craft), Parker has always gravitated to the European scene. As he describes in an unwontedly personal liner-note, bassist Peter Kowald, promoter and label boss Jost Gebers and pianist Alex von Schlippenbach were largely responsible for widening his musical horizons, in terms of playing partnerships. The Schlippenbach trio with Lovens is the perfect counterbalance to the more familiarly documented work with Guy and Lytton. The textures are more open and more concerned with radical harmonics. Lovens and Lytton are occasionally confused – verbally – even by people who know the scene well. They couldn't be mixed up even on the briefest hearing. Lovens is immensely detailed, a microsurgeon of the pulse, while Lytton tends to favour broader and more extended areas of sound, opening and unfolding like an anatomist. The long opening piece with Schlippenbach, 'Hero Of Nine Fingers', is supremely well argued, with Parker and the the pianist trading ideas at a dazzling pace. This isn't energy playing, but it generates its own energies moment to moment. The only quibble is that disc one is only 45 minutes in length (and disc two only 40); however, we are not awarding the ultimate accolade on durations, but on sheer brilliance of conception and execution. The remaining pieces with Guy and Lytton are closer to the language of *Atlanta* and *Imaginary Values*, but no less valuable for that. Guy seems particularly focused on this celebratory occasion. Rising 50 himself, he has regularly rethought his musical parameters, and one can almost hear him refining his language as he plays. Lytton is flawless on the long 'In Exultation', though he's the one musician on the set who probably isn't well served by the sound. The occasion, recorded in Dingwalls Club in north London, was very special. These documents are no less so. It would be hard to imagine music less of its moment *and* less ephemeral.

****** Breaths And Heartbeats**

Rastascan BRD 019 *Parker; Barry Guy (b); Paul Lytton (d).* 12/94.

*****(*) Obliquities**

Maya MCD 9501 *Parker; Barry Guy (b).* 12/94.

Breaths And Heartbeats is unusual, not so much in the way it was performed, but in the way that it involves post-sequence editing. The trio recorded material in three blocks, two sessions with saxophone, bass and drums and one on orchestral percussion. After the event, the percussion 'breaths' were attached to the 'heartbeat' tracks according to a certain formal symmetry. Parker points out that the album can be played in a different order so long as the final track is number 12 each time. Performances are shorter and more uniform in duration here than usual, though 'Breath And Heartbeat 3' is over ten minutes in length. The sound is wonderful, as it is on *Obliquities*. Asking what difference Lytton's absence makes to the music is the wrong question. This is not the trio-minus-percussion. This is a very differently configured relationship, a free give-and-take of ideas founded on years of shared experience. Essentially, tenor and contrabass, soprano and chamber bass are paired in order to ensure that the tessitura – the basic pitch-range – is aligned to greatest effect. The exchange of material is so fast and responsive that it is difficult to keep track of where it begins and where it is going, a perfect musical correlative of the uncertainty principle. Both are records that require time and a certain suspension of expectation. They pay huge aesthetic dividends.

***** Improvvisazioni**

CD ADA 02.11 *Parker; Antonello Salis (p, acc); Mauro Orselli (d, perc).* 1/95.

Frantic as his Italian partner's drumming and keyed figures are, this is a more conventional, almost jazz-based setting for Parker than most of his recent projects. Salis has a wonderfully limber touch on the accordion particularly, and his taut, breathy tones are a perfect complement to Evan's harmonic overblowing. Orselli, by contrast, often sounds as if he's about to break into bebop figures or some other regular groove. There is an almost militaristic cast to his snare work, accentuated by the hollow acoustic in which the set was taped. An interesting record and well worth tracking down, but not an essential Parker project.

***** The Redwood Sessions**

CIMP 101 *Parker; Joe McPhee (t); Barry Guy (b); Paul Lytton (d).* 6/95.

Not a quartet record; McPhee guests on the final jam, 'Then Paul Saw The Snake', a performance that suggests future collaboration may yield something. As it is, this has the feel of afterthought. The trio sound less intensely focused than usual, perhaps because they were playing in baking heat. This was the disc that kicked off CIMP's *audio-vérité* series, recorded in the Spirit Room in Rossie, New York (Cadence is based in Redwood, hence the title), and it underlines the label's unvarnished sound more than later sessions were to do, perhaps because windows had to be left open. The twitcher among us surfaces to point out that an American robin and some kind of babbler can be heard singing outside. Low recording levels are part of the ethos, but a concert experience and a home-listening experience are different, and some may find it hard to focus sufficiently on some of the quietest passages. These, though, are wider questions, not to do with these performances; they are non-vintage Parker/Guy/Lytton, fine in their way but lacking the intellectual command of previous discs.

****** Chicago Solo**

Okkadisk OD12017 *Parker (ts solo).* 11/95.

Remarkably, after eight discs of solo soprano saxophone, this is the first time Parker has committed himself to a full programme of tenor-playing. The results are, as one would expect by this juncture, extraordinary, music of intense focus and a fearsome weight and intensity of tone. Four of the tracks are dedications to musicians Parker has worked with or been associated with over the years – Chris McGregor, Lee Konitz, trombonist George Lewis and 'Mr' Braxton. No evident thematic connection to any of them, though the tiny Braxton tribute includes elements that are reminiscent of the American. Probably redundant at this point in time to start taxonomizing the differences between Parker's soprano and tenor work. The range of overtones is perhaps more restricted, the line more direct, the pace and delivery of ideas more measured. No mistaking, though, the integrity of the performances or the identity of the performer.

***** Tempranillo**

New Contemporary Music NCM 4 *Parker; Agusti Fernandez (p).* 11/95.

A measure of the international dimension of Parker's career is that, less than a week after the Chicago recording, he is in the studio again, this time in Barcelona. Probably hard to get hold of, but as heady as the vinous elixir of the title. Fernandez is a fiery Mallorcan who is superficially reminiscent of Borah Bergman and plays in a similar hinterland between jazz and new music. At moments, he sounds as if he might be playing scored pieces by Xenakis or Stockhausen; at others, some passionate folk theme seems about to announce itself. Parker goes about his music with the same intensity as ever, listening, responding, interpolating new ideas. The studio sound is very good, with a resonant piano and a vibrant space round the saxophone. It's to be hoped that a few of these at least get into general circulation.

****** Towards The Margins**

ECM 453514-2 *Parker; Philipp Wachsmann (vn, vla, elec); Barry Guy (b); Paul Lytton (d); Walter Prati, Marco Vecchi (elec).* 5/96.

The triumphant representation of 'synergetics', stripped of the awkward eclecticism of the Ulrichsberg project. Here the system yields unexpected surpluses when the sound of Parker's long-established trio, now increasingly often augmented with other voices, is confronted by a responsive technology which behaves – within the limits of its capability – like a listening musician. Without Wachsmann's presence one suspects that the degree of actual interaction would seem secondary rather than central to this music, but his highly attuned sensibility helps move the electronic elements from the periphery to the centre, without in any way de-emphasizing Parker's instrumental role (soprano throughout), or that of Guy and, above all, Lytton, who seems ever more important in this context. Though there is no mistaking that the Electro-Acoustic Ensemble performs like a regular (rather than an *ad hoc*) agglomeration, these are still difficult performances to analyse. Relative to a jazz tradition, they seem to advance a long-standing exploration of the limits of time. Relative to contemporary composition, they seem to relate to the whole modernist rejection of linear progress in favour of simultaneity, the physical presence of music as masses. This was an exciting step in Parker's progress, magnificently recorded and mastered, and compelling from start to finish. None of the pieces is very long (only two are over seven minutes), but even in the tiny space of 'The Regenerative Landscape', a tribute to AMM who pioneered some aspects of the idiom, the amount of musical information is formidable. 'Field And Figure' and the closing 'Contra-Dance' are Parker/Guy collaborations and perhaps the strongest things on the set.

*****(*) Natives And Aliens**

Leo CD LR 243 *Parker; Marilyn Crispell (p); Barry Guy (b); Paul Lytton (d).* 5/96.

As on the set with Fernandez, interesting to hear Parker, so long devoted to the microtonal devastation of Western harmony, working in the context of an instrument with fixed pitches. Not that it holds Crispell back. She creates huge, resonant chords which are difficult to analyse with any precision but into which the entire trio seems to be subsumed, as if the sound-box of the piano has become an environment rather than another instrument.

Lytton continues to develop with almost every release. His work on 'Sumach' (many of the titles are named after trees, invasive species in particular) is compellingly musical, the leaf-work to the roots, trunk and branches suggested by Crispell, Guy and Parker. If any is the alien, then – by virtue of instrument, nationality and artistic temperament – one would have thought it was Crispell, except that she naturalizes so instinctively. There is a fierce melancholy to some of Parker's playing, which is new and slightly unsettling. On the basis of it alone, this isn't a vintage performance, but the group has almost never sounded more unified and of equal weight.

****** At The Vortex (1996)**

Emanem 4022 *Parker; Barry Guy (b); Paul Lytton (d, perc).* 6/96.

Those who were there still talk about this midsummer encounter at north London's 'listening jazz club'. Those who weren't will probably have tired of hearing about it and will be relieved that they too can now sample this extraordinary session. Because Guy and Lytton both live abroad, this isn't a group that gets together very often and every chance to hear them is rather special. Parker has often said that he regards the soprano saxophone as his first instrument, but on the first set he once again demonstrates what a formidable tenor-player he is as well. His gruff, low tones are ideally complemented by Guy's floating harmonics and Lytton's impeccably musical percussion. The second opens on a long soprano solo, an introduction that unleashes the saxophonist's signature sound, a long, continuous line using circular breathing and high-order harmonics, whose partials would defy all but the most mathematically minded of analysts. For some reason, this set seems less of a group effort than its predecessor. Guy is rather low in the mix and here and there seems to lose definition on an otherwise well-recorded disc. As so often in the past, the real dynamic is between Parker and Lytton, now two generations on from the Coltrane/Ali sessions that established the modalities of this extraordinary music.

***** Mars Song**

Victo 42 *Parker; Sainkho Namtchylak (v).* 96.

Though rooted in Tuvan tradition (a tradition normally resistant to female participation), Namtchylak is completely *sui generis* on the free-music scene. Her radical extension of throat singing has led her to a new vocal language that is, in its way, the equal of Parker's extension of the saxophone. This is a powerful and sometimes forbidding performance, probably best taken one track at a time to allow the duo's ferocious interactions to sink in. 'Time, That Other Labyrinth' clocks at more than 20 minutes and is as exhausting to listen to as it must have been to perform, except that both performers, Parker particularly, seem to have developed a weightless clarity to their music that allows them to explore areas of enquiry that genuinely seem beyond human scope. Powerful music, but best approached cautiously and with an open mind.

****(*) Monkey Puzzle**

Leo CD LR 247 *Parker; Ned Rothenberg (as, bcl).* 5/97.

Recorded at a mini-festival organized in memory of the late Sergei Kuryokhin, this was a frank and flat disappointment, a dialogue of the deaf in which two hugely talented players conspicuously failed to trade in their artistic differences. The release was distinguished only by a cryptic crossword for which the label offered as prize an unreleased CD-R of further material from the concert. 1 down, Abominable Snowman loses personal identity after going north. Russian declines! (4)

*****(*) London Air Lift**

FMP CD 89 *Parker; John Russell (g); John Edwards (b); Mark Sanders (d).* 12/96, 3/97.

This group only convened during the latter part of 1996, but it has become a reasonably regular ensemble since then. The title, and the quite brief second piece, are ironic references to British improvisers' continuing dependence on Jost Gebers's excellent label to have their work heard. The two younger players in the line-up have had very different musical experiences from Parker and Russell, but they fit into this concept seamlessly. Edwards solos on the title-track and leads off 'The Drop', a tough, stringy sound that owes nothing to rock music and electronics except density and expanse. 'Half And Half' is a reference to Sanders's mixed parentage, but it's started by Russell, an acoustic guitar loyalist who always manages to combine a classical delicacy with the fire of rock. As ever, Parker shifts from soprano to tenor, playing with a lightness and speed that sometimes get buried in the sheer density of detail he generates in solo and in duo formats. Within a more conventional group configuration he is happier to allow the line to declare itself. His tone more than ever recalls the late Coltrane, iron-hard, harmonically free, rhythmically complex. An artist in his pomp.

***** Strings with Evan Parker**

Emanem 4032 3CD *Parker; Peter Cusack (g, bouzouki, elec); Phil Durrant, Philipp Wachsmann (vn); Kaffe Matthews (vn, elec); Marcio Mattos, Mark Wastell (clo); Rhodri Davies (hp); John Edwards (b); Hugh Davies (strings, elec); other personnel.* 1/97–5/00.

The title gently reminds us of those rather controversial 'Parker With Strings' dates that Bird made so much of, but there's little of that here. Evan originally convened a large improvising group to play some pieces and then, almost a year later, reconvened a string ensemble with the idea of directing improvisations. Parker only plays sporadically on these three discs. 'Single Headed Serpent' is an ensemble performance on to which Parker dubs a soprano solo, yielding 'Double Headed Serpent'. Including the former and some obvious workshop items, like the very formulaic *arco* and pizzicatto 'Ghost Series' seems a little redundant. There is very little here that might justify a triple-album format. The various sub-groups who perform on the second disc turn in some remarkable music, but what this has to do with Parker, other than as an enabler and inspiration, is difficult to gauge. Even allowing for the 'with … ' branding (Emanem boss Martin Davidson isn't trying to pass this off as an *echt* Parker release), this seems a rather dubious product.

****** Most Materiall**

Matchless MRCD 33A/B 2CD *Parker; Eddie Prévost (perc).* 2 & 4/97.

Given his immense respect for the pioneering example of AMM, and their long experience of the British scene, it is surprising that Parker and Prévost have not recorded in a duo setting before. The immediate and obvious source of comparison is Coltrane's late masterpiece with Rashied Ali, *Interstellar Space*, which was recorded exactly 30 years before. For all his attraction to the stillness of Korean court music, Prévost has remained grounded in modern jazz, and recent experience in rock groups has greatly strengthened and simplified the sense of pulse he derived from Roach and Blackwell. Similarly, Parker has always been Coltrane's man. In practice, this is much as one would expect: a tough, extended exploration of sonorities and structures. The titles are all derived from the work of Francis Bacon, which explains the curious spelling of 'materiall', and they underline once again Parker's capacious understanding of English natural philosophy. Prévost bows cymbals to create complex harmonic shapes. Parker exploits his circular breathing to create huge, spooling lines, which then break up multiphonically. There are tongue-slaps and toneless sounds from the saxophone, richly tuned, quasi-melodic figures from the kit, an unfailing procession of vividly exploratory ideas. Essential listening for anyone interested in the work of either man.

*** At Les Instants Chavires

PSI 02.06 *Parker; Barry Guy (b); Paul Lytton (perc).* 12/97.

***(*) Live At 'Les Instants Chavires'

Leo CD LR 255 *Parker; Noël Akchoté (g); Joel Casserley, Joel Ryan (elec).* 12/97.

Recorded in Montreuil just a few days before Christmas 1997, this continues Parker's trio work and his recent exploration of electronic interfaces. The two discs were recorded on consecutive days. On December 19, Parker, Guy and Lytton performed a superb trio set that must be one of the finest in their long association. There is a hiatus in the middle of track four, which actually continues as track five, after a real time interruption in which the direct-to-hard-disc recording failed. *Caveat.* The music is seamless and logical enough not to suffer. Guy is titanic, playing like an orchestral continuo player one moment, a drummer possessed the next. Lytton is his extraordinary self and Parker pushes into areas on tenor and soprano that he has not previously explored.

The next day's music was almost as good, pitching him in with the rich jazz sound of Akchoté (who has also appeared with The Recyclers) and with two sound-processors who are kitted up to respond in real time to Parker's powerful, pungent saxophone improvisations. This is a record which either needs to be swallowed whole, absorbed as if it were a straightforward monolith of sound, or else responded to with care and attention. It is both intensely physical and intellectually detailed, constantly challenging at every level.

**(*) Unity Variations

Okka 12028 *Parker; George Graewe (p).* 98.

Not this time the Unity Theatre, but the Unity Temple in Chicago and a night at the Empty Bottle Festival of Improvised Music. Parker has less of a bond with Graewe than his countryman and fellow-saxophonist John Butcher and there is something rarefied, abstract and almost remote in these relatively short improvisations. It's reminiscent of the later mismatch with pianist Patrick Scheyder and it fuels our conviction that, Alex von Schlippenbach apart, Parker isn't comfortable around piano-players.

***(*) Drawn Inward

ECM 547209 *Parker; Phillip Wachsmann (vn, elec); Barry Guy (b); Paul Lytton (perc); Lawrence Casserley, Walter Prati, Mario Vecchi (elec).* 99.

Regrettably, an entry for this record was first garbled and then omitted in our last-but-one and last editions. The reconvened Electro-Acoustic Ensemble sounds ever more like a lasting association for Parker, a fruitful line of enquiry that will take many years to work through. They start out, unexpectedly, with a tribute to crooner Johnny Hartman, who Parker may have first experienced through the singer's Impulse! album with John Coltrane. It's a beautiful opening and it strongly confirms what we have previously thought: that this is very much a collaborative project and not just an Evan Parker project. Wachsmann and Guy are absolutely central to the multidimensional harmonic language, while Lytton's percussion is ever more subtly dramatic. The three sound processors create a virtual environment in which the trio functions and with which it interacts with increasing complexity. By the time these 12 short tracks are over (only 'Collect Calls (Bugged)' is over ten minutes and most are very short by normal improvisation standards), the ensemble has acquired its own unique identity.

**** After Appleby

Leo 283/284 2CD *Parker; Marilyn Crispell (p); Barry Guy (b); Paul Lytton (d, perc).* 6/99.

A free-music supergroup, playing in a number of internal permutations but coming together forcefully on three long pieces, 'Blue Star Kachina', 'Where Heart Revive' and 'Capnomantic Vortex'. The set consists of a studio disc, together with a long live performance recorded the following day. Crispell has been quieter recently than half a decade before and it's tempting to suggest that this is really her album. Her duets with Guy and particularly with Lytton are masterpieces of delicate concentration. However, it's Evan who dominates the long pieces, locked in dialogue with the sounds around him, constantly listening and responding and wasting nothing on empty gesture. His powers of concentration remain formidable.

***(*) The Two Seasons

Emanem 4202 2CD *Parker; John Edwards (b); Mark Sanders (d).* 2 & 7/99.

***(*) Foxes Fox

Emanem 4035 *Parker; Steve Beresford (p); John Edwards (b); Louis Moholo (d).* 7/99.

Marking an unexpected return to a species of free bop, the *Two Seasons* trio has its stylistic lineage in '60s groupings like Amalgam and the more pulse-driven versions of SME. Parker plays tenor for most of the album, including just one soprano piece on the July set. The sound at London's Vortex club is quite busy and intense, and it suits this music particularly well. Edwards amplifies his double bass, which gives him a wide range of articulations, and Sanders has always been an extremely active player, setting off patterns in entirely unexpected directions. Edwards is back on *Foxes Fox*, but it is unclear whether his bass has any amplification on this studio recording. The line seems straighter and the dynamics less varied, except on his opening duet with Moholo. This is a collective album rather than a Parker. There are four quartet numbers, but there are also four on which Evan does not appear at all. Beresford is as cleverly inventive as ever and is sparkling with ideas on his two duets with Edwards and

Moholo. Emanem have generally been associated with archive releases, often of mixed sound-quality. Here the standard of recording and mixing is very good indeed.

**** Brot & Honig**

True Muze 0003 *Parker; Heinz-Erich Godecke (tb, didgeridoo); Hannes Wienert (ss); Alexander Dannullis (g); Michael Haas (bjo); Nicola Kruse (vn, tenor vn); Peter Niklas Wilson (b); ensemble.* 10/99.

Parker spent almost a week workshopping with the members of the TonArt Ensemble before conducting them in this disappointing performance. Both pieces, the title-track and 'Syrah & Papidoux', come out at almost exactly the same 37-minute length. Parker himself shines momentarily on the latter, which has far more musical drama, but as a whole this is a very spiritless and unengaging work and only very dedicated fans should trouble to track down this hard-to-find release.

***** 2 × 3 = 5**

Leo CDLR 305 *Parker; Alexander von Schlippenbach (p); Barry Guy (b); Paul Lovens, Paul Lytton (d).* 8/99.

The odd arithmetic is easily explained. This was a one-off meeting of two groups, Parker's own and the Schlippenbach Trio, of which Parker is also a long-term member. The resulting quintet plays one long piece that explores much of their common musical ground and opens up new areas of improvising language. The key element is the interplay between the two drummers, both of them subtle masters of percussion craft, and the austerely brilliant Schlippenbach, who fires off starbursts of sound throughout. Parker and Guy stick to a relatively pedestrian course. Both are, of course, virtuosic in execution, but on this occasion the Englishmen are less compellingly brilliant than they have been in trio contexts. Parker for once seems to rely on set-piece figures and repetitive ideas; Guy can make his contrabass talk, but this time at least it seems discursive rather than poetic. A marvellous occasion and a rare, possibly unrepeatable, chance to hear these players together, but not the most commanding record in the Parker discography.

****(*) Evan Parker/Patrick Scheyder**

Leo LRCD 326 *Parker; Patrick Scheyder (p).* 99.

One of the few disappointments in Leo's eventful catalogue and one of the few dead spots in Parker's increasingly compelling discography. These saxophone/piano duos (described in the liner-notes as 'Coltrane meets Chopin') actually sound like a dialogue of the deaf. The two players come from different performing disciplines and neither seems able to broker a neutral space, let alone viable creative territory. There is some lovely playing from both, not least on 'Dancing With Dr Dee', a further reference to Parker's fascination with pre-modern science-magic, but not enough to make the record sing as a whole.

***** Rangirua**

Leo LRCD 314 *Parker; Richard Nunns (Maori instruments).* 10/99.

A one-off relic of a tour to New Zealand in October 1999 and an encounter with local musician Nunns and his *taonga puoro* instruments. The record is worth it as much for the beautiful photographs of these hand-carved traditional instruments as it is for the music, which is oddly vague and evanescent, like a murmured conversation.

****** Dark Rags**

Potlatch 200 *Parker; Keith Rowe (g, elec).* 12/99–1/00.

***** Solar Wind**

Touch 035 *Parker; Lawrence Casserley (elec).* 00.

As a key member of AMM, Rowe is an equally important figure in British improvisation, and though the two have met and performed together before, this is a rare opportunity to hear two of the finest sound artists of their generation in duo. As ever, Parker blows long, seemingly unfeasible streams of notes, this time caught up in great loops and catenaries of sound that make inventive and sometimes surprising use of dynamics; we have rarely heard Evan play so quietly for so long. Rowe's electronics are never merely an ambient backdrop to the main action. Frequently one senses that it is he who is dictating the musical direction, and subsequent hearings bring the guitarist's role to the foreground. An utterly fascinating and genuinely enjoyable record. Not much to do with ragtime on first hearing, but the spirit of this densely virtuosic music isn't so very far removed.

The duo performance with Casserley, though equally beautiful, makes an interesting point of comparison. The fleetness and freedom of Rowe's table-top guitar isn't matched even by real-time electronics. There is something willed and deliberate about the work with Casserley; still powerful, still admirable in its way but certainly not as flowingly potent.

***** Chicago Tenor Duets**

Okka 12033 *Parker; Joe McPhee (ts).* 00.

Definitive, even iconic, as his soprano-playing has become, it is still intensely exciting to hear Parker on tenor. His roots in Coltrane, Rollins and Warne Marsh become instantly more evident. In company with multi-instrumentalist McPhee (restricted to another tenor on this occasion), he sounds much more jazz-based than usual, which is to say that there is a bluesy colouration to these improvisations, even if there are no pre-set structures or chord sequences. The sound isn't very good, but in more detailed passages it is difficult to prevent two such intense players seeming to fall over each other, or to include some of the quieter dynamics. All credit, though, to Bruno Johnson and John McCortney for their efforts.

***** The Needles**

Leo LRCD 348/349 2CD *Parker; Phillip Wachsmann (vn); Teppo Hauto-aho (b).* 6/00–5/01.

Taken from a live set at the Kerava Jazz Festival in Finland (the first outing for this interesting trio) and from a subsequent studio recording, *The Needles* is a fairly exhaustive examination of this group's potential. Parker had worked with strings before and there are moments when, unusually for Wachsmann, he and his fellow player seem to do little more than provide backgrounds for the saxophone. That may have something to do with the slightly tentative approach of the 2000 encounter. On the studio record, there is more interaction from the start. 'The Needles' and 'Devil's Punchbowl', named after geographical/geological forms, are immensely powerful performances, packed with criss-crossing lines and unexpected condensations, where all three players erupt into the same space simultaneously, as fiercely co-ordinated as a SWAT squad.

Some have suggested that the live performances are reminiscent of Albert Ayler's work with a violinist. We hear the connection, but suspect it's a false trail, since Parker seems little interested in Albert's radical simplification of melody and line;

to the contrary, he splinters it into a thousand pieces and the violin's overtones are an ideal corollary.

These are wonderful performances. 'A Punky And A Song' is probably the best of the live date, initially minimal and almost hypnotic, later developing in intensity, much like the relationship itself.

***(*) Lines Burnt In Light

Psi 01.01 *Parker (ss solo).* 10/01.

This release launched Parker's own label, the first time he had been involved in such a venture since the early days of Incus with Derek Bailey. Two of the three tracks included are concert pieces, part of a recital in St Michael and All Angels Church in London, but the first is essentially a rehearsal piece, recorded before the audience arrived. As ever, Parker fires off incredible streams of notes, but here he is able to use the church acoustic almost like a studio reverb, building layers of harmonics to almost unbelievable levels.

Parker had for a time set aside his interest in solo performance and this is a welcome return to a format that represents one of the central strands of his creative output. The central piece 'Line 2' has a fearsome intensity and directness; the third element is more discursive and somewhat less focused, but dynamically it is the climax of the record and no one – committed Parker fan or newcomer – will leave the experience unmoved and unimpressed.

** Parker Haslam Edwards

Slam 314 *Parker; George Haslam (bs, tarogato); John Edwards (b).* 9/00.

A fairly lowly marking because this is not strictly a Parker record, nor is it a trio record, but instead it is a series of solos (two from Haslam on baritone and tarogato respectively, one each from Parker and Edwards), a saxophone/bass duet, and one trio-piece for two saxophones and a bass. Haslam and Parker are very different musically, a distance even greater than that between Parker and Dunmall, and though the trio piece allows them to find some common ground, as a whole the record seems the product of a loose confederation rather than a genuine alliance. Evan's soprano solo is almost generic. He is instantly identifiable and yet one cannot be quite sure whether this is a new performance or one from the now-substantial back catalogue of such work. That is as much as anything a measure of how surely he has marked out this musical territory as his own.

***(*) Dividuality

Maya MCD 0101 *Parker; Barry Guy (b); Lawrence Casserley (elec).* 01.

Unexpectedly, Casserley dominates this electro-acoustic set. Both Parker and Guy seem very happy to set aside their usual hyperactivity and dwell in the mirrored halls that their new associate creates around them. 'Aulos' features just Parker and electronics (there are a couple of tracks where Guy similarly takes the foreground) and it is fascinating to hear a player who has made such inventive use of real-time harmonics ceding some responsibility to another performer. Casserley, though, is a genuinely creative and *listening* musician and his treatments are always thoroughly responsive and idiomatic.

The trio tracks are consistently good, especially the two long pieces, 'Shifting' and 'Transmute'. Here the logic and dynamics of the group are put to maximum effect. A powerful, haunting record, *Dividuality* lives on in the mind long after the final tones have faded.

**(*) Free Zone Appleby 2002

PSI 03.02/03 *Parker; John Rangecroft (cl); Neil Metcalfe (f); John Edwards (b); Phillip Wachsmann (vn, elec); Sylvia Hallett (vn, sarangi, v); Marcio Mattos (clo); Mark Sanders (perc).* 7/02.

Not to be confused with the earlier *After Appleby*, not least because it's a very dull and shapeless old dog compared to that record. There is no coherence to the parts and no hint of beauty in the sound, almost as if Parker's continuing immersion in sound synthesis and real-time processing has left him impatient of larger instrumental associations. Still a riveting duo player, as can be heard at various points here, he seems diffident and even awkward in the ensemble sections, and it's only Edwards who seems able or willing to drive the music on, picking up on the challenge of Parker's strings associations and running with that; one might have expected Mattos to be there with him, but he's exceedingly off-colour on this, while Hallett and Wachsmann are respectively in and out of character, she whimsical, he scratchy and unfocused.

***(*) Alder Brook

Leo LRCD 379 *Parker; Hans Anliker (tb); Peter A. Schmid (bcl, cbcl, cb-tubax, tarogato); Jurg Solothurnmann (ss, as); Reto Senn (cl, bcl, tarogato).* 9/02.

Recorded in a large water tank in Switzerland, this is a beautifully crafted and simply very beautiful record. The natural acoustic offers harmonic effects very similar to Parker's recent processings, but there is real charm in hearing him in company with other horns. It is very much a collaborative effort with Swiss ensemble September Winds, though Parker is the obvious star turn. He is absent from the opening trio by Anliker, Schmid and Senn, and elsewhere in the quintet passages keeps a somewhat lower-than-usual profile. There is a wonderful central passage where he joins Schmid on his double-bass 'tubax' for a duo and a trio section with Solothurnmann on soprano. The balancing of horns is done with virtuosic skill and, unlike his unhappy Appleby performance of two months previously, Parker demonstrates what a brilliant ensemble-player he can be. It's a beautifully weighted programme, pitched somewhere between the Vienna Art Orchestra's more open-plan moments and the experimentalism of the '60s New York loft scene (Parker sounds unaccountably like Sam Rivers in some places; that distinctive wail). Strongly recommended.

**** Memory/Vision

ECM 1852 *As for Electro-Acoustic Ensemble records above.* 10/02.

It's now a decade since the Electro-Acoustic Ensemble was first convened and seven years since its ECM debut on *Towards The Margins*. Before he began working with sound processors Walter Prati and Marco Vecchi, Parker had explored an interim stage in this evolution on 1991's *Process And Reality*, which used multi-tracking and overdubbing to create a music that went beyond the linear dimensions and vertical harmony of the solo performances. That record was inspired by Alfred North Whitehead. *Memory/Vision* is inspired by and dedicated to the late Charles Arthur Muses, who died in 2000. Muses was the founder of chronotopology and an influential thinker in the admittedly arcane field of hypernumber arithmetics and imaginary vector analysis in virtual dimensions. These ideas and processes obviously recommend him strongly to a musician of Parker's briskly scientistic approach. What one actually hears on *Memory/Vision*, which was commissioned for the Huddersfield Contemporary Music Festival, is a dramatic utopics, a real-time analysis of sound orders that goes as far beyond Whitehead's 'process' as Whitehead goes beyond tune-a-day diatonics.

On this first live recording of the Ensemble, signal processor Lawrence Casserley and computer processor Joel Ryan have been added to the original line-up of Parker, Prati, Vecchi, violinist Philipp Wachsmann, pianist Agusti Fernandez, bassist Barry Guy and percussionist Paul Lytton. The pace and dynamic of the music is strongly reminiscent of the kind of work Evan was doing in 2002 with September Winds. There the combination of other wind players and a notably resonant acoustic contributed to ensemble music of a very high order. *Memory/Vision* was first performed and then recorded only weeks later, and it is clear how consistent Parker's ideas are at the moment and how searching his musical quiddities. In keeping with Muses's ideas, he seems to be 'shaping' time rather than measuring it. The single continuous performance has both a monumental quality and a strong sense of process and flux, like a sculpture made of plasma rather than stone or bronze.

In the past, on *Towards The Margins* and *Process And Reality*, Parker has paid tribute to forerunners like AMM and Conlon Nancarrow, both practitioners of a music that moves beyond human instrumentality and which dispenses with the ego-tainted problems of 'expression' and 'performance'. *Memory/Vision* seems unwilled, internally perfect even when its exterior shapes look perverse. It's the test of very great music that it comes to the ears with an aura compounded of surprise and inevitability. After 70 minutes of this amazing work, it's hard to think that there was a time before you started listening to it.

William Parker

DOUBLE BASS

The creative heir of Jimmy Garrison and Paul Chambers, and directly influenced by '60s avant-gardists like Sirone and Alan Silva, Parker has emerged as one of the most inventive bassist/leaders since Mingus. His brooding, sepia-tinted tone first emerged in the Improvisers Collective in New York, an experimental workshop which later transmuted into the Mingus-like Little Huey Creative Music Ensemble.

*** Through Acceptance Of The Mystery Peace

Eremite 12 *Parker; Toshinori Kondo (t, ahn); Arthur Williams (t); Jemeel Moondoc (as); Will Connell Jr (as, f); Daniel Carter (as, ts, f, t); Charles Brackeen, John Hagen (ts); Rozanne Levine, Henry Warner (cl); Peter Kuhn (bcl); Ramsey Ameen, Billy Bang, Polly Bradfield, Jason Hwang (vn); Trinstan Honsinger (clo); Dennis Charles (d); Roger Baird (perc).* 79.

An important early record by the bassist, originally on Centering, and now reissued with one new track. In many respects, it looks forward to the larger bands of the '90s, but here Parker develops his ideas with a series of smaller ensembles and with more emphasis than later on free blowing. Kondo is an interesting figure who has made an intermittent impact. On trumpet here, he's reminiscent of Leo Smith in declamatory form – which is much of the time – but with a roundness of tone that almost suggests cornet. He's also featured on alto horn. The smaller groups favour strings and could almost be playing classical pieces. The bigger ensembles, though, are the surest indication of what was to come.

*** Song Cycle

Boxholder BXH 017 *Parker; Yukio Fujiyama (p); Ellen Christi, Lisa Sokolov (v).* 91–93.

At around the same time, saxophonist David Murray was expressing interest in writing songs. Typically, Parker put the wish into action and created this strange and powerful set of songs dedicated to particular inspirations in Parker's life. The reissue was dedicated to the late Jeanne Lee, who would have been a wonderful interpreter. Christi's voice is fine, though, and the material is so full of ideas and potential that one can imagine almost any one of these items having a vivid repertory life. Outstanding are 'Cloud And See Fading As Rain Falls', sung by Sokolov, and 'Falling Shadows', which has Parker duetting with Christi; the highlights of a wonderful album.

*** In Order To Survive

Black Saint 120159 *Parker; Lewis 'Flip' Barnes (t); Grachan Moncur III (tb); Rob Brown (as); Cooper-Moore (p); Dennis Charles (d).* 4 & 6/93.

***(*) Compassion Seizes Bed-Stuy

Homestead 231 *Parker; Rob Brown (as); Susie Ibarra (d).* 7/96.

Dominated by 'Testimony Of No Future', one of three tracks recorded at Club Roulette, and almost 40 minutes in length. Developed from the simplest ideas generated in a rhythm section dominated by Parker and Cooper-Moore (who has been an important and loyal associate), it is an immensely involving piece that opens up acres of improvisational territory for all the soloists. 'Anast In Crisis, Mouth Full Of Fresh Cut Flowers' is transparently and gloriously influenced by Cecil Taylor, an impression reinforced on 'Testimony Of The Stir Pot'. The closing piece, 'Square Sun', was recorded on another occasion at the Knitting Factory and is very different emotionally and stylistically. Parker uses his bow to good – even comic – effect, and trumpeter Barnes (reminiscent of Hugh Ragin in style) covers the generations, drawing in everything from Cootie Williams to Leo Smith. Moncur is as wise and philosophical as usual.

After the Black Saint album, Parker groups seem to have been known as In Order To Survive. *Compassion* is tighter, more focused and more obviously improvisational than parts of the previous disc, which seems workshopped round simple predetermined ideas. The tracks on the later album are more developed and feature some of the bassist's very best writing. The opening sequence of pieces, 'Compassion', 'Malcolm's Smile', 'For Robeson' and 'Holiday For Hypocrites', is worthy of Mingus, and the playing is strongly reminiscent of a Mingus Jazz Workshop until Parker's subtle bass overtones and harmonics start to come through. The later stretches of the album are more discursive.

*** Testimony

Zero In [no number] *Parker (b solo).* 12/94.

Solo contrabass performance is a stern discipline, mastered by few. Parker pays full tribute to the great Barre Phillips as his mentor, and much of this live recording from the Knitting Factory recalls Barre's rich, balletic solo works. The album is, however, dedicated to the less well-known and now sadly deceased French bassist Beb Guerin, and it is interesting to note how much in tonal colour and sense of musical architecture Parker resembles other European contrabass players like Jean-François Jenny-Clark and Henri Texier. The opening 'Sonic Animation' is in places not much more than a repository of sound-sources, animated by no other impulse. The sheer physical effort of playing Parker's favourite instrument, with its famously wide divide between strings and fingerboard, is balanced by the intensity and massiveness of his tone, and it's only with 'Testimony' itself, the brief sketch of 'Light #3' and 'Dedication' (a tribute to two more familiar spirits who died young) that this starts to pay real expressive dividends. By no means an undemanding listen, *Testimony* goes to the very core of what Parker is about, both musically and emotionally.

***** Sunrise In The Tone World**

Aum Fidelity 2 2CD *Parker; Lewis 'Flip' Barnes, Richard Rodriguez (t); Roy Campbell (t, flhn); Masahiko Kono, Alex Lodico, Steve Swell (tb); Dave Hofstra (tba); Chris Jonas (ss); Marco Eneidi (as); Ben Koen, Assif Tsahar (ts); Richard Keene (ts, ob); Joe Ruddick, David Sewelson (bs); Vinny Golia (reeds); Gregg Bendian (vib); Jason Hwang (vn); Akira Ando (clo); Susie Ibarra (d); Lisa Sokolov (v).* 97.

***** Flowers Grow In My Room**

Centering 1002 *Similar to above.* 95.

The bassist's work with the Improvisers Collective led directly to the foundation of the Little Huey Creative Music Orchestra, and these large-scale compositions and group improvisations are close to the heart of Parker's turbulent music. Their roots are in Trane's *Ascension*, in Mingus's sprawling big bands and Sun Ra's Arkestra; but they also have strong affinities with Butch Morris's conducted improvisation and with Anthony Braxton's mythic-realist fantasy pieces. The two long tracks, 'Bluest J' and 'Huey Sees Light Through A Leaf', are guilty of moments of lassitude and self-indulgence but for the most part they fulfil Parker's creative imperatives, and some of the shorter tracks like 'Sunship For Dexter' and 'Voice Dancer Kidd' are as beautiful as they are challenging, pointing out beyond the bassist's influences to a new aesthetic for large-band performance.

Flowers Grow In My Room has a slightly uncertain existence and we are unsure whether it is still generally available. However, it is another important chapter in Parker's development and that of the Little Huey Creative Music Orchestra, and well worth tracking down.

***** Lifting The Sanctions**

No More 6 *Parker (b solo).* 97.

As before on his solo projects, Parker favours the bow over pizzicato and creates a dazzling soundscape that shows once again how engaged and committed a player he is, not just technically but also emotionally and intellectually. Experiencing this album without preconception and with gently suspended attention is akin to listening to philosophical argument in an unfamiliar tongue. The logic and the wisdom are evident, even if the components of the language remain a secret. As before, too, there is a discursive quality to the opening piece, 'Emory', but this soon leads into deeper and more evocative territory in 'Rainbow Escaping', 'Mary Waiting' and, above all, the monumental 'Macchu Picchu'.

*****(*) Posium Pendasem**

FMP CD 105 *Parker; Rob Brown (as, f); Assif Tsahar (ts, bcl); Cooper-Moore (p); Susie Ibarra (d).* 4/98.

****** The Peach Orchard**

Aum Fidelity 10 2CD *As above.* 98.

This is the point at which Parker's massive investment in his instrumental technique, in thoughtful musicianship and in the collective aesthetic of In Order To Survive pays off, as one knew it would. Recorded during the Workshop Freie Musik in Berlin, the fascinating *Posium Pendasem* suggests how close Parker has always been to the very different and un-American freedoms of European improvisation. Peter Kowald's presence as author of the liner-notes is a further reinforcement. Divided into three pieces, at 51 minutes, 13 minutes and 30 seconds, and one and a half minutes respectively, the album gives a reasonable impression of how In Order To Survive function structurally over different durations. Inevitably, the longest track, 'Posium Pendasem #7', is the most intensely involving. There are acres of space for individual improvisation, but the real substance of the piece is evident when the group is improvising collectively, as in the middle section, when the horns seem to develop a strangely symmetrical counterpoint to what in a more conventional jazz line-up would have been the rhythm section. It's unfair at this stage in his career to heap more 'influences' on Parker, all the more so when he is showing not so much influence as a desire to continue the work of others; but these moments strongly recall Cecil Taylor's intense – and ironically bass-less – trios of the '60s. Fabulous music, in every sense of the word, dense and thoughtful, brightly coloured and abstract by turns.

The Peach Orchard is better still and arrayed across two full CDs of complex, mediated performance. Ibarra's long introduction to 'Moholo' (a tribute to South African drummer, Louis) is fine testimony to her growing skills and vision, while Cooper-Moore, who now plays only in Parker's company, creates a vivid and almost skittish accompaniment to the otherwise dark-toned 'Leaf Dance'. The first disc ends with a passionate elegy for a lost Eden. 'The Peach Orchard' is, along with a repeated version of 'In Order To Survive' at the end, the closest one comes to the essence of the group, highly individualistic but also profoundly collective in approach. Tsahar joins the group at the start of the second half with a mournful bass clarinet/piano duet on 'Posium Pendasem #3', another page from that astonishingly fertile workbook. William Parker is at the peak of his powers, and these two recent albums should be priority purchases for anyone who wants to confirm the durability of creative jazz at the turn of a new century.

***** Zen Mountains, Zen Streets: A Duet For Poet And Improvised Bass**

Boxholder 1 / 2 2CD *Parker; David Budbill (v, whistling, perc, other instruments).* 10/98.

Parker's interest in language, poetry and song is already well attested. This mammoth selection is the most rugged example of it yet. Harking back to the poetry and jazz experiments of the '50s, it puts Budbill's Whitmanesque lyrics into a strong musical context which is very similar to the kind of 'little instrument' improvisation pioneered by the AACM musicians in the '60s and early '70s. There are trumpets and flutes, even a touch of valve trombone, as well as bass and percussion, and one wonders whether it mightn't have been more effective to put Budbill in a more structured musical context. Parker moves all over his fretboard in search of sounds and patterns that will enhance the spoken word. The poet does not so much declaim or theatricalize his work as give it an air of almost ritual presence. It's effective enough, but by the time one turns to the second disc, it's with the air of a weary traveller

*** Painter's Spring

Thirsty Ear 57088 *Parker; Daniel Carter (as, ts, cl, f); Hamid Drake (d).* 00.

*** Piercing The Veil

AUM Fidelity 17 *As above, except omit Carter.* 4/00.

Painter's Spring is a deeply satisfying record that sees Parker harnessing the dynamic of his larger groups to the idiom of the free-jazz trio. Apart from 'Balm In Gilead' and Duke's 'Come Sunday', all the tunes are by Parker himself. They combine harmonically rich accompaniments – reminiscent of Matthew Shipp, who acts as producer – with brisk, stabbing figures that often imply, rather than state, melodic directions. Carter (not to be confused with namesake James) is a very impressive performer, but it's the leader's thunderous dialogues with Hamid Drake which capture the attention. Their interaction on the three-part 'Foundation' suite – which is obviously drawn from something larger and more free form since the sections are numbered one, four and two, and presented in that order – is quite breathtaking.

Those same energies are harnessed on the duo record as well. Drake is a maximalist in such settings and here he peppers the sound environment with a myriad of tiny effects that are too well structured and meaningful to be merely haphazard. Parker himself more than makes up for the absence of a conventional horn with long, singing lines and percussive, almost reed-like, effects. He is now such a master of his instrument that he seems able to create almost any sound he wants or needs on the contrabass. Another astonishing record from a modern master.

**** Mayor Of Punkville

Aum Fidelity 15 2CD *Parker; Roy Campbell (t, flhn); Lewis 'Flip' Barnes, Richard Rodriguez (t); Masahiko Kono, Alex Lodico, Steve Swell (tb); Chris Jonas (ss); Ori Kaplan (as); Charles Waters (as, cl); David Sewelson (bs); Cooper-Moore (p); Dave Hofstra (b, tba); Andrew Baker (d); Aleta Hayes (v).* 7–11/99.

The Little Huey Creative Music Orchestra has become one of the most compelling large units on the scene and this remarkable performance clinches Parker as a composer of large-scale dramatic works. The title-piece and the equally long 'I Can't Believe I Am Here' are structured around deceptively simple ideas, melodic cells and simple ostinatos which open up improvising possibilities for the soloists. Parker includes two curious 'interludes' which sound like rehearsal material, but with 'Three Steps To Noh Mountain' he demonstrates a capacity for jewel-like perfection and a pristine logic, even in a small span. There is so much to admire here that it's virtually impossible to single out tracks but, along with those already mentioned, 'Oglala Eclipse' and the closing 'Anthem' are outstanding.

**** O'Neal's Porch

Aum Fidelity 22 *Parker; Lewis 'Flip' Barnes (t); Rob Brown (as); Hamid Drake (d).* 5/00.

After the majestic sweep of *Mayor Of Punkville*, this is an almost straightahead post-bop session. Parker and Drake establish a telepathic rapport on the opening 'Purple' and the album just drives on from there. 'Sun', 'Song For Jesus' and the title-track rely on harmonic ideas and rhythmic displacements that will inevitably conjure up the spirit of Eric Dolphy. Eric's feel for the blues suffuses 'Rise' and 'Moon' though Rob Brown has his own very distinctive voice and is most certainly not a copyist. Parker has been bolder and will write more ambitious music, but he will find it challenging to top this one for sheer listenability and intrigue. One of *the* jazz albums of 2000.

*** Raincoat In The River

Eremite MITE 036 *Parker; Lewis Barnes, Richard Rodriguez (t); Roy Campbell Jr (t, flhn); Alex Lodico, Masahiko Kono, Steve Swell (tb); Dave Hofstra (tba); Rob Brown, Ori Kaplan (as); Charles Waters (as, cl); Darryl Foster (ss, ts); David Sewelson (bs); Shiau-Shu Yu (clo); Andrew Barker, Guillermo E. Brown (d); Leena Conquest (v).* 2/01.

Disappointing sound for such ambitious and beautiful music. Perhaps it's because Parker favours so much lower-register writing that the balance has to be so flat. Soloists sound rather remote and as if enclosed in booths. Like some of Anthony Braxton's large-scale works, this seems to have a narrative component, though one so enigmatic that it is hardly worth trying to reconstruct it. Leena Conquest's vocals are an acquired taste, in any case. With just a couple of exceptions, the Little Huey Creative Music Orchestra is made up of young and relatively unknown names, so there are few familiar playing personalities to listen up for, though Steve Swell does have a couple of characteristic moments near the beginning. The core of the album comes with 'Anast Crossing The Lake Of Light' and the title-piece and there's a marked falling-off after that, but only because the final track, 'A Painter's Celebration', seems out of place there.

*** Bob's Pink Cadillac

Eremite MITE 32 2CD *Parker; Perry Robinson (cl, ocarina); Walter Perkins (d, perc).* 01.

Like Anthony Braxton and David Murray before him, Parker seems fated to have almost every new project and line-up preserved on record. It affords a wonderful picture of how a creative career evolves, but it's difficult to keep pace, particularly when, as with this set, the records come in twos. What's immediately exciting about *Bob's Pink Cadillac* is a full glimpse of the recently resurgent Robinson, who has been out of the picture for far too long. His high, keening approach is the antithesis to what you'd normally expect on a Parker record, but it's very effective, and the suite of clarinet themes that make up the second disc, 'Ebony Fantasy', pushes Perry to the front. The best work, it has to be said, is on the first disc. 'Blue Flower' and 'Fence In The Snow' are both viscerally powerful, a fascinating blend of '60s-style freedom and Parker's contemporary structures. Worth getting, but only if you really feel up to two hours plus of this kind of music.

***(*) Raining On The Moon

Thirsty Ear THI 57119 2 *Parker; Lewis Barnes (t); Rob Brown (as, f); Hamid Drake (d); Leena Conquest (v).* 10/01.

When this was released, there was much talk of Parker's 'retro' taste taking him back to a sound that would not have been out of place on some AACM project of the late '60s. The lineage is very much that and, in a curious way, it's Leena Conquest's vocal which cements the comparison. There is something refreshingly sanguine and upbeat about all the music on the record. 'Hunk Pappa Blues' and the following 'Song Of Hope' provide as enjoyable an intro as you'll hear in many a year, while 'Raining On The Moon', 'James Baldwin To The Rescue' and 'Donso Ngoni' mix the light-hearted and sombre in perfect proportion.

****(*) Eloping With The Sun**
Riti 7 *Parker; Joe Morris (bjo, banjolele, banjouki); Hamid Drake (frame d).* 02.

Released on Morris's label, so he presumably called the shots. The idea here was that each musician would leave their main instrument at home and bring along something else. One might have expected Parker to tote his shakuhachi (for portability if nothing else) but he opted for the Middle Eastern stringed zintir, on which he gets a pleasant, adaptable, but ultimately rather boring sound. Morris switches to banjo, banjolele and hybrid banjouki, while Drake makes the least concession by abandoning his kit for a frame drum. It's interesting enough and some of the pieces have a genuine charm, but it's hard to see this as an important Parker record, rather an agreeable experiment that probably doesn't merit a CD afterlife.

***** ... And William Danced**
Ayler 44 *Parker; Anders Gahnhold (as); Hamid Drake (d, perc).* 4/02.

Recorded live in Stockholm on the same visit that yielded Jemeel Moondoc's *Live From The Glenn Miller Café*, which featured Parker and Drake as the rhythm section. The saxophonist is an able and in some regards highly original player, and it is his presence that seems to keep the set to a jazzier and more groove-driven approach. Parker's bass-playing is as strong and sure-footed as ever and it's Drake who seems slightly off-line at times on this, often when Gahnhold is soloing and the tempo becomes stiffer than usual. Just three long improvisations and lots of good music in them, but not a priority for Parker fans.

*****(*) Scrapbook**
Eremite 57133 *Parker; Billy Bang (vn); Hamid Drake (perc).* 6/03.

This is Parker's Violin Trio, a song-based group that takes two elements of his career and fuses them brilliantly. There is plenty of open improvisation to be found, but it's the structure of these six songs that is intriguing. The best of them is also the longest, 'Sunday Morning Church', on which Bang plays a heart-achingly mournful solo against Parker's bass ostinati. 'Dust On A White Shirt' is more mysterious, an exploration of the quotidian so intense that it becomes almost surreal. The final 'Holiday For Flowers' is short enough to release as a single and almost as catchily done. A fascinating turn for the bassist, who has never sounded more engaged and straightforward.

Horace Parlan (born 1931)

PIANO

Veteran Pittsburgh hard-bopper, active in the USA through the '60s but since 1973 an expatriate living in Denmark. His blues-based style is solidity incarnate.

***** Arrival**
Steeplechase SCCD 31012 *Parlan; Idrees Sulieman (flhn); Bent Jaedig (ts); Hugo Rasmussen (b); Ed Thigpen (d).* 12/73.

***** No Blues**
Steeplechase SCCD 31056 *Parlan; Niels-Henning Orsted Pedersen (b); Tony Inzalaco (d).* 12/75.

***** Frankly Speaking**
Steeplechase SCCD 31076 *Parlan; Frank Strozier (as); Frank Foster (ts); Lisle Atkinson (b); Al Harewood (d).* 2/77.

****** Blue Parlan**
Steeplechase SCCD 31124 *Parlan; Wilbur Little (b); Dannie Richmond (d).* 11/78.

***** Musically Yours**
Steeplechase SCCD 31141 *Parlan (p solo).* 11/79.

***** The Maestro**
Steeplechase SCCD 31167 *Parlan (p solo).* 11/79.

***** Like Someone In Love**
Steeplechase SCCD 31178 *Parlan; Jesper Lundgaard (b); Dannie Richmond (d).* 3/83.

*****(*) Glad I Found You**
Steeplechase SCCD 31194 *Parlan; Thad Jones (flhn); Eddie Harris (ts); Jesper Lundgaard (b); Aage Tanggaard (d).* 7/84.

****(*) Little Esther**
Soul Note 121145 *Parlan; Per Goldschmidt (bs); Klavs Hovman (b); Massimo De Majo (d).* 3/87.

Parlan's most moving single performance is arguably the unaccompanied 'Lament For Booker Ervin', posthumously tacked on to the Ervin album of that title. None of his other solo recordings evinces that much intensity or attention to detail. A middle-order bop pianist in a highly oversubscribed field, Parlan catches the attention only for his tough bass chords and highly restricted melody figures (an attack of infantile paralysis crabbed his right hand) which contributed substantially to *Mingus Ah Um* and accorded closely with the bassist/composer's preference for highly rhythmic and unorthodox pianists. Parlan has developed a blues-influenced repertoire, marked by a substantial inclusion of Thelonious Monk themes, heavily left-handed melodies like 'Lullaby Of The Leaves' and throbbing swingers like Randy Weston's 'Hi-Fly', both of which recur throughout his recorded work, and in particular a wilderness of minimally differentiated Steeplechase sessions. Most of these have now returned on CD.

Perhaps the best of Parlan's earlier group work was made for Blue Note in the '60s. The pick of those, *Happy Frame Of Mind*, which featured his friend Ervin, was briefly available on CD (784134) but has subsequently disappeared again. The excellent 1960 sessions with the Turrentine brothers are no longer available. Like other American players of the time, facing a slackening demand for jazz recording, Parlan emigrated to Scandinavia, where he has pursued a workmanlike and unspectacular career, documented by Steeplechase from *Arrival* onwards with almost redundant thoroughness, although the sequence ends in the '80s. The only high spots that call for separate treatment are the very fine 1978 trio with Wilbur Little and Dannie Richmond (also, of course, a Mingus man) and the much later *Glad I Found You*, where Parlan and the late Thad Jones shrug off a rather diffident setting to produce some sparkling performances. *Frankly Speaking* offers a rare glimpse of Frank Strozier, briefly visible as a Steeplechaser at the time; and the solo sets, *Musically Yours* and *The Maestro*, each have their felicities, particularly the gentler tracks on the second disc. For the rest, cautious sampling is perhaps the best bet. Although he rarely resorts to cliché, Parlan is still somewhat repetitive in the structuring of his solos, and he's rarely as challenging as like-minded figures such as Roland Hanna and Jaki Byard. The discography seems to have come to a stop, and with his early work still in limbo, Parlan is very much in the shadows as far as his standing goes.

Phil Parnell

PIANO

Big-toned Brit, making his debut.

★★★ Dear Jo

Slam CD 227 *Parnell; Dave Green (b); Johnny Vidacovich (d); Paul Clarvis (perc).* 10/96.

A strong and sometimes gripping jazz gig which introduces Parnell as a fine two-handed player who likes to mix harmonic sophistication with lots of energy. Hear him on 'The Touch Of Your Lips' and a couple of the originals and you're reaching for American parallels to explain how he sounds, though there's no obvious influence foremost. The key element on the set is Green, who is dependable, inventive and unobtrusive. Nice record.

John Parricelli (born 1959)

GUITAR

After a start in local rock bands in his native Worcester, Parricelli came to London and was soon involved in the Loose Tubes axis during the '80s. He's been a regular and trusted, versatile musician in many contexts ever since.

★★★ Alba

Provocateur PVC 1021 *Parricelli; Mark Lockheart (ts); Dudley Phillips (b); Martin France (d).* 9/99.

A deserved feature outing for this prolific sideman. He's often worked with Mark Lockheart, and their partnership here offers some echoes of the Scofield–Lovano sound familiar from many New York records. It's an accomplished set, but, as far as the most interesting writing goes, it rather runs out of steam after the first three tracks: 'Shore Song' is a beatbox mood-piece that disperses the more musicianly results of the first half, and some of the other tunes dawdle in the backwaters of English pastorale, which so many musicians seem hung up on. The best stuff is when Parricelli and Lockheart engage in more fruitful lines of dialogue.

Joe Pass (1929–94)

GUITAR

Already working with pro bands when in high school, Joseph Passalaqua toured with Charlie Barnet before naval service, then grappled with a drug problem and played small gigs in Los Angeles. Cleaning up in the early '60s, he worked with George Shearing and others and became internationally known after signing with Norman Granz's Pablo operation, for which he made scores of albums as leader and sideman. Revered by other players for a consummate technique, he helped restore a 'traditional' modernism as something valuable, after the inroads of rock had taken their toll on the respectability of the open-tone electric sound.

★★★ Joy Spring

Pacific Jazz 835222-2 *Pass; Mike Wofford (p); Jim Hughart (b); Colin Bailey (d).* 2/64.

Pass became the most significant 'classic' guitar stylist since Wes Montgomery. He first recorded as a member of a Synanon Rehabilitation Centre house-band, and the string of albums he made for Pacific Jazz during the '60s are all currently out of general circulation – except this one, which didn't even emerge until the '70s. It's a typical Los Angeles club date from 1964, handling some bop and standard set-pieces. Pass's style is fully formed: only the warmth and finesse of his later years are missing, and that may be as much due to the recording, which is no more than respectable. He builds long and quite fanciful lines out of 'Joy Spring' and 'Relaxin' At Camarillo' and comfortably overcomes some tuning problems on 'The Night Has A Thousand Eyes'. This is an inadequate look at this point in his career but, in the absence of *Catch Me!* and *For Django*, it's all there is.

★★★ Portraits Of Duke Ellington

Pablo 2310-716 *Pass; Ray Brown (b); Bobby Durham (d).* 6/74.

★★(★) Tudo Bem!

Original Jazz Classics OJC 685 *Pass; Don Grusin (p); Oscar Castro-Nueves (g); Octavio Bailly (b); Claudio Slon (d); Paulinho Da Costa (perc).* 5/78.

★★★(★) Chops

Original Jazz Classics OJC 686 *Pass; Niels-Henning Orsted Pedersen (b).* 11/78.

★★★ Checkmate

Pablo 2310-865 *Pass; Jimmy Rowles (p).* 1/81.

★★★ Ira, George And Joe

Original Jazz Classics OJC 828 *Pass; John Pisano (g); Jim Hughart (b); Shelly Manne (d).* 11/81.

★★★ Eximious

Pablo 2310-877 *Pass; Niels-Henning Orsted Pedersen (b); Martin Drew (d).* 5–7/82.

★★★ We'll Be Together Again

Original Jazz Classics OJC 909 *Pass; J. J. Johnson (tb).* 10/83.

★★ Whitestone

Pablo 2310-912 *Pass; Don Grusin, John Pisano (g); Abe Laboriel, Nathaniel West, Harvey Mason (d); Paulinho Da Costa (perc); Armando Compean (v).* 2–3/85.

★★★ One For My Baby

Pablo 2310-936 *Pass; Plas Johnson (ts); Gerald Wiggins (p, org); Andy Simpkins (b); Albert 'Tootie' Heath (d).* 4/88.

★★★ Summer Nights

Pablo 2310-939 *Pass; John Pisano (g); Jim Hughart (b); Colin Bailey (d).* 12/89.

★★★ Appassionato

Pablo 2310-946 *Pass; Jim Hughart (b); Colin Bailey (d).*

★★★ Duets

Pablo 2310-959 *Pass; John Pisano (g).* 2/91.

★★★ Joe Pass In Hamburg

ACT 9100-2 *Pass; NDR Big Band and Radio Philharmonic.* 4/90–2/92.

***** Live At Yoshi's**

Pablo 2310-951 *Pass; John Pisano (g); Monty Budwig (b); Colin Bailey (d).* 1/92.

***** Nuages – Live At Yoshi's Vol. 2**

Pablo 2310-961 *As above.* 1–2/92.

*****(*) Finally**

Emarcy 512603-2 *Pass; Red Mitchell (b).* 2/92.

***** My Song**

Telarc CD-83326 *Pass; John Pisano (g); Tom Ranier (p); Jim Hughart (b); Colin Bailey (d).* 2/93.

His long series of albums for Pablo helped Pass become both a major concert attraction and a benchmark player for jazz guitar. Pass smooths away the nervousness of bop yet counters the plain talk of swing with a complexity that remains completely accessible. An improvisation on a standard may range far and wide, but there's no sense of him going into territory which he doesn't already know well. There's nothing hidden in his music, everything is absolutely on display, and he cherishes good tunes without sanctifying them. His tone isn't distinctive but it is reliably mellifluous, and he can make every note in a melody shine. Compared with Tal Farlow or Jimmy Raney, Pass took few risks and set himself fewer genuine challenges, but any guitarist will recognize a performer who has a total command over the instrument.

Pass effectively became the house guitarist for Pablo and, besides his own sessions, there are very many guest appearances with Oscar Peterson, Milt Jackson and the rest of the company stable. One could complain that Pass made too many records, but even taking a few deletions into account it amounts to only about one a year under his own name. The problem is more that his favourite context tended to be insufficiently various to make one want to own more than one of them.

Although he recorded extensively as a soloist, there are also many group albums in the catalogue. *Chops* is plenty of fun for the sheer expertise on display, Pass and NHOP basically doing little more than showing off how well they can play, but with enough nous to make it sound good. The meeting with J. J. Johnson on *We'll Be Together Again* is a little sleepy, but these are two sly old dogs, and you can almost hear them kidding each other on the blues, 'Naked As A Jaybird'. Johnson deadpans his way through it and for once Pass sounds like the assertive one; still, it's hard to think of a more sheerly mellifluous partnership. Shelly Manne is a useful presence on *Ira, George And Joe*, and this set of Gershwin tunes is nicely varied: Pass almost twangs his way through 'Bidin' My Time' and 'It Ain't Necessarily So', makes a waltz out of 'Love Is Here To Stay' and does a beautifully slow take on 'Lady Be Good'.

Of the trio sets, the Ellington album with Ray Brown and Bobby Durham is a shade disappointing. *Summer Nights* is something of a tribute to Django Reinhardt, and Pass sounds contented and thoughtful, while *Appassionato*, which benefits from a wider and more modern sound on CD, chooses terser material than usual – 'Grooveyard', 'Relaxin' At Camarillo', 'Nica's Dream' – and finds a cutting edge which some of Pass's records pass by. *Eximious* is a mixed set of standards and jazz themes, most of them adroitly handled, although Drew doesn't seem like the ideal drummer for the situation and the studio sound is a bit glaring. *Live At Yoshi's* is a solid club set, recorded in California, with a boppish tinge that gets a little extra juice out of 'Doxy' and 'Oleo'. The second helping on *Nuages* turns out much the same, with the closing 'Cherokee' a characteristic flourish from all hands.

The odd records out are *One For My Baby*, which sets the guitarist up in a sort of down-home kind of roadhouse band with mixed success, although Johnson contributes a few lively solos; the two Latin-styled albums, both of which have their finesse swamped by Don Grusin's penchant for light-music triviality, prettily though everyone plays; and *In Hamburg*, which sets Joe against both big band and strings on two occasions. Some of the charts are prosaic and this kind of situation isn't really Joe's thing, but he treats the occasion graciously enough and on a superior arrangement like Herb Geller's 'Love For Sale' there's a degree of excitement.

There is some poignancy about *Finally*, given that it's among the last recordings by both Pass and Mitchell, but the sheer good humour and craftiness of the playing make it a special item in the Pass list. Mitchell's knack of elevating an ordinary playing situation brings out the best in both men, and there's an extra twist in such staples as 'Blue Moon' and 'Have You Met Miss Jones?'. 'I Thought About You', done at a tempo that approximates syrup dripping off a spoon, is very fine. The other duo albums are equally effective and suggest how much Pass responded to the format. *Checkmate* is a typical Rowles session, with forgotten sweeteners like 'So Rare' and 'Marquita' in the programme, and since both men share an approach that mixes the respectful with the inventive they get along just fine. Pass plays with the minimum of amplification and it helps to offset any chord-clashing problems. There was a long-standing and fruitful liaison with fellow guitarist Pisano, and *Duets* documents their sympathies very candidly. Whether playing acoustic or electric, there's a good deal of bite about this pairing, with little of the sonorous fluff that sometimes gets stuck to guitar duets. Recorded very close up, the music has much presence and sting.

His first for Telarc reunited him with Pisano, and the rhythm section generate some civilized heat. It's still a bit restrained, but a couple more records by this group might have seen them reaching beyond the norm. Instead, Pass's passing closed the chapter.

CORE COLLECTION

****** Virtuoso**

Pablo 2310-708 *Pass (g solo).* 12/73.

This original *Virtuoso* album remains definitive: Pass never sounded sharper or warmer on a set of standards, played with all the expertise the title suggests.

*****(*) Virtuoso # 2**

Pablo 2310-788 *Pass (g solo).* 10/76.

***** Virtuoso # 3**

Original Jazz Classics OJC 684 *Pass (g solo).* 5–6/77.

***** Virtuoso # 4**

Pablo 2640-102 2CD *Pass (g solo).*

***** At the Montreux Jazz Festival 1975**

Original Jazz Classics OJC 934 *Pass (g solo).* 7/75.

***** Montreux '77**

Original Jazz Classics OJC 382. *Pass (g solo).* 7/77.

***** I Remember Charlie Parker**

Original Jazz Classics OJC 602 *Pass (g solo).* 2/79.

***** Blues Dues (Live At Long Beach City College)**
Original Jazz Classics OJC 964 *Pass (g solo).* 1/84.

***** University Of Akron Concert**
Pablo 2308-249 *Pass (g solo).* 85.

***** Blues For Fred**
Pablo 2310-931 *Pass (g solo).* 2/88.

***** Virtuoso Live!**
Pablo 2310-948 *Pass (g solo).*

***** What Is There To Say**
Pablo 2310-971-2 *Pass (g solo).* 9/90.

***** Songs For Ellen**
Pablo 2310-955 *Pass (g solo).* 8/92.

***** Unforgettable**
Pablo 2310964-2 *Pass (g solo).* 8/92.

Pass's solo records are almost a category by themselves, and their importance in re-establishing the eminence of straightahead jazz guitar now seems clear. At a time when traditional jazz guitar playing was being sidelined by the gradual onset of fusion, Joe's solo work reaffirmed the virtues of the unadorned electric guitar, and the subtleties and harmonic shrewdness of his playing are like a long drink of water after much of the overheated guitar-playing of the '70s and '80s.

Following on from the original, the three subsequent *Virtuoso* volumes are replays with lightly diminishing returns; *Virtuoso #4* has now made it to a double-CD, with some extra tracks, although with the emphasis here on the acoustic guitar, some may see this as a makeweight to the others.

Concert situations don't seem to affect Pass's concentration: he played with the same careful diligence as in the studio, so the live solo albums sound much alike. Both Montreux albums are good, but *Montreux '77* is interesting for its emphasis on blues – four of the seven tracks – and how much Pass can get out of the form. *Blues Dues* includes a 'Round Midnight' which makes one wish that Pass had looked at this repertoire more often. *University Of Akron Concert* includes one of his extended Ellington medleys, a favourite device. *Virtuoso Live!* is in most respects just another solo album, but the pieces chosen reflect Pass's concern to try and wriggle free of his own routines. 'Mack The Knife' appears as a ballad, delivered with a superb touch, and the chopped rhythms of 'Stompin' At The Savoy' show how he could find a new tone, even in such a warhorse as that. *What Is There To Say* is a recent issue of previously unheard material, live at Hollywood's Vine Street Bar & Grill. Joe sounds in strong form, not dwelling too long on the ballads and making even the likes of 'Old Folks' and 'Come Rain Or Come Shine' muster a little urgency as they go.

Of the other studio dates, *I Remember Charlie Parker* is a slight disappointment, Pass a little quiescent; *Blues For Fred* has some charming material, associated with Fred Astaire; and *Songs For Ellen* is Pass at his gentlest. From those same final sessions *Unforgettable* has just emerged. Played on a nylon-strung acoustic, it is Joe at his most winsome, even if rhythmically it's a little deliberate.

***** The Best Of Joe Pass**
Pablo 2405-419 *Pass; as albums above.*

****** Guitar Virtuoso**
Pablo 4423 4CD *Pass; as albums above.*

The Best Of is a respectable cross-section from the Pablo albums, but it has been superseded by the handsome, smartly chosen and very pleasurable four-disc collection, *Guitar Virtuoso*, which puts Pass's virtues into a clear light as both leader and sideman. Looking through this very long and hard-to-differentiate discography, it's hard to argue with the suggestion that if you have this one, you have all the Pass you need.

Jaco Pastorius (1951–87)

BASS GUITAR, STEEL DRUMS

Tried several instruments before settling on bass, and played rock, soul and reggae before looking at jazz. He acquired enough of a reputation to have cut a solo record before joining Weather Report in 1976, where he stayed until 1982. His fretless-electric bass style, soloistic and virtuosic, was hugely influential, but his personal life went dramatically downhill in the mid-'80s and he died following a beating outside a night club in 1987.

***** Jaco**
DIW 312 *Pastorius; Paul Bley (p); Pat Metheny (g); Bruce Ditmas (d).* 6/74.

Le demi-dieu de la basse: the unofficial subtitle of a recent compilation of Pastorius's music suggests the magnitude of the cult that has grown up around him after his pointless, wasteful death, beaten senseless by a club bouncer following one of his legendary binges. There was never any doubt about Jaco's brilliance, even before he became a member of Weather Report and became sanctified as the Jimi Hendrix of the bass guitar. The quartet with Metheny and Paul Bley is pretty much how you'd expect it to sound at that vintage. Metheny's playing is articulate but not profound, and a great pianist (albeit on an electric instrument) finds himself lost away in a rumbly sound-mix. Even so, Pastorius is the voice who commands the attention, nimble, precise and already experimenting with chords and harmonics.

*****(*) Jaco Pastorius**
Sony Jazz EK 64977 *Pastorius; Randy Brecker, Ron Tooley (t); Peter Graves (btb); Peter Gordon (frhn); Hubert Laws (picc); Wayne Shorter (ss); David Sanborn (as); Michael Brecker (ts); Howard Johnson (b); Alex Darqui, Herbie Hancock (p, ky); Richard Davis, Homer Mensch (b); Bobby Oeconomy, Narada Michael Walden, Lenny White (d); Don Alias (perc); Othello Molineaux, Leroy Williams (steel d); Sam and Dave (v); strings.* 75.

This was the first time anyone attempted to groom Jaco for big stardom. It puts him into an appropriately epic setting and demonstrates with tiny gestures just how completely in command he was when focused and straight, not just of his own instrument, but of an entire musical conception. But for oddities like the vocal contribution of soulmen Sam and Dave, which doesn't really work, and an understandable desire to show off as many different facets of his musical personality as possible, this might stand as Pastorius's best memorial. In the end, it doesn't quite add up to a great album. The solo 'Portrait Of Tracy' is exquisite and there is an early and very wonderful performance of the Charlie Parker tune 'Donna Lee', a tune dedicated to a bassist of a previous age, and a very courageous one by all accounts. Perhaps too many different line-ups on show for one record.

***(*) Word Of Mouth

Warner Bros 3535 *Pastorius; Bill Reichenbach (tb); Tom Scott (bcl); Toots Thielemans (hca); Jack DeJohnette (d, perc).* 80.

A brilliant example of Jaco's gift for sound, with a rich blend of horn sounds within the confines of the small group. DeJohnette's drumming is the key additional element here, intensely musical and endlessly responsive to the long, winding bass-line. Jaco seems at ease and plays more quietly and with less percussive an attack. Some of his mid-range tones might almost be made by a cello. A lovely record, full of surprises.

*** The Birthday Concert

Warner Bros 954290 *Pastorius; Dan Faulk, Brett Murphy, Melton Mustafa, Brian O'Flaherty (t); Russ Freeland, Peter Graves, Mike Katz (tb); Dave Bargeron (tb, tba); Peter Gordon, Jerry Peel, Steve Rothstein (hn); Dan Bonsanti, Neal Bonsanti, Michael Brecker, Greg Lindsay, Bob Mintzer (sax); Randy Emerick (bs); Paul Hornmuller, Othello Molineaux, Oscar Salas, Bobby Thomas (perc).* 12/81.

Jaco's 30th birthday, celebrated in a club in his native Fort Lauderdale. The band seems to have been a mixture of visiting guests, like Brecker, and local stalwarts. It's the usual mix of virtuosic grandstanding and ambitious ensemble-playing. Perhaps moved by the occasion (though there are other possible explanations), Jaco plays less than usual and with less than usual precision. Not much more than five years later he would be dead. Perhaps if there had been more years, less weight would now be put on sessions like this. As it is, every crumb and every contrivance must be made to count. Not a great sound, with the brasses in particular recorded thinly and inadequately.

*** Invitation

Warner Brothers 16662 *Pastorius; Randy Brecker, Elmer Brown, Forrest Buchtel, Jon Faddis, Ron Tooley (t); Wayne Andre (tb); Dave Bargeron (tb, tba); Peter Gordon, Brad Warnaar (frhn); Peter Graves, Bill Reichenbach (btb); Alex Foster (ss, as, ts, picc, f); Mario Cruz (ss, as, ts, cl, f); Bob Mintzer (ss, ts); Randy Emerick (as, bs, f); Paul McCandless (ts, ob, eng hn); Toots Thielemans (hca); Peter Erskine (d, perc); Don Alias, Othello (perc).* 82.

Another live concert and another hand-picked big band. Jaco steps out front for a Hendrix-influenced version of 'Amerika' (sic) and is prominently featured as soloist, with the massed horns roaring and murmuring behind him. It's a slightly unsettling sound, but such is the level of his inventiveness that it never palls. As if to show off his jazz chops, Jaco medleys a couple of his own compositions with John Coltrane's 'Giant Steps', *the* modern test piece in the jazz musician's harmony and counterpoint class. He comes off just fine. Gil Evans's 'Eleven' is another of the repertory pieces, but for the most part Pastorius sticks to an eclectic mix of originals ('Liberty City', 'Continuum', and things like Pee Wee Ellis's 'The Chicken', a riff he'd been playing for most of his career. It's a great record and a feast for electric-bass fans.

***(*) Punk Jazz

Big World BW 1001 *Pastorius; Jerry Gonzalez (t, perc); Alex Foster, Butch Thomas (sax); Michael Gerber (p); Delmar Brown (ky); Hiram Bullock (g); Kenwood Dennard (d).* 3/86.

Pastorius's wish to be considered a jazz man (albeit a punk jazz man) surfaced regularly through the final few years, when as often as not personal circumstances dictated a less sophisticated approach. 'Donna Lee' reappears here, but without the boppish authenticity of the Epic session (reissued on Sony). The remainder of the set is good, hot-sauce electric jazz, surprisingly conventional when set alongside the 'punk' aesthetic of Zorn, Lindsay, Marclay and company.

**(*) Honestly

Jazzpoint JP 1032 *Pastorius (b solo).* 3/86.

***(*) Live In Italy

Jazzpoint JP 1037 *Pastorius; Bireli Lagrene (g); Thomas Borocz (d).* 3/86.

*** Heavy'N Jazz

Jazzpoint JP 1036 *Pastorius; Bireli Lagrene (g); Serge Bringolf (d).* 12/86.

The untitled improvisations on *Honestly* frequently seem no more than a Sears catalogue of exotic harmonies and effects, put together with diminishing logic and questionable taste. Needless to say, the Italian crowd cheer it to the echo, although they don't respond at all to a quote from 'My Favorite Things', and they don't rise to 'America The Beautiful' or the riff from 'Purple Haze' either, so what does that suggest about their musical expectations? The trio was recorded at the same time, a very different line-up and sound from the group with Bullock and Dennard, but it has its own distinctive strengths. Lagrene's romanticism is closest in spirit, and the two guitarists trade lines with fire and discipline. In contrast to Metheny's Wes Montgomery fixation, Lagrene is in thrall to his countryman, Django. His opening improvisation more or less focuses the mind on what he's doing thereafter, to the virtual exclusion of a slightly subdued and acoustically recessed Pastorius. They do creditable versions of 'Satin Doll', Joe Zawinul's Weather Report theme 'Black Market', and Bob Marley's reggae classic 'I Shot The Sheriff', which underlines Pastorius's childhood closeness to Caribbean music of all sorts.

**** Punk Jazz: The Jaco Pastorius Anthology

Warner Bros / Rhino 8122 73779 2 2CD *Pastorius solo and with various groups: Wayne Cochran's C C Riders; Little Beaver; Pat Metheny/Paul Bley/Bruce Ditmas; Trilogue; Weather Report; Airto Moreira/Flora Purim; Michel Colombier; Joni Mitchell; Mike Stern; Brian Melvin.* 68–86.

As Jaco Pastorius Inc, run by the late bassist's children, starts to mop up the bootlegs and unauthorized releases, the contours of their father's remarkable story becomes clearer. This sumptuous and beautifully mastered set touches all the obvious bases: the stint with Weather Report ('Birdland' inevitably), working with Joni Mitchell ('Goodbye Pork Pie Hat', 'Dry Cleaner From Des Moines'), Pat Metheny, Paul Bley, and a generous sampling of Jaco's small groups and big bands with Warners. The real plus, though, is the early material, and for collectors the previously unreleased cuts. We first hear Jaco in his bedroom, playing all the parts – guitar, drums, saxophone, bass – on Pee Wee Ellis's 'The Chicken', a tune that turned up again later in his career; this, though, from 1968 or 1969 when he was still a teenager. We also hear him with Wayne Cochran's C C Riders and with Little Beaver. Then there's the free-form jazz stuff with Paul Bley and Pat Metheny from the Improvising Artists' *Jaco*. There are later tracks with pianist Michel Colombier which may not be known to some listeners. More familiar are 'Amerika' (the ultimate electric-bass feature) and the glorious moment on *Word Of Mouth* when Toots Thielemans plays harmonica on Bach's 'Chromatic Fantasy'. Poignantly the track listing goes right up to the autumn of 1986, less than a year before Jaco's pointless death, when he played with the Brian Melvin Trio for what was to be the 1990 release *Standards Zone,* a cover of Joe Henderson's 'Out Of The Night' that once again cements Jaco's jazz credentials.

For anyone who has only just heard of Jaco Pastorius, this will be a revelation. For serious collectors, the issue of 'Okonkole Y Trompa' from the 1982 tour is a very definite plus, as is that amazing bedroom track. Portrait of the genius as a young man fated not to grow old.

Don Patterson (1936–98)

ORGAN

Switched from piano to organ after hearing Jimmy Smith, and began recording for Prestige in the '60s. Associations included Sonny Stitt and, latterly, Al Grey, and he was still performing in the '80s.

***** Legends Of Acid Jazz**
Prestige 24178 *Patterson; Booker Ervin (ts); Leonard Houston (as); Billy James (d).* 5/64.

***** Just Friends**
Prestige 24237 *Patterson; Booker Ervin, Houston Person (ts); Pat Martino (g); Billy James (d).* 7/64–8/67.

***** Boppin' And Burnin'**
Original Jazz Classics OJC 983 *Patterson; Howard McGhee (t); Charles McPherson (as); Pat Martino (g); Billy James (d).* 2/68.

***** Dem New York Dues**
Prestige 24149 *Patterson; Blue Mitchell, Virgil Jones (t); Junior Cook, Houston Person, George Coleman (ts); Pat Martino (g); Billy James, Frankie Jones (d).* 6/68–6/69.

While he had a skilled grasp of bebop as it might work on the organ, Patterson was in the end an also-ran in the Hammond gang, though he cut plenty of albums for Prestige as both leader and sideman, several of them sampled here. The *Acid Jazz* entry is his debut for the label, *The Exciting New Organ Of Don Patterson,* with a couple of extras from the same session. Ervin is his usual blustery and beefy self, and they work up a fair head of steam on the likes of ''S About Time'. *Boppin' And Burnin'* moves forward four years, but Patterson's style hasn't changed a whit. His huge and overcooked solo on 'Pisces Soul' has all the clichés piled on, one after another, but played with an intensity that persuades (or bludgeons) the listener into thinking that it's burnin', all right. McGhee, as ever in this period, is wildly inconsistent and makes 'Donna Lee' into a splashy mess. Nevertheless, McPherson is ironclad, and the most exciting player is Martino, who sounds ferociously hungry. *Dem New York Dues* pulls together the LPs *Opus De Don* and *Oh Happy Day!*. More of the same, although the two different horn line-ups introduce the sort of variety which collectors of this music tend to prefer. The newest arrival is *Just Friends,* which doubles up *Don Patterson/Booker Ervin* from 1964 and *Four Dimensions,* with Person and Martino, from 1967; the faithful Billy James is on both. Critiquing these kinds of dates is either difficult or foolhardy, but we do enjoy Ervin when he's got no agenda other than blowing on a pick-up date and he earns the stars.

Big John Patton (1935–2002)

ORGAN

Born in Kansas, Patton played piano for Lloyd Price in the '50s, then switched to organ and made a string of Blue Note records as leader and sideman. Less visible in later years, he made a minor comeback in the '80s, appearing on some John Zorn dates.

*****(*) Along Came John**
Blue Note 31915 *Patton; Fred Jackson, Harold Vick (ts); Grant Green (g); Ben Dixon (d).* 4/63.

***** Let 'Em Roll**
Blue Note 89795-2 *Patton; Bobby Hutcherson (vib); Grant Green (g); Otis Finch (d).* 12/65.

***** Got A Good Thing Goin'**
Blue Note 80731-2 *Patton; Grant Green (g); Hugh Walker (d); Richard Landrum (perc).* 4/66.

Patton was one of the most entertaining of the players who followed in Jimmy Smith's footsteps, and a pile of Blue Note albums became his principal legacy. Most of them are out of print again, although there are plenty of tracks anthologized on sundry Blue Note compilations. *Along Came John* is probably his great moment, and even that can be boiled down to 'The Silver Meter', an irresistible loping groove. It sounds like a proper band, with Green, Jackson and Vick doing good business without showing off.

Let 'Em Roll is a somewhat atypical date from 1965. Hutcherson is a surprise presence, but Grant is on hand to make sure nothing too unusual happens. They all get particularly busy on 'The Turnaround' to good effect. *Got A Good Thing Goin'* is one of his last strong records: pop tunes are starting to encroach, but the group burn through 'Ain't That Peculiar' as if it were a hard-bop staple.

Mario Pavone

DOUBLE BASS

A frequently encountered presence on New York's downtown scene and a familiar from a few of the steady groups of that environment.

***** Sharpeville**
Playscape 090885 *Pavone; Pete McEachern (tb); Mark Whitechage (as); Thomas Chapin (as, f, af); Marty Ehrlich (ss, as, cl, f, af); Michael Musillami (g); John Betsch, Pheeroan akLaff (d).* 1–9/85.

***** Toulon Days**
New World 80420 *Pavone; Steve Davis (tb); Thomas Chapin (as, f); Marty Ehrlich (cl, f); Joshua Redman (ts); Hotep Idris Galeta (p); Steve Johns (d).* 11/91.

*****(*) Song For (Septet)**
New World 80452 *As above, except Peter McEachern (tb) replaces Davis; Peter Madsen (p) replaces Galeta; add Bill Ware (vib).* 3/93.

*****(*) Dancer's Tales**
Knitting Factory Works KFW 205 *As above, except omit Ware.* 2/96.

Pavone has a big, ringing sound and a seemingly bottomless supply of ideas. A regular in Thomas Chapin's trio, he is probably best known in that context, but he has also worked with Bill Dixon, Anthony Braxton and Paul Bley. The distinctive feature of the albums he has released under his own name is the prominence given to trombone, either Steve Davis or Peter McEachern; the latter is responsible for the arrangement of 'Recovery', perhaps the best track on *Dancer's Tales*, and he brings a sharp-edged, slightly sour quality to the solo work. Until the reissue of *Sharpeville*, where he makes an early showing on 'Bass Ballad', Pavone didn't really seem to emerge as a soloist until *Song For (Septet)*, but there his fleet, Mingus-influenced approach begins to pay dividends; 'George On Avenue A' might well be something from the great man's notebook. 'Foxwood Shuffle' on *Dancer's Tales* is an explicit homage and an exceptional piece of work, as is the piece for Julius Hemphill, 'Lunch With Julius'.

Sharpeville was originally issued on his own label and it significantly alters the shape of his available output. Again with McEachern and Chapin, it's a work of real emotional power, particularly the title-piece, which is dedicated to the victims of one of the most infamous episodes of the apartheid years in South Africa. The mournful undertheme is almost a passacaglia and provides the horns with great scope for passionate improvisation, especially from Chapin.

*****(*) Remembering Thomas**
Knitting Factory 257 *Pavone; Peter Madsen (p); Matt Wilson (d).* 99.

Thomas Chapin's death left a hole in the New York scene and left his regular playing partners bereft. It's hardly surprising that Pavone should have returned to the studio to record this lovely tribute as part of what became known as the Nu Trio. They play four Chapin tunes, of which the closing 'Insomnia' and 'Aeolus' are the most effective, but there is also a mix of other material, including Monk's 'Raise Four' and Gary Peacock's 'Miracles'. Nothing by Madsen, which seems surprising, given his palpable gift for sophisticated structures. The group play very much as a trio, with a measure of freedom in the ensembles and lots of fine support during the solo passages.

****** Totem Blues**
Knitting Factory 292 *Pavone; Art Baron, Peter McEachern (tb); Mike DiRubbo (ss, ts, cl); Jimmy Greene (ts); George Sovak (ts, cl); Peter Madsen (p); Matt Wilson (d).* 8/00.

This is a stunning record, full-voiced, thoughtful and rippling with musical muscle. Most of the credit falls to the 'rhythm section', effectively a group-within-a-group since Madsen and Wilson have worked with Pavone as the Nu Trio. Their ability to lay out the structure of a song and leave the horn soloists to build skyscrapers on it is consistently impressive. 'Bass Song' is another of Pavone's self-reflexive ideas, ever more sophisticated, and 'Poet O Central Park' is a Chapin composition, a by now customary though never less than sincere tribute to a fallen comrade. 'Totem' is the best cut, a hauntingly atavistic theme built round the bass's spiralling harmonies. The range of textures offered by the brass and woodwind players is extraordinary and subtler than most 'multi-instrumental' configurations allow. Intelligent music for deep listeners.

***** Motion Poetry**
Playscape 052880 *Pavone; Michael Musillami (g); Peter Madsen (p); Michael Sarin (d).* 5/00.

***** Op.Ed**
Playscape 20981 *As above.* 2/01.

Chapin's 'Poet O Central Park' again has a prominent place in this elegant collaboration between four of the late saxophonist's closest associates. Motion Poetry is also the name of the group and there is no doubt that this is intended to be a meeting of equals, though Pavone and the guitarist share all the writing responsibilities. Musillami shows his quality with 'Archives', a theme that fits very closely the group's elegant dissonance and rhythmic tension. The only off-putting element is the opening improvisation, 'Foody', which just sounds like a warm-up and at just two minutes duration might easily have been dropped.

Op.Ed is more of the same, though that might seem to imply a comfortable resting on laurels when it's if anything an edgier and more effortful set than its predecessor. 'Bass Song' puts in a reappearance and Musillami's 'Today The Angels' calls for regular airings in future. Another fine album, perhaps lacking some of the finish of *Motion Poetry* but making up for that in sheer musicality.

****** Mythos**
Playscape *Pavone; Steven Bernstein (t); Tony Malaby (ts); Peter Madsen (p); Michael Sarin, Matt Wilson (d).* 2–11/01.

*****(*) Orange**
Playscape 061083 *As above, except omit Sarin, Wilson; add Gerald Cleaver (d).* 03.

The Nu Trio plus two. The addition of a trumpeter gives a new spiky edge to the music and seems to drive Madsen, who grows with every session to ever greater heights of invention. Wilson and Sarin have also both grown with this music and they bring quite distinct characters to the music: Sarin's edgy and combative, Wilson's more flamboyant but also unexpectedly dry and uninflected in places. Pavone sounds in solid voice, and there is a new forthrightness to his playing, as if the mourning period that followed Tom Chapin's death has passed and given way to new resolution. Even so, 'Sky Piece' is probably the best track, closely followed by 'Isobars'. 'Crutch For The Crab' is a Richard Twardzik obscurity, and meat and drink to Madsen. Not perhaps the most representative Pavone album of the current bunch, but its quality speaks for itself.

On *Orange*, Cleaver's more direct delivery evens out the tempos and in some respects simplifies the music. Some will prefer the linear quality of this album to some of its predecessors, but it lacks the depth and character of *Mythos*. 'Sky Tango' is a long, slowly developing piece, largely improvised in the later stages. 'Goorootoo' is the other large-scale essay, almost African in some aspects, very New York in others. Pavone has established himself as one of the city's most interesting and creative players and as a composer who demands the closest attention and greatest respect.

Cecil Payne (born 1922)

BARITONE AND ALTO SAXOPHONES, FLUTE

The powerfully voiced New Yorker gave up playing alto and switched to the big horn in 1946 while working with J. J. Johnson. If bebop seemed resistant to the tenor saxophone, it was even more so to the baritone. Payne, though, established a limber, articulate approach while with Dizzy Gillespie, and he has continued to make convincing bop-tinged jazz ever since, albeit with a lighter tone which owes a debt to Lester Young.

***** Stop And Listen To ...**
Fresh Sound FSR CD 193 *Payne; Clark Terry (t); Bennie Green (tb); Duke Jordan (p); Ron Carter (b); Charli Persip (d).* 3/61–3/62.

***** Performing Charlie Parker Music**
Collectables COL-5794 *As above, except omit Green.* 3/61.

Payne cut his teeth as a soloist with Dizzy Gillespie's late-'40s Cuban-bop big band. Along with the lighter-sounding Leo Parker, he did much to adapt the hefty baritone to the rapid transitions and tonal extremities of bebop. *Stop And Listen To ...* does little more than confirm his authority and demonstrate how comfortably he could function in company as demanding as this. Both are New York City sessions, recorded at a time when Payne seemed to be bent on proving that Charlie Parker's music *could* be played convincingly on the big horn. You want him to be right, but there are moments when it all falls apart rather badly. The Kenny Drew material on the 1962 date is more his speed, but of course it lacks that whirling intensity one gets from Parker. The Collectables edition offers only the earlier set of Parker material, although American readers should find this one easier to get hold of than the Fresh Sound.

***** Cerupa**
Delmark DE 478 *Payne; Freddie Hubbard (t); Eric Alexander (ts); Harold Mabern (p); John Ore (b); Joe Farnsworth (d).* 93.

*****(*) Scotch And Milk**
Delmark DE 494 *As above, except omit Hubbard; add Marcus Belgrave (t), Lin Halliday (ts).* 96.

*****(*) Payne's Window**
Delmark DE 509 *As above, except omit Halliday, Ore; add Steve Davis (tb), John Webber (b).* 8/98.

***** Chic Boom Live At The Jazz Showcase**
Delmark DE-529 *As above, except add Jim Rotondi (t).* 00.

Payne's recent work for Delmark has been something of an Indian summer. The formula is pretty much the same on all three records: a weighty, two-saxophone front line (with the addition of Halliday as a pacemaker on *Scotch And Milk*), and guest brass in the very different shapes of Freddie Hubbard, Marcus Belgrave and, most effective of all, Steve Davis. The rhythm section is anchored by Mabern, who is one of the great post-bop pianists, a bridge between Duke Jordan and the younger generation. Eric Alexander is a Mabern pupil and has absorbed much of the pianist's vast knowledge of the idiom, creating solos that bespeak historical awareness as well as formidable technique.

Cecil himself continues to plough his own thoughtful furrow. The skirling bebop reel that begins 'Scotch And Milk' is an indication of how receptive he is to ideas from outside the bebop mainstream, but his strength remains the driving swing of 'Et Vous Too, Cecil?' on the same album. *Payne's Window* (title-track courtesy of the impressive Davis) is probably the best of the bunch by a nose. Cecil reprises his King tribute from *Zodiac*, adds Miles's 'Tune Up' and Gershwin's 'Delilah' and restates his commitment to the Minton generation in 'Spiritus Parkus'. *Chic Boom*, though, shows the old warrior starting to sound fallible: the band is still in top form, but Payne's solos have a fragility which suggests his powers are fading.

Nicholas Payton

TRUMPET

Payton's ripe, rather full trumpet-sound is markedly different from Wynton Marsalis's, and it is his writing that most resembles Wynton's, essays in traditional harmony with a hard, modern edge. Payton lacks both the skyrocketing movement between pitches and the other's delicacy of touch with a ballad, but he seems to be moving on a fruitfully parallel course and it will be interesting to see how he responds to the challenge.

***** From This Moment**
Verve 527073-2 *Payton; Mulgrew Miller (p); Monte Croft (vib); Mark Whitfield (g); Reginald Veal (b); Lewis Nash (d).* 95.

***** Gumbo Nouveau**
Verve 531199-2 *Payton; Jesse Davis (as); Tim Warfield (ts); Anthony Wonsey (p); Reuben Rogers (b); Adonis Rose (d).* 96.

Verve have taken a slightly odd route with Payton, pushing him into situations which are obviously intended to increase his profile, but which seem to do no more than blunt his real strengths. A head-to-head with the venerable Doc Cheatham is the most obvious example, but then there was *Fingerpainting*, a homage to the compositional genius of Herbie Hancock with Mark Whitfield and Christian McBride (under whose name it is reviewed). Then there was the music for Robert Altman's thoroughly bogus *Kansas City* (a kind of *Nashville* with heroin and horns); the fairest thing that can be said about it is that at least the music was exuberantly played. So, a strange start for Payton.

Produced by Delfeayo Marsalis on *From This Moment*, he could hardly fail to sound a *little* like Wynton. Payton is a traditionalist who, in addition to developing his own book of songs, has shown a deep interest in classic jazz, as witness the material on *Gumbo Nouveau*. Interestingly, by the time he gets into the swing (and swing is the word) of both these crisp, uncomplicated sets, one has forgotten all about the Marsalis connection and begun to concentrate on the young man's bright, storytelling voice. He makes no demands on himself that he can't comfortably fulfil, and his best solos occupy that middle register which so many younger players seem to think is either dull or sissy. The material is all carefully thought out and, having seen service with Elvin Jones, he has a brilliant grasp of how to pace a set, one of Elvin's less well-publicized gifts. The band are pretty familiar now and go about their business with precision and enthusiasm. Needless to say, the recordings are absolutely up to standard.

*****(*) Payton's Place**
Verve 557327-2 *Payton; Wynton Marsalis, Roy Hargrove (t); Joshua Redman, Tim Warfield (ts); Anthony Wonsey (p); Reuben Rogers (b); Adonis Rose (d).* 9/97, 1/98.

He was obviously going to make a record called *Payton's Place* sooner or later. This is more like the real thing, working with a tough young band and with the chance to blow alongside a more appropriate trumpet partner than Cheatham. Marsalis stops long enough for two tunes, 'Brownie A La Mode' and the self-explanatory 'The Three Trumpeteers' (on which Hargrove also guests). Roy is the unexpected choice of partner on 'With A Song In My Heart' and shows a side of his playing which rarely surfaces in his own work, bright, fleet and softly lyrical. Josh Redman comes in on 'A Touch Of Silver' and continues to prompt questions as to how great he really is. This is a very lacklustre performance. The basic group is in no way overshadowed by the visiting stars. Warfield and Wonsey are both developing by the session, and newcomer Adonis Rose (since embarked on a recording career of his own) is a great find. The interaction on Wayne Shorter's 'Paraphernalia' (a favourite of Payton's) suggests directions he might want to explore with a working band, some shift of emphasis that might allow him to broker a synthesis of classic jazz and the challenging harmonics of '60s Blue Note and beyond. As things stand, he sounds as if he might just get prematurely stuck in a style and a market niche – the perils of early success.

***(*) Nick@Night

Verve 547598-2 *Payton; Tim Warfield (ss, ts); Anthony Wonsey (p, hpd, cel); Reuben Rogers (b); Adonis Rose (d).* 5/99.

The title might suggest an e-mail address, and there is an urgency of communication about this very fine set. Payton's writing has come on in leaps and bounds, utilizing unfamiliar registers and altered harmonic patterns to give the album a hint of strangeness. That's evident on the title-track, on the two improvised interludes and on material like 'Somnia' and 'Little Angel'. The crepuscular feel is sustained in pieces by Wonsey and Rose, both fine composers in their own right. The pianist makes use of harpsichord and celeste colours but concentrates on soft, minor intervals that leave several of the tracks melodically but not harmonically resolved, a tinge of ambiguity that suits Payton's developing style very well indeed.

*** Dear Louis

Uptown/Universal 549419 *Payton; Paul Stephens, Roy Vega (t, flhn); Vincent Gardner (tb); Bob Stewart (tba); Tim Warfield (ss, ts, f); Bill Easley (as, cl, f); Scott Robinson (bs, cbsax, bcl, f); Anthony Wonsey (p); Peter Bernstein (g); Walter Payton, Reuben Rogers (b); Adonis Rose (d); Dr John, Dianne Reeves (v).* 00.

Payton's centenary tribute to Pops includes enough identifiable transcriptions of the Ur-texts – 'Potato Head Blues', 'West End Blues' – to draw in those who might otherwise be suspicious. Unlike Wynton, Nicholas hasn't got the kind of dominant musical personality that might overpower these tunes; instead he pays them respectful deference and allows memories of the great originals to settle in the mind. Vocals from Dianne Reeves and Dr John are reminders of what an important vocalist Armstrong also was, but only because they are so resolutely off the money.

The ensembles are the best aspect of this commissioned suite, beautifully arranged and vividly voiced. Scott Robinson adds weight to the bottom end of the horn arrangements and Payton's bright ringing tone cuts through. A more than worthy tribute to the great man.

*** Sonic Trance

Warners 48447 *Payton; Tim Warfield (ss, ts): Kevin Hays (p, ky, rec, v); Karriem Riggins (syn, samples); Vicente Archer (b); Adonis Rose (d); Daniel Sadownick (perc).* 03.

The move to Warners has sparked an astonishing change in Payton's approach, from the boppish swing of his earlier records to something like Miles Davis's electric fusion. In a curious way, it seems a more dated record than the more traditional sessions of the Verve years, but there is a growing market for such stuff and so it presumably makes sense. Payton's trumpet is often half-drowned in washes of electronic processing and there are times when he finds it hard to make himself heard through an insistently funky beat, but he is too good a player to lose his way and tracks like 'Fela 1', the opening track proper after a strange 'Praalude', is packed with ideas. It also seems to be one of a number of tributes to an eclectic range of other musicians. 'Shabba Unranked' is another. Best track is 'Two Mexicans On A Wall: Too Much Tequila', but by the time you get there, there have already been too many pauses for salt and lime, tiny trackettes which don't so much refresh as irritate. Best of the rest of the group is saxophonist Warfield, who follows Payton's lead in blurring and blending his lines into long abstract washes of colour, almost without harmonic significance. Rose is an increasingly confident drummer, and Kevin Hays, handed the toughest job on the gig, handles himself very well indeed. Intriguing, but where to from here?

Gary Peacock (born 1935)

DOUBLE BASS

Played bass in army bands before going to California in 1958, then to New York in 1962, where he became immersed in the new free scene, particular associations including Albert Ayler and Paul Bley. Studied macrobiotics and other sciences during a sabbatical from music. Most recently associated with the Keith Jarrett 'Standards Trio'.

***(*) Tales Of Another

ECM 827418-2 *Peacock; Keith Jarrett (p); Jack DeJohnette (d).* 2/77.

*** December Poems

ECM 531029-2 *Peacock; Jan Garbarek (sax).* 78.

**(*) Shift In The Wind

ECM 829159-2 *Peacock; Art Lande (p); Eliot Zigmund (d).* 2/80.

Peacock's career has rarely hewn to the centre. After a brief apprenticeship in Europe, he moved to the West Coast and worked with the likes of Bud Shank and Shorty Rogers, before absorbing himself in the challenging formal structures of Don Ellis, Bill Evans, Jimmy Giuffre and George Russell, all the while maintaining a powerful involvement in avant-garde transformations of early jazz, notably with Albert Ayler, Roland Kirk and Steve Lacy. His playing style combines elements of Jimmy Blanton's and Wilbur Ware's sonority with something of Oscar Pettiford's rapid disposition of wide intervals. Peacock's own records have been rather mixed and can't be taken as representative of his abilities. The earliest, *Tales Of Another*, is performed by the band that was to become known as Keith Jarrett's 'Standards Trio' six years later. In the late '60s, Peacock had turned his back on the music scene and gone to Japan to study macrobiotics. However uncertain he may have been about a return to bass playing (and he may have been persuaded by ECM chief, Manfred Eicher), there is a wonderful coherence to his solo work on 'Vignette' (with piano rippling underneath) and on 'Trilogy I/II/III' which quashes any suggestion that this is another Jarrett album, politely or generously reattributed; it is, in fact, his last appearance but one as a sideman. Even so, the pianist is clearly at home with Peacock's music and there is a level of intuition at work which became the basis of their later standards performances, but it is unmistakably Peacock's record.

December Poems is almost claimed by the saxophonist, who at this point in his career was rapidly settling into the stark, echoey style ECM cemented for him. It's interesting to hear him in this duo in a rather drier and less responsive acoustic and with a good deal more definition on the lower frequencies. Peacock sets the agenda throughout, though in performance terms he does find himself consistently overshadowed. Sadly, he never sounds quite so poised or concentrated again. *Shift In The Wind* is merely enigmatic, and there seems to be little positive understanding among the trio (beyond, that is, an agreement not to tread on one another's toes).

***** Voice From The Past / Paradigm**

ECM 517768-2 *Peacock; Tomasz Stańko (t); Jan Garbarek (ts, ss); Jack DeJohnette (d).* 8/81.

***** Guamba**

ECM 833039-2 *Peacock; Palle Mikkelborg (t, flhn); Jan Garbarek (ts, ss); Peter Erskine (d, d syn).* 3/87.

The later quartets further obscure Peacock's playing, and though *Voice From The Past* is particularly good, it is chiefly memorable for the atmospheric interplay of Garbarek and Stańko. Mikkelborg's hyperactive style dissipates much of the concentration of Peacock's writing on *Guamba*, and Erskine seems a poor substitute for DeJohnette's brilliant out-of-tempo colorations. However, the 1987 record stands up pretty decently after a decade, and renewed acquaintance prompts a reassessment of Erskine's contribution in particular. Cruder, yes, but perhaps deliberately so, an attempt to roughen up the texture of music that had become a little hidebound in his pursuit of esoteric harmonies. Peacock himself also comes through very strongly and is clearly pushing himself into new territory.

***** Oracle**

ECM 521350-2 *Peacock; Ralph Towner (g).* 5/93.

The comparison with Glen Moore rises with *Oracle*, which some listeners may find reminiscent of Towner's *Trios/Solos* project with his fellow Oregonian. And the contrast holds good. Peacock is driven and propulsive where Moore is happy to dwell on particular areas of sound. This isn't a criticism but a description. Where one might criticize *Oracle* is in its rather haphazard alternation of moods and its rather indistinct programme. There is a floaty, New Age quality to some parts, and then the duo throws in something almost violent as if to offer a sufficient contrast. This isn't an effective way to make records, and the final verdict has to be that, good as *Oracle* is in parts, it doesn't cohere. Lately, Peacock seems to have been happy enough to settle for a sideman role again.

Curtis Peagler (1929-1992)

ALTO AND TENOR SAXOPHONES

He grew up in Ohio and studied music at the Cincinnati Conservatory after working in territory bands and backing singers. Toured with Ray Charles and for several years with Count Basie. Recorded infrequently under his own name but deserves notice.

***** Disciples Blues**

Prestige PRCD-24263-2 *Peagler; William Kelly (normaphone, euph); Billy Brown (p); Lee Tucker (b); Wilbur Jackson, Roy McCurdy (d).* 59, 60.

The Modern Jazz Disciples were sponsored by Eddie 'Lockjaw' Davis, who helped to get them these dates for Prestige. What makes the line-up distinctive isn't so much Peagler's boppish alto but his colleague William 'Hickey' Kelly's use of the normaphone, which is basically a valved trombone curved like a member of the saxophone family. It's prominent from the off with a brisk version of 'After You've Gone', though Peagler also does some nifty business on the same theme. 'Right Down Front' was the title-track of their second and last LP, but 'Disciples Blues' itself is the best thing on this not quite complete compilation of the band's work; 'Autumn Serenade' is missing and seems an odd omission when something as formulaic as 'My Funny Valentine' might have been dropped to solve the duration problem. Peagler is unlikely to enjoy much of a renaissance, unless his Pablo disc is reissued.

Duke Pearson (1932–80)

PIANO

Named after Ellington and sharing some of the great man's piano chops and big-band sound, the Atlantan had a stint as MD and producer at Blue Note, but never entirely fulfilled his potential, drifting away from the music as multiple sclerosis progressively hampered his technique.

***** Honeybuns**

Koch 8519 *Pearson; Johnny Coles (t); Garnett Brown (tb); James Spaulding (as); George Coleman (ts); Les Spann (f); Bob Cranshaw (b); Mickey Roker (d).* 5/65.

*****(*) Sweet Honey Bee**

Blue Note 95974-2 *Pearson; Freddie Hubbard (t); James Spaulding (as, f); Joe Henderson (ts); Ron Carter (b); Mickey Roker (d).* 12/66.

Pearson's stint at Blue Note has meant that his name is scattered through this book, though there is perplexingly little under his own name. His natural life was uncomfortably fated. As a young man he was thwarted in his ambitions to become a trumpeter by dental problems, and his health failed while he was still in his 40s.

Back in circulation after a long time in limbo, this Atlantic session reissued by Koch isn't absolutely compelling, but it does suggest some of the ways in which the pianist makes a smallish band sound like a much bigger unit. Some of it comes from the arranging, which is very richly textured in the middle register, but the recording is also very impressive, the horns arranged in a V-formation that gives the soloist a lot of presence but with plenty of backweight from the ensemble. Duke's originals, 'Heavy Legs' and 'Is That So', are wonderfully imagined, as is the title-track, which features a strong contribution from trumpeter Coles. Big George Coleman is in great shape, blowing his trademark choruses with freedom and great harmonic control. Spaulding is a little more anonymous. Comparing the sound with the original LP, the remastering sounds a little muffled when the dynamics peak; even so, this is a welcome return for a long-absent record.

The new RVG edition of *Sweet Honey Bee* restores another Pearson session which has been off the racks for decades. As Bob Blumenthal's note suggests, the highlights are the lushly voiced melodies of 'Sudel' and 'Gaslight', the former a tune which Pearson had recorded some years earlier with a different group. Hubbard and Henderson eat up their solo opportunities without sundering the essentially easy-going feel which was Pearson trademark, and while not all the material is up to this standard, as a showcase for the pianist as writer and group-leader, this is surely the best thing available at present.

*** Introducing Duke Pearson's Big Band

Blue Note 94508 *Pearson; Randy Brecker, Burt Collins, Joe Shepley, Marvin Stamm (t); Jimmy Cleveland, Julian Priester, Kenny Rupp (tb); Benny Powell (tb, btb); Garnett Brown (btb); Jerry Dodgion (as, f, picc); Al Gibbons (as, f, bcl); Pepper Adams (bs, cl); Bob Cranshaw (b); Mickey Roker (d).* 12/67.

Pearson was always most interesting on a larger scale. He has an idiosyncratic touch as an arranger, imposing a personal touch on material as varied as Chick Corea's 'Tones For Joan's Bones', tunes by Joe Sample and standards as varied as 'Days Of Wine And Roses' and 'Here's That Rainy Day'. Nicely voiced and crisply recorded with a strong live presence, this is an album that repays the closest attention.

Mary Pearson

VOCALS

Striking debut by adventurous American singer.

*** You And I

Arkadia 71325 *Pearson; Lynne Arriale, Fred Hersch, David Lahm (p); John Hart (g); Harvie Swartz (b); Steve Davis (d).* 00.

It may look like a group line-up, but the questionably grammatical title is perfectly literal. This is a series of duets with instrumentalists which showcases Pearson's boldly rhythmic approach. One obvious line of descent is Sheila Jordan's highly regarded duos with bassist Swartz and, as if to confirm the lineage, Mary sings 'What Are You Doing The Rest Of Your Life', which Jordan so memorably covered on Roswell Rudd's *Flexible Flyer* disc. The really intriguing performance, though, is her strange, enervated take on 'Thou Swell'; Davis's percussion accompaniment gives the song an almost neurotic edge, but it also confirms the singer's grasp of metrical shift.

Arriale is her partner on 'The More I See You', Davis is back for 'Lazy Afternoon', Hersch is his usual inventive self on 'Over The Rainbow' and a wonderful 'Take Five', Swartz comes in on 'How Long Has This Been Going On?', and it's Hart who does his stuff on 'What Are You Doing ...' The pace throughout is slow but unmannered, with the exception of 'Thou Swell', which is almost brisk. If this is a measure of what Pearson is capable of, we should be hearing much more from her.

Jeremy Pelt (born 1976)

TRUMPET, FLUGELHORN

New Yorker Pelt plays with unashamed nostalgia for the great days of Blue Note. His bright sound recalls both Lee Morgan and Donald Byrd.

*** Profile

Fresh Sound New Talent 127 *Pelt; Jaleel Shaw (as); Jimmy Greene (ts); Robert Glasper (p); Mike Moreno (g); Gerald Cannon (b); Ralph Peterson (d).* 02.

*** Insight

Criss Cross 1228 *Pelt; Jimmy Greene (ss, ts); Myron Alden (as); Rick Germanson (ky); Vincente Archer (b); Ralph Peterson (d).* 5/02.

Pelt may favour a retro sound, but he doesn't lack the confidence to inscribe the idiom in his own terms. Most of the material on these first forays as leader is original, and promisingly individual. The debut album is full of strong, committed writing and some more than competent playing from all concerned. Peterson is the oldest member of the group and holds things together from the drum chair, cementing an occasional impression that one is listening to a forgotten incarnation of the Messengers. The long 'Jigsaw' is an excellent band workout, but Jeremy also sounds as if he might fit right in at a south of the border wedding with his bright phrasing on the Latinish 'We Share A Moon'. The two saxophonists are more anonymous but Greene has listened to the same basic repertoire and he clearly knows his stuff.

The follow-up CD benefits from better sound and from a more confident and less pushy approach. The Blakey influence is there in tunes like 'Ides Of March' and 'The Glass House', but there is a new depth of emotion in the ballad 'In My Grandfather's House', which suggests that Pelt's forte may well be a more sombre-toned and thoughtful approach. Two eminently listenable records by a promising young talent, still not yet 30.

Clarence Penn (born 1968)

DRUMS

In-demand sideman with a strong musical personality.

***(*) Penn's Landing

Criss Cross 1134 *Penn; John Swana (t, flhn); Ron Blake (ts); Rodney Whitaker (d).* 97.

*** Play-Penn

Criss Cross 1201 *As above, except add Jesse Van Ruller (g).* 5/01.

Interesting that Penn's debut album should have been a pianoless quartet. The opening 'C.P. Time' is a fairly routine barnburner, with not much sophistication, but it does illustrate how Penn's awareness of his drums' tuning can take the place of a harmony instrument. Add to that Rodney Whitaker's singing tone and brilliantly placed accents, and the absence of a keyboard player isn't noticed at all. The title-track is another Penn original and a more sophisticated idea. Blake's 'Re: Evaluation' and the bassist's tribute to Tony Williams are probably the best themes on a record that bids fair for an extended run of good solo projects from Mr C.P.

The sequel is impressive enough, and the arrival of labelmate Van Ruller doesn't detract from our point about Clarence's harmonic openness. Mostly the guitarist lays single lines and fills rather than strict comping. His intro to 'You Must Believe In Spring' is superb. Penn's 'Blues For Paris' seems to be a variation on a Charlie Parker (same initials, so he's allowed) tune, presumably 'Blues For Alice'. There's not so much sheer excitement about this record, perhaps because they've got used to playing with each other, but it's a fine set none the less.

Ken Peplowski (born 1958)

CLARINET, ALTO AND TENOR SAXOPHONES

Strongly influenced by Benny Goodman, Peplowski plays clarinet with the same acidity and precision. A soloist of some imagination, he favours short, percussive sequences interspersed with longer and more detailed elaborations of the theme.

****** Grenadilla**

Concord CCD 4809-2 *Peplowski; Kenny Davern (cl); Marty Ehrlich (cl, bcl); J. D. Parran (cbcl); Scott Robinson (acl); Ben Aronov (p); Howard Alden (g); Greg Cohen (b); Chuck Redd (d).* 12/97.

Peplowski is by now a veteran of the swing-repertory school which has kept that side of American jazz robust during otherwise lean times, from the '80s onwards. He has a very big discography on Concord but of late the label has decimated much of it, and we can only hope that they bring some discs back via their current twofer-reissue series. This one is the earliest survival. Grenadilla is the wood from which the majority of quality clarinets are made. Like any other rainforest tree, it is endangered, and Peplowski dedicates this remarkable album to its preservation. Perhaps even more importantly, though, he makes the record an expression of his own desire to preserve jazz tradition even as he pushes it forward into a new generation. Here, the guests represent wildly different aspects of contemporary clarinet-playing.

Working together for the first time, Peplowski and the veteran Kenny Davern combine on the New Orleans Rhythm Kings' 'Farewell Blues', a tune first recorded in 1922. Davern's calm delivery complements Peplowski's own characteristically fervid statement; ironically, he has seldom sounded more like Benny Goodman's descendant. At the opposite end of the spectrum are Marty Ehrlich's 'The Reconsidered Blues' and 'The Soul In The Wood' and Greg Cohen's brief, powerful 'Variations', on which Parran, Robinson and Ehrlich again guest. At first blush, Ehrlich might seem the arch-modernist, but his moody clarinet and bass clarinet (no accident that his publishing imprint is called Dark Sounds) is hooked back into a long and remarkably conservative line. In Peplowski's company his roots show through strongly.

The rest of the original writing is credited to Ben Aronov, who continues to surprise. He is composer of the two quartet tracks and the opening 'Benny's Pennies' (no real relation to the Tristano number) on which Alden makes the first of several strong contributions. At the end of the album, 'Farewell Blues' is sandwiched between two classics which show the guitarist and the leader at their intuitive best: Victor Herbert's 'Indian Summer' and, done as a drummerless, pianoless trio, 'Cry Me A River'. An exquisite end to a remarkable album.

*****(*) Last Swing Of The Century**

Concord CCD 4864-2 *Peplowski; Conte Candoli, Bob Millikan, Randy Sandke (t); Eddie Bert, Bobby Pring (tb); Joe Romano, Jack Stuckey (as); Scott Robinson, Rickey Woodard (ts); Ben Aronov (p); Frank Vignola (g); Richard Simon (b); Frank Capp (d).* 11/98.

Recorded in Japan as part of the 14th Fujitsu/Concord Jazz Festival, this is a tribute to the music of Benny Goodman, the artist who most thoroughly shaped Peplowski's increasingly protean style. Encouraging to note that, even on an occasion like this, he is much more than a respectful copyist. Listening to him shape a solo on 'Stealin' Apples', 'King Porter Stomp' and even 'Moon Glow', it becomes obvious that Ken is ever on the lookout for ways to recast classic idiom. He subtly reworks those now slightly shopworn phrases, sometimes subverts them entirely and then, just to prove that he's no wrecker, restates them with absolute fidelity to the originals.

The band sounds a touch under-rehearsed and perhaps not entirely at ease with the material. The redoubtable Candoli is the obvious exception; he delivers crisp, shining solos on 'Between The Devil And The Deep Blue Sea', 'Moon Glow' and 'Don't Be That Way'. Aronov is the anchor, as ever, and he lifts the ensembles more than once, though he isn't best placed in the mix.

***** Ellingtonian Tales**

Mainstem MCD 0021 *Peplowski; John Horler (p); Phil Lee (g).* 2/01.

Peplowski is a regular visitor to Britain and he cut this on one of his trips. The compositions come from both Ellingtons (Duke and Mercer), Hodges and Strayhorn, and there are a few arcane choices along with the obvious ones. They start with a trio, but mostly it's clarinet or tenor with either guitar or piano, and while there's a lot of good tale-spinning along the way, the record feels overly respectful, and (though many of the tempos are slow) a bit hurried – as if they had just put down the lead sheets and started playing.

Art Pepper (1925–82)

ALTO AND TENOR SAXOPHONES, CLARINET

Pepper's first notable jobs were with the Benny Carter and Stan Kenton big bands. After army service, he rejoined Kenton and stayed until 1951. He was a premier name among Californian saxophonists in the '50s, cutting several leadership records, but his career was constantly interrupted by his dependence on narcotics and several spells in prison. He was finally rehabilitated at Synanon at the end of the '60s. In 1975, he made his comeback album and gradually forged a new career as a surviving master of West Coast bebop alto, curtailed only by his eventual death in 1982. His book, Straight Life, is a definitive jazz autobiography.

**** Complete Lighthouse Sessions**

Jazz Factory 22836 *Pepper; Shorty Rogers (t); Frank Patchen (p); Howard Rumsey (b); Shelly Manne (d).* 12/51.

****(*) Complete Surf Club Sessions**

Jazz Factory 22835 2CD *Pepper; Hampton Hawes (p); Joe Mondragon (b); Larry Bunker (d, vib).* 2/52.

****(*) Complete Straight Ahead Sessions**

Jazz Factory 22847 2CD *Pepper; Sonny Clark (p); Harry Babasin (b); Bobby White (d).* 3–5/53.

***** The Art Pepper Quartet**

Original Jazz Classics OJC 816 *Pepper; Russ Freeman (p); Ben Tucker (b); Gary Frommer (d).* 8/56.

Pepper's remains one of the most immediately identifiable alto sax styles in post-war jazz. If he was a Parker disciple, like every other modern saxophonist in the '40s and '50s, he tempered Bird's slashing attack with a pointed elegance that recalled something of Benny Carter and Willie Smith. He was a passionate musician, having little of the studious intensity of a Lee Konitz, and his tone – which could come out as pinched and jittery as well as softly melodious – suggested something of the duplicitous, cursed romanticism which seems to lie at the heart of his music. After a brief period with Californian big bands, he began recording as a leader and sideman on the Hollywood studio scene of the early '50s.

We are listing the various Jazz Factory releases a little reluctantly, in the absence of any other current edition of this music. Each catches Pepper on various Californian gigs (two at the Lighthouse, one at the Surf Club). The sound on each is between poor and diabolical, the playback speed is open to question, and there's the inevitable crowd noise; yet each in its way has some memorable Pepper, working over standards and bebop themes with power-packed intensity, even in the climate of Californian cool. The Lighthouse set with Rogers, where Pepper is merely one of the band, is probably the weakest, the Surf Club dates are the scruffiest, but if you can listen through the detritus you'll hear some classic Pepper.

The OJC release is drawn from a session for the Tampa label, with five alternative takes beefing up the playing time. This is Pepper entering his greatest period, and the quality of his thinking and playing is already nearing that of the remarkable Contemporary sessions, though the rather brief tracks clip the wings of some of the solos.

***** The Return Of Art Pepper**
Blue Note 46863-2 *Pepper; Jack Sheldon (t); Red Norvo (vib); Gerald Wiggins, Russ Freeman (p); Leroy Vinnegar, Ben Tucker (b); Shelly Manne, Joe Morello (d).* 8/56–1/57.

****** Modern Art**
Blue Note 46848-2 *Pepper; Russ Freeman, Carl Perkins (p); Ben Tucker (b); Chuck Flores (d).* 12/56–4/57.

****** The Art Of Pepper**
Blue Note 46853-2 *As above, except omit Freeman.* 4/57.

Pepper's sessions for Aladdin, collected on the three Blue Note albums, have been overshadowed by his records for Contemporary (below). *The Return Of Art Pepper* (the altoist had been in prison for narcotics offences, a problem that would plague his career) puts together a fair if patchy quintet session with Jack Sheldon – the two ballad features without Sheldon, 'You Go To My Head' and 'Patricia', are easily the best things – with a set originally led by Joe Morello, with Red Norvo in the front line. The really valuable records, though, are the two quartet discs. *Modern Art* is a deceptively quiet and tempered session: the opening 'Blues In' is a seemingly hesitant, improvised blues which typifies the staunchless flow of Pepper's ideas, and the following 'Bewitched' and a quite exceptional reworking of 'Stompin' At The Savoy' are so full of ideas that Pepper seems transformed. Freeman responds with superbly insightful support. Yet the succeeding *Art Of Pepper* is even better, with bigger and more up-front sound and with Carl Perkins spinning along in accompaniment. 'Begin The Beguine' is both beguiling and forceful, the dizzying lines of 'Webb City' are an entirely convincing tribute to Bud Powell, and the melodies unravelled from 'Too Close For Comfort' and 'Long Ago And Far Away' – which Pepper returns to on the Contemporary sessions – show a lyrical invention few players of the day could have matched.

*****(*) The Way It Was!**
Original Jazz Classics OJC 389 *Pepper; Warne Marsh (ts); Ronnie Ball, Red Garland, Dolo Coker, Wynton Kelly (p); Ben Tucker, Paul Chambers, Jimmy Bond (b); Philly Joe Jones, Gary Frommer, Frank Butler, Jimmy Cobb (d).* 11/56–11/60.

****** Modern Jazz Classics**
Original Jazz Classics OJC 341 *Pepper; Pete Candoli, Jack Sheldon, Al Porcino (t); Dick Nash (tb); Bob Enevoldsen (vtb, ts); Vince DeRosa (frhn); Herb Geller, Bud Shank (as); Charlie Kennedy (ts, as); Bill Perkins, Richie Kamuca (ts); Med Flory (bs); Russ Freeman (p); Joe Mondragon (b); Mel Lewis (d).* 3–5/59.

*****(*) Gettin' Together**
Original Jazz Classics OJC 169 *Pepper; Conte Candoli (t); Wynton Kelly (p); Paul Chambers (b); Jimmy Cobb (d).* 2/60.

****** Smack Up**
Original Jazz Classics OJC 176 *Pepper; Jack Sheldon (t); Pete Jolly (p); Jimmy Bond (b); Frank Butler (d).* 10/60.

****** Intensity**
Original Jazz Classics OJC 387 *Pepper; Dolo Coker (p); Jimmy Bond (b); Frank Butler (d).* 11/60.

Pepper's records for Contemporary, all of which have been reissued in the OJC series, make up a superlative sequence. *The Way It Was!* remained unissued until the '70s, but the first half of it – a session with Warne Marsh, which secures a brilliant interplay on 'Tickle Toe' and exposes all Pepper's lyricism on 'What's New' – is as good as anything in the series (the other tracks are out-takes from the succeeding sessions). *Modern Jazz Classics* is in some ways more prosaic, with Marty Paich's arrangements of Monk, Gillespie, Giuffre, Mulligan and more working from the by now over-familiar West Coast glibness, yet the sound of the ensemble is beautifully rich; Paich conjures new things out of 'Bernie's Tune' and 'Anthropology', and Pepper – who also brings out his clarinet and tenor – alternately glides through the charts and dances his way out of them. There isn't a great deal to choose between the three remaining sessions: *Smack Up* finds Pepper playing Ornette on 'Tears Inside' as well as a memorable version of Duane Tatro's haunting 'Maybe Next Year', and the appropriately titled *Intensity* is a wistful series of ballads and standards in which Pepper, a peculiarly astringent romantic, seems to brood on the words of the songs as well as their melodies and changes: 'Long Ago And Far Away', for instance, seems a perfect transliteration of the song's message. Throughout these records, the saxophonist's phrasing, with its carefully delivered hesitations and sudden flurries, and his tone, which sometimes resembles a long, crying ache, communicate matters of enormous emotional impact. They demand to be heard. Remastering of all of them is well up to the fine OJC standards.

CORE COLLECTION

****** Meets The Rhythm Section**
Original Jazz Classics OJC 338 *Pepper; Red Garland (p); Paul Chambers (b); Philly Joe Jones (d).* 1/57.

The playing of the quartet on this CD beggars belief when the circumstances are considered: Pepper wasn't even aware of the session till the morning of the date, hadn't played in two weeks, was going through difficult times with his narcotics problem and didn't know any of the material they played. Yet it emerges as a poetic, burning date, with all four men playing above themselves.

****(*) Art Pepper Quartet '64 In San Francisco**
Fresh Sound FSCD-1005 *Pepper; Frank Strazzeri (p); Hersh Hamel (b); Bill Goodwin (d).* 5–6/64.

Devastated by his personal problems, Pepper didn't make another studio record (aside from a Buddy Rich session) until 1973. These tracks come from a 1964 TV appearance and another at a San Francisco club. Not long released from prison, his style had changed dramatically: hung up on Coltrane and a fear that his older style would be out of touch, he sounds to be in a bizarre transition from the former, lyrically confident Pepper to a new, darker, often incoherent style based round tonal investigations and timbral distortions as much as anything. It's a trait he would rationalize with his 'normal' self in the '70s, but here he's finding his way. He's still musician enough to make it an intriguing document, though, with the first version of 'The Trip' and a long 'Sonnymoon For Two'. The sound is rough, not much better than an average bootleg, but Pepperphiles will want to hear it. There is also an interview track with presenter Ralph Gleason.

★★ I'll Remember April
Storyville STCD 4130 *Pepper; Tommy Gumina (polychord); Fred Atwood (b); Jimmie Smith (d). 2/75.*

★★★(★) Living Legend
Original Jazz Classics OJC 408 *Pepper; Hampton Hawes (p); Charlie Haden (b); Shelly Manne (d). 8/75.*

★★★ The Trip
Original Jazz Classics OJC 410 *Pepper; George Cables (p); David Williams (b); Elvin Jones (d). 9/76.*

★★(★) A Night In Tunisia
Storyville STCD 4146 *Pepper; Smith Dobson (p); Jim Nichols (b); Brad Bilhorn (d). 1/77.*

★★(★) No Limit
Original Jazz Classics OJC 411 *Pepper; George Cables (p); Tony Dumas (b); Carl Burnett (d). 3/77.*

★★★ Tokyo Debut
Galaxy GCD-4201-2 *Pepper; Clare Fischer (p); Cal Tjader (vib); Bob Redfield (g); Rob Fisher (b); Peter Riso (d); Poncho Sanchez (perc). 5/77.*

Pepper's re-emergence blossomed into the most remarkable comeback of its kind. He became a symbol of jazz triumph-over-adversity, and though in the end it didn't last very long, there was a stubborn, furious eloquence about his later playing that makes all his records worth hearing, even when he struggles to articulate a ballad or has to fight to get his up-tempo lines in shape. The earlier sessions, following the *Living Legend* set, continue his struggle to digest Coltrane and reconcile that influence with his honourable past achievements: on both *The Trip* and *No Limit* he gets there some of the time, and the former at least includes his haunting blues line, 'Red Car'. But *Living Legend* itself is the one to hear first. 'Lost Life' is one of his gentle-harrowing ballads, a self-portrait rigorously chewed out, and the whole session seems imbued with a mixture of nerves, relief and pent-up inspiration which the other players – an inspiring team – channel as best they can. The two Storyville discs chronicle a couple of live dates with local players in the rhythm sections. *I'll Remember April* is marred by a gymnasium sound and Gumina's odd-sounding polychord, but Pepper blows very hard throughout. *A Night In Tunisia* is better – Dobson is a useful player, and there is another strong version of 'Lost Life' – but the studio albums merit prior attention.

Tokyo Debut documents Pepper's first tour of Japan, which started with the utmost trepidation and ended in triumph. The Cal Tjader group is the unlikely support, with Fischer playing an ugly-sounding electric piano; but Pepper, who was honoured by every audience throughout the trip, pours himself into the music. 'Cherokee' is chorus after chorus of ideas and, when Tjader joins in for three numbers, the altoist fits comfortably with the lite-bossa grooves.

★★ Hersh Hamel's Songbook
Fresh Sound FSR-CD 150 *Pepper; Pete Robinson (ky); Hersh Hamel (b); Steve Strazzeri (d); Linda McCrary, Judy Brown, Brenda Burns (v). 75.*

More like a series of soul demos than anything else, this material was written by Hamel and features Pepper as the guest soloist. The three-woman singing team perform anonymously, the music's scarcely anything at all – and yet Pepper plays with something approaching his usual intensity a lot of the time. For completists.

★★(★) Renascence
Galaxy 4202 *Pepper; Ed Kelly (p); Kenny Jenkins (b); Bard Bilhorn (d). 9/75.*

Pepper has to push the house rhythm section through what he wants them to do on this gig, which was clearly a pick-up date and little more. Somebody had a tape machine rolling, so here it is. Art sounds ready to get into his comeback period, but it hasn't quite started yet here.

★★★(★) Thursday Night At The Village Vanguard
Original Jazz Classics OJC 694 *Pepper; George Cables (p); George Mraz (b); Elvin Jones (d). 7/77.*

★★★ Friday Night At The Village Vanguard
Original Jazz Classics OJC 695 *As above. 7/77.*

★★★ Saturday Night At The Village Vanguard
Original Jazz Classics OJC 696 *As above. 7/77.*

★★★ More For Les: At The Village Vanguard Vol. 4
Original Jazz Classics OJC 697 *As above. 7/77.*

★★★(★) The Complete Village Vanguard Sessions
Contemporary CCD-4417-2 9CD *As above. 7/77.*

Pepper's four nights at New York's Village Vanguard were filleted down to four single LPs (and, subsequently, CDs) in the past, but Contemporary have gone for broke and brought together every note of the engagement in a single nine-disc set. This provides more than five hours of extra music. The new material includes alternative versions of tunes played in other sets plus three entirely fresh pieces: a jangling 'Stella By Starlight', a notably impressive blues called 'Vanguard Max' and 'Live At The Vanguard'. Pepper specialists can compare the different versions of 'Goodbye', 'Blues For Heard' and 'For Freddie' at their leisure, but the main point of the set is the way it documents one of the major performers of the era with unflagging candour. Pepper was always a fascinating man to see and hear in concert – his sometimes obsessive talking with audiences is given full rein with the announcements here – and playing through these discs will remind all who saw him of his enduring struggle with his own demons, as well as the sometimes cruel beauty of his music-making. Besides him, there is the blue-chip rhythm section to listen to. The less committed will settle for the remaining single discs, of which the first is probably the single best. Excellent location recording.

★★★ Live In Japan Vol. 1
Storyville STCD 4128 *Pepper; Milcho Leviev (p); Bob Magnusson (b); Carl Burnett (d). 3/78.*

***** Live In Japan Vol. 2**
Storyville STCD 4129 *As above.* 3/78.

***** Art Pepper Today**
Original Jazz Classics OJC 474 *Pepper; Stanley Cowell, Cecil McBee (b); Roy Haynes (d); Kenneth Nash (perc).* 12/78.

***** Landscape**
Original Jazz Classics OJC 676 *Pepper; George Cables (p); Tony Dumas (b); Billy Higgins (d).* 7/79.

*****(*) Straight Life**
Original Jazz Classics OJC 475 *Pepper; Tommy Flanagan (p); Red Mitchell (b); Billy Higgins (d); Kenneth Nash (perc).* 9/79.

****** Winter Moon**
Original Jazz Classics OJC 677 *Pepper; Stanley Cowell (p); Howard Roberts (g); Cecil McBee (b); Carl Burnett (d); strings.* 9/80.

***** One September Afternoon**
Original Jazz Classics OJC 678 *As above, except omit strings.* 9/80.

***** Art 'N' Zoot**
Pablo 2310-957-2 *Pepper; Zoot Sims (ts); Victor Feldman (p); Barney Kessel (g); Ray Brown, Charlie Haden (b); Billy Higgins (d).* 9/81.

***** Arthur's Blues**
Original Jazz Classics OJC 680 *Pepper; George Cables (p); David Williams (b); Carl Burnett (d).* 8/81.

***** Goin' Home**
Original Jazz Classics OJC 679 *Pepper; George Cables (p).* 5/82.

***** Tete-A-Tete**
Original Jazz Classics OJC 843 *As above.* 4–5/82.

The later records for Galaxy are in some ways all of a piece, and it's rather appropriate that the Fantasy group have chosen to issue a colossal boxed set of the whole output (see below). Pepper remained in fragile health, however robustly he played and carried himself, and the sense of time running out for him imparted an urgency to almost everything he played: ballads become racked with intensity, up-tempo tunes spill over with notes and cries. Studio and live dates are the same in that respect. Of these many late albums, the best should be in all general collections: *Straight Life*, with another fine quartet; *Landscape*, a sharp set by the band Pepper worked with most frequently in his last years; and above all the profoundly beautiful *Winter Moon*, a strings album which far surpasses the norm for this kind of record, Pepper uncorking one of his greatest solos against the rhapsodic sweep of Bill Holman's arrangement on 'Our Song'. The two Japanese live albums are also well worth seeking out.

The meeting with Zoot Sims is an oddity, a UCLA concert in which Zoot had three features, Art one, and they jammed together on a pair of tunes. Pepper's 'Over The Rainbow' is one of his typical slowburns on a ballad, while Zoot breezes affably through 'In The Middle Of A Kiss' and digs in surprisingly hard on 'The Girl From Ipanema'; but the main point of interest is hearing them together on the old bebop jam, 'Wee'. It's good. The sound is much better than it was on an unauthorized European release.

Arthur's Blues is a distillation of nearly an hour of previously unreleased music, taken from the complete Galaxy set listed below. Like so much later Pepper, it's full of interesting music while falling short of essential, although the gripping title-track is a prototypical blues workout by a man desperate to play his soul out in the time he had left. The two duo sessions with Cables, his favourite accompanist, are neither more nor less 'naked' than the quartet music, since Pepper never spared himself or his listeners from his versions of the truth. 'Over The Rainbow' (*Tete-A-Tete*) and 'Don't Let The Sun Catch You Cryin'' (*Goin' Home*) are among his final ballads and set down the closing thoughts of an unbowed spirit.

*****(*) The Hollywood All-Star Sessions**
Galaxy 4431 5CD *Pepper; Jack Sheldon (t); Bill Watrous (tb); Sonny Stitt, Lee Konitz (as); Bob Cooper (ts); Russ Freeman, Milcho Leviev, Pete Jolly, Lou Levy, Mike Lang (p); Bob Magnusson, Tony Dumas, Chuck Domanico, John Heard, Monty Budwig (b); Carl Burnett, Roy McCurdy, Shelly Manne, John Dentz (d).* 3/79–1/82.

*****(*) Art Standards**
Galaxy 4203-2 *As above.* 3/79–1/82.

This, at least, is close to prime Pepper, after a lot of very average reissues of late in the quest for little-known revivals. The saxophonist cut these various dates with other leaders as part of a series meant to rekindle West Coast memories of a couple of decades earlier; so he's next to the likes of Stitt, Konitz, Jolly, Levy and Sheldon, who take it in turns to helm the session. They were released on vinyl only in Japan and have been very collectable ever since.

Cut over a period of nearly three years, they actually find Pepper in a number of different moods, situations and capabilities; the final dates, with Konitz, were set down only months before Art's death. Laurie Pepper's detailed and candid reminiscences in the booklet are an interesting sidelight on the music, but in the end it stands by itself. Numerous tracks stand out as something special – a quartet reading of 'Out Of Nowhere', for instance, sounds as fine as anything in the later Pepper discography – but in its entirety, the set stands as one of Pepper's most revealing legacies. The sessions with Stitt are sometimes tiresomely combative, those with Konitz often just plain strange (two completely individual altoists, remote from each other), but in the end there's the peculiar heat and intensity which Pepper always seemed to create – especially when paired with figures from his own past. The *Art Standards* release fillets the set for a sensible one-disc compilation.

***** Laurie's Choice**
Fresh Sound FSR-CD 192 *Pepper; Milcho Leviev, George Cables (p); Bob Magnusson, David Williams, Tony Dumas (b); Carl Burnett (d).* 78–81.

Odds and ends from Laurie Pepper's tape collection, this is probably for Pepper fanatics only. There are three terrific performances out of five: an almost definitive disquisition on his ballad, 'Patricia', from a 1980 Georgia concert, a tough 'Kobe Blues' and a long and thoughtful handling of Joe Gordon's 'A Song For Richard', apparently the only existing live version. There's also some prime bebop in 'Allen's Alley'. On the down side is the sound, which is often amateurish and unbalanced, and we have to question whether some of these tunes have been mastered at the right speed: a Tokyo reading of 'Straight Life', for instance, sounds unreasonably fast.

*****(*) San Francisco Samba**
Contemporary 14086-2 *Pepper; George Cables (p); Michael Formanek (b); Eddie Marshall (d).* 8/77.

***** In Copenhagen 1981**
Galaxy 2GCD-8201-2 2CD *Pepper; Duke Jordan (p); David Williams (b); Carl Burnett (d).* 7/81.

Fantasy continue to turn up previously unreleased live tapes of Pepper, and both of these will please his admirers. The outstanding one is the Keystone Korner date from 1977. Following his Village Vanguard recordings, Pepper had flown to San Francisco with Cables, but Formanek (then not yet out of his teens) and Marshall were hired guns for the date. There are just four tunes on the disc, but it earns the stars for the stunning treatment of 'Blue Bossa' which opens proceedings, 16 minutes of staunchless invention. Marshall was an inspired choice for the drumstool. After Elvin at the Vanguard he's relatively straight-ahead, but he drives the group with such energy that the leader is obliged to think hard and play up to his best. There is a fast, hard blues and an intense 'Here's That Rainy Day', while the closing 'Samba Mom-Mom' is another powerhouse, if a slightly less convincing one. Dusty recording, but the feel comes through.

The Copenhagen session is also good, with Jordan guesting on piano, and a set-list that includes more bebop staples than Pepper would have liked. As a result, he is rather more focused and less wilful than on some of his regular dates of the period. But two discs and two and a half hours of music is too much, and there are unavoidable dead patches. Best shot is probably a marathon 'Besame Mucho' in which the playing has unanswerable vim.

****** The Complete Galaxy Recordings**
Galaxy 1016 16CD *As above OJC/Galaxy albums.* 77–82.

A vast and surprisingly playable archive – most such monuments seldom come off the shelf, but Pepper's resilience, febrile invention and consistency of commitment make this music endure far beyond expectations. There are dead spots, inevitably, and it's a costly undertaking, but there is also a lot of music still unavailable elsewhere, including many alternative takes, out-takes and Japanese-only issues.

****** The Art Of the Ballad**
Prestige 11010 *Pepper; as various OJC albums above.* 77–81.

Pepper at his best was one of the masters of ballad playing, and this skilful compilation offers a splendid selection of some of his most intense and heart-on-sleeve performances from Fantasy's catalogue. An excellent buy for those who'd wish for only a few Peppers.

Ivo Perelman

TENOR SAXOPHONE, TROMBIVO, CELLO, PIANO

Brazilian saxophonist marching towards the freest free jazz he can find, without letting go of some elements of both hard bop and his native song.

***** Children Of Ibeji**
Enja 7005-2 *Perelman; Don Pullen, Paul Bley (p); Brandon Ross (g); Fred Hopkins (b); Andrew Cyrille (d); Guilherme Franco, Manolo Badrena, Frank Colon, Mor Thiam (perc, v); Flora Purim (v).* 5–7/91.

***** Bendito Of Santa Cruz**
Cadence CJR 1076 *Perelman; Matthew Shipp (p).* 1/96.

*****(*) Blue Monk Variations**
Cadence CJR 1066 *Perelman (ts solo).* 2/96.

***** Cama De Terra**
Homestead HMS237-2 *Perelman; Matthew Shipp (ts); William Parker (b).* 6–7/96.

*****(*) Geometry**
Leo LR 248 *Perelman; Borah Bergman (p).* 6/96.

****** Sad Life**
Leo Lab 027 *Perelman; William Parker (b); Rashied Ali (d).* 6/96.

***** Slaves Of Job**
CIMP 126 *Perelman; Dominic Duval (b); Jay Rosen (d).* 10/96.

***** Revelation**
CIMP 134 *As above, except add Rory Stuart (g).* 10/96.

***** Sound Hierarchy**
Music & Arts CD-997 *Perelman; Marilyn Crispell (p); William Parker (b); Gerry Hemingway (d, v).* 10/96.

***** En Adir**
Music & Arts CD-996 *As above.* 10/96.

**** Strings**
Leo LR 249 *Perelman; Joe Morris (g).* 12/96–4/97.

Perelman is a Brazilian who has burst into a prolific streak of recording almost from nowhere. He is already shrugging off comparisons with Gato Barbieri (perfectly plausible), Ayler (same syntax, different agenda) and David Murray (well, he made a lot of records to begin with, too). Perelman's methodology is to grab hold of a theme and shake it asunder via his hugely powerful tone: whatever the surroundings in terms of group or material, Perelman takes himself off into the red at a moment's notice. It's frequently exciting and at times enthralling, though one questions whether he needs to be documented at this length and in these sometimes indulgent circumstances.

Children Of Ibeji was an arresting start. The sound of the record is unfocused, but Perelman is already more than a match for the formidable rhythm section of Pullen, Hopkins and Cyrille, and the auxiliary percussionists add to the air of wildness. The most interesting piece, though, is a duet with Bley, cooler and restrained yet strikingly effective.

There were an astonishing nine albums recorded in 1996 alone. *Bendito Of Santa Cruz* is mostly made up of Brazilian folk-tunes, and it's hard not to recall the Barbieri–Dollar Brand session of many years earlier – though Perelman is strong enough to outface memories of the older saxophonist. Shipp is very much second fiddle here, as he is on the subsequent *Cama De Terra*, and Borah Bergman is a more creative partner (opponent?) on the subsequent *Geometry*; but all three records show how much Perelman enjoys having a pianist behind him. He clearly likes to be the single voice out front, but the harmonic anchors offered by a piano are a useful succour, and Bergman in particular is wily enough to find ways of both supporting and undercutting the mighty sound of the tenor. *Slaves Of Job* and the 'bonus' *Revelation*, cut on a whim as a jam session with Stuart sitting in, are strong entries which don't quite enter the front rank: Duval and Rosen are too busy and tend to overplay their hands, and Stuart is a distraction. Perelman plays lustily enough to earn the stars, but these are basically inadequate showcases for him. The two discs with Crispell, Parker and Hemingway also offer some fine playing without quite gelling as a good framework for the saxophonist. Crispell is too strong a personality to settle for the kind of subsidiary role that Perelman needs, and Hemingway's rhythms are too bracingly inventive – they offer Perelman a distraction rather than fed lines. *En Adir*, a collection of traditional Jewish songs, is an interesting departure, but it's only intermittently effective.

The one outright miss is *Strings*, where Perelman plays cello (his apprentice instrument) in a series of duets with Morris. The guitarist tries his best to make something of the situation, but Perelman is so self-absorbed in what he's playing that nothing very meaningful happens, and his cello-playing is frankly not up to the tenor-work. *Blue Monk Variations* is a vivid footnote to the other records. Warming up by himself in a studio, Perelman came up with some 36 minutes of solo tenor based around 'Blue Monk' – three full interpretations and three variations. Unencumbered by the need to 'perform' as such, Perelman presents some of his least self-conscious and surprising playing. He turns the tune inside out three times, in quite distinct ways on each occasion, and while this is as plangent as the rest of his work there's a vein of introspection which is absent in the rest of what he's done so far.

The essential disc, though, is surely *Sad Life*. With Ali and Parker he is playing with musicians on the highest level, and they secure a propulsion and intensity which has its independent life without either overpowering or standing subservient to the leader. In the title-tune (which he starts by playing through a mouthpiece), 'Caiapo' and the ambivalent 'Hoedown', Perelman is giving us his most emotive and convincing playing.

*****(*) The Hammer**
Leo LR 286 *Perelman; Jay Rosen (d).* 3/98.

***** The Alexander Suite**
Leo LR 258 *Perelman; Jason Hwang (vn); Ron Lawrence (vla); Tomas Ulrich (clo); Dominic Duval (b).* 5/98.

***** Brazilian Watercolour**
Leo LR 266 *Perelman; Matthew Shipp (p); Rashied Ali (d); Guilherme Franco, Cyro Baptista (perc). n.d.*

The Hammer is blissful uproar of the sort which Perelman the saxophonist was born to make. Coltrane and Ali never got anywhere near this much violence on *Interstellar Space*, and the duo compounds it by having most of these pieces run to only a few minutes each in duration, purist punk onslaught. The sleeve-notes are going a country mile too far when they say that at the end, 'there is exactly nothing left anywhere in the world'; but it is a splendid battle royal. We are less convinced by the often similarly inclined chaos of *The Alexander Suite*. This eight-part work runs more of a textural gamut, but the noisier sections tend to run aground on incoherence – mere fury is not necessarily an end in itself, even when played by virtuosos, and for once Perelman's force of character doesn't legitimize the results.

Brazilian Watercolour is, by Perelman's standards, easy listening. Half of it is leftovers from the *Bendito Of Santa Cruz* session with Shipp, half a set of interpretations of Brazilian favourites such as 'Desafinado', in which the saxophonist is surrounded by percussion. A game of two halves, with the expected mixed results.

*****(*) Sieiro**
Leo LR 271 *Perelman; Tomas Ulrich (clo); Dominic Duval (b); Jay Rosen (d).* 3/98.

*****(*) The Seven Energies Of The Universe**
Leo LR 309 *Perelman; Joseph Scianni (p); Jay Rosen (d).* 4/98.

Perelman overcomes the often gloomy Ulrich–Duval axis by steamrollering over them. But the strings have a part to play – joining in the high-end screeching of 'Rush Hour' and as conservatory counterpoint in the mordantly beautiful 'Santana'. 'Assimptotica' debuts Perelman's use of the trombivo, apparently a trombone played with a saxophone mouthpiece, which at least puts him in the Eddie Harris lineage. A great set all round.

The Seven Energies Of The Universe might almost be Perelman's *Love Supreme*, named for the Hebrew alphabet as preserved in the Torah. It certainly puts up the same kind of religious intensity, though this is less about a search for ecstasy. As turbulent as Perelman's music is, there's rarely any sense of merely surrendering to chaos, and Scianni in particular provides an almost analytical weight and substance to the trio's directions. His brief solo episode in the longest piece, 'Fruition', is fascinating in itself. Another demanding Perelman essay, but it's compelling stuff.

****** The Ventriloquist**
Leo LR 345 *Perelman; Louis Sclavis (bcl, ss); Christine Wodrascka (p); Paul Rogers (b); Ramon Lopez (d).* 6/01.

A tough call for Perelman: his first encounter with another horn-player, and in a band of considerable talents too. It's surely an atypical set for him, since this is very much a group record where he either cannot, or chooses not to, dominate. Sclavis has numerous ways of playing, but for the most part here he chooses to take on Perelman at his own game, and there are some flagrantly exciting results (though uncredited, Sclavis plays some soprano as well). Rogers, who is too little heard from these days, and Lopez make a superbly powerful team. And then there's Wodrascka: she plays on three tracks (on which Sclavis sits out), and when Perelman says that he 'can hear the urgency of her music screaming to get out', he's not wrong. This is probably the best record the saxophonist has put his name on so far.

*****(*) Suite For Helen F**
Boxholder 038/039 2CD *Perelman; Mark Dresser, Dominic Duval (b); Gerry Hemingway, Jay Rosen (d).* 3/02.

Dedicated to painter Helen Frankenthaler, this seven-part work is spread across two CDs, credited to Perelman's Double Trio. He's playing with two teams of huge experience here, and perhaps it frees him up to take whatever course he wishes, secure in the knowledge that any path taken will be unstintingly followed. In moments such as the overwhelming climax to 'Part 1', that impression certainly hits home. But the set has much diversity along the way, textured in fine detail as well as blusteringly apocalyptic, and it helps that the studio mix is notably clear. Not a bad place at all for the curious to investigate what Perelman can do.

Danilo Perez (born 1966)

PIANO

Born in Panama, Perez studied at the National Conservatory and then went to Berklee. Played with the Dizzy Gillespie group, 1989–92, and with his own groups from 1993.

***** Panamonk**
Impulse! 11902/051190-2 *Perez; Avishai Cohen (b); Terri Lyne Carrington, Jeff Tain Watts (d); Olga Roman (v).* 1/96.

***** Central Avenue**
Impulse! 12812/051281-2 *Perez; Aquiles Baez (cuatro, perc); John Patitucci, John Benitez (b); Jeff Ballard, Jeff Tain Watts (d); Ray Spiegel, Pernell Saturnino, Miguel Anga Diaz (perc); Raul Vital, Lyciana Souza (v).* 98.

Perez is the most convincing of the several pianists to emerge from South America to stake a place in contemporary American jazz. However, his technical expertise still sometimes gets the better of him, as it does with such contemporaries as Chucho Valdes. On *Panamonk*, which synthesizes Monk's music with Perez's own composing, he plays 'Evidence' and 'Four In One' side by side in what amounts to a circus performance. Perez's Monk isn't terribly convincing, since he hits the piano so hard that all the abruptness in Monk's music is intensified to the point of absurdity, but he does much better by some of his own themes: 'Hot Bean Strut' and the pretty 'September In Rio', with a wordless vocal by Roman, are worth returning to.

Central Avenue self-consciously strives for a pan-global-jazz effect: setting 'Impressions', for instance, to three different rhythms, or recording the Panamanian folk singer Raul Vital by himself and then constructing a jazz background in the studio. When he settles himself away from such persiflage and focuses on the piano, with the excellent Patitucci and either Ballard or Watts in support, the best music breaks out: the three-part 'Rhythm In Blue' suite, the opening 'Blues For The Saints', and the solo farewell of 'Smoke Gets In Your Eyes'. Perez looks to be having a hard job separating his music from its marketing.

****(*) Motherland**
Verve 01043-2 *Perez; Diego Urcola (t); Chris Potter (ss, as); Regina Carter (vn); Kurt Rosenwinkel (g); Aquiles Baez (g, cuatro); Richard Bona (b, v); Carlos Henriquez, John Patitucci (b); Brian Blade, Antonio Sanchez (d); Greg Askew, Louis Bauza, Richard Byrd, Luisito Quintero (perc, v); Ricuarte Villarreal (perc); Claudio Acuña, Luciana Souza (v).* 00.

Perez may be entirely sincere about this project, which is weighed down with titles such as 'Suite For The Americas', 'Song To The Land' and 'Panama Libre', but sincerity won't cut it if the music's not up to it; and this feels inflated and borderline pretentious for much of the way. Themes are often stated as wordless vocals, and Bona's feature on 'Prayer' is smooth jazz going to church. A host of Verve guest-stars (Potter, Carter, Rosenwinkel, Acuna) have been drafted in to assist when what's needed is a coherent group empathy and some sense that Perez is distilling his ideas. On this showing, he's confused.

***** ... Till Then**
Verve 7614129 *Perez; Donny McCaslin (ss); John Patitucci, Ben Street (b); Brian Blade, Adam Cruz (d); Lizz Wright (v).* 2/03.

A cover-sticker quotes Wayne Shorter: 'Daniel Perez has all of the attributes ... greatly needed in these uncertain times.' To which one might add, when were the times ever 'certain'? Nevertheless, this is surely his best record for Verve. Calmer, more considered all the way, Perez still sometimes lets his lightning fingers get ahead of his judgement, but in these mostly brief and songful pieces, he distils some of his expertise into music which has point and grace. There are still drawbacks, traceable to Tommy LiPuma's interfering production: Lizz Wright makes two meaningless appearances. But the record works best when the pianist lets his imagination loose, as in the unexpectedly dark and steely deconstruction of Stevie Wonder's 'Overjoyed'.

Perfect Houseplants

GROUP

Centred on Mark Lockheart's tenor, this is a contemporary British group with a hint of local folk tradition.

***** Clec**
EFZ 016 *Mark Lockheart (sax); Huw Warren (p, acc, clo); Dudley Phillips (b); Martin France (d).* 94.

***** Snap Clatter**
Linn AKD 063 *As above.* 8/96.

This imaginative British group has never quite managed to dig itself out of the hole that yawns for intelligent 'name' bands (one thinks of Roadside Picnic and Itchy Fingers). They certainly deserve to. All four players are gifted craftsmen and, if Lockheart and Warren are the main writers, the balance of responsibilities seems very evenly shared around. In common with many of their contemporaries, they have introduced a folk element – sometimes almost subliminally – into a jazz context. Because it *is* almost subliminal, it works very well indeed. The first (deleted) album was slightly mannered but unmistakably fresh and inviting. It isn't until *Snap Clatter*, though, that the mix of technical facility, informed writing and convincing playing seems properly balanced. Lockheart's saxophone sound has always had a beguiling quality, but it is on the more recent discs that it becomes central to the Houseplants' concept. As Warren grows in stature on his own account, he too becomes more significant, and the shift from the first to third records is very telling: lots of space, a steady flow of ideas and a relaxed, almost insouciant quality to the playing.

***** New Folk Songs**
Linn AKD 130 *As above, except add Pamela Thorby (recorder).* 00.

The title encapsulates the PH itinerary and their problem: jazz rarely manifests itself as any kind of folk music, and even when it does it gets called unsympathetic names. But the Houseplants are making a kind of crossover which seems both very British and dependent on the universal improvising skills of Lockheart and Warren. The saxophonist's sound has got warmer and more appealing as he's grown into it, and his playing on a piece such as 'Old Song New Song' is a pleasure to follow. Warren is similarly appealing for much of the way. Yet their premise here is, more than ever, to make something curiously Anglo-Saxon out of it, as if it were a visit to a jazz craft-fair. Titles such as 'The Barford Angel', 'Earl's Slog' (not much like 'That's Earl Brother', for sure) and 'Dunwhich And The Sea' tell some of the story, Thorby's recorders tell a bit more, and it's unlikely that American readers will be anything but baffled by it all. They are, at least, unique. Warren has subsequently gone on to other adventures.

Bill Perkins (1924–2003)

TENOR AND BARITONE SAXOPHONES, FLUTE, BASS CLARINET

Born in San Francisco, Perkins studied music and engineering after military service. Much touring with Kenton and Herman, and then much studio work in the late '50s, '60s and '70s. Latterly he assumed much eminence as an original West Coaster and as a faithful Lester Young descendant.

***** Quietly There**

Original Jazz Classics OJC 1776 *Perkins; Victor Feldman (p, org, vib); John Pisano (g); Red Mitchell (b); Larry Bunker (d).* 11/66.

This was one of only two sessions that the veteran West Coast reedman made under his own name in the '60s. Gentle, pretty, but closely thought out, this is easy-listening jazz as it could be at its best. The nine tracks are all Johnny Mandel compositions, and Perkins devises a different setting for each one, some decidedly odd: baritone sax and organ for 'Groover Wailin'', for instance, which mainly proves that Feldman was no good as an organist. But Perkins's grey, marshy tone makes a charming matter of 'The Shining Sea', the flute-and-vibes treatment of 'A Time For Love' is ideal, and tempos and textures are subtly varied throughout. A welcome reissue of a little-known record.

***** The Front Line**

Storyville STCD 4166 *Perkins; Gordon Goodwin (ss, ts); Pepper Adams (bs); Lou Levy (p); Bob Magnusson (b); Carl Burnett (d).* 11/78.

Perkins plays tenor, flute and baritone here, with another baritone expert in attendance in the shape of Adams. The latter's memorable 'Civilization And Its Discontents' gets a stringent reading here, but space is otherwise evenly split between the horns, and one could use more of Perkins's own playing.

***** I Wished On The Moon**

Candid CCD79524 *Perkins; Metropole Orchestra.* 11/89–4/90.

*****(*) Warm Moods**

Fresh Sound FSR-CD 191 *Perkins; Frank Strazzeri (p).* 11/91.

In the '90s, Perkins was offered a brief flurry of recording opportunities. Rob Pronk's arrangements for *I Wished On The Moon* give Bill his chance at a big band/strings album and, though the arrangements have more mush than backbone, the saxophonist breezes through the charts with an old pro's ease. The *Warm Moods* session is altogether tougher. Perkins chooses to use baritone for most of the record (with two forays into bass clarinet and a single clarinet reading of 'Sweet Lorraine') and his faintly peevish sound on the horn sits nicely with Strazzeri's energetic bop lines. When they get to a ballad like 'You Know I Care' the leathery sound unravels into tenderness. Warmly recommended.

***** Perk Plays Prez**

Fresh Sound FSR 5010 *Perkins; Jan Lundgren (p); Dave Carpenter (b); Paul Kreibich (d); Jack Sheldon (v).* 6/95.

Clearly a labour of love for Perkins and realized with great finesse, this tribute to his original inspiration has been very carefully handled. He is paying homage to the Lester Young specifically of the late '30s, and he re-creates entire Young solos – such as those of 'Shoe Shine Boy', 'Taxi War Dance' and 'Let Me See' – before adding improvisations of his own. As gracefully as it's done, there's a vague sense of redundancy about the exercise, given that Perkins's own solos seem strong enough to stand alone – and to have their own context. A bigger problem is the studio sound, which puts the saxophonist too far back: delicate as his tone is, he doesn't need to be overpowered by the rhythm section, even when it's playing as complicitly as here.

Rich Perry

TENOR SAXOPHONE

Born in Cleveland, Perry was touring with the Glenn Miller Orchestra in 1975 and then moved to New York, where he has since performed in a wide range of small groups and big bands. One notable recent gig has been as one of the principal soloists in the Maria Schneider Orchestra.

***** To Start Again**

Steeplechase SCCD 31331 *Perry; Harold Danko (p); Scott Colley (b); Jeff Hirshfield (d).* 4/93.

****** Beautiful Love**

Steeplechase SCCD 31360 *Perry; Jay Anderson (b); Victor Lewis (d).* 10/94.

*****(*) What Is This?**

Steeplechase SCCD 31374 *Perry; Fred Hersch (p); Jay Anderson (b); Tom Rainey (d).* 4/95.

***** Left Alone**

Steeplechase SCCD 31421 *Perry; Frank Kimbrough (p); Jay Anderson (b); Billy Drummond (d).* 4/97.

We were rather cool about Perry's debut on his first appearance in this guide, but the subsequent records and a greater familiarity with his work have proved that to be an over-cautious judgement. Previously hidden in big-band sections and sideman roles for some 20 years, the tenorman's absolute command goes with a soft-edged tone and an undemonstrative delivery that creates a paradox at the centre of his style. Other commentators have cited Getz, Marsh and Rollins among his models, yet Perry doesn't sound much like anyone else, while at the same time not quite standing out as an individual. The main characteristic of such a player is consistency, and there is little to choose between his work on each of these four records. Instead, more depends on the context. *Beautiful Love* is easily the pick of the four, since without a piano the skill and judicious intensity of the sax-playing comes through more clearly. There are truly marvellous improvisations on 'Prisoner Of Love', 'All The Things You Are' and 'I Fall In Love Too Easily' at the heart of the record, and for once eight quite lengthy tracks don't seem a moment too long. Anderson and the superb Lewis are also in good order. The debut *To Start Again* still sounds a little ordinary, despite some exemplary work from Danko; we prefer *What Is This?*, which drafts in Hersch, whose playing is at its liveliest. They take Thad Jones's 'What Is This?' at a terrific clip, and there is some exceptionally genuine interplay between piano and tenor on the ballads. *Left Alone* is a shade behind again, perhaps because Kimbrough is no real match for either Danko or Hersch. The set-list, which includes tunes by Bley, Coleman, Shorter, Waldron and Andrew Hill, is typical of Perry's imagination. Although we have ranked the four discs a notch apart from each other, nobody who wants to hear the leader will be disappointed by any of them.

*****(*) So In Love**

Steeplechase SCCD 31447 *Perry; Renee Rosnes (p); Peter Washington (b); Billy Drummond (d).* 9/97.

***** Canções Do Brasil**

Steeplechase SCCD 31463 *Perry; Harold Danko (p).* 4/98.

*****(*) Doxy**

Steeplechase SCCD 31473 *Perry; George Mraz (b); Billy Hart (d).* 11/98.

Perry's albums continue to work thoughtful variations on the blowing date. The duet album with Danko consists of Brazilian songs, but beyond that the discs are focused around the players and their abilities, rather than any overriding concepts. *So In Love* benefits hugely from Rosnes, Washington and Drummond as the supporting team. The pianist is going through a purple patch with recording, and she sounds as lucid and imaginative as she does on her own records. Perry picks excellent tunes – Steve Swallow's 'Eiderdown', Ron Carter's 'Little Waltz', Alec Wilder's 'Moon And Sand' – and noses round them, looking for counter-melodies and improvisations that seem to run in a sort of parallel with the theme.

The collaboration with Danko invites comparison with Stan Getz–Kenny Barron and similarly minded duos. Perry and Danko aren't looking for that kind of comparison; if anything, this takes an opposite stance to the view of Brazilian music as sweetly romantic and sensuous. Their quiet and introspective path through the nine themes – nothing obvious here, either, with no Jobim but Gismonti, Francis Hime and Toninho Horta all represented – has a mournful and sometimes abstracted air. The results are a little dry, but not unpleasurable.

The return to a trio format produces another fine session for Perry. He is not a great communicator on the saxophone, in the same way as a master of the trio situation like Rollins, but that is more a matter of his preference for a sound and a manner that never buttonholes the listener. It is intriguing to hear him improvising on 'Blue In Green', Bill Evans's oblique classic, where he finds an almost chilly peacefulness. Much of this music has a take-it-or-leave-it quality, but it's not a bad change from the in-your-face tactics of many modern saxophonists.

*****(*) O Grande Amor**

Steeplechase SCCD 31492 *Perry; George Colligan (p); Doug Weiss (b); Darren Beckett (d).* 12/99.

*****(*) Hearsay**

Steeplechase SCCD 31515 *Perry; Steve Lampert (t); Dennis Irwin (b); Jeff Hirshfield (d).* 3/01.

This is becoming an exceptionally rewarding sequence, and there's good evidence that *O Grande Amor* is another upturn. One reason is Colligan, who seems incapable of being boring and is prepared to push Perry a fraction harder than some of his predecessors on the piano stool; looking at the illustrious list this is quite something. The tunes are a jazz musician's choicest – 'Nardis', 'The Peacocks', 'On Green Dolphin Street' and the like – one or two of them possibly too familiar, but you'd hardly think so from the freshness of playing in both ensemble and solo. Just a few dead spots hold back a top rating.

Hearsay rings a few useful changes. Perry brought two tunes, but most of them are by Lampert, an old playing-partner. The feel is of seamless, endless improvising over harmonic points spare enough to let the improviser go where his instincts take him. The rhythm-playing recalls the Tristanoite brushes-on-a-phonebook approach, the better to focus on the melodic stream. It's doubtless too dry for some tastes, but not for ours.

*****(*) At Eastman**

Steeplechase SCCD 31533 *Perry; Clay Jenkins (t); Harold Danko (p); Jeff Campbell (b); Rich Thompson (d).* 3/01.

Typical that this should be a recital by what is effectively a faculty group at Eastman School of Music: it's a vintage master-class, with Perry, his old compadre Danko and the others investigating the likes of 'Bemsha Swing', 'Doxy' and 'Stella By Starlight' – cool, nimble, melodious, but in its riskless way, quite chancey. 'Bemsha Swing' in particular is made into an almost classical dissertation on Monk, without falling into the juiceless inertia that that description suggests. As with all Perry's records, you either get with the style, or not.

Houston Person (born 1934)

TENOR SAXOPHONE

Born in Florence, South Carolina, Person was a relatively late starter. He worked for a time with Johnny Hammond before establishing his own guitar- and organ-based groups, with whom he has recorded extensively. Person is in the Coleman Hawkins mould, a fine ballad-player with a low, urgent tone.

***** Trust In Me**

Prestige 24264 *Person; Cedar Walton (p); Alan Dawson (vib); Bob Cranshaw, Paul Chambers (b); Frankie Jones, Lenny McBrowne (d); Ralph Dorsey (perc).* 6–10/67.

***** Blue Odyssey**

Original Jazz Classics 1045 *Person; Curtis Fuller (tb); Pepper Adams (bs); Cedar Walton (p); Bob Cranshaw (b); Frankie Jones (d).* 3/68.

***** Goodness!**

Original Jazz Classics OJCCD 332 *Person; Sonny Phillips (org); Billy Butler (g); Bob Bushnell (b); Frankie Jones (d).* 8/69.

***** Legends Of Acid Jazz**

Prestige 24179 *As above, except add Cecil Bridgewater, Thad Jones, Virgil Jones, Ernie Royal (t), Garnett Brown (tb), Harold Vick (ts), Grant Green (g), Idris Muhammad, Bernard Purdie (d).* 10/70–4/71.

Though Person's Muse catalogue has not yet come back on line, his stock remains high as a forefather of the acid jazz movement, a lineage explicitly celebrated on the Prestige compilation. It's pretty straightahead stuff: blaring brass, chugging organ, square-four rhythm and the beefy sound of Houston's tenor over the top, inexhaustible, reliable, seldom anything other than squarely on the beat and on the case. The gospelly side of his playing personality is surprisingly much in evidence on these two dance-orientated sets. 'Lift Every Voice And Sing' on *Legends* has the power to bring a lump to the throat, and there are moments on both discs when Person, sounding like a latter-day Ike Quebec, negotiates some quite subtle interchanges with the rhythm-players. One either goes for this aural equivalent of soul food or one doesn't.

Trust In Me brings back the LP of that title together with the slightly earlier *Chocomotive.* The latter set has Alan Dawson for once on vibes, and hits a pretty extraordinary groove on the title-track: blues in the jazz-locomotive tradition. But much of the rest is mere Prestige piece-work, with Houston receiving an unfortunate echoey sound in the mix. He sounds better on the later session, and eats up Parker's 'My Little Suede Shoes'.

Blue Odyssey isn't particularly bigger in ambition, but it does use a larger group. The use of lower horns gives the front line a bit of useful gravitas and Cedar Walton sits down and thinks about the charts, so it's a notch higher than the expected blow –

although, in the end, not that much, and in some ways Person followers would rather hear him having space to himself.

***** Person-ified**
HighNote HCD 7004 *Person; Richard Wyands (p); Ray Drummond (b); Kenny Washington (d).* 11/96.

*****(*) My Romance**
HighNote HCD 7033 *As above.* 6/98.

Having taken his A&R and production nous from Muse to HighNote, Person turned in some of the best recorded work of his career, a pungent mix of jazz, gospel and blues with a first-rate rhythm section. Person the balladeer has often tended to the gruff and heavy-handed, but here he is convincingly romantic on 'Stranger On The Shore' and 'Gentle Rain', and when he says 'I'll Never Stop Loving You', one is inclined to believe him. Wyands is excellent in support and the Van Gelder sound flatters the pianist more than the rest of the group. Richard sounds uneasy only on the Ammons-inspired 'Blue Jug', which isn't his speed or style. Elsewhere he's immaculate, and it's hard to fault the other two either; Washington always gives of his best and Drummond could probably carry a whole orchestra on those broad shoulders.

The same group reconvened 18 months later to record a slightly quieter but even better album. Right from the opening 'But Beautiful' it is obvious that Person is completely in command of his idiom. The pace is very gentle and determinedly romantic, and 'Laura' and 'Stairway To The Stars' are both superlative performances. Wyands occasionally chafes at the pace, but he too is a natural balladeer and it is hard to fault his exquisitely tailored solos or his rhythm work with Drummond and Washington.

***** The Opening Round**
Savant SCD 2005 *Person; Joey DeFrancesco (org); Rodney Jones (g); Tracy Wormworth (b); Bernard Purdie (d).* 2/97.

From the same group of labels, Savant is devoted to a rootsier sound and this boisterous album comes in its 'Groove Masters' series. It's been some little while since Houston went back to the saxophone–organ–guitar format but it still fits him like a glove, and his solos on 'Sweet Sucker' and 'When A Man Loves A Woman' are pure delight. The band has a tight R&B feel to it, but also considerable intelligence, and DeFrancesco is adept at shifting registers within a couple of measures, keeping the music open and stimulating.

***** Soft Lights**
High Note HCD 7049 *Person; Richard Wyands (p); Russell Malone (g); Ray Drummond (b); Grady Tate (d).* 4/99.

Person and ten ballads in a programme that almost recalls the old mood-music sax and strings dates of the '50s and '60s. There's no orchestra and the band actually hit the odd shuffle here and there, but the point of it is to hear a veteran of a vanishing saxophone generation working over some timeless smoochers. He does what has to be done.

***** Dialogue**
High Note HCD 7072 *Person; Ron Carter (b).* 8/00.

***** Sentimental Journey**
High Note HCD 7101 *Person; Richard Wyands (p); Russell Malone (g); Peter Washington (b); Grady Tate (d).* 5/02.

Houston and Ron have done the duo session before, and even if this doesn't really seem like Person's kind of thing, they make a good go of it. The quartet date is much the same, with ballads to the fore. Approaching 70, Person has nothing to prove, no new words to say, but it's what he does: a jazz journeyman's notes on a long and busy working life.

Ake Persson (1932–75)

TROMBONE

Born in Hässleholm, Sweden, Persson was something of a prodigy on trombone, and he soon acquired a reputation for excellence in big-band work. He played with German radio bands, the Quincy Jones orchestra, the Clarke–Boland band and even with Duke Ellington on one of his European tours. He took his own life in 1975.

***** 'The Great' Ake Persson**
Four Leaf Clover FLC CD 127 *Persson; Frank Rosolino, Bob Burgess (tb); Carl-Erik Lindgren, Hacke Bjorksten (ts); Arne Domnérus (as); Lars Gullin (bs); Ingemar Westberg, Gosta Theselius, Bengt Hallberg, Rob Pronk, Reinhold Svensson, Claes-Goran Fagerstadt (p); Bengt Carlsson, Gunnar Johnson, Simon Brehm, Don Bagley, Georg Riedel (b); Nils-Bertil Dahlander, Egil Johansen, Sven Bollhem, Jack Noren, Kenneth Fagerlund, Stan Levey (d).* 8/51–1/57.

A welcome homage to one of the greatest of European trombonists. Persson was still a teenager when he made the earliest tracks here, and his mellifluous sound and effortless phrasing were already in place. The CD gathers together small-group dates with Domnérus and Hallberg, a three-trombone frontline with Rosolino and Burgess, two very fine tracks by The Modern Swedes – Persson quite outstanding on 'Penta' – and the better part of a 1957 quintet date with Gullin in which Persson is overdubbed into a trombone section. Most of this is vintage Swedish cool and much of it seems relatively slight in stature, the tracks coming off EPs and the like, with many of the tunes coming in at under three minutes apiece. But it pays tribute to the earlier work of an impeccable musician who virtually disappeared into big bands and orchestras for much of the remainder of his career. Hans Fridlund's note offers a poignant appreciation of the man who died by his own hand in 1975.

Bent Persson (born 1947)

TRUMPET

Born in Karlskrona, Persson has worked with many European groups who need a trumpeter playing in the classic style. He has an uncanny ability to evoke the sounds of stylists long gone.

***** Louis Armstrong's 50 Hot Choruses Vol. 1–2**
Kenneth CKS 3411 *Persson; Karin Kristensson, Björn Larsson (t); Jens Lindgren, Hans Brandgärd (tb); Claes Brodda, Jan Böstrom (cl, ts); Lars-Göran Olsson, Hakan Kritensson (cl, as); Jan Akerman (cl, ss, ts); Göran Eriksson (cl, as, bj); Anders Lindén, Keith Nichols, Morten Gunnar Larsen, Ulf Lindberg, Ray Smith (p); Johan Lepistö (g); Tommy Gertoft, Klas Lagerberg (bj); Carl Jakobsson, Mats Jungner, Bo Juhlin (tba); Christer Ekhe (d, v); Bertil Ekman (d).* 1/89–11/92.

***** Louis Armstrong's 50 Hot Choruses Vol. 3–4**
Kenneth CKS 3413 *As above.* 1/89–11/92.

***** Swinging Straight**
Sittel SITCD 9218 *Persson; Dicken Hedrenius (tb); John Högman (ts); Ulf Johansson (p); Göran Lind (b); Ronnie Gardiner (d).* 12/94.

***** Jazz, Blues And Stomps**
Kenneth CKS 3417 *Persson; Frans Sjöström (bsx); Jacob Ullberger (g, bj).* 9–11/01.

Persson can sound like any bygone trumpeter he cares to – and he's been asked to play in just that way, on a number of revivalist dates. The most extraordinary was the project to record the fabled solos and breaks which Louis Armstrong recorded on to wax cylinders for the Melrose Publishing company in 1927. The cylinders were lost long ago, but many of the solos and breaks were transcribed at the time, and Persson re-created them on new recordings of the tunes (plenty of which were never recorded by Armstrong himself). The Kenneth company undertook this project as far back as the '70s and the final recordings were all due to be issued on CD, although so far only the first and third sets appear to have emerged. Backed with various groups of players sympathetic with the idiom, Persson does his copycat stuff and plays other parts 'in the style'. More detailed notes would have been an asset to the listener, since it's not clear what's written and what's being improvised, and as freely as the players often work, there's a pervasive sense of something unreal about the whole project. Armstrong scholars, though, will find it intriguing at least.

Persson's chameleonic abilities perhaps tell against his other records having a character of their own. Instead, *Swinging Straight* is purely pleasurable mainstream, buoyed up by a sense of enjoyment that is often hard to find on equivalent American dates. Persson here comes on like one of the great Basie trumpeters, and Hedrenius's rascally trombone and Högman's burly tenor merely add to the fun. The Hot Jazz Trio are rather more classic in style, with Sjöström's cavernous bass sax filling all the bottom end, and the music's performed with affectionate warmth.

Oscar Peterson (born 1925)

PIANO, ORGAN, ELECTRIC PIANO, CLAVICHORD

Few musicians have done more to popularize jazz – real jazz as opposed to a dilution – than Oscar Peterson. The big Canadian has been a stalwart on the scene for longer than half a century. Spotted by Norman Granz, he became a regular at Jazz At The Philharmonic events and has always been a big festival draw. His occasionally showy multi-note approach owes much to Art Tatum, but it was Nat Cole who was the most powerful and lasting influence. In recent years, Peterson's playing career was hampered by ill-health, but with characteristic patience and application he has returned to the studio and to performance.

****(*) The First Recordings**
Indigo IGOCD 2070 *Peterson; Armand Samson (g); Bert Brown (b); Russ Dufort, Franck Gariepy, Roland Verdon (d).* 4/45–7/46.

***** Oscar Peterson, 1945–1947**
Classics 1084 *As above, except add Albert King, Auston Roberts (b), Clarence Jones, Mark Wilkinson (d).* 4/45–12/47.

According to Lalo Schifrin, Oscar Peterson is the Liszt of modern jazz, Bill Evans its Chopin; this refers back to the much-quoted assertion that the Hungarian conquered the piano, while the Pole seduced it. Certainly, all through his career Peterson has seemed to have all the technical bases covered, working in styles from Tatum-derived swing to bebop, stride to near-classical ideas. What is extraordinary about him is how quickly and completely he matured as a stylist and how consistently he has been able to sustain piano jazz of the highest quality right through his career. Peterson left his native Canada in 1949 at the behest of Norman Granz, who became his main sponsor. However, he had already established a successful recording career before that, signing for RCA Victor in Montreal. Peterson was already known round the city as the Brown Bomber of Boogie Woogie, and it is that style which dominates these early sides. There are clinkers aplenty on the faster tracks, though buried so deep in the precocious rush of notes that they scarcely register as anything other than slubs and craquelure on what is already a fantastically rich canvas. 'Blue Moon', recorded in April 1946, is hugely accomplished, as is 'China Boy' and the somewhat later 'East Of The Sun'. A bass-playing Brown would play a huge role in his later career, but it was Bert Brown who supported on these early sides and, though he's not well registered even in these remasterings, it's obvious that Peterson relied heavily on him. The Tatum influence is less evident than one might have expected, given the consensus about Oscar's sources, but it is undeniably and unmissably present, and on tracks like 'I Got Rhythm' and 'The Sheik Of Araby' it is the dominant voice. Peterson had not yet quite attained an expressive personality of his own, but it is waiting in the wings.

The Classics compilation – and somehow it seems odd to find Oscar covered by the French label – pushes the story on into 1947 and some further recordings for Victor in Canada. There is a fine 'Ghost Of A Chance' from April and a wonderful version of 'Stairway To The Stars', taped just before Christmas. Deft and virtuosic as they are, these early sessions are likely to be of interest to committed fans only.

***** This Is Oscar Peterson At The Piano**
RCA 63990 2CD *Peterson; Ben Johnson (g); Bert Brown (b); Albert King, Auston Roberts (b, v); Frank Gariepy, Roland Verdon, Mark Wilkinson (d).* 45–49.

***** The Complete RCA Recordings**
Jazz Factory 22830 2CD *As above.* 45–49.

The RCA set is an important release which clears up a long-standing discographical blunder and also completes the picture of the young Peterson's work for the Canadian division of RCA. It transpires that the so-called *Complete Young Oscar Peterson* released in 1994 (a) wasn't and (b) consisted largely of alternate takes rather than release masters. We haven't managed to check whether this mistake has been duplicated in other releases, but it has certainly been rectified on this beautifully packaged and documented set and the results are quietly revelatory. Peterson was still a developing player at this time and the exigencies of 78 rpm recording mean that most of the songs are short, showy and lacking in development. There are 49 cuts on the set, of which 17 are alternates. The preferred versions seem to be slightly faster and crisper, though not necessarily always more musical. There are few obvious clinkers, though once or twice Oscar's supporting players slip up and only deft footwork from the pianist keeps the track on line. An important issue and a thoroughly enjoyable one; good to have the record put straight.

The Jazz Factory release is a good budget option, but there are question marks about the provenance and the remastering.

***** Oscar Peterson, 1949–1950**
Classics 1198 *Peterson; Ben Johnson (g); Ray Brown, Major Holley, Auston Roberts (b); Clarence Jones (d).* 49–50.

***** Oscar Peterson, 1950**
Classics 1250 *Peterson; Ray Brown, Major Holley (b).* 50.

***** Oscar Peterson, 1950–1952**
Classics 1323 *Peterson; Irving Ashby, Barney Kessel (g); Ray Brown (b).* 50–52.

****(*) Get Happy**
Dreyfus FDM 36738 2 *As above.* 49–52.

Under Norman Granz's wing, Peterson began to record steadily from 1949 onwards, working mainly just with a bass-player, which put him under some pressure rhythmically. These are still the work of a young man, not so much technically callow as expressively inexperienced. When he 'does' one of his predecessors and idols on 'Salute To Garner' (August 1950), the effect is still rather sarcastic and superior and not at all affectionate, but then the 24-year-old had been propelled into stardom very suddenly and it was difficult for him to keep his equilibrium. There are some lovely things here, mostly on the 1950 volume. When Ray Brown took over for that August session, the harmonic vocabulary suddenly doubles in size and the left-hand lines become ever more subtle and evocative. The Carnegie Hall set from 16 September 1950 explains exactly why Granz signed him: excitement, sophistication and a likeable humour.

The Dreyfus trawls through some of this early material, out of chronological sequence and with a dispiriting absence of clear discographical information, which might lead some potential purchasers to think this was a free-standing issue of later vintage.

***** 1951**
Just A Memory 9501 *Peterson; Auston Roberts (b).* 3–7/51.

Twenty beautifully executed miniatures, presumably kept down in length on the instructions of the Canadian Broadcasting Commission who taped these performances for relay on a famously tight schedule. Roberts certainly isn't a playing partner of the quality of Major Holley or Ray Brown, but he has an inherent musicality and a genuine instinct for swing, and these are lovely cuts, albeit frustratingly brief.

***** The President Plays With The Oscar Peterson Trio**
Verve 521451-2 *Peterson; Lester Young (ts); Barney Kessel (g); Ray Brown (b); J. C. Heard (d).* 52.

Flawlessly lyrical piano-playing, but nothing much from Pres but the shards and fragments of a musical mind that had very little left to say. Some of the tunes are stunning. 'Tea For Two' is a revelation and 'On The Sunny Side Of The Street' is as fresh and uncomplicated as a spring morning. Much of the rest, though, is as empty as after-dinner conversation between generations who aren't at odds but who don't quite understand each other.

***** Jazz Masters 37: Oscar Peterson Plays Broadway**
Verve 516893-2 *Peterson; Clark Terry (t); Irving Ashby, Herb Ellis, Barney Kessel (g); Ray Brown (b); Gene Gammage, Alvin Stoller, Ed Thigpen (d).* 3/50–8/64.

*****(*) Jazz Masters 16: Oscar Peterson**
Verve 516320-2 *Peterson; Roy Eldridge (t); Sonny Stitt (as); Stan Getz, Flip Phillips, Ben Webster, Lester Young (ts); Lionel Hampton (vib); Milt Jackson (vib); Herb Ellis, Barney Kessel (g); Ray Brown (b); J. C. Heard, John Poole, Buddy Rich, Alvin Stoller, Ed Thigpen (d); Fred Astaire, Ella Fitzgerald, Anita O'Day (v).* 52–61.

***** The Duke Ellington Songbook**
Verve 559785-2 *Peterson; Barney Kessel (g); Ray Brown (b); Ed Thigpen (d).* 52, 59.

***** The George Gershwin Songbook**
Verve 529698-2 *As above, except omit Thigpen.* 11 & 12/52.

***** Jazz At The Philharmonic, Hartford 1953**
Pablo 2308240 *Peterson; Roy Eldridge, Charlie Shavers (t); Bill Harris (tb); Benny Carter, Willie Smith (as); Flip Phillips, Ben Webster, Lester Young (ts); Herb Ellis (g); Ray Brown (b); J. C. Heard, Gene Krupa (d).* 5/53.

*****(*) At Zardi's**
Pablo Live 2620118 2CD *Peterson; Herb Ellis (g); Ray Brown (b).* 55.

No single moment ever gave a clearer impression of Oscar Peterson's fabled technique than a tiny incident on one of those all-star Jazz At The Philharmonic events released in rafts by the Pablo label. Count Basie has just stated the opening notes of a theme in his inimitable elided style when there is a pause and then – presto! – showers of sparkling notes. Any suspicions about what the Count might have ingested during his few bars of silence are allayed by the liner-note. What had happened, quite simply, was that Basie had spotted Oscar Peterson standing in the wings and had dragged him on for an unscheduled 'spot'.

Peterson has been almost as prolific as he is effusive at the piano. He appears on literally dozens of albums in solo and trio settings, but also with horn-led groups and orchestras. He is one of the finest accompanists in swing-orientated jazz, despite which he served no real apprenticeship as a sideman, being introduced to an American audience (he was born and raised in Canada) by impresario and record producer Norman Granz in 1949. He has ridden on the extraordinary momentum of that debut ever since, recording almost exclusively for Granz's labels, Verve and, later, Pablo. The earliest material available here suggests how complete he was as an artist, even at the very beginning. He quickly became a favourite at JATP events and the *Hartford 1953* sessions anticipate the walk-on/walk-off sensation he was to become in the '70s.

Peterson is perhaps best as a trio performer. During the '50s these tended to be drummerless, and with a guitarist. Barney Kessel sounds rather colourless and Herb Ellis is much more responsive to Peterson's technique, as was his much later replacement, Joe Pass. After 1960, the stalwart Ray Brown was joined by a drummer, first by Ed Thigpen then by Louis Hayes. This coincided with Peterson's consolidation as a major concert and recording star; his early work, influenced primarily by Nat Cole, is now rather less well known. Of the mid-'50s sets, *At Zardi's* and the excellent *Jazz Masters* compilation (which covers the early years of the later trio as well) are certainly the best.

There has long been a critical knee-jerk about Peterson's Tatum influence. This was very much a later development. Tatum died in 1956 and only then does Peterson seem to have taken a close interest in his work. Even then it overlay the smoothed-out, ambidextrous quality he had found in Cole. With the turn of the '60s and international stardom, Peterson's style changes only in accordance with the context of specific performances, particularly between the big, grandstanding, 'all star' events and more intimate occasions with his own trio, where he demonstrates an occasional resemblance to Hampton Hawes and, more contentiously, to Bill Evans.

His debt to Duke Ellington is less obvious, but something of Duke's urbane phrasing crept into Oscar's playing in the '50s and one can hear him both surrender to it and resist it strongly on the Ducal songbook, one of the best of the sequence but also one of the most exposed. Oscar's solo on 'Prelude To A Kiss' is about as raw-nerved as he gets. Peterson's powerfully swinging style does on occasion tend to overpower his melodic sense and he is apt to become repetitious and, less often, banal. After four decades in the business, though, he understands its workings better than anyone. Above all, Peterson *delivers.*

***** 1953 Live**

Jazz Band 2111 *Peterson; Barney Kessel (g); Ray Brown (b).* 53.

Not strictly a Peterson album since the trio was opening for the Buddy DeFranco group at the Blue Note in Chicago and are only featured on two short sets before the clarinettist took over. Two versions of 'Heat Wave', the second longer and better than the first, a nice 'The Man I Love', 'The Continental', 'Anything Goes' and a tune given as 'Mood' on the sleeve and introduced by Oscar as a Miles Davis composition, but surely Denzil Best's 'Move'. As a further insight into Peterson's early years in the US, this is a valuable find, but it's not an essential purchase, unless you also have a passion for DeFranco.

*****(*) At The Stratford Shakespearean Festival**

Verve 513752-2 *Peterson; Herb Ellis (g); Ray Brown (b).* 8/56.

*****(*) At The Concertgebouw**

Verve 521649-2 *As above.* 9 & 10/57.

Unlike the Ahmad Jamal and Nat Cole trios, which also dispensed with drummers in favour of piano, guitar and bass, the Peterson group never sounded spacious or open-textured – the pianist's hyperactive fingers saw to that. Here, though, for once Peterson seemed able to lie back a little and let the music flow under its own weight, rather than constantly pushing it along. Peterson has described how during the daytime Brown and Ellis sat and practised all the harmonic variables that might come up during a performance. A sensible precaution, one might have thought, given a player with Peterson's hand-speed. The irony is that his vertical mobility, in and out of key, was never as rapid as all that, and there are occasions here, as on 'How High The Moon' and the closing 'Daisy's Dream' (both from Stratford), where it appears that Ellis and Brown manage to anticipate his moves and push him into configurations he hadn't apparently thought of.

The other concert is augmented with material from Los Angeles a fortnight later, suggesting a quick return to the United States. However, the 'Concertgebouw' material was actually recorded in Chicago. The Dutch concert given by the trio earlier in 1957 was never actually taped, but presumably it sounded classier on the sleeve to pretend that it had. One other mistake has been corrected from the CD. The track originally labelled 'Bags' Groove' clearly wasn't and has now been retitled 'Bluesology'.

***** Tenderly**

Just A Memory 9146 *Peterson; Herb Ellis (g); Ray Brown (b).* 58.

***** Vancouver 1958**

Just A Memory 9148 *As above.* 58.

These resurfaced in 2002 and 2003 and add to the image of a trio of almost telepathic understanding, at this stage about one year from its eventual dissolution. Brown is magisterial throughout both sets and on the opening 'How High The Moon' (*Vancouver 1958*), he reminds us that he once played with Charlie Parker. 'The Music Box Suite' is the other long track, but it's a bit of a filler and it's 'The Golden Striker' that stands out from the rest of the set. 'The Music Box Suite' is also on *Tenderly* and no more compelling in this version. The sound, from two performances at the Orpheum Theatre, isn't perfect but as a slice of archive these are hard to beat and they fill in another significant chapter in the Oscar Peterson story.

*****(*) The Ultimate Oscar Peterson**

Verve 539786-2 *Peterson; Clark Terry (t, v); Milt Jackson (vib); Herb Ellis (g); Ray Brown (b); Ed Thigpen (d); Ernie Wilkins Orchestra.* 8/56–8/64.

Like Penguin's own classic 'Poets on Poets' series, these *Ultimate* compilations are selected by the musicians' peers, in this case not another piano-player but the man who has anchored Peterson's groups over so many years, bassist Ray Brown. Given the range of material he has to select from, any choice is going to be controversial, but it's hard to argue with these ten tracks from *The Trio* ('Sometimes I'm Happy', 'In The Wee Small Hours Of The Morning' and 'Chicago'), *At The Stratford Shakespearean Festival* ('Love You Madly' and 'Noreen's Nocturne'), *Very Tall* ('Reunion Blues'), *The Jazz Soul* ('Waltz For Debby'), the big-band *Bursting Out* with Ernie Wilkins ('Blues For Big Scotia'), *West Side Story* ('Jet Song'), and *Trio + 1* ('Mumbles' with Clark Terry, inevitably). Tomorrow, asked again, you might well pick ten different tracks but, as these things go, this is a nicely balanced and not altogether predictable selection, and if you had never previously made Peterson's acquaintance it would at least take you some way towards a rounded picture of the artist.

*****(*) On The Town**

Verve 543834 *Peterson; Herb Ellis (g); Ray Brown (b).* 7/58.

This live Toronto recording was reissued by Verve in 2001. The trio opens with a sparkling 'Sweet Georgia Brown', which must count as one of the most grabbing intros Oscar ever played to a concert. From there, the pace never drops for a second; even the ballad performances seem fired up and packed with musical information. Not that this is a coldly technical set. It's as warm as summer and 'Joy Spring' and 'Love Is Here To Stay', the latter one of two bonus cuts, are both delightfully soulful.

*****(*) Plays My Fair Lady & The Music From Fiorello**

Verve 521677-2 *Peterson; Ray Brown (b); Gene Gammage (d).* 11/58, 1/60.

*****(*) A Jazz Portrait Of Frank Sinatra**

Verve 825769-2 *Peterson; Ray Brown (b); Ed Thigpen (d).* 5/59.

***** Plays The Cole Porter Songbook**

Verve 821987-2 *As above.* 7 & 8/59.

*****(*) The Jazz Soul Of Oscar Peterson**

Verve 533100-2 *As above.* 7 & 8/59, 9/62.

****** Plays Porgy & Bess**

Verve 519807-2 *As above.* 10/59.

Not to be confused with the later duo interpretation featuring Joe Pass, the Gershwin set is brilliantly spontaneous jazz, apparently recorded after the sketchiest of run-throughs. Peterson has played 'I Wants To Stay Here' (or 'I Loves You, Porgy', as it is more commonly known) many times in his career (see *Tristeza*, below), but nowhere with the pure feeling and simplicity he gives it on this disc. The two apostrophes to Bess at the end are heartfelt and utterly compelling, with liquid left-hand figures and an unstoppable flow of melody ideas. As pianist Benny Green indicates in a special introductory note to the reissue, Ray Brown gets less solo space here than on many of the trio's records, unlikely to be a symptom of unfamiliarity with the material, more probably because Peterson makes the session so forcibly his own. Brown's contribution to the fiery 'There's A Boat Dat's Leavin' Soon For New York' is beyond reproach, however, and his intro to 'I Got Plenty O' Nuttin'' is masterful.

With Peterson, nothing fundamental rests on the quality of the material he has to work with. His almost alchemical transformation of the songs from *Fiorello* beggars belief. *My Fair Lady* offers more familiar melodies and the element of surprise is proportionately less. However, these are some of his most lyrical and melody-centred interpretations, often sticking quite close to the line. The Porter and Sinatra records are slightly odd in that Peterson does very little more than run through the songs, chorus by chorus, adding very little in the way of improvisational embellishment. The shortest track on the Sinatra is under two minutes, the longest on either just three and a half, the average about two minutes forty-five. This gives the performances a slightly abrupt air that's only partly mitigated by the sheer empathy the pianist feels with the tunes. Though Peterson's admiration for Sinatra comes through strongly, the Porter tribute isn't a great record, and there are signs that it was made to order as part of a burgeoning catalogue of 'songbook' projects; but its value lies precisely in its terseness, Peterson's brilliant feel for song form.

The Jazz Soul rounds out the picture and completes CD coverage of this classic period, pairing the disc of that name with a later session called *Affinity*. The latter is fairly adventurous for the time, including 'Waltz For Debby' and a complex, freighted version of 'Tangerine'. The pace drops thereafter, but these are special tracks and it's a wonder that they weren't made available to a new generation of listeners sooner.

***(*) Plays The Harold Arlen Songbook

Verve 589 103 2 *Peterson; Herb Ellis (g); Ray Brown (b); Ed Thigpen (d).* 11/54, 7 & 8/59.

Actually two albums, brought together as part of Verve's Master Edition series. The earlier set, released in 1954 as *Plays Harold Arlen*, was a lightly skipping progress through themes as diverse as 'I've Got The World On A String', 'As Long As I Live' and 'Between The Devil And The Deep Blue Sea'. The first and last of these also feature on the 1959 set, where Thigpen had come in to replace the guitarist, leaving Oscar freer from rhythmic duties to indulge his amazing harmonic understanding and probe both songs that bit more deeply. Almost all the cuts are under three minutes, all the same, and frequently Oscar's overpacked solo is over before you've quite caught up with his opening idea. An enjoyable kind of frustration. The Master Edition is issued with original artwork and liner-notes, a very attractive package.

**** The Song Is You: Best Of The Verve Songbooks

Verve 531558-2 2CD *Peterson; Herb Ellis, Barney Kessel (g); Ray Brown (b); Ed Thigpen (d).* 52, 53, 54, 59.

An absolute joy and delight, whether as an introduction to the work of this period or as a spare copy for car or personal stereo. A Verve Take 2 compilation which really does bring together the best of these years. 'Lover', 'Tea For Two', 'Come Rain Or Come Shine': everyone will have favourites, and most tastes will be catered for. Excellent value.

*** Live At CBC Studios, 1960

Just A Memory 9507 *Peterson; Ray Brown (b); Ed Thigpen (d).* 60.

For some reason, this session wasn't released on disc for almost 40 years, doubly odd in that it comes amid an otherwise quiet moment in Oscar's output. The performances are disciplined and swinging. 'Dancing On The Ceiling' and 'Blues For Big Scotia' stand out, but the real importance of this late release is historical rather than strictly aesthetic, filling in another stage in OP's development.

***(*) The London House Sessions

Verve 531766-2 5CD *As above.* 61.

Five CDs of quality live performance, beautifully registered, remastered and packaged and effortlessly musical from start to finish – but, given the price, for the hardcore Peterson fan only. It would be pointless to unpick a set as densely filled with extraordinary music, but 'Whisper Not' on disc one, 'On Green Dolphin Street' on two and four, 'I Remember Clifford' on three, and the closing 'Confirmation' on the final disc would be our desert island pick. *The Trio*, listed below, is one disc of highlights.

*** The Trio – Live From Chicago

Verve 539063-2 *As above, except omit orchestra.* 9 & 10/61.

*** The Sound of the Trio

Verve 543321 *As above.* 61.

Ideal for anyone who doesn't want to fork out for the complete London House sessions which, though desirable, are expensive. The latter of these is from the Master Edition, beautifully packaged.

CORE COLLECTION

**** Night Train

Verve 521440-2 *Peterson; Ray Brown (b); Ed Thigpen (d).* 12/62.

After 30 years, *Night Train* is well established as a hardy perennial and is certainly Peterson's best-known record. Dedicated to his father, who was a sleeping-car attendant on Canadian Pacific Railways, it isn't the dark and moody suite of nocturnal blues many listeners expect but a lively and varied programme of material covering 'C-Jam Blues', 'Georgia On My Mind', 'Bags' Groove', 'Honey Dripper', 'Things Ain't What They Used To Be', 'Band Call', 'Hymn To Freedom' and a couple of others. Though by no means a 'concept album', it's one of the best-constructed long-players of the period and its durability is testimony to that as much as to the quality of Peterson's playing, which is tight and uncharacteristically emotional. The beautifully remastered reissue has six extra tracks, including a fascinating rehearsal take of 'Moten Swing' and an alternative of 'Night Train', which is called 'Happy Go Lucky Local'.

***** The Silver Collection**

Verve 823447-2 *Peterson; Ray Brown (b); Ed Thigpen (d); Nelson Riddle Orchestra.* 8/59 & 63.

*****(*) Very Tall**

Verve 827821-2 *As above, except add Milt Jackson (vib).* 9/61.

***** West Side Story**

Verve 821575-2 *As above, except omit Jackson.* 1/62.

***** Plus One**

Verve 558075 *As above, except add Clark Terry (t, flhn).* 8/64.

***** We Get Requests**

Verve 521442-2 *As above, except omit Terry.* 10 & 11/64.

We Get Requests reverses the polarity established by *Night Train* totally. Cool but technically effusive, Peterson gets all over two sets of (mostly) romantic ballads, played with a portrait of Nat Cole perched on the soundboard in front of him. The 'requests' are pretty much of their time, mostly songs that either started out as soft pop or, like 'The Girl From Ipanema', made their way there via the charts. *The Silver Collection* has four excellent trio tracks fighting for their lives among nine syrupy orchestrations that might have worked for another pianist but which are emphatically not in Peterson's line of sight. The *West Side Story* covers are interesting because they put the weight of emphasis on all the unlikeliest tunes. The 'Jet Song' receives the most developed interpretation but, while 'Maria' and 'Somewhere' are both consummately polished performances, they lack the commitment and graceful intelligence Peterson normally brings to romantic ballads. As a whole, and even upgraded to the highest standard of digital remastering, the record is a little lightweight and uninvolving.

So different is Peterson from John Lewis's unemphatic keyboard approach that there's not the remotest chance that *Very Tall* might be mistaken for an MJQ record. One of the great improvisers in modern jazz, Jackson is the undoubted star of the session, finessing 'On Green Dolphin Street' with a subtle counterpoint and adding a tripping bounce to 'A Wonderful Guy'. Excellent stuff. Watch out for *Reunion Blues*, not currently around, which saw Peterson and the vibist get together again.

Plus One, now available in a Master Edition, is aptly named. Terry never gets more involved than his guest star role would imply, and there are occasions when (to be frank) he sounds more like a revelling gatecrasher. He slides into a sombre, almost remorseful mood on 'They Didn't Believe Me', giving his flugelhorn that celebrated bone-china fragility, before bouncing back with a second wind on a Peterson original (averaging one or two per disc around this time) called 'Squakay's Blues', dedicated to the redoubtable Joanie Spears, who managed the big man's career at this time.

Almost all these records are now available as 20-bit digital transfers, filling out the sound. Anyone who hasn't yet upgraded from vinyl will be delighted with the difference. Anyone who already has a CD copy may wonder if it's really worth the outlay.

***** Paris Jazz Concert**

Malaco Jazz 1208 *Peterson; Roy Eldridge (t); Ray Brown, Sam Jones (b); Louis Hayes, Ed Thigpen (d).* 61–69.

The title is misleading because this isn't a tape of a single concert but of a sequence of Paris appearances in the '60s. The mastering is pretty suspect and, though some of the performances are above average, it's not a record that casual Peterson listeners need bother about.

***** Olympia, Mai 1957, Avril 1960, Février 1961, Mars 1963**

Trema 710597 *Peterson; Roy Eldridge (t); Herb Ellis (g); Stuff Smith (vn); Ray Brown (b); Jo Jones, Ed Thigpen (d).* 5/57, 4/60, 2/61, 3/63.

*****(*) Olympia 1663/Th. Champs Élysées 1964**

Trema 71908 *As above; omit Ellis, Jones.* 63, 64.

***** Th. Champs Élysées 20 Mars 1965 – Pleyel 29 Mars 1965**

Trema 710599 *As above; add Sam Jones (b); Louis Hayes (d).* 3/65.

A fine haul of live dates from France, and a chance to hear Oscar in some interesting guest company. The earliest set features some fine playing from Eldridge and the effervescent Stuff Smith, and there is an emotional reunion in 1960 with Herb Ellis, who'd moved on from the Peterson trio a couple of years before. Eldridge is in absolutely phenomenal form on the Olympia 1963 date, playing fierce, edgy stuff on 'Mainstem' and a superb 'But Not For Me'. The remainder of the date is just Oscar with the trio, but he obviously likes the Parisian air and plays with a relaxed bravura that culminates on a superb extended reading of 'Yours Is My Heart Alone' and 'Blues For Big Scotia'. The third volume sees an unusual variation in the core trio with Jones and Hayes, who worked with Oscar for a time, significantly reshaping some of his most familiar strategies.

It should be noted that the sound on all these discs is not wonderful and there are passages where the piano is obviously not in good shape.

****(*) Immortal Concerts, Part 1**

Giants Of Jazz 32032 *Peterson; Ray Brown (b); Ed Thigpen (d).* 64.

****(*) Immortal Concerts, Part 2**

Giants Of Jazz 32042 *As above.* 64.

Poor recordings, but fine performances from a group which doesn't seem to have had a bad night. The second volume is the more interesting of the two, with a wonderful interpretation of 'Waltz For Debby' (Peterson briefly paying explicit tribute to Bill Evans) and a stunning 'I Remember Clifford'. Volume one, recorded in Ljubljana, is less compelling in terms of material – 'Wheatland' stands out – but probably a crisper and more coherent gig.

***** Girl Talk**

MPS 821 842 2 *Peterson; Ray Brown, Sam Jones (b); Bobby Durham, Louis Hayes (d).* 64, 66.

Between 1963 and 1968 Peterson recorded a series of six LPs for the MPS label in the Villingen home of German producer, Hans Georg Brunner-Schwer. It's not quite the same sort of relationship as existed between Bud Powell and Francis Paudras. Peterson was successful, fit and hip to the realities of the music business. What is different about these recordings is the degree of relaxation (and, to a certain degree, of risk) in the performances.'On A Clear Day You Can See Forever' and 'Moon River' are the outstanding tracks, but both rhythm sections perform with ease and confidence, with Hayes getting the nod in the percussion department, an astonishingly lyrical player when he has material like this to work with.

***** With Respect To Nat**

Verve 557486-2 *Peterson; John Frosk, Joe Newman (t); Ernie Royal, Danny Stiles (t, flhn); Wayne Andre, Jimmy Cleveland, J. J. Johnson (tb); Tony Studd (btb); Seldon Powell, Jerome Richardson (f); Jerry Dodgion, Phil Woods (as); Mervin Halladay (bs); Hank Jones (p); Herb Ellis, Barry Galbraith (g); Ray Brown, Richard Davis (b); Mel Lewis (d).* 65.

Nat Cole was always Peterson's biggest influence and his approach to the trio format was very much in the Cole template. This, then, is both a very sincere tribute and an example of the anxiety of influence. Oscar's vocal stylings are rougher and more abrupt than Nat's, but his piano-playing is right in the groove and performances like 'When My Sugar Walks Down The Street' and 'What Can I Say After I Say I'm Sorry?' are first-rate. The various backgrounds and arrangements, largely organized by the redoubtable Manny Albam, could hardly be bettered.

***** Soul Espanol**

Verve 314 510 439 2 *Peterson; Sam Jones; Louis Hayes (d); Henley Gibson, Marshall Thompson, Harold Jones (perc).* 12/66.

This is basically a bossa nova record with a somewhat more varied rhythmic vocabulary, so very much in line with market forces of the time. The title is slightly misleading none the less. Oscar contributes two fine, idiomatic sambas, but most of the material is Brazilian rather than Spanish and the main composers are Tom Jobim and Luis Bonfa. The additional percussion does little more than clutter up the sound and certainly gets in the way of a rather recessed piano sound. Not up to Oscar's usual scratch and a strange record to get out of the vaults for this restricted release treatment; it will be on the market until 2005 only.

****** Exclusively For My Friends**

MPS 513830 4CD *Peterson; Ray Brown, Sam Jones (b); Bobby Durham, Louis Hayes, Ed Thigpen (d).* 63–68.

***** Exclusively For My Friends: The Lost Tapes**

MPS 529096 *As above, except omit Hayes.* 5/65, 11/67, 10/68.

'Love Is Here To Stay' on Volume 2 is one of the most interesting performances Peterson ever put on disc. Essentially a tribute to Tatum, it is full of harmonic ambiguities and stretched-out metres, and there is more musical meat in it than in the over-long 'I'm In The Mood For Love' on the first volume, which at 17 minutes begins to pall slightly. The highlight there is 'Like Someone In Love', which Peterson turns into a grand romantic concerto, closing with quotes from *Rhapsody In Blue.* The sessions were played before a small invited audience of friends and admirers, and the recordings are clearly aimed at connoisseurs, offering the nearest thing to a candid portrayal of Peterson musing on his art. There are unexpected touches of modernity, as in 'Nica's Dream' with Sam Jones and Bobby Durham on Volume 2, and there are perhaps too many knowing quotes (mostly from Ellington, but also from Basie's single-finger intros and even, less obviously, from Monk on 'Lulu's Back In Town'). The piano sounds big and resonant and the recordings are immediate and appropriately intimate.

By 1968, the magic of these sessions had perhaps worn a little thin and the *Lost Tapes* material suggests that it may be possible to have too much of a good thing. The solo pieces on Volumes 3 and 4 are rarely as acute as the group tracks, and there are signs that Peterson is simply not concentrating on 'Someone To Watch Over Me', which opens the last disc. A hint of self-indulgence at last? It should be noted that the six MPS LPs were: *Action, Girl Talk, The Way I Really Play, My Favourite Instrument, Mellow Mood* and *Travelin' On.* The reappearance of the missing tapes wasn't quite drama of Watergate proportions and doesn't add significantly to the tally on this handsome compilation. Peterson aficionados will be delighted with an 11-minute version of 'Tenderly', played with Brown and Thigpen, and with an unexpected run-through of Bobby Timmons's 'Moanin'' from a later session with Jones and Durham. For the most part, though, this is an item for completists, though of course it stands up on its own quite respectably as a Peterson record. If there were fewer of them around, it would be most desirable.

****(*) Motions And Emotions**

MPS 821289 *Peterson; Sam Jones (b); Bobby Durham (d); orchestra; Claus Ogerman (cond).* 69.

***** Hello Herbie**

MPS 821846 *As above, except add Herb Ellis (g); omit orchestra and Ogerman.* 11/69.

***** Tristeza On Piano**

MPS 817489 *As above, except omit Ellis.* 70.

***** Three Originals**

MPS 521059 2CD *As for above three discs.* 69–70.

***** Tracks**

MPS 523498 *Peterson (p solo).* 11/70.

Later sessions for Brunner-Schwer, though *Tristeza* was recorded in a New York studio. What's lost there, and in the others to an extent, is the gentle experimentalism of the private sessions. Peterson sounds as if he's on auto-pilot, and it's probably no coincidence that the track-listing veers strongly away from the earthbound, 'Down Here On The Ground' notwithstanding. 'Nightingale' is a rare self-written piece; 'Tristeza' and 'You Stepped Out Of A Dream' are equally moody.

Motions And Emotions is disappointing because the repertoire is so bland. The mixture of Lennon-McCartney, Mancini, Jim Webb, Bobby Gentry and Bacharach needs more leavening than even Peterson can give it; though professionally rehearsed and recorded, the strings are as gooey as always. As such, it represents a serious stumbling-block to any unqualified recommendation for the two-CD compilation, *Three Originals.* Most listeners might be prepared for two, rather better, originals. *Hello Herbie* is certainly worth having, if only for Peterson's great reading of Hampton Hawes's 'Hamp's Blues' and the Wes Montgomery tune, 'Naptown Blues', both of which catch him at his best. The reunion with Ellis is also a happy one; their interplay on 'Seven Come Eleven', a theme associated with Benny Goodman and Charlie Christian, is spot on.

The solo performances on the oddly titled *Tracks* have the musing, unself-conscious quality that was the other side of Peterson's prodigious keyboard showmanship. Things like 'A Little Jazz Exercise' and the reworkings of 'Basin Street Blues' and 'Honeysuckle Rose' are so chock-full of ideas that any aspirant jazz pianist will want to study them. For more casual listeners, these are valuable as solo performances, of which there are surprisingly few, relative to the huge mass of issued trios.

★★★(★) Two Originals

MPS 533549 *Peterson; Jiri Mraz (b); Ray Price (d).* 70.

Omitting just one track, 'Just Friends', for reasons of space (though it's hard to see how it would have caused problems), this is a compilation of *Walking The Line* and *Another Day*, two of the better Peterson albums of the early '70s. The line-up is slightly unfamiliar, but Mraz, who would become an American citizen and plain George in just a couple of years, brings his usual lyrical touch to the sessions, and he plays like a dream on 'I Didn't Know What Time It Was' and 'It Never Entered My Mind', two of the outstanding tracks, one from each album. Peterson himself is somewhat reflective and seems on occasion to be deliberately restricting the onrush of notes, not out of tiredness or diffidence but perhaps just to open up a little space. The piano sounds immaculately cared for and responsive and is perhaps a touch closer-miked than usual, unless this is just a side-effect of remastering. Whatever the reason, it's very attractive.

★★★(★) The Will To Swing

Verve 847203-2 *Peterson; Herb Ellis, Barney Kessel (g); Ray Brown, Sam Jones, Niels-Henning Orsted Pedersen (b); Louis Hayes, Buddy Rich, Ed Thigpen (d).* 54–71.

Another compilation drawn from Verve's vast holding of Oscar material. This is a good one, covering a vintage period and with an emphasis very strongly on jazz rather than popular entertainment. The version of 'Waltz For Debby' opening the second disc should be played to anyone who doubts OP's serious credentials as a modernist. Drawn from studio performances and live concerts, the sound is quite mixed and the levels seem unusually ill-adjusted, but as an introduction to Peterson's pianism this is hard to beat.

★★★ Swinging Cooperations

MPS 539085 *Peterson; Milt Jackson (vib); Ray Brown, Niels-Henning Orsted Pedersen (b); Louis Hayes (d).* 7 & 10/71.

The first astonishment here is that the first track of *Reunion Blues*, the first of two MPS discs compiled on this reissue, should be the Jagger-Richards rocker, 'Satisfaction'. The second is the way in which Oscar dispatches it. Everything else is pretty much by the book. Milt Jackson's 'Reunion Blues', written for the occasion, is unfamiliar, but scarcely a surprise. The better material is from the other LP, which reappears shorn of one track for space reasons. Charles Chaplin's 'Smile' has always been a favourite tune of Oscar's, and the trio with NHOP and Louis Hayes gives it a delicacy and warmth which sometimes disappear when jazz musicians try to make the tune swing. Oscar's 'Wheatland' is a delight, and versions of 'Younger Than Springtime' and 'Soft Winds' find the old romantic in top form.

★★★ Solo

Pablo 972 *Peterson (p solo).* 72.

Oscar Peterson solo albums are surprisingly thin on the ground and so this 2002 issue of unreleased material is particularly welcome. Apparently recorded live in Israel, probably from broadcast material, it features Oscar working through some 14 themes in not much over an hour. Though known mainly for his treatment of standard material, Peterson is an overlooked composer and 'Blues Of The Prairies' and 'Hogtown Blues' (both from his largely forgotten *Canadiana Suite*) are excellent performances. 'Body And Soul' and 'Here's That Rainy Day' are the best of the rest, not least because on both Oscar has to negotiate a slightly temperamental piano that sounds slightly out of tune. A valuable issue, though, and certain to be of interest to OP collectors.

★★★(★) History Of An Artist

Pablo 2625702 2CD *Peterson; Irving Ashby, Herb Ellis, Barney Kessel, Joe Pass (g); Ray Brown, Sam Jones, George Mraz, Niels-Henning Orsted Pedersen (b); Bobby Durham, Louis Hayes (d).* 12/72–5/74.

This collects some of Oscar's earliest trio dates for Pablo, and the original double-LP of *History Of An Artist* served notice of what would amount to a fine comeback on record during the '70s. Some great music here.

★★★ The Trio

Original Jazz Classics OJC 992 *Peterson; Joe Pass (g); Niels-Henning Orsted Pedersen (b).* 73.

★★★ The Good Life

Original Jazz Classics OJC 627 *As above.* 73.

For some fans this is Peterson's best vintage and most effective partnership. *The Trio* concentrates largely on blues material, with a withers-wringing 'Secret Love' as a curtain-piece. On the other album, 'Wheatland' needs the rhythmic drive that Ed Thigpen brought to the tune on *Compact Jazz*; but by and large the drummerless trio is a setting that suits Peterson's Tatum-esque delivery. Only five tracks, and little sense of significant development on any of them as Peterson's technique becomes increasingly pleased with itself.

★★★ Jazz In Paris: Oscar Peterson And Stéphane Grappelli, Volume 1

Verve 013028 *Peterson; Stéphane Grappelli (vn); Niels-Henning Orsted Pedersen (b); Kenny Clarke (d).* 9/73.

★★★ Jazz In Paris: Oscar Peterson And Stéphane Grappelli, Volume 2

Verve 013030 *As above.* 9/73.

A brilliant partnership and a lovely set of standards that see Oscar and Stéphane gently spar their way through. There's nothing too demanding about these sides, but unless you're averse to the wheedling tone of Grappelli's violin, they're hugely entertaining, and a long 'My One And Only Love' and the lesser-known 'Flamingo' on the first volume and the unexpected 'Blues For Musidisc' on the second are must-have items for any serious Peterson collector.

★★★ Oscar Peterson In Russia

Pablo 2625711 2CD *Peterson; Niels-Henning Orsted Pedersen (b); Jake Hanna (d).* 11/74.

The real meat of this journey was the duos with NHOP. Their trip down Green Dolphin Street is a revelation, one of the partnership's genuinely shining moments. Hanna is a rather pushy, forceful drummer for this context, but he has his strengths and, with temperatures outside doubtless plummeting, his push through 'Take The "A" Train' and 'Do You Know What It Means To Miss New Orleans' must surely have been welcome. Oscar redresses the balance with lovely readings of 'Someone To Watch Over Me' (solo) and 'Georgia On My Mind' (trio).

★★★ Oscar Peterson & Dizzy Gillespie

Pablo 2310740 *Peterson; Dizzy Gillespie (t).* 11/74.

★★★(★) Oscar Peterson & Roy Eldridge

Original Jazz Classics OJC 727 *Peterson; Roy Eldridge (t).* 12/74.

★★★(★) Oscar Peterson & Harry Edison

Original Jazz Classics OJC 738 *Peterson; Harry 'Sweets' Edison (t).* 12/74.

★★★ Oscar Peterson & Clark Terry

Original Jazz Classics OJCCD 806 *Peterson; Clark Terry (t).* 5/75.

★★★ Jousts

Original Jazz Classics OJCCD 857 *As the four discs above, except add Jon Faddis (t).* 11/74–6/75.

This instrumentation goes all the way back to 1928, when Louis Armstrong and Earl Hines recorded 'Weather Bird'. There are, inevitably, hints of a later Bird in Gillespie's blues style, but there is also a slackness of conception similar to what overtook Armstrong in later years, and Peterson's overblown accompaniments don't help. The ballads are better, but only because they're prettier.

Eldridge pushes a little harder (and, incidentally, sounds prettier than Diz), and the slightly later session is on balance the more compelling. There is still a feeling of Buggins's turn and mix-and-match about a lot of these sessions, but the two players' artistry does show through. Peterson's switch to organ was a happy stroke and might have been usefully extended to the album as a whole, rather than to selected tracks. The closing 'Blues For Chu' is a small master-stroke.

Of the three, Sweets is closest in conception to Armstrong, and the opening 'Easy Living' reverberates back and forth across almost half a century of the music. There are some lovely things later on in the set as well: 'Willow Weep For Me', where Sweets squeezes low, throaty tones out of his trumpet, and 'The Man I Love', a straight, unabashed performance.

The Clark Terry sequence as a whole seems the drabbest of the bunch. There's surprisingly little feeling of communication between two men who must have worked together literally dozens of times – or perhaps that's the problem. Oscar breezes away delightedly at 'Makin' Whoopee', 'Satin Doll' and 'Slow Boat To China', but there's not much in the way of bonhomie from Clark, who's had better days in the studio and seems intent on shouting his partner down.

Jousts brings together additional material from all four sessions, and from a date with Dizzy's spiritual son, Jon Faddis, who'd certainly pass for J. B. Gillespie on his tracks. A good buy for anyone who wants to sample the sequence, or who simply doesn't want to shell out for the set; needless to say, genuine enthusiasts will have other reasons for wanting it.

★★★ The Giants

Original Jazz Classics OJCCD 898 *Peterson; Joe Pass (g); Ray Brown (b).* 12/74.

At the end of a fantastically busy spell for Oscar, he squeezed in this thoughtful trio set. Oscar's on organ for just two of the numbers, but the best of the playing comes on a stretched-out version of 'I'm Getting Sentimental Over You', where his touch and ability to select a telling phrase are almost uncanny. There's also an interesting version right at the end of the album of Quincy Jones's 'Eyes Of Love', which should have appeared more often in Oscar's bag.

★★★★ À La Salle Pleyel

Pablo 2625705 2CD *Peterson; Joe Pass (g).* 5/75.

Two brilliant solo sets, with both players on cracking form, followed by duo performances that must count as among the best these giants ever recorded. Peterson's playing on 'Tenderly' is exquisite and his shaping of an Ellington medley headed up by 'Take The "A" Train' is almost uncannily good. Pass responds in kind, but it's when they get together that the sparks really begin to fly. 'If' is astonishing, both players picking up on passing notes and constructing new ideas almost at quantum speed. 'Honeysuckle Rose' should be studied by anyone interested in jazz improvisation. The whole thing will be enjoyed by anyone who's ever been remotely moved by jazz.

★★★ The Oscar Peterson Big 6 At The Montreux Jazz Festival 1975

Original Jazz Classics OJCCD 931 *Peterson; Milt Jackson (vib); Toots Thielemans (hca); Joe Pass (g); Niels-Henning Orsted Pedersen (b); Louie Bellson (d).* 7/75.

Notable for the inclusion of Parker's 'Au Privave', a bebop classic that has been a favourite of the pianist's but which still sits rather awkwardly alongside Peterson's usual diet of blues and swing. In the event, it's an effective enough performance, though the logic of his solo is rather lost in the showers of notes he plays. Thielemans underlines how good an improviser he can be, but Pass is very muted.

★★★ Porgy And Bess

Original Jazz Classics OJC 829 *Peterson; Joe Pass (g).* 1/76.

Peterson's choice of clavichord for the *Porgy And Bess* session looked initially promising but ultimately suggests nothing more than a way of freshening up rather stale performances. It's perhaps the least-known of the keyboard family, covering between three and five octaves (Peterson seems to be using the larger model) and distinguished from the piano and harpsichord by the fact that the strings are struck (rather than plucked, as with the harpsichord) by metal tangents which can be left in contact with the string rather than rebounding, altering its distinctive vibrato. Peterson certainly hasn't mastered that aspect of the instrument and plays it with a pianist's 'clean' touch that loses him the delicious, bluesy wavers and bends it could have brought to these rather stolid Gershwin interpretations.

★★★ Montreux '77

Original Jazz Classics OJC 383 *Peterson; Ray Brown, Niels-Henning Orsted Pedersen (b).* 7/77.

★★★ Montreux '77

Original Jazz Classics OJC 378 *Peterson; Dizzy Gillespie, Clark Terry (t); Eddie 'Lockjaw' Davis (ts); Niels-Henning Orsted Pedersen (b); Bobby Durham (d).* 7/77.

The first of these is an intriguing two-bass experiment from the much-documented 1977 festival, where Peterson had become a recognized draw. Brown tends to take on some of the responsibilities of a guitarist, alternating his familiar 'walk' with clipped strums reminiscent of Herb Ellis's guitar and leaving the darker sonorities to the great Dane. The material, with the exception of 'There Is No Greater Love', is perhaps not ideally suited to the two string-players and they're often left with a rather subsidiary role. Peterson was just about blown out of sight by Tommy Flanagan's excellent performance earlier in the weekend, but he's generally in good if undemanding form. He can also be heard on other sets from the same event: with Roy

Eldridge (OJC 373), Eddie 'Lockjaw' Davis (OJC 384) and on an *All-Star Jam* (OJC 380); there are festival highlights on OJC 385.

***(*) The London Concert

Pablo 2620111 2CD *Peterson; John Heard (b); Louie Bellson (d).* n.d.

A delight to hear Peterson and the ebullient Bellson in this context and away from the crowded stages they occupied at festivals. Above all, and despite his occasional flash grandstanding, Bellson is a great accompanist, and for much of the time here he happily restricts himself to that role, just laying off the odd deadly fill and take that! riposte as the mood hits him. Heard is a quieter partner but, as always in a Peterson group, absolutely central to the sound. A great evening, marked by more fireworks than usual for this vintage.

*** The Paris Concert

Pablo 2620112 2CD *Peterson; Niels-Henning Orsted Pedersen (b); Joe Pass (g).* 10/78.

Again, much of the interest focuses on two Parker tracks, 'Donna Lee' and 'Ornithology', both of which receive the kind of scalping treatment meted out by the army barber at boot camp. There's a 'who's next?' feel to the succession of tracks that makes you wish someone had shouted out 'Excursion On A Wobbly Rail' or 'Three Blind Mice' ... *anything* to wrong-foot the man. Playing without drums, as he did a lot around this time, Peterson seems rhythmically yet more commanding, but he also opens up his phrasing quite noticeably, highlighting the stresses and accents.

***(*) Skol

Original Jazz Classics OJC 496 *Peterson; Stéphane Grappelli (vn); Joe Pass (g); Niels-Henning Orsted Pedersen (b); Mickey Roker (d).* 7/79.

Peterson as group player. He defers more than usual to his colleagues – 'Nuages' and 'Making Whoopee' have Grappelli's thumbprint on them, after all – and contributes to a surprisingly rounded performance. The music is still on the soft side, but Peterson is as unfailingly sensitive as an accompanist as he is as a leader, and his solo spots are all the more striking for being tightly marshalled. A good choice for anyone who prefers the pianist in smaller doses, or who enjoys Grappelli. The fiddler suffers broadly similar critical problems. A player of consummate skill and considerable improvisational gifts, he has been somewhat hijacked by television and has come (quite wrongly) to seem a middle-of-the-road entertainer rather than a 'legitimate' jazzman. There is still probably more thought and enterprise in just one Grappelli solo than in a whole raft of albums by Young Turk tenor-saxophone-players.

***(*) Digital At Montreux

Pablo 2308224 *Peterson; Niels-Henning Orsted Pedersen (b).* 7/79.

Very much a middle-market package for the hi-fi enthusiast who wants to watch the dials glow and twitch. This is a rather dead spell in Peterson's career, and listening to him negotiate 'Caravan' or 'Satin Doll' for the umpteenth time is a little like watching a snooker professional clear the table according to the book. One longs for a few near-misses. Collectors and dial-twitchers only.

***(*) The Personal Touch

Pablo 2312135 *Peterson; Clark Terry (t, flhn); Ed Bickert, Peter Leitch (g); Dave Young (b); Jerry Fuller (d); orchestra conducted by Rick Wilkins.* 1 & 2/80.

Rick Wilkins's orchestrations aren't as drowningly fulsome as one might have feared, and both Peterson and Clark Terry are forceful enough players to rise above them. All the same, it's hard to see how a fairly unenterprising set would have been much different for quintet alone. Peterson's brief switch to electric piano (listen to 'The World Is Waiting For The Sunrise' for a quick sample) underlines the instrument's limitations rather than the player's.

*** Live At The Northsea Jazz Festival

Pablo 2620115 *Peterson; Toots Thielemans (hca); Joe Pass (g); Niels-Henning Orsted Pedersen (b).* 7/80.

The sprawling Northsea Festival has some of the chaotic glamour of the old JATP packages. Though not a pianist who generally sounds good around horns, Peterson gives Thielemans a lot of space and respect, weaving counterlines round his plangent figures on 'Like Someone In Love' and 'Caravan' (a gorgeously exotic performance). It's a quieter, less dynamic set than many of the festival albums from the period (which suits Thielemans) but isn't particularly reflective. The Nat Cole references are well to the forefront if you care to look for them.

***(*) Nigerian Marketplace

Pablo 2308231 *Peterson; Niels-Henning Orsted Pedersen (b); Terry Clark (d).* 7/81.

The title-track has a vivid 'live from Lagos' bustle about it that carries on into 'Au Privave', by now established as Peterson's favourite Charlie Parker item. The middle of the programme is on much more familiar turf with 'Nancy', 'Misty' and, perhaps more surprisingly, Bill Evans's lovely 'Waltz For Debby'. Peterson hasn't shown a great deal of interest in Evans's book (and it's difficult to judge whether his occasional Hawes and Evans touches show a direct influence), but he handles this theme with characteristic amplitude and not too much depth. Newcomer Clark performs well if rather busily.

*** A Royal Wedding Suite

Original Jazz Classics OJCCD 971 *Peterson; strings.* 81.

Cynics have been known to ask if a 'Royal Divorce Suite' was ever written, which would be funny if the aftermath hadn't been so tragic. A great anglophile, Oscar obviously wrote this from the heart, but it's not one of his happier moments and apart from 'Lady Di's Waltz', which has surfaced subsequently, none of these themes has entered his repertoire. Reissued in 1998, possibly inspired by the death of the former Princess of Wales, it's a collectors' item only.

*** Freedom Song

Pablo 26401001 *Peterson; Joe Pass (g); Niels-Henning Orsted Pedersen (b); Martin Drew (d).* 2/82.

There are few places in the world where Peterson has not recorded, but there are no fans more vociferous in their support than the Japanese. These dates were recorded in Tokyo and they find him in cracking good form. 'Now's The Time' reinforces his attachment to bebop, and the medley 'Hymn To Freedom'/'The Fallen Warrior'/'Nigerian Marketplace' is one of his grandest conceptions. Reservations? Two. The sound is not all it might be, a little muffled and indistinct; and the band is not playing anything like as well as the leader's performance requires. Two cheers.

***** Two Of The Few**
Original Jazz Classics OJC 689 *Peterson; Milt Jackson (vib).* 1/83.

We are declared sceptics when it comes to piano/vibraphone duos, but this one is a winner from start to finish. Perhaps because the session was run down and recorded at short notice, there's not much originality in the material, which consists entirely of well-worn standards. The closing 'Here's Two Of The Few' is great, though, and worth the price on its own. CD certainly brings out the definition of both instruments, so perhaps we're slowly being converted.

****(*) A Tribute To My Friends**
Pablo 2310902 *Peterson; Joe Pass (g); Niels-Henning Orsted Pedersen (b); Martin Drew (d).* 11/83.

***** If You Could See Me Now**
Pablo 2310918 *As above.* 11/83.

The tribute album nods in the direction of Fats Domino, Dizzy Gillespie, Ella and others who've crossed the big man's path over the years. There's a slight air of the end-of-contract, A&R meeting about it: how do we find a new wrinkle? *If You Could See Me Now* includes 'Limehouse Blues' and the bassist's feature, 'On Danish Shore'. These are about the best things on offer, but it's a thin set altogether.

***** Live At The Barbican**
BBC 7001 *Peterson; Niels-Henning Orsted Pedersen (b); Martin Drew (d).* 84.

NHOP almost steals the show more than once on this excellent London live set, which was issued on CD more than a decade later. That isn't to say that Oscar isn't in fine form. His blending of 'Falling In Love With Love' and 'Rockin' In Rhythm' is done without missing a beat and his versions of 'Time After Time' and 'Satin Doll' are both exquisite. The sound is a little too precise, lacking in atmosphere for a live gig, but there are intelligent liner-notes and a valuable interview with OP, recorded by the BBC's Geoffrey Smith. Worth having for that alone.

****(*) Oscar Peterson Live!**
Pablo 2310940 *Peterson; Joe Pass (g); Dave Young (b); Martin Drew (d).* 11/86.

*****(*) Time After Time**
Pablo 2310947 *As above.* 11/86.

***** Oscar Peterson + Harry Edison + Eddie 'Cleanhead' Vinson**
Pablo 2310927 *As above, except add Harry 'Sweets' Edison (t); Eddie 'Cleanhead' Vinson (as).* 11/86.

The first of these related sessions consists largely of the deutero-classical 'Bach Suite', a more gainly and authentic pastiche than anything of Jacques Loussier's, but with an awful predictability about it as well. 'City Lights', 'Perdido' and 'Caravan' are tacked on at the end to keep the strict-constructionists happy. Better on harpsichord? *Time After Time* restores the balance considerably. An original 'Love Ballade' revives Peterson's reputation as a melodist, and the closing 'On The Trail' allays any doubts about failing stamina. The material with Edison and Vinson fails to live up to past encounters with the trumpeter, and there are odd occasions when Vinson seems to get in the way. It is, though, a hard session to fault on any more serious ground, and the 'Stuffy' and 'Satin Doll' work-outs are top class.

****(*) The Composer**
Pablo CD 2130 970 2 *Peterson; Joe Pass (g); Niels-Henning Orsted Pedersen, David Young (b); Martin Drew (d); orchestra.* 74–86.

Self-explanatory, but slightly beside the point. The two opening selections from *Royal Wedding Suite* are hardly Oscar's best work; indeed 'Lady Di's Waltz' makes the toes curl for the title alone. Better work follows, including the Allegro from *The Bach Suite*, 'Hogtown Blues' and 'Place St Henri' from *Oscar Peterson In Russia* and a couple of other tracks. Inessential.

***** Oscar Peterson Plays Duke Ellington**
Pablo 2310966 *As above.* 67–86.

Apart from the inclusion of 'The Lady Of The Lavender Mist', a real Ellington obscurity, the material here is quite predictable. Oscar's interest in Duke's music for piano was scarcely a surprise, and Pablo had plenty to trawl for this elegant compilation. The tracks also include items written by Strayhorn and Mercer but, given the quality of the playing and the authority with which Oscar approaches the Ellington songbook, no one is going to quibble about copyrights.

****** Piano Moods: The Very Best Of Oscar Peterson**
Verve 557462 2CD *Peterson; Milt Jackson (vib); Ray Brown, Sam Jones, Jiri Mraz (b); Bobby Durham, Gene Gammage, Louis Hayes, Ray Price, Ed Thigpen (d).*

An impeccable 33-track compilation, questionable only for the absence of anything with guitarists Ellis or Kessel, but good enough on its own terms to overcome any quibbles or cavils. Piano jazz of the very highest order. Strongly recommended, even if you have most of the constituent records.

*****(*) Live At The Blue Note**
Telarc CD 83304 *Peterson; Herb Ellis (g); Ray Brown (b); Bobby Durham (d).* 3/90.

***** Saturday Night At The Blue Note**
Telarc CD 83306 *As above.* 3/90.

***** At The Blue Note: Last Call**
Telarc CD 83314 *As above.* 3/90.

***** Encore At The Blue Note**
Telarc CD 83356 *As above.* 3/90.

Whatever stiffness has crept into Peterson's fingers over the last few years has served only to increase the feeling he injects into his playing. It's hard to relate 'Peace For South Africa' on the first volume to the torrents of sound he conjured up in his big-hall Pablo days. This is quieter, more intimate and more thoughtful, and the ballad medley at its centre shows genuine melodic inventiveness. A must for Peterson fans, and 'Honeysuckle Rose' offers a good – albeit second-gear – impression of the Tatum-derived technique which overlaid his earlier commitment to Nat Cole.

The second volume was recorded the following night. It's a more varied, less familiar programme, but the playing is pretty much by the numbers. The 'final' visit and the almost inevitable *Encore* are even more subdued and formal. The elegance of Peterson's segues begins to pall long before the end. Fans will value 'It Never Entered My Mind' on the last but one, but more casual purchasers might want to plump for the first volume and leave it at that, even if it means missing the *Encore* performance of 'I Wished On The Moon' which, though brief, is exquisite.

*** Side By Side

Telarc 83341 *Peterson; Itzhak Perlman (vn).* 94.

These jazz-meets-classical encounters hardly ever work, usually because many accomplished classical players couldn't swing even if you hanged them. Perlman, though, has always had a mischievous streak, even when the context is otherwise solemn, and on this *tête-à-tête* he brings his own catchy humour and bright musical intelligence to staples like 'Makin' Whoopee' and 'Mack The Knife'. Perhaps inevitably, it's most effective when Oscar is looking after the bottom end, but there's plenty to enjoy throughout.

***(*) The More I See You

Telarc CD 83370 *Peterson; Clark Terry (t, flhn); Benny Carter (as); Lorne Lofsky (g); Ray Brown (b); Lewis Nash (d).* 1/95.

Leaving aside the guitarist and the drummer, who are mere boys, the collective age here is 295. That's a lot of jazz experience to squeeze on to one disc. Peterson was still battling his way back to health and playing at this time, and the presence of even older men must have been some sort of stimulus to fold up his bed and play. There are some extraordinary moments, as when Terry duets with himself, trumpet and flugelhorn in opposite hands, in an episode from Ferde Grofé's *Grand Canyon Suite*, and the interplay between Peterson and Brown on 'In A Mellow Tone', but it's hard to make invidious comparisons. Lofsky is a young Canadian guitarist who has been generously sponsored by Oscar over the last few years. This was a summit conference and, while there is a certain amount of polite jockeying (these are not small egos on display), most of it is generously good-natured and no one can question the veracity of the music played. That it should have followed so swiftly on the heels of serious illness just makes it more special.

*** An Oscar Peterson Christmas

Telarc 33372 *Peterson; Jack Schantz (flhn); Dave Samuels (vib); Lorne Lofsky (b); Dave Young (b); Jerry Fuller (d).* 1–7/95.

Tommy Smith's too thin, Wynton Marsalis too prickly. White beard notwithstanding, no jazz musician is closer to the physical form and smiling character of St Nicholas than Oscar Peterson. Christmas discs are always a bit of an enigma and something of an embarrassment. Do you only play them once a year, or do you stick them on ironically during a heatwave? Oscar's is predictably genial and, equally predictable, brilliantly done. He was still in convalescence after suffering that alarming stroke and the pace and articulation aren't as demanding as they once were, but that is not to say that these 14 holiday tunes aren't completely musical and entertaining. The orchestral accompaniment isn't too intrusive and the band is absolutely up to the mark, with some nice horn features and a guest spot by vibist Samuels. Our favourite? the relatively little known 'What Child Is This?'

*** Marian McPartland's Piano Jazz

The Jazz Alliance 12033 *Peterson; Marian McPartland (p, v).*

First released in 1996, this is a wonderful souvenir of Oscar's appearance on fellow pianist McPartland's insightful NPR series, where she spoke to fellow-practitioners about the piano's role in jazz. Divided between conversation and performance, it's not a record that you'd want to listen to very frequently, but it's full of insights into Peterson's technique and full of warmth and humour.

***(*) Oscar Peterson Meets Roy Hargrove And Ralph Moore

Telarc 83399 *Peterson; Roy Hargrove (t); Ralph Moore (ts); Niels-Henning Orsted Pedersen (b); Lewis Nash (d).* 96.

Moore has previously guested as 'fourth leg' to the Ray Brown trio and, though Telarc artist Brown isn't present on this occasion (we gather he was touring), it's a further chance to hear Peterson once again in the company of the big Viking who anchored his band for so many years. The two horn men occupy a good deal of the foreground, perhaps still compensating a little for Oscar's post-stroke change of pace. Hargrove isn't articulating at his best and a couple of times on 'My Foolish Heart' drifts perilously close to playing flat. 'Here's That Rainy Day' conjures up an extraordinary range of ghosts, from Miles to Bill Evans, and Oscar seems to quote someone's idea, some half-remembered phrase, in the middle of his statement. A lovely album.

***(*) Oscar & Benny

Telarc 83406 *Peterson; Benny Green (p); Ray Brown (b); Greg Hutchinson (d).* 97.

Old cats teach young cats how it's done. This was, in effect, Oscar guesting with the current Ray Brown trio, and the two seniors steal the show in almost every department. There's never been any doubt that Benny Green learned a good deal from Peterson (and more directly from Peterson than from *his* sources, as is often suggested) and here there are moments when you might almost be listening to overdubs of the old man. Brown's huge, emphatic tone and crisp high-note runs are a perfect complement and the rhythmic profile is so full that there isn't much for Hutchinson, one of the best young mainstreamers on the scene at the moment, to do with his time, other than keep it. 'Scrapple From The Apple' is the stand-out track, confirming that Oscar is back from his brush with the Reaper and playing as well as ever. That doesn't necessarily mean as fast or as fluently, but with bags of feeling, which was the only question mark over him in the past.

*** A Tribute To Oscar Peterson: Live At Town Hall

Telarc 83401 2CD *Peterson; Clark Terry (t, v); Stanley Turrentine (ts); Benny Green (p); Milt Jackson (vib); Herb Ellis (g); Ray Brown, Niels-Henning Orsted Pedersen (b); Greg Hutchinson (d); Shirley Horn, Manhattan Transfer (v).* 97.

More interesting as an event than as music. This is one of those feel-good moments it would be churlish to quibble over. Few people in the business are regarded with such genuine affection as Oscar Peterson, and it is no surprise that so many were prepared to turn out and pay tribute in this way. The unlikely inclusion is Turrentine, but he turns out to be one of the stars of the show, alongside the two bassists and the redoubtable Shirley Horn, who gets better every time she opens her mouth.

*** Oscar In Paris

Telarc 83414 2CD *Peterson; Lorne Lofsky (g); Niels-Henning Orsted Pedersen (b); Martin Drew (d).* 97.

Back to business. Recorded live at the Salle Pleyel, on a piano that classical players purr over. Good to hear the effortlessly swinging Martin Drew bring his very distinctive touch to the group. He and NHOP have always performed well together and with the addition of an in-form Lofsky, whose career seems to be taking off, they create a well-balanced group performance. The emphasis is still on ensembles and there are a couple of points when Oscar sounds tired and lacklustre. Generally, though, he is playing with precision and formidable hand-speed. We'd question that this Telarc was worth a double CD, but with a treasure like Peterson on your hands you'd probably want to release his warm-ups as well.

*****(*) A Summer Night In Munich**
Telarc 83450 *Peterson; Ulf Wakenius (g); Niels-Henning Orsted Pedersen (b); Martin Drew (d).* 7/98.

Oscar rather tastelessly described this as his 'NATO Quartet'. The actual performances are a good deal more harmonious than that antagonistic title suggests and the latter-day versions of things like 'Nigerian Marketplace', 'Hymn To Freedom' and 'When Summer Comes' are very good. Wakenius fills the shoes of Ellis and Kessel very well indeed, and it would have been interesting to hear piano and guitar duet more spaciously. Drummer Martin Drew takes a well-earned solo on the closing 'Sushi'.

*****(*) The Very Tall Band Live At The Blue Note**
Telarc 83443 *Peterson; Milt Jackson (vib); Ray Brown (b); Karriem Riggins (d).* 11/98.

Almost four decades after he recorded *Very Tall*, Oscar, Milt and Ray (and the title could have referred to the bassist only ironically) met up again for an old pals night at the Blue Note, which was becoming Oscar's second home. Peterson's technique is still far from being as florid and fiery-paced as it used to be, but he retains his ability to communicate a melody and to invest tunes as various as 'I Remember Clifford' and 'Nature Boy' with his unmistakable character. As if making up for his shorter stature, Brown is the hero of the session, claiming a wonderful bass solo medley which doesn't pall at seven and a half minutes and playing a wonderful introduction to 'Blues For Jr'. Milt Jackson's health was causing serious concern at the time and he sounds unusually inward and clenched, rarely cutting loose with those long, rippling, piano-like lines. Drummer Karriem Riggins comes on for the closing 'Caravan' and brings a thoroughly satisfying record to an appropriate climax. Life in the old dog(s) yet.

***** Trail Of Dreams – A Canadian Suite**
Telarc 83500 *Peterson; Ulf Wakenius (g); Niels-Henning Orsted Pedersen (b); Martin Drew (b); Michel Legrand (strings).* 4/00.

Not to be confused with the 1964 small group record *Canadiana Suite*, on which such Peterson classics as 'Wheatland' and 'Hogtown Blues' were first heard. This is a sumptuous orchestral work designed to evoke his native land in rather more grandiose terms. The music is such that Peterson has little opportunity to improvise at any length, leaving much of the action to Michel Legrand's string orchestra. One the other hand, everything both Peterson and Legrand do tends to swing and this is unmistakably a jazz record. The closing hymn to Canada is very moving and rounds off a satisfying musical experience. A pity nobody has thought to reissue *Canadiana Suite* in the West, though it is occasionally available as a Japanese import.

***** Oscar's Ballads**
Telarc 83504 *As for Live At The Blue Note, A Tribute To Oscar Peterson, A Summer Night In Munich, Meets Ralph Moore And Roy Hargrove, Trail Of Dreams – A Canadian Suite.* 90–00.

A decade's worth of Peterson at his most expressive. Starting off with 'Harcourt Nights' from *Trail Of Dreams* seems a funny and potentially off-putting tack, given the wonderful jazz ballads that come along later in the set and earlier in his discography, but track order can always be dealt with at home. The main question is: with nothing new to sweeten the deal, who is going to want a rehash of such recent material? For the record, 'When Summer Comes' and 'Love Ballade' from *A Summer Night In Munich* and 'Ecstasy' from the Hargrove and Moore encounter are well worth sampling if you haven't come across them before.

***** A Jazz Odyssey**
Verve 589 780 2 *Peterson; Harry 'Sweets' Edison, Roy Eldridge, Dizzy Gillespie, Charlie Shavers, Clark Terry (t); Sonny Stitt (as); Stan Getz, Coleman Hawkins, Flip Phillips, Lester Young (ts); Herb Ellis, Barney Kessel (g); Ray Brown, Major Holley, Sam Jones (b); Bobby Durham, Louis Hayes, Gus Johnson, Jo Jones, Buddy Rich, Max Roach, Alvin Stoller, Ed Thigpen (d); Ella Fitzgerald, Billie Holiday (v).* 50–70.

In 2002, Oscar published his autobiography *A Jazz Odyssey*. This is the aural equivalent, a fairly predictable but none the less entertaining trawl through the Verve catalogue. Another one. This has the advantage of featuring him as accompanist to some of the jazz greats, as the personnel listing reveals. Most serious collectors will have the material already, but if you've only come at Oscar recently or if you were moved by the book, this takes you some of the way along his long professional road.

Ralph Peterson (born 1962)

DRUMS, TRUMPET

Peterson emerged as one of the busiest and most inventive drummers on the New York scene of the '80s. He made several records for Blue Note as a leader, all currently out of print, and has since gone on to lead various editions of his group, The Fo'tet.

***** The Reclamation Project**
Evidence 22113-2 *Peterson; Steve Wilson (ss); Bryan Carrott (vib); Belden Bullock (b).* 11/94.

*****(*) The Fo'tet Plays Monk**
Evidence 22174-2 *As above.* 11–12/95.

Peterson is a very fine drummer, wonderful to hear live, and challenging and provocative as a leader. While peripherally associated with the black hard bop of the '80s, he is more often thought of as a musician who can move from inside to out in New York's avant-garde company. A fireball of energy on any recording, he isn't so much noisy as determined to make something happen from the kit at every moment in the music.

There are a bundle of earlier Blue Note albums in the deletions file, but Peterson has since started recording for Evidence with the group he calls The Fo'tet. *Reclamation Project* takes the sombre theme of recovery from substance abuse and turns it into a thematic thread. Peterson is back in his more demanding groove here, delivering tunes in 9/8 and 14/8, setting

Carrott and Wilson hugely difficult rhythmic tasks as improvisers – and somehow making it click. His innate sense of swing sees him through even the most potentially awkward situations. That said, this is a dark and sometimes introverted record, and some may find it hard to find a way inside.

The Fo'tet Plays Monk is a more prosaic project, but Peterson was clearly keen to take this out of the normal tribute furrow. Of the 11 tunes, only 'Epistrophy' and 'Well You Needn't' are obvious. Songo and second-line rhythms add some multicultural spice, and the sheer sizzle of the playing is exciting: Wilson's serpentine playing is worth a close listen, but the star improviser is Carrott, who seems as imaginatively at home in these settings as Milt Jackson was with Monk himself. 'Played Twice', 'Light Blue' and 'Brilliant Corners' are peerless. Only the two originals, one apiece by the leader and Carrott, seem less than absorbing.

*****(*) Back To Stay**
Sirocco SLJ 1006 *Peterson; Ralph Bowen (ss); Michael Brecker (ts); Bryan Carrott (vib, mar); Belden Bullock (b). 5–6/99.*

A new edition of the band (Brecker plays only a cameo role), but the leader's energy remains unstinting, the tunes are full of detail, and Carrott, by now almost as important to this group as Peterson, blends solo and ensemble roles with unassuming panache. The instrumentation continues to offer a strikingly different sonic palette, and the approach to repertory pieces such as 'Soul Eyes' and 'Miles' Mode' is similarly unclichéd.

***** Triangular 2**
Sirocco SJL 1009 *Peterson; David Kikoski (p); Gerald Cannon (b). 12/99.*

*****(*) The Art Of War**
Criss Cross 1206 *Peterson; Jeremy Pelt (t, flhn); Jimmy Greene (ss, ts); Orrin Evans (p); Eric Revis (b). 1/01.*

*****(*) Subliminal Seduction**
Criss Cross 1225 *As above. 12/01.*

If you're not prepared to play your socks off when Peterson's on the stand, you'll be simply blown away. That point comes across as strongly as ever on these three releases. Kikoski's not a player to be intimidated and he's a pianist who manages to impose a kind of calm even in the midst of heated music: on the slightly reharmonized 'Night And Day' he manages to keep the song sounding songful, even while the drums are pushing, shoving and goading all the way. Cannon is an unobtrusive presence whose lines look for simplicity. There are times when you want to hear Peterson cool off and just swing a little less ingeniously. Not the greatest set these men have been involved with, but plenty to enjoy.

The Art Of War offers a more straightforward group than *The Fo'tet* and the programme alternates fast, hard-hitting swingers and more temperate pieces, though as ever the drummer stokes things up throughout. It helps that he has soloists as exciting as Pelt and Greene out front. Not everything they play comes off, but they don't mind being impolite and both men get off some daredevil moves. Evans, as he is on his own records, is a creative and dynamic fulcrum. Hot and imposing music.

They pick up exactly where they left off with *Subliminal Seduction*. Pelt is the man to follow at fast tempos, but Greene outdoes him at the steadier pace of 'Tears I Cannot Hide', and 'I Only Miss Her When I Think Of Her' is tenor balladry of a high order.

Le Petit Jazzband De Mr Morel

GROUP

A band of French revivalists led by Jean-Pierre Morel.

*****(*) Farewell Blues**
Stomp Off CD1343 *Jean-Pierre Morel (c); Alain Marquet (cl); Daniel Huck (ss, as, v); Michel Bescont (ts); Bernard Thévin (p); François Fournet (bj); Gérard Gervois (tba). 3/97.*

***** Delta Bound**
Stomp Off CD1344 *As above, except add Gabriel Conesa (tb). 3–10/98.*

*****(*) Cafe Capers**
Stomp Off CD 1389 *As above, except add Jean-François Bonnel (cl), Nicolas Montier (as, ts); Jacques Schneck (p), Nicolas Peslier (bj). 9/00–6/02.*

The group is actually a reassembling of a band named Charquet & Co which Morel had run in Paris in the early '80s. They're expert revivalists, perfectly at home in idiomatic '20s-style playing but with sufficient personality to make the music swing to their own beats. *Farewell Blues* is a very rare item in the Stomp Off catalogue since it's a reissue of a record from another label, in this case Morel's own operation. A smart mix of familiar material such as Ellington's 'Stevedore Stomp' and 'Shout 'Em Aunt Tillie' with more obscure pieces, the record is tight, hot and graceful in turn. Each of the players makes a strong contribution, but we might single out the superbly heated playing of tenor saxophonist Bescont, who sounds like himself without moving even a step beyond the saxophone language of the '20s. Tied to the beat but rocking with it, this is a very enjoyable set.

We don't find the follow-up, *Delta Bound*, quite so good, though it's not easy to say why: the band is almost the same (trombonist Conesa substitutes for Huck on a few tracks) and the material is of the same stripe. This time, though, some of the ensembles seem a little congested, and in at least one case – Morton's 'Grandpa's Spells' – the performance doesn't do the best justice to the subject-matter. But they're back to their best for *Cafe Capers*. Recorded at seven different sessions, with various guests dropping in and out, the programme is expertly chosen and paced, and there are some beautiful rarities for period connoisseurs to savour – the Dixie Rhythm Kings' 'Congo Love Song' and Joplin's 'Fig Leaf Rag' among them. Splendidly entertaining.

Umberto Petrin

PIANO

Contemporary Italian pianist, in the post-bop idiom but brushing up against the avant-garde.

***** Ooze**
Splasc(h) 384-2 *Petrin; Guido Mazzon (t); Tiziano Tononi (d). 4–5/92.*

Petrin has taken a long, hard look at jazz-piano history and synthesized a very idiosyncratic method. Many of these 15 tracks are miniatures, several last only a minute or two, but the opening treatment of Ornette Coleman's 'Street Woman' – which sounds like Earl Hines playing a Coleman tune – or the bleak, ghostly farewell of Donald Ayler's 'Our Prayer', with Mazzon making a guest appearance, display real understated authority. Though there are avant-garde flourishes here and there, Petrin has more conservative manners and, in reflective, almost rhapsodic pieces such as 'Mesty' or the slow but incisive look at 'Round Midnight', he approaches the serene radicalism of Paul Bley. Tononi adds very spare percussion parts to four tracks. The record has a disjointed and sometimes half-realized feel, but how many pianists making their debut would offer such an uncompromising programme?

*****(*) Wirrwarr**
Splasc(h) 481-2 *Petrin; Giancarlo Schiaffini (tb); Daniele Patumi (b); Tiziano Tononi (d).* 2/96.

*****(*) Monk's World**
Splasc(h) 619-2 *Petrin (p solo).* 3/97.

Petrin's progress is fascinating to hear. *Wirrwarr* is a programme of originals, aside from two surprising choices of Coltrane tunes – 'Ogunde' and 'After The Rain'. The long title-track is a fiercely argued creation, pianist and drummer engaging in a multi-layered dialogue over a steadying bass vamp. Schiaffini makes a cameo appearance on two tracks only, with 'Contiene Une Linea Di Lunghezza Infinita' about as far out as Petrin will ever go. If he is following the Varèsean doctrine of 'intelligent structures of sound moving freely in space', as the sleeve-note suggests, they remain sometimes hard to fathom. Which may be why, anchored by the familiarity of the tunes, his Monk recital stands out as his most clearly satisfying record. His own tune, 'Inscape', reappears from *Wirrwarr* along with two other originals, but otherwise these are gentle but inquiring treatments of several of the less frequently encountered themes from the Monk repertory: 'Brilliant Corners', 'Introspection', 'Green Chimneys', played to elicit not so much the quirks in Monk's music as its underlying, almost shy embrace of the ballad form.

*****(*) Voir Loin**
Splasc(h) 832-2 *Petrin; Assif Tsahar (ts, bcl); Giovanni Maier (b); Roberto Dani (d); Milo De Angelis (v).* 4/01.

Although Petrin's music continues to keep hold of an inscrutable side, this is a very impressive set. Some may find his ingenuities a little exasperating, with one surprise following another, but much of this is very lyrical music: sample 'Nervosa Evidenza, Pietre, Iridi, Carver', most of which revolves around a single melodic lick, yet enters into all sorts of tangential complexities too. His treatment of Monk's 'Evidence', despatched in 70 seconds, is the most radical since the stylings of *Gaslini Plays Monk*, and jazz history is further reshaped in the stark recasting of Ornette Coleman's 'Lorraine'. And perhaps it is just as well that 'As The Doors Swing Open, Crack Or Slam' is followed by 'Please, Relax ... '. Tsahar appears as if out of nowhere on two tracks. Remarkable.

***** Reuniao**
Splasc(h) 846-2 *Petrin; Pedrino Figueiredo (ss, f); Renato Borghetti (acc); Daniel Sà (g); Susie Georgiadis (v).* 9/01.

Petrin shares top billing here with Borghetti, and with no rhythm section, Figueiredo adding sweetly melancholy soprano and flute, and material drawn from largely non-jazz sources, this is the pianist's gentlest and most accommodating record. Georgiadis sings on one track. Some moments of darkness, but this is more music to evoke an unspecific nostalgia – often very pretty, although an interlude away from Petrin's challenging agenda.

Michel Petrucciani (1962–99)

PIANO

Born in Montpellier, he played in his father's band and began recording after moving to Paris, aged 17. Moved to the USA in 1982 and recorded for Blue Note, later for Dreyfus. A diminutive man handicapped by an obscure bone disease, he triumphed over any disability and became one of the most popular of concert performers, playing in a romantic post-bop style.

*****(*) Days Of Wine And Roses**
Owl 548288-2 2CD *Petrucciani; Lee Konitz (as); Robin McClure (b); Jean-François Jenny-Clark (b); Aldo Romano (d).* 4/81–1/85.

There's a freshness and quicksilver virtuosity about Michel Petrucciani's early records which is entirely captivating, and they still sound terrific: a shame that his Concord discs have gone. While he is an adoring admirer of Bill Evans – 'Call me Bill,' he once suggested to Jim Hall, who demurred – his extrovert attack places Evans's harmonic profundity in a setting that will energize listeners who find Evans too slow and quiet to respond to. Petrucciani was already a formidable talent when he began recording and, while some of these discs have been criticized for being the work of a pasticheur, that seems a curmudgeonly verdict on someone who enjoys the keyboard so much.

He made six albums for the independent Owl Label (now since acquired by the Universal Group) and *Days Of Wine And Roses* compiles a double-CD from this material. These sessions feel like his most European music; originals such as 'Eugenia' and 'Mike Pee' combine his brightness of touch with a more reflective feel in which the overall choice of tracks trades heavily. A contrast to the sometimes forced ebullience of his later music.

***** Pianism**
Blue Note 746295-2 *Petrucciani; Palle Danielsson (b); Eliot Zigmund (d).* 12/85.

*****(*) Power Of Three**
Blue Note 846427-2 *Petrucciani; Wayne Shorter (ss, ts); Jim Hall (g).* 7/86.

***** Michel Plays Petrucciani**
Blue Note 848679-2 *Petrucciani; John Abercrombie (g); Gary Peacock, Eddie Gomez (b); Roy Haynes, Al Foster (d); Steve Thornton (perc).* 9–12/87.

Petrucciani's first three albums for Blue Note provided a variety of challenges. *Pianism* is another excellent batch of six work-outs by the trio who made the earlier live album (the now deleted *Live At The Village Vanguard*), and if Zigmund and Danielsson sometimes sound a little underwhelming, that's partly due to the leader's brimming improvisations. *Power Of Three* is a slightly fragmented but absorbing concert meeting of three masters, skittish on 'Bimini' and solemnly appealing on 'In A Sentimental Mood'.

Plays Petrucciani is an all-original set which lines the pianist up against two magisterial rhythm sections, with Abercrombie adding some spruce counterpoint to two pieces. The smart hooks of 'She Did It Again' suggest that the pianist would have had a good living as a pop writer if he had decided to quit the piano, but the more considered pieces show no drop in imagination, even if some of the themes seem to be curtailed before the improvisations really start moving.

***** Live**

Blue Note 780589-2 *Petrucciani; Adam Holzman (ky); Steve Logan (b); Victor Jones (d); Abdou M'Boup (perc).* 11/91.

***** Promenade With Duke**

Blue Note 780590-2 *Petrucciani (p solo).* n.d.

***** Marvellous**

Dreyfus FDM 36564-2 *Petrucciani; Dave Holland (b); Tony Williams (d); Graffiti String Quartet. n.d.*

The 1991 live album documents Petrucciani's 'fusion' band – not really any kind of jazz-rock, more a sitting of his famous virtuosity inside stiffer beats, with the dubious gratification of Holzman's synthesizer colourings. 'Miles Davis Licks' opens with boogie figures, then turns into a clever steal of some of the later Davis clichés. The sound of the band feels more dated than the rest of Michel's music, and the best moments come when the others stay as far in the background as possible, as in the elegant reading of 'Estate'.

Michel's promenade is more with Strayhorn and Petrucciani than with Ellington. Beautifully played and recorded, but it's rather sombre after the elated feel of his earlier sessions. Although some of his other Blue Note albums have disappeared, there is a French edition which boxes all seven of them together, but availability is somewhat limited.

Marvellous matches him with the formidable team of Holland and Williams, who play up the music's dramatic qualities to the hilt: a graceful tune like the 3/4 'Even Mice Dance' gets thumped open by Williams's awesome drumming. The pianist revels in the situation, though, and produces some of his most joyful playing. Yet it hardly squares with the string quartet parts, arranged by Petrucciani but more of a distraction than an integral part of such fierce playing.

*****(*) Au Théâtre Des Champs-Élysées**

Dreyfus FDM 36570-2 2CD *Petrucciani (p solo).* 11/94.

The opening 'Medley Of My Favourite Songs' might be a quintessential Petrucciani performance, 40 unbroken minutes of a piano master in full flow, lightning flashes of humour illuminating an otherwise seamless sequence. Maybe he never quite recaptured the effortless excitement of the early discs, and to that extent the energy of his playing is mitigated somewhat by his sense of proportion; but there's a great deal to enjoy across these two discs: a lovely, thoughtful 'Night Sun In Blois', a finger-busting Monk medley, and a beautifully distilled 'Besame Mucho' to close on.

***** Both Worlds**

Dreyfus FDM 36590-2 *Petrucciani; Flavio Boltro (t); Bob Brookmeyer (vtb); Stefano Di Battista (ts, ss); Anthony Jackson (b); Steve Gadd (d).* 96.

Almost a complete departure from his other work, this rather mysteriously seemed to set out to tame Petrucciani by placing him squarely in a band format, where he flourishes only intermittently as a soloist, and even then without his usual *brio.* He wrote all nine tunes but the arrangements are all Brookmeyer's, who brings his trademark quirks to a nevertheless very interesting line-up. The soloists are all strong enough, and there's a particularly appealing piano–soprano duet on 'Petite Louise', yet this could all use a shot of Michel letting go.

*****(*) Concerts Inédits**

Dreyfus FDM 36607-2 3CD *Petrucciani; Niels-Henning Orsted Pedersen, Louis Petrucciani (b); Lenny White (d).* 7/93–8/94.

Petrucciani's passing robbed jazz of one of its most charismatic spirits, especially in performance, and these sets are reminders of how much an audience would respond to him. The three-disc set offers him in solo, duo and trio settings: it's somewhat patchy, since the solo disc has a rather hard and unattractive piano sound, and the trio set (with Louis Petrucciani and White, cut at a Japanese concert) doesn't entirely benefit from the drummer's energies. But the duo record with NHOP is a delight, two virtuosos at the top of their game without overpowering the listeners with how much they can play.

CORE COLLECTION

****** Solo Live**

Dreyfus FDM 36597-2 *Petrucciani (p solo).* 2/97.

***Solo Live* is a marvellous Frankfurt concert recording. Michel warms up with a sequence of shorter pieces before stretching out on 'Trilogy In Blois' and 'Caravan'. He was always rethinking material: the 'Besame Mucho' here is entirely different from the treatment on *Concerts Inédits.* The final 'She Did It Again'/'Take The "A" Train' medley is showstopping, but each note seems to matter as part of the flow. This great communicator will be sorely missed.**

John Petters

DRUMS, VOCAL

Essex-based drummer working in the traditional idiom.

***** Mixed Salad**

Jazzology JCD-176 *Petters; Ben Cohen (t); Len Baldwin (tb); Wally Fawkes (cl, ss); Martin Litton (p); Paul Sealey (g); Annie Hawkins (b).* 11/85–7/86.

****(*) Boogie Woogie And All That Jazz**

Rose RRCD003 *Petters; Neville Dickie (p); Mickey Ashman (b).* 7/93.

***** Stompin' At The Savoy**

Rose RRCD 1025 *Petters; Trevor Whiting (cl); Nick Dawson (p).* 6/01.

****(*) Bing – The Road To Rhythm And Romance**

Rose RRCD 1028 *Peters; Trevor Whiting, James Evans (cl, ts, as); Martin Litton (p); John Day (b).* 9/02.

***** Tailgate Ramble – A Salute To Kid Ory**

Rose RRCD 1029 *Petters; Cuff Billett (t, v); Mike Pointon (tb); James Evans (cl, ts); Martin Litton (p); Tim Phillips (g); Keith Donald (b).* 9/03.

****(*) Swinging Down Memory Lane 2**

Rose RRCD 1030 *Petters; James Evans (cl, ts); Nick Dawson (p, v); Keith Donald (b); Val Wiseman (v).* 10/03.

There's nothing very 'authentic' about these records, but how much authenticity can a drummer from Harlow give to traditional jazz? In fact Petters brings a great sense of fun to these sessions, and it's disappointing that the earlier discs should be let down by their circumstances. The Jazzology date features some memorable playing on both 'Shim-Me-Sha-Wabble' and 'Out Of The Galleon', with the veteran Cohen sounding wonderfully lyrical, and Fawkes and Baldwin playing their part. The music never seems to hit quite the same high after those two tracks, and Litton's 'Wolverine Blues' is perfunctory; but the music is excellent trad, and it's a pity that the tinny sound and poor balance detract. *Boogie Woogie And All That Jazz* is a session of rag, boogie and novelty piano, in which Dickie does all the playing and Ashman and Petters keep straight, simple time. Some of it sounds more like B Bumble and the Stingers than James P. Johnson, and the tunes are often ones that many will never want to hear again, but it's righteous. Recorded in Eastleigh.

For his next, Petters went to the Goodman book, and turned in as likeable a homage to BG's trio music as one could wish for. Whiting and Dawson are hardly on the level of Goodman and Wilson, but Petters himself puts in all his best Krupa licks, and the music has plenty to enjoy. Petters says he was switched on to jazz by watching an old Bing movie, so his tribute album is a fair cop – he doesn't sound much like him, and the music's all right, but it's a bit like the afternoon shift on the old Light Programme. The Ory Tribute CD is very good though, perhaps the pick of all these records. The band don't do anything that hasn't been done as well by many another traditional outfit, but Billett and Pointon get the feel just right and the music goes with a proper kind of swing.

Swinging Down Memory Lane 2 is, unfortunately, drifting back to the middle of the track again. Val Wiseman's good, but Nick Dawson might think about sticking to piano.

Oscar Pettiford (1922–60)

BASS, CELLO

Like Charlie Haden's, Pettiford's playing career began in a family orchestra, under the tutelage of his father, Harry 'Doc' Pettiford. As with his contemporary, Charles Mingus (who was also of mixed blood), there was an undercurrent of anger and frustration. Pettiford's wonderfully propulsive bass-playing marks a middle point between Mingus and Jimmy Blanton. Had he lived longer, he might now be acknowledged the more influential player, but he didn't live to see 40 and spent his last years as a European exile.

*** The New Oscar Pettiford Sextet

Original Jazz Classics OJCCD 1926 2 *Pettiford; Red Rodney (t); Earl Swope (tb); Julius Watkins (frhn); Al Cohn, Phil Urso (ts); Serge Chaloff (bs); Walter Bishop, Barbara Carroll, Jan Johansson (p); Terry Gibbs, Louis Hjulmand (vib); Charles Mingus (b); Denzil Best, Percy Brice (d).* 3/49–12/53.

It may seem faint or even sarcastic praise to say that these 1953 recordings mark the high-water mark of the cello as a jazz instrument, but not so. Pettiford's facility on the instrument is unparalleled, even by such gifted doublers as Ron Carter, and the freedom and fluency of his solo line on 'Pendulum At Falcon's Lair' is genuinely exhilarating. Oscar's placing of notes, his unfailing harmonic awareness and sheer musicality will win over all but the hardest-hearted sceptics. Oscar switches to bass for the lovely 'Tamalpais Love Song', a stately and rather mysterious composition on which what would have been the cello part is taken by french horn. 'Low And Behold' and the boppish 'Jack The Fieldstalker' are both virtuosic displays, but the album is leavened by a bright and pungent version of Quincy Jones's 'Stockholm Sweet'nin''. Two of the tracks feature Louis Hjulmand on vibes and Jan Johansson on piano; Hjulmand's originals, 'Fru Buel' and 'I Succumb To Temptation', are not the strongest things on the record and were excluded from the original Debut Records ten-inch release. The CD also includes four tracks recorded in 1949 under the leadership of Serge Chaloff and arranged by Shorty Rogers. Slim pickings at the moment for this significant musician, whose work as a sideman will be found in many other entries: his ABC-Paramount albums of the later '50s could do with CD revival.

Barre Phillips (born 1934)

DOUBLE BASS, ELECTRONICS

Inspired by Ornette Coleman, the young San Franciscan moved east in 1962, and six years later he recorded the first-ever solo-bass jazz record, Journal Violone, a discipline which has been a staple of his work ever since.

**** Mountainscapes

ECM 843167-2 *Phillips; John Surman (bs, ss, bcl, syn); John Abercrombie (g); Dieter Feichtener (syn); Stu Martin (d).* 3/76.

**** Three Day Moon

ECM 847326-2 *Phillips; Terje Rypdal (g, g syn, org); Dieter Feichtener (syn); Trilok Gurtu (perc).* 3/78.

*** Journal Violone II

ECM 847328-2 *Phillips; John Surman (ss, bs, bcl, syn); Aina Kemanis (v).* 6/79.

***(*) Camouflage

Victo 08 *Phillips (solo).* 5/89.

*** Aquarian Rain

ECM 511513-2 *Phillips; Alain Joule (perc).* 5/91.

***(*) Uzu

PSF CD 75 *Phillips; Yoshizawa Motoharu (b).* 96.

Phillips's first album of solo bass improvisations was originally intended as material for an electronic score, but composer Max Schubel thought the bass parts stood more than adequately on their own. Nearly 25 years later, Phillips produced an album which does make significant use of electronic processing of instrumental performance. The effect suggests that Schubel's instincts were sound, for *Aquarian Rain* is the most diffuse and least focused album the bassist has released. Phillips's own description of the process of 'collective composition', by which tapes were sent back and forth between his French home in Puget-Ville and the Studio Grame in Lyon where Jean-François Estager and James Giroudon worked the filters and gates, may have yielded exemplary music for live performance (a suite called 'Brick On Brick' was created, incorporating pieces like 'Inbetween I And E' and 'Promenade De Mémoire'), but it sounds rather stilted and contrived when digitalized and fixed. Enthusiasts for the bassist's work will find much of value but, compared to the duos with Guy, these interchanges with percussionist Joule lack even that tiny spark of electricity which rescues processed improvisation of this sort from becoming acoustic set-dressing.

It's galling to note that Phillips's very best record is *still* out of the ECM catalogue. The solo *Call Me When You Get There* from 1983, with its lyrical journeyings and unfussy philosophical musings, covers similar musical territory to the much earlier but almost equally fine *Mountainscapes*, a suite of subliminally interrelated pieces which demonstrate the astonishing transformations visited on basic musical perspectives by very slight changes in the angle of vision. Almost all of Phillips's output operates in that way. Whatever is being hidden on the solo *Camouflage*, it can scarcely be the artist himself. Recorded in almost disturbing close-up (an effect necessarily heightened by CD reproduction), one can almost hear the bassist thinking as he investigates the sometimes fugitive tonalities of his instrument. Something of the same relationship between *Call Me* and *Mountainscapes* applies (recognizing the lapse in time) between *Camouflage* and *Journal Violone II*. The 1979 trio again makes use of Surman's melancholy soliloquizing, but in a rather more colouristic way that is reminiscent of *Three Day Moon*. This is Phillips's most accessible work on record but is by no means unrepresentative. Rypdal is an intelligent partner and Feichtener adds (as he had on *Mountainscapes*) some highly individual flourishes. One questions Gurtu's role, though: too effusive and individual a player, surely, for this selfless idiom.

Looking at Phillips's career only in the context of his recent solo work or of his improvisational activities with Derek Bailey's Company collective tends to cast it as something rarefied and dauntingly inward of gaze (the duo *Figuring* with Bailey – *q.v.* – Incus CD05, might attract that charge) but it's as well to remember that Phillips was Archie Shepp's bass-player at the 1965 Newport Festival and that, with Surman and the late Stu Martin, also on *Mountainscapes*, he was a member of The Trio, one of the most dynamic free-jazz units of the late '60s. There is a dancer's grace and concentration in Phillips's playing, an internal balance and rhythm that, as on *Camouflage*'s 'You And Me', make it virtually impossible to separate man and instrument.

There are problems on *Uzu*. Motoharu has so thoroughly wired himself up to what is described as a 'homemade electric vertical five string bass' that it is genuinely difficult to work out what one is listening to. This is a problem only if you take a close interest in the technical dimensions of music like this. For most people, the album will be a vivid, arresting experience, well worth a bit of patience.

*** Jazzd'aia

Bleu Regard 1956 *Phillips; Serge Pesce (g); Jean-Luc Danna (d, perc, acc, v)*. 98.

At first hearing this seems very different to Phillips's usual fare and might be mistaken for cellist Ernest Reijseger's recent collaborations with Italian players on folk-based improvisation. Gradually, though, Phillips's personality comes through and this ends on a beautiful and provocative note that guarantees a second and subsequent note. Well worth tracking down.

*** Trignition

Nine Winds 1086 *Phillips; Vinny Golia (reeds); Bertram Turetzky (b)*. 98.

A delightful *mésalliance*. Golia is a remarkable player, who seems at ease with just about every member of the extended reed family. However, one wonders whether he's quite up to the task of playing with two such thoughtful and idiosyncratic bassists. Our immediate reaction was how wonderful it might have been if they had gone for broke and invited the now deceased Peter Kowald along as a third contrabass virtuoso. What we have instead is a record on which Golia overlays some stunning bass work with some rather mundane, often chordally inspired improvisation. Phillips and Turetzky are quite easy to separate, both in stereo terms and in sound and basic technique, and their interplay is consistently fascinating.

*** Play 'Em As They Fall

Eyewill SKCY1002 *Phillips; Kaou Imai (g)*. 99.

At first hearing, one might think this was a duet with Derek Bailey, but very quickly it's clear that the guitarist is working to very different agenda from the veteran English improviser. Imai is a member of the Taj Mahal Travellers, a cultish group whose work falls outside jazz. Here, though, he's completely in tune with the bassist, and their communication is almost telepathic. Probably hard to find, but worth a while on the Internet to get hold of a copy.

**** Journal Violone 9

Emouvance emv 1015 *Phillips (b solo)*. 3/00.

This has now become one of the most important solo instrumental recording projects of recent years. It will be difficult for anyone to reconstruct the progress of Phillips's engagement with his bass, but each record is self-sufficient, and this one is a quiet masterpiece. One does not listen to it for 'technique' but purely for the musical logic and occasional delightful illogic that Phillips applies. He begins, without the bow, on 'Time, Our Time', a 17-minute *tour de force* that should whet appetites for the rest of the record. 'Windwalk' is the other long piece, though it's the shorter studies that thereafter command attention, particularly 'Dear Doctor' and the two shortest pieces, 'J.B.'s Present' and 'Nellie's Fire'. Beautifully recorded and mixed, each track has its own dynamic and distinctive sound. Thoroughly recommended, especially if you haven't encountered Phillips solo before. The avant-garde intensity may have dimmed, but the music has taken over regally.

**** After You've Gone

Victo 91 *Phillips; Joelle Leandre, William Parker, Tetsu Saitoh (b)*. 7/03.

A formidable agglomeration of contemporary bass-players, convened in honour of the late Peter Kowald. The playing is exceptionally intense, featuring all four players most of the time, which means that some of the detail is inseparable, unless you're already very familiar with the individual idioms. Most of the tracks are longer than ten minutes. 'Whoop Yer Tal' is incredibly detailed and virtuosic; by contrast, 'P.S. – Te Queremos' is a mournful threnody to the departed bass master. A stunning performance by any standard and a feast for bass aficionados.

Flip Phillips (1915–2001)

TENOR SAXOPHONE

Born in Brooklyn, Joseph Phillips had a rather uneventful time in big bands, before joining Woody Herman in 1944. He then became closely identified with the travelling Jazz At The Philharmonic concerts, jousting with the likes of Illinois Jacquet and playing in the shouting style, the opposite of the cooler Lester Young method towards which younger tenormen were moving. From 1960 he was living and working outside music in Florida, although he still played gigs. In his old age he was a grand reminder of an earlier time.

****(*) The Claw**

Chiaroscuro CR(D) 314 *Phillips; Clark Terry (t); Buddy Tate, Al Cohn, Scott Hamilton (ts); John Bunch (p); Chris Flory (g); Major Holley (b); Chuck Riggs (d).* 10/86.

***** Try A Little Tenderness**

Chiaroscuro CR(D) 321 *Phillips; Dick Hyman (p); Howard Alden, Bucky Pizzarelli (g); Bob Haggart (b); Ronnie Traxler (d); strings.* 6–7/92.

With sundry major-label compilations of Flip's early work already missing in action, it's only the work of his old age which is reasonably accessible. Flip is in good spirits for both these disparate sessions for Chiaroscuro. *The Claw* is a tenors-all-out jam session on board the SS *Norway* during the 1986 Floating Jazz Festival: they didn't look too far afield for the material ('Topsy', 'Flying Home', and so forth) and in the end it sounds too much like a parade of tenor solos to make for a satisfying record. But Flip and Al Cohn especially come up with a few remarks that evade the rules of the tenor extravaganza. Phillips gets to make his strings album on *Try A Little Tenderness* and, with canny arrangements by Dick Hyman and the saxophonist in his ripest form, the music is sly enough to sidestep most of the clichés of the situation, or at least to make them enjoyable. A nice indulgence for the old warrior.

***** Swing Is The Thing!**

Verve 543477-2 *Phillips; James Carter, Joe Lovano (ts); Benny Green (p); Howard Alden (g); Christian McBride (b); Kenny Washington (d).* 10/99.

At almost 85 Flip went back home to Verve with this enjoyable stroll through tunes and music he knew well. There are inevitable shortcomings in his control, but the big tone is pretty much still there and none of this is giving him much trouble. Having Carter and Lovano come in on a few tracks does little other than introduce unfair contrast, though, even if Carter's exuberant sprint through his 'Where Or When' solo is nicely countered by Flip's deliberate shifting down a gear. Altogether a pleasing farewell for a distinctive voice.

Sonny Phillips (born 1936)

ORGAN

Phillips was born in the Deep South, but left Alabama to study with Ahmad Jamal. He was inspired to play organ by Jimmy Smith and became a soul-jazz stalwart, appearing as sideman and making a few records of his own. Phillips still lives in California but rarely plays, even though contemporary acid jazz has revived his reputation.

***** Legends Of Acid Jazz**

Prestige *Phillips; Virgil Jones (t); Rusty Bryant, Houston Person (ts); Joe Boogaloo Jones, Melvin Sparks (g); Bob Bushnell, Jimmy Lewis (b); Bernard Purdie (d).* 10/69, 7/70.

All the Sonny Phillips you'll ever need, though to be strictly honest there isn't much more under his own name. This compilation, which capitalizes on the revived vogue for soul jazz, brings together two of his sets for Prestige, *Sure 'Nuff* and *Black On Black*, though oddly nothing from the other 1970 set *Black Magic*. It's musical soul food, hot and greasy, which makes the appearance of Sonny Rollins's bebop staple 'Oleo' an ironic exception to the norm. There's some fine playing from the leader, who never sounds like a Smith clone, from Houston Person and the ever-powerful Pretty Purdie. The best of it is very good indeed; the rest never falls below entertaining; all of it is very danceable, which guarantees Phillips longevity as a club favourite.

Simon Picard

TENOR SAXOPHONE

Fearsomely gifted British reedman with a no-holds-barred approach to free playing.

***** News From The North**

Intakt 028 *Picard; Paul Rogers (b); Tony Marsh (d).* 91.

Veterans both, Rogers and Marsh are good enough to listen to on their own. Picard is the lord of misrule on this tough, disruptive set, which really takes off with the second piece, 'Plump But Expansive', a showcase for Picard's hard (over)-blowing and Rogers's bow work. 'Shenanigan' is exactly as it sounds it might be, while 'Nervy', 'B'zoo' and the title-piece shift the balance of the trio back and forth. Uncompromising music, but a set which repays frequent hearings.

Enrico Pieranunzi (born 1949)

PIANO

The Italian is an elegant performer and an often unexpected composer, a storyteller who very seldom lapses into abstraction. His piano style is a hybrid of Bill Evans and Herbie Hancock, with boppish accents that recall Bud Powell rather than Monk.

****(*) Jazz Roads**

CAM 504162-2 *Pieranunzi; Birch Johnson (tb); Riccardo del Fra, Marc Johnson (b); Giampaolo Ascolese, Roberto Gatto, Joey Baron (d).* 80–01.

*****(*) Isis**

Soul Note 121021 *Pieranunzi; Art Farmer (flhn); Massimo Urbani (as); Furio Di Castri (b); Roberto Gatto (d).* 81.

***** Deep Down**

Soul Note 121121 *Pieranunzi; Marc Johnson (b); Joey Baron (d).* 2/86.

*****(*) No Man's Land**

Soul Note 121221 *Pieranunzi; Marc Johnson (b); Steve Houghton (d).* 5/89.

***** Seaward**

Soul Note 121272 *Pieranunzi; Hein van de Geyn (b); André Ceccarelli (d).* 3/94.

***** Flux And Change**

Soul Note 121242 *Pieranunzi; Paul Motian (d).* 95.

***** Ma L'Amore No**

Soul Note 121321 *Pieranunzi; Enrico Rava (t); Lee Konitz (ss); Piero Leveratto (b); Mauro Beggio (d); Ada Montellanico (v).* 2/97.

***** Don't Forget The Poet**

Challenge CHR 70065 *Pieranunzi; Bert Joris (t, flhn); Stefano D'Anna (ss, ts); Hein Van De Geyn (b); Hans van Oosterhout (d).* 3/99.

Pieranunzi is not an extravagant virtuoso; his self-effacing manner recalls something of Hancock, but he uses all the ground-breaking modern discoveries in modality, rhythm and the broadening of pianistic devices to his own ends. As with the Space Jazz trio, which he apparently leads with the bassist Enzo Pietropaoli, he is an exponent of post-modern jazz, sounding perfectly self-aware yet concerned to introduce elements of abstraction and emotional flow alike.

Jazz Roads reissues an early record, with an unexpected choice of Birch Johnson's trombone as lead voice and occasional synthesizer touches. It feels rather dated, and Johnson, while agile enough, doesn't have much to say. There's a bonus in the form of a new version of one of the compositions, 'From E To C', by the current trio with Johnson and Baron.

Seaward is perhaps the straightest blowing album of Pieranunzi's current catalogue and thus the most welcoming for listeners who don't know his work. There are a few originals on the set, but it is dominated by standards and jazz tunes: 'Stardust', 'I Hear A Rhapsody', Wayne Shorter's joyous 'Footprints'. Van de Geyn and Ceccarelli are a dream rhythm section, loose, disciplined and responsive.

Isis is transformed by the presence of Farmer and by a couple of gorgeous solos from the ill-fated Urbani, who provided Pieranunzi with a solo voice that chimes perfectly with his own. The duo album with Motian contains no fewer than 23 standard and original songs arranged into two long suites. It's a persuasive combination and is handled with imagination and skill.

Ma L'Amore No is essentially a collaboration with the singer Ada Montellanico, but it is also graced by two fine guest instrumentalists in Rava and Konitz, both of them playing as beautifully and elegantly as ever. Most of the songs are Italian, though universally communicable; but the addition of the neglected Gershwin classic 'Who Can I Turn To', and the Beatles' 'Fool On The Hill' adds a special dimension. The quintet session from 1999 was the first of its kind for some years, and Enrico takes the opportunity to showcase 11 compositions which range from the gently ironic lyricism of 'With My Heart In A Song' to the more acerbic language of the title-piece.

*****(*) Un'alba Dipinta Sui Muri**

EGEA SCA 070 *Pieranunzi (p solo).* 7/98.

*****(*) Con Infinite Voci**

EGEA SCA 071 *Pieranunzi (p solo).* 7/98.

*****(*) Canto Nascosto**

EGEA SCA 080 *Pieranunzi (p solo).* 9/00.

It would be a bit overheated to say that controversy rages over whether Pieranunzi is better heard solo or in a trio context. While these solo sets tend to follow the same pace and measured delivery, by the same token if any one appeals then they all will. The task facing a pianist with such a delicate, nuanced touch is to introduce enough robustness to stop the music merely drifting into background pleasantries. That doesn't mean playing a stomp every now and again, which may be a relief to him; Enrico's unlikely to do a Jelly Roll Morton album any time soon and, indeed, there is scarcely anything here which hasn't come out of his own head. But 'Blu Laggiù', from *Un'alba Dipinta Sui Muri*, is a fine example of how even a ruminative solo can generate its own kind of interior heat.

The first two discs were recorded at Umbia Jazz on the same day and clearly found Pieranunzi in his finest form. *Canto Nascosto* is a studio set which perhaps leans more heavily than usual on the pianist's classical manners; he played the solos on five different pianos (for annotators: two Steinways, a Borgato, a Fazioli and a Kawai) and the music-room serenity of the playing seems to have becalmed some of his flair. But it is intensely beautiful piano-playing.

***** Daedalus' Wings**

Challenge CHR 70069 *Pieranunzi; Bert van den Brink (p).* 3/99.

About as remote from Ralph Sutton and Dick Hyman as you could imagine, and to that extent it's unlikely to convert sceptics to either Pieranunzi or Van Den Brink's cause. However, despite the dreamy opener, 'Woods', most of this is quite pointed, even taut, and only rarely luxuriates in the resonance of two keyboards. Each man does a solo 'I Can't Get Started' and there are some oddball miniatures which they seem to have made up on the spot. A long Ellington medley wraps things up. Extravagant piano sound, which some may find irritatingly oversized.

***** Plays The Music Of Wayne Shorter**

Challenge CHR 70083 *Pieranunzi; Hein van de Geyn (b); Hans van Oosterhout (d).* 2/00.

***** Racconti Mediterranei**

EGEA SCA 078 *Pieranunzi; Gabriele Mirabassi (cl); Marc Johnson (b).* 2/00.

The Shorter record – as happens so often when this composer gets the full treatment – is hit and miss. Pieranunzi, surprisingly, does best by the more forceful pieces, such as 'E. S. P.' and 'Deluge', which the trio open out with a lusty enjoyment. 'Nefertiti' is mined for its sombre lyricism, but a couple of the slower pieces feel merely droopy.

With Mirabassi and Johnson, Pieranunzi revisits some of the material from the solo records as well as some new pieces. There are times, again, when this sounds more like a chamber recital than any kind of jazz record, but Johnson's roving lines are as ear-catching as always and the sound of the trio is so beguiling that only the stone-hearted would disapprove.

***** Alone Together**

Challenge CHR 70070 *Pieranunzi; Eric Vloeimans (t); Philip Catherine (g); Hein van de Geyn (b); Joe LaBarbera (d).* 3/00.

****** Play Morricone**

CamJazz 504425-2 *Pieranunzi; Marc Johnson (b); Joey Baron (d).* n.d.

Philip Catherine prefers swinging to stately European philosophizing and *Alone Together* is Pieranunzi's most conventionally swinging set for a long time. Vloeimans sits in on three tunes in a programme of rather obvious standards. It's all well done, but it does enter a crowded category and never transcends it.

The Morricone set is practically a dream date for Pieranunzi. He doesn't need to elaborate too much on such melodies and Italians-by-proxy Johnson and Baron add delicate muscle to the pianist's impeccable authenticity. We wish he'd done the theme from *Moscow Farewell*, but there could always be a second volume. Yes, please!

****** Current Conditions**
CAM 7756-2 *Pieranunzi; Marc Johnson (b); Joey Baron (d).* 11/01.

*****(*) Play Morricone 2**
CAM 7763-2 *As above.* 6/02.

Current Conditions is a live set by this most wonderful group. It benefits from the frisson of a performance but doesn't lose any of the sensitivity and nuance which they muster in the studio. A beautiful set of themes and a good location sound, and one of those rare CDs where 70 minutes of music doesn't feel a second too long.

Their second helping of Morricone is most welcome, although frankly it does sound a shade behind the first, possibly because the material is a whit less fresh this time (and they still haven't done *Moscow Farewell*). The studio mix also doesn't seem all that kind to Johnson. That said, still much glorious music.

***** Fellini Jazz**
CAM 7761-2 *Pieranunzi; Kenny Wheeler (t): Chris Potter (ss, ts); Charlie Haden (b); Paul Motian (d).* 3/03.

Something of a disappointment. It looks like a wonderful group, but Wheeler sounds tired and Haden's not the right man for this gig, his lines too slow and elemental. Motian at least doesn't try to hijack the date, as he often does in a sideman role, although he is mixed quite far down. It's a pity, because Pieranunzi's arrangements of various Fellini film-pieces (mostly by Nino Rota) are done with his usual grace and flair, and Potter is rather good, especially on 'La Città Del Donne'.

Billie Pierce (1907–74)

PIANO, VOCAL

AND

De De Pierce (1904–73)

CORNET

Billie was a touring pianist in the '20s, but she settled in New Orleans with her husband, De De, and they worked frequently as a duo, securing a measure of fame in revivalist circles in the '60s and early '70s.

***** Billie Pierce (With Raymond Burke)**
American Music AMCD-76 *Billie Pierce; Jack Delany (tb); Raymond Burke (cl); Roy Zimmerman (p); Chink Martin (b); Paul Barbarin (d).* 7/50–3/54.

***** Gulf Coast Blues**
Arhoolie 488 *Pierce; Pierce; Brother Randolph (wbd); Lucious Bridges (perc, v).* 10/59.

**** With Kid Thomas Valentine 1960**
504 CD 36 *Pierce; Pierce; Kid Thomas Valentine (t).* 60.

****(*) In Binghamton, N.Y.**
American Music AMCD-80 *Pierce; Pierce.* 10/62.

****(*) In Binghamton, N.Y. Vol. 2**
American Music AMCD-81 *Pierce; Pierce; Albert Warner (tb); Willie Humphrey (cl); Cie Frazier (d).* 10/62.

****(*) In Binghamton, N.Y. Vol. 3**
American Music AMCD-82 *As above.* 10/62.

***** New Orleans: The Living Legends**
Original Blues Classics OBC 534 *Pierce; Pierce; Albert Jiles (d).* 1/61.

The Pierces were a familiar husband-and-wife team in New Orleans dance-halls for many years. Though De De also worked in the Preservation Hall Jazz Band, it's his recordings with Billie that remain his best legacy; so far, these have made it to CD. Arhoolie's *Gulf Coast Blues* finds them near their best. It's very spare, and Billie's playing dominates the more diffident De De, but it's less wayward than some of their later records. The session with Kid Thomas sitting in as guest is very ramshackle-sounding, but the spirit abides, and it's a curiously moving document even with all the fluffs and effortful playing. The Binghamton discs were cut at a college concert. The music is often all over the place, and De De is so unpredictable that Willie Humphrey, who arrives in time for the second volume, seems to be trying to watch him all the time; but, for all the rackety playing, it becomes oddly exhilarating after a while.

On the OBC, the programme is nearly all simple, slow blues, taken at a stately tempo by Billie's piano, with cornet elaborations by De De that are modestly ambitious: he plays a much more improvised line than the standard New Orleans lead horns and, though he cracks a lot of notes and sometimes loses his way, he works hard at his playing. Billie's high vocals are sometimes hard to take, since she hardly varies her delivery (she once accompanied Bessie Smith, but sounds more like Clara Smith). This is deep New Orleans music.

On her own – or, at least, without De De – Billie's earlier recordings are something of a surprise. She sounds stronger and more individual, a blend of classic-blues singer and the more songful voice that she used for the likes of 'When The Saints'. The 1950 session, a private recording, features her in the sole company of Raymond Burke, who's in playful form, and the 1954 band date has her fronting a capable group with everyone in high spirits. None of these tracks was issued before and the sound in this first mastering is more than good enough – a pleasing discovery.

Dave Pike (born 1938)

VIBRAPHONE, MARIMBA

Born in Detroit, Pike began on drums and later switched to vibes. West Coast work in the '50s preceded a move to New York in 1960 and three years with Herbie Mann. His band, The Dave Pike Set, became popular in Germany, where he lived for several years, and then he toured South America. Pike returned to California in the mid-'70s.

***** It's Time For Dave Pike**
Original Jazz Classics OJC 1951 *Pike; Barry Harris (p); Reggie Workman (b); Billy Higgins (d).* 1–2/61.

Pike's approach was both backward-looking, to the styles of Milt Jackson and Hamp, and also irretrievably time-locked, and though he returned to the States and to favour after an increasingly barren sojourn in Europe he's never quite recovered from the feeling that he's merely a bebop copyist on a lumpy and stiff-jointed instrument. Said album has finally returned via the OJC imprint, and while it has its notable moments – the terse ballad 'It's Time', the vintage bop bluster of 'Hot House' – the record feels as if it's going nowhere, which is what Pike did, until his unexpected resurgence in the '90s.

***(*) Carnavals

Prestige 24248 *Pike; Clark Terry (flhn); Leo Wright (as, f); Tommy Flanagan (p); Kenny Burrell, Jimmy Raney (g); Ahmed Abdul-Malik, George Duvivier, Chris C. White (b); Rudy Collins, William Correa (d); Ray Barreto, Jose Paulo (perc).* 9–12/62.

This is the Pike set to go for, a compilation of two 1962 albums, *Bossa Nova Carnival* and *Limbo Carnival* (note change of spelling). Both records are dance-oriented, but none the worse for that, and they underline Pike's (or his producers') genius for simpatico line-ups. The first album was all Donato material, quality writing delivered with a measure of authenticity. The second record was more original in focus, with a touch of bebop ('My Little Suede Shoes'), some pop ('La Bamba'), a couple of songs associated with Harry Belafonte, and a knock-off of Sonny Rollins's 'St Thomas'.

*** Jazz For The Jet Set

Atlantic 8122 73527-2 *Pike; Clark Terry, Melvin Lastie, Martin Shellar (t); Herbie Hancock (org); Billy Butler (g); Bob Cranshaw, Jimmy Lewis (b); Bruno Carr, Grady Tate (d).* 66.

The Atlantic date, four years later, is programmed as a desperate jazz-meets-pop enterprise, yet there's far more to enjoy than a glance at the cover (a stewardess – sometimes these images sell records, you know) might suggest. Terry may have been hired to lead the trumpet section, but he also gets in some typically puckish solos, and Pike himself sounds hungry just to be out front and to play on a record with his name on it.

**(*) Pike's Groove

Criss Cross CRISS 1021 *Pike; Cedar Walton (p); David Williams (b); Billy Higgins (d).* 2/86.

Pike disappeared to Europe for a while (an MPS compilation of his German recordings has been and gone), but eventually returned to the US. There he mainstreamed himself to a degree, threw off some of the trendier accessories and addressed his undoubted talent to straight, swinging jazz. *Pike's Groove* is lifted almost bodily by a superb rhythm section, but the overall result is curiously unsatisfying.

*** Peligroso

Cubop 32 *Pike; Carl Saunders (t); Rich Pullin (tb); Michael Turre (bs, f); Theo Saunders (p); Bobby Matos, Robertito Melendez (perc).* 00.

And as if to confirm his renaissance, Pike swings back with another delicious Latin-tinged set. Again, it's the band as a whole that merits attention, though this time the solo space is more obviously dominated by the leader. The ensembles are tight, flexible and always flowing and Michael Turre fills the all-important bass role with aplomb. Not so easy to pick out tracks this time, but the title-track opens the set in adventurous spirit, and following it with Wayne Shorter's 'Beauty And The Beast' was an excellent stroke; Pike's occasional dissonances here are cleverly placed.

Roberta Piket (born 1965)

PIANO

The daughter of a composer who studied in Vienna, Piket is a composer-pianist in a familiar post-bop style.

*** Unbroken Line

Criss Cross CRISS 1140 *Piket; Scott Wendholt (t); Donny McCaslin (ts, ss); Javon Jackson (ts); Michael Formanek (b); Jeff Williams (d).* 4/96.

*** Speak, Memory

Fresh Sound FSNT 088 *Piket; Masa Kamaguchi (b); Jeff Williams (d).* 2/00.

Piket's father took part in the Spanish Civil War and then emigrated to America after the great War Against Fascism. Roberta imbibed a solid classical training from him and she retains a capacious understanding of all sorts of modern music. Her compositional gifts are evident from the very start of *Unbroken Line*. 'Brookland' sounds derivative of too many things for it to be indebted to any of them. 'The Long, Long Wait' was seemingly inspired by a session Piket heard involving her premier jazz influence, Richie Beirach; it's a meditation on *ars longa, vita brevis*, heartfelt and touched by a proper humility. 'Daily Affirmation' is based on Charlie Parker's 'Confirmation', though it develops in directions Bird hadn't dreamt of. The closing 'Unbroken Line' is a fierce blowing tune, and belated evidence that the composer isn't overly hung-up on her classical training. Only two standard treatments, but Irving Berlin's 'Always' and the pairing of 'You'll Never Walk Alone' and 'Some Enchanted Evening' are sensitively reworked. The supporting cast are excellent, almost all of them veterans of Criss Cross's superb catalogue. Jackson brings the most, in terms of ideas, but this is a showcase for the leader.

Piket's entry in the demanding, hugely oversubscribed trio category is decorously played, and the balance between originals and covers works well. 'Up, Up And Away' (a choice which, she says, engenders 'scepticism and dismay' among would-be listeners) evolves into a rousing set-piece by its end, and the two originals, 'Hands' and 'Speak, Memory', benefit from her forceful delivery. On slower pieces such as 'Lost In The Stars' she tends to weigh the notes too ponderously, and the music can sometimes recede into a trudge.

Jean-Michel Pilc

PIANO

A consistently inventive and intelligent player, Pilc has not yet received the critical attention he deserves.

**** Together: Live At Sweet Basil, Volume 1

Challenge 73195 *Pilc; François Moutin (b); Ari Hoenig (d).* 00.

**** Together: Live At Sweet Basil, Volume 2

Challenge 73196 *As above.* 00.

A certain understandably sentimental devotion to the late Michel Petrucciani camouflaged the inescapable conclusion that Pilc is the finest French pianist since Martial Solal. The flow of invention on these mostly standards-driven sets is remarkable. 'Tea For Two' and the title-piece are on both sets and offer an insight into how Pilc approaches the reharmonization of a familiar tune. We'd strongly recommend investing in both volumes, if only for the two-minute delight of 'My Köln Concert', a solo excursion that pokes gentle fun at the pretentious giantism of Keith Jarrett's most famous improvisation.

Pilc's approach is evident from the very start of 'Softly, As In A Morning Sunrise', a dawn which might promise storms or hot sun, and probably both. 'C Jam Blues' is a *tour de force* worthy of Liszt, while 'Tea For Two' and 'Bye Bye Blackbird' nod in the direction of both Tatum and Bartók. 'My One And Only Love' is a rare mood piece. Volume 2 – the Köln joke aside – is more of the same high-quality stuff. 'On Green Dolphin Street' and 'My Funny Valentine' are substantially deconstructed, but Pilc saves his best stroke for last, with a headlong reading of Miles Davis's 'All Blues'. Moutin and Hoenig both play their part to the hilt. The bassist's solo spots are delicately nuanced and Hoenig's sense of time is imaginatively elastic. We can't endorse these recordings highly enough. State-of-the-art jazz piano.

*** The Long Journey

Challenge 73216 *Pilc; Hein van de Geyn (b).* 01.

A very different project from the trios and very much a meeting of equals. Van De Geyn is a superb bassist and an immensely intelligent musician. His sophisticated lead-lines on Wayne Shorter's 'Footprints' are delightful, like footprints on a high wire. On the opening 'Nardis', he might almost be Scott LaFaro and on more familiar themes like 'My Funny Valentine' he finds more new things to say than seems possible. By contrast, and certainly in contrast to his usual approach, Pilc is quieter and here and there less assured. His romanticism is of an austere sort and there are few outbreaks of virtuosity, as on the trio records. Great stuff, though, and well worth sampling.

**** Welcome Home

Dreyfus 36630 *Pilc; Francois Moutin (b); Ari Hoenig (d).* 9/01.

Again, one wonders at the fuss raised round latter-day piano trios like Esbjörn Svensson's admittedly fine EST, when Pilc's superb trio still languishes in relative obscurity outside his native country. They get off to a rollicking start with another remake of a Miles Davis classic. This time, 'So What' is rendered almost unrecognizable. The repertoire is more modern this time out, with Coltrane's 'Giant Steps' and 'Cousin Mary', and Monk's 'Rhythm-A-Ning' stretching the harmonic language and the dynamics further still. The Monk tune is almost apocalyptic, an impression heightened by having it follow 'Scarborough Fair'. And just to show that they haven't gone over entirely to the new school, there's a loving deconstruction of 'I Got It Bad (And That Ain't Good)'.

The interplay between piano and bass is as dramatic as ever; Moutin's phrasing becomes more inventive with every appearance. We can only repeat our recommendation.

*** Cardinal Points

Dreyfus 36649 *As above; add Sam Newsome (ss); James Genus (b); Abdou Mboup (perc).* 02.

This was a shrewd decision at this stage in the trio's career. The addition of new voices opens out the language and broadens the palette considerably. The four parts of 'Trio Sonata' and the other originals show how much Pilc is prepared to extend his standards into new compositional strategies. 'Mood Indigo' is there to remind us and them where it all comes from. This one takes a bit of time to get used to and given the unfamiliarity of the material, more time to absorb.

Courtney Pine (born 1964)

TENOR, ALTO AND SOPRANO SAXOPHONES, BASS CLARINET, FLUTE, ALTO FLUTE, KEYBOARDS

Born in London, Pine played funk and reggae as a teenage saxophonist, then became interested in John Coltrane. Always an organizer, he became a focal point for young London musicians in the '80s, helped form the Jazz Warriors big band and had an unprecedented hit album with his debut release. He has since investigated various jazz and popular black-music forms and remains among the most widely known of British jazz musicians.

*** Modern Day Jazz Stories

Antilles/Talkin' Loud 529 428 *Pine; Eddie Henderson (t); Geri Allen (p, org); Mark Whitfield (g); Charnett Moffett (b); Ronnie Burrage (d, perc); DJ Pogo (turntables); Cassandra Wilson (v).* 95.

British readers will have had a difficult time of it separating Pine the musician from Pine the marketing phenomenon since – after the success of his first record – he was fruitfully presented as the face of young British jazz in the '80s. It was a move that brought unprecedented attention to the music in the UK, but the fall-out has been a certain suspicion among many who are wary of media hype, as well as a problem in evaluating the records purely on their musical worth. Fortunately, Pine himself is a saxophonist of clear and outstanding capabilities; whatever flaws these records may have, his own contributions are of a consistently high standard.

His '80s albums have drifted out of print at present, so newcomers will have to start with *Modern Day Jazz Stories*. This one found Pine consolidating and developing his own kind of fusion. He has the experience of Geri Allen to guide him and 'hook up the chords', and with guest contributions from Eddie Henderson and Mark Whitfield and the ferocious bass of Charnett Moffett to root the whole session it has a powerfully evocative quality. Pine keeps the turntable manipulations relatively far back in the mix and places himself just left of centre. Interestingly, the most effective track on the album is a setting of Langston Hughes's poem 'The Negro Speaks Of Rivers', which Pine originally heard on a Gary Bartz album of the early '70s. He has made something very contemporary and immediate out of Hughes's timeless lines.

*** Underground

Talkin' Loud 537745-2 *Pine; Nicholas Payton (t); Cyrus Chestnut (ky); Mark Whitfield (g); Reginald Veal (b); Jeff 'Tain' Watts (d); DJ Pogo (turntables); Jhelisa (v).* 3/97.

His vision is so populous and rich in its ambition that the plain truth is that Pine doesn't make enough records. Eight albums in nearly 15 years was simply an inadequate showing for a man who should be as prolific as David Murray in his pomp. That way we could rack one like this in his enjoyable second division, instead of having to settle for it as his premier set in a five-year period. 'All the tracks started off as breaks or loops from classic records from the period 1964–97' – but to get the consent would have been cripplingly difficult and expensive, so Pine reharmonized them and re-created them in real time. It was taking the long way round, but the results are often exciting, even thrilling – listen to 'Oneness Of Mind'. Unfortunately the track fades just as it's getting going, and that sense of the cup being dashed from the lips recurs throughout *Underground*. There are sublime pop melodies like 'Invisible (Higher Vibe)', fragments of impressive solos. DJ Pogo putters around in the background, creating his own underfelt of scratched voices and sounds. Every so often, Pine pulls off a head-turning solo. But the album never establishes its own world. Jazz, hip-hop, soundtrack music, hip easy-listening – it's all part of Courtney's multi-kulti aesthetic, and you can hear him straining to make it all synthesize. Give this talented man his own label and let him keep on doing it – it might be the only way he'll make his masterpiece.

****(*) Back In The Day**

Blue Thumb 543580–2 *Pine; Alex Pushkin (t); Lewis Latimer (tb); Mary Secole (as); Robert Mitchell (p); Cameron Pierre (g); Sheema Muhkersee (sitar); Robert Fordjour (d); DJ Pogo (turntables); Eska Mtungwezi, Kele Le Roc, MC Mello, Blak Twang, London Community Gospel Choir (v).* n.d.

Bits and pieces. In terms of impact, this is weedier and less intrusive than the last one. Most of it seems tailored for radio. A fine improvisation such as the soprano solo on 'Brotherman' sits sweetly inside an untroubling groove, and the same thing happens with the tenor outing on the subsequent 'Keep It Real'. With the record pieced together second by second by Pine at home, there's no pretence at real-time intensity, and some of the improvising seems weirdly frozen in its setting. At the same time, it's never as trenchant and radicalized as the finest of Pine's inspirational sources. Like many prodigious talents, he's still struggling to focus everything he's got into a single great record.

*****(*) Devotion**

Destin-E 777 001 *Pine; Byron Wallin (t); Dennis Rollins (tb); Chris Jerome (ky); Robert Mitchell (p); Shemma Mukherjee (sitar); Cameron Pierre (g); Peter Martin (b); Robert Fordjour (d); Yousuf Ali Khan (tabla); Thomas Dyani (perc); David Mcalmont, Carlene Anderson, Jacqui Dankworth (v).* n.d.

It still seems extraordinary that, nearly 20 years into his recording career, Pine has so far essayed only nine studio albums proper. If his last couple of records have been a jumble, then so is this one; the difference is, it's more joyous, more focused, less bitty. 'Osibisa', for instance, is a cheering homage to those heroes of '70s funk, and the title-track nods to Courtney's reggae roots, perhaps even more significant to him than his jazz sources. It's less of a one-man studio show, and organized more around his working band. As always, there are guest vocals, broadly from the soul idiom, with David Mcalmont doing a neat job on John Martyn's lovely 'Bless The Weather', but the most encouraging thing is how the music works to frame the leader's own playing to its best advantage – he's never sounded more exciting than he does on the likes of 'U.K.'. As his American audience falls away, he's concentrating more and more on a British perspective and, spared any overweening ambitions, this one sounds fine.

Alberto Pinton

BARITONE SAXOPHONE, CLARINET, BASS CLARINET, ALTO FLUTE

Free-thinking woodwinds man, specializing in the lower frequencies, and though an Italian he has close ties with Sweden – hence these albums on a Swedish indie label.

***** Common Intent**

Moserobie CD 003 *Pinton; Kyle Gregory (t, flhn, picc-t); Salvatore Maiore (b); Roberto Dani (d).* 8/01.

***** Terraferma**

Moserobie CD 008 *As above.* 11/02.

Although Pinton's tunes can sometimes sound sketchy and unfinished, both he and Gregory are basically melodic players who enjoy free space without feeling the need to fill it up with a lot of sound and fury. 'Improvisation III/IV', on the earlier disc, is a good instance of how the group can build inventively on a clean canvas. Both sets also make maximum use of resources: 15 pieces are despatched in 50 minutes on *Common Intent*, which makes the record seem somewhat longer than it actually is. Not that Pinton is shy about using the big horn to get out some aggression: 'C-Melody', from the same disc, is tough stuff. Gregory rarely goes as far out and he makes a likeable foil for the leader.

Terraferma follows a rather similar pattern. As with the first set, though, the lack of anything for the rhythm players to get their hands dirty on, the absence of any kind of groove playing, does become a tad wearing, and one might wish for something a little more smiling among the tunes: titles such as 'Stoneface', 'Fragment' and 'Paradox' do tell of the music's tendency to gloom.

Armand Piron (1888–1943)

VIOLIN, VOCAL, BANDLEADER

Piron was born in New Orleans and began leading bands there in the first decade of the new century. He joined forces with Clarence Williams in music publishing and only rarely left his native city, continuing to work there until his death.

***** Piron's New Orleans Orchestra**

Retrieval RTR 79041 *Piron; Peter Bocage (t); John Lindsay (tb); Lorenzo Tio Jr (cl, ts); Louis Warnecke (as); Steve Lewis (p); Charles Bocage (bj, v); Bob Ysaguirre (tba); Louis Cottrell (d); Esther Bigeou, Ida G Brown, Lela Bolden, Willie Lewis (v).* 12/23–3/25.

For the most part they were recorded in New York, but Piron's band was a New Orleans outfit and as such was one of the few to be documented in the '20s. This splendid reissue is a model of its kind: the sleeve-notes sum up years of research into the performers' activities, and this latest remastering of a set of terrifically rare originals is excellent. That said, the disc isn't a revelation. Piron's group was a more genteel, proper orchestra than some New Orleans bands of the time, pitching itself somewhere between ragtime, society music and the glimmers of early jazz: though 1923 is early in jazz recording history, they still sound a much less modern band next to Oliver or Fletcher Henderson from the same year (one should compare their treatment of 'Doo Doodle Oom' with Henderson's 1923 Vocalion version). A few tracks, including the very first, 'Bouncing

Around', brew up a potent mix of syncopation, with Tio's wriggling clarinet-breaks and Bocage's urbane lead making their mark over an ensemble rhythm that is almost swinging. But there is surprisingly little development between the earliest and the latest tracks by the orchestra.

John Pizzarelli (born 1960)

GUITAR, VOCAL

Performed with his father as a guitar duo, then began working as a solo and with his own trio from 1990, gaining extra recognition as a vocalist.

***** My Blue Heaven**
Chesky JD38 *Pizzarelli; Clark Terry (t, v); Dave McKenna (p); Bucky Pizzarelli (g); Milt Hinton (b); Connie Kay (d).* 2/90.

***** All Of Me**
Jive 63129 *Pizzarelli; Randy Sandke, John Frosk, Anthony Kadleck, Michael Ponella (t); Jim Pugh, Rock Ciccarone, Michael Davis (tb); Paul Faulise (btb); Walt Levinsky, Phil Bodner (as); Scott Robinson (ss, ts, f); Frank Griffith (ts); Sol Schlinger (bs); William Kerr, Lawrence Feldman (f); Ken Levinsky (p); Bucky Pizzarelli (g); Martin Pizzarelli (b); Joe Cocuzzo (d); Gordon Gottlieb (perc, vib); strings.* 91.

***** Dear Mr Cole**
Jive 63182-2 *Pizzarelli; Benny Green, Ray Kennedy (p); Christian McBride, Martin Pizzarelli (b); John Guerin (d).* 94.

***** After Hours**
Jive 63191-2 *Pizzarelli; Randy Sandke (t); Harry Allen (ts); Ray Kennedy (p); Bucky Pizzarelli (g); Martin Pizzarelli (b); Joe Cocuzzo (d).* 95.

John Pizzarelli follows in father's footsteps by using a guitar style that owes an obvious debt to paternal influence: quick, clean picking, a Django-like tone and a penchant for the humorous aside in the middle of otherwise terse improvisations. While this makes for solid, gratifying mainstream, Pizzarelli isn't really a young fogey: there's a coolness about his manner which detaches him a little from the material and, while some of his song choices are as neo-classic as one can get, he sounds a little dreamier than the Concord crew of mainstreamers. Besides, he sings – and this is what has determined his career in recent years. Pizzarelli was doing this sort of thing long before the likes of Harry Connick, and his singing and playing are accomplished in their own right; but the tenor of the later records is unmistakably tuned to seeking an audience that likes singers rather than players.

My Blue Heaven is beautifully recorded and shrewdly programmed, with Clark Terry tossing in some characteristic obbligatos and the instrumental pieces – including a very sharp-witted 'Don't Get Around Much Any More' – finding a real, spontaneous zest. *All Of Me* is Pizzarelli's initial stab at the big time: cleverly pitched between the big-band charts and the nucleus of the singer and the rhythm section, it's an artfully realized but legitimate musical success by dint of Pizzarelli's trust of the material. His three original songs are, though, no special achievement.

Dear Mr Cole looks promising: with the nucleus of Green, McBride and Pizzarelli himself as a dream trio, Nat Cole tunes as the repertoire, and a perfectly intimate studio-mix, this was set up to be a classic. But the opening 'Style Is Coming Back In Style' with the other rhythm section is so blissful that the rest is almost a disappointment and, as cleverly as the trio plays, it's just a shade too neo-classic to wholly convince, despite some lovely moments.

After Hours moves the concept to a full-fledged ballad album. Sandke and Allen blow sweetly apposite obbligatos and John's working trio play with intuitive rightness: on a couple of less obvious choices such as 'Coquette' and 'Mam'selle', the pitch is flawlessly right. Because he's singing so quietly and without undue emphasis, it's easy to miss how effective Pizzarelli has become at this music, too. Yet the album still seems to slip uneventfully by – through its very nature, perhaps. If some of these gradings look harsh, it should be noted that in many ways this is the best sequence of vocal records of recent times, even though the individual albums miss out on masterpiece status, and a couple have now been deleted.

***** Our Love Is Here To Stay**
RCA 67501-2 *Pizzarelli; Tony Kadleck, Ron Tooley, Jim O'Connor, Glenn Drewes (t); Jim Pugh, John Mosca, Wayne Andre, Alan Raph, Ed Neumeister (tb); Andy Fusco, Chuck Wilson, Gary Keller, Scott Robinson, Kenny Berger, Tom Christiansen (reeds); Peter Gordon, John Clark (frhn); Ray Kennedy (p); Martin Pizzarelli (b); Dennis Mackrel, Danny D'Imperio (d).* 2/97.

Another good one, another not-quite-great one, and, while some have ridiculed Pizzarelli's discography, his class and poise seem unfazed. Don Sebesky's arrangements return him to a big-band setting and it's a kick to hear them go at 'Avalon' and 'Kalamazoo'. Some of the charts, though, are as rote as they come. Again, much more voice than guitar, but we like the singing, too.

****** Kisses In The Rain**
Telarc 83491 *As above, except omit Allen.* 6/99.

A new label, but nothing new in the music – John's dusting off more old standards, coming up with new ones of his own, and they're trying to get the feel of how the band do a live set in the context of a studio session. But nothing has to be new, anyway, since the pleasure in the record is how good this group have become at making such repertory their own. Pizzarelli's getting a bit old to be a young smoothie at this point, but fogeydom doesn't beckon either. It's character and wit that rule this music. Aw, give the man four stars – he's earned them.

*****(*) Let There Be Love**
Telarc CD-83518 *Pizzarelli; Harry Allen (ts); Ken Peplowski (cl); Dominic Cortese (acc); Ray Kennedy (p); Bucky Pizzarelli (g); Jesse Levy (clo); Martin Pizzarelli (b); Tony Tedesco (d).* 7/00.

*****(*) The Rare Delight Of You**
Telarc CD-83546 *Pizzarelli; George Shearing (p); Reg Schwager (g); Neil Swainson (b); Dennis Mackrel (d).* 10/01.

Love them or not, Pizzarelli's albums are copper-bottomed class, and we're not tired of them yet. *Let There Be Love* has another basketful of picked tunes, the voice is in fine shape, Allen and Peps put in some of their stuff, Bucky takes a solo or two ... hey, you know what's going to happen, and it does, and it sounds great.

Hard to know whether to file the next one under Pizzarelli or Shearing. John guests with the quintet, and while the climate is tempered a little to accommodate George, it doesn't hurt: 'Lost

April' has a hushed, old-world elegance of a sort which rarely turns up on the regular Pizzarelli sessions. But the up-tempo tunes are just as satisfying.

***** Live At Birdland**

Telarc CD-83577 2CD *Pizzarelli; Ray Kennedy (p); Martin Pizzarelli (b); Grover Kimble (v).* n.d.

*****(*) Bossa Nova**

Telarc CD-83591 *Pizzarelli; Harry Allen (ts); Ray Kennedy, César Camargo Mariano (p); Martin Pizzarelli (b); Paulinho Braga (d); Jim Saporito (perc); Daniel Jobim, Chiara Civello (v); strings.* 5/03.

The inevitable live album has been a long time in coming, but it's a fine souvenir of John's live set, two discs of good songs performed with a suave blend of showbiz and jazz feeling. The between-song schtick and bits of live business may deter this from returning to the player too often, though that's hardly the fault of the performers. As a record of one of America's most accomplished club acts, it works fine.

The *Bossa Nova* set is beautifully produced by Russ Titelman, and might turn out to be Pizzarelli's biggest success if some of these very poppy tracks become airplay hits. There's less guitar than ever (?) before, but he has a real feel for the right groove, and the slushy romanticism of this kind of music comes easily to him. Here and there – especially on a surprising 'Fascinatin' Rhythm' – the band hit a real groove.

Lonnie Plaxico (born 1960)

DOUBLE BASS

Widely travelled bass man, with experience in mainstream and M-Base modern. His most high-profile gig was with the Messengers, but he has also sustained a solo career.

****(*) Emergence**

Savant 2019 *Plaxico; Ralph Alessi, Larry Lunetta (t); Don Braden (ss, ts); Tim Hegarty (ts); Jason Moran (p); Eric Lewis (p, org); Lionel Cordew (d, perc); Jeff Haynes (perc).* 2/00.

There's a sophomoric cleverness to Plaxico's debut as leader, an insistence on showing off every aspect of his playing personality that becomes increasingly off-putting as *Emergence* progresses. The resonant titles – 'Emancipation', 'Delusion', 'Libertarian' – don't seem to have a substantial correlative in the music, and one finds oneself admiring the sophistication of the charts without enjoying the noise they make. Braden is in fine form, but Plaxico's own switching from acoustic to electric instruments is just a further symptom of his desire to pitch camp in both hard-bop and fusion camps. Neither is secured and ultimately the record falls rather than succeeds on its own eclecticism.

****(*) Mélange**

Blue Note 32355 *Plaxico; Lew Soloff (t, flhn); Tim Ries (ss, ts); George Colligan (p, org); Lionel Cordew (d).* 7/01.

Another album that flatters to deceive and very quickly runs out of energy. The opening sequence, which includes the title-tracks, suggests fine, funky hard bop mixed with fusion and a few added contemporary elements. The remainder of the set meanders through reworked ideas – too many of Plaxico's 'compositions' seem like reworkings of the same idea – and grandstanding gestures from the bassist, who is best heard in other people's bands. The Blue Note imprimatur and the first-rate band don't save the day.

***** Live At The 5:01 Jazz Bar**

Orchard 802211 *Plaxico; Alexander Pope Norris (t); Marcus Strickland (ts); George Colligan (org, ky); Nathaniel Townsley (d).* n.d.

Caught live, Plaxico's real strengths come through strongly. His command of line and harmonic variation are nowhere more clearly heard than on 'Too Young To Go Steady', not because it's the strongest track, but because the tune is familiar enough for his creative rethink to be obvious; similarly on Tower Of Power's brilliant 'Squib Cakes', first covered on the Blue Note album, which hasn't been picked up by anyone else except, we think, Rob McConnell. 'Emergence' is given a fresh outing and the other originals are tough, focused and thoroughly entertaining. Colligan has a lot to do with the success of the record, as convincing on organ as he always has been on piano.

***** Rhythm & Soul**

Sirocco 1023 *Plaxico; Alex Sipiagin (t); George Colligan (p, org); Arene Lomax (p); Billy Kilson (d); Jeff Haynes (perc); Amelia Lomax (v).* 02.

Lonnie gets better and better. Here, the band is schooled and adept in the leader's ideas. The bassist is hard-edged and funky one moment ('Weather Report'), softer and more expansive the next (Mal Waldron's 'Soul Eyes'). He's never out of the groove and never wastes a note. And yet, the overall impression is still of something rather too polished and contrived, music that doesn't come from the heart but from the head. A new live album was tabled for release shortly before we went to press. It will be interesting to see if it confirms the pattern of past albums and reflects Lonnie at his best.

King Pleasure (1922–81)

VOCAL

Born plain Clarence Beeks, Pleasure won an amateur night at the Apollo in 1951 and went on to scoop enormous success with 'Moody's Mood For Love', a vocalese version of James Moody's saxophone solo on 'I'm In The Mood For Love'. But his career didn't last long and there are no records after the '50s.

*****(*) King Pleasure Sings**

Original Jazz Classics OJC 217 *Pleasure; Ed Lewis (t); J. J. Johnson, Kai Winding (tb); Charles Ferguson, Lucky Thompson (ts); Danny Bank (bs); Jimmy Jones, John Lewis, Ed Swanston (p); Paul Chambers, Percy Heath, Peck Morrison (b); Kenny Clarke, Joe Harris, Herbie Lovelle (d); Betty Carter, Jon Hendricks, Eddie Jefferson, The Dave Lambert Singers, The Three Riffs (v).* 12/52–12/54.

***** Golden Days**

Original Jazz Classics OJC 1772 *Pleasure; Matthew Gee (tb); Teddy Edwards, Harold Land (ts); Gerald Wiggins (p); Wilfred Middlebrooks (b); Earl Palmer (d).* 4/60.

Eddie Jefferson claimed to have invented the practice of fitting lyrics to bop solos, but it was Pleasure who garnered the praise and what cash was going. (Just to confirm Jefferson's luck, he was blown away outside a Detroit club in 1979, just as his career was reviving; Jefferson, Jon Hendricks and The Three Riffs all feature on two 1954 tracks from *Sings*.) The earlier of the two

OJCs is shared with Annie Ross, who sings the classic vocalization of Wardell Gray's 'Twisted', along with 'Moody's Mood For Love' and Pleasure's 'Parker's Mood' the best-known vocalese performance. Pleasure has something of Ross's honeyed smoothness of tone but combines it with a more biting articulation that can sound remarkably like Charlie Parker's alto saxophone (or, more frequently, the smooth tenor sound of Teddy Edwards and Lucky Thompson). Using less sophisticated arrangements and generally less witty lyrics than Jon Hendricks's for Lambert, Hendricks and Ross, Pleasure more often relies on the quality of the voice alone. The accompaniments are generally good, but the Quincy Jones backings to 'Don't Get Scared' and 'I'm Gone' are exceptional.

The later *Golden Days* is a decent record, marked out by some adventurous improvisation from the singer and rugged solos from both Land and Edwards, although the steam had gone out of Pleasure's career at this point (it was made for the small Hi Fi label). Vocalese has always been something of an acquired taste, though interest in it has grown over the last few years. These two records are key texts in the revival.

Steve Plews (born 1961)

PIANO

The Englishman came to full-time music late, but for the last decade has combined jazz with classical composition and music promotion. He leads the Ascension jazz ensemble.

***** Secret Spaces**
ASC CD3 *Plews; Jeff Clyne (b); Trevor Tomkins (d).* 93.

Imagine the classic Bill Evans trio taken on three decades and exposed to Keith Jarrett's standards trio, Esbjörn Svensson and a handful of other contemporary influences along the way. You're now close to what Plews does, but not quite there. His elaborate, classically influenced style sounds written-out in places, but the strong swing imparted by Tomkins and Clyne overcomes any reservation. Fine modern jazz.

Paul Plimley

PIANO, MARIMBA

Canadian pianist. Studied classical music in his youth, but since the late '70s has been immersed in Canada's free-music scene and has toured and performed internationally with a wide range of players. Also composes; has led an octet.

*****(*) Everything In Stages**
Songlines SGL 1503-2 *Plimley (p solo).* 4/95.

Plimley has created a formidable body of work. *Everything In Stages* is another contrast: 17 pieces, many very brief episodes, many examining one, often minute, aspect of the piano – technique, vocabulary, structure. Plimley makes one think about the whole nature of the instrument here, its physicality and resonances, and though it can be tough going it's many times more absorbing than the typical piano record.

*****(*) Sensology**
Maya MCD9701 *Plimley; Barry Guy (b).* 1/95.

****** Ivory Ganesh Meets Doctor Drums**
Songlines SGL 1523-2 *Plimley; Trichy Sankaran (perc).* 4/86–4/98.

*****(*) Safecrackers**
Victor 066 *Plimley; Lisle Ellis (b); Scott Amendola (d).* 1/99.

The meeting with Guy (at a Vancouver concert) is a joyful occasion, for all the high-velocity counterpoint. Both players can touch on the academy when they want to, and that introduces such elegant episodes as the beginning of 'Short Steps Until It Finally Dawned', but the impression of brief, snatched-up tracks such as 'Hand Held Hot Coals' is of sheer high spirits. There is an excellent gag at the end of the record, too, luckily explained in the sleeve-notes.

Ivory Ganesh Meets Doctor Drums is world jazz of a high order. Sankaran brings the almost courtly grace of his tabla rhythms to a platform which Plimley builds and demolishes and rebuilds with his usual ebullience, and the miracle is that this is one (ahem) fusion which doesn't seem forced, overcooked or blighted by mutual incomprehension. It helps that Plimley thinks hard about the piano's status as a percussion instrument, but he's helped enormously by Ganesh's superb responsiveness to each situation. Each man also gets some intriguing solos and, aside from the enormous 'Jhampalaya II', most of the tracks are actually quite short and resolved in very specific ways.

His latest trio debuts on *Safecrackers*. New drummer Amendola fits right in, and this is probably also the best sound Plimley's had in a studio. A surprising bit of audio-vérité at the end of 'An Exhilaration Of Larks, And Their Discovery Of Fire' (yes, his titles are becoming too arch for their own good) and an unexpected sign-off with Claude Thornhill's 'Snowfall'. Plimley likes to surprise, and he's still doing it.

Paul Plummer and Ron Enyard

TENOR SAXOPHONE (PLUMMER) DRUMS (ENYARD)

Plummer, a former sideman with George Russell in the early '60s, and Enyard, a drummer from the Great Lakes area, have worked together extensively during the past 25 years.

*****(*) Trio And Quartet**
Quixotic 5005 *Plummer; Enyard; Steve Corn (org); Tony Byrne (g); Lou Lausche (b).* 80–81.

**** Driving Music: A Great Concert Vol. 1**
Cadence CJR 1075 *Plummer; Enyard; Al Kiger (t); Charlie Wilson (p); Lou Lausche (b).* 3/84–4/97.

**** Driving Music: A Great Concert Vol. 2**
Cadence 1078 *As above.* 3/84–4/97.

Trio And Quartet reissues two LPs, *Detroit Opium Den* (Resound) and *Acoustic Jazz Trio* (Jewel), the latter especially fondly remembered by collectors. The trio session featured Plummer, Lausche and Enyard in four swing-to-bop workouts that balanced simple, straightahead time with Plummer's striking, almost argumentative lines and shapes. Might almost have been a Marsh–Tristano situation, but for the saxophonist's distinctive mix of short and long phrasings. The other tracks, though, are just as interesting: Corn's cool approach to the Hammond, akin to that of contemporary players such as Dan Wall, is surprisingly ahead of its time; Byrne plays his part, and the simmering treatment of the likes of 'Freddie Freeloader' and even 'Greensleeves' is very effective.

You can hear why Bob Rusch wanted to reissue this music, but his judgement over the much later concert tapes found on the two Cadence releases was less sure. Plummer is here reunited with his old Russell colleague Al Kiger, and they both have some fine moments; a lot of this, though, is routine, the sound is often rough and distant, some of the tunings seem suspect, and Wilson is, to say the least, an eccentric pianist. Both discs are padded out with two enormous piano soliloquies (dating from 1984) which suggest that Wilson has a lot of technique and little idea of what to do with it.

Pekka Pohjola

BASS, PIANO

Pohjola played bass in the Finnish prog-rock group Wigwam, and concurrently ran a solo career based more around instrumental jazz-rock. This is a one-off from the '70s.

★★★(★) Harakka Bialoipokku

Love LRCD 116 *Pohjola; Bertil Löfgren (t); Pekka Pöyry (ss, as); Eero Koivistoinen (sno, ss, ts); Paroni Paakkunainen (as, bs, picc); Coste Apetrea (g); Tomi Parkkonen (d).* 11/74.

This one will be fondly remembered by many British readers, since it was once issued by Virgin records as *B The Magpie*, less of a mouthful for non-Finnish speakers. Pohjola's later adventures in instrumental music are more rock than jazz, but here he enlisted a group of fine horn players and the results are a melodious and attacking series of themes where each of the saxophonists has a chance to shine. 'The Madness Subsides' is a beautiful interlude where Apetrea solos over a haunting piano lick and Pohjola plays a breathtaking bass solo as a coda. Love have been making a scrupulous job of the remastering of their old catalogue and this echo of the '70s from the top of the world sounds very fine.

Pony Poindexter (1926–88)

ALTO SAXOPHONE

Born in New Orleans, Poindexter toured with Billy Eckstine and worked with Lambert, Hendricks and Ross. After moving to Europe, he became a regular member of Annie Ross's band and recorded on his own account. After returning to the US in the late '70s, he drifted into obscurity.

★★★ Pony's Express

Koch International 8591 *Poindexter; Eric Dolphy, Gene Quill, Sonny Red, Phil Woods (as); Dexter Gordon, Jimmy Heath, Clifford Jordan, Sal Nistico (ts); Pepper Adams (bs); Tommy Flanagan, Gildo Mahones (p); Ron Carter, Bill Yancey (b); Elvin Jones, Charli Persip (d).* 5/62.

Slim pickings from such a substantial career, but this is a very useful representation of an artist who is otherwise almost unavailable on record. The set features the saxophonist – dedicatee of Neal Hefti's 'Little Pony' – in a series of line-ups and much of the interest lies in the other personnel. There is, for instance, a fine Eric Dolphy solo on 'Lanyop' which adds to his sadly truncated discography and a remarkable chase with Dexter Gordon on an unexpected version of 'Struttin' With Some Barbecue'. The material could hardly be more varied: 'Mickey Mouse March', 'Basin Street Blues', the bebop classic 'Salt Peanuts' and Kenton's 'Artistry In Rhythm'. Poindexter's surprisingly lyrical alto is heard to best effect on 'Skylark', which is probably the outstanding cut of the set and demonstrates that whatever his limitations the saxophonist was more than a one-trick pony.

Kerry Politzer

PIANO

Politzer is an alumna of the New England Conservatory and a prizewinning songwriter. Her nimble approach is backed by increasing substance.

★★(★) Yearning

Cap 952 *Politzer; Eric Rasmussen (ss, as); Pete Smith (g); Howard Britz (b); Andrea Valentini (d).* 00.

★★★ Watercolour

Polisonic 01 *Politzer; Dan Fabricatore (b); Scott McLemore (d).* 1/01.

Politzer's rapid-fire Brazilian debut had reviewers reaching for comparisons with Eliane Elias. In practice, Kerry is a less virtuosic player, despatching tunes with brisk efficiency and rarely dwelling on an improvisation. The opening 'Twist Of Samba' establishes her credentials but it is the piano–guitar duet with Smith ('Tug Of War') which unveils the extent of her chops. 'Yearning' is a longer ballad and a rather drabber performance. The closing 'Piece For Charlie' is unaccompanied piano and a defiant promise of better things to come.

Watercolour is an awful name for a jazz album and invites snippy comments about pastel piano and wishy-washy playing. In point of fact, the sequel is a much better effort. Stripped to a trio, Politzer's group delivers 11 originals (including another very brief tune for the mysterious Charlie, this time a romantic waltz) and a notably brooding version of 'A Foggy Day'. The playing is more expansive and less obviously Latinized. Nice sound, too. Hard to gauge where Politzer may go next, but she has the chops to make a career of it.

Jimmy Ponder (born 1946)

GUITAR

Pittsburgh-born, and still based there, Ponder began in soul bands but preferred straightahead. He's worked with many organ-players and is a redoubtable sideman, and an occasional leader.

★★★ Ain't Misbehavin'

High Note HCD 7041 *Ponder; Don Braden (ts); John Hicks (p); Dwayne Dolphin (b); Cecil Brooks III (d).* 6/98.

★★★ Thumbs Up

High Note HCD 7080 *Ponder; Dave Pellow (b); Cecil Brooks III (d).* 7/00.

Ponder doesn't seem completely comfortable as a leader and there's the feeling that he sometimes has to be coaxed through these sessions, but even in the distinguished company of the first date he still sounds like the most interesting performer. Although he'll sometimes turn in a boppish performance in the classic manner – 'Three Little Words' is one such – much of his playing is a sometimes stiff but notably personal twisting of R&B licks into jazz shapes. The opening 'On Broadway' is almost as unlike the Benson version as you could expect to hear. Hicks and the rhythm section centre the music, but Braden sounds exhausted and even in the duet of 'Who Can I Turn To' he can barely get started.

The trio session hits a good groove. Blues lines and a few standards, and the closing 'Funk Wit Dis' gives Brooks a chance to see how his kit works. Probably the one to get to hear Ponder in close-up.

Valery Ponomarev (born 1943)

TRUMPET, FLUGELHORN

A Muscovite under Clifford Brown's spell, Ponomarev defected in 1973 and joined Art Blakey in 1977. His group, Universal Language, was an interesting hard-bop band of the '80s and '90s.

*****(*) Means Of Identification**
Reservoir RSR 101 *Ponomarev; Ralph Moore (ts); Hideki Takao (p); Dennis Irwin (b); Kenny Washington (d).* 4/85.

***** Trip To Moscow**
Reservoir RSR CD 107 *As above.* 4/85.

Universal Language is a rather wonderful band name for a man who left Russia during the deep freeze of the Brezhnev years in order to play jazz in the West. A version of the story was adapted for the movies in a Robin Williams vehicle called *Moscow On The Hudson*. Less manic than Williams, the trumpeter nevertheless shares a great sense of humour and a palpable joy at being able to play and play freely. *Means Of Identification* is certainly the place to begin with him. As will be seen from the names, Universal Language is a multiracial outfit – black, white, Japanese, Slavic – united by the Esperanto of hard bop. When Ponomarev was with the Messengers, Art let him loose on 'I Remember Clifford' night after night. It's the outstanding performance here, a flowing, feeling solo on what the trumpeter considers to be one of the greatest jazz compositions ever. His admiration is evident, as it is for Art Blakey himself in 'Envoy', a fresh and soulful original. The opening 'Dialogue' pits him against Moore, an exciting duel which recalls the great Blue Note recordings. No surprise that this session was made at the Van Gelder studio in Englewood Cliffs. Originally the group included guitarist Kevin Eubanks, but Takao came in at short notice, apparently sight-read the charts with ease and kept his place. Irwin is a former Messenger, beautifully featured on 'Mirage'. Washington has his moment on 'Dialogue' and keeps things tight throughout.

Almost inevitably, the follow-up isn't quite so forceful. 'For You Only' combines sinew and tenderness, and much of the second album seems devoted to underlining the point that Ponomarev isn't just a fast-valve showman but a player of real expressive range. The point is well made, but one could have done with a little variation in the pace and content.

****** A Star For You**
Reservoir RSR CD 150 *Ponomarev; Bob Berg (ts); Sid Simmons (p); Ken Walker (b); Billy Hart (d).* 4/97.

Perhaps the vintage Universal Language to date. Hart is as revelatory as ever, a hugely musical drummer who always has ideas to impart and energy in superfluity. Ponomarev makes it clear that this is a set very much dedicated to the spirit and memory of Art Blakey, perhaps because the 25th anniversary of his arrival in America wasn't so far away. The opening 'Commandments From A Higher Authority' is absolutely in the spirit of the Messengers' great days, a wheeling, driving theme which never quite comes to rest but exudes authority in every measure. 'Uh Oh' was apparently a Blakey vocal mannerism. It's a more jocular idea, and the trumpeter has fun trading figures with Hart. Bob Berg is the key addition to this group, superb on 'Dance Intoxicant' and the long standard, 'We'll Be Together Again', adding a warm-toned confidence to every track. Simmons and Walker get to show why they got the call, playing with intelligence and taste, never over-fussy, but subtle when the tune calls for another dimension. Back at Van Gelder's place, the band gets exactly the sound it deserves: rich and ringing, with plenty of space round the horns and kit, but not so much that you feel the guys are working in parallel rather than as a unit. Highly recommended.

***** The Messenger**
Reservoir RSR 166 *Ponomarev; Michael Karn (ts); Sid Simmons (p); Martin Zenker (b); Jimmy Cobb (d).* 8/00.

Another fine, polished album from Valery, who as he approaches 60 sounds more and more relaxed in his delivery without losing the bite and fire he brings to his trumpet work. On flugelhorn, he tends now to be noticeably mellower, and his ballad-playing has a wistful quality that is genuinely moving. 'Stardust', these days a signature piece for Wynton Marsalis, receives an archetypal reading, full of warmth, but with a gently ambiguous quality that suggests the singer is enchanted and slightly nonplussed. Of the originals, 'Escape From Gorki Park' and 'Messenger From Russia' are the best, both of them well-structured hard-bop themes with individual touches in the harmony.

Jean-Luc Ponty (born 1942)

VIOLIN, ELECTRIC VIOLIN, KEYBOARDS

Classically trained, Ponty was a violin prodigy who found himself sidetracked by jazz. By the end of the '60s he had made an international name for himself with festival and club work. Playing with Frank Zappa and the Mahavishnu Orchestra led him into fusion, and his own '70s recordings were pioneer efforts in the idiom. His star waned somewhat in the '80s and '90s, and he has dabbled in a jazz-inflected world music.

***** Jazz Long Playing**
Emarcy 548150-2 *Ponty; Michel Portal (f); Eddy Louiss (p, org); Gilbert Rovere, Guy Pedersen (b); Daniel Humair.* 64.

****(*) Live At Donte's**
Pacific Jazz 35635-2 *Ponty; George Duke (p); John Heard (b); Al Cecchi (d).* 3/69.

***** King Kong**
Pacific Jazz 895392-2 *Ponty; Vince DeRosa, Arthur Maebe (fr hn); Ernie Watts (as, ts); Ian Underwood (ts); Jonathan Meyer (f); Gene Cipriano (ob, cor); Donald Christlieb (bsn); Gene Estes (vib, perc); George Duke (p); Frank Zappa (g); Milton Thomas (vla); Harold Bemko (clo); Buell Neidlinger, Wilton Felder (b); Art Tripp, John Guerin (d).* 3/69.

Ponty's earlier work should be better represented than it currently is. He was a pioneer of the violin in both a modern straightahead format and in the fusion of the '70s and '80s. The 1964 session with an impressive line-up is a bit of a hotchpotch of swing, bop, Parisian cool and even (via Louiss's organ licks) a little soul-jazz. But already Ponty was an exhilarating soloist when he got some space.

While he acknowledges Stuff Smith and Grappelli as inescapable influences, it's clear from the dusty 1969 tracks that he was by then more specifically in thrall to Coltrane and the long-form soloists of the decade. His solos have a spiralling excitement and a surprisingly far-sighted feel that suggest he is challenging his formidable technical prowess as he goes. The problem with the record is a very flat sound that does the musicians no favours. Interesting to hear subsequent fusion kingpin Duke as a Tynerish pianist, too, but in truth the rhythm section isn't up to all that much.

King Kong is almost as much a Frank Zappa project as a Ponty record. Zappa wrote and arranged all the music, he plays guitar on 'How Would You Like To Have A Head Like That', and his 'Music For Electric Violin And Low-Budget Orchestra' is a typical piece of Zappa folderol. It was all pretty demanding stuff in 1969 but it hasn't weathered all that well, and Ponty himself sounds unsure whether he should be improvising as a rock or a jazz player.

***** Aurora**

Atlantic 19158-2 *Ponty; Patrice Rushen (ky); Daryl Stuermer (g); Tom Fowler (b); Norman Fearington (d).* 12/75.

***** Imaginary Voyage**

Atlantic 19136-2 *Ponty; Allan Zavod (ky); Daryl Stuermer (g); Tom Fowler (b); Mark Craney (d).* 7–8/76.

**** Enigmatic Ocean**

Atlantic 19110-2 *Ponty; Allan Zavod (ky); Allan Holdsworth, Daryl Stuermer (g); Ralphe Armstrong (b); Steve Smith (d).* 6–7/77.

***** Cosmic Messenger**

Atlantic 19189-2 *Ponty; Allan Zavod (ky); Peter Maunu, Joaquin Lievano (g); Ralphe Armstrong (b); Casey Scheuerell (d).* 78.

****(*) Mystical Adventures**

Atlantic 19333-2 *Ponty; Chris Rhyne (p); Jamie Glaser (g); Randy Jackson (b); Rayford Griffin (d); Paulinho Da Costa (perc).* 8–9/81.

**** Fables**

Atlantic 81276-2 *Ponty; Scott Henderson (g); Baron Browne (b); Rayford Griffin (d).* 7–8/85.

****(*) Tchokola**

Columbia 468522-2 *Ponty; Yves Ndjock (g); Guy Nsangue (b); Brice Wassy (d); Abdou M'Boup (perc, v).* 91.

****(*) No Absolute Time**

Atlantic 82500 *Ponty; Wally Minko (ky); Martin Atangana, Kevin Eubanks (g); Guy Nsangue (b); Moktar Samba (d); Abdou M'Boup, Sydney Thiam (perc).* 12/92–3/93.

***** The Very Best Of Jean-Luc Ponty**

Atlantic/Rhino 79682 *As Atlantic albums above.* 75–85.

***** The Best Of Jean-Luc Ponty**

Columbia 507609-2 *Ponty; Grover Washington (ss); Clara Ponty (p); Wally Minko, Patrice Rushen (ky); Pat Thomi, Jamie Glaser, Yves Ndjock, Martin Atangana (g); Kemo Kouyate (hp, perc); Guy Nsangue, Baron Browne (b); Raymond Griffin, Brice Wassy (d); Abdou M'Boup, Moustapha Cisse (perc, v).* 6/87–3/91.

Ponty had always amplified his violin, but by the '70s he was making it a major part of his aesthetic, trying out echo and other effects to colour an approach which had fundamentally changed little since his earliest recordings. He had recorded a session with Frank Zappa, *King Kong*, in 1969, and Zappa's punishingly difficult kind of instrumental rock was a significant influence on the sort of fusion that Ponty recorded once he signed with Atlantic in 1975. Tunes were built out of complicated riffs or trance-like harmonic patterns, with modal solos played at blistering speed to create the excitement. Unusually, though, the music is more interesting than the average fusion band of the period allows, since the lyrical tang of the leader's violin sustains the mood of most of the records.

The earlier records, especially *Aurora* and *Imaginary Voyage*, are the best, if only because the sound of the group is at its freshest. Players like Stuermer and Zavod are capable technicians, but it's always Ponty whose fire ignites the music. Some of the Atlantics from this period are currently out of print, and after *Mystical Adventures* the music grew a little stale. *Fables* returns to a quartet format, but Ponty seems uninterested in the overall sound. A label switch brought him to Columbia, with mixed consequences: *Tchokola* was an attempt at a new kind of fusion, with Afropop players from different schools, and the results were an interesting but uneasy alliance. There were two other albums for Columbia, and all three have been filleted to produce the label's own idea of *The Best Of*, which does a decent job at picking the modest highlights of a relatively uneventful period (and ends on a charming Chopin transcription).

No Absolute Time, though, was his best record for years. Jazz-rock is cast aside in favour of a glittering kind of electric world music: all the tracks simmer over a polyrhythmic base, drawn equally from human hands and drum machines, and Ponty's violin and keyboard effects are hummably rich and pleasing.

Atlantic's previous best-of, *Le Voyage*, an excellent two-disc set with several of the highlights from his many albums for the label, seems to have been axed, but there is another compilation available from the same source – docked a notch, though, for cutting back to a single disc and dumping some of our favourites.

****(*) Live At Chene Park**

Atlantic 82964-2 *Ponty; Chris Rhyne (ky); Jamie Glaser (g); Baron Browne (b); Michael Barsimanto (d).* 6/96.

Ponty returns to Atlantic with a solid if basically uneventful live set, the kind of thing that comes in the middle of a contract rather than at the beginning. The material's a nice blend of nuggets from the various parts of a fruitful career, but its rather old-fashioned feel is a step backwards. We await more from this likeable and gifted musician.

****(*) In Concert**

Le Chant Du Monde 274 1185 *Ponty; William Lecomte (ky); Guy Nsangue Akwa (b); Thierry Arpino (d); Moustapha Cisse (perc).* 10/99.

More of the same. Nobody seems ready to sponsor another studio set by Ponty, so here's a second stop-gap live affair, and it all seems pretty pointless. It's time this talented man was given something interesting to do.

Odean Pope (born 1938)

TENOR SAXOPHONE

Pope was born in the intriguingly named Ninety Six, North Carolina, but moved to Philadelphia as a child. He worked with Max Roach and in an inventive band called Catalyst before forming his own Saxophone Choir.

***(*) The Saxophone Choir

Soul Note 121129 *Pope; Robert Landham (f); Julian Pressley, Sam Reed (as); Bootsie Barnes, Arthur Daniel, Bob Howell (ts); Joe Sudler (bs); Eddie Green (p); Gerald Veasley (b); Dave Gibson (d).* 10/85.

**** The Ponderer

Soul Note 121229 *Pope; Byard Lancaster, Julian Pressley, Sam Reed (as); Glenn Guidone, Bob Howell, Middy Middleton, John Simon (ts); Joe Sudler (bs); Eddie Green (p); Tyrone Brown, Gerald Veasley (b); Cornell Rochester (d).* 3/90.

*** Epitome

Soul Note 121279 *As above, except omit Lancaster, Veasley, Rochester; add Robert Landham (as); Dave Burrell (p); Craig McIver (d).* 10/93.

'I tried to imagine what it would sound like if I played at the bottom range of my instrument like Coltrane played at the top.' This is pretty much what Odean Pope has done. If he sounds less like his fellow-Philadelphian (the City of Brotherly Love shaped Trane, even if he wasn't born there) and more like Sam Rivers or even Jimmy Heath, Pope is nevertheless profoundly influenced by some less exposed aspects of Coltrane's approach: its concern with ensembles rather than its torrential outpouring of personal feelings, its rootedness rather than its God-bothering excursions. Pope is a profoundly modest individual who aligns himself with the pianist Ibn Hassan Ali's belief that Coltrane's music is a not-quite-conscious expression of some higher state. Behind Pope's Saxophone Choir is the fiery, inchoate music of *Ascension*, but also something of the voicing of the later Ellington orchestras, as they negotiated with 'world music'.

Pope has not been prolific. He rehearses the Choir meticulously and then records live in the studio with no overdubs. The charts are intricate and demanding, a broad orchestral sound punctuated with episodes from a roster of players who, like the leader himself, are not well known outside this context. Byard Lancaster, also a Philadelphian, has an earthy wail redolent of Jackie McLean and Ornette Coleman, and he blends perfectly with Pope's multiphonics on 'The Ponderer', title-piece on the best of the Choir albums. Like the others, it has a strong internal consistency and is almost written like a continuous symphonic work, from 'Overture' to the Spanish-tinged 'Phrygian Love Theme'. Eddie Brown's 'One For Bubba' serves as an encore piece and a chance for the rhythm section to do its stuff.

Pope has tremendous gifts as a composer, layering rhythmic figures and harmonies in a way that parallels some of Ornette's 'harmolodic' experiments, but still making sense; Ellington again doesn't seem far away on 'The Saxophone Shop', the slightly ragged opener on the 1985 album. *Epitome* is the most ambitious but also the weakest of the bunch. The addition of Dave Burrell was inspired, opening up a rich, almost gospelly vein, and the recruitment of Craig McIver, in place of Rochester, was to be a particularly fruitful one for Pope. 'Zanzibar Blue' is the outstanding track.

***(*) Collective Voices

CIMP 124 *Pope; Tyrone Brown (b); Craig McIver (d).* 8/96.

Unexpected to hear Pope in this context after years with the Choir. Brown and McIver are alumni, but Pope's association with the bassist goes all the way back to a criminally undervalued band called Catalyst which they founded in 1972 (vinyl browsers might be lucky enough to turn up their stuff even now). Brown was the inspiration for the Eddie Brown original, 'One For Bubba', which ends *The Ponderer*, and his funky, loose-shouldered bass-lines are the foundation of this small group. He contributes three strong originals to this session: one of them a tribute to classical bassist Gary Karr, and another, 'El Monte', arranged as a duo for bass and saxophone.

Pope has worked in various Max Roach groups over the years, but he is not immediately thought of as a small-group player. The Coltrane influence is ever more deeply and inextricably enmeshed in a very personal idiom. On 'Collective Voices' and the two takes of 'You And Me' one can chart the extremes, the one dry and quite abstract, the other keeningly immediate and expressive. The overall impression, as ever, is of music that has been very carefully thought out. There are no throwaway gestures and, if one occasionally longs for a more unfettered and spontaneous expression, it's worth being reminded that there are bins full of cut-price free-for-all jazz in every store, but very little that reflects as much care and perspicacity as this.

*** Changes & Chances

CIMP 191 *Pope; Dave Burrell (p).* 1/99.

Two fascinating individualists who seem to come from opposite ends of the musical spectrum, yet find a great deal of common territory. If the history of jazz really is 'Three Four vs. Four Four' as the opening cut suggests, then the result is an amicable and thoroughly stimulating draw. 'Changes' and 'Chances' are no less thoughtful exercises, but a touch academic in conception. The really expressive writing is by Burrell, who is restricted to just two numbers, 'Full Moon In The Village' and 'Early On'. Interesting to put this disc on after one of Burrell's duets with David Murray, a saxophonist with a more groove-driven concept. This, by contrast, is rather esoteric and in places rather forbidding. Unusually, it was recorded away from CIMP's home base (the Spirit Room at Rossie, New York), down in Chester, Pennsylvania. The sound is rather different but still bare-bones and unadorned.

*** Ebioto

Knitting Factory KFR 245 *Pope; Tyrone Brown (b); Craig McIver (d).* n.d.

Pope's heavy, at times almost battle-weary, sound sits pretty well with the kind of elemental backdrop offered by Brown and McIver. Coltrane and some earlier spirits are again deep inside his playing, but the rather cloudy sound doesn't help him and the music unfolds in an effortful manner. He may sound like an individual in an age of soundalike saxophonists, but he still needs context, and the thin material here doesn't help much.

*** Nothing Is Wrong

CIMP 294 *Pope; Khan Jamal (vib); Arthur Harper (b); Allen Nelson (d).* 8/03.

Some piquancy of contrast between these players although, as with the previous date, Pope's almost lumbering delivery can ground the music at points where it needs to take flight. Jamal tends to riff and play scales behind him rather than offer notable counterpoint. But somehow the music makes an impression: the title-track is an energizing free piece which really hits home, and some of the best playing comes from drummer Allen Nelson, a veteran performer.

Michel Portal (born 1935)

SAXOPHONES, CLARINET, BASS CLARINET, BANDONEON

Portal grew up in Bayonne, France, and earned his reputation working with visiting Americans in Paris, ranging stylistically from swing and bop to the avant-garde. He is also a highly accomplished classical musician, with a very pure and controlled tone on all his instruments. He is the favourite clarinettist of composers like Pierre Boulez and Luciano Berio.

*****(*) ¡Dejarme Solo!**

Dreyfus Jazz Line 849231 *Portal (sax, clarinets, perc, acc solo).* 79.

In 1970 Portal was working with John Surman, and a decade later he too was exploring solo performance. The solo record will certainly recall some of Surman's work, not least in its confident incorporation of folk themes, but there is a jaggedness and angularity to Portal's attack that are very different from the Englishman's softer and more accommodating accents. The record and the individual tracks are quite brief and enigmatically poetic. There are no wasted gestures. Portal has a remarkable ability to make even extremes of sonority, as from sopranino to contrabass clarinet, sound perfectly natural and idiomatic. It is a great pity that he did not release more material in this vein.

***** Arrivederci Le Chouartse**

hatOLOGY 622 *Portal; Leon Francioli (b); Pierre Favre (d, perc).* 80.

This live date was the first time that Favre and Portal had played together in some considerable time and there is a real air of expectation as bass and percussion set up a long, enigmatic introduction before Portal enters and whirls the trio away on a half-hour-long improvisation that must count as one of the best in his recorded career, full of classical and jazz references, but driven by his own impeccable logic. The rest of the set consists of two improvisations linked somewhat tenuously and designed to showcase Portal's clarinet-playing. Though the association with Favre is probably deeper as well as longer, he works off the bassist's cues more often than not, weaving together unrelated phrases and sixteenth-note figures into long lines of melody that spin out and round the hall before being picked up by one of the others and reinterpreted. Francioli is masterful, capable of everything from classical abstraction to rolling, funky ostinati that would do a Detroit or Philly session-man proud. It's beautifully recorded and packed with atmosphere. Out of circulation for a while, it's a welcome reappearance in the hatHUT catalogue.

***** Fast Mood**

RCA 344102 *Portal; Martial Solal (p).* 82.

The Solal discography contains many duo sessions of this sort, but few with this degree of quiet sophistication. Portal is his ideal partner and the music speaks for itself. Something is slightly odd about the balance and positioning of the two voices, with the piano often sounding behind the reeds in the stereo picture, with a resultant loss of detail. However, it's a minor consideration, given how fine this music is.

***** Cinémas**

Label Bleu LBLC 6576 *Portal; Paolo Fresu (t); Laurent Dehors, Guillaume Orti (sax); Rita Marcotulli (p, syn); Andy Emler (syn); Ralph Towner (g); Nguyen Lê (g, syn); Richard Galliano (acc); Michel Benita, Linley Marthe, François Moutin (b); Tony Rabeson, Aldo Romano (d, perc); Mino Cinelu, Doudou N'Diaye Rose (perc); Juan Jose Mosalini Et Son Grand Orchestre de Tango.* 95.

Portal describes this project as 'various kinds of music for the cinema outplayed with jazz musician friends'. *Out*playing may distort a little in the translation, but it is clear that Portal has given his chums free rein to reinterpret these seven movie themes and one television score, the music for Michel Polac's much-admired *Droit de réponse.* This is played with just Mino Cinelu in accompaniment. Other tracks, like 'Champ D'Honneur', find Portal in a horn-led sextet, or backed by Doudou N'Diaye Rose's tambours, or indeed, on 'Docteur Petio', with a whole tango orchestra. The results are beguiling and thoroughly unexpected, though the sheer range of styles may be bewildering for anyone who hasn't encountered Portal's brand of stylistic eclecticism before.

****** Dockings**

Label Bleu LBLC 6604 *Portal; Markus Stockhausen (t); Bojan Zulfikarpasic (p); Bruno Chevillon, Steve Swallow (b); Joey Baron (d).* 6/97.

A quiet masterpiece from an all-star band. Portal's daring in using such strong musical personalities so delicately and sparingly more than pays dividends, and it would be hard to imagine a record of such poise and grace. Baron and Swallow happily move between insistent ostinato figures and more or less free time, leaving Chevillon to anchor the basic metre. Bojan Z is as usual tasteful and responsive, and the two horns are deployed with great subtlety. Though there isn't a vibraphone, the most obvious model for the sound is the Dolphy group of *Out To Lunch!* (Eric is the dedicatee of the second track) but rendered ever more abstractly lyrical. Stockhausen has the penetrating intensity of a Freddie Hubbard, but with a softer and more plangent quality. The mourning dove timbre of Portal's clarinet on 'Dolphy', building in intensity over Baron's pattering accompaniment, is matched only by their interaction on 'Ida Lupino', this time with Portal on bandoneon. A truly marvellous record, thoughtfully swinging and emotionally focused.

**** Minneapolis**

013511-2 *Portal; Tony Hymas (ky); Vernon Reid (g); Sonny Thompson (b, v); Michael Bland (d).* 7/00.

Once past the disastrous 'M. P. On The Run', where Sonny Thompson's rap is an unfortunate recall of Miles Davis's 'Man With The Horn', the music settles down into a plausible kind of fusion, at least. After the subtle eloquence of *Dockings*, though, this is an embarrassing mistake. Portal can't assert himself in these settings and his playing, for all its eagerness to get involved, is simply not right.

Position Alpha

GROUP

Swedish all-sax quartet/quintet of the '80s and '90s, a European pioneer of the form.

♛ **** The Great Sound Of Sound

Dragon DRCD 307 *Mats Eklöf (bs, bsx, cl, tb); Sture Ericson (as, ts, ss, f); Thomas Jaderlund (as, ss, bcl, f); Jonny Wartel (sno, ss, as, ts, cl, t); Jonas Akerblom (ss, as, bs, alto horn).* 10/84.

*** Greetings From The Rats

Dragon DRCD 199 *As above, except add Erik Balke (saxes, v), Per Ekblad (d); omit Eklöf, Wartel.* 6/90.

** Titbits

Dragon DRCD 252 *As above, except Eklöf and Wartel return; add Jonny Axelsson (perc); omit Balke and Akerblom.* 8/93.

One of the great saxophone-band records, *The Great Sound Of Sound* is welcome at last on CD. By going one better than the host of saxophone quartets – and having a fifth member – Position Alpha created a huge sonority that is employed to devastating effect on a set recorded live in Gothenburg. Vast pieces like 'The Dada Zone' (and 'The Mama Zone') are comical in one way, disturbing in another: when one of their knees-up tempos dissolves into a flaring argument between the horns, it sounds like jazz tradition going sour before us. The tango, 'Riviera II', shows they can beat the big-band-section imitations beloved of the American sax groups with their eyes shut, and their two Mingus pieces are madly exhilarating, as bleakly humorous as the composer's own. There are stunning individual contributions when one of them gets hold of a solo, but it's the great sound of their sound that counts, recorded with raw immediacy and perfectly surviving the transfer from vinyl. A great favourite of ours which should be rescued from obscurity.

The rest of their output is inexplicably disappointing. Almost immediately, they began to move away from their first format, with very mixed results. *Greetings From The Rats* interspersed recitations by band members into the music and introduced a drummer, to no great purpose; there are a few real successes, such as 'Lexikon', but not enough. *Titbits* finds the group a shadow of its old self. Another live set, and this time the drummers often threaten to take over altogether; the saxophones sound distant and uninvolved.

*** Yeti

Dragon DRCD 350 *Mats Eklöf, Fredrik Ljungkvist, Jonny Wartel (saxes); Per-Ake Holmlander (tba, tb, nafir); Henrik Wartel (d).* 11/00.

Reconvened in the new century, the group has some new members but is still looking to recapture some of its early freshness. There are interesting moments for the reeds in the more composed passages, but little of the exhilarating wildness of yore; it sounds symptomatic of the times catching up with a group, since there's much other music in this vein being made elsewhere. Eklof's three pieces still create the odd frisson, though.

Chris Potter (born 1970)

TENOR, ALTO AND SOPRANO SAXOPHONES, BASS CLARINET, ALTO AND CHINESE WOOD FLUTES

Born in Columbia, South Carolina, Potter studied at Manhattan School and was gigging with Red Rodney when barely into his 20s. He has since become a prolific sideman and has already made many discs under his own name.

***(*) Presenting Chris Potter

Criss Cross Jazz 1067 *Potter; John Swana (t, flhn); Kevin Hays (p); Christian McBride (b); Lewis Nash (d).* 12/92.

***(*) Sundiata

Criss Cross Jazz 1107 *Potter; Kevin Hays (p); Doug Weiss (b); Al Foster (d).* 12/93.

Potter has grown into one of the major saxophonists of today. The astonishingly confident and full-blooded debut shows his prowess with any one of his chosen horns, and there's amazingly little to choose between his alto- (which he's subsequently all but given up) and tenor-playing. Both of them are muscular in the post-bop manner but full of surprising stylistic twists that make one think of both Parker's generation and the elegant elaborations of Benny Carter and Hodges. The breakneck opener, 'Juggernaut', is a typical young man's manifesto, but just as impressive are the various approaches to Monk's 'Reflections', Davis's 'Solar' and the five originals by the leader. One could single out Potter's consistently powerful tone, his reluctance to go too far out for effect or the thematic weight applied to all his improvisations; it's the way all this is combined that is impressive. He also gets the best out of the sometimes erratic Swana as a front-line partner, and Hays, McBride and Nash are a superb team. *Sundiata* is a shade behind: a little of Potter's playing exuberance seems to have been held back, and on a set-piece like 'Body And Soul' his lines of thinking are a mite too calculated to convince. That said, there's still plenty of terrific music. Foster, Weiss and Hays don't miss any tricks, and when the group take on another immortal tenor situation by tackling Rollins's 'Airegin' there's a sense of new adventure to go with Potter's insistent classicism.

**** Chris Potter/Kenny Werner: Concord Duo Series: Vol. 10

Concord CCD 4695 *Potter; Kenny Werner (p).* 10/94.

Potter and Werner go at some of these duos like a couple of boy racers. 'Istanbul (Not Constantinople)' is very fast and funny. But the main point here – with due respect to Werner, who plays excellent things – is to hear Potter at full stretch and in clear space, surprisingly freeish at some points, always concerned with the weight of his sound, and eliding bar lines and turning handsome phrases much in the manner of the young Rollins. He plays soprano on two and bass clarinet on one, but the tenor's the thing, and it's interesting to hear how *much* he plays; rather than soloing and resting, both men are playing together almost constantly. The results are witty, full-blooded and with a serious 'modern' bent, since the tunes are either originals, tough jazz pieces or oddball standards.

***(*) Moving In

Concord CCD 4723 *Potter; Brad Mehldau (p); Larry Grenadier (b); Billy Hart (d).* 2/96.

Although Mehldau was a hired gun for the date, this is an intriguing meeting between two of the sharpest players of their generation. The pianist leaves centre-stage to Potter but manages to get in some of the most telling solos, distilling his usual inquiring lyricism into brief, intense passages. Potter sounds very fine and, though some of his writing (the only non-original is 'A Kiss To Build A Dream On') is a trifle cryptic, the delivery is grand and powerful enough to spin a convincing whole out of a disjunctive collection of pieces.

*****(*) Unspoken**
Concord CCD 4775 *Potter; John Scofield (g); Dave Holland (b); Jack DeJohnette (d).* 5/97.

Potter does his inevitable all-star date and makes it sound easy. 'Seven Eleven' and 'Et Tu Brute?' are brainy blowing vehicles which sum up an aspect of the saxophonist's approach: he likes form but always finds ways to get round it. One could argue that his bandmates are close to the record-too-far zone and sometimes there's the feeling that we've heard Sco, Dave and Jack do this groove so often that it's a comfortable stroll where it should be an urgent sprint. As quartet music, though, this is cut and delivered at a very high level, and the two tunes which the guitarist sits out give Potter the chance to seal his stature.

*****(*) Vertigo**
Concord CCD 4843-2 *Potter; Joe Lovano (ts); Kurt Rosenwinkel (g); Scott Colley (b); Billy Drummond (d).* 4/98.

Vertigo is another step in 'helping me get to the next level'. As fine as many of the records under his own name are, nothing feels like a flat-out masterpiece so far, and his numerous sideman appearances betoken a player who loves to take gigs but is in some ways shy of asserting himself as the major personality on a record. Rosenwinkel (who worked with Potter in the Paul Motian Electric Bebop Band) is one of the most challenging players he's recorded with, and he makes more sense in this context than the ubiquitous Lovano, whose appearance on three tracks is more of a distraction than a help to the leader. Potter's solo intro to 'Act III, Scene I' sets out his stall, but the subsequent piece itself is an undeveloped episode. Better – outstanding, in fact – are the knotty improvisations he conjures out of the likes of 'Fishy'. There's still a studiedly cool quality to Potter's writing and group arranging, but the improvisation he spins out of it remains rich and satisfying.

***** This Will Be**
Storyville 101 4245 *Potter; Kasper Tranberg (c); Peter Fuglsang (f, bcl); Kevin Hays (p); Jacob Fisher (g); Scott Colley (b); Billy Drummond (d).* 3/00.

Potter was the most youthful winner of the Jazzpar prize when he collected it in 2000, and the celebratory concerts certainly have a forward-looking and optimistic feel. The leader's quartet play two pieces and an encore, and in the middle is 'Jazzpar Suite', which features the extra musicians in a six-part work. It's a pity that Potter's small group didn't get to play the entire programme, since their pieces are far and away the most creative music on show; in comparison, the septet music seems laboured. The record's uncomplicated sound captures something of Potter's in-person presence, though.

*****(*) Gratitude**
Verve 549433-2 *Potter; Kevin Hays (p); Scott Colley (b); Brian Blade (d).* 9/00.

If Potter's major-label move held any fears for him, you wouldn't know from this confident sprint through the history of jazz saxophone, conceived as a salute to a string of masters old and new. Some of the jumping around from horn to horn – he gets through six of them here, including a debut on Chinese wood flute – underlines that this would be a record pitched as a coming-out, even after all those listed above. It's still rather coolly conceived, too. The opening dedication to Coltrane, 'The Source', avoids the master's grandest gestures and scales him down to a kind of pocket-size, and 'Sun King' is Rollins refracted through 'an odd-meter context' that needs all four men to keep their eye unswervingly on the pulse. Here, and in the best of the session, one gets the exultant feel of players at the top of their game, even if they're not necessarily saying anything strikingly original as they go. Hays, who's been somewhat in shadow since his Blue Note albums, performs well, and Colley and Blade are top-notch. But at a few key points, Potter's concept gets away from him; he brings little of interest to the Parker piece, 'Star Eyes', and the flute tune 'Vox Humana' sits oddly with the rest. It should be interesting to follow his progress at the home of Diana Krall.

****(*) Traveling Mercies**
Verve 018243-2 *Potter; Kevin Hays (ky); John Scofield, Adam Rogers (g); Scott Colley (b); Bill Stewart (d).* 1/02.

Just at the moment when Potter might have asserted himself with an uncomplicated jazz record which trusted in his own powers as a player, he offers a complicated, often dreary set of themes that want to emphasize Potter the composer. Bits of sampling and electronic noise distract, Scofield arrives for three conquering-hero solos, and though there are passages which offer rewards – the powerful solo on 'Migrations', for one – the record feels overburdened with importance. He might like to think back to those first Criss Cross dates of a decade earlier, and reflect on what made them work.

Bud Powell (1924–66)

PIANO

It was a life and career clouded by physical and mental illness, and by the death of a brother, Richie, in the same car accident that took Clifford Brown, but during its short, troubled span Bud Powell created some of the most intense piano jazz in the literature. He grew up in New York City and from the age of 16, sponsored by Thelonious Monk, was jamming at Minton's Playhouse, the crucible of bebop. Though he adopted certain devices of older piano-players Art Tatum and Teddy Wilson, Monk was his main influence. Powell attempted to extend his linear, horn-derived, but still thoroughly pianistic approach by using unfamiliar intervals. At its greatest and also at its most troubled, his music is dark and alienated. Much of this is purely harmonic, but it also reflects the chronic mental disturbance Bud suffered after receiving a beating – racially motivated – in 1945, from which he never entirely recovered.

***** Bud Powell, 1945–1947**
Classics 1003 *Powell; Kenny Dorham, Fats Navarro, Freddie Webster (t); Sonny Stitt (as); Frank Socolow, Morris Lane (ts); Eddie de Verteuil (bs); Al Hall, Curley Russell (b); Kenny Clarke, Irv Kluger, Max Roach (d).* 45–47.

****** The Complete Bud Powell On Verve**
Verve 521669-2 5CD *Powell; Ray Brown, George Duvivier, Percy Heath, Curley Russell, Lloyd Trotman (b); Art Blakey, Kenny Clarke, Osie Johnson, Max Roach, Art Taylor (d).* 5/49–2/51, 54–56.

*** Bud Powell, 1949–1950

Classics 1170 *Powell; Fats Navarro (t); Sonny Rollins (ts); Ray Brown, Tommy Potter (b); Curley Russell, Buddy Rich, Max Roach (d).* 49–50.

**** Tempus Fugue-It

Properbox 1022 4CD *Powell; Miles Davis, Kenny Dorham, Leonard Hawkins, Fats Navarro, Tommy Stevenson, George Treadwell, Freddy Webster, Cootie Williams, Lammar Wright Sr (t); Edward Burk, Ed Glover, Bob Horton, J. J. Johnson (tb); Charlie Parker, Cecil Payne, Frank Powell, Sonny Stitt, Eddie Cleanhead Vinson (as); Eddie 'Lockjaw' Davis, Dexter Gordon, Morris Lane, Lee Pope, Sonny Rollins, Frank Socolow, Sam 'The Man' Taylor (ts); Leo Parker, Eddie de Verteuil (bs); Leroy Kirkland (g); Ray Brown, Leonard Gaskin, Norman Keenan, Tommy Potter, Carl Pruitt, Curley Russell, Ted Sturgis (b); Wallace Bishop, Art Blakey, Kenny Clarke, Al Hall, Roy Haynes, Irv Kluger, Sylvester Payne, Buddy Rich, Max Roach (d); Sarah Vaughan (v).* 44–50.

*** Mad Bebop

Savoy 17183 *Similar to above.* 44–47.

*** The Complete 1946–1949 Roost/Blue Note/Verve Swing Masters

Definitive 11145 3CD *As above.* 46–49.

**** The Ultimate Bud Powell

Verve 539788-2 *As above.* 49–56.

***(*) The Best Of Bud Powell On Verve

Verve 523392-2 *As above.* 49–55.

The chronology of Bud Powell's issued records is slightly complex. It was, in any case, an intermittent career and, more than most of his peers – certainly more than Parker – Bud suffered on the stand. Good and bad, 'early' and 'late' are inextricably mixed. The first Classics volume brings together some remarkable 1946 sessions with Kenny Dorham, Fats Navarro and Sonny Stitt that immediately point to how remarkable the 22-year-old already was, albeit in a raw-toned and unfinished way. The earliest things are with a group fronted by tenor man Frank Socolow, but then follow those fine Be Bop Boys sides, followed by the trio dates with Curley Russell and Max Roach which mark the emergence of Bud as a significant solo voice.

Mad Bebop is a piece of shrewd repackaging, with tracks cut for other leaders repackaged (and beautifully remastered from original acetates and source tapes) as if they were Bud's. The same period is also well covered on the beautifully packaged *Tempus Fugue-It*, which picks up Bud's story at around the same point and takes it on to a recording with the Charlie Parker quintet in 1950 and the band he co-led with Sonny Stitt at around the same time. In between, some astonishingly good music that works well when heard in chronological order like this. 'Dance Of The Infidels' from the Blue Note dates is a classic and seems enlarged by this broader context. As do the others.

By the end of this remarkable progress, Bud has created a new language for jazz piano, rooted on harmonic centres but moving ever wider beyond them, rhythymically subtle and virtuosic (he frequently has to move ahead of his section players) and driven by a passionate modernism, which comes out strongly on the peerless Blue Notes. There is a hint of manic intensity as well. Listening to these discs one after the other is a wearying experience, not because there are dull spots (very few) but because Powell seems keyed to an unbearable pitch every time he touches the keyboard.

The sheer erratic brilliance of the Blue Note recordings has tended to cloud the remarkable work that Powell did for Norman Granz. The Verve set documents his solo playing just before that catastrophic breakdown of 1951, and takes him through to rather calmer waters. There is no indication that neglect was ever part of Powell's problem. He was well looked after by Verve and they have done him proud with this magnificent five-CD package.

Powell's virtuosity shines through the bustling 'Parisian Thoroughfare' (a piece which, like 'Un Poco Loco', always precisely reflects his mood at the moment of playing) and 'A Nightingale Sang In Berkeley Square', which draws heavily on a Tatum influence. No single session on this set really outweighs the Blue Notes below, but cumulatively and collectively this sits beside them, one of the pillars of this most complex man's life-work.

The Classics option is always there and the 1949–50 volume includes mostly good trio sets from this fertile period. There are a couple of horn-led dates as well, with Navarro and Sonny Rollins, but most serious purchasers should consider a more measured (and inevitably expensive) approach to this period via the Definitive complete masters or the Properbox.

Selected by fellow pianist Chick Corea, the *Ultimate* compilation is an excellent introduction to Bud's Verve output and an ideal purchase for anyone who doesn't want to shell out for the full set. The best-of set contains a lot of overlap – 'Dance Of The Infidels', 'Parisian Thoroughfare', 'Tempus Fugue-It' – but perhaps inevitably gives more emphasis to standards than to Bud originals.

CORE COLLECTION

**** The Amazing Bud Powell: Volume 1

Blue Note 781503 *Powell; Fats Navarro (t); Sonny Rollins (ts); Tommy Potter (b); Roy Haynes (d).* 8/49, 5/51.

**** The Amazing Bud Powell: Volume 2

Blue Note 781504 *Powell (p solo), and with George Duvivier, Curley Russell (b); Max Roach, Art Taylor (d).* 5/51 & 8/53.

Despite the linking name and numbered format and the existence of a magnificent boxed set (below), the Blue Note CD transfers can quite comfortably be bought separately; indeed *Volume One* – with its multiple takes of 'Bouncing With Bud' (one of which was previously on *The Fabulous Fats Navarro: Volume 1*), the bebop classic, 'Ornithology', and Powell's own barometric 'Un Poco Loco' – was out of print for some time, and the fourth volume was issued only in 1987, after which the whole series was made available again at a very acceptable mid-price. *Three* and *Four* have only just reappeared, even though they have to some extent been superseded by the magnificent *Complete* which is a must for every Powell enthusiast and is denied a crown only because it does have its dark and troublous moments and isn't perhaps the kind of thing you'd want to spend extended periods of time with. The multiple takes of 'Un Poco Loco' are perhaps the best place for more detailed study of Powell's restless pursuit of an increasingly fugitive musical epiphany. 'Parisian Thoroughfare' contrasts sharply with the unaccompanied version, above, and is much tighter; Powell had a more-than-adequate left hand; however, since he conceived of his music in a complex, multilinear way, bass and drums were usually required – not for support, but to help proliferate lines of attack. The quintet tracks are harshly tempered, but with

hints of both joy and melancholy from all three front-men; Navarro's almost hysterical edge is at its most effective, and Powell plays as if possessed.

Volume 2 contains one of the most famous Powell performances: the bizarre, self-penned 'Glass Enclosure', a brief but almost schizophrenically changeable piece. There are also alternative takes of 'A Night In Tunisia', 'It Could Happen To You', 'Reets And I' and 'Collard Greens And Black Eyed Peas' (better known as 'Blues In The Closet', see below).

***(*) Jazz At Massey Hall

Original Jazz Classics OJC 111 *Powell; Charles Mingus (b); Max Roach (d).* 5/53.

Jazz At Massey Hall is the rhythm section's spot from the classic Parker/Gillespie concert in Toronto, which has become a trig point for bop fans. (Any lucky dog who owns the 12-CD compilation of Mingus on Debut will already have it.) If for no other reason, these tracks redirect attention to the enormous influence all three players had on bebop. Powell's schizophrenic opposition of delicate, high-register lines and thudding chords is most obvious on 'Cherokee'. He displaces 'Embraceable You' entirely, losing his two colleagues in the middle choruses as he works out his own romantic agony.

*** From Birdland (New York City 1956) *[sic]*

Musidisc 550202 *Powell; Oscar Pettiford (b); Roy Haynes (d).* 2/53.

Some mistake surely? Well, yes. These live tracks, confidently attributed to Birdland and three years later, are identical to the dates of 7 and 14 February, which were taped at the Royal Roost. Even the personnel is wrong and it shouldn't take a seasoned bebop listener too long to work out that they're not listening to Paul Chambers and to a much lighter and busier drummer than Art Taylor. Not the best recording of the period. Some of those below are better; but an interesting set, and the two longish standards performances – 'Tea For Two' and 'Lover Come Back To Me' – throw light on Bud's debt to Tatum and Teddy Wilson.

**** Bud Plays Bird

Roulette 8 37137 *As above.* 10 & 12/57, 1/58.

Roulette was the label associated with Birdland, and these newly discovered masters, uncovered by the tireless Michael Cuscuna, are the most significant addition to the Powell discography since the release of Francis Paudras's extensive memorial album of Powelliana. Appropriately enough, given the provenance, all the tracks (except for 'Salt Peanuts') are Parker compositions. This is one of the most allusive and far-reaching of all Powell's recordings. He has rarely demonstrated his sheer musical intelligence so clearly, freely associating between harmonically or melodically similar material, at times almost eliding passages which are too familiar and replacing them with new ideas, as on 'Relaxing At Camarillo' and the finger-breaking 'Shaw 'Nuff'. His introduction to 'Yardbird Suite' is actually the opening of Tadd Dameron's 'Our Delight'; 'Big Foot' (aka 'Drifting On A Reed') invokes Dizzy's 'Oop-Pop-A-Da' and (as Ira Gitler very perceptively notes) Allen Eager's 'Meeskite' as well. 'Ornithology' and 'Scrapple From The Apple' are both magnificent, coming from the later and better December and January sessions, by which time the trio seems to have got its balance back. Powell plays inspired piano throughout, but it seems to have taken time to get Duvivier and Taylor, and particularly the bassist's characteristic low-end lines, accurately recorded. There are a number of incomplete and rejected takes from this session. Perhaps they will be issued in future in a more compendious issue, but for the moment applause to Cuscuna and Roulette for releasing a well-balanced album, and not an unedited slice of archive. All Bud Powell fans will want this record.

*** The Amazing Bud Powell, Volume 4: Time Waits

Blue Note 21227 *Powell; Sam Jones (b); Philly Joe Jones (d).* 5/58.

*** The Amazing Bud Powell, Volume 3: Bud!

Blue Note 35585 *Powell; Curtis Fuller (tb); Paul Chambers (b); Art Taylor (d).* 8/58.

Time Waits is perhaps the least interesting of the Blue Notes, which may be why it appears out of chronological sequence. Compared to Chambers and Taylor, the two Joneses offer fairly crude accompaniment and Philly's rush through things, audible on alternate takes of 'John's Abbey' and 'Sub City', blunts one or two of these tracks. Bud himself is playing with fire and considerable intelligence and his solos on 'Time Waits' and the mournfully titled 'Dry Soul' are the old mix of extraordinary harmonic gravity with vigorous counterpoint. Flashes of genius, still. *Bud!* is back in circulation with an extra track. Otherwise known as volume three of *The Amazing Bud Powell*, it consists of five Powell compositions played by the trio and three standards with the addition of Curtis Fuller, who makes an interesting lead voice. The real drama lies in the former tracks, though, and while there is nothing of quite the scarifying intensity of 'Glass Enclosure', the charge that he brings to 'Frantic Francies', 'Bud On Bach' and 'Keepin' In The Groove' is astonishing.

**** The Amazing Bud Powell, Volume 5: The Scene Changes

Blue Note 46529 *Powell; Paul Chambers (b); Art Taylor (d).* 12/58.

The cover photograph is heartbreakingly symbolic: a lowering Bud looks down at sheet music on the piano in front of him, rapt, private, shut away with his thoughts, while round his left shoulder a little boy peers guardedly, like his own lost younger self. These 1958 performances for Blue Note were an attempt to rekindle the fires. All the material is original and, though most of it harks back to the bop idiom rather than forward to anything new, it contains some of his most significant statements of any period. 'Comin' Up', of which there is also an alternative take, is in the released version his longest studio performance, and one of his most exuberant and playful, almost Latinate in feel. 'Down With It' is generic bebop and not a particularly effective idea, a long melody-line over orthodox changes, and only really distinguished for Chambers's fine *arco* solo. There was an earlier tune called 'Crossin' The Channel'; this, though, is Bud's alone and is the most formally constructed piece in the set, the one item that marks him down as a significant composer. 'The Scene Changes' is the final track on the original LP. It's a curious piece in that it looks back more than forward, almost as if the next scene were fated to be like the last. So it was to prove in Bud's life.

**** The Complete Blue Note And Roost Recordings

Blue Note 830083 4CD *Powell; Fats Navarro (t); Curtis Fuller (tb); Sonny Rollins (ts); Curley Russell, Tommy Potter,*

George Duvivier, Paul Chambers, Sam Jones, Pierre Michelot (b); Max Roach, Roy Haynes, Art Taylor, Philly Joe Jones, Kenny Clarke (d). 47–63.

The box set draws a line under Powell's genuinely amazing Blue Note career. Now that all of these records are available individually, the package is perhaps less attractive, but it does offer some additional music and information and as an object, it's decidedly top drawer.

***(*) **Round About Midnight At The Blue Note**
Dreyfus Jazz Line 849227 *Powell; Pierre Michelot (b); Kenny Clarke (d).* 4/61.

Michelot and fellow-exile Clarke are as attentive as courtiers, and Bud himself sounds unusually focused and responsive to what they in turn are doing, frequently making space for Michelot's miniature counter-melodies. Very much a straight bebop gig, it also points strongly to Bud's debt to Thelonious Monk, which is evident on 'Monk's Mood', 'Round Midnight' and 'Thelonious'. Was God in the house that night?

*** **A Tribute To Cannonball Adderley**
Columbia CK 65186 *Powell; Idrees Sulieman (t); Julian 'Cannonball' Adderley (as); Don Byas (ts); Pierre Michelot (b); Kenny Clarke (d).* 12/61.

***(*) **A Portrait Of Thelonious**
Columbia CK 65187 *Powell; Pierre Michelot (b); Kenny Clarke (d).* 12/61.

Two sessions produced in Paris by Cannonball Adderley. His role was more complicated than the average producer's for, in addition, the first record is a tribute to him, and he also plays on one previously unheard track. The collaboration with Byas was a happy one for Bud, who was in better shape at this time than he had been in a couple of years, and certainly he is playing with confidence and passion. The trumpeter plays on only a few of the tracks and the quartets are frankly better. Byas's pre-bop stylings and instinct for the blues don't always sit entirely easily with Bud's approach, but they manage to broker some common ground and Bud puts more blues feel into his playing than usual. 'Jackie, My Little Cat' appears in an alternative take which is actually better than the release version, and there is a previously unissued retake of 'Cherokee' which has a lot going for it as well, not least that cameo by Cannonball. Sulieman makes his most significant intervention on the Dameron tune, 'Good Bait', tackling it with aplomb. 'All The Things You Are' is awash with memories of days with Bird and Dizzy, as saxophonist and piano-player swap quotes, and doubtless reminiscences as well.

Recorded two days later, the Monk record is no less accomplished. Powell had been in on this particular story almost from the beginning; at 19, as a member of the Cootie Williams Orchestra he performed on the first recorded version of 'Round Midnight' and had subsequently gone on to become the other major piano innovator in the bebop revolution. The eight tunes recorded (there is also an unreleased take of 'Squatty') come from pretty much across the spectrum of Monk's output. 'Monk's Mood' is the longest track and one of the very best, with feeling support from Michelot, who it is known practised and rehearsed on his own for some time before these sessions and who certainly sounds absolutely on song for them. Clarke is his usual relaxed but hard-driving self and on 'Ruby, My Dear' he excels himself, playing with taste and imagination. These were rather special moments in Powell's life. In the city which had become his other home, with sensitive playing companions and a producer who knew the material inside out as well, he could hardly fail, though in the past equally well-starred sessions had come to naught.

(*) **At The Golden Circle: Volume 1
Steeplechase SCCD 36001 *Powell; Torbjørn Hultcranz (b); Sune Spångberg (d).* 4/62.

(*) **At The Golden Circle: Volume 2
Steeplechase SCCD 36002 *As above.*

**** **Swedish Pastry**
Steeplechase SCCD 37045 2CD *As above.* 4/62.

(*) **At The Golden Circle: Volume 3
Steeplechase SCCD 36009 *As above.*

** **At The Golden Circle: Volume 4**
Steeplechase SCCD 36014 *As above.* 4/62.

*** **At The Golden Circle, Volume 5**
Steeplechase SCCD 36017 *As above.* 4/62.

*** **Budism**
Steeplechase SCCD 30007/9 3CD *As above.* 4 & 9/62.

We're now firmly in the era of an important discographical sub-genre: the Bud-Powell-live-in-Europe album. There are a great many of these. Some are good, others awful, but the majority don't really stand up on their own terms. Steeplechase have long been guilty of excessive documentation. One sharply edited disc from the 19 April 1962 gig would have been more than adequate, but now at least the label has put out the first two volumes in a budget edition as *Swedish Pastry.* The Stockholm session finds Powell wavering between the hesitant and the near-brilliant, without ever quite capturing the quality of the previous decade. The rhythm section play about as much part in the music as Rosencrantz and Guildenstern do in *Hamlet* – though, like most Scandinavian players, they seem well enough versed in the idiom. Volume 3 has a second version of 'I Remember Clifford' from later in the residency; the last three all come from 23 April and are of more than passing interest, but by this stage the whole exercise seems rather redundant. Four volumes of Powell at his *best* would still call for stamina. Volume five is probably a disc too far, especially when it makes room for a ludicrous Powell vocal on 'This Is No Laughing Matter', which probably wouldn't have been any better if it had been on-mic. There is, however, a fine 20-minute version of 'Straight, No Chaser' which makes up for it somewhat. Most buyers can safely stick to *Swedish Pastry* as a good representation of this tour.

There is no certainty about the dating of the material on *Budism.* With the exception of ten tracks which are known to come from the autumn residency, there is no firm dating; however, listening to the tracks one by one, instinct suggests that they may well all come from the later period. There are a few small rhythmic devices which don't seem to be audible on the earlier sessions, most notably a sharp trill near the start of 'Dance Of The Infidels' on disc three (one of the definite September tracks), which crops up again on 'Epistrophy' and 'Off Minor' on the uncertainly provenanced disc one. Amorphous as the changes are, one might fudge it by saying that *Budism* is a more 'Monkish' selection, stylistically speaking, than the earlier Steeplechases. That may well recommend it.

*** **Bouncing With Bud**
Delmark DD 406 *Powell; Niels-Henning Orsted Pedersen (b); William Schiopffe (d).* 4/62.

Recorded three days after the later Golden Circle session, this has the pianist nosing again at 'I Remember Clifford', apparently dissatisfied with something in the theme. Otherwise it's quite predictable fare, played with discipline but not much passion. This material was originally issued on Sonet, with just one track ('Ruby My Dear', absent from this issue) released on Delmark.

***** Live In Lausanne 1962**
Stretch 9038 *Powell; Bob Jaquillard (b); Mike Stevenot (d).* 62.

What's frustrating about this set from that same heavily documented year is that Bud plays no originals, presumably because his Swiss sidemen were unfamiliar with them. Good to hear him on standards and repertory pieces, though, and the piano seems fair to decent. A brisk run-through of some bebop classics, though, and a great version of 'All God's Chillun Got Wings', which Bud seems to enjoy playing. It's mic'ed quite close, so Bud can be heard murmuring and wailing through his solos, but neither this nor a very muddy mix detract from the modest pleasure this unusual live date offers.

***** Paris Sessions**
Pablo 2310972 *Powell; Dizzy Gillespie (t); Zoot Sims, Barney Wilen (ts); Guy Hayat, Pierre Michelot, Gilbert Rovere (b); Kenny Clarke, Kansas Fields, Jacques Gervais (d).* 57–64.

***** Parisian Thoroughfares**
Pablo 0976 *Powell; Clark Terry (t, flhn); Peanuts Holland (t); Eric Peter, Zoot Sims, Barney Wilen (ts); Rene Thomas (g); Pierre Michelot (b); Kenny Clarke, Daniel Humair (d).* 57–64.

In our first edition, we reviewed the complete vinyl edition of Paris recordings made of Bud by his friend and protector (and character in *Round Midnight*) Francis Paudras. This is a very good one-volume sampling of tracks which found Bud mostly happy and if not playing with the fiery intensity of previous years, certainly still playing well. The choicest cuts here are a live 'Taking A Chance On Love' with Zoot Sims on tenor and a poorly recorded but exciting version of 'How High The Moon' with Dizzy Gillespie. There are lots of short, atmospheric tracks to enjoy and despite the headlong pace of 'Be Bop', a feeing of calm as Bud approached the end of his short life.

Parisian Thoroughfares offers a taste of how Powell played live over the same period. It's a sketchy album, mostly poorly recorded and with an awful lot of Bud singing to himself thanks to unhappy mic placements. It's also probably better value for the guest stars – the irrepressible Terry on 'Miguel's Party', Wilen, Zoot, guitarist Thomas – than for the pianist himself. On the other hand, any vestiges of this short life's achievements are welcome and the opening 'Yesterdays' (austere in its beauty) and 'Omicron' (recorded for French television) are worth having even if the rest palls.

Gerard Presencer

TRUMPET, FLUGELHORN

Brilliant young British horn man who's made a stir as a sideman and in his own right.

***** Platypus**
Linn AKD 079/139 (SACD) *Presencer; Jason Rebello (p); John Parricelli (g); Andrew Cleyndert (b); Jeremy Stacey (d); Chris Fletcher (perc).* 00.

***** The Optimist**
Linn AKD 069/ 166 (SACD) *Presencer; Graham Harvey, Jim Watson (p); John Parricelli (g); Jeremy Brown, Laurence Cottle, Orlando Le Fleming (b); Jeremy Stacey (d, perc, prog); Miles Bould (perc); Jacqui Dankworth (v); Heavy Horns (brass).* 00.

***** Chasing Reality**
Act 10897 *Presencer; Joe Locke (vib); Geoff Keezer (p); Tommy Wadlow (ky); Adam Goldsmith, John Parricelli (g); Jeremy Brown (b); Chris Dagley (d).* 01.

Presencer plays flugelhorn throughout the debut album, with a warm, fat tone that sits nicely with Rebello's Fender Rhodes and Parricelli's tastefully old-fashioned jazz guitar. Much of the material is by the trumpeter, but 'Still Moanin'' is a wonderful variation on the Bobby Timmons classic: part respectful, part satirical. The rhythm section plays with unfussy authority and the SACD sound is magnificent. It's also available on a regular edition. *The Optimist* was widely reviled for its apparent sell-out to jazz fusion, but listen closely to Presencer's endlessly inventive phrasing and to his sharp writing and such dismissive comments seem irrelevant and prejudicial. He is every bit as impressive on these albums as he seemed as a youngster, making his way as guest horn man on other people's discs. The opening sequence of 'Blah De Blah' and 'Dr Jekyll' puts him in the Donald Byrd camp, a trumpeter whose subtlety is disguised by his affection for a groove.

Chasing Reality was also intended for Linn, but a tape was sent to Siegfried Loch at ACT and was taken up. The music came out of a commission from Birmingham Jazz and was broadcast by the BBC. It's a typical British jazz project: complex, thoughtful and unexpectedly swinging and funky. The other solo voices are hard to keep down and Presencer's own personality comes through strongly, even if the material is forbiddingly impersonal.

André Previn (born 1929)

PIANO

A transplanted Berliner, like Marty Grosz, Previn is slightly better known as a conductor than as a jazz pianist. He's useful, though.

***** Double Play!**
Original Jazz Classics OJC 157 *Previn; Russ Freeman (p); Shelly Manne (d).* 4 & 5/57.

***** Pal Joey**
Original Jazz Classics OJC 637 *Previn; Red Mitchell (b); Shelly Manne (d).* 10/57.

***** Gigi**
Original Jazz Classics OJC 407 *As above.* 4/58.

***** Like Previn!**
Original Jazz Classics OJCCD 170 *Previn; Red Mitchell (b); Frank Capp (d).* 58.

***** André Previn And His Pals**
Fresh Sound FSR CD 106 *As above, except add Leroy Vinnegar (b), Shelly Manne (d).* 6 & 8/58.

***** Plays Songs By Vernon Duke**
Original Jazz Classics OJC 1769 *Previn (p solo).* 8/58.

A concentrated period of activity for Contemporary, and what a gift he must have been for the label, turning up immaculately rehearsed, straight, clean, unimpeachably professional, and then laying down first-take performances one after the other. One suspects there never will be a box of André Previn out-takes and alternatives, and yet there's nothing unswinging or unspontaneous about any of these performances. 'No Words For Dory', on *Like Previn!* touches an expressiveness one would not expect from him in this context.

The label quickly cottoned on to the show-based and song-book approaches as quick and effective ways of selecting and theming material. *Gigi* is predictably skittish and playful, though not without its moments of tenderness. *Pal Joey* offers more of real musical substance, including the deathless 'I Could Write A Book' and the less well-known 'What Is A Man?'. The Duke portfolio is the only one on which the pianist's classical training becomes evident, turning 'Cabin In The Sky' and 'Autumn In New York' into tiny symphonic statements and 'April In Paris' into an elegant, impressionistic tone-poem.

Double Play! had cast him in a more straightahead formula and repertoire, and in retrospect it almost seems the best of the bunch, because the most uncomplicatedly jazz-driven. Ever after, a Previn And His Pals album always seemed to need an angle or a spin; though, as the Fresh Sound compilation suggests, he could deliver the goods in a live context without strain or self-consciousness.

★★★ King Size!
Original Jazz Classics OJC 691 *Previn; Red Mitchell (b); Frank Capp (d).* 11/58.

★★★ Plays Songs By Jerome Kern
Original Jazz Classics OJC 1787 *Previn (p solo).* 2 & 3/59.

★★★ West Side Story
Original Jazz Classics OJC 422 *As for Pal Joey.* 8/59.

★★★(★) Plays Songs By Harold Arlen
Original Jazz Classics OJC 1840 *Previn (p solo).* 5/60.

The pace didn't slacken into 1959 and 1960, though increasingly the approach seems deliberate and even over-programmed. Previn dropped the 'And Pals' tag, and went out for a time as Trio Jazz, though he was also increasingly committed to the idea of solo performance. His minimal opening statements on 'Something's Coming' on *West Side Story* give way to a brash and tightly belted solo which exactly suits the emotional temper. Typically, though, it degenerates into rather technical figuring, octave jumps and altered chords which are impressive without being very involving. *King Size!* suffers in much the same way, almost too clever, and the fact that Red Mitchell also had a formidable musical brain only reinforced the impression, as the two attempt to outdo one another.

The songbook albums are again most impressive, though interestingly here there is now more unvarnished jazz than in the trios. The Kerns are magnificent. 'All The Things You Are' is little less than a summation of everything Previn had learned about jazz piano, though it's the harmonic shifts on 'Why Do I Love You?' and on Arlen's 'For Every Man There's A Woman' that tug at the heart-strings.

★★(★) Like Love
Collectables 6681 *Previn; orchestra.* 60.

André's diary for 1960 must have been packed pretty solid. His trio work for Columbia seemed to be selling briskly but this project gave him an opportunity to show off his arranging skills. These are mostly softly romantic cuts, without the element of surprise which crept into many of the small-group sessions. All of the songs have a love theme, which is hardly original, though nor is it a guarantee of banality. Dare we say in this case: background music?

★★★ Give My Regards to Broadway
Collectables 6695 *Previn; Red Mitchell (b); Frank Capp (d).* 60.

★★★ Camelot / Thinking Of You
Collectables 6086 *As above; add Herb Ellis (g); Ray Brown (b); Shelly Manne (d).* 60.

★★★ 4 To Go! / The Light Fantastic
Collectables 5892 *As above.* 12/63.

Two pairs of André's Columbia LPs, teamed on useful compilation sets, plus the more eclectic *Give My Regards*, which ranges over a number of shows and composers. *Camelot* has never been one of our favourite Broadway shows and songs like 'The Simple Joys Of Maidenhood' haven't quite forced their way into the jazz mainstream. However, Previn as ever makes a very decent case for them in jazz terms, and while this is certainly not a classic set, it's worth having if you like his thing.

Of the second pairing, the second album was a tribute to Fred Astaire and includes such obvious picks as 'Nice Work If You Can Get It', 'A Foggy Day' and 'Puttin' On The Ritz'. Previn sounds easy and charming, and it's left to Red Mitchell to sound some of the more robust tones. The earlier *4 To Go!* is a delight and it's astonishing that Columbia have not seen fit to reissue it, even if only for Previn's deft work on 'Oh, What A Beautiful Morning'.

(★★★★) The 4 Horsemen Of The Apocalypse
Rhino 77764 *Previn; MGM Studio Orchestra; Eileen Wilson (v).* 62.

Previn's soundtrack for Vincente Minnelli's Second World War epic was drastically cut along with the release version of the film and was then further diluted on the soundtrack album. This set restores the whole score, though it mystifyingly puts the 'Entr'acte' at the very beginning. The movies were in Previn's blood and on this he indulges the full spectrum of moods and styles, from moody *noir* passages to ensembles that shout full-screen action. The jazz component is quite high, considering, and cast interesting light on Previn's other work of the period. Vocalist Wilson is there for only a single track.

★★★ After Hours
Telarc 83002 *Previn; Joe Pass (g); Ray Brown (b).* 3/89.

★★(★) Uptown
Telarc 83303 *As above, except Mundell Lowe (g) replaces Pass.* 3/90.

★★(★) Old Friends
Telarc 83309 *As above, except omit Lowe.* 8/91.

Previn's renaissance as a jazz pianist was hailed as a return to an old love, but it was also, of course, the resort of a man who had been bruised by orchestral politics more subtly cut-throat than anything the Medicis would have dared. These don't quite have the bounce and the freshness of old and very quickly sound formulaic. Listening back after a gap of some years doesn't change the impression, though Lowe's long-neglected gifts are a source of delight and interest on *Uptown*. Best to stick with the Contemporarys.

★★★ A Classic American Songbook
DRG 5222 *Previn; Thomas Stevens (t).* 1/92.

A delightful set of readings from a fairly predictable roster of songs. Stevens is like Wynton Marsalis in reverse, a fine classical player who also has a deep grasp of jazz, and though he doesn't swing too many numbers, he has the ability to reinvest these hoary old songs ('My Funny Valentine', 'Bewitched, Bothered and Bewildered', 'Easy Living', 'Stardust'/'Skylark') with real emotion and dramatic presence. As show tunes should be.

***(*) Jazz At The Musikverein

Verve 537704 *Previn; Mundell Lowe (g); Ray Brown (b).* 6/95.

***(*) Show Boat

Deutsche Grammophon 453 860 *As above, except add Grady Tate (d).* 96.

***(*) We Got Rhythm: A Gershwin Songbook

Deutsche Grammophon 453 493 *Previn; David Finck (b).* n.d.

A long way from the club in *The Subterraneans* where a very young Previn played himself soundtracking Kerouac's troglodyte hipsters to the Musikverein in Vienna. Listening to him tackle 'What Is This Thing Called Love?' revives the complaint that he was never called on or never willing to do a Cole Porter songbook for Contemporary. It's an exquisite, feeling performance, like everything on this record. 'Hi Blondie' is an original, but a tune that might have sprung unbidden out of some forgotten '30s show. 'Satin Doll' is equally lovely and the medley that begins with 'Prelude To A Kiss' is a fitting end to the set, just to be followed by a roistering 'Sweet Georgia Brown'. Where Red Mitchell might have tinkered with the harmonics, and Mundell Lowe has had his own bout of experimentalism, Brown plays it straight and true, pushing along the beat with that huge, authoritative tone. We can vouch for the impact of this group live; engineer Andrew Wedman and producers Elizabeth Onstrow and Alison Ames (how often are we able to credit two women in the role, even in the late '90s?) deliver a rich, authentic sound, full of atmosphere and not missing a single detail.

We're not aware of ever having listed any Deutsche Grammophon releases, either, and it's nice to welcome the blue-chip classical label. *Show Boat* contains some wonderful music, and this group (especially with the addition of the utterly musical Tate) does it every justice. This is Lowe's big moment; recorded strong and very full, he leaves no doubt what we all missed when he was out of the picture.

The Gershwin date is interesting in that it followed an all-Mozart programme Previn was conducting at Tanglewood. The next day he and that fine bassist David Finck simply wandered down to the Florence Gould Auditorium in Seiji Ozawa Hall, Lenox, Massachusetts, got up a pot of coffee and started running through some tunes. Here and there Previn doesn't sound note-perfect, but he has the musical nous to profit from occasional slips, and the best of these tracks are quite exceptional. Edward Jablonski's liner-notes on the individual songs are an added plus (little details like the three-times failure of 'The Man I Love', the best track here, but a flop initially and canned from *Lady Be Good!* and *Strike Up The Band*), but the real delight is the simple lyricism and creative sophistication Previn brings to a composer whose work he seems to understand with his very nerve-ends.

*** We Got It Good And That Ain't Bad: An Ellington Songbook

Deutsche Grammophon 3456 *Previn; David Finck (b).* 4/99.

You'd be forgiven for thinking this was a latter-day Oscar Peterson set. The speed of invention (notably on 'Take The "A" Train' and 'I Didn't Know About You') is reminiscent of the big Canadian, but André is more identifiably himself on the slower tracks. He gives 'Isfahan' a delightful reading, and 'Chelsea Bridge' is almost a classical étude, without lapsing into a 'classical' style of playing. His swing is easy and always on the edge and Finck is an ideal accompanist for a session of this kind, often hovering in the background when he realizes there's no need to push things along.

*** Live At The Jazz Standard

Decca 013220 *Previn; David Finck (p).* 10/00.

Teamed up with bassist Finck, Previn turns in a breezy and confident set that kicks off in the most emphatic way imaginable with a cover of Gerry Mulligan's 'Westwood Walk'. Son Lukas Previn is credited as composer of 'Bye Bye Sky', which is a lovely theme. Much of the rest is standard fare, 'What Is This Thing Called Love?', 'My Funny Valentine' and so on, but Previn executes even these tired warhorses with wit, verve and undimmed enthusiasm. His obvious delight in the closing take of 'I Got Rhythm' is so infectious most listeners will recue the track and hear it through again. Splendid stuff from a born-again jazzman.

Bobby Previte (born 1957)

DRUMS, PERCUSSION

Previte arrived in New York in the early '80s and quickly established himself as a versatile bandsman, composer and leader, most closely associated with the downtown circle, but up and ready for anything in music. His own bands have included Weather Clear, Track Fast and Latin For Travelers.

***(*) Too Close To The Pole

Enja 9306-2 *Previte; Cuong Vu (t, v); Curtis Hasselbring (tb, v); Andrew D'Angelo (as, bcl, v); Jamie Saft (ky); Lindsey Horner (b, v).* 96.

Previte's drumming has a strangely loose, unfettered quality that sometimes camouflages very effectively the absolute steadiness of the beat he is laying down. Since he started recording under his own name, he has shown an ability to function in all sorts of contexts, drawing on music outside jazz and stamping everything with a wry, slightly mischievous personality. The records often sound like soundtracks to an imaginary movie, with a multiplicity of characters, an enigmatic story-line and no particular axe to grind. Moody reprises loom out of nowhere and disappear again.

This is Previte's racetrack band (Weather Clear, Track Fast) coming through for a determined late challenge – probably from a position one or two off the stands rail, although the leader's five originals are as idiomatic as anything in this well-spoken milieu of free bop and beyond. Vu and Hasselbring are well drawn, and the lesser-known D'Angelo is running well off a light weight; but it's Previte himself, clearly a long way from being in the handicapper's grip, who is the paciest runner.

***** Euclid's Nightmare**
Depth Of Field DOF 1-2 *Previte; John Zorn (as).* 3/97.

A nostalgic back-to-the-roots exercise by two now-venerable mandarins of their (ahem) scene. Few of these 27 miniatures manage to breast the two-minute barrier and perhaps that's a pity, since they often seem to be starting something which then stops. Or maybe we should just hear the thing as a continuous piece with its interstices decided on at random. Zorn is often a lot quieter and sweeter than one expects. Previte taps out one swinging tattoo after another.

*****(*) My Man In Sydney**
Enja 9348-2 *Previte; Jamie Saft (ky); Marc Ducret (g); Jerome Harris (b, g, v).* 1/97.

Boisterous good fun from a warm-to-hot quartet, coming to you from the sun-soaked pleasure zone of Sydney, Australia, in high summer (actually, it was cut in a place called The Basement Club). Saft's little battery of keyboards – Hammond, Fender Rhodes and Mini-Moog – induce a nicely nostalgic feel of late-'70s fusion, which Harris and Ducret undercut with their howlin' guitars; all the while, Previte is drumming up a storm of varied rhythms from the back, the side, anywhere he feels like he can roll it forward. The sound-mix is appropriately thick and humid. As brainy bar-bands go, there can't be many to touch this one.

*****(*) Just Add Water**
Palmetto PM 2081 *Previte; Ray Anderson, Joseph Bowie (tb); Marty Ehrlich (ts); Wayne Horvitz (p); Steve Swallow (b).* 6/01.

Previte, like many another veteran of a once avant-garde kind of scene, has accrued his own dynasty of associations and integrities by now, which means that a new set from him is, if not quite predictable, at least in a familiar bag. Ehrlich and Horvitz, for instance, both go way back with him. Downtown irony is more or less a thing of the past now, so Ehrlich's ballad solo on 'Nice Try' sounds unaffected and genuine, while the various kinds of funk beat served up in ''63' and ''53 Macerate' are signature Previte frolics. He likes to have fun with his music, but don't be surprised if this sounds better than many a more serious contemporary set 20 years hence.

***** Counterclockwise**
Palmetto PM 2091 *Previte; Curtis Fowlkes (tb); Marty Ehrlich (ts); Wayne Horvitz (p); Timothy Young (g); Steve Swallow (b).* 10/02.

This time, though, some of the fun seems to have ebbed away. Previte's still edging closer to a kind of stasis: his players do his bidding, and they can play anything from the complicated funk of '877-Soul' to the sweeter strains of 'Patricia'. Yet while it works as all-of-a-piece, one waits for something to stand up or stand out.

Eddie Prévost (born 1942)

DRUMS, PERCUSSION

Conventional start in British trad and bebop, then co-founded AMM in 1965 and has been among the leaders of British improv since. Writings suggest his position as a foremost theoretician of the scene, and his own Matchless label has documented a broad range of work.

***** Silver Pyramid**
Matchless MRCD40 *Prévost; large ensemble.* 5/69.

Eddie Prévost was once nicknamed 'the Art Blakey of Brixton', and though he has long since outstretched his early jazz influences – Roach rather than Blakey, and above all Ed Blackwell – he still has deeper roots in jazz drumming than almost any of his free-music peers. The only arguable exception is his exact contemporary, Han Bennink, but Prévost has also explored traditions like Korean court music and, in recent years, the further reaches of noise-rock with groups like God.

His main area of activity remains the long-standing collective AMM, and *Supersession* has to be heard in a similar context, one in which individual expression is less important – indeed almost irrelevant – against the interactions of the ensemble. The *Silver Pyramid* disc is the record of a remarkable Music Now event at the Roundhouse in London, featuring work by some of the leading avant-garde composers of the day and centring on Prévost's title-piece and totem object, a prismatic reflector that somehow channels a whole improvisational language. Work by Cage, Christian Woolf, Christopher Hobbs, Cornelius Cardew, LaMonte Young and others, played by a floating ensemble of improvisers, among whom Keith Rowe (Prevost's bellwether for four decades) is enticingly prominent. As an aural experience, it's less compelling than AMM recordings of the time. It is none the less an important document of a critical moment in creative music in Britain.

****** Live: Volumes 1 & 2**
Matchless MRCD 01/02 *Prévost; Gerry Gold (t); Geoff Hawkins (ts); Marcio Mattos (b).* 77.

*****(*) Continuum + 1983/84**
Matchless MRCD 07 *Prévost; Larry Stabbins (ts, ss); Veryan Weston (p); Marcio Mattos (b).*

****** Supersession**
Matchless MR 17 *Prévost; Evan Parker (ss, ts); Keith Rowe (g, elec); Barry Guy (b, elec).* 9/84.

Prévost's jazz origins are still quite clearly audible on *Live*, the album which inaugurated his own Matchless label, and one on which he delivers, as an obstetrician might, one of the best recordings of this period of British free jazz.

Gold and Hawkins make a marvellous partnership, ranging from austere fury to jovial rave-ups which occasionally recall the more experimental of Mingus's workshop bands. Gold in particular has a clear, emphatic signature, idiosyncratic enough to make one wonder why he hasn't been recorded more often.

Prévost is one of the most articulate exponents of the music. He is the author of a book called *No Sound Is Innocent*, where he argues the existence of an aesthetic in which music is inseparable from the realm of ideas and social exchanges. The quartet might seem conventionally distant from what he has done with AMM and with other groups, but it does illustrate how generously he opens himself to situations in which hierarchies collapse. There is no 'front line' here, no 'rhythm section'. It is the musical equivalent of total football, everyone contributing at every level.

That is presumably also the aim of *Supersession*, a punning name which combines the idea of the supergroup – the core of AMM plus two of the leading British improvisers of recent years – with a Hegelian concept in which thought constantly 'supersedes' the last level of organization. Some will say this is meta-jazz, too rarefied to bother with. Unfortunately (for them) it is as viscerally exciting as anything Art Blakey ever did.

The quartet with Stabbins and Mattos is not unrepresentative, but it certainly touches on different interests and loyalties. Stabbins is undeservedly neglected. He is a fascinating player who has learned much from Coltrane and earlier tenor-players, but who has a sound and an approach to phrasing which is entirely his own. Mattos is a giant, a player of great spirituality. Prévost himself is in great form, crisp, disciplined, but wild as well.

*****(*) Loci Of Change – Sound And Sensibility**
Matchless MRCD 32 *Prévost (solo).* 9/96.

Evan Parker describes this as 'social music', while simultaneously suggesting that it is both 'lonely' and 'intimate'. This is just about right. Prévost gives no sense, and almost certainly wouldn't welcome the notion of expressive, let alone confessional, music, but *Loci Of Change* does presuppose a very direct involvement on the listener's part. It is necessary to surrender oneself to Prévost's music, to its particular language. This does not require a suspension of all other associations, nor does it require a technically literate understanding of the instrumentarium – idiophones, membraphones, harmonics, overtones. It simply calls for a level of responsiveness which allows these six very different pieces to make their undogmatic point.

*****(*) Touch – The Weight, Measure And Feel Of Things**
Matchless MRCD 34 *Prévost; Tom Chant (ss); John Edwards (b).* 3/97.

*****(*) The Virtue In If**
Matchless MRCD 43 *As above.* 99.

This is Prévost's most interesting project outside AMM, a mostly quiet and very centred trio which harks back to the free jazz of the '60s (groups like Trevor Watts's Amalgam) but which also touches on the expanded language and dissolved categories of the '90s. Chant's curious birdcall effects and Steve Lacy-influenced chirrups and yelps are never foregrounded to the detriment of the other two instruments. Edwards is a hugely underrated player, perhaps damned to the shadow of the showier and more histrionic Paul Rogers, but absolutely critical to the disciplines of this music. Prévost himself is better than ever, hinting at a pulse, refusing to allow it to be taken. Ten years ago, there was some reason to fear that music of this kind had outlived its natural span. This makes it relevant again.

The second trio record shows a step forward in terms of concentration of sound. Prévost is unbelievably responsive to his two colleagues, making room for them and playing with a delicacy and grace that is breathtaking. Again, the almost ritual quality of his work comes to the fore, as if we are present at some mysterious event which unfolds according to arcane and hermetic principles.

***** Concert, v.**
Matchless MRCD 37 *Prévost; Veryan Weston (p).* 6/98.

The first reaction to this music might be that it is private, inward and uncommunicative, but both these experienced players have the ability to make any performance sound eavesdropped. Weston has a touch that at first hearing seems formal, almost constrained, but also fraught and strange. Prévost has dabbled in other musics over the last few years and plays with eclectic authority. For us, though, this is an instance of the law of diminishing returns. What must have been a riveting concert performance palls rather quickly.

****** Material Consequences**
Matchless MRCD 48 *Prévost (perc solo).* 01.

*****(*) Seventh of May 2001 – The Matchless Day**
Matchless MRCD 47 2CD *Prévost (perc solo); Tom Chant (sax); John Edwards (b).* 5/01.

There have been few enough opportunities to hear Prévost perform outside a group context. This is riveting stuff, rhythmic, intensely lyrical and focused. It is perhaps best to listen to the album as a single, undifferentiated performance. There is a quality of ritual about some passages, a sense of time suspended as enigmatic mysteries are unfolded or some arcane mathematics unfolds. It is one of the most moving performances Prévost has chosen to release and demands constant and attentive listening.

The other record is not strictly Prévost's, though disc one includes another, briefer solo recital and disc two has material with his most recent trio. The Freedom of the City event as a whole has yielded other material on Emanem Records, but this was the best of it and the set will be welcomed by anyone who has admired and appreciated Prévost's work, not just as a performer but also as dramaturge of Matchless.

*****(*) The Blackbird's Whistle**
Matchless MRCD 56 *Prévost; Tom Chant (ts, bcl); John Edwards (b).* 10/03.

Conceived as a meditation on a musical and philosophical encounter in Italo Calvino's *Mr Palomar*, this delightful set extends the language of Prévost's now well-established trio. Chant's tenor-playing on the opening 'Twirls Of Modulation' is robustly jazz-centred, but still free of constraint and absolutely idiomatic in this context. Prévost's drumming is, as ever, poised between freedom and a recognizable pulse, which takes this music closer to a free-jazz idiom than his still better-known work with AMM. His solo on that same opening track is a model, virtuosic as it moves between 9/8 and other equally difficult counts, and endlessly musical. Edwards is a still unacknowledged star, a bassist of real resource and power, whose limber woody tone commands attention in any context. The final eponymous section is as good a trio performance as you'll hear this or any year.

*****(*) Imponderable Evidence**
Matchless MRCD 57 *Prévost; Evan Parker (ts).* 11/03.

Received too late to include in Parker's already capacious entry, this is too good to omit and Prévost's co-authorship justifies its inclusion here. Perhaps because his partner does always imply elements of pulse, Parker always plays subtly differently in the drummer's presence and here, restricted to tenor, that's very evident again. Subtitled 'the subtleties of glance, of gesture, of tone', it's very much in line with the duo's deceptively well-mannered philosophical explorations. The five tracks are entitled 'exhibits' as if these pieces were raw evidential material in some overridingly pressing case or quiddity. The urgency of enquiry is compelling from start to finish. Vintage times for Prévost and for his doughty label.

Sam Price (1908–92)

PIANO, VOCAL

Played piano in his native Texas before going to Kansas, Chicago and New York. House pianist for Decca from 1938, playing blues and boogie styles, then worked in clubs, Europe, Texas again, and back in New York. Often visited Europe in later years and also ran his own clubs and commercial companies.

★★★ Sam Price 1929–1941

Classics 696 *Price; Douglas Finnell, Joe Brown, Eddie 'Moon' Mullens, Shad Collins, Bill Johnston, Chester Boone, Emmett Berry (t); Bert Johnson, Floyd Brady, Ray Hogan (tb); Fess Williams (cl, as); Lem Fowler (cl, v); Don Stovall (as); Ray Hill, Lester Young, Skippy Williams (ts); Percy Darensbourg (bj); Duke Jones, Ernest 'Bass' Hill, Billy Taylor (b); Wilbert Kirk, Harold 'Doc' West, Herb Cowens, J. C. Heard (d); Yank Taylor, Ruby Smith, Jack Meredith (v).* 9/29–12/41.

Aside from two 1929 tracks, all this material dates from 1940–41, when Price was recording regularly for Decca with his 'Texas Bluesicians'. It might have been recorded in New York, but the music is authentic southern swing, fronted by the pianist from Honey Grove, Texas. Many of the 24 tracks are features for his simple, blues-to-boogie playing and amiable vocals, which tend to predominate as the sessions go by, but there's also some fine playing from the horns. 'Sweepin' The Blues Away' includes excellent work by Brown and Stovall, and a 1941 session actually features the Lester Young band, though Young himself has only a few bars here and there in the limelight. Remastering is quite good, though the two 1929 tracks are noisy and some surface hiss is intrusive on a couple of later tracks.

Julian Priester (born 1935)

TROMBONE

A Chicagoan, Priester worked in R&B and big bands before coming to New York in 1958, joining the Max Roach group until the early '60s and subsequently freelancing. Moved to California in the '70s and is sighted occasionally; a couple of scarce ECM albums await reissue.

★★★(★) Keep Swingin'

Original Jazz Classics OJCCD 1863 *Priester; Jimmy Heath (ts); Tommy Flanagan (p); Sam Jones (b); Elvin Jones (d).* 1/60.

★★★ Out Of This World

Milestone 47087 *Priester; Walter Benton (ts); Charles Davis (bs); McCoy Tyner (p); Sam Jones (b); Art Taylor (d).* 7/60.

Priester has always been scarce as a leader. Apart from his 1977 ECM record, *Polarization* (and its predecessor *Love, Love*), which has acquired almost cult status with vinyl collectors, he remains virtually unknown in that capacity. To some extent, the eclipse must be due to the instrument he plays, which has almost always been B-list. Priester's apprenticeship was with Muddy Waters and Bo Diddley, playing blues and R&B, but in 1954 he was recruited by Sun Ra, which must have helped to reinforce his distinctive combination of swing with a dark, sometimes almost fey abstraction. Though the debut album is edged with shadows, it's basically a straightahead blowing set, short, well-crafted tunes with nicely defined shapes. The three on which Heath sits out give the leader a little more space. The closing 'Julian's Tune' is perhaps the clearest indication, though here more recent associations with Lionel Hampton and Max Roach are evident as well. They open with Heath's '24-Hour Leave', which establishes the atmosphere. 'The End' is a Priester original, strongly vocalized and with the blues running through it. Charles Davis is the composer of '1239A' which, though brief, is as strong on atmosphere as the rest of the set. Priester's own other originals are 'Bob T's Blues', which sounds like a studio run-down, and 'Under The Surface', another that plumbs his darker side. An excellent debut.

Out Of This World pairs Priester's *Spiritsville* with an album of Walter Benton material named after the Arlen-Mercer song. Priester remains firmly rooted in orthodox hard bop and, while there is some interest in hearing the young McCoy Tyner working his apprenticeship, there isn't much of any great moment to report. The remastering is nice and the set is useful as an introduction to the under-recorded Benton, but as a Priester set it's a bit thin.

Marcus Printup

TRUMPET

Studied at Georgia State, then played with Marcus Roberts and the Lincoln Center Jazz Orchestra, before striking out on his own account.

★★★(★) The New Boogaloo

Nagel Heyer 2019 *Printup; Wycliffe Gordon (tb); Walter Blanding (ts); George Colligan, Eric Lewis (p); Vicente Archer (b); Donald Edwards (d).* 11/01.

Printup emerged with two Blue Note albums in the '90s, but those have disappeared and this new excursion for Nagel Heyer is a fresh start for the trumpeter from Georgia. One problem with the earlier discs was a shortage of strong material, and Printup's seven themes here remedy that at once. From the beginning, 'The Bullet Train' is a ferocious blues with a requirement for the bassist to play the same figure throughout; and the tendency for the players to play to a strut rhythm edges over into most of the pieces. What comes out is often akin to a brainy kind of soul-jazz, softened by Printup's own rather romantic tone, then buoyed up again by the feelgood time which Archer and Edwards bring to even lyrical themes such as 'Sardinian Princess'. It helps that the leader can call on the services of several colleagues from the Lincoln Center gang: Gordon proves again that he's the boss trombonist of the moment, with stunning plunger-mute work on 'The Weeping Prince', and Blanding's tenor is a beautifully dark, finely felt voice. Plus the bonus of George Colligan, a pocket genius at the piano, who shares keyboard duties with Eric Lewis across the session. A strong comeback for a figure who once looked to have lost his way.

Don Pullen (1944–95)

PIANO, ORGAN, COMPOSER

A long spell with R&B groups and singers eventually led Pullen to the Charles Mingus band of the mid-'70s, and thereafter a long association with George Adams. His early death cut short a career which seemed full of music but which now seems to belong to an increasingly distant and sadly unfashionable corner of the jazz past.

*****(*) Solo Piano Album**
Sackville SKCD2-3008 *Pullen (p solo).* 2/75.

***** Capricorn Rising**
Black Saint 120004 *Pullen; Sam Rivers (ts, ss, f); Alex Blake (b); Bobby Battle (d).* 10/75.

***** Healing Force**
Black Saint 120010 *Pullen (p solo).* 76.

*****(*) Warriors**
Black Saint 120019 *Pullen; Chico Freeman (ts); Fred Hopkins (b); Bobby Battle (d).* 4/78.

***** Milano Strut**
Black Saint 120028 *Pullen; Famoudou Don Moye (d, perc).* 12/78.

****** Evidence Of Things Unseen**
Black Saint 120080 *Pullen (p solo).* 9/83.

*****(*) The Sixth Sense**
Black Saint 120088 *Pullen; Olu Dara (t); Donald Harrison (as); Fred Hopkins (b); Bobby Battle (d).* 6/85.

Don Pullen's solo records demand comparison with Cecil Taylor's. Pullen's traditionalism is more obvious, but the apparent structural conservatism is more appearance than fact, a function of his interest in boogie rather than Bartók, and he routinely subverted expected patterns. The classic Sackville session, recently reissued on CD, makes the point, although it sometimes reinforces an impression of Pullen as a performer interested in large masses of sound, sometimes to the detriment of forward progress. That in turn led him back to the organ, on which he created huge, sustained chords and swirling textures, as on the duo record with Moye. *Evidence Of Things Unseen* is by far the best of the solo discs, though the recently reissued *Solo Piano Album* will have its supporters as well. *Evidence* bespeaks the same dark-and-light opposition as Andrew Hill or Ran Blake, though Pullen was more of a free player than either, and certainly less of an ironist than Blake.

He favoured exotic dissonances within relatively conventional chordal progressions and, to that extent, was a descendant of Monk. His tribute album is very uneven, with completely wrong-headed effects on 'Round Midnight' and some of the aimlessness that creeps into his duos with George Adams.

Of the groups with horns, the best are those fronted by Freeman and Dara, where Pullen develops spiky, almost spasmodic graph-lines of improvisational material in the midst of inventive and often rather Ivesian structures; the technique is reminiscent of Mingus, with whom Pullen played in the mid-'70s. Rivers is too floaty and ethereal to be entirely effective in this context, though he noticeably tailors his approach to Pullen's cues. Now that all of his latter-day work for Blue Note has been remaindered, Pullen is suddenly a figure who belongs to a somewhat remote past. A strong best-of compiled from those later sets would help correct this misleading impression, but so far, nothing doing.

Ike Quebec (1918–63)

TENOR SAXOPHONE

Quebec began his career as a dancer but developed a tenor style that was somewhat influenced by Basie's Herschel Evans. His recording career came in two phases, early and late, though 'late' was to be depressingly early. Ike succumbed to lung cancer at 45 and left behind a small but significant legacy of recordings, plus a creative thumbprint on many of Blue Note's most distinctive bop recordings.

*****(*) Ike Quebec, 1944–1946**
Classics 957 *Quebec; Buck Clayton, Jonah Jones (t); Tyree Glenn, Keg Johnson (tb); Johnny Guarnieri, Roger 'Ram' Ramirez, Dave Rivera (p); Napoleon Allen, Bill De Arango, Tiny Grimes (g); Milt Hinton, Grachan Moncur, Oscar Pettiford (b); J. C. Heard (d).* 7/44–8/45.

***** The Strong Tenor Of Mister Quebec, 1943–1946**
EPM Musique 159602 *Similar to above.* 43–46.

Blue Note's last recording date in Hackensack and first in its new headquarters at Englewood Cliffs were both by Ike Quebec. Little known to younger fans, the saxophonist was nevertheless a figure of considerable influence at the label, acting as musical director, A&R man and talent scout (Dexter Gordon and Leo Parker were two of his 'finds'). He was also an important Blue Note recording artist, producing some marvellous sessions for the label just after the war and steering the label in the direction of a more contemporary repertoire. Mosaic had already issued a compilation of mid-'40s work by Quebec and John Hardee. *The Complete Blue Note 45 Sessions* brought together 27 popular sides Quebec made for the thriving jukebox market. By no means wholly organ-dominated, as such 45s tended to be, the sessions strongly featured Quebec's still-underrated tenor style, which sounds like a cross between Evans, Wardell Gray and Dexter Gordon. 'Blue Harlem', recorded for Blue Note in July 1944 in the company of Roger 'Ram' Ramirez, creator of 'Lover Man', was a jukebox hit and pretty much sums up the Quebec sound. The early cuts were made in collaboration with guitarist Tiny Grimes, who was also much involved in Charlie Parker's early career. The compilation includes a couple of rejected takes, of 'Blue Turnin' Grey Over You' and 'The Day You Came Along', alongside the released singles, of which 'Topsy'/'Cup Mute Clayton' (featuring Buck, of course), 'Mad About You' and 'Facin' The Face' (which features Oscar Pettiford in an early appearance) are by far the best. Much of the same material is covered on the EPM compilation.

*****(*) It Might As Well Be Spring**
Blue Note 21736 *Quebec; Freddie Roach (org); Milt Hinton (b); Al Harewood (d).* 12/61.

***** Blue And Sentimental**
Blue Note 784098 *Quebec; Sonny Clark (p); Grant Green (g); Paul Chambers (b); Philly Joe Jones (d).* 12/61.

***** Ballads**
Blue Note 56690 *Quebec; Sonny Clark (p); Earl Van Dyke, Freddie Roach, Sir Charles Thompson (org); Grant Green, Willie Jones (g); Milt Hinton, Sam Jones (b); Art Blakey, Al Harewood, Louis Hayes, J. C. Heard, Wilbert G. T. Hogan (d).* 9/60–3/62.

It Might As Well Be Spring is pretty squarely in the tenor–organ tradition, except that Quebec has opted to record some gently expressive standards, not just the title-track but also 'Lover Man', 'Ol' Man River' and 'Willow Weep For Me', as well as his own compositions, 'A Light Reprieve' and 'Easy – Don't Hurt'. Digital remastering has restored a bit of detail to the sound, and Roach is the one who benefits most, a surprisingly subtle player who always has plenty to say and doesn't sound as if he's merely stoking up a fairground calliope. Much to enjoy, and probably spot-on at this length. We're not sure that extra material would make a substantial difference.

Quebec has several times teetered on the brink of major rediscovery, but each time interest has flagged. He is, admittedly, a rather limited performer when set beside Gordon or any of the other younger tenor-players emerging at the time, but he has a beautiful, sinuous tone and an innate melodic sense, negotiating standards with a simplicity and lack of arrogance that are refreshing and even therapeutic. *Blue And Sentimental*, with fine performances on 'Minor Impulse', 'Don't Take Your Love From Me' and 'Count Every Star', is an excellent place to make his acquaintance, and once again sophisticated remastering has made a world of difference to the accessibility of the music.

Ballads is a fairly predictable compilation of laid-back themes drawn from four of Quebec's later albums for Blue Note, padded out with a single track, 'Born To Be Blue', which was recorded under Grant Green's leadership. An attractive package, and very welcome when these sessions are still only patchily available.

***** Bossa Nova Soul Samba**

Blue Note 52443 *Quebec; Kenny Burrell (g); Wendell Marshall (b); Willie Bobo (d); Garvin Masseaux (shekere).* 10/62.

Recorded a matter of months before Ike's death from lung cancer and when he was already showing signs of waning powers, this was made at a time when 'Latin' albums – and particularly *bossa nova* sessions – were more or less *de rigueur*. Almost uniquely for the time, there is nothing by Jobim in the programme, and the range of material is quite broad and imaginative. 'Me'N'You' and 'Blue Samba' are both strong originals, suggesting that Ike might well have moved fruitfully in this direction, had he been granted a little more time.

Paul Quinichette (1916–83)

TENOR SAXOPHONE

His nickname was the Vice Pres, and Quinichette was one of the very few who, without turning into a slavish Lester Young copyist, managed to convey something of the great man's tone and spirit. He was out of the business for many years, working as an electrical engineer, but he left behind some strong and individual albums.

***** Complete Dawn Sessions**

Blue Moon/Dawn DCD 106 *Quinichette; John Carisi, Renauld Jones, Thad Jones, Joe Newman, Gene Roland (t); Henry Cooker, Bob Swope (tb); Dick Meldonian (as); Bill Graham (as, bs); Nat Pierce (p); Freddie Green, Doyle Salathiel (g); Eddie Jones, Wendell Marshall, Oscar Pettiford, Dudley Watson (b); Osie Johnson, Walter Nolan, Sonny Payne (d); Sylvia Pierce (v).* 7/56–8/57.

***** On The Sunny Side**

Original Jazz Classics OJC 076-2 *Quinichette; Curtis Fuller (tb); John Jenkins, Sonny Red Kyner (as); Mal Waldron (p); Doug Watkins (b); Ed Thigpen (d).* 57.

***** For Basie**

Original Jazz Classics OJC 978-2 *Quinichette; Shad Collins (t); Nat Pierce (p); Freddie Green (g); Walter Page (b); Jo Jones (d).* 10/57.

Very much a middle-order batsman, Quinichette was best in the loose, jam-session format that Prestige favoured in the later '50s, and in the easy, open-ended cuts for Dawn. More often than is entirely comfortable, the man from Denver sounds overpowered by his colleagues. Trumpeter Gene Roland, hardly the most dominant of presences, is in great form on the August 1957 sets on the Dawn compilation. The larger formats consign Paul entirely to the shadows. He is more convincing on the Prestige dates. The eponymous 'On The Sunny Side Of The Street' and the Basie material on the other OJC are quite strong, but on both occasions the band is more impressive than the leader. On the former, he is paired with just Jenkins and rhythm, and he shapes some elegant and persuasive solos, but there isn't much to chew on here.

John Rae

DRUMS

Edinburgh-based drummer with a blend of post-bop and Scottish music.

***** Celtic Feet**

Caber 010 *Rae; Phil Bancroft (sax); Brian Kellock (p); Eilidh Shaw (vn); Simon Thoumire (concertina); Mario Caribé (b).* 6/99.

***** Beware The Feet**

Caber 018 *As above, except add Kevin MacKenzie (g); Guy Nicholson (perc).* 11/00.

Mr Rae used to run a jazz collective round Edinburgh which at times seemed the only bulwark north of the border against trad, funk and lite jazz. Edinburghers – and Irvine Welsh readers – will understand a title like 'Power Of The Radge', a celebration of in-your-face, up-front *thrawn*-ness. No one will mistake the sheer rhythmic power of Rae's small band. Anchored by pianist Kellock and light-toned bassist Caribé, it weaves a complex rhythmic and textural spell, from the unexpected stride opening to the astonishing rhythmic coup of the closing 'Slumber Jack' – 17/16, indeed! Thoumire's mournful concertina and the now patented saxophone sound of Phil Bancroft provide the spot colour, but it's Rae's ideas and sheer punch that make this such an engaging record. Hard to categorize (as is probably the intention) but, as the election celebration of 'May 7th' underlines, full of the confidence of a country and a music reinventing itself.

The sequel is an equal delight. There is a greater emphasis on traditional music, but Kellock's joyous imitation of Fats Waller on the opening 'Boogie Celt' establishes a jazz feel right from the beginning; laughter of pure delight in the studio at the end. 'Sing For Your Supper' is a good example of how Rae intends to use folky themes as the basis for adventurous improvisation; Bancroft's solo on it is topped only by MacKenzie's brilliant guest spot on the next track, played in a weavy Latin rhythm. The rest unfolds more or less familiarly, sometimes reminiscent of older crossover Celtic experiments by the likes of John Surman or Ken Hyder, but with considerable originality and unflagging imagination.

Boyd Raeburn (1913–66)

BASS, TENOR AND BARITONE SAXOPHONES

Began bandleading at 20, and by the '40s was in charge of a challenging group with many prominent modernists and some innovative arrangers. But the records weren't hits and he reverted to sweeter fare, leaving music altogether in 1957.

***** More 1944–1945**
Circle CCD 113 *Louis Cles, Ewell Payne, Pincus Stavitt, Benny Harris, Stan Fishillsen, T. D. Allison, Dizzy Gillespie (t); Earl Swope, Pullman Pederson, Bob Swift, Trummy Young, J. K. Corman, O. C. Wilson, W. C. Robertson (tb); John Bothwell, Hal McKusick (as); Angelo Tompros, Joe Megro, Al Cohn (ts); Serge Chaloff (bs); George Handy, George Hendelman, Ike Carpenter (p); Dennis Sandole, John Payuo, Steve P. Jordan (g); Andy Delmar, Mort Oliver, Oscar Pettiford (b); Don Lamond, Shelly Manne (d); Don Darcy, Marjorie Wood Hoffman (v).* 6/44–1/45.

***** March Of The Boyds**
Hep 22 *Raeburn; Gordon Boswell, Pete Candoli, Norman Faye, Conrad Gozzo, Wes Hensel (t); Eddie Bert, Dick Noel, Hal Smith, Britt Woodman, Ollie Wilson, Freddie Zito (tb); Lloyd Oto, Al Richman, Evan Vail (frhn); Harvey Estrin, Allen Fields (as); Harvey Klee (as, f); Wilbur Schwartz (as, cl); Frank Socolow (as, ts); Ralph Lee, Lucky Thompson, Shirley Thompson (ts); Hy Mandel (bs); Harry Babasin, Clyde Lombardi (bsx); Gus McReynolds (sax); Jules Jacob (eng hn, ob, ts); Michael 'Dodo' Marmarosa, Dale Pierce (p); Sam Herman, Tony Rizzi (g); Gail Laughton (hp); Tiny Kahn, Irv Kluger, Jackie Mills (d); Doug Jones (perc); David Allyn (v).* 45–46.

***** The Transcription Performances 1946**
Hep CD 42 *Similar to above.* 45–46.

In 1944 an unexplained fire at the Palisades Pleasure Park in New Jersey destroyed the instruments and music of one of the most challenging big bands of the period. Typically of Boyd Raeburn, his re-formed band and new book were even more adventurous than what had gone before. Musically, the Circle material from the apocalyptic year is typical of the leader's adventurous spirit and of the willingness of his players to push the boat out a little and take risks. Often exhilarating stuff. Raeburn's was a musicians' band, held in the highest esteem by his peers, regarded with some suspicion by those who believed that bands were for dancing. Raeburn had an intelligent awareness of classical and 20th-century forms and was as comfortable with Bartók and Debussy as he was with Ellington and Basie. The bands were clangorous, neither 'sweet' nor 'hot', but a curious admixture of the two, and arrangements were full of awkward time-signatures and tonalities. Tunes such as 'Tonsilectomy', 'Rip Van Winkle' and 'Yerxa', from earlier and (as yet) not reissued sessions, are among the most remarkable of modern-band pieces. Hal McKusick was a featured soloist and the Raeburn bands of the time (like Kirk's or McShann's) are well worth scouring for the early work of prominent modernists. It may be that simple market forces pushed Raeburn back in the direction of the swing mainstream.

Hep's set of transcriptions comes in decent sound and is something of a mixed bag: vocal features for David Allyn blend in with some of the maverick arranger George Handy's outlandish work. 'Cartaphilius' is a typically extraordinary Handy piece, the sort of thing Stan Kenton must have enjoyed. In sum, this is an inconsistent body of work, but Raeburn deserves a better shake than jazz history has so far given him.

Hugh Ragin (born 1951)

TRUMPET

Born in Houston, Ragin studied in Colorado and formed associations with some of the leading avant-gardists of the '70s, becoming a regular sideman with Anthony Braxton, Roscoe Mitchell and David Murray. He has since returned to Colorado to teach, and in consequence has been heard from less frequently of late.

*****(*) Sound Pictures For Solo Trumpet**
Hospscotch HOP 13 *Ragin (t solo).* n.d.

A rare sighting for Ragin as both leader and solo architect. As we've remarked elsewhere, solo trumpet is a tough discipline for a record, and it's to Hugh's credit that he makes this set as engaging to a listener as it is. 'For The Joy Of Sound Space & Music' makes a dazzling start, the trumpet treated with delay to evoke a whirling kaleidoscope. But the largest part of the disc is given over to the nine 'Rhythm Units', which are based around some of Leo Smith's pioneering themes for the solo trumpeter, an intriguing piece of repertory – although, given that they involved a very patient and even ordering of sounds, taken as a sequence they're stiff work for the uncommitted listener. The 'Ballad For Miles' is a poignant muted display; some variations on Paganini include the most virtuosic work on the disc; and a Braxton dedication starts slow and gets mercurial. Interesting as the 'Rhythm Units' are, it's Ragin's own themes which offer the most rewarding music here.

Ram Ramirez (1913–94)

ORGAN

Born in Puerto Rico, Ramirez was working as a pianist on the New York scene from the early '30s, and he switched to organ – supposedly following the example of Wild Bill Davis – in the early '50s. He remained a fixture on the club circuit for many years, although he seldom recorded.

*****(*) Live In Harlem**
Black & Blue BB 927.2 *Ramirez; Ronnie Coles (d).* 60.

Recorded at Frank's Steak House in New York, this is a priceless example of the kind of music which was still being played nightly at dozens of American clubs and eateries in simpler times. The opening 'Robbins' Nest' is luxuriantly spread across 25 minutes, and Ramirez simply plays chorus after chorus of sparse, almost parsimonious licks that develop their own irresistible momentum and logic, beautifully sustained. He sounds unlike any of the prevailing models on the instrument of the day, and is all the better for it. All Coles has to do is keep steady, steady time. Somebody in the audience – allegedly Bill Davis! – shouts out encouragement, but it sounds as if Ramirez is engrossed in his own world anyway. After that, the three remaining tracks are something of an anti-climax, but for a record steeped in New York atmosphere, this is hard to better.

Mark Ramsden

SAXOPHONES

Underrated British reedman with fingers in several musical pies.

*** **Tribute To Paul Desmond**
33Jazz 041 *Ramsden; Dave Cliff (g); Andy Hamill (b); Gary Hammond (perc).* 98.

*** **Above The Clouds: Saxophone And Organ**
Naxos 86041 *Ramsden; Steve Lodder (org).* 00.

Effectively co-led by Ramsden and Cliff, this is pretty much what it says, a more or less literal homage to Desmond and by extension his employer Dave Brubeck. 'Desmond Blue' and 'Take Five' are vivid enough, though the latter palls when set alongside drummer Simon Goubert's epic re-reading on his *Haiti*. Ramsden's more adventurous work features on the Naxos set with Lodder. His soprano sound is bright and penetrating, but there is too little musical substance to these meditations, which sit at least partly outwith a jazz idiom.

Freddy Randall (1921–99)

TRUMPET

A Londoner, Randall started out with a comedy group but formed his own traditional band in the late '40s. He recorded extensively for Parlophone in the '50s but, after a spell of illness, faded from the scene. He returned to more active duty in the '70s but continued to work sparingly and, away from music, he ran an old people's home.

***(*) **Vintage Freddy Randall 1949–1951**
Lake LACD170 *Randall; Geoff Love, Eddie Harvey, Norman Cave (tb); Cliff Townsend, Bruce Turner (cl); Laurie Gold (ts); Pat Rose (bs, cl); Freddy Gardener (bs); Dill Jones, Al Mead, Stan Butcher (p); Don Cooper, Vic Lewis (g); Hank Hobson, Danny Heggarty, Ron Stone, Ted Palmer (b); Max Abrams, Harry Miller, Lennie Hastings (d).* 2/49–10/51.

**** **Freddy Randall And His Band**
Lake LACD123 *Randall; Roy Crimmins, Norman Cave, Dave Keir (tb); Archie Semple, Dave Shepherd, Al Gay (cl); Betty Smith (ts); Dave Fraser, Harry Smith (p); Ron Stone, Ken Ingerfield, Jack Peberdy (b); Lennie Hastings, Stan Bourne (d).* 3/53–7/55.

A pair of records to convert unbelievers to the energy and vitality of the best British trad. Randall's groups weren't rough-and-ready outfits. He led by example, his trumpet-playing crackling with conviction and imagination alike, and his groups were hard-bitten but swinging in their doughty way. Randall liked the sound of the Chicagoan brassmen rather than the New Orleans strain beloved by Ken Colyer, and his jazz has an incendiary quality to it which eluded many of his contemporaries. Not that there isn't a sense of fun in the tracks on the second CD, chosen by Paul Lake from the 70-odd sides he made for Parlophone between 1953 and 1955. 'Professor Jazz' still raises a smile, and anyone who calls one of his originals 'My Tiny Band Is Chosen' has a reserve of wit as well as commitment. A model reissue, in excellent sound, and it is a pity that Randall himself did not live to see it happen. The earlier set is not quite as strong, perhaps. The 1949 session for Tempo suffers a bit from the band going off at too frantic a pace, though it's certainly exciting. The first sessions for Parlophone fill up the rest of the disc, and the Randall horn burns out of the speakers.

Doug Raney (born 1957)

GUITAR

Doug's career kicked off at the age of 18 when he worked with his dad, Jimmy Raney, and pianist Al Haig. A couple of years further on, Doug and Jimmy formed what was to be a long-standing duo. Both have recorded extensively, a substantial body of swinging, thoughtful and emotionally understated but unmistakably powerful jazz.

*** **Introducing Doug Raney**
Steeplechase SCCD 1082 *Raney; Duke Jordan (p); Hugo Rasmussen (b); Billy Hart (d).* 9/77.

*** **Cuttin' Loose**
Steeplechase SCCD 31105 *Raney; Bernt Rosengren (ts); Horace Parlan (p); Niels-Henning Orsted Pedersen (b); Billy Hart (d).* 8/78.

*** **Listen**
Steeplechase SCCD 31144 *As above, except omit Parlan; replace NHOP with Jesper Lundgaard (b).* 12/80.

Raised to the family craft, Doug Raney quickly established his own identity and a more contemporary idiom that also seemed to draw on swing guitar (missing out, that is, much of the bebop influence his father has sustained). Less robust rhythmically than his father, Raney slots more conventionally into a horn-and-rhythm set-up. CD doesn't always flatter his technique, which sounds slightly scratchy and lacks Jimmy Raney's smooth, Jim Hall-like legato. However, now that the Steeplechase catalogue is back in better shape, fine early records like *Introducing* are back in circulation, broadening the picture considerably; with Raney Junior, bulk is what it's about, fewer moments of sheer glory than the old man, but in their stead a dogged brilliance that begins to impinge only over many records. He's an artist who needs to be listened to steadily and whole.

The closing 'Moment's Notice' on *Listen* is one of Raney's best performances on record. There is a steady modal shift on his theme statements, and the soloing is robust without losing the tune's innate romanticism. Rosengren's Coltrane-isms are reasonably well assimilated, and he modulates well, as on *Cuttin' Loose*, between a smooth swing and a more aggressive modernism.

*** **I'll Close My Eyes**
Steeplechase SCCD 1166 *Raney; Bernt Rosengren (ts, af); Horace Parlan (p); Jesper Lundgaard (b); Ole Jacob Hansen (d).* 7/82.

*** **Meeting The Tenors**
Criss Cross Criss 1006 *Raney; Bernt Rosengren (ts, f); Ferdinand Povel (ts); Horace Parlan (p); Jesper Lundgaard (b); Ole Jacob Hansen (d).* 4/83.

*** **Lazy Bird**
Steeplechase SCCD 31200 *Raney; Bernt Rosengren (ts); Ben Besiakov (p); Jesper Lundgaard (b); Ole Jacob Hansen (d).* 4/84.

***(*) **Blue And White**
Steeplechase SCD 31191 *Raney; Ben Besiakov (p); Jesper Lundgaard (b); Aage Tanggaard (d).* 4/84.

The first few years of the '80s saw Raney trying to consolidate and managing only to mark time. These are not very compelling albums if one comes to them first and without an awareness of the robust thinking that lies beneath their rather bland surfaces. *Blue And White* is probably the best of them, dominated by titanic performances of Jimmy Heath's 'Gingerbread Boy' and John Coltrane's 'Straight Street'. The three previous records are only exceptional for the contributions of Bernt Rosengren, one of the great unsung heroes of European jazz and at this period a somewhat dark and brooding performer, even on relatively lightweight material. Raney understandably defers to him more often than not, taking more of a back-seat role on these discs than he had before and would subsequently.

*****(*) Something's Up**
Steeplechase SCCD 31235 *As above, except replace Tanggaard with Billy Hart (d).* 2/88.

***** Guitar Guitar Guitar**
Steeplechase SCCD 31212 *Raney; Mads Vinding (b); Billy Hart (d).* 7/85.

*****(*) The Doug Raney Quintet**
Steeplechase SCCD 31249 *Raney; Tomas Franck (as); Bernt Rosengren (ts); Jesper Lundgaard (b); Jukkis Uotila (d).* 8/88.

Things pick up sharply again with the neutrally titled 1988 album, which is intended to give the signal that here is a working band, under the command of its leader, playing full-on and undistractable. It's certainly a major lift on the rather shambolic essays of the early part of the decade. Besiakov is nowhere near as commanding a player as Parlan, but he has sharpened considerably over the four years since his last recording with Raney and lends a genuine presence to 'Good Morning Heartache' and 'Upper Manhattan Medical Group'.

The '88 quintet album is excellent in every department. There is another fine version of 'Speedy Recovery' (also on *Something's Up*). The extra horn and the absence of piano restores certain harmonic responsibilities to the guitar, but it also generates a very different texture through which he has to play with just a little more force than usual. It's difficult to know where else to start with Raney. The late-'80s albums are completely accomplished. Follow the stars.

***** Blues On A Par**
Steeplechase SCCD 31341 *Raney; George Cables (p); Steve LaSpina (b); Adam Nussbaum (d).* n.d.

It's always tricky to pitch two harmony instruments together, but Cables is such a subtle and swinging player that guitar and piano sound like two aspects of a single personality. The programme is more predictable than usual, with just the title-track as an original. 'When Sunny Gets Blue' is stretched out very much longer than usual, and it offers space to the whole group. Kenny Dorham's 'La Mesha' is delivered crisply and without fuss, setting up Charlie Rouse's 'Pumpkin's Delight' as a strong and big-voiced ending. Doug's delight in melody is most evident in the opening pair of tracks, 'I Concentrate On You' and 'Estate', which in a scant quarter of an hour run a remarkable range of ideas. He sounds more than usually relaxed and the guitar is nicely mixed with the rest of the group.

***** Back In New York**
Steeplechase SCCD 31409 *Raney; Kenny Barron (p); Peter Washington (b); Kenny Washington (d).* 95.

*****(*) Raney '96**
Steeplechase SCCD 31397 *Raney; Ben Besiakov (p); Lennart Ginman (b); Herlin Riley (d).* 7/96.

Rising 40, Raney was perhaps anxious to show that he hadn't got ring-rusty working in exile over in Europe, so the Manhattan session was something of a confidence-boosting exercise. It's certainly not as good a record as the four-oh celebration that is *Raney '96*, one of his strongest group albums yet, opening uncompromisingly with 'Giant Steps' and closing on 'Afro Blue', with material by Pat Martino, Wes Montgomery, Charlie Parker (an unexpected 'Moose The Mooche') and Bill Evans (a graceful 'Re: Person I Knew'). We've no technical reason for it, but Raney has become fuller-voiced and more resonant in recent years, and most noticeably on this album. The guitar seems to be the same favoured Gibson, but there are perhaps more upstroke notes and harmonics, filling in the background sound and creating harmonic shadows, where before all was sunlight and space. Whatever the reason, we like it; our favourite Raney album to date.

*****(*) The Backbeat**
Steeplechase SCCD 31456 *Raney; Joey DeFrancesco (org); Billy Hart (d).* 98.

Raney hasn't previously experimented with the traditional guitar/organ funk format, but this delicious set, named after the Horace Silver tune, suggests he can do the Wes Montgomery/Grant Green stuff with the best of them. Unlike *Raney '96*, the recording is flatter and less detailed, but with lots of extra bass, which suits the material perfectly. Duke's 'Prelude To A Kiss' is exquisite, a trio performance of near-perfect balance. Nothing else quite comes up to this standard and the record could possibly seem one-dimensional ... but only to cheerless cynics.

***** You Go To My Head**
Steeplechase SCCD 31474 *Raney; Jay Anderson (b); Billy Hart (d).* 99.

Steeplechase have always erred on the side of generosity in recording and issuing favoured artists. This is an album straight off the house production-line, a confident and uncomplicated performance that might sound a touch drab on second and subsequent hearings. All eight tracks kick in at about the same length and it might have been better to have given the trio its head on a couple of the stronger items – 'I Hear A Rhapsody', 'Triste', say – which suggest that there was much more to be said than is delivered. Never less than competent, Raney has been more arresting.

Jimmy Raney (1927–95)

GUITAR

Kentucky-born, Raney synthesized Charlie Christian with Lester Young to create long, cool, improvisational lines which have been hugely influential on guitarists of a later generation. Though now overtaken in terms of sheer quantity by his son Doug, with whom he has performed in duo and group contexts, Jimmy's work demands the closest attention.

***** Jimmy Raney Visits Paris**
Fresh Sound FSR-CD 89 *Raney; Roger Guerin (t); Bobby Jaspar (ts); Maurice Vandair (p); Jean-Marie Ingrand (b); Jean-Louis Viale (d).* 2/54.

****** A**

Original Jazz Classics OJC 1706 *Raney; John Wilson (t); Hall Overton (p); Teddy Kotick (b); Art Mardigan, Nick Stabulas (d).* 5/54–3/55.

Of the bop-inspired guitarists Raney perhaps best combined lyricism with great underlying strength. Essentially a group player, he sounds good at almost any tempo but is most immediately appealing on ballads. *A*, which contains some of his loveliest performances, remains an overlooked classic. Overton anticipates some of the harmonic devices employed by Hank Jones (below), and bebop bassist Kotick plays with a firm authority that synchronizes nicely with Raney's rather spacious and elided lower-string work. Wilson adds a dimension to the lovely 'For The Mode' and to four more romantic numbers, including 'A Foggy Day' and 'Someone To Watch Over Me'.

The Paris session has him lining up with some of the city's premier boppers, which may not mean all that much to anyone bar the natives. Yet there's the cool, almost mentholated tenor of Jaspar to add interest, and Raney is clearly engaged and up to play. The sound is a bit dusty.

*****(*) Raney '81**

Criss Cross Criss 1001 *Raney; Doug Raney (g); Jesper Lundgaard (b); Eric Ineke (d).* 2/81.

*****(*) The Master**

Criss Cross Criss 1009 *Raney; Kirk Lightsey (p); Jesper Lundgaard (b); Eddie Gladden (d).* 2/83.

****** Wisteria**

Criss Cross Criss 1019 *Raney; Tommy Flanagan (p); George Mraz (b).* 12/85.

The early '80s saw some vintage Raney on record. The quartet with Hank Jones is valuable largely for the inclusion of alternative takes that give a clearer idea of how subtly the guitarist can shift the dynamic of a piece by holding or eliding notes, shuffling the rhythm and increasing the metrical stress. *'81* includes some rejected takes, of 'Sweet And Lovely', 'If I Should Lose You' and 'My Shining Hour' most obviously, which offer convincing demonstration of his speed of thought and suggest once again what an underrated player he was by all except jazz guitar groupies, who presumably know their way round this stuff already.

The Master offers second takes of 'The Song Is You' and 'Tangerine' (but not, unfortunately, the vibrant 'Billie's Bounce'), revealing how thoughtful an accompanist Lightsey is. The rhythm-players are slightly too stiff for him, but he compensates by breaking up their less elastic figures with single-note stabs and scurrying runs at the next bar-line.

Flanagan's right hand is lost in a rather woolly mix, but the material on the marvellous *Wisteria* more than makes up for any purely technical shortcomings. From the opening 'Hassan's Dream', with its big, dramatic gestures, to 'I Could Write A Book', the drummer-less group plays at the highest level and 'Out Of The Past' is very special indeed.

***** Guitar Moments**

Steeplechase SCCD 37031/32 *Raney; Doug Raney (g); Michael Moore (b); Billy Hart (d).* 4/79.

*****(*) Nardis**

Steeplechase SCCD 31184 *Raney; Doug Raney (g).* n.d.

If you can't hire 'em, breed 'em. Raney's partnership with his son, Doug, has been one of the most productive and sympathetic of his career. Their duos are masterpieces of guitar interplay, free of the dismal call-and-response clichés that afflict such pairings, and often unexpectedly sophisticated in direction. Generally, the repertoire is restricted to standards, but Jimmy is also an impressive composer and frequently surprises with an unfamiliar melody.

Guitar Moments is a budget reissue of two LP/CDs, *Duets* and *Stolen Moments*. The closing 'My Funny Valentine' from the first album would melt a heart of stone, and Doug Raney, with the lighter, less strongly accented style that was so responsive to Chet Baker's needs, is particularly good on 'My One And Only Love' and 'Have You Met Miss Jones'. The addition of rhythm doesn't alter the basic conformation of the music, but it does increase the tempo and spices up the slightly unlikely samba. The curtain number is that old duo warhorse, 'Alone Together'. *Nardis* is a tribute to the late Bill Evans. Elegantly crafted and wisely paced, it is perhaps the best representation of how he and Doug have created a rich and vigorous language almost by swapping generational roles. Doug sounds like the traditionalist and Jimmy like the radical, and on 'I Can't Get Started' the dialogue is intensely absorbing. Recommended.

*****(*) But Beautiful**

Criss Cross Criss 1065 *Raney; George Mraz (b); Lewis Nash (d).* 12/90.

This is the master at work, to be sure. Raney plays with consummate ease and elegance, as perfectly balanced and utterly tasteful as ever. It's a great pity that he hasn't recorded more in this format. Mraz and Nash are both excellent, as always, and contribute considerably to the direction of Raney's solos, which do still have a tendency to drift and turn hazy at the edges. Mraz is formidably disciplined without losing expressiveness. The recording is very close and soft, picking up all the overtones in both sets of strings. By contrast, Nash is a little recessed.

John Rangecroft

CLARINET

Veteran British free improviser, rarely heard from on record of late.

*****(*) Blythe Hill**

Slam 228 *Rangecroft; Marcio Mattos (b); Stu Butterfield (d).* 10/96.

Cultivated free playing by three old hands who know each other well – Butterfield and Rangecroft played together in Cirrus in the late '60s, and Mattos joined them in the '70s. This is a rare sighting of the trio on record. It's chamberish, British free – Rangecroft is well known as a saxophonist, but he sticks to clarinet here, getting a rather cultured sound and seldom looking for extremes. The title-piece is a soberly beautiful exploration, and perhaps only on the long 'Altair' does the music show signs of sagging.

François Raulin

PIANO

Elegant chamber jazz from a rising star.

***** Trois Plans Sur La Comète**

hatOLOGY 582 *Raulin; François Corneloup (ss, bs); Bruno Chevillon (b, v).* 00.

Raulin can be drily abstract one moment and meltingly romantic the next. This fine trio set, which sounds like a Europeanized version of Jimmy Giuffre's '50s trio, is an excellent introduction to two very fine players; Chevillon will be known to most from his work with Louis Sclavis. The highlight is 'Calligraphies', which starts with a Satie-esque stillness and then whirls off into a wildly erotic dance, executed by Corneloup's soprano. The saxophonist is on baritone for 'Soho', which also features an unexpected touch of prepared piano. Raulin always seems keen to explore new sonorities. His touch is very varied and his occasional Bill Evans-isms are no more than way-stones on a very idiosyncratic path. Immediately accessible and enjoyable music if you don't mind music that marches to no drummer whatsoever.

Enrico Rava (born 1943)

TRUMPET, FLUGELHORN

Rava was born in the international city of Trieste and grew up in Turin, which in the '60s was to be a meeting-place for American musicians. Deeply influenced by Miles Davis, he gravitated towards the avant-garde with Gato Barbieri's group, and later with Steve Lacy; Rava was also a member of the Globe Unity Orchestra. His interest in free jazz has, though, always been tempered by an awareness of other genres and styles, anything from classical music and pop to electronics.

***** Il Giro Del Giorno In 80 Mondi**

Black Saint *Rava; Bruce Johnson (g); Marcello Melis (b); Chip White (d).* 2/72.

'Around The Day In 80 Worlds'; it's a fascinating variation on the Jules Verne title. This is funkier than Rava's slightly later ECM albums, driven along by Bruce Johnson's guitar, and quite explicitly influenced by Miles Davis's electric experiments, which were still quite fresh and new in 1972. As ever, Rava wasn't far behind the pace of what was going on in the US. Apart from Carla Bley's 'Olhos De Gato', all the tunes are Rava originals, and as befits a debut solo album, he tries to cover as many bases as possible. The title track, 'CT's Dance' (presumably that well-known terpsichorean Cecil Taylor) and 'Xanadu' are the most substantial pieces, reaching from the bright, bouncing figures of the first couple to a more misterioso approach. Often overlooked in favour of *The Pilgrim And The Stars,* this is one that deserves a fresh listen.

****** The Pilgrim And The Stars**

ECM 847322-2 *Rava; John Abercrombie (g); Palle Danielsson (b); Jon Christensen (d).* 6/75.

*****(*) The Plot**

ECM 523282-2 *As above.* 8/76.

****** Enrico Rava Quartet**

ECM 523283-2 *Rava; Roswell Rudd (tb); Jean-François Jenny-Clark (b); Aldo Romano (d).* 3/78.

For a time, these seemed the definitive Rava albums, unlikely to be bettered, so perfectly balanced are they. The trumpeter's distinctive manner is a combination of sustained, curving notes, unmistakably coloured, with sudden rhythmic tangents. In combination with Abercrombie's guitar and the top-flight Scandinavian rhythm section, he creates a sound-world all his own. Reconvening the same band two years later yielded a more subtle album, structurally and compositionally, but *The Plot*'s narrative sophistication ('Amici', 'The Plot' itself) consistently yields to the sheer pictorial poetry evident on 'Foto Di Famiglia', a Rava–Abercrombie collaboration that might have come from the same sessions as the earlier record. Anyone interested in the progress of European jazz should take notice of it at least.

The eponymous *Quartet* album paired him – often literally – with the waywardly brilliant Rudd. Their unison lines on the upbeat 'The Fearless Five' would be useful evidence for anyone wanting to disprove the old *canard* about ECM's supposed New Ageist failings. Both men are in cracking form, but they save their most expressive and lyrical statements for the long 'Lavori Casalinghi', co-written with Graciela Rava, which opens the set. There are strong things on 'Tramps' as well, but here it's the remarkable rhythm section of Jenny-Clark and Romano which catches the ear; their interaction could hardly be bettered on either side of the Atlantic, and the bassist in particular is given a lot to do, covering for the absence of a harmony instrument. 'Round About Midnight' is a hokey party-piece for the two horns on their own.

***** Rava String Band**

Soul Note 121114 *Rava; Augusto Mancinelli (g); Giovanni Tommaso (b); Tony Oxley (d); Nana Vasconcelos (perc); string quartet.* 4/84.

*****(*) Secrets**

Soul Note 121164 *Rava; Augusto Mancinelli (g, g syn); John Taylor (p); Furio Di Castri (b); Bruce Ditmas (d).* 7/86.

In the early '80s, Rava worked with (mainly) Italian bands, relying heavily on Mancinelli's Abercrombie-derived guitar. Tony Oxley's recorded contribution is restricted to the less than wholly successful *String Band* project, which reflects Rava's growing interest in formal composition for orchestral groups. *Secrets* gains immeasurably from the presence of another Englishman, John Taylor, whose cultured accompaniments and understated soloing are probably more widely recognized outside the British Isles.

*****(*) Nausicaa**

EGEA SCA 037 *Rava; Enrico Pieranunzi (p).* 3/93.

Some of the playing is, of course, exquisitely lovely, but it's not all rhapsodizing by any means: Rava's brassiness dispels Pieranunzi's occasional tendency to noodle, and there's no preening from the trumpet at all. 'Overboard', for instance, is an almost violent interchange. A very fine duet.

***** Rava, L'Opera Va**

Label Bleu LBLC 6413 *Rava; Francesco Fiore (as); Richard Galliano (acc); Battista Lena (g); Lorenzo Colitto, Giorgio Sasso (vn); Luca Peverini, Bruno Tomasso (b); Palle Danielsson (b); Jon Christensen (d).* 93.

Attempts to jazz up opera arias are either doomed to failure from the off, or perversely they work well. Something of the structure of an aria, which is after all a composed 'improvisation' derived from the preceding narrative and discursive material, is actually very similar to what a jazz soloist does with a theme or head. Rava knows this repertoire so intimately that the tunes are second nature to him, even relatively unfamiliar – in the sense of rarely whistled – things like the intermezzo from *Manon Lescaut* and the tiny fragments he chooses from Puccini's *La Fanciulla Del West* (usually translated as *The Girl Of The Golden West*). The group is larger than usual, and Rava's reliance on harmony instruments is subtly different from other projects. It's a delightful record. The trumpeter is on top form, hitting big top notes and wringing every drop of drama out of his selections from *Tosca*, which is clearly a personal favourite.

*** Electric Five

Soul Note 121214 *Rava; Gianluigi Trovesi (as, cl, bcl); Domenico Caliri, Roberto Cecchetto (g); Giovanni Maier (b); U. T. Gandhi (d).* 9/94.

It is, of course, a sextet; Rava follows the practice of excluding himself from his line-ups, almost as if the group was a separate entity. That's how the Electric Five comes across here. Their ensembles are very much a background against which Rava sings, prays, prowls and occasionally mourns bitterly. We've always found this a very moving record but one which lacks some essential element of expressive circuitry to make it a great one. The non-Rava tracks are, interestingly, 'Milestones' and 'Boplicity', which Miles always credited to his mother rather than himself, rather than anything from the electric period. This makes a certain sense, since it's the Miles of earlier years who affects Rava's trumpet-playing, even as he borrows the energies of the post-*In A Silent Way/Bitches Brew* records.

*** Carmen

Label Bleu LBLC 6579 *Rava; Gianluigi Trovesi (cl, bcl); John Schroeder (g); Enzo Pietropaoli (b); Michel Godard (tba); Han Bennink (d); orchestra.* 5/95.

A curiosity, really, with the famous melodies transposed for (and occasionally vandalized by) an interesting line-up. Bruno Tommaso's arrangements walk a slightly sticky line between pastiche and honourable revision, though with Bennink in the line-up there's not much danger of reverence overtaking matters. Rava might be the principal soloist, but it doesn't really feel like his record: more a pageant in which he has a leading role.

*** Noir

Label Bleu LBLC 6595 *Rava; Stefano Di Battista (sax); Roberto Ceccheto, Domenico Caliri (g); Maier Giovanni Girolamo (b); Umberto Trombetta (d).* 6/96.

The electric group on *Noir* is vibrant, if a little overcooked. The better tracks are when Di Battista plays and the pace is a little less frenetic. Rava's model is obviously the Miles Davis of the early '70s, and to that extent he does a good job, but it is an old-fashioned sound. The CD comes with a comic book – or 'graphic novel' – which may delight some purchasers.

***(*) D.N.A.

Giants Of Jazz CD 53302 *Rava; Mario Rusca (p); Lucio Terzano (b); Tony Arco (d).* 12/96.

Though associated with budget reissues, the Italian-based Giants Of Jazz has also started to issue newly recorded sessions, and it seems appropriate that Rava should be one of the first artists so documented. With the exception of four themes by pianist Rusca, who is reminiscent of compatriot Enrico Pieranunzi, all the tunes are standards, and it's fascinating to hear Rava, now 35 years into his career, return to the repertoire he must first have heard on Miles Davis records. The phrasing and articulation still betray an influence, but the voice is entirely the Italian's own. Play 'Out Of Nowhere' or 'My Foolish Heart' back to back with Prestige-era Miles, and the differences are marked.

**** Duo En Noir

Between The Lines btl 004 *Rava; Ran Blake (p).* 9/99.

A tribute to the late Art Farmer, recorded live in Frankfurt and issued on Franz Koglmann's new label, *Duo En Noir* represents one of the most creative pairings of Rava's career. The material is surprisingly varied, in the first ten minutes ranging from 'Nature Boy' to Bernard Hermann film music, and taking in modern themes like Al Green's gospelly love song 'Let's Stay Together', as well as 'There's A Small Hotel'. Needless to say, given the instincts of both musicians, none of the material is played entirely straight. Blake can occasionally sound brittle and abstract, but there is real warmth to his playing here, while Rava sounds as if he uses best extra-virgin instead of valve oil, a lovely, compelling tone that recalls the great swing trumpeters and, of course, Art Farmer himself.

***(*) Shades Of Chet

Label Bleu LBLC 6629 *Rava; Paolo Fresu (t, flhn); Stefano Bollani (p); Enzo Pietropaoli (b); Roberto Gatto (d).* 5/99.

It's some indication of the esteem in which Chet Baker is still held in Europe that such a project – featuring two brassmen whose playing is surely superior to Baker's on almost every level – should have been countenanced. Yet from the off it's clear that the Chet connection is a mere flag of convenience. Fresu has always been much more of a Miles-man anyway, and this is a back-to-the-roots exercise for both men, each having ranged far and wide since their original inspirations. 'Doxy' is an object lesson in returning to vintage repertory and investing it with a wealth of wider experience. The rhythm section offer fine support, and this is altogether a record that turns a genre exercise into something personal and distinctive.

*** Live At Birdland Neuberg

Challenge 71011 *Rava; Franz Lauber (as); Michael Flugel (p); Dietmar Fuhr (b); Dejan Terzic (d).* 7/00.

This club has become a favourite for live recordings and one can see why, given the rich, immediate sound of this fine date with pianist Flugel's band. They kick off with Rava's 'Diva', a lovely idea in double waltz-time that has long been one of the trumpeter's favourites. He finishes with another, 'Serti Angoli Secreti', title-track of one of his records. 'My Funny Valentine', 'East Broadway Run Down' and 'You Don't Know What Love Is' are maybe included in deference to the home band, likened in the liner-notes to four hungry German lions meeting a grey Italian wolf, but Enrico has no problems with the Rollins tune and slips into Chet Baker mode for 'MFV' with just Flugel and Fuhr in support to begin with. 'Secrets' is another original, a performance that grows in intensity virtually all the way, but allowing young Lauber to strut his boppish stuff to his heart's content. Nicely recorded and a useful reminder that Enrico is still able to play straight bop and modal jazz when the fit moves him.

*** Montreal Diary / B – Live At Montreal Jazz Festival

Label Bleu LBLC 6645 *Rava; Stefano Bollani (p).* 7/01.

*** Plays Miles Davis

Label Bleu LBLC *As above; add Paolo Fresu (t); Enzo Pietropaoli (b); Roberto Gatto (d).* 7/01.

A fruitful visit to Canada. The duos with Bollani are delightful, and the stripped-down version of 'Serti Angoli Secreti' is one of the best he's given of this beautiful composition. Bollani is very much an accompanist but he knows how to create shapes behind the trumpeter that draw attention to themselves as well as enhancing the horn-lines. He's on hand again on the Miles set, coming on somewhere closer to Bill Evans than to Wynton Kelly or Al Haig. That comes out on 'Blue In Green' and perhaps explains why he sounds a bit sticky on 'Bye Bye Blackbird'. Rava has been identified as a Miles-and-Chet clone, but, while there is a strong influence, he's a much more individual, more classically inspired player than either. His Miles stylings are less slavish than, say, Freddie Hubbard's on the VSOP tours, and Hubbard is no mean stylist himself. Two very attractive albums that again underline Rava's basic grounding in modern jazz. They clear the way very effectively for what was to be his best record since that far-off ECM classic …

**** Easy Living

ECM 1760 *Rava; Gianluca Petrella (tb); Stefano Bollani (p); Rosario Bonaccorso (b); Robert Gatto (d). 6/03.*

Never a maximalist, Rava seems content to play less and less on his own records, much like fellow trumpeter and stablemate Tomasz Stańko who has also adopted a similar reserve, keeping his counsel in order to deliver maximum impact. This is Rava's first album for ECM in 17 years, a long absence from the imprint that delivered his first classic LP, *The Pilgrim And The Stars*. This is potentially another, a beautiful, quiet and mostly quite reserved album of songs. He is on record as thinking it's his best work, and at 60 he uses the occasion to revisit a lot of his music past. There are high trills reminiscent of the Dixieland he used to play, bebop figures which are irresistibly reminiscent of young Miles Davis, and freer and more abstract shapes as well. Apart from the title standard, everything is original. 'Hornette And The Drum Thing' is especially fascinating, full of teasing quotes and allusions, but absolutely on its own terms as well. This is a record that will grow in stature with repeated hearings.

Freddie Redd (born 1927)

PIANO

Still best remembered for his Blue Note set of music from The Connection, Redd is a journeyman hard-bopper of honest service, with a modest showing on record.

*** Piano: East/West

Original Jazz Classics OJC 1705 *Redd; John Ore (b); Ron Jefferson (d). 2/55.*

*** San Francisco Suite

Original Jazz Classics OJC 1748 *Redd; George Tucker (b); Al Dreares (d). 10/57.*

Redd's amiable West Coast bop soundtracks an unscripted (but you've seen it) Bay Area movie: bustling streetcars, pretty girls flashing their legs, sudden fogs and alarms, an apology for a narrative. The *San Francisco Suite* is cliché from start to finish, but the hackneyed moods are done unpretentiously and engagingly. He was a lot more coherent when there was a real narrative to deal with. Redd was one of several jazzmen drawn to Jack Gelber's drugs drama *The Connection*, and in Jackie McLean he had a player who knew both the music and the life inside out, the one illuminating and shadowing the other; but the Blue Note album which documents the music has once again been cut from the catalogue.

Rob Reddy

ALTO AND SOPRANO SAXOPHONES

New York saxman with his boisterous little big band.

*** Post-War Euphoria

Songlines SGL 1512-2 *Reddy; Eddie E. J. Allen (t); Josh Roseman (tb); Jef Lee Johnson (g); Dom Richards (b); Pheeroan akLaff (d). 1/96.*

Reddy calls his group the Honor System; their album, recorded in New Jersey, is a rumbustious event, almost a party record if you think recent downtown New York jazz should be played at parties. Tracks like 'The Pipe Smoker' and 'Same Old' rattle and roll along, the ensemble making a lot of noise and driven by akLaff's falling-downstairs drum parts which are as exuberant as they should be. Rather than handing out solos, Reddy breaks his group down into twos and threes and fours, so there's a broad range of duets and ensembles scattered through a lot of music (over 70 minutes) and they're all playing to the max. The drawback is that nothing peaks or stands out, which makes the disc, for all its spirited blowing (and Reddy himself, while not the most renowned name here, is probably the most vivid voice), fade into the background when it should collar the attention.

***(*) Songs That You Can Trust

Koch 7876 *As above. 2/99.*

The glib judgement (a route we never countenance, of course) is that this is more of the same. Reddy has assembled exactly the same group, a feat in itself in these peripatetic circles, and they're called on to blast their way through material which calls for the group to create its own relentless dynamic, rather than following by-the-numbers structures. The results, though, are as enlivening as the first record, and endowed with extra wit, grace and point. 'Prayer 1' is a genuinely affecting dirge. 'Count Your Blessings', which takes an age to get going and makes it worthwhile in the end, shows that Reddy's prepared to take his time. The best of this proposes an ensemble music worthy to stand beside Threadgill and Shannon Jackson, which in this book is high praise.

*** However Humble

Koch 8579 *Reddy; Jeff Lee Johnson (g, sitar); Charles Burnham (vn, mand); Rufus Cappadocia (clo); Dom Richards (b); Hearn Gadbois (perc). 5/00.*

***(*) Seeing By The Light Of My Own Candle

Knitting Factory KFW 291 *Reddy; John Carlson (t); Charles Burnham (vn); Dom Richards (b); Guillermo Brown (d). 3/01.*

The first set is by Quttah, the second by Sleeping Dogs, and aside from never sticking to a band name for very long, Reddy's certainly up for variety. The Koch album, though, isn't as varied as it might be, and the string-laden personnel seem to get hung up on slow, almost droning pieces, which even the more bustling rhythms below can't quite bring aloft. In context, Johnson's occasional outbursts sound overheated.

Sleeping Dogs are back in the Threadgill/Jackson pocket, and the mix of trumpet, violin and reeds is an effectively pungent brew. This set is more mediated and sensitive than the earlier ones, without losing its cerebral funkiness; Reddy's juxtapositions yield results which occasionally grow almost ecstatic, as in 'Rjoc'.

Dewey Redman (born 1931)

TENOR AND ALTO SAXOPHONES, CLARINET, MUSETTE

Redman grew up in Ornette Coleman's home town and was the anchor member of one of Ornette's most incendiary bands. Dewey was almost 30 before he opted for a full-time musical career, and to some extent has never quite caught up with the slow start. His output as leader is quite small but has filled up in recent years. He has also been a member of Keith Jarrett's American quartet and of the Ornette repertory band, Old And New Dreams.

★★★(★) Musics
Original Jazz Classics OJCCD 1860-2 *Redman; Fred Simmons (tb); Mark Helias (b); Eddie Moore (d).* 10/78.

★★★ Redman And Blackwell In Willisau
Black Saint 120093 *Redman; Ed Blackwell (d).* 8/80.

★★★(★) Living On The Edge
Black Saint 120123 *Redman; Geri Allen (p); Cameron Brown (b); Eddie Moore (d).* 9/89.

Redman's strong Middle Eastern influence is perhaps most evident on the duets with Blackwell, where the musette introduces a subtle microtonal dimension which builds on Dewey's vocalized approach on single-reeded horns. Blackwell's chops are so finely attuned in contexts like this that it is hard at moments to imagine that there are two musical personalities at work. It is also hard, though, to avoid the impression that this is a sheared and foreshortened Ornette session.

At the opposite end of the decade, *Living On The Edge* preserves much of the menace Redman generated on the (now deleted) Impulse! session *Ear Of The Beholder*, but with a new simplicity of emotion and with a tone notably less forced than on previous outings. There are strong parallels between Redman's quiet accommodation and Pharoah Sanders, though the Texan has retained more of the fire and fight of his youth. Allen is an ideal partner in that she is willing to examine intervals that fall outside the usual geometry of blues and bebop, but she also has an unfailing rhythmic awareness that keeps Redman within bounds.

The OJC set, originally recorded for Galaxy, features the band which Redman alternated with the Ornette repertory group, Old And New Dreams. *Musics* combines a samba, a stirring march, interludes on musette and autoharp and a totally unexpected version of Gilbert O'Sullivan's 'Alone Again (Naturally)'. Moore has a whale of a time, and the rich harmonic landscape introduced by Simmons (a very underrated musician) stands duty for piano and sometimes a whole horn section. An unexpected and highly enjoyable record.

★★★(★) In London
Palmetto PM 2030 *Redman; Rita Marcotulli (p); Cameron Brown (b); Matt Wilson (d).* 10/96.

Recorded live at Ronnie Scott's club, Redman sounds rejuvenated and adventuresome with a band that splits down naturally into two pairs, himself and long-standing oppo Brown up against the young Italian Marcotulli and Wilson. The Mid-Westerner is the first white drummer to be hired by the saxophonist, and he repays the confidence handsomely. The band actually work from a different axis on 'Tu-Inns', the most adventurous tune on the set. Piano and bass take off darkly, building up a steady, brooding ostinato against which saxophone and drums enter with an explosion of sound. As ever, Redman mixes outside and relatively mainstream styles, giving 'The Very Thought Of You', his tribute to Dexter Gordon, a loose, swinging energy and Sammy Cahn's 'I Should Care' an easy, melodic interpretation. 'Portrait In Black And White' is an unexpectedly straightforward Jobim cover, but what's interesting about each of these middle-of-the-road numbers is how carefully they're juxtaposed with the more adventurous material. Tunes like 'I-Pimp', 'Kleerwine' and 'Elevens' suggest that Redman hasn't abandoned his loyalty to the avant-garde. A remarkable record, characterized by some daring group-interaction. The sound is a bit uninflected, but the performances more than make up for any technical insufficiency.

★★(★) Momentum Space
Verve 559944-2 *Redman; Cecil Taylor (p); Elvin Jones (d).* 98.

After all this time, they must have been astonished to be asked, or perhaps mildly peeved. The result is a flat, chaotic sampling of deutero-radical approaches with most of the power sucked out. Cecil at least sounds as though he's having fun here and there, but Dewey and Elvin honk and thrash away without much purpose, and 'Life', 'As', 'It', 'Is' is as ungainly a sequence as these remarkable gentlemen can ever have consigned to record. That said, the sound is very good indeed, well up to the standard you'd hope for and expect, and it's wonderful to hear the supertrio at all, even if they are crashing gears much of the time. Don't blink, it'll be gone by the time you do.

Don Redman (1900–64)

ALTO AND SOPRANO SAXOPHONES, OTHER INSTRUMENTS, BANDLEADER

Joined Fletcher Henderson in 1923 as arranger and reed-player, then was lured away to McKinney's Cotton Pickers. Led his own band, 1931–40, before writing for other bandleaders. Toured with a post-war big band in 1946, and later freelanced for New York orchestras in the '50s. One of the pioneer jazz arrangers and a fine multi-instrumentalist.

★★★(★) Don Redman, 1931–1933
Classics 543 *Redman; Henry 'Red' Allen, Shirley Clay, Bill Coleman, Langston Curl, Reunald Jones, Sidney De Paris (t); Claude Jones, Benny Morton, Fred Robinson, Gene Simon (tb); Jerry Blake (cl, as, bs); Robert Cole, Edward Inge (cl, as); Harvey Boone (as, bs); Robert Carroll (ts); Horace Henderson, Don Kirkpatrick (p); Talcott Reeves (bj, g); Bob Ysaguirre (bb, b); Manzie Johnson (d, vib); Chick Bullock, Cab Calloway, Harlan Lattimore, The Mills Brothers (v); Bill Robinson (tap dancing).* 9/31–5/36.

★★★(★) Shakin' The Africann
Hep CD 1001 *Basically as above.* 9/31–12/32.

★★★ Don Redman, 1933–1936
Classics 553 *As above.* 33–36.

★★★ Chant Of The Weed
Topaz TPZ 1043 *As above, except add Tom Stevenson, Robert Williams (t), Quentin Jackson (tb), Carl Frye, Edward Inge (cl, as, bs), Eddie Williams, Gene Sedric (ts).* 28–38.

★★★(★) Doin' What I Please
ASV/Living Era 5110 2 *As above.* 25–38.

Redman remains one of the essential figures of the pre-war jazz period. He started out as lead saxophonist and staff arranger with Fletcher Henderson's band, infusing the charts with a breathtaking simplicity and confidence, eventually leaving in 1928 to front the highly successful McKinney's Cotton Pickers. This was his most celebrated music, but some of the music under his own leadership in the '30s surpassed his earlier charts, even if the recordings are inconsistent. The material on the two Classics discs is the core of Redman's output. The earlier of the pair features the band's remarkable theme-tune, 'Chant Of The Weed', Redman's brilliant and justly celebrated arrangement of 'I Got Rhythm' and two cuts of the title-track. The band at this time also featured Harlan Lattimore, one of the few genuinely challenging singers of the era, who was once described by George T. Simon as sounding like a rather hip Bing Crosby; one man or the other is spinning in his coffin even now. The arrangements are well up to scratch, and there is more impressive work from Lattimore. Bojangles Robinson tip-taps on one version of the title-piece, but the better cut features the Mills Brothers and Cab Calloway.

The Topaz compilation is, as the Topazes always are, a useful fast run-through of the career, without much depth of focus at any point. The obvious things are there – 'Chant Of The Weed', 'Shakin' The African', 'Nagasaki' – and there aren't any glaring chronological gaps. A very worthwhile purchase. *Shakin' The Africann* (sic) is also a good sampling of Redman's activities just after leaving McKinney's Cotton Pickers. There are fine versions of the bizarre 'Chant Of The Weed', which deserves to be considered on its considerable musical daring as well as for its celebration of the jazz man's favourite relaxant. The set ends with two versions of 'Doin' The New Low Down' with tap dancing from Bojangles Robinson and on the other version a slightly crazed vocal from Cab Calloway. The ASV Living Era set is beautifully remastered and sounds as good as any of these compilations. Given that it's got all the major cuts, including 'Chant Of The Weed', 'Shakin' The African' and 'Nagasaki', it's probably the only Redman record a casual buyer will ever need.

***** Don Redman, 1936–1939**

Classics 574 *Redman; Harold Baker, Mario Bauza, Shirley Clay, Sidney De Paris, Otis Johnson, Reunald Jones, Tommy Stevenson, Carl Warwick, Robert Williams (t); Benny Morton, Gene Simon (tb); Quentin Jackson (tb, v); Rupert Cole (as, cl); Eddie Barefield, Harvey Boone, Pete Clarke, Carl Frye, Edward Inge (as, bs, cl); Robert Carroll, Joe Garland, Gene Sedric (ts); Eddie Williams (ts, v); Bob Ysaguirre (bs, bsx); Don Kirkpatrick, Nicholas Rodriguez (p); Clarence Holiday, Bob Lessey, Talcot Reeves (g); Bill Beason, Big Sid Catlett (d); Manzie Johnson (d, vib); Harlan Lattimore, Laurel Watson, Three Little Maids (v).* 5/36–3/39.

The beginning of the swing era saw Redman softening and commercializing his approach somewhat. These sides, however, still stand apart from the generic big-band music of the time. They're harmonically gritty, exuberantly voiced, and elegantly arranged and conducted with an emphasis on precision and timing. And yet, what made the Redman band of the early '30s so distinctive has largely gone and the material and treatment are not so very different from any other band on the scene. Some nice tracks, though, including Morton's 'Milenberg Joys' and a bizarre version of the Gilbert and Sullivan singalong classic 'The Flowers That Bloom In The Spring'. Possibly too many tra-la-las for most jazz fans as commercially acceptable vocals took over.

***** For Europeans Only**

Steeplechase SCCD 36020 *Redman; Peanuts Holland (t, v); Allan Jeffries, Bobby Williams (t); Jackie Carman (tb); Tyree Glenn (tb, vib); Pete Clarke (as, bs, cl); Chauncey Haughton (as, bs); Ray Abrams, Don Byas (ts); Billy Taylor (p); Ted Sturgis (b); Buford Oliver (d); Inez Cavanaugh (v).* 9/46.

***** Swiss Radio Days, Volume 11: Live From Geneva, 1946**

TCB 2112 *As above.* 46.

Just after the war, Redman took an all-star band to Europe, hoping to capitalize on a revived enthusiasm for big-band jazz and swing there. Redman was also shrewd enough to introduce some elements of bebop into the mix. In many respects, it's not the band of old, but the quality of soloists guarantees some interest. Amazingly, they don't do 'Chant Of The Weed', which perhaps didn't have the resonance in Switzerland or Scandinavia that it would have had back home. There are, though, fine versions on the Steeplechase of 'The World Is Waiting For The Sunrise', 'Laura' and the Tadd Dameron title-track, and Don Byas, very much a fixture in Europe after this, takes some very fine solos. Poor sound, but given that the set is taken from privately recorded acetates, it's better than it deserves to be. The Swiss set is from a radio broadcast, so the sound is somewhat better. Similar repertoire, but one senses a certain lack of snap and commitment in the playing. These were among the last things that Redman did, though he lived on for another 18 years.

Joshua Redman (born 1969)

TENOR, ALTO AND SOPRANO SAXOPHONES

Dewey Redman's son became a figurehead for the young American jazz movement of the '90s. After winning the 1991 Thelonious Monk Competition, he began making a series of high-profile albums for Warner Bros. Despite an eclectic choice of material, Redman has so far preferred to work in straightahead settings and he brings an almost purist approach to his own recording.

****** Joshua Redman**

Warner Bros 945242-2 *Redman; Kevin Hays, Mike LeDonne (p); Christian McBride, Paul LaDuca (b); Gregory Hutchinson, Clarence Penn, Kenny Washington (d).* 5–9/92.

****** Wish**

Warner Bros 945365-2 *Redman; Pat Metheny (g); Charlie Haden (b); Billy Higgins (d).* 93.

*****(*) Mood Swing**

Warner Bros 9362-45643-2 *Redman; Brad Mehldau (p); Christian McBride (b); Brian Blade (d).* 3/94.

***** Spirit Of The Moment – Live At The Village Vanguard**

Warner Bros 945923-2 2CD *Redman; Peter Martin (p); Christopher Thomas (b); Brian Blade (d).* 3/95.

Joshua Redman's first albums caused a sensation: few discs from this period have communicated such sheer joy in playing as these. Although he had already made some interesting sideman appearances, the saxophonist's eponymous set was a stunning debut: a canny blend of bop, standards, the odd tricky choice (Monk's 'Trinkle Tinkle') and young man's fancy (James Brown's 'I Got You (I Feel Good)'), all of it buoyed up on the kind of playing that suggests an instant maturity. His lean tone turned out to be as limber or as weighty as he wished, his phrasing had plenty of spaces but could cruise at any bebop height, and his invention sounded unquenchable. The euphoric but controlled feeling extends to his sidemen, Hays, McBride and Hutchinson (two odd tracks were drafted in from other sessions). Beautifully recorded, too.

Wish was an equally splendid follow-up: a little more self-conscious with the starry support group, and a couple of the tunes (Eric Clapton's 'Tears In Heaven'?) seemed a little too modish; but the more open harmonics of Metheny's guitar and the gravitas of Haden and Higgins framed the younger man's improvisations with great eloquence. The bonus live versions of 'Wish' (from the first album) and a roughly sketched 'Blues For Pat' add a further dimension and extend the joyousness of Redman's playing.

After such a start, *Mood Swing* had huge expectations to live up to. It's still a very impressive record, but it's just arguable that the sheer *joie de vivre* of the playing on the first two records has been suspended in favour of a more considered, careful methodology. Not that Redman holds much back in his solos, or that his group are any less imposing. Mehldau, in fact, gives notice that he is a star in the making himself: his contributions, allusive, mischievous and profound by turns, are as substantial as the leader's own. And McBride and Blade are superfine. But here and there are traces of a self-conscious eloquence that suggest a spirit in transition.

Spirit Of The Moment might also be a snapshot analysis of work in progress. There are inevitable recalls of the great Rollins records of nearly 40 years before, especially when Redman tackles 'My One And Only Love' and 'St Thomas'. But this is more exhaustive – two CDs of close to 80 minutes apiece – and more prone to longueurs. As good as the group is, it doesn't really match either the quartet on *Mood Swing* or Redman's previous touring band of McBride, Blade and Eric Reed. Perhaps, too, the days of a new voice setting down an instantaneous great document, as Rollins once did, are as long gone for jazz as is, say, the idea of rock giants cutting their debut set in an afternoon (cf. the Beatles). Gripes aside – and when a man makes a start as powerful as Redman's, one can't help but be anticipatory – there's still much great jazz here.

*****(*) Freedom In The Groove**

Warner Bros 46330-2 *Redman; Peter Martin (p); Peter Bernstein (g); Christopher Thomas (b); Brian Blade (d).* 4/96.

It was hard to imagine Redman making a less than enjoyable record at this point. He has such a fine sound, fertile imagination and ambitious delivery that he is a kind of celebration of the core jazz language in himself. But his stance is inevitably becoming more mediated and arranged as he goes on. His own sleeve-note essay, which details the background to his musical tastes and his viewpoint on eclecticism, may be entirely from the heart, but in the context of a major-label jazz disc it can't help but read like a press flak's handout. The ten originals on the disc are a catchy set of variations on various forms – a touch of the blues, a couple of groove tunes, a modal blow, a Coltrane-ish prayer – that he has absorbed along the way. The solos are uniformly (perhaps *too* uniformly – the odd stumble might humanize him a little) handsome and eloquent, and of course his group is a talented one. He benefits further from Matt Pierson's shrewd production and a really splendid studio sound from James Farbar. At this point, Redman can't surprise us; he can only play his best strokes. For many, that will be enough.

*****(*) Timeless Tales For Changing Times**

Warner Bros 9362-47052-2 *Redman; Brad Mehldau (p); Larry Grenadier (b); Brian Blade (d).* 98.

It was a good idea for Redman to do an album of modern-day cover-versions: he's young enough to empathize with an audience that knows about Prince and Stevie Wonder (although his choices of pop material are actually rather old-fashioned and conservative, with names like Joni Mitchell and Bob Dylan in the composer credits) but determined enough to make them part of an uncompromised jazz record. Mehldau especially is a like-minded conspirator in this. The result is an intelligent and incisive repertory record. Wonder's 'Visions' and Mitchell's 'I Had A King' are vehicles in which the improvisations grow plausibly out of the song structure. There's no sense that the players use some motif from the song as a peg on which to hang increasingly remote solos: Redman has arranged the material too assiduously for that. He plants 'Summertime' and 'Yesterdays' in there as if to democratize the set-list, too. This record didn't excite as much attention as his earlier sets, but it feels like a genuine step forward for him.

***** Beyond**

Warner Bros 9362-47465-2 *Redman; Mark Turner (ts); Aaron Goldberg (p); Reuben Rogers (b); Gregory Hutchinson (d).* 5/99.

The one entirely satisfying piece here is 'Leap Of Faith', where guest tenor Turner engages in a thinkers' duel with the leader, a compelling interchange of views that turns a neat circle across nine minutes. The other pieces, though, never break out of their cryptic skin. 'Balance' and the very long 'Twilight ... And Beyond' are particularly perverse in the way that they turn into mere bombast after their careful development, as if Redman felt that he had to reach catharsis of some kind. In the circumstances, his new group makes no definite impression on music that needs to provide listeners with more of a map than Redman has here.

*****(*) Passage Of Time**

Warner Bros 9362-47997-2 *Redman; Aaron Goldberg (p); Reuben Rogers (b); Gregory Hutchinson (d).* 6/00.

Although the material still feels difficult to figure out, this is a more relaxed, affable, yet more powerful, set than the last one. With a year of growth in it, the quartet sound both more confident and more generously outgoing, and though Redman overreaches here and there, as in the overcooked climax to 'Before', he sounds as if he's playing within himself, to prosperous effect. Where next?

*****(*) Yaya^3**

Loma 9362-48277-2 *Redman; Sam Yahel (org); Brian Blade (d).* 1/02.

***** Elastic**

Warner Bros 9362-48279-2 *As above, except add Bashiri Johnson (perc).* 3/02.

As Redman has begun to have the spotlight shifted off him, his records have got lighter, less heavy with meaning. The Yaya^3 set is almost an interlude in his work, the album co-credited to the three players, and the music realized as a sort of post-mod take on the organ–sax combo (others, such as Larry Goldings, have already been there, but never mind). It's often enjoyable in a curiously giddy way, the simple grooves of, say, 'One More Once' taken to the edge of turbulence by the sax solo before being suddenly righted by Yahel and Blade. As usual, the drummer's very busy, but he's not *too* smart, and 'Hometown' especially has a near-classic feel to it, presumably just what they were striving (if that's not too effortful a word) for.

The difficulty with *Elastic* is just that: there's too much striving. Same line-up, with a bit of extra percussion; Yahel fingers some other keyboards; but somehow the fresher feel of the other record (even if it was made only two months earlier) has been staled. Redman's records are always going to yield pleasure, if only to hear a premier saxman stepping up to deliver, but this isn't a good place to start listening to him.

Dizzy Reece (born 1931)

TRUMPET

A Jamaican, Reece was working in Europe from 1949, basing himself in London from 1954, then settling in New York from 1959. Though a frequently encountered name in bop circles, he recorded comparatively little.

***** A New Star**

Jasmine JASCD 615 *Reece; Sammy Walker, Tubby Hayes, Ronnie Scott (ts); Tony Crombie, Harry South, Johnny Weed, Terry Shannon (p); Dave Goldberg (g); Lennie Bush, Pete Blannin (b); Phil Seamen, Bill Eyden (d).* 5/55–7/56.

*****(*) Progress Report**

Jasmine JASCD 620 *Reece; Tubby Hayes (ts, bs); Sammy Walker (ts); Victor Feldman, Norman Stenfalt (p); Lloyd Thompson, Lennie Bush (b); Phil Seamen (d).* 12/56–10/58.

*****(*) Asia Minor**

Original Jazz Classics OJC 1806 *Reece; Joe Farrell (ts, f); Cecil Payne (bs); Hank Jones (p); Ron Carter (b); Charli Persip (d).* 62.

Reece established his base of operations in Europe for a long while and became a regular partner of British players like Tubby Hayes and Victor Feldman. His rare British sessions have at last been revived as part of Jasmine's reissue programme from the '50s Tempo label. Rather than following the pattern of the original LPs, the CD editions follow eight sessions chronologically (including tracks issued at the time on various EPs). This is seminal British hard bop, with all its flaws and virtues alike. Reece wasn't a bruising player: he kept the fireworks under restraint, even as snapping little phrases suddenly broke out of his line of thought. *A New Star* has lots of rough edges, and it's not until the final quartet session on the disc that Reece really makes a distinctive impression. *Progress Report* has a more finished feel to it, and there are interesting Reece originals such as 'The Gypsy' and 'A Variation On Monk'. Of the other players, Feldman and the inevitable Hayes make their mark, but Reece usually makes the strongest impression, even if there's a sense that his mind is occasionally wandering in the middle of a solo.

His Blue Note dates *Star Bright* and *Blues In Trinity* show him in his very best light, but so far neither has been generally available on CD (keep an eye out for Japanese or Connoisseur editions). Even at a somewhat later stage, Reece is slightly difficult to pin down stylistically. Though he can play skyrocketing top-note lines, there's something curiously melancholy about his work on *Asia Minor*, a recording which recalls some of the South African players. His trump card here is, of course, the marvellous band he has round him, all of whom contribute to this very welcome calling-card from a dedicated practitioner who has been unjustly neglected in recent years.

Eric Reed (born 1970)

PIANO

Reed came to prominence as a member of the Wynton Marsalis group, with whom he still plays. Born in Philadelphia, he moved to Los Angeles at 11 and was playing with Gerald Wilson when still only 16.

****(*) Soldier's Hymn**

Candid CCD 79511 *Reed; Dwayne Burno (b); Gregory Hutchinson (d).* 11/90.

Although intended as a showcase debut for Reed, *Soldier's Hymn* is much more of a trio record. Originals like the title-piece (present in two different versions) and 'Coup De Cone' are conscious evaluations of the manner of a Jazz Messengers rhythm section (Art Blakey is the album's dedicatee), and elsewhere Reed's chord-based solos and call-and-response interplay suggest the influence of Ahmad Jamal or even Ramsey Lewis. This works out well on the less ambitious pieces – 'Soft Winds' is an impressive update of the old Benny Goodman tune – but on the more portentous tracks, such as 'Things Hoped For' or the half-baked medley which Reed does as a solo turn, the music sounds more like a demo session than a finished record.

*****(*) Happiness**

Nagel-Heyer 2010 *Reed; Marcus Printup, Mike Rodriguez (t); Wycliffe Gordon, Dion Tucker (tb); Wessell Anderson, Julius Tolentino (as); Wayne Escoffery (ts, as); Walter Blanding (cl); Barak Mori (b); Rodney Green (d); Enato Thoms (perc).* 12/00.

Back with an independent after a spell with Impulse!, and unencumbered with major-label considerations, Reed delivers a sunny, bluesy, muscular, free-spirited kind of set. The Marsalis legacy still hangs heavy with him: much of this is for a Wynton-like septet, purloining bits and pieces from jazz gone by, finessed through modern manners. 'Crazy Red' sounds as if it could have come out of, say, Lucky Millinder's book, but it's dressed up in contemporary energy. The rhythm section plays in a way that blends deep swing with trickier, cooler stylings, and soloists like Printup, Gordon and Anderson are pledges of quality – they're raring to play hot, but Reed has them under close command. This kind of set will be the new mainstream.

*****(*) E-Bop**

Savant SCD 2051 *Reed; Marcus Printup (t); Walter Blanding Jr (ts); Rodney Whitaker (b); Rodney Green (d).* 10/00.

***** Mercy And Grace**

Nagel Heyer 2030 *Reed (p solo).* 10/01.

***** Merry Magic**
MaxJazz MXJ 302 *Reed; Steve Nelson (vib); Barak Mori (b); Rodney Green (d); Erin Bode, Paula West (v).* 4/02.

Three contrasting records. *E-Bop* delights in its classic post-bop vocabularies, recalling any number of Blue Note/Prestige shootouts while still sticking to a contemporary ground which the players and their solos stake fierce claim on. Printup and Blanding reassert their right to head up an adventurous front line, but major credit goes to Reed for fertile material and bandleading chutzpah. He ends with a Monk double-header of 'Evidence/Think Of One', done solo, which closes the neocon circle.

Mercy And Grace is all solo, all spirituals and hymns, and dedicated to Reed's late father. A quiet interlude, soberly done, and the listener feels intrusive, even as Reed plays with open heart.

The MaxJazz album is Christmas music, made with suitable merriment, yet thoughtful too: something about the piano–vibes combination seems to be a natural for festive music, and the record's no throwaway, loaded with charm, but necessarily for certain temperaments at certain times of the year.

Ruben Reeves (1905–55)

TRUMPET, BANDLEADER

Reeves was a Chicagoan who taught music during the day. He led his own recording band for a brief period at the end of the '20s, but the records were indifferently received and he later joined the Cab Calloway band. He played as section-man for various leaders after the war, but quit the business in 1952.

***** The Complete Vocalions 1928–1933**
Timeless CBC 1-039 *Reeves; Fats Robins, James Tate, Cicero Thomas (t); Eddie Atkins, William Franklin, Gerald Reeves, John Thomas (tb); Darnell Howard, Fred Brown (cl, as); Fess Williams, Omer Simeon (cl); Ralph Brown (as); Franz Jackson, Norval Morton (ts, f); Clarence Lee, Bobby Wall, Joe McCutchin (vn); Jimmy Prince, Eddie King (p); Cecil White (g); Lawrence Dixon (bj, v); Elliott Washington (bj); Harry Gray (tba); Sudie Reynaud (b); Jasper Taylor, Richard Barnes (d); Blanche Calloway (v).* 4/28–12/33.

Ruben 'River' Reeves was seen by Vocalion as a rival to Louis Armstrong, and the 15 titles he made in 1929 are a sort of riposte to Armstrong's Hot Seven and Five sides. As with Jabbo Smith, Reeves was both like and unlike Armstrong: a similar *brio* but not quite the same mastery of execution, and he stumbles at moments when Louis would simply soar. But he was still a very good trumpet-player and, with bandsmen like Simeon and Howard also on hand, the music is a splendid evocation of small-group Chicago jazz at a great moment in time. The records sold poorly and Reeves returned to the studios as a leader on only one further occasion, to cut the four 1933 titles which close the disc. The band is much bigger, but the leader still sounds commanding and fiery. He spent the rest of his career doing section work before becoming a bank guard. This is his story (aside from one lost master, 'Bottoms Up') and, judged on solos like those in 'Papa Skag Stomp' and 'Head Low', it bears plenty of retelling. Excellent remastering in what is one of the best-presented reissue series of the period.

Rufus Reid (born 1944)

DOUBLE BASS

The Georgian is a stalwart sideman who has appeared on dozens of dates for other leaders. He had a long-standing association with pianist Akira Tana. A firm time feel and generous tone are his calling cards.

***** Perpetual Stroll**
Sunnyside 1027 *Reid; Kirk Lightsey (p); Eddie Gladden (d).* 1/80.

***** Seven Minds**
Sunnyside 1011 *Reid; Jim McNeely (p); Terri Lyne Carrington (d).* 84.

Rufus has been unfortunately overlooked since our first edition, where his Theresa LP *Perpetual Stroll* received a warm review. It's back in circulation as a Sunnyside CD and it's good to renew acquaintance. The outstanding track, and the best indication of Reid's talents as leader as well as sideman, is his performance of Oscar Pettiford's 'Tricotism'. Brief as it is, and tucked away right at the end of the record, it's a dazzlingly good piece and an excellent choice for Rufus's style of bass-playing. Lightsey and Gladden worked with him as Dexter Gordon's group, and so the empathy is clear.

The other '80s record is, if anything, even better. The tracks are longer and more developed and the opening title-track holds out a promise that it amply fulfilled. 'Tone For Joan's Bones' is a surprise inclusion but the trio makes hay with the Chick Corea classic. Nothing of quite the standard of the Pettiford tune, but music-making of the highest calibre. A pity that the live *Corridor To The Limits*, featuring yet another trio, is unavailable.

***** Double Bass Delights**
Double Time 117 *Reid; Michael Moore (b).* 96.

***** The Intimacy Of The Bass**
Double Time 158 *As above.* 99.

The early '90s were a quiet time for Reid as far as solo projects were concerned, so these are valuable returns to the studio. In company with the sonorous Moore, who has a fleeter and somehow stringier delivery, he makes short work of 13 mostly short themes, including 'Satin Doll', 'Stompin' At the Savoy', his old favourite 'Stardust' and a fine duo version of 'Seven Minds', all on the earlier album. The second disc is more varied in material. The original 'Almost But Maybe' pitches bowed bass against a brisk plucked accompaniment. Moore's 'When I Wage Battle Next' is an unexpected gem, packed with emotion. There are also fine Strayhorn and Miles interpretations. All-bass records make for demanding listening, but this one is immediately accessible and consistently attractive.

*****(*) The Gait Keeper**
Sunnyside 1106 *Reid; Fred Hendrix (t, flhn); Rich Perry (ts); John Stretch (p); Montez Coleman (d).* 12/02.

Great title for a bassist's session and a thoroughly impressive album. It's the first he's made with a horn-led group and without swamping his distinctive lead playing it opens up all sorts of new harmonic possibilities. The opening track 'The Meddler' is a superbly convoluted idea, with some surprise elements. 'Seven Minds' is reprised at the end of the set, as if to keep Rufus's best-known composition in view, but the most effective and affecting track is 'Ode To Ray', a tribute to fellow bassist Ray Brown, who died not long before this date was recorded.

At 60, Rufus Reid hasn't yet accumulated as many credits, but is heading in that direction. With the Tana–Reid material out of catalogue these records are an important reminder of what makes him a first-call sideman and a thoroughly respected musician.

Ernest Reijseger (born 1954)

CELLO, VOICE

The Dutchman has been a regular on the European improvising scene, a founder member of the Clusone 3 and a frequent collaborator with percussionist Gerry Hemingway.

***** Colla Parte**
Winter & Winter 910 012 2 *Reijseger (clo, v).* 2 & 3/97.

*****(*) Colla Voche**
Winter & Winter 910 037 2 *Reijseger; Alan Purves (perc); Tenore de Orosei, Tenore de Concordu (v).* 99.

*****(*) I Love You So Much It Hurts**
Winter & Winter 910 077 2 *Reijseger; Franco d'Andrea (p).* 00.

***** Janna**
Winter & Winter 910 094 2 *Reijseger; Serigne Gueye (perc); Mola Sylla (v).* 01.

Unlike fellow instrumentalist Tristan Honsinger, Reijseger has never committed himself absolutely to abstract music and has always retained a measure of melody and euphony in his cello-playing. Though there are earlier records, the solo Winter & Winter set is the earliest readily available and it's a fine place to make the Dutchman's acquaintance. Apart from Abdullah Ibrahim's 'Gwidza', all the compositions are his own and some seem to be meditations on non-figurative canvases by the German artist Thomas Argauer, some of which are included in the liner booklet. The playing, and occasional singing, is delightful, ranging from idiomatic *arco* work to softer, strummed passages and gently percussive stops. 'Ricercare', 'Ritornello' and 'Toccata' are all cheerfully non-canonical.

Reijseger has worked with the Scottish percussionist Alan 'Gunga' Purves before, on the brilliantly punning *Cellotape & Scotchtape*, but *Colla Voche* moves into a new dimension with the addition of two Sardinian vocal groups. The Sard dialect and accent is as distinct from Italian as Scots is from English and that imparts a very special, indefinable quality to these performances which are among Reijseger's very best on record. Though mostly the two improvisers work along with the choir on a mixture of new and traditional music there are some interludes as well, as when singer Patrizio Mura plays harmonica in an impromptu trio with cello and percussion. Wonderful.

The duets with d'Andrea are much more conventional, very much in the familiar line of horn–piano sets. That's not to say the two don't make beautiful music. 'In A Sentimental Mood' and 'Night And Day' start proceedings on relatively familiar ground, though the rest of the album ranges more freely and eclectically. Reijseger seems to concentrate on keeping his cello within the range of a tenor singing voice, which heightens the songbook feel of the record. D'Andrea solos sparingly and often with affecting reticence, but no mistaking the emotion.

The trio set with Senegalese poet Sylla takes the Dutchman off in a new direction entirely, exploring some of the often overlooked shared ground between European and African music. Sylla's poetry dominates the set, but there is ample space for Reijseger to improvise and his understanding of new rhythms, touched in by Gueye with notable lack of fuss and occasion, is fascinating to watch unfold. A fine record, though inevitably more restricted in appeal than most of its predecessors.

Django Reinhardt (1910–53)

GUITAR, VIOLIN

One of the few genuine legends of the music, Jean Baptiste Reinhardt was born at Liverchies in Belgium. He was something of a prodigy and played professionally before his teens. When he was 18, though, a fire in his caravan seriously damaged his hand and for the rest of his life he had to negotiate two clawed fingers on his fretting hand. The Django legend developed between the wars with the success of the Quintette Du Hot Club De France. As a gypsy, he survived the Second World War only through the patronage of a Luftwaffe officer who admired his music. After the Liberation, Django became an international hero, travelling to America to work with Duke Ellington. As erratic as he was brilliant, he seemed foredoomed to a short and glittering career, and he died aged just 43 at Samois, near Paris.

*****(*) Django Reinhardt, 1934–1935**
Classics 703 *Reinhardt; Pierre Allier, Gaston Lapeyronnie, Alphonse Cox, Maurice Moufflard, Alex Renard (t); Marcel Dumont, Isidore Bassard, Pierre Deck, René Weiss, Guy Paquinet (tb); André Ekyan (cl, as); Amédée Charles (as); Charles Lisée (as, bs); Andy Foster (as, cl, bsx); Maurice Cizeron (as, cl, f); Noël Chiboust, Alix Combelle (ts); Stéphane Grappelli (vn, p); Michel Warlop (vn); Jean Chabaud (p); Roger Chaput, Joseph Reinhardt (g); Roger Chomer (vib); Juan Fernandez, Roger Grasset, Louis Pecqueux, Louis Volas (b); Maurice Chaillou (d, v); Bert Marshall (v).* 3/34–3/35.

****** Django Reinhardt, 1935–1936**
Classics 739 *Reinhardt; Bill Coleman, Alex Renard (t); George Johnson (cl); Maurice Cizeron (as, f); Alix Combelle (ts); Garnet Clark (p); Stéphane Grappelli (vn); Pierre Feret, Joseph Reinhardt (g); June Cole, Lucien Simoens, Louis Vola (b); Freddy Taylor (v).* 9/35–10/36.

****** Swing From Paris**
ASV CD AJA 5070 *Reinhardt; Stéphane Grappelli (vn); Roger Chaput, Pierre Ferret, Joseph Reinhardt, Eugène Vées (g); Robert Grassnet, Tony Rovira, Emmanuel Soudieux, Louis Vola (b).* 9/35–8/39.

***** Django Reinhardt, 1937**
Classics 748 *Reinhardt; Stéphane Grappelli (vn); André Ekyan (as); Marcel Bianchi, Pierre Ferret (g); Louis Vola (b).* 4–7/37.

*****(*) Django Reinhardt, 1937 – Volume 2**
Classics 762 *Reinhardt; Stéphane Grappelli, Paul Bartel, Josef Schwetsin, Michel Warlop (vn); Philippe Brun, Gus Deloof, André Cornille, André Pico (t); Guy Paquinet, Josse Breyère (tb); Jean Magnien (cl); Charles Blanc, Max Lisée, André Lamory (as); Charles Shaaf (ts); Maurice Cizeron (f); Georges Paquay (f, d); Pierre Zepilli (p); Louis Gaste, Joseph*

Reinhardt, Eugène Vées (g); Eugène D'Hellemmes (b); Maurice Chaillou (d). 9–12/37.

*****(*) Django Reinhardt, 1937–1938**

Classics 777 *Similar (i.e. Hot Club De France) to Classics above, except add Jean-Louis Jeanson (tb, vn), André Lluis (as, cl), John Arslanian (cl, bcl, ts, bs), Adrien Mareze, Noël Chiboust (ts), Larry Adler (hca), Roger Pirenet, Roger Du Hautbourg (vn), Bob Vaz (p), André Taylor (d), Gregoire Coco Aslan (perc), André Dassary (v).* 12/37–6/38.

*****(*) Jazz Masters 38: Django Reinhardt**

Verve 516393-2 *Similar to above.* 38–53.

****** Bruxelles / Paris**

Musidisc 403222 *As above, except add Raymond Fol (p).*

***** Django Reinhardt, 1938–1939**

Classics 793 *Similar to above, except add Bob Stewart (c), Barney Bigard (cl, d), Billy Taylor (b).* 6/38–4/39.

*****(*) Django Reinhardt, 1939–1940**

Classics 813 *Similar to above, except add Frank Big Boy Goudie (t), André Ekyan (as), Charles Lewis, Joe Turner (p), Marceau Sarbib, Lucien Simoëns (b), Tommy Benford, Charles Delaunay (d).* 5/39–8/40.

One of the Christian-name-only mythical figures of jazz, Django embodies much of the nonsense that surrounds the physically and emotionally damaged who nevertheless manage to parlay their disabilities and irresponsibilities into great music. Django's technical compass, apparently unhampered by loss of movement in two fingers of his left hand (the result of a burn which had ended his apprenticeship as a violinist), was colossal, ranging from dazzling high-speed runs to ballad-playing of aching intensity.

Pity the poor discographer who has to approach this material. The Reinhardt discography is now as mountainous as his native Belgium is flat. All we can hope to do is point out a few accessible passes. There is also a problem with titles: the principle seems to be that anything with 'Paris' or 'swing', either in conjunction or separately, will sell records; and there is the additional problem that Django's name has become so iconic that it alone is often deemed enough. There are huge numbers of compilations on the market, some of them of questionable authority and quality, often inaccurately dated and provenanced and with only notional stabs at accurate personnels. But this is a glass house we are entering ...

Classics – who do their usual thorough job – devote a whole CD to the output of just one month in 1937; the tally for the year as a whole is staggering. Unusually for this label, there is quite a bit of material which strictly belongs to other artists, prominently trumpeter Brun, but which features significant amounts of Django and so is included. The series begins with Django's first recordings with the Michel Warlop orchestra in 1934, reaching on into the classic Hot Club sessions over the next couple of years. In bulk, though, the music begins to sound slightly tired and dated, and Django's astonishing technique almost *too* perfect.

The other Classics are no less exhaustive, and the 1938–9 volume, with its roster of guests, is a most valuable indicator of his standing *vis-à-vis* the original begetters of a music he had graced for several years not fully appreciated outside Europe. Other curiosities in the run include four tracks with the late harmonica genius Larry Adler.

The Verve is valuable for the breadth of its coverage. Some will quibble at the lack of earlier material, but the fact that it carries the story right up to the year of Django's death gives the picture a certain valuable symmetry, and the music is, of course, quite wonderful. The Hot Club reunion of 1946 in London is well represented, and some care has been taken to give a reasonable balance of material over the final years, including the poignant 'Night And Day' of March 1953, when the shadows were beginning to draw in.

The ASV is beautifully remastered by Colin Brown, an example of how historical recordings can be restored without intrusive sweetening or inauthentic balances. At 66 minutes, it's also excellent value. It's good to be reminded how extraordinarily forceful the drummerless Hot Club could sound. Even with the chugging background, 'Appel Direct' is remarkably modern, and it's easy to see why Django continues to exert such an influence on guitarists of later, technically more sophisticated generations. The titles are confusingly similar, but this is the best single-volume option.

Most of the other volumes scoot ahead in time and are not as coherent, either artistically or technically, for that reason. The Musidisc offers a more extensive sample of the important sessions of 21 May 1947 (with Hubert Rostaing and the reconstituted Hot Club; the albums share 'Just One Of Those Things') and of 8 April 1953, the month before his death (with Martial Solal; they share a marvellous 'I Cover The Waterfront'), as well as good-quality material from 1951: 'Nuits De St Germain-Des-Prés', 'Crazy Rhythm', 'Fine And Dandy'.

Bruxelles/Paris has a marginally tougher version of 'Nuages'. In 1947, Django was battling with amplification (not always successfully), coping with the repercussions of a not entirely ecstatic reception with Ellington in the USA (ditto), and slipping backwards into the moral vagrancy that undoubtedly shortened his life. On the better tracks, on 'Blues For Barclay', 'Manoir De Mes Rêves', 'Mélodie Du Crépuscule' and 'Nuages', his instincts seem to be intact. He picks off clusters of notes with tremendous compression, holds and bends top notes like a singer and keeps a deep, insistent throb on the bottom string that, when it makes it up through the lo-fi hiss and drop-out, is hugely effective.

***** Rare Django**

Disques Swing SWC 8419 *Similar to items above.* 28–38.

A useful little compilation that takes in some very early and quite naïve recordings along with more familiar material from later years. Hearing Django do 'If You Knew Susie' is a reminder of how joyous and wicked he could be when the spirit moved him.

***** The Swing Sessions: Volume 1**

Frog 50 *Reinhardt; Bill Coleman (t, v); Benny Carter (t, as); Philippe Brun, Shad Collins, Bill Dillard (t); Dicky Wells (tb); André Ekyan (as); Coleman Hawkins (ts); Alix Combelle (ts, cl); Eddie South, Michel Warlop (vn); Stéphane Grappelli (vn, p); Marcel Bianchi, Roger Chaput, Pierre Ferret, Louis Gaste (g); Dick Fulbright, Eugène D'Hellemes, Wilson Myers, Louis Vola (b); Bill Beason, Tommy Benford, Maurice Chaillou (d).* 37.

***** The Swing Sessions: Volume 2**

Frog 52 *As above; add Christian Wagner (cl, as); Frank 'Big Boy' Goudie (cl, ts); Emile Stern (p); Joseph Reinhardt, Eugène Vées (g); Paul Cordonnie, Lucien Simoëns (b); Jerry Mengo (d).* 37.

The first volume brings together all the cuts Django made for Charles Delaunay's Swing label in 1937. For much of the time he's effectively Coleman Hawkins's rhythm guitarist and there's not much of the frantic interplay associated with the Hot Club. He also provides rhythm for violinist Eddie South, but there are some fine small-group sessions as well, where the guitarist is the front-man and unmistakably the star. Some dazzling play from the guitarist; however familiar some of this material is, it's good to hear it in label context like this. Volume 2 rounds out the story nicely and includes the remarkable 'Interprétation Swing Du Premier Mouvement Du Concerto En Re Mineur De Jean Sebastien Bach', a fascinating reading of the D minor concerto by Django, Eddie South and Stéphane Grappelli.

CORE COLLECTION

**** The Classic Early Recordings In Chronological Order

JSP Jazz Box JSPCD 901 5CD *As for the above, with some variations.* 34–39.

The first thing to note about these marvellous and superbly priced compilations is that they are not strictly chronological at all, but 'piecewise continuous'. Prompted by the poor quality of the existing reissues (and the shortcomings of the Classics volumes are well documented), remastering engineer Ted Kendall, who learned his craft under the tutelage of the great John R. T. Davies, has cleaned away the 'audio rubble' and restored these great recordings to something like pristine condition. All but the first two tracks on disc one, of which there are no original pressings, have been taken from excellent-quality 78s. We have compared in detail 15 tracks from various Classics volumes with their equivalents here, and it is clear that a whole generation of Django listeners have grown up with insecurely pitched renditions, with problems ranging from intermittent flattening of tone to consistently slow transfers, often resulting in tunes being heard a quarter-tone adrift. It would be redundant simply to detail the tracks we have sampled with very close attention. Even a cursory listen suggests that the JSP box, which is issued at a bargain price, is a much more attractive proposition. The arrangement of material is logical enough. Disc one consists of the Hot Club recordings of 1934 and 1935, with Stéphane Grappelli strongly featured. Disc two corrals the London Deccas and, though Kendall has had to compromise here and there with vinyl and one corroded metal master (only the sharpest ears will notice), the quality remains very high indeed. Disc three is discographically trickier since some of the material was never issued on 78. Kendall has clarified a few troublesome points, confirming for instance that a supposed alternative take of 'Time On My Hands' from March 1939 is simply a dub of the original release. Disc four steps back in time to the Decca and HMV recordings made between March 1935 (the earliest of them with Coleman Hawkins) and the first Swing label releases of 1937. The last disc rounds up some additional material from 1935 along with the fine 1937 HMVs. The detail shouldn't put anyone off. These are quite splendid jazz records which belong in every collection, and Ted Kendall has done a demanding job with taste and precision.

**** Volume 2 – Paris and London: 1937–1948

JSP CD 504 A-D 4CD *As above and below, again with some variations.* 37–48.

This second volume covers material from Paris and London over the period indicated, a period during which recording quality probably improved exponentially, not that anyone told the majority of reissue producers that. Kendall's impeccable work has restored these precious sides as well.

*** All Star Sessions

Blue Note 31577 *Reinhardt; Rex Stewart (c); Pierre Allier, Noël Chiboust (t); Barney Bigard (cl); Benny Carter (t, as); Guy Pacquinet (tb); Fletcher Allen, André Ekyan, Charles Lisée (as); Coleman Hawkins, Bertie King (ts); Alix Combelle (cl, ts); York deSouza, Stéphane Grappelli (p); Len Harrison, Eugène D'Hellemmes, Billy Taylor (b); Tommy Benford, Maurice Chaillou, Robert Montmarche (d).* 35–39.

Nothing here that isn't available elsewhere, but the transfers are very good indeed and the supporting documentation is sound. Grappelli isn't heard on violin, interestingly enough, so the usual Hot Club echoes aren't there. Some sessions are under other leadership and Django doesn't feature at all prominently in the ensemble led by Hawkins; elsewhere he has to vie for prominence with other soloists. All in all, though, a very attractive set.

*** Swing From Paris

Emarcy 159 853 2 *Reinhardt; Stéphane Grappelli (vn); Pierre Ferret, Joseph Reinhardt, Eugène Vées (g); Louis Vola, Tony Rovita, Emmanuel Soudieux (b).* 35–39.

*** Django Et Compagnie

Emarcy 549 241 2 *Reinhardt; Michel Warlop Orchestra; Nitta Rette Et Son Trio Hot; André Pasdoc & Orchestra; Yvonne Louis & Orchestra; Micheline Day Et Son Quatuor Swing; Wal-Berg Et Son Jazz Français.* 35–37.

*** Swing '39

Emarcy 159 854 2 *As above; omit Vées, Vola, Rovita.* 3–5/39.

If ever an artist represented Universal's 'Jazz In Paris' series it is surely Django. Nothing on these volumes that hasn't appeared before or that should represent any surprise to seasoned listeners. The middle set has Django in some less well-known company and mostly in the role of accompanist, so it's of historical interest first and foremost. But they are nice sets, attractively packaged and with highly professional sound.

*** Django Reinhardt, 1940

Classics 831 *Reinhardt; Philippe Brun, Pierre Allier, Aimé Barelli, Christian Bellest, Alex Renard, Al Piguillem (t); Guy Paquinet, Gaston Moat, Pierre Deck (tb); Hubert Rostaing (cl, ts); Alix Combelle (bs); André Ekyan (as); Charles Lewis, Raymond Wraskoff (p); Pierre Ferret, Joseph Reinhardt (g); Emmanuel Soudieux, Francis Luca (b); Pierre Fouad (d).* 2–10/40.

*** Django Reinhardt, 1940–1941

Classics 852 *Reinhardt; Pierre Allier, Aimé Barelli, Christian Bellest, Jean Heutchel, Severin Luino, Georges Wallez (t); André Cauzard, Maurice Gladieu, Guy Paquinet (tb); Hubert Rostaing, Christian Wagner (cl); Alix Combelle (cl, ts, glock); Max Blanc, Charles Lisée, Pierre Martineau (as); Roger Allier, Noël Chiboust, Georges Jacquemont (ts); Léo Chauliac, Paul Colot (p); Joseph Reinhardt (g); Tony Rovira (b); Pierre Fouad (d); Charles Trenet (v).* 12/40–3/41.

*** Django Reinhardt, 1941–1942

Classics 877 *Similar to above, except add Raymond Chantrain, Georges Clais, Paul D'Hondt (t); Sus Van Camp, Jean Damm (tb); Louis Billen, Jo Magis (cl, as); Jeff Van*

Herswingels, Jack Demany (ts); Arthur Saguet (ts, bs, cl); John Ouwerckx, Jim Vanderjeught (p); Arthur Peeters (b); Josse Aerts (d). 4/41–3/42.

***** Django Reinhardt, 1942–1943**

Classics 905 *Similar to above, except add Alex Caturegli, Lucien Devroye, Maurice Giegas, Janot Morales, Maurice Moufflard, Alex Renard (t), Nick Ferrar, Maurice Gladieu, Louis Melon, Pierre Remy (tb), Gérard Léveque (cl), Bobby Naret, Guy Plum (cl, ts), Robert Mavounzy, Robert Merchez (as), Charles Hary, Benny Pauwels (f, cl, ts), André Lluis, Fud Candrix (cl, ts), Emile Deltour, Chas Dolne, Jean Douillez, Walter Feron, Raymond Goutard, Paulette Izoird, Sylvio Schmidt (vn), Eugène Vées (g), Jean Storne (b), Pierre Fouad, Gaston Léonard (d), Nelly Kay (v).* 5/42–7/43.

***** Django Reinhardt, 1944–1946**

Classics 945 *Reinhardt; Alex Caturegli, Herb Bass, Christian Bellest, Robin Gould, Roger Hubert, Bernie Privin, Jerry Stephan, Lonnie Wilfong (t); Bill Decker, Don Gardner, Shelton Heath, John Kirkpatrick, Marcel Librecht, Pierre Remy (tb); Jim Hayes, Hubert Rostaing (cl, as); Desiré Duriez, Roger JeanJean, André Lluis, Joe Moser (as); Bernie Cavalière, Noël Chiboust, Peanuts Hucko, Gaston Rahier, Bill Zickefoose (ts); Ken Lowther, Yves Raynal (bs); Stéphane Grappelli (vn); Leo Chauliac, Larry Man, Mel Powell (p); Roger Chaput, Alan Hodgkiss, Jack Llewellyn, Joseph Reinhardt (g); Bob Decker, Coleridge Goode, Josz Schulman, Lucien Simoëns (b); Bill Bethel, Ray McKinley, Jerry Mengo (d); Sgt Jack Platt (cond).* 11/44–5/46.

The war years obviously brought a certain non-musical poignancy, and the remarkable story of how Django was protected by a jazz-loving Luftwaffe officer, but the coldest and most detached audition still reveals a shift in Django's playing towards something altogether more inward, secretive, less joyous, and even when there are no obvious shadows gathering there is a hint of darkness and doubt. Again there is a good deal of non-Django (or non-lead) material included, largely stuff by Ekyan and Brun; and the latter's session from February 1940, recorded in Paris, has the fascinating discographical footnote of a playing role for Charles Delaunay, who was operating under the aka of H. P. Chadel.

With the war in progress, Django was cut off from many of his greatest sources of inspiration, Grappelli only most obviously, but it also caught him at his peak of popularity and on 13 December 1941 he made the recording of 'Nuages' that was to cement him in jazz history for ever. Even after more than half a century, and the despoliation of a thousand buskers, it's still a wonderful performance. Django had recorded the piece earlier, but he was dissatisfied with the result – and his judgement, as ever, was sound. It's certainly the highlight of the 1940 and 1941 Classics volume. The dating is a little misleading, because only one item from March 1941 is included, a Charles Trenet song – 'La Cigale Et La Fourmi' – with the Quintette Du Hot Club De France accompanying. A track credited to 'Festival Swing 1941', a Charles Delaunay-sponsored event, was actually recorded on Boxing Day 1940, as was the celebratory 'Django's Music' line-up originally issued on Swing 95. Most of the remaining material is under the nominal leadership of trumpeter Pierre Allier or clarinettist Christian Wagner, and though Django's personality shines through every time, these are more workaday sessions and not strictly part of the core discography.

The end of 1942 saw Django's behaviour becoming ever more erratic. On another Delaunay tour in the south and Algiers, he refused to play matinées and simply left the party. Delaunay managed to get the remaining players back to the mainland just before the Allied invasion of 8 November 1942. Django had been recording with the Stan Brenders Orchestra, an undemanding gig that in no way stretched or challenged him. In the spring of 1943, though, he made some Hot Club sides with Léveque and Lluis sharing the front line, and he also recorded a trio and a couple of improvised solos for the Swing label. The remainder of the year was taken up with collaborations with Fud Candrix and a few sides with a big band, never Django's strongest suit.

The Liberation of Paris was a key moment in the early autumn of 1944 and immediately opened up the jazz and swing scene. The first recordings represented are a session by Noël Chiboust's orchestra, appropriately enough entitled 'Welcome' (Django doesn't play on the first part), but the real delights had to wait until 1945, the beginning and end of the year, when Django recorded with a 'mystery' Hot Club featuring Peanuts Hucko, Mel Powell and Ray McKinley, and then in November with an American swing band under the direction of Sergeant Jack Platt. 'Djangology' and 'Manoir De Mes Rêves' from the latter session are professional enough, but it's interesting to hear Django playing American standards on the January 1945 session, including a wonderful 'How High The Moon'.

Sentimentally, if not always musically, the reunion with Grappelli was always going to be an important moment. They met up in London in January 1946 and recorded four sides for Swing and another four (including a reworked and extremely disappointing 'Nuages') for Decca the following day. The old magic simply wasn't there, though everyone seems upbeat and keen to play. The British rhythm section had been well versed in Hot Club idiom, but they lack the Gauloise-wreathed cool and sophistication of their cross-Channel counterparts, and the songs never quite come off. Back in Paris in May, there was a date with Rostaing. Again, Django sounds jaded and almost indifferent, and he even fluffs a couple of chord changes on 'Yours And Mine' and 'On The Sunny Side Of The Street'. It had been a long war, but with its passing went the last tension and urgency in Django's playing. Thereafter, he was to become a replica of himself, capable of extraordinary things, but with a critical element missing. Listening to the span of the Classics issues to date, one can't help hearing a fall.

***** Django Reinhardt, 1947**

Classics 1001 *Reinhardt; Jo Boyer, Vincent Casino, Louis Ménardi (t); André Lafosse, Guy Paquinet (tb); Hubert Rostaing, Michel De Villers (as, cl); Jean-Claude Fohrenbach (ts); Stéphane Grappelli (vn); Eddie Bernard (p); Joseph Reinhardt, Eugène Vées (g); Ladislas Czabancyk, Willie Lockwood, Emmanuel Soudieux (b); Al Craig, Pierre Fouad (d).* 3–7/47.

***** Django Reinhardt, 1947 – Volume 2**

Classics 1046 *Reinhardt; Gérard Léveque, Maurice Meunier, Hubert Rostaing (cl); Stéphane Grappelli (vn); Eddie Bernard (p); Joseph Reinhardt, Eugène Vées (g); Emmanuel Soudieux (b); Fred Ermelin, André Jourdan, Jacques Martinon (d).* 7–11/47.

*****(*) Swing De Paris**

Arco 3 ARC 110 *Reinhardt; Gérard Léveque, Maurice Meunier, Hubert Rostaing (cl); Joseph Reinhardt, Eugène Vées (g); Eddie Bernard (p); Ladislas Czabancyk, Emmanuel Soudieux (b); André Jourdan, Jacques Martinon (d).* 7–11/47.

***(*) Pêche À La Mouche

Verve 835419-2 *Reinhardt; Vincent Casino, Jo Boyer, Louis Menardi, Rex Stewart (t); André Lafosse, Guy Paquinet (tb); Michel De Villers (as, cl); Hubert Rostaing (cl); Jean-Claude Forenbach (ts); Eddie Bernard, Maurice Vander (p); Joseph Reinhardt, Eugène Vées (g); Will Lockwood, Ladislas Czabancyk, Pierre Michelot, Emmanuel Soudieux (b); Al Craig, Ted Curry, André Jourdan, Jean-Louis Viale (d).* 4/47–3/53.

Django's visit to the United States made a big impact on him, both positive and negative. It certainly reinforced the feeling of isolation and aggressive independence that increasingly became part of his character. It may also have reminded him that jazz was, after all, an American music. However, it did expose him to a whole raft of new influences – not least bebop – which henceforward were to play a part in his music. Though there is nothing that definitively points to a bebop influence, the phrasing is terser and the attack more forceful. Also the grouping of phrases on tunes such as 'Lover Man' (March), 'Just One Of Those Things' (May) and 'Blues For Barclay' (July, all Classics 1001) points to a more modern idiom.

The most pressing business of all was to record a reunion of the Hot Club after Grappelli's return from wartime exile in England. The violinist had often pronounced himself irritated by Django's 'monkey business', and the reunion did not seem likely to be long-standing. In the spring, Django reconvened his wartime quintet with Hubert Rostaing and recorded a score of sides in Paris and Brussels. There was a further meeting with Grappelli in November, but it's a strangely flat-footed and unamiable encounter which might have waited for more complete coverage in a later Classics volume.

Prefaced by a track each – 'Pêche À La Mouche' and 'Minor Blues' – from Django's quintet and orchestra, the 1947 sessions for Blue Star with the re-formed Hot Club are not classics like the great sides of the previous decade, but they have a spontaneity and ease that are both attractive and aesthetically satisfying. Producer Eddie Barclay gave Django a free hand to play what he wanted, and the music that emerged was bright, flowing and often thoughtful, with a rough edge that is only partially explained by the technical limitations of the recording.

There is one further session from 1947, under the leadership of Rex Stewart, which again might have served to remind Django of the huge cultural distance between him and the Americans. He plays with immense elegance on 'Night And Day' but never sounds as though he's on top of what Stewart is doing harmonically.

The later recording, which was issued as a ten-inch LP, not as 78s, saw the shadows move a little closer round the guitarist, but Django's solo on 'Brazil' is, as noted by Pierre Michelot, quite astonishing in its fiery grace, and he seems to have overcome some of the amplification problems he had been having since the war. He tackles 'Night And Day' again, on his own terms this time, and there are beautiful versions of 'Nuages' and 'Manoir De Mes Rêves'. He isn't a musician whose work divides easily into 'early' and 'late', but it's clear that the period between these two recordings was one of personal and artistic change and, in some respects, retrenchment. Django had made a great many miscalculations and had to spend too much time compensating for them.

As ever, the Classics are hard to beat for literal chronology and completeness, but the sound is very much better on the other compilations and, unless exhaustive documentation is required and pure sound is at a discount, these are the priority purchases.

*** Django's Blues

Emarcy 013 545 2 *Reinhardt; Hubert Rostaing (cl); Joseph Reinhardt, Eugène Vées (g); Emmanuel Soudieux (b); André Jourdan (d).* 7 & 10/47.

Another in Emarcy's 'Jazz In Paris' series and two lateish sets from the reconvened Hot Club quintet. Two takes of 'I'll Never Smile Again' from July 1947 suggest that Django is still thinking musically and still taking pains, but there is a slackening of concentration on all these sides and certainly little of the tense drama of the classic sessions of a decade earlier.

**(*) Echoes Of France

Dreyfus FDM 36726 2 *Various personnels and dates.*

No one would deny Francis Dreyfus his right to choose and issue a personal selection of Django performances, but one might reasonably expect a bit more detail. Lack of discographical data is a problem with this now well-established series. It may not worry a casual purchaser, but a little more effort might have made a nicely packaged and mastered set a more attractive proposition for serious collectors.

***(*) Djangology 1949

Bluebird/BMG ND90448 *Reinhardt; Stéphane Grappelli (vn); Gianni Safred (p); Carlo Recori (b); Aurelio De Carolis (d).* 1–2/49.

A final opportunity to hear Reinhardt and Grappelli playing together, albeit with a dud rhythm section. In an intelligent sleeve-note (which includes useful track-by-track comments on all 20 CD items), guitarist Frank Vignola warns against making comparisons between these rather edgy and competitive sessions and the great days of the pre-war Quintette Du Hot Club. The most evident token of changing musical times, and a legacy of Django's relatively unsuccessful American trip, is a boppish cast to several of the tracks, most significantly the Ur-text of bebop, 'I Got Rhythm'. Fortunately for the session, both Django and Grappelli got rhythm to spare, for the local musicians are a positive hindrance. On 'All The Things You Are' Safred chords morosely in the background while Recori and de Carolis go off for a *grappa*. Django's frustration comes through in places, but it's clear that at least some of the aggression is directed at his one-time junior partner who now claims his full share of the foreground. For all its shortcomings, this is a worthwhile addition to the discography.

*** Django Reinhardt, 1947–1951

Classics 1317 *Reinhardt; Bernard Hullin (t); Hubert Fol (as); Hubert Rostaing (cl); Raymond Fol (p); Henri Baumgartner, Rene Ferret, Joseph Reinhardt, Eugène Vées (g); Pierre Michelot, Emmanuel Soudieux, Louis Vola (b); Fred Ermelin, Pierre Lemarchand, Arthur Motta (d).* 47–51.

Very nearly the end of the story and it's clear that the fires are going out and that Django's personal problems are winning. There is still some fine and fiery playing, and tracks like 'Belleville', 'Micro (Mopping the Bride) Danse Nuptiale', 'Bricktop' and 'To Each His Own Symphony' are worth having, as well as a couple of fine versions of 'Nuages', one late one stretching to well over six minutes.

★★★(★) Django In Rome
JSP 919 4CD *Reinhardt; André Ekyan (as, cl); Stéphane Grappelli (vn); Gianni Safred (p); Carlo Pecori (b); Aurelio de Carlis (d).* 49–50.

An often forgotten corner of Django's later *Wanderjahre* with Grappelli, lovingly restored by Ted Kendall who has single-handedly done more for Django's posthumous reputation than anyone. Though some of the settings are a little flat and uninspired, courtesy of a local rhythm section, there are some lovely things here, and with 90 tracks spread over four CDs no one will complain about the value.

★★★★ Intégrale Django Reinhardt: Volume 1 – 1928–1934
Frémeaux et Associés 301 2CD *As for many items above.* 28–34.

★★★(★) The Complete Django Reinhardt: Volume 18 – 1949–1950, I'll Never Be The Same
Frémeaux et Associés 318 2CD *As for many items above.* 49–50.

These are but two examples from a massive and comprehensive documentation of the great guitarist's work from his coming out to the end of his active career, all in 18 well-packed volumes. The language seems to have switched from French to English part way through. There is nothing to be said about the music that hasn't been said before. This is certainly the definitive source for Django fans who are prepared to make the investment. Judging by what we have heard and read, none will be disappointed by either sound quality or documentation.

★★★(★) Volume 1: 1934–1935
Naxos 8021505 *As for many items above.* 34–35.

★★★★ Volume 3: 1936–1937
Naxos 8120686 *As for many items above.* 36–37.

★★★★ Volume 4: 1937
Naxos 8120698 *As for many items above.* 37.

★★★★ Volume 2: 1938–1939
Naxos 8120575 *As for many items above.* 38–39.

Now that Django's music is out of copyright, there is an unstaunchable flow of compilations and reissues. Naxos are pioneers of ultra-budget releases and these will appeal strongly to anyone who doesn't want to spend too much on a Django collection. The chronological sequence shouldn't trouble anyone, nor should the sound-quality, which is excellent, and these highly accessible sets allow the listener to trace the development of Django's virtuosic style, culminating in the extraordinary epiphanies of 1937, when streams of notes seems to fly off the guitar in vivid counterpoint and with an ever-deepening harmonic awareness.

Emily Remler (1957–90)

GUITAR

Studied at Berklee from 1974, then spent three years in New Orleans before returning to NYC and playing in her own small group. Also worked in a duo with Larry Coryell.

★★★ Firefly
Concord CCD 4162 *Remler; Hank Jones (p); Bob Maize (b); Jake Hanna (d).* 4/81.

★★★★ East To Wes
Concord CCD 4356 *Remler; Hank Jones (p); Buster Williams (b); Marvin 'Smitty' Smith (d).* 5/88.

Remler's senseless early death (from heart failure while on tour in Australia) deprived us of a talent that seemed on the point of breakthrough. While her early role-models were conservative ones in terms of her instrument – Christian and Montgomery, specifically – her tough-minded improvising and affinity with hard-hitting rhythm sections let her push a mainstream style to its logical limits. *Firefly* was her debut for the label and is fluent if a little anonymous, although she handles the diversity of 'Strollin'' and 'In A Sentimental Mood' without any hesitation. Some of her albums have now been deleted, but the best example of her work is the impeccable Montgomery tribute, *East To Wes*. Smith proves to be an ideal drummer for the guitarist, his busy cymbals and polyrhythmic variations on the bebop pulse perfectly cast to push Remler into her best form: 'Daahoud' and 'Hot House' are unbeatable updates of each tune. Jones, imperturbable as ever, takes a cool middle course. While conceived as a Montgomery homage, Remler's playing actually shows how unlike Wes she really was: harder of tone, her solos more fragmented yet equally lucid. Hopefully, Concord will follow their current procedure and reissue some of her other albums as mid-price twofers.

The Remote Viewers

GROUP

British explorers previously associated with B Shops For The Poor.

★★(★) Low Shapes In Dark Heat
Leo Lab CD 049 *Adrian Northover (ss, as); Louise Petts (as, syn, v); David Petts (ts, syn).* 2 & 7/98.

★★★ Obliques Before Pale Skin
Leo Lab 061 *As above, except add theremins to instrumentation for Northover, Petts and Petts.* 6 & 7/99.

★★★(★) Persuasive With Aliens
Leo Lab 067 *As above.* 1–2/00.

★★★(★) Stranded Depots
Leo Lab CD 076 *As above.* 00.

★★★(★) The Minimum Programme Of Humanity
Leo LR 342 *As above.* 11–12/01.

★★★ Sudden Rooms In Different Buildings
GE 5 *As above.* 6/01–1/03.

The CIA and NASA still, we understand, take remote sensing very seriously, but what are we to make of these enigmatic trios? At moments, we might be dealing with a conventional saxophone quartet who, in the absence of the senior and most sensible member, muck about in the studio for a couple of afternoons, but then Louise Petts's remarkable voice and strange, associative lyrics kick in and the spell is cast.

This is music of great privacy. Even when a familiar theme does emerge – and *Low Shapes* includes a tender version of the theme from television's *Callan* – the associations are not necessarily shared. The effect is somewhat akin to a session by Bristol's lamented Startled Insects, but produced by and guesting John Zorn and the sound-crew of *The X-Files*.

The second album opens with a minimally unaccompanied reading of Jimmy Van Heusen's 'It Could Happen To You', continues with Madonna's 'Secret' and ends with a gorgeous version of Dmitri Tiomkin's 'Wild Is The Wind'. What happens in between defies straightforward description, beyond the fact that it is a richer acoustic mix, with few of the London Saxophone Quartet mannerisms that made the debut so quirkily old-fashioned in places.

Surreal and funky, weary with the world but helplessly fascinated by its many strangenesses, the music has wound on through three more sets for Leo (interestingly, the group has moved from the more arcane Leo Lab sector to the main label with album five). As they've grown and gone deeper into whatever it is they're doing, The Viewers are now able to impose themselves on source material which might seem a complete wrong turning: so we get David Bowie on *Persuasive With Aliens* (and an Agatha Christie reference), Gordon Jenkins and Satie on *Stranded Depots*, and texts by Bertolt Brecht on the often very disquieting *The Minimum Programme Of Humanity*, which makes a greater play with electronics and synthesized percussion. Points of reference might be Annette Peacock, Edith Sitwell and N. F. Simpson, but we advise adventurous listeners to discover for themselves. The latest *Sudden Rooms In Different Buildings*, after Petts's opening vocal on David Sylvian's 'Ghosts', abandons song form – perhaps any form – completely and all but disappears under corrosive electronic weather. Will they return?

Henri Renaud (born 1925)

PIANO

Legendary French player, probably best known for his 1953 recordings with Clifford Brown. Became head of jazz for CBS France and largely gave up playing from 1965.

***** The Complete Legendary**

Saturne Picture Discs PJC 222008 *Renaud; Bobby Jaspar, Sandy Mosse (ts); Jimmy Gourley (g); Pierre Michelot (b); Pierre Lemarchand (d).* 6/51.

Renaud is an important figure in French jazz, less cerebral and less celebrated than Martial Solal but a consistent champion of home-grown jazz. He had the benefit of two visiting Americans – Gourley and Mosse – on the Saturne sessions, which were originally issued as picture discs with infamously bad sound, and they bring something fresh and spontaneous to a session that is otherwise a little tramlined. Like his fellow saxophonist, Jaspar is very much a Lester Young disciple, soft-toned and occasionally a little diffident, but capable of some fine flourishes.

Don Rendell (born 1926)

TENOR AND SOPRANO SAXOPHONES, FLUTES

Played with John Dankworth from 1950, then in big bands and with his own group. The Rendell–Carr Quintet of the '60s is a much-remembered outfit, and he has been an avuncular presence since, teaching rather more than performing live.

***** Meet Don Rendell**

Jasmine JASCD 613 *Rendell; Dickie Hawdon (t, flhn); Ronnie Ross (ts, bs); Damian Robinson (p); Ashley Kozak, Sammy Stokes, Pete Elderfield (b); Derek Hogg, Benny Goodman, Don Lawson (d).* 6/54–5/55.

***** Don Rendell Four And Five & Rendell–Carr Quintet 1964–68**

Spotlite SPJ-CD 566 *Rendell; Ian Carr (t, flhn); John Mealing, Michael Garrick (p); Dave Green (b); Trevor Tomkins (d).* 1/64–7/68.

*****(*) Space Walk**

Redial 538 806-2 *Rendell; Stan Robinson (ts, cl, f); Peter Shade (vib, f); Jack Thorncroft (b); Trevor Tomkins (d).* 72.

The veteran British saxophonist currently has his best-ever showing in terms of CD availability. The Jasmine set reissues his very scarce output for the Tempo label: one ten-inch album and a few EP tracks. At this point, Rendell was an easy-going Lester-man; four quartet tracks where he plays some sinuous variations on standards show him at his best. At faster tempos there is a hint of a boppish bite, but really only a hint. As usual with records from this vintage, some welcome glimpses of the likes of Hawdon and Ross.

The Spotlite album at last brings some of the work of a very important British group to circulation: both of these sessions, a 1964 studio date and a live set from four years later, have never appeared before. The group's empathy and crisp ensemble sound are at least as important as the solos, the more so since the 1964 tracks are clipped rather closely, many not even breaking the three-minute barrier. Carr's attactive sound survives the slightly dry studio mix and Rendell's more assertive tenor has three tracks to itself. The three tracks from an Antibes Festival set are much more open-ended; original material throughout, and on Garrick's interesting 'Voices' Rendell does some beautiful work on flute and tenor; however, the rather swimmy live sound isn't very helpful. This album should really stand as a pendant to the group's various studio albums: there are new editions of some of them on BGO but they did not arrive in time for this edition.

Though many who know and appreciate his work will think of Rendell as a mainstream player, he was also deeply influenced by John Coltrane's 'sheets of sound' period, this long before Trane became the orthodoxy in jazz saxophone. That is immediately evident on *Space Walk*'s opening 'On The Way', though it is Stan Robinson who takes the first – and equally Coltrane-inspired – solo, leaving Don to come in later, sounding rather distant and as yet uncertain. The opening number segues into 'Antibes', a remembrance of the Rendell–Carr Quintet's appearance at the south of France festival. The key component here, and just one of the album's many brilliant instrumental twists, is the trio of flautists. Rendell is one of those rare saxophone-players who are equally and in some lights more convincing on flute.

'Street Called Straight' is an example of how expressive he can be on what is usually treated as a 'double' or colour instrument. It's one of two tracks here inspired, unlikely as it sounds, by St Paul's wanderings in the Mediterranean. The other is Stan Robinson's 'Earoaquilo', which evokes the stormy wind that brings in cold air from the continent. As a vibesman, Peter Shade belongs up there with Bill LeSage, Frank Ricotti and Tubby Hayes, and he makes an important contribution to this imaginative and unusual record, not least the title-track, which is almost a vibraphone feature.

***** Live At The Avgarde Gallery Manchester**

Spotlite SPJ-CD 401 *Rendell; Pete Martin (t); Joe Palin (p); Ian Taylor (b); Gordon Beckett (d).* 74.

***** Just Music**

Spotlite SPJ-CD 402 *Rendell; Barbara Thompson (ss, ts, f); Peter Lemer (p); Steve Cook (b); Laurie Allan (d).* 1–6/74.

Rendell made a sometimes awkward transition to the '70s, and these Spotlite reissues are interesting rather than essential. The Manchester set, recorded with a pick-up rhythm section, is a fine feature for his playing, although it sometimes demonstrates that the sum of his various influences was at this point in a slight state of flux. *Just Music* is an early example of Thompson on record, and the two front-liners share eight horns between them. Some of the writing stiffens the mobility of the group, and it's occasionally up to the excellent Lemer to wake up matters with his argumentative comping. Two sets very much of their British time.

Melvin Rhyne (born 1936)

ORGAN

Rhyne's reputation stems from his work with Wes Montgomery for Riverside. It took some considerable time to establish a separate identity, but in his mid-50s things started to happen and since then there has been a steady procession of strong, idiosyncratic albums.

***** Organ-izing**

Original Jazz Classics OJCCD 1055 *Rhyne; Blue Mitchell (t); Johnny Griffin (ts); Gene Harris (p); Andy Simpkins (b); Albert Tootie Heath (d).* 3/60.

This feels less like a studio album than a good-quality tape of a live set. It's basically an extended jam on four solid, bluesy themes, with ample space for all the guests to solo, which Griff does with his usual abandon. Harris is more circumspect but even with the Hammond to contend with, he produces some fine things. The longest – and probably best – track is Adderley's 'Barefoot Sunday Blues'. It was to be a long time before Mel fronted another session.

***** The Legend**

Criss Cross 1059 *Rhyne; Brian Lynch (t); Don Braden (ts); Peter Bernstein (g); Kenny Washington (d).* 12/91.

***** Boss Organ**

Criss Cross 1080 *Rhyne; Joshua Redman (ts); Peter Bernstein (g); Kenny Washington (d).* 1/93.

The Legend was Rhyne's first recording as a leader since his comeback and rediscovery. It was done impromptu after the organist had finished a Criss Cross session for trumpeter Brian Lynch. Whether the title is entirely deserved is a matter for debate, but Mel certainly enjoyed an enviable reputation among fellow players and he plays with a robustly insouciant confidence. Rhyne immediately sounds different from the prevailing Jimmy Smith school of organ players. Instead of swirling, bluesy chords, he favours sharp, almost staccato figures and lyrical single-note runs that often don't go quite where expected. The format for the session is the same as that for the classic Montgomery recordings, and Kenny Washington makes a particularly strong impact. The set opens with Eddie 'Lockjaw' Davis's 'Licks A-Plenty', kicks along with 'Stompin' At The Savoy', Wes Montgomery's 'The Trick Bag' and Dizzy Gillespie's 'Groovin' High'; there are two evocative ballads, 'Serenata' and 'Old Folks', and the session closes with a long 'Blues For Wes', with Lynch and saxophonist Braden sitting in.

Another young horn-player makes a vital contribution to the later *Boss Organ*. Few saxophonists have been more comprehensively hyped than Joshua Redman. He lives pretty much up to billing on this set, swanking through tunes by Stevie Wonder and Wes Montgomery as if he grew up playing them. Rhyne sounds relaxed and laid-back – almost too unhurried since, as the set advances, it begins to drag ever so slightly. Enjoyable, though, and a convincing consolidation of the fine form of *The Legend.*

*****(*) Stick To The Kick**

Criss Cross Criss 1137 *Rhyne; Ryan Kisor (t); Eric Alexander (ts); Peter Bernstein (g); Kenny Washington (d).* 12/94, 12/95.

***** Mel's Spell**

Criss Cross Criss 1118 *Rhyne; Peter Bernstein (g); Kenny Washington (d); Daniel Sadownick (perc).* 12/94, 12/95.

*****(*) Kojo**

Criss Cross Criss 1164 *As above.* 12/97.

By the latter half of the '90s, a Melvin Rhyne record was as predictable and as reliable as a No. 12 bus, and these must have delighted existing fans. The band on *Stick* … offers a scaled-down version of a big-band sound and it would be intriguing to hear Mel working with a full-size ensemble. Apart from Dameron's 'Lady Bird' and Bud Powell's 'Wail', all the material is by Rhyne himself. He writes themes rather than songs, but themes with a very definite shape and structure. The other two albums are much looser in concept and feature considerably more standards material. Mel shows how readily he can switch between bebop ('Blue'N'Boogie') and a swing ballad like 'In A Sentimental Mood', both on *Kojo*; on *Mel's Spell* he weaves a delicious programme of tunes, from Bird's 'Billy's Bounce' to Frank Sinatra's 'This Love Of Mine'. As ever, Gerry Teekens gives Mel a big and very natural sound. The organ–guitar–drums trio is not difficult to record, technically speaking, but it calls for a measure of taste and balance which isn't always on call.

***** Classmasters**

Criss Cross 1183 *Rhyne; Eric Alexander (ts); Peter Bernstein (g); Kenny Washington (d); Daniel Sadownick (perc).* 12/99.

Mel's earned the right to call a tune 'Rhyne, Rhythm And Song', although composing isn't really his thing, perhaps, and after that one's done the rest of the set is given over to other writers. It unfolds like a live situation where songs and composers occur to Rhyne as he goes on, so we get two Legrand tunes, a Turrentine blues, 'Don't Explain', 'Well You Needn't' and then a couple of McCoy Tyner pieces. He has a way of voicing a line that makes you think of the old compliment about 'making the organ speak' and some of the slower pieces are the best. Nothing especially stands out, though, and the session's really just an enjoyable cruise.

Buddy Rich (1917–87)

DRUMS, VOCAL

A child performer in vaudeville, Rich was a bandleader by the time he was 11. He worked in many of the big swing bands of the '30s and spent six years with Tommy Dorsey before leading his own group in the late '40s (it foundered financially). He freelanced through the '50s, sang and did some acting, and spent five years with Harry James, before re-forming a big band in

1966. Against the run of the time, it was an international success, and he toured with it for the rest of his life, although heart problems interrupted an otherwise tireless working schedule. A ruthless man, peerless in his technique, Rich has been idolized by many as the archetypal swinging jazz drummer.

★★★ His Legendary 1947–48 Orchestra

Hep CD 12 *Rich; Tommy Allison, Stan Fischelson, Phil Gilbert, Charlie Shavers, Charlie Walp, Dale Pearce, Frank LePinto, Doug Mettome (t); Mario Daone, Bob Ascher, Chunky Koenigsberger, Rob Swope, Jack Carmen, Lou McGarity (tb); Peanuts Hucko (cl); Hal McKusick, Eddie Caine, Jerry Therkeld (as); Allen Eager, Mickey Rich, Ben Larry, Warne Marsh, Al Sears, Jimmy Giuffre (ts); Harvey Levine (bs); Harvey Leonard, Jerry Schwarz, Buddy Weed (p); Joe Mooney (acc); Terry Gibbs (vib); Gene Dell, Remo Palmieri (g); Trigger Alpert, Tubby Phillips, Charlie Leeds, Nick Stagg (b); Stan Kay, Big Sid Catlett (d); Ella Fitzgerald (v).* 10/45–10/48.

★★★ The Legendary 46–48 Orchestras Vol. 2

Hep CD 56 *As above, except add Bitsy Mullens, Pinky Savitt, Louis Oles (t), Earl Swope, Johnny Mandel, Al Lorraine (tb), Les Clarke, Jerry Thirkeld (as), George Berg, Mickey Rich (ts), Sid Brown (bs), Tony Nichols (p), Jimmy Johnston (b), Stan Kay (d), Dottie Reid (v).* 3/46–10/48.

★★★ Buddy Rich 1946–1948

Classics 1099 *Similar to above discs, except add Red Rodney (t).* 1/46–10/48.

Rich, probably the most renowned big-band drummer of all time, had a rough time as a bandleader in the late '40s, but somehow he held on until 1949. Hep's sets of airshots, V-Discs and the like find various editions of the group in vigorous form. Some of the charts are routine, but others make the most of the impressive sections, and there are some fine soloists on the first disc, particularly Allen Eager on 'Daily Double' and 'Nellie's Nightmare'. There is one small-group track with Charlie Shavers on trumpet and a fairly hilarious 'Blue Skies' where Rich scats along with Ella Fitzgerald. The second disc leans more towards the 1948 orchestra, which is more commercially directed, with vocals and ballads tending to take over; but the opening 'Let's Blow' is prototypical of the excitement that Rich was after in a big band. The sound is fair to good on both discs, but the clout of the orchestra still comes through when they hit hard enough.

Classics bring together three sessions for V-Disc and three for Mercury. It duplicates eight titles with Hep 56, but the balance of the Mercury titles is well worth having: 'Dateless Brown' and 'Desperate Desmond' are flag-wavers of real excitement. Rich shows how appealing a vocalist he could be on 'Baby, Baby All The Time', and bop gets a modest look-in on 'Oop-Bop-Sha-Bam'. An interesting cross-section of titles, with a few soloists – such as Red Rodney – to surprise.

★★★(★) Swingin' New Big Band

Pacific Jazz 835232-2 *Rich; Bobby Shew, John Sottile, Yoshito Murakami, Walter Battagello (t); Jim Trimble, John Boice (tb); Dennis Good, Mike Waverley (btb); Gene Quill (as, cl); Pete Yellin (as, f); Jay Corre, Marty Flax (ts, cl, f); Steve Perlow (bs, bcl); John Bunch (p); Barry Zweig (g); Carson Smith (b).* 9–10/66.

★★★ Big Swing Face

Pacific Jazz 837989-2 *As above, except add Chuck Findley (t), Ron Myers (tb), Ernie Watts (as, f), Quin Davis (as), Robert Keller (bs), Ray Starling (p), Richard Resnicoff (g), James Gannon (b), Cathy Rich (v); omit Boice, Quill, Yellin, Perlow, Bunch, Zweig and Smith.* 2–3/67.

★★★(★) The New One!

Pacific Jazz 494507-2 *Rich; Chuck Findley, Russell Iverson, John Sottile, Yoshito Murakami (t); Jim Trimble, John Boice, Robert Brawn, Jack Spurlock, Sam Burtis (tb); Ernie Watts, James Mosher (as, cl, f); Robert Keller, Pat LaBarbera (ts, cl, f); Jay Corre (ts, cl); Meyer Hirsh, Frank Capi (bs, bcl); Ray Starling, Russell Turner Jr (p); Richie Resnicoff (g); James Gannon, Ronald Funoldi (b).* 6–12/67.

★★★(★) Mercy, Mercy

Pacific Jazz 854331-2 *Rich; Al Porcino, Bill Prince, Ken Faulk, Dave Culp (t); Jim Trimble, Rick Stepton, Peter Graves (tb); Art Pepper, Charles Owens, Don Menza, Pat LaBarbera, John Laws (reeds); Walt Namuth (g); Gary Walters (b); Tony Bennett (v).* 7/68.

★★★ Swingin' New Big Band / Keep The Customer Satisfied

BGO BGOCD169 *Rich; Bobby Shew, John Sottile, Yoshito Murakami, Walter Battagello, John Giorgani, John Madrid, Mike Price, George Zonce (t); Jim Trimble, John Boice, Rick Stepton, Tony Lada (tb); Larry Fisher, Mike Waverley (btb); Gene Quill (cl, as); Richie Cole, Jimmy Mosher, Pete Yellin (as, f); Jay Corre, Marty Flax (cl, ts, f); Pat LaBarbera (ss, ts, f); Don Englert (ts, f); Steve Perlow (bs, bcl); Bob Suchoski (bs); John Bunch, Meredith McClain (p); Barry Zweig (g); Rick Laird, Carson Smith (b).* 9/66–2/70.

The late '60s were scarcely vintage times for big bands, but Rich, who was used to stopping at nothing, drove a limousine outfit through the period with concessions that didn't really bother him much. They had items like 'Uptight' and 'Ode To Billie Joe' in the book, but they still played the likes of 'In A Mellotone' and 'Sister Sadie', and among the technique-laden sections there were players who could step out and play an individualist's solo: Don Menza, Jay Corre, Bobby Shew, and – on *Mercy, Mercy* – Art Pepper, who has a wounded feature on 'Chelsea Bridge'. The Pacific albums are nearly all taken from live dates, from Hollywood or Las Vegas, and since the band thrived in performance they are among Rich's most characteristic testaments. There's nothing subtle about the arranging or the musicianship: all is speed, bravado, intensity. Not to say that the band didn't have different strokes at its disposal: some of the charts on *Swingin' New Big Band* (by a variety of hands, including Oliver Nelson, Bill Holman and Phil Wilson) are as elegant as they are assertive. But Rich's rule meant that the band had to fire on all cylinders and there were no pastel shades involved. He even makes 'Ode To Billie Joe' (*Mercy, Mercy*) into a stormer. There's little to choose between the discs, which have been handsomely reshaped by Pacific with numerous unissued bonus tracks on each disc and some fine discoveries among them. We especially like *Mercy, Mercy* for the stunning treatment of Joe Zawinul's title-track and for the contributions of Pepper and Menza. *The New One!* includes material written for a TV series, *Away We Go*, that Rich worked on during 1967: the theme-tune is a typical barnstormer and, although the sound seems compressed on this reissue, there's plenty to hear, with Watts taking some storming solos – listen to the preposterously over-fast but thrilling treatment of Wes Montgomery's 'Naptown Blues'. In sum, these are probably the necessary Rich albums for the library – considering that his catalogue is still neglected on CD and there is perhaps no obvious classic album in it. The BGO set couples the original *Swingin' New Big Band* with a lesser effort from 1970, and we prefer the Pacific edition.

***** Buddy And Soul**

BGO BGOCD 23 *Rich; Sal Marquez, Nat Pavone, Dave Culp, Bob Yance, Mike Price, Darryl Eaton, Ken Faulk, Oliver Mitchell (t); Rick Stepton, Vince Diaz, Don Switzer (tb); Ernie Watts, Joe Romano, Richie Cole, Don Menza, Pat LaBarbera, Joe Calo, Don Englert (reeds); Dave Lahm (ky); Herb Ellis, Dave Dana, Freddie Robinson (g); Bob Magnusson (b); Victor Feldman (perc).* 1–6/69.

Live or in the studio, Rich's band hit very hard. Anachronistic in the age of Hendrix and Jefferson Airplane (Rich's choice of a tune called 'Love And Peace' probably didn't express what he thought about rock's ascendance), they made up in personal firepower what they lacked in stage amplification. There's some dreadful, modish material and some things which Rich made into valid vehicles through sheer force of will. Big-band jazz out of its time, and presumably for ever.

Tim Richards (born 1952)

PIANO

A familiar presence on the British contemporary scene, most of Richards's work can be found under the listing for his band, Spirit Level; these are outings under his own name.

*****(*) The Other Side**

33 JAZZ 037 *Richards; Kubryk Townsend (b); Kenrick Rowe, Andreas Trillo (d).* 97.

... but the other side of what? This is Richards's other project, working apart from the horn-fronted Spirit Level, and interestingly he gravitates to a mostly standards repertoire, or rather to a body of jazz tunes which take their cues in turn from standards material, things like Miles Davis's and Victor Feldman's 'Seven Steps To Heaven', Hampton Hawes's 'Blues The Most' and Big John Patton's 'String Bean'. Rowe (a Spirit Level regular) is used only on seven of the 15 tracks, a very different percussionist from the stylish but forceful Trillo, about whom we know very little, except that his roots seem to be in the swing era, reminiscent of Shelly Manne rather than anything more recent. Richards switches to electric keyboard for Eddie Harris's 'Freedom Jazz Dance' and demonstrates once again the ability to give amplified piano considerable personality.

***** Shibop**

FMR CD61 *Richards; Sigi Finkel (ss, ts); Phil Scragg (b); Marc Parnell (d).* 99.

***** Twelve By Three**

33 Jazz 072 *Richards; Dominic Howles (b); Matt Home (d).* 01.

The Austrian saxophonist was Richards's most sympathetic partner in years and the Soundscape group that made *Shibop* felt like his most effective outfit since Spirit Level. The material is all original, eight elegantly crafted songs with plenty of open space for both pianist and saxophonist to range across. Rugged support from Scragg and Parnell. The trio with Howles and Home are less ambitious, but the session highlights Richards's endlessly buoyant, blues-flavoured playing much more prominently.

Jerome Richardson (1920–2000)

SAXOPHONES, WOODWINDS, FLUTES

Richardson started working in his teens, and subsequently rarely stopped. He worked with Marshall Jones, Quincy Jones, led his own group at Minton's, and was a charter member of the Thad Jones–Mel Lewis band. He recorded only rather rarely under his own name.

***** Midnight Oil**

Original Jazz Classics OJC 1815 *Richardson; Jimmy Cleveland (tb); Hank Jones (p); Kenny Burrell (g); Joe Benjamin (b); Charli Persip (d).* 11/58.

*****(*) Roamin' With Richardson**

Original Jazz Classics OJC 1849 *Richardson; Richard Wyands (p); George Tucker (b); Charli Persip (d).* 11/59.

The quiet Texan was always more than a journeyman multi-instrumentalist. It took him some time to assert himself in his own voice. He became a leader only on moving to New York City in 1953, having served an apprenticeship with Jimmie Lunceford, Lionel Hampton and Earl Hines. *Oil* was an earlier session on New Jazz, predating *Roamin'* by a few months, as rare as hen's teeth and reissued without fanfare. The interesting thing about the 1959 band is that all four are individualists, and each is encouraged to bring something to the session. Wyands in particular asserts himself on tracks like 'Warm Valley' and 'Poinciana', the latter a solitary outing on flute, the former with his very distinctive, Mulligan-influenced baritone. His only other horn this time out is tenor saxophone ('Friar Tuck' and 'Candied Sweets').

In the past, we've argued that Richardson's one great stock-in-trade was the simple variety of his resources. Certainly on both records he could rely on an absolutely solid band and indulge a little decorative work here and there. Further acquaintance, though, confirms that he was an able, often thoughtful soloist, and his traded lines with Cleveland and the more boppish Burrell will be a revelation to those who have heard him only as a utility band player.

Alex Riel (born 1940)

DRUMS

The Copenhagen-born Riel has been the most rock-solid fixture in the city's jazz scene for more than 40 years, accompanying seemingly every visitor and occasionally leading his own dates.

***** The Riel Deal**

Stunt STUCD 19604 *Riel; Jerry Bergonzi (ts); Kenny Werner (p); Jesper Lundgaard (b).* 1/95.

***** Unriel!**

Stunt STUCD 19707 *Riel; Jerry Bergonzi, Michael Brecker (ts); Niels Lan Doky (p); Mike Stern (g); Eddie Gomez (b).* 3/97.

***** D. S. B. Kino**

Stunt STUCD 19811 *Riel; Harry 'Sweets' Edison (t); Roger Kellaway (p); Mads Vinding (b).* 3/98.

***(*) Rielatin'

Stunt STUCD 19918 *Riel; Jerry Bergonzi, Michael Brecker (ts); Kenny Werner (p); Mike Stern (g); Christian Minh Doky (b).* 10/99.

*** Live At Jive

Stunt STUCD 01202 *Riel; Lutz Büchner (ts); Carsten Dahl (p); Jesper Lundgaard (b).* 3/00.

***(*) Celebration

Stunt STUCD 00232 *Riel; Kenny Werner (p); Jesper Lundgaard (b).* 9/00.

Alex Riel loves life and jazz, and as an unrivalled exponent of wordplay in more than one language he probably set up most of these punning titles himself. None of these sets is exactly a world-beating classic but they all benefit from the man's enormous bonhomie and a style that is as swinging and band-lifting as you'll find on any stand. *The Riel Deal* is a live gig where Bergonzi and Werner get into some heavyweight chopsmanship. The even more stellar cast made *Unriel!* in New York, with Niels Lan Doky producing, and though some of the playing has a slightly faceless, superstar feel to it, it's an imposing set.

The set with Harry Edison is sometimes a bit discomforting since the old man is clearly a long way from the force he was; yet, as if to compensate, Alex himself plays quite beautifully and there's some super stuff from Kellaway too. *Rielatin'* rematches some of the big guys from New York, and this one is a bit looser and more fun: the two tenors have a joyful romp through the old Ben Webster favourite 'Did You Call Her Today?', and Brecker relaxes more than he often does.

Live At Jive debuts a new quartet co-led with Büchner. It's a bit of a hard-bop potboiler, but if nothing else you can always listen to what Riel's playing. We slightly prefer his 60th birthday set, released as *Celebration*; Werner at the keyboard again, and he thrives in an environment where the swinging sounds less portentous than it does on some of his own-name records. 'Siciliana' is Alex's birthday solo – may there be many more.

Barry Ries

TRUMPET, FLUGELHORN

Ries is a seasoned player, with credits embracing the Lionel Hampton Band and Joe Lovano's recent Nonetet. His debut as leader was much belated.

*** Solitude In The Crowd

Justin Time 137 *Ries; Joe Lovano (ts); Michael Cochrane (p); Dennis Irwin (b); Billy Drummond, Yoron Israel (d).* 98.

Listeners might conclude that Ries is better served in a crowd than out front on his own. The playing here is mostly workmanlike and unexceptional, though Lovano's presence adds a gruff energy to the music. The opening 'Akasha' is a longish workout that doesn't ever catch fire and the best of the music is reserved for the end of the set, a reading of Monk's 'Ugly Beauty' (tough for the trumpeter) and a composition by bassist Irwin that puts his leader's originals in the shade. Nice to see him get his moment in the spotlight but Barry's real contribution is fated to be more anonymous than this.

Tim Ries (born 1959)

TENOR AND SOPRANO SAXOPHONES

Born in Detroit, Ries started on trumpet but is now playing post-bop saxophone.

***(*) Universal Spirits

Criss Cross CRISS 1144 *Ries; Scott Wendholt (t); Ben Monder (g); Scott Colley (b); Billy Drummond (d).* 10/97.

*** Alternate Side

Criss Cross 1199 *Ries; Greg Gisbert (t, flhn); Michael Davis (tb); Larry Goldings (p, org); Ben Monder (g); Stacey Shames (hp); John Patitucci (b); Billy Drummond (d).* 6/00.

One afternoon in Paris, Tim Ries saw Ornette Coleman being interviewed in a hotel lobby. Not knowing a better way to introduce himself, he took out his soprano and played the early Coleman tune, 'Jayne'. Ornette stood up and applauded, as well he might have done, for the version included here is excellent. Ries's kinship with trumpeter Wendholt is almost twin-like, a mutual understanding that beams out from the very first number, a deceptively simple circle-of-fifths thing called 'Indeed', which has been in his book for many years. Other pieces on the set are derived from his classical side as well, most obviously the Bach 'Sonata No. 2: Siciliano', which is something he has played on flute with his wife, harpist Stacey Shames. A strongly personal record, almost every tune seems – and feels – associated with some strong emotion. 'Guardian Angel' relates to his mother's recovery from life-threatening illness, 'St Michel' to a chance escape from a terrorist bomb in Paris; 'When I'm Through' is a lullaby for his daughter, and again shows indications of being written for a chamber group rather than a jazz band. As ever on Criss Cross, the band is tailor-made. Monder and Colley are friends, and Billy Drummond has the ability to fall in with almost any line-up thrown at him.

Alternate Side is a good, if in the end slightly disappointing, follow-up. Too much of it falls into what is often (and generally incorrectly) attributed as the Criss Cross hard-bop convention, of which '4637' might be a perfectly idiomatic example. Goldings warms things up at the B-3 and Davis gets in the odd surprising jab, but Ries himself sounds less individual this time and may do better in a less busy band.

Knut Riisnaes (born 1945)

TENOR AND SOPRANO SAXOPHONES

Norwegian post-bop saxophonist of wide experience, one of the two Riisnaes sax-playing brothers.

***(*) Confessin' The Blues

Gemini GMCD 63 *Riisnaes; Red Holloway (as, ts); Kjell Ohman (p, org); Terje Venaas (b); Egil Johansen (d).* 8/89.

*** The Gemini Twins

Gemini GMCD 75 *As above.* 1/92.

Gifted with a huskily rich and weighty tone, Riisnaes is an Oslo-born jazzman who, like so many musicians from northern Europe, deserves a far wider reputation than he has (his brother, Odd, is also a fine tenorman). His celebrated *Flukt* LP won a Norwegian Grammy award but it's currently *still* out of print. *Confessin' The Blues* is a fine place to start, though. The session was organized to document Red Holloway's visit to the

Oslo Jazz Festival in 1989, and the sympathetic interplay among all five men belies the hasty circumstances of the occasion. While there are some straightforward blowing tracks, such as an ebullient 'Billie's Bounce', the highlight is probably the almost indecently languorous stroll through 'All Blues' at the beginning, which is paced out by both tenormen to sumptuous effect. If Holloway is the more perkily bluesy of the two saxophonists, Riisnaes emerges as at least his equal, taking a solo 'My Romance' which methodically opens out the melody to superb effect. The rhythm section, with Ohman playing mostly organ, is absolutely on top of things, and the digital sound is excellent. They have a return match on *The Gemini Twins*, which is a mild disappointment since nothing hits the peaks of the previous record. Riisnaes's solo ballad treatment of 'Tribute To Melvin' and the ultra-slow 'Yesterdays' still make the record substantial.

★★★(★) Touching

Resonant RM8-2 *Riisnaes; Dag Arnesen (p); Terje Gewelt (b); Frank Jakobsen (d).* 2/01.

Riisnaes enters the new century with a powerful if conventional record. He brought only the title-piece to the date – the rest are standards, a Jarrett tune, a couple of Arnesen themes and one by Gewelt – and the quartet approaches the occasion with a no-nonsense manner which might have sounded severe if it weren't for the lyricism which touches all of the playing. Riisnaes has never had a better sound in a studio – all the subtleties in his delivery are caught evocatively – and Arnesen, a sometimes unremarkable player on other records, plays beautifully both solo and in accompaniment. 'You Know I Care' has a superb treatment, and Jarrett's 'Love No 1' is fashioned as a coolly serious ballad.

Herlin Riley

DRUMS

Guaranteed prominence and possibly brickbats as successor to Jeff 'Tain' Watts in the Wynton Marsalis group, Riley has proved himself ably and has taken steps to carve out a solo career in addition.

★★★ Watch What You're Doing

Criss Cross 1179 *Riley; Ryan Kisor (t); Wycliffe Gordon (tb); Victor Goines (ts, bs); Farid Barron (p); Rodney Whitaker (b).* 00.

Riley looks as if he's been storing up some of this material for some time. It's got the easy structure and quietly challenging time feel of work that has been adequately road-tested. For this debut recording, he has a like-minded group of Young(ish) Turks and a sound that settles comfortably into the middle and lower register, certainly the latter when Goines picks up his baritone. Ironically, the best track on the set – or at least the most attractive piece of writing – is bassist Whitaker's tribute to John Lewis. Otherwise, the charts are pretty much of a muchness. A couple of standards, or possibly the odd Marsalis tune, might have lifted a perfectly agreeable and unexceptionable session an extra notch. After all, the Marsalis group is the uncamouflaged model for the set.

Howard Riley (born 1943)

PIANO

Born in Huddersfield, Riley played in local clubs before moving south and finding his own way to completely free playing. A long and distinguished discography charts this direction and his occasional glances back into bebop repertory.

★★★(★) Angle

Columbia 494433-2 *Riley; Barbara Thompson (f); Barry Guy (b); Alan Jackson (d).* 12/68–1/69.

♛ ★★★★ The Day Will Come

Columbia 494434-2 *As above, except omit Thompson.* 3–4/70.

★★★★ Flight

Future Music FMR CD 26 *Riley; Barry Guy (b); Tony Oxley (d).* 3/71.

★★★(★) Synopsis

Emanem 4044 *As above.* 73.

Howard Riley's two CBS recordings – the result of the label's brief outbreak of enthusiasm for British improvisation – immediately marked out the 25-year-old as a musician of considerable originality. The reappearance of *Synopsis* adds significantly to the picture. All that is now required to complete the picture of these early years is the reissue of the three-LP *Facets* on Impetus.

For Riley himself, the key thing about these recordings was that they represented a working band. Other improvising musicians of the time were happy to issue what were effectively public rehearsals. By contrast, these records by the Howard Riley Trio are terse, focused improvisations on written themes. Only *Synopsis* features extended tracks; otherwise, none is longer than 8½ minutes. The fully notated flute-and-piano duets, 'Three Fragments', on *Angle* stand somewhat apart, but are unmistakably from the same hand. Riley is the only credited composer on the earlier album, which perhaps accounts for its thoughtful and rather reserved character.

The introduction of Barry Guy as co-composer on the brilliant *The Day Will Come* is the key factor in our very high rating for this record. It is worth noting that, whatever the public persona Guy has now, in 1969 Chris Wellard thought nothing of describing him in his liner-note to the first record, *Angle*, as 'rumbustious and violent'. It is he who balances the rather tender and melancholic cast of Riley's playing. His *arco* solo on 'Angle' is astonishing, and he drives the following track, 'Aftermath', into territory new in British jazz at the time. On the later album Guy tunes like 'Sad Was The Song', 'Playtime' and the title-track present genuine improvisational challenges. Of the trio members, Jackson is the one who seems to have been eclipsed by the passing years. He is a drummer of great control and precision, inch-perfect on fast numbers like 'Angle' without compromising a robustly swinging presence which recalls Phil Seamen but also has ties right back to the days of Dave Tough. These are key recordings, even if to some extent they eclipse some of the work that followed.

Some months on from *The Day Will Come*, *Flight* represents a development of Riley's trio language, expanded considerably through the use of Guy's pedal and amplifier and drummer Oxley's astonishing range of amplified percussion effects. Even playing acoustically, his trademark device of exchanging sticks and mallets for knitting needles generates a light, skittering sound that blends perfectly with the piano. All three men contribute material. Oxley's 'Cirrus' is a personal *tour de force*; Riley's opening 'Motion' is a fair representation of his parallel interest in 'legitimate' composition. Pianist and bassist are jointly credited for 'Two Ballads'. Riley's technique is utterly assured, his sense of time is gnomic rather than metronomic, and his dynamics – ranging from huge clusters to the tiniest mosaic effects – bring a constantly shifting intellectual drama.

Synopsis is riveting from start to finish. Guy's sound-world is gloriously idiosyncratic and utterly different from that of any other bass-player of the time. At the same time, Oxley seems to have broken the bounds of jazz percussion in the most joyous and intelligent way. It's possible to luxuriate in these performances without concerning oneself too much about the structures involved, which are looser and less concentrated than on earlier recordings. We still value *The Day Will Come* most highly, but the Riley trio was a wonder and a joy. Even for those who never saw them perform, these sides are a valuable document.

***(*) Singleness

Jazzprint JPVP110 *Riley (p solo).* 74.

The spirit of Thelonious Monk was not far distant when this lovely recording was made. Riley is still audibly in touch with the language of bebop, especially on the blues-soaked 'Item' and the appropriately titled 'Introspective', which takes the conventions of bop piano, slows them down, and subjects them to rigorous scrutiny. 'Inside' and 'Boeotian' are threatening, the former calling on jangly plucked strings, the latter a hectic rhythm that could be dedicated to the cult of Pan. 'Gypsum' is, by contrast, almost folksy. The piano sounds like a modern instrument, but an impeccably well-behaved one.

***(*) Overground

Emanem 4054 *Riley; Barry Guy (b); Tony Oxley (d).* 8/74–11/75.

Only recently released, this reveals another facet of a classic trio. Oxley is experimenting with electronics and Guy exploits a measure of amplification, but the real dynamism comes from Riley himself, occasionally amplified, overdubbed on 'Recognition' and strongly foregrounded on the ferociously beautiful 'Pages'. All three players are already pushing at the 'jazz' envelope and though in later years Riley was to reveal more and more of his bop lineage, this period sees him and his like-minded colleagues exploring new territory. Guy is in stunning form on 'Loops' and Oxley's straight percussion is alternately precise and wayward, but never dull.

*** The Toronto Concert

Jazzprint JVP 11 *Riley (p solo).* 77.

You might be forgiven for looking at the liner-notes sceptically, for this isn't by any means typical Riley. There is a Liszt-like bravura which almost overwhelms keyboard and audience alike, an outpouring of ideas that, contrary to Howard's usual approach, is delivered at high volume and without the kind of shading he normally favours. There are, of course, quieter passages on both 'Sonority' and the shorter 'Finite Elements' (just two tracks) but they seem less important overall. As ever, Riley gives his free improvisations impressive form, building an architecture that is completely satisfying even if in this case oddly baroque in execution. The source tape is good quality and every note rings out round an estimably quiet auditorium, though of course the Canadians are famous for behaving themselves in public.

***(*) Trisect

Jazzprint JPVP 116 *Riley (p solo).* 5/80.

An extended exercise in three-part overdubbing, *Trisect* is rigorous without becoming bloodlessly analytical. Organized into 'Introduction' and 'Coda' with four related 'Phases' and a 'Transition' passage, the whole album feels structured and logical, but still quintessentially free. Riley's attack has never seemed more spontaneous. Echoes of Bill Evans's *Conversations With Myself* are accidental rather than wilful.

*** Organic

Jazzprint JVP 115 *Riley; Barry Guy (b); John Stevens (d).* 81.

Riley and Guy had worked in trio form before, but with Alan Jackson or Tony Oxley rather than Stevens, though he in turn had partnered Guy in Amalgam with Trevor Watts. So there are intersecting family trees here. Stevens's lighter, simpler drumming actually suits the trio very well indeed, even on those few occasions when the music seems more conventionally jazz-inspired and possibly even predetermined if not actually notated. Riley is spacious and mercurial, leaving lots of room for Guy's extraordinarily rich harmonics. The middle track, also by far the shortest on the set, sounds like a hangover from Riley's early Columbia trios; the other two are more obviously improvised with a resultant increase in both energy and formlessness. They hit dead spots, as free improvisers almost always do, but this is a very fine record. Originally issued as part of a three-LP set with *Trisect* and *First Encounter*, it works very well on its own.

**(*) First Encounter

Jazzprint JPVP 114 *Riley; Keith Tippett (p).* 5/81.

***(*) In Focus

Jazzprint JVP 121 *As above.* 84.

On the face of it an unlikely partnership, Tippett as spontaneous and emotional as Riley is analytical and outwardly reserved. In practice, this was a very tentative first meeting, with both players clinging to a familiar language and with little sign of real communication. The two players are not difficult to distinguish and this tends to reinforce an impression of music conducted on tramlines, fated never to converge, even on the closing (presumably encore) blues.

The second encounter is very much more interesting and coherent. There are moments of uncontrolled activity, as at the climax to part two, but it all sounds much more like a dialogue and less like a scuffle. The test is that, stereo positioning apart, it's often difficult to tell who is playing at any moment. Tippett is still more inclined to get inside the piano; Riley is more given to quasi-classical gestures, even if these come from Henry Cowell rather than Chopin; but there is a consistency of language that isn't evident on *First Encounter* and the record is all the better for it, a genuinely pleasing experience rather than an interesting historical document.

***(*) Feathers With Jaki

Slam CD 215 *Riley; Jaki Byard (p); Mario Castronari (b); Tony Marsh (d).* 81–91.

The idea of Riley playing Monk in the company of Jaki Byard would have struck even sympathetic fans as an unlikely one. This, though, is one of the forgotten classics of jazz in Britain, an anomalous but highly creative encounter somewhat akin to the fabled meeting of Cecil Taylor and Mary Lou Williams, though far less acrimonious.

Byard is the more obviously Monk-like in conception and execution, and is far more deeply rooted in blues tonality. However, it's Riley who tends to keep the music on line and within touching distance of the original. The sound-quality isn't all that good, and no better – as we remember it – than the original LP. Released by Leo Records, it's now been compiled with a later Spotlite recording by Riley's Feathers Trio. Some good stuff on that, but people will want this one for the Riley/Byard encounter.

*****(*) Procession**

Wondrous WM 0101 *Riley (p solo).* 4/90.

***** The Heat Of Moments**

Wondrous WM 0103 *As above.* 4/91–4/92.

*****(*) Beyond Category**

Wondrous WM 0104 *As above.* 2/93.

You might well ask what has happened to the work of the mid- and later '70s and of the '80s. Familiar story: neglect and deletion. Riley has been indebted to Brian Miller of Wondrous for issuing these well-recorded, highly atmospheric sessions which, though taped in a studio, somehow suggest a live ambience. The first two consist of nothing but originals, though as ever written with a strong awareness of the jazz-piano tradition; we wonder how many listeners ambushed by 'April Again', the lead item on *Procession*, would guess who the player was. Similarly 'Inseparable' and the long 'Tell Me', while 'Striding' hints at a different tradition again.

It was some time before Riley committed himself wholeheartedly to solo performance. There is no discomfort in any of these, but nor is there the muscly, overdetermining sweep of some who have tackled the discipline. Instead, a rigorous and almost deliberate approach, which becomes a touch enervated on *The Heat Of Moments.* This is a much more abstract performance. Apart from the title-track and 'Zig Zag' (which inescapably recalls Byard), most of the pieces are short and introspective. 'Mirror Image' has nothing to do with the Zawinul composition, but coincidentally reflects the Austrian's combination of 'correctness' and an earthy, folksy groove.

Beyond Category is devoted to the music of Monk and Ellington, two of the obvious jazz influences on Riley's work. This came along at a time when he was placing greater emphasis on form and less on freedom, and one can hear him working inside the songs, pushing at their boundaries, appending footnotes and marking sources. Of the 17 tracks only two are over five minutes long, suggesting a considerable concentration of effort and thought.

*****(*) Interchange**

Jazzprint JPVP109 *Riley; Keith Tippett (p).* 12/93.

Riley mentions that the first piano duo he remembers hearing was an old 78 of James P. Johnson and Clarence Williams, and he points to the combination of subtlety and 'orchestral' power the instrumentation yields. Though Johnson and Williams are mostly replaced by latter-day mentors, that same combination of virtues is audible all the way through this.

It's difficult to say how the later album differs, except as a function of how both men have changed as individuals over the years. Tippett probably allows more space than he did; Riley has a more forcible attack. However, only someone particularly anxious to separate two voices is going to worry about who is playing what line at a particular moment. The status of the title isn't entirely clear, but what one hears is almost an hour of continuous creative interchange, highly responsive and respectful. The digital recording is of very high quality, though perhaps a little intimately mic'ed for some tastes.

*****(*) Wishing On The Moon**

Future Music FMR CD 14 *Riley; Mario Castronari (b); Tony Marsh (d).* 95.

****** Descending Circles**

Blueprint BP221 *Riley; Elton Dean (as, saxello); Mario Castronari (b); Mark Sanders (d).* 10/95.

The mid-'90s saw Riley perhaps shifting emphasis back to group playing (often with Dean as co-leader, but also with Art Themen) and at the same time taking a greater interest in composition. There is a more tightly reined and briskly registered attack, a more straightforward approach to the chords, and a freely melodic approach that often suggests a standard lies somewhere behind the theme, an enigma being subjected to fresh variation, but never openly declared.

The trio with Castronari and Marsh is as different from the early-'70s group as its very different personnel would suggest. Both are forceful players who are also capable of sitting out when required, or heading off on parallel courses of their own. The integrity and cohesion of the older group isn't there, but in its place there's a sparkle and lightness of touch which carries over into the quartets as well. Dean is marvellous in these contexts, and his writing for the group is different enough from Riley's to maintain interest. 'Descending Circles' is an almost definitive Riley composition: sturdy, well rooted, harmonically fascinating, but with a usefully problematic shape and direction. The group sound less secure on two spontaneous improvisations. This isn't Castronari's bag, one suspects, though he throws himself into it with a will. Playing with a horn pushes Riley further than usual into a chords mode, but with no sign that he feels constrained or uncomfortable. An earlier record, *All The Tradition,* is listed under Dean's leadership.

*****(*) Classics (Live)**

Slam CD222 *Riley; Art Themen (ss, ts); Mario Castronari (b); Trevor Tomkins (d).* 5/96.

Co-led with saxophonist Themen, who famously combines his jazz activities with a career as an orthopaedic surgeon, this is a further attempt by Riley to build bridges between repertory jazz and freer forms of improvisation. Monk has always been a profound inspiration (as he was on Themen's regular employer Stan Tracey) and it's no surprise to hear them both tear into 'Straight, No Chaser' with such gusto. 'Body And Soul' has long been the tenor-player's test-piece, but here Themen deconstructs it rather than simply exploring its changes. It's a refreshing and powerfully spontaneous performance. Riley seems to have some difficulties with the piano, though they may be of his own making, since his playing is so intense in places the keys must have warped. As ever, he plays through them, constructing unexpected chords and stringing together powerfully melodic phrases that are both unpredictable and wholly logical.

*****(*) Air Play**

Slam 244 *Riley (p solo).* 4/00.

Riley reasserts his debt to Monk from the off, with the resounding title-track. A couple of the tracks are available in alternative versions, suggesting how far the pianist has moved from free improvisation back into the discipline of theme-and-solo, except that often the theme announces itself only well into the piece. Most of the tracks are short, intense and clearly directed. Riley has rarely sounded more in sympathy with the piano masters.

*****(*) Duology**
Slam CD249 *Riley; Lol Coxhill (ss).* 3/02.

On paper again, this doesn't sound an altogether probable encounter, except that both pianist and saxophonist come to free improvisation with a deep understanding of jazz that surfaces at unexpected intervals. The two longest items on the set, 'Two Timing' and 'Interplay', are excellent examples of how much both these players have invested of themselves in this music. Coxhill's deceptively shrill approach disguises a real sensitivity to nuance, while Riley's 'classicism' is classical the way Thelonious Monk was classical. The CD was recorded over two sessions in the famous Holywell Room at Oxford, the first of them a private recording session. There is a small difference in acoustic between that session and the concert tape, testimony to what a sensitive recording space the Holywell is. It certainly brings out the best in these remarkable musicians.

Sammy Rimington (born 1942)

CLARINET, ALTO AND TENOR SAXOPHONES, VOCAL

Born in London, he began playing with Ken Colyer and other trad stalwarts around 1960. Moved to the USA in 1965, subsequently to New Orleans, and played and recorded with many masters of the New Orleans style. Returned to Europe in the '70s and investigated jazz-rock, but stayed mainly with traditional jazz styles and by the '90s was as eminent as many of his former heroes.

***** Clarinet King In Norway**
Herman HJCD 1001 *Rimington; Andy Finch (p); Ole Olen (b); Søren Houlind (d).* 12/77.

***** The Exciting Sax Of Sammy Rimington**
Progressive PCD-7077 *Rimington; David Paquette (p, v); Walter Payton (b); Placide Adams, Stanley Stephens, Ernest Elly (d).* 4/86–4/91.

*****(*) One Swiss Night**
Music Mecca 1021-2 *Rimington; Freddy John (tb); Jon Marks (p); Koen De Cauter (g, bj); Karl-Ake Kronquist (b); Sven Stahlberg (d).* 11/91.

***** More Exciting Sax Of Sammy Rimington**
Progressive PCD 7088 *Rimington; Phamous Lambert (p); Lloyd Lambert (b); Ernie Elly (d).* 5/94.

****(*) Watering The Roots**
Jazz Crusade JCCD-3011 *Rimington; Big Bill Bissonnette (tb); Sarah Bissonnette (ts); Eric Webster (bj); Ken Matthews (b); Colin Bowden (d).* 1/95.

Rimington has had a strange career: a stalwart with Ken Colyer, a transplantation to Louisiana where he became a bosom friend of Capt. John Handy, a flirtation with jazz-rock and now occasional sightings in sundry pick-up groups, like these. The two Progressive albums feature him exclusively on alto, where he sounds like Handy but phrases as if he were brother to Johnny Hodges: the result is a queer hybrid, soaked in a woozy kind of romanticism. Engagingly done, although the sound-mix (with the piano in the distance, the drums right up front) doesn't assist on the earlier disc. The second sounds better and goes along at a jollier pace, with Rimington this time sounding more like a jump-band hornman on a featured night of his own. *One Swiss Night* catches him with a second-rate band (John's trombone is especially unhealthy) on dull material, but there is one real surprise, a very Websterish reading of 'My Funny Valentine' on tenor. *Watering The Roots* finds Sammy back in England. Bissonnette organized and sponsored the recording, and it's fair enough that he plays on it, but he can't summon the authority to stand in the front line and is painfully outclassed by the clarinettist. The material this time goes back to New Orleans purism, and the only one earning stars is Rimington. He deserves a break in better company and on a proper budget.

The Herman album resuscitates a set made by Rimington's quartet at the end of a 1977 tour. He sticks to clarinet, and his own playing, from the beautifully inflected 'Hymn For George Lewis' to the bodacious 'Lou-Easy-An-I-A', is excellent. But the rhythm section is hamfisted, and Rimington needs another horn as some kind of context.

****(*) Live At Wettingen**
Jazztime JTCD-004 *Rimington; Earl Warren, Vittorio Castelli (cl); David Paquette (p, v); Guido Cairo (p); Johnny Rohrberg (bj); Alberto Contre, Karel Algoed (b); Didier Geers (d).* 9/83.

***** Plays Spirituals And Hymns**
Jazztime JTCD-002 *Rimington; Freddie John (tb); Jon Marks (p); Brian Turnock (b); Didier Geers (d).* 10/84.

***** Live In Switzerland**
Sam 002 *As above, except John Coles (bj), Michel Verstraeten, Sven Stahlberg (d) replace Turnock and Geers.* 87.

***** Live At Meilen Jazzclub**
Jazztime JTCD-003 *As above, except Karl-Ake Kronqvist (b) replaces Coles and Verstraeten.* 10/97.

Jazztime and Rimington's own label Sam have begun issuing archive performances, and these are four examples. The Wettingen concert is rather noisily recorded and a bit slipshod here and there; Sammy's turn on the singing saw is also best heard only once. A version of 'Mood Indigo' at the end seems to be by a different band, with Warren and Castelli joining in. *Spirituals And Hymns* is a good mix of dirges and up-tempo pieces, even if again the sound isn't terrific; and nor is it on *Live In Switzerland*, although this seems to have been a happy occasion and the band play well. Rimington is so obviously the star of his own groups that the merely capable players he works with don't seem to set him too much in the way of challenges. At least the 1997 gig at Meilen was better recorded, and there are some interesting tune choices to go with the more familiar material.

***** Live 'In Store' At The Louisiana Music Factory**
504 CDS 74 *Rimington; Clive Wilson (t); Lester Caliste (tb); Bob Broockman (p); Les Muscutt (bj); Gerald Adams (b); Frank Oxley (d).* 1/98.

Recorded at one of the leading record stores in the French Quarter, here's a recent Rimington crew tackling a dozen favourites from the NO book. Broockman has been playing in the city since the '40s, but this was his first record date; Caliste works for the Post Office but plays nights. Wilson and Rimington are old playing companions from many years before, in the

Barry Martyn band. Inevitably, the feel is good-natured fun, and any blemishes are easily forgiven. Not the record Rimington fans have necessarily been waiting for, but good-hearted.

***** The Whitewater Session**

PEK Sound PKCD-071 *Rimington; Ken Pye (t); Stan Stephens (tb); Rachel Hayward (bj); Tony Sharp (b); Dion Cochrane (d).* 12/96.

***** Very Live At Pakefield Rose**

RRCD 1020 *Rimington; Cuff Billett (t); Mike Pointon (tb); Nick Dawson (p); Louis Lince (bj); Annie Hawkins (b); John Petters (d).* 3/99.

****(*) Reed My Lips**

Jazz Crusade JCCD-3045 *Rimington; Bill Sinclair (p); Emil Mark (bj); Colin Bray (b); Big Bill Bissonnette (d).* 4/99.

Rimington these days tends to be the star of whichever group he's in, and he seems to operate a Bill Davison-type role: turn up, tune in, off we go. Except he rarely gives less than his best, and he's easily the main man on at least two of these three. *The Whitewater Session* finds him sitting in with Ken Pye's Creole Serenaders in Newby Bridge, Cumbria. The band is basic British trad, but Rimington usually manages to raise everyone's game, and this is a spirited and surprisingly passionate outing. The Pakefield date sets him up with a John Petters group, which bridges trad and Gene Krupa-styled swing in the leader's own drumming if nothing else. Billett is in good heart and Rimington puts down a vintage 'Burgundy Street Blues'. The weakest of the three is the studio date *Reed My Lips*, made in Wallingford, Connecticut. Rimington is fine, but Sinclair's more enthusiastic than accurate and Bissonnette's drumming is close to appalling.

Sam Rivers (born 1923)

TENOR AND SOPRANO SAXOPHONES, FLUTE, PIANO, VOCAL

Born in El Reno, Oklahoma, he studied composition and viola in Boston and played sax in local bands. Backed R&B singers and show groups, but also worked with Miles Davis (1964) and Cecil Taylor (1968–73), composed, and led his own occasional bands and sessions. Ran Studio RivBea, a focal point for New York jazz in the '70s, and has been one of the major teachers in American jazz. In the '90s, as an honoured veteran, he finally began recording more frequently, especially his big-band writing.

***** Fuchsia Swing Song**

Blue Note 90413 *Rivers; Jaki Byard (p); Ron Carter (b); Tony Williams (d).* 12/64.

Rivers's debut on Blue Note was a shrewd attempt to blend marketable hard bop with an altogether more abstract and edgy approach to composition. The title-tune here might have made it on to jukeboxes, but the others, with the possible exception of the evergreen 'Beatrice' (dedicated to his then wife) are chewier fare. 'Ellipsis' is probably the telling title. For all the formidable chording and time-keeping of a vintage band, the tracks move in quite unexpected directions, both harmonically and rhythmically and few of the tunes are genuinely memorable, which is why they haven't turned up in other bandleaders' songbooks.

A valuable reissue and a useful insight into the early career of an enigmatic genius.

*****(*) Trio Live**

Impulse! IMP 12682 *Rivers; Arild Andersen, Cecil McBee (b); Barry Altschul (d).* 8 & 10/73.

Rivers was content to leave a significant measure of freedom in his trio performances. Larger units tended to have more structure, but these recordings, albeit highly developed, are the sketchpads on which he worked out ideas. Even so, there is a clear continuity between these multisectioned works and the long-form compositions showcased on the much later big-band *Inspiration*, the same blend of structure and freedom. Most of this material, recorded weeks apart at the Molde Jazz Festival in Norway and at Yale University, has been heard before, but on a bizarre range of Impulse! compilations. Presented as performed, it reveals the organization even in Sam's most free-floating work. The two sets, 'Suite For Molde' and the Yale piece, 'Hues For Melanin', are subdivided according to the leader's choice of horn. The long soprano section of 'Hues' was formerly available on *Impulse! Artists On Tour*; the flute section was issued on *The Drums*; the remainder, and the soprano and flute sections of 'Suite For Molde' were issued on a Rivers record called *Hues*, with the remainder released as *No Energy Crisis*.

These are now collectors' items. The beauty of having the material on one format is that it is possible to track the progress of improvisations. Rivers characteristically trades ideas from one instrument to another. The most obvious traffic is between the tenor and flute. Sam often recasts a phrase many minutes later, allowing it to resettle into a new instrumental idiom. It's a fascinating process, and anyone with the technical wherewithal to scoot back and forth from one track to another will learn a great deal about his musical thinking.

***** Crystals**

Impulse!/Universal 589760 *Rivers; Ahmed Abdullah, Sinclair Acey, Martin Banks, Jothan Callins, Ted Daniel, Joe Dupars, Ronald Hampton, Virgil Jones, Marvin Hannibal Peterson, Michael Ridley, Richard Williams, Yusef Yancey (t, flhn); Ashley Fennell, Bill Campbell, Charles Greenlee, Vincent Holmes, Charles Stephens (tb); Richard Dunbar, Julius Watkins (frhn); Howard Johnson, Bob Stewart (tba); Joe Daley (tba, euph); Roland Alexander, Bill Barron, Anthony Braxton, Ron Bridgewater, Bobby Capers, Paul Jeffrey, Fred Kelly, Bob Ralston, Bill Saxton, John Stubblefield, Jens Ware, Monty Waters (sax, woodwind); Ronnie Boykins, Stafford James, Hakim Jami, Reggie Workman (b); Andrew Cyrille, Warren Smith (d); Horace Arnold, Roger Blank, Sonny Brown, Billy Hart, Maurice McKinley, Steve Solder (perc).* 74.

A titanic big-band project that showcases Sam's approach to atonal composition. The strong impression is of an overscored and carefully written-out performance, with little or no room for spontaneous soloing or much in the way of improvisation. The sheer density of sound is often off-putting, though digital transfer has cleaned it up somewhat. If as the cover suggests (and the new edition has deluxe packaging) the aim is to present musical ideas as faceted and crystalline, Rivers has mostly succeeded, but one does feel that attention is quickly drawn to surfaces rather than to anything of substance underneath. 'Exultation', 'Earthsong' and 'Postlude' all have touches of Ellington in the scoring, but such is the Duke's grip on jazz scoring on this scale that it would be surprising if there weren't. A brave and commendable effort but not an album that even the most devoted fan is going to reach for very often.

★★★(★) Colors

Black Saint 120064 *Rivers; Marvin Blackman (ts, f, ss); Talib Kibwe (f, cl, ts, ss); Chris Roberts (ss, f); Steve Coleman (as, f); Bobby Watson (as, f); Nat Dixon (ts, cl, f); Eddie Alex (ts, picc); Jimmy Cozier, Patience Higgins (bs, f).* 9/82.

This spectacular convocation of New York reed-playing talent went under the name Winds Of Manhattan. Dominated by flutes and without a rhythm section, it creates a sound that is absolutely consistent with everything Rivers had been doing over the previous 20 years, but scaled up dramatically. The usual interest in wave-forms, flux and unity, dispersement and integration, come together again in these complex charts. Rivers is unmistakably the leader, in that he determines the basic concepts, but the music as a whole is democratic and very broadly based. Those familiar with Coleman or Watson or even with the distinctive Kibwe may well be able to pick out their voices, but this is not the point of the exercise, and *Colors* is best listened to as an orchestral piece, relatively undifferentiated and a long way removed from conventional theme-and-solos jazz.

★★★★ Portrait

FMP CD 82 *Rivers (ts, ss, f, p, v solo).* 6/95.

A self-portrait presumably and of the artist at over 70, espousing what he describes in a notably effusive liner-note as an 'uninhibited emotion-driven free-flowing river of vibrant, bold, melodic inventions'. It's a piece of text that runs dangerously close to self-review: 'dazzling', 'musical perfection', 'eloquently phrased' and so on. What saves it is there is hardly a word with which one might disagree. These unaccompanied essays, with their characteristic one-word titles – 'Image', 'Reflection', 'Shadow' and overlong 'Cameo' – are magnificently crafted and thoroughly imbued with the creator's personality. Full attributions are given for all the instruments used, Keilwerth saxophones, a Bosendorfer Imperial and a Gemeinhardt flute, while under 'voice' it says laconically 'Sam Rivers', which is a version of 'model's own' on the fashion pages. Again, it makes complete sense, for this is the most thoroughly individual thing he has done for many years, a magnificent testament to his creative range, his generosity of spirit, and his great, great intelligence.

★★★(★) Concept

RivBea 50101 *Rivers; Doug Mathews (b); Anthony Cole (d).* 2–7/96.

A mixture of studio material recorded at the bassist/producer's homebase and live tracks from Florida, this is a tightly constructed record which has presumably been selected from a wide range of available material. The playing is consistently fascinating. The sound is underpowered and there are occasions when Rivers disappears into the background for no readily discernible reason. Interesting to note that the track titles here are entirely abstract – 'Aspect', 'Concept', 'Notion' – and the music has something of that quality as well, certainly nothing like as personalized, even confessional as on the FMP session. If that stands as Rivers's highest achievement of recent times, this must be accounted a more tentative project. Though clearly drawing on the shared experience of a working trio, it lacks the intimacy and the quickfire response one might expect from such a unit, working over a six-month period. It would be fascinating to hear some of the material that wasn't released; perhaps over the course of a live set or a day in the studio the logic and the dynamics would make more sense. A fine achievement nevertheless.

★★★★ Inspiration

RCA Victor 7432 164717 2 *Rivers; Ralph Alessi, Ravi Best, Baikida Carroll, James Zollar (t); Ray Anderson, Art Baron, Joseph Bowie (tb); Joseph Daley (bhn); Bob Stewart (tba); Steve Coleman, Greg Osby (as); Chico Freeman, Gary Thomas (ts); Hamiet Bluiett (bs); Doug Mathews (b); Anthony Cole (d).* 9–10/98.

★★★ Culmination

RCA 68311 *As above.* 9/98.

Trimmed of backgrounds and presumably many of the possible solos, these quarter-scale representations are powerful and convincing, and it's difficult to imagine some of them – and most obviously the atonal cluster pieces, 'Nebula' and 'Whirlwind' on *Inspiration* – sustaining interest and coherence over the full duration. The oldest piece represented is, almost inevitably, 'Beatrice', in which the main theme has always come garlanded with secondary subjects. Thirty years after its composition, this is its definitive incarnation, an anniversary tribute.

Rivers explains the enormous impact Dizzy Gillespie's solo work with the Eckstine orchestra made on him when he was in the Navy, listening to USO discs between watches. 'Inspiration' is a set of variations on Dizzy's 'Tanga', written while Sam was a member of the Gillespie touring orchestra. By contrast, 'Vines' is an exercise in harmonic minimalism, all the activity taking place over one admittedly ambiguous chord. 'Solace' is a later poem to Bea, no less lyrical, but more quietly accepting.

The all-star band consists largely of players who, individually and severally, have worked with Rivers before. Our only quibble is with the use of an electric bassist; Doug Matthews is an immaculate technician, but he doesn't seem to create quite the right sound for this ensemble. There are fine solo statements by tubist Stewart and the ever-distinguished Bluiett. No indication is given as to who the other soloists are. Sam, of course, is distinctive and prominently featured, but it may take a moment or two to decide whether Bowie or Anderson, Freeman or Thomas, Osby or album producer Coleman are occupying front-of-stage. That in part is testimony to the sheer originality of Rivers's concept: that he can mould a orchestra of highly individual performers so that it sounds like the expression of a single, idiosyncratic imagination.

Culmination is a no less interesting record, but once again the sheer richness of musical material is difficult to take on board in a single hearing, and a second disc of this challenging work may prove a bridge too far for all but the most dedicated listeners. The central grouping of 'Revelation', 'Culmination' and 'Ripples' would have filled an old-fashioned LP and given the most devoted Rivers fans meat and drink for weeks. At an hour, the disc is almost too generously packed, and one tires a little of having to work out who is soloing and exactly how thematic material is being deployed.

★★★ Fluid Motion

Isospin Labs 42058 *Rivers; Jonathan Powers (t); David Manson (tb); Doug Mathews (b); Anthony Cole (d).* 02.

Much of the material here seems to be by trombonist Manson and the whole has little feel of a Rivers session, though Sam's dry and laconic saxophone style is well to the fore. The recording and mastering leave something to be desired and there are distortions here and there which would be forgivable in louder passages but which seem to occur even when the dynamics are quite gentle. Now that the Rivers discography is looking healthier than for some years, this can safely be overlooked in favour of some of the more compelling sessions.

Max Roach (born 1924)

DRUMS, PERCUSSION

All revolutions in jazz are, on closer inspection, revolutions in the rhythm section. The fierce metres of bebop, with the accent taken away from the bass drum and given to the hi-hat instead, were created by Kenny Clarke, Art Blakey and Max Roach. In terms of long-term influence, Roach may be the most important of the three and he has continued to create a radical, often politically engaged brand of jazz in which the drum is primal and at the centre of the action. His group, M'Boom, took this to the extreme, but it is also true of Roach's more conventional personnels.

*** Max Roach

Original Jazz Classics OJCCD 202 *Roach; Idrees Sulieman (t); Leon Comeghys (tb); Gigi Gryce (as); Hank Mobley (ts); Walter Davis Jr (p); Frank Skeete (b).* 4 & 10/53.

***(*) Brownie Lives!

Fresh Sound FSRCD 1012 *Roach; Clifford Brown (t); Sonny Rollins (ts); Richie Powell (p); George Morrow (b).* 4 & 5/56.

Half a century of extraordinary music-making. With Kenny Clarke and Art Blakey, Roach was in at the birth of the revolution that was bebop but, unlike either of them, he continued to develop a language for the drums that took account of melody and – more obviously than either of his contemporaries – of sound-colour as well. Stylistically, he stands mid-way between swing drummers like Jo Jones, Dave Tough, Gene Krupa and Big Sid Catlett and the avant-garde of the '60s. If Krupa made the drummer a 'high-price guy', as he claimed with some justification, Roach set jazz percussionists free as instrumentalists in their own right. Some of his best solo performances now have to be dug out of samplers, but there is plenty around from the early days.

The eponymous 1953 session gives little indication of what is to follow and there are spells where Roach sounds oddly unlike himself. No mistaking the flashes of originality in the writing, even though most of the themes are orthodox bebop. Even at this juncture, the horns sound carefully arranged, almost orchestral in timbre – though, as he was to do later, Roach also breaks the band up into constituent parts. Six of the tracks are for quartet only, though brass and a second saxophone bring a rather special extra dimension to 'Sfax' and 'Orientation'.

Roach's career as leader really took flight only when he formed the now legendary – though, in the event, tragically short-lived – quintet with Clifford Brown. Their rapport was immediate and, for much of the period after Brownie's death, one senses Roach searching for a trumpeter to take his place, something he achieved briefly with the equally short-lived Booker Little. Roach himself missed the road accident which killed Brown and Richie Powell, but his career faltered badly. The live *Brownie Lives!* comes from a residency at Basin Street in New York, just six weeks before the tragic events of that summer. Understandably billed as a tribute to the trumpeter, it's arresting for what it tells us about the co-leader. Roach is magnificent throughout and, with digital remastering, occupies his proper place in the mix. He improvises constantly, shifting and recalibrating the rhythms on 'I Get A Kick Out Of You' and on his brilliant young colleague's 'Daahoud'; the energy passing between the two is palpable. A very exciting set, though one probably has to look under Brown's name for the best of their association.

CORE COLLECTION

**** Alone Together

Verve 526373-2 2CD *Roach; Clifford Brown, Kenny Dorham, Booker Little, Tommy Turrentine (t); Julian Priester (tb); Ray Draper (tba); George Coleman, Harold Land, Hank Mobley, Paul Quinichette, Sonny Rollins, Stanley Turrentine (ts); Herbie Mann (f); Ray Bryant, Jimmy Jones, Richie Powell, Bill Wallace (p); Barry Galbraith (g); Joe Benjamin, Bob Boswell, Nelson Boyd, Art Davis, Milt Hinton, George Morrow (b); Boston Percussion Ensemble; Abbey Lincoln (v).* 9/56–10/60.

A very valuable compilation both with and, later, without Brownie, and an excellent introduction for anyone who hasn't caught up with Roach. Fans of the drummer may well feel that it's better representative of his work than of the trumpeter's – which seems fair, given the relative weight of material. There are two tracks from *Max Roach + 4* and just one from *Jazz In 3/4 Time*. Most of the rest is later, some of it from less well-known records like *The Many Sides Of Max* (1959, with Little, Priester and Coleman) and *Quiet As It's Kept* (1960, with the Turrentines and Priester again). 'Max's Variations' is based on 'Pop Goes The Weasel' and is performed with the Boston Percussion Ensemble, a foreshadowing of later drum orchestra projects like M'Boom. On balance, a very good record indeed, pointing the way to most of the directions Roach was to take over the next few years. Serious enthusiasts should not settle for anything less than the full run of original albums, but for almost everyone else there can't be any better place to start.

**** Deeds, Not Words

Original Jazz Classics OJCCD 304 *Roach; Booker Little (t); Ray Draper (tba); George Coleman (ts); Art Davis, Oscar Pettiford (b).* 9/58.

Roach was bruisingly committed on *Deeds, Not Words*, a superb statement that makes a nonsense of generic pigeonholes like 'hard bop' but which also feels like the apotheosis of that often derided style. Draper's chesty valvings are not much more than a footnote in recent jazz, but he has booked his place and this is one of his more successful appearances, fulfilling an important role in this piano-less group that was to stay together successfully for two years. The CD also includes a duo featuring Roach with Oscar Pettiford which was made during a Sonny Rollins session; no idea why it turns up, unrelated, here.

CORE COLLECTION

♛ **** We Insist! Freedom Now Suite

Candid CCD 79002 *Roach; Booker Little (t); Julian Priester (tb); Walter Benton, Coleman Hawkins (ts); James Schenck (b); Ray Mantilla, Thomas Du Vall (perc); Abbey Lincoln (v).* 8 & 9/60.

Some works of art are inseparable from the social and cultural conditions which spawned them, and *We Insist!* is certainly one of these, a record that seems rooted in its moment. Within a few short years, the civil rights movement in the USA was to acquire a more obdurate countenance. On the threshold of the Kennedy years, though, this was as ferocious as it got. The opening 'Driva' Man' (one of Oscar Brown Jr's finest moments as a lyricist) is wry and sarcastic, enunciated over Roach's deliberately mechanical work rhythms and Coleman Hawkins's blearily proud solo, just the kind of thing you might expect from a working stiff at the end of the longest shift in history. It's followed by 'Freedom Day', which, with 'All Africa', was to be part of a large choral work targeted on the centenary of the Emancipation Proclamation. 'Freedom Day' follows Roach's typically swinging address, but is distinguished by a Booker Little solo of bursting, youthful emotion, and a contribution from the little-regarded Walter Benton that matches Hawkins's for sheer simplicity of diction.

The central 'Triptych' – originally conceived as a dance piece – is a duo for Roach and Lincoln. 'Prayer', 'Protest' and 'Peace' was not a trajectory acceptable to a later generation of militants, but there is more than enough power in Lincoln's inchoate roars of rage in the central part, and more than enough ambiguity in the ensuing 'Peace', to allay thoughts that her or Roach's politics were blandly liberal. The closing 'Tears For Johannesburg' has more classic Little, and also good things from Priester and Benton. It follows 'All Africa', which begins in a vein reminiscent of Billie Holiday, briefly degenerates into a litany of tribal names and slogans, and hinges on a 'middle passage' of drum music embodying the three main Black drum traditions of the West: African, Afro-Cuban and Afro-American. Its influence on subsequent jazz percussion is incalculable, and this extraordinary record remains listenable even across four decades of outwardly far more radical experimentation.

*** Members, Don't Git Weary

Koch International 8514 *Roach; Charles Tolliver (t); Gary Bartz (as); Stanley Cowell (p); Jymie Merritt (b); Chief Bey (v).* 10/60.

Coming so soon after *Freedom Now!*, this is inevitably something of an anti-climax, and it's perhaps more interesting in parts than as a whole. As a showcase for the burgeoning talents of Tolliver, Bartz and Merritt, it's almost an extended audition. Gary is trenchant and intense in his solo spots and Tolliver's bright, metallic tone has rarely since been heard to such advantage, even though his solo building is rather predictable. Andy Bey's vocal on the title-track takes a bit of getting used to, but it's attractively hokey. Roach plays his familiar 3/4s and 6/8s against a straight backbeat, giving the album, as so often with this transitional artist, a feeling of belonging to two generations simultaneously.

**** It's Time

Impulse! 051185-2 *Roach; Richard Williams (t); Julian Priester (tb); Clifford Jordan (ts); Mal Waldron (p); Art Davis (b).* 62.

It's Time was always a magnificent-*sounding* record, bright and brash and very accurately balanced. Poor Richard Williams has long been destined for the footnotes, recording just one impressive record under his own name but contributing to some remarkable sessions for other leaders. Here he sounds at his best, picking off clean, single-note lines when out front, blurring his sound most attractively when in the ensembles, and contributing a steady run of ideas. Priester also has one of his finest moments, a wonderful solo on 'Another Valley' which modulates between A major and A minor and carries an almost biblical authority. In contrast to his rather laid-back approach on *Speak, Brother, Speak*, Waldron is taut and ambiguous. A fine group record in every way. Only Roach's feature sounds padded, and perhaps a little too discursive.

***(*) Speak, Brother, Speak

Original Jazz Classics OJCCD 646 *Roach; Clifford Jordan (ts); Mal Waldron (p); Eddie Khan (b).* 10/62.

Driven by the same impulse as *We Insist! Freedom Now*, this is even more explicitly hooked into the civil rights movement of the time. The four band members are credited as co-composers of the long title-piece, a 25-minute epic based on a blues progression with a suspended interlude which serves to introduce each of the soloists in turn; they then preach on a 'text' suggested by the change in metre. It's a fascinating exercise, though not perhaps the band to have tried it out with. Waldron sounds diffident and uncomfortable, and Khan has little of substance to offer. 'A Variation' is more conventionally driven by a harmonic idea, and both the pianist and Jordan immediately seem easier with it. It must have been fascinating to have been at the Jazz Workshop in San Francisco when this was being recorded. How much more material was taped that day? Will we ever be able to hear it?

*** The Max Roach Trio Featuring The Legendary Hasaan

Atlantic 82273 *Roach; Hasaan (p); Art Davis (b).* 12/64.

The legend of Hasaan – who was also known as Ibn Ali, and who comes out as a strange hybrid of Abdullah Ibrahim and Ahmad Jamal – hasn't really stretched much beyond this record. This was a time when Atlantic were anxious to graft any amount of marketable exotica on to jazz performances and, while the familiar 3/4 and 6/8 variations are intriguingly varied with unfamiliar intervals and metres, the result is never much more than interesting, and only mildly so.

***(*) Drums Unlimited

Atlantic 7567 81361 *Roach (d solo) and with Freddie Hubbard (t); Roland Alexander (ss); James Spaulding (as); Ronnie Mathews (p); Jymie Merritt (b).* 10/65, 4/66.

The group tracks are little more than a change of pace around Roach's three solo features. The title-track is a meticulously structured and executed essay in rhythmic polyvalence that puts Sunny Murray's and Andrew Cyrille's more ambitious works in context; the second is a further exploration of the inner algebra of 3/4, adding nothing much more than further curlicues; while the last of the pieces is a heart-felt tribute to one of the swing-era drummers who has exerted a strong pull on Roach, Big Sid Catlett. Some of that era also creeps into the writing on 'In The Red', a fascinating idea performed by the group in a rather lacklustre way. Of the additional players, only Hubbard seems sufficiently relaxed, with an autonomous and often implicit pulse. Spaulding and Alexander are inclined to fall into rather mechanical cadences, almost as if afraid of losing a count that is already so capacious and undogmatic that one could claim any amount of freedom in it.

*** Lift Every Voice And Sing

Koch Jazz 8516 *Roach; Cecil Bridgewater (t); Billy Harper (ts); George Cables (p); Ruby McClure (b, v); Eddie Mathias (b); Ralph McDonald (perc); J. C. White Singers (v).* 71.

This lost Atlantic classic might well have come from the legendary Stax label with the Staples Singers. Roach and former wife Abbey Lincoln have always been interested in the power of gospel and spirituals, and these arrangements of traditional material, some of them by William Bell, some by Lincoln, some by Roach, come at the end of a period in which the music business was rediscovering some of the lost dimensions of black American music. Billy Harper is or should have been a storefront preacher, and Bridgewater, a longtime Roach collaborator, could dep for the Archangel Gabriel. 'Motherless Child', 'Troubled Waters' and 'Joshua' are the strongest and most developed tracks, with the voices beautifully arranged and recorded. Koch have done sterling service of late, bringing sets like this back from oblivion.

**** Birth And Rebirth

Black Saint 120024 *Roach; Anthony Braxton (as, ss, sno, f, cl, cbcl).* 9/78.

**** Historic Concerts

Soul Note 121100 2CD *Roach; Cecil Taylor (p).* 12/79.

In 1972 Roach wrote an article in the journal *Black Scholar* called 'What Jazz Means To Me'. It's a curious piece in retrospect, half confident and assertive, half elegiac. Users of this book will be well used to finding hiatuses in the careers even of major figures and will be aware that gaps in the discography usually have more to do with industry values or vicissitudes in the reissue programme than with prison sentences, decades spent in the shadow of junk or (though it happens) spells away from the music. Roach founded his percussion ensemble, M'Boom, in 1970 and it occupied much of his time in the coming years. However, the 12-year gap in the discographical record at this point does seem excessive for a musician of his stature.

The duets with Braxton are a key point. In their anxiety to sort-code music, critics couldn't decide who was climbing into whose pigeonhole, whether *Birth And Rebirth* was a better example of the reedman's accommodation to the mainstream, or of Roach's avant-garde credentials. In the event, of course, they met exactly head-to-head. Braxton, even of this vintage, is still making respectful gestures towards bop, and Roach is constantly looking for points beyond orthodox time-signatures. The sound is mainly very good, not as sharp and present as the hatART set (deleted), but musically far superior. The reunion has a more contrived, less spontaneous quality. A suite of four notionally connected arguments, used as the basis for extended improvisation, it calls on a wider range of sounds, not least from Braxton's flute and contrabass clarinet. The prevailing mood is combative rather than genuinely dialectical, abrasive rather than organic and coherent.

By contrast, the summit with Taylor, recorded at the McMillin Theatre at Columbia University, is still exhilarating. Both men warm up in their respective corners, before launching into a huge, 40-minute fantasy that sees neither surrendering a whit of individuality. As was noted at the time, it was the perfect occasion to test the cliché about Roach the melodic percussionist and Taylor the percussive pianist and, like all successful sound-bites, it proves to be both helpful and misleading. For much of the opening duet, Roach fulfils a conventional drummer's role, sustaining a time-feel, accelerating and arresting the pace of development, filling and embellishing; it is Taylor who creates the grandly insane melodies that spring away for whole minutes at a time. The second segment unravels more than a little, and there are symptoms of weariness in Roach's soloing. A recorded interview with the participants makes this a valuable historical document.

*** Pictures In A Frame

Soul Note 121003 *Roach; Cecil Bridgewater (t, flhn); Odean Pope (ts, f, ob); Calvin Hill (b).* 1 & 9/79.

*** In The Light

Soul Note 121053 *As above.* 7/82.

This was to be the basis of Roach's working band in the '80s, a period during which he turned back once again to standards. At this stage, though, the writing is still strong and rather sombre, accurately pitched – or they were well recruited – to meet the players' sensibilities. The arrangements almost sound as if they were intended for a much larger group with a wider array of timbres at its disposal. Some of the pieces have an almost vestigial quality, as if there are horn-lines still to be overlaid, and a good many are for subdivisions of the group, as if Roach is still experimenting with the constituents of the jazz ensemble. Through it all pulses a strength and determination one immediately recognizes as Roach's artistic signature.

The later of this pair already sounds less tentative and a good deal more straightforwardly linear. Pope concentrates on tenor, less on the oboe and flute doubles which give the earlier disc much of its tone-colour. Bridgewater favours a more open sound than before or since. The key tracks are two Monk covers – 'Ruby, My Dear' and 'Straight, No Chaser' – with Roach repositioning the rhythmic commas like the master he is.

**(*) Collage

Soul Note 121059 *Roach; Kenyatte Abdur-Rahman (xy, cabassa, perc); Eddie E. J. Allen (woodblocks, perc, cym); Roy Brooks (steel d, slapstick, musical saw, perc); Joe Chambers (xyl, mar, vib, b mar); Eli Fountain (cowbell, xyl, crotales, orchestral bells); Fred King (tym, concert bells, vib); Ray Mantilla (bells, chimes, perc); Warren Smith (b, mar, perc); Freddie Waits (concert tom-toms, gongs, bass d, shaker).* 10/84.

We can vouch for the sheer vitality and exuberance, and for the sheer thoughtfulness, of M'Boom's live output. Unfortunately, though perhaps not surprisingly, it does not transfer easily to record. Roach is not very prominent, restricting himself to snare, bass and marimba for much of the time and leaving it to the ever-inventive Chambers, Waits and Mantilla (each of whom can confidently be picked out of the mix on occasion) to add the substance and flesh to what is otherwise a rather sparse document.

*** Live At Vielharmonie

Soul Note 121073 *Roach; Cecil Bridgewater (t, flhn); Dwayne Armstrong (ts); Phil Bower (b); string quartet.* 11/83.

***(*) Easy Winners

Soul Note 121109 *Roach; Cecil Bridgewater (t, flhn); Odean Pope (ts); Tyrone Brown (b); Ray Mantilla (perc); string quartet.* 1/85.

Roach was much interested at this point in doubling a basic horn-and-rhythm jazz group with the acme of classical ensembles, the string quartet. At the same time, he seemed particularly concerned with exploring aspects of his own personal history, and the 1983 German concert celebrates two of his most important collaborators, Booker Little and, on 'Bird Says', Charlie Parker. The sound isn't absolutely *comme il faut* and there are problems in the balance of the strings, something that was later taken care of in studio settings. Armstrong has a rather blunt and wearying tone when compared to the assertive Pope, and Bower's electric bass was an unhappy compromise, especially when placed in front of acoustic strings.

Roach's daughter Maxine plays viola with the Uptown String Quartet on *Easy Winners*. The album contains a further memorial to Little and a later, much tougher and more coherent version of 'Bird Says'. The reappearance of Mantilla, who'd performed on *We Insist!* and with M'Boom seems a little surprising, but our initial prejudice has been overcome: he does add an extra dimension. The balance between the two quartets is very much better this time, with lots of space round the strings, who lift their game and establish a real presence.

***** Scott Free**
Soul Note 121103 *Roach; Cecil Bridgewater (t, flhn); Odean Pope (ts); Tyrone Brown (b).* 5/84.

***** It's Christmas Again**
Soul Note 121153 *As above, except add Lee Konitz (as), Tony Scott (cl), Tommaso Lana (g).* 6/84.

Scott LaFaro also died in a motor accident in 1961, within four months of Booker Little, and doubtless reviving memories of the wasted promise of Clifford Brown, whose departure left an unfillable gap in Roach's life. *Scott Free* is a hefty two-part suite which sustains interest, not just for Roach's astonishing ability to give even minute changes in the metre all the drama of major instrumental statements, but because his partners are by now so well attuned to what he is doing. Bridgewater and Pope play with considerable dash and eloquence, weaving strong contrapuntal lines and trading ideas at a high rate of resolution.

It's Christmas Again stands up very well. The guest performers appear only on a single track, and even if it weren't included this would be a successful record. The only reason we can't rate them any higher is that both discs have a curiously unmemorable quality. So absorbed and inward is the playing that it doesn't always communicate very openly, and many listeners will struggle to remember the music, even if they remember having been impressed by it. A measure perhaps of the extent to which Roach was re-examining his procedures during this fertile and prolific period.

*****(*) Survivors**
Soul Note 121093 *Roach; Donald Bauch, Guillermo Figueroa (vn); Louise Schulman (vla); Christopher Finckel (clo).* 10/84.

*****(*) Bright Moments**
Soul Note 121159 *Roach; Odean Pope (ts); Tyrone Brown (b); Uptown String Quartet.* 10/86.

Survivors continues the strings experiment and takes it a step further by dispensing with a jazz group altogether. This is territory the Kronos Quartet were exploring around the same time, and they must have kicked themselves that they didn't follow up a collaboration with Ron Carter by setting up an encounter with a drummer who sounds more and more as if he is moving away from jazz strictly conceived and out into new territory. 'The Drum Also Waltzes' is an old idea given fresh impetus and a very unexpected sound, but the best of the material is in the vibrant 'Billy The Kid' and the African-influenced 'Smoke That Thunders'. Roach experiments with dotted rhythms and stretched-out passages of suspended harmony in which he is the only active presence. This was to become a regular feature of his work in the '90s.

Bright Moments is necessarily something of a compromise, a step back towards a more conventional jazz idiom and line-up, but by this stage Roach has worked out exactly how and where the two instrumentations clash and merge, and he has devised a language conducive to maximizing their respective strengths. A fine record.

*****(*) Beijing Trio**
Asian Improv 0044 *Roach; Jon Jang (p); Jiebing Chen (erhu).* 98.

There have been previous attempts to synthesize jazz with Asian musics, but this brilliant trio scores highly in exploring common ground rather than exotic differences. Jang is a superb player, deeply grounded in the music of both traditions, and Roach is as responsive to new rhythms as ever. The *erhu* – a kind of two-stringed fiddle – has to stand in for a double bass, which it does with surprising fidelity, and Jiebing Chen deliberately lowers the register of the instrument in places to yield a sound that is surprisingly close (a chance resemblance that rehearings have only confirmed) to *Money Jungle*, a trio with Duke Ellington and Charles Mingus, on which Roach also played. This is a very challenging and unexpected record, more than just a blandly diplomatic meeting of cultures, a piece of genuine improvisation and experiment. Mostly highly recommended. For Max's latest appearance on record, though, look under Clark Terry's entry.

David Thomas Roberts

PIANO

A ragtime scholar and practitioner at work in California.

*****(*) Folk Ragtime: 1899–1914**
Stomp Off 1317 *Roberts (p solo).* 94–96.

The title sounds like a college thesis, but the contents are thoroughly delightful. These are ragtime strains from areas long since left to archivists, and Roberts (and Trebor Tichenor, whose superb notes help to bring the history of the music to life) does us a service by performing them with such elegance and particularity. The composers represented include Charles H. Hunter, Thomas E. Broady, Calvin Lee Woolsey and John William 'Blind' Boone, and the tunes have titles like 'A Bran Dance Shuffle', 'Felix Rag (A Phenomenal Double Ragtime Two Step)' and 'A Tennessee Tantalizer'. For those who know only the likes of Joplin, these embroidered trifles from a neglected treasure-chest of American music will be almost shocking. Roberts honours their composers by playing them with a seemingly flawless touch. Nothing is too fast or heavy, tempos are judged to the finest degree and the recording is excellent. Our only hesitation is that 72 minutes of this kind of music is a lot at a single sitting: you may prefer to sample these a few rags at a time.

Hank Roberts (born 1954)

CELLO, FIDDLE, 12-STRING GUITAR, VOICE

Though somewhat removed from the scratch-and-scrabble of more avant improvising cellists, Roberts has a style that identifiably owes something to post-Hendrix guitarists like Bill Frisell. He is a member of the string group Arcado but has also recorded quite extensively as leader.

*** **Black Pastels**
Winter & Winter 919016-2 *Roberts; Ray Anderson, Robin Eubanks (tb); Dave Taylor (btb); Tim Berne (as); Bill Frisell (g, bj); Mark Dresser (b); Joey Baron (d).* 11–12/87.

(*) **Birds of Prey
Winter & Winter 919036 *Roberts; Mark Lampariello (g, v); Jerome Harris (b, v); Vinnie Johnson (d, v); D. K. Dyson (v).* 1–2/90.

*** **I'll Always Remember**
Level Green 22002 *Roberts; Peter Chwazik (b, elec); Bill King (d).* 5/97.

Roberts's first JMT date has now been reissued on Winter & Winter. It stands up well enough, though it already feels of its slightly green time, when a fusion of post-bop with country music sounded raw and a bit peculiar (Frisell, who is of course on the record, has taught us all differently since). The brass-players are what makes the difference to Roberts's splintery music; a bleak touch of almost medieval darkness.

The much-later trio album sounds as if most of the material was spontaneously composed in rehearsal or in the studio, which is not to denigrate it but to suggest that this feels more of a blowing band than previous units. Certainly the middle tracks, leading up to the wonderfully titled 'Our Meeting With Other Worldly Spirit Creatures At The Campfire', must have been worked on collectively. Longer items, 'Living Bicycles/ Jersey Devil' and 'Trees', are more formally structured but without losing the fresh and responsive cast of the short tracks. The sound isn't top notch, with some distortion on Hank's cello here and there, but it captures the group as it is and as it does.

Birds Of Prey hasn't worn particularly well. The ideas are quite strong, but the execution seems half-hearted and Roberts's cello is a difficult voice to integrate with a group as linear and literal as this. The vocals don't add much and the only track that really stands out is the relatively short 'Angels And Mud'.

Luckey Roberts (1887–1968)

PIANO

Started as a child performer in vaudeville, then played piano in Baltimore bars and began writing ragtime-to-jazz pieces which were popular in New York, where he set the pace for Harlem pianists from around 1912. Led his own band and wrote prolifically, with many show scores being produced. Figured in the revival of the '40s but never recorded much, and eventually ran his own bar in the city.

***(*) **The Circle Recordings**
Solo Art SACD-10 *Roberts (p solo).* 5/46.

*** **Luckey & The Lion – Harlem Piano**
Good Time Jazz GTJCD-10035 *Roberts; Willie 'The Lion' Smith (p).* 58.

Charles Luckeyeth Roberts was a giant of Harlem stride piano, and he was also one of its least-documented performers, at least so far as records are concerned. One of the titles on the Circle session, 'Shy And Sly', was cut for Columbia as far back as 1916 but was never issued; aside from a few cameo appearances, it wasn't until the '40s that he got himself properly on record. The six tracks on the Solo Art CD sound like a man making up for lost time: they explode with sheer bravado, rhythms taken at a helter-skelter pace, trills and runs and horn-like outbursts folded into each of the pieces. 'Pork And Beans', which Willie 'The Lion' Smith also liked to play, is the one to try first. But this is all there is of Roberts on this CD: the rest is devoted to early tracks by Ralph Sutton.

Luckey joined forces with The Lion for the 1958 album: they share the date rather than playing together. It's a piquant contrast. Roberts was already an old man, but much of his particular flair is intact on the splendid locomotive piece, 'Railroad Blues', and 'Complainin'' is a chuckle. Not much evidence, in sum, for a piano legend but, given the extravagances of Luckey's style, maybe that's all for the best.

Marcus Roberts (born 1963)

PIANO

Learned piano from the age of eight, studied in his native Florida, then joined the Wynton Marsalis group in 1985 and stayed until 1991, although he continues to be closely identified with the Marsalis 'clan'. Recorded extensively by BMG, then by Columbia.

(*) **Gershwin For Lovers
Columbia 477752-2 *Roberts; Reginald Veal (b); Herlin Riley (d).* 93.

Roberts was first acknowledged as the gifted pianist in the Wynton Marsalis group, but he has long since gone on to making his own way as a thoughtful and accomplished pianist-composer – even if the association with Marsalis still sticks to him like a limpet. Perhaps he exacerbates the situation by using musicians closely associated with the Marsalis axis, and by following tenets that the trumpeter has particularly espoused. Either way, Roberts has been in thrall to a specific notion about the jazz tradition all through an interesting if rather studied career on record. His several albums for Novus have been supplanted by a more recent association with Columbia. His first for the label is 'intended to be part of a romantic evening', says the artist, but there's an awful lot of foreplay here. While there may be some of the pianist's best work – in a fine solo on 'They Can't Take That Away From Me' and a closing trot through 'But Not For Me', where the tempo finally picks up – there's some terribly serious music to get through as well. The intractably slow delivery of the earlier tunes on the record isn't just a matter of ballad tempos. It's a conceptual trudge, too. For all the interesting touches here and there, the bald reality is that Roberts and company don't even swing for much of the time.

*** **Time And Circumstance**
Columbia 484451-2 *Roberts; David Grossman (b); Jason Marsalis (d).* 3/96.

***** Blues For The New Millennium**

Columbia CK 68637 *Roberts; Marcus Printup, Randall Haywood (t); Ronald Westray, Vincent Gardner (tb); Richard Brown (ts, ss); Stephen Riley (ts); Ted Nash (cl, f, bs); Sherman Irby (as); Roland Guerin, Thaddeus Exposé (b); Ali Jackson, Jason Marsalis (d).* 10/96–5/97.

Time And Circumstance is a suite of 14 pieces concerning a personal relationship, and with its various imbalances – some of the extracts are suffocatingly long, others perplexingly brief, and there is a great deal of space allotted to bass and drums – Roberts can scarcely be accused of avoiding a personal touch. Yet he seems too generous in handing out space to musicians who are less interesting than he is, and Grossman in particular gets more than his share. Thelonious Monk haunts Roberts's composing, but that's an awkward shade to assimilate without seeming like a copyist, and Marcus doesn't quite avoid the difficulty. As always, it seems, the disc is simply too long, and could have usefully lost 20 minutes; but there remains a lot of interesting playing.

Blues For The New Millennium is Roberts's most specific homage to old times, with covers of Jelly Roll Morton and Robert Johnson along with his own musings on past and present jazz. The musicianship is impeccable and the delivery impressive, but Roberts's most familiar problem surfaces again: he's studied this stuff so hard that there's no sense of spontaneity left in it, and there are numerous bands on labels like Stomp Off that have all the freshness and unforced energy which the pianist can't quite extract from his forces. Recorded and mixed with fine clarity and zing, the music has a polish that evades many a smaller-budget project, but it's hardly any more convincing.

*****(*) In Honor Of Duke**

Columbia CK 63630 *Roberts; Roland Guerin (b); Jason Marsalis (d); Antonio Sanchez (perc).* 4/99.

Since he is in many respects a conservative, Roberts's penchant for organizing his records in difficult, almost abstruse ways is surprising. This sequence of originals, gathered together as an Ellington homage, resists expectation most of the way through. Bass and drum parts are granted an almost cussed independence. Swinging passages suddenly fall away into near-silence. Rather than programming it in a fast-mid-slow-mid-fast style, it feels like a single, varied pulse, and Roberts musters an appealing lightness much of the way. His records have rarely been fun and they have often sunk under the weight of their pretensions, but that never happens here. His bag of Ellington quotations is effectively rustled and will tempt knowledgeable listeners into a spot-the-lick parlour game, but he doesn't forget about Monk and Coltrane either. Earnest support from Guerin and Marsalis on what sounds like Roberts's best record.

***** Cole After Midnight**

Columbia 69781 *Roberts; Roland Guerin, Thaddeus Exposé (b); Jason Marsalis, Leon Anderson (d).* 6/98.

Half-Nat Cole, half-Cole Porter, and you have to admire the subversive conceit. Roberts has been experimenting in live situations with variations on the rhythm section, and sure enough there are tracks here with two drummers and two bassists. The record does tend to feel like an uncomfortable halfway-house between radical homage and an almost petulant individuality.

Tom Roberts

PIANO

Originally from Pittsburgh, Roberts is a regular in traditional groups of many kinds and spent six years working in New Orleans. He currently bases himself in New York, where he walks his dog, Bix.

*****(*) In The Lion's Den**

Stomp Off CD 1392 *Roberts (p solo).* 3–4/03.

A beautiful repertory record. Roberts is an expert on Harlem stride, and this homage to Willie 'The Lion' Smith features 20 of The Lion's tunes, from such famous pieces as 'Echoes Of Spring' to rarities such as 'Sparklets' and 'Hot Things'. Smith was the most lyrical of all the Harlem stride masters, and Roberts is exacting in his quest to point up the detail and exquisite touch in the likes of 'Zig Zag', 'Concentratin'' and, perhaps above all the other tracks, the almost tragically lovely 'Tango A La Caprice', with its three charming themes. There is plenty of hot stuff too, but the lingering impression left by the music is of a poignant farewell to an epoch of piano-playing which has long since vanished. If there's a criticism, it's that – as is the Stomp Off way – the record is almost too much of an indulgence, and is best heard a few tracks at a time.

Herb Robertson (born 1951)

TRUMPET, FLUGELHORN, POSTHORN, OTHER INSTRUMENTS

A familiar figure on New York's so-called downtown scene in the '80s and '90s, Robertson is on many of the key records from that movement and has a few of his own too.

*****(*) Transparency**

Winter & Winter 919002 *Robertson; Tim Berne (as); Bill Frisell (g); Lindsey Horner (b); Joey Baron (d).* 85.

****** Shades of Bud Powell**

Winter & Winter 919019 *Robertson; Brian Lynch (t); Robin Eubanks (tb); Vincent Chancey (frhn); Bob Stewart (tba); Joey Baron (d).* 1/88.

***** X-Cerpts: Live at Willisau**

Winter & Winter 919013 *Robertson; Tim Berne (as); William Gust Tsilis (vib); Lindsey Horner (b); Joey Baron (d).* 1/88.

A maverick presence on a whole range of downtown projects, Robertson often gives the impression that he only took up the trumpet that afternoon and discovered he had an aptitude for it. His tone is raw, breathy and of a sort to make orthodox brass-teachers throw themselves out of upper-storey windows. However, he's never less than wholly musical and his tight, often pinched sound, which often sounds as if it's coming from a pocket or piccolo trumpet, is instantly attractive.

Over the last couple of years, Winter & Winter have been reissuing the JMT catalogue in a striking new livery. *Transparency* is one of the best returns yet, a bright, brash album with an impressive range of tonalities and timbres. Berne and Frisell are significant contributors, and on two of the long tracks, 'Flocculus' and 'Floatasia', they combine with Herb so confidently and assertively as to suggest this was a permanent band and he a more experienced leader.

Arranging Bud Powell for a brass ensemble was a genius idea that works brilliantly and yields one of Robertson's own best recorded performances. His level of playing here is almost uncanny as he makes the horn sing on 'Un Poco Loco', 'Hallucinations' and others. Sterling support, too, from Eubanks, Lynch and Stewart.

The live album has some wonderful moments but the three long tracks are each overcooked in some significant regard, either in the complexity of the chart or the seemingly wilful perversity of what is done with it. As always, Robertson and Berne turn in some fiery and effective playing, but too much of it sounds thrown away.

*****(*) Certified**

Winter & Winter 919048 *Robertson; David Taylor (btb); Mark Goldsbury (ss, ts, cl); Ed Schuller (b); Phil Haynes (d, perc).* 3/91.

The line-up changed quite significantly for *Certified.* Goldsbury's introduction was slow to gel, but here his multi-instrumentalism (reminiscent of Marty Ehrlich) gives a new timbral sophistication to the music and allows Robertson to concentrate on new areas of sound. The rhythm section hasn't the flexibility and wit of the Horner–Baron partnership, but Schuller and Haynes are both brightly gifted players and they dig in manfully on 'Cosmic Child' and 'Seeking Seeds In The Blue Bazaar', the two most ambitious tracks, which need a strong pulse to prevent them from fragmenting utterly.

Great to have all these albums back in circulation again. A wonderful initiative from Winter & Winter.

***** Falling In Flat Space**

Cadence CJR 1065 *Robertson; Dominic Duval (b); Jay Rosen (perc, v, etc.).* 2/96.

*****(*) Sound Implosion**

CIMP110 *As above.* 3/96.

The story of these two discs is that *Falling In Flat Space* was sent in to Cadence on spec. Producer Bob Rusch offered the trio a recording and subsequently decided to release the first session as well. It has to be said that, given CIMP's *audio vérité* approach, there isn't much to choose between actual session and presumed demo. Like all the label's output, the sound is raw and very immediate. Strictly, this is a collaborative trio. *Sound Implosion* begins with a long solo statement from Duval, an expert craftsman who seems unfettered by the example of any previous bass-player and who sounds much more European (Peter Kowald and Paul Rogers spring to mind) than any North American. Rosen and Robertson both call on a huge range of ancillary sounds – whistles, posthorns, voice, toys, and so on – to vary the weave.

On *Falling In Flat Space* the main interest lies in three long improvisations in the middle of the set. Almost everything else is preparatory or somehow unachieved. Of the three, 'The Double Stop' is most impressive, but there is also 'We Can't Get Started', an uncredited standard which nods to Mingus here and there. *Sound Implosion* follows the same course: long and short pieces (the latter more successful here) and a wholly unexpected re-creation of Jimmy Van Heusen's 'Deep Purple'. Two excellent free-jazz records which trumpet enthusiasts will want to compare with recent projects by Dave Douglas and Paul Smoker.

****(*) Knudstock 2000**

Cadence CJR 1117 *Robertson; Frank Grasso (picc t); Steve Swell (tb, p); Bob Hovey (tb); Bob Ackerman (as, ts, cl, f); Knud Jensen (ts); Jim Hart (g, t); Hans Tammen (g); Chris Lough (b); Tom Sayek, Herb Fisher (d).* 2/00.

***** Brooklyn–Berlin**

CIMP 218 *Robertson; Vinny Golia (cl, sop-cl, as, bcl); Ned Rothenberg (cl, bcl); Ken Filiano (b); Phil Haynes (d).* 2/00.

****(*) Ritual**

CIMP 222 *Robertson; Phil Haynes (d).* 2/00.

****(*) Music For Long Attention Spans**

Leo LR 315 *Robertson; Steve Swell (tb); Bob Hovey (tb, perc, v); Hans Tammen (g); Chris Lough (b); Tom Sayek (d).* 6/00.

Robertson now bases himself in Berlin and this flurry of recording was done on a trip home. It's a mostly disappointing lot, though Robertson himself is rarely to blame. The *Knudstock* session is a shambolic free-blow, three pieces (one which runs for nearly 40 minutes) for 11 musicians, all of them in an unruly mood. Not harsh enough for genuine assaultive shocks, yet without many redeeming features. *Brooklyn–Berlin* is a quintet session that benefits from three virtuoso horn-players. Golia and Rothenberg wrangle out a truce between themselves, and Robertson gets in some fine moments, but even here some of the pieces ramble past their useful lifespan. The duo set with Haynes was done while everyone else was on a long break at the same sessions. The sleeve-notes highlight an almost mystical experience but, in the cold light of the CD player's digital read-out, it's nothing like as special. Far too much atmosphere, not enough musical result: compare similar sessions by Phil Minton and Roger Turner to hear much more satisfying music.

Music For Long Attention Spans sounds like a challenge, and Herb's poem(!) on 'The Status Quo' sounds like a snook cocked at commercial attitudes, audiences who won't listen and the like. OK, but give us more compelling music than this. It's a typical free-jazz jumble, Hovey and Swell barging into each other, and Robertson playing what are easily the most interesting things, yet seldom getting them across all the surrounding blah. Some merit, much malarkey.

Donald Robinson (born 1953)

DRUMS

A member of the group What We Live and a regular in Glenn Spearman's music, Robinson is an experienced performer in contemporary American free music.

***** Straight Lines Skewed**

CIMP 213 *Robinson; Marco Eneidi (as); Lisle Ellis (b).* 10/00.

Ellis and Robinson are a practised team and their duo passages here are particularly good. Eneidi plays with a kind of strangulated force that throws out terrific energy and his shrilling contribution to, say, 'Brush Up' certainly stirs the blood. But he often sounds oddly isolated from the other two, and, for a trio, there's a surprising sense of compartmentalizing as they go forward. The altoist's relentless astringency does make the collective playing hard work for the listener, although (as so often with sessions from this source) in smaller doses the music's effective.

Jim Robinson (1892–1976)

TROMBONE

Robinson took up the trombone while serving with the US army in France. He played in and around New Orleans for most of his long life, and was a favourite with most of the bandleaders for his old-fashioned style, rarely playing anything that sounded like a solo, and hitting his notes hard. Much of his best work is with George Lewis or Bunk Johnson, but he led some sessions at least nominally.

***** Jim Robinson's New Orleans Band**

Original Jazz Classics OJC 1844 *Robinson; Ernest Cagnolotti (t); Louis Cottrell (cl); George Guesnon (g); Alcide 'Slow Drag' Pavageau (b); Alfred Williams (d).* 1/61.

***** Plays Spirituals And Blues**

Original Jazz Classics OJC 1846 *As above, except add Annie Pavageau (v).* 1/61.

***** Classic New Orleans Jazz Vol. 2**

Biograph BCD 128 *Robinson; Kid Thomas Valentine, Ernest Cagnolotti, Tony Fougerat (t); John Handy (as); Sammy Rimington, Albert Burbank, Orange Kellin (cl); Dick Griffith, George Guesnon, Al Lewis (bj); Dick McCarthy, Alcide 'Slow Drag' Pavageau, James Prevost (b); Sammy Penn, Cie Frazier, Louis Barbarin (d).* 8/64–12/74.

***** Birthday Memorial Session**

GHB BCD-276 *Robinson; Yoshio Toyama (t); Paul 'Polo' Barnes (cl); James Miller (p, v); Keiko Toyama (bj); Chester Zardis (b); Cie Frazier (d).* 73.

The doyen of New Orleans trombonists – along with Louis Nelson – Robinson had turned 80 by the time the last of these records was made, but his simple, perfectly appropriate playing wasn't too bothered by the passing of time, and he performs much as he did on all the sessions he appeared on over a space of some 35 years. The two OJCs were originally a part of Riverside's New Orleans Living Legends series and were among the first occasions when Robinson had been asked to perform as a leader. Cagnolotti and Cottrell weren't much more interested than Jim in taking a lead, and as a result the front line sounds reserved here and there; but the two discs – neatly split between NO standards on the first and gospel and blues tunes on the second – are as tough and genuine as most such sessions from this period. The Biograph disc puts together three sessions stretching across ten years. The first is a noisy and quite exciting gathering of generations – Valentine and Robinson on one side, Rimington and Handy on another – with boisterous music resulting, and the four tracks from the following year are in the same mould; but it's on the closing 'Gasket Street Blues', which features one of Robinson's rare, unaffected solos, that the man himself stands out most clearly.

On *Birthday Memorial* the band play with undimmed enjoyment of the occasion. The presence of the Toyamas, the Japanese couple who lived and worked on Bourbon Street for a spell in the late '60s, invigorates the other old-timers involved on the date, with Yoshio's admiration for Bunk Johnson letting him fit into the group without any sense of strain.

Justin Robinson

ALTO SAXOPHONE

Teamed with veteran players – Gary Bartz, Eddie Henderson, Bobby Watson – on his Verve debut, Robinson shone promisingly but didn't quite capture the spotlight. His sharp, Jackie McLean-influenced alto seems ever more relevant.

***** The Challenge**

Arabesque 137 *Robinson; Ron Blake (ts); Stephen Scott (p); Dwayne Burno (b); Dion Parson (d).* 98.

Robinson was a schoolmate of pianist Stephen Scott, who also appeared on the debut *Just In Time* and who had his own brief flirtation with Verve. 'Master Scott' is the leader's affectionate thank you. This is a more settled project than the now deleted first record. Not having to make so much room for guest spots (Blake appears on four tracks), Robinson digs in and shows his stuff. The pace is brisk and often intense, with just one ballad on the set, the mournful 'Love Thy Father'. His take on Herbie Hancock's 'Maiden Voyage' is fresh and original and he shows a fine turn with the pen on new material liked 'Adnil', the brief, intense 'Cognitive Activity' and the longer, more passionate 'No More Sacrifices'. Rodney Kendrick's 'A Little Sweeter' is an inspired choice of material. Some claim to hear an Eric Dolphy influence, but if Robinson is still processing his original inspirations, it is surely Jackie McLean who springs to mind, especially on the blues.

Spike Robinson (1930–2001)

TENOR SAXOPHONE

An American who came to Britain on a navy posting in 1951, Robinson was a frequent visitor to the UK and made most of the records under his own name under British auspices. He started on alto but became a cool midstreamer in the style of the Lester Young school.

*****(*) At Chesters Vol. 1**

Hep CD 2028 *Robinson; Eddie Thompson (p); Len Skeat (b); James Hall (d).* 7/84.

***** At Chesters Vol. 2**

Hep CD 2031 *As above.* 7/84.

Although he played tenor subsequently, Robinson was an altoman entirely under Parker's spell when he made some early tracks in London in 1951. Robinson's switch to tenor may have deprived us of a fine Bird-man, but his command of the bigger horn is scarcely less impressive on what were comeback recordings. His models were Getz, Sims and – at the insistence of some – Brew Moore, but Robinson was deft enough to make the comparisons sound fully absorbed. These two live records, made in Southend on a 1984 British visit, are wonderfully light and swinging, as if the tenor were an alto in his hands. Volume 1 has the edge for a couple of ethereal ballads and the swing which is piled into 'Please Don't Talk About Me When I'm Gone'. Vivid location recording.

***** Three For The Road**

Hep CD 2045 *Robinson; Janusz Carmello (t); David Newton (p); Louis Stewart (g); Paul Morgan (b); Mark Taylor (d).* 7/89.

****(*) Stairway To The Stars**

Hep CD 2049 *Robinson; Brian Kellock (p); Ronnie Rae (b); John Rae (d).* 10/90.

Robinson continued on his steady way. *Three For The Road* makes for an amiable blowing match between a seasoned cast: nothing fancy, and nothing untoward. *Stairway To The Stars*, though, is a trifle dull – Robinson never plays with less than a professional commitment, but on this occasion he sounds as though he might have been a bit tired.

***** Spike Robinson And George Masso Play Arlen**

Hep CD 2053 *Robinson; George Masso (tb); Ken Peplowski (cl, ts); John Pearce (p); Dave Green (b); Martin Drew (d).* 10/91.

Consistency became Robinson's most obvious virtue: this is another dependable, likeable record, with Masso and Peplowski (who's on only two tracks) as foils. The trombonist plays quirkily enough to make one think of Bill Harris, and it's a strong counterpoint to Spike's gentlemanly playing. 'This Time The Dream's On Me' and 'My Shining Hour' work particularly well. But the snug, tasteful rhythm section keep dragging the music back into formulaic mainstream.

***** Plays Harry Warren**

Hep 2056 *Robinson; Victor Feldman, Pete Jolly (p); Ray Brown, John Leitham (b); John Guerin, Paul Kreibich (d).* 12/81–8/93.

Spike's 'modern' career came full circle with this release, which couples a reissue of his 1981 set for Discovery with a new date made in 1993 with a different American rhythm section. There's an almost seamless transition between the two dates and the playing is as handsome as one might expect – though, without another horn out front, Robinson sometimes lets himself drift off – as charmingly as ever. At nearly 80 minutes, another overloaded CD.

***** Young Lions Old Tigers**

Jazzizit 0022 *Robinson; Derek Nash (ss, as, ts, bs, perc); Nick Weldon (p); Rob Richenburg (b); Pete Carter (d).* 5/00.

Spike's passing lends a little sadness to this genial date, which showed him not so much jousting with Nash as lending a helping hand in sundry two-sax workouts. It's very good-natured, but it should have dawned on anyone following Spike's work by now that that was his whole style, a gentlemanly delivery of a kind which is vanishing all too quickly. British audiences in particular do miss him.

Andrew Robson (born 1969)

ALTO AND SOPRANO SAXOPHONES

Young Australian saxophonist leading an open-ended trio music.

***** Scrum**

Rufus RF031 *Robson; Steve Elphick (b); Hamish Stuart (d).* 5/96.

*****(*) Sunman**

Rufus RF062 *As above.* 11/99.

*****(*) On**

ABC Jazz 066634-2 *As above, except add Alister Spence (p).* 12/01.

Robson's fierce trio plays a tough and tender variation on post-bop sax-and-rhythm. The debut suggests that he's closer to the hard-bop masters than to the free school, even when the music nudges at tonality, and there's a clever interplay between the musicians on the title-track, which epitomizes the co-operative feel of the date. Robson isn't shy with his writing – there are ten originals here – but perhaps a familiar melody or two might have thrown the rest of the music into slightly sharper relief. 'Margaret Island' is an evocative and pensively lyrical farewell.

Sunman introduces soprano to Robson's range. Recorded in Sydney's summer heat, some of it has a suitably parched quality, but the trio pace themselves beautifully: hear the steadily intensifying 'Chant', or the patient lines of 'Sierra's Waltz'. Robson sometimes suggests Lee Konitz in his improvising, worrying out details from the core of his themes, and with Elphick playing plenty of melody on his bass there's a nice richness to the music.

Robson's switched labels and brought in pianist Spence for *On*. A fresh set of ten originals give the players plenty to chew on, and if Robson's writing still doesn't quite have the knack of real memorability, it sets his own playing into a very agreeable light. Spence adds harmonic weight and gives the leader a break from carrying the solos, and the others punch up to their weight. A classy set which offers real pleasure.

Betty Roche (born 1920)

VOCAL

Originally from Wilmington, Delaware, Roche sang in Harlem with the Savoy Sultans and Hot Lips Page and enjoyed two spells with the Duke Ellington orchestra – though she made no studio records with Duke. Her LP career was confined to three albums.

***** Singin' And Swingin'**

Original Jazz Classics OJC 1718 *Roche; Jimmy Forrest (ts); Jack McDuff (org); Bill Jennings (g); Wendell Marshall (b); Roy Haynes (d).* 1/61.

***** Lightly And Politely**

Original Jazz Classics OJC 1802-2 *Roche; Jimmy Neeley (p); Wally Richardson (g); Michael Mulia (b); Rudy Lawless (d).* 1/61.

Roche had two separate spells with Duke Ellington, in the '40s and again in the early '50s, but she made only a handful of sides with the orchestra: her set-piece was a version of 'Take The "A" Train' which incorporated a long scat episode. Duke liked her style: 'she had a soul inflexion in a bop state of intrigue'. Her Bethlehem tracks of the '50s have been available but are now out of print (although, with the Bethelehem catalogue currently enjoying one of its several reissue programmes, that may change soon enough). These 1961 sessions are a modest but enjoyable memento of her art. Bop appears on *Singin' And Swingin'* with 'Billie's Bounce', but her huskier ballad delivery takes some of the slush out of 'When I Fall In Love', and her Anita O'Day influence shows through in a certain wry sidelong delivery of some of the lyrics. That trait is more exposed on the cooler, slower *Lightly And Politely*. Some of the lyrics she seems to phrase in abruptly chopped sections, a little like Abbey Lincoln, and it lends a curious detachment to heartbroken stuff like 'Jim'. By the end of the record, however, one feels that she has made the songs her own in an odd sort of way.

Mart Rodger

CLARINET, C MELODY SAXOPHONE, VOCAL

A veteran Manchester jazzman, Rodger played clarinet with the Canal Street Ragtimers in the '70s before deciding to form his own New Orleans-style group following a visit to the Crescent City in 1984. Manchester Jazz has been recording and playing live in their local patch ever since.

★★★(★) **Makin' Whoopee**
Bowstone OWSCD 2602 *Rodger; Allan Dent (t); Terry Brunt (tb); Alec Collins (p); Tim Roberts (bj); Colin Smith (b); Pete Staples (d); Marion Montgomery (v). 93.*

★★★ **T'Aint Nobody's Bizness If We Do**
Bowstone OWSCD 2603 *As above except add Paul Munnery (tb), Roy Chappell (v), omit Montgomery. 95.*

★★★ **Mart Rodger Manchester Jazz**
Jazzology JCD-313 *As above except add Charlie Bentley (bj, g), omit Munnery, Roberts and Chappell. 97.*

★★★ **Manchester Delighted**
Bowstone OWSCD 2604 *As above. 97.*

★★★ **Moments Like This**
Bowstone OWSCD 2605 *As above. 01.*

Regulars at Mart's Monday-night gig in Manchester will find any of these a more than acceptable souvenir of the work of this doughty and long-standing pillar of the British trad establishment. Everyone else should at least enjoy the playing of the MJ gang, which is a sprightly and unpretentious take on various traditional styles. The various CDs have certain thematic threads to them. *T'Ain't Nobody's Bizness* is a collection of band favourites, many of them relatively unfamiliar to non-specialists (including pieces as diverse as 'Kater Street Rag' and 'Along The Road To Gundagai'!); *Manchester Delighted* aims to replicate one of their characteristic live sets; and the Jazzology disc might be a calling card for the band for American audiences. *Moments Like This*, the most recent, is a collection of some of their most-requested numbers.

The band play with infectious and smiling enthusiasm. Perhaps we could do without some of their vocals, and they could use a genuinely outstanding soloist (Terry Brunt's loveable trombone shenanigans aren't quite what we mean), but it's hard to fault the spirit of the playing. Our favourite is the set with Marion Montgomery: she sings on six tracks, and does the job so beguilingly that she brings a touch of class to the occasion which Mart's mob may not necessarily need, but it does help matters along.

Claudio Roditi (born 1946)

TRUMPET, FLUGELHORN, VOCAL

Born in Rio, he studied at Berklee in 1970, then moved to New York in 1976. Worked frequently with Paquito D'Rivera, but is also heard in numerous sideman roles and big-band duties, playing a mix of Latin and unadorned hard-bop styles.

★★ **Two Of Swords**
Candid CCD 79504 *Roditi; Jay Ashby (tb); Edward Simon, Danilo Perez (p); Nilsson Matta, David Finck (b); Duduka Fonseca, Akira Tana (d). 9/90.*

Roditi's bright tone and fizzing delivery have served him well in several bands. This one isn't terrible, but it's just a potboiler. Roditi splits the session between a 'jazz' and a 'Brazilian' group, and both perform in much the same direction, although the Brazilian band has Ashby in the front line to add some tonal colour. Roditi's fat-toned flugelhorn gets a little more exposure than usual, but the music lacks much character. Another CD which doesn't really justify its 72-minute length.

★★(★) **Milestones**
Candid CCD 79515 *Roditi; Paquito D'Rivera (cl, as); Kenny Barron (p); Ray Drummond (b); Ben Riley (d). 11/90.*

An absolutely top-class band with everybody feeling fine and playing hard – yet the results are, as with the record above, vaguely disappointing. One can't fault the virtuosity of either of the horn-players – D'Rivera, especially, gets off some breathtaking flights on both alto and clarinet – but the final impression is of too many notes and too much said. The jam-session material doesn't assist matters much – the ballad, 'Brussels In The Rain', is the only departure from familiarity – and with playing time at almost 70 minutes it does start to sound like too much of a good thing. The live recording is clear if a little dry.

★★★(★) **Free Wheelin'**
Reservoir RSRCD 136 *Roditi; Andres Boiarsky (ss, ts); Nick Brignola (ss, bs); Mark Soskin (p); Buster Williams (b); Chip White (d). 7/94.*

★★★ **Samba – Manhattan Style**
Reservoir RSRCD 139 *Roditi; Jay Ashby (tb); Greg Abate (as); Andres Boiarsky (ss, ts); Helio Alves (p); John Lee (b); Duduka Fonseca (d). 5/95.*

Roditi doing a tribute to Lee Morgan sounds like a recipe for overcooking it. Yet *Free Wheelin'* comes close to being exactly the classic album the trumpeter might have in him. This is the best band he's had in the studio: Boiarsky is a heavyweight, and the rhythm section, especially the inimitable Williams, are right there with the horns. But it's Roditi's concentration of his own powers that impresses here. Without trading in any of his fire, he keeps all his solos tight and impeccable, which makes flare-ups like those on 'Trapped' and 'The Joker' all the more exciting. 'The Sidewinder' follows the original arrangement – in his notes Roditi confesses that he couldn't see any point in messing around with the original charts – and still sounds entirely different from Morgan's original. Nine of the ten tunes are from Morgan's own pen, but the new twist on 'A Night In Tunisia' – with trumpet overdubs and a two-soprano section – is a startling departure. Brignola guests on three and is a welcome visitor. Still slightly exhausting at 70 minutes, but a good one.

Samba – Manhattan Style is a notch lower, with a less impressive cast. The gentler aspects of Roditi's playing bring lustre to pretty melodies such as 'Fone Da Saudade', and the sweetness of samba infects the best of the music, although one feels that there's too much padding, and the studio sound does nothing for the lower frequencies.

★★(★) **Double Standards**
Reservoir RSR 148 *As above, except add Hendrik Meurkens (hca), Gil Goldstein (p), Marty Ashby (g), David Finck (b), Chip White (d). 9–10/96.*

Double Standards is a disappointment after the last couple of records. Cut as a pure blowing session in the studio, with standbys like 'Bye Bye Blackbird' and 'So What' in the programme, there's nothing wrong with the music but it has no pressing need to exist; only Roditi's shy vocal on 'Desafinado' breaks out of the general blandness.

***** Three For One**
Nagel Heyer 2028 *Roditi; Klaus Ignatzek (p); Jean-Louis Rassinfosse (b).* 11/02.

In temperate surroundings, Roditi turns in a graceful performance. The programme is mostly originals, shared between trumpeter and pianist, and there's an agreeably cool and patient demeanour to the playing, though no shortage of sunshine: Ignatzek's 'Avocado' makes a buoyant finale.

Red Rodney (1927–94)

TRUMPET

His given name was Robert Chudnick, which wasn't quite the right handle, nor was his shock of ginger hair quite the right look for the early days of bebop. And yet Red was one of the most responsive trumpeters Charlie Parker worked with. Unfortunately he also responded to and imitated Bird's other habits, and Rodney's career was punctuated with narcotics problems. To his credit, he put these behind him and sustained a second career right through to his death in the mid-'90s.

***** First Sessions: Volume 3**
Prestige PCD 24116 *Rodney; Jimmy Ford (as); Phil Raphael (p); Phil Leshin (b); Phil Brown (d).* 9/51.

Rodney was the red-haired Jewish boy in Charlie Parker's happiest band. Though diffident about his own talents, the young Philadelphian had done his learning up on the stand, playing with the likes of Jimmy Dorsey while still a teenager. Rodney was perhaps the first white trumpeter to take up the challenge of bebop, which he played with a crackling, slightly nervy quality. It sat well with Parker, and Rodney was an integral part of Bird's quintet in 1950 and 1951, having first worked with him slightly earlier than that. Rodney was not a prolific recording artist, and his career succumbed from time to time to one of the more common jeopardies of life on the road, but there is some excellent stuff on disc. The early Prestige material dates from Rodney's time in the Parker band, and it has the nervy exuberance you'd expect. Ford is a very average player, and each number seems to mark time when he solos.

*****(*) Red Rodney Quintets**
Fantasy 24758 *Rodney; Jimmy Ford (as); Ira Sullivan (ts); Phil Raphael, Norman Simmons (p); Phil Leshin, Victor Sproles (b); Phil Brown, Roy Haynes (d).* 52, 55.

In our last edition we lamented the absence of Rodney's best work, the 1955 *Modern Music From Chicago.* It now forms half of this valuable set, along with a slightly less compelling release, *Broadway.* The trumpeter is in great form on the first set, blowing intricate and deeply felt solos, especially on his own 'Red Is Blue'. Roy Haynes helped invent bebop rhythm, and he sounds totally in command of the idiom here, with Ira Sullivan and Norman Simmons filling out the harmony richly.

The earlier group has a much less distinguished line-up (most of them called Phil) and though there are some good things – 'Red Wig' and 'Coogan's Bluff' – there is nothing to match the delightful muted solo on 'Laura' which remains the outstanding moment on *Chicago.* If you buy only one Red Rodney record, this could be the one.

*****(*) Red Giant**
Steeplechase SCCD 31233 *Rodney; Butch Lacy (p); Hugo Rasmussen (b); Aage Tanggaard (d).* 4/88.

***** One For Bird**
Steeplechase SCCD 31238 *Rodney; Dick Oatts (as); Garry Dial (p); Jay Anderson (b); John Riley (d).* 7/88.

****(*) Red Snapper**
Steeplechase SCCD 31252 *As above.* 7/88.

Nowhere was bebop accorded higher sentimental status than in Scandinavia. House bands and rhythm sections have excellent chops (the same is true of Japanese players) but with a strongly authentic 'feel' as well. Of these 1988 sessions *Red Giant* is undoubtedly the best, with Rasmussen, Tanggaard and the rough-diamond Lacy all contributing substantially. Compare the versions of 'Greensleeves' and a curiously but effectively tempoed 'Giant Steps' with those on *Red Snapper,* which seem merely curious. The original material on *Red Snapper* is perhaps more interesting, but there's little doubt where Rodney's heart lies. At 60-plus, he sounded chastened but undeterred, and his playing reveals a depth of reference that was seldom there previously.

***** The Tivoli Session**
Steeplechase SCCD 37025 *Rodney; Dick Oatts (ts); Garry Dial (p); Jay Anderson (b); James Madison (d).* 89.

Notable largely for a wonderful medley of 'Greensleeves' and John Coltrane's 'Giant Steps', this is a long and for the most part successful foray in Rodney's late, sophisticated style. The more demanding the material – like Cedar Walton's 'Ugetsu' – the more comfortable the band manage to sound. Red was still reliving the great days of bebop, as the frequent Diz and Bird quotes suggest, but he managed to broker something more contemporary as well, and this is one of the freshest and most stimulating of the later records.

Adam Rogers

GUITAR

Well-respected sideman with impressive credentials making an overdue debut as leader. He is a charter member of fusion group Lost Tribe.

***** Art Of The Invisible**
Criss Cross 1223 *Rogers; Edward Simon (p); Scott Colley (b); Clarence Penn (d).* 12/01.

*****(*) Allegory**
Criss Cross 1242 *As above.* 12/02.

Like many a debut CD, *Art Of The Invisible* suffers from trying to do too much, or at least to show how many different dimensions there are to Rogers's playing and writing. Most listeners will be aware of his skills already, so the drastic shifts from relatively accommodating blues-based themes to the freedom of 'The Aleph' is more off-putting than impressive. That said, the guitarist's coming out is more than welcome, since his considerable light has been under a bushel for some years. He has assembled a like-minded band, with a nicely rugged sound, and has led them through some challenging territory. The high-energy 'In Broad Daylight' is among the best things here, with some ferocious playing from the leader, but he's probably at his best on the more brooding numbers like 'Cathedral' and the closing 'The Unvanquished'. A very impressive start.

Wisely, Rogers stays with the same line-up for *Allegory*, which in every way is a more coherent and polished effort. Perhaps it lacks the runaway energy and unfettered emotion of its predecessor, but it's a more successful album for that. 'Phyringia', 'Orpheus' and 'Purpose' are very ambitious pieces, played at durations that demand a great deal of the players' attention (though there may be an edit in 'Purpose'; the mood and timbre shift subtly and unaccountably unless two performances have been digitally spliced). Simon keeps out of the guitarist's way. He's an old-fashioned player in lots of ways but still capable of adding something to the fusion-driven material.

Rogers has a long career ahead of him. These records, and his sideman work, already represent a considerable achievement. We're sure he'll build on it.

Paul Rogers (born 1956)

BASS

British free-music bassist and improviser, now based in France.

**** Listen

Emanem 4078 *Rogers (b solo).* 10/89–5/99.

Rogers stands squarely in a formidable tradition of European bass improvisers, enormously skilful with and without the bow. His pair of discs for Rare Music have become as scarce as their label-name suggests, but Martin Davidson's initiative in releasing this set on Emanem is very welcome. It opens with almost 40 minutes of unflagging invention in a single piece recorded at a French concert. Rogers makes the bass sound as it is, a big, resonant, capacious instrument. He isn't shy of melodic patterns or conventional timbres, although he makes these elements part of a rushing flow which evolves so quickly that it asks the listener to be very alert, and there's a notable skill in avoiding prearranged figures. Two smaller pieces, encores possibly, spin off into smaller orbits. Then comes music from a London pub gig of ten years earlier: same man, but a four- rather than a five-string instrument; less well-recorded, but here the musician engages in an abrasive, even violent monologue. This can stand with the best solo-bass albums.

Shorty Rogers (1924–94)

TRUMPET, FLUGELHORN

Milton Rogers came from Massachusetts, but he is forever seen as a kingpin figure in the West Coast jazz of the '50s and after, scoring several of the classic big-band dates of the period and subsequently writing a lot of music for TV and Hollywood. His own playing was lithe if unremarkable, but his love for jazz was demonstrated by his final years, spent in various reunion editions of his old outfits.

CORE COLLECTION

**** The Sweetheart Of Sigmund Freud

Giant Steps GIST 009 2CD *Rogers; Conrad Gozzo, Maynard Ferguson, Pete Candoli, John Howell, Ray Linn (t); Harry Betts, Bob Enevoldsen, Jimmy Knepper, Milt Bernhart (tb); John Graas (frhn); Art Pepper, Bud Shank, Jimmy Giuffre, Bob Cooper, Bill Holman, Bill Perkins (reeds); Marty Paich, Russ Freeman, Hampton Hawes (p); Gene Englund (tba); Curtis Counce, Don Bagley, Joe Mondragon (b); Shelly Manne (d); also orchestras led by Woody Herman, Red Norvo, Stan Kenton, Maynard Ferguson, Louie Bellson and Howard Rumsey.* 5/46–7/53.

Much influenced by the Davis–Mulligan–Lewis *Birth Of The Cool*, and even claiming a revisionist role in the creation of that movement, Shorty Rogers turned its basic instrumentation and lapidary arranging into a vehicle for relaxedly swinging jazz of a high order. His arrangements are among the best of the time. If they lack the gelid precision that Lewis and Mulligan brought to *Birth Of The Cool*, Rogers's charts combine the same intricate texture with an altogether looser jazz feel. While never an especially memorable soloist himself, he could call on the top players of the day on a regular basis.

Rogers seemed to be in the studios all the time in the '50s and early '60s and, although his Atlantic albums are currently out of circulation, several of his RCA sets have made a comeback. The classic *Cool And Crazy* sessions (alias *The Big Shorty Rogers Express*) have now been gathered in on this set, along with another disc of early Rogers charts for Herman, Norvo and Kenton, plus a few later dates with Ferguson and Rumsey. It is a quite irresistible package, excellently remastered and with a fine sleeve-note. The tracks which made up the original ten-inch *Cool And Crazy* still act as a benchmark in the appreciation of West Coast jazz, and their energy and ingenuity seem completely undimmed a half-century on.

***(*) Shorty Rogers And His Giants

RCA 74321 60989-2 *Rogers; Milt Bernhart (tb); John Graas (frhn); Art Pepper (as); Jimmy Giuffre (ts); Hampton Hawes (p); Joe Mondragon (b); Gene Englund (tba); Shelly Manne (d).* 1/53.

**** Shorty Rogers Courts The Count

RCA 74321 63818-2 *Rogers; Conrad Gozzo, Maynard Ferguson, Harry 'Sweets' Edison, Clyde Reasinger, Pete Candoli (t); Milt Bernhart, Harry Betts, Bob Enevoldsen (tb); John Graas (frhn); Herb Geller, Bud Shank (as); Bob Cooper, Jimmy Giuffre (ts, bs); Zoot Sims, Bill Holman (ts); Bobby Gordon (bs); Marty Paich (p); Curtis Counce (b); Shelly Manne (d).* 2–3/54.

*** Collaboration

RCA ND 74398 *Rogers; Milt Bernhart (tb); Bud Shank (as, f); Bob Cooper (ts, ob); Jimmy Giuffre (bs); André Previn (p); Al Hendrickson (g); Joe Mondragon (b); Shelly Manne (d).* 3–6/54.

***(*) Wherever The Five Winds Blow

RCA ND 74399 *Rogers; Jimmy Giuffre (ts); Lou Levy (p); Ralph Pena (b); Larry Bunker (d).* 7/56.

***(*) Plays Richard Rodgers

RCA 74321 433882 *Rogers; Conte Candoli, Pete Candoli, Harry 'Sweets' Edison, Maynard Ferguson, Al Porcino (t); Milt Bernhart, George Roberts, Bob Burgess, John Haliburton, Frank Rosolino (tb); Jimmy Giuffre (cl, bs); Herb Geller (as); Bill Holman, Jack Montrose, Bill Perkins (ts); Pepper Adams (bs); Pete Jolly (p); Sam Rica (tba); Red Mitchell (b); Stan Levey (d).* 1–4/57.

***** Portrait Of Shorty**

RCA 74321 61105-2 *Rogers; Al Porcino, Conrad Gozzo, Don Fagerquist, Conte Candoli, Pete Candoli (t); Frank Rosolino, George Roberts, Harry Betts, Bob Enevoldsen (tb); Herb Geller (as); Bob Cooper (ts, bs); Richie Kamuca, Jack Montrose (ts); Pepper Adams (bs); Lou Levy (p); Monty Budwig (b); Stan Levey (d).* 7–8/57.

***** Gigi In Jazz**

RCA 74321 125882 *Rogers; Bill Holman (ts); Larry Bunker (vib); Pete Jolly (p); Buddy Clark, Ralph Pena (b); Mel Lewis (d).* 1/58.

***** Chances Are, It Swings**

RCA 74321 433902 *Rogers; Don Fagerquist, Pete Candoli, Conte Candoli, Ollie Mitchell, Ray Triscari, Al Porcino (t); Bob Enevoldsen (vtb); Harry Betts, Dick Nash, Kenny Shroyer (tb); Paul Horn, Bud Shank (cl, as, f); Bill Holman, Richie Kamuca (ts); Chuck Gentry (bs); Gene Estes, Red Norvo (vib); Pete Jolly (p); Howard Roberts, Barney Kessel (g); Joe Mondragon, Monty Budwig (b); Mel Lewis (d).* 12/58.

***** The Wizard Of Oz**

RCA 74321 453792 *Rogers; Don Fagerquist, Al Porcino, Conte Candoli (t); Harry Betts, Kenny Shroyer, Frank Rosolino (tb); Bob Enevoldsen (vtb); Bud Shank (f, as); Herb Geller (as, ts); Bill Holman (ts); Jimmy Giuffre (bs, cl); Larry Bunker (vib); Pete Jolly (p); Barney Kessel (g); Joe Mondragon (b); Mel Lewis (d).* 2/59.

***** The Swinging Nutcracker**

RCA 74321 421212 *Rogers; John Audino, Conte Candoli, Ray Triscari, Jimmy Zito (t); Harry Betts, Frank Rosolino, Kenny Shroyer (tb); Jimmy Giuffre (cl); Art Pepper (as); Bud Shank (as, f); Richie Kamuca, Harold Land, Bill Perkins, Bill Holman (ts); Chuck Gentry (bs); Pete Jolly, Lou Levy (p); Joe Mondragon (b); Frank Capp, Mel Lewis (d).* 5/60.

*****(*) An Invisible Orchard**

RCA 74321 49560-2 *Rogers; Ray Triscari, Ollie Mitchell, Stu Williamson, Conte Candoli, Al Porcino (t); Harry Betts, Frank Rosolino (tb); Kenny Shroyer, Marshall Cran, George Roberts (btb); Bud Shank, Paul Horn (as); Bill Perkins, Harold Land (ts); Bill Hood, Chuck Gentry (bs); Pete Jolly (p); Emil Richards (vib); Red Mitchell (b); Mel Lewis (d).* 2–4/61.

Of the subsequent sessions, there is frankly little to choose between them, each built around some sort of concept, most of them obvious from the titles. The *Collaboration* was with André Previn, who is co-credited. *Wherever The Five Winds Blow* is a small-group date of sheer finesse, the quintet breezing over the material like a polished sailboat. *Chances Are, It Swings* is a mixed bag of orchestral charts, while *Gigi In Jazz* returns to the small-group format. We have so far been spared (shame!) the reappearance of *Shorty Rogers Meets Tarzan* from the same period. In a way, this music was as much cursed as illuminated by its Californian sunshine. Revisionist critics looked down their noses at it for many years, claiming all sorts of outrages: clinical, studio-bound playing, smoothness over passion, the suppression of more radical Californian jazz, etc. At this distance, the virtues of the music now seem more apparent, as they are in the New York jazz of three decades earlier. Rogers had the wit to turn many of the less promising tunes into tongue-in-cheek set-pieces that are not so far from the more irreverent repertory excursions of more recent years. Rather than creating a climate for memorable improvising, Rogers stitched the solos into a detailed fabric. Each man was usually called on for no more than a few appropriate bars, and the result was a language of excellence in miniature. In players such as Shank, Holman, the Candolis, Bernhart and Cooper, Rogers had performers who could eat up these opportunities, and it spawned a discipline which today's West Coast jazz – via the numerous 'occasional' big bands that still record for labels such as Sea Breeze – continues to work from. While the music has some period feel, its vitality survives.

Later additions to the range have all but completed RCA's Rogers output in reissue form (we're still waiting for *Tarzan* though!). The original *Shorty Rogers And His Giants* is by a fresh-sounding nonet, and Shorty sounds as if he's raring to go with his charts. *Courts The Count*, though, is better still, a great favourite of ours, and sounding better than ever in this transfer. Shorty scored nine Basie chestnuts, such as 'Taps Miller', 'Tickle Toe' and 'Jump For Me', and somehow managed to pay homage without once sounding like the Basie band itself. Check, for instance, the brooding 'Topsy', a brilliant bit of recasting. *Portrait Of Shorty* is more routine, but the playing remains full of sparkle.

An Invisible Orchard collects three sessions for an album that was never released at the time: an ambitious suite of compositions that remain in the Rogers pocket but find him clearly looking for new directions within his accustomed style. The opening 'Inner Space' is certainly one of his most challenging efforts, a maze of interwoven lines that still hold the trademark Rogers clarity and lightness. Most of the eight pieces feel like transitional music, between the sun-soaked optimism of his earlier charts and a darker – or at least more abstruse – feel. There are hints, for instance, of a John Lewis influence, most obviously in the MJQ-like opening of 'La Valse'. An intriguing departure which RCA shelved at the time of its production.

***** Bossa Nova / Jazz Waltz**

Collectables COL-CD-7504 *Rogers; Joe Burnett, Ollie Mitchell (t); Ken Shroyer, Richard Leith (tb); Paul Horn, Bud Shank (f, as); Bill Hood (bsx); Larry Bunker (vib); Pete Jolly, Lou Levy (p); Laurindo Almeida (g); Joe Mondragon (b); Shelly Manne, Mel Lewis (d); Milt Holland, Emil Richards, Chico Guerrero (perc).* 62.

This wraps up the pair of albums Shorty made for Reprise, one a set of bossa nova tunes, the second a rather less fashionable set of themes all played in three. While both were clearly conceived by the company as not much more than quota quickies, it was typical of Rogers to introduce all sorts of interesting touches, even into what was quickly to become a hackneyed bossa nova concept: try his delightful version of 'One Note Samba'. The waltz collection is a little less inventive-but still has plenty of inimitable Rogers touches, particularly in the brass-scoring (and the use of Bill Hood's bass sax). Excellent remastering.

*****(*) America The Beautiful**

Candid CCD 79510 *Rogers; Bud Shank (as); Conte Candoli (t); Bill Perkins (bs, ts, ss); Bob Cooper (ts); Pete Jolly (p): Monty Budwig (b); Larance Marable (d).* 8/91.

***** Eight Brothers**

Candid CCD 79521 *Rogers; Conte Candoli (t, flhn); Bud Shank (as); Bill Perkins (ts, ss, bs); Bob Cooper (ts); Pete Jolly (p); Monty Budwig (b); Larance Marable (d).* 1/92.

There is then something of a hiatus. For much of this period, Rogers concentrated on film music. His '80s comeback found him in strong voice and, alongside Bud Shank, in musically conducive company. *America The Beautiful* is certainly the pick of these. Shank's solo intro to 'Lotus Bud' is huskily beautiful and is surpassed only by Bill Perkins's eerily cadenced soprano solo on another of Bud's tunes 'Un Poco Loco'. 'Here's That Old Martian Again' continues a series of similar conceits, done in reassuringly un-alien blue rather than green, but with a hint of 'Blue In Green' in the shift across the line. The Lighthouse All Stars play beyond themselves, with big credits to drummer Marable. Recommended.

The other one is rather less interesting. Rogers doesn't always sound a naturally confident player alongside the other Lighthouse chapter members, and his solos on these latter-day recordings are genial but rarely memorable.

Bryce Rohde

PIANO

Originally from Adelaide, Rohde co-founded the Australian Jazz Quintet and subsequently moved to the US in 1965, although he regularly returns to Australia and sometimes records there.

***** Turn Right At New South Wales**
Music In The Vines (no number) *Rohde; Bruce Cale (b); Lee Charlton (d).* 00.

Rohde's piano is an interesting agglomeration of styles, from Tristano to Bill Evans, and he admits to a distinct George Russell influence. This likeable if thinly recorded set has plenty of ideas in music which is primarily ruminative but has some darker and surprisingly oblique currents running through it, even though the titles suggest a paean to the Australian big country. The interested might also like to investigate, on the same rather homemade-looking label, *Short Way Home*, a love set from 1978, and *Always Come Back Here*, a duo session with Cale.

Dennis Rollins

TROMBONE

Bad British 'boneman.

***** Badbone**
Rae CD 1001 *Rollins; Jay Phelps (t); Nick Ramm, Alex Wilson, Kwame Yeboah (ky); David Okumu (g); Courtney Thomas (b); Donald Gamble (perc); Mo Mason (v); other vocalists.* n.d.

***** Make Your Move**
Sound CD 1002 *Rollins; Benet McLean (ky); Johnny Heyes (g); Peter Martin (b); Perry Melius (d).* n.d.

Rollins has made a substantial career for himself as the Fred Wesley of British rock and soul, adding brassy funk and soul to a whole range of albums. His own work hasn't suffered, though there's a journeyman quality to his albums to date which doesn't reflect the sophistication of the live set. The Badbone record is agreeable, even if there isn't much hardcore improvisation to get your teeth into. The 'Badbone Theme' is great fun and there are a couple of strong, well-developed tracks in '(I Say ...) It's Alright' and 'Red Cent'. Keyboards predominate over a sliding, funky bass. Otherwise, a fairly routine outing that won't creep back on to your player too often.

The second album is brighter and mostly better. Ironically, for such a fine live player, Rollins's finest moment is on 'Soul Journey' where he's overdubbed several times. Less successful is an attempt to put a jazz spin on Tracey Chapman's 'Fast Car'. The rhythm guys are good and tight and there's mercifully little vocal input. Good things are sure to come from Dennis's band, though for the most part they're not translating to CD.

Sonny Rollins (born 1930)

TENOR AND SOPRANO SAXOPHONES

Born Theodore Walter Rollins, the New York saxophonist recorded as a teenager with Bud Powell and J. J. Johnson, later with Miles Davis and Thelonious Monk, before working in Max Roach's group for two years. Since 1957 he has been his own leader. Recording associations have been with Prestige, Blue Note, RCA, Impulse! and, since 1972, Milestone. Two famous sabbaticals from public appearances (1959–61 and 1968–71) have been the only interruptions in a prolific and inspirational career in concert and on record. Although famously inscrutable at times, Rollins's music has been – in its virtuoso command of the horn and in the calibre of his improvising – enormously influential.

*****(*) Sonny Rollins With The Modern Jazz Quartet**
Original Jazz Classics OJC 011 *Rollins; Miles Davis, Kenny Drew, John Lewis (p); Percy Heath (b); Art Blakey, Kenny Clarke, Roy Haynes (d).* 1/51–10/53.

***** Moving Out**
Original Jazz Classics OJC 058 *Rollins; Kenny Dorham (t); Thelonious Monk, Elmo Hope (p); Percy Heath, Tommy Potter (b); Art Blakey, Art Taylor (d).* 8–10/54.

Rollins's most important early session is with Miles Davis on *Bags' Groove* (OJC 245). The nine 1951 tracks on OJC 011 are cursory bop singles, and the MJQ – despite the headline billing – appear on only three tracks, in a meeting that took place a second time on an Atlantic album some years later. One track, 'I Know', has the novelty of Miles Davis on piano. *Moving Out* is more substantial, though it still stands as a stereotypical blowing date, even with a single track – 'More Than You Know' – from a session with Monk. The most interesting contributor here is probably Hope, whose off-centre lyricism still turns heads.

*****(*) Work Time**
Original Jazz Classics OJC 007 *Rollins; Ray Bryant (p); George Morrow (b); Max Roach (d).* 12/55.

*****(*) Sonny Rollins Plus 4**
Original Jazz Classics OJC 243 *Rollins; Clifford Brown (t); Richie Powell (p); George Morrow (b); Max Roach (d).* 3/56.

****** Tenor Madness**
Original Jazz Classics OJC 124 *Rollins; John Coltrane (ts); Red Garland (p); Paul Chambers (b); Philly Joe Jones (d).* 5/56.

*****(*) Sonny Rollins Plays For Bird**
Original Jazz Classics OJC 214 *Rollins; Kenny Dorham (t); Wade Legge (p); George Morrow (b); Max Roach (d).* 10/56.

****** Tour De Force**
Original Jazz Classics OJC 095 *Rollins; Kenny Drew (p); George Morrow (b); Max Roach (d); Earl Coleman (v).* 12/56.

*** Sonny Rollins Volume 1

Blue Note 81542 *Rollins; Donald Byrd (t); Wynton Kelly (p); Gene Ramey (b); Max Roach (d).* 12/56.

An astounding year's work on record. Rollins was still a new and relatively unheralded star when he was working through this series of sessions, and – in the aftermath of Parker's death – jazz itself had an open throne. There was a vast distance between Rollins and the tenorman who was winning most of the polls of the period, Stan Getz, but though Sonny evaded the open-faced romanticism and woozy melancholy associated with the Lester Young school, he wasn't much of a Parkerite, either. Rollins used the headlong virtuosity of bop to more detached, ironical ends. The opening track on *Work Time* is a blast through 'There's No Business Like Show Business', which prefigures many of his future choices of material. Parker would have smiled, but he'd never have played it this way. Still, Rollins's mastery of the tenor was already complete by this time, with a wide range of tones and half-tones, a confident variation of dynamics, and an ability to phrase with equal strength of line in any part of a solo. If he is often tense, as if in witness to the power of his own creative flow, then the force of the music is multiplied by this tension. The most notable thing about the records is how dependent they are on Rollins himself: Roach aside, whose magnificent drum parts offer a pre-echo of what Elvin Jones would start to develop with John Coltrane, the sidemen are often almost dispensable. It is Rollins who has to be heard.

If *Work Time* is just a little sketchy in parts, that is only in comparison with what follows. *Plus 4* is one of Rollins's happiest sessions. With both horn-players in mercurial form, and Roach sensing the greatness of the band he is basically in charge of, the music unfolds at a terrific clip but has a sense of relaxation which the tenor man would seldom approach later in the decade. His own piece, 'Pent-Up House', has an improvisation which sets the stage for some of his next advances: unhurried, thoughtful, he nevertheless plays it with biting immediacy. *Tenor Madness* features Coltrane on, alas, only one track, the title-tune, and it isn't quite the grand encounter one might have wished for: but the rest of the record, with Miles Davis's rhythm section, includes surging Rollins on 'Paul's Pal' and 'The Most Beautiful Girl In The World'.

Plays For Bird, though it includes a medley of tunes associated with Parker, is no more Bird-like than the other records, and a reading of 'I've Grown Accustomed To Her Face' establishes Rollins's oddly reluctant penchant for a tender ballad. *Sonny Rollins* ended the year in somewhat more desultory fashion – the session seems to return to more conventional horns-and-rhythm bebop – but *Tour De Force*, recorded two weeks earlier, is almost as good as *Colossus*, with the ferocious abstractions of 'B Swift' and 'B Quick' contrasting with the methodical, almost surgical destruction of 'Sonny Boy'. The OJC reissues are all remastered in splendid sound.

CORE COLLECTION

♛ **** Saxophone Colossus

Original Jazz Classics OJC 291 *Rollins; Tommy Flanagan (p); Doug Watkins (b); Max Roach (d).*

The undisputed masterpiece from this period is *Saxophone Colossus* and, although Rollins plays with brilliant invention throughout the above albums, he's at his most consistent on this disc. 'St Thomas', his irresistible calypso melody, appears here for the first time, and there is a ballad of unusual bleakness in 'You Don't Know What Love Is', as well as a rather sardonic walk through 'Moritat' (alias 'Mack The Knife'). But 'Blue Seven', as analysed in a contemporary piece by Gunther Schuller, became celebrated as a thematic masterpiece, where all the joints and moving parts of a spontaneous improvisation attain the pristine logic of a composition. If the actual performance is much less forbidding than this suggests, thanks in part to the simplicity of the theme, it surely justifies Schuller's acclaim.

***(*) Way Out West

Original Jazz Classics OJC 337 *Rollins; Ray Brown (b); Shelly Manne (d).* 3/57.

***(*) Sonny Rollins Volume 2

Blue Note 97809 *Rollins; J. J. Johnson (tb); Horace Silver, Thelonious Monk (p); Percy Heath (b); Art Blakey (d).* 4/57.

***(*) The Sound Of Sonny

Original Jazz Classics OJC 029 *Rollins; Sonny Clark (p); Percy Heath (b); Roy Haynes (d).* 6/57.

**** Newk's Time

Blue Note 76752 *Rollins; Wynton Kelly (p); Doug Watkins (b); Philly Joe Jones (d).* 9/57.

Rollins continued his astonishing run of records with scarcely a pause for breath. A visit to Los Angeles paired him with Brown and Manne on a session which, if it occasionally dips into a kind of arch cleverness, features some superb interplay between the three men, with Rollins turning 'I'm An Old Cowhand' into a jovial invention. The CD edition includes three alternative takes. One of the compelling things about this sequence is the difference in drummer from session to session: Blakey's inimitable pattern of rolls and giant cymbal strokes sounds, for once, a little inappropriate, with Philly Joe Jones using the same kind of drama to far more effect on *Newk's Time*. The undervalued player here, though, is Haynes, whose playing on *The Sound Of Sonny* is ingeniously poised and crisp. The Blue Note Volume 2 finds Rollins a little cramped by his surroundings, but Johnson's sober playing is a far more apposite accompaniment than Byrd's was, its deadpan line a wry rejoinder to the tenor parts. The new RVG edition is very punchy. *The Sound Of Sonny* is unexpectedly cursory in its treatment of some of the themes: after the longer disquisitions which Rollins had accustomed himself to making, these three- and four-minute tracks sound bitten off. But the grandeur of Rollins's improvisations on 'Just In Time' and 'Toot-Toot-Tootsie' is compressed rather than reduced, and a solo 'It Could Happen To You', though a little snatched at, celebrates the breadth of his sound. We are somewhat divided on the merits of *Newk's Time*. If Rollins is arguably self-absorbed on some of the studio session, the extraordinary motivic development of 'Surrey With The Fringe On Top' is one of his most powerful creations, and 'Blues For Philly Joe' takes the work done on 'Blue Seven' a step further. The new RVG edition, as with other Blue Note classics of the period, dusts off this music beautifully and restores its power anew.

CORE COLLECTION

♛ **** A Night At The Village Vanguard

Blue Note 99795 2CD *Rollins; Donald Bailey, Wilbur Ware (b); Pete LaRoca, Elvin Jones (d).* 11/57.

The live material, originally cherry-picked for a single peerless LP, has now been stretched across two CDs, and in its latest incarnation the in-person feel is heightened by the addition of some more of Sonny's announcements. In the past we felt that the abundance of this material slightly checked the power-packed feel of the original LP, but in the new RVG edition the sound is extraordinarily deep and immediate, and the sheer impact of Rollins on top form is close to overwhelming – hence our upgrading to crown status, since this is a model example of a classic record given its proper treatment. Working with only bass and drums throughout leads Rollins into areas of freedom which bop never allowed, and while his free-spiritedness is checked by his ruthless self-examination, its rigour makes his music uniquely powerful in jazz. On the two versions of 'Softly, As In A Morning Sunrise' or in the muscular exuberance of 'Old Devil Moon', traditional bop-orientated improvising reaches a peak of expressive power and imagination. Overall, these are records which demand a place in any collection.

***** The Essential Sonny Rollins On Riverside**
Riverside FCD-60-020 *Rollins; Kenny Dorham (t); Ernie Henry (as); Sonny Clark, Thelonious Monk, Hank Jones, Wynton Kelly (p); Percy Heath, Paul Chambers, Oscar Pettiford (b); Max Roach, Roy Haynes (d); Abbey Lincoln (v).* 56–58.

***** The Best Of: The Blue Note Years**
Blue Note 93203 *As the Blue Note albums above.* 56–57.

****** The Complete Prestige Recordings**
Prestige 4407 7CD *As the appropriate discs above.* 51–56.

Each of the two best-ofs scores lower marks only because the original albums are indispensable. But the Riverside set does include tracks which are otherwise under the leadership of Dorham or Monk. The *Complete Prestige* set, on the other hand, is an abundant feast for those who'd prefer to have the nine original albums compressed to a seven-disc edition.

*****(*) The Freedom Suite**
Original Jazz Classics OJC 067 *Rollins; Oscar Pettiford (b); Max Roach (d).* 2/58.

*****(*) The Sound Of Sonny / Freedom Suite**
Riverside CDJZD 008 *Rollins; Sonny Clark (p); Percy Heath, Paul Chambers, Oscar Pettiford (b); Roy Haynes, Max Roach (d).* 6/57–2/58.

***** Sonny Rollins And The Contemporary Leaders**
Original Jazz Classics OJC 340 *Rollins; Hampton Hawes (p); Victor Feldman (vib); Barney Kessel (g); Leroy Vinnegar (b); Shelly Manne (d).* 10/58.

Although we have been taken to task over this assertion, we still aver that Rollins hasn't shown a great deal of interest in composition. Some of his early bop-orientated themes remain in the repertory, but he has based most of his improvising around other people's tunes for much of the past 40 years. Nevertheless, 'The Freedom Suite' takes a stab at an extended work, although its simple structure makes it more of a sketch for an improvisation than anything else. The engineers caught his sound with particular immediacy on this date, and it's more a celebration of his tone and dynamic variation than a coherent, programmatic statement (Orrin Keepnews's sleeve-notes seem deliberately to fudge the directness of whatever Rollins was trying to say about black freedom). A somewhat neglected record, and one worth further pondering as regards its importance in the Rollins canon. The (British) Riverside CD usefully couples both *The Freedom Suite* and *The Sound Of Sonny*. Despite a self-conscious clustering of stars for the *Contemporary Leaders* date, Rollins takes a determined path through one of his most bizarre programmes: 'Rock-A-Bye Your Baby', 'In The Chapel In The Moonlight', 'I've Told Ev'ry Little Star'.

*****(*) Sonny Rollins And The Big Brass**
Verve 557545-2 *Rollins; Nat Adderley (c); Clark Terry, Reunald Jones, Ernie Royal (t); Frank Rehak, Billy Byers, Jimmy Cleveland (tb); Dick Katz, John Lewis (p); Don Butterfield (tba); Henry Grimes, Percy Heath (b); Roy Haynes, Connie Kay, Specs Wright (d).* 7–8/58.

A rare sighting on Verve (actually the original edition came out on Metrojazz), this is coupled with the even more unfamiliar tracks cut with John Lewis, Percy Heath and Connie Kay, which was once a shared LP with a Teddy Edwards session on MGM. Ernie Wilkins's charts are lively and chrome-laden (with no softening reeds and in this very bright transfer, this is sometimes metal-machine music) and, while Rollins responds to them, it's not really the kind of thing he does best. But there are three good trio tracks with Grimes and Wright, and Sonny even essays a solo 'Body And Soul', though it seems comparatively unadventurous.

Rollins had already worked with the MJQ, on a 1953 Prestige date, but these four live tracks are memorably effective – Lewis might be temperamentally very different from Rollins, but his obliquities are so subtly apt and resourceful that it makes one wish they had worked together much more often. And the saxophonist is in huge, hearty voice on each track, 'I'll Follow My Secret Heart' (which Lewis sits out) and 'You Are Too Beautiful' offering almost indecently full-bodied oratory.

*****(*) St Thomas**
Dragon DRCD 229 *Rollins; Henry Grimes (b); Pete LaRoca (d).* 3/59.

Rollins's European tour of 1959 brought about no 'official' recordings, but some radio and concert material has survived. The Dragon set is formidable, although the studio programme which makes up most of the record isn't quite up to the storming concert recording of 'St Thomas' which opens it. A feeling persists throughout these 1959 records that Rollins is coming to the end of a great period, having balanced his own achievements within a straight-bop milieu and realized that, as a singular figure, he is remote from the ideas of interplay within a group (and particularly between horns) which almost everyone else in jazz was pursuing.

*****(*) The Bridge**
RCA 0902 668518-2 *Rollins; Jim Hall (g); Bob Cranshaw (b); Mickey Roker, Ben Riley, Harry T. Saunders (d).* 1–5/62.

***** What's New?**
RCA Victor Gold 74321 796262 *Rollins; Jim Hall (g); Bob Cranshaw (b); Ben Riley (d); Willie Rodriguez, Dennis Charles, Franck Charles, Candido Camero (perc).* 4–5/62.

***** Our Man In Jazz**
RCA 74321 19256-2 *Rollins; Don Cherry (t); Bob Cranshaw, Henry Grimes (b); Billy Higgins (d).* 7/62–2/63.

***** Sonny Meets Hawk**
RCA Victor Gold 74321 748002 *Rollins; Coleman Hawkins (ts); Paul Bley (p); Bob Cranshaw (b); Roy McCurdy (d).* 7/63.

***** The Standard Sonny Rollins**
RCA 74321 22109-2 *Rollins; Herbie Hancock (p); Jim Hall (g); David Izenson, Teddy Smith, Bob Cranshaw (b); Stu Martin, Mickey Roker (d).* 6–7/64.

*****(*) The Complete RCA Victor Recordings**
RCA 09026 68675-2 6CD *As above discs; add Thad Jones (c).* 1/62–9/64.

The saxophonist disappeared for two years, before returning to the studio with a new contract from RCA. The CD era has seen this music emerging in a confusing series of editions and, while RCA have reverted to some of the original LPs for their programming, different territories have released their own editions. This seems to be the picture at the moment, but prospective buyers should be prepared for confusion!

The Bridge started him off. On the face of it, little had changed: though Ornette Coleman's revolution had taken place in the interim, the music sounded much like the old Rollins. But this is his most troubled and troubling period on record. The treatment of 'God Bless The Child' is starkly desolate in feeling, and Rollins plays with a puzzling melancholy throughout. Hall, though, is an unexpectedly fine partner, moving between rhythm and front-line duties with great aplomb and actually finding ways to communicate with the most lofty of soloists. It's an often compelling record as a result.

A new edition of *What's New?* plugs a gap, though this includes some titles from the same sessions as *The Bridge*. 'If Ever I Would Leave You' and especially 'The Night Has A Thousand Eyes' are magisterial Rollins, long, fertile with ideas, and with a typical mating of laziness and urgency; but the almost laborious distortions of 'Jungoso' (with only bass and percussion accompaniment) dismayed many Rollins admirers, and even the first appearance of the crowd favourite, 'Don't Stop The Carnival', now sounds tame.

The meetings with Cherry and Hawkins are both hit and miss. *Our Man In Jazz* was hailed as Rollins's head-on collision with the new thing, as exemplified by Cherry, but hardly anything the two men play bears any relation to the other's music: recorded live, they might as well be on separate stages. On an exhaustively long 'Oleo', the tenorman's pent-up outburst could almost be an expression of rage at the situation. Cherry, peculiarly, sounds like a pre-echo of the older Rollins in his crabby, buzzing solo on 'Doxy'. Three brief studio tracks at the end are an almost irrelevant postscript.

The encounter with Hawkins is much more respectful, even if Rollins seems to be satirizing the older man at some points, notably in his weirdly trilling solo on 'Yesterdays'. Again, though, there's relatively little real interplay, aside from a beautifully modulated 'Summertime'. *The Standard Sonny Rollins* sets him alongside either Jim Hall or Herbie Hancock plus rhythm section: aimless, encumbered by his own genius, Rollins sounds bored with whatever tune he's playing but can't help throwing in the occasional brilliant stroke.

The *Complete* edition spreads all the above music across six CDs, together with the unissued fragments which went to make up *Alternatives* (now seemingly in limbo) and a few other stray items. Awkward though some of the music often is, few sets document a major artist in both triumph and adversity as scrupulously as this; along with the Prestige and Blue Note editions, this is essential to Rollins followers. The original sessions always sounded particularly handsome on original vinyl; as clean as this edition is, it seems to have lost some warmth in the transition.

*****(*) On Impulse!**
Impulse! 051223-2 *Rollins; Ray Bryant (p); Walter Booker (b); Mickey Roker (d).* 7/65.

*****(*) Alfie**
Impulse! 051224-2 *Rollins; Jimmy Cleveland, J. J. Johnson (tb); Phil Woods (as); Oliver Nelson, Bob Ashton (ts); Roger Kellaway (p); Kenny Burrell (g); Walter Booker (b); Frankie Dunlop (d).* 1/66.

*****(*) East Broadway Rundown**
Impulse! 051161-2 *Rollins; Freddie Hubbard (t); Jimmy Garrison (b); Elvin Jones (d).* 5/66.

Rollins's Impulse! records numbered only a handful and they tend to be somewhat overlooked. The new editions of *On Impulse!* and *Alfie*, while not quite demanding a re-evaluation, sound better than ever, and the former in particular, with 'On Green Dolphin Street' and especially 'Three Little Words' transformed into great Rollins set-pieces, is a must. *Alfie* is arguably slighter stuff, with only the main theme – a swaggering line in the tradition of 'Sonnymoon For Two' – offering much meat to the soloist. But this unusual situation for Rollins is one he seems to have enjoyed, and there are some surprisingly unencumbered and witty solos. Nelson, who arranged, had to do little more than keep the horns out of Sonny's way, but it's interesting to conjecture what impact Kellaway – who contributes a handful of intriguing remarks – might have had on the situation. *East Broadway Rundown* still sounds disappointing, with Garrison and Jones no kind of dream match for the leader. The long title-track spends a lot of time going nowhere: only a gnarled 'We Kiss In A Shadow' approaches the real Rollins.

***** Next Album**
Original Jazz Classics OJC 312 *Rollins; George Cables (p); Bob Cranshaw (b); David Lee (d); Arthur Jenkins (perc).* 7/72.

**** Horn Culture**
Original Jazz Classics OJC 314 *Rollins; Walter Davis Jr (p); Yoshiaki Masuo (g); Bob Cranshaw (b); David Lee (d); James Mtume (perc).* 6–7/73.

****(*) The Cutting Edge**
Original Jazz Classics OJC 468 *Rollins; Rufus Harley (bagpipes); Stanley Cowell (p); Yoshiaki Masuo (g); Bob Cranshaw (b); David Lee (d); James Mtume (perc).* 7/74.

**** Nucleus**
Original Jazz Classics OJC 620 *Rollins; Raul De Souza (tb); Bennie Maupin (ts, bcl, lyr); George Duke (p); Bob Cranshaw, Chuck Rainey (b); Roy McCurdy, Eddie Moore (d); James Mtume (perc).* 9/75.

***(*) The Way I Feel**
Original Jazz Classics OJC 666 *Rollins; Oscar Brashear, Chuck Findley, Gene Coe (t); George Bohannon, Lew McCreary (tb); Marilyn Robinson, Alan Robinson (frhn); Bill Green (ss, f, picc); Patrice Rushen (ky); Lee Ritenour (g); Don Waldrop (tba); Alex Blake, Charles Meeks (b); Billy Cobham (d); Bill Summers (perc).* 8–10/76.

***** Easy Living**
Original Jazz Classics 893 *Rollins; George Duke (ky); Charles Icarus Johnson (g); Paul Jackson, Byron Miller (b); Tony Williams (d); Bill Summers (perc).* 8/77.

****(*) Don't Stop The Carnival**
Milestone 55005 *Rollins; Donald Byrd (t, flhn); Mark Soskin (p); Aurell Ray (g); Jerry Harris (b); Tony Williams (d).* 4/78.

****(*) Milestone Jazzstars In Concert**

Milestone 55006 *Rollins; McCoy Tyner (p); Ron Carter (b); Al Foster (d).* 9–10/78.

***** Don't Ask**

Original Jazz Classics OJC 915 *Rollins; Mark Soskin (ky); Jerome Harris (b); Al Foster (d); Bill Summers (perc).* 5/79.

Rollins returned to action with *Next Album*, a very happy album which sounded much more contented than anything he'd recorded in over a decade. 'Playin' In The Yard' and 'The Everywhere Calypso' were taken at a joyous swagger, 'Poinciana' showcased his debut on soprano, and 'Skylark' was the tenor *tour de force* of the record, the saxophonist locking into a persuasively argued cadenza which shook the melody hard. But at root the album lacks the sheer nerve of his early music. This reining-in of his darker side affects all of his '70s records to some degree. *Horn Culture* makes a more oppressive use of the electric rhythm section, none of whom plays to Rollins's level, and while the two ballads are pleasing, elsewhere the music gets either pointlessly ugly ('Sais') or messy with overdubs and overblowing ('Pictures In The Reflection Of A Golden Horn'). *The Cutting Edge*, recorded at Montreux, is a muddle, with only a lovely reading of 'To A Wild Rose' to save it.

Nucleus and *The Way I Feel* both court outright disaster. The former has at least some interesting material, and Rollins's very slow path through 'My Reverie' is perversely compelling; but the band have his feet chained, and none of the tracks takes off. The latter, with its dubbed-in horn-section, is plain feeble. The best of *Easy Living* – 'My One And Only Love', a merry treatment of Stevie Wonder's 'Isn't She Lovely' and the bleak title-piece – earns a better rating, but Rollins is still surrounded by players who don't belong with him, even Williams.

Don't Stop The Carnival has two great set-pieces, a ravishing 'Autumn Nocturne' and a fine display of virtuosity on 'Silver City', but the mismatched band – Williams tending towards extravagance, and Byrd prefiguring his astonishing total decline of the '80s – let him down. The *Jazzstars* live session is another disappointment, with the all-star group playing well but to no special purpose and with nothing to show at the end of the record. The almost sublime frustration of this period was provided by reports of (unrecorded) concerts where Rollins was reputedly playing better than ever. *Don't Ask* is initially a groaner – with a track called 'Disco Monk' and the boogaloo thump of 'Harlem Boys' – but there are some unpredictably enjoyable moments since Rollins is actively enjoying what seem to be inappropriate situations for him. 'My Ideal' is another of his peculiarly bitter ballads. These are curmudgeonly ratings – but we're talking about Sonny Rollins and, next to his masterpieces, these are intensely disappointing records.

***** Love At First Sight**

Original Jazz Classics OJC 753 *Rollins; George Duke (p); Stanley Clarke (b); Al Foster (d); Bill Summers (perc).* 5/79.

***** Sunny Days, Starry Nights**

Milestone 9122 *Rollins; Clifton Anderson (tb); Mark Soskin (p); Russel Blake (b); Tommy Campbell (d).* 1/84.

Rollins began the '80s with a session that intercut some of his old philosophies with supposed modernists like Duke and Clarke, though both are called on to perform in neo-traditional roles. The result is a diffident rather than a genuinely contrary record: not bad, with a nice 'The Very Thought Of You' and a sweet original called 'Little Lu', but the perfunctory retread of the ancient Rollins classic 'Strode Rode' shows up the lightweight cast and situation. *Sunny Days, Starry Nights* features the nucleus of the band he kept for many years, built around Soskin and Anderson. Nobody else is remotely on Rollins's level, and he seems to prefer it that way: certainly his best performances have arisen out of a certain creative isolation. This is another good-humoured date, with the melody of 'I'll See You Again' coming in waves of overdubbed tenor and jolly themes such as 'Kilauea' and 'Mava Mava' tempting the leader out of himself; it's as enjoyable as any of his later records.

****(*) The Solo Album**

Original Jazz Classics OJC 956 *Rollins (ts solo).* 7/85.

This still sounds like a curious failure. Since Rollins's solo cadenzas had always been luminous moments in his best concerts, hopes were high that this one-man recital would be a classic. Yet so much of it seems like aimless wool-gathering, the very opposite of Rollins at his best, that one assumes it was an occasion he didn't really want to take part in. A good opportunity to study his tonal characteristics at length, but on a purely musical level this was a great disappointment.

*****(*) G Man**

Milestone 9150 *Rollins; Clifton Anderson (tb); Mark Soskin (p); Bob Cranshaw (b); Marvin 'Smitty' Smith (d).* 8/86–4/87.

***** Dancing In The Dark**

Milestone 9155 *As above, except Jerome Harris (b, g) replaces Cranshaw.* 9/87.

***** Falling In Love With Jazz**

Milestone 9179 *As above, except add Branford Marsalis (ts), Tommy Flanagan (p), Bob Cranshaw (b), Jeff 'Tain' Watts, Jack DeJohnette (d); omit Smith.* 6–9/89.

***** Here's To The People**

Milestone 9194 *As above, except add Roy Hargrove (t), Al Foster (d), Steve Jordan (perc); omit Marsalis and Flanagan.* 91.

The live show which produced the title-track of *G Man* caught Rollins in his most communicative form: it might not be his most profound playing, but the sheer exuberance and tumbling impetus of his improvising sweeps the listener along. *Dancing In The Dark* seems tame in comparison, though the leader plays with plenty of bite: tracks such as 'Just Once', though, seem to have been designed more for radio-play than anything else, and the band's snappy delivery of 'Duke Of Iron' is a well-crafted routine, not a spontaneous flourish. The two studio sessions follow a similar pattern, with the guest horn-player on each date doing no more than blowing a few gratuitous notes. *Falling In Love With Jazz* has a quite irresistible version of 'Tennessee Waltz', and there are two Rollins flights through 'Why Was I Born?' and 'I Wish I Knew' on *Here's To The People*, where his tone seems grouchier and less tractable than ever before. Both discs, though, sound excessively studio-bound, suggesting that Rollins could use a change of scene here. In his 60s, though, he is probably content to work at his own whim, which – on the basis of the extraordinary catalogue listed above – he has surely earned.

***** Old Flames**

Milestone MCD-9215-2 *Rollins; Jon Faddis, Byron Sterling (flhn); Clifton Anderson (tb); Alex Brofsky (frhn); Tommy Flanagan (p); Bob Stewart (tba); Bob Cranshaw (b); Jack DeJohnette (d).* 7–8/93.

This is a sombre record after the sequence of mostly cheerful Milestones that Rollins delivered in the previous ten years or so. The only upbeat piece is 'Times Slimes', a title directed at corporate greed and its effect on the environment; the major set-pieces, 'I See Your Face Before Me' and Franz Lehár's 'Delia', are wrenchingly slow, tragic laments. Rollins is in magisterial voice, his tone veering between exasperation and wistfulness; but the session still lacks the urgency and incisiveness he once brought to even his most wayward playing. He is a different musician now. Jimmy Heath's stentorian brass charts on two tracks lend a little variation, and Flanagan's thoughtful presence is an unobtrusive bonus.

*** + 3

Milestone 9250 *Rollins; Tommy Flanagan, Stephen Scott (p); Bob Cranshaw (b); Jack DeJohnette, Al Foster (d).* 8–10/95.

Another strange one. Sonny's tone has never been grainier or more fogbound, he uses repetitions obsessively, cracks some notes as wilfully as Miles Davis, and states a written melody with seemingly intentional cruelty. The two different rhythm sections – Cranshaw is common to both – adopt a mediatory role, yet both manage to sound relatively faceless, imposing though these players are. Rollins turns 'Cabin In The Sky' into one of his tragic vehicles, complete with roving cadenza, and he defaces 'Mona Lisa'; but some of these pieces sound merely charmless – especially the two originals, which purport to be funky in an elephantine way. The most enigmatic figure in jazz continues to go his own way.

***(*) Global Warming

Milestone 9280 *Rollins; Clifton Anderson (tb); Stephen Scott (p); Bob Cranshaw (b); Idris Muhammad, Perry Wilson (d); Victor See Yuen (perc).* 1–2/98.

The good-humoured 'Island Lady' and the sunny-sounding title-track militate against a mood which is meant to be about planetary crisis: '*Global Warming* is my *Freedom Suite* of 1998,' says Rollins. One turns instead to an elaborate 'Mother Nature's Blues' and a strangely queasy ballad called 'Echo-Side Blue' for the leader's darkest thoughts; with 'Change Partners' as the sole standard, this is an unbalanced and rather enigmatic set altogether. Anderson gets more space than he has ever had on a Rollins record and makes quite assertive use of it; Scott, now a Rollins regular, is the most inventive band pianist he's had for a long time. The result is a fractious and unpredictable album which sometimes has Rollins straining on the horn – some of his forays into a false register sound like a real effort – yet which has a greater share of inspirational tenor than any other disc he's put his name on in ten years.

**** Silver City

Milestone 2501-2 2CD *As Milestone albums above.* 72–95.

Rollins has been fortunate in his repackaging, and this two-disc set – with a revealing interview essay – is a notably effective round-up of the pick of many mixed albums. His inconsistency and contrariness are part of what makes Rollins great, and to that extent the many individual Milestone albums, for all their faults, will remain in most collections. For less committed Rollins acolytes, this should be a first choice: there's nothing amiss here and, while a third disc would surely have covered the remaining high-spots, this one stands very fairly by itself.

CORE COLLECTION

**** This Is What I Do

Milestone MCD-9310-2 *Rollins; Clifton Anderson (tb); Stephen Scott (p); Bob Cranshaw (b); Perry Wilson, Jack DeJohnette (d).* 5–6/00.

It's a commonplace that jazz has for the most part lost its small legion of charismatic figures who have shouldered its great innovations, embodied its major advances. Who are the surviving giants? Cecil Taylor, Ornette Coleman ... Sonny Rollins. If Taylor's massive advances exemplify the jazz of a once and future era, Rollins belongs to a bygone golden age, an almost classical figure. He is, perhaps, jazz's Sinatra, absolutely 'traditional', even conservative now, yet so enormously individual that he dictates his own space in his culture. He may have tried modish flavours from time to time, but if they didn't fit with him he simply discarded them. Each new session is nothing more than a set's worth of Rollins, blowing as lustily as he felt at that point. His bandsmen have included distinguished players – Stephen Scott is the best pianist he's had for years, and DeJohnette, who plays on four of the six tracks, is hardly a mere sideman – but they are little more than framing devices for the saxophone.

More than ever, this set dismisses ornamentation. The studio sound is unsparing on the players, with a new immediacy in the mix: Rollins's records of recent times have seldom sounded so close and alive. The material is *sui generis*: a new calypso, 'Salvador'; a more-or-less blues, 'Charles M'; a surprising memento of a nearly forgotten tenorman, 'Did You Hear Harold Vick?'; and three improbable standards, two of them all but unknown to jazz repertory. He makes 'Sweet Leilani' into something approaching a gospel piece, and 'The Moon Of Manakoora', a choice to gladden the hearts of Dorothy Lamour fans, is fractious and regal. Here and throughout, the tenor tone has an almost crusty grandeur, the old supreme-steel sound mottled and scarred, but superbly resilient. His solos no longer sweep through numberless choruses, instead focusing around fragments of the material. The rhythmic chops have been hurt by the passage of time, perhaps, but there's a compensating sense that he's phrasing everything to his own particular clock. If anything, he has gone back to the performer whose sets he always tried to catch after his own night's work, Billie Holiday. 'A Nightingale Sang In Berkeley Square', with the leader lagging imperiously behind the beat, might almost be a late-period Holiday interpretation.

The others do their duty, and often handsomely. Scott gets off some shapely and even ingenious solos. Anderson is the patient colourist, and he has some nice muted work on 'Charles M'. But nothing they do is anything other than an intermission, while we impatiently await the saxophonist's return. *This Is What I Do* is unmistakable, and great Sonny Rollins.

Wallace Roney (born 1960)

TRUMPET, FLUGELHORN

In the '80s, three young trumpeters seemed to divide the known world between them. While Wynton Marsalis and Terence

Blanchard parcelled out the mainstream tradition, Roney established himself as the eclectic heir of Miles Davis. He is married to, and has regularly recorded with, pianist Geri Allen.

***** Misterios**

Warner Bros 245641 *Roney; Ravi Coltrane, Antoine Roney (ts); Geri Allen (p); Gil Goldstein (ky); Clarence Seay (b); Eric Allen (d); Waltinho Anastacio, Steve Barrios, Steve Thornton (perc); woodwinds; strings.* 93.

*****(*) Village**

Warner Bros 46649 *Roney; Michael Brecker, Pharoah Sanders (ts); Antoine Roney (ts, ss, bcl); Geri Allen, Chick Corea (p); Robert Irving III (syn); Clarence Seay (b); Lenny White (d); Steve Berrios (perc).* 12/96.

Roney's contract with Warner Bros opened him up to big-budget production and glossy packaging. Inevitably, this did blunt the urgency of his work to a degree. *Misterios* is swamped in superfluous sound but does contain some beautiful playing. 'Michelle', the Lennon-McCartney staple, is an unexpected choice but one which works well with just horn and rhythm. Brother Antoine appears on three cuts, including Jaco Pastorius's '71+' and Pat Metheny's 'Last To Know', one of a pair of compositions by the guitarist. Coltrane Jr makes a guest appearance on Astor Piazzolla's 'Muerte', which is medleyed with an excerpt from Bach's *Art Of The Fugue*, but does nothing of any great consequence. *Village* very much picks up where the currently deleted *Quintet* left off, though, in an effort to boost sales and profile, Warners have teamed him up with an all-star band which doesn't really do him any great favours. Two of the tracks, the title-piece and 'Oshiririke', are collectively composed, and they suggest that some attempt was made to loosen the constraints of what had become a rather formulaic session. Guest pianist Chick Corea's 'Affinity' is the lead-off tune and Chick gives way to Mrs Roney only mid-set, though he turns up as second keyboard on Fender Rhodes on Lenny White's 'EBO'. The drummer is a revelation, playing wonderful cross-patterns and fills and setting up grooves you could launch ships down. Brecker and Sanders have cameo parts, though Pharoah makes full use of the spotlight on a theme dedicated to him. An excellent record, but less coherent and focused than its plainly named predecessor.

****** No Room For Argument**

Stretch 9033 *Roney; Antoine Roney (ss, ts); Geri Allen (p, ky); Adam Holzman (p, org, ky); Buster Williams (b); Lenny White (d).* 4/00.

This is a most impressive tapestry of styles and sounds, incorporating free-form passages, straight(ish) bop and some intriguing spoken-word samples from African-American heroes Malcolm X and Martin Luther King Jr. Wallace pays homage to John Coltrane in a version of the 'Acknowledgement' section from *A Love Supreme*; Buster Williams takes that famous bass-line and makes it triumphantly his own. 'Straight No Nothing' and 'Midnight Blue' are both originals but are clearly intended to make direct reference to the modern jazz canon. In terms of trumpet-playing, Wallace refers quite explicitly to Miles, Dizzy, Booker Little and Freddie Hubbard, but the voice is now most distinctively his own and the impact of the album as a whole is considerable. Chick Corea produces and Glen Kolotkin engineers with a delicate touch. Even if you've not been convinced hitherto, this is a formidable achievement and well worth having.

Adonis Rose (born 1974)

DRUMS

Young drummer entering the vanguard of today's post-bop.

***** Song For Donise**

Criss Cross Criss 1146 *Rose; Nicholas Payton (t); Tim Warfield (ts); Anthony Wonsey (p); Reuben Rogers (b).* 12/97.

***** The Unity**

Criss Cross 1173 *As above.* 6/99.

Rose first came to notice with Nicholas Payton's band on the trumpeter's *Gumbo Nouveau* disc for Verve. This session returns the compliment: more or less the same line-up and with Payton and Wonsey the main composers. One might suspect that Payton, a Wayne Shorter devotee, also brought in 'E.S.P.', but this is the best pointer to Rose's own debt to the late Tony Williams. He has the same dry, rippling delivery, and a generous amount of the same innate musicality. On 'Love Walked In', which is for piano trio only, he cements the connection with a beautifully crafted performance. Perhaps inevitably, the session is dominated by the two horn men. The cast returns for another go on *The Unity* and, while this is perhaps just another good day at the office, the music continues to breathe and expand as these young performers become ever more masterful in their skills. Payton gets a huge sound on 'I Remember You', which sounds as if it must be an uncredited flugelhorn, and Wonsey, who plays modestly for much of the way, digs in hard on his own mockingly titled 'Smooth Jazz'.

Noah Rosen

PIANO

Originally from Brooklyn, Rosen studied at Bennington College, sought out Andrew Hill as a mentor, then moved to base himself in Paris, where he has been since 1991.

*****(*) Trips Jobs And Journeys**

Cadence CJR 1152 *Rosen; Didier Levallet (b); Makoto Sato (d).* 9/00.

Rosen's playing is steady and methodical, yet fearsomely powerful. He makes a nearly monolithic way through these five trio pieces (recorded live at Parisian club La Fenêtre). The music has a themeless feel to it, but the underlying structures are there – actually, they often seem to sit right on top of the music in a kind of hide-in-plain-sight scenario. Rosen's left hand is so fierce that there's an irresistible feel of another expatriate, Mal Waldron (as Bob Rusch's sleeve-note avers), although it's not an influence which Rosen claims for himself. He hardly plays fast at all, preferring to accumulate thunderous voicings around clusters which he belts out of the keyboard, and it sets a problematic task for bass and drums, who tend to scuttle at the edges or cling on for dear life. Rusch also suggests that it feels more like a solo than trio set, and given the pianist's intensive use of both hands it's hard to disagree. Over the course of an hour-plus of music, the fixed intensities can get a little exhausting, but what a forceful and unhackneyed opening to a recording career, which clearly needs further sponsorship.

Bernt Rosengren (born 1937)

TENOR AND ALTO SAXOPHONES, FLUTE, TAROGATO, PIANO

Rosengren led Swedish hard bop as its premier young tenorman in the late '50s. He acquired some international exposure in the '60s with George Russell and others, but he has basically remained tied to his native scene as a player and bandleader, and a fair spread of his career is currently available on CD.

***** Bombastica!**

Dragon DRCD 287 *Rosengren; Lasse Werner (p); Kjell Samuelson (p); Torbjørn Hultcrantz, Göran Pettersson (b); Sune Spangberg (d).* 2/59–6/60.

***** Stockholm Dues**

EMI 792428-2 (Swed.) *Rosengren; Lalle Svensson (t); Claes-Goran Fagerstadt, Lars Sjøsten (p); Bjorn Alke, Torbjørn Hultcrantz (b); Bo Skoglund (d); Nannie Porres (v).* 3–4/65.

****** Notes From The Underground**

EMI 136462-2 (Swed.) *Rosengren; Maffy Falay (t, darbuka); Bertil Strandberg (tb); Tommy Koverhult (ss, ts, f); Gunnar Bergsten (bs); Bobo Stenson (p); Torbjørn Hultcrantz, Bjorn Alke (b); Leif Wennerstrom (d); Okay Temiz, Bengt Berger (perc); Salih Baysal (v, vn).* 9/73.

Rosengren has been a force in Swedish jazz for some 40 years and is still undervalued on the world stage. Wider availability of his earlier records would still be welcome. *Bombastica!* restores a session which was an early example of Swedish music crossing the Atlantic, since it was released in the US on Jazzland. There are extra, unissued tracks and four pieces from a rare EP by Lasse Werner. It's a nice example of European hard bop, although not all that hard, and often more swing than boppish in its inclinations, though Rosengren's sound, a light variation on Rollins at this point, is sweetly caught.

Stockholm Dues is a decent approximation of a genre hard-bop record, but it's let down by the thick, clattery sound and some occasionally scrappy playing; Porres's singing on some tracks is also an uneasily acquired taste. But Rosengren's muscular, assured playing stands out when he takes centre stage, with Svensson a solid partner. There are several tracks added to what was the original LP issue.

Notes From The Underground is far superior and stands as an important record of its time. Rosengren varies the tracks from 11 players down to quartet, with the members of the Turkish-Swedish group Sevda also on hand – an early example of a jazz–world fusion that retains its potency. The big group plays with enormous gusto on Rosengren's charts, the rhythms rolling underneath, and the points of reference – Coltrane/Sanders and the McCoy Tyner groups of the early '70s – are subsumed in the force of Rosengren's delivery. Crucial is his partnership with Koverhult, the latter now entirely neglected but a tenorman capable of the force and intensity of the leader's own best playing. The Rachmaninov arrangement which opened the original double-album has been lost but that means all the music can now be fitted on to a single CD. Splendid remastering, and the title is a somewhat ironic comment on the state of live jazz in Stockholm at the time.

***** Surprise Party**

Steeplechase SCCD 31177 *Rosengren; Horace Parlan (p); Doug Raney (g); Jesper Lundgaard (b); Aage Tanggaard (d).* 3/83.

***** The Hug**

Dragon DRCD 211 *Rosengren; Carl Fredrik Orrje (p); Anders Ullberg (g); Torbjørn Hultcrantz (b); Leif Wennerstrom (d).* 5/92.

*****(*) Full Of Life**

Dragon DRCD 205 *Rosengren; Krister Andersson (ts, cl); Goran Lindberg (p); Sture Nordin (b); Bengt Stark (d).* 3/91.

*****(*) Bent's Jump: Summit Meeting Live At Bent J**

Dragon DRCD 233 *As above.* 7/93.

The Steeplechase session, rather glibly dismissed in our first edition, is standing up rather better than we previously allowed. Admittedly not much more than one of the label's in-house blowing dates, the calibre of the band is nevertheless considerable and the easy-going authority of the playing is hardly disappointing. *The Hug* is an agreeable, lightly swinging programme of standards and a few originals which all involved take affably enough, though scrutiny of any passage reveals that nobody's asleep. Rosengren's tone and phrasing are a nice balance of strength and a certain vulnerability which can sometimes give his solos a dozing quality they don't deserve. He is in more commanding form on the two albums by the band Summit Meeting. *Full Of Life* is a studio date, while *Bent's Jump* was recorded at the establishment squired by Bent J. Jensen, one of the great jazz-club owners. The live session has an ounce more snap to it, although the sound is somewhat documentary-standard. The music is a sinewy variation on midstream hard bop, and the two saxophonists – neither exactly a pugilist – forge an amicable front line that transcends jam-session clichés.

***** Porgy And Bess**

Liphone 3167 *Rosengren; Carl Fredrik Orrje (p); Per-Ola Gadd (b); Bengt Stark (d).* 1/96.

*****(*) Plays Evert Taube**

Arietta ADCD 19 *Rosengren; Håkan Nyqvist (t, flhn, frhn); Sven Berggren (tb); Tommy Koverhult (ss, f); Gunnar Bergsten (bs); Peter Nordahl (p); Patrik Boman (b); Jesper Kviberg (d).* 99.

In the light of Joe Henderson's take on the Gershwin score, Rosengren's *Porgy And Bess* seems a much more modest affair, tenor and rhythm section working patiently through the score – taken surprisingly literally by the leader – with no grand set-pieces. But the saxophonist's maturity is as considerable as Henderson's and, even when he sounds comparatively diffident, he makes one hear fresh things in what is now a thoroughly jazzed piece of Americana. As a bonus there is some particularly thoughtful playing by Orrje.

Taube's name may not be too familiar to non-Swedish audiences, but he was the country's national poet and a songwriter who dominated Swedish radio for many years. Rosengren has arranged 12 of Taube's songs, chosen from 40 years of the composer's work. A graceful rather than a memorable melodist, Taube seems somewhat hidden in Rosengren's arrangements, an elusive simplicity built over by the saxophonist's writing. He is keen to give everyone something to do, even when there's a soloist out front, and the horns are almost continuously involved. The waltz metre of 'Personligt Samtal' is decorated by some intense solos, but one never feels that the music has lost its founding character. A strong and typically individual set by a true individualist.

Kurt Rosenwinkel

GUITAR, KEYBOARDS, DRUMS, VOCAL

A ubiquitous presence on the New York club scene of the late '90s, Rosenwinkel has progressed rapidly from sideman to leader status with these sets.

*****(*) East Coast Love Affair**
Fresh Sound FSNT 016 *Rosenwinkel; Avishai Cohen (b); Jorge Rossy (d).* 7/96.

***** Intuit**
Criss Cross 1160 *Rosenwinkel; Michael Kanan (p); Joe Martin (b); Tim Pleasant (d).* 8/98.

***** The Enemies Of Energy**
Verve 543042-2 *Rosenwinkel; Mark Turner (ts); Scott Kinsey (ky); Ben Street (b); Jeff Ballard (d).* 99.

The debut has a beautiful feel – the three men were recorded in Smalls' Club, where Rosenwinkel has had a regular gig, and the sound of the record is close, almost humid. The interplay lifts the material to a high level of invention – when they fade 'All Or Nothing At All', it sounds as though they could have gone on in that groove for hours yet. Rosenwinkel plays with a clean, almost classical sound and his melody lines are spacious and paced to suit whatever tempo they've chosen – he never seems to feel he has to rush through his phrases. Cohen and Rossy are just as generous of spirit on a very enjoyable set. It's certainly more successful than the subsequent Criss Cross, which is all right but basically uneventful. The bebop tunes are given a going-over which sounds like a lot of other records, and it feels like routine.

The Enemies Of Energy is by Rosenwinkel's regular band. The music's a curious blend of straightahead, fusion, prog-rock instrumentals and even folk music, with Rosenwinkel accompanying his own vocal on 'The Polish Song'. Kinsey's keyboards bring in what sound like clavinet and analogue synthesizers. Rosenwinkel and Turner have their moments, but this feels like a patchwork in search of a clear pattern, and what might sound a lot more vivid and convincing in a live situation seems very tame in the studio.

*****(*) The Next Step**
Verve 549162-2 *Rosenwinkel; Mark Turner (ts); Ben Street (b); Jeff Ballard (d).* 5/00.

Rosenwinkel's second for Verve goes back to the feel of his first record. In many ways, it's penny-plain music: he uses a straightforward sound, and the quartet play in a heads-down, get-on-with-it manner. It's all about content, very little variety, nothing to show off. Rosenwinkel and Turner match each other solo for solo, while Street and Ballard push on tirelessly behind them. It has a Tristano-ite logic and cool-headedness. There's nothing to listen for except rigorous thought and intensity; it's abstruse, but entirely coherent. An extraordinary record for a major record company to release.

****(*) Heartcore**
Verve 589776-2 *Rosenwinkel; Mark Turner (ts, bcl); Andrew D'Angelo (bcl); Mariani Gil (f); Ethan Iverson (ky); Ben Street (b); Jeff Ballard (d).* n.d.

Despite the personnel listing, this is almost a solo album by Rosenwinkel: playing keyboards and drums, singing and programming, he's orchestrated these tracks to cushion his guitar solos in lush surroundings. Turner, Iverson and the others play what amount to cameo roles. It's skilfully done, but in a way there's too much skill involved: as with the flabbier parts of *The Enemies Of Energy*, a lot of it sounds like prog-rock without the hooks, which leaves the record beached in a territory which is all texture and no point. There are many moments worth rescuing, but it's likely most listeners won't even get that far.

Renee Rosnes (born 1962)

PIANO

Canadian-born Rosnes has maintained a consistent output for Blue Note throughout the '90s and is one of the most reliable names on the current roster, an adventurous player and composer who maintains close links with the label's classic repertoire.

*****(*) Ancestors**
Blue Note 34634 *Rosnes; Nicholas Payton (t); Chris Potter (ts, ss, af); Peter Washington (b); Al Foster (d); Don Alias (perc).* 10/95.

This is the record that marks Rosnes's maturity as a composer. In 1994, she had met her biological mother and learnt more about her Indian heritage; at almost the same moment her adoptive mother succumbed to a late-diagnosed cancer. These extremes of joy and pain are reflected in 'Ancestors' itself, a swinging, confident piece with a measure of tragedy at its centre, and also in 'The Ache Of The Absence', 'Lifewish', 'The Gift' and 'Chasing Spirits', which give the latter stages of this fine record the feel of a loosely connected suite.

This is the first time she has recorded with a brass instrument. Payton's solo on 'The Ache' is immaculate, only matched by Potter's restless idea on 'Chasing Spirits'. Washington and Foster (the latter another stalwart of the Henderson band) cannot be faulted on any count, and the sound, masterminded by Bob Belden, is pristine.

****** As We Are Now**
Blue Note 56810 *Rosnes; Chris Potter (ts, ss); Christian McBride (b); Jack DeJohnette (d).* 3/97.

This time, Rosnes has few items of personal agenda on show. 'The Land Of Five Rivers' is a small exception, a portrait of the northern Indian landscape her ancestors left to go to Canada. The disc gets off to a roaring start with 'Black Holes', an original that sits well for both piano and horn. Nothing could be of greater contrast than the haunted title-piece, named after a May Sarton novel and almost as beautiful. Tony Williams's 'Pee Wee' was written for the Miles Davis album *Sorcerer* and was included on the album just a couple of weeks after the drummer's untimely death. Rosnes has the gift of turning strong emotion into compelling music. No mistaking the strength of her feelings, or the ability to convert and transform it.

****** Art & Soul**
Blue Note 99997 2 *Rosnes; Scott Colley (b); Billy Drummond (d); Richard Bona (perc); Dianne Reeves (v).* 2/99.

As ever, Rosnes draws on the past and makes it sound fresh, friendly and contemporary. Beginning with 'Blues Connotation' (a clever, eleven-and-a-half-bar blues by Ornette Coleman) was a master stroke, for its off-centre phrasing and hectic pace leave the listener slightly winded and pleasantly punchy for the rest of a fine set. Following it up with a romantic reading 'With A Little Help From My Friends' was even more clever. Rosnes has the gift of taking shop-worn tunes and making them sound as if they were being written on the spot, and the musing quality she brings to the Beatles song, this time with minimal accompaniment from Colley and Drummond, is spot-on.

Wayne Shorter's 'Footprints' features lyrics by Kitty Margolis and a strong vocal by Dianne Reeves, who also features on 'Fleurette Africaine', a Duke Ellington tune first recorded on the *Money Jungle* session with Charles Mingus and Max Roach. Richard Bona's *kalimba* adds a delightful and unexpected dimension. 'Little Spirit' is a love-song for Renee's baby son, and the closing piece is an arrangement of a Bartók children's song (though you might have guessed Chick Corea). Rosnes is playing at her very best.

***** Life On Earth**

Blue Note 33997 *Rosnes; Conrad Herwig (tb); Doug Purviance (btb); Walt Weiskopf (ss, ts); Steve Nelson (mar); David Gilmore (g); Laura Oatts, Laura Seaton (vn); Ralph Farris (vla); Erik Friedlander, Sachi Patitucci (clo); Christian McBride, John Patitucci (b); Billy Drummond, Jeff 'Tain' Watts (d); Zakir Hussain (tabla); Duduka DaFonseca (perc); Mor Thiam (v, djembe); Kevin Tarrant (v).* 01.

This is a very ambitious record. Two years away from the studio have given Rosnes time to develop some very interesting ideas, but also perhaps so much time that she has rather overcooked her comeback disc. *Life On Earth* has a curious world-music quality, underlined by the percussion of Duduka DaFonseca and the brilliant Zakir Hussain, but it still bears the stamp of Renee's own lyrical style. Husband Billy Drummond is once again an influential component, but Jeff Watts does some distinguished work as well. 'Icelight' and 'Nana' are outstanding tracks, but the album as a whole lacks cohesion and ultimately disappoints.

*****(*) With A Little Help From My Friends**

Blue Note 26584 *Rosnes; Joe Henderson, Branford Marsalis, Walt Weiskopf (ts); Chris Potter (ss, ts, bcl); Wayne Shorter (ss, ts); Ron Carter, Ira Coleman, Scott Colley, Christian McBride, Peter Washington, Buster Williams (b); Jack DeJohnette, Billy Drummond, Al Foster (d); Don Alias (perc); Dianne Reeves (v).* 88–95.

A lot of Renee's earliest stuff is now either out of print or only available in certain territories. This very valuable compilation brings together some of her best Blue Note material but also adds some unreleased tracks and a wonderful version for trio of 'With A Little Help From My Friends'. We quibble about some of the choices but, as a quick introduction to Renee's recording career, it's a very attractive purchase indeed.

***** And The Danish Radio Big Band**

Blue Note 90799 2 *Rosnes; Henrik Bolberg, Thomas Fryland, Anders Gustafsson, Thomas Kjaergaard, Benny Rosenfeld (t, flhn); Steen Hansen, Annette Husby, Peter Jensen, Vincent Nilsson (tb); Axel Windfeld (btb, tba); Nicolai Schultz (as, f); Michael Hove (as, cl, f); Uffe Markussen (ts, cl, bcl, f); Bob Rockwell (ts, cl); Flemming Madsen (bs, bcl); Anders Lindvall (g); Thomas Ovesen (b); Soren Frost (d); Ethan Weisgaard (perc).* 12/01.

There is a hint of retrospection to this elegantly polished set as well. Instead of writing brand-new charts for her gig with the big band, Renee has dusted off some favourite themes from earlier in her career and given them a new bulk and presence. 'Ancestors' is the most obvious example, but also 'Black Holes' and the funky 'Bulldog's Chicken Run' from *Where We Are Now*. This is fine as far as it goes, but the feeling here is very much a big-budget remake rather than a genuinely new project. Jim McNeely's arrangements are spot-on, and the soloists are good without exception, notably trombonist Peter Jensen on 'Ancestors'. Renee herself plays with fire and commitment and even brings a touch of steel to a clever arrangement of the English song 'Early One Morning', which is scored without woodwinds.

Frank Rosolino (1926–78)

TROMBONE

Though he was also fondly remembered as a comic vocalist, it's Rosolino's fast, responsive trombone-playing which established his reputation. He worked in an array of big bands, including Gene Krupa's, before joining Howard Rumsey's Lighthouse All Stars, with whom he worked during the latter half of the '50s. His eventual suicide was all the more poignant for seeming so totally out of character.

****** Frank Rosolino/5**

V.S.O.P. #16 *Rosolino; Richie Kamuca (ts); Vince Guaraldi (p); Monty Budwig (b); Stan Levey (d).* 6/57.

*****(*) Free For All**

Original Jazz Classics OJC 1763 *Rosolino; Harold Land (ts); Victor Feldman (p); Leroy Vinnegar (b); Stan Levey (d).*

*****(*) Fond Memories Of ...**

Double-Time Records DTRCD 113 *Rosolino; Louis Van Dyke (p); Jacques Schols (b); John Engels (d); Metropole Orchestra.* 6/73, 5/75.

***** Thinking About You**

Sackville 5007 2CD *Rosolino; Ed Bickert (g); Don Thompson (b); Terry Clarke (d).* 76.

*****(*) Frank Talks**

Storyville 8284 *Rosolino; Thomas Clausen (p); Bo Stief (b); Bjarne Rostvold (d).* 78.

Coming of age in Gene Krupa's post-war band, Rosolino developed a style that seemed to combine elements of bop harmony with the more durable virtues of swing. A wonderfully agile player with a tone that could be broad and humane, almost vocalized one moment, thinly abstract the next, Rosolino brings a twist of humour to almost everything he plays.

Rosolino/5 is close to the best of the available records: three Rosolino standards, mostly in modified blues forms, together with 'Thou Swell', 'They Say', the old groaner 'Cherry' and Bill Holman's topically titled 'Fallout'. Typically, almost every track involves some manipulation of time or harmony, with 'Thou Swell' falling unexpectedly in threes, and 'How Long' cast in a long, yearning line that puts maximum emphasis on the interplay between Rosolino and the superlative Kamuca, who has rarely sounded better on disc.

The OJC rounds out a fine session done for the Specialty label with some valuable alternative takes ('There Is No Greater Love', 'Chrisdee' and 'Don't Take Your Love From Me') and some great performances from the band that belie the undisciplined mood suggested by the title. Land is a more muscular soloist than Kamuca, but no less responsive to the mood of the session, and capable of some extremely delicate and detailed passage-work.

The Dutch session was recorded at the radio studios in Hilversum at a time when Rosolino was spending most of his time on this side of the Atlantic, often working with Conte Candoli. The Metropole Orchestra are featured on only three tracks, including the superlative 'Corcovado', and though there are no real quibbles about the rhythm section, they aren't entirely well adapted to Rosolino's fast, elegant later style. *Fond Memories* was a limited-edition pressing, but copies should still be in circulation, and they are well worth snapping up.

The CD reissue of *Thinking About You* is vastly expanded. Originally just four longish tracks, it now includes the whole of a long Toronto set which paired Frank with some of Canada's finest jazz musicians. Bickert is especially good and comes through strongly in the remastering. Some of the tracks are overlong and loose; the opening 'Sweet And Lovely' is almost a quarter of an hour in duration, and it's to be doubted whether any but the most devoted of fans will want a full double-CD of this stuff. But it's engaging enough, and Frank was in fine voice, no sign yet of the shadows that were to overtake him later. His solos on 'My Old Flame' and a mellow 'Round Midnight' are among his best on record.

The Storvyville session, recorded less than three months before his death, finds him buoyant and persuasive on a Copenhagen club date. Ably supported by Thomas Clausen, who takes some very effective solos, he strolls through five long tunes of which the first and last, the poignantly named 'Blue Daniel' and 'Waltz For Diane', are originals. The middle cuts are probably longer than is strictly effective, with something of the Buggins's turn of solos one tends to find on sessions like this; but there is plenty for fans of the trombonist to enjoy in a record that seems to have surfaced only in 1998. Rosolino's end could hardly have been grimmer or more bitterly ironic for a man who had played on a record called *The Most Happy Fella* and who is remembered above all for his good humour; in the liner-note to *Fond Memories of ...*, J. J. Johnson speaks of his 'infectious giggle'. In the autumn of 1978, suffering from depression, he murdered his children, then took his own life.

Ned Rothenberg (born 1956)

ALTO SAXOPHONE, BASS CLARINET, SHAKUHACHI

A charter member of the New Winds ensemble, Rothenberg has embraced many branches of the music, from Dolphy-influenced post-bop to formal composition and improvisation on solo horn. A versatile instrumentalist and one of the few Westerners to sound convincing on shakuhachi, the traditional Japanese bamboo flute.

*****(*) Port Of Entry**

Intuition INT 3249 2 *Rothenberg; Jerome Harris (g, b); Samir Chatterjee (tabla, perc).* 10/97, 3/98.

Rothenburg's alto saxophone-playing – particularly unaccompanied – bears some comparison with Anthony Braxton's but is much more precise in articulation, just as its content is rather more diffuse. Though *Port Of Entry* is strictly credited to the group, Sync, it is very much a Rothenberg project. His basic idea, inspired by Pat Metheny, is that creative musicians are stretched only by working in contexts, modes and idioms in which they are not adept. In this trio, he has to pit himself against the kind of complex Carnatic rhythms which are basic ABC to a player like Chatterjee but which sit oddly for a Westerner. Jerome Harris is a natural-born blues player whose work falls naturally into blues forms, and yet on 'Lost In A Blue Forest', Rothenberg has him work out of normal range by playing an acoustic bass guitar with bottleneck and pick; very effectively, too.

*****(*) Tools Of The Trade**

CIMP 248 *Rothenberg; Denman Maroney (p).* 6/01.

In the notes, Maroney annotates exactly what he uses on the piano on each rack – knives, bars, bowls, screwdrivers – with a surgeon's (torturer's?) precision. There is surprisingly little torment. Actually, a lot of the interplay is no more difficult or bound up in obfuscation than many a mainstream date. Even Rothenberg says that the pieces are 'pieces', not just excerpts of a never-ending whole, and that sense of finished work permeates what's otherwise free-thinking improvising. Rothenberg uses various clarinets and one alto saxophone, and his precise kind of technique imposes a useful, if unorthodox, order. A curious but very interesting pairing.

Jim Rotondi (born 1962)

TRUMPET, FLUGELHORN

From Butte, Montana, Rotondi played in high school jazz groups and graduated in music from North Texas State. He moved to New York in 1987, toured with Ray Charles, and started recording.

***** Introducing Jim Rotondi**

Criss Cross 1128 *Rotondi; Eric Alexander (ts); Larry Goldings (p, org); Dwayne Burno (b); Billy Drummond (d).* 12/96.

*****(*) Jim's Bop**

Criss Cross 1156 *Rotondi; Eric Alexander (ts); Harold Mabern (p); John Webber (b); Joe Farnsworth (d).* 10/97.

***** Excursions**

Criss Cross 1184 *Rotondi; Steve Davis (tb); Eric Alexander (ts); David Hazeltine (p); Peter Washington (b); Kenny Washington (d).* 12/98.

No more and no less than three excellent '90s hard-bop dates. Whether such a prospect quickens the pulse or induces a yawn will be up to individual readers, since there's nothing in Rotondi's music that is strikingly new. He doesn't write much – only six of the 24 compositions across the three discs are his, and two of those share a credit with Alexander – and his methods are based around clean, graceful improvising, with a flugelhorn sound much like Freddie Hubbard's on ballads. Alexander, his front-line cohort on all three dates, is always a fail-safe partner in the studios and three different rhythm sections each do their swinging duty – interesting to spot old-timer Mabern in fast company on *Jim's Bop*. Farnsworth really kicks the fast ones along on that date, and it's full of spark. *Excursions* is just slightly disappointing in that Davis doesn't seem to add much except extra weight (and another solo) to all of the tunes.

***** Destination Up!**

Sharp Nine 1022-2 *Rotondi; Steve Davis (tb); Mulgrew Miller (p); Joe Locke (vib); Peter Washington (b); Joe Farnsworth (d).* 3/01.

Same as before, basically, with a little brightness injected by the reliable Joe Locke. Brightness is something that this style, and Rotondi's version of it, does cry out for, since otherwise it all tends towards clean, unsurprising mechanics. Davis is a downbeat presence, but luckily he's only on two tracks – though his composition 'Evening Shades Of Blue' is the longest and least interesting piece on the record. Rotondi gets hotter elsewhere, the solo on 'Last Ditch Wisdom' turning out particularly pellucid. Miller, who's had a quiet time of it lately, has a few characteristic, strong passages.

Charlie Rouse (1924–88)

TENOR SAXOPHONE

Rouse spent the '60s in the company of Thelonious Monk and remained a devoted interpreter of the great man's work. He began his career with Billy Eckstine and Dizzy Gillespie and played for some time in R&B bands as well. Rouse is an immediately identifiable soloist, but his legacy of recordings as leader is patchy.

***** Jazz Modes**
Biograph 134/135 *Rouse; Julius Watkins (frhn); Gildo Mahones (p); Janet Putnam (hp); Paul Chambers, Oscar Pettiford, Martin Rivera, Paul West (b); Ron Jefferson, Art Taylor (d); Chano Pozo (perc); Eileen Gilbert (v).* 7–12/56.

***** Mood In Scarlet**
Dawn CD 1345 *As above.* 7-12/56.

*****(*) Takin' Care Of Business**
Original Jazz Classics OJC 491 *Rouse; Blue Mitchell (t); Walter Bishop (p); Earl May (b); Art Taylor (d).* 5/60.

Rouse always played saxophone as if he had a cold in the head. There were those who questioned whether his slightly adenoidal, wuffling tone was ever appropriate to Thelonious Monk's music. However, Rouse became one of Monk's most loyal and stalwart supporters, and an essential part of some of Monk's finest quartet recordings. Rouse also carried the banner posthumously in his band Sphere, and in such tribute recordings as the not entirely successful *Epistrophy*, recorded just a month before his death (and currently deleted).

For a time in the late '50s Rouse co-led a group called Les Jazz Modes with french horn master, Julius Watkins. The material, available again on Biograph and Dawn, is more interesting as a historical artefact than as a listenable record, but there are episodes and occasional tracks which recommend it.

***** Bossa Nova Bacchanal**
Blue Note 90416 *Rouse; Freddie Hubbard (t); McCoy Tyner (p); Kenny Burrell, Chauncey Westbrook (g); Bob Cranshaw, Larry Gales (b); Willie Bobo, Billy Higgins (d); Carlos 'Patato' Valdes (perc); Garvin Masseaux (shekere).* 11/62, 65.

Rouse isn't the obvious tenor for a Latin project like this, and the album's success is largely down to some wonderful percussion work from Masseaux on shekere and to Patato Valdes, also to the supremely elegant guitar work of Burrell and Westbrook. Charlie's solos on top of this are a bit rough and ready, though he brings a distressed grandeur to the classic 'Samba De Orfeu', which is the centrepiece of the set. 'Un Dia' and 'Merci Bon Dieu' are less familiar themes and Rouse explores them both at first tentatively and then with audibly growing confidence. Never the most effusive of soloists, he has the engaging ability to reinvent even his own ideas on the stand, working at an idea until it's clear to him. Some of this is lost in the studio, without benefit of alternates, and oddly the advertised bonus track on this reissue, 'One For Five', comes from a different session altogether, taped in 1965 with Hubbard, Tyner, Cranshaw and Higgins. If you know Charlie Rouse only as a Monk sideman, or from the tribute group Sphere, this will be a pleasant revelation.

***** Social Call**
Uptown 2750 *Rouse; Red Rodney (t); Albert Dailey (p); Cecil McBee (b); Kenny Washington (d).* 1/84.

Inevitably, this is pretty much a bebop date. 'Half Nelson', available in two takes here, as are 'Social Call' and 'Darn That Dream', is taken at a relaxed swing and both horns allude to Charlie Parker and Miles Davis in their solos. Albert Dailey is a neglected figure, largely because he has recorded so little under his own name. He's hugely authoritative here, and plays with relaxed power against McBee's gigantic bass-lines. Washington sounds as if he comes from a later generation and that's all to the good, given how authentic the rest of the set is. The bonus cuts are a genuine asset, as always with Rouse, showing how he thinks his way through the changes quite deliberately. A fine showing from the saxophonist, though to hear the real Rouse, best turn to the Monk entry.

ROVA

GROUP

An American all-saxophone group, its name derived from the surname initials of the players, although Andrew Voigt has been replaced by Steve Adams (ROAA would be harder to pronounce). Though their music seeks an exact balance between composition and improvisation, they have lately been written for extensively by many different composers.

***** Favourite Street**
Black Saint 120076-2 *Larry Ochs, Bruce Ackley, Andrew Voigt, Jon Raskin (reeds).* 11/83.

*****(*) Beat Kennel**
Black Saint 120176-2 *As above.* 4/87.

ROVA's first five albums were cut over a period of 12 months, but all – save *The Bay*, listed under Andrea Centazzo's entry – are still missing in action. Along with the World Saxophone Quartet, they pioneered the all-sax ensemble as a regular and conceptually wide-ranging unit. Whereas WSQ were more concerned with updating the swinging vitality of the big-band sax section, though, ROVA sought out remoter climes, specifically building on the discoveries of the Chicago avant-garde and claiming such composer-performers as Steve Lacy and Roscoe Mitchell as major influences. Their early work can be rather hard going: deliberately eschewing conventional notions about swing, prodding at the boundaries of sound and space, many of their '80s records are notebooks which frequently throw up as many failures as successes.

Steve Lacy was only belatedly recognized as a major patrician influence on a wide spectrum of modern players, and ROVA's homage to him on *Favourite Street* paid overdue tribute. The bony rigour of Lacy's themes focuses ROVA's meandering, no matter how adventurous their earlier trips had been: Lacy's music is a good way to clear the head of distractions, either as listener or as performer, and in their thoughtful elaborations on seven favourite themes they clear away some of the more baroque elements of their work. The subsequent *Beat Kennel* appears to build on this: in 'The Aggregate' and 'Sportspeak', their assured rhythms and tone-colours pull them closer to a jazz tradition, and in their vibrant reading of a Braxton composition they create distinctive jazz repertory.

***** Electric Rags II**
New Albion NA027 *As above, except Steve Adams (reeds) replaces Voigt.* 3/89.

***** This Time We Are Both**
New Albion NA 041 *As above.* 11/89.

***** For The Bureau Of Both**
Black Saint 120135-2 *As above.* 2–9/92.

Steve Adams replaced Andrew Voigt, but otherwise ROVA's universe remained constant: a teeming cosmos of saxophone sounds. *Electric Rags II* is properly co-credited with the composer, Alvin Curran, who devised a 30-section work, designed to be performed in a random order and played in tandem with a computerized system of electronics that makes various adaptations to each man's playing. This can work in real and deferred time. The concept, one of many such which grew up as computers and electronics were increasingly brought into new music, is absorbing but the results often seem like a jumble which the players may or may not be in charge of. There are many rich and even funny moments, but it seems like little more than an entertaining (and, at this distance, already somewhat dated) one-off.

Now that Hat's *Saxophone Diplomacy* is deleted, *This Time We Are Both* is the only evidence of ROVA's work in the former Soviet Union. A snapshot of their second excursion into the era of *glasnost*, the six pieces make up a typical concert of that time – the frolicsome 'Third Terrain', the sombre 'The Freedom Of Information' and their epic 'The Unquestioned Answer'. Held back somewhat by the fair but less than ideal sound – this is a group that needs all the sonic detail in place.

For The Bureau Of Both seems like a transitional record. Pieces such as 'Streak' take off from energetic riffs, but again one feels that their hearts are more involved in a big work like the 18-minute 'The Floater'.

*****(*) The Works Vol. 1**
Soul Note 120176-2 *As above.* 7–9/94.

This seemed like a breakthrough record which their subsequent albums have built on. Like any group of long-standing experience, ROVA knew themselves well enough by now to discover new things in old chapters. There are just three compositions here, each a lengthy exploration and each concerned with both minutiae – of timbre, tempo, texture – and long-form considerations, such as the progressive weight of a piece, its sustainable intensities and its capacity to decay. Ochs's 'When The Nation Was Sound' is both one of their most ambitious and most approachable pieces, while the themes by Jack DeJohnette and John Carter are exemplary pieces of repertory and revisionism, ROVA-style.

*****(*) The Works Vol. 2**
Black Saint 120186-2 *As above.* 8/95.

*****(*) John Coltrane's Ascension**
Black Saint 120180-2 *As above, except add Dave Douglas, Raphe Malik (t); Glenn Spearman (ts); Chris Brown (p); Lisle Ellis (b); Donald Robinson (d).* 12/95.

It might seem churlish to deny the group their unreserved fourth star, but the quality of their records keeps going up and it's more an encouraging sign that a group of some 20 years' standing can still suggest their best is yet to come. *The Works Volume Two* consists of three long works: Tim Berne's 'The Visible Man' is solid sax-band repertory, but the two stronger pieces are Fred Ho's indignant-to-explosive 'Beyond Columbus And Capitalism', an intensely vivid piece of revolutionary rhetoric in sound, and Jon Raskin's fairly monumental 'Appearances Aren't Always What They Seem'. While the Ho piece has its fallibilities, Raskin knows the virtues of the band so well that his piece musters an almost visionary sweep, passing from bright contrapuntalism to fantastical convolutions to a moving coda that is among their most sheerly beautiful moments.

The sheer audacity of trying to re-create 'Ascension' in its entirety is justified by the uplifting result. Augmented by a rhythm section (Ochs takes a solo spin with them on 'Welcome', to introduce the record), the group employ Coltrane's theme but take the inevitable departures with both the solos and what seems to be spontaneous counterpoint. Trane and his men were taking early steps in a new world; these players have a fund of preconceived knowledge. The result is a realization which makes up in assured power what it might lack in 'pure' freedom. Douglas is a crucial element, injecting a lyrical passage before Raskin's almost brutal alto solo, but everyone plays their part. Bravo!

CORE COLLECTION

****** Bingo**
Victo CD 056 *Bruce Ackley, Steve Adams, Larry Ochs, Jon Raskin (saxes).* 9/96.

They've become a great repertory group – the five pieces here are from commissions involving Lindsay Cooper, Barry Guy and Fred Frith, plus one of Larry Ochs's most colourful originals – and they are, if not exactly reinventing themselves, at least reconsidering how they respond to each other, how the balance of their group can change, how they sound when they play soft or loud, how they start and end a piece, and what they can do to make their music new *and* better. The result is a considered and exceptionally satisfying record which has as much freshness in it as detail and maturity. Who's to say they won't be even better, twenty years hence?

*****(*) The Works Vol. 3**
Black Saint 120196-2 *As above.* 3–7/97.

Studio commissions from Muhal Richard Abrams and Robin Holcomb and a live-in-Turkey original by Steve Adams make up this third volume. Holcomb's 'Laredo' is in the Copland tradition and Abrams's 'Quartet #1' is in the modern Chicagoan tradition. Adams's 'The Gene Pool' is a classic ROVA situation, initiatives and responsibilities passed around the quartet quickly and creatively. More than good enough to stand beside the others.

Keith Rowe

GUITAR

Guitarist and founder-member of AMM, Rowe is as much a sound-sculptor as an improviser.

****** A Dimension Of Perfectly Ordinary Reality**
Matchless MRCD19 *Rowe (g solo).* 89.

***** Dial: Log-Rhythm**
Matchless MRCD36 *Rose; Jeffrey Morgan (as). 97.*

There has been an intermittent but often heated debate in British improvisation about 'instrumentalism', about whether music is a function of specific and idiomatically delimited technical resources or whether musical instruments should be an invisible and ultimately dispensable conduit for sound. Keith Rowe – and his colleagues in AMM – work at the sharp end of the debate. To describe him as a 'guitarist' is misleadingly simplistic. Rowe's deconstruction and reinvention of the guitar is one of the most radical sound strategies in contemporary music. He plays the instrument flat on a table and uses a range of articulation devices and electronic interventions to shape the sound – or, rather, to let the sound shape itself.

It's virtually impossible to describe what he does in terms of conventional technique, beyond saying that both these performances are thoughtful, intense and often very beautiful; above all, like the music of AMM, it is quite without expressive ego. The duo with Morgan doesn't strike us as the best starting-point for listeners who have no previous history with either Rowe or AMM. The saxophonist is emphatically his own man and the record is very much a meeting of equals. For a more revealing insight into how Keith Rowe functions, the earlier album is definitive, a whirling, almost violent foray into pure sound. Make some time for it.

***** Harsh**
Grob 209 *Rowe (g solo). 99.*

The three tracks are somewhat misleadingly labelled since 'Extremely' is less harsh than 'Very' while 'Quite' has some moments of real estrangement. These solo pieces, recorded in Germany, offer as good an account as any of Rowe's tautly disciplined sound-world. This is music that demands attention and will refuse to be consigned to the background.

***** The World Turned Upside Down**
Erstwhile 005 *Rowe; Taku Sugimoto (g); Gunter Muller (d, elec). 10/00.*

Named after either Christopher Hill's book on the English Civil War or a pub on the Old Kent Road in London, this recital actually took place in Paris, as part of the Instant Chavires festival. The key participant, apart from Rowe, is Muller, who deploys his 'selected percussion' with great delicacy and control. The guitarist is less compelling a presence, though much of Rowe's output for the next couple of years was to be with fellow guitarists. Here he is streets ahead of his colleague in virtually every respect, outthinking and out playing him. Rowe's intensity of concentration is less evident in group situations, but all the more important when he is listening not just to himself but to others.

***** Grain**
Zarek 06 *Rowe; Burkhard Beins (perc). 00.*

***** Weather Sky**
Erstwhile 018 *Rowe; Toshima Nakamura (mixing board). 00.*

***** Rabbit Run**
Erstwhile 027 *Rowe; Thomas Lehn (syn, elec); Markus Schmickler (sound manipulation). 00.*

Rowe's recorded output increased exponentially around 2000. These collaborations are entirely typical of his work of the time but not necessarily his best performances. In company, Rowe's impact seems to be diminished and Nakamura's gentle manipulation of his sound is almost surplus to requirements. More interesting, though ultimately no more relevant, is producer Markus Schmickler's detailed sampling and reshuffling. Your 'Random' button might well be called into play for this one, but whether the aleatory approach makes any more of the music is a matter for debate. Strong records, but not vintage Rowe performances.

***** Flypaper**
Staubgold 32 *Rowe; Oren Ambarchi (g). 01.*

***** Thumb**
Grob 432 *As above; add Sachiko M (elec). 01.*

Australian Ambarchi was probably the first to come out as a card-carrying Rowe disciple. Like most such encounters – and one thinks of the late Peter Kowald's encounters with young bassists – these sets waver uneasily between respectful discipleship and a pointless mimicry. Nevertheless, Rowe is incapable of making an uninteresting sound and there is more than enough material on these albums to intrigue anyone concerned with the extended language of guitar.

****** Duos for Doris**
Erstwhile 030 *Rowe; John Tilbury (p). 02.*

Not to be confused with Stockhausen's very early composition *Chore Für Doris.* That was dedicated to the composer's wife. This superb duo is dedicated to the pianist's mother, who died just a few days before the recording took place. How much of the emotion that surrounded her death seeped into the music can only be guessed at. However, these are powerful and deeply felt exchanges between two men who have worked together many times as part of AMM but who have never enjoyed a public dialogue quite as close as this one. Tilbury is in superb form, sounding at one moment as if he might be reading from Stockhausen's later *Klavierstücke* and the next as if conjuring up the spirit of Henry Cowell. Rowe concentrates as ever on small movements and this time a relatively narrow band of sonorities, certainly on the monumental 'Cathnor'. A superb record; thoroughly recommended.

Jimmy Rowles (1918–96)

PIANO, VOCAL

Had much big-band experience during the '40s before settling in Los Angeles, where he did years of studio work interleaved with club gigs, occasional feature recordings, and much work as accompanist to singers, including Billie Holiday and Peggy Lee. Decamped for New York in the '70s but eventually returned West. A character player in the music, but a player full of wit and sly humour and with an encyclopaedic knowledge of the American songbook.

*****(*) Piano Playhouse**
VSOP 31 *Rowles; Carl Perkins, Paul Smith, Lou Levy, Gerald Wiggins (p). 9/57.*

***** Weather In A Jazz Vane**
VSOP 48 *Rowles; Lee Katzman (t); Bob Enevoldsen (vtb); Herb Geller (as, bs); Bill Holman (ts, bs); Monty Budwig (b); Mel Lewis (d). 12/58.*

*****(*) Our Delight**

VSOP 99 *Rowles; Max Bennett, Chuck Berghofer (b); Larry Bunker, Nick Martinis (d).* 4/68.

***** Shade And Light**

Black & Blue 946.2 *Rowles; George Duvivier (b); Oliver Jackson (d).* 7/78.

*****(*) Ellington By Rowles**

Cymbol CYMCD 1 *Rowles (p solo).* 11/79.

Rowles's discography is very scattered and many of his own-name records are out of print. This rather motley bunch still include a lot of fine music. *Piano Playhouse* was an initiative by the Mode label to put five pianists together for an album of solos (ironically, the label went bust before it could be released). Rowles gets to do a blues, a fast 'Jordu', a serene 'That Old Devil Called Love' and a brief 'Laugh Clown Laugh', although the record also has delightful glimpses of Carl Perkins and the others. *Weather In A Jazz Vane* is a fairly conventional West Coast kind of date, arranged by Bill Holman, and the horns make a grander impression than Rowles, who tends to be confined to the rhythm section. *Our Delight* is a souvenir of one of his regular club gigs of the '60s, at The Carriage House on Burbank, and though the recording is of mediocre amateur standard the surviving pieces have a lot of definitive Rowles, including 'Moon Of Manakoora' and 'America The Beautiful'.

Shade And Light, part of Black & Blue's trove of French recordings, has a knockabout quality best realized in Jimmy's vocals on the likes of 'When The Morning Glories Wake Up In The Morning' and if paired with the Ellington set one gets a rounded look at this maverick talent. The Cymbol album takes a more serious and considered look at a baker's dozen of Ellington nuggets, and though one might have wished for Rowles to have done his archaeological bit and dug up some rarer stuff, he does manage to strip some of the overpolished layers off the likes of 'Satin Doll' and 'Sophisticated Lady', the playing often beautifully inventive.

Gonzalo Rubalcaba (born 1963)

PIANO, KEYBOARDS

A Cuban émigré pianist, Rubalcaba created a minor sensation with his early appearances and was quickly signed up by Blue Note, for whom he recorded through the '90s.

****(*) Discovery: Live At Montreux**

Blue Note 795478-2 *Rubalcaba; Charlie Haden (b); Paul Motian (d).* 7/90.

****** The Blessing**

Blue Note 797197-2 *As above, except Jack DeJohnette (d) replaces Motian.* 5/91.

***** Diz**

Blue Note 830490-2 *Rubalcaba; Ron Carter (b); Julio Barreto (d).* 12/93.

***** Antiguo**

Blue Note 837717-2 *Rubalcaba; Reynaldo Melian (t); Felipe Cabrera (b); Julio Barreto (d); Giovanni Hidalgo, Dagoberto Gonzalez (perc); Lazaro Ros, Maridalia Hernandez (v).* 6/95–7/96.

***** Inner Voyage**

Blue Note 499241-2 *Rubalacaba; Michael Brecker (ts); Jeff Chambers (b); Ignacio Berroa (d).* 11/98.

Rubalcaba is perhaps the most singular of those Cuban musicians who have made an impact on the American jazz scene of late. While he plays with as much grandstanding power as any of his countrymen, there is a compensating lightness of touch which one sometimes misses in the perpetually ebullient tone of most Cuban jazz. However, *Discovery*, a record of his sensational debut appearance at the Montreux Festival of 1990, suffers from an excess of tumult which finally makes the record wearisome, impressively played though it all is. From the first terrifically overheated workout on Monk's 'Well You Needn't', it sounds as if Rubalcaba is out to impress at any cost, and Motian and Haden can only anchor him as best they can. Much exhilaration, but not a record to play often.

The subsequent studio record, *The Blessing*, is a huge step forward. The pianist rations his outbursts to a handful and instead negotiates a thoughtful but no less compelling way through a delightful programme. Haden's 'Sandino' emerges with just the right note of troubled dignity, 'Giant Steps' is reharmonized and made new through brilliant use of repetition, DeJohnette's charming 'Silver Hollow' rivals the composer's own version, and 'The Blessing' and 'Blue In Green' remodel Coleman and Evans. Best of all, perhaps, is a beautifully chiselled treatment of 'Besame Mucho' which eliminates all sense of kitsch that the tune may possess, suggesting instead a flinty sort of romanticism. Rubalcaba's touch and finesse are marvellous throughout, and DeJohnette is clearly the ideal drummer for the situation, his unassuming virtuosity meeting all the challenges head on.

Diz is Rubalcaba's 'pure' bebop album, nine themes from the heartland of the repertory done partly as a tribute to Dizzy Gillespie. Appropriately enough, perhaps, it is not much like any traditional bebop record, infused with suggestions of Latin polyrhythms even when they aren't always directly stated. The dark colours of, say, 'Bouncing With Bud' are the elements that dominate. Yet this is all too knowing a record. Carter's elegant lines work well, but Barreto's drumming is aggravatingly ingenious, and it spurs the pianist on to some pointlessly clever improvising. For all his dazzle, Rubalcaba can be hard to warm to.

Antiguo is another mightily ambitious undertaking, this time a fusion of his core Cuban-American jazz, involving a trio of bata drummers, an Afro-Cuban choir, the Dominican pop diva Maridalia Hernandez, and the almost shamanic chanting of Lazaro Ros. A heady mixture, to which Rubalacaba's battery of keyboards – 11 synths and samplers are credited – adds even more spice and/or bulk. Some of this is reminiscent of Chick Corea's *My Spanish Heart* (from 1976 – hardly a forward-looking music to cite!), with the babble of synths mixed with the voices to often unconvincing effect, and it's hard to comprehend to which principles Rubalcaba is being faithful; it doesn't sound like any useful development out of the ingredients which he is stirring together. That said, the record is undeniably very pretty and songful a lot of the time.

Inner Voyage is yet another side of this interesting if frustrating talent. Played often at a slow-to-mid tempo, this is trio jazz of surpassing restraint, a somewhat surprising feat of concentration from this frequently explosive musician. Brecker comes in on two tracks and puts matters on edge somewhat, but more typical is the almost tortoise-like pace chosen for 'Here's That Rainy Day'.

*****(*) Supernova**
Blue Note 31172-2 *Rubalcaba; Carlos Henriquez (b); Ignacio Berroa (d); Luis Quintero, Robert Quintero (perc).* 00.

After Rubalcaba's long and difficult sequence of records, listeners may find this a minor revelation. He has never balanced the different sides of his personality as well as he does here with a 'basic' instrumentation; the percussive elements fall neatly into place, and tunes such as 'El Cadete Constitucional' and the title-piece (the latter in two absorbingly different renditions) bring melody and rhythm into a confluence which is both joyful and darkly enigmatic. Henriquez is often almost as impressive as the leader, taking an independent line while still playing for the group. Definitely the best place to start in approaching this restless talent.

Roy Rubenstein

TROMBONE

English traditional trombonist working with contemporaries from both sides of the Atlantic in his Chicago Hot Six.

***** Shout 'Em!**
Delmark DE-227 *Rubenstein; Bob Nabors (c); Norrie Cox (cl); Jack Kuncl (bj); Dick Pierre (b); Ken Lowenstine (d); Katherine Davis (v).* 12/93–1/94.

Somehow this expatriate 'bone man has ended up leading his Chicago Hot Six on that city's most eminent local label. Traditional music played without a trace of self-consciousness, though not necessarily the better for it: the dynamic is unvaryingly even and some of the tempos are a bit too gentlemanly. 'Shout 'Em Aunt Tillie', a choice piece of early Ellington, gets a splendid treatment, and 'Pontchartrain Blues' counts as rarely heard Jelly Roll Morton. Katherine Davis sings on four numbers and her surprisingly small, intimate voice suits the situation. Excellent recording.

Roswell Rudd (born 1935)

TROMBONE, TRUMPET, FRENCH HORN, VOCALS

Born in Connecticut, Rudd made his professional debut with Eli's Chosen Six and, despite his adherence to the avant-garde, his approach always suggested a return to the primordial simplicities of early jazz. His trombone style recalls the more expressionist methods of an earlier age, using slurs and growls, blustering swing and a big, sultry tone.

*****(*) Regeneration**
Soul Note 121054 *Rudd; Steve Lacy (ss); Misha Mengelberg (p); Kent Carter (b); Han Bennink (d).* 6/82.

It has been a matter of intense frustration that Rudd made so few records since his work with the New York Art Quartet and Archie Shepp in the '60s announced a marvellously vivid and unpredictable spirit in the new jazz of the period, and certainly one of the most imaginative trombone-players since J. J. Johnson. Only the German Albert Mangelsdorff has made a comparable impact on the unfashionable horn, though Mangelsdorff's star is, if anything, more securely positioned above the horizon. One of the difficulties with Rudd is that he has often preferred to work with other leaders, such as Cecil Taylor, or the 'comeback' recordings made under the leadership of Allen Lowe. Much of his best work of recent years has been in the company of the British saxophonist Elton Dean.

Regeneration is very satisfying although, for a demonstration of Rudd's latter-day style, Enrico Rava's *Quartet* album for ECM is a more representative and comprehensive example. Like the two CIMP sessions below (titles self-explanatory), it's a tribute to the pianist and composer with whom Rudd worked in the early '60s. For 35 years since Nichols's death in 1963, Rudd has been the keeper of the spirit, campaigning with Steve Lacy and an increasing constituency of players against Nichols's marginalization. Lacy and Rudd used to work together in a unit which performed only Thelonious Monk material, and so it's no surprise to hear three Monk tunes here alongside the same number of Nichols pieces.

****** The Unheard Herbie Nichols: Volume 1**
CIMP 133 *Rudd; Greg Millar (g, perc); John Bacon Jr (d, vib).* 11/96.

*****(*) The Unheard Herbie Nichols: Volume 2**
CIMP 146 *As above.* 11/96.

The CIMP session was a chance to concentrate on Nichols entirely, and to dig out some of the most obscure material in his legacy. There are some surprises in instrumentation as well. On 'Some Wandering Bushmen', Rudd played trumpet on the initial take before reprising the same tune on his more familiar horn. On the long 'Jamaica' (Volume 1) he plays percussion, and elsewhere on the same disc gets out the little-used mellophone. The biggest surprise of all, though, comes at the end of Volume 2, when Roswell sings the lyric to 'Vacation Blues'.

Most of this material is genuinely unknown and unheard, even to those who do know 'Shuffle Montgomery' and 'Lady Sings The Blues'. It seems extraordinary that tunes like 'Freudian Frolics', the far from lightweight 'Tee Dum Tee Dee', 'Prancin' Pretty Woman', and 'Karna Kanji' are not in the wider repertoire. The trio is well balanced and very responsive, with Millar taking part at least of the accompanist's role. He and Bacon duet on 'Dream Time', leaving Rudd to play 'One Twilight' and 'Passing Thoughts' unaccompanied, the latter a long, virtuosic performance that must count as one of his most extraordinary statements on record. These are important statements, largely because of the slighted legacy of one of the great jazz composers, but also because Rudd himself is so badly under-represented in the catalogues. Anyone who has admired either man will be drawn to these and, while we favour the first volume, both are strongly recommended.

Howard Rumsey (born 1917)

BASS

Studied in Los Angeles, then formed a small group with Stan Kenton and subsequently joined the Kenton orchestra. Formed the Lighthouse All Stars, a revolving group of West Coast leading lights, which performed regularly at the Hermosa Beach Lighthouse Club, then promoted other Californian concerts in the '50s and '60s.

*****(*) Sunday Jazz À La Lighthouse**
Original Jazz Classics OJC 151 *Rumsey; Shorty Rogers (t); Milt Bernhart (tb); Jimmy Giuffre, Bob Cooper (ts); Hampton Hawes, Frank Patchen (p); Shelly Manne (d).* 7/52–2/53.

***** Volume 3**

Original Jazz Classics OJC 266 *As above, except add Rolf Ericson (t), Frank Rosolino (tb), Bud Shank (as, f), Herb Geller (as), Max Roach, Stan Levey (d), Carlos Vidal, Jack Costanza (perc).* 7/52–8/56.

****** Sunday Jazz À La Lighthouse Vol. 2**

Original Jazz Classics OJC 972 *As above, except add Chet Baker (t), Russ Freeman, Lorraine Geller, Claude Williamson (p); omit Rosolino, Levey, Vidal, Costanza, Geller, Hawes, Patchen.* 3–9/53.

***** Oboe / Flute**

Original Jazz Classics OJC 154 *Rumsey; Bob Cooper (ob, cor); Bud Shank (f, af); Buddy Collette (f); Claude Williamson, Sonny Clark (p); Max Roach, Stan Levey (d).* 2/54–9/56.

***** In The Solo Spotlight**

Original Jazz Classics OJC 451 *Rumsey; Conte Candoli, Stu Williamson (t); Frank Rosolino (tb); Bob Enevoldsen (vtb); Bud Shank, Lennie Niehaus (as); Bob Cooper, Richie Kamuca (ts); Bobby Gordon, Pepper Adams (bs); Claude Williamson, Dick Shreve (p); Stan Levey (d).* 8/54–3/57.

***** Volume 6**

Original Jazz Classics OJC 386 *Rumsey; Conte Candoli (t); Frank Rosolino (tb); Stu Williamson (vtb); Bud Shank (as); Bob Cooper (ts); Claude Williamson (p); Stan Levey (d).* 12/54–3/55.

***** Lighthouse At Laguna**

Original Jazz Classics OJC 406 *Rumsey; Frank Rosolino (tb); Bud Shank (as, f); Bob Cooper (ts); Claude Williamson, Hampton Hawes (p); Barney Kessel (g); Red Mitchell (b); Shelly Manne, Stan Levey (d).* 6/55.

***** Music For Lighthousekeeping**

Original Jazz Classics OJC 636 *Rumsey; Conte Candoli (t); Frank Rosolino (tb); Bob Cooper (ts); Sonny Clark (p); Stan Levey (d).* 10/56.

***** Mexican Passport**

Contemporary 14077-2 *As for OJC* 151, 266, 406 *and* 636 *above.* 52–56.

Rumsey was of no major significance as a bassist, but he was a canny organizer, and his Lighthouse All Stars – the name which all these CDs go under – offered the pick of the West's best in the mid-'50s. Their Sunday-afternoon concerts are still talked about by veterans of the Hermosa Beach scene, effectively 12-hour jam sessions that started in the afternoon and went on into the small hours. There are live sessions on OJCs 151, 972 and 406 (though the latter was cut at Laguna Beach) and part of OJC 154; the rest are studio dates. To catch the excitement of these sessions, the best is *Sunday Jazz À La Lighthouse Vol. 2*: a buzzing crowd, bandstands full of the hottest players; with 25 minutes of previously unreleased material, this one's a best buy. Sound is at times more atmospheric than accurate, but it's a terrific document of those sessions. The first volume is also excellent, with some fine work by Hawes, but the *Laguna* set is more like a formal concert, with a guest spot by Kessel and two tracks by the Hawes–Mitchell–Manne trio.

The studio dates are more in the familiar West Coast language and are rather more efficiently styled. Considering the stellar line-up, *In The Solo Spotlight* is a shade disappointing, with too many of the features emerging as glib showcases. While none of the others really stands out, followers of the style will find much to satisfy, not least in the consistently superb drumming by Manne and Levey. *Mexican Passport* compiles the various Latinesque tracks which the band made across their albums.

Jimmy Rushing (1903–72)

VOCAL

Raised in Oklahoma, Rushing started as a pianist, but began singing and making a name for himself in that capacity around the South-West of the USA in the mid-'20s. His greatest successes were with the Count Basie orchestra of the '30s and '40s, his huge physical presence partnering the great voice. A gentle and genial man, he worked right up until his death from leukaemia in 1972.

***** Mr Five By Five**

Topaz TPZ 1019 *Rushing; orchestras of Walter Page, Bennie Moten and Count Basie.* 11/29–4/42.

Jimmy Rushing began recording in 1929, with Bennie Moten, and carried on for 40-plus years. Many of his finest performances are with Count Basie and are listed under the bandleader's name, but this collection creams off some of his best features for Bennie Moten and Basie. It's useful to have the original takes of Rushing favourites like 'Sent For You Yesterday' and 'Harvard Blues' all in one place. That said, the remastering is erratic – not one of the best discs in the usually solid Topaz series – and the formulaic nature of his Basie discs makes an unbroken sequence less appetizing. With his Vanguard recordings back out in the cold, though, this is as good a place as any to start hearing this great blues/jazz man. *Jimmy Rushing Swings The Blues* (CDS RPCD 637) covers similar ground.

CORE COLLECTION

****** Rushing Lullabies**

Columbia CK 65118 *Rushing; Buck Clayton, Emmett Berry, Bernie Glow, Mel Davis, Doc Cheatham (t); Dicky Wells, Vic Dickenson, Urbie Green, Frank Rehak (tb); Rudy Powell, Earl Warren (as); Coleman Hawkins, Buddy Tate (ts); Danny Bank (bs); Nat Pierce, Ray Bryant (p); Sir Charles Thompson (org); Danny Barker, Skeeter Best (g); Milt Hinton, Gene Ramey (b); Jo Jones, Osie Johnson (d).* 2/58–6/59.

Coupling the original albums *Rushing Lullabies* and *Little Jimmy Rushing And The Big Brass*, this is a connoisseurs' set of jazz singing, one of the ripest and most enjoyable examples of Rushing on record from what should have been a period of great success for him. These albums have never been widely known, but they date from a vintage period of mainstream playing, the band almost peerless in its personnel with a host of strong soloists headed by Hawkins and Tate. Some of the material dates back to the original jazz age, some – 'Good Rockin' Tonight', handled with a sort of smiling tolerance – a nod to rock'n'roll, but Rushing sings all of it with his singular blend of blues and jazz in a serene counterpoint that survives the years. A model reissue in excellent sound.

***** Five Feet Of Soul**

Roulette 81830-2 *Rushing; Ernie Glow, Markie Markowitz, Joe Newman, Snooky Young (t); Billy Byers, Jimmy Cleveland, Willie Dennis, Urbie Green (tb); Gene Quill, Phil Woods (as);*

Budd Johnson, Zoot Sims (ts); Sol Schlinger (bs); Patti Bown (p); Freddie Green (g); Milt Hinton (b); Gus Johnson (d). 1/63.

Five Feet Of Soul was the singer's only session for Roulette (although it was actually issued on Colpix), and really isn't much more than a studio quickie – Al Cohn arrangements for a band full of session-rats, and tunes that Jimmy must have known backwards by 1963. Al copies The Count for the feel and sound, and the likes of Snooky Young and Zoot Sims throw off the righteous obbligatos. He's in hearty voice, though occasionally it gets away from him: he starts 'Trouble In Mind' mightily, but by the end the troubles seem to be getting to the tonsils. Some of them are faster than he'd like – 'Oooh! Look-A-There' is rattled off in a couple of minutes, and you start wondering how much better it might have sounded recast as a slow blues. He saves some of his best for his own lyrics, and 'Please Come Back' and 'Did You Ever' work out just fine. Not vintage Rushing, but with little enough by him around, a welcome renewal.

*** Who Was It Sang That Song?

New World 80510-2 *Rushing; Buck Clayton (t); Dicky Wells (tb); Julian Dash (ts); Sir Charles Thompson (p); Eugene Ramey (b); Jo Jones (d).* 10/67.

*** Gee Baby, Ain't I Good To You?

New World 80530-2 *As above.* 10/67.

Recorded in a studio that had once been a hotel ballroom, this 'jazz party' is a boisterous affair. The stellar personnel suggest a special occasion, but the pretty awful recording (not helped by the fact that the original stereo masters were destroyed, and the tracks were reconstructed from indifferent mono tapes) and the sometimes ramshackle playing are discouraging. Even so, Rushing is indomitable, Clayton is elegant, Wells idiosyncratic and the unlikely presence of Dash is a surprising plus. The best of it could have been boiled down to a single CD, but there is little enough of LP-era Rushing available to make every surviving disc worth having.

*** Every Day I Have The Blues

Impulse! 547967-2 *Rushing; Clark Terry (t); Dicky Wells (tb); Buddy Tate, Bob Ashton (ts); Hank Jones, Shirley Scott (org); David Frishberg (p); Hugh McCracken, Wally Richardson, Kenny Burrell (g); George Duvivier, Bob Bushnell (b); Grady Tate, Joe Marshall (d).* 67–68.

Although Jimmy himself remains in fine voice, this is a misconceived Bob Thiele production. It couples two Impulse! albums which mixed together some genuine blues with faddish tunes such as 'Berkeley Campus Blues' (which complains about student sit-ins) and some attempted funky stuff from the guitarists. The imperturbable Rushing carries on regardless, but this was hardly his ideal setting, although there are compensations in the cameos from Terry, Wells and Tate.

George Russell (born 1923)

COMPOSER, BANDLEADER, PIANO, ORGAN

George Russell's significance within jazz is rather tough to evaluate. For many years he was almost entirely marginalized by the critical and commercial establishment. After graduating in his native Cincinnati, he suffered a long illness during which he overturned much of what he and his teachers had thought about harmonics. Russell is responsible for what remains the most significant single theoretical treatise written about the music. The Lydian Chromatic Concept of Tonal Organization, completed in the early '50s, was the direct source of the modal or scalar experiments of John Coltrane and Miles Davis. Russell spent most of the '60s in Europe, reworking his treatise and writing little music. Recognition has been slow and hard-won.

CORE COLLECTION

**** Jazz Workshop

Koch 7850 *Russell; Art Farmer (t); Hal McKusick (as, f); Bill Evans (p); Barry Galbraith (g); Milt Hinton (b); Teddy Kotick (b); Joe Harris, Osie Johnson, Paul Motian (d).* 3–12/56.

However important Russell's theories are, they are even now not securely understood. Sometimes falsely identified with the original Greek Lydian mode, *The Lydian Chromatic Concept* is not the same at all. In diatonic terms, it represents the progression F to F on the piano's white keys; it also confronts the diabolic tritone, the *diabolus in musica*, which had haunted Western composers from Bach to Beethoven. Russell's conception assimilated modal writing to the extreme chromaticism of modern music. By converting chords into scales and overlaying one scale on another, it allowed improvisers to work in the hard-to-define area between nontonality and polytonality. Like all great theoreticians, Russell worked analytically rather than synthetically, basing his ideas on how jazz *actually was*, not on how it could be made to conform with traditional principles of Western harmony. Working from within jazz's often tacit organizational principles, Russell's fundamental concern was the relationship between formal scoring and improvisation, giving the first the freedom of the second, freeing the second from being literally esoteric, 'outside' some supposed norm.

Russell's theories also influenced his own composition. 'A Bird In Igor's Yard', a celebrated early piece, was a (rather too) self-conscious attempt to ally bebop and Stravinsky – it was also a young and slightly immature work – but it pointed the way forward. Russell's music always sounds both familiar and unsettlingly alien. His versions of staples like Charlie Parker's 'Au Privave', Thelonious Monk's equally precocious 'Round Midnight', and Miles Davis's almost oriental 'Nardis' on *Ezz-thetics* create new areas for the soloists to explore; in Don Ellis and Eric Dolphy he has players particularly responsive to expansions of the harmonic language (Dolphy in particular preferred to work the inner space of a piece, rather than to go 'out'). 'Ezz-thetic' first appeared on the classic 1956 *Jazz Workshop* sessions, now restored to CD and currently on the Koch imprint. It is one of the key pieces in an astonishing collection, including several pieces that stand as almost unique avenues of thought in the jazz language: 'Night Sound', 'Round Johnny Rondo', 'Knights Of The Steamtable' and 'Concerto For Billy The Kid', the latter including one of Bill Evans's most remarkable solos on record.

*** New York, N. Y.

Impulse! 051278-2 *Russell; Art Farmer, Doc Severinsen, Ernie Royal, Joe Wilder, Joe Ferrante (t); Bob Brookmeyer (vtb); Frank Rehak, Jimmy Cleveland, Tom Mitchell (tb); Hal McKusick, Phil Woods (as); John Coltrane, Al Cohn, Benny Golson (ts); Sol Schlinger, Gene Allen (bs); Bill Evans (p);*

Barry Galbraith (g); Milt Hinton, George Duvivier (b); Charli Persip, Max Roach, Don Lamond (d); Al Epstein (perc); Jon Hendricks (v). 58–59.

****** Jazz In The Space Age**

Chess GRP 18262 *Russell; Ernie Royal, Al Kiger, Marky Markowitz (t); Frank Rehak, Dave Baker (tb); Bob Brookmeyer (vtb); Jimmy Buffington (frhn); Walt Levinsky, Hal McKusick (as); Dave Young (ts); Sol Schlinger (bs); Bill Evans, Paul Bley (p); Barry Galbraith, Howard Collins (g); Milt Hinton (b); Don Lamond, Charli Persip (d).* 5–8/60.

****** At The Five Spot**

Verve 112287-2 *Russell; Alan Kiger (t); Dave Baker (tb); Dave Young (as); Chuck Israels (b); Joe Hunt (d).* 9/60.

****** Stratusphunk**

Original Jazz Classics OJC 232 *As above.* 10/60.

****** Ezz-thetics**

Original Jazz Classics OJC 070 *Russell; Don Ellis (t); Dave Baker (tb); Eric Dolphy (as, bcl); Steve Swallow (b); Joe Hunt (d).* 5/61.

*****(*) The Stratus Seekers**

Original Jazz Classics OJC 365 *Russell; Dave Baker, Don Ellis (t); John Pierce (as); Paul Plummer (ts); Steve Swallow (b); Joe Hunt (d).* 1/62.

***** The Outer View**

Original Jazz Classics OJC 616 *Russell; Garnett Brown (tb); Paul Plummer (ts); Steve Swallow (b); Pete LaRoca (d); Sheila Jordan (v).* 8/62.

As a very good start to a Russell collection there's a strong case to be made for *Ezz-thetics*, with its fine Dolphy contributions (coincidentally or not, the year of the saxophonist's death also marked the beginning of Russell's long exile in Europe and a mutual alienation from the American scene). But all these early Russells, with the exception of the slightly less achieved *The Outer View*, are indispensable. His regular sextet is responsible for most of the music on the various OJCs, and the improvising on *Stratusphunk* and *The Stratus Seekers* matches the composing and arranging in terms of insight and creativity.

The best of the lot may be *At The Five Spot*; despite the implication of the title it's a studio, rather than live, album. Opening with the early Miles Davis blues variation 'Sippin' At Bell's', they get the easy music out of the way first. The rest are originals by Russell and Baker, two early Carla Bley tunes and Coltrane's 'Moment's Notice'. The album was made after three weeks of six-nights-a-week playing, so the players were ready for it, and the fierce (though oddly melodious) complexities of both the themes and the improvising are entirely mastered. Chuck Israels, in the notes, remembers seeing audiences full of fellow musicians and artists: 'jazz at this time was connected to intelligent society, just as the work of writers and painters was'. Perhaps it's no wonder that this little masterpiece has scarcely been available in the 40 years since it was released, and even now is only available as a Verve limited-edition release.

The slightly earlier *New York, N. Y.* and *Jazz In The Space Age* yoke what sound like conceptual-modern album titles to what is actually the first application of Russell's mature music to a big-band setting. 'Manhattan', from the former, is almost a programme-piece, with a narration by Jon Hendricks that now seems charmingly of its time, and a solo by Coltrane. Both sets apply what's to be heard in the more concentrated sextet music in a more expansive setting. *Jazz In The Space Age*, in particular, is as fine as any of Russell's music from this period; 'Dimensions', a sequence of freely associated moods indigenous to jazz, outstrips whatever Gil Evans was doing for Miles Davis, and 'The Lydiot', with its framework for solos by both Evans and Bley, is similarly intriguing. To what extent these records are 'important' is, as with all of Russell's work, hard to say, since they have had very little discernible impact on jazz. They remain, however, indispensable music.

****(*) Othello Ballet Suite / Electronic Organ Sonata No. 1**

Soul Note 121014 *Russell; Rolf Ericson (t); Arne Domnérus (as); Bernt Rosengren (ts); Jan Garbarek (ts); Jon Christensen (d); others unknown.* 1/67.

Conducting the exuberant big bands of the '80s, Russell bore a striking physical resemblance to the choreographer, Merce Cunningham. There was a dancemaster's precision to his gestures that was communicated through his music as well. Russell's conception of harmonic space is somewhat like a modern choreographer's. The *Othello Ballet Suite* is only the most obvious example of how his imagination turns on movement – in this case, the curiously inward movements of Shakespeare's play – and on the formation of black identity in the West. The music is more stately than passionate, with an almost ritualistic quality to its development. Russell's orchestration is curiously reminiscent of Ravel, and it cloys in consequence; the saxophones sound slightly out of pitch. The *Electronic Organ Sonata* is rather superficial, too obvious an essay in Russell's harmonic and structural ideas to be entirely involving. The sound on both pieces, though, is good, and both are highly significant in his development of a non-canonical but systematic musical language.

*****(*) The Essence Of George Russell**

Soul Note 121044/5 2CD *Russell; Maffy Falay, Bertil Lövgren, Palle Mikkelborg, Palle Boldtvig, Jan Allan, Lars Samuelsson, Stanton Davis (t); George Vernon, Gunnar Medberg (tb); Runo Ericksson, Olle Lind (btb); Arne Domnérus (as, cl); Claes Rosendahl (ts, ss, as, f); Lennart Aberg (ts, ss, f); Bernt Rosengren (ts); Erik Nilson (bs, bcl); Bengt Egerblad (vib); Rune Gustafsson, Terje Rypdal (g); Bengt Hallberg (p); Arild Andersen, Roman Dylag (b); Jon Christensen (d); Rupert Clemendore (perc).* 66, 67.

***** Electronic Sonata For Souls Loved By Nature**

Soul Note 121034 *Russell; Manfred Schoof (t); Jan Garbarek (ts); Terje Rypdal (g); Red Mitchell (b); Jon Christensen (d).* 4/69.

***** Electronic Sonata For Souls Loved By Nature 1980**

Soul Note 121009 *Russell; Lew Soloff (t); Robert Moore (ts, ss); Victor Gomer (g); Jean-François Jenny-Clark (b); Keith Copeland (d, perc).* 6/80.

****(*) Trip To Prillargui**

Soul Note 121029 *Russell; Stanton Davis (t); Jan Garbarek (ts); Terje Rypdal (g); Arild Andersen (b); Jon Christensen (d).* 3/70.

For all the quality of the performances, these are conceptually woolly and rather abstract works that add no more than grace-notes to Russell's remarkable compositional output. In the triumvirate of great arrangers, Russell is closer to the open texture of Gil Evans than to Quincy Jones's lacquered surface. There is a sense, though, with these performances that surface is all that matters. The original *Electronic Sonata*, which is included on the big-band *Essence* as well as on the self-titled small-group recording, has a depth of perspective and firmness of execution that the still-puzzling 1980 revision totally lacks. Conceived for tapes and ensemble, the piece is again chiefly concerned with the relationship between scored and improvised materials. *Trip To Prillargui* is beautifully played but sounds curiously emptied of significance, and it yields no more on repeated hearings; the transfer to CD has made a big difference, but it's still less than compelling.

***** Listen To The Silence**

Soul Note 121024 *Russell; Stanton Davis Jr (t); Jan Garbarek (ts); Bobo Stenson (p); Webster Lewis (org); Bjornar Andresen, Terje Rypdal (g); Arild Andersen (b); Jon Christensen (perc); Sue Auclair, Gailanne Cummings, Kay Dunlap, David Dusing, Joyce Gippo, Ray Hardin, Don Hovey, Don Kendrick, Dan Windham (v).* 6/71.

Episodically fascinating, this series of otherwise untitled 'Events I–IV' has something of the feel of rehearsal material worked up quickly for performance. The harmonics are unmistakably Russell's and as challenging as ever, but the players are left with little opportunity to swing the ideas or to invest them with any kind of expressive presence, and they remain as neutrally beautiful as snapshots inside a cloud chamber or of cultures in a Petri dish. Significantly, the main interest is in the developing voices of particular soloists, Garbarek, Rypdal and Christensen, all of whom would learn much from the experience with Russell, but who already seemed to be chafing. The project does underline how brilliant a writer for voices Russell was (a gift even he seems to have underestimated) and how exceptional an engineer Jan Erik Kongshaug was and was to be in the coming decade when he became the man more or less directly responsible for another chimera of new music, the 'ECM sound'.

****(*) Vertical Form VI**

Soul Note 121019 *Russell; Americo Bellotto, Bertil Lövgren (t, flhn); Hakan Hyquist (t, flhn, frhn); Jan Allan (t, frhn); Ivar Olsen (frhn); Bengt Edvarsson, Jorgen Johansson, Lars Olofsson (tb); Sven Larsson (btb, tba); Arne Domnérus (cl, as, ss); Jan Uling (f, as, ts); Lennart Aberg, Bernt Rosengren (f, as, ts, ss); Erik Nilsson (f, bcl, bs); Rune Gustafsson (g); Bjorn Lind (electric p); Vlodek Gulgowski (electric p, syn); Monica Dominique (electric p, cel, org, clavinet); Stefan Brolund, Bronislaw Suchanek, Lars-Urban Helje (b); Lars Beijbom, Leroy Lowe (d); Sabu Martinez (perc).* 3/77.

If we're looking for appropriate visual analogies, *Vertical Form VI* is less like an upright menhir than another kind of standing stone. The dolmen has a huge, slabby top perched on unfeasibly skinny supports. By that analogy Russell's piece has considerable mass and gravitational force, but seems to rest on nothing more than the bare uprights of theory, with little or no emotional engagement. The band is well drilled and produces a big, generous sound. Once encountered, though, the music seems just to sit there, much involved with its own enigma and a few intelligent guesses about its origins. Towards the end of the '70s and during the following decade, Russell began to receive some of the attention he had long deserved.

*****(*) New York Big Band**

Soul Note 121039 *Russell; as above, plus: Stanton Davis, Terumasa Hino, Lew Soloff (t); Gary Valente (tb); Dave Taylor (btb); John Clark (frhn); Marty Ehrlich (as); Ricky Ford (ts); Roger Rosenberg (ts); Carl Atkins (bs, bcl); Mark Slifstein (g); Stanley Cowell, Gotz Tangerding (p); Ricky Martinez (electric p, org); Cameron Brown (b); Warren Smith (d); Babafumi Akunyon (perc); Lee Genesis (v).* 77–78.

*****(*) Live In An American Time Spiral**

Soul Note 121049 *Russell; Stanton Davis, Tom Harrell, Brian Leach, Ron Tooley (t); Ray Anderson, Earl McIntyre (tb); Marty Ehrlich (as, f); Doug Miller (ts, f); Bob Hanlon (bs); Jerome Harris (g); Jack Reilly, Mark Soskin (ky); Ron McClure (b); Victor Lewis (d).* 7/82.

New York Big Band includes a vital (in every sense) performance of the epochal 'Cubana Be, Cubana Bop', written in collaboration with Dizzy Gillespie and first performed in 1947. With its structural and not just decorative use of African and Caribbean metres, the piece opened out a whole new direction for jazz writing, paving the way for *The African Game* 25 years later. *Big Band* also includes two sections from *Listen To The Silence* and a wonderful and unexpected 'God Bless The Child' that derives something from Dolphy's long engagement with the piece.

The main piece on *Live* is a concert performance of 'Time Spiral'. Concerned again with the larger, almost meta-historical movements of human life, the charts have a slightly dense philosophical feel on the studio album, but they open up considerably in a live setting. The album also includes a fine reading of 'Ezz-thetic' and the faintly ironic 'D.C. Divertimento', given force by a (mostly) young and enthusiastic band.

***** The London Concerts: Volumes 1 & 2**

Label Bleu 6527 2CD *Russell; Stuart Brooks, Ian Carr, Mark Chandler (t); Pete Beachill, Ashley Slater (tb); Andy Sheppard, Chris Biscoe, Pete Hurt (reeds); Brad Hatfield, Steve Lodder (ky); David Fiuczynski (g); Bill Urmson (b); Steve Johns (d).* 89.

Somewhat as he had in Scandinavia two decades earlier, Russell found young British players (and some of their elders) hanging on his every compositional idea, and more than willing to work with him. These recordings, originally on Stash, were the first discs since the early part of the decade, a bizarre neglect of the man some would consider one of the half-dozen most important composers to have graced the music. Whether that valuation stands up to these oddly confected discs, which contain another performance of the 'Electronic Sonata', is very much a matter of personal judgement. We tend to think rather not. The band is absolutely on the case, but the material sounds either diffuse or ridiculously knotty, needing something of the looseness and relaxation that Gil Evans got out of British players. It is rather baffling to look back on the Russell discography, since it seems to suggest a brilliant early phase that has almost completely disintegrated into unsuitable and unproductive music. While there are worthwhile things among the later records, as noted, Russell's dazzling small-group music of the '50s and early '60s now seems like a prematurely closed chapter which jazz would do well to take another look at.

Hal Russell (1926–92)

SAXOPHONES, TRUMPET, VIBRAPHONE, DRUMS, BANDLEADER

Born in Detroit, Russell played drums in big bands before spending most of the '50s and '60s in Chicago, playing behind numerous visitors and forming a pioneer free-jazz group with

Joe Daley. Later applied himself to trumpet, sax and vibes and formed the NRG Ensemble in the late '70s, which performed his music until his sudden death, five weeks after cutting The Hal Russell Story.

*** Elixir

Atavistic Unheard Music UMS 203 *Russell; Spider Middleman, Mars Williams (sax); George Southgate (vib); Russ Ditusa (b). 3/79.*

*** Generation

Chief 5 *Russell; Chuck Burdelik (cl, as, ts); Charles Tyler (as, cl, bs); Brian Sandstrom (g, b, t); Curt Bley (b); Steve Hunt (d, vib). 9/82.*

***(*) Conserving NRG

Principally Jazz PJP CD 02 *Russell; Brian Sandstrom (t, g, b, perc); Chuck Burdelik (ts, as, perc); Curt Bley (b); Steve Hunt (d, vib, perc). 3/84.*

There was nothing else in the jazz of its period quite like Hal Russell's NRG Ensemble. Playing just one instrument is considered rather wimpish, especially when the old man drifts back and forth between vibes, cornet and high-register, Ayler-influenced saxophone. Arguably, no one made a comparable impact so late in his career, other than Joe Maneri, who trod similar territory. Russell actually set out as a drummer; he was recruited by Miles Davis in 1950 and by the radical Chicagoan Joe Daley (now little known outside free-jazz circles in the United States) a decade later. Towards the end of the '70s he took up trumpet again for the first time since his student days and learned to play the saxophone.

The Unheard Music disc catches Russell immediately before the NRG Ensemble was convened and playing with a surreal three-saxophone outfit known as Chemical Feast. Included in the programme from the Elixir Gallery were two Ornette Coleman tunes 'Broadway Blues' and 'Airborne', as well as his own bizarre 'Four Free', 'Kahoutek' and 'Manas'. There's still a strong element of theatre about the groups of the time, a Fluxus sensibility which doesn't time-travel all that well, but these are very important documents in the pre-history of NRG.

Given the band's fierce underground reputation, *Generation* and *Conserving NRG* are slightly disappointing, sounding forced where the later *Finnish/Swiss Tour* appears spontaneous, disorderly where the later things conform to some logic. Nevertheless it's powerful stuff, the sound is better, and there isn't that much of Russell available. Watch out for 'Generation' itself, and the scissorhands 'Poodle Cut'. The sound on both records is rather slipshod, presumably due to the exigencies of performance, but both are perfectly listenable.

***(*) The Finnish/Swiss Tour

ECM 511261-2 *Russell; Mars Williams (ts, ss, didjeridu); Brian Sandstrom (b, t, g); Kent Kessler (b, didjeridu); Steve Hunt (d, vib, didjeridu). 11/90.*

*** Naked Colours

Silkheart SHCD 135 *Russell; Joel Futterman (p, rec); Jay Oliver (b); Robert Adkins (d). 91.*

*** Hal's Bells

ECM 513781-2 *Russell (all instruments). 5/92.*

***(*) The Hal Russell Story

ECM 517364-2 *Russell; Mars Williams (ts, as, bsx, f, didjeridu, bells, v); Brian Sandstrom (b, g, t, toys, perc); Kent Kessler (b, tb); Steve Hunt (d, tim, vib, perc). 7/92.*

In its blend of forceful, rock-inflected ostinati, extreme dynamics and broadly satirical approach, the NRG Ensemble bears some kinship to Frank Zappa's Mothers Of Invention; in his liner-note to *The Finnish/Swiss Tour*, Steve Lake also notes Russell's physical resemblance to Charles Ives, which isn't so far away, either. A record of the Ensemble's first and rather surreal European itinerary, and the leader quotes from Keith Jarrett, and for 'Linda's Rock Vamp' dons Prince of Darkness shades over his prescription specs, as the liner-booklet shows, in dubious homage to his former employer. The band have the huge, dark sound of the mid-'70s Miles Davis units, the days when Miles was Abstract Expressionist rather than Neo-Figurative. 'Compositions' are treated as reference points, and performances frequently develop into all-out jams which nevertheless give off a strong aura of control. The sheer *size* of the sound suggests a much larger outfit. Sandstrom's stripped guitar-playing, Steve Hunt's ferocious time-keeping and the occasional use of twinned basses generate astonishing volume, with Mars Williams (formerly of the rock band Psychedelic Furs) overblowing furiously beside the leader on the powerful 'Temporarily'. 'For MC' is for didjeridus, electric guitar and cornet; the Zappa-sounding 'Hal The Weenie' is also an Ayler-ish invocation of ghosts and spirits.

His final legacy was two quite extraordinary 'concept' albums for ECM, the first a multitracked solo effort, the second a potted autobiography in music and cartoon narrations shouted through a paper megaphone. The tunes on both are a mixture of reworked standards and themes worked out on the spot for the session. Those in *Hal's Bells* range from vibraphone solos – the lovely 'I Need You Know' – to 'group' pieces like 'Kenny G', a curious name-check for Bill Clinton's favourite saxophonist, arranged for tenor, vibes and drums, to the more radical 'For Free' (saxophones, trumpets, vibes and drums), which harks back to his days with the Joe Daley group. Some of these tracks plod a little. Certainly, few of them have the all-out energy of the material on *Story*, a record which compresses 40 years of music-making into a standard-length CD. Russell's biography is no more linear and sequential than anything else he ever did, but it takes him from childhood fantasies right through to middle-aged fantasies of moving 'beyond the barlines / beyond the changes / beyond the time / tiptoeing in some wild and lonely space'. Underneath all the clamour, it is the loneliness and isolation that show through. Though the NRG Ensemble had become Russell's mouthpiece, it is on the solo session that his curiously vulnerable personality emerges with greatest clarity. It comes through again on the quartet co-led with Futterman, a loyal supporter and interpreter who provides all the compositional material for the session, though Russell wholly dominates it. A figure to put alongside Ives and Ruggles, Nancarrow and Moondog and Harry Partch, Russell is a genuine American original.

Luis Russell (1902–63)

PIANO, BANDLEADER

Born in Panama, Russell was working in New Orleans in the early '20s, but his major break came as the resident bandleader at the Saratoga Club in New York in 1928. In 1935 his band became the full-time backing group for Louis Armstrong, but it was sacked in 1940 and Russell led a band of diminishing importance thereafter. At the time of his death he was driving cars and teaching piano.

★★★★ The Luis Russell Collection, 1926–1934

Collector's Classics COCD-7 *Russell; Louis Metcalf, Henry 'Red' Allen, Bill Coleman, Otis Johnson, George Mitchell, Leonard Davis, Gus Aiken (t); Bob Shoffner (c); Kid Ory, J. C. Higginbotham, Vic Dickenson, Preston Jackson, Dicky Wells, Nathaniel Story, Jimmy Archey (tb); Albert Nicholas (cl, ss, as); Charlie Holmes (ss, as); Darnell Howard, Henry Jones (cl, as); Bingie Madison (cl, ts); Barney Bigard, Teddy Hill, Greely Walton (ts); Will Johnson (g, bj); Lee Blair (g); Johnny St Cyr (bj); Bass Moore (tba); George 'Pops' Foster (b); Paul Barbarin (d); Walter Pichon, Sonny Woods, Chick Bullock, Palmer Brothers (v).* 3/26–8/34.

★★★★ The Luis Russell Story

Retrieval RTR 79023 2CD *Similar to above.* 1/29–8/34.

★★★★ Luis Russell 1926–1929

Classics 588 *Similar to above.* 3/26–12/29.

★★★★ Luis Russell 1930–1931

Classics 606 *Similar to above.* 1/30–8/31.

★★★★ Luis Russell & His Orchestra

Topaz TPZ 1039 *As above discs, except add Louis Armstrong (t, v), Eddie Condon (bj), Lonnie Johnson (g).* 1/29–8/34.

Russell led one of the great orchestras of its period, having originally put it together in New Orleans in 1927, with such young local stars as Allen, Nicholas and Barbarin in attendance. Their 18 essential sides from seven remarkable sessions in New York are variously available on the Classics and Topaz CDs. The band had secured a prime Harlem residency at the Saratoga Club. This was a sophisticated outfit, first because of its soloists – with Higginbotham dominating the earlier sides and Allen, Nicholas and Holmes adding their own variations to the later ones – and second because of its increasing stature as an ensemble. 'Louisiana Swing', 'High Tension', 'Panama' and 'Case On Dawn' all show the orchestra swinging through the more advanced new ideas of counterpoint and unison variation while still offering chances for Allen and the others to shine as soloists.

The Collector's Classics CD fills in various gaps in the Russell discography. There are two small-group sessions from 1926, the first having a Mortonesque sound through the presence of Mitchell, Ory and Nicholas in the front line, the second a fine example of Chicago music moving out of the barrelhouse and into the front parlour. 'Broadway Rhythm' and two takes of 'The Way He Loves Is Just Too Bad' come from a Banner session of 1929 featuring the full band, and the final two sessions for Victor (1931) and Banner (1934) appear in full. If the ten tracks suggest Russell's hard-bitten swing was softening a little with the era of smooth big bands just around the corner, there is still some memorable playing on the likes of 'Hokus Pokus'. The Classics discs cover similar ground, although the remastering seems to be spottier. However, the new two-disc Retrieval set surpasses all previous editions. Though it doesn't include the 1926 tracks, it offers the two sessions which Russell covered to help out King Oliver (under whose name the titles were issued), and Russell-associated dates by the Jungle Town Stompers and J. C. Higginbotham's Six Hicks; there are also several alternative takes making a total of 48 tracks. Remastering and annotation are up to Retrieval's high standards.

Topaz's compilation cherrypicks the best of Russell's orchestral sides but stirs in two tracks from when the band backed Louis Armstrong and also adds Armstrong's Savoy Ballroom Five classic, 'Mahogany Hall Stomp'. A strong single disc.

★★(★) Luis Russell 1945–1946

Classics 1066 *Russell; Chester Boon, John Swan, Emory Thompson, James Mitchell, Rex Kearney, George Scott, Bernard Flood (t); Luther Brown, Austin Lawrence, Charles Williams, Charles Stocvall, Thomas Brown, Nathaniel Allen (tb); Sam Lee, Clarence Grimes (as); Esmond Samuels, Andy Martin, Troy Stowe (ts); Howard Robertson (bs); Howard Biggs, John Motley (p); Ernest Lee Williams (g); Don Richmond, Nathan Wodley, Leslie Bartlet (b); Roy Haynes (d); Milton Biggs, Lee Richardson (v).* 45–46.

Russell's later sides are all but unknown, and deservedly so on this evidence. An unidentified Eckstine-styled vocalist pours himself over four tracks, there are some strictly routine big-band shouters, and a general feeling of pointlessness pervades. For hardcore collectors only!

Pee Wee Russell (1906–69)

CLARINET, TENOR SAXOPHONE

Charles Ellsworth Russell, a jazz original, came from Missouri and played in the New York school of hot music in the '20s, with Nichols, Mole and the others. From the '30s he was better known as a member of the Eddie Condon gang, but his later playing suggested his disaffection for that style of jazz, and in his final decade he played in increasingly mainstream-to-modern settings, though by the end of the '60s he was largely back with traditional music. Alcoholism, illness and depression prevented him from ever making a more solid base for his career.

★★★ The Land Of Jazz

Topaz TPZ 1018 *Russell; Red Nichols (t, c); Leo McConville, Manny Klein, Henry 'Red' Allen, Max Kaminsky, Marty Marsala (t); Bobby Hackett (c); Miff Mole, Tommy Dorsey, George Brunies, Vernon Brown (tb); Brad Gowans (vtb); Fud Livingston (cl, ts); Jimmy Lord (cl); Happy Caldwell, Bud Freeman, Gene Sedric (ts); Adrian Rollini (bsx); Lennie Hayton, Fats Waller, Arthur Schutt, Jess Stacy, Joe Bushkin, Teddy Wilson, Frank Froeba (p); Jack Bland, Eddie Condon, Allan Reuss, Dick McDonough, Eddie Lang (g); Al Morgan, George 'Pops' Foster, Artie Shapiro, Sid Weiss (b); Vic Berton, Zutty Singleton, George Wettling, Johnny Blowers, Lionel Hampton (d); Billy Banks (v).* 8/27–9/44.

★★★ Jack Teagarden / Pee Wee Russell

Original Jazz Classics OJC 1708 *Russell; Max Kaminsky (t); Dicky Wells (tb); Al Gold (ts); James P. Johnson (p); Freddie Green (g); Wellman Braud (b); Zutty Singleton (d, v).* 8/38.

Russell's music is tyremarked by his many years in Dixieland, which he came to hate, with the Condon gang, who sent him up for much of the time, and by his own fatalism and poor habits. There's a danger in patronizing his home-made approach to playing, and he *was* inconsistent, but his best music is exceptional. He began with the New York players of the '20s – Nichols, Mole, Beiderbecke – but was more readily linked with Condon's Chicagoans in the '30s and '40s. The Topaz compilation starts with Nichols, adds four tracks with Billy Banks, including the immortal 'Oh Peter', but bulks up with various Condon line-ups for Commodore from 1938. Pee Wee sounds fine on 'Tappin' The Commodore Till' and a lovely slow solo on 'Sunday'. But the four outstanding items are by a quartet with Russell, Jess Stacy, Sid Weiss and George Wettling, culminating in the almost gargled 'D.A. Blues'. Sound is variable – some of the Commodores have a low-fi resonance – but mostly good.

The 1938 session (the rest of the CD features a Teagarden-led group) features a surprising line-up on five standards and a blues, two tracks featuring Russell and the rhythm section alone. Kaminsky and Wells are the most confident-sounding voices, but it's Russell's queer sense of line and wobbly pitch that take the ear. His partnership with Johnson is just one of a series of unlikely alliances he formed with pianists on record, which would later include George Wein and Thelonious Monk.

****** Swingin' With Pee Wee**

Prestige 24213-2 *Russell; Buck Clayton, Ruby Braff (t); Vic Dickenson (tb); Bud Freeman (ts); Tommy Flanagan, Nat Pierce (p); Wendell Marshall, Tommy Potter (b); Osie Johnson, Karl Kiffe (d).* 2/58–3/60.

A valuable and long-awaited reissue of a classic Russell session, *Swingin' With Pee Wee* is one of his best latter-day records. Clayton handled the arranging duties, and the rhythm section, with Flanagan, Marshall and Johnson, was about the most modernistic Russell had had behind him at this point. The result is a stylish and triumphant assimilation of his clarinet into a vibrant mainstream setting. His dissertation on his great blues, 'Englewood', is but one example of Pee Wee at his best – and Clayton matches him in the calibre of his playing. Even more of a bonus are the tracks from the 1958 date for Counterpoint, *Portrait Of Pee Wee*, with Braff and Dickenson – not quite as good, but it only adds to the merits of an excellent reissue.

*****(*) Jazz Reunion**

Candid CS 9020 *Russell; Emmett Berry (t); Bob Brookmeyer (vtb); Coleman Hawkins (ts); Nat Pierce (p); Milt Hinton (b); Jo Jones (d).* 2/61.

Russell's quixotic progress is still inadequately represented on CD. The *Reunion* was with Hawkins – one of the tracks, 'If I Could Be With You One Hour Tonight', they'd recorded together as far back as 1929 – and it caught both men in excellent form, Hawkins's solos delivered in his most leathery, autumnal manner which makes Russell's nagging at notes sound minimalist. Jones, in particular, reads everybody's moves superbly, although Berry and Brookmeyer especially seem rather irrelevant.

***** With Alex Welsh And His Band**

Lake LACD 157 *Russell; Alex Welsh (t); Roy Crimmins, Roy Williams (tb); John Barnes (bs, cl); Fred Hunt (p); Jim Douglas (g); Ron Mathewson (b); Lennie Hastings (d).* 11/64–7/66.

This is an ounce better than some of the surviving recordings of visiting Americans with British trad groups, in the main because Russell himself sounds in good fettle, even though he was back to playing the kind of Dixieland which he professed to have become tired of. At least he gets his own blues, 'Pee Wee's Blues', with just the rhythm section. As so often, Williams is the standout among the local men and the rhythm section is nothing special. Respectable sound.

***** Ask Me Now!**

Impulse! 755742-2 *Russell; Marshall Brown (vtb, bt); Russell George (b); Ronnie Bedford (d).* 65.

Russell's 'modern' album set him to work on Monk and Coleman tunes and a few standards, with Brown playing what might be termed the Don Cherry role. It's a curious set: Pee Wee plays everything his way, and he blithely walks through Coleman's 'Turnaround' as if he's blowing on standard changes. It's a fun record, and it's strange to reflect that it was made in the same period that he cut the sessions with Welsh listed above. In the end, it sounds as if Russell is telling us that he can play this stuff if he wants to – although it's not, you know, really him.

Paul Rutherford (born 1940)

TROMBONE, PIANO

A Londoner, Rutherford played in RAF bands, then studied at the Guildhall. A prime mover in both the Spontaneous Music Ensemble, Iskra 1903 and London Jazz Composers' Orchestra, as well as playing solo, Rutherford is a major part of British free music.

****** Chapter One: 1970–1972**

Emanem 4301 3CD *Rutherford; Derek Bailey (g); Barry Guy (b).* 70–72.

***** Buzz Soundtrack**

Emanem 4066 *As above.* 71.

Rutherford was the guiding spirit behind Iskra 1903 – named after Lenin's revolutionary newspaper *The Spark* – and even if he had not recorded another note, this fact alone would place him at the very heart of British improvisation since 1970. The early performances documented on *Chapter One* are typical of the group's highly concentrated output. More intensely focused and, residually at least, more jazz-inflected than either AMM or the more radical excursions of the Spontaneous Music Ensemble, Iskra 1903 represent a wonderfully challenging auditory experience. So densely interwoven are the lines and so convincingly vocalized is Rutherford's tone that one almost feels one is listening to a passionate discourse, perhaps one of those unrecorded speeches Lenin made from the back of a truck in the months before the Bolshevik Revolution. The sound is mostly very clear and faithful, though there are a couple of tracks which sound muddied and uncertain. *Buzz Soundtrack* is a less essential purchase and not at all typical of the group's output. The music was written for a film by Michael Grigsby and once again underlines Rutherford's affection for blues and jazz, though there is very little overt jazz-phrasing to be heard. This may well be seen as the trombonist's *L'Ascenseur Pour L'Échafaud*: a minor project but one which sparked all manner of stylistic explorations.

***** Sequences 72 & 73**

Emanem 4018 *Rutherford; Kenny Wheeler (t, flhn); Malcolm Griffiths, Paul Nieman, Geoff Perkins (tb); Dick Hart (tba); Dave White (ss, as, bs, bcl, cbcl); Trevor Watts (ss, as); Evan Parker (ss, ts); Howard Riley (p); Derek Bailey (g); Barry Guy (b); Tony Oxley (elec); Maggie Nicols, Norma Winstone (v).* 9/72–5/74.

★★★★ The Gentle Harm Of The Bourgeoisie

Emanem 4019 *Rutherford (tb solo). 7–12/74.*

The trombone is said to be the musical instrument closest to the human voice. When Paul Rutherford spoke or sang through his horn, it sounded like no instrument anyone had ever heard, a sound as lyrically potent and as expressively stressed and freighted as a whole ensemble. Rutherford was part of some of the most important improvising groups of the '60s, co-founding the Little Theatre Club with Trevor Watts and John Stevens and joining their Spontaneous Music Ensemble, as well as Watts's Amalgam and the London Jazz Composers' Orchestra, and founding Iskra 1903, his own electro-acoustic trio, with LJCO bassist and composer Barry Guy and guitarist Derek Bailey, which re-formed in 1980 with violinist Philipp Wachsmann. It's worth labouring the genealogy to underline just how central Rutherford has been to the scene and to point up just how important recent reissues have been.

Rutherford's solo performances, documented on *The Gentle Harm Of The Bourgeoisie*, are as wryly subversive as the title suggests. Devotedly recorded by Martin Davidson at the Unity Theatre, it's now infinitely more listenable than on muddy LP. Rutherford's grasp of multiphonics is already assured; additional sounds and overtones come from mutes, microphone knocks and from spittle in the horn, part and parcel of the process. The two long tracks, 'Elaqust' from July 1974 and 'Osirac Senol' from the week before Christmas, are definitive.

Sequences 72 & 73 is a historic release, a first chance to hear Rutherford's work as composer/conductor. Iskra 1912 never performed in public and these studio recordings were never released. The two 'Sequences' were recorded a year apart, while Rutherford recorded the short solo 'Non-Sequence' in the late spring of 1974. The main difference between the main pieces is that Derek Bailey's stereo guitar was overdubbed on to the latter, which also featured Tony Oxley on live electronics, replacing the saxophones of Trevor Watts, who was one of the main soloists on the 1972 session, duetting with Guy. The brass-players are sometimes required to play chorally, sometimes improvising freely. The other main soloist in 1972 was Evan Parker, who is heard on tenor a year later.

With no drummer, there is no definite pulse and, as so often in Rutherford's music, it is the human voice, wordless on this occasion, which provides the unifying principle. Quite why these extraordinary works have had to wait until now for release is a mystery only if one chooses to forget how marginalized this music has been, and how little critical press its creator has had, since they were recorded.

★★★(★) Trombolenium

Emanem 4072 *Rutherford (tb solo). 86–95.*

Almost a decade's worth of solo performance from one of the great masters of British improvisation. The sound-quality varies hugely, or rather the acoustics do, and it is interesting to hear how responsive Paul is to his environment, piling on the notes when the ambience is dry and allowing the decays to fade gently when playing in a small Italian church. No mistaking that this is a tough and involving listen, possibly one that should be taken a track at a time rather than attempted in one sitting.

★★★ Rogues

Emanem 4007 *Rutherford; Paul Rogers (b). 11/88.*

★★★(★) ISKRA / NCKA 1903

Maya MCD 9502 *Rutherford; Philipp Wachsmann (vn); Barry Guy (b). 10/92.*

Rogues involves two-thirds of a trio that also included drummer Nigel Morris. The involvement of a percussionist meant that this was a very different set-up from Iskra 1903, in either of its incarnations, and Morris's absence on the 1988 disc changes the language quite considerably. None of this material appeared on LP and it was finally issued almost a decade after the performances, which were recorded at a pub called the Cannonball in Adderley Street, Birmingham. Debates about documenting such music still rage, but the opening 'Rogues 1' is as riveting as it must have been on the night. The rest of the disc is less compelling.

The Iskra 1903 disc was also recorded live, in Vancouver. It once again underlines Rutherford's genius for creating contexts in which fellow-musicians thrive. His own playing is calm, positive and completely tuneful, if by that one means a basic musicality that goes beyond mere melodism. The sound is quite crisp, for a concert recording, and though Wachsmann's amplified violin tends to dominate, the basic unity of the trio is always evident.

★★★(★) Chicago 2002

Emanem 4082 *Rutherford; Jeb Bishop (tb); Lol Coxhill (ss); Mats Gustafsson (ts); Fred Lonberg-Holm (clo, elec); Kent Kessler (b); Kjell Nordeson (d). 4/02.*

Rutherford live at the Empty Bottle in Chicago. He plays a tremendous 30-minute solo, and that's followed by a septet where he and fellow Brit Coxhill met up with some local guys and two (regular) visitors from Scandinavia. The group pieces aren't so much tentative as surprisingly deferential, with noted power-players Bishop and Gustafsson often throttling back to give clearer space to the visitors. An enjoyable blow.

Terje Rypdal (born 1947)

ELECTRIC GUITAR, GUITAR, SOPRANO SAXOPHONE, FLUTE, OTHER INSTRUMENTS AND EFFECTS

Born in Oslo, Rypdal played rock in the '60s before teaming with George Russell and Jan Garbarek. A pioneer of electric-guitar 'impressionism', he's spent almost 30 years with the ECM label and recorded there in a range of settings, with several (unlisted) recent records in particular more concerned with contemporary composition than jazz.

★★★ Terje Rypdal

ECM 527645-2 *Rypdal; Sveinung Hovensjo (b); Jon Christensen (d). 72.*

★★★ What Comes After

ECM 839306-2 *Rypdal; Erik Niord Larsen (ob, eng hn); Sveinung Hovensjo, Barre Phillips (b); Jon Christensen (perc, org). 8/73.*

★★★ Whenever I Seem To Be Far Away

ECM 843166-2 *Rypdal; Odd Ulleberg (frhn); Erik Niord Larsen (ob); Pete Knutsen (p, mellotron); Sveinung Hovensjo (b); Jon Christensen (perc); Helmut Geiger (vn); Christian Hedrich (vla); strings of Südfunk Symphony Orchestra, conducted by Mladen Gutesha. 74.*

★★★(★) Odyssey

ECM 835355-2 *Rypdal; Torbjørn Sunde (tb); Brynjulf Blix (b); Svein Christiansen (d).* 8/75.

★★★(★) After The Rain

ECM 523159-2 *Rypdal; Inger Lise Rypdal (v).* 76.

★★★(★) Waves

ECM 827419-2 *Rypdal; Palle Mikkelborg (t, flhn, elec); Sveinung Hovensjo (b); Jon Christensen (d, perc).* 9/77.

In the later '80s, Terje Rypdal was increasingly seen at the head of an impressive train of opus numbers; two classical releases, *Undisonus* and *Q.E.D.*, appeared on ECM in the '90s. 'Straight' composition was, in fact, his third string. His professional career had begun as a rock performer, in the pit band at a Scandinavian production of *Hair!* (chilblains were doubtless a problem) and as accompanist to his sister, Inger Lise Rypdal (who added soft vocal colours to the otherwise solo *After The Rain*). In the '70s, under the influence of George Russell (directly) and of Jimi Hendrix (less so), Rypdal made a series of highly atmospheric guitar-led albums which combined elements of classical form with a distinctive high-register sound and an improvisational approach that drew more from rock music than from orthodox jazz technique. (It's worth noting that *After The Rain* refers to a Rypdal composition, not Coltrane's.)

If there is an 'ECM sound', in either a positive or a more sceptical sense, it may be found in the echoey passages of these albums. Rypdal's music is highly textural and harmonically static, its imagery kaleidoscopic rather than cinematic. At worst, Rypdal's solo excursions sound merely vacuous. The debut is pretty typical of his combination of power and lyricism, though in future years the two strands were increasingly separate, carried in different works and by different kinds of ensemble. In the '70s, Rypdal had more or less single-handedly pioneered a style of guitar-playing which grafted a rock attack over large-scale orchestral washes. 'Silver Bird Is Heading For The Sun' on *Whenever I Seem To Be Far Away* is reminiscent of Pink Floyd's woollier moments, yet it has a harmonic outline that is almost worthy of Bill Evans, and that is true to Rypdal's range of sources. The long title-track (which Rypdal calls an 'image', a useful generic description of his work) is, on the other hand, highly effective in its balance of winds, guitar and strings. ('Live' strings are more effective than the cumbersome and now outmoded mellotrons and 'string ensembles' that the guitarist uses elsewhere.)

Waves and *Odyssey* are the most interesting of this group, although we are still rather partial to *After The Rain*, which evokes a particular time in record-making and has some shamelessly pretty moments. Rypdal favours brass with an almost medieval quality and, despite Mikkelborg's baroque embellishments, the trumpeter fits that prescription surprisingly well. Hovensjo and Christensen don't play as an orthodox rhythm section but as a shifting backdrop of tones and pulses; the bassist doubles on a six-stringed instrument which is effectively a rhythm guitar. Despite being technically dated in some ways, these albums seem to have come round again, addressing a post-modernist desire to embrace the last-but-one technology and a gentler, more sentimental range.

★★★(★) Descendere

ECM 829118-2 *Rypdal; Palle Mikkelborg (t, flhn, ky); Jon Christensen (d, perc).* 3/79.

★★★(★) Terje Rypdal/Miroslav Vitous/Jack DeJohnette

ECM 825470-2 *Rypdal; Miroslav Vitous (b, p); Jack DeJohnette (d).* 6/78.

★★★ To Be Continued

ECM 847333-2 *As above.* 1/81.

There have always been charges that Rypdal is not 'really' an improviser, just a high-powered effects man. At the root of the misconception is a prevailing belief that improvisation takes place only on a vertical axis, up and down through chord progressions and changes. Rypdal's genius is for juxtapositions of textures, overlays of sound that act as polarizing lenses to what his companions are doing. A broad, open chord laid close over a drum pattern takes the 'percussive' stringency out of DeJohnette's line, making him sound as if he were playing piano (as in other and later company he might well be) or adding harmonics to Vitous's huge bass-notes. There is also, of course, a great deal of straightforward interplay which in itself helps refute the charge that Rypdal is a mere techno-freak.

The other trio is less conventional in format, though Mikkelborg's palette-knife keyboard effects mean that there's very little sense of 'missing' piano or bass. The trumpeter, who has an approach broadly similar to Rypdal's, tends to lay it on a little thick, and there is a suspicion of either muddle or overkill on a couple of tracks. That apart, *Descendere* still sounds fresh and vital and stands out as a high-point in Rypdal's output.

★★★ Eos

ECM 815333-2 *Rypdal; David Darling (clo, 8-string electric clo).* 5/83.

The scorching power chords of the opening 'Laser' tend to mislead, for this is a remarkably subtle and sophisticated record, making the fullest use of the players' astonishing range of tone-colours and effects. Darling conjures anything from Vitous-like bass strums to high, wailing lines that are remarkably close in timbre to Rypdal's souped-up guitar. He is still mostly reliant on rock-influenced figures played with maximum sustain and distortion, but his rhythm counts are consistently challenging, and the pairing of instruments sets up an often ambiguous bitonality. The title-track wavers a bit at over 14 minutes, but the two closing numbers, 'Mirage' and 'Adagietto', are particularly beautiful.

★ Chaser

ECM 827256-2 *Rypdal; Born Kjellmyr (b); Audun Kleive (d).* 5/85.

★★ Blue

ECM 831516-2 *As above.* 11/86.

★★★ The Singles Collection

ECM 837749-2 *As above, except add Allan Dangerfield (ky).* 8/88.

It may say something about Rypdal's psychic economy that, at a time when his scored, formal music was achieving new heights of sophistication and beauty, he should have gone on the road and on record with a power trio of minimum finesse. *Chaser* is a harsh, clunking slice of nonsense that does Rypdal no credit at all. *Blue* at least shows signs of thought, notably on 'The Curse' and 'Om Bare'. How many people have been thrown by the ironically titled *Singles Collection*? It's not utterly improbable that Rypdal might have been sneaking out the odd seven-incher over the years, but this is a wholly new album of wry, generic samples. Basically, it's a tissue of rock guitar styles, with the changing of stylistic season marked by Dangerfield's progress from apoplectic Hammond to a rather underprogrammed synth. Rypdal has expressed interest in Prince's music (and 'U.'N.I.' is presumably a reference to the Small One's trademark elision of titles) but it isn't clear whether he is drawn more to Paisley Park production techniques or to Prince's Carlos Santana-derived (rather than Hendrix-derived) guitar-playing. Rypdal emerges as a surprisingly good *pasticheur*, and there is plenty to think about in this slightly odd, deliberately regressive set. It's certainly the best of these three.

***** If Mountains Could Sing**
ECM 523987-2 *Rypdal; Born Kjellemyr (b); Audun Kleive (d); Terje Tonnesen (vn); Lars Anders Tomter (vla); Oystein Birkeland (clo); Christian Eggen (cond).* 1 & 6/94.

Half a dozen tracks by the shortly to be disbanded Chaser trio, and five more augmented by strings. As one might expect by this stage in the game, the whole is elegant and richly textured, though the specifics are less than compelling. Rypdal's full-on guitar is over-emphatic when in company with the strings, and Manfred Eicher's fabled production values are less secure than they might be. No indication when individual tracks were made, though it must be assumed that the strings sessions were recorded at a separate session. Whatever the case, Rypdal sounds very different, somewhat dry and percussive. There is some lovely material, though. The title-track and the wry 'But On The Other Hand' stand out, and 'Foran Peisen', for trio alone, is as good as Rypdal has done with this line-up.

*****(*) Skywards**
ECM 533768-2 *Rypdal; Palle Mikkelborg (t); Terje Tonnesen (vn); David Darling (clo); Christian Eggen (p, ky); Paolo Vinaccia (d, perc); Jon Christensen (d).* 2/96.

Skywards was made to mark Rypdal's 25-year association with ECM. In a rare liner-note, Rypdal concedes that *If Mountains Could Sing* had not been an easy album to record and repeats his weariness with the increasingly formulaic Chasers. The idea was to put together a celebration orchestra of old colleagues and create an album that would illustrate both continuity and progress. The main piece is a specially written 'Sinfonietta', subtitled 'Out Of This World', and a couple of the other works – 'Remember To Remember' and 'Shining' – bear a close relation to pieces in Rypdal's classical catalogue. 'Into The Wilderness' was originally written for a film soundtrack. Though a much more disparate album, it is also more successful than its predecessor. The larger group, with Mikkelborg a key component, is superb on 'Shining', the trumpeter's main feature. The reunion with Darling is also a fruitful one, and on 'Remember To Remember' the combination of string sounds finally comes right in the small-group context. Not quite the epochal retrospective it might have been, but a fine album nevertheless.

****** Lux Aeterna**
ECM 1818 *Rypdal; Palle Mikkelborg (t); Iver Kleive (org); Annar Folleso (vn); Ashild Stubo Gundersen (v).* 7/00.

An absolutely stunning record, whatever musical category you feel it belongs in. The chamber orchestra opening is punctuated by a note from Mikkelborg which instantly conjures up that cliché about Miles Davis being able to change the direction of a performance with a single tone; the reality is that Mikkelborg really does. Here Rypdal plays with layers of harmonic tensions, overlapping ideas and introducing instruments with infinite care. How much improvising goes on is neither clear nor immediately relevant. The impact of *Lux Aeterna* is both free and formidably structured. The live recording from the Molde Festival captures the music with precision and a suprising intimacy.

***** rarum: Selected Recordings – Volume 7**
ECM 014201 *As above.* 74–85.

A decade's worth of Rypdal's more jazz-based material for ECM. His classical work isn't particularly important here, but the second movement of his 'Double Concerto' is included and makes perfect sense in – or rather out of – context. The opening choice of 'Silver Bird Is Heading For The Sun' is a shrewd one and will draw in listeners who haven't previously experienced Terje's guitar work. A dozen other tracks offer a decent overview, and though 'Chaser' seems slightly jarring after the more impressionistic and ethereal stuff, it helps round out the picture. A nice buy.

Harvie S

BASS

The 'artist formerly known as' Harvie Swartz has been a familiar sideman and educator on the New York scene for the past two decades; and he has a special interest in Latin rhythms.

***** Eye Contact**
Ondine Music, no number. *S; Ray Vega (t); Michael Brecker (ts); Daniel Kelly (p); Bruce Arnold, Haru Takauchi (g); Gregor Huebner (vn); Adam Weber (d); Renato Thomas (perc).* 2/01.

A likeable set of melodious groove tunes which S steers with his usual big sound. Some of it veers a little close to a Latinized smooth jazz but there's enough improvisational chops on show to keep the faith and the leader has come up with worthwhile material. Brecker sits in on two tracks and he and Vega sound best on 'From The Ashes'.

Marc Sabatella

PIANO

Elegant keyboard technician, Colorado-based, who dabbles in free improvisation.

***** Second Course**
Cadence 1095 *Sabatella; Hugh Ragin (t); Peter Sommer (ts); Erik Turkman (b); Roger Barnhart (g); Thomas Van Schoik (d).* 97.

***** The Spanish Inquisition**
Golden Horn 22 *As above, except omit Ragin, Barnhart.* 7/98.

***** Falling Grace**
Outside Shore 1001 *As above, except omit Sommer.* 03.

Perhaps because he works at some distance from the obvious centres of improvised music, Sabatella has pursued a markedly individual course. His interest in free-form playing is balanced by a fascination with large-scale and open-ended structures, which is why he kicks off this set with a version of Mingus's 'The Shoes Of The Fisherman's Wife Are Some Jive Ass Slippers', one of the composer's less frequently covered pieces. He also pays homage to Keith Jarrett on the epic 'Everything That

Lives Laments' which first put in an appearance on *Mourning Of A Star* in 1971. His occasional use of alto and soprano recorders might also be thought a nod to Jarrett's multi-instrumentalism, but it's the shape of those early Jarrett bands that seems to have influenced Sabatella. Here he makes use of Ragin and the excellent Sommer to create a flowing, melodic language that offers ample scope for improvisation within very definite but elastic parameters.

Hence the title of the second CD, which is not about the Catholic Church's most feared enforcers but taken from the Monty Python line 'Nobody expects the …'. Sabatella's improvisations are never predictable or by rote and this quartet (also known as The Spanish Inquisition) is full of delightful surprises. The personnel is ideally suited to the leader's needs and his unexpected Brubeck influence is well supported on the opening 'Blue Honda A La Truck', with Sommer in an improbable Paul Desmond role. 'Or Not' is another deft abstraction, with a touch of Cecil Taylor. For the most part, though, these are fluid inventions that betray their influences only incidentally.

The live trio date also kicks off with a Jarrett tune, this time 'Lucky Southern'. They also do Charlie Haden's 'First Song', the title-piece by Steve Swallow and, more surprisingly, 'Stella By Starlight'. The chemistry is close and at moments explosive, though some of the fire has gone out of Sabatella's playing since the debut record and here he sounds more like a conventional jazz pianist with an adventurous repertoire.

Dino Saluzzi (born 1935)

BANDONEON, FLUTE, PERCUSSION, VOICE

Saluzzi was born in Argentina, in Salta province. He worked for the house orchestra of the national radio station, Radio El Mundo, in the '50s, and worked for a time with Gato Barbieri. His interest has ranged between tango, folkloric music, jazz and classical forms, and he uses the bandoneon in a markedly orchestral way, conjuring everything from single voices to whole sections and infusing the whole with tremendous longing and nostalgia.

***** Kultrum**

ECM 821407-2 *Saluzzi (solo).* 11/82.

*****(*) Andina**

ECM 837186-2 *As above.* 5/88.

Though it was the Argentinian master, Astor Piazzolla, who sparked a revival of interest in bandoneon and accordion, it has been Dino Saluzzi who has performed some of the most significant new music on an instrument that has always held a peculiar fascination for the avant-garde; this partly because of its slightly kitsch image, but also because it permits an astonishing range of harmonic and extra-harmonic devices (wheezes, clicks, terminal rattles) that lend themselves very readily to improvisational contexts.

Saluzzi's compositions and performances (and he is usually best heard solo) cover a wide spectrum of styles, from sombre, almost sacred pieces (like 'Choral' on *Andina*, his best record), to a semi-abstract tone-poem like 'Winter' on the same album, which takes him much closer to the exploratory work of radical accordionist, Pauline Oliveros. *Kultrum* is well worth hearing, and sets the agenda for what is to be a life's work, a whole album of pieces united by the composer's cross-cultural philosophy, but it is also a very inward work, darkly private and not always as communicative as one might like. As a first exposure to Saluzzi, *Andina* is the one to plump for; richly and intimately recorded, although doubtless less authentic in idiom, it has infinitely greater presence than the later album.

*****(*) Once Upon A Time … Far Away In The South**

ECM 827768-2 *Saluzzi; Palle Mikkelborg (t, flhn); Charlie Haden (b); Pierre Favre (d).* 7/85.

***** Volver**

ECM 831395-2 *Saluzzi; Enrico Rava (t); Harry Pepl (g); Furio Di Castri (b); Bruce Ditmas (d).* 10/86.

***** Mojotoro**

ECM 511952-2 *Saluzzi; Celso Saluzzi (bandoneon, perc, v); Felix Cuchara Saluzzi (ts, ss, cl); Armando Alonso (g, v); Guillermo Vadalá (b, v); José Maria Saluzzi (d, perc, v); Arto Tuncboyaciyan (perc, v).* 5/91.

***** Cité De La Musique**

ECM 533316-2 *Saluzzi; José M. Saluzzi (g); Marc Johnson (b).* 96.

Saluzzi tends to recede a little in a group setting, perhaps because European ears have not been conditioned to listen to button accordion as anything other than a bland portable organ useful for dancing and local colour. Both Rava and (especially) Mikkelborg are rather dominant players and occupy more than their fair share of the foreground. *Once Upon A Time* is better because Haden and Favre are so responsive; *Volver* takes a bit of getting used to.

At first hearing, remarkably similar to one of Edward Vesala's accordion-led pieces, 'Mojotoro' is dedicated to the universalization of musical culture. It draws on tango, Bolivian *Andina* music, Uruguayan *Candombe* and other folk forms, travelling between deceptively spacious but highly intricate bandoneon figures and passionate saxophone outcries which suggest a hybrid of Gato Barbieri with another ECM alumnus, Jan Garbarek. The multi-part 'Mundos' is less effective than the title-piece, and the strongest performances are on the more conventionally structured pieces, 'Tango A Mi Padre' and Pintin Castellanos's wonderful *milonga*, 'La Punalada'. Instrumental colours are expertly handled, but the main drama comes from the interaction between Saluzzi and his kinsman, 'Cuchara', who is a marvellously evocative clarinettist.

Cité De La Musique is big on atmosphere, but a disc with no real centre, and one finds oneself wandering through it, a little disorientated culturally, not at all clear what idiom one's dealing with and where one's being led. Johnson is superb as ever, but no sense of engagement beyond a pro's refusal to be thrown or wrongfooted.

***** Rios**

Intuition 2156 *Saluzzi; David Friedman (vib, mar); Anthony Cox (b).* 95.

A rare foray away from ECM and one of the least accessible and appealing of Saluzzi's albums. The music is a mixture of denatured tango and bossa nova on the one hand and a curiously abstract jazz-based improvisation on the other. It isn't exactly colourless, and Friedman's 'Penta Y Uno' is fascinatingly done, but there is little of the atmosphere Saluzzi gets when recording for ECM.

***** Kultrum – Rosamunde Quartet**
ECM 457854-2 *Saluzzi; Andreas Reimer, Simon Fordham (vn); Helmut Nicolai (vla); Anja Lechner (clo).* n.d.

The original *Kultrum* (above) was for unaccompanied bandoneon, but Saluzzi has always regarded the work as an ongoing and ever-expanding project rather than as a fixed opus number, and on this beautifully modulated album he emphasizes the orchestral dimensions of the piece with the addition – or, rather, the integration – of the Rosamunde Quartet. These are experienced practitioners of modern and contemporary repertoire and, like their colleagues, Kronos, are untroubled by non-Western rhythms. Easy to assume that Saluzzi uncritically embraces the tango tradition, but in 'Salon De Tango', he suggests that his country's national form is escapist and passive. 'Milonga De Los Morenos' touches on the genre's African influences while 'Miserere', now almost a repertory piece, touches on a wider range of emotions than grief. Indeed, on this version it seems closer to anger. The development of *Kultrum* continues apace and deepens every time Saluzzi returns to it.

*****(*) Responsorium**
ECM 1816 *Saluzzi; José Maria Saluzzi (g); Palle Danielsson (b).* 11/01.

Very similar in conception to *Cité De La Musique*, but the addition of Danielsson adds something quite unexpected, a harmonic richness that one would not have thought a Saluzzi project needed. In contrast to Johnson, who is a more quietly propulsive player, the Swede ventures into areas of tonality that are otherwise unexplored in the bandoneonist's work. Both father and son are playing beautifully and the set has a quiet elegance that doesn't in any way belie its more spiritual side. Recommended.

Perico Sambeat (born 1962)

ALTO AND SOPRANO SAXOPHONES, FLUTE

Played on the Valencia scene in the '80s before visiting and performing in London and New York, subsequently associating with several major players; former sideman in the Guy Barker group.

***** Uptown Dance**
EGT 565 *Sambeat; Michael Philip Mossman (t, picc-t, tb); David Kikoski (p); Bill Morning (b); Keith Copeland (d).* 5/92.

***** Dual Force**
Jazz House JHCD 031 *Sambeat; Steve Melling (p); Dave Green (b); Stephen Keogh (d).* 12/93.

The Spaniard plays with unstinting energy. He loves the sound of bebop alto to the extent that he could have stepped on to a bandstand with Stitt or Cannonball and come off just fine. The tightly packed solo on 'The Menace', on the earlier of these two sessions, shows what he can do and reveals that Coltrane was probably an influence as well. But the context, on this date in particular, is more modern and prickly than that: the compositions by the underrated Mossman establish a lean, angular world of unusual shapes and harmonies, and Sambeat seems to thrive on them. The brassman is in excellent voice himself, Kikoski is bright and alert, and the result is a cut above the average. The Jazz House disc, recorded during a season at Ronnie Scott's, is more cursory: as sole horn, Sambeat carries it and, though his colleagues play well, it's no more than a workmanlike result.

***** Jindungo**
Fresh Sound New Talent FSNT 029 *Sambeat; Bruce Barth (p); Joe Martin (b); Jorge Rossy (d).* 95.

*****(*) Ademuz**
Fresh Sound FSNT 041 *Sambeat; Mike Leonhart (t); Mark Turner (ts); Brad Mehldau (p); Kurt Rosenwinkel (g); Joe Martin (b); Jorge Rossy (d); Guillermo McGill, Enric Canada (perc); Enrique Morente (v).* 8–11/95.

Sambeat was associated early on with new majors such as Mehldau, Turner and Rosenwinkel, and they're all here on the simmering, thickly textured *Ademuz*, excitingly delivered, if overcrowded with detail and noise. The percussion team is involved most of the way through and they set much of the feel of the music, from the polyrhythmic undergrowth of the title-track to the more closely argued layers of 'Expedición'. The leader makes as much of an impression as anyone in his solos, often sailing out of the hyperactivity in the rhythm section with aplomb. The other players are sometimes crowded for space and never make the impression they do on their later records, but this is still a charismatic and frequently exciting record.

The earlier disc has Barth as co-leader and is a much more tentative effort because of it. Sambeat still sounds full of confidence and fire but he lacks some of the polish that comes through on the second disc.

*****(*) Perico**
Lola/Chrysalis 7243 5 33204 2 *Sambeat; Bernardo Sassetti (p); Javier Colina (b); Marc Niralta (d); Israel Piranha Suarez, Pepe Moto (perc).* 01.

This is Sambeat's most explicitly Iberian album. He adds flamenco *palmas* to a couple of tracks, notably the delightful 'De Camino', which begins with handclaps before moving off into a beautiful modal idea that could have been inspired by Miles Davis. Right from the off, ballads dominate the record. 'Drume Negrito' is a soprano feature for the leader and 'Diddi' is another beautiful idea. The hand percussion is an attractive feature but certainly not a distraction and this is no faux-flamenco gig but a solid jazz set with some interesting colours; and you can't get closer to a 'Spanish tinge' than with flamenco.

***** Friendship**
ACT 9421 2 *Sambeat; Brad Mehldau (p); Kurt Rosenwinkel (g); Ben Street (b); Jeff Ballard (d); Carmen Canela (v).* 03.

Sambeat's ideas often seem rooted in what his fellow players are doing and right from the beginning of 'Memoria Du Un Sueno' he is locked in tight with Mehldau, who is of course an old sparring partner. In comparison to pianists David Kikoski and Steve Melling, with whom Sambeat has worked before, Brad usually likes to let space and silence do much of the work for him. Here, however, he seems to be striving.

Rosenwinkel, Street and Ballard do their stuff competently but without much drama and the record would not have been very different had they missed the subway across town. There is a sameness about the tracks that might have been avoided had Perico picked up his soprano more often. He reserves it for 'Actors', which comes right after the only standard of the set, 'Crazy She Calls Me', and marks a belated change of pace. He gets a drier, sourer sound with the straight horn, which is what this album needs. Just one vocal from Canela, on 'Matilda'; nice enough.

David Sanborn (born 1945)

ALTO AND SOPRANO SAXOPHONES

Sanborn is one of the most widely known instrumentalists of today, principally through his signature alto saxophone sound, which has appeared on hundreds of recordings in the past three decades. He took up the horn partly as therapy for a polio condition which he went through as a child. He worked with rock and R&B bands in the '60s before leading a long series of albums which bridged jazz with instrumental pop and R&B. He has expressed his distaste for the 'smooth jazz' school of recording and tries to distance himself from being considered an influence on it.

****(*) Taking Off**

Warner Bros 927295-2 *Sanborn; Randy Brecker (t); Tom Malone (tb); Peter Gordon, John Clark (frhn); Michael Brecker (ts); Howard Johnson (bs, tba); Don Grolnick (ky); Steve Khan, Buzzy Feiten, Joe Beck (g); Will Lee (b); Chris Parker, Rick Marotta (d); Ralph Macdonald (perc); strings.* 75.

**** Heart To Heart**

Warner Bros 3189-2 *Sanborn; Jon Faddis, Lew Soloff, Randy Brecker (t); Michael Brecker (ts); Mike Mainieri (vib).* 1/78.

***** Voyeur**

Warner Bros 256900-2 *Sanborn; Tom Scott (ts, f); Michael Colina (ky); Hiram Bullock, Buzzy Feiten (g); Marcus Miller (b, g, ky, d); Buddy Williams, Steve Gadd (d); Lenny Castro, Ralph Macdonald (perc).* 81.

**** As We Speak**

Warner Bros 923650-2 *Sanborn; Bill Evans (ss); Bob Mintzer (bcl); Robert Martin (frhn); Don Freeman, Lance Ong, George Duke (ky); James Skelton (org); Michael Sembello (g, v); Buzzy Feiten (g); Marcus Miller (b); Omar Hakim (d); Paulinho Da Costa (perc).* 82.

Whatever palatable, easy-listening trimmings are applied to David Sanborn's records, his own contributions always cut deeper than that. 'I'm pushing for the limit,' he says about his playing, whether in the studio or on the concert stage. He had a particular sound by the time of *Taking Off*, having already worked in rock and blues bands for ten years, and, while he is shy of jazz as a basis for his own music, his high, skirling tone and succinct phrasing have inspired countless other players. The problem with *Taking Off* and *Heart To Heart* is context: other than delivering a vague format of funky instrumentals, there's little for Sanborn to bite on here, and the original tunes aren't much more than '70s funk clichés. *Voyeur* is the album that raises the game a notch: the sound assumes a hard gleam, and a tightness that would be constricting for most players replaces any sense of a loose gait. The altoman thrives in the context, cutting sharp circular patterns like a skater on ice, with the prettiness of 'It's You' and 'All I Need Is You' balancing the bright, airless funk of 'Wake Me When It's Over'. *As We Speak*, though, was a disappointing repeat run, with sentimental fluff courtesy of guitarist-singer Sembello taking up too much room.

***** Backstreet**

Warner Bros 923906-2 *Sanborn; Marcus Miller (ky, g, b, perc); Michael Colina (ky); Hiram Bullock (ky, g); Buzzy Feiten (g); Steve Gadd (d); Ralph Macdonald (perc).* 83.

***** Straight To The Heart**

Warner Bros 925150-2 *Sanborn; Randy Brecker, Jon Faddis (t); Michael Brecker (ts); Don Grolnick (ky); Hiram Bullock (g); Marcus Miller (b, ky); Buddy Williams (d); Errol Bennett (perc).* 84.

**** A Change Of Heart**

Warner Bros 925479-2 *Sanborn; Michael Brecker (syn); Marcus Miller (ky, g, b); Don Grolnick, Rob Mounsey, Michael Colina, John Mahoney, Michael Sembello, Bernard Wright, Philippe Saisse, Ronnie Foster, Randy Waldman (ky); Mac Rebennack (p); Hiram Bullock, Hugh McCracken, Nicky Moroch, Carlos Rios (g); Anthony Jackson (b); Mickey Curry, John Robinson (d); Paulinho Da Costa, Mino Cinelu (perc).* 87.

*****(*) Close-Up**

Reprise 925715-2 *Sanborn; Marcus Miller (ky, g, b); Richard Tee, Ricky Peterson (p); Hiram Bullock, Nile Rodgers, Steve Jordan, Jeff Mironov, G. E. Smith, Paul Jackson (g); Andy Newmark, Vinnie Colaiuta, William House (d); Paulinho Da Costa, Don Alias (perc); Michael Ruff (v).* 88.

Marcus Miller had been playing and composing for Sanborn's records before, but with *Backstreet* he began producing as well, intensifying further the almost abstract neo-funk which the saxophonist had behind him in the mix. *Backstreet* featured some agreeable tunes as well as the beat, though, and in the title-piece, 'A Tear For Crystal' and 'Blue Beach' Sanborn wrung the most out of each situation. His sound was sometimes almost frozen in the still space of the studio but his tone remained uniquely capable of emoting in this context. Cut before a studio audience, *A Change Of Heart* simulated one of Sanborn's live shows and, while it has some tedious features, it's a rare chance to hear the leader in more extended solos than usual, and they are strong enough to belie his insistence that a jazz context is inappropriate for him.

A Change Of Heart was a false step. Four different producers handle the eight tracks, and the result is a mish-mash of styles where each man tries to affix Sanborn's trademark wail in his own setting. Only Miller's work is truly effective, although Michael Sembello gave Sanborn one of his most insistently catchy melodies in 'The Dream'; the rest is over-produced pop-jazz. *Close-Up*, however, was a brilliant return to form. This time Miller handled the whole project and turned in tunes and arrangements which took Sanborn to the very limit of this direction. Having experimented with different keyboard and drum-programme sounds on the earlier records, Miller built backing tracks of maze-like complexity which barely gave the saxophonist room to breathe, yet the exciting riff-tune, 'Slam', the sweet melodies of 'So Far Away' and 'Lesley Ann' and the staccato snap of 'Tough' squeezed Sanborn into delivering some of his smartest ideas. It's a little like a modernization of West Coast jazz, where soloists were required to put a personal stamp on 16 bars in the middle of a skin-tight arrangement. The sound is artificially brilliant but entirely suitable for the music.

***** Another Hand**

Elektra 61088-2 *Sanborn; Art Baron (tb, btb); Lenny Pickett (cl, ts); Terry Adams, Mulgrew Miller (p); Leon Pendarvis (org); Bill Frisell, Marc Ribot, Al Anderson, Dave Tronzo (g);*

Greg Cohen, Charlie Haden, Marcus Miller (b); Joey Baron, Steve Jordan, Jack DeJohnette (d); Don Alias (perc); Syd Straw (v). 90.

A striking if sometimes uneasy change of direction. After working with a wide range of players on his American TV series, *Night Music*, Sanborn (and producer Hal Willner) sought out less familiar territory and came up with this curious fusion of jazz, R&B and the kind of instrumental impressionism which participants Frisell and Ribot have been associated with. Sanborn sounds interested but not entirely sure of himself at some points, and seems happiest on the rhythmically less taxing pieces such as the infectious lope of 'Hobbies' and two tracks with the Millers and DeJohnette. The film-music medley arranged by Greg Cohen emerges as a queer pastiche. Possibly more important to its maker than to his audience, but well worth hearing.

★★★(★) Upfront

Elektra 61272-2 *Sanborn; Earl Gardner, Laurie Frink, Randy Brecker, Paul Litteral, Herb Robertson (t); Dave Bargeron, Art Baron (tb); Stan Harrison (as); Lenny Pickett, Arno Hecht (ts); Crispin Cioe (bs); Richard Tee (org); John Purcell (ts, saxello); William Patterson, Eric Clapton (g); Marcus Miller (b, ky, g, bcl); Steve Jordan (d); Don Alias, Nana Vasconcelos (perc).* 91.

Looser, funkier, free-flowing where the last one was bound up in itself, this is Sanborn sounding comfortable and in charge. His own playing doesn't change so much from record to record, but he sounds a lot happier back here in Marcus Miller's grooves than he did on Hal Willner's on the previous disc. The hip, updated treatment of Ornette's 'Ramblin" works out a treat, with Herb Robertson adding squittery trumpet, but the whole record has a lot of fine playing – in a live-in-the-studio atmosphere – that stands up to plenty of listening.

★★★ Hearsay

Elektra 61620-2 *Sanborn; Earl Gardner, Michael Stewart (t); John Purcell, Lenny Pickett (ts); Marcus Miller (bcl, ky, g, b); Ricky Peterson (org, p); William Patterson, Dean Brown, Robben Ford (g); Steve Jordan (d); Don Alias (perc).* 93.

Still seeking a live-in-the-studio sound, Miller produces a great set of grooves here for Sanborn to blow over; a revision of Marvin Gaye's 'Got To Give It Up' and a gorgeous 'The Long Goodbye' are two highlights among many. But the man himself sounds merely capable. One longs for a single killer solo, or for one of the other horns to step up and push him into his best form.

★★★ Pearls

Elektra 61759-2 *Sanborn; Don Grolnick (ky); Kenny Barron (p); Marcus Miller, Christian McBride, Mark Egan (b); Steve Gadd (d); Don Alias (perc); Oleta Adams, Jimmy Scott (v); strings.* 94.

Sanborn's strings album is an elegant vehicle for his sound. The choice of material is safe rather than surprising, but it's interesting that the old-fashioned pieces – 'Willow Weep For Me' or 'Come Rain Or Come Shine' – don't suit him nearly as well as the 'mature' modern pop of Sade's title-tune – where he gets a nice note of menace in – or Leon Russell's 'Superstar'. Scott and Adams take a vocal apiece, to no great effect, and the sound is glassy rather than warm, but the overall effect is pleasing enough.

★★★ The Best Of David Sanborn

Warner Bros 9362-45768-2 *As various discs above.* 75–93.

Sanborn's hits collection covers seven of his Warners albums and is a neat survey of his most commercially successful years. As a pocket primer on the most copied and insidiously influential sax sound of its era, very effective.

★★★ Songs From The Night Before

Elektra 61950-2 *Sanborn; Randy Brecker (t); John Purcell (bcl, f); George Young (ss, cl, f); Dave Tofani (ts, f); Ricky Peterson (ky); Paul Peterson, Phil Upchurch, Dean Brown (g); Pino Palladino (b); Steve Jordan (d); Don Alias (perc).* 96.

Ricky Peterson has worked with Sanborn before, but here he produces a whole set for the nominal leader. The results are just sweet enough for the radio and sufficiently gritty for Sanborn to get creative. An affecting melody like 'Rikke' sits next to a tersely funky take on Eddie Harris's 'Listen Here', and further down the list is Wayne Shorter's 'Infant Eyes'. Sanborn remains peerless at grafting a serious player's heart and soul on to moves that would otherwise be mere fluff: his kind of urban night music, shrewdly suggested by this disc's packaging, can pass by unnoticed but still present an authoritative and lived-in hinterland to 'real' jazz. Like his other recent records, though, this one misses a pressing reason to exist.

★★★(★) Inside

Elektra 7559-62346-2 *Sanborn; Wallace Roney (t); Michael Brecker, Lennie Pickett (ts); Ronnie Cuber (bs); Gil Goldstein (p); Ricky Peterson (org); Marvin Sewell, Dean Brown, Bill Frisell, Fareed Haque (g); Hank Roberts (clo); Marcus Miller (b, bcl, ky, v); Gene Lake (d); Don Alias (perc); Cassandra Wilson, Sting, Lalah Hathaway, Eric Benet (v).* 98.

Sanborn has another go at making heavyweight music that they'll still play on the radio. Back with Marcus Miller at the desk, he gets close to delivering his best record. Warm, without the phoney radiance of smooth jazz, the settings which Miller devises are just idiosyncratic enough to refuse to let the record slip into the background and, if Sanborn himself sometimes drifts through the music rather than commanding it, he plays his parts with real sensitivity and effort. His own tune, 'Lisa', one of two writing credits, is the prettiest thing on the record. Miller writes in real horns – Brecker and Cuber play only charts, but they're easy to spot – and plays his brainy-sidekick role just right.

★★★ Timeagain

Verve 655782-2 *Sanborn; Randy Brecker (t, flhn); Lawrence Feldman (af, bf); Ricky Peterson (ky); Gil Goldstein (p); Mike Mainieri (vib); Russell Malone (g); Christian McBride (b); Steve Gadd (d); Don Alias, Luis Quintero (perc); Lani Groves, Arnold McCuller, David Lasley, Valerie Pinkston (v); strings.* n.d.

Now in situ at another jazz label, Sanborn *almost* goes all the way and nearly makes a full-on jazz record. The listed personnel are together on most of the tracks (Brecker, Feldman and the vocalists aside). The material includes old jazz hits such as 'Cristo Redentor', 'Harlem Nocturne' and Stanley Turrentine's 'Sugar', and the groove they all lock into for 'Comin' Home Baby' is hard to resist. Producer Stewart Levine rekindles memories of his long stint with The Crusaders. And the saxophonist never sounds less than keen. All that said, the music feels regressive: compared to *Songs From The Night Before* and *Inside*, this one feels more like an executive's idea of a strong

Sanborn project than one conceived by the man and his closest allies, and they're kidding us that these top-price session players can really act like a band (which The Crusaders were, after all). Still worth more than a thousand smooth-jazz entries, though.

Angelica Sanchez

PIANO

Gifted young player, making her recorded debut.

★★★ Mirror Me

Omnitone 2203 *Sanchez; Tony Malaby (ts); Michael Formanek (b); Tom Rainey (d).* 02.

She might be the most interesting young female piano-player to come along since Francesca Tanksley. Her compositions – and this live set consists of nothing but – are sharply original in a Wayne Shorter mode and her playing is fleet and elegant, using a lot of the keyboard in every solo and modulating evenly between quite different and difficult harmonic areas. A name to watch.

David Sánchez (born 1969)

TENOR AND SOPRANO SAXOPHONES

Born in Guaynabo, Puerto Rico, Sánchez played salsa before turning to jazz, and he studied with Kenny Barron. Encouraged by Dizzy Gillespie, he won a contract with Columbia.

★★★ Sketches Of Dreams

Columbia 508619-2 *Sánchez; Roy Hargrove (t); Danilo Perez, David Kikoski (p); Larry Grenadier (b); Adam Cruz (d); Milton Cardona, Jerry Gonzalez, Leon Parker (perc).* 94.

When he made his first record (*Departure*, currently deleted), Sánchez was already in his mid-20s, still young but not a raw and untamed stripling, and there was a callowness in it which is only briefly engaging. Sanchez has a big, broad, old-fashioned sound that some have likened to Johnny Griffin but which in approach borrows much from Rollins and very little from Coltrane, unusually for a player of his generation. Once again on *Sketches Of Dreams* what makes this album is the sterling support from Perez, Grenadier and Cruz, who turn what might have been an exercise in individualist showmanship into a jazz album.

★★★(★) Street Scenes

Columbia 485137 *Sánchez; Kenny Garrett (as); Danilo Perez (p); John Benitez, Larry Grenadier, Charnett Moffett (b); Horacio Hernandez, Clarence Penn (d); Milton Cardona, Richie Flores (perc); Cassandra Wilson (v).* 2–3/96.

On *Street Scenes* Sánchez concentrates more on his tenor-playing and on constructing well-shaped and logical solos, a little less on texturing and ornamentation. It's all the better for it. Effective guest slots from Kenny Garrett and Cassandra Wilson (on 'Dee Like The Breeze'), but a slightly more functional role for Perez, whose own career was moving apace. This throws more light on the leader himself, and Sánchez sounds like a man comfortably in control of his thing. His exchanges with Garrett on 'Los Cronopios' are both traditional saxophone-duel stuff and highly contemporary, almost ironic. It may or may not be significant that the best track of all is 'Four In One', performed by an unadorned quartet – just Sánchez, Perez and rhythm. Moffett and Hernandez are used only on the title-track, subtitled 'Downtown', a strong rhythmic idea that outstays its welcome by a couple of minutes.

★★★(★) Obsesión

Columbia CK 69116 *Sánchez; John Clark (frhn); George Young (as, ff); Dale Kreps (as, af); Tom Christensen (ts, ob); Andres Boiarsky (ss, ts, cl); Roger Rosenberg (bs, bcl); Edsel Gomez (p); John Benitez (b); Adam Cruz (d); Richie Flores, Jose Gutierrez, Hector Matos, Pernell Saturnino (perc); strings.* 12/97–1/98.

Branford and Delfeayo Marsalis were on hand to produce what turns out to be Sánchez's most wholly Latin date of the bunch, and a first attempt to deal with other composers' work. Four of the tracks are from Puerto Rican musicians, two from Brazil (including Jobim's 'Omorro Nao Tem Vez'), and the set is rounded out with Ray Bryant's 'Cuban Fantasy', arranged for big band. The overall sound is very big, almost grandiose; but here and there Sánchez sounds slightly pinched, almost as if playing on a borrowed horn. His solo development, though, has never been better and there is a depth of focus which hasn't been evident on previous records. With extra woodwinds and strings in the mix, the arrangements are both capacious and nicely detailed. The focus, though, remains on Sánchez himself.

★★★(★) Melaza

Columbia 62085 *Sánchez; Miguel Zenón (as); Edsel Gomez (p); Hans Glawischnig (b); Adam Cruz, Antonio Sánchez (d); Pernell Saturnino, Hector Matos, William Cepeda (perc).* 2/00.

★★★★ Travesía

Columbia 85948 *As above, except omit Cruz, Matos and Cepeda.* 5–6/01.

The earlier of these is an overtly political statement from the young Puerto Rican. The title of the album refers to one of the island's greatest exports, the molasses that comes from sugar cane, a sweetness that comes not out of strength but out of exploitation and cruelty. Sánchez is a wiser artist than to lard his music with editorialized commentaries, but he does make it clear what passion and anger lie behind these themes.

The working band is now a more than competent vehicle for his ideas and Branford Marsalis's hand at the production desk is a guarantee of quality as well. There are guest percussionists and Adam Cruz sits in for a couple of tunes, but the basic lineup is the key. The sound is rich and detailed, and the writing strong enough to support the ideas being communicated. 'Against Our Will' is a brilliant jazz theme and David's solo is one of his most accomplished to date; it has the feel of a first take – fresh, strong and intense – but also very polished, so it may be that much of this material was worked through carefully beforehand. Glawischnig is the composer of 'Orbitando' which sees David switch to his soprano horn, though the highlight of the number is a storming solo from Pernell Saturnino, who lives up to his name. Miguel Zenón also contributes a track, 'El Ogro', which underlines just how strong a working unit this has become. Diversity and unity of purpose in one coherent package.

Travesía shares a vivid sound and some brilliant compositional ideas. This time it doesn't have the same ideological baggage and in some respects is the better for it, since it delivers a more various and pleasurable product. For the first time quite this explicitly, Sanchez explores aspects of Puerto Rican folk music, casting three pieces in *bomba* and *plena* forms and melding them beautifully with the jazz idiom. He also throws in 'River Tales', a brooding melody in double waltz time. A more than confident consolidation on the strengths of its predecessor.

Pharoah Sanders (born 1940)

TENOR SAXOPHONE

Originally Farrell Sanders (and persuaded to make the change by none other than Sun Ra), John Coltrane's latter-day playing partner has run the gamut, from stretched-out bop to high-intensity trance music to a late and unexpected role as a disco hero. A powerful soloist and something of an enigma in the recent history of the music.

***** Pharoah's First**
ESP Disk 1003 *Sanders; Stan Foster (t); Jane Getz (p); William Bennett (b); Marvin Patillo (d, perc).* 9/64.

*****(*) Izipho Zam**
Charly CDGR 226 *Sanders; Sonny Fortune (as); Lonnie Liston Smith (p); Sonny Sharrock (g); Cecil McBee, Sirone (b); Howard Johnson (tba); Billy Hart, Majid Shabazz (d); Chief Bey (African d); Tony Wylie (perc); Leon Thomas (v, perc).* 1/69.

***** Karma**
Impulse! 051153-2 *Sanders; Julius Watkins (frhn); James Spaulding (f); Lonnie Liston Smith (p); Ron Carter, Richard Davis, Reggie Workman (b); William Hart, Freddie Waits (d); Nathaniel Bettis (perc); Leon Thomas (v, perc).* 2/69.

**** Jewels Of Thought**
Impulse! 051247-2 *Sanders; Lonnie Liston Smith (p, f, perc); Richard Davis, Cecil McBee (b, perc); Roy Haynes (d); Idris Muhammad (d, perc).* 10/69.

*****(*) Deaf, Dumb, Blind, Summun, Bukmun, Umyun**
Impulse! 051265-2 *Sanders; Woody Shaw (t, perc, v); Gary Bartz (as, perc); Lonnie Liston Smith (p, perc); Cecil McBee (b); Clifford Jarvis (d); Nathaniel Bettis (perc, v); Anthony Wiles (perc).* 7/70.

***** Thembi**
Impulse! 051253-2 *Sanders; Michael White (vn, perc); Lonnie Liston Smith (p, perc); Cecil McBee (b, perc); Roy Haynes (d); Clifford Jarvis (d, perc); Nat Bettis, Chief Bey, James Jordan, Majid Shabazz, Anthony Wiles (perc).* 11/70, 1/71.

If the Creator does, indeed, have a master plan, then the role he has written for Pharoah Sanders is a complex one. Like those other great saxophonists, Snub Mosley and Bill Clinton, he hails from Little Rock, Arkansas, and in the '60s, while Snub was getting by and Bill was obstinately refusing to inhale, Sanders was swallowing great draughts of air to produce some of the most raucously beautiful saxophone sounds of the decade. Having worked with John Coltrane during the latter's last years, he had acquired licence to stretch harmonics to the utmost, but always, unlike Coltrane, over a hypnotically simple ground, which is why in later years Sanders was able to reinvent himself as the wicked uncle of the club and dance scene.

An ESP Disk recording was almost *de rigueur* for anyone in the New York avant-garde. Sanders's is better than most, though it suffers from a very anonymous band. As usual, the leader plays with enough intensity to weld metal, albeit with a softer and broader tone than Coltrane's. Like his sometime employer, he was taken up by Impulse! and given a freer hand than was strictly good for him. Unlike the admirably disciplined Trane, Pharoah never knows when an idea has run its course, and the half-hour plus of 'The Creator Has A Master Plan' (which is basically all there is of *Karma*) palls rather quickly. The saxophone part is pretty much front and centre throughout, and though Bob Thiele's production gives due weight to the other instruments, there is no mistaking that it's Pharoah's gig. The short 'Colors' is a makeweight, but on reflection contains as much of promise as the main event. Like other Impulse! products of the time, it feels like slim pickings at less than 40 minutes; surprising that there wasn't at least some out-take material to pad it out.

Summun, Bukmun, Umyun consists of just two pieces, and it is pretty short measure in contemporary CD terms. Lonnie Liston Smith's adaptation of 'Let Us Go Into The House Of The Lord' is altogether more engaging than the title-piece, which is overstocked with yodelling cries and aimless percussion. Bartz sounds in good voice and it is intriguing to hear Woody Shaw in this company; not his usual turf, though as ever he responds very positively to a free environment.

Izipho Zam is interesting but timelocked, a shambolic and rather undisciplined group performance which doesn't really give any of the soloists except Fortune and the irrepressible Sharrock much room to express themselves. Even well remastered, *Thembi* obstinately refuses to move us, a bland and strangely mechanical run-through of the familiar ethnic/free clichés of the period, with an over-emphasis on small instruments and not enough on straight playing. This was more about wearing funny hats than making music. *Jewels Of Thought* is even weaker still, two great slabs of ambient sound which again bear the stamp of Lonnie Liston Smith as co-composer. Perhaps it was his influence that blunted these early records. Certainly Sanders seems all too willing to shed the ferocity and sheer strength of his work with Coltrane.

*****(*) Black Unity**
Impulse! 051219-2 *Sanders; Hannibal Marvin Peterson (t); Carlos Garnett (ts); Joe Bonner (p); Stanley Clarke, Cecil McBee (b); Norman Connors, Billy Hart (d); Lawrence Killian (perc).* 11/71.

Skimpy as to length, but packed with interest. The line-up alone should be tweaking interest already; Garnett, Bonner, McBee and Hart have never enjoyed the celebrity they deserve, and here they contribute to a fascinating collage of sound, dark splashes of colour which never sound virtuosic but which contribute to an intensely vivid and dramatic canvas. Garnett in particular is stunning, a lighter sound almost in alto range. Again, it's tempting to wonder how much material from the session was left on the cutting-room floor. We have two versions of Coltrane's 'Ascension' and a first draft of Ornette's 'Free Jazz', and though the differences are not critical in either case, the fascination remains.

***** Journey To The One**
Evidence ECD 22016 *Sanders; Eddie Henderson (flhn); Joe Bonner, John Hicks (p); Paul Arslanian, Bedria Sanders (harmonium); Mark Isham (syn); Chris Hayes, Carl Lockett (g); James Pomerantz (sitar); Yoko Ito Gates (koto); Ray Drummond, Joy Julks (b); Randy Merrit, Idris Muhammad*

(d); Phil Ford (tabla); Babatunde (perc); Claudette Allen, Donna Dickerson, Bobby McFerrin, Vicki Randle, Ngoh Spencer (v). n.d.

A club classic. In purely artistic terms, this was something of a false start. Learning that he was to make an album of ballads was a little like learning – and we're struggling now for a suitably bathetic comparison – that Carlos the Jackal was doing voluntary work with the elderly. What's quickly apparent is that the gentler, more linear and melodic Sanders is not fundamentally different from the high-octane screamer, just differently modulated. As was to be the norm from here on in, the key track is a Coltrane cover, in this case 'After The Rain'. Players of the quality of Bonner, Hicks and Henderson add materially to the mix. The piano-players are required to generate an almost tranced quality, bedding Sanders's breathy excursions. This is such a well-trodden set now that it's hard to reach an objective conclusion; strong, vibrant jazz.

***** Rejoice**

Evidence ECD 22020 *Sanders; Danny Moore (t); Steve Turre (tb); Bobby Hutcherson (vib); John Hicks (p); Joe Bonner (p, v); Peter Fujii (g, v); Lois Colin (hp); Art Davis (b); Jorge Pomar (b, v); Billy Higgins, Elvin Jones (d); Babatunde, Big Black (perc); Flame Braithwaite, William S. Fischer, Mira Ishida, B Kazuko, Bobby London, Sakinah Muhammad, Carol Wilson Scott, Yvette S. Vanterpool (v).* n.d.

Cluttered by spurious vocals, but packed with interesting episodes. The basic group is hard to fault, but it's rarely heard in isolation and there is always someone running interference. The brasses aren't heard to advantage; a pity, because one can imagine someone like Eddie Henderson thriving in this company. The two Coltrane items are 'Moment's Notice' and 'Central Park West', the latter interesting for being one of the few originals on which Trane did not solo. Sanders turns it into a moody, brooding excursion.

***** Shukuru**

Evidence ECD 22022 *Sanders; William Henderson (p); Ray Drummond (b); Idris Muhammad (d); Leon Thomas (v).* n.d.

***** Live**

Evidence E22223 *Sanders; John Hicks (p); Curtis Lundy (b); Idris Muhammad (d).* 4/81.

****(*) Heart Is A Melody**

Evidence ECD 22063 *Sanders; William Henderson (p); John Heard (b); Idris Muhammad (d); Paul Arslanian (bells, whistle); Chief Bey, Flame Braithwaite, Cort Cheek, Janie Cook, William S. Fischer, Mira Hadar, Debra McGriffe, Jes Muir, Kris Wyn (v).* 1/82.

Henderson becomes a key player in the early '80s, an able and fluent player with a touch of the Herbie Hancock. Sanders appears to be rethinking his strategy around this time, turning back to standards-playing for the first time in many years. That tenor saxophonist's shibboleth, 'Body And Soul', on *Shukuru* is intelligently performed, with few new ideas, but a sympathetic synthesis of much of what has gone on between Byas and Coltrane concentrated into a relatively straightforward melodic response.

The live set was reissued in 2003. Added to the original release material, taped in LA and Santa Cruz, is a long track recorded at around the same time in San Francisco. 'Doktor Pitt' makes the album, a big-voiced, dramatic piece with some of Sanders's best playing from this period. It seems odd that it hasn't been made available before, though bootlegs do exist. Of the other material, another extended improvisation, 'Pharomba', stands out brightly. Still, one can't help feeling that in these years Sanders marked time musically.

***** A Prayer Before Dawn**

Evidence ECD 22047 *Sanders; William Henderson (p, syn); John Hicks (p); Lynn Taussig (sarod, chandrasarang); Alvin Queen (d); Brian McLaughlin (tabla).* 9/87.

The cover of *A Prayer Before Dawn* shows the middle-aged Sanders with white fringe beard and anomalously black hair framing a benevolently owlish expression far removed from the contorted scowl of former years. With accommodation has come productivity, a steady string of unscary and mostly very palatable records. The sound is drier and less physical than Timeless had started to give him, but very effective on its own terms. Coltrane cover: 'After The Rain' again – torrential, fresh, brand-new.

***** Africa**

Timeless 253 *Sanders; John Hicks (p); Curtis Lundy (b); Idris Muhammad (d).* 87.

***** Moon Child**

Timeless SJP 326 *Sanders; William Henderson (p); Stafford James (b); Eddie Moore (d); Cheikh Tidiane Fale (perc).* 10/89.

*****(*) Welcome To Love**

Timeless SJP 358 *Sanders; William Henderson (p); Stafford James (b); Eccleston W. Wainwright (d).* 7/90.

Henderson and James aren't quite in the Hicks/Lundy mould, but you can readily hear the kind of thing Sanders is after, a hypnotic groove that allows the horn to float almost at will. Interestingly, the saxophonist stays very much on the comfortable side of the chords; even given all the leeway in the world, Sanders no longer wants to tread the outside edge. *Moon Child* is the straightest jazz album he'd made for years, anticipating the trim, angular contours of the later *Crescent With Love*. At this juncture, though, he sounds almost restrained, holding out if not holding back. *Welcome To Love* is more elaborate, embellished, and much of the credit has to go to the estimable Eccleston W. Wainwright, who ought to be executive vice president of his own firm with a name like that, but certainly can't be short of work playing as he does.

*****(*) On Timeless**

CD SJP 253/326/358 3CD *As for Moon Child, Welcome To Love.* n.d.

A valuable gathering-in of Pharoah's work for the Dutch label, though on the face of it it seems odd that they should have opted for this approach, with no additional tracks or out-takes, rather than a more conventional compilation or best-of. Hearing these albums back-to-back doesn't significantly relocate them. The 'Timeless years' were strong but relatively uneventful in terms of big stylistic shifts.

****** Crescent With Love**

Evidence ECD 22099 2CD *Sanders; William Henderson (p); Charles Fambrough (b); Sherman Ferguson (d).* 10/92.

The 25th anniversary of Coltrane's death spawned a rash of tribute albums, few of them as apostolically convincing as this. A perfectly balanced band, with Henderson growing in stature almost as you listen to him and Fambrough showing once again what a responsive and intelligent player he can be in the right company. Five Coltrane tunes, opening with 'Lonnie's Lament', 'Wise One', 'Naima', 'Crescent' and closing disc two with 'After The Rain', these interspersed with 'Misty', 'Too Young To Go Steady', 'Feeling Good', Pietro Piccioni's 'Light At The Edge Of The World' and one original, Henderson's 'Softly For Shyla'. Sanders sounds thoughtful and even a little wistful, as befits a tribute to his friend, but he never lets his playing drift into sentiment. A strong, creative record, perhaps the only one of the recent batch that can be considered essential.

***** Spirits**

Meta 4 *Sanders; Hamid Drake (d, tabla, perc); Adam Rudolph (perc, f, djembe).* 00.

This is one of the most satisfying of Sanders's recent recordings. It is effectively a suite of tone poems for saxophone and percussion, drifting seamlessly from one idea to the next, but constantly evoking some aspect of the African heartland. The long opening 'Sunrise' is the most substantial single piece. Some of the later cuts – in so far as they can be separated out – are more amorphous, even a little bland and New Ageish, but in context they all work beautifully and Pharoah is blowing with a magisterial ease and authority. A challenging format, but the bearded one more than rises to the challenge.

**** With A Heartbeat**

Evolver 2015 *Sanders; Graham Haynes (c); Nicky Skopelitis (g, sitar); Jeff Bova (ky); Bill Laswell (b, ky); Trilok Gurtu (tabla, v).* 02.

It's almost embarrassing to reveal that the title is quite literal. This is a set of improvisations and arrangements played over a recording of a heartbeat made by the improbably named Dr Jean-Louis Zink. As a side-project for a cardiologist, it must have been a gas; as a jazz record it falls pretty short. Laswell is the dominant presence, though he seems to resent someone else's pulse taking over the music and gives the unfortunate donor a scary bout of arrythmia. Though he plays well, these days Sanders plays well within himself and there is a feeling that on this one he just showed up, blew and went for supper. Graham Haynes impresses, though.

Randy Sandke (born 1949)

TRUMPET, CORNET, GUITAR

Born in Chicago, he learned trumpet and followed the music of idols such as Bix and Louis. Worked for ASCAP in New York but began playing jazz again and found himself in demand in swing/mainstream circles. In the '90s he took on an ambassadorial role for the styles he loved, playing at repertory concerts but also recording more outré material on his own records.

***** Stampede**

Jazzology JCD-211 *Sandke; Dan Barrett (tb, c); Ken Peplowski (cl); Scott Robinson (bsx, c); Ray Kennedy (p); Marty Grosz (g); Linc Milliman (tba); Dave Ratajczak (d).* 12/90.

***** Wild Cats**

Jazzology JCD-222 *As above, except Mark Shane (p), James Chirillo (g), Jack Lesberg (b) replace Robinson, Kennedy, Grosz and Milliman.* 7/92.

When it comes to versatility, Sandke's the man, and it lines him up alongside Guy Barker, Wynton Marsalis and a select few in a trumpet section that could play more or less anything in pretty much any style. As ever, the problem with that skill lies in how to sound like yourself. Sandke is getting there, but on some of the earlier records his accomplishments can sound hollow. Sandke's New Yorkers account for the first four discs. This is a repertory group in the manner of those helmed by Marty Grosz and Keith Ingham, and with a similar cast of performers, so there's little to surprise anyone who's heard the many records in this burgeoning genre. *Stampede* is a bit brisker than *Wild Cats*, but the latter gives the soloists some extra room and Sandke sounds more relaxed; he constructs a very fetching solo out of 'Wild Cat' itself, for instance. On all four discs there is first-class support from both Peplowski and Barrett, spirits in close kinship to the leader. Sandke himself is rather variable – some of his solos sound almost pernickety in their attempts to please period feel, others better their environment.

****** The Re-Discovered Louis And Bix**

Nagel-Heyer CD 058 *Sandke; Jon-Erik Kellso, Nicholas Payton (t); Wycliffe Gordon, Dan Barrett (tb); Ken Peplowski (cl, ts); Kenny Davern (cl); Chuck Wilson (as); Scott Robinson (ts, Cmel, bsx); Dick Hyman (p, cel); Howard Alden, James Chirillo (g, bj); David Ostwald (tba); Peter Washington, Greg Cohen (b); Joe Ascione (d).* 6–9/99.

With all of his Concords suddenly deleted, it's a bit of a jump to Sandke's next. Other albums by the New York All Stars are listed under that name, but Sandke gets top billing here – as well he might. A stunning bit of revivalism, this aligns eight Armstrong pieces – some little-heard, others virtually unknown and unrecorded – and seven similarly associated with Beiderbecke. It starts with a bristling piece in the Oliver Jazz Band style called 'Papa What Are You Trying To Do To Me I've Been Doing It For Years', moves through Hot Seven and big-band styles to something in the manner of the All Stars. The Bix material (abetted by Hyman's scholarship) is at least as fascinating, with Goldkette and Venuti material of varying stripes. The playing is little short of superlative by all hands: outside of the great Keith Nichols projects, this kind of living history has seldom been presented with this mix of individual panache and proper homage. One of the best projects this label's realized to date, going several notches above their frequently polite mainstream manners.

*****(*) Inside Out**

Nagel Heyer 2025 *Sandke; Ray Anderson, Wycliffe Gordon (tb); Ken Peplowski (cl, ts); Marty Ehrlich (ss, cl, bcl, af); Scott Robinson (ss, bs, cbsx, bcl, f, theremin); Uri Caine (p); Greg Cohen (b); Dennis Mackrel (d).* 1/00.

Had this been released by a major American label it would likely have been greeted with all kinds of ballyhoo. Instead, Sandke's audacious project, aligning himself and Peplowski alongside the likes of Ehrlich, Anderson and Caine, thereby lining up the new mainstream and New York's downtown side by side, barely got a mention in most parts of the jazz press. Sandke put in three of his own tunes and scored 'Creole Love Call' but he also got everyone else to contribute a tune and the compatability of the playing, even when the music's kicking at doors which some of these players don't care to open, is wonderful. As an ensemble they get a gorgeous sound, the reeds making up a voluptuously rich range and the rarity of two trombones in a nine-piece band also makes its mark. One or two of the pieces are more jokey than good-humoured – Gordon's 'Sam Bone' is just a bit of nonsense for himself and Anderson – but Ehrlich's 'Like I Said', Sandke's 'Inside Out' and Cohen's 'Trapianti Di Scimmia' alone make the record special.

Arturo Sandoval (born 1949)

TRUMPET, FLUGELHORN, KEYBOARDS, PERCUSSION, VOCAL

A Cuban expatriate, Sandoval created a storm of interest in the '80s, seeming to ride in on a fresh wave of Latin jazz creativity. His subsequent progress has been much less interesting.

****(*) No Problem / Just Music**

Jazz House JHCD 6601 2CD *Sandoval; Hilario Duran Torres (p, ky); Jorge Chicoy (g); Jorge Reyes Hernandes (b); Bernardo Garcia Carreras (d); Reinaldo Valera Del Monte (perc).* 8/86–8/88.

****(*) Straight Ahead**

Jazz House JHCD 007 *Sandoval; Chucho Valdes (p); Ron Mathewson (b); Martin Drew (d).* 8/88.

**** Flight To Freedom**

GRP 059634-2 *Sandoval; Ed Calle (ts, f); Chick Corea, Mike Orta, Danilo Perez, Richard Eddy (ky); Rene Luis Toledo (g); Anthony Jackson, Nicky Orta (b); Dave Weckl, Orlando Hernandez (d); Long John, Portinho (perc).* 91.

In person, Sandoval is one of the most ebullient trumpet ambassadors since Dizzy Gillespie, his great mentor. On record, this Cuban exile and scintillating virtuoso is a less convincing figure. *No Problem* is a fair sample of the kind of music he serves up at Ronnie Scott's on his regular visits and, while the playing bubbles with Latin fire and brilliance, battle fatigue tends to overtake the listener. Sandoval may be a great technician, but it's often hard to detect any reason for the galloping runs other than a love of showmanship. The band provide zesty accompaniment. In the studio, with Valdes and a British rhythm section, the atmosphere seems calmer until they go into the trumpet machismo of 'Mambo Influenciado', which shows that Sandoval doesn't need a live audience to prod him into going over the top. *Just Music* (now doubled up as a twofer with the first set) was recorded around the same time and is another mixed bag of kitsch and genuine music-making. The GRP set was his first 'American' statement after defecting to the USA, and the irony is that it often falls into international muzak: GRP house-bands provide faceless backing tracks which the trumpeter dances over with a sometimes light but more often crashingly heavy footfall.

***** I Remember Clifford**

GRP GRP-96682 *Sandoval; Ernie Watts, David Sánchez, Ed Calle (ts); Felix Gomez (ky); Kenny Kirkland (p); Charnett Moffett (b); Kenny Washington (d).* 91.

Tribute albums are becoming a bore, but this is easily the best record under Sandoval's name. The material is all in dedication to Clifford Brown, and most of it emanates from Brownie's own repertoire, including 'Joy Spring', 'Daahoud' and the like. The up-tempo pieces are as thrilling as Sandoval can make them: 'Cherokee' is taken at a preposterously fast tempo, and the trumpeter still pulls off a solo which outpaces everybody else. Watts and Sánchez also fire off some exciting solos of their own, and the rhythm section is absolutely on top of it, with Kirkland at his most dazzling. Yet there remains a gloss of routine on the music, which can sound utterly unyielding, and the production decision to create some trumpet parts by feeding them through a harmonizer only adds to the sense of a spirit tamed by the demands of making successful records.

**** Dream Come True**

GRP 059702-2 *Sandoval; Bill Watrous (tb); Ernie Watts (ts); Michel Legrand, Otmaro Ruiz (ky); Brian Bromberg (b); Peter Erskine, Aaron Sefarty (d); Carlos Gomez, Mitchell Sanchez (perc); strings.* 93.

**** The Latin Train**

GRP 059820-2 *Sandoval; Dana Teboe (tb); Ed Calle (ts, bs, f); Kenny Anderson (as); Otmaro Ruiz (p); Rene Toledo (g); David Enos (b); Aaron Sefarty (d); Manuel Castrillo, Luis Enrique, Edwin Bonilla, Carl Valldejuli (perc); Joe Williams, Celia Cruz, Oscar D'Leon, Luis Enrique, Vicente Rojas, Laura Pifferrer, Cheito Quinones (v).* 1/95.

Gimcracked around Sandoval's prodigious but exhausting talents, these albums are a stifling bore, and they show Sandoval already with nowhere interesting to go. *Dreams Come True* just about gets by on the basis of 'Dahomey Dance', which at least gives Watts and Watrous something useful to do; the rest, heavingly arranged by Legrand, is charmless. So is most of *The Latin Train*, which seems about as feelingful and sincere as a Las Vegas wedding. The frantic high-note playing and souped-up arrangements go nowhere fast. For diehard fans only.

****(*) Swingin'**

GRP 059846-2 *Sandoval; Clark Terry (t); Dana Teboe (tb); Michael Brecker, Ed Calle (ts); Eddie Daniels (cl); Joey Calderazzo (p); Mike Stern (g); John Patitucci (b); Gregory Hutchinson (d).* 1/96.

Well, the supporting cast is terrific, and Sandoval probably stands as tall as any of them on this set of bebop and hard-bop covers and copies. But it's hard to see why anyone would want to invest in this kind of xeroxed imitation.

**** Americana**

N-Coded Music NC-4205-2 *Sandoval; Jason Carder (flhn); Dana Teboe (tb); Ed Calle (as, ts, ss, cl); Charles McNeill (ts); Doug Bickel (p); Richard Eddy Martinez, Jim Gasior (ky); Dan Warner, Danny Toledo (g); Dennis Marks (b); Ernesto Simpson (d); Luis Enrique (perc).* n.d.

Smooth jazz in all but name, this set of pop tunes from the songbooks of Sting, Janet Jackson and so forth musters some respectable music – 'Englishman In New York' not bad, 'All Night Long' good enough to compete with Herb Alpert. But the ballads are melted slush.

**** My Passion For The Piano**

Columbia 507615-2 *Sandoval; Ed Calle (ts); Dennis Marks (b); Ernesto Simpson (d); Samuel Torres (perc).* n.d.

Sandoval usually gives himself a turn at the piano in his live shows, and this time he's cut a whole record at the keyboard. It's all-acoustic, and when he's playing a ballad such as 'Romántico', he at least gets something out of the melody. But it's the same as with his trumpet-playing: far, far too many notes, and he doesn't exactly have a light touch.

**** Best Of Arturo Sandoval**

Milan/WEA 5050466 3099-2 *Sandoval; other personnel unlisted.* n.d.

Not too sure where this gathering of tracks comes from or the likely date – and frankly, we're disinclined to spend too much time researching it – but if you want a sampling of Sandoval in various situations this works well enough. There's an excruciating 'Maria', and overblown concert treatments of 'My Funny Valentine' and 'A Night In Tunisia'. The closing blues is surprisingly restrained, for Arturo.

Marit Sandvik (born 1956)

VOCAL

Norwegian vocalist from the far north of Europe.

****** Song, Fall Soft**

Taurus TRCD 834 *Sandvik; Oystein Blix (tb); Jorn Oien (p); Konrad Kaspersen (b); Trond Svarre Hansen (d).* 3/95.

Jazz from Tromsø, at the northern tip of Norway, an unlikely home for bebop for many years and a self-sufficient community of players, many of whom have passed into local legend. Sandvik's strong, lean voice is perfectly at ease, whether torching 'Cry Me A River' (her startling entrance takes the breath away), scatting the melody of Jimmy Raney's 'Motion' or duetting with Hansen on a beautiful 'Up Jumped Spring'. She never struggles for a note, has a perfectly clear sense of where a melody's going and uses the most subtle dynamics in all her vocals. She writes lyrics for Wayne Shorter's 'Fall' (transmogrified into the title-piece) and three graceful originals by Oien, whose exquisite touch and insight stand in a fine tradition of Norwegian jazz. Blix is a surprise choice for a front-line partner, but his sober agility works superbly in the context, and Kaspersen and Hansen do everything they have to. Jan Erik Kongshaug also gives them all a wonderful sound. A quite marvellous record.

***** Even Then (Mother Song)**

Taurus TRCD 843 *Sandvik; Henning Gravrok (ss, ts); Eivind Valnes (p); Sigurd Ulveseth (b); Finn Sletten (d).* 7/02.

The belated follow-up disappoints only because it feels more prosaic. Sandvik's singing is still coolly commanding and she again puts together a strong programme of originals, jazz tunes and just a couple of standards, while the band (again from the north of the country) play with sensitive aplomb. Yet something has disappeared. She does very well with Abbey Lincoln's 'Throw It Away' and 'I Know You' is a beautiful original. Perhaps something in the production, which feels more muted, has made a difference; or perhaps the record needs more time.

San Francisco Starlight Orchestra

GROUP

A band of devotees of the more 'orchestral' style of '20s dance music, sometimes hot, sometimes in a sweeter vein. They play regularly in their home town and are meticulous about period detail.

***** Doin' The Raccoon**

Stomp Off CD1271 *Bob Schulz (c, v); Bruce Vermazen (c); Brent Bergman, Gene Isaeff (tb); John Howard (cl, as, bs); John Pedone (as, cl); Robert Young (ts, ss, bsx, cl, c); Alan Hall (p); Ray Landsberg, Ed Rosenback (vn, v); Jeremy Cohen, Su Jacobsen, Pamela Carey (vn); Dave Frey (bj); Jim Brennan (tba); Hugh O'Donnell (d).* 12/92–7/93.

***** Cheerful Little Earful**

Stomp Off CD1296 *As above, except add Gloria Isaeff (vn), Janine-Marie Braddock (v); omit Bergman, Jacobsen.* 2–4/95.

***** Rose Colored Glasses**

Stomp Off CD1334 *As above, except omit Young and Cohen; add Brian Campbell (cl, ts, bsx).* 9/97–3/98.

***** Sunny Side Up**

Stomp Off CD1364 *As above except add Chris Kive (ob).* 8/00–2/01.

An institution in the city, this contentedly time-locked outfit re-creates the symphonic jazz of Paul Whiteman, blending hot-dance arrangements of period material with the sweetness of a violin section. They are stricter and more genteel than most of the Stomp Off repertory bands and, with their specific commitment which goes as far as using period instruments when possible (Schulz even blows on Bix Beiderbecke's cornet on the first disc), probably unique. Since they go as far as including a Rudy Wiedoeft number, jazz listeners may find it all a bit much, but the second disc's quota of hot tunes includes 'Bessie Couldn't Help It' and 'Baltimore'. *Rose Colored Glasses* continues in more or less identical fashion, with a few licks of the exotic: 'Rumba Negro', 'Maori (A Samoan Dance)'. *Sunny Side Up* gets as archaic as The Six Brown Brothers' 'That Moaning Saxophone Rag' while also going almost modernistic with Ellington's 'Harlem Flat Blues' and Redman's 'Chant Of The Weed'. They sail contentedly on.

Eivin Sannes (born 1937)

PIANO

Born in Hønefoss, Sannes turned pro in 1957. His regular gig as the house pianist in Bergen's Hotel Neptun during the '60s was a focal point for Norwegian jazz.

***** Sandu**

Gemini GMCD 67 *Sannes; Sture Janson (b); Ronnie Gardiner (d).* 5/90.

***** Jubilee**

Gemini GMCD 93 *Sannes; Atle Hammer (t); Harald Gundhus (ts, f); Jesper Thilo (ts); Arvid Genius (vib, v); Sture Janson, Niels Pallesen (b); Edward Olsen (d); Sven Erik Nørregaard, Sergio Gonzalez (perc).* 6–7/97.

Sannes comes from, in his own words, 'the generation that will always be grateful to the great composers – Duke Ellington, Van Heusen, Benny Golson and many others'. The veteran Norwegian pianist plays 15 standards on *Sandu* with a lot of engaging sparkle. His manner is poised between swing and the cooler end of bebop – one of his early inspirations was Pete Jolly – and while there's nothing to startle a casual listener here, the tracks are delivered with fine, unassuming candour. A duet with Janson on 'Lulu's Back In Town' is particularly crisp and witty, but there's something good in all the tracks, and though he can be a little too fond of arpeggios and the occasional commonplace, some unusual tunes – Buster Bailey's 'Peruvian Nights' and Victor Feldman's 'Azule Serape', which bookend the record – add fresh interest.

Sannes celebrates 40 years of playing on *Jubilee*, with plenty of old friends on hand, four new originals and some Monk,

Dameron and standards. A nice stroll through his back pages. Nothing fancy, but much to enjoy.

★★★ Together

Gemini GMCD 99 *Sannes; Harald Johnsen (b); Eyvind Olsen(d); Inge Stangvik (v).* 12/98–1/99.

As much Stangvik's record as Sannes's, this is a lightweight but fetching mix of vocals on standards, a few originals by the singer, and a few pieces for the trio. Stangvik has one of those Scandinavian voices which makes the English language sound coolly sexy, and she has an inventive take on many of the melody lines. Sannes placidly follows and leads as the fancy takes him.

Mongo Santamaria (1922–2003)

PERCUSSION

Born in a poor quarter of Havana, Santamaria moved to the USA in 1950, originally to work with Cal Tjader, and became a hugely influential force in hybridizing the rhythms of Latin American music with jazz. In his own groups he adapted the charanga line-up to accommodate saxophones and brasses. His composition 'Afro Blue', still occasionally credited in error to John Coltrane, is a modern classic.

★★★ Sabroso

Original Jazz Classics OJCCD 281 *Santamaria; Louis Valizán (t); Jose Chombo Silva (ts); Rolando Lozano (f); Vince Guaraldi (p); Cal Tjader (vib); Felix Pupi Legarreta (vn); Al McKibbon, Victor Venegas (b); Willie Bobo (perc); Pete Escovedo, Bayardo Velarde (v).* 59.

★★★ Arriba!

Fantasy 24738 *Santamaria; Rolando Lozano (f); Jose Chombo Silvo (ts); Joao Donato (p); Felix Pupi Legarreta (vn); Victor Venegas (b); Cuco Martinez (perc); Rudy Calzado (v).* 59.

★★★ Our Man In Havana

Fantasy FCD 24729 2 *Santamaria; Armandito El Fine (t); Julio (f); Paquito (f, p); Nino Rivera (tres); Willie Bobo (perc); Bol, Pepito (b); Gustavito (guiro); Yeyito (perc); Mario Arenas, Carlos Embales, Cheo Junco, Macuchu, Armando Raymact, Luis Santamaria, Merceditas Valdés (v); Cuban All Stars.* 60.

Santamaria is now regarded more as a catalyst than as a significant performer in his own right, but his work is well worth hearing, and he has stuck to his last over the years. *Sabroso*, which includes in the line-up Santamaria's old boss, Cal Tjader, is nicely balanced between traditional *charanga*, with its flute-and-violin front line, and a more contemporary jazz sound. Bobo and vocalist Escovedo are effectively co-leaders, providing a lot of the drama of the set.

Arriba! sticks doggedly to the same formula, a generous array of 22 themes by the leader, band members Lozano and Legarreta, with the Gillespie/Pozo classic 'Manteca' thrown in as an example of reciprocal influence.

The personnel on *Our Man In Havana* remains somewhat obscure, largely because many of the players are identified only by their first names. It's remotely possible that political pressures have something to do with this. The music is certainly very much on first-name terms: hot, intimate and joyous, with a greater admixture than before of traditional elements. The two main vocalists, Embales and Valdés, are classic exponents of the repertoire and flautist Julio and *tres* player Nino Rivera add to the chemistry.

★★★ Watermelon Man

Milestone 47075 *Santamaria; Marty Sheller (t); Mauricio Smith (f); Bobby Capers, Pat Patrick (f, sax); Jose Chombo Silva (ts); Rodgers Grand (p); Felix Pupi Legarreta (vn); Victor Venegas (b); Frank Hernandez, Ray Lucas (d); Willie Bobo, Joseph Gorgas, Kako (perc); Rudy Calzado, La Lupe, Osvaldo Chihuahua Martinez (v).* 12/62, 9/63.

By the first years of the '60s, Santamaria was working in what was identifiably a jazz idiom, with strong Latin inflexions, rather than the other way round. Herbie Hancock's 'Watermelon Man', played very much in the spirit of the original but rhythmically much looser and more elaborate, delivered the percussionist his first major hit. From this point on, his reputation was firmly established. The horn voicings are very jazz-orientated and the track lengths were carefully tailored to radio and jukebox requirements. It would be good to hear longer versions of almost all of these tunes, not least the Cannonball Adderley/Joe Zawinul collaboration 'Cut That Cane'. The reissue includes six previously unissued tracks from a live Californian set recorded in 1962. These don't add much to a record that is already classic Santamaria.

★★★ At The Black Hawk

Fantasy FCD 24734 *Santamaria; Jose Chombo Silva (ts); Pat Patrick (sax, f); Rolando Lozano (f); Joao Donato (p, tb); Victor Venegas (b); Willie Bobo (perc); Rudy Calzado (v).* 62.

There was still something of a split in Santamaria's market placing at this time, so Fantasy divided the material from the Black Hawk into two slightly different album packages. The jazz-inflected *Mighty Mongo* and the more Cuban *Viva Mongo!* are paired up on this fine CD reissue. Santamaria's sidemen were also getting used to the idea of playing like jazz musicians, and saxophonist Jose Chombo Silva unveils a range of influences from Hawkins to Coltrane, which makes slightly more sense when you see tunes like 'Body And Soul' and 'All The Things You Are' slipped into the programme for the first time.

★★★ Mongo At The Village Gate

Original Jazz Classics OJCCD 490 *Santamaria; Marty Sheller (t); Pat Patrick (as, f); Bobby Capers (ts, f); Rodgers Grand (p); Victor Venegas (b); Frank Hernandez (d); Julian Cabrera, Osvaldo Chihuahua Martinez (perc).* 9/63.

The live records have always been the best measure of Santamaria's work, and even though the registration on this Symphony Sid-hosted event isn't of the absolute best, the whole disc is shot through with a sense of excitement and the tunes are allowed to find their own length rather than be tailored for radio and jukebox. Santamaria's feature on 'My Sound' was the sort of thing that American players from Dizzy Gillespie onwards were to find so inspirational.

★★(★) Mongo Introduces La Lupe

Milestone MCD 9210-2 *Santamaria; Alfredo 'Chocolate' Armenteros, Marty Sheller (t); Pat Patrick (as, f); Bobby Capers (ts, f); Rodgers Grand, Rene Hernandez (p); Victor Venegas (b); Kako, Osvaldo Martinez, Frank Valerino (perc, v); La Lupe (v).* 63.

La Lupe is a bit of an acquired taste and just a touch overdone. She features on only half the tracks, leaving the rest to a rather generic and formulaic instrumental recording which Santamaria fans will treasure and most others find irritatingly inconsequential. This was the band's high-water mark and it was overproducing furiously. Marty Sheller and Chocolate Armenteros exchange some high-note stuff that would have done Dizzy Gillespie proud, and the usual range of saxophonists and percussionists, not forgetting the ever-present Rodgers Grand, provide deft accompaniment. For enthusiasts only, though.

*** Greatest Hits

Fantasy 24753 *As above.* 58–63.

The first of a series of anthologies and compilations which manage, big hits apart, not to step on each other's toes. This rounds up Mongo's first records for Fantasy, up to the point when 'Watermelon Man' propelled him into the pop charts. It's worth having if you don't own or wouldn't find the occasion to play the original releases. There are no new or unissued selections, just a nicely packaged and well-sequenced choice.

*** Skins

Milestone 47038 *Santamaria; Paul Serrano, Marty Sheller (t); Nat Adderley (c); Hubert Laws (f, picc, ts); Al Abreu, Pat Patrick (sax, f); Bob Capers (as, bs); Chick Corea, Rodgers Grand (p); Jose De Paulo (g, perc); Victor Venegas (b); Ray Lucas (d); Julio Collazo, Carmelo Garcia, Wito Kortwright, Osvaldo Chihuahua Martinez, To-Tiko (perc); Carmen Costa, Marcellina Guerra, Elliott Romero (v); chorus.* 64, 72.

Skins has always been the best place to start for those who are not ready for the undiluted Santamaria of earlier years. The album still has a lot to recommend it, and the presence of Adderley and Chick Corea, who learned a great deal from Santamaria's music, will recommend it to jazz fans. There is a preponderance of vocal music on the later set which is rather wearing when mixed up as loud as it is; very much in the style of the time but unnatural to contemporary tastes.

*** Mongo 70 / Mongo At Montreux

Collectables 6401 *Santamaria; Israel Gonzalez (t); Raymond Maldonado (t, perc); Carter Jefferson, Grant Reed (ts, f); Trevor Lawrence (bs); Roger Glenn (f, vib); Neal Creque, Eddie Martinez (p); Eric Gale (g); Edward Rivera (b); Steve Berrios (d, perc); Angel Allende, Osvaldo Martinez, Armando Peraza (perc).* 70.

In their usual way, Collectables put together two albums from the start of the '70s (note: this is a different Montreux performance from the one below). The 1970 appearance pitted him with cousin Armando Peraza and a steaming band that must have been as good to watch as they are to listen to. The Santamaria magic always worked less well in the studio and there are lapses on the *70* disc.

*** Summertime

Original Jazz Classics OJCCD 626 *Santamaria; Dizzy Gillespie (t); Tommy Villarini (t, perc); Doug Harris (ts, f); Allan Hoist (ts, clo); Toots Thielemans (hca); Milton Hamilton (p); Lee Smith (b); Steve Berrios (d, perc).* 7/80.

*** Montreux Heat

Pablo 5317 *As above.* 7/80.

Coming back to this record after several years, we find our enthusiasm somewhat diminished by what now seems an overlong and indulgent set on which Mongo, Dizzy and Toots stretch out over four tunes, including the percussionist's otherwise evergreen 'Afro Blue' and the title-piece. Dizzy has articulation problems throughout and yet seems bent on hitting the heights every time he takes a solo. The opening tune, Alphonse Mouzon's 'Virtue', is the best thing on the album, its crisp promise unfulfilled.

*** Mambo Mongo

Chesky 100 *Santamaria; Eddie E. J. Allen (t); Jimmy Cozier (as); Craig Rivers (ss, as, ts); Hubert Laws, Dave Valentin (f); Dario Eskenazi (p); Johnny Almendra Andreu (perc); Eddie Rodriguez (perc, v).* 3/92.

Later Santamaria albums were arranged and conducted by trumpeter Marty Sheller, who had been part of the early American bands. Here, having switched to a new label, he seems to have captured something like the feel of the old group, but only very episodically and with no consistency, and the record jumps in and out of focus on almost every number. William Allen and Hilton Ruiz are also credited as composer/arrangers, and it is Ruiz's 'Caribbean Sunrise' which gives the first half of the record its optimistic bounce. The group also tackles a composition by Onaje Allan Gumbs, 'Are They Only Dreams', a softly dreamlike theme with an edgy second subject which is darker than Santamaria's usual fare.

***(*) Mongo Returns

Milestone 9245 *Santamaria; Eddie E. J. Allen (t, flhn, as, bs, f); Roger Byam (ss, ts, f); Robert DeBellis (as, bs, f); Mel Martin (picc, f, af, bf); Oscar Hernandez (p, ky); Hilton Ruiz (p); John Benitez (b); Robby Ameen (d); Greg Askew (d, shekere); Johnny Almendra Andreu (d, perc); Louis Bauza, Steve Berrios (perc, g).* 6/95.

... and returns to Fantasy Records in some triumph with one of his most vivid sets for some considerable time. Once again, Marty Sheller is in charge of the arrangements, and with Hilton Ruiz on board as pianist and bringing with him the charts for 'Free World Mambo', the stage was set for something quite special. The nods in the direction of pop music are still evident in Stevie Wonder's 'You've Got It Bad, Girl' and Marvin Gaye's 'When Did You Stop Loving Me', but these sound entirely consistent with the style and working practice of the band. A cracking record, recommendable to fans and newcomers alike.

*** Brazilian Sunset

Candid 79703 *Santamaria; Eddie E. J. Allen (t, flhn); Jimmy Cozier (as, bs, f); Craig Rivers (ts, f); Ricardo Gonzalez (p); Johnny Almendra Andreu (d, perc); Eddie Rodriguez (perc).* 2/96.

Santamaria's 75th birthday was already behind him when this lovely, low-key record was made. The reprise of 'Watermelon Man' was a forgivable indulgence and 'Summertime' might well have been segued into 'Autumn Leaves', so thoroughly is the record suffused with a ripe nostalgia. Immaculately produced by Alan Bates and Mark Morganelli, it's flawless product, even if a long way removed from the excitement of the early years.

***(*) Skin On Skin: The Mongo Santamaria Anthology, 1958–1995

Rhino 75689 *As for many of the above.* 58–95.

A skilfully selected compilation that picks its way round existing anthologies and makes light of a 15-year gap covering most of the '70s and '80s. As a one-stop introduction to 'Afro Blue', 'Summertime', 'Para Ti', 'Manteca' and 30 others you really couldn't hope to do better.

***** Mucho Mongo: Soca Me Nice / Ole Ola**
Concord Jazz CCD 4999 *Santamaria; Ray Vega (t, flhn); Bobby Porcelli (as, bs, f); Mitch Frohman (ts, f); Bob Quaranta (p); Johnny Almendra Andreu, Bobbi Cespedes, Claudia Gomez, Humberto Nengue Hernandez (perc); Angelo Mark Pagen (v).* 5/88–5/89.

Reissued in 2001, *Mucho Mongo* is an attractive compilation of characteristic Santamaria material. A couple of pop songs, including the Beatles' 'Day Tripper', are included to leaven the diet of percussion-heavy Latin themes. As so often, there is very little material by Santamaria himself, though there is no mistaking whose personality dominates proceedings.

Bernardo Sassetti

PIANO

A Portuguese pianist who spent some time in London in the '90s and is familar to British audiences from his work in the Guy Barker group, Sassetti bases himself in Lisbon.

****** Nocturno**
Clean Feed CF 008 *Sassetti; Carlos Barretto (b); Alexandre Frãzao (d).* 7/02.

A beautiful and unexpectedly compelling record. Sassetti's work with Guy Barker alerted us to his fine touch and lovely melodic sense, but this set trumps all that material. After a rapt reading of 'A Time For Love' to commence matters, it works through seven originals and two pieces (one played twice) by Federico Mompou, each lit by the most luminous touch at the keyboard and enlivened by outstanding work from bassist and drummer. Listeners looking for something a bit more virile and swinging might deem the music to be a little on the light side but it's a measure of the group's working powers that these serene waters actually conceal some quite hard and purposeful musical thinking. Either way, a truly wonderful set from a label which usually specializes in much noisier music.

Tom Saunders

CORNET, VOCAL

A Wild Bill Davison disciple who recorded with his mentor on several occasions, Saunders follows in that fiery tradition of hot cornet-playing.

***** Call Of The Wild**
Arbors ARCD 19146 *Saunders; Bill Allred (tb); Chuck Hedges (cl); Rick Fay (ts); Johnny Varro (p); Paul Keller (b); Warren Sauer (d).* 4/95.

***** Exactly Like You**
Nagel-Heyer 023 *Saunders; Dick Sudhalter (c, t, flhn); Bill Allred, Roy Williams (tb); Chuck Hedges (cl); Danny Moss (ts); John Barnes (bs, cl); Johnny Varro (p); Marty Grosz (g, v); Isla Eckinger (b); Butch Miles (d); Jeanie Lambe (v).* 9/95.

Saunders calls his group the Wild Bill Davison Legacy Band, since much of their material pays tribute to the cornetist. The Arbors date is a studio session brimming with boisterous *joie de vivre*, running through (and over) some of Bill's favourite tunes, from 'Running Wild' to 'On The Alamo'. There's nothing fancy here, and the band have the chops and the know-how to keep it short of mere Dixieland blarney. *Exactly Like You* captures a concert from Hamburg in which the band was joined by guests Sudhalter, Williams, Barnes and Grosz for a run-through of some more Davison chestnuts (plus Grosz doing one of his Fats Waller numbers). This is a notch above the usual mainstream jam since most of the players are genuine virtuosos and there is some terrific playing on several of the tunes. 'Exactly Like You' is a strong feature for the reedmen, and the other horns take it in turns in the front line before an all-hands-on-deck finale. Lambe comes on only for, oddly enough, 'Milenberg Joys'. In a close call for individual honours, Allred just takes them ahead of Hedges, but acolytes of the genre will enjoy the whole show.

Savannah Jazz Band

GROUP

British trad from the north of England.

****(*) Savannah Jazz Band**
Lake LACD29 *Tony Smith (t, v); Brian Ellis (tb); Martin Fox (cl); Jack Cooper (bj); Tony Pollitt (b); John Meehan (d).* 6/92–1/93.

****(*) It's Only A Beautiful Picture ...**
Lake LACD51 *As above.* 1/95.

***** Out In The Cold**
Lake LACD82 *As above, except add Dave Morrell (tb); Ellis plays (p).* 1/97.

***** Nothing Blues**
Lake LACD112 *As above, except omit Morrell; Ellis plays (tb).* 11/98.

Based in Huddersfield, which is some way from Savannah, the SJB play unreconstructed trad somewhat in the Ken Colyer tradition: absolutely no frills, not many solos, and no shame about the vocals. Smith cracks too many notes to provide a really purposeful lead, and it's left to the bustling clarinet of Fox to make the biggest impression. These aren't bad records, but they sound pretty ramshackle when compared with the best of the new American traditionalists. The first has a more acidic sound-mix, but at least that has some fizz, which the second is a little short on.

The two later records emerge rather better, partly owing to a more sympathetic sound, particularly on *Nothing Blues*, and partly through what must be a course of pep pills for whoever decides the tempos. Ellis was too ill to blow trombone on the earlier date, and he adds some clattery piano instead. However, we really must ask Mr Smith to give someone else a go at the vocals, if there have to be any!

Jarmo Savolainen (born 1961)

PIANO

Contemporary Finnish pianist working both on his home patch and on American turf.

★★★(★) Songs For Solo Piano
Beta BECD 4023 *Savolainen (p solo).* 12/89–6/90.

When Savolainen first turned up in the USA, one seasoned critic refused to accept that somewhere in his east Finnish ancestry there wasn't at least one antecedent from south of the Mason-Dixon line. This is perhaps slightly overstating the case, but there certainly isn't much of your copywriter's 'Nordic chill' about this gifted piano stylist. He comes from the same quarter of the country as percussionist Edward Vesala, but he is much more obviously steeped in jazz and in a wide range of idioms, from blues and swing to bebop and the fringes of the avant-garde. The solo record provides an ideal opportunity to sample him at close quarters. First records always invite questions about influences. The two improvisations and 'Song No. 1' recall a spectrum of American players from Chick Corea to Keith Jarrett, though here and there one can hear the impact of other, perhaps less prominent stylists: Hampton Hawes, Wynton Kelly, even a touch of Teddy Wilson. 'Lowlands', 'The Word' and the opening 'Ode For Opportunists' are all well-crafted originals. The piano – apparently a model-D Steinway – is superb and has been given the sort of presence, reserved but by no means distant, that a classical player would be delighted with.

★★★★ True Image
A Records AL 73031 *Savolainen; Tim Hagans (t); David Liebman (ss); Kari Heinila (ts); Ron McClure (b); Billy Hart (d).* 3/94.

★★★(★) Another Story
A Records AL 73112 *Savolainen; Tim Hagans (t); Kari Heinila (ts); Anders Jormin (b); Markku Ounaskari (d).* 8/97.

True Image was made in New York and is packed with solid, four-square jazz. There are two groups involved, a larger group fronted by Hagans and Heinila and a quartet with Liebman which represented the first time for three years he had played with old Quest colleagues McClure and Hart; 'smooth as glass' was his delighted estimate of the reunion. The soprano coaxes the pianist out of his relative reserve and there are some lovely exchanges on the cleverly constructed 'Things Are The Way They Are', which may be related to 'All The Things You Are', albeit distantly.

The follow-up was taped in Helsinki and is altogether more relaxed, though less tautly focused. For the first time, Savolainen relies almost entirely on originals, with just one standard and one composition by Heinila among the 11 that make up this generously proportioned set. This sounds like a working group, though it seems clear that some of the material hasn't been fully assimilated. One would like to hear a tighter and more focused performance of 'Another Story' and 'Rapids', which blunt an otherwise impressive opening section. Nicely balanced and mixed, and a positive sign that Savolainen is growing in stature as both composer and performer.

★★★(★) Grand Style
A Records AL 73207 *Savolainen; Eric Vloeimans(t); Uffe Krokfors (b); Markku Ounaskari (d).* 4/00.

Dominated again by Savolainen originals, this is an ambitious set, often stark in its emotional pulse, but vigorously played, often powerful and surprising. Bringing in Vloeimans was a masterstroke: he blows his heart out, even on material which may have seemed abstruse and unfamiliar, and with the leader switching between acoustic piano and a heavily FX-ed Fender Rhodes, the band often feels like a pocket Weather Report; it's fitting that the one cover is Shorter's 'Non-Stop Home' (originally on *Sweetnighter*), here reconfigured as a lonely ballad. Fascinating stuff.

The Savoy Sultans

GROUP

Cooper was a modest saxophonist, but he led the very popular Savoy Sultans for many years, including a residency at New York's Savoy Ballroom from 1937 to 1946.

★★★ Al Cooper's Savoy Sultans 1938–1941
Classics 728 *Cooper; Pat Jenkins (t, v); Sam Massenberg (t); Rudy Williams (as); Ed McNeil, Sam Simmons, Irving 'Skinny' Brown, George Kelley (ts); Oliver Richardson, Cyril Haynes (p); Paul Chapman (g, v); Grachan Moncur (b); Alex 'Razz' Mitchell (d); Helen Procter, Evelyn White (v).* 7/38–2/41.

The Sultans usually played opposite the Chick Webb band at Harlem's Savoy Ballroom, and visiting bands were wary of competing with them, since they were so popular with the dancers. The records are another matter: simple head arrangements, average solos and merely capable playing make one wonder why they were held in such high regard. However, playing through these 24 tracks, one can hear some of the simple appeal of what wasn't really a big band but a small, mobile, flexible unit which covered whatever base the customers wanted. Pat Jenkins is the best soloist. Transfers start out very clean, but some of the tracks have plenty of original surface noise.

Jeremy Sawkins

GUITAR

Part of the Rufus family of Australian contemporary players, Sawkins works in an open-ended modern idiom.

★★★ Southpaw
Rufus RF054 *Sawkins; Miroslav Bukovsky (t); Julian Gough(ts); Alister Spence (p); Adam Armstrong (b); Fabian Hevia (d).* n.d.

Though he introduces licks from elsewhere, here and there, Sawkins follows a free-thinking modal idiom for the most part, and the music's very likeable, if hardly blisteringly original: the title-piece sounds like a classic Scofield line, and 'Thanks To John' is a flimsy acoustic noodle. They do better when Sawkins, Gough and Spence have something to bite on. 'The Blues' is a notably haunting variation, and they end on a delicately shaded 'Dolphin Dance'.

Martin Schack born 1975

PIANO

Talented keyboard man with vigorous compositional style.

***** Headin' Home**

Storyville 1014253 *Schack; Tom Harrell (t, flhn); John Ellis (ss, ts); Joshua Ginsburg (b); Niclas Campagano (d).* 02.

Martin showcases some of his subtle compositions on his debut set. 'The City' is a bustling opening shot, an evocation of New York that doesn't rely on spurious sound effects. 'Keep Them Chords Comin'' is a clever, convoluted idea, apparently inspired by a comment of Dave Liebman's and written for him and Hal Galper, though taken very confidently here by Ellis and the composer. The obvious plus of the album, leaving aside Schack's own undoubted competence, is the guest appearance of Tom Harrell on four tracks. The best of these is the fulsome 'Dedication to Tom Harrell', which gives all the soloists plenty to work on. 'Headin' Home' itself is less engaging, and there are dead spots on 'To Elvin And Cleve', a dedication to the great drummer and one of his talented pupils, Cleve Pozar. Lots to mull over and lots to enjoy on this niftily produced first chapter in what promises to be an interesting career.

Ken Schaphorst (born 1960)

COMPOSER, ARRANGER, TRUMPET, FLUGELHORN, PIANO

Wrote and studied in the Boston area during the '80s, co-founding the Jazz Composers Alliance in 1985 and forming his own big band. Since 1991 has directed jazz studies at Lawrence University, Wisconsin.

****** Purple**

Naxos Jazz 86030-2 *Schaphorst; Dave Ballou, John Carlson, Andy Gravish, Cuong Vu (t, flhn); Jose Roseman, Curtis Hasselbring (tb); Dave Taylor, Chris Cresswell (btb); Doug Yates (as, cl, bcl); Jay Brandford (as, cl); Donny McCaslin, Seamus Blake (ts); Andy Laster (bs, cl); John Medeski (ky); Uri Caine (p); Brad Shepik (g); Drew Gress (b); Jamey Haddad, Dane Richeson (d).* 1/98.

Schaphorst's four earlier big-band records have been tough to find, and this one certainly deserves a wider hearing. He's a conservative radical, hewing to familiar forms and techniques – blues lines, writing with Ellingtonian concern for individuals, making the band a big swinging entity when it has to be – but insisting that there are fresh wrinkles on the old language. So he uses Caine and Medeski as a double-act, bolsters the rhythm section as an independent entity by having two drummers much of the way, and makes sure that the band works on several levels, players constantly called on to switch roles as soloists, ensemble foot-soldiers, accompanists and section-shouters. The soloists are a very talented team – any band that can boast Blake, Caine, Medeski, Ballou and Shepik in its number is never going to be starved of improvisers – and, rather than stepping out to assert themselves, they serve to heighten the contrast of individual voices within this hugely impressive outfit. Each of the nine pieces sets up its own world without seeming to stand aside from its siblings, which suggests that Schaphorst's writing and scoring is, for all its multiplicity of elements, very definitely on one track. David Baker's excellent studio sound will be the envy of many other big-band leaders. This is one of the jewels in the Naxos list: get it before they delete it.

***** Indigenous Technology**

Accurate AC-5049 *Schaphorst; Matt Turner (clo); Dave Richardson (marim, perc).* 11/99.

A pretty strange record but not unrewarding. The music is a mix of chamber forms, completely free playing and miniaturized post-bop. None of the three players makes much of an impact as an instrumental voice and parts of this album are little short of exasperating, although others are dryly beautiful. An unpredictable entry.

Mario Schiano (born 1933)

ALTO AND SOPRANO SAXOPHONES, SHEKERE, ORGAN

A pioneer of Italian free music, Schiano recorded with Gruppo Romano in the '60s but spent much of the next two decades in comparative obscurity. In the '90s he recorded frequently and now holds a singular place in his country's contemporary jazz and improvising doctrine.

***** Gruppo Romano Free Jazz 1966/67 Schiano Trio 1969/70**

Splasc(h) 509-2 *Schiano; Giancarlo Schiaffini (tb, bari-flhn, ocarina); Bruno Tommaso (b, p); Marcello Melis (b); Franco Pecori (d).* 6/67–4/70.

***** Original Sins**

Splasc(h) 502-2 *Schiano; Giancarlo Schiaffini (tb); Franco D'Andrea (p); Marcello Melis, Bruno Tommaso (b); Franco Pecori, Paul Goldfield, Franco Tonani, Marco Cristofolini (d).* 3/67–4/70.

*****(*) Sud**

Splasc(h) 501-2 *Schiano; Massimo Bartoletti, Roberto Antinolfi, Gaitano Delfini (t); Guido Anelli, Ruggero Pastore (tb); Eugenio Colombo, Tommaso Vittorini, Massimo Urbani, Maurizio Giammarco, Toni Formichella (reeds); Domenico Guaccero (ky); Bruno Tommaso, Roberto Della Grotta (b); Alfonso Alcantara Vieira, Michele Iannacone (d); Mandrake (perc).* 1/73–5/78.

**** De Dé**

Splasc(h) 510-2 *Schiano; Alessandro Sbordoni(p, f, syn, vib, perc); Domenico Guaccero (vib, syn, f, perc, v); Bruno Tommaso (b, org, perc).* 2–9/77.

Schiano is a weathered veteran of Italy's tiny and often nearly invisible free-jazz movement. His uncompromising but fundamentally lyrical and persuasive alto-playing is relatively unstartling, but persistence and a readiness to meet and collaborate with improvisers from other territories has resulted in what's now an extensive discography. Splasc(h) have taken up his cause of late, and these reissues of previously obscure early works fill in a number of details of prehistoric Italian free playing. The earliest CD covers the pioneering Gruppo Romano Free Jazz, originally a trio, then a quartet with Schiaffini, then back to a trio with Tommaso replacing Melis. 'No going back,' says Pecori (now a journalist) in his sleeve-notes, but the scratchy, exuberant music smacks of an excitement which is worth rekindling. The 1967 session is blemished by very poor sound; the 1970 date has something of a free-bop feel, with Schiano even turning in a performance of 'Moonlight In Vermont' along the way. A worthwhile piece of history. *Original Sins* is an interesting patchwork of bits and pieces – 'Beat Suite' is the best excerpt, a dynamically varied trio work-out by Schiano, Tommaso and Pecori – *Sud* is of more consistent quality. A mix of quick-fire quintet pieces and rolling, blustering sketches for a big band, the record finds a fine and spontaneous balance between its elements, uses the synthesizer with rare integrity for the period, and is a valuable glimpse of some important players (apart from Schiano, there are major contributions by Vittorini and Giammarco) from a largely 'unavailable' period of Italian jazz. The clinker in this batch is *De Dé*, which sounds more like a lot of messing about than anything very musical; a live 'version' of the long title-piece has little relevance to the studio incarnation.

*****(*) Unlike**
Splasc(h) H 309-2 *Schiano; Co Strieff (as); Evan Parker (ts); Alexander von Schlippenbach (p); Jean-Marc Montera (g); Maarten van Regteren Altena, Joelle Léandre (b); Paul Lovens (d).* 3/90.

*****(*) Uncaged**
Splasc(h) H 357-2 *Schiano; Giancarlo Schiaffini (tb); Marcello Melis (b); Famoudou Don Moye (d); Mauro Orselli (bells).* 4/91.

***** And So On**
Splasc(h) H 368-2 *Schiano; Paul Rutherford (tb); Ernst Reisjeger (clo); Leon Francioli (b); Gunter Sommer (d, etc.).* 10/91.

Uncaged and *And So On* are full-length sessions by groups assembled for the occasion, with old friend Moye in usefully alert form on the former date, binding together the memorable interplay between Schiano and the perennially undervalued Schiaffini, whose mix of trombone grotesqueries and hard-bitten commentary is something to treasure. The live date, recorded at Rome's Alpheus Club, features a sober but intensely active group with Reisjeger and Sommer the wild cards, countering the more meditative work of the two horns (Reisjeger gets a suitably demented solo piece as an encore). *Unlike* finds Schiano in three group-settings: there are two brief duets with Strieff and two numbers apiece with a quartet and a quintet, the latter the Von Schlippenbach Trio with Léandre as a further guest. Perhaps surprisingly, it's the quintet pieces which turn out for the best: Altena's brilliant yet discreet responses to Schiano and Lovens mitigate the more glaring noises made by Montera on guitar. The group with Léandre, Parker, Von Schlippenbach and Lovens follows the vocabulary laid down by the nucleus of that group, and Schiano has a harder time making himself felt. But all of these records have points of absorbing interest.

***** Meetings**
Splasc(h) H 418 *Schiano; Irène Schweizer, Giorgio Gaslini (p); Philipp Wachsmann (vn); Clenert Ford (g, v); Bruno Tommaso, Barry Guy (b); Paul Lovens (d); Archie Savage, Pamela Fries (v).* 1/80–10/93.

*****(*) Blue Memories**
Splasc(h) H 449-2 *Schiano; Renato Geremia (ts, cl, f, vn, p); Joelle Léandre (b, v).* 10/94.

*****(*) Used To Be Friends**
Splasc(h) H 452-2 *Schiano; Paul Rutherford (tb); Ernst Reijseger (clo); Peter Kowald (b); Paul Lovens (d).* 10/95.

****** Social Security**
Victo 043 *Schiano; Sebi Tramontana (tb); Evan Parker (ss, ts); Barry Guy (b); Paul Lovens (d).* 5/96.

***** The Friendship Of Walnuts**
Splasc(h) H 611-2 *Schiano; Conrad Bauer (tb); Pasquale Innarella (frhn); Roberto Ottaviano (ss, ts); Ernst-Ludwig Petrowsky (cl, as); Vittorino Curci (ts, v, tape); Giuseppe Guarrella (b); Fabrizio Spera (d).* 6/96.

Plenty of music and most of it more than worthwhile. Schiano's own playing remains an element rather than a premier voice in all these ensembles and sometimes he seems like an anti-virtuoso when in company with the likes of Parker and Rutherford. With the smaller groups of *Meetings* and *Blue Memories* this is more problematic, but only in so far as the music occasionally misses a lead when it needs one to be taken. *Meetings* sweeps together a jittery set by the Action Trio of Schiano, Gaslini and Tommaso, two sextet pieces from a Rome concert ('Three Little Songs' part two is particularly effective) and two peculiar gospel tracks on which Schiano plays organ and Archie Savage vocalizes. *Blue Memories* is a friendly joust with Geremia (switching instruments all the time) and Léandre – not bad, if prone to meandering.

Used To Be Friends brings together a superb group for five improvisations where Schiano's good humour seems to set the tone. This is a vivid and often lighthearted encounter. A phone message from Evan Parker interrupts part two, but the man himself is present at the Victoriaville Festival set on *Social Security*, a surpassingly powerful quintet in very fine voice, with the unexpected power and breadth of the little-known Tramontana matching the other four all the way. These two sets are something of a match, but the Victo one has the edge, and the sound is slightly better. *The Friendship Of Walnuts* assembles a bigger ensemble for a single, dense collective. Schiano is something of a bystander here, with such power-players as Ottaviano, Petrowsky and Curci on hand, but the principal music comes from the inimitable Bauer, hugely inventive and accomplished. Another disc where the sound is less than ideal, although improv veterans won't be too troubled by it.

***** Supposing That ...**
Splasc(h) 838 *Schiano; Luca Venitucci (p, acc); Giovanni Maier (b); U. T. Gandhi (d).* 10/01.

A lively set from Rome's Counter-Indications Festival in 2001. Schiano's playing is reasserted as the central voice this time, and while he does like to drop in the occasional clownish touch, quoting from glaringly inappropriate sources in the middle of otherwise free passages, that's Italian free playing for you. Venitucci tends to act as referee at the piano and Gandhi thinks about whether to play in time or not. An entertaining reminder that Schiano is still around.

Lalo Schifrin (born 1932)

PIANO, ARRANGER

Born in Buenos Aires, Schifrin studied music in Paris in the '50s, then began film soundtrack work and moved to New York. Wrote for and toured with Dizzy Gillespie in the early '60s, then with Quincy Jones, and eventually focused entirely on film and TV scoring; many famous signature-themes are his. Back with big-band work in the '90s, seemingly for his own amusement.

***** Tin Tin Deo**

Fresh Sound FSR-CD 319 *Schifrin; Clark Terry (t); Jimmy Cleveland (tb); Leo Wright (as, f); Seldon Powell (ts, f); Jerome Richardson (bs); Felipe Yanez (p); Jimmy Raney (g); Frank Schifano, Art Davis (b); Rudy Collins (d); Antonio Diaz Mena, Miguel Avila, Victor Allende, Willie Rodriguez (perc).* 62.

***** Piano, Strings And Bossa Nova**

Verve 589763-2 *Schifrin; Jim Hall (g); Chris White (b); Rudy Collins (d); José Paulo, Carmen Costa (perc); strings.* 10/62.

**** Black Widow**

CTI ZK 65128 *Schifrin; Jon Faddis (t); Wayne Andre, Billy Campbell, Barry Rogers (tb); Dave Taylor (btb); Pepper Adams, Joe Farrell (saxes); Hubert Laws, George Marge (f); Clark Spangler (ky); Eric Gale (g); Andy Newmark (d); Don Alias, Carlos Martin, Carter Collins, Sue Evans (perc); Patti Austin (v); strings.* 3/76.

Schifrin has spent most of his career in Hollywood, but his arrangements have made a mark on some fine albums, none more so than Dizzy Gillespie's *Gillespiana*. The 1962 sessions on *Tin Tin Deo* follow a similar style to the Gillespie project, in a slightly smaller format. There are some great spots for Terry and Wright in the orchestral tracks, but the eight pieces for sextet are slighter stuff and rely heavily on a moody Latin base – prescient of what would interest him later. *Piano, Strings And Bossa Nova* is sumptuously crafted MOR, the then-popular fad for bossa nova tunes plundered for high-octane mood-music which actually muster some good grooves along the way, although any suggestion that there was some real jazz content here would surely have made Lalo laugh

Schifrin's more recent records aren't so much any kind of Third Stream as sumptuous examples of high-grade jazz schmaltz. *Black Widow* is a survival from a grim period for jazz, but Schifrin's charts have a grain of wit about them that manages to just about peek through the discofied situations, mewling solos and general inconsequentiality (this was 1976, after all). Since our last edition Atlantic have deleted the *Jazz Meets The Symphony* recordings from the catalogue, but Schifrin admirers should be advised that these sessions can now be found on a small-circulation label called Aleph.

Alexander von Schlippenbach (born 1938)

PIANO

The founder of the vast collective Globe Unity was born in Berlin and studied music there under the composer Bernd Alois Zimmerman. He played with trumpeter Manfred Schoof and recorded extensively with other improvisers. The Schlippenbach Trio has been making music for nearly 30 years, though Globe Unity now seems to be in abeyance. Schlippenbach is percussive and intense, but also aware of structure and responsive to traditional jazz piano as well as free music.

***** The Living Music**

Atavistic/Unheard Music Series UMS/ALP231 *Schlippenbach; Manfred Schoof (t); Paul Rutherford (tb); Peter Brötzmann (ts); Michel Pilz (cl); Buschi Niebergall (b); Han Bennink (d).* 4/69.

Schlippenbach's clean, atonal lines are far more reminiscent of Thelonious Monk than of Cecil Taylor, the figure who is usually adduced as ancestor for this kind of free music. By 1970 Schlippenbach had to some extent turned away from total abstraction and was showing an interest not only in formal compositional principles (serialism, orthodox sonata form, aspects of *ricercare*) but also in renewing his own initial contact with early and modern jazz, blues and boogie-woogie. These interests were still obvious even underneath the radical freedoms of his influential collective Globe Unity Orchestra. They became much clearer in his work with the later Berlin Contemporary Jazz Orchestra, in which he uses the conventionally swinging drummer Ed Thigpen and trumpeter Benny Bailey among the free men. Schlippenbach's conception of freedom has nearly always resulted in densely layered explorations of tonality, with a pronounced rhythmic slant. It's this that renders him surprisingly accessible as a performer.

Recorded in April 1969 and initially released on his own Quasar label, *The Living Music* is an important manifesto that lent its name to the influential Free Music Production label's inaugural workshop the following year. The session was taped on the same day as Peter Brötzmann's superb *Nipples* and the saxophonist is a dominant presence on this disc as well, though comparatively restrained in the context of Schlippenbach's deceptively cool and well-behaved formations. The recording is about on par for the time, which means not much separation and not much detail in the busier sections. An important document, none the less.

*****(*) Live 1976/77**

FMP CD 111 *Schlippenbach; Sven-Ake Johansson (b).* 4/76–11/77.

****** Smoke**

FMP CD 23 *Schlippenbach; Sunny Murray (d).* 10/89.

The partnership with Johansson is a long-standing one and this reissue fillets highlights from the LPs *Live At The Quartier Latin* and *Kung Bore*. Schlippenbach asserts his own ideas on the tradition in a comprehensive (if ultimately affectionate) deconstruction of two Monk tunes, but mostly this is a rushing music filled with lightning juxtapositions and rapidly evolved pieces that confound normal ideas about development. Johansson's singing on the final track is something which has occupied him more frequently in recent years, to the dismay of some.

Despite being tossed with insulting casualness into that overstuffed category, Schlippenbach is a very different kind of player from Taylor. By the same token, Sunny Murray is a very different kind of player *now* from what he was when he played with Taylor back in 1960. *Smoke* is an intriguing collaboration, in which both men hang up their 'free music' armour and get down to what sounds like a set of phantom standards. There are a dozen or more teasing echoes, more elusive than allusive, but only one outwardly identifiable theme, Monk's 'Trinkle Tinkle'. Beautifully recorded and superbly played, it warms slowly from a rather misterioso opening. Only on 'Down The Mission' does the Taylor parallel make complete sense. Elsewhere, Monk and even Herbie Nichols seem more valid points of reference. Murray's 'Angel Voice' uses material that he has developed over two decades; cymbal overtones create an illusion of choral effects, studded by tight accents and the familiar polydirectional lines.

★★★(★) **Hunting The Snake**
Atavistic Unheard Music Series 213 *Schlippenbach; Evan Parker (ss, ts); Paul Lovens (d).* 9/75.
★★★★ **Elf Bagatellen**
FMP CD 27 *As above, except omit Kowald.* 5/90.
★★★(★) **Physics**
FMP CD 50 *As above.* 6/91.

The Schlippenbach Trio with Parker and Lovens has been one of the most lasting and creative associations in European free jazz. Schlippenbach's catalogue has slumped with the disappearance of FMP's vinyl catalogue; two other great records, *Detto Fra Di Noi* and *Das Höhe Lied*, were released on Paul Lovens's small Po Torch label, which may now be difficult to find, and have not been on CD. Missing and mourned is the magnificent *Pakistani Pomade*, garlanded with top rating in our first edition. However, *Hunting The Snake* admits a previously unheard broadcast, with an extra presence in Kowald's bass. It has a carefree, even slightly humorous (or just well-humoured) quality, at least more so than some of the trio's most intense recordings, and having Kowald on board certainly varies the pace. *Elf Bagatellen* almost merits *Pakistani Pomade*'s crown, not just for its markedly improved sound, but also for the sheer untrifling intensity of the trio's performances. Like the earlier record, this is a studio performance rather than a live set, and it acts as a very conscious summation of the trio's near two-decade career. It is, inevitably, rather more predetermined than a more spontaneous performance, and there are shards of melody scattered throughout. 'Sun-Luck: Revisited' refers to 'Sun-Luck Night-Rain', one of the finest pieces on the 1972 album, while 'Yarak: Reforged' provides a similar gloss on a piece from *Payan*, a rare recording for a label other than FMP, in this case Enja. Parker and Lovens have rarely played better together, and if Schlippenbach seems a trifle mild-mannered in places, the richness of the sound more than compensates for a slight drop in pulse-rate. Tremendous stuff.

The more recent *Physics* by the same trio doesn't quite rise to the heights of its predecessors, but it is a dramatic performance all the same. Taped at the 1991 free-music workshops at the Akademie der Künst in Berlin, it has a freewheeling, exploratory quality which is one of the graces of European improvised music. Schlippenbach structures 'The Coefficient Of Linear Expansion' with magisterial control. At nearly 45 minutes, it has the compression and exactitude of a piece one-tenth that length, and yet it seems to imply all sorts of realities that lie outside the confines of the work.

★★★(★) **The Morlocks**
FMP CD 61 *Schlippenbach; Henry Lowther, Thomas Heberer, Axel Dörner (t); Jörg Huke, Marc Boukouya, Sören Fischer (tb); Ute Zimmermann (btb); Tilman Denhard (ts, f, picc); Darcy Hepner (as); Evan Parker (ts, ss); Walter Gauchel (ts); Claas Willecke (bs, f); Aki Takase (p); Nobuyoshi Ino (b); Paul Lovens (d, perc).* 7/93.

This is perhaps more strictly a Berlin Contemporary Jazz Orchestra record, but since it consists entirely of Schlippenbach pieces and bears his signature all over it, there is some justification for covering it here. Unlike many of his contemporaries, Schlippenbach has never let go of the term 'free jazz', and it is interesting to compare the harmonic language of many of the pieces here – not least the opening dedication to his companion, Aki Takase – with the work of Ornette Coleman. There are moments in 'The Morlocks' itself when he seems to be playing with the parameters of pitch, duration and attack in a way that is very similar to Ornette's. Elsewhere, as on 'Rigaudon Nr 2 Aus Der Wassertoffmusik', he uses graphic scores and a much more gestural approach that now sounds slightly old-fashioned. On the magnificent 'Marcia Di Saturno', though, he constructs a dense landscape that is much closer to the neo-tonality of his American contemporaries; bassist Nobuyoshi Ino introduces it with a brooding grace before saxophonist Gauchel develops the difficult central elements. This record establishes Schlippenbach much more clearly as a composer. It is worth comparing its language to that of the London Jazz Composers' Orchestra under Barry Guy, which is simultaneously more abstract but also more orthodoxly jazz-centred.

★★★(★) **Complete Combustion**
FMP CD 106 *Schlippenbach; Evan Parker (ss, ts); Paul Lovens (d, perc).* 4/98.

The Schlippenbach Trio is still the best response to the rather trite suggestion that the only improvised music that 'really' works comes as a result of chance encounters. In point of fact, the trio has recorded very rarely down the years, but the players' familiarity and understanding is a key element in the process of creation. To suggest that the relationship is telepathic is to multiply concepts unnecessarily and to drift into the metaphysical. As this remarkable live recording underlines, the real key is dialectic, a testing and synthesis of ideas in the crucible of live performance. Having dabbled with something close to Webernian organization on *Elf Bagatellen*, the group has gone back to its former freedom but with a new dynamic implicit in Evan Parker's opening and the slow involvement of the other players. The ability of individual players to drop back and listen, to maintain silence and wise counsel has always been one of the group's great strengths. It is evident here on 'Complete Combustion', less so on 'Fuels 1–7', a sequence of shorter pieces that explore other areas of the group's shared language. Taken together, and lest anyone doubt its vitality, they reaffirm the creative energy of free music.

★★★★ **Digger's Harvest**
FMP CD 013 *Schlippenbach; Tony Oxley (d).* 11/98.

Fascinating to compare this with the Schlippenbach–Murray duo that made *Smoke* a decade before. All but the first and last tracks are very short and highly focused. The titles are drawn from the names of poisonous plants, and there is a sharp and sometimes toxic edge to these improvisations. Oxley is the dominant presence almost throughout, not because he filibusters a more prominent place than his playing partner but quite simply because what he plays is more immediately compelling. Yet Schlippenbach is worth listening to with some care as well. His phrasing on 'Digger's Harvest' and on a couple of the short tracks is quite without precedent in this music: taut, elegant, and persuasive without undue rhetoric. A fine record, whoever you buy it for.

CORE COLLECTION

★★★★ **Swinging The Bim**
FMP CD 114/5 2CD *Schlippenbach; Evan Parker (ts, ss); Paul Lovens (d, saw).* 11/98.

Evan Parker's sleeve-note touches on a number of pertinent issues. How can such a long-standing group retain its creative life? How much is new? His counter-assertion is 'that the

unknown can only be approached from the known', which is, broadly speaking, what happens on these two sets from Amsterdam's BIM-Huis. We might add that searching for new things to 'say' about such music can often be nearly as frustrating and demanding as the playing of it. So: across two substantial sets, the trio certainly swung the Bim.

*****(*) Broomriding**
Psi 03.05 *Schlippenbach; Rudi Mahall (bcl); Tristan Honsinger (clo); Paul Lovens (perc).* 02.

The presence of material by Eric Dolphy should be no surprise given the instrumentation and at moments this recalls nothing more than a freer and more classically aligned version of Dolphy's work with bassist/cellist Ron Carter. Mahal's bass clarinet is better recorded than Eric could ever have dreamed of and this release on Evan Parker's own label (aided by the redoubtable Martin Davidson of Emanem) is immaculately recorded and mastered, allowing every delicate inflection of piano, cello and percussion to come through as well. An album to savour slowly.

Larry Schneider (born 1950)

TENOR, ALTO AND SOPRANO SAXOPHONES

Born in New York, Schneider came up as one of the post-bop tenors of the '70s, working with Horace Silver and others, but he decamped to San Francisco, where the weather is better for his other passion, tennis.

*****(*) Just Cole Porter**
Steeplechase SCCD 31291 *Schneider; Andy LaVerne (p); Mike Richmond (b); Keith Copeland (d).* 8/91.

*****(*) Blind Date**
Steeplechase SCCD 31317 *As above.* 4/92.

Schneider has played a sideman role in many situations, and these albums commence a belated recognition of an accomplished saxophonist. He's emblematic of a generation of hard-bop tenor-players who came of age in the '70s, before the fashionable new interest in the form, which leaves his playing untainted by technical strivings and nicely weathered by his experience. The album of Cole Porter tunes is close to being a definitive gallery of standards, with Schneider in riveting voice on 'What Is This Thing Called Love?', knowingly tender on 'Every Time We Say Goodbye'. *Blind Date* brings the quartet together again on four standards, two originals by LaVerne and Charles Mingus's 'Peggy's Blue Skylight'. Schneider likes long improvisations and, more often than not, makes them work. The best solos here, such as the grand, sprawling oratory on the title-tune and the flaring urgency that grows out of 'Autumn Leaves', are usefully anchored by a rhythm section that hears him very clearly, with LaVerne a comparably mature voice.

***** Bill Evans ... Person We Knew**
Steeplechase SCCD 31307 *Schneider; Andy LaVerne (p).* 3/92.

***** Mohawk**
Steeplechase SCCD 31347 *As above, except add Steve LaSpina (b), Anton Fig (d).* n.d.

A couple of concept albums. Schneider and LaVerne duet on the Evans legacy with considerable potency at times, although the record runs aground a bit on the bare concept. 'Dream Gypsy' is the outstanding performance, evocative of the kind of hushed intensity Evans used to create with Jim Hall, and some of the other pieces are ingenious – the tense contrapuntal lines of 'Israel' and the unfolding melodies of 'Show Type Tune' in particular. Others seem half-done, and Schneider's tone takes on a querulous edge that doesn't always seem right for the music. *Mohawk* tackles nine Charlie Parker tunes, and Schneider turns to the alto for the whole date. He sounds more like Lee Konitz at many moments, especially on the solo version of 'Donna Lee', and while this is an enjoyable repertory record, some of the settings come out as rather cute; the dead-slow tempo for 'Yardbird Suite' or the Latin temperament of 'Scrapple From The Apple' are two such.

***** Ali Girl**
Steeplechase SCCD 31429 *Schneider; Alexander Sipiagin (flhn); Dave Stryker (g); Jay Anderson (b); Billy Drummond (d).* 9/97.

Back after a break, Schneider delivers something of a hotchpotch date. Four of the six tunes are done on soprano, on which he again suggests a Konitzian bent: try the first chorus of his solo on 'I'm Old Fashioned'. The tracks extend into long, somewhat rambling excursions, with good work by all hands, but without cutting a deep impression. Sipiagin sits in on two tunes, one of which, 'The Way You Look Tonight', brings out the tenor and the best solo of the session.

***** Ornettology**
Steeplechase SCCD 31461 *Schneider; Scott Wendholt (t); Mike Richmond (b); Billy Drummond (d).* 4/98.

Eight Ornette Coleman tunes, making an interesting pendant to the Charlie Parker record, although this doesn't convince as something that Schneider had any pressing need to record. If anything, the quartet take a rather glib and unruffled path through the likes of 'The Disguise' and 'When Will The Blues Leave'. Energetic playing and creative improvising, but the uncommitted might ask why the record had to be made.

*****(*) Summertime In San Remo**
Splasc(h) 809-2 *Schneider; Andrea Dulbecco (vib); Sandro Gibellini (vib); Dodo Goya (b); John Arnold (d).* 8/97.

*****(*) Lemon Lips**
Splasc(h) 833-2 *Schneider; Gaspare Di Lieto (p); Dario Deidda (b); Amedeo Ariano (d).* 8/00.

Italian air seems to do Schneider some good. Both of these are very satisfying. He plays tenor in San Remo, mostly soprano in Salerno (*Lemon Lips*, recorded live). The softer mix of the quintet session suits a band where Dulbecco's vibes drift hazily around the edges, although Schneider's favourite Parker blues 'Mohawk' gets a tenor treatment as intense as any he's done. More typical, perhaps, is an almost louche passage through 'You Don't Know What Love Is'. The quartet date is played fast and hard, Schneider's soprano tone full-bodied and convincing, and Di Lieto gets in plenty of stuff of his own.

***** Jazz**
Steeplechase SCCD 31505 *Schneider; Andy LaVerne (p); Steve LaSpina (b); Matt Wilson (d).* 3/01.

A bit cheeky using a title like that, but it's jazz all right, not so pure, not so simple, even if the band and chosen material may strike some as entirely generic. Laverne brought a 'How Deep Is The Ocean' variation called 'Portrait Of Dorian Mode', and they approach some of their material sideways, such as the teasing what's-this-coming intro to 'Old Folks'. Schneider could probably use a more idiosyncratic pianist than LaVerne to keep him off the relatively straight and narrow, but as ever he manages a few solos which look to stand taller than his more practised ones.

Maria Schneider (born 1960)

COMPOSER, ARRANGER, BANDLEADER

After lessons from Bob Brookmeyer and a stint as assistant to Gil Evans, the lady from Windom, Minnesota, had the best possible grounding in big-band jazz – and yet setting out on her own, as she did in 1989, was brave in the extreme, but a Monday-night residency at Visiones in New York gave her the platform she needed.

*** **Evanescence**
Enja ENJ 8048-2 *Schneider; Laurie Frink, Greg Gisbert, Tim Hagans, Tony Kadleck (t); Larry Farrell, John Fedchock, George Flynn, Keith O'Quinn (tb); Rick Margitza (ts); Rich Perry (ts, f); Mark Vinci (picc, f, cl); Tim Ries (ss, f, cl); Scott Robinson (bsx, bcl); Bill Hayes (flexatone); Kenny Werner (p); Jay Monder (g); Jay Anderson (b); Dennis Mackrel (d); Emedin Rivera (perc). 10/92.*

***(*) **Coming About**
Enja ENJ 9069-2 *As above, except omit Anderson, Hayes, Mackrel, Rivera; add Rock Ciccarone (tb); Charles Pillow (eng hn, cl); Frank Kimbrough (p); Tony Scherr (b); Tim Horner (d). 11/95.*

*** **Allegresse**
Enja 3306 *Schneider; Dave Ballou, Laurie Frink, Greg Gisbert, Ingrid Jensen (t, flhn); Tony Kadleck (t, picc-t, flhn); Rocky Ciccarone, Larry Farrell, Keith O'Quinn (tb); George Flynn (btb, tba); Rick Margitza (ss, ts, f); Tim Ries (ss, cl, t, picc-t, flhn); Charles Pillow (ss, as, ts, cl, picc, f, ob, eng hn); Rich Perry (ts, f); Scott Robinson (bs, bsx, cl, bcl, af); Frank Kimbrough (p); Ben Monder (g); Tony Scherr (b); Tim Horner (d); Jeff Ballard (perc). 7/00.*

Schneider's characteristic voice is closer to her teacher Brookmeyer's than to the more obvious Svengali, a rich fabric of sound that is alert to nuance but still capable of great power. Her use of a relatively straightforward rhythm section belies the sophistication of the metre, and often the horns are playing improbable counts over a basic 4/4. Schneider was blessed from the very start by a team of time-served craftsmen with enough musical individuality to temper the slightly too accurate placing of the charts.

By the time the second album appeared – and this may be implicit in the title – Schneider had the confidence to turn her vessel into the wind and let it go. Her suite, 'Scenes From Childhood', is largely written and works well on its own terms, but it is tracks like 'Love Theme From *Spartacus*' and 'Giant Steps' which really show her mettle.

You'd be forgiven for thinking that *Allegresse* was a Brookmeyer set, except that there's a freedom and romantic abandon in tunes like 'Hang Gliding' which aren't part of the trombonist's bag. The arrangements here manage to sound both crisply accurate and open-ended, putting more and more weight on the personality of the soloists, almost as if she has been studying classic-period Ellington and emulating his wonderful balance of authoritarianism and laissez-faire. 'Nocturne', the very long, suite-like 'Dissolution' and 'Sea Of Tranquility' are all impressive new charts. All power to her for keeping a big band going even this long.

Rob Schneiderman (born 1957)

PIANO

Born in Boston, Schneiderman grew up in California and moved to New York in 1982, influenced by old-school beboppers. He also has a doctorate in mathematics and teaches the subject at Berkeley.

(*) **New Outlook
Reservoir RSR 106 *Schneiderman; Slide Hampton (tb); Rufus Reid (b); Akira Tana (d). 1/88.*

*** **Smooth Sailing**
Reservoir 114 *As above, except add Billy Higgins (d); omit Hampton and Tana. 2/90.*

*** **Radio Waves**
Reservoir 120 *Schneiderman; Brian Lynch (t); Ralph Moore (ts); Gary Smulyan (bs); Todd Coolman (b); Jeff Hirshfield (d). 5/91.*

*** **Standards**
Reservoir 126 *Schneiderman; Rufus Reid (b); Ben Riley (d). 3–8/92.*

*** **Dark Blue**
Reservoir 132 *Schneiderman; Brian Lynch (t); Ralph Moore (ss, ts); Peter Washington (b); Lewis Nash (d). 5/94.*

***(*) **Keepin' In The Groove**
Reservoir 144 *Schneiderman; Rufus Reid (b); Akira Tana (d). 1/96.*

***(*) **Dancing In The Dark**
Reservoir 152 *Schneiderman; Brian Lynch (t); Gary Smulyan (bs); Rufus Reid (b); Billy Hart (d). 5/97.*

'Beautiful and abstract and I'm curious about it.' Rob Schneiderman was talking about mathematics – more specifically his specialist subject of Low Dimensional Topology, not much investigated by jazz musicians – and making the comparison with music. He is up to eight albums in his series for Reservoir now and, while there's no masterwork here, they offer a genuine kind of modern bop that can be very satisfying. Slide Hampton was an unusual choice as the sole horn on *New Outlook*, and his mild-mannered fluency suits Schneiderman's approach perhaps a little too well: the music tends to settle down into blandishments of the kind that have been committed to record many times before. Despite a couple of interesting ideas, such as the prickly waltz tempo chosen for Alec Wilder's 'While We're Young', the music never quite lifts off the ground. Maybe the pianist just prefers the kind of knowing, grooving accompaniment that's second nature to Reid and Higgins, because they all sound much happier on *Smooth Sailing*, a blithe mix of standards and new tunes.

Good spirits also prevail on the next date, with three horns in the front line. Lynch is a little overwhelmed by the beguiling Moore and the big, tough sound of Smulyan's baritone, but Schneiderman resolves any difficulties with intelligent if sketchy arrangements. But then it's back to the trio for the rather aristocratic treatment of *Standards*, in which Schneiderman gives up on his own writing for a day at least. Riley is such a wily drummer – very different from Higgins – that he's often barely there, but it suits the occasion. Schneiderman plays interesting things, as he does on all these records, without making one think that it's of great consequence. *Dark Blue* is soundly professional without generating much excitement, and the preponderance of themes based on blues doesn't lift it far enough out of routine; Lynch and Moore, though, guarantee good value. A beguiling 'People Will Say We're In Love' is the highlight.

The next two are a point ahead. Nothing extraordinary about *Keepin' In The Groove*, with only one original among a clever choice of jazz tunes, but it's played with such enjoyment that the feel is infectious. Reid and Tana are an a winning team – hear the drummer's wonderful brushwork on 'Four' and 'Bebop' – and they light up a trio music which Schneiderman refuses to clutter with awkward lines or mere verbosity. The good form carries on into *Dancing In The Dark*. The horns make an impeccable duo, and Lynch is at his best – catch his fabulous solo on 'Broken Dreams'. Smulyan doesn't miss out, and Schneiderman brought some of his best writing to the date in 'Broken Dreams', 'Oval Essence' and 'Late Breakthrough'.

*****(*) Edgewise**

Reservoir 165 *Schneiderman; Ray Drummond (b); Winard Harper (d).* 7/00.

Album number eight is a beauty. The trio is surely Schneiderman's best setting – he likes grooving situations, with enough space to develop an argument, and is a man for the co-operative art. Although he'd never before recorded with Drummond or Harper, the threesome sounds happy and in accord. Bud Powell is one of the major texts here: there are three Powell originals, plus Monk's 'In Walked Bud', and the Oscar Pettiford line which Powell loved to play, 'Blues In The Closet', as well as an original by the leader called 'Bud Powell Boulevard'. Yet Schneiderman is as unlike Powell as it's possible to be: a calm logician, with his feelings mostly under wraps, he makes the likes of 'Cleopatra's Dream' into rational vehicles. But that only helps to expose the calibre of the composer's inspiration. On 'Just One Of Those Things', taken at a fast pace, he's still able to expose all the detail of his improvising while carrying us along with the flow. The result is a lucid and absorbing essay on bebop as a contemporary language – and let's pause for a moment to salute the industry of Reservoir, who've allowed an unfashionable and largely 'unknown' player to build a very good discography across eight records.

Manfred Schoof (born 1936)

TRUMPET, FLUGELHORN

A key figure on the European free scene, Schoof played with Gunter Hampel and the George Russell Orchestra, as well as less structured formations. He has a second career as a classical composer but most of his jazz-related recordings – including a beautiful disc for ECM – are currently out of print.

***** European Echoes**

Atavistic/Unheard Music Series ALP232 *Schoof; Enrico Rava, Hugh Steinmetz (t); Paul Rutherford (tb); Peter Brötzmann, Gerd Dudek, Evan Parker (ss, ts); Fred van Hove, Alexander von Schlippenbach, Irène Schweizer (p); Derek Bailey (g); Arjen Gorter, Peter Kowald, Buschi Niebergall (b); Han Bennink, Pierre Favre (d).* 6/69.

Schoof was a charter member of Alexander von Schlippenbach's sprawling Globe Unity Orchestra and this album, the first to be issued on the influential Free Music Production label, was recorded not long after another recent Atavistic reissue, Schlippenbach's *The Living Music*, and shares some of its personnel.

Important as it was in the development of European free music, *European Echoes* makes uncomfortable listening. The larger ensembles come across as undifferentiated blocks of sound from which individual contributions are hard to separate. Given Schoof's orchestral style – a hybrid of Richard Strauss and Karlheinz Stockhausen – this may be a description rather than a criticism. There are moments of great beauty, as when Derek Bailey uses his swell pedal to mimic an entire orchestral section or when Schlippenbach, Fred van Hove and Irène Schweizer play a seemingly scored section towards the end of what was the first LP side, a passage that anticipates some of Barry Guy's later work with Schweizer and the London Jazz Composers' Orchestra. But a difficult and challenging listen all the same and one that will appeal more to initiates of European free than to a casual listener who would be better advised to track down some of Schoof's out-of-print small-group work.

Bob Schulz

CORNET, VOCALS

Schulz is under the spell of Bob Scobey, as both a cornetist and a bandleader, and his Frisco Jazz Band play very much in a modern-day styling of the Californian revivalists.

****(*) Thanks Turk!**

Stomp Off 1288 *Schulz; Tom Bartlett (tb, v); Kim Cusack (cl); Ray Skjelbred (p); Scott Anthony (bj); Bill Carroll (tba); Wayne Jones (d).* 5–6/94.

***** Travelin' Shoes**

Stomp Off 1315 *As above, except Steve Pistorius (p) and John Gill (bj, v) replace Skjelbred and Anthony.* 5/96.

***** Bob Schulz And His Frisco Jazz Band**

GHB BCD-406 *Schulz; Tom Bartlett, Bob Mielke (tb); Bill Napier (cl); Ray Skjelbred (p); Scott Anthony (g, bj, v); Bill Carroll (tba); Bill Maginnis (d).* n.d.

Schulz and his men are a sound team of Turk Murphy/Bob Scobey followers, and they hardly put a foot wrong here on *Thanks Turk!* – keen, well-rounded interpretations of many Murphy favourites. Plenty of it goes back to the original masters of the '20s, and there are some rag tunes like 'Smokey Mokes' and 'Swipsey Cake Walk'. Twenty numbers done in this vigorous and chanceless way are a bit of a bore, though, and one eventually longs for one of the players to take the session by the scruff of its neck. It never happens, although Bartlett's rather crabby trombone has a go here and there.

Travelin' Shoes gets off on the good foot with a knockout treatment of 'Pretty Baby', and while this is another disc that trades heavily on the Scobey/Murphy style (to the extent of using several of their original charts), it's an ounce more personal, and Mike Cogan engineers an excellent sound for the band. Even Bob's vocals are in the spirit.

The GHB set is, we suppose, more of the same, and again the band are growing into their own style, which takes them a slight remove from the Murphy model. 'Brother Lowdown' is a great one.

***** Oh! Play That Thing!**
Jazzology JCD-326 *Schulz; Bob Havens (tb); Tom Fischer (cl); Mark Shane (p); Marty Grosz (g, v); Mike Karoub (b); Hal Smith (d).* 4/00.

Schulz recants! The sleeve-notes say that his 'instincts tend more toward the Chicago style', and as if to prove it here he leads his Chicago Rhythm Kings through a pretty straightforward show of Windy City revivalism. The band certainly stretch out a bit more than the Stomp Off outfits, and with reliable heads such as Grosz and Smith along for the ride, the music's cheery and enjoyable without exactly pushing for immortality. Two points for applause: they play the verse to 'Limehouse Blues', and Grosz sings the exceptionally scarce 'Believe It, Beloved'.

Manfred Schulze (1934–96)

BARITONE SAXOPHONE

Schulze worked out of the GDR and formed his first Brass Quintet as early as 1969. Interested as much in the writing of Hindemith, Schoenberg and Bach as in free improvisation, he brought a striking mix of disciplines to bear on what was original and surprising music.

*****(*) Viertens: Nummer 12**
FMP CD 87 *Schulze; Johannes Bauer (tb); Manfred Hering, Dietmar Diesner, Heiner Reinhardt (reeds).* 5/85–7/86.

*****(*) Konzertino**
FMP CD 70 *Paul Schwingenschlögl (t); Johannes Bauer (tb); Manfred Hering (ss, as, cl); Heiner Reinhardt (ss, ts); Gert Anklam (bs).* 9/94.

To call Schulze underrated would be an understatement. He worked in comparative isolation in the GDR, rarely recorded or travelled, and worked patiently at a synthesis of improvising with quite specific and formal structures for reeds and brass. The '80s recordings are marvellously choleric, the stiff, severe textures peeling open to reveal powerful improvisatory ideas. 'Nummer 12' is a long concert-piece, but rather better and more focused are the two studio tracks, 'Viertens' and the sly 'B-A-C-H'. Bauer aside, these players are not often encountered, but they give the music their all.

The later disc is a Berlin concert performed almost as a tribute to Schulze, who by this time was too ill to play himself. The group has a somewhat jazzier feel, the solos emerging more conventionally out of the group's interaction, and some of the dour distinction of the earlier disc has dissipated; but there's a compensating verve to the playing, and Schwingenschlögl adds some useful brassy fizz.

Irène Schweizer (born 1941)

PIANO

Irène Schweizer is a pioneering figure in European free jazz. She founded her innovative trio as long ago as 1963 and since then has worked with most of the major figures of European modernism. Her style is complex, dense and intellectually generous, and on her day few pianists in the world can equal her for sheer drama.

****** The Storming Of The Winter Palace**
Intakt CD 03/2000 *Schweizer; George E. Lewis (tb); Joelle Léandre (b); Gunter Sommer (d, perc); Maggie Nicols (v).* 5/86, 3/88.

The great Mary Lou Williams asserted that working with men ... you automatically become strong, though this doesn't mean you're not feminine. Schweizer has almost inevitably been saddled with a 'female Cecil Taylor' tag, one that has been harder to shift as a result of her series of duets with drummers, encounters which invite all manner of yin–yang nonsense. As a sometime percussionist herself, Schweizer makes instinctive guesses as to how her own keyboard language might meld with untuned instruments. That is evident in her important sequence of recordings with percussionists, but it is also a component of her other work in a variety of groups and as a solo pianist.

The Storming Of The Winter Palace is a welcome reissue of a classic LP. Recorded at the Moers Festival in 1986 and at the Taktlos Festival in Zurich two years later, it documents a group with formidable powers. Schweizer is very much the key element, assembling and unpicking a series of small-scale themes and ideas like some intellectual *tricoteuse.* Maggie Nicols's ability to break down narrative song into its constituent elements, semantic nonsense, and still leave you feeling that you've heard a story and been serenaded as well continues to amaze, as does George Lewis's ability to make even a disassembled trombone sound like the most musical thing on the planet. The two 'rhythm' players are supreme craftspersons and crafty supremos of free music. Sommer is not so much a minimalist as a miniaturist, able to invest tiny ideas with enormous significance, as effective in what he does not do as most drummers are in a full-scale assault on the kit. Léandre rumbles away in the background – and, to be truthful, too much in the background acoustically to represent fully her part in this music.

The earlier Moers piece is the most developed of the three included. 'Now And Never' makes few references to any musical forms outside itself, but it quickly establishes its own internal logic and Schweizer sustains a high level of concentration, contention and flow, reinforcing the impression that everything she does is a miniature concerto for piano, like 'Theoria', the piece written for her by Barry Guy and performed with the London Jazz Composers' Orchestra. 'The Storming Of The Winter Palace' is dominated to a degree by Nicols, who is at her most angrily playful. A relatively short piece, it is also highly condensed and impacted, with a great deal of musical information to absorb. 'Living On The Edge', which follows, is more intense but also more verbose and with a few flat moments. Taken together, though, this represents a wonderful documentation of an important group.

***** Irène Schweizer/Louis Moholo**
Intakt CD 006 *Schweizer; Louis Moholo (d).* 11/86.

****** Irène Schweizer/Gunter Sommer**
Intakt CD 007 *Schweizer; Gunter Sommer (d).* 2/87.

*****(*) Irène Schweizer/Andrew Cyrille**
Intakt CD 008 *Schweizer; Andrew Cyrille (d).* 9/88.

★★★★ Irène Schweizer/Pierre Favre

Intakt CD 009 *Schweizer; Pierre Favre (d).* 2/90.

It is enormously difficult to make qualitative judgements among these superb sets. They are extraordinarily various in approach, though it seems clear that the Europeans are much closer in basic conception to Schweizer than the two Americans, as one might expect. Sommer and Favre are melodic players, moving round the kit much as she moves across the keyboard. Moholo creates a network of cross-rhythms that Schweizer herself likens to Elvin Jones's playing with Coltrane, but there is nothing to build on it, and one is left with an impression of two artists working at right angles, making beautiful sounds but in isolation one from the other. With Favre, the level of interaction is such that one almost seems to be hearing a meta-instrument, a source of sound which is neither one voice nor the other, but a genuine synthesis of the two. With Sommer, the connection is more dialectical, but the result is still entirely sympathetic: two voices in conjunction, mutually responsive. Andrew Cyrille was a long-standing collaborator of Cecil Taylor's and is a leader in his own right. It is difficult to gauge what is wrong on this session. One senses that Schweizer is very aware of the Taylor lineage and deliberately tries to steer away from it, though the clusters and clumped runs she falls into are immediately and inescapably redolent of the American pianist. This remarkable series of duets was not finished in 1990. A later record with Han Bennink was still to come and is reviewed below, but the bulk of the series was in place by the end of the '80s. Hearing it somewhat later, and transferred to CD, suggests more consistency than difference. Schweizer never for a moment diverges from her robust, assured approach. It is her playing partners who are required to rethink their language.

★★★★ Piano Solo: Volume 1

Intakt CD 020 *Schweizer (p).* 5/90.

★★★(★) Piano Solo: Volume 2

Intakt CD 021 *As above.*

Schweizer is not a natural unaccompanied performer. The most communicative of players, she needs no one to play against, but she simply functions better in an environment where there is an element of interchange and reciprocity. That having been said, these are excellent discs. Brief and apparently inconsequential structures are delivered without elaboration and there is a meditative stillness to much of the music. 'The Ballad Of The Sad Café', a title derived from Carson McCullers's soft-tough story, is a masterpiece of unsentimental expression, played with an affecting combination of gentleness and iron-clad certainty. 'Sisterhood Of Spit' is a name that refers to an all-female collective of the '70s. It's dedicated to the late Chris McGregor, whose Brotherhood Of Breath was a lasting example of the possibility of reconciling lyrical expressiveness and hard-edged improvisational freedom, and also to saxophonist Dudu Pukwana. It both reflects and ironizes the spirit they evoked. Recorded at home in Switzerland, both records are faithfully and accurately registered, picking up Schweizer's softest figures and sustains, and handling the loudest and most impactful moments without distortion.

★★★ Les Diaboliques

Intakt CD 03 *Schweizer; Joelle Léandre (b); Maggie Nicols (v).* 4/93.

★★★ Splitting Image

Intakt CD 048 *As above.*

Three of the most consistently neglected figures on the European scene, united on one powerful record. Schweizer is the centre of gravity to which Léandre and Nicols lean and steer. Her touch is softer and more spacious than on the solo discs, deliberately leaving space open, not packing the time with information but allowing her playing partners room to breathe. Nicols, so often acerbic, gives herself the chance to unpack her sometimes cluttered ideas. Unfortunately, she loses impetus as a consequence. Léandre is well recorded and has a good deal to say, but is inclined to repeat herself. The second record from the same group, who subsequently called themselves Les Diaboliques, is every bit as good. Some evidence that Léandre is jockeying for prominence in what is already a tightly constructed group, but generally the level of interaction is as close and responsive as one might wish. Another intriguing disc, though on balance we'd probably just plump for the first one by the trio.

★★★★ Irène Schweizer/Han Bennink

Intakt CD 010 *Schweizer; Han Bennink (d).* 1/95.

Our admiration for Bennink is probably in breach of the second and third commandments. On this, he is supreme, the ideal foil to Schweizer's full-voiced and pointed delivery. Recorded live, as is much of this remarkable series, it shows two artists of markedly different temperament – Schweizer is both more 'serious' and more unaffectedly playful – negotiating a comfortable middle ground. Of all the piano–drums duets, this is the one that sounds as if it might be the result of prior negotiation.

★★★(★) Many And One Direction

Intakt CD 044 *Schweizer (p).* 4/96.

The title says it all: a critical moment in a career which seems to have combined an eclectic range of ideas with an absolute solidity of purpose. This solo record is beautifully engineered and played with an immaculate touch. One wonders a little how much Schweizer is attempting to say and how much she simply wants her listeners to luxuriate in the sound. Either way, this is an immensely strong performance, marred only by a reliance on predetermined outlines which she does a good deal to disguise and hide, to no real purpose.

★★★★ Chicago Piano Solo

Intakt CD 065 *Schweizer (p solo).* 2/00.

Schweizer's fourth solo for Intakt was recorded at a concert at Chicago's Empty Bottle, already a hallowed venue for American free playing (though six nights a week, it's rock). The excellent sound (no rough live mixes here) highlights the pianist's impeccable touch, the evenness of her attack in high-velocity sequences, and the absolute crispness (and decision) in the way she gets from one to phrase to another. It's difficult to guess how much Irène plays is spontaneously created, to what extent she reconvenes material previously explored (which, of course, every improviser does anyway), but the logic of her playing is rare and seemingly invincible: there's nothing here which doesn't seem to fit or stand as superfluous. The one interpretation, of Don Cherry's 'Togetherness One', is fine enough to wish that she would tackle a full recital of repertory. In the meantime, another great one from the modest Swiss giant.

★★★★ Ulrichsberg

Intakt CD 084 *Schweizer; Pierre Favre (d).* 5/03.

Schweizer and Favre are history all by themselves: as the fascinating sleeve-notes reveal, they go all the way back to Montreux 1966. This festival set was recorded in its entirety and stands as a wonderful souvenir of a long-standing friendship and working relationship which is, as Favre regretfully admits, reconvened only occasionally. What one marvels at is the clarity and purpose in the playing. There's no clatter or rhetorical fog: both musicians call on their powers of instinct and intellect to divine a music which sounds deep and complex and at the same moment entirely transparent. Irène says how much she delights in 'our joy in playing', and there's scarcely a moment here where that isn't manifest.

Louis Sclavis (born 1953)

BASS CLARINET, TENOR AND SOPRANO SAXOPHONES

Born in Lyons, Sclavis studied there and toured with the Workshop of Lyons improvising group. His playing is a blend of free forms, contemporary compositional structures, theatre music and folk strains, a mix which has grown increasingly personal.

★★★★ Clarinettes

IDA 004 *Sclavis (solo), and with Christian Rollet, Christian Ville (perc).* 9/84–1/85.

★★★(★) Chine / Chamber Music

Label Bleu 6656/7 2CD *Sclavis; Yves Robert (tb); Michel Godard (tba); François Raulin (p, syn, perc); Philippe Deschepper (g); Dominique Pifarély (vn); Bruno Chevillon (b); Christian Ville (d, perc).* 7–9/87.

Louis Sclavis has attempted to create an 'imaginary folklore' that combines familiar jazz procedures with North African and Mediterranean music, French folk themes and music from the *bal musette.* Early exposure on the mostly solo *Clarinettes* confirmed word-of-mouth reports from France that he was a performer to be reckoned with. Unlike Sidney Bechet, who may have been a dim ancestral influence, his clarinet work is a great deal more forceful than his soprano-saxophone-playing, and Sclavis is one of the foremost of a growing number of younger jazz musicians who have rescued the clarinet from desuetude as an improvising instrument. His bass-clarinet work is particularly original, drawing little or nothing from the obvious model and condensing most of Sclavis's virtues: melodic invention, timbral variation, rhythmic sophistication. Perhaps the most striking track on *Clarinettes* is 'Le Chien Aboie Et La Clarinette Basse' – a husky duo with percussionist Ville which puns on a French gypsy saying: the dog barks '*et le caravane passe*'. For all his interest in European folk and popular themes, Sclavis considers himself unequivocally a jazz musician. A duo version of 'Black And Tan Fantasy' on the same album suggests he has much to contribute to standards-playing. Most of his work, however, has been original and this, coupled with his obvious straining at the conventions of the orthodox jazz ensemble (particularly as regards the drummer, whom Sclavis considers to be excessively dominant), seemed at first to hold back his development as a soloist. *Chine* is a fine and original set of pieces, but its unfamiliar tonal components only partially mitigate an overall lack of development. *Chamber Music*, as the title implies, throws still more weight on compositional values, but there are signs that Sclavis was working through his dilemmas. In Chevillon he has an understanding and highly effective foil whose rhythmic awareness makes light of settings without a part for a drummer or percussionist. These two fine records are now available on a double CD, and anyone who wants to investigate earlier, pre-ECM Sclavis would be well advised to start here.

★★★(★) Rouge

ECM 511929-2 *Sclavis; Dominique Pifarély (vn); François Raulin (p, syn); Bruno Chevillon (b); Christian Ville (d).* 9/91.

★★★★ Ellington On The Air

IDA 032 *As for Chine Chamber Music, except omit Deschepper, Ville; add Francis Lassus (d, perc).* 12/91–2/92.

★★★(★) Acoustic Quartet

ECM 521349-2 *As for Rouge, except omit Raulin, Ville; add Marc Ducret (g).* 93.

★★★★ Les Violences De Rameau

ECM 533128-2 *As for Rouge, except add Yves Robert (tb), Francis Lassus (perc).* 96.

Sclavis's ECM debut is a challenging and surprisingly abstract set that rarely allows itself to settle into a jazz groove. *Rouge* establishes Sclavis as an enterprising and thought-provoking composer. If it does so at the expense of rhythmic energy (a strategy consistent with his ambivalence about jazz percussion), it doesn't short-change in other departments. The first four tracks are moodily atmospheric, with a strong suggestion of North African music: 'Nacht' is particularly effective, with dissonant flashes of multi-tracked clarinet echoed by the softly bouncing thunder of Ville's bass drum, before giving way to an evocative solo by Chevillon. Pifarély comes into his own on 'Reeves', teasing out a long unison statement with Sclavis and then soloing on his own 'Moment Donné'. Several tracks sound as if they are through-composed, and apart from the later stages of 'Les Bouteilles' and a delicious waltz-tag on the title-piece, the emphasis is all on textures and rather brooding melodic outlines rather than on linear development. The longest track 'Face Nord' echoes 'Reflet' in the way it suspends Sclavis's high, swooping clarinet-lines over a dense chordal background (that on 'Face Nord' suddenly erupts into a convincing simulacrum of a flat-out electric guitar solo, all done on Raulin's imaginatively programmed synth).

The ECM follow-up is once again impressionistic rather than dynamic. The drummerless *Acoustic Quartet* is listed as co-led by Pifarély, and he certainly plays an increasingly prominent role in the music, as does Chevillon, another long-standing accomplice. Ducret has a less functional role and is used for broad (and not always very subtle) background effects, where a more adventurous leader and/or producer might have preferred a starker profile. Pifarély contributes three compositions, including the long 'Seconde', and the violinist's writing has matured very quickly. However, Sclavis's touch on 'Sensible' and 'Rhinoceros' is flawless, and the brief 'Beata' is incomparably lovely. Attractive as it all is, one misses the edgy, improvisational sound that energizes the Ellington session. The interplay between Sclavis and the admirable Robert adds a dimension that has been missing for some time. The programme is an imaginative exercise in re-creation. Ellington themes are interleaved with associated originals by Sclavis, Chevillon, Raulin and others. 'Jubilee Stomp' yields 'J'Oublie';

though not itself included, 'Mood Indigo' suggests Chevillon's 'Indigofera Tinctoria' and Andy Emler's 'Mode Andy Go'; a snatch of 'Caravan' introduces 'Caravalse'; and so on. The verbal puns aren't screamingly witty, but the music is always intelligently allusive and manages to suggest new angles on Ellington without lapsing into pastiche. Indeed, it's very clear that Sclavis has picked precisely those themes which most emphatically suit his own compositional style.

Nothing could have prepared anyone, though, for his turn to the mysterious music of Rameau for the next record. This is a perfect illustration of his eclectic, omnivorous approach to French music, a virtuosic appropriation of a composer who has never been warmly appreciated outside France but who reveals on closer inspection an almost Gothic concentration of expression which is, yes, violent. A now familiar line-up, augmented significantly by the wonderful Robert, broods through fascinating charts which are neither obscure nor transparent.

***** Ceux Qui Veillent La Nuit**
Label Bleu LBLC 6596 *Sclavis; Bruno Chevillon (b); François Merville (d, perc).* 96.

Surprisingly, Sclavis had not recorded in this format before. Otherwise it's pretty much another clarinet album, apart from some strong soprano saxophone on the opening 'Dernier Regards' (was that intended as a farewell?). The title-piece toys with the same North African sonorities that influenced *Clarinettes* and there are hints of something similar, though subtly different, on the beautiful 'Qumran', a stunning bass-clarinet solo. 'L'Ombre' and 'Procession' are strong ideas as well and strong trio performances. A fine album.

*****(*) Trio De Clarinettes Live**
FMP CD 39 *Sclavis; Jacques Di Donato (cl, bcl); Armand Angster (cl, bcl, cbcl).* 11/90.

*****(*) Et On Ne Parle Du Temps**
FMP CD 66 *Sclavis; Ernst Reijseger (clo).* 7/94.

Sclavis on free ground, although the trio of clarinets is actually quite strictly worked out. There is even a Pierre Boulez piece, 'Domaines', to go with the five-part 'Berliner Suite' which otherwise comprises the record. Timbral exercises, counterpoint, call-and-response: their materials are classic, even if the feel of the record is, perhaps inevitably, more reminiscent of European chamber music than the style once evoked by Clarinet Summit. For specialist tastes, a delightful record.

With Reijseger, Sclavis has some of the clearest space he's ever had on record to demonstrate what a master he is of the clarinet family. The music is brimful of great technique from both men, without (much) resorting to show-off proficiency. Here and there are either dead spots or bits of machismo, but mostly this is a witty and often thrilling duel between top players.

****** L'Affrontement Des Pretendants**
ECM 159927 *Sclavis; Jean Luc Capozzo (t); Vincent Courtois (clo); Bruno Chevillon (b); François Merville (d).* 9/99.

A new group sound for Sclavis, with Capozzo's trumpet very much to the forefront and creating an atmosphere of almost unbearable grief on the long 'Hommage À Lounes Matoub', Sclavis's threnody to the brilliant Algerian political singer who was murdered the year before this recording was made. Trumpet then gives place to cello and it is more than five minutes before the whole band is involved, but what a track it is. Sclavis takes a solo on soprano and manages to nod in the direction of John Coltrane while taking off in his own somewhat classical idiom. Other tracks are more conventional. 'Distances' is a slice of idiosyncratic bebop, while 'Contre Contre' and the title-piece (which lacks an explicit programme) are very much in line with his now familiar polystylistic approach. Immensely impressive and emotionally engaging music from the French master.

***** Dans La Nuit**
ECM 589524 *Sclavis; Dominique Pifarély (vn); Vincent Courtois (clo); Jean-Louis Matinier (acc); François Merville (d, mar).* 10/00.

Written, as has been somewhat fashionable of late, as the soundtrack to a silent movie, this is an attractively low-key and delicate disc from Sclavis. It certainly lacks the power and authority of recent sets, but the musicianship, hinged this time on the clarinettist and accordionist Matinier, is of sufficient merit to hold the attention. The sound is as good as ever, but Sclavis's own production levels out the different voices, making the overall impact quite orchestral.

*****(*) Napoli's Walls**
ECM 1857 *Sclavis; Mederic Collignon (pkt-t, hn, perc, elec, v); Hasse Poulsen (g); Vincent Courtois (clo, elec).* 12/02.

Between 1987 and 1995, artist Ernest Pignon-Ernest created a body of work inspired by and intended for the streets of Naples, the city you see and die. Its themes were death and decay, the eternal feminine and the continuity of cultures from pagan to Christian to neo-pagan. Sclavis's music perfectly reflects these concerns and in Collignon he has found a collaborator – one part Don Cherry, two parts Herb Robertson – who empathizes totally with his vision. Most of the tracks are dedications – to the artist, to Charles Mingus, to the children of Naples and the world – but the music runs together as a continuous suite that makes complete sense without a programme.

John Scofield (born 1951)

GUITAR

Studied at Berklee 1970–73, then with Billy Cobham and Charles Mingus on record. With Dave Liebman and under his own leadership, he began recording regularly, then joined Miles Davis in 1982, staying until 1985. Subsequently he has recorded many discs for Blue Note and Verve and has been in huge demand as a sideman. Seen by many as the quintessential, most widely read and flexible contemporary jazz guitarist.

**** Electric Outlet**
Gramavision GR 8045 *Scofield; Ray Anderson (tb); David Sanborn (as); Pete Levin (ky); Steve Jordan (d).* 4–5/84.

****** Still Warm**
Gramavision GR 8508 *Scofield; Don Grolnick (ky); Darryl Jones (b); Omar Hakim (d).* 6/85.

***** Blue Matter**
Gramavision 18-8702 *Scofield; Mitchel Forman (ky); Hiram Bullock (g); Gary Grainger (b); Dennis Chambers (d); Don Alias (perc).* 9/86.

***** Loud Jazz**
Gramavision 18-8801 *As above, except Robert Aries, George Duke (ky) replace Forman; Bullock omitted.* 12/87.

***** Pick Hits Live**

Gramavision 18-8805 *As above, except omit Duke and Alias.* 10/87.

*****(*) Flat Out**

Gramavision 18-8903 *Scofield; Don Grolnick (org); Anthony Cox (b); Johnny Vidacovich, Terri Lyne Carrington (d).* 12/88.

John Scofield was perhaps the last of Miles Davis's sidemen to break through to a major career, but his first records for Enja (all currently deleted), all made prior to his joining Davis in 1982, bespeak a substantial talent already making waves. He had played with a diverse group of leaders – Charles Mingus, Lee Konitz, Gary Burton, Billy Cobham – before forming his own band. Scofield's six Gramavision albums are a coherent and highly enjoyable body of work. *Electric Outlet* was a false start: the band seems gimcracked around a dubious idea of highbrow pop-jazz, Sanborn and Anderson are there only for colour, and the attempted grooves are stiff and unyielding. But *Still Warm* solved matters at a stroke. Steve Swallow's production clarified the sound without overpowering the fluidity of Scofield's arrangements, Grolnick added thoughtful keyboard textures, and Jones and Hakim (colleagues from the Miles Davis band) were tight and funky without being relentlessly so. Scofield's own playing here assumes a new authority: tones are richer, the hint of fuzz and sustain is perfectly integrated, and his solos are unflaggingly inventive: for a single sample, listen to the sharp, hotly articulated solo on 'Picks And Pans'.

The band which the guitarist then formed with Grainger and Chambers bolstered the funk-fusion side of his playing. The drummer, especially, is a thunderous virtuoso in the manner of Billy Cobham, and the next three albums are all fired up with his rhythms. Scofield's writing revolves around ear-catching melodic hooks and a favourite device of a riff repeated over a shifting harmonic base, and the two studio albums are full of naggingly memorable themes. But the music was formulaic in the end. The live record is a feast of hard-nut jazz-funk showmanship, but it starts to sound clenched by the end. *Flat Out* comes as a welcome change of pace. Vidacovich and Carrington, who split chores between them through the record, are swinging but no less busy drummers: hear the consummately controlled rave-up on 'The Boss's Car' (a cheeky rip-off of Bruce Springsteen's 'Pink Cadillac'). Two standards, a Meters tune and a rollicking turn through 'Rockin' Pneumonia' also lighten the programme.

****** Time On My Hands**

Blue Note 792894-2 *Scofield; Joe Lovano (ts); Charlie Haden (b); Jack DeJohnette (d).* 11/89.

*****(*) Meant To Be**

Blue Note 795479-2 *Scofield; Joe Lovano (ts, cl); Marc Johnson (b); Bill Stewart (d).* 12/90.

Scofield's transfer to Blue Note moved his career and his music substantially forward. Lovano is an inspired choice of front-line partner, renegotiating the jazz roots of Sco's approach without surrendering the feisty attack which the guitarist amplified through his Gramavision records. *Time On My Hands* provides some of his best writing, including the lovely ballad of 'Let's Say We Did' and the twining melodies of 'Since You Asked'. 'Fat Lip' is acoustic jazz-rock which Haden and DeJohnette jump on with brilliant ferocity. Superb studio sound throughout. If *Meant To Be* seems a shade less invigorating, it's only because it seems like a second run through the same territory. Both are very highly recommended.

*****(*) Grace Under Pressure**

Blue Note 7981672 *Scofield; Randy Brecker (flhn); Jim Pugh (tb); John Clark (frhn); Bill Frisell (g); Charlie Haden (b); Joey Baron (d).* 12/91.

Though given a mixed reception on its release, this is a strong and thoughtfully realized continuation of Scofield's work for Blue Note. If he's starting to seem over-exposed as a player, turning up in countless guest roles as well as on his own records, the ten themes here display a consistent strength as a writer: variations on the blues, slow modal ballads, riffs worked into melodies, Scofield makes them all come up fresh, and he creates situations where the rhythm-players can line the music with intensities and colours of their own. There are hard, swinging solos on the title-track and 'Twang', and if the interplay with Frisell can sometimes seem more like cheese and chalk, there are piquant contrasts which sometimes blend with surprising effectiveness: 'Honest I Do' is the kind of haunting, downbeat melody that Scofield has made his own. The brass are used sparingly to underscore a few tracks.

*****(*) I Can See Your House From Here**

Blue Note 827765-2 *Scofield; Pat Metheny (g); Steve Swallow (b); Bill Stewart (d).* 12/93.

For his second meeting with another leading guitarist, Scofield uncorked some more of his best writing: the title-piece and 'No Matter What' are typically serpentine, elegant, feelingful tunes to which the slick playing only adds. This is far more collaborative than the record with Frisell, with Metheny taking several writing credits himself, and, while it occasionally softens in the face of Pat's tendency to turn to marshmallow, it's good.

***** Hand Jive**

Blue Note 827327-2 *Scofield; Eddie Harris (ts); Larry Goldings (p, org); Dennis Irwin (b); Bill Stewart (d); Don Alias (perc).* 10/93.

Scofield's final Blue Note albums round off the most enjoyable run of guitar records in recent years. Perhaps no genuinely fresh ground is broken here, but just by shuffling his options the guitarist finds new ways of walking over old paths. The fashion to turn back to the guitar/organ combos of the '60s has already grown stale, but Scofield's take on the genre turns the emphasis around: not surprisingly, it's the guitar-player who takes the limelight rather than a licks-bound organist, and in any case Goldings is the most interesting new organ man on the scene. *Hand Jive* blends the chugging groove beloved of the old school with the leaner rhythms of Irwin and Stewart, Sco's pop-tune sensibility, Goldings's feel for line and colour and the surprise choice of maverick tenorman Harris. The result is excellent fun. His final date for the label, *Groove Elation*, which we slightly preferred of these two, has apparently gone to the dead-letter office.

CORE COLLECTION

****** Quiet**

Verve 533185-2 *Scofield; Randy Brecker (t, flhn); Wayne Shorter (ts); Charles Pillow (f, cor, ts); Lawrence Feldman (f, ts); John Clark, Fred Griffin (frhn); Roger Rosenberg (bcl); Howard Johnson (bs, tba); Steve Swallow (b); Bill Stewart, Duduka Fonseca (d).* 4/96.

Having already tried numerous settings for Blue Note, Scofield's Verve debut was different again. Playing acoustic

guitar exclusively is one departure; setting it against the mournful sound of low brass and woodsy reeds is another. The horn charts are just witty enough to inject a certain wryness and just eerie enough to lend a sometimes other-worldly air to the likes of 'After The Fact'. The addition of Shorter, playing his now unaccustomed tenor on three tracks, seems like an unlikely bonus, but he fits in uncannily well. Scofield's own playing is made to seem less conspicuous by his playing acoustic, yet it lends a certain piquancy to his improvising. And then there is Swallow, co-producing and seeming to direct much of the playing with high, light bass-lines of the utmost ingenuity and relevance. The result comes close to Scofield's finest hour.

*****(*) A Go Go**

Verve 539979-2 *Scofield; John Medeski (ky); Billy Martin (b); Chris Wood (d).* 97.

Opportunism, maybe, but this is a shrewd match, and if the MM&W trio sometimes seem at a loss for substance on their own records, Scofield hands it to them on a plate with his ten originals here. The difference between tunes such as 'Green Tea' and 'Hottentot' and any other organ blues or Bo Diddley shuffle is the degree of harmonic/melodic sophistication which Scofield has slid in. *A Go Go* emerges as not so much a fun record with brains as a loosely intense essay on the common ground in jazz, rock and funk. The dead drum sound and buzzing keyboards which are the trio's trademarks remain. It's a 'fusion' which suggests that neither side is merely buying in to the other.

***** Bump**

Verve 543430-2 *Scofield; Mark Degli Antoni (ky); David Livolsi, Tony Scherr (b); Kenny Wollesen, Eric Klab (d); Johnny Durkin, Johnny Almendra (perc).* 99.

Not bad, but Scofield's edging away from jazz and into a hinterland of rock does seem vaguely disappointing. As his tone gets more clotted and the phrasing more hook-orientated, the results are bitty and insubstantial over the course of a CD. For all the cleverness of the playing – and there is plenty – this feels fundamentally lightweight, even if his intentions seem more honourable than many who are seeking a way out of their niche.

***** Works For Me**

Verve 549281-2 *Scofield; Kenny Garrett (as); Brad Mehldau (p); Christian McBride (b); Billy Higgins (d).* 1/00.

Given a spacious studio mix by James Farber, this one-time-only all-star date seeks to restore Scofield's endangered jazz status. Unfortunately, it's kept out of the top grade by the easy-going, overly respectful mien, as if these guys were so humbled by each other that they forgot to really dig in and play. There is the usual cute-to-clever bag of Scofield compositions, and hearing McBride and Higgins together was always going to be a treat, but this is in the end no more than a nice blow.

**** Uberjam**

Verve 589356-2 *Scofield; Karl Denson (f, ts); John Medeski (ky); Avi Bortnick (g, samples); Jesse Murphy (b); Adam Deitch (d).* 01.

Publicity suggested that Scofield sees this as taking jazz to a 'new place'; if so, he might be dismayed to hear that '70s rock got there a long time ago. Based around nattily funky small-combo licks, the music's more like a string of commercials for equipment suppliers: there's a different sound on every track, and if the leader sought to impose his signature on the whole, he failed. The nadir comes with the 'Blue Moon' quotes in the title-track. If *A Go Go* had some promise of an interesting fusion, this one buries it.

***** Up All Night**

Verve 065596-2 *Scofield; Avi Bortnick (g); Andy Hess (b); Adam Deitch (d).* 03.

Better, if still not exactly enthralling. Some of the extraneous clutter of the last record has been wiped off, and there are moments for Scofield nuts to savour: the improvising on 'Creeper' and 'Whatcha See Is Whatcha Get', for instance. But there's still too much which sounds anaesthetized by special FX, both in Scofield's own kit and with Bortnick's loops and samples, which serve mainly to dampen the leader's individualism. And Hess and Deitch are going nowhere.

*****(*) Oh!**

Blue Note 42081-2 *Scofield; Joe Lovano (ss, ts); Dave Holland (b); Al Foster (d).* 7/02.

This might more properly be listed under Lovano's name – he's the Blue Note guy here, after all – but Scofield comes first in the rubric (and there was reputedly plenty of flying fur over *that*). It's a supergroup record for sure, but a pleasingly good-natured one. Even on an agitated piece such as 'Shorter Form' the group glide through it. This is certainly the most challenging material Scofield's had put in front of him for some time (with the possible exception of Tommy Smith's international band record), although there are pieces which are little more than vamps too. Lovano, like Scofield, has played on so many records that it's hard to hear him making defining statements any more, although he sounds as if he enjoyed this. Holland and Foster are a top team. Doesn't torch any souls, but it's luxury class.

Hazel Scott (1920–81)

PIANO

Originally from Trinidad, Scott was a child performer in New York and was playing in clubs while still in her middle teens. She jazzed the classics and sang in an amiable blues style, but her marriage to Adam Clayton Powell brought her into disrepute during the McCarthy era and she retreated to France, before returning to the US around 1960. Though she largely left jazz behind, she still appeared in public into the '70s.

***** Hazel Scott 1939–1945**

Classics 1308 *Scott; Nat Natoli, Yank Lawson, Pee Wee Erwin (t); John Owens (tb, t); Danny Polo (cl); Hymie Schertzer (as, bs); Pete Brown (as); Joe Dixon (ts); Ellis Larkins (p); Albert Harris, Carl Kress (g); Pete Barry (b, v); Leonard Gaskin (b); Arthur Herbert, J. C. Heard, Johnny Blowers, Sid Catlett (d).* 12/39–5/45.

Scott is largely forgotten today, but she was a V-Disc favourite during the war years and was the first black American woman to have her own TV show. This CD collects her first four sessions for Decca, plus a 1939 sextet set for Bluebird and four titles made for V-Disc. Six numbers feature her jazzing such classics as the Minute Waltz and the Rachmaninov C sharp minor prelude, but more appetizing are boogie-woogie and blues features which show a smart dexterity, although the music is sometimes a bit top-heavy with grace notes. Still, it's charming to hear her having such evident fun with 'Body And Soul', and a duet with the ebullient Sid Catlett on 'C Jam Blues' really swings the house. The Bluebird titles have a nice bluesy feel and good spots for Danny Polo and Pete Brown, although by 1945 she was becoming more of a straight ballad singer. Reproduction is a typically mixed Classics bag: some of the Decca titles are surfacey, one of the V-Discs is evidently from a very poor original, but the other one is crisp and clear.

Jimmy Scott (born 1925)

VOCAL

A hormone problem kept Scott's voice unusually high-pitched as he grew up. He sang around Cleveland in the '40s and joined Lionel Hampton in 1950, hob-nobbing with the boppers and recording plenty of songs, but after 1960 he was plagued with contractual difficulties and lost his way. Returned in the late '80s, and finally achieved cult eminence with a string of records in the '90s.

***** Everybody's Somebody's Fool**

Decca/GRP 050669-2 *Scott; orchestras led by Lionel Hampton, Billy Taylor, Lucky Thompson.* 1/50–8/52.

Scott's early records had been almost forgotten by all but a handful of vocal followers, but his return to prominence in the '90s awakened enough interest for these sides to be trawled out of the Decca vaults. His high but unmannered voice will remind you of many female singers, but there's a musing quality to his style at this point which sets delicacy alongside a pleading, contrite sensibility. He made a speciality out of ballads full of entreaties, such as the title-track, his first hit with Lionel Hampton, and not all of this material is worthwhile raw matter for his extraordinary voice. The last four tracks, with an octet led by Thompson, open on a heart-sick 'Why Was I Born?', but he doesn't do too badly by 'The Bluest Blues', an unreleased track from the same session.

*****(*) The Source**

Atlantic 8122-73526-2 *Scott; David 'Fathead' Newman, Joe Gentle (ts); Junior Mance (p); Eric Gale, Billy Butler (g); Ron Carter (b); Bruno Carr (d); Cissy Houston (v); strings.* 70.

A collectors' piece, this sole entry for Atlantic starts with an awesomely melodramatic slope through 'Exodus', where Scott's control is extraordinary. His voice was probably at its peak around this time, and he handles the programme with a serene mastery that's something to hear. Though there are glances at pop with 'On Broadway' (done as a wistful stroll) and 'Our Day Will Come', Scott treats every song with a respectful, gripping intensity, and the accompaniments – even the string charts – exude class and sympathy.

****** All The Way**

Sire/Warner Bros 926955-2 *Scott; David 'Fathead' Newman (ts); Kenny Barron (p); John Pisano (g); Ron Carter (b); Grady Tate (d); strings.* 92.

****** Dreams**

Sire/Warner Bros 9362-45629-2 *Scott; Patience Higgins, Red Holloway (ts); Mitchell Froom (org); Junior Mance (p); Milt Jackson (vib); Rick Zunigar (g); Ron Carter (b); Peyton Crossley (d).* 2/94.

*****(*) Heaven**

Warner Bros 9362-46211-2 *Scott; Jacky Terrasson (p); Hill Greene (b); Joseph Bonadio (d).* 4/96.

***** Holding Back The Years**

Birdology 3984-27577-2 *Scott; Pamela Fleming (t); Bruce Kirby (ts); Gregorie Maret (hca); Michael Kanan (p); Matt Muniseri (g); Ghill Green (b); Victor Jones (d); strings.* 98.

Absent from recording studios for many years, Scott's comeback was little short of astounding. *All The Way* presents the voice as withered but strong, stretched and vibrato-laden but peculiarly youthful, even as it suggests a lifetime's experience and the wear of many disappointments. Some notes he grabs at, shouting them, but his control seldom falters and even a bar of struggle seems to be part of a song's overall plan. It can sometimes be an exhausting listen, since Scott either compels the attention or drives you away, but there's no singing like it listed elsewhere in this book. Both *All The Way* and *Dreams* can boast blue-chip accompanists and the most handsome of standards in the song-list. We slightly prefer the second, with impeccable cameos from Jackson and a quiet, nocturnal feel to the occasion, but the string arrangements on the first will appeal to many, and the emotion of Scott's return feels palpable throughout this one.

Heaven is a surprise match with Terrasson, and one which works far better than the pianist's deluded encounter with Cassandra Wilson, although even here Jacky can't always resist his impulse to overplay. The material is a curious mix of secular pop (the Talking Heads title-track), gospel-soul, folk themes and spirituals, all of it one way or the other about heaven. Very bare-bones in presentation, and the most exposed Scott has ever left himself, it's hard to be unmoved, often by his frailties as much as by his vocal powers. By now the voice is becoming thinner and less able to do its owner's bidding, and the idea of *Holding Back The Years* was unreasonable. Against a sort of soft-rock/lounge backing, Jimmy takes on ten songs from contemporary rock writers. It's not that the likes of Elvis Costello, Mick Hucknall and Bryan Ferry songs are beyond him, but he doesn't have the kind of narcissism which those performers invest in their own material to make it work for them. Against the odds, he still makes more of this project than anybody might have expected.

***** Mood Indigo**

Milestone 9305 *Scott; Hank Crawford (as); Grégoire Maret (hca); Cyrus Chestnut, Michael Kanan (p); Joe Beck (g); George Mraz, Hilliard Greene (b); Grady Tate, Victor Jones (d).* 99.

****(*) Over The Rainbow**

Milestone 9314 *Scott; Bob Kindred, David 'Fathead' Newman (ts); Justin Robinson (as); Grégoire Maret (hca); Larry Willis, Michael Kanan (p); Joe Beck (g); Joe Locke (vib); George Mraz (b); Grady Tate, Clarence Penn (d).* 11/00.

*****(*) But Beautiful**

Milestone 9321 *Scott; Wynton Marsalis, Lew Soloff (t); Eric Alexander, Bob Kindred (ts); Renee Rosnes (p); Joe Beck (g); George Mraz (b); Lewis Nash, Dwayne Boradnax (d); Freddy Cole (v).* 8/01.

Now with Milestone, Scott has completed three albums already. There's something too strained about the settings on the first two records. The accompaniments are sympathetic but too tight, too professionally tuned, and on *Over The Rainbow*, in particular, he sounds up against it. Jimmy can supply his own dramatics, and he doesn't need the almost preposterous arrangement of 'Strange Fruit' to do it for him.

Yet *But Beautiful* is another great one. The unlikely ministering angel is Renee Rosnes, who arranged six of the ten tracks, and recognized that Scott needs a warm simplicity, not tailored melodrama. It's mostly about the rhythm section, with the horns using their discretion (King Wynton is on one track, and sounds great); but it all has to be in the service of the singer, and Jimmy responds with a wonderful effort. Even though the voice is becoming too frayed for comfort now, it's still an artist in command.

***** Moonglow**

Milestone 9332 *Basically as above two discs.* 3/00–8/01.

Judging from the dates and line-ups, these are offcuts from the sessions for the last two albums. Which might suggest this as second-rate Scott, but it doesn't work out like that: 'Yesterday' is more wistful than tragic, and 'Since I Fell For You' – with David Newman in good shape – has a light, bluesy bounce. 'I Thought About You' is charming. Jimmy's voice is still more tattered than trenchant, but on its own terms the record has much to enjoy.

Ronnie Scott (1927–97)

TENOR SAXOPHONE

There have been musician-run jazz clubs before – Shelly's Manne Hole, Ali's Alley, Fred Anderson's Velvet Lounge – but none with quite the charisma of Ronnie Scott's in London's Soho. Unlike the others, Ronnie's career as proprietor and MC eclipsed his playing, which is a shame because he was a fine tenor-player and, in the opinion of Charles Mingus, quite the best and bluesiest of the 'white boys'.

***** Boppin' At Esquire**

Indigo 2125 *Scott; Ralph Sharon (p); Pete Chilver (g); Jack Fallon (b); Jackie Dougan (d).* 48.

****** When I Want Your Opinion, I'll Give It To You**

Ronnie Scott's Jazz House JHAS 610 *Scott; Stan Tracey (p); Ernest Ranglin (g); Malcolm Cecil, Rick Laird (b); Jackie Dougan, Chris Karan, Ronnie Stephenson (d).* 12/63–4/65.

*****(*) The Night Has A Thousand Eyes**

Ronnie Scott's Jazz House JCAS 614 *Scott; Sonny Stitt (ts); Stan Tracey (p); Malcolm Cecil (b); Jackie Dougan, Ronnie Stephenson (d).* 5/64.

It was always ironic that Ronnie Scott should have become a virtual brand name, and a substantial proportion of the Japanese and American tourists who filed into the Frith Street club never got a chance to hear him play. Originally Ronald Schatt, he was a pastmaster at the chewish chive, but also a musician soaked in the blues and capable of compelling emotion in a solo. He disliked recording and did it only sparingly, though a couple of his records have acquired almost iconic status in Britain and on the Continent.

The early bop material on Indigo underlines what an able exponent of the idiom Ronnie was. There had been very few top-flight bop tenor-players, and Ronnie is as convincing as any of the Americans. His solos on 'How High The Moon' and 'Scrapple From The Apple' are particularly effective, with altered chords in some of the choruses showing how Ronnie was keen to push the limits of the new form. Other tracks are shorter and more intensely focused. Worth setting this one as a blindfold test and seeing how many people plump for a Brit, let alone Ronnie.

When I Want Your Opinion (a typical Scott line) brings together material from the early to mid-'60s when the club really was the crucible of modern jazz in Britain. The various groups, with either Malcolm Cecil or Rick Laird (later to join the Mahavishnu Orchestra and then to give up music for photography) were boppish in idiom, but closer in feel to the swing era. If there is a saxophonist Scott resembles on these tracks, then it must be the Janus-faced Don Byas, who also recorded at the club towards the end of his life. The presence of Ernest Ranglin brings a bouncy playfulness to 'Ronnie's Blues' from December 1963. A couple of months later, he's missing, and Chris Karan has been replaced by Jackie Dougan. Stan Tracey is the piano-player on all the tracks with keyboard (there are two trios, with just Laird and Dougan or Stephenson) and he brings his usual abrupt lyricism to 'Bye Bye Blackbird' (recorded in 1965) and a touch of deadpan humour to 'I'm Sick And Tired Of Waking Up Tired And Sick', a Scott original that in 1997 seemed unbearably ironic.

The great joy of being Ronnie Scott was, of course, being allowed to cry *and* sing at your own party. The 1964 encounters with Sonny Stitt are the first of his encounters with visiting Americans to be released by Les Tomkins and Jazz House. Just three long tracks, but some roaring Scott performances, which show him to be no slouch in any company. 'The Night Has A Thousand Eyes' kicks off with Sonny's bright, exuberant solo, switches to Scott for a long, beautifully shaped statement which feeds off the American's in the wittiest and most sardonic way, leaving it to Stitt to round out the solos. Unfortunately, tape problems mean that the number has to be faded at the end. Scott takes the initiative on 'A Sonny Day For Ronnie', recorded later in the month, and leaves Stitt eating dust; honours are even again in the exchange of eights, but it's definitely the club owner's moment. Perhaps rightly, Stitt takes charge on 'Bye Bye Blackbird', a performance that throws in some classic bebop phrasing along the way.

****** Live At Ronnie Scott's**

Columbia 494439 2 *Scott; Kenny Wheeler (t, flhn); Chris Pyne (tb); Ray Warleigh (as); John Surman (ss, bs); Gordon Beck (p, org); Ron Mathewson (b); Kenny Clare, Tony Oxley (d).* 69.

This was the group known simply as The Band, a kind of house outfit that had the time to develop some pretty sophisticated charts and an enviable level of empathy on the stand. Ronnie himself is in great form in front of the home crowd (most of whom, needless to say, had travelled a good way to be there). His solo on the opening 'Recorda Me' is up there with any of composer Joe Henderson's and his long, burning statement on 'Macumba' bracket the album beautifully. Warleigh plays with his usual headlong appetite, and Surman blisters the paintwork on Laurie Holloway's 'King Pete', which sees him shift to soprano. Wheeler is as calmly tasteful as ever but, even in this congenial company, manages to suggest a great deal of passion under the unflustered exterior. The rhythm section is fascinating. Beck has never received due credit and remains something of a figure apart. His comping is as solid as railway sleepers, underpinning solos of terse originality. Mathewson switches between upright and electric bass, the latter sounding rather dated in this context. The real key to the band's headlong pace is the twinned drumming of Clare and Oxley; Tony cut his jazz teeth at Ronnie's and provides the turbulent, swirling groove on which the set is constructed. It's possible to hear Kenny laying accents and paradiddles in the middle of Tony's sweeping runs, content to let him do the assault course and to stay laid back and cool himself. A final word for Chris Pyne, who blows dour and strong on Kenny Wheeler's 'Second Question', using a big virile tone that sounds deeper in pitch than it is just because the tone is so broad. A strong album from a band in top form.

*****(*) Never Pat A Burning Dog**

Ronnie Scott's Jazz House JC 012 *Scott; Dick Pearce (t); Mornington Lockett (ts); John Critchinson (p); Ron Mathewson (b); Martin Drew (d).* 10 & 11/90.

Never Pat A Burning Dog (seems obvious, but you never know) will appeal to those who have worn out their copy of *Serious Gold*, Scott's late-'70s Pye album, though they may also be surprised at how far his harmonic thinking has developed since then. A muted, almost elegiac set (recorded live at the club) begins with a stunning version of McCoy Tyner's 'Contemplation', full of glassy harmonies and tender, dissonant flourishes. Scott's choice of material is typically adventurous and tasteful: Jimmy Dorsey's 'I'm Glad There Is You', David Sanborn's 'White Caps', Cedar Walton's 'When Love Is New', a slightly unsatisfactory reading of Freddie Hubbard's 'Little Sunflower' with the less than inspiring Lockett in for Pearce, and two standards, 'All The Things You Are' and the under-recorded 'This Love Of Mine'. Scott's tone is deep and subtly modulated, and his phrasing has the kind of relaxed precision and inner heat one associates with Paul Gonsalves or Zoot Sims. Despite the variety of material, it's a remarkably consistent set, perhaps even a little unvaried in treatment.

The records will never quite make up for the loss of his presence. Scott was an original, a wise old business head whose love of the music was the best excuse for occasional peevishness and an unsmilingly literal approach to the small print on a contract.

Shirley Scott (1934–2002)

ORGAN, PIANO

Born in Philadelphia, she studied trumpet and piano, then began working with Lockjaw Davis and switched to organ. Formed her own trio in 1960, often working with Stanley Turrentine, who was her husband for a time. Visible in the '90s on TV with Bill Cosby, when she was still playing organ and piano.

***** Workin'**

Prestige 24126-2 *Scott; Eddie 'Lockjaw' Davis (ts); Ronnell Bright (p); Wally Richardson (g); George Duvivier, Peck Morrison (b); Arthur Edgehill, Roy Haynes (d); Ray Barretto (perc).* 5/58–3/61.

*****(*) Like Cozy**

Prestige 24258 *Scott; George Duvivier, George Tucker (b); Arthur Edgehill (d).* 10/58–9/60.

***** Legends Of Acid Jazz**

Prestige 24200-2 *Scott; Stanley Turrentine (ts); Herb Lewis, George Tucker (b); Roy Brooks, Otis Finch (d).* 6–11/61.

***** Legends Of Acid Jazz – Soul Sister**

Prestige 24233-2 *Scott; Lem Winchester (vib); Kenny Burrell (g); George Duvivier, Eddie Khan (b); Otis Finch, Arthur Edgehill (d).* 6/60–2/64.

*****(*) Soul Shoutin'**

Prestige 24142-2 *Scott; Stanley Turrentine (ts); Major Holley, Earl May (b); Grassella Oliphant (d).* 1–10/63.

***** Blue Flames**

Original Jazz Classics OJC 328 *As above.* 8/65.

Shirley Scott was used to heavy company. In 1955, in her native Philadelphia, she was working in a trio with John Coltrane. Wider recognition came with her association with Eddie 'Lockjaw' Davis, which led to dozens of albums for Prestige, Impulse!, Atlantic and Cadet through the '70s. There are currently only a few CD revivals of this prodigious output. Scott wasn't a knockabout swinger like Jimmy Smith and didn't have the bebop attack of Don Patterson, but there's an authority and an unusual sense of power in reserve which keep her music simmering somewhere near the boil. She is a strong blues-player and a fine accompanist, and her right-hand lines have a percussive feel that utilizes space more than most organ-players ever did. *Like Cozy* is one of the best places to hear her, since there's no horn-player in attendance, and from the opening slink through 'Sweet Lorraine' she sounds fearless about running the show. The original albums (*Shirley Scott Trio* and *Like Cozy*) were pitched as late-night sounds and most of the tracks are taken at a slow lope but, with the blues hovering around every measure and Shirley's engagingly odd phrasing (she plays piano on several tracks too), this is a very enjoyable revival.

She was also married to Stanley Turrentine, and they made a number of records together: *Soul Shoutin'* brings together the contents of the original albums *The Soul Is Willing* and *Soul Shoutin'*, and this one gets the nod as the pick of the reissues. The title-track off *The Soul Is Willing* is the near-perfect example of what this combination could do, a fuming Turrentine solo followed by a deftly swinging one by Scott. In comparison, *Blue Flames* seems like short measure, but this kind of jazz is perhaps best sampled a few tracks at a time in any case, including these two – nothing more nor less than some cooking tenor and organ on some blues and a ballad or two. *Workin'* is a compilation of four sessions that cover some of Shirley's earlier dates and includes one bruiser with Lockjaw Davis – good stuff, if a notch below *Soul Shoutin'*. The two *Acid Jazz* sets bring back four more of the two dozen or so original LPs that Scott made for Prestige: the first couples *Hip Soul* and *Hip Twist*, the second brings together *Soul Sister* and, oddly, the much later *Travelin' Light*. The first one has another heaping helping of Turrentine, while the second relies on the not terribly interesting Winchester and the admirable Burrell. Little to choose, really, since while her cast-list varied Scott herself played with unshakeable consistency.

***** Talkin' Verve**

Verve 549539-2 *Scott; Thad Jones, Clark Terry (t); Urbie Green, Melba Liston (tb); Phil Woods (as); Jerome Richardson, Stanley Turrentine (ts); Attila Zoller (g); Ron Carter (b); Mel Lewis, Grady Tate (d).* 63–71.

Not bad as a compilation of Shirley's work for Impulse! (she was never on Verve, despite the series title). There's a drift towards pop material, and the Oliver Nelson charts seem like leftovers from his work for Jimmy Smith. It also suggests that we're unlikely to see the original albums returning any time soon.

***** Blues Everywhere**
Candid CCD79525 *Scott; Arthur Harper (b); Mickey Roker (d).* 11/91.

***** Skylark**
Candid CCD 79705-2 *As above.* 11/91.

For once Scotty handles the acoustic keyboard for an entire date, and what comes out is a fat, funky, authoritative trio date somewhat in the style of Red Garland. Harper and Roker can sleepwalk through this kind of music and, since it keeps on swinging for nearly an hour, it's a tribute to Shirley that they stayed awake. Their second set is laid down on the subsequent *Skylark*, and one can safely say it's more of the same: two enjoyable records, but only a relative will need both of them. Fine, live recording from Birdland in New York.

***** A Walkin' Thing**
Candid CCD79719 *Scott; Terell Stafford (t); Tim Warfield (ts); Arthur Harper (b); Aaron Walker (d).* 11/92.

Harper survives from the last two trio records, but otherwise this was a hot young group that Shirley's in charge of. The feel is vintage Prestige/Blue Note (done at Van Gelder's, unsurprisingly) and if some of the tracks are a bit of a long stretch nobody sounds unhappy about it. It suits Warfield and Stafford to take their time on the title-piece especially. Scott presides with unblinking authority.

Tony Scott (born 1921)

CLARINET, BARITONE SAXOPHONE, PIANO, ELECTRONICS, VOCAL

Born A. J. Sciacca, he worked as a New York sideman in the '40s and '50s and led his own groups from 1953, playing his own version of bop on the clarinet. Left for Europe and Asia in 1959, and turned to investigating various ethnic musics, although jazz remains in his make-up. Now based in Italy, though his activities rarely reach international audiences.

*****(*) The Complete Tony Scott**
RCA 74321 421322 *Scott; John Carisi, Thad Jones, Jimmy Nottingham, Clark Terry, Wendell Culley, Jimmy Maxwell, Joe Newman, Bernie Glow (t); Henry Coker, Quentin Jackson, Benny Powell, Sonny Truitt, Bill Hughes (tb); Gigi Gryce (as); Frank Foster, Zoot Sims, Frank Wess (ts); Danny Bank, Sahib Shihab, Charlie Fowlkes (bs); Bill Evans (p); Freddie Green (g); Les Grinage, Milt Hinton (b); Osie Johnson, Paul Motian (d).* 12/56.

Scott's position as a master of his instrument has never been in question, but it was that instrument's own status which bebop and after was disputing, and excellent records like this one have been comparatively lost as a result. A dozen miniatures handsomely crafted for a crack studio band, with Scott incisively making his way through and around the music, never encumbered by the task but going at it with a degree more passion than these situations would customarily demand.

****** A Day In New York**
Fresh Sound FSR CD 160/2 2CD *Scott; Clark Terry (t); Jimmy Knepper (tb); Sahib Shihab (bs); Bill Evans (p); Henry Grimes, Milt Hinton (b); Paul Motian (d).* 11/57.

In 1959 Tony Scott turned his back on America, wounded by the death of several friends (Hot Lips Page, Billie Holiday, Charlie Parker, Lester Young) and by what he considered the 'death' of the clarinet in jazz terms. Since then he has been a wanderer, exploring the culture and music of the East, trading in the sometimes aggressive assertions of bebop for a meditative approach to harmony that at its best is deeply moving, at its least disciplined a weak ambient decoration.

Scott enjoyed a close and fruitful relationship with Bill Evans, and perhaps his best recorded work is the session of 16 November 1957 with the Evans trio and guests, tackling a copious roster of originals and well-worn standards (including a lovely 'Lullaby Of The Leaves' with Knepper). The clarinettist's opening statements on Evans's 'Five' are almost neurotically brilliant and a perfect illustration of how loud Scott could play. 'Portrait Of Ravi' and 'The Explorer' are Scott originals, directed towards the concerns that were increasingly to occupy him. Evans's light touch and immense harmonic sophistication suited his approach ideally. Scott was at the top of his professional tree and enjoyed great critical acclaim. More recent years have found him a relatively forgotten figure. But he is unmistakably an original.

***** Music For Zen Meditation**
Verve 521444-2 *Scott; Hozan Yamamoto (shakuhachi); Shinichi Yuizi (koto).* 2/64.

***** Tony Scott**
Verve V6-8788 *Scott; Beril Rubenstein (p, org); Attila Zoller (g); Collin Walcott (sitar); John Berbarian (oud); Milt Hinton, Richard Davis (b); Souren Baronian (dumbek); Jimmy Lovelace (d); Steve Pumilia (perc).* 11/67.

***** Music For Yoga Meditation And Other Joys**
Verve 835371-2 *Scott; Collin Walcott (sitar).* 68.

Scott's absorption in Buddhist thinking ultimately resulted in some intriguing cross-cultural experiments like these. His interest in Indian *raga* (as in his ahead-of-the-pack dedication to Ravi Shankar on the Fresh Sound, above) and in African musics (below) bespeaks certain philosophical premises which are rather difficult to judge on purely artistic grounds. How efficacious *Music For Zen Meditation* may be for its professed purpose is beyond the scope of this book to determine, but it's slightly disappointing to note how quickly Scott seemed prepared to abandon the taut harmonic arguments of his work with Evans, LaFaro and Motian in favour of the bland affirmations here. Nevertheless these discs have remained hugely popular in their way over the years, Verve even placing *Zen Meditation* in their Master Edition series. The lesser-known *Tony Scott* has just been reissued, and it acts as a strange staging post between Scott's jazz past and his then-present: there's a 'Homage To Lord Krishna' with Walcott and an 'Ode To An Oud', but there's also a coolly impressive 'Blues For Charlie Parker', quartet tracks with Rubenstein, Davis and Lovelace, and a duet with Davis on 'Sophisticated Lady' where Scott plays baritone. An early crossover into world music which must have seemed potent in their day; now they're charming period-pieces for hippie reminiscence.

★★★(★) **African Bird**

Soul Note 121083 *Scott; Glenn Ferris (tb); Giancarlo Barigozzi (f, bf); Chris Hunter (as, f); Duncan Kinnel (mar); Rex Reason (kalimba); Robin Jones, Karl Potter (perc); Jacqui Benar (v).* 81–5/84.

Conceived and performed before 'World Music' had become a sneer, *African Bird* is a largely convincing synthesis of Scott's African and Afro-American concerns into a suite of songs with an impressive level of coherence and developmental logic. To all intents and purposes it is a solo record, with largely incidental colorations from all but Barigozzi and Kinnel, who both play beautifully. For a flavour of where Scott has been since 1960, this is ideal.

Al Sears (1910–90)

TENOR SAXOPHONE

Joined the Chick Webb band in 1928, then led his own group for much of the '30s. A famous spell with Ellington, 1944–9, then in the '50s he started his own publishing house and played in rock'n'roll shows.

★★(★) **Swing's The Thing**

Original Jazz Classics OJC 838 *Sears; Don Abney (p); Wally Richardson (g); Wendell Marshall (b); Joe Marshall (d).* 11/60.

A minor Ellingtonian, Sears did rather better out of music publishing and became one of the few jazzmen to make money out of rock'n'roll. His Websterish sound is seldom more than a fair copy of the master, and on this plain and unremarkable date he ambles through some blues, some Ellington, and quite a decent take on 'Out Of Nowhere'. The band are very ordinary, and perhaps the curious should go to some of Ellington's '40s records to hear Sears at his most effective.

Gene Sedric (1907–63)

CLARINET, TENOR SAXOPHONE

Best known for his association with Fats Waller, Sedric also worked for Don Redman and Mezz Mezzrow, among others. Made a modest splash on his own account with a lively and accurately pitched clarinet sound.

★★★ **Gene Sedric 1938–1947**

Classics 1181 *Sedric; Herman Autrey, Henry Mason (t); Henry Duncan (p); Freddie Lee Jefferson (p, d); Albert Casey (g); Lincoln Mills (acc, v); Cedric Wallace (b); Wilmore Slick Jones (d); Myra Johnson, Ruby Smith (v).* 11/38–1/47.

Good-natured jazz from the man from St Louis. Sedric recorded a few sides on his own account in 1938 and then again in 1946 and that was just about it as far as solo recordings are concerned. He plays and sings some greasy blues and solos briskly on both clarinet and tenor, but he was never a virtuoso and it's hard to get too excited about any of these cuts. It's the association with Ruby Smith towards the end of the period covered that probably works best. 'The Wail Of The Scromph' and 'Music To My Sorrow' are both intriguing originals.

Janet Seidel

VOCAL, PIANO

Raised in a small South Australian country town, Seidel began singing in the '80s and has since recorded frequently and risen to the top of her native jazz scene.

★★(★) **Winter Moon**

La Brava LB 0002 *Seidel; Tom Baker (c, as, ts, v); Ian Date (g); David Seidel (b); Billy Ross (d).* 93.

★★(★) **Doodlin'**

La Brava LB 9504 *As above, except add Glenn Henrich (vib).* 6–7/94.

★★★ **The Art Of Lounge**

La Brava LB 9702 *Seidel; Tom Baker (c); Paul Williams (cl, ts); Col Nolan (p, org); Kevin Hunt (p); David Seidel (b); John Morrison, Len Barnard (d); Ian Bloxsom (perc); David Mcleod (v); strings.* 2–8/97.

★★★(★) **The Way You Wear Your Hat**

La Brava LB 9801 2CD *Seidel; Bob Jeffery (saxes, f); Kevin Hunt (p, acc); David Seidel (b); Billy Ross (d).* 9/98.

★★★ **Love Letters**

La Brava LB 0034 *Seidel; William Galison (hca); Kevin Hunt (p); Chuck Morgan (g); David Seidel (b); Adam Pache, Len Barnard (d).* 2/00.

★★★(★) **Don't Smoke In Bed**

La Brava LB 0050 *Seidel; Don Burrows (cl, as, f); Kevin Hunt (p); Chuck Morgan (g); David Seidel (b); Adam Pache (d).* 3/02.

Janet Seidel is Australia's first lady of jazz singing. She's not an ambitious singer: there're very few liberties taken with melody or time, she doesn't scat much if at all, and she's never too far from the beat. The pleasure in her voice is in her perfect tuning, accurate intonation and obvious pleasure in working through a lyric. There aren't many shadows in her music, but it isn't annoyingly upbeat either: she's gracious and affectionate with her songs. There are times where she might seem more like a cabaret singer than a jazz cat, but she isn't really an entertainer in that sense and she keeps a proper jazz group behind her (including her bassist-brother David) all the way through these albums. *Winter Moon* and *Doodlin'*, the latter really a duet record with the late Tom Baker, are a rather modest start: her singing's already pleasing, but the production on both discs is very flat and they tend to drift past without making much impression. *The Art Of Lounge* sounds much better, with some suitably luscious string charts, and if it's only a beat away from MOR that scarcely seems to matter on quality material such as 'I Got Lost In His Arms' and 'The Sweetest Sounds'. *The Way You Wear Your Hat* is perhaps the best place to hear her, since it offers a sparky studio set and a live disc made the day before (where it's rather a shock to hear her say 'Thank you very much' in a South Australian twang).

Love Letters puts Galison up as featured guest and if your taste runs to harmonica in this setting it may appeal rather more than it does to us. *Don't Smoke In Bed*, though, is a beauty: doing a Peggy Lee homage seems a bit tired at this point, but Janet clearly loves the material and there are quite gorgeous versions of 'Street Of Dreams' and the title-song among others.

Trygve Seim

TENOR AND SOPRANO SAXOPHONES

Young Norwegian reedsman with some fresh ideas on life after jazz.

★★★★ Different Rivers

ECM 159521-2 *Seim; Arve Henriksen (t, v, trumpophone); Øyvind Braekke (tb); Hild Sofie Tafjord (frhn); Nils Jansen (sno, bsx, cbcl); Håvard Lund (cl, bcl); Stain Carstyensen (acc); Berbnt Simen Lund, Morten Hannisdal (clo); David Gald (tba); Per Oddvar Johansen (d); Sidsel Endresen (v).* 98–99.

Seim's debut is little short of amazing. Not since Edward Vesala's *Lumi* has there been such a riveting opening to an ECM session as 'Sorrows'. Seim's music seems to follow a direct route from the great early discs by Garbarek, Arild Andersen and Vesala. There are no guitars and no keyboards; Seim is interested in human breath, the sound in wind instruments. In the magnificent 'Ulrika Dans' he leads nine musicians through a carefully shaded score that's a small masterpiece of writing for horns, hoisted aloft by Johansen's brilliant drum part and illuminated by the leader's own tenor solo. He seems to have a knack for making a band sound conversational and ritualistic at the same moment. 'Different Rivers' itself is a splicing of two versions of the same piece, with the musicians doubling on different instruments, a seamless montage which seems different on every hearing. In the stately procession of 'Breathe', over Sidsel Endresen's recitation, everything is sublimated into long cathedral chords that suggest a never-ending echo. A pretty extraordinary start.

★★★(★) The Source And Different Cikadas

ECM 014432-2 *Seim; Arve Henriksen (t); Øyvind Braekke (tb); Frode Haltli (acc, b-t); Christian Wallumrod (p); Odd Hannisdal, Henrik Hannisdal (vn); Marek Konstantynowicz (vla); Morten Hannisdal (clo); Finn Guttormsen (b); Per Oddvar Johansen (d).* 11/00.

'The Source' is the group led by Seim and Braekke, and the Cikada Quartet are the chief collaborators here. Again, Seim is exploring just how human he can make these instruments, what voicings he can conjure from a hypersensitive (in the best sense) cast of players. When part of a Łutosławski string quartet slips into the programme it fits right in, but jazz survives too, in the stately, dead-slow swing of 'Mmball' or the deadpan amusement of 'Fort-Jazz'. The final improvisation 'Tutti Free' closes the circle, and if it looks as if it was a cop-out bringing in a piano, it should be noted that Wallumrod (superb anyway) plays on only five of fifteen tracks. If this isn't quite the transfixing experience which the debut was, it's still very fine.

Esmond Selwyn

GUITAR

Gifted British guitarist making own-name debut.

★★★ Follow That

Slam CD 240 *Selwyn; Paul Sawtell (ky); Bill Coleman (b); Robin Jones (d).* 11/99.

And we're confident that he will follow this promising but flawed first shot with something better still. Selwyn has a lovely touch and his ballad-playing on 'Prelude To A Kiss' is to die for. He's also assembled a very capable and responsive band. Perhaps the music needs a touch more dynamic variation, but no complaints: this is a name to watch.

Archie Semple (1928–74)

CLARINET

Edinburgh-born, Semple worked with Alex Welsh's band for some ten years from 1954. A nervous breakdown ruined his career and he played little after 1964.

★★★ Night People

Lake LACD 187 *Semple; Alex Welsh (t); Fred Hunt (p); Jack Fallon (b).* 60–61.

Semple had only a few turns in the limelight, and two of them – the LPs *Jazz For Young Lovers* and *Night People* – are reissued here. Half of the tracks are by Semple, Hunt and Fallon alone, but Archie's old boss Alex Welsh is on the rest. The music may be played by a group of trad stars, but it's more like – as the title suggests – a series of nocturnes, tranquil ballads given a musing and respectful treatment. A lot of the way, the clarinettist hardly bothers to depart from the melodies, and it's all in the breathy, slightly gargled tone which used to call up comparisons with Pee Wee Russell. The tracks with Welsh are a little saltier, and to that end a shade more satisfying. Our relatively modest grading is down to the slightly indigestible nature of the record: these were the sort of albums best played a side at a time, and 22 tracks in this vein is perhaps too much of a certain good thing. The originals are these days very rare, though, and Paul Adams of Lake is to be congratulated on bringing them back. A reissue of Semple's *It's Right Here For You* will be a future treat in this series.

Boyd Senter (1897–?)

CLARINET, ALTO AND TENOR SAXOPHONES

Born in Nebraska, Senter first learned piano, then switched to clarinet. He made many records as a soloist in the '20s and worked in Detroit during the '30s, eventually selling sports equipment and hardware items as well as playing.

★★★ Jazzologist Supreme 1928–1930

Timeless CBC 1-032 *Senter; Phil Napoleon, Mickey Bloom, James Migliore (t); Bill Haukenheiser (c); Tommy Dorsey, Charlie Butterfield, Ray Stilwell, Herb Winfield (tb); Fud Livingston (cl, ts); Jimmy Dorsey (as); Jack Russell, Frank Signorelli (p); Eddie Lang, Carl Kress (g); Dan Calker (bj, g); Ward Lay (b); Vic Berton, Stan King, Walter Meyer (d).* 3/28–6/30.

Senter is a wryly beloved figure among collectors of early jazz. The 'Jazzologist Supreme' was shameless in producing some horrible sounds on the clarinet, and his most outlandish playing makes even Ted Lewis sound like Artie Shaw. Yet even in the midst of his barnyard phrasing and jackass effects, one can often discern a surprisingly tough and hard-bitten musician. He must have had some sense of humour about his music – why else would he name his band The Senterpedes? – and on the sessions where he's joined by the likes of Napoleon, Lang and the Dorseys there is the obvious compensation of some hot and classy New York jazz to set beside Senter's vaudevillian routines. In any case, tracks like 'Prickly Heat' and 'Mobile Blues' muster their own peculiar intensity. This is by no means a comprehensive edition of Senter's music (he even recorded several masters for Paramount) but it is a useful and excellently remastered group of his OKeh recordings. Brian Rust's sleeve-notes reveal that The Boss Of The Stomps eventually retired to selling saw blades and fishing tackle in Mio, Michigan.

Eddie Severn

TRUMPET

Gifted Scot, recently somewhat eclipsed by Colin Steele.

***** Moments In Time**

Caber 016 *Severn; Phil Bancroft (ss, ts); Paul Harrison (p); Mario Caribe (b); Tom Bancroft (d).* 01.

Severn's credentials are impeccable, as is his playing. With a rich, broad tone, he is capable of tackling anything from rugged bebop to a subtly inflected ballad. As with most debut albums, *Moments In Time* attempts too much and doesn't do enough of it thoroughly. There are, though, moments to savour here, notably Bill Evans's 'Very Early' and a wonderful version of Herbie Hancock's 'Dolphin Dance'. Smart to build in this repertory stuff rather than pack the date with 'originals', though 'The Lost World' (with P. Bancroft on soprano) is a delight. The saxophonist shows up for one other tune and another interesting choice, Harold Land's 'Rapture'. Severn is an established player who will one day make a genuinely significant statement.

Sextet Of Orchestra USA

GROUP

Kurt Weill splinter group from vintage big band.

***** Mack The Knife**

Koch 8588 *Thad Jones (c); Nick Travis (t); Michael Zwerin (tb); Eric Dolphy, Jerome Richardson (as, bcl); Jimmy Raney (g); Richard Davis (b); Connie Kay (d).* 1–6/64.

Convened by Mike Zwerin and formerly on RCA, this is a thoughtful and still durable reworking of Weill themes by a group of seasoned jazz hands who – Zwerin, Jones and Davis particularly – understood better than most the trade-off between jazz and various European musics. Recorded towards the tail end of the Third Stream experiment, it has some faintly grandiose classical pretensions, but what's wonderful about these recordings of 'Moritat', 'Alabama Song', 'Pirate Jenny' and others is how idiomatic and also freshly original they sound. Dolphy completists will want it, not least for his bass-clarinet-playing on the opening 'Alabama Song', one of the highlights of Eric's short career, and poignantly close to the end of his life. Travis and Richardson were on hand to make up the numbers at the later session.

Bud Shank (born 1926)

ALTO SAXOPHONE, FLUTE, PENNY WHISTLE

Originally a tenor-player, Shank switched to the smaller horn while working with Charlie Barnet and Stan Kenton, adding the flute to his armoury. The Ohioan's light, tender touch was a significant component of the Lighthouse All Stars sound, and Shank was the founder of the L.A. 4. Like many of the cool West Coast school, he turned to bebop rather late in his career.

***** Jazz In Hollywood**

Original Jazz Classics OJC 1890 *Shank; Shorty Rogers (flhn); Jimmy Rowles, Lou Levy (p); Harry Babasin (b); Roy Harte, Larry Bunker (d).* 3/54–9/54.

***** Cool Fool**

Fresh Sound FSRCD 148 *Shank; Maynard Ferguson (t); Bob Brookmeyer, Bob Enevoldsen (tb); Claude Williamson (p); Joe Mondragon (b); Shelly Manne (d).* 54, 55.

***** Bud Shank & Bill Perkins**

Blue Note 93159 *Shank; Bill Perkins (as, ts, f); Hampton Hawes, Jimmy Rowles (p); Red Mitchell, Carson Smith, Ben Tucker, Leroy Vinnegar (b); Mel Lewis, Shelly Manne (d).* 5/55–58.

***** Live At The Haig**

Candid CCD 71030 *Shank; Claude Williamson (p); Don Prell (b); Chuck Flores (d).* 56.

***** Blowin' Country**

Blue Note 94846 *Shank; Bob Cooper (ts, bcl, ob); Claude Williamson (p); Don Prell (b); Chuck Flores (d).* 11/56–6/57.

***** Bud Shank Quartet**

Fresh Sound FSR CD 129 *Shank; Claude Williamson (p); Don Prell (b); Chuck Flores, Jimmy Pratt (d).* 11/56–4/58.

Bud Shank has been the quintessential West Coast altoman for more than 40 years. He has appeared on numberless sessions but his playing has remained sharp, piercingly thoughtful and swinging in a lean, persuasive way. For a long spell he was considered cool to the point of frigidity, and his later work has grown fiercer and more inclined to collar the listener; but the early albums have a kind of snake-eyed ingenuity which has its own appeal. The trombones album is material originally released on ten-inch LPs, good for a glimpse of Ferguson and Brookmeyer in their early years but disappointing as a Shank set. *Jazz In Hollywood* is an interesting find, two rather rare albums for the Nocturne label combined on one disc. One was Shank's debut, with a quintet including frequent partner Rogers; the other features a trio date for Lou Levy. *Live At The Haig* is a strong set, marked by some fine Shank alto and some very good piano-playing from Williamson. *Quartet* rounds up some stray TV and South African dates, including one where Shank tries out the penny whistle. None of these is exactly vintage Bud.

The two Blue Notes, originally on Pacific, were reissued in 1998. Both are effectively co-led sessions with Bill Perkins and Bob Cooper respectively, though the Perkins material is drawn from a number of mid- to late-'50s dates and includes a trio version of 'I Hear Music' with just Hampton Hawes and rhythm. Though bitty, it's a fine record. Bob Cooper brings his usual range of alternative horns to his session. The title comes from a Shank tune and doesn't refer to country and western music. Most of the tunes are familiar enough, but the set includes the lovely 'Two Lost Souls', the Steve Allen theme, and a delightful short version of 'I've Grown Accustomed To Her Face'.

***** California Concert**

Original Jazz Classics OJC 948 *Shank; Shorty Rogers (flhn); George Cables (p); Monty Budwig (b); Sherman Ferguson (d).* 5/85.

In more recent years Shank deployed a tougher bebop idiom, still with the same lyrical edge and softness of tone but with sharper and more incisive phrasing, and a shorter line. *California Concert* is relatively tame, but it's one of the few examples of these old friends playing together in their later years.

****** Lost In The Stars**

Fresh Sound FSRCD 18 *Shank; Lou Levy (p).* 12/90.

*****(*) I Told You So!**

Candid CCD 79533 *Shank; Kenny Barron (p); Lonnie Plaxico (b); Victor Lewis (d).* 6/92.

***** Lopin'**

Hep CD 134 *Shank; Don Lanphere (ts); Denny Goodhew (as); Marc Seales (p); Doug Miller (b); John Bishop (d).* 92.

*****(*) New Gold!**

Candid CCD 79707 *Shank; Conte Candoli (t); Bill Perkins (ts, ss); Jack Nimitz (bs); John Clayton (b); Sherman Ferguson (d).* 12/93.

Lost In The Stars is a Sinatra songbook, marked by the quirky brilliance of Levy (an accompanists' accompanist) and by Shank's attractive alto sound which sounds as if it's been in and out of retirement as often as the man himself. 'This Love Of Mine', a much-overlooked standard, is played masterfully, with just the right balance of sentiment and cynicism.

Lopin' is a nice bright set, taken at a comfortable pace. Goodhew is an underrated player and Seales is worthy of notice too, but it's Shank who dominates, sounding relaxed and unhurried whenever he takes a solo. Nice sound, very faithfully captured, with lots of room round the players.

New Gold! sees him steering comfortably towards his 70th birthday. Shank's own playing is exemplary, but it is Perkins who shapes the music round himself on this date. Though the varied package of songs suits Shank perfectly, he doesn't shine quite as brightly as he had on the previous *I Told You So!*, a splendidly gritty performance with a fine rhythm section.

***** Plays The Music Of Bill Evans**

Fresh Sound FSR 5012 *Shank; Mike Wofford (p); Bob Magnusson (b); Joe LaBarbera (d).* 3/96.

Bud and Linda Shank were sorting through their music room when they came across a folder of charts which Bill Evans had put together for a date that never happened. This quartet session picked up the threads. Some of the tunes are beautifully handled, and Bud's original 'Evanescent' is a particular highlight. However, some of them are too stridently delivered ('Funkellero' is steamrollered), as if Shank were for once trying too hard, and the record is a bit too long.

*****(*) By Request**

Milestone 9273 *Shank; Cyrus Chestnut (p); George Mraz (b); Lewis Nash (d).* 97.

The veteran altoman is still in formidable form on this meeting with another top-flight trio. Eleven standards are dealt with minus fuss or circumstance, and if he substitutes a rough intensity for some of the guile of his younger self, the music seems very alive.

***** After You, Jeru**

Fresh Sound FSRCD 5028 *Shank; Mike Wofford (p); Bob Magnusson (b); Joe LaBarbera (d).* 12/98.

With the exception of the title-piece, which closes the record, the whole album is devoted to Mulligan compositions. Shank's tenderest statement for years will appeal even to those who are unconvinced by his light and undramatic playing. The album strengthens as it advances and the closing sequence, with 'Night Lights', 'Theme For Jobim' and the title-piece in close proximity, is very fine indeed. Otherwise, rather low-key.

****** Silver Storm**

RAW 301 *Shank; Conte Candoli (t); Bill Perkins (ts); Bill Mays (p); Bob Magnusson (b); Joe LaBarbera (d).* 9/99.

This album hides a complete surprise. Nestled away in the middle is 'Perkolator', a slice of dissonant free-jazz that is as unlike the other tracks on this pretty straightahead hard-bop session as you could imagine. It's the kind of stroke Shank has been able to pull over the years, and now in his 70s he's disinclined to put on pipe and slippers. There is nothing low-key about the session, which swings briskly from the off, with all three horn-players anxious to show that they've as much energy as ever. Bud's in great form on Gerry Mulligan's 'Idol Gossip' and he burns through his solos on 'My Shining Hour', 'Cotton Blossom' (which sounds familiar, though not under that name) and 'Yardbird Suite'. Candoli and Perkins are in cracking form, too, and Bill's easy lope on the slower numbers is the perfect foil to Shank's impatience. What about 'Perkolator', though? If it's there as a joke, it's a very good one and it'll always win you double points at a blindfold session.

***** On The Trail**

RAW 202 *Shank; Conte Candoli (t); Jay Thomas (ss, ts); Bill Mays (p); Bob Magnusson (b); Joe LaBarbera (d).* 01.

Conte Candoli died just before Christmas 2001. This was the last time he and Shank played together and, while it's by no means a vintage performance, it's a very effective and sometimes moving reminder of their long association. The Count is bright and almost antagonistic on the opening title-number, but for the most part he prefers a lower, softer register and a more spacious approach to theme statements and solos. Perhaps it's wishful hindsight, but Bud seems to give him lots of room, keeping his own solo statements relatively compact except on 'Tommyhawk' and the delightful 'California Medley'. We've listed it separately from the session above because, similar as the two groups are, they're in very different form here, far less hectic and almost elegiac.

Artie Shaw (born 1910)

CLARINET

Arthur Arshawsky was born in New York and was a dance-band musician before forming his own ensemble in 1936. His orchestra became one of the major swing-era big bands, and his use of strings and arrangements blending commercialism with interesting musical values was almost unique of its kind. But Shaw was a contrary soul, critical of any pandering to audiences, and he formed and disbanded several orchestras during the period 1939–44. As a clarinettist, he was as accomplished as Benny Goodman and, like Goodman, was the major soloist in his own band. He had several marriages, became a gifted writer of fiction and was interested in psychoanalysis. But he was entirely disillusioned with the business of music, and after 1949 he rarely performed again. In the '80s and '90s he returned to conducting, although he himself no longer played.

**(*) Artie Shaw 1936

Classics 855 *Shaw; Willie Kelly, Lee Castaldo, Dave Wade, Zeke Zarchy (t); Mark Bennett, Mike Michaels, Buddy Morrow (tb); Tony Zimmers, Tony Pastor (ts); Fulton McGrath, Joe Lippman (p); Wes Vaughan, Tony Gottuso, Gene Stultz (g); Hank Wayland, Ben Ginsberg (b); Sammy Weiss, George Wettling (d); Peg La Centra (v); Julie Schechter, Lou Klaymann, Sam Persoff, Jimmy Oderich, Jerry Gray, Frank Siegfield, Bill Schumann, Ben Plotkin (strings).* 6–11/36.

*** In The Beginning

Hep CD 1024 *As above.* 6–12/36.

*** Artie Shaw 1936–1937

Classics 886 *Shaw; Lee Castle, Zeke Zarchy, John Best, Malcolm Crain, Tom Di Carlo (t); Buddy Morrow, Harry Rodgers, George Arus (tb); Les Robinson, Art Masters, Harry Freeman (as); Tony Pastor (ts, v); Fred Petry (ts); Joe Lippman, Les Burness (p); Tony Gottuso, Al Avola (g); Ben Ginsberg (b); Sam Weiss, Cliff Leeman (d); Peg La Centra (v); Jerry Gray, Sam Persoff, Bill Schumann (strings).* 12/36–7/37.

*** The Chant

Hep 1046 *As above.* 12/36–8/37.

*** Artie Shaw 1937

Classics 929 *As above, except add Jules Rubin (ts), Dolores O'Neil, Nita Bradley, Bea Wain, Leo Watson (v); omit Castle, Zarchy, Morrow, Masters, Petry, Lippman, Gottuso, Weiss, Gray, Persoff, Schumann, La Cetra.* 8–12/37.

*** Non-Stop Flight

Hep 1048 *As above.* 8–12/37.

Among the most picaresque of jazz figures, Shaw has had an amazing life which makes his records seem tame. They form a unique part of the jazz literature, although his real successes were comparatively few and his ambitions always outran his achievements. One problem was having relatively lightweight bands. Certainly his sessions for Brunswick, which represent the start of his story on record and which are collected here, have only himself as any kind of soloist, and with haphazard material and the oddly backward rhythm section, it's unsurprising that Shaw was considered minor league at the start of the swing era. But there are glimmers of light, and there is the then extraordinary sound of the string section meeting the band on numbers like 'Sugar Foot Stomp' and 'Sobbin' Blues'. Shaw's second band (his 'New Music') arrived in 1937 and soon sounded like a sleeker and more powerful unit, though the great finesse of the Victor sides was yet to become apparent – even Shaw's playing is hit and miss. 'Nightmare', which would later be his first theme, showed a more interesting direction, and with the hiring of Leo Watson as vocalist, the band seemed a much hipper outfit.

The Classics and Hep releases follow a similar course, but while Hep's transfers are usually clean and clear, the Classics tracks are another motley lot – some with huge amounts of surface noise, some very loud, others muddy. None of this is deathless material, but the Hep records are clearly the ones to get.

***(*) Artie Shaw 1938

Classics 965 *Shaw; Chuck Peterson, John Best, Claude Bowen, Bernie Privin (t); George Arus, Ted Vesley, Harry Rodgers, Russell Brown, Les Jenkins (tb); Les Robinson, Hank Freeman, George Koenig (as); Tony Pastor (ts, v); Ronnie Perry, Georgie Auld (ts); Les Burness, Bob Kitsis (p); Al Avola (g); Sid Weiss (b); Cliff Leeman, George Wettling (d); Billie Holiday, Helen Forrest (v).* 7–12/38.

**** Artie Shaw 1939

Classics 1007 *As above, except add Buddy Rich (d); omit Bowen, Vesley, Brown, Koenig, Burness, Leeman, Wettling and Holiday.* 1–3/59.

***(*) Artie Shaw 1939 Vol. 2

Classics 1045 *Similar to above.* 3–8/39.

***(*) Artie Shaw 1939–1940

Classics 1087 *Shaw; Chuck Peterson, Billy Butterfield, Harry Geller, Bernie Privin, Charles Margulis, Manny Klein, George Thow (t); George Arus, Les Jenkins, Harry Rogers, Randall Miller, Bill Rank, Babe Bowman (tb); John (Jack) Cave (frhn); Les Robinson, Hank Freeman, Blake Reynolds, Bud Carlton, Jack Stacey, Ben Kanter, Lyle Bowen (as); Tony Pastor (ts, v); Georgie Auld, Dick Clark, Happy Lawson (ts); Joe Krechter (bcl); Morton Ruderman (f); Phil Nemoli (ob); Bob Kitsis, Stan Wrightsman, Lyle Henderson (p); Al Avola, Bobby Sherwood (g); Sid Weiss, Jud DeNaut (b); Buddy Rich, Carl Maus, Spencer Prinz (d); Helen Forrest, Pauline Byrne, Martha Tilton (v); strings.* 8/39–5/40.

Although 'Begin The Beguine' made him a success – Shaw switched the original beguine beat to a modified 4/4, and its lilting pulse was irresistible – the huge hit he scored with it was greeted with loathing when it dawned on him what it meant in terms of fawning fans and general notoriety. He never seemed satisfied with his bands, and the four different orchestras on the Bluebird compilation played through a series of break-ups and disbandments by the leader. The second band, with arrangements by Jerry Gray and with Buddy Rich powering the rhythm section, was a harder-hitting outfit than the original Shaw 'New Music'. But best sides are still scattered, although the new Shaw-selected box (listed at the end of this entry) rectifies matters somewhat.

Classics have the first four Victor sessions with its first disc (in reasonable if sometimes rather brutal-sounding remasters). A generous 24 tracks make an impressive disc. It starts with 'Begin the Beguine' and goes on through many of Shaw's most enterprising records. Billie Holiday turns in her one Shaw appearance on 'Any Old Time' and there are ten appealing vocals by Helen Forrest. But it's the gusto of the band and Shaw's piercing solos one remembers, a quite astonishing advance on the music of only a little over a year earlier. This sounds like a swing master close to full command.

Classics 1007 carries on the story in style – these are good-sounding transfers. One is impressed with how often Shaw got a musical result of one sort or another. Listen to the way the band makes the melody line of 'The Man I Love' sing, or how Shaw makes the most of even a bit of hokum like 'The Donkey Serenade'. Only ten of the 22 tracks sport a vocal – a very low strike-rate compared to most other white bands of the day – and even then Shaw could boast the admirable Helen Forrest as his singer. It's sometimes disappointing that there weren't more interesting soloists to emerge from the band, but Shaw by himself is always worth listening to. Track for track, this is a marvellous portrait of a swing band.

Classics 1045 sees a slackening in the quality of the material, but Shaw still delivers some excellent individual records such as 'One Foot In the Groove' and 'Out Of Nowhere', as well as the hit coupling of 'Traffic Jam' and 'Serenade To A Savage'. Even on the more routine songs, the band's accomplished playing draws its own rewards, and Forrest's singing is a further bonus. Classics 1087 has its own share of indifferent material – despite featuring 'Oh! Lady Be Good', a terrific chart and one of Shaw's biggest hits – and Forrest has to sing some real fluff on the first four sessions, after which Shaw broke up the band and retreated to Mexico. He was back in Los Angeles only months later with a new band, this time with strings attached. It was a recording outfit only and never appeared live; but the experiment worked, since it gave Shaw another big hit in 'Frenesi'. Mainly good transfers again, although here and there we detected a strange hint of speed wobble in the sound.

***** Live In 1938–39 Vol. I**

Phontastic CD 7609 *Shaw; Chuck Peterson, Claude Bowen, John Best, Bernie Privin (t); George Arus, Russell Brown, Harry Rodgers, Les Jenkins (tb); Les Robinson, Hank Freeman, Tony Pastor, Ronnie Perry, Georgie Auld (reeds); Les Burness, Bob Kitsis (p); Al Avola (g); Sid Weiss (b); Cliff Leeman, Buddy Rich, George Wettling (d); Helen Forrest (v).* 11/38–1/39.

***** Live In 1938–39 Vol. II**

Phontastic CD 7613 *As above, except omit Bowen, Brown, Burness, Perry, Wettling and Leeman.* 1–3/39.

***** Live In 1939 Vol. III**

Phontastic CD 7628 *As above.* 2–5/39.

*****(*) King Of The Clarinet 1938–39**

Hindsight HBCD-502 3CD *As above discs.* 11/38–11/39.

***** 1938–39 Old Gold Shows**

Jazz Hour 1009 *Probably as above discs.* 38–39.

Airshots by the 1938–9 band. The Phontastics offer a broad survey. Like all such ancient history, there is period charm (the announcements, the hysterical applause) as well as period dross and even a decent amount of good music. Some of the tracks are too short to have much impact, but there are some more extended pieces that show the band at full stretch: a fast and sassy 'Carioca' and a long treatment of 'The Chant' that prefigures something of 'Concerto For Clarinet'. These are both on Volume III, but there are interesting things on the first two discs as well, notably otherwise unrecorded items such as 'The Yam' (Volume I), Shaw playing Ellington with 'Diga Diga Doo' (Volume II) and some alternative versions of hits like 'Back Bay Shuffle' (also Volume II). The sound is very mixed: quite sharp and clear on some pieces, very fusty on others. These are mainly for Shaw specialists. Hindsight's three-disc set may be a first choice for those wanting a generous survey: splendidly packaged and annotated, with interesting comments on most of these versions by Shaw himself, they underline how this band's airshots throw a strikingly different light on how a big band worked outside the studios. (Shaw himself has recently commented how he prefers the band's airshot versions of some of their best-known numbers.) The sound isn't as bright as on some of these reissues, but there's a lot to enjoy across the three discs. Jazz Hour's compilation is another good one, and it has some more strong material: 'In The Mood', 'Back Bay Shuffle' and 'Copenhagen', among others. Very clean sound for the period.

***** Hollywood Palladium 1941**

Hep 19 *Shaw; Billy Butterfield, George Wendt, Jack Cathcart, Steve Lipkins, Lee Castle, Hot Lips Page, Max Kaminsky, Bobby Hackett (t); Vernon Brown, Bruce Squires, Morey Samuel, Ray Conniff, Jack Jenney, Elmer Smithers (tb); Charlie DiMaggio, Les Robinson, Neely Plumb (as); Jerry Jerome, Bus Bassey, Georgie Auld, Mickey Folus (ts); Johnny Guarnieri (p); Al Hendrickson, Mike Bryan (g); Jud DeNaut, Ed McKimmey (b); Nick Fatool, Dave Tough (d); strings.* 7/40–9/41.

***** In Hollywood 1940–41 Vol. 2**

Hep 55 *Similar to above.* 9/40–3/41.

Two further discs of airshots, culled from numerous Hollywood broadcasts, where Shaw was working on films and the Burns and Allen show. Most of the arrangements are by either Lennie Hayton or Ray Conniff, and the various bands on display – some with strings, some not – make light work of them. The first disc is slightly more interesting, with an alternative version of 'Concerto For Clarinet' and some rousing work by Hot Lips Page and Georgie Auld on the final tracks. The second, though, has a very fine treatment of 'Star Dust'. The material is taken from surviving acetates, and some of those on the first disc haven't worn as well as they might. Interesting footnotes for the Shaw specialist.

***** Artie Shaw 1940**

Classics 1127 *Shaw; Harry Geller, Manny Klein, George Thow, Billy Butterfield, George Wendt, Jack Cathcart (t); Jack Jenny, Vernon Brown (tb); John (Jack) Cave (frhn); Ben Kanter, Lyle Bowen, Jack Stacey, Bus Bassey, Neely Plumb (as); Happy Lawson, Les Robinson, Jerry Jerome (ts); Joe Krechter (bcl); Lyle Henderson (p); Johnny Guarnieri (p, phchd); Bobby Sherwood, Al Hendrickson (g); Jud Denaut (b); Spencer Prinz, Nick Fatool (d); Pauline Byrne, Jack Pearle, Anita Boyer (v); strings.* 5–12/40.

***** Artie Shaw 1940–1941**

Classics 1167 *As above, except add Henry 'Red' Allen (t), Ray Conniff, J. C. Higginbotham (tb), Benny Carter (as), Sonny White (p), Jimmy Shirley (g); Billy Taylor (b), Shep Shepherd (d), Lena Horne (v), omit Geller, Klein, Thow, Cave, Kanter, Bowen, Stacey, Lawson, Krechter, Henderson, Sherwood, Prinz, Byrne, Pearle.* 12/40–6/41.

***** Artie Shaw 1941–1942**

Classics 1206 *Shaw; Hot Lips Page (t, v); Lee Castle, Steve Lipkins, Max Kaminsky (t); Jack Jenney, Ray Conniff, Morey Samuel (tb); Les Robinson, Gene Kinsey, Charlie DiMaggio (as); Georgie Auld, Mickey Folus (ts); Johnny Guarnieri (p); Mike Bryan (g); Eddie McKimmey (b); Dave Tough (d); Bonnie Lake, Paula Kelly, Georgia Gibbs (v); strings.* 9/41–1/42.

The final session by the West Coast band opens Classics 1127. Then comes the first date by the Gramercy Five, Shaw's new small-group-within-a-big-band, which pursued his chamberish ideals further. 'Special Delivery Stomp' and 'Summit Ridge Drive' were its first titles, and remain two of the best. After this, Shaw formed his fourth new orchestra, and its first four sessions yielded an excellent 'Stardust', Elington's 'Pyramid' and William Still's portentous but interesting two-parter 'Blues'.

Classics 1167 has more by the Gramercy Five and some very good orchestra tracks – 'Who's Excited' and 'Georgia On My Mind'. The main interest here is in the two-part 'Concerto For Clarinet' – one of the classic set-pieces of the swing era, kitsch though it may have been – and a final all-star session in which Shaw's clarinet features alongside Henry Allen, J. C. Higginbotham and Benny Carter.

Classics 1206 takes the story on into 1942 – and another new orchestra. The jazz content is under tighter control here, and mood pieces of the order of 'Suite No. 8' and 'Beyond The Blue Horizon' bridge Shaw's ambition with his dancers' requirements. But Lips Page's arrival and occasional feature is a warmer ingredient, and there are one or two more swinging charts such as 'Just Kiddin' Around' and 'Deuces Wild'. Throughout all three discs, Shaw's own playing retains its tough consistency, seemingly oblivious to its various settings, or at least, adaptable to any of them. As usual, the Classics transfers are dependable if a little short on overall sparkle.

****** Artie Shaw 1945**

Classics 1277 *Shaw; Roy Eldridge, Stan Fishelson, Bernie Glow, George Schwartz (t); Gus Dickson, Bob Swift, Ollie Wilson, Harry Rodgers (tb); Lou Prisby, Rudy Tanza (as); Herb Steward, Ralph Roselund, John Walton (ts); Chuck Gentry (bs); Dodo Marmarosa (p); Barney Kessel (g); Morris Rayman (b); Lou Fromm (d); Dorothy Allen.* 6–9/45.

*****(*) Artie Shaw 1945–1946**

Classics 1330 *As above, except add Ray Linn, Paul Cohen, Zeke Zarchy, Clyde Hurley, Manny Klein (t); Fred Fox, Jack Kirksmith, James Decker, Harry Parshal (flhn); Elmer Smithers, Hoyt Bohannon, Joe Howard (tb); Les Robinson, Heinie Beau, Deacon Dunn, Don Raffell, Chuck Gentry, Herman Berardinelli, Joe Krechter, Skeets Herfurt, Harold Lawson (saxes); Harold Lewis (f); Gordon Pope (ob); Jules Seder, Charles Graveer (bsn); Tommy Todd, Mark McIntyre, Milt Raskin (p); Al Hendrickson, Dave Barbour (g); Phil Stephens, Art Shapiro, Morris Rayman (b); Nick Fatool, Lou Singer (d); Kitty Kallen, Hal Stevens, Mel Torme, The Mel-Tones (v); strings.* 7/45–6/46.

***** 1945 Spotlight Bands Broadcasts**

Jazz Unlimited 201 2088 *Unlisted personnel but likely as above discs.* 9–10/45.

The sheer beauty of Shaw's big-band sound comes through most strongly, perhaps, on his mid-'40s dates, and there's hardly a track on Classics 1277 in particular which doesn't luxuriate in it: the reed section is sublime, the trumpets almost golden. There were few vocals to distract (only four on the whole disc) and besides Shaw himself there's Eldridge and Marmarosa, and the set ends on Eddie Sauter's remarkable chart for 'The Maid With The Flaccid Air'. Perhaps the likes of 'Lament' did aspire to be high-quality mood-music, in the then-burgeoning Thornhill manner, but that's Shaw for you.

Classics 1330 isn't quite as good, since half-way through the band depart Victor (where they were handsomely recorded, too) and move to Musicraft, with a newish personnel and banks of strings. The final Victor sessions have some more excellent music, though, and there are four sides with the Gramercy Five. Mel Torme's arrival doesn't hurt, either. The transfers on both discs sound fine. The Jazz Unlimited set collects five broadcast dates from 1945. Dusty sound, but there are plenty of good spots for Eldridge and the leader.

****(*) The Artistry Of Artie Shaw**

Fresh Sound FSCD 2012 *Shaw; Don Fagerquist, Dale Pierce, Vic Ford (t); Sonny Russo, Fred Zito, Angie Callea, Zoltan Cohen (tb); Herbie Steward, Frank Socolow (as); Al Cohn, Zoot Sims (ts); Danny Bank (bs); Gil Barrios (p); Jimmy Raney (g); Dick Nivison (b); Irv Kluger (d).* 12/49.

Considering the personnel and the possibilities – of Shaw meeting the early cool movement, if not bebop – this is a disappointment. Yet more radio transcriptions, these make a so-so fist out of charts that include pieces from the hands of Johnny Mandel and Tadd Dameron. Shaw is his impeccable self as soloist but the others don't get much room, and the rhythm section's dour.

CORE COLLECTION

****** Self Portrait**

Bluebird 09026-63808-2 5CD *As discs above; add Roy Eldridge, Stan Fishelson, Bernie Glow, George Schwartz, Manny Klein, Ray Linn, Clyde Harley (t); Harry Rogers, Gus Dixon, Ollie Wilson, Bob Swift, Si Zentner (tb); Rudy Tanza, Lou Prisby, Skeets Herfurt (as); Herbie Steward, Jon Walon (ts); Chuck Gentry (bs); Dodo Marmarosa, Milt Raskin, Hank Jones (p); Barney Kessel, Tal Farlow, Dave Barbour (g); Morris Rayman, Artie Shapiro, Tommy Potter (b); Lou Fromm, Nick Fatool, Irv Kluger (d); Mel Torme, Mel-Tones, Lillian Lane, Ralph Blane, Kitty Kallen (v).* 9/38–6/54

Selected by Shaw himself, and discussed by the leader in conversation with Richard Sudhalter, this is an impressive shot at the definitive Shaw collection – even if some of it might be thought subject to its maker's own caprices. He sometimes chooses broadcast versions of tunes over their studio originals, and the notes are boastful and self-deprecating at the same moment – inimitable Shaw. His choices reflect his ambitions, though fortunately that seems to have allowed the inclusion of his greatest hits along the way, and it does take the story up to the final sessions of 1954, which are otherwise currently unavailable. We find the remastering by Dennis Ferrante something of a mixed blessing. The later material sounds excellent, but some of the original Bluebird pressings from the late '30s are very hard to get undistorted sparkle from, and this problem doesn't seem to have been completely overcome.

Ian Shaw (born 1962)

VOCAL, PIANO

Born in Wales, Shaw studied music in London where since the late '80s he has worked almost constantly. Performing in musicals as well as clubs he has gained recognition as one of the leading British vocalists of his day, though he prefers to drift betweeen categories rather than be called a jazz singer per se.

*****(*) In A New York Minute**

Milestone 9297-2 *Shaw; Iain Ballamy (as, ts); Cedar Walton (p); David Williams (b).* 9/98.

Shaw has recorded other albums in Britain, but this is the only one likely to receive international distribution. Luckily, it's also his most accomplished and compelling work. The bare-bones accompaniment of Walton and Williams is a setting which would make almost any singer sound good; it takes Shaw close to greatness. Though he's flirted with soul, pop and supper-club styles in the past, he folds all his expertise into a bullseye delivery in these songs. He doesn't really swing in the manner of a Torme descendant and tends to fashion his own tightrope relationship with the beat, which in the past has often seemed jerky. But the urgent mannerisms of 'Standing In the Dark' have taken on a conviction which presents an artist in his maturity and his prime; and the passionate embrace of many of these lyrics recalls a cadre of singers (Mark Murphy is the obvious reference-point) who could mix beat-poetry slickness with torch-song sensuality. The songs are beautifully chosen, from the title-piece (thankfully, Fran Landesmann's song, not Don Henley's lugubrious effort of the same title) to a graceful 'Wouldn't It Be Loverly', to a slow, chastening 'Last Night When We Were Young'. Icing on this cake: Iain Ballamy's sax contributions, which are marvellous.

***** Soho Stories**
Milestone 9316-2 *Shaw; Lew Soloff (t); Papo Vasquez (tb); Eric Alexander, Bob Kindred (ts); Steve Rubie (f); Cedar Walton, James Pearson (p); Joe Beck (g); Chip Jackson (b); Mark Fletcher (d).* 9/00.

Joel Siegel's notes won't please patriotic Britons ('British jazz players don't swing'), even if he's meant to be building up Shaw. And this time the music does site the singer, a little uncomfortably, as a Welshman in New York. The various instrumentations are as accomplished as you'd expect from such top-line professionals, but they quieten Shaw's individuality. The best songs are the least adorned; 'I Never Went Away' is beautifully paced and handled. Yet some of them – the hipsterish 'Be Sure I'll Let You Know', and Janis Ian's awfully melodramatic 'Ruby' – may make the uncommitted wince. Shaw has better records in him yet.

Lee Shaw

PIANO

Contemporary American pianist drawing mostly on the virtuoso end of bop language.

***** Essence**
CIMP 125 *Shaw; Mike DeMicco (g); Rich Syracuse (b).* 9/96.

***** A Place For Jazz**
Cadence CJR 1149 *As above except Jeff Siegel (d) replaces DeMicco.* 11/01.

While we are happy to applaud CIMP's unvarnished recording procedures in principle, *Essence* is one that could have beneficially used a little sweetening. Shaw and her group were recorded live in a club setting, and it does tend to sound as if somebody's pro-Walkman captured the gig. Which is a pity, since the pianist is a gifted and rather intense performer. Art Tatum is cited in the sleeve-notes, which isn't too fanciful, and, allied with a bopper like DeMicco, the music has a virtuosic flavour which is sublimated in tunes like the fast, exhilarating 'Holiday'. Shaw's fundamental lyricism is another plus: she seldom sounds as if she's running through the material with anything less than full commitment. A very interesting encounter.

The concert captured on *A Place For Jazz* was a poignant one, since it took place only two weeks after the death of Stan Shaw, Lee's husband of 40 years' standing. Again, there is some finely accomplished and vigorous playing, with a moving climax in a rendition of Cole Porter's 'I Love You'. Bob Rusch has let his heart rule his head in releasing it, perhaps, since the recording is a poor amateur one which has required a lot of cleaning up and is still a long way from what one expects these days, and for all the merit in the music one feels frustrated that Shaw still waits for a proper representation in the CD era.

Woody Shaw (1944–89)

TRUMPET

Father sang gospel music, and young Woody studied trumpet at 11. Worked with the Eric Dolphy band until 1964, then played in Europe, with Horace Silver, Max Roach and eventually, in the '70s, his own regular bands. Despite his talent and influence on many younger players, his career never really had much luck, and nor did he.

***** Blackstone Legacy**
Contemporary 762728 *Shaw; Gary Bartz (as); Bennie Maupin (ts, bcl); George Cables (p); Ron Carter, Clint Houston (b); Lenny White (d).* 12/70.

*****(*) Song Of Songs**
Original Jazz Classics OJCCD 1893-2 *Shaw; Emmanuel Boyd (ts, f); Bennie Maupin, Ramon Morris (ts); George Cables (p); Henry Franklin (b); Woodrow Theus II (d).* 9/72.

Woody Shaw's career judgement was almost as clouded as his actual vision. A classic under-achiever, his relatively lowly critical standing is a result partly of his musical purism (which was thoroughgoing and admirable) but more largely of his refusal or inability to get his long-term act together. A sufferer from *retinitis pigmentosa* (which severely restricted his sight-reading), he fell under a subway train in the spring of 1989 and died of his injuries.

Woody made his recording debut with Eric Dolphy at the age of 19 in what are usually thought of as the *Iron Man/Jitterbug Waltz* sessions. One reviewer was convinced that 'Woody Sho" was a *nom de session* for Freddie Hubbard, inexplicably when you listen to his Navarro- and Morgan-inspired attack and phrasing. It was Dolphy who taught Woody to play 'inside and outside at the same time', but it was listening to the classics that awakened a player with perfect pitch to the subtler nuances of harmony. Like all imaginative Americans, Woody was violently stretched between opposites and inexorably drawn to the things and the places that would destroy him. Europe drew him for all the usual non-musical reasons, but there is a sense, too, that Woody's foreshortened career represented a sustained fugue from the racially constrained job-description of the 'jazz musician'.

However hardly won, Woody's technique sounded effortless, which disguised the awful disquiet at the root of his music. His influences were not settling ones: at the one extreme Debussy, the most inside-and-outside of the pre-Schoenberg composers; at the other his Newark friend, the organist Larry Young, with whom he recorded the superb *Unity* and who taught him, across the grain of the earlier Hubbardly aggression and linearity, the value of accepting a measure of chaos in music.

Woody's best-known composition was actually premiered on Larry Young's Blue Note classic, *Unity*, but his own version of 'The Moontrane' is currently out of print. The eponymous album, like the rest of Woody's output for Muse, has vanished with the demise of 32 Jazz, leaving the Shaw discography depressingly thin again. Woody's debut as leader was *Blackstone Legacy*. He'd already recorded *Cassandranite/In The Beginning* for Muse, but these sides weren't released until the '80s. The

1970 album is a valuable reappearance, but it is very much tied up with a seismic shift in jazz that followed Miles Davis's *Bitches Brew* experiments and it stands as a rather isolated performance, dense, brooding, overproduced and somewhat slack in execution. Shaw *does* sound like free-range Hubbard on the title-track and 'New World', but he is already finding a voice of his own, somewhere between Miles and the harder-edged boppers. Bartz and Maupin provide strong support and some lovely textures and Cables demonstrates his underrated mastery of the Fender Rhodes.

Song Of Songs was his second record as leader. Wonderful it is, but also undeniably timelocked, heavily dependent on George Cables's electric piano effects, but also swinging and propulsive. Woody's four compositions are still not fully assimilated, and not many contemporary players would attempt something as sardonic as 'The Goat And The Archer'. Redundant as it may be to make the point again, had Shaw been picked up by a sensitive label and producer at this point, afforded the players and the studio time his exacting concept demanded, then who knows what he might have achieved. As it is, these two albums are among the best he did until the brief starburst of the '80s.

***** Live: Volume 1**

High Note 7051 *Shaw; Carter Jefferson (ss, ts); Larry Willis (p); Stafford James (b); Victor Lewis (d). 77.*

***** Live: Volume 2**

High Note 7089 *As above; add Steve Turre (tb). 77.*

***** Live: Volume 3**

High Note 7102 *As above; add Mulgrew Miller (p). 77.*

Imaginatively kicking off with Joe Bonner's 'Love Dance', the first volume is a strong blowing set from what was at the time a pretty settled band, caught at the Keystone Korner. The interaction with Willis (composer of 'Light Valley') and underrated saxophonist Jefferson works very well indeed, and the only longueur on an otherwise strong disc is Lewis's featured 'Why'. And well we might ask.

We had reservations about the value of another two volumes in this sequence and they have been borne out. There is strong playing on all three sets, notably 'Rahsaan's Run' and 'What Is This Thing Called Love?' on Volume 2 and 'Little Red's Fantasy' on Volume 3, but we'd question that any but committed Shaw fans will want the whole set. A judicious double CD would have sufficed, even if it meant missing some interesting work from Steve Turre and Mulgrew Miller, who sat in for part of the residency.

****** Rosewood**

Columbia CK 65519 *Shaw; Steve Turre (tb, btb); Janice Robinson (tb); Carter Jefferson (ss, ts); James Vass (ss, as); Joe Henderson (ts); Frank Wes (f, picc); Art Webb (f); Onaje Allan Gumbs (p); Lois Colin (hp); Clint Houston (b); Victor Lewis (d); Sammy Figueroa, Armen Halburian (perc). 12/77.*

Not for nothing was *Rosewood* voted Best Jazz Album of 1978 in *Down Beat.* It is one of the most ambitious projects Shaw was ever involved in, and though he wrote only one of the pieces performed by the large-scale Concert Ensemble, his hand is evident throughout a well-balanced and expansive set.

Woody's sole writing credit is the title-piece, an idea to set alongside 'The Moontrane' and 'Song Of Songs' as among his very best. The other titles are Victor Lewis's intriguing 'The Legend Of Cheops', Allan Gumbs's 'Every Time I See You' and Clint Houston's nondescript 'Sunshowers'. Significantly, this last is the only track not to feature the splendid Joe Henderson, who graces both the larger ensemble and the small group which delivers 'Rahsaan's Run' and 'Theme For Maxine', another tribute to Mrs Shaw. In Joe's company, Shaw sounds blithe and thoughtful at the same time, riveting bright points of sound into Joe's leathery tone.

A less thoroughly compelling statement than *Song Of Songs*, this immaculately produced CBS session underlines what Shaw might have done if health and inclination had lent his career more shape and consistency.

*****(*) Bemsha Swing Live**

Blue Note CDP 7243 8 29029 2 *Shaw; Geri Allen (p); Robert Hurst (b); Roy Brooks (d). 2/86.*

Ten years after his death, Shaw sounds more than ever like a lost genius, someone whose career was never adequately steered or sufficiently appreciated. These live sessions from Baker's Keyboard Lounge in Detroit are dominated by Monk tunes, and it is fascinating to compare Woody's handling of the bebop keyboard legacy with his reinterpretations of Sonny Clark material at the Mount Fuji Jazz Festival later on that same summer. Fascinating, too, to hear him in the presence of a player of Geri Allen's sensibilities. The long unravelling of 'Well, You Needn't' exposes a few longueurs and what seem to be repetitions in Woody's playing. Closer examination, though, suggests that he was deliberately exploring tiny modulations. His improvisations have a shifting, almost fugitive quality by this stage, but it is still easy to overlook their subtleties.

Allen was probably doing some of her most interesting work at this stage, harmonically adventurous, percussive and rhythmically very tight. There are moments when Hurst and Brooks disappear into the background, leaving the piano to carry the load. 'Bemsha Swing' itself is a cracking opener, and there are also strong interpretations of Wayne Shorter's rarely covered 'United', Woody's own 'Ginseng People' and 'In A Capricornian Way', and a closing reading of 'Star Eyes' that shows how much Shaw learned from earlier boppers like Fats Navarro and Howard McGhee. A strong live set.

George Shearing (born 1919)

PIANO, ACCORDION, VOCAL

Born blind to a poor London family, Shearing trained as a classical pianist but turned to jazz, partly on the advice of his teacher. He played dance-band gigs before settling in the USA in 1946. His quintet, first formed in 1949, lasted for many years and won a huge following for its numerous albums, all of them in a light music smooth-jazz mould. He later worked extensively with Mel Torme and still plays in solo and small-group situations.

***** The London Years**

Hep CD 1042 *Shearing; Leonard Feather (p); Carlo Krahmer (d). 3/39–12/43.*

Shearing's early recordings are in some ways slight, given that he glossed over bop's passion with a tinkling niceness that suggested a clever pianist merely toying with the music. But the occasional parallels with Lennie Tristano suggest the more profound direction Shearing could have gone in; that he chose a more temperate kind of commercial climate leaves one of those might-have-beens that jazz is full of. His earliest records are in any case a showcase of swing piano, recorded in London in the early years of the war. The Hep CD collects 25 tracks and is an enjoyable, witty sequence of solos (there are two early tracks with Krahmer and one with Feather on piano, where Shearing squeezes a few dolorous blues chords out of the accordion). There are many entertaining bits of Tatum, Waller and Wilson in the pianist's style, and these tracks might surprise anyone unfamiliar with his first period.

*****(*) Verve Jazz Masters: George Shearing**
Verve 529900-2 *Shearing; Marjorie Hyams, Cal Tjader, Joe Roland, Don Elliott (vib); Chuck Wayne, Dick Garcia (g); John Levy, Al McKibbon (b); Denzil Best, Marquis Foster, Bill Clark (d); Armando Peraza (perc).* 49–54.

These are the MGM recordings which established the Shearing quintet as a commercial force. Clever rather than profound, appealing rather than attention-grabbing, the front line of piano, vibes and guitar was a refreshing sound which, when allied to memorable themes such as 'Lullaby Of Birdland', proved immensely popular. Shearing had been listening closely to bebop and synthesized what he needed from it to make a cool, modern sound. At this distance, away from any controversy about its standing, the results are smoothly enjoyable on any level. This compilation brings together the expected hits and the slightly more challenging material such as 'Conception', which was once covered by Miles Davis (although Shearing has recently complained that Miles got the bridge wrong!).

*****(*) Quintets At Newport**
Pablo 5315-2 *Shearing; Nat Adderley (t); Cannonball Adderley (as); Emil Richards (vib); Toots Thielemans (g); Al McKibbon (b); Percy Brice (d); Armando Peraza (perc).* 7/57.

While this is shared with a brief set by the Cannonball Adderley quintet, the Shearing music (from the 1957 Newport Festival) is the more remarkable. They open with a furiously fast Ray Brown tune, 'Pawn Ticket', which is enough to leave the leader out of breath for his following announcement. Thereafter it's more like business as usual until the Adderleys themselves sit in for a tumultuous blues, 'Soul Station', which once again leaves George breathless. Coupled with five strong Adderley numbers, this is all in wonderful high spirits.

***** Two For The Road**
Concord CCD 4128 *Shearing; Carmen McRae (v).* 80.

***** Alone Together**
Concord CCD 4171 *Shearing; Marian McPartland (p).* 3/81.

**** Grand Piano**
Concord CCD 4281 *Shearing (p solo).* 5/85.

**** Plays The Music Of Cole Porter**
Concord CCD 42010 *Shearing; Barry Tuckwell (frhn); strings.* 1/86.

***** Breakin' Out**
Concord CCD 4335 *Shearing; Ray Brown (b); Marvin 'Smitty' Smith (d).* 5/87.

****(*) A Perfect Match**
Concord CCD 4357 *Shearing; Neil Swainson (b); Jeff Hamilton (d); Ernestine Anderson (v).* 5/88.

***** Piano**
Concord CCD 4400 *Shearing (p solo).* 5/89.

***** Duets**
Concord CCD 2121-2 2CD *Shearing; Hank Jones, Marian McPartland (p); Jim Hall (g); Neil Swainson, Don Thompson (b); Donny Osborne, Jeff Hamilton (d); Ernestine Anderson, Mel Torme, Carmen McRae (v).* 80–88.

Shearing has always been on the periphery of jazz rather than all the way inside it, even when he's been making records with genuine jazz musicians. Someday we will set aside the time to go through all the various Capitol albums of the '50s and early '60s, and make a jazz judgement on them all. But that will have to wait until a later edition. In the '80s his many records for Concord put some focus on his work and drummed up a few more worthwhile situations. Some of his best playing will be found on records under Mel Torme's name, but a few others listed here are also worth hearing. When Shearing sets aside his incessant borrowings from other players and eschews middlebrow ideas of what's tasteful to play in the jazz idiom, he can come up with some nice ideas: the partnership with McPartland finds him adapting to the far greater range of that player with some success, and he even holds his own in the trio with Brown and Smith. Carmen McRae's recital finds her in good, typically grouchy form, and Shearing accompanies with deference and good humour.

The albums that lose their way are those where he has to provide most of the musical interest himself. Having said that, the solo disc *Piano* finds him in an unusually effective, ruminative mood. The Cole Porter set is MOR prettiness. The *Duets* compilation is a nice stroll through these back pages.

***** I Hear A Rhapsody**
Telarc 83310 *Shearing; Neil Swainson (b); Grady Tate (d).* 2/92.

A new label and a live album from New York's Blue Note must have galvanized the expatriate Englishman a little. The boppish moments he essays on 'Birdfeathers' and 'Wail' are some of his most convincing in years. Swainson and Tate are right there with him, too.

***** Walkin'**
Telarc 83333 *As above.* 2/92.

***** How Beautiful Is Night**
Telarc 83325 *Shearing; Robert Farnon Orchestra.* 93.

***** That Shearing Sound**
Telarc 83347 *Shearing; Steve Nelson (vib); Louis Stewart (g); Neil Swainson (b); Dennis Mackrel (d).* 2/94.

It seems almost impertinent to say it, but Shearing seems to be getting better, at least as far as the calibre of his records is concerned. Certainly Telarc is eliciting some of his most enjoyable music in years. None of these is a masterpiece exactly, but each shows the man's persuasive craftsmanship at its best. *Walkin'* is a second helping from the Blue Note engagement which produced the earlier disc, and the programme is intriguing – 'That's Earl Brother', 'Pensativa', 'Celia' and, above all, 'Subconscious-Lee', which is dark enough to be genuinely Tristano-esque. Measure for measure, this must be one of his best records. *How Beautiful Is Night* recalls his Capitol days, although Farnon's arrangements are so luxurious and so sumptuously recorded that one surrenders to the sheer comfort. *That Shearing Sound* debuts a new band, and with Nelson and Stewart in the line-up it looks very promising. That said, they both bow amiably enough to Shearing's sometimes tyrannical arrangements, which in the main elongate the style of his '40s quintet to double-length tunes. On its own terms, smartly enjoyable.

***** Paper Moon**
Telarc CD-83375 *Shearing; Louis Stewart (g); Neil Swainson (b). 3/95.*

***** Favorite Things**
Telarc CD-83398 *Shearing (p solo). 3/96.*

Paper Moon is in dedication to Nat Cole, and when they start 'Straighten Up And Fly Right' with the kind of rocking swing that Shearing enjoys, one looks forward to a felicitous occasion. Somehow, though, as graciously as it's done, the disc in the end falls victim to the routine which is the other side of Shearing's jazz. Stewart seems a bit subdued in support. *Favorite Things* has a parlour-piece where a touch of Scarlatti turns into the title-song, and when 'Angel Eyes' turns up as a dark and mysterious creature, it again seems like something special's happening. This time, though, there are too many slow ones, and when George gets Garneresque on the penultimate 'P.S. I Love You' it's almost a shock.

*****(*) Reflections: The Best Of George Shearing 1992–1998**
Telarc CD-83513 *As various Telarc albums above. 92–98.*

***** Back To Birdland**
Telarc CD-83524 *Shearing; Don Thompson (vib); Reg Schwager (g); Neil Swainson (b); Dennis Mackrel (d). 10/00.*

The compilation catches George at his wisest and wittiest most of the way, ending suitably enough on the piece which the MJQ used to refer to as 'England's Carol'. At Birdland again, he's not taking things too hard, and the group looks after him, although he still manages to turn over a few wrinkles even in 'Lullaby Of Birdland'; his introductory routine to this one is worth hearing by itself.

Jack Sheldon (born 1931)

TRUMPET, VOCAL

Florida-born, Sheldon moved to Los Angeles as a teenager and has been there ever since. He was an anchorman trumpeter in much of the West Coast jazz of the '50s, and in the '60s he did both acting and stand-up comedy as well as jazz. He has latterly returned to a modest jazz career, though his onstage persona is that of a Hollywood man.

***** The Entertainers**
VSOP 90 *Sheldon; Frank Rosolino (tb); Howard Roberts (g); Joe Mondragon (b); Shelly Manne, Stan Levey (d); Johnny Mercer (v). 3/64–3/65.*

***** Live At Don Mupo's Gold Nugget**
VSOP 101 *As above, except omit Rosolino, Manne, Mercer. 4/65.*

***** Playing For Change**
Uptown 2743 *Sheldon; Don Sickler (flhn); Jerry Dodgion (as); Barry Harris (p); Rufus Reid (b); Ben Riley (d). 5/86.*

Sheldon has been something of a polymath: an ingenious comedian, a very hot cool-school trumpeter, a slight but charming vocalist – and for two of those attributes he owes something to Chet Baker. But he works best with a straight man, or at least a foil – in the Curtis Counce group of the '50s, or on an early Jimmy Giuffre LP, he fires up on the challenge of the other horns. Still, the two VSOP albums are a truthful record of Sheldon's stage routine in his prime – a probably unique blend of proper bebop, crooning (Johnny Mercer helps out on one disc) and comic patter. The latter is still best sampled on his old Capitol LP, *Ooo – But It's Good!*, even though it's impossible to find. But the Richard Burton parody (presumably he couldn't do Sean Connery) on 'Creamfinger' from *Golden Nugget* may still raise a smile, and there is actually some more than capable instrumental work from Sheldon and Howard Roberts on both this set and *The Entertainers*. It's a unique band that can handle the skit on 'The Girl From Ipanema' one minute and play six minutes of heated bebop on 'Steeplechase' the next. For an even earlier taste of Sheldon, try to find *The Quartet And The Quintet* (Pacific Jazz 93160-2), released in 1998 in a 'Connoisseur' limited edition. It picks up his 1955 sessions for Jazz:West (very rare in their vinyl form) but disappeared from most racks in a flash.

Playing For Change is no-nonsense small-band bop and, with Dodgion going through the gears and the rhythm section in prime shape, this is crisply cooked and flavoursome playing.

Brad Shepik

GUITAR, SAZ, BANJO, CUMBUS

Shepik – whose real name Schoeppach he has altered to aid in universal pronunciation – is a New York guitarist whose deep interest in various European and Middle Eastern musics he imports into what are otherwise characteristic metropolitan energies.

***** The Loan**
Songlines 1518-2 *Shepik; Peter Epstein (ss); Tony Scherr (b); Kenny Wollesen (d); Seido Salifoski (perc). 5/96–4/97.*

*****(*) Short Trip**
Knitting Factory KFW 290 *Shepik; Scott Colley (b); Tom Rainey (d). 12/00.*

Shepik's band The Commuters (on Songlines) is inspired by 'Turkish, Persian, Balkan and African music traditions'. So far, so world-music takeaway, but at least the guitarist knows his noodles and there's a sprightly, almost carefree feel to much of *The Loan*, as if the group were only interested in transporting the most joyous aspects of those traditions into their home ground. A piece such as 'Gastibelza', with its bubbling solo lines, reminds of the helium lift of Afropop guitars, even as they're whirling their way around Eastern scales. Yet they still feel as if they're just visiting, somehow: for all the lightness of touch – or maybe because of it – the music doesn't linger so long in the mind.

Short Trip is a different kind of roots music: Shepik links up with two hardcore jazz-club veterans and the playing's right in the guitar-trio pocket, with the unflappable Colley casting a huge shadow over the tunes and nimble-but-muscular Rainey swinging very hard. Shepik leaves his ethnic axes in the closet and aside from the final piece (from the Sudan) plays only his own, straightahead stuff. It might sound more conservative but it's the better record.

Archie Shepp (born 1937)

TENOR, ALTO AND SOPRANO SAXOPHONES, PIANO, VOCAL

Archie Shepp is one of the major intellectuals of modern jazz. A passionate and articulate spokesman for the music and its ethnic-national ramifications, he is also a significant playwright. His early saxophone style resembled Ben Webster with a carborundum edge, but – like another sometime Trane associate, Pharoah Sanders – Shepp's approach has grown gentler and more lyrical down the years; he also plays piano and sings.

★★★★ New York Contemporary Five

Storyville 8209 *Shepp; Don Cherry (c); John Tchicai (as); Don Moore (b); J. C. Moses (d).* 11/63.

Archie Shepp once declared himself something 'worse than a romantic, I'm a sentimentalist'. Shepp has tended to be a theoretician of his own work, often expressing his intentions and motivations in off-puttingly glib and aphoristic language. He has, though, consistently seen himself as an educator and communicator rather than an entertainer (or even an Artist) and is one of the few Afro-American artists who has effected any sort of convincing synthesis between black music (with its tendency to be depoliticized and repackaged for a white audience) and the less comfortable verbal experiments of poets like LeRoi Jones (Imamu Amiri Baraka). The dialectic between sentiment and protest in Shepp's work is matched by an interplay between music and words which, though more obvious, is also harder to assess. A playwright who also wrote a good deal of influential stage music, Shepp devised a musical style that might be called dramatic or, at worst and later in his career, histrionic.

Though strongly associated in most people's minds with John Coltrane (he worked on the augmented *Love Supreme* sessions and on *Ascension*), Shepp's most potent influence among the modernists was the radical populism of Ornette Coleman. Unlike Coltrane, the Texan saw no need to dismantle or subvert the tradition in order to use it, and Shepp was much affected by Ornette's rediscovery of the freedoms inherent in earlier forms. Fortunately, early work with The New York Contemporary Five (which grew out of a Coleman-influenced quartet co-led with trumpeter Bill Dixon) is now available on CD. The group had an influence out of all proportion to its brief life-span. As often with Shepp projects, there was no piano-player. The longest piece on the album is non-member Bill Dixon's elaborate 'Trio', but all the front-men are credited composers – Tchicai with 'Mick' and 'Wo Wo', Cherry with 'Consequences' and Shepp himself with 'Funeral' – but the twin presences which define this almost complete reissue of the band's studio work are Ornette Coleman and Thelonious Monk. The horns tackle 'O.C.' and 'When Will The Blues Leave' with aching intensity, and the absence of a harmonic centre leaves both open to the wildest flights. Shepp establishes himself as the *de facto* leader with towering solos; Storyville have his name and picture, as they say in Hollywood, 'over the title'. The Monk tunes are treated almost as throwaways, but their influence, melodic, lyrical and nakedly expressive, permeates the album as a whole and points out the direction Shepp would take in later years.

★★★ The House I Live In

Steeplechase SCC 6013 *Shepp; Lars Gullin (bs); Tete Montoliu (p); Niels-Henning Orsted Pedersen (b); Alex Riel (d).* 11/63.

The tenor on *The House I Live In* is very different from what people normally think of as the Shepp of the '60s. Pre-radical, though, he sounds like a player long steeped in swing and blues. Though primarily of historical interest, this hasn't made the much-needed transition to CD in step with a Gullin rediscovery or a comprehensive reassessment of Shepp's career, and may therefore sound like a rather enigmatic one-off. The opening 'You Stepped Out Of A Dream' is perhaps the best of the set, the closing 'Sweet Georgia Brown' giving off the air of a hastily agreed encore. Shepp and NHOP met again on record in 1980, below.

CORE COLLECTION

★★★★ Four For Trane

Impulse! 051218-2 *Shepp; Alan Shorter (t); Roswell Rudd (tb); John Tchicai (as); Reggie Workman (b); Charles Moffett (d).* 8/64.

One of the classic jazz albums of the '60s, and a fascinating glimpse into how thoroughly different what was already thought of as the Coltrane revolution might sound. Shepp immediately sounds more deeply soaked in the blues than the man he is paying tribute to here; Shepp's interpretation of 'Cousin Mary' is stunningly good, and his entry on 'Syeeda's Song Flute' is one of those musical moments that stay embedded in the skin like a bee-sting, painful and pleasurable by turns. Without a harmony instrument, the group has a loose, floating quality which Coltrane himself would never have attempted. The sound is totally open and without walls. Shorter, Rudd and Tchicai (who was to play such a significant part on Trane's *Ascension*) are all in spanking form, and the altoist's solo on the unforgettably titled 'Rufus (Swung; His Face At Last To The Wind, Then His Neck Snapped)' has a raw urgency that recalls the very roots of this music. This is Shepp's only composition of the set and, following the love ballad, 'Naima', it makes a dramatic end to a set of powerful and committed music, as if Coltrane's dark twin had risen up and gained speech.

★★★(★) Fire Music

Impulse! 051158-2 *Shepp; Ted Curson (t); Joseph Orange (tb); Marion Brown (as); David Izenzon, Reggie Johnson (b); Joe Chambers, J. C. Moses (d).* 2 & 3/65.

One of the best of Shepp's albums (though sounding rather brittle on CD), *Fire Music* is the saxophonist's most balanced synthesis of *agitprop* and lyricism, avant-gardism and traditionalist deference. 'Hambone', the long opening track, is a blues-rooted but unconventional theme, cast in irregular time-signatures, tough and citified. At the opposite extreme, there is a slightly kitsch 'Girl From Ipanema' with a reworked bridge; Shepp's colonization of pop tunes is less subversive than Coltrane's (for the most obvious comparison, see 'My Favorite Things' on *New Thing*, below) because he always remains half sold on the sentiments therein, but he makes a persuasive job of the Jobim tune. 'Los Olvidados' is dedicated to the youthful underclass of the city, the 'forgotten ones', those who will not be beguiled by Sandy Becker's 'Hambone' television character. The main focus of the piece is on Marion Brown's desolate middle passage, conjuring up thwarted promise in a hectic but unheeding environment; Shepp's own solo, as became his norm, is a rather pat summing-up, musical Method-acting, that slightly detracts from the sophistication of the composition. 'Malcolm,

Malcolm – Semper Malcolm', scored for just Shepp, Izenzon and Moses and dominated by Shepp's sonorous recitation, is a brief foretaste of the later but no more convincing 'Poem For Malcolm', below. Clipped and re-dedicated from a longer and more ambitious work, it runs a slight risk of being ironized by 'Prelude To A Kiss' and the Jobim tune that follow; Shepp's ironies, though, are maintained not just between but also within compositions.

***(*) On This Night

Impulse! GRP 11252 *Shepp; Bobby Hutcherson (vib); Henry Grimes, David Izenzon (b); Rashied Ali, Joe Chambers, J. C. Moses (d); Ed Blackwell (perc); Christine Spencer (v).* 3 & 8/65.

On This Night has a slightly complicated discographical history, explained by a laudable desire to get Impulse! releases back into some semblance of chronological order. 'Malcolm' is repeated from *Fire Music*, a slightly unnecessary duplication; two takes of 'The Chase' and the alternative take of 'The Mac Man' were originally released on a sequel called *Further Fire Music*; a further take of 'The Chase' was around for some time on a compilation called *The Definitive Jazz Scene: Volume Three.* Anyone who has a vinyl copy of *On This Night* will now look in vain for 'Gingerbread, Gingerbread Boy', which has been moved, quite logically, to the *New Thing At Newport* document (again, below).

So much for the background. Having the March and August 1965 sessions together on one CD makes good sense, even though they are presented in reverse chronological order. It's a big, brawling record, announced by Shepp's out-of-kilter piano and Christine Spencer's churchy voice on the opening 'On This Night (If That Great Day Would Come)'. As well as those items mentioned above, there is a brief excursion on Ellington's 'In A Sentimental Mood', a fine 'The Original Mr Sonny Boy Williamson' and, one of Shepp's quirkily poetic titles, 'The Pickaninny (Picked Clean – No More – Or Can You Back Back Doodlebug)' ... and your guess is probably as good as ours. Hutcherson makes an important contribution, as do the various drummers, with Moses making his presence felt very strongly on the five trio tracks with Izenzon from the March session which yielded the classic 'Malcolm'.

*** New Thing At Newport

Impulse! 543414-2 *Shepp; Bobby Hutcherson (vib); Barre Phillips (b); Joe Chambers (d).* 7/65.

With the classic Coltrane Quartet on the other side of the original album, this gave an explicit and, in the circumstances, slightly ironic blessing to Shepp's emergence as one of the leading lights of the New Thing. Again, the balance of apparently contradictory motivations is just about right, with a less than wholly subversive 'My Favorite Things' set against the inner furies of 'Call Me By My Rightful Name' and 'Skag', and the surreal 'Rufus (Swung His Face At Last To The Wind ...)' from *Four For Trane.* On the whole, though, the music is far from radical in impact, and Shepp's spoken interpolations serve, as throughout his career, to mitigate any slight shift towards abstraction at this stage. Perhaps because of the circumstances and the eventual packaging of the music, Shepp's Newport performance has been somewhat overrated. Again piano-less, the quartet takes a sharp, percussive edge from Hutcherson's tightly pedalled vibes. Phillips fares deservedly better on the CD and can be heard for the remarkable influence he was on the group. Shepp sounds quite self-consciously like a latter-day descendant of Webster and Hawkins, aggravating swing rhythms and phraseology with devices borrowed from R&B and early rock (and, more immediately, from the unabashed populist radicalism of Ornette Coleman). On the other side, Coltrane already sounds tired, but with the understandable weariness of a man whose path would be hard to follow.

***(*) Mama Too Tight

Impulse! 051248-2 *Shepp; Tommy Turrentine (t); Grachan Moncur III, Roswell Rudd (tb); Howard Johnson (tba); Perry Robinson (cl); Charlie Haden (b); Beaver Harris (d).* 8/66.

'I play music out of an overwhelming need to play ...', and yet *Mama Too Tight* is also the best possible illustration of Shepp the control freak, the master-musician who needs to retain his hold on the reins. The largeish ensemble, with brasses and clarinet, allows him to develop orchestral textures at the same time as he pushes forward his increasingly lyrical approach. The overlapping trombones on 'Basheer' (one of a group of portraits of black artists) suggest twin preachers, exegete and commentator, and on 'Mama Too Tight' itself the two slidemen could almost be prophets crying in the wilderness, not quite in agreement, but united in adversity. Turrentine's high, chiming sound (which Shepp himself rightly likens to that of Fats Navarro) cuts through the ensembles. The rhythm section, again minus piano, is utterly musical, fulfilling an orchestral function, and Johnson's part on 'A Portrait Of Robert Thompson (As A Young Man)', a suite of pieces which begins with Ellington's 'Prelude To A Kiss', elevates the tuba to the front rank of horns. This is one of Shepp's quieter albums, one on which he is content to take a back seat to the ensemble. In direct ratio, it is also one of his most impressive as a composer, a disc that demands – and repays – a bit of work.

**** The Way Ahead

Impulse! 051 272 2 *Shepp; Jimmy Owens (t); Grachan Moncur III (tb); Charles Davis (bs); Dave Burrell, Walter Davis Jr (p); Walter Booker, Ron Carter (b); Beaver Harris, Roy Haynes (d).* 1/68.

A great deal of fuss was made when in the '90s Ornette Coleman used a piano-player for the first time in decades. No less significant was Shepp's reintroduction of a keyboard here, and typically he opts for the maverick traditionalism of Dave Burrell, who brings his usual intelligence and sense of history to the blues, 'Damn If I Know'.

This 1998 reissue includes the whole of *The Way Ahead* with a couple of tracks from the relatively obscure *Kwanza*, which pitched Shepp up against baritone saxophonist Charles Davis, a somewhat ungainly encounter. The main album stands at a curious point in the career, looking as much back as it does ahead, and Shepp seems to be exploring the potential of free soloing over quite settled harmonic foundations, even if in Burrell's hands and given the heterodoxy of Moncur and Jimmy Owens, these are more challenging than usual. The trombonist contributes two fine compositions, 'Frankenstein' and 'New Africa', one from each album. And there is also a long version of Cal Massey's 'Bakai'. Historically, this is an important release, filling in a missing part of the picture. Anyone who knows only the later, romantic/sentimental Shepp will certainly recognize the voice, if not its particular mood. Anyone who still prefers to regard him as a Coltrane epigone might be gently persuaded that Archie was always about different things.

*** Yasmina, A Black Woman

Le Jazz 51 *Shepp; Lester Bowie (t); Clifford Thornton (c); Arthur Jones (as); Hank Mobley (ts); Roscoe Mitchell (bs, bsx); Dave Burrell (p); Malachi Favors, Earl Freeman (b); Philly Joe Jones, Sunny Murray, Art Taylor (d); Laurence Devereaux (balafon).* 8/69.

Originally issued on Affinity, this intriguing set brings together members of the Art Ensemble, radical drummer Sunny Murray and, most improbably, hard-bop tenor Hank Mobley, whose driving approach complements Shepp unexpectedly well on 'Sonny's Back'. It's a slightly schizophrenic album. The title-piece, at 20 minutes, is ambitious in both structure and development and is full of avant-garde gestures, some of which will seem a little dated at this distance. At the opposite extreme, 'Body And Soul' is a generic tenor work-out, and yet Shepp manages to stamp a measure of individuality on both ends of the spectrum. The CD should not be too difficult to find and, while it takes some time to adjust the ear to a mix of styles, it's a rewarding experience.

*** Blasé / Live at the Pan African Festival

Varese 061156 *Shepp; Clifford Thornton (c); Lester Bowie (t, flhn); Grachan Moncur III (tb); Dave Burrell (p); Chicago Beau, Julio Finn (hca); Alan Silva, Malachi Favors (b); Philly Joe Jones, Sunny Murray (d); Jeanne Lee (v).* 69.

Originally issued on Actuel, this is a ropy recording of a very fine band on a somewhat average and a rather better day for most concerned. Shepp is in wonderful form throughout, though there is distortion here and there on his best solos, but the other front-liners are not at all well represented and the more complex charts are muddied and uneven on the festival cuts. Shepp was already deeply involved in what became his life's project: finding the beauty and delight which nestled in the darkness of the African-American experience. The version of 'There Is A Balm In Gilead' is delightful and affecting, but the long 'Brotherhood' rambles excessively as it drifts across different styles of black music. 'Sophisticated Lady' is an interesting homage to Ellington, lyrical but strangely acerbic as well.

***(*) Looking At Bird

Steeplechase SCCD 31149 *Shepp; Niels-Henning Orsted Pedersen (b).* 2/80.

Never short of a handy phrase and ever mindful of a need to resist the condescending nomenclature of 'jazz', Shepp prefers to consider bebop as the baroque period of Afro-American classical music. Given the brutal accretions of his approach, it's an accurate but still slightly misleading designation. His Parker readings are irregular pearls with a raw, slightly meretricious beauty but with only questionable currency as serious re-examinations of the tradition. There is a rather better version of 'Now's The Time' (one of Parker's most traditionally rooted tunes and the one to which Shepp seems to be drawn) on the later *I Didn't Know About You*. The great NHOP cut his teeth on this repertoire and sounds completely at home with it, bouncing and singing through a more or less predictable roster of bebop anthems. It's probably easier for bass-players who don't have to negotiate a dense and anxiety-inducing archaeology of previous readings to make their own statements, but the Dane does seem to encourage Shepp to some of his most relaxed and probing performances in the bebop canon. (It's worth listening to this in the context of two saxophone–bass duo takes of 'Davis' with Buell Neidlinger on Cecil Taylor's *Cell Walk For Celeste*, Candid 9034.)

***(*) Goin' Home

Steeplechase SCCD 31079 *Shepp; Horace Parlan (p).* 4/77.

*** Trouble In Mind

Steeplechase SCCD 31139 *As above.* 2/80.

Parlan's slightly raw, bluesy style suits Shepp almost perfectly. The earlier of these, a moving compilation of gospel tunes, is by far the better and more concentrated. *Trouble In Mind*, which takes the same line on 11 blues staples, is perhaps a little too earnest in its pursuit of authenticity but achieves a chastened dignity.

**(*) I Know About The Life

Sackville SK 3062 *Shepp; Kenny Werner (p); Santi Debriano (b); John Betsch (d).* 2/81.

**(*) Down Home New York

Soul Note 121102 *Shepp; Charles McGhee (t, v); Kenny Werner (p, v); Saheb Sarbib (b); Marvin 'Smitty' Smith (d, v); Bartholomew Gray (v).* 2/84.

**(*) Live On Broadway

Soul Note 121122 *Shepp; George Cables (p); Herbie Lewis (b); Eddie Marshall (d); Royal Blue (v).* 5/85.

After about 1975, Shepp's reputation held up more robustly in Europe than in the USA, in part because it may have been easier to sustain the mien of cool, magisterial fury when removed from the company of younger black Americans who either did it better or who rejected the premisses and methodology. Smith takes a more pragmatic line on American racism, and he plays on *Down Home New York* with a brisk self-confidence that rather shames the leader's dull rhythmic sense and increasingly formulaic phrasing.

Perhaps because the rhythm section is less ebullient, Shepp plays better on *Live On Broadway*, but 'My Romance', 'A Night In Tunisia', 'Giant Steps' and a vocal 'St James Infirmary' still leave the residual impression of an illustrated lecture. *I Know About The Life*, the earliest of the group, is simply drab.

** Mama Rose

Steeplechase SCCD 31169 *Shepp; Jasper Van't Hof (ky).* 2/82.

Successive recordings of 'Mama Rose' (and there seem to be droves of them) are probably the most useful gauge of Shepp's progress or decline. The version with Van't Hof is vulgarly overblown and recorded in horrible close-up. Nothing here on a par with Shepp's longer-standing partnership with Horace Parlan.

***(*) California Meeting

Soul Note 121122 *Shepp; George Cables (p); Herbie Lewis (b); Eddie Marshall (d); Royal Blue (v).* 5/85.

An intriguing live programme with a very good band. Cables is the co-star, negotiating 'Giant Steps' with what sounds like a bow to Tommy Flanagan along the way. Marshall and Lewis do a very respectable job and, though the vocals won't be to everyone's taste, Shepp is blowing strongly on both tenor and soprano. 'A Night In Tunisia' is one of his strongest performances of the '80s, a reaffirmation of his belief that bop is the baroque phase of modern jazz.

★★(★) Little Red Moon

Soul Note 121112 *Shepp; Enrico Rava (t, flhn); Siegfried Kessler (p, syn); Wilbur Little (b); Clifford Jarvis (d).* 11/85.

A mystifyingly dull record, which many will be attracted to on the prospect of hearing Shepp do 'Naima' and 'Whisper Not' in the company of the ever-inventive Rava. The individual components, and not least Shepp's solos on the title-track and the Benny Golson tune, are absolutely fine, but the parts certainly don't add up to anything of substance. Serious collectors and devoted Sheppherds only.

★★★ St Louis Blues

Jazz Magnet 2006 *Shepp; Richard Davis (b); Sunny Murray (d); Leopoldo Fleming (perc).* 99.

To characterize this set as predictable is more description than criticism. It is a signature Shepp album: overblown, slightly mawkish, poised between traditionalism and the ragged tatters of the avant-garde. Working again without a piano obliges Archie to sketch in the contours of a song much more exactly – 'St Louis Blues', 'God Bless The Child', Dorham's 'Blue Bossa' – but also frees him to wander over the changes. Murray and Davis are deft and sympathetic partners, but one wonders what they might have done with this material without Shepp; Davis is superb on his own 'Total Package' but occasionally sounds a little remote when the saxophonist drifts off into the wide blues yonder. 'Steam' is an old favourite, but sounds a little cursory and bland. 'Limbuke' is a collaboration with guest percussionist Fleming. Archie sings robustly on 'St Louis Blues' but it's a very casual vocal take.

★★★(★) Live In New York

Verve 013482 *Shepp; Roswell Rudd (tb); Grachan Moncur III (tb); Reggie Workman (b); Andrew Cyrille (d).* 9/00.

The rather plain title is presumably meant to remind us of Shepp and Rudd's '60s encounters, documented on the Impulse! *Live In San Francisco.* That they haven't recorded together since is less surprising, given the trombonist's virtual disappearance and late renaissance. This set, though, makes the years fall away. Both are palpably older and more mellow. Archie's 'Steam', long a signature piece, now carries a slightly world-weary tinge, and he would hardly have played or sung anything quite as nostalgically lyrical as 'Deja-Vu' back in 1966; but the set is meant to show what both men have been doing more recently. Shepp's 'Hope No. 2', which closes the set, is a major statement, though it bears a more than fleeting resemblance to some of David Murray's work. By the same token, Roswell offers up a long interpretation of 'Slide By Slide', highlighting the recent evolution of his writing and playing.

The band is a joy for anyone who remembers these guys first time round, but even if you don't they all play like masters: a little safe and little too much under control, but pungent nevertheless. Moncur hasn't sustained much of a presence since his Blue Note years, but he sounds just the same, blowing dark counterpoints to the other two horns and very much fulfilling the pianist's natural role. In that he's supported by Workman, who couldn't be better or more honourably named; he builds rock-solid edifices for 'Pazuzu' and 'Ujamma', another two recent Shepp compositions. Cyrille isn't as hyperactive as in the old days, but his touch is as deft as ever and he must wish there had always been recording engineers like Chris Anderson.

★★★ Hungarian Bebop

Budapest Music 66 *Shepp; Mihaly Dresch (ss, ts); Kalman Balogh (cimbalom); Ferenc Kovacs (vn); Matyas Szandai (b).* 02.

The title-tune isn't really bebop, and one suspects that Dresch and his sidemen have a very different cultural perspective on jazz to Shepp's, but the results, recorded on tour in Eastern Europe, are very engaging. The presence of violin and cimbalom offers a few stray echoes of Archie's early '70s work, when new sonorities and little instruments were very much part of the language of the time. 'Steam' is included, almost *de rigueur*, and Archie plays with magisterial calm and possibly a small lump in the throat. The saxophone duets on 'Buzai Song' (apparently a folk-tune) are worth the price of admission alone.

Andy Sheppard (born 1957)

TENOR AND SOPRANO SAXOPHONES, FLUTE

Born in Warminster, Wiltshire, he came to some prominence in the '70s bands Sphere and Spirit Level, before spending time in Paris, returning in time to catch star-status in the '80s jazz boom and recording for Antilles and Blue Note. His reputation settled down in the '90s and he pursued a career as a film and TV composer along with small-group work with Steve Lodder.

★★★ Inclassificable

Label Bleu LBLC 6583 *Sheppard; Steve Lodder (syn); Nana Vasconcelos (perc).* 10/94.

Sheppard is a British saxophonist who had a fruitful time in the '80s and early '90s. Unfortunately, his Antilles and Blue Note albums are currently out of print. Sheppard lasted no longer with Blue Note than most of his European contemporaries, but one has to pause to wonder, before lambasting the label for short-sightedness, whether such a response is anything more than a knee-jerk. This is a troublingly diffuse album by an artist too mature to speak about in terms of 'promise'. Anyone who has heard a version of the group in concert will realize that the record is no more than a shadowy version of the live act, and should perhaps be comforted by that. This might have been an ideal occasion for a festival or concert recording. In the studio it sounds thin and stilted, and Sheppard's unmistakable gifts are short-sold.

★★★ Learning To Wave

Provocateur PVC 1016 *Sheppard; Steve Lodder (ky); John Parricelli (g); Chris Laurence (b); Paul Clarvis (d, perc, tabla); Shalda Sahai (tabla).* 6/98.

A decade adrift stylistically, *Learning To Wave* is by no means the revelatory shift of direction Sheppard implies. The title refers to a trip to Africa where children would appear out of nowhere to wave at passing cars. Some of that relaxed spontaneity is evident in Andy's contemplative playing, which nowadays is muzzled by a broad fusion reverb. Relaxed as it is obviously meant to sound, there is a tense quality to the album, too much of the embattled, isolated individualist in Sheppard's playing and writing. A few more – and rawer – sessions with strangers might work wonders at this stage. The impression is of a man comfortable with his sound and playing entirely within himself. As previously, his soprano is the more convincing horn, delicately balanced between Wayne Shorter's minimalist gestures and Grover Washington's light, funky groove.

Lodder is loyalty itself, a craftsman who just occasionally rises above himself and does something of real moment. Sheppard has said that he wrote much of the material on guitar, which puts Parricelli's role in a different light. The guitarist is easily overlooked in a group setting, sometimes too tasteful for his own good; here, he doesn't put a foot wrong. *Learning To Wave* is a *nice* record; only a curmudgeon would snipe at it. Sadly, that's the business we're in.

*****(*) Dancing Man And Woman**
Provocateur PVC 1020 *Sheppard; Steve Lodder (ky); John Parricelli (g); Chris Laurence, Steve Swallow (b); Paul Clarvis (perc); Kuljit Bhamra (tabla).* 9/99.

Shrewd and subtle compositions from Sheppard and crisp and committed playing from the band make *Dancing ...* a thoroughly compelling record. Andy's range as a writer and player gets broader all the time. There are lots of unexpected rhythms, cranky melodies and some wonderfully inflected musical atmospheres. 'Tippi' (which is reprised at the end), 'Sugar Beach Hotel', 'Oscar And Lucinda' and the title-track make up the bulk of the session and each is memorable in its own way, either bright and funky or more thoughtful and winsome.

***** Nocturnal Tourist**
Provocateur PVC 1029 *Sheppard (sax, wind syn, ky, g); Stephane San Juan (perc).* 02.

***** P.S.**
Provocateur PVC 1034 *Sheppard; John Parricelli (g).* 1/03.

The duo with Parricelli is the result of a long-standing friendship and artistic association. Sheppard's eclectic approach is kept in check by the guitarist's estimably clear and almost pragmatic lines, though in turn he increases his usual level of energy for the gig. Not a free-form gig, but comparable in interesting ways to Andy's set of duets with Keith Tippett. The other album is inspired by collaborations with a whole range of musicians over the last few years, including Northumbrian piper Kathryn Tickell. It sees Sheppard in almost one-man-band mode, exploring wind synthesizer, keyboards and guitar as well as saxophone; he weaves strong melody into found sound and sampled rhythms, mostly on original themes but also including a fine version of the old chestnut 'I Wish I Knew'. Sheppard still sounds very distinctively himself, but with a new range of options that should yield interesting dividends in the years ahead.

Joya Sherrill (born 1927)

VOCALS

The New Jersey-born singer was a precocious talent, greatly admired by Duke Ellington, for whom she wrote the lyrics for 'Take The "A" Train'. Her solo career never really took off, and she is best remembered as an agile, precise interpreter of the great man's music.

***** Sings Duke**
Verve 547266-2 *Sherrill; Ray Nance (c, v); Cootie Williams (t); Johnny Hodges (as); Paul Gonsalves (ts); Ernie Harper, Billy Strayhorn (p); Joe Benjamin, John Lamb (b); Shep Shepherd (d).* 65.

Billy Strayhorn's presence at the piano determines the emotional temperature of this smooth and oddly unemphatic set. How different it might have been if Duke himself had been around on the day, except that Joya was never the most rhythmic and harmonically astute of singers. Her great strength was an ability to pitch a song and to invest even the slightest of lyrics with tough, terse emotion. Inevitably and unfairly, much of the interest comes from the players. Gentlemen that they are, Nance and Hodges and Gonsalves pay court with the deepest seriousness, but with a slight reserve. The better material comes early on, with 'Mood Indigo' and 'Prelude To A Kiss', but once Sherrill's voice becomes familiar the impact is lost, and attention switches to the background. An attractive set, and a convincing tribute to Duke's songwriting skills.

Bobby Shew (born 1941)

TRUMPET, FLUGELHORN

Worked in several big bands and Las Vegas groups in the '60s, then settled in California and has since taught, done session-work and played in occasional small-group settings.

*****(*) Playing With Fire**
MAMA MMF 1017 *Shew; Tom Harrell (t, flhn); Kei Akagi (p); John Patitucci (b); Roy McCurdy (d).* 9/86.

***** Heavyweights**
MAMA MMF 1013 *Shew; Carl Fontana (tb); George Cables (p); Bob Magnusson (b); Joe LaBarbera (d).* 95.

***** Salsa Caliente**
MAMA MMF 1023 *Shew; Sal Cracchiolo (t, flhn); Arturo Velasco (tb); Justo Almario (ts, f); Mark Levine (p); Eddie Resto (b); Jose 'Papo' Rodriguez, Ricardo 'Tiki' Pasillas, Michito Sanchez (perc).* 5/98.

***** Play The Music Of Reed Kotler**
Torii (no number) 2CD *Shew; Gary Foster (as, ts, f, af); Bill Cunliffe (p); Darek 'Oles' Oleszkiewicz (b); Paul Kreibich (d).* 01.

A pros' pro, Shew has spent much of his career in top-notch big bands and studio work. These records for MAMA are brimming with virtuoso playing without resorting to soulless cliché. The session with Harrell sat on the shelf for many years until Shew persuaded MAMA to release it. Hastily prepared, the music crackles with ebullience and spontaneity: the choruses on the opener, 'Prelude And Blues', are so exciting that the rest of the date struggles to match up. It does, although here and there one wishes they'd had time to finesse the situation a little more. Still, the two brassmen are as *simpatico* as blood brothers, and this should go down as a great two-trumpet record.

The meeting with trombonist Fontana is more considered all round: a less explosive rhythm section, and the interplay between the two horns is more about warmth and elegance than fireworks. To that extent it's a less compelling record, but some may prefer the sonorities which Shew and Fontana create almost without trying.

Salsa Caliente is a back-to-my-roots exercise for Shew, who grew up in New Mexico surrounded by Latin music. Sent on its way with a crisply cooked 'Cubano Chant', this is an affectionate and warm-blooded set. Mark Levine brought three attractive originals to the session and the playing is classy, if arguably a little too tailored and clean. Shew is a master at sounding hot and inspired without losing his cool, and he does tend to outclass the other soloists. Also useful: Bobby's recipes for guacamole and red chilli sauce, in the sleeve booklet.

The Torii set (which has no apparent catalogue number) is an indulgence for the composer Reed Kotler, who wrote all 21 tunes on the double-CD and presumably paid for the whole thing too. It's not much more than a long, easy stroll in the park for Shew and Foster and at least the compositions let them play pretty. The horns vary the pace by picking up different instruments from tune to tune, although the preponderance of mid-tempos doesn't encourage riveted listening.

Matthew Shipp (born 1961)

PIANO

Born in Wilmington, Delaware, he began on piano at the age of five. Studied at Berklee and the New England Conservatory but didn't begin recording until the '90s. A musician who has absorbed a great deal of music, Shipp is situated in the avant-garde but can probably be a principal in whatever area of improvisation he chooses.

*****(*) Sonic Explorations**
Cadence CJR 1037 *Shipp; Rob Brown (as).* 11/87–2/88.

***** Points**
Silkheart SHCD 129 *Shipp; Rob Brown (as); William Parker (b); Whit Dickey (d).* 90.

*****(*) Circular Temple**
Infinite Zero 32758-2 *As above, except omit Brown.* 10/90.

***** Zo**
213 61 21315-2 *Shipp; William Parker (b).* 93.

***** Prism**
hatOLOGY 549 *Shipp; William Parker (b); Whit Dickey (d).* 3/93.

***** Critical Mass**
213 CD003 *Shipp; Mat Maneri (vn); William Parker (b); Whit Dickey (d).* 9/94.

***** Before The World**
FMP CD81 *Shipp (p solo).* 6/95.

****(*) Thesis**
hatOLOGY 506 *Shipp; Joe Morris (g).* 11/97.

Already in his forties, Shipp has been around long enough to know what he's about, yet these albums show a steady progress of discovery that suggest he is taking his time in a productive and rather exciting way. The FMP date, for instance, is a record of his first solo concert (in Berlin) and he clearly came to it as a mature yet naturally open player. He has assembled a repertory cast of companions as the personnels suggest and the players clearly know each other's moves pretty well. *Sonic Explorations* counts almost as an archive release. Though rather more akin to a straightforward free session than some of Shipp's subsequent music, there's much detailed interplay between piano and saxophone, with Brown's beautiful tone and ripping phrasing pushing the pianist into an accompanying role at times. They end on two notably destructive takes on 'Oleo' and 'Blue In Green'.

The two 1990 albums take some cues from the avant-garde past – Taylor, Bley and Shipp's personal favourite, Andrew Hill – while going their own way in a quite dramatic fashion from moment to moment. Shipp likes to worry at individual motifs or gradually to open out blocks and progressions which can take a long and absorbing time in yielding their numerous details. Dickey's light but propulsive rhythms scurry the music along and Brown's fundamentally lyrical lines add further nuances. *Points* is a shade behind the trio date since it just runs out of steam here and there, while the second disc could if anything be even longer. *Zo* seems more specifically experimental in that Shipp and Parker seem to want to plunge into the darkest (and sometimes the dreariest) corners they can find, deep left-hand chords set on top of juddering bass vamps; their version of 'Summertime' is a bit excruciating, but some of the improvisations are full of a kind of slow, concentrated energy. *Critical Mass* takes a similar form, though this one is divided into a tripartite meditation on a church mass, components developed into a quartet music that seems to be both slow and stately and densely churning. Shipp never sprints through his music the way Taylor does, and his decision to use players like Parker and Maneri rather than saxophonists lends a somewhat baroque feel to his ensembles. An interesting record but rather dour work for the listener.

Prism is a recent appearance, although it was briefly available on a tiny American label called Brinkman. The two long pieces suggest, as usual in this period, that Shipp was trying out, discarding and picking up again all manner of ideas – too many for the listener to impose a clear idea of what he was about. Parts of 'Prism I' certainly have the feel of Shipp as part of a continuum of post-bop piano, while the second piece (after an introductory solo passage which might be the most interesting thing on the record) seems to be all over the place formally and stylistically.

***** The Multiplication Table**
hatOLOGY 516 *Shipp; William Parker (b); Susie Ibarra (d).* 7/97.

***** Strata**
hatOLOGY 522 *Shipp; Roy Campbell (t); Daniel Carter (as, ts, f, t); William Parker (b).* 12/97.

***** Gravitational Systems**
hatOLOGY 530 *Shipp; Mat Maneri (vn).* 5/98.

The trio music of *The Multiplication Table* is sometimes as dry as its title. Ellington's 'C Jam Blues' is a desiccation across 13 minutes, and 'Autumn Leaves' a turmoil. But this is an absorbing group in other ways, particularly with Ibarra adding her own ideas about free swing to the firmly established Parker–Shipp axis. The problem is with the recording, which has the piano too far back, the drums too far forward and the bass often lost. *Strata* debuts Shipp's Horn Quartet in a 14-part piece. Campbell is a diehard free-jazz man and he puts some warmth into the surroundings. There are times, though, when even he and Carter seem to find their environment inscrutable. *Gravitational Systems* is as close to chamber music as Shipp is ever going to get, and when they do a rough-and-*tumbe* 'Greensleeves' early on, it's a strange moment, quickly righted by the following 'Series Of Planes'. Shipp ends with a solo 'Naima', not one of his most remarkable transformations.

***** Expansion, Power, Release**
hatOLOGY 558 *Shipp; Mat Maneri (vn); William Parker (b).* 11/99.

*****(*) New Orbit**
Thirsty Ear 57095-2 *Shipp; Wadada Leo Smith (t); William Parker (b); Gerald Cleaver (d).* 01.

While Shipp and Parker are present on both of these, they're entirely different from each other. The trio record functions somewhat in the manner of a classical ensemble, with some Viennese references slipping into the design, but the pianist is at his freshest and most beguiling on what is a compact, smartly delivered set of mostly short pieces. *New Orbit* is a meeting of masters, stark, sometimes abrasive, with Smith's playing at its most imperial over Shipp's regimen of blocks and clusters, the music gathering a cumulative power across the ten pieces, though never seeming to suggest any formal codification. The music is becoming more obviously accessible, yet more mysterious at the same time – a fascinating agenda.

***** Nu Bop**

Thirsty Ear 57114-2 *Shipp; Daniel Carter (as, f); William Parker (b); Guillermo Brown (d); Chris FLAM (syn).* n.d.

Shipp is an artistic director at Thirsty Ear and has been involved in other electronic records, but this is his first full-scale try at integrating his own playing with the electronic mixing and programming of FLAM. As a record, it's hit and miss. The mordant piano solo 'ZX-1' doesn't work in the context, and it does seem like a huge and not too productive jump from the music of the previous two records to the splintery funk of 'Nu Bop' and 'Space Shipp', although 'Nu Abstract' sounds like a much more inventive blending of Shipp's most outside ideas with synthetic soundscaping. As an investigative start, fine, but don't expect revelations.

***** Songs**

Splasc(h) 840.2 *Shipp (p solo).* 11/01.

From 'Angel Eyes' to 'Almighty Fortress Is Our God', Shipp's songbook could have been any contemporary pianist's flick back through the archives, although it is, inevitably, *sui generis.* It's a vivid showcase for his thoughts on repertory, but there are times when his dichotomous approach – thundering out the melody at maximum volume and foot-dragging tempo, then splintering it into freely-shaped pieces – gets plain wearisome.

***** Equilibrium**

Thirsty Ear TH 571272 *Shipp; Khan Jamal (vib); William Parker (b); Gerald Cleaver (d); FLAM (syn, elec).* n.d.

If this sounds like an advance on the previous *Nu Bop*, it also holds some of the same question marks and distractions. FLAM never seems fully integrated into music which retains its power through old-fashioned jazz staples such as improvisational interplay (especially between Shipp and Jamal, who rarely finds his right niche on record and sounds good here) and rhythmical momentum – swing, even. Here and there one can even detect Shipp's admiration for Bill Evans, not often talked of as any kind of influence on him.

Wayne Shorter (born 1933)

TENOR AND SOPRANO SAXOPHONES

Shorter worked with Art Blakey and Miles Davis and recorded on his own account, but it was an association he made while working with Maynard Ferguson that led to one of his most significant creative relationships. For more than a decade, with Joe Zawinul, he was half of the central axis of the profoundly influential Weather Report. Shorter has something in common with John Coltrane, but his characteristic approach is more staccato and elided, and with a more delicately lyrical tone on soprano saxophone.

*****(*) Introducing Wayne Shorter**

Vee Jay VJ 007 *Shorter; Lee Morgan (t); Wynton Kelly (p); Paul Chambers (b); Jimmy Cobb (d).* 11/59.

***** Second Genesis**

Vee Jay 016 *Shorter; Cedar Walton (p); Bob Cranshaw (b); Art Blakey (d).* 10/60.

***** Wayning Moments**

Vee Jay 014 *Shorter; Freddie Hubbard (t); Eddie Higgins (p); Jymie Merritt (b); Marshall Thompson (d).* 62.

Anyone who has encountered Shorter only as co-leader of Weather Report will know him primarily as a colourist, contributing short and often enigmatic brush-strokes to the group's carefully textured canvases. They may not recognize him as the formidable heir of Rollins and Coltrane (scale up and repitch those brief soprano saxophone statements, and the lineage becomes clear). They will emphatically not know him as a composer. As Weather Report's musical identity consolidated, Joe Zawinul largely took over as writer. However, much as Shorter's elided 'solos' (in a group that didn't really believe in solos) still retained the imprint of a more developed idiom, so his compositions for the early records – 'Tears' and 'Eurydice' in particular – convey in essence the virtues that make him one of the most significant composers in modern jazz, whose merits have been recognized by fellow-players as far apart as Art Blakey, Miles Davis ('ESP', 'Dolores', 'Pee Wee', 'Nefertiti') and Kirk Lightsey (a challenging tribute album).

Known as 'Mr Weird' in high school, Shorter cultivated an oblique and typically asymmetrical approach to the bop idiom. His five years with the Jazz Messengers are marked by an aggressive synthesis of his two main models, but with an increasingly noticeable tendency to break down his phrasing and solo construction into unfamiliar mathematical subdivisions. Working with Miles Davis between 1964 and 1970 (a period that coincides with his most productive phase as a solo recording artist), he moved towards a more meditative and melancholy style – with an increasing dependence on the soprano saxophone – which is consolidated on the fine *Super Nova* (below), where he also makes unusually inventive use of the Jekyll–Hyde guitar partnership of McLaughlin and Sharrock. Shorter's recordings at this time relate directly to his work on Miles's *In A Silent Way* and to his work with Weather Report over the following decade.

Shorter's earliest recordings, for Vee Jay, have been available only rather intermittently over the years. The current issue, though, has restored them and re-established their place in the canon, correcting a number of mistakes which surrounded previous releases. On *Introducing,* he sounds in thrall to the Coltrane of the time, and possibly John Gilmore as well. The 26-year-old, who had seriously considered giving up music altogether, turns in five strong originals and a short but blistering version of Weill's 'Mack The Knife'. This CD version includes four alternatives, which add little to the picture but helpfully reinforce the impression of a searching performer who has sufficient lateral vision to keep himself one step ahead of the game. Morgan was at his best in 1959, playing with punch and fire and, like Kelly, with a grasp of the blues which was never vouchsafed to the session leader.

Second Genesis is unfortunately titled, for it is all too obviously another visit to a well that has already been drained. The band, anchored by the Chief Messenger, is superb, but Shorter himself has little enough to say, pushing through his five originals with nervy attention, a detailed, almost deliberate style very different from later work. He's at his best, interestingly, on the two Richard Rodgers compositions which close the album, 'Getting To Know You' and 'I Didn't Know What Time It Was', the latter almost serving as self-definition for a player who works across the bar-lines and, as often as not, ignores the basic count and tonality.

Wayning Moments catches him on the brink of what was to be a purple patch for Blue Note. Hubbard is a lesser performer than Morgan on this material, though he does bring an occasional flicker of ambiguity which does the music no harm. The original album is padded out with alternative takes for every (very short) track, a rather dull reduplication of effort that will excite only those who are already firmly wedded to this period. Higgins is a drab pianist whose approach to the changes is signalled with lights, flags and telegrams, robbing even these short tracks of any drama whatsoever. Listeners would be well advised to stick to the earlier discs, or to hold fire for the classic Blue Notes.

★★★(★) Night Dreamer

Blue Note 84173 *Shorter; Lee Morgan (t); McCoy Tyner (p); Reggie Workman (b); Elvin Jones (d).* 4/64.

★★★(★) Juju

Blue Note 99005 *As above, except omit Morgan.* 8/64.

Shorter's most individual work remains the group of albums made for Blue Note in the mid-'60s, ending in 1970 with the low-key *Odyssey Of Iska. Juju* and the undervalued and compositionally daring *Night Dreamer* pit him with one version of the classic Coltrane quartet. This is Shorter at his most Coltrane-like, and happening across these records again is a slightly startling experience. The lines are much fuller than typical Wayne, with lots of accidentals and grace notes. 'Virgo' on the first record is an object lesson in how Trane influenced slightly younger players, but even on the debut for Blue Note, the emphasis falls very much on Shorter the composer. 'Charcoal Blues' and 'Armageddon' are instantly identifiable as his work, and the little exotic accent of 'Oriental Folk Song' is a touch that was to be reproduced in almost all the records which followed.

New takes of 'JuJu' and 'House Of Jade' on the second album (available in a Rudy van Gelder tribute edition) offer valuable insights into how thoughtful and experimental a player Shorter was at this period, already trying to marry the sheer energy and drive of hard bop with something altogether more lateral and evocative. The Coltrane influence seems less evident four months later, and the absence of Lee Morgan emphasizes a more brooding and melancholy strain which was to become the Shorter signature.

CORE COLLECTION

★★★★ Speak No Evil

Blue Note 99001 *Shorter; Freddie Hubbard (t); Herbie Hancock (p); Ron Carter (b); Elvin Jones (d).* 12/64.

For us, this is by far Shorter's most satisfying record. The understanding with Hancock was total and telepathic, two harmonic adventurers on the loose at a moment when, with John Coltrane still around as a tutelary genius, the rules of jazz improvisation were susceptible to almost endless interrogation.

This album created a template for a host of imitators, but so far no one has ever produced a like recording with such strength *and* internal balance. There has always been some controversy about Freddie Hubbard's role on the session, with detractors claiming that, unlike Shorter, the trumpeter was still working the hand dealt him in the Messengers and was too hot and urgent to suit Shorter's growing structural sophistication. In fact, the two blend astonishingly well, combining Hubbard's own instinctive exuberance on 'Fee-Fi-Fo-Fum' with something of the leader's own darker conception; interestingly, Shorter responds in kind, adding curious timbral effects to one of his most straight-ahead solos on the record. As with *Adam's Apple* (see below), much of the interest lies in the writing. Shorter has suggested that 'Dance Cadaverous' was suggested by Sibelius's 'Valse Triste', (which he plays on *The Soothsayer*, also below). 'Infant Eyes' is compounded of disconcerting nine-measure phrases that suggest a fractured nursery rhyme, and the title-piece pushes the soloists into degrees of harmonic and rhythmic freedom that would not normally have been tolerated in a hard-bop context. Set *Speak No Evil* alongside Eric Dolphy's more obviously 'revolutionary' *Out To Lunch!*, recorded by Blue Note earlier the same year, and it's clear that Shorter claims the same freedoms, giving his rhythm section licence to work counter to the line of the melody and freeing the melodic Hancock from merely chordal duties. It's harder to reconstruct how alien some of Shorter's procedures were because, by and large, he does remain within the bounds of post-bop harmony, but it's still clear that this is one of the most important jazz records of the period.

★★★(★) The Soothsayer

Blue Note 84443 *Shorter; Freddie Hubbard (t); James Spaulding (ss, as); McCoy Tyner (p); Ron Carter (b); Tony Williams (d).* 3/65.

★★★(★) Etcetera

Blue Note 33581 *Shorter; Herbie Hancock (p); Cecil McBee (b); Joe Chambers (d).* 6/65.

★★★★ Adam's Apple

Blue Note 46403 *Shorter; Herbie Hancock (p); Reggie Workman (b); Joe Chambers (d).* 2/66.

Adam's Apple would be remembered for 'Footprints' if for nothing else. It's Wayne's one deathless contribution to the repertory and it still pops up in delightful surprise on the CD. In fact, the 1966 record is a series of surprises. Shorter's interest in Latino styles – supposedly 'a departure' when *Native Dancer* came along – is already well in place with 'El Gaucho', but there is another side on show as well, in the rollicking, head-back laddishness of Jimmy Rowles's '502 Blues'. It takes a moment or two to register who is playing.

The Soothsayer and *Etcetera* weren't released until the end of the '70s, a sign perhaps that interest in Shorter had switched over almost entirely to his work with Weather Report. Though certainly not of the same quality as the two albums that bracketed them, both are strong and challenging sets. It's no surprise that *Etcetera* might have frightened the corporate horses; it's certainly Shorter's freest recorded session, powerfully argued and vividly recorded, but demanding when set up against 'Footprints' and 'Fee-Fi-Fo-Fum'. With no extra horns, the emphasis falls squarely on saxophone and piano, though McBee and the redoubtable Chambers go about their work with admirable focus and concentration. As so often, Shorter includes one piece by another composer, this time, intriguingly, Gil Evans's 'Barracudas'.

The sextet also makes for compelling listening. 'Angola' (included in two versions) and 'Lady Day' are definitive Shorter compositions, and the closing arrangement of Sibelius's 'Valse Triste' demonstrates yet again how wide and attentive was his awareness of other musics.

*** Schizophrenia

Blue Note 32096 *Shorter; Curtis Fuller (tb); James Spaulding (ss, as, f); Herbie Hancock (p); Ron Carter (b); Joe Chambers (d).* 3/67.

*** Super Nova

Blue Note 84332 *Shorter; Walter Booker, John McLaughlin, Sonny Sharrock (g); Miroslav Vitous (b); Chick Corea (vib, d); Jack DeJohnette (d, perc); Airto Moreira (perc); Maria Booker (v).* 9/69.

Schizophrenia is a title that has come back to haunt Wayne Shorter. It's easy and largely pointless to underscore his eccentricity as a performer. He can be gnomic to the point of uncommunicativeness, but the opening 'Tom Thumb' does show him continuing to tread a path between straightforward hard bop and freer elements. With Hancock and Carter again on board, the balance of forces is rock solid, and the two extra horns are used pretty much in that capacity, filling out ensembles and filling in short, accented statements. Spaulding contributes one original to an album that isn't marked by any of the highs of past discs, though 'Miyako' is a beautiful thing.

**** The Best Of Wayne Shorter

Blue Note 91141 *Shorter; Freddie Hubbard (t); Curtis Fuller (tb); James Spaulding (as); Herbie Hancock (p); Ron Carter, Reggie Workman (b); Joe Chambers, Elvin Jones, Tony Williams (d); collective personnel.* 12/64–3/67.

Earlier versions reflected the rather enigmatic valuation Blue Note placed on one of the label's most brilliant but complex talents. As an introduction, or simply as a distillation of the Capitol years, it's hard to fault now. The track-listing runs in full: 'Speak No Evil', 'Infant Eyes', 'Tom Thumb', 'Lost', 'Adam's Apple', 'Footprints' (of course!), 'Virgo', 'JuJu' and another of the tunes that appealed so much to Miles Davis, 'Water Babies'. Hard to fault and a truly excellent buy.

***(*) Native Dancer

Columbia 467095 *Shorter; Milton Nascimento (g, v); Herbie Hancock (p); Airto Moreira (perc); with Dave McDaniel, Roberto Silva, Wagner Tiso, Jay Graydon, Dave Amaro (instrumentation not listed).* 12/74.

A decade to the month after *Speak No Evil* finds Shorter in a bland samba setting which does more to highlight Nascimento's vague and uncommitted vocal delivery than the leader's saxophone-playing. There is a hint of the old Shorter in the oblique introduction to 'Lilia' and some fine tenor work on 'Miracle Of The Fishes', but much of the rest could have been put together by a competent session *pasticheur.* Reviewers tended to go one way or the other on *Native Dancer*, but the consensus was that it was a 'surprise' and a 'new departure'. In fact, Shorter had long shown an interest in Latin American rhythms and progressions; 'El Gaucho' on *Adam's Apple*, above, is one of his finest compositions, and *Native Dancer* is almost exactly contemporary with Weather Report's Pan-American *Tale Spinnin'*. The 'surprise' lay in the lush, choking arrangements and unnecessary verbiage. Shorter encountered similar resistance when his '80s band flirted with discofied funk-jazz, stripped-down settings that pushed his distinctive tenor sound to the forefront again.

*** Atlantis

Columbia 481617-2 *Shorter; Jim Walker (picc, f); Yaron Gershovksy, Michiko Hill (p); Larry Klein (g, ky, b); Joseph Vitarelli (ky, synclavier); Michael Hoenig (synclavier); Ralph Humphrey (d); Alex Acuña (d, perc); Lenny Castro (perc); Diana Acuña, Dee Dee Bellson, Nain Brunel, Troye Davenport, Sanaa Lathan, Edgy Lee, Kathy Lucien (v).* 85.

Shorter hadn't recorded under his own name for nearly a decade, and his return was something of a shock. *Atlantis* was marked out by wacky funk rhythms and a dense electronic sound that was at odds with Shorter's spare, elided sound. Almost all the material is written by the leader, but it takes a couple of listens to cut through the incidentals and hear how consistent the strategies are with Shorter's classic work for Blue Note. The band isn't so much undistinguished as determinedly anonymous, delivering a highly processed sound that stands at the apex of a weirdly extended stylistic triangle embracing those early acoustic sets and Wayne's work with Weather Report. The studio sound is sharp and clinical, and often intriguingly at odds with the emotional temperature of the writing.

*** High Life

Verve 529224-2 *Shorter; Rachel Z (ky); David Gilmore (g); Marcus Miller (b, bcl); Will Calhoun, Terri Lyne Carrington (d); Lenny Castro, Airto Moreira, Munyungo Jackson, Kevin Ricard (perc); brass and strings.* 95.

Shorter's return to active duty is a solid, colourful, gregarious session. Marcus Miller's production is characteristically multi-textured and inventive, and there are plenty of spots for Shorter the soloist to make a mark on what are generally more flexible fusion settings than he's enjoyed for some years. But the lack of either compositional depth or attention-grabbing melodies tells against the record making a deeper impact, and there's nothing here to challenge the best of the Weather Report era.

*** Footprints Live!

Verve 589769 *Shorter; Danilo Perez (p); John Patitucci (b); Brian Blade (d).* 01.

Recorded on tour in Europe in 2001, this captures Shorter's quartet working through some of his best-known themes, 'Masqualero', 'Sanctuary', 'Footprints', as well as less familiar material like the original 'Aung San Suu Kyi' and Sibelius's 'Valse Triste'. There is something slightly truncated and incomplete about some of these performances and Perez is not the ideal piano-player for this very demanding material, but it is great to hear Wayne sounding so open-hearted and in charge.

***(*) Alegría

Verve 543558 *Shorter; Chris Gekker, Jeremy Pelt, Lew Soloff (t); Bruce Eidem, Jim Pugh, Steve Davis, Papo Vasquez, Michael Boschen (tb); Marcus Roja (tba); Chris Potter (bcl, ts); Brad Mehldau, Danilo Perez (p); John Patitucci (b); Brian Blade, Terri Lyne Carrington (d); Alex Acuña (perc); woodwinds, strings.* 02.

Shorter looked to be heading for a technical knockout until *Footprints Live!* signalled his return to the terse, phlegmatic post-bop of earlier years. All that remained then was the follow-up punch, and the saxophonist's critical comeback would look secure. *Alegría* is it. With some reservations.

The obvious problem is that Shorter's first all-acoustic studio album for 35 years (!) doesn't present a consistent line-up throughout. There is such a difference between Perez's swinging but slightly one-dimensional playing and Mehldau's more harmonically ambitious approach. The two pianists' differences could have been brokered into an interesting contrast, but instead one feels the album shifting in tone and intention from track to track, which is less satisfactory. That said, the individual components are very good indeed.

The opening could hardly be more promising, with Shorter on soprano kicking into 'Sacajawea' with more power and commitment than has been heard from him in some time. There are older pieces in the set, and the now expected classical essay in the shape this time of Leroy Anderson's 'Serenata' and Villa-Lobos's 'Bachianas Brasileiras No. 5', a theme that lends itself perfectly to Shorter's playing. 'Angola' and 'Orbits' are both familiar ideas given unfamiliar readings, the latter slowed down to the point where the line seems to break down into its components. 'She Moves Through The Fair' seems an odd choice, but it works well and serves as the best possible contrast to the stone groove of the opening track.

Wally Shoup (born 1944)

ALTO SAXOPHONE

Working modestly out of the American Pacific North-West, Shoup is an experienced free player only recently offered much in the way of documentation.

***** Fusillades And Lamentations**

Leo LR 364 *Shoup; Reuben Radding (b); Bob Rees (d).* 3/02.

****(*) Live At Tonic**

Leo LR 369 *Shoup; Paul Flaherty (ts, as); Thurston Moore (g); Chris Corsano (d).* 9/02.

Shoup's playing sounds oddly isolated: on both sets here, he appears to be working almost privately, glancing off the other players and creating unison statements by accident. He works patiently and fretfully at the horn, making every phrase sound like something he's had to prise free of his instrument. On the trio disc, bass and drums follow him as best they can, and it's absorbing work.

The live session will appeal to those who enjoy Flaherty's habitual roaring, and Shoup stands up to him as best he can. Moore tries to overpower everybody with his usual shedload of feedback and untempered noise, but he sounds like a beginner next to the saxophonists, and the raw live sound doesn't exactly assist.

Tad Shull (born 1955)

TENOR SAXOPHONE

Took up sax at 11, studied with Dave Liebman and then in Boston, moving to New York in 1978, playing more with swing stylists than with hard boppers.

*****(*) Deep Passion**

Criss Cross Criss 1047 *Shull; Irving Stokes (t); Mike LeDonne (p); Dennis Irwin (b); Kenny Washington (d).* 11/90.

***** In The Land Of The Tenor**

Criss Cross Criss 1071 *As above, except omit Stokes.* 12/91.

Shull is a big-toned tenor specialist out of Norwalk, Connecticut. His first models were Don Byas and Coleman Hawkins, moving on to Johnny Griffin and Lockjaw Davis. Having taken the trouble to get himself a decent sound and to learn the changes inside out, he's not afraid to tackle ungarnished D flat blues. 'The Eldorado Shuffle' brings *Deep Passion* to a rambunctious, shouting close and *In The Land Of The Tenor* ends in much the same way, with another elastic blues, Lucky Thompson's little-heard 'Prey-loot'.

Thompson also makes his mark on the quieter side of Shull's playing, but he's shown no sign of picking up the soprano, even for tunes which might seem to lie comfortably for the small horn. There's plenty of evidence that Shull keeps his ears open. Though an unabashed traditionalist, he doesn't look the kind of guy who's going to be prepared to grind out 'Body And Soul' every night. On *Deep Passion* (the title-track is another Thompson song) he digs out Mary Lou Williams's 'Why' and Babs Gonzales's 'Soul Stirrin''. A year later, he's working equally enterprising material: Kurt Weill's lovely 'This Is New', Hank Jones's 'Angel Face' and Ellington's 'Portrait Of Bojangles'. The band fits him like an old jacket. LeDonne's a great player who also writes a decent tune; 'Tadpole' and 'Big Ears' on the first record are down to him. Irwin and Washington can't be faulted. It's a pity, though, that Stokes was dropped or couldn't make it to the 1991 session. Despite a tendency to drift into a Wynton-as-Pops mode at inopportune moments, he adds a dimension that's missed the second time around. A shame that we haven't had a new record from Shull for several years now.

Alan Silva (born 1939)

DOUBLE BASS, VIOLIN, CELLO, PIANO, SYNTHESIZERS

Silva's CV is a relatively unusual one. He was born in Bermuda and raised in New York, where he took lessons in piano and violin, before showing an interest in jazz trumpet. Led into jazz by Donald Byrd, he eventually took up double bass at the late age of 23. He was a member of the Sun Ra Arkestra, but his main body of work has been with his own Celestrial Communication Orchestra (see separate entry).

***** Skillfullness**

ESP/Get Back 1091 *Silva; Becky Friend (f); Dave Burrell (p); Mike Ephron (p, org); Karl Berger (vib); Lawrence Cooke (perc); other personnel.* 3/68.

Silva was powerfully influenced by the collective improvisation of John Coltrane's *Ascension* and by his time with Sun Ra. He modelled his work very largely on those experiences, playing down the solo element considerably. Here, on the record he made before moving to France, he utilizes a much smaller ensemble (some members of which went unidentified) to create a gentle blueprint for the ecstatic sound he sought with the Celestrial Communication Orchestra. These are surprisingly delicate pieces, on which Friend and Berger feature strongly. Silva moves from bass to violin and piano, though it's Burrell who most effectively nails down the group's unique free/traditional with piano-playing that hints at stride and ragtime, as well as classical influences. A valuable insight into Silva's early post-Sun Ra career.

*****(*) In The Tradition**

In Situ 166 *Silva; Johannes Bauer (tb); Roger Turner (d, perc).* 4/93.

Silva's discovery of synthesizers was an important moment in his career. This wonderful trio shows how musically and inventively he embraced technology. His wry understanding of what 'standard' means in a jazz context is reflected in the track listing: 'Standards 1–9'. Silva deals with neither orthodox tunes nor straightforward chord sequences, but manages to sound as if he has absorbed the Broadway songbook as well as the solo sequences of *Free Jazz* and *Ascension*.

Turner and Bauer are utterly *simpatico* and any reservations we have about this record stem from an unlovely mix and from a tendency to repeat ideas with irrelevant embellishment rather than moving on.

*****(*) A Hero's Welcome: Pieces For Rare Occasions – Volume 1**

Eremite MTE 017 *Silva; William Parker (b).* 3/98.

Two modern giants of the bull fiddle, united in a project of awesome power. Silva's ambitions to write orchestrally have finally been fulfilled. He uses MIDI keyboards and old-fashioned acoustic piano to create a body of sound that occupies a mid-territory between Duke Ellington or Charles Mingus and Edgard Varèse. The five relatively brief sections might almost be movements in a romantic symphony, were the language and articulation not so unmistakably American.

Parker is by now beyond reproach and beyond categorization; but what is surprising is how thoroughly and how completely Silva still thinks/plays like a bass-player, even if nowadays his imagination ranges right across the strings and beyond.

****(*) Alan Silva & The Sound Visions Orchestra**

Eremite MTE 026 *Silva; Roy Campbell (t, flhn); Taylor Ho Bynum, Stephen Haynes, Raphe Malik (t); Art Baron, Steve Swell (tb); Bill Lowe (btb, tba); Mark Taylor (frhn); Elliot Levin (ss, picc); Rob Brown, Ori Kaplan (as); Sabir Mateen (ts, cl, f); Kidd Jordan, Andrew Lamb (ts); Scott Currie (bs); J. D. Parran (bsx, acl); William Connell Jr (bcl, f); Karen Borca (bsn); Mark Hennen (p); Joe Daley (tba); Wilber Morris (b); Jackson Krall (d); Steve Dalachiunsky (v).* 5/99.

Some fine moments in the three free-speaking pieces by the orchestra, but judged as a record this one doesn't come over too well. The recording quality simply isn't good enough to handle such a complex entity, and some absorbing solos and ensemble passages get lost in the mix. Silva's synthesizer sits awkwardly with the rest of the ensemble, and Dalachinsky's (barely audible) poetry at the start of the first piece rekindles old beatnik memories.

***** Transmissions**

Eremite MTE 027 *Silva; Oluyemi Thomas (bcl, Cmel, f, perc).* 10/99.

Silva sticks to bass here, with the elusive Thomas, a free-music veteran who's only seldom recorded. Some of the duos (divided into five, though they run as a continuous sequence) are simple, almost sweetly beatific, such as 'Lofty Flight'. Most of the interest, though, centres around Silva's often brilliant work, as in 'Offering To The Exalted One'. Thomas has things to say, but he rarely comes over as a significant force.

Judi Silvano

VOCALS

Born in Philadelphia, Silvano is an adventurous singer still unfairly best known for her work on husband Joe Lovano's records. Her own deserve close investigation.

***** Dancing Voices**

Orchard 5776 *Silvano; Tim Hagans (t); Joe Lovano (ss, ts, perc); Salvatore Bonafede, Kenny Werner (p); Scott Lee (b); Jeff Hirshfield (d); Val Hawk, Spencer McLeish (v).* 97.

An ambitious debut from a singer who scats confidently but who is also able to carve the lyrical core out of a jazz theme (like Charlie Haden's 'Silent Longing') and give it new life as a song. She pays tribute to another jazz couple, Abbey Lincoln and Max Roach, on 'Living Room' and dabbles in something more experimental with husband Joe and bassist Lee on the strange 'Trio Freeyo'. Lincoln's records are probably the best point of comparison, but Silvano's is a less theatrical and less self-absorbed voice.

***** Songs I Wrote, Or Wish I Did**

JSL 3 *Silvano; Joe Lovano (ts); Larry Goldings (org); Vic Juris (g); Essiet Okun Essiet (b); Victor Lewis (d).* 6/99.

Shouldn't that be 'Wish I *Had*'? No matter. Silvano's own compositions stand up well here. 'You're My One', which we assume is dedicated to Joe, is an easy Latin swinger, with a lot of musical matter. 'Hey Boy' is a more adventurous scat. Goldings is the new element in the equation here. He gives Judi a funky basis on which to improvise, and mimics some of her more adventurous slides from note to note. There is some lovely guitar, appropriately enough, on Jim Hall's 'Something Tells Me' but, contrary to our previous reservations, the star turn is one of the tracks featuring Joe Lovano, a wonderful interpretation of 'A Flower Is A Lovesome Thing'.

***** Riding A Zephyr**

Soul Note 121348 *Silvano; Mal Waldron (p).* 11/00.

The most minimal accompaniment this time, and from one of the great accompanists. Mal's own 'Soul Eyes' is the outstanding track in a quieter and more intimate set than Silvano has previously attempted. The tempos are generally more relaxed, the emotional temperature somewhere between wistful and romantic. There's an awful tribute to Waldron, a piece which might have gone down fine at a party but not on a CD. Apart from that, very hard to fault. Silvano remains a singer to watch.

Horace Silver (born 1928)

PIANO

Born in Norwalk, Connecticut, he toured with Stan Getz in 1950, then moved to New York and worked with Art Blakey from 1952. Formed own quintet from 1956 and he has largely worked in that format ever since. Spent nearly 30 years with Blue Note, then stints with Columbia and now Impulse!. The defining stylist of hard-bop piano, mixing bebop licks with gospel influences, and an influential composer, as well as one of the most enduring of small-group leaders.

*****(*) Horace Silver Trio**

Blue Note 91725 2 *Silver; Percy Heath, Gene Ramey, Curley Russell (b); Art Blakey (d); Sabu Martinez (perc).* 10/52–11/53.

*****(*) Horace Silver And The Jazz Messengers**
Blue Note 46140-2 *Silver; Kenny Dorham (t); Hank Mobley (ts); Doug Watkins (b); Art Blakey (d).* 11/54.

Horace Silver's records present the quintessence of hard bop. He not only defined the first steps in the style, he also wrote several of its most durable staples, ran bands that both embodied and transcended the idiom and perfected a piano manner which summed up hard bop's wit and trenchancy and popular appeal. The first outcroppings of that can be heard in the *Trio* album, with its first versions of 'Horacescope', 'Opus De Funk' and 'Ecaroh' – funkier and less many-noted than the preceding wave of bop pianists. Silver's borrowings from the swing masters are still in evidence here. The new RVG edition sounds very fine.

The Blue Note *Jazz Messengers* album might be the one that started it all: two sessions, originally issued as a brace of ten-inch LPs, with a definitive hard-bop cast. While the finest music by this edition of the original Jazz Messengers was probably recorded at the Café Bohemia the following year (listed in Art Blakey's entry), this one is still fresh, smart but properly versed in the new language (or, rather, the new setting for the old language). The album sets out Silver's own expertise: a crisp, chipper but slightly wayward style, idiosyncratic enough to take him out of the increasingly stratified realms of bebop piano. Blues and gospel-tinged devices and percussive attacks give his methods a more colourful style, and a generous good humour gives all his records an upbeat feel.

CORE COLLECTION

****** Blowin' The Blues Away**
Blue Note 95342-2 *Silver; Blue Mitchell (t); Junior Cook (ts); Gene Taylor (b); Louis Hayes (d).* 8/59.

Picking a favourite record out of Silver's run of Blue Notes is an invidious task. After many hours of cogitating, we have finally come down on this album, because it seems more than any other to exemplify all his virtues as pianist, composer and leader. The title-track goes off like a typhoon. The ten-bar ballad 'Peace' is one of his most haunting and most-covered themes. 'Sister Sadie' is a soul-jazz classic which other bandleaders were quick to cover. 'The Baghdad Blues' finds him guying various kinds of jazz exoticism. And he ends the record with another version of one of his most durable pieces, 'Melancholy Mood'. It's a typical Blue Note, a characteristic Silver session, but every part of it is powerful enough to transcend what would become clichés of the idiom; and the band all play superbly.

*****(*) Six Pieces Of Silver**
Blue Note 25648-2 *Silver; Donald Byrd (t); Hank Mobley, Junior Cook (ts); Doug Watkins, Gene Taylor (b); Louis Hayes (d); Bill Henderson (v).* 11/56–6/58.

*****(*) Further Explorations**
Blue Note 56583-2 *Silver; Art Farmer (t); Clifford Jordan (ts); Teddy Kotick (b); Louis Hayes (d).* 5/57.

***** Horace-Scope**
Blue Note 84042-2 *Silver; Blue Mitchell (t); Junior Cook (ts); Gene Taylor (b); Roy Brooks (d).* 7/60.

*****(*) The Tokyo Blues**
Blue Note 53355-2 *As above, except Joe Harris (d) replaces Brooks.* 7/62.

***** Silver's Serenade**
Blue Note 21288-2 *As above, except Roy Brooks (d) replaces Harris.* 5/63.

****** Song For My Father**
Blue Note 99002-2 *As above, except add Carmell Jones (t), Joe Henderson (ts), Teddy Smith (b), Roger Humphries (d).* 10/64.

*****(*) Cape Verdean Blues**
Blue Note 84220-2 *Silver; Woody Shaw (t); J. J. Johnson (tb); Joe Henderson (ts); Bob Cranshaw (b); Roger Humphries (d).* 10/65.

****** The Jody Grind**
Blue Note 84250-2 *Silver; Woody Shaw (t); James Spaulding (as, f); Tyrone Washington (ts); Larry Ridley (b); Roger Humphries (d).* 11/66.

***** In Pursuit Of The 27th Man**
Blue Note 35758-2 *Silver; Randy Brecker (t, flhn); Michael Brecker (ts); Dave Friedman (vib); Bob Cranshaw (b); Mickey Roker (d).* 10–11/72.

Although Silver went on to record some 25 further albums for Blue Note, only the above are currently available as CD reissues. *Six Pieces Of Silver*, in its RVG edition, is the latest addition to the pile, an early one: a vintage Silver ballad in 'Shirl', his classic 'Senor Blues' (with a Bill Henderson vocal version from two years later as a bonus), and typical Silver small-combo music in 'Cool Eyes' and 'Camouflage'. It's hard to pick the best of the albums since Silver's consistency is unarguable: each album yields one or two themes that haunt the mind, each usually has a particularly pretty ballad, and they all lay back on a deep pile of solid riffs and workmanlike solos. Silver's own are strong enough, but he was good at choosing sidemen who weren't so characterful that the band would overbalance: Cook, Mitchell, Mobley, Shaw, Jones and Spaulding are all typical Silver horns, and only Johnson (who was guesting anyway) and Henderson on the above records threaten to be something rather more special. Two of the two choicest records, though, are surely *Song For My Father* – with its memorable title-tune, the superb interplay of Jones and Henderson, and the exceptionally fine trio ballad, 'Lonely Woman' – and *The Jody Grind* – which hits some sort of apex of finger-snapping intensity on the title-tune and 'Mexican Hip Dance'. *Blowin' The Blues Away* includes the soul-jazz classic 'Sister Sadie', sounding very hot in its new RVG edition; and although this and each of the two subsequent albums with this line-up has its merits, our favourite of the three might be *The Tokyo Blues*, with its material inspired by a trip to Japan and the band playing at the top of its game. The somewhat earlier *Further Explorations* marks the start of the long association between Farmer and Jordan, who were still recording together with memorable results in the '80s.

The Cape Verdean Blues presents Henderson, Shaw and Johnson on three tracks for one of Silver's most full-bodied front lines. A more recent reappearance is *Silver's Serenade*, a typically solid if unremarkable set of Silverisms. His piano solo on the title-piece is a compendium of quotes and licks that he shapes with a kind of diffident aplomb, as if he knows that this stuff comes so easily he could do it in his sleep. The rougher 'Let's Get To The Nitty Gritty' is a more wholehearted groover. In the end, Silver's albums miss the intensity that came as second nature to Blakey's Jazz Messengers: his blues are chirpier, less driven, and to that extent the records feel less significant. But in their in-the-pocket rightness, they perhaps define the Blue Note sound better than any other.

In Pursuit Of The 27th Man was one of his final Blue Notes. While the label was going to pieces around him, Silver's constancy was extraordinary: with the Breckers out front, he still cut the better part of a characteristic Horace session, with 'Nothin' Can Stop Me Now' at least woven from all his classic threads. Some tracks, though, follow an MJQ instrumentation, with Silver and vibist David Friedman plaiting their lines.

*****(*) Paris Blues**
Pablo 5316-2 *Silver; Blue Mitchell (t); Junior Cook (ts); Gene Taylor (b); Roy Brooks (d).* 10/62.

Away from Rudy Van Gelder's, the Silver group never sounds quite the same. This is a set of their contemporary hits – 'Tokyo Blues', 'Filthy McNasty' and the like – from a gig at the Paris Olympia. Both Mitchell and Cook play some beautiful stuff and the recording (despite the away-from-home locale) is actually very fine. More relaxed, less taut than the Blue Note records, a valuable look at the band *en vacances*.

****** Retrospective**
Blue Note 495576-2 4CD *As Blue Note albums above, plus Randy Brecker, Charles Tolliver, Cecil Bridgewater, Tom Harrell (t); Tyrone Washington, Stanley Turrentine, Michael Brecker, Harold Vick, Bennie Maupin, George Coleman, Bob Berg, Larry Schneider (ts); Dave Friedman (vib); Bob Cranshaw, John Williams, Larry Ridley, Ron Carter (b); John Harris Jr, Mickey Roker, Al Foster (d); Bill Henderson, Chief Bey, Gail Nelson (v); brass, chorus.* 10/52–11/78.

A superbly chosen anthology of Silver's many albums for Blue Note, with the first three discs full of peerless stuff and the fourth making the most of his patchy and often misdirected later work. It samples many otherwise out-of-print records and introduces several players whose Silver age is often forgotten, such as Harrell, Berg and Schneider. The booklet has some glorious Frank Wolff photography as a bonus. The perfect introduction to the master.

*****(*) Jazz Has A Sense Of Humor**
Verve 050293-2 *Silver; Ryan Kisor (t); Jimmy Greene (ss, ts); John Webber (b); Willie Jones III (d).* 12/98.

Informally dedicated to Fats Waller, the music on the Verve album looks from the titles and the lyrics printed on the sleeve (mercifully they are not sung, by anyone) as if they are harbingers of a comedy album. But that's just Horace kidding us around. Actually, the music is as sprightly and righteous as many of his better old records. Solo for solo, Kisor and Greene may not be up to their premier forebears, but this feels more like a genuine Horace Silver band than any of his last few (deleted) efforts. Some of the faster tempos seem too quick – a gutbucket mid-tempo was usually the ideal Silver pace – but never mind, the band clicks.

Silver Leaf Jazz Band

GROUP

Led by trumpeter Chris Tyle, this is a modern group playing New Orleans and vintage Chicago styles.

****(*) Streets And Scenes Of Old New Orleans**
Good Time Jazz GTJCD-15001-2 *Chris Tyle (t, v); David Sager (tb); Jacques Gauthé (cl); Tom Roberts (p); John Gill (d, v).* 5/93.

***** Jelly's Best Jam**
Good Time Jazz GTJCD-15002-2 *Chris Tyle (t); John Gill (tb); Orange Kellin (cl); Tom Roberts, Jelly Roll Morton (p); Vince Giordano (b); Hal Smith (d).* 10/93.

*****(*) Sugar Blues**
Stomp Off CD1298 *Chris Tyle, Leon Oakley (c); John Gill (tb); Mike Baird (cl); Steve Pistorius (p); Clint Baker (bj); Marty Eggers (b); Hal Smith (d).* 4/95.

***** Here Comes The Hot Tamale Man**
Stomp Off CD1311 *Chris Tyle (c, v); Mike Owen (tb); Orange Kellin (cl); Tom Fischer (as); Steve Pistorius (p); Craig Ventresco (g, bj); Mike Eggers (b); Hal Smith (d).* 3/96.

Chris Tyle leads this group of New Orleans wannabees. Even though the group is based in the city, few of them are authentic NO musicians, and followers of this axis of traditional players will recognize many of the names. They got off to a somewhat ordinary start with *Streets And Scenes Of Old New Orleans*: the best numbers are the more obscure pieces, including several by Johnny Wiggs. Tunes as hoary as 'Perdido Street Blues' and 'Tin Roof Blues' have been done more vividly elsewhere. But the subsequent Jelly Roll Morton set, *Jelly's Best Jam*, is much more like the right thing: a shrewd blend of familiar and less hackneyed Morton titles is arranged with enough élan to sidestep mere copycat tactics, and the inclusion of four of Morton's 1938 piano solos offers a ghostly echo of the master's presence.

The two Stomp Off discs follow a similar line of homage without artifice. *Sugar Blues* is a tribute to King Oliver that walks a very difficult line. Tyle's aim was to fashion the sound of the Oliver Creole Jazz Band and put it to use not only on Oliver's repertoire but also on contemporary tunes that he might have played. It's fascinating to hear them tackle 'If You Want My Heart' and 'That Sweet Something, Dear', two famous 'lost' Oliver records, as well as the cornet–piano duet on 'The Pearls' and set-pieces like 'Eccentric'. Tyle is a shrewd judge of tempos and he gets amazingly close to a hi-fi treatment of Oliver's band sound. Not everything convinces, but this is a mostly splendid record.

Even tougher to pull off is the Freddie Keppard homage, *Here Comes The Hot Tamale Man*. With so little surviving evidence to go on, Tyle has still managed to weave together 19 tracks and a sound that seems like a plausible echo of Keppard's terse, often relentless music. His own cornet-playing certainly seems to catch much of the blaring intensity of Keppard himself, and though the rest of the band seem rather less characterful they create convincing treatments of the likes of the title-piece and 'Messin' Around'. Tyle's vocals aren't quite so effective, but he's surely allowed some indulgence.

♛ ****** New Orleans Wiggle**
GHB BCD-347 *Chris Tyle (c, v); Orange Kellin (cl); Steve Pistorius (p); John Gill (d).* 99.

The name of the group – Chris Tyle's Silver Leaf Jazz Band of New Orleans – is now a proud declamation, and Tyle is right to feel chuffed with this quartet and their rugged, sweet, hot music. The four men are by now all masters of the style they set out to inhabit, which isn't really Dixieland, revivalism or even 'New Orleans': it's a modern methodology applied to classic principles, and the results are entirely of their own time. The material goes as near in as 'St Louis Blues' and as far out as Lovie Austin's 'Stepping On The Blues' – a mix of populism and connoisseurship which ought to appeal to anybody. Tyle and Kellin play with stinging spirit and not *too* much finesse,

Pistorius finds all the right feeds and stomps with superb élan, but if one player stands out it's Gill, whose tumbling bravado and dazzling sticksmanship make the quartet into an orchestra. Recorded without needless echo, the sound is as evocative as it should be. Essential, and our only disappointment is that there's been no new record to celebrate in our latest edition.

Sonny Simmons (born 1933)

ALTO AND TENOR SAXOPHONES, COR ANGLAIS

Born Huey Simmons in Louisiana, he moved to California as a boy and took up alto sax. Worked with Prince Lasha for many years and made his recording debut with Lasha's group. Associated with the '60s avant-garde but made only a handful of records and dropped from sight in the '70s, reappearing in the '90s with some new records.

***** Music From The Spheres**

Abraxa/ESP 103 *Simmons; Barbara Donald (t); Bert Wilson (ts); Michael Cohn (p); Joony Booth (b); James Zitro (d).* 66.

A valuable reissue of Simmons's second ESP record, this is immediately marked by the leader's obvious empathy with trumpeter Donald. They work superbly together on the opening 'Resolutions', an enterprising modal composition that sounds like no one else playing at the time. On 'Balladia' the group sound is reminiscent of the classic Ornette–Cherry quartet, though the piano is a giveaway, suggesting a different harmonic approach. Despite that, the main influence on Simmons himself is Eric Dolphy at his most abstract and frantic. Bert Wilson guests on 'Dolphy's Days', but the best thing on the set is the ambitious 'Zarak's Symphony', a strangely vulnerable and elusive idea that isn't allowed to outstay its welcome. Simmons's first ESP session, *Staying On The Watch*, apparently still hasn't reappeared.

***** Manhattan Egos**

Arhoolie CD 483 *Simmons; Barbara Donald (t); Michael White (vn); Juma (b, perc); Kenny Jenkins (b); Paul Smith, Eddie Marshall (d); Voodoo Bembe (perc).* 2/69–11/70.

A reissue of the original Arhoolie LP, with four live quartet tracks dating from the following year. Simmons was a powerful exponent of full-on energy playing, and his solos have retained their fuming energy and directness. The rest of his group is less honoured by the recording, which zeroes in on Donald's fluffs and the clumsy rhythms. The live material fares better in that White's playing, while less relentless than Simmons's, has a raddled elegance to it. A document of its time.

****** Transcendence**

CIMP 113 *Simmons; Michael Marcus (stritch, manzello); Charles Moffett (d).* 4/96.

*****(*) Judgement Day**

CIMP 117 *Simmons; Michael Marcus (manzello, Cmel); Steve Neil (b); Charles Moffett (d).* 5/96.

Two almost desperately powerful records by an angry man. The sleeve-notes say something about the saxophonist's resolve and intensity, revealing the strained circumstances of both sessions, and the bloody virulence of the playing can at times seem as exhausting to listen to as it was to perform. Moffett's swing and jazz time are one leavening agent; the lovely sound of Marcus's horns intertwining with Simmons is another. But these are severely beautiful records altogether, which CIMP's unadulterated sound enhances. The second gets a marginally lower rating if only because Neil sometimes seems an unnecessary addition to the other three. Simmons plays alto on the first, a very dark tenor on the second, and despite evident problems he is awesome.

***** The Cosmosamatics**

Boxholder BXH 022 *Simmons; Michael Marcus (ss, ts, bcl, f); James Carter (bsx); Karen Borca (bsn); William Parker (b); Jay Rosen (d); Samir Chatterjee (tabla).* 2/01.

*****(*) The Cosmosamatics II**

Boxholder BXH 030 *Simmons; Michael Marcus (ss, ts, bcl, f); Curtis Lundy (b); Jay Rosen (d).* 8/01.

Simmons and Marcus had been playing partners for some time when they made the association official by founding this fiery group. The first album kicks off strongly with 'Quasar', on which Parker opens up his usual vein of aural astonishment. Simmons is playing with the same intensity he brought to his early ESP work, but now with a bleakly funky edge. 'Mingus Mangus' brings in tenor-star Carter, but this time with the booming tonality of his bass saxophone. The other guest spots are less happy. The bassoon – Illinois Jacquet notwithstanding – has never been a comfortable jazz instrument, and while Simmons is very committed to double-reeded horns in this context, his recruitment of Borca doesn't quite repay the confidence. She and Chatterjee both feature on the spacey 'Beyond The Inner East', and while they bring some nice textures, they aren't really part of the main action.

The follow-up album is dominated by the spirit of Eric Dolphy, still the most obvious, but only the most obvious, influence on Simmons's work. One track is a tribute to him, but again the lead-off number, 'Fusionanatomy', is the most powerful statement of the set. Parker is missing, but Lundy brings his own singing tone to the session, especially on 'Cosmic Curtis', and the smaller, more coherent group makes sense for music of this stamp. Two intriguing records.

*****(*) Live In Paris**

Arhoolie 506 2CD *Simmons; Jean-Jacques Avenel (b); George Funky Brown (d).* 01.

This is an interesting release, in that it seems to represent an effort on Simmons's part to write himself on to a larger page of jazz history. In addition to his usual, cosmically inclined originals, he includes 'My Favorite Things', 'Hot House', 'Salt Peanuts' and 'Round Midnight' in a long and high-coloured set, playing with a conscious nod to both Parker and John Coltrane. The trio is a high-energy unit, with Avenel playing the rich, flowing bass-lines one is accustomed to from European players (Jenny-Clark and Dave Holland both spring to mind) while Brown lives up to his soubriquet in every bar. The sound is intermittent, as if machines were switched during the set, but as a live recording it is very acceptable and a further welcome glimpse of Simmons taking care of business.

Edward Simon (born 1969)

PIANO

Born in Venezuela, Simon has emerged as one of the more innovative Chick Corea disciples on the scene.

***** Beauty Within**

Audioquest 1025 *Simon; Diego Urcola (t); Anthony Jackson (b); Horacio Hernandez (d).* 93.

***** The Process**
Criss Cross 1229 *Simon; John Patitucci (b); Eric Harland (d).* 03.

The debut album is now almost a decade old, and still Edward Simon hasn't broken through to the reputation he deserves. That, though, may be put right by the appearance of his Criss Cross debut. It's a strong set, with a distinctive Latin tinge that is reminiscent of Chick Corea's less abstract compositions. Simon has a very diligent touch, plays his lines cleanly and keenly and constructs meaningful solos. Fast forward to his 'Woody'N'You' feature on *The Process* to see how quickly he has advanced harmonically. There, too, he has the sterling advantage of the quicksilver Patitucci, who saw service with the Corea group and understands the idiom inside out. Good as the Criss Cross is, we retain an affection for the earlier record with its trundling bass-guitar lines and exuberant swing. Trumpeter Urcola is only on hand for three tracks and his presence somewhat blunts the impact of Simon's coming out. The pianist has a nice touch as a composer, responsive to its main influence but bluesier and romantic without being blowsy.

Ken Simon (born 1948)

TENOR SAXOPHONE

American saxophonist moving in an uncompromising free-jazz direction, mostly.

****(*) The Twilight Of Time**
Cadence CJR 1082 *Simon; Vattel Cherry (b); David Pleasant (d).* 7/97.

***** Another Side**
CIMP 217 *Simon; Jorge Sylvester (ss, as); Greg Maker (b); Barry Altschul (d).* 2/00.

The cover photo of *The Twilight Of Time* looks like Monument Valley, and Simon and his team are like high plains drifters, free-jazz outlaws in an otherwise lawbound time. Romanticism apart, this isn't all that good: the saxophonist doesn't so much build on Albert Ayler's legacy (specifically recalled in 'Albert's Ladder') as flatten it. He's a brutally aggressive player and, since he doesn't have a great deal to say, it's wearisome. Cherry and Pleasant do their best to illuminate, but it's difficult work.

There's an almost apologetic air about *Another Side*, since it arose out of a situation where CIMP boss Bob Rusch heard a tape of Simon playing standards. Since two of the four themes worked on are 'Syeeda's Song Flute', and 'Yesterdays', this is almost Simon going pop. Despite the reference points, there's still a considerable amount of windbag playing. Any opportunity to hear Altschul – still masterful – is welcome, though, and at least there's some light, shade and space in the music. Sylvester is more of a free-bopper than the leader, and he's a useful contrast.

Pete (La Roca) Sims (born 1938)

DRUMS

A New Yorker, Sims – he got his nickname through playing in timbale bands – was an accomplished hard-bop drummer who came to prominence in the late-'50s Sonny Rollins group. Dismayed at the decline of jazz in the late '60s, he left music and studied as an attorney; but he has since returned, although not to full-time performing.

***** SwingTime**
Blue Note 854876-2 *Sims; Jimmy Owens (t); David Liebman, Lance Bryant (ss); Ricky Ford (ts); George Cables (p); Santi Debriano (b).* 2–3/97.

Blue Note collectors will always remember him as Pete La Roca, the nickname he picked up through his expertise as a *timbale* player in Latin bands, 40 years ago; but he prefers plain Pete Sims. The unsung hero of many a hard-bop date, with only the much-liked *Basra* to his name on Blue Note (recently available again briefly as a Connoisseur edition), Sims has had something of a minor resurgence. The drummer has bided his time between occasional gigs and work as an attorney. The return to the studios on *SwingTime* offers a set of likeable, splashy hard bop, something of a contradiction in terms, given the strictness of the genre, but convincing enough. Though he has to split soprano duties with Bryant, Liebman is easily the outstanding player, getting an especially pithy solo into 'Susan's Waltz'. Owens is all right and Ford sounds almost outlandishly larger-than-life on tenor. Sims himself ('I'm really a kettle drummer') isn't shy about leading, although the Newley-Bricusse tune, 'The Candyman', perhaps wasn't his best idea.

Zoot Sims (1925–85)

TENOR, ALTO, SOPRANO AND BARITONE SAXOPHONES, VOCAL

A Californian, and one of Woody Herman's 'Four Brothers' saxophonists in the '40s, Sims continued to play in big-band situations on several tours, but from 1950 was primarily a solo artist who worked in almost countless studio and live situations. One of his most frequent collaborators was fellow tenorman, Al Cohn. Instantly recognizable, and among the most consistently inventive and swinging of musicians, Sims was a paradigmatic jazzman. He died of cancer in 1985, having played for as long as he was able.

***** Zoot Sims Et Henri Renaud**
Emarcy 013037-2 *Sims; Jon Eardley, Jean Liesse, Nat Peck (t); Phillippe Benson (as); Sandy Moss, André Ross (ts); Jean-Louis Chautemps (bs); Fats Sadi (vib); Henri Renaud, Bernard Peiffer (p); Jimmy Gourley (g); Benoît Quersin, Eddie De Haas (b); Charles Saudrais, Pierre Lemarchand, Jean-Louis Viale (d).* 52–56.

***** Quartets**
Original Jazz Classics OJC 242 *Sims; John Lewis, Harry Biss (p); Curley Russell, Clyde Lombardi (b); Don Lamond, Art Blakey (d).* 9/50–8/51.

***** East Of The Apple**
Jasmine JASMCD 2598 *As above, except add Jimmy Woode, Dick Hyman, Gerry Wiggins (p); Simon Brehm, Charlie Short, Pierre Michelot (b); Jack Noren, Ed Shaughnessy, Kenny Clarke (d).* 4/50–8/51.

*****(*) Zoot!**
Original Jazz Classics OJC 228 *Sims; Nick Travis (t); George Handy (p); Wilbur Ware (b); Osie Johnson (d).* 12/56.

Like Jack Teagarden, Zoot Sims started out mature and hardly wavered from a plateau of excellence throughout a long and prolific career (oddly enough, Sims's singing voice sounded much like Teagarden's). As one of Woody Herman's 'Four Brothers' sax section, he didn't quite secure the early acclaim of Stan Getz, but by the time of these sessions he was completely himself: a rich tone emboldened by a sense of swing which didn't falter at any tempo. He sounded as if he enjoyed every solo, and if he really was much influenced by Lester Young – as was the norm for the 'light' tenors of the day – it was at a far remove in emotional terms. *Quartets* sets up the kind of session Sims would record for the next 35 years: standards, a couple of ballads, and the blues, all comprehensively negotiated with a rhythm section that strolls alongside the leader: neither side ever masters the other. 'Zoot Swings The Blues' has Sims peeling off one chorus after another in top gear, while a seemingly endless 'East Of The Sun' shares the solos around without losing impetus. The original Prestige recording is grainy. Ten of these tracks are also on *East Of The Apple*, which is bulked out by two Stockholm sessions and one from Paris. Sound on these isn't too good either (the Paris date is so hissy that everyone will be turning down their treble control) but Sims does his usual cheerful swinging.

Zoot! goes up a notch for the inspirational pairing of Sims and Travis, a minor figure who probably never played as well on record as he does here: 'Taking A Chance On Love' is a near-masterpiece, and Ware and Johnson play superb bass and drums. The Emarcy set belongs more to Renaud than to Sims, since the saxophonist is only on four quartet tracks, with Jon Eardley. Still, they're four fine pieces, after-hours jamming and Sims sounding free as a bird.

*****(*) The Modern Art Of Jazz**
Dawn DCD 101 *Sims; Bob Brookmeyer (vtb); John Williams (p); Milt Hinton (b); Gus Johnson (d).* 1/56.

***** Zoot Sims Goes To Jazzville**
Dawn DCD 103 *Sims; Jerry Lloyd (t); John Williams (p); Bill Anthony, Knobby Totah (b); Gus Johnson (d).* 8–9/56.

*****(*) That Old Feeling**
Chess GRP 18072 *Sims; John Williams (p); Knobby Totah (b); Gus Johnson (d).* 10–11/56.

The Dawn material has been out in various incarnations, often compiled as one CD, but these are surely the definitive editions, with previously unreleased tracks as a bonus. *The Modern Art Of Jazz* is a cracking session with Brookmeyer, both horns ebullient throughout, and though the sound is a bit cavernous it's very listenable. *Zoot Sims Goes To Jazzville* sets him alongside the little-known Lloyd, who does nothing to disgrace himself and has a light though rather short-breathed style. Zoot plays alto on four tracks, and a surprise choice is Monk's 'Bye-Ya'. The original LP programme is bolstered by six extra tracks, four of them 'new'.

That Old Feeling collects two sessions originally released on Argo and ABC-Paramount, including a date where Zoot overdubbed alto and baritone to make a one-man sax section. Unlike other such experiments, this one worked out well. Zoot's utter professionalism, coupled with his easy-going style, seems to have transcended the artifice of the situation, and a couple of tunes – 'Minor Minor' and 'Pegasus' – are lucid gems. But there is also a sumptuous ballad feature on 'The Trouble With Me Is You'.

*****(*) Americans Swinging In Paris**
EMI France 539646-2 *Sims; Jon Eardley (t); Henri Renaud (p); Benoit Querson (b); Charles Saudrais (d).* 3/56.

Zoot and Jon Eardley in absolutely prime form on a Paris stop-over. Renaud and Querson do well and the 18-year-old Charles Saudrais does nothing wrong. Eardley blats a few notes here and there as if his lip wasn't quite on that day but Zoot is magisterial and the very vivid remastering catches his sound beautifully.

***** Either Way**
Evidence ECD 22007-2 *Sims; Al Cohn (ts); Mose Allison (p); Bill Crow (b); Gus Johnson (d); Cecil 'Kid Haffey' Collier (v).* 2/61.

One of the earlier collaborations between these two tenor masters, *Either Way* suffers from a foggy sound-mix and the less-than-desirable presence of Collier, whose singing on three tunes wastes valuable saxophone time (on what is a short CD anyway). But there is still some great duelling on 'The Thing', 'I'm Tellin' Ya' and a honeyed 'Autumn Leaves', plus the bonus of Allison at the piano.

***** Recado Bossa Nova**
Fresh Sound FSR-CD 198 *Sims; Spencer Sinatra (f, picc); Phil Woods (cl); Gene Quill (cl, bcl); Sol Schlinger (bcl); Ronnie Odrich, Phil Bodner, Jerry Sanfino (reeds, f); Jim Hall, Kenny Burrell, Barry Galbraith (g); Milt Hinton, Art Davis (b); Sol Gubin (d); Ted Sommer, Willie Rodriguez, Tommy Lopez (perc).* 8/62–63.

Zoot's entry in the bossa nova craze. Al Cohn and Manny Albam did a perfect pro's job in arranging everything from 'Bernie's Tune' to 'Cano Canoe' for Sims to blow on, and the results are finely manicured without encumbering the saxophonist. He takes some typically swinging, unruffled solos.

***** Zoot Sims In Copenhagen**
Storyville STCD 8244 *Sims; Kenny Drew (p); Niels-Henning Orsted Pedersen (b); Ed Thigpen (d).* 8/78.

A characteristic club date with Zoot. Drawbacks: the rhythm section play well but are too generously featured; the material is stuff Zoot did many times over; the sound is a bit rough here and there. The plus is that Sims is playing close to the top of his latter-day game, which ought to be good enough for anybody.

****** Zoot Sims And The Gershwin Brothers**
Original Jazz Classics OJC 444 *Sims; Oscar Peterson (p); Joe Pass (g); George Mraz (b); Grady Tate (d).* 6/75.

***** Soprano Sax**
Original Jazz Classics OJC 902 *Sims; Ray Bryant (p); George Mraz (b); Grady Tate (d).* 1/76.

****(*) Hawthorne Nights**
Original Jazz Classics OJC 830 *Sims; Oscar Brashear (t); Snooky Young (t, flhn); Frank Rosolino (tb); Bill Hood, Richie Kamuca, Jerome Richardson (reeds); Ross Tompkins (p); Monty Budwig (b); Nick Ceroli (d); Bill Holman (arr).* 9/76.

*****(*) Warm Tenor**
Pablo 2310-831 *Sims; Jimmy Rowles (p); George Mraz (b); Mousie Alexander (d).* 9/78.

*****(*) For Lady Day**
Pablo 2310-942 *As above, except Jackie Williams (d) replaces Alexander.* 4/78.

***** Just Friends**

Original Jazz Classics OJC 499 *Sims; Harry 'Sweets' Edison (t); Roger Kellaway (p); John Heard (b); Jimmie Smith (d).* 12/78.

***** The Swinger**

Original Jazz Classics OJC 855 *Sims; Ray Sims (tb, v); Jimmy Rowles (p); John Heard, Michael Moore (b); Shelly Manne, John Clay (d).* 11/79–5/80.

***** Passion Flower**

Original Jazz Classics OJC 939 *Sims; Bobby Bryant, Al Aarons, Oscar Brashear, Earl Gardner (t); J. J. Johnson, Britt Woodman, Grover Mitchell, Benny Powell (tb); Frank Wess (as, f); Marshal Royal (as); Plas Johnson, Buddy Collette (ts); Jimmy Rowles (p); John Collins (g); Andy Simpkins, John Heard, Michael Moore (b); Grady Tate, Shelly Manne, John Clay (d).* 8/79–5/80.

****** I Wish I Were Twins**

Original Jazz Classics OJC 976 *Sims; Jimmy Rowles (p); Frank Tate (b); Akira Tana (d).* 7/81.

*****(*) The Innocent Years**

Original Jazz Classics OJC 860 *Sims; Richard Wyands (p); Frank Tate (b); Akira Tana (d).* 3/82.

***** Blues For Two**

Original Jazz Classics OJC 635 *Sims; Joe Pass (g).* 3–6/82.

***** On The Korner**

Pablo 2310-953 *Sims; Frank Colett (p); Monty Budwig (b); Shelly Manne (d).* 3/83.

*****(*) Suddenly It's Spring**

Original Jazz Classics OJC 742-2 *Sims; Jimmy Rowles (p); George Mraz (b); Akira Tana (d).* 5/83.

***** Quietly There**

Original Jazz Classics OJC 787 *Sims; Mike Wofford (p); Chuck Berghofer (b); Nick Ceroli (d); Victor Feldman (perc).* 3/84.

**** The Best Of Zoot Sims**

Pablo 2405-406 *As above Pablo albums.*

When Sims signed to Norman Granz's Pablo operation, he wasn't so much at a crossroads as contentedly strolling down an uneventful path. For a man who could fit effortlessly into any situation he chose – admittedly, he never chose a situation that might cause much trouble – Sims could have spent his final years as a nebulous figure. But his Pablo albums set the seal on his stature, sympathetically produced, thoughtfully programmed and with enough challenge to prod Zoot into his best form. *Gershwin Brothers* is a glorious sparring match with Peterson, rising to an almost overpowering charge through 'I Got Rhythm' via a simmering 'Embraceable You' and a variation on Coltrane's approach to 'Summertime'. It's the ravishing tone which makes the session with Pass so attractive: with drums and bass cleared away, the tenor sound is swooningly beautiful. A pity, though, that Pass sounds so perfunctory throughout. The sessions with Jimmy Rowles at the piano, though, are indispensable examples of Zoot at his best. *Warm Tenor* is only a shade behind, and the recently discovered set of tunes associated with Billie Holiday, *For Lady Day*, is another plum choice, with an amble through 'You Go To My Head' that dispels the happy-sad clouds of Holiday's *œuvre* with a smouldering lyricism. *Suddenly It's Spring* is another that betrays Rowles's affection for unlikely material – 'In The Middle Of A Kiss', 'Emaline', even Woody Guthrie's 'So Long' – and though the playing seems a shade too relaxed in parts, it's still delightful music. *The Swinger* reunites Zoot with brother Ray and they make a joshing, harmless team: 'Now I Lay Me Down To Dream Of You' is sweetness personified. *I Wish I Were Twins* is at last on CD, and it's another great one. Perhaps new rhythm section Frank Tate and Akira Tana push Rowles a little too much, but there is a little masterpiece in their version of 'Georgia'. *The Innocent Years* substitutes Wyands for Rowles, and this is a swinging session: Zoot does an earthy blues on soprano, plays 'Over The Rainbow' as a fast samba and takes 'The Very Thought Of You', which was one of his favourite vehicles for soprano, at his patented easy lope.

Soprano Sax was one of his earliest Pablos but is only recently on CD. Zoot grew to like his second horn and he sounds just like himself on it, a pinchier, tinier Zoot but still a perfect lyricist on 'Baubles, Bangles And Beads' and his favourite 'Bloos For Louise'. *Passion Flower* features him with a big band scored by Benny Carter on nine Ellington tunes. The charts are frankly functional rather than inspiring, but Zoot tended to find his inspirations from within anyway and he seems chipper enough.

The only real disappointment is *Hawthorne Nights*, which finds Zoot a tad perfunctory for once on a generally uninspiring set of Bill Holman charts. *On The Korner* finds him in a San Francisco club, still enjoying himself, with 'Dream Dancing' and the surprisingly urgent soprano rendition of 'Tonight I Shall Sleep' of special interest; Frank Colett plays fine supporting piano. Although only a year away from his death when he made *Quietly There*, a set of Johnny Mandel themes, Sims was still in absolute command. Feldman's percussion adds a little extra fillip to the likes of 'Cinnamon And Clove', although Sims himself sounds undistracted by anything: his winding, tactile improvisation on the melody of 'A Time For Love', to pick a single instance, bespeaks a lifetime's preparation. The *Best Of* is a mysteriously ill-chosen retrospective: better to pick any one of the albums with Rowles if a single disc is all that's required.

CORE COLLECTION

****** If I'm Lucky**

Original Jazz Classics OJC 683 *Sims; Jimmy Rowles (p); George Mraz (b); Mousie Alexander (d).* 10/77.

***If I'm Lucky* is, narrowly, the pick from the Pablo stable of recordings, for its ingenious choice of material – '(I Wonder Where) Our Love Has Gone' counts as one of Sims's most affecting performances – and the uncanny communication between saxophonist and pianist throughout.**

***** Elegiac**

Storyville STCD 8238 *Sims; Bucky Pizzarelli (g).* 11/80.

A live date comes out of the shadows of a large discography. *Elegiac* follows the same format as *Blues For Two*, this time with the more muscular style of Pizzarelli in the partnership. Some of the playing is nearly ferocious, such as the whipcrack treatment of 'Limehouse Blues', and it's interesting to hear Sims blow on some of his latter-day favourites in this context. But it has to be docked a point for the very grey sound of what must have been an amateur recording.

Hal Singer (born 1919)

TENOR SAXOPHONE

Grew up in Tulsa, and served an apprenticeship with Jay McShann before joining Lucky Millinder's band and ultimately Duke Ellington's. Then Singer had an R&B hit with 'Cornbread', which earned him his nickname. He played rock'n'roll for a while, and emigrated to Europe, but jazz and America's heartland were his first loves.

***** Blue Stompin'**

Original Jazz Classics OJCCD 834 *Singer; Charlie Shavers (t); Ray Bryant (p); Wendell Marshall (b); Osie Johnson (d).* 59.

Uncomplicated jazz with an R&B flavour from the man they called 'Cornbread'. The plus on these 1959 sessions is Shavers, who plays bright, excitable trumpet on most selections, and stars on his own 'Windy'. The 11-minute 'Midnight' is a typical Singer workout, but it's interesting to listen again and hear just how subtle and logical his solo-building can be. Entertaining stuff from one of the industry's great characters.

Alex Sipiagin

TRUMPET, FLUGELHORN

Sought-after big-band player with experience in the George Gruntz outfit and the Mingus Big Band, making a strong start to a solo recording career.

***** Images**

TCB 98602 *Sipiagin; Josh Roseman (tb); Dave Binney (as); Chris Potter (ts); Kenny Wollesen (p); Gil Goldstein (p, acc); Adam Rogers (g); Scott Colley (b); Jeff Hirshfield (d).* 98.

The most convincing token of Sipiagin's originality is the lovely pealing version of the traditional Russian theme 'Novgorod Bells' on the first album. Alex has a somewhat unorthodox take on the blues and blues-derived jazz, very competent with the changes, but always sounding as if he's learned it retranslated from some other source. Which is all to the good, with so many drab Browniephiles and Milesians cluttering the scene. He is a genuine original, and his 'Little Dancer' is a lovely composition. The band is well weighted and strong-voiced, and Alex gives his fellow players plenty of the limelight.

*****(*) Steppin' Zone**

Criss Cross 1202 *Sipiagin; Chris Potter (ts); David Kikoski (p); Scott Colley (b); Jeff 'Tain' Watts (d).* 6/00.

The Criss Cross debut feels like a homecoming. Much of the huff and effort that lay behind the first record has been brokered into brisk, confident playing, with Alex very much at the heart of the action. The only thing that's been stepped on is a strange version of George Shearing's 'Conception', which is almost unrecognizable. Scott Colley's 'Catalyst' opens and closes the date, two different interpretations that hint at the shifting mood of the album. The longest piece is Kikoski's 'Spacing', which is a latter-day 'Giant Steps' in zero gravity and the thinnest harmonic atmosphere – original, engaging and a great theme to blow on. As on the first record, Sipiagin includes a Pat Metheny composition; 'Missouri Uncompromised' is not as immediately engaging as 'Midwestern Night Dream' on *Images*, but it has more going for it as an improvisation theme. Another fine record from the trumpeter and a secure berth at what is currently the top-drawer label.

*****(*) Hindsight**

Criss Cross 1220 *Sipiagin; Chris Potter (ts); Adam Rogers (g); Boris Kozlov (b); Gene Jackson (d).* 5/01.

No piano this time, but Rogers fits into the mix beautifully, playing horn-like lead lines and the open, capacious chords that fuel the long, blues-inspired title-track. Alex seems to like opening and closing albums with the same theme. Here it's a long, then longer still, version of Bill Evans's 'Very Early', a more obvious curtain piece than an opener, but beautifully done in both places. Kozlov is a bit of a revelation. His harmonic understanding is best attested on 'Hindsight', but elsewhere his subtle understanding of the rhythm is an important factor in the group's and the album's success. Sipiagin continues to play beautifully, and his duet with Rogers on 'Light Blue' (on flugelhorn this time) is simply gorgeous. We also like what he's done with Mingus's 'Reincarnation Of A Love Bird', familiar material for Alex, but done with a fullness of sound that briefly makes the quintet sound like, well, a Mingus band; Kozlov's well to the fore here as well.

***** Mirrors**

Criss Cross 1236 *Sipiagin; Josh Roseman (tb); Seamus Blake (ts); Donny McCaslin (ss, ts); David Kikoski (p); Adam Rogers (g); Boris Kozlov (b); Jonathan Blake (d).* 6/02.

Piano and guitar this time, and a much fuller sound throughout the set. This isn't perhaps the killer punch we'd hoped for after the steady progress of the previous records. It's a solid, very thoughtful set, marked out again by strong originals – 'Def I' and 'Def II' (this time placed next-to-last) – and an even more powerful closing track, 'Mood One', and the immensely thoughtful 'Travel', which follows a slice of Mingus's *Tijuana Moods*, suggesting that that music, on which Alex has worked with the Mingus Big Band, is very much part of his personal itinerary. It's a powerful statement, as are the other new pieces, but somehow the album doesn't quite gel.

Blaise Siwula (born 1950)

ALTO AND SOPRANO SAXOPHONES

Originally from Detroit, Siwula has been in the thick of New York's free scene since arriving there in 1989, although he had hitherto recorded little prior to these sets for Cadence and CIMP.

****(*) Dialing Privileges**

CIMP 197 *Siwula; Dom Minasi (g); John Bollinger (d).* 3/99.

****(*) Badlands**

Cadence CJR 1120 *Siwula; Vattel Cherry (b); Jeff Arnal (d).* 1–5/00.

***** Tandem Rivers**

Cadence CJR 1157 *Siwula; Adam Lane (b).* 3/02.

Siwula is a peculiar mix of ancient and modern. He has a broad, almost New Orleansian vibrato, which he uses either on unfancy melodic motifs or huge exhalations of sound. It's free playing somewhat in the Ayler tradition, but without the subtexts of spirituals and blues. *Dialing Privileges* matches him against the scrabbled 12-string guitar of Minasi (often barely audible) and the tight, sometimes militaristic drumming of

Bollinger. Here and there they get quite funny, as in the chicken-strut climax of 'Trawler', and the free-for-all format hides away a few engaging tunes. Tough work, but not unrewarding.

Badlands intersperses five brief alto solos with five (much longer) live trio tracks. The solos are far more interesting: some of them seem, inevitably, like studio exercises, but the curious feel that the vibrato lends suggests playing which is being reproduced at a pace faster than real time. The trio music tends to run along well-worn freakout grooves, and perhaps the most interesting thing is Arnal's opening solo on 'Freedom In Wind'.

Tandem Rivers is much gentler and more amenable, with Siwula picking up the soprano for some of the way. The two musicians work at a level of genuine melodic dialogue, and while one feels that they've said most of what they have to after half an hour or so, the record doesn't entirely outstay its welcome.

Greg Skaff

GUITAR

Mainstream guitarist, formerly a Stanley Turrentine sideman, with a nicely individual style.

***** Blues And Other News**

Double Time 111 *Skaff; Bruce Barth (p); Tony Scherr (b); Greg Hutchinson (d).* 96.

*****(*) Blues For Mr T**

Khaeon 200307 *Skaff; Mike LeDonne (org); Joe Farnsworth (d).* 03.

A big gap between the first and second records, but no obvious explanation why. The market is pretty saturated with discs like these – competent, even clever, originals delivered with confidence and, in the case of the second album, a hint of class. Unfortunately, not much else to lift them out of the slush pile. Skaff's sound is meaty and resonant, occasionally reminiscent of Larry Coryell in his more straightahead style, but also sufficiently individual not to sound like a cloned manner. 'In Walked Bud' on the first album is probably the best single thing on either set, but the second disc is ahead by a short nose if you're tempted to sample Skaff's work. On it, he reprises the sax–organ–guitar sound of the Turrentine group but, as so often with younger players, tries to do it in a lo-fat style that rather misses the point. The title-piece pays overt tribute, but the inclusion of 'Isfahan', one Freddie Hubbard and one lovely McCoy Tyner tune ('Inception') suggests that Greg is trying to push the boat out a bit. 'Super 80' has a Coltrane influence, but doesn't deliver on its promise.

Alan Skidmore (born 1942)

TENOR SAXOPHONE

Son of saxophonist Jimmy, he played with big bands and blues groups in the '60s. Formed his own band at the end of the '60s, but has since followed a journeyman route, playing with many leaders; an accomplished stylist with his influences fully assimilated.

****** After The Rain**

Miles Music MMCD 084 *Skidmore; Colin Towns Mask Symphonic; Radio-Philharmonie Hannover des NDR; individual personnels not listed.* 98.

Like his saxophonist father, Jimmy, who was a stalwart of the British mainstream scene in the '50s and early '60s, Alan Skidmore is much less well known than he ought to be. In a wilderness of clones, he stands out – admittedly older and therefore wiser – as one of the few who have submitted the Coltrane legacy to thoughtful consideration, rather than taking it as licence for frenzied harmonic activity and emotional streaking. Skidmore is rather poorly represented on record, though he can also be heard on a growing range of reissued British jazz records from the Golden Age of the late '60s and early '70s.

Coltrane is the dominant presence on the big-band album as well. Three of the pieces are Trane compositions ('After The Rain', 'Naima' and 'Central Park West'), and four more ('Nature Boy', 'Nancy', Fred Lacey's 'Theme For Ernie' and 'In A Sentimental Mood') were recorded by him at one time or another. Any doubts about putting jazz improvisers in strings settings should by now have been thoroughly dispelled. Here the backgrounds are as unobtrusive and subtly shaded as one could wish for, giving the album an intimate, quietly reflective feel rather than syrupy excess. The German orchestra's underpainting on 'Nature Boy' is breathtaking, a brief overture to an unaccompanied statement of Eden Ahbez's haunting melody. Palle Mikkelborg is the conductor and he organizes the sound with his usual deft touch. Engineer Manfred Kietzke has Skidmore well out in front and slightly off-centre, which gives his solos even greater presence.

***** The Call**

Provocateur Records PVC 1018 *Skidmore; Colin Towns (ky); Steve Melling (p); Arnie Somogyi (b); Gary Husband (d); Madosini Manqineni (mouth bow); Mandla Lande, Michael Ludonga, Simpawe Matole, Zandisile Mbizela, Dizu Zungula Plaatjies, Mzwandile Qotoyi (perc, v); Dizu Kudu Horn Band.* 4 & 5/99.

***** Ubizo**

Provocateur PVC 1036 *Skidmore; Ingolf Burkhardt (t, flhn); Steve Melling (p); Colin Towns (ky); Arnie Somogyi (b); Stephen Keogh (d); Mandla Lande, Michael Ludonga, Risenga Makondo, Simpiwe Matole, Mzwandile Qotoyi (perc).* 10/02.

Back in the days of SOS, his saxophone trio with John Surman and Mike Osborne, Skidmore liked nothing more than getting in behind the drumkit for a couple of numbers. Though his playing career has been almost entirely focused on the saxophone, Skid professes to be a drummer at heart and *The Call* sees him reunited with South African group, Amampondo, whom he first met on a trip to the Cape in 1994.

Five years later, Colin Towns of Provocateur Records organized a return trip and a recording session. Skidmore fits into the distinctive triplet rhythm of the African group with consummate ease. Years of standing on bandstands with the late Dudu Pukwana presumably alerted him to the possibilities of this kind of music and, though the dedication of the record is once again to John Coltrane, it is Dudu's spirit which shines through at every turn. Trane's ballad playing informs 'Bridges Of Sand', a delicate duo with Towns, and the strangely moving 'Migration', which also features Arnie Somogyi's sonorous bass; but it is the numbers with Amampondo and on 'Rwakanembe' the Dizu Kudu Horn Band which catch the attention. Kudu horn is one of your more recherché jazz instrumental categories – but what an infectious sound, and what a delightful album.

Ubizo was recorded following a short UK tour. It features a strong blend of original and traditional African themes. The title again means 'The Call', but this time Skidmore's clarion is less immediately compelling and the music, if not the playing, seems more willed and self-conscious. Nevertheless, Skidmore's achievement as the first British jazz musician to visit South Africa since the fall of apartheid is a signal one, and his approach to this music is joyous and full-hearted.

Steve Slagle (born 1951)

ALTO AND SOPRANO SAXOPHONES

Born in Los Angeles, Slagle's family moved east in the '60s and he studied at Berklee from 1970. Early work included playing with Lionel Hampton (lead alto), Woody Herman (on tenor), Jack McDuff and the Carla Bley Band.

*** The Steve Slagle Quartet

Steeplechase SCCD 31323 *Slagle; Tim Hagans (t); Scott Colley (b); Jeff Hirshfield (d).* 11/92.

***(*) Spread The Word

Steeplechase SCCD 31354 *As above.* 4/94.

***(*) Reincarnation

Steeplechase SCCD 31367 *Slagle; Kenny Drew Jr (p); Cameron Brown (b); Jeff Hirshfield (d).* 10/94.

Slagle has hitherto been best known by association – as a sideman with Carla Bley and in the Mingus Big Band, for instance – but his several albums as a leader deserve a hearing. *Quartet* features some difficult writing by the leader: 'Leadbelly Sez' is a tricky eight-bar blues, and 'Mondo' might suggest a leaning towards the original Ornette Coleman quartet. Colley and Hirshfield work very capably behind the horns, and Hagans plays thoughtfully. The quartet return for *Spread The Word*, and this time it manages to suggest an eloquent kind of free playing that actually owes little to Coleman's quartet. The improvising has an air of long-breathed virtuosity about it, the many-noted solos rooted in bebop but coloured by the freedoms of what came after. If the leader's convolutions suggest a struggle with form, Hagans's calm and lucid playing reconciles structure with freedom, and the contrast between the two styles makes the music compelling and rounded at the same time.

Slagle's own work suggests a link between hard-bop stylists and the free players of a generation later, which some of his own sleeve-notes on *Reincarnation* also allude to. The opening track here is a long, sinewy extemporization on Charles Mingus's 'Reincarnation Of A Lovebird', and Slagle recalls how it struck him as a link between Parker and Dolphy. If you add Jackie McLean to the mixture, it could almost come up as Slagle himself, and this twisting solo is certainly one of the best things he's done on record. There are fine ballads in 'Soultrane' and 'Bess, You Is My Woman Now', and though one misses some of the interaction which Hagans created on the other discs, Slagle takes the weight on his own shoulders very convincingly. In the circumstances, Drew's excellent work is something of a bonus.

*** Our Sound!

Double-Time DTRCD-107 *Slagle; Dave Stryker (g); Bill Moring (b); Tony Reedus (d).* 4/95.

***(*) Alto Blue

Steeplechase SCCD 31416 *Slagle; Ryan Kisor (t); Scott Colley (b); Gene Jackson (d).* 4/97.

The Double-Time session, taken down more or less on the hoof, is a swinging, genuine date with plenty to listen to – Stryker is a good partner, offering harmonic leads without tying the leader down, and Reedus stokes the rhythms with a good deal of fire. 'Theme For Ernie' is a persuasive rendering of the dedication to Ernie Henry. But a couple of choices seem less effective: Mingus's 'Haitian Fight Song' doesn't really convince as a quartet tune and 'Little Rootie Tootie' seems arbitrarily done. Keeper: the duet on 'Lush Life'.

Alto Blue is more like it and arguably Slagle's best to date. The music is all blues, either in form or feeling, and with Kisor matching or even outplaying the leader on some pieces the content is way up. Slagle's three originals work beautifully and his flute feature on 'Detour Ahead' is clean as a whistle. Colley and Jackson vary the rhythms and sponsor the horns without getting in their way, and the studio sound catches them all to a tee.

*** New New York

Omnitone 12005 *Slagle; Joe Lovano (ts); Joe Locke (vib); Dave Stryker (g); Cameron Brown (b); Gene Jackson (d).* 6/00.

Well, not *that* new. Essentially this is a continuation of the Steeplechase work, with perhaps a slightly more packaged and conceptually considered feel to it – and nothing wrong with that. But Slagle is a typical New York jazzman of today, for sure, playing with bands of many stripes, in and out of jazz, and stewing up all this experience when it comes to helming his own date. So there's a juicy amount of rhythmic and textural detail, without quite establishing a defining course or a particularly cathartic moment. It's mostly quartet music, with Locke and Lovano taking a guest turn apiece, the vibesman sounding coolly efective on 'What Goes Around Comes Around'. Highly enjoyable, without pitching even close to classic status.

Don Sleet (1938–86)

TRUMPET

Sleet worked in California in the '50s and '60s and spent some years with the San Diego Symphony, but his boppish delivery brought him this one date as a leader in the studios.

*** All Members

Original Jazz Classics OJC 1949 *Sleet; Jimmy Heath (ts); Wynton Kelly (p); Ron Carter (b); Jimmy Cobb (d).* 3/61.

Long a collectors' favourite, it's nice to welcome a CD edition of this pleasing date. It is, in truth, no great masterpiece: the quintet play within themselves, Carter's bowed solos are an annoyance, and not much really sticks in the mind. But Sleet, for all his share of fluffs (surprising for someone with as much classical experience – maybe he was nervous), shies away from the obvious. He sounds as if he wants to be Miles Davis for much of the way, with long vibratoless notes and a touch of the Davis preening on ballads, but he'll suddenly throw in an excitable phrase or follow a sequence of short remarks with a long, handsomely executed line. Heath sounds full and resonant in his solos and brought in the title-track; there are also two Clifford Jordan tunes. A shame that the leader never had another chance out front.

Carol Sloane (born 1937)

VOCAL

American vocalist who made some Columbia albums in the early '60s, re-emerging in the '80s as a more jazz-directed singer, recording for independent labels.

***** Love You Madly**

Contemporary 14049-2 *Sloane; Art Farmer (flhn); Clifford Jordan (ts); Kenny Barron, Richard Rodney Bennett (p); Kenny Burrell (g); Rufus Reid, Akira Tana (d).* 10/88.

***** The Real Thing**

Contemporary 14060-2 *Sloane; Phil Woods (as); Mike Rienzi (p); Rufus Reid (b); Grady Tate (d, v).* 5/90.

*****(*) Sweet And Slow**

Concord CCD 4564 *Sloane; Frank Wess (ts, f), Stefan Scaggiari (p); John Lockwood (b); Colin Bailey (d)* 4/93.

Carol Sloane's quiet, considered style of singing isn't so much conversational as conspiratorial. She takes as many liberties with a melody as many a more flamboyant singer, and she has the ability to swing in her easeful way; but since her voice often resembles a sung whisper, one could mistake her delicacy for reserve. She actually rises to the challenge of the material with consistent aplomb. These are not especially varied albums and it's hard to pick out a singular gem, but consistency is her long suit. Like many such singers, she has been around long enough to be a veteran but has built up a significant catalogue in the CD era only by dint of sympathetic labels such as Concord. The two Contemporary albums, though, are just as strong. *Love You Madly* has the support of the Art Farmer group which made some superb sets for Contemporary. While it stays in the background, there are some lovely moments, especially when Burrell plays a couple of softly-softly duets with Sloane. Bennett does a turn only on 'Norwegian Wood', which seems to have strayed in from another record altogether. *The Real Thing* is handsomely arranged by Rienzi and has Woods turning in five typically flawless solos in support. Tate sings a duet on 'Makin' Whoopee'. *Sweet And Slow* benefits from the trio's eloquent support, with Wess as a bonus and this might be the best place to hear her.

***** The Songs Sinatra Sang**

Concord CCD 4725 *Sloane; Byron Stripling, Greg Gisbert (t); Steve Turre (tb); Bill Easley (ss, as, ts); Scott Robinson (bs, bcl, bsx); Frank Wess (ts, f); Bill Charlap (p); Ben Brown, Sean Smith (b); Dennis Mackrel, Ron Vincent (d).* 3/96.

***** The Songs Ella & Louis Sang**

Concord CCD 4787 *Sloane; Clark Terry (t, flhn, v); Bill Charlap (p); Marcus McLaurine (b); Dennis Mackrel (d).* 5/97.

Sloane's very own songbook series. These are records to admire, gracefully achieved, although they're never much more than the sum of their parts. *Sinatra* is a little burdened by its horn charts which sound a bit tacked on: Sloane does best by a long and slow, but successful, 'One For My Baby' and the gentle coda of 'Young At Heart'. She obviously likes Charlap, and he does good service on both discs. *Ella & Louis* is a tailor-made opportunity for Terry to do his thing, with horn and with voice, and they clearly had fun on chestnuts like 'I Won't Dance' and 'Blueberry Hill'. However, both principals, without being uncharitable, don't have quite the chops that they once did.

***** I Never Went Away**

High Note HCD 7085 *Sloane; Bill Easley (ts, cl, f); Norman Simmons (p); Paul Bollenback (g); Steve LaSpina (b); Kenny Washington (d).* 6/01.

A new label for Carol, and a very gracious beginning. Norman Simmons, who did much work with Joe Williams in his later years, is the anchor here, and he's assembled a sympathetic team. The songs have not a single hackneyed choice among them, unless you count 'Cotton Tail', which is in any case set to Jon Hendricks's lyrics. Sweetly enjoyable, although in the end it's a record by a vocalist in her autumnal years.

Bill Smith (born 1926)

CLARINET

Born in Sacramento, Smith studied under Darius Milhaud at Mills College and at the Juilliard School. He was a member of Dave Brubeck's influential Octet and has worked with Brubeck again in more recent years. His advanced ideas are unique and still overlooked, largely because his own recording career has been so slight.

*****(*) Folk Jazz**

Original Jazz Classics OJCCD 1956 *Smith; Jim Hall (g); Monty Budwig (b); Shelly Manne (d).* 2 & 11/59.

Far ahead of its time in its integration of modern modal jazz and folk music, this sees Smith take a group of traditional songs, all the way from 'Greensleeves' to American classics like 'Nobody Knows The Trouble I've Seen', 'Go Down Moses' and 'Nobody Knows You When You're Down And Out', and subjects them to gently swinging, harmonically subtle arrangement. Hall's clean comping takes the place of a piano and sounds more open and folkish, while Budwig plays with typical subtlety. Highpoints of the album include a version of 'Black Is The Colour of My True Love's Hair' which rivals Luciano Berio's in *Folk Songs*. Smith's lean clarinet introduction is inch-perfect and the best possible introduction to the clarinettist's work. Reissued in 2003, this is a valuable rediscovery.

Hal Smith (born 1953)

DRUMS

A pro since the late '70s, Smith is from Indiana but is associated with many West Coast revivalist groups and New Orleans bands of today, leading the Frisco Syncopators and the Down Home Jazz Band.

***** Milneburg Joys**

GHB BCD-277 *Smith; Chris Tyle (c); David Sager (tb); Jacques Gauthé (cl, ss); Steve Pistorius (p); Amy Sharpe (bj); Bernie Attridge (b).* 6/89.

Smith and Tyle were at this point co-leaders of the Frisco Syncopators, one of the several fine American trad groups currently revisiting the classic repertoire with unusual aplomb, although both can also be found on numerous other projects. Though they take their cue from Bob Scobey's original Frisco Jazz Band, the group is actually New Orleans-based, and their approach seasons chestnuts such as 'Skid-Dat-De-Dat' and 'Panama' with enough sharpness to lend a fresh point of view. The rhythm of the group attains a nice blend of sleekness and ragged drive, and in the clean-toned Tyle and the adept Pistorius they have two excellent soloists. The studio sound eschews the accustomed murk of trad recordings in favour of a crisp and punchy attack that gives the record extra zip, although most of the vocals are the usual acquired taste in this setting.

Harrison Smith

TENOR AND SOPRANO SAXOPHONES, BASS CLARINET

British bop-to-free saxophonist with a wide CV.

***** Outside Inside**

Slam CD 231 *Smith; Liam Noble (p); Jeremy Brown (b); Winston Clifford (d).* 3/98.

Smith belongs to a generation of British players for whom rapid transition between free music and a settled groove presents no difficulty. Sparingly recorded for a musician of his experience, he plays with maturity and presence on this session as leader. Opening with bass clarinet on 'Inside Outside' was a bold stroke, but his long unfolding statement holds the attention throughout. He switches to soprano for 'Adventures With DP', a more tuneful and expressive horn for Smith than the tenor, on which he always sounds a little forced.

A freer conception informs the two-part 'Cliffhanger/For U', and Smith revels in the space to develop a raw-textured but sensitive solo that instantly identifies itself as British and of a certain vintage. The supporting band is always on hand with a complementary idea. Noble has a thoughtful touch and Clifford is unfailingly musical.

Ian Smith

TRUMPET

Cousin of trumpeter Jimmy Deuchar, Smith started out in rock bands, including Real Wild West, before becoming disillusioned and turning to more creative music. He is a member of the London Improvisers Orchestra and other groups.

*****(*) Tryst**

Red Toucan 9311 *Smith; Brian Godding (g, syn); Marcio Mattos (b, clo, pedal steel); Mark Sanders (d); Thebe Lipere (perc).* 97.

On his debut improv recording, Smith and producer Steve Beresford subtly deployed the players into various smaller units, keeping the full group for just one track, which as it turns out is the weakest on the record. The opening trio with Godding and Lipere is a strong sign that something different is happening; Smith's short, staccato phrases and occasional long tones are very distinctive and have no single antecedent. They're at work again on a long quartet track with Godding, Mattos and Sanders, the most jazz-like cut here, and on the very beautiful 'Close The Light' with Lipere and an inspired Mattos. Smith and Beresford generously give Godding a solo spot on 'The Laughing Police Force', which acts as a little intermezzo before the final sections of the record. 'Jive Rhapsody' is delightful and the closing 'Tin Foil', for just Mattos and Smith, rounds out a brilliant set.

****** Daybreak**

Emanem 4059 *Smith; Gail Brand (tb); Oren Marshall (tba); Veryan Weston (org); Derek Bailey (g).* 01.

If *Tryst* was an impressive starting-point, *Daybreak* is a small miracle. The basic chemistry is the same – solos, duos and small groups with only occasional use of ensemble – but what a wealth of sound from such unexpected instrumentation. Wherever his sound comes from, namesake Leo Smith, Bill Dixon or the Gabriels of forgotten jazz bands and orchestras, Smith is in love with brass. That comes across on the delicious trio with Marshall and Brand, 'Falange, Flanginha, Falangeta', as well as the opening duet with the brilliant tubist. Weston plays a breathy chamber instrument, and if you know your Wilhelm Reich you'll love the title of 'Function Of The Organ', another of Smith's generous solo-spots-cum-interlude. The veteran Bailey is the trumpeter's partner on 'Coffee' and makes light of the fact that timbrally he is odd man out on this date. Derek is back with Smith and Marshall on the closing 'Go On'. It's a stunning album, one of the unexpected treasures of the Emanem catalogue and something that anyone interested in contemporary trumpet-playing and structured improvisation should sample.

Jabbo Smith (1908–90)

TRUMPET, VOCAL

Born Cladys Smith in Pembroke, Georgia, Smith was a dashing figure in late-'20s Chicago and was signed by Brunswick as a rival to Louis Armstrong. His career was damaged by drink and a poor attendance record at his own gigs, and by 1940 he was barely visible, subsequently taking jobs outside music. Came back in the '70s and was on Broadway in New York in the '80s, reformed and intact.

****** Jabbo Smith 1929–1938**

Classics 669 *Smith; Omer Simeon, Willard Brown (cl, as); Leslie Johnakins, Ben Smith (as); Sam Simmons (ts); Millard Robins (bsx); Cassino Simpson, Kenneth Anderson, Alex Hill, William Barbee, James Reynolds (p); Ikey Robinson (bj); Connie Wainwright (g); Hayes Alvis, Lawson Buford (tba); Elmer James (b); Alfred Taylor (d).* 1/29–2/38.

****** Ace Of Rhythm**

Topaz TPZ 1072 *Similar to above, except add Louis Metcalf (t), Joe 'Tricky Sam' Nanton (tb), Otto Hardwick (ss, as, bs), Garvin Bushell (as, bsn), Harry Carney (cl, bs), Rudy Jackson (cl, ts), James P. Johnson, Duke Ellington (p), Fats Waller (org), Wellman Braud (b), Sonny Greer, Walter Bishop (d).* 11/27–2/38.

Until his rediscovery in the '60s, Smith was legendary as Armstrong's most significant rival in the '20s, a reputation built almost entirely on the records reissued on these discs. He had already made a name for himself with Charlie Johnson's orchestra, but it was the 20 sides he cut with his Rhythm Aces that have endured as Smith's contribution to jazz. The Classics CD includes all of them, together with four tracks from a single 1938 session by Smith's then-eight-strong group. Smith's style is like a thinner, wilder variation on Armstrong's. He takes even more risks in his solos – or, at least, makes it seem that way, since he's less assured at pulling them off than Louis was. Some passages he seems to play entirely in his highest register; others are composed of handfuls of notes, phrased in such a scattershot way that he seems to have snatched them out of the air. If it makes the music something of a mess, it's a consistently exciting one. Organized round Smith's own stop-time solos and dialogue with the rhythm, with the occasional vocal – a quizzical mix of Armstrong and Don Redman – thrown in too, the records seem like a conscious attempt at duplicating the Hot Five sessions, although in the event they sold poorly. Simeon is curiously reticent, much as Dodds was on the Hot Fives, and alto-players Brown and James do no more than behave themselves. The livewire foil is, instead, the extraordinary Robinson, whose tireless strumming and rare, knockout solo (as on 'Michigander Blues') keep everything simmering. Shrill and half focused, these are still lively and brilliant reminders of a poorly documented talent (who reappeared in his 70s as a festival and stage performer).

The Topaz CD isn't a clear-cut alternative, since it substitutes eight tracks where Smith was a sideman for three of the 1938 cuts and five of the lesser Rhythm Aces pieces. There are two appearances with Ellington (odd to hear Smith doing the Miley part on 'Black And Tan Fantasy') and two rollicking pieces with an Ikey Robinson group. Specialists may prefer to have the Rhythm Aces sides complete, but measure for measure *Ace Of Rhythm* offers a better portrait of Jabbo in his prime.

Jimmy Smith (born 1925)

ORGAN

Studied piano and bass in Philadelphia, but he switched to organ in the early '50s and arrived in New York with a trio in 1956. Many albums for Blue Note, 1957–61, and Verve, 1962–73. Opened his own club in 1975 and quit touring, but returned to it in the '80s and is still performing. His style – bebop lines rooted in the blues, punchily delivered – set the tone for all the organists who came after him, and helped create the soul-jazz genre.

*****(*) A New Sound ... A New Star ... Jimmy Smith At The Organ Vols 1–3**
Blue Note 57191-2 2CD *Smith; Thornel Schwartz (g); Bay Perry, Donald Bailey (d).* 2–6/56.

***** Home Cookin'**
Blue Note 53360-2 *Smith; Percy France (ts); Kenny Burrell (g); Donald Bailey (d).* 7/58–6/59.

***** Standards**
Blue Note 21282-2 *Smith; Kenny Burrell (g); Donald Bailey (d).* 8/57–5/59.

***** Cool Blues**
Blue Note 35587-2 *Smith; Lou Donaldson (as); Tina Brooks (ts); Eddie McFadden (g); Art Blakey, Donald Bailey (d).* 4/58.

****(*) Crazy Baby**
Blue Note 84030-2 *Smith; Quentin Warren (g); Donald Bailey (d).* 3/60.

*****(*) Open House/Plain Talk**
Blue Note 84269-2 *Smith; Blue Mitchell (t); Jackie McLean (as); Ike Quebec (ts); Quentin Warren (g); Donald Bailey (d).* 3/60.

***** Back At The Chicken Shack**
Blue Note 46402-2 *Smith; Stanley Turrentine (ts); Kenny Burrell (g); Donald Bailey (d).* 4/60.

****(*) Midnight Special**
Blue Note 84078-2 *As above.* 4/60.

***** I'm Movin' On**
Blue Note 32750-2 *Smith; Grant Green (g); Donald Bailey (d).* 1/63.

***** Prayer Meetin'**
Blue Note 76754-2 *Smith; Stanley Turrentine (ts); Quentin Warren (g); Sam Jones (b); Donald Bailey (d).* 6/60–2/63.

***** Rockin' The Boat**
Blue Note 76755-2 *Smith; Lou Donaldson (as); Quentin Warren (g); Donald Bailey (d); John Patton (perc).* 2/63.

Jimmy Smith got going rather late as a jazz organist. Astonishingly enough, he allegedly didn't even touch the instrument until he was 28, but he quickly established and personified a jazz vocabulary for the organ: tireless walking bass in the pedals, thick chords with the left hand, quick-fire melodic lines with the right. It was a formula almost from the start, and Smith has never strayed from it, but he so completely mastered the approach that he is inimitable. At his best he creates a peerless excitement, which is seldom sustained across an entire album but which makes every record he's on something to be reckoned with.

Smith made a great stack of albums for Blue Note. As with all the long-serving artists on the label, their availability has been frustratingly inconsistent. This seems to be what's around at the moment. His first three albums have been collected on the twofer, *A New Sound ...*, and welcome it is since it catches much of the initial raw excitement that Smith was after. Pet licks and his familar great flourishes, delighting in the noise-making capacity of the organ, still sound at their most fresh and swinging here. *Cool Blues* sat on the shelf until 1980. Again recorded at Smalls', Lou Donaldson and Tina Brooks guest, with Blakey on drums on a few tracks. More of a potboiler, although any memento of Brooks, even in a routine blowing context, is something to keep.

It was disappointing, though, to hear how quickly Smith's albums became formulaic. *Home Cookin'* has the little-known Percy France on tenor, but more significant is the presence of Burrell, the organist's favourite partner. A solid one, with five bonus tracks on the CD edition. *Crazy Baby* is discouragingly rational. *Back At The Chicken Shack* has Turrentine confronting Smith to periodically powerful effect – the title-blues in particular blows very warmly – but, for all its 'classic' status, this is an album we've never really been impressed by. *Midnight Special* was recorded at the same session and is ... more of the same. *I'm Movin' On* is notable mainly for the sole recorded appearance of Smith with guitarist Grant Green – though the programme never quite gets off the ground and what should have been the big steamer, 'Back Talk', resolves itself into a series of clichés.

Smith rarely recorded with more than one horn in attendance, and the front line on *Open House/Plain Talk* marked a welcome change of pace. Regulation hard bop, perhaps, but plenty of smoke and cinders, and just as an alternative to the usual Smith programme this is one to hear. *Prayer Meetin'* is more secular blues than sanctified gospel, but either way Turrentine gets in a righteous blow. Two extra tracks from an abandoned 1960 session fill out the CD. This has now emerged in a new RVG edition, as has *Rockin' The Boat*, which was actually recorded one day earlier, with Lou Donaldson (making a rare solo appearance on a Smith date) and John Patton apparently playing tambourine. Solid.

Standards is a discovery – seven cuts from a previously unheard 1959 date plus five from earlier sessions, all with Burrell and Bailey. With the tempos mostly idling and the emphasis on ballads, this is almost as much Burrell's album as it is Smith's, and it underlines how fine a partner for the organist the guitarist has always been: economical, bluesy, adroit. A sleeper but a good one.

CORE COLLECTION

**** Groovin' At Smalls' Paradise

Blue Note 99777-2 2CD *Smith; Eddie McFadden (g); Donald Bailey (d). 11/57.*

On *Groovin' At Smalls' Paradise* Smith in his element in a club setting and, while McFadden also gets plenty of space (and doesn't do badly, in his modest way), the master's big, sprawling solos are definitive: 'After Hours' is perhaps the classic Smith blues performance, although the entire record works to a kind of bluesy slow burn. The original albums have been turned into a double-CD and, in the Rudy van Gelder edition remastering, the years fall away. This is the Smith album to get.

**** Bashin'

Verve 539061-2 *Smith; Joe Newman, Ernie Royal, Doc Severinsen, Joe Wilder (t); Jimmy Cleveland, Urbie Green, Britt Woodman (tb); Tom Mitchell (btb); Jerry Dodgion, Phil Woods (as); Bob Ashton, Babe Clark (ts); George Barrow (bs); Barry Galbraith, Quentin Warren (g); George Duvivier (b); Donald Bailey, Ed Shaughnessy (d). 3/62.*

*** Any Number Can Win

Verve 557447-2 *Smith; Jimmy Maxwell, Joe Newman, James Sedlar, Charlie Shavers, Snooky Young (t); Jimmy Cleveland, Paul Faulise, Melba Liston, Kai Winding (tb); Jerry Dodgion, Marvin Halladay, Budd Johnson, Seldon Powell, Jerome Richardson, Phil Woods (reeds); Kenny Burrell, Vince Gambella, Billy Mure (g); Bob Bushnell, Art Davis, George Duvivier, Milt Hinton (b); Bobby Donaldson, Ed Shaughnessy (d); Doug Allen, George Devens, Art Marotti (perc). 7/63.*

*** The Cat

Verve 810046-2 *Smith; Ernie Royal, Bernie Glow, Jimmy Maxwell, Marky Markowitz, Snooky Young, Thad Jones (t); Billy Byers, Jimmy Cleveland, Urbie Green (tb); Ray Alonge, Jimmy Buffington, Earl Chapin, Bill Correa (frhn); Tony Studd (btb); Kenny Burrell (g); George Duvivier (b); Don Butterfield (tba); Grady Tate (d); Phil Kraus (perc). 4/64.*

*** Got My Mojo Workin' / Hoochie Coochie Man

Verve 533828-2 *Smith; Joe Newman, Ernie Royal, Richard Williams, Snooky Young (t); Quentin Jackson, Melba Liston, Tom McIntosh, Britt Woodman (tb); Donald Corrado, Willie Ruff (frhn); Jack Agee, Romeo Penque, Phil Woods, Jerome Richardson, Jerry Dodgion, Bob Ashton (reeds); Buddy Lucas (hca); Kenny Burrell, Billy Butler, Barry Galbraith, Bill Suyker (g); Don Butterfield (tba); George Duvivier, Bob Cranshaw, Ron Carter, Ben Tucker, Richard Davis (b); Grady Tate (d); Bobby Rosengarden (perc). 12/65–2/66.*

**(*) Peter And The Wolf

Verve 547264-2 *Smith; Joe Newman, Ernie Royal, Snooky Young, Richard Williams (t); Quentin Jackson, Britt Woodman, Tom McIntosh (tb); Dick Hixson, Tony Studd (btb); Jimmy Buffington, Willie Ruff (frhn); Bob Ashton, Danny Bank, Jerry Dodgion, Jerome Richardson, Stan Webb (reeds); Billy Butler, Barry Galbraith (g); Richard Davis (b); Harry Breuer, Bobby Rosengarden, Grady Tate (d); Oliver Nelson (cond). 5/66.*

Smith might have felt, after 20 albums or so, that he'd done all he could do at Blue Note. But one thing he hadn't done was act as a soloist within a big band. Verve's first step with him was to set up just such a situation, and with Oliver Nelson's sinister chart for 'Walk On The Wild Side' Smith immediately struck into exciting new terrain. It's actually only one of four witty and successful charts on the *Bashin'* album. Just as good is the wryly engaging lope through 'Ol' Man River', for instance, which gives Smith's sardonic humour full rein. The rest of the album is more ordinary small-group workouts, and it's a pity that Nelson, clearly in top form, couldn't have scored the whole thing. In its Master Edition form, this is an essential Smith record.

Somehow, the feel and freshness of this set was never recaptured at Verve. *The Cat* pits him against Lalo Schifrin charts, which are interesting but never as good; and the pop-to-blues material which makes up the two albums, *Got My Mojo Workin'* and *Hoochie Coochie Man*, is more notable for Smith's grunted approximations of the lyrics than the sometimes cheesy arrangements. Nelson didn't click with it this time. Nor did he fare especially well with the preposterous idea of re-creating Prokofiev's *Peter And The Wolf*, one of Creed Taylor's inspirations. At least it only runs for some 33 minutes.

The odd one out here is *Any Number Can Win*. The charts this time were by Billy Byers and Claus Ogerman, and they did a decent job: 'The Ape Woman'(!) is genuinely menacing and 'Georgia On My Mind' played with much feeling, though the title-track is a pinball-arcade jingle.

**(*) Christmas Cookin'

Verve 513711-2 *Smith; Quentin Warren, Kenny Burrell, Wes Montgomery (g); Bill Hart, Grady Tate (d); orchestra directed by Bill Byers. 6/64–9/66.*

***(*) The Dynamic Duo

Verve 521445-2 *Smith; Wes Montgomery (g); Grady Tate (d); Ray Barretto (perc); Oliver Nelson orchestra. 9/66.*

*** Further Adventures Of Jimmy And Wes

Verve 519802-2 *As above. 9/66.*

***(*) Walk On The Wild Side: The Best Of The Verve Years

Verve 527950-2 2CD *As above discs, plus Steve Williams (hca), George Benson, Arthur Adams, Quentin Warren, Eric Gale, Thornel Schwartz, Vince Gambella (g), Wilton Felder, Ron Carter, Bob Bushnell (b), Buck Clarke (perc), Paul Humphrey, Billy Hart, Bernard Purdie, Mel Lewis (d), orchestras directed by Oliver Nelson, Johnny Pate and Thad Jones, strings. 3/62–2/73.*

The Christmas album is one of the best in a hapless genre: great cover-art, and the music isn't too hopeless. Smith's meeting with Montgomery isn't so much a battle of the giants as a genial bit of backslapping. The sessions produced enough for two albums and although some of the material is a bit thin – 'Baby It's Cold Outside' and 'King Of The Road' – the sound of the group, Montgomery's funky lyricism matched with Smith's extravagant blues, is a delight and, with Oliver Nelson charts abetting a few tracks, they rekindle some of the excitement of the early Smith Verve dates.

Verve's two-disc best-of is a very useful sweep through what is a very mixed catalogue and, as far as this period is concerned, this should satisfy all but the most obsessive Smith devotee. Aside from obvious choices like the title-tune, the compilers choose a smart mix of small groups and big bands. One or two nuggets, such as an alternative take of 'OGD' from the date with Montgomery, will tempt collectors, and there are a few rescued obscurities: two tracks from the orchestral collaboration with Thad Jones, *Portuguese Soul*; a live blues from 1972, 'Sagg Shootin' His Arrow', with a band including Arthur Adams and Wilton Felder; the title-track off Johnny Pate's set of charts, *Groove Drops*; and 'The Boss' with George Benson and Donald Bailey. Good stuff, and a slightly superior choice to the *Verve Jazz Masters 29* compilation from the same source (Verve 521855-2).

***(*) Live! Root Down

Verve 559805-2 *Smith; Steve Williams (hca); Arthur Adams (g); Wilton Felder (b); Paul Humphrey (d); Buck Clarke (perc).* 2/72.

A valuable glimpse of Smith at a period where his music was at a comparatively low point, or at least in danger of being bypassed by more fashionable black idioms. Cut at the Bombay Bicycle Club(!) in Los Angeles, the master suffers no loss of energy and has a crew of top LA session-men in tow. Wilton Felder's Jazz Crusaders were probably much more successful than Smith at this point, but Felder sounds as if he's enjoying the gig. Adams plays a mess of rock-funk guitar (plenty of wah-wah licks along the way) and Steve Williams walks on to blow some blues harp on 'After Hours'. As unpromising as it might look, this is actually a terrific Smith date, and a rare example of Smith's idiom in successful transition. Its new incarnation is complicated: all six original tracks were edited for the original LP, but three only have been restored to their full length. There's also a bonus extra version of the title-track, which is two seconds longer than the other take.

***(*) All The Way Live

Milestone 9251-2 *Smith; Eddie Harris (ts); Kenny Dixon (d).* 8/81.

An off-the-cuff meeting between Smith and Harris at San Francisco's Keystone Korner produced some delightful music. They stuck to the blues and some standards, and Harris couldn't resist turning on his swaggering circular lines and lexicon of bebop licks. They suit Smith just fine, although, since he plays as imperturbably as ever, one wonders whether he'd change his style even if the ghost of Buddy Petit got up on stage to jam.

*** Prime Time

Milestone M 9176 *Smith; Curtis Peagler (as, ts); Herman Riley, Rickey Woodard (ts); Phil Upchurch, Terry Evans (g); Andy Simpkins (b); Michael Baker, Frank Wilson (d); Barbara Morrison (v).* 8/89.

*** Fourmost

Milestone MCD 9184-2 *Smith; Stanley Turrentine (ts); Kenny Burrell (g); Grady Tate (d, v).* 11/90.

**(*) Sum Serious Blues

Milestone MCD-9207-2 *Smith; Oscar Brashear (t); George Bohannon (tb); Maurice Spears (btb); Buddy Collette (as); Herman Riley (ts); Ernie Fields (bs); Mick Martin (hca); Phil Upchurch (g); Andy Simpkins (b); Michael Baker (d); Marlena Shaw, Bernard Ighner (v).* 1/93.

Smith has adapted rather cautiously to changing times. He still sticks to straightahead Hammond, but he or his producers vary the other ground rules, with mixed results. *Prime Time* and *Fourmost* are simple blowing records with muscular solos by the horns on the former and a rather more stately contribution from Turrentine on the latter. *Sum Serious Blues* is produced by Johnny Pate as a throwback to some of Smith's Verve sessions of the '60s – some blues, a new version of 'The Sermon', a couple of vocals from Shaw and Ighner. Probably no more systematized than any of the older records, but it doesn't sound as spontaneous, either.

*** Damn!

Verve 527631-2 *Smith; Roy Hargrove, Nicholas Payton (t); Abraham Burton (as); Tim Warfield, Mark Turner, Ron Blake (ts); Mark Whitfield (g); Christian McBride (b); Bernard Purdie, Art Taylor (d).* 1/95.

*** Angel Eyes

Verve 527632-2 *As above, except add Gregory Hutchinson (d); omit Burton, Warfield, Turner, Blake, Purdie, Taylor.* 1/95.

Having gone back to Blue Note, Smith then returned to Verve with *Damn!*, an enjoyable if finally somewhat programmed session in which the old man spars alongside rather than with a bulging personnel of young Turks. The chosen themes blend bebop and funk, but it's a little stiff in the joints. *Angel Eyes* is a rerun with the dials set on 'ballad'. Thoughtfully programmed, with the instrumentation carefully varied between solos, duos, trios and one performance by the whole sextet, this is a genuine piece of work that has much appeal, if finally succumbing a little to the same conceptual fatigue that besets the other record: Smith's best music has always had more spit in it than this can muster.

*** Ultimate Jimmy Smith

Verve 547161-2 *Smith; as Verve albums above.* 62–95.

*** Jimmy Smith's Finest Hour

Verve 543598-2 *Smith; as Verve albums above.* 62–95.

The first was (supposedly) selected by Grover Washington; the second is in Verve's latest series of rehashes. They duplicate each other in the title listings, and both overlap hugely with the superior two-disc compilation *Walk On The Wild Side*, which is also still available. Each is very playable, but both are docked notches for wasting our time.

**(*) Dot Com Blues

Blue Thumb 543978-2 *Smith; Darell Leonard (t); Joe Sublett (ts); Dr John (p, v); B. B. King, Taj Mahal, Keb' Mo' (g, v); Russell Malone (g); Reggie McBride (b); Harvey Mason (d); Etta James (v); The Texicali Horns.* 00.

Smith hasn't really changed label ties again, since Blue Thumb is part of the vast Universal/Verve holding. Designed to place blues over jazz in the playing pecking order, this has its moments. But the trumped-up list of guest stars offers about as much rootsiness as a Hollywood manicure parlour. Smith may yet have a great autumnal record in him, but not when he's given an agenda like this.

Johnny 'Hammond' Smith (1933–97)

ORGAN

Began on piano but switched to Hammond organ in the '50s and was one of the school of Chicago organ-combo leaders, popular in the '60s, quiet in the '70s, popular again in the '80s and '90s.

****(*) That Good Feelin' / Talk That Talk**

BGP 0612 *Smith; Oliver Nelson (ts); Thornel Schwartz (g); George Tucker (b); Art Taylor, Leo Stevens (d); Ray Barretto (perc).* 11/59–4/60.

****(*) That Good Feelin'**

Prestige 24164 *Smith; Thornel Schwartz (g); George Tucker (b); Leo Stevens (d).* 9–11/59.

****(*) Talk That Talk**

Prestige 24151 *Smith; Oliver Nelson (ts); Lem Winchester (vib); Eddie McFadden (g); George Tucker, Wendell Marshall (b); Art Taylor, Bill Erskine (d); Ray Barretto (perc).* 4–10/60.

***** Black Coffee**

Milestone 47072 *Smith; Sonny Williams (t); Seldon Powell, Houston Person (ts); Eddie McFadden (g); Leo Stevens (d).* 11/62–63.

****(*) Good 'Nuff**

Prestige 24282-2 *Smith; Willis Jackson, Houston Person, Earl Edwards (ts); Eddie McFadden, Floyd Smith (g); Leo Stevens, John Harris (d).* 6/62–5/65.

***** Open House**

Milestone 47089-2 *Smith; Thad Jones (t, c); Virgil Jones (t); Seldon Powell (ts, f); Houston Person (ts); Eddie McFadden (g); Bob Cranshaw (b); Leo Stevens, Luis Taylor (d); Ray Barretto (perc).* n.d.

***** The Soulful Blues**

Prestige 24244 *Smith; Virgil Jones (t); Houston Person (ts); Thornell Schwartz, John Abercrombie (g); Jimmy Lewis (b); John Harris, Grady Tate (d).* 3/67–6/68.

****(*) Soul Flowers**

Prestige 24235 *Smith; Earl Edwards, Houston Person (ts); Wally Richardson (g); Jimmy Lewis (b); John Harris (d); Richard Landrum (perc).* 9/67–1/68.

**** Legends Of Acid Jazz**

Prestige 24177 *Smith; Virgil Jones (t); Rusty Bryant (as, ts); Wally Richardson (g); Bob Bushnell, Jimmy Lewis (b); Bernard Purdie (d).* 5–12/69.

Smith (who actually changed his name to Johnny Hammond at one point) made dozens of albums, yet he is one of the least followed of the organists who came in the wake of Jimmy Smith. These reissues mostly couple up his various albums for Prestige to convenient if hardly compelling effect. For the record, *Black Coffee* puts that original alongside *Mr Wonderful*; *Talk That Talk* is next to *Gettin' The Message*; *That Good Feelin'* is that album plus his debut, *All Soul*; *The Soulful Blues* puts together *Ebb Tide* and *Nasty*; *Legends Of Acid Jazz* doubles up *Soul Talk* and *Black Feeling*; and *Soul Flowers* couples that one with *Dirty Grape*. The (British) BGP set puts together the two albums of its title. All good-value packages, but Smith is strictly second division in the Hammond league. To be fair, Prestige didn't give him much of a chance at making any kind of classic. The material is all blues or obvious standards, the sidemen are scarcely a scintillating lot (Nelson hardly bothers to stick the horn in his mouth on the three tracks he plays on) and Smith himself is a decent but undemonstrative player on an instrument where one has to be indecent and extremely demonstrative. The soulful clichés of the 1969 sessions are no more and no less discouraging than the earlier ones, really, and our preference is for the *Black Coffee* set, which has two good saxophone-players and some of the best material. *The Soulful Blues* may tempt the curious for its glimpse of the young John Abercrombie paying some early dues in Smith's 1968 band. A few sparks. The newest pair are *Good 'Nuff*, which doubles up *Johnny 'Hammond' Cooks With Gator Tail* and *The Stinger* – not much cop; and *Open House*, which pairs the LP of that name with *A Little Taste*. These albums were originally made for Riverside rather than Prestige, though that didn't make much difference. At least the earlier of the two can boast the super-reliable Thad Jones and Seldon Powell on the team, even if they're not exactly stretching.

Johnny Smith (born 1922)

GUITAR

Not to be confused with Johnny 'Hammond' Smith, the Kentuckyan made his name with 'Moonlight In Vermont' but never scaled those heights again and was pretty much out of the business after the '50s.

*****(*) Moonlight In Vermont**

Roulette Jazz 93091 *Smith; Stan Getz, Paul Quinichette, Zoot Sims (ts); Sanford Gold (p); Bob Carter, Arnold Fishkind, Eddie Safranski (b); Morey Feld, Don Lamond (d).* 3/52, 8/53.

'Moonlight In Vermont' with Stan Getz made Smith a star and kept him in the public eye longer than his quiet, thoughtful jazz would have done otherwise. These early cuts are probably his best work on record, all of them made with formidable sidemen. The jazz content is pretty high, certainly relative to the crossover stuff Smith did later; 'Cherokee' and 'Lullaby Of Birdland' are impeccably crafted, and even when the guitarist tackles pop-classical tunes such as Lehar's 'Vilia', he takes a challenging path through them. This reissue includes just about everything he recorded over this crucial period (some work with organist Joe Mooney has been dropped), although they seem to be in slightly different order to the last reissue and certainly the alternative take of 'Jaguar' has been dropped down the listing.

***** The Sound Of The Johnny Smith Guitar**

Blue Note 31792 *Smith; Hank Jones, Bob Pancoast (p); George Duvivier, George Roumanis (b); Mousie Alexander, Ed Shaughnessy (d).* 61.

Anyone seriously interested in Johnny Smith has to get hold of the Mosaic box of his Roost recordings. The Blue Note, though, offers a good appreciation of his quiet and unflusterable talent, a technique honed on violin and viola lessons when a boy. With two different groups, of markedly different quality as you'd guess from the personnel, Smith weaves subtle counterpoints and variations on standards as varied as 'Misty' and 'Embraceable You' to more challenging bop pieces like 'Un Poco Loco' and even a rare version of John LaPorta's 'Blues Chorale'. Smith is often close to the clarinettist's classical vein, but however little he seems to favour orthodox changes playing, he's still a jazzman to the core.

Joshua Douglas Smith (born 1982)

TENOR SAXOPHONE

Gifted young tenorist who's studied with George Garzone and has studied the saxophonists of the past.

★★★ **Major Incident**

Steeplechase SCCD 31545 *Smith; Adam Fernandez (p); Justin Marx (b); David Christian (d).* 4/03.

Even if Smith weren't 21, this would still be an impressive record. Because he is, the temptation is either to let him off on its few lapses or to pick them apart as assiduously as teachers Garzone and Ron McClure might have done. McClure was responsible for getting the Steeplechase gig and listening to *Major Incident* it's pretty clear that this group (collective age still comfortably under the 100) is ready for the studio. Boldly, and possibly wisely since detractors will always pick up on standards-playing, Joshua has gone for an all-original set-list, mostly by himself, but also including Marx's excellent 'Napoleon Complex' and 'Right Coast' and three tunes, including the long title-piece, by Fernandez.

Keith Smith (born 1940)

TRUMPET, VOCAL

London-born, Smith spent time in New Orleans, California and New York, in traditional and mainstream company, before returning to Britain. His Hefty Jazz group was the backbone of many jazz-package shows which he ran in the '80s and '90s.

★★(★) **Keith Smith And His Climax Jazz Band**

GHB BCD-27 *Smith; Mike Sherbourne (tb); Frank Brooker (cl, ts); Jon Marks (p); Brian Turnock (b); Barry Martyn (d).* 65.

★★(★) **Mr Hefty Jazz**

Lake LACD 67 *Smith; Jimmy Archey, Hugh Watts (tb); George Lewis (cl); John Handy (as); Alton Purnell, Lars Edegran (p); George Guesnon, Ron Simpson (bj); George 'Pops' Foster, Alcide 'Slow Drag' Pavageau (b); Freddy Moore (d, v); Cie Frazier (d).* 4/65–9/66.

★★(★) **Keith Smith & Jimmy Archey**

GHB BCD-217 *Smith; Jimmy Archey (tb); Dranell Howard (cl); Captain John Handy (as); Lars Edegran, Alton Purnell (p); Ron Simpson (bj); George 'Pops' Foster (b); Freddy Moore (d, v); Cie Frazier (d).* 3–9/66.

★★★ **Swing Is Here Again**

Lake LACD 80 *Smith; Vic Dickenson, Bob Havens, Tom Artin, Johnny Mortimer, Russell Moore (tb); Peanuts Hucko, Johnny Mince (cl); Bruce Turner (as, cl); Benny Waters, Al Gay (ts); Barney Bates, Stan Greig, Dick Cary, Nat Pierce, Johnny Guarnieri (p); Jim Douglas (g); Peter Ind, Major Holley, Arvell Shaw, Harvey Weston (b); Barrett Deems, John Cox, Bobby Worth, Oliver Jackson (d).* 11/78–10/83.

Unrepresented on CD until recently, Smith is a British trad-to-swing trumpeter who has often found himself in exalted company, as a look at the personnels of the two Lake compilations will attest. He has had a rather picaresque career (Lake's sleeve-notes tell how he was hustled out of a successsful fish-and-chip-shop operation in New Orleans by the local Mafia) and the records are a somewhat motley gathering of tracks. GHB's session by his Climax Jazz Band is very average British trad of the day, enlivened somewhat by guest drummer Martyn, who insists on playing New Orleans style even on inappropriate pieces like 'West End Blues'. Some boisterous playing is sabotaged by a complete lack of finesse. Smith's trumpet-style – originally an Anglophile version of Henry Allen, but also soaked in Armstrong and others – is decent enough, but the interest on the other discs is sparked by his companions. *Mr Hefty Jazz* features three sessions in which Smith was the unlikely kibitzer on dates with Lewis, Archey, Handy and others – in Canada, New Orleans and an attic in Plaistow! Quite good fun, but the recording quality (especially on the five tracks recorded at San Jacinto Hall in New Orleans) is sometimes dreadful. There's more from the Canadian session on *Keith Smith & Jimmy Archey*, along with five titles cut with a different back line in London the same year. Better sound overall and quite lusty playing, but it doesn't amount to much for a general listener. *Swing Is Here Again* is a better bet, pulling together 16 tracks from six different dates, and the pearls are the five pieces with the irresistible Dickenson from a session in Nice. At least these are all in good sound, although the remainder of the CD offers little more than a group of mementoes from a busy life.

Roger Smith

GUITAR

An improviser of uncompromising dedication, Smith was a member of the Spontaneous Music Ensemble for longer than its co-founder, Trevor Watts, and yet is still often referred to as a relative newcomer. He employs a distinctive scrabbled attack and softly percussive tone.

★★★★ **Spanish Guitar**

Emanem 4083 *Smith (g solo).* 1/80–7/97.

★★★(★) **Unexpected Turns**

Emanem 4014 *Smith (g solo).* 12/93–7/96.

★★★ **Extended Plays**

Emanem 4032 *As above.* 93–97.

★★★ **S&M**

Incus CD 24 *Smith; Neil Metcalfe (f).* 7–12/95.

★★★(★) **Green Wood**

Emanem 4073 *Smith (g solo).* 1/02.

Not even the most cursory listener would mistake Roger Smith for fellow free guitarist Derek Bailey. Though Smith has studied with the acknowledged master of free-form guitar improvisation and has performed alongside Bailey in one version of the Spontaneous Music Ensemble, they could hardly be more different in approach. For a start, Smith favours a gut-strung Spanish guitar, rejects amplification and approaches the music with a good deal more stylistic baggage. Where Bailey sets out with no pre-set formulae or destination, Smith often seems to be deconstructing something, albeit remote rather than familiar. Occasionally he will seem to be winding up towards some melancholy flamenco theme; elsewhere there is almost an African tinge; quite often, it sounds as though he is picking his way through something heard only fragmentarily and in an unknown idiom, but still recognizably a song.

The solo records give the best available account of his approach to date, though some will argue that his best work was within the confines of the SME, where he worked for nearly 20 years under the tutelage of John Stevens and made an often undervalued contribution to that remarkable group. Heard alone, Smith sounds remarkably delicate, creating lines which seem to head for some point of resolution. Most of the pieces are short, and only on the 11-minute 'Guitar In Top [sic]', one of half-a-dozen tracks recorded around Christmas 1994, does he seem to ramble. One suspects that Smith is by instinct a miniaturist, which is why the ironically titled *Extended Plays* both is and is not a good representation of his work.

The duos with Metcalfe see him paired with another unsung acoustic player and fellow member of the SME. Stevens coached his playing colleagues to listen to one another with a particular kind of *in*attention (he used the analogy of peripheral vision) and it sounds very much as though Metcalfe and Smith have taken that lesson to heart. These are not monologues, but neither are they conversations in any strict sense. Their reactions to each other suggest a melancholy abstraction, like Beckett's tramps. Though in both cases the sound is very faithful, these are lo-fi recordings. *Unexpected Turns* includes a whole range of ambient effects, from bird chatter to domestic clanks and rumbles. *S&M* is a little drier, which suits it quite well. This music, though, is not about production values. *Green Wood* is another home recording, from Smith's kitchen in Wood Green. His central heating system intrudes here and there, in what are otherwise minutely detailed soliloquies. Martin Davidson titled the pieces; the last, 'Arse Myth', is apparently how the artist sometimes signs letters.

Spanish Guitar restores Smith's first solo record, made for the LMC label in 1980, to which Davidson has added five pieces recorded at various gigs from the '90s. It is, in a way, an excellent sampler of his solo work, the often unabashedly lyrical matter of the earlier solos mixing with some more harsh adventures in the later pieces, two of which involve a squeaking chair, traffic noise and (pretty shocking, for Smith) a practice amplifier on one solo.

Stuff Smith (1909–67)

VIOLIN, VOCALS

Played with Alphonso Trent in the '20s, then in a band with Jonah Jones which was a big success on 52nd Street. Career petered out in the '40s, although musicians were still impressed; and from the '50s he based himself in California and Europe. A capricious temper and a liking for alcohol did him few favours.

*****(*) Stuff Smith & His Onyx Club Boys 1936**
Classics 706 *Smith; Jonah Jones (t, v); Buster Bailey (cl); George Clark (ts); Sam Allen, James Sherman, Clyde Hart, Raymond Smith (p); Bernard Addison, Bobby Bennett (g); John Brown, Mack Walker (b); Cozy Cole, Herbert Cowens, John Washington (d).* 2/36.

***** Stuff Smith 1939–1944**
Classics 1054 *Smith; Jonah Jones (t); George Clarke (ts); Sam Allen, Eric Henry, Jimmy Jones (p); Bernard Addison, Luke Stewart (g); Mary Osborne (g, v); John Brown (b); Herbert Cowens, John Levy (d); Stella Brooks (v).* 6/39–9/44.

***** The Stuff Smith Trio – 1943**
Progressive PCD 7053 *Smith; Jimmy Jones (p); John Levy (b).* 11/43.

*****(*) Stuff Smith/Dizzy Gillespie/Oscar Peterson**
Verve 521676-2 2CD *Smith; Dizzy Gillespie (t); Wynton Kelly, Carl Perkins, Oscar Peterson (p); Red Callender, Curtis Counce, Paul West (b); Oscar Bradley, Frank Butler, J. C. Heard, Alvin Stoller (d); Gordon Family (v).* 1–4/57.

***** Cat On A Hot Fiddle**
Verve MGVS-9067 *Smith; Paul Smith, Shirley Horn (p); Red Mitchell, Lewis Powers (b); Sid Bulkin, Harry Saunders (d).* 8–10/59.

***** Live At The Montmartre**
Storyville STCD 4142 *Smith; Kenny Drew (p); Niels-Henning Orsted Pedersen (b); Alex Riel (d).* 3/65.

****(*) Hot Violins**
Storyville STCD 4170 *Smith; Poul Olsen (vn); Svend Asmussen (vn, v); Kenny Drew, Jorgen Borch (p); Erik Molbach, Niels-Henning Orsted Pedersen (b); Makaya Ntoshko, Alex Riel, Bjarne Rostvold (d).* 3/65–2/67.

What would have been Hezekiah Leroy Gordon Smith's 90th birthday prompted a certain reassessment of his work. Those who remember his final performances in Scandinavia are themselves fewer on the ground these days, and emphasis has fallen on the earlier and better work. It's hard to imagine how Billy Bang's or Leroy Jenkins's mordant new-wave fiddling would have come about had it not been for his example. Initially influenced by Joe Venuti, Smith devised a style based on heavy bow-weight, with sharply percussive semiquaver runs up towards the top end of his range. His facility and ease on a swinging 1943 version of Dvořák's 'Humoresque', included on Classics 1054, is jaw-dropping. Like many '20s players, Smith found himself overtaken by the swing era and re-emerged as a recording and concert artist only after the war, when his upfront style and comic stage persona attracted renewed attention. Even so, he had a thriving club career in the meantime, most famously at the Onyx Club on 52nd Street, and managed to hold his ground while the bebop revolution, which he either anticipated, or was left untouched by, depending on your point of view, went on around him.

The Classics disc covers some important early material. This is when Smith's talent was at its most buoyant. 'I'se A Muggin'' and the associated musical numbers game are pretty corny (corny enough to be omitted from the Topaz compilation, which warns that the song 'goes on a bit'), but they retain their appeal over five decades like all the Vocalion sides, and Smith's astonishing fiddle technique lifts them up out of the mere novelty class. Jonah Jones makes a big impact, with a slithery, burping style that's hard to categorize and which shouldn't fit these sessions as well as it seems to. Sensibly, Classics have restricted this first volume to things Smith made under his own name. Future releases will include sessions for Alphonso Trent which are much less typical, though the second item here from the French label includes some excellent small-group sessions made after Smith's return east from the Coast.

The 1943 trio is a good representation of what he was about in the pre-war years, an exhaustive documentation of the session of 17 November with incomplete takes and false starts included alongside the release versions. Three full versions of 'Minuet In Swing' suggest that Smith went at a solo in a fairly deliberate way, attempting to maintain an energy level rather than rethinking his approach every time. On the other hand, an unissued 'Bugle Call Rag' – or 'Rage', as here – shows that he could be thoughtful even on lighter material.

Verve have, of course, always had a gift for picking up artists relatively late in their career and injecting new life into them. The sessions with Diz and Oscar are beautifully recorded, if not sublimely musical, and one values the record – a generously filled two-CD set – for the glimpses of the under-recorded Perkins as much as anything. It was pleasing to find a new reissue of *Cat On A Hot Fiddle* in 2004. This rare album is scarcely known at all, and what a line-up: Shirley Horn and Red Mitchell alongside the forgotten Harry Saunders and Sid Bulkin. The session has a rather cheap feel to it and Stuff was rather unkindly recorded but there are still moments of sly insouciance from the old warrior.

The later European sessions, recorded within a couple of years of Smith's death in Munich, are worth hearing. Less good is *Hot Violins*, made shortly before 'the cat that took the apron strings off the fiddle' was taken back into the fold. They're pretty tired, and it gets a bit dispiriting listening to Smith being cut by guys who're doing no more than playing his licks back at him. Asmussen does a party piece with a tenor violin on 'Caravan'; pitched somewhere between viola and cello, it makes a pretty noise, but it's hard not to feel so-what-ish about it.

Tab Smith (1909–71)

ALTO AND TENOR SAXOPHONES

Talmadge Smith's first break came in joining Lucky Millinder in 1936, before moving to Count Basie in 1940. Ran his own small groups at the end of the '40s and became involved in early R&B. Moved from music to real-estate development in the '60s.

*** Jump Time

Delmark DD-447 *Smith; Sonny Cohn (t); Leon Washington (ts); Lavern Dillon, Teddy Brannon (p); Wilfred Middlebrooks (b); Walter Johnson (d); Louis Blackwell (v).* 8/51–2/52.

*** Ace High

Delmark DD-455 *As above, except add Irving Woods (t), Charlie Wright (ts).* 2/52–4/53.

Smith jobbed around the Harlem big bands of the '30s and eventually found a niche with Count Basie. But he won his wider fame as an R&B soloist in the '50s and for a while jockeyed with Earl Bostic on the nation's jukeboxes. This pair of CDs collects a stack of such performances, offering a chronological survey of his output for the United label. Backed by an unobtrusive small group, Smith works through ballads, the blues and more roisterous outings. His sound is more graceful than Bostic's: he always seems to have something in reserve, and the hollow sound he sometimes gets in the alto's upper register reminds that he often made use of the soprano, too, although not here. Given the sameness of the format and the repetitive formulas Smith had to apply, these are surprisingly engaging CDs, although one or the other will be more than enough for all but the most devout followers. Very clean remastering.

Tommy Smith (born 1967)

TENOR SAXOPHONE

In Scotland and beyond, Smith was something of a legend before he left his teens. Since then, he has processed influences – Rollins, Garbarek, George Coleman, Michael Brecker, Branford Marsalis – faster than the critical establishment has been able to typecast him. These days, he writes complex long-form tunes and plays like nobody but himself: intense, lyrical and thoroughly versed in more of the tradition than most saxophonists manage in a lifetime.

*** Reminiscence

Linn AKD 024 *Smith; Terje Gewelt (b); Ian Froman (d).* 7/93.

With a perversity that went all the way round to inevitable, Blue Note dispensed with Tommy Smith as soon as he had made one wonderful album – *Paris* – for them. As with Stan Tracey, it was too hard to market an 'Englishman' in North America. The confusion over accent isn't altogether risible for, in performance as in speech, Smith tends to shift between Scottish, American and Scandinavian tonalities. His highly individual sound, heard in his precocious teens on small-label sets like *Taking Off* and *Giant Strides*, has been replaced in more recent years by a simulacrum of Jan Garbarek's tense, keening sound, and then even more recently by a seeming return to the classic voices: Webster, Hawkins and Pres.

For the moment, though, on these his first records for Glasgow-based Linn, he simply sounds glad to be home, relaxed in the company of Gewelt and Froman, former colleagues in Forward Motion, and able to take some pleasure in his playing. There are still moments which suggest an ambition that outstrips not technique but the maturity to make it count, as on 'Emancipation Of Dissonance', and the awkward 'Ally' (which refers back to an earlier composition). In this rather spare and unforgiving context he can be a little dry and discursive, and his colleagues are no more expansive. However, one does constantly feel that Smith is on the brink of a new direction, and that this curiously titled disc (curious for a 27-year-old to be retreading and rethinking his own career) is a clearing of the ground for something new.

***(*) Misty Morning And No Time

Linn AKD 040 *Smith; Guy Barker (t, monette); Julian Arguëlles (sax); Steve Hamilton (p); Terje Gewelt (b); Ian Froman (d).* 12/94.

The trio is significantly augmented for the next record, which is certainly the most ambitious thing Smith had attempted thus far in terms of composition. *Misty Morning* was made in collaboration with the veteran Scottish poet, Norman MacCaig (since decesased), a notably plain-spoken and unfussy craftsman with a bottomless humanity and humour. Though the level of direct contact seems to have been quite slight, less than with Edwin Morgan on *Beasts Of Scotland* later, it seems also to have made a significant impact on Smith, allowing him to mix complexity (and the band baulked anxiously when they first saw these charts) with a directness of expression that is immediately appealing.

Barker is inspirational, tackling each of the compositions as if they were familiar standards and bringing a very individual sound to 'Memorial', a threnody for the poet's dead daughter, and one of the most directly emotional pieces Smith has yet written. Arguëlles grows in stature every time one hears him, and his interplay with the leader on 'Estuary', a dappled theme which also makes use of Barker's liquid-sounding monette (an instrument not unlike Art Farmer's flumpet), is quite exceptional in its tact and taste. This was the breakthrough album. Afterwards, Smith has sounded less self-conscious, less driven, more focused and expressive.

★★★(★) Beasts Of Scotland

Linn AKD 054 *Smith; Guy Barker (t, flhn); Andy Panayi (as, f); Steve Hamilton (p, syn); Alec Dankworth (b); Tom Gordon (d, perc).* 96.

Playfully conceived, but revealing a core of solid invention, this was another poetic collaboration. Edwin Morgan is no less direct and unliterary than MacCaig, but he is also more immediately responsive to the music of his words, and this has allowed Smith to work at a new level again, creating tunes that are miniature tone-poems, evocative of the supposed subject-matter and at the same time utterly separate from it without ever sounding abstract.

He makes no attempt to evoke the fauna and avifauna of Scotland in sound-effects. 'Seal' has a slippery harmonic structure, but no more of it than that relates to the title. By the same token, 'Salmon' and 'Conger Eel' swim free of any programme, taut, elegant structures from Smith that throw up few opportunities for extended improvisation. 'Midge' may require a small gloss for non-Scottish listeners: a tiny insect, troublesome only in the plural and in the female gender, which has a healthy summer appetite for human blood. It's the most appealing idea and music of the set, though we rather liked Morgan's inclusion of the wolf as a beast of Scotland; there is a lobby for its reintroduction, and if it is as heroic as Smith makes it sound, then the sooner the better ...

★★★(★) Azure

Linn AKD 059 *Smith; Kenny Wheeler (t, flhn); Lars Danielsson (b); Jon Christensen (d).* 96.

A collaborative album, with compositions by the ever-tougher Christensen and some wonderful playing by Wheeler. As on the early Blue Note sessions, Smith is in some danger of being eclipsed by his 'sidemen', and the album is at some risk of disappearing into sub-ECM impressionism, but the rigour of compositions like the opening 'The Gold Of The Azure' and 'The Calculation' lift the set.

★★★★ The Sound Of Love

Linn AKD 084 *Smith; Kenny Barron (p); Peter Washington (b); Billy Drummond (d).* 97.

Who can this wise old man be, with the deep, breathy delivery, the chastened romanticism and the ability to combine passion and introspection? Whatever bruises Smith picked up during the Blue Note days are put right here. A top-drawer American band, seemingly almost unrehearsed, and a bag of songs by Ellington and Strayhorn, from the opening 'Johnny Come Lately', through 'Chelsea Bridge', 'Isfahan', 'Prelude To A Kiss' to a delightful closing 'Cottontail'. Crowd-pleasing romance and a more naked and unaffected Smith than we've ever had a chance to hear before. Barron is a giant of the music, and should be knighted, sanctified and nationalized without delay. His playing on 'Duke Ellington's Sound Of Love' (a Mingus composition and the only non-Duke and Sweet Pea tune on the album) is jaw-dropping: profound, lyrical and totally in tune with both the piece and the saxophonist. Marvellous album. If you can make room for only one by T. Smith, this should be it.

★★★★ Blue Smith

Linn AKD 110 *Smith; John Scofield (g); James Genus (b); Clarence Penn (d).* 1/99.

... But then again, you wouldn't want to be without this one, either. Smith has spoken warmly about working with Scofield: the absolute distinctiveness of his guitar-playing; the complete musicality; the sheer intelligence. Nevertheless, all the compositions here are his own. The liner-photos of the band are time-coded a quarter past midnight and there's a late-night feel to these splendid performances: nothing wee-small-hours and either over-mellow or frenetic; just relaxed, fluent and adult.

Smith's growing stature as a composer is evidenced above all in the relative simplicity of these tunes. Whereas in the past his besetting vice was an over-elaboration of the line, here the emphasis is on the scaffolding rather than the curlicues. 'Eany Meany Miny Mo', 'Blacken' Blue' and 'Hubba Hubba' are convincingly personal but unfussy and clean-limbed. Scofield's driving lines and rich harmonics are an essential ingredient, but Smith has rarely played better. Genus and Penn are magnificent, not so laid back as to suggest the horizontal but certainly not in a hurry for the last subway train.

Smith throws in one standard, 'Amazing Grace', and gives that weary old tune – Scottish? Virginian? – a remarkable dignity. Graceful and amazing.

★★★(★) Spartacus

Spartacus STS 001 *Smith; Kenny Barron (p); James Genus (b); Clarence Penn (d).* 9/00.

Smith launched his new label with this elegant New York session that is, appropriately, co-credited to or 'featuring' Kenny Barron. The pianist makes his presence felt from the opening sections of Jimmy Rowles's 'The Peacocks' and is secure, expressive and constantly inventive from there on. The title-track is another typical Smith composition: brooding, complex and unexpectedly airy, effortlessly idiomatic writing for the saxophone. Much of the rest of the session is upbeat and swinging – 'The Lady Is A Tramp', 'I Want To Be Happy', 'Bye Bye Blackbird' – but with some delightful, sepia-tinged passages on tunes like 'It Never Entered My Mind' (a subliminal quote from Coltrane there) and 'When I'm All Alone'. The studio sound is rich and very faithful, with lots of room round the individual players.

★★★ Into Silence

Spartacus STS 003 *Smith (ss, ts, bells).* 10/01.

Recorded in the acoustic of Hamilton Mausoleum in central Scotland, this solo set is intensely atmospheric but ultimately quite a tough listen. Other saxophonists have attempted unaccompanied performance in similar settings – Barbara Thompson has done it in an abbey cloisters, for instance – but the obvious influence is Garbarek again, except that Smith has given the set his own special stamp, using traditional Scottish themes, original ideas, and a cover of Coltrane's 'Naima' which is almost the best thing on the record. The long, long decay – we reckon some fifteen seconds – allows him to experiment with harmonics and with multiple lines, but over time the ambience overpowers the playing. One for certain moods, or to be sampled one track at a time, we reckon, but further testimony to Smith's continuing willingness to experiment.

★★(★) Alone At Last

Spartacus STS 004 *Smith; Kenny Barron (p); Steve Hamilton (syn); James Genus, Aiden O'Donnell (b); John Blease (d); Edwin Morgan, Groven Myrhen (v).* 00–02.

It's unlikely that another label would have authorized release of an album as haphazard as this, certainly by a living musician, but no fan of Smith's would want to be without most of this material. There is a reworking with the American band which made *Spartacus* of 'Ally the Wallygator', one of his best-known compositions and a couple of pieces – 'Cumhaichean' most notably – which clinch his much-discussed but often unevidenced devotion to the 'Nordic' sound of Jan Garbarek. Some of the material comes from festival commissions and there are inspired interventions by Scotland's finest living poet Edwin Morgan, who has been a tutelary figure in Smith's recent career. A couple of tracks don't merit inclusion by any respectable standard. It's hard to think there isn't something better in the saxophonist's tape library than 'Over The Rainbow'. The Celtic stuff is consistently interesting but doesn't sit altogether comfortably with the straighter jazz performances. The first, tiny hint of indulgence from the chairman of the Spartacus board.

*** The Christmas Concert

Spartacus STS006 *Smith; Gareth Williams (p); Orlando Le Fleming (b); Sebastian De Krom (d).* 12/01.

Frankly, the odds were longer on a Wynton Marsalis hip-hop album. Needless to say, the emphasis is on improvisation rather than Yuletide cheer and there is some astoundingly good playing all round. Williams is a vivid and original pianist, who manages to be simultaneously intriguing and unobtrusive. His rhythm section colleagues rightly opt for the latter quality, but manage to keep up a brisk pace throughout. 'God Rest Ye, Merry Gentlemen' is a heavyweight tenor workout, and contrasts strongly with 'Silent Night' and 'I'll Be Home For Christmas', the strongest cut of the set. Smith's improvisational language grows with every passing season and it's encouraging to find that he doesn't even take Christmas off.

**** Bezique

Spartacus STS 007 *Smith; Brian Kellock (p).* 07/02.

Brian Kellock's route to jazz stardom was slower and quieter than Smith's, as perhaps suits their respective personalities, but here the pianist demonstrates his quality with every phrase. Recorded live at the 2002 Edinburgh International Jazz Festival, the set was a long-awaited collaboration that delivered magisterially. The choice of material, which includes Chick Corea's 'Bud Powell' and Bill Evans's 'Very Early', looks as though it might have been Brian's but in performance he keeps for the most part to an uneffusive structural role, blocking in themes and harmonic variations and leaving Smith to explore the outer reaches. 'Parker 51' is a fearsome duet, not instantly recognizable as either man but at every turn a convincing demonstration of their shared ability to react at speed. 'Lush Life' is inevitably something of a coda to such a powerful cut, but it sees both Smith and Kellock back in more familiar roles and it's such a feeling and intelligent performance that one's immediate reaction is to cue back to track one and listen to the whole astonishing thing over again.

Wadada Leo Smith (born 1941)

TRUMPET, FLUGELHORN, PERCUSSION

Born in Mississippi, Smith became part of the radical AACM group before founding the Creative Construction Company with Anthony Braxton and Leroy Jenkins. A subtle theoretician, he has rarely enjoyed adequate opportunity to put his ideas into practice and remains undervalued.

CORE COLLECTION

**** Divine Love

ECM 529126-2 *Smith; Lester Bowie, Kenny Wheeler (t); Dwight Andrews (af, bcl, ts, perc); Bobby Naughton (vib, mar, perc); Charlie Haden (b).* 9/78.

Heard the one about the Rastafarian trumpeter who went to live in Iceland? There's no punchline, because it isn't a joke. It seems an unlikely destination for Smith, except that his conception of jazz as a world music seems to need no definite cultural location, but shifts steadily from one to the next. Given the level of indifference at home, Iceland seemed as good a berth as any for a while.

Since the '70s Smith has organized his music according to the principles of 'rhythm-units', which seem to call for a mystical equivalence of sound and silence, and of 'ahkreanvention', a method of notating improvised music. 'Tastalun' on *Divine Love* is the first of these pieces Smith had an opportunity to record, three muted trumpets weaving an extraordinary extended spell. So closely integrated is the playing by Smith and guests Wheeler and Bowie that it is difficult – and probably pointless – trying to sort out who is playing which line.

The basic group, on both this record and the one below, is Smith with Naughton and Andrews. *Divine Love* opens on a long meditation for alto flute, Andrews at his atmopsheric best, before Smith's tight, compressed sound comes through. The title-piece is another of his ritual works, like the earlier *Mass For The World* and *Budding Of A Rose*, issued on Moers but sadly no longer available. Naughton's vibes are a key element on this record, not least because there is no conventional percussion part. He opens the last track pitched against Charlie Haden's bass, marking the pauses that constitute the work's stately rhythm unit. Andrews's bass clarinet intones ancient wisdoms while Smith sounds elevated, rapt, almost tranced.

***(*) Go In Numbers

Black Saint 120053 *Smith; Dwight Andrews (af, bcl, ts, perc); Bobby Naughton (vib, mar, perc); Wes Brown (b, odurgyaba f).* 1/80.

This is a live recording, from the Kitchen in New York, of the group Smith called New Dalta Ahkri. In terms of its duration, it's better value for money than the decidedly skimpy *Divine Love* (above), which was reissued on CD with no extra tracks.

The two major statements on the Black Saint album occupy most of its length. Naughton and Wes Brown open 'Go In Numbers' with a desolate meditation that sounds like the funeral march of some lost leader. Smith's opening figures seem to contain half-remembered elements of Ives's *The Unanswered Question*. Elsewhere he sounds uncannily like a slowed-up version of Don Cherry, an influence that was to seem ever more pressing in years to come.

***(*) Procession Of The Great Ancestry

Chief CD6 *Smith; John Powell (ts); Bobby Naughton (vib); Louis Myers (g); Joe Fonda, Mchaka Uba (b); Kahil El'Zabar (d, perc).* 2/83.

'Seven mystical poems of jazz in 17 links', dedicated to some of the honoured shades of Afro-America, including fellow-trumpeters Miles, Dizzy, Roy Eldridge and Booker Little, with a special paean to Gabriel's right-hand man, the Revd Martin

Luther King Jr. As in *The Mass On The World*, this is conceived as a long seamless ritual, much of it conducted in duet with Naughton, whose vibes have never sounded more like mystical bells.

Smith makes no attempt to pastiche any of his musical ancestors. Stylistically, it would be difficult to determine merely by listening who was being celebrated in which piece, except that there is probably more of Miles in the title-track, which begins the procession proper. What Diz would have thought of a title like 'Celestial Sparks In The Sanctuary Of Redemption' is fortunately not recorded. A wonderful record, despite its slightly overcooked poetics. May be difficult to find, but well worth the search.

*****(*) Kulture Jazz**

ECM 519074-2 *Smith (solo).* 10/92.

Another attempt to commune with the ancestors. The honour'd shades are Billie Holiday, Trane, Ayler and Pops, but this time there is much greater emphasis on Smith's poetic writing, which, like Cecil Taylor's, has become ever more important relative to pure instrumentalism. One longs for more trumpet in place of the barrage of percussion and little instruments that clogs the album.

Interestingly, Smith's name is one that often comes up when supporters are (rightly) trying to debunk the notion of ECM as purveyors of nothing but pastelly Nordic chamber music. It was brave of them to go back to him after a gap of almost 25 years, but sadly this one dates far more quickly than *Divine Love*, which was a welcome reissue, seeming to coincide with quarter-centenary celebrations.

*****(*) Tao-Njia**

Tzadik TZ 7017 *Smith; Dorothy Stone (f, af, picc); Martin Walker (cl, bcl); Vicki Ray (p, cel); Mika Noda (vib, perc); Robin Lorentz (vn); Erika Duke (clo); David Philipson (bansuri, perc); Harumi Makino Smith (v).* 11 & 12/95.

***** Light Upon Light**

Tzadik TZ 7046 *Smith; Bill Powell, Marty Walker (cl, bcl); Dorothy Stone (picc, f, af); Allan Vogel (ob); Vicki Ray (p); Robin Lorentz (vn); Karen Elaine Bakunin (vla); Erica Duke-Kirkpatrick (clo); Bertram Turetzky (b); Arthur Jarvinen (perc, mar, vib); I. Nyoman Wenten (gender barung); John Parsons (gender parembung); Mark Trayle (elec); Harumi Makino Smith (v).* n.d.

In the spring of 1995 Smith unveiled a large-scale, multi-ensemble piece called *Odwira*. It was the clearest sign of how far he has moved from small-group improvisation to a new conception of himself as a composer, albeit a heterodox one. In this regard, and in some respects only, his career closely parallels that of Anthony Braxton.

Recent years have seen Smith personally and musically involved with Oriental culture, and this is strongly reflected in *Tao-Njia*. Acoustically, it is one of his most remarkable records, a rich montage of sounds that are at once new and immediately familiar, bearing Smith's stamp from the very first overdubbed passages of 'Another Wave More Waves'. Here, once again, the dominant exchange is between trumpet and vibraphone, no longer Bobby Naughton but Mika Noda, and pairs of low drums performed by David Philipson, two members of his Nda-Kulture Ensemble. They are augmented by members of new-music and crossover specialists California E.A.R. for 'Tao-Njia' itself. As on *Kulture Jazz*, this is essentially a text piece, recited by Harumi Makino Smith against a wind-and-string ensemble, Smith's trumpet and pre-recorded *mbira*. It's the only questionable part of the record, over-long, slightly indulgent and not always very clearly articulated.

The remainder is taken up by 'Double Thunderbolt', one of many recent memorials to the late Don Cherry. It borrows his 'Symphony For Improvisers' tag for the second and fifth movements, opening with Smith on bamboo flute and ending – 'A Falcon Ascends In A Moonbow Lightbeam' – with magnificent solo muted trumpet. A piece to cherish, utterly true to Cherry's great gifts, and to Smith's.

The second record extends this phase of Smith's compositional career. Two of the pieces are performed by the E.A.R. Ensemble and the New Century Players, one of them, 'Nur' written for bassist Turetzky. 'Hetep: Serenity: Tranquility 2' is for Bakunin's viola, while the last two pieces are complex soundscapes for electronics, samples and Smith's keening trumpet. Almost a new-music record and certainly some way removed from Smith's more jazz-based recording, but fascinating none the less.

***** Condor, Autumn Wind**

Wobbly Rail WOB 001 *Smith; Harumi Makimo Smith (v).* 11/97.

A very intimate, almost private musical experience that will either command or repel. So much of Smith's creative energy has gone into tributes to other musicians – and here again Dizzy Gillespie, Marion Brown and Albert Ayler are honoured – that one wonders whether he makes such obeisances with all due self-confidence or whether something like that old American principle, the 'anxiety of influence', is at work.

'Condor' is a further gesture of respect to Diz and is very fine, but the real meat of the album – and the most positive answer to the question above – is in the first three tracks. Haiku-simple and unfussily played, they show the Smiths at their unaffected best.

*****(*) Yo Miles!**

Shanachie 5046 2CD *Smith; Bruce Ackley, Steve Adams, George Brooks, Lary Ochs, Jon Raskin (sax); Oluyemi Thomas (bcl); Paul Plimley (p, org); John Medeski (org); Bob Bralove (ky); Nels Cline, Henry Kaiser, Freddy Roulette, Elliott Sharp (g); Chris Muir (g, elec); Michael Manring (b, g); Wally Ingram, Lukas Ligeti (d, perc).* 1/98.

Why listen to reprocessed Miles when there is a whole shelfload of the real thing? If the answer seems self-evident, it might be worth spending an hour with Smith, guitarist Henry Kaiser and band on this generous two-CD pastiche of Miles's electric phase. Smith's trumpet-playing is rawer and more intense than anything Miles ever attempted. One is tempted to say it is also more harmonically astute. What it lacks is the eggshell fragility of the original, which is what most fans will instinctively value most.

The material is predictable enough, mostly *Jack Johnson* and *Big Fun* vintage funk. Smith turns 'Calypso Frelimo' into a dark, squally ride, and the ABC groove of 'Ife' – perhaps the most ubiquitous staple of the electric years – into a sprawling essay in time-changes and minimal harmonics. 'Miles Dewey Davis III – Great Ancestor' is an original and in some respects the most stretching piece on the record.

Kaiser's part is harder to quantify and assess. Unlike John McLaughlin and later guitarists, he doesn't command much of a front role, but he underpins the ensembles with real understanding. The guest musicians, who include the members of the ROVA Saxophone Quartet, are used to great effect, and Kaiser and fellow-guitarist Chris Muir produce with a feel for the grooves and timbres that Teo Macero would enjoy.

★★★★ Red Sulphur Sky

Tzadik TZ 7070 *Smith (t, flhn solo).* 01.

This is a devastatingly beautiful recital, calling on all of Smith's technique as well as his wonderfully poetic musical personality. 'The Medicine Wheel' and 'Evening Glow As Shining Outward' are the closest things to pure jazz, partly because of the articulation and attack, partly because of the harmonic language implied, but it is the title-track which really captures the ear, quoting a whole range of themes and styles as it goes. There are no studio effects on the album, just the sound of a masterful instrumentalist who is in complete command of his instrument and his sound. On 'AFMIE: Purity And Poverty', he digs deep into his Miles Davis bag but still comes up with something utterly new and original. A delightful record, warm and compelling.

★★★(★) Reflectativity

Tzadik TZ 7060 *Smith; Anthony Davis (p); Malachi Favors (b).* 99.

★★★(★) Golden Quartet

Tzadik TZ 7604 *As above, except add Jack DeJohnette (d).* 00.

The *Reflectavitity* session reworks a piece from 1972, which has lain in Smith's work bag ever since, unacknowledged and only now recast as a tribute to Duke Ellington. The other dominant influences on this extraordinary record are Thelonious Monk (surely namechecked in the most sincere way on 'Blue Flag'), Charlie Parker and Anthony Braxton, with whom Smith has worked many times and with whom he shares something of an aesthetic. The playing is very powerful and very compelling.

On 'Celestial Sky And All The Magic', Smith demonstrates again how much he owes to Miles Davis, but also how far he has travelled beyond. His muted introduction is as delicately moving as his rapid-fire exposition on 'America's Third Century Spiritual Awakening' is rousing. The opening 'DeJohnette' is a Milesian tribute to a band member and affords the drummer lots of space to spread out and show his wares. Jack is an utterly compelling soloist and his ability to understand where Smith is coming from generates the key relationship of the set. Davis is sympathetic enough, but he doesn't quite have the chops to equal Smith.

★★★ The Year Of The Elephant

Pi Recordings 4 *Smith; Anthony Davis (p, syn); Malachi Favors Mahgostut (b); Jack DeJohnette (d, syn).* 9/02.

A surprisingly straightahead jazz record, strongly influenced by electric-period Miles Davis. DeJohnette plays crisp, flowing lines, and Favors, always a fascinating groove-player, lays down beefy lines that sound at times more like bass guitar. Smith and Davis are the more 'outside' half of the equation, but the trumpeter tends to restrict himself to yawing, almost anguished figures that on the duet with Davis, 'Kangaroo's Hollow', flirt with abstraction. The opening 'Al-Madinah' promises that this is not going to be an unduly complex or tortuous album, and 'The Zamzan Well A Stream Of A Pure Light' is milder and more circumspect than anything Smith has done in recent years. 'Miles Star In 3 Parts' is interesting, with Davis playing a bass vamp under the trumpet. The pianist and DeJohnette both deploy synthesizers, but in the most conventional and unassuming way, almost as if they had planned on having a Hammond in studio. An attractive album, but not a particularly ear-grabbing one. A must, all the same, for Smith fans.

★★★ Luminous Axis

Tzadik TZ 7083 *Smith; William Winant (d, perc); John Bischoff, Ikue Mori, Tim Perkis, Mark Trayle (elec).* 03.

A suite of miniatures and longer improvisations, with the trumpet keening out across spare and sometimes almost subliminal electronic backgrounds. Curated by John Zorn, who may well have introduced Mori to the proceedings, it's a questing, continuously evolving set that demands a lot of attention, even when it seems mildest. Smith plays well and with a lot of gentle spirit.

★★★ Organic Resonance

Pi Recordings 6 *Smith; Anthony Braxton (reeds).* 4/03.

Widely admired on first release, this is a curiously disappointing set that – somewhat like Braxton's '70s duos with Derek Bailey – never seems to find the two players on common ground. It's a live recording, consisting of two Smith compositions bracketing Braxton's 'Compositions 314/315'. Smith, as ever, paints broad brush, while Braxton's pieces are faster-moving, rhythmically complex tessellations of very simple materials. There's an almost conversational intimacy to much of the music, a warmth that is instantly engaging but in the long haul curiously unsatisfying.

Willie 'The Lion' Smith (1895–1973)

PIANO, VOCAL

A founder-member of the New York stride pianists, Smith served in the First World War, then haunted the toughest New York clubs. He led occasional bands, toured, and became a self-appointed living historian and raconteur in his old age. He wrote Echoes of Spring.

★★★(★) Willie 'The Lion' Smith 1925–1937

Classics 662 *Smith; Dave Nelson, Frankie Newton (t); June Clark, Jabbo Smith, Ed Allen (c); Jimmy Harrison (tb); Buster Bailey (cl, ss, as); Cecil Scott, Herschel Brassfield (cl); Prince Robinson, Robert Carroll (ts); Edgar Sampson (as, vn); Pete Brown (as); Buddy Christian, Gus Horsley (bj); Jimmy McLin (g); Bill Benford, Harry Hull (tba); Ellsworth Reynolds, John Kirby (b); O'Neil Spencer (d, v); Eric Henry (d); Willie Williams (wbd); Perry Bradford (v).* 11/25–9/37.

★★★★ Willie 'The Lion' Smith And His Cubs

Timeless CBC 1-012 *As above, except omit Clark, Harrison, Robinson, Christian, Benford, Jabbo Smith, Brassfield, Sampson, Horsley and Hull.* 4/35–9/37.

★★★ Willie 'The Lion' Smith 1937–1938

Classics 677 *Smith; Frankie Newton (t); Pete Brown (as); Buster Bailey (cl); Milt Herth (org); Jimmy McLin (g); Teddy Bunn (g, v); John Kirby (b); O'Neil Spencer (d, v).* 9/37–11/38.

★★★(★) Willie 'The Lion' Smith 1938–1940

Classics 692 *Smith; Sidney De Paris (t); Jimmy Lane, Johnny Mullins (as); Perry Smith (ts); Joe Bushkin, Jess Stacy (p); Bernard Addison (g); Richard Fulbright (b); George Wettling, Puss Johnson (d); Joe Turner, Naomi Price (v).* 11/38–11/40.

One of the great Harlem pianists and an unrivalled raconteur, Willie Smith came into his own when an old man, reminiscing from the keyboard. But these more youthful sessions stand up very well and are surprisingly little known. Classics 662 opens with two of his few appearances on record in the '20s; each of the pair of sessions is by a pick-up group, both with Jimmy Harrison and one with Jabbo Smith in the front line. Typical small-group Harlem jazz of the period, with Perry Bradford shouting the odds on two titles. The remainder – and all of the Timeless CD – is devoted to sessions by Smith's Cubs, an excellent outfit: with Ed Allen, Cecil Scott and Willie Williams on washboard on the first eight titles, they can't help but sound like a Clarence Williams group, but the next three sessions include Dave Nelson (sounding better than he ever did on the King Oliver Victor records), Buster Bailey, Pete Brown and Frankie Newton, effecting a bridge between older hot music and the sharper small-band swing of the late '30s. Smith plays a lot of dextrous piano – he also has a 1934 solo, 'Finger Buster', a typical parlour show-off piece of the day – and the music has a wonderful lilt and sprightliness. The Timeless transfers are clearly superior and include a lot of alternative takes: this is the disc to get if you just want the Cubs tracks, but the other tunes on the Classics disc are also worth hearing. Classics 677 is made up mostly of tracks by Milt Herth, a Hammond organist who had Smith, Spencer and Bunn making up his group. Herth is always getting in the way, but The Lion usually pushes some decent stride piano into the tunes, and there are two fine 1938 solos, 'Passionette' and 'Morning Air', which show something of his penchant for novelty piano of the Roy Bargy genre. Classics 692 starts with a three-piano date featuring Smith, Stacy and Bushkin, before a marathon session that produced 14 piano solos in one day – originals and show tunes, done in the manner of courteous syncopation that trademarks Smith's style. The rest of the disc includes a rare small-band session and a pair of blues, partnering Smith with Joe Turner. Exemplary, although docked a notch for less-than-ideal remastering.

***** Music On My Mind**
Emarcy 014032-2 *Smith (p, v solo).* 11/65.

The Lion's irrepressible showmanship often got in the way of his piano-playing when it came to his later records. Most of them were done for whatever label would have him, and as a result most of them are now out of print. In Paris, in 1965, he mixed up 'Shine', James P. Johnson, 'Summertime' and Chopin, alongside a bouquet of his own evergreens. Delicate and boisterous music in good sound.

Paul Smoker (born 1941)

TRUMPET

Paul Smoker is a Mid-West academic who plays free-form jazz of surpassing thoughtfulness. Though by no means averse to tackling standards, he creates a lot of his own material, cleaving to quasi-classical forms which, coupled with a tight, rather correct diction, sometimes recall Don Ellis.

****(*) Halloween 96**
CIMP 129 *Smoker; Vinny Golia (bs); Ken Filiano (b); Phil Haynes (d).* 10/96.

***** Halloween – The Sequel**
Nine Winds NWCD 0207 *As above.* 4/97.

*****(*) Standard Deviation**
CIMP 186 *Smoker; Steve Salerno (g); Thomas Ulrich (clo); Jay Rosen (d).* 9/98.

Interesting that the liner-notes to *The Sequel* record document some difficulties getting the sound right and the group properly balanced. Smoker has always depended on a very careful spatial distribution and a rather subtle internal balance. We're not convinced he got it with Golia, but we're not convinced that the baritonist is his natural playing partner either. *Halloween 96* is an entirely free-form set, five longish improvisations played at high temperature but lacking the analytical poise of Smoker's attack on standard material. Golia always has interesting things to say, as does Smoker, but this too often sounds like an amiable encounter between two men who really have nothing musical in common.

The return fixture is this time largely based on composition rather than free improvisation. The exceptions are two brief takes of 'That Was For Albert', a collective composition that bears some wispy traces of Ayler's own open-formed melodies. The sound is much better than on the CIMP, a label that prides itself on rough-hewn immediacy and no polish. The smoother surface does this music no disservice at all.

Smoker subtly adjusts the tonalities on *Standard Deviation*, which is really what the title is about. 'Speak Low' is shifted into a very unbluesy B major and 'Stormy Weather' into G flat. He also overturns the usual order of head and solo, placing rubato melody statements over strict-time accompaniments and vice versa. All four group members introduce songs and Rosen, who is among the most ubiquitous performers in the CIMP catalogue, is especially good in his introduction to 'Stormy Weather'. Unlike the earlier set with Golia, Smoker modulates the dynamics and expressive range with genuine mastery. 'Speak Low' is as delicate a version as you'll ever hear, and his approach to 'Beyond The Blue Horizon' is exquisitely weighted. Smoker's recent engagement with jazz harmonics is similar to that of Franz Koglmann (another who has suffered from the deletion of hat ART's 6000 catalogue) but is unmistakably more American in emphasis and, one almost hesitates to say, more expressive as well.

***** Large Music 1**
CIMP 219 *Smoker; Bob Magnusson (as, ts); Ken Filiano (b); Lou Grassi (d).* 3/00.

***** Large Music 2**
CIMP 226 *As above.* 3/00.

*****(*) Mirabile Dictu**
CIMP 233 *Smoker; Steve Salerno (g); Ken Filiano (b).* 9/00.

Magnusson has been all bother and bluster on some of his recordings that we've encountered, but Smoker seems to have been a mollifying presence and he plays with more point on the two *Large Music* sets, both cut during a marathon at the CIMP studio. Grassi is propulsive enough but he's not the most subtle or imaginative drummer, and with a musician as thoughtful as Smoker, his playing won't really do. In spite of the sometimes aggravating surroundings (listen to the difference between Smoker's remarkable low-register playing on 'Hold On, Hold On' and Grassi's insensitive batterings), there's still plenty of food for thought in both CDs.

Mirabile Dictu is a fascinating trio encounter, which reveals all kinds of interesting *détente* when Smoker is in the chair. The chattering 'Open Season', mood-painting title-piece and 'Elegy' (a homage to Lester Bowie in which Smoker outdoes its dedicatee) all work superbly. There are one or two slow spots elsewhere, but closing on a funereal, entirely straight 'The Meaning Of The Blues' (which probably shocked the CIMP team) was a masterstroke.

***** Brass Reality**

Nine Winds 0241 *Smoker: Herb Robertson (t, vtb, tba); David Taylor (tb, tba); Phil Haynes (perc).* 6/97.

It's as well not to be put off by the seemingly functional titles – 'Solo Prelude', 'Fanfare And Procession', 'Waltz' – or by what might seem like workshop ideas ('Harmon City'). All of these are fully realized and often very powerful statements by three virtuosic players; Haynes is very much in support. Robertson's sheer range of sound is extraordinary and he exploits it to the full on the 'Fractals' tracks and on the delightful 'Alice's Legacy'. Smoker is less of an exhibitionist, but he will convert many with this performance.

***** Duocity**

Cadence CJR 1155/56 2CD *Smoker; Dominic Duval, Ed Schuller (b).* 5–10/01.

Two live duos taped at the Bop Shop in Rochester, New York. This kind of session can make for tough listening, but Smoker's willingness to mix bluesy wails and smears with entirely abstract patterns, as he does on 'Didgerotics' with Schuller, keeps even uncommitted listeners onside and eventually won over. Schuller is a less lyrical player than his fellow bass-man. He alternates tough, hard-scrabble figures with didjeridu effects, long slides up and down the scale with precisely plucked melody lines and remote harmonics. The long central piece, 'Hypnotics/Bassoptic Mutetics/Nostematics', is completely virtuosic from start to finish but also rivetingly dramatic. Nothing of quite that ambition or calibre from the duo with Duval, but he is the more obviously listenable of the two bassists and the shorter tracks reveal their structure more readily. Great stuff, even if not to every taste.

Gary Smulyan (born 1956)

BARITONE SAXOPHONE

Already a veteran of big-band section playing, Smulyan worked with Woody Herman and Mel Lewis before making these leadership dates in the '90s. Very much in the Pepper Adams mould, he's become perhaps the leading American exponent of post-bop baritone.

***** The Lure Of Beauty**

Criss Cross 1049 *Smulyan; Jimmy Knepper (tb); Mulgrew Miller (b); Ray Drummond (b); Kenny Washington (d).* 12/90.

A staunch section player, Smulyan has as good a grasp of baritone technique as any of the younger players of what's still a rare instrument. It was a smart idea to bring Jimmy Knepper to this session, a frequent associate of Pepper Adams and a player whose manner is individual enough to lift the music out of the hard-bop rut which several Criss Cross sessions have fallen into. The group work up a great head of steam on 'Canto Fiesta', the rhythm section grooving hard enough to sustain the feel over more than ten minutes, and there are a couple of pretty (if functional) ballad performances; but at 74 minutes the record could have lost a couple of items and been none the worse for it.

***** Homage**

Criss Cross 1068 *Smulyan; Tommy Flanagan (p); Ray Drummond (b); Kenny Washington (d).* 12/91.

It was a pleasing notion to pay tribute to Smulyan's acknowledged master, Pepper Adams, who wrote all eight themes here. Having Flanagan, an old Detroit friend of Adams's, along as well was another good idea. Smulyan is both similar to and different from the older player, less ornery than Adams but given to a comparable stoniness and scepticism with the tender approach: on a ballad such as 'Civilization And Its Discontents' his refusal to turn to a sanctimonious vibrato adds to the power of the improvising, even with Flanagan's featherbed chords to hand. The hard-bop lines of 'Claudette's Way' are reeled off with unassuming strength: this is a baritone man who understands the weight and gravitas of the instrument without having to insist on it. Smulyan doesn't always convince one that the tunes are that good, but it's an impressively substantial record.

***** Saxophone Mosaic**

Criss Cross 1092 *Smulyan; Dick Oatts (ss, as, f); Billy Drewes (as, cl, f); Ralph Lalama (ts, cl, f); Rich Perry (ts); Scott Robinson (bs, bcl); Mike LeDonne (p); Dennis Irwin (b); Kenny Washington (d).* 12/93.

George Coleman's 'Apache Dance', which opens the record, features all the horns, but it's the exception. For the most part, Bob Belden's arrangements use this six-sax team for colour, and for something which Smulyan himself can bed down in. He peels off long, heated solos on every track, as if under pressure to make the baritone dominate the line-up, and it's an effective strategy. But here and there one wishes the other horns had taken a greater part, though everyone comes back in again on the closing 'Fingers'.

***** With Strings**

Criss Cross 1129 *Smulyan; Mike LeDonne (p); Peter Washington (b); Kenny Washington (d); strings.* 12/96.

Baritone plus strings is a rare arrangement. Bob Belden's charts are sound and gracious, and Smulyan does well enough by them, although he hardly strikes one as the ideal player for the situation: Chaloff or Mulligan, perhaps, but Smulyan is more out of the impassive Pepper Adams end of the horn. The programme is mostly built around originals, too, which gives the listener few enough footholds in coming to terms with the tunes. It's appealingly done, but one feels that Criss Cross (on their debut session with strings) might have gone all out for the emotional ticket and handed Smulyan a programme of familiar ballads.

***** Blue Suite**

Criss Cross 1189 *Smulyan; Earl Gardner, Greg Gisbert, Scott Wendholt (t); John Mosca, Jason Jackson (tb); Douglas Purviance (btb); John Clark, Fred Griffith (frhn); Bill Charlap (p); Bob Stewart (tba); Christian McBride (b); Kenny Washington (d).* 12/99.

A musicians' record. After a brisk charge through Oliver Nelson's 'Interlude', the record is made up of the seven-part 'Blue Suite', composed and arranged by Bob Belden to feature

Smulyan in front of big brass and rhythm sections. The material is all based on blues and Belden sneaks in numerous reference points – from Ellington, Mingus, Coltrane, Basie and elsewhere – as if he's working the aisles of a jazz supermarket. It's all cleverly done, but what comes out is the kind of date which has the players smiling knowingly and leaving the listeners not quite warmed enough. Long solos slow matters down. But Smulyan still plays with great chutzpah.

Jim Snidero (born 1958)

ALTO SAXOPHONE

Snidero is a talented musician and a passionate musical advocate and educator who has created his own latter-day synthesis of hard bop. A seasoned player with an impressive track record working for everyone from Toshiko Akiyoshi to Frank Sinatra, he now has an extensive discography as leader as well.

****(*) Mixed Bag**

Criss Cross 1032 *Snidero; Brian Lynch (t); Benny Green (p); Peter Washington (b); Jeff 'Tain' Watts (d).* 12/87.

*****(*) Blue Afternoon**

Criss Cross 1072 *As above, except replace Watts with Marvin 'Smitty' Smith (d).* 12/89.

Washington-born Snidero has never quite managed to locate himself stylistically. An immensely able player who seems to have processed a good deal of the jazz history of preceding generations, he is not yet a man with a definite voice and presence. We were assured that *Mixed Bag*, the title, shouldn't be taken too literally, but that is exactly what it is. 'Pannonica' lacks the sort of ironic detachment that Monk requires, and Snidero's introductory cadenza on 'Blood Count', a haunting Strayhorn theme, is one of the very best things he has done, but it stands somewhat apart among this material.

Blue Afternoon is better, not just because it features the splendid Smith, but also because the material is better judged. Wayne Shorter's 'Infant Eyes' and Mal Waldron's 'Soul Eyes' are key peformances, and Snidero's occasional Coltraneisms are reasonably in keeping with the music being played. Briskly paced and well recorded.

*****(*) San Juan**

Red Records 123265 *Snidero; Steve Nelson (vib); Kevin Hayes (p); Dennis Irwin (b); Billy Hart (d).* 10/94.

The year 1994 marked something of a breakthrough for Snidero. There is a sharpness and precision about his playing which wasn't always or consistently in evidence before, and the standard of writing seems to be on a new plane. All tracks, except for a sensitive reading of Kenny Dorham's 'La Mesha', are by him, and they're very good indeed. It's remarkable that music written in an idiom that was already probably 30 years past its sell-by should sound so fresh and immediate, and so well paced. Though no one is likely to mistake it for a period piece, this is the kind of album Blue Note was turning out in its heyday. 'Introspect', 'Mystery' and 'The Web' are bold and intelligent conceptions, and only with the closing 'To Whom It May Concern' does either conception or execution start to seem a little formulaic. A word of recognition for Steve Nelson, a Red stalwart who provides much of the impetus on these cuts. He is a player worthy of closer attention, but also perhaps still in need of a broader stage.

*****(*) Vertigo**

Criss Cross 1112 *Snidero; Walt Weiskopf (ts); David Hazeltine (p); Peter Washington (b); Tony Reedus (d).* 12/94.

Opportunity knocked, as for so many interesting players of this generation, in the shape of Gerry Teekens and Criss Cross. The result is both engaging and challenging. Snidero kicks off with some new material, including the excellent original 'A.S.A.P.', before switching to standards, cracking interpretations of 'Ah-Leu-Cha' and 'Skylark' which open up the band and allow them and tenorist Weiskopf (who has already established a presence on the label) to show their paces as a collective. Hazeltine isn't the most confident soloist on the planet, but he has Washington to lean on, and he turns in a more than competent set. The group sounds well rehearsed and sympathetic.

*****(*) Standards + Plus**

Double Time Records DTRCD 139 *Snidero; Mike LeDonne (p); Dennis Irwin (b); Kenny Washington (d).* 97.

Not clear what is intended by the 'Plus', other than entirely warranted enthusiasm for a strong, vibrant set. All nine tracks – it's a generously proportioned record – are based on standard material, to which Snidero or the label have interestingly and usefully attached dates of composition, ranging from 1929 for Vincent Youmans's 'Without A Song' to Sylvester Kynor's 'Bluesville', penned 30 years later.

He opens with 'You And The Night And The Music', handled in a manner that suggests Coltrane's deconstruction of 'My Favorite Things', the original Atlantic version rather than the more radical live performances which followed on. 'Round Midnight' and Benny Golson's 'Along Came Betty' are almost as good. LeDonne is a very talented accompanist without being distinctive as a solo voice. Confusingly, this time out it's the other (unrelated) Washington on drums – and what a strong and confidence-inspiring presence he is. Snidero is certainly going places. One wonders whether it would be so very hard to assemble a regular recording band. He certainly has the cachet and the experience now to call in a few favours. If not, it's a harder world than we thought.

****** The Music Of Joe Henderson**

Double Time Records DTRCD 152 *Snidero; Joe Magnarelli (t); Conrad Herwig (tb); David Hazeltine (p); Dennis Irwin (b); Kenny Washington (d).* 12/98.

Jim Snidero the jazz scholar comes to the fore on this fine disc, which is none the worse and none the less individual for being devoted to the great Joe H. There is every sign that Snidero has analysed these remarkable compositions in close detail and not just blandly covered them. He delves into rarely explored territory like the maverick blues, 'If', which Joe recorded on the 1967 Milestone album, *The Kicker*, and he brings no less insight to the more familiar 'Recorda-Me' and 'Punjab', which have become pretty much repertory pieces. The band is sympathetic and sounds exceedingly well prepared to tackle challenging material. Magnarelli and Herwig have the combined precision and big tone one expects of good ensemble players and the rhythm section does its job fluently. Snidero's solos are considered but in no way pat or pre-formed. Interestingly, it is Henderson's rhythmic complexity rather than his harmonics which seem to intrigue the altoist. Henderson has a very distinctive way of splitting perfectly ordinary time-signatures up into unexpected fractions and, equally, making very complex metres sound as basic as four-to-the-floor. Snidero picks up those cues on the closing 'Black Narcissus' and 'Afro-Centric' in particular, two tunes which open him up to new and fascinating opportunities.

*****(*) Strings**

Milestone MCD 9326 2 *Snidero; Renee Rosnes (p); Cenovia Cummings, Mark Feldman, Joyce Hammann, Sue Lorentsen, Laura Seaton, Paul Woodiel (vn); Kenji Bunch, Ralph Ferris (vla); Tomas Ulrich, Mary Wooten (clo); Paul Gill (b); Billy Drummond (d).* 11/01.

It might seem odd to suggest that it was a covers album that exposed Snidero's gifts as a composer/arranger but that was the long-term effect of the Henderson project. It prompted a fresh look at some of Snidero's earlier work – which stands up well to a return visit – and it paved the way for this remarkable set, which establishes the saxophonist as a genuinely significant figure in jazz composition.

This is not a 'with strings' project in the usual sense, with a few jazz stylings drenched in maple-syrup section work. The smallish orchestra is tightly drilled and commendably rhythmic. Husband and wife team Billy Drummond and Renee Rosnes anchor every track and apart from the long-form 'River Suite', which perhaps owes something to Snidero's association with Toshiko Akiyoshi (he has also worked with the Mingus Big Band, but that seems a less important influence here), the individual cuts are well shaped, tuneful and logical in structure. It isn't a tough listen, but the music is more challenging than at first appears and right from the opening track, 'Slipping Away', Jim is in command. Toning down some of his post-bop mannerisms reveals a mellifluous soloist with touches of Hodges and Paul Desmond. It's unlikely, given the economics of such projects, that he'll make many records with these forces, but *Strings* opens up a new facet of an already fascinating career.

Valaida Snow (1903–56)

TRUMPET, VOCALS

Now something of a forgotten figure, Valaida was a multi-instrumentalist raised in a musical family. She worked with Noble Sissle and Eubie Blake and enjoyed a stage and film career. At the start of the Second World War she was in Scandinavia and was captured by German forces in Denmark. Internment scarred her mentally and physically and her post-war career was a long slow decline. Snow died of a stroke after coming offstage at the Palace Theater in New York.

***** Valaida Snow: 1933–1936**

Classics 1158 *Snow; Walter Fuller, Duncan Whyte (t); Jock Fleming, Wallace Franklin, Louis Taylor (tb); Jimmy Mundy (ts); Freddy Gordon (as, ts); Darnell Howard (as, cl); Cecil Irwin (ts, cl); Omer Simeon (as, bs); Billy Mason (p); Lawrence Dixon (g); Dick Escott, Alan Ferguson, Sam Molyneux, Quinn Wilson, Joe Young (b); Max Bacon, Wallace Bishop, George Elrick (d).* 33–36.

***** Valaida Snow: 1937–1940**

Classics 1122 *Snow; Bengt Artander, Johnny Claes, Gunnar Green, Winstrup Olesen (t); Sture Green (tb); Kai Moeller (cl); Derek Neville (as, bs); Lulle Ellboj, Gunnar Wallberg (as); Reggie Dare, Rudolf Eriksson (ts); Gun Finlay, Leo Mathiesen, Willard Ringstrand (p); Norman Brown, Helge Jacobsen (g); Louis Barreiro, Roland Bengtsson, Christian Jensen (b); Kai Fischer, Olle Stahlin, Ken Steward (d).* 37–40.

Revisionist and feminist histories of jazz have occasionally attempted to reawaken interest in Valaida Snow. She was a formidable musician with an occasionally original take on swing, but even with the best will in the world she can hardly be deemed a major figure. These sides, which have also been available on two Harlequin sets, are engaging enough. Some were recorded in London, with competent dance-band players; others come from later in Snow's European *Wanderjahre*. Valaida's own compositions, songs like 'I Want A Lot Of Love' and 'Imagination' on the earlier volume, are less effective showcases for her talent than more familiar themes like 'Nagasaki' and 'Tiger Rag' on the second, but they do underline her basic musicality.

Unlike Louis Armstrong, who generously praised her, she is a much less effective singer than she is a trumpet-player. Her horn sound was rich and full and on 'St Louis Blues', recorded in Scandinavia with saxophonist Lulle Ellboj's band, she makes even the most jaded listener sit up; worth trying this one in a blindfold test. As usual, Classics' mastering is somewhat perfunctory, but anyone interested in the byways of swing will enjoy these two discs which restore a neglected and curiously engaging figure.

Elmer Snowden (1900–73)

BANJO

History is fickle. Snowden was the leader of a band called the Washingtonians that after his departure became the Duke Ellington Orchestra. He worked in and around the business all his life, as agent, promoter, teacher and occasionally still as a player.

***** Harlem Banjo**

Original Jazz Classics OJCCD 1756 2 *Snowden; Cliff Jackson (p); Tommy Bryant (b); Jimmy Crawford (d).* 12/60.

There's a certain irony in Snowden's choice of 'It Don't Mean A Thing' to kick off this 1960 record, a very rare sample of his work in the LP era. His banjo-playing is percussive, tuneful and surprisingly swinging, and the set as a whole is an object lesson for those revivalists who think that a jiggling banjo and soggy drumbeat is all that's required for authentic jazz. The programme is mostly blues and rags. 'Tishomingo Blues', 'Sweet Georgia Brown', 'C Jam Blues', 'Twelfth Street Rag' and 'Bugle Call Rag' are the essential cuts. Not much more than a historical footnote to a player who never achieved much public recognition, but a delightful set for anyone who isn't allergic to Elmer's instrument.

Martial Solal (born 1927)

PIANO

Born in Algiers, Solal moved to France in his early 20s, worked with Django Reinhardt and became a valued accompanist for visiting or exiled Americans such as Sidney Bechet and Don Byas. He is a remarkable composer, creating complex themes out of simple intervals and brief melodic cells. At times, Solal has headed big bands and has written for film, but his main contribution is as a small-group and solo performer.

*****(*) Sans Tambour Ni Trompette**

RCA 7432 137511 *Solal; Gilbert Rovere, Jean-François Jenny-Clark (b).* 10/70.

As the title suggests, Solal dispensed with the services of both horn-player and drummer to experiment with a new kind of trio: virile, calm but searching, and at every turn indicative of a technique that was still uncovering new areas of concern and ever-wider circles of capability. There was nothing else quite like this in 1970, and had it been performed or recorded in New York, it would have caused a sensation. The two long tracks 'Sequence Tenante' and 'Unisson' might almost be Debussy dancing with Art Tatum. The two bass-players anchor the harmonies, often at some remove one from the other, while Solal dances on top. By any standards these are astonishing performances and recognition is long overdue for them.

*****(*) En Solo**

RCA Victor 74321 47789 2 *Solal (p solo).* 11/71.

Beautifully remastered from a slightly muddy and indefinite recording, this offers yet more testimony to Solal's multi-faceted gifts as an improviser. All but two of the pieces are originals. 'Ah! Non!', 'Mercredi 13' and 'Jazz Antagoniste' are typical Solal ideas, fitted together like mosaic or cloisonné out of tiny shards of melody or sometimes, as on 'Fa Mi Re Do', out of minimal harmonic material. The two standards, 'What Is This Thing Called Love' and 'Darn That Dream', are played with a mixture of reserve and impressive emotion, particularly the latter, which must count as one of Solal's most focused and convincing interpretations of another composer's work.

***** Duo In Paris**

Dreyfus Jazz Line 19016 *Solal; Joachim Kühn (p).* 10/75.

*****(*) Bluesine**

Soul Note 121060 *Solal (p solo).* 1/83.

Bluesine is a lovely record, and an excellent place to sample Solal's solo style. Though he remains something of a specialized taste, he is utterly distinctive as a piano-player, owing much to Monk and Bud and even, in some lights, to Oscar Peterson, but remaining absolutely his own man. The recording quality here is impeccable: very full and resonant, but with lots of attention to detail as well. A good place to start, with a mixture of original and standard material.

The earlier record with Kühn is more difficult to pin down, largely because these are both players with a markedly individual, not to say idiosyncratic, approach, and hearing them in conjunction can be slightly disconcerting. Kühn is more obviously a romantic; or perhaps that should be a more obvious romantic. He is also, on occasion, an obfuscator. Solal's romanticism is more strait-laced and unaffected, and he comes out of these duos well ahead.

****** Plays Hodeir**

OMDCD 5008 *Solal; Roger Guérin, Eric Le Lann, Tony Russo, Bernard Marchais (t); Jacques Bolognesi, Christian Guizien (tb); Marc Steckar (tba); Jacques Di Donato (cl); François Jeanneau (cl, ts, ss); Jean-Pierre Debarbat (ts, ss); Jean-Louis Chautemps (bcl, as, ss); Pierre Gossez (bs, cl); Pierre Blanchard (vn); Hervé Derrien (clo); Philippe Mace (vib); Christian Escoudé (g); Césarius Alvim (b); André Ceccarelli (d).* 3 & 4/84.

*****(*) Martial Solal Big Band**

Dreyfus Jazz Line 849230 *As above, except add Patrick Artero (t), Hamid Belhocine, Glenn Ferris, Denis Deloup (tb), Patrice Petitdidier (frhn), Philip Legris (tba), Pierre Mimran, Roger Simon, Jean-Pierre Solves (sax, f), Philippe Nadal (clo), Frédéric Sylvestre (g).* 12/83, 5/84.

It's the larger ensembles of the '80s that really stand out in Solal's recording career: the Gaumont *Big Band* session of 1981 (long deleted) and the truly superb Hodeir set, recorded at Radio France three years later. Trumpeter Roger Guérin is there of course and is, as always, striking, notably on the closing Monk tribute, 'Comin' On The Hudson'. 'Transplantation I' is a companion-piece to 'Flautando' (not included here) and features Debarbat's ringing tenor. 'D Or No' is for sextet and, like the full-band 'Le Désert Recommence', highlights Solal at his most ironically Gallic. It is difficult to judge whether Solal is more effective with the larger unit or whether the angular movement of his compositions sounds better with a small ensemble. Simple preference will probably dictate future choices; both should certainly be sampled if at all possible.

*****(*) Just Friends**

Dreyfus FDM 36592 *Solal; Gary Peacock (b); Paul Motian (d).* 7/97.

****** Balade Du 10 Mars**

Soul Note 121340 2 *As above, except omit Peaock; add Marc Johnson (b).* 3/98.

When Solal made his American debut in 1963 at the Newport Jazz Fetival, Paul Motian was in the group. Over the last couple of years, the association has been revived and has produced some of the best music of the pianist's career. Martial celebrated his 70th birthday with Paul and Gary Peacock and has rarely sounded more blues-based and swinging, eliding at least some of his subtler, 'European' configurations to produce what is arguably his most straightahead album ever. This is not to say that it lacks individuality. No one who has listened to him with any attention will mistake who the soloist is on 'Willow Weep For Me' or 'You Stepped Out Of A Dream', though it is not until halfway through the record, and a markedly original 'Hommage À Frédéric Chopin', that something of a more familiar Solal comes through.

Balade Du 10 Mars is even better. The free-form improvisation on Motian's 'Gang Of Five' is the most outside playing Solal has done on record for many years. 'Round Midnight' is a duet for piano and drums, recalling the same piece on the Newport record, which RCA should think hard about reissuing. Johnson stands in for Gary Peacock on this occasion, and as might be expected, the rhythm is looser and less rugged. As before, echoes of the classic Bill Evans trio are everywhere and it would be wonderful to hear either version of this group tackle 'Gloria's Step' or 'Waltz For Debby'. Martial's touch is as deft and lyrical as ever, but there is a new and welcome hint of wildness to the playing, as if finally he feels relaxed enough in his own technique to cut loose and challenge the harmonic rules. Unusual to hear Solal concentrate so absolutely on standards and jazz repertory. 'Night And Day', 'Softly, As In A Morning Sunrise', 'Almost Like Being In Love', 'The Lady Is A Tramp' and 'My Old Flame' round out the programme, with a fine, unhackneyed interpretation of 'Round Midnight' and just one other original, 'The Newest Old Waltz', coming in right at the end. A marvellous modern-jazz record by one of the masters.

***** Jazz'n (e)motion**

BMG/RCA 74321 55935 2 *Solal (p solo).* 1/98.

A wonderful writer of film music himself, Martial here explores the screen fantasies of fellow composers, from Charles Trenet's

music for the Truffaut classic *Baisers Volés* to 'Over The Rainbow' and 'The Shadow Of Your Smile' from *The Sandpiper*. He caresses the melodies and in some cases improvises only rather sparingly, preferring to stay within the confines of the original conception. There are exceptions: 'Carioca' from *Flying Down To Rio* is jazzed up considerably and 'Strike Up The Band' is inspired more by Busby Berkeley than by the Gershwins. Fine, moody stuff, but if anyone wants examples of Solal's own film-writing, they will need to look elsewhere. Apart from 'Hommage À Tex Avery', written for an imaginary movie, there is nothing.

★★★★ Plays Ellington

Dreyfus 36613 *Solal; Roger Guérin, Eric LeLann, Tony Russo (t); Jacques Bolognesi, Denis Leloup (tb); Didier Havet (tba); Sylvain Beuf, Jean-Louis Chautemps (sax); Jean-Pierre Solves (bs, f); Patrice Caratini (b); François Merville, Umberto Pagnini (d).* 12/97.

Here Solal presents himself as part of Dodecaband, a medium-sized line-up that is instantly recognizable in terms of ensemble voicings rather than individual voices as an Ellington-inspired outfit. Martial himself is rather modest as a soloist, allowing the charts to speak for themselves, as they do eloquently and often with brilliance. 'Caravan' is spun out to a wonderful length and has rarely seemed such an epical idea. 'Take the "A" Train' is almost as extended but transformed into something quite new and almost atonal in places.

Solal's brilliance is in retaining enough of the original and yet adding a wholly new dimension to these familiar themes. He has not received and probably never will receive the kind of adulation that was Duke's, but on the strength of this set many will begin to wonder why even at its centenary the Ellington name is internationally known and that of Solal is still relatively marginal.

★★★★ Contrastes: The Jazzpar Prize

Storyville 4242 *Solal; Jesper Riis, Benny Ronsenfeld (t); Vincent Nilsson (tb); Tomas Franck, Michael Hove, Flemming Madsen, Ufe Markussen (reeds); Thomas Ovesen, Mads Vinding (b); Daniel Humair, Jonas Johansen (d).* 99.

In 1999 Solal was the deserved winner of the coveted Jazzpar Prize. The award makes provision for a performance by the winner's group – here a trio with Vinding and Humair – and with the Danish Radio Jazz Orchestra. As a brilliant small-group player and orchestrator, Solal rises to the challenge with utmost confidence and enthusiasm. The trio cuts are as thoughtful and intense as anything he has ever put on record and the ensemble tracks reveal something of his astonishing gift for complex voicings. One can imagine some of these players going off after the event and copying out parts, the like of which they'd never heard before. The two most formidable pieces are 'Ritournelle No. 1', a magnificent conception that hints at Ravel and Debussy, and the more dramatic 'Mythe Décisif', which calls on some virtuosic playing from the pianist.

★★★(★) NY – 1 Live At The Village Vanguard

Blue Note 84391-2 *Solal; François Moutin (b); Bill Stewart (d).* 9/01.

Agreeable to find the great pianist securing one of his rare American releases for such a distinguished American label. In his 70s, some of the daring has gone out of his music – or perhaps it has simply become more an accepted part of jazz-piano vocabulary. What endures is the sense that he knows everything he's going to do in a performance while keeping the whole thing fresh and spontaneous, that curious sense of inevitability which he has used to underpin even the most outlandish parts of his playing over four or five decades. Moutin and Stewart do their best to keep up, although one feels that in many ways Solal defers to anyone he's playing with, as if he could run rings round them if it were any kind of cutting contest.

Lew Soloff (born 1944)

TRUMPET, FLUGELHORN

Classically trained at the Juilliard and Eastman schools, Soloff has become a first-call trumpeter for big bands and smaller ensembles, offering anything from nimble negotiation of complex charts to old-fashioned high-note pyrotechnics. He spent a fruitful time as a member of R&B band, Blood, Sweat & Tears. Influenced by that, and by leaders as diverse as Gil Evans and Thad Jones, he has devised a style of his own, terse, well structured and, underneath the toughness, very affecting.

★★★ With A Song In My Heart

Milestone MCD 9290 *Soloff; Mulgrew Miller (p); Emily Mitchell (hp); George Mraz (b); Victor Lewis (d).* 1/98.

As the years go by, Soloff takes on more and more of the easy lyrical style of his sometime boss, Clark Terry. That influence, direct or unconscious, is dominant on *With A Song In My Heart*. Lew's soloing has a featherlight mobility but delivered with a full, brassy tone. The choice of material is also challenging, with standards like the Andantino from Tchaikovsky's Fourth Symphony set against standards like 'Come Rain Or Come Shine' and 'With A Song In My Heart', Soloff originals 'Istanbul' and 'One For Emily', and film composer Dmitri Tiomkin's 'Deguello', one of two tracks on which the selfsame Emily Mitchell plays. A session-man par excellence.

Mark Soskin (born 1953)

PIANO, KEYBOARDS

After playing in rock groups, Soskin studied music in Colorado and at Berklee. His most important jazz association was with Sonny Rollins, in whose group he worked through the '80s. His own recording career has been sparse but effective.

★★★ Five Lands (Cinqueterra)

TCB 98402 *Soskin; Walt Weiskopf (ss, ts); Joe Locke (vib); John Abercrombie (g); Erik Friedlander (clo); Harvie Swartz (b).* 98.

★★★ 17 (Seventeen)

TCB 2065 *Soskin; Tim Hagans (t, flhn); Billy Drewes (ss, ts); Jay Anderson (b); Matt Wilson (d); Daniel Sadownick (perc).* n.d.

Soskin's ability to swing a jazz tune was evident not just from his work with Sonny Rollins and Billy Cobham, but also from his own early solo records on Vartan and other labels. He's still not often in the studio under his own steam, but these two recent TCB discs are important reminders of his pedigree. Often said to be influenced by Cedar Walton, he often sounds more like a spiced-up Kenny Barron, and it's KB who seems the main influence on the excellent *17 (Seventeen)* (we're not clear why the addiction to brackets). On 'Un Poco Loco' he turns the Bud Powell theme inside out, demonstrating some of his own characteristic harmonic devices. Augmented chords and unusual chordal progressions appear in '17' itself, and notably in 'Elysian Fields'. The earlier album is more impressionistic, a set of duos with mostly like-minded players who fail to deliver the same challenge as the group set, or indeed the same intensity of focus as on Soskin's excellent deleted solo record on Vartan. Good stuff, but not so much to our taste.

Eddie South (1904–62)

VIOLIN

South learned violin as a child and received a considerable music education before playing in Chicago and New York in the '20s. Worked on the black theatre circuit in the early '30s as a chamber-jazz act before touring Europe. On radio and even TV in the '40s and '50s, but gradually drifted from sight.

***** Eddie South 1923–1937**

Classics 707 *South; Jimmy Wade (c); Williams Dover (tb); Clifford King (cl, bcl, as); Arnett Nelson (cl, as); Vernon Roulette (cl, ts); Teddy Weatherford, Antonia Spaulding (p); Walter Wright, Stéphane Grappelli, Michel Warlop (vn); Everett Barksdale (g, bj, v); Django Reinhardt, Mike McKendrick, Roger Chaput, Sterling Conaway (g); Louis Gross (bb); Wilson Myers, Milt Hinton, Paul Cordonnier (b); Edwin Jackson, Jimmy Bertrand, Jerome Burke (d).* 12/23–11/37.

***** Black Gypsy, 1927–1934**

Frog 36 *Similar to above.* 27–34.

***** Eddie South 1937–1941**

Classics 737 *South; Charlie Shavers (t); Buster Bailey (cl); Russell Procope (as); David Martin, Stanley Facey (p); Stéphane Grappelli (vn); Django Reinhardt, Isadore Langlois, Eddie Gibbs, Eugene Fields (g); Paul Cordonnier, Doles Dickens, Ernest 'Bass' Hill (b); Specs Powell, Tommy Benford (d); Ginny Sims (v).* 11/37–3/41.

South wasn't simply one of the most accomplished of jazz violinists; he might have been one of the best-schooled of all jazz musicians of his time, given a thorough classical grounding that, unusually, blossomed into a hot rather than a cool improviser's stance. If his reputation rests on his Paris recordings of 1937 (available on Classics 707), there are some interesting footnotes to an unfulfilled career in the other tracks listed here. The first Classics disc starts with a very rare 1923 track by Jimmy Wade's Moulin Rouge Orchestra: awful sound (it was recorded for Paramount), but South's intensely blue violin still cuts through the ensembles.

In 1928 South visited Hungary and became enamoured of gypsy music. From then on, it played an important part in his style and it's very much the key sound on *Black Gypsy*, a compilation that pretty much reduplicates the coverage of the Classics set, though obviously the shorter purview means a more focused look at these Victor recordings of the 1927–34 period. Not much to choose between them in terms of sound or packaging, though the Classics probably has more user-friendly notes.

South's slightly later Chicago and New York sessions are well played if comparatively lightweight – on songs such as 'Nagasaki' or 'Marcheta' he sounds almost like a vaudevillian – but the three sessions with Grappelli and Reinhardt are fascinating, the guitarist driven into his best form, the violinist playing his finest solos on 'Sweet Georgia Brown' and 'Eddie's Blues', and the date culminating in the extraordinary improvisation on Bach's D Minor Concerto for two violins by South, Grappelli and Reinhardt together. A further 1938 session in Hilversum has some more strong playing by South's regular quintet, but his final titles from 1940–41 belabour the material, which seems designed to cast South as a romantic black gypsy and sends him back to vaudeville. He seldom recorded again, despite a fair amount of broadcasting, and must be accounted as a talent out of his time.

***** The Dark Angel Of The Fiddle**

Soundies 4120 *South; Billy Taylor (p); Eddie Brown, LeGrand Mason (b); Connie Jordan (d).* 58.

A valuable set of radio transcriptions for Standard and Jubilee, these show in the same vaudevillean mode as earlier recordings, but with his classical technique even more evident. Billy Taylor is an excellent partner, harmonically astute, rhythmically just a little ahead of the boss and dynamically soft enough to keep South pretty much to the forefront. Two versions of 'Rhapsody In Blue', a nice 'Paganini In Rhythm' and a very swinging 'Cherokee' all stand out, but the real hit is the gypsy-inspired 'Tzigani In Rhythm'. There is some distortion on many of these tracks, especially the three Jubilee cuts, but they're a valuable record of an intriguing star.

South Frisco Jazz Band

GROUP

A clan of Californian followers of the Murphy–Watters methods, this great institution of its scene began playing in the late '50s and has now elected to go into voluntary retirement.

****** Sage Hen Strut**

Stomp Off 1143 *Dan Comins, Leon Oakley (c); Jim Snyder (tb); Mike Baird (cl, ss, as); Bob Helm (cl, as); Robbie Rhodes (p); Vince Saunders (bj); Bob Rann (tba); Bob Raggio (d, wbd).* 11/84.

*****(*) Broken Promises**

Stomp Off 1180 *As above, except omit Helm.* 9/87.

*****(*) Got Everything**

Stomp Off 1240 *As above, except add Bob Helm (cl, ss, v), Jack Mangan (d).* 11/89–9/91.

*****(*) Big Bear Stomp**

Stomp Off 1307 *As above, except add Lloyd Byassee (d); omit Helm, Raggio and Mangan.* 10/95.

*****(*) Emperor Norton's Hunch**

Stomp Off 1342 *As above, except Brian Shaw (t), Charlie Bornemann (tb), John Gill (d, v) replace Comins, Snyder and Byassee.* 2–3/98.

The South Frisco Jazz Band (and by South Frisco they usually mean Los Angeles) have been playing as a group, on and off, since around 1960. Formed in the spirit of the Lu Watters and Turk Murphy groups, they approach traditional material with a zest, flair and ingenuity that shame most British trad groups and manage to combine a faithful feel with a certain irreverence: this isn't corny or the work of pasticheurs, but it's very good fun. The band has made a fair number of records over the years and these CDs are a good representation of what the line-up can do. The two-cornet front line plays a fiercely hot lead on most of the tunes, abetted by Snyder's choleric trombone and Baird's authentically quivering reed parts. Helm, a sideman with Murphy, sits in on two of the discs. The material is all original archaeology. When they play Jelly Roll Morton, it's 'Little Lawrence' or 'If Someone Would Only Love Me' rather than 'Wolverine Blues', and there are tiny tributes scattered through the discs to the likes of Roy Palmer, Richard M. Jones and Natty Dominique. There are plenty of rags, too. Of these discs, *Sage Hen Strut* takes a very narrow lead for the choice of material and the complete absence of vocals (not quite the group's strong point, though they don't do much singing). *Big Bear Stomp* doesn't sound like one of their absolute best, but they still turn in enough winners – try Lovie Austin's 'Rampart Street Blues' – to please admirers of the other records.

Emperor Norton's Hunch features three personnel changes, although Gill is a very familiar name in these sorts of surroundings, and sadly it is likely to be their final record: the band members live too far apart to be able to play regularly, and after 42 years they deserve a bit of a rest. So this is a typically spirited farewell – not their greatest, but again liberally sprinkled with hotter-than-that playing. Until the Sage Hen struts again!

Sune Spångberg

DRUMS

Part of the community of Young Turks who made up Swedish modernism in the '50s, Spångberg played on many important dates and has been a significant presence in that scene ever since. He worked extensively with the group, ISKRA, in music education.

****(*) Two Absent Friends**

Dragon DRCD316 *Spångberg; Arne Forsén (p); Ulf Akerhielm (b).* 2/96.

***** Live At Café Aguéli**

Dragon DRCD 328 *Spångberg; Johan Setterlind (t); Carl Fredrik Orrje, Göran Strandberg, Claes-Göran Fagerstadt, Ake Johansson (p); Ludvig Girdland (vn); Ivar Lidell, Owe Gustavsson (b); Nannie Porres (v).* 9/97–8/98.

Spångberg has been a singular witness in the music. He was with Bud Powell at The Golden Circle and he drummed on Albert Ayler's first record. His sleeve-notes to *Two Absent Friends* muse on a broad vista of Swedish jazz history but pay special note to the two dedicatees who provided the music here, Lasse Werner and Kurt Lindgren. Both composers had much inspiration in them and these 12 tunes are an attractive lot. More than that, one feels the music is haunted by a number of ghosts, not just Werner and Lindgren but also Torbjorn Hultcrantz, Jan Wallgren and Allan Olsson. It's a pity, then, that the results are finally not so distinguished. The trio muster only a rather clumsy empathy which detracts from the occasion, and Akerhielm's several *arco* solos seem insecure; nor is the balance, with Spångberg sounding too crisp and up-front in the mix, properly effective. Some fine material is deposited here, but it's not as well served as it might have been.

The live CD, cut at various sessions at the small Café Aguéli, is much more like it. The sound is rough, close-up and atmospheric, and the various combinations of musicians make an interesting match, old-timers such as Johansson and Fagerstadt next to young players like Orrje and Setterlind. Roots music as it's being played today.

Muggsy Spanier (1906–67)

CORNET

Recording as a teenager, Francis Spanier was off to a quick start in his native Chicago. He worked with Ted Lewis and Ben Pollack in the '20s and '30s, before forming his Ragtime Band in 1939. The records are classics but the band was a commercial failure. He stuck with Dixieland through the '40s and '50s, before moving west to join Earl Hines in 1957 and leading modest small groups up until his death.

CORE COLLECTION

****** Muggsy Spanier 1939–1942**

Classics 709 *Spanier; Ruby Weinstein, Elmer O'Brien (t); Ford Leary, George Brunies (tb, v); Rod Kless (cl); Karl Kates, Joe Forchetti, Ed Caine (as); Ray McKinstrey, Bernie Billings, Nick Caizza (ts); George Zack, Charlie Queener, Joe Bushkin (p); Bob Casey (g, b); Pat Pattison (b); Marty Greenberg, Al Hammer, Don Carter, Al Sidell (d); Dottie Reid (v).* 7/39–6/42.

Spanier's 1939 Ragtime Band recordings are among the classic statements in the traditional-jazz idiom. Bob Crosby's Bob Cats had helped to initiate a modest vogue for small Dixieland bands in what was already a kind of revivalism at the height of the big-band era, and Spanier's group had audiences flocking to Chicago clubs, although by December, with a move to New York, they were forced to break up for lack of work. Their recordings have been dubbed 'The Great Sixteen' ever since. While there are many fine solos scattered through the sides – mostly by Spanier and the little-remembered Rod Kless – it's as an ensemble that the band impresses: allied to a boisterous rhythm section, the informal counterpoint among the four horns (the tenor sax perfectly integrated, just as Eddie Miller was in the Bob Cats) swings through every performance. The repertoire re-established the norm for Dixieland bands, and even though the material goes back to Oliver and the ODJB, there's no hint of fustiness, even in the rollicking effects of 'Barnyard Blues'. 'Someday Sweetheart', with its sequence of elegant solos, is a masterpiece of cumulative tension, and Spanier himself secures two finest hours in the storming finish to 'Big Butter And Egg Man' and the wah-wah blues-playing on 'Relaxin' At The Touro', a poetic tribute to convalescence (he had been ill the previous year) the way Parker's 'Relaxin' At Camarillo' would subsequently be. His own playing is masterful throughout – the hot Chicago cornet-sound refined and seared away to sometimes the simplest but most telling of phrases.

The Classics CD adds eight tracks to the definitive 16 by Muggsy's big band, none of them outstanding but all grist to the Spanier collector's mill. Since RCA have let their own edition apparently slip out of circulation, this is the only option.

*****(*) Muggsy Spanier 1944**

Classics 907 *Spanier; Miff Mole, Lou McGarity (tb); Pee Wee Russell (cl); Boomie Richman (ts); Ernie Caceres (bs); Gene*

Schroeder, Dick Cary, Jess Stacy (p); Eddie Condon, Hy White (g); Bob Casey, Bob Haggart, Sid Weiss (b); Joe Grauso, George Wettling (d). 4–10/44.

***** Muggsy Spanier 1944–1946**

Classics 967 *Spanier; Lou McGarity, Vernon Brown (tb); Pee Wee Russell, Peanuts Hucko (cl); Bud Freeman, Nick Caizza (ts); Ernie Caceres (bs); Gene Schroeder, Dave Bowman, Nick Rongetti (p); Eddie Condon, Carl Kress, Hy White (g); Bob Haggart, Bob Casey, Trigger Alpert (b); Joe Grauso, Charlie Carroll, George Wettling (d).* 12/44–9/46.

*****(*) Manhattan Masters**

Storyville STCD 60-51 *Spanier; Lou McGarity, Miff Mole (tb); Pee Wee Russell (cl); Ernie Caceres (bs); Gene Schroeder, Nick Rongetti (p); Carl Kress, Fred Sharp, Allan Hanlon (g); Bob Casey, Jack Lesberg, Bob Haggart (b); Joe Grauso, Charles Carroll (d).* 3/45.

***** The Complete V-Disc Sessions**

Jazz Unlimited JUCD 2049 *Spanier; Yank Lawson (t); Lou McGarity, Bill Mustarde (tb); Pee Wee Russell (cl, v); Peanuts Hucko (cl); Boomie Richmond, Bud Freeman (ts); Jess Stacy, Dane Bowman, Buddy Weed (p); Hy White, Carmen Mastren (g); Bob Hagart, Trigger Alpert (b); George Wettling, Ray McKinley (d).* 10/44–10/45.

Muggsy's sessions for Commodore, V-Disc, Disc and an almost unknown date for Manhattan make a very welcome addition to his CD listing. The Commodores could probably sound better than they do here, but at present this is their only accessible edition. All the music on Classics 907 is vintage Spanier, with standouts including 'Lady Be Good', a superb 'Snag It' and a very fine 'Sweet Sue', with a solo by Miff Mole on the latter that proves he was far from the lost soul his post-'20s reputation would have one think. Besides Spanier, the standout player is Pee Wee Russell: connoisseurs of the bizarre will relish his vocal on the V-Disc 'Pee Wee Speaks'. The subsequent volume is just a shade behind, perhaps, although there is so little surviving Spanier that it's a necessary disc for followers. Both docked a notch for unpleasing sound: they should be better than this.

The six Manhattan tracks reappear on the Storyville edition, along with a dozen other pieces which were done at the same sessions, although under the nominal leadership of either Miff Mole or Pee Wee Russell. The tracks were made at the instigation of Nick Rongetti of Nick's in Greenwich Village (he even gets to play a solo on 'That's A Plenty'!). It's Condonesque Dixieland without Condon, and although the principals are all in hearty fettle it doesn't have the spark of greatness about it. But always good to hear Spanier and the excellent Mole, who was well out of the limelight at this stage: his fine solo on 'I Can't Give You Anything But Love' makes one regret his later decline all the more.

The V-Disc material on Jazz Unlimited duplicates the Classics sessions but has a number of extra takes of some titles, and also includes material from four Bud Freeman dates.

***** At Club Hangover 1953–54**

Storyville STCD 6033 *Spanier; Ralph Hutchinson (tb); Darnell Howard, Chico Gomez (cl); Mel Grant, Red Richards (p); Truck Parham (b); Barrett Deems, Cuz Couzineau (d).* 4/53–11/54.

Not a great time for Dixieland, but Spanier kept the faith and these were serviceable bands. Like the pro that he was, he plays and leads with assurance, and the only real disappointment is the choice of tunes which lines up warhorse after warhorse. The lovely playing on 'Moonglow' and 'If I Had You' makes one wish that they had other tunes on the set-list.

*****(*) In New Orleans 1938–1955**

American Music AMCD-109 *Spanier; Julian Lane, Ralph Hutchinson (tb); Bujie Centobie, Darnell Howard (cl); Armand Hug, Red Mackie, Floyd Beam (p); Edmond Souchon (g, bj, v); Chink Martin, Truck Parham, Sherwood Mangiapanne (b); Monk Hazel, Barrett Deems (d).* 38–8/55.

The real surprise here is four previously unknown 1938 transcriptions where Spanier is heard with a New Orleans group (including such stalwarts as Armand Hug, Chink Martin and Monk Hazel) in extended versions of four pieces. Despite the imperfect sound Muggsy comes through loud and clear and he sounds in cracking form: these tracks count as some of his most exciting surviving playing. The 1955 tracks with Mackie, Souchon and Mangiapanne are very rough and ready but as ever Spanier makes some strong remarks. The disc is rounded off by five tracks by the band heard on the above Storyville disc, although these don't duplicate any tunes and they are in excellent sound. A hotchpotch, but quite essential for Spanier fans.

Les Spann (1932–89)

GUITAR, FLUTE

Primarily a guitarist, with a style that blended bop and blues stylings in a very personal way, Spann's associations with Dizzy Gillespie and Quincy Jones brought him some renown, but he drifted from view at the end of the '60s.

***** Gemini**

Original Jazz Classics OJC 1948 *Spann; Julius Watkins (frhn); Tommy Flanagan (p); Sam Jones (b); Albert 'Tootie' Heath (d).* 12/60.

Spann's only album as leader is likeable but spotty. When he plays flute, and harmonizes with Watkins on melody lines, it's sonorously effective on the opening 'Smile'. But his guitar got a bad deal in the mix, and it sounds thin and hidden a lot of the way. 'Con Alma' is poor, and 'Q's Dues Blues' is sloppy. Watkins was presumably chosen so as not to overwhelm the leader with a 'real' front-line horn; if so, it was a mistake. All that said, there is some lively improvising, and the curious contrast in the leader's guitar and flute styles is used quite effectively, with a smart rhythm section.

James Spaulding (born 1937)

ALTO AND SOPRANO SAXOPHONES, FLUTE

Studied at Chicago Cosmopolitan School and worked with both Sun Ra and Freddie Hubbard. A versatile instrumentalist, much in demand as a sideman, Spaulding has never achieved fame as a leader.

***** The Smile Of The Snake**

High Note HNCD 7006 *Spaulding; Richard Wyands (p); Ron McClure (b); Tony Reedus (d).* 12/96.

***** Escapade**

High Note HNCD 7039 *Spaulding; John Hicks (p); Ray Drummond (b); Kenny Washington (d).* 4/99.

Spaulding's earlier work for Muse is long deleted and shows no sign of reappearing. These later sessions are marked by the same easy musicianship that has marked his extensive discography. Though he is no writer, Spaulding has a gift for spotting unusual and creative material. He begins *The Smile Of The Snake* with a Clifford Jordan number, 'Third Avenue', and programmes material by Richard Wyands, Geoff Keezer and Donald Brown, who is composer of the title-track. This is hardly repertory fare and the unfamiliarity of the material is either intriguing or off-putting depending on your level of curiosity. The group performs beautifully, with McClure particularly prominent. As ever, Spaulding gives his flute a lot of prominence; there is an argument that it is his stronger horn.

Escapade is a less winning set in some respects, but the inclusion of two Kenny Dorham tunes – 'La Mesha' and the title-piece – suggests that Spaulding remains an eclectic who's drawn to a strong melody. A couple of standards, 'Just One Of Those Things' and 'It Could Happen To You', suggest he's less at ease playing changes over relatively familiar terrain, but that shouldn't suggest that James is a dull or dilettante player, just that his improvising instincts are set a little left of the norm.

Martin Speake (born 1958)

ALTO SAXOPHONE

Speake studied in London and came to prominence with the all-sax group, Itchy Fingers; he has subsequently tried a variety of settings but seems most at home in a quartet.

***** Trust**

33 Records 33 JAZZ 035 *Speake; John Parricelli (g); Steve Watts (b); Steve Arguëlles (d).* 11/96.

Speake's recording debut as leader was in 1994 with a disc called *In Our Time*, which was released on Danny Thompson's The Jazz Label, which as far as we can gather is now in abeyance. *Trust* almost seems like back to square one. It features the same group, sounding very much in sympathy, but cleaving to essentially the same concept. As before, Arguëlles is the bedrock for Speake's muscular but tuneful ideas, playing with a bright, clean articulation that comes across very strongly. Tunes like 'Golden Rooster', 'The Heron' and 'The Accidental Flamboyant' are colourful and witty. The ballad forms are less secure, but only because Speake seems inclined to be reserved. It makes sense with this music to have guitar rather than piano. Parricelli's chiming, slightly edgy sound works very well indeed and contrasts nicely with Watts's dark, woody bass-lines.

***** Hullabaloo**

Linn AKD 191 *Speake; John Parricelli (g); Mick Hutton (b); Tom Skinner (d).* 12/99.

*****(*) Secret**

Basho SRCD 3-2 *Speake; Nikki Iles (p); Duncan Hopkins (b); Anthony Michelli (d).* 10/00.

Speake's delivery works a rather unusual combination of directness and deference. Some have suggested a Konitz connection, but he's more like, say, Richard Tabnik, a Tristanoite of a more severe bent. His music rarely collars the attention and relies on a purposeful accrual of interesting details and conversational touches. *Hullabaloo* is about as inappropriate a title as one could get, since the quartet is more interested in playing quietly and carefully. Parricelli is an effective partner for the altoist and they circle patiently around each other, somewhat in the manner of Jan Garbarek and Bill Connors. But there are times when the record could use a jolt of something.

One way to contrast these sessions is to compare the two versions of 'J.T.'s Symmetrical Scale', which is on both discs. That on *Secret* is much more forceful and pungent, and the later record benefits greatly from the presence of both Michelli and Iles. The drummer's a pushy but not overbearing player and gooses some of the playing just enough to make it fly, when a more discreet player could have left it on the ground. But it's Iles who draws the ear, and the record is as much hers as Speake's, with five of her own originals and playing which really puts substance and weight into what might otherwise turn into spindrift.

***** Exploring Standards**

33Jazz 090 *Speake; Mick Hutton (b); Tom Skinner (d).* 4/01.

***** My Ideal**

Basho BRCD 7-2 *Speake; Iverson (p).* 12/02.

The 'standards' record is attractively weighted towards a jazz connoisseur's choice of tunes – Paul Bley's 'Big Foot', Frank Rosolino's 'Blue Daniel', Sonny Rollins's 'Strode Rode' – so any sense that this would be some nice album of Gershwin tunes is derailed at the outset. That said, the trio's approach isn't terribly exciting: it's a recital of these pieces rather than any kind of revisionist approach, and Speake seems to almost deliberately distance himself from any sort of plangency of interpretation. The record is coolly attractive in its way, but they have some way to go before they can muster the kind of individuality which the masters of that approach displayed.

The meeting with Iverson is a trifle bizarre. Speake intones the melodies of the chosen standards – this time, a typical songbook selection of 'So In Love', 'Stardust' and the like – while the pianist contrives to subvert and undercut him at every step of the way, with accompaniments which are often extraordinarily imaginative yet far from what one considers supportive. Give Speake his due, he carries on regardless, but his almost hooting timbre and poker-faced delivery does seem a strange counterweight. Here and there – as in 'Loverman' – there's a more conventional dialogue.

Glenn Spearman (1947–98)

TENOR SAXOPHONE

Spearman's death from liver cancer in 1998 was not unexpected, but it left a sense of things undone and of a major talent not yet properly recognized. His sound was soaked in the blues, and bears comparison with an eclectic range of masters from Illinois Jacquet to Coltrane and Shepp.

***** Utterance**

Cadence CJR 1103 *Spearman; John Heward (d, kalimba, v).* 10/90.

*****(*) Mystery Project**

Black Saint 120147 *Spearman; Larry Ochs (ts, sno); Chris Brown (p, DX7); Ben Lindgren (b); Donald Robinson, William Winant (d).* 8/92.

****** Smokehouse**

Black Saint 120157 *As above.* 11/93.

Spearman was over 40 before the first of these was recorded, so not surprisingly he already sounds settled into a strong and individual voice. He started out as a Coltrane-influenced screamer but quickly recognized that a more thoughtful delivery might well bear dividends. A 1981 duo with drummer Donald Robinson has been compared to Trane and Rashied Ali's *Interstellar Space*, and Spearman was to return to the same format with *Utterance*, a sequence of duos with drummer John Heward. By that time Spearman had come under the tutelage of Frank Wright, with whom he had bunked and woodshedded in France, and it was clear that he was striking out in a new direction. The Coltrane influence is still there, but it has been subsumed into something altogether more linear. After a period with trumpeter Raphe Malik's sextet, Spearman founded his Double Trio.

Dedicated to Ornette Coleman (and to the structured freedom on Ornette's *Free Jazz*), *Mystery Project* consists of a large three-part suite, in which the direction of the music is dictated not so much by notated passages as by the distribution of the personnel. As in Rova man Larry Ochs's 'Double Image', the basic group is a palette from which various colours and shadings can be drawn. Spearman's personal colour-code would seem to be black and red. He's a fierce player, overblowing in the upper register and virtually incapable of anything less than full throttle. He never sacrifices subtlety to power, though. This is intelligent music that never palls or sounds dated.

The follow-up record has the same line-up and makes similarly effective use of doubled instruments. It's a long – 75-minute – suite with an intermission built in, not because an LP version required a break, but because the music is so unremittingly present that one couldn't absorb any more without some surcease. Spearman's time in Europe opened up many interesting compositional ideas to him, but these performances are squarely in the tradition of the '60s avant-garde, and their strength comes from Spearman's profound conviction that the ideas adumbrated at that time are far from exhausted but still constitute a *lingua franca* for improvisation. The 'in-take' and 'out-take' of 'Axe, Beautiful Acts' exude a fierce poetry that is worthy of Cecil Taylor.

**(*) Free Worlds

Black Saint 120207 *Spearman; Raphe Malik (t); Marco Eneidi (as); Paul Plimley (p); John Baker (syn); Donald Robinson (d); Tim Witter (tabla); Shafquat Ali Khan, Don Paul, U. R. Routhier, Dhyani Dharma Mas (v).* 94, 95.

A valuable posthumous release that is more instructive than genuinely satisfying. Spearman's freedom seems more than a little forced on these sessions from 1994 and 1995, and there is less melodic control than on the later sessions which were to represent his premature last word. 'Pipes, Spirits And Bronze' and 'Raga Sharmati' are not entirely successful takes on the subcontinental improvising tradition; these performances will dismay conservatives without offering much nourishment to those of a more experimental bent. Good to have this record out there, but it isn't one that is going to make or break Glenn's posthumous reputation.

*** The Fields

Black Saint 120197 *Spearman; Larry Ochs (ss, ts); Chris Brown (p); Lisle Ellis (b); Don Robinson, William Winant (d).* 96.

The Spearman Double Trio was an interesting formal experiment, but it may have foundered on the strong creative personality of his fellow-saxophonist, who always seems ready to hi-jack this session and take it off in a different direction. Ochs's 'Melts' and Spearman's 'Sound Section' are the two main statements on the record, and are kept well apart at the beginning and end respectively. The supporting cast is strong and supportive, though very often the band seem to be playing set charts while the two horns duel in the foreground.

***(*) th

CIMP 148 *Spearman; Christopher Cauley (as); David Prentice (vn, vla); Dominic Duval (b); John Heward (d, perc, v).* 5/97.

It was no surprise when Spearman turned up on CIMP. It's a label whose blunt, unvarnished ethos entirely matches his own. This group is co-led with drummer Heward, who duets with the saxophonist (and on this occasion kalimba-player and vocalist) on the extraordinary 'Summoning', which has no precedent in either's work to date. Prentice sits out a couple of tracks and 'Initiation' is a trio with Spearman, Duval and Heward, thus varying the sound of this remarkable group.

The long 'Irreversible Blues' which opens the set has a fascinating asymmetrical structure, while '3 For John' (Heward? Coltrane?) is more of an exercise in extended harmonics and sprung rhythm. The other long track, 'Moment In Time', has a more conventional structure, but is no less challenging as an idea. As with everything else recorded at the Spirit Room in Rossie, the sound makes no compromises. One wishes there had been a few tucks and stitches here, though once again no complaints that the label has failed to deliver on its promise: 'what you hear is exactly what was played'.

*** Let It Go

Red Toucan 9308 *Spearman; James Routhier (g); Lisle Ellis (b); Don Robinson (d).* 6/97.

G-Force was one of Spearman's groups of this time – there was also the trio Surya, which is represented on a collaborative disc – and it's a typically strong line-up. 'Geronimo's Song', 'Almost Shaft' (Isaac Hayes?) and 'Mixed Bag' are the main statements, and Spearman is at his incendiary best. The group is mixed up a bit loud and Routhier's guitar is intrusive, though generally he gives the set a flexible and open-ended harmonic foundation, ably abetted by Ellis.

*** Live At Fire In The Valley

Eremite 10 *Spearman; William Parker (b); Paul Murphy (d).* 97.

Attributed to Trio Hurricane, this strong festival set derives much of its compelling power from bassist Parker, but it is Spearman compositions which dominate. 'Initiation' and 'Blue For Frank And John' almost exhaust the energies of the group, with each of the three members receiving generous solo space, but the enthusiasm of the crowd spurs them on and an improvised encore is a worthwhile bonus. Some of the playing is a little opaque, and here and there Spearman surrenders expression to sheer dynamic force.

*** Blues For Falasha

Tzadik 7130 *Spearman; Larry Ochs (ss, ts); Chris Brown (p); Lisle Ellis (b); Don Robinson, William Winant (d).* 97.

Few artists better represented the cultural collisions of John Zorn's 'Radical Jewish Culture' imprint than Spearman, whose parents were Jewish and black. Unlike some titles in this Tzadik series, there is little overtly Judaic music played, most of it on 'Rituals', which seems to be Spearman's attempt to think his way back into a forgotten ancestry for the blues. 'The Old Book' makes explicit reference but does less with it musically, and the rest of the album is familiar enough from Spearman's earlier work with the Double Trio.

***** Working With The Elements**

CIMP 181 *Spearman; Dominic Duval (b).* 7/98.

***** First And Last**

Eremite MTE015 *Spearman; Matthew Goodheart (p); Rashid Bakr (d).* 7/98.

Spearman died less than three months after these sessions and, to be frank, his failing health is all too evident. The live Eremite record is the saxophonist's last earthly word and it is an unhappy affair, dominated by Goodheart and at moments barely coherent. Recorded at the 1998 Fire In The Valley, it weaves awkwardly between intense insight, notably on the opening 'Intertextual Reference', and a prosy banality.

On the studio set for CIMP, Duval holds things together as often as not, and even his meandering personal feature, 'Sass Bolo', is more focused and articulate than a lot of the music involving Glenn. There are flashes here and there of the player who made *Smokehouse*, but they are few and far between.

Apart from 'Series Series' and 'Augh Oh', most of the pieces are very short. Some of them almost seem abortive, as if Spearman is unable or unwilling to follow through on his own premisses. A sad end to a remarkable career, but things to cherish even as the curtain falls.

Chris Speed (born 1967)

TENOR SAXOPHONE, CLARINET

Studied classical piano and clarinet, then added sax in high school. Worked with Jim Black in Boston, and formed the bands Humna Feel and Pachora. Based in New York since 1992.

***** Yeah No**

Songlines SGL 1517-2 *Speed; Cuong Vu (t); Skuli Sverrisson (b); Jim Black (d).* 7–12/96.

*****(*) Deviantics**

Songlines SGL 1524-2 *As above.* 10/98.

Speed has been a valuable and provocative presence on other people's records. His own set tends towards the fragmentary and emerges as an entertaining collection of, well, fragments. The frantic 'Scribble Bliss', the ghostly 'The Dream And Memory Store', the intense and purposeful 'Merge' – each uses the resources of the quartet to good ends without quite suggesting a particular vision. On its own terms, this is a sharp, funny exploration of some of the musics that Speed's come across – jazz and everything else. In many ways the key player is Black, whose nutty rhythms are what really bring the group to life, as boisterous as the horns are.

Deviantics pushes the ideas a little harder into a more coherent shape. This has elements of post-bop in it, but Vu is a strange player, as likely to play against the grain of whatever's going on as to follow it, and the stew of influences is getting thicker and richer. Sverrisson's odd 'Tulip' is a very curious melange, and the following 'Wheatstone' is a storming modal blow. 'Valya' has an East European feel. An unpredictable but often genuinely exciting set.

***** Iffy**

Knitting Factory KFW 275 *Speed; Jamie Saft (ky); Ben Perowsky (d).* 12/99.

*****(*) Emit**

Songlines SGL 1532 *Speed; Cuong Vu (t); Skuli Sverrisson (b); Jim Black (d, melod).* 3/00.

It seems strange for a clarinet-player to be fronting a power trio, but Speed uses that horn almost as much as the tenor on *Iffy*. Saft and Perowsky are strong in support – strong enough, in fact, to seem as if they're completely involved even though they're not really allowed to exploit solo space. The clarinet's reediness (Speed certainly isn't one for *chalumeau*) brings on a kind of stark folkiness to some of it; elsewhere there are boppish and soul-jazz tinges. Smart and enjoyable without exactly knocking the listener over.

His regular gang on Songlines are rather better value. This is quite a harsh set, and there seem to be some electronics bubbling away at the bottom of the mix on a few tracks, unless it's Sverrisson or Black fiddling with an effects unit. Speed's knack for a clarion melody, though, stops matters from getting too dark or abstract – 'Constance And Georgia' is one such example. Black can play with what sounds like absolute fury, but somehow without overwhelming everyone else, and Vu continues a one-man advance in trumpet sound and technique. Speed often referees more than dominates, but it's an exciting record.

***** Astereotypical**

Winter & Winter 910082-2 *Speed; Brad Shepik (g, saz); Skuli Sverrisson (b, g); Jim Black (d).* 2/02.

Credited to 'Pachora', but Speed takes the lion's share of the writing, and it's really the same band as last time except Shepik comes in for Vu. That said, the music often trades in the Balkan-terpsichorean feel which Shepik delights in, even if it does develop some of the threads from Speed's earlier sets. With a dozen pieces despatched in just over 50 minutes, there's no hanging about, and with Speed exclusively on clarinet the tracks settle into what might be called a hip idea of Balkan wedding music. The line to earth is Black, who often finds his way back to a basic rock feel. Thickly textured, yet almost perversely insubstantial.

Alister Spence

PIANO, SAMPLER

Australian pianist, with long service in the group Clarion Fracture Zone.

*****(*) Three Is A Circle**

Rufus RF055 *Spence; Lloyd Swanton (b); Toby Hall (d).* 4/00.

***** Flux**

Rufus RF065 *As above.* 7/03.

The trio have worked together in Clarion Fracture Zone and know each other's moves well enough to make an ambitious programme on the first record seem straightforward. Spence thinks in orchestral terms: a piece such as 'Speak And Say Nothing' has a very grand design indeed, yet it's carried across eight minutes with no strain. It's quite close, sometimes claustrophobic music, especially in the more abstracted moments, but there's an underlying melodicism which stops it short of getting too forbidding. Samplers are deftly used on three tracks, but this is very much a thinking take on acoustic, jazz piano-trio language.

The skilful group interplay carries over into the second album, but there are effortful lines in *Flux* which the inward-looking material has to carry, and in almost 70 minutes of music the playing doesn't seem to communicate a great deal other than skill. The final 'Let It Ring', for instance, is 'written as an excuse to use the sustain pedal', but more evocative melodic materials would have been preferable. While the record has plenty to savour from moment to moment, the entirety of it feels wanting in something.

Sphere

GROUP

Formed as a Monk repertory band, and named after the great man – his middle name – Sphere was a good festival draw and a less secure recording outfit. Though Rouse and Riley could claim apostolic connection to the great man, Williams became the de facto leader.

*****(*) Four In One**
Elektra 62601 *Charlie Rouse (ts); Kenny Barron (p); Buster Williams (b); Ben Riley (d).* 2/82.

***** Flight Path**
Elektra 62602 *As above.* 83.

*****(*) On Tour**
Red RR 123191 *As above.* 85.

***** Pumpkin's Delight**
Red RR 123207 *As above.* 86.

The spooky thing about Sphere is that the very day the band went into the studio to fulfil a long-standing arrangement to record an album of Monk tunes the great man's death was announced. He had been living in effective retirement for some time, but his work was slowly leaching into the jazz mainstream. The group made no attempt to pastiche his sound. Barron wisely sticks to what he knows best and only very rarely throws in a direct quote; unconsciously, one suspects. Rouse's slightly adenoidal sound is always attractive, and in some respects these are among his very best recordings and certainly up to the standard of his playing with Monk himself.

The first record took on something of the mystique surrounding Monk's death, an almost apostolic quality that doesn't quite come through when it's heard in retrospect. It is, though, a vivid and beautifully produced representation of 'Light Blue', 'Evidence', 'Eronel', a particularly fine 'Monk's Dream', 'Reflections' and the title-track, which heads off the disc.

The second album is very different in that, apart from 'Played Twice', all the tunes are originals by band members, perhaps signalling that this is not merely a Monk tribute band but a working unit with its own personality. On those terms, it works pretty well. Rouse's 'Pumpkin's Delight' is a clever, elaborate theme and became a staple of their performances. Barron contributes 'El Sueno' and the title-piece, but Williams carries the day with the delightful ballad 'Christina', dedicated to his niece, and one of his most beautiful creations. Again, the sound is very good. The two Reds were recorded in Italy, in Umbria and Bologna. The earlier of the pair is slightly surprising in including only one Monk composition. Williams and Barron are represented by two compositions each, the strongest of which are Williams's 'Dual Force' and the pianist's thoroughly Monkian 'Spiral'. The Umbrian set is recorded roughly but is very immediate and faithful to the live experience. Not a great record, but a thoroughly enjoyable one.

Spirits Of Rhythm

GROUP

Originally the Sepia Nephews and the Five Cousins, the group was expanded in the early '30s with the arrival of Teddy Bunn. Favouring humorous or nonsense lyrics with use of the tiple (a kind of small Latin American guitar with variable tuning), the group were still formidable musicians and sustained a career right through the '30s and the war years before disbanding.

***** The Spirits Of Rhythm 1933–1945**
Classics 1028 *Leonard Feather (p); Teddy Bunn, Ulysses Livingston (g); Leo Watson, Wilbur Daniels, Douglas Daniels (tiple, v); Wilson Myers, Wellman Braud, Red Callender (b); Virgin Scoggins, Georgie Vann (d, v); Red McKenzie, Ella Logan (v).* 10/33–1/45.

The Spirits are now treasured largely for nurturing the guitar-playing of Teddy Bunn, one of the undoubted giants of the instrument in jazz before Charlie Christian and Wes Montgomery revolutionized it, ironically often smoothing out the very features which made it different from the horns and piano. No less a musician than Derek Bailey has pointed to Bunn as an early influence. The Spirits were, however, essentially a singing group, not quite a novelty act but not a million miles from it. Watson and the two Daniels boys sang jovial scat lines, accompanying themselves on tiples, while Bunn kept up a solid but ever-changing background. The sound is light and delicate, an almost harp-like backing for voices. Like Freddy Guy, for whom he once depped in the Ellington band, and Freddie Green, who did a similar job for Basie, Bunn understood the workings of a group instinctively and, despite being wholly self-taught, had the uncanny ability to anticipate even non-standard changes.

The Classics set contains the group's entire output. There are two versions of 'I Got Rhythm', both of them featuring Bunn quite strongly; but the outstanding track is 'I'll Be Ready' on which he plays crisp melodic breaks without a single excess gesture. Watson's full-on madness was better displayed elsewhere, but he has his moments here (one bizarre piece from 1934, 'Dr Watson And Mr Holmes'). There are three titles with the 'Swingin' Scots Lassie' Ella Logan and a final date from 1945 where Bunn is the only survivor from the original line-up. A wacky footnote in jazz history.

Spontaneous Music Ensemble

GROUP

One of the most radical and thoughtful improvisation groups to emerge on the British scene in the '60s, SME (sometimes changed to Orchestra) evolved, like AMM, out of free jazz and quickly developed a performance philosophy that eschewed any predetermined structure or materials and any of the familiar supports of melody, harmony or rhythm. That said, at the heart of the group were a melodist and a master of rhythmical pulse, co-founders Trevor Watts and John Stevens. In later years,

Watts's central position fell to Roger Smith and saxophonist John Butcher, but Stevens stayed at the helm until his untimely death.

***** Challenge**

Emanem 4053 *Kenny Wheeler (t, flhn); Paul Rutherford (tb); Trevor Watts (ss, as, picc); Evan Parker (ss); Bruce Cale, Jeff Clyne, Chris Cambridge (b); John Stevens (d).* 3/66 & 4/67.

***** Withdrawal**

Emanem 4020 *Kenny Wheeler (t, flhn, perc); Paul Rutherford (tb, perc); Trevor Watts (as, f, ob, perc, v); Evan Parker (ss, ts, perc); Derek Bailey (g); Barry Guy (b, p); John Stevens (d).* 9 & 10/66, 3/67.

*****(*) Summer 1967**

Emanem 4005 *Evan Parker (ts, ss); Peter Kowald (b); John Stevens (d).* 67.

****** Karyobin**

Chronoscope CPE 2001 *Kenny Wheeler (t, flhn); Evan Parker (ss); Derek Bailey (g); Dave Holland (b); John Stevens (d).* 2/68.

Asked to say what had been important to him about 1968, Derek Bailey made the typically perceptive and clear-sighted point that the year of revolutions had really made much less difference to the way things were, in either politics or culture, than a whole string of dates in the previous decade. For admirers of British improvised music, though, 1968 saw the emergence of the SME from the rather constricting cocoon of 'free jazz' into an approach that placed all its weight on a collectively generated, non-hierarchical sound with no preconceived structures of any sort.

The publication of 11 previously unissued SME tracks in 1997 was something of a nostalgia trip for anyone who has followed the British improvisation scene with affection. What is instantly noticeable is that the personnel then corresponds exactly to the front rank of senior players now, with the sad exception of the late John Stevens. Even more striking is that all of them, with the partial exception of Watts, have continued to mine the same musical lode for most of the intervening 30 years. *Withdrawal*, though, does catch them on the cusp. The group had made an LP for the now extinct Eyemark label in the spring of 1966, working in a vein that was unmistakably free jazz. It has now been rescued from obscurity by the redoubtable Martin Davidson, and *Challenge* helps to fill out an important gap in the documentation of SME, and in turn the development of British free music. There is still a strong emphasis on written material, much of it palpably influenced by Eric Dolphy, whose jittery, thoughtful style is the obvious source of Watts's already distinctive approach. Stevens is a strong writer, and 'Little Red Head' is an idea that someone should consider dusting down; tough and direct, it smacks strongly of the drummer's musical personality. Interestingly, it's Rutherford – that chronically overlooked genius of the trombone – who is the most distinctive soloist; like Watts, he sounds deeply rooted in the blues, but he also knows how to use huge portamento effects which give an orchestral richness to the group. Parker was not yet on board, but an extra track, 'Distant Little Soul', features him for the first time, recognizable but still somewhat diffident on soprano, contributing to a piece on which Stevens and Watts have already struck out for new territory, marking the shift away from free jazz to free music.

A matter of months later, creating music for a 35-minute film made by George Paul Solomos, they seem to have moved out into new and more abstract territory. (How often has it happened, as is often noted of Miles Davis and *L'Ascenseur pour l'échafaud*, that a film or theatre project allows artists to explore new territory, new sounds, by yoking the music to another artistic artefact?) Part One is very much a feature for Kenny Wheeler, who had been sceptical about becoming involved in free music. It is far from dry, this startling sound, but it is already a long way removed from even a distant memory of bebop or swing. Guy provides dark shifting drones; Parker is not yet quite the skyscraping genius of later years, and it is the still-undervalued Rutherford and Watts (who took over the running of the SME during Stevens's sojourn on the continent) who dominate the ensembles. Bailey performs on some of the later tracks only, having been invited to join SME after its inception. Remarkable as the music is, the photographs (by Evan Parker and Jack Kilby) are a delight. Parker was reportedly overawed by his playing companions; it may be that he was also having second thoughts about the Zapatisto moustache.

Summer 1967 is significant not just in documenting one of Evan Parker's earliest recordings; it also preserves his and Stevens's first meeting with a player whom both were later to credit with opening up whole new areas of improvisational language to them. Kowald is a central figure in the European free movement, a generous, open-minded player who never for a moment stops listening to what is going on around him. This doesn't happen in a confrontational-conversational way, but with a constant awareness of what is going on in what Stevens was later to describe, using an analogy from his other art-form, as 'peripheral vision', an ability to pick up fleeting clues and render them as significant as the apparent focal point. That to a degree is what the SME has always been about, whatever its exact personnel and instrumentation.

Until Martin Davidson's excavations in the tape archive, the first significant product of the SME's change in philosophy was *Karyobin*, a strikingly light-toned and unaggressive exploration of group identity that lasts 49 minutes but contains within it arrays and patterns of musical sound which suggest infinity. The title is the collective name of the birds which inhabit paradise, living in harmony with one another. *Karyobin* has been a collectors' item on vinyl for many years. It transfers to CD pretty well, de-emphasizing the horns and drums slightly and letting Holland and Bailey come through with a bit more definition.

***** For You To Share**

Emanem 4023 *Trevor Watts (ss, v); John Stevens (perc, v); audience members perform various instruments.* 1 & 5/70.

****** Face To Face**

Emanem 4003 *Trevor Watts (as); John Stevens (d).* 73.

A few years further on, SME was functioning as a duo. Stevens and Watts were later to part company, somewhat acrimoniously, but for the duration of their partnership they created music of astonishing harmoniousness; 'harmony' would be the wrong word. *For You To Share* is interesting in that audience members join the two musicians in the collaborative, non-virtuosic philosophy of the AACM in Chicago. This isn't one of their strongest encounters, and is something of a timepiece (the CND symbol on the cover is a giveaway). Again, though, it is the delicacy of Stevens's percussion that is notable, while Watts's keening cries have an emotional pull that makes nonsense of attempts to relabel this sort of music 'abstract'. Small wonder that so many of these players were profoundly affected by the work of Samuel Beckett, in whom abstraction and the most passionate humanitarianism were wedded.

*** Mouthpiece

Emanem 4039 *John Stevens; no personnel listed.* 5–11/73.

***(*) SME+ = SMO

Emanem 4062 *Evan Parker, Bob Turner, Trevor Watts (ss); Robert Calvert (sno); Dave Decobain, Herman Hauge, Ye Min (as); Martin Mayes (frhn); Chris Turner (hca); Peter Drew (p); Ian Brighton (g); Robert Carter, Nigel Coombes, Stephen Luscomb (vn); Lindsay Cooper, Jane Robertson, Colin Wood (clo); Angus Fraser (b); John Stevens (perc, c).* 1/74.

The October 1973 performances are credited to the Spontaneous Music Orchestra, which was essentially SME plus the members of a larger workshop group known as Free Space. No definite details about the musicians involved are known or given, but anyone familiar with this period in British improvisation will be able to make informed guesses about at least some of the players. As with much of Emanem's recent catalogue, all these performances are previously unissued, so they strike with something of the force of the original concerts, which were all in and around London; the two most substantial works were recorded at the SME's spiritual home, the Little Theatre Club, and at Ealing Technical College. Since much of the music was workshopped, there is on occasion a faintly tentative air and sometimes, as in the two versions of 'Sustained Piece', too dogged an application to a single informing idea, on this occasion quite literally the sustaining of blown or sung tones. 'One Two' is the closest the group came to a fixed beat or groove, with players opting whether to play on the first or second count. 'Mouthpiece' required the orchestra to begin with unvoiced mouth sounds, move on to vocalized sounds and only then to their instruments. This is perhaps the least involving part of the disc, albeit a valuable documentation of John Stevens's working philosophy.

The later of the two records again features an augmented SME, and the work of two consecutive nights, first at the Little Theatre Club and then at St John's, Smith Square, part of an evening devoted to the two different aspects of Stevens's music: jazz-based and improvised. The St John's performance was previously issued, the other not; and this latter piece is an edit that cuts out what Martin Davidson refers to as an 'unsatisfactory' start. The main piece, though, is satisfactory in every regard and is wonderful to hear again. It begins in a soft mêlée of tight, high horn sounds with growling drones behind, a structured section in which individual players are required to 'Search & Reflect', listen and respond to the work of players around them. This then develops into a 'Sustained' passage of longer-held tones. Evan Parker is very prominent, but gradually Trevor Watts unfreezes the tableau and leads the music to a powerfully joyous climax. A remarkable work, and one of SME/SMO's finest documented moments.

***(*) Quintessence 1

Emanem 4015 *Evan Parker, Trevor Watts (ss); Derek Bailey (g); Kent Carter (clo, b); John Stevens (perc, v).* 10/73, 2/74.

*** Quintessence 2

Emanem 4016 *As above.* 10/73–2/74.

Kent Carter first came to Britain in 1973 with Steve Lacy (who was himself to become an important overseas player in Derek Bailey's Company project). Despite coming from a radically different musical background, Carter fitted into the SME concept quite seamlessly. He recorded with Stevens and Watts at the Little Theatre Club in October of that year, and then joined the quintet (hence the title) form of the SME for the Institute of Contemporary Arts concert held the following February. *Quintessence 1* contains the first set from that occasion, together with three trios from the Little Theatre. The remainder of the ICA date is on Emanem 4016. The stereo separation of the two sopranos, cello and guitar leaves Stevens's kit very much in the foreground, and there are moments when the performance sounds almost like a concerto for percussion. His lifelong interest in the aural equivalent of 'peripheral vision' seems already to be in play here, and it makes for fascinating listening. His awareness of his colleagues' playing is instinctive, but it is not studied. He seems to respond to them almost as someone might who is reading during conversation, not rudely or detachedly, but because he is able to. The trio sessions, which have not previously been issued, don't quite match up in quality and are rather disappointing, though once again not because Carter is out of sympathy with the music.

*** Low Profile

Emanem 4031 *Nigel Coombes (vn); Colin Wood (clo); Roger Smith (g); John Stevens (d, c, v).* 11/77, 2/84, 10/88.

A mixed bag of SME performances, recorded in performance over a decade. Wood is heard only on the 1977 gig from Derby College of Further Education, which consists of the fragmentary 'Immediate Past Present' and a half-hour set rejoicing in the title, 'The Only Geezer An American Soldier Shot Was Anton Webern'. Like the much later 'Kitless With Elbow', it features Stevens's often very effective cornet (often it was bugle instead) and voice. Unusually, Smith uses an amplified guitar on the title-piece, a rare resort to electricity by a player who has almost always prepared a soft and unprocessed sound. This is by no means a major SME document, but it adds to the documentation and fills in the story from a time when the group was not heavily documented.

*** Hot And Cold Heroes

Emanem 4008 *As above, except omit Wood.* 80, 91.

There is at this point something of a jump in the documentation, and the final item belongs to a rather later SME. Of all the players associated with the group, the one who seems most wholly defined by the experience, and yet the one constitutionally least adjusted to its collectivist, ego-less philosophy, is Coombes. The material on *Hot And Cold Heroes*, unlike the other records, has not been available before. Despite its obvious importance, it lacks their sheer impact and should perhaps not be considered a priority find. *Karyobin* and *Face To Face* are, in our view, essential.

Brett Sroka

TROMBONE

Born in Lexington, Massachusetts, Sroka taught himself composition by dissecting Ellington scores. On his instrument, he carries some debt to Britt Woodman and Steve Turre.

*** Hearsay

Fresh Sound New Talent FSNT 140 *Sroka; Avishai Cohen (t); Aaron Stewart (ts); Jason Moran (p); John Sullivan (b); Eric Harland (d).* 2/01.

This is very much a band project. A strong line-up is well featured and drummer Harland effectively hi-jacks 'Tabula Rasa' as a percussion spot. For all his acknowledged influences, Sroka sounds more like Jimmy Knepper than anyone, noticeably on the opening title-track, a long Ellington-inspired workout which flags a little in the middle. Cohen is a bright and pungent trumpeter and cuts through some of the muddier arrangements. The production brings the rhythm section – and especially Moran – well to the fore and here and there some of the horn detail is lost in a cluster of piano and bass tones. Otherwise, though, a very strong set from a leader who knows his own mind and who will very soon be playing and writing in an idiom he can genuinely call his own.

Larry Stabbins (born 1949)

TENOR SAXOPHONE

Stabbins has dabbled in most contemporary forms and has perhaps paid the price for his versatility, being slow to record under his own name.

*** Monadic

Emanem 4093 *Stabbins (ts solo).* 02.

Larry's belated debut is in one of the most difficult improvising disciplines of all. Solo saxophone records are tricky blighters. For every *For Alto* or *The Snake Decides*, there are a dozen egotistical nightmares, front room rehearsals posing as product. At first glance, *Monadic* looks likely to fall into that trap. Beginning with 'Breathing' and some toneless exhalations, it only gets around to 'Playing' 13 tracks later and the only live-with-audience piece of the set, which was recorded in an otherwise empty Red Rose in London. However, the titles shouldn't be off-putting because Stabbins is too thoroughly musical a performer ever to fob us off with mere exercises. There are nods throughout to others who have gone down this tough road – Braxton and Evan Parker, of course, also Steve Lacy – but the sheer expressiveness of tracks like 'Thinking', 'Shaking', 'Speaking' and 'Playing' bespeak an underexposed musical imagination. The relatively modest rating undersells the record and is provisional. Time to hear more of Larry Stabbins, alone and in sympathetic company.

Jess Stacy (1904–94)

PIANO

Born in Missouri, Stacy went to Chicago in the '20s and was a fixture on the scene until he joined Benny Goodman in 1935, with whom – aside from a spell with Bob Crosby – he stayed for a decade, an association he is best remembered for. He later became a Condonite and, after a gradual decline in work, left music to sell cosmetics in 1961. He returned to the festival circuit in the '70s.

**** Jess Stacy 1935–1939

Classics 795 *Stacy; Billy Butterfield (t); Les Jenkins (tb); Hank D'Amico, Irving Fazola (cl); Eddie Miller, Bud Freeman (ts); Allen Hanlon (g); Israel Crosby, Sid Weiss (b); Gene Krupa, Don Carter (d); Carlotta Dale (v).* 11/35–11/39.

**** Ec-Stacy

ASV AJA 5172 *Stacy; Bobby Hackett, Muggsy Spanier (c); Charlie Teagarden, Harry James, Ziggy Elman, Chris Griffin, Yank Lawson, Lyman Vunk, Max Herman, Billy Butterfield, Pee Wee Irwin, Anthony Natoli, Nate Kazebier, Bunny Berigan, Ralph Muzillo (t); Floyd O'Brien, Red Ballard, Joe Harris, Murray McEachern, Elmer Smithers, Buddy Morrow, Will Bradley, Jack Satterfield (tb); Benny Goodman, Johnny Hodges, Pee Wee Russell, Danny Polo, Hymie Schertzer, Bill De Pew, Dick Clark, Arthur Rollini, George Koenig, Vido Musso, Bud Freeman, Dave Mathews, Noni Bernardi, Matty Matlock, Art Mendelsohn, Eddie Miller, Gil Rodin, Sal Franzella, Henry Ross, Larry Binyon, Julius Bradley, Arthur Rando (reeds); Nappy Lamare, Allan Reuss, Frank Worrell, Ben Heller (g); Israel Crosby, Sid Wess, Artie Shapiro, Harry Goodman, Bob Haggart (b); Specs Powell, Gene Krupa, George Wettling, Ray Bauduc, Mario Toscarelli, Buddy Schutz (d); Lee Wiley (v).* 11/35–6/45.

One of the great piano masters of the '30s gets his due at last with these two very strong compilations of his early work. There is a duplication of three of the early solo pieces, but the chronological Classics compilation concentrates on Commodore and Varsity material from 1938–9, while the ASV disc covers sideman work with Benny Goodman, Bob Crosby, Lionel Hampton, Bud Freeman and Pee Wee Russell for an exceptionally well-rounded portrait of a man who appeared in many interesting situations. His unassuming virtuosity went with a deceptively romantic streak – 'the intensity of Hines with the logic of Bix', as Vic Bellerby puts it – and his impeccable touch and undercurrent of blues feeling, even if tempered by a rather civilized irony, give him a rare position among the piano-players of the era. The Classics set includes two splendid blues-based fantasies in 'Ramblin'' and 'Complainin'', the excellent solo session from 1939 and two engaging band dates, while the ASV offers several rarities, including an aircheck version of Beiderbecke's 'In A Mist', three 1944 duets with Specs Powell and the beautiful 'Down To Steamboat Tennessee' with Muggsy Spanier and Lee Wiley. Transfers are mostly very fair. Both discs are a strongly recommended portrait of a remarkable personality.

*** Tribute To Benny Goodman

Koch 8506 *Stacy; Ziggy Elman (t); Ted Vesely, Murray McEachern (tb); Heinie Beau (as); Babe Russin, Vido Musso (ts); Charles Gentry, Joe Koch (bs); Allen Reuss, Al Hendrickson (g); Morty Corb, Artie Shapiro (b); Nick Fatool (d).* 10/54–10/55.

Stacy reputedly walked out of the studio sessions for *The Benny Goodman Story* without taking up the offer of a solitary feature, and these sessions (originally for Atlantic) might be seen as his own version of the tale. 'The Famous Sidemen', as they were credited, include plenty of old friends and the inevitable choices – from 'When Buddha Smiles' to 'Sing Sing Sing' – come up sprightly, if not exactly fresh. Four tracks by Stacy with the rhythm section to himself are among the best things.

*** Stacy Still Swings

Chiaroscuro CR(D) 133 *Stacy (p solo).* 7/74–7/77.

The veteran Condonite (as he later became) quit professional music in the '50s but came back to festivals and studios very occasionally. This congenial, easy-going set of solos was among the last he made: nothing much has changed over the years except the tempos, and even then he was never exactly a tornado at the keyboard. His own tunes, such as 'Lookout Mountain Squirrels', are charming but robust; his standards are an old-fashioned choice.

Terell Stafford (born 1966)

TRUMPET, FLUGELHORN

American trumpeter with his own take on the post-bop vernacular.

*** Time To Let Go

Candid CACD 79702 *Stafford; Tim Warfield (ts); Steve Wilson (as, ss); Edward Simon (p); Steve Nelson (vib); Michael Bowie (b); Victor Lewis (d); Victor See-Yuen (perc).* 95.

**** Centripetal Force

Candid CACD 79718 *Stafford; John Clark (frhn); Ron Blake, Tim Warfield (ts); Russell Malone (g); Stefon Harris (vib); Stephen Scott (p); Ed Howard (b); Victor Lewis (d); Daniel Moreno (perc).* 10/96.

Stafford was a regular member of Bobby Watson's group, Horizon, which also numbered Simon and Lewis, and he comes to this debut project with a sensibility very much marked by Watson's small-group/big-sound idea. The opening 'Time To Let Go' is an emphatic statement of intent, and the other two originals 'Qui Qui' and 'Why?' are in the same bag. Stafford isn't just another latter-day run-of-the-mill bopper. Though he draws on a range of influences running from Fats Navarro and Clifford Brown to mid-period Miles and Lee Morgan, he already has a distinctive inflexion and on Stephen Scott's lovely 'Was It Meant To Be', he carves out a very personal phraseology which points onward to the follow-up disc.

Centripetal Force is exactly what's at work here, a group which is working very closely and sympathetically. Again Tim Warfield brings his clean, youthful sound, but on just one track this time. Second time out, Stafford has at his disposal two of the brightest young guys on the scene, vibist Stefon Harris and pianist Stephen Scott, who sounds more comfortable on this session than he has on a couple of recent projects under his own name. A version of 'Daahoud' is a special dedication, but it also points up the Brown influence again. Though the whole band is never heard together, the richer palette suits the trumpeter admirably and he produces some magnificent statements on 'I'll Wait' and 'Skylark', a back-to-back pair that are as sheerly refreshing as anything from the last few years. Thad Jones's 'A Child Is Born' is for trumpet and guitar, and 'My Romance' is an elegant trumpet solo. Fine stuff from a highly intelligent young musician.

*** Fields Of Gold

Nagel Heyer 2005 *Stafford; Antonio Hart (as); Bill Cunliffe (p, org); Kiyoshi Kitagawa (b); Rodney Green (d).* 00.

This is a beautifully balanced jazz set. Stafford goes funky on 'Ms Shirley Scott', though it's Cunliffe's organ which pays the most explicit tribute; it goes cool and almost modal on 'I Believe In You' and brings an entirely original sound and presence to the traditional 'If I Perish', which has a chilling beauty and delicacy of touch.

Of the originals, Hart's 'Flashdance' and the leader's 'Dear Rudy' are the most plausible, though Terell isn't yet entirely fledged a composer. A nod, though, to Kitagawa, whose credit for 'Sagittarius' is perhaps more generous than strictly good programming; as an accompanist, however, the bass-player is very impressive – strong-voiced, disciplined and firmly across the beat. More good stuff. If you stumbled across this in a club, you'd go home very happy indeed. Whether it merits repeated outings remains to be seen.

***(*) New Beginnings

Max Jazz 402 *Stafford; Jesse Davis, Dick Oatts (as); Steve Wilson (ss, as); Harry Allen (ts); Mulgrew Miller (p); Derrick Hodge (b); Dana Hall (d).* 6/03.

It's not clear how this represents new beginnings. As a consolidation of Stafford's work, though, it's hard to fault. He sounds assured, relaxed and on top of his material. The saxophones bed his sound nicely in the ensembles, and the trade-off of solo ideas is thoughtful and exciting by turns. There aren't too many players of his generation who'd start an album with a Fletcher Henderson composition. 'Soft Winds' is a lovely thing, but it conceals some surprises in Stafford's opening statement. He throws down the gauntlet to Jesse Davis (ever more polished) and the genial Harry Allen before taking the theme up and out.

The only disappointment on the record is the three-part 'New Beginnings Suite', which begins with a dreary funk theme called 'Selah' and doesn't really recover. There's no obvious connection between the three compositions, and they could just as easily have been programmed as free-standing tracks. The spiritual 'He Knows How Much You Can Bear' (usually '*We* Can Bear' and associated with Mahalia Jackson, Solomon Burke and others) is handled with delicate stoicism and there's another Stephen Scott arrangement on 'Kumbaya'. Scott's role shouldn't be underestimated, but Pamela Watson, wife of former boss Bobby, contributes charts as well. This is a very polished and elegant record. The standard 'The Touch Of Your Lips' has a richness to the voicings that makes it seem a much grander and more portentous theme.

Mattias Ståhl

VIBRAPHONE

Young Swedish vibesman leading a new quartet.

***(*) Ståhls Blå

Dragon DRCD 361 *Ståhl; Joakim Milder (ss, ts); Flip Auguston (b); Thomas Stronen (d).* 6/01.

Anyone looking at the instrumentation and expecting a nice, easy-going chamber session will be knocked down straight away by the explosive 'Blues För Mor' which opens the disc like an unruly typhoon. They're an interesting brew of personalities: the patient, occasionally blustering Milder, the unpredictable Ståhl, and a rhythm section that can play flat out as easily as it does simple, limber swinging. The key man here may be Stronen, yet another in a new breed of Scandinavian drummers (see also Per Oddvar Johansen and Jarle Vespestad) who can play hard and fast and light and easy, at any dynamic, without any apparent effort. Some of the material is a bit on the inscrutable side, but this is a terrific band.

Tomasz Stańko (born 1942)

TRUMPET

One of the central figures and influences in Polish jazz, leading his own groups since 1962 and effecting his own blend of inside and out, mainstream and avant-garde.

*** Music For K

Power Bros 00131 *Stańko; Zbigniew Seifert (as); Janusz Muniak (ts); Bronislaw Suchanek (b); Janusz Stefanski (d).* 1/70.

***(*) Balladyna

ECM 1071 *Stańko; Tomasz Szukalski (ts, ss); Dave Holland (b); Edward Vesala (d).* 12/75.

It may seem an odd thing to say, but Tomasz Stańko is an artist first and a musician only second. He is a man whose imagination is fired as much by words – Joyce, Lautréamont – and by visual images as by music. He is certainly not confined to jazz formulae, and at first hearing his music might seem to have more kinship with the abstract experimentalism of the Polish avant-garde than with orthodox or even free jazz. This is deceptive, for the trumpeter is deeply versed in the defining elements of jazz. His first big influence was Chet Baker, he says, though subsequently Miles Davis (who was to play an important part in the creative breakthrough of Stańko's generation of musicians) would become almost as important.

Totally free playing has never played a large part on the Polish scene and even when the setting is abstract there is still an underlying jazz 'feel', expressible both as a pulse and as dimly familiar harmonies and structures. Though some important records for Edward Vesala's Leo Records in Finland (not to be confused with Leo Feigin's London-based imprint) have not appeared on CD, the even earlier *Music For K* is still around, a forceful, sometimes inchoate session, with as much emphasis on Seifert's raw, emotive alto (this is before the ill-fated young genius made his shift to violin) as there is on Stańko's own rather fragile sound. The rhythm section is not really up to the task, though Stefanski is an accurate and unfussy percussionist, always absolutely on the beat. 'Cry' is the closest thing to American jazz of the time, but it is 'Music For K', dedicated to the late Krzysztof Komeda (who would be the inspiration for the later *Litania*) which really establishes Stańko's credentials as composer and *auteur*. He dominates this piece entirely, even when not in the foreground, and it points forward to the quieter, slower conception that he shares with the Finnish percussionist who joins him on the 1975 disc.

Stańko had jammed with Vesala some time previously and shyly revealed himself as a composer. It was to be some time, though, before his quality as both writer and performer became more widely known. *Balladyna* was his breakthrough album, a very personal statement given a high production gloss by ECM. Szukalski is a workmanlike player with, one suspects, a somewhat limited range. Stańko was fortunate in his other colleagues, however. Vesala is cautious in his approach to free music, but Holland seems to move between freedom and structure without a blink. The collectively written 'Tale' is rather weak, but Vesala's 'Num', three more Stańko compositions and an improvised duet with Holland give the record a solid impact and set the scene for the masterful ECM sessions of the '90s.

***(*) Bluish

Power Bros 00113 *Stańko; Arild Andersen (b); Jon Christensen (d).* 10/91.

There is a gap in the story which accounts for most of the '80s. When this superb record appeared, Stańko was still largely unavailable, with *Balladyna* not yet on CD and little available on widely distributed labels. The Rybnik-based Power Bros did manage to broker some distribution outside Poland, and *Bluish* awakened many listeners to the buried treasure that awaited them in Stańko. Working with northern Europe's premier rhythm section, he sounds more effusive than ever before, though with the same melancholy edge that made him such a haunting successor to both Chet and Miles.

The opening 'Dialogue' with Andersen recalls the duo with Holland on the earlier record. Stańko is not playing entirely free but is certainly not working within a fixed metre and his long, meditative lines are very compelling. The title-piece begins in a more straightforward idiom, before breaking down into a superb solo from Christensen which is marked by hesitations and silences.

Part two of 'If You Look Enough' (it comes first for some reason) is an eerie, out-of-tempo meditation, punctuated by brass smears and growls. The first part (placed last in the set) has the same chordal structure with a nagging insect-like chitter from Christensen. The drummer creates remarkable effects with damped cymbals on the long 'Bosanetta', a tune that recalls one of Vesala's tango pastiches, as does the succeeding 'Third Heavy Ballad', on which Stańko plays with a quiet lyricism that is reminiscent of Kenny Wheeler's work for ECM, the label that would shortly transform the enigmatic Pole's career.

**** Bossanossa And Other Ballads

GOWI CDG 08 *Stańko; Bobo Stenson (p); Anders Jormin (b); Tony Oxley (d).* 3 & 4/93.

This group was the highlight of the 1993 Jazz Jamboree in Warsaw, playing the material recorded on this record. Most of the material had been around for some time. 'Sunia' had been a staple of sets with Freelectronic, Stańko's free/fusion group. This is the definitive version, with wonderful interplay between Stańko's frail lead line and Oxley's metallic patterns. The Englishman resembles Vesala in his ability to register strong pulse in an otherwise free setting, but he is a lighter, more abstract player and ideal for this material, which is both unremittingly sombre and more playful.

Stenson was to become a key element in Stańko's musical thinking. Here he brings an uneasy cast to 'Maldoror's Love Song' and 'Die Weisheit Von Isidor Ducasse', two pieces which reflect Stańko's fascination with the proto-surrealist and arch-decadent Lautréamont. The trumpeter uses a big, unfettered tone and long sinuous lines that anticipate and overlap the pianist's statements by several bars, creating a shifting surface across which the group lays out its sound. A wonderful record that caused a sensation when it was released, it stands up absolutely with passing time.

*** Matka Joanna

ECM 531693-2 *Stańko; Bobo Stenson (p); Anders Jormin (b); Tony Oxley (d).* 5/94.

Not hugely compelling music, written for a 1960 film by Jerzy Kawalerowicz, *Matka Joanna Od Aniolow* ('And The Angels'). Stańko uses this found text as a basis to create 'images' for the group. Whether these turned out to be constraining rather than liberating isn't entirely clear, but the impression is of a less than wholehearted performance from all except Oxley, who steals the record with his focused abstractions. Stenson doesn't have his best day and often does little more than shadow the leader's keening monologues.

CORE COLLECTION

♛ **** Leosia

ECM 1603 *As above.* 1/96.

***Leosia* is one of the finest jazz records of recent times, a work of immense creative concentration made by a band at the peak of its powers. Stańko has probably played better, but never with such instinctive support from his colleagues. As was the norm with ECM sessions at this time, considerable emphasis is put on the component members of the ensemble and on subdivisions of the basic group. Oxley, Jormin and Stenson are the begetters of 'Trinity' and bassist and drummer collaborate on the similarly constructed 'Brace'. 'No Bass Trio' is self-explanatory, and very fine, but the real action comes around these tracks, on the numbers drawn from *Bossanossa* and on the long title-piece which ends the album on a creative high, a long, perfectly weighted theme that seems to have no beginning or end.**

**** Litania

ECM 537551-2 *Stańko; Bernt Rosengren (ts); Joakim Milder (ts, ss); Bobo Stenson (p); Terje Rypdal (g); Palle Danielsson (b); Jon Christensen (d).* 96.

Stańko had been a key member of Krzysztof Komeda's group in the '60s, and given an increasing awareness of the pianist's eminence as a composer, some kind of tribute record had long seemed on the cards. For *Litania*, he summoned up a remarkable septet, co-fronted by the veteran Rosengren (one of the giants of European jazz) and the younger Milder, who is perhaps the weak link on the session.

They kick off with Komeda's 'Svantetic', one of his most lateral ideas and one of his best. There are three versions of 'Sleep Safe And Warm' from the soundtrack to *Rosemary's Baby* (only two of them involving Rypdal) and a striking performance of 'Ballada' from *Knife In The Water*, another Roman Polanski film for which Komeda wrote music. No room for 'Crazy Girl' or 'Astigmatic', which may be held in reserve for a follow-up session. What we have, though, is the clearest evidence both of Komeda's skill as a composer and of Stańko's ability to convey both the atmospherics of this neglected music and its ironclad structure. He is playing with absolute conviction and immense authority, and with a tone that conveys technical mastery coupled with total self-confidence.

Milder earns his place as a second-string soloist. Stenson and Christensen make one another play harder and with a more abrupt attack. Little of the pianist's tendency to drift off the pace, and certainly a very emphatic performance from Christensen. As a now-legendary London performance amply proved, the absence of Rypdal would make little difference. He is included as a colourist, and while he makes some lovely shapes on 'The Witch' and 'Sleep Safe And Warm', he is by no means integral to the music. Stańko's finest hour came with *Leosia*, but this is still an important, even historic record.

**** From The Green Hill

ECM 547336-2 *Stańko; John Surman (bs, bcl); Dino Saluzzi (bandoneon); Michelle Makarski (vn); Anders Jormin (b); Jon Christensen (d).* 8/98.

Leosia was Stańko's apotheosis as composer and bandleader. *Litania* was a full-hearted tribute to his great mentor and friend. *From The Green Hill* is quite simply the most beautiful record he has ever made, a fragile, almost folkish disc, which is also a wonderful group performance. Reprising Komeda's 'Litania' as a bandoneon solo, with Saluzzi playing organ chords, was a stroke of genius, emphasizing the suite-like nature of the record and its continuity with Stańko's recent work.

The association with Surman is particularly happy. The saxophonist opens and signals the end of the album with his own theme 'Domino', which takes him back to a signature hybrid of folk and church music. He also leads into Stańko's 'Quintet Time' with a bass-clarinet figure which recalls the old days with the Trio, before the track opens out into a restless free form that allows Christensen to express a quiet fury. The trumpeter plays some mournful high notes and smears reminiscent of the classic cornet-players, though the dynamic of the piece is his usual brooding synthesis of Miles and Chet. 'Pantronic' sees Stańko donning Komeda's compositional mantle, while the title-piece might almost be a nod of appreciation in Surman's direction, so similar is it to some of the saxophonist's own themes.

Makarski is used rather sparingly, which is a pity, but probably wise. Her role in the group is episodic rather than structural and, if anything, she gains from being slightly marginalized. Jormin has emerged as a considerable player and composer, but he has a quieter time as well, some of his strengths cancelled out by the presence of Saluzzi.

***(*) Soul Of Things

ECM 016374-2 *Stańko; Marcin Waslewski(p); Slawomir Kurkiewicz (b); Michel Miskiewicz (d).* 8/01.

Almost a Stańko 'genre' record, 13 variations on an original theme, with the trumpeter exploring each melodic delicacy as it emerges from the design, sometimes with an almost studied vulnerability, sometimes momentarily fierce. His Polish team play it straight and supportive, though the leader allows space for their own musings too. A little dry, and for all its conventional beauties probably not the record to convert anyone to Stańko's music.

**** :rarum: Selected Recordings

ECM 000180202 *As for ECM recordings above.*

A generous selection from the ECM catalogue provides a good introduction to Stańko's work. Highlights of the dozen tracks include 'Balladyna', Komeda's 'Litania' and the collaboration with Edward Vesala 'Together'. Anyone sufficiently intrigued should probably dive straight in and explore *Balladyna* or the lovely *Matka Joanna*, but this is still a fine way to start.

Johnny St Cyr (1890–1966)

GUITAR, BANJO

Born in New Orleans, St Cyr is on many of the classic '20s records by Armstrong and Morton. Thereafter he mixed music with working as a plasterer, though in the last decade of his life he played with many revivalist groups on the West Coast.

*** Johnny St Cyr

American Music AMCD-78 *St Cyr; Thomas Jefferson (t, v); Percy Humphrey (t); Jim Robinson, Joe Avery (tb); George Lewis (cl); Jeanette Kimball (p, v); Leo Thompson (p); Ernest McLean (g); Richard McLean, Fran Fields (b); Paul Barbarin, Sidney Montague (d); Jack Delany, Sister Elizabeth Eustis (v).* 7/54–5/55.

The doyen of New Orleans rhythm guitarists was seldom noted as a group leader, but American Music have pieced together a CD's worth of material. The first two tracks are rather dowdy treatments of 'Someday You'll Be Sorry' by a band with Percy Humphrey, Lewis and Robinson; but more interesting are the five previously unheard pieces by a quintet in which protégé Ernest McLean is featured rather more generously than Johnny himself, both men playing electric. The rest of the disc is jovial New Orleans music, fronted by the hearty Jefferson and the imperturbable Percy Humphrey. St Cyr, as always, is no more inclined to take any limelight than Freddie Green ever was, so it's nice to have a disc under his name. Remastering is from sources that were a lot cleaner than AM often have access to, so sound is good.

Colin Steele

TRUMPET

Scottish trumpeter working in his native scene and sorting out a mix of post-bop with more localized strains.

***(*) Twilight Dreams

Caber 024 *Steele; Julian Arguëlles (ts, as); Dave Milligan (p); Brian Shiels (b); John Rae (d).* 9/00.

**** The Journey Home

Caber 029 *As above, except Aidan O'Donnell (b) replaces Shiels.* 12/02.

Steele's quintet is one of the best advertisements for the new jazz being made in Scotland, and these records are confident, polished and passionate statements from a very gifted leader. The first record is full of stylish themes and crisply committed playing, just occasionally settling into a merely capable routine but taking much from the strong front line of Steele and Arguëlles, the latter turning in some of his most constructive and melodious work on record. It's trumped, though, by the superb *The Journey Home.* Steele notes that after years searching for a voice in 'the American jazz idiom', he's simply looked back to personal roots and measured his steps in local country. In the epic-length title-track he brings it all back home with a vengeance. The 'Lament For Miles' sounds more like something with a whiff of Islay air about it, and when Arguëlles – outstanding again throughout – has the audacity to throw in an uillean skirl or two along the way, the lament has travelled a long way from Alton, Illinois. Topping it off is Milligan, who finds orchestral comps and solos of delicious poise and inventiveness, and Rae, the Scottish Art Taylor. Essential new jazz.

John Stein

GUITAR

The Boston-based guitarist is a fairly unreconstructed hard bopper, albeit at the quieter and gentler end of the spectrum.

*** Hustle Up!

Tightly Knit 172 *Stein; Bruce Alan Torff (p); Dave Limina (org); Marshall Wood (b); Les Harris, Dave Hurst (d).* 95.

*** Green Street

Challenge 73158 *Stein; David 'Fathead' Newman (as, ts, f); Ken Clark (org); Dave Hurst (d).* 99.

*** Portraits And Landscapes

Jardis 20029 *Stein; Bill Thompson (as, ts, f); Larry Goldings (org, p); Keala Kaumeheiwa (b); Greg Conroy (d).* 12/99–1/00.

*** Conversation Pieces

Jardis 20140 *Stein; David 'Fathead' Newman (ts, f); Keala Kaumeheiwa (b); Greg Conroy (d).* 3/01.

Some listeners will not get past the first couple of minutes of Stein's debut recording, an ultra laid-back and uninspired recording of 'Poor Butterfly'. It would be a pity if they didn't, because John is an effective performer who writes imaginatively. His own 'Eleanor's Folly' is next up and immediately the level of interest rises. Curious programming. Overall, the tone is too laid-back to distinguish this set from dozens of similar ones, but when Stein is playing to his strengths, the results are very effective indeed.

The second album calls up David 'Fathead' Newman, who unusually doubles on alto, which gives the set a plangent, boppish quality. As on the debut, Hammond represents an important component of the sound, but there is little clichéd 'organ trio' stuff in evidence here. The title-piece is the most formulaic but there is always intelligence behind Stein's playing, and he makes a well-established form sound brand-new.

By the turn of 2000 Stein had his conception pretty well down pat and *Portraits And Landscapes* sounds like the work of a man who enjoys going to the office. As ever, he avoids blurry chords and over-elaborate lead lines, leaving it to the impressive Goldings (who also doubles on piano) to fill in the backgrounds. The Latinate 'Rio Con Brio' gives Thompson a chance to show off his skill on flute, though for the most part he sticks to tenor in the time-honoured way. Fathead comes back for the most recent album of the four, which features a stripped-down line-up. Once again, the material is mostly Stein originals, but here the revelation is bassist Kaumeheiwa, who manages to combine delicate countermelodies (on 'Sao Paulo', the token south-of-the-border number) with some full-on accompaniment on things like 'The Willie Walk'.

Hugh Steinmetz (born 1943)

TRUMPET

A pioneer on the Danish free scene in the '60s, Steinmetz played in The Contemporary Jazz Quartet and made these sessions under his own leadership at the same time. He later played in more conventional studio and big-band dates but still leads a large band which plays what he calls 'experimental compositions'.

*** NU!

Steeplechase SCCD 36027 *Steinmetz; Karsten Vogel (as); Niels Harrit (ts, f); Per Aage Brandt (p); Steffen Andersen (b); Bo Thrige Andersen (d).* 3–4/66.

This couples the original Debut album *NU!* with six tracks from a slightly earlier date which have never been previously issued (they were essentially rehearsals for the 'proper' session, done in the cellar of somebody's home), so there are basically two versions of the same set of music here. While this scarcely counts as a forgotten classic, it's a thoroughly worthwhile rediscovery which fills in a little history. Certainly any admirer of, say, the New York Contemporary Five or early Amalgam will find plenty to take in here. Steinmetz agrees that he was working under a strong Don Cherry influence, 'but it was within my own style', and some of the keening melancholy which came to typify Scandinavian timbres during the '70s comes through in the likes of 'NGO' and the very Coleman-esque 'One For Carl'. Harrit, these days a chemist and teacher, is a strong contributor and there's some thoughtful work from Brandt, now a distinguished professor of linguistics, who had one of the most difficult roles in the group but makes a good fist of what he needed to do. Steinmetz himself is more obviously lyrical. In its way, one of the more challenging records to appear on Steeplechase.

Bobo Stenson (born 1944)

PIANO

Born in Västerås, Sweden, Stenson has been a major figure on the Stockholm post-bop scene since 1966. Work with Jan Garbarek and Charles Lloyd was the prelude to his own considerable ECM albums.

*** Very Early

Dragon 304 *Stenson; Anders Jormin (b); Rune Carlsson (d).* 86.

These days, Stenson is virtually the house pianist at ECM, adding his effortlessly eclectic touch to the groups of Charles Lloyd, Tomasz Stańko, and others. If this isn't quite the mainstream, it's certainly closer to it than seemed likely at one time. As co-founder of Rena Rama in 1971, he seemed embarked on an effort to hybridize jazz with Balkan and Indian folk-music, a somewhat quixotic enterprise in the event, but one which coloured his work for many years, and which can still be heard on *Dansere*, on which he co-leads with Jan Garbarek.

Stenson's career began with Borje Frederiksson, and after a brief apprenticeship under the Swedish tenor saxophonist, he branched out with high-profile gigs for Stan Getz (in Africa, of all places) and Red Mitchell. Increasingly in the last ten years he has been associated with ECM's efforts to reshape and redefine modal jazz.

Very Early is a rare chance to hear him away from ECM and it is a wonderful record. The repertoire ranges from original themes, notably 'Coming On A Bike', to repertory compositions by John Coltrane (a fine modal 'Satellite'), a favourite Ornette Coleman ('Ramblin'') and Bill Evans's title-track, which as fine a piece of piano-trio jazz as you'll hear in many a long year. Stenson substantially reworks the theme and develops harmonic ideas beyond any Evans explored. His own writing shows little of the interest in Asian musics that had influenced his early career.

**** Reflections

ECM 523160-2 *Stenson; Anders Jormin (b); Jon Christensen (d).* 5/93.

A much earlier ECM date, *Underwear*, remains out of print, which is a pity. *Reflections* is as fine a performance as one would have expected, given the more than telepathic understanding between these players. Stenson and Jormin are temperamentally so close as to function almost like a single creative organism, an effect perhaps most noticeable on the bassist's two compositions, 'NOT' and 'Q', enigmatic titles which reflect his rather oblique musical personality. The title actually refers to Duke Ellington's 'Reflections In D'. The only other non-original is 'My Man's Gone Now', played as if through the prism of Miles and Gil Evans.

Stenson's two main compositions are 'The Enlightener', a shape-shifting meditation erected on a tricky mode which oddly (and not just the title) recalls recent work by Geri Allen, and '12 Tones Old', a clever reworking of age-old harmonic ideas. The final and longest piece 'Mindiatyr' is the closest to how this group might sound in a club context. It's to be hoped that it might be possible to hear such a recording in the not too distant future.

**** War Ophans

ECM 1604 *Stenson; Anders Jormin (b); Jon Christensen (d).* 5/97.

The trio blossoms. Stenson's approach to two more Ornette themes, including the title-track, shows how thoughtfully he approached (for a pianist) challenging repertoire like this. He frequently changes the key and tonal character of a piece completely and in that Jormin is an able collaborator, developing the melody and adding his own counter-themes. Christensen is faultless throughout, one of the most thoroughly musical percussionists of his generation. The opening 'Oleo De Mujer Con Sombrero' by Silvio Rodriguez is a surprise and a delight.

CORE COLLECTION

**** Serenity

ECM 543611 2CD *Stenson; Anders Jormin (b); Jon Christensen (d).* 4/99.

This is a towering achievement and the culmination of Stenson's steady progress as a composer and performer. The integration of free jazz, serialism and atonality, elements of bebop and an almost folkish lyricism yield a double set of great power and almost inexhaustible invention. The pianist and his two associates both contribute originals, and there is a wonderful version of Wayne Shorter's 'Swee' Pea', but it is the reworking of themes by Charles Ives, Alban Berg and Hanns Eisler that impress most thoroughly.

In Berg's 'Die Nachtigall', Stenson takes the basic row and transforms it into a softly lyrical jazz theme that sounds like nothing else in the canon. He does something similar with Eisler's 'Die Pflaumenbaum', though here the music already seems more susceptible to such treatment. It is interesting how French some of the leader's keyboard strategies are; the

sources notwithstanding, his harmony seems to draw on Debussy and Ravel more than anyone and his melodic touch owes little to the Austro-German school.

Jormin and Christensen, both of whom are represented early on by strong compositions – 'T.' and 'North Print', and 'East Print' respectively – adding their idiosyncratic touches to a sequence of pieces that demands patient and attentive listening. *Serenity* is the record that confirms Stenson's growing importance and the growing authority of this remarkable trio.

***** :rarum: Selected Recordings**
ECM 014214-2 *Stenson; Don Cherry, Tomasz Stańko (t); Jan Garbarek, Charles Lloyd (ss, ts); Arild Andersen, Palle Danielsson, Anders Jormin (b); Jon Christensen, Billy Hart, Tony Oxley, Okay Temiz (d).* 71–99.

A fine survey of Stenson's work for the label, including dates with other leaders – Garbarek, Lloyd and notably Stańko ('Morning Heavy Song') – but also touching on some of his own finest performances. Good to have 'Oleo De Mujer Con Sombrero' from *War Orphans* and some material from the deleted *Underwear* but perhaps a touch surprising that there is no room for his wonderful Ornette Coleman interpretations, always such an important part of Stenson's live performances.

Mike Stern (born 1954)

GUITAR

Stern came to prominence as the guitarist in one of Miles Davis's 'comeback' bands of the early '80s. He often seemed loud and unsubtle in that context, but he was probably no worse than any other fusion-directed guitarist of the day. He has since expanded his range through a long series of albums for Atlantic, and for much of the late '80s and early '90s he co-led a popular touring band with Bob Berg.

***** Time In Place**
Atlantic 781840-2 *Stern; Bob Berg, Michael Brecker (ts); Don Grolnick (org); Jim Beard (ky); Jeff Andrews (b); Peter Erskine (d); Don Alias (perc).* 12/87.

***** Jigsaw**
Atlantic 782027-2 *Stern; Bob Berg (ts); Jim Beard (ky); Jeff Andrews (b); Peter Erskine, Dennis Chambers (d); Manolo Badrena (perc).* 2/89.

*****(*) Standards (And Other Songs)**
Atlantic 782419-2 *Stern; Randy Brecker (t); Bob Berg (ts); Gil Goldstein (ky); Jay Anderson, Larry Grenadier (b); Ben Perowsky (d).* 92.

*****(*) Is What It Is**
Atlantic 82571-2 *Stern; Michael Brecker, Bob Malach (ts); Jim Beard (ky); Will Lee, Harvie Swartz (b); Ben Perowsky, Dennis Chambers (d).* 93.

***** Between The Lines**
Atlantic 82835-2 *Stern; Bob Malach (ts); Jim Beard (ky); Lincoln Goines, Jeff Andrews (b); Dave Weckl, Dennis Chambers (d).* 95.

***** Give And Take**
Atlantic 83036-2 *Stern; David Sanborn (as); Michael Brecker (ts); Gil Goldstein (ky); John Patitucci (b); Jack DeJohnette (d); Don Alias (perc).* 97.

Perhaps Stern has still not quite shaken off his association with Miles Davis, where he created a mixed impression as something of a metalhead guitarist in the early '80s. But his own discography is considerable by now, even if he still lags some way behind those inveterate recording artists, John Scofield and Bill Frisell, in first-call credibility. Mostly his Atlantic albums offer a musicianly, muscular style of fusion which is tougher than the smooth-jazz format, but not quite challenging enough to interest a wider constituency.

The problem on several of the earlier albums is the material, which can be little more than a springboard for solos – and these are tidy and intermittently powerful (especially Berg's) on the earlier sets. Chambers and Erskine provide other interest with their interactive parts, but while the band acquired a substantial reputation on the live circuit, it's too much a rational and unsurprising group in the studios. *Time In Place*, *Jigsaw* and the deleted *Odds Or Evens* all followed a similar brief – commendably turned out, but nothing to get really excited about. The following *Standards (And Other Songs)* recast Stern as a 'serious' improviser at the moment when he might have drifted back towards jazz-metal. Instead, with seven standard jazz or show tunes dominating the programme, Stern cooled off the pace without surrendering all his fire-power. His best solos here have a fluency and resonance that might have got him his job with Davis in the first place.

At this point, though, Stern's music begins to sound more assured and whole, to go with the inventiveness of the solos. *Is What It Is* returns to original themes: Jim Beard's production orchestrates the keyboards and rhythm instruments into a thick, almost juicy, studio mix, which Stern's guitar noses through and occasionally screams over. Brecker and Malach lend heavyweight sax support, but the fundamental text is attractively lyrical in tunes such as 'What I Meant To Say'. *Between The Lines*, again produced by Beard, follows a similar path, though there's a sense of diminishing returns, and while the record scores big on texture, this time individual parts don't always impress beyond a surface attraction. It also goes on for too long, at 70 minutes. But 'Wing And A Prayer' at least is among the prettiest tunes Stern has given us.

For *Give And Take*, Stern enlisted Gil Goldstein as producer and another starry cast of performers. This time the music turns back to straightahead, with tunes like 'Giant Steps' and 'Oleo' in the set-list, and the sparse production floats the guitarist to a central point, where he peels off some of his most lucid solos. Brecker has a couple of cameos and Sanborn turns up to blow on a blues; but the record never seems like more than the sum of its parts, for all the virtuous playing.

*****(*) Play**
Atlantic 7567-83219-2 *Stern; Bob Malach (ts); John Scofield, Bill Frisell (g); Jim Beard (ky); Lincoln Goines (b); Ben Perowsky, Dennis Chambers (d).* 12/98–1/99.

Both tougher and more colourful than many of its predecesors, this is a candidate for Stern's very best at Atlantic. Jim Beard returns as producer, and with his shrewd keyboard touches he puts aside any wispiness in Stern's writing besides getting a real presence out of all the players on each track. The first three have the leader swapping punches with Scofield, and four of the next seven have Frisell as conversationalist. Stern has continued to hone his knack for coming up with fetching, hooky tunes, and pieces such as 'All Heart' can double as smart mood-music as well as players' vehicles. Malach gets off some burning solos on 'Tipatina's' and 'Link' which in the context seem like an unlooked-for bonus.

***** Voices**

Atlantic 7567 83483-2 *Stern; Bob Franceschini, Michael Brecker (ts); Jim Beard (ky); John Herington (g); Richard Bona (b, v); Lincoln Goines, Christian Minh Doky (b); Dennis Chambers, Vinnie Colaiuta (d); Arto Tuncboyaciyan(perc, v); Elizabeth Kontomanou, Philip Hamilton (v).* n.d.

Jim Beard gets 'extra, extra special thanks' from the artist, and no wonder: this time it's a Jim Beard album in all but name. The orchestrated voices and keyboards have Beard's signature all over them, even when he's copping licks and textures from Zawinul, Davis or whomever, and Stern is a bit of a bystander on his own set. But that can't altogether hurt: the guitarist needs guiding hands to get the best out of him. Placed in their proper compartment, his hooks and solos make their modest mark, but his (his?) decision to involve singers on a more prominent basis sidelines him a lot of the way. Expert pop-jazz, and in its way, probably as good as it gets.

John Stevens (1940–94)

DRUMS, PERCUSSION, BUGLE

Worked in RAF bands, 1958–64, and then in London's modern scene, becoming interested in completely free playing and co-founding Spontaneous Music Ensemble. Led other bands – Splinters, Dance Orchestra, Away, Freebop, Folkus – in the '70s and '80s and was tireless in his encouragement of young players. A difficult and tempestuous man but one of the most significant figures of his age.

***** Application, Interaction And ...**

Hi 4 Head HF002 *Stevens; Trevor Watts (as); Barry Guy (b).* 72.

*****(*) No Fear**

Hi 4 Head HF001 *As above.* 5/77.

***** Live At The Plough**

Ayler aylCD-007 *Stevens; Mike Osborne (as); Paul Rogers (b).* 3/79.

Stevens was one of the key British jazz musicians of his era, a protean figure who seemed at ease in a bewildering range of musics, from hard-edged free improvisation, through semi-rock and traditional jazz, and even latterly encompassing classical composition. He was also a gifted educator who has left his mark on a whole generation of young British players. He came from an art-school background, and several CD covers bear witness to his skill as a graphic artist. Initially inspired by Phil Seamen, his most obvious stylistic debts are to Kenny Clarke's proto-bop and to Elvin Jones. His Spontaneous Music Ensemble/Orchestra (see separate entry) was one of the most influential improvising groups of its period, while other Stevens groups such as Splinters, the rock-defined Away and the Dance Orchestra were more concerned with pre-structured forms. Stevens, it has to be said, claimed never to see any difference.

The early *Application, Interaction And ...* is an excellent example of the empathy that once flowed between Stevens and Watts, whose strong, emotive alto sound is one of the definitive voices of British free jazz. This unit also worked and recorded as Amalgam, sometimes with Jeff Clyne on bass, so the music drew on a wide and common experience. The two long improvisations and 'encore' were, like *No Fear,* recorded for a '70s Spotlite release. Remastered, they sound fresh and direct, with the music moving steadily from tonal centres towards complete freedom, though never the ecstatic abandon of American fire music.

The same trio is in great form on the May 1977 set. The opening title-track is one of the best recorded moments in British free jazz, a pungent and fiery theme that shouts defiance. 'The Id' is spontaneously improvised and frankly a bit shambolic compared to the written pieces, of which the next best is Watts's delightful 'Speed From The Light'. Repeated listens demonstrate how central Guy (often poorly audible on the early releases) was to this music. His constant reconfiguration of harmony and his brilliant grasp of long pulse define many of these tracks.

The Ayler release is a precious glimpse of one of the many weekly gigs which John ran at a pub named The Plough in Stockwell, South London, in the late '70s. One of the authors spent many a tempestuous evening there and it's a nostalgic pleasure to be reminded of them via this set, which has its poignant side: Stevens is gone, Osborne hasn't played for many years, and even Paul Rogers has left the British scene. This is a typical Plough set of swinging, ragged but hugely compelling freebop. As soon as the drummer kicks into his shuffle-beat on 'Blue Rondo', underscoring Ossie's wailing, the years roll back. Sadly, this is only from a poor amateur tape – Rogers is often close to inaudible, and it needs a sympathetic ear all round. But the music is still memorably intense, the British equivalent perhaps of New York's Loft Jazz of a similar era.

***** A Luta Continua**

Konnex LC 5056 *Stevens; Jon Corbett (t, tb); Alan Tomlinson (tb); Paul Rutherford (tb, euph); Robert Calvert (ts); Trevor Watts (as, ss); Lol Coxhill (ss); Elton Dean (saxello); Dave Cole, Nigel Moyse, Martin Holder, Tim Stone, Mark Hewins (g); John Martyn (g, v); Jeff Young (org); Paul Rogers, Nick Stephens, Ron Herman, Andre Holmes (b); Francis Dixon, Richie Stevens (perc); Pepi Lemer, John Martyn (v).* 5/77–12/81.

***** Mutual Benefit**

Konnex LC 8718 *Stevens; Jon Corbett (t); Robert Calvert (ts, ss); Nigel Moyse, Tim Stone (g); Jeff Young (p, org); Ron Herman, Nick Stephens (b).* 5/77–5/80.

The Dance Orchestra tracks on *A Luta Continua* (the war-cry of the Portuguese anti-fascist movement) embrace groups of very different sizes; like the SME, the Orchestra was always intended to be a flexible ensemble, the only constants being Stevens, trumpeter Jon Corbett and saxophonist Trevor Watts, who was co-leader of the SME. As always, and unusually in free-jazz circles, Stevens put considerable emphasis on vocals, and the October 1979 tracks that make up about half the disc even include parts by folk-rocker John Martyn. There is also an unexpected emphasis on guitar, sometimes used as a conventional harmony instrument (Stevens only rarely called on a piano player, though he liked to feature Jeff Young on organ), sometimes (as on 'Birds') used quite abstractly.

Though *Mutual Benefit* is nominally an Away record, there is considerable overlap between the two, both in style and in personnel (and two tracks from the same May 1977 recording session). Stevens's crisp, almost militaristic accents create passages of dissipated melody over which the other players are relatively free to improvise. The striking thing about his playing is that he was always able to give the sense – or illusion – of a regular metre or pulse, even when it was clear from the most casual listening that what Stevens was playing was anything but regular. It is easy to be seduced by parts of *Mutual Benefit* into thinking that not much is going on, but, like Ornette Coleman's experiments with electric groups, there is a great deal of complexity behind the rather one-dimensional exterior.

***** Touching On**

Konnex KCD 5023 *Stevens; John Calvin (sax); Dave Cole, Allan Holdsworth, Nigel Moyse (g); Jeff Young (p); Ron Mathewson, Nick Stephens (b).* n.d.

****** New Cool**

The Jazz Label TJL 006 *Stevens; Byron Wallen (t); Ed Jones (ts); Gary Crosby (b).* 8/92.

Touching On is a free-ish jazz-rock session that reflects Stevens's talents only inadequately. Perhaps the most interesting tracks are those featuring Allan Holdsworth, one of many artists who receive a dedication on *Mutual Benefit.* This process was far from incidental or *ex post facto* to Stevens. Almost everything he did, whether it was with long-standing colleagues like Trevor Watts or with college students, was specifically designed with individuals in mind.

To the end of his life, Stevens continued to bring forward gifted young players. The SME evolved constantly, as its specific ethos demanded, but so too did Stevens's other groups, and *New Cool*, recorded at the Crawley Jazz Festival, is an excellent example of how seriously he took his mission to lead younger musicians at an accelerated pace through some of the major epiphanies of his own career. Of the four tracks, two are reworkings of Ornette and John Coltrane material, 'Ramblin'' and 'Lonnie's Lament' respectively. The listener doesn't need to be aware of this to enjoy or appreciate this music, which is immensely accessible, but it adds a significant dimension once the connection becomes obvious. As always, Stevens is thinking about old friends as well, in this case the two South Africans, Johnny Mbizo Dyani and Dudu Pukwana, whose own early deaths he was to echo all too soon thereafter.

*****(*) One Time**

Incus 22 *Stevens; Derek Bailey (g); Kent Carter (b).* 92.

To our knowledge, this is the only documented encounter between these three. Carter's low-tuned bass is the unexpected element, but it provides the fulcrum for some quiet and detailed performances that rank among Stevens's best of the time. Bailey's ants-marching scribble creates a line that the others follow in their own way, especially on 'Not A Dry Glass In The House', but again it is Carter who reels things in.

***** Blue**

That's Jazz 2008 *Stevens; Byron Wallen (t, flhn); Paul Rutherford (tb, euph); Iain Ballamy, Ed Jones, Evan Parker (ss, ts); Mike Pyne (p); Phil Lee (g); Jeff Clyne, Ron Mathewson (b).* 92.

Posthumously released, this ensemble set takes a bit of getting used to. The blues hover round it, not least when Paul Rutherford is playing, but there is no obvious structure to hang on to and some of the solo passages are rather attenuated. Curiously, for a musician of Stevens's dynamism, the ideas being developed are also quite monolithic. For years, he had been interested in the notion of peripheral hearing (rather than vision), noting and responding to events that took place at the very edges of conscious attention. That discipline works well with a small ensemble, but there are signs here that the players have too much to absorb, an excess of input restricting the output.

Bob Stewart (born 1945)

TUBA

The man from Sioux Falls has challenged Howard Johnson's crown as tubist of choice. He's made a couple of fine albums of his own as well.

*****(*) First Line**

Winter & Winter 919014 *Stewart; Stanton Davis Jr (t); Steve Turre (tb, shells); Kelvyn Bell (g); Idris Muhammad (d); Arto Tuncboyaciyan (perc).* 87.

***** Goin' Home**

Winter & Winter 919026 *Stewart; Earl Gardner, James Zollar (t); Steve Turre (tb); John Clark (frhn); Jerome Harris (g); Ed Blackwell, Buddy Williams (d); Frank Colon (perc).* 12/88.

Stewart has the ideal combination of sounds for a tuba lead. His rhythm lines are snappingly strong and full-voiced, while his upper register is bright and burnished. Even so, very few specialists on this instrument have ever managed to sound like any other than a slowed-down trombone and it's the speed and clarity of Stewart's articulation which is so impressive. *First Line* is now more than 15 years old, but has recently reappeared as part of W&W's comprehensive reissue of the JMT catalogue. It's good that they're making space for work like this. The three-brass front line was an interesting idea at a time when the saxophone was king once again, but Lester Bowie's Brass Fantasy had paved the way and there's a cheerful confidence to Stewart's group. Turre is as fine as ever (even if he overdoes the conches) and Davis is an exceptional player. Muhammad delivers his usual funky thing. There are a couple of originals, including the brief opening track, which serves as a statement of intent. The best things, however, are a couple of traditional themes, including 'Sometimes I Feel Like A Motherless Child', and a pair of compositions by Arthur Blythe, Stewart's one-time employer and a too rarely heard composer. Bob saves best for last, though, with his own haunting 'Hambone', which should be on every jazz DJ's playlist at least once in a while.

The second album doesn't quite match up to the same standard. The playing is superfine and the choice of repertoire – 'Sweet Georgia Brown', Billy Harper's 'Priestess', a couple of good charts from the leader – is as inventive as before. It just lacks zing and surprise, almost as if the First Line Band had found a formula and was happy to merchandise it one more time. There was to be a further album from Stewart, *Then And Now* in 1996, but it doesn't seem to be available currently and we're both unsurprised and disappointed that the impetus was allowed to drop. These are worth having, though.

Grant Stewart

TENOR SAXOPHONE

One of Criss Cross's posse of gunslinging tenormen.

***** Downtown Sounds**

Criss Cross 1085 *Stewart; Joe Magnarelli (t); Brad Mehldau (p); Peter Washington (b); Kenny Washington (d).* 92.

***** More Urban Tones**

Criss Cross 1124 *Stewart; Chris Byars, Jay Collins (ts); Peter Bernstein (g); Peter Washington (b); Billy Drummond (d).* 10/96.

***** Buen Rollo**

Fresh Sound New Talent FSNT 053 *Stewart; Fabio Miano (p); Chris Higgins (b); Marc Miralta (d).* 00.

With some vintages, you can judge the contents very accurately by looking at the label. That was the feeling when Stewart's debut came out. It's tough-tender hard bop, played with intelligence and resolutely unsurprising. 'Smada', 'Sweet And Lovely' and 'Intimacy Of The Blues' are the most interesting tracks, while the original themes are fairly generic. The second album is, if anything, more callow than the first, and the tenor-heavy format doesn't do Stewart himself any real favours. But a nice enough hard-bop record, played as if Alfred Lion were still alive. The Fresh Sound date exposes Stewart more than he's been before and by and large he comes out on top, but he's not a player you'd pick out of a crowd.

Rex Stewart (1907–67)

CORNET, KAZOO, VOCALS

The good-natured Philadelphian had two stints with Fletcher Henderson, interrupted by doubts about his own ability to fill the shoes of Louis Armstrong, who was his greatest influence. A pioneer of half-valving and of a loquacious, vocalized style, Stewart was a persuasive and engaging soloist.

***** An Introduction To Rex Stewart: His Best Recordings, 1926–1941**

Best of Jazz 4005 *Stewart; Langston Curl, Joe Smith, Russell Smith, Bobby Stark (t); Ed Cuffee, Jimmy Harrison, Claude Jones, Benny Morton (tb); Don Redman (cl, as); Benny Carter, Edward Inge (as); Coleman Hawkins (cl, ts); Prince Robinson (ts); Fletcher Henderson (p); Todd Rhodes (p, cel); Charlie Dixon, Dave Wilborn (bj); Ralph Escudero, Billy Taylor (b); Cuba Austin, Kaiser Marshall (d).* 5/26–11/30.

*****(*) Rex Stewart: 1934–46**

Classics 931 *Stewart; Stafford Simon (t); Lawrence Brown, George Stevenson, Sandy Williams (tb); Tyree Glenn (tb, vib); Earl Bostic, Tab Smith (as); Barney Bigard, Rudy Powell (cl, as); Pete Clarke, Bingie Madison, Al Sears (ts); Cecil Scott (ts, bs); Harry Carney (bs, cl); Mike Colucchio, Johnny Guarnieri, Eddie Heywood, Billy Kyle, Roger 'Ram' Ramirez, Dave Rivera (p); Brick Fleagle, Ulysses Livingston (g); Wellman Braud, Wilson Myers, Junior Raglin, Billy Taylor, Sid Weiss (b); J. C. Heard, Jack Maisel, Bazeley Perry, Keg Purnell, Dave Tough (d).* 12/34–2/46.

*****(*) Rex Stewart And The Ellingtonians**

Original Jazz Classics OJC 1710 *Stewart; Lawrence Brown (tb); Barney Bigard (cl); Billy Kyle (p); Brick Fleagle (g); Wellman Braud, John Levy (b); Cozy Cole, Dave Tough (d).* 7/40–46.

*****(*) Rex Stewart: 1946–1947**

Classics 1016 *Stewart; Lawrence Brown, Sandy Williams (tb); John Harris (cl, as); Al Sears, Vernon Story (ts); Harry Carney (bs); Don Gais, Eddie Heywood, Jimmy Jones, Billy Kyle (p); Ulysses Livingston (g); Simon Brehm, Fred Ermelin, John Levy, Junior Raglin (b); Uffe Baagh, Cozy Cole, Ted Curry, Keg Purnell (d); Honey Johnson, Joya Sherrill (v).* 1/45–12/47.

*****(*) Rex Stewart: 1947–1948**

Classics 1057 *Stewart; Sandy Williams (tb); Hubert Rostaing (cl); John Harris (cl, as); Vernon Story (ts); Don Gais (p, cel); Django Reinhardt, Jean-Jacques Tilché (g); Ladislas Czabanyck, Lucien Simoens (b); Ted Curry (d); Honey Johnson, Louie Williams (v).* 12/47–1/48.

***** Trumpet Jive!**

Prestige PCD 24119 *Stewart; Tyree Glenn (tb, vib); Earl Bostic (as); Cecil Scott (ts, bs); John Dengler (bsx, wbd, kazoo); Wilbert Kirk (hca, perc); Dave Rivera (p); Jerome Darr, Brick Fleagle, Chauncey Westbrook (g); Junior Raglin (b); J. C. Heard, Charles Lampkin (d).* 7/45–3/60.

The poet John Keats once wrote about the way very great artists erect a Great Wall across their respective genres, Shakespeare in the drama, Milton in the poetic epic. For trumpeters of the '20s, Louis Armstrong fell into that category. His achievement was so primal and so pre-eminent that it was extraordinarily difficult to see a way round or over it. Rex Stewart, a self-confessed Armstrong slave (though he also loved Bix), experienced the problem more directly than most when he took over Armstrong's chair in the Fletcher Henderson orchestra.

The early material on Best Of Jazz gives little real impression of what was to come, except that Stewart's solo forays are bright and peppy, with a chattery, button-holing quality that makes them stick out from the ensemble. Other cuts have him with McKinney's Cotton Pickers and the Ellington band, before the cornetist began to make records under his own name in the mid-'30s. There are inevitable overlaps in the compilations which follow, but this is a decent introduction to his work over a relatively long period, and it is more evenly remastered than the Classics discs, which are, as usual, somewhat rough and ready.

In reaction to the inevitable but invidious comparisons, Stewart developed his distinctive 'half-valving' technique. By depressing the trumpet keys to mid-positions, he was able to generate an astonishing and sometimes surreal chromaticism which, though much imitated, has only really resurfaced with the avant-garde of the '60s. As a maverick, Stewart was ideal for the Ellington orchestra of the mid-'30s, though the Black and Blue sessions seem, despite the august company, to step back a generation to the sound of the Hot Sevens. Stewart was never to lose that loyalty. On the Prestige, he can be heard singing in obvious (and authentic) imitation of Pops, but also taking in a good deal of what he had learnt with Henderson.

The early Classics disc brings together all the material Stewart recorded under his own name over a busy decade in which he spent most of his time working for other leaders. The very earliest cuts, with George Stevenson and Rudy Powell, were made for Vocalion just before Christmas 1934. There is no mistaking Stewart, even at this early period and even before he developed the harmonic richness of later years. It's only somewhat later, in the recordings of the mid-'40s, that he manages to combine it with the fullness of tone that was to be his trademark. Recording in turn for Keynote, Capitol, Parlophone and Mercury, Stewart created a body of work that was tantalizingly individual, out of all proportion to its actual amount.

As an original Ellingtonian, Stewart was revered in Europe and in 1947 went back to France and Scandinavia, where he laid down sessions for Blue Star, Cupol and Baronet. These represent the greater bulk of the two later Classics sets, credited to Rex Stewarts Orkester and other groups. The only additional material consists of four cuts done in New York for the short-lived HRS, and anomalously on the volume dated 1946/1947, a single, rejected take of 'Blue Jay' for Capitol recorded with the Big Eight in Los Angeles in January 1945. Half a dozen effective standards included on the same disc were recorded at the Salle Pleyel in Paris and originally released on three 78-r.p.m. discs. On these Rex sounds in buoyant and enthusiastic form, punching out the notes like a stapler. Generally, though, the voice was mellower, and the December 1947 tracks on Classics 1057 are the most relaxed and conversational work yet heard from him on record. Difficult to pick out individual tracks, largely because these sessions work best by accretion, piling on anecdotal detail at a leisurely pace rather than going for the big dramatic finish or large-scale romancing. Hard not to pick out his encounter with Django Reinhardt on 10 December 1947 for a brace of matey cuts. With Hubert Rostaing also on board, 'Confessin'' and 'Night And Day' are minor classics of post-war swing.

After Paris, Rex moved on through Europe, making some important recordings in London; these will presumably form the bulk of the next Classics issue. It was probably from Django Reinhardt, though, that he first heard the Hot Club staple, 'Nagasaki'; the cornetist returned to it in 1960, as part of the *Happy Jazz* session repackaged with Wingy Manone material on Prestige. (*Trumpet Jive!* was the name of a Manone LP.)

Stewart's vocalized style had few imitators, though Clark Terry gave it a more contemporary slant, bridging the gap with the modernists. In later life, Stewart became one of the most persuasive writers on jazz and his *Jazz Masters of the '30s* is required reading for students of the period. His ability to give convincing demonstrations of changes in trumpet-playing became a component of his act, and the later, Rudy van Gelder-recorded session on *Trumpet Jive!* is just such a date, with Stewart sending himself up on his own 'Rasputin' and 'Tell Me'.

Robert Stewart

TENOR SAXOPHONE

Oakland boy who claims a Pharoah Sanders influence, but has thrived despite it.

***** Judgement**

World Stage 1013 *Stewart; Eric Reed (p); Mark Shelby (b); Billy Higgins (d).* 94.

***** Beautiful Love**

Red 123273 *Stewart; Eric Tillman (p); Jeff Littleton (b); Brett Sanders (d).* 10/94.

Stewart was taken up by the Italian-based Red Records and made some interesting statements while under their wing, but has never quite managed to get his head over the parapet as far as media attention is concerned. The better of these is probably *Beautiful Love*, where he goes the standard tenorist's route of 'Body And Soul', a Benny Golson tune ('Five Spot After Dark' on this occasion) and two contrasting takes of 'Speak Low'. The addition of Higgins on *Judgement* is obviously a plus, but even there something seems to be missing. There are a couple of out-of-catalogue Warner albums, where some attempt was made to groom and market Stewart for a bigger audience, but nothing seems to have come of it.

***** Nat The Cat: The Music Of Nat King Cole**

Red 123292 *Stewart; Ed Kelly (p); Mark Shelby, Mark Williams (b); Billy Higgins, Sly Randolph (d).* 00.

Shameless. And bravo. This is an out-and-out attempt to make a saleable middle-market disc by taking one of jazz's best-loved names and playing his work in the style of the great swing saxophonists. Stewart doesn't hesitate to lay on the breathy vibrato, and his Websterish phrasing is very convincing. Listen to him on 'The Sand And The Sea' and 'Mona Lisa' and you might be listening to the soundtrack of some elegant '50s romantic comedy thriller.

Slam Stewart (1914–87)

DOUBLE BASS, VOICE

Studied in Boston and heard violinist Ray Perry singing along to his own lines; Slam adapted that to his bass-playing. Worked in a duo with Slim Gaillard and with Art Tatum and many others. Keeping busy to the end.

****(*) Slam Stewart 1945–1946**

Classics 939 *Stewart; Erroll Garner, Billy Taylor, Johnny Guarnieri (p); Red Norvo (vib); Bill D'Arango, Mike Bryan, Chuck Wayne, John Collins (g); Harold 'Doc' West, Morey Feld (d).* 1/45–4/46.

Stewart was already a star when he appeared in the movie, *Stormy Weather*, in 1943. During the '30s he had been a stalwart of the New York scene, playing with Art Tatum and forming an evergreen partnership (love it, hate it; it sold records) with Slim Gaillard which exploited the less serious side of Stewart's virtuosic self-harmonizing on bass and vocals. However corny he now seems, few modern bass-players have taken up the technical challenge Stewart posed (though Major Holley had a stab), and the purely musical aspects of his work are of abiding value. The Classics disc shuffles together five early sessions under his own name. Erroll Garner was working for Slam at The Three Deuces when they made the January 1945 date which has its apotheosis in the absurd 'Dark-Eyesky'. There are a dozen tracks with a quintet including Red Norvo, and Stewart is relatively back-seat on these for at least some of the time. For the most part, these sessions impart a harmless kind of chamber jazz which is frankly boring after a few tracks. The very oddity of Stewart's technique is initially off-putting, but on repeated listening its complexities begin to make an impact. It's perhaps a shame that Stewart wasn't able – or didn't choose – to record with more of the younger modern bassists. If Mingus and Pettiford are now thought to have set the instrument free, much of what they did was already implicit in Stewart's work of the '30s.

Sonny Stitt (1924–82)

ALTO, TENOR AND BARITONE SAXOPHONES, VOCAL

A quick learner of the bebop vernacular, it is open to dispute as to how much Stitt absorbed from Charlie Parker – they met early on – and how much he developed for himself. He played tenor in a band he co-led with Gene Ammons from 1950, and thereafter drifted between that and the alto, very occasionally picking up the baritone. A definitive example of the 'road musician', always available to play with local rhythm sections or jam with Jazz At The Philharmonic, Stitt made scores of records and, arguably, diluted his reputation with an approach that was simultaneously dedicated and careless.

***** Sonny Stitt / Bud Powell / J. J. Johnson**

Original Jazz Classics OJC 009 *Stitt; J. J. Johnson (tb); Bud Powell, John Lewis (p); Curley Russell, Nelson Boyd (b); Max Roach (d).* 10/49–1/50.

****(*) Prestige First Sessions Vol. 2**

Prestige 24115 *Stitt; Alfred 'Chippie' Outcalt, Matthew Gee (tb); Gene Ammons (bs); Kenny Drew, Duke Jordan, Junior Mance, Clarence 'Sleepy' Anderson (p); Tommy Potter, Earl May, Gene Wright (b); Art Blakey, Teddy Stewart, Wesley Landers, Jo Jones (d); Larry Townsend (v).* 2/50–8/51.

****(*) Sonny Stitt 1950–1951**

Classics 1291 *Similar to above.* 2/50–2/51.

***** Kaleidoscope**

Original Jazz Classics OJC 060 *Stitt; Bill Massey, Joe Newman (t); Kenny Drew, Charles Bateman, Junior Mance, John Houston (p); Tommy Potter, Gene Wright, Ernie Shepard (b); Art Blakey, Teddy Stewart, Shadow Wilson (d); Humberto Morales (perc).* 2/50–2/52.

***** Sax O'Bebop**

Proper PROPERBOX 65 4CD *As various discs above.* 46–52.

Considering the size of his discography – there are at least 100 albums under Stitt's own name – the saxophonist still has relatively little left in the catalogue, although the desultory nature of many of his records suggests that perhaps it is better this way. Stitt took every opportunity to record, often with undistinguished pick-up groups, and while his impassive professionalism meant that he seldom sounded less than strong, his records need careful sifting to find him genuinely at his best. Originally, he was acclaimed as a rival to Charlie Parker, and the derivation of his style, which may have been arrived at quite independently of Bird, is a famously moot point. Whatever the case, by the time of the 1949 sessions on OJC 009, he was in complete command of the bop vocabulary and playing with quite as much skill as any man in the milieu. This disc finds him exclusively on tenor, which he plays with a rather stony tone but no lack of energy. Powell contributes some superb playing on such up-tempo pieces as 'All God's Children Got Rhythm', and the 1950 group with Johnson and Lewis, though less obviously hot, finds Stitt at his best on the urgent improvisation on 'Afternoon In Paris'. Both the Prestige collection and *Kaleidoscope* bring together bits and pieces from the early days of the label and, though some of the tracks sound foreshortened, Stitt dominates throughout both discs. He occasionally played baritone, too, and there's a surprisingly full-blooded ballad treatment of 'P.S. I Love You' on *Kaleidoscope* which suggests that his use of the bigger horn was by no means offhand. The boxy sound of the originals carries over into all the CD issues. Classics 1291 is pretty much a straight duplication of the Prestige material. Proper's collection in their bargain four-disc series offers much of it, too, as well as sundry bebop dates where Stitt lined up alongside some of the stars of the day. It's an indiscriminate collection but will appeal to bargain-hunters.

*****(*) New York Jazz**

Verve 517050-2 *Stitt; Jimmy Jones (p); Ray Brown (b); Jo Jones (d).* 9/56.

Still young and at the peak of his powers – 'lean, plunging Sonny Stitt', Nat Hentoff's note calls him – this is the Stitt that's most worth remembering and listening to again. He is helter-skelter on 'I Know That You Know', casts lyrical alto spinners on 'If I Had You' and cruises through 'Alone Together' in lightly bruised tenor mode. It's lushly melodic, yet the different astringencies he gets out of alto and tenor put an acidly personal edge on the improvising. Here and there one still gets the notion that he's just laughing at both us and the material, but this is surely the real Stitt.

***** Jazz Masters 50**

Verve 527651-2 *Stitt; Lee Katzman, Jack Sheldon, Dizzy Gillespie (t); Frank Rosolino (tb); Sonny Rollins (ts); Amos Trice, John Lewis, Jimmy Jones, Lou Levy, Oscar Peterson, Bobby Timmons, Jimmy Rowles (p); Skeeter Best, Paul Weeden, Herb Ellis (g); Al Pollan (tba); George Morrow, Percy Heath, Ray Brown, Paul Chambers, Leroy Vinnegar, Edgar Willis, Buddy Clark, Tommy Bryant (b); Lennie McBrowne, Charli Persip, Billy James, Stan Levey, Ed Thigpen, Kenny Dennis, Lawrence Marable (d); strings.* 1/56–2/62.

Verve's compilation series reached number 50 with this useful Stitt collection, picking a dozen tracks, no fewer than eight of which come from out-of-print Stitt albums. But all the best moments here – save perhaps the lovely ballad-with-strings 'Time After Time' from 1961 – are from familiar records: *Sonny Side Up* with Gillespie and Rollins and *Sits In With The Oscar Peterson Trio.* Stitt's own-name dates weren't any more commanding then than his later sets for Prestige. Of course there's still much exemplary alto and tenor, and the remastering gets the most out of Sonny's impeccable tone and delivery.

*****(*) Sonny Stitt Sits In With The Oscar Peterson Trio**

Verve 849396-2 *Stitt; Oscar Peterson (p); Herb Ellis (g); Ray Brown (b); Ed Thigpen, Stan Levey (d).* 10/57–5/58.

A memorable meeting. Stitt plays alto and tenor here, and sounds unusually at ease with a pianist who might have brought out his most sparring side. Instead, on the likes of 'Moten Swing' and 'Blues For Pres', they intermingle their respective many-noted approaches as plausibly as if this were a regular band (in fact, they never recorded together again). The CD includes three tracks from a session a year earlier, previously unreleased, with a storming 'I Know That You Know' emerging as the highlight. Excellent CD remastering.

***** Sonny Stitt And The Top Brass**

Atlantic 80802-2 *Stitt; Reunald Jones, Blue Mitchell, Dick Vance (t); Jimmy Cleveland, Matthew Gee (tb); Willie Ruff (frhn); Perri Lee (org); Duke Jordan (p); Joe Benjamin (b); Philly Joe Jones, Frank Brown (d).* 7/62.

A slight departure from what would become Stitt's '60s routine, this set of charts by Tadd Dameron and Jimmy Mundy has him fronting a brass-heavy band. Still no masterpiece, but it's pleasing to hear Stitt being asked to make his way through 'On A Misty Night' rather than his usual book of standards and blues; and Blue Mitchell also has a few moments to himself.

***** Stitt Plays Bird**

Atlantic 8122-73716-2 *Stitt; John Lewis (p); Jim Hall (g); Richard Davis (b); Connie Kay (d).* 1/63.

This had the makings of a classic: nobody knew Bird's music better than Stitt, and with an outstanding group behind him there might have been some defining thesis on this material in the offing. Yet Sonny doesn't really nail it, as if he can't be bothered a lot of the way. The articulation is slurred here and there and the contrast between his workaday intensities and the customary precision of Lewis (as well as Hall's ingenuities) is not a fruitful one. Still, even when he's coasting Stitt has rewards to offer – he's fine on 'My Little Suede Shoes', especially – and the band give him warm support. The booklet for this new edition includes some little-seen and excellent photos of Stitt.

***** Salt And Pepper**

Impulse! 12102 *Stitt; Paul Gonsalves (ts); Hank Jones (p); Milt Hinton, Al Lucas (b); Osie Johnson (d).* 6–9/63.

This couples the original *Salt And Pepper* together with Stitt's other Impulse! album, *Now!*. Neither was exactly a masterpiece but they have their moments. The tracks with Gonsalves find the saxophonists running themselves ragged on the blues, and when they finally get to a really rather gorgeous 'Star Dust' it makes the rest of the date seem like a waste. *Now!* is at its best on simple little pieces like 'Estralita', and Jones adds his usually seigneurial presence.

****(*) Sonny's Blues**

Jazz House JHAS 603 *Stitt; Dick Morrissey (ts); Terry Shannon, Harry South (p); Ernest Ranglin (g); Phil Bates, Rick Laird (b); Benny Goodman, Bill Eyden (d).* 5/64.

Sonny at work in London, with variations on the Ronnie Scott house band – Dick Morrissey sits in on a long blues and Ernest Ranglin on another. Sonny sings a tribute to his 'adopted mother' before going into 'My Mother's Eyes'. It's all a bit ragtag, and the sound is not much better than bootleg level, but it's a nice souvenir for those who may have sat in one of Sonny's audiences back then.

****(*) Sonny Stitt Meets Brother Jack**

Original Jazz Classics OJC 703 *Stitt; Jack McDuff (org); Eddie Diehl (g); Art Taylor (d); Ray Barretto (perc).* 2/62.

***** Soul Classics**

Original Jazz Classics OJC 6003 *Stitt; Virgil Jones (t); Jack McDuff, Don Patterson, Gene Ludwig, Leon Spencer (org); Hank Jones (p); Pat Martino, Grant Green, Billy Butler, Melvin Sparks, Eddie Diehl (g); Leonard Gaskin, George Duvivier (b); Idris Muhammad, Art Taylor, Billy James, Randy Gillespie (d).* 2/62–2/72.

***** Soul People**

Prestige 24127-2 *Stitt; Booker Ervin (ts); Grant Green, Vinnie Corrao (g); Don Patterson (org); Billy James (d).* 8/64–9/69.

***** Night Letter**

Prestige 24165-2 *Stitt; Jack McDuff, Gene Ludwig (org); Pat Martino (g); Leonard Gaskin (b); Herbie Lovelle, Randy Gillespie (d).* 9/63–10/69.

**** Made For Each Other**

Delmark DD-426 *Stitt; Don Patterson (org); Billy James (d).* 7/68.

****(*) Legends Of Acid Jazz**

Prestige 24169-2 *Stitt; Virgil Jones (t); Don Patterson, Leon Spencer (org); Melvin Sparks (g); Idris Muhammad (d).* 1/71.

***** Legends Of Acid Jazz Vol. 2**

Prestige 24236 *Stitt; Charles McPherson (as); Don Patterson (org); Pat Martino (g); Bill James (d).* 9/68.

Whatever the state of jazz's declining fortunes in the '60s, Stitt worked and recorded incessantly, if often carelessly. A lot of run-of-the-mill albums for Roulette and Cadet are currently unavailable; these Prestige dates scarcely break the mould. With McDuff in tow, Stitt strolls unblinkingly through a programme of rootless blues. *Soul People* has some natty sparring with Booker Ervin, never one to shirk some cheerful sax fisticuffs and, though the ballad medley is a bit dragging, 'Flying Home' isn't. A 1969 'Tune Up' and one track with Patterson in the chair fills up the disc. *Soul Classics* collects tracks from eight sessions over a decade and is a truthful picture of Stitt's ups and downs. Four tracks feature the saxophonist with his varitone horn, a gimmick which didn't last; but more encouraging is the tough 'Night Crawler' with Patterson and a dark-blue 'Goin' Down Slow' with a surprise guest-slot by Hank Jones.

Made For Each Other is a desperately routine set of tracks that Stitt plays his varitone sax on throughout: missable. *Night Letter* and the two *Legends Of Acid Jazz* discs, though they sound like compilations, actually put together six complete original albums. The first couples a spunky 1963 date with Jack McDuff, *Soul Shack*, with the 1969 *Night Letter*, where Martino's guitar sneaks in some of the best licks. The second fits together *Turn It On!* with the modishly titled *Black Vibrations*, each by more or less the same group (Patterson comes in for two titles). *Acid Jazz Vol. 2* pairs a Stitt date with Patterson, *Soul Electricity!*, and a Patterson date with Stitt, *Funk You*, which also brings in Charles McPherson. They were recorded only a day apart! Stitt is still using the varitone on 'his' session, but the other one has some nicely struck sparks. Not much really changes across the seven years the discs span, although the later group is the more self-consciously funky and garners a lower mark as a result. Stitt himself never had to pretend about soul.

***** The Boss Men**

Prestige 24253 *Stitt; Don Patterson (org); Billy James (d).* 9–12/65.

****(*) Brothers-4**

Prestige 24261 *Stitt; Don Patterson (org); Grant Green (g); Billy James (d).* 9/69.

More sweepings from Stitt's endless round of '60s sessions, all with Patterson. *The Boss Men* includes the LP of that name alongside *Night Crawler*. The later date is a marathon session, originally split across three albums. The varitone sax comes in again on the second one and is missable, but the earlier set is par for its course.

****(*) Back To My Own Home Town**

Black & Blue 59574-2 *Stitt; Gerald Price (p); Don Mosley (b); Bobby Durham (d).* 11/79.

***** The Good Life**

Evidence ECD 22088-2 *Stitt; Hank Jones (p); George Duvivier (b); Grady Tate (d, v).* 11/80.

Stitt died in 1982 from cancer, but he betrayed only a few signs of failing powers up to the end. Although he went right on recording through the '70s, there's not that much around just now. The pick-up date in France (Black & Blue) is as rote as one might imagine. *The Good Life* was recorded in Japan and works out better. Stitt could hardly have felt more comfortable than with this rhythm section; it's a pity, given his vast knowledge of standards, that they couldn't have chosen a more interesting set of tunes to play on. 'Angel Eyes' is a splendid tenor performance and with the title-ballad it makes up a pleasing valediction.

Kathy Stobart (born 1925)

TENOR, BARITONE AND SOPRANO SAXOPHONES

First lady of British saxophone-players; just don't tell Barbara Thompson.

***** Saxploitation**

Spotlite Jazz SPJ 403 *Stobart; Joe Temperley (ts, bs); Mike Pyne (p); Dave Olney (b); Tony Mann (d).* 3/76.

In recent times more closely associated with Humphrey Lyttelton's band, Kathy recorded this cheerfully swinging set back in the day. Her multi-instrumentalism has rarely been commented upon, but it's very impressive, especially when she hefts the bulky baritone. It's good, solid English fare, or Scots/English if you take account of Joe Temperley's strong contribution and, at a time when only the British avant-garde were garnering much attention, a sign that mainstream was thriving alongside.

Markus Stockhausen (born 1957)

TRUMPET, FLUGELHORN, SYNTHESIZER

Son of Karlheinz, he has pursued a career as a fusionesque trumpeter and sound-scaper, creating a kind of brainy mood-music with an improvisational edge.

****(*) Cosi Lontano ... Quasi Dentro**

ECM 837111-2 *Stockhausen; Fabrizio Ottaviucci (p); Gary Peacock (b); Zoro Babel (d).* 3/88.

***** Aparis**

ECM 841774-2 *Stockhausen; Simon Stockhausen (sax, syn); Jo Thones (d, electric d).* 8/89.

*****(*) Despite The Fire-Fighters' Efforts ...**

ECM 517717-2 *As above.* 7/92.

***** Sol Mestizo**

ACT 9222 *Stockhausen; Philip Catherine (g); Chano Dominguez (p); Simon Stockhausen (ky, ss); Jochen Schmidt (b); Enrique Diaz (b, v); Thomas Alkier (d); Filipe Mandingo (perc); Juanita Lascarro, Alexandra Naumann, Pia Miranda (v).* 2/95.

Markus Stockhausen came to prominence as Michael, the main soloist in his father's opera, *Donnerstag*, the first part of the colossal *Licht* cycle, which bids fair to become the twenty-first century's *Ring*. As an improvising performer he has the same purity of tone all through the range but lacks entirely the dramatic force he draws from his father's global conception on 'Michaels Reise Um Die Erde'. Though the material is quite impressive, the conventional quartet set-up on *Cosi Lontano* ... suits his approach not one bit. His solos are vague and unanchored and, without Peacock's patient figuring, it would all fall apart.

In recent years, Stockhausen has continued to experiment with his own brand of theatricality and world music. *Sol Mestizo* is a set of pieces written by the Chilean, Enrique Diaz. On the face of it a strange project for Stockhausen, it actually works very well, and his trumpet-playing (minus the quarter-tone effects of the earlier record) is quite straightforward and often very upbeat, reminiscent of some early bebopper experimenting with free rhythms.

Markus and half-brother Simon have also constituted two-thirds of a group called Aparis. The eponymous record and the very impressive *Despite The Fire-Fighters' Efforts* ... are more straightforwardly impressionistic and altogether more successful. Neo-funk tracks like 'High Ride' on the former sit rather uneasily, but Thones's acoustic and electric drums and Simon's intelligent sequencing bring a propulsive energy to even the quieter, watercoloured pieces. No clear indication why they've used a shot of Windsor Castle ablaze on the cover of the second group record, and there's a persistent avoidance of the dramatic climaxes individual pieces seem to promise, as if every piece, not just the album title, ends with a string of ellipses. Increasingly impressive, though it's hard to shake off the feeling that this is just relaxation from working in the old man's shop.

Stockholm Jazz Orchestra

GROUP

Founded in 1983 to showcase some of the best straightahead musicians in Sweden's capital, under the general leadership of Fredrik Norén, the SJO frequently invite guest conductors and soloists to work with them.

***** Dreams**

Dragon DRCD 169 *Jan Kohlin, Fredrik Norén, Lars Lindgren, Stig Persson, Gustavo Bergalli (t, flhn); Bob Brookmeyer (vtb); Mikael Råberg, Bertil Strandberg, Mats Hermansson (tb); Sven Larsson (btb); Dave Castle (ss, as, cl); Håkan Bröstrom (ss, as, f); Ulf Andersson, Johan Alenius (ss, ts, cl); Hans Arktoft (bs, bcl); Anders Widmark (ky); Jan Adefeldt (b); Johan Dielemans (d).* 8/88.

***** Jigsaw**

Dragon DRCD 213 *As above, except Peter Asplund (t, flhn), Anders Wiborg (tb), Johan Hörlén (ss, as, cl, f), Jan Levander (ts, cl, f), Joakim Milder (ts), Jim McNeely (p), Martin Löfgren (d) replace Lindgren, Brookmeyer, Larsson, Bröstrom, Alenius, Widmark and Dielemans.* 3/91.

***** Live At Jazz Club Fasching**

Dragon DRCD 269 *As above, except add Bob Mintzer, Per Johansson (ts), Neta Norén (bs), Göran Strandberg (p), Jukkis Uotila (d), Rafael Sida (perc); omit Milder, McNeely, Löfgren.* 4/94.

***** Sound Bites**

Dragon DRCD 311 *As above, except add Patrik Skogh (t, flhn), Dick Oatts (as), Hector Bingert, Marcus Lindgren (ts), Alberto Pinton (bs, bcl), Jim McNeely (p); omit Mintzer, Johansson, Norén, Strandberg, Sida, Levander, Kohlin, Persson, Andersson, Arktoft.* 9/95.

Originally a rehearsal band, and now an occasional enterprise under a nominal leadership from Fredrik Norén, the SJO recorded the first two CDs to celebrate working with guest arrangers: *Dreams* with Bob Brookmeyer and *Jigsaw* with Jim McNeely. While the two sessions are unalike in tone and delivery, each is rewarding. Brookmeyer, who spends much time as a resident composer with West German Radio, knows European orchestras, and his themes make the most of the prowess of the band: difficult scoring in 'Missing Monk' and 'Cats' is dispatched without much effort by the group, and while the soloists take a lesser role they're perfectly in tune with Brookmeyer's quirkily structured pieces. Some of them resemble no more than eccentrically linked episodes, but there are many striking passages – the first three tracks are an informal suite, with 'Lies' a particularly intriguing patchwork – which deserve a close listen.

Jigsaw is a more conventional record. One gets the feeling that McNeely is a more meticulous and thoroughgoing composer than Brookmeyer, but a less inspirational one. The modern orchestral bop of 'Off The Cuff', for instance, or the concerto for Milder in 'The Decision' are convincing and tersely wound set-pieces, but the freewheeling demeanour of the earlier record is missed. Still, it may suit some tastes better. *Sound Bites* is a second turn for McNeely, and with guest soloist Oatts the orchestra sounds in vigorous spirits at a Stockholm concert. Although McNeely brought four of his own themes to the concert – the opening 'Pete's Feet' is probably the best – the most interesting scores are 'Yesterdays', scored with accumulating power around Oatts's soprano, and 'In A Sentimental Mood', something of a concerto for Hörlén. Oatts aside, there are few soloists: this is one band where the ensemble itself is what counts.

The live album has Bob Mintzer as guest conductor-soloist. The stays are a bit looser and there's a frolicsome feel to some of the music, although Mintzer's scores are rather tough and sometimes unyielding; so it winds up as much like their studio work. Star soloist: Peter Asplund on 'Elvin's Mambo'.

Ole Stolle (born 1940)

TRUMPET, FLUGELHORN, VOCAL

Danish disciple of Louis Armstrong, who spent nearly 20 years with Papa Bue's Vikings and now fronts his own small swing groups.

*** It Ain't Necessarily So

Music Mecca 2054-2 *Stolle; Jørgen Svare (cl); Søren Kristiansen (p); Ole Skipper Mosgaard (b); Mikkel Find (d).* 11/97.

*** Trioen

Music Mecca 2078-2 *Stolle; Jacob Fischer (g); Jesper Lundgaard (b).* 4/98.

Stolle's basic take on Louis Armstrong is embellished by a liking for Roy Eldridge and Sweets Edison, plus a little of himself, and small-band swing's immortality is affirmed by these likeable sessions. Svare is a fellow Papa Bue veteran but the rhythm section is a generation younger, and Kristiansen especially settles for no clichés. When Stolle lands himself in hot water on a few high notes it tends to add to the fun, though a few less obvious tunes could have helped.

Ole takes a holiday from the quintet for the trio date. Fischer and Lundgaard are smooth and impeccable, and Stolle is rowdy, which usefully roughs up the session. His singing is less than fabulous, though.

Goran Strandberg (born 1949)

PIANO

A Stockholm native, Strandberg has been busy on his local scene since the early '70s, although he has recorded as a leader only seldom.

*** Gentle Stream

Dragon DRCD 322 *Strandberg; Hans Backenroth (b); Bengt Stark (d); Rafael Sida (perc).* 5/98.

Strandberg appeared in our early editions with some vinyl entries but this characteristically self-effacing player has had a quiet time of it since (at least as a leader) and it's a pleasure to welcome this more recent session. Our verdict on the earlier records – 'stripped-down hard bop' – still holds good to some extent, but on this mix of standards and originals he takes a generally more expansive course. Encouraged perhaps by Stark, who's a more knockabout drummer than Rune Carlsson was, the pianist takes a looser, less stitched-up progress through 'Danny's Return', which borrows a lick from 'Londonderry Air', and finds a humorous side to 'King Porter Stomp'. Strandberg may have softened some of the more pointed aspects of his playing, and not everything here really compels the attention, but it's a satisfying set.

Billy Strayhorn (1915–67)

PIANO, COMPOSER, ARRANGER

He began writing for Duke Ellington in 1939, first as lyricist, then as collaborator. He occasionally played piano while Duke directed, and made some own-name band recordings in the '50s and '60s, but the importance of 'Swee' Pea' was as a composer and right-hand man to Ellington.

***(*) Great Times!

Original Jazz Classics OJC 108 *Strayhorn; Duke Ellington (p); Wendell Marshall, Lloyd Trottman (b); Oscar Pettiford (b, clo); Jo Jones (d).* 9–11/50.

They were like two aspects of a single complex self. Where Duke Ellington was immodest, priapic and thumpingly egocentric, his longtime writing and arranging partner, Billy Strayhorn, was shy, gay and self-effacing. It's now very difficult, given the closeness of their relationship and their inevitable tendency to draw on aspects of the other's style and method, to separate which elements of an 'Ellington–Strayhorn' composition belong to each; but there is no doubt that Swee' Pea, as Ellington called him, made an immense impact on his boss's music. Even if he had done no more than write 'Lush Life' and 'Take The "A" Train', Strayhorn would still have been guaranteed a place in jazz history. It's about time that the excellent small-group session, *Cue For Saxophone*, was back on CD.

Strayhorn was not an outstanding pianist by himself and he wasn't, of course, an instinctive performer. In fairness, the 1950 *Great Times!* may be credited to Strayhorn's account. In performance terms he's overshadowed by his boss, playing much more 'correctly' and inside the key than the Duke found comfortable. It's easier to separate them on the inevitable '"A" Train' and 'Oscalypso', when Strayhorn switches to celeste.

Co Streiff

SOPRANO AND ALTO SAXOPHONES, PERCUSSION

Gifted Swiss saxophonist and composer, more interested in mood and texture than in virtuosic soloing.

****(*) Twin Lines**
Intakt 073 *Streiff; Irène Schweizer (p).* 7/99–8/00.

***** Qattara**
Intakt 078 *Streiff; Christoph Gantert (t, perc); Tom Varner (frhn); Tommy Meier (ts, bcl, pipe); Ben Jeger (p, ky, acc); Christian Weber (b); Fredi Flukiger (d).* 7/02.

The biggest and most unexpected influence on Streiff's sextet writing is the Art Ensemble Of Chicago. On *Qattara*, she includes themes by Roscoe Mitchell ('Nonaah') and Joseph Jarman ('Blues For Zen'), as well as fragments by Sun Ra and the like-minded Andrew Cyrille, but the bulk of the writing is her own and fellow saxophonist Tommy Meier's.

The album draws something from an eye-opening (and nearly fatal) trip through the Egyptian and Libyan deserts, but one suspects that more straightforward music influences are paramount. There is a pervasive African feel, not just in the use of bass drones, balafon and Meier's shawm-like bagpipe chanter, but also in Streiff's preference for short, almost folksy thematic statements, what Roscoe Mitchell refers to as vamps.

Meier is the more obviously jazz-based player, perhaps because he is playing tenor. Streiff has a wilder and more erratic tone, which suits material like 'Darb El-Mahashas' perfectly. The horns play intriguing unison lines on 'Message From Thule' and the title-track. Keyboard man Ben Jeger favours the old-fashioned Farfisa, wah-wah clavinet and accordion, while bassist Christian Weber is happy to set aside conventional lines for a more atmospheric approach. The Sextet is a highly thoughtful working unit and *Qattara* is a powerful statement of Streiff's collaborative approach. Tom Varner is listed as 'musical assistant' and contributes horn to two tracks.

The duo album is either attractively low-key or disappointingly undramatic, depending on your point of view, and, critically, your expectation of fellow-Swiss Irène Schweizer, who has rarely sounded more constrained. Here she seems happy to play straight accompaniment to Streiff's attractively uncomplicated melodies. The effect is pleasant but unmemorable. Dry as the landscape is, *Qattara* seems a much more refreshing place to start.

Marcus Strickland

TENOR AND SOPRANO SAXOPHONES

Young New York saxophonist, part of a burgeoning wave of players in what may formulate itself as a fresh modern mainstream.

***** At Last**
Fresh Sound FSNT 101 *Strickland; Robert Glasper (p); Brandon Owens (b); E. J. Strickland (d).* 8–12/00.

***** Brotherhood**
Fresh Sound FSNT 152 *As above, except add Jeremy Pelt (t).* 4/02.

Strickland's foggy, almost diffident sound isn't the sort of playing set to buttonhole anybody's attention, but there are plenty of details and wrinkles which suggest that he'll have much more to say than he does on the comparatively uneventful quartet date. Significant, perhaps, that the only covers he chooses to play are from Wayne Shorter and Joe Henderson, both quizzical musicians with a kinship to his own manner. His brother E. J. plays tight, propulsive drums, but the most interesting player here may turn out to be Glasper, whose 'Three For Her' and 'Joy Song' are absorbing pieces.

Album two is basically by the same group, although Pelt arrives for two tracks. He livens up Strickland to the extent that one wishes the whole album might have been a quintet set, although that clearly isn't what the leader's after. It's music where a cerebral intensity tries to sit comfortably with more visceral playing, and credit to Strickland for giving a tough task a good shot.

String Trio Of New York

GROUP

Led by bassist Lindberg, the Trio represents a dogged refusal to accept the casual consensus that a jazz group necessarily includes a horn, a piano and a set of drums. The personnel has changed – and changed very successfully – but the group's future was threatened when Lindberg suffered serious wrist damage, now successfully overcome.

***** First String**
Black Saint 120031 *Billy Bang (vn); James Emery (g); John Lindberg (b).* 79.

***** Area Code 212**
Black Saint 12048 *As above.* 81.

***** Common Goal**
Black Saint 120058 *Billy Bang (vn, yokobue, f); James Emery (g, soprano g, mand): John Lindberg (b).* 11/81.

*****(*) Rebirth Of A Feeling**
Black Saint 120068 *As above.* 11/83.

In the interests of neatness it would be convenient to shorthand these albums: 'with Billy Bang – good; without – not'. Despite a general critical consensus to that effect, the reality isn't so simple. Though Bang's ducks-and-drakes approach to tonality was a vital component of the STNY's first four albums, Burnham is a perfectly adequate replacement, and it's clear that much of the impetus of the band comes from the bassist, who is also an impressive writer.

The first two albums are fresh, bright and still eminently listenable, but there is a slight feeling that the members are pulling in too many directions at once. It took some time for STNY to establish a collective identity. But all credit to Black Saint for deciding to record an outfit as out of kilter with the mainstream as this one.

Rebirth Of A Feeling claims the attention more than any of the previous or later discs. Centred round Bang's 'Penguins An' Other Strange Birds' (a gloriously wacky piece) and the long, rather more brooding 'Utility Grey', which was written by Lindberg, it's a superb record which can be recommended warmly to anyone who hasn't yet encountered the STNY.

Whatever the merits of the post-Bang STNY (and they are considerable), there's no doubt that their best albums are those involving him.

★★★(★) Intermobility

Arabesque AJ018 *As above, except replace Bang with Regina Carter (vn). 7/92.*

★★★(★) Octagon

Black Saint 120131 *As above.* 11/92.

There was a further change of personnel after 1990, with Regina Carter coming in for Burnham. She's not a particularly imaginative player (certainly not when placed against someone like Britain's Sylvia Hallett), but *Intermobility* restored a little of the buzz and fire, a few of the raw edges; and *Octagon* is an ambitious record nevertheless, covering a startling range of contemporary compositions (Marty Ehrlich, Muhal Richard Abrams, Mark Helias, Leo Smith and Bobby Previte are all credited), and Carter's own 'Forever February' is one of the loveliest things they've done, which bodes well for future projects.

★★★(★) Blues ...?

Black Saint 120148-2 *As above.* 10/93.

Not clear what the question mark is about, except that the Trio seems to be interrogating the blues rather than merely rehashing them. 'Cobalt Blue', 'Red Shift' and 'Speedball' represent a toughening of the band's sound, while an intriguing montage of Charlie Parker tunes suggests how readily this personnel adapts to bebop as well. The addition of 'Freddy Freeloader', Miles's relaxed blowing theme from *Kind Of Blue*, adds a further dimension to a thoroughly unexpected and highly attractive record.

★★★★ Faze Phour

Black Saint 120168 *As above, except omit Carter; add Diane Monroe (vn). 11/97.*

Another change of personnel, but – more important – a token of successful recovery from Lindberg's career-threatening arm injury. The idea of *Phaze Four* is a retrospective of what is now two decades of activity, with re-recordings of three earlier pieces alongside new material. As ever, the group also covers some repertory material, on this occasion Monk's 'Straight, No Chaser' (highly successful), Duke's 'In A Sentimental Mood' (oddly not), and Mingus's rise-and-fall tone-poem, 'Pithecanthropus Erectus' (which succeeds on pure cheek). Monroe fits very comfortably into a now settled partnership. By no means a player of Bang's dramatic presence, she is none the less capable of fireworks, on the opening 'Frozen Ropes' and her own 'Groovin' Roots'. As ever, the sound is very strong, nicely balanced and richly textured.

Jan Strinnholm (born 1936)

PIANO

Born in Stockholm, he started playing boogie piano in school, then was inspired by Coltrane and Bill Evans. He has worked modestly in the leading mainstream-modern circles of Swedish jazz since.

★★★ Strinnholm – 95

Sittel SITCD 9224 *Strinnholm (p solo). 3/95.*

A rare CD for the Swedish veteran. Most of these are originals, sprightly or ruminative as the fancy takes him, and the long, thoughtful but quite pointed improvisation, 'Step By Step', which starts the record, is characteristic of his style, romantic but with a lean streak. He's managed to filter bebop, Coltrane, Evans and Jarrett (all honoured in his sleeve-note) into a manner which isn't so much distinctively individual as gracious in the way it displays his experience. Well done.

Frank Strozier (born 1937)

ALTO SAXOPHONE

Born in Memphis, and subsequently moved to Chicago, New York and LA, never quite making it as a big name on the scene. He even briefly switched to piano in the hope of a breakthrough. He has a fine blues tone and considerable musical intelligence.

★★★ Fantastic Frank Strozier

Koch 8550 *Strozier; Booker Little (t); Wynton Kelly, Billy Wallace (p); Paul Chambers, Bill Lee (b); Jimmy Cobb, Vernell Fournier (d).* 12/59–2/60.

★★★ Cool, Calm And Collected

Koch 8552 *As above, except omit Little, Kelly, Chambers, Cobb.* 10/60.

★★(★) Cloudy And Cool

Vee-Jay 013 *As above.* 60.

Strozier's early work for Vee-Jay has come back into circulation. Apart from Kelly's 'WK Blues' and Little's 'Waltz Of The Demons' almost all the material on the debut album is Strozier's own and in a fairly orthodox hard-bop idiom. 'A Starling's Theme' hints at his quiet originality, while 'Runnin'' is almost self-consciously generic. It may also have been a reference to the fact that he was working with Miles Davis's rhythm section. They blend together beautifully, leaving it to Strozier and the remarkable, ill-fated Little to roughen up the surface with some dramatic playing.

The extra material is pretty lame and forgettable, but any additional glimpses of Strozier in this period have to be welcome. That pretty much goes for the whole of *Cool, Calm And Collected* and the well-named *Cloudy And Cool*, two more sessions for Vee-Jay that weren't actually released until the early '90s. Because all the takes are included, the first of the pair set is extremely repetitive and ultimately rather dull. Surely a good double CD culling the best of this period might have been a better option.

★★★(★) Long Night / March of the Siamese Children

Milestone 47095 *Strozier; George Coleman (ts); Pat Patrick (bs, f); Chris Anderson, Harold Mabern (p); Bill Lee (b); Al Dreares, Walter Perkins (d).* 9/61–3/62.

There was probably a touch of wilful perversity about Frank Strozier's career. Who else made a jazz standard out of 'March Of The Siamese Children' from *The King And I*? Who else promised so much only to disappear so completely into obscurity? These two albums were made with Orrin Keepnews, and hearing them again does raise the question why they have remained out of catalogue for so long. Strozier came to rely on Mabern and Spike Lee's father Bill, but another curiosity of this compilation is the work of Pat Patrick, best known as a Sun Ra acolyte.

Long Night is by far the better of the pair. George Coleman is in superb form, revealing with every chorus what an original grasp of harmony he has. 'Happiness Is A Thing Called Joe' is another of the rarities Frank digs up for the date, and Coleman is inside the tune like a terrier. Strozier doubles on flute effectively. The later tracks don't have the same punch, though the themes are equally oddball, but taken together this adds a significant dimension to the career.

***** Remember Me**

Steeplechase SCCD 31106 *Strozier; Danny Moore (flhn); Howard Johnson (tba); Harold Mabern (p); Lisle Atkinson (b); Michael Carvin (d).* 11/76.

***** What's Going Out**

Steeplechase SCCD 31420 *As above, except omit Johnson, Atkinson, Carvin; add Stafford James (b); Louis Hayes (d).* 77.

As an album title, *Remember Me* has a slightly plangent sound when you think that Strozier hadn't made a record in his own name since 1962. All the stranger when one hears how original his sound could be, especially in this augmented format, with lots of action in the lower registers. Strozier himself liked to play around the low end of his horn, punctuating these passages with gospelly wails that are somewhat reminiscent of Jackie McLean. Moore and Mabern accentuate that impression and the redoubtable Howard Johnson brings his unique touch to the bass lines, though Atkinson is no mean performer or writer. It's very much Strozier's gig, though. 'For Our Elders' is a remarkable piece, post-bop of a unique stamp and a good place to begin the rehabilitation of a neglected reputation.

The second Steeplechase date feels like something of an afterthought. There is nothing of the sheer power of 'For Our Elders', and only 'Chelsea Drugs' and the feeling 'Psalm For John Coltrane' match up to the previous album. There is still some excellent playing, though, and the recruitment of Hayes at the drum kit was an inspired stroke; a much more swinging delivery than Carvin.

Dave Stryker (born 1957)

GUITAR

Born in Omaha, Stryker took up guitar at ten and began playing in local rock bands. Moved to Los Angeles, then to New York in 1980. Worked with Jack McDuff, Lonnie Smith, Jimmy Smith and Stanley Turrentine, then led his own dates.

***** Stryke Zone**

Steeplechase SCCD 31277 *Stryker; Marc Cohen (p); Ron McClure (b); Ronnie Burrage (d).* 10/90.

****** Passage**

Steeplechase SCCD 31330 *Stryker; Steve Slagle (ss, as); Joey Calderazzo (p); Jay Anderson (b); Adam Nussbaum (d).* 3/91.

*****(*) Blue Degrees**

Steeplechase SCCD 31315 *Stryker; Rick Margitza (ts); Larry Goldings (org); Jeff Hirshfield (d).* 4/92.

***** Full Moon**

Steeplechase SCCD 31345 *Stryker; Steve Slagle (as, f); Jay Anderson (b); Jeff Hirshfield (d).* 10/93.

Stryker did long service in the pressure-cooker atmosphere of Jack McDuff and Jimmy Smith groups, and while he prefers a slightly blurred tone over the crisp lines of many modern guitarists, he has a knack for cutting through any ensemble. 'Jungle' on *Passage* is an example of how he digs into a solo – the leering bent notes and swaggering delivery are a startling display. But the fast, bop lines of 'It's You Or No One' on the same record show he has the necessary language down pat. Consistently energetic and persuasive, there's little to choose between these records as regards his own playing. *Stryke Zone* is a shade behind for a rhythm section that doesn't quite strike best sparks, and the next two Steeplechases are the place to start. *Passage* is an all-round programme – there's a brief, pretty 'I Fall In Love Too Easily' as a nice change of pace – with both intensity and finesse. *Blue Degrees* is just a touch cooler – Goldings, the only organ-player ever to feature on a Steeplechase date at that point, is more of a pastel player than a bar-burner – but the undervalued Margitza is a welcome presence, and Stryker is full of ideas again.

Full Moon is perhaps a mite disappointing as the next in the sequence. Ornette Coleman's 'The Sphinx' makes a hurried, splashy opening, Coltrane's 'Wise One' is mush for flute and acoustic guitar, and not till Slagle's 'Leadbelly Sez' do they really dig in. But there's still some marvellous playing on Wayne Shorter's 'Deluge' and two slow-to-mid blues.

***** Stardust**

Steeplechase SCCD 31362 *Stryker; Joey DeFrancesco (org); Adam Nussbaum (d).* 10/94.

***** Nomad**

Steeplechase SCCD 31371 *Stryker; Randy Brecker, Bill Warfield, Bob Millikan, John Eckert, Tony Kadleck, Bud Burridge (t); Tim Sessions, Jeff Nelson (tb); Steve Slagle, Andy Fusco, Bob Hanlon, Alex Stewart, Walt Weiskopf, Bob Parsons (reeds); Joel Weiskopf (p); Scott Colley, Lynn Seaton (b); Jeff Hirshfield, Grisha Alexiev (d).* 8/94.

*****(*) The Greeting**

Steeplechase SCCD 31387 *Stryker; Bruce Barth (p); Scott Colley (b); Tony Reedus (d); Daniel Sadownick (perc).* 11/95.

***** Blue To The Bone**

Steeplechase SCCD 31371 *Stryker; Brian Lynch (t); Conrad Herwig (tb); Rich Perry (ts); Bob Parsons (bs); Bruce Barth (p, org); Jay Anderson (b); Billy Drummond (d).* 3/96.

Stryker's good run continues on these latest Steeplechases, though there's a certain sense of diminishing returns, and not many will want to own all of these. *Stardust* sets him up with Joey DeFrancesco on the kind of gig he cut his teeth on, and with the organist in his usual bumptious form, the session slips by in friendly style, though it presses few demands on the listener. *Nomad* is perhaps the most disappointing record, given that this was a rare opportunity to be a featured soloist with a big band. There's nothing wrong with the record, yet there seems so little to remember: the arrangements feel perfunctory, if not exactly hurried, and soloists like Brecker and Slagle do no more than they have to. Stryker plays handsomely enough, but it feels like a mishandled project. *The Greeting* is more satisfying in every way: Stryker's originals are a sound lot, Barth is a good new companion, and the guitarist finds his most melodic and purposefully aggressive form, though the closing cover of a Sonny Sharrock tune scarcely competes with that departed master.

Blue To The Bone tries another variation by sticking to straight-up blues with a horn section and Barth turning to the organ. Again, Stryker knows this terrain well, and there's no lack of feeling or grit in the delivery: his bottleneck intro to

'Bayou Blues' is an arresting touch, and Slagle's chart for 'Messenger' is very sharp. In the end, though, this feels like an LP-length project getting tuckered out over a CD's duration.

*** All The Way

Steeplechase SCCD 31455 *Stryker; Scott Colley (b); Bill Stewart (d).* 4/97.

Stryker grasps the nettle of a trio session (mystifyingly described as 'a seldom-explored milieu' in the sleeve-notes). The playing is comely and expansive rather than particularly biting – Stewart is much more delicate here than he is with Pat Metheny – and each of the eight standards receives a good-natured interpretation. Stryker concentrates on little details, like his paraphrases of the melody of 'All The Way', which are sweetly done.

**(*) Blue To The Bone II

Steeplechase SCCD 31465 *Stryker; Brian Lynch (t); Clark Gayton (tb, btb); Steve Slagle (as, f); Bob Parsons (bs); Bruce Barth (p, org); Jay Anderson (b); Adam Nussbaum (d).* 4/98.

*** Shades Of Miles

Steeplechase SCCD 31480 *Stryker; Brian Lynch (t); Steve Slagle (ss, as); Billy Drewes (ss, ts, bcl); Marc Copland, Larry Goldings (org); Terry Burns (b); Billy Hart (d); Manolo Badrena (perc).* n.d.

***(*) Changing Times

Steeplechase SCCD 31510 *Stryker; Steve Slagle (ss, as); Bill Morning (b); Tim Horner (d); Manolo Badrena (perc).* 12/99.

Blue To The Bone II has its moments, but as before it has a pointless feel to it. Steeplechase aren't good at this kind of record, which needs a much bigger and walloping sound to make it work, and the date has a session-man ennui about it.

Turning the Miles Davis early-fusion music into a repertory exercise doesn't seem like a much better idea, and though the band is stuffed with good players, as an ensemble they have nothing particular to say. Lynch steers well clear of Davis-isms, to his credit, and the soloists work capably when tracks such as 'Topaz' and 'Sienna' come to the boil.

Changing Times is easily the best of these three and simply returns Stryker to his strengths: thoughtful small-combo music, with no special agenda, but deftly coloured and smartly played. Horner's not too tasteful a drummer and Badrena puts in some odd amusing touches, so the session's usefully roughed-up, which suits Slagle as well.

*** Blue To The Bone III

Steeplechase SCCD 31524 *Stryker; Brian Lynch (t, flhn); Clark Gayton (tb); Steve Slagle (as); Bob Parsons (bs); James Williams (p); Jay Anderson (b); Tim Horner (d).* 3/01.

The third entry by Blue To The Bone has plenty to enjoy – not least Clark Gayton's playing, particularly on 'For Jack And T', a dedication to the then recently departed Turrentine and McDuff. As with the first two albums, though, the record doesn't pack enough punch to really convince, which may not be Stryker's fault. The studio sound is still too polite – it needs a socking R&B smack, not this nice jazz feel. Since the band does its share of live work, maybe an in-your-face live set is what's needed now.

Dick Sudhalter (born 1938)

CORNET, TRUMPET, FLUGELHORN

A jazz writer of great acumen and distinction, Sudhalter is a cornetist and trumpeter whose lyricism owes much to Bix Beiderbecke, of whom he has written the definitive biography.

*** With Pleasure

Audiophile ACD-159 *Sudhalter; Dan Barrett (tb); Bob Reitmeier (cl, as, ts); Dan Levinson (cl, ts); Joe Muranyi (cl); David Frishberg (p, v); James Cirillo (g); Howard Alden (g, bj); Putter Smith (tba, b); Bill Crow (b); Eddie Locke, Dick Berk (d).* 3/81–4/94.

*** After Awhile

Challenge 70014 *Sudhalter; Roy Williams (tb); Jim Shepherd (tb, bsx); John R. T. Davies (as); Al Gay (ts); Keith Nichols (p, tb); Mick Pyne (p); Nevil Skrimshire, Paul Sealey (g); Dave Green, Jack Fallon (b); Allan Ganley, Jack Parnell (d); Chris Ellis (v).* 5–6/94.

Sudhalter's Bixian brass stylings have tended to take a back seat to his jazz scholarship, but he is a lyrical player and a rare example of a musician/historian who can make his enthusiasms take on a personal cast when he plays. These good-natured sessions make no great demands on the listener, but they're enjoyable for all that. The first reissues a 1981 date with eight extra, subsequent tracks, and it blends the echoes of a vanished Chicago with a few more modern licks: Sudhalter cuts from such ancient cloth as 'Madame Dynamite' and 'Boneyard Shuffle' and reshapes a Beiderbecke legacy such as 'Slow River' into a winsome duet with Frishberg. The Challenge album goes to the other side of the Atlantic – to the Bull's Head in Barnes, in fact – and brings on an English team for a similarly inclined session. The material isn't quite so arcane here, but the playing probably isn't quite as vivacious either.

*** Melodies Heard ... Melodies Sweet

Challenge CHR 70055 *Sudhalter; Roger Kellaway, Sy Johnson (p); Frank Vignola, James Chirillo (g); Ed Saindon (vib); Marshall Wood (b); Joe Cocuzzo (d); Barbara Lea (v).* 5–8/98.

It is, indeed, sweet and melodious music, and Sudhalter's own playing has never sounded better. Six duets with his old friend Kellaway are good enough to wish for an entire album by the duo, and the concept – songs by jazzmen – is lightly worn, since the tunes are an unhackneyed and likeable lot. But it never feels like much more than an amiable time-passer, graciously though everyone plays – perhaps too graciously. Lea sings two lyrics, and the others come and go at the leader's suggestion.

Ira Sullivan (born 1931)

TRUMPET, FLUGELHORN, PECKHORN, SAXOPHONES

Sullivan is something of an enigma, a transitional figure between bop and free music whose restless style and intriguing multi-instrumentalism may well have had an impact on the nascent AACM generation in Chicago. Sullivan's reluctance to travel restricted him to Florida for much of his career.

***(*) Nicky's Tune

Delmark DD 422 *Sullivan; Nicky Hill (sax); Jodie Christian (p); Vic Sproles (b); Wilbur Campbell (d).* 58.

***** Blue Stroll**

Delmark DD 602 *As above, except omit Hill; add Johnny Griffin (ts).* 59.

Sullivan started out as a bopper, but one who assiduously avoided the basic, standards-based repertoire in favour of new material; this, it seems, was the condition he imposed when he went on the road with Red Rodney. These two albums for Delmark are all that's generally available of his fairly modest own-name output.

The earlier of the pair is dedicated to the equally enigmatic Nicky Hill, one of those catalytic players who remained little known outside a small circle. Like all of Ira's output, it's a slightly puzzling and forbidding experience if you approach it expecting basic changes and contrafacts on 'I Got Rhythm', 'Cherokee' and 'How High The Moon'. Ira's harmonic sense is unimpeachable and his understanding with the excellent Christian is intuitive and sympathetic. Trumpet is the dominant voice on both records, but the saxophones and peckhorn are deployed to excellent effect. This was the period when Ira was losing patience with the formulae of bebop, even his own individual brand, and was striking out in the direction of free jazz. There are atonal and polytonal episodes on *Nicky's Tune*, fewer on the set with Griff, who barges and blusters his way through his solos, tossing out tags and quotes as if to remind the others what else was going on in the world. Two powerful records by an almost forgotten figure.

Joe Sullivan (1906–71)

PIANO

Studied in Chicago and then worked in the local scene during the '20s and early '30s. Joined Bob Crosby in 1936 but was sidelined by illness. Worked in group and solo situations in the '40s, but was playing solo in San Francisco in the '50s and, despite a couple of modest comebacks, finally drifted into obscurity.

***** Joe Sullivan 1933–1941**

Classics 821 *Sullivan; Ed Anderson (t); Benny Morton (tb); Edmond Hall, Pee Wee Russell (cl); Danny Polo (ts, cl); Freddie Green (g); Billy Taylor, Henry Turner (b); Yank Porter, Zutty Singleton, Johnny Wells (d); Joe Turner, Helen Ward (v).* 9/33–3/41.

This collects all of Sullivan's piano solos of the period, plus the two dates by his Café Society Orchestra and a 1941 trio date for Commodore with Pee Wee Russell and Zutty Singleton. Sullivan had a terrific left hand and his style was a personal blend of boogie-woogie and stride language, imbued with a shot of local Chicago blues. Not a great melodist, perhaps, which gives some of the dozen solos here a certain sameness, and the band tracks are nothing very special; but the intensity of Sullivan's style has weathered the years well enough and his bluff passion gives the music bite. Transfers are variable, but the music survives the surface noise and boomy bass patterns.

*****(*) Joe Sullivan 1944–1945**

Classics 1070 *Sullivan; Archie Rosatie (cl); Ulysses Livingston (g); Artie Shapiro (b); Zutty Singleton (d).* 11/44–12/45.

Twenty of these 24 tracks are solos, and they're some of Sullivan's best work. Two obscure sides for Sunset are rocking boogie-woogie pieces. There are eight tracks made for Capitol EPs and an undated session that was later issued on Folkways. Sullivan's virtues shine through – his almost violent swing, the Irish humour, the no-nonsense improvising – and it's an enjoyable disc. Four quintet tracks are nothing special. This sound isn't terrible, but don't expect hi-fi.

****(*) Piano Solo**

Storyville STCD 8234 *Sullivan (p solo).* 8/53–11/73.

Richard Hadlock's notes detail Sullivan's last years in a touching and funny way. He worked regularly at San Francisco's Club Hangover in the '50s but, after that closed, he worked rarely, and basically he drifted away. This collects 18 tracks, many from the Hangover, and some from a session which Hadlock recorded privately. Sullivan's ornery playing strikes sparks, but there are stumbles too, and the sound is often pretty awful, with crowd noise at times close to overpowering. A characterful memento, but it needs a tolerant ear.

Maxine Sullivan (1911–87)

VOCAL

Born Marietta Williams, Sullivan was singing in New York when Claude Thornhill did arrangements of a couple of Scottish songs for her and started a craze for jazzing folk material. She worked with John Kirby, Benny Goodman and others, then as a solo, before retiring to be a nurse during the '50s. She came back around 1960 and thereafter sang (and sometimes played valve-trombone) in a career which stretched into the '80s.

***** Maxine Sullivan 1937–1938**

Classics 963 *Sullivan; Manny Klein, Charlie Spivak, Frankie Newton, Charlie Shavers (t); Bobby Hackett (c); Jack Lacey (tb); Buster Bailey (cl); Jimmy Lytell, Paul Ricci (cl, as); Toots Mondello, Jess Carneol, Pete Brown (as); Babe Russin (ts); Eddie Powell (bs, f); Claude Thornhill (p); Artie Bernstein, John Kirby (b); Chauncey Morehouse, O'Neil Spencer, Buddy Rich (d).* 6/37–6/38.

*****(*) Maxine Sullivan 1938–1941**

Classsics 991 *Sullivan; Bobby Hackett (c); Lloyd Reese, Charlie Shavers, Doc Cheatham, Lincoln Mills, Sidney De Paris (t); Vic Dickenson, Jimmy Archey, Joe Britton (tb); Slats Long, Chester Hazlett (cl, as); Buster Bailey, Leo Trammel, Reggie Merrill, Eddie Powell (cl); Benny Carter (t, as); Floyd Turnham, Russell Procope, Ernie Purce, Eddie Barefield (as); Bud Freeman, Buddy Banks, Fred Williams, Ernie Powell (ts); Carl Prager (bcl); Harold Goltzer (bsn); Mitch Miller (ob); Milt Rettenberg, Eddie Beal, Walter Gross, Billy Kyle, Sonny White (p); Ken Binford, Herb Thomas (g); Ed Brader, Red Callender, Frank Carroll, John Kirby, Charles Drayton (b); Ed Rubsam, Oscar Bradley, Cary Gillis, O'Neil Spencer, Al Taylor (d).* 12/38–4/41.

***** More 1940–1941**

Circle CCD-125 *Sullivan; Charlie Shavers (t); Buster Bailey (cl); Russell Procope (as); Billy Kyle (p); John Kirby (b); O'Neil Spencer (d).* 10/40–11/41.

*****(*) Maxine Sullivan 1941–1946**

Classics 1020 *Sullivan; Charlie Shavers, Emmett Berry, Shorty Rogers, Joe Newman, Neal Hefti (t); Al Grey, Trummy Young, Alton Moore, Sandy Williams (tb); Buster Bailey, Hank D'Amico (cl); Russell Procope (as); Willard Brown (as, bs); Tony Scott (cl, as); Dexter Gordon, Don Byas (ts); Billy Kyle, Kenneth Billings, Teddy Wilson, Sonny White (p); Samuel*

Persoff, Samuel Rand, Joseph Breen (vn); Laura Newell (hp); Everett Barksdale, Freddie Green, Tony Colucci (g); Red Norvo (vib); John Kirby, Cedric Wallace, Billy Taylor, John Simmons, Harry Patent (b); O'Neil Spencer, Morey Feld, Specs Powell, J. C. Heard (d); strings. 6/41–46.

*****(*) The 'Le Ruban Bleu' Years**

Baldwin Street BJH-303 *Similar to above, except add Ellis Larkins (p), Everett Barksdale (g), Beverley Peer (b), Jimmie Lunceford Orchestra (personnel unidentified).* 44–49.

'Loch Lomond' was the novelty hit which launched Maxine Sullivan's career, part of a faintly ludicrous vogue for turning folk tunes and 'light music' into swing vehicles. The song (and 'Darling Nellie Gray', 'It Was A Lover And His Lass' and so forth) still works, though, because of Sullivan's transparent, almost ghostly singing. She didn't really swing her material so much as give it a lilting quality, floating it on phrasing that was measured and controlled without sounding excessively polite. Her version of 'St Louis Blues' sounds mousy next to a voice like Bessie Smith's, but the demure melancholy with which she invests it is surprisingly compelling. She also finds a particular tranquil beauty in 'Easy To Love', 'Moments Like This' and 'Spring Is Here'. All these are on Classics 963, which covers her successful first years in the studios. A disc's worth of this is a lot in one go, though, and we find the Classics transfers inconsistent and surely muddier than they should be.

Classics 991 picks up the story and starts with three sessions for Victor, then two with John Kirby's small group which was an almost ideal setting for Max. There are some good, forgotten songs here such as 'I'm Happy About The Whole Thing' and 'Kinda Lonesome', as well as the expected updates of such as 'Drink To Me Only With Thine Eyes'. But the Kirby dates, with their gentle jig-jog rhythms and pastel tones, suit her wonderfully well. 'If I Had A Ribbon Bow' is a definitive piece of Sullivan. Classics 1020 carries on with ten more charming titles with Kirby, before an interesting and obscure date for Beacon, two titles with Teddy Wilson, four with a Benny Carter band and six with a chamberish group that remade several of her earlier successes. The sound on these last titles is very muddy, on the rest average-to-good. Sullivan's singing remains rather demure and unconfected but, taken a few tracks at a time, she is irresistible.

The Baldwin Street release (Le Ruban Bleu was a supper club where Sullivan sang for several seasons from 1943) duplicates many of the tracks with Classics 1020 but also adds six splendid tracks with an Ellis Larkins trio (in surfacey sound), a pair of songs with a 1949 studio orchestra ('Cry, Buttercup, Cry' a choice rarity) and some AFRS transcriptions with the Lunceford orchestra. A collectors' delight!

The Circle CD collects a series of transcriptions by the John Kirby group, six of which feature Sullivan. Some of them continue the folk-towards-jazz theme, and Kirby's willowy band are perhaps all too suitable as a backing group, but the music exudes an undeniable period charm. Excellent sound, given the source.

CORE COLLECTION

****** Close As Pages In A Book**

Audiophile 203 *Sullivan; Bob Wilber (ss, cl); Bernie Leighton (p); George Duvivier (b); Gus Johnson Jr (d).* 6/69.

Sullivan retired in the '50s but later returned to regular singing (she also played flugelhorn and valve-trombone) and by the '80s was as widely admired as she had ever been. Her manner didn't change much but, as recording improved, her intimate style and meticulous delivery sounded as classic as any of the great jazz singers. In her 70s there was inevitably a decline in the strength of her voice, but careful production ensured that her albums sounded very good.

This record was long a collectors' favourite, and it makes a welcome return on CD. The dozen songs are perfectly delivered – thoughtful, graceful, introspective without being introverted, this is peerless jazz singing, and the accompaniments by Wilber and his team are as *simpatico* as one could wish.

***** Sullivan Shakespeare Hyman**

Audiophile 250 *Sullivan; Rusty Dedrick (t, flhn); Dick Hyman (p, hpd); Bucky Pizzarelli (g); Milt Hinton (b); Don Lamond (d).* 6/71.

***** The Queen: Like Someone In Love**

Kenneth CKS 3402 *Sullivan; Bent Persson (t); Jens Lindgren (tb); Goran Eriksson (as); Erik Persson, Claes Brodda (ts); Bjorn Milder (p); Mikael Selander (vn, g); Ronnie Holmqvist, Anders Rabe (g); Olle Brostedt (b, g); Goran Lind (b); Sigge Dellert (d).* 10/78–5/83.

*****(*) The Queen: Something To Remember Her By**

Kenneth CKS 3406 *Sullivan; Bent Persson (t); George Vernon (tb); Claes Brodda (cl, ts); Goran Eriksson (as); Erik Persson (ts, bs); Bjorn Milder (p); Mikael Selander (g); Olle Brostedt (g, b); Goran Lind (b); Sigge Dellert (d).* 10/78–7/84.

The Shakespeare collection was the last word on Sullivan's 'Elizabethan' direction and it sounds better, at least, than Cleo Laine's efforts in this field. The pick of these, though, may be the beautiful *Something To Remember Her By* collection on Kenneth, cut in Sweden with local players. The sessions cover a six-year period, but Maxine sounds entirely at ease throughout, whether swinging on 'You Were Meant For Me' or strolling through 'Thanks For The Memory'. The band are very fine, too, with Brodda's Websterish tenor and Eriksson's sinuous alto particularly impressive. The recording is rather dry but otherwise sounds very good. This was meant to be the first of five such volumes (and is numbered five!) but so far only *Like Someone In Love* (numbered one in the sequence) has emerged as a follow-up. Not quite so good, this one, suggesting that the best tunes had already been cherrypicked for the previous release.

***** Great Songs From The Cotton Club**

Mobile Fidelity MFCD 836 *Sullivan; Keith Ingham (p).* 11/84.

***** Enjoy Yourself!**

Audiophile ACD 154 *Sullivan; Herman Foretich (cl, ts); Sil Austin (ts); Dardanelle (p, v); Dan Wall (p); Bob Shaw (g); Ike Isaacs, Bob Haggart (b); Steve Ellington, Bryan Childers (d).* 2/78–5/85.

*****(*) Love ... Always**

Baldwin Street BJC-201 *Sullivan; Seldon Powell (ts, f); Dick Hyman (p); Major Holley (b); Mel Lewis (d).* 12/85.

****(*) Spring Isn't Everything**

Audiophile ACD 229 *Sullivan; Loonis McGlohon (p); Jim Stack (vib); Terry Peoples (b); Bill Stowe (d).* 7/86.

***** Highlights In Jazz**

Storyville STCD 8276 *Sullivan; Doc Cheatham (t); Bill Watrous (tb); Phil Bodner (cl); Buddy Tate (ts); Derek Smith (p); Milt Hinton (b); Butch Miles (d).* 3/87.

Max never slowed down: she recorded 16 albums in the '80s, and *Spring Isn't Everything*, one of her last sessions, features a 'songbook' recital (the tracks are all by Harry Warren) which finds her still in excellent shape. Unfortunately the studio balance doesn't favour her at all. Better to turn to the two Concord dates with Hamilton's smooth neo-classic band, which do as fine a job for her as they do for Rosemary Clooney, and what was an award-winning album with Keith Ingham, dedicated to tunes associated with the Cotton Club. *Enjoy Yourself!* pairs a farly routine 1978 session with a group led by Ike Isaacs with a superior 1985 set under Bob Haggart's watchful eye, which goes with a good swing. She's given marvellous support on *Love ... Always*, with Hyman in top form and the admirable and unjustly neglected Seldon Powell filling in many of the backgrounds. She makes as much of more modern songs like 'He's Got Away' and 'Two For The Road' as she does of the more familiar standards: a fine example of latter-day Sullivan. The Storyville set is a New York concert, cut only weeks before she died. The studio records are better, but it's hard to listen to this set and not be moved by her still-indomitable artistry, which here closes with a ten-minute 'St Louis Blues'.

Stan Sulzmann (born 1948)

TENOR, ALTO AND SOPRANO SAXOPHONES, ALTO FLUTE

Worked on the London scene in the '60s and formed a long-standing quartet in 1970. Lately a frequent partner of pianists John Taylor and Marc Copland, and composing for larger groups.

***** Treasure Trove**

ASC CD 7 *Sulzmann; Nikki Iles (p); Martin Pyne (perc).* 10/95.

A classic case of a Talent Deserving Wider Recognition who has failed to break through to the audiences his ability and commitment would seem to merit. Sulzmann's showing in the CD era has been consistently self-effacing and underachieved. *Treasure Trove* benefits from the presence of Nikki Iles. She has something of Geri Allen's richness of texture and rhythmic awareness and, good as she is in a larger group setting, she comes across most formidably in settings like this one. Pyne is restricted to just one number, on which Sulzmann also airs his beautifully toned alto flute, and it was a good notion not to clutter this partnership with any other guest slots. The range of Sulzmann's reeds and Iles's intelligently varied attack, in combination with fascinating material (all originals, except Paul Simon's 'I Do It For Your Love' and Bill Evans's 'Since We Met'), contribute to a satisfying set that could perhaps have done with a bit more studio presence.

***** Birthdays, Birthdays**

Village Life 99108VL *Sulzmann; Patrick White, Henry Lowther, Noel Langley, Kenny Wheeler, Derek Watkins (t); Mark Bassey, Pete Beachill, Jeremy Price, Nichol Thomson, Richard Henry, Sarah Williams (tb); Ray Warleigh, Martin Hathaway, Julian Siegel, Pete Hurt, Mick Foster (saxes); Pete Saberton (p); Frank Ricotti (vib); John Parricelli (g); Tim Wells (b); Paul Clarvis (d).* 7–8/99.

Sulzmann conducts and composes but plays very little on this record (he's credited only with 'toy saxophone' on a single track). Played with great gusto by a strong team of British pros, the music is expertly put across if somewhat hard to follow at times: 'Little Dog' seems like a bundle of bits and pieces, and the bebop line of 'Newness' searches for a context for itself. Some of the scores sound overcrowded with incident. But when, as on the ingenious 'Midnight', everything locks into place, the results are impressive. Stan should have given himself more to do as a player, too.

Torbjørn Sunde (born 1954)

TROMBONE, VOCALS

Norwegian composer and arranger, who enjoys West Coast cool and funkier sounds.

***** Meridians**

ACT 9263 2 *Sunde; Jens Petter Antonsen (t); Morten Halle (as); Peter Wettre (ts); Eivind Aarset, Børge Petterson-Øverleir, Terje Rypdal (g); Jon Balke (p); Bugge Wesseltoft (ky); Geir Holmsen, Bjørn Kjellemyr (b); Rune Arnesen, Per Oddvar Johansen (d); Manolo Badrena, Joakin Nordin, Celio De Carvalho (perc).* 98.

***** Where Is The Chet**

Orchard 802889 *Sunde; Jens Antonsen (t, flhn); Trude Eick (frhn); Morten Halle (ts, f); Havard Lund (bcl); Jon Eberson (g); Rob Waring (vib); Aslak Hartberg (b).* 03.

Meridians was garlanded with praise when it first appeared, and it stands up strongly even five years on. Sunde's track record, which ranges from Edward Vesala and Terje Rypdal albums to Rickie Lee Jones, has stood him in good stead as he assembles a highly eclectic and individual disc. Apart from 'Kjaere Maren', all the compositions and arrangements are by Sunde. 'Confronting Hemispheres' and 'Vertigo' are typical of a strain of Norwegian jazz that is big on atmosphere and less strong in the swing department. Indeed, for all the percussionists involved, it's a remarkably static project, with a rather motoric quality that grates on second and subsequent hearings.

The follow-up is an imaginative revisiting of the Chet Baker songbook by a group with interesting ideas and a delightfully modulated range of voices. Sunde is always interesting, and his arrangements for this drummerless octet is thoughtful as well as romantic. His singing is very different to Chet's broken whisper but effective in its more functional way. The real delight of these cuts is the horn ensemble, which gets to places in these familiar tunes that makes them seem brand-new.

Sun Ra (1914–93)

PIANO, CLAVIOLINE, CELESTE, ORGAN, SYNTHESIZER

The most mysterious figure in the history of jazz was, depending on your angle of vision, either a fearsome avant-gardist or a traditionalist in the line of Fletcher Henderson, for whom he wrote many arrangements early in his career. The truth about Sun Ra was that he was both those things. The man born Herman 'Sonny' Blount in Alabama grew up steeped in the blues. Even when he founded his famous Arkestra, with its theatrical approach to jazz, and became a leading presence on the Chicago improvisation scene, his work was always grounded in melody and in blues changes. Sun Ra's claim to come from Saturn was doggedly sustained, one of the great metaphors of Black American music.

★★★(★) **Sound Sun Pleasure!!**

Evidence ECD 22014 *Sun Ra; Hobart Dotson, Akh Tal Ebah, Art Hoyle (t); Bob Northern (flhn); Marshall Allen, Danny Davis (as); John Gilmore (ts); Charles Davis, Pat Patrick (bs); Danny Ray Thompson (reeds); Stuff Smith (vn); Ronnie Boykins, Victor Sproles (b); Robert Barry, Nimrod Hunt, James Jackson, Clifford Jarvis (d); Hatty Randolph, Clyde Williams (v).* 53–60.

★★★(★) **Supersonic Jazz**

Evidence ECD 22015 *Sun Ra; Art Hoyle (t); Julian Priester (tb); James Scales (as); Pat Patrick (as, bs); John Gilmore (ts); Charles Davis (bs); Wilburn Green, Victor Sproles (b); Robert Barry, William Bugs Cochran (d); Jim Herndon (perc).* 56.

★★★(★) **Visits Planet Earth / Interstellar Low Ways**

Evidence ECD 22039 *Sun Ra; Phil Cohran, Art Hoyle, George Hudson, Lucious Randolph, Dave Young (t); Julian Priester, Nate Pryor (tb); James Spaulding (as); Marshall Allen (as, f); Pat Patrick (as, bs, space f, bells, solar d); John Gilmore (ts, bells, solar d); Charles Davis (bs); Ronnie Boykins, Victor Sproles (b); Robert Barry, William Bugs Cochran, Edward Skinner (d); Jim Herndon (perc).* 56, 58, 60.

★★★★ **We Travel The Spaceways / Bad And Beautiful**

Evidence ECD 22038 *Sun Ra; Art Hoyle, Walter Strickland (t); Phil Cohran (t, space harp, perc); Julian Priester, Nate Pryor (tb); James Scales, James Spaulding (as); Marshall Allen (as, bells, flying saucer, perc); John Gilmore (ts, cosmic bells, perc); Pat Patrick (bs, perc); Ronnie Boykins, Wilburn Green (b); Tommy Hunter (d); Robert Barry (d, perc); Edward Skinner (perc).* 56, 58 or 59, 59 or 60, 61.

★★★ **Angels And Demons At Play / The Nubians Of Plutonia**

Evidence ECD 22066 *Sun Ra; Bill Fielder, Lucious Randolph (t); Phil Cohran (t, zither); Bob Bailey, Julian Priester, Nate Pryor (tb); James Spaulding (as); Marshall Allen (as, f); Pat Patrick (as, bs); John Gilmore (ts, cl, bells); Charles Davis (bs); Ronnie Boykins, Wilburn Green (b); Robert Barry, Jon Hardy (d); Jim Herndon (perc).* 56, 60.

A much-maligned and very influential figure, Sun Ra was either born in Chicago under the earth-name Herman Poole 'Sonny' Blount, as the birth-roll insists, or on Saturn, as the man himself often claimed. Uncertainty about his seriousness (and sanity) tended to divert attention from a considerable three-decade output, which included well over 100 LPs. Because much of it remained inaccessible during his lifetime, critical responses were apt to concentrate on the paraphernalia associated with his Arkestra big band, rather than on the music. Nevertheless, he was one of the most significant bandleaders of the post-war period. He drew on Ellington and Fletcher Henderson (for whom he did arrangements after the war), but also on the bop-derived avant-garde, and was a pioneer of collective improvisation. Though rarely acknowledged as an instrumentalist, he developed a convincing role for the synthesizer and was a strong rather than subtle piano-player. The solo recordings, some of which have been reissued (see below), are only now being appreciated.

Above all, Sun Ra maintained a solitary independence from the music industry, a principled stance that certainly cost him dear in critical and commercial terms. For the first time in many years, it's possible again to get hold of important material self-released on the El Saturn label. These discs are being reissued *in toto* by Evidence (who work out of Conshohocken, Pennsylvania), a colossal project that will presumably take several years. Sound-quality is remarkably good, given the often shaky balance of the original masters and the fact that they've been subjected to uncertain storage conditions. The original El Saturn titles have been preserved wherever possible, even when this has led to rather cumbersome doubling up. One of the drawbacks of Evidence's programme is the out-of-sequence pairing of sessions, rendering a strictly chronological review impossible. A more orderly approach or a separate chronological listing might have been helpful, even though exact recording dates remain a matter of controversy.

The '50s were in many respects a golden age for Sun Ra and the Arkestra. The music is frankly experimental (in the sense that both leader and players are clearly working through ideas on the stand) and the sci-fi apparatus was already part and parcel of American culture through the latter half of the decade. Chants like 'We Travel The Spaceways' began to sound more artful and mannered as the years went by, but for now they manage to sound almost spontaneous. There was always a suspicion that titles like 'Rocket Number Nine Take Off For The Planet Venus' were simply a diversionary addition to a fairly conventional jazz tune.

The bands themselves are terrific, of course. The original *Sound Sun Pleasure!!* has been filled out for CD by material from the 1950s which was released in 1973 as *Deep Purple*. The earliest material appears to come from as early as 1953, a useful round-number indicator of Sun Ra's remarkable longevity, and features violinist Stuff Smith on the lo-fi, home-recorded title-track. *Supersonic Jazz* comes from the same period. Again, it is a set of originals combining conventional harmony and orchestrations with a thoroughly individual 'voice' (conveyed in occasional devices like Wilburn Green's use of electric bass on 'Super Blonde' and the closing 'Medicine For A Nightmare') and a striking gentleness that contrast sharply with the often brutal aspect of contemporaneous hard bop. So good is Julian Priester's own brief 'Soft Talk' (the only non-Sun Ra composition) that one immediately wishes for more. All the Evidence reissues have original cover-art, crude by present standards but wildly unconventional in the late '50s and '60s when a pretty girl with a low-IQ expression was generally considered essential to successful music marketing.

Bad And Beautiful, recorded during 1961, is thought to be the first Arkestra disc to be made in New York City. Chronologically it belongs after the last of the Chicago discs, *Fate In A Pleasant Mood*, which is discussed below. There is no doubt that the pace slackened somewhat after this point, allowing greater concentration on detail and on refining the Arkestra sound. Compare the version of Sun Ra's bluesy 'Ankh' here with a harder-edged performance on *Art Forms For Dimensions Tomorrow*, below. There are three standards on the session – the Previn/Raksin title-track, 'And This Is My Beloved' and 'Just In Time' – played in a rather more mannered and deliberate style than later in his career, but with no outer-space embellishments.

(A word about personnels. There may seem a degree of redundancy in listing every player on every available Arkestra recording, except, of course, those which offer no breakdown. Despite the improbable but common misconception that Sun Ra commanded the loyalty of a single group of musicians for nearly four decades, personnels changed very rapidly. Instrumentations are also remarkably capricious. Most players doubled on percussion and vocals at some time or other. At various stages, others may be credited with a secondary instrument only: Gilmore on bass clarinet, Allen on oboe, and so on. We have tried to note these in accordance with the details given on the disc, recognizing all the while that these are often unreliable in the extreme. It is sometimes possible to hear uncredited instruments, and former Arkestra members have taken convincing issue with specific attributions. These, however, are matters for the specialist. Apart from normalizing inconsistent spelling, details above and below are as given.)

CORE COLLECTION

♛ **** Jazz In Silhouette

Evidence ECD 22012 *Sun Ra; Hobart Dotson (t); Julian Priester (tb); Marshall Allen, James Spaulding (as, f); John Gilmore (ts); Charles Davis (bs); Pat Patrick (bs, f); Ronnie Boykins (b); William Bugs Cochran (d).* 58.

This marvellous record will surely some day be recognized as one of the most important jazz records since the war. The closing 'Blues At Midnight' is sheer excitement. The baritone solo on the short 'Saturn', most probably Patrick, is an extension of Sun Ra's brilliantly individual voicings. The great surprise of this recording (though presumably no surprise to those who have taken the Saturnian aesthetic fully on board) is its *timelessness*. Listening to 'Enlightenment', given an uncharacteristically straightforward reading, it's very difficult to guess a date for the performance. As Francis Davis suggests in a useful liner-note, it is ideal 'blindfold test' material that might have been recorded at any point from the '40s to the late '80s. Only the long drum passage on 'Ancient Aiethopia' and the astonishing Dotson solo and chants that follow sound unequivocally 'modern'. Inevitably, the next track, 'Hours After', is orthodox swing.

*** Sound Of Joy

Delmark DS 414 *Sun Ra; Art Hoyle, Dave Young (t); John Avant, Julian Priester (tb); Pat Patrick (as, bs); John Gilmore (ts); Charles Davis (bs); Victor Sproles (b); William Bugs Cochran (d); Jim Herndon (perc).* 56.

*** Sun Song

Delmark DD 411 *As above, except omit Avant, Priester, Sproles; add James Scales (as); Richard Evans, Wilburn Green (b); Robert Barr (d).* 7/56.

As with other recordings of this period, the exact personnels are not definitively known. It seems that Priester was only involved on a couple of tracks on *Sound Of Joy* and there is some argument as to whether he even played on them; Delmark have suggested that Avant was the slide-player. There were also extra cuts made with singer Clyde Williams. These, though, are discographical quibbles. The music is classic period Arkestra and 'El Is A Sound Of Joy' and 'Overtones Of China' are important early recordings, strangely reminiscent in conception and structure of some of Ellington's more impressionistic pieces.

Sun Song may be a confusing title to those who collected Sun Ra LPs, because this one used to be called *Jazz By Sun Ra*. It has also appeared on Sonet and possibly other labels. It's a good-quality studio recording, apparently made at Universal in Chicago in July 1956. Revel's 'Possession' was a favourite item at the time, with a similarly spacey sound, but 'Street Named Hell' 'Future' and the (new) title-track are all excellent.

**** The Singles

Evidence ECD 22164 2CD *Sun Ra; The Nu Sounds; The Cosmic Rays; Mr V's Five Joys; Arkestra/Arkistra, including: Fred Adams, Phil Cohran, Akh Tal Ebah, Art Hoyle, Lucious Randolph, Michael Ray, Walter Strickland, E. J. Turner (t); Jothan Collins (flhn, v); Tyrone Hill, Julian Priester (tb); Marshall Allen (as, ob); James Spaulding (as); Danny Davis (f, acl, d, perc, v); Mickey Boss, John Gilmore (ts); Pat Patrick, Danny Ray Thompson (bs); Buddy Guy, Sam Thomas (g); Ronnie Boykins, Wilburn Green, Victor Sproles (b); Luqman Ali, Robert Barry, William Bugs Cochran, Alvin Fielder, Clifford Jarvis, C. Scoby Stroman (d); Jim Herndon (perc); Lacy Gibson (v, g); Sam Bankhead, David Henderson, Little Mack, Juanita Rogers, Yochanan (v); other personnel unidentified or uncertain.* 54–82.

An eye-opening title to be sure, but from the early '50s to the mid-'70s Sun Ra issued a huge array of singles, aiming to some extent for a jukebox market and airing his never-to-fade enthusiasm for doo-wop, R&B and funk (an affection echoed by Anthony Braxton, another who is often thought of as an ultra-modernist, but who claims Frankie Lymon and the Teenagers as an influence). This is a key document in African-American music, underlining how much of a continuum there is between popular forms and the avant-garde, even during a period when separatist tendencies seemed to dominate. Included are sessions made in the later '60s with the 'space-age vocalist' Yochanan, with early groups like the Nu Sounds and the Cosmic Rays (a sort of club version of the early Arkestra), and for vocalists like Lacy Gibson. Everyone will find favourites. Ours include a 1968-ish basement recording (without Sun Ra himself) and then a later radio station recording of 'I'm Gona Unmask The Batman', a glorious piano–drums duo with Luqman Ali on 'Rough-House Blues', 'Great Balls Of Fire' with the Arkestra in 1958, and the outrageously hokey 'Daddy's Gonna Tell You No Lie' with the Rays a couple of years earlier. Sound-quality is as variable as elsewhere in the Saturn canon, but the sheer energy and verve of the performances more than make up for technical deficiencies. *Jazz In Silhouette* still remains our recommended Sun Ra record, but this runs it a close second, and it has the sterling advantage of tracing the Arkestra's and its leader's progress over more than two decades. There is some padding out with live and rehearsal material, but for the most part it documents one of the most extraordinary and unexpected creative adventures of recent times.

*** Music From Tomorrow's World

Atavistic Unheard Music 237 *Sun Ra; Phil Cochran (c); George Hudson (t); Gene Easton (as); Marshall Allen (as, f); John Gilmore (ts); Ronald Wilson (bs); Ronnie Boykins (b); Robert Barry, Jon Hardy (d); Ricky Murray (v).* 60.

A fascinating pair of sessions from 1960, rescued from oblivion by Atavistic curator John Corbett. The first set is a live date from the well-named Wonder Inn; the other was taped at Chicago's Majestic Hall, and is presumably a rehearsal, like so many of the Arkestra's recorded sessions. Sound-quality is variable, particularly on the latter set, and there is a certain amount of dinner-hour interruption on the first date, but the music is consistently interesting throughout and it's remarkable to think of diners sitting down to these sounds in 1960. Having said that, Ricky Murray's vocal on ''S'Wonderful', a long-term Sun Ra favourite, is absolutely conventional, though the Arkestra's vocal accompaniments are cheerfully eccentric. Sun Ra plays piano and electric piano throughout, with none of the space-organ effects of later years. There are also versions on the earlier date of 'How High The Moon' and 'It Ain't Necessarily So', though the highlight of that portion of the album is the opening 'Angels And Demons At Play', a never bettered performance. On the Majestic date, 'Possession' is a composition by Harry Revel, who also took an interest in the exotic and the cosmic.

***(*) When Angels Speak Of Love

Evidence ECD 22216 *Sun Ra; Walter Miller (t); Marshall Allen (as, ob, perc); John Gilmore (ts, perc); Pat Patrick (bs, perc); Robert Cummings (bcl); Ronnie Boykins (b); Clifford Jarvis (d).* 63.

One of the best albums of this period and the title-track is one of his best compositions; it resurfaces on the label's *Greatest Hits* package. The record wasn't released for some years after recording, presumably for budgetary reasons, but it must have arrived in the middle of a music scene rather more ready for these outer-edge sounds than it would have been in the otherwise unexpectedly conservative year of 1963. Having said that, this is by no means the most way-out of Sun Ra's discs of the period and as such may appeal more to jazz fans who find the chants and pink noise mystifying. The leader's free-form playing is tempered by some lovely, almost balladic touches.

*** Monorails And Satellites

Evidence ECD 22013 2 *Sun Ra (p solo).* 66.

Before considering the Arkestra recordings of the '60s, it is worth interpolating a comment about the solo material. There has always been a convention that Sun Ra's 'real' instrument was the collective sound of the Arkestra itself. While it has been contextualized with reference to the Henderson and Ellington orchestras or, looking forward, to Gil Evans and AACM, it's very rare to find the leader's piano-playing contextualized in the same way. With that in mind, it's worth noting that in the year *Monorails And Satellites* was made, Andrew Hill released *Andrew!* and Cecil Taylor *Unit Structures* on Blue Note; Chick Corea released his debut, *Tones For Joan's Bones*; *Solo Monk* had appeared the year before, and fellow-Chicagoan Muhal Richard Abrams's *Levels And Degrees Of Light* was still some months away. How does Sun Ra fare, compared to these? The immediate and obvious response is that *Monorails And Satellites* sounds rather old-fashioned, but at a second hearing there are aspects which are entirely unprecedented: great blocks of pure sound, a tonal richness and uncertainty that suggest Scriabin rather than James P. Johnson. There are few warp-speed runs on *Monorails*: rather, a gently spacey version of 'arranger's piano' that always seems to suggest cues for an absent band. The title-track certainly sounds like a direct transcription of Arkestra charts, as does the opening 'Space Towers'. 'The Galaxy Way', though, is entirely pianistic, a remarkable performance by any measure. Only one standard this time around: a surprisingly smooth version of 'East Street'.

*** Fate In A Pleasant Mood / When Sun Comes Out

Evidence ECD 22068 *Sun Ra; Phil Cohran, George Hudson, Walter Miller, Lucious Randolph (t); Teddy Nance, Bernhard Pettaway, Nate Pryor (tb); Danny Davis (as); Marshall Allen (as, f, bells, perc); John Gilmore (ts); Pat Patrick (bs); Ronnie Boykins (b); Jon Hardy (d); Clifford Jarvis (d, perc); Tommy Hunter (gong, perc); Theda Barbara (v).* 60, 62–63.

**** Cosmic Tones For Mental Therapy / Art Forms For Dimensions Tomorrow

Evidence ECD 22036 *Sun Ra; Manny Smith (t); Ali Hassan (tb); John Gilmore (ts, bcl, dragon d, sky d); Pat Patrick (bs, f); Marshall Allen (as, ob, astro space d); Danny Davis (as, f); Robert Cummings (bcl); James Jackson (f, log d); Ronnie Boykins, John Ore (b); Clifford Jarvis, C. Scoby Stroman (d, perc); Thomas Hunter (perc).* 61–62, 63.

**** Other Planes Of There

Evidence ECD 22037 *Sun Ra; Walter Miller (t); Ali Hassan, Teddy Nance (tb); Bernhard Pettaway (btb); Marshall Allen (as, ob, f); Danny Davis (as, f); John Gilmore (ts); Ronnie Cummings (bcl); Pat Patrick (bs); Ronnie Boykins (b); Roger Blank, Lex Humphries (d).* 64.

This is where the outer-space stuff begins with a vengeance. Sun Ra briefly experimented with the Hammond, producing huge, blocky areas of sound. Curiously, it wasn't an instrument that greatly attracted him, and recorded instances are surprisingly rare (there is another on *We Travel The Spaceways*). He coaxes extraordinary percussive effects from it on 'Moon Dance', the first highlight of *Cosmic Tones*. The other, unquestionably, is John Gilmore's long solo on 'Adventure-Equation'. It's a rare outing for Gilmore on bass clarinet (duties normally assigned to Robert Cummings), the only instrument he's credited with on this album. There has to be some doubt about this, as about most of these personnel details; but there is no doubt about the quality of the solo, which is his most compelling on record until 'Body And Soul' on *Holiday For Soul Dance*, several years later. The album is awash with echo effects and thunderous reverb, apparently devised by drummer Thomas Hunter, who claimed production and engineering credits. The 1961–2 *Art Forms* material is a good deal more straightforward in terms of pure sound, and the playing is absolutely up to standard. The band turns in a sterling performance of 'Ankh' (see *Bad And Beautiful*, above) which includes steaming solos from Patrick and trombonist Ali Hassan. Highly recommended.

Fate / Sun is a less appealing compilation but it does catch the Arkestra at a critical juncture. *Fate In A Pleasant Mood* documents the last Arkestra to be based in Chicago; it therefore strictly precedes the first of the New York sessions, *Bad And Beautiful*, which is listed above. Following a trip to Canada in the spring of 1961, a long-standing Arkestra began to break up, leaving only a rump of loyal adherents: Gilmore, Allen, Boykins and, despite having set out on a solo course, Pat Patrick, who signed up for a second term. Sun Ra began recruiting new members, including the teenage Danny Davis, who makes a solid impact on *When Sun Comes Out*. Gilmore sounds jaded and tentative on this record, and there is little of the spark of the earlier band, less still of its inspired weirdness. The appearance of Theda Barbara on 'Circe' is a foretaste of how important singers like June Tyson were to become in years to come.

Other Planes Of There is a long-overlooked masterpiece, but certainly also an oddity in the canon. In effect, it is Sun Ra's concerto for Arkestra. His own piano introduction touches bases all the way from Bud Powell to Cecil Taylor, and there are wonderful solos from Danny Davis, Gilmore and Marshall

Allen (on oboe). The rest of the record consists of shorter, jazzier segments, with another thoughtful solo from Gilmore on 'Sketch' and a more sensuous statement from Patrick on 'Pleasure'. *Other Planes* stands apart from the other recordings in this group. The instrumentation is straighter and the structures more obviously polyphonic. It shows how adaptable Sun Ra's concept still was in the mid-'60s.

*** The Heliocentric Worlds Of Sun Ra: Volume 1

ESP/Calibre 1014 *Sun Ra; Chris Capers (t); Teddy Nance (tb); Bernard Pettaway (tb, btb); Marshall Allen (as, picc, perc); John Gilmore (ts, tympani); Pat Patrick (bs, perc); Danny Davis (f, af); Ronnie Boykins (b).* 4/65.

*** The Heliocentric Worlds Of Sun Ra: Volume 2

ESP/Calibre 1017 *As above, except add Walter Miller (t); Jimmy Johnson (perc, tympani).* 11/65.

For a time, these were the only Sun Ra records generally known. Their mainstream celebrity in the UK was down to a brilliant article by Richard Williams in *Sounds* magazine, expressing a mixture of bafflement and awe at Sun Ra's aesthetic. Heard in retrospect, neither volume of *The Heliocentric Worlds* seems earth-shaking, and yet this is probably the best work of the period. Sun Ra's range of space effects is extraordinarily vivid; as well as piano, he plays electronic celeste, marimba, cello and tympani. On 'The Sun Myth' (Volume 2) he introduces part of the theme on bongos. Otherwise, the mood is sombre, ritualized and mysterious. John Gilmore's tympani duet with bassist Ronnie Boykins on 'Of Heavenly Things' (Volume 1) is, perversely, one of the best and most dramatic things the saxophonist ever did. Percussion dominates throughout both volumes, though there is a shift on the second part towards a more discursive and linear style of composition, and a feeling that some of these tracks have not been quite as fully worked out as on the first disc. These shouldn't be seen as a two-part set, because there is actually very little connection beyond title and personnel between the two sessions.

CORE COLLECTION

**** The Magic City

Evidence ECD 22069 *Sun Ra; Walter Miller (t); Chris Capers (t, perc); Ali Hassan, Teddy Nance (tb); Bernhard Pettaway (btb); Marshall Allen (as, f, picc); Danny Davis (as, f); Harry Spencer (as); John Gilmore (ts); Pat Patrick (bs, f); Robert Cummings (bcl); Ronnie Boykins (b); Roger Blank, Jimhmi Johnson (d); James Jackson (perc).* 65.

This record is about a futuristic place trapped in the present, rather than a past civilization swallowed up by history. 'The Magic City' was a promotional slogan for Birmingham, Alabama, to boost it as a commercial centre. References to slavery and race in an accompanying poem are bound up with imagery borrowed from the Bible or *Paradise Lost*, suggesting the rootedness of Sun Ra's fantastical vision in contemporary reality and in Afro-American tradition. The piece itself was collectively improvised, though the confident synchronization of small-group sections within the main piece strongly suggests either an element of 'conduction' or of predetermined sequences. This was the period of Ornette's *Free Jazz* and, more to the point, of Coltrane's huge *Ascension*, and *The Magic City* stands up remarkably well in that company.

**** Atlantis

Evidence ECD 22067 *Sun Ra; Akh Tal Ebah, Wayne Harris (t); Ali Hassan, Charles Stephens (tb); Bob Northern (frhn); Marshall Allen (as, ob, Jupiter f, perc); Danny Davis (as); John Gilmore (ts, perc); Robert Cummings (bcl); Pat Patrick (bs, f, perc); Robert Barry, Clifford Jarvis (d, perc); James Jackson (perc).* 67, 69.

As befits its majestic programme, the 22-minute 'Atlantis' is for the biggest Arkestra yet. Sun Ra himself plays (often simultaneously) both piano and clavioline. He claimed the latter gave him the 'purest' sound he'd ever had from an electric instrument. Oddly, though economics may have had something to do with it (the Arkestra was still a shoestring operation and busted instruments were not always repaired or replaced), at the time of this recording he was using squeaky little keyboards like the Hohner Clavinet or the Gibson Kalamazoo organ (a sound immortalized by Ray Manzarek of the Doors). *Atlantis* gained wider-than-usual currency, following reissue on the Impulse! label. Four tracks are for Sun Ra with Gilmore, Robert Barry and Clifford Jarvis only. A fifth, 'Bimini', adds Allen, Patrick and Jackson on percussion. These were supposed by some observers to be Sun Ra's nod in the direction of Thelonious Monk, but Cecil Taylor seems a more likely point of reference. The main piece starts *in medias res* (just like *Paradise Lost*) and rumbles hellishly before Sun Ra kicks in with a quite extraordinary organ solo that must count as one of his most significant instrumental passages. Ali Hassan plays a dadaist trombone solo before the piece is turned on its head with a skittish beat and the chant: 'Sun Ra and band from outer space have entertained you here.' It's an odd gesture, given the emotional temperature of what goes before, but that was Sun Ra ...

(***) The Ark And The Ankh

IKEF 004 *Sun Ra; Henry Dumas (v).* 66.

An extended interview with scholar Dumas, who takes Sun Ra through a spectrum of subjects, ranging from the Egyptological origins of black American culture to the political and cultural role of Malcolm X. Essential for Sun Ra specialists; too detailed and eccentric for all others.

***(*) Holiday For Soul Dance

Evidence ECD 22011 *Sun Ra; Phil Cohran (c); Danny Davis, Hobart Dotson, Akh Tal Ebah, Wayne Harris (t); Ali Hassan (tb); Marshall Allen, Danny Ray Thompson (as); John Gilmore (ts); Pat Patrick (bs, b); Robert Cummings (bcl); Bob Barry (d); James Jackson, Carl Nimrod (perc); Ricky Murray (v).* 68–69.

*** My Brother The Wind, Volume II

Evidence ECD 22040 *Sun Ra; Akh Tal Ebah, Kwame Hadi (t); Marshall Allen (as, ob, f); Danny Davis (as, acl, f); John Gilmore (ts, perc); Pat Patrick, Danny Ray Thompson (bs, f); James Jackson (ob, perc); Alejandro Blake (b); Clifford Jarvis, Lex Humphries (d); Nimrod Hunt (hand d); William Brister, Robert Cummings (perc).* 69, 70.

Predictably, *My Brother The Wind, Volume II* was followed many moons later by volume one. Sun Ra's organ really does sound 'intergalactic' on this one, but he also checks out that ubiquitous squealer of the late '60s, the Mini-Moog. His approach, inevitably, is heterodox in the extreme. Instead of making the synth sound like anything else, he homes in unerringly on its 'own' sound – shrill, with loads of vibrato – and then pushes all the buttons to get right into its uptight psyche:

angry bleeps, TV shut-down hiss, off-station crackles. The band, unfortunately, have begun to plod a bit, though the (uncredited) appearance of June Tyson on 'Walking On The Moon' – no relation to the pop hit – marks a hitherto undocumented association that was to last until the '90s (Tyson died shortly after Sun Ra in 1993).

Holiday is a more appealing album, largely because the band get their act together. It's entirely a standards set, but for the brief snippet of cornetist Cohran's 'Dorothy's Dance', which may have been conceived in homage to Oz. Sun Ra's opening solos on 'Holiday For Strings' and 'I Loves You, Porgy' amply confirm his *bona fides* as a 'straight' swing soloist. He shows a surprisingly light touch and gently alternates emphasis on left- and right-hand figures which again bear only a fleeting and misleading resemblance to Monk's. Gilmore's solo on 'Body And Soul', the tenor saxophonist's proving-ground, suggests something of what Coltrane found in his work. Much less well-known, Hobart Dotson also emerges strongly as an underrated player deserving of reassessment. Boykins's unexplained absence leaves the bottom end a bit straggly. Alejandro Blake is at best only a stop-gap replacement; at several points he's audibly flummoxed by what's going on and chugs out bland ostinato figures or else – what the hell! – goes quietly mad.

★★★(★) Nuits de la Fondation Maeght: Volume 1

Universe 80 *Sun Ra; Akh Tal Ebah (t, co); Kwame Hadi (t); Absolom Ben Shlomo (as, f, cl); Danny Davis (as, f, perc); Marshall Allen (as, f, cl, ob); Pat Patrick (as, ts, bs, f, cl, bcl, perc); John Gilmore (ts); Danny Ray Thompson (bs); Robert Cummings (bcl, d); James Jacson (f, cl, ob, perc); Danny Thompson (f, bsn); Alan Silva (b, vn, clo); Nimrod Hunt (d); Rashied Salim IV (d, vib); John Goldsmith, Lex Humphries (d, perc); June Tyson, Verta Grosvenor, Gloristeena Knight (v).* 6/70.

★★★ Nuits de la Fondation Maeght: Volume 2

Universe 81 *As above.* 6/70.

Like Cecil Taylor and Albert Ayler, Sun Ra played one of his most stirring live sets at this prestigious Parisian arts centre. These are fantastic recordings, once available on Jazz View but out of circulation for a time. 'Enlightenment' is sung by Sun Ra and June Tyson. The short keyboard piece 'The Stargazers' is an opportunity to hear Sun Ra solo, but it's what follows in the titanic 'Shadow World' that makes the first volume so compelling. So much of the talk about the Arkestra's soloists falls on John Gilmore that there's too little said about Marshall Allen's brilliance. In sound, he sits somewhere between Johnny Hodges and Eric Dolphy; his solo here is simply stunning and one of the highlights of the whole Arkestra canon. The final track of Volume 1, 'The Cosmic Explorer', is a disappointment, a whirl of seemingly random noise in places.

Volume 2 is more shambolic, but there are fine Sun Ra moments on 'Spontaneous Simplicity' and the multi-part 'Black Myth'. It makes sense to have both and with some judicious editing this would make a fine single CD, but if the budget presses, Volume 1 stands well on its own. The sound is better than on the Jazz View issue, which sounded as if it were taken direct from vinyl copies.

★★★(★) Space Is The Place

Evidence ECD 22070 *Sun Ra; Kwame Hadi (t, vib, perc); Wayne Harris (t); Marshall Allen (as, f, ob, bsn, kora, perc); Danny Davis (as, f, acl, perc); Larry Northington (as, perc); John Gilmore (ts, perc, v); Eloe Omoe (bcl, perc); Danny Ray Thompson (bs, perc); Lex Humphries (d); Ken Moshesh (perc); June Tyson (v).* 72.

In 1968, the year of upheaval in America as elsewhere, Sun Ra and the Arkestra made their first trip to the West Coast. Perhaps surprisingly, they were met with a wholly lukewarm response. Three years later, Sun Ra taught a course entitled 'The Black Man In The Cosmos' at the University of California, Berkeley, developing ideas that were to influence Anthony Braxton (Braxton wasn't on the course – but, then, hardly anyone was). Sun Ra felt rejected by the university and by California in general, and he returned east in high dudgeon. It was a repeat of the stormy Montreal trip.

However, Sun Ra had been spotted by producer Jim Newman, who suggested making a feature film loosely based on the mythology implicit in the Berkeley course. *Space Is The Place* cast Sun Ra as a cosmic equalizer, John Shaft in an even more outrageous suit, locked in combat with the Overseer, an interplanetary super-pimp who symbolizes the exploitation of the black races. As with a lot of experimental cinema of the time (a good example is Conrad Rooks's ill-fated *Chappaqua*, for which Ornette Coleman wrote the music), the soundtrack was far more interesting than the film itself. Using material from the previous few years – 'Outer Spaceways Incorporated', 'Calling Planet Earth', 'Space Is The Place' – Sun Ra compiled a brisk montage of Arkestra music. Sixteen tracks was unusually quick turnover, but it works remarkably well and the playing is tight and enigmatic. Tracks like 'Mysterious Crystal' were almost unprecedented in the Arkestra canon, combining a huge array of elements into something that simply cannot be characterized by reference to any other music. A setting like this was tailor-made for June Tyson, who sings hypnotically on 'Blackman'. Marshall Allen switches from his occasional oboe to bassoon to suggest the creaking evil of 'The Overseer', while Danny Davis switches to alto clarinet (anticipating Hamiet Bluiett's experiments on that unfamiliar horn by many years). The movie may still be circulating in obscure art-houses. Whatever the case, the music stands up amazingly well.

★★★(★) Space Is The Place

Impulse! IMP 12492 *Sun Ra; Akh Tal Ebah (t, flhn); Kwame Hadi (t); Marshall Allen, Danny Davis (as, f); John Gilmore (ts, v); Danny Ray Thompson (bs, v); Pat Patrick (bs, b, v); Eloe Omoe (bcl, f); Lex Humphries (d); Atakatune, Odun (perc); Cheryl Banks, Judith Holton, June Tyson, Ruth Wright (v); all Arkestra members also play percussion.* 10/72.

There is inevitable confusion over Sun Ra album titles, with so many overlaps and elsewhere a relatively limited permutation of space-related concepts. This one, entirely different from the record above, was engineered by Baker Bigsby for the Blue Thumb label and issued under those auspices in 1972, at a moment when Sun Ra seemed on the brink of mainstream recognition. It's a rather smooth performance by Arkestra standards, and almost too formulaically representative of what the group was about. Sun Ra plays piano only on 'Images', a small-group performance with Tal Ebah and Gilmore in close attendance, but with Patrick on bass. Elsewhere he plays the Farfisa 'Space' organ, and perhaps what is lacking on the album as a whole is the range of sounds that he might have been able to add with a Mini-Moog or some other synth of the time. To describe a Sun Ra album as 'spacious' is to risk being misunderstood, but that is how it comes across, open-textured, uncluttered and rather proper. A good point of entry for anyone who really doesn't want to fight their way past the hiss and crackle of the classic El Saturns, and there is much to enjoy on the title-track which dominates the set; but not one of his greatest moments.

***** Life Is Splendid**

Total Energy 3026 *Sun Ra; Akh Tal Ebah (t, flhn, v); Lamont McLamb (t); Marshall Allen, Danny Davis (as, f); Larry Worthington (as); John Gilmore (ts, perc); Pat Patrick (bs); Danny Ray Thompson (bs, f); Leroy Taylor (bcl); Lex Humphries, Robert Underwood, Alzo Wright (d); Russell Branch, Stanley Morgan (perc); Cheryl Bank, Judith Holton, June Tyson, Ruth Wright (v).* 9/72.

*****(*) Outer Space Employment Agency**

Total Energy 3021 *Sun Ra; Intergalactic Orchestra.* 9/73.

These were recorded in successive years at the Ann Arbor Blues And Jazz Festival. This was the town in Michigan where Sun Ra had had his first, uneasy encounter with the student hippie movement, an aspect of his fan-base he found troubling and unsatisfactory. In 1972 Slug's saloon in New York City, a regular Arkestra location, had closed its doors, and over the next few years the ensemble was more mobile and in some respects more responsive to changes of mood. The pity is that the opening of the 1972 Ann Arbor performance is missing. Proper balances were achieved only some minutes into a 40-minute suite of Arkestra staples. June Tyson and the leader are the dominant voices, and the huge swoops and wails of Sun Ra's organ are as exciting as any in the documentation, and it's a shame that the whole continuous performance can't be heard in its (doubtless dramatic) entirety. Memory may be deceptive, but we seem to recall that an edit of 'Life Is Splendid' was once included on an Atlantic sampler of performances from Ann Arbor. It would have hurt less if the meters had failed to calibrate the following year. This shaky recording is no less typical of the Arkestra's performances of the period and as such is valuable as a document of Sun Ra's work of the early '70s. He and June Tyson are the main elements, with the band behind producing a wild and often chaotic backdrop of pure sound, often according to no discernible harmonic or rhythmic logic. The long closing medley, which includes the title-piece, is more accessible than the rest of the record and the sound is inexplicably better in the middle section, following a rather obvious edit point. Were there multiple tape sources, or can it be that tapes of another performance have been collaged?

***** Live In Paris At The 'Gibus'**

Universe 79 *Sun Ra; Akh Tal Ebah, Kwame Hadi (t, flhn); Marshall Allen (as, picc, f, ob); Danny Davis (as, acl, f); John Gilmore (ts, perc); Danny Thompson (bs, f); Eloe Omoe (bcl, f); James Jacson (bsn, f, perc); Alzo Wright (vla, clo, d); Ronnie Boykins (b); Thomas 'Bugs' Hunter (d); Aralamon Hazoume, Odun, Makhtar Samba, Shahib (perc); Cheryl Bank, June Tyson, Ruth Wright (v).* 73.

From the busiest and most fertile period in Sun Ra's career since the '50s. A certain cult reputation made Arkestra performances a big draw and in Europe his eclectic mix of free jazz and swing was accepted with scarcely a murmur. Here, 'King Porter Stomp' is sandwiched between the long, open-plan 'Ombre Monde' and 'Salutations From The Universe'. As usual, there is a good deal of chanting and stage business that doesn't quite come across on record, but the version of 'Spontaneous Simplicity' at the beginning is an excellent earnest of what is to follow.

***** Concert For The Comet Kohoutek**

ESP/Calibre 3033 *Sun Ra; personnel similar to above.* 10/73.

Those young enough only to remember the arrival of Hale-Bopp will not be aware that the appearance of Kohoutek (which appears on the cover of Weather Report's *Mysterious Traveller*) was a cause for much foreboding and anxious speculation about the fate of the planet. Typically, Sun Ra greeted the planetary wanderer with cheerful gusto. This is one of the best live dates from the Arkestra of this period, a similar group to the Ann Arbor line-up, and with every bit as much energy. There is some very drab passage work and the chants are as irritating as ever, but buried away in this session is some of the music that makes Sun Ra a great American outsider. The sequence running from 'Unknown Kohoutek' to 'Discipline' is the place to sample.

***** The Great Lost Sun Ra Albums: Cymbals / Crystal Spears**

Evidence 22217 *Sun Ra; Akh Tal Ebah, Kwame Hadi (t, perc); John Gilmore (ts); Marshall Allen (as, f, picc, ob); Elmo Emoe (bcl, perc); Ronnie Boykins (b); Clifford Jarvis (d); Odun (perc).* 73.

***** Pathways To Unknown Worlds / Friendly Love**

Evidence 22218 *As above, except add James Jacson (d).* 73–74.

In the early '70s Sun Ra struck a deal with Impulse! Records to release both new material and back-catalogue Saturn albums. The understanding was inevitably short-lived, given the composer's incurable perversity and the label's desire to turn a small profit, even on marginal material. These two records are making their first (official) appearance on CD in this format. Both may have had some circulation before as unofficial releases. Neither is 'great' nor quite as 'lost' as the blurb would have it and neither substantially changes the picture of Sun Ra at this period. What impact they might have had if they had managed to get release at the time is imponderable but one suspects that Sun Ra would have continued to plod his lonely course as an outsider figure.

Cymbals is interesting in that it is effectively a small-group recording, mostly played quietly and intimately, a moment of downtime in the bowels of the mothership. Ra's keyboard effects are less baroque than usual; grander gestures are saved for the ensembles of *Crystal Spears*, which thumps along very familiarly. 'Sunrise In The Western Sky' is a rousing anthem and perhaps the most extravagantly beautiful thing on the record.

The other disc brings together some material that had already seen the light of day, but the remaining tracks that should have made up *Friendly Love* were seemingly rejected by Impulse! and are only now being heard. Robert L. Campbell has done sterling work in reconstructing these sessions and some of the extremely unusual instrumentation involved, which includes space mellophone and Neptunian libflecto! Pointless to look either of those up in *Grove*!

***** Greatest Hits: Easy Listening For Intergalactic Travel**

Evidence ECD 22219 *As above.* 56–73.

Since there weren't any chart hits – in the terrestrial charts at any rate – these selections were apparently made from fans' choices, though how the fans were polled isn't clarified, and one suspects this is a reasonable label compromise. There are 18 tracks from nearly 20 years of music making. 'Saturn', 'We Travel The Spaceways' and 'When Angels Speak Of Love' are probably the best-known Sun Ra compositions represented, but there is also a fine 'I Loves You, Porgy' and 'Round Midnight' is given the Arkestra treatment as well. A good single-CD introduction to the soundworld of Sun Ra.

*** The Solar Myth Approach: Volumes 1 & 2

Varese 061159 *Sun Ra; Akh Tal Ebah (t, mel); Kwame Hadi (t); Ali Hassan, Charles Stevens (tb); John Gilmore (ts, perc); Marshall Allen (as, picc, f, ob); Pat Patrick, Danny Ray Thompson (bs, f); Ronnie Boykins (b); Lex Humphries, Clifford Jarvis (d, perc); James Jacson (d, perc, f, ob); Nimrod Hunt (perc); Artie Jenkins (v).* 75.

This is a very good way in to Sun Ra's work as an innovative electronic keyboardist. The emphasis is for once very much on the leader and less so on the ensembles. Even such luminaries as Gilmore and Allen are relatively out of the picture, though both create typically powerful solos from time to time. It is Sun Ra's shimmering organ and Moog figures which capture the ear. It seemed at the time – and this was recorded for the European Byg/Actuel stable – that the Arkestra's music might well soundtrack the latest phase of the cultural revolution, but it never quite made it into the mainstream. The reissue of material like this underlines how very much of his moment Sun Ra could be; there are echoes here of everything from progressive rock to some of the classical experiments of the time. A valuable musical document.

***(*) Live At Montreux

Universe 75 / P-Vine 22032 *Sun Ra; Ahmed Abdullah, Chris Capers, Al Evans (t); Vincent Chauncey (frhn); Reggie Hudgins (ss); Marshall Allen, Danny Davis (as, f); John Gilmore (ts); Pat Patrick (bs, f); Eloe Omoe (bcl); James Jacson (bsn, perc); Tony Bunn, Hayes Burnett (b); Larry Bright, Clifford Jarvis (d); Stanley Morgan (perc); June Tyson (v).* 7/76.

Long out of print, and surprisingly so, since this is a very fine live date and infinitely superior to some of the lo-fi recordings that have circulated freely over the years. There are some edits on the set, and an unexpected fade towards the end of 'On Sound Infinity Spheres', though only very serious collectors will be troubled by this. The show the Arkestra gave in Switzerland is much superior to the one released on hatART some years later. It's pretty much standard fare, all of it heading for the curtain call of 'We Travel The Spaceways' (but managing to touch on 'Take The "A" Train' along the way) which begins with a fine piano introduction and includes a superb alto solo from Allen. 'House Of Eternal Being' and the rambunctious 'Gods Of The Thunder Realm' are the best of a set that, for us, could do with more tidying up, but a very welcome return to the catalogue; it's also available, without that fade, on P-Vine. A pity we can't see the dancers who were very much part of the Sun Ra experience at this time.

*** A Quiet Place In The Universe

Leo CD LR 198 *Sun Ra; probably Ahmed Abdullah (t); Akh Tal Ebah (t, v); Craig Harris (tb); Vincent Chauncey (frhn); Marshall Allen (as, picc); Pat Patrick (as); John Gilmore (ts); Danny Ray Thompson (bs, f) Luqman Ali (d); Atakatune, Eddie Thomas (perc); Eloe Omoe (bcl, f); James Jackson (bsn, f, perc); June Tyson (v).* 76–77.

We have to declare ourselves a touch confused about this one. According to a liner-note, tracks 3–6 ('Images', 'Love In Outer Space', 'I'll Never Be The Same' and 'Space Is The Place') have already been released on *A Night In East Berlin*, CD LR 149. The last of these four is ubiquitous, but none of the other tracks matches, and the listed personnels differ, and the suggested dates differ, so we are in the dark. This tape was no more illuminating than usual, found with just a number but believed (by expert Chris Trent) to be 1976 or 1977. If so, and it seems likely, this fills a long gap in the current discography. The sound is murky and congested, and there is considerable to-ing and fro-ing even though it does appear to be a concert documentation. 'I Pharaoh' is a slice of music theatre which homes in close on the leader and sounds to us as if it may not have been recorded at the same time or from the same position as the rest ...? The plus, as always, is the Gilmore solo, this time on the title-track, which is unusually arranged and followed by a french-horn solo from Vincent Chauncey. Some good music, then, but outstanding questions about the exact provenance.

*** Solo Piano Recital: Teatro La Fenice, Venezia

Golden Years of New Jazz GY 21 *Sun Ra (p solo).* 11/77.

The tapes are only of bootleg quality and there had been some deterioration in storage before Leo Feigin released them in his archive series. As a performance, it's very good indeed, and adds significantly to the remarkably small body of Sun Ra solo recordings. There are a couple of free improvisations, unremarkable except in that they cast light on his compositional procedures, mostly repetitive structures that disguise a lot of movement; one wonders if the some of the so-called American minimalists ever paid attention to Sun Ra recordings. 'Outer Spaceways Inc' and 'Love In Outer Space' are both familiar pieces, 'Angel Race' probably less so. 'Take The "A" Train' and 'St Louis Blues' are superb, but the real highlight is a sturdy deconstruction of 'Honeysuckle Rose' that ends up sounding like another tune entirely. Wonderful.

*** Lanquidity

Evidence ECD 22220 *Sun Ra; Michael Ray (t, flhn); Julian Priester (tb); Marshall Allen (as, f, ob); John Gilmore (ts, perc); Danny Ray Thompson (bs, f); Eloe Omoe (bcl, f); James Jacson (f, bsn, ob); Disco Kid, Dale Williams (g); Richard Williams (b); Tahmaha, June Tyson (v); Artaukatune, Luqman Ali (perc).* 78.

An unusual item in the Sun Ra discography, since it is to all intents and purpose an album of relatively conventional grooves over which the leader and a couple of the horns lay some out-of-whack lines. Originally recorded for the small Philly Jazz label and long out of circulation, it's more of a curiosity than a key Arkestra recording, but it's certainly worthy of a listen. The title-track is oddly moving, almost elegiac and 'Twin Stars Of Thence' has some lovely playing by the leader.

**(*) Sunrise In Different Dimensions

hatOLOGY 568 *Sun Ra; Michael Ray (t); John Gilmore (ts, cl, f); Chris Henderson, Eric Walker (d).* 2/80.

Recorded live in Switzerland, which explains the unusual label for a Sun Ra disc, this isn't the most inspiring of his albums of the time. There's something faintly leaden about the Arkestra's performance, though the Henderson-tinged versions of 'Limehouse Blues', 'King Porter Stomp' and even 'Take The "A" Train' are thoroughly enjoyable. A lot of music for your money, but none of it top-drawer Sun Ra.

*** Nuclear War

Atavistic Unheard Music 40242 *Sun Ra; unknown personnel.* 9/82.

This was supposed to have been issued in England by Y Records, who went out of business before the record could be pressed. Originally released in Greece and later licensed by John Corbett of Atavistic, this is a worthy enough later-period Arkestra record. 'Drop Me Off In Harlem', 'Sometimes I'm Happy' and 'Smile' are fascinating examples of his standards arrangements of the period. By contrast, the originals are fairly dull.

***(*) Cosmo Sun Connection

Recommended ReR SR1 *Sun Ra; Tyrone Hill (tb); Marshall Allen (as, f); Eloe Omoe (as, bcl); John Gilmore (ts, perc); Danny Ray Thompson (bs, f); Rollo Radford (b); Atakatune (perc); other personnel unidentified.* 84.

The story on this undated but apparently 1984 recording is an interesting one. Recommended imported a good deal of Sun Ra material into Europe during the '70s and '80s. Pressings were paid for up front, but on one occasion money had been so tight in the Arkestra that ReR's front man, Chris Cutler, arrived to find his advance had been spent and no discs were forthcoming. To purge his debt, Sun Ra gave Cutler the master-tape of *Cosmo Sun Connection*; Cutler in turn is turning over proceeds to the Arkestra as a gesture of respect and to help a group which now finds itself leaderless and in no small debt.

Musically, it isn't a classic, though performances of 'Fate In A Pleasant Mood' and the title-track are absolutely typical of what the group was doing in this period. Gilmore makes a commanding figure throughout, though it's Marshall Allen (better recorded and sounding full of beans) who steals his thunder on occasion. Hints of funk and rock-influenced, straight-eight patterns give the record an immediate impact that will recommend (no pun intended) it to those who find some of the floatier, ritual stuff hard to swallow.

*** The Sun Ra Arkestra Meets Salah Ragab In Egypt

Leo/Golden Years of New Jazz GY 1 *Sun Ra; Tyrone Hill (tb); Marshall Allen (as, f); Danny Ray Thompson (as, bs, perc); John Gilmore (ts, perc); Eloe Omoe (as, bcl, perc); James Jackson (bsn); Rollo Radford (b, perc); Claude Broche, Chris Henderson, Clifford Jarvis (d); Matthew Brown, Salah Ragab (perc).* 71, 72–74, 75, 83, 84.

Given how thoroughly his philosophy was based on the ancient Egyptian civilizations and their thought-practice, the prospect of playing in Egypt was obviously a very beguiling one for Sun Ra. The Arkestra played at the Ballon Theatre in Cairo in 1971, a performance documented on a rare Thoth Intergalactic LP, but despite the confusing dates on the disc all of the Sun Ra material comes from two further visits in 1983 and 1984 when he played in the company of drummer (and later head of Egypt's military music) Salah Ragab. The remainder of the album consists of much earlier material by Ragab and his small group ('Oriental Mood') and by the Cairo Jazz Band ('Ramadan', 'A Farewell Theme') and the Cairo Free Jazz Ensemble ('Music For Angela Davis'), performances which do not involve either Sun Ra or any Arkestra members. Like the item below, this was originally released on Praxis but has now been licensed to Leo Feigin's new Golden Years of New Jazz imprint. The Egyptian players seem to be as much impressed by American innovations as Sun Ra was by ancient Nilotic culture; the final piece at least, but for some unexpected tonalities, might be the work of an American or even European improvising ensemble of the time. The Arkestra was so completely *sui generis* that it's hard to be surprised by any variation in its 'usual' practice. Ragab certainly brings a fresh rhythmic awareness to the tracks where he is featured, and one can imagine American musicians heading home with unsuspected subdivisions of 13/8 and 11/8 ringing in their ears.

***(*) Live At Praxis '84

Leo/Golden Years of New Jazz GY 5 2CD *Sun Ra; Ronnie Brown (t, flhn, perc); Marshall Allen (as, cl, f, ob, kora, perc); Eloe Omoe (as, bcl, contra-acl, f, perc); John Gilmore (ts, cl, perc, v); Danny Ray Thompson (bs, as, f, perc); James Jackson (bsn, f, ob, perc, v); Rollo Radford (b); Don Mumford (d, perc); Matthew Brown, Salah Ragab (perc).* 2/84.

Trimmed down from a triple LP recorded in concert in Athens, Greece, this double set is one of the best live recordings of the Arkestra at any period, certainly in terms of giving an accurate impression of how a set developed round swing standards, free-for-all improvisation and ritual chanting. The ability to swing from 'Mack The Knife', 'Cocktails For Two' and 'Satin Doll' back to 'Theme Of The Stargazers' is consistently jaw-dropping and the band had rarely sounded as exuberant, with some of the more intriguing textures coming from what are described as 'electric valve-instruments'. There is less emphasis than even five years before on Sun Ra himself as an instrumentalist. Increasingly, he seemed to be the dramaturge and guiding spirit who held the whole remarkable thing together.

***(*) A Night In East Berlin / My Brothers The Wind And Sun No. 9

Leo CD LR 149 *Sun Ra; Michael Ray, Ahmed Abdullah (t); Tyrone Hill (tb); Pat Patrick (as); Marshall Allen (as, f); John Gilmore (ts, perc, v); Danny Ray Thompson (bs, perc); Kenny Williams (bs); Eloe Omoe (as, bcl); James Jackson (bsn, perc); Bruce Edwards (g); Billy Bang, Owen Brown Jr (vn); June Tyson (vn, v); John Ore, Rollo Radford (b); Luqman Ali, Earl Buster Smith (d); ?Pharoah Abdullah (perc); Art Jenkins (v).* 6/86, 1/88 or 90.

In true Leo Records style, the origins of these tapes are shrouded in uncertainty, and the disc fades in on the opening of the East Berlin set, as if the mikes weren't on quick enough. Whatever the technical shortcomings, there's no mistaking the quality or beauty of the music. 'Mystic Prophecy' highlights two of the Arkestra's pillars, Marshall Allen and John Gilmore, and Gilmore is pressed into vocal duty with his boss in the absence of June Tyson, who seems not to have made the trip on this occasion.

The material on *My Brothers The Wind And Sun No. 9* was originally released in an extremely limited edition on an El Saturn white-label release with just a number and (in some cases) a few hand-written comments. Like the East German material, titles weren't known till later. It's thought this may have been recorded at the Knitting Factory in New York City, and there is apparently further material from that time. Good news, because this is a steamingly good band, fierce and propulsive in the slipstream of Sun Ra's synth and with the additional bonus of Billy Bang in the ensembles and soloing. Regrettably, this being *samizdat*-land, it's interrupted by the end of the tape. The most valuable single item on the disc is the quasi-atonal 'The Shadow World', a most unexpected conception even for this most unexpected of groups. No surprise that it should again feature Allen and Gilmore.

*** Reflections In Blue

Black Saint 120101 *Sun Ra; Randall Murray (t); Tyrone Hill (tb); Pat Patrick (as, cl); Marshall Allen (as, f, ob, picc); Danny Ray Thompson (as, cl, bcl); John Gilmore, Ronald Wilson (ts); James Jackson (bsn, African d); Carl LeBlanc (g); Tyler Mitchell (b); Thomas Hunter, Earl Buster Smith (d).* 12/86.

***(*) Hours After

Black Saint 120111 *As above.* 12/86.

*** Love In Outer Space

Leo CD LR 180 *Sun Ra and his Arkestra; no personnel details.* 12/83.

The '80s were a period of steady and often unimaginative consolidation. Sun Ra's music had, at last, become a *style*. Even so, the Arkestra were still able to create an astonishing impact in performance. There are powerful moments on *Love In Outer Space*, which was recorded at a concert in Utrecht. The closing 'Space Is The Place' still sounds positive and challenging, and there are outrageous versions of 'Big John's Special' and 'Round Midnight'.

Of later '80s performances, *Reflections In Blue* and, from the same sessions, *Hours After* concentrate exclusively on mainstream composition (though the latter is punctuated by a chaotic 'Dance Of The Extra Terrestrians' and 'Love On A Far Away Planet', which are more typical of past snippets from the Arkestra's anarchic shows).

*** Second Star To The Right: Salute To Walt Disney

Leo CD LR 230 *Sun Ra; Michael Ray (t, v); Tyrone Hill, Julian Priester (tb); Marshall Allen (as, cl, f); Eloe Omoe (as, cl, bcl); Noel Scott (as, cl, f); James Jackson (bsn, ob, v); Bruce Edwards (g); Arthur Joonie Booth (b); June Tyson (vn, v); Earl 'Buster' Smith (d); Elson Nascimento Santos (perc).* 4/89.

*** Stardust From Tomorrow

Leo CDLR 235/236 2CD *As above.* 4/89.

Sun Ra plays Disney. Of course. Initially this sounds so perverse as to go all the way round to being inevitable. A&M had done an album of Disney covers which included the Arkestra doing 'Pink Elephants On Parade' from *Dumbo*, but this Austrian concert goes the whole hog. Marshall Allen provides alto solos of surreal beauty in the opening chant on 'Forest Of No Return' and to the Sun Ra-introduced 'Someday My Prince Will Come'. The leader even quotes a couple of Miles Davis tags on his long, delicate opening, before horns, vocalists June Tyson and a falsetto Michael Ray, and then the rhythm come in behind him. 'Frisco Fog' isn't Disney and, perversely, it's the best band track on the date, a driving, train-time number that gets the sections properly worked out. 'I'm Wishing' is pretty good but takes an age to get under way. The title-tune gives Hill a lot of space, and 'Hi Ho! Hi Ho!' features Scott on alto and clarinet. Sun Ra experts seem to think 'Zip-A-Dee-Doo-Dah' is from *Sleeping Beauty* but, apart from that, it's good to have what is effectively a private bootleg recording so fully documented. The sound is awful; someone coughs right in the mic at one point and there is only a rather artificial balance on some tracks. The piano is clearly audible, though, and no complaints about the quality of the music.

Stardust From Tomorrow was recorded in concert at the Jazzatelier in Ulrichsberg, Austria. It's a fascinating document of the Arkestra at work and in its pomp. The mix of material is breathtaking: untitled composition/improvisations by the leader, 'Prelude To A Kiss', Noble Sissle and Fletcher Henderson's 'Yeah, Man' and the crowd-pleasing 'We Travel The Spaceways' to round off the night. It sounds as if it has been recorded through the mixing desk, and while the balance is pretty decent, there's too much emphasis on horns and percussion and not nearly enough on the main man. Otherwise, though, a fine set.

**** Mayan Temples

Black Saint 120121 *Sun Ra; Ahmed Abdullah, Michael Ray (t, v); Tyrone Hill (tb); Noel Scott (as); Marshall Allen (as, f); John Gilmore (ts, perc); James Jackson (bsn, perc); Jothan Callins (b); Clifford Barbaro, Earl 'Buster' Smith (d); Ron McBee, Elson Nascimento Santos, Jorge Silva (perc); June Tyson (v).* 7/90.

As Francis Davis points out in his liner-note, this studio session restores the emphasis to Sun Ra's piano-playing. Illness would shortly curtail his ability to play acoustic keyboards this crisply. His introductions and leads are absolutely in the line of Ellington, and the voicings are supple, open-ended and often quietly ambiguous, leaving considerable emphasis on the soloists. As always, Gilmore is a giant and Marshall Allen's searing solo on 'Prelude To Stargazers' is a model of controlled fury. Ra re-records 'El Is A Sound Of Joy' (see *Supersonic Jazz*, above), a late-'50s theme that sounds completely contemporary and brings a freshness and simplicity to 'Alone Together' that is quite breathtaking. 'Discipline No. 1' is a lovely ballad, illustrating Sun Ra's ability to give simple material an unexpected rhythmic profile (Davis rightly points to the example of Mingus in this case) and the closing 'Sunset On The Night On The River Nile' is one of his very best space anthems. Few Sun Ra albums give a better sense of his extraordinary versatility; this is far preferable to the majority of recent live sets.

***(*) Live At The Hackney Empire

Leo CD LR 214/215 2CD *Sun Ra; Michael Ray (t, v); Jothan Callins (t); Tyrone Hill (tb); Marshall Allen (as, f, picc, ob); Noel Scott (as, bcl); John Gilmore (ts, cl, perc, v); Charles Davis (bs); James Jackson (bsn, perc); India Cooke (vn); Kash Killion (clo); John Ore (b); Clifford Barbaro, Earl Buster Smith (d); Talvin Singh (perc, v); Elson Nascimento Santos (perc); June Tyson (v).* 10/90.

This concert was recorded as part of a documentary project originally for Britain's Channel 4. Originally, there was a projected backdrop and other effects, but so far the finished work – by Chris Foster and Dave Hayes – has not materialized. It has nevertheless bequeathed us some excellent music, if unsurprising in content by Arkestra standards, until the second set, at any rate. All the familiar names are present and all in good form: Gilmore, Allen (glorious on 'Prelude To A Kiss') and Tyson. Disc two begins with a violin improvisation, before Davis, Cooke, Allen and others solo over 'Discipline 27-II'. There is then a version of 'East Of The Sun' (vocalist, Gilmore), a beautiful rendition of a Sun Ra favourite, 'Somewhere Over The Rainbow', and a rapid charge through the Sissle/Henderson anthem 'Yeah Man!' and 'Frisco Fog'. A now-familiar mixture of the strange and the traditional, this is a highly attractive set.

(★★★) Pleiades

Leo CD LR 210/211 2CD *Sun Ra; Jothan Callins, Michael Ray (t); Tyrone Hill (tb); Marshall Allen (as); John Gilmore, Noel Scott (ts); Charles Davis (bs); James Jackson (ob, d); India Cooke (vn); Kash Killion (clo); John Ore (b); Clifford Barbaro, Earl Chinna Smith (d); Elson Nascimento Santos (perc); Talvin Singh (tabla); June Tyson (v, vn); unidentified symphony orchestra.* 10/90.

It is a measure of Sun Ra's belatedly growing reputation that this concert was able to take place at all. Recorded in Paris, it features a mainly unfamiliar Arkestra and all-too-familiar repertoire (with the exception of Chopin's 'Prelude In A Major'!) in an acoustic that is Jupiterian in resonance. The recording falls so far below acceptable standards that *Pleiades* seems to represent a return to the snap, crackle and pop of the old El Saturns (and of Leo's original, *samizdat* catalogue). One wonders how good and faithful servants like Gilmore and Allen viewed the music by this stage; Tyson's enthusiasm, though, is undimmed, and it is significant that she should have survived Sun Ra by such a short time.

★★(★) Friendly Galaxy

Leo CD LR 188 *Sun Ra Arkestra; no personnel details.* 4/91.

★★★ At The Village Vanguard

Rounder 12125 *Sun Ra; John Gilmore (ts); Chris Anderson (p); Bruce Edwards (g); John Ore (b); Earl Chinna Smith (d).* 91.

The rest should have been silence, but just as the concert appearances (and the word is used advisedly) continued to the bitter end, so too will offcuts and live sessions continue to emerge. Few of the later dates do Sun Ra's memory any credit. Ill and tired, he plays a largely symbolic role in the proceedings, fronting shrunken ensembles that no longer seem to have the concentration to play ensemble music. The absence of Gilmore on the last session, whatever the reason, has to be seen as symbolic. He is present on the Rounder Records disc, which documents the moment when Sun Ra led a sextet at the Village Vanguard. The leader is doing little more than adding shades and gestures to the group, and the presence of guitarist Bruce Edwards probably renders most of them irrelevant. The plaudits go to Chris Anderson, who sounds very much as Sun Ra must have done in the Fletcher Henderson years, hooked confidently into swing, but looking ever outward for something new. Gilmore makes his presence known in brief flashes, but the old dark fire has gone.

There will be other releases, and continued debate about the enigma that was Sun Ra. As for his place in history, one must conclude that, for the moment at least ... destination unknown.

★★(★) A Song For The Sun

El Ra 99021 *Fred Adams, Dave Gordon, Michael Ray (t); Dick Griffin, Tyrone Hill (tb); Marshall Allen (as, f); Noel Scott (as); Charles Davis (bs); Bruce Edwards (g); John Ore (b); Luqman Ali (d); Jorge Silva, Ted Thomas (perc).* 99.

Given how other-worldly much of the Sun Ra oeuvre was, a ghost Arkestra might have worked better than both. There are plenty of familiar names in the line-up, and no one had more right to front such a band than the permanently under-rated Marshall Allen, but in the absence of John Gilmore, June Tyson and Sun Ra, this seems no more than a slick copycat outfit with very little originality. What's most telling is that the once virtuosic balance between free-form jazz and swing is now self-conscious and awkwardly executed. Anyone interested in the afterlife of the band would be better tracking down some of the live issues that have appeared since the leader's final transition.

Monty Sunshine (born 1928)

CLARINET

Born in London, Sunshine is a key figure in British trad of the '50s and onwards. He was a featured soloist in the Chris Barber band, and his departure in 1960 to form his own group and play in a relatively strict New Orleans style was a minor sensation at the time. In the past four decades he has pursued his own take on this music, and he found a big following in Europe, especially Germany.

★★★ The Full Monty Sunshine

Upbeat URCD 184 *Sunshine; Rod Mason, Ian Hunter-Randall (t); Graham Stewart (tb, v); Charlie Galbraith (tb); Johnny Parker, Barney Bates (p); Dickie Bishop (bj, g); Duncan Chalmers (bj); Gerry Salisbury (bg, tba); Ron Russell (b); Nick Nicholls, Geoff Downs (d); Beryl Bryden (v, wbd); George Melly (v).* 7/61–4/67.

★★★ Just A Little While To Stay Here

Lake LACD 70 *Sunshine; Ken Colyer (t, v); Alan Gresty (t); John Beecham, Ron Brown (tb), Barry Dew, Lonnie Donegan (bj, v); Ken Bartin (bj, g, v); Pete Sayers (g, v), Tony Bagot, Mickey Ashman (b); Geoff Downs (d).* 80–87.

An auld licht traditionalist, Sunshine stood firm when the Chris Barber band began to shift its ground in the late '50s to accommodate the growing vogue for skiffle and the blues. Sunshine had contributed materially to the group's success and was the featured soloist on the big hit, 'Petite Fleur'. Leaving Barber certainly punched holes in his marketability, but he has commanded a loyal following in both Britain and continental Europe throughout the past three decades.

The earlier Sunshine is well represented on Chris Barber records and on some useful trad compilations, but to some extent he has remained in the shadow of more eminent colleagues. *The Full Monty Sunshine* takes three snapshots of the band as it stood at the beginning and in the middle of the '60s. A 1961 BBC broadcast finds the group in enjoyably rowdy form, with a couple of mighty vocals from Beryl Bryden for good measure, although when asked for a bit of finesse on 'I Keep Calling Your Name' the group sounds a bit woeful. Three titles from a year later (with George Melly guesting this time) are a little smarter, but the ten 1967 titles (from an NDR radio session) are handled much more crisply and authoritatively, even if some of the excitement of the earlier days has been tempered. The BBC material is a little rough soundwise, but the German tracks are bright and clear. The obvious fillip on *Just A Little While* ... is the presence of Colyer and Donegan (and perhaps, for some tastes, country singer Pete Sayers as well) on a couple of tracks each. But for them, this would be a slightly pedestrian set. There are live tracks from London, Hamburg and Cologne, and all of the material was previously issued on the German Pinorrekk label.

***** New Orleans Hula**
Lake LACD 47 *Sunshine; Alan Gresty (t); Johnny Beecham (tb); Barry Dew (bj, v); Tony Bagot (b); Geoff Downs (d).* 4/85.

Originally released (on vinyl) on Stomp Off, this catches the 1985 edition of the Sunshine band in good fettle. At this point, Gresty had already been in the group for many years and the line-up had settled down into a form which has largely remained constant since. In his notes, Paul Adams suggests that it's the 'danceable' feel of the playing which sets the Sunshine band apart, and the easy-going jog which they like to work at certainly finds an effective point between plodding and belting along. The set could use a track which really collars the listener, but it's a likeable session.

***** Live At The Worker's Museum, Copenhagen**
Music Mecca CD 1096 *Sunshine; Arne Mathiesen (t, v); Finn Frosig (tb, v); Preben Danielsson (cl, as, ss); Jorgen Juncker (bj); Ebbe Wettlaufer (b); Morten Pedersen (d).* 3/96.

Sunshine has been as much admired in Scandinavia as the other British traditionalists, and this lively set catches him with 'Pee Dee' Danielsson's group playing Kid Ory tunes (a fine version of 'Savoy Blues') and some traditional gospel, ending unexpectedly with 'When I Grow Too Old To Dream', which has a delightful elegiac quality that crept back into Sunshine's work over the '90s. The sound is a bit cavernous, but decent enough for all but the fussiest of purchasers, and a bit of lift in the bass helps a good deal.

***** You Are My Sunshine**
Timeless TTD 609 *Sunshine; Alan Gresty (t); John Beecham (tb); Barry Dew (bj, v); Tony Bagot (b); Tony Scriven (d).* 4/96.

***** Live At The BP Studienhaus**
Timeless TTD 620 *As above.* 9/97.

This line-up has acquired plenty of seasoning by now, and they sound as comfortable as you'd expect; but there's a degree of literacy and easy-going determination which set the Sunshine band apart from many traditional outfits: they're less drilled than Barber's group but won't submit to the sloppiness of weekend trad. There are too many obvious tunes on both these discs – surely Sunshine must be exhausted with the likes of 'Just A Little While To Stay Here' and 'Put On Your Old Grey Bonnet'? – and the singing won't really do. But the group are still enjoying themselves, and the live album has a genuine *joie de vivre* rare in this often relentless genre. Sunshine's clarinet is still finding unexpected paths, too: listen to his pretty outrageous solo on 'Yellow Dog Blues' from *You Are My Sunshine.*

The Sunshine Boys

GROUP

Joe and Dan Mooney were a vaudeville duo, popular on American radio in the '20s and early '30s.

*****(*) The Sunshine Boys**
Retrieval RTR 79039 *Joe Mooney (p, v); Mannie Klein, Tommy Gott (t); Tommy Dorsey, Charlie Butterfield (tb); Jimmy Dorsey, Benny Goodman (cl, as); Hymie Wolfson (ts); Irving Brodsky (p); Cornell Smelser (acc, xy); Joe Venuti (vn); Eddie Lang, Dick McDonough, Carl Kress (g); Ward Ley, Hank Stern (b); Dan Mooney, Bruce Yantis (v).* 29–31.

A charming rediscovery. Joe and Dan Mooney have entirely disappeared into obscurity. They began working together in radio from 1926, and recorded these 23 sides between 1929 and 1931. The material is all modern pop of the order of 'I'm Crooning A Tune About June', 'Would You Like To Take A Walk?' and 'Boy! Oh! Boy! I've Got It Bad'. Dan sings most of the leads, Joe plays piano and harmonizes, and although there are six titles with a full band – two with Ben Selvin, and four with Irving Mills – most of them have no more than two or three other players in the studio. As these include Tommy Dorsey, Joe Venuti, Eddie Lang and Dick McDonough, though, the results are in the chamber-jazz mould beloved of New York studios of the day. The Mooneys also engage in plenty of polite scatting, much in the mould of Paul Whiteman's Rhythm Boys, and most of the up-tempo titles go with a real and unaffected swing. Nicely mastered from decent originals, it sounds great. Their disappearance is mysterious. No photograph of the pair exists, and while Joe continued in the business on and off until his death in 1975, Dan seems to have vanished completely after they split up the duo in 1936.

Klaus Suonsaari (born 1959)

DRUMS

Suonsaari is a Finn who led one of his country's leading groups, Blue Train, in the '80s, before these leadership dates.

*****(*) Reflecting Times**
Storyville STCD 4157 *Suonsaari; Tom Harrell (t, flhn); Bob Berg (ts); Niels Lan Doky (p); Ray Drummond (b).* 3/87.

***** Inside Out**
Soul Note 121274 *Suonsaari; Scott Wendholt (t, flhn); Scott Robinson (ts, ss, f); Renee Rosnes (p); Steve Nelson (vib); Ray Drummond (b).* 3/94.

A Finnish drummer who sounds not a bit like Edward Vesala (but is a physical ringer for Bill Frisell). The Storyville record obviously gains visibility from the other band members, but it is the leader's clean, unaffected swing, reminiscent of Billy Hart or Billy Higgins, that strikes even the casual listener straight away, and it has become clear that he is not just a facile time-keeper but is also a very thoughtful musician, contributing several numbers to *Inside Out*, a very polished record which is disappointing only relative to earlier promise. Something doesn't quite gel about it. Despite the bright opening, we have not heard the best from him yet.

***** Something In Common**
Storyville 4218 *Suonsaari; Jukka Perko (ss, as); Jerry Bergonzi (ts); Niels Lan Doky, Jarmo Savolainen (p); Mike Mainieri, Severi Pyysalo (vib); Ray Drummond, Eerik Siikasaari (b); Bobby Sanabria (perc).* 98.

Another powerful set from the drummer, this time with a larger group and some quite adventurous arrangements. Two basic groups are involved, similarly configured but each with its own definite character. The combination of saxophone, vibes and percussion defines much of the record, an intensely rhythmic sound that also allows a sophistication of harmonics as well, especially when a bassist of Ray Drummond's stamp is involved in the ensembles. Pyysalo's 'Burning Bridges', Bergonzi's 'Jab', Savolainen's 'Inseparable' and the standard 'If I Were A Bell' are the only tracks not by Suonsaari, whose writing is, as usual, inventive and unexpected. 'Motion', 'Blues For G' and 'Happy People' are worth sampling. Klaus has a good website with some interesting musical downloads.

★★★(★) With Every Breath I Take

Storyville 4241 *Suonsaari; Scott Robinson (Cmel, ts, bsx, theremin); Geri Allen (p); Jules Thayer (b).* 99.

The title-piece is a delightful thing, artfully executed and completely idiomatic, but it's the originals and arrangements (including a theme by Shostakovich) which catch the attention here. 'Skar' is collectively improvised and very impressive. 'The Amorphous Them' and 'Imaginary Day' are showcases for the drummer, as is 'Visions', though it has a more elaborate structure. Robinson creates a wide range of sounds on his horns and theremin, but it is Geri Allen who holds the set together with some of her most straightforward playing in years, almost as if she is happy to subsume personal considerations for the duration. 'Subsumption' opens the set and prompts the thought that all the players involved were happy to leave egos and other agenda parked at the door. Attractive, selfless music that reflects well on all concerned.

John Surman (born 1944)

BARITONE AND SOPRANO SAXOPHONES, BASS AND ALTO CLARINETS, SYNTHESIZERS, PIANO, RECORDER

Born in Tavistock, Devon, he studied in London and quickly came to prominence as a leading force in the new British jazz of the '60s. Major associations with Mike Westbrook, Mike Gibbs, John McLaughlin and SOS, as well as his own solo records, before the sequence of ECM albums which has brought him further renown in the '80s and '90s.

★★★ John Surman

Deram 844 884-2 *Surman; Kenny Wheeler (t, flhn); Malcolm Griffiths, Paul Rutherford (tb); Tom Bennellick (frhn); Mike Osborne (as); Russell Henderson (p, b); Dave Holland, Harry Miller (b); Stirling Betancourt, Alan Jackson (d); Errol Phillip (perc).* 69.

★★★(★) How Many Clouds Can You See?

Deram 844 882-2 *Surman; Harry Beckett (t, flhn); Malcolm Griffiths, Chris Pyne (tb); George Smith (tba); Mike Osborne (as); Alan Skidmore (ts); John Warren (bs, f); John Taylor (p); Harry Miller, Barre Phillips (b); Alan Jackson, Tony Oxley (d).* 70.

♛ ★★★★ Tales Of The Algonquin

Deram 844 883-2 *Surman; Harry Beckett, Martin Drover, Kenny Wheeler (t, flhn); Danny Almark, Malcolm Griffiths, Ed Harvey (tb); Mike Osborne (as, cl); Alan Skidmore (ts, af); Stan Sulzmann (as, ss, f); John Warren (b, f); John Taylor (p); Harry Miller, Barre Phillips (b); Alan Jackson, Stu Martin (d).* 71.

John Surman first came to notice in Mike Westbrook's group, and it was a direct result of his performances on the Westbrook albums *Celebration* and *Marching Song* that persuaded producer Peter Eden to record him for Deram. The first of these makes slightly unexpected listening, being largely devoted to calypso jazz in the Sonny Rollins mode, played accurately and with some exuberance but hardly representative of what are now thought to be Surman's great strengths – his ability to combine power with a fragile delicacy on both baritone and soprano, and to move between sophisticated vertical improvisation and diatonic folk.

At the same time Surman was developing a more individual style in a trio with Dave Holland and Alan Jackson, and the second half of the debut record was devoted to large-scale arrangements of trio material. Unfortunately that is very much the impression the album creates. The ensembles sound padded-out rather than organic, though by the closing 'Dance', inspired by Coltrane's *Africa/Brass*, the mix is a good deal richer and more coherent.

How Many Clouds Can You See? marks a dramatic step forward. The slow, brooding opening track 'Galata Bridge' builds steadily to a climax of frenzied energy before calming and then building again to a more measured peak, almost as if the ensemble have crossed the bridge in question, which is in Istanbul and straddles two very different cultures. The Middle Eastern influence is replaced by a folksy Celticism on 'Caractacus', the name of the Pictish chieftain who faced down the Romans; this is a feature for Surman and drummer Jackson. After that comes a first Surman collaboration with the Canadian composer John Warren, who was to play an important part on the third and last Deram recording. 'Premonition' is a powerful trade-off between free jazz and more classically orientated structures and was an important pointer to what was to come later.

The final two tracks, the multi-part 'Event' and the title-piece, are small-group pieces, reflecting the kind of work Surman was doing with The Trio. The closing part of 'Event', 'Circle Dance', is powered along by drummer Oxley's vivid use of dynamics and his ability to combine a strong pulse with apparent freedom from steady metre. It is another key moment, and one regrets that Surman was to have few chances in future years to work in this vein with players of Oxley's and Phillips's stature.

Surman's time with Deram ended with his very best album to date, a full-scale collaboration with Warren. *Tales Of The Algonquin* is a masterpiece, conceived on a grand scale, meticulously executed and marked by superb soloing from Surman, Skidmore and the always wonderful Osborne. The set opens with four unrelated themes by Warren. Surman produces a boiling soprano solo on the up-tempo 'With Terry's Help', which exploits double time and displaced harmonies. 'The Dandelion' is perhaps the stand-out track of the album, though it is Mike Osborne's plaintive, keening solo which gives it its power. By contrast, the connected pieces which give the album its title are slightly too fey and impressionistic. 'Shingebis And The North Wind' is adventurous even by the standards of those blithely experimental days. Again Surman takes a back seat, this time to trumpeter Harry Beckett, who solos with an elemental sadness. Surman sounds most sure-footed in the immediate company of his Trio colleagues Phillips and Martin and produces his own most effective playing with them on 'The Adventures Of Manabush'. *Tales* is a record that has enjoyed almost legendary status among British jazz fans. It is one of the most welcome reissues of the last decade and a must for admirers of British modern jazz.

★★★★ Where Fortune Smiles

Sequel Records NED CD 302 2CD *Surman; John McLaughlin (g); Karl Berger (vib); Dave Holland (b); Stu Martin (d).* 71–76.

In 1971 Surman left Europe for the USA, apparently exhausted by his touring schedule with The Trio and anxious to break new creative ground. He had already worked with Dave Holland and had been an important presence on John McLaughlin's debut recording, *Extrapolation*. He had also met and worked with Karl Berger, who makes such a significant contribution to *Where Fortune Smiles*. Once, this album was spoken of in the same breath as McLaughlin's *My Goal's Beyond*, which documented the guitarist's commitment to Sri Chinmoy and his philosophy, but *Extrapolation* is a far better point of comparison. It has the same mix of torrential intensity and sweet, song-like gentleness. The opening two tracks are the best point of comparison. Surman's 'Glancing Backwards' is a fiery 12-note figure, traded between saxophone, guitar and vibes, marked by the feedback-laden rock sound of Jimi Hendrix and his followers. Ironically, McLaughlin's 'Earth Bound Hearts' is a gentle, semi-acoustic feature for Surman's soprano.

The album never quite regains its initial intensity. Much of its energy is burnt out in the first nine minutes. The title-piece is introduced by Berger, whose solo sounds like Fender Rhodes, and developed by a laid-back McLaughlin; no Surman at all. As on the opening track, Holland is masterly and is now mixed very far forward for CD. The closing 'Hope' is a solemn chorale for baritone and accompaniment, a fitting end to an oddly balanced but still entrancing record.

The brief second half of this budget-priced twofer is a duo session which technically belongs to drummer Stu Martin and is derived from music he wrote for radio. We have covered it in more detail under Martin's name. The two discs don't quite sit comfortably together. If we were bound for a desert island – and with rising sea levels who knows where the next edition will be datelined? – a two-CD set of *Where Fortune Smiles* with *Extrapolation* would be a priority purchase.

★★★ **Westering Home**

FMR CD 19 *Surman (all instruments).* 72.

★★★(★) **Morning Glory**

FMR CD 21 *Surman; Malcolm Griffiths (tb); John Taylor (p); Terje Rypdal (g); Chris Laurence (b); John Marshall (d).* 73.

Westering Home was an early and only intermittently convincing version of the multi-tracked solo projects that Surman was to make his staple in the '70s and '80s. He uses a variety of horns, piano and percussion to construct an evocative collage which, despite the pibroch and hornpipe elements, remains centred in jazz. It is a record that should perhaps be dusted down only now and again, as a reminder of the many and complex elements that go into the making of this very gifted artist.

Morning Glory was the name of and sole release by an unfortunately short-lived group that could and should have been allowed to develop further. Surman is both front man and chief composer, though he seems to have gone through some sort of creative crisis at this time, abandoning his signature baritone in favour of soprano and bass clarinet. Rypdal is the colourist and decorator, providing great washes of sound. Griffiths's brass tones seemed unfashionable in 1973 but sound much more idiomatic and relevant now. As so often, Laurence and Marshall – two absurdly underrated players – provide the dynamism.

★★★ **Upon Reflection**

ECM 825472-2 *Surman (ss, bs, bcl, syn).* 5/79.

★★★(★) **The Amazing Adventures Of Simon Simon**

ECM 829160-2 *Surman; Jack DeJohnette (d, perc, p).* 1/81.

★★★(★) **Such Winters Of Memory**

ECM 810621-2 *Surman; Karin Krog (v, ring modulator, tambura); Pierre Favre (d).* 12/82.

★★★ **Withholding Pattern**

ECM 825407-2 *Surman (ss, bs, bcl, rec, p, syn).* 12/84.

★★(★) **Private City**

ECM 835780-2 *As above.* 12/87.

★★★(★) **Road To St Ives**

ECM 843849-2 *As above.* 4/90.

★★★★ **Adventure Playground**

ECM 511981-2 *Surman; Paul Bley (p); Gary Peacock (b); Tony Oxley (d).* 9/91.

★★★(★) **The Brass Project**

ECM 517362-2 *Surman; Henry Lowther, Stephen Waterman, Stuart Brooks (t); Malcolm Griffiths, Chris Pyne (tb); David Stewart, Richard Edwards (btb); Chris Laurence (b); John Marshall (d); John Warren (cond).* 4/92.

Surman turned an absence of satisfying commissions to (creative) advantage on a series of multi-tracked solo projects on which he improvised horn lines over his own synthesizer accompaniments. In the early '60s he had modernized baritone-saxophone-playing, giving an apparently cumbersome horn an agile grace that belied its daunting bulk and adding an upper register much beyond its notional range (somewhat as Eric Dolphy had done with Surman's second instrument, the bass clarinet, and Albert Mangelsdorff with the trombone).

Upon Reflection quickly established the rather withdrawn, inward mood that became almost a vice on *Withholding Pattern* (it's hard not to read too much into the titles), but it also revived the folkish mode of Surman's solo *Westering Home*, which had mixed free passages with piano songs and even a sailor's dance on what sounds like harmonica. Surman's work of the '80s under the aegis of ECM has updated that experiment and allied it to the stark and unadorned 'Northern' sound associated with Jan Garbarek and the better parts of Rypdal. This is at its coolest and most detached on *Private City*, which was based on dance scores and sounds rather inconsequential outside that context.

Withholding Pattern is a curious combination of mock jauntiness ('All Cat's Whiskers And Bee's Knees') and similar untypical abstraction, with some of his best baritone-playing for years, marred by bland waterdrop synthesizer patterns. 'Doxology' reflects an early interest in church music which re-emerges in the 'organ' opening to 'Tintagel' on *Road To St Ives*. The 1990 album isn't intended to be directly evocative of places, but it is one of Surman's warmest and most humane performances, in which the absence of 'live' accompaniment seems less constricting. Surman is a highly rhythmic player, but his multi-tracked backgrounds are often very unresponsive.

This wasn't a problem on Surman's live and studio collaborations with percussionist and keyboard player, Jack DeJohnette. *The Adventures Of Simon Simon* re-creates the quasi-narrative style of Surman's '70s duo collaborations with The Trio drummer, Stu Martin, who died suddenly in 1980. DeJohnette's more explicit jazz background gives the music a more linear thrust, and less of the '(with)holding pattern' stasis that sometimes creeps into it and creeps again into the otherwise excellent collaboration with singer Sheila Jordan and percussionist Pierre Favre.

Much of Surman's compositional energy in recent years has been directed towards his Brass Project, and a record was long overdue. It represented his first opportunity to work in the studio with Canadian composer-arranger John Warren since they recorded the magnificent *Tales Of The Algonquin* at the end of the '60s. Unfortunately, comparison between the two records doesn't reflect all that positively on *The Brass Project*. Nevertheless it's a fine record. Surman's gently bucolic themes are played with just the right mixture of exuberance and reserve, and the voicings are often very subtle.

A faint sense that Surman has spent the last decade profitably marking time in an idiom that suited ECM's high-shine production had been shattered by the previous year's *Adventure Playground*, not so much a Surman album as a series of intimate collaborations in a freer mode than has been the saxophonist's norm over the past few years. The standard of playing is very high indeed (most noticeably from Bley and Oxley) and strongly suggests that Surman has still got a great deal to contribute at the sharper end of the music.

***(*) Stranger Than Fiction

ECM 521850-2 *Surman; John Taylor (p); Chris Laurence (b); John Marshall (d).* 12/93.

This was very nearly a re-formation of the Morning Glory group. Without a second horn or Rypdal's clangorous guitar-playing, the emphasis is very squarely on Surman and Taylor and on light-footed country airs with a countervailing shadow. The long 'Triptych', with which the record closes, is a masterpiece of abstract invention, relieving any doubt that they are content merely to spin out uncomplicated melodies. Careful listening suggests that Laurence and Marshall are much more important to the group than appears at first sight, supplying an unshakeable foundation and a subtle hint to the frontmen that stopping to muse is tempting but ultimately insufficient.

**** Nordic Quartet

ECM 527120-2 *Surman; Vigleik Storaas (p); Terje Rypdal (g); Karin Krog (v).* 8/94.

Surman and long-time partner Krog are a gifted team. The interesting thing about this record is how much of the emphasis is devolved to the little-known Storaas (an elegant stylist with a few forgivable Keith Jarrett touches) and to even-handed group improvisation. Krog's voice is much jazzier than the setting strictly suggests, and her phrasing imposes a certain discipline on the opening 'Traces', 'Unwritten Letter' and 'Wild Bird'. Surman often functions as her accompanist and commentator, working off the vocal line. Rypdal is, as usual, more detached and abstract, but there is a compelling logic to the music that overcomes its cool detachment and draws the listener into its world.

CORE COLLECTION

***(*) A Biography Of The Rev. Absalom Dawe

ECM 523749-2 *Surman (solo).* 10/94.

Dawe was an ancestor of Surman's and his part in this is limited to providing a certain thematic glue to a further set of solo improvisations which nowadays place less emphasis on synthesized ostinati and much more on the detailed interplay of horn lines. Adding alto clarinet to his armoury has given Surman an important new timbre and pitch, and many of these pieces seem – at first hearing and without undue thought – to be lighter and more plain-spoken than some of the earlier ECMs. It is the same mix of jazz, folk and church themes, however, the only difference lying in the more relaxed, less stressed opposition of tension and release, and in the significance accorded to individual lead-lines. Surman is now a master of this demanding craft.

*** Proverbs And Songs

ECM 537799-2 *Surman; John Taylor (org); Salisbury Festival Chorus; Howard Moody (cond).* 1/96.

Richly and resonantly recorded in the magnificent acoustic of Salisbury Cathedral, but flat and desiccated for all that. Surman's exchanges with Taylor are episodically involving, but the vocal settings have an overpowering quality that neutralizes some iron-hard instrumental ideas. It has always been understood that Surman's writing drew much from the Anglican tradition, and here is the proof. Unfortunately, in making the influence explicit he loses much of the subtlety that informed earlier records.

**** Coruscating

ECM 543033-2 *Surman; Rita Manning, Keith Pascoe (vn); Bill Hawkes (vla); Nick Cooper (clo); Chris Laurence (b).* 1/99.

This is almost a double concerto for Surman and long-time friend and partner Chris Laurence. They are the main soloists in a string-based suite which was written to celebrate 30 years of ECM and only recorded after a thorough workout during the summer festival season. Given that, the performances are lovely and beautifully integrated, with just the right weight and dynamic. Combined with the instrumentation, the pastoral quality of the writing means that it is not the most funky of swinging albums you'll ever hear, but we defy anyone not to be moved by the sheer beauty of 'At Dusk', 'An Illusive Shadow' or 'Crystal Walls'. No electronics this time out, but Surman dabbles in exotica with an outing for his contrabass clarinet, an instrument previously only associated with Anthony Braxton. Typically, John makes it sound like a piece of delightful old farm technology, a mill wheel or feed grinder turning slowly ... Lovely stuff.

***(*) Invisible Nature

ECM 016376 *Surman; Jack DeJohnette (d, elec perc, ky).* 11/00.

This is now a long-standing and very sympathetic partnership. DeJohnette's range of sound is enormously impressive and he often takes the lead on these tracks – especially 'Song For World Forgiveness' – leaving Surman to create ostinati and free-form lines in the background ... though strictly there is no background and no foreground in music as spontaneously conceived and executed as this. Surman is magnificent on 'Mysterium', a deeply spiritual theme that sounds very close to some of the saxophonist's classic compositions of the '70s, combining classical harmonies with jazz energy.

***(*) Free And Equal

ECM 017065-2 *Surman; Jack DeJohnette (d, p); London Brass.* 6/01.

A dramatic and successful extension of the long-standing Surman–DeJohnette partnership, this draws on John's lasting love of brass and brass choirs. Once again, it's a live recording, from the Meltdown Festival on London's South Bank, and this may be the key to its success, since one can't imagine a piece like 'Back And Forth' or indeed the title-track working quite as well in a studio atmosphere. Surman's improvising is immaculately true to the line of each composition, not so much an embellishment as a completion of its logic.

***** :rarum: Selected Recordings**
ECM 014197-2 *As for ECM records above.* 76–99.

Listening to these tracks in isolation prompts an unexpected realization and that is how well Surman albums, and not just the solo projects, have been constructed over the years. Certainly the material from the solo projects fares less well here than work with the *Adventure Playground* group and the duos with DeJohnette, but anyone who has followed Surman's career may find these selections rather too random and bitty. For the newcomer, however, there can be few better ways to make his acquaintance.

Rowland Sutherland

FLUTE

Former Jazz Warrior explores an eclectic Latin groove.

***** Coast To Coast**
FMR CD 101 *Sutherland; Byron Wallen (t); Kevin Robinson (t, flhn); Fayyaz Virji (tb); Joe DeJesus (tb, perc); Mark Donlon (p, ky); Nick Cohen, Geoff Gascoyne, Dudley Phillips (b); Winston Clifford (d); Richard Ajileye (perc).* 01.

With a clean, strong sound that occasionally recalls Herbie Mann, Sutherland is well equipped to lift this debut set of Brazilian-tinged themes by the band he calls Mistura, which he has been working with since the late '80s. The supporting cast is equally strong, with some fiery playing from Wallen and the still-unsung Virji. Some of the arrangements could do with tidying up, but as a representation of what this band can do live, *Coast To Coast* is an excellent calling card.

Ralph Sutton (1922–2001)

PIANO

Sutton played with Jack Teagarden while still a college student, and after the war worked for many years as Eddie Condon's intermission pianist. Turned up in Dixieland and trad groups of varying kinds and was a founder member of The World's Greatest Jazz Band in 1968. He enjoyed an Indian summer of recording and gigging in the '80s and '90s and was recognized as perhaps the last original master of stride piano.

***** Wondrous Piano**
Arbors ARCD 19297 *Sutton; Hugh Cregg (d).* 10/61.

***** Quartet With Ruby Braff**
Storyville STCD 8243 *Sutton; Ruby Braff (c); Milt Hinton (b); Mousie Alexander (d).* 2/68.

***** Live At Sunnie's Rendezvous 1969**
Storyville STCD 8286 *Sutton; Al Hall (b); Cliff Leeman (d).* 2/69.

*****(*) Live At Sunnie's Rendezvous Vol. 2**
Storyville STCD 8281 *As above, except add Bob Wilber (ss, cl).* 2/69.

Sutton was one of the premier stride- and swing-piano players in jazz for 50 years, although it's only comparatively recently that he got on record as a leader in a big way. *Wondrous Piano* is a recent retrieval from a cache of family recordings; Sutton running through some tunes in a bar, with Hugh Cregg (actually a doctor) playing modest drums. A nice example of his early-mature style on a bunch of songs he'd carry on playing for decades more.

The Storyville sessions date from a period when he performed at a club run by his wife in Aspen. The sound is imperfect on each, and the relaxations of a club set mean that they lack the focus of his studio dates. Nevertheless this is swinging music. Braff sounds typically forthright and unpretentious on his appearance, tersely handling the dozen repertory tunes with his hard-bitten lyricism. There are too many solo spots for Hinton, but the rhythm section do well. The trio date is marginally better for Sutton himself: a lot of Waller tunes here, though the best thing is the suitably aggressive 'Dog Ass Blues'. The second helping from Sunnie's adds Bob Wilber to the fun, and he is in excellent enough form to hitch this one up a notch: 'Dardanella' is divine.

***** With Ted Easton's Jazzband**
Jazzology JCD-159 *Sutton; Bob Wulffers (t); Henk Van Muyen (tb); Frits Kaatee (cl, as, ts); Jacques Kingma (b); Ted Easton (d).* 70s.

No clear date on this session, which was recorded at the (empty!) New Orleans Jazz Club in Scheveningen. Easton's group play a good Dutch copy of trad-to-swing mainstream, and it's a setting which Sutton seems to like: 'Blues In My Heart' is arranged almost as a concerto for him, and he gets four characteristic solos to himself.

****(*) Live At Haywards Heath**
Flyright 204 *Sutton (p solo).* 11/75.

***** Trio And Quartet**
Storyville STCD 8210 *Sutton; Lars Blach (g); Hugo Rasmussen (b); Svend Erik Norregaard (d).* 5/77.

***** Last Of The Whorehouse Piano Players: The Original Sessions**
Chiaroscuro CR(D) 206 *Sutton; Jay McShann (p); Milt Hinton (b); Gus Johnson (d).* 12/79.

*****(*) In Concert**
Nif Nuf 43/016 *Sutton; Ruby Braff (c); Rob Jeffery (b); Laurie Kennedy (d).* 10/81.

*****(*) Partners In Crime**
Sackville SKCD 2-2023 *Sutton; Bob Barnard (t); Milt Hinton (b); Len Barnard (d).* 8/83.

****** At Café Des Copains**
Sackville SKCD 2-2019 *Sutton (p solo).* 6/83–1/87.

*****(*) More At Café Des Copains**
Sackville SKCD2-2036 *Sutton (p solo).* 1/88–1/89.

*****(*) Eye Opener**
Solo Art SACD 122 *Sutton (p solo).* 4/90.

***** Easy Street**
Sackville SKCD2-2040 *Sutton; Bob Barnard (t); Len Barnard (d).* 5/91.

Sutton was a great favourite with British audiences and two of the solo albums were cut in England. The Flyright record finds him in relaxed, ambling form, and there is his usual mixture of romping stride and tinkling, wayward balladry, but the piano is in bad shape and the sound isn't much of an improvement on what was a rotten LP issue. Much better to go to either the Sackville or the Solo Art sessions. *Eye Opener* was recorded (on a Steinway) at a church hall in Woking, and besides Sutton chestnuts like the title-piece (a famous piece of virtuosity) there is a charming Willard Robison medley and mothballed stride fantasies such as 'Rippling Waters' and 'Clothes Line Ballet'. This one was last listed on J&M but has been reissued on Solo Art.

The quartet date with the Barnard brothers has a timeless feel, since the trumpeter seems wholly unself-conscious about an Armstrong influence, and their opening romp through 'Swing That Music' shows how beautifully swing repertory can turn out when delivered in the right hands. Sutton's accompaniments are as sharp as his solos: when he leans in and clears the decks, his huge two-handed manner gives the clearest impression of what stride masters such as Waller and Johnson would have sounded like if they'd been recorded on contemporary equipment. *Easy Street* is a rematch with perhaps just the slightest shine taken off: there's some handsome playing, but a vague sense of routine about some of the tunes. The solo record from Café Des Copains, drawn from a series of broadcasts over a five-year period, uses scarce material – 'Russian Lullaby', 'Laugh Clown Laugh' and a rollicking 'Somebody Stole My Gal', with its rhythms cunningly displaced – which Sutton relishes, acknowledging the melodies but steamrollering past them into areas of what might be called 'pure' stride piano. The second helping on *More* concentrates on two shows a year apart and gets a slightly lower mark since the material is rather more familiar this time.

The 1979 date was originally issued as two LPs on ChazJazz and it also includes two previously unreleased tracks. The meeting of Sutton and McShann is the occasion for much musical backslapping, and while their styles aren't exactly complementary, Sutton tones down enough to make McShann's wry kind of blues seep through. They both sing, although Ralph sticks to Fats Waller ham on 'Truckin''. Lots of fun.

The Nif Nuf record features a duet concert with Braff which was the last date of an Australian tour, this one coming from Thebarton Town Hall in Adelaide. Ruby is in an extravagant good humour, judging from his announcements, and the pairing is completely simpatico. For some reason, Jeffery and Kennedy arrive for the final track.

Storyville have reissued *Trio And Quartet* after several years in the vinyl scrapyard. Recorded on one of Ralph's Scandinavian tours, this is a typically amiable encounter which finds Blach, Rasmussen and Norregaard as capable if not especially effective bystanders. Sutton tends to go his own way.

***** Sunday Session**

Sackville SKCS2-2044 *Sutton; Milt Hinton (b); Butch Miles (d).* 12/92.

***** Echoes Of Swing**

Nagel-Heyer CD 038 2CD *Sutton; Jon-Erik Kellso (t); Bill Allred (tb); Antti Sarpila (cl, ss); Jack Lesberg (b); Gregor Beck (d).* 3/97.

Sackville's disc was recorded in Switzerland, and it sets the trio to work on another familiar programme of jazz tunes and standards. Good stuff, but even though Miles is a surprise choice of drummer (and he does fine), there's much that is polished routine about the occasion. At this point Sutton was never going to do anything startling, but with so many CDs of his around, this is really just another one. So too the Nagel-Heyer concert disc, even though recording Sutton with a band was something of a rarity. The horns play handsomely and good spirits abide across both discs, but with so much mainstream being recorded, again this falls into the middleweight bracket.

***** Sweet Sue**

Nagel-Heyer CD 057 *Sutton; Jon-Erik Kellso (t); Brian Ogilvie (cl, ts); Marty Grosz (g, v); Dave Green (b); Frank Capp (d).* 10/99.

***** The Music Of Fats Waller Vol. 2**

Nagel Heyer CD 086 *As above.* 10/99.

A set of Waller tunes given a good going-over in one of the regular Nagel-Heyer concerts/record dates. Sutton takes a relatively minor role as band pianist and the spirited work of Kellso and Ogilvie takes precedence, although Grosz does his usual scene-stealing, dedicating 'It's A Sin To Tell A Lie' to Kenneth Starr (historians will be scratching their heads over that one soon enough). Volume 2 is much the same again, although it sounds as if the well was starting to run dry as far as the best performances were concerned.

***** Revelations**

Nif Nuf 43/012 *Sutton; Kenny Davern (cl); Bill Polain (d).* 8/88.

***** At Bob Barnard's Jazz Party 1999**

Nif Nuf 43/003 *Sutton; Bob Barnard (c); Peter Gaudion (t); Ed Wilson (tb); John McCarthy (cl); Kenn Jones, Danny Moss (ts); Marty Grosz, John Scurry (g); Len Barnard (d).* 4/99.

Sutton was a regular visitor to Australia and these sets come from two of his trips. *Revelations* is in the main a duet record with Davern (recorded on a day off in Bridgewater Mill), with local man Polain sitting in on four tracks. Davern doesn't quite sound at his best but Sutton sweeps all before him and there is one rarity, 'Should I?'. Alternative takes pad out what was originally a cassette release.

There are several CDs available now made up from various sets at Bob Barnard's regular Jazz Parties, and this is Ralph's entry. There are duo, trio and small-group performances and the music brims with festival good humour, although the unwary should be warned that there are some wild swings in fidelity and volume: one of us nearly had his ears blown off in the transition between tracks two and three.

***** A Pair Of Kings**

Arbors ARCD 19245 *Sutton; Johnny Varro (p); Phil Flanigan (b); Ed Metz Jr (d).* 1/00.

The expected high jinks in a concert of piano duets, with Flanigan and Metz along for the ride. Ralph gets to do a 'Farewell Blues' by himself, which, given his passing, seems a poignant choice on what is at present the last disc in this listing.

Tierney Sutton

VOCALS

Singer trying to mix standards with genuine jazz material.

***** Introducing Tierney Sutton**

A Records AL 73111 *Sutton; Buddy Childers (flhn); Christian Jacob, Michael Lang (p); Trey Henry (b); Ray Brinker (d).* 8/95–4/96.

***** Blue In Green**

Telarc CD-83522 *Sutton; Christian Jacob (p); Trey Henry, Ken Wild (b); Ray Brinker, Joe LaBarbera (d).* 11/00.

Ms Sutton's star potential doesn't seem to have developed much since this release: her big, rangy voice, on this showing, limited only by a fairly conservative approach to some reasonably adventurous material. That she has the capacity to tackle it more imaginatively is hinted at at every turn. A medley of Wayne Shorter's 'Footprints' and 'My Favorite Things', coming late in the set, was an opportunity to cut loose and try something different. Chick Corea's 'High Wire' was another strong choice, though probably the best two things are the closing 'If I Were A Bell' and 'In The Wee Small Hours Of The Morning', on which Lang co-stars.

The Telarc album is a belated follow-up. Sutton does have some head-turning mannerisms: singing a phrase half through her mouth, half down her nose; swallowing a word just as it's about to emerge; rushing and then laying back on the beat; going from coy to seductive inside one phrase. Given all this apparent artifice, it's surprising that any songs emerge unscathed, but several of these are handled with great skill, not least the title-track – a jazz untouchable which Sutton puts her fingerprints all over. It is, in fact, a Bill Evans tribute record, and it's Evans at his most hushed and interior which suits her best. A very individual vocal set.

***** Something Cool**

Telarc CD-83548 *Sutton; Christian Jacob (b); Trey Henry (b); Ray Brinker (d).* 3/02.

The title-track is another untouchable, if you're any kind of June Christy fan, and it's similarly hard for her to put any kind of mark on 'Walkin' After Midnight' or 'The Best Is Yet To Come'. Yet minus strings, fancy charts or superstar guests, Sutton gives it all her best shot, and the record is likeable in its way. Too many of these are either overly familiar or tied to another voice: she needs to figure out a set-list which is neither.

Esbjörn Svensson (born 1964)

KEYBOARDS

Born in Västeras, Svensson studied music in Stockholm and began working in the local scene in the mid-'80s. He formed his current trio in 1993.

***** When Everyone Has Gone**

Dragon DRCD 248 *Svensson; Dan Berglund (b, whistle); Magnus Öström (d, v).* 7–9/93.

***** Mr And Mrs Handkerchief**

Prophone PCD 028 *As above.* 3/95.

***** E.S.T. Live**

ACT 9295-2 2CD *As above.* 3/95–7/99.

****** Trio Plays Monk**

ACT 9010-2 *As above, except add Ulf Forsberg, Ulrika Jansson, Elisabeth Arnberg, Ulrika Edstrom (strings).* 96.

Svensson's early records are comparatively modest, but he was already telling an attractive story at the piano. The sound of *When Everyone Has Gone* is lightly impressionistic post-bop, nodding at Keith Jarrett's Standards Trio but scaling down the grand gestures to a more manageable size. The trio play together in a loose but cleanly focused way that gives a degree of relaxation to themes which might sound merely uptight. 'Mohammed Goes To New York Part Two' is a catchy piece of Scandinavian funk, much in the style of Niels Lan Doky, but Svensson's heart is probably more in the ballads: 'Waltz For The Lonely Ones' is particularly charming. He also uses the electronic keyboards with such restraint that they acquire an almost ghostly quality at the back of the music. *Mr And Mrs Handkerchief* dispenses with the electronics, but this time Svensson alternates between upright and grand pianos: the homely quality of the upright lends an oddly clattery quality to his work, an almost perverse note when one hears the delicacy of his touch on, say, 'The Day After'. As if in compensation, Berglund plays with a degree more urgency this time. *E.S.T. Live* resurrects a live set from the same period: as with the rest of the earlier work, germs that would multiply into the later brilliancies are everywhere, but there's also an over-elaboration and a self-conscious showing-off that spoils the flow a little. A bonus track from 1999 has four years of growth, and it's startling.

Any reservations about the trio's calibre are brushed aside by the superlative Monk tribute album. Svensson chooses nothing unusual from the canon – only 'Eronel', given a beautifully lyrical turn, might be deemed scarce – so it's all the more astonishing what freshness and urgency he and his partners bring to the material. The secret is in the rhythmic frameworks, each of them unexpected to some degree: march, funk or parade times are introduced to melodies which have otherwise grown stale in the jazz repertory, and it's amazing what this does to the likes of 'I Mean You' and 'Rhythm-A-Ning'. There is a choice string arrangement lent to 'Round Midnight' which is in all ways wholly unhackneyed, while they even manage to find a right-sounding pulse for the intractable 'Little Rootie Tootie'. Svensson is no genius at the keyboard, but he comes up with some glorious ideas: he seems to think no further ahead than the next note in every part of the extended 'Bemsha Swing', yet so spontaneous is the improvisation that it carries all before it. Berglund and Öström, recorded in a kind of hot close-up, are just as fine. An outstanding disc.

****** Winter In Venice**

Superstudio 74321 539612 *Svensson; Dan Berglund (b); Magnus Öström (d).* 10/97.

****** From Gagarin's Point Of View**

ACT 9005-2 *As above.* 5–11/98.

Did we say no genius? Svensson may be out to prove us wrong. Working in comparative isolation in Stockholm, he was here producing piano-trio records ready to take on the best of whatever the rest of the jazz world can retaliate with. *Winter In Venice* is a radiant set. The Jarrett comparison comes up again (in one way unfortunately so, as Svensson has some of the singalong bug) since the meditative beauty of the title-piece, for one, recalls the pared-away melodicism of the old master's mid-period improvising. And a track such as 'At Saturday' even suggests a smidgen of gospel-funk. But Svensson is content to adopt a less-is-more position almost throughout. Many would have taken the opportunity to turn several of these pieces into marathon shows of rhetoric, but the trio let only one track break the six-minute barrier. Berglund and Öström are by now fully in tune with the group conception and they're superbly responsive, the drummer finding almost pinpoint details in his playing.

From Gagarin's Point Of View continues in the same vein, perhaps even more inventively. If jazz musicians are going to effect any kind of rapprochement with rock or dance music, then one way might be via the kind of fusion which the trio suggests in 'Dodge The Dodo', where Öström plays a sort of hip-hop beat at the kit and Svensson still lets the melodious theme determine the end result. It's just one of 11 diverse, ingenious compositions. The shaping of these episodes into a sequence may strike some as a bit too artful, but it's the act of musicians who are of a generation that knows about their vast range of options and still want to play acoustic jazz. At any rate, Svensson does more than enough here to show why, along with such performers as Jason Moran, Guus Janssen, Yosuke Yamashita and Brad Mehldau, he's helping to keep the piano-trio situation full of new music.

***(*) Good Morning Susie Soho

ACT 9009-2 *As above.* 3–4/00.

*** Strange Place For Snow

ACT 9011-2 *As above.* 4–12/01.

Good Morning Susie Soho develops the work of the previous records, perhaps not to quite such a high level, but it can scarcely be called a disappointment. 'Thoughts Of A Septuagenarian' alone would make the record substantial, and in 'The Wraith' Svensson continues to explore how a dappling of electronics might embellish and amplify what he's doing at the piano. 'Do The Jangle' is virtuosity placed at the service of the music, and underlines how important Berglund and Öström are to the overall result.

But *Strange Place For Snow* feels as if the balance is shifting towards a more pat, less organic and spontaneous kind of jazz. Svensson has always been in danger of flirting with pop mannerisms – he does the Jarrett singalong when he feels like it, and a few of his gospel and blues licks could easily grow tiresome if he doesn't keep a vigilant grip on himself – and on a number of tracks here, the music either outstays its welcome or hints at a crowd-pleasing cliché. The finale of the title-track, for instance, is charming, but it could have been lifted off a Camel record. In performance Svensson is still a marvellous, bountiful performer. The records are going to need a careful hand.

*** Seven Days Of Falling

ACT 9012-2 *As above.* n.d.

E.S.T. have been gathering in awards and surprising sales at a steadily increasing pace, and this best-selling set continues the success story. It's not hard to understand why Radiohead's audience finds it a lot easier to relate to this music than to a 'typical' piano-trio record: the group increasingly involve the studio as an integral part of their art, and however the electronic dapplings of 'Seven Days Of Falling' and 'Mingle In The Mincing-Machine' are contrived, they place a reassuringly abrasive edge on music which is often otherwise all too dependent on simple gospel licks and forms. 'Did They Ever Tell Cousteau?' even sounds like a nattily decorated dance track. Svensson, Berglund and Öström still make an exhilarating sound, as they do on the comparatively straightforward 'Elevation Of Love', but those who loved the earlier records may be wondering where they're headed now.

Ewan Svensson

GUITAR, GUITAR-SYNTHESIZER

Contemporary Swedish guitarist, seeking his own path through the fusion and modal-bop fields which are currently the instrument's main areas.

*** Present Directions

Dragon DRCD 218 *Svensson; Palle Danielsson (b); Magnus Gran (d).* 9/90–6/91.

Anyone fluent in the vocabulary of Scofield and Abercrombie will find Svensson's conversation easy to follow. If he seldom sounds strikingly individual, he follows the language with great skill. Across 12 compositions and over an hour of music on *Present Directions*, he alternates between fast, neatly picked solos and broader, expressive washes via the guitar-synthesizer. What makes the difference is the exacting support offered by Danielsson, as strong a bassist as one could ask for in this setting, and Gran's busy and intelligent drumming.

*** Reflections

Dragon DRCD 239 *Svensson; Ove Ingemarsson (ts); Harald Svensson (p); Matz Nilsson (b); Magnus Gran (d).* 11/92–1/93.

*** Next Step

Dragon DRCD 284 *As above, except omit Harald Svensson.* 11/94.

More mood(y) electric jazz from Svensson, this time abetted by Ingemarsson. The compositions are thoughtful, if rather lacking in melody, but the duet with Harald Svensson on 'Boat Trip' is very pretty, and the leader has plenty to say beyond the usual unreeling of fast licks. The subsequent *Next Step* pares the music back to a quartet, Ingemarsson sticking to straightahead tenor; and his bluff authority cuts through any chaff that Svensson might have been tempted by. They move very easily through the 11 tunes. Nothing special to make the record stand out from its predecessors, though.

*** Streams

Dragon DRCD 291 *Svensson; Yasuhito Mori (b); Magnus Gran (d).* 9/95–2/96.

In his unemphatic way, Svensson has put together a strong catalogue of records, even if none of them stands out as an essential. Back in the trio format, and alternating only between a cool-toned electric and (on two tracks) an acoustic instrument, he patiently explores another 13 tunes with Mori's lines shadowing his and with Gran the soul of discretion. The writing, however, sounds particularly enticing: anonymous though it sounds, 'Piece IV' is ingeniously memorable, and some of the mood pieces are done at precisely the right temperature.

*** Figures

Dragon DRCD 356 *As above.* 11/99–12/00.

Recorded at two sessions over a year apart, Svensson's latest continues his patient progress. An original such as 'Still Raining' personifies his melodious, faintly melancholy style: with his electric tone now a clean, big, resonant chime, his arpeggios can sound like a clarion of bells. Sometimes, though, he'll find an unexpectedly arresting line or two, as in his surprisingly tough extemporization on Bill Evans's 'Time Remembered'. It's not startling, but it keeps the listener interested, even if the record hardly qualifies as memorable. Mori is becoming a more assertive member of this group and some of his solos take the initiative from the leader.

Steve Swallow (born 1940)

BASS GUITAR

Early work with Paul Bley and Jimmy Giuffre, then with Stan Getz and Gary Burton for the rest of the '60s. Spent some time in California before returning east and switched from double bass to bass guitar as his sole instrument. Latterly a central figure in the Carla Bley circle. His own records are musicianly but often suggest that he's not that bothered about them.

*****(*) Home**
ECM 513424-2 *Swallow; David Liebman (ss, ts); Steve Kuhn (p); Lyle Mays (syn); Bob Moses (d); Sheila Jordan (v).* 9/79.

***** Carla**
XtraWatt 833492-2 *Swallow; Carla Bley (org); Larry Willis (p); Hiram Bullock (g); Victor Lewis (d); Don Alias (perc); Ida Kavafian (vn); Ikwhan Bae (vla); Fred Sherry (clo).* 86–87.

*****(*) Swallow**
XtraWatt 511960-2 *Swallow; Steve Kuhn (p); Carla Bley (org); Karen Mantler (ky, hca); Gary Burton (vib); Hiram Bullock, John Scofield (g); Robby Ameen (d); Don Alias (perc).* 9–11/91.

***** Real Book**
XtraWatt 521637-2 *Swallow; Tom Harrell (t, flhn); Joe Lovano (ts); Mulgrew Miller (p); Jack DeJohnette (d).* 12/93.

***** Deconstructed**
XtraWatt 537119-2 *Swallow; Ryan Kisor (t); Chris Potter (sax); Mick Goodrick (g); Adam Nussbaum (b).* 95.

Swallow is one of the most accomplished bassists of recent times. A man of real generosity of spirit, he has largely sublimated his own ambitions in the service of others, not least his partner Carla Bley. The writing on *Carla* barely reflects the quality of classics like 'Arise Her Eyes' and 'Hotel Hello', which represent Swallow's other main contribution to modern jazz. But for the absence of the dedicatee's abrasive melodic mannerisms, this might just as well be a Carla Bley album (which will be sufficient recommendation for Bley fans).

For *Home* Swallow set a group of poems by Robert Creeley, tiny snapshots of ordinariness that deliver their meanings precisely and without embellishment. Much the way Swallow plays. It might be that these pieces would work better with a less developed accompaniment, perhaps just voice, bass and piano, but the scoring is never allowed to overpower the lyric.

There's a touch of sameness about the writing on the eponymous *Swallow*, but the bassist's arrangements are impeccable and he's seldom sounded better. The tunes are mostly mid-tempo Latino grooves with plenty of solo scope. Guest players Burton and Scofield don't figure all that prominently and the most arresting voice is Karen Mantler's harmonica; her brief solo on 'Slender Thread' sets the bassist up for one of his delicate, single-note constructions, built up over Bley's organ chords and a soft shuffle beat. It could do with just one ripping tune, but that isn't Swallow's forte. On its own perfectly respectable terms, this is a beauty.

Real Book is a modest adventure for an all-star (though arguably over-familiar) band of heroes. Harrell and Lovano are dependably excellent, and the session has class and aplomb from moment to moment; but this kind of meeting of heavyweights isn't necessarily Swallow's best thing, and the music misses some of his most interesting quirks.

Deconstructed is an attempt to strike some new chords. Using a trumpeter and saxophonist of airier bent makes a difference to the shape of the songs, and spreading the harmonic business across two guitars gives the music a spacious quality which is very appealing. However, nothing develops and there is hardly a tune which goes anywhere more interesting than its own initial premisses.

***** Always Pack Your Uniform on Top**
ECM 543506 *Swallow; Barry Ries (t); Chris Potter (ts); Mick Goodrick (g); Adam Nussbaum (d).* 4/99.

Steve's intro to the opening track 'Bend Over Backward' is about the most prominent thing he does on the whole album; he prefers as ever to stay very much part of the ensemble. Yet there is no doubt whatsoever that it is Swallow who is steering the music and guiding it into territory that challenges his fellow players without throwing down a confrontational gauntlet. The second track 'Dog With A Bone' is as fast-paced and boppish as anything the bassist has recorded and the crowd at Ronnie Scott's in London must have put down their drinks and moved to the front of their seats to see if the band really could pull it off. It does and returns with 'Misery Loves Company' which is rhythmically subtle and full of unexpected colorations. Steve also plays an unaccompanied introduction on 'Reinventing The Wheel', but thereafter he is happy to slip back into the group, its motor and fifth column all in one.

***** Damaged In Transit**
XtraWATT 11 *Swallow; Chris Potter (ts); Adam Nussbaum (d).* 12/02.

Swallow's self-effacing tactics may in some senses be admirable, but here he is really pushed into the background: this set is all about Potter, and to some extent his dialogue with Nussbaum, with the compositions and bass-playing a poor third. Potter's tenor work here is individual and purposeful, and in some of his interactions with the drums he is building on some very distinguished prior jazz traditions. But one may well ask – why is all this happening on a Steve Swallow record?

John Swana (born 1962)

TRUMPET, FLUGELHORN

Raised in Philadelphia, where he still lives, Swana began listening to jazz in high school, then sat in at the local clubs. His experience is with big bands, organ combos and the current post-bop mainstream.

***** Introducing John Swana**
Criss Cross 1045 *Swana; Billy Pierce (ts); Benny Green (p); Peter Washington (b); Kenny Washington (d).* 12/90.

***** John Swana And Friends**
Criss Cross 1055 *Swana; Tom Harrell (t, flhn); Billy Pierce (ts); Mulgrew Miller (p); Ira Coleman (b); Billy Drummond (d).* 12/91.

*****(*) The Feeling's Mutual**
Criss Cross 1090 *Swana; Chris Potter (ts, as, f); Dave Posmontier (org); Steve Giordano (g); Billy Drummond (d).* 12/93.

Swana is a staunch modern traditionalist, firmly in the mould of such bygone masters as Lee Morgan and Kenny Dorham, and though he also cites Tom Harrell as a key influence it's his silvery tone and ready fluency that mark him out as an accomplished player. These are meaty, enjoyable records that just miss out on indispensability: little about the first two lingers long in the mind. *Introducing* pairs him with a near-perfect companion in the useful Pierce, who manages to play muscular tenor without quite falling into muscle-bound moves. The rhythm section are characteristically full of *brio*, but the material comes out sounding the same, even with such diverse composers as Wayne Shorter, Kenny Dorham and Swana himself. *John Swana And Friends* adds Harrell to the front line, and his arrangements of some of the jazz tunes – a tart reharmonization of 'Oleo', for instance – introduce a fresh twist. Yet the music never quite catches fire as it might, and Harrell's lovely playing on 'Darn That Dream' puts Swana in the shade.

The Feeling's Mutual is a more relaxed and convincing step forward. With the estimable Potter turning in fine support, Swana takes some of his best solos on his originals here, but more important is the way he's organized the group: Posmontier and Giordano (friends from Philadelphia) steer well clear of organ–guitar-band clichés, and instead the music has an open, modal feel that material like Chick Corea's 'Litha' seems tailored for. A surprising 'When Johnny Comes Marching Home' and a yearning ballad called 'Autumn Landscape' use the same virtues for different results. A very good Criss Cross.

★★★(★) In The Moment
Criss Cross 1119 *Swana; Steve Davis (tb); Eric Alexander (ts); Kenny Barron (p); Peter Washington (b); Kenny Washington (d).* 12/95.

Swana has been lucky in his sidemen, and that proves true again here: the rumbustious Davis and Alexander are a sound contrast in styles to the leader's more wistful and cajoling manner, and the rhythm section is absolutely blue-chip. The originals are a quite characterful lot, particularly the engaging ballad 'Martha' and the muted set-piece for the leader on 'Ballad Of The Sad Young Men' has genuine class about it.

★★★(★) Philly–New York Junction
Criss Cross 1150 *Swana; Joe Magnarelli (t, flhn); Eric Alexander (ts); Joel Weiskopf (p); Peter Washington (b); Kenny Washington (d).* 6/98.

★★★(★) Tug Of War
Criss Cross 1163 *Swana; Chris Potter (ts, ss, f); David Hazeltine (p); Dwayne Burno (b); Byron Landham (d).* 12/97–12/98.

Both of these are, in their way, no more than massively confident genre entries, rendered skilful by the great expertise of the players and informed by their pleasure at playing together; but the lack of a grand concept – which is the Criss Cross 'what you hear is what you get' trademark – adds to rather than subtracts from the results. The sextet session benefits from the piquancy of having Swana and Magnarelli together in the front line, and the horns are used in some interesting ways across the course of the date; but the quality of the solos, plangent but relaxed, is what you remember. Sample the title-track to hear how much they extract out of a relatively straightforward blowing tune.

Tug Of War is distinguished not only by the partnership of Swana and Potter, five years on from *The Feeling's Mutual*, but also by the excellent original material, idiomatic within a fairly conservative hard-bop tack, but fresh and imaginative, too. For once a 70-minute record doesn't seem too long – it's neatly paced, and even though the two halves of the record were made almost exactly a year apart, there's nothing disjointed between the dates. Swana and Potter both play some beautiful solos, but they are often almost aced out of it by Hazeltine's ability to surprise.

★★★ Philly Gumbo
Criss Cross 1203 *Swana; Bootsie Barnes (ts); Sid Simmons (p); Mike Boone (b); Byron Landham (d).* 6/00.

Yes, it's another genre entry. Barnes is an interesting new face in Swana's line-up – a laid-back and seemingly unaggressive character with a penchant for mooching around the bottom end of the tenor. Swana's own playing gets leaner, more accurate, maybe a touch more Milesian as he goes on. A 'local' jazz record that reports from the Philly scene. Sounds as if all's well.

★★★(★) On Target
Criss Cross 1241 *Swana; Jesse Van Ruller (g); John Patitucci (b); Eric Harland (d).* 12/02.

And that's the impression reinforced by the new one as well. 'Philly Jazz' is a hometown tribute, a clever late-night burner that is deceptively unsophisticated until it's been heard once or twice. Indeed, that's very much the impression of the album as a whole. Swana is the main voice out front, but Patitucci and Van Ruller break up the rhythmic and harmonic expectations, allowing him to range freer and lighter than before. Harland replaces Byron Landham and Kenny Washington and brings a springier metre which makes sense of the new material. The opening 'Through My Eyes' is a naggingly familiar slice of Blue Note hard bop (Swana notes an unintended echo of Donald Byrd), which gives way to the delicate sophistication of 'Mud Puppy' (muted) and 'Sweet Sadness'. The title-track is a brisk and striking theme from an increasingly confident composer.

Steve Swell (born 1954)

TROMBONE

Born in Newark, Swell is a contemporary trombonist, going his own way through free and post-bop styles of playing.

★★★(★) Observations
CIMP 108 *Swell; Chris Kelsey (ss).* 2/96.

★★★(★) Out And About
CIMP 116 *Swell; Roswell Rudd (tb); Ken Filiano (b); Lou Grassi (d).* 6/96.

★★★ Moons Of Jupiter
CIMP 149 *Swell; Mark Whitecage (as, cl); Dominic Duval (b); Jay Rosen (d).* 5/97.

Fine records helmed by a distinctive and impassioned improviser. Swell isn't a virtuoso trombonist in the manner of Rutherford or Christmann, but he's a powerful, vocal player whose energies ignite each of these occasions. The duo with Kelsey is a long-standing rehearsal partnership, and they read each other's moves with brilliant empathy. These are long, almost Tristano-like lines of counterpoint, each following a determined plan that has the feel of extemporization, and if the format is a little monochromatic there's nothing routine in their conversation. *Out And About* sets up an encounter with a godfather of free trombone. Rudd seems less than the force he was, and Swell is clearly the stronger participant, but the music is more an affectionate, collaborative joust than a cutting contest. Swell's tone has a raucous, overheated timbre when he warms up, and set beside Rudd's more constricted delivery, the results are more reminiscent of a couple of old Dixieland tailgaters going at it than anything 'avant-garde'. Filiano and Grassi enter into the spirit with the necessary gusto.

Moons Of Jupiter gets off to a tumultuous start with the overwhelmingly powerful 'For Henry Darger'. The rest of the record never quite measures up to the opening; as good as the horns are, they don't quite click with the long-standing partnership of Duval and Rosen, and it turns out as a free-bop date with flashes of brilliance. As so often with CIMP releases, both Duval and (on the previous disc) Filiano suffer from inaudibility – these records simply don't give the bassist a chance.

***** Atmospheels**

CIMP 184 *Swell; Will Connell (as, cl, bcl); Lou Grassi (d).* 8/98.

***** Flurries Warm And Clear**

CIMP 203 *Swell; Ned Rothenberg (as, cl, bcl); Tomas Ulrich (clo).* 7/99.

Two different trios. Connell is an unexposed veteran – now in his 60s, he came up through the Horace Tapscott groups of the '60s and has recorded only rarely – and he plays buzzsaw solos on alto which are rampant in a not very purposeful way. With no bassist, Grassi seems unsure of how to make the music go forward, and it tends to clump around his bass-drum pedal. That said, there are still some corking improvisations from the leader, such as his long, blaring take on 'Folk Tune'.

Track three, 'Acoustic Rumble', pretty much sums up the second disc. It's chamber jazz of a growly, unbeautiful temperament. Ulrich drones and slides around the other two, and a lot of the music is a dense weave. Three duos lighten the texture, and briefer, snappier pieces such as 'Consume This' perk the listener up.

***** Particle Data Group**

Cadence CJR 1139 *Swell; Bruce Eisenbeil (g); Gregg Bendian (vib).* 9/00.

An unique instrumentation for sure, and an altogether strange record: several tracks (with titles such as 'Diagnostic Placements') barely break the one-minute barrier, while others drift hazily on towards eight minutes or so. It doesn't feel like free jazz, even though all the tracks are apparently improvised: it's more like modern composition where the lines and responses are absolutely articulated and decided. Spacious, stark, but sometimes soothingly melodious, it recalls some of the earlier experiments of Leo Smith, without the serenity.

***** This Now!**

Cadence CJR 1159 *Swell; Matt Lavelle (t); Jemeel Moondoc (as); Cooper-Moore (p); Wilber Morris (b); Kevin Norton (d).* 11/01.

A talented group – or, at least, a group full of talented players – boiling through a gig at New York's Roulette one November night. Of the three pieces, the most interesting is the middle one, 'BA-1', which features some particularly creative interplay between everyone bar Norton, who keeps quiet a lot of the way and lets the various voices rise and fall. Having Cooper-Moore in the group introduces the rarity of a piano into Swell's music and he plays in a neoclassic free-jazz style which actually works very well. 'Tryarhythmic' rattles along as a kind of free-bop boogaloo – too long, but a nutty adventure as far as it goes.

****(*) Poets Of The Now**

CIMP 272 *Swell; Ursel Schlicht (p); Tom Abbs (b, tba); Geoff Mann (d, c).* 7/02.

***** Still In Movement**

CIMP 285 *As above, except omit Schlicht.* 3/03.

Poets Of The Now was meant as a showcase for Schlicht, but Swell gets a co-credit as leader. Arguably, he overdoes it here, on a session where the capable pianist seems to be looking for space and Swell keeps barging in. With Abbs and Mann both doubling on brass instruments – notably on 'Barbara Ellen' – the piano often sounds to be shunted off to the side, and where Schlicht starts to make real progress, as on the final 'Orbicularis Orbis', Swell for once sounds like the outsider. Too many interesting points dispersed across too much terrain.

Unsurprisingly, the trio situation of *Still In Movement* works better. Swell's tunes are utilitarian pieces to get the group into a mood or a groove, and they battle it out across nine pieces. The problem may be that Swell eventually runs out of enough ammunition to sustain his role as sole horn across the whole record (a needlessly marathon 71 minutes): at half-way, you feel they've said their piece, and the rest traverses similar ground.

Aki Takase (born 1948)

PIANO

Once a student of Yosuke Yamashita, Takase emerged in the '80s as a pianist working in an area which touched on post-bop but more often looked towards an entirely free vocabulary.

*****(*) Piano Duets Live In Berlin 93/94**

FMP OWN-90002 *Takase; Alexander von Schlippenbach (p).* 3/93–12/94.

Takase rises out of jazz-piano history with unique intensity and panache. Her earlier music (there are vinyl-only releases and several departed Enja CDs) suggested a pianist who was involving herself in earlier methods only reluctantly – most of the music leapt into the darkness of free playing at the earliest opportunity.

The record with Schlippenbach is meticulously balanced, opening with two long pieces by AVS, centred with four Monk tunes and ending with two extended variations on Takase themes. Even the two pairs of compositions share affinities: 'Na, Na, Na, Na ... Ist Das Der Weg?' and 'Tales Of Something' both come out of overlapping, building-block figures that achieve a terse complexity, and 'The Morlocks' (recorded before the orchestral version on the FMP CD of that title) and 'Chapelure Japonaise' are whirlwinds of prepared-piano turbulence. The Monk tunes – each pianist takes one solo – are like a breathing space, and Frank Zappa's 'You Are What You Is' is like a roistering encore. For catholic tastes, perhaps, but an impressive record.

*****(*) Duet For Eric Dolphy**

Enja 91209-2 *Takase; Rudi Mahall (bcl).* 5/97.

Mahall is by no means intimidated by the fact that David Murray has already played this duettist role on a Takase record.

He's a mercurial player, making light of the lumbering reputation of the bass clarinet, with a slightly pinched tone and a quacking approach to a line. Ten Dolphy tunes – a big chunk of his *œuvre*, in fact – are whistled through, along with three originals and a peg-leg treatment of 'I'm Confessin''. Miniaturized into briefly explosive or bittersweet episodes, it's an inventive, droll record.

*****(*) Le Cahier Du Bal**

Leo LR 319 *Takase (p solo).* 1/01.

In dedication to her friend, the dancer Anzu Furukawa: 'I just thought of her, as if she were dancing on the keyboard instead of my fingers, jumping, stopping, bending gently.' Percussive as ever, Takase doesn't have fairy fingers, and while some of her spontaneous melodies have their delicacy, they're picked, chopped, hammered and chiselled out of the keyboard. They whirl, they pirouette ... what a dazzling sound!

****** The Dessert**

Leo LR 370 *Takase; Rudi Mahall (bcl, cbcl).* 12/02.

A return match for this pairing, and five years on their merrymaking remains infectious. Most of the tracks are named for something likely to be served at table and the playing is suitably flavoursome and impeccably cooked. Thirteen compositions all have their own special detail and quality, and some of the performances, such as 'Panna Cotta', are so beautifully modulated that – for all that this is set down in quite a rough and unlovely acoustic – one can't imagine them being bettered. As a kind of encore, they uncork four brief improvisations, whose scattershot qualities underscore how fastidiously the preceding tunes were performed.

Akira Tana (born 1952)

DRUMS

Co-leader of the group TanaReid, with bassist Rufus Reid, Tana is based in New York and has long experience of the local scene.

*****(*) Moon Over The World**

Sons Of Sound SSPCD 018 *Tana; Ted Lo (p); Rufus Reid (b).* 3/93.

Tana's small-band records with Rufus Reid are currently deleted, which leaves this 1993 trio date, first issued in Japan and only getting a belated US release in 2004. In a very crowded genre, this makes an unassumingly generous case for a listen. Lo, who bides his time between Hong Kong and New York, plays with uncommon grace and sensitivity, fingering out the Chinese folk melody of the title-track with respectful restraint and showing his colours as a ballad-player throughout the set: Reid's 'No Place Like The End Of The World' brings out a particularly fine piano part. Tana himself resists the temptation to play too hard and the music has a lyrical momentum which is very charming.

Francesca Tanksley

PIANO

Able Billy Harper associate who was unaccountably slow to make her debut as leader.

*****(*) Journey**

DreamCaller 7168 *Tanksley; Clarence Penn (b); Newman Baker (d).* 8/01.

Anyone who heard Chessie Tanksley's work with the Billy Harper group would probably have assumed that the young pianist had a solo career already going. Tanksley's debut as a leader is all the better for being belated. Fellow Harper sidemen Penn and Baker offer able support on this elaborately constructed set of originals. Judy Brady is featured on 'Prayer', but 'Journey Without Distance', 'Trickster' and 'In Grace' establish Chessie's credentials as a melodist and her ability to give a solo the richest of textures. Less sure is her rhythmic sense, which is why she relies so much on her colleagues, but this is a side issue on *Journey*. It's an album that brings her into the spotlight at last. Better things will follow.

Horace Tapscott (1934–99)

PIANO

Tapscott's music and his views on integration and racial equality cannot be separated, and yet he rarely composed anything resembling programme or agit-prop music, preferring to let the free flow of creativity do the job of discourse for him. Inevitably, given his views, he was held apart from the critical mainstream and, despite a substantial body of recording from the time of his comeback in 1978 onwards, most of it was for his own label. He remains, perversely, best known for the compositions and arrangements on Sonny Criss's 1968 album, Sonny's Dream.

♛ ** The Dark Tree**

hatOLOGY 2-2053 2CD *Tapscott; John Carter (cl); Cecil McBee (b); Andrew Cyrille (d).* 12/89.

There was, inevitably, a darker side to the cool 'West Coast sound' and to the conventionally sunny image of California. One hardly thinks of Eric Dolphy or Charles Mingus as 'West Coast' players, yet that is what they were, and they conveyed a fundamental truth about the region's culture that is reflected in Horace Tapscott's still painfully unrecognized work. Tapscott was first and always a community musician. His decision to remain in Los Angeles as a performer/activist undoubtedly thwarted wider recognition, but so too did the fact that he conformed to no readily marketable pigeonhole; 'West Coast Hot' was considered something of a pleonasm in the business, and there was a measure of suspicion regarding Tapscott's political agenda. In 1961 he helped establish the Union of God's Musicians and Artists Ascension, out of which grew the Pan-Afrikan People's Arkestra, both attempts to find uncompromised work for talented, young, black musicians. Their work is fiercely disciplined, built up out of deceptively simple elements, but with subtle polychordal shadings that reflect Tapscott's solo work and his intriguing duos and trios with members of the PAPA. Much of this work has been issued on his own Nimbus label, but its status and availability have always been troublingly hard to pin down. Readers should refer to our first (1992) edition for a listing of LP releases.

The Dark Tree is special in having two neglected giants of modern jazz working with instinctive sympathy, intelligence and bottomless expression. Both pianist and clarinettist are entirely at ease with brusque, angular melodies and more sweepingly lyrical passages. Tunes like 'Lino's Pad' exploit unusual and often difficult time-signatures, combinations of metre which present no problems to players as deft as McBee and Cyrille. Alternative versions of 'The Dark Tree' can be found elsewhere, notably on a valuable Novus/BMG compilation called *West Coast Hot* which pops up every now and then and is well worth the search. These two versions, though, are the key statements; one can't say 'definitive' of a piece that is defined by its fugitive, experimental quality, but the interplay between Carter and Tapscott is astonishing and one's only regret is that they didn't choose to tape or release a duo version as well. According *The Dark Tree* the clinching accolade of a crown might seem belated enthusiasm, but the record has been out of circulation for some time and returns now, in the wake of Horace's death, with redoubled impact. The recording sounds as fresh and densely textured as ever. A genuinely important reissue.

★★★(★) aiee! The Phantom

Arabesque AJ0119 *Tapscott; Marcus Belgrave (t); Abraham Burton (as); Reggie Workman (b); Andrew Cyrille (d).* 6/95.

★★★(★) Thoughts Of Dar Es Salaam

Arabesque AJ 0128 *Tapscott; Ray Drummond (b); Billy Hart (d).* 96.

Arabesque took on Tapscott in the mid-'90s, perhaps conscious that time might be slipping away for one of the sleeping giants of the music. The oddly named *aiee! The Phantom* is unmistakable Tapscott: big, pounding motifs, with horns punching away over the top. The long pieces, 'Mothership' and a reprise of an older theme 'Drunken Mary/Mary On Sunday', are very impressively voiced and crafted, almost like scaled-down versions of big-band arrangements. The only quibble relates to Burton, who usually punches his weight but sounds out of place here. It isn't that he can't keep pace with Tapscott's slewing harmonics and rapid-rotation rhythm; it's simply that he doesn't have much to add in his own voice.

Tapscott had never shied away from standards but he rarely played them in common times. The slightly strange thing about *Thoughts Of Dar Es Salaam* is that there is scarcely an oblique or asymmetrical time-signature to be heard. Despite a trio perfectly capable of tackling anything he threw at them, Horace stays in ordinary metres throughout, leaving Hart and Drummond to embellish and vary at will, but not straying on his own account. Recent years had seen him re-examining aspects of bebop. 'So What' on *Among Friends* is a vivid example, and 'Now's The Time' on the trio record is a powerful restatement of how much unexplored acreage Horace had found in bop. Some of the tunes would seem pointlessly cranky when executed in any way other than straightforwardly, and Tapscott seems to have wakened to the potential of clear and clean-edged melody. For many listeners, *Thoughts* will be a first exposure to his work. As such, it's potentially misleading, and they should certainly not neglect to follow through with *The Dark Tree*.

Gregory Tardy (born 1966)

TENOR AND SOPRANO SAXOPHONES, CLARINET

After signing to Impulse! and subsequently getting a dismissal from the label, this American tenorman looks to rebuild.

★★★(★) Abundance

Palmetto PM 2075 *Tardy; Miguel Zenon (as); George Colligan (p); Sean Conly (b); Woody Williams (d).* 3/01.

Tardy's progress on record unfortunately was in keeping with his name, since Impulse! didn't stick with him after a ballyhooed signing earlier in the '90s. This belated follow-up is a New York quartet record of class and power. The leader pushes his sound much harder, shouting at some phrases and generally getting away from any notions of major-label accessibility. Whether that entirely suits him or not is contentious. The opening 'Plan B', with counterpoint from Zenon in his only appearance of the date, feels rather crudely violent at first, but the hook sticks in the mind and repeat plays reveal subtleties. Colligan is an asset to seemingly any situation, and he plays a strong part in the record's success. The originals aren't exactly an immortal bunch, but as props for the improvising they do their job; and the neoclassic interlude, 'The Very Thought Of You', overcomes its tepid pace with an immaculate performance.

Buddy Tate (1915–2001)

TENOR SAXOPHONE, CLARINET

Tate was the replacement for the late Herschel Evans in the Basie band, which shows how much faith the Count placed in him. Born in Sherman, Texas, he'd worked with the Clouds Of Joy before that and was later to become a solo artist, though most of Buddy's solos are scattered over recordings by others. He had formidable control in the upper register of his instrument and can frequently sound as if he were playing something other than a tenor.

★★★ Buddy Tate 1945–1950

Classics 1207 *Tate; Emmett Berry, Forest Powell (t); Ted Donnelly (tb); J. J. Johnson, Glenn Tyree, Charles Q. Price (as, v); Frank Sleet (as); Charlie Thomas (ts); Bill Doggett, Frank Whyte (p); Louis Speiginer, Freddie Green (g); Benny Booker, Walter Page, John Simmons (b); Edward Smith, Chico Hamilton, Pete McShann, Shadow Wilson (d); Jimmy Witherspoon (v).* 8/45–4/50.

Buddy Tate was one of the greatest and most durable of swing tenor men, a major performer for over half a century and a much-loved and amiable man; but the records under his own name are perhaps a little disappointing in the light of his grand reputation, and his reticent standing as a leader may be the reason why he's never quite secured the wider fame of some of his peers. His great records were made with Basie – whom he joined following Herschel Evans's death in 1939 – and his old friend from the band, Buck Clayton; in 1947 he was still with the band but did some moonlighting in an anonymous ensemble which cut 12 of the 25 tracks here (the others are by even less identifiable groups, though there's a nice early blues from Witherspoon). The music is unpretentious but mostly forgettable jump-band music, typical of the day, although there's an interesting Karl George session with some fine work by J. J. Johnson which raises the interest level.

★★★(★) Jive At Five

Storyville STCD 5010 *Tate; Doc Cheatham (t); Vic Dickenson (tb, v); Johnny Guarnieri (p); George Duvivier (b); Oliver Jackson (d).* 7/75.

Tate's records in the '70s have a desultory, pick-up feel to them, but there's still plenty of ingratiating music in some of them. Perhaps the best of them is the all-star date on *Jive At Five*, which benefits from a perfectly balanced front line: the upright, proper Cheatham, the louche Tate, the almost lascivious-sounding Dickenson. Each man's ballad feature is a treat, and Guarnieri supports and embellishes beautifully.

★★★(★) **The Ballad Artistry Of Buddy Tate**
Sackville SKCD-3034 *Tate; Ed Bickert (g); Don Thompson (b); Terry Clarke (d).* 6/81.

★★(★) **Just Jazz**
Reservoir RSR CD 110 *Tate; Al Grey (tb); Richard Wyands (p); Major Holley (b, v); Al Harewood (d).* 4/84.

The Ballad Artistry is surely Tate's best latter-day record. By sticking mostly to slow tempos and never forcing the pace, the supporting trio provides just the right sort of intimacy and cushioning detail to let Tate relax and, though he still has his doubtful moments, most of his solos are controlled, ruminative, nicely eloquent. It's much like a vintage Ben Webster date. Bickert is in excellent form, unobtrusively filling all the harmonic space round the saxophonist, and Thompson and Clarke both play well. An immaculate 'Darn That Dream' and the pleasing choice of Ellington's 'Isfahan' provide the highlights. The Reservoir disc is a reissue of an earlier LP with a couple of alternative takes to beef up playing time. Nothing very exciting here, but dependable playing from the principals, and Grey in particular taking a witty role.

Art Tatum (1910–56)

PIANO, CELESTE

Born in Toledo, Ohio, and almost blind from birth, Tatum travelled widely in the '30s on the club circuit. He recorded as a soloist and accompanist until he formed a trio in 1943. A master of every kind of jazz-piano style, he nevertheless was not interested in composing himself and preferred to work endless variations on standard material, often following a formula on familiar tunes but varying it to infinitesimal degrees. He influenced pianists and other instrumentalists alike, all of them impressed by the depth of his rhythmic and harmonic thinking within his self-imposed boundaries. He died from uraemia in 1956.

★★★(★) **Art Tatum 1932–1934**
Classics 507 *Tatum (p solo).* 3/33–10/34.

★★★(★) **Art Tatum 1934–1940**
Classics 560 *Tatum; Lloyd Reese (t); Marshal Royal (cl); Bill Perkins (g); Joe Bailey (b); Oscar Bradley (d); Adelaide Hall (v).* 10/34–7/40.

The enormity of Tatum's achievements makes approaching him a daunting proposition even now. His very first session, cut in New York in 1933, must have astonished every piano-player who heard any of the four tracks (available on Classics 507, and also the Columbia reissue listed below). 'Tiger Rag', for instance, becomes transformed from a rather old-fashioned hot novelty tune into a furious series of variations, thrown off with abandon but as closely argued and formally precise as any rag or stomp at one-quarter of the tempo. If Tatum had only recorded what is on these first CDs, he would be assured of immortality; yet, like Morton's early solos, they are both achievements in their own right and sketchbooks for the great works of his later years.

There are just a few distractions in the music leading up to 1940: Adelaide Hall sings a couple of vocals on one session, and Tatum's Swingsters record one 1937 session (which also includes Tatum on celeste).

★★★★ **The Standard Transcriptions**
Music & Arts CD-919 2CD *Tatum (p solo).* 35–45.

★★★★ **The Standard Transcriptions 1935–1945**
Storyville STCD 8260/1 2CD *Tatum (p solo).* 35–45.

Tatum's transcription discs for radio were made at different sessions over a period of several years and have survived as rather indifferently stored acetates. They are as valuable in their way as the later sessions for Norman Granz: briefer, many solos almost casually tossed off, and some blemished by the poor recording (Tatum never received the kind of studio sound which his work demanded), but it's a magnificent archive, spread over two lengthy CDs. Some of them, such as 'I Wish I Were Twins', have the melody abstracted into a monstrously fast chunk of stride piano; others, like 'The Man I Love', become tender but firm ballads, while others begin at a medium tempo before hurtling forward in double-time. Trifles such as Dvořák's 'Humoresque' are treated with Tatum's peculiar knowing gaucheness, while his versions of such pieces as 'I'm Gonna Sit Right Down And Write Myself A Letter' are like destructive tributes to such colleagues as Waller and Johnson: immensely superior in terms of technique, Tatum nevertheless pays them a kind of offhand homage by adopting elements of their manner to his own vast vocabulary. 'All God's Chillun Got Rhythm', meanwhile, prefigures Powell and bebop intensity. Highly recommended ... however, collectors now face a tricky choice between the Music & Arts set and a new Storyville edition of the same music. It's complicated by what seems to be an inconsistency between the sets. The earlier solos are better served by the Storyville set, but after that, honours are difficult to award; while Don Asher's essay on the Music & Arts set is highly entertaining, some may prefer the more scholarly Storyville notes. In the end, either set should provide much pleasure to Tatum admirers, although those expecting hi-fi should be warned that many of the tracks (on each set!) still suffer inferior sound.

★★★(★) **Art Tatum 1940–1944**
Classics 800 *Tatum; Joe Thomas (t); Edmond Hall (cl); Oscar Moore, John Collins, Tiny Grimes (g); Billy Taylor, Slam Stewart (b); Eddie Dougherty, Yank Porter (d); Joe Turner (v).* 7/40–44.

★★★ **Art Tatum 1944**
Classics 825 *Tatum; Tiny Grimes (g); Slam Stewart (b).* 5–12/44.

★★★(★) **Art Tatum 1945–1947**
Classics 982 *Tatum (p solo).* 5/45–1/47.

Tatum's 1940 solos are another superb sequence. There is a first revision of 'Tiger Rag', which first appeared at his debut session, and particularly imaginative interpretations of 'Lullaby Of The Leaves', 'Moon Glow' and, improbably enough, 'Begin The Beguine'. The Classics *1940–1944* disc goes on to take in ten trio tracks with Grimes and Stewart, a format that took up much of the pianist's time in the '40s. It didn't so much cramp his style as push it into a formula to a degree that some will be dissatisfied by. In a sense, though, it was characteristic of the man. Grimes and Stewart were mere mortals next to the pianist, but their earthbound playing kept Tatum within reach of a paying audience. The *1944* Classics disc covers trio sessions for the Asch and Comet labels in rather murky sound, as well as a single solo date for Asch that includes a version of 'Sweet And Lovely', one tune he never recorded commercially again. The low-fi sound keeps this one within specialist realms.

These are also on Classics 982, which is otherwise filled out by 11 solos for V-Disc and a January 1947 session for Victor. It is oddly moving to hear Tatum himself introduce his V-Disc solos and hope that the servicemen enjoy hearing the tunes, whatever they may think of the piano-playing. One or two unusual choices, such as '9.20 Special' and 'I'm Beginning To See The Light', make these solos of extra interest, and the Victor date is valuable because Tatum was recorded this well only rarely.

*****(*) The Art Of Tatum**
ASV AJA 5164 *Tatum; Oscar Pettiford (b); Big Sid Catlett (d).* 8/32–10/44.

A useful collection of early Tatum solos, with a single concert track with Pettiford and Catlett to round it off. The compilers have taken a generous sample, and though some will still find ASV's remastering rather fudgy this may appeal to any who want only a single example of the man's earlier work.

*****(*) In Private**
Fresh Sound FSR-CD 127 *Tatum (p solo).* c. 48.

***** The Complete Capitol Recordings Of Art Tatum**
Capitol 821325-2 2CD *Tatum; Everett Barksdale (g); Slam Stewart (b).* 7/49–12/52.

In Private comes from a tape allegedly made at Buddy Cole's house around 1948. There are many stories of Tatum doing even more impossible things at after-hours sessions, but he must have felt he was being watched at this one, since there is nothing strikingly different from his everyday genius here. But the disc comes in unusually clean sound: there is a notably fine 'Over The Rainbow', and a couple of tunes – 'You're Driving Me Crazy' and 'Sittin' And A Rockin'' – are ones he didn't often record.

The Capitol sessions date from the period when Tatum was working with a trio, but Barksdale and Stewart actually appear on only some of the tracks. These are mostly fine rather than great Tatum performances: from most other pianists they would be astonishing work, but ranked next to his other recordings these are on a lower flame. There are hints of the routine which he would often settle into on particular tunes, and one or two tracks where he sounds relatively indifferent to the occasion. On others – 'Someone To Watch Over Me' or 'Somebody Loves Me', both on the first disc – he is the great Tatum.

*****(*) Masters Of Jazz Vol. 8: Art Tatum**
Storyville STCD 4108 *Tatum (p solo).* 8/32–1/46.

*****(*) Over The Rainbow**
Dreyfus 36727-2 *Tatum (p); Tiny Grimes (g); Slam Stewart (b).* 4/40–9/49.

The Storyville disc is a hotchpotch of solos covering the '30s and '40s. The music is unimpeachable but it makes little sense as a chronological compilation. Dreyfus's *Over The Rainbow* is another matter. Concentrating on Tatum's '40s solos (only four tracks out of 21 are by the trio), it's well programmed, attractively packaged and agreeably remastered, and makes an introduction that should intrigue a generation that knows nothing of Tatum.

***** Piano Starts Here**
Columbia 501655-2 *Tatum (p solo).* 33–49.

Tatum's debut solo session turns up again here, this time as a prelude to nine solos from a 1949 Gene Norman concert. There is one unusual choice – 'The Kerry Dance'. Valuable as always, but probably for completists only, since sound is again no better than fair. In an astonishing show of cheapness, Columbia don't seem to have even bothered to try and remaster any of the material properly for their new edition; and there are no notes, only a reprint of the back cover of the 1968 American LP issue, dedicated to listing some of their other releases of that moment, including *Eddie Gronet's TV Polka Party*!

*****(*) Live 1944–45**
Storyville 101 8332 *Tatum; Tiny Grimes (g); Slam Stewart (b); Murray McEachern Orchestra; Mel Torme, The Mel-Tones, Jack Martin, Martha Stewart (v).* 8/44–10/45.

(***) Live 1945–1949
Storyville 101 8333 *Tatum (p solo).* 45–11/49.

(***) Live 1949–1951
Storyville 101 8334 *Tatum; Bill Carter (t); Bill Povey (as); Johnny Ord (ts); Ned Ciashine (acc); Murray Lauder (b); Don Hilton (d).* 11/49–7/50.

Storyville's archive releases of live Tatum material take in broadcasts of every description – on shows fronted by Mildred Bailey, Perry Como, Faye Emerson and others – with occasional guest bands or vocalists, but in the main featuring Tatum as a solo act. Most of the 1944–5 sessions are in decent enough sound, but thereafter quality is very modest: on the 1945–9 disc, nine tracks made at a party are top-notch Tatum, but the sound isn't much better than dreadful, and on the 1949–51 discs there are Toronto recordings and a 1950 set from Café Society Downtown which are similarly harsh. If you can deal with the fidelity there's the expected payload of impeccable playing, but these are really for Tatum diehards only.

****** The Art Tatum Solo Masterpieces Vol. 1**
Pablo 2405-432 *Tatum (p solo).* 12/53.

****** The Art Tatum Solo Masterpieces Vol. 2**
Pablo 2405-433 *Tatum (p solo).* 12/53.

****** The Art Tatum Solo Masterpieces Vol. 3**
Pablo 2405-434 *Tatum (p solo).* 12/53.

****** The Art Tatum Solo Masterpieces Vol. 4**
Pablo 2405-435 *Tatum (p solo).* 4/54.

****** The Art Tatum Solo Masterpieces Vol. 5**
Pablo 2405-436 *Tatum (p solo).* 4/54.

****** The Art Tatum Solo Masterpieces Vol. 6**
Pablo 2405-437 *Tatum (p solo).* 1/55.

****** The Art Tatum Solo Masterpieces Vol. 7**
Pablo 2405-438 *Tatum (p solo).* 1/55–56.

♛ ** The Complete Pablo Solo Masterpieces**
Pablo 4404 7CD *As above seven discs.* 12/53–1/55.

Tatum's extraordinary achievement was set down in no more than four separate sessions over the course of a little over a year. Twenty years after his first solo records, this abundance of music does in some ways show comparatively little in the way of 'progression': he had established a pattern for playing many of the tunes in his repertoire, and changes of inflexion, nuance and touch may be the only telling differences between these and earlier variations on the theme. But there are countless small revisions of this kind, enough to make each solo a fresh experience, and mostly he is more expansive (freed from playing-time restrictions, he is still comparatively brief, but there can be a major difference between a two-and-a-half-minute and a four-minute solo) and more able to provide dynamic contrast and rhythmic variation. He still chooses Broadway tunes over any kind of jazz material and seems to care little for formal emotional commitments: a ballad is just as likely to be dismantled as it is to be made to evoke tenderness, while a feeble tune such as 'Taboo' (Vol. 7) may be transformed into something that communicates with great power and urgency. Tatum's genius (these records were originally known as *The Genius Of Art Tatum*) was a peculiar combination of carelessness – even at his most daring and virtuosic he can sometimes suggest a throwaway manner – and searching commitment to his art, and those contradictory qualities (which in some ways exemplify something of the jazz artist's lot) heighten the power of these superb solos.

While it is invidious to single out particular discs, we suggest that the uncommitted start with discs four and six. The boxed-set edition includes all the music, and demands a fifth star. It is tantalizing to conjecture what Tatum might have done in contemporary studios, for his whole discography is marred by inadequate recording – even these later solos are comparatively unrefined by the studio – but the CD versions are probably the best to date. Still, surely this is a moment to go back to the best original sources and give us a new overview of this profound body of work.

****** 20th Century Piano Genius**
Verve 531763-2 2CD *Tatum (p solo).* 4/50–7/55.

***** Ultimate Art Tatum**
Verve 559877-2 *Tatum (p solo).* 4/50–7/55.

Even though these were privately recorded at the home of Tatum admirer Ray Heindorf, the sound is a lot better than on many of his regular sessions – a reminder of one of the most unfortunate aspects of jazz on record, that we cannot hear Tatum in hi-fi on a good piano. Out of 39 performances, 13 come from a 1950 occasion and the rest date from July 1955, late in the pianist's life, though he shows no lessening of his powers. The quite crisp fidelity lets one hear the precision and exactness of Tatum's runs, his mercurial fingerings and his almost off-hand genius rather better than usual, and in, say, 'Yesterdays', he seems to be thinking, creating and moving on so quickly that one understands anew all the disbelieving praise that has helped to build his legend. For all its informality, this isn't a bad place to start hearing Tatum, though the Pablo discs remain the cornerstones. The *Ultimate* collection is well chosen by Hank Jones, but it's somewhat pointless, given that the two-disc set gives everything here plus plenty more.

****** The Tatum Group Masterpieces Vol. 1**
Pablo 2405-424 *Tatum; Benny Carter (as); Louie Bellson (d).* 6/54.

*****(*) The Tatum Group Masterpieces Vol. 2**
Pablo 2405-425 *Tatum; Roy Eldridge (t); Larry Simmons (b); Alvin Stoller (d).* 3/55.

*****(*) The Tatum Group Masterpieces Vol. 3**
Pablo 2405-426 *Tatum; Lionel Hampton (vib); Buddy Rich (d).* 8/55.

*****(*) The Tatum Group Masterpieces Vol. 4**
Pablo 2405-427 *As above.* 8/55.

*****(*) The Tatum Group Masterpieces Vol. 5**
Pablo 2405-428 *Tatum; Harry 'Sweets' Edison (t); Lionel Hampton (vib); Barney Kessel (g); Red Callender (b); Buddy Rich (d).* 9/55.

****** The Tatum Group Masterpieces Vol. 6**
Pablo 2405-429 *Tatum; Red Callender (b); Jo Jones (d).* 1/56.

****** The Tatum Group Masterpieces Vol. 7**
Pablo 2405-430 *Tatum; Buddy DeFranco (cl); Red Callender (b); Bill Douglass (d).* 2/56.

****** The Complete Pablo Group Masterpieces**
Pablo 4401 6CD *As above eight discs.* 6/54–8/56.

The overall quality isn't so consistently intense, since Tatum's partners are sometimes either relatively incompatible or simply looking another way: the cheery Hampton and Rich, for instance, work well enough in their trio record, but it seems to lighten the music to an inappropriate degree. Yet some of this music is undervalued, particularly the trio session with Callender and Douglass, the group working in beautiful accord. The sextet date with Edison, Hampton and Kessel is comparatively slight, and the meeting with Eldridge, while it has moments of excitement, again sounds like two virtuosos of somewhat contrary methods in the same room.

The meetings with Carter, DeFranco and Webster, though, are unqualified masterpieces. The Carter session is worth having just for the astonishing 'Blues In C', and elsewhere Carter's aristocratic elegance chimes perfectly with Tatum's grand manner, their differing attitudes to jazz eloquence a rare match. With DeFranco, whose virtuosity is not so different from Tatum's own, the way the ingenuities of each man unfold can make one chuckle out loud; Tatum must have loved this session. As music to study, live with and simply enjoy, this is the most approachable of all of Tatum's series of recordings: he finds the company stimulating and manages to vary his approach on each occasion without surrendering anything of himself.

CORE COLLECTION

****** The Tatum Group Masterpieces Vol. 8**
Pablo 2405-431 *Tatum; Ben Webster (ts); Red Callender (b); Bill Douglass (d).* 9/56.

Even after the awesome achievement of the solo sessions, Tatum wasn't finished yet. Norman Granz recorded him in eight different group-settings as well. The meeting with Webster might on the face of it have been unlikely, but this time the contrasts in their styles create a moving alliance, the heavy, emotional tenor floating poignantly over the surging piano. The new 24-bit reissue of the Webster session (apparently only in Europe) is, to our ears, inferior to the 1990 mastering, and reminds us that the various bit-upgrades which CD is going through at present are not the cure-all they're often marketed as.

Art Taylor (1929–94)

DRUMS

Taylor began working on the New York scene in 1950 and became one of the most prolific drummers of the hard-bop movement. He moved to Europe in 1963 and later began interviewing musicians, resulting in the book, Notes and Tones. He returned to New York in the '80s and became a senior figure and group leader until his death.

***** Taylor's Wailers**

Original Jazz Classics OJC 094 *Taylor; Donald Byrd (t); Jackie McLean (as); John Coltrane, Charlie Rouse (ts); Ray Bryant, Red Garland (p); Wendell Marshall, Paul Chambers (b).* 2–3/57.

*****(*) Taylor's Tenors**

Original Jazz Classics OJC 1852 *Taylor; Charlie Rouse, Frank Foster (ts); Walter Davis (p); Sam Jones (b).* 6/59.

Art Taylor was a prolific visitor to the studios in the '50s, drumming for Red Garland, John Coltrane, Miles Davis and many others on countless sessions, most of them for Prestige. The company gave him a few shots at a leadership date and, while the first is a well-cooked hard-bop session, it doesn't go much further than that. The album is actually compiled from two sessions, one with Coltrane, who works up his patented head of steam on 'C.T.A.', and another with Rouse, whose more circumspect passions are rather well caught in his solo on 'Batland'. 'Off Minor' and 'Well You Needn't' feature in Thelonious Monk's own arrangements, but the band sound no more committed here than elsewhere, with Byrd his usual blandly confident self. The leader's own playing is authoritative, although some of his mannerisms leave him a degree short of the single-minded drive of Art Blakey.

Taylor's Tenors is a cracker. Rouse didn't often have to play in two-tenor situations, but he acquits himself with honour against Foster, who moves like a particularly dangerous big cat through Taylor's flashing rhythms. 'Rhythm-A-Ning' and 'Little Chico' both go off like a rocket, 'Cape Millie' and 'Straight No Chaser' cool off, but the pots are on again for 'Dacor'. Forty minutes or so of this sort of thing is enough; and this is just right. A.T. carried on bandleading into the '90s, but later entries for Enja and Verve are currently out of print.

Billy Taylor (born 1921)

PIANO

Born in North Carolina but moved to New York in the '40s and worked in various contexts, eventually running a trio for most of the '50s. From the '60s he was more involved in teaching and generally broadcasting the good word about jazz, a role he has followed with peerless energy.

****(*) Cross-Section**

Original Jazz Classics OJC 1730 *Taylor; Earl May (b); Percy Brice (d); Charlie Smith, Jose Mangual, Ubaldo Nieto, Machito (perc).* 5/53–7/54.

***** The Billy Taylor Trio With Candido**

Original Jazz Classics OJC 015 *Taylor; Earl May (b); Percy Brice (d); Candido (perc).* 9/54

***** Billy Taylor Trio**

Prestige 24285-2 *Taylor; Earl May (b); Percy Brice (d).* 12/54–4/55.

****(*) Billy Taylor With Four Flutes**

Original Jazz Classics OJC 1830 *Taylor; Phil Bodner, Herbie Mann, Frank Wess, Jerome Richardson, Bill Slapin, Jerry Sanfino, Seldon Powell (f); Tom Williams (b); Albert 'Tootie' Heath, Dave Bailey (d); Chano Pozo (perc).* 7/59.

***** Custom Taylored**

Fresh Sound FSR-CD 205 *Taylor; Henry Grimes (b); Ray Mosca (d).* 3/60.

While he has become best known as one of the most experienced and respected forces in jazz education in America, Billy Taylor's talents as a piano-player should be recognized more than they are. He played with everyone from Stuff Smith to Charlie Parker on 52nd Street in the '40s, and having worked with Machito stood him in good enough stead to make these early Latin-flavoured outings sound plausible. Taylor's affinities are essentially with bop, but his sensibility is akin to Teddy Wilson's: cultivated, gentlemanly, his improvisations take a leisurely route through his surroundings, alighting only on points which are germane to the setting, but managing to suggest a complete grasp of the material and task at hand. *Cross-Section* features eight tracks by his trio with May and Brice and four with Machito's rhythm section: daintily cast, the music is very engaging and, although the second session is transparently fixed to feature Candido – whose conga and bongo solos tend to bore when heard at length – the slow and almost luxuriant reading of 'Love For Sale' and the swinging 'Mambo Inn' suggest Taylor's careful preparation for the date. There is no dramatic sense of Latin–jazz fusion on either of these records, just a calm and logical pairing of one genre with another. *With Four Flutes* dates from five years later and counts as one of the sillier ideas of the day, given that the massed flutes on each track do little more than try to outwhistle one another. Even so, they get up a fair head of steam on 'St Thomas', and Taylor himself keeps urbane order. The new *Trio* couples a pair of sets by Billy's regular group of the day, one recorded live at New York's Town Hall, which closes on a marathon 'How High The Moon', the other at Rudy Van Gelder's. The studio set is typical Taylor: unfancy, brightly swinging and seldom looking for anything more profound than a few chipper melodic lines over some helpful chords; the three minutes of 'It's A Grand Night For Swinging' just about sums him up.

The trio fly through the dozen originals on *Custom Taylored* with fine aplomb. Originally done for a radio transcription service, and curtailed in running time, the crispness and snap of these blues and riff pieces comes fizzing through. Lightweight, maybe, but one of Billy's most enjoyable sessions.

***** Music Keeps Us Young**

Arkadia 71601 *Taylor; Chip Jackson (b); Steve Johns (d).* 8/96.

Back to straightahead for this trio date, and Taylor gives no suspicion of boredom, even when he gets to his old favourite, 'I Wish I Knew How It Would Feel To Be Free'. A couple of tracks find him wandering to no special purpose, but when given a melody like 'Wouldn't It Be Loverly' he knows how to make it sing.

***** Ten Fingers – One Voice**

Arkadia 71602 *Taylor (p solo).* 8/96.

Billy celebrated his 75th by delivering a rare solo album. He's such a genial, big-hearted player that even when he's doing little more than ornament a melody, he's very listenable. There's not much to get excited about with 'Tea For Two' or 'Laura', but the original ballad, 'Can You Tell By Looking At Me?', could charm a statue.

Cecil Taylor (born 1930)

PIANO, VOICE

Taylor learned piano at six and went on to study at New York College and New England Conservatory. Worked in R&B and swing-styled small groups in the early '50s, then led his own band with Steve Lacy from 1956. Although he had few opportunities to work in either clubs or concerts, Taylor acquired a reputation as the most daring of artists, with his music leaving tonality and jazz rhythm and structure behind (meanwhile he was still frequently working as a dishwasher). Occasional records, trips to Europe and finally, from 1969, a steady group with more international bookings allowed him more exposure. Academia began to recognize him and he taught in colleges. In the late '70s and '80s his work was steadily more admired and acknowledged, and his poetry and writing also came to the fore. By century's end he had built up a much more substantial discography, numerous awards of various kinds, and the reputation properly due a grandmaster of the music. Throughout his career, both on and off record, there has been no suspicion of any compromises at any point on his most singular path.

CORE COLLECTION

**** Jazz Advance

Blue Note 84462-2 *Taylor; Steve Lacy (ss); Buell Neidlinger (b); Dennis Charles (d).* 9/56.

Taylor's first record remains one of the most extraordinary debuts in jazz, and for 1956 it's an incredible effort. The pianist's '50s music is even more radical than Ornette Coleman's, though it has seldom been recognized as such, and, while Coleman has acquired the plaudits, it is Taylor's achievement which now seems the most impressive and uncompromised. While there are still many nods to conventional post-bop form in this set, it already points to the freedoms in which the pianist would later immerse himself. The interpretation of 'Bemsha Swing' reveals an approach to time that makes Monk seem utterly straightforward; 'Charge 'Em' is a blues with an entirely fresh slant on the form; Ellington's 'Azure' is a searching tribute from one keyboard master to another. 'Sweet And Lovely' and 'You'd Be So Nice To Come Home To' are standards taken to the cleaners by the pianist, yet his elaborations on the melodies will fascinate any who respond to Monk's comparable treatment of the likes of 'There's Danger In Your Eyes, Cherie'. Lacy appears on two tracks and sounds amazingly comfortable for a musician who was playing Dixieland a few years earlier. And Neidlinger and Charles ensure that, contrary to what some may claim, Taylor's music swings. The CD reissue sounds very well.

***(*) Looking Ahead!

Original Jazz Classics OJC 452 *As above, except Earl Griffith (vib) replaces Lacy.* 6/58.

The most pensive of Taylor's early records may be the best place to start in appreciating his music. The A minor blues of 'Luyah! The Glorious Step', Griffith's charming 'African Violet' and the remarkable fantasy on 'Take The "A" Train', 'Excursion On A Wobbly Rail', mark the pianist's transitional explorations of jazz form, while 'Toll' embarks on a new journey towards his own territory. 'Wallering', named in tribute to Fats Waller, is a wonderfully constructed improvisation on 'two improvised figures that are simultaneous', as Taylor says in the sleeve-note. Griffith combines edginess with inborn lyricism, which works surprisingly well in context, and Neidlinger and Charles swing the music without inhibiting Taylor's search for rhythmical freedom.

***(*) Love For Sale

Blue Note 94107-2 *Taylor; Ted Curson (t); Bill Barron (ts); Buell Neidlinger (b); Dennis Charles (d).* 4/59.

The three Cole Porter songs that open the record are starting-points for interpretations which are as radical as any standard had been subjected to at this point in jazz. Taylor keeps a toehold on melody or harmony, but no more than that and, as his phrase-lengths become ever more unpredictable, his shaping of the material transforms not just the songs but the way jazz after bop could improvise on received forms. Even Coleman's version of 'Embraceable You' is nothing like as dramatic as what Taylor does with 'Get Out Of Town'. The three originals that close the disc, with Curson and Barron joining the group, are in some ways less striking, since the horns remain tied to hard-bop language, even though Curson is clearly more responsive than the awkward Barron. Another fascinating stop in the patient transition from jazz orthodoxy to Taylor's mature music.

**** The World Of Cecil Taylor

Candid CCD 79006 *As above, except Archie Shepp (ts) replaces Griffith.* 10/60.

***(*) Air

Candid CCD 79046 *As above.* 1/61.

**** Jumpin' Punkins

Candid CCD 79013 *As above, except add Clark Terry (t), Roswell Rudd (tb), Steve Lacy (ss), Charles Davis (bs), Billy Higgins (d).* 1/61.

***(*) New York City R&B

Candid CCD 79017 *As above.* 1/61.

***(*) Cell Walk For Celeste

Candid CCD 79034 *As above.* 1/61.

The 1961 recordings for Candid – some of them under the nominal leadership of Neidlinger – secure a final balance between Taylor's insistent unshackling of familiar organization and his interest in standard material. *The World Of Cecil Taylor* introduced Shepp into the pianist's difficult universe, and it is a memorable encounter: Shepp's scrawling tenor battles through 'Air' with courageous determination, but it's clear that he has little real idea what's going on, and Taylor's own superbly eloquent improvisation makes the saxophonist seem like a beginner. It's even more apparent on the alternative takes of the piece (there were 18 attempts at it in the studio), many of which are on the Mosaic boxed set of this music (now out of print) and three of which are on *Air* (a collection of alternatives which includes two different takes of 'Number One' and one of 'Port Of Call'). But the same sessions also included the lovely and (for Taylor) surprisingly impressionistic 'Lazy Afternoon' and the blues fantasy of 'O.P.'. The larger band tackles only two tunes, both by Ellington, 'Things Ain't What They Used To Be' and 'Jumpin' Punkins', though they sound more like the Monk ensembles of *Monk's Music* than any Ellington band. Finally, there are the trio pieces: 'E.B.', which approximates a sonata and includes a superb piano improvisation, and the wholly improvised yet seemingly finished 'Cindy's Main Mood' are outstanding. The original records are *The World* and *New York City R&B*, but the various collections of out-takes are equally revealing.

★★★(★) Mixed

Impulse! 051270-2 *Taylor; Ted Curson (t); Roswell Rudd (tb); Jimmy Lyons (as); Archie Shepp (ts); Henry Grimes (b); Sunny Murray (d).* 10/61.

The three pieces here (the rest of the disc is given over to a Roswell Rudd session which Taylor is not involved in) were originally released under Gil Evans's name on the LP *Into The Hot*. Still poised between some measure of hard-bop language and his own developments, the music has a somewhat jolted feel, as if three tracks and 22 minutes simply wasn't sufficient to project the wealth of ideas Taylor had going on; even though this is the first disc to feature such collaborators as Lyons and Murray, everything is still trying to fall into place. The outstanding track, though, is 'Mixed', the only one to feature Curson and Rudd as well as the rest of the group. With its cross-ply of riffing, intense variations in dynamics, richness of voicing and juggernaut momentum, this proposes a group music very different from what would come later. As with the John Carisi music which made up the rest of the original *Into The Hot* LP, it feels like an unexplored nook in the music.

♛ ★★★★ Nefertiti, The Beautiful One Has Come

Revenant 202 2CD *Taylor; Jimmy Lyons (as); Sunny Murray (d).* 11/62.

It's taken a long time for these recordings to appear on CD, and many newcomers to the music may wonder why they caused such fascination. The drawbacks are numerous: the original recording was never very effective; Taylor seems to be playing one of the poorest pianos Copenhagen had to offer; Murray's drums sound thin and rattly a lot of the time. Nevertheless, these sessions from the Café Montmartre should be accounted among the greatest live recordings in jazz. Taylor is still working his way out of jazz tradition and, with Murray at his heels, the playing has an irresistible momentum that creates its own kind of rocking swing, the pulse indefinable but palpable, the rhythm moving in waves from the drummer's kit. Lyons shapes his bebopper's vocabulary into gritty flurries of notes, a man caught in a squall and fighting his way through it and over it. He would become Taylor's most dedicated interpretative colleague, but here he is sharing in the discovery of a fierce new world. Melody has a part to play: the two versions of 'Lena' measure out a beleaguered lyricism, for instance. Group interaction is a matter, sometimes, of clinging tight and hanging on, but this was a trio that had already done a lot of work together, and in the multiple layers of the monumental 'D Trad, That's What' and 'Call' the musicians seem to touch on an inner calm to go with the outward intensity. The Revenant release runs to two discs and includes some previously unheard extra material (admittedly in even more terrible sound!).

★★★(★) Unit Structures

Blue Note 84237-2 *Taylor; Gale Stevens Jr (t); Jimmy Lyons (as); Ken McIntyre (as, bcl, ob); Henry Grimes, Alan Silva (b); Andrew Cyrille (d).* 5/66.

Unit Structures is both as mathematically complex as its title suggests and as rich in colour and sound as the ensemble proposes, with the orchestrally varied sounds of the two bassists – Grimes a strong, elemental driving force, Silva tonally fugitive and mysterious – while Stevens and McIntyre add other hues and Lyons improvises with and against them. The title-piece is a highly refined but naturally flowing aggregation of various cells which create or propose directions for improvisation, combinations of players and tonal and rhythmical variations. Blue Note's recording wasn't ideal for this music, but it's good enough.

★★★★ Conquistador!

Blue Note 76749 *Taylor; Bill Dixon (t); Jimmy Lyons (as); Cecil Taylor (p); Henry Grimes, Alan Silva (b); Andrew Cyrille (d).* 10/66.

An all but flawless record. Dark, difficult, unique, yet operating at an artful tangent to some of the other 'difficult' Blue Note music of the period, this is Taylor at his most devious. Dixon and Lyons are deployed as a kind of 'classic' Blue Note front line, while still playing music which, say, Freddie Hubbard and even Eric Dolphy would have found close to impossible. It still suggests a level akin to but distant from the other 'avant-garde' record which appeared on the label at this time.

★★★(★) Dark To Themselves

Enja 2084-2 *Taylor; Raphe Malik (t); Jimmy Lyons (as); David S. Ware (ts); Marc Edwards (d).* 6/76.

★★★(★) Air Above Mountains

Enja 3005-2 *Taylor (p solo).* 8/76.

Originally edited to fit LP length, *Dark To Themselves* is a complete set from the 1976 Lubljana Festival. With no bassist, Taylor supplied all the bottom end himself, and the horns parade themselves over his figures. Edwards works hard, although he is scarcely a match for the drummers who've held down this role before and since. More than in many of Taylor's concert recordings, the music here suggests not darkness but incandescence – the flaring trumpet of Malik has a prominent role in the first 20 minutes, and the brilliance of Taylor's playing in this section is radiant.

Two months later, Enja also recorded Taylor at the Moosham Castle Open Air Festival in Austria, with 73 minutes of solo piano (once excerpted for LP release). Decent recording but a so-so piano. Still crowded, colossal.

★★★★ Cecil Taylor Unit

New World NW 201 *Taylor; Raphe Malik (t); Jimmy Lyons (as); Ramsey Ameen (vn); Sirone (b); Ronald Shannon Jackson (d).* 4/78.

★★★★ 3 Phasis

New World NW 203 *As above.* 4/78.

This was a superb group, full of contrast but bursting with the spirit of Taylor's music and exultant in its ability to make it work. The two New World albums are studio recordings, but they're performed with the intensity of a live set. These are colourful records: Ameen is a key member of the group, his fiddling vaguely reminiscent of Michael Sampson with Albert Ayler (a group which Jackson also played in), and there are moments when he aspires to a very close kinship with the pianist. But textures are only one part of this music. Malik and Lyons play bright or wounded or bitingly intense lines, and they play their part in a group chemistry which sometimes has the players contrasting with one another, sometimes combining to push the music forward, sometimes providing a textured background to Taylor's own sustained flights of invention. After the ferocity of his playing and organization in the late '60s, there is more obvious light and shade here, the freedoms more generously stated, the underlying lyricism more apparent. If there's a slight problem, it's with Jackson, who – ingenious and masterful though he is – hasn't quite the same grasp of Taylor's designs as Sunny Murray or Andrew Cyrille.

****** Winged Serpent (Sliding Quadrants)**
Soul Note 121089 *Taylor; Enrico Rava, Tomasz Stańko (t); Jimmy Lyons (as); Frank Wright (ts); John Tchicai (ts, bcl); Gunter Hampel (bs, bcl); Karen Borca (bsn); William Parker (b); Rashid Bakr (d); Andre Martinez (d).* 10/84.

An important and insufficiently recognized record. Taylor's four compositions here begin from melodic cells: an eight-note motif starts 'Taht', a sort of riff (which at one point seems ready to turn into a locomotive piece, very much in an Ellingtonian tradition!) emerges in 'Womb Waters', but mainly these are exploding, brilliantly coloured ensemble improvisations where the horns (all very well caught by the recording) make superbly euphoric collective statements. Densely characterized though Taylor's music is, these musicians make their way into it with the highest courage, and the results are extraordinarily compelling.

CORE COLLECTION

**** For Olim
Soul Note 121150 *Taylor (p solo).* 4/86.

By now, Taylor had built an impressive discography of solo recordings and there is nothing rote in this further addition to it. 'Olim' is the only long piece at some 18 minutes in duration; the others are sometimes only a couple of minutes long, isolating an idea, delivering it up, and then closing it down. What emerges most clearly from such a session is the refinement of his touch, sometimes obscured by the messier live mixes he's had to contend with, the absolute integration of favourite devices – clusters, call-and-response – into a peerless mastery of the techniques available to the pianist, and his communicative abilities: nothing here does anything but speak directly to an attentive listener.

***** Live In Bologna**
Leo LR 100 *Taylor; Carlos Ward (as, f); Leroy Jenkins (vn); William Parker (b); Thurman Barker (d, mar).* 11/87.

***** Live In Vienna**
Leo LR 174 *As above.* 11/87.

(***) Chinampas
Leo LR 153 *Taylor (speech).* 11/87.

Carlos Ward is hardly the man one thinks of when citing Taylor's saxophonists, and he is scarcely a match for Jimmy Lyons; but his more directly responsive and familiar lines make an agreeable change in their way, and Jenkins is a formidable presence on both records, adding rustic colours and primeval textures to the mix, which also includes marimba and bell sounds from Barker. Frankly, though, these concert sets haven't worn well, and we must admit that there are many better examples of Taylor's work in this entry.

Chinampas may appeal only to hardcore Taylor devotees, since there is no piano, simply the man reading some of his poetry. It's a fascinating adjunct to a monumental body of work; but, inevitably, it's of limited appeal.

****** Erzulie Maketh Scent**
FMP CD 18 *Taylor (p solo).* 7/88.

****** Pleistozaen Mit Wasser**
FMP CD 16 *Taylor; Derek Bailey (g).* 7/88.

****** Leaf Palm Hand**
FMP CD 6 *Taylor; Tony Oxley (d).* 7/88.

****** Spots, Circles And Fantasy**
FMP CD 5 *Taylor; Han Bennink (perc, etc.).* 7/88.

****** Regalia**
FMP CD 3 *Taylor; Paul Lovens (perc).* 7/88.

****** Remembrance**
FMP CD 4 *Taylor; Louis Moholo (d).* 7/88.

****** The Hearth**
FMP CD 11 *Taylor; Evan Parker (ss, ts); Tristan Honsinger (clo).* 7/88.

****** Riobec**
FMP CD 2 *Taylor; Gunter Sommer (d).* 7/88.

***** Legba Crossing**
FMP CD 0 *Heinz-Erich Godecke (tb); Ove Volquartz (ss, ts, bcl); Joachim Gies (as); Brigitte Vinkeloe (as, ss, f); Daniel Werts (ob); Sabine Kopf (f); Harald Kimmig (vn); Paul Plimley (p); Alexander Frangenheim, Uwe Martin, George Wolf (b); Lukas Lindenmaier, Peeter Uuskyla, Trudy Morse (v).* 7/88.

****** Alms/Tiergarten (Spree)**
FMP CD 8/9. *Taylor; Enrico Rava (t, flhn); Tomasz Stańko (t); Peter Van Bergen (ts); Peter Brötzmann (as, ts); Hans Koch (ss, ts, bcl); Evan Parker (ss, ts); Louis Sclavis (ss, cl, bcl); Hannes Bauer, Wolter Wierbos, Christian Radovan (tb); Martin Mayes (frhn); Gunter Hampel (vib); Tristan Honsinger (clo); Peter Kowald, William Parker (b); Han Bennink (d).* 7/88.

This unprecedented set of records still seems like a towering achievement, and it may stand as the apex of Taylor's latter-day work, creating resonances and establishing links and influences which may reverberate through European free playing for years to come. A document of his visit to a celebratory festival of his music in Berlin, it matches him with several of the finest European improvisers in a series of meetings that had, at that time, relatively few precedents. Although groupings such as Derek Bailey's Company had allowed a certain amount of Euro-American co-operation among improvisers, it was rare indeed for a player of Taylor's magnitude to be involved in such a celebration. An unparalleled inspiration to all these players, the fact of his presence seems to make most of them play above themselves.

Originally issued as a single boxed set, and now available as individual records, no collection should be without at least some of these, as examples of the expressive power and liberating energy which this central figure has introduced into jazz and 20th-century music in general. We would single out the encounters with Bailey, Parker/Honsinger, Oxley, Moholo and Bennink as particularly brilliant examples of Taylor's adaptive capabilities and his partners' own contributions, but every one of these records is both thought-provoking and individually inspiring to any listener prepared to give themselves over to Taylor's music.

Only the Workshop record, *Legba Crossing*, which Taylor merely directs, is in any way less than essential, although even here it is absorbing to follow how Taylor's methodology is brought to bear on the situation. The climactic concert with the full orchestra, *Alms/Tiergarten*, is a monumental event, the colossal sonic impact tempered by Taylor's own unflinching, instinctual control and a grasp of dynamics and dramatic possibility which is breathtaking. It is also, in the circumstances, deeply moving. So often in this area of jazz, above all others, the rewards for the players are minimal beyond the satisfaction in the music itself. The force of Taylor's presence in this situation has a legitimizing power which will remain an emotional matter to both the musicians and the hardy followers of this neck of the jazz woods, for ever off the familiar, accepted paths. As a collective achievement this stands as one of the major jazz recording projects and, were the original boxed set still available (it is now a prized collectors' item in its original form), we would have no hesitation in awarding it a crown.

★★★★ In East Berlin
FMP CD 13/14 2CD *Taylor; Gunter Sommer (perc).* 6/88.

★★★★ Looking (Berlin Version)
FMP CD 28 *Taylor (p solo).* 11/89.

★★★(★) Looking (Berlin Version) Corona
FMP CD 31 *Taylor; Harald Kimmig (vn); Muneer Abdul Fataah (clo); William Parker (b); Tony Oxley (d).* 11/89.

★★★★ Looking (The Feel Trio)
FMP CD 35 *Taylor; William Parker (b); Tony Oxley (d).* 11/89.

The duets with Sommer were recorded a month prior to the Berlin sessions: thunder and lightning, light and shade, and brimful of music, even across two long CDs. The three editions of *Looking* take a *Rashomon*-style look at the same piece of music, one solo (dense, heavily contoured, lots of pedal-sustain), one trio (magnificent interplay with Parker and Oxley, who became a frequent Taylor confrère), and one with the somewhat more awkward string stylings of Kimmig and Fataah, the latter meshing unconvincingly with Parker. The incredible richness of event continues, with barely a pause, in what was a remarkable period for the man.

★★★★ Celebrated Blazons
FMP CD 58 *Taylor; William Parker (b); Tony Oxley (d).* 6/90.

Does Taylor swing? The old litmus test comes to mind, since Taylor's ever-widening horizons sound more in touch and touched by jazz tradition than ever. Oxley's drumming is a more European flavour than anything Taylor's other regular drummers have created, yet it only serves to emphasize the huge rhythmic resources of the leader's own playing. Where Cyrille's magnificent breakers would sometimes obscure the keyboard, Oxley's playing – a unique blend of lumpen momentum and detailed percussive colour – reveals more of it. Parker, too, is coming into his own, deflecting off what the others do while speaking his own piece. Nearly an hour of music, and it swings.

★★★★ Olu Iwa
Soul Note 121139-2 *Taylor; Earl McIntyre (tb); Peter Brötzmann (ts, targato); Frank Wright (ts); Thurman Barker (mar, perc); William Parker (b); Steve McCall (d).* 4/86.

On the shelf for eight years before release, and with Wright and McCall both gone in the interim, this already has the feel of history about it. Some of the music, too, has one reflecting on Taylor's own history: the presence of Barker's marimba harks back to Earl Griffith on the ancient *Looking Ahead!*, and the small group with horns reminds one of *Unit Structures*. But the two sprawling pieces here (the first is almost 50 minutes; the second, where the horns depart, is nearly 30) have moved far on from those days. Alternately hymnal, purgatorial, intensely concentrated and wildly abandoned, the first theme is a carefully organized yet unfettered piece that again disproves Taylor's isolation (it's firmly within free-jazz traditions, yet sounds like something no one else could have delivered). The second, despite the absence of the towering Brötzmann, superb in the first half, is if anything even more fervent, with the quartet – a one-time appearance for this band on record – playing at full stretch. Another great one.

★★★ Iwontunwonsi – Live At Sweet Basil
Sound Hills SSCD-8065 *Taylor (p solo).* 2/86.

Another one from the archives, and perhaps less than essential, given that Taylor's '80s music is relatively widespread and in circulation. Basically a piano solo of some 45 minutes, this unspools some of the master's favourite methods into a typically Byzantine exploration of the keyboard. In the heavy company of some of the above discs, though, this one's a middleweight.

★★★★ Double Holy House
FMP CD 55 *Taylor (p, v, perc).* 9/90.

Taylor's quietest, most beguiling record ever is a profound meditation on some of the well-springs of what he does. It starts with a beautiful prelude at the piano before an extended recitation of poetry, accompanied by tiny splashes of percussion, and eventually a return to the piano – although the voice and percussion were actually recorded later, the act seems spontaneously whole. Eventually the accustomed intensity of Taylor in full flow breaks through, and with his accompanying cries the music searches through vocal and non-vocal tradition with a master's aptitude. Outstanding, again.

★★★(★) Melancholy
FMP CD 104 *Taylor; Tobias Netta (t); Jorg Huke, Thomas Wiederman (tb); Wolfgang Fuchs (sno, bcl); Harri Sjöström (ss); Volker Schott (as); Evan Parker (ts, ss); Thomas Klemm (ts); Barry Guy (b); Tony Oxley (d).* 9/90.

★★★★ Nailed
FMP CD 108 *Taylor; Evan Parker (ss, ts); Barry Guy (b); Tony Oxley (d).* 9/90.

A performance by the 'Workshop Ensemble', and to that extent perhaps only a rough cut of the kind of big-scale group music which Taylor might achieve, given limitless time and resources. But it is still enough to have other composers and arrangers slack-jawed, with three pieces that put an evolving structure through complex changes and developments. If the middle section, 'Sphere No. 2', seems like a bonding of improvisers, then 'Sphere No. 3' expands to a glorious reconciliation of free solos and composed and implicit structures. Besides Taylor himself, superb contributions from Guy, Parker and Klemm – but it's as a group performance that this works best.

Nailed is the third episode from the same event. Parker and Guy are frequent playing-partners, and although Oxley works with them comparatively rarely, they have much shared history; and he is a regular Taylor confrère too. As a quartet, they make a distinguished group, and only a few minutes into the first of two pieces, 'First', it's clear that the music has a special ration of power and exercised skills. Free-jazz blowouts have been commonplace for decades, but the exciting thing about the intensity which the quartet reaches ten minutes into this piece is the clarity, even at such a tumultuous level of activity. For once, FMP secures a recording of fine accuracy and detail, and the consequence is a mighty document indeed.

CORE COLLECTION

★★★★ The Tree Of Life
FMP CD 98 *Taylor (p solo).* 3/91.

A gorgeously lyrical and handsomely realized recital, decently recorded, and one of Taylor's most sheerly enjoyable records. For readers who aren't prepared to entertain the pianist on the basis of the sheer amount of work involved – and it's a viewpoint which even we have some sympathy with – this might even be the record to start with. It's no great departure for the man, 70 minutes or so of often rapt and sometimes even quizzical playing, and it tends towards the distilled feel of much of his latter-day music: having got much of the thunder behind him, or having the means to explore it via his various larger groupings, by himself he seems more content to sit and muse on aspects of a voluminous art. And this is the result.

★★★ Always A Pleasure
FMP CD 69 *Taylor; Longineau Parsons (t); Harri Sjöström (ss); Charles Gayle (ts); Tristan Honsinger (clo); Sirone (b); Rashid Bakr (d).* 4/93.

As always, there are marvellous moments. But we would count this among Taylor's less successful group concerts (Berlin, again, in 1993). While Honsinger, Sirone, Bakr and – surprisingly – Parsons seem right in tune, Sjöström isn't, and Gayle is frankly completely in the wrong world for this occasion. He simply can't get through the way he does on his own records, and he's reduced to what seems like ranting from the sidelines. The closing segment lets the group find a sort of peaceful reconciliation with itself, and it's nearly worth sorting through some of the prior confusion to get to the coda.

★★★(★) Qu'a: Live At The Iridium Vol. 1
Cadence CJR 1092 *Taylor; Harri Sjöström (ss); Dominic Duval (b); Jackson Krall(d).* 3/98.

★★★ Qu'a Yuba: Live At The Iridium Vol. 2
Cadence CJR 1098 *As above.* 3/98.

The instrumentation for these New York club sets goes back to Taylor's first group with Steve Lacy. Sjöström at times seems to be thinking about that, some of his remarks having a playful irony that suggests his illustrious forebear, but in other respects the music is inevitably a long, long way distant from such ancient history. The saxophonist does better here than he did on the earlier, FMP session without finally making a convincing case for his presence. Duval isn't particularly well placed in the mix, and his *arco* playing has an unpleasant buzz which suggests a tinny bass amplifier. Krall, though, is inventive and often delicately propulsive: his brushwork halfway through the first set is impeccable. Taylor's intensity seems as trenchant as ever. Whatever the shortcomings of the two discs in either musical or recording terms, his own contributions remain worthy of the listener's best attention.

★★★★ The Willisau Concert
Intakt CD 072 *Taylor (p solo).* 9/00.

One of the pleasures of recent times has been superior piano sound on gramophone records, and the opportunity to hear Cecil Taylor in as excellent fidelity as this, in concert, on an excellent piano, reminds one of all the missed opportunities of his early years, when such an acute keyboard practitioner had to settle for poor pianos and even poorer recordings. Never mind: here he is at 71(!), the music-making still something to marvel at, the energy levels amazing, and the results fine enough to account for a lot of enjoyable future study. Or just play it once, as John Cage might have advised, and be overwhelmed.

★★(★) Cecil Taylor/Bill Dixon/Tony Oxley
Victo 082 *Taylor; Bill Dixon (t); Tony Oxley (d).* 5/02.

A strange one, from Victoriaville 2002. Dixon's penchant for noodling to himself (here he also uses a digital reverb device, with annoyingly trivial results) tends to close him off from the other two, and the record works best if one tunes him out. Difficult, though.

David Taylor (born 1944)

BASS TROMBONE

A specialist in the low-brass range, Taylor is a busy sessioneer who is as likely to be found on a contemporary-composition date as any jazz-associated recording.

★★(★) Doppelganger
CIMP 269 *Taylor; Dominic Duval (b); Jay Rosen (d).* 5/02.

A rare outing in the limelight for this prolific musician, who usually works under someone else's orders. The trio rattle through 14 tracks and the feel is somewhat reminiscent of an old FMP date from the '70s. So some of it works, and a lot doesn't. Curiously, some of the short tracks sound as if they should be longer, while the longer ones could use some pruning. Taylor is master of the bass trombone, but he seems to think in sentences rather than paragraphs and when he's stuck for his next move he tends to bluster. Duval and Rosen make appropriate noises, and at least there's some humour, often a rare commodity in CIMP releases.

John Taylor (born 1942)

PIANO

A Mancunian, Taylor arrived in London in 1964 and was soon in the thick of the local scene. Led his own groups in the late '60s and '70s and co-formed Azimuth in 1977. An internationalist as a performer, much admired overseas, his most notable partnerships have been with vocalist Norma Winstone and trumpeter Kenny Wheeler.

★★★(★) Pause, And Think Again
FMR CD 24 *Taylor; Kenny Wheeler (t); Chris Pyne (tb); Stan Sulzmann (as); John Surman (ss); Chris Laurence (b); Tony Levin (d); Norma Winstone (v).* 71.

★★★ Ambleside Days
Ah Um 013 *Taylor; John Surman (ss, bs, bcl, syn).* n.d.

★★★ Blue Glass
Jazz House JHCD 020 *Taylor; Mick Hutton (b); Steve Arguëlles (d).* 6/91.

Much admired, Taylor is under-recorded as a leader, though one should also weigh his work with Azimuth in the balance. He started out as an accompanist, established and sustained a reputation with his first wife, Norma Winstone, and is still routinely described as if his gifts are best suited to a supportive role. In fact, Taylor is a riveting solo performer and an exceptional writer. Typically, he likes to spin out long lines of melody, braced by a firm but flexible rhythmic base. He sounds effortlessly fluent but never less than thoughtful. It's ironic that the most immediately arresting of these records was made a quarter of a century ago. Anyone familiar with Azimuth will hear powerful echoes throughout *Pause, And Think Again*, particularly when Winstone and Wheeler occupy the foreground. Even more impressive than the soloing, though, are the tightly marshalled but intriguingly open-ended ensembles, especially on the two title-pieces, which sandwich a thing called 'White Magic'.

The record with Surman belongs every bit as much to the saxophonist. The two men share an interest in pastoral ideas, and it is fascinating to listen to them both steer as close as could be to mere prettiness before pulling suddenly away with something arresting and unexpected but also entirely appropriate. Much the same applies to the live set from Ronnie Scott's jazz club. Like 'White Magic', 'Blue Glass' is a good example of Taylor's gifts as a sound-painter, but it is his treatment of standards – 'Spring Is Here', 'How Deep Is The Ocean' – that catches the attention first time around. There is also a new version of 'Clapperclowe' from *Ambleside Days*, cast very differently for the trio format.

*****(*) Rosslyn**

ECM 1599 *Taylor; March Johnson (b); Joey Baron (d).* 4/02.

One rather hoped that having former Bill Evans bass-man in the trio Taylor might consider programming some Evans material, particularly given that he has been compared to the American many times. In fact, what one gets is a set that is Evans-like in temperament rather than content. Taylor doesn't pack this first solo set for ECM with original material, but brings in compositions by Ralph Towner (the lovely 'Tramonto') and Kenny Wheeler ('Ma Bel') as well as a standard, 'How Deep Is The Ocean', to which he gives a slyly Jarrett-like spin. His original themes, each of them with a folkish tinge, are swung much harder by this group than one imagines would be the case with British sidemen, and Taylor seems to be lighter in spirit and faster in response here than on previous records. However, all *Rosslyn* really does is clinch his pedigree as one of the finest pianists in Europe (and he spends much of his time in Europe rather than England).

****** Insight**

Sketch 1064 *Taylor (p solo).* 4/03.

Insight may be the kind of title, and those pastoral evocations exactly the kind of track, that put off jazz snobs. The important thing to register about this superb release is that Taylor has never sounded so completely like a jazz player. Even when he alludes to Bartók or Debussy, even when his inspiration is a long way removed from the blues, his playing has never been more aware of tradition and never more completely individual. 'Evans Above' is a miracle of harmonic invention, while Taylor's interpretation of Steve Swallow's 'Vaguely Asian', complete with strums inside the soundbox, is quietly virtuosic. The other highlight, perhaps pointedly meant, is Kenny Wheeler's 'Everybody's Song But My Own'. A magnificent album, superbly paced and recorded.

Martin Taylor (born 1956)

GUITAR

Taylor was closely associated with Stéphane Grappelli in his pomp and has shown an instinctive feel for the Hot Club de France idiom while simultaneously carving out a richly expressive solo sound that draws on every aspect of the jazz guitar tradition, up to (but probably not including) the electric fusion of the '70s. He veers between unaccompanied performance and a more spacious group sound.

****(*) Taylor Made**

Wave CD 17 *Taylor; Peter Ind (b); John Richardson (d).* 79.

***** Triple Libra**

Wave CD 24 *Taylor; Peter Ind (b).* 81.

Awesomely but unassumingly gifted, Taylor is the kind of artist who gives the music a good name. In straightforward technical terms, he is probably a match for any guitarist of today. His lines seem so cleanly articulated that there is no distance between thought and execution. Perhaps too much so. These aren't very exciting records; the studio sound is as blemish-free as the playing, and one never quite gets that little flicker of danger that would lift them up a notch. The debut album confirms all of that. Precocious, able, even facile, but not yet with a story to tell. Taylor tackles 'On Green Dolphin Street' with an assurance that is uncanny and brings a crisp precision to George Benson's 'My Latin Brother', a more contemporary sound. Taylor only really begins to sound like himself on the follow-up *Triple Libra*, where he chips in with 'Green Eyes', an early sign of compositional gifts, along with a superb version of Chick Corea's 'Windows'. Long out of circulation, these records are a welcome addition to the catalogue, though – relative to what follows – they should be considered a priority only for confirmed Taylor fans.

***** Sketches – A Tribute To Tatum**

P3 014 *Taylor (g solo).* 83, 78.

Recorded in Edinburgh (and in the case of the final three tracks, in London five years before), these catch Taylor at the end of his precocious youth and on the cusp of turning into the formidable star of today. His technique is dazzling and his interpretations of such things as 'Old Man River' and 'Honeysuckle Rose' are to die for. The bonus tracks from 1978 are 'All The Things You Are', 'Cotton Tail' and 'Misty', of which only the last betrays a whiff of callowness, forgivable at 22.

***** Don't Fret**

Linn AKD 014 *Taylor; David Newton (p); Dave Green (b); Allan Ganley (d).* 9/90.

***** Change Of Heart**

Linn AKD 016 *Taylor; David Newton (p); Brian Shiels (b); John Rae (d).* 6/91.

Change Of Heart includes a blues, 'You Don't Know Me', that Taylor takes to the cleaners, but the anodyne brilliance of the playing takes some of the pith out of the playing, and certainly undermines the conviction of the rock-orientated 'Angel's Camp'. The earlier record is more solidly in the jazz camp, thanks mostly to Ganley's civil adaptation of Art Blakey's beat; but the more four-square Rae does no harm to the second session. Taylor was advancing by leaps and bounds all through the '80s and the contrast between these and the Wave sessions above is breathtaking. Technically there isn't much in it. Expressively, he's already on a different plane.

*** Artistry

Linn AKD 020 *Taylor (g solo).* 5/92.

Recorded with superb polish and clarity, this solo recital is almost too good to be true. The title is exactly right, for one feels that the main aim isn't so much musical as technical, a chance to show off untarnishable gifts rather than to make anything more personal of these songs. Taylor is an endlessly expressive player in a live context, but a chill descends whenever he enters a studio. Not all the tunes are ballads, yet they all seem to come out that way: sensitive, shimmering and rhythmically so even that the notes fold into one another with little apparent variation. Other guitarists will love and treasure it. We've found it hard to sustain interest.

*** The Linn Box

Linn AKD 115 *Taylor; as for Don't Fret, Change Of Heart, Artistry.* n.d.

A nicely repackaged three-volume set that brings together Martin's first three records for Linn. There's no new material on offer, so Taylor collectors are unlikely to be attracted, but newcomers will find the box an invaluable primer.

*** Reunion

Linn AKD 022 *Taylor; Stéphane Grappelli (vn).* 92.

Or: *Old Art And Young Hector.* This fascinating creative friendship has been closely documented in a couple of rather moving television programmes. It's difficult to tell which moves most, the youthful exuberance of an old fiddle-player who worked with Django and long ago passed his biblical span, or the improbably coiffed young man who seems to understand and appreciate the older language almost as well as Grappelli himself. The best of this is wonderful, but it's a little bit unrelieved unless you buy wholeheartedly into the idiom. Grappelli is as flagrantly inventive as ever; it's impossible to stop and wonder if what he just did was legitimate or even possible, because he's done another half-dozen unexpected things in the meantime. Taylor is fleet-fingered and wise, and on tunes like 'It's Only A Paper Moon' and 'Hotel Splendid' demonstrates how fast his own harmonic intelligence operates.

**** Spirit Of Django

Linn AKD 030 *Taylor; Dave O'Higgins (ts, ss); John Goldie (g); Jack Emblow (acc); Alec Dankworth (b, cabassa); James Taylor (perc).* 6–8/94.

Given the association with Grappelli, the naming of this group was no surprise, and nor was much of the repertoire. Taylor had decided to give up unaccompanied performance for a while and concentrate on a group sound. It must have been difficult to sustain the level of highly exposed creativity he was bringing to solo concerts. What the group allows him to do is work within a much bigger harmonic and timbral framework, allow his guitar to thread together ideas rather than sustain them all. In Dave O'Higgins (one of the best of the younger generation of British saxophonists) and the seasoned Jack Emblow, he has partners who are absolutely in sympathy with what he is doing. In Dankworth, he has a bass-player who can sustain the tempo in a drummerless group (son James has only a bit part at this stage) but who can also lend himself to the other parameters of the music as well. On 'Night And Day' and 'Honeysuckle Rose', he is creating as much of the musical movement as anyone else. Taylor intended the record to be a tribute to his own father, as well as to the artistic parent namechecked in the title. Playing acoustically and in a setting that juxtaposes Django material ('Nuages', 'Minor Swing', 'Swing 42') against originals and Taylor's own celebrated reworking of Robert Parker's 'Johnny And Mary' theme, he sounds very different from the solo artist, less busy and layered, but instantly identifiable as himself. A masterly record, and probably his best to date.

***(*) Portraits

Linn AKD 048 *Taylor; Chet Atkins (g).* 7–12/95.

Notwithstanding Taylor's apparent desire to leave this kind of thing aside for a while, this is an excellent record, and the chance to play with another of the great legends of modern music must have been irresistible. Atkins went around afterwards saying what a privilege it had been for him to play with Martin, when everyone might have supposed the gratitude flowed the other way. They're first heard together on 'Sweet Lorraine' and one can hear at once where some of Taylor's clean-picked lines come from – not from Django after all. He tries a couple of interesting overdubs, but as before it is the solo tracks where the real action lies. A version of Earl Klugh's 'Kiko' and a closing version of Bill Evans's lovely 'Very Early' are the real gems.

***(*) Years Apart

Linn AKD 058 *Taylor; Gerard Presencer (flhn); Dave O'Higgins (sax); John Goldie (g); Stéphane Grappelli (vn); Jack Emblow (acc); Terry Gregory (b); James Taylor (perc); Claire Martin (v).* 96.

The second Spirit Of Django album lacks the impact of the first, but it's still a highly appealing and beautifully crafted performance. The basic group plays wonderfully well, but one wonders if, Grappelli aside, the guest performances from Presencer and Martin (and a further cameo from son James) don't dilute the whole rather than enhance it. 'Manoir De Mes Rêves' is worth waiting for, sealing a habit of finishing albums with the strongest number. The title-piece is wonderful, too, with one of Taylor's most nakedly expressive lines.

*** Two's Company

Linn AKD 081 *Taylor; duets with Bob Barnard, Ian Date, George Golla, James Morrison, Johnny Nicol, Jim Pennell, Suzanne Wyllie, Peter Zog.* 97.

To all intents and purposes another solo album. The motley assortment of guests don't add very much to what Martin himself is doing. If the album signals anything – and, with no fewer than 17 tracks, it signals it with great insistence – it is that Taylor may be moving away from swing and closer to a more mainstream jazz style, at least for this project. That's suggested in 'Royal Garden Blues' as much as in the following 'You Stepped Out Of A Dream' and 'Willow Weep For Me'. As ever, the closing track is the killer, a glorious rendition of 'My Foolish Heart'.

**** Gold

Linn AKD 064 *Taylor; as for the above.* 90–97.

We're not usually enthusiastic about 'best of' compilations, but this magnificently remastered career retrospective on special, gold-coated pressings offers a good selection of tunes (14 of them, with all the obvious ones included) and pristine, shiny sound. Kicking off with 'Johnny And Mary' was inevitable, given its prominence as an advertising theme, and Linn have wisely gone for a pretty straightforward sample thereafter, including 'Minor Swing', 'Paper Moon', 'Nuages' and 'I Got Rhythm.' A perfect starter for anyone who hasn't any of Taylor's previous albums. We should note that up to *Two's Company* Linn have also issued high-quality cassettes of all the albums, and that there is a memorial disc of Martin's association with the late Stéphane Grappelli; that we have covered under the violinist's entry.

*** Gypsy

Linn AKD 090 *Taylor; Dave O'Higgins (sax); Jack Emblow (acc); John Goldie, Terry Gregory (g); James Taylor (perc).* 96–97.

The most recent disc from Spirit Of Django has a steady-as-she-goes feel. The group is now well enough established to have struck off in some new directions, but *Gypsy*, which was recorded on tour in England with three studio tracks added, has a faintly recycled quality. Taylor is as good as always, and these cuts have presumably been selected to show him at his best. However, the group doesn't always gel and the two subsidiary guitarists go about their business with a slightly grim determination, as if they were being paid by the chord.

*** Kiss And Tell

Columbia 495387 2 *Taylor; Randy Brecker (flhn); Jay Ashby (tb, v); Kirk Whalum (ss, ts); George Garzone (ts); Matt Rollings (p, org); Brian Siewert (ky); Pat Bergeson (g); John Catchings (vn); Kristin Wilkinson (vla); David Davidson (clo); Eddie Gomez, Chris Kent (b); Al Foster (d); Eric Darken (perc).* 99.

Major-label interest was long overdue, but Taylor wastes no time in flash grandstanding and instead delivers a musical set that covers just about every aspect of his playing approach. His solo style is represented on 'Mona Lisa', a performance that would have made his dad proud. There are ancestral influences, too, on the guitar/piano duet, 'Ginger', an old tune written for his great-grandfather, the boxer Ginger Stewart, and on 'The Nearness Of You', a duet with tenor saxophonist Kirk Whalum, who played it with the dying Arnett Cobb. And there is a hint of godparental influence on 'Sunstep', which revives memories of the association with Grappelli.

**** In Concert

Milestone 9306 *Taylor (g solo).* 6/98.

Having broken his duck as far as live releases were concerned with *Gypsy*, Taylor repeated the experiment with a new label. Whether or not Milestone producer Jay Ashby had anything to do with the selection of material, this is a very much more straightahead set than usual. Martin sticks to standard material throughout – no pop songs or Hot Club repertoire – and plays in a relatively conventional, Joe Pass-influenced style. The best of the songs are very good indeed. A brief, brisk 'I Got Rhythm' demonstrates how completely on top of his material he is. Taylor had moved away somewhat from unaccompanied playing at this time, but this gig, recorded at Manchester Craftsmen's Guild, is a near perfect example of what he is capable of in this format. Delightfully recorded in a clear and warm acoustic, this is quintessential jazz guitar, effortlessly musical and intelligent.

***(*) Stepping Stones

Linn 166 *As for Linn releases above.* 90–97.

A nice selection from Taylor's years with the Scottish label. It kicks off, almost inevitably, with the 'hit' version of 'Johnny and Mary' and finds room for a duet with Grappelli on 'Hotel Splendid'. For the rest, it's a good blend of solo and group material and will provide a very attractive way in to Martin's career.

** Nitelife

Sony 85909 *Taylor; Jim Reid (ss); Jim Horn(as, ts, bs); Kirk Whalum(ts); Brian D. Stewart, John Stoddart (ky); Steve Buckingham(g); David Hungate, Viktor Krauss (b); Chester Thompson (d).* 00.

We could not and would not grudge Martin a measure of commercial success, but his second for Sony is an overproduced mish-mash of fashionable gestures and poppy arrangements which do little more than mask the unalloyed beauty of his guitar-playing. The blame has to be laid at the feet of producers Steve Buckingham and Kirk Whalum. While the guitarist picks out the line of Earth, Wind & Fire's 'That's The Way Of The World', the mix buries it in fuzz and mush. The same thing happens on Dionne Warwick's 'Déjà Vu'. Taylor has shown often enough that he can take pop material – 'Johnny And Mary' is the best example – and give it a highly inventive spin without resorting to the effects desk. This is a real disappointment.

**(*) Gypsy Journey

P3 1056 *Taylor; Jermaine Landsberger (p); Davide Petrocca (b); Scotty Gottwald (d).* 11/02.

This is a rather disappointing release from Taylor, whose last appearance on P3 was in the company of Steve Howe and several million dollars' worth of unique guitars, all of them from the collection of the late Scott Chinery. This is a rather bland and formulaic album and the group, a recent convocation, is only intermittently responsive to Taylor's needs, at least in the studio. Technically, they are fine, and may well be a more interesting live proposition. This, though, is Taylor's most uninvolving project for some time.

John Tchicai (born 1936)

ALTO, SOPRANO AND TENOR SAXOPHONES, FLUTES, BASS CLARINET

It is often assumed that Tchicai is African-American, an impression cemented by his part in John Coltrane's masterpiece of new jazz, Ascension, but the saxophonist is half-Danish, half-Congolese. He started out on violin and, after switching to saxophone, was noticed by Archie Shepp and others on the European festival circuit. Originally rather dry and papery in tone, Tchicai has become more emotionally nuanced over the years and nowadays recalls no one more than Sidney Bechet.

*** The Real Tchicai

Steeplechase SCCD 31075 *Tchicai; Pierre Dørge (g); Niels-Henning Orsted Pedersen (b).* 3/77.

***** Ball At Louisiana**
Steeplechase SCCD 31174 *Tchicai; Pierre Dørge (g).* 11/81.
***** Timo's Message**
Black Saint 120094 *Tchicai; Thomas Dürst, Christian Kuntner (b); Timo Fleig (d, perc).* 2/84.
****** Grandpa's Spells**
Storyville STCD 4182 *Tchicai; Misha Mengelberg (p); Margriet Nabrier (syn); Peter Danstrup (b); Gilbert Matthews (d).* 3/92.

Tchicai moved to the United States in the early '60s and joined Archie Shepp and Bill Dixon in the New York Contemporary Five; but he went on to lead a more significant, if less well-known, group with percussionist Milford Graves and trombonist Roswell Rudd, known as the New York Art Quartet. In the following year he played alongside fellow altoist Marion Brown (whom he somewhat resembles in approach) on John Coltrane's epic *Ascension*, before returning to Europe to work on a number of individual projects.

Tchicai has now been a presence in the European avant-garde for more than a quarter of a century, although his few records and occasional appearances have marginalized him more than somewhat. Though most obviously influenced by Ornette Coleman and, to a lesser extent, Eric Dolphy, Tchicai's very individual tonality has more often been likened to that of Lee Konitz, and his performing style has followed a similar trajectory, turning away from a rather cool and dry approach towards a rootsier and more forceful delivery. The two Steeplechases are rather dry affairs in which the moments of beauty feel as forced as hothouse blooms. Dørge and NHOP try to eke some energy out of the saxophonist, but he often seems curiously ill at ease. That said, there are some striking moments, especially on some of the ballads on the later disc, on which NHOP is absent.

The '80s saw Tchicai shift away from alto saxophone. His tenor and soprano work was initially competent but rather anonymous, and it really came into its own only during the following decade, as on the excellent *Grandpa's Spells*. For the most part, the '70s had been a time of consolidation, of teaching and of research into Eastern musics, but he returned to performance with a group called Strange Brothers. Among the more recent material, there is a fine 'Stella By Starlight' on *Timo's Message*, but again the weight of interest falls largely on Tchicai's now quite varied compositional style, which include calypso and rock elements.

Grandpa's Spells foreshadows Tchicai's growing interest in electronics. The basic quartet is augmented with intelligently deployed sequences that give pieces like 'Community Bells' a rich, almost orchestral texture. There are two old-fashioned improvisations from the group, with Mengelberg well to the fore, a hint of the 'fusion' direction on 'Heksehyl', some folky stuff using traditional melodies ('Fran Engeland Till Skottland'), a touch of Carl Nielsen, and two Jelly Roll Morton compositions.

***** Love Notes From The Madhouse**
8thhb 80001 *Tchicai; Aaron Getsug (bs, v); Margriet Naber-Tchicai (ky, v); Jeff Parker (g, v); Fred Hopkins (b); Benita Haastrup (d, perc, v); Yusef Komunyakaa (v).* 9/97.

Jazz and poetry have been long-standing bedfellows, but this remarkable collaboration between Tchicai and poet Yusef Komunyakaa redefines the relationship. With the exception of Billy Strayhorn's 'Bloodcount', everything is conceived by the players. 'Dolphy's Aviary' is a remarkable musical and verbal history of recent jazz, and the terse, allusive lyrics are wonderfully complementary to the music. Not suited to every taste, but worth exploring.

***** Infinitesimal Flash**
Buzz 76010 *Tchicai; Francis Wong (ts, f); Adam Lane (b); Mat Marucci (d).* 99.

The opening 'Kippiology', a Johnny Dyani theme, is full-flushing energy music, which might suggest that Tchicai has gone full circle; but thereafter the quartet follow more diverse paths. The partnership with Wong offers some interesting wrinkles, with the Chinese-American taking a major compositional role, and also adapting the traditional melodies 'Autumn Moon' and 'Alishan', which prove to be effective vehicles for Tchicai's soprano and tenor respectively. That said, neither saxophonist really cuts that deeply, and the sleeve-note suggestion that they're akin to a Marsh–Konitz dialogue is distinctly flattering.

**** Hope Is Bright Green Up North**
CIMP 278 *Tchicai; Pierre Dørge (g); Lou Grassi (d).* 10/02.

Dørge and Tchicai are old colleagues and some of their dialogue is rewarding, but the record is completely unbalanced by Grassi, who thrashes around seemingly with very little attention paid to whatever else is going on. A misfire.

Jack Teagarden (1905–64)

TROMBONE, VOCAL

A Texan, Teagarden took the trombone to new levels, with his impeccable technique, fluency and gorgeous sound, allied to a feel for blues playing which eluded many of his white contemporaries. He was also a fine, idiosyncratic singer. He was with Ben Pollack for five years from 1928, with Paul Whiteman in the '30s, and finally led his own swing orchestra, though it left him broke in the end. He joined the Louis Armstrong All Stars in 1946, stayed till 1951, then led small groups of his own and toured for the rest of his life. He died in New Orleans, worn out by drink.

***** I Gotta Right To Sing The Blues**
ASV AJA 5059 *Teagarden; Leonard Davis, Red Nichols, Ray Lodwig, Manny Klein, Charlie Teagarden, Ruby Weinstein, Sterling Bose, Dave Klein, Harry Goldfield, Nat Natoli, Frank Guarente, Leo McConville, Charlie Spivak (t); Jack Fulton, Glenn Miller, Ralph Copsey, Bill Rank (tb); Benny Goodman (cl); Mezz Mezzrow, Arthur Rollini, Charles Strickfadden, Benny Bonaccio, John Cordaro, Chester Hazlett, Jimmy Dorsey, Art Karle, Eddie Miller, Matty Matlock, Joe Catalyne, Pee Wee Russell, Max Farley, Happy Caldwell, Arnold Brilhart, Bernie Day, Sid Stoneburn, Babe Russin, Larry Binyon, Gil Rodin, Irving Friedman, Adrian Rollini, Min Leibrook (reeds); Red McKenzie (kz, v); Fats Waller (p, v); Joe Sullivan, Jack Russin, Lennie Hayton, Arthur Schutt, Gil Bowers, Joe Moresco, Roy Bargy, Vincent Pirro, Howard Smith (p); Joe Venuti, Matty Malneck, Mischa Russell, Harry Struble, Walt Edelstein, Alex Beller, Ray Cohen (vn); Carl Kress, Jack Bland, Nappy Lamare, Eddie Lang, Dick McDonough, Perry Botkin, Mike Pingitore, George Van Eps (g); Treg Brown (bj, v); Eddie Condon (bj); Artie Bernstein, Art Miller, Jerry Johnson, Harry Goodman, Al Morgan (b);*

Norman McPherson (tba); Ray Bauduc, George Stafford, Herb Quigley, Stan King, Gene Krupa, Josh Billings, Larry Gomar (d). 2/29–10/34.

Teagarden's star is somehow in decline, since all his greatest work predates the LP era and at this distance it's difficult to hear how completely he changed the role of the trombone. In Tea's hands, this awkward barnyard instrument became majestic, sonorous and handsome. By the time he began recording in 1926 he was already a mature and easeful player whose feel for blues and nonchalant rhythmic drive made him stand out on the dance-band records he was making.

This compilation features 12 different bands and 18 tracks, which points up how easily Teagarden could make himself at home in bands of the period. One celebrated example is the treatment meted out to a waltz called 'Dancing With Tears In My Eyes', under Joe Venuti's leadership: Teagarden contravenes everything to do with the material and charges through his solo. Two early sessions under his own name have him trading retorts with Fats Waller on 'You Rascal You' and delivering his original reading of what became a greatest hit, 'A Hundred Years From Today'. Stricter jazz material such as two tracks by The Charleston Chasers is fine, but no less enjoyable are such as Ben Pollack's 'Two Tickets To Georgia', where Teagarden's swinging outburst suggests that he treated every setting as a chance to blow. One or two of the transfers are noisy, but most of the remastering is agreeably done.

*** A Hundred Years From Today

Conifer 153 *Teagarden; Charlie Teagarden, Claude Whiteman, Sterling Bose, Frank Guarente (t); Pee Wee Russell, Benny Goodman (cl); Chester Hazlett, Jimmy Dorsey, Rod Cless (cl, as); Joe Catalyne, Max Farley, Dale Skinner, Mutt Hayes (cl, ts); Frankie Trumbauer (cmel); Bud Freeman (ts); Adrian Rollini (bsx); Casper Reardon (hp); Fats Waller (p, v); Joe Meresco, Terry Shand, Charlie LaVere (p); Walt Edelstein, Joe Venuti, Lou Kosloff (vn); Nappy Lamare (g, v); Dick McPartland, Perry Botkin, Frank Worrell (g); Artie Bernstein, Eddie Gilbert, Art Miller (b); Stan King, Bob Conselman, Larry Gomar, Herb Quigley (d).* 10/31–9/34.

*** Jack Teagarden 1930–1934

Classics 698 *As above, except add Gene Austin (v).* 10/30–3/34.

*** Jack Teagarden 1934–1939

Classics 729 *Teagarden; Charlie Teagarden, Charlie Spivak, Carl Garvin, Alec Fila, Lee Castaldo (t); Jose Gutierrez, Mark Bennett, Charles McCamish, Red Bone (tb); Benny Goodman (cl); Clint Garvin, Art St John (cl, as); John Van Eps, Hub Lytle (cl, ts); Ernie Caceres (cl, ts, bs); Frankie Trumbauer (Cmel); Terry Shand, John Anderson (p); Casper Reardon (hp); Allan Reuss (g); Art Miller (b); Herb Quigley, Cubby Teagarden (d); Meredith Blake, Linda Keene (v).* 9/34–7/39.

The two Classics discs take their usual chronological survey of Teagarden's work up to the middle of 1939. The tracks by the 1931 band are mostly spirited stuff: a hot 'Tiger Rag', a couple of items in which Fats Waller and Tea swap banter – and some feeble tracks with Gene Austin singing. The 1933 date is another heated one, with a front-rank group of Chicagoans on hand, although Classics 698 ends on a couple of dreary sessions. Classics 729 opens with Casper Reardon's famous harp party-piece, 'Junk Man', before moving to the first sessions by the big band Teagarden formed after leaving Paul Whiteman. He never had much luck as a bandleader, but this wasn't a bad group: decent if second-division swing, always suddenly illuminated when the leader took a solo. The Conifer disc is a mixed bag of 17 tracks, all issued under Teagarden's leadership. Some of the tunes are more vocal than instrumental and reveal the leader's peculiar ability to swing even at indolent tempos. Adequate sound.

**(*) Jack Teagarden 1939–1940

Classics 758 *Teagarden; Charlie Spivak, Carl Garvin, Lee Castle, John Fallstitch, Tom Gonsoulin, Frank Ryerson (t); Jose Gutierrez, Mark Bennett, Charles McCamish, Eddie Dudley, Seymour Goldfinger, Joe Ferrall (tb); Clint Garvin, Art St John (cl, as); John Van Eps, Hub Lytle (cl, ts); Jack Goldie, Tony Antonelli, Joe Ferdinando (as); Larry Walsh (ts); Ernie Caceres (bs); John Anderson, Jack Russin, Nat Jaffe (p); Allan Reuss, Dan Perri (g); Art Miller, Arnold Fishkind, Benny Pottle (b); Cubby Teagarden, Dave Tough, Ed Naquin (d); Kitty Kallen (v).* 3/39–2/40.

*** Jack Teagarden 1940–1941

Classics 839 *Teagarden; John Fallstitch, Tom Gonsoulin, Sid Feller, Pokey Carriere (t); Rex Stewart (c); Jose Gutierrez, Seymour Goldfinger, Joe Ferrall (tb); Art St John, Jack Goldie, Danny Polo, Tony Antonelli, Joe Ferdinando, Larry Walsh, Benny Lagasse, Art Moore, Art Beck (reeds); Barney Bigard (cl); Ben Webster (ts); Billy Kyle, Ernie Hughes, Nat Jaffe (p); Dan Perri, Brick Fleagle (g); Arnold Fishkind, Billy Taylor (b); Ed Naquin, Paul Collins, Dave Tough (d); Lynn Clark, David Allen, Marianne Dunne, Kitty Kallen (v).* 2/40–1/41.

Teagarden was struggling to find success with this band. Most of the records tend towards undemanding, commercial swing, vocalists Kallen and Allen begin to dominate, and even the leader's peerless phrasing was starting to figure less. The first disc is brightened by a mere handful of instrumentals, though there is a fine 'Wolverine Blues' and 'The Blues' is vintage Tea. Classics 839 gets its stars mainly from the session by the Teagarden Big Eight, a small group which featured the trombonist sparring with Rex Stewart on four good (if hardly earthquaking) titles. The rest is pretty dreary, with the likes of 'Fatima's Drummer Boy' plumbing the depths of material. Transfers are clean but not very lively.

***(*) Jack Teagarden 1941–1943

Classics 874 *Similar to above, except add Billy May, Art Gold (t); Jimmie Noone, Heinie Beau (cl); Dave Matthews (ts); Joe Sullivan (p); Dave Barbour (g); Artie Shapiro (b); Zutty Singleton (d); Bing Crosby, Mary Martin (v).* 1/41–11/43.

Three more sessions by the big band, a couple of tracks with Bing Crosby and two small-group dates for Capitol make up this CD. It's a curious jump from 'Prelude in C Sharp Minor' to 'Chicks Is Wonderful', but the three Decca sessions are among the best vehicles for Teagarden, who plays and sings with serene authority on 'Blue River', 'Black and Blue', 'The Blues Have Got Me' and especially 'Nobody Knows The Trouble I've Seen'. The seven titles by The Capitol International Jazzmen bring together an unlikely band – May, Teagarden, Noone (making his farewell on record), Matthews, Sullivan – but it worked out very well, with the various soloists shining in different degrees. One of the best of the Classics Teas.

***(*) Jack Teagarden 1944–1947

Classics 1032 *Teagarden; Bobby Hackett (c); Clair Jones, Bob McLaughlin, Val Salata, Tex Williamson, Max Kaminsky, Ray Norden, Jerry Rosen, Andy Marchese, Jerry Redmond, Nyles Davis, Lee Castle, Carl Garvin, Frank Ryerson (t); Fred Keller, Ray Olsen, Wally Wells, Palmer Combatelli, Jack Lantz, Chuck Smith, Kenny Martin, Mark Bennett, Eddie Dudley, Jose Gutierrez (tb); Art Lyons, Peanuts Hucko (cl); Ernie Caceres, Vic Rosi, Clint Garvin (cl, as); Dale Stoddard, Bob Derry, Dale Jolley, Bert Noah, Merton Smith, Ray Skieraski, Leon Radcliffe, Ray Tucci (as); Howard Gilbertson, Ken Harpster, Nick Caiazza, Johnny McDonald, Cliff Strickland, Hub Lytle, John Van Eps (ts); Clark Crandall, Art St John (bs); Don Seidel, Bill Clifton, Norma Teagarden, Bob Carter, Nick Tagg, Gene Schroeder, Jack Russin (p); Herb Ellis, Charles Gilruth, Eddie Critchlow, Chuck Wayne, Allan Reuss (g); Jimmy Lynch, Felix Giobbe, George 'Pops' Foster, Lloyd Springer, Jim Hearne, Jack Lesberg, Bonnie Pottle (b); Frank Harrington, Cozy Cole, George Wettling, Bobby Fisher, Dave Tough (d); Wingy Manone, Christine Martin (v).* 11/39–10/47.

Starting with a couple of 1939 V-Discs that were missed off an earlier volume, this is a mix of rare and familiar Teagarden. His 1944 session for Commodore includes a duet with Wingy Manone on 'Rockin' Chair'. There are six sides from his own label, Teagarden Presents, two Dixieland titles and four by his latest big band. A V-Disc of 'Body And Soul', with a largely unknown rhythm section, is classic Tea. Four Victor titles by Teagarden's Big Eight, including Kaminsky and Hucko, swagger along, and Tea sounds in good heart. A hotchpotch but an excellent one.

*** Club Hangover Broadcasts

Arbors ARCD 19150/1 2CD *Teagarden; Jackie Coon (t); Jay St John (cl); Norma Teagarden, Lil Hardin Armstrong, Don Ewell (p); Kas Malone (b); Ray Bauduc (d).* 4/54.

Four broadcasts by a Teagarden small group in San Francisco. With the big band and the Armstrong All Stars behind him, Tea sounds settled enough, though there are no vocals from him – a by-product of an old cabaret tax law. The material is all Dixieland chestnuts and the band suffers a little under Ray Bauduc's crashing drums, but there are some nice glimpses of the leader at his best, even if they are only glimpses (and often ones where Tea isn't very well mic'ed). Clean sound, though Coon and Bauduc (and Malone) usually sound louder than everyone else. Ewell and Armstrong are the intermission pianists and get a couple of solos each.

** Jack Teagarden And His All Stars

Jazzology 199 *Teagarden; Dick Oakley (c); Jerry Fuller (cl); Don Ewell (p); Stan Puls (b); Ronnie Greb (d).* 58.

Teagarden drifted through his final years in a way that looks as careless and slipshod as some of Armstrong's later efforts: the numerous renditions of 'St James Infirmary' and 'Rockin' Chair' (both included here) eventually sound as fatigued as his perennially tired voice. The Jazzology release is a well-recorded club date, made in Cleveland in 1958, but it features a dusty band and a leader content to amble along. There is much better Teagarden from the '50s still awaiting reissue. Verve briefly reissued his Willard Robison collection in their Elite Edition, and admirers who missed it should check out the Teagarden bins to see if any copies remain.

***(*) Mis'ry And The Blues

Verve 9860310 *Teagarden; Don Goldie (t); Henry Cuesta (cl); Don Ewell (p); Shay Torrant (org); Stan Puls (b); Barrett Deems (d).* 6/61.

Tea's final great album is a welcome addition to the catalogue. By this time his career had settled into a routine of one-nighters which he seemed to care little for, and his working and recording bands were scarcely becoming for him. Yet this date worked out exceptionally well. Goldie has often been criticized, and he can't help showing off on the likes of 'Basin Street Blues', but it would have been no good having a trumpet in the front line sounding as tired as the leader, and he does bring a James-like energy to proceedings. Ewell is very good, Cuesta does nothing to disgrace himself, and even Deems is on good behaviour. Creed Taylor secured an excellent studio sound which is attractively brought out in the remastering. Best of all, the material is unhackneyed enough to persuade Tea into giving it his best shots: 'Froggie Moore' and 'Dixieland One-Step' were already ancient history, but a lot more interesting than 'The Saints' and 'I Don't Want To Miss Mississippi', and the title-track especially inveigles some fine singing from him.

Clare Teal

VOCAL

Teal grew up listening to show tunes and sang on jingles and commercials before embarking on a jazz singing career. She has quickly become a popular figure among the numerous performers working the standards idiom in the UK.

**(*) That's The Way It Is

Candid CCD 79767 *Teal; Trevor Whiting (ss, as, ts, cl); Martin Litton (p); Nils Solberg (g); Richard Jefferies, John Day (b); Rod Brown (d).* 1–3/01.

*** Orsino's Songs

Candid CCD 79783 *As above, except add Malcolm Earl Smith (tb), Alan Barnes (as, cl); Ian Shaw, Nick Hannan, Dan Chambers, Ella Trace (v); omit Jefferies.* 3/02.

*** The Road Less Travelled

Candid CCD 79794 *Teal; Mark Crooks (cl, bcl, as, ts); Simon Wallace (p, org); Martin Litton (p); Nils Solberg (g); Melvin Duffy (pdl steel); John Day (b); Rod Brown (d); Jamie Cullum (v).* 5/03.

Teal takes a confident course through these three sessions, which progress from a kind of novelty jazz feel to the more secure synthesis of country-singer-songwriter of *The Road Less Travelled.* She sounds more like a show singer than any kind of jazz diva, though in an age when there are busloads of chanteuses trying to be Billie, maybe that's no bad thing. She has a very big, white tone that puts a huge spotlight on the likes of 'Night And Day' (*That's The Way It Is*) and the originals on the debut are a sometimes uncomfortable mix of cute and sickly. But the opening of *Orsino's Songs*, a smoochy stroll through 'California Dreamin'', opted for a smart approach to repertory, and the originals have got better – and at least she's writing some of her own stuff and not merely plundering the songbooks. *The Road Less Travelled* sounds more upfront, less home-made, and the band are edging towards a kind of pop-country feel – although the likes of 'So Blue' make her sound more like k d lang than anybody from the jazz idiom.

Joe Temperley (born 1929)

BARITONE AND SOPRANO SAXOPHONES, BASS CLARINET

Born in Fife, he played in dance-band sax sections in the '50s before spending seven years with Humphrey Lyttelton from 1958. In 1965 he moved to New York and became familiar in American big bands as well as doing much session-work. He has enjoyed an Indian summer with his stay in the Lincoln Center Jazz Orchestra in the '90s and beyond.

***** Nightingale**
Hep CD 2052 *Temperley; Brian Lemon (p); Dave Green (b); Martin Drew (d).* 4/91.

***** Concerto For Joe**
Hep CD 2062 *As above, except add Steve Sidwell, Eddie Severn, Gerard Presencer (t); Gordon Campbell, Nichol Thomson (tb); Peter King (as); Duncan Lamont (ts); Brian Kellock (p); Alec Dankworth (b); Jack Parnell (d).* 9/93–7/94.

Temperley has seldom figured in record dates in the UK since his move to America and there has been very little under his own leadership, but *Nightingale* was an opportune session. A seamless, singing manner belies the difficulties of the instrument and, though his sometimes bubbly timbre at fast tempos may not be to all tastes, there's a genuineness about his improvisations. There's a beautiful Ellington rarity in 'Sunset And A Mocking Bird', in which Temperley's sound never makes one think of Harry Carney. He ends on an *a cappella* 'My Love Is Like A Red, Red Rose' that sums up the sound he can get from the horn. The weakness lies in the rhythm section: nothing very wrong, but the sheer ordinariness of the playing is unfortunate. *Concerto For Joe* is an agreeable continuation. Jimmy Deuchar's composition for Temperley is the centrepiece of the record, performed by the saxophonist with the big group, and it's a substantial if not quite deathless performance. Elsewhere there are more quartet tracks with the previous group. Temperley sounds well enough but, in the end, as with the previous disc, a certain flavour of routine militates against its acquiring essential status.

***** Double Duke**
Naxos 86032-2 *Temperley; Wycliffe Gordon (tb); Eric Reed (p); Rodney Whitaker (b); Herlin Riley (d).* 10/98.

Naxos have snared an impressive line-up for this one, an Ellington homage with Temperley supported by several of the Marsalis teamsters. It's a good blow, but frankly the leader is outdone by his fellow players, and Gordon's ripe range of styles with both open horn and plunger mute borders on the cartoonish at times (notably in an outrageous handling of 'Black And Tan Fantasy' and the closing 'Danny Boy'). 'Creole Love Call' is played so slowly that it's below a crawl.

***** Easy To Remember**
Hep CD 2083 *Temperley; Toby Coe (ss); Frank Griffith (cl); John Pearce (p); Andy Cleyndert (b); Steve Brown (d); strings.* 4/01.

A sweetly melodious jog around a string of familiar standards – perhaps too familiar, with 'Just Friends', 'That Old Feeling' and 'East Of The Sun' the kind of things which listeners will know as well as the players at this point. Frank Griffith's charts do well enough by the soloists (Coe as much as Temperley) but, as with the first record listed, it's at the very end that Temperley has his finest moment: a poignant 'Hielan' Laddie' in memory of his brother.

Tenor Triangle

GROUP

Saxophone triumvirate or troika from the Criss Cross stable.

***** Tell It Like It Is**
Criss Cross 1089 *Eric Alexander, Ralph Lalama, Tad Shull (ts); Melvin Rhyne (org); Peter Bernstein (g); Kenny Washington (d).* 3/93.

***** Aztec Blues**
Criss Cross 1143 *As above.* 2/94.

So much of Melvin Rhyne's issued work seems to come from impromptu jams or in studio overtime that it's no surprise to hear him backing this in-house project, which feels very much like the old tenor battles of a past age. In practice, Alexander, Lalama and Shull are all too intelligent, and possibly just a little too alike, to indulge in cutting contests. Their separate statements on the shibboleth 'Body And Soul' (*Tell It Like It Is*) are equally philosophical and with a similar world-weariness. It works better when they're not all vying for attention, and the ballad medley on the same album is delightful for that reason.

The second disc is pretty much more of the same. If you like loads of saxophones in formation, it's great. If you'd rather focus on one or other of these individualists, the Criss Cross catalogue beckons.

Ten Part Invention

GROUP

Nearly-big band operating out of Sydney and employing many of the leading musicians on the Australian scene.

*****(*) Unidentified Spaces**
Rufus RF 056 *Miroslav Bukovsky (t, flhn); Warwick Alder (t); James Greening (tb, btb); Berbie McGann, Sandy Evans, Bob Bertles, Ken James (reeds); Paul McNamara (p); Steve Elphick (b); John Pochée (d).* 5/00.

This bristling biggish band is an impressive showcase for some of the major players on the Sydney scene. Led by Pochée, they include veterans such as McGann and Bertles alongside Evans and Greening. The music's sometimes in the manner of groups such as the Hieroglyphics Ensemble, but there are plenty of sections which sit comfortably in a shouting big-band tradition to go with the more exotic touches. Bertles, McGann and Evans are among the more familiar soloists, and the writing, shared between several hands, is consistently strong, with Evans's title music the centrepiece. If you want to know about Australian jazz today, this would be a very fair place to start.

Paul Termos (1952–2003)

ALTO SAXOPHONE

Dutch virtuoso who worked mainly in a new music idiom but also recorded some powerful post-bop jazz.

***** Paul Termos Sessions: Volume 1**
X-Or 015 *Termos; Misha Mengelberg (p).* 02.

★★(★) Paul Termos Sessions: Volume 2
X-Or 016 *Termos; Wiek Hijmans (g).* 02.

It might seem opportunistic that this remarkable player's first appearance in these pages should have followed his early death, but until these records were released in the final weeks of his life, there was little in print that merited inclusion in a jazz guide. The early *Death Dance Of Principles* (released on Geest-Gronden, who also collaborated on these releases) is effectively a classical project, as are the pieces on *Works.*

Sessions belatedly unveil Termos the improviser. With Mengelberg he is witty and teasing, steering the music in the direction of Tristano-ish jazz and then away again into the outer reaches. His innate rhythmic sense and ability to manipulate tones almost infinitely give the music a fluid and densely textured quality, either the legacy or the source of his fine writing for ensemble and orchestra. With Hijmans, especially on the epic opening 'Longplay', he takes a more aggressive and forceful stance, in which the guitarist's amplified sound overpowers any hint of subtlety. Some of the shorter pieces are quite incendiary and unfocused and one misses the brightly intelligent empathy he instantly strikes up with the pianist on Volume 1.

Jacky Terrasson (born 1966)

PIANO

Born in Berlin, of French and American parents, Terrasson grew up in Paris and attended the Lycée Lamartine. He moved to New York in 1990 and won the Thelonious Monk Competition in 1993, thereafter signing to Blue Note.

★★★ Jacky Terrasson
Blue Note 829351-2 *Terrasson; Ugonna Okegwo (b); Leon Parker (d).* 7–8/94.

★★★ Reach
Blue Note 835739-2 *As above.* 95.

Terrasson gathered much acclaim from an early stage, and these debut records as a leader are notably single-minded efforts. He never approaches a tune from any predictable point: on the first disc, there are versions of 'I Love Paris', 'My Funny Valentine' and 'Bye Bye Blackbird' which are so revisionist as to be almost unrecognizable at times. Yet he sticks to otherwise familiar paths of harmony and rhythmic patterns which call to mind influences ranging from Ahmad Jamal to Bill Evans. The problem with both discs is a slightly exasperating ingenuity which seems less at the service of the music and more about creating a sensation. Terrasson's writing has a greater showing on the second set, *Reach,* though it often sounds to be more about motifs and vamps than full-scale structures. Okegwo and Parker perform well, but theirs is a largely subsidiary role, rather than one where a true trio music is called for.

★★(★) Rendezvous
Blue Note 855484-2 *Terrasson; Lonnie Plaxico, Kenny Davis (b); Mino Cinelu (perc); Cassandra Wilson (v).* 1–4/97.

Anyone expecting something of the order of, say, *The Intimate Ella* from this collaboration is likely to be sorely disappointed. Perhaps it's inevitable, with two such self-regarding artists as Terrasson and Wilson, that their shared record is simultaneously inflated and introverted, to the virtual exclusion of an audience. There are quite preposterous versions of 'It Might As Well Be Spring' and 'If Ever I Would Leave You' which take melodic and rhythmic displacement to extraordinary lengths and, while they get away with 'Old Devil Moon' and 'Tennessee Waltz', the rest of the record is pretty much a trudge, including Terrasson's own features. Wilson's following may find this a lot more entertaining than we do, possibly, but this isn't a record to convert anybody.

★★★ Alive
Blue Note 859651-2 *Terrasson; Ugonna Okegwo (b); Leon Parker (d).* 6/97.

Caught live at New York's Iridium Club, the Terrasson trio deliver a typically larger-than-life set. The music has much presence and numerous surprising moments, but again we are unconvinced by Terrasson's musical decisions. His attractive original 'Cumba's Dance' is gradually speeded up to a nonsensical tempo. Tony Williams's 'Sister Cheryl' goes from quiet reflection to great intensity, but with no real logic, and 'Nature Boy' is made merely eccentric. At its best, as on the opening 'Things Ain't What They Used To Be', the trio offer a persuasive revision of their materials. But for a lot of the time Terrasson appears to be such a crowd-pleaser, conscious or otherwise, that the uncommitted will be bewildered by his music.

★★(★) Smile
Blue Note 42413 *Terrasson; Sean Smith, Remi Vignolo (b); Eric Harland (d).* 6/02.

A pretty discouraging continuation. Terrasson continues to take on standards with the grace and discretion of a bulldozer, and even though he moves a lot faster, the final result is still something ground into submission. 'Nardis' is at least sweetly done, even if he manages to suggest a solipsism which Bill Evans would have frowned at. There are lighter moments elsewhere which suggest that Jacky's real commercial future might be with smooth jazz.

Clark Terry (born 1920)

TRUMPET, FLUGELHORN

Also known as 'Mumbles' after his famously indistinct scat style, Terry was born in St Louis and managed to hold down a seat in both the Basie and Ellington bands, before disappearing into the studios and broadcasting, like many of his generation. He reappeared in the '70s and added flugelhorn to his armoury as he became an ever more expressive soloist, widely featured at festivals and capable of sustaining interest entirely on his own.

★★★ Serenade To A Bus Seat
Original Jazz Classics OJC 066 *Terry; Johnny Griffin (ts); Wynton Kelly (p); Paul Chambers (b); Philly Joe Jones (d).* 4/57.

Though not reducible to his 'influences', Terry hybridizes Dizzy Gillespie's hot, fluent lines and witty abandon with Rex Stewart's distinctive half-valving and Charlie Shavers's high-register lyricism; he is also a master of the mute, an aspect of his work that had a discernible impact on Miles Davis. Miles, though, remained unconvinced by Terry's pioneering development of the flugelhorn as a solo instrument; later in his career he traded four-bar phrases with himself, holding a horn in each hand. An irrepressible showman with a sly sense of humour, Terry often fared better when performing under other leaders. His encounter with the Oscar Peterson Trio in 1964 is often judged his best work, and it's hard to see where and when he played better. The 'early' – he was 37 – *Serenade To A Bus Seat* combines a tribute to civil-rights activist Rosa Parks with pungent versions of 'Stardust' and Parker's 'Donna Lee'. Terry isn't an altogether convincing bopper, but he's working with a fine, funky band, and they carry him through some slightly unresolved moments.

****** Daylight Express**

Chess GRP 18192 *Terry; Paul Gonsalves (ts); Mike Simpson (sax, f); Willie Jones (p); Remo Biondi (g); Jimmy Woode (b); Sam Woodyard (d).* 7–8/57.

Slotted into the middle of his contract with Riverside (which yielded most of the OJCs), these insecurely dated sessions from the summer of 1957 yielded two LPs for Argo: *Out On A Limb* and (under Gonsalves's name) *Cookin'*. The ten tracks with the saxophonist, which include the previously unissued 'The Girl That I Call Baby', are far and away the most interesting things on the record. Clark sounds rather restrained in his presence, concentrating on a quietly lateral lyricism, whereas on the early session, which was produced, you'll be glad to know, by Daddy-O Daylie, he goes for broke every time, demonstrating an iron lip on 'Trumpet Mouthpiece Blues' and positively ripping up tunes like 'Daylight Express' and 'Taking A Chance On Love'. The songs are all very short, with the exception of the 'Mouthpiece' feature, and the impact is not dissimilar to having an express train shoot past in front of you. Interesting to compare with the more measured approach on the Gonsalves session. A very welcome reissue, which comes as part of GRP's bid to restore all the Leonard Chess 'Legendary Masters'.

***** Duke With A Difference**

Original Jazz Classics OJC 229 *Terry; Quentin Jackson, Britt Woodman (tb); Tyree Glenn (tb, vib); Johnny Hodges (as); Paul Gonsalves (ts); Jimmy Jones, Billy Strayhorn (p); Luther Henderson (cel); Jimmy Woode (b); Sam Woodyard (d); Marion Bruce (v).* 7 & 9/57.

In 1957 Terry was most of the way through his eight-year stint with Ellington (he'd already worked with Charlie Barnet and Count Basie and was bound for a staff job with NBC, the first black man to get his feet under that rather clubby table) and a successful partnership with trombonist Bob Brookmeyer. It's the slide-brass men he cleaves to on this mildly impertinent tribute to his boss. He undercuts both Jackson and Hodges on a beautifully arranged 'In A Sentimental Mood' (which features Strayhorn on piano and Luther Henderson on celeste) and cheerfully wrecks 'Take The "A" Train' in spite of Gonsalves's best efforts to keep it hurtling along the rails. Marion Bruce's vocals are nothing to write home about, but the band is as good as the form book says it ought to be.

****** In Orbit**

Original Jazz Classics OJC 302 *Terry; Thelonious Monk (p); Sam Jones (b); Philly Joe Jones (d).* 5/58.

Terry's solitary excursion on Monk's *Brilliant Corners*, a vivid 'Bemsha Swing', underlined the degree to which Monk himself still drew sustenance from swing. *In Orbit* is firmly Terry's album. If the material is less stretching, the arrangements are surprisingly demanding, and the interplay between flugelhorn (used throughout) and piano on 'One Foot In The Gutter' and the contrasting 'Moonlight Fiesta' is highly inventive.

***** Top And Bottom Brass**

Original Jazz Classics OJC 764 *Terry; Don Butterfield (tba); Jimmy Jones, Sam Jones (b); Art Taylor (d).* 2/59.

The title is self-explanatory, the results patchy. Terry's own ability to dive down into lower registers means that this bold attempt at chiaroscuro is both likely to work and also unnecessary, indeed it might almost seem as if it neutralizes one of the trumpeter's great assets. The material is kept pretty simple and straightforward: 'Mardi Gras Waltz' is delightful and some of the interchanges on 'Top'N'Bottom' are well worth hearing again. A sidebar rather than a classic Terry album.

***** Clark Terry And His Orchestra Featuring Paul Gonsalves**

Storyville 8322 *Terry; Paul Gonsalves (ts); Raymond Fol (p); Jimmy Woode (b); Sam Woodyard (d).* 59.

Clark was in the final stages of his association with Duke Ellington when this small group session was made in Europe. The competent Raymond Fol was in Duke's chair and does a very decent job. The set kicks off with the life-on-the-road epic 'Serenade To A Bus Seat', includes a couple of takes of Monk's 'Pannonica' and some jammed material. Gonsalves is an ideal playing partner: his rich harmonic awareness coaxes ever more adventurous ideas out of Terry and their duels on 'Clark Bars' and the second, previously unreleased take of the Monk tune are enormously impressive.

****** Color Changes**

Candid CCD 79009 *Terry; Jimmy Knepper (tb); Julius Watkins (frhn); Yusef Lateef (ts, f, eng hn, ob); Seldon Powell (ts, f); Tommy Flanagan, Budd Johnson (p); Joe Benjamin (b); Ed Shaughnessy (d).* 11/60.

Terry's best record, and ample evidence that swing was still viable on the cusp of the decade that was to see its demise as anything but an exercise in nostalgia. What is immediately striking is the extraordinary, almost kaleidoscopic variation of tone-colour through the seven tracks. Given Lateef's inventive multi-instrumentalism, Powell's doubling on flute and Terry's use of flugelhorn and his mutes, the permutations on horn voicings seem almost infinite. 'Brother Terry' opens with a deep growl from Terry, a weaving oboe theme by composer Lateef and some beautiful harmony work from Watkins (who a matter of days later was to make such a contribution to Benny Bailey's superb Candid session, *Big Brass*) who interacts imaginatively with Knepper on Terry's 'Flutin' And Fluglin''. Again arranged by Lateef, this is a straightforward exploration of the relation between their two horns; Terry has written several 'odes' to his second instrument, and this is perhaps the most inventive. 'Nahstye Blues', written by and featuring Johnson, in for the unsuitably limpid Flanagan, comes close to Horace Silver's funk. Terry is slightly disappointing, but Lateef turns in a majestic solo that turns his own cor anglais introduction completely on its head. The closing 'Chat Qui Pêche' is an all-in, solo-apiece affair that would have sounded wonderful in the Parisian *boîte* it celebrates and brings a marvellous, expertly recorded record to a powerful finish. Needless to say, it comes highly recommended.

*****(*) Mellow Moods**

Prestige PCD 24136 *Terry; Lester Robertson (tb); Budd Johnson (ts); George Barrow (bs); Junior Mance (p); Eddie Costa (p, vib); Joe Benjamin, Art Davis (b); Charli Persip, Ed Shaughnessy (d).* 7/61, 5/62.

Following on from the last item, this confirms that a purple patch was in progress. A calmer, less frantic record all round, it showed off Terry's abilities as a balladeer as well as a fast action man. Mance is a good accompanist on the earlier session, a quartet with just Terry and rhythm. Inevitably there is slightly less of him on the other date, but this almost-big band generates an impressive body of noise when it gets going, and the settings laid out for him on 'If I Were You' and 'It's Fun To Think' are completely irresistible.

*** Spanish Rice

Impulse! 143602 *Terry; Joe Newman, Ernie Royal, Snooky Young (t, flhn); Everett Barksdale, Barry Galbraith (g); George Duvivier (b); Grady Tate (d); Julio Cruz, Frank Malabe, Chano Pozo, Bobby Rosengarden (perc); Chico O'Farrill (cond).* 7/66.

Co-led with the late Chico O'Farrill and inevitably slanting towards Latin tunes – 'The Peanut Vendor', 'Macarena', 'Mexican Hat Dance' – this is a jolly set, enlivened by Clark's full-voiced trumpet and flugelhorn. He does some fine blues playing on 'Joonji', which is probably the strongest track, but there's also some rich arranging and playing on Dizzy's 'Tin Tin Deo'. The tracks are all very short and no one has much chance to rev up and really get going. Clark and Chico do the title-tune as a comic routine. Reissued in 2004, but something of a period piece and only really for stone fans of the principals.

*** Live At The Wichita Jazz Festival

Vanguard 79335 *Terry; Greg Bobulinski, Dave Carley, Paul Cohen, Oscar Gamby, Jimmy Nottingham (t); Chuck Connors, Sonny Costanzo, Janice Robinson, Jimmy Wilkins (tb); Jack Jeffers (tb, btb, tba); Frank Wess, Chris Woods (as); Jimmy Heath, Ron Odrich, Ernie Wilkins (ts); Charles Davis (bs); Arnie Lawrence, Phil Woods (reeds); Duke Jordan, Ronnie Matthews (p); Wilbur Little, Victor Sproles (b); Ed Soph (d, perc).* 74.

*** Live! At Buddy's Place

Universe 60 *Similar to above.* 74.

A surprisingly modern programme from the revitalized Terry. On the first he includes Kenny Dorham's 'Una Mas' and, even more unexpectedly, Wayne Shorter's complex 'Nefertiti', alongside the easy swing of 'Take The "A" Train' and the delightful 'Mumbles'. The arrangements are by Ernie Wilkins, Phil Woods, Jimmy Heath and Allan Foust, and the latter also contributes the long curtain-piece, 'Cold 'Tater Stomp'. The section aren't always entirely together and there is some definite slackness in the horns but, like many a festival gig, it relies more on atmosphere than on formal accuracy. This was the outfit he called the Big B-a-d Band. It was both of those things.

*** Live At Montmartre, 1975

Storyville STCD 8358 *Terry; Ernie Wilkins (ts); Horace Parlan (p); Mads Vinding (b); Bjarne Rostvold (d); Richard Boone (v).* 6/75.

Wilkins didn't have quite the cachet in this room that Dexter Gordon built up over the years, but in company with Clark he was still quite a draw. It's Boone who does the best of the vocal work on this, though the best of the playing comes on the three long tracks, 'Bye Bye Blackbird', 'Satin Doll' and 'Misty', all of which are exquisite. Clark is playing with great enthusiasm and Parlan opens up possibilities for him that a more literal piano player would not spot. Vinding is a master at this kind of gig and even if Alex Riel wasn't on hand, Rostvold is a worthy replacement. Clark's best solo is on the opening track, which seems a pity, but he's in fine form.

*** Funk Dumplin's

Music Mecca 2055 *Terry; Kenny Drew (p); Red Mitchell (b); Ed Thigpen (d).* 8/78.

Recorded in Denmark with three distinguished expats, the highlight of this is a vocal with Mitchell on 'Snavset Blues', which proves the bassist to be every bit as much of a ham as the leader. The material is fresh and unhackneyed and the sound is quite decent for the time. The LP was on the Danish Matrix imprint and is now presumably quite scarce, so this is a very welcome reappearance.

***(*) Intimate Stories

Challenge 70050 *Terry; Horace Parlan (p); Red Mitchell (b).* 7/78.

By contrast, this is a straightforward instrumental set, with some astonishingly good playing from all three members of this drummerless group. Parlan can blow hot and cold, but is superb on 'What Will I Tell My Heart?', 'Blue Moon' and 'Days Of Wine And Roses'. Mitchell resists the temptation to sing, as does Clark except for a bit on 'The Perils Of Pauline' and collectors will enjoy every note of it.

*** Swiss Radio Days Jazz Series: Volume 8 – Lucerne 1978

TCB 2082 *Terry; Chris Woods (as, f, v); Horace Parlan (p); Victor Sproles (b); Bobby Durham (d).* 12/78.

This is a familiar series that maintains a pretty high quality. The band is interesting, with Woods's boppish alto and flute blending well with Terry's warm brass tone and some inspired playing from Parlan, who was going through a purple patch around this time. The tracks are mostly quite short, presumably for scheduling reasons, but the best of them contain some strong soloing from Clark. He couldn't resist singing and there is a strong version of 'I Want A Little Girl' as well as some daft back-and-forth stuff with Woods on 'Lemon Drop'. The sound is less than pristine, and we wonder if the source tapes were second generation.

CORE COLLECTION

**** Memories Of Duke

Original Jazz Classics OJC 604 *Terry; Joe Pass (g); Jack Wilson (p); Ray Brown (b); Frank Severino (d).* 3/80.

Obvious, really, but exquisitely done. The interplay between Pass and Brown touches unsuspected areas of 'Cotton Tail' and 'Sophisticated Lady' (compare the version with Red Mitchell, below) and, though Severino might have been dispensed with for at least a couple of the softer tracks, the overall sound is excellent.

*** Yes, The Blues

Original Jazz Classics OJC 856 *Terry; Eddie 'Cleanhead' Vinson (as); Harmonica George Smith (hca); Art Hillery (b); J. C. Heard, Roy McCurdy (d).* 1/81.

Somewhat dominated by Vinson's raw blues line (especially on the closing 'Kidney Stew', the saxophonist's signature-tune), this isn't the best place to catch up with Terry, but it is a hugely entertaining album which sounds as if it might have originated in a spontaneous jam and certainly benefits from a live ambience. Vinson may require reassessment in the years ahead, for here he has certainly negotiated an intriguing path between country blues and orthodox swing, a route mastered by very few others.

★★(★) Squeeze Me

Chiaroscuro CRD 309 *Terry; Virgil Jones (t); Al Grey, Britt Woodman (tb); Haywood Henry, Red Holloway, Phil Woods (reeds); John Campbell (p); Marcus McLaurine (b); Butch Ballard (d).* n.d.

Good arrangements, but a rather knotted sound that strips some fine horn-players of any real individuality. The rhythm section sounds under-rehearsed and the tempo is always either lagging behind or rushing to catch up. Disappointing.

★★★ The Clark Terry Spacemen

Chiaroscuro 309 *Terry; Virgil Jones (t); Al Grey, Britt Woodman (tb); Phil Woods (as); Red Holloway (ts); Haywood Henry (bs); John Campbell (p); Marcus McLaurine (b); Butch Ballard (d).* 2/89.

Often with Chiaroscuro, the closing 'Jazzspeak' interview is almost the most interesting aspect of the set. Here, the music matches up to the anecdote pretty well, which by this stage in Terry's career is pretty impressive. Nearly all the horn guys get some respectable solo space, including the late Henry, but it's Clark who commands most of the foreground. He's in sparkling form on 'For Dancers Only'. Worth tracking down.

★★★(★) Live At The Village Gate

Chesky JD 49 *Terry; Jimmy Heath (ts, ss); Paquito D'Rivera (as); Don Friedman (p); Marcus McLaurine (b); Kenny Washington (d).* 11/90.

Recorded three weeks short of Terry's 70th birthday, this is a good-natured set of uncomplicated jazz. Terry alternates his trumpet ('my driver') and flugelhorn ('putter'), favouring a soft, blurred-edge tone that in no way compromises the clarity of his bop-influenced lines. Jimmy Heath is dry without being sterile and takes a lovely solo on 'Pint Of Bitter', a dedication to the late Tubby Hayes. D'Rivera shows up for only a single track, the appealing 'Silly Samba'. The recording is impeccably handled, with a light sound that still captures the live ambience; on 'Keep, Keep, Keep On Keepin' On', Terry has the entire audience singing along, and so he can't resist throwing them 'Hey Mr Mumbles' at the end. 'If Sylvester Stallone can make *Rocky* 3, 4, 5, I don't see why I can't make Mumbles 8, 9 and 10.'

★★★(★) The Hymn

Candid 799770 *Terry; Jesse Davis (as); Don Friedman (p); Marcus McLaurine (b); Sylvia Cuenca (d).* 93.

A pretty archetypal set from Clark, recorded at Birdland. He kicks off with the fast swing of the title-tune, throws in 'Ow!', some trumpet and flugelhorn juggling on 'On The Trail' and even finds time to do some serious harm to the vocal of 'On The Sunny Side Of The Street'. Young Davis plays well in his boppish manner and the rhythm section, all of whom were to get to know Terry pretty well, do their jobs with aplomb. A fine record of a great entertainer still in his prime.

★★★ Shades Of Blues

Challenge 70007 *Terry; Al Grey (tb); Charles Fox (p); Marcus McLaurine (b).* 5/94.

Apart from the closing trilogy ('Parker's Mood', McShann's 'Hottie's Blues' and Handy's 'St Louis Blues') and a mostly polite early inclusion of Al Grey's 'Salty Mama', all of the themes are original blues, simple and unpretentious but played with maximum variation. Clark's vocal on 'Whispering The Blues' is very much in the 'Mumbles' tradition, light, buoyant and deceptively clever. The interplay with Grey is more challenging than might at first appear, with every conceivable variation on conventional blues changes.

★★★ Reunion

D'Note Classics 2001 *Terry; Brian Gould (tb, v); Howard Dudune (as, ts, cl); PeeWee Claybrook (ts); Dean Reilly (b); Harold Jones (d).* 95.

And you didn't know that they'd ever been apart. Clark and tenorman Claybrook go back many years, and this friendly, uncomplicated session is pitched square in the middle of common musical ground. Duke and Strayhorn's 'Isfahan' has an unfamiliar cast but works well, and there is a lively version of 'Jitterbug Waltz'.

★★★ Top And Bottom Brass

Chiaroscuro 347 *Terry; Don Butterfield (tba); David Glasser (as); Red Holloway (ts); Jimmy Jones, Willie Pickens (p); Sam Jones, Marcus McLaurine (b); Sylvia Cuenca, Art Taylor (d).* 11/95.

Red Holloway can't spent much time ashore these days, having tapped into the jazz cruise sector. In a curious way, though, the key element here is the 'bottom brass' of tubist Don Butterfield. Clark's chocolatey flugelhorn is the main voice, and his quarter-hour ballad medley will be a constant source of delight. Recorded on the SS *Norway*, the music seems brisk and oxygenated – or ozoned – and Terry is in cracking form.

★★★ Express

Reference 73 *Terry; Bob Lark (t); Jason Aspinwall, Amir El-Saffar, Eric Nelson, Vance Thompson, Gil Wukitsch (t, flhn); Steve Bradley (tb); Dave Hutten (as, f); Mark Colby (ts); Rob Denty (ts, cl); Jeff Erikson (bs, cl); Michael Stryker (p); Sharay Reed (b); Tom Hipskind, James Ward (d).* 12/95.

Amiable big-band swing with a few modern touches from Terry and the well-drilled DePaul University Big Band under the direction of Bob Lark. The programme is dominated by Ellington and Strayhorn tunes, of which 'Star-Crossed Lovers' and the closing 'Something To Live For' are by far the most vivid. Clark's warm tone isn't always matched by the band, which can sound a touch mechanical when the tempo drops; but the faster tunes are pitch-perfect and the disc is enjoyable from start to finish.

★★★ Jazz Matinee

Hanssler Classics 93036 *Terry; Karl Farrent, Claus Reichstaller, Thomas Vogel (t, flhn); Marc Godfroid (t); Peter Weniger (ss, ts) Bernd Rabe (as); Klaus Wagenleiter (p); Decebel Badila (b); Jorg Gebhardt (d).* 98.

Recorded in Stuttgart with members of the SWR Big Band, this finds Clark in relaxed and mellow form but still able to turn in a storming solo on the likes of 'Big Bad Blues' and 'The Zinger'. The Germans are exceedingly good and competent players and they take some very worthwhile solo spots. By and large, though, the emphasis is on the American guest star and no way were they going to let him off stage without a version of 'Mumbles'; Clark obliges right at the end, in Ernie Wilkins's arrangement.

*** The Good Things In Life

Mons 874437 *Terry; George Robert (as); Dado Moroni (p); Isla Eckinger (b); Peter Schmidlin (d).* 2/96.

Recorded live in Switzerland, and a great deal of fun. The band play straight man for the most part. Robert is a fine saxophonist in a boppish vein, which might explain why fellow-altoist Phil Woods's 'Somebody Done Stole My Blues' is the first number. Clark's tone is rich and fruity throughout and he gets to do his 'Mumbles' routine as part of the encore 'Steppin' On The Roaches'. Some good playing in between, though; just listen carefully to Isla Eckinger, who's one of the underrated bass-players in Europe.

*** Ritter Der Ronneburg, 1998

Mons 874335 *Terry; Paul Kuhn Orchestra.* 9/98.

Another live set, this time from a castle in Germany with a band of talented locals. Terry is the main star, and plays some extended solos on 'Robbins' Nest', 'Perdido' and 'There Is No Greater Love', but he's joined by some challenging players, particularly tenorist Gustl Mayer who brings something of his own to 'Body And Soul'. 'Take The "A" Train' and Basie's 'The King' bookend the set, which is nicely recorded.

***(*) One On One

Chesky 198 *Terry; Monty Alexander, Geri Allen, Kenny Barron, Tommy Flanagan, Don Friedman, Eric Lewis, Marian McPartland, Junior Mance (p).* 99.

Something of the range and sophistication of this lovely album of trumpet and piano duets can be gauged from the roster of accompanists. A word of advice. Buy it, stick it in the machine and sit back without the notes. Second time around, you can start to work out who's at the piano. Given that at least two of Clark's partners are – seemingly deliberately – playing out of character, it won't be as easy as you might think. And that's all the help you're getting.

*** Uh Oh!

Nagel-Heyer 2003 *Terry; Roy Hargrove (t); Benny Powell (tb); Dave Glasser (as); Frank Wess (ts, f); Barry Harris (p); Peter Washington (b); Curtis Boyd (d).* 6/99.

This isn't strictly a Terry record, but regular Dave Glasser's first solo album billed as the Glasser/Terry/Harris project. The other horns only come as guests on some tracks, and the line-up varies from quartet to septet on wonderful arrangements of Strayhorn's 'Intimacy Of The Blues' and Duke's 'Blue Rose', which give Glasser a chance to do his Johnny Hodges thing. Clark's own act – and particularly the trumpet/flugelhorn chase – sounds oddly tired on someone else's record, but he contributes the title-tracks to the set and maybe claims full authorship that way. Great to hear Barry Harris in such good form and to be reminded what a great drummer the veteran Curtis Boyd has always been. Benny Powell and Frank Wess bring their own authority.

*** Live On QE2

Chiaroscuro 365 *Terry; David Glasser (as); Don Friedman (p); Shirley Horn (p, v); Marcus McLaurine (b); Sylvia Cuenca(d); Etta Jones, Vanessa Rubin, Carrie Smith (v).* 5/00.

*** Herr Ober

Nagel-Heyer 68 *As above, except omit Horn, Jones, Rubin, Smith.* 99.

The cruise-ship circuit has become a happy hunting-ground for musicians of Clark's generation and this sounds like a very relaxed and easy set on the big liner. The guest singers will be the main draw for many purchasers and Shirley Horn's spot on 'But Beautiful' is a definite high point. Etta Jones makes a lovely job of 'East Of The Sun, West Of The Moon' and 'Etta's Fine And Mellow Blues'. Clark himself eases solos out of his flugelhorn as if he were drawing taffy. Parker's 'The Hymn' is an unexpected inclusion and very effective it is too.

Herr Ober catches the old fellow back in Germany with an appearance at the Birdland Neuburg. The group is very strong and responsive to the leader. Clark scats like a youngster on two takes of the title-track, but the main attractions are versions of 'Jumpin' At The Woodside' and 'Taking A Chance On Love'. Well up to scratch.

***(*) Friendship

Eighty Eights/Columbia 51086 2 *Terry; Don Friedman (p); Marcus McLaurine (b); Max Roach (d).* 3/02.

A meeting between two old masters. Terry and Roach duet on several tracks, including the startling opening 'Statements' which sounds like an angelic summons. There are also a number of group tracks, on which Friedman is featured fairly prominently, possibly to cover for Clark's shaky articulation; he doesn't quite pull off the opening theme of 'Let's Cool One' and some of his notes aren't absolutely hit on the head. 'Brushes And Brass' is another duo track, which touches on 'Salt Peanuts', 'Singing In The Rain' and even hints at Miles's 'Jean-Pierre'. 'Simple Waltz' is delightful and could only be by those two great men, with Roach splintering melodies from his cymbals, Clark finding a rich, warm sound for a simple but lovely line. And so it goes, down to 'The Nearness Of You', which rounds out the set. Producer Yasohachi '88' Ito gets a nice, intimate sound for the duos, though the piano seems up very high on the group tracks. A word again for bassist McLaurine, very much the hired hand on this, but a fine evocative player.

TEST

GROUP

New York improvisers playing hardcore free jazz.

***(*) TEST

AUM Fidelity AUM012 *Daniel Carter (as, ts, f, t); Sabir Mateen (cl, as, ts, f); Matthew Heyner (b); Tom Bruno (d).* 8/98.

***(*) Live / TEST

Eremite MTE021 *As above.* 11/98.

This quartet seem ready to spearhead a back-to-the-roots exercise in New York free jazz, playing long and loud (though not unlyrical) sets of unfettered improvisation. The notes to the AUM Fidelity release suggest that TEST can be heard at the corner of 57th and 5th, and they've also been known to do subway gigs. This is classic street music: tough, sweepingly passionate, but informed and articulate playing. The Eremite disc has one long set from Baltimore and a brief postscript from a Boston show which is a riotous coda to the disc. Rough, live sound, but the spirit is unquenchable and there is some feelingful and exciting interplay among the four players, each of whom suggests that he has a good grasp of long form in improvising. *TEST* isn't much less intense, although there's a serene interlude called 'Alen's Flight Preparation' where the horn players pick up flutes and play a whispery dialogue. Carter, who occasionally turns to the trumpet but is more often on sax, and Mateen are both driven but not without their melodious side, and it sweetens or at least lightens what might otherwise have been an overdose of grim.

Henri Texier (born 1945)

DOUBLE BASS

'It's a sound you feel safe with, like you could lie down on it and go to sleep'; and there is a pillowing security and strength in Texier's sound which amply confirms his fellow-player's assessment. Influenced by the great Wilbur Ware, Texier has a strong, full sound that nearly always sounds better at lower tempos, when its sheer weight and fullness become more evident. Like Charlie Haden, though, he can also play nimbly and melodically.

***** La Companera**
Label Bleu LBLC 6525 *Texier; Michael Marre (t, flhn); Louis Sclavis (cl, ts); Philippe Deschepper (g); Jacques Mahieux (d).* 2/83.

***** Paris-Batignolles**
Label Bleu LBLC 6506 *As above, except replace Marre with Joe Lovano (ts).* 5/86.

The earlier of these records was noted as much for Sclavis's contribution as for the leader's. In 1983, he was not much known outside France, but there were already mutterings about his ingenious and fiery, folk-based improvisations. Interesting as he was at this stage, it's only when Marre makes up the complement that the record really catches light. *Paris-Batignolles* is higher-octane stuff from the start. Lovano's remarkably traditional sound melds perfectly with this group, both on the faster dance-tunes and on the brooding laments. Texier isn't caught so well or so fully on this live recording from the Amiens Jazz Festival, but his presence is consistently evident in the reactions of fellow-players, who always seem easier and open-hearted in his presence.

****** Izlaz**
Label Bleu LBLC 6515 *Texier; Joe Lovano (ts, ss, cl, f, perc); Steve Swallow (b); Aldo Romano (d).* 5/88.

***** Colonel Skopje**
Label Bleu LBLC 6523 *As above, except add John Abercrombie (g).* 7/88.

Texier's Transatlantik Quartet allowed a promising relationship with Lovano to cement and brought in the rock-tinged, free-swinging bass guitar of Steve Swallow. The sound is wonderfully open and unstuffy. 'Ups And Downs' is superb, though it bears no relation to Bud Powell's composition of that name, and the only quibble about this set is that the sound-mix is awry, pushing up bass and drums too far and making Lovano sound as if he's out back somewhere, waiting to get in. *Colonel Skopje* is a ragbag, too various to hang together convincingly, though Abercrombie's presence guarantees some interesting moments, as always.

*****(*) Respect**
Label Bleu LBLC 6612 *Texier; Bob Brookmeyer (vtb); Lee Konitz (as); Steve Swallow (b); Paul Motian (d).* 4–5/97.

Superior, beautifully crafted jazz from a dream line-up. The interplay between Texier and Motian is immaculate, particularly on the drummer's own 'In The Year Of The Dragon', and the blend of horns has a dreamy precision. Konitz is well settled into a purple patch, spinning off quicksilver lines on his own 'Thingin'', which manages to sound as if it was made up on the spot. Brookmeyer's cool, slightly reserved approach probably won't appeal to everybody, but it's combined with a flawless sense of structure and a certain wry humour. Certainly the pairing of voices on 'Lee And Me' is as tongue-in-cheek as 'Idyll', Bob's other composition, is sincere and unalloyed. Texier himself has seldom been heard to greater advantage. The acoustic in Amiens's Studio Gil Evans is both intimate and capacious, and the bass, which never calls for much in the way of electronic boosting, is as resonant and present as if he were standing between your speaker cabinets, playing live.

***** Mosaic Man**
Label Bleu LBLC 6608 *Texier; Glenn Ferris (tb); Sebastien Texier (as, cl); Bojan Zulfikarpasic (p); Tony Rabeson (d).* 9/98.

This is the Azur Quintet, nowadays very much centred on Texier and his son, Sebastien. The bass still remains the axis on which the music turns, freeing up Bojan Z's role considerably and allowing the two horns to range quite widely. Apart from 'Mosaic Man' itself and 'Cap d'Espérance', the songs are mainly quite short. As ever, Henri doesn't indulge himself in long solo features, preferring to register a presence with rich, double-stopped chords and fleet, muscular melody-lines. Not our favourite to date of his own recordings, but a fine showing nevertheless.

Toots Thielemans (born 1922)

HARMONICA, GUITAR, WHISTLING

If you were a young Belgian jazz fanatic in the early '40s, you took up guitar in emulation of Django. Thielemans recorded 'Bluesette' in 1961, after working with George Shearing; his first hit had him playing guitar and whistling, but he subsequently became the pre-eminent harmonica player in jazz, with a facility and depth of expression that rivals any conventional horn-players. A festival favourite, Thielemans tended to avoid the studio in later years.

*****(*) Man Bites Harmonica**
Original Jazz Classics OJC 1738 *Thielemans; Pepper Adams (bs); Kenny Drew (p); Wilbur Ware (b); Art Taylor (d).* 12/57.

Thielemans frequently finds himself in the awkward and unsatisfactory position of coming first in a category of one or consigned to 'miscellaneous instruments'. Though ubiquitous in the blues, the harmonica has made remarkably little impact in jazz, and there are no recognized critical standards for his extraordinary facility as a whistler. Thielemans's pop and movie work has tended further to downgrade his very considerable jazz credentials. Surprisingly, to those who know him primarily as a performer of moodily atmospheric soundtrack pieces (*Midnight Cowboy* pre-eminently) or as composer of the undemanding 'Bluesette', his roots are in bebop and in the kind of harmonically liberated improvisation associated with John Coltrane. That's perhaps most obvious in the dark, Chicago-influenced sound of *Man Bites Harmonica*, which includes a wonderful 'Don't Blame Me'. The rather dark-toned group is not the setting one expects for him, but it is wonderfully effective.

***** Aquarela Do Brasil**
Verve 830391-2 *Thielemans; Elis Regina (v); Orquesta Elis Cinco.* 69.

This belongs as much to the singer as to Toots, but for lovers of Latin jazz it's a jewel of an album, lush and overproduced, but full of enchanting moments, from the inevitable Jobim ('Wave') to Toots's little posy, 'Five For Elis'. There is a light and joyous touch to everything the two principals attempt and it's almost a pity that this couldn't have been recorded with just a couple of guitarists and a melodic bass player. 'Honeysuckle Rose' is robbed of much of its intimacy by the big sound.

***** The Silver Collection: Toots Thielemans**
Polydor 825086 *Thielemans; Ferdinand Povel (ts); Rob Franken (ky); Wim Overgaauw, Joop Scholten (g); Victor Kaihatu, Niels-Henning Orsted Pedersen (b); Bruno Castellucci, Evert Overweg (d); Ruud Boos Orchestra; collective personnel, other details unknown.* 4/74–4/75.

In addition to the inevitable 'Bluesette', there are good solo performances of 'Muskrat Ramble', 'The Mooche' and a slightly off-beam 'You're My Blues Machine' on *The Silver Collection*, a useful sample which establishes his bop *bona fides* with 'My Little Suede Shoes' and is marred only by a set of rather dreary band arrangements by Boos.

*****(*) Images**
Candid 71007 *Thielemans; JoAnne Brackeen (p); Cecil McBee (b); Freddie Waits (d).* 9/74.

****(*) Live**
Polydor 831694 *Thielemans; Wim Overgaauw, Joop Scholten (g); Rob Franken (electric p); Victor Kaihatu, Rob Langereis (b); Bruno Castellucci (d); Cees Schrama (perc).* 4/75.

***** Live In The Netherlands**
Original Jazz Classics OJC 930 *Thielemans; Joe Pass (g); Niels-Henning Orsted Pedersen (b).* 7/80.

These live sets appear to confirm a long-standing belief that Thielemans is not always a successful studio performer but needs the resistance and charge of a live audience. *Images* is one of the best records he ever made. The group is stunningly inventive and the version of 'Giant Steps' is all the proof anyone will ever need of the chromatic harmonica's place in the jazz canon. Other compositions are by Toots and pianist Brackeen, who is in very good form. The Netherlands trio is a record that grows in stature with every hearing, and Toots's bop-tinged solos on 'Thriving On A Riff' and 'Someday My Prince Will Come' are a revelation. NHOP and Pass are both in splendid form and the interplay of melodic lines creates entirely new contrafacts out of familiar materials. Ellington's 'The Mooche' is a guitar solo, brief but evocative and with a steely edge.

The third of the group stands up less well as the years go by, largely because the accompanying musicians are so sturdy and unresponsive. Toots delivers his usual unflappable set, but the backgrounds could certainly be more exuberant.

****** Only Trust Your Heart**
Concord CCD 4355 *Thielemans; Fred Hersch (p); Marc Johnson, Harvie Swartz (b); Joey Baron (d).* 4–5/88.

*****(*) Footprints**
Emarcy 846650 *Thielemans; Mulgrew Miller (p); Rufus Reid (b); Lewis Nash (d).* 89.

The later '80s marked a considerable revival of Thielemans's jazz playing. A studio jazz recording led by Thielemans was by then a rarity, but *Only Trust Your Heart* is his masterpiece. Restricted on this occasion to harmonica, the playing is superb. The choice of material (and Fred Hersch's arranging) is impeccable and challenging and the production first rate, with Thielemans front and centre and the band spread out very evenly behind him. The set kicks off with a marvellous reading of Wayne Shorter's 'Speak No Evil', includes 'Sophisticated Lady', Monk's 'Little Rootie Tootie' and Thad Jones's 'Three And One', transposed unfamiliarly high to bring it within the range of Thielemans's instrument, which takes on the slightly yodelling timbre of soprano saxophone. Throughout, Thielemans's solo development merits the closest attention, particularly on the original 'Sarabande', the better of two duets with Hersch. The pianist's other composition, 'Rain Waltz', deserves wider distribution. Allegedly nearly all first takes, each of the dozen tracks represents Thielemans's undervalued art at its finest.

***** Concerto For Harmonica**
TCB 94802 *Thielemans; Matthie Michel (t, flhn); Michel Weber (as, cl); Yvan Ischer (ss, ts); Christian Gavillet (bs, bcl); Fred Hersch (p); Antoine Ogay (b); Big Band de Lausanne.* 12/95.

Christian Gavillet's 'concerto' for Toots is really just a suite of thematically connected melodies with very little structural logic beyond that. That, though, is sufficient to conjure one of the Belgian's finest performances, though he saves the really good stuff for a couple of encores with just Hersch in accompaniment. As ever, the sound of the harmonica floats away above the well-drilled Swiss band, which is under the direction of Charles Papasoff. Other featured soloists include Gavillet himself, a fine baritonist in a pre-Mulligan style, and trumpeter Michel, who has a soft, almost liquid tone. A delightful evening's music.

****(*) The Live Takes**
Narada 49455 *Thielemans; Michael Herr, Kenny Werner (p, ky); Jay Anderson, Ray Drummond, Michel Hatzigeorgiou (b); Adam Nussbaum (d).* n.d.

A gentle, perhaps rather too laid-back compilation of concert performances which see Toots ease his way through some familiar standards like 'Stardust' and some more obscure things like Pastorius's 'Three Views Of A Secret'. The best of the record probably comes in the first ten minutes with a lovely reading of 'I Loves You, Porgy'. Thereafter the pace drifts. Toots fans will lap it up, but the unconverted may find it all a bit predictable and slow.

*****(*) Toots Thielemans & Kenny Werner**
Uptown/Universal 014722 *Thielemans; Kenny Werner (p, syn).* 6/01.

There are some wonderful performances on this live (but exceedingly clean) recording. Toots tackles modern jazz classics like Hancock's 'Dolphin Dance' and Bill Evans's 'Time Remembered' and 'Very Early' with the greatest aplomb, but also adds something unique to Chaplin's 'Smile' and to medleys saluting Sinatra, Michel Legrand and the movies of Walt Disney. Werner alternates piano and synthesizer, but rarely allows his electronic keyboard to crowd the sound, leaving plenty of space for Toots's plangent sound to swell and settle. Astonishingly for a live recording, there are no audience interruptions and no detectable edits or dubs. A very fine record indeed, and testimony to a very sympathetic partnership.

Ed Thigpen (born 1930)

DRUMS

Born in Chicago but raised in St Louis, Thigpen played in R&B and jazz groups from 1948. His most famous associations have been with Oscar Peterson (1959–65) and Ella Fitzgerald (1965–72), but he has lived in Sweden for most of the past 30 years and teaches and performs there still.

***** Easy Flight**
Stunt STUCD 19912 *Thigpen; Johnny O'Neal (p); Tony Purrone(g); Marlene Rosenberg (b).* 11/89–1/90.

*****(*) It's Entertainment!**
Stunt STUCD 19816 *Thigpen; Carsten Dahl (p); Jesper Bodilsen(b).* 5/98.

*****(*) The Element Of Swing**
Stunt STUCD 01222 *As above, except add Joe Lovano (ts, bcl).* 10/01.

A master of crisp, swinging drumming, Thigpen dominates these sessions but in a generous way: he plays for the music, and while the drumming is a masterclass in itself, the results are always enjoyable. The first set was made in Chicago and is more routine, although the quartet plays well; but *It's Entertainment!* is a cracking live set from the Copenhagen Jazzhouse. Dahl and Bodilsen introduce telling variations on standards such as 'Softly As In A Morning Sunrise', but it's Thigpen – using brushes much of the time – who really puts the heart and power into the music. His long improvised journey on 'Cosmic Voyage' is a lot more entertaining than many more serious free-form episodes.

The gig with Lovano came at the end of a brief tour. The saxophonist is in prime form, imperious on his own 'Emperor Jones' and traditionally inclined on 'Chelsea Bridge', though again the drummer keeps scene-stealing without overdoing it; follow his impeccable brushwork on 'Emperor Jones', as one example.

Jesper Thilo (born 1941)

TENOR SAXOPHONE, CLARINET, TRUMPET

From Copenhagen, Thilo was working in the Danish mainstream from the early '60s and is a big-sounding player, almost equally influenced by swing and bop styles.

***** Jesper Thilo Quartet With Clark Terry**
Storyville STCD 8204 *Thilo; Clark Terry (t); Kenny Drew (p); Jesper Lundgaard, Mads Vinding (b); Svend-Erik Norregaard, Billy Hart (d).* 12/80.

***** Jesper Thilo Quintet Featuring Harry Edison**
Storyville STC-CD 4120 *Thilo; Harry 'Sweets' Edison (t); Ole Kock Hansen (p); Ole Ousen (g); Jesper Lundgaard (b); Svend-Erik Norregaard (d).* 2/86.

****(*) Shufflin'**
Music Mecca CD 1015 2 *Thilo; Ole Kock Hansen, Søren Kristiansen (p); Henrik Bay (g); Jesper Lundgaard, Hugo Rasmussen (b); Svend-Erik Norregaard (d); Ann Farholt (v).* 9/90.

*****(*) Jesper Thilo Quintet Featuring Hank Jones**
Storyville STCD 4178 *Thilo; Hank Jones (p); Doug Raney (g); Hugo Rasmussen (b); Svend-Erik Norregaard (d).* 3/91.

***** Plays Duke Ellington**
Music Mecca CD 1025-2 *Thilo; Søren Kristiansen (p); Hugo Rasmussen (b); Svend-Erik Norregaard (d); Ann Farholt (v).* 4/92.

***** Don't Count Him Out**
Music Mecca CD 1035-2 *As above.* 3/93.

*****(*) Movin' Out**
Music Mecca 1045-2 *Thilo; Ben Besiakov (p); Jesper Lundgaard (b).* 4/94.

***** Together**
Music Mecca 1975-2 *Thilo; Søren Kristiansen (p); Niels Pallesen (b); Svend-Erik Norregaard (d).* 10/95.

***** Jesper Thilo / Ann Farholt Meets Thomas Clausen**
Music Mecca 2025-2 *Thilo; Thomas Clausen (p); Henrik Bay (g); Mads Vinding (b); Svend-Erik Norregaard (d); Ann Farholt (v).* 10/96.

*****(*) Thank You Mr Hat!**
Music Mecca 2045-2 *Thilo; Henrik Bolberg (t); Søren Kristiansen (p); Niels Pallesen (b); Svend-Erik Norregaard (d).* 11/97.

Thilo plays the kind of straightahead swing that the Scandinavians have now virtually patented: he's a tenorman in the noble tradition, a plain speaker and a reliable journeyman. The early session with Terry is coupled with a quartet date from the same month, and though this is no more than a friendly chug through a familiar programme the front line has real class. The set with Edison would be by far the more impressive were it not for the dullness of the accompaniments; however, the trumpeter does kick-start 'There Will Never Be Another You' and there are some graceful moments on a romantic medley recorded on a later – and better – night. *Shufflin'* is very much in the same vein, a professional club set that doesn't really bear frequent repetition at home. The bebop flourishes on 'How High The Moon', with Ann Farholt's rather strained voice acting as second horn, are quite dramatic, and there are enough imaginative flourishes on a long roster of standards to sustain interest; but, again, nothing to write home about.

The more recent records count among his best. The meeting with Hank Jones benefits hugely from Hank's benign but slyly alert presence, whether prodding a soloist or taking a typically suave improvisation of his own. Raney, too, plays very well. The first two Music Mecca albums are focused round Ellington and Basie repertoire and, though some of the choices are a little too familiar in each case, the quintet plays them with fine enthusiasm and Thilo musters some of his sharpest improvising (his clarinet-playing on 'Duke's Place' is also a neat surprise). Farholt's singing is much more assured and the studio sound is very crisp on each record.

It seems almost cheeky to suggest that Thilo is improving. But it's hard to avoid the feeling that *Movin' Out* is his best record. The lighter feel of a drummerless trio suits him and, though he stands in a mainstream tenor tradition, he has a more airy approach to an improvisation than some masters of the style; boppish without really sounding 'modern', his solos have a fleetness which defies cliché. 'Blue Monk' turns a contemporary blues into a masterclass of the style. Besiakov is perhaps no more than a good prop, but this is a cracker of a record.

There is some flab on *Together* – too many bass solos and perhaps too many tracks overall – but otherwise Thilo is still in top form. 'Donna' is full-on bebop, still synthesized through a swing man's dedications, and it's intriguing to hear how he makes Joe Henderson's 'Recorda-Me' into the kind of full-blooded declamation which the more oblique hard-boppers would shy away from. The rhythm section is good, if not quite in the front rank, and it may be time to hear Thilo trading punches with an all-American band.

Thank You Mr Hat! is by the same group, with a couple of years' worth of extra seasoning and trumpeter Bolberg stepping in on the final four tracks. They're all in great shape, too. Jesper sweeps all before him – cop the wondrous invention on a long, luxuriant 'Sweet Lorraine' – but the others are swinging like champions too. The ten tracks are all in the old-favourite category, but it's conceived as a tribute to the wonderful Arnvid Meyer (or 'Mr Hat', as J. C. Higginbotham christened him) and the days when Arnvid's small-group swing dominated the Danish jazz scene (with Thilo in the band). A warm tribute to a great man.

A surprise to hear Thilo taking out the trumpet for 'September Song' on *Meets Thomas Clausen*. But he's soon back on tenor for the cheeky 'Five Bebop Tunes', a beefy 'It Might As Well Be Spring', a grouchy 'Svinninge Blues'. Clausen follows keenly, but one's reaction may depend on how much Farholt appeals – she's all over the record and sometimes seems over-confident.

*****(*) 40th Anniversary Collection**
Music Mecca CD 2105-2 2CD *As Music Mecca discs listed above.* 92–97.

The best of Jesper, or at least the pick of his Music Mecca albums, generously pillaged for a little over two hours of music in this double-disc compilation. Arguably too much from the Ellington and Basie discs, but if you wanted one Thilo record for the collection we wouldn't dissuade you from snapping this one up.

***** Jesper Thilo Meets Jake Hanna**
Music Mecca 2075-2 *Thilo; Søren Kristiansen (p); Jake Hanna (d).* 6/98.

*****(*) Flying Home**
Music Mecca 3015-2 *Thilo; Jan Lundgren (p); Lars Erstrand (vib); Jesper Lundgaard (b); Nils-Bertil Dahlander (d); Ann Farholt (v).* 8–9/99.

*****(*) Nothing To Declare**
Music Mecca 3050-2 *Thilo; Olivier Antunes (p); Jens Skou Olsen (b); Svend-Erik Norregaard (d); Ann Farholt (v).* 11/00.

The meeting with Jake Hanna is from a gig at the Copenhagen Jazz House, a very happy occasion by the sound of it, even if nothing very extraordinary happens. Hanna's cymbal work on 'China Boy' will be a lesson for aspiring drummers.

Flying Home is another gig, with an all-star group in Malmö. Thilo shares top billing on both this and *Nothing To Declare* with Ann Farholt, so if it's the man's tenor you've come to hear you may feel antsy during the vocals, though that would be unfair on the singer, who's progressed from 2025-2. From a gorgeous 'They Can't Take That Away From Me' onwards, there's so much playing out of the top drawer – Erstrand and Lundgren matching Thilo blow for blow – that it breezes past the typical on-the-hoof club-session.

The band on *Nothing To Declare* made the (studio) session as a celebration of a trip to Beijing earlier in that year (hence the opening 'On A Slow Boat To China'). Farholt's smoochy contralto makes an agreeable impression here and we can forgive the odd bar of trying too hard. Again, though, the playing throughout is replete with class; Thilo's built his sound into one of the great mainstream voices, and it's unalloyed pleasure to hear him tackling these tunes (though he miscredits 'If You Were The Only Girl In The World' to Noël Coward in his sleeve-note!).

Gary Thomas (born 1961)

TENOR SAXOPHONE, FLUTE

Thomas was one of the most assertive and acerbic of the M-Base musicians, with a punchy, insistent tone that is most forceful on his own records but which has also contributed materially to records by other leaders, including Uri Caine, Peter Herborn and John McLaughlin.

***** By Any Means Necessary**
Winter & Winter 919031 *Thomas; Greg Osby (as); Tim Murphy, Geri Allen (ky); Mick Goodrick, John Scofield (g); Anthony Cox (b); Dennis Chambers (d); Nana Vasconcelos (perc).* 5/89.

***** While The Gate Is Open**
Winter & Winter 919037 *Thomas; Greg Osby (as); Kevin Eubanks (g); Anthony Cox, Dave Holland (b); Dennis Chambers (d).* 11/89.

**** The Kold Cage**
Winter & Winter 919049 *Thomas; Mulgrew Miller (p); Michael Cain, Tim Murphy (syn, p); Anthony Perkins (syn); Paul Bollenback, Kevin Eubanks (g); Anthony Cox (b); Dennis Chambers (d); Steve Moss (perc); Joe Wesson (v).* 3–6/91.

***** Found On Sordid Streets**
Winter & Winter 910 002 *Thomas; George Colligan (org); Paul Bollenback (g); Howard Curtis (d); Steve Moss (perc); Pork Chop, No Name (v).* 2/96.

***** Pariah's Pariah**
Winter & Winter 910 033 *As above, except omit Moss, Pork Chop, No Name.* 99.

Thomas's first record for the newly founded W&W label wisely attempted to do no more than consolidate the sound he had been trading in for years at JMT. As if to prove it, the early JMTs have been reissued by W&W and the first of them here is the archetypal M-Base record, rhythmically rugged, harmonically subtler than it sounds at first, ultimately less alienated from the post-bop mainstream than you might think. The surprise on *While The Gate Is Open* was that Thomas, seemingly so resistant to anything not as fresh as today's papers, was still willing to work with standards. His readings of 'Epistrophy' and 'Star Eyes' are wonderfully engaging. We have to reverse our position somewhat on *The Kold Kage.* What once seemed vital and relevant now seems a polystylistic shambles, unredeemed by any informing logic. Thomas's desire to harness for jazz all the energies of hip hop and other street musics is admirable enough, but fails in the execution. Interesting to have it around again, though. The work has matured considerably by the time of *Found On Sordid Streets*. Thomas reworks 'Exile's Gate' and includes Terri Lyne Carrington's 'The Eternal Present', a tune that sounds as if it's been around longer than any of these guys. The raps are still pretty hokey and not entirely convincing, but this is a solid performance from all concerned.

The follow-up album is no less tough and uncompromising, but without the raps Thomas's tenor comes through stronger than ever, and on 'Zero Tolerance' and 'Vanishing Time', which represent the real climax of the album, he is playing at his peak, phrasing fast and with real control and definition.

René Thomas (1927–75)

GUITAR

Though Belgian, Thomas made his mark on the Parisian scene of the '50s, before spells in New York and Canada. His later stint with Stan Getz and Eddie Louiss brought him his widest exposure.

***** The Real Cat**
Emarcy 549400-2 *Thomas; Serge Monville (ts); René Urtreger, Roland Ronchaud(p); Benoît Quersin, Jean-Marie Ingrand (b); Jean-Louis Viale, José Bourguignon (d).* 54–56.

*****(*) Guitar Groove**
Original Jazz Classics OJC 1725 *Thomas; J. R. Monterose (ts); Hod O'Brien (p); Teddy Kotick (b); Albert 'Tootie' Heath (d).* 9/60.

***** Meeting Mr Thomas**
Emarcy 549812-2 *Thomas; Jacques Pelzer (as, f); Lou Bennett(org); Gilbert Rovère, Benoît Quersin (b); Charles Bellonzi (d).* 3/63.

A fatal heart attack cut short a career that was already rather overshadowed by a more colourful and charismatic guitarist, Thomas's Belgian compatriot, Django Reinhardt. Though Django must have been the unavoidable comparison when Thomas moved to North America, there really wasn't very much in common between them and Thomas's modernist credentials allowed him to fit into the American scene more comfortably than his illustrious predecessor. *Guitar Groove* is a fine product of his American sojourn and is one of the high points of a poorly documented career. The original, 'Spontaneous Effort', combines firm, boppish melody with an easy swing. Monterose is too raw-throated for 'Milestones' but slots into 'Ruby My Dear' with impressive ease. He sits out for 'Like Someone In Love' and O'Brien joins him on the bench for the duration of 'How Long Has This Been Going On?'. The sound is better balanced on these tracks than when the horn is present, but overall it sounds very good indeed.

The two Emarcy reissues are a welcome showing of material recorded either side of Thomas's American sojourn. It's all very cool and very light, a restraint which carries over into the 1963 sessions as much as in the briefer, just slightly less relaxed 1954–6 quintets. Lou Bennett adds a little bluesy heat to the later dates, but it's very little, and the point of interest on both discs is how cleanly Thomas appropriated the nutrients in the Farlow–Raney axis – no garlicky grooves, just frothily enjoyable bopping.

Barbara Thompson (born 1944)

SAXOPHONES, FLUTES, SOPRANINO RECORDER, KEYBOARDS

At 20, Thompson joined Neil Ardley's orchestra, where she met her future husband, Jon Hiseman. They, together with Colin Dudman, have been the basic line-up of Paraphernalia, a band that has now lasted for nearly three decades in different forms.

***** A Cry From The Heart**
VeraBra CDVBR 2021 *Thompson; Pete Lemer (ky); Paul Dunne (g); Phil Mulford (b); Jon Hiseman (d, perc).* 11/87.

*****(*) Breathless**
VeraBra CDVBR 2057 *Thompson; Pete Lemer (ky); Malcolm MacFarlane (g); Jon Hiseman (d).* 90.

***** Everlasting Flame**
VeraBra CDVBR 2058 *Thompson; Pete Lemer (ky); Malcolm MacFarlane (g); Paul Westwood (b); Jon Hiseman (d); Hossam Ramzy (perc); Anna Gracey Hiseman, London Community Gospel Singers (v).* 93.

***** Shifting Sands**
Intuition INT 3174 2 *Thompson; Pete Lemer (ky); Billy Thompson (vn); Paul Westwood (b); Jon Hiseman (d).* 98.

***** Thompson's Tangos**
Intuition 3290-2 *As above, except Dave Ball (b) replaces Westwood.* 00.

***** In The Eye Of A Storm**
Intuition 3338-2 *As various discs above.* 83–03.

An astonishingly talented multi-instrumentalist, Thompson encompasses straightahead jazz, rock and fusion, but she incorporates an interest in ethnic, formal and elements of ambient and 'New Age' music. She is difficult to categorize and has therefore rarely received the critical attention she merits. Thompson is a forceful soloist who regularly introduces unusual harmonic juxtapositions by playing two instruments simultaneously. Thompson's band, Paraphernalia, has never perhaps been as effective in the studio as in a live setting. The band featured on both *Breathless* and *Everlasting Flame* also has a strong rock tinge, but it provides Thompson with a solid platform for some of her most evocative solos on record and some of her most imaginative writing. 'The Night Before Culloden' and 'Tatami' on the later disc identify how far away from orthodox jazz she has felt able to work. They also, less encouragingly, help identify the essential bittiness of the records. Paraphernalia's live performances tend to be much more focused.

Shifting Sands is even more of a family affair, with Billy Thompson joining the line-up and acquitting himself extremely well. As often, Barbara has assembled a loosely themed programme, concerned with change and decay, illusion and continuity. The last of these, at least, is the key to her work, a steady and clear-sighted application to creative music.

Thompson's Tangos starts with four pieces in the mode suggested by the title, and proceeds through a pensive reading of 'Naima' and some further originals which depend significantly on Lemer's keyboard colourings. It's an entertaining set, if not quite one of her best, and it's sad to report that illness has obliged her to largely curtail further playing. *In The Eye Of The Storm* is a compilation from some 20 years of work, but despite the title it's based around Barbara's ballad-playing, and some excellent tracks would have been more interestingly counterpointed by some of her brisker material.

Lucky Thompson (born 1924)

TENOR AND SOPRANO SAXOPHONES

Legend has the young South Carolinan obsessively practising saxophone fingerings on a broom handle before he had a proper horn. Thompson has always seemed an outsider, drawing on the swing era, involved in bebop, but also prefiguring much of what went on in the '60s and '70s, after his playing career was effectively over.

***** Smooth Sailing**
Indigo IGO CD 2104 *Thompson; John Best, Buck Clayton, Karl George, Conrad Gozzo (t); J. J. Johnson, Shorty Rogers, Dicky Wells, Gerald Wilson (tb); Marshall Royal (as, cl); Jewell Grant, Herb Hoise, Dick Norris (as); Gordon Reeder (ts); Leon Beck (bs); Stuff Smith (vn); Wilbert Baranco, Eddie Beal, Sammy Benskin, Bill Doggett, Erroll Garner, Bob Mosley, G. Styles (p); Irving Ashby, Frank Davenport, Freddie Green, Al Hendrickson, Barney Kessel, Charlie Norris, Gene Phillips (g); Red Callender, Al Hall, John Kitzmiler, Charles Mingus, Oscar Pettiford, Rodney Richardson, Bob Stone (b); Edward Hall, Bob Hummell, Jackie Mills, Roy Porter, Alvin Stoller, George Wettling, Shadow Wilson, Lee Young (d); David Allyn, Ernie Andrews, Marion Abernathy, Sylvia Sims (v).* 12/44–6/47.

***** Lucky Thompson: 1944–1947**
Classics 1113 *As above.* 44–47.

***** The Beginning Years**
IAJRC CD 1001 *Thompson; Frank Beach, Karl George, Al Killian, Chuck Peterson, Charlie Shavers (t); Lyle Griffin, Sidney Harris, J. J. Johnson, Charles Maxon, Si Zentner (tb); Rudy Rutherford (cl); Marshal Royal (as, cl); Jewell Grant, Hal McKusick, Clint Meagley, Eddie Rosa (as); Stan Getz (as, ts); L. Beck, Butch Stone (bs); Wilbert Baranco, Eddie Beal, Bill Doggett, Michael 'Dodo' Marmarosa, Bob Mosley, Jimmy Rowles (p); Frank Davenport (cel); Irving Ashby, Freddie Green, Al Hendrickson, Barney Kessel, Charles Norris, Gene Phillips, Tony Rizzi (g); Harry Babasin, Red Callender, Arnold Fishkind, Charles Mingus, Oscar Pettiford, Rodney Richardson, Bob Stone (b); Edward Hall, Don Lamond, Roy Porter, Alvin Stoller, Shadow Wilson, Lee Young (d); Marion Abernathy, David Allyn, Ernie Andrews, Estelle Edson (v); other personnel uncertain.* 45–47.

****** Accent On Tenor Sax**
Fresh Sound FSCD 2001 *Thompson; Ernie Royal (t); Jimmy Hamilton (cl); Earl Knight, Billy Taylor (p); Sidney Gross (g); Oscar Pettiford (b); Osie Johnson (d).* 54.

***** Lucky Thompson With Gerard Pochonet & His Quartet**
Fresh Sound FSR CD 86 *Thompson; Martial Solal (p); Michel Hausser (vib); Jean-Pierre Sasson (g); Pierre Michelot, Benoît Quersin (b); Gerard Pochonet (d).* 3/56.

Thompson's disappearance from the jazz scene in the '70s was only the latest (but apparently the last) of a strangely contoured career. A highly philosophical, almost mystical man, he reacted against the values of the music industry and in the end turned his back on it without seeming regret. The beginning was garlanded with promise. He recorded with Charlie Parker just after the war (a rare example of that chimera, the bebop tenor player), but then returned to his native Detroit, where he became involved in R&B and publishing. Like Don Byas, whom he most resembles in tone and in his development of solos, he has a slightly oblique and uneasy stance on bop, cleaving to a kind of accelerated swing idiom with a distinctive 'snap' to his softly enunciated phrases and an advanced harmonic language that occasionally moves into areas of surprising freedom.

The material on *The Beginning Years* includes Thompson's debut as leader, an autumn 1945 session with J. J. Johnson in the line-up and a magnificent performance of 'Irresistible You' which is the earliest indication of Lucky's skills as a balladeer. Everything else on the disc is for other leaders, much of it straightforward accompaniment for singers, with just occasional flashes of saxophone brilliance. It's an album that is more interesting than genuinely enjoyable, worth picking up by anyone who's been intrigued by the later, more individual sessions and who wants to see where Lucky is coming from. Nicely detailed session notes help the listener navigate a rather bitty disc.

The Indigo compilation mostly features Thompson under other leaders – Freddie Green, Oscar Pettiford, Bob Mosley, Karl George, Frank Davenport and Ike Carpenter – but does also include 'Test Pilots' from 1944 with Stuff Smith and Errol Garner, a September 1945 all-stars session with J. J. Johnson, and six tracks recorded for Down Beat with the equally fugitive Dodo Marmarosa on piano. The sound quality is generally pretty poor, but there are enough glimpses of Thompson as a solo voice to make this a valuable documentation of a career that has yet to be fully assessed.

Thompson's best performances as leader are always when he has first-rate partners to bounce off, as with *Accent On Tenor Sax.* Thompson's rich, driving style coaxes some astonishing playing out of Jimmy Hamilton, who contributes 'Mr E-Z' to the session. Thompson's tenor has a smooth, clarinet quality on 'Where Or When', gliding over the changes with total ease. One curious characteristic is Thompson's preference for soloing at least a couple of choruses without harmonic accompaniment, a device that is most obvious on *Lord, Lord ...* but is common to all the records to some degree. Though very far back in the mix, Pettiford and Johnson play superbly, and the bassist checks in with one fine composition, 'Kamman's A'Comin''. For the last four tracks, including a superb 'Mood Indigo', Ernie Royal comes in on trumpet and Earl Knight replaces the guesting Billy Taylor.

*****(*) Modern Jazz Group**
Emarcy 159823 *Thompson; Fred Gerrard, Roger Guerin (t); Benny Vasseur (tb); Jean-Louis Chautemps (ts); William Boucaya (bs); Henri Renaud (p); Benoît Quersin (b); Christian Garros (d).* n.d.

*****(*) Lucky In Paris**
High Note HJCD 7045 *Thompson; Martial Solal (p); Michel Hausser (vib); Gilbert Gassin (b); Gerard Pochonet (d); Gana M'Bow (perc).* 1/59.

Originally released in France and France only on Symphonium Records, *Lucky In Paris* catches Lucky in a transitional phase, sounding broody and reflective but also revelling in the company of Martial Solal and Gérard Pochonet, and still playing his soprano in the limber, expressive way that sets his approach to the instrument apart from what would become the orthodoxy of John Coltrane's style. Thompson sounds much closer to Johnny Hodges and, in places, to Lester Young, as in his wonderfully lyrical interpretation of 'We'll Be Together Again'. This was, strictly speaking, Pochonet's group and he commands his fair share and more of the spotlight, even on a short track like 'Tea For Two'. The interplay of piano and saxophone on 'Pennies From Heaven' is exquisite. Why this record was never released internationally seems incomprehensible. It catches Lucky ranging more freely than ever over the chords and reshaping melodies like that of 'Have You Met Miss Jones?' but already betraying a reticence that would all too shortly become permanent.

The Emarcy release is part of a larger series celebrating the work of American musicians in Paris. It finds Lucky in strong and relaxed form, blowing some exquisite bop solos but also stretching out into something altogether more challenging. The accompaniments are well crafted and well rehearsed, testimony to the quality of musicianship round Paris at the time.

****** Lord, Lord, Am I Ever Going To Know?**
Candid CCD 79035 *Thompson; Martial Solal (p); Peter Trunk (b); Kenny Clarke (d).* 61.

This is the Lucky Thompson record to have, eight originals recorded in Paris with musicians who understood his wants and shared his musical and spiritual values. It is astonishing that this material has lain unheard for so long; only the title-track had been issued before and the other song titles were chosen by Alan Bates and Mark Gardner for release in 1997. The title-track is a loping tenor blues, crafted with great care and sophistication. The ballad that follows, 'Love And Respect', is the first of the soprano numbers, light-toned and limber. The real *tour de force* is the unaccompanied 'Choose Your Own', which has Lucky switching back and forth between tenor and soprano with seamless precision. As Gardner points out, with great justice, Thompson never believed he had even scratched the surface in his career, a statement denied by the vivid and intense improvisation on the final number which Bates and Gardner have called 'Scratching The Surface'. It's an extraordinary piece, and one that it would be interesting to play blindfold to some jazz commentators. Almost all will guess at a later date than 1961 and suggest someone in the nascent avant-garde, though it's by no means an 'outside' performance itself. The CD opens with a recording made in 1968, a message from Thompson to delegates at what was to have been a symposium in Coventry (ironic location, in the circumstances) dedicated to Lucky's work. What we hear is a man of surpassing modesty, but with a burning conviction as well. He asks us to rethink our priorities and take a more careful look at some of our idols' feet. He offers blessings and warm wishes and the the next thing we hear is 'Lord, Lord, Am I Ever Gonna Know?'. Presumably he found his own answer to that. The sorry tailpiece to the story is that the planned symposium was cancelled for lack of interest. Thompson took himself outside little more than a decade after this, and what followed was silence.

****** Lucky Strikes**
Original Jazz Classics OJC 194 *Thompson; Hank Jones (p); Richard Davis (b); Connie Kay (d).* 9/64.

Lucky Strikes is tighter and more precise. In the meantime Thompson had made significant bounds in his understanding of harmonic theory, and he attempts transitions that would have been quite alien to him a decade earlier. All his characteristic virtues of tone and smooth development are in place, though. He subtly blurs the melodic surface of 'In A Sentimental Mood' (a curious opener) and adjusts his tone significantly for the intriguing 'Reminiscent', 'Midnite Oil' and 'Prey Loot'.

*****(*) Happy Days**
Prestige PRCD 24144 *Thompson; Tommy Flanagan, Hank Jones (p); Wendell Marshall, George Tucker (b); Dave Bailey, Jack Melady, Walter Perkins (d).* n.d.

***** Lucky Meets Tommy**
Fresh Sound FSRCD 199 *Thompson; Tommy Flanagan (p); Frank Anderson (org); Wally Richardson (g); Willie Ruff (b); Oliver Jackson, Walter Perkins (d).* 65.

Flanagan was the ideal piano partner for Thompson, a fluent melodist who doesn't lack for rhythmic drive and who constantly flirts with harmonic freedom. He's easily the more convincing of the two piano players on *Happy Days*, as upbeat and joyous a session as the name suggests, but with a softer and more poignant side as well. 'Long Ago And Far Away' and 'Dearly Beloved' are among the best things Thompson recorded; his own solos are crafted with intelligence and taste and he's never less than wholly responsive to those around him. The Fresh Sound is, as usual for this imprint, better musically than it is technically.

***** Soul's Nite Out**
Ensayo ENYCD 3471 *Thompson; Tete Montoliu (p); Eric Peter (b); Peer Wyboris (d).* 5/70.

Thompson has something of a cult following, not least in Barcelona, where local fans and musicians have long regarded him as up there with the very greats. That is where *Soul's Nite Out* was recorded, on a symbolically potent May Day in 1970. Thompson concentrates very largely on soprano, as so often at this time, switching to his tenor for Duke's 'I Got It Bad' and three other numbers. The tunes are all surprisingly short and solos rarely run to more than a few choruses, but there is no mistaking the inventiveness and sophistication of his playing. Montoliu and the locally celebrated rhythm section provide a fertile base.

Malachi Thompson (born 1941)

TRUMPET, VOICE

A player who mixed hard bop with free playing in about equal measure, Thompson is of the generation which fuelled the new music of Chicago in the '60s, although his fundamentally more conservative line is at a tangent to those explorers. He overcame a serious illness and began a long series of Delmark recordings, and his two principal bands are Freebop and Africa Brass.

***** Spirit**
Delmark DD-442 *Thompson; Carter Jefferson (ts); Albert Dailey (p); James King (b); Nasar Abadey (d); Randy Abbott (perc); Leon Thomas, Arnae Burton (v).* n.d.

***** The Jaz Life**
Delmark DD-453 *Thompson; Joe Ford (ss, as); Carter Jefferson (ts); Kirk Brown (p); Harrison Bankhead (b); Nasar Abeday (d); Richard Lawrence (perc).* 6/91.

***** Lift Every Voice**
Delmark DE-463 *Thompson; David Spencer, Kenny Anderson, Bob Griffin, Elmer Brown (t); Edwin Williams, Bill McFarland, Ray Riperton (tb); Steve Berry (btb); Carter*

Jefferson (ts); Kirk Brown (p); Harrison Bankhead (b); Ayreeayl Ra (d); Richard Lawrence, Enoch (perc); voices. 8/92.

***** New Standards**

Delmark DE-473 *Thompson; Steve Berry (tb); Joe Ford (as); Ron Bridgewater, Sonny Seals, Carter Jefferson (ts); Kirk Brown (p); Yosef Ben Israel, John Whitfield (b); Ayreeayl Ra, Nasar Abaday (d); Dr Cuz (perc).* 4/93.

***** Buddy Bolden's Rag**

Delmark DE-484 *Thompson; David Spencer, Kenny Anderson, Phillip Perkins, Lester Bowie, Zane Massey (t); Edwin Williams, Bill McFarland, Ray Riperton, Steve Berry (tb); Ari Brown (ts); Harrison Bankhead (b); Darryl Ervin (d); Richard Lawrence, Dr Cuz (perc).* 94.

***** 47th Street**

Delmark DE-497 *Thompson; Steve Berry (tb); Joe Ford (ss, as); Carter Jefferson, Billy Harper, Ron Bridgewater (ts); Kirk Brown (p); Harrison Bankhead, John Whitfield (b); Dana Hall, Nasar Abaday (d); Dr Cuz (perc); Marian Hayes, Mae Koen, Dianne Madison, Byron Woods, Dan Porter (v).* 4/93–9/96.

With 20 years of recording behind him and no real recognition on a world stage, Thompson has been quietly building up a catalogue of records for Delmark in his home base of Chicago. Despite a serious illness diagnosed as lymphoma in 1989, he has come back with a personal take on new Chicagoan developments which bespeaks a courageous outlook. If he is not an especially outstanding technician or any kind of innovator, his music is a skilled synthesis of several threads from the Chicagoan repertory.

That said, none of these discs really marks itself out from the others, and each has its share of disappointments as well as successes. *Spirit* dates from the early '80s and is relatively sketchy, but his long association with Carter Jefferson provides a confident front line and Dailey's dignified piano parts lend extra weight. *The Jaz Life* was almost a comeback album after his illness and peaks on the splendid swagger of Thompson's arrangement of the Ray Charles chestnut, 'Drown In My Own Tears'. *Lift Every Voice* is the first album to feature his big brass ensemble, which shares duties with his regular Freebop Band, and 'Elephantine Island' and 'Old Man River' make sonorous waves. Sometimes, though, it seems as if Thompson isn't sure what to do with the orchestra. He is back on safer ground with *New Standards*, which looks at some choice pieces of modern repertory. Freebop's slightly ragged edges are at least a change from the smart orthodoxy of most modern revivalists, but they could use a grain of extra finesse here and there. This was Jefferson's last album (he died in 1993) and his fine tenor improvisation on Booker Little's 'We Speak' is a poignant farewell.

Buddy Bolden's Rag brings back Africa Brass, with Bowie, Massey and Ari Brown as guests: Brown gets off a knockout solo on 'Harold The Great', Bowie makes some mysterious noises on a revised 'Nubian Call' and the brass play with real enthusiasm. Though one still feels that Thompson's collaring of this genre misses some of the visionary clout which Brass Fantasy has brought to this kind of big-band music, and the leader's own solos miss the ripe authority of Bowie himself, it's an entertaining set. *47th Street* is a dedication to Chicago's black community and the title-piece and 'Mystery Of Jaaz [*sic*] Suite' feature the singers, to rather merry effect. Thompson has a strong band here – though there are four tracks left over from 1993, including Jefferson's final recordings – and even if, as before, there's a faulty, sometimes unkempt feel to the ensembles, the music has spirit. Thompson's own playing seems to have got slower and more thoughtful, and hence more effective. His little chorus with the mute on 'CJ's Blues' is very beguiling.

***** Freebop Now!**

Delmark DE-506 *Thompson; Steve Berry (tb); Billy Harper, Sonny Seals, Carter Jefferson (ts); Oliver Lake (as); Kirk Brown (p); Harrison Bankhead, John Whitfield, James Cammack (b); Richard 'Drahseer' Smith, Nasar Abadey, Hamid Drake (d); Tony Carpenter (perc); Amiri Baraka, Larry Smith, Sharese Locke (v).* 4/93–5/98.

***** Rising Daystar**

Delmark DE-518 *Thompson; Steve Berry (tb); Gary Bartz (as, ss); Sonny Seals (ts); Kirk Brown (p); Harrison Bankhead, John Whitfield, James Cammack, Fred Hopkins (b); Dana Hall, Nasar Abadey (d); Tony Carpenter (perc); Dee Alexander (v).* 8/97–6/99.

Thompson continues an interesting if erratic series of discs. *Freebop Now!* is half good, and the good's mostly in the first half, with Berry and Harper turning in some spirited work in celebration of some 20 years of the Freebop Band. But the record turns awkward in the latter stages, with a long piece based around a science-fiction story which in turn is based on an Amiri Baraka poem. It's not something to return to.

Rising Daystar is a more conventional date, but Thompson should resist the temptation to try too many things over the course of a record. There are basically three different groups here, a quintet, a septet, and a trio in which Thompson flexes his bardic (and scat) chops over rhythms by Hopkins and Hall. 'Surrender Your Love' is a fairly hopeless stab at jazzing a pop-soul tune, vocalized by Alexander. Otherwise, playing honours are again taken by Bartz, Berry and Kirk Brown. Thompson himself leads from the front but, in a long solo like the one he takes on the title-tune, it suggests that he needs to pace himself better.

***** Timeline**

Delmark DE-421 *Thompson; Carter Jefferson, Sonny Seals, Jesse Taylor (ts); Harold Barney, Kirk Brown, Rafik Raheem (ky); Marvin Horn, John Thomas (g); Aaron Dodd (tba); James King, Paul Ramsey, Curtis Robinson Jr (b); Nasar Abadey, Greg Bandu, Bob Crowder, Bill Salter (d); Drake Colley, Penny Jeffries, Karen McPherson, Miambi Steele Scat City Singers, Bill Striggles (v).* 5/72–8/88.

A retrospective of Thompson's work in the '70s and '80s. A lot of it has dated badly: pseudo-fusion keyboards, singers and poetry that might best have been left in the notebook. Fine trumpet work is sometimes sidelined by the surroundings. At its best, however, in the most conventional small-band free-bop settings, all flourishes. The set is as much a tribute to Carter Jefferson as to Thompson, since the saxophonist has many of the best moments.

Sir Charles Thompson (born 1918)

PIANO

Journeyman pianist and arranger who worked for numerous leaders, on both the East and West coasts in the '40s and '50s.

One of the new 'mainstream' figures of the '50s, he visited Europe often in the '80s and has enjoyed an Indian summer of late with new recordings.

***** Hey There**

Black & Blue 922-2 *Thompson; Major Holley (b); Ed Thigpen (d).* 3/74.

***** Robbins' Nest Live At The Jazz Showcase**

Delmark DE-526 *Thompson; Art Hoyle (t); Eric Schneider (ts, as, cl); Eddie de Haas (b); Charles Braugham (d).* 8/00.

***** I Got Rhythm**

Delmark DG-537 *As above, except omit Hoyle.* 5/01.

Thompson's vintage sessions for Vanguard – harbingers of the entire mainstream style – have never been satisfactorily available on CD for very long, and share the now-you-see-them fate which seems to attend everything cut for that label. These later dates are one and two generations further along. Sir Charles is broadly in the Basie lineage but he's busier and heftier with it and, while he sustains the trio music plausibly enough, these aren't sensational records. The 1974 Black & Blue music benefits from a swinging performance by Ed Thigpen, which gets Thompson working harder than usual himself, and several of these pieces are pretty exciting. Twenty-six years on and into his 80s, the old man's still in good nick, opening with his great hit 'Robbins' Nest' and going through some standards and jazz pieces from his own heyday. The trio tracks are, in truth, nothing special at all, but when Schneider sits in on five tracks (and Hoyle on one) everything goes up a notch, his beefy sound really stirring the coals. He does the same thing on the subsequent set, recorded in the following year at the same venue.

Claude Thornhill (1909–65)

PIANO, ARRANGER

Formally trained, Thornhill began working for New York bands in the mid-'30s and led some groups of his own, before touring with his orchestra from 1940. After war service, he re-formed the orchestra in 1946; having already had an association with Gil Evans since the late '30s, he hired him and Gerry Mulligan to write many of the band's arrangements. Worked through the '50s with various-size groups, though playing dance music rather than jazz.

***** Snowfall**

Hep CD 1058 *Thornhill; Joe Ahuano, Ralph Harden, Bob Sprentall, Rusty Dedrick, Conrad Gozzo (t); Bob Jenney (tb, v); Tasso Harris (tb); Vincent Jacobs, Dick Hall (frhn); Irving Fazola (cl); Dale Brown, George Paulsen, Jack Ferrier, Bill Motley (cl, as); Hammond Russum, John Nelson (cl, ts); Hal Tennyson, Ted Goddard (cl, as, bs); Allen Hanlon (g); Don Whitaker, Harvey Sell (b); Gene Lemen, Ray Hagan, Nick Fatool (d); Dick Harding, Jane Essex, Kay Doyle (v).* 9/40–7/41.

***** Buster's Last Stand**

Hep CD 1074 *As above, except add Louis Mucci, Randy Brooks, Steve Steck, Jackie Koven (t), Buddy 'Bud' Smith (tb), Mike Glass (frhn), Danny Polo (cl), Bob Walters (cl, as), Carl Swift (cl, ts), Marty Berman (cl, bcl, bs), Buddy Dean (cl, bs), Conn Humphreys (as), Barry Galbraith, Chuck Robinson (g), Marty Blitz (b), Lou Fromm (d), Terry Allen, Buddy Stewart, Martha Wayne, Lillian Lane (v); omit Motley, Tennyson, Hanlon, Whitaker, Essex and Doyle.* 3/41–7/42.

****(*) Autumn Nocturne**

Hep CD 1060 *Similar to above two discs.* 8/41–2/42.

*****(*) The Transcription Performances 1947**

Hep CD 60 *Thornhill; Ed Zandy, Emil Terry, Louis Mucci, Paul Cohen, Red Rodney (t); Tak Takvorian, Allan Langstaff, John Torick (tb); Walt Weschler, Sandy Siegelstein, Al Anthony (frhn); Danny Polo, Lee Konitz (cl, as); Mickey Folus (cl, ts, bs); Mario Rollo (cl, ts); Bill Bushey (cl, bs); Barry Galbraith (g); Bill Barber (tba); Joe Schulman (b); Billy Exiner (d); Fran Warren, Gene Williams (v).* 9–12/47.

***** The 1948 Transcription Performances**

Hep CD 17 *Thornhill; Louis Mucci, Emil Terry, Ed Zandy, Johnny Vohs, Bob Peck, Johnny Carisi, Gene Roland (t); Allan Langstaff, Johnny Torick, Leon Cox (tb); Walter Weschler, Sandy Siegelstein, Al Antonucci, Addison Collins (frhn); Danny Polo, Lee Konitz, Gerry Mulligan, Mickey Folus, Jerry Sanfino, Brew Moore, Jet Rollo (reeds); Barry Galbraith, Joe Derise (g); Bill Barber (tba); Russ Saunders, Joe Shulman (b); Bill Exiner (d); The Snowflakes(v).* 4–10/48.

With the revival of interest in mood-music mandarins like Martin Denny and Arthur Lyman, it's not inconceivable that Thornhill's work could catch the ear of those seeking something in the classic easy-listening style. He was a pianist and arranger who formed a band in 1939, struggled with it for three years, then re-formed it after his war service. It was never a striking commercial success, though Thornhill's interest in a meticulousness of sound – subtle section-work, carefully filtered reed textures, the static bass harmony provided by Barber's tuba parts – resulted in little classics like his theme, 'Snowfall'. But his relationship to jazz is rather hazy, given the formalized tone of the band, and though there were major cool-school players in the orchestra and it features much of the early work of Gil Evans and Mulligan as arrangers, many of the recordings are exotically ephemeral.

The earliest studio recordings have been restored to print by Hep's excellent compilation, *Snowfall*, and from the first tracks it's clear why Thornhill was so popular with audiences seeking sweet music. There seems to be the scent of freesias and the feel of lace-work around such scores as 'Alt Wein' and 'Love Tales', dappled by the leader's piano. He stacks up clarinets, quietly, or threads the reed section around simple brass comments which can't even be called riffs. A piece such as 'Portrait Of A Guinea Farm' is as exotic as society music would ever get. 'Snowfall' itself is a flawless miniature. But there are also numerous vocal features, such as 'Mandy Is Two', which may bring on impatience in the listener. The sleeve-note suggests that Thornhill's band was 'too musical' to secure wider success, but that was not a problem which bothered such musical orchestras as Ellington or Goodman. *Buster's Last Stand* takes the story a step further, and though the track listing looks unpromising – 'Funiculi-Funicula', 'Pop Goes The Weasel' – these titles actually bring on some of the band's most spirited playing, with some surprising solos as well as strong ensemble work. Several of the 1942 sessions have a lugubrious feel which can be traced to the post-Pearl Harbor climate, but the title-piece, credited jointly to Evans and Thornhill and arranged by Evans, is extraordinary. Though ostensibly a straightforward riff-tune, it stands as a kind of homage to Basie (via Thornhill's deft piano interlude) and Ellington, played with almost shrill intensity.

Autumn Nocturne fills in more gaps, although it is probably the least interesting of the three sets in jazz terms: most of it is in Thornhill's primmest light-orchestral mode, and even the Gil Evans charts have very little going on.

The first volume of transcriptions is the best place to follow Thornhill's placid truce between jazz – either late swing or early bebop – and a more circumspect kind of orchestration. 'Robbins' Nest' is Basie done by stealth; 'Anthropology' is bebop tied up in a chocolate box. These are two of the 11 Gil Evans charts on the CD, intriguing examples of his early work and already showing departures from everyone else's thinking. There are also a couple of Gerry Mulligan arrangements, though these are somewhat green, and the rather raffish version of 'Oh You Beautiful Doll' shows that Thornhill had a sense of humour too. Hep CD 17 continues the story, with further transcriptions in excellent sound (better than that on the 1947 disc). There is a further treatment of 'Anthropology', Mulligan's first take on 'Godchild', and a number of standards relayed through the veils of sound which continued to be Thornhill's speciality. One feels, though, that the pieces he liked best were things like 'Spanish Dance', 'Adios' and 'La Paloma', where his aspirations to have a unique-sounding group weren't troubled by any mild leanings towards bop terminology. 'Royal Garden Blues' is a jazz standard almost as Mantovani might have played it. In the end, Thornhill's benign music is little more than an entertaining cul de sac.

Henry Threadgill (born 1944)

ALTO AND TENOR SAXOPHONES, CLARINET, BASS FLUTE

Describing an artist as 'uncategorizable' is both a feeble shorthand and a truism, but in the case of Henry Threadgill it's also an inevitable recourse, because the Chicagoan's dense, chewy music really is sui generis. Formerly leader of Air and New Air, he started to create denser and more carefully structured compositions in the '80s, using bizarre instrumentations and voicings, and yet his playing is always visceral and compelling.

*****(*) Spirit Of Nuff ... Nuff**

Black Saint 120134 *Threadgill; Curtis Fowlkes (tb); Edwin Rodriguez, Marcus Rojas (tba); Masujaa, Brandon Ross (g); Gene Lake (d).* n.d.

Threadgill's Very Very Circus appears to be the culmination of a cycle in his work. *Spirit of Nuff ... Nuff* (his titles are nothing if not enigmatic) deploys the band in a way that recalls '60s experiments with structures and free improvisation, but with far more discipline. Threadgill's writing has been quite muted in emotional timbre; 'Unrealistic Love', in which Threadgill's solo is announced by a long guitar passage, is typical. The arrangements on 'First Church Of This' (on which he plays flute) and 'Driving You Slow And Crazy' (which opens with a fractured chorale from the brasses) are consistently inventive, but it's increasingly clear that Threadgill, like Anthony Braxton, has now almost reached the limits of what he can do with a more or less conventional jazz instrumentation. It will be interesting to see whether he is able to develop a new instrumental idiom or whether he will choose – or be forced – to remain within the conventions.

*****(*) Song Out Of My Trees**

Black Saint 120 154 *Threadgill; Ted Daniel (t); Myra Melford (p); Amina Claudine Myers (org, hpd); James Emery, Ed Cherry, Brandon Ross (g); Dierdre Murray, Michelle Kinney (clo); Jerome Richardson (b); Gene Lake, Reggie Nicholson (d).* 8/93.

Song Out Of My Trees is for the most part dominated by strings, though the title-track is played over organ (Amina in testifyin' mood) and guitar. By using soprano and alto guitars in addition, tracks like 'Crea' take on a rich harmonic coloration that is quite difficult to pin down. On the superb 'Grief', Threadgill switches to a line-up of accordion, harpsichord and two cellos, a dazzling mixture of sounds and textures. Perhaps structural concerns have been downplayed to some extent here in the search for a new timbral language. It's a fascinating process to watch at close quarters, but slightly wearying after a few listens.

*****(*) Everybody's Mouth's A Book**

PI 1 *Threadgill; Brandon Ross (g); Bryan Carrot (vib, mar); Stomu Takeishi (b); Dafnis Prieto (d).* 01.

***** Up Popped The Two Lips**

PI 2 *Threadgill; Jose Davila (tba); Liberty Ellman(g); Tarik Benbrahim (oud); Dana Leon (clo); Dafnis Prieto (d).* 01.

The PI label has offered some patronage to a musician who has been fairly disastrously neglected by American labels and currently has scandalously little in the catalogues. Two sharply contrasting bands illustrate different stages of Threadgill's current practice. Make A Move is an amplified unit, hinged on Brandon Ross's and Stomu Takeishi's electric guitars and sounding not unlike a freaked-out version of Ornette's Prime Time, if such a thing is imaginable. The writing is as quirky and cranky as ever, with some delirious playing from the leader on alto and flute. 'Don't Turn Around' is amazing, a headlong flurry of sound from start to finish but governed as ever by Henry's unquantifiable musical vision.

The other group represented on these debut PI releases is Zoo-Id. It's a lighter and more acoustic sound, with an emphasis on strings and brasses, and the improvising language is even less obviously Western as a result; except when on 'Do The Needful', he seems to push early jazz through some strange prism. 'Dark Block' and 'Around My Goose' are somewhat confused stylistically. We are sceptical about *Up Popped The Two Lips*, but the Make a Move set is a winner.

The Three Sounds

GROUP

Formed in 1955, the group lasted until the '70s, playing light variations on bop and the blues and recording dozens of albums.

***** Black Orchid**

Blue Note 821289-2 *Gene Harris (p); Andy Simpkins (b); Bill Dowdy (d).* 2–6/62.

***** Standards**

Blue Note 821281-2 *As above.* 10/59–6/62.

At one time, every jazz label had a piano trio like this – Red Garland at Prestige, Erroll Garner at Columbia, Ramsey Lewis at Chess. Harris, Simpkins and Dowdy were the Blue Note version. Standards, simple variations on the blues or mild gospelesque outings, a steady, steady tempo that the drummer simply ticked off on number after number, and the pianist never letting the melody get too far away from the listener. This is as easy-going as jazz after bebop has ever been, and it's undeniably pleasant on the ear. But it's hard to imagine anyone wanting more than one Three Sounds album, as popular as they were; and even though vintage Blue Note vinyl remains in high demand among collectors, this is the group that nobody much collects. One reason is, they recorded an awful lot of sessions for the label. The original programme for *Black Orchid* has been expanded with seven previously unissued tracks, doubling the length of the disc, while *Standards* has nearly an hour of never-before-released. It is all much the same as everything else they did, and Harris carried on in much the same vein for Concord. The Three Sounds are perhaps the one remaining Blue Note group yet to be accorded extensive CD restoration – surely it can't be for much longer.

Steve Tibbetts (born 1954)

GUITAR, MANDOLIN, SITAR, KEYBOARDS, KALIMBA

Based in St Paul, Minnesota, Tibbetts is a guitar-impressionist, creating big aural landscapes using electronic and studio enhancements, with regular collaborator Marc Anderson doing rhythmic duties.

****(*) Northern Song**
ECM 829378-2 *Tibbetts; Marc Anderson (perc).* 10/81.

***** Bye Bye Safe Journey**
ECM 817438-2 *Tibbetts; Bob Hughes (b); Marc Anderson, Steve Cochrane, Tim Wienhold (perc).* 83.

***** Yr**
ECM 835245-2 *As above.* 80.

***** Exploded View**
ECM 831109-2 *As above, except add Marcus Hughes (perc), Claudia Schmidt, Bruce Henry, Jan Reimer (v); omit Cochrane and Wienhold.* 85–86.

***** Big Map Idea**
ECM 839253-2 *Tibbetts; Michelle Kinney (clo); Marc Anderson, Marcus Wise (perc).* 87–88.

*****(*) The Fall Of Us All**
ECM 521144-2 *As above, except add Mike Olson (syn), Jim Anton, Eric Anderson (b), Claudia Schmidt, Rhea Valentine (v); omit Kinney.* 93.

Steve Tibbetts and Marc Anderson are musicians whose methodical, dreamy patchworks of guitars and percussion are surprisingly invigorating, taken a record at a time. Tibbetts's favourite device is to lay long, skirling electric solos over a bed of congas and acoustic guitars; at its best, the music attains a genuinely mesmeric quality. While their pieces are mostly short in duration, an interview included in the notes to *Big Map Idea* reveals that many are excerpts from much longer jamming situations, and Tibbetts's self-deprecating stance – 'When I tape four hours of sound, only ten minutes have any potential, and only 30 seconds ends up being used' – is refreshing. Anderson is clearly as important an influence in the music, and his pattering, insinuating rhythms are an appealing change from the usual indiscriminate throb of world-music situations. *Bye Bye Safe Journey* is perhaps the best of the earlier albums: Tibbetts plays at his most forceful and there's very little slack in the music. 'Running', which features the ingenious use of a tape of a child running, shows how inventively Tibbetts can use found sound. *Yr* is a reissue of his first album, previously available on an independent label, and *Northern Song* is a bit too quiet and rarefied. *Big Map Idea* opens with a charming treatment of Led Zeppelin's 'Black Dog' and, although some of the tracks suggest that Tibbetts has been listening to Bill Frisell – dreaminess overtaking the rhythmic impetus at times – it is a landscape of his own.

In a way, Tibbetts and Anderson are as consistent as a hard-bop band: the differences between their records are more a matter of nuance and small variation than of any dramatic development. *Exploded View* and *Big Map Idea* continued the run of their '80s work with patient inevitability, the tracks following one another like a sequence of snapshots or episodes from work in progress. The only striking difference was a greater interest in the use of (wordless) voices. *The Fall Of Us All*, Tibbetts's first album of the '90s, sounds bigger and more powerful than anything that went before. Rhythm is the presiding element for much of the record, Anderson playing a grander role than ever before, and the big, digital soundstage is nearly overwhelming at times. This is large-scale impressionism, and in 'Full Moon Dogs' or 'All For Nothing' Tibbetts has created some of his most imposing and vivid music.

***** A**
Hannibal HNCD 1438 *Tibbetts; Knut Hamre (hardingfele); Turid Spildo (hardingfele, v); John Siegfried (hp, b); Steve Hassett (p); Ray Gilles (jublang, suling); Karla Ackerman (vn); Amy Morton (vla); Emily Khorana (clo); Anthony Cox (b); Marc Anderson (d).* 99.

Tibbetts on his travels again, this time to Norway for a meeting with the Hardanger fiddle-player, Knut Hamre. The droning sound of the two hardingfele players is austerely beguiling, and for once Tibbetts is rather outdone in terms of texture: these multi-string instruments really do muster orchestral sonority by themselves. That said, the record could use a little injection of pace, or something to outflank the fiddles, since they will eventually weary any who are less than devoted to the style.

*****(*) A Man About A Horse**
ECM 1814 *Tibbetts; Jim Anton (b); Marc Anderson, Marcus Wise (perc).* n.d.

His first ECM record in a decade – and it's as if he's picking up where *The Fall Of Us All* left off. Mighty, big-sky soundscapes, great guitar washes over polyrhythmic flow, with studio resources used to simply build and build the gestures into towering statements. It sounds formulaic, and it is – but it would be hard to mistake this music for anyone else's, and it shows how sensitive and idiosyncratic Tibbetts's work really is. A welcome return.

Bobby Timmons (1935–74)

PIANO, ORGAN, VIBRAPHONE

If he had done nothing else in his short career, Timmons would have been guaranteed immortality for writing 'Moanin'', the gospelly tune that became a Jazz Messengers hit. Otherwise a permanent underachiever, haunted by self-doubt and alcoholism, the Philadelphian rarely lived up to his potential.

***** This Here Is Bobby Timmons**
Original Jazz Classics OJC 104 *Timmons; Sam Jones (b); Jimmy Cobb (d).* 1/60.

*** **Easy Does It**
Original Jazz Classics OJC 722 *As above.* 3/61.

*** **Soul Time**
Original Jazz Classics OJC 820 *Timmons; Blue Mitchell (t); Sam Jones (b); Art Blakey (d).* 8/60.

***(*) **In Person**
Original Jazz Classics OJC 364 *Timmons; Ron Carter (b); Albert 'Tootie' Heath (d).* 10/61.

*** **Sweet And Soulful Sounds**
Original Jazz Classics OJC 928 *Timmons; Sam Jones (b); Roy McCurdy (d).* 6–7/62.

***(*) **Born To Be Blue**
Original Jazz Classics OJC 873 *Timmons; Ron Carter, Sam Jones (b); Connie Kay (d).* 8–9/63.

*** **The Prestige Trio Sessions**
Prestige 24277-2 *Timmons; Sam Jones, Keter Betts (b); Ray Lucas, Tootie Heath (d).* 6–8/64.

*** **Workin' Out**
Prestige 24143-2 *Timmons; Wayne Shorter (ts); Johnny Lytle (vib); Keter Betts, Ron Carter (b); Jimmy Cobb, William Peppy Hinnant (d).* 10/64–1/66.

*** **From The Bottom**
Original Jazz Classics OJC 1032 *Timmons; Sam Jones (b); Jimmy Cobb (d).* 64.

** **Quartets And Orchestra**
Milestone 47091-2 *Timmons; Jimmy Owens (t, flhn); Hubert Laws (f, ts); James Moody (ts, asa, f); Joe Farrell (ss, ts, f); George Barrow (bs); Eric Gale, Howard Collins, Joe Beck (g); Ron Carter, Bob Cranshaw (b); Billy Higgins, Jimmy Cobb, Jack DeJohnette (d).* 67–68.

This Here is a pun on 'Dat Dere', Timmons's second-best-known tune, to which Oscar Brown Jr subsequently added a lyric. Timmons will for ever be remembered, though, as the composer of 'Moanin'', recorded by the Jazz Messengers in 1958 on a marvellous album of that name and a staple of live performances thereafter. *This Here* was recorded two years later, just before his second stint with Art Blakey. It features both the hit tracks; as a disc, it is probably less good value than a now-deleted Milestone compilation, also called *Moanin'*, which includes material from the January 1960 session, together with excellent tracks recorded over the next three years. *Easy Does It* is slightly shop-soiled and untidy round the edges, though 'Groovin' High' is splendid. Only those who really appreciate Timmons's piano-playing need consider it a priority purchase.

Timmons's characteristic style was a rolling, gospelly funk, perhaps longer on sheer energy than on harmonic sophistication. The live *In Person* is surprisingly restrained, though Timmons takes 'Autumn Leaves' and 'Softly, As In A Morning Sunrise' at an unfamiliar tempo. The drummer is probably better suited to Timmons's style than Cobb, but there's nothing between Carter and Jones. Timmons's handling of more delicate material here is rather better than expected and certainly better than on *This Here*; there, 'My Funny Valentine' (also on the Milestone *Moanin'*) and 'Prelude To A Kiss' leave a lot to be desired, and the unaccompanied 'Lush Life' (a song whose subject-matter was rather close to home) is uncomfortably slewed. Traces of Bud Powell in his approach at this time slowly disappeared over the next few years. 'Sometimes I Feel Like A Motherless Child', from an August 1963 session on the Milestone *Moanin'*, is perhaps the most typical if not the best trio performance on record.

Timmons never sounds quite right in a group with horns, which is why *Soul Time* and the Prestige material with a young Wayne Shorter seem so unsatisfactory. There are excellent things on *Born To Be Blue* and on *Sweet And Soulful Sounds*, and there are even things to take out of *From The Bottom* where Bobby turns to organ for a retread of 'Moanin'' and to vibes for the delightfully paced 'Quiet Nights' and 'Someone To Watch Over Me'. These were recordings made late in the Riverside story and not released until some time later; they have had to wait even longer for CD reissue. *Prestige Trio Sessions* doubles up a couple of albums which had a negligible impact at the time. Timmons sounds good, playing bluesy variations on the soul-jazz formula, but he never makes as much of an impression as Horace Silver in this repertoire and he can't muster Red Garland's implacable calm.

Quartets And Orchestra is a sad finale. The 'orchestra' session has negligible charts by Tom McIntosh and cooing (unidentified) singers on '60s pop material, while the quartet music is better, but still profoundly uneventful.

Keith Tippett (born 1947)

PIANO, OTHER INSTRUMENTS

Bristol-born Tippett has been a key figure of the British avant-garde for more than 30 years. He played bebop and traditional jazz before attempting a more experimental course with his own groups, Ovary Lodge, Ark and the huge Centipede; more recently he has been a key member of the improvising group Mujician. He also worked with Amalgam, Ninesense and other leaders' groups, but gradually his distinctive approach came to be focused on solo performance, using spontaneous 'preparations' to turn his piano into a whole orchestra of effects. Some of his work has veered towards classical composition, but his basic language is undetermined by any organizing principle except his unfailing sense of beauty.

(*) **You Are Here ... I Am There
Disconforme 226 *Tippett; Marc Charig (c); Nick Evans (tb); Elton Dean (as); Jeff Clyne (b); Alan Jackson (d).* 69.

*** **Dedicated To You, But You Weren't Listening**
Disconforme 227 *Tippett; Marc Charig (c); Nick Evans (tb); Elton Dean (as); Gary Boyle (g); Roy Babbington, Neville Whithead (b); Phil Howard, Bryan Spring, Robert Wyatt (d); Tony Uta (perc).* 71.

Though routinely likened to Cecil Taylor (he actually *sounds* much more like Jaki Byard), Tippett is unique among contemporary piano improvisers. He shows little interest in linear or thematic development but creates huge, athematic improvisations which juxtapose darks and lights, open-textured single-note passages and huge, triple-*f* *ostinati* in the lowest register. On *Mujician III*, his most accomplished work, these sustained rumbles persist so long that the mind is drawn inexorably towards tiny chinks in the darkness, like points of light in a night sky.

His first album, *You Are Here ... I Am There* was a disappointment, though it's a collectable item these days. Its reappearance helps complete a picture of Tippett poised between rock and jazz. Apart from Dean's 'Stately Dance For Miss Primm', there's a strained cast to much of the music, possibly too ambitious for its own good, but not yet with the breadth of vision or the responsive players needed to lift it. The next album is much more like the thing, a set that paves the way for the ambitious big, bigger and biggest band experiments of the next few years. When critics discuss the harmonic inventiveness of modern jazz and the experiments of big-band composers on both sides of the Atlantic (and sometimes composers who've made an Atlantic voyage), no one ever mentions pieces like 'Gridal Suite' (an Elton Dean term) and 'Green And Orange Night Park' on this hugely underrated record. Tippett knew the sound he was after and knew the players who might deliver it. This was his first real attempt to go after it. It's more than a historical document – it is genuinely involving jazz.

***** Septober Energy**

Disconforme 1034 *Tippett; Marc Charig (c); Nick Evans (tb); Elton Dean, Dudu Pukwana (as); Karl Jenkins, Gary Windo (reeds); John Marshall, Robert Wyatt (d); many (!) others.* 71.

A masterwork or a shambles, depending on your point of view. The idea was to assemble an ensemble of 50 players (called Centipede: 100 legs) to follow through Tippett's vision of a massive free-jazz ensemble that would have the friendly spontaneity of a small group. It didn't quite work out like that, but it was a magnificent achievement in its way. We've found it more or less unlistenable now, and it's a record that's more talked about than listened to, but we cherish it as a unique moment in modern British music.

*****(*) Frames: Music For An Imaginary Film**

Ogun 010/011 2CD *Tippett; Marc Charig (t, thn, thumb p); Henry Lowther (t); Dave Amis, Nick Evans (tb); Elton Dean (as, saxello); Trevor Watts (as, ss); Brian Smith (ts, ss, af); Larry Stabbins (ts, ss, f); Stan Tracey (p); Steve Levine, Rod Skeaping, Philipp Wachsmann, Geoffrey Wharton (vn); Tim Kramer, Alexandra Robinson (clo); Peter Kowald (b, tba); Harry Miller (b); Louis Moholo (d); Frank Perry (perc); Maggie Nicols, Julie Tippetts (v).* 5/78.

The reappearance of *Frames* was the first in a wave of valuable Tippett reissues, where previously the discography had depended almost entirely on his solo recordings. Like Centipede, the big band he called Ark went in pairs of players, a huge, warm-hearted sound which has been expertly remastered by Steve Beresford. This vast soundtrack in four parts has the seamless, orchestral quality of the solo performances, but with a vastly enlarged palette of sound. Pointless to identify soloists in music as selfless as this, but a word for the twinned basses of Peter Kowald and the late Harry Miller near the beginning, and for the astonishing percussion-plus-electric-violin passage that begins Part Two, originally the second side of the LP release. All in all a staggering record, one of the very finest large-scale projects to be released in Britain in the craven, cowardly '70s.

****** Mujician I / II**

FMP CD 56 *Tippett (p solo).* 12/81, 6/86.

****** Mujician III (August Air)**

FMP CD 12 *As above.* 6/87.

*****(*) Une Croix Dans L'Océan**

Victo CD 046 *As above.* 95.

Though he is still remembered for such quixotic projects as the 50-strong Centipede band, for whom he wrote *Septober Energy*, and for the later Ark, Tippett is still best heard as a solo and duo performer. It may turn out that the three *Mujician* albums made for FMP during the '80s (the word was his daughter's childish version of her father's vocation) will be regarded as among the most self-consistent and beautiful solo improvisations of the decade and a significant reprogramming of the language of piano. Though there are unmistakable gestures to the presence of Cecil Taylor (especially on the first album), the differences of basic conception could hardly be greater.

Tippett has always insisted that listeners should not concern themselves with *how* particular sounds are made in his performances, but absorb themselves in what he clearly sees as a highly emotional and spontaneous process in which 'technique' is not separable from the more instinctual aspects of the music. In addition to now relatively conventional practices like playing 'inside', he makes use of distinctive sound-altering devices, such as laying wood blocks and metal bars on the strings, producing zither and koto effects. Though there are similarities, this is very different from John Cage's use of 'prepared piano'. Cage's effects, once installed, are immutable; Tippett's are spontaneous and flexible.

The long 'August Air' is one of the essential performances of the decade. It seems to complete a cycle whose development can only be experienced and intuited, not rationalized. The transfer of the two first *Mujician* discs to CD allows the sequence to be heard as a whole and, though a goodly span of time separates the three records, they make sense heard as a continuous sequence, an extended dialogue with the piano and with Tippett's musical sources. These are beautiful records, unaffected and sincere, though not so laden with ego that they make sense only as confessionals.

*****(*) Twilight Etchings**

FMP CD 65 *Tippett; Willi Kellers (d); Julie Tippett (v).* 10/93.

****** Couple In Spirit II**

ASC CD 12 *Tippett; Julie Tippett (v).* 96.

Though the British label ASC have finally done something to redress the scandalous lack of interest in Tippett's work back home, it should be said that both of these records were recorded in Germany, at the Total Music Meeting in Berlin in 1993 and at the Stadtgarten in Cologne, now a key venue for new music, three years later. Tippett's performances with his wife Julie are always rather special, and both of these records bespeak the closest empathy and understanding. The addition of Kellers does nothing to blunt it, and indeed he seems to have an intuitive grasp of what drives these two deeply committed musicians, adding his own commentaries, his wilfully insistent pulse and his unfailing instinct for the appropriate gesture. Two very good records; not Tippett at his best or most characteristic, but well worth having.

***** Friday The 13th**

Resurgent 4737 *Tippett (p solo).* 6/97.

One of the most majestic and sonorous of Tippett's solo piano performances, this one was recorded in Japan, where you might have expected him to reduce the dynamics and play in the quieter, filigree mode he sometimes favours. Not a bit of it. From the opening, Keith pounds away at the bass end, creating a tidal wave of sound far more impressive than the Hokusai image of Fuji about to be swamped. It's also a very beautiful recording, which delivers its subtleties slowly and almost covertly.

***** Linuckea**

FMR CD70 0600 *Tippett; Christopher George, David Le Page (vn); Malcolm Allison (vla); Philip Sheppard (clo); Martha Sheppard (v).* 3/00.

Tippett has long been drawn towards a more classical idiom and this long-form piece – 'Linuckea' weighs in at 36 minutes, the other item, 'Let The Music Speak', at less than ten – is an intriguing exploration of piano with string quartet. All the signature Tippett devices are present: rolling melodic figures, pure sound and some treatment of the piano; but what is striking is how much more formal and architectural he sounds in this context. The recording quality is superb and Tippett is ideally balanced with the quartet.

Cal Tjader (1925–82)

VIBRAPHONE, DRUMS, PERCUSSION, VOCAL

Though originally from St Louis, Tjader based himself in California and, after high-profile stints with Dave Brubeck and George Shearing, led his own groups from 1954. His essentially lightweight blend of Latin, Cuban and bebop styles became popular in the late '50s and '60s, and he helped pioneer the salsa idiom, at least from a jazz perspective. His many records kept him in the public ear, but he died in Manila at only 56.

***** Extremes**

Fantasy 24764 *Tjader; Allen Smith (t); Vince Guaraldi, John Marabuto, Hank Jones (p); Jack Weeks, Monty Budwig (b); Shelly Manne (d).* 8/51–9/77.

***** Mambo With Tjader**

Original Jazz Classics OJC 271 *Tjader; Manuel Duran (p); Carlos Duran (b); Edgard Rosalies, Bayardo Velarde (perc).* 9/54.

***** Tjader Plays Mambo**

Original Jazz Classics OJC 274 *Tjader; Dick Collins, John Howell, Al Porcino, Charlie Walp (t); Manuel Duran (p); Carlos Duran (b); Edgard Rosalies, Bayardo Verlade (perc).* 8–9/54.

***** Tjader Plays Tjazz**

Original Jazz Classics OJC 988 *Tjader; Bob Collins (tb); Brew Moore (ts); Sonny Clark (p); Eddie Duran (g); Al McKibbon (b); Eugene Wright (vib); Bobby White (d).* 12/54–6/55.

***** Los Ritmos Calientes**

Fantasy FCD-24712-2 *Tjader; Joe Silva (ts); Jerry Sanfino, Jerome Richardson (f); Vince Guaraldi, Richard Wyands, Manuel Duran (p); Al McKibbon, Bob Rodriguez, Eugene Wright (b); Roy Haynes, Al Torres (d); Willie Bobo, Armando Peraza, Luis Kant, Armando Sanchez, Mongo Santamaria, Bayardo Velarde (perc).* 54–57.

***** Black Orchid**

Fantasy FCD-24730-2 *Similar to above, except add Paul Horn (f), Luis Miranda (perc).* 54–57.

***** Cal Tjader Quartet**

Original Jazz Classics OJC 891 *Tjader; Gerald Wiggins (p); Eugene Wright (b); Bill Douglass (d).* 5/56.

***** Latin Kick**

Original Jazz Classics OJC 642 *Tjader; Brew Moore (ts); Manuel Duran (p); Carlos Duran (b); Luis Miranda, Bayardo Velarde (perc).* 56.

****(*) Jazz At The Blackhawk**

Original Jazz Classics OJC 436 *Tjader; Vince Guaraldi (p); Gene Wright (b); Al Torres (d).* 1/57.

**** Latin Concert**

Original Jazz Classics OJC 643 *Tjader; Vince Guaraldi (p); Al McKibbon (b); Willie Bobo, Mongo Santamaria (perc); strings.* 9/58.

***** Monterey Concerts**

Prestige P24026 *Tjader; Paul Horn (f); Lonnie Hewitt (p); Al McKibbon (b); Willie Bobo, Mongo Santamaria (perc).* 4/59.

***** Blackhawk Nights**

Fantasy 24755 *Tjader; Jose 'Chombo' Silva (ts); Vince Guaraldi, Lonnie Hewitt (p); Al McKibbon, Victor Venegas (b); Willie Bobo (d); Mongo Santamaria (perc).* 59.

***** Plays Harold Arlen & West Side Story**

Fantasy 24775-2 *Tjader; Buddy Motsinger (p); Al McKibbon, Red Mitchell (b); Willie Bobo, Johnnie Rae (d); orchestra arranged by Clare Fischer.* 6–10/60.

Cal Tjader was a great popularizer whose musical mind ran rather deeper than some have allowed. As a vibes-player, he was an able and not quite outstanding soloist, but his interest in Latin rhythms and their potential for blending with West Coast jazz was a genuine one, and his best records have a jaunty and informed atmosphere which denigrates neither side of the fusion. He made a lot of records, and many of them have been awarded reissue, which makes it difficult to choose particular winners. Tjader helped to break Willie Bobo and Mongo Santamaria to wider audiences, and the steps towards an almost pure salsa sound are documented on most of the records listed above. The earlier records are feet-finding, in a way, but they have a freshness which later became more of a routine. Tjader plays either vibes or percussion, but he's the kit drummer on *Tjader Plays Tjazz*, which has four very flat ballad features for quartet but sparkles a bit more on six quintet tunes with Sonny Clark and Brew Moore. Tjader's excellent solo on 'Jeepers Creepers' shows how good he could be in a straightahead small band, but that was not his destiny. *Cal Tjader Quartet* is the most conventional of all his records, but in the end it's little more than a capable vibes-plus-rhythm date.

Latin Kick, which has Brew Moore again guesting on tenor, is a good one, and *Jazz At The Blackhawk* is another un-Latin event in which Tjader sounds at ease on standard material. *Blackhawk Nights* couples the original *A Night At The Blackhawk* with *Live And Direct*, which is at least a moneysaving option. Tjader's live recordings aren't much more charged than his studio ones and display how he relied as heavily on bop language as anything 'Latin'. *Latin Concert*, though, starts to run the formula down, and the intrusion of strings marks the inevitable move towards wallpaper which Tjader seemed shameless enough about later on. Two recent compilations, *Los Ritmos Calientes* and *Black Orchid*, collect the residue of Tjader's Fantasy sessions from the period, and they're effectively split between authentic Latin themes (on Fantasy 24712) and Tjaderized jazz and show-tune standards (Fantasy 24730). Not bad. A new arrival is *Plays Harold Arlen & West Side Story*, which couples the two sessions suggested by the title. The first is a typical Tjaderization of the Arlen songbook, but the second finds him secreted within Clare Fischer arangements for a full orchestra, and the results, if you can imagine it, are like an astringent lounge music.

Extremes is an interesting conceit on Fantasy's part. It couples Tjader's first two sessions, which were issued as a single ten-inch LP, with his last for the label, *Breathe Easy*, which was originally released in 1977. The early tracks have a novelty feel to them, with Tjader playing bongos on one track and kit drums on another, and they're over very quickly. The later session has elements of prototype-smooth about it, with Hank Jones on electric piano part of the time, but some of it ('When Lights Are Low' especially) is much more vigorous, and it's all so melodious that it stands fast.

***** El Sonido Nuevo**

Verve 519812-2 *Tjader; Barry Rogers (tb, perc); Julian Priester, Jose Rodriguez, Mark Weinstein (tb); George Castro (f, perc); Jerry Dodgion (f); Derek Smith (org); Lonnie Hewitt, Chick Corea, Eddie Palmieri, Al Zulaica (p); unknown (g); Stan Appelbaum (cel); Bobby Rodriguez, Stan Gilbert, George Duvivier (b); Tommy Lopez, Manny Oquendo, Carl Burnett, Grady Tate (d); Armando Peraza, Ismael Quintana, Ray Barretto (perc).* 11/63–3/67.

Held in high esteem as the album which commenced the real fusion of Latin and jazz called salsa, *El Sonido Nuevo* (here with six extra tracks picked from *Breeze From The East* and the otherwise unavailable *Along Comes Cal*) draws its power more from pianist Eddie Palmieri and his arrangements than anything Tjader does. The title-track illustrates the difference: Tjader embellishes the percussive onslaught below with pretty figures, then Palmieri comes in and intensifies it with his hard, percussive piano parts. Many of the tracks are still too short, in the fashion of the day, and one longs for a decisive blast from the ensemble; but next to much of Tjader's work it's impressive. The bonus tracks are softer and a good deal sweeter.

**** Amazonas**

Original Jazz Classics OJC 840 *Tjader; Raul De Souza (tb); Hermeto Pascoal (f); Egberto Gismonti, Dawilli Gonga (ky); Aloisio Milanez (p); David Amaro (g); Lis Alves (b); Roberto Silva (d).* 6/75.

****(*) The Grace Cathedral Concert**

Fantasy 9677 *Tjader; Lonnie Hewitt (p); Rob Fisher (b); Pete Riso (d); Poncho Sanchez (perc).* 5/76.

***** Here And There**

Fantasy 24743 *Tjader; Clare Fischer (p); Bob Redfield (g); Rob Fisher (b); Pete Riso (d); Poncho Sanchez, Carmelo Garcia (perc).* 9/76–6/77.

*****(*) Cuban Fantasy**

Fantasy 24777-2 *As above, except omit Garcia.* 6/77.

****(*) La Onda Va Bien**

Concord CCD 4113 *Tjader; Roger Glenn (f, perc); Mark Levine (p); Rob Fisher (b); Vince Lateano (d); Poncho Sanchez (perc).* 7/79.

Tjader returned to Fantasy in 1970, after his spell with Verve, and pretty much picked up where he'd left off. *Amazonas* includes heavyweights like Pascoal and Gismonti in the group, but it's flimsy stuff. *Here And There* couples the original LPs *Guarabe* and *Here*, the former studio, the latter live; this was an effective partnership with Fischer, even if the material sticks to Tjader's preference for the soft option. However, the leftover live tracks which make up *Cuban Fantasy* push the more polite music of the studio albums to one side and really hit a very hot groove: this has claims to be one of the best of Tjader's later sessions, even if the music didn't emerge until 2004! The cathedral concert, though, is another lightweight match.

Tjader had something of a comeback when he joined Concord, though the music wasn't that different from what he'd been doing 20 years earlier. Cleaner, crisper recording and highly schooled musicianship put a patina of class on these records, but it still emerges as high-octane muzak from track to track.

*****(*) Cal Tjader's Greatest Hits**

Fantasy 24736 *Tjader, plus personnel as Fantasy and OJC albums listed above.* 54–76.

Purists may prefer *El Sonido Nuevo*, but for us this is the Tjader album to have, 20 of his most characteristic pieces covering the modest spectrum of his work.

Skeets Tolbert (1910–?)

CLARINET, ALTO SAXOPHONE, VOCAL

Born in Charlotte, North Carolina, Tolbert moved to New York and gigged around during the early '30s. He formed his 'Gentlemen Of Swing' in 1939 and made a success of the group until he decided to move to Houston, Texas, in the mid-'40s, when he became involved in union work and teaching rather than playing.

***** Skeets Tolbert 1931–1940**

Classics 978 *Tolbert; Lester Mitchell, Joe Jordan, Carl Smith (t); Leslie Johnakins (as, bs); Lem Johnson (ts, cl); Otis Hicks, Ernest Parham (ts); Freddy Jefferson, Jimmy Gunn, Clarence Easter, Red Richards (p); Guy Harrington (bj, v); Harry Prather (tba, b); Bill Hart, Hubert Pettaway (d); Babe Hines, Babe Wallace (v).* 5/31–3/40.

***** Skeets Tolbert 1940–1942**

Classics 993 *As above, except add Wingy Carpenter (t, v), Buddy Johnson, Herbert Goodwin (p), John Drummond (b), Larry Hinton (d), Nora Lee King, Jean Eldridge, Yack Taylor (v); omit Johnakins, Mitchell, Jordan, Jefferson, Gunn, Easter, Harrington, Prather, Hart, Hines and Wallace.* 10/40–7/42.

An interesting footnote in New York's swing era, Tolbert's career on record began with the territory band of Dave Taylor, who cut the two early tracks which start the first Classics CD. The remaining sides on both CDs are very different: up-market, black, small-group swing. Tolbert's style is a polished variation on the kind of material that might otherwise have gone to Fats Waller or Louis Jordan. His groups were drilled but relaxed outfits and they featured some good players: the outstanding one is probably trumpeter Carl 'Tatti' Smith, but Tolbert himself was no slouch on alto, and the rhythm sections are able, swinging teams. Wingy Carpenter turns up on two later sessions and Buddy Johnson is on one. When they play a blues, as on 'Harlem Ain't What It Used To Be' (an ironic title, since Tolbert never played in Harlem), they do it with some sensitivity, not slickness. Most of the material is made up of relatively undistinguished novelty songs, but nothing descends to any sort of embarrassment and Tolbert's music had no mugging in it. Taken a few tracks at a time, these are very enjoyable records and, since the originals are rather rare and little-known, this is an excellent initiative by Classics.

Viktoria Tolstoy

VOCAL

Swedish singer who started out in the standards suit and has moved on to originals.

*****(*) Blame It On My Youth**

Kaza/EMI 532620-2 *Tolstoy; Jakob Karlzon (p, org vib, marim); Mattias Svensson (b); Rasmus Kihlberg (d); strings.* 7/01.

***** Shining On You**

ACT 9701-2 *Tolstoy; Nils Landgren (tb, v); Toots Thielemans (hca); Bror Falk, Esbjörn Svensson, Daniel Karlsson (p); Lars Danielsson (clo, b); Christian Spering, Dan Berglund (b); Wolfgang Haffner, Jonas Holgersson, Magnus Ostrom (d); strings.* 6–9/03.

Though she looks like the classic Swedish blonde, Tolstoy's voice isn't in the ice-maiden bracket and she has a firm, clear style which doesn't go in for affectation. *Blame It On My Youth* is mostly standards, but gains individuality from Joakim Milder's inventive production and the superb playing by Karlzon's trio – as well as the singer's communion with the material. 'Midnight Sun' gets an imaginative and dramatic reworking, the title-piece is very well sung, and though we could have done without Elvis Costello's hateful 'Baby Plays Around' there aren't many steps that could be counted as false.

The ACT album is all originals and is, unfortunately, much more chilly. Esbjörn Svensson wrote the music and it's not quite as interesting as his trio material. Tolstoy does her best with it and at least it gravitates towards art song rather than mere pop material.

Tolvan Big Band

GROUP

Contemporary Swedish big band, drawing its personnel mainly from the region around Malmö; directed since 1979 by saxophonist Helge Albin.

****** Plays The Music Of Helge Albin**

Naxos Jazz 86025-2 *Peter Asplund (t, flhn); Roy Wall, Anders Gustavsson, Christer Gustavsson, Fredrik Davidsson (t); Vincent Nilsson, Olle Tull, Ola Akerman, Ole Nordqvist (tb); Björn Hängsel (btb); Per Bäcker, Helge Albin (as, f); Cennet Jönsson (ss, ts, bcl); Inge Petersson (ts, f); Bernt Sjunnesson (bs, f); Jorgen Emborg (p); Lars Danielsson (b); Lennart Gruvstedt (d).* 11/97.

Anyone ever caught raising an eyebrow at the idea of Swedish big bands competing with the rest of the jazz world might do well to ponder the attention-grabber slipped into these sleeve-notes: that Sweden, a country with fewer people than New York City, is home to 500 big bands. Hard to say where the Tolvan crew rank in the list, but it must be pretty close to the top, and it's disappointing that at present their occasional records have largely slipped into obscurity. At least Naxos here snapped up a terrific session for their 'new' jazz label, which unfortunately they have since abandoned. Helge Albin wrote everything here and it is as rich, eventful and satisfying an orchestral record as you could wish to find in the current jazz environment. Albin keeps everyone on their toes by involving the orchestra as a constantly shifting entity, sections working together or in contrast, brass and reeds in sumptuous counterpoint or brawling opposition and, though he is missing a couple of the best soloists from the earlier records, there is ample compensation in the presence of Asplund. At Naxos price, an outrageous bargain – but get it before it disappears.

Alan Tomlinson

TROMBONE

A brilliant deconstructionist of his instrument, Tomlinson plays free improvisation with humour, intelligence and real delicacy.

***** Trap Street**

Emanem 4092 *Tomlinson; Steve Beresford (elec); Roger Turner (d, perc).* 02.

Astonishingly, this is Tomlinson's first album for more than 20 years. It is strictly a trio project, but Beresford and Turner are somewhat better represented on record and *Trap Street* offers what for some will be a first glimpse of the trombonist's technique, which is not so much extended as elastically stretched.

He conjures a vast range of sounds from his instrument, few of them conventionally associated with brass playing. There are clicks, whistles and long, flatulent tones; more rarely, he explores the trombone's vocal properties with what sounds like rarefied speech. Beresford is a brilliant pianist and arranger, but here he concentrates on tiny electronic effects, while Turner largely gives his drum kit the day off and contents himself with a grab-bag of sound-producing objects.

The tracks, named after London postal districts, are short but not enigmatically so. Each seems to have its own logic and its own natural duration. Like label-mate Paul Rutherford (also grievously under-recorded as a solo artist), Tomlinson has managed to combine abstract improvisation with genuine drama and feeling.

Jim Tomlinson

TENOR SAXOPHONE

Young British tenorman whose style is bound up in the cool, post-Lester saxophone manner.

***** Only Trust Your Heart**

Candid CCD 79758 *Tomlinson; Guy Barker (t); John Pearce (p); Colin Oxley (g); Simon Thorpe (b); Steve Brown (d); Stacey Kent (v).* 10/98.

****(*) Brazilian Sketches**

Candid CCD 79769 *As above, except add Dave Newton (p), Chris Wells (d); omit Brown.* 01.

Humphrey Lyttelton's sleeve-note describes Tomlinson's sound as 'softly articulated but capable of becoming steely at moments, in a way reminiscent of Stan Getz'; and that Getzian feel is the saxophonist's starting point. Some may feel it's where he finishes up, too, since he seldom departs from the shadow of the inspiration, and the programme is based around a ballad feel that rarely moves above mid-tempo. Tomlinson's comely sound is so unwavering that the entire record is a pleasure, but it could arguably use a little more of that steel. His group plays with impeccable discretion, Oxley having a more central role than Pearce, but when Guy Barker comes in on three tracks his more experienced demeanour adds a fresh dimension. The outstanding track features their collected thoughts on a Johnny Mandel tune called 'Just A Child'. Stacey Kent's three vocals are suavely accomplished, although she tends to distract from the balance of the record.

The Brazilian follow-up is eventually a bore. This time Tomlinson seems to invite the Getz analogy more than ever while trying to set himself just sufficiently aside from the source. Despite some graceful playing the record ends up sounding like muzak much of the way.

Pietro Tonolo (born 1959)

SOPRANINO, SOPRANO AND TENOR SAXOPHONES

Studied classical violin, then switched to saxophone, and has since become a principal in the contemporaty Italian movement.

***** Slowly**
Splasc(h) 327-2 *Tonolo; Roberto Rossi (tb, shells); Piero Leveratto (b); Alfred Kramer (d).* 5/90.

*****(*) Tresse**
Splasc(h) 386-2 *Tonolo; Henri Texier (b); Aldo Romano (d).* 5/92.

Tonolo's accomplished midstream tenor works a creditable contemporary groove across both these sessions. *Slowly* features tight, almost disciplined interplay between trombone and tenor, while bass and drums cut a neoclassic hard-bop groove on tunes such as 'Misterioso' and 'Introspection'. *Tresse* is a further step forward in that Tonolo (on tenor exclusively this time) creates a wide range of settings with his distinguished partners without really stepping far from familiar signposts. They are conventionally swinging on 'You're The Top', thrillingly intense on 'Gammon', airily lyrical on 'For Heaven's Sake'. Tonolo doesn't seem like a grandly ambitious spirit – several of these pieces are finished inside five minutes – but he has a hip, versatile mind.

***** Simbiosi**
Splasc(h) 431-2 *Tonolo; Paolo Birro, Rita Marcotulli, Danilo Rea, Riccardo Zegna (p).* 6/94.

***** Disguise**
Splasc(h) 492-2 *Tonolo; Giampaolo Casati (c, t); Roberto Rossi (tb); Gianluigi Trovesi (as, picc, bcl); Riccardo Zegna (p, d); Pietro Ciancaglini (b); Alfred Kramer, Luigi Bonafede (d).* 12/96.

Simbiosi is an album of duets with four different pianists. The readiest empathy comes with Marcotulli, with the simply gorgeous soprano/piano duet on 'Finestre', but there are several productive combinations throughout the record. Sometimes, though, as in the effortful version of 'The Fool On The Hill', one feels that Tonolo is trying too hard to make his point, and a more judicious hand on the tiller might have made the record more effective. *Disguise* also seems, at times, like too ponderous an exercise, with Tonolo drawing on famous melodies by Satie, Beethoven, Handel, Prokofiev and others for his 'disguised' material. While there are some interesting developments out of the themes, some of it emerges as merely cute, and the ensembles seem needlessly wayward and lacking in focus.

***** Un Veliero All'Orizzonte**
EGEA SCA 060 *Tonolo; Bebo Ferra (fg); Alfredo Minotti, Umberto Vitiello (perc, v); Maria Pia De Vito (v).* 5/97.

***** Sotto La Luna**
EGEA SCA 069 *Tonolo; Danilo Rea (p).* 7/98.

Tonolo's first releases for the handsome EGEA label are engaging, brightly toned sets which fall just short of anything compelling or indispensable. *Un Veliero All'Orizzonte* is an 'imaginary voyage', a world trip of the sort which is a modest obsession in recent Italian jazz, where the saxophonist tends to voice melodies and make commentaries rather than dominate. Maria Pia De Vito makes a couple of compelling appearances but much of the action is left to Ferra and the two (singing) percussionists, who come over as very worldly. The duet with Rea is from an Umbria Jazz concert. If anything, this belongs more to the pianist, and again Tonolo is required to be more of a recitalist than an improviser. Some lovely Italian melodies along the way earn the stars.

***** Portrait Of Duke**
Label Bleu LBLC 6628 *Tonolo; Gil Goldstein (p); Steve Swallow (b); Paul Motian (d).* 5/99.

A centenary homage where Tonolo fronts something of an all-star band. The surprise package is Goldstein, who spends so much time as a hired-gun accordion player these days that his piano skills tend to go unremarked, yet he plays some of the most interesting things here. Swallow reasserts his princely status on the electric bass and Motian is his customary grand self, which leaves Tonolo a little high and dry in asserting his own role. Still, some surprise choices of tune ('Blue Rose', 'Angelica') and the interpretations confound a few expectations, too – such as 'Dancers In Love', a duet for soprano and (he had to pick it up eventually) accordion.

*****(*) Retrò**
EGEA SCA 082 *Tonolo; Luciano Titi (bandoneon); Bebo Ferra (g); Piero Leveratto (b).* 11/00.

The instrumentation is chamber-jazz again, but this is a good deal tougher and more lively than the previous EGEA sets, recorded in a fierce close-up which puts an extra edge on the playing. Every so often there's the sense that we're listening to a film-score from *Cinecitta*, but the energy and light in the playing refuse to let things settle down too cosily and the brevity of the individual pieces helps.

***** Autunno**
EGEA SCA 084 *Tonolo; Paolo Birro (p).* 4/01.

A more even-handed duet situation than the one with Rea listed above, but the result tends towards the same end: a reflective meander across some untroubled waters, most of them with a suitably autumnal shading. While Tonolo clearly isn't looking to shake any leaves off the trees with these releases, perhaps the material needs to offer a few more imperatives.

Mel Torme (1925–99)

VOCAL, DRUMS

A child performer, Torme graduated from radio work to touring, and his group, the Mel-Tones, were popular in the '40s. Had solo hits and became a nightclub performer in the '50s. A gifted songwriter, passable drummer and capable arranger, Torme was a versatile man, and he was enduringly popular and prolific until a stroke stopped him performing in 1997.

***** The Best Of The Capitol Years**

Capitol 799426-2 *Torme; Red Norvo (vib); Howard Roberts, Tal Farlow (g); Peggy Lee (v); studio orchestras.* 1/49–5/52.

The young Torme's voice was honey-smooth, light, limber, ineffably romantic and boyish; and it's amazing how many of those qualities he kept, even into old age. His '40s material for Musicraft seems to be back in the deletion racks, but this is a pleasing miscellany from his tenure with Capitol, very cleanly remastered. There are four previously unreleased tracks with Norvo and Farlow in support and a couple of duets with Peggy Lee, as well as two songs that find Mel himself at the piano. Some of the material is less than top-of-the-line, and most of the arrangements heave rather than glide, but Torme's rhythmic panache and tonal sweetness turn back the years.

*****(*) Torme**

Verve 44006556628 *Torme; Marty Paich Orchestra.* 6/58.

***** Ole Torme!**

Verve 314589517-2 *Torme; Billy May Orchestra.* 3–4/59.

*****(*) Swingin' On The Moon**

Verve 511385-2 *Torme; Russell Garcia Orchestra.* 60.

This is arguably Torme's greatest period on record, and it captures the singer in full flight. His range had grown a shade tougher since his '40s records, but the voice is also more flexible, his phrasing infinitely assured, and the essential lightness of timbre is used to suggest a unique kind of tenderness. Marty Paich's arrangements are beautifully polished and rich-toned, the french horns lending a distinctive colour to ensembles which sound brassy without being metallic. There may be only a few spots for soloists but they're all made to count, in the West Coast manner of the day.

Swingin' On The Moon is a more rote affair and a record of one 'moon' song after another may strike some as a concept that belongs in outer space; but everything Torme did in this period was delightful, and so is this.

The two earlier discs are a recent revival. *Torme* is like a dry run for *Shubert Alley* (below), and it's not far behind – how rarely have singers been so simpatico with the jazz orchestra that's been backing them. Even the miserable 'Gloomy Sunday' gets a respectable treatment. Designed as a low-key sort of record, it's only the preponderance of downbeat songs that keeps this off the top rating. Contrariwise, the Billy May charts for *Ole Torme!* are flippant, but Mel dignifies them with careful and detailed singing, strolling right past the tasteless chart for 'Malaguena' and salvaging most of the others. At this point it was inconceivable that Torme could make a poor record.

CORE COLLECTION

****** Mel Torme Swings Shubert Alley**

Verve 8215812 *Torme; Al Porcino, Stu Williamson (tb); Frank Rosolino (tb); Vince DeRosa (frhn); Art Pepper (as); Bill Perkins (ts); Bill Hood (bs); Marty Paich (p); Red Callender (tba); Joe Mondragon (b); Mel Lewis (d).* 1–2/60.

***Shubert Alley* is loaded with note-perfect scores from Paich and a couple of pinnacles of sheer swing in 'Too Darn Hot' (a treatment Torme kept in his set to the end) and 'Just In Time', as well as a definitive 'A Sleepin' Bee'. Deleted, shamefully enough, in Europe, but it should still be in American print.**

***** My Kind Of Music**

Verve 543795-2 *Torme; studio orchestras directed by Geoff Love, Tony Osborne, Wally Stott.* 7/61.

Made on a visit to Britain, this one is a mild disappointment: Mel's cushioned in cosy English arrangements, and one misses already the snap of the Paich sessions. Not that he gives less than a pro's performance; but it's a shade too comfortable.

***** Prelude To A Kiss**

Fresh Sound FSR-CD 109 *Torme; Don Fagerquist (t); Vince DeRosa (frhn); Hynie Gunker (as, cl); Ronnie Lang (as, bs, cl); Bob Enevoldsen (ts, bcl); Stella Castellucci (hp); Bill Pilman (g); Joe Mondragon (b); Mel Lewis (d); strings.* n.d.

Vinyl collectors will remember this one with some affection, issued on minor labels at budget price for several years. Originally interspersed with dialogue between Mel and an unnamed female admirer (sadly expunged from this release, though a little of it survives before the final track), the music and singing are actually pretty marvellous, arranged by Marty Paich in the style of the great Bethlehem and Verve sessions. Mel sounds terrific on the likes of 'One Morning In May' and 'I'm Getting Sentimental Over You'. Docked a notch for brevity, and for cutting the chat.

***** That's All**

Columbia CK 65165 *Torme; studio orchestras directed by Robert Mersey, Dick Hazard, Mort Garson, Pat Williams.* 64–66.

****(*) Right Now!**

Columbia CK 65164 *Torme; studio orchestras directed by Mort Garson, Shorty Rogers, Ernie Freeman, Arnold Goland.* 66–67.

Torme didn't look back kindly on his '60s recordings, and there's an apologetic air about both these packages; even so, there's a lot of very appealing singing. *That's All* was a ballad album of some distinction, with lovely versions of 'P.S. I Love You' and 'The Nearness Of You', and it is extended by various singles and rarities to a 24-track disc. 'I Remember Suzanne' is a pretty period-piece and there's one of his sweetest readings of 'The Christmas Song'; the rest shows quality-control thinning a little. *Right Now!* is less distinguished, a set of contemporary pop covers to which Torme brings his customary care and diligence; in the end one wonders why anyone thought such a refined singer should be trying to make a go of the likes of 'Secret Agent Man'. Worth keeping, though, are 'All That Jazz' and 'Wait Until Dark'.

***** At The Red Hill / Live At The Maisonette**

Rhino R2 7295 *Torme; Jimmy Wisner (p); Ace Tesone (b); Dave Levin (d); Al Porcino Orchestra.* 3/62–9/74.

A couple of live situations, a dozen years apart. At Pennsauken, New Jersey, home of the Red Hill, Mel delivers a typical club set: one might compare the two versions of 'Mountain Greenery', the first a hepcat's delivery, the second a showbiz master's. Both sets are great fun but neither really counts as classic Torme.

***** An Evening With George Shearing And Mel Torme**

Concord CCD 4190 *Torme; George Shearing (p); Brian Torff (b).* 4/82.

***** Top Drawer**
Concord CCD 4219 *Torme; George Shearing (p); Don Thompson (b).* 3/83.

***** An Evening At Charlie's**
Concord CCD 4248 *As above, except add Donny Osborne (d).* 10/83.

****(*) Mel Torme–Rob McConnell And The Boss Brass**
Concord CCD 4306 *Torme; Arnie Chycoski, Erich Traugott, Guido Basso, Dave Woods, John McLeod (t, flhn); Rob McConnell, Ian McDougall, Bob Livingston, Dave McMurdo (tb); Ron Hughes (btb); George Stimpson, Jim McDonald (frhn); Moe Koffman (ss, as, cl, f); Jerry Toth (as, cl, f); Eugene Amaro (ts, f); Rick Wilkins (ts, cl); Robert Leonard (bs, bcl, f); Jimmy Dale (p); Ed Bickert (g); Steve Wallace (b); Jerry Fuller (d); Brian Leonard (perc).* 5/86.

***** A Vintage Year**
Concord CCD 4341 *Torme; George Shearing (p); John Leitham (b); Donny Osborne (d).* 8/87.

***** In The Studio And In Concert**
Concord CCD2-4928-2 2CD *Torme; Warren Luening, Jack Sheldon (t); Bob Enevoldsen (vtb); Lou McCreary (tb); Gary Foster (as); Ken Peplowski (ts); Bob Efford (bs); Pete Jolly (p); Jim Self (tba); Chuck Berghofer (b); Jeff Hamilton (d); Joe Porcaro, Efrain Toro (perc).* 8/88.

***** Two Darn Hot**
Concord CCD2-2118-2 2CD *Torme; John Campbell (p); Bob Maize (b); Donny Osborne (d); Frank Wess Orchestra.* 8–11/90.

**** Mel And George Do World War Two**
Concord CCD 4471 *Torme; George Shearing (p); John Leitham (b).* 90.

***** The Complete Concord Recordings**
Concord CCD7-2144-2 7CD *As various discs above.* 4/82–2/90.

Torme's contract with Concord gave him the chance to record a long run of albums that should provide his final legacy as a singer. Even though most singers would be thinking about easing up at this stage, Torme's workload and enthusiasm both seemed limitless. The voice has throttled back a little, and there is a greyness at the edges, but he still makes his way to high notes very sweetly and will sometimes cap a song with an extraordinary, long-held note that defies the rules on senior singers.

If there's a problem with these records, it's the formulaic settings which Concord tend to encourage for some of their regulars. The duo setting with Shearing is actually a good one, since both men seem to admire each other's work to the point where some of the sessions threaten to slip into mutual congratulations; and context is given to both Shearing's sometimes dinky playing and Torme's romantic sweeps. Of their records together, both *Top Drawer* and *An Evening With* are splendid, and *An Evening At Charlie's* isn't far behind; but there are too many live albums here, when Torme can slip into an ingratiating showmanship and an intrusive audience distracts from what is really a close and intimate kind of jazz singing. The World War Two disc founders on the terrible material, charmingly though the principals deal with it.

The two 1990 concert sessions find Torme in ebullient form, delivering a gorgeous 'Early Autumn' and two equally distinctive ballads in 'Wave' and 'Star Dust' on *Two Darn Hot.*

The *Complete* edition with Shearing is loaded with great music, and we give it a rather modest mark only because seven discs is a long haul for anybody and it would be useful for the label to spend some time sitting down and preparing a genuinely effective compilation from their work together.

**** Nothing Without You**
Concord CCD 4516 *Torme; Guy Barker (t, flhn); Chris Smith (tb); John Dankworth (ss, as, cl); Ray Swinfield (as, cl); Ray Loeckle (ts, f, bcl); David Roach (ts, f); Jamie Talbot (bs, bcl, cl); John Colianni (p); Larry Koonse (g); John Leitham (b); Donny Osborne (d); Martyn David (perc); Cleo Laine (v).* 3/91.

****(*) Christmas Songs**
Telarc CD-83315 *Torme; John Colianni (p); John Leitham (b); Donny Osborne (d).* 4/92.

****(*) Sing, Sing, Sing**
Concord CCD 4542 *As above, except add Ken Peplowski (cl), Peter Appleyard (vib).* 11/92.

These records are a disappointing set. *Nothing Without You* is shared with Cleo Laine, whose voice isn't quite the come-hither instrument it once was, and the mawkish atmosphere and over-cute situations make this one dispensable to all but obsessive devotees of either singer. The Christmas album is fair game for a man who wrote 'The Christmas Song' but otherwise it goes the seasonal way of all such projects. *Sing, Sing, Sing* finds Mel with two Concord regulars sitting in with his rhythm section at the 1992 Fujitsu Festival, with a 14-minute Benny Goodman medley as the centrepiece. Fair enough, but there are already plenty of live Torme albums in the catalogue and this adds little to the list.

****(*) The Great American Songbook**
Telarc 83328 *Torme; Bob Milikan, Ross Konikoff, John Walsh, Frank London (t); Tom Artin, Rich Willey, Timothy Newman (tb); Jack Stuckey (as, cl, f); Adam Brenner (as, cl); Jerry Weidon, Jeff Rupert (ts, cl); David Schumacher (bs, bcl); John Colianni (p); John Leitham (b); Donny Osborne (d).* 10/92.

***** Velvet And Brass**
Concord CCD 4667 *Torme; Arnie Chycoski, Steve McDade, John MacLeod, Guido Basso, Kevin Turcotte (t, flhn); Alastair Kay, Bob Livingston, Jerry Johnson (tb); Ernie Pattison (btb); Rob McConnell (vtb); Gary Pattison, James MacDonald (frhn); Moe Koffman, John Johnson, Rick Wilkins, Alex Dean, Bob Leonard (reeds); David Restivo (p); Reg Schwager (g); Jim Vivian (b); Ted Warren (d); Brian Leonard (perc).* 7/95.

The Telarc album is yet another live offering from Torme: he retains his usual high standards without suggesting that the record demands a place in any but the most devoted admirer's archive. There is a very fine 'Stardust', as good a version as he's ever done, but the medleys and more routine moments don't amount to much. The Concord set offers a return bout with Rob McConnell's Boss Brass, a group he loves to sing with, and this time the record is a keeper. Torme is in remarkably good shape for a 70-year-old and, though one tends to credit singers with the mere ability to keep singing at such a stage in their careers, this is a project with some challenge in it. McConnell's band play with some discernment and several of the songs depart from convention: 'Autumn Serenade', 'High And Low' and, especially, 'If You Could See Me Now'.

★★★★ **The Mel Torme Collection**

Rhino R2 71589 4CD *Torme; various orchestras and small groups.* 44–85.

Rhino's four-disc retrospective of one of the most accomplished of vocalists is so consistently enjoyable that one overlooks the sometimes spotty remastering and occasionally idiosyncratic selection. It starts with mid-'40s work with the Mel-Tones, picks some of his best Musicraft sides, then follows with some of the finest of his Capitol, Bethlehem and Verve sides, before going choosily through the '60s. The '70s are largely ignored altogether, while the '80s are covered by a handful of cameo appearances. There are many delights along the way, including a lovely 1947 transcription of 'Three Little Words', the singer at his youthful peak; some of his best work with Marty Paich; three tracks from the disgracefully ignored *Torme Meets The British* Philips album of 1957; a previously unheard 'Walkin' Shoes' with Shorty Rogers; a virtuoso live Gershwin medley from 1975; and his extraordinary guest appearance with Was (Not Was) on 'Zaz Turned Blue'. One is impressed over and over again by Torme's musicianship, but the most agreeable aspect of the set is his enjoyment of the singer's art, an effortless pleasure that he insists we share.

Ralph Towner (born 1940)

CLASSICAL GUITAR, 12-STRING GUITAR, PIANO, SYNTHESIZER

Studied music at Oregon University and guitar in Vienna in the '60s; then in New York from 1969, playing in various groups, coming to prominence in Oregon. Has also pursued a solo career as stand-alone acoustic guitarist and occasional pianist, with a long sequence of ECM discs to his name.

★★★(★) **Trios/Solos**

ECM 833328-2 *Towner (solo) and with Paul McCandless (ob); Glen Moore (b); Collin Walcott (tabla).* 11/72.

★★★★ **Diary**

ECM 829157-2 *Towner (solo).* 4/73.

'Only tenuously connected with jazz', it says in *Grove*, so what's he doing here, and at this length? Two things cement Towner firmly to this music, both of them occurring at the start of the '70s. The first was an astonishing 12-string solo on 'The Moors', a stunning guest spot by the 31-year-old on Weather Report's *I Sing The Body Electric*, still one of the finest fusion records ever made. The second was the formation of Oregon, a group which brought to a jaded scene a fresh acoustic sound – not unmixed with technical awareness – and a hint of other improvising traditions. There had never been (and probably never again will be) a group quite like it: four earnest, professorial types from the far North-West, playing oboe, cor anglais, french horn, gut-strung guitar, stand-up bass, tablas and sitar; indeed *Grove* suggests some '60 to 80' instruments in all (why the imprecision in the count isn't clear).

The other important thing that happened to Ralph Towner was the emergence of the ECM label. If anyone creates what has sometimes been parodied as 'the ECM sound' – cool, acoustic, European, very spacious and classical in intent – then it's surely Towner. *Trios/Solos* was effectively an Oregon record, documenting some of the sub-pairings that presumably went on in the rehearsal room and certainly featured in concerts. Though not usually standards or jazz repertory players, Towner and Moore give a persuasive reading of Bill Evans's 'Re: Person I Knew', though curiously it's Moore who almost steals the album with his solo 'Belt Of Asteroids', a fantastic unaccompanied performance.

The other album is a genuine solo performance. Like the abstract blues '1 × 12' and 'Suite: 3 × 12' on *Trios/Solos*, it finds him trying to cut a trail between the two great 'twelves' of modern music: the blues and Viennese dodecaphony, which he studied in Europe in 1963 and 1967; the addition of 12-string guitar gives the mix an almost mystical quality. *Diary* is for some fans *the* Ralph Towner record. It is certainly very beautiful and, as with Oregon, there is no anxiety about using studio effects (apart from the churchy ECM acoustic) when required; 'Icarus' is a highly effective overdub. 'Silence Of A Candle', though, one of the genuine classics from the early days of Oregon, is almost thrown away on piano, a little too heavy-handed for such a glorious piece. This is odd, because Towner aims to play guitar 'pianistically'. He once told Joachim Berendt that his aim was to treat his first instrument as if it was a piano trio – not piano, violin, and cello, presumably, but a trio like Evans's. His ability to work simultaneous lines, sustain rich harmonics and drones (especially on the 12-string) and even get a percussive counterpoint out of the snap of the strings and the thud of the sound-box is what makes his solo playing so rich and multi-dimensional.

★★★★ **Solstice**

ECM 825458-2 *Towner; Jan Garbarek (ts, ss, f); Eberhard Weber (b, clo); Jon Christensen (d).* 12/74.

★★★ **Sound And Shadows**

ECM 829386-2 *As above.* 2/77.

Solstice was an attempt to hybridize the Oregon aesthetic, unmistakably American, with the new European jazz that ECM was sponsoring. Almost every separate element was both in place and subtly transformed: Paul McCandless's keening oboe into Garbarek's taut, stressed soprano sound; Moore's huge, woody bass into Weber's multiphonic sound; Walcott's unusual counts into Christensen's uninterruptable flow.

'Distant Hills', on the later and rather disappointing *Sound and Shadows*, is the best point of comparison between the groups, and one surely has to come down in favour of the original. It's only really when Weber and Christensen are given their head, as on the bassist's marvellous 'Piscean Dance', that the pace exceeds the most accommodating medium tempo, but this isn't theme-and-solos jazz, but a new and still not quite secure hybrid. Garbarek sounds wonderful throughout, alternating tenor and soprano, as Towner moves between guitar and piano. This must have been a riveting group live.

★★★ **Matchbook**

ECM 835014-2 *Towner; Gary Burton (vib).* 75.

Odd title for a record #1. What resonances do book matches have? ... throwaway advertisement, fugitive memories, perhaps of faraway places, a touch of something illicit, a spark of flame? There is nothing of that here. It's been suggested that some of the best material on the session was ditched because it was too raw. If so, then some pungent bathwater was thrown away to rescue a very douce baby indeed. Towner often does little more than accompany Burton's nagging, slightly troubled melodies, and even these fail to catch light. A decade later, the sparks still wouldn't fly ...

***(*) Batik

ECM 847325-2 *Towner; Eddie Gomez (b); Jack DeJohnette (d).* 78.

As a title this was equally unfortunate, for quite clearly the aim was to relocate Towner in what was unmistakably a jazz context, much as was to happen to Jan Garbarek with *Star* in 1991. The results are patchy but good. DeJohnette has some difficulty adjusting to the minimalist approach and he sounds impatient here and there, before his impeccable musicianship reasserts itself. It's meat and drink to Gomez, however, who sounds closer to Glen Moore than anyone might have expected, recalling some of their finest moments together. 'Batik' itself is overlong and slightly shapeless, but it does maximize the space for improvisation, and it includes some strong exchanges between Towner and Gomez in particular. We had quibbles about the original sound, but the balance is ideal on CD, with Towner pushed well forward.

*** Old Friends, New Friends

ECM 829196-2 *Towner; Kenny Wheeler (t, flhn); David Darling (clo); Eddie Gomez (b); Michael DiPasqua (d, perc).* 7/79.

Friends either grow closer with age, or they disappear altogether. This collaboration has fared rather better than expected. Gomez is again the star, but Kenny Wheeler's unexpectedly forceful soloing catches the attention early on and becomes the most obvious focus. Towner tries out some slightly unusual articulations, and at a couple of points sounds as if he's detuned a top string. This time around, we'll skip the obvious comparison and not mention Oregon at all.

***(*) Solo Concert

ECM 827268-2 *Towner (g solo).* 10/79.

**(*) Blue Sun

ECM 829162-2 *As above.* 12/82.

Towner never seemed to be a natural stage performer, certainly not without the mutual-support mechanism of the group. Working alone, he could seem and sound diffident and introverted. Not so on the 1979 disc, recorded at concerts in Munich and Zurich. There is fire and some passion in the playing. Miles Davis's 'Nardis', a rare jazz piece, is idiomatic but also unmistakably Towner's conception, and one can almost hear the trumpet-line come floating in over the top at a couple of points. 'Ralph's Piano Waltz', written for Towner by John Abercrombie, has rarely sounded better. None of the tracks outstays its welcome, with the possible exception of the opening 'Spirit Lake', not one of his stronger ideas; don't be put off by it, for what follows is very good indeed. *Blue Sun* is a frank disappointment, an album with almost no character and none of the intensity of the earlier solo disc.

**(*) Slide Show

ECM 827257-2 *Towner; Gary Burton (vib, mar).* 5/85.

Odd title for a record #2. What resonances do slide shows have? ... fleeting images, rather personalized memories, no real narrative flow or development. Yes, pretty much the same again, a decade on, from this highly talented but seriously inward-looking duo. This may have been involving, even moving, to play. As a listening experience, unfortunately it never gets anywhere.

*** City Of Eyes

ECM 827754-2 *Towner; Markus Stockhausen (t, picc t); Paul McCandless (ob, eng hn); Gary Peacock (b); Jerry Granelli (d).* 90.

At first blush, this is very close to *Old Friends, New Friends.* Stockhausen is a masterful performer, with instinctive taste and a greatly under-appreciated ability to bury himself in other people's ideas (perhaps a legacy of his apprenticeship with Papa Karlheinz). The blending of wind sounds is often quite exceptional, unfamiliar as they are in this sort of context. Peacock is very much in the same mould as Gomez, and they are probably the two double-bassists who give Glen Moore his sound. Granelli remains the weak point, a formulaic player who either hasn't a clue what is expected of him here or else who chooses to stick to his own tried-and-tested patterns, irrespective of what's going on around him.

*** Open Letter

ECM 511980-2 *Towner; Peter Erskine (d).* 7/91.

We were unduly hard on this one in the distant past. The point at issue was a track like 'Infection', a duo between Towner and Erskine which seemed to trade in everything each is good at, in favour of a drab 'jazz' style which suits neither. Towner never sounds convincing playing heavyweight lines, and the percussion doesn't do much more than accentuate the fact. However, his own increasingly confident use of the Prophet synth adds a very significant dimension to much of this. If it seems slightly pointless at this stage in Towner's career to push him out into darker and deeper waters – the cover seems to feature a pall of volcanic ash, maybe an ironic reference back to the peaceful seascape of *Diary* – then perhaps it has to be asked who is doing the pushing, artist or label?

***(*) Lost And Found

ECM 529347-2 *Towner; Denny Goodhew (ss, sno, bs, bcl); Marc Johnson (b); Jon Christensen (d).* 5/95.

Sorry, but look at that line-up. If this isn't another attempt to recapture – forget about 'the ECM sound' – 'the Oregon sound', then frankly we give up. It's even constructed very much the way early Oregon records were, with tiny carved images (one track is called 'Scrimshaw') interspersing longer, almost narrative pieces. And as has become ECM's practice in recent years, the leader opens the set himself, a solo 'Harbinger' that doesn't quite prepare one for the astonishing 'Trill Ride' with Johnson, a duo which avoids all the pitfalls of *Open Letter* and which yet manages to make the guitarist sound tough and aware. Johnson himself is simply masterful, and if anyone wants a crash course in one branch of modern bass-playing Towner's discography affords some valuable reference points. Goodhew and Christensen don't put in an appearance until 'Elan Vital', but they make an immediate difference to the sound. Goodhew is a bright, propulsive player with a delightful touch on the higher horns and a nice judgement of space on the baritone and bass clarinet. He leads off the collaborative 'Soft Landing' on sopranino and contributes two strong pieces elsewhere, 'Flying Cows' (a baritone feature and quite the jazziest thing Towner's been involved with for years) and 'Midnight Blue ... Red Shift', which deserve to be covered. 'Soft Landing' is one of the freer things Towner has done in recent years, and he should be reassured that it's an experiment worth repeating. As so often before, though, the real drama is what passes between guitar and bass. No piano these days; in the presence of a player like Johnson, it really isn't necessary.

★★★★ A Closer View

ECM 531623-2 *Towner; Gary Peacock (b). 12/95.*

A wholly involving and deeply resonant set, two great string players meditating on their instruments. Peacock has an immense tone, but it's the *detail* that one notices primarily, shakes, soft strums (as on 'Moor'), delicate harmonics and bent tones (on 'Infrared' and the seemingly improvised 'From Branch To Branch' and 'Postcard To Salta'). As with much of ECM's recent output, this is a genuinely collaborative project, and Towner often sounds as though he is playing accompaniment to the contrabass. He is also playing with firmer attack and a greater use of dissonance than usual, and there are signs too that he may have been listening to classical flamenco, evidenced not so much in the harmonic shapes he uses as in the overall shape and texture of his performances. A fine album.

★★★(★) Ana

ECM 537023-2 *Towner (solo). 3/96.*

To mark 25 years with the label – an astonishing achievement in itself – a quietly magisterial release that will delight anyone who enjoys Towner's music and will surprise no one, whether they admire him or not. Again, there is no piano part and no overdubs, simply a recital of virtuosic guitar-playing. The set closes with a sequence, 'Seven Pieces for Twelve Strings', which sums up much of what Towner has done over the years. Phrase-shapes reminiscent of 'The Moors' with Weather Report swap places with rich passages entirely in harmonics and, on 'Sage Brush Rider', an almost country feel. There is, to be fair, one surprise: 'Veldt', a strummed, percussive piece which might almost be something by South African composer Kevin Volans. It rounds off the first half of a highly effective record. Towner's ability to tell stories, and tell them quietly and without rhetoric, remains unchecked.

Colin Towns (born 1948)

KEYBOARDS, ARRANGER

Born in London, Towns taught himself music and began writing as a teenager. Worked in rehearsal bands and jazz-rock groups, but began writing for film in the late '70s, a career which has brought him wider eminence and many commissions. Founded the Mask Orchestra in 1991 to play his big-band compositions and has recently started his own label, Provocateur.

★★★★ Nowhere And Heaven

Provocateur PVC 1013 2CD *Towns; John Barclay, Graham Russell, Henry Lowther, Guy Barker, Gerard Presencer (t); Mark Nightingale, Richard Edwards, Peter Beachill, Pat Hartley (tb); Roger Williams (btb); Peter King (as); Jamie Talbot (as, ss, cl); Alan Skidmore, Nigel Hitchcock (ts, ss); Alan Barnes (bs); Julian Arguëlles (bs, ss); Phil Todd (bcl); Andrea Hess (clo); Dudley Phillips (b); Clark Tracey (d); Maria Pia De Vito (v). 96.*

★★★ Still Life

Provocateur PVC 1015 *Towns; Julian Arguëlles (ts, ss); John Parricelli (g); Dudley Phillips (b); Ralph Salmins (d). 98.*

★★★(★) Dreaming Man With Blue Suede Shoes

Provocateur PVC 1017 *As above discs, except add Dave Hartley (p), Norma Winstone (v); strings, brass, woodwind. 97–98.*

Towns has been so busy with film and TV work that most will have missed his jazz credentials – at least until the formation of the Mask Orchestra and these superb albums. The Orchestra collects many of the best London-based players, and they're given some tremendous challenges by these imaginative and uncompromising scores. The simple charge would be that Towns is writing jazz film-music, something meant to accompany something else, but even if that were true it would be a welcome departure from the familiarities of modern big-band albums. Instead, an example such as the title-track to *Nowhere And Heaven* is a fully formed and stand-alone score for a team of jazz players working within a strikingly personalized idiom. Towns constantly involves the orchestra, rather than resigning it to a subsidiary role behind soloists or making it a trained animal going through practised tricks. He subtly differentiates tonal colour and space, balances the weight of different sections within a composition, and has a fine grasp of dynamics – the ear is constantly teased, without any recourse to avant-garde flourishes. Towns keeps an absolute grip on what he wants his players to do, so there's nothing 'free' in this music.

Perhaps most telling of all is Towns's understanding of modern studios: the ingenious *recording* of all of this music is shaped as often by his way with a studio desk as it is by the inflexions of the players, with occasional keyboard flavourings and mixes that throw fresh light on what can sound quite different in a live context. The two-disc *Nowhere And Heaven* is a huge sprawl of almost two and a half hours, not all of similar calibre, but there's enough here to fascinate and return to time and again for fresh listening. *Still Life* is more song-based and features Maria Pia De Vito throughout: the appeal may depend on how one responds to her voice. This is a less ambitious undertaking for Towns; but the quintet's playing is full of character, and Arguëlles and Parricelli are both outstanding.

Dreaming Man With Blue Suede Shoes is different again, introducing the Mask Symphonic with a full orchestral complement as well as the basic Mask Orchestra. The title-track is a self-portrait, the least this generous entrepreneur can allow himself. It's also an extraordinarily complex and big-scale integration of soloists, jazz rhythm section, rock electricity and improvising soloists, a theme which to a greater or lesser degree is followed throughout the record. Most such projects founder on hubris. Just slightly, here and there, the ambitions of this one threaten to topple it over, but what other composer-arranger is trying anything like this (as well as paying for it himself)? Bravo!

★★★(★) Another Think Coming

Provocateur PVC 1028 *Towns; John Barclay, Derek Watkins, Graham Russell, Henry Lowther, Guy Barker, Stuart Brooks (t, flhn); Andy Wood, Mark Nightingale, Pete Beachill, Richard Edwards, (tb); Roger Williams (btb, tba); Peter King, Andy Mackintosh (ss, as); Alan Skidmore, Nigel Hitchcock (ts, ss); Phil Todd (bs, bcl, ss, as); Dave Hartley (p); John Parricelli (g); Dudley Phillips (b); Ian Thomas (d); Paul Clarvis (perc). 7/01.*

Towns sets his players extraordinary tasks – the brass writing in the opening 'Heated Think Tank' alone must have taxed to the max the collective lip of that section – but he likes to have fun with his music, too, and this is perhaps his wildest record to date. The transformation of 'I Am The Walrus' is something its composer would surely have enjoyed, full of leering horns and replete with a staggered ending which just hangs together. The immediate contrast comes with 'Prayer', over a secular, martial beat, which is more quietly sinister than penitent. 'Andrew Hill And Far Away' takes a lick from that composer and turns it into something else. 'Hot Lips' is three minutes of expert raving. Towns puts enough in to these records that they repay many plays with new finds, but even as one-off experiences they're hard to resist. The players are among the best Britain has to offer, as usual.

Tino Tracanna

SOPRANO, ALTO AND TENOR SAXOPHONES

Studied in Bologna, then joined the Franco D'Andrea group in 1981 and stayed 13 years. Also a regular in the Paolo Fresu Quintet, and leader of his own groups and projects.

***** 292**

Splasc(h) 322-2 *Tracanna; Paolo Fresu (t, flhn); Massimo Colombo (ky); Marco Micheli (b); Francesco Sotgiu (d); Naco (perc); Mariapia De Vito, Marti Robertson (v).* 6/90.

Tracanna is another member of Italy's contemporary jazz vanguard, and he debuted with two briskly entertaining albums for Splasc(h) (the first, *Mr Frankenstein Blues*, isn't yet on CD). The second record is more considered than his first and more confidently finished. Tracanna plays soprano as his first horn here, although there's a startling, helter-skelter alto solo on 'P.F.C. Concept', and his meditations on 'Argomenti Persuasivi' and the pretty ballad, 'Notti Eluse Ed Attese Deluse' (which also appears as a song, delivered by De Vito), are very well done. Fresu and Colombo are suitably challenging partners.

***** Quartetto**

Splasc(h) 618-2 *Tracanna; Massimo Colombo (p); Paolino Dalla Porta (b); Francesco Petreni (d).* 7/96.

A dozen originals by the leader, here dividing his time equally between tenor and soprano, each thoughtfully dispatched by his regular quartet. The record as a whole is somewhat unstartling, rather careful, and to that extent one could count it as slightly disappointing: there's nothing to denote the individuality Tracanna has sounded on the earlier discs, or with Paolo Fresu. But the playing has a fine polish to it.

*****(*) Gesualdo**

Splasc(h) 677-2 *Tracanna; Claudio Pontiggia (frhn); Riccardo Parrucci (f); Glorioa Merani (vn); Alessandro Franconi (vla); Filippo Burchietti (clo); Paolino Dalla Porta (b); Francisco Petreni (d); Fulvio Maras (perc); Maria Pia De Vito (v); Corrado Guarino (cond).* 4/98.

Five madrigals by Gesualdo, from the late 16th century, plus some in-the-spirit originals by Tracanna and Guarino. The composer is very far away from jazz in all senses, but his melodies endure and Guarino, who did most of the arranging, takes care not to manhandle him. Pontiggia and Tracanna get plenty of space to improvise in the appropriate passages and the latter is almost as imposing a presence as the co-leader, getting a sound like a frisky crumhorn. De Vito (familiar from Colin Towns's records) was an inspired choice for the vocal role, idiomatic but open to a freer expression.

***** Nudes**

Splasc(h) 703-2 *Tracanna; Paolino Dalla Porta (b).* 10/99.

A demanding format, which Tracanna approaches on soprano and tenor. Gracefully played, the performers working from compositions rather than a free form, the situation is not quite as exposed as the title suggests. The playing has style, but it's not the most engaging of records.

Clark Tracey (born 1961)

DRUMS

The younger Tracey began playing drums in his father's group from 1978, and over many years and thousands of gigs he's developed into a failsafe and superbly accomplished drummer in a tough, straightahead style.

*****(*) Full Speed Sideways**

33 Jazz 018 *Tracey; Mark Nightingale (tb); Nigel Hitchcock (as); Dave O'Higgins (ts); John Donaldson (p); Arnie Somogyi (b).* 2/94.

An exciting straightahead record by a group abrim with talent. Tracey's tunes are meaty enough to give the players plenty to chew on, and they set up one knockout solo after another from the three horns, with the more studious Donaldson acting as the cool drink of water. It's unfancy, and some would call it routine, but it would take a real sourpuss to sneer at the likes of 'The Revenge Of Sam Tacet', even if Hitchcock gets so over-excited in his fast solos that he sounds like he's about to fall off the stand. Clark's own playing is copybook, refining a Blakey influence to the point where inessentials are banished and the remaining tools are sharp, cutting and wholly right for the job.

*****(*) Stability**

Linn ADK 159 *Tracey; Guy Barker (t); Andy Sheppard, Tommy Smith, Tim Garland (ts); Iain Ballamy (ss, ts); Nigel Hitchcock (as); Gareth Williams (p); Arnie Somogyi (b); Christine Tobin (v); Locrian String Quartet.* 12/00.

A stellar line-up of British talent, and hearing the tenors and Barker getting stuck into 'Gone' offers a formidable start to the record. If the programme feels a bit too deliberately diverse, Tracey cramming in everything he can think of doing (leading, drumming, arranging, writing and even playing a solo piano on 'Melancholia', plus doing five string quartet charts), there's not much wrong with any of it. The muscle and swing of his straightahead work is channelled into a wider frame of reference, and it might almost be a mature player's manifesto for further research. And there's the bonus of hearing several of the finest British horn-players in their unselfconscious pomp: Smith on 'The Peacocks', Barker on 'Ugly Beauty', Ballamy on 'Lounge Blues'.

Stan Tracey (born 1926)

PIANO, SYNTHESIZER

Worked in dance bands before playing jazz in the '50s and working with Ted Heath, 1957–9. House pianist at London's Ronnie Scott Club 1960–7, backing many visiting players, and then a group leader of numerous units, from trio and quartet to big band. The pioneer modernist and composer-leader in post-war British jazz, and one of its most significant figures for close on five decades.

***** Little Klunk / Showcase**
Jasmine JASCD 639 *Tracey; Ike Isaacs, Ray Dempsey (g); Kenny Napper, Johnny Hawksworth (b); Phil Seaman, Ronnie Verrell (d).* 5/58–5/59.

****** Under Milk Wood**
Jazzizit 9815 *Tracey; Bobby Wellins (ts); Jeff Clyne (b); Jackie Dougan (d).* 5/65.

Stan Tracey is one of Britain's few genuinely original contributions to world jazz. The persistent notion that Tracey only plays a rather second-hand, olde-worlde version of his original mentors, Duke Ellington and Thelonious Monk (or what one critic called 'white man's blues'), is completely misleading. While elements of Monk's style – the insistent, percussive left hand, the quirky melodism – and of Duke's capacious structural understanding remain components of Tracey's work in all its various forms and outlets, he has brought something entirely original to the music.

The surprise reappearance here is of the first two sessions under Stan's name, now reissued as a two-on-one on Jasmine. While more than 'prentice work, the standard treatments of *Showcase* (where Tracey plays vibes on some tracks) and the originals of *Little Klunk* find him still working towards the style which would be in more authoritative hands on his '60s Columbias. He is at his most Monkian on the likes of 'Li'l Ol' Pottsville', but his improvising doesn't yet have the mastery of variation which he later displayed. The other players are also more serviceable than inspiring.

Under Milk Wood remains one of the most distinctive records of its era, a setting of Dylan Thomas which uses spare, unadorned jazz material to somehow evoke the eccentric light of the original play. A pioneering work which is a rare instance of jazz accommodating an outside inspiration in a way that honours the qualities of each side of the equation. Its leanness is a Tracey characteristic which has sometimes been dissipated by his big-scale orchestrations. Wellins's somewhat legendary solo on 'Starless And Bible Black' remains compelling, but it shouldn't overpower the impact of the rest of a record which should be listened to in its entirety.

***** Laughin' And Scratchin'**
Jazz House JHAS 608 *Tracey; Rick Laird (b); Ronnie Stephenson, Bill Eyden (d).* 8–10/65.

A surprisingly rare glimpse of Stan on his regular gig at Ronnie Scott's, in the period when he led what was effectively the house rhythm section. The sound is scruffy, with drums thin and bass often scarcely registering, but it's the piano we want to hear and it comes through clearly enough. The blues improvisation 'At Random' shows what Tracey could conjure out of the elementals, and the methodical break-ups of 'Sweet And Lovely' and 'I'm Getting Sentimental Over You' are object lessons in digging into the matter of standards without merely getting as remote from them as possible. Solos by the others are a distraction and the audio quality is tiresome, but this is in other respects two nights of work from a fine vintage.

***** Genesis**
Steam SJCD 114 *Tracey; Guy Barker, Steve Sidwell, John Barclay, Henry Lowther, Alan Downey (t); Malcolm Griffiths, Geoff Perkins, Pete Smith, Pete Beechel (tb); Peter King, Jamie Talbot (as); Tony Coe (ts, cl); Art Themen (ts); Phil Todd (bs); Roy Babbington (b); Clark Tracey (d).* 1/87–8/89.

***** We Still Love You Madly**
TAA 004 2CD *As above, except add Chris Pyne (tb), Alan Skidmore (ss, ts); omit Downey, Smith, Beechel, Coe.* 7/86–12/88.

Genesis is still the only one of Tracey's large-scale suites to be available on CD at this juncture. Unlike *Milk Wood*, which makes no obvious attempt to be programme music (a re-recorded vocal version with a later band was signally unsuccessful), to a large extent *Genesis* is constrained by its attempt to express the Creation myth as sound. There are moments of pure invention, as on 'The Sun, Moon & Stars', with Themen and Guy Barker to the fore, but there is something slightly plodding about the rest. One wonders, if Tracey had simply been writing nine discontinuous pieces with no overarching theme, whether they would not have been executed more successfully.

The Ellington set reissues two albums, one of orchestral treatments and the other of solo and (with Roy Babbington) duo interpretations. The orchestral pieces are played with fine spirit but sometimes get bogged down in too many long solos by the horns. The playing has a rackety quality which Duke might have enjoyed more than many a more pompous homage, although there are arguably too many over-familiar choices from the canon. The duo record is more personal, and on the solos in particular (especially 'Prelude To A Kiss'), Stan and Duke work closely together. But the session is sabotaged by a pretty awful piano sound which the CD remastering has done little to improve. The producers should have done better than this.

*****(*) For Heaven's Sake**
Cadillac SGCCD 04 *Tracey; Gerard Presencer (t); Andrew Cleyndert (b); Clark Tracey (d).* 9/95.

Billed as 'The New Stan Tracey Quartet', this set was cut before they'd played any gigs, and its freshness, even on a set made up largely of standards and Monk tunes, is very appealing. As ever, it's the spareness in Tracey's music which makes the deepest impression; Monk is winnowed down to his essence in 'Crepuscule With Nellie' and 'Bright Mississippi', and the pianist sets out standards such as 'Just Friends' as skeletal keyboard blueprints, which the other players decorate to give the music its light. Presencer, then 23, is mercurial but already mature, his own 'Blah De Blah De Blah' a modest but intriguing original, and his solos beautifully toned and supple. Cleyndert and Clark read the old man's moves handsomely. Very little waste, and one can only regret that the quartet didn't make another record when they'd played some more.

*****(*) Solo: Trio**
Cadillac SGCCD 06 *Tracey; Andrew Cleyndert (b); Clark Tracey (d).* 1–6/97.

When you get right down to it, the only true way to hear Stan Tracey is solo. He does the bass; he does the percussion; he does the rip-note, blue-edge melody lines. He does the lot. The solo tracks here are the best available example of Tracey's rough and chunky style. Monk's 'Ask Me Now' bruises lesser players, and the harmonic permutations of 'Body And Soul' are so deeply stacked that only someone of Tracey's individuality can seem to work something entirely new. The trios aren't quite as compelling, and there are a couple of tracks – the original 'Lover's Freeway' and a duff 'Round Midnight' (on which we have declared a moratorium) – which really don't cut the mustard. No fault of the rhythm-players, who are spot-on. It would just have been good to have had more of the main man.

★★(★) Duke Ellington – The Durham Connection
33 Jazz 049 *Tracey; Tony Fisher, Henry Lowther, Gerard Presencer, Derek Watkins, Patrick White (t); Malcolm Griffiths, Mark Nightingale, Roger Williams (tb); Alan Barnes (cl, as); Peter King (as); Mornington Lockett, Art Themen (ts); Jay Craig (bs); Andrew Cleyndert (b); Clark Tracey (d); Tina May, Niall Hoskin, Teresa Troiani (v); Durham Cathedral Choir.* 2/98.

Not our favourite among Tracey's heftier projects. This is a collection of Ellington's sacred music, and while the playing is as fine as the personnel would lead you to expect, the singing (May excepted) is all too British and buttoned-up. We would much prefer to hear the pianist's own big-scale works given this kind of recording.

★★★(★) Suspensions And Anticipations
psi 04.02 *Tracey; Evan Parker (ts).* 9/03.

We continue to fret at the unavailability of so much of Stan's best work – from the Columbias of the '60s to various Steam LPs of the '70s and '80s – but here he is at 77, mixing it up with one of the few British musicians who can lay equal claim to rightful space on a global stage. Pianist and saxophonist are both readily identifiable as themselves, even though neither plays in his most accustomed style: Parker is trimmer, less voluminous; Tracey is elliptical and set aside from his familiar rough-and-tumble swing. Sometimes they circle watchfully round one another, sometimes they're chummily gladiatorial, but it's a dialogue where there are few blind turnings and much bounteous discourse. Three solos – two for piano, one for tenor – let each man stretch his legs before the next bout.

Theo Travis (born 1964)

TENOR AND SOPRANO SAXOPHONES, FLUTE

British saxophonist moving easily between post-bop, fusion and, most recently, free idioms.

★★★ 2 a.m.
33 Records 33JAZZ 011 *Travis; David Gordon (p); Mark Wood (g); Rob Statham (b); Ichiro Tatsuhara (d); Robin Jones (perc).* n.d.

★★★ View From The Edge
33 Records 33JAZZ 019 *Travis; Tony Coe (ts, bcl); David Gordon (p); Mark Wood (g); Jeff Clyne, Rob Statham (b); John Marshall, Ichiro Tatsuhara (d).* 6/94.

★★★(★) Secret Island
33 Records 33JAZZ 033 *Travis; David Gordon (p); John Etheridge (g); Rob Statham, Dave Sturt (b); Marc Parnell, Andrew Small (d); Gary Hammond (perc).* 5–6/96.

'Brummagem' used to be the cant for anything shoddily built, ersatz or second-hand, but there is nothing but cleanly smelted strength and quality in the work of this Birmingham-born saxophonist. An able composer as well as improviser, Travis contributes all but one tune to his debut recording; there was an earlier cassette release, but this may be hard to track down now. He plays the eclecticism card a little too forcefully but impresses with tunes which range from the hectic clatter of 'Sex, Food And Money (Part Two)' and 'Nightmare In New York' to the calmer lyricism of 'Shore Thing', a strain which comes out more strongly on *Secret Island.*

The two follow-up albums are poised and confident and allow Travis to settle down to making well-rounded sets rather than showcasing as many disparate aspects of his talent as possible. *View From The Edge* is closer to the dynamic of the first album. Guest appearances from Coe, Clyne and Marshall are an additional fillip, and the addition of guitarist Wood points forward to a later trio for the same label. With the exception of 'Love For Sale', all the pieces are by Travis, and the set is dominated by the long, opening 'Fort Dunlop' (the great tyre factory in Birmingham), 'Freedom' and the closing 'The Purple Sky', which includes all the guest performers except Coe.

Secret Island is a mellower and less abrasive record than the other two. John Etheridge is a key presence, with a folksy approach to jazz playing. None of the other guests, Hammond, Sturt or Small, makes anything like the same impact. As with all of 33's catalogue, the sound is good, slightly over-emphatic and mixed as if a rock or pop session, with too much emphasis on volume at the expense of subtlety.

★★★ Bodywork
33 JAZZ 036 *Travis; Mark Wood (g); John Marshall (d).* 9/97.

Thirteen 'wholly spontaneous' improvisations, as the sleeve-notes state: it's conservative but often exciting playing. Travis can't shake off the forms of late-Coltrane improvising, and Marshall is a drummer who has a clock in his head, so even if they're making these up, it's really only Wood who sounds genuinely unfettered, and even he bows to the overall sense of preordained resolution. Nevertheless, these are clever and attractive pieces, reminiscent of much British experimentation of the '70s – and none the worse for revisiting that modest alcove.

★★★ Passion Dance
Jazz House JHCD 059 *Travis; David Gordon(p); Andy Hamill (b); Marc Parnell (d).* 7/99.

★★★ Berlin Vibe
Symbol 20001201 *Travis; Roger Beaujolais (vib); Stefan Weeke (b); Björn Lücker (d).* 12/00.

★★★(★) Heart Of The Sun
33JAZZ 063 *Travis; Palle Mikkelborg (t, flhn); Stuart Curtis,(cl, bcl); David Gordon (p, org); Mark Wood (g); Stefan Weeke, Andy Hamill (b); Björn Lücker, Marc Parnell (d).* 6/00–5/01.

Passion Dance is a live set from Ronnie Scott's – a progress report from Travis's quartet, nothing very fancy, with one or two old favourites such as 'Nightmare In New York' given a going-over and nice takes on Tubby Hayes's 'Off The Wagon' (on flute) and McCoy Tyner's title-piece.

Berlin Vibe was made after a tour by the band, and its appeal may depend on one's taste for the use of vibes: it brings out the sunniness in Travis's music, and an obvious vehicle such as 'Bags Groove' is confected into something sweet but blues-less. A mild, enjoyable listen, but hardly essential.

Theo's heart is in darker places if the tone of *Heart Of The Sun* (scarcely a representative title) is anything to go by. A lot of this is close to ECMish mood-painting, and when the huge sound of the tenor looms out of the speakers on the opening 'All I Know', it's a bit of a surprise after some of the lighter climes of the recent records. Mikkelborg is a heavyweight guest and appears on four tracks, but Travis goes toe-to-toe with him and makes at least as strong an impression; the gritty late-Miles sound of 'Fast Life' is particularly effective. The sound of the record is a curious hybrid of atmospheric distances and instruments in very hot close-up – intriguing, and actually surprisingly effective for the music.

*****(*) For The Love Of Open Spaces**
Pillow Mountain PMR 0014 *Travis; Steve Lawson (b).* 7/03.

Lusciously beautiful without descending into New Age claptrap, the music here walks an awkward line with great confidence. Both musicians make extensive use of loop technology (although, as they proudly say, no synths or midi-triggered sounds), and the result is a series of mood-poems crafted with skill and a capacious melodic bent. Lawson gets a bit rocky here and there and maybe a couple of pieces stay around a little too long, but in what is often a threadbare genre they've done very well.

The Trio

GROUP

A group of brief but significant life, who galvanized British listeners with their 1970 debut and became a 'power trio' benchmark.

****** The Trio**
BGO BGOCD 231 *John Surman (bs, ss, bcl); Barre Phillips (b); Stu Martin (d).* 3/70.

***** Conflagration**
Sequel Records NED CD 303 *As above, except add Harry Beckett, Kenny Wheeler (t, flhn); Marc Charig (c); Nick Evans, Malcolm Griffiths (tb); Mike Osborne (as, cl); Stan Sulzmann (as, f); Alan Skidmore (ts, ss); Chick Corea, John Taylor (p); Dave Holland (b); John Marshall (d).* 71.

For years, aficionados of British jazz have misted over at the mere mention of this 1970 record. Like John McLaughlin's *Extrapolation*, on which Surman also played, it was a salutary reminder of how good that scene could be when it got its act together. Though occasionally discussed as if it was a Surman record, this was a genuinely collaborative group, with all three members contributing material. (In point of fact, it is Phillips who can claim the lion's share of credits.)

A wonderfully welcome CD reissue, it will captivate new listeners as well as those who spent the early '70s nodding sagely to 'Incantation' and 'Caracticus', the evergreen 'Green Walnut' and '6's And 7's', 'Silvercloud' and 'Dee Tune'. Surman's multi-instrumentalism isn't overdone and Phillips's melodic bass is always tasteful. The late Stu Martin is the least-known member of the group, his career cut short by a fatal heart attack. This wasn't necessarily his personal finest hour, but he contributes in full measure to a classic recording.

If a big-band version of The Trio sounds like a bad Irish joke, things had gone seriously awry by the time *Conflagration* was recorded. The album was billed as 'featuring' John Surman, and whether it was his own project, a trio encounter or a collaborative big band remains unclear. It has always been a record that yields slightly less than the sum of its admittedly impressive parts. The presence of Chick Corea was a sign of the saxophonist's growing international reputation, but Corea's addition adds little light and not much heat. The British improvisers represented are not having the best of days either, though honourable mentions to the brilliant Mike Osborne, trumpeter Harry Beckett and drummer John Marshall, all of whom shine through the heat-haze.

Trio AAB

GROUP

One of the several bands involving the Bancroft brothers.

***** Cold Fusion**
Caber 004 *Phil Bancroft (sax); Kevin MacKenzie (g, syn); John Speirs (b); Tom Bancroft (d, perc, elec); Gina Rae (v).* 8/97–4/98.

*****(*) Wherever I Lay My Home That's My Hat**
Caber 021 *As above, except omit Speirs, Rae.* 9/00.

Cold Fusion is a relaxed and free-flowing expression of the Bancroft brothers' musical interests. Like the physical process that gives the album its title, it's room-temperature modern jazz that doesn't aspire to the structural complexities of Tom Bancroft's big-band writing (also available on Caber, their own label) or to the more driven and rock-tinged approach of MacKenzie's own projects. Phil Bancroft's 'Untitled' is a musing saxophone solo that confirms his developing expressiveness. There is a fine version – albeit mistitled – of Ornette's 'When Will The Blues Leave' and an unexpected reading of murdered hip-hopper Tupac Shakur's 'I Ain't Mad Atcha'. 'Abstract' is a delightful tone-poem seemingly built on a traditional melody, which surfaces at the close. Speirs and singer Gina Rae (who comes from Scotland's other musical dynasty) only appear on two numbers, Rae providing a backing vocal for the Tupac piece.

Trio AAB are certainly a more commanding outfit in a live setting and there's some of that edge and danger on the splendidly titled sequel. Interestingly, it's very much an exploration of influences and ancestral debts, and thoroughly dominated by Phil's compositions. 'Bibo' is a gushingly intense celebration of life, tinged by Ornette's raucous hymn-singing, while 'Fall' is in a more conventional Trane bag. It's hard not to experience this as an intensely personal record. It seems to have lain unmixed for some time, but that has only concentrated the emotional charge. On 'Jam' and 'Some Of The Things I'm Not' (no prizes for guessing the source), the trio is working at a supercharged level, intuitive, consistently intelligent and drivingly swinging. Great stuff.

Lennie Tristano (1919–78)

PIANO

Blinded as a child, Tristano learned piano, saxophone and cello and studied music in Chicago. Worked in trios in New York in the '40s, then with a sextet, but gradually abandoned live work for full-time teaching from 1951. Created a doctrinal school of thought which placed rigorous thought and construction ahead of mere emoting in jazz; once controversial, now a part of the language.

★★★★ The Complete Lennie Tristano
Mercury 830921-2 *Tristano; Billy Bauer (g); Clyde Lombardi, Bob Leininger (b).* 10/46–5/47.

(★★★) Live At Birdland 1952
Jazz Records JR-1CD *Tristano; Lee Konitz (as); Warne Marsh (ts); Billy Bauer (g); Arnold Fishkind (b); Jeff Morton (d).* 45–52.

(★★★) Wow
Jazz Records JR-9 *As above, except omit Fishkin and Morton.* 50.

★★★(★) Live In Toronto
Jazz Records JR-5 *As above, except add Peter Ind (b), Al Levitt (d).* 6/52.

★★★(★) Manhattan Studio
Jazz Records JR-11 *Tristano; Peter Ind (b); Tom Weyburn (d).* 55–56.

★★★★ Lennie Tristano / The New Tristano
Rhino/Atlantic R2 71595 *Tristano; Lee Konitz (as); Gene Ramey, Peter Ind (b); Jeff Morton, Art Taylor (d).* 55–61.

★★★ Continuity
Jazz Records JR-6 *Tristano; Lee Konitz (as); Warne Marsh (ts); Henry Grimes, Sonny Dallas (b); Paul Motian, Nick Stabulas (d).* 10/58–6/64.

★★★ Note To Note
Jazz Records JR-10 *Tristano; Sonny Dallas (b); Carol Tristano (d).* 64–65.

If Charlie Parker can be made to seem the Schoenberg of modern jazz, then Tristano is certainly its Webern; he represents its 'difficult' phase. Whereas most horn-led post-bop delved into uncomfortable psychic regions and cultivated a scouring intensity, Tristano ruthlessly purged his music of uncontrolled emotion, in sharp contrast to the highly expressive playing of Bill Evans. Perhaps because his basic instruction to his horn-players – the best-known of whom were, of course, Lee Konitz and Warne Marsh – was that they should use a deliberately uninflected and neutral tone, concentrating instead on the structure of a solo, Tristano has remained a minority taste, and a rather intellectual one. This is a pity, because Tristano's music is always vital and usually exciting. Though he abandoned the rhythmic eccentricities of bop in favour of an even background count, his playing is far from conventional, deploying long sequences of even semiquavers in subtly shifting time-signatures, adding sophisticated dissonances to quite basic chordal progressions. If his emphasis on structural rigour and technical (rather than emotional) virtuosity still alienates some listeners, there is a problem for the beginner in the nature of the Tristano discography, much of which involves indifferent live recordings and posthumously released private tapes. However, far from being the cerebral purist of legend, the blind Tristano was fascinated by every possibility of music-making and was a pioneer in studio overdubbing and in speeding up half-speed recordings to give them a cool, almost synthesized timbre.

The key track in this regard was 'Requiem', perhaps the most striking item on the 1955 Atlantic sessions, reissued on the indispensable Rhino CD. His overdubbing and multi-tracking would influence the Bill Evans of *Conversations With Myself.* But the latter part of the album offers a rare club date with Lee Konitz: the saxophonist sounds dry and slightly prosaic on 'If I Had You' and much more like his normal self on a beautiful 'Ghost Of A Chance'. Tristano's own solos are derived, as usual, from the refined and twice-distilled code of standard material. The original Atlantic LP has also been reissued as *Lennie Tristano*, as listed.

This is the essential Tristano CD, but the early sessions on the Mercury disc are almost as important. They catch Tristano just before bebop – specifically, Powell and Parker – had had a significant impact on his playing, so his style, refracted through Tatum and Hines, is like a mysterious, charged yet inscrutable distillation of swing piano's most elaborate settings. One is sometimes reminded of Tatum's (or Nat Cole's) trio recordings, yet Tristano's ideas, while harmonically dense, adapt bop's irresistible spontaneity better than either of those peers. Eleven of the 19 tracks are previously unreleased alternative takes, and the five versions of 'Interlude' (alias 'A Night In Tunisia') are as varied as Parker's Dials. In Bauer he had one of his most sympathetic partners: often lost to jazz history, the guitarist's lines are unfailingly apt yet fresh. Comparison between each take shows how insistent Tristano already was on making his music new from moment to moment. Some of the surviving masters were in imperfect shape, with occasional high-note distortions, but it won't trouble anyone used to music from this period.

The New Tristano is an essential record. The multiple time-patterns secured on most of the tracks suggest a vertiginous, almost mathematical piano music that moves beyond its scientific sheen to a point where the ingenuities acquire their own beauty: 'I can never think and play at the same time. It's emotionally impossible.' Howsoever the conjoining of technique, interpretation and feeling may work for the listener, this is remarkable piano-jazz, and the contrasting ballads of 'You Don't Know What Love Is' and 'Love Lines' suggest a world of expression which jazz has seldom looked at since.

The Jazz Records releases are from tapes kept in the Tristano family archive. Both *Live At Birdland 1952* (which also includes four early piano solos from 1945) and *Wow* are tarnished by terrible sound, the discs apparently made from wire recordings: more's the pity, since both feature the musicians in what is, even through the detritus of the flawed sound, masterful music. That becomes clearer on the considerably superior (if still imperfect) sound of the 1952 Toronto concert. Any who might doubt Tristano's ability to outswing any of the regular bebop pianists should lend an ear to the astonishing solo on the first piece, his favourite 'Lennie's Pennies'. Throughout, the group work with uncanny accord, improvisations moving seamlessly from one man to the next, yet set within a palpable groove by Ind (though he's nearly inaudible) and Levitt.

Manhattan Studio derives from worktapes from Tristano's New York studio over a year or two. Much of this is prime Tristano, the up-tempo pieces especially: 'Momentum', 'I'll Remember April' and, above all, 'All The Things You Are', which is like a working primer on bebop piano, are riveting examples of the man's artistry, and he's assisted by Ind's simply melodic solos and Weyburn's steady beat. This was previously available on an Elektra LP, *New York Improvisations*, and it has to be said that the indifferent sound hasn't been much improved by the CD transfer.

The concert fragments on *Continuity* are in better sound. There are four pieces from 1958 with Marsh, Grimes and

Motian, including an 'Everything Happens To Me' which fades after 50 tantalizing seconds, and some 24 minutes from 1964 with Marsh, Konitz, Dallas and Stabulas. The playing is of a typically high order, with a fine '317 East 32nd', but the snapshot documentation is finally rather frustrating, and the Konitz *Live At The Half Note* set on Verve, even with Bill Evans in for Tristano, may appease less specialist appetites.

The duos with Dallas date from the early '60s. Five improvisations cover 40 minutes, and the overdubbed drums (hardly sacrilege – Carol Tristano merely centres the rhythm, never doing more than mark time) fill out an otherwise rather dry recording. Like all the Jazz releases, there's a half-finished quality: rigorous though Tristano was, such notebook survivals inevitably lack the precise brilliance of such as *The New Tristano*. But there are insights enough here to make this a valuable pendant to the other solo music.

CORE COLLECTION

****** Lennie Tristano**

Atlantic 7567-80804-2 *Tristano; Lee Konitz (as); Gene Ramey, Peter Ind (b); Art Taylor, Jeff Morton (d).* 55.

Perhaps the best way to sample Tristano is in the almost distilled form of this classic record, discussed above. While the coupling with *The New Tristano* offers more music, in this latest mastering and minus excess baggage, here is the purest of the purist, with his most sympathetic collaborators.

Gianluigi Trovesi (born 1944)

ALTO AND SOPRANO SAXOPHONES, ALTO AND BASS CLARINETS, PICCOLO

Studied at Bergamo from 1960 and in a jazz environment was first noticed as a member of Giorgio Gaslini's groups in the '70s. He has become a familiar name in many European jazz situations since then, although his own music is a deeply personalized take on jazz, classical and native Italian music of several sorts.

*****(*) Roccellanea**

Splasc(h) H 506-2 *Trovesi; Paolo Fresu (t, flhn); Giancarlo Schiaffini (tb); Paolo Damiani (b); Ettore Fioravanti (d).* 12/83.

****(*) Dances**

Red 181 *Trovesi; Paolo Damiani (b, clo); Ettore Fioravanti (d).* 1/85.

****(*) Les Boîtes À Musique**

Splasc(h) H 152 *Trovesi; Luciano Mirto (elec); Tiziano Tononi (perc).* 3/88.

Trovesi is a key figure in Italy's new jazz, as performer, composer and organizer. *Roccellanea*, for instance, came about as part of a research project into jazz and its relationship with indigenous Mediterranean culture. That issue has been largely taken up since by the splendid efforts of Peppo Spagnoli's Splasc(h) label to document the Italian scene in all its variety, and it's appropriate that the session in question appears in the label's 'Italian Jazz Classics' series. Co-credited to Trovesi and Damiani, the disc consists of two long-form pieces in which the quintet explore a score that offers a superbly vivid blend of writing and improvising. Originally played by the two leaders with Manfred Schoof, Connie Bauer and Gunter Sommer, the three locals who substituted on the recording session are more than up to the job. Since Damiani uses an amplified bass that sounds rather like one of Eberhard Weber's old set-ups, the music has a pleasantly dated feel which the playing refutes: the three horn-players criss-cross to great effect, Fresu's more conventional lines ameliorating the expressionism of the other two.

This is a more useful survival than the other two projects, which gave a somewhat misleading impression of Trovesi as a lugubrious stylist. Luciano Mirto is credited as 'computer operator', and he establishes harsh, jangling washes of sound which Trovesi decorates with a mirthless sort of intensity while Tononi patters away in the background. Interesting, but the genre has been handled with better results elsewhere. *Dances* ends on the track 'Sorry I Can't Dance', which suggests a sense of humour, though the playing here often seems curiously effortful – even though bass and drums employ a wide variety of rhythms.

****** From G To G**

Soul Note 121231-2 *Trovesi; Pino Minafra (t, flhn, didjeridu, v); Rodolfo Migliardi (tb, tba); Marco Remondini (clo); Roberto Bonati, Marco Micheli (b); Vittorio Marinoni (d); Fulvio Maras (perc).* 5/92.

From G To G is a small classic. Without sacrificing any of his intensities, Trovesi has created a colourful, unpredictable, brilliant marshalling of devices drawn from jazz and far beyond. While there are hints of Italian folk music and remote echoes of ancient masters of Italian composition, the synthesis leads inexorably to a real Italian jazz. 'Herbop' uses two themes which are split and reshaped continuously through 18 minutes of music, soloists and ensemble set in perfect balance. 'Now I Can' and 'Hercab' are satirical without being heavy-handed and without losing an underlying severity which Trovesi uses to pare off any fat in the music. But the finest piece is probably 'From G To G' itself, a long, serenely effective dirge in memory of a friend, with a memorable solo from Minafra. The brass-player turns in some of his most lucid work here, Migliardi is rumbustious on tuba and urgently expressive on trombone; but it's Trovesi himself who leads from the front, his alto solos elegantly moving forward from Dolphy and Coleman into a sonority that again suggests the tradition of Italian song. Very fine indeed.

***** Let**

Splasc(h) H 429 *Trovesi; Giancarlo Schiaffini (tb, euph, elec); Walter Prati (elec); Fulvio Maras (perc, elec).* 1/92.

This deconstructivist free-with-electronics session isn't really Trovesi's forte, and he plays more of a willing second fiddle to Schiaffini, whose short-breathed monologues and wheezing electronics (abetted by Prati) fill in most of the space. Pitched somewhere between improvisation and shapeless sound-blocks, the music aspires to dialogue here and there – notably in the horn conversation of 'Allegro, Adagio, Quasi Vivo' – and climaxes in the epic 'Canzona Duodecima', which seems to reprise everything else that's happened in 11 packed minutes.

*****(*) Radici**

Egea SCA 050 *Trovesi; Gianni Coscia (acc).* 95.

*****(*) In Cerca Di Cibo**

ECM 543034-2 *As above.* 2/99.

A gently harmonious collaboration, Trovesi sticking to clarinets, with Coscia's accordion creating both a lovely harmonic undertow and rippling breakers of arpeggios that counterpoint all the reed player's lines. Some of it is café society, some classical rigour, some folk-tune, some dance: 'Antica Mazurka' is a little of all of that, sonorously spread across eight minutes.

The sequel appeared on ECM and may be even finer. 'Django', one of the great melodies in jazz, starts in muted respect and eventually takes an almost shockingly bowdlerized turn. 'Lucignolo' is a marvellous dance for the two instruments, and 'Celebre Mazurka Alterata' is a simply gorgeous piece of music-making.

*****(*) Les Hommes Armés**
Soul Note 121311-2 *As for From G To G.* 5/96.

For all its ingenuities, this is just a degree less welcoming and appealing than its predecessor. Much of it revolves around the ancient European melody of 'L'Homme Armé', out of which came pieces by numerous composers (and Trovesi makes direct reference to the *Kyrie* from Dufay's Mass on the theme at one point). Five tunes – 'Tango', 'Tengo', 'Tingo', 'Tongo' and 'T'Ungo' – are used to interlude the big pieces, which are themselves broken up into diverse fragments; and then there's a crackpot version of 'Mood Indigo' and a tribute to Eric Dolphy, based on a reharmonization of 'Miss Ann'. Trovesi's team play with their usual aplomb but, as delightful as it often is from moment to moment, the record never quite coheres or compels the way *From G To G* did.

****** Around Small Fairy Tales**
Soul Note 121341-2 *Trovesi; Emilio Soana (t); Andrea Dulbecco (vib); Marco Esposito (b); Vittorio Marinoni (d); Orchestra di Camera di Nembro Enea Salmeggia; Bruno Tommaso (cond).* 1/98.

Wonderfully vivid and colourful music, informed by jazz but just as much in debt to the strains he associates with his birthplace of Nembro, this is fashioned somewhat as a suite, the eight pieces arranged by Bruno Tommaso to feature the orchestra alongside the rhythm section and Trovesi's own solos. Swooningly romantic in places, but usually with a hint of tartness underneath via Trovesi's own parts, this is enjoyable as soundtrack escapism or as an intelligent and highly crafted blending of consonant ingredients.

*****(*) Dedalo**
Enja 9419 *Trovesi; Markus Stockhausen(t, flhn); Tom Rainey (d); Fulvio Maras (perc); WDR Big Band.* 5–6/01.

There's a dazzling studio sound, Markus Stockhausen on hand to put in some fine solos, and outstanding rhythm from Rainey and Maras. But this is one of Trovesi's finest hours. Some of these themes – 'From G To G', 'Dance For A King' – will be familiar from earlier records, but the invincible skills of the WDR Big Band are a great boon to such a situation: they're not mavericks like the Vienna Art Orchestra, or regimentally drilled in the manner of many American big bands, but a supremely accomplished ensemble that know European music. Maybe they're less completely simpatico than the group on *Around Small Fairy Tales*, but this is a different kind of record. Energizing, surprising, impolite and completely entertaining.

****** Fugace**
ECM 066583-2 *Trovesi; Massimo Grego (t, elec); Beppe Caruso (tb); Gianluigi Trovesi (picc, acl, as); Marco Remondini (clo, elec); Roberto Bonati, Marco Michell (b); Vittorio Marinoni (d); Fulvio Maras (perc, electronics).* 6/02.

In concert, this is a rowdy, knockabout group, but the studio tempers and polishes them and refines Trovesi's material into something memorable and even unique. Four examples of the 'Siparietto' (or 'Curtain Call') break up the action latterly, which suggests how this is all designed for stage performance, but any of these pieces can stand alone too. The Ottetto boasts typically bumptious Italian-school soloists in Greco and Caruso, but it's perhaps the abundant string- and rhythm-players which really make the group motor. Electronics play a greater role than in any previous Trovesi recording, and they're integrated into compositional concerns that round up the world- and folk-music elements of earlier projects and subsume them into an overall design which is in the end more juicily jazz-directed than many of Trovesi's previous albums. And the maestro himself is in fine fettle as an instrumentalist.

Erik Truffaz

TRUMPET

Born on the Franco-Swiss border, Truffaz has often worked in Geneva but counts himself a French musician. Began in a modal post-bop style, but has more recently experimented with electronic textures and is a rare European signing to Blue Note.

***** Nina Valéria**
Plainisphare/Elephant EL 2204 *Truffaz; Maurice Magnoni (ss, ts); Pierre-Luc Vallet (ky); Marcello Giuliani (b); Marc Erbetta (d).* 92.

***** Out Of A Dream**
Blue Note 855855-2 *Truffaz; Cyrille Bugnon (as, ts); Patrick Muller (p); Marcello Giuliani (b); Marc Erbetta (d).* 97.

***** The Dawn**
Blue Note 493916-2 *As above, except add Nya (v); omit Bugnon.* 12/97.

*****(*) Bending New Corners**
Blue Note 522123-2 *As above.* 4/99.

***** The Walk Of The Giant Turtle**
Blue Note 583885-2 *As above, except omit Nya.* n.d.

The rather dreamy and attractively melodic acoustic music of the Plainisphare set (now reissued on their Elephant subset) didn't altogether suggest that Truffaz was going to go the way he has – although even there he investigated a dance-directed beat in 'Paysage D'Ombres'. More typical was the pretty ballad feel of 'Patience D'Azur' and the title-track, his own muted playing having a Milesian introversion. The Blue Note debut, *Out Of A Dream*, carried on in this vein. If anything, it isn't quite as strong compositionally as *Nina Valéria*, although the sound is undeniably fuller and brighter. But there's nothing here that marks much of an advance on the earlier set, and Bugnon makes little impression. *The Dawn* is altogether different. The album is barely under way before in comes Nya, a self-conscious (and sometimes embarrassing) mix of rapper, beat poet and talkover artist. The words are the expected blend of hipsterese, which listeners raised on Lord Buckley and Eddie Jefferson will find strictly old hat, and a more contemporary outlook, although little dates as quickly as a recorded rapper. The music, though, is an often strikingly effective translation of mild hip-hop beats – played in real time by the rhythm section – to a fundamentally acoustic small-group sound. What makes it work is the starkness of the sound: there's no distracting keyboard clutter, Truffaz has to play the sole horn, and his own delivery is quite skinned-back and pointed. The improvised groove of 'Round-Trip' is bleakly effective. It doesn't feel like a very substantial record, but it's starting something.

Bending New Corners carries it on. Muller makes more extensive use of Fender Rhodes, often with thick sustain and wah wah to grant it an even more fashionably retro sound. All but one of the themes are credited as group compositions, and there's a sense that the band grow these tracks out of collective blowing on simple motifs. If anything, Truffaz himself takes an even lower profile as soloist-leader and, although some of the music sounds like a cleaner, sweeter edition of a lot of old electric Miles Davis stuff, the abstractions of 'More' – followed by the beatbox noodling of 'Less' – are looking towards something else. Even Nya sounds more confident and genuine on his four appearances. Difficult to see how this music will develop without either descending into self-parody or changing into dance music (the group have already been playing at rock festivals), but that's for Truffaz to figure out.

The Walk Of The Giant Turtle starts at an appropriately slow pace and occasionally, though not all that often, gets out of first gear. The best episodes are the ambient-styled tracks, where Truffaz decorates a pretty veil of sound with Milesian musings. It's nice, but it's hard to feel passionate about music which is as determinedly retro as any revivalist bop session.

Frankie Trumbauer (1901–56)

C-MELODY AND ALTO SAXOPHONES, CLARINET, CORNET, VOCAL

'Tram' was one of the master saxophonists of his era, coming to prominence with the Benson Orchestra of Chicago in the early '20s and striking up a famous partnership with Bix Beiderbecke. After the '20s his star descended, despite regular work with Paul Whiteman; an accomplished pilot who often flew himself to gigs, Trumbauer spent his later years working in aviation and playing only rarely.

**** Frankie Trumbauer 1927–1928

Classics 1186 *Trumbauer; Bix Beiderbekce (c); Charlie Margulis (t); Bill Rank (tb); Pee Wee Russell (cl); Jimmy Dorsey (cl, as); Don Murray (cl, bs); Doc Ryker, Charlie Strickfaden (as); Adrian Rollini, Min Leibrook (bsx); Paul Mertz, Itzy Riskin, Frank Signorelli, Tom Satterfield (p); Matt Malneck (vn); Eddie Lang, Carl Kress (g); Chauncey Morehouse, Harold McDonald (d); Seger Ellis, Irving Kaufman, Jerry Macy, John Ryan, Les Reis, Bing Crosby (v).* 2/27–1/28.

***(*) Frankie Trumbauer 1928–1929

Classics 1216 *Trumbauer; Bix Beiderbecke, Andy Secrest (c); Charlie Margulis (t); Bill Rank (tb); Charles Strickfaden (as); Izzy Friedman (cl, ts); Min Leibrook (bsx); Rube Crozier (bsn); Lennie Hayton, Roy Bargy (p); Kurt Dieterle, Miscah Russell, Matt Malneck, Joe Venuti (vn); Eddie Lang, George Rose, Snoozer Quinn (g); Harold McDonald, Stan King, Chauncey Morehouse, George Marsh (d); Scrappy Lambert, Noel Taylor, Marlin Hurt, Smith Ballew (v).* 4/28–5/29.

*** Frankie Trumbauer 1929–1931

Classics 1245 *Trumbauer; Charlie Margulis, Nat Natoli, Harry Goldfield (t); Andy Secrest (c); Bill Rank (tb); Rosy McHargue (cl, as); Charles Strickfaden (as); Izzy Friedman, Fud Livingston (cl, ts); Min Leibrook (bsx); Matt Malneck, Mischa Russell, Kurt Dieterle (vn); Lennie Hayton, Dave Rose, Hoagy Carmichael (p); Eddie Lang (g); John Tobin (bj); Dan Gaybe (b); Bob Conselman, George Marsh (d); Smith Ballew, Art Jarrett (v).* 9/29–6/31.

*** Frankie Trumbauer 1932–1936

Classics 1275 *Trumbauer; Max Connett, Vance Rice; Nat Natoli, Charlie Teagarden, Bunny Berigan, Ed Wade (t); Joe Harris, Jack Teagarden, Glenn Miller (tb); Johnny Mince (cl); Gail Stant, Mac Elstead, Benny Bonacio, Charles Strickfaden, Artie Shaw, Joe Cordaro (cl, as); Harold Jones, Mutt Hayes, Larry Binyon (ts); Herman Crane, Roy Bargy (p); Leon Kaplan, Frederick Saping (vn, g); Craig Leitch, Dick McDonough, Lionel Hall, George Van Eps (g); Charles McConnell, Art Miller, Artie Bernstein (b); Leroy Buck, Herb Quigley, Jack Williams, Stan King (d); The Nitecaps, Helen Rowland, Johnny Blake, Johnny Mercer, Dick Robertson (v).* 4/32–4/36.

**(*) Frankie Trumbauer 1936–1946

Classics 1331 *Trumbauer; Ed Wade, Charlie Teagarden, Russ Case, Dick Dunne, Howard Lamont, Pee Wee Erwin (t); Wayne Williams (t, v); Jack Teagarden (tb, v); Del Menton, Bernie Bahr, Jack Lacey (tb); Artie Shaw, Matty Matlock (cl); Joe Cordaro (cl, as); Bill Stegmeyer (cl, ts); Mutt Hayes, Eddie Miller (ts); Johnny Ross, Joe Sches, Joe Kiefer, Connie Blessing (cl, as, ts); Carl Kress, John Kreyer (g); Roy Bargy, Rene Faure, Dave Bowman (p); Art Miller, Trigger Alpert, Bob Haggart (b); Stan King, Ray Bauduc, Dave Becker, Johnny Blowers (d); Fredda Gibson (aka Georgia Gibbs) (v).* 4/36–3/46.

These five discs contain what amounts to a complete edition of Trumbauer's music under his own name. An influence on Benny Carter (who felt he was never Trumbauer's equal) and Lester Young, he still sounds remarkable on his best records: a cool, almost neutral tone, and a way of slipping through the most contorted phrases in such a way as to make them graceful and as natural as breathing. It's a moot point as to whether it's his solo or Bix's which makes 'Singing The Blues' (1927) the classic it is. The first two discs here include all his sessions with Beiderbecke, and even though many of the sides get bogged down in poor vocals, effects and even blackface hokum (as in 'Dusky Stevedore' and the like), the best music is as good as white jazz got in the '20s: they often save the best for the ride-out chorus, which usually goes with a real swing, and besides Bix and Tram there's Bill Rank, Min Leibrook and Eddie Lang to listen to. These sides are easily available elsewhere in Beiderbecke editions, but this isn't a bad way to get them.

The later music is discouraging in the way it declines in quality, but what happened to Trumbauer was the same thing that happened to many of his peers: the times passed him by, and he belonged to an age before the swing era. Classics 1245 is the first without Beiderbecke and although there are still some good sides – 'Manhattan Rag', 'Happy Feet', 'Choo Choo' – the sound is slipping towards dance-band routine. In 1932, Trumbauer assembled a new orchestra of his own (up till this point he'd been a fixture in the Paul Whiteman Orchestra) and their only eight titles open Classics 1275. In their way they're pretty extraordinary: 'Sizzling One-Step Medley' includes an orchestration of a typical Tram solo which takes the breath away, and there's quite a vocal by Johnny Mercer. Some of the other side are pop tunes, but 'Business In Q' is exciting and Trumbauer's solos suggest that, given time, he could have taken his music much further. The 1934–36 tracks are by what was basically a studio aggregation drawn from Whiteman's band and there are plenty of good moments for both Tram and Teagarden, although in the end the records – almost forgotten today – are sidebars in the swing era. The final disc starts out in the same vein, but the 1940 tracks are dreary and a closing octet session from 1946 sounds inevitably anachronistic, Tram's era seemingly long gone. Considering how renowned his early music was, it's still surprising to reflect on how little-known the later sessions remain.

Vassilis Tsabropoulos

PIANO

A brilliant keyboard technician who has explored free jazz and aspects of the Greek Orthodox liturgy.

*****(*) Achirana**

ECM 1689 *Tsabropoulos; Arild Andersen (b); John Marshall (d).* 99.

***** Akroasis**

ECM 1737 *Tsabropoulos (p solo).* 3/02.

Anyone fearing the spiky modernism of Skalkottas or Xenakis can be reassured. These – the first of the pair particularly – are beautifully textured and thoughtfully harmonic jazz records. If the term continues to mean something, then it has to embrace music of this type. On *Akroasis*, the pianist has taken aspects of the Easter vigil service and woven them into a seamless sequence of hymns and meditations which the composer wisely recommends should be heard as an entirety rather than as separate tracks. The effect is very beautiful and spiritually engaging.

The earlier record is superficially reminiscent of a late Bill Evans trio, particularly on tunes like 'Song For Phyllis' and 'The Spell', but a more convincing parallel might be Paul Bley's trios with Kent Carter and Barry Altschul. 'Diamond Cut Diamond' and 'Mystic' are very much in that demanding mould and here the key protagonist is Andersen, who anchors the music in recognizable tonal territory when it seems in danger of disappearing into total abstraction.

Assif Tsahar

TENOR SAXOPHONE

Contemporary free-form saxophonist, who's made himself into a significant leader and organizational figure in New York circles.

****(*) Shekhina**

Eremite MTE04 *Tsahar; William Parker (b); Susie Ibarra (d).* 7/96.

Passionate free playing that runs dry on Tsahar's lack of variation. His delivery is all post-Ayler howling and wailing – the relatively pacific 'Hidden Heart' is a piece of bruised lyricism and a welcome change – and he does it well enough, but the constant overblowing turns into what seems like the same phrase in gruelling rotation. The redoubtable Parker and the interesting Ibarra do their best to shift the scenes around him, but it's heavy going. Recorded at the Fire In The Valley festival in Amherst, Massachusetts.

***** The Hollow World**

Hopscotch HOP 3 *Tsahar; Herb Robertson, Cuong Vu (t); Vincent Chancey (frhn); Chris Jonas (ss); Rob Brown (as); Joe Daley (tba); Susie Ibarra (d).* 3/99.

The Brass Reeds Ensemble is responsible for this one, a live New York concert from 1999. Tsahar seeks no startling breakthroughs in terms of group sound or organization: much of it derives straight from the language of free jazz as it stood at least 30 years earlier, even if there's a sense of knowing which was either denied to or ignored by their illustrious forebears. As a kind of repertory exercise, it provides plausible material for these skilled and experienced performers. If there's a wild card in the troupe, it might be Chancey, whose impolite sounds keep breaking past the others. But the most powerful presence is surely Ibarra, who develops a never-ending solo with a simultaneous concern for the momentum of each piece and the needs of her fellow players.

***** The Labyrinth**

Hopscotch HOP 12 *Tsahar; Matt Lavelle, Nate Wooley, Marianne Giosa (t); Reut Regev (tb); Charles Waters (cl); Oscar Noriega (bcl); Sabine Arnaud, Muriel Vergnaud (f); Melinda Rice, Jean Cook, Katie Pawluk (vn); Stephanie Griffin, Jessica Pavone (vla); Okkyung Lee, Jonah Sacks (clo); Terence Murren, Byrne Klay, Todd Nicholson (b); Tatsuya Nakatani (perc).* 2/02.

This one's by the New York Underground Orchestra. They follow ten 'paths', all composed and conducted by Tsahar, although he doesn't take an instrumental role himself. The balance of the instrumentation is unusual to say the least, and the numinous string section does inculcate the feel of sombre sinfonietta music into the whole: the fourth section, for one, sounds like a straight piece of composed chamber music, and it would have been interesting to know how much of the concert recording was improvised and how much written (the notes are clueless on this aspect). While much of it is stiff and slow-moving, Tsahar certainly accrues some absorbing textures and juxtapositions along the way, and jazz does survive in some of the solos, especially those of the trumpeters.

Bruce Turner (1922–93)

CLARINET, ALTO SAXOPHONE

Born in Saltburn, Turner joined the Humphrey Lyttelton Band in 1953, which outraged trad purists. He formed his own Jump Band in 1957 (the recordings are all out of print), then disbanded it and joined Acker Bilk in 1966. He rejoined Lyttelton in 1970.

***** That's The Blues, Dad**

Lake LACD49 *Turner; Kenny Baker, Terry Brown (t); Keith Christie (tb); Wally Fawkes (cl); Jimmy Skidmore (ts); Harry Klein (bs); Dill Jones, Lennie Felix, Al Mead (p); Ike Isaacs, Cedric West, Fitzroy Coleman (g); Frank Clarke, Jim Bray, Major Holley, Danny Haggerty (b); Benny Goodman, Stan Greig, Don Lawson, Phil Seamen, Billy Loch (d).* 2/55–1/58.

*****(*) The Jump Band Collection**

Lake LACD 184 *Turner; Terry Brown, John Chilton (t); Pete Strange (tb); Bruce Turner (cl, as); Al Meade, Collin Bates (p);*

Danny Haggerty, Jim Bray (b); Billy Loch, John Armatage (d); Long John Baldry (v). 8/57–2/62.

Turner was a much-loved fixture in British trad-to-swing circles. In later years he became more like the modernist that trad fans were afraid had been imported into the Humphrey Lyttelton band in the early '50s, but on these dates his affection for Hodges, Carter and other masters of swing alto is more obvious. Paul Adams's meticulous compilation *That's The Blues, Dad* puts together tracks by groups co-led by Turner and Fawkes, the Jazz Today group with Kenny Baker and Keith Christie, and Turner's own Jump Band. None of these bands was destined for immortality, and Fawkes and Turner stand out like beacons of inventiveness, but they all made light, amiable work out of a small corner of the music. Adams has done his best with a mix of surviving vinyl and master tapes, and the sound is as good as one can hope for.

Better still, though, is the surprising discovery of the tracks on *The Jump Band Collection*. This makes a much stronger case for Turner's Jump Band as an important and relatively neglected part of British jazz. It is hard to define the band's sound, since it seems to flicker between allegiances to Ellington, Basie, the Vanguard sessions and – with unexpected choices of material such as 'Cushionfoot Stomp' – echoes of the trad background which Turner had largely left behind. His playing on both alto and clarinet has the chameleonic quality which Lyttelton always most valued him for, and the start of any solo opens an enjoyable guessing game as to who he's going to sound like here. The other players also acquit themselves well, even if the personnel on the seven tracks from 1957 is itself speculative. Most of these tracks are previously unissued, and despite sometimes indifferent sound this is a valuable piece of archive work from Lake.

Joe Turner (1907–90)

PIANO, VOCAL

Born in Baltimore, Turner played piano in New York in the '20s but spent much of the '30s in Europe. After military service he returned to Europe and seldom went back.

***(*) Stride By Stride Vol. 1

Solo Art SACD 106 *Turner (p, v).* 12/60.

Turner was one of the least well-known of the great Harlem stride pianists, since he did very little recording in the USA and decamped for Europe in the '40s. His albums reveal an often self-effacing, gentlemanly stylist, fond of an occasional vocal but concentrating on the keyboard, playing the tunes with a modest amount of elaboration and voicing his lines with a certain restraint: he seldom goes for the hurricane kind of stride, and when he plays something like 'Boogie' (on *Stride By Stride Vol. 1*) it's relatively perfunctory. 'Tea For Two' was one of his favourites: there's a memorable version on *Stride By Stride Vol. 1* (once issued on vinyl on 77, and emanating from a Swiss club session), and this is the best place to hear him. Actually, until some of his later recordings are repackaged, it's more or less the only place.

Mark Turner (born 1965)

TENOR SAXOPHONE

Raised in California, Turner took up alto in high school and switched to tenor before attending Berklee, where he met such current colleagues as Kurt Rosenwinkel. He moved to New York in 1990.

**** Yam Yam

Criss Cross 1094 *Turner; Seamus Blake, Terence Dean (ts); Brad Mehldau (p); Kurt Rosenwinkel (g); Larry Grenadier (b); Jorge Rossy (d).* 12/94.

***(*) Consenting Adults

Criss Cross 1177 *Turner; Brad Mehldau (p); Peter Bernstein (g); Larry Grenadier (b); Leon Parker (d).* 12/94.

***(*) Two Tenor Ballads

Criss Cross 1182 *Turner; Tad Shull (ts); Kevin Hays (p); Larry Grenadier (b); Billy Drummond (d).* 12/94.

Turner's debut album was almost nothing like the traditional tenor/rhythm date and he has the character to make such a contrary effort almost entirely successful. Warne Marsh is his most acknowledged influence, and the sinuous lines of most of his improvisations are both like and unlike that tenor master. His own tunes are off-centred, oblique, never quite going the way one expects; with the equally unpredictable Rosenwinkel as the other main horn – if one discounts the superlative Mehldau, that is – the music emerges as a seamless yet intriguingly episodic sequence. In one striking departure, the tenors of Blake and Dean join in on 'Zurich' in a remarkable, almost ghostly interweaving of saxophone sound. This was certainly a very impressive start.

Recorded during the same week but both unreleased until 2000, the other Criss Cross discs are a welcome addition to the Turner canon. *Consenting Adults* is credited to MTB and, while its pick-up nature places it behind both the debut and the discs listed below, there's still much impressively achieved playing here. Parker introduces some unexpected touches, such as the rocking pulse with which he underpins the second version of 'Little Melonae', and Mehldau squeezes in a coolly spacious trio ballad. *Two Tenor Ballads* is more like a typical Criss Cross blowing date, even if pitched at a deliberately laid-back level, but Turner and Shull make a surprisingly compatible team, the more classic sound of the latter a piquant counter to Turner's timbre.

**** Mark Turner

Warner Bros 9 46701-2 *Turner; Joshua Redman (ts); Edward Simon (p); Christopher Thomas (b); Brian Blade (d).* 12/95.

Turner's first for a major (though it was produced by Gerry Teekens, like the last one – so was originally meant for Criss Cross?) is not quite the departure the debut was: it's more in a specific tenor-plus-rhythm vocabulary, perhaps. But what a vocabulary! Redman guests on three tracks and creates a quite sublime contrapuntalism, complementary rather than competitive, though some terrific sparks are struck on the fade to the opening 'Mr Brown'. Maybe the solos on this one reach a tad self-consciously for the limits, but these are players who know what they're doing. Tristano's '327 East 32nd Street' is another fine pair-off, but the grandest set-piece is on a rather obscure Ornette Coleman tune, 'Kathelin Gray'. Simon contributes a gorgeous solo to this one and the tenors work together like their operatic counterparts, stately, full-throated and in rapturous counterpoint.

Turner has the rest of the date to himself – though Simon, Thomas and Blade are the most resourceful of teams behind him – and, while there's no more of his own writing, the improvisations on 'Autumn In New York' and Coltrane's '26-2' are proof of his composer's mind. He has one of the most appealing tenor sounds of recent times, flitting around the highest reaches of the horn without sounding thin or stretched, and hearing him nourish a melody line with it is very satisfying.

**** In This World

Warner Bros 9362-47074-2 *Turner; Brad Mehldau (p); Kurt Rosenwinkel (g); Larry Grenadier (b); Brian Blade, George Rossy (d).* 6/98.

A superb continuation, with Turner and Mehldau seemingly reading each other's minds at some points. An original such as 'Lennie Groove' is straight out of its inspiration, yet settled squarely into a more contemporary, multi-levelled climate of expression. Turner's confidence in his altissimo range is growing all the time, his tone lean but never under strain, and when he improvises at speed the absence of cliché can be thrilling, even as he projects an implacable sense of calm. Rossy sits alongside Blade on the final pair of tracks while Rosenwinkel is on only three tracks but is also a telling contributor. Quite a dense and demanding record, but immensely satisfying.

*** Ballad Session

Warner Bros 9362-47631-2 *Turner; Kevin Hays (p); Kurt Rosenwinkel (g); Larry Grenadier (b); Brian Blade (d).* 10/99.

Disappointing at this stage to find Turner being asked to make a record like this, since it is (on the face of it) a passive retreat from the concerns of the previous two. Ten ballads of varying pedigree, impeccably played; but it's not until the second half of the record that it really makes an impression, starting with a haunting recitation of Bobby Hutcherson's 'Visions', then into three further jazz themes. Here Turner's winsome tone and Rosenwinkel's nimble counterpoint come into their own. But the opening standards seem merely droopy, for all the finesse of the playing.

***(*) Dharma Days

Warner Bros 9362-47998-2 *Turner; Kurt Rosenwinkel (g); Reid Anderson (b); Nasheet Waits (d).* 1–2/01.

Minus piano, and minus any semblance of commercial considerations, this is Turner's toughest record. Like the saxophonist, Rosenwinkel chooses to eschew any sense of gimmickry, and the playing is refined almost to the point of asceticism: the tunes are made up of nine Turner originals which ask for the most acute thinking. It's not obviously a showcase for virtuoso playing, yet the performances are fiercely demanding of the players. Turner sounds to have expanded further his mastery of a high, light sound, which doesn't prevent him from exploring the horn's lower ranges. If it seems unlikely to find him cast as any kind of leader, then the inevitable point of comparison should be with such past masters as Konitz and Marsh: complete individuals who managed to sustain their singularity across an enormous body of work. Enlightened listeners will be fortunate if Turner manages the same. His subsequent abandonment by Warner is very disappointing.

Steve Turre (born 1948)

TROMBONE, SHELLS

An in-demand brassman throughout the '70s, '80s and '90s, Turre's occasional albums as leader have investigated a series of increasingly fanciful fusions of idiom, with his shell-playing often taking a strong role.

*** In The Spur Of The Moment

Telarc CD-83484 *Turre; Ray Charles, Stephen Scott, Chucho Valdes (p); Peter Washington, Buster Williams, Andy Gonzalez(b); Peter Turre, Jack DeJohnette, Horacio 'El Negro' Hernandez(d); Quartette Indigo.* 8–10/99.

*** TNT

Telarc CD-83529 *Turre; James Carter, Dewey Redman, David Sanchez(ts); Mulgrew Miller, Stephen Scott (p); Buster Williams, Peter Washington (b); Victor Lewis, Lewis Nash (d); Giovanni Haidalgo(perc).* 11/00.

Turre's albums have always been mix 'n' match affairs, and his new efforts for Telarc are no exception. *In The Spur Of The Moment* pulls off the coup of bringing Ray Charles into a quartet setting for four tracks. There are two other trios in support of Turre as well: the one with Chucho Valdes is predictably souped-up, with the pianist sounding like he's been at the rocket fuel again, while the one with Stephen Scott is the best of the lot, and 'Something For John' is the outstanding piece on the whole set. Good bits and pieces, but as an album it doesn't really hang together.

Nor, frankly, does *TNT*. Again, it's three groups (though Scott, Washington and Nash are common to two) and three tenors, but the obsessive variation in sound and style merely distracts from the good stuff on the record, which includes a nicely chirpy 'Puente Of Soul' with Sanchez. Turre himself sounds bleary on the slower pieces and the tenormen tend to traipse on and off without really getting into whatever spirit was supposed to fuel the thing.

*** One4J

Telarc CD-83555 *Turre; Joe Alessi, Steve Davis, Robin Eubanks, Andre Hayward, Douglas Purviance (tb); Renee Rosnes, Stephen Scott (p); Peter Washington (b); Victor Lewis (d); Abou M'Boup (perc).* n.d.

Not bad. Turre tips his slide to J. J. Johnson, and brings along five fellow bone-men to help him out. Joe Alessi, who is lead trombone for the New York Philharmonic, does rather show up some of the others in terms of tone and technique. Mostly it's about celebrating the trombone as a plausible front-line instrument, with tracks involving the sort of two-bone workouts which Kai and J.J. once did, as well as all of them getting stuck into 'El Camino Real' and a nippy 'Wee Dot' for four horns. Besides the playing, the record does remind one of Johnson's composing skills, since eight of the tunes are by him. The album does eventually pall a bit, even though it's perhaps meant to prove the trombone's staying power.

Stanley Turrentine (1934–2000)

TENOR AND SOPRANO SAXOPHONES

Father Thomas played with the Savoy Sultans, and brother Tommy was a hard-bop trumpeter. 'Mr T' worked in R&B bands in the '50s before joining Max Roach and then cutting albums for Blue Note from 1960, and with Shirley Scott for Prestige. Had crossover success in the '70s but moved back to more straightahead playing and latterly divided his time between both situations.

***** Blue Hour – The Complete Sessions**
Blue Note 24586-2 2CD *Turrentine; Gene Harris (p); Andrew Simpkins (b); Bill Dowdy (d).* 6–12/60.

*****(*) Up At Minton's**
Blue Note 28885-2 2CD *Turrentine; Horace Parlan (p); Grant Green (g); George Tucker (b); Al Harewood (d).* 2/61.

***** Rough 'N' Tumble**
Blue Note 24552-2 *Turrentine; Blue Mitchell (t); James Spaulding (as); Pepper Adams (bs); McCoy Tyner (p); Bob Cranshaw (b); Mickey Roker (d).* 7/66.

*****(*) The Best Of Stanley Turrentine: The Blue Note Years**
Blue Note 93201-2 *Turrentine; Blue Mitchell (t); Curtis Fuller, Julian Priester (tb); James Spaulding (as); Pepper Adams (bs); Herbie Hancock, Gene Harris, Les McCann, Horace Parlan, McCoy Tyner (p); Shirley Scott, Jimmy Smith (org); George Benson, Kenny Burrell, Grant Green (g); Ron Carter, Bob Cranshaw, Major Holley, Herbie Lewis, Andy Simpkins, George Tucker (b); Bill Dowdy, Otis Finch, Al Harewood, Clarence Johnston, Jimmy Madison, Mickey Roker, Grady Tate (d).* 60–84.

Turrentine's bluesy soul-jazz enjoyed considerable commercial success in the '60s and after. His forte was the mid-tempo blues, often in minor keys, played with a vibrato as broad as his grin. A long sequence of Blue Note albums started as far back as 1960 (*Look Out!*) and ended in 1969 with *Ain't No Way*, but their availability seems to confound expectation, and Stan The Man's records seem to come and go from that catalogue with bemusing rapidity. So snap up *Rough 'N' Tumble* quickly if you want it. Typical Turrentine, the big blue sound sailed over Duke Pearson's functional but effective horn charts, with Green and Tyner getting in some artful fills here and there. Very enjoyable, if scarcely any kind of classic.

At least the twofer *Up At Minton's* seems to be more of a fixture, the original pair of albums spread across a mid-price double-CD. A pity that brother Tommy, who'd been on *Jubilee Shout* a month earlier, didn't make the date, but it's a fine opportunity to hear Stan stretching out with a willing team, as well as some splendid work from Green, whose star seems to have risen dramatically again in the last few years – sad that it had to be a posthumous acclaim. *Blue Hour* offers the 1960 date where The Three Sounds backed Turrentine on his debut session (originally shelved because the producer felt Mr T had outplayed his hit act) and all the tracks from *Blue Hour* itself: Harris does sound more subdued than usual here and there, and two discs of low-flame cooking is a bit of a marathon, but track for track it's soulful and satisfying.

The Blue Note *Best Of* is thoroughly recommended, picking nine longish tracks (the shortest are a lovely, brief 'God Bless The Child' from the excellent *Never Let Me Go* and the previously unreleased 'Lonesome Lover', a Max Roach composition). Worth searching out.

***** Sugar**
CTI/Epic 5051732 *Turrentine; Freddie Hubbard (t); Hubert Laws (f); Johnny 'Hammond' Smith (p, org); Lonnie Liston Smith (p); Butch Cornell (org); George Benson (g); Ron Carter (b); Billy Kaye, Billy Cobham (d); Pablo Landrum, Airto Moreira (perc).* 11/70–7/71.

The sleeve-notes describe the second track, 'Sunshine Alley', as 'post-boogaloo', but this set is really a transition between Turrentine's long-standing hard-bop self and the amiable guy of his '70s sets for Fantasy. Creed Taylor let the band dig in on the three tracks (which let the entire LP run for a miserly 25 minutes) and there's some decent blowing by what was becoming the CTI in-house team. Hardly epochal, though, and certainly no great advance on what Stanley had been doing at Blue Note. There's a woozy 'bonus' live version of 'Sugar' by a similar group to the studio line-up.

**** Pieces Of Dreams**
Original Jazz Classics OJC 831 *Turrentine; Sonny Burke, John Miller, Gene Page (ky); Ray Parker, Dean Parks, David T. Walker (g); Ron Brown (b); Ed Moore, Ed Greene (d); Gary Coleman, Joe Clayton (perc); strings, voices.* 7/74.

**** Everybody Come On Out**
Original Jazz Classics OJC 911 *Turrentine; Oscar Brashear, Paul Hubinon, Bob Findley (t); George Bohannon, Charley Loper (tb); Lew McRearey (btb); Buddy Collette, Bill Green (reeds); Joe Sample (ky); Lee Ritenour, Craig McMullen (g); Paul Jackson (b); Harvey Mason (d); Bill Summers (perc); strings.* 3/76.

****(*) The Best Of Mr T**
Fantasy 7708 *Turrentine; Freddie Hubbard (t); Cedar Walton (p); Paul Griffin, Patrice Rushen, Joe Sample (ky); Cornell Dupree, Eric Gale, Ray Parker Jr, Lee Ritenour (g); Ron Carter (b); Jack DeJohnette, Harvey Mason (d).* n.d.

Despite a partial return to jazz structures in subsequent decades, Turrentine moved over almost permanently to pop, like his collaborator on the thumping *Straight Ahead*, George Benson. His albums for Fantasy in the '70s are a dull and dated lot, with only a few phrases poking through the candied, synthetic gloom to suggest that Mr T is actually in there somewhere. In the '90s, he went back to his original strengths, perhaps only to find that his voice had faded away more than he realized: a couple of deleted albums for Musicmasters were close to useless.

29th Street Saxophone Quartet

GROUP

Four New York-based saxophonists of different backgrounds, who rehearsed at Jim Hartog's apartment on ... 29th Street.

*****(*) Live**
Red RR 123223 *Ed Jackson, Bobby Watson (as); Rich Rothenberg (ts); Jim Hartog (bs).* 7/88.

***** Milano New York Bridge**
Red 123262-2 *As above.* 11/92–12/93.

At once the most fun and the most coherent and self-challenging of the saxophone quartets, 29th Street was first put together at the behest of Jackson and Hartog, who both met Rich Rothenberg independently of each other and then persuaded Bobby Watson to enlist. If Watson was in many ways the key member of the group – his are the most distinctive improvisations, and his romantic streak softens the edges of some of their repertoire to beneficial effect – there was an exceptional uniformity of ideas and abilities in this band. Since they never doubled on other instruments, there's a special concentration on individual and collective timbre, raised to a very high level, and their interaction became so advanced that they're close to that fabled point where improvisation and structure merge into one. Yet it's a high-spirited, funky and contagiously exciting group to listen to.

It's cheering to hear that this fine group has reformed in 2003/4 but so far this has yet to yield any recorded results and there still isn't much in the catalogue. *Live* is arguably their most vivid record. While there are occasional flaws – at least by their own prodigiously high standards – the sheer exuberance of the playing is phenomenal. Hartog's 'New Moon' must be the prettiest of all their ballads, and the way Jackson's yelping alto leads into the collective barnstorming of Kevin Eubanks's 'Sundance' is enough to elicit cheers from any listener. *Milano New York Bridge* is not quite one of their best: mostly jazz standards, tightly arranged and a bit airless in parts.

McCoy Tyner (born 1938)

PIANO, KOTO, DULCIMER, FLUTE, PERCUSSION

Born in Philadelphia, Tyner worked with local players until meeting John Coltrane in 1959. He joined the Coltrane quartet in 1960 and stayed for six years, simultaneously making his own records for Impulse!. After a spell with Blue Note, he commenced a long association with Milestone and began leading medium-sized groups as well as working in a trio situation. In the '80s and '90s he made records for several labels, in solo, small-group and big-band settings. His grand style, uncompromisingly based around familiar tonalities and all the qualities of the acoustic piano, remains a major influence on contemporary pianists.

*****(*) Inception**
Impulse! 051220-2 *Tyner; Art Davis (b); Elvin Jones (d).* 1/62.

***** Nights Of Ballads And Blues**
Impulse! 051221-2 *Tyner; Steve Davis (b); Lex Humphries (d).* 3/63.

*****(*) Plays Ellington**
Impulse! 051216-2 *Tyner; Jimmy Garrison (b); Elvin Jones (d); Willie Rodriguez, Johnny Pacheco (perc).* 12/64.

Tyner was still with John Coltrane's group when he started making records under his own name. While these early sessions add little to what he was doing with the saxophonist, they do reveal what the pianist was doing more clearly than the engine-room of the Coltrane band could allow. Impulse! have now reorganized his output into a clear sequence of single-disc reissues. *Inception* was Tyner's debut as a leader. He had yet to build his playing into the massive, orchestral concept which came later. His variations on his own 'Inception' and 'Blues For Gwen' are beautifully bright and lively, echoing Coltrane's own comment in the sleeve-note on how the pianist would use unusual clusters to illuminate his structures. *Reaching Fourth* came back briefly but has been deleted again. *Nights Of Ballads And Blues* is all jazz standards or pop tunes, and it is perhaps a degree more ordinary, yet the playing is unfailingly strong. The Ellington album is disappointing: Tyner's romanticism emerges, but his interpretative bent seems untested by the likes of 'Satin Doll' – it works better on the *Ballads And Blues* version – and the addition of the percussionists on four tracks seems like nothing but a gimmick. This is a very attractive sequence in the Impulse! digipak format, and though we find that Rudy van Gelder's piano sound remains cloudy and unsympathetic, the records probably sound as good as they ever will.

CORE COLLECTION

****** The Real McCoy**
Blue Note 97807-2 *Tyner; Joe Henderson (ts); Ron Carter (b); Elvin Jones (d).* 4/67.

A key album in Tyner's discography. On the face of it, the music might be a direct extension of the Coltrane group, with Henderson substituting for Trane. But with Tyner calling the tunes, it sounds quite different: dynamics are much more varied, form is more finely articulated and, while the band pushes at the limits of tonality and metre alike, it never quite breaches them. The opening 'Passion Dance' is a definitive Tyner composition: structured round a single key but pounding through a metre which the leader noted as 'evoking ritual and trance-like states', it gathers power through the piano and saxophone statements until it sounds ready to explode; yet the concluding regrouping and subsequent variations are resolved immaculately. 'Contemplation', 'Four By Five' and 'Search For Peace' explore this brinkmanship further, through 3/4, 4/4 and 5/4 rhythms and fragments of melody which are enough to fuel all of the band's manoeuvres. Henderson is superbly resolute in avoiding cliché, Carter and Jones work with dramatic compatibility, and Tyner's own playing exults in some of his discoveries learnt over the previous three years. His grand pedal-chords and fluttering right-hand lines establish the classic patterns of call-and-response which have dominated his manner ever since, and the sound he gets is peculiarly translucent, enabling one to hear through the clusters and follow all of his complex lines. Very highly recommended. It has been remastered as part of the Rudy van Gelder Edition and sounds better than ever.

***** Asante**
Blue Note 93384-2 *Tyner; Gary Bartz (ss, as); Andrew White (as, ob); Hubert Laws (f, af); Ted Dunbar (g); Buster Williams, Herbie Lewis (b); Billy Hart, Freddie Waits (d); Mtume (perc); Songai (v).* 7–9/70.

This sounds like a transitional record, two 1970 sessions (originally withheld for release until later in the decade) which see Tyner feeling his way towards the pan-cultural feel of his best music of the coming decade. Songai's wordless vocals are the most dated element, and some of the percussion parts seem like tacked-on polyrhythms, but the three earlier tracks with Laws, White and Bartz making a vividly colourful front-line are more encouraging, especially the bright weave of interdependent lines in 'Forbidden Land'. Exoticism from a more innocent time.

***** Sahara**
Original Jazz Classics OJC 311 *Tyner; Sonny Fortune (ss, as, f); Calvin Hill (b, perc); Alphonse Mouzon (d, t, f).* 1/72.

Another important record for Tyner. After leaving Blue Note (several of his last sessions for them are currently missing), his career floundered until he was signed by Milestone: his first release, *Sahara*, was a poll-winning record which established his course for the '70s. Mouzon couldn't have played the way he does but for Elvin Jones, yet his choked cymbals and relentless emphasis of the beat are very different from Jones's polyrhythmic swells. Fortune plays with uproarious power and velocity, and his solo on 'Rebirth' is electrifying; but his is essentially a decorative role, while the pianist drives and dominates the music. The group acts as the opposing face to Cecil Taylor's brand of energy music: controlled by harmonic and metrical ground-rules, nobody flies for freedom, but there is a compensating jubilation in the leader's mighty utterance. 'Sahara' and 'Ebony Queen' best express that here, although the piano solo, 'A Prayer For My Family', is a useful oasis of calm. Later Tyner records would be better engineered and realized, but this one remains excitingly fresh.

***** Song For My Lady**

Original Jazz Classics OJC 313 *As above, except add Charles Tolliver (flhn), Michael White (vn), Mtume (perc).* 9–11/72.

*****(*) Echoes Of A Friend**

Original Jazz Classics OJC 650 *Tyner.* 11/72.

****(*) Song Of The New World**

Original Jazz Classics OJC 618 *Tyner; Virgil Jones, Cecil Bridgewater, Jon Faddis (t); Garnett Brown, Dick Griffin (tb); Julius Watkins, Willie Ruff, William Warnick III (frhn); Hubert Laws (picc, f); Sonny Fortune (ss, as, f); Harry Smyles (ob); Kiane Zawadi (euph); Bob Stewart (tba); Juni Booth (b); Alphonse Mouzon (d); Sonny Morgan (perc); strings.* 4/73.

*****(*) Enlightenment**

Milestone MCD-55001-2 *Tyner; Azar Lawrence (ss, ts); Juni Booth (b); Alphonse Mouzon (d).* 7/73.

*****(*) Atlantis**

Milestone MCD-55002-2 *Tyner; Azar Lawrence (ss, ts); Juni Booth (b); Willy Fletcher (d); Guilherme Franco (perc).* 8–9/74.

***** Trident**

Original Jazz Classics OJC 720 *Tyner; Ron Carter (b); Elvin Jones (d).* 2/75.

**** Fly With The Wind**

Original Jazz Classics OJC 699 *Tyner; Hubert Laws (f, af); Paul Renzi (picc, f); Raymond Duste (ob); Linda Wood (hp); Ron Carter (b); Billy Cobham (d); strings.* 1/76.

*****(*) Focal Point**

Original Jazz Classics OJC 1009 *Tyner; Gary Bartz (cl, sno, ss, as); Joe Ford (ss, as, f); Ron Bridgewater (ss, ts); Charles Fambrough (b); Eric Gravatt (d); Guilherme Franco (perc).* 8/76.

Following the success of *Sahara*, Tyner embarked on a regular schedule of recording and found himself a popular concert draw at last. The music certainly sounded at home among 'progressive' trends in rock and beyond, although the pianist's beefy romanticism had a lot more profundity in it than most such music-making. *Song For My Lady* varied the cast of the previous disc by adding Michael White and Charles Tolliver to two open-ended pieces, but it was the lyricism of the title-track and Tyner's solo outing, 'A Silent Tear', which were most impressive. *Echoes Of A Friend* is a solo tribute to John Coltrane which resounds with all the grand exhortation which the pianist can wring from the keyboard. *Atlantis* and *Enlightenment* are two huge, sprawling concert recordings which will drain most listeners: Tyner's piano outpourings seem unstoppable, and Lawrence comes on as an even fierier spirit than Fortune, even if both are in thrall to Coltrane. The *Enlightenment* set, cut at Montreux, is marginally superior, if only for the pile-driving 'Walk Spirit, Talk Spirit'. But *Atlantis* is still very strong, with a majestic turn through 'My One And Only Love' and another torrential group-performance on the title-piece.

It was this kind of incantatory concert form which began to make Tyner's output sound overcrowded with effort: without the ability to soar away from structure, the music could seem bloated, as if packed with steroids. His other Milestone records of the period compensate with varied settings. *Song Of The New World* adds brass and string sections, *Fly With The Wind* sets up an orchestra behind him. But the latter seems to have its energy papered over with the strings, and *Song Of The New World* uses the extra musicians to no very bountiful purpose. *Trident* reunited Tyner with Elvin Jones, but the results were genial rather than passionate. *Focal Point* looks to secure the firepower in the studio which the band generated in concert; the horns are made even more massive via overdubbing, and this sometimes leads to stiffness in the ensemble sound. 'Parody' is an exultant duet for piano and drums. A neglected album in Tyner's canon, and we were a little surprised to find how well it's aged in this new CD edition.

Some fine albums from the period are (still) currently deleted – including *The Greeting* and *Passion Dance* – and though they all contain music of lesser power than *Enlightenment*, Tyner's search for strength and tenderness in equal measure remains compelling.

*****(*) Supertrios**

Milestone MCD 55003-2 *Tyner; Ron Carter, Eddie Gomez (b); Tony Williams, Jack DeJohnette (d).* 4/77.

***** Quartets 4 × 4**

Milestone MCD-55007-2 *Tyner; Freddie Hubbard (t); Arthur Blythe (as); Bobby Hutcherson (vib); John Abercrombie (g); Cecil McBee (b); Al Foster (d).* 3–5/80.

Shrewdly balanced between show-tunes, jazz standards and Tyner originals, the double-trio event, with Tyner meeting Gomez and DeJohnette on one date and Carter and Williams on the other, is a memorable one. Almost 15 years after his first trio records, Tyner's methods have taken on an invincible assurance, and with musicians like these he is working at his highest level. The session with Carter and Williams is slightly the more invigorating, with pianist and drummer working trenchantly through 'I Mean You' and 'A Moment's Notice', which stands out among many versions the pianist has played.

The album of quartets, with Abercrombie, Hubbard, Blythe and Hutcherson taking turns as the star guest, is pretty disappointing, given the personnel. Everyone plays politely rather than with any pressing need to communicate anything, and as a result it's perhaps the meeting with Hutcherson, most thoughtful of musicians, which comes off best.

*****(*) Uptown/Downtown**

Milestone M 9167 *Tyner; Virgil Jones, Earl Gardner, Kamau Adilifu (t); Robin Eubanks (tb); Steve Turre (tb, didjeridu); John Clark (frhn); Joe Ford, Doug Harris (ss, as); Ricky Ford, Junior Cook (ts); Howard Johnson (tba); Avery Sharpe (b); Louis Hayes (d); Steve Thornton (perc).* 11/88.

A memorable departure for Tyner, which he built on with his subsequent Birdology albums. The six charts here amplify the sweep of his groups of the '70s, and the miracle is that it comes across as expansive and uncongested. Although he hardly seems like a big-band pianist, his own solos seem able to raise the already grand sound of the orchestra to an even higher level, and the choice of horn soloists – Joe Ford, Turre, Cook, Ricky Ford – makes for a thrillingly coloured and barnstorming effect. Five of the pieces are Tyner originals, the sixth is by Steve Turre, and nothing misfires; even the live sound is good enough to expose the few touches of under-rehearsal which slip through.

*****(*) Things Ain't What They Used To Be**

Blue Note 935982 *Tyner; George Adams (ts); John Scofield (g).* 89.

Tyner returned to Blue Note as a solo artist, and the albums are prized examples of a great player in his late prime. Alas, the splendid *Revelations*, a solo 'studio' recital in New York's Merkin Hall, has been deleted for the moment. *Things Ain't What They Used To Be* is more of the same, although Scofield and Adams duet on some tracks. Tyner sees no reason to check his regular flow, and as a result the three pieces with Scofield sound too full, but the duet with Adams on 'My One And Only Love' is gloriously realized, and some of the solos – particularly his latest thoughts on 'Naima' – are Tyner at his finest.

****** Soliloquy**

Blue Note 796429-2 *Tyner (p solo).* 2/91.

Tyner's third solo outing for Blue Note completes a triptych that sums up his art: rushing, open-hearted, grand of gesture, ineffably romantic, muscular, florid. He still takes every chance to overplay his hand, but that is his way: 'Willow Weep For Me', for instance, is about as aggressive a version of this tune as has ever been recorded. Yet his best melodies – either written or improvised out of tunes by Powell, Coltrane and, surprisingly, Dexter Gordon – are as communicative as they are powerful. He has written for long enough to make his own choices of tune a reflection on his own dynasty: 'Effendi' dates back to his earliest Impulse! sessions, 'Española' – a haunting use of the Spanish tinge – is brand new, and both are performed with fine evocative skill. Like its predecessors the album was recorded at Merkin Hall in New York, and the piano sound is superb.

****** Manhattan Moods**

Blue Note 828423-2 *Tyner; Bobby Hutcherson (vib, mar).* 12/93.

They've met before with auspicious results, but this encounter is pure bliss from first to last. Instead of the instruments cancelling each other out, as is often the case in this kind of situation, the keyboard and vibes entwine to create textures of ecstatic beauty – limpid, resonant, revealing. Tyner allows Hutcherson to take centre stage for much of the time, even if the piano is slightly the more forward in the mix, and Bobby responds with some of his most rapt playing. One could complain that they might have chosen some fresher tunes to play, but the results tend to sweep aside reservations. The closing look at 'For Heaven's Sake' is on a par with Hutcherson's superlative version with Kenny Barron (discussed under the pianist's name).

***** Infinity**

Impulse! 11712 *Tyner; Michael Brecker (ts); Avery Sharpe (b); Aaron Scott (d); Waltinho Anastacio (perc).* 94.

***** Prelude And Sonata**

Milestone MCD-9244-2 *Tyner; Joshua Redman (ts); Antonio Hart (as); Christian McBride (b); Marvin 'Smitty' Smith (d).* 11/94.

Infinity marked the return of Impulse! as a 'new' jazz label, and it's fitting that it should be Tyner who started it off. This isn't one of his greatest: Brecker could have been the fall-guy here, cast in the Coltrane role, but he manages to sidestep too many of the comparisons without finally convincing that he needn't walk in giant steps. *Prelude And Sonata* is basically a ballad album, bookended with pieces of Chopin and Beethoven; it's interesting to note that McBride and Smith – for all their star status – are no more an appropriate match for Tyner than the undervalued Sharpe and Scott. The saxophonists play well, but this kind of session has become a commonplace which Tyner doesn't respond to especially well. He plays professionally on both records without ever getting into his top gear.

*****(*) McCoy Tyner And The Latin All-Stars**

Telarc CD-83462 *Tyner; Claudio Roditi (t, flhn); Steve Turre (tb, shells); Gary Bartz (ss, as); Dave Valentin (f); Avery Sharpe (b); Ignacio Berroa (d); Giovanni Hidalgo, Johnny Almendra (perc).* 7/98.

He's gone to yet another new label, and it's amusing to find that this fresh start has found him, if anything, returning to his glory days of the '70s Milestone bands. Bartz goes all the way back to *Asante*, and the rest of the group know better than to try and upstage the master. If anyone can make a 'Latin-Jazz' album without submitting to the tyranny of that rhythm, it's Tyner – all he really does is fit the expected sunshine-shuffle into his own thunderous drive, and the result is his most characteristic set for years. Valentin plays a few silly solos, but he's largely rendered harmless by the situation, and there's some excellent work from the other horns, especially Turre. Tyner's latest thoughts on 'Afro Blue' are a highlight, and the farewell parade through 'Blue Bossa' sends us out with a cheer.

*****(*) McCoy Tyner With Stanley Clarke And Al Foster**

Telarc CD-83488 *Tyner; Stanley Clarke (b); Al Foster (d).* 4/99.

All-star again, underlined by all three names appearing in the album title. Clarke divides his time between electric and stand-up instrument, and one piece, 'I Want To Tell You 'Bout That', gets a version with each option (predictably, the 'electric' rendition is zippier). These are three individual stylists still in top fettle, and the record is no disappointment, even if it's clear that at this point McCoy is going to spend the rest of his career musing on what he's already achieved.

*****(*) Jazz Roots**

Telarc CD-83507 *Tyner (p solo).* 6/00.

Whatever music Tyner has left in him, it feels like its most personal cast is going to come out when he's playing solo. If there's little left for him to discover in a group situation, by himself he can touch on reserves and refinements which are going to brighten and invigorate even a tired old concept like this, a homage to 'the jazz piano legends of the 20th century'. There are bows made in the direction of Powell, Evans, Hines, Tatum, Jarrett and Corea; although none of them sound like

McCoy 'doing' the player in question, even if he gets, say, the Hines insouciance down pretty well on 'Blues For Fatha'. It's the great ebullience, the intensely dark sonorities lit up by sudden fireworks and the big man's tenderness (especially on the finale to 'My Foolish Heart') which really strike home.

*****(*) Land Of Giants**
Telarc CD-83576 *Tyner; Bobby Hutcherson (vib); Charnett Moffett (b); Eric Harland (d).* 12/02.

The title recalls an old lament, 'there were giants in those days', and it might suggest a poignant nod to a jazz continuum passing into history. After all, Tyner and Hutcherson, once the fieriest of young turks, are suddenly elder statesmen with their groundbreaking days far behind them. And some of these tunes are the matter of autumnal reflection, for sure: 'December', 'For All We Know' and 'Contemplation' among them. But Moffett and Harland are young(ish) men with remits of their own, and they play some stirring stuff behind the old masters – at times the music reaches a very fast boil. The drummer in particular overplays, although one feels that that has to be better than mere respectful timekeeping, which would send everything to sleep. Jack Renner's engineering creates a big stage with depth and immediacy, and helps sort out what must be a crowded live sound. Maybe it is, in the end, just a jog round the park for virtiuoso players, but it's a very satisfying listen.

Hiromi Uehara

PIANO

A Japanese piano scholar who was turned on to Oscar Peterson by her mother, Uehara is an Ahmad Jamal protégée now working in the US.

***(*) Another Mind**
Telarc SACD-63558 *Uehara; Jim Odgren (as); David Fiuczynski (g); Mitch Cohn, Anthony Jackson (b); Dave DiCenso (d).* 9/02.

The SACD sound on this mostly acoustic disc is stunning, but the music's more numbing than anything. Uehara (although her record company would prefer her first name to be highlighted) presides over what's really a tumultuously busy fusion record, driven into hyperdrive by DiCenso's infuriatingly overcooked drumming. By accenting her left-hand lines more than usually, she at least gets a heavier texture than one normally expects from the piano–bass–drums trinity. Mostly, though, this is energy and technique flailing all over the place. The closing piano solo makes a welcome respite.

Federico Ughi (born 1972)

DRUMS, VOCALS

Grew up in Rome and started his career early before moving to England and then the US, where he studied with Paul Bley. His most robust association, following the group After Breakfast, has been with multi-instrumentalist Daniel Carter.

***** The Space Within**
Slam CD 236 *Ughi; Steve Buckley (as); Rachel Musson (ts); Matthew F. Morris (bs).* 10/98.

***** Astonishment**
577 Records 577-1 *Ughi; Daniel Carter (t, as, f, cl).* 3/01.

****(*) ULERS Two**
577 Records 577-2 *Ughi (d, v, sounds).* 8/01.

*****(*) South Of Brooklyn**
577 Records 577-3 *Ughi; Daniel Carter (as); Nathan Hanson (ts, elec); Matt Glassmeyer (ts, sounds); Sean Moran (g); Dan Fabricatore (b).* 02.

Ughi is a notably delicate player, much more interested in the accidentals and overtones he can conjure from his kit than he is in power and circumstance. The duets with Carter are superb and somewhat reminiscent in quality, if not in basic idiom, of Bill Dixon's duets with Tony Oxley. Federico likes to play with soft mallets or with the tips of his fingers. On *ULERS Two* there is a quiet heartbeat, sometimes interspersed with impatient rapping, as he accompanies soundscape material – the title refers to 'Unrehearsed live editing of recorded sound' – taped on a one-hour journey from the Piazza S. Cosima to Via Alberico II in Rome. It's lovely stuff, though the improvised quotient is obviously much less than on his free-jazz projects.

South Of Brooklyn celebrates his move to the United States and immediately conjures up a much funkier, more rhythmic personality. The groups here, with Carter very much a presence, are young, curious and cheerfully over the top when it seems appropriate and sometimes when it doesn't. The album scampers by as insouciantly as the sessions must have done, but one is constantly aware of Ughi's level of concentration and his determined approach to the source material. Of the supporting players, guitarist Moran stands out shiningly, though the saxophonists are equally impressive.

Saxophones are very much in the foreground on *The Space Within*, a series of duets recorded in London before Ughi's departure for America. These are patchy sessions, sometimes brilliant as when he locks horns with Buckley, occasionally drab and uncommunicative, but no one can miss the enthusiasm and care with which Ughi approaches any playing situation. A player for the future.

Gebhard Ullmann (born 1957)

TENOR AND SOPRANO SAXOPHONES, BASS CLARINET, FLUTE, BASS AND ALTO FLUTES, PICCOLO

An eclectic reed specialist who shuttles between Berlin and New York, Ullmann is at home in many contemporary settings and performs regularly with several different groups, working mainly from his own prolific composer's book.

*****(*) Basement Research**
Soul Note 12171-2 *Ullmann; Ellery Eskelin (ts); Drew Gress (b); Phil Haynes (d).* 11/93.

Ullmann's albums from the '90s are a diverse lot. The meeting with the Eskelin/Gress/Haynes trio on *Basement Research* is different again. Ullmann is stepping into a trio environment where the players already know one another well, and he's welcomed cautiously, though there's some provocative duelling for space. If Eskelin is the further out of the two players, Ullmann's primarily cool extremism is still cutting-edge, and the tracks in which the two both play tenor have a splendidly combative element.

*** Ta Lam

Songlines SGL 1520-2 *Ullmann; Dirk Engelhardt (ss, ts, bcl); Thomas Klemm (ts, f); Jürgen Kupke (cl); Joachim Litty (acl, bcl, as); Heiner Reinhardt (bcl); Volker Schlott (ss, as, f); Hans Hassler (acc).* 8/91–3/94.

What an extraordinary record *Ta Lam* is. Ullmann summons a great phalanx of reed-players (and overdubs himself on five other tracks, playing nine different horns) in a collection of pieces that blend free-for-all uproar with a lumbering, symphonic delivery that is sometimes too weighty for its own good. A bizarre arrangement of 'Mack The Knife' will turn enough heads, but what about the crescendo (and diminuendo) of 'Think Tank', or the way odd-man-out Hassler scampers in and around the saxophone army? Beautifully recorded, this is an intriguing disc, and its ration of near-misses shouldn't stop the curious from investigating.

***(*) Kreuzberg Park East

Soul Note 121371-2 *Ullmann; Ellery Eskelin (ts); Drew Gress (b); Phil Haynes (d).* 5/97.

A return match for this quartet. Stylistically, this is a more diverse record, with Ullmann the composer keen to display his range, which stretches from the stealthy whisperings of 'Flutist With Hat And Shoe' to the vertiginous contrapuntal melodies of 'Almost Twenty-Eight'. It's all meat and drink to Eskelin and the others, who remain unfazed by whatever the leader throws their way. Good-humoured and rarely without an absorbing moment.

*** The Clarinet Trio Oct. 1, '98

Leo Lab CD 058 *Ullmann; Jürgen Kupke (cl); Theo Nabicht (bcl).* 9–10/98.

***(*) Translucent Tones

Leo LR 339 *As above.* 8/01.

Clarinet and two bass clarinets, in another packed record of miniatures – 19 despatched inside 55 minutes. There is some overdubbing here and there to give the reeds even more weight, but mostly they rely on the attractive ambience of an old chamber-music hall in Berlin. Since nothing outstays its welcome, none of the pieces have their impact blunted; though dropping in 'Tea For Two' half-way through is a flippancy which doesn't really chime with an otherwise often severe outlook. For specialist tastes, but well done. As is the successor: since it's not a band convened all that often, one suspects, it's hard to detect what might be considered conventional growth and maturing, but the wit is an ounce sharper, the ballad-lines a degree warmer, the reflexes a measure quicker.

**(*) Variations On A Master Plan

Leo LR 371 *Ullmann; Michael Jefry Stevens (p); Joe Fonda (b); Han Bennink (d).* 3/01.

**(*) Spirals

482 Music 482-1028 *As above, except George Schuller (d) replaces Bennink.* 3/03.

Ullmann calls this group Conference Call. The first record gets off to a very slow start which Bennink seems to be trying to kick some life into. Thereafter it does rather meander along, and Ullmann seems curiously reluctant to take any kind of lead, as if he weren't sure what the point of the group was. Schuller arrives for the second record and immediately takes a strong role: he contributes the first and last pieces, and they're two of the longest. Ullmann again sounds oddly bleary and the group doesn't suggest itself as one of his better vehicles. If this is a conference call, not everyone's listening properly.

James Blood Ulmer (born 1942)

GUITAR, VOCALS

Born in South Carolina, Ulmer sang gospel, played in funk groups, and then studied with Art Blakey and Ornette Coleman in turn; the former influence is often understated by commentators on his music, but it is certainly there. Some of the guitarist's work borders on the hard-edged black rock sound of bands like Living Color, but his jazz and blues chops are undeniable.

CORE COLLECTION

**** Odyssey

Columbia 485101 *Ulmer; Charles Burnham (vn); Warren Benbow (d).* 3–5/83.

Often described as a student of Ornette Coleman's still-unassimilated 'harmolodics' – a theory which dispenses with the normal hierarchy of 'lead' and 'rhythm' instruments, allowing free harmonic interchange at all levels of a group – Ulmer had actually started to devise similar ideas independently. In the late '60s he played with organists Hank Marr and Big John Patton, promoting a harsh modern derivative of soul-jazz. His work with drummer Rashied Ali (who rejoined one of the more abstract of Ulmer's late-'80s bands, Original Phalanx/Phalanx) brought him to the attention of Ornette Coleman.

Ulmer's contract with Columbia petered out after three albums, and so far only the final one has made it to CD. It's a classic New York record of the period. Given a beefy, up-front sound (at last), Ulmer slimmed his group down to a bass-less trio, added the almost shamanistic sound of Charles Burnham's fiddle, and set the group to rock and roll over eight rootsy chunks of American music. 'Church' and 'Little Red House' reach back to gospel, blues and country dance as transmogrified into electrical storms, the whine of the violin mingling with the bite and twang of Ulmer's chording to superb effect. 'Are You Glad To Be In America?' reappears as a kind of slow lament. The essential Ulmer record.

***(*) Memphis Blood: The Sun Sessions

Label M 5728 *Ulmer; Vernon Reid (g); Charles Burnham (vn); David Barnes (hca); Aubrey Dayle (d).* 4/01.

*** No Escape From The Blues: The Electric Lady Sessions

Sindrome 9312 *Ulmer; Olu Dara (pocket t); Leon Gruenbaum (p, org, mca, ky, v); Vernon Reid (g, bj, sitar); Charles Burnham (vn, mn, v); David Barnes (hca, v); Mark Anthony Peterson (b); Aubrey Dayle (d); John Kruth (tamboura); Queen Esther Marrow, Memphis Blood Jugband Singers (v); May Smullyan Jenkins (tap).* 02.

In 2001 Ulmer and band began to tour not clubs and concert halls but some of the legendary studios of American music. The Sun session is – at last – a confrontation with the early fathers of the blues. The date opens with a version of 'Spoonful' and includes a further five Willie Dixon songs, as well as material by Sonny Boy Williamson (including 'Fattening Frogs For Snakes'), T-Bone Burnett and John Lee Hooker. Black rocker

Vernon Reid almost steals the show here and there, but he is mixed somewhat back of Blood; he takes the lead on Otis Rush's 'Double Trouble'. Burnham is astonishing on 'Little Red Rooster', using a wah-wah pedal on his violin. The overall impression is of familiar melodies and structures passed through a prism. The distortions are most effective when they are least mannered, and Ulmer is by now sussed enough to know when not to push his luck. A vivid and intense record from a player at the top of his powers.

The Electric Lady date is more shambolic but full of the same vivid energy. 'Are You Glad To Be In America' is reprised, but the real gem is the closing version of 'The Blues Had A Baby And Called It Rock'N'Roll', which is completely over the top. There's not much finesse to the album but it's vintage Ulmer. Nice guest spots from Dara and the others. It's somehow unlikely that he'll be moving on the Rudy Van Gelder's in Englewood Cliffs, but we'll wait and see.

Hans Ulrik (born 1965)

TENOR AND SOPRANO SAXOPHONES, CLARINET

Copenhagen-based modernist who used his time in America in the '80s to make a string of useful contacts, several of whom play on his records.

***** Day After Day**

Storyville STCD4189 *Ulrik; Niels Lan Doky (p); John Abercrombie (g); Gary Peacock (b); Adam Nussbaum (d); Mino Cinelu (perc).* 12/91.

***** Strange World**

Stunt STUCD 19406 *Ulrik; Lars Jansson (p); Lars Danielsson (b); Anders Kjellberg (d); Marilyn Mazur (perc); Mona Larsen (v).* 5/94.

*****(*) Jazz And Mambo**

Stunt STUCD 19818 *Ulrik; Jacob Christoffersen (ky); Niclas Knudsen (g); Anders Christensen (b); Mikkel Hess (d); Rune Olsen, Ignacio Guerra Acosta (perc).* 6/98.

***** Shortcuts**

Stunt STUCD 00032 *Ulrik; John Scofield (g); Lars Danielsson (b); Peter Erskine (d).* 3/99.

Like his fellow countryman Niels Lan Doky, Ulrik's writing marries jazz thinking with a feel for an instrumental pop hook. 'Ordinary People' and 'Message Returned' on the Storyville album are like that, yet on several of the other tracks there's a po-faced approach to ballad tempos which can make his heavy 'Nordic' sound seem oppressive. It helps that he has a crack band in support. *Strange World* has the considerable plus of Lars Jansson in the band, and in a likeable set of tunes Ulrik again banks on catchiness, overdubbing saxophone lines and employing Larsen's wordless voice on two tracks. Mazur's presence is more of a cameo than anything, and the music hinges on the give-and-take between saxophonist and pianist. It's a pleasing record, but it could use a knockout punch somewhere in the dozen tracks.

Jazz And Mambo feels so different that it might be by another leader altogether. The material is almost all standards – Ulrik sneaks in one original at the end – and the band plays off a crunching rather than a light mambo beat, with Knudsen's hard-nut guitar and Christoffersen's Hammond licks all over the music ('Moon River', done on clarinet, is a sweet intermission). The record's mix is completely different, too – upfront and in your face. It doesn't assert Ulrik as any more of an individual, but it's the most enjoyable set under his name.

Shortcuts is one of the records made under the ongoing sponsorship of the Jazzpar Prize, with Ulrik getting his chance at an all-star session. Very good, but with the ubiquitous Scofield on hand, we feel we've heard it all before. At least Ulrik feels like he's balancing the sound of his earlier and later records with confidence.

UMO Jazz Orchestra

ENSEMBLE

Founded in 1975, and with a range that embraces everything from light standard swing to the avant-garde, UMO is one of the world's great jazz orchestras. The key to its success has been a careful blend of inch-perfect section-work, some genuinely individual solo voices, and an intriguing leaven of guest musicians.

***** UMO Plays The Music Of Muhal Richard Abrams**

UMO CD 101 *Anders Bergcrantz, Chuck Findley, Heiki Haimila, Esko Heikkinen, Simo Salminen (t); Juhani Aaltonen, Mikael Långbacka, Mircea Stan, Markku Veijonsuo (tb); Kari Heinila, Eero Koivistoinen, Pentti Lahti, Pertti Paivinen, Teemu Salminen (sax); Seppo Kantonen (p); Kirmo Lintinen (syn); Lars Danielsson (b); Klaus Suonsaari (d); Mongo Aaltonen (perc).* 5/88.

This, it hardly needs saying, exemplifies the chewier and more adventurous side of UMO's remit. Since the composer himself supervised the sessions, we have to assume that he was relatively pleased with the results, but the results are rather flat and mechanical and without the fire that a Chicago outfit might have brought to the proceedings. But then, the Windy City hasn't been in any rush to offer Abrams recording opportunities of this sort. Among the pieces included are 'Ritob', 'Fotex', 'Melancholia' and 'Symtre' and there is a fine Abrams arrangement of Duke's 'Melancholy' for contrast.

As ever, the section-work is impeccable and there are some good solo spots from the likes of Lahti (a genuine national treasure) and Bergkrantz. The rhythm section could do with a more relaxed approach, but all credit to the recording engineers in Helsinki and to remix wizard Dave Baker who gave the record its undeniable gloss.

*****(*) UMO Jazz Orchestra**

Naxos Jazz 86010 *Anders Bergcrantz, Esko Heikkinen, Teemu Mattsson, Timo Paasonen, Mikko Pettinen (t, flhn); Markku Veijonsuo (tb); Mikko Mustonen (tb, euph); Pekka Laukkanen (tb, tba); Mikael Långbacka (btb); Eero Koivistoinen (ts, ss); Manuel Dunkel (ts, f); Jouni Jarvela (as, ss, cl); Pentti Lahti (as, ss, f); Pertti Paivinen (bs, bcl, f); Teemu Salminen (ts, bcl, cl, f); Seppo Kantonen (p); Kirmo Lintinen (syn); Markku Kanerva, Jarmo Saari (g); Hannu Rantanen, Pekka Sarmanto (b); Markus Ketola (d); Mongo Aaltonen (perc); Bino Nkwazi, Jarmo Saari (v); Kari Heinila, Kirmo Lintinen (cond).* 5/97.

All credit to the team at Naxos Jazz as well. This was an enterprising signing and it could prove to be good business for both Naxos and UMO. Most of the material is original, with compositions from conductor Heinila and saxophonist Koivistoinen the most prominent. There are two arrangements of jazz tunes, Miles's 'All Blues' (a feature for excellent trumpeter

Bergcrantz and vocalist Nkwazi) and a more unexpected version of John Coltrane's 'Equinox' on which Koivistoinen manages to avoid the remotest hint of pastiche Trane.

Nicely paced, with a well-judged selection of tunes, this makes for an ideal introduction to what the band do and do best. And at a throwaway price, it should be pretty nearly irrestistible to big-band fans.

**** Electrifying Miles

A Records AL 73153 *Tim Hagans (t); Esko Heikkinen, Teemu Mattsson, Timo Paasonen, Mikko Pettinen (t, flhn); Pekka Laukkanen, Mikko Mustonen, Marku Veijonsuo (tb); Mikael Långbacka (btb); Pentti Lahti (ss, as, f); Jouni Jarvela (ss, as, cl); Teemu Salminen (ts, cl, bcl, f); Janne Murto (ts, f); Pertti Paivinen (bs, bcl, f); Jukka Hakokongas, (elp, org); Jarmo Savolainen (p, elp, syn); Raoul Björkenheim (g); Harri Rantanen, Pekka Sarmanto (b); Markus Ketola, Aussi Nykanen (d); Mongo Aaltonen (perc); Eero Koivistoinen (cond).* 4/97.

Guest soloist Tim Hagans did his apprenticeship in the Stan Kenton band, and if this Miles Davis tribute has another stylistic source it is the Kenton orchestra. The most effective aspect of the project is that Hagans is able to suggest enough of Miles's spirit without sounding like a slavish acolyte. He solos on every track, most effectively on 'Spanish Key' and 'Sanctuary', where he shares the front line with the second tune's arranger, Raoul Björkenheim. It, of course, is a Wayne Shorter composition, as are 'Prince Of Darkness' and 'Nefertiti', and it seems that conductor Eero Koivistoinen (a trumpeter himself) was drawn rather to these more complex, long-lined items in the Miles *œuvre* than to the trumpeter's own rather less elaborate themes. 'What It Is' is a Miles/John Scofield collaboration, played briefly and simply as a feature for Hagans.

Other soloists acquit themselves well. The Olympic Rhythm Section, led by Björkenheim and the two keyboard players, is a fair simulacrum of the *Bitches Brew* band. Pertti Paivinen's Maupin-influenced bass clarinet on 'Spanish Key' is very effective, and he returns with fresh ideas on 'Calypso Frelimo' right at the end of this fine album, which is one of the very best large-scale Miles tributes on the shelves.

***(*) Ellington Tribute

Finlandia 3984 27857-2 *Esko Heikkinen, Teemu Mattsson, Timo Paasonen, Tero Saart (t); Pekka Laukkanen, Vesa-Matti Mattsson, Mikko Mustonen, Markku Veijonsuo (tb); Jouni Jarvela, Mikko Jarvinen, Pentti Lahti, Janne Murto, Pepa Paivinen, Teemu Salminen (reeds); Kirmo Lintinen (p); Pekka Sarmanto (b); Mikko Hassinen, Markus Ketola (d).* 7–8/97.

In 1985, UMO performed a programme of Ellington compositions with Mercer Ellington wielding the baton, an association which he repeated in 1995, not long before his death. UMO's grip on the charts is hard to fault, though again there is a soulless clank to some of the playing, relieved only by sterling solos from Lahti, Heikkinen and the underrated Mustonen. Taking the Williams part in 'Concerto For Cootie', the trumpeter shows his true mettle and his thoughtful absorption of the classic recordings.

The overture blends together 'Things Ain't What They Used To Be', 'Sophisticated Lady', and a great reading of 'Perdido'. They save '"A" Train' for last, which confirms an upbeat tone for this early and prescient centenary tribute. Concentrating on the more rhythmic side of Duke's legacy is no bad thing, but it would have been good to have had a greater admixture of moodier themes and solos.

*** Selected Standards

Beta BECD 4029 *Esko Heikkinen, Timo Paasonen, Antero Priha, Simo Salminen (t, flhn); Markku Johanson (flhn); Pekka Laukkanen, Mikael Långbacka, Mikko Mustonen, Markku Veijonsuo (tb); Pentti Lahti (ss, as, picc, f); Jukka Perko (ss, as, cl); Sonny Heinila (ts, f); Teemu Salminen (ts, f, cl); Pertti Paivinen (bs, bsx, bcl); Kirmo Lintinen (p); Jarno Kukkonen (g); Pekka Sarmanto (b); Markko Timonen (d); Mongo Aaltonen (perc); Bill Carson (v).* n.d.

It does exactly what it says on the spec. A set of bright, elegantly executed standard themes, somewhat lacking in surprises but marked out by fine musicianship right through the band. Paivinen's baritone solo on 'My Shining Hour' is a revelation, and Kukkonen's complementary solo makes this the outstanding track of the set, though a rascally 'Love For Sale' (complete with rap) and a feeling interpretation of 'Darn That Dream' round out an excellent album.

By this stage in the game, one looks for somewhat more from UMO. This is motor show jazz: sleek, shiny and somewhat mechnical.

***(*) Day Dreamin'

FSR FSRCD 02 *Esko Heikkinen, Timo Paasonen, Mikko Pettinen, Tero Saarti (t); Mikael Långbacka, Pekka Laukkanen, Mikko Mustonen (tb); Ulf Johansson (tb, p, v); Jouni Jarvela, Pentti Lahti, Janne Murto, Pepa Paivinen, Teemu Salminen (reeds); Mikael Jakobsson (p); Larry Coryell (g); Pekka Sarmanto (b); Markus Ketola (d); Ricardo Padilla, Yamar Thiam (perc); Annika Hultman (v); Kirmo Lintinen (cond).* 4/98.

Never slow to capitalize on a winning formula, UMO followed up the fine Ellington tribute with a set devoted to Billy Strayhorn. Larry Coryell isn't the first and most obvious guest soloist, but he fits into place with almost casual ease, playing beautiful solos on 'Day Dream', 'Absinthe' and 'Blood Count', and in duo with fellow-soloist Johansson on 'Lotus Blossom', the trombonist momentarily switching to piano.

The other important element is the vocal styling of Annika Hultman. A slightly characterless singer when intense emotion is called for, she has an elegant and buoyant approach to harmony, which makes her an exceptional band vocalist. Drifting back and forth across the beat doesn't always do her favours and occasionally makes her seem mannered, but there is no doubting her musicianship.

Fans of Coryell will welcome the chance to hear him in this context but, as ever, the real hero is the ensemble, this time out under the direction of Kirmo Lintinen, one of at least half a dozen conductors from the ranks of UMO.

***(*) One More Time

Challenge 75027 *As above, except add Kenny Wheeler (t, flhn); Norma Winstone (v).* 00.

***(*) Transit People

Naxos 86067 *Similar to above.* 00.

UMO's association with creative modern composers mean that a project fronted by Canadian trumpeter Kenny Wheeler was almost a dead certainty. *One More Time* is very largely devoted to Wheeler composition, though vocalist Winstone is also represented by 'Sea Lady'. The charts are beautifully arranged and executed and, as solo voices, Wheeler and Winstone are absolutely perfect for the UMO sound. Less obviously challenging than some of their releases to date, this is nonetheless a wonderful opportunity to hear the band doing what it does best.

UMO continue their exploration of the modern jazz canon on *Transit People*, with covers of Mongo Santamaria's 'Afro-Blue' and John Coltrane's classic 'Naima', the latter a theme that lends itself gracefully to big-band arrangement. There are originals as well from band members Savolainen, Sarmanto and Koivistoinen, but what one remembers is the sheer authority of the playing, which would lift almost any material. UMO are flying high and it seems only a matter of time before they receive the international recognition they so obviously deserve.

Massimo Urbani (1957–93)

ALTO SAXOPHONE

A brilliant prodigy, Urbani was working at 17 with Giorgio Gaslini's quartet. He subsequently played in whatever context he fancied. A Roman who was careless about taking care of himself or his career, he died following a heroin overdose, and his surviving recordings are now precious mementoes of one of the most masterful bebop saxophonists to have emerged from Europe.

***** 360 Degrees Aeutopia**

Red RR 123146-2 *Urbani; Ron Burton (p); Cameron Brown (b); Beaver Harris (d).* 6/79.

*****(*) Dedications To Albert Ayler And John Coltrane**

Red RR 123160-2 *Urbani; Luigi Bonafede (p); Furio Di Castri (b); Paolo Pellegatti (d).* 6/80.

*****(*) Easy To Love**

Red RR 123208-2 *Urbani; Luca Flores (as); Furio Di Castri (b); Roberto Gatto (d).* 1/87.

*****(*) Out Of Nowhere**

Splasc(h) H 336-2 *Urbani; Paul Rodberg (tb); Giuseppe Emmanuele (p); Nello Toscano (b); Pucci Nicosia (d).* 4/90.

****** The Blessing**

Red RR 123257-2 *Urbani; Maurizio Urbani (ts); Danilo Rea (p); Giovanni Tommaso (b); Roberto Gatto (d).* 2/93.

Urbani's senseless death robbed Europe of a player whose records are a flawed testament to a bopper of enormous guts and facility. Marcello Piras describes him as a 'wastrel genius' in his notes to the Splasc(h) issue. Certainly Urbani's earlier records sometimes failed to live up to the reputation he had as a *Wunderkind* in the '70s, but these recent reissues still make an impressive group. The opening of the first Red album consists of an astonishing outburst of alto on 'Cherokee', at a suitably hectic tempo, and though matters cool off somewhat from that point, Urbani's grip seldom lets go. Cameron Brown is superb at the bass, but Beaver Harris's splashy drumming isn't right for the group. The *Dedications* set poses an intriguing premiss, although Urbani never really tackles Ayler head-on, except in some of his distortions. It's more about linking Parker and Coltrane. There is a lustrous, acerbic 'Naima' as well as one of his fighting bebop miniatures in 'Scrapple From The Apple'. *Easy To Love* is a relatively straightforward programme of standards, apart from the opening 'A Trane From The East'; Urbani burns through them.

The final offerings, both taken down almost by chance, are a memorable and even chastening last statement. The Splasc(h) record, cut at Rodberg's studio with the trombonist sitting in on two tunes, is simple, standard fare, with a very modest rhythm section, but Urbani's herculean playing comes through all the more strongly as a result, utterly tempestuous on 'There Is No Greater Love' and surprisingly lyrical on 'Alfie'. Highly recommended; but the final session for Red is even stronger. For all the glances in the direction of Coltrane, Urbani was a diehard bopper to the end; but his brother, Maurizio, looked forward in other directions, and his two appearances offer a tart contrast in styles on a pair of originals by Tommaso. Otherwise Urbani's coruscating tone and energy command all the attention, even with the impressive Rea in the group: two takes of 'What's New' are brimming with ideas, and a solo 'Blues For Bird' is an astonishing tribute to Parker.

****(*) Go Max Go**

Philology W 187.2 *Urbani; Riccardo Zegna (p); Luciano Milanese (b); Gianni Cazzola (d).* 8/81.

***** Live In Ancona At Strabacco '84**

Philology W 221.2 *Urbani; Carlo Gargioni (p); Marco Cempini (b); Massimo Manzi (d).* 11/84.

***** Live At The Supino Jazz Festival 1987**

Philology W 228.2 *Urbani; Luca Flores (p); Pino Sallusti (b); Gianpaolo Ascolese (d).* 8/87.

***** Urlo**

Elicona 3343-2 *Urbani; Carlo Atti (ts); Massimo Farao (p); Piero Leveratto (b); Gianni Cazzola (d).* 10/88.

***** Round About ... Max**

Sentemo SNT 30392 *Urbani; Gianni Lenoci (p); Pasquale Gadaleat (b); Antonio Di Lorenzo (d); strings.* 11/91.

Urbani admirers will welcome any survivals of this unrepeatable talent, even as spotty live recordings or modestly prepared studio dates. Philology have unearthed three live dates from the '80s. *Go Max Go* is sourly recorded and unflattering in the extreme to Urbani's tone, so it's a tribute to his inspiration that the disc is still as enjoyable as it is. 'Solar' has some helter-skelter amazement, and in the favourite context of a Parker blues, Massimo burns very brightly. The *Ancona* date is a bit cleaner and the quartet bounce through a typical Max set: 'Red Cross' is a power-packed start, and the pace rarely lets up from there. The *Supino* set is again disappointingly recorded and has too much space for the others, even if Flores handles himself very well. The highlight is, perhaps, a memorably sculpted intro to 'Body And Soul'.

Urlo is a brief quartet date with three originals by Farao and Leveratto balanced by three standards and a blues. Urbani coasts here and there, but there is the unpredictable launching into sheer passion that makes his music so exhilarating from moment to moment. *Round About ... Max* includes two tracks with a string section, along with five other standards. The recording is pretty atrocious for something made in the '90s – the bass frequencies are negligible, and even Urbani sounds thin at times – but his outlandish solo treatment of 'Days Of Wine And Roses' is a gem, and a duet with Lenoci on 'Invitation' was worth preserving.

René Urtreger

PIANO

French veteran with a Bud Powell influence bordering on obsession.

★★★(★) **Jazz In Paris: Joue Bud Powell**
Universal/Emarcy 14182 *Urtreger; Benoit Quersin (b); Jean-Louis Viale (d).* 55.

★★★ **Move**
Black & Blue 864 *Urtreger; Yves Torchinski (b); Eric Dervieu (d).* 95.

★★★ **Onirica**
Sketch SKECD 329 *Urtreger (p solo).* 6/00.

René's Bud thing has stayed with him throughout his career. You'd never think it was the original playing – there is a very different cast to Urtreger's phrasing – but the spirit is caught perfectly. The solo record is quite interesting, but the trios are better and the early date, originally on Barclay and now larded with Ernest Hemingway quotes, is a lovely slice of Parisian jazz when the city did seem a moveable feast. 'Dance Of The Infidels' and 'Budo' are both splendid and René has a nice original as well, just to show his obsession has some bounds.

Allan Vaché (born 1953)

CLARINET

The younger of the two Vaché brothers is a clarinettist of great facility whose work as a sideman in mainstream situations has recently been built on by a plentiful supply of leadership dates.

★★★ **Jazz Im Amerika Haus: Vol. 3**
Nagel-Heyer 013 *Vaché; Warren Vaché (c); Johnny Varro (p); Jim Douglas (g); Frank Tate (b); Mike Masessa (d).* 8/94.

★★★ **Swing Is Here**
Nagel-Heyer 026 *Vaché; Antti Sarpila (cl, ss); Mark Sahen (p); Len Skeat (b); Joe Ascione (d).* 10/95.

★★★ **Summit Meeting**
Nagel-Heyer 027 *As above, except add Ken Peplowski (cl, ts).* 10/95.

★★★ **Allan Vaché's Florida Jazz Allstars**
Nagel-Heyer 032 *Vaché; David Jones (c); John Allred (tb); Johnny Varro (p); Bob Leary (g); Bob Haggart (b); Ed Metz Jr (d).* 3/96.

★★★ **Swing And Other Things**
Arbors ARCD 19171 *Vaché; Warren Vaché (c); Johnny Varro (p); John Cocuzzi (vib); Bucky Pizzarelli (g); Frank Tate (b); Ed Metz Jr (d).* 6/96.

Hitherto less well-known than his brother Warren, Allan Vaché seems to be taking his place in the fold of mainstreamers looked after by Nagel-Heyer and Arbors. A fluent technician, he gets all over the clarinet with indecent rapidity and can handle the most overheated of tempos with no apparent trouble. If anything, his playing seems to egg on the rhythm section into going ever faster. On the first, live album above, it helps him to hit a few clinkers along the way, but even when he gargles a note it just gets swallowed up in the flow. The songbook of the '20s and '30s (with the occasional later tune) is what he loves and, while he sometimes chooses a comparative rarity, most of these tunes will be well known to even the uninitiated.

There's very little to choose among the five discs. *Jazz Im Amerika Haus Vol. 3* is perhaps the weakest, if only because of characteristic live-album longueurs; but it's still a good blow and is the one chance to hear the brothers together at length. *Florida Jazz Allstars* is our favourite, if only for a quite beautiful treatment of Bob Haggart's 'My Inspiration': Vaché should work at this tempo more often. Jones and Allred have their own moments of exultation, too. *Swing Is Here* is rather exhaustingly full of clarinet, and a problem with both this and *Summit Meeting* is the sound, which has very little bottom (Skeat often disappears altogether). The latter, though, has the bonus of Peplowski joining in, sometimes on tenor, to add further piquancy to the front line: his gorgeous solo treatment of 'These Foolish Things' smokes the other two. The tempos are sometimes almost manically fast and the record's too long at almost 80 minutes, but there's lots to enjoy.

Perhaps the Arbors disc is the best place to hear Vaché as the featured man (Warren sits in on only 'Cheek To Cheek'). His penchant for noodling around the very highest register can be annoying: he gets the notes all right, but the tone goes as thin as a pencil. Some agreeable choices of tune and a charming ballad in 'Nancy With The Laughing Face'.

★★★(★) **Revisited!**
Nagel Heyer 044 *Vaché; David Jones (c); Bob Leary (g, v); Phil Flanigan (b).* 6/97.

★★★ **Raisin' The Roof**
Nagel Heyer 054 *Vaché; Jim Galloway (ss); John Bunch (p); Howard Alden (g); Michael Moore (b); Jake Hanna (d).* 12/98.

The group subject to the revisitation is the Bechet–Spanier Big Four, and this is one re-creation which works out exceedingly well. For once, Vaché's full-flushing manner doesn't seem overpowering, even in this slimmed-down context: Bechet himself was no shrinking violet, and he might have approved of some of the clarinet fusillades on offer. Jones plays the Muggsy role very well. Neither man is a ringer for their respective forebears, so the record is more than just a slavish homage.

Raisin' The Roof is another good one, but again there's an impression that there's just too much playing going on here, and a little restraint wouldn't have hurt. Galloway gets caught up in it and his normally more relaxed style gets squeezed, while the otherwise imperturbable campaigners in the rhythm section sail serenely on. 'Dream' is nice, but at nine minutes it's far too long.

★★★(★) **Allan And Allen**
Nagel Heyer 074 *Vaché; Harry Allen (ts); Eddie Higgins (p); Phil Flanigan (b); Eddie Metz (d).* 1/00.

Allen likes a slugging match as much as anybody and this one does go with a real punch. Nothing you won't have heard before from either man and the opening steam through 'Lover Come Back To Me' says it all inside seven minutes, but even if you just take it as pure showboating it's fine entertainment. If anyone takes first playing honours it's probably Eddie Metz, who keeps things swinging hard without losing his cool for a second.

Warren Vaché (born 1951)

CORNET, TRUMPET, FLUGELHORN, VOCAL

Born in Rahway, New Jersey, Vaché was deeply influenced by Louis Armstrong. He has worked with the Benny Goodman

Band and in the house band at Eddie Condon's, but his most enduring association has been with like-minded saxophonist Scott Hamilton. Vaché's slightly dry, pungent tone is estimably controlled; even when he opts to play slightly sharp, it is always with dramatic intent.

***** First Time Out And Encore '93**

Audiophile ACD 196 *Vaché; Kenny Davern (ss); Bucky Pizzarelli, Wayne Wright (g); Michael Moore (b); Connie Kay (d).* 11–12/76, 4/93.

Warren Vaché came to prominence re-creating the solos of Bix Beiderbecke and ever since has been addicted to the backward glance. He is one of the leading swing players of the last couple of decades and is arguably the first cornetist since Ruby Braff (with whom he has shared a couple of labels over the years) to try to build on the example of Pops. But whereas Ruby is always incisive, pugnacious and sometimes downright filthy, Vaché has a curiously mild approach to swing which consistently fails to excite. He has the facility to play extremes of pitch very quietly and with estimable control, but this is not the same as being equipped to play great jazz. For us, he remains a triumph of technique over content.

'Nepotism be damned!' cried his father, writing the sleeve-note for young Warren's debut. Paired with an 'encore' from a decade and a half later, the 1976 session presents a calm and competent young brass-player with a thoroughly old-fashioned delivery. It doesn't suggest much more than that. The duo tracks with Bucky Pizzarelli stem from both dates, and there is nothing to choose between the two. 'When It's Sleepy Time Down South' from 1993 is a brilliant closer, but by then it's hard to be excited. The group tracks with Davern, Moore and Kay, recorded a fortnight after the debut, are more adventurous, and Davern is in splendid form, but there is little to get the teeth into.

****** Iridescence**

Concord 4153 *Vaché; Hank Jones (p); George Duvivier (b); Alan Dawson (d).* 1/81.

The peacock feather on the cover might suggest self-regarding display. The contents offer no such thing, just wonderfully mellow jazz. Vaché's tone is almost creamy here, but the single kind, nothing too cloying. These are superb cuts, with not a dull spot anywhere and this is unhesitatingly a library must-have. 'Softly, As In A Morning Sunrise' is innocent enough to begin with, but Warren's solo lifts it dramatically, as he does with virtually everything that follows. Jones and Duvivier are authoritative and the bassist is particularly well captured, seeming to shadow the cornet in ensembles and adding extra buttresses of harmony on Hank's title-tune and the closing 'Autumn In New York'. It remains a Vaché triumph, though, and all one wishes for is a cameo from brother Allan on 'The More I See You', which seems to cry out for a second horn line.

***** My Shining Hour**

Nagel-Heyer 5006 *Vaché; Allan Vaché (cl); Brian Lemon (p); Dave Cliff (g); Dave Green (b); Allan Ganley (d).* 6/94.

A great set from the Hamburg club, featuring Warren and his brother with a British rhythm section of the highest quality. There are some shaky moments, particularly when Allan is featured (perhaps he was having reed problems), but the overall quality is high and the best of the tracks – 'Poor Butterfly', 'Isfahan' – are as good as any Warren has committed to record.

***** Stardust**

Zephyr ZECD19 *Vaché; Derek Watkins (t); Brian Lemon (p); Dave Cliff (g); Dave Green (b); Martin Drew (d).* 95.

Another fine swing record with a transatlantic provenance. Zephyr do these sets wonderfully well, with none of the spurious polish some labels still give swing, and without the egregious roughness that some mistake for authenticity. The two trumpeters could hardly be more different, yet Watkins understands this repertoire according to his own lights and his touch on the ballads in particular is the equal of Warren's. The cornet/trumpet debate won't delay us here. A blind man running for his life could tell the difference.

****** An Affair To Remember**

Zephyr ZECD 8 *Vaché; Brian Lemon (p).* 12/95.

*****(*) Warren Plays Warren**

Nagel-Heyer CD 033 *Vaché; Randy Sandke (t); Kenny Drew Jr (p); Murray Wall (b); Jimmy Cobb (d).* 5/96.

Vaché's love affair with the music of Harry Warren has now been documented twice over. The Zephyr disc is superb, largely because Lemon is in crisply brilliant form. There is an inevitable overlap of material – 'Nagasaki', 'I Only Have Eyes For You', 'September In The Rain' and others – but the difference of setting and the imaginative arrangements by fellow trumpeter Sandke on the German recording mean that almost nothing sounds repetitive or trite. Vaché's tone has broadened, but is also much sharper and more emphatic in attack than it was. With Lemon, he is able to indulge that long-standing ability to soften the dynamic even while exploring the outer reaches of his range. His tone is fat and fruity and the close miking on the Zephyr set gives a very immediate and authentic version of what he's about.

***** Live At The Vineyard**

Challenge 70026 *Vaché; John Bunch (p); Phil Flanigan (b).* 10/96.

A luscious concert date from the Vaché trio. His tendency to play slightly sharp is noticeable here on occasion, where he's clearly not tuning too precisely to Bunch's unembellished chords, but there's nothing off-putting about it, and it lends a certain urgency to 'A Time For Love' and the durable 'Cherokee'. Warren has interesting comments about cornet vis-à-vis trumpet and also about his great predecessor Roy Eldridge in the course of a set that has a delightful immediacy and warmth of presence.

****** Shine**

Zephyr ZECD24 *Vaché; Tony Coe (ts, ss, cl); Alan Barnes (as, bs, cl); Brian Lemon (p); Dave Cliff (g); Dave Green (b); Allan Ganley, Clark Tracey (d).* 1 & 5/97.

***** Memories Of You**

Zephyr ZECD 21 *As above, except omit Coe.* 5/97.

***** Jumpin'**

Zephyr ZECD27 *As above.* 5/97.

Glorious stuff, though mostly because Barnes and Coe are in such good form. *Shine* begins and ends with versions of 'Shine' itself, and Zephyr's recent practice of including alternatives makes complete sense. Vaché's tone seems particularly relaxed and conversational in this company, and his soloing on 'Stella By Starlight', 'Pee Wee's Blues' (the great Erwin was his teacher) and 'Don't Get Around Much Any More' are exemplary. We have emoted sufficiently elsewhere about this rhythm section.

They are hard to beat on a session of this kind, but with a front-line of genuinely international quality, even they have to take a back seat. Coe is missed on the second album but the chemistry with Barnes is sufficient to see it through, and rarities like 'You're Mine, You' from two of the creators of 'Body And Soul' and 'Serenata' make this an intriguing listen for students of traditional jazz and swing.

****** Mrs Vaché's Boys**
Nagel-Heyer 50 *Vaché; Allan Vaché (cl); Eddie Higgins (p); Howard Alden (g); Phil Flanigan (b); Ed Metz Jr (d).* 9/99.

The opening 'Just Friends' is as thrilling a performance as you'll hear from a family band, and it's a pity that nothing that follows quite matches it. Warren is in fantastic form on a new version of Miles Davis's 'All Blues' and his flugelhorn-piano reading of 'London By Night' with Higgins is equally wonderful. Indeed, you run out of superlatives for this set. The brothers' interplay is boundless and the rhythm section, with Alden very much to the fore, exudes excitement. Glorious.

***** Swingtime!**
Nagel-Heyer CD 059 *Vaché; Randy Reinhart (t); John Allred, Matt Bilyk (tb); Chuck Wilson (as, cl); Harry Allen, Rickey Woodard (ts); Alan Barnes (bs, as, cl); Steve Ash (p); Murray Wall (b); Jake Hanna (d).* 1/00.

Vaché ushered in the new century with an unashamed exercise in swing nostalgia. This is a beautifully balanced band, with a lot of middle weight and players who are prepared to improvise in the middle register rather than skyscrape. 'Jumpin' At The Woodside' is a delight and Harry Allen's arrangement of 'Stompin' At The Savoy' would have had the original creators nodding with delight. Vaché is the main soloist, but Barnes and Woodard are featured, as is the very good John Allred.

*****(*) What Is There To say?**
Nagel-Heyer 056 *Vaché; Joe Puma (g); Murray Wall (b); Eddie Locke(d).* 5/99.

*****(*) The Best Thing For You**
Zephyr ZECD 31 *Vaché; Brian Lemon (p); Dave Cliff (g); Dave Green (b); Allan Ganley (d).* 2/01.

Warren is going through a very purple patch, and even if this kind of mainstream has been very exposed by these labels of late, one can hardly complain about the calibre of the music. The quartet date for Nagel-Heyer features a working group, and Puma is the kind of player Vaché works with particularly well, finding surprising harmonic feeds when another might just strum away. Their duet on the title-track is a beauty. Back with the Zephyr gang, it's the cornetist who ensures that the music goes up a notch from the typical mainstream jog, and it restores some of the more lively elements of small-group swing before it was smoothed out. Nice to find someone reviving 'Sweet Pumpkin', too.

CORE COLLECTION

♛ ** 2gether**
Nagel-Heyer 2011 *Vaché; Bill Charlap (p).* 12/00.

An unqualified delight. 'We wanted to play some nice old tunes, and at tempos you don't hear any more. Guys I admire did it – maybe it's because nobody dances.' Vaché's remarks recall an era in jazz now gone, as does the music – except, then or now, it was rarely played with as much finesse, joyous invention and unassuming charm as this. Many of these pieces are as close to perfection as you can imagine a duet could ever be. Warren's tone, whether tightly muted or luxuriously open, speaks directly to the listener, and his playing has taken on a mantle which goes back past Braff and Hackett, maybe to Armstrong himself. Yet it's modern music – there's no whiff of mustiness, or stale old repertory here. Charlap, who sometimes seems like a merely fail-safe executant on some records, is equally inspired, turning in swinging accompaniments at every tempo, every line logical but never falling in quite the place you expect. No record surveyed for this edition has given us more pleasure. One of the great discs of the CD era.

Kid Thomas Valentine (1896–1987)

TRUMPET

Although originally from elsewhere in Louisiana, Valentine became one of New Orleans's most characteristic trumpeters, leading his Algiers Stompers from 1926, working extensively with George Lewis, then playing at home and on tour for the rest of a very long and busy life.

****** Kid Thomas And His Algiers Stompers**
American Music AMCD-10 *Valentine; Bob Thomas, Harrison Barnes (tb); Emil Barnes (cl); George Guesnon (g, bj); Joseph Phillips (b); George Henderson (d).* 9/51.

**** At The Tip Top**
American Music AMCD-97 *Valentine; Louis Nelson (tb); Edmund Washington (as); Joe James (p); Burke Stevenson (b); Sammy Penn (d).* 6/57.

***** Dancing Tonight**
American Music AMCD-115 *Valentine; Charlie DeVore (t); Louis Nelson (tb); Emanuel Paul (ts); Joe James (p); Burke Stevenson (b); Sammy DeVore (d).* 8/57.

***** Larry Borenstein Collection Vol. 8**
504 CD 37 *Valentine; Louis Nelson (tb); Edmund Washington (as, v); Joe James (p); Burke Stevenson (b); Sammy Penn (d, v).* 57.

***** The Dance Hall Years**
American Music AMCD-48 *Valentine; Louis Nelson (tb); Emanuel Paul (cl, ts); Joe James, James 'Sing' Miller (p); Burke Stevenson, Joseph Butler (b); Sammy Penn (d); 'Pa' (v).* 59–3/64.

*****(*) Kid Thomas Valentine's Creole Jazz Band**
American Music AMCD-49 *Valentine; Louis Nelson (tb); Emanuel Paul (ts); Joe James (p); George Guesnon (bj); Alcide Pavageau (b); Sammy Penn (d).* 5/59.

*****(*) Sonnets From Algiers**
American Music AMCD 53 *Valentine; Louis Nelson (tb); Paul 'Polo' Barnes (cl); Emanuel Paul (ts); Joe James (p); George Guesnon (bj); Sammy Penn (d, v).* 7/60.

****(*) Kid Thomas' Dixieland Band 1960 With Emanuel Paul**
504 CD33 *Valentine; Louis Nelson (tb); Emanuel Paul (ts); Joe James (p, v); Joseph Butler (b); Sammy Penn (d, v).* 9/60.

***** Kid Thomas And His Algiers Stompers**
Original Jazz Classics OJC 1833 *As above, except add Emil Barnes, Albert Burbank (cl), Homer Eugene (p).* 8/60–1/61.

****(*) Kid Thomas And His Algiers Stompers**
Original Jazz Classics OJC 1845 *As above, except omit Burbank, Eugene.* 1/61.

***** Kid Thomas And Emanuel Paul With Barry Martyn's Band**

GHB BCD-257 *Valentine; Cuff Billett (t); Pete Dyer (tb); Emanuel Paul, Bill Greenow (ts); Richard Simmons (p); Terry Knight (b); Barry Martyn (d).* 64.

Thomas Valentine arrived in New Orleans rather late, in 1922. By the time he made his first records, almost 30 years later, he had led bands all over Louisiana but remained based in the city, where he continued to play for a further 35 years. He approached this awesome career with a Zen-like simplicity, reducing the New Orleans sound to its essentials and creating a lifetime's work from them. A fascinating lead-trumpeter, his methods – including a severe observance of the melody, a blunt, jabbing attack and a vibrato that sounds like an angry trill – manage to create high drama and lyrical depth alike, and though he seldom took solos he was such a strong lead voice that he tended to dominate every band he played in.

He made a lot of records during his long life. The first (1951) sessions have survived in excellent sound and find Valentine and Barnes in their first prime. There are two trombonists, since Bob Thomas had to leave after three numbers, and the changed balance of the front-line tells much about the sensitivity of the New Orleans ensemble. Alden Ashforth's excellent notes chronicle the whole session in detail. The most characteristic is *The Dance Hall Years*, where Thomas plays with his regular working band (usually called The Algiers Stompers) at a couple of dance sessions, one identified only to the late '50s, the other dated precisely to March 1964. The material is familiar New Orleans stuff and a few blues. The seven earlier tracks are dustily recorded but the remainder sound good, although there seems to be no audience present. Nelson and Paul are in strong form and the band drives along with the ramshackle but perfectly appropriate rhythm that makes this music tick. The 504 CDs are drawn from the Larry Borenstein archives. The 1957 set is notable for Ed Washington's full-on style, with its scattershot approach to pitch, and on a typical set of staples he puts some nervous energy into the occasion. The later disc is a less significant survival: the band sounds shop-worn in parts and the sound is rather dusty, though Thomas rouses them on occasion.

Two recent 'discoveries' on American Music are of somewhat dubious merit. *At The Tip Top* is in very shabby sound and the performances are ramshackle in the extreme. The main saving grace here is the hugely entertaining sleeve-notes by Charlie DeVore. *Dancing Tonight* is only slightly better, a neighbourhood dance (one wonders how anyone came to even record it) where Valentine's band do their stuff but little is created that makes one want to go through it again, some 50 years later. Much better is *Kid Thomas Valentine's Creole Jazz Band*. This time the band gets an excellent sound, which shows up all their problems as well as their virtues, and one can hear saxophone and brass timbres which a jazz band will likely never sport out front again. The whole band play well and the session is a tribute to the enthusiasm of the English jazz fan Mike Slatter, who made it happen in the first place.

The two OJCs are more from Riverside's *New Orleans: The Living Legends* series, and they're surprisingly disappointing in some ways. Though clearly recorded, the band sound shrill – especially the clarinets – and some of the tempos seem either too hurried or down to a crawl. OJC 1833 is the better of the two. Better still, though, is the almost contemporaneous *Sonnets From Algiers*. This time the slightly acid and very up-front sound catches the raw charisma of the group, and the familiar set-list includes some particularly characterful takes on 'Ballin' The Jack' and 'Milenberg Joys'. The session with Barry Martyn and his British team is a spirited, affectionate meeting between men of vastly different backgrounds, and while Martyn anchors the pulse, his colleagues don't do so well, with Dyer especially blasting all before him to no real purpose. Thomas and Paul, though, fashion a more graceful partnership.

CORE COLLECTION

♛ ** Kid Thomas–George Lewis Ragtime Stompers**

GHB BCD-5 *Thomas; Jim Robinson (tb); George Lewis (cl); Emanuel Sayles (bj); Alcide 'Slow Drag' Pavageau (b); Sammy Penn (d).* 11/61.

This wonderful session could stand as the perfect introduction to classic New Orleans playing. For one thing the sound is superb, better than on most of Valentine's other records, and it lets us hear the balance of the front line – Valentine's curt lead, Lewis's lovely rococo embellishments, Robinson's doughty support. The rhythm team is unimpeachable. The tunes are obvious, but just what was needed for the day. As a group, the sextet swing along with the indefinable rightness which this music, at its best, delivers like no other style of jazz. Essential!

*****(*) The December Band Vol. 1**

GHB BCD-197 *Valentine; Jim Robinson (tb); Sammy Rimington (cl); Captain John Handy (as); Bill Sinclair (p); Dick Griffith (bj); Dick McCarthy (b); Sammy Penn (d).* 12/65.

*****(*) The December Band Vol. 2**

GHB BCD-198 *As above.* 12/65.

****(*) Red Wing**

GHB BCD-189 *Valentine; Big Bill Bissonnette (tb); Sammy Rimington (cl, as, ts), Bill Sinclair (p); Dick Griffith (bj); Dick McCarthy (b); Art Pulver (d).* 3/66.

*****(*) Kid Thomas At Moose Hall**

GHB BCD-305 *Valentine; Bill Connell (cl); Dick Griffith (bj); Dick McCarthy (b); Big Bill Bissonnette (d).* 67.

***** At Moose Hall 1968**

Jazz Crusade 3065 *Valentine; Louis Nelson(tb); Manny Paul (ts); Charlie Hamilton (p); Joseph Butler (b, v); Sammy Penn (d).* 10/68.

***** Same Old Soupbone!**

Jazz Crusade JC-3001 *Valentine; Louis Nelson (tb); Emanuel Paul (ts); Charlie Hamilton (p); Joe Butler (b); Sammy Penn (d).* 10/68.

****** Kid Thomas In California**

GHB BCD-296 *Valentine; Big Bill Bissonnette (tb, v); Captain John Handy (as); Cyril Bennett (p); Jim Tutunjian (b); Sammy Penn (d); Carol Leigh (v).* 2–3/69.

*****(*) Spirit Of New Orleans 4**

Music Mecca 1059-2 *Valentine; Percy Humphrey (t); Louis Nelson, Jim Robinson (tb); Orange Kellin, Albert Burbank (cl); Emanuel Paul (ts); Charlie Hamilton (p); Niels Richard Hansen (bj); Chester Zardis, Joseph Hutler (b); Cie Frazier, Alonzo Stewart (d).* 71–72.

It was quite an occasion at Moose Lodge Hall in December 1965 when Valentine and cohorts took to the stage. From the

23-year-old Rimington to the venerable Valentine and Robinson, the band swung mightily through their sets, spread rather generously across two CDs. Handy especially seems in unquenchably high spirits, Rimington isn't overawed once, and the comparatively youthful rhythm section sound as if they were prepared to play all night. As one example, listen to the tempo that develops on 'Ice Cream'. Great New Orleans music, and we regretfully hold back a single notch due to the sometimes disappointing sound-quality, which often has soloists disappearing off-mic.

At Moose Hall and *In California* were both recorded by Bissonnette, a stalwart crusader for New Orleans jazz who usually worked out of Connecticut. Forced to switch from his usual trombone to drums for the earlier session, he drafted in local hero Connell and booked Thomas to play the session, which suffers from an imperfect location sound and plenty of clinkers by the players, yet still offers much great Thomas. He was obliged to play more solos than usual, which he never liked doing, but somehow he took to the task with great relish, even though the rhythm section plays a lot faster and with more bounce than he was used to. As Bissonnette notes, there is more Kid Thomas on this one record than on two or three of his regular dates.

In California is one of the best available discs. Bissonnette secured a very good sound, recording mostly at Earthquake McGoon's, and the front-line partnership of Thomas and Handy strikes many sparks. 'Say Si Si' and 'Rose Room' are tunes less often encountered in the Thomas discography, and Penn's drumming is an outstanding show of maverick New Orleans timekeeping. Carol Leigh contributes two sweet-toned but convincing vocals. Highly recommended.

Jazz Crusade is Bissonnette's own label and *Same Old Soupbone!* is salvaged from a local TV appearance by Thomas's band. A good if comparatively routine Thomas date by his standard band, playing much of their usual material. The title is a favourite saying of the leader's, the sort of thing he would say to shrug off compliments or questions. The 1968 set at Moose Hall, from the same label, is solid without challenging the better Valentine dates.

Music Mecca's compilation of two different LPs (plus four previously unreleased tracks) has Thomas sharing the billing with a Percy Humphrey-led band. The Humphrey tracks are slightly better since he is in great form, but Thomas's tunes fare well, with the Europeans Kellin and Hansen fitting in without a murmur. Bright but effective sound.

The dud in this batch is *Red Wing*. Yet another date at Moose Hall, but the band sound a bit out of sorts, Bissonnette is very poor on trombone, and the sound is scruffy. Only Rimington, reliable as usual, does well.

***** Kid Thomas & Earl Humphrey With Orange Kellin's New Orleans Joymakers**

GHB BCD-353 *Valentine; Earl Humphrey (tb); Orange Kellin (cl); Lars Edegran (p); Sylvester Handy (b); Lester Alexis (d).* 70.

***** Live In Denmark Vol. 1**

Storyville STCD 6026 *Valentine; Louis Nelson (tb); Soren Sorenson (ts); Erik Hansen, Jon Marks (p); Niels Richard Hansen (bj); Derek Cook (b); Keith Minter (d).* 12/72–1/74.

***** Live In Denmark Vol. 2**

Storyville STCD 6027 *As above.* 12/72–1/74.

***** Live In Denmark Vol. 3**

Storyville STCD 6028 *As above.* 12/72–1/73.

***** Live In Denmark Vol. 4**

Storyville STCD 6029 *As above.* 12/72–1/73.

Kid Thomas was an inveterate traveller to the end of his life, and there are plenty of surviving tour recordings. The GHB disc was cut in South Carolina and is the only opportunity to hear Valentine with the third of the famous Humphrey brothers, trombonist Earl. Perhaps not the most immortal of sessions, but with Thomas away from his usual sidemen, he plays a little more sideways than normal, and with Humphrey responding, there's plenty of interest. The Danish session is selected from five nights of recording in Copenhagen and has Valentine and Nelson together with a European outfit. Sorenson sounds like he learned to play at Emanuel Paul's knee, and he helps make up a boisterous front line; but listen to Valentine's circumspect playing on 'Yellow Dog Blues' to hear how, at 77, he was still formidably inventive. The second volume includes eight previously unheard tracks. Excellent sound. Four from these marathon sessions have so far been released, and there's still two to come!

Johnnie Valentino

GUITAR, MANDOLIN

Valentino is a dark-toned eclectic who experiments restlessly but has not yet found a completely sympathetic context for his compositions.

***** Searching Souls**

Nine Winds NWCD 0233 *Valentino; Wadada Leo Smith (t); Billy Drewes, Andy Laster (cl); Vinny Golia (cl, bcl); Rick Rossi (bcl); Kermit Driscoll, Trevor Ware (b); Mick Rossi (d, p).* 00.

If one were to isolate the most melancholy overtones of Bill Frisell's playing and intensify them fourfold, one would be close to Valentino's sound. These are strange cuts, made with a flexible group that is actually more consistent and more consistently interesting than some critics have suggested. The mood of the songs can be gauged from titles like 'Dark Matter', 'Nono', the Monk cover 'Ugly Beauty' and 'Vapor Burn', but then right at the end along come 'My Old Kentucky Home', cleverly arranged in something like the Frisell style by drummer Mick Rossi, and the closing 'Spiritual Blessing' and some of the clouds disappear.

Ken Vandermark (born 1964)

SAXOPHONES, CLARINETS

Born in Warwick, Rhode Island, Vandermark played trumpet into his teens, then switched to saxophone. Studied and led bands in Boston and Montreal, then relocated to Chicago and spent the '90s working in the local scene there running a string of bands, organizing gigs and generally making significant waves.

***** Big Head Eddie**

Platypus PP 001 *Vandermark; Todd Colburn (g); Kent Kessler (b); Michael Zerang (d).* 2/93.

★★★(★) Solid Action
Platypus PP 002 *As above, except Daniel Scanlan (c, g, vn) replaces Colburn.* 5/94.

★★★(★) Standards
Quinnah Q08 *Vandermark; Mars Williams (saxes); Kevin Drumm (g); Jim Baker (p, syn); Daniel Scanlan (g, vn); Kent Kessler (b); Steve Hunt, Hamid Drake (d).* 7/94.

★★★ Caffeine
Okkadisk 12002 *Vandermark; Jim Baker (p); Steve Hunt (d).* 94.

★★★(★) International Front
Okkadisk 12005 *Vandermark; Kent Kessler (b); Curt Newton (d).* 9/94.

★★★ Blow Horn
Okkadisk OD12019 *Vandermark; Mats Gustafsson (ts, bs, flageolet); Kent Kessler (b); Steve Hunt (d).* 10/95.

★★★★ Utility Hitter
Quinnah Q09 *Vandermark; Mars Williams (reeds); Kent Kessler, Nate McBride (b); Hamid Drake, Curt Newton (d).* 9/95.

★★★(★) Hoofbeats Of The Snorting Swine
Eighth Day Music EDM 80001 *Vandermark; Mars Williams (ss, as, ts, cl).* 3/95–2/96.

★★★(★) Single Piece Flow
Atavistic ALP47 *Vandermark; Jeb Bishop (tb, g); Mars Williams (saxes); Kent Kessler (b); Tim Mulvenna (d).* 8/96.

Vandermark has charged straight to the front of free music in America – and not from New York, either. One could call him an archetypal post-modernist, working in rock, R&B and jazz alike, except with Vandermark there's nothing cool or once-removed about his expressiveness. He's a full-on energy player a lot of the time, a canny organizer of groups and musical forms, a man perhaps destined to make things happen. While he's primarily a tenor saxophonist, he often picks up both bass and B-flat clarinets, and he espouses European models as readily as American ones – Evan Parker arabesques might invade a solo as plausibly as Dolphyesque skirlings and Lockjaw Davis-like pugilistics. Vandermark likes structure – most of these records start off from compositions, sometimes of considerable complexity – but his music can take off into the most provocative and open-ended byways. He also knows a lot of great players, most of them stalwarts of a scene which Vandermark himself has been crucial in documenting and bringing to wider attention.

Names are often dropped all over these records, but when someone like George Clinton or Witold Lutoslawski is cited it never means that Vandermark is about to get either funky or neo-classical. What he loves is jazz language in the raw, and this is how the earlier discs sound. *Big Head Eddie* is a nifty set of tunes, sparked by Colburn's scrawling guitar lines, lurid and alive if not quite focused yet. *Solid Action* is Vandermark's first shot at greatness, with Scanlan a tremendously exciting figure on all three of his instruments, and the wild landscaping of 'Bucket' and 'Catch 22' balanced by the fuming, rocked-over 'Leadfoot'. An exciting disc.

Standards is experimental in that it sets Vandermark up as a member of four different trios: sax with (respectively) bass/drums, saxes/drums, keyboards/guitar and guitar/drums. Each has something interesting to yield and some of it sounds almost glaringly new and alive. *Caffeine* and *International Front* are by two trios, one named Caffeine, the other Steelwool. With Baker and Hunt, Vandermark is slightly too exposed, and for all the interesting music here, this doesn't quite have the vividness of some of his other discs. The Steelwool Trio, with long-time compadre Kessler (also a colleague in the NRG Ensemble) in great fettle, is a roughly shod power-trio that finds each man vying for attention: muscular, exhilarating, unrepentant.

Our favourite of these earlier discs is the monumental *Utility Hitter* by the Barrage Double Trio: three guys from Chicago meet three from Boston, and it's a mutual slugfest of sensitivity and ingenuity. The dedications to Mingus, Andrew Hill, Ornette, Cherry and Ayler (the latter a huge, brawling outrage) are marvellous, but so is the revisionist hard-bop-as-raging-fury of their tribute to Griffin and Lockjaw, 'Over And Both'.

Blow Horn is a day at Uberstudio in Chicago. Gustafsson more usually crosses horns with Vandermark from his position in the AALY Trio, and 'Dedication' carries on that shouting tradition. Hunt and Kessler sometimes get drowned out (not something one can often say about a drummer going full tilt), although they're good enough to listen to by themselves, which happens on the first two minutes of 'Blow Horn For Service' at least. Not our favourite of these records, but still plenty of action.

Hoofbeats Of The Snorting Swine finds Vandermark locking horns with frequent sparring-partner Williams (the record is credited to Cinghiale). Typical Vandermark in that it feels as if the duo is running (or careering) down composed lines, even as they blow right away from them. Williams is at least an equal partner here, sharing the writing duties and matching the other man at every step. A dialogue for two epic sensibilities.

Single Piece Flow debuts The Vandermark Five, with Jeb Bishop an intriguing booking. Almost temperate in parts, there's some exemplary use of the group as a unit, with a piece like 'The Mark Inside' offering a sort of jaundiced twist on jazz tradition. When Vandermark offers dedications to the likes of Johnny Hodges and Gil Evans, it's the tribute of a fan, but one isn't always sure what homage he's paying. As prolific as he has already been in a short space of time, there's little to suggest a man who'll be content to be a career jazz musician.

★★★ Steam
Eighth Day Music EDM 80010 *Vandermark; Jim Baker (p); Kent Kessler (b); Tim Mulvenna (d).* 4/96.

A 'traditional' quartet, though hardly of any traditional stripe, dedicated to a modern repertory of Dolphy, Coleman, Braxton ... and yet for this debut, they decided, frustratingly, to play an all-original programme. The usual quota of interest, but it would have been more exciting to see how they dealt with a set of covers, especially as there's been no follow-up to date.

★★★(★) The DKV Trio With Fred Anderson
Okkadisk OD12014 *Vandermark; Fred Anderson (ts); Kent Kessler (b); Hamid Drake (d).* 12/96.

★★★(★) Baraka
Okkadisk OK 12012 *As above, except omit Anderson.* 2/97.

★★★ Deep Telling
Okkadisk OD12027 *As above, except add Joe Morris (g).* 4/98.

★★★(★) Live In Wels & Chicago 1998
Okkadisk OD12030 2CD *As above, except omit Morris.* 11/98.

This is the DKV Trio, one of Vandermark's most regularly assembled projects. The album with Anderson is beautifully focused. The older man is a less multi-faceted player than either Vandermark or some of the other horn men on these records, but he fits gracefully into the trio's set-up and there is some muscleman playing which doesn't descend into posturing. *Baraka* has its moments of stasis – the title-track runs for more than 35 minutes, and it needs plenty of resources to sustain that – but there is still an awful lot to listen to. Morris guests on *Deep Telling* and the results are quieter and more inward-looking in feel. There are three quartet tracks and five by differing combinations of the four players. *Wels & Chicago* features two concerts, recorded in the same month but geographically a continent apart – and the music is sometimes prone to traversing a great distance without saying a great deal. The 30-minute 'Open Door' is out of steam well before the end. But the Wels set, basically framed around Don Cherry's 'Complete Communion Suite', is a stunning example of free repertory, the original materials ingeniously transplanted to this situation.

***** Straight Lines**
Atavistic ALP115 *Vandermark; Jeb Bishop (tb); Kent Kessler (b); Tim Mulvenna (d).* 9/98.

Vandermark's Joe Harriott Project is an overdue salute to that departed master, but the record is under-rehearsed and unfinished in feel. It could be that the group are a shade too respectful of Harriott's themes, since their playing feels a bit stiff and uncertain, something that a Vandermark record has never been in the past. Bishop is arguably the strongest voice and some of his solos are cracklingly inventive responses to the material.

*****(*) Target Or Flag**
Atavistic ALP106 *Vandermark; Jeb Bishop (tb, g); Mars Williams (saxes); Kent Kessler (b); Tim Mulvenna (d).* 10/97.

****** Simpatico**
Atavistic ALP107 *As above, except Dave Rempis (as) replaces Williams.* 12/98.

More reports from The Vandermark Five. This seems to be Vandermark's principal outlet as far as writing and arranging are concerned. Dedications to the likes of Shelly Manne, Jack Montrose and Curtis Counce betray his affection for the urbane precision of prime West Coast jazz, and his own pieces make the point of following some of the precepts (counterpoint, tonal contrast) which that school lived by. Except they're channelled through a combative and inclusive perspective which takes in all the more expected freedoms. Obsessive work is making the band (and its leader) into ever more expressive and capable players, so a tough slice of free bop such as 'Attempted, Not Known' on *Target Or Flag* holds no terrors. Bishop seems to be as at home on guitar as he is on trombone (one of the less frequently encountered examples of doubling). Rempis is a surprise substitute for Williams on *Simpatico*, and since he plays only alto it slightly narrows the tonal palette – though this supercharged and superbly focused set is surely the group's best to date.

*****(*) Design In Time**
Delmark DE-516 *Vandermark; Robert Barry, Tim Mulvenna (d).* 99.

Vandermark goes through the card here, playing jump-band tenor on 'Green Chimneys', unchained howling on 'Angels', even New Orleans clarinet on 'Cut To Fit'. Barry and Mulvenna make an unapologetically swinging team, playing at least as much time as they do free, and with Coleman, Monk and Ayler among the composer-credits, this is an amenable place to acquaint a newcomer with Vandermark's methods.

***** Transatlantic Bridge**
Okkadisk OD 12040 *Vandermark; Axel Dörner (t); Jeb Bishop (tb); Dave Rempis (as, ts); Jim Baker (p); Fred Lonberg-Holm (clo); Kent Kessler (b); Paul Lytton, Tim Mulvenna (d).* 2/00.

***** Spaceways Incorporated**
Atavistic ALP 120 *Vandermark; Nate McBride (b); Hamid Drake (d).* 1/00.

***** Version Soul**
Atavistic ALP 132 *As above.* 8/01.

The nonet music of *Transatlantic Bridge* is Vandermark at his most composerly, although he seems to back off from a really detailed involvement with directing the group, since the four long pieces have extended solos which pad out the music: more interesting would have been to hear the ensemble minus the lengthy extemporizing. 'RM' may catch out the unwary since it features a minute of silence halfway through (Marcel Duchamp, the dedicatee, may have enjoyed the point).

Spaceways Incorporated offers 'thirteen cosmic standards' by Sun Ra and George Clinton. The Ra pieces have a melodious folky feel, Vandermark often playing them in a mild clarinet setting, while the Clinton tunes are given a rollocking via electric bass, Drake thundering out funk beats and Vandermark in R&B tenor mode. Might have been interesting to have heard them the other way around. The encore set is this time all-original. 'Reasonable Hour' is a beautiful dedication to Serge Chaloff, and there's funk in more than one style ('Meters', for instance). A light sidebar in the oeuvre.

*****(*) Burn The Incline**
Atavistic ALP 121 *Vandermark; Jeb Bishop (tb, g); Dave Rempis (as, ts); Kent Kessler (b); Tim Mulvenna (d).* 12/99.

*****(*) Acoustic Machine**
Atavistic ALP 128 *As above.* 1/01.

****** Airports For Light**
Atavistic ALP 140 *As above, except Tim Daisy (d) replaces Mulvenna.* 8/02.

The Vandermark Five continue to be the leader's keynote ensemble. The records are settling almost into a repertory feel: for all the sometimes flaming intensity (actually notably pared back on these two sets), the quintet could be a variation on the classic hard-bop band. Vandermark's tunes certainly rise to the challenge that nobody's writing catchy jazz pieces any more: 'Roulette' on *Burn The Incline* or 'Fall To Grace' and 'Coast To Coast' on *Acoustic Machine* easily hook into the memory. His dedications often contain a note of mimicry: 'Coast To Coast', for Stan Getz, isn't so far from the Getz–Brookmeyer group, and 'License Complete' is very akin to 'Hard Blues'-era Julius Hemphill. New recruit Dave Rempis fits right in, and Bishop picks up the guitar for some of *Burn The Incline. Airports For Light* goes further and deeper, with Bishop especially in top fettle. A modern-day band for the jazz ages.

****** Crossing Division**
Okkadisk OD 12037 *Vandermark; Jeb Bishop (tb); Ingebrigt Haaker-Flaten (b); Paal Nilssen-Love (d).* 3/00.

The group which toured Europe in 2003. This might be the closest to straightforward freebop Vandermark's been in recent times, though the superb work from bass and drums tends to explode conventions, and throws the melodious soloing into sharper relief. There are a couple of Roswell Rudd tunes, but Bishop's 'Bookworm' is even better. A classic entry.

*****(*) Free Jazz Classics Vols. 1 & 2**

Atavistic ALP 137 2CD *Vandermark; Jeb Bishop (tb, g); Dave Rempis (as, ts); Kent Kessler (b); Tim Mulvenna (d).* 00–01.

Previously available as bonus CDs on earlier Vandermark Five records, these live sets of greatest hits from the avant-garde make a feasible sampler of the group's work in the area of cover versions. Composers called up include Braxton, Dolphy, Coleman, Hemphill, Giuffre and the inevitable Cherry and everything is played with a righteous mix of dedication and irreverence.

*****(*) Trigonometry**

Okkadisk OD 12042 2CD *Vandermark; Kent Kessler (b); Hamid Drake (d).* 3/01.

The latest report from DKV, from two gigs (Rochester, NY, and Kalamazoo, MI). Although Vandermark's note insists that it's primarily an improvising unit, they work from a base of material which appears to 'arrive' during each set. The first has lots of Don Cherry, as does the second, though there's also Ellington, Ayler, etc. Given Drake's tremendous strength this is always one of the most virile of Vandermark's groups, and these were clearly two great gigs.

*****(*) Two Days In December**

Wobbly Rail WOB012 2CD *Vandermark; David Stackenas (g); Sten Sandell (p); Raymond Strid (d); Kjell Nordeson (perc).* 12/01.

Just two days playing with these guys: Vandermark plays one set with each man. 'There are elements of styles defined as Free Jazz, Free Improvisation, New Music, Blues, Jazz etc, but there are many times I think we found something which is personal and does not fit into the categories that are set by 20th century expectations.' It is easy to both agree and diasagree: they don't find their way to anywhere 'new' here, yet, like everything Vandermark seems to put his fingers on, it's definitely his and their own.

*****(*) Dual Pleasure**

Smalltown Supersound STS 068 *Vandermark; Paal Nilssen-Love (d).* 7/02.

Europe's premier drummer meets Chicago's leading ambassador. It's some conversation. Listening to Nilssen-Love by himself is exhilarating; with Vandermark going full tilt alongside for an hour (well, they're not at full blast *all* the time), it's dizzying, if not quite deafening. Bravo!

***** Furniture Music**

Okkadsik 12046 *Vandermark (cl, bcl, ts, bs solo).* 8/02.

Alone at last! But Vandermark thrives so much on the interactions of group playing, especially with drummers, that one might anticipate some dry bones here. His dedications to Parker (Evan) and Brötzmann do have a certain copycat feel, too. Elsewhere, though, the ruminative Vandermark comes out. 'Immediate Action' is one small gem among several.

*****(*) Furnace**

Wobbly Rail WOB013 *Vandermark; Havard Wiik (p); Ingebrigt Haker Flaten (b).* 10/02.

Here he goes with yet another trio, Free Fall – and the dedication should be obvious, with a glance at the instrumentation. Ken sticks to B-flat and bass clarinets and the echoes of the great Giuffre trio are loud enough. Still, has anyone else thought of emulating and building on that distinguished group? Wiik is a more interventionist pianist than Bley, and of course Vandermark doesn't settle for chalumeau and woodsy shadows. The result is a fascinating departure and homage in one.

Eric Van der Westen (born 1963)

BASS

Dutch bassist leading a substantial, local post-bop outfit.

*****(*) Working Dreamer**

Bvhaast CD 9212 *Van der Westen; Chris Abelen, Hans Sparla (tb); Erwin Vann (ss, ts, bcl); Paul Van Kamenade (as); Paul De Leest (cl, ts); Ge Bijvoet (p); Pieter Bast (d).* n.d.

Van der Westen might have been listening to David Murray's Octet when he made this – his own musters a lot of the same *brio*, with rollicking counterpoint and horns-answering-horns music. His 'Ballad For John Carter' is a dirge Murray would be proud of; the conflation of Mingus melodies in 'The Underdog' is prime jazz repertory; and the five-part 'Out Of Time, Out Of Space' gets the most out of a little big band. But naturally, he puts a Europeanized spin on it too. The record may be on Bvhaast and these might be Dutchmen at work, but it's tellingly different from, say, a Willem Breuker band – more streamlined, less soberly comic. A nice absence of trumpets, a lot of good reeds, and a very good record.

***** Me, Myself And I**

Challenge CHR 70077 *Van der Westen; Angelo Verploegen, Reiner Winterschladen, Laurent Blondiau (t); Hans Sparla, Joost Buis, Louk Boudestein (tb); Miguel Boelens (ss, as, ts); Erwin Vann (ss, ts); Mete Erker (ts, bs); Jeroen Van Vliet (p); Thorsten Grau (d).* 11/99.

Van der Westen's salute to Charles Mingus is no ordinary homage. Briefly: he commissioned eight composers (including himself) to each write a new piece for his Quadrant quintet plus seven extra horns, each writer receiving a Mingus theme as a guide. Seven minutes of music was allowed for each composition, with spaces for improvisation to take it up to the 14-minute mark if need be. Of the eight composers involved, four came from 'contemporary classical' and four from jazz. It took two years to get to the rehearsal stage and the works were eventually premiered at a sequence of Amsterdam concerts; five of them got as far as this live CD.

The bassist deserves stars for chutzpah alone. But the results are often fascinating, if inconsistent. The most remarkable piece is probably Chiel Meijering's 'Min(g)us One', based around several Mingus themes, and sustained via minimalistic repetitions and a thickly clotted ensemble which nevertheless produces a smooth, almost hypnotic momentum. The chief difficulty with some of the pieces is the awkward integration of free and written passages, which some of the composers had a hard time with. Roderik de Man's 'Changin' Sue' sounds to be too self-consciously 'Mingusian' to convince. At the end, van der Westen contributes a second piece of his own, 'The Underdog'. Well worth hearing.

*****(*) Rush Hour**

EWM 75106 *Van Der Westen; Mete Erker, Erwin Vann (ss, ts); Jeroen Van Vliet (p); Thorsten Grau (d).* 2/01.

This seems like more of a watercolour after the crowded canvases of the previous two. It's also a very playable and attractive record. Quadrant play this without augmentation and Van der Westen has given them a set of yearning, wistful themes which the twinned timbres of Vann and Erker make into haunting motifs. The changes of 'Could It Have Happened' are beautifully explored by all hands and the reggae-like beat of 'Flow' sounds entirely plausible as handled here.

Fred Van Hove (born 1937)

PIANO, CHURCH ORGAN

Classical studies in his native Antwerp, then he worked in dance orchestras before becoming interested in free jazz, playing extensively with Peter Brötzmann in the '60s and early '70s. Many associations across the spectrum of free playing since then, although discs under his own leadership are comparatively few in number.

***** Lust**

Wimprotwee 100494 *Van Hove; Ivo Vander Borght (d).* 4/94.

***** Passing Waves**

Nuscope CD 1001 *Van Hove (p solo).* 5/97.

*****(*) Flux**

Potlatch P 2398 2CD *Van Hove (p solo).* 1/98.

Van Hove's almost ancestral status in European free music isn't acknowledged by his available discography: a stack of vinyl from the '70s and '80s has yet to get even a sniff of CD reissue, and recent sightings (in front of microphones, at least) have been rare. The two solo sets arrived almost simultaneously. The scarcity of his records is compensated for by their dense, sometimes super-concentrated content. Interesting to conjecture on what he learned from Taylor, or if – as with his early collaborator Peter Brötzmann – he arrived at his style mostly independently of American influence. Either way, as far back as the earliest FMPs he was projecting a fiercely individual aesthetic on free-jazz piano, and by now it is quite his own, while inevitably steeped in the unorthodoxies of the style. The two sets are quite unalike, since the Potlatch (live) is made up of two long, continuous sets while the Nuscope is a more prepared set of ten studio pieces. The latter takes a specific starting-point for most of the tracks – a billiard ball on the strings or the qualities of an arpeggio – and fashions it quite deliberately. The former simply lets Fred go at the keyboard, and he works through big structures with the kind of block-follows-block linearity that marks him out, perhaps, as old school. That said, his pianism (on which Georg Graewe comments admiringly in a sleeve-note to *Passing Waves*) is so refined that the concert disc in particular is mostly spellbinding. Some of *Passing Waves* is more interesting for its formal ideas than for their execution, but *Flux* is often as exciting as it is profound.

Lust came out of a theatre piece of the same title. As with many such documents, one feels that there's a vital element missing, and the brief vocal intrusion of the actors on one track underlines it. Taken simply as a sequence of duets, though, there are some absorbing dialogues, which Borght is more than up to playing his part in: 'Tafeltjesballade', for instance.

***** PijP**

WIMprovier 140497 *Van Hove; Johannes Bauer, Konrad Bauer (tb).* 4/97.

The only record of trombone and church organ duets in the catalogue, we suspect. Johannes and Connie do one each, and Fred takes a solo in the middle. Van Hove recorded improvisations on an organ in the '70s, so this isn't exactly new ground for him. The horn-players battle manfully against what are basically impossible odds, and it's all amusing high jinks, really. The solo sounds like a horror-film soundtrack.

Jesse Van Ruller

GUITAR

Promising young Dutchman with a good head of steam as a recording artist.

***** Here And There**

Criss Cross 1217 *Van Ruller; David Hazeltine (p); Nat Reeves, Franz Van Geest (b); Joe Farnsworth, Willie Jones III (d).* 1/02.

***** Circles**

Criss Cross 1235 *Van Ruller; Seamus Blake (ts); Sam Yahel (org); Bill Stewart (d).* 12/02.

Reminiscent in places of label-mate Peter Bernstein, Van Ruller plays flowing, efficient jazz guitar without too much embellishment and with a certain impatience for complexity where simplicity will do just as well. Konitz's 'Subconscious-Lee' on the first album is a good indication of how his mind works, but there are even better tracks, such as the opening 'The Best Things In Life Are Free' and Buster Williams's delightful and rarely covered 'Christina'. A brief version of Monk's 'In Walked Bud' is marked by wit and intelligence. The two rhythm sections are broadly similar in conception, though Jones is probably the more propulsive and effective drummer.

The second album steams straight into sax/guitar/organ soul-jazz, but demolishes expectations with a set of Van Ruller originals which emphasize the subtler side of this particular configuration. 'Zoab', '33 Waltz' and the closing 'Secret Champ' are all fine themes, each with a touch of mystery. The group sounds well rehearsed and sympathetic, and only on the solitary standard, 'Gone With The Wind', is there any sign of flagging. The only other tune not by Van Ruller is Blake's very good 'Black Dahlia'. Another very satisfying set, and buried among all those seventh and ninth progressions there is something rather special lurking. We'll look forward to future projects.

Jasper Van't Hof (born 1947)

PIANO, KEYBOARDS, DRUMS

The gifted Dutchman worked with flautist Chris Hinze and with Archie Shepp and has had a special fondness for working with violinists, most obviously Jean-Luc Ponty and the late

Zbigniew Seifert. Sometimes showy and over-effusive, Van't Hof has a powerful sense of structure and writes challenging charts reminiscent of Chick Corea in more formal mode.

*****(*) Blau**

ACT 9203 *Van't Hof; Bob Malach (ts); Wayne Krantz (g), Nicholas Fiszman (b), Philippe Allaert (d).* n.d.

Malach turned out to be a highly responsive partner and is even more dominant in the group with Krantz, an imaginatively constituted outfit that should have recorded more. Van't Hof favours long, ripplingly arpeggiated lines and richly augmented chords, but he is also capable of playing spare, funky lines. It may seem like a very long shot, but play their duets back to back with David Murray's collaborations with Dave Burrell: there is the same stark melody combined with all the harmonic elegance and daring that one could ask for.

*****(*) At The Concertgebouw – Solo**

Challenge CHR 70010 *Van't Hof (p solo).* 12/93.

Boxing Day 1993 and the most prestigious concert venue in the Netherlands. Jasper rises to the occasion grandly. His rippling opening statement on 'Equivalent' (which may have been written for the occasion) establishes a mood for the rest of the evening: lyrical, gracious and not a bit self-indulgent. Interesting to compare the versions here of 'Prelude To A Kiss' and 'Dinner For Two' with those on his earlier solo album *Solo Piano* (Timeless SJP 286). The first and obvious point is that the Concertgebouw piano is a better and more responsive instrument, but the hushed expectancy with which Jasper invests the Ellington melody is quite entrancing. He ends with a wonderful reading of Horace Silver's 'Peace', rounding off a thoroughly satisfying performance. Why, then, the rather hesitant valuation? Simply because there is little texture to the set, no highs and lows, no light and shade, and no drama. Technically accomplished, but not vital enough for most listeners.

*****(*) Tomorrowland**

Challenge CHR 70040 *Van't Hof; Bob Malach (ts); Jean-François Jenny-Clark (b).* 9/96.

Jasper made very substantial claims for this record, suggesting that it represented a new genre, related to but different from African-American jazz. Bold as the writing is, and splendidly as it is executed, it's hard to swallow his claim that VOJ – as he chooses to call this new style – has made a qualitative step beyond bebop. The writing is, as one would expect, both thoughtful and intense, and three longish tracks space through the record – 'Wildcard', 'Round About' (which may have been influenced by Monk) and 'The Quiet American' are all markedly individual. Jenny-Clark and Malach are admirably responsive. The bassist has never enjoyed the kind of attention his attentive, detailed playing deserves. Like Barre Phillips, he is able to combine an old-fashioned sound (reminiscent of Wilbur Ware) and unfailing swing with what often sounds like complete freedom. Malach, too, follows no known school, and the drummerless trio has a marked independence of direction that is consistently fascinating. The harmonic language and experimental metres are certainly food for thought – but as to founding a new idiom, we don't think so.

*****(*) Un Mondo Illusorio**

Challenge CHR 70059 *Van't Hof (org solo).* 8/98.

Completely *sui generis*, this astonishing record is certainly at the boundaries of jazz, VOJ, or any other identifiable idiom. Van't Hof has long included organ in his armoury, but these performances on the instrument at Chiesa di Santa Maria delle Rose in Bonefro, Italy, are unique, provocative and sometimes bewilderingly idiosyncratic. Consisting of 17 short études or thematic improvisations, the album explores an astonishing range of tonalities and timbres, from the percussive snaps and clicks of 'Dimenarsi Da Maniaco' to huge, shimmering tone-clusters reminiscent of classical composer-organists Jehan Alain and Olivier Messiaen. The mood of the recording is almost entirely thoughtful and reflective, with little in the way of dynamic variation. Van't Hof's concentration is palpable, but so too is his shrewd sense of humour. While these are far from lightweight pieces, there is a sense of play about them. We are, it hardly needs to be said, a long way from Art Tatum, and anyone who demands an element of swing will be put off from the outset; but, should you like to think you have open ears and mind, *Un Mondo Illusorio* is a very worthwhile experience.

***** Tempo Brutto**

Intuition 3309 *Van't Hof; Charlie Mariano (as); Steve Swallow (b).* 01.

Not strictly a Van't Hof album at all but a series of collaborative duos involving all three players as leaders and composers. Mariano is in sparkling form and fans of his work will be drawn to this record, which includes some delicately weighted solos and some wonderful melodic lines. Van't Hof is fine on the title-track and makes some telling interventions, but there are better representations of his work than this.

Tom Varner (born 1957)

FRENCH HORN

At work in the New York scene for some 20 years, Varner, whose background is Missourian, specializes in what is still a rarity in jazz, the french horn.

***** Tom Varner Quartet**

Soul Note 121017-2 *Varner; Ed Jackson (as); Fred Hopkins (b); Billy Hart (d).* 8/80.

***** Jazz French Horn**

Soul Note 121176-2 *Varner; Jim Snidero (as); Kenny Barron (p); Mike Richmond (b); Victor Lewis (d).* 10/85.

****** The Mystery Of Compassion**

Soul Note 121217-2 *Varner; Steve Swell (tb); Dave Taylor (btb); Matt Darriau, Ed Jackson (as); Rich Rothenberg, Ellery Eskelin (ts); Jim Hartog (bs); Mark Feldman (vn); Mike Richmond (b); Tom Rainey (d).* 3/92.

****** Martian Heartache**

Soul Note 121286-2 *Varner; Ed Jackson (as); Ellery Eskelin (ts); Pete McCann (g); Drew Gress (b); Tom Rainey (d); Dominique Eade (v).* 3/96.

Varner's decision to apply french horn as a weapon in the New York avant-garde might once have seemed improbable but with every kind of instrument pressed into service in that milieu, no longer. There is the inevitable feel from time to time that it's a trombonist we're listening to, but Varner has taken pains to develop his own vocabulary on an often intractable brass instrument. The *Quartet* album is more like uneventful free-bop, depending on satisfying solos to make its modest impact.

Jazz French Horn continued along similar lines, but the band is excellent and even as a repertory exercise it's very well done.

The later Soul Note records are something else entirely. On *The Mystery Of Compassion*, Varner's alarming juxtapositions make coherent sense without losing their capacity to surprise, and the players involved respond with a passionate intensity which is rare even among these driven musicians. The central group is a quintet made up of Varner, Jackson, Rothenberg, Richmond and Rainey. On all-out barnstormers like 'How Does Power Work?' and '$1000 Hat' they play with unstinting panache. 'The Well' is a concerto-like piece for Feldman, and 'Death At The Right Time' uses a tentet to create a bemusing recall of Coltrane's 'Ascension'. Varner's own improvising has never been better – he actually makes the instrument assert its personal qualities – and he closes the record on a sombre antiphonal piece for low brass called 'Prayer' which makes a moving coda to the rest.

Martian Heartache is probably even better. Varner packs 15 pieces into the record, again based around the core quintet, with McCann arriving only for the fascinating 'Erva Etc'. Sculpted with absolute precision but loose and swinging in feel, the music never turns fragmentary or episodic; even the shortest pieces are fully realized, composed and uncluttered. Varner plays a gracious role as leader, offering terrific opportunities for the horns to make characterful statements, without letting anybody blemish their book by spinning out rhetoric. Jackson and Eskelin are more than equal to the task.

**** The Window Up Above

New World 80552-2 *Varner; Dave Ballou (c); Mark Feldman (vn); Pete McCann (g); Steve Alcott, Lindsey Horner (b); George Schuller (d); Thirsty Dave Hansen (v).* 5/98.

A complete departure for Tom, but just as powerful and surprising a record. It's a ramble through 200 or so years of American songwriting, going as far back as the earliest public-domain folk-tunes and as far forward as Ellington, George Jones and Hank Williams (the latter two voiced by Thirsty Dave Hansen). If he treats 'I Got It Bad' relatively straight, it's to emphasize the lieder element in the tune. 'Kingdom Coming' gets a blues injected into it, and 'When Jesus Wept' is gradually, but logically, broken down into a strange lament. 'Abide With Me' gets its first jazz treatment, as a sweet waltz, since Monk's horn arrangement. And so on. No track seems silly or forced, and Varner makes every melody count. Excellent work from the little-known McCann, playing a Frisell-like role a lot of the way, and cameos from Feldman and Ballou add to the pleasure of a mature and beautifully sustained record.

*** The Swiss Duos

Unit UTR 4218 *Varner; George Gruntz, Christoph Baumann, Hans Feigenwinter, Gabriella Friedli (p).* 8/98.

Varner meets the local pianists, on a Swiss visit. The use of Hans Hassler's hymn as an interleaving between many of the duets is rather tiresome, and it does tend to detract from what's otherwise an interestingly diverse series of engagements. The horn stands back, or at least pat, when Gruntz gets going. With Baumann Varner's harsh, even splenetic at times, and with Feigenwinter he reprises his old favourite 'What Is This Thing Called First Strike Capability'. Mixed, but rarely less than involving.

**** Second Communion

Omnitone 12102 *Varner; Dave Ballou(c); Tony Malaby (ts); Pete McCann (g); Cameron Brown (b); Matt Wilson (d).* 9/00.

A brilliant piece of repertory, recasting Don Cherry's entire *Complete Communion* in a fresh interpretation by an admirable band. Ballou's finest moment probably comes on 'Cherryco' but he takes the Cherry 'role' with individual aplomb and Varner himself has rarely played with more decision and adventure, pushing the horn into difficult areas with great skill. Brown and Wilson, crucially, evoke the kind of smart but free-flowing swing which kept Cherry's music buoyant, and there is a poignant farewell to the trumpeter which Varner plays solo.

Dimitrios Vassilakis

SOPRANO AND TENOR SAXOPHONES

A leading figure on the burgeoning Greek jazz scene, he initially studied engineering before moving to London. Draws on a wide array of influences, from Balkan folk to roots reggae.

***(*) Secret Path

Candid 79765 *Vassilakis; Craig Bailey (as); George Contrafouris (p, tb); Dimitrios Kalatzis (p); Kostas Konstaninou (b); Spyros Panayotopolous (d, perc); Arco String Quartet.* 3–7/98.

A remarkable major-label debut for the young Greek saxophonist, who conjures amazing depths of colour and harmonic resonance from his group, augmented on some tracks by Bailey and by the string quartet. The themes – 'Afro-Diti', 'Mind Of Blue' – are all inspired by modern jazz of a broadly modal sort, but filtered through a unique imagination and delivered by a powerfully individual voice. 'Triptych' is a powerful tenor statement, but there is room for balladry of an idiosyncratic sort on 'Ammos Soma' and 'A Puppet's Dream'.

*** Labyrinth: Daedalus Project

Candid 79776 *Vassilakis; Dave Liebman, Andy Sheppard (ss, ts); George Contrafouris (p); Emmanuel Saridakis (p, org); Marc Johnson (b); Jamey Haddad, Ralph Peterson (d, perc); Theodossi Spassov (kaval).* 9/00.

There's something slightly rum about a concept album that purports to tell the story of Theseus, the Minotaur and the Labyrinth, Ariadne's thread, Pasiphae's dance and Icarus's flight and then ends with a run-through of the Miles Davis/Bill Evans staple 'Blue In Green'. Slightly more logic to the inclusion of King Crimson's 'Epitaph', though why it comes second in the set and not last is equally puzzling. That said, this is a fine group, Vassilakis is a consistently interesting and often very impressive player, and it is clear that he is looking for universal significance in these old mythologies rather than mere colour. Liebman has been an important influence on Vassilakis and is always open-minded enough to bring something individual and philosophically challenging to a date like this. The ethnic element is largely restricted to Bulgarian Spassov's kaval but it has a more important structural role than is initially obvious. We found the record enjoyable and provocative as soon as we stopped thinking about its apparent agenda.

Sarah Vaughan (1924–90)

VOCAL, PIANO

Studied piano as a child, then joined the Earl Hines band in 1943 as vocalist. Left with Billy Eckstine to sing in his new band and went solo in the late '40s, usually working live with a trio or small group; sang on record mostly with orchestras, especially from the mid-'50s. Had many crossover hits during that decade but was always seen as a jazz vocalist, one of the most gifted, with a big range and variety of tone, a bopper's way with scat – though she rarely used it – and the stage presence of a forbidding diva. Never as popular as Holiday or Fitzgerald – and, some would say, better than either.

***** Sarah Vaughan 1944–1946**

Classics 958 *Vaughan; Dizzy Gillespie, Freddy Webster, Shorty McConnell, Gail Brockman, Boonie Hazel, Clarence Brereton, George Treadwell, Al Aaron, Danny Blue, Art House, Al Porcino, Neal Hefti, Sonny Rich, George Schwartz (t); Gerald Valentine, Trummy Young, Tracy Allen, Mike Datz, Rude De Luca, Gus Dixon, Johnny Mandel, Taswell Baird, Howard Scott, Alfred 'Chippie' Outcalt, Dicky Wells (tb); Aaron Sachs, Buster Bailey, Tony Scott (cl); Charlie Parker, Scoville Brown, Leroy Harris, John Jackson, Bill Frazier, Russell Procope, Lou Prisby, Gene Zanoni, Leroy Harris, Sam Zittman (as); Don Byas, Dexter Gordon, Gene Ammons, Flip Phillips, Ben Webster, Al Cohn, Irv Roth (ts); Cecil Payne, Serge Chaloff, Leo Parker, Cecil Scott (bs); Al Haig, Jimmy Jones, Bud Powell, Leonard Feather, John Malachi, Billy Kyle, Freddy Jefferson, Roy Kral, Harvey Leonard, Tadd Dameron (p); John Collins, Remo Palmieri, Bill D'Arango, Connie Wainwright, Chuck Wayne, Barry Galbraith (g); Al McKibbon, Curley Russell, Ted Sturgis, Tommy Potter, Jack Lesberg, John Kirby, Gene Ramey, Ted Sturgis, Joe Pillicane, Ed Cunningham (b); Pete Glover, Big Sid Catlett, Kenny Clarke, Art Blakey, Morey Feld, Max Roach, Bill Beason, Ed Nicholson, Art Madigan (d).* 9/44–7/46.

*****(*) The Divine Sarah Vaughan: The Columbia Years 1949–1953**

Columbia 465597 2CD *Vaughan; Miles Davis, Billy Butterfield, Taft Jordan, Andrew Ferretti, Bernie Privin, Yank Lawson, Carl Poole, Ziggy Elman (t); Will Bradley, Jack Satterfield, William Rausch, Benny Green, John D'Agostino, William Pritchard (tb); Tony Scott (cl); Hymie Schertzer, Art Drelinger, George Kelly, Toots Mondello, Al Klink, Bill Versaci, Richard Banzer, Bill Hitz, Budd Johnson (saxes); Jimmy Jones (p); Freddie Green, Al Caiola, Mundell Lowe (g); Frank Carroll, Eddie Safranski, Jack Lesberg, Billy Taylor, Bob Haggart (b); J. C. Heard, Terry Snyder, Norris Shawker, Bill Coles (d); strings; studio orchestras led by Percy Faith, Paul Weston and Norman Leyden.* 1/49–1/53.

Her vocal on the 1946 Dizzy Gillespie Sextet record of 'Lover Man' was Sarah Vaughan's banner arrival. Yet she'd already cut several fine sides – four with a Dizzy Gillespie small group, including a fine vocal version of 'Night In Tunisia' – and there were several other scattered appearances, all of which seem to have been gathered up on the intriguing if finally slightly disappointing Classics CD. A later session with Bird and Dizzy includes a terrific 'Mean To Me', with Parker shadowing her almost like Lester with Billie, but the remaining sessions are motley in nature and Vaughan seems to get only doleful ballads to sing. 'All Too Soon', with a Tony Scott group, is a nice one, with some lovely Ben Webster, and overall the best performances earn the stars, although remastering seems very spotty. But her sessions for Musicraft and Columbia were her first significant body of records, following her stint with the Billy Eckstine Orchestra.

The bulk of the Columbias are scarcely jazz-orientated sessions, with full orchestras and hefty ballads, but two sessions from May 1950 put Vaughan in front of a small band that included Miles Davis, Tony Scott and Budd Johnson for eight fine tracks. Vaughan's musical insight – she was a more than capable pianist – and involvement with bop's early days gave her a hip awareness that went with a voice of vast range and power, and her early Billy Eckstine influence – both singers use vibrato to the same enormously ripe effect – makes her sound like a close relation of Eckstine on all these tracks. Far from disguising the operatic qualities of her voice, Vaughan insists on them, sometimes dispersing the sense of a lyric while luxuriating in the depth of her own voice. Luckily, the material on the Columbia sessions is good enough to withstand such indulgence, and it's a very enjoyable double set, acceptably if not outstandingly remastered.

***** Sarah Vaughan 1951–1952**

Classics 1296 *Vaughan; orchestras led by Norman Leyden, Percy Faith, Paul Weston.* 1/51–12/52.

One lush ballad after another, with the occasional flash of religion ('A City Called Heaven'). Many of the tracks are predictably gorgeous, but even the great voice is often almost smothered by the orchestrations.

CORE COLLECTION

♛ ** Sarah Vaughan**

Verve 543305-2 *Vaughan; Clifford Brown (t); Paul Quinichette (ts); Herbie Mann (f); Jimmy Jones (p); Joe Benjamin (b); Roy Haynes (d).* 12/54.

The session with Clifford Brown was a glorious occasion, and the kind of date that occurred far too infrequently during the rest of Sarah's career. A blue-chip band (even Mann doesn't disgrace himself) on a slow-burning set of standards that Vaughan lingers over and details with all the finesse of her early-mature voice: 'Lullaby Of Birdland' (the master take is a composite, and there is a 'partial alternative' take here too) is taken at a pace that suspends time or lets it drift, and the very slow pace for 'Embraceable You' and 'Jim' doesn't falter into a trudge. In the past we have wondered if the many slow tempos were perhaps *too* many, but in this superb new remastering it is very difficult to find any flaw in what should be recognized as one of the great jazz vocal records. We are upgrading it to crown status as a result.

****** Swingin' Easy**

Emarcy 514072-2 *Vaughan; Jimmy Jones, John Malachi (p); Richard Davis, Joe Benjamin (b); Roy Haynes (d).* 54–57.

Swingin' Easy isn't far behind, though. With just a rhythm section in support, Vaughan is at her freest and most good-humoured: it's worth having just for the cheeky, sublime 'Shulie A Bop', but there's also a gorgeous 'Lover Man' and a shivery 'Linger Awhile'.

*****(*) Sings George Gershwin**

Verve 557567-2 2CD *Vaughan; Hal Mooney Orchestra.* 57.

***** Golden Hits**
Mercury 824891-2 *Vaughan; Hal Mooney Orchestra.* 58.

*****(*) Sings Broadway: Great Songs From Great Shows**
Verve 526464-2 2CD *As above discs.* 3/54–1/56.

*****(*) Jazz Masters 42: The Jazz Sides**
Verve 526817-2 *As above.* n.d.

Vaughan's later Mercury sessions are sometimes a shade self-conscious – not in any sense an embarrassment to Vaughan but in the way that she can get hung up on the sound of her own voice, the criticism most often levelled at her. Musicality and the comparative brevity of each piece usually win through, though, and while her 'songbook' collections miss some of the simple swing and infectiousness of the contemporaneous Ella Fitzgerald records in the same style, Vaughan's grandness and the lavish Mercury recording make these rich sonic experiences. At the moment Universal seem to be rethinking their Vaughan holdings, and the individual albums which are out there are few in number. The Gershwin set competes but loses out to the Fitzgerald counterpart, though that is scarcely a disgrace. *Golden Hits* offers a fine cross-section of material, although the occasional stuffiness of the studio orchestra discourages any hint that Vaughan might use the occasions as springboards for more idiomatic jazz singing. Her coloratura tones and sweeping phrasing work instead to a different aesthetic, and one that is as individually creative.

Sings Broadway is an intelligent compilation from this era, with a 'songbook' approach to the material and scarcely a dud track among it all. Some may prefer the *Jazz Masters* choice from her more jazz-directed sessions, but it's still no substitute for *Sarah Vaughan* or *Swingin' Easy.*

*****(*) At Mister Kelly's**
Emarcy 832791-2 *Vaughan; Jimmy Jones (p); Richard Davis (b); Roy Haynes (d).* 57.

*****(*) Sassy Swings The Tivoli**
Mercury 832788-2 2CD *Vaughan; Kirk Stuart (p); Charles Williams (b); Georges Hughes (d).* 7/63.

The best of these live sessions is the earliest *At Mister Kelly's.* Most singers can't wait to get out of clubs and into concert halls, but the 'intimacy' of the situation can be a boon, and with this excellent trio Vaughan sounds completely relaxed. Nineteen songs, some of them dashed off, but she dashes better than most. The later date is very good rather than great. *Tivoli* is a solid balance between the unbridled grandeur of her range and the more loose-limbed jazz-musician stance; despite the grandiloquence of her voice, most of her best records have been done with small groups rather than orchestras.

*****(*) Ultimate Sarah Vaughan**
Verve 539052-2 *Vaughan; various groups.* 54–67.

*****(*) 'Round Midnight: Sarah Vaughan**
Verve 510086-2 *As above.* n.d.

*****(*) Verve Jazz Masters: Sarah Vaughan**
Verve 518199-2 *As above.* n.d.

None of these compilations holds a candle to either *Sarah Vaughan* or *Swingin' Easy*, even though they take tracks from both. But each has enough classics – 'Shulie A Bop', 'Dreamsville' on *Ultimate*, 'April In Paris', 'Jim', 'Darn That Dream' on *'Round Midnight*, 'Say It Isn't So' and 'Lonely Woman' on *Jazz Masters* – to satisfy a seeker after a run-through of Sarah's Emarcy/Mercury period.

****** After Hours**
Roulette 855468-2 *Vaughan; Mundell Lowe (g); George Duvivier (b).* 7/61.

A comparatively little-known record, yet one of her finest. With the skeletal accompaniment of Lowe (who plays only a single solo on the date) and Duvivier, Vaughan muses over 11 standards (there is a previously unheard try-out take on 'Through The Years') which find her by turns playful and profound. A light, gorgeous 'Easy To Love' looks back to her bebop days, there's a starkly effective 'My Favorite Things', and 'Vanity' – just one among several fascinating choices of song – is immaculately modulated. The remastering gets the most out of the great voice.

*****(*) Snowbound / The Lonely Hours**
EMI 855394-2 *Vaughan; orchestras arranged and conducted by Don Costa and Benny Carter.* 63–64.

***** Sweet 'N' Sassy**
Roulette 31793-2 *Vaughan; Lalo Schifrin orchestra.* 6/63.

*****(*) Ballads**
Roulette 37561-2 *As Roulette albums above.* 60–63.

The first album has Vaughan getting indecently comfortable in Costa's very deep-pile orchestrations; the second has her finding a soupçon of civilized blues in Benny Carter's charts. Carter is scarcely trying too hard here, but he still finds a few interesting quirks, such as the low brass for 'You're Driving Me Crazy', and Vaughan is at her most perfectly controlled on 'Look For Me, I'll Be Around'. The Costa tracks are a shameless wallow by all concerned. As a coupling, this works rather well in showing off Vaughan's two sides of the time.

Sweet 'N' Sassy is typical of the Roulette output: a mixed bag of familiar songs and try-outs, some of which are pretty trying. She gives them all her best attention, pro that she was, but Lalo Schifrin's charts don't do a tremendous amount to help. 'Lazy Afternoon' buzzes with junebug sound effects. She sounds ready to throw everything into 'I Got Rhythm' but the track's over inside two minutes. Bold remastering, though.

The Ballads collection makes an appealing buy. Roulette may not have encouraged Sarah's most creative side but their microphones caught much of the luxuriance of her mature voice, and there's nothing less than enjoyable here.

***** It's A Man's World**
Verve 589487-2 *Vaughan; Joe Mooney Orchestra.* 1/67.

The concept here is songs with 'Man' in the title (or, at least, a man's name). It's not recorded what Sassy thought about that. In the wasteland of her '60s records, this one's as fair as any. 'Trouble Is A Man' and 'Jim' are given regal embellishments, and the Mooney group at least has some decent jazz players in it.

*****(*) How Long Has This Been Going On?**
Pablo 2310-821 *Vaughan; Oscar Peterson (p); Joe Pass (g); Ray Brown (b); Louie Bellson (d).* 4/78.

*****(*) Duke Ellington Song Book One**
Pablo 2312-111 *Vaughan; Waymon Reed (t, flhn); J. J. Johnson (tb); Eddie 'Cleanhead' Vinson (as, v); Frank Wess (ts, f); Frank Foster, Zoot Sims (ts); Jimmy Rowles, Mike Wofford (p); Joe Pass, Bucky Pizzarelli, Pee Wee Crayton (g); Andy Simpkins, Bill Walker (b); Grady Tate, Charles Randell (d); big band.* 8–9/79.

★★★(★) Duke Ellington Song Book Two
Pablo 2312-116 *As above.* 8–9/79.

★★★★ Copacabana
Pablo 2312-125 *Vaughan; Helio Delmiro (g); Andy Simpkins (b); Grady Tate(d).* 10/79.

★★★ Send In The Clowns
Pablo 2312-230 *Vaughan; Sonny Cohn, Frank Szabo, Willie Cook, Bob Summers, Dale Carley (t); Booty Wood, Bill Hughes, Denis Wilson, Grover Mitchell (tb); Kenny Hing, Eric Dixon, Bobby Plater, Danny Turner, Johnny Williams (saxes); George Gaffney (p); Freddie Green (g); Andy Simpkins (b); Harold Jones (d).* 2–5/81.

★★★★ Crazy And Mixed Up
Pablo 2312-137 *Vaughan; Sir Roland Hanna (p); Joe Pass (g); Andy Simpkins (b); Harold Jones (d).* 3/82.

Vaughan's Pablo albums will endure as some of her most finely crafted music. *How Long Has This Been Going On?* introduced a new note of seriousness into her recording career after several years of indifferent efforts and a seemingly careless approach to the studios. The voice has never been better or more closely recorded, and the picked session players and uniformly strong material make these albums the most consistent of her career. *How Long* has the odd flaw, but there are beautiful readings of 'I've Got The World On A String' and the title-tune, and when Vaughan takes it in turns to do a duo with each member of the band it's a marvellous display of her ability. The Ellington albums gave her – at last – the opportunity to stamp her identity on the greatest of jazz songbooks, and while again there are a few disappointments – a second-class 'Solitude' that should have been a classic, the sometimes overbearing heft of Bill Byers's arrangements and the slightly problematic balance – there are some exceptionally bountiful treatments, of 'In A Sentimental Mood', 'I'm Just A Lucky So-And-So' and 'Chelsea Bridge' to cite three. Both discs stand as a worthy counterpoint to Fitzgerald's celebrated Ellington collaboration.

Send In The Clowns features the Basie orchestra minus Basie, and while it's good – the gliding 'All The Things You Are' and a lovely 'Indian Summer' especially – the hard power of the band and Vaughan's own superhuman technique sometimes secure a coldness rather than any warmth of interpretation. *Copacabana* is the neglected album of the bunch, with the sparest of accompaniments to support the great, glowing voice, and the bossa/samba material proving unexpectedly strong for Vaughan. Best of all, perhaps, is *Crazy And Mixed Up*, a disappointingly short (about 32 minutes) but ideally paced and delivered set of standards with the most sympathetic of accompaniments.

★★★(★) Linger Awhile
Pablo 2312-144-2 *Vaughan; Waymon Reed (t); Frank Foster (ts); Jimmy Jones, Roland Hanna, Mike Wofford, Jimmy Rowles, Oscar Peterson(p); Joe Pass, Bucky Pizzarelli (g); Richard Davis, Andy Simpkins, Ray Brown (b); Roy Haynes, Grady Tate, Louie Bellson (d); Count Basie Orchestra.* 7/57–2/81.

The first eight tracks are quite a discovery, Vaughan live at the 1957 Newport Festival. Girlish and almost flirtatious at some points, the dark mocha tones are there on 'Black Coffee' and the virtuosity of 'All Of Me' is inimitable. The rest offers eight alternative takes from her Pablo albums, many of them fine enough to make one want to return to the neglected original albums. As an album it doesn't really hang together, but as a feast of rare Vaughan for devotees it's excellent.

Charlie Ventura (1916–92)

TENOR SAXOPHONE

Born Charles Venturo in Philadelphia, worked a day job in a navy yard but jammed after hours with local players. Worked with Gene Krupa, 1942–6, then ran his own big band and small group, as well as JATP appearances. Led a 'Bop For The People' group from the late '40s but, despite a later spell with Krupa, drifted from sight in the '60s.

★★★ Live At The Three Deuces
High Note HCD 7066 *Ventura; Bill Harris (tb); Ralph Burns (p); Bob Leininger, Curley Russell (b); Dave Tough (d).* 47.

★★★ Live At The Three Deuces Vol. 2
High Note HCD 7082 *As above, except add Ray Abrams (ts), Ed Shaughnessy (d), Teddy Walters (v).* 47–52.

★★★ Charlie Ventura 1945–1946
Classics 1044 *Ventura; Howard McGhee, Red Rodney, Buck Clayton (t); Barney Bigard (cl); Willie Smith (as); Arnold Ross, Bill Rowland, Harry Fields (p); Barney Kessel, Dave Barbour, Eddie Yance (g); Artie Shapiro, Red Callender, Billy Hadnott, Al Hall, John Levy (b); Specs Powell, Nick Fatool, Gene Krupa (d).* 3/45–3/46.

★★★ Charlie Ventura 1946–1947
Classics 1111 *Ventura; Red Rodney, Neal Hgefti, Stan Fishelson, Jack Palmer, Al Stearns, Fern Caron, Charlie Shavers (t); Bob Ascher, Al Lorraine, Leo Checchi, Saul Kaye, Bill Harris (tb); Tony Scott, Aaron Sachs (cl, as); Barney Bigard (cl); Charlie Kennedy, Ed Scalzi, Murray Williams (as); Dan Cappi, Nick Jerrett, Barney Marino (ts); Tony Ferina (bs); Tony Aless, Milt Raskin, Teddy Napoleon, Ralph Burns, Hank Jones, Mary Lou Williams (p); Marjorie Hyams (vib); Allan Reuss, Billy Bauer, Bill D'Arango (g); Red Callender, Clyde Lombardi, Curly Russell, Chubby Jackson (b); Dave Tough, Nick Fatool, Ellis Tollin, Stan Levey (d); Marianne Dunne, Jack Palmer, Buddy Stewart, Lilyann Carol (v).* 4/46–4/47.

★★★(★) Charlie Ventura 1947–1948
Classics 1149 *Ventura; Norman Faye, Conte Candoli (t); Kai Winding, Benny Green (tb); Boots Mussulli (as, bs); Ben Ventura (bs); Lou Stein, Roy Kral (p); Bob Carter, Gus Cole, Chubby Jackson, Kenny O'Brien (b); Shelly Manne, Ed Shaughnessy (d); Buddy Stewart, Jackie Cain (v).* 9/47–4/49.

★★★(★) Charlie Ventura 1949
Classics 1215 *Ventura; Conte Candoli (t, v); Benny Green (tb, v); Boots Mussulli (as, bs); Roy Kral (p, v); Teddy Kaye, Dave McKenna (p); Kenny O'Brien, Red Mitchell (b); Ed Shaughnessy(d); Jackie Cain, Betty Bennett, Beverley Brooks, Jimmy Vanelli (v).* 4–9/49.

★★★ Charlie Ventura 1949–1951
Classics 1309 *Ventura; Stan Fishelson, Johnny Mandel, Dale Pierce, Red Rodney, Conte Candoli, Ed Bagley, John Cabot, Dick Sherman, Rolf Ericson, Pete Ventura (t); Mort Bullman, Benny Green, Bart Varsalona, Bob Ascher, Billy Byers, Jack Hitchcock (tb); Ray Beckenstein, Frank Socolow, Andy Cicalese, Tom Mace, Art Friedman, Charlie Kennedy (as); Al Cohn, Al Young, Hervey Estrin (ts); Manny Albam, Ben*

Ventura (bs); Lou Stein, Joe Scusa, Tony Aless, Jimmy Wisner, Ralph Burns (p); Barry Galbraith, Sam Herman (g); Curley Russell, Jimmy Johnson, Ace Tesone, Chubby Jackson (b); Ed Shaughnessy, Chick Keeny (d); Lucy Reed, The Honeydreamers, The Blentones, Betty Bennett (v). 12/49–8/51.

Ventura was very popular in his day, but has since been entirely marginalized in jazz's history. Unfairly so, on the evidence of the early sessions, since his playing had chutzpah and skill, even if he was entirely derivative of Coleman Hawkins and took on the bop vernacular as only a sideline to his main swing language. Classics 1044 collects five sessions for Sunset, Black & White, Savoy and Lamplighter, and while his own playing is enjoyable, there is rather more interesting playing from McGhee, Rodney and even the young Barney Kessel. The first Black & White session sounds rough, but otherwise the transfers seem good.

As Ventura progressed through the '40s, he began to build an audience and a style which managed to make some kind of integration between bop and the 'swingtet' music which was one of the 52nd Street threads of the period. Classics 1111 is a transitional set, since it includes two sessions by quite a commercial big band, plus sextet/septet dates for Crystalette, Emarcy and National – featuring swing players such as Shavers, Bigard and Bill Harris – as well as one with Red Rodney. It was the Ventura septet, sometimes billed under the banner 'Bop For The People', which really brought him a following. Classics 1149 includes several of the group's key sessions, but at this distance the principal ingredient is the singing of Jackie Cain and Roy Kral. Buddy Stewart's bopping tones are heard on the first session (including a nice 'Baby, Baby All the Time'), but it's the harmonizing of Jackie and Roy which really gives these sessions their flavour, bop lines as pop tones. As such, they've retained a lot of period charm and with Ventura's own brief solos making their mark (listen to the way he bubbles up out of 'F.Y.I.') the music holds up very well. Ventura signed to Victor in 1949, and his first session yielded Cain's classic reading of 'Lullaby In Rhythm', with 'For Boppers Only' to follow.

Much of Classics 1215 is taken up with Ventura's set from a 1949 Gene Norman concert, and you can believe that the cats were swinging. One might argue that this is bop with all the passion and, perhaps, blackness steamed out of it but the sheer high spirits of the gig are still infectious, and besides Ventura, Cain and Kral there is sterling stuff from Conte Candoli and Benny Green. The set is rounded out with two further studio dates for Victor: tongue-twisting fun on 'Boptura' and 'Ha!', and a very early appearance from Dave McKenna at the piano. Ventura's music in his period has sometimes been called vulgar, but it's hardly any such thing. In comparison, Classics 1309 is almost tame, with the first 14 titles (all for Victor) smoothing the way from bebop to dance orchestra. Six quintet titles for Clef (with Conte Candoli) follow, which are so-so, but the quartet date which ends the disc has Charlie blowing smooch tenor while backing singers coo along behind him.

The *Three Deuces* sets are airshots in very average sound (and the provenance of some of them is suspect, since at least one track actually comes from a Carnegie Hall concert!). But the music is fascinating: rare glimpses of the superb Bill Harris at some length, and very strange piano from Ralph Burns, who comes on as a mixture of Monk and Garner. The final track on disc two is from five years later and is a long jam on 'Broadway'.

***** High On An Open Mike**

Fresh Sound FSR-CD 314 *Ventura; Dave Hildinger, Dave McKenna (p); Billy Bean (g); Richard Davis (b); Mousie Alexander (d).* 57.

The thrill isn't exactly gone, but Ventura's day was over as far as jazz prominence was concerned by the time of these 1957 sessions. If his own playing is more capable than pleasing at this point, there are moments for McKenna, Bean and even Davis that are worth hearing.

Joe Venuti (1903–78)

VIOLIN, PIANO

Born in Philadelphia (he once claimed it was on board a ship bound for the USA), he befriended Eddie Lang as a boy and they worked together on the New York dance-band and small-group jazz recording scene until Lang's death. Formed his own band in the '30s, then returned from war service to feature regularly on radio. Out of favour in the '60s but made a great comeback in 1967–68, and then he made regular appearances and records until his death. A legendary practical joker and a pioneer of jazz violin.

***** Four String Joe**

Jazz Archives 160132 *Venuti; Ray Lodwig, Fuzzy Farrar, Tommy Gott, Leo McConville, Charlie Teagarden (t); Jack Teagarden, Miff Mole, Spiegel Wilcox, Bill Rank (tb); Danny Polo(cl, bs); Benny Goodman (cl); Doc Ryker (as); Max Farley (cl, as); Alfie Evans (cl, as, bs); Arnold Brilhart (cl, as, f); Harold Sturr (cl, ts); Frankie Trumbauer (Cmel, bsn); Bud Freeman, Pat Davis (ts); Don Murray (bs, cl); Adrian Rollini (bsx, gfs, hfp, p, cel); Rube Bloom (p, v); Itzy Riskin, Frank Signorelli, Joe Sullivan, Phil Wall, Lennie Hayton, Irving Brodksy (p); Charlotte Laughton, Charlotte Tinsley (hp); Eddie Lang, Vincent Terri, Dick McDonough (g); Howdy Quicksell, Tony Colucci (bj); Arthur Campbell (tba); Steve Brown, Ward Lay, Larry Breen (b); Chauncey Morehouse, Vic Berton, Neil Marshall, Louis Singer (d); Annette Hanshaw (v).* 9/26–10/46.

***** Joe Venuti 1926–1928**

Classics 1211 *Venuti; Manny Klein, Fuzzy Farrar, Leo McConville (t); Charlie Butterfield (tb); Arnold Brilhart, Max Farley, Jimmy Dorsey (cl, as); Fud Livingston (cl, ts); Herb Spencer(ts); Don Murray (cl, bs); Adrian Rollini (bsx, gfs, hfp); Rube Bloom (p, v); Arthur Schutt, Frank Signorelli (p); Eddie Lang (g); Tony Colucci (bj); Hank Stern, Joe Tarto (b); Paul Graselli, Justin Ring, Chauncey Morehouse (d); Scrappy Lambert, Billy Hillpot (v).* 9/26–7/28.

***** Joe Venuti 1928–1930**

Classics 1246 *As above, except add Andy Secrest, Charlie Margulis, Harry Goldfield, Ray Lodwig (t), Bill Rank, Glenn Miller, Jack Teagarden, Tommy Dorsey (tb), Izzy Friedman (cl, ts), Charles Strickfaden (as, bs), Rube Crozier (ts, ob), Lennie Hayton (p), Stan King (d), Smith Ballew, Irene Beasley, Frank Luther (v); omit Murray, Colucci, Stern, Ring, Lambert, Hillpot.* 9/28-9/30.

****** Joe Venuti 1930–1933**

Classics 1276 *Venuti; Charlie Teagarden, Manny Klein, Ray Lodwig (t); Jack Teagarden (tb, v); Tommy Dorsey (tb); Pete Pumiglio (cl, bs); Jimmy Dorsey (cl, as, bs, t); Arnold Brilhart (as); Bud Freeman (ts); Adrian Rollini (bsx, gfs, p, vib); Frank*

Signorelli, Lennie Hayton, Irving Brodsky, Phil Wall (p); Eddie Lang, Dick McDonough (g); Joe Tarto, Ward Lay (b); Paul Graselli, Neil Marshall (d); Harold Arlen, Hoagy Carmichael, Smith Ballew (v). 10/30-5/33.

Venuti wasn't the only violinist to play jazz in the '20s, but he established the style for the instrument as surely as Coleman Hawkins did for the saxophone. He was a key figure on the New York session scene of the era and appears on many dance-band records alongside Beiderbecke, Trumbauer and the Dorseys; but his most important association was with Eddie Lang, and although their partnership was curtailed by Lang's death in 1933, it was a pairing which has endured like few other jazz double-acts.

Four String Joe is quite an interesting cross-section of material: besides a few good Blue Four and duo titles, there's Jean Goldkette's tremendous 'My Pretty Girl', all four titles from the all-star session of 1931 with Teagarden and Goodman, and a curious finale in a 1946 chamber version of 'Tea For Two'. Transfers are unfortunately not very good and certainly erratic.

Classics have begun a Venuti survey. These are mostly duo and Blue Four titles to start with, though there are six rather dreary titles by the Venuti New Yorkers, where the large dance-band play very stiff and ordinary charts. Again, the transfers don't have much sparkle.

Classics 1246 follows a similar patttern, although there are some super tracks: Rube Bloom taking the most extraordinary vocals on 'The Blue Room' and 'Sensation', Frankie Trumbauer playing bassoon on 'Runnin' Ragged', and Jack Teagarden's sensational solo on the otherwise half-dead 'Dancing With Tears In My Eyes'. Classics 1276 follows on with sessions for Victor, OKeh, Columbia and Vocalion. Besides the strange feat of having two of the greatest American songwriters as featured vocalists, there's a greater emphasis on small groups here, and there are at least two classic dates: the magnificent tracks by the Lang-Venuti All Stars from October 1931, and the February 1933 session where Jimmy Dorsey played trumpet – and where Lang and Venuti played together for the last time.

***(*) Joe Venuti And Zoot Sims

Chiaroscuro CRD 142 *Venuti; Spiegel Wilcox (tb); Zoot Sims (ts); Dick Hyman, John Bunch (p); Bucky Pizzarelli (g); Milt Hinton (b); Cliff Leeman, Bobby Rosengarden (d).* 5/74–5/75.

**** Alone At The Palace

Chiaroscuro CRD 160 *Venuti; Dave McKenna (p).* 4/77.

Venuti's Indian summer in the studios is currently represented by only a few records. He remained in such good form to the end of his playing life that all his final records are worth hearing at least. Perhaps the partnership with Zoot Sims has been a shade overrated, since Sims's bluff swing is no different from anything he plays on his own records and occasionally sounds a little glib, whereas Venuti's own playing – coloured by unexpected bursts of pizzicato, oddball kinds of bowing and resinous streams of melody that seem to go on for ever – is of a different order. *Sliding By* (now deleted) continued a profitable association with Dick Hyman, but it's *Alone At The Palace* which is Venuti's valedictory masterpiece. McKenna's granitic swing and authority are just the kind of bedrock the violinist loved, and whether they play 'At The Jazz Band Ball' or 'Runnin' Ragged' (almost exactly 50 years after Venuti's original version) or a slush-free 'Send In The Clowns', it's all superbly achieved. The CD reissue of the original LP includes four new tracks and three alternative takes, all equally welcome, and the sound is admirably clear.

Edward Vesala (1945–99)

DRUMS, PERCUSSION, OTHER INSTRUMENTS

Grew up in a remote part of Finland, taking up drums at 20. Played rock and studied music before travelling through Asia and returning to the local Finnish jazz scene. Toured with Tomasz Stańko, 1975–80, then with his own Sound And Fury Ensemble. His death at the end of the century was a severe loss to European music.

CORE COLLECTION

♛ **** Lumi

ECM 831517-2 *Vesala; Esko Heikkinen (t, picc t); Tom Bildo (tb, tba); Pentti Lahti (as, bs, f); Jorma Tapio (as, cl, bcl, f); Tapani Rinne (ts, ss, cl, bcl); Kari Heinilä (ts, ss, f); Raoul Björkenheim (g); Taito Vainio (acc); Iro Haarla (hp); Häkä (b).* 6/86.

Vesala produced one unqualified masterpiece, *Lumi*. Even its cover, of a shrouded, Golem-like figure on an empty road under a threatening sky, suggests something of Vesala's distinctive combination of almost Gothic intensity and sheer playfulness. A re-recording of 'The Wind' shows how much he has advanced since 1974. It is spare, subtly voiced, less dependent on literal reference than its predecessor, but not a whit less evocative. 'Frozen Melody' is a superb exercise in static harmony; Vesala works variations on a descending repetition of four notes of the same pitch, gradually unpicking the rhythmic implications.

***(*) Nan Madol

ECM 829376-2 *Vesala; Kaj Backlund (t); Mircea Stan (tb); Charlie Mariano (as, f, nagaswaram); Juhani Aaltonen (ts, ss, f); Pentti Lahti (ss, bcl); Seppo Paakkunainen (ss, f); Sakari Kukko (f); Elisabeth Leistola (hp); Juhani Poutanen (vn, alto vn); Teppo Hauta-aho (b).* 4/74.

***(*) Rodina

Love Records LRCD 189 *Vesala; Tomasz Stańko (t); Mircea San (t, tb); Juhani Aaltonen (ss, as, ts, picc, f, af); Pekka Poyr (ss, as, f, cl); Tomasz Szukalski (ss, ts); Pentti Lahti (bs, bcl); Pekka Rechardt (g); Esa Helasvuo (p); Pekka Sarmanto (b); Irina Milan (v); strings, choir.* 5/76.

Edward Vesala bore an uncanny physical resemblance to Richard Brautigan and wove narratives and textures which, like the late American novelist's, are magically suffused, wry and tender by turns. Vesala was one of the few percussionists capable of sustaining interest as a solo performer; an early '80s recording of extracts from the Finnish epic *Kalevala* rivets the attention despite the minimalist accompaniment and the fact that no English translation is provided. Despite this, Vesala has been sparing of solo tracks on his records – the brief 'Call From The Sea' on *Nan Madol* is an exception – preferring to elevate his light, pulse-driven but often non-metrical drumming until it occupies the forefront of a piece. Recording later with ECM greatly enhanced his capacity in this regard. Vesala's groups have a unique sound compounded of folk and popular references with a grasp of orchestration that, for all his commitment to themes and solos, is more typical of through-composed concert music. He favours extremes of timbre, alternating very dark themes that exploit sombre modes and tonalities with light, airy arrangements of flutes, soprano saxophones and harp. Typically, though, he reverses the expressive polarity, investing light-toned pieces like 'The Wind' (on *Nan Madol*, re-recorded later) with a sinister quality, often reserving darker instrumentation for tongue-in-cheek compositions based on popular forms.

Rodina has recently been issued on the Finnish Love Records label and is a welcome reminder of the percussionist's larger ambitions of the time and his early embrace of a bold 'world-music' strategy which incorporated Turkish, African and Oriental elements. Broad, string-based compositions at slow, sweeping tempos, sit alongside relatively free improvisations (the duet 'Dady and Komba' with Stańko is a CD bonus) and powerful recitations. Vocalist Irina Milan is something of an acquired taste, and the opening track 'Lapsellein' is rather too close to soft art-rock to appeal to every listener or to many jazz purists; but it is entirely of a piece with Vesala's aesthetic. The disc has many high points, but the high, fanfare-like trumpet calls of 'Satujen Satu' have a heart-breaking majesty and beauty, underpinned by almost Aboriginal drones. Soloists of the calibre of Stańko, fellow-Pole Szukalski, Stan, and Aaltonen guarantee a high level of musical interest. A most welcome reissue with three bonus cuts (mostly rough versions of existing tracks) which offer an intriguing insight into Vesala's working methods.

****** Ode To The Death Of Jazz**

ECM 843196-2 *Vesala; Matti Riikonen (t); Jorma Tapio (as, bcl, f); Jouni Kannisto (ts, f); Pepa Päivinen (ts, ss, bs, f, cl, bcl); Tim Ferchen (mar, bells); Taito Vainio (acc); Iro Haarla (p, hp, ky); Jimi Sumen (g); Uffe Krokfors (b).* 4–5/89.

****** Invisible Storm**

ECM 511928-2 *Vesala; Matti Riikonen (t); Jorma Tapio (as, bcl, f, bf, perc); Jouni Kannisto (ts, f); Pepa Päivinen (ts, ss, bs, f, af); Jimi Sumen (g); Pekka Sarmanto (b); Marko Ylönen (clo); Mark Nauseef (perc).* 5–6/91.

***** Nordic Gallery**

ECM 523294-2 *Vesala; Matti Riikonen (t); Tapani Rinne (cl); Jorma Tapio (as, bcl, acl, bf); Jouni Kannisto (ts, f); Pepa Päivinen (ts, ss, bs, bsx, f, af, picc); Iro Haarla (hp, p, ky, acc, koto); Petri Ikkela (acc); Jimi Sumen (g); Pekka Sarmanto (b); Kari Linsted (clo).* 93–94.

Vesala worked slowly and never recorded prolifically, although a lack of resources to prepare and create his music also took its toll. Each of his records was a superb balance of careful organization and arrangment and all-out freedom.

'A Glimmer Of Sepal', on *Ode To The Death Of Jazz*, is based on tango rhythms and illustrates Vesala's interest in extreme stylistic repetitions. This is evident in 'Winds Of Sahara', which begins in spooky 'ethnic' mode, wobbles a bit, and then breaks into a camel-racing flag-waver of Maynard Ferguson proportions. 'Calypso Bulbosa' evokes similar incongruities. The opening four tracks of *Invisible Storm* contain the most powerfully dramatic music Vesala committed to record. It opens with an extraordinary recitation, 'Sheets And Shrouds', a cracked voice in an unfamiliar tongue (Finnish has a quality that is both ancient and curiously Asian) before giving way to 'Murmuring Morning', a slow chorale highlit by Ylönen's cello, and then exploding in the thudding fury of 'Gordion's Flashes'. The fourth piece – and each is successively longer – also features a spoken vocal; 'Shadows on the Frontier' is in English but preserves the tranced quality of the opening. Though there is no explicit reason to connect them, they do seem to cohere in a way that later tracks do not. Of these, 'Somnamblues' is another of Vesala's brilliant generic parodies, and the closing 'Caccaroo Boohoo' is drily witty. The longest single item, 'The Wedding Of All Essential Parts', and the title-track are less impressive, but only relative to Vesala's now absurdly high standard. His melodic inventiveness grows apace, concentrating on sinuously extended figures that evade conventional rhythmic resolution but underneath which there beats a powerful, even dramatic, pulse. *Lumi* (above) remains the record of choice, but it's hard to put *Invisible Storm* lower than essential in terms of contemporary recording. Needless to say, the studio work and mastering are impeccable.

The final disc of the group was the only real disappointment. Newcomers may well still be entranced by the sheer unexpectedness of Vesala's sound-world in this series of still landscapes and wry portraits, but anyone who has followed his course over a few discs will surely find *Nordic Gallery* formulaic and repetitive, a reworking of elements rather than anything new. Vesala's passing was a blow to the music, and the restoration of several, at present vinyl-only, albums would be some consolation.

Vienna Art Orchestra

ENSEMBLE

The brainchild of composer and arranger Matthias Ruegg, and founded in 1977, the VAO attempt to forge a synthesis between jazz and 20th-century compositional language, between the avant-garde and popular music. Not a conventional big band in section terms, the ensemble favour an open, improvisational sound rather than massed instruments. Five years into the VAO's history, Ruegg also formed the Vienna Art Choir.

****** The Minimalism Of Erik Satie**

hatOLOGY 560 *Bumi Fian, Hannes Kottek (t, flhn); Christian Radovan (tb); Harry Sokal (ss, ts, f); Wolfgang Puschnig (bcl, as, sno, f); Roman Schwaller (ts, cl); Woody Schabata (vib); Johj Sass (tba); Wolfgang Reisinger (perc); Lauren Newton (v); Matthias Ruegg (cond).* 9/83–3/84.

A classic of its era – though in some ways its impact has been dispersed by subsequent work by others, it remains a benchmark recording and a welcome reissue. Most of the tracks briefly articulate a Satie theme before proceeding to work variations on it. The orchestral voicings are bright and spare, with most of the space devoted to solo material. The most remarkable sections are devoted to essays on Vexations, which are by a 'minimalist' VAO – only Lauren Newton, in a Berberian-derived vocalise, Roman Schwaller's tenor sax and Wolfgang Puschnig on bass clarinet, each duetting with vibesman Woody Schabata, who maintains a steady chordal pulse below. The closing passage with Puschnig, easily his finest hour on record, is extraordinary.

***** All That Strauss**

TCB 20052 *Thorsten Benkenstein, Matthieu Michel, Rudi Pitz, Bumi Fian (t); Robert Bachner, Christian Radovan (tb); Charly Wagner (btb); Arkady Shilkloper (frhn); Michel Portal, Wolfgang Puschnig, Klaus Dickbauer, Florian Brambock,*

Harry Sokal, Andy Scherrer, Heinrich von Kalnein, Herwig Gradischnig (reeds); Bertly Mayer (hmca); Alegere Correa (g); George Breinschmid (b); Mario Gonzi (d); Ingrid Oberkanins (perc); Anna Lauvergnac (v); Matthias Ruegg (cond). 1/00.

***** Artistry In Rhythm**

TCB 01102 *As above, except add Jurain Bartos, Thomas Gansch (t), Tom Varner (frhn), Adrian Mears, Christian Muthspiel (tb), Ed Partyka (tba), Franck Tortiller (vib), Wolfgang Muthspiel (g), Robert Riegler (b), Jojo Meyer (d); Patrice Heral (perc); omit Pitz, Wagner, Portal, Puschnig, von Kalnein, Mayer, Correa, Breinschmid, Gonzi, Oberkanins, Lauvergnac.* n.d.

***** Duke Ellington's Sound Of Love**

TCB 99802 *Thorsten Benkenstein, Bumi Fian, Thomas Gansch, Matthieu Michel (t); Robert Bachner, Christian Muthspiel (tb); Charly Wagner (btb); Arkady Shilkloper (frhn); Florian Brambock, Klaus Dickbauer, Andy Scherrer, Harry Sokal (reeds); Wolfgang Muthspiel (g); George Breinschmid (b); Mario Gonzi (d); Anna Lauvergnac (v).* 99.

***** A Centenary Journey**

Quinton 0104 *As above, except omit Wagner, Wolfgang Muthspiel; add Ed Partyka (tb); Herwig Gradischnig (reeds); Martin Koller (g); Robert Riegler (b); Thomas Lang (d).* 11/00.

***** Art & Fun 25**

Emarcy 017 072-2 2CD *As various discs above.* 77–02.

The better part of 20 years of VAO work is currently in the deletions file, which does give this entry a foreshortened feel at present. Ruegg carries on, though, with many of the long-standing members of the team still in tow. The TCB albums aren't especially pitched as major VAO works. The Strauss set has its moments (guest stars include Portal and the returning Puschnig) and is thrown out as a counterpart to the traditional New Year's Day concert in Vienna. But Strauss doesn't yield so easily to Ruegg's irreverent ministrations, and some of this is either too much or too little. *Artistry In Rhythm* is a whistlestop European tour – in fact, it doesn't stop at all until the end, since all the pieces run together. The titles suggest a jokiness ('Madrid Madness', 'London Rushes In The Tube'), but humour isn't Ruegg's strong point and a lot of this sits rather mildly in a continuum of jazz orchestration.

Having said that, there's a refreshing verve and sardonic grimace to the album of Ellington covers. As the title implies, this is Duke through a very specific filter, though the Charles Mingus composition which gives the album its title isn't actually included in the set. The highlights are brash, unapologetic readings of such revered classics as 'Blood Count', usually played slower in memory of composer Billy Strayhorn, 'Come Sunday', 'Warm Valley' and 'Mood Indigo', though you know you're not in the presence of another run-of-the-mill Ellington set when the VAO kick off with 'Red Garter' and then run the 'A' train off the rails with a wildly out of control interpretation driven by Dickbauer's bass clarinet and Breinschmid's roiling bass. We feared last time that Matthias Ruegg might be running out of creative steam. Listening to the horns gathering for a final rough wooing of 'Sophisticated Lady' you suspect he's found a second wind. There's a suspicion, however, that creating a remix album out of the VAO's back catalogue might be an admission of creative block, or else a symptom of superficial trendiness. *Art & Fun* justifies its title, though. Ruegg has re-arranged many of the Orchestra's past successes and morphed them into a brand new musical reality. There's also a genuine remix disc masterminded by Martin Koller.

The 'centenary journey' isn't (yet) the band's 100th birthday, but that of the music they play and in this set, with its competing/complementing rhythm sections – acoustic and electric – the VAO attempt nothing less than a surreally potted history of jazz all the way from Jelly Roll Morton to the rock and hip-hop flavoured crossovers of recent years. It's a less successful experiment than, say, *The Minimalism Of Erik Satie* – not because the charts are less effective and the soloists less compelling, but really because the element of surprise has gone. This should be and often is a plus. When in the middle of 'Roll On Jelly' and 'Steam Stomp' the register seems to switch radically, seasoned listeners will no longer feel disorientated. Newcomers should ideally start earlier in the Orchestra's history, but this isn't a bad introduction if you come across it first.

Steen Vig (1946–94)

TENOR AND SOPRANO SAXOPHONES

The exuberant Swede covered many musical styles from Dixieland to modern but died unseasonably early.

***** Blue Boat**

Storyville 4192 *Vig; Mighty Flea Conners, Ole Fessor Lindgreen (tb, v); Cornell Dupree (g); Hugo Rasmussen (b); Thorkild Moller (d).* 4/93.

He didn't live long enough to establish a reputation outside Scandinavia, but this set conveys something of the warmth, sense of fun and sheer musicality of Steen Vig. He opens with the Bechet rarity of the title and continues with a programme of classic, traditional and repertory pieces that gives a fine band lots to do. Dupree is a key component of the sound, but it is Vig's bossy tenor and Bechet-inspired soprano which dominate proceedings, when he can get a word in edgeways round the trombones. Nothing profound or provocative; just entertaining music. Nine months later, on the first day of 1994, Vig passed away.

Frank Vignola (born 1965)

GUITAR, BANJO

Frank is a smoothly accomplished guitar-player. There is only a slight and subtle rock influence on his playing style, which is immediately identifiable while hard to define, drawing on the fusion guitarists of an earlier generation, notably Al DiMeola, while retaining its individuality.

*****(*) Off Broadway**

Nagel-Heyer 2006 *Vignola; Randy Sandke (t); Frank Wess (ts, f); Roland Hanna (p); John Goldsby (b); Joe Ascione (d).* 12/99.

Vignola's smooth and unstressed sound disguises a wealth of subtlety that emerges only over time. His Concord records are currently unavailable but here Frank reconvenes his set-up at Nagel-Heyer, Europe's new centre of mainstream, and if you started at track two, a perfectly respectful treatment of 'Stars Fell On Alabama', you might think that this is entirely in the label's most familiar midstream pocket. Actually, it's a surprising, even unguessable set as it goes from track to track. Six of the 15 tracks are originals by Ascione, with the blazing 'The Return' and the staccato funk of 'Sing That' only two of the several startling episodes. Sandke and Wess are carefully positioned at various points: Wess has to execute a popping flute line on the title-piece, and they're asked to play a smart, fat-free treatment of Horace Silver's 'Cookin' At the Continental'. Vignola himself shows off a lot of chops – on both electric and a twangy acoustic – without actually crossing the border into merely showing off. Brushing up against the 80-minute barrier, it's probably too much on one disc – but high marks to the leader for a lot of pungent music-making.

*****(*) Blues For A Gypsy**
Acoustic Disc 43 *Vignola (g solo).* 6/01.

The gypsy in question might be Django Reinhardt, except that this lovely set of acoustic blues and jazz is so unpretentiously universalized that Vignola's title-tune could stand as a quiet anthem for all outsiders and displaced peoples. It's a lovely thing, and a gentle surprise after the scurry of the opening 'Donna Lee'. There's a nice mix of familiar material – 'Laura', 'Limehouse Blues', 'Misty', Django's 'Manoir De Mes Rêves' – with originals like 'Fishing With Django' and 'Train Ride' (the last of which has a threatening pulse that suggests it refers to the last train ride many of Reinhardt's people ever took). Frank plays supremely well and this makes up for the disappearance of his Concord records.

Mads Vinding (born 1948)

BASS

Vinding was performing at Copenhagen's Café Montmartre while still a teenager. Has probably played with every jazz visitor to Denmark and has long been in the thick of his local scene.

*****(*) The Kingdom (Where Nobody Dies)**
Stunt STUCD 19703 *Vinding; Enrico Pieranunzi (p); Alex Riel (d).* 3/97.

*****(*) Daddio Don**
Stunt STUCD 19813 *As above, except Roger Kellaway (p) replaces Pieranunzi.* 3/98.

***** Six Hands Three Minds One Heart**
Stunt STUCD 00052 *As above, except Carsten Dahl (p) replaces Kellaway.* 6/99.

They're his gigs, but the admittedly slight overplaying of the bassist's role in these sessions stops them short of reaching the highest level – a piano trio does tend to depend on the pianist taking the leading steps. Still, there's lots to listen to. The contrast between the first two discs is particularly interesting: Pieranunzi's aristocratic-romantic touch is inimitable, but Riel and Vinding don't let him wander off down too many introspective byways, and the surprisingly tough and individual treatment of 'My Foolish Heart', for one, begs for the repeat button. Kellaway is entirely different – extravagant, mercurial in his thinking, and humorously elaborate on standards such as 'How Deep Is The Ocean'. But there's rarely been a more deeply thought-out version of 'Blue In Green' as the one which starts the session, and 'Daddio Don' and 'Seven' are typical Kellaway originals, making light work of their unorthodox feel. Two absorbing sets.

Dahl is an impressive younger talent, though inevitably he finds it hard to displace the memory of what his predecessors at the keyboard managed. This feels like a more self-consciously 'modern' date, Dahl extracting ideas which tend to encrypt the likes of 'I Hear A Rhapsody' and 'All Blues' rather than opening them out. Since it was recorded live (at Copenhagen Jazzhouse), showmanship plays a part too. Worthwhile, but start with the other two.

Biggi Vinkeloe

ALTO SAXOPHONE, FLUTE

Born in Germany, raised in France, and now seemingly based in Sweden, Vinkeloe is a free-bop saxophonist.

***** Mbat**
LJ 5209 *Vinkeloe; Barre Phillips (b); Peeter Uuskyla (d).* 4/93.

***** One Way Out**
Slask 8433 *As above.* 7/97.

*****(*) Slowdrags And Interludes**
LJ LJCD5219 *As above, except Peter Kowald (b) replaces Phillips.* 1/99.

Vinkeloe's sparse delivery and pierced tone recall Jimmy Lyons, and her compositions are more like dissembled bits of melody than anything else ('Fragments' is one of them). So Phillips, who plays free but never surrenders a melodic line, is a good partner for her on *Mbat.* When they find their way to counterpoint on the title-track, the music feels like it's reached its reward. Some of the eight pieces wind on rather aimlessly, but it's pleasing music in its benign, muted way. *One Way Out* is a more pointed and more confident continuation, peaking on the long title-piece.

Carved up into 19 sections, the music on *Slowdrags And Interludes* has a more ritualistic feel to it, with 12 brief 'Interludes' interspersing the handful of longer pieces. They sound like improvisations with a splash of preordained structure (and, since there are individual composer-credits, that may be the case), and with Uuskyla's rhythms – more often tattoos or cymbal-crashes in stark, open space – as simple and open as the leader's melodies, it's left to the incomparable Kowald to provide the textural density, which he does, superbly. Kowald may not be the humorist that Phillips is, but he has far more in the way of technique and ideas. Concentrated, without sounding dense, the record rewards patient study.

***** Maghzen**
Slask SLACD 023 *Vinkeloe; Barre Phillips (b).* 8/00.

***** Desert Sweets**
Balance Point Acoustics BPA 004 *Vinkeloe; Mark Warner (tba, tb); Damon Smith (b).* 4/01.

Recorded in the attractive acoustic of the Chapelle Ste-Philomène, *Maghzen* picks up the dialogue between Vinkeloe and Phillips. Some of the best music comes in the four brief 'Kumo' pieces where Vinkeloe uses the flute, getting an acid-drop lyricism which Phillips counterpoints by bouncing the bow off the strings. The alto–bass exchanges find a kind of bruised melancholy that takes the ear, although Vinkeloe's disjunctive way with ideas does rather undermine the thematic hold of the longer tracks. Sampled a few minutes at a time this is very worthwhile.

The trio setting, though, suits Vinkeloe best – as it does so many improvisers. *Desert Sweets* has even more tracks than *Slowdrags And Interludes*, all 22 of them. The sleeve-notes make great play of the fact that Vinkeloe works to a slightly different-to-standard tuning and has the rest of the band follow her (matters which haven't impeded either Jackie McLean or Lee Konitz), but most listeners will simply enjoy the curious combination of alto/flute, trombone/tuba and bass spelling out a sequence of often startling episodes. This time, though, there are intimations of further development which are simply shut down by the deliberate brevity of many of the tracks.

Leroy Vinnegar (1928–99)

DOUBLE BASS

Moved to California in the '50s and became one of the most in-demand session-men in Los Angeles studios, playing on a vast number of jazz and pop sessions alike.

*****(*) Leroy Walks!**
Original Jazz Classics OJJCD 160 *Vinnegar; Gerald Wilson (t); Teddy Edwards (ts); Victor Feldman (vib); Carl Perkins (p); Tony Bazley (d).* 6–9/57.

***** Leroy Walks Again!**
Original Jazz Classics OJCCD 454 *Vinnegar; Teddy Edwards (ts); Mike Melvoin (p); Victor Feldman (p, vib); Roy Ayers (vib); Ron Jefferson, Milton Turner (d).* 8/62.

***** Jazz's Great 'Walker'**
Vee Jay VJ 022 *Vinnegar; Mike Melvoin (p); Bill Goodwin (d).* 64.

****(*) Walkin' The Basses**
Contemporary 14068 *Vinnegar; Geoff Lee (p); Mel Brown (g); Curtis Craft (d).* 92.

***** Integrity: The Walker Live At Lairmont**
Jazz Focus JFCD009 *Vinnegar; Gary Harris (ss, ts); Dan Faehnle (g); Mel Brown (d).* 5/95.

Given the unimaginative range of titles, it seems almost redundant to say that Vinnegar was one of the great exponents of walking bass, his talent an ability to invest a solid four beats to the bar with a seeming infinity of harmonic and rhythmic variations. Indianapolis-born, he moved to Los Angeles 45 years ago and established himself as first-call bass-player for jazz and even the occasional rock gig; he even once did sessions for the bass-less Doors.

The Vee Jay album opens with a textbook demonstration of Vinnegar's double-stopping, playing two notes simultaneously. Merely doing this is impressive enough; investing it with a degree of musicality is something else entirely. Because he rarely solos, here or on the OJCs, much of the interest rests on what his band members are doing, but CD has been generous to him, pushing the bass up in the mix.

The earliest of the albums is probably still the most appealing. Gerald Wilson went on to find his forte in bandleading and large-scale arrangement, but, compared to the bland cut-outs which pass for solos from Hill on the 1962 session, his solos are well crafted and full of ideas and Edwards is as urbane and funky – if you can be both urbane and funky – as ever.

Vinnegar returned to recording as leader in 1992 with *Walkin' The Basses*. There had been stories of ill-health, perhaps even of retirement, but the Lairmont set, recorded in Bellingham, Washington, sees those lines pumping out with the regularity of a Stairmaster. It's basically a bebop set, with Bird's 'Segment', Hampton Hawes's 'Me Ho' and a cracking version of Freddie Hubbard's 'Little Sunflower'. Persuasive testimony to one of the unsung giants of the music.

Eddie 'Cleanhead' Vinson (1917–88)

ALTO SAXOPHONE, VOCALS

Played in swing bands in the '30s and '40s, but later best known as an R&B-directed alto-man and singer, although he wrote several bop staples such as 'Tune Up'. A memorable live face at festivals in the '70s and '80s.

***** Cleanhead And Cannonball**
Milestone 9324 *Vinson; Nat Adderley (c); Cannonball Adderley (as); Joe Zawinul (p); Sam Jones (vb); Louis Hayes (d).* 9/61–2/62.

***** Jumpin' The Blues**
Black & Blue 959.2 *Vinson; Jay McShann (p, v); Gene Ramey (b); Paul Gunther (d).* 3/69.

***** I Want A Little Girl**
Original Jazz Classics OJC 868 *Vinson; Martin Banks (t); Rashied Jamal Ali (ts); Cal Green (g); Art Hillery (p, org); John Heard (b); Roy McCurdy (d).* 2/81.

A hugely entertaining singer and saxophonist, Vinson became a festival favourite in the '70s, guesting with anyone who thought they could take his pace, and playing Parker-tinged R&B with disconcerting self-possession. Some claim to find a Louis Jordan influence in Vinson's work, but this may have more to do with his performing personality than with any stylistic borrowing. The catalogue's a bit thin on Cleanhead at the moment (if not quite bald). He was going through a rough patch when he made the album with the Adderleys, and sounds as if he was more than pleased to have been asked. It's probably no more than typical fare for both men, but the quintet accomodate Cleanhead amicably and it's an entertaining session. The Montreux Festival set on *Jumpin' The Blues* includes a terrific 'Now's The Time' and some smoothly Parkerish solos on themes of his own and Ellington's 'C Jam Blues'. The Paris set with McShann is more about the pianist than Vinson, who doesn't even come on until nearly halfway, then delivers 'Mr Cleanhead Blues', which was inevitable even in 1969.

The OJC features Vinson the festival personality with slightly heavy-fisted bands. *I Want A Little Girl* runs through a bag of blues numbers and contains a surprising 'Straight, No Chaser' and an excellent version of Pettiford's 'Blues In The Closet'.

Miroslav Vitous (born 1947)

DOUBLE BASS, GUITAR, SYNTHESIZERS

Vitous studied classical music in his native Prague before going to America to study at Berklee. He worked with a variety of leaders, including Art Farmer and Miles Davis, before joining Weather Report as founding bassist. A professor and sometime head of jazz at the New England Conservatory, Vitous has maintained a quiet career, recording somewhat sporadically in later years.

***(*) Infinite Search

Collectables 6176 *Vitous; Joe Henderson (ts); Herbie Hancock (p, ky); John McLaughlin (g); Joe Chambers, Jack DeJohnette (d).* 10/69.

*(*) Magical Shepherd

Wounded Bird 2925 *Vitous; Herbie Hancock (p, ky); Jack DeJohnette, James Gadson (d); Airto Moreira (perc); Cheryl Grainger, Onike (v).* 76.

**(*) Guardian Angels

Evidence 22055 *Vitous; Mabumi Yamaguchi (ss); Kenny Kirkland (p, syn, ky, g); John Scofield (g); George Ohtsuke (d).* 11/78.

After leaving Weather Report in 1973, having recorded three classic albums (he appears only briefly on *Mysterious Traveller*, the group's fourth release), Vitous experimented with various 'lead' and 'piccolo' basses, but he doesn't seem to have acquired the confidence in their use that made Stanley Clarke and a later Weather Report member, Jaco Pastorius, such charismatic figures (compare Vitous's and Pastorius's work with guitarist Bireli Lagrene, and that becomes clear).

It took Vitous some time to re-establish the musical identity stamped all over his marvellous pre-Weather Report solo debut, *Infinite Search*, long deleted but now available again as a Collectables reissue. The line-up is a usual suspects of jazz fusion, and the sound, produced by Herbie Mann, draws heavily on the energy of Miles's *Bitches Brew* and Herbie Hancock's own early crossover experiments. For some reason, the reissue rejigs the track listing, putting Eddie Harris's 'Freedom Jazz Dance' first. It's certainly the most familiar and accessible item on the set, but not necessarily the most characteristic, since most of the rest is an experiment in atmospheres rather than a blowing session. The tiny 'Mountain In The Clouds' lent its name to an Atlantic reissue; beware discographies which imply these are different albums. Vitous is at his best on another long track, 'I Will Tell Him On You', where his bass-playing delivers the kind of impact that persuaded Joe Zawinul and Wayne Shorter he was the man to anchor Weather Report.

Magical Shepherd was a blatant but ill-advised bid for crossover success. The freaked-out guitar lines – Miroslav is pictured on the front in goatskins clutching a double-neck, while gazing out at the star-clouds – generate much more heat than light and the funk of tracks like 'New York City' clearly don't suit his temperament. We'll pass over the singing in silence. These were strange times. Let that cover be your guide.

There's a different kind of awkwardness to the fusion idiom of *Guardian Angels*, which alternates rather ineffectually between jazz rock and softer, more impressionistic pieces. There are some delightful and unexpected sonorities, not least from the use of baritone guitar, but it's a patchy project, only of interest as a pointer to later work.

***(*) First Meeting

ECM 519280-2 *Vitous; John Surman (ss, bcl); Kenny Kirkland (p); Jon Christensen (d).* 5/79.

**** Journey's End

ECM 843171-2 *As above, except add (bs) to Surman; omit Kirkland; add John Taylor (p).* 7/82.

***(*) Emergence

ECM 827855-2 *Vitous (solo).* 9/85.

The first of the ECMs is a return to the thoughtful music-making of *Infinite Search* (which was reissued as *Mountain In The Clouds*). Once again Vitous attempts to reintegrate the classical and folk-impressionistic elements on the earlier record into a much more coherent performance. Kirkland sets aside his electronic keyboards and turns in a performance of rippling grace. No problems with the recording-quality on *Journey's End* – the sound is rich and warm. That's also true of *First Meeting*, except that Kirkland's approach doesn't seem altogether appropriate for tunes like 'Silver Lake' and 'Beautiful Place To', too obviously jazz-based and funky and lacking Taylor's floating lyricism. Surman still wasn't playing any baritone when the first record was made, and its deep, rich sound is much missed. *Emergence* is both a step forward and a summation. 'Morning Lake Forever' relates back to a composition on the first Weather Report record, and there's a new solo version of 'When Face Gets Pale' from *Miroslav Vitous Group*, which still hasn't appeared on CD. It begins with an 'Epilogue', which suggests a degree of self-reassessment, and though the 'Atlantis Suite' is rather too floating in conception (like the pretentiously titled 'Concerto In Three Parts' on *First Meeting*) there is a new solidity of purpose to his playing. Originally influenced by Scott LaFaro's remarkable performances with the Bill Evans Trio, Vitous has returned to something close to those singing lines. Though *Emergence* is a triumph, Vitous's best work still has to be sought out on the albums of other leaders, notably Chick Corea and Jack DeJohnette.

**** Universal Syncopations

ECM 038506 2 *Vitous; Wayne Bargeron (t); Valery Ponomarev (t, flhn); Isaac Smith (tb); Jan Garbarek (ts); Chick Corea (p); John McLaughlin (g); Jack DeJohnette (d).* 3/00–3/03.

It's been a decade since Miroslav's last studio album and with this he comes back with a bang. *Universal Syncopations* feels almost like a career survey, recorded over nearly three years and bringing back together some of the key players and associations of the bassist's career. The most important of all is, of course, with ECM Records, and label-mate Jan Garbarek is the key presence on the album. His solos, particularly on 'Univoyage' and, out of character, on 'Tramp Blues' are breathtaking enough to re-cue and listen to again and again.

Mclaughlin and DeJohnette are back from the band that made *Infinite Search* nearly 35 years (!) ago, though it seems that Herbie Hancock couldn't be persuaded to take part. His replacement is Chick Corea, who brings a much lighter, brighter and more thoughtful line to pieces like 'Beethoven', which one can imagine Herbie cutting up, and 'Bamboo Forest', which is saved from impressionism by some beautifully structured ensemble playing.

The brass players are less familiar in this kind of idiom and company, but they acquit themselves magnificently, content for the most part to lay down big metallic sheets of harmony over which Vitous's latter-day post-fusion dances gracefully along. A remarkable record and one of Garbarek's best jazz performances in some considerable time.

Cuong Vu

TRUMPET

The son of a Vietnamese pop singer mother and multi-instrumentalist father, Vu moved to Seattle when he was six. He swapped saxophone for trumpet and developed a remarkably powerful voice. In style, his recorded work ranges freely between Miles-influenced impressionism and a species of advanced rock, with a few more abstract soundscapes interspersed.

*** **Bound**

OmniTone 12002 *Vu; Jamie Saft (ky); Stomu Takeishi (b); Jim Black (d, perc).* 8/99.

(*) **Pure

Knitting Factory 266 *Vu; Stomu Takeishi (b); John Hollenbeck (d).* 00.

** **Come Play With Me**

Knitting Factory 298 *As above, except add Laurent Brondel (g, lap steel).* 5/01.

Cuong Vu has yet to improve on his debut recording, which opens with some of the fiercest trumpet playing you'll hear ('Two') and manages an easy transition to pop sweetness on the title-track, which was co-written with Holly Palmer and features a surprisingly effective vocal. 'Our Bridge' finds him in yet another mode, darker and more mysterious, and not unlike Wadada Leo Smith's 'Procession of the Great Ancestry'. Saft's Fender Rhodes has a thoroughly fresh and contemporary quality, but regular collaborator Takeishi always sounds as if he's just blown in from a '70s tribute gig. Black is essentially a rock drummer, but his successor Hollenbeck is always interesting to listen to.

The two subsequent albums are not up to the same standard, and there is a troubling and not fully explained emphasis on birth, childhood and innocence running through the titles: 'Amniotic', 'Vini's Lullaby' and 'Safekeeping' (*Come Play With Me*). Guitarist Laurent Brondel sits in for the first of these, on electric and lap steel, an interesting variation of sound that might have been developed further. The album opens very lamely indeed with the impressionistic 'Dreams, Come Play With Me' which goes nowhere, and both records see Cuong Vu settle into some of the formulae associated with '70s jazz-rock: soft tones and arpeggiations build to a chaotic climax and then revert to stillness and silence again.

Philipp Wachsmann (born 1944)

VIOLIN, VIOLA, ELECTRONICS

Ugandan-born Wachsmann studied with Nadia Boulanger and went on to devise his own form of neo-classicism within free music. A brilliant sound-sculptor, he has mainly been heard in other leaders' improvising ensembles, like the London Jazz Composers' Orchestra, Iskra 1903 and, more recently, Gush and Evan Parker's Electro-Acoustic Ensemble. Wachsmann also runs his own label, Bead Records.

***(*) **Eleven Years From Yesterday**

FMR CD-2-100988/Bead CD 01 *Wachsmann; Peter Jacobsen (p, hpd, syn); Ian Brighton (g); Marcio Mattos (b, clo); Trevor Taylor (perc).* 10/88.

Typical of the violinist's intrepid synthesis of neo-classicism and pure sound, a tightrope walk between Stravinsky and Varèse, these group improvisations are delicately executed by a highly sympathetic group of musicians who share many of Wachsmann's concerns. Jacobsen's keyboard work is astonishing, combining formality with the most unhierarchical approach imaginable.

Wachsmann deploys his electronics with virtuosic precision, never introducing an effect merely for its own sake, much as Georg Trakl, from whose death-songs all the titles are derived, never used a word but for maximum expressive impact. The three central pieces – 'On Sombre Boat He Rode', 'Down The Shimmering Torrents' and 'Full Of Purple Stars' – are exquisite group creations and it's only during the very last track that the pace and expression seem to flag, an example of more not necessarily being a good thing.

*** **Icarus**

FMR CD15 V1298 *Wachsmann; Mark Wastell (clo); Roger Curphy (b); Trevor Taylor (perc, elec); Carol Ann Jackson (v).* 8/95.

*** **Chathuna**

Bead CD 03 *Wachsmann (solo).* 10/96.

Icarus flies a little too close to the sun of pure abstraction. The wax melts and eventually the music takes a disappointing tumble. The five improvisations seem to call for some stronger structural rationale than each receives. Wachsmann's playing is as focused and provocative as ever, and there are a couple of occasions, notably on the two long closing tracks, where one would like to extract his playing and hear the violinist on his own, as he is on *Chathuna*.

It was conceived in collaboration with artist Sarah Eckel, whose work is shown on the cover, and was recorded in the Synagogue at Oerlinghausen. In recent times, Wachsmann has talked about a hidden pulse in his music. That is clearly audible here. 'Point Of Departure', the opening piece, has nothing to do with Andrew Hill's jazz masterpiece; but the underlying metre and the carefully layered harmonics come from broadly the same tradition. Though Wachsmann has seemed the least jazz-based and most academic of the British-based free-music specialists, that may now be changing, or it may always have been illusory.

Easy to hear from this how readily he would fit into saxophonist Evan Parker's electronic project. Wachsmann shares Evan's interest in complex mathematical procedures and high-harmonic improvisation, where the calculus of sound is the key concern.

**** **Some Other Season**

ECM 1662 *Wachsmann; Paul Lytton (perc, elec).* 10/97.

The two brightest sparks in Parker's Electro-Acoustic Ensemble went back into the studio as a duo. Lytton dusted off a lot of his old percussion and together they cut a modern masterpiece. The unexpected jazz feel creeps in again, notably on 'Shuffle' and 'Whispering Chambers', though it's the latter (and not 'Shuffle', as producer Steve Lake suggests) which bears the obvious kinship to Monk.

As expected, and as is now very much part of the ECM ethos, both solos and duos were recorded. Lytton does some wonderful things, 'Leonardo's Spoon', 'Nu Shu' and 'Shell', while Wachsmann seems more comfortable this time out working in partnership, though he saves his very best and straightest playing of the set for the penultimate solo, 'From The Chalk Cliffs'.

Steve Waddell

TROMBONE, VOCAL

Aussie trombonist and bandleader, a relative youngster among the seasoned pros of the game; his Creole Bells band plays in the trad style that mixes Lu Watters and Graeme Bell.

*** **Egyptian Ella**
Stomp Off CD 1230 *Waddell; Bob Pattie (c); Dafydd Wisner-Ellix (cl, ss, perc, v); Doug Rawson (p); John Brown (bj); Fred Clark (tba).* 12/90–2/91.

*** **Along The Road**
Stomp Off CD 1301 *As above, except Eric Holroyd (c), Mike Edwards (cl, as, v), Tony Orr (bj) replace Wisner-Ellix and Brown.* 6/95.

***(*) **Waltzing Matilda**
Stomp Off CD 1348 *As above, except add Hans Karssemeyer (p), Richard Opat (d, wbd); omit Rawson.* 3/98.

Steve Waddell's Creole Bells come from Melbourne, Australia, and they offer an amiable continuation of the kind of down-under trad that Graeme Bell initiated some 40 years earlier. The absence of a drummer on the first two discs frees the group from the tyranny of the trad beat to some degree, although Fred Clark's gruff bass-lines are suitably ponderous. Waddell's noisy trombone and the scratchily hot solos by Pattie give the group its character, and the material is inventively chosen; on the minus side, at times the vocals are close to hopeless, though the later discs fare better in this regard! *Along The Road* focuses on local composers like Roger Bell and Ian Pearce and is a nice change of menu, but it's *Waltzing Matilda* which shows them at their best. The two-cornet front line (Holroyd is still listed only as a guest – when's he joining full time?) is in cracking form, Karssemeyer (who died in 1999) plays excellent piano, but above all the arrival of Richard Opat really lights a fire under the group's collective tail.

Ulf Wakenius

GUITAR

Swedish guitarist moving between mainstream and more fusion-oriented situations.

*** **First Step**
Imogena IGCD 034 *Wakenius; Ove Ingmarsson (ts); Lars Jansson (ky); Lars Danielsson (b); Raymond Karlsson (d).* 10/92.

(*) **Enchanted Moments
Dragon DRCD 278 *As above, except omit Ingmarsson.* 10/95–3/96.

*** **Live**
Dragon DRCD 347 *Wakenius; Ake Johansson (p); Yasuhito Mori (b); Magnus Gran (d).* 4/99.

Wakenius's playing impresses without quite suggesting a recording artist of striking originality. As a technician, he plays the electric instrument with a precision and attention to tone that imply a cool head no matter what the situation. The 'local' band on the Imogena session surrenders nothing to the all-star outfit on an earlier record, and each has its share of invigorating music, but the first Dragon date specifically turns down the intensity with Wakenius sticking to acoustic over a series of sometimes anodyne backings. His treatment of 'Blame It On My Youth' on *First Step* presaged the quiescent music of this second disc, but some of it is all too pretty and unembellished. Yet when he gives himself the space to improvise a chorus, as on the translucent version of 'Cry Me A River', one wonders why he bothers with the smooth-jazz prettiness of much of the rest.

Live opens with a dedication to Wes Montgomery, 'The Greatest Of Them All', and by himself Wakenius creates a benign pastorale. But that's quickly displaced by 'Notes To J.C.', some 20 minutes of full-on hard-bop quartet music. Wakenius doesn't really sustain these long solos beyond their sheer momentum, but it's exciting to hear when propelled by Mori and the bullish Gran. Plenty to enjoy.

*** **Forever You**
Stunt STUCD 03192 *Wakenius; Carsten Dahl (p); Lars Danielsson (b, clo, p); Morten Lund (d).* 5/03.

Wakenius sticks to an acoustic instrument for his Stunt debut, and a programme of lyric pieces is dispatched in handsome style. Metheny's 'Always And Forever' is a typical selection, and as gracefully played as it is, it does suggest that the music's in hock to records already made by more renowned players and groups – specifically, much of this sounds like Metheny working with a vintage Jarrett trio (and Dahl's singalong style reinforces the impression).

Terry Waldo

PIANO, VOCAL

Veteran Ohio-based traditionalist whose several groups have worked at the ragtime and '20s end of the music.

*** **Hot House Rag**
Delmark DE-239 *Waldo; Roy Tate (t); Jim Snyder (tb); Frank Powers (cl, ts); Bob Sundstrom (bj); Mike Walbridge (tba); Wayne Jones (d).* 1/71.

*** **Kinky And Sweet**
Stomp Off CD 1339 *Waldo; Dan Levinson (cl, as); Craig Ventresco (g, bj); Marty Eggers (b); Pete Devine (wbd, perc).* 6/97.

***(*) **Let It Shine**
Stomp Off CD 1377 *Waldo; Peter Ecklund, Simon Wettenhall (t); Tom Artin (tb); Dan Levinson (cl, Cmel); Peter Martinez (cl, as, ts); Evan Christopher (cl, as); Craig Ventresco (g, bj); Cynthia Sayer (bj); Tom Marion (bj, g, mand); Greg Cohen (b); Paul Monat, Mike Wallbridge, Louise Anderson (tba); Pete Devine (d, wbd, jug); Janet Kline, Colleen Hawks, Eddy Davis, The Subway Trio (v).* 8/81–9/01.

Waldo's various bands certainly make some noise. He's not the most dainty of pianists and that certainly suits The Gutbucket Syncopators, the band that play quite furiously throughout *Hot House Rag* was recorded live at Deibel's Bier Stube in Columbus. The music's often incredibly clunky, but the head of steam which they get up on the likes of 'At The Jazz Band Ball' is about as exciting as this kind of revivalism gets. The two Stomp Offs present various other kinds of nostalgia. *Kinky And Sweet* has Terry guesting with the trio Bo Grumpus, and they basically play rags and '20s music in a string-band style: frolicsome, although 20 tracks of this sort of thing will strike most as a bit much. *Let It Shine* is better: a nice mix of groups (including a nod back to an old track by the Syncopators), much more jazz-oriented, and the sensational vocal by Janet Kline on 'Happy Feet' is alone worth having the CD for.

Mal Waldron (1926–2003)

PIANO

Waldron has effectively had two careers, divided by a catastrophic nervous breakdown in 1963. Up to that point, he had worked with Ike Quebec, Charles Mingus and, most memorably, Billie Holiday, with whom he stayed until her death in 1959. He also established himself as a distinctive recording artist with a darkly lyrical style. After his illness he had to begin afresh, and he emerged from the shadows with a new sound: percussive, minor-keyed and often long-lined, and much influenced by his move to Europe.

*****(*) Update**

Soul Note 121130-2 *Waldron (p solo).* 3/86.

An immensely gifted and prolific player whose professional roots are in the raw soul-jazz of Big Nick Nicholas and Ike Quebec, Waldron typically builds up solos from relatively simple ideas (his classic, much-covered 'Soul Eyes' could hardly be less elaborate), paying great attention to colour and shading, and to space. He favours block chords rather than rapid single-note runs, a style which has lent itself equally to large ensembles and smaller blowing groups (he worked with Mingus and Coltrane in the mid-'50s and early '60s), sensitive accompaniment (he spent more than two years with Billie Holiday), and free playing. Though it's clear that Waldron's main influences are Bud Powell and Thelonious Monk, he has developed independently and sounds quite unlike either. Until relatively recently he has not been a prolific solo performer, and this record is by no means his best music; but it does allow closer inspection of his compositional and improvising style and it helps establish the brand identity of one of the labels which have consistently supported his work, Enja giving him a darker and more lugubrious sound, Soul Note a sunnier, clearer focus. Unfortunately, the Enja vinyl catalogue has taken a pasting and, while it may be possible to find vinyl copies like *Mingus Lives*, recorded one week after the great bassist's death, *Black Glory*, *A Touch Of The Blues*, *Hard Talk* and *What It Is* (all of which are reviewed in the first edition of the *Guide*), there is as yet no sign of them on compact disc.

Update is unusual in including a standard (in addition to 'Night In Tunisia', there is a very individual gloss on a Frank Loesser tune); Waldron has generally preferred to spin his own material out of dark, minor intervals and from an area in the centre of the keyboard, using extremes of pitch only for dramatic contrast and colour effects. *Update* also further adjusts Waldron's polite reserve *vis-à-vis* free playing, which he explored with the 1969 *Free At Last* trio, below. Taken together, 'Free For C.T.' and 'Variations On A Theme By Cecil Taylor' firmly underscore Waldron's rugged individualism and refusal to be colonized by what has become the most invasive of contemporary piano styles. The variations are subtly rhythmic and beautifully proportioned. This is an important album in Waldron's career, coming at a time when his group performances were also at a peak. It merits the closest attention.

***** Mal – 1**

Original Jazz Classics OJC 611 *Waldron; Idrees Sulieman (t); Gigi Gryce (as); Julian Euell (b); Arthur Edgehill (d).* 11/56.

***** Mal – 2**

Original Jazz Classics OJC 671 *Waldron; Bill Hardman (t); Jackie McLean, Sahib Shihab (as); John Coltrane (ts); Julian Euell (b); Art Taylor, Ed Thigpen (d).* 4–5/57.

***** Mal – 3: Sounds**

Original Jazz Classics OJC 1814 *Waldron; Art Farmer (t); Eric Dixon (ts); Calo Scott (clo); Julian Euell (b); Elvin Jones (d).* 58.

*****(*) Mal – 4**

Original Jazz Classics OJC 1856 *Waldron; Addison Farmer (b); Kenny Dennis (d).* 9/58.

****** Impressions**

Original Jazz Classics OJC 132 *Waldron; Addison Farmer (b); Albert 'Tootie' Heath (d).* 59.

Despite Sulieman's and Gryce's bursting expressiveness, the first OJC is a low-key selection from Waldron's Prestige period, which saw the pianist concentrating on sophisticated harmonic patterns and cross-rhythms. The sound – as they used to say about serving girls – is no better than it ought to be, but, given the anonymity of the rhythm section, not much is lost. A fine 'Yesterdays' picks things up a bit at the end. All the same material can also be found on a high-gloss Coltrane on Prestige set (16 CDs for Gold Card types) and, if anything, sounds rather sharper there.

The later tracks with Coltrane and McLean are inevitably of greatest interest. Waldron made substantial strides as a composer towards the end of the '50s and that's reflected in his solo construction, too. In 1957, Coltrane had finally decided to rid himself of a deeply rooted drug and alcohol dependency. It isn't reading too much into basically conventional performances to suggest that his solos have a new maturity, coupled with an emotional vulnerability, which McLean seems to comprehend better than the rather single-minded Shihab, but round which Waldron steals with unfailing tact and supportive ease. No classic tracks, though 'Don't Explain' (with McLean) and 'The Way You Look Tonight' (with Shihab) are a cut above the rest.

Mal – 3 already shows signs of the tremendous stresses and tensions that make *Impressions* such a darkly wonderful record; there is even a track at the beginning of the 1958 disc called 'Tension', as if to signal what's coming. There is something extremely uncomfortable about listening to Waldron at this period. The echoes of Bud Powell are unmistakable and faintly sinister, given the breakdown in Waldron's health just a couple of years later. 'Champs Elysées' and 'With A Song In My Heart' are both outwardly sanguine but, all the way through, Waldron is inverting harmonies, throwing in minor-key variations, generally changing the emotional temper. It's a stern experience, but a rewarding and chastening one. *Mal – 4* skins the line-up back to a trio and is again rather Janus-faced in its delivery: compare the opening 'Splidium-Dow' with the subsequent 'Get Happy' (!), interestingly enough another favourite of Powell's. These are scarce and rather little-known records in their original form and deserve to be in wider currency.

*****(*) Free At Last**

ECM 831332-2 *Waldron; Isla Eckinger (b); Clarence Beckton (d).* 11/69.

To call Waldron 'unmelodic' is a description, not a criticism. He has rarely written memorable tunes, concentrating instead on subtly coded tonal cells out of which, as his career has continued, longer and longer improvisations can be developed. *Free At Last* was a conscious attempt to come to terms with free jazz;

in Waldron's own words, it represented his desire to play 'rhythmically instead of soloing on chord changes'. At the same time, Waldron utterly rejects any notion of free jazz as 'complete anarchy or disorganized sound'. At first glance, these half-dozen tracks are disappointingly constrained and modest in scope. The long 'Rat Now' (a typical Waldron pun) and 'Rock My Soul' point a way forward for extended improvisation that does not depend on chord sequences; but, interestingly, both have the same 'feel' as more conventionally harmonic music because Waldron's clusters always seem to gravitate towards specific resolutions. A useful trivia question, especially for anyone who wields the 'ECM sound' *canard* too freely, is to ask what the label's very first release was. If one quality characterizes ECM's output, it has been a search for new principles of organization in jazz, its only constraint a rejection of anarchic disorganization. *Free At Last* was a fine send-off.

*** Up Popped The Devil

Enja ENJ 2034 *Waldron; Carla Poole (f); Reggie Workman (b); Billy Higgins (d).* 12/73.

One of Waldron's darker and more intense sessions, with few glimpses of the light and humour that often pervaded his work. 'Changachangachang' is a curious piece, not unlike 'Giant Steps' in some respects, but marked by the same countervailing vamps and minor episodes that are also part of 'Snake Out' and the title-track. One for enthusiasts only.

**** Live At Dreher

hatOLOGY 4-596 4CD *Waldron; Steve Lacy (ss).* 8/81.

These are the encounters that sparked off what was to be one of the most fruitful relationships in either musician's life. Lacy's dry, intense sound was perfectly complemented by Waldron's darker sonority, though each shared enough of the other's characteristics (notably a wicked sense of humour) to ensure that this was never merely a union of opposites. The two original discs – *The Peak, Round Midnight* – are now amalgamated in a four-CD set which covers the span of their residency at Dreher and allows the closest possible examination of their interplay on themes like 'Hooray For Herbie', 'Let's Call This' and 'Herbe d'Oublie' (two very different versions of the latter tunes, three of 'Round Midnight'). Monk, with whom they met and played some of the material 25 years earlier, is obviously the common ground between the two; Lacy was a pioneering exponent of Monk compositions and Waldron has the dark blue intensity to bring them alive. These are almost flawless performances, a peak in modern jazz.

*** Dedication

Soul Note 121178-2 *Waldron; David Friesen (b).* 11/85.

Something of an oddity, but an enjoyable one. Friesen's floating, soft-edged bass-lines (played on an amplified, bodyless instrument, credited as 'Oregon bass') actually work rather well over Waldron's dark mutterings, and the set as a whole has a coherence and unity that begin to sound slightly repetitive only on subsequent hearings.

**** Sempre Amore

Soul Note 121170-2 *Waldron; Steve Lacy (ss).* 2/86.

Sempre Amore is dedicated to Ellington–Strayhorn material, which must have made an intriguing change from Lacy's specialized diet of Monk.

***(*) The Git Go

Soul Note 121118-2 *Waldron; Woody Shaw (t, flhn); Charlie Rouse (ts, f); Reggie Workman (b); Ed Blackwell (d).* 9/86.

**** The Seagulls Of Kristiansund

Soul Note 121148-2 *As above.* 9/86.

Two top-flight sets from a single night of a fine week's engagement at the Village Vanguard in New York City. All six compositions are Waldron's and his playing is supremely economical, sketching in tonal centres with a minimum of elaboration, soloing on the faster tracks with a positive touch, shading beautifully on the slow 'Seagulls Of Kristiansund'. This shows a side of Waldron's work which some critics have likened to American minimalism: a slow accretion of almost subliminal harmonic and rhythmic shifts steadily pile up until the music seems ready to overbalance. Perhaps oddly – for subsequent releases from live or studio sessions rarely match up to the original albums – the second album is more appealing. *The Git Go* consists of no more than the title-piece and an overlong 'Status Seeking', which seems to have lost much of the terse discipline Waldron brought to it on *The Quest.* On the second album, Waldron kicks off 'Snake Out' with a menacing bass pulse that builds up almost unbearable tension before loosing Woody Shaw on one of his most unfettered solos. Rouse's solo is more compact and provides a taut bridge between Shaw and Waldron, who plays lyrically over a bleak vamp. Blackwell and Workman both solo effectively, though the drummer's finest moment comes at the end of 'Judy', the middle track of the set and a tribute to Waldron's great supporter, Judy Sneed. Shaw's solo is astonishing. Blackwell shines again on 'Seagulls', producing non-metrical effects on his splash cymbal; Workman's foghorn and seabird effects are straight out of Mingus's bag. *The Git Go* has some *longueurs*, but its successor is thoroughly and straightforwardly enjoyable, and should be tried for size.

**** Our Colline's A Tresure

Soul Note 121198-2 *Waldron; Leonard Jones (b); Sangoma Everett (d).* 4/87.

Still on a high. Waldron's handling of 'The Git Go' is markedly different from that on the Village Vanguard sessions, tighter in conception, if not in length, and with most of the solo space inevitably restored to the composer. The opening 'Spaces' is a superb example of direct motivic improvisation and lets in Jones for the first of several fine contributions. Everett, a neighbour of Waldron's in Munich, is less well known but sounds more than competent. The title-piece (and the misspelt word is probably deliberate) is dedicated to a young French friend of Waldron's, who may grow up to 'tresure' the beautiful waltz-tune better than she will the picture on the cover.

**** Crowd Scene

Soul Note 121218 *Waldron; Sonny Fortune (as); Ricky Ford (ts); Reggie Workman (b); Eddie Moore (d).* 6/89.

***(*) Where Are You?

Soul Note 121248 *As above.* 6/89.

'Crowd Scene' is a large-scale piece that attempts to capture the point at which individual elements begin to cohere and act in unison, as a collectivity. Waldron has always liked to describe himself as a parcel of disparate elements, held together by chance, everyday necessities, good luck, rather than by any pressing philosophy; and something of that seems to underline this piece. 'Yin And Yang', the other long track, perhaps represents a more specific and settled viewpoint, but one that in no way contradicts the first. Like 'Crowd Scene', it's held together by riffs and *ostinati*, rather than by any single principle of development. The two saxophonists, who managed to dramatize a sense of diversity and questioning plurality in the first piece, are not so much opposites as two sides of a single reality in the second, playing in close intervals but with markedly different timbres. The effect is very powerful, and engineer Kazunori Sugiyama has done a marvellous job capturing it so accurately. For once, it's good to have Waldron in the studio. Much would have been lost in a club or concert hall. There's a bit of padding on the second disc; only a second and longer take of 'Where Are You?' takes it up over the 50-minute mark. However, what there is is so good that no casual purchaser will feel short-changed. 'Waltz For Marianne' is gorgeous, with Workman playing a prominent role. One feels that, with a little judicious editing, an absolutely top-flight single CD could have been made out of these.

*****(*) Waldron–Haslam**

Slam 305 *Waldron; George Haslam (bs).* 2/94.

***** Two New**

Slam 306 *Waldron; George Haslam (bs, tarogato).* 4/95.

Spells of indifferent health have slowed up Waldron's recording regimen of late. These engaging duet records with British baritone man Haslam don't have the gravitas and sheer monumentality of the best Waldron, but their friendly dialogue has its own rewards and at some moments – especially in the two improvised pieces on the first disc, 'Catch As Catch Should' and 'Motion In Order' – there is the trademark dry, lyrical intensity which is in all of the pianist's best work. Though Haslam might have been outclassed, especially in having to step into the shoes of some of Waldron's other horn partners, his light, flexible lines make an attractively serene counterpoint. Excellent recording on both discs.

***** Travellin' In Soul-Time**

BVHaast CD 9701 *Waldron; Toru Tenda (f); Jeanne Lee (v).* 96.

Recorded live in Tokyo, Nagasaki and Kobuchizawa, this remarkable trio combine traditional Japanese material with some of Mal's most culturally ambiguous work, pieces like 'Black Rain' (who could guess at its provenance?) and the perennial 'The Seagulls of Kristiansund', which has never sounded fresher or more unexpected. Jeanne Lee was not just a wonderful singer but a masterful musician, and her contribution to this album is bound to invite comparison with Mal's interaction with Billie Holiday. The additional element of Toru Tenda's delicate but piercing flute (serving a similar role to Steve Lacy's soprano saxophone in past encounters) makes for a fresh and unexpected collection of performances that suggest Waldron still refuses to stand still but continues to explore fresh musical and cultural territory.

***** Into The Light**

Materiali 90116 *Waldron; Christian Burchard (vib); Dieter Serfas (d).* 99–00.

The association between Waldron and Burchard has been a happy and creative one. The addition of Serfas on some tracks adds an intriguing dimension. The long opening track 'From Darkness Into the Light' tends to the diffuse and lacks a moment of genuine dramatic transition, but it contains some compelling playing and once it gives way to the terse 'Waters From the Waters' most listeners will be hooked.

Mal plays direct on his piano strings (on 'Left Alone') and creates a deeply brooding atmosphere on 'Embryo Solo', which seems to be an edit from a longer performance, but for the most part his delivery is a familiar lyricism. Burchard has a wonderful moment right at the end of the set with 'Giesing', but it is Mal's playing which will stay in the mind.

Dan Wall

ORGAN

Best known for his work with guitarist John Abercrombie's trio, Wall is very much his own man, influenced by – but independent of – the example of Jimmy Smith and Larry Young.

*****(*) On The Inside Looking In**

Double-Time DTRCD 175 *Wall; Jerry Bergonzi (ts); Mick Goodrick (g); Billy Drummond (d).* 4/00.

Wall was excellent on Bergonzi's albums for the same label, and the tenorman returns the favour here. With Goodrick playing lines of nearly pernickety precision and Drummond's sensible time and groove, the music sits as something almost rarified, a professorial distillation of the organ/tenor combo tradition. But the sense of power idling in reserve introduces a keenness into the music which is surprisingly persistent. Even unpromising titles such as 'The New Blues' and '5 Minute Funk' offer up fresh ideas.

Thomas 'Fats' Waller (1904–43)

PIANO, ORGAN, VOCAL

The son of a clergyman, Waller worked in vaudeville until the mid-'20s and began composing with lyricist Andy Razaf, as well as making occasional sideman appearances with bands like the Ted Lewis group. His fame came with the 'Fats Waller And His Rhythm' sessions for Victor, which began in 1934 and proceeded through hundreds of titles. A nonpareil humorist and lampooner of trite pop tunes, Waller's own best songs were strong enough to have remained in the standard repertory. His piano style, which emerged from stride, was percussive and swinging, yet often delicate or even whimsical. He died of pneumonia while on an overnight train.

****(*) Classic Jazz From Rare Piano Rolls**

Biograph BCD 104 *Waller; James P. Johnson, Lawrence J. Cook (piano rolls).* 3/23–1/29.

***** Low Down Papa**

Biograph BCD 114 *Waller; James P. Johnson (piano rolls).* 5/23–6/31.

Thomas Waller was already deputizing for James P. Johnson and playing film and stage-show accompaniments when he started making piano-rolls for the QRS company in 1923. These two discs transfer some of his many rolls to CD. Most of the tunes are typical light blues novelties of the day, and they're played with a crisp, courtly demeanour, although individuality is to some extent suppressed by the machinery of the roll system: certainly Waller's first piano records show much more idiosyncrasy than any of these tracks. There are a couple of items with Johnson, Waller's great mentor, and one on the earlier disc which was credited to Waller but is actually by Lawrence Cook. Ebullience and good humour are persistent here to the point of becoming exasperating, and perhaps these pieces are best sampled a few at a time: there are only a few genuinely Walleresque touches, such as the abrupt doubling of tempo in 'Your Time Now' on *Low Down Papa*. The rolls have been brightly recorded, although *Low Down Papa* is less glassy and generally has the better selection of themes.

★(★) Fats At The Organ

ASV AJA 5007R *Waller (org solo).* 23–27.

A unique record, if a bizarre one. Waller made several pipe-organ solos early in his career, but this set consists of organ transcriptions of piano-roll solos: Waller is heard twice-removed. If the piano-roll discs listed above sound artificial, it's hard to hear much of Waller in here except in the merry rhythmic gait of the original rolls: all the choices of registration are made by Ronald Curtis – admittedly after studying Waller's original organ records – and any authenticity that remains comes off a second-best to whatever a 78 can produce.

★★(★) Fats Waller 1922–1926

Classics 664 *Waller; Clarence Williams (kz, v); Clarence Todd (kz); Justin Ring (perc); Sara Martin, Alberta Hunter, Anna Jones, Porter Grainger, Rosa Henderson, Alta Browne, Bertha Powell, Caroline Johnson (v).* 10/22–4/26.

This is fantastically obscure music, 19 tracks of classic blues and vaudeville singers accompanied by Waller, plus two 1922 solos and two tracks with the Jamaica Jazzers (Clarence Williams and Clarence Todd blowing through their kazoos). Those accustomed to listening to the earliest blues reissues will know what to expect in terms of sound-quality; everyone else may be in for a shock (and even Classics themselves have apologized for it on the sleeve). On its own terms, fascinating, with the almost unknown titles by Alta Browne, Bertha Powell and Anna Jones especially interesting.

★★ The Complete Early Band Works 1927–29

Halcyon HDL 115 *Waller; Tom Morris (c); Charlie Gaines, Henry 'Red' Allen, Leonard Davis (t); Jack Teagarden, Jimmy Archey, J. C. Higginbotham (tb); Arville Harris (cl, as, ts); Albert Nicholas, Charlie Holmes (cl, as); Larry Binyon (ts); Bobbie Leecan (g); Will Johnson, Eddie Condon (bj); George 'Pops' Foster, Al Morgan (b); Eddie King, Gene Krupa, Kaiser Marshall (d); The Four Wanderers (v).* 5/27–12/29.

★★(★) Fats Waller 1926–1927

Classics 674 *As above discs, except add Alberta Hunter, Maude Mills (v).* 11/26–6/27.

★★★ Fats Waller 1927–1929

Classics 689 *As above discs, except add Bert Howell (vn, v), Lou Raderman, Howard Nelson (vn), David Martin (clo), Chuck Campbell (tb), J. Lapitino (hp), Gene Austin, Andy Razaf, Juanita Chappelle (v).* 11/27–6/29.

★★★(★) Fats Waller 1929

Classics 702 *As above discs.* 6–12/29.

Waller doesn't sing anywhere on the Halcyon disc, and given the nightmarish vocals by The Four Wanderers on two tracks, perhaps he was numbed into silence. The seven tracks by Fats with Tom Morris's Hot Babies are a garish mismatch of pipe organ and cornet-led hot band, and since the resonances and overtones of the organ tamp down everything the other players do, it's hard to imagine how anyone could have thought that the group would work. The eight tracks by Fats Waller & His Buddies are merely loose-knit New York jazz of the period (1929).

The Classics discs go forward with Waller's 1926–27 organ solos – beautiful, lilting creations – as well as some of the Morris Hot Babies tracks and more accompaniments to Mills and Hunter. There is some very strange stuff on Classics 689 – three tearful tributes to the lately departed Florence Mills, where Waller plays respectful piano, and a version of 'Chloe' with violin, organ and piano. It ends with Gene Austin singing 'Maybe – Who Knows?'. In between, though, are several classic piano solos and 'I Ain't Got Nobody', one of the best of his organ records. Remastering on all these is mixed but quite an improvement over Classics 664. The 1929 disc offers a great run of his finest piano solos (see below): still not the best sound, but it's a strong one-disc primer on early Waller.

★★(★) You Rascal You

ASV AJA 5040 *Waller; Henry 'Red' Allen, Leonard Davis, Bill Coleman, Herman Autrey, Charlie Gains, Charlie Teagarden, Sterling Bose (t); Jack Teagarden (tb, v); Charlie Irvis, Tommy Dorsey, J. C. Higginbotham, Charlie Green (tb); Arville Harris, Ben Whittet, Artie Shaw, Albert Nicholas, Larry Binyon (cl, as); Gene Sedric, Larry Binyon (cl, ts); Bud Freeman (ts); Al Casey, Dick McDonough (g); Eddie Condon (bj); Billy Taylor, George 'Pops' Foster, Artie Bernstein (b); Stan King, Kaiser Marshall, Harry Dial (d).* 3/29–11/34.

★★★ Fats Waller 1929–1934

Classics 720 *As above.* 12/29–11/34.

Waller's early band sides, picked out in this ASV cross-section of 1929–34 sessions, suggested a mercurial talent pondering on its ultimate direction. The two sides by Fats Waller's Buddies are frantic small-band New York jazz of the day (1929), with little of the slyness of the Rhythm sides represented by seven 1934 tracks. The guest-star role he takes on a Jack Teagarden version of 'You Rascal You' offers little more than inspired mugging, entertaining as it is. A few solos, including the enchanting 'My Fate Is In Your Hands', suggest the other side of Waller's art, and the complexity of his personality. Mixed reproduction again, alas: some sides sound very dull, others are clear and strong. Much the same applies to the Classics version of this material.

★★★ Fats Waller 1934–1935

Classics 732 *Waller; Herman Autrey, Bill Coleman (t); Floyd O'Brien (tb); Gene Sedric (cl, ts); Mezz Mezzrow (cl, as); Al Casey (g); Billy Taylor, Charles Turner (b); Harry Dial (d, vib).* 9/34–1/35.

★★★(★) Fats Waller 1935

Classics 746 *As above, except add Rudy Powell (cl, as), James Smith (g), Arnold Bolling (d); omit Mezzrow and Taylor.* 1/35–6/35.

★★★(★) Fats Waller 1935 Vol. 2

Classics 760 *As above, except omit Coleman, Sedric, Dial.* 6–8/35.

★★★(★) Fats Waller 1935–1936

Classics 776 *As above, except add Benny Morton (tb), Emmett Matthews (ss), Bob Carroll, Gene Sedric (ts), Hank Duncan (p), Yank Porter (d); omit Powell, Smith.* 11/35–2/36.

★★★ Fats Waller 1936

Classics 797 *As above, except add Slick Jones (d); omit Morton, Matthews, Caroll, Duncan.* 6–9/36.

***** Fats Waller 1936–1937**

Classics 816 *As above, except omit Bolling, Porter.* 11/36–3/37.

***** Fats Waller 1937**

Classics 838 *As above, except add Bunny Berigan (t), Tommy Dorsey (tb), Dick McDonough (g), George Wettling (d).* 3–6/37.

Waller worked hard in the studios, and though his material has been traditionally looked down upon, he did usually make the most of it, even if the relentless clowning, yelled asides, importuning of soloists and general mayhem obscured much of what his hands were doing at the keyboard. This is often knockabout music, but whenever he gets to a good melody or does one of his own better tunes – such as the 12-inch master of 'Blue Turning Grey Over You' – its underlying seriousness rises to the surface. Autry and Sedric, the most ubiquitous yet least recognized of horn-players, are always ready to heat things up. Bill Coleman's presence on a few early sessions introduces some of his elegant horn, and the almost forgotten Rudy Powell replaced Sedric on several of the 1935 dates.

Much order has now been imposed on these sessions. Classics have set out a comprehensive survey of Waller's Rhythm recordings and his various solos. The Classics CDs are easy to follow, but three deleted RCA sets of this material were attractively packaged and the remastering (much improved on the earlier standards of the Bluebird reissues) is generally better. Waller fans may want to seek these out, though it's possible that the parent company may redo them yet again.

Classics 732 includes four piano solos as well as the session which produced 'Serenade For A Wealthy Widow'; 'Baby Brown' is another good one. Classics 746 has 'Rosetta', 'I'm Gonna Sit Right Down And Write Myself A Letter', the outstanding 'Dinah' and 'Sweet And Slow'. Either this or the following Classics 760 might be a good one to sample: the latter includes several more of the best Rhythm tracks, with one of the best ever versions of 'Somebody Stole My Gal'. Classics 776 has the fruits of a session involving a 12-piece band, which even has a second pianist, Hank Duncan, who brings on a joshing cutting contest on 'I Got Rhythm'. Also on this disc is a particularly fine session that produced 'The Panic Is On', 'Sugar Rose' and 'West Wind'. There is still a decent quota of good music on Classics 797, but this and the next two see the Rhythm formula wearing dangerously thin and some truly dreadful material coming under assault. There are many pickings here, but they're camouflaged by a lot of nonsense. By the time the Classics sequence reaches its end, this stands as a fairly monumental set, but follow the stars in the meantime for Waller's better moments.

*****(*) Fats Waller 1937 Vol. 2**

Classics 857 *Waller; Herman Autrey, Paul Campbell (t); Gene Sedric, Caughey Roberts (cl, ts); Al Casey, Ceele Burke (g); Charles Turner, Al Morgan (b); Slick Jones, Lee Young (d).* 6–12/37.

***** Fats Waller 1937–1938**

Classics 875 *As above, except add John 'Bugs' Hamilton, Courtney Williams (t), George Robinson, John 'Shorty' Haughton (tb), William Alsop, James Powell, Fred Skerritt (as), Lonnie Simmons (ts), Cedric Wallace (b).* 12/37–7/38.

***** Fats Waller 1938**

Classics 913 *Waller; Dave Wilkins, Herman Autrey (t); George Chisholm (tb); Alfie Kahn, Gene Sedric (cl, ts); Ian Sheppard (ts, vn); Al Casey, Alan Ferguson (g); Len Harrison, Cedric Wallace (b); Hymie Schneider, Edmundo Ros, Slick Jones (d); Adelaide Hall (v).* 8–12/38.

***** Fats Waller 1938–1939**

Classics 943 *Waller; Herman Autrey (t); Gene Sedric (cl, ts); Coco Heimel, Al Casey (g); Candy Hall, Cedric Wallace (b); Slick Jones, Johnny Marks (d).* 12/38–4/39.

***** Fats Waller 1939**

Classics 973 *As above, except add John 'Bugs' Hamilton (t), Chauncey Graham (ts), John Smith (g), Larry Hinton, Max Lewin (d); omit Heimel, Hall, Marks.* 6–11/39.

Waller's progress with his Rhythm is documented further here. The humour grows less manic, more formulaic, and sometimes even gentle in its delivery; the material continues to be a mix of worthy and throwaway; and the tenor of each session is usually rather light and fresh, since Waller disliked doing more than the minimum rehearsal before setting down a take. Classics 857 starts with five rather sweetly engaging solos, including 'Keepin' Out Of Mischief Now' (an almost definitive version), and some excellent Rhythm tracks make this one a very good entry in the series. Classics 875 includes eight titles where the Rhythm group was augmented into an orchestra. Waller is uncharacteristically reserved on some of his vocals but there are fine versions of 'Skrontch' and 'The Sheik Of Araby'. There's also a curious date where Ceele Burke plays steel guitar and Waller sings 'Why Do Hawaiians Sing Aloha?'

Waller visited Europe twice in the late '30s, and he recorded in London on both trips. Two sessions in 1938 found him handling organ and piano with a British band, cutting six organ solos (including a surprisingly bleak and unsettling 'Deep River') and backing Adelaide Hall for two further songs (all on Classics 913). Two Rhythm dates back in New York round off the disc. The following year, he worked alone or with drum-only support. There are six wistful miniatures, the 'London Suite', and a rather mournful 'Smoke Dreams Of You', which go to suggest the reflective side of Waller's art which rarely made it to record yet which is always touted by supporters as his shamefully overlooked inner self. Whatever the case, these are slight but charming pieces, and they're on Classics 973, along with three more dates with the Rhythm. On one, they do a polite remake of 'Bond Street' from the London Suite. Classics 943 includes a bizarre two-title date where Waller plays electric organ behind Gene Austin, who sounds like he's doing a Waller impersonation. It also offers three very rare tracks from his 1939 London visit, including 'Cottage In The Rain' – unfortunately dubbed from a very poor master. Transfers tend to be respectable rather than outstanding.

***** Fine Arabian Stuff**

High Note HCD 7053 *Waller (p, org, v solo).* 11/39.

Waller plays the likes of 'The Old Oaken Bucket', 'Oh! Susanna' and 'Go Down Moses', guying the lyrics without mercy yet often playing the melodies with improbable delicacy. These are 16 transcription performances for radio programming and much of the way it's vintage Fats, but the sound has a thick mist of echo over it which isn't very appealing.

***** Fats Waller 1939–1940**

Classics 1002 *Waller; John 'Bugs' Hamilton (t); Gene Sedric (cl, ts); John Smith, Al Casey (g); Cedric Wallace (b); Slick Jones (d); Una Mae Carlisle (v).* 39–40.

***** Fats Waller 1940–1941**

Classics 1030 *As above, except omit Smith and Carlisle; add Catherine Perry (v).* 7/40–3/41.

*****(*) Fats Waller 1941**

Classics 1068 *As above, except add Herman Autrey, Bob Williams (t), George Wilson, Ray Hogan (tb), Jimmy Powell, Dave McRae (as), Bob Carroll (ts), Charles Turner (b), Arthur Trappier (d); omit Perry.* 5–12/41.

***** Fats Waller 1942–1943**

Classics 1097 *Waller; Herman Autrey, John 'Bugs' Hamilton, Joe Thomas, Nathaniel Williams, Benny Carter (t); Herb Flemming, George Wilson, Slim Moore (tb); Gene Sedric, Gene Porter (cl, ts); Jackie Fields, George James (as); Bob Carroll (ts); Al Casey, Irving Ashby (g); Cedric Wallace, Slam Stewart (b); Arthur Trappier, Zutty Singleton (d); Deep River Boys, Ada Brown (v).* 3/42–9/43.

If Waller was ultimately trapped by his non-stop funny-man image, the routine of the Fats Waller And His Rhythm records at least helped to focus a talent that was sometimes in danger of merely running ragged. The dozens of throwaway tunes he lampooned may have had little intrinsic merit, and he often falls back on favourite lines and devices, but like Armstrong in the same period Waller remains an inimitable talent, and the space limitations of the records often result in performances full of compressed excitement. The later sessions are unpredictable in this respect, since he often goes gentle when one expects a shot of uproar. It is certainly untrue to say that the Rhythm recordings declined in quality. The 1941–42 sessions include some of the finest sides the band made, and Hamilton, Sedric and Autrey, all minor figures who nevertheless played handsomely at the right moment, lend a more urgently swinging touch to the music than anything provided by, say, the Louis Jordan band. (Compare Waller's 'Your Socks Don't Match' or 'Don't Give Me That Jive' (both on Classics 1068), two very Jordanesque tunes, with any of the alto-man's records. Next to Jordan's calculating burlesques, Waller's wit sounds wholly spontaneous.)

Since RCA's multi-disc overview seems to be gone for the moment, these Classics volumes – which finally complete the Waller story after 21 CDs! – take first place. Pick of the four is surely Classics 1068, which has the Rhythm augmented by horns for the session that produced the terrific 'Chant Of The Groove', as well as five piano solo tracks and superior singles such as 'Buck Jumpin'' and 'Clarinet Marmalade'. Classics 1097 offers the final four Victor dates and includes Fats singing 'That's What The Well Dressed Man In Harlem Will Wear' in front of the Victor First Nighter Orchestra and Benny Carter playing trumpet on the last session. Ten titles for V-Disc, with Fats alone at the piano or the organ, make a fine conclusion to the series, with the chilling farewell of 'Sometimes I Feel Like A Motherless Child' making an eerie finale to his career on record. Sound is mostly more than acceptable on all four discs.

****(*) The Alternative Takes Vol. 1 1923–1929**

Neatwork RP 2003 *As appropriate discs above.* 7/23–8/29.

***** The Alternative Takes Vol. 2 1929–1938**

Neatwork RP 2004 *As appropriate discs above, except add Peggy Dade (v).* 8/29–3/38.

***** The Alternative Takes Vol. 3 1938–1941**

Neatwork RP 2005 *As appropriate discs above.* 38–41.

The first volume starts with a barely listenable Paramount from 1923, with Waller backing Anna Jones, before five organ solos and various alternatives with the Tom Morris Hot Babies and the Louisiana Sugar Babes. Four piano solos wrap it up. Not a tremendous amount of interest here, unless you're a Waller completist. The other two volumes are rather more worthwhile. Although most of them offer alternatives from the various Rhythm sessions, the second volume starts with eight solos and also offers two tests, where Fats backs the (admittedly indifferent) singing of Peggy Dade, and a scarce orchestral title in 'Marie'. Sound-quality is variable, but aside from a couple of stinkers most of them are clean enough.

****(*) Misbehavin' Badly**

Giant Steps G15T006 *Waller; Charlie Gaines, Herman Autrey, John Hamilton, Benny Carter (t); Charlie Irvis (tb); Arville Harris, Eugene Cedric, Gene Porter (ts, cl); Al Casey, John Smith Jr, Irving Ashby (g); Charles Turner, Cedric Wallace, Slam Stewart (b); Allen 'Yank' Porter, Elmore 'Slick' Jones, Arthur Trappier, Zutty Singleton (d); Ada Brown (v).* 29–43.

There are seven tracks here culled from a hotchpotch of Waller's Victor sessions, but most of it is dedicated to his solo V-Disc recordings. Everything here is otherwise available in the Classics sequence, and by itself the disc makes few pressing claims on likely purchasers.

Jan Wallgren (1935–96)

PIANO

Originally from Norway, Wallgren spent most of his life in Sweden. A bopper in the '50s and '60s, he was an eclectic who turned to prolific composing and brought a dedicated knowledge of classical and folk forms to his writing and playing.

*****(*) Standards And Blueprints**

Dragon DRCD 246 *Wallgren (p solo).* 4/87–2/93.

****** Raga, Bebop And Anything**

Dragon DRCD 303 *Wallgren; Magnus Broo (t); Nils Landgren (tb); Håkan Bröstrom (ss, as); Jonas Knutsson (ss, as, bs); Lennart Aberg (ss, ts); Christian Spering (b); Anders Kjellberg (d).* 4/95.

Wallgren's *Blueprints*, listed in our first edition in its vinyl form, is an album we have returned to often, and its CD incarnation adds six standards and a conflation of Monk and Powell. The veteran bebopper-turned-composer wore his heart on his sleeve here, with the jazz pieces sitting beside dedications to Berg, Webern and Schoenberg, and while it is principally a recital of tiny miniatures – some of which might blow away on a puff of wind – the beauty of his touch brings most of it to life, with the dozen 'Hints And Suggestions' particularly fine. His version of the Lennon–McCartney tune 'Blackbird' is about as eloquent as the Beatles have ever been in a jazz setting.

The group record takes its title from an advertisement once placed to advertise a Wallgren concert ('Wallgren: Raga, bebop and anything'). Like so many Scandinavian composers, his music is inseparable from a heritage that a jazz vocabulary has only tempered. Chorale and passacaglia forms are as prevalent here as the blues, and in company with a front-rank band the leader sets out a rich programme of nine themes, none of them alike with each other. Cancer took him in the summer of 1996, and this stands as a memorial to a rare imagination. There are other fine Wallgren recordings which await CD restoration: *Steel Bend Rock, Love Chant* and *Ballade An Der Ruhr* among them.

Per Henrik Wallin (born 1946)

PIANO

An explosive post-bop stylist, the Swede led many record dates during the '70s and early '80s but was badly injured in a 1988 accident and has since recorded only occasionally.

****** Coyote**
Dragon DRCD 320 *Wallin; Tørbjörn Hultcrantz (b); Erik Dahbäck (d).* 8/86–10/87.

*****(*) Dolphins, Dolphins, Dolphins**
Dragon DRCD 215 *Wallin; Mats Gustafsson (ss, ts, bs); Kjell Nordeson (d).* 8/91.

Wallin's extensive discography has been seriously depleted by the disappearance of vinyl. He is a fascinating pianist, taking whatever he wants from free- and post-bop piano language. A bravado delivery, involving tumultuous climaxes and moment-by-moment contrast, makes him hard to follow or even like at times, but he is surely a European original. *Coyote* documents some radio sessions by his power trio of the '80s. Massive pieces like 'The Strange Adventures Of Jesper Klint' go through lightning changes of mood, spinning through amazing pyrotechnics from the keyboard but always under precarious but particular control. Compared to some of his other groups, the bassist and drummer are much in tune with his style and help rather than hinder. A belated but splendid release.

Hospitalized after a crippling accident in 1988, Wallin astonishingly came back with seemingly none of his power depleted. The shade most closely evoked here is Thelonious Monk, since 'Nu Nu Och Då Nu Går Då Och Nu' sounds like a perversion of 'Round Midnight', and other Monkish melodies drift through the remaining tunes. But the level of interplay here – confrontational and conspiratorial in equal proportion – goes against the impression given by much of his earlier work, that Wallin is best by himself, although his long solo 'J.W.' is a wonderfully expressive tribute to a painter friend. Gustafsson is gothically powerful and jagged, Nordeson works with military intensity, and it's all splendidly recorded.

***** Blues For Allan**
Flash Music FLCD-8 *Wallin; Peter Janson (b); Leif Wennerström (d).* 4–12/98.

His second record of the '90s finds Wallin at Club Fasching with a new trio – Janson, who plays in the Aaly Trio, is a great find. 'Thelonious' is so dramatically reharmonized that Monk himself might have raised an eyebrow. For once, Wallin's playing is too relentless: the pair of blues pieces are almost teeth-grindingly tensed up. 'Ryssland' is a desolate tribute to the Russian people. 'Sweet And Lovely' is neither, although the record as a whole is a good antidote to too many perfumed piano recitals.

***** 9.9.99**
Stunt STUCD 00202 *As above.* 9/99.

As ever, Wallin picks over his Monk songbook obsessively: there are six more renditions here. When he does Bud Powell's 'Elegy', it seems disorientating, because it feels it should be a Monk credit. In the end this is no primed masterpiece but (as the title suggests) a day's work, as singular as any other day's. Wallin isn't likely to settle for making himself into repertory, but it depends how he's documented from this point onwards.

*****(*) Proklamation I & Farewell To Sweden**
hatOLOGY 563 2CD *Wallin; Peter Janson (b); Leif Wennerström, Sven-Åke Johansson (d).* 3/00–2/01.

A duo set with Johansson recorded in Wallin's apartment and a trio session at the Bimhuis in Amsterdam. The ten improvisations by the duo (really a single piece, banded on the CD) are conciliatory, rather different from the battleground which Wallin sometimes makes out of his preferred standards and jazz themes, although hints of Ellington and Monk keep breaking in. At the Bimhuis it's more like business as usual for the trio. Janson and Wennerström have grown into their roles and the group sounds like a purposeful entity even in a piece as difficult as Monk's 'Work'. They also centre what would otherwise be badly scarred versions of 'Embraceable You' and 'Answer Me My Love'. It's hard to tell if Wallin is smiling inside at this kind of creative desecration. A track at a time, it's certainly exhilarating.

*****(*) One Knife Is Enough**
Caprice CAP 21722 *Wallin (p solo).* 1/82–3/03.

Caprice have reissued Wallin's 1982 solo set under this title and added another eight tracks cut in 2003. One way to compare them is to try out the two versions of 'April In Paris'. The lick which he uses almost as a punctuation device in the earlier treatment is entirely absent, and maybe he's a little kinder on the melody, but otherwise he sounds as vehement as he was 20 years earlier. Wallin is a hard listen as a soloist: crabby, stubborn and not a great one for letting in light, he pounds his way through the compositions. Taken a couple of tracks at a time, though, the results are undeniably compelling, and when he does soften just a little – as on 'My Pearl Just Left' – a strange poignancy comes out.

George Wallington (1924–93)

PIANO

Born in Sicily, Wallington was involved in the first wave of bebop, working with Gillespie and others. Though he made a series of recordings between then and 1957, he subsequently left the music business altogether and returned for one album and a few concerts in the mid-'80s.

*****(*) The George Wallington Trios**
Original Jazz Classics OJC 1754 *Wallington; Chuck Wayne (mandola); Charles Mingus, Oscar Pettiford, Curley Russell (b); Max Roach (d).* 9/52–5/53.

More so even than Joe Albany or Dodo Marmarosa, George Wallington is the underrated master of bebop piano: his name is still best known for his composing 'Lemon Drop' and 'Godchild'. His speed is breathtaking, his melodies unspooling in long, unbroken lines, and he writes tunes which are rather more than the customary convoluted riffs on familiar chord-changes. The OJC *Trios* disc is all piano, bass and drums, and there are marvellous, flashing virtuoso pieces like the ultrafast 'Cuckoo Around The Clock', although the elegance of 'I Married An Angel' is a harbinger of Wallington's later work.

***** Live! At Café Bohemia**
Original Jazz Classics OJC 1813 *Wallington; Donald Byrd (t); Jackie McLean (as); Paul Chambers (b); Art Taylor (d).* 9/55.

***** Jazz For The Carriage Trade**
Original Jazz Classics OJC 1704 *As above, except Phil Woods (as), Teddy Kotick (b) replace McLean and Chambers.* 1/56.

*****(*) The New York Scene**
Original Jazz Classics OJC 1805 *As above, except Nick Stabulas (d) replaces Taylor.* 3/57.

Some of these are merely serviceable hard-bop entries, prosaic stuff after the fine fierceness of the earlier records; but some of the music takes exception. Wallington's playing seemed to turn inwards and his improvisations are at an altogether cooler temperature. Byrd muddles through the first two dates and is approaching his faceless self on the later one, yet this anonymity throws some of Wallington's own contributions into sharper relief – almost like Freddie Hubbard on some of the more outré Blue Notes of the next decade. Woods hits every note he needs to with his usual accuracy on his appearances; McLean is his customary tart mid-'50s self on the earliest date. *Café Bohemia* and *Carriage Trade* are tough and darting but finally straight-ahead in their demeanour; it's *The New York Scene* that looks a little further out, thanks to Wallington's material and his own solos, which have begun to skin bebop language back to something more elemental. A shame that he chose at this point to quit jazz altogether.

***** The Pleasure Of A Jazz Inspiration**
VSOP 84 *Wallington (p solo).* 8/85.

Tempted back into the studios, Wallington created this 'jazz tone poem' in eight parts. Bebop figures drift through some of the themes: 'Writing In The Sand' is very like Powell's 'Parisian Thoroughfare'. But the slower pieces are unusually dark, with the harmonies of 'Memory Of The Heart' almost impenetrably dense, and there's a hint of sourness that goes with the pleasure. Wallington sounds rusty here and there, and much of the old exhilaration has dissipated, but it's an interesting if eccentric postscript to a frustrating career.

Bob Wallis (1934–91)

TRUMPET, VOCAL

A Yorkshireman, Wallis moved to London and played with Acker Bilk before forming his own Storyville Jazzmen, who were popular during the trad boom. Latterly made a new career in Switzerland.

****(*) The Pye Jazz Anthology**
Castle CMDDD 484 2CD *Wallis; Avo Avison (tb); Al Gay (cl, ts, ss); Pete Gresham (p); Hugh Rainey (bj); Brian Kirby (b); Ken Buckner (d).* 60–63.

***** Live In Leipzig 1976**
Dine-A-Mite DJKCD-002 2CD *Wallis; Mike Sherbourne (tb); Andre Beeson (cl, as); Ian Armit (p); Ken Ames (g, bj); Bernie Cash (b); George Collier (d).* 9/76.

Wallis was a bit of a second-division leader in the trad years, at least next to the Three B's, but he did manage a couple of hits and worked steadily enough. The Storyville Jazzmen made several records for Pye, and the Castle set collects most of the tracks. Bob's singing gets a bit wearisome and the studio tracks never really capture the pandemonious feel the band could usually generate live, but it's a fair souvenir of their work.

The Leipzig live set was not recorded at a very propitious period for British trad, but the music is surprisingly better than expected. The faster pieces go off at a scatterbrained pace yet everyone manages to keep up, even if Ian Armit has to contend with a modest piano. Too many vocals again, but Wallis fans will understand.

Jack Walrath (born 1946)

TRUMPET, FLUGELHORN, VOCAL

Montana-born, Walrath worked in Charles Mingus's group during the '70s, having attended Berklee and worked in a variety of R&B units. Strongly influenced by bebop, he has a clear-edged and intense sound and great humour, which comes across on many of his recordings.

*****(*) In Europe**
Steeplechase SCCD 31172 *Walrath; Glenn Ferris (tb); Michael Cochran (p); Anthony Cox (b); Jimmy Madison (d).* 7/82.

Walrath is a brassy, upfront kind of trumpet-man and has been a stalwart in some strong repertory bands. As a leader, he's never had tremendous impact on record. The brass front line on the Steeplechase is ringingly present, and Ferris's old-fashioned tone is a huge asset on 'Duesin' In Dusseldorf' and 'At Home In Rome', two of four Walrath originals on a relatively short-measured release that will leave most purchasers calling for more. Cox and Madison make an interesting partnership, not always absolutely squarely on the metre, but lateral enough to keep a step ahead of a notably capricious leader.

***** Hipgnosis**
TCB 01062 *Walrath; David Fiuczynski (g); Hill Green (b); Cecil Brooks III (d); Dean Bowman (v).* 3/95.

****** Solidarity**
ACT 9241 *Walrath; Ralph Reichert (sax); Buggy Braune (p); Christian Havel (g, v); Andreas Henze (b); Joris Dudli (d).* 8/95.

Walrath's long-standing passion for horror films is reflected in the name of his working band, The Masters of Suspense. They are featured on *Hipgnosis*, an unusual set in that it puts considerable emphasis on lyrics and vocal performance. These suggest that Walrath remains under the influence of the great Charles Mingus, at whose former home he wrote the piece 'Mingus Piano'. The 'Sweet Hip Gnosis' suite which it brings to an end is much involved with Walrath's other fascination in esoteric philosophy, a rich and complex group of distantly related pieces that cohere more and more securely each time they are heard. The Mingus association is cemented by 'Eclipse' but is omnipresent, detectable even on a Walrath original like 'Blues Sinistra'.

Solidarity is the closest of the surviving records to the Muses, a blues-soaked and – as Jack points out – very American-sounding recording that could again almost be a Mingus offshoot. Reichert's father owns the Hamburg club where the recording was made; it's an atmospheric place and a strong, smouldering set. The two-part 'Hamburg Concerto' and the title-track bespeak anew Walrath's ability to give long forms the immediacy and the visceral punch of a simple blues, while

'Hot-Dog For Lunch', 'Political Suicide' and 'Psychotic Indifference' underline his more capricious and satirical side. Reichert claims joint honours, and his father's production yields up a sound which favours the horns over the rest of the group – not overwhelmingly so, but with a definite edge. Good stuff.

*****(*) Journey, Man!**

Evidence 22150 *Walrath; Bobby Watson (as); Craig Handy (ss, ts); Kenny Drew Jr (p); Ray Drummond (b); Victor Lewis (d).* 11/95.

Jack called this band Hard Corps and used it to mark a return to pretty orthodox hard bop. Whether this was out of frustration or a genuine desire to explore that slightly tired idiom is hard to determine, but the playing on *Journey, Man!* – from the horns in particular – suggests an exuberant embrace of the old style. 'Butt! (Tails From The Backside)' veers close to parody, but 'Pete's Steps', derived from Coltrane's 'Giant Steps', is both generic and spot on. 'Bouncin' With Ballholzka' flirts with elements of freedom, while 'When Love Has Gone (It Comes Out Like This)' is an exquisite ballad, pitched in a middle register and showing a side of Walrath's playing that is all too rarely highlighted.

*****(*) Get Hit In Your Soul**

ACT 9246 2 *Walrath; Bill Bickford (g); Miles Griffith (v); WDR Big Band.* 96–98.

A joyous celebration of the music and the spirit of Charles Mingus, which of course Walrath experienced at first hand. Miles Griffith serves to remind us that Mingus's recitations and songs were never an incidental aspect of what he was about but were absolutely central to it, and 'Oh Lord, Don't Let Them Drop That Atomic Bomb On Me' is the proof: passionate, wry and intense. However, the real surprises on the album are Jack's compositions. The opening 'Motley As An Amorphous Hangdown' is brassy and roiling, while his arrangement of the famous Egyptian 'Hymn To Aten' alongside Psalm CIV touches new areas of expression for the trumpeter.

Danny Walsh

ALTO AND TENOR SAXOPHONE

Bright newcomer who has made an impact with vibist Joe Locke, now striking out on his own.

***** D's Mood**

Steeplechase SCCD 31428 *Walsh; Joey Calderazzo (p); Dave Stryker (g); Jay Anderson (b); Billy Drummond (d).* 00.

Walsh is relatively unusual in doubling alto and tenor saxophones. He doesn't have a particularly distinctive voice on either, but the keener, more plangent sound of the alto suits him better, in this setting at least. He can be forgiven 'Danny Boy', which he's probably been playing since the beginning of his career, and he makes good on his early promise with fine readings of 'Shiny Stockings' and a long 'You Stepped Out Of A Dream'. The originals aren't quite there yet, but we hope for good things from a young man working a crowded scene.

Priska Walss (born 1964)

TROMBONE, ALPHORN

A delightful new voice, and since 1991 half of Duo Frappant with college friend Gabriela Friedli.

****** Intervista**

Intakt CD 087 *Walss; Gabriela Friedli (p, org).* 00–02.

This is as fresh and inviting a disc as any to appear on the European scene in recent years. Walss's trombone technique has little to do with the deconstructions of players like George Lewis and Vinko Globokar. Instead, she favours a bright, vocal tone, sometimes almost in tailgating style, which contrasts sharply with the mournful drones of the alphorn on tracks like 'Furggelti' and 'Lisblueme', the latter a wonderful duet between thundercloud and pianistic waterdrops. On 'Clara', Priska uses her mute to create a bluesy wah-wah in the middle distance over Friedli's meditative one-note 'accompaniment' (which actually sits well forward of the horn); she then has her moment for a short Daffy Duck monologue before Friedli comes back in canon to bring the piece to an unexpectedly conventional but satisfying end. Organ is used sparingly, as in the wheezy pulse running through 'Fil Bleu', and throughout the attention falls squarely on the horn player who is going to be one of the most interesting new voices of coming years. Find her also on Urs Voerkel's Intakt work, but catch up with this one without delay.

Cedar Walton (born 1934)

PIANO

Dallas-born Walton has impressive credentials. After a stint in the military, he worked with Kenny Dorham and J. J. Johnson before joining the Jazz Messengers (and, unusually, rejoined the outfit a few years later). He also served a tour as house pianist for the Prestige label. He has a confident feel for the blues but favours a kind of angular lyricism.

*****(*) Cedar!**

Original Jazz Classics OJCCD 462 *Walton; Kenny Dorham (t); Junior Cook (ts); Leroy Vinnegar (b); Billy Higgins (d).* 7/67.

*****(*) Soul Cycle**

Original Jazz Classics OJCCD 847-2 *Walton; James Moody (ts, f); Rudy Stevenson (bs); Reggie Workman (b); Albert 'Tootie' Heath (d).* 68.

*****(*) Cedar Walton Plays Cedar Walton**

Original Jazz Classics OJC 6002 *As Cedar!, except add Blue Mitchell (t), Clifford Jordan (ts), Bob Cranshaw, Richard Davis (b), Jack DeJohnette, Mickey Roker (d).* 7/67–1/69.

***** Spectrum**

Prestige PRCD 24145-2 *As above.* 7/67–1/69.

Walton has only slowly been recognized as a significant jazz composer. Tunes like 'Bolivia', 'Ojos De Rojo', 'Maestro' and 'Ugetsu' rival McCoy Tyner's work for sophisticated inventiveness. During the '70s Walton was anchoring Clifford Jordan's Magic Triangle band. They seem to have struck up an immediate rapport on these earlier sessions, made for Prestige, for which label Cedar was house pianist for a time. *Plays* contains a useful sample of the earlier quartet and quintet stuff with

Dorham and Cook, but the compilation misses a fine trio, 'My Ship'. Paired with the characteristically blunt Mitchell, Jordan takes the direct route to goal, with no sign of his irritating tendency to mark time in mid-solo. 'Higgins Holler' and 'Jake's Milkshakes' also feature sterling work by DeJohnette, who still sounds rather eager to please. There's an excellent trio performance of Walton's 'Fantasy In D', related to 'Ugetsu', with Roker and Cranshaw. Though there's good stuff on OJC 462, the compilation has to be a better bet. By and large *Spectrum* runs a few variants on the same sessions and the same material and, heard afresh, it has much to recommend it; but the reappearance of *Soul Cycle*, with Moody and Stevenson, is the real find, a brisk, expressive session which is paced just about perfectly and contains one gem of a performance in 'My Cherie Amour'.

*****(*) First Set**

Steeplechase SCCD 31085 *Walton; Bob Berg (ts); Sam Jones (b); Billy Higgins (d).* 1 & 10/77.

*****(*) Second Set**

Steeplechase SCCD 31113 *As above.* 1 & 10/77.

***** Third Set**

Steeplechase SCCD 31179 *As above.* 1 & 10/77.

This was a vintage period for Walton, who was beginning to shake off a tendency to blend with his surroundings. This is the band that went out as Eastern Rebellion, documented on Timeless and elsewhere, though these discs seem to be credited to Walton alone. His European gigs were models of tough contemporary bop and, though the incidence of covers is higher than one might expect, given the strength of his writing, the standard of performance is consistently high, and for once Steeplechase's exhaustive documentation seems justified. Berg, who replaced George Coleman in the group, turns in an excellent performance of Coltrane's 'Blue Train' on *Second Set*, avoiding the usual pastiche of Trane's lonesome solo and turning the theme into something altogether tougher and more locomotive. There are several good Monk performances, but the opening 'Off Minor' on *First Set* is the most dynamic. There certainly wasn't enough strong material for three discs, and these sessions suggest an obvious occasion for editing and repackaging.

***** Bluesville Time**

Criss Cross Criss 1017 *Walton; Dale Barlow (ts); David Williams (b); Billy Higgins (d).* 4/85.

Williams and Higgins were the ground floor of Walton's fine '80s groups. The drummer's ability to sustain and develop a pattern became increasingly important to the pianist as he simplified and reduced his delivery. Barlow compares very favourably with the inventive Bob Berg, who had played for a time in Walton's other group, Eastern Rebellion (see above). The material is excellent – 'Naima' and 'I Remember Clifford' alongside distinctive originals like 'Rubber Man' and 'Ojos De Rojo' – but the playing, Higgins apart, isn't quite crisp enough.

*****(*) The Trio: Volume 1**

Red 123192 *Walton; David Williams (b); Billy Higgins (d).* 3/85.

***** The Trio: Volume 2**

Red 123193 *As above.* 3/85.

***** The Trio: Volume 3**

Red 123194 *As above.* 3/85.

Recorded live in Bologna, these represent a compelling mixture of originals ('Ojos De Rojo', 'Jacob's Ladder', 'Holy Land'), standards ('Lover Man', 'Every Time We Say Goodbye') and challenging repertoire pieces (Ellington's 'Satin Doll', Fred Lacey's 'Theme For Ernie', S. R. Kyner's 'Bluesville'). Walton's brilliant phrasing and inbuilt harmonic awareness keep thematic material in view at all times, and his solos and accompaniments are always entirely logical and consistently developed. About Higgins there is very little more to add but that he has inherited and fully deserved the mantle of Elvin Jones. Williams offers firm, unobtrusive support but isn't a very exciting soloist.

****** Manhattan Afternoon**

Criss Cross 1082 *Walton; David Williams (b); Billy Higgins (d).* 12/92.

*****(*) Cedar's Blues**

Red Records RR 123179 2 *As above, except add Curtis Fuller (tb), Bob Berg (ts).* 93.

***** Off Minor**

Red Records RR 123242 2 *Walton; David Williams (b).* 93.

Manhattan Afternoon is a tremendous record. With just two originals tucked away in the middle of the set, Walton sticks to a programme of fairly routine standards and repertoire pieces – Monk's 'I Mean You' isn't his most played piece, though – and dispatches them all with consummate skill. His very first solo, on 'There Is No Greater Love', is replete with unexpected angles, and the soft harmonic displacements recur later on John Lewis's 'Afternoon In Paris'. Williams and Higgins fit the music like a glove. Strongly recommended.

The quintet record was recorded live in Bologna. It showcases four Walton themes, including a brief but powerful take of 'Ugetsu' and an unexpectedly romping 'Fiesta Espanola'. The only standard of the session is 'Over The Rainbow', executed without a shred of sentimentality. Berg is on fine form, but it's Fuller, so often the bridesmaid, who captures the attention, even when slightly off-mic.

The duos with Williams are strongly tinged with Monk's angular harmonics. The bass-player is a rich source of harmonic ideas as well as being a strong, rhythmic anchor. A highly effective record, though probably only of interest to converts.

****** The Composer**

Astor Place TCD 4001 *Walton; Roy Hargrove (t); Vincent Herring (as); Ralph Moore (ts, ss); Christian McBride (b); Victor Lewis (d).* 1/96.

Not since *Cedar Plays Cedar* has there been such a full-blooded attempt to establish Walton's credentials as a writer, and yet what one remembers from this crisply recorded set isn't the writing at all but some fantastic playing from a band that sounds as if it works together every week. 'Hindsight' and 'Underground Memoirs' are both crafted and well scaffolded, but it's the horns that make it, and often Walton lies back and comps while the youngsters flutter about in the foreground. It's well worth concentrating on his line for a moment or two, doing what he does and filtering out any extraneous signal in favour of a direct line to the chords.

****** Roots**

Astor Place TCD 4010 *Walton; Terence Blanchard (t); Scott Whitfield (tb); Don Sickler (t, flhn); Bobby Porcelli (as);*

Joshua Redman (ts); Willie Williams (ss, ts); Gary Smulyan (bs); Ron Carter (b); Lewis Nash (d); Ray Mantilla (perc). 1/97.

As on the previous Astor Place set, Walton sticks to original material, confident now that his pianism is not just a technical resource but the basis of a broad musical vision. Unlike the previous album, though, this is a retrospective of compositions that go back many years. 'Mode For Joe', 'Ojas De Rojo' (which features Josh Redman in great form), and 'Fantasy In D' (which includes one of three fine contributions from Whitfield) are all well known from previous records, but here they have a fresh and incisive quality that makes them sound new-minted. The larger ensemble is of the highest quality, building on the strengths of a magnificent trio. Carter is allowed to come forward strongly in the mix and Nash, kept off to the side, is less intrusive than on some of his recorded appearances. Walton's arrangements are sure-footed and confidently shaped and, even when fully voiced, sound as stark and raw-boned as any blues. A fine album from a master composer.

***(*) The Promise Land

High Note HCD 7081 *Walton; Vincent Herring (as, f); David Williams (b); Kenny Washington (d).* 3/01.

The missing 'D' off the 'Promise' is correct as listed, odd though that may appear, and otherwise this is a sure-footed set from a veteran leader. The quartet has been a stable working band for Walton for some time, so Herring's involvement with the material has a completeness which takes the music a notch above the usual horn-meets-rhythm section feel of a pickup date. Cedar's writing has the casual elegance of someone who's grown into his composing and knows what he wants from it, and the playing has a dash of wit to go with the expected fluency and strength.

*** Latin Tinge

High Note HCD 7099 *Walton; Cucho Martinez (b); Ray Mantilla (perc).* 6/02.

Cedar went back to his own book for three of the Latinate pieces here, and filled in the gaps with the likes of 'Tres Palabras' and 'Besame Mucho'. It's a light, airy record, not much more than a repertory exercise, but enacted with good grace.

David S. Ware (born 1949)

TENOR SAXOPHONE, SAXELLO, STRITCH

Studied in Boston but settled in New York and played with Cecil Taylor in the '70s. Drove taxis in the '80s before a comeback with European recordings which over the next decade led to something like star status in the American avant-garde, culminating in a record deal with Columbia.

**(*) Surrendered

Columbia 63816 *Ware; Matthew Shipp (p); William Parker (d); Guillermo E. Brown (d).* 99.

Ware grew up in New Jersey, attended Berklee for a couple of years at the end of the '60s and then formed his own group, Apogee, before moving to New York City. He has worked extensively with drummer Andrew Cyrille and with Cyrille's mentor, Cecil Taylor. Other leaders have included trumpeter Raphe Malik and pianist Barry Harris. Since the late '80s, though, Ware has recorded a good many albums under his own name, all of them in a fierce, modernist style that makes much use of overblowing and multiphonics. Though he once carried alto and baritone as well as his tenor, he seems to have abandoned the big horn. Albert Ayler is only the most obvious source for the sound; Pharoah Sanders is unmistakably another, and Ware seems to have borrowed more than the alto-related stritch from Roland Kirk. Most of his '80s and '90s work has abruptly been deleted.

Perhaps at the behest of the label, Ware stays much more strictly within the changes on this, his final recording for Columbia. Here and there he betrays a Charles Lloyd influence that has surfaced in the past, though rarely as evidently as now. It's by no means an unwelcome manifestation, but what is disturbing about this set is how derivative David sounds for a man turning 50.

Beaver Harris's 'African Drums' is in double waltz time, but seems awkwardly pitched throughout. The originals are mostly free in structure but based on identifiable chords. Lloyd's 'Sweet Georgia Bright' and 'Glorified Calypso' coax some fine playing out of the leader and some great exchances with Shipp but this is not the happiest item in Ware's discography, and one strongly senses that he needs new challenges and a more sympathetic working environment.

**(*) Live In The Netherlands

Splasch 43297 *Ware (ts solo).* 00.

The first plus of this one is that it doesn't outstay its welcome; just 40 minutes of concentrated improvisation. The first drawback is that the performances have a curious quality of inwardness and abstraction, almost as if we were listening to David in rehearsal rather than communicating to a live audience. Generically titled as '4th, 5th, 6th and 7th Dimensional', they draw on blues ideas, John Coltrane phrases and some of Albert Ayler's and Charles Gayle's extreme saxophone dynamics that make for challenging listening. Not, in our view, a priority item, but one that is certainly full of interest for students of improvisation and of the tenor saxophone.

***(*) Corridors & Parallels

Aum Fidelity 19 *Ware; Matthew Shipp (org, syn); William Parker (b); Guillermo E. Brown (d).* 2/01.

In sharp contrast to the disappointing *Surrendered*, this explores new sonic territory. The most obvious outward change is Shipp's unfamiliar use of electronic keyboards to create great swirls and whorls of sound-colour, very different even from his usual polytonal accompaniment. Driven along by Brown and the redoubtable Parker, the band sounds as if it might have been hanging out in some of New York's trendier downtown clubs before going into the studio.

Many of the pieces are short, some as little as half a minute, and the impression is of an album built up in mosaic, brightly coloured fragments of musical information gradually cohering into something much larger. Outstanding among the new writing is 'Straight Track', the moment on the record when you recognize that David is involved in something new; but equally impressive are the dance-like 'Superimposed' and the eulogy, 'Mother, May You Rest In Bliss', which is clearly a very personal and deeply felt theme. The sound-balance is awkward in places, especially when the keyboard textures are densest, but the overall effect is very strong indeed.

****** The Freedom Suite**

Aum Fidelity 23 *Ware; Matthew Shipp (p); William Parker (b); Guillermo E. Brown (d).* 7/02.

*****(*) Threads**

Thirsty Ear THI 57137 2 *As above, except add Daniel Bernard Roumain (vn); Mat Maneri (vla).* 10/03.

There have been reworkings of John Coltrane's *A Love Supreme* and Eric Dolphy's Five Spot recordings with Booker Little, so why not a re-exploration of Sonny Rollins's barely pioneered *Freedom Suite*? Recorded in 1958, Rollins's trio masterpiece edged into areas of harmonic and rhythmic freedom that make it one of the most important records of its era and also one of the least securely understood. Ware's decision to add Matthew Shipp was a wise one. The pianist probes the implications of the line much more quickly than a trio without harmony instrument would have done, though it has to be said that Parker is working a quantum speed in every passage, finding overtones and rhythmic cells that nobody else could have anticipated.

Thematically, the album could hardly be better timed. As a cultural and political concept, freedom has never been more ambiguous. What Ware seems to be saying is that it is a quality found within rather than without. At every stage, this music turns in on itself as completely as Rollins's original turned outward. That is not to say that it is less communicative, merely that it communes at a different level.

The string ensemble record works some further variations on the same ideas, except that Shipp's switch to synthesizer and the addition of Roumain and Maneri extend the harmonic and timbral potential of the group a hundredfold. Ware seems surprisingly contained here, and there are few flights on the saxophone. For the most part, he seems content to direct a powerful ensemble through some intricate passage work. 'Sufic Passages' is the key piece, an exciting groove that gets everybody on board and whirls away to who knows where. As with the earlier record, Brown's drumming is a key element: solid but relaxed, powerful but still capable of great subtlety.

Wilbur Ware (1923–79)

DOUBLE BASS

Self-taught, he played in swing and bop groups in the '40s, and with hard-boppers in the '50s, most famously with Thelonious Monk (1957–8). He influenced a school of bassists exemplified by Charlie Haden. Records as leader are very few in number.

*****(*) The Chicago Sound**

Original Jazz Classics OJC 1737 *Ware; John Jenkins (as); Johnny Griffin (ts); Junior Mance (p); Wilbur Campbell, Frank Dunlop (d).* 10–11/57.

Though much of what Ware did stemmed directly from Jimmy Blanton's 'Jack The Bear', he developed into a highly individual performer whose unmistakable sound lives on in the low-register work of contemporary bassists like Charlie Haden. Ware's technique has been questioned but seems to have been a conscious development, a way of hearing the chord rather than a way of skirting his own supposed shortcomings. He could solo at speed, shifting the time-signature from bar to bar while retaining an absolutely reliable pulse. Significantly, one of his most important employers was Thelonious Monk, who valued displacements of that sort within an essentially four-square rhythm and traditional (but not European-traditional) tonality; the bassist also contributed substantially to one of Sonny Rollins's finest recordings. He grew up in the sanctified church and there is a gospelly quality to 'Mamma-Daddy', a relatively rare original, on *The Chicago Sound*. The only other Ware composition on the record, '31st And State', might have come from Johnny Griffin's head; the saxophonist roars in over the beat and entirely swamps Jenkins, whose main contribution to the session is a composition credit on two good tracks.

Though the Ware discography is huge (with numerous credits for Riverside in the '50s), his solo technique is at its most developed on his own record. 'Lullaby Of The Leaves' is almost entirely for bass, and there are magnificent solos on 'Body And Soul' (where he sounds *huge*) and 'The Man I Love'. One wonders if a couple of alternative takes mightn't have been included on the CD. Ware's impact was enormous, and one record (albeit a fine one) seems a poor trawl.

Tim Warfield

TENOR SAXOPHONE

Like other Criss Cross artists, Warfield has managed to bring a classic hard-bop style up to date. He has a full, emphatic tone which oscillates between terse R&B and a more loquacious version of Wayne Shorter's gnomic approach.

***** A Cool Blue**

Criss Cross 1102 *Warfield; Terell Stafford (t); Cyrus Chestnut (p); Tarus Mateen (b); Clarence Penn (d).* 12/94.

*****(*) A Whisper In The Night**

Criss Cross 1122 *As above, except add Stefon Harris (vib).* 12/95.

***** Gentle Warrior**

Criss Cross 1149 *As above, except omit Harris; add Nicholas Payton (t).* 12/97.

***** Jazz Is ...**

Criss Cross 1227 *Warfield; Nicholas Payton (t); Cyrus Chestnut (p); Stefon Harris (vib); Tarus Mateen (b); Clarence Penn (d).* 1/01.

Warfield's four Criss Cross records are as solidly accomplished as anything on the label but are also rather lacking in personality. If the label is the '90s equivalent of Blue Note – and we have argued that point often enough – these records partake of some of the classic imprint's incidental shortcomings: formulaic repetition, generic writing, and over-reliance on a narrowly collegiate personnel.

Stafford always sounds like a man who wishes he were in charge of things and his contributions have an impatient quality that is briefly engaging on *A Cool Blue*, less effective subsequently. The second record is by some way the shortest and most concentrated of the four, and one feels that quality control has won out. The two standards – 'Speak Low' and 'Bye Bye Blackbird' – give the set a balance that isn't reflected elsewhere, but it also benefits from two of Warfield's best compositions, 'Tin Soldier' and 'I've Never Been Blue Before', which are definitive of his approach.

While we like *Gentle Warrior* and admire its softer and more subtly inflected approach, it cries out for an reprise of Harris's wonderful vibes-playing, and the alternation of trumpet-players is less than effective, largely because Payton and Stafford are too similar in approach. After something of a gap, he's returned with *Jazz Is* ... The unanswered question hangs over the music, too. It feels like a very written record: Payton and Harris play well, but they're obliged to work through difficult and rather charmless pieces which Warfield has some trouble in communicating to the unconvinced listener. It's much more about Warfield the composer than the improviser, although there is still some powerful stuff from what is, after all, an impressive line-up.

Washboard Rhythm Kings

GROUP

Although the name suggests some early rural blues outfit, they were actually a New York-based group who recorded many sessions in the city during the early '30s, styling themselves in the manner of early small-band swing.

***** Washboard Rhythm Kings Vol. 1**
Collectors Classics COCD-17 *Dave Page (t); Ben Smith (as); Jimmy Shine (as, v); Carl Wade (ts); Eddie Miles (p, v); Steve Washington (bj, g); Teddy Bunn (g); Jimmy Spencer (wbd); Jake Fenderson, The Melody Four (v).* 4/31–3/32.

***** Washboard Rhythm Kings Vol. 2**
Collectors Classics COCD-18 *As above, except add Taft Jordan (t), Wilbur Daniels (bj), Leo Watson, George 'Ghost' Howell (b, v), H Smith (wbd).* 32.

***** Washboard Rhythm Kings Vol. 3**
Collectors Classics COCD-19 *As above, except add Valaida Snow (t), John 'Shorty' Haughton (tb), Jerome Carrington (as), Bella Benson, Lavada Carter (v).* 10/32–8/33.

There are plenty of unidentified names to add to the various personnel listed above, which gives some idea of how little is known about this group, which recorded around New York for a period of a couple of years at the beginning of the '30s. Smith, Wade and Miles seem to have been the mainstays of the band, which otherwise fluctuated between a quartet and a group running to ten pieces. While a washboard may have been appropriate for the earlier tracks, which sounded about as down-home as a band working in New Jersey could be, by the time of the final session in August 1933 it was anachronistic for a group that was playing quite a tough and respectable small-group swing. The material is a peculiar blend of blues, jazz themes and pop tunes: 'Please Tell Me' (*Vol. 1*), for instance, is a mixture of Ellington's 'Stevedore Stomp' and Blind Blake's 'Diddy Wah Diddy'. The earlier stuff is attractively rough and unpretentious, the later tracks more ambitious; but all of it makes up a valuable backwater in the recording of jazz at the end of the first golden age. John R. T. Davies has done the transfers on all three discs and they are from mainly superb originals.

Dinah Washington (1924–63)

VOCAL

Born Ruth Lee Jones in Tuscaloosa, Alabama, Washington joined Lionel Hampton in 1943, then went solo as an R&B artist, finally aspiring to a grand torch singer role in the '50s, making many records for Emarcy, Mercury and Roulette. She finally referred to herself as 'The Queen', and her gospel-and-blues methodology undeniably influenced a generation of soul singers who followed her. Married seven, eight or nine times, she died from an accidental pill overdose.

***** Mellow Mama**
Delmark DD 451 *Washington; Karl George (t); Jewell Grant (as); Lucky Thompson (ts); Milt Jackson (vib); Wilbert Baranco (p); Charles Mingus (b); Lee Young (d).* 12/45.

Whether or not she counts as a 'jazz singer', Washington frequently appeared in the company of the finest jazz musicians and, while she was no improviser and stood slightly apart from such contemporaries as Fitzgerald or Vaughan, she could drill through blues and ballads with a huge, sometimes slightly terrifying delivery. Her start came with the Lionel Hampton band, and after leaving him she made these dozen tracks for Apollo Records in the company of a band organized by Lucky Thompson. While Washington herself sounds comparatively raw and unformed, the jump-blues material doesn't demand a great range, and she swings through the likes of 'My Voot Is Really Vout' as well as the more traditional 'Beggin' Mama Blues'. Thompson's team sound as if they're having fun, and the remastering is quite clear.

***** Complete 1943–1951 Mercury Master Takes**
Jazz Factory JFCD 22841 4CD *Washington; groups and orchestras led by Gus Chappell, Tab Smith, Gerald Wilson, Chubby Jackson, Dave Young, Rudy Martin, Teddy Brannon, Lionel Hampton, Cootie Williams, Mitch Miller, Teddy Stewart, Jimmy Carroll, Walter Buchanan, Nook Shrier and Ike Carpenter; The Ravens (v).* 12/43–10/51.

In the absence of any issue of this material by the Verve Group, this Spanish release is the only option. Washington was given some dreary material and a lot of 'jive' pieces of the order of 'Shuckin' And Jivin'', and the accompanying groups range from awful to hot to sweet. Only a real fanatic will want all this music, but the great voice never flags.

***** Queen Of The Juke Box 'Live' 1948–1955**
Baldwin Street BJH-310 *Washington; Wynton Kelly, Junior Mance (p); Percy Heath, Keter Betts (b); Art Blakey, Al Jones, Ed Shaughnessy, Jimmy Cobb (d); Dizzy Gillespie Orchestra; Paul Williams's Hucklebuckers (v).* 10/48–7/55.

Not quite as good as the later Baldwin Street airshot collection (see below), but this is still a must-have discovery if you're a Dinah admirer. Two songs from the Royal Roost with a woozy-sounding Dizzy Gillespie band, then four Birdland dates with Wynton Kelly. She tells Symphony Sid to 'take your teeth out' and fends off requests for 'Tennessee Waltz' ('I didn't bring my ukelele'). Some of the songs are forgettable, but she does a terrific 'Cold Cold Heart'. Two songs from a soundtrack and a Basin Street session from 1955 fill out the disc. Sound is about average for this kind of material.

***** The Queen Sings**
Proper PROPERBOX 43 4CD *Washington; various accompaniments, largely as discs listed above.* 12/43–10/51.

If this is the Washington music you want, Proper's four-disc box makes a tempting bargain. The nasty-gal R&B stylings finally get a bit wearisome across 109 tracks, but that was her style in that period.

★★★(★) After Hours With Miss D

Verve 605622 *Washington; Clark Terry (t); Gus Chappell (tb); Rick Henderson (as); Eddie Chamblee, Eddie 'Lockjaw' Davis, Paul Quinichette (ts); Clarence 'Sleepy' Anderson, Junior Mance (p); Jackie Davis (org); unknown (g); Keter Betts (b); Ed Thigpen (d); Candido Camero (perc).* 6/53–6/54.

A neglected record, overdue for reissue in this form, which vies with the next disc for a place as the essential Washington disc for the jazz library. 'Blue Skies' (here in two extended versions) and 'Bye Bye Blues' are fast swingers which Dinah smokes through, and crisp, jukeboxy singles such as 'Pennies From Heaven' offer her style in smaller but no less well-cooked portions. Terry and Jaws help out in the blowing department and one stand-out is Junior Mance, who really plays hard. A welcome revival.

★★★(★) Dinah Jams

Emarcy 814639-2 *Washington; Clifford Brown, Clark Terry, Maynard Ferguson (t); Herb Geller (as); Harold Land (ts); Junior Mance, Richie Powell (p); Keter Betts, George Morrow (b); Max Roach (d).* 8/54.

Washington's major 'jazz' record is fine, but not as fine as the closely contemporary Sarah Vaughan record with a similar backing group, and therein lies a tale about Washington's abilities. She claimed she could sing anything – which was probably true – but her big, bluesy voice is no more comfortable in this stratum of Tin Pan Alley than was Joe Turner's. Still, the long and luxuriant jams on 'You Go To My Head' and 'Lover Come Back To Me' are rather wonderful in their way, and there is always Clifford Brown to listen to.

★★★(★) For Those In Love

Emarcy 514073-2 *Washington; Clark Terry (t); Jimmy Cleveland (tb); Paul Quinichette (ts); Cecil Payne (bs); Wynton Kelly (p); Barry Galbraith (g); Keter Betts (b); Jimmy Cobb (d).* 55.

★★★ Dinah!

Emarcy 842139-2 *Washington; Hal Mooney Orchestra.* 55.

★★★(★) The Swingin' Miss D

Verve 558074-2 *Washington; Quincy Jones Orchestra.* 55.

★★★ In The Land Of Hi-Fi

Emarcy 826453-2 *Washington; Hal Mooney Orchestra.* 4/56.

★★★ The Fats Waller Songbook

Emarcy 818930-2 *Washington; Ernie Royal, Johnny Coles, Joe Newman, Clark Terry (t); Melba Liston, Julian Priester, Rod Levitt (tb); Eddie Chamblee, Jerome Richardson, Benny Golson, Frank Wess, Sahib Shihab (reeds); Jack Wilson (p); Freddie Green (g); Richard Evans (b); Charli Persip (d).* 10/57.

★★★ Sings Bessie Smith

Verve 538635-2 *Washington; Blue Mitchell, Fip Ricard, Clark Terry (t); Melba Liston, Quentin Jackson, Julian Priester (tb); Eddie Chamblee, Harold Ousley (ts); Charles Davis, McKinley Easton, Sahib Shihab (bs); Wynton Kelly, James Craig, Jack Easton (p); Paul West, Robert Lee Wilson (b); Max Roach, James Slaughter (d).* 12/57–7/58.

★★★ What A Diff'rence A Day Makes!

Verve 543300-2 *Washington; studio orchestra, including Jerome Richardson (reeds), Charles Davis (bs), Joe Zawinul (p), Milt Hinton (b), Panama Francis (d).* 59.

★★★ Unforgettable

Mercury 510602-2 *Washington; studio orchestra.* 59–1/61.

★★★(★) Verve Jazz Masters: Dinah Washington

Verve 518200-2 *As above Emarcy discs, plus Quincy Jones Orchestra.* 55–61.

★★★ Verve Jazz Masters: Sings Standards

Verve 522055-2 *As above.* 52–58.

★★★ 'Round Midnight: Dinah Washington

Verve 510087 *As above, except add Nook Shrier Orchestra, Eddie Chamblee Orchestra, Tab Smith Orchestra, Jimmy Cobb Orchestra.* 10/46–12/61.

★★★ Ultimate Divas: Dinah Washington

Verve 539053-2 *As above.* 52–61.

★★★★ The Dinah Washington Story

Mercury 514841-2 2CD *As above discs.* 43–59.

Washington's studio albums for Emarcy are a good if fairly interchangeable lot: the quality of the backing doesn't much affect the calibre of her singing, and a frowsy studio orchestra is as likely to generate a great vocal as a smoking jazz ensemble. *For Those In Love* is a stand-out from this pack, since the accompaniment is as classy as that on the *Dinah Jams* session, and at least one track – a perfectly realized 'I Could Write A Book' – is a stone classic. The new edition of *What A Diff'rence A Day Makes!* sounds particularly glowing, in audio terms, but the usual problems with Washington's albums apply: a fine performance of 'I Thought About You' is marred by the cooing backing vocals, and Belford Hendricks's arrangements are little more than feebly functional. Fewer problems with *The Swingin' Miss D*, since Jones uses a crack jazz orchestra, and though Dinah doesn't seem to be any more excited by them than by any of her other accompanists, it's a record full of classy, genuine music-making. *Sings Bessie Smith*, which couples a studio date with an Eddie Chamblee orchestra and three live tracks from a Newport session, is something of a curio. It's never as good as the similarly directed session by Lavern Baker for Atlantic, and as ever Washington seems ambiguous about her material: as if singing blues is beneath her, she almost camps it up at times. But there are some dark, truthful moments too.

The Dinah Washington Story still sweeps the board as a first choice from this area: a 40-track double set that creams off all the most interesting songs from the period, with a few from her earliest days to round out the picture. The other compilations will do fine for anyone wanting a one-disc representation of Dinah's albums from this period. Anyone wanting a complete Washington collection from her Mercury years is directed to the several multi-disc sets available in the USA comprising *The Complete Dinah Washington On Mercury Volumes 1–7*. Each is a three-disc set, and in total they cover the period 1952–61 as comprehensively as anyone would wish.

★★(★) In Love

Roulette 797273-2 *Washington; studio orchestra.* 62.

★★(★) Back To The Blues

Roulette 854334-2 *Washington; studio orchestras.* 7–11/62.

★★★ The Best Of Dinah Washington

Roulette 799114-2 *Washington; studio orchestras.* 62–63.

The Roulette albums merely continue what was a disappointing decline on record, even though it's hard to define exactly where the problem lies. Washington sings mightily and with no lack of attention throughout all these records, and an improvisational gleam resides at the heart of many of these songs, especially 'Do Nothin' Til You Hear From Me' (*In Love*). But the relentlessly tasteful orchestrations by Don Costa and Fred Norman turn down the heat all the way through, and Washington can sound curiously alone and friendless on a lot of the tracks. *Back To The Blues* is arguably the most disappointing, since she makes so little out of promising vehicles such as 'How Long, How Long Blues' and 'Don't Come Running Back To Me' – although when abetted by harps and cooing vocal support, perhaps it's no surprise. Washington's legacy is something of a conundrum: a great pop singer with a dilettante's touch, she is difficult to see clearly.

*****(*) Live At Birdland 1962**

Baldwin Street BJH 301 *Washington; Joe Zawinul (p); Jimmy Rouser (b); Al Jones (d).* 61–62.

A fascinating postscript to the Washington discography, this collects three Birdland broadcasts, two with the listed trio, one with unknown tenor, organ and drums. The great voice is scaled down, more intimate and more moving. There are several medleys – she liked to talk to friends when working Birdland, so she would try to shorten sets by stringing as many songs together as possible! – and Zawinul is clearly keeping his ears wide open so as not to miss any cues. Symphony Sid jumps in here and there with announcements. One of her most likeable entries and something that will surely delight Washington admirers: sound is a bit boxy and flat, but very listenable.

Grover Washington Jr (1943–99)

ALTO, SOPRANO, TENOR AND BARITONE SAXOPHONES

The early death of Grover Washington was a shock. Grover's joyous, soaring saxophone had turned up in some unexpected contexts over the years but the man from Buffalo was an underrated improviser whose abilities were perhaps critically eclipsed by the million-selling success of records like Mister Magic. Sadly, one of Grover's early R&B employers, organist Charles Earland, died within weeks of him, further underlining how untimely a loss it was.

***** Discovery: The First Recordings**

Prestige 11020-2 *Washington; Virgil Jones, Gary Chandler (t); Sonny Phillips, Butch Cornell, Leon Spencer Jr, Charles Earland, Johnny 'Hammond' Smith (org); Boogaloo Joe Jones, James Clark, Maynard Parker, Melvin Sparks (g); Jimmy Lewis (b); Jesse Kilpatrick, Bernard Purdie, Eddie Gee, Idris Muhammed (d); Buddy Caldwell (perc).* 9/70–8/71.

The title and packaging is a bit of a cheat, since they hint that this may be a newly-found set of Washington recordings. In fact, it's his first appearances on albums by Johnny 'Hammond' Smith, Boogaloo Joe Jones and Charles Earland. Admirers of the suave voice of the later music may be dismayed to hear the honking, aggressive stylist of these blustering sets of organ-combo R&B. Joe Jones's 'No Way' in particular is an almost manic performance. A misleading but very entertaining start.

*****(*) Inner City Blues**

Motown 530577 *Washington; Bob James (arr); collective personnel.* 9/71.

****** Mister Magic**

Motown 530103 *Washington; Randy Brecker, Jon Faddis, Marvin Stamm (t); Eric Gale (g); Gary King, Ralph Upchurch (b); Harvey Mason Sr (d); Ralph MacDonald (perc).* 11/74.

***** The Millennium Collection**

Motown 157617 *Washington; Randy Brecker, Jon Faddis, John Frosk, Bernie Glow, Thad Jones, Irwin Markowitz, Bob Millikan, Alexander Otey, Ernie Royal, Alan Rubin, Marvin Stamm (t, flhn); Paul Faulise, Santo Russo (tb); Alan Raph (btb); Ray Alonge, James Buffington, Fred Klein (frhn); Gerry Niewood (as); Jerry Dodgion (ts); Pepper Adams, Don Ashworth, Phil Bodner (bs); Arthur Clarke (bs, f); Hubert Laws (f, picc); Romeo Penque (woodwinds); Hilary James (p, ky); Jorge Dalto (p); Jay Berliner, Gene Bertoncini, Cornell Dupree, Eric Gale, Steve Khan (g); John Blake (vn); Ron Carter, Richard Davis, Anthony Jackson, Marcus Miller, George Mraz, Idris Muhammad (b); Billy Cobham, Pretty Purdie (d); Phil Kraus, Ralph MacDonald, Airto Moreira (perc); strings.* n.d.

Much exploited for television signature-tunes, programme stings and advertising, Washington's brand of smooth, contemporary soul-jazz rarely won over the more sober jazz critics, who like to think he's just another pop musician. There is, however, no getting away from Washington's consummate musicianship and taste. He has a lovely, melting tone, even on the treacherous soprano, and is capable of writing simple, beautiful ballads, like the Grammy-winning 'Just The Two Of Us', which appeal to pop and jazz fans alike.

The Marvin Gaye covers on *Inner City Blues* (including the title-track) and a delicate interpretation of Bill Withers's 'Ain't No Sunshine' pushed the album in the direction of a younger pop and soul audience, but there is no mistaking the leader's jazz background. Washington derives much from Cannonball Adderley – and sometimes from Earl Bostic in his gentler mode – and his solos are logically shaped and suffused with the blues.

Mister Magic is pure pleasure. The title-track has a soaring, timeless quality that still makes people smile. The theme is held suspended just so long and then it's as if someone has shaken a storm of butterflies out of a basket. It was a staple on British television for many years as signature-tune to a current affairs programme. Billy Strayhorn's 'Passion Flower' is the other key performance and a sign that Washington could bring something special and individual to repertory material; one wishes passionately that he had made more records in this vein.

****(*) Feels So Good**

Motown 5177 *Washington; Randy Brecker, Jon Faddis, John Frosk, Bob Millikan (t, flhn); Barry Rogers (tb); Alan Raph, David Taylor (btb); Bob James (p, ky); Eric Gale (g); Louis Johnson, Larry King (b); Steve Gadd, Jimmy Madison, Kenneth Rice (d); Ralph MacDonald (perc); strings.* 75.

***** Feels So Good / A Secret Place**

Raven 153 *As above, except add John Gatchell (t); Gerry Niewood (ss, as, ts); Dave Grusin (ky); Steve Khan (g); Anthony Jackson, George Mraz (b); Harvey Mason (d).* 75, 76.

Begins with Bob James's strange 'The Sealion' and includes Grover's own 'Knucklehead' and an arrangement of 'It Feels So Good'. The strings are no more intrusive than usual and James's charts make sense to everyone concerned, so the album floats by at speed. Given the duration, that's not an illusion, though this set is available on Raven along with *A Secret Place* from the following year. It was never such a compelling record, though there is an interesting version of Herbie Hancock's 'Dolphin Dance' which is worth having.

***** Live At The Bijou**

Motown 37463 0239 2 *Washington; Leslie Burrs (f); James Sid Simmons (ky); Tyrone Brown (b); Millard Vinson (d); Doc Gibbs (perc).* 78.

Live albums by Grover Washington are rare indeed, and this one offers what is presumably a pretty accurate impression of how the band sounded in a club context. 'Mr Magic' doesn't have the same airborne quality as on the original, studio set. The double-LP format is over-generous and a spot of judicious editing wouldn't have gone amiss.

*****(*) Paradise**

Elektra 60537 *Washington; James Sid Simmons (p); Tyrone Brown, Richard Lee Steacker (g); John Blake (vn); Millard Vinson (d); Doc Gibbs (perc).* 79.

***** Winelight**

Elektra K252262 *Washington; Paul Griffin, Richard Tee (p); Bill Eaton, Ed Walsh, Raymond Chew (syn); Eric Gale (g); Marcus Miller (b); Steve Gadd (d); Robert Grenidge, Ralph MacDonald (perc); Bill Withers, Hilda Harris, Yvonne Lewis, Ullanda McCullough (v).* 6–7/80.

***** Come Morning**

Elektra 562 *Washington; Richard Tee (p); Paul Griffin (syn); Eric Gale (g); Marcus Miller (b); Steve Gadd (d); Ralph MacDonald (perc); Grady Tate, Yvonne Lewis, Vivian Cherry, Ullanda McCullough, Frank Floyd, Zack Sanders, William Eaton (v).* 6–9/81.

***** The Best Is Yet To Come**

Elektra 60215 *Washington; Jon Faddis (t); Frank Wess, Alex Foster (ts); Mona Goldman-Yoskin (f); Teddi Schlossman, Richard Tee (p); James Lloyd, Paul Griffin, Billy Childs, Dexter Wansel (ky); James Herb Smith, Eric Gale, Lee Ritenour, Richard Lee Steacker (g); Marcus Miller, Cedric Napoleon, Abe Laboriel (b); Yogi Horton, Harvey Mason, Darryl Washington (d); Victor Feldman, Kevin Johnson, Leonard Gibbs, Ralph MacDonald (perc); Patti Labelle, Bobby McFerrin, Carla Benson, Evette Benton, Lucille Jones (v).* 82.

***** Anthology Of Grover Washington Jr**

Elektra 60415 *As above discs.* n.d.

*****(*) Love Songs**

Warners 8122-76693-2 *As various albums above.* 79–84.

A time-served session-man with Prestige, Washington tended to make albums the way American football is played. Players are called on for cameo performances in highly specialized roles and are then dispensed with. The sound is teased and plucked and sprayed into shape but manages, unlike most commercial pop product, to sound relatively unconfected and even, on some of the earlier discs, quite spontaneous. We've never warmed to *Paradise*, which is thinly arranged and produced. *Winelight* and *Come Morning* at least sound as if they have had some money spent on them, though not necessarily in the most tasteful way possible. The only real constant is Washington himself. He phrases a little like Cannonball Adderley, who was the main inspiration behind 1975's wonderful *Mister Magic*. There's nothing that good in this batch, but we are rather taken with the recent *Love Songs* compilation. Listening again to the likes of 'Winelight' and 'Just The Two Of Us' reminds of how much Grover managed to sneak some genuinely soulful playing into what were otherwise anodyne early-'80s black-pop settings. If he sounds smooth – and this kind of music did set the controls for the awful blight which is the smooth-jazz movement – it's never slick, and minus some of the merely mundane pieces on the regular studio albums, this set offers a lot of simple pleasure.

****(*) Strawberry Moon**

Columbia CK 40510 *Washington; Joey DeFrancesco (p); James Lloyd (p); Jason Miles (syn); B. B. King (g, v); Michael J. Powell, Richard Lee Steacker (g); Tyrone Brown, Gerald Veasley (b); Jim Salamone, Darryl Washington (d, perc); Doc Gibbs (perc); Jean Carne, Elizabeth Hague, Spencer Harrison (v).* 87.

****(*) Then And Now**

Columbia CK 44256 *Washington; Igor Butman (ts); Tommy Flanagan, Herbie Hancock, James Sid Simmons (p); Richard Lee Steacker (g); Ron Carter, Gerald Veasley (b); Marvin 'Smitty' Smith, Grady Tate, Darryl Washington (d); Miguel Fuentes (perc).* 88.

**** Time Out Of Mind**

Columbia CK 45253 *Washington; Bill Jolly, Donald Robinson, Jim Salamone, James Sid Simmons, Philip Woo (ky); Richard Lee Steacker (g); Ronnie Foster (g, ky, etc.); Gerald Veasley (b); Darryl Washington (d); Daryl Burgee, Miguel Fuentes, Doc Gibbs (perc); Spencer Harrison, Paula Holloway, Phyllis Hyman (v).* 89.

There are parallels between Washington's move to Columbia and Miles Davis's move *from* Columbia to Warner Bros. In both cases, the logic seemed to be to throw as much production as possible at the album, get as much of the personnel plugged in as the studio boards would take and then crank up all the levels.

Strawberry Moon has an interesting vignette from B. B. King ('Caught A Touch Of Your Love') and some typically smooth playing from the leader, who excels on 'The Look Of Love'. Otherwise, there isn't much that's genuinely arresting. A year later, *Then And Now* suggested possibilities which no one seemed inclined to pick up on. The addition of Flanagan and Hancock (not to forget big Ron Carter and the two distinguished drummers) plus the inclusion of jazz and standard material seemed to signal some desire to return to the jazz mainstream. Performances of 'Stella By Starlight' and Hancock's 'Just Enough' are encouraging, though Grover for once seems a little constrained by his sidemen and fails to take flight.

It wasn't to be repeated. *Time Out Of Mind* is the most disappointing of all Washington's later records, an overspiced gumbo of funk and fusion gestures, for once unredeemed by the leader's trademark saxophone.

****(*) Next Exit**

Columbia CK 48530 *Washington; Ite Jerez (t); Lewis Khan (tb); John Bolden, Terry Bolden (ky, perc); Curtis Dowd Jr, Sergio George (ky); Randy Bowland, Rodney Millon, Richard Lee Steacker (g); Reuben Rodriguez, Gerald Veasley (b); Darryl Washington (d); Lalah Hathaway, Nancy Wilson, Four Tops (v); additional vocals; strings.* 92.

Much of the emphasis is on guest vocalists, but there is enough instrumental interest on 'Take Five (Take Another Five)', the disarming opener, on Grover's 'Next Exit' and 'Summer Chill' to sustain attention and, as ever, the orchestrations are gorgeous. After his death, Grover's album titles all suddenly seemed ironic, except maybe this one which hinted (as does the music) that the road ahead might not be infinite.

***** All My Tomorrows**

Columbia CK 64319 *Washington; Eddie Henderson, Earl Gardner (t, flhn); Robin Eubanks (tb); Bobby Watson (as);*

Bobby LaVell (ts); Jimmy Cozier (bs); Hank Jones (p); Romero Lubambo (g); George Mraz (b); Billy Hart, Lewis Nash (d); Freddy Cole, Jeanie Bryson (v). 94.

A look at that personnel is enough to make one think that Washington had recanted. Mostly these are sensible, lush (well, we'd hardly expect 'harsh') charts by dependable hands such as Slide Hampton, placing Grover in a more jazzed environment than usual but not doing anything to trip him up or let him come to harm. It merely underlines the smooth appeal of his saxophone playing, here displayed on soprano, alto and tenor alike. And we wouldn't wish anything else: we have enough hard-bop saxmen as it is. If Grover could put even a drop of soul into the smooth-jazz scenario, there was no point standing in his way.

***** Soulful Strut**

Columbia CK 57505 *Washington; Mac Gallohon, Andy Gravish, Tim Ouimelte, Jimmy Powell (t); Herb Hubel (tb); Aaron Heick (sax, f); Dale Kelps (as, bcl, f); Rick DePofi (ts); Donald Robinson (p); Charlie Ernst, George Whitty (ky); Dan Shea (ky, b, d); Steve Bargonetti, Bob Ward (g, ky); Randy Bowland, Dan Huff, Ray Obiedo, Paul Pimsler, Richard Lee Steacker, Chris Taylor (g); Gary Haase (b, d, arr); Gerald Veasley (b); Steve Gadd, Omar Hakim, Peter Michael, Richie Morales (d); Cyro Baptista, Pablo Batista, Joe Bonadio, Norberto Goldberg, Roger Squitero (perc); Lindiwe Diamini, NtombKhona Diamini, Sandy Griffith, Wayne Hernandez, Amanda Homi, Bakithi Khumalo, Claytoven Richardson, Katherine Russell, Wincy Terry, Jeanie Tracy (v).* 96.

Just because classic Blue Notes didn't carry credits for 'grooming' doesn't mean we should be too snooty about this one, which does. The ten tracks, which lean heavily on arranger Gary Haase, are a touch too primped and correct, but the authority of Grover's saxophone cuts through even the most viscous of background arrangements and 'I Can Count The Times' and 'Mystical Force' are positively honeyed. As so often, he is the only truly individual solo voice, though Washington and Haase have attempted to pull some of the horns up through the mix. The sheer size of personnel suggests how meticulously this and similar albums have been assembled, a dot-and-wash approach to production which is also a long way removed from live recording round a stereo pair. A delight for anyone who appreciates professionally executed soul-jazz, and a goldmine – surely? – for any remix artist and sampler on the lookout for instrumental nuggets.

***** Breath Of Heaven – A Holiday Collection**

Sony 68527 *Washington; Billy Childs (p); Adam Holzman (syn); Hiram Bullock, Richard Lee Steacker (g); Dawn Andres (clo, v); Will Lee, Gerald Veasley (b); Victor Lewis, Steve Wolfe (d); Pablo Batista, Bashiri Johnson (perc); Lisa Fischer (v).* 97.

As Christmas – sorry, *holiday* – albums go, this is a winner. Two takes of 'Breath Of Heaven' and 'A Child Is Born' are outstanding, but 'Away In A Manger' and 'Christmas Waltz' will banish any signs of Bah, humbug from the opening bars.

***** Aria**

Sony 61684 *Washington; Terence Blanchard (t); Billy Childs (p); Ron Carter (b); Orchestra of St Luke's.* 99.

Apparently, Washington had always dreamed of making an album of operatic highlights arranged for the saxophone. It's a strange set, complicated by the fact of posthumous release. He must have read some of these scores when at music school and probably listened to them a thousand times. The melodies are all caught very simply and without much variation, which works for most of the Puccini pieces. Some of the others are more challenging, like Massenet's 'Pourquoi Me Reveiller?' and the Delibes 'Flower Duet' but, despite some fine interaction with Blanchard on a solitary Gershwin selection – 'My Man's Gone Now' – and some great work with Carter and Childs, it doesn't feel very much like a jazz record.

***** The Best Of Grover Washington Jr**

Motown 530620 *Various personnels.* 71–86.

***** Prime Cuts – The Columbia Years 1987–1999**

Columbia 69722 *As above.* 87–99.

****(*) The Ultimate Collection**

Hip-O 53888 *As above.* 11/99.

***** Les Incontournables**

WEA International 34797 *As above.* 03/00.

There seems to be a plethora of Washington compilations around, probably a good option for anyone who only wants to sample one period or who perhaps likes just a couple of songs: 'Mister Magic' and 'Winelight' maybe. Ratings for these are pretty much in line with the album reviews above, but the Columbia set and the Motown sampling are both very good.

Rosella Clemmons Washington

VOCAL

Based in Philadelphia, Washington sings and works in her locality and has so far made these two albums, released by the Cadence operation.

**** Just Peace**

Cadence CJR 1116 *Washington; Cecil Bridgewater (t); Bill Meek, Dawn Crist (ky); John Blake (vn); Tyrone Brown (b); Dave Brown (d).* 5–9/97.

***** Rosella ... A Good Place To Start**

CIMO 224 *Washington; Tyrone Brown (b); Bill Meek (perc).* 5/00.

Washington has a vast, almost operatic voice, and her difficulty is in scaling it down and using it in a way that doesn't obliterate her material. She can hit low notes that would have given Sarah Vaughan trouble and can sweep across a sky of high Cs. Making it all sound musical is another matter. The first album has a home-made feel: the keyboard parts sound like they're off an unproduced demo, almost every track rambles on for too long, 'Since I Fell For You' is cooked to death (no wonder Grover Washington, who plays the solo, complained that she left him no room) and there are inappropriate beats – as on a discofied 'Summertime'. One might think that Washington really wanted to be a soul queen or a gospel diva. Yet in moments of repose the voice is certainly impressive.

Bob Rusch didn't like the sound of the record either, so he decided to record Washington in the bare-walls ambience of the CIMP studio with only a bassist for company (Meek is on only two tracks). It's certainly a strange setting for a standards-singer, even if the instrumentation is familiar from some of Sheila Jordan's work. Washington isn't remotely in that class, but tamed by the environment she turns in a much stronger performance. Brown is a capable rather than outstanding accompanist and writes some of the material. The singer does best on a sparer piece such as 'Deep River', and the overripe lyric of 'Lush Life' does suit her rather well. A curious set which may well appeal to those brave enough to give it a try.

Sadao Watanabe (born 1933)

ALTO, SOPRANINO AND SOPRANO SAXOPHONES, FLUTE

Born in Tochohi, he joined the Toshiko Akiyoshi band in 1953 and took it over when she left for Berklee. Studied in the USA and founded the first Japanese jazz school in 1965. A patrician figure at home, he divides his playing time between a version of soft Brazilian fusion and more firmly centred bebop.

***(*) Round Trip

Universe 46 *Watanabe; Chick Corea (p); Miroslav Vitous (b); Jack DeJohnette (d).* 7/76.

Like most Japanese of his generation (the composer Toru Takemitsu told a similar story), Sadao Watanabe heard nothing but Japanese traditional and German martial music during his teens, and was exposed to Western popular music only through American forces radio; he also cites Norman Granz's Jazz At The Philharmonic broadcasts as a big influence. Watanabe had already largely rejected Japanese music (his father was a teacher of *biwa*, a lute-like instrument), and by the time he was 20 he was sufficiently adept on the alto saxophone to join Toshiko Akiyoshi and perform in America.

He subsequently recorded with both Chico Hamilton (who was always on the look-out for unusual tonalities) and Gary McFarland, who turned Watanabe on to the fashionable sound of bossa nova. Perhaps because he encountered jazz at a relatively advanced stage in its development, Watanabe seemed able to take virtually any of its stylistic variants (swing, bop, Latin, Afro and, later, fusion) on their own terms. Though his recent recordings have tended to be heavily produced, middle-market fusion, Watanabe has recorded with an impressive array of American heavyweights including (to mention only the piano-players) Chick Corea, Herbie Hancock, Cedar Walton and Richard Tee. In 1967 he collaborated with Toshiko Akiyoshi's ex-husband, Charlie Mariano, producing three fine albums of standards and oriental themes.

Round Trip is very different from the later, more eclectic work. In keeping with the jazz of the time, it's floating and impressionistic, though Watanabe's Parker-inspired solos somewhat confound the occasional comparisons between this and Wayne Shorter in early Weather Report. Joe Farrell in Chick Corea's *Return To Forever* would perhaps be a better analogy. Chick brings a touch of class to *Round Trip*, but so, too, do Vitous and DeJohnette. The opening title-track is the only weak link on the set. It's too long and rambling and, as the name suggests, seems to travel a long way to get back to the original point. 'Nostalgia' and the atmospheric 'Pastoral' are more like the thing. Watanabe plays flute and soprano throughout this fine record. It's worth noting that though this is the earliest survivor, Sadao had been recording for almost a decade already.

*** I'm Old Fashioned

Sony International 4008 *Watanabe; Hank Jones (p); Ron Carter (b); Tony Williams (d).* 5/76.

*** Birds Of Passage

Elektra 60748 *Watanabe; Freddie Hubbard (flhn); Hubert Laws (f); George Duke, Russell Errante (ky); Dan Huff, Paul Jackson (g); Abraham Laboriel (b); Vinnie Colaiuta, John Robinson, Carlos Vega (d); Alex Acuña, Paulinho Da Costa (perc); collective personnel.* 5/77.

It's good to have further reminders of Watanabe's bebop roots and to balance out the highly produced crossover records of later years. Billed as 'the Great Jazz Trio', his colleagues on *I'm Old Fashioned* are as deft a rhythm section as you'd find and it would be taxing most blindfold testees to recognize that the saxophonist on the opening 'Confirmation' was not American. 'I Concentrate On You', 'I'm Old Fashioned' and 'Chelsea Bridge' are the other star turns, and there's a version of a Japanese television theme, which is surprisingly good and consistent with the bop idiom of the rest. *Birds Of Passage* marks a shift within the year to a much more produced and smoothed-out sound, though interestingly Watanabe still comes across as a bopper.

**(*) Rendezvous

Elektra/Asylum 60371 2 *Watanabe; Don Grusin (ky); Richard Tee (p, ky); Barry Eastmond (syn); Dori Caymmi, Eric Gale (g); John Patitucci (b); Marcus Miller (b, syn); Peter Erskine, Steve Gadd (d); Ralph MacDonald (perc); Roberta Flack (v); strings.* 2/83–4/84.

*** Sweet Deal

Elektra 61120 *Watanabe; Robbie Buchanan, Russell Ferrante (ky); Paul Jackson Jr (g); Abe Laboriel, Neil Stubenhaus (b); William Kennedy, Michael Shapiro, Carlos Vega (d); Alex Acuna, Paulinho da Costa (perc); Warren Wiebe (v).* 84.

This is almost purposefully bland in *Rendezvous*' attempt to give jazz-funk a sophisticated, supper-club sound. There are some fine players here, but the results are unlikely to be of interest to most jazz fans. *Sweet Deal* is more enterprising, suggesting that Watanabe is preparing to make one of his occasional forays back into straight – i.e. bop-based – jazz.

**(*) Front Seat

Elektra 60906 4 *Watanabe; Robbie Buchanan, George Duke (ky); Oscar Castro-Neves, Paul Jackson Jr (g); Jimmy Haslip, Abe Laboriel, Neil Stubenhaus (b); Jeff Porcaro, J. R. Robinson, Carlos Vega (d); Alex Acuna, Paulinho da Costa, Efraim Toro (perc); Patti Austin, Alex Brown, Carl Carwell, Syreeta Wright (v).* 5/90.

One of the least appalling records from this period. The title-track and 'Miles Apart' are the closest to being vintage Watanabe, but even these have a warmed-up taste to them. Trivia-spotters will have noticed the presence of Jeff Porcaro, the drummer of rock group Poco, who despite an elaborate rumour did *not* die (two years after this) of an acute reaction to weedkiller spray, but from rather more familiar rock-star causes. It's perhaps telling that this is the most interesting thing we can find to say about this record.

*** Night With Strings

Elektra Asylum 61539 *Watanabe; Soichi Noriki (p); Marc Johnson (b); Peter Erskine (d); strings.* 11/93.

Watanabe sounds good with strings, but only when they are as well-drilled and as finely tuned as the smallish group arranged by Noriki to accompany this lovely trio session with two top-drawer Americans. Johnson's tone is gorgeous and Erskine is a big softy at heart, for all his occasional bluster. There's a strong Sinatra feel to this, with 'In The Wee Small Hours Of The Morning' and 'Violets For Your Furs' both prominently featured. Not much grit to the improvisation, and an emphasis on loveliness of tone rather than complexity of line, but with results as beguiling as this, who's complaining?

*****(*) Remembrance**

Verve 547440-2 *Watanabe; Nicholas Payton (t, flhn); Robin Eubanks (tb); Cyrus Chestnut (p); Romero Lubambo (g); Christian McBride (b); Billy Drummond (d).* 1/99.

By the sharpest contrast with the 1997 and 1998 discs, *Remembrance* teams Watanabe with ranking jazz players and strong improvising charts, all of them originals. The real hero of the set (as so often where he is present) is McBride. He rattles off titanic solos on 'Dim Blue' and 'Forest Song' but, more importantly, provides a solid architecture for the whole set.

Watanabe's chops are still in excellent shape. Never a profound soloist, he nevertheless manages to shape elegant statements over blues chords and mid-tempo boppish themes. His tone has always sounded slightly sharp, less than a quarter-tone, but enough to sustain its exotic character. On 'Aquarian Groove' and 'Going Back Home', he is reminiscent of Sonny Fortune, elsewhere of the largely forgotten Carlos Garnett.

****(*) Sadao 2000**

Verve 543676-2 *Watanabe; George Whitty (ky); Mike Stern (g); Richard Bona (b, g, perc, v); Jonathan Joseph (d); Café (perc).* 00.

The old campaigner goes on. There's too much input from the likes of the annoying Bona, and Whitty is as individual as a Rich Tea biscuit, but Sadao still manages to sneak in the odd turn of phrase which lets you know that, no matter how crummy his surroundings, he's still Watanabe.

Steve Waterman

TRUMPET, FLUGELHORN

Studied at Trinity College of Music and now a respected player and educator, whose credits include work with John Surman's Brass Project, Carla Bley's Big Band and his own groups.

***** Destination Unknown**

ASC ASCD 4 *Waterman; Liam Noble (p); Jeff Clyne (b); Paul Clarvis (d).* 95.

***** Out Of Touch**

ASC ASCD 32 *As above, except omit Clarvis; add Russell Van Der Berg (sax); Richard Newby (d, perc).* 99.

Two albums' worth of fine, intelligent writing from one of the quietest talents on the British scene, consistently undervalued at home, but widely appreciated by senior musicians for his clear, strong tone and alert improvisations. All the material on these albums is by the trumpeter. The two groups are anchored on the empathy between Noble and the veteran Clyne, who is an inspirational figure for a whole generation of young British jazzmen. Well worth sampling; we probably favour the first album by a whisker.

Ben Waters

PIANO

Bright young British boogie-woogie specialist.

***** Shakin' In The Makin'**

Jazzizit JITCD 0230 *Waters; Derek Nash (ss, as, ts, bs); Jools Holland (p); Colin John (g); Chris Lonergan, Dave Swift, (b); Sam Kelly (d); Roger Bastable (v).* 01.

Good-natured boogie from a first-rate band, and a chance to hear the charismatic Mr Holland do his stuff without opening his mouth. Colin John is a charismatic presence onstage and off, and Waters has a real feel for this repertoire and style.

Benny Waters (1902–98)

ALTO AND TENOR SAXOPHONES, CLARINET, VOCAL

He studied in Boston before spending several years from 1925 with Charlie Johnson, then with Henderson, Hopkins, Lunceford and others through the '30s and '40s. From 1955 he was mostly in Europe, touring relentlessly, and he carried on doing this into a charismatic old age.

***** When You're Smiling**

Hep 2010 *Waters; Roy Williams (tb); Joe Temperley (bs); Alex Shaw (p); Ron Mathewson (b); Martin Drew (d).* 8/80.

****(*) Hurry On Down**

Storyville STCD 8264 *Waters; Paul Sealey (g); Erica Howard (b); John Cox (d).* 4/81.

***** Benny Waters–Freddy Randall Jazz Band**

Jazzology JCD-124 *Waters; Freddy Randall (t); Jim Shepherd (tb); Stan Greig (p); Paul Sealey (g, bj); Tiny Winters, Mike Durrell (b); Laurie Chescoe (d).* 12/82.

Waters was an indomitable personality, among the oldest practising jazzmen, and though his recent records tend to be too accommodating for a man who doesn't like to act his age, there is much vigorous work on clarinet and alto. Like Benny Carter or Doc Cheatham, he sounds like a survivor from another age, raising his voice among us with few concessions to his surroundings. His tone, vibrato and delivery are antiquarian, but none of this suggests frailty, more an enduring style.

These British recordings, made when Waters was a mere lad and only pushing 80, are likeable stuff. *When You're Smiling* is prime British mainstream, courtesy of Williams, Temperley and the rhythm section, and even without Waters there would be plenty to listen to. Benny is in grand spirits on the title-piece and Williams has three features where he makes trombone playing seem like the easiest thing on earth. *Hurry On Down*, with respectable if sometimes charmless backing from Paul Sealey's trio, is all right, but Waters usually sounds better with another hornman standing at his elbow. The meeting with Freddy Randall and a more trad-orientated crew is good enough, though some of the rhythms plod and there's too much solo space given to the sidemen; Randall's brusquely hot solos and Waters's sometimes impish humour are the reasons to listen.

Bill Watrous (born 1939)

TROMBONE

One of the great trombone technicians, Watrous can play extraordinarily fast, prefers a steady pace, and produces a tone so smooth it could be spread on toast. He worked in swing groups and show bands in the '70s before moving to California and majoring in studio work and arranging.

***** Bone-ified**
GNP Crescendo GNPD 2211 *Watrous; Shelly Berg (ky); Lou Fischer (b); Randy Drake, Tom Cummings (d).* 92.

****(*) A Time For Love**
GNP Crescendo GNPD 2222 *As above, except add Dennis Farias, Wayne Bergeron, Ron Stout (t), Doug Inman, Bob McChesney, Rich Bullock (tb), Sal Lozano, Phil Feather, Bill Liston, Bruce Eskovitz, Bob Carr (saxes), Dave Carpenter (b); omit Cummings.* 93.

***** Space Available**
Double-Time DTRCD-124 *Watrous; Dennis Farias, Wayne Bergeron, Bob Summers, Darrel Gardiner, Steve Huffsteter (t); Doug Inman, Bob McChesney, Wendell Kelly, Rich Bullock (tb); Sal Lozano, Phil Feather, Bill Liston, Gene Burkurt, Bob Carr (reeds); Shelly Berg (p); Trey Henry (b); Randy Drake (d).* 12/96.

Watrous remains among the most accomplished trombonists alive. His occasional albums, though, are almost too classy for their own good. The main thing he needs is context, and the GNP albums don't really pull this one off. Berg's flashy piano and frequent recourse to string-synthesizer parts make a much too fulsome contribution out of what he has to do and, despite some typically fluent and thoughtful solos by the trombonist, the album makes only a modest impression. *A Time For Love* is all Johnny Mandel tunes. The big band appears only here and there, Berg goes back to the synthesizer, and the mood is more like light music than a jazz situation. Watrous salvages something, but maybe he just wants to treat these projects as extensions of his studio routine.

Space Available puts him in the surroundings of the Refuge West Big Band, an institution in Sherman Oaks, California, for a number of years and an awesomely proficient machine when it comes to tackling difficult scores and multi-storeyed frameworks. Watrous loves this kind of situation and he has a solo on every tune, his familiar style – a plummy, fat tone, phrasing that seems to have no discernible joins in it and a way of getting from one end of an improvisation to the other without any hint of faltering – still intact. In a way it's a pity that more members of the band aren't heard from in a solo capacity, since it could use a jolt of surprise here and there: one sometimes feels that proficiency is everything here and, if nothing sounds soulless, there's nothing to set the heart on fire either. 'The Road Goes Ever Onward' has some rather extraordinary textures in it and Watrous will always make jaws drop with some of his playing: try the way he turns 'My Foolish Heart' into a *bel canto* aria for the horn.

Bobby Watson (born 1953)

ALTO AND SOPRANO SAXOPHONES

Watson learned his trade as saxophonist and musical director with the Jazz Messengers, establishing himself as a soloist of real authority, with a keening, blues-drenched sound. Most of his recording has been for European labels.

***** Round Trip**
Red RR 123187-2 *Watson; Pietro Bassini (p); Attilio Zanchi (b); Giampiero Prina (d).* 2/85.

***** Beatitudes**
Evidence ECD 22178 *Watson; John Hicks (p); Curtis Lundy (b); Marvin 'Smitty' Smith (d).* 87

****** The Year Of The Rabbit**
Evidence ECD 22210 *Watson; Irving Stokes (t); Art Baron (tb); Bill Easley (ts, cl); Jim Hartog (bs); Mulgrew Miller (p); Lawrence Lucie (g); Curtis Lundy (b); Kenny Washington (d).* 2/87.

Few contemporary saxophonists are more instantly recognizable than the brilliant Kansan. Watson's hard, bright sound and trademark descending wail (a device that seems increasingly mannered as years go by) were first acclaimed in a vintage Jazz Messengers line-up. Watson went on to work in Charli Persip's Superband and to co-found the 29th Street Saxophone Quartet. Though the quartet has been internationally successful, Watson's recording career has been intermittent to say the least. Most of his best work has been for the Italian Red label. Most of Watson's titles from the late '70s to mid-'80s have so far failed to make the transition to CD (the loss of *Estimated Time Of Arrival*, named after his theme-tune, leaves a bit of a hole).

However, the very good *Beatitudes*, co-led with Lundy, is still around. With typical perversity, both his Blue Note discs with Horizon have disappeared from the catalogue, which makes the Red catalogue all the more important.

Round Trip is a slightly disappointing record and certainly contains no inkling of the majesty of *Love Remains*, but hindsight invests it with an impressive confidence. The Ornette-composed title-track kicks off a set which contains almost nothing of Watson's own – only the closing 'All The Thing Of Jo Maka' bears his name – and not enough of his signature blues. Miles's and Bill Evans's 'Blue In Green' and Lee Morgan's 'Ceora' don't seem quite the right repertoire for this group, however confidently they're played.

The Year Of The Rabbit is a heartfelt, beautifully disciplined tribute to Johnny Hodges. All the great songs are there and, not surprisingly, it's 'Isfahan' that steals the show, one of the most evocative and sympathetic accounts of that great song *not* performed by Rabbit himself.

CORE COLLECTION

♛ ** Love Remains**
Red CD 123212 *Watson; John Hicks (p); Curtis Lundy (b); Marvin 'Smitty' Smith (d).* 11/86.

***Love Remains* is Watson's one certain masterpiece, a startlingly poised performance. From the Parker-influenced 'Mystery Of Ebop' to the solemnly funky 'Dark Days (Against Apartheid)', it has a complete unity of purpose. The title-piece, jointly credited to Bobby and Pamela Watson, is built round a three-note motif which means the same thing in any**

language. Hicks's solo is a perfect foil for Watson's slightly plangent second entry, while Lundy and Smitty Smith sustain a dark bass pulse. Lundy's 'Sho Thang' is the only non-Watson composition, a weak interlude before Pam Watson's 'The Love We Had Yesterday' rounds off the set. If the '80s threw up maybe a baker's dozen of essential jazz albums, *Love Remains* comes in somewhere near the top.

***(*) This Little Light Of Mine

Red RR 123250 *Watson (as solo).* 93.

The solo saxophone album was a challenge Watson had resisted for many years. The results are inevitably patchy, and it isn't the kind of set that makes for comfortable listening straight through. Better to concentrate on one track at a time and savour Watson's deft phrasing and sinuous developments. A few of the pieces are little more than workouts: 'These Foolish Things', 'Body And Soul', and a quick run through the 'Giant Steps' changes. 'Misterioso', 'Donna Lee' and Joe Henderson's 'Recorda Me' are more developed, but some of the most interesting ideas emerge out of traditional material; there are two takes of Apostoloy Kaldara's 'Mes'Tou Bosporou' and the title-track is an old spiritual Watson's preacher grandfather used to sing. *This Little Light* doesn't quite take him full circle, but it sets out certain agenda that he could usefully spend the next ten years addressing.

**** Quiet As It's Kept

Red RR123284-2 *Watson; Terell Stafford (t); Orrin Evans (p); Lenny Argese, Greg Skaff (g); Curtis Lundy (b); Ralph Peterson (d); Marlon Simon (perc); Pamela Watson (v).* 98.

The hair is grizzled these days but, a decade on, from *Love Remains*, Watson is playing with the same maturity and grace. He was never a turbulent player, but the distinctive keening swoop which used to punctuate solos has given way to a mellower and more measured slide down the scale. The calm reflection of 'Always A Friend' represents a new dimension in his music. The title-track is vintage Watson, identifiable from the very first bars and as ably constructed as ever. 'Nubian Breakdown' is a more fragmentary and alienated piece, and perhaps a nod in the direction of Arthur Blythe, though it also resembles some of Sonny Fortune's African-inspired pieces. The mood of 'Back Home Again With You' and 'Watch The Children Play' is touchingly sombre. Stafford is used on only three tracks, including 'Nubian Breakdown' and the intriguing folk-song arrangement 'Nanatsu-No-Ko'. For balance, that seems about right, for Terell is a dominant presence wherever he plays and this is an album which truly belongs to Bobby Watson. The use of guitar is something of a departure, and it's elegantly done; Skaff's rapid articulation on the first track is revelatory. As in the past, Pamela Watson shares in the plaudits, credited as co-composer on 'Concentric Circles' and adding a vocal to 'Afternoon In Ottobrun'. A remarkable musical partnership. *Quiet* isn't a classic, but it is a very special record, easily Watson's best for years.

***(*) Live At Someday In Tokyo

Red 123290 *Watson; Tokyo Leaders Big Band.* 00.

This project set out to recreate Watson's Tailor Made group with a Japanese personnel. The results are extraordinary, with long passages of free-form improvisation and some absolutely riveting ensemble work on compositions such as 'Dual Conversation', 'Karita' and 'Unfold'. Watson himself sounds in absolutely wonderful form and plays like a man who is enjoying himself immensely. The live sound is remarkably good, though it does favour the soloist over the orchestra to perhaps too flattering a degree.

** Old Friends – New Point

City Light 4 *Watson; David Basse, Angela Hagenbach, Old Friends (v).* 01.

Like David Murray, Watson has long expressed an interest in writing songs as well as jazz themes. One wishes he had given it a go. This is a pretty cheesy vocal set, marred by an awful choice of material – including 'Wichita Lineman', which belongs to Jimmy Webb and Glen Campbell through all eternity – and a blunt, ugly sound-mix. It will appeal to anyone who enjoys Basse's and Hagenbach's brand of post-Manhattan Transfer jazz pop, but not for mainstream Watson fans.

*** Live And Learn

Palmetto 2083 *Watson; Orrin Evans (p); Curtis Lundy (b); Montez Coleman (d).* 9/01.

A label debut and a pretty solid return to form. Though he has been consigned to minor imprints for most of his career, Watson is still capable of delivering a magisterial performance every time he enters a studio. On tunes like 'Landmarks Lost' and pianist Evans's composition 'Why Not' (which seems to make reference to Miles's 'So What'), he plays with presence and authority. Evans isn't a John Hicks, but he solos with logic and with something to say. Lundy, as ever, is the mainstay, a firm, sure-footed player who combines reliable timekeeping with beauty of tone and the occasional flash of brilliance, as on 'Landmarks Lost'. A fine album, though not yet the devastating statement Watson has always seemed capable of.

Eric Watson (born 1955)

PIANO

Expatriate American pianist working from France.

***(*) Silent Hearts

Free Flight 1434 *Watson; Mark Dresser (b); Ed Thigpen (d).* 10/98.

Watson is an interesting player, but he's hard to characterize: influences such as Monk, John Lewis and Mal Waldron seem to drift in and out of his music, 'classical' influences stand in the margins, and his composing favours dark, sluggish structures that mysteriously relax into moments of pure lyricism. Intriguing – but sometimes hard to take over the course of a record, and the hint of gallows humour suggested by his titles ('New Canaan Con Man', 'Substance Abuse') never really surfaces.

Much of his early work has disappeared, but this is Watson's best record by a mile up to this point. Centred by the swinging rhythms of Dresser and Thigpen – an unlikely but superb combination – the pianist comes up with eight strong originals and allows himself the indulgence of memorable melodies and considerable amounts of light and shade. That renders the thunderous explosion which takes place halfway through the one marathon performance, 'Punchin Paich Patch', all the more effective. A terrific piano trio record.

**** Full Metal Quartet

Owl 159572-2 *Watson; Bennie Wallace (ts); Mark Dresser (b); Ed Thigpen (d).* 12/99–1/00.

Bennie Wallace joins in the fun and his bleary, hollering sound soon locks in with the trio's work. The music here is ostensibly some kind of suite, though the nine components sound perfectly able to function by themselves, and the balance between solo, quartet and rhythm-section music is secured with real mastery. By himself, Wallace can get discomfortingly turgid – as we have said above – but that's never an option with Dresser and Thigpen, the 'out' tendencies of the former impeccably balanced by the unfussy, deep swing of the veteran drummer. Wallace wouldn't have been anybody's first thought for this gig, yet he eats up the complexities in a piece such as 'Wear And Tear', and in what might have been an excessively brainy, inward-looking session he adds blood and fire. A superb quartet record.

*** Sketches Of Solitude

Night Bird 1005 *Watson (p solo).* 8/01.

Watson's experience in classical recital always seems to put a difficult spin on his solo playing. 'The Peacocks' honours Jimmy Rowles's melody but, stretched across ten minutes, the reading is eventually airless. 'Blue In Green' is a requiem, and the gentler plains of Mal Waldron's 'Left Alone' suit him better. The last four tracks are all his own originals, and if titles such as 'The Girl Who Never Sang' and 'Daughter Of Darkness' suggest that Michael Mantler's nodding in approval, the music is harmonious enough, if often crawlingly slow. If your taste is rooted in keyboard sonority, Watson's your man.

Jeff 'Tain' Watts (born 1960)

DRUMS

Watts emerged from the group of players centred around the Marsalis brothers in the '80s, an association which continues, although he has also subsequently worked in a wider circle.

***(*) Citizen Tain

Columbia CK 69551 *Watts; Wynton Marsalis (t); Delfeayo Marsalis (tb); Kenny Garrett (as); Branford Marsalis (ss, ts); Kenny Kirkland (p); Eric Revis, Reginald Veal (b).* 6–8/98.

*** Bar Talk

Columbia 508157-2 *Watts; Ravi Coltrane, Branford Marsalis, Michael Brecker (ts); Gregoire Maret (hca); David Budway, Joey Calderazzo (p); Henry Hey (ky); James Genus, Eric Revis (b); Robert Thomas Jr (perc).* 12/01–1/02.

Watts stood out as one of the leading new drummers of his time when he worked in the first Wynton Marsalis Quintet, and since then he's become among the most eminent sticksmen of his generation. Watts always makes noise as a player, not as a composer, and his favourite devices – thumping interpolations on the toms, crash-cymbal strokes that seem to linger in their own time, and an iron-faced swing – are well in evidence on his every appearance. For *Citizen Tain,* Watts not only manages to reassemble the Marsalis family for the final track (when producer Delfeayo also sits in), but he writes some good tunes, has Wynton and Branford recalling the explosive excitement of their original quintet on 'The Impaler', and provides settings for Kirkland that make one regret that fine player's early death. Some of the music is a shade too keen to impress the listener, but this is in most respects a powerful and assured document of these players at this time.

Bar Talk has a lot of similar muscle-flexing but somehow comes out less impressive, possibly because the Brecker–Coltrane–Marsalis front line (diffused across various tracks, of course) do their usual thing, and nobody feels the need to do much more than turn up and play. Given the virtuosity on show, that doesn't hurt, but it doesn't make for immortal results, either.

Trevor Watts (born 1939)

ALTO AND SOPRANO SAXOPHONES

Played in RAF bands in the early '60s, then moved in London free-music circles and co-founded SME. More recently, in his Moiré Music group, has investigated fusions of jazz with other musics.

*** With One Voice

FMR CD 108 *Watts; Simon Picard (ts); Veryan Weston (p); Lianne Carroll (ky, v); Richard Granville-Smith (acc); Colin Gibson (b); Liam Genockey (d); Kofi Adu, Nana Tsiboe (perc).* 88.

*** A Wider Embrace

ECM 521351-2 *Watts; Colin McKenzie (b); Nana Tsiboe, Nee-Daku Patato, Jojo Yates, Nana Appiah, Paapa J. Mensah (perc).* 4/93.

***(*) Moiré

Intakt CD 039 *Watts; Colin McKenzie (b); Paapa J. Mensah (d, perc, v).* 3/95.

A stalwart of the British free-jazz scene, and a founder member of both Amalgam and the Spontaneous Music Ensemble (both listed separately), Watts has to some extent turned his back entirely on abstract music in order to explore the strongly rhythmic, non-European language of his two main groups of the '80s, the Drum Orchestra and (as on the first two of these) Moiré Music. The word 'moiré' refers to the shimmering patterns one sees in watered silk, and what Watts was trying to do was to create such patterns musically by overlaying rhythmic patterns and textures in live performance.

Moiré Music performances have tended to be either entrancing or dull. On *With One Voice,* originally an Arc LP, the manifesto is in the album title, a desire to weave the band, saxophones, keyboards (including accordion) and percussion, into a single, sinuous unit. As a record, it falls very much on the former side. The ECM album inclines to the latter but is still eminently listenable, and techno buffs can marvel at the way engineer Gary Thomas and Steve Lake at ECM managed to get so many drums sounding good. Watts's studies in African percussion music have occasionally resulted in illustrated lectures. While there is a wealth of ethnomusicological detail attached to this recording, it is altogether more flowing, and Watts is playing singingly and with passion. Unfashionable he may be, even as a negative example, but this is territory opened up by Ginger Baker in the years after Cream. Though some aspects of the music have still not been thought through, it's a significant performance.

The tight, fierce trio on the Intakt disc gives a better sense of how his current work relates back to British free-movement projects like Amalgam. Mensah is a big presence, bringing a pungent vocal attack as well as wild percussion, and McKenzie's bass lines weave to and fro like oiled rope.

*****(*) Live at the Athens Concert Hall**

Arc CD 08 *Watts; Colin McKenzie (g); Greg Leppard, Marc Parnell (d); Ali Laazane, Roberto Pla (perc); Nana Tsiboe (perc, v); Paapa J. Mensah (djembe).* 2/98, 11/99.

Supplemented with 'Mrs Robinson', which was recorded in Beijing more than a year later, this Greek appearance features the basic Moiré Music group with Tsiboe and Parnell on percussion; Mensah and Pla appear only in China. Live, the group is even more compelling than in the studio. Watts sounds entranced on 'Seamless', 'Tribute To Don Cherry' and 'Gentle Love' and his soprano-playing can rarely have been so compelling. McKenzie is hugely inventive, rhythmically supple and driven, sometimes reminiscent of Steve Swallow but with hints of Jack Bruce's rolling-thunder approach as well. The sound isn't absolutely pristine but any flaws are more than compensated for by the sheer vigour of the playing.

****** Trevor Watts and the Celebration Band**

Arc CD 010 *Watts; Rob Leake (ss, ts); Marcus Cummins (ss, as); Amy Metcalf (ts); Geoff Sapsford (g); Roger Carey (b); Giampaolo Scatozza (perc); Jamie Harris (djembe, djarabouka, perc).* 4/01.

The Moiré concept transferred to something much closer to the multi-horn lines of Watts's earlier groups. This sounds very unlike orthodox British free-bop but the basic idiom is still audible in the rich, shifting mix. Guitar and bass guitar thicken up the harmonies wonderfully and Sapsford is a real find. '8 In 7' kicks off proceedings in the most arresting way; at 13 minutes it could hardly be more ambitious, and yet it passes as vividly as a jewelled miniature. 'Spring Sunrise' is more reflective but 'Out Of The Street' restores the energy, bringing an outstanding album to a climax. A real treat.

***** 6 Dialogues**

Emanem 4069 *Watts; Veryan Weston (p).* 02.

And a real surprise in this one, too. Weston and Watts have been working together for some time, notably in the Moiré Music project. This, though, is Trevor's first free-improvisation record since the '70s. When he parted company with John Stevens, he took a very different musical road, and enthusiasts for British improvisation of the 'Golden Age' will immediately warm to the sound of Watts's plangent alto following an uncharted course on 'Unrest Assured'. The companion piece, 'Rest Unassured', is better still, as is the soprano outing on 'Split Frequencies', all of which shows that his chops haven't been in any way compromised by more than two decades of playing riffs and minimal ostinati. Weston has immediate rapport and understanding and when the two nudge away at a single idea for some minutes, as they do on the three closing tracks, it's hard to resist. Fans will still be reaching for their Amalgam reissues, but this gives fair promise that Trevor Watts can still deliver wholly improvised music.

Chuck Wayne (1923–97)

GUITAR, BANJO

Wayne was much involved on 52nd Street in the '40s and later played in George Shearing's quintet and with Tony Bennett. Latterly a CBS staffer and teacher, he rarely procured a high profile but managed to lead a few sessions of his own.

*****(*) Morning Mist**

Original Jazz Classics OJC 1097 *Wayne; Joe Williams (b); Ronnie Bedford (d).* 12/64.

This Prestige date is as unassuming as its leader's career. Wayne had good bop chops but rarely took the Tal Farlow course of high speed around all the turnbacks, and his delivery is nice and easy without ever losing a certain piquancy: on 'Li'l Darlin'', for instance, he picks a slightly quicker tempo than usual and throws off a witty, bluesy solo. There's a lot of octave playing of the melodies throughout, but nothing meant to send a listener to sleep, and Williams and Bedford are asked to stay surprisingly on their toes. As a final flourish, Wayne picks up the banjo for the last track, Stephen Sondheim's 'Lovely', and actually plays convincing bebop on it. The only disappointing thing is the album's duration, which doesn't even reach a miserly 30 minutes.

Weather Report

GROUP

Along with Miles's electric band, of which Joe Zawinul was a member, the Mahavishnu Orchestra and Return To Forever, Weather Report were key players in the development of fusion music. The spare atmospherics of the early albums gave way to a funkier and more dance-based approach, largely determined by Joe's rock-solid, harmonically subtle bass-lines and chord progressions and by Wayne Shorter's minimal approach. The personnel kept changing, but the basic concept remained consistent and strong for 15 years.

***** Weather Report**

Columbia 468212 *Joe Zawinul (ky); Wayne Shorter (ts, ss); Miroslav Vitous (b); Alphonse Mouzon (d); Airto Moreira (perc).* 71.

*****(*) I Sing The Body Electric**

Columbia 468207 *Joe Zawinul (ky); Wayne Shorter (ts, ss); Miroslav Vitous (b); Eric Gravátt (d); Dom Um Romao (perc); with Ralph Towner (g); Wilmer Wise (t, picc t); Hubert Laws (f); Andrew White (eng hn); Joshie Armstrong, Yolande Bavan, Chapman Roberts (v).* 72.

****** Live In Tokyo**

Columbia 489208 2CD *Joe Zawinul (ky); Wayne Shorter (ts, ss); Miroslav Vitous (b); Eric Gravátt (d); Dom Um Romao (perc).* 1/72.

Weather Report is one of the great jazz groups of its time. 'Birdland' on *Heavy Weather* (below) is one of only a tiny handful of contemporary jazz tunes that everyone seems to have heard. Though it has tended to overshadow the rest of the group's output, it encapsulates perfectly the formula that made the group so successful: solid part-writing from Joe Zawinul, Wayne Shorter's enigmatic saxophone sound, a free-floating personnel round the Zawinul–Shorter cadre, and great product marketing (Weather Report covers were consistently eye-catching and aesthetically pleasing). A much-talked-about boxed set of all the group's Columbia recordings seems unlikely to ever appear, although the individual albums have been steadily upgraded, a few at a time, in new masterings.

From its inception until its demise in 1986, Weather Report was a flexible ensemble. After the first album, it was unmistakably Zawinul's flexible ensemble. From that point, Zawinul claimed the majority of composition credits (though Shorter, Pastorius and others chipped in) and steered the band's increasingly rhythm-orientated conception. Zawinul compositions are typically riff-centred bass-clef ideas, built up in layers by the rest of the band. Those who had followed Shorter's developing career were alternately baffled and horrified by the exiguous squeaks and tonal smears that suddenly were passing for solos (solos, it had been pointed out, were not the Weather Report way; 'we always solo and we never solo'). The first album was a set of fey acrylic sketches, clearly derived from the pastel side of the 1969–70 Miles Davis band (in which both Zawinul and Shorter saw service) but much rawer in tone. The opening 'Milky Way' is a pleased-with-itself set of FX on electric piano and soprano saxophone; 'it has to do with overtones and the way one uses the piano pedals?' Yeah? That's great, man. Most of the rest is in similar vein. Many years later, Vitous rejigged his folksy 'Morning Lake' and made something of it. The recording is thin and erratic, which is a shame, for Shorter's closing 'Eurydice' introduces some promise.

Everything about *I Sing The Body Electric* was very 1972: the title lifted from Whitman via Ray Bradbury, the brilliant sci-fi artwork (an overdue hand, please, for Ed Lee, Jack Trompetter and Fred Swanson), the psychobabble liner-note ('There is flow. There is selflessness'). There was also a band on the brink of premature extinction. Side one is more or less an extension of the debut album. The (presumably) anti-war 'Unknown Soldier' is almost prettified. The only thing that redeems it from banality is a tense cymbal pulse that on the live second side erupts into some of the most torrential and threatening percussion of the period. Zawinul is on record as thinking that Gravátt was the finest drummer the group ever had. On 'Vertical Invader' he plays with a clubbing hostility that somehow intensifies the impression that the group was heading off in four or five (Dom Um Romao was only a part-timer) directions at once. These days, Gravátt works as a prison guard. *Plus ça change.*

The live material from Japan had been known from the second side of *I Sing The Body Electric* but, as anyone who managed to catch the group at this time knows (and they played memorable gigs in Europe as well, not least at Ronnie Scott's in London), the live impact was fearsome and cumulative. Listening to *Live In Tokyo* over the span of two whole discs confirms for sure that at this point this was not merely a studio-confected band, good on atmospheres but lacking in sheer fire and funk. The ferocity of Gravátt's drumming, the soaring brilliance of Vitous's bass playing, and (as always) the Zawinul–Shorter axis made this one of the great groups of the time. Much of the second disc was drawn from the group's first album, and though 'The Moors', medleyed with 'Eurydice', hasn't the frail beauty of the studio version it has certainly acquired a new strength and gravitas.

***(*) Sweetnighter

Columbia 485102-2 *Joe Zawinul (ky); Wayne Shorter (ts, ss); Miroslav Vitous (b); Alphonso Johnson, Eric Gravátt (d); Dom Um Romao (perc).* 73.

Sweetnighter was in some ways a consolidating record, though nowadays it yields up considerable treasures, not least the stunning 'Boogie Woogie Waltz', which is the band's single most accessible track before 'Birdland'. The tracks were subject to a degree of post-production which was much more marked than that on the first records, and the glistening studio sound, given an almost juicy reverb on the keyboards and percussion, suddenly brought the group's sound on to much firmer ground, and made the point that from this marker onwards this was very much a band whose best work would be done in studios. 'Boogie Woogie Waltz' and '125th Street Congress' were seemingly endless jams that secured a suitably hypnotic feel, and Vitous's farewell piece 'Will' is peculiarly beautiful, circling around Zawinul's piano lick.

CORE COLLECTION

**** Mysterious Traveller

Columbia 507657-2 *Joe Zawinul (ky); Wayne Shorter (ts, ss); Miroslav Vitous (b); Ismael Wilburn (d); Dom Um Romao (perc).* 73–74.

This is still perhaps the most sheerly beautiful of the Weather Report records, from the wild joy of 'Nubian Sundance' with its synthed crowd-noises to the quietness of 'Blackthorn Rose', a lyrical, delicate piece of music that suggests this may have been the point of maximum closeness between the band's onlie begetters, Zawinul and Shorter. Some of the material was recorded at Zawinul's home, with his kids romping in the background, and only later put together in the studio, and it is this balance between improvisational immediacy and brilliantly crafted overdubbing that gives the record its lasting freshness and power.

***(*) Tale Spinnin'

Columbia 507656-2 *As above, except Alphonso Johnson (b) replaces Vitous; omit Romao, Wilburn; add Leon Ndugu Chancler (d), Alyrio Lima (perc).* 74.

***(*) Black Market

Columbia 507658-2 *Joe Zawinul (ky); Wayne Shorter (ts, ss); Alphonso Johnson, Jaco Pastorius (b); Chester Thompson, Narada Michael Walden (d); Alex Acuña, Don Alias (perc).* 76.

***(*) Heavy Weather

Columbia CK 65108 *Joe Zawinul (ky); Wayne Shorter (ts, ss); Jaco Pastorius (b); Alejandro Neciosup Acuna (d, perc); Manolo Badrena (perc).* 76.

**(*) Mr Gone

Columbia 468208 *Joe Zawinul (ky); Wayne Shorter (ts, ss); Jaco Pastorius (b); Tony Williams, Steve Gadd, Pete Erskine (d); Manolo Badrena (perc); Denice Williams, Jon Lucien (v).* 78.

*** Night Passage

Columbia 468211 *Joe Zawinul (ky); Wayne Shorter (ts, ss); Jaco Pastorius (b); Peter Erskine (d); Robert Thomas Jr (perc).* 80.

*** Weather Report

Columbia CK 48824 *As above.* 82.

*** 8:30

Columbia 476908 2CD *As above.* 83.

***** Procession**

Columbia CK 65453 *Joe Zawinul (ky); Wayne Shorter (ss, ts); Victor Bailey (b); Omar Hakim (d); Jose Rossy (perc).* n.d.

***** Sportin' Life**

Columbia CK 39908 *As above.* 84.

Ever afterwards, Weather Report albums were inclined to look like audition sessions for new drummers. Steve Gadd, Tony Williams and Peter Erskine all played on *Mr Gone*, suggesting a band that was going in too many directions at once. *Tale Spinnin'*, in its new mastering, sounds fresher and more vibrant than we had previously remembered, with the epic melody of 'Lusitanos' a forgotten Shorter highlight and Zawinul relishing his keyboard effects on 'Freezing Fire'. *Black Market* seems to combine the virtues of earlier albums: atmospheric tone-poetry, thudding, joyous rhythms. With Pastorius arriving in time to cut the funky 'Barbary Coast', Zawinul has the engine-room tuned to his obvious satisfaction. 'Black Market' is a wonderful, thunderous tune that completely blows out Shorter's rather wimpy 'Three Clowns' and utterly piffling figures; galling, because on 'Cannon Ball', dedicated to Julian Cannonball Adderley – for whom Zawinul played and wrote 'Country Preacher' and 'Mercy, Mercy, Mercy' – Shorter signs in again with some chunky tenor.

Heavy Weather was the breakthrough album in market terms. It allegedly shifted in excess of 400,000, largely on the strength of 'Birdland', a whistleable, riffy tune dedicated to the New York jazz club. No one had ever danced to 'Orange Lady' or 'Surucucú'; suddenly, Weather Report was big – a fact that comfortably disguised the detail that, 'Birdland' and 'A Remark You Made' apart, *Heavy Weather* was nothing much. Onstage, the band went decidedly *nouveau riche*, tossing around techno-nonsense, indulging in pointless virtuosity.

All except Shorter. He is widely taken to be *Mr Gone* (at high school, they'd called him 'Mr Weird'), but he shows his taste, maintaining virtual silence on the band's worst record, lower than which it took them some time to dive. *Night Passage* was better, but it was already obvious that a decade was more than enough and the band had done most of its best work. The decision to repeat the eponymous title of the first album for the 11th was, on the face of it, puzzling; but in some ways this overlooked record does hark back to the first couple, where atmosphere and degree of abstraction were still very much the key.

The final settled line-up still created most of its best work. *Procession* is particularly good, though often overlooked, and the electronically distorted voices of Manhattan Transfer on 'Where The Moon Goes' reprises their imaginative and still stirring intepretation of 'Birdland'.

***** This Is This**

Columbia CK 40280 *Joe Zawinul (ky); Wayne Shorter (ss); Carlos Santana (g); Victor Bailey (b); Peter Erskine, Omar Hakim (d); Mino Cinelu (perc).* 85.

A curtain-call and a slightly sad farewell to one of the most influential groups of recent times. The photo of Zawinul and Shorter shaking hands on the back cover underlined the strong impression that this was a farewell project. For most of the album, Joe's keyboard and wind-synth figures replace much of the saxophone work of the past, while guest performer Santana creates some astonishing effects on 'The Man With The Copper Fingers', a track that anticipates much of what Zawinul was to do with his future groups. Erskine is also on the fringes, though his hand is also evident in the production, and he hands over drumming responsibilities to the much less expressive Hakim.

***** The Jaco Years**

Columbia CK 65451 *As above.* 75–80.

****** The Best Of Weather Report**

Columbia 507659-2 *As various albums above.* 73–84.

As a survey of Pastorius's contribution as a composer, *The Jaco Years* makes some sense, but Weather Report and Jaco fans will almost certainly have the material already. The solo workout on 'Slang' is a predictable curtain-call, but as a whole *The Jaco Years* merely underlines the impression that WR was Zawinul's band, with Shorter as his secret sharer, and all other participants, even Pastorius, as bit-players. Affirmed further by the new *Best Of Weather Report*, which is an exceptionally well-chosen set, rescuing hidden beauties such as 'Elegant People' from *Black Market* and – a daring one for those who know only the pop high of 'Birdland' – the full original 'Boogie Woogie Waltz'. The salutary point about it is that there are only two tracks made after 1976. The earlier set made sense when circulation of some of the earlier discs was patchy, but since these are now squarely in the marketplace, it seems a touch redundant. However, for anyone who want just a flavour of those early, more abstract years this is a good buy.

*****(*) Live And Unreleased**

Columbia Legacy C2K 65526 2CD *Wayne Shorter (ss, ts); Joe Zawinul (ky); Victor Bailey, Alphonso Johnson, Jaco Pastorius (b); Peter Erskine, Omar Hakim, Chester Thompson (d); Alex Acuna (d, perc); Manolo Badrena, Jorge Rossy (perc).* 75–83.

Though half of *I Sing The Body Electric* was a concert recording (since completed on a separate CD release), Weather Report didn't issue a full-scale live album until *8:30* in 1980. These present tapes have been closely supervised by Zawinul and Shorter but so good are they and so electrifying was WR as a touring outfit that one wonders why there haven't been more live sessions over the years. The only thing missing here is the torrential drumming of Eric Gravátt; otherwise an exemplary representation of the band in its best years. The reappearance of early material like 'In A Silent Way' (segued with 'Waterfall' from the first album), mini-medleys of compositions like 'Dr Honoris Causa' (dedicated to Herbie Hancock), 'Directions', a rumbustious 'Cucumber Slumber' and a stupendous 'Man In The Green Shirt' make this an essential purchase for WR fans and a chance to ease the conscience and clear those illicit C-90s off the shelf. Nicely packaged, too, which you can't say about any of the bootlegs.

Chick Webb (1909–39)

DRUMS

Born in Baltimore, the diminutive Webb had already been bandleading for some time in New York when he took over at the Savoy ballroom in 1933. He kept the most competitive band in the city there for six years, hiring Ella Fitzgerald as his band singer in 1935, but TB of the spine eventually killed him. Fitzgerald took over his band after his death.

****** Chick Webb 1929–1934**

Classics 502 *Webb; Ward Pinkett, Louis Bacon, Taft Jordan (t, v); Edwin Swayzee, Mario Bauza, Reunald Jones, Bobby Stark,*

Shelton Hemphill, Louis Hunt (t); Robert Horton, Jimmy Harrison, Sandy Williams, Ferdinand Arbello, Claude Jones (tb); Hilton Jefferson, Louis Jordan, Benny Carter (cl, as); Pete Clark, Edgar Sampson (as); Elmer Williams (cl, ts); Wayman Carver (ts, f); Don Kirkpatrick, Joe Steele (p); John Trueheart (bj, g); Elmer James (bb, b); John Kirby (b); Chuck Richards, Charles Linton (v). 6/29–11/34.

***(*) **Rhythm Man 1931–1934**
Hep CD 1023 *As above.* 31–34.

***(*) **Chick Webb 1935–1938**
Classics 517 *As above, except add Nat Story, George Matthews (tb), Chauncey Houghton (cl, as), Ted McRae (ts), Tommy Fulford (p), Bill Thomas, Beverley Peer (b); omit Bacon, Swayzee, Jones, Hemphill, Hunt, Horton, Harrison, Arbello, Carter, Kirkpatrick, Richards, Linton.* 6/35–8/38.

Between them, these CDs include virtually all of Webb's studio recordings aside from those with vocals by Ella Fitzgerald, which Classics have released under her name. The two tracks by The Jungle Band of 1929 sound almost primitive in comparison to the ensuing sessions, driven as much by Trueheart's machine-like banjo-strumming as by Webb; but its use of the reeds and Webb's already exciting playing point a way out of the '20s, and by the time of the 1931 session – which includes a memorable arrangement by Benny Carter of his own 'Blues In My Heart' and a valedictory appearance by Jimmy Harrison, who died not long afterwards – Webb was running a great band, which eventually (in 1933) won him a long-running residency at Harlem's Savoy Ballroom. Edgar Sampson handled the best of the earlier arrangements, and the leader could boast fine soloists in Taft Jordan (later to join Ellington), Sandy Williams, Bobby Stark and Elmer Williams, as well as a rhythm section that was almost unrivalled for attack and swing. Webb's own mastery of an enormous drum-kit allowed him to pack a whole range of percussive effects into breaks and solos which never upset the momentum of the band. His distance from the showmanship of Gene Krupa, who would far surpass him in acclaim, was complete. Some of the best examples of what he could do are on the second Classics disc, including the terrific drive of 'Go Harlem' and the breaks in 'Clap Hands! Here Comes Charley'. Once Fitzgerald had started singing with the band and began to secure a wider fame, though, some of the zip went out of their playing, and although the weakest material is confined to the Fitzgerald CDs, the closing tracks on Classics 517 show them cooling off.

Choosing among these discs is a matter of individual taste. The two Classics CDs offer uninterrupted coverage, but their reproduction, though quite listenable, is second-best to the Hep disc. Hep's excellent survey covers only the period 1931–4 and misses many of the best tracks, but it is still a fine set in excellent sound.

Eberhard Weber (born 1940)

BASS, CELLO, OCARINA, KEYBOARDS

Learned cello as a boy but soon switched to bass and played many gigs in the '60s, although only as a part-timer, since he also worked in film and television. Early associations with Wolfgang Dauner and Volker Kriegel led to his own composing and bandleading, and a long tenure with ECM beginning in 1973. He was a pioneer in using bass with electronics, playing an adapted upright model.

***(*) **The Colours Of Chloe**
ECM 833331-2 *Weber; Ack Van Rooyen (flhn); Rainer Bruninghaus (ky); Peter Giger, Ralf Hubner (d); strings.* 12/73.

Having played straightahead jazz bass through the '60s, Weber delivered this uncannily beautiful album to Manfred Eicher's ECM operation and won himself an award or two. If some passages now suggest a cooler version of *Tubular Bells*, with the overlapping themes of 'No Motion Picture' hinting at the tranquillizing pomposity of progressive rock, the singular beauty of the textures and Weber's discovery of a new world based around massed cellos and subtle electronic treatments remains insidiously affecting. While the improvisational content is carefully rationed against the measure of the themes, Bruninghaus and Weber himself emerge as thoughtful and surprisingly vigorous virtuosos. If the CD offers few improvements over the excellent original vinyl edition, the recording itself still sounds splendid.

CORE COLLECTION

**** **Yellow Fields**
ECM 843205-2 *Weber; Charlie Mariano (ss, shenai); Rainer Bruninghaus (ky); Jon Christensen (d).* 9/75.

Weber's masterpiece is essentially a period piece which nevertheless still seems modern. The sound of it seems almost absurdly opulent: bass passages and swimming keyboard textures that reverberate from the speakers, chords that seem to hum with huge overtones. The keyboard textures in particular are of a kind that will probably never be heard on record again. But there's little prolixity or meandering in this music. Weber builds keenly around riffs and rhythmical figures, and solos – Mariano sounding piercingly exotic on the shenai, heartbreakingly intense on soprano – are perfectly ensconced within the sound-field. The key element, though, is the inspirational series of cross-rhythms and accents which Christensen delivers, rising to an extraordinary crescendo towards the close of 'Sand-Glass', a sprawling performance built from simple materials. And the leader's own bass never sounded better.

** **The Following Morning**
ECM 829116-2 *Weber; Rainer Bruninghaus (ky); Oslo Philharmonic Orchestra.* 8/76.

*** **Silent Feet**
ECM 835017-2 *Weber; Charlie Mariano (ss, shenai); Rainer Bruninghaus (ky); John Marshall (d).* 11/77.

(*) **Fluid / Rustle
ECM 829381-2 *Weber; Gary Burton (vib, mar); Bill Frisell (g, bal); Bonnie Herman, Norma Winstone (v).* 1/79.

The anchorless drifting of *The Following Morning* was an inexplicably disappointing continuation, rhythmically dead and texturally thin, with Weber and Bruninghaus circling dolefully through their material and badly missing a drummer. *Silent Feet* introduced John Marshall, formerly of Soft Machine, into the Colours band which Weber was touring with and, while his stiffer virtuosity wasn't the same thing as Christensen's sober flair, he restored some of the punch to Weber's music. The record hasn't the memorable tunes and perfect empathy of the earlier discs, though. Nor is *Fluid / Rustle* much more than enervating, with Burton's blandly effortful playing and Frisell's as-yet-unfocused contributions adding little to Weber's pretty but uninvolving pieces.

*****(*) Little Movements**
ECM 159492-2 *Weber; Charlie Mariano (ss, f); Rainer Bruninghaus (ky); John Marshall (d).* 7/80.

****(*) Later That Evening**
ECM 829382-2 *Weber; Paul McCandless (ss, cor, ob, bcl); Lyle Mays (p); Bill Frisell (g); Michael DiPasqua (d).* 3/82.

Little Movements was a return to form. Some of its worldly metres and textures (especially in 'Bali' and 'Dark Spell') have become a commonplace, perhaps even a cliché in recent years, but at the time it felt like fresh ground and the quality of the playing by all hands has kept its lustre. The opening 'The Last Stage Of A Long Journey' remains especially fine, and Weber has gone back to this piece in the last few years (see below). *Later That Evening* isn't quite so good, with Mays a poor substitute for Bruninghaus, and McCandless missing Mariano's acute sense of context, but it has its moments.

*****(*) Chorus**
ECM 823844-2 *Weber; Jan Garbarek (ss, ts); Manfred Hoffbauer (cl, f); Martin Kunstner (ob, cor); Ralf Hubner (d).* 9/84.

***** Orchestra**
ECM 837343-2 *Weber; Herbert Joos, Anton Jillich, Wolfgang Czelusta, Andreas Richter (tb); Winfried Rapp (btb); Rudolf Diebetsberger, Thomas Hauschild (frhn); Franz Stagl (tba).* 5–8/88.

Weber has lacked a valuable context in recent years: having patented one of the most gorgeous of bass sounds, he doesn't seem to have much else to say with it. *Chorus* is heavy on the brooding-spirit element, with Garbarek delivering some of his most stentorian commentaries on what are less than riveting themes, as Weber and Hubner toil away in the background. As a sequence of mood-music cameos, it may appeal strongly to some, but it's a depressing listen over the course of an entire record. *Orchestra* may disappoint any who've attended Weber's highly entertaining solo concerts. He splits the album between bass soliloquies and counterpoint with a chilly brass section, yet the prettiest piece on the disc is the synthesizer tune, 'On A Summer's Evening'.

****** Pendulum**
ECM 519707-2 *Weber (b solo).* 93.

Weber's second solo record is all bass this time and finds much of the beguiling and unexpectedly light-hearted feel of his one-man concerts. Ironically, it is much more studio-orientated: where *Orchestra* was overdub-free and essentially live, *Pendulum*, while remaining a solo meditation, is carefully edited for maximum effect. Weber's bass remains a unique sound in the music, and here he finds an almost perfect balance between the mixed blessing of bass opulence and the sing-song quality of his best melodies. Overlapping riffs or vamps counter the steady onward flow of the improviser's ideas, and in 'Street Scenes', 'Children's Song No. 1' and 'Pendulum' itself he secures a marvellous, patient equilibrium. His sleeve-notes are remarkably self-aware and offer some useful signposts for working through this encounter with 'my life-long preoccupation – also my old adversary'. Weber's best for many years.

***** Endless Days**
ECM 013420-2 *Weber; Paul McCandless (ob, cor, bcl, ss); Rainer Bruninghaus (ky); Michael DiPasqua (d).* 00.

Weber told his band that 'you can play anything, as long as it doesn't sound like jazz', a recipe which we admire if not exactly condone. The old firm duly work their way through music which seems to have had its improvisational element thinned to the point of absence, yet it is unmistakably Weberian. McCandless's reeds aren't exactly jazzy to start with and DiPasqua (who is otherwise in retirement!) has a role which sometimes resembles a tympanist more than a kit drummer. Weber fans will, of course, want to hear it and have it, but we miss the sense of melodious power which used to light up Eberhard's older records. At least the closing 'The Last Stage Of A Long Journey' sends us on our way rejoicing.

*****(*) :rarum: Selected Recordings**
ECM 014202-2 *Weber; Jan Garbarek (ss, f, ts); Paul McCandless (ss, cor); Charlie Mariano (ss); Rainer Bruninghaus (ky); Lyle Mays (p); Gary Burton (vib); Bill Frisell, Pat Metheny (g); Steve Swallow (b); Jon Christensen, Danny Gottlieb, John Marshall, Michael DiPasqua, Marilyn Mazur (d); Norma Winstone (v).* 12/74–4/00.

Weber's choice from his voluminous ECM archive is one of the most surprising in this series. Five of the ten tracks are not from his own albums, and he leaves aside both *The Colours Of Chloe* and *Yellow Fields*. Instead, there are collaborations with Burton, Towner – the superlative 'Nimbus' from *Solstice* – Metheny and Garbarek. The title-pieces from *Silent Feet* and *Fluid / Rustle* are welcome reminders of somewhat neglected records, as is Garbarek's 'Gesture'. Everywhere, that huge, signature sound is a constant.

Ben Webster (1909–73)

TENOR SAXOPHONE

Born in Kansas City, he played violin, then piano, before taking up sax at Budd Johnson's suggestion. Joined Bennie Moten in 1931 and worked with many bands before gaining his greatest eminence with Duke Ellington from 1940. Left in 1944, rejoined 1948–9, then worked as a freelance through the '50s. Settled in Europe from 1964 and eventually died in Amsterdam, having long since been an unpredictable if beloved character. His unique timbre on the tenor – breathy, swooningly romantic – is high on most lists of favourite sounds in jazz.

***** The Horn**
Progressive PCD-7001 *Webster; Hot Lips Page (t); Clyde Hart (p); Charlie Drayton (b); Denzil Best (d).* 2/44.

***** Ben Webster 1944–1946**
Classics 1017 *As above, except add Emmett Berry, Dick Vance (t), Walter 'Foots' Thomas, Budd Johnson (ts), Marlowe Morris, Johnny Guarnieri, Jimmy Jones (p), Oscar Pettiford, Al Hall, John Simmons (b), Big Sid Catlett, Cozy Cole, David Booth (d).* 2/44–1/46.

*****(*) Ben Webster 1946–1951**
Classics 1253 *Webster; Idries Sulieman, Bill Coleman, Richard Smith, Maynard Ferguson (t); Tony Scott (cl); Benny Carter (as); Argonne Thornton, Al Haig, Jimmy Jones, Buster*

Moten, Gerry Wiggins (p); Bill De Arango, Johnny Rogers (g); John Kirby, Lloyd Anderson, Al Hall, John Simmons (b); Sid Catlett, Denzil Best, Jesse Price, George Johnson (d). 5/46–12/51.

★★★★ King Of The Tenors

Verve 519806-2 *Webster; Harry 'Sweets' Edison (t); Benny Carter (as); Oscar Peterson (p); Barney Kessel, Herb Ellis (g); Ray Brown (b); Alvin Stoller, J. C. Heard (d).* 5–12/53.

★★★★ Soulville

Verve 521449-2 *Webster; Oscar Peterson (p); Barney Kessel, Herb Ellis (g); Ray Brown (b); J. C. Heard, Stan Levey (d).* 5/53–10/57.

★★★★ Ben Webster Meets Oscar Peterson

Verve 521448-2 *Webster; Oscar Peterson (p); Ray Brown (b); Ed Thigpen (d).* 59.

Thirty years after his death, his sound still haunts every tenor saxophonist who tackles a ballad. Ben Webster, often identifiable via a single, signature note, played jazz like few other musicians ever have. As he got older and less partial to any tempo above a very slow lope, he pared his manner back to essentials which still, no matter how often one hears them, remain uniquely affecting. Sometimes, all he does is play the notes of a melody, in a time that is entirely of his own choosing, and still he makes it uniquely absorbing. The best of his early work is with Duke Ellington – he remained, along with Paul Gonsalves, one of only two tenormen to make a genuine impression on Ducal history – but his records as a solo player, from the early '50s onwards, are a formidable legacy.

The Horn is a collection of WBC transcriptions featuring Ben as nominal leader of a quintet with Hot Lips Page. The flow of the music is somewhat jolted by the programme, which includes various false starts and alternatives for the sake of completeness, and Lips Page takes a subsidiary role; but Webster's playing is already graceful and creating its own time and space. The remastering is occasionally cloudy but mostly good. Classics 1017 starts with the same session, minus the various alternatives, then proceeds through some excellent small-group music. There's a rare glimpse of Marlowe Morris on two 1944 titles (with lots of surface noise), before four titles by Walter Thomas – nice jump-band music; four quartet titles for Savoy, including an 'I Surrender Dear' which prefigures the great ballad interpretations of the '50s; and four titles by an Al Hall quintet with Dick Vance on trumpet – not very remarkable. Webster collectors will want to hear this music, but the remastering isn't up to much. Classics 1253 moves the story on as far as his first Mercury session in 1951. There are small-group dates for Haven, Wax and Capitol with some interesting sidemen (Bill Coleman, although he seems to be on the other side of the studio, and Tony Scott). The four titles with Bus Moten are good bluesy fun. By the time of the Mercury date, he's moving towards his grandest years, and 'Old Folks' is a vintage performance.

By 1953 Webster was ready to make his mark on the LP era – 78-r.p.m. duration was too short for such a patient improviser – and Norman Granz began recording him for his labels. *King Of The Tenors* blends a date with Oscar Peterson plus rhythm section with another where Edison and Carter sit in too, though the spotlight is always on Webster. 'Tenderly' has never been more tender, 'That's All' is sheer heaven, but 'Jive At Six' is a good piece of studio knockabout. Peterson may seem an unlikely partner, but just as Webster played superbly next to Art Tatum, so he mastered the potentially open floodgates of Peterson's playing. On *Soulville* there are lustrous ballads in 'Where Are You' and an eerily desolate 'Ill Wind', while 'Boogie Woogie' brings out the raucous side of the tenorman. Three previously unissued tracks from the sessions are also included on the CD. *Meets Oscar Peterson* is just as fine, with two melting ballads in 'The Touch Of Your Lips' and 'In The Wee Small Hours Of The Morning' and a lissom 'This Can't Be Love'. In its latest incarnation, as a Verve Master Edition with excellent sound, it stands as one of the indispensable mainstream jazz albums of the '50s.

CORE COLLECTION

★★★★ Music For Loving

Verve 527774-2 2CD *Webster; Harry Carney (bs); Teddy Wilson, Billy Strayhorn, Leroy Lovett (p); Billy Bauer (g); Ray Brown, George Duvivier, Wendell Marshall (b); Jo Jones, Osie Johnson, Louie Bellson (d); horns and strings.* 3/54–9/55.

Impeccably prepared, this and the following two-disc reissues are among Webster's most handsome records. The strings sessions, mostly arranged by Ralph Burns, may sound a little thin to ears used to digital grandeur, but the writing is beguiling, and Webster sweeps through what must have been an ideal setting for him. Hidden away at the end of the package, almost as a bonus, is the rare album which Harry Carney recorded with strings, a fine date in its own right.

★★★★ The Soul Of Ben Webster

Verve 527475-2 2CD *Webster; Art Farmer, Harry 'Sweets' Edison, Roy Eldridge (t); Vic Dickenson (tb); Johnny Hodges (as); Harold Ashby (ts); Jimmy Jones, Oscar Peterson, Billy Strayhorn (p); Mundell Lowe, Barney Kessel, Herb Ellis (g); Milt Hinton, Ray Brown, Jimmy Woode (b); Dave Bailey, Alvin Stoller, Sam Woodyard (d).* 3/57–7/58.

The Soul Of Ben Webster puts together three original LPs: the title album, Harry Edison's *Gee Baby Ain't I Good To You*, and Johnny Hodges's *Blues A-Plenty*. With three superb bands on hand, the music is a blueprint for small-group swing, and Webster contributes some of his most rounded and accomplished playing: the mesmerizing drift through 'Chelsea Bridge', for instance. His own date featured Ashby as second tenor, and there's a palpable camaraderie. Some of the Hodges titles are a bit slight, but this is altogether an indispensable issue.

★★★(★) Ben Webster And Associates

Verve 543302-2 *Webster; Roy Eldridge (t); Coleman Hawkins, Budd Johnson (ts); Jimmy Jones (p); Les Spann (g); Ray Brown (b); Jo Jones (d).* 4/59.

A belated arrival for a blustery, swaggering jam session for Ben and some top-dog pals. Tempos such as those chosen for 'De-dar' and 'Young Bean' are much faster than he would have liked but, with Hawkins and Johnson on hand, he wasn't going to take anything lying down, and the playing is vociferous and full of splendour. 'Time After Time' is a peerless Ben ballad. The remastering has left a lot of tape-hiss intact, but the music has great presence.

★★★(★) Verve Jazz Masters 43: Ben Webster

Verve 525431-2 *As Verve records above, except add Ella Fitzgerald (v), Johnny Otis Orchestra.* 12/51–11/59.

A choice selection from Webster's Verve years. Besides some of the staples from the albums listed above, there's Ella doing 'In A

Mellow Tone' from the *Ellington Songbook* sessions and a 1951 version of 'Star Dust' with Johnny Otis that seems to float skyward, star-dusted indeed.

*****(*) The Warm Moods**

Warner Bros 8122-73721-2 *Webster; Donn Trenner (p); Alfred Lustgarten, Lisa Minghetti (vn); Cecil Figelski (vla); Armond Kaproff (clo); Don Bagley (b); Frank Capp (d).* 1/60.

This rather scarce and somewhat forgotten Webster date goes about as far as anyone could in pushing the Webster envelope. The strings amount to no more than a quartet (unless you count Don Bagley's bass, but he plays it like a jazzman does). They're arranged by Johnny Richards, a man who was never satisfied unless he gave his players a tough assignment. The tunes are a queer lot: 'The Sweetheart Of Sigma Chi'? 'The Whiffenpoof Song'? Still, Ben just moseys through it. This was 1960, and he wasn't quite as indolent as he later became: he's pretty near the beat, and the notes which are more like huffs of air than something somewhere on the scale were yet to take over his phrasing. He can't be bothered to do much more than embellish the melodies, although here and there, as on the closing chorus of 'But Beautiful', he starts out on a promising solo – and then the song's over. The remastering is particularly excellent.

***** At The Renaissance**

Original Jazz Classics OJC 390 *Webster; Jimmy Rowles (p); Jim Hall (g); Red Mitchell (b); Frank Butler (d).* 10/60.

At The Renaissance finds Webster in unusual company and, while Rowles reads him like a good book, the others sometimes sound a little too smartly present and correct. 'Gone With The Wind', though, is a beauty.

****(*) Live! Providence, Rhode Island, 1963**

Storyville STCD 8237 *Webster; Mike Renzi (p); Bob Petterutti (b); Joe Veletri (d).* 12/63.

***** Soulmates**

Original Jazz Classics OJC 390 *Webster; Thad Jones (c); Joe Zawinul (p); Richard Davis (b); Philly Joe Jones (d).* 9–10/63.

Ben enjoyed himself in Providence: a gig which included 'My Romance', 'Embraceable You' and 'Danny Boy'. The local rhythm section plays respectfully but the sound is from an average, amateur tape. *Soulmates* offers a strange pairing with the young Joe Zawinul, with Jones sitting in on four tracks, although Webster was happy with any pianist who stood his ground. Highlights include a poignant reflection on Billie Holiday's 'Trav'lin' Light' and the title blues.

*****(*) At Montmartre 1965–1966**

Storyville 101 8347 *Webster; Kenny Drew, Atli Bjørn (p); Niels-Henning Orsted Pedersen (b); Alex Riel, Rune Carlsson (d).* 1/65–5/66.

Vintage Ben from a place he loved to play in, with men he could trust. The rhythm section do little other than frame the great sound, but that's what we've come to hear. The fidelity flickers in and out of focus at times, though no serious problems.

***** Ben And Buck**

Storyville STCD 8245 *Webster; Buck Clayton (t); Camille De Ceunyck (p); Tony Vaes (b); Charlie Pauvels (d).* 6/67.

Webster and Clayton could have been a dream team, but they actually don't play together all that much here. Most of the set is a feature for one or other of them and, when they do work together, it's usually at the kind of tempo Webster didn't like (anything over slow). Still, the individual features are often wonderful, and it's a shame that the inadequate sound doesn't catch the range of Clayton's lovely tone.

***** Masters Of Jazz Vol. 5: Ben Webster**

Storyville 4105 *Webster; Palle Mikkelborg, Perry Knudsen, Palle Bolvig, Allan Botschinsky (t); Per Espersen, Torolf Moolgaard, Axel Windfeld, Ole Kurt Jensen (tb); Uffe Karskov, Jesper Thilo, Dexter Gordon, Sahib Shihab, Bent Nielsen (reeds); Ole Kock Hansen, Kenny Drew (p); Ole Molin (g); Niels-Henning Orsted Pedersen, Hugo Rasmussen (b); Ole Steenberg, Albert 'Tootie' Heath, Bjarne Rostvold (d); strings.* 68–70.

***** Plays Ballads**

Storyville STCD 4118 *As above, except add Erling Christensen, Flemming Madsen (reeds), William Schiopffe (d), John Steffensen (perc).* 7/67–11/71.

***** Gentle Ben**

Ensayo ENY-CD 3433 *Webster; Tete Montoliu (p); Eric Peter (b); Peer Wyboris (d).* 11/72.

***** Baden 1972**

TCB 02102 *Webster; Dexter Gordon (ts); Kenny Drew (p); Bo Stief (b); Ed Thigpen (d).* 11/72.

****(*) My Man**

Steeplechase SCCD 31008 *Webster; Ole Kock Hansen (p); Bo Stief (b); Alex Riel (d).* 4/73.

Webster's final years found him based in Copenhagen, and his manner was by now so *sui generis* that it's tempting to view the later work as a single, lachrymose meditation on the same handful of favourite ballads and Ellington tunes. But Ben's own subtle variations on himself create felicitous differences between each stately rendition of 'Prelude To A Kiss' or 'Old Folks'. He was lucky in his accompanists: while several of the rhythm sections sound anonymous in themselves, Webster's knack of helping them raise their game elicits some exceptionally sympathetic playing from almost everybody. The two Storyville albums collect scatterings from several sessions over a five-year period, including dates with strings, some heavenly ballads and a couple of dates with Teddy Wilson at the piano; both mixed bags, but plenty of vintage Webster. *My Man* is a middling session, recorded on a typical late night at the Café Montmartre and a bit too relaxed. Montoliu, a favourite of the saxophonist, is on hand for the Barcelona studio date, *Gentle Ben*, which catches Ben's sound beautifully. Peter and Wyboris are less than ideal, but otherwise this is a bountiful example of late Webster. The radio broadcast from Baden is a potboiler, and though Ben enjoyed Dexter's company, this probably wasn't his sort of thing at this stage. That said, there's some lovely playing on a 'Blues In F', and Gordon does a surprisingly bleak turn on 'Didn't We'. Ed Thigpen kicks off 'Sunday' at an insane tempo, and Webster doesn't seem best pleased, but he gets through it. Anyone who loves the sound of Ben Webster will find something to enjoy in all these records.

***** Ultimate Ben Webster**

Verve 557537-2 *Webster; as various Verve albums listed above.* 52–59.

Chosen by James Carter, the tracks are a strange gathering in the end. Entries with R&B group The Ravens and Dinah Washington are collectable curios, not parts of anything 'ultimate', and since the most recent track dates from 1959, there's nothing from the old Webster in his Lear period – Carter could have picked something off *Big Ben Time* (otherwise deleted), for instance, which would at least have honoured the many years Ben spent in Europe.

Joel Weiskopf (born 1962)

PIANO

Syracuse-born, Weiskopf is a New York-based midstream-modernist with a wide range of experience, including a year with the Woody Herman orchestra and numerous sideman dates.

***** The Search**
Criss Cross 1174 *Weiskopf; Peter Washington (b); Billy Drummond (d).* 12/98.

***** New Beginning**
Criss Cross 1204 *Weiskopf; John Swana (t); Walt Weiskopf (ts); John Patitucci (b); Jeff Brillinger (d).* 1/01.

***** Change In My Life**
Criss Cross 1232 *Weiskopf; John Patitucci (b); Brian Blade (d).* 02.

The younger of the two Weiskopf brothers is a sunny player. His treatments of Shorter ('Edda'), Gershwin ('Bess You Is My Woman Now') and Monk ('Criss Cross') aren't so much lightweight as light-filled, the melodies articulated with a free, zesty airiness. His original 'Song For The Lost', with its unusual melodic structure, is the most inventive of his own pieces: on the title-track he tends to get a bit lost in rhetoric, and the tune outstays its welcome. He has superb cohorts in Washington and Drummond, the latter's cymbal-play in 'Song For The Lost' being especially ear-catching.

New Beginning is about Weiskopf's spiritual enlightenment, and it does tend towards perkiness rather than anything tougher: 'One For Gerry' is the prissiest kind of blues. Planting Weiskopf with a reputation as the Ned Flanders of Criss Cross isn't entirely fair, though: the playing throughout is crisp and smart. ***Change In My Life*** would seem to have the same or similar agenda. This is a first chance to hear him in a hornless trio and some of the restrictions of his playing become evident. Again, there isn't much blues feel, just a faux-toughness that creeps into the solos once or twice. The writing is good, though, and Patitucci is a master at this kind of gig, reprising some of the things he used to do for Chick in his few features.

Walt Weiskopf (born 1959)

TENOR SAXOPHONE

Weiskopf was an alto-player until, aged 20, he was offered a tenor chair in the Buddy Rich band. He has much other big-band and section experience and is based in New Jersey.

****** Simplicity**
Criss Cross Jazz 1075 *Weiskopf; Conrad Herwig (tb); Andy Fusco (as); Joel Weiskopf (p); Peter Washington (b); Billy Drummond (d).* 12/92.

***** A World Away**
Criss Cross 1100 *Weiskopf; Larry Goldings (org); Peter Bernstein (g); Bill Stewart (d).* 12/93.

Weiskopf is an experienced section-player (with Buddy Rich and Toshiko Akiyoshi) but these records are a lot more ambitious than the usual sideman-steps-out date. A couple of satisfying sessions for the small indie Iris led him to Criss Cross, where he opened his account with the splendid *Simplicity*. More than ever, Weiskopf chooses to assert his writing over his playing, with his own solos relatively discreet and deferential. The brimming, complex melodies of 'Subordination', the artfully overlapping horns of 'Brazilia' and the wholly original revision of 'Lazy Afternoon' are among the most interesting moments, but there's nothing here to disappoint. Fusco and Herwig are modest personalities too, but their relative mildness lets the calibre of Weiskopf's writing come through, and his rhythm section, ably led by brother Joel, is keenly alert.

A World Away puts the emphasis more keenly on Weiskopf's own playing, and for once the setting doesn't seem just right for him. Goldings, Bernstein and Stewart are old hands at the organ–guitar groove, and though clichés are displaced by the leader's typically penetrating writing, the music misses the firm centre of the previous discs. One compensation is another ingenious standard choice, 'The Long Hot Summer'.

*****(*) Night Lights**
Double Time DTRCD 106 *Weiskopf; Joel Weiskopf (p); Drew Gress (b); Steve Davis (d).* 10/95.

*****(*) Song For My Mother**
Criss Cross 1127 *Weiskopf; Joe Magnarelli (t); Conrad Herwig (tb); Jim Snidero (as, f, af); Anders Bostrom (f, af); Scott Robinson (bs, bcl, f); Joel Weiskopf (p); Peter Washington (b); Billy Drummond (d).* 12/95.

More excellent jazz. *Night Lights* has Weiskopf seeing what he can find within the confines of tenor, rhythm and standards. The trio seem to light on just the right tempo in all the tunes, and whether balladeering on 'Some Other Time' or taking a somewhat cryptic fast turn through 'You Go To My Head', Weiskopf uses his vibratoless tone and lean, twisty phrasing to fine effect. He also picks some intriguing tunes: 'Moonlight On The Ganges', 'Camelot', 'With The Wind And The Rain In Her Hair'.

Song For My Mother returns him to a nine-strong line-up. There's a surprise emphasis on Bostrom's flute, though he's not especially remarkable as a soloist; and it's the varied ways the leader marshals his horns that make the session well out of the ordinary for Criss Cross blowing. 'Where Is Love' is spine-tingling ballad-playing, and 'High Noon' a real head-turner.

*****(*) Anytown**
Criss Cross 1169 *Weiskopf; Renee Rosnes (p); Joe Locke (vib); Doug Weiss (b); Tony Reedus (d).* 12/98.

Weiskopf says that his aim this time was to try and sustain longer solos than on his previous records – a recipe for trouble, given the existential meanderings of too many saxophonists. But the seven originals are among his most absorbing work too, and the band is absolutely off the top shelf. The title-track is a furiously paced start which cools off only for the first part of Rosnes's solo. 'Blues In The Day' isn't a blues but a complex unison theme, 'Scottish Folk Song' is a folkish melody cleverly harmonized, and the 'Naima'-like 'Adrienne' is a tender but unsentimental ballad line. Here and there Reedus makes too much noise, but there is very little to find fault with on another great Weiskopf session, longer solos and all.

*****(*) Siren**
Criss Cross 1187 *Weiskopf; Joe Magnarelli (t, flhn); Conrad Herwig (tb); Jim Snidero (as, f); Anders Bostrom(f, af); Scott Robinson (bs, bcl); Joel Weiskopf (p); Doug Weiss (b); Billy Drummond (d).* 12/99.

Back to the nonet, and with all these voicings at his disposal, the leader adds and subtracts players in a way that might feel overworked, as if obliged to keep everybody involved. But he knows large-group music well enough to skirt that problem. The writing is instead dedicated to a kind of connoisseurship. There's a rather ingenious harmonizing of 'Baby Won't You Please Come Home' for the horns, while the piano takes the chance for an extravagant solo underneath; a teasingly brief essay in minimalism, 'Glass Eye'; and lush playing situations in 'Sire' and 'Separation'.

David Weiss

TRUMPET

Respected arranger and producer, with a credit on O Brother, Where Art Thou?, Weiss has been slow to record under his own name.

***** Breathing Room**
Fresh Sound New Talent FSNT 110 *Weiss; Craig Handy (as); Marcus Strickland (ts); Xavier Davis (p); Dwayne Burno (b); E. J. Strickland (d).* 2/01.

Already known for his film and session work and for the New Jazz Composers Octet disc issued on the same label a couple of years earlier, Weiss has nothing to prove and takes this 'debut' set very much in that spirit. Seemingly influenced by Wayne Shorter (he includes two of Wayne's more impenetrable themes here), he favours lateral chord progressions and unfamiliar tonalities. 'Getaway' is stunning and if it's the shape of things to come, it's a very exciting prospect, a thick, dark piece with something for everyone to do. Handy comes in for four tracks and makes an immediate impression, though the tenor-playing Strickland is a more than competent player. Fine group sound and a set that leaves you asking for more.

Michael Weiss

PIANO

Not to be confused with the electronica musician of the same name, Michael is a thoughtful stylist with a faintly sombre demeanour at the keyboard.

***** Presenting Michael Weiss**
Criss Cross 1022 *Weiss; Tom Kirkpatrick (t); Ralph Lalama (ts); Ray Drummond (b); Kenny Washington (d).* 4/86.

*****(*) Milestones**
Steeplechase SCCD 31449 *Weiss; Paul Gill (b); Joe Farnsworth (d).* 5/99.

*****(*) Soul Journey**
Sintra 2003 *Weiss; Ryan Kisor (t, flhn); Steve Davis (tb); Steve Wilson (as); Paul Gill (b); Joe Farnsworth (d); Daniel Sadownick (perc).* n.d.

It's hard to know whether Weiss has been more influenced by Bill Evans or early Herbie Hancock. There's a definite strain of melancholy, but when you hear what he does with 'My Melancholy Baby' at the top of *Presenting*, you wonder how deep it runs. He doesn't seem the kind of piano-player who'd relish the hard-bop format of that first record, but he pulls it off in style, though often working counter to the expressive direction of the rest of the band.

And so to Steeplechase, and at last a piano trio album. This is the first occasion on which one feels Weiss shakes off his torpor and produces an album that really reflects his talents. It's marked by some unexpected charts, like McLean's 'Walter Davis Ascending' and 'Little Melonae', both of which sit beautifully for the piano, as well as Kenny Dorham's 'Buffalo'. Farnsworth is now part of the operation and the same strictures apply, though so does the same enjoyment of his beetling style.

And having got that out of his system, and worked through a few of his compositional mentors, Weiss turns in a septet album packed with his own compositions. These are not earth-shaking, and with most of them an ancestral strain is evident. What's wonderful about them is the arranging, with every line clearly voiced (and clearly executed by these guys). 'Soul Journey', 'Cheshire Cat' and 'El Camino' are the outstanding cuts. Perhaps a couple of standard arrangements, or maybe new versions of things like 'Little Melonae' and 'Buffalo' from the previous album, would have helped

Don Weller (born 1940)

TENOR SAXOPHONE

A much-liked fixture on the British club scene for 30 years, Weller has been relatively sparsely recorded: his groups Major Surgery and the Weller–Spring Quartet are unrepresented on CD. His artful playing is very much his own, and his writing has recently taken much more prominence.

*****(*) 'Live'**
33 Jazz 032 *Weller; Gerard Presencer, Henry Lowther, Steve Waterman, Patrick White (t); Mark Nightingale, Malcolm Griffiths, Pete Beachill, Andy Fawbert (tb); Peter King, Nigel Hitchcock (as); Art Themen, Mornington Lockett (ts); Alan Barnes (bs); David Newton (p); Andrew Cleyndert (b); Bryan Spring (d).* 10/96.

The most sterling of sidemen and a formidable leader too, Weller has had a thin time of it in the CD era, and this great saxophonist has only this to show in the racks for what has been a splendid and unexpected initiative: a big band of British majors playing only Weller originals. Alternately rousing, hummable and charmingly songful, the material is exceptionally strong, and makes one wish that Don had had this opportunity before now. Passages such as the collective shout on 'Four By Three' and the tenor solo threaded against the ensemble on 'Bongate Song' are both exhilarating and thought-provoking. A relatively rough live recording and a sometimes wayward relationship between horns and rhythm section (and some under-rehearsal) makes the record short of a triumph. They have done other live work since, and the music deserves a well-resourced studio recording. But it really is time that a sympathetic label and producer got together to enable Don to set down his signature record.

Bobby Wellins (born 1936)

TENOR SAXOPHONE

A veteran Glaswegian modernist, Wellins won renown with the Stan Tracey group of the '60s and has worked his personal variations on small-group hard bop since.

***** Making Light Work**
Hep 2070 *Wellins; Pete Jacobsen (p); Kenny Baldock (b); Spike Wells (d).* 83.

***** Nomad**
Hot House HHCD 1008 *Wellins; Jonathan Gee (p); Thad Kelly (b); Spike Wells (d); Claire Martin (v).* 4/92.

****** Don't Worry 'Bout Me**
Cadillac SGCCD 05 *Wellins; Graham Harvey (p); Alec Dankworth (b); Martin Drew (d).* 2/96.

****** The Satin Album**
Jazzizit JITCD 9607 *Wellins; Colin Purbrook (p); Dave Green (b); Clark Tracey (d).* 7/96.

***** The Best Is Yet To Come**
Jazzizit 124 *Wellins; Liam Noble (p); Simon Thorpe (b); Dave Wickins (d).* 7/00.

As long ago as 1965, Bobby Wellins guaranteed his moment of jazz immortality with a solo on Stan Tracey's instrumental rendition of *Under Milk Wood.* 'Starless And Bible Black' remains the key reference-point for Wellins, a moment of brooding lyricism not without a hint of self-mockery, and it is a characteristic common to the residents of Llareggub and Glasgow that they don't take themselves too seriously, even when they are pouring their hearts out. Wellins is a consummate ballad-player, breathy and very immediate, with, as fellow-Scot and fellow saxophonist Tommy Smith has pointed out, a lot of 'air', not so much in his tone as in his shaping of a solo.

Unfortunately – though he himself now speaks of it with calm and some amusement – Wellins's health and career went off the grid for a good many years, and so the discography is startlingly thin. Comeback discs like *Birds Of Brazil,* reviewed in an earlier edition, are no longer available, and only with his 60th birthday did Wellins begin to establish himself as a recording artist. The 1983 Hep has made a reappearance with a couple of good bonus tracks. It's worth having not just for Bobby's delightfully chastened romanticism, but also because Jacobsen is one of the best accompanists in Europe, though rarely mentioned in despatches. *Nomad* is frankly disappointing, not so much because the saxophonist is below par as because the group behind him lacks definition and a bit of colour in its cheeks. To be fair to them, Wellins has picked some fairly chewy material: Hank Mobley's 'This I Dig Of You', Brownie's 'Sandu' and Monk's 'Little Rootie Tootie'. He doesn't hang around waiting for stragglers on any of them.

The next two albums were recorded only months apart, indication that Wellins was marking his 60th year with a burst of activity. Some of the most impressive work on *Nomad* was with singer Claire Martin. Wellins has always had a particular affection for voices. What he does is almost vocalese in reverse, taking the words out of the line, but retaining their emotional as well as their more strictly musical significance. That is what lies behind *The Satin Album,* an extended gloss (no pun intended) on Billie Holiday's 1958 LP, *Lady In Satin.* This is an altogether stronger group than on the Hot House release, and Wellins's interplay with Green is remarkable. 'I Get Along Without You Very Well' has the familiar self-possession and humour; but what follows, 'For All We Know', a wry plea of *carpe diem,* lifts the album at mid-point to a new height of emotional and philosophical sophistication.

The Cadillac disc was recorded live at the Vortex in north London, and it has all the presence and intimacy of that upper room. No American player could map out any more of the side-tracks and by-ways of these seven standards (a Wellins original, 'Tracery', closes the set) with any more subtlety, and yet not lose contact with the song itself. 'How Deep Is The Ocean' is masterful: beauty, exhilaration and the abyss all compressed into 12 minutes; even 'Lover Man' has a kind of majesty.

The most recent album is a tribute to Tony Bennett, who though no kind of jazz singer, has something of the same feel and presence as Wellins, a voice that always sounds up close and personal, always with a message for each specific listener, incapable of blandness or generality.

Dicky Wells (1907–85)

TROMBONE

Worked with various New York bands in the early '30s – and made some memorable records in Paris – before spending eight years with Count Basie from 1938. Thereafter he turned up in various small groups, although alcohol troubled him and his playing was inconsistent. He was a gifted writer and was still playing in the '80s.

****** Dicky Wells 1927–1943**
Classics 937 *Wells; Bill Coleman, Shad Collins, Bill Dillard, Kenneth Roane, Gus McLung (t); Frankie Newton (t, v); John Williams, Fletcher Allen (cl, as); Cecil Scott (cl, ts, bs); Howard Johnson (as); Lester Young (ts); Don Frye, Ellis Larkins (p); Django Reinhardt, Roger Chaput, Freddie Green (g); Hubert Mann, Rudolph Williams (bj); Chester Campbell, Mack Walker (tba); Richard Fulbright, Al Hall (b); Lloyd Scott, Bill Beason, Jo Jones (d).* 1/27–12/43.

The important tracks here are the dozen Wells headed up in Paris on two memorable July days in 1937. The first two groups feature the trombonist with Bill Coleman and Django Reinhardt, with Dillard and Collins making up a three-man trumpet-section on three titles. With no piano and Reinhardt driving all before him, the ensembles have a sound at once mercurial and light and limber, with quite magnificent playing from Coleman and Wells. There isn't a note out of place on 'Between The Devil And The Deep Blue Sea', 'Sweet Sue', the blues 'Hangin' Around Boudon' and 'Japanese Sandman'. The next session is comparatively lightweight, but it ended on what were effectively two trombone solos with rhythm accompaniment, and Wells's seven choruses on 'Dicky Wells Blues' make up one of the great pieces of trombone improvisation on record. His sound introduces a sober gaiety into the instrument's lugubrious temperament, and his vibrato and colouristic use of sudden shouting notes make every chorus fresh and surprising.

The disc opens with seven tracks with which Wells made his debut, with Lloyd Scott and Cecil Scott: lively if unexceptional New York jazz of the '20s. It ends on a septet date for Signature, from 1943, with Coleman, Young and Larkins (playing the Basie role). They take 'I Got Rhythm' far too fast, but there's compensation in the next three titles, with Dicky playing a beautiful slow introduction to 'I'm Fer It Too'. Wells can be heard to useful effect on many Basie records, but he seldom stepped out front again and he never surpassed those wonderful Paris dates.

Dick Wellstood (1927–87)

PIANO

Worked in Chicago and New York in the '50s and became a young upholder of swing and mainstream values, prized as band player and accompanist. A witty writer and dry humourist, his early death when still in great form was a loss to the music.

***** Dick Wellstood And His Famous Orchestra Featuring Kenny Davern**
Chiaroscuro CRD 128 *Wellstood; Kenny Davern (cl, ss).* 81.

***** Dick Wellstood And His All-Star Orchestra Featuring Kenny Davern**
Chiaroscuro CRD 129 *As above.* 81.

A jobbing musician who was content to play supper-club dates, parties and tribute recordings to great predecessors like Waller, James P. Johnson and Art Tatum, Dick Wellstood is easily underestimated. Always up for a gig though he may have been, he was also a practising lawyer, and his easy, engaging stride approach masks a steel-trap understanding of every wrinkle of piano jazz, an eclecticism that allows him to play in virtually every idiom, from early ragtime to quasi-modal compositions from the shores opposite bop. He has a decent touch with a Monk tune, as he shows on the second of the discs above. Regrettably, much of his work has bloomed and faded in highly unappreciative settings and company, and he is not well represented in the current catalogue. There is a distinct shortage of CD material for so active and undemanding a player.

At the keyboard, he sounds most like a younger version of James P. Johnson, setting up big and forceful alternations in the left hand against a characteristic tremolo in the melody line. He favours huge, raw bass-figures and counters their jagged outlines with wonderfully subtle fills and footnotes. The personnels above are not incomplete, despite the titles. The 'orchestra' business is one of Wellstood's jokes, as are originals like 'Fat As A Bastard'. In his late fifties he tempered his approach slightly, enough to admit an occasional ballad, though often in very improbable keys.

****** Live At The Sticky Wicket**
Arbors ARCD 19188 2CD *Wellstood (p solo).* 11/86.

How often do we manage to laugh aloud in the course of the lonely pilgrimage that is the *Penguin Jazz Guide*? Frankly, not that often, which makes this a particularly well-loved point in the journey. Wellstood's undentable good humour, lacking the sardonic bite of a Mose Allison or the surreal waywardness of a Slim Gaillard, has nevertheless warmed us many times over the past few years. Intended as a memorial and retrospective, this long set was recorded at the eponymous club in Hopkinton, Massachusetts, a location unknown to us, but graced by the great man's presence on this night. The programme is remorseless: 'St James Infirmary', 'Ain't Misbehavin'', 'The Entertainer', 'Maple Leaf Rag', 'Prelude To A Kiss', in fact, 32 tracks that cover a vast gamut of jazz history, played with unaffected exuberance. A sheer delight from start to finish.

*****(*) A Night In Dublin**
Arbors ARCD 19241 *Wellstood (p solo).* 2/77.

What it says on the box: Dick in an Irish bar, recorded by Ralph O'Callaghan on his then new reel-to-reel tape recorder, the tape sitting on his shelf for the next 23 years. Not quite as good as the Sticky Wicket marathon, but it's not far off, and the sound has been neatly cleaned up.

Alex Welsh (1929–82)

CORNET, VOCALS

Despite the surname, Welsh was a Scot. He didn't entirely look the part but was nevertheless a fine cornetist, influenced by Wild Bill Davison (though he emphatically denied this). When he died in 1982, Humphrey Lyttelton described the Welsh band's impact as a combination of 'romanticism and rage', a near-perfect characterization of its leader's buttoned-up ferocity.

*****(*) Live At The Royal Festival Hall 1954–55**
Lake LACD 8 *Welsh; Roy Crimmins (tb, v); Ian Christie, Archie Semple (cl); Fred Hunt (p); Nevil Skrimshire (g); Frank Thompson, Tom Page, Chris Staunton (b); Pete Appleby, Lennie Hastings (d).* 10/54–4/55.

***** It Has To Be**
Lake LACD 145 *As above, except add George Melly, Dickie Valentine (v).* 4–11/55.

***** Vintage Alex Welsh 1955-1956**
Lake LACD 179 *Welsh; Roy Crimmins (tb); Archie Semple (cl); Fred Hunt (p); Nevil Skrimshire (g); Hugh Carey, Billy Lock, Tom Page, Chris Staunton, Frank Thompson (b); Lennie Hastings (d); George Melly, Neva Raphaello (v).* 2/55–4/57.

***** Dixieland To Duke**
Lake LACD 92 *Welsh; Roy Crimmins (tb); Archie Semple (cl); Fred Hunt (p); Nigel Sinclair (g); Chris Staunton (b); Billy Lock, Johnny Richardson (d).* 2/57–3/58.

***** Music Of The Mauve Decade**
Lake LACD 62 *Welsh; Roy Crimmins (tb); Len Doughty (vtb); Archie Semple (cl); Harry Gold (bsx); Fred Hunt (p); Bill Reid (b); Johnny Richardson (d).* 59.

****(*) Vintage Alex Welsh Band 1962**
Jazzology JCD0-308 *Welsh; Roy Crimmins (tb); Archie Semple (cl); Fred Hunt (p); Tony Pitt (g); Bill Reid (b); Lennie Hastings (d).* 1/62.

Welsh's combination of, as Humphrey Lyttelton put it, 'romanticism and rage' was a unique and much-loved part of British jazz for many years. He made many records, and there is a better CD showing at present than there has been for some time. Lake have brought back most of the '50s recordings, which are often disconcertingly mixed: the Festival Hall sets are crashingly enthusiastic and will rekindle some happy memories, but some of the studio sessions on the likes of *Dixieland To Duke* and *Mauve Decade* walk an awkward line between crude Dixieland, trad and a more personal, bluesy synthesis. A good best-of from the period would probably be a welcome solution, provided it included 'New Orleans Masquerade' and 'You've Been A Good Old Wagon' from the *1955-1956* set by the Dixielanders. Jazzology have turned up a 1962 session from West Bridgeford's Dancing Slipper – foggy recording doesn't help, and the band aren't as together as on some nights, but Alex has some decent moments and it's loaded with atmosphere.

*****(*) Strike One**
Lake LACD 107 *Welsh; Roy Williams (tb); John Barnes (as, bs, cl, v); Fred Hunt (p); Jim Douglas (g, bj); Ron Mathewson (b); Lennie Hastings (d). 6/66.*

***** Just One More Chance**
Upbeat jazz URCD 191 *Welsh; Roy Williams (tb); John Barnes (as, bs, cl); Al Gay (ss, ts); Fred Hunt (p); Jim Douglas (g, bjo); Ron Mathewson, Ronnie Rae, Harvey Weston (b); Lennie Hastings (d). 66–72.*

***** Eddie Miller With Alex Welsh**
Jazzology JCD-298 *Welsh; Roy Williams (tb); John Barnes (as); Al Gay (ts, cl); Eddie Miller (ts); Fred Hunt (p); Jim Douglas (g); Ron Rae (b); Lennie Hastings (d). 4/67.*

****(*) Oh, Baby!**
Upbeat URDC 175 *Welsh; Roy Crimmins (tb); Al Gay (ss, ts, cl); Fred Hunt (p); Jim Douglas (g, d); Denny Wright (g); Ron Rubin, Pete Skivington (b); Roger Nobes (d, vib); Laurie Chescoe (d). 12/79–10/81.*

The band changed markedly in approach during the '60s, a period during which the once teetotal Welsh acquired a famous thirst for vodka, moving away from the ragged, Chicagoan 'Condon style' towards a more orthodox swing approach. The sessions on *Just One More Chance* were recorded for the BBC's Jazz Club. Though the rhythms seem quite mechanical, there is some formidable playing throughout the band: notably from Welsh himself, with the mute on 'I Wished On The Moon', from Roy Williams on that same tune and from the wonderful Barnes. The band's enormous success at Antibes in 1967 and at later American festivals seemed to do no more than reinforce internal divisions. The Lake sets are pretty much definitive of what the band was about, and *Strike One* is a cracking listen by any standard. Eddie Miller joined the band for a 1967 gig in Manchester: he squeaks all over 'Oh Baby', but things settle down after that, and by the end the band sound in great heart.

Oh, Baby! resurrects a couple of BBC broadcasts from the end of Alex's life. The leader still commands respect but there's an air of pointlessness around it all which makes for sometimes sad listening. It's the faithful Fred Hunt, still there after nearly 30 years, who probably plays the best things.

Scott Wendholt (born 1965)

TRUMPET, FLUGELHORN

Contemporary post-bop trumpeter leading his own variations on a familiar theme.

***** The Scheme Of Things**
Criss Cross Jazz 1078 *Wendholt; Vincent Herring (ss, as); Kevin Hays (p); Dwayne Burno (b); Billy Drummond (d). 1/93.*

***** Through The Shadows**
Criss Cross 1101 *Wendholt; Don Braden (ts, f); Bruce Barth (p); Ira Coleman (b); Billy Drummond (d). 12/94.*

***** From Now On ...**
Criss Cross 1123 *Wendholt; Steve Armour (tb); Steve Wilson (as); Tim Ries (ts, ss); Bruce Barth (p); Larry Grenadier (b); Billy Drummond (d). 12/95.*

***** Beyond Thursday**
Double-Time DTRCD-128 *Wendholt; Dave Berkman (p); Tony Scherr (b); Adam Watson (d). 6/97.*

***** What Goes Unsaid**
Double-Time STRCD0164 *Wendholt; Eric Alexander (ts); Anthony Wonsey (p); Dennis Irwin (b); Billy Drummond (d). 12/99.*

Wendholt has built up a solid little discography, even if none of the discs really stands up as indispensable. In almost 70 minutes of good, substantial post-bop on *The Scheme Of Things* there is plenty to enjoy, yet not much to remember. The most striking thing is the contrast between Herring (who has had a working quintet with the trumpeter) and Wendholt: the saxophonist's sour, blue playing is a piquant alternative to the polished, processional manner of some of Wendholt's solos. The leader isn't terribly well served by the recording, and he sounds a bit thin on Freddie Hubbard's 'Birdlike', the sort of tune where a trumpeter should stand tall. But there is some impressive improvising, and his favourite device, a fast trill, comes in for clever use.

The writing on *Through The Shadows* is one point of advance; the other is the band which man for man is arguably no stronger than the first but seems a more purposeful group for Wendholt's ideas. 'Totem' and the title-piece are especially strong, and the mid-tempo for Duke Pearson's 'You Know I Care' elicits a solo of real finesse and control by Wendholt. The third Criss Cross date is split between sextet tracks with Armour and Wilson and a quartet with Ries. Some of this sounds a bit rushed, as if the label's usual one-day-in-the-studio strategy put a strain on both groups, but there's little gainsaying the skill and crispness of the best playing.

Beyond Thursday is another one-day quickie, reuniting Wendholt with a rhythm section he used to play with at Augie's in New York. Being sole horn is a challenge he seems to rise to: this is probably his best showcase as a soloist, and the mix of clean, long notes and bubbling phrases which he pursues on 'The Party's Over' becomes the thematic thread of the date. Berkman plays Fender Rhodes, and its interesting sonorities work unexpectedly well, dark one moment, light and pneumatic the next. There's nothing extraordinary here, but it's handsomely done.

What Goes Unsaid goes back to unflashy post-bop of a conservative nature. Alexander sounds comparatively quiet here next to some of his own recent outings, and it's Wendholt himself who ranks as the most creative player on the date. The inward-looking cast of his playing, though, suggests that he may always find it problematic to make a date of his own leadership stand out from a lot of similar records.

Kenny Werner (born 1951)

PIANO

A Brooklynite, Werner studied at Manhattan School and Berklee, then went to Brazil, before returning to gigs with Archie Shepp and, in the '80s, the Mel Lewis band. Led his own trio from 1981.

****(*) Meditations**
Steeplechase SCCD 31327 *Werner (p solo). 12/92.*

****(*) Copenhagen Calypso**
Steeplechase SCCD 31346 *Werner (p solo). 10/93.*

Werner is a beguiling player, perfectly at home in either a solo, trio or rhythm-and-horns date, and if on his earlier discs he can seem a little becalmed in his playing it does gradually draw an attentive listener in.

Meditations is not bad, but Werner's return to the solo recital (there is a forgettable Enja record in the deletions pile) is prettily nondescript. There are three numbered 'Meditations' and a 'Contemplation Suite', all leaves from the same tree, judiciously played, charmingly articulated, but rhythmically and melodically mundane. The best interpretation is a dense revision of 'Giant Steps': Aki Takase and Dick Wellstood have done it, but piano-solo treatments are comparatively rare, and this one's a vivid nod to Coltrane. Monk and Debussy are mistakenly alluded to in the sleeve-notes: Werner is not in their league, but he's worth hearing.

The Copenhagen set also has a vague air of Coltrane hovering around it, with 'Ballad For Trane' and 'Naima' in the programme, but again it's rather bland.

*****(*) A Delicate Balance**
RCA 516942 *Werner; Dave Holland (b); Jack DeJohnette (d).* 6/97.

The opening Monk tribute, 'Amonkst', is a bit obvious, but thereafter Werner's lines impress for their fastidious search for the unexpected, swinging on 'Ivoronics' and 'Footsteps', blossoming on 'Lorraine' and ending cryptically on the themeless 'Melodies Of 1997'. It must be tempting to overplay with Holland and DeJohnette behind you, but for the most part he tempers force with restraint. Bassist and drummer are a nonpareil partnership at this point and they don't disappoint.

*****(*) Unprotected Music**
Double-Time DTRCD-139 *Werner; Marc Johnson (b); Joey Baron (d).* 12/97.

A spare day of studio time brought forth this session of trio improvisations, new ground for Werner as far as an entire date is concerned, although there's one standard ('It's Alright With Me'), 'Greensleeves' is tailgunner for 'Hell Realm', and 'Tribute To Sonny' turns out to be akin to a Rollins calypso. Not free as in European improv, then; but these are more like wide-ranging thinkers than blank-canvas players anyway. Though titles such as 'Vague Wanderings' don't inspire confidence, Werner's lyricism resonates throughout, and it's a show of three considerable musicians enjoying themselves.

*****(*) Beauty Secrets**
RCA 74321 699042 *Werner; Dave Ballou (t); Joe Lovano, Toby Malaby (ts); Mark Feldman, Todd Reynolds, Victor Schulz, Heidi Stubner (vn); Mary Wooten (clo); Drew Gress, Johannes Weidenmuller (b); Billy Hart, Ari Hoenig (d); Betty Buckley (v).* 4–5/99.

Werner's second for RCA is a sometimes bemusing mixture. It opens with four pieces for trio (Werner, Gress and Hart), one of which, the title-track, is distinguished by a piano introduction of sublime beauty. There's a duet with Lovano, a quintet track with Malaby, Weidenmuller, Ballou and Hoenig, a quartet with Feldman added to the core trio (the superb collective improvisation 'Goblins'), then a version of 'Send In The Clowns' sung by theatre vocalist Betty Buckley. The finale is a 12-minute piece that seems like light concert-music, with extensive written parts for the strings and Werner reading out a poem. While some of this seems hugely overblown, full marks to Werner for ambitiousness, and the smaller and more concentrated tracks are fine enough to persuade that he's on an impressive streak.

***** Form And Fantasy**
Night Bird NBM 1001-2 *Werner; Johannes Weidenmuller (b); Ari Hoenig (d).* 11/00.

***** Beat Degeneration**
Night Bird NBM 1009-2 *As above.* 11/00.

Live sets from Paris. Werner's frustrating taste for light music invades too many of the tracks on the first disc, and when he does Eric Clapton's 'Tears From Heaven' you feel like paying your tab and leaving – but then you would miss a power-packed finale on 'Lonnie's Lament'. A very mixed bag, but the good stuff is enticing.

The second set is all originals. Werner's fast ones are a lot more useful than the slower pieces, which tend to send him back to his Bill Evans shoes and make the listener droop. There are some curious juxtapositions, rhythmically speaking, and a sense that something highbrow is going on. Again, certainly not a record to miss if you're a Werner admirer, but difficult to recommend generally.

Frank Wess (born 1922)

TENOR SAXOPHONE, FLUTE

A native of Kansas City, Wess became a stalwart of the Basie woodwind section and an impressive solo star in his own right. His tenor approach is somewhat influenced by Lester Young, and perhaps by Don Byas as well, but Wess's real importance as an instrumentalist is in making the flute a valid solo voice. He plays with a strong, correct tone and is a nimble improviser.

***** The Long Road**
Prestige 24247 *Wess; Thad Jones, Al Aarons (t); Oliver Nelson (ts); George Barrow (bs); Tommy Flanagan, Gildo Mahones (p); George Duvivier, Buddy Catlett (b); Osie Johnson, Roy Haynes (d); Ray Barretto (perc).* 3/62–1/63.

Wess's Prestige albums are little known and it's no surprise that they've waited this long for reissue. This disc couples *Southern Comfort* and the curiously titled *Yo Ho! Frank Wess/Poor You, Little Me.* Neither is, frankly, anything that special: the first employs an eight-strong line-up, but Oliver Nelson's writing is routine and little more than a prop for the solos, while the second is mostly about Wess's prettifying flute solos, with the CD's title-track taking an appropriately long time to get done.

***** Surprise! Surprise!**
Gemini GMCD 84 *Wess; Norman Simmons (p); Joe Cohn (g); Lynn Seaton (b); Jackie Williams (d).* 8/93.

***** Surprise! Surprise!**
Chiaroscuro 350 2CD *Wess; Frank Foster, Jimmy Heath, Flip Phillips (ts); Richard Wyands (p); Lynn Seaton (b, v); Winard Harper (d).* 95.

The Gemini disc was recorded at Oslo's Rainbow Studio and engineered by Jan Erik Kongshaug, who is responsible for most of ECM's output. Predictably, it sounds as good as they get, even though on this occasion the band Wess assembled has some creaking elements. It would be unfair to point to individuals, beyond saying that the rhythm section don't sound so much unrehearsed as rather stiff and unswinging. Wess switches to flute for the brand-new 'Equal Parts', but for once he fails to convince, and it is his tenor solo on Ettore Stratta's 'Forget The Woman' which takes the laurels. Joe Cohn, son of saxophonist Al, wins credit for his elegant soloing and solid accompaniment.

Confusingly, the Chiaroscuro set has the same title as the earlier disc. This double set was recorded as part of a jazz cruise – nice work if you can get it – and the addition of a couple of guest stars lifts the gently relaxed mood up a notch. Among the walk-ons is Jimmy Heath on a long, long version of 'All The Things You Are', while the veteran Flip Phillips turns the engines back to full ahead for a steaming version of 'Cottontail'. The outstanding moment, though, is the renewed partnership with old Basie compadre Frank Foster for a powerfully sweeping version of 'My Funny Valentine', a showcase for Wess's flute. Seaton takes a couple of vocals and Wyands makes his presence felt with some excellent solo choruses, notably on 'Friendship' ... which is probably the keynote of the album. A lot of good music for your money.

***** Without A Doubt**
Koch 7896 *Wess; Mark Egan (ts); Frank Vignola (g); Joe Ascione (d).* 10/00.

Frank was approaching 80 when this was recorded. It's nominally co-led with guitarist Vignola who's done everything from this kind of bop-tinged jazz to pop music, but always seems to produce his best when so challenged. Wess sticks to flute for much of the way, largely because Egan handles the tenor parts, but his flute-playing is so idiomatic and so characterful that there's no feeling he's stuck to a 'second' instrument. Boldly, most of the material is new, but sounds well-seasoned and played in.

Bugge Wesseltoft

PIANO, KEYBOARDS, ELECTRONICS, VOCALS

Active as a keyboard player in Norwegian jazz since the beginning of the '90s, Wesseltoft is seeking out new fusion forms with his own groups.

*****(*) New Conception Of Jazz**
Sonet 537251-2 *Wesseltoft; Jens Petter Antonsen, Erlend Gjerde, Sjur Miljeteig (t); Vidar Johansen (ss, bcl); Trude Eick (waldhorn); Ingebrigt Håker Flaten, Sveinung Hovensjø, Bjørn Kjellemyr (b); Audun Kleive (d, elec); Rune Arnesen, Anders Engen (d).* 1/95–8/96.

***** It's Snowing On My Piano**
ACT 9260-2 *Wesseltoft (p solo).* 10/97.

***** Sharing**
Jazzland 538278-2 *Wesseltoft; Erlend Gjerde, Nils Petter Molvaer (t); Vidar Johansen (ss); Ingebrigt Håker Flaten (b); Anders Engen, Paal Nilssen-Love (d); Olle Abstract, Pål Strangefruit (turntables); Jan Bang (d prog); Sidsel Endresen (v).* 98.

Wesseltoft first made an impact a decade ago when he recorded with Arild Andersen and Jan Garbarek. Those associations give only a partial impression of what he is about, for alongside the classically tinged filigree he has created his own intriguing synthesis of jazz, funk and hip-hop, a project which goes out under the umbrella title New Conception of Jazz.

There is nothing on either NCOJ record which would have astonished Miles Davis or perturbed the M-Base collective in its heyday. Wesseltoft's strength doesn't lie in the originality of the approach so much as in the distinctive character of the soundscapes he creates, intimate and lyrical with a strangely off-kilter quality which is either immediately beguiling or irritating. The earliest record is certainly the most adventurous, a sometimes edgy, questioning album that, in 'Spectre Supreme' and 'Modular' in particular, asks fascinating questions about where jazz is going at the end of the '90s. Though the emphasis is largely on texture and pure sound, there is also some great linear playing, as on 'Trio' with Kjellemyr and Arnesen.

Sharing is content to rest on a settled formula – or, rather, a settled eclecticism. It's a much more polished record, technically assured and superbly cast. Sidsel Endresen, with whom Bugge has recorded before, contributes a delightful vocal to 'You Might Say', one of the less heavily treated items on the set. A bonus three-track disc came with the limited-edition first release. It included one all-acoustic track, 'Tune In', which underlines once again what a god Miles was and is to this generation of Scandinavian players. Not so much a matter of sound or syntax, more the confidence to place sounds and gestures and let them stand for nothing but themselves. Saxophonist Vidar Johansen is a sensitive and responsive partner with a very similar approach, but it would have been good to have heard more of Nils Petter Molvaer, who has gone on to make his own new synthesis of styles. The young trumpeter is magnificent on 'Breen'N'Glue'.

The other album is Wesseltoft's debut as a solo pianist. It is, ahem, a Christmas record, a mixture of traditional themes like 'Stille Nacht', 'O Little Town Of Bethlehem' and 'In Dulci Jubilo' and original compositions. Magnificently recorded by Jan Erik Kongshaug at Rainbow Studios in Oslo, it might just as readily belong in the catalogue of another, rather more celebrated label. If Erik Satie had known how to ski, this is how he would have sounded.

***** Moving**
Jazzland 013534-2 *Wesseltoft; Håkon Kornstad (ts); Ingebrigt Håker Flaten, Marius Reksjø (b); Anders Engen (d); Paolo Vinaccia (perc); Jonas Lönna (turntables).* 11/01.

Wesseltoft is being built up into a kingpin figure of Oslo's 'Underground', but marketing aside the music's interesting, if – as intimated above about the first record – scarcely groundbreaking or subversive. It's jazz fusion as chill-out music, the beats propulsive but restrained, even as they inevitably set the pace. Much of it could have been lifted from any number of fusion records from many different periods and sources, but that's not the point: context is everything. What Wesseltoft attempts is to inject some tough musical – even improvisational – thinking into soundscapes which are still overseen by a tyrannical beat. It's a music where soft, insidious details attempt to count for much. In that sense, it probably asks a lot of its audience, many of whom may be prepared to settle for the beat.

****(*) Film'Ing**
Jazzland 9866123 *Wesseltoft; Vidar Johansen, Joshua Redman (ts); Dhafer Youssef, Oyen Groven Myrhen (v).* 02.

Several albums down the track, the pianist is still oscillating between bedroom-album soundscapes and a brisk Nordic version of Miles's jazz-funk; beguilingly so on 'O Ye', where the saxophonist (presumably special guest Joshua Redman) dons Kenny Garrett's skivvies. It's the best thing on the album by some distance. Wesseltoft is credited not with piano but with 'piano sounds' and even when the track title promises 'Piano', what you get is collaged and pitch-shifted out of immediate recognition.

The overall impression is of slowly morphing ostinati couched in an approximation of jazz tonality but handled without swing and with no obvious harmonic progression. The saxophone on 'Piano' (presumably this time Vidar Johansen) is closer to the Garbarek sound, austerely focused and folkish in idiom. Elsewhere there are touches of brass, acoustic bass, percussion and programming, and fugitive vocals from Dhafer Youssef and Oyen Groven Myhren.

Kate Westbrook

VOCALS, TENOR HORN, PICCOLO

Although closely associated with her husband's work, Kate is a fine writer and performer in her own right, with a brilliant approach to text.

****(*) Goodbye, Peter Lorre**

Femme/Line FECD 9.01060 *Westbrook; John Alley, Mike Westbrook (p); Fine Trash (v).* 96.

*****(*) Love Or Infatuation**

ASC CD 20 *Westbrook; Mike Westbrook (p).* 5/97.

We have always been rather curmudgeonly about Kate Westbrook's highly theatrical vocal style. Out of context, it can jar. In its place, though, it is a powerful vehicle for strong lyrics, better at tough affirmation than at more reflective inscape. Kate has worked most frequently in the context of husband Mike's various groups, but she has run her own group, the Skirmishers, and these two albums find her working pretty much on her own account, albeit using material by other hands.

Goodbye, Peter Lorre is an odd, awkward hybrid, recommendable only to established fans, but Kate's interpretations of the songs of Friedrich Hollaender on *Love Or Infatuation* are absolutely first rate. Hollaender himself may be unfamiliar as a name, but everyone knows songs like 'Falling In Love Again' from *The Blue Angel* and 'You've Got That Look' and 'The Boys In The Backroom' from *Destry Rides Again.* Westbrook isn't Dietrich, and she doesn't attempt to be. What she does instead is a clever pastiche, relocating the songs both harmonically and dramatically for her own musical personality. As ever, Mike is a sympathetic and often arresting accompanist. Sadly, for the moment at least, this seems to be a limited-edition release.

****** Cuff Clout**

Voiceprint VP 310 *Westbrook; Stuart Brooks (t); Andy Grappy (tba); Tim Holmes (sno, ss); Barbara Thompson (ss); Peter Whyman (ss, as); Alan Barnes (as); Chris Biscoe (ss, as); Mike Carr (org); Laka Daisical (p, ky); John Alley, Errollyn Wallen (p); Pete Lemer (syn); Billy Thompson (vn); Steve Brown, Jon Hiseman, Sebastian Rochford (d); Neil Percy (perc); John Winfield (v).* 11/01.

Alarmingly subtitled a 'neoteric music hall', this astonishing piece of work is a loosely organized entertainment by Kate's Skirmishers, a group of doughty (ir)regulars who snipe away at all signs of pretension, injustice and cruelty. Hence pieces about the invention of barbed wire, a narrative turning of the tables that makes Toad's washerwoman the heroine rather than the overblown amphibian himself, along with sundry bittersweet love songs. The composers concerned (all working to Kate's texts) are as various as Eleanor Alberga, Barbara Thompson, Jenni Roditi, James MacMillan and Errollyn Wallen. A floating personnel supports Kate and fellow vocalist John Winfield. Starring items are Thompson's strange rock-rap 'Oceans, Straits, Currents and Seas' and Chris Biscoe's 'Joseph F. Glidden of De Kalb, Illinois', a tale of the man who first exploited mankind's cruellest invention. It's all stirring and moving stuff, and one looks forward to seeing it staged.

Mike Westbrook (born 1936)

COMPOSER, PIANO, TUBA

Studied painting but turned to music and, on arriving in London in 1962, set about composing and arranging for groups of many different shapes and sizes: the Concert Band, Cosmic Circus, Brass Band and others. Worked widely in theatre, occasionally in TV, and has frequently worked on major, revisionist settings of British icons from Blake to the Beatles. A man of many talents.

****** Celebration**

Deram 844 852-2 *Westbrook; Dave Holdsworth (t, flhn); Malcolm Griffiths (tb); Dave Perrottet (vtb); Tom Bennelick (frhn); George Smith (tba); John Surman (ss, bs, bcl); Mike Osborne (as); Bernie Living (as, f); Dave Chambers (ts, cl); Harry Miller (b); Alan Jackson (d).* 7–8/67.

*****(*) Release**

Deram 844 851-2 *As above, except omit Perrottet, Bennelick, Smith, Chambers; add Paul Rutherford (tb); Nisar Ahmed (George) Khan (ts).* 8/68.

*****(*) Marching Song**

Deram 844 853-2 2CD *As for both albums above, except omit Perrottet, Smith, Chambers; add Kenny Wheeler (t, flhn); Greg Bowen, Tony Fisher, Ronnie Hughes, Henry Lowther (t); Mike Gibbs, Eddie Harvey (tb); Martin Fry (tba); Alan Skidmore (ts, f); John Warren (as, bs, f); Brian Smith (ts); Barre Phillips (b); John Marshall (d).* 69.

It's tempting to suggest that, were Mike Westbrook American or German rather than English, his career might already have been garlanded with the praise it so conspicuously deserves. Britain's neglect of one of its most distinguished contemporary composers amounts to a national disgrace. Westbrook's regular groups – the early Concert Band, the mixed-media Cosmic Circus, the jazz-rock Solid Gold Cadillac and, most recently, the Brass Band – have drawn from a startling range of musical and performance backgrounds.

The Concert Band was probably the most straightforwardly jazz-influenced of all, Ellingtonian in sound and in intention, profoundly engaged and committed – as the anti-war agenda of these early discs underlines – and already theatrical in ways that suggested Westbrook had been listening to Charles Mingus's long-form works as well. Like both Mingus and Ellington, Westbrook has the ability to make what on paper look like relatively conventional horn voicings sound utterly original. The more abstract and expressionist tone-poems of subsequent years, and most notably *Metropolis*, retreated slightly from that dramatic premiss, but it has never been absent in 30 years' music-making.

Westbrook's early recordings for Deram have only just returned to the catalogue, sounding fresh and vigorous on CD. He had founded his original concert band as early as 1958, recruiting John Surman shortly thereafter, and then expanding the group to something like the ensemble that started giving concert performances of *Celebration* and *Marching Song*, both of which were shortened for recording.

Surman is the main soloist and co-composer on the first album, mostly on baritone, but checking in with a roiling soprano solo on 'Awakening', which also features Mike Osborne. Ossie, sounding close to his best on these recordings, is the main soloist on another Surman composition, 'Image'. Hints of Westbrook's later interest in the possibilities of rock rhythms surface on 'A Greeting'. By contrast, his limited exploration of free improvisation is evident on 'Echoes And Heroics', an intense ostinato over which Surman and Osborne, Malcolm Griffiths and Dave Holdsworth improvise at high intensity.

As the title hints, *Release* extended Westbrook's interest in freedom. Though hailed by his admirers as an advance on *Celebration*, it has always seemed to us a less accomplished album, rather bitty and perhaps rather too intent on dramatic impact. A continuous concert linked by cadenzas, it this time mixes in standards as well: 'Lover Man', 'Flying Home', 'Gee, Baby, Ain't I Good To You', 'Sugar' and, unexpectedly, 'The Girl From Ipanema'. It is almost as if Westbrook wants to ensure that, however far he ventures in the direction of the avant-garde, it will be clear where his root loyalties lie. Two versions of 'Folk Song' and 'Take Me Back' confirm the absolute importance of John Surman to the mission, and it's still the saxophone-players who take the bulk of solo space.

As its military theme perhaps dictates, brass begins to dominate on *Marching Song*: a long, fraught exploration of how patriotism corrodes into horror and disillusion. First heard at the Camden Festival in the spring of 1969, it may well have been inspired by 50th anniversary commemorations the previous November of the end of the First World War. In the opening sequence, over a background of not altogether crowd noises, the band marches off round the stereo field while trumpeter Dave Holdsworth expresses the individual soldier's enthusiasm for the cause. A quieter section immediately follows, almost as if doubts and fears are already present. Bernie Living's overdubbed solo has a restless, almost schizophrenic quality. The twinned basses create a bed for Surman and Osborne, performing powerfully again. Huge ensemble chords signal a further change of mood, opening up a singing soprano feature by Surman which seems to nod in the direction of John Coltrane (though 'My Favorite Things' rather than 'Naima', as Mike Hennessey suggests in his sleeve-note). Paul Rutherford is the featured soloist on 'Other World', before the drums kick in with 'Marching Song' itself. The drama is kept balanced until, in 'Conflict', the apocalypse is unleashed. This is some of the most violent music you'll encounter within these pages, an angry, despairing statement which is all the more powerful for its sheer physicality. George Smith's tuba solo is completely *sui generis*, a quite remarkable statement. 'Requiem' and 'Memorial' document the inevitable aftermath, but with a weary, disillusioned tonality which is far more disturbing even than what has gone before.

These albums established Westbrook as a major presence on the European scene. In future years, recordings were harder to come by and much of his best work was limited to one-off festival performances and occasional broadcasts. That he was able to get such splendid results in the studio was testimony to his and the band's commitment.

*** Metropolis

BGO CD 454 *Westbrook; Nigel Carter (t); Harry Beckett, Dave Holdsworth, Henry Lowther (t, flhn); Kenny Wheeler (t, flhn, mel); Malcolm Griffiths, Paul Nieman, Derek Wadsworth (tb); Paul Rutherford (tb, euph); Geoff Perkins (btb); Mike Osborne (as, cl); Ray Warleigh (as, f); Alan Skidmore (ts, ss); George Khan (ts); John Warren (bs); John Taylor (p); Gary Boyle (g); Harry Miller (b, clo); Chris Laurence (b); Alan Jackson, John Marshall (d); Norma Winstone (v).* 8/71.

We always considered this a modern classic, a near-perfect example of Westbrook's ability to create musical structures and contexts flexible enough to be performed by anything from a conventional small combo to the largest big band. The material that makes up *Metropolis* had been played by forces ranging from a quartet to 25 musicians by the time it was recorded. In retrospect, it sounds strangely bitty, fragmentary rather than cohesive, and much less securely rehearsed and performed than the Deram records above on which Westbrook's reputation rests.

Essentially, it is a further attempt on that modernist cliché, a sonic evocation of the urban dream/nightmare. It opens with a chaotic septet improvisation, two plangent trombones, two saxophones and rhythm, before kicking off into a driving, rock-tinged riff which surfaces here and there throughout the record, opposed to a softly questioning, rising figure which has always seemed to us a latter-day version of the nightingale in Berkeley Square.

The suite restarts with a second improvisation in which Ray Warleigh's flute segues seamlessly into Norma Winstone's voice, which is used instrumentally throughout. Malcolm Griffiths, Henry Lowther and, before them, Alan Skidmore and Dave Holdsworth all solo effectively in the early stages of the disc. Where Charles Mingus would have cheerfully mixed genres and juxtaposed elements, Westbrook tries to create a work out of whole cloth. Heard again after a gap of some years, *Metropolis* comes across as repetitive and episodic, an awkward hybrid of free jazz and fusion. Its moments of beauty – like Winstone's first entry, Skidmore's first solo and Harry Beckett's mournful coda – are breathtaking, but the album as a whole has lost its early impact. We would also draw attention to what sound like tape problems here and there. Westbrook's own solo on Part Seven is disconcertingly detuned and Mike Osborne's feature shortly afterward lacks Ossie's usual consistency of tone: presumably a problem that arose in remastering, for it is certainly not evident on the original LP.

*** The Orchestra Of Smith's Academy

Enja ENJ 9358-2 *Westbrook; Graham Russell, Stuart Brooks, Noel Langley, James McMillan, Lee Butler (t); Paul Nieman, Adrian Lane, Mike Kearsey (tb); Tracy Holloway (tb, euph); Chris Biscoe, Alan Barnes, Peter Whyman, Dave Bitelli, Alan Wakeman, Chris Caldwell (saxes); Pete Saberton (ky); David Maric (p); Anthony Kerr (vib); R. Farrer (mar); Phil Boyden, Dominique Pifarély (vn); Frank Schaefer (clo); Tim Maple (g); Andy Grappy (tba); Malcolm Moore, Steve Berry (b); Peter Fairclough, Simon Pearson (d); Kate Westbrook (v).* 9/92–7/95.

In 1992 Westbrook was offered a retrospective at the Catania Festival in Sicily. This album represents the middle night of three and music all written round the matrix of what he calls the 'Smith's Hotel Chord', which Westbrook discovered at the hostelry of that name in Glasgow during a 1983 tour (although the set included on this CD was actually recorded some weeks later, in England). Developing materials out of the chord, Westbrook often liked to place different rhythmic cycles side by side, as on the innovative recreation of '*I.D.M.A.T. (It Don't Mean A Thing)*' and the exquisite harmonies of 'So We'll Go No More A-Roving', which reworks Westbrook's original 'Smith's Hotel Chord' as a feature for Chris Biscoe's emotive alto.

The most interesting aspect of the set is its dependence on the blues, albeit in heterodox forms. 'Checking In', a feature for Anthony Kerr, Dominique Pifarély and Pete Saberton, has a 24-bar structure. 'Measure For Measure' is a bizarre 12-bar form grafted on to classical sonata with free elements superadded. Very strange. 'Blighters' is another feature for Kate Westbrook, adapted from a text by Siegfried Sassoon.

Kerr and Pifarély are reunited to front 'Viennese Waltz'. As throughout the album, solos are recorded much less effectively than ensembles, and the violinist in particular sounds as if he is standing on the brink of a vast empty water tank. A valuable glimpse at an important moment in Westbrook's career.

****(*) Stage Set**
ASC CD 9 *Westbrook; Kate Westbrook (v).* 11/95.

*****(*) Bar Utopia**
ASC CD 13 *Westbrook; Andy Bush, Noel Langley (t); Paul Edmonds, James McMillan (t, flhn); Mark Bassey, Tracy Holloway, Adrian Lane (tb); Andy Grappy (tba); Dave Bitelli (as, ts, cl); Peter Whyman (as, ss, cl); Chris Biscoe (as); Alan Wakeman (ts); Karen Street (ts, acc); Chris Caldwell (bs); Anthony Kerr (vib); Stanley Adler (clo); Steve Berry (b); Peter Fairclough (d); Kate Westbrook, John Winfield (v).* 10/96.

The Westbrooks have continued to plough what seems a lonely furrow in the mid-'90s. Their particular brand of music theatre, whether miniaturized and personalized, as in *Stage Set*, or else scaled up ambitiously, as in *Bar Utopia*, consistently receives critical garlands ... and no support. The big-band set has all the Westbrook signatures: subtle ideas, bravura theatrical writing and ample space for improvisation. The overture is dedicated to Jelly Roll Morton and his 1926 recording, 'The Chant', a household god who doesn't entirely explain what happens subsequently. The three distinct groups who perform on 'Bar Utopia' itself are nicely distributed, and solo space throughout the record is always subordinate to structural dictates.

We are not great fans of *Stage Set*. Hampered by Kate Westbrook's increasingly mannered singing and by the rather sparse setting, it engages neither mind nor emotions, as *Bar Utopia* does on occasion.

*****(*) Platterback**
PAO 10530 *Westbrook; Kate Westbrook, John Winfield (v); Karen Street (v, acc); Stanley Adler (v, clo).* 98.

A bittersweet tale of five travellers *en route* from Stiltsville to Platterback, this is the most engaging piece of music theatre the Westbrooks have created for years. It is also an intriguing shift in musical language, with accordion and cello (the latter always a Westbrook favourite) taking the place of horns and woodwinds.

As before, the piece draws on a whole range of styles, from Ellington-tinged jazz to cabaret song and quasi-serial structures. It evokes a landscape crowded with story and with cultural associations. John Winfield's voice is an engaging foil to Kate Westbrook's and, with three other vocalists in the line-up, the emphasis is very largely on texts and words; but it is their integration with an often minimalist backing that makes them so powerfully effective.

****** Chanson Irresponsable**
Enja 9456 2 *Westbrook; Stuart Brooks (t, flhn); Jane Hanna (frhn); Chris Biscoe (as, acl); Peter Whyman (as, ss, cl, bcl); Karen Street (ts, acc); Dave Bitelli (bs, cl); Neil McTaggart, Mark Wilson (vn); David Lasserson (vla); Chris Allan (clo); Tim Harries (b); Sebastian Roachford (d); Matthew Sharp, Kate Westbrook (v).* 02.

This musically ambitious work takes as its starting point the distinctive song of one of the most popular bird migrants to Britain, the sedge warbler. Westbrook's transcription and transformation of its song isn't Messiaen-like, either in intent or outcome, but has something of the same concentration and mystery. The vocalists and saxophonists develop the song and the piece moves through the various stages of the birds' reorientation and nesting. It ends with one of them being killed by a domestic cat and the New Orleans-style funeral that follows. The texts, by Kate, are sung in a variety of European languages. It's a clever and funny idea and musically one of the Westbrooks' most interesting works for some years, a purple patch that also yielded Kate's *Cuff Clout*.

*****(*) L'Ascenseur/The Life**
Jazzprint JPVP 130 *Westbrook; Chris Biscoe (ss, as, ts, bs, picc); Kate Westbrook (thn).* 9/02.

To mark the 20th-anniversary tour, a journeying set that sees the Westbrooks and their adopted range far afield – Rome, Duisberg, Western Australia – absorbing impressions of places, plants and people. The original conception was by Kate, but the piece was developed by the trio and it has a cheerfully eclectic cast, along with a good deal of harmonic subtlety. It's perhaps less raw and more polished than works of the past, but marks another fascinating stage in the couple's creative evolution.

Randy Weston (born 1926)

PIANO

Strongly influenced by Monk, from whom he had lessons, the impressively proportioned Weston – he is 6 foot 5 – spent the late '60s and early '70s in North Africa, an experience that coloured his playing from then on. His solo approach is a cross between Monk and Abdullah Ibrahim, but Weston is best known for the joyous 'Hi-Fly', a classic jazz tune.

*****(*) Solo, Duo, Trio**
Milestone MCD 47085 *Weston; Sam Gill (b); Art Blakey (d).* 4/54, 1/55.

These sides were originally released on 10″ and 12″ Riverside sets. The duos with Sam Gill were issued as *Plays Cole Porter In A Modern Mood* and even now they are startling reinventions of songs that even in a jazz context can seem tired and hackneyed. Weston's percussive delivery and rhythmic hardness transform the tunes and Gill's fine melodic sense creates a second tier of interest even in the most seemingly literal interpretation, as on 'In The Still Of The Night'.

The trios with Blakey are inevitably yet more upbeat. The influence of Monk and Tadd Dameron is immediately obvious here but it is Weston's soloing which really grabs the attention, sonorous, intensely logical but never predictable, and harmonically adventurous. These are important restorations to the Weston discography and strongly recommended to lovers of piano jazz who are not willing to pay the price for the Mosaic set of early Weston recordings.

***** Get Happy**

Original Jazz Classics OJCCD 1870 *Weston; Sam Gill (b); Wilbert Hogan (d).* 8/55.

***** With These Hands ...**

Original Jazz Classics OJCCD 1883 *Weston; Cecil Payne (bs, as); Ahmed Abdul-Malik (b); Wilbert Hogan (d).* 3/56.

*****(*) Jazz A La Bohemia**

Original Jazz Classics OJC 1747 *Weston; Sam Gill (b); Al Dreares (d).* 10/56.

***** The Modern Art Of Jazz**

Dawn DCD 107 *Weston; Ray Copeland (t); Cecil Payne (as, bs); Ahmed Abdul-Malik (b); Wilbert Hogan, Willie Jones (d).* 11/56.

Weston cuts such an impressive figure that his rather marginal critical standing remains an enigma. Though dozens of players every year turn to the joyous 'Hi-Fly' theme, few of them seem to have probed any deeper into Weston's output, which is considerable and impressive. Like many players of his generation, his main initial influence was Thelonious Monk. In later years, though, Weston was to explore African and Caribbean musics, somewhat in the manner of Dollar Brand/Abdullah Ibrahim and Andrew Hill, and to attempt larger-scale structures of a sort pioneered by James P. Johnson and Duke Ellington. Though a ruggedly beautiful performer, it is as a composer that he is most seriously underrated. For the clearest sense of what Weston gained – harmonically, rhythmically, spiritually – from his trip to Africa, it's necessary only to compare the excellent *Carnival* (currently deleted) with the much earlier *Jazz A La Bohemia* and *With These Hands*, which was recorded in the spring of the same year. It isn't the case that Weston passively 'discovered' African rhythms and tonalities on one of his early-'60s study trips. Art is seldom the product of accidents. As one can clearly hear from the Africanized inflexions of the Riverside sessions, Weston went in search of confirmation for what he was already doing. Abdul-Malik had a turn of phrase that was very different from anyone else of the time. 'You Go To My Head' on *A La Bohemia* has a quality quite unlike the average standards performance of the time, and Payne's rather solemn-sounding baritone here and on the other 1956 recordings can almost suggest the buzz and thump of Central African drones. Among younger-generation players, probably only Billy Harper had the right combination of traditionalism and modernist, post-bop technique, though later Weston was to record successfully with the new avant-traditionalist of tenor saxophone, David Murray.

After his Riverside contract expired, Weston recorded for Dawn with a somewhat augmented band. *The Modern Art of Jazz* was a valuable reissue for filling in a further aspect of the story. Both technically and artistically less appealing than the preceding discs, it does represent a very important step in Weston's development into the 'world' artist he became, and the originals, 'Loose Wig', 'A Theme For Teddy' and 'J.K. Blues', are all foretastes of a vein he was to refine in coming years.

***** African Rhythms**

Comet CD 028 *Weston; Henri Texier (b); Art Taylor (d); Niles Azzedin Weston, Reebop Kwaaku Ba (perc).* 6/69.

This reissues a couple of obscure French sessions, *African Rhythms* and *Niles' Little Bag*. Several of his familiar pieces are revised here for trio and percussion, although the ancillary drumming gets a bit tiresome at times and the solo 'Pam's Waltz' is easily the most impressive thing on offer. Well worth hearing, given that Weston has only a modest showing in the current catalogues.

***** African Nite**

Owl 014 732 2 *Weston (p solo).* 9/75.

Less compelling than the above, but another welcome return to catalogue for a '70s solo recording that had disappeared. The Owl disc is distinguished by lovely sound and what sounds like a rather special piano. 'Jejuka' anticipates some of what lay ahead; 'Portrait of Myriam Makeba' (sic) is an affectionate backward glance.

***** Ancient Future / Blue**

Mutable Music 17508/2 2CD *Weston (p solo).* 3/83–6/01.

A valuable reissue of two sets that have been out of circulation for some time. At first blush, Weston sounds similar to the Abdullah Ibrahim of the period, but listen longer to things like 'Isis' and 'Ballad For T' (both on *Ancient Future*) and it's clear that all sorts of other inputs are at work. Apart from anything else, Weston does not follow Ibrahim's practice of reinforcement by repetition; he allows melodic figures to do their work and then lets them go. This is a very attractive package packed with 23 mostly short tracks.

***** Khepera**

Verve 557821-2 *Weston; Benny Powell (tb); Talib Kibwe (as, f); Pharoah Sanders (ss, ts); Alex Blake (b); Victor Lewis (d); Chief Bey (perc, v); Neil Clark (perc); Min Xiao Fen (pipa, gong).* 2/98.

Weston's Verve albums have lately been under the axe. This augmented trio session, with the emphasis very much on African sounds and rhythms, is more or less a world-music project, with very little space for jazz improvisation. 'Anu Anu' and 'The Shrine' are the tracks which maintain most connection with Weston's earlier career, but this time he seems self-consciously bent on an 'ethnic' sound and feel. The results are perfectly attractive and the record yields up new subtleties every time, but it's not the most compelling performance by the pianist himself, who sounds almost jaded here and there.

****** Spirit: The Power of Music**

Sunnyside 3015 *Weston; Benny Powell (tb); Talib Kibwe (as, f); Alex Blake (b); Neil Clarke (d, perc); Master Gnawa Musicians of Marrakech and Tanger.* 9/00.

This reunion with the Gnawa Masters was recorded in Brooklyn, but far from being a carefully packaged re-run of a successful collaboration it feels like a climactic encounter that clinches a lot of unfinished business. Weston begins the set alone on 'Receiving The Spirit', which serves as ritual prologue to the truly astonishing music that is to follow. He is joined by the band, who build up the energy still further, Kibwe in particularly vibrant form. Then the Moroccans enter and the music audibly lifts onto a new plane. There is genuine spirit in these performances, which are difficult to verbalize and impossible to forget. One of the most important and most moving releases from Weston in many years and an ideal place to make his acquaintance.

Petter Wettre (born 1967)

TENOR, ALTO AND SOPRANO SAXOPHONES, BASS CLARINET

Norwegian saxophonist whose small-group work – which we have previously listed as The Trio – sets a formidable standard in terms of modern post-bop-into-free playing.

*****(*) Pig Virus**
Curling Legs CD 28 *Wettre; Håvard Wiik (p); Terje Gewelt (b); Per Oddvar Johansen (d).* 9/96.

****** Meet The Locals**
Resonant RM3-2 *Wettre; Ingebrigt Håker Flaten (b); Jarle Vespestad (d).* 98.

*****(*) In Color**
Resonant RM 5-2 *As above, except add David Liebman (ss, ts).* 10/99.

Wettre is some saxophonist. While he can drive with enormous power and velocity, his ability to throttle back, stop on a dime or simply enunciate a difficult line with almost insolent ease sets him aside from mere overblowing merchants of freedom. The quartet music of *Pig Virus* sets a demanding agenda to start with – check the two-minute manifesto of 'Sann' which opens the disc, Wettre and Johansen rolling up their sleeves and going off at express pace. The subsequent tracks calm down a little, but there's a menacing sense of something waiting to explode in even the quieter corners of this music. Wettre has a beautifully clear, open tone that lets him articulate his lines so sweetly that their blowtorch qualities are at times mollified.

Meet The Locals must go down as one of the most attention-grabbing group debuts in years, and played blindfold it should have listeners everywhere demanding to know who this is. That it actually emerges from Oslo, where the most internationally familiar tone has been set by Jan Garbarek's plaintive wail, is all the more startling. This is clipped, tough, overdriven saxophone trio music, deriving from quite closely wrought hard-bop structures yet all but bodily hurled into free space by the fantastic impetus which the threesome work up on 'Meet The Locals', 'Chasing The Girl' (a scarcely recognizable derivative of Joe Henderson's 'Inner Urge') and 'Cold Turkey'. Vespestad is the most swinging drummer imaginable for the situation, pushing the other two as hard as he can possibly go (and that includes when he's going at a simply brushed four) while the supremely assured Wettre peels off line after line. It may sometimes be pattern-playing at this kind of velocity, but Wettre keeps his cool to an amazing degree, the tone utterly secure and the breath-control phenomenal. Flaten stands his ground in the middle and even gets in a growling feature of sorts with 'A Bored Broad Abroad'. Maybe the concluding 'The Epidemic Of Self-Pity' is, at 32 minutes, an ounce overweight, but the record has already earned its four stars.

If *In Color* seems like a disappointment, that may be because the livid excitement of the debut is too much mollified by the presence of Liebman. Always the consummate professional, the American digs the situation, but he adds little to the occasion except extra weight and sometimes even gets in the way. That proviso aside (and Liebman is only on five of ten tracks anyway), it's another hothouse of excitement. The very close-up sound which the group favours puts an intimacy on a style of playing which too often now is recorded with a festival-stadium respectability. It works best if the band feels as if it's on top of you; on, say, 'Next Level', the crispness and deep bottom of the sound involve the listener as few such records do. These are fabulous records: get them.

***** The Only Way To Travel**
BP 00007 *Wettre; Per Oddvar Johansen (d).* 00.

***** The Mystery Unfolds**
BP 01009 *Wettre; Trygve Seim (ss); Jørgen Munkeby (f); Mahatma Bubb (shenai); Ingebrigt Håker Flaten (b); Jarle Vespestad (d).* 2/01.

Wettre can sometimes remind of that ultrasecure technician Tubby Hayes – like Tubby, he never seems to stumble, but he's not quite as glib. *The Only Way To Travel* is a set of duets which only occasionally drift towards Coltrane territory; the title-piece has a kind of incantatory Trane feel to it, and here and there the music settles into the kind of introspective territory engendered by Norwegian air. By himself on 'Big Dipper', though, Wettre suddenly doesn't seem to have anything very interesting to say.

The Mystery Unfolds is strong, though some of the lift-off ebullience of *Meet The Locals* already seems to have been dispersed – in the name of progress, possibly. The modest appearances by the additional players add little but a bit of extra colour. Variety, in fact, is what the album is tuned to: bass clarinet and bass, Wettre moving indecisively between alto and tenor. 'As Time Goes By Part 2' thrills in the manner of the earlier discs, but otherwise the whole seems vaguely disappointing.

*****(*) Household Name**
Household DAA 001 *Wettre; Håvard Wiik (p); Palle Pesonen (g); Per Zanussi (b); Anders Mogenson (d).* 4/02.

***** Live At Copenhagen Jazzhouse**
Household DAA 002 *Wettre; Anders Christensen (b); Anders Mogenson (d).* 11/02.

Wettre's such a powerful player that he sets himself problems – the right fellow players, situations, material, context. The quintet of *Household Name* (none of them are) offer some new challenges. Wiik accompanies the tenor alone on a monumental 'Lush Life', and there's the wry feel of tracks such as 'Former Teen Sensation'. While coming up with material isn't a problem, making it strong enough to withstand the delivery may be. The live set is good enough but, again, some of the delirious velocity and impact of the first record has gone astray.

What We Live

GROUP

A striking improvisational group, driven by strong empathies and formidable technique. Later recordings see the group collaborate with a variety of guest instrumentalists.

***** What We Live**
DIW 909 *Larry Ochs (sno, ts); Lisle Ellis (b); Donald Robinson (d).* 4 & 6/94, 6/95.

****(*) What We Live Fo(u)r**

Black Saint 120156-2 *As above, except add Glenn Spearman (wood f), Ben Goldberg (bcl), Paul Plimley (p), William Winant (vib), India Cooke (vn), Miya Masaoka (koto).* 6/94.

*****(*) Never Was**

Black Saint 120169 *As for What We Live.* 6 & 7/96.

*****(*) Trumpets**

Black Saint 120189-2 *As above, except add Dave Douglas, Wadada Leo Smith (t).* 11/96, 3/98.

*****(*) Quintet For A Day**

New World 80553-2 *As above.* 4/98.

The trio was formed in 1994 in the Bay Area, always with the proviso that other participants would become involved as circumstances dictated. The first album and *Never Was* are the only two on which the founding members play without guest spots. The language is intense but surprisingly relaxed, as if the high intensity of East Coast free jazz were tempered with Californian sunshine. There is hardly a note on either album on which one feels the group is straining for effect.

Ellis is the main composer and his ideas sound very much like a milder version of Cecil Taylor's ferocious polytonality. Ochs is a much more impressive soloist than any of his colleagues in the ROVA saxophone quartet, and he is one of the very few contemporary players who has managed to make a decent fist of the treacherously pitched sopranino saxophone. The main pieces on *Never Was* are fierce and intense, but also compellingly lyrical. The understanding between Ochs and Ellis on 'Strength In Numbers' recalls some of the exchanges between Taylor and Jimmy Lyons, and Robinson has certainly listened carefully to the torrid playing of '60s innovators Sunny Murray, Andrew Cyrille and Milford Graves.

We find the guest-studded 1994 album shambolic and unfocused. It seems perverse to get the late Glenn Spearman in and then restrict him to wood flute. Few of the other cameos add a great deal to the sum. The two trumpet sessions are a different matter. On *Trumpets* the two horn men appear on alternate tracks, Smith's burning intensity chequered with Douglas's thoughtful cool; Dave's playing on 'Orbital' and 'Song Of Roland' is breathtaking. They play together on every track on *Quintet For A Day* and here there is a more measured texture, a combination of long and short, almost imagistic tracks. What We Live is a group that requires a measure of commitment and patience, not because the music is alienating or harsh, but precisely because it is so accessible that it can easily seem shallower and less mediated than it actually is. Give these fine records an early audition.

***** Especially The Traveller Tomorrow**

Metalanguage MLX 2002 *Larry Ochs (sno, ts); Lisle Ellis (b); Donald Robinson (d).* 4/00.

Disc number six returns the group to its basic trio format. Ochs seems almost wilfully addicted to a sound that keeps its distance from lyrical saxophone beauty, yet taken a frame at a time, the music sounds severely beautiful. The rigour and wasteless feel of the playing is satisfying yet curiously puritanical, like a Coltrane group purged of its exultation and dependent on a step-by-step path to enlightenment. Across the 32-plus minutes of the title-track, it's a hard journey.

Kenny Wheeler (born 1930)

TRUMPET, FLUGELHORN

The brilliant Canadian trumpeter and composer came to London in the '50s and very quickly became associated with the avant-garde, playing in some of the most advanced groups of the day. It was clear, though, that his limpid, very pure tone was also amenable to other styles and that his interests veered to composition every bit as much as to free improvisation. Wheeler's body of work for the ECM label is definitive of its devotion to advanced musical language, great purity of sound and a constant trade-off between experimentalism and accessibility.

*****(*) Gnu High**

ECM 825591-2 *Wheeler; Keith Jarrett (p); Dave Holland (b); Jack DeJohnette (d).* 6/75.

****** Deer Wan**

ECM 829385-2 *Wheeler; Jan Garbarek (ts, ss); John Abercrombie (g, electric mand); Ralph Towner (12-string g); Dave Holland (b); Jack DeJohnette (d).* 7/77.

*****(*) Double, Double You**

ECM 815675-2 *Wheeler; Michael Brecker (ts); John Taylor (p); Dave Holland (b); Jack DeJohnette (d).* 5/83.

***** Flutter By, Butterfly**

Soul Note 121146 *Wheeler; Stan Sulzmann (ss, ts, f); John Taylor (p); Billy Elgart (d).* 5/87.

****** The Widow In The Window**

ECM 843198-2 *Wheeler; John Taylor (p); John Abercrombie (g); Dave Holland (b); Peter Erskine (d).* 2/90.

Wheeler has been a fixture on the British jazz scene since 1952, when he emigrated from his native Canada and did section work with some of the best bandleaders of the time, joining John Dankworth in 1959 and staying until the mid-'60s. Initially influenced by the bop trumpet of Fats Navarro and his equally short-lived descendant Booker Little, Wheeler also took on board the clipped abstractions and parched romanticism of trumpeter and flugelhorn-player Art Farmer. Under this combination of interests, Wheeler turned towards free playing, joining John Stevens's influential Spontaneous Music Ensemble, Alexander von Schlippenbach's Globe Unity Orchestra and Anthony Braxton's superb early-'70s quartet. More recently, Wheeler has played with Norma Winstone and her pianist husband, John Taylor, in the impressionistic Azimuth, and he became the latest permanent recruit to the United Jazz + Rock Ensemble in 1979.

It was possible in 1990 to wonder at Wheeler's threescore years because he became a leader only rather late in his career. Famously self-critical, the trumpeter seemed to lack the basic ego-count required to front a working band. Association with Manfred Eicher's musician-friendly ECM made an enormous difference to Wheeler's self-perception, and since 1975 he has regularly recorded for the label whose painstaking technical virtues match his own. With ECM, Wheeler has also made enormous strides as a composer; standards are now very rare in his recorded work and the Dietz/Schwartz 'By Myself' on ECM 843152-2 seems a significant exception. 'Ana', on *The Widow In The Window*, had already been given a notable reading by the Berlin Contemporary Jazz Orchestra (ECM 841777-2).

Significantly, *Around 6*, the most abstract of the albums he has made for the label, is currently deleted. The best of those that remain is undoubtedly *Deer Wan*. It includes Wheeler's most atmospheric brass effects and some of his most unfettered playing. The opening 'Peace For Five' is a straightforward blowing theme, with fine solos by each of the players. The three remaining tracks are more elliptical but no less impressive, and only the relatively brief '3/4 In The Afternoon', featuring one of Ralph Towner's off-the-peg 12-string spots, is a mild disappointment.

Deer Wan's predecessor on ECM is distinguished by being Keith Jarrett's last session as a sideman. There is some evidence that the pianist was less than happy with the music, but he produces three startling performances that are matched by Wheeler's distinctive phraseology and impeccable tone. An important album for the trumpeter, it's still marked by a degree of diffidence which persists through the later work. *Flutter By* utilizes the softly falling figures one has heard in Wheeler's work from the outset but which increasingly play a structural role in the composition. *Widow In The Window* recaptures – but for Garbarek – the sound of *Deer Wan*, while adding a new solidity of conception. This group of records (and *Music For Large And Small Ensembles* below) signal Wheeler's emergence as a major jazz composer. Late in the day by some standards, but none the less welcome.

CORE COLLECTION

****** Music For Large And Small Ensembles**
ECM 843152-2 2CD *Wheeler; Alan Downey, Ian Hamer, Henry Lowther, Derek Watkins (t); Hugh Fraser, Dave Horler, Chris Pyne, Paul Rutherford (tb); Julian Arguëlles, Duncan Lamont, Evan Parker, Ray Warleigh (sax); Stan Sulzmann (ts, f); John Taylor (p); John Abercrombie (g); Dave Holland (b); Peter Erskine (d); Norma Winstone (v).* 1/90.

Music For Large And Small Ensembles **contains some of Wheeler's most distinctive scores and is perhaps the best place to gain an understanding of how Wheeler's particular grasp of tonality and instrumental colour works in a mixture of scored and improvised settings. As in Azimuth, he uses Norma Winstone's voice to increase the chromaticism of his arrangements and further humanize unwontedly personal and self-revealing pieces, full of folk echoes and deeply embedded North American themes (the 'Opening' to 'Sweet Time Suite' sounds like a variant on a cowboy tune, and there's a wide-open quality to the voicings that can be heard in fellow-Canadian Leonard Cohen's eclectic jazz–buckskin–*musette*–rock syntheses). The trios that conclude disc two (there are also three duets which do not involve Wheeler as a player) are closer to his free-abstract work than to the thematic improvisations on his best-known ECM records.**

****** Angel Song**
ECM 533098-2 *Wheeler; Lee Konitz (as); Bill Frisell, Dave Holland (b).* 95.

*****(*) Siren's Song**
Justin Time JTR 8465 *Wheeler; John Taylor (p); Norma Winstone (v); Maritime Jazz Orchestra.* 96.

Two misconceptions here. First, *Angel Song* was widely thought to be a co-led project with Konitz; while it is as collaborative as much of the label's recent output, with much emphasis on internal relationships within the group, it has Wheeler's stamp all over it: a delicate, floating sound with a sting and hard ideas scattered through it. By the same token, *Siren's Song* (a seeming paucity of album-title ideas at the moment) is not really an Azimuth project and is not so billed. What it is is a form of jazz *concerto grosso* with the trio ranged against a well-schooled and precise Canadian orchestra. They provide texture and depth of focus, but they also feed and re-feed Wheeler's more searching musical cues, creating a back and forth of ideas that is actually a lot more thoughtful than first appears. *Angel Song* is the one to have from this period, and it is probably the more accessible too. Frisell's soft-edged phrasing melds with Holland's unusually deep-rooted figures, creating a symmetry that fires both hornmen to some of their best recorded work in years.

***** Moon**
EGEA SCA 086 *Wheeler; Gabriele Mirabassi (cl); John Taylor (p).* 2/01.

Many beautiful moments for this long-standing partnership (Mirabassi appears on three out of nine tracks), but there's a sense of an impeccable jog around the track at this point, and some of the lustre has finally begun to fade from Kenny's sound. More could have been made from Mirabassi's involvement, perhaps: the pieces which he plays on have an extra vitality which some of the others lack.

*****(*) Dream Sequence**
psi 03.04 *Wheeler; Ray Warleigh (as, f); Stan Sulzmann (ts); John Parricelli (g); Chris Laurence (b); Tony Levin (d).* 9/95–1/03.

Pieced together from sessions across a four-year spell and then topped off with a solo cut in 2003, this is a predictably eloquent, lyrical, slightly mournful Wheeler session. Nothing surpasses the beautiful opener, 'Unti', one of those stop-start Wheeler compositions where every melodic motif is carefully weighted in the line, each cadence voiced with pristine assurance. The other pieces all have their merits, although some of them do tread water in Kenny's own immaculate realm, and the solo piece does suggest again that the once incomparable sound has tarnished a little. Sonic star turn: Ray Warleigh's flute-playing.

Rodney Whitaker (born 1968)

DOUBLE BASS

Wynton Marsalis once autographed a fragment of score for Rodney with the words: 'Listen to Jimmy Blanton'. Whitaker, who teaches at Michigan State University, has been a member of the Marsalis-led Lincoln Center Orchestra for some time and has demonstrated that, subconsciously at least, he has already absorbed much of Blanton's language. A copper-bottomed soloist with a big tone, he is an asset to bands of any size.

*****(*) The Brooklyn Session: Ballads And Blues**
Criss Cross 1167 *Whitaker; Wycliffe Gordon (tb); Ron Blake (ss, ts); Stefon Harris (vib); Eric Reed (p); Carl Allan (d).* 12/98.

The Detroit jazz community is said to be one of the tightest in the United States, built on mutual support and respect. Rodney Whitaker was quickly picked out as a young man to watch and foster, and his early reputation won him a place in Donald Washington's group Bird/Trane/Sco/Now!, a cumbersome handle for a working band, but a reasonable shorthand for the influences at work. Whitaker is quite open about his own biggest influence: the intense, short-lived genius of Paul Chambers informs much of what he does.

The debut for Criss Cross is very much a tribute to Rodney's greatest single ancestral influence, the precocious but ever more impressive legacy of Chambers. Mr PC is represented by three tracks, the ubiquitous 'Whims Of Chambers', which every bass player takes in with his mother's milk, 'Ease It', and 'The Hand Of Love', the last of which is a long way from the prevailing bebop idiom of the time, and a delicately phrased song which bears surprising kinship to the Motown material Rodney grew up with. Like many young players of his generation, he has kept an active lookout for new 'standards' and perhaps the most striking solo performance on the record is Whitaker's *arco* phrasing on the Carly Simon song, 'The Way They Always Said It Should Be'. Miles would have approved. Crisply recorded with a nice live feel, *Ballads And Blues* is a sterling performance which represents a bright young talent at his very best.

***** Yesterday Today And Tomorrow**

Sirocco Jazz SJL 1007 *Whitaker; Wynton Marsalis (t); Wycliffe Gordon (tb); Wessell Anderson (sno, as); Victor Goines (ss, ts, bcl); Farid Barron (p); Herlin Riley (d); Dianne Reeves (v).* 12/99.

Whitaker doesn't impose too much of himself on this date – only five of the 12 tunes are his originals, and extended bass features are noticeable by their absence. It's an outgoing record in feel, even with the heavyweight company of several of the LCO regulars, notably boss Wynton on three tracks (Anderson is credited only with sopranino, but he presumably handles the alto parts on two other tracks). Goines is the most featured voice, a polished-mahogany sound on tenor, and every track seems to boast a particularly pointed solo or statement by the ensemble. Overall, though, we felt that the music could use a little more relaxation. Marsalis, as so often these days, seems to be conducting some sort of masterclass when he solos and some of that propriety seeps into the whole enterprise. The most peppery moment comes in Gordon's solo on 'Hurricane Andrew', although Reeves takes an effectively sultry cameo on 'Mood Indigo'.

David White

GUITAR

Guitarist whose preference for a simple tone and no effects in a contemporay setting is a refreshing change from the norm.

***** All Stories Are True**

Cadence CJR 1057 *White; Valery Ponomarev (t); Tim Armacost (ts); Calvin Hill (b); Victor Jones (d).* 5/93.

***** Object Relations**

CIMP 117 *As above, except Shingo Okudaira (d) replaces Jones.* 6/96.

*****(*) Double Double**

CIMP 168 *White; George Garzone, Tim Armacost (ss, ts); John Lockwood (b); Joris Dudli (d).* 2/98.

Likeable, oddball neo-bop, but not without its problems. White's muffled, sometimes bluesy sound is a refreshing change from the standard Montgomery/Scofield options, and he has a Tristano-like sense of selflessness: some of his solos sound completely 'inside'. *All Stories Are True* takes on some interesting structures, too, such as the various metres of 'Iconoclasts' and the contrary 'Hot Issues In An Open House'. Ponomarev and Armacost come up with some strong improvisations in support. But the rhythm section often seem unaware of what's going on and where everybody's headed. Hill especially is very busy, yet oblivious to the rest of the music, and both he and Jones are given an unpleasant studio sound. *Object Relations* picks up the baton three years later, with Okudaira in for Jones, and the results are much the same, though the CIMP sound is just as unsuitable. Armacost and Ponomarev have their moments, although some of these pieces seem inflated beyond their useful length.

The latest album is a clear notch ahead. Garzone is a valuable addition to any band, and he seems to encourage Armacost to raise his game, too. The results are dominated by the two saxmen, who play generously but are part of a strong quintet which White, Lockwood and Dudli fill out more than dutifully. This time White takes more of a back seat as a soloist; but his tunes are fertile ground for the horns, and the one standard, 'Love Thy Neighbour', is beautifully handled.

Michael White (born 1954)

CLARINET

White is from a musical New Orleans family and is dedicated to the original music of his home, playing in the grand traditions of the city. At home, he also plays in brass bands as well as his own groups.

***** Shake It & Break It**

504 CDS 6 *White; Greg Stafford (c); Reginald Koeller (t); Freddie Lonzo (tb); Sadie Goodson Cola (p, v); Frank Moliere (p, v); Les Muscutt (g); Walter Payton Jr, Chester Zardis (b); Frank Parker, Stanley Stephens (d).* 1/81–5/87.

We were rather cool in our first edition on what was White's debut recording, and Frank Moliere's piano still sounds awful, but perhaps we've grown more tolerant of New Orleans 'idiosyncrasies' down the years. The music is played with undeniable spirit, and there is now the bonus of five tracks from a 1987 session, recorded in the cavernous-sounding Olivier House, with Cola and Zardis (who had played together in Buddy Petit's band, 60 years earlier!) in attendance. Stafford plays carefully and the stage belongs mostly to White, who sounds very good.

***** A Song For George Lewis**

Basin Street BSR051-2 *White; Greg Stafford (t, v); Mark Braud (t); Lucien Barbarin (tb); Rickie Monie (p); Detroit Brooks (bj); Kerry Lewis (b); Shannon Powell (d).* 2/00.

***** Jazz From The Soul Of New Orleans**

As above, except add Clyde Kerr (*t*), Steve Pistorius (*p*), Herman Lebeaux (*d*), Thais Clark, Juanita Brooks (*v*); omit Braud and Powell. 2/02.

White made a couple of records under the Antilles imprint in the '90s, but these seem to be his only recent showing as a leader. Made as a homage to Lewis on the occasion of his centenary, the baker's dozen tunes will be familiar to acolytes of the clarinettist, though there are two originals by White. It's one of the better things to appear on the New Orleans label, Basin Street. The difficult thing about playing this old-time sound is making it true to its spirit of entertaining a crowd without succumbing to slickness or showboating. Sometimes White and his men sound as if they might be playing down to their material a little, and on a test-piece such as 'Burgundy Street Blues' the clarinettist seems to be deliberately avoiding Lewis as a direct model. But it's still good to hear this music smartly recorded and played with obvious skill and affection.

The follow-up carries the torch onwards. White is clearly steeped in the right stuff, but to suggest that he's any kind of maverick leader would be a mistake. The presence of Pistorius, who plays in many such bands, underscores the sense that White's music has to take its turn with every other revivalist group. It's good enough.

Mark Whitecage (born 1937)

ALTO AND SOPRANO SAXOPHONES, CLARINET, ALTO AND SOPRANO CLARINETS, SYNTHESIZER, ELECTRONICS, VOCAL

A free-thinking alto saxophonist who made some discs in the '70s with John Fisher, Bobby Naughton and Leo Smith, Whitecage has only recently resurfaced as a recording artist. His idiosyncratic methods move between chamber-like forms and entirely free improvisation.

*****(*) Free For Once**
CIMP 106 *Whitecage; Dominic Duval (b); Jay Rosen (d).* 1/96.

****** Caged No More**
CIMP 119 *As above, except add Tomas Ulrich (clo).* 7/96.

Whitecage is a somewhat reclusive figure whose appearances on record have been unfortunately rare. On alto he plays long, almost pure streams of melody which impart a graceful beauty to a free-bop methodology which makes these discs both exciting and serenely attractive. Even when he's playing at a heated full stretch, Whitecage seems to want to talk about agreeable things, and it makes these fundamentally uncompromising sessions temperate enough to avoid the raging exhaustion that sometimes afflicts this area of jazz. *Free For Once* is still a shade too long, but there's an almost terpsichorean feel to the music which Rosen and Duval pick up on (it's not only on 'Two Horn Tango' that they fall into a tango rhythm). Whitecage has so much to say on the horn that he sustains the date. *Caged No More* is a notch better, though, and Whitecage was right to feel proud of it. Ulrich's cello adds pith and sinew to the group's sound, and the players frequently hit a stride that balances lyricism, intensity and creative flux in an unusually harmonious accord.

***** 3 + 4 = 5**
CIMP 155 *As above, except add Joseph Scianni (p).* 6/97.

*****(*) Consensual Tension**
CIMP 157 *Whitecage; Sabir Mateen (as, ts, cl, f); Joe Fonda (b); Harvey Sorgen (d).* 7/97.

***** Research On The Edge**
CIMP 193 *Whitecage; Sabir Mateen (as, ts, cl, f); Chris Dahlgren (b); Jay Rosen (d).* 2/99.

Having found a patron in Robert Rusch of Cadence/CIMP, Whitecage seems to be making up for lost time as far as record-making is concerned. *3 + 4 = 5*, recorded at Dunn Hall in Potsdam, NY, continues the good work of the previous disc, but the balance of the group is sent slightly askew by the addition of Scianni and, for all its 'naturalness', the recording is unkind to both Ulrich and Duval, who simply can't be heard properly for much of the session.

Consensual Tension introduces Whitecage's 'Other Quartet', and a splendid one it is: Mateen is a more restless and argumentative soul and, while Whitecage adds lyrical and sometimes rococo flights to the mix, Mateen is gritty and cutting. Fonda and Sorgen – they manufacture a nice, slithering shuffle on 'Joe's Groove' – fill in the backgrounds and sometimes push their way to the front. It's very free, but the way they play 'Oleo', a spontaneous fancy in the studio, proves how this thinking has plenty of formal knowledge stirred into it.

Whitecage's 'Other Other Quartet' (we hardly dare guess what the next group will be called) picks up the baton for *Research On The Edge*. This is more like unvarnished energy music: the first three tracks are huge blow-outs ('Green St Rundown' runs almost half an hour) and, mightily as the four men play, there are passages when sound and fury stand in for communicable creativity, or so it seems. Not that they are playing full-tilt all the time: there is the usual cycle of attack and decay in each piece. When they do 'Well You Needn't' at the end, the music almost gets funky, and it freshens the listener up. Enjoyable, but probably not the best representation of Whitecage's work.

***** The Paper Trail**
Acoustics ELE 413 *Whitecage; Dominic Duval (b); Jay Rosen (d).* 4/95.

****(*) Moon Blue Boogie**
Acoustics ELE 408 *Whitecage; Sabir Mateen (as, ts, cl, f); Tomas Ulrich (clo); Chris Dahlgren (b); Jay Rosen (d).* 12/98–2/99.

****(*) Fractured Standards And Fairy Tales**
Acoustics ELE 409 *Whitecage; Dominic Duval (b); Jay Rosen (d).* 10/99.

****(*) Fractured Again**
Acoustics ELE 412 *As above.* 10/99.

***** No Respect**
Acoustics ELE 414 *As above.* 5/01.

**** Ducks On Acid**
Acoustics ELE 415 *Whitecage (cl, as, syn, elec, v solo).* 12/02.

A pile of sessions all released on Whitecage's own Acoustics label. *The Paper Trail* is old enough to count as archive material. Like all the trio sets here, it's terrific when the band hit a grooving freebop feel, less sure when Whitecage moves into overblowing and chaos beckons (though it doesn't quite overtake the music). *Moon Blue Boogie* is split between trio and quartet tracks and is drawn from live New York recordings. Again, there are some tough, concentrated moments and other passages where raggedness and disintegration spoil things. Mateen is a good foil, but when he and Whitecage are both going full blast the listener tires. The next two come from consecutive nights of live work in France. The title-piece of *Fractured Standards* has some clever touches, where familiar jazz pieces drift in and out between the improvisations. Whitecage is starting to use electronics more regularly, and given that he has a rather attractive tone on the undoctored horn, some may see this as a mixed blessing. *No Respect* follows the pattern of the other trio discs – 'Dolphin Dance' and 'Round Midnight' get into the setlist, though not unscarred, and again it's when the group leave the effects-making and such behind them and concentrate on playing music that they hit home. *Ducks On Acid* presents Whitecage's 'virtual combo', where he uses electronic gizmos to sub for other musicians. Better left in the notebook.

Tim Whitehead (born 1950)

TENOR SAXOPHONE

Born in Liverpool, he studied law but turned to music in the '70s. Early groups South Of The Border and Borderline brought him local renown, then a spell with Loose Tubes, followed by his own small bands in the '90s.

***** Silence Between Waves**
Jazz House JHCD 033 *Whitehead; Pete Jacobsen (ky); Arnie Somogyi, Steve Watts (b); Dave Barry (d).* 1–4/94.

*****(*) Personal Standards**
Home Made HMR047 *As above, except add Liam Noble (p), Davide Mantovani, Sam Burgess (b), Milo Fell (d); omit Watts.* 98–99.

Whitehead has fashioned a convincing and evocative English tone to his playing and writing. Although recorded in the less than pastoral surroundings of Ronnie Scott's Club, *Silence Between Waves* is quartet music that is redolent of Albion's greenest meadows as well as market-town England. Jacobsen is a willing collaborator, his hard-bitten solo on 'Southend' no less effective than his meditative introduction to 'The Sky Seas Me', but it's otherwise very much the saxophonist's show, traversing the range of the tenor saxophone with broad-shouldered ease and drawing long, melodic lines in his solos rather than falling back on licks. That said, the record is far too long and could comfortably have surrendered 20 of its 80 minutes, heightening the impact of the best playing.

Personal Standards suffers the same drawback, to a degree: Whitehead can sustain long solos persuasively enough, but some of these pieces still outstay their most effective duration. Nevertheless a very impressive record overall. The saxophonist selected pop material for the most part, 'My Girl', 'Dancing In The Street', 'Lovely Day' and 'What's Going On' being among the most familiar choices, and while these are conservative interpretations they showcase a magnificent saxophone timbre: the leader has never had a better sound in a studio. Although the other players give their best, Whitehead is an almost overpowering presence in this company, and the hallmark of the record is the way he personalizes what is sometimes unpromising material.

Mark Whitfield

GUITAR

Though superficially from the same mould as Kevin Eubanks and Hiram Bullock, Whitfield is much more deeply suffused with the blues. His phrasing is attractively old-fashioned without ever sounding like pastiche, and his arrangements are always absolutely contemporary.

***** True Blue**
Verve 523591-2 *Whitfield; Nicholas Payton (t); Branford Marsalis (ss, ts); Kenny Kirkland (p); Rodney Whitaker (b); Jeff Tain Watts (d).* 94.

*****(*) Forever Love**
Verve 533921-2 *Whitfield; Jim Pryor (p); Roland Guerin (b); Donald Edwards (d); Diana Krall (v).* 96.

These seem to be all that survives of Whitfield's run of albums for Verve, and they are superficially very different. The earlier album was recorded in Hollywood with a top-drawer roster of Polygram artists and a very definite emphasis on the blues. And yet it's the later album with its relatively unfamiliar line-up and more showbizzy programme which has the jazz vibe.

True Blue made the classic corporate mistake of garlanding new and relatively untried talent with bankable names. Whitfield barely comes across at all, and his guests are able to offer only cameo contributions. Even so, some of the tracks – an unexpected 'Ba-Lue Bolivar Ba-Lues Are' and a cracking version of Trane's 'My Syms' – are strongly impressive and Whitfield makes his mark as a composer as well.

The later record is the one we'd recommend, even against the obvious draw of Marsalis, Kirkland and Payton. It's a gentler album, more thoughtful and less obviously bent on making an impact. It's also beautifully executed and having Diana Krall on board is never a disadvantage, though it would have been good to hear her on piano as well. Standout tracks: that mid-section which sequences 'My One And Only One', 'Nature Boy' and 'It Never Entered My Mind', the last respectfully aware of Miles and John Coltrane. Super stuff. At present, though, Whitfield's recording career as leader seems becalmed.

Wesla Whitfield

VOCAL

California-based vocalist, singing the great American songbook.

***** Seeker Of Wisdom And Truth**
Cabaret CACD 5012 *Whitfield; Mike Greensill (p); John Goldsby (b); Tim Horner (d).* 11/93.

***** Teach Me Tonight**
High Note HCD 7009 *Whitfield; Noel Jewkes (as, ts, bs, cl, bcl); Mike Greensill (p); Michael Moore (b); Joe LaBarbera (d).* 1/97.

Whitfield has a strong and clear voice – perhaps too strong, since it often feels like she's bearing down on a song, if not quite wrestling it to the ground. Her penchant for very long notes without vibrato can make a lyric seem enormously extended, and because she usually likes to sing the verse as well this can sometimes tell against her. Nor does she exactly strike one as a swinging vocalist. All this carping aside, she can often turn in uncommonly affecting performances on improbable tunes; if her style appeals, her records will appeal very strongly.

The discography is looking a bit foreshortened by the absence of her Landmark albums. *Seeker Of Wisdom And Truth* is a decent one – the Astaire medley is delightful, 'The Boy Next Door' has a nice ambiguity about it, and 'I Want To Talk About You' is very fine. *Teach Me Tonight* has an obvious benefit in the personnel: Jewkes is a master multi-instrumentalist, Moore and LaBarbera are unimpeachable, Greensill knows her better than anybody. Doubts about some of the interpretations will nag the uncommitted, but how about the rubato intro to 'Almost Like Being In Love', or the shoulder-shrug 'I Fall In Love Too Easily'?

★★★(★) With A Song In My Heart

High Note HCD 7040 *Whitfield; Mike Greensill (p); Michael Moore (b).* 5/99.

Whitfield (formerly Weslia, now Wesla, apparently due to confusion over how her name is pronounced) goes absolutely her own way. Her pronunciation has become even more idiosyncratic, swallowing some consonants, hitting long, loud notes when you expect a little leniency – listen to the curt ending of 'Spring Is Here' – and turning some songs into curiously abstract meditations. The result, in these Rodgers and Hart performances, is a set of 18 interpretations which stand resolutely aside from so many other versions of this familiar material. It helps that Greensill and Moore come up with unusual frameworks of their own, never merely comping; but it's Whitfield's show and she makes it her own.

★★★(★) Let's Get Lost

High Note HCD 7065 *Whitfield; Ken Peplowski (cl, ts); Gary Foster (ts, cl, bcl, af); Mike Greensill (p); Michael Moore (b); Joe LaBarbera (d).* 3/00.

It's hard to pin down what appeals about Wesla's records, since they continually seem to go against expectations of how a song will or should sound. She shouldn't even try and do 'Too Young To Go Steady', but it comes out extraordinarily well. 'It's Me Remember' is easier to like, because there's no other version that we even know of, but what about the austerity of 'Blame It On My Youth'? And she doesn't even see herself as being really a jazz singer, though here she's in top jazz company for sure. Definitely one to refresh jaded ears.

★★★(★) The Best Thing For You Would Be Me

High Note HCD 7091 *Whitfield; Marty Wehner (tb); Gary Foster (as, ts, cl, f); Mike Greensill (p); John Wiitala (b); Vince Lateano (d).* 5/01.

★★★ September Songs

High Note HCD 7114 *Whitfield; Gary Foster (saxes, f); Mike Greensill, Tommy Flanagan (p); John Wiitala, Peter Washington, Michael Moore (b); Vince Lateano, Tootie Heath (d); Kronos Quartet.* 5/00–6/01.

The first is a Berlin programme. Wehner and Foster add jazz cred again, and they've chosen some good tunes – we'd much rather enjoy 'Not For All The Rice In China' than 'God Bless America', anyway. Berlin's a long-ago guy in American songwriting these days (even if he did outlive most of his peers), and the old-fashioned grace of some of these tunes suits Wesla well.

The trouble with *September Songs* is that it's too fancy. The Kronos Quartet show up for three tracks; Tommy Flanagan's trio accompany on three others; five have just Moore and Greensill. The record feels bitty and too long, and Whitfield's not the kind of binding personality that overcomes such problems. That said, she does very well with a few of these: 'I Know Why And So Do You' suits her oddball enunciation particularly well.

Putte Wickman (born 1924)

CLARINET

One of the godfathers of post-war Swedish jazz, Wickman styled himself a swing player at first but – despite the unfashionable nature of his instrument – he increasingly adopted a personal take on the cooler side of bebop language. Essentially he has worked in whatever context he liked for the past 40 years, though he led a dance band for a time in the '60s.

★★★ Young, Searching And Swinging

Phontastic CD 9304 *Wickman; Gosta Torner (t); George Vernon (tb); Arne Domnérus, Sven Gustafsson (as); G. Bjorklund, Gosta Theselius (ts); Charlie Norman, Bob Laine, Reinhold Svensson, Gunnar Svensson (p); Johan Adolfsson (acc); Fred Eriksberg, Stan Carlberg, Kalle Lohr, Rolf Berg, Rune Gustafsson (g); Sune Svensson, Bo Kallstrom (vib); Thore Jederby, Simon Brehm, Roland Bengtsson, Yngve Akerberg, Hans Burman (b); Ake Brandes, Bertil Frylmark, Georg Oddner, Jack Noren, S. Bollhem, Robert Edman, Sture Kallin (d).* 3/45–2/55.

★★★ The Sound Of Surprise

Dragon DRCD 289 *Wickman; Lars Sjøsten (p); Sture Nordin (b); Pelle Hulten (d).* 1/69.

★★★ Bewitched

Bluebell ABCD 051 *Wickman; Claes Crona (p); Mads Vinding, Ove Stenberg (b); Bjarne Rostvold, Nils-Erik Slorner (d).* 9/80–7/82.

★★★ Desire / Mr Clarinet

Four Leaf FLC-CD 101 *Wickman; Lars Samuelsson (t); Bjorn J-Son Lindh (ky, f); Janne Schaffer (g); Teddy Walter (b); Magnus Person, Per Lindvall (d).* 4/84–6/85.

★★★(★) The Very Thought Of You

Dragon DRCD 161 *Wickman; Red Mitchell (b).* 12/87–1/88.

★★★★ Some O' This And Some O' That

Dragon DRCD 187 *Wickman; Roger Kellaway (p); Red Mitchell (b).* 6/89.

Putte Wickman is still, after more than five decades, completely at home among Sweden's jazz masters. An impeccable swing player who followed cool developments in the '50s, Wickman has spent time away from jazz but seems fully aware of every kind of development in the music. Some of his earlier recordings have been restored to circulation by *Young, Searching And Swinging*, which compiles 22 tracks from various playing situations – though all small groups – over his first ten years in the studio. Many are with pianist Reinhold Svensson, who partnered the clarinettist in a quartet for several years. The format doesn't move far beyond the small-band sides by Goodman and Shaw, and could even seem anachronistic at a time when bop had taken a grip, but Wickman's essentially cool stance allowed wrinkles of modernism to sidle into the music. By the time of the final sextet tracks that persona is firmly in place. Some of the earlier tracks sound a little grey, but remastering is mostly good.

The Dragon reissue goes some modest way towards filling in a large gap in the Wickman story on record. A snapshot of a quartet show at Stockholm's Pawnshop Club, in front of an irresponsibly noisy audience, this finds Wickman (at probably the least fashionable point in jazz history for his kind of music) in a rich vein of invention. Like his contemporary, Buddy DeFranco, he seems to have the gift of playing jazz on the instrument that transcends its time-frame. The surroundings are discouraging but the music has a doggedly creative spirit.

Bewitched covers two trio sessions – Crona plays on both – in which Putte investigates two sets of standards. The 1980 session is better by a whisker: Stenberg plays with real drive and there's an interesting version of Bernie Senensky's 'Another Gift' which makes one wish that Wickman would look at contemporary tunes more often. The music tends to be sleepy on melody statements, then gradually wakes up when the leader probes his way through a solo. The Four Leaf CD reissues a pair of albums in which the clarinettist works in a soft-fusion setting: it's slight stuff, the playing vitiated a little by the context, but Wickman finds things to say, and the music remains disarmingly pretty.

The two later Dragons find Wickman in splendid fettle. The duo set with Mitchell is momentarily troubled by the bassist's capricious streak: his fascination with the lowest register sometimes strays into indulgence, and the huffing momentum won't be to all tastes. But Wickman goes on spinning out memorable improvisations, and they devise some unexpected variations on the (standard) material: Basie's 'Topsy' becomes rather intense and brooding, and the Ellington themes have no sniff of routine in them. When Kellaway joins in, the music spreads itself out (eight pieces take 72 minutes here, whereas there are 13 in 68 minutes on the duo record), and Kellaway's extravagant imagination is perfectly checked by Wickman's insidious, wily lines. The recording is sometimes a little flat, since both discs were made in Red Mitchell's apartment rather than a studio, but it suits the intimacy of the music.

*****(*) Putte Wickman In Trombones**

Phontastic NCD 8826 *Wickman; Olle Holmquist, Bertil Strandberg, Anders Wiborg, Urban Wiborg, Nils Landgren (tb); Gösta Rundqvist (p); Sture Akerberg, Christian Spering (b); Peter Ostlund (d).* 5–6/92.

***** In Silhouette**

Phontastic NCD 8848 *Wickman; Butch Lacy (p); Rune Gustafsson (g); Jesper Lundgaard (b); Arne Tangaard (d).* 6/94.

Putte likes trombones: they make a sound he 'can pull over himself like a comforting down quilt'. *In Trombones* is a little reminiscent of an oddball West Coast date of 40 years earlier, but the excellent charts – Strandberg, Rundqvist, Bo Sylven – create a leaner tone on some tracks; others have the clarinet bedding down in deep-pile trombone luxury. Wickman still sounds brilliantly zestful and alert: the clarinet solos on 'Ebony Dance' remind that, even when some have been talking about the clarinet finding its modern feet via Braxton and Byron, Putte Wickman's been here all the time.

In Silhouette is a mixed bag where Wickman again does his best work on the originals, and the relatively pale interpretations of some of the standards suggest that he should always be given fresh challenges. Gustafsson, another wily veteran by now, has his own ideas and gets just enough space to sneak them in.

***** Interchange**

Phontastic NCD 8852 *Wickman; Claes Crona (p); Olle Steinholtz (b); Rune Carlsson (d).* 6/84–8/96.

These veterans were in good form on the June day in 1984 when the first dozen of these tracks were made, and it was a shrewd idea of Anders Ohman to recall Putte and Claes to the studios to cut five further duets for the CD reissue. As he says, they pick up from where they left off as if it was the same session. A nice mix of standards and jazz themes, each given a soft but incisive treatment, with the combination of clarinet and piano a particularly attractive one in timbral terms.

Gerald Wiggins (born 1922)

PIANO

Though born a New Yorker, Wiggins has made most of his music on the West Coast, particularly as an accompanist to singers or in piano-trio situations.

***** The Gerald Wiggins Trio**

VSOP 28 *Wiggins; Joe Comfort (b); Bill Douglass (d).* 56.

****(*) Music From Around The World In Eighty Days In Modern Jazz**

Original Jazz Classics OJC 1761 *Wiggins; Eugene Wright (b); Bill Douglass (d).* 56–57.

***** Wiggin' Out**

Original Jazz Classics OJC 1034 *Wiggins; Harold Land (ts); Jackie Mills (d).* 9/60.

***** Relax And Enjoy It!**

Original Jazz Classics OJC 173 *Wiggins; Joe Comfort (b); Jackie Mills (d).* 61.

Gerry Wiggins began with swing big bands, but he has pursued much of his career as an accompanist, originally with Lena Horne. On his own, with an appropriate rhythm section, he plays light, undemanding but beguiling swing-to-cool piano, rarely challenging the listener and preferring to make a few well-chosen remarks rather than dramatically refashioning a tune. The earliest of these four is the liveliest: *Trio*, originally on the Tampa label, suggests a keen kinship with Garner and Peterson. Ellington's 'I Don't Know What Kind Of Blues I Got' is authoritative, and all the up-tempo pieces are played with dexterity and plenty of punch. The *Eighty Days* material is typical of many records that were worked up from popular contemporary film and show material, and while it's not bad it sounds as perfunctory as most such genre entries. *Relax And Enjoy It!* has worn well enough, although this amiable recital of a few standards will probably appeal only to the piano-trio collector who must have everything.

Wiggin' Out is something different: Wig plays Hammond organ on this one, with the surprise presence of Harold Land. It's the tenorman who earns the stars, mostly, since Wiggins isn't exactly Jimmy Smith at the organ and the music is a bit lead-footed under Mills's stewardship. But some pleasing moments survive – catch Land's lean and pointed solo on 'A Night In Tunisia'.

*****(*) Wig Is Here**

Black & Blue BB 952.2 *Wiggins; Major Holley (b); Oliver Jackson, Ed Thigpen (d).* 3/74–3/77.

This is the second CD edition of this material, and we were rather pleased to be reacquainted with it. There's nothing here to startle or even surprise, but as a faithful documenting of Wig's rocking swing, his chuckling good humour and unaffected bluesiness, it works uncommonly well. Thigpen drums on the earlier session, Jackson on the later one, and there's little to choose between them in terms of quality. The latest remastering brings exceptionally clean and upfront sound.

Bob Wilber (born 1928)

SOPRANO, ALTO AND TENOR SAXOPHONES, CLARINET

Born in New York, Wilber studied with both Sidney Bechet and Lennie Tristano as a teenager. He worked in various Dixieland–

swing–bop situations in the '50s and '60s, mostly as a freelance, before joining the World's Geatest Jazz Band in 1968 and forming Soprano Summit in 1973 with Kenny Davern. Other repertory projects connected with King Oliver and Bechet followed. He announced his retirement in 1995 but still seems to be recording.

***** Live At The Illiana Jazz Club**
Storyville STCD 8254 *Wilber; Kenny Davern (ss, cl); Marty Grosz (g); Eddie De Haas (b), Bob Cousins (d).* 11/76.

*****(*) Summit Reunion**
Chiaroscuro CR(D) 311 *Wilber; Kenny Davern (cl); Dick Hyman (p); Bucky Pizzarelli (g); Milt Hinton (b); Bobby Rosengarden (d).* 5/90.

***** Summit Reunion – Jazz Im Amerika Haus Vol. 5**
Nagel-Heyer 015 *Wilber; Kenny Davern (cl); Dave Cliff (g); Dave Green (b); Bobby Worth (d).* 9/94.

*****(*) Yellow Dog Blues**
Chiaroscuro CR(D) 339 *As CR(D) 311 above.* 3/95.

Once upon a time everyone tried to play soprano sax like Sidney Bechet. Now that everyone tries to play soprano like either Coltrane or Steve Lacy, Bob Wilber seems like something of a throwback. Since he actually played with Bechet and has done more than anyone to keep that master's music in circulation, there's no 'authenticity' problem here. Wilber still seeks the wide, singing tone of his mentor, but he long since became his own man, and even where there is a specific homage – as in *On The Road* (below), which was made by his band, Bechet Legacy – he still sounds like himself. This is an impressive run of records. The *Soprano Summit* discs are by a popular double-act with Davern. *Live At Illiana* finds them on a good night in Chicago, and though it's another live album, there's still much fun.

The band was dissolved for a while, and in the interim Davern chose to give up soprano in favour of clarinet alone. Their reunion album is very strong, the more piquant since there's a regular contrast between the horns rather than a doppelgänger effect. The group carried on into the '90s, though the concert set from the Amerika Haus is a potboiler – Wilber and Davern seem to be jogging through this one rather than striking sparks. However, *Yellow Dog Blues* is much more like it; everyone seems in the highest of spirits and Davern and Wilber run good-natured rings round each other; listen also for the marvellous things Hyman is playing in the ensembles. Three perfect choices: 'I'll See You In C-U-B-A', 'Hindustan' and 'The Japanese Sandman'.

***** Bob Wilber And The Scott Hamilton Quartet**
Chiaroscuro CR(D) 171 *Wilber; Scott Hamilton (ts); Chris Flory (g); Phil Flanigan (b); Chuck Riggs (d).* 6–7/77.

**** The Music Of King Oliver**
GHB BCD-201 *Wilber; Bob Zottola, Glenn Zottola (t); Tom Artin (tb); Mark Shane (p); Chris Flory (bj); Phil Flanigan (b); Chuck Riggs (d).* 5/81.

*****(*) On The Road**
Jazzology JCD-214 *Wilber; Glenn Zottola (t); Mark Shane (p); Mike Peters (g, bj); Len Skeat (b); Butch Miles (d).* 11/81.

***** Ode To Bechet**
Jazzology JCD-142 *As above, except add Vic Dickenson (tb, v), Reggie Johnson (b), Joanne 'Pug' Horton (v); omit Skeat.* 8/82.

*****(*) The Duet**
Progressive PCD 7080 *Wilber; Dick Wellstood (p).* 3/84.

***** Bechet Legacy**
Challenge CHR 70018 *Wilber; Randy Sandke (t); Mike Peters (g); John Goldsby (b).* 1/84.

****** Dancing On A Rainbow**
Circle CCD-159 *Wilber; Wallace Davenport (t); David Sager (tb); Clarence Ford (cl, ts, bs); Dave Bodenhouse (p); Danny Barker (g); Dewey Sampson (b); Freddie Kohlman (d); Joanne 'Pug' Horton (v).* 12/89.

*****(*) Moments Like This**
Phontastic NCD 8811 *Wilber; Antti Sarpila (ss, ts, cl); Ulf Johansson (tb, p, v); Sture Akerberg (b); Ronnie Gardiner (d).* 5/91.

Wilber's other projects are perhaps rather more interesting. *On The Road* is a very fine salute to Bechet, uncovering many rarities in the material and with top-notch support from Zottola in particular. The CD remastering is a bit bright. The King Oliver record is very disappointing: the tempos feel infernally polite, the ensemble jig-jogs along and there's little evidence of Oliver's powerful spirit infecting anybody here. *Ode To Bechet*, though it welcomes Vic Dickenson to the ranks in a guest role, is a slight disappointment: the material seems a bit taut, and Dickenson can't really find an effective way in. *Bechet Legacy* puts similar material into a concert situation, and though Sandke isn't much like Muggsy Spanier, the instrumentation inevitably evokes the Bechet–Spanier small group. Another astute piece of revivalism. Better still, though, is *Dancing On A Rainbow*. This is an exemplary mainstream outfit, with Sager's quirky trombone and Ford's ripe gallery of reeds lending character as well as precision, and Wilber's Ellington archaeology is spot-on. It was a shrewd idea to bring back 'Love In My Heart' and 'Charlie The Chulo', but all the material turns out well. The 1977 album with Scott Hamilton is merely OK mainstream, with the tenor-man still in his copycat phase, but the recent *Moments Like This* sets up Wilber with another young disciple, the Swedish reeds-man, Sarpila. Johansson does his usual trick of doubling trombone and piano, and it sounds like a happy occasion.

The 1984 duets with Dick Wellstood have made a welcome transition to CD. Wellstood's slightly macabre imagination might not be to all tastes, as in his transformation of 'I've Got You Under My Skin' into a stride showcase, but he was a thinking player and had the executive powers to match. Wilber, more of a literalist, makes a nice balance, and the disc has some superb moments, although on a recent reacquaintance we admit we found the studio sound very fierce.

***** Horns A-Plenty**
Arbors ARCD 19135 *Wilber; Johnny Varro (p); Phil Flanigan (b); Ed Metz Jr (d).* 3/94.

*****(*) Bean**
Arbors ARCD 19144 *Wilber; Harry Allen, Tommy Whittle, Antti Sarpila (ts); Mick Pyne (p); Dave Green (b); Clark Tracey (d).* 10/94.

*****(*) Nostalgia**
Arbors ARCD 19145 *Wilber; Ralph Sutton (p); Bucky Pizzarelli (g); Bob Haggart (b); Butch Miles (d).* 3/95.

***** The Hamburg Concert – Tribute To A Legend**
Nagel-Heyer CD 028 *Wilber; Randy Sandke (t); Mark Shane (p, v); Dave Cliff (g); Dave Green (b); Butch Miles (d); Joanne 'Pug' Horton (v).* 10/95.

★★★ Memories Of You: Lionel And Benny

Black & Blue 897-2 *Wilber; Dany Doriz (vib); Georges Arvanitas (p); Eddie Jones (b); Butch Miles (d).* 11/95.

★★★ Bufadora Blow-Up

Arbors ARCD 19187 *Wilber; Charlie Bertini, Wendell Brunious, Jon-Erik Kellso, Bob Merrill (t); Dan Barrett, George Masso, Paul O'Connor (tb); Shoeless Henry Aaron, Jerry Jerome, Brian Ogilvie, Scott Robinson, Chuck Wilson (saxes); Dick Hyman (p); Howard Alden (g); Phil Flanigan (b); Ed Metz Jr (d); Joanne 'Pug' Horton (v).* 3/96.

★★★(★) What Swing Is All About

Nagel-Heyer 5007 *Wilber; Antti Sarpila (cl, ts); Mark Shane (p); Phil Flanigan (b); Joe Ascione (d); Joanne 'Pug' Horton (v).* 9/96.

Although Wilber had announced his retirement from active duty, he seems to have been busier than ever with making records. These are rather a mixed lot. *Horns A-Plenty* finds him switching between clarinet and four saxes on a typically arcane set of tunes, with a few lightweight originals floating in among the likes of 'Just A Rose In A Garden Of Weeds'. Not bad, but the music's pleasantries tend to leave no impression. *Bean* puts a four-man tenor team through its paces on a tribute to Coleman Hawkins. Wilber concentrates on Hawk's music from the '30s and early '40s, and there are some ingenious reductions and embellishments on what are in several cases neglected originals. The team is recorded in a dry but very effective acoustic, and some of the unison passages are played wonderfully, with Wilber and Whittle emerging as the most Hawk-like. *Nostalgia* is mostly ballads and tunes from bygone albums. If Wilber were British, he might have thought twice about doing 'The Lambeth Walk' here; and a couple of the classical pieces recall the days of Rudy Wiedoft. Stately stuff. If Wellstood were still alive, he might have lent a Machiavellian touch at the piano, but Sutton, admirable though he is, is no such ironist.

The Hamburg Concert is another Bechet Legacy project, with a string of tunes associated with the great man and played with the expected brio by the band – a little too much brio, perhaps. Butch Miles is on his most bumptious form, and though that actually gives the music a sometimes welcome kick it occasionally seems to egg the normally meticulous Sandke into overplaying what he seems to be hearing as a supercharged Armstrong role. It's still agreeable to hear a contemporary band playing 'Egyptian Fantasy' and 'Dans La Rue D'Antibes'.

Memories Of You takes an amiable canter through the Goodman–Hampton book. Nothing happens beyond the obvious, a smiling delivery of the expected staples, although Butch Miles, who hates to doze at the kit, keeps things moving.

The big-band date comes from Wilber's feature spot at the 1996 March of Jazz Festival in Florida. It falls easily on the ear, and as a soloist Wilber works sunnily in this context, but his writing for the band is nothing very special – he likes the reed section, and that's about it. A better choice is *What Swing Is All About*, another concert set on Nagel-Heyer but measured with particular grace and balance by Wilber and cohorts. Sarpila proves to be very *simpatico* in the front line and the material, though saddled with a few overbaked chestnuts, comes up fresh.

★★★ A Perfect Match

Arbors ARCD 189193 *Wilber; Britt Woodman (tb); Dick Hyman (org); James Chirillo (g); Phil Flanigan (b); Joe Ascione (d).* 8/97.

★★★ Everywhere You Go There's Jazz

Arbors ARCD 19202 *Wilber; Bent Persson (t, c); Don Barrett (tb); Antti Sarpila (cl, ss, as, ts); Dick Hyman (p); Peter Appleyard, Lars Erstrand (vib); Dave Cliff (g); Dave Green (b); Ed Metz Jr (d); Joanne 'Pug' Horton (v).* 3/98.

Since Wilber and Hyman share the billing on *A Perfect Match*, hopes are raised of a sax–piano duet record. Instead, it's a Hodges tribute, with Hyman playing organ in the Wild Bill Davis style. A nice repertorial jog, and frankly not much more than that, although the surprise presence of Britt Woodman is a nostalgic note. The International March Of Jazz All-Stars tackle the other disc, and a formidable line-up it is, although some of it is less than inspiring: 'Mood Indigo' is merely silly in three, and some of the pieces are too groomed to work up much interest. But this time Hyman gets in some apposite remarks, and Barrett and Horton are both very fine on 'Music Maestro Please'.

★★★ You Ain't Heard Nothin' Yet!

Jazzology JCD-328 *Wilber; Kenny Davern (cl); Mark Shane (p); Bucky Pizzarelli (g); Frank Tate (b); Hal Smith (d).* 4/99.

★★★(★) Summit Reunion In Atlanta

Jazzology JCD-385 *Wilber; Kenny Davern (cl); Johnny Varro (p); James Chirillo (g); Frank Tate (b); Joe Ascione (d).* 4/01.

As with (in another field) Fairport Convention, this band has so many reunions that it seems like it's on permanent recall. The rhythm section is, though, subject to change. *You Ain't Heard Nothin' Yet!* is all Jolson-associated material, although it doesn't, alas, do 'Mammy' (or 'Yaaka Hula Hickey Dula', or 'Quarter To Nine', or ...). Tightly organized, with most pieces around the four- or five-minute mark, the set percolates nicely enough but could use a little more abandon – it's not as if Jolie was exactly a reserved performer, after all.

The Atlanta set (the packaging suggests it's a live set, but it was done in a studio) is much more like it, with both principals in very warm order. Chirillo could use a better sound in the microphones, especially as he's generously featured, but Varro fits in in fine style and it's the horns everyone's come to hear.

★★★(★) Fletcher Henderson's Unrecorded Arrangements For Benny Goodman

Arbors ARCD 19229 *Wilber; Jean Imbert, Eric Robert, Phillippe Luadet, Ron Dixon, Jacques Sallent (t); Laurent Hotta, Didier Pascal, Michel Chalot (tb); Paul Chéron, Stéphane Lourties (as); Michel Pastre (ts); Guy Robert (bs); Tierry Ollé (p); Henri Chéron (g); Pierre-Luc Puig (b); Jean-Luc Guiraud (d).* 7/99.

★★★(★) More Never-Recorded Arrangements For Benny Goodman

Arbors ARCD 19282 *As above, except Jean-François Bonnel and Gérard Barbie (ts, cl) replace Pastre.* 10/02.

The Tuxedo Big band assist Wilber on these first-time (re)creations, explained by the somewhat prosaic titling. The orchestra secure an amazingly lifelike copy of the vintage Goodman orchestra on the first disc, and with a trove of 'new' charts by his most formative arranger, the old master's sound comes convincingly back to life here. On disc two, it's a wider range of hands involved – including Benny Carter, Eddie Sauter and Buck Clayton – but handled with the same aplomb. Wilber is the principal soloist, but the rest of the band are no slouches and get plenty of feature spots along the way. Any Goodman fan will surely welcome these records, and the sound is exemplary on both. A nice collaboration between a French band and (for once) an American label.

Barney Wilen (1937–96)

SOPRANO, ALTO, TENOR AND BARITONE SAXOPHONES

Born in Nice, Wilen made a big impact on Parisian audiences when still a teenager and played with Miles Davis in 1957. A stop-start career saw him working as an engineer and film-maker as much as playing sax. Toyed with free and jazz-rock but returned to straightahead playing in the '80s.

*****(*) Jazz Sur Seine**

Emarcy 548317-2 *Wilen; Milt Jackson (p); Percy Heath (b); Kenny Clarke (d); Gana M'Bow (perc).* 58.

***** Newport '59**

Fresh Sound FSR-CD 165 *Wilen; Clark Terry (t); Toshiko Akiyoshi, Bud Powell, Ewald Heidepriem (p); Tommy Bryant, Eric Peter, Karl Theodor Geier (b); Roy Haynes, Kenny Clarke, Eberhardt Stengl (d).* 59.

Basically a tenor player, Wilen made his name when Miles Davis chose him to play in a group he was fronting in Europe in 1957. But Wilen had already garnered a reputation with visiting Americans for a considerably accomplished technique and a real mastery of hard-bop forms. At last one of his French albums has come back, on Emarcy; the rhythm section is familiar, but Milt Jackson plays piano. There's some beautiful playing by the saxophonist, his tone veiled but wonderfully singing, on the blues, 'Nuages' and 'Epistrophy'. Wilen's subsequent visit to play at Newport in 1959 is commemorated by the Fresh Sound CD, although there's only 20 minutes of music from that occasion. Akiyoshi plays exuberant bebop piano in support and Wilen's even, supple tenor works patiently and impressively through 'Passport' and 'Barney's Tune', with what was then a rare appearance of the soprano on 'Round Midnight', in which his tonal control is impressive. Two other tracks of unclear date find him with Powell (very subdued), Terry and Clarke; Wilen's solo on 'No Problem' is typically artful – since the recording is subject to some vagaries of balance, he seems to emerge from the shadows here. There is also another 'Round Midnight' with a German rhythm-section. The sound is very mixed throughout but it's listenable enough.

Don Wilkerson (1932–86)

TENOR SAXOPHONE

Not strictly a 'Texas tenor', Louisiana-born Wilkerson might just as well have been. A veteran of blues and R&B sessions with the likes of Ray Charles and B. B. King, he also recorded as a leader, mostly generic hard-bop and soul-jazz, but played with great personality. Don's small output has yet to be widely explored.

***** The Texas Twister**

Original Jazz Classics OJCCD 1950 *Wilkerson; Nat Adderley (c); Barry Harris (p); Sam Jones, Leroy Vinnegar (b); Billy Higgins (d).* 5/60.

Wilkerson's debut as leader came thanks to the enthusiasm of Cannonball Adderley, who produced sympathetically. *The Texas Twister* isn't quite as headlong as the title suggests and there are subtleties to be found amid the blowing-session clichés. A superb line-up guaranteed a very professional product, with Nat Adderley and pianist Harris in especially good form. Wilkerson's only writing credit is the predictable 'Jelly Roll'. He comes across better on more challenging ideas, notably Adderley's breezy title-track.

*****(*) The Complete Don Wilkerson On Blue Note**

Blue Note 24555 2CD *Wilkerson; Johnny Acea, Sonny Clark (p); Grant Green (g); John Patton (org); Lloyd Trotman, Butch Warren (b); Willie Bobo, Ben Dixon, Billy Higgins (d).* 5 & 6/62, 7/63.

Don's three sessions for the Blue Note label, which relied as heavily on this kind of fare as on more advanced music, are handily gathered on to one set. The three sets he made with Alfred Lion and Rudy van Gelder were actually released out of sequence. *Elder Don* was recorded a month before the cuts on *Preach, Brother!* but released only somewhat later, and one can see why. The playing on the latter record is much crisper and more together, almost as if the band melded only after that first 'rehearsal'. Sonny Clark is also a much more compelling player than Johnny Acea, while Billy Higgins is a more appropriate rhythm man than the talented but miscast Willie Bobo.

The outstanding cut on the May 1962 session is a beautiful reinterpretation of Bob Wills's Texas swing classic, 'San Antonio Rose', which sits delightfully with Wilkerson's own 'Lone Star Shuffle'. His writing confidence is much higher on *Preach, Brother!* and, while there are no lost classics in the set-list, 'Camp Meeting', 'Homesick Blues' and 'Pigeon Peas' are all strong items.

The final session for Blue Note was recorded a year later and saw Don return to a more straightforward format and a simpler accompaniment. Green is still present and still playing with a forceful grace, but Patton and Dixon offer a more secure and predictable platform for the leader. No particularly outstanding tracks from this session; but if you've bought into the concept, much to enjoy.

Andreas Willers (born 1957)

GUITAR

Fine Austrian player with a distinctive sound.

***** Tin Drum Stories**

Between the Lines btl 10179 *Willers; Horst Nonnenmacher (b); Horst Griener (d, dictaphone).* 12/00.

***** In The North**

Between the Lines btl 10196 *As above; omit Griener; add Yves Robert (tb); Paul Bley (p).* 10/02.

Anyone chancing across the first album might think they were listening to Joe Morris or, glimpsing the cover, a freer and funkier than usual disc by label-mate James Emery. In fact, this trio set, which follows a couple of earlier Sound Aspects records, is inspired by Günter Grass's great novel *Die Blechtrommel.* Quite how it's inspired and how these terse lines tie up with Grass's tale of the imagination and control can't be determined easily, but it's a very engaging set. Griener is an interesting player, who may have been given a tin drum on his fourth birthday, but it's Willers's single-note lines which keep the set from complete abstraction, cutting trajectories across Nonnenmacher's moaning bass.

The appearance of 'The Train And The River' and variations on his 'Yggdrasil' on *In The North* makes the album a kind of tribute to Jimmy Giuffre. Bley has rarely sounded more rarefied in recent years, closer to his own free-jazz self than the modified bop of most of his current projects. That's not to say it's not engaging and entertaining music, but it requires a determined suspension of expectations to make it work. Cool and thoughtful as you'd expect

Bruce Williams

ALTO SAXOPHONE

Vivid player; comes out of bebop but with free and funky overtones.

***** Brotherhood**

Savant 2004 *Williams; Russell Gunn (t); Alan Palmer (p); Dwayne Dolphin (b); Cecil Brooks III (d).* 7/97.

***** Altoicity**

Savant 2025 *As above; omit Palmer, Dolphin; add Marc Cary (p); Gerald Cannon (b).* 5/00.

Williams isn't well-known and can be slightly anonymous in a solo, but his two issued albums are worth having for the sheer energy and dexterity he brings to mostly original programmes. The first group, anchored by Savant man Brooks, is probably the better of the two by a whisker, mostly because the material is more inviting. On McLean's 'Jackie's Tune', he lifts the curtain on one obvious influence. 'Portrait Of Jennie', 'Out Of Nowhere' and 'I Can't Get Started' are all despatched with some thought, but it's originals like 'Memory Of Waterford' and 'Ichi-Wuda' which stick in the mind.

The replacement of Palmer with Cary adds a measure of sophistication to the rhythm section, but that isn't necessarily what this music needs. Williams's lines are strong and simple enough to deserve relatively unembellished performance. If you enjoyed the first date, and the leader's burnished tone, you'll probably want the second disc as well.

Buster Williams (born 1942)

DOUBLE BASS

One of the key sidemen in modern jazz, Williams was born in Camden, New Jersey. Originally coached in drums as well as bass, his eventual career was mapped out for him when he first heard Oscar Pettiford's bass improvisations. Williams has a rock-solid grounding in harmony, counterpoint and orchestration, gained at the Combs College of Music, Philadelphia, at the very end of the '50s and aired on just about every recording he has made since then.

*****(*) Somewhere Along The Way**

TCB 97602 *Williams; Gary Bartz (as); Carlos McKinney (p); Stefon Harris (vib); Lenny White (d).* 11/96.

*****(*) Lost In A Memory**

TCB 99252 *As above, except omit Bartz, McKinney; add Geri Allen (p).* 97.

The little genius has graced many records over the years but, unlike many a gifted sideman, has also created a body of work under his own name. Buster's harmony is impeccable and he has a rhythmic sense that is unfailing, feeling and utterly original. Williams worked with singers for many years – Dakota Staton, Nancy Wilson, Betty Carter – and always shows an instinct for the dimensions of song. His own compositions, like 'Toku-Do', call out for lyrics and a tough-but-tender singing voice. Williams loves to play melody lines, scampering tunes almost too urgent for coherence. *Somewhere Along The Way* unveils the bones of a line-up that was to express Williams's music with real confidence. Vibist Stefon Harris cut his teeth in this band, filling the role that Roy Ayers had performed in the past. Gary Bartz had a similar background in Miles's band and is exceptional on 'Summertime' (*Somewhere*). Without a horn, the recent *Lost In A Memory* is even more focused and at times very intense. A couple of horn-led tracks might have made sense, but Buster's playing is so good that one wouldn't have it any other way.

***** Live At The Montreux Jazz Festival, 1999**

TCB 20152 *Williams; Mulgrew Miller (p); Steve Nelson (vib); Carl Allen (d).* 7/99.

Buster's leads on 'Toku-Do' are the first and best reminder of what a formidable player he is. Of bassist-led bands, only Ray Brown's could come up to this standard at the time. With Miller and Nelson online, Buster had a unit which was capable of graceful swing and thoughtful interplay, as one hears on 'The More I See You' and 'You And The Night And The Music', the two most substantial cuts. The live sound is very good, but also sounds quite artificial in places, perhaps because the bass is mixed so high and forward. It has the unfortunate effect of flattening out the vibes and piano right hand; no complaints, though, for a set of consistently excellent jazz.

*****(*) Houdini**

Sirocco SJL 1014 *Williams; Geri Allen(p); Lenny White (d).* 3/00.

A lucid essay on the modal forms of the kind of jazz which Williams grew up playing and which he clearly feels still have endless possibilities. Aside from a couple of standards, the only non-Williams originals are Hancock's 'Sorceror' and Shorter's 'Fall', which gives a close idea of the terrain Buster's moving through. Allen is masterful in this music and if White might seem an unlikely choice, he's a regular playing partner of Geri's and the trio have a serene empathy. Unlikely to garner much attention, in a world full of piano-trio records, but Sirocco deserve praise for making it happen.

***** Joined At The Hip**

TCB 21202 *Williams; Steve Wilson (as); Carlos McKinney (p); Ali Muhammad Jackson (d).* 5/02.

A tight, remarkably punchy bop set that reminds you how hard it was to hear Tommy Potter and Curley Russell in the heyday of bebop; even Mingus had to re-record one of his greatest performances. 'Yardbird Suite' gets it off to a rollicking start, and Wilson shows his class from the whistle without ever trying to sound like Bird. McKinney is a more modest player than Mulgrew Miller or Geri Allen, but he has time and formidable technique on his side and he's always right on the leader's tempo. 'Scrapple From The Apple' and 'Moose The Mooche' are two more Parker favourites, the former seeing Buster explore an extended line and altered chords. Buster's bass sounds sharper and cleaner-lined than on any previous recording, which suggests some finessing of the technology.

Clarence Williams (1893–1965)

PIANO, JUG, VOCAL

Born outside New Orleans but playing there in his early days, Williams was a smart hustler who was already earning money from publishing by 1916. He later owned his own publishing house in New York, while organizing countless recording sessions as A&R man for OKeh and playing either piano or jug on his own dates (his wife, Eva Taylor, sang on many, too). His Blue Five sessions ran on into the '30s, but he eventually left the business in 1943 and ran a shop in Harlem.

***** Complete Sessions Vol. 1 1923**
EPM/Hot 'N Sweet FDC 5107 *Williams; Thomas Morris (c); Charlie Irvis, John Mayfield (tb); Sidney Bechet (cl, ss); Buddy Christian (bj); Sara Martin, Eva Taylor, Lawrence Lomax, Rosetta Crawford, Mamie Smith, Margaret Johnson (v).* 7–11/23.

*****(*) Complete Sessions Vol. 2 1923–1925**
EPM/Hot 'N Sweet FDC 5109 *As above, except add Louis Armstrong, Bubber Miley (c), Aaron Thompson (tb), Buster Bailey, Lorenzo Tio (cl, ss), Don Redman (as), Virginia Liston, Maureen Englin, Sippie Wallace (v); omit Martin, Lomax, Crawford and Smith.* 11/23–3/25.

****(*) Clarence Williams 1921–1924**
Classics 679 *Similar to above two discs.* 10/21–11/24.

***** Complete Sessions Vol. 3 1925–26**
EPM/Hot 'N Sweet 15122 *As above, except add Johnny Dunn, Big Charlie Thomas, Edward Allen (c), Joe 'Tricky Sam' Nanton, Jimmy Harrison, Jake Frazier (tb), Bob Fuller (cl), Coleman Hawkins (cl, ts, bs), Leroy Harris (bj), Cyrus St Clair (tba), Clarence Todd (v); omit Thompson, Tio, Liston, Englin, Wallace.* 7/25–4/26.

***** Clarence Williams 1924–1926**
Classics 695 *Similar to above.* 12/24–1/26.

***** Clarence Williams 1926–27**
Classics 718 *Williams; Tommy Ladnier, Jabbo Smith, Ed Allen, Bubber Miley, Tom Morris, Louis Metcalf (c); Jimmy Harrison, Joe 'Tricky Sam' Nanton (tb); Buster Bailey (cl); Arville Harris, Don Redman (cl, as); Coleman Hawkins (ts); Fats Waller (p); Leroy Harris (bj); Cyrus St Clair (bb); Eva Taylor (v).* 3/26–4/27.

***** Clarence Williams 1927**
Classics 736 *Williams; Ed Allen (c); Henry 'Red' Allen, Ed Anderson (t); Charlie Irvis (tb); Buster Bailey (ss, cl); Carmelo Jari, Arville Harris, Ben Whittet, Albert Socarras (cl, as); Leroy Harris (bj); Cyrus St Clair (bb); Floyd Casey (wbd); Clarence Lee, Evelyn Preer (v).* 3–9/27.

Williams was of negligible importance as a musician – he wasn't a great pianist, handled vocals with clumsy enthusiasm, and often resorted to blowing a jug on his Jug Band records – but he was a brilliant hustler and a master at making record dates come together. At his very first session, on the first CD listed above, he secured the services of Sidney Bechet (also making his debut), and in fact Bechet appears on every track on this disc. Later sessions brought in Armstrong alongside Bechet, Bubber Miley, Lorenzo Tio and others. The material was mostly novelty tunes ('Who'll Chop Your Suey When I'm Gone?') or vaudeville blues, with the occasional tougher piece – such as Sippie Wallace's two tracks on volume two – and some instrumentals by Williams's Blue Five.

Both Classics and Hot 'N Sweet have undertaken complete series, but the latter quickly came to a halt. The Classics discs got off to an indifferent start with the first two discs, which had very mixed reproduction, although Classics 718 and 736 are more consistent and quite lively. Musically, the later sides are hotter, though Bechet makes a striking impact throughout the first disc, and his partnership with Armstrong on 'Cake Walking Babies From Home', 'Mandy Make Up Your Mind' and a few others is exhilarating enough to cut through the acoustic recording. Hot 'N Sweet's volume two is perhaps the best disc to sample, although the third volume introduces cornetist Ed Allen, Williams's most loyal sideman, who seldom recorded elsewhere, and includes some rollicking band sides. The first Classics disc starts off with some ancient 1921 material in which Williams is basically a band singer on six tracks, historical curios more than anything. Classics 718 has several tracks where Williams and The Blue Five are accompanying the sweet-voiced Eva Taylor, but there is more jazz on Classics 736: three different versions of Williams's hit, 'Cushion Foot Stomp', the knockabout 'Old Folks Shuffle', a Brunswick date with Henry Allen and Ed Anderson as a two-trumpet front line, and two versions of another Williams favourite, 'Shootin' The Pistol'.

***** Clarence Williams 1927–1928**
Classics 752 *Williams; Ed Allen, Joe 'King' Oliver (c); Ed Cuffee (tb); Arville Harris, Benny Waters, Albert Socarras, Buster Bailey (cl, as); Coleman Hawkins (ts); James P. Johnson (p); Leroy Harris (bj); Cyrus St Clair (tba); Floyd Casey (d, wbd).* 10/27–8/28.

*****(*) Clarence Williams 1928–1929**
Classics 771 *As above, except add Ed Anderson (c), Ben Whittet (cl, as), Ernest Elliott (cl), Claude Hopkins (p), Charlie Dixon (bj), Kaiser Marshall (d); omit Hawkins, Johnson.* 8/28–1/29.

***** Clarence Williams 1929**
Classics 791 *As above, except add James P. Johnson (p), Russell Procope (cl, as); omit Anderson, Elliott, Hopkins, Dixon, Marshall.* 1–5/29.

*****(*) Clarence Williams 1929–1930**
Classics 810 *As above, except add Ed Anderson, Charlie Gaines, Leonard Davis, Henry 'Red' Allen (t), Geechie Fields (tb), Frank Robinson (bsx, hca, v), Prince Robinson (cl, ts).* 6/29–4/30.

***** Clarence Williams 1930–1931**
Classics 832 *Williams; Ed Allen, Bill Dillard, Ward Pinkett, Henry 'Red' Allen, Charlie Gaines (t); Jimmy Archey (tb); Albert Socarras (cl, as, f); Henry Jones (as); Arville Harris, Prince Robinson, Bingie Madison (cl, ts); Fred Skerritt (bs, as); Gene Rodgers, Herman Chittison (p); Lonnie Johnson (g); Goldie Lucas (g, bj); Ikey Robinson, Leroy Harris (bj); Cyrus St Clair (tba); Richard Fulbright (b); Bill Beason (d); Floyd Casey (wbd); Eva Taylor, Clarence Todd (v).* 5/30–2/31.

****** Dreaming The Hours Away**
Frog DGF14 *Similar to appropriate discs above.* 5/26–9/28.

*****(*) Whoop It Up**
Frog DGF17 *Similar to appropriate discs above.* 2/29–2/31.

*****(*) Shake 'Em Up**

Frog DGF37 *As for appropriate discs above.* 2/27–5/29.

*****(*) Speakeasy – QRS Recordings Vol 1**

Frog DGF48 *Williams; Ed Allen, Joe 'King' Oliver (c); Ed Cuffee (tb); Buster Bailey (cl); Bennie Moten, Arville Harris (cl, as); Benny Waters (cl, ts); Leroy Harris (bj); Cyrus St Clair (tba); Anna Bell, Katherine Henderson (v).* 8–11/28.

Williams's music doesn't have any great variety in it: his basic configurations were the Washboard and Jug Bands, the Jazz Kings sides, a few stray piano solos, the occasional vocal where he's accompanied by another (James P. Johnson on one occasion) and some ensemble dates which are simply credited to the Williams Orchestra. The more knockabout material was reserved for the jug or washboard situations, but some of these also have a gentleness about them. Although Casey's irresistible beat and St Clair's parping lines provide a steady momentum, Williams could often find unexpected subtleties in some of his line-ups, pairing reeds together or providing space for the faithful Ed Allen to play one of his tight, incisive solos. Allen is the unsung hero of most of these dates, unfailingly consistent and interesting, and though a few star names turn up here and there – notably King Oliver, Eddie Lang and James P. – it's Williams's repertory cast – Allen, Harris, St Clair, Casey, Whittet, Cuffee and a few others – who make the most of the music. Because the playing is fun and unpretentious, these tracks have often been undervalued over the years, but at the same time it's hard to pick out special highlights. We award a token extra notch for Classics 771 (some excellent individual tracks) and Classics 810 (a particularly nice variety of bands and approaches), but if you enjoy one of these discs, you'll enjoy them all. The transfers (from unlisted sources, as usual) vary almost from track to track, and some sound very sludgy, but the music shines through on the best of them.

Frog's two compilations of Williams's Columbia sessions completely outclass the Classics discs. Superb sound from what seem to be mint copies of the originals make these model reissues. *Dreaming The Hours Away* is particularly outstanding since it includes several of the best Jazz Kings sides and 11 tracks – mostly accompaniments to the likes of Ethel Waters, Lucille Hegamin and Lizzie Miles – which aren't included in the Classics sequence. The sound on *Whoop It Up* is just as good, and although the only 'new' tracks are a pair of accompaniments to singer Bertha Idaho, these sessions are again some of Clarence's best; the Columbia studios were his most congenial home. These are certainly the discs to get if you want only a couple of Williams CDs.

Frog's two newest Williams sets are slightly more specialized. *Shake 'Em Up* gathers all his Brunswick, Victor, Paramount and Grey Gull sides from 1927–9, with alternative takes: it's a good sampler, in effect, of vintage Williams, with a handful of classics ('Cushion Foot Stomp', 'Shooting The Pistol') and some merely good ones, including his Victor solo date of February 1929. Transfers are quite astonishingly good, from beautiful originals! The disc which is even more of an achievement, though, is *Speakeasy*, since this gathers in 25 tracks culled from Williams's sessions for QRS – records which are in some cases stupendously rare. Even John R. T. apologizes for the sound on some tracks, but mostly it's fine, and Williams collectors should be delighted. It also includes several tracks with blues singers Bell and Henderson, which are absent from the Classics sequence. Bravo to Frog!

***** Clarence Williams 1933**

Classics 845 *Williams; Ed Allen (c); Albert Nicholas, Cecil Scott (cl); Herman Chittison, Willie 'The Lion' Smith (p); Ikey Robinson (bj, g); Cyrus St Clair (tba); Willie Williams, Floyd Casey (d, wbd); Eva Taylor, Clarence Todd (v).* 5–11/33.

***** Clarence Williams 1933–1934**

Classics 871 *As above, except add Charlie Gaines (t, v), Louis Jordan (as, v), James P. Johnson (p), Roy Smeck (bj, g), Dick Robertson, Chick Bullock, Little Buddy Farrior (v); omit Nicholas, Chittison, Smith, Robinson, Williams, Taylor, Todd.* 12/33–6/34.

***** Clarence Williams 1934**

Classics 891 *As above, except add Willie 'The Lion' Smith (p), Richard Fulbright (b), Ikey Robinson (bj, v), Eva Taylor, Clarence Todd (v); omit Gaines, Jordan, Robertson, Bullock, Farrior.* 7–10/34.

***** Clarence Williams 1934–1937**

Classics 918 *As above, except add Wilbur De Paris (tb), Prince Robinson (ts), Jimmy McLin (g), William Cooley, Chick Bullock (v); omit Smith, Robinson, Todd, Johnson.* 9/34–4/37.

****(*) Clarence Williams 1937–1941**

Classics 953 *Similar to above, except add James P. Johnson (p), Cozy Cole (d), Babe Matthews (v).* 4/37–10/41.

***** Clarence Williams And His Orchestra Vol. 1**

Timeless CBC 1-056 2CD *As appropriate discs above.* 5/33–6/34.

***** Clarence Williams And His Orchestra Vol. 2**

Timeless CBC 1-057 2CD *As appropriate discs above.* 6/34–4/37.

The Depression cut down so many survivors of the '20s that Williams's endurance seems remarkable. He actually made more records in 1934 than in some of his peak years. This is a little-known sequence of sessions, many of the originals very rare and while nothing much changes from the earlier music, an almost repertorial feel takes over as one goes through the tracks. The principal voices remain those of Ed Allen and Cecil Scott, the most loyal of sidemen, whose respective styles grow more polished down the years without losing the old-fashioned heat that must have seemed anachronistic by the mid-'30s. Along with Casey (still playing washboard) and the similarly faithful St Clair, Williams went serenely on. There is the odd difference between dates: a 1934 Decca session with Willie 'The Lion' Smith (Classics 891) is brighter and rather louder than the others. But as late as the final Vocalion session, of May 1935 (Classics 918), the group are still playing disciplined, impeccable small-group jazz in the manner of a decade earlier. Transfers are in the usual inconsistent Classics style.

The pair of Timeless two-CD sets are a first choice if this is the Williams vintage you're looking for. Several extra takes are included (not an especially revealing bonus, admittedly), and transfers and documentation beat the Classics discs hands down.

The final disc is something of a curiosity. Most of it is taken up with radio transcriptions of uneventful gospel material from 1937. There's a 1938 trio date which Williams hardly seems to take part in, and a final pair of titles with James P. and Eva Taylor from 1941.

Cootie Williams (1910–85)

TRUMPET

Not many musicians can have had not one but two concertos written for them by as august an artist as Duke Ellington, but that was Cootie's good fortune, in 1940 and again in 1963, when he rejoined the Ellington orchestra. Having replaced Bubber Miley, he developed a solo style that seemed to cover every creative eventuality, grainy, intense, and making use of the mutes. Cootie's recordings as leader are less well known but are still the source of some wonderful jazz.

*****(*) Cootie Williams 1941–1944**
Classics 827 *Williams; Milton Fraser, Joe Guy, Harold 'Money' Johnson, Ermit V. Perry, George Treadwell (t); Louis Bacon (t, v); Ed Burke, Jonas Walker, Robert Horton, George Stevenson, Sandy Williams, Lou McGarity (tb); Charlie Holmes, Les Robinson (as); Eddie 'Cleanhead' Vinson (as, v); Eddie 'Lockjaw' Davis, Bob Dorsey, Lee Pope, Greely Walters (ts); John Williams, Skippy Martin, Eddie De Verteuil (bs); Johnny Guarnieri, Kenny Kersey, Bud Powell (p); Artie Bernstein, Norman Keenan (b); Butch Ballard, Jo Jones, Vess Payne (d); Pearl Bailey (v).* 5/41–8/44.

****(*) Cootie Williams 1945–1946**
Classics 981 *Williams; Billy Ford, Otis Gamble, Harold 'Money' Johnson, Ermit V. Perry, George Treadwell (t); Gene Redd (t, vib); Ed Burke, Robert Horton, Edward Johnson, Dan Logan, Julius Watson (tb); Rupert Cole, John Jackson, Frank Powell, Daniel Williams (as); Eddie 'Cleanhead' Vinson (as, v); Chuck Clarke, Everett Gaines, Eddie Johnson, Lee Pope, Sam Taylor (ts); Bob Ashton, George Favors, Eddie De Verteuil (bs); Arnold Jarvis (p); Sam Allen, Leroy Kirkland, Pee Wee Tinney (g); Jimmy Glover, Norman Keenan, Carl Pruitt (b); Butch Ballard, Sylvester Payne (d); Johnny Mercer, Bob Merrill, Tony Warren (v).* 2/45–7/46.

***** Cootie Williams 1946–1949**
Classics 1105 *Williams; Billy Ford (t); Bob Merrill (t, v); Edward Burke, Edward Johnson, Julius Watson (tb); Rupert Cole (as); Willis Gator Jackson (ts); Bob Ashton (bs); Arnold Jarvis (p); Mundell Lowe (g); Norman Keenan, Leonard Heavy Swain (b); Butch Ballard (d); Billy Mack, Eddie Matthews, The Balladeers (v).* 46-49.

****(*) The Big Challenge**
Fresh Sound FSRCD 77 *Williams; Rex Stewart (c); Bud Freeman, Lawrence Brown, J. C. Higginbotham (tb); Coleman Hawkins (ts); Hank Jones (p); Milt Hinton (b); Gus Johnson (d).* 4 & 5/57.

Ellington wrote 'Do Nothing Till You Hear From Me' as a 'Concerto For Cootie', a feature for the young growler he recruited at 19 as a replacement for Bubber Miley. During the '30s Williams showed himself of all the Ellingtonians the one most capable of sustaining an independent career. His high, bright trumpet was to be replaced by even more agile players, but no one with the sheer musical intelligence of Cootie.

The Classics compilations do not include material recorded under any other leader, so the tracks with Hamp's band or Barney Bigard's Jazzopators (previously available on a Topaz compilation) are not included. As so often in this valuable and clearly documented series, one is apt to be distracted from the leader's achievement by early sightings of soon-to-be-important players. Bud Powell's appearance with the Williams Orchestra marked an important phase in his career, and the band also made the first recordings of two Thelonious Monk compositions, 'Fly Right' (aka 'Epistrophy') and 'Round Midnight', the latter from the August 1944 date covered on both discs. Cootie's own contributions go their growling, alternately chipper and sombre, way. Some will undoubtedly favour the orchestra sides with Vinson playing and singing, and Lockjaw beginning to make his move. These are delightful recordings and even the rather muddy Classics sound can't blunt their appeal.

The second Classics volume is full of anticipations of Cootie's later swing to R&B. His bands of 1945 and 1946 are full of names who would play a part in a later chapter of American music: Gene Redd was the father of singer Sharon Redd and Gene Jr of Kool & The Gang; Sylvester Payne was the father of Basie's drummer; Eddie Vinson puts in an appearance as vocalist on 'Juice Head Baby' and 'When My Baby Left Me'. Excellent as many of these cuts are, they are far short of the quality of Williams's work with Duke. 'Echoes Of Harlem' comes from a 1946 session with Johnny Mercer as vocalist; elsewhere Bob Merrill takes on vocal duties. We find these dates pall on subsequent hearings, but Cootie's admirers will find enough of the real thing to make this a worthwhile purchase.

The later Classics set takes up the story just as Cootie was looking for commercial success with vocal sides for Capitol, Majestic and Mercury. They're not the most profound things you'll ever hear and some of them are decidedly lame, almost novelty records, but the sound of Cootie's trumpet does cut through when he takes a feature and he sounds in good lip still.

By the late '50s, when *The Big Challenge* was set up (and set up is the operative term), Williams was working with a rock'n'roll group, a drab routine that had significantly blunted the edge of his tough, brassy sound. Much of his most effective playing on the set seems to derive from the man in the opposite corner. He duplicates Rex Stewart's half-valved style and gruff swoops authentically but also rather redundantly, because the cornetist is in excellent, pungent form. Williams plays most convincingly on 'Walkin' My Baby Back Home', where he throws in a muted solo even the Duke would have liked. The two tenors compare more straightforwardly, trading choruses on 'Alphonse And Gaston' with the polite brutality of a Larry Holmes fight. The closing 'I Knew You When' is a carefully matched head arrangement that allows Williams and Stewart to slug it out to a finish. Not altogether inspiring stuff and a sorry reminder of the way in which Williams's independent career, thwarted by the draft and the recording ban, was short-circuited into blandly commercial sessions that offered little scope for his towering talent.

Jessica Williams (born 1948)

PIANO

Jessica Williams will one day tell her own remarkable story, which begins in Baltimore and stretches to the West Coast. Her style is very much her own, but is compounded of many elements of the jazz piano tradition, including Art Tatum, Dave Brubeck, Bill Evans and a lyrical edge reminiscent of Hampton Hawes. Prolific, perhaps over-prolific, Williams has astonishingly made 60 LPs and CDs.

***** The Next Step**
Hep CD 2054 *Williams (p solo).* 4/93.

***** In The Pocket**

Hep CD 2055 *Williams; Jeff Johnson (b); Dick Berk (d).* 4 & 7/93.

***** A Song That I Heard**

Hep CD 2061 *As above.* 3/94.

The first of the Hep records is called *The Next Step* with good reason. It is by no means a recording debut and catches a mature artist at work. Great plaudits to label boss Alastair Robertson for having the foresight to sign her up at a point in the story when Williams was not a well-known name outside Baltimore and California. Heard unaccompanied, her style is complex, clever and slightly overwrought, too laden with quotations and parallel ideas. Her experience as a drummer and Hammond player, and her long experimentation with synthesizers can be detected in a taste for dense chord-clusters overlain on a driving beat. Often, as on the second and third Hep discs, one wonders what is really required of the bassist and drummer, so ahead of the game does she seem.

Originals like 'The Quilt', inspired by the AIDS memorial quilt, and 'Bongo's Waltz', which is dedicated to her dog, suggest a strong compositional talent, though as time goes by one begins to detect a formulaic quality, too much dependence on certain harmonic quirks. 'A Gal In Calico' on *In The Pocket* is a *tour de force*; legacy of many years playing bars and clubs round Baltimore, it underlines her talent for spotting the interrelatedness of thematic material, because buried in the texture one can spot a whole procession of tiny, almost subliminal tags from Rodgers and Hammerstein, Porter and Gershwin songs. 'I Remember Bill', from the same set, is a tender memoir of another potent influence.

***** Arrival**

Jazz Focus JFCD 001 *Williams (p solo).* 94.

***** Momentum**

Jazz Focus JFCD 003 *Williams; Jeff Johnson (b); Dick Berk (d).* 2/94.

***** Inventions**

Jazz Focus JFCD 008 *As above.* 1/95.

An almost exact repetition of her recording pattern for Hep, Williams's first three records for Jazz Focus sound somewhat like more of the same. For our taste, the Canadian label gives her a warmer sound, with less space between the instruments, which helps to mitigate a feeling that the rhythm lines are merely superadded and are not integral.

Alarmingly, *Inventions* comes with the generic subtitle, 'Explorations In Music', which was to appear on some of the later Jazz Focus discs. Much of her 'exploration' involves nothing more than walking in the footsteps of those who have gone before. There is a foray into Coltrane's harmony on 'Last Trane' and a nod in the direction of Toshiko Akiyoshi (both *Inventions*), but where she is strongest is when the melody lines are simple and clearly directed and the harmonic language is her own.

On balance, the Hep album is probably the stronger of the two solos, but that may simply be the vestige of genuine surprise when it first emerged.

***** Encounters**

Jazz Focus JFCD 005 *Williams; Leroy Vinnegar (b); Mel Brown (d).* 10/94.

No nonsense about 'explorations', and for a change a rhythm section which really does offer Williams some challenges. Recorded live at Atwater's club in Portland, Oregon, *Encounters* kicks off with a wonderful version of John Coltrane's 'Equinox', not necessarily the kind of repertoire you'd associate with the veteran walker Vinnegar, but all grist to his mill. Randy Weston's 'Berkshire Blues' is equally unexpected but no less effective, and Brown really comes into his own at this point. We suspect that the tracks are not in the order played; there is a certain slackening of pace and a more tentative quality to the tunes after 'If I Were A Bell'. Williams's own 'The Sheikh' is very much a personal feature, but the two standards which follow, 'Wrap Your Troubles In Dreams' and 'Say It Over And Over Again', are quite nondescript and unfocused.

*****(*) Gratitude**

Candid CCD 79721 *Williams (p solo).* 6/95.

We like *Gratitude* as much as anything she has committed to record. There are two Coltrane tunes in the programme – the blues 'Mr Syms' and 'Like Sonny' – and reprises of her own 'Last Trane' and 'The Sheikh'. She was presumably listening to Trane a good deal at the time, and also to Monk, who is represented again by 'Justice', a marvellous reading, and by a thoroughly individual interpretation of the tired old piano warhorse 'Round Midnight', which is suddenly fresh as a colt again. The two standards are 'I Cover The Waterfront' and 'Nice Work If You Can Get It', both of them dispatched briskly and without indulgence.

*****(*) Intuition**

Jazz Focus JFCD 010 *Williams (p solo).* 6/95.

****** The Victoria Concert**

Jazz Focus JFCD 015 *As above.* 9/95.

The studio album is more thoroughly suffused with the blues than Williams has seemed for a while, not just as a matter of strict harmony but in feel and emotional pressure as well. 'Holocaust Blues' is a dark, strong original, boldly placed first in the set. Billy Cobham's and George Duke's 'Heather' is an entirely unexpected inclusion, but a great find. Otherwise, Monk is the presiding deity, with both 'Green Chimneys' and 'Monk's Dream' covered.

The live album is joyous, open-hearted and at points quite intense. Opening with 'I Want To Be Happy' is some kind of statement of intent, and even blues material like 'Mr Syms', a theme which always seems to have the corners of its mouth slightly turned down, is given a buoyant and almost rambunctious feel. At a quarter of an hour, 'Straight, No Chaser' is a work-out of Marine Corps proportions, a real harmonic and rhythmic assault course. Williams, as ever, passes with flying colours (if that isn't mixing military services) but the likely reaction is going to be: So what? – a lot of effort expended for very little real musical return. Even with that one quibble, a fine, beautifully styled album, though perversely Jessica looks more sombre on the cover than on any previous release.

***** Joy**

Jazz Focus JFCD 014 *Williams; Jay Thomas (t, ts, f); Hadley Caliman (ts); Jeff Johnson (b); Dick Berk, Mel Brown (d, perc).* 11/95, 1/96.

*****(*) Jessica's Blues**

Jazz Focus JFCD 018 *As above, except omit Caliman, Berk.* 10/96.

Williams's decision to record with horns wasn't altogether surprising, but it takes a moment or two to adjust to the sheer busyness of the sound. Thomas is a talented and adaptable player, shifting from trumpet on the opening 'Joy', which is retrospectively dedicated to the late Don Cherry, to flute on 'Infinite Circle', to trumpet and flute on a reworked 'The Quilt', and back to trumpet again on the Hancock-like 'Dharma Dance', which also features more straightahead tenor from Hadley Caliman.

Williams seems to thrive on these larger-scale arrangements, and she plays with an attractive simplicity that would not be out of place in more restricted settings as well. Unembellished melody statement is the key to *Jessica's Blues.* It is also a more coherent package, having been recorded in a single session rather than over a period of time and with slightly different personnel from its predecessor.

*****(*) Encounters II**

Jazz Focus JFCD *Williams; Leroy Vinnegar (b); Mel Brown (d).* 10/96.

A happy reunion with the veteran walker and at the same club in Portland that hosted their earlier meeting. By this stage in the game, nothing that Williams might choose to play should evince any surprise, but it's a little startling to come across Rahsaan Roland Kirk's 'Haunted Melody' upsides with Basie's 'The "M" Squad' and 'Mack The Knife'. 'Empathy' is a highly effective original, with a curious turn in the melody line which strongly suggests the Monk influence is still strong.

Someone had obviously done a bit of homework on the acoustic at Atwater's. The bass and drums are better balanced than on the original *Encounters,* and there's a bit more air round the piano. A fine record; certainly one to consider.

*****(*) Higher Standards**

Candid CCD 79736 *Williams; Dave Captein (b); Mel Brown (d).* 11/96.

*****(*) Jazz In The Afternoon**

Candid CCD 70750 *As above.* 2/98.

***** Blue Fire**

Jazz Focus 35 *As above; add Scott Hall (ts).* 5/99.

***** Some Ballads, Some Blues**

Jazz Focus 38 *As above; omit Hall.* 00.

A pure standards album always seemed a likely bet. It's slightly surprising that it should have been so long in coming, but Williams has chosen to bide her time and craft it carefully. Our suspicion is that a very great deal more than is actually released was recorded, so technically secure is the playing and so well sequenced the results. Surely it wasn't all as good as this? The downside is that it comes across as an album of peaks and climaxes, with hardly any basic passage-work.

'Mack The Knife' is again very good indeed, but the high points of the album are 'A Night In Tunisia', which is recast as funky post-bop, and 'East Of The Sun (And West Of The Moon)', which can't be faulted on any count whatsoever. Captein is a less effusive and insistent player than either Vinnegar or Johnson, but he takes his place in the trio with great assurance.

By the time of *Jazz In The Afternoon,* which was recorded live at Chemekata College, Oregon, the trio is functioning like a band that has been working together for years. Williams is once again brilliant on 'Straight, No Chaser', though one wonders how often one would want to buy a record like this just to hear her *not* repeating ideas. Her own 'I Remember Dexter' is another slightly self-conscious attempt to write herself into jazz history, and a not entirely successful one.

Blue Fire has some lovely things. Jessica's tribute to the late Kenny Kirkland is heartfelt without being fulsome. She kicks off with the title-track, playing inside the piano and adding a few percussion touches as well. Saxophonist Hall joins the trio for this one and pairs Jessica on a fine duo version of 'Everything Happens To Me', which is miscredited on the album. 'The Vision' is a lovely modal idea which inhabits territory somewhere between McCoy Tyner and Bill Evans.

The ballads and blues record is precisely that, entertaining rather than profound but thoughtful as ever. The only non-originals are 'You Don't Know What Love Is', 'My Foolish Heart' and 'When I Fall In Love'. All the rest are Williams compositions, some of them settled in the black keys or in particular tonalities as if they emerged out of technical exercises but always expressive and stimulating.

***** In The Key Of Monk**

Jazz Focus JFCD 029 *Williams (p solo).* 5/97.

Emphatically not an album of Monk covers, but an attempt to create a seamless suite of meditations on the great pianist and composer. Williams's own pieces, like 'The House That Rouse Built' (a reference to Monk's saxophonist Charlie) and 'Monk's Hat', veer close to pastiche but are strong enough in themselves to sustain some rather over-the-top playing. The best of the album is in the opening ten minutes, with 'Bemsha Swing', 'Just A Gigolo' and 'Reflections' rattled off with drive, swing and great charm. The rest is a touch laboured and will probably appeal only to devoted Williams fans.

***** Ain't Misbehavin'**

Candid 79763 *Williams (p solo).* 99.

Much has been made of the acoustic and the piano in the Maybeck Recital Hall beloved of Concord Records. The Holywell Room in Oxford is no slouch in the same regards and this delightful solo performance is one of Williams's best. The Fats Waller tune brings out her wicked side, while the rest of the package demonstrates how thoughtful and exploratory a recitalist she is. How many contemporary pianists would include two Roland Kirk-associated pieces, 'Black Diamonds' and 'The Eulipians'? Who else does Sonny Rollins's 'Paul's Pal', before ending the set with Coltrane's 'After The Rain'? Jessica's allusive soloing is sometimes too self-conscious, but these are thoroughly attractive interpretations and anyone who enjoys jazz piano will find much pleasure in *Ain't Misbehavin'.*

*****(*) I Let A Song Go Out of My Heart**

Hep 2082 *Williams (p solo).* 9–10/00.

Williams's tribute to the compositions of Duke Ellington was one of many released in and around the centenary year, but typically hers is more individual, more imaginative and in many regards truer to the source material than most. 'Satin Doll' and 'In A Sentimental Mood', which come together near the middle of the set, are quite extraordinary performances but some of the briefer statements, like 'C Jam Blues' and the title-piece, are equally satisfying and powerful. Williams also builds in three short 'interludes', which are obviously intended as meditations on Ellington's favoured themes and harmonies.

*****(*) This Side Up**

Maxx Jazz 203 *Williams; Ray Drummond (b); Victor Lewis (d).* 8/01.

Latest in a series of piano recitals from this small label, it catches Williams and a superb trio in sparkling form. Almost all the material is her own and is played, 'Miles to Go' and 'I Remember Dexter' in particular, with enormous energy and compression of mood. The opening track, 'The Judge', is a tribute to the late Milt Hinton and, true to form, Drummond drops in a couple of sly quotes. Jessica's affection for Roland Kirk is reflected in 'Theme For The Eulipians' and 'Black Diamonds', which have become regular components of her work-book.

*****(*) All Alone**

Maxx Jazz 206 *Williams (p solo).* 8/02.

Williams seems to be having more fun with her playing as the years go by. She opens with a frankly sentimental 'As Time Goes By', continues with Ellington and Irving Berlin, including the title-piece. She gets inside the piano and footers with the strings on 'The Sheikh', which adds to her palette without sounding self-conscious or histrionic. The recording is very close and faithful, with a lot of detail, and Williams has rarely sounded happier at work.

Joe Williams (1918–99)

VOCAL

Raised in Chicago, he sang in clubs in the city from the late '30s and later toured with Andy Kirk. His hit version of 'Every Day' made his reputation, then he played with Count Basie, 1954–60. After that he worked as a soloist, usually with a trio that included Junior Mance and latterly Norman Simmons.

***** Together / Have A Good Time**

Roulette 31790-2 *Williams; Harry 'Sweets' Edison (t); Jimmy Forrest (ts); Frank Strazzeri, Sir Charles Thompson(p); Tommy Potter, Joe Benjamin (b); Clarence Johnston, Charli Persip (d); orchestra.* 2–7/61.

***** A Swingin' Night In Birdland**

Roulette 95335-2 *Williams; Harry 'Sweets' Edison (t); Jimmy Forrest (ts); Hugh Lawson (p); Ike Isaacs (b); Clarence Johnston (d).* 6/62.

***** At Newport '63 / Jump For Joy**

Collectables COL-2706 *Williams; Clark Terry (t, flhn); Howard McGhee, Bernie Glow, Thad Jones, Snooky Young (t); Urbie Green, Quentin Jackson (tb); Phil Woods, George Dorsey, Walt Levinsky (as); Jerome Richardson, Phil Bodner, Romeo Penque (ts, f); Coleman Hawkins, Zoot Sims (ts); Danny Bank (bs); Junior Mance, Bernie Leighton, Hank Jones (p); Kenny Burrell (g); Bob Cranshaw, Milt Hinton (b); Mickey Roker, Sol Gubin (d); Willie Rodriguez (perc).* 2–7/63.

*****(*) Me And The Blues / The Song Is You**

Collectables COL-2703 *Williams; Thad Jones, Clark Terry (t); Urbie Green (tb); Phil Woods, Jerome Richardson (as), Seldon Powell, Ben Webster (ts); Danny Bank (bs); Hank Jones (p); Barry Galbraith (g); Milt Hinton (b); Osie Johnson (d); Frank Hunter Orchestra.* 11/63–64.

***** Finest Hour**

Verve 549674-2 *Williams; Med Flory, Lanny Morgan (as); Ray Reed, Jay Migliorio (ts); Jack Nimitz (bs); Norman Simmons (p); Henry Johnson, Kenny Burrell, Ted Dunbar (g); Bob Badgley, Paul West, Charles Ables (b); Gerryck King, Dennis Mackrel, Steve Williams (d); Shirley Horn (v); Count Basie Orchestra.* 55–90.

Williams followed on from Billy Eckstine in bringing in a new sophistication to the black male singer's stance. Though he made his name singing blues with Count Basie (and their albums together are classics – turn to the Basie entry for details), Williams preferred superior standards and original material. His current CD showing is only so-so, with Verve having deleted most of its material and a sparse showing from both Roulette and RCA.

The two-on-one *Together / Have A Good Time* is nice, but a little disappointing; too many of these songs don't really suit Joe as either singer or stylist, and though the Basie-ish backings are skilful, they don't warm him up the way the Count's full band always did. Sweets Edison still sneaks in some agreeable stuff in what are really rather polite settings. In comparison, the Birdland date sounds a bit scrappy, with Edison's group lowering rather than raising the tone, for once, but Williams is in fine voice at least.

The two Collectables discs usefully pick up four of Joe's RCA albums. His set from the 1963 Newport Festival has a starry backing group – Terry, Sims, Hawkins, McGhee, Mance – but the playing is often raggedy. When Williams essays a typically suave 'April In Paris' and Hawkins turns in a fine solo, it's all undone by the flatfooted playing of the rhythm section. *Jump For Joy*, with helpful charts by Oliver Nelson and Jimmy Jones, works better for him, although it feels a bit harried: none of the tracks gets close to three minutes, and one feels that material like the fast-bossa 'You Perfect Stranger' would sound better if Joe had more time and space to elaborate. His range of dark tones does get some impressive showings, though.

Me And The Blues might be the best of his '60s records. The material is either in the blues form or cast in a bluesy-pop mould, and Joe eats it all up, whether it's 'Rocks In My Bed' (with a Ben Webster cameo), 'Work Song' or a limo-class 'Kansas City'. The mighty voice is right at the front of the mix, and the way he wraps himself around a line that takes his particular fancy is sheer delight. If ever an album made a case for the black-tie blues, it's this one. *The Song Is You*, which starts with nothing less than Franz Lehar's 'Yours is My Heart Alone', sounds like a full-blooded pitch at the Eckstine camp, although since Mister B had already started to move towards soul at this point, it all feels a bit late. The fulsome Frank Hunter arrangements set Williams a challenge which he offsets with his most operatic voice.

The *Finest Hour* compilation has the drawback of not leaving the compilers much to work with – the early days with Basie, and later stuff from his final contract with Verve. Track for track, it's enjoyable enough.

****(*) Joe Williams With The Count Basie Orchestra**

Telarc CD-83329 *Williams; Frank Foster (ts); Count Basie Orchestra.* 11/92.

***** Here's To Life**

Telarc 83357 *Williams; strings conducted by Robert Farnon.* 8/93.

Williams endured marvellously well, even into his 70s. The top end lost much of its old limber power and there might be a shake where once all was honey-smooth, but he still phrased with the assurance of a singer who knows where the pulse is all the time, and he could hit a note with the same regal potency.

By the time of his Telarc dates, though, the voice was finally sounding a little frayed. His appearance with the Foster/Basie ensemble is a nostalgic one, and he handles himself with dignity and an almost Zen calm on the slower ones. Farnon's limousine of an orchestra is the most gorgeous thistledown for Joe to get comfortable in. He gives himself a few tough ones, several surprising high notes here and there, and generally makes a go of a situation that most singers approaching his age wouldn't even have thought about.

John Williams

BARITONE AND TENOR SAXOPHONES, RECORDER

Unsung stalwart of the British scene.

***** Baritone Band**

Spotlite SPJ 564 *Williams; Steve Waterman (flhn); John Surman (ss, bs); Alan Wakeman (ss, bs, cl); Andy Panayi (ts, bs, f); Chris Biscoe (as, bs, acl); Jay Craig (bs); John Horler (p); Jim Richardson, Tim Wells (b); Trevor Tomkins (d).* 5 & 7/97.

Gerry Mulligan used to say that he never found the baritone cumbersome. Both physically and harmonically, he found it perfectly weighted and balanced and highly responsive to his needs as a musician. That's borne out amply in this lovely baritone project. Sensibly, the front line guys all double on other horns, so the textures are as varied and rich as could be, but it's the big saxophone that remains the focus. Williams's arrangements are as thoughtful as ever and his occasional features underline what an underrated figure he's been even on the British scene.

***** Tenorama**

Spotlite SPJ 572 *Williams; Steve Waterman (t); Bob Sydor (as, ts, cl); Renato D'Aiello, Phil Day, Dave Gelly, Don Rendell, Karen Sharp (ts); John Horler, Mark Latimer (p); Mario Castronari, Jim Richardson (b); Asaf Sirkis, Trevor Tomkins (d).* 10 & 11/02.

Two sessions from Williams's flexible saxophone outfit. His own baritone holds very much to the middle register, anchoring solid arrangements that rely on subtle chord shadings and detailed melodic patterns. The effect is too interesting to be soporific, but there isn't much high drama about these tenor-driven dates, apart from some very fine Steve Waterman trumpet on the October session, and some lovely guest playing from the great Don Rendell. Don, as well as D'Aiello and pianist Latimer, are Spotlite artists in their own right.

Mary Lou Williams (1910–81)

PIANO

Williams grew up in Pittsburgh and played professionally from her early teens. Along with her husband, John Williams, she joined Terrence Holder's Clouds Of Joy orchestra, shortly to be taken over by Andy Kirk, for whom Mary Lou arranged and performed. Her later style shows a deep understanding of jazz history, a profound spiritual dimension and a grasp of structure and harmonic logic that bears comparison with Duke Ellington's.

*****(*) Mary Lou Williams 1927–1940**

Classics 630 *Williams; Harold 'Shorty' Baker, Henry McCord, Earl Thompson (t); Bradley Bullett, Ted Donnelly (tb); Edward Inge (cl); Earl Buddy Miller (cl, as); Dick Wilson (ts); John Williams (as, bsx); Ted Robinson, Floyd Smith (g); Joe Williams (bj); Booker Collins (b); Robert Price, Ben Thigpen (d).* 1/27–11/40.

*****(*) Key Moments**

Topaz TPZ 1016 *Similar to above.* 29–40.

****** Mary Lou Williams 1944**

Classics 814 *Williams; Bill Coleman (t, v); Frankie Newton, Charlie Shavers, Dick Vance (t); Vic Dickenson, Trummy Young (tb); Claude Greene, Edmond Hall (cl); Remo Palmieri (g); Al Hall, Al Lucas (b); Jack Parker, Specs Powell (d); Nora Lee King (v).* 2–11/44.

***** Roll 'Em**

Solo Art 014 *Williams; Al Lucas (b); Jack 'The Bear' Parker (d).* 44.

****** Mary Lou Williams 1944–1945**

Classics 1021 *Williams; Bill Coleman (t); Claude Greene (cl); Joe Evans (as); Coleman Hawkins (ts); Margie Hyans (vib); Mary Osborne (g); Jimmy Butts, Al Lucas, Edie Robinson, Bea Taylor (b); Denzil Best, Eddie Dougherty, Bridget O'Flynn, Jack Parker (d); Josh White (v).* 11 & 12/44, 6/45.

*****(*) Mary Lou Williams 1945–1947**

Classics 1050 *Williams; Irving Kusting, Edward Sadowski, Leon Schwartz (t); Allan Feldman, Martin Glaser (ss); Mauricio Lopez (as, bs); Orlando Wright (ts); Frank Roth (p); John H. Smith Jr (g); Mary Osborne (g, v); Margie Hyams, Bridget O' Flynn (vib, d); Grachan Moncur, Milton Orent, June Rotenberg (b); Rose Gottesman, Jack Parker (d).* 45, 2, 7 & 10/46, 47.

Duke Ellington described her as 'perpetually contemporary'. Mary Lou Williams's career encompassed weary days of travel with Andy Kirk's Clouds Of Joy band (she began as a part-time arranger and only grudgingly won recognition as a piano-player), staff arranging for Ellington, and band-leading. Having divorced John Williams, who had taken her on the road with Kirk, she married trumpeter Harold Baker and co-led a group with him.

The earlier Classics compilation covers some intriguing early stuff, including sides made with Jeanette's Synco Jazzers as Mary Leo Burley (her stepfather's name) when she was only 16, and two good solo sides recorded for the Brunswick label in Chicago in 1930. There are also two useful solos from rather later; 'Mary's Special' from April 1936 has her doubling on celeste, and there's a fine 'Little Joe From Chicago', recorded for Columbia in October 1939. The next decade saw Mary move out as an artist in her own right, and the Classics compilation (1944) includes much of the best of that material, including 'Little Joe From Chicago', 'Roll 'Em' and a piece from a jam session organized by the photographer and film-maker Gjon Mili. The disc includes some excellent solos as well as forgettable work accompanying singer Nora Lee King.

The complete World Broadcast performance with Lucas and Parker appears on Solo Art and is worth tracking down, even if the sound isn't wonderful. The sheer vibrancy of this trio makes technical quibbles seem irrelevant.

The appearance of further Classics volumes helps to fill out the story even more. In 1945, Mary Lou was completing work on her *Zodiac Suite* and also presenting a regular radio programme on which she performed excerpts from the extended work. They are included here under the generic title 'Signs Of The Zodiac' and performed either solo ('Pisces', 'Capricorn', 'Sagittarius', 'Aquarius' and 'Libra') or with a quartet. Most of the material on this volume was recorded for the Asch label, the only exceptions being two *astronomically* inspired piano solos for Selmer in France and a fascinating single track, 'Timmie Time', recorded some time in 1945 with an all-female group. The remaining tracks were recorded just before Christmas 1944 with an orchestra co-fronted by trumpeter Bill Coleman.

The zodiac pieces mark the emergence of Williams as a more than usually ambitious composer, but there are signs of her breaking free of conventional swing harmonics in a piece like the alarmingly titled 'Carcinoma'. The remaining tracks from the session sound flat and uninflected and one wonders whether Williams and her players – Coleman apart – were at odds about the material. Even the closing 'Lady Be Good' sounds perfunctory, though it closely anticipates Coleman Hawkins's later and better-known 'Rifftide' variant.

The Girl Stars reappear at the start of Classics 1050, making one wonder why it was necessary to split off 'Timmie Time' on the previous issue. Dominated by Williams and Mary Osborne, who sounds superficially like Charlie Christian, the group had more than novelty appeal, and tunes like 'Rumba Rebop', 'Boogie Misterioso' and 'Fifth Dimension' (the latter pair from a July 1946 session for Victor) are full of musical interest. Later that year Williams was working in a trio with June Rotenberg and Bridget O'Flynn (who had swapped drums and vibes duties with Margie Hyams) and recorded a neat selection of standards, including the Dvořák 'Humoresque' and 'All God's Chillun Got Rhythm'. A couple of tracks find her not playing but directing the rather mournful Milton Orent and Frank Roth Orchestra; 'Lonely Moments' is rather effective, but again the band seem either baffled or resentful of some of Mary Lou's alternative changes. Two tracks from 1947 are with a drummerless group including the emergent Kenny Dorham and on bass Grachan Moncur Senior, the father of the '60s trombonist. The return to circulation of the original *Zodiac Suite* sections is an important development, especially when coupled with the live performance below. For the most part, though, these two issues show Williams working hard at expanding her jazz vocabulary into new areas and coming to terms with the rhythmic demands of bebop, a music which she embraced only somewhat cautiously.

***(*) The Zodiac Suite

Smithsonian Folkways SF CD 40810 *Williams; unidentified big band, featuring Ben Webster (ts); New York Philharmonic Orchestra.* 12/45.

On New Year's Eve 1945/6, Williams gave a remarkable performance of her *Zodiac Suite* with the New York Philharmonic at Town Hall. It's a sequence of dedications to fellow musicians (identified by their astrological characteristics) and combines straight orchestral writing of a slightly bland, film-soundtrack sort with jazz interpolations and occasional sections ('Taurus' and 'Gemini', significantly) where the two seem to coincide. Williams had been profoundly dissatisfied with a partial reading of the music, recorded in 1957 for Norman Granz's Verve label, and the rediscovery of the 'lost' tapes from the Town Hall concert is a significant addition to the discography. The sound isn't always very reliable, with occasional crackles and some loss of resolution in the string parts, but Williams is caught in close-up and the piece remains a key moment in the recognition of jazz as an important twentieth-century music, not 'classical', but with its own history and logic.

**(*) Mary Lou Williams 1949–1951

Classics 1260 *Williams; Idrees Sulieman (t); Mundell Lowe (g); George Duvivier, Carl Pruitt, Billy Taylor Sr (b); Denzil Best, Bill Clark, Al Walker (d); Kenny Pancho Hagood, Dave Lambert Singers (v).* 49–51.

This will be followed by a further Classics volume that takes the story into the early '50s and a period when Mary Lou was starting to think about getting out of jazz for a while, which she subsequently did. These are not classic dates, though there is some strong playing on both piano and organ. Mary Lou's touch seems less assured and her solos are overcomplicated and muddy in conception.

*** I Made You Love Paris

Verve 13141 *Williams; Nelson Williams (t); Ray Lawrence (ts); Buddy Banks (b); Jean-Louis Viale (d); Beryl Bryden (v).* 54.

The horn-players on this are pretty ropy and Bryden is something of an acquired taste, but fortunately much of the material is either solo or trio. It's almost worth having the set for 'Nicole' alone, a strange, out-of-whack blues that shows what an unexpected and exciting player/composer Williams was even at this point in her life when she was preparing to drop out of jazz for a period. The solo 'I Made You Love Paris' is very fine and beautifully textured. At the other extreme, Bryden's vocal on 'Rock Me' by Piano Red is unpleasingly vulgar.

*** Nite Life / From The Past

Chiaroscuro 103 *Williams (p, v solo).* 71.

There were few more articulate historians of the music than Mary Lou and unlike the majority of Chiaroscuro 'Jazzspeaks', which tend to be amiable recollections of past times, sentimental and self-aggrandizing by turns, hers is thoroughly intelligent and revelatory. This is an ideal introduction to her art, not just for that half-hour interview but also because it includes some of her best themes, re-recorded at the age of 61: the stride of 'Nite Life', 'Little Joe From Chicago', 'My Mama Pinned A Rose On Me', 'What's Your Story, Morning Glory?', many of them with alternate performances. The latter-day variations on 'Nite Life' are perhaps a little overdone and self-important, but they do underline how secure was Williams's technique. The sound quality is bright and detailed, though there are a couple of dead spots on the piano.

**** Zoning

Smithsonian Folkways SF CD 40811 *Williams (p solo).* 74.

***(*) Live At The Cookery

Chiaroscuro CRD 146 *Williams; Brian Torff (b).* 11/75.

*** Embraced

Pablo 2620-108 *Williams; Cecil Taylor (p).* 77.

*** Solo Recital/Montreux Jazz Festival 1978

Original Jazz Classics OJC 962 *Williams (p solo).* 78.

There followed a period away from the USA, living in France (where she recorded for Vogue), and then away from music altogether, during which time she worked with drug addicts.

Renewed activity from the late '50s onwards included lecture-recitals on the history of jazz, large-scale sacred compositions – *Mary Lou's Mass* and *Black Christ Of The Andes* – reflecting her conversion, and stormy contact with the new avant-garde, as on her remarkable if often bemusing collaboration with Cecil Taylor. *Embraced* gives off little sense of the hostilities behind the scenes, but it underlines her ability to play from almost any stance within the black-music tradition: gospel, blues, swing, bop, free.

Williams was treated dismissively by male colleagues for much of her career (Kirk finds room for only half a dozen references in his autobiography, and his acknowledgement of her 'tremendous influence' seems rather *pro forma*). In the '70s she was releasing material on her own label, Mary Records, including the superb *Zoning* (since reissued on Smithsonian Folkways) and the huge *Mary Lou's Mass*. The *Solo Recital* from Montreux in 1978 is a defiant showcase performance and its extensive coverage of signature compositions is particularly valuable to have in one place, even if her own playing may not have been what it once was. The rather earlier *Live At The Cookery* is perhaps a better bet, though. Jon Bates has done an excellent job of bringing the sound up to current standards and there's a minimum of distortion and extraneous noise ('I'm recording. If you talk too loud, it'll be on the record'). It's not clear why she tolerated Brian Torff thudding away relentlessly in her left ear, but Williams had always tended to be a right-sided player and, here more than ever, concentrates on a middle and upper register. Her playing is superb throughout and there are vintage performances of 'Roll 'Em', 'The Surrey With The Fringe On Top' (an odd favourite of hers), 'The Man I Love' and Johnny Hodges' 'The Jeep Is Jumping'.

CORE COLLECTION

****** Free Spirits**

Steeplechase SCCD 31043 *Williams; Buster Williams (b); Mickey Roker (d).* 7/75.

As a straightforward performance, *Free Spirits* is a much better record than those above. Williams's health was still robust (it began to break down towards the end of the '70s) and her playing is much sharper and surer, also more relaxed and swinging. Typically, she mixes standards ('Temptation', 'Surrey With The Fringe On Top') with jazz staples (Miles's 'All Blues', Bobby Timmons's gospel-tinged 'Dat Dere') and her own work, 'Ode To Saint Cecilie', 'Gloria', 'Blues For Timme', unexpectedly adding two John Stubblefield compositions (two takes each of 'Baby Man' and 'Free Spirits') and a promising 'Pale Blue' by bassist Buster Williams, who provides a perfect complement to her light left hand.

****** At Rick's Café American**

Storyville STCD 8285 *Williams; Milton Suggs (b); Drashear Khalid (d).* 11/79.

There are few surviving records from Williams's last period, when she was playing not just with great majesty and grace, but with a return of her characteristic salty wit. This is a fairly standard programme, light on her own compositions – only 'What's The Story, Morning Glory' – but resolutely upbeat, even when the blues mood is strongest. 'Surrey With The Fringe On Top' and 'The Jeep Is Jumping' both make an appearance, buoyant and well thought out. 'St James Infirmary' is one of her best recorded performances, and the closing version of her friend Billy Taylor's 'A Grand Night For Swinging' must have sent the Chicago crowd smiling into the night. Competent as her young sidemen are, a greater admixture of solo playing would have been welcome, but an excellent record nevertheless: wise, witty and full of gentle experience.

Richard Williams (born 1931)

TRUMPET

A singleton in the jazz catalogue, Williams's one album is a thin reflection of a busy career as sideman to Charles Mingus and others.

***** New Horn In Town**

Candid 9003 *Williams; Leo Wright (as); Richard Wyands (p); Reggie Workman (b); Bobby Thomas (d).* 11/60.

Like Fats Navarro and Clifford Brown, Williams managed to combine great technical brilliance and a biting tone with a sweeping lyricism, probably best heard here on an unexpected 'Over The Rainbow'. The opening 'I Can Dream, Can't I?' draws quite explicitly from Brown's successful version of the standard, but the phrasing is Williams's own. 'I Remember Clifford' follows at once, with a fat, sentimental tone that sounds almost like flugelhorn, were it not so exact in articulation; Wright plays flute underneath. The three Williams originals don't bespeak a major compositional talent, but the closing 'Renita's Bounce' asks to be played again, and there are some good things about the jokey 'Blues In A Quandary', which never quite reaches a resolution; 'Raucous Notes', a version of his high-school nickname, shows how accurate he can be at speed. Richard Wyands's 'Ferris Wheel' is in keeping with his bouncing accompaniments.

Williams remained a well-kept secret from jazz fans throughout his career and it's a shame he recorded nothing more under his own name.

Roy Williams (born 1937)

TROMBONE

Born in Bolton, Williams played in different groups during the trad era but his stay with Alex Welsh (13 years, from 1965) made him more renowned. Currently freelances and can lay fair claim to being Britain's most distinctive mainstreamer on his instrument.

***** Something Wonderful**

Hep CD 2015 *Williams; Eddie Thompson (ky); Len Skeat (b); Jim Hall (d).* 3/80–5/81.

***** Royal Trombone**

Phontastic 7556 *Williams; John McLevy (t); Arne Domnérus (as, cl); Putte Wickman (cl); Nisse Sandström (ts); Bengt Hallberg (p); Rune Gustafsson (g); Len Skeat, Georg Riedel (b); Rune Carlsson (d).* 12/83.

Williams first emerged as a second-eleven man in British trad, but his stay with the Alex Welsh band of the '60s (and, subsequently, with Humphrey Lyttelton) revealed a much more accomplished and versatile performer than anything most of his colleagues could aspire to. He has a lovely, creamy sound on the trombone which, with its relatively quiet dynamic and effortless delivery, has drawn comparisons with Jack Teagarden that are surprisingly near the mark. These albums are typically relaxed, but inimitably Williams. The trombonist and John McLevy were visiting Sweden for the Phontastic sessions and teamed up with an all-star group of locals. Standards make up most of the menu, although Hallberg pens a crafty twist on 'Exactly Like You' called 'Accurately Like You', and there's a lot of variation in voicings and instrumentations: 'I'm Old Fashioned' is a duet for trombone and piano. Wickman aces out Williams from time to time and has a serene 'I Remember Clifford' to himself, but the guest leader plays admirably throughout. The CD issue adds some tracks to the original LP release but leaves out some that were on the matching album, *Again!*.

Something Wonderful relies on Williams's class to see it through, since the material is over-familiar and Thompson's trio uninvolving, although there's a serenely effective duo for piano and trombone on 'It Never Entered My Mind'.

***** Standard Time**

Sine SND0021 *Williams; Bob Hudson (p); Pete Heron (b); Derek Bush (d).* 9/95.

*****(*) Interplay**

Sine SND0038 *As above, except add John Barnes (bs), Geoff Pearson (b); omit Heron.* 10/96.

Williams has seldom found himself in ideal recording situations: one wonders what records might have resulted from some pre-production and pairing him with a crack rhythm-section. These are pleasing enough without being startling. *Standard Time* has him mulling over 12 standards with Hudson's decent if workmanlike trio, and it's an amiable hour or so of music, if slightly bothered by the very loud bass. *Interplay* finds him back with old sparring partner Barnes, and this is a lot more energizing. The horns circle round each other like dancing masters and some of the dialogue has a gem-like sparkle to it. The material is, again, a trifle overworked but they do sound very good on the likes of 'Squatty Roo'.

****(*) Weavers Of Dreams**

Raymer Sound RSCD684 *Williams; Frank Brooker (ts, ss); Billy Harper (p); Dave Turner (b); Nigel Cretney (d).* 9/98.

***** 'S Wonderful**

Raymer Sound RSCD770 *As above.* 8/02.

One night at the Falcon Hotel, Bude. Brooker's band (which has apparently played in Siberia) tend to get in Williams's way more than help him out and there are some distinctly wayward moments, as well as a sound that isn't handing out favours. Despite it all, the trombonist still manages some typically literate and persuasive solos. And four years later, they did it all in Bude again – although this time at the Strand Hotel. The others are about the same, but if anything Williams is even better, and there are a couple of visits to the rarer end of the Ellington archive in 'A Lull At Dawn' and 'Black Butterfly'.

Tony Williams (1945–97)

DRUMS

A prodigy on drums, he was working with Miles Davis at 17 and played on key '60s dates such as Dolphy's Out To Lunch. Later investigated the wilder shores of fusion in Lifetime, but by the '80s he was a revered senior figure, increasingly interested in composing and investigating acoustic music again. He died suddenly at 52.

CORE COLLECTION

*****(*) Life Time**

Blue Note 99004 *Williams; Sam Rivers (ts); Herbie Hancock (p); Bobby Hutcherson (vib, mar); Ron Carter, Richard Davis, Gary Peacock (b).* 8/64.

Tony Williams's death following a relatively innocuous surgical procedure was doubly shocking, first for the unnecessary waste of life, and more importantly because it came at a time when his career was in marvellous resurgence. Williams had his baptism of fire in the Miles Davis band while still in his teens; everyone who owns it treasures the live recording from the south of France on which the MC announces '*Le jeune Tony Williams à la batterie ... il a dix-sept ans*'. Somewhat as Denardo Coleman did for his father, Tony gave Miles a raw and unfinished sound, one that didn't know it was breaking the rules. It was clear even then that he would go places, and recordings under his own name weren't slow in coming, even if they have slipped in and out of circulation ever since.

Williams's early Blue Notes are intense, sometimes rather inward-looking explorations of the rhythmic possibilities opened up by bebop. Much of what he had learnt to date was concentrated into *Life Time* (not to be confused with the later jazz-rock group, listed separately). This album has now been issued in Blue Note's RVG edition, dedicated to the achievement of engineer Rudy van Gelder. Compare the crisp attacks and precise, undistorted cymbal sound with what Williams had to put up with in later years and judge how worthy the tribute is on both sides. On 'Memory', Williams turns in a remarkable trio performance with Hancock and Hutcherson (and it should be remembered that his most shining moment before this point was on Eric Dolphy's *Out To Lunch!* session, on which Hutcherson and Davis both played). Rivers's angular approach was ideally suited to the young drummer's multidirectional approach and attack.

Williams's own drumming at this period may have suffered slightly from a division of attention between playing, writing and bandleading, but one suspects that what he was after was a sound, rather than a mere outlet for virtuosity, and on these excellent records he found it.

*****(*) Spring**

Blue Note 746135 *Williams; Sam Rivers, Wayne Shorter (ts); Herbie Hancock (p); Gary Peacock (b).* 8/65.

The addition of Shorter on *Spring* underlines the impression that Williams was always happiest with a rather enigmatic lyricism. It's another delightful album and, while it lacks the resonance that comes with the doubled basses on the above *Life Time*, it has a big, rich sound that reverberates through the memory for many hours after every hearing.

***** Wilderness**

Ark 21 8 54571 *Williams; Michael Brecker (ts); Herbie Hancock (p); John Van Tongeren (ky); Pat Metheny, Lyle Workman (g); Stanley Clarke (b); David Garibaldi (perc); orchestra.* 12/96.

A curious record, though testimony to the obvious conclusion that in the last few years of his life Williams was going in almost as many directions musically as there were days in the week. *Wilderness* is a large-scale poem to the frontier, both the physical emptinesses of America and the spiritual richness that could be discovered through them. Alternating small-group (albeit supergroup) and orchestral pieces, it's a step on from the thematic approach of now-deleted *The Story Of Neptune*.

The overture is 'Wilderness Rising', a Copland-influenced idea which outstays its promise by a couple of minutes. The first of the group tracks puts things into a more familiar context, but John Van Tongeren's co-compositions on some tracks take the music off in directions that one senses Williams finds fascinating but isn't entirely clear how to articulate.

Metheny always has the air of the young, well-off kid on the block who wants to play with the older, tougher guys and then somehow manages to shame them with a moment or two of pure grace. He did it with Ornette on *Song X*, and he pulls it off again here, adding such lovely orchestral effects that one wonders why the strings and woodwinds were needed at all. On the short 'Wilderness Island', he brings a wonderful touch to the climax of Williams's best solo feature. The only uncomfortable element is Clarke's very '70s-sounding bass, though Stan's to be applauded for a lovely, accomplished orchestration on 'Harlem Mist '55'.

****** Young At Heart**
Columbia CK 69107 *Williams; Mulgrew Miller (p); Ira Coleman (b).* 96.

In his last couple of years, Williams straddled extremes. He effectively reconvened Lifetime in the guise of Arcana, a boiling trio with Bill Laswell and Derek Bailey (and, later, other guitarists), and he at last got down to making a trio record in a straight jazz idiom. Given its place in the canon, *Young At Heart* has to seem replete with ironies. It is not Williams's greatest record, but it is ample reminder that he was first and foremost a jazz man and one of the very greatest of the last 30 years.

Sticking pretty much to standards, though a version of his own 'Neptune' stands out, this is as even-handed a project as one could wish. Miller is superb, efficient, lyrical and note-perfect, and Ira Coleman stamps his personality on the music more than he has to date. The best of the tracks are the most familiar themes: 'On Green Dolphin Street', 'Body And Soul' (a lovely contribution from Coleman) and 'You And The Night And The Music'. Williams hadn't been known as much of a standards player, but he caresses these as if they were second skin.

Williams's death was a grievous loss to jazz, and an unnecessary waste. His legacy is rich and complex. What is painful is the recognition that he was only just entering into a new phase, a new level of creativity.

***** Ultimate Tony Williams**
Verve 559704 *As above; and as for Lifetime entry.* 69–72.

This is obviously not the 'ultimate' career survey. Without something from Williams's Blue Notes and Columbias, a full picture isn't possible; but it does offer a picture of the drummer in some of his most powerful settings, notably the Lifetime years with John McLaughlin and Larry Young. And the set has the sterling advantage of having been selected, as the *Ultimates* are, by a fellow practitioner, in this case drummer Jack DeJohnette, who is one of Williams's most distinguished heirs. His selections range from the slight 'Some Hip Drum Shit' to the turbulent 'Via The Spectrum Road', and concentrates mostly on Williams compositions, though Carla Bley's 'Vashkar' is also given prominence. At a budget price, this is well worth having.

Larry Willis (born 1940)

PIANO

Born in New York, he played hard bop with Jackie McLean in the '60s before trying fusion, soul-jazz and crossover in the '70s, spending a period with Blood Sweat & Tears. Moved back into straightahead in the '80s and has numerous sideman credits.

***** Just In Time**
Steeplechase SCCD 31251 *Willis; Bob Cranshaw (b); Kenny Washington (d).* 7/89.

***** Heavy Blue**
Steeplechase SCCD 31269 *Willis; Jerry Gonzalez (t, flhn); Joe Ford (ss, as); Don Pate (b); Jeff Tain Watts (d).* 12/89.

***** Let's Play**
Steeplechase SCCD 31283 *Willis; Santi Debriano (b); Victor Lewis (d).* 1/91.

*****(*) How Do You Keep The Music Playing?**
Steeplechase SCCD 31312 *Willis; David Williams (b); Lewis Nash (d).* 4/92.

****(*) Unforgettable**
Steeplechase SCCD 31318 *Willis (p solo).* 5/92.

Something of a journeyman whose stints with Blood Sweat & Tears and numerous high-profile leaders have kept him involved but out of the spotlight, Willis came into his own with the fine series of Steeplechase sessions. He plays at the gentler end of hard-bop piano, writes tunes that often wind up somewhere near the blues, and often picks compositions that have been neglected by others. *Just In Time* is a solid start, but *Heavy Blue* is a more interesting date for the contrasting horns: Gonzalez sounds handsomely lyrical on flugelhorn and is countered by Joe Ford's bruising alto solos, which are always bursting into double-time runs. Willis's five originals here are all worthwhile. The next two trio albums, *Let's Play* and *How Do You Keep The Music Playing?*, might be the best places to hear Willis's own playing. The first has lovely readings of 'Who Can I Turn To?' and 'Bess, You Is My Woman Now', and Lewis is in fine form, though Debriano is a bit overbearing at times. *How Do You Keep The Music Playing?* finds Willis distilling the lightest of tones out of Wayne Shorter's usually impenetrable 'Dance Cadaverous'; he throws in some gentlemanly funk on 'Slick Rick' and even makes 'Ezekiel Saw The Wheel' fit the programme. Williams and Nash are a near-perfect team. The only disappointment in this stack is the Steeplechase solo disc, dedicated to Nat Cole ballads and, finally, a bit soporific. By himself, Willis expands his voicings and makes some of these tunes sound too weighty and formal, though there are still some pleasing variations.

Cassandra Wilson (born 1955)

VOICE, GUITAR, SARDO

Born in Jackson, Mississippi, Wilson's emergence in the '80s was as a peripheral member of the so-called M-Base group of New

York musicians. Following a number of records for JMT, she signed to Blue Note and scored major successes with her first releases for the label.

****(*) Point Of View**
Winter & Winter 919004-2 *Wilson; Grachan Moncur III (tb); Steve Coleman (as, perc); Jean-Paul Bourelly (g); Lonnie Plaxico (b); Mark Johnson (d).* 12/85.

**** Days Aweigh**
Winter & Winter 919012-2 *Wilson; Steve Coleman (as); Rod Williams (ky); Jean-Paul Bourelly (g); Kevin Bruce Harris, Kenneth Davis (b); Mark Johnson (d).* 5/87.

*****(*) Blue Skies**
Winter & Winter 919018-2 *Wilson; Mulgrew Miller (p); Lonnie Plaxico (b); Terri Lyne Carrington (d).* 2/88.

****(*) Jumpworld**
Winter & Winter 919033-2 *Wilson; Graham Haynes (t); Robin Eubanks, (tb); Steve Coleman (as); Rod Williams (ky); David Gilmore (g); Kevin Bruce Harris, Lonnie Plaxico (b); Mark Johnson (d); James Moore (v).* 7–8/89.

***** Live**
Winter & Winter 919047-2 *Wilson; James Weidman (ky); Kevin Bruce Harris (b); Marc Johnson (d).* 90.

Wilson's early records contain all the seeds of the success she has enjoyed at Blue Note, but with one exception they rarely cohere as albums of any particularity or sustained success. Most are awkward compromises between a more traditional jazz singing role and the funk and rap influences which dominate today's commercial black music. Her own compositions were flavourless vehicles for her style, marked by rambling melodies, vaguely prescriptive lyrics and rhythmical staggers; the early records (up to *Blue Skies*) are an occasionally exciting but often unfocused attempt at finding a balance. She shows a marked Betty Carter influence rhythmically, but the timbre of her voice is cloudier, and it can throw an interesting spin on otherwise familiar songs. *Blue Skies*, now reissued on Winter & Winter, is the least typical but easily the best of her JMT records: though made up entirely of standards with a conventional rhythm section, the recital finds Wilson investing the likes of 'Shall We Dance?' with a wholly unfamiliar range of inflexions and melodic extensions which is captivating. Her third-person version of 'Sweet Lorraine' is peculiarly dark and compelling and, while some of the songs drift a little too far off base, it's a remarkable record, and it makes the ensuing *Jumpworld*, a return to self-consciously 'modern' music, sound all the more contrived. The live session confirms that Wilson can sustain a concert set which is essentially a seamless, ongoing vocal improvisation, but the slipshod attention to quality-control, as far as the material is concerned, is a point which seems to afflict most of what she does. Winter & Winter have now reissued much of her JMT catalogue, but the new editions basically affirm that the music belongs very much to its time and has mostly dated badly.

***** Blue Light 'Til Dawn**
Blue Note 781357-2 *Wilson; Olu Dara (c); Don Byron (cl); Tony Cedras (acc); Charles Burnham (vn); Gib Wharton (steel g); Brandon Ross, Chris Whitley (g); Lonnie Plaxico, Kenny Davis (b); Lance Carter, Bill McClellan (d); Cyro Baptista, Jeff Haynes, Kevin Johnson, Vinx (perc).* n.d.

Wilson's debut for Blue Note was hailed in many quarters (mostly by rock critics) as a masterpiece, and it's certainly a clear step forward from her earlier records: Brandon Ross's production clarifies all the colours of her voice for the first time, and the inventive textures involving Dara, Byron, Burnham and Baptista create digital fantasies on country blues and string-band forms. Yet Wilson again makes peculiar labour out of some of the songs: Joni Mitchell and Robert Johnson tunes stagger under her mannerisms, and it's on the simpler, more straightforward arrangements, such as a lovely glide through Van Morrison's 'Tupelo Honey', that it all comes together.

***** New Moon Daughter**
Blue Note 837183-2 *As above, except add Graham Haynes, Butch Morris (c); Gary Breit (org); Kevin Breit (g); Mark Anthony Peterson (b); Dougie Bowne (d); omit Dara, Byron, Davis, Carter, McClellan, Johnson, Vinx.* 95.

The same again, only more polished, a shade more inventive, as well as a fraction more arch: 'Last Train To Clarksville' was a cute idea for a cover, and Wilson takes it over, but her improvisation on the fade suggests that she doesn't really know what to do with it. 'Strange Fruit' is harrowing in a deadpan, designerish way, and the Robert Johnson tunes again don't fit. Where she really puts her mark on the music is in her own writing: the calm, serenely pretty 'Until' is outstanding, and so are 'Memphis' and 'Find Him'. Jazz as art-song, and pretty damn accomplished.

*****(*) Traveling Miles**
Blue Note 54123-2 *Wilson; Olu Dara (c); Steve Coleman (as); Vincent Henry (hca); Eric Lewis (p); Regina Carter (vn); Doug Wamble, Marvin Sewell, Pat Metheny, Kevin Breit (g); Stefon Harris (vib); Cecilia Smith (mar); Dave Holland, Lonnie Plaxico (b); Marcus Baylor, Perry Wilson (d); Jeffrey Haynes, Mino Cinelu (perc); Angelique Kidjo (v).* 12/97–9/98.

There's always going to be a preening quality in Wilson's vocals, and non-believers will probably find it as hard to warm to this record as to her previous sets. But as a tribute to Miles Davis, this seems like the most creative and thought-through of the many genuflections to the master since his passing. For once – although even this seems self-conscious at times – Wilson seems less like the epicentre of the music and more like a graceful sound which drifts through a record that is, as usual, heavy on texture and feel and light on improvisational input. There is no trumpet on the record at all – Dara's cornet makes only a couple of ghostly appearances – and most of the weight is carried by the guitarists. It seems strange to hear the likes of 'Run The Voodoo Down' and 'Blue In Green' adorned with lyrics, although Wilson's poetry is more useful as atmosphere than as substance. But this is surely the best singing she has put down on record, wistful without becoming studied, and 'Time After Time' is a pop interpretation which surpasses any of those she tried on the previous Blue Note albums.

***** Belly Of The Sun**
Blue Note 35072-2 *Wilson; Olu Dara (t); Rhonda Richmond (p, v); Boogaloo Ames (p); Kevin Breit (g, bj, bizouki); Marvin Sewell, Jesse Robinson (g); Mark Peterson (b); Xavyon Jamison (d); Cyro Baptista, Jeffrey Haynes (perc); India Arie, Jewell Bass, Patrice Moncell, Henry Rhodes, Vasti Jackson (v).* n.d.

Wilson's Mississippi roots are the linchpin for a project which was apparently conceived as a straight blues record. This doesn't much square with the inclusion of the likes of Bob Dylan's 'Shelter From The Storm', Jimmy Webb's 'Wichita Lineman' or A. C. Jobim's 'The Waters Of March', none of which she delivers with any real conviction. Walking a studied line between rootsy authenticity and a digital fantasy on old-time sounds (Baptista and Haynes conjure all sorts of queer percussive noises), the music just about coheres, though nothing works as well as Wilson's simple recitation of 'Darkness On The Delta' against the rickety piano of Boogaloo Ames (who died just before the record was released). Let's call it a 'characteristic' offering from a minor-major artist.

*** Glamoured

Blue Note 81860-2 *Wilson; Grégoire Maret (hca); Brandon Ross (g, bj); Fabrizio Sotti (g); Calvin Jones, Reginald Veal (b); Herlin Riley, Teri Lyne Carrington (d); Jeffrey Haynes (perc).* 12/02–3/03.

A dozen years ago she was on top of jazz singing, but first Diana Krall and now Norah Jones have usurped the throne, and Wilson sounds dressed up with few places left to go. Fabrizio Sotti has done much of the arranging and he thins out the backings: less exotica, more guitars, bass and drums, clearly delineated (even Wilson does some twanging). As ever, the material is a wholly unpredictable mix, from 'Lay Lady Lay' to 'Honey Bee', and in at least one instance – the beguiling acoustic funk of 'What is It?' – there's a search for a hit single (or at least a track that will go down well on radio). It's an appealing enough set, but the singer's mannerisms and solipsistic way with almost every lyric leave the listener unconvinced much of the time.

Garland Wilson (1909–54)

PIANO

Apart from a short time at the beginning of his career and during the war years, Wilson spent most of his time in Europe where he recorded in his familiar stride style with Nat Gonella and others.

*** Garland Wilson 1931–1938

Classics 808 *Wilson; Michel Warlop (vn); Nina Mae McKinney (v).* 31–38.

*** Harlem Piano In Montmartre

Verve 548 321 2 *Wilson; Danny Polo (cl); Herman Chittison, Charlie Lewis (p); Emmanuel Soudieux (b); Jerry Mengo (d); Arita Day, Nina Mae McKinney (v).* 51.

Because Wilson's career was spent away from the US, he's rarely been accorded much attention. His playing is buoyant and effective, with a strong sense of melody and little in the way of harmonic sophistication. The Gitanes set is shared with Chittison and Lewis and offers no more than a sampling. Better, if you're interested in him at all, to opt for the Classics set, which covers the key years from his departure from America to the year before he returned at the start of the war. This has pretty much everything Wilson recorded as a leader (the Verve set rounds out the story); most of them are solos, but there are a couple of vocals with McKinney and two duos with violinist Warlop, who appears right at the end on 'Limehouse Blues' (very Grappelli-like) and 'You Showed Me The Way'. Garland's two-handed approach is very effective, if a little lacking in subtlety, but he has an ability to squeeze nuances out of tunes – 'Bei Mir Bist Du Schon', 'Your Heart And Mine' – that no one else hears and his originals – 'Blues En Si Bemol', 'The Blues Got Me', 'The Way I Feel', 'You Rascal You' – are endlessly entertaining. A minor figure, to be sure, but not to be overlooked.

Gerald Wilson (born 1918)

TRUMPET, BANDLEADER

Studied in Detroit then joined Jimmie Lunceford, before forming own band. Has worked in Los Angeles music ever since, arranging, accompanying, bandleading in many kinds of music.

*** Gerald Wilson, 1945–1946

Classics 976 *Wilson; James Anderson, Emmett Berry, Hobart Dotson, Red Kelly, Fred Trainor, Snooky Young (t); Ralph Bledsoe, Vic Dickenson, Robert Huerta, Melba Liston, Isaac Livingstone, Alton Moore (tb); Edward Hale, Leo Trammel, Floyd Turnham (as); Eddie 'Lockjaw' Davis, Vernon Slater, Olis West (ts); Maurice Simon, Charles Waller (bs); Jimmy Bunn (p); Williams Edwards, Buddy Harper, Benny Sexton (g); Arthur Edwards, Robert Rudd (b); Henry Tucker Green (d); Estelle Edson, Dick Gray, Pat Kay, Betty Roche, Thrasher Sisters (v).* 5/45–46.

Gerald Wilson joined the Jimmie Lunceford Orchestra just around the time America joined the Second World War. After a stint in the Navy, the talented young trumpeter and composer decided to form his own band. It was a progressive outfit whose faintly experimental air has long since been eclipsed by Stan Kenton's more abrasive approach, but these early recordings are full of interest.

As often with Classics releases, much of the interest lies in identifying stars of the future in embryo. Melba Liston debuts as a soloist on a reading of 'Come Sunday', recorded for Excelsior in 1945, while the irrepressible Snooky Young features on a rather later 'One O'Clock Jump'. Wilson's own contributions as a player are less dramatic. He also features on 'Come Sunday', urbane, unflustered and conscientious but hardly incendiary. His main role is as arranger, turning in crisp, intelligent charts which anticipate the work of later years. There is already a signature Wilson sound: slightly dark, overtoned, regular without being robotic. Anyone who has turned on to the fine bands of the '70s and '80s will find much of interest in these sides. Even where the sound is less than pristine, the content is always involving.

***(*) State Street Sweet

Mama MMF 1010 *Wilson; Ron Barrows, Bob Clark, George Graham, Tony Lujan, Bobby Shew, Frank Szabo, Snooky Young (t); Thurman Green, Alex Iles, Charlie Loper, Ira Nepus (tb); Maurice Spears (btb); John Stephens, Randall Willis (as); Plas Johnson, Carl Randall, Louis Taylor (ts); Jack Nimitz (bs); Brian O'Rourke (p); Eric Otis, Anthony Wilson (g); Trey Henry (b); Mel Lee (d).* 95.

Wilson's appearance at the Monterey Jazz Festival in 1963 was something of a revival meeting. After running a successful band during the '40s, he more or less dropped out of jazz for a decade, returning to the fray only at the start of the '60s. Wilson had cut his teeth with the Jimmie Lunceford Orchestra, where he had replaced Sy Oliver as staff arranger. There he acquired skills which have lasted him to this day. One of the great orchestrators in jazz, he leans heavily on the blues, but integrates swing, bebop, rock and some classical influences. *State Street Sweet* is a lovely record marked out by well-honed skill and a sure hand at recruiting players. Bobby Shew is excellent on 'The Serpent' and guest Plas Johnson has a brief starring role on 'Come Back To Sorrento'.

****** Theme For Monterey**

MAMA MMF 1021 *Wilson; Ron Barrows, Oscar Brashear, David Krimsley, Carl Saunders, Snooky Young (t); Leslie Benedict, George Bohannon, Isaac Smith, Maurice Spears (tb); Scott Mayo, Jack Nimitz, Carl Randall, John Stephens, Louis Taylor, Randall Willis (sax); Brian O'Rourke (p); Eric Veliotes, Anthony Wilson (g); Trey Henry (b); Mel Lee (d).* 97.

Wilson was a natural choice for the keynote new work at the 40th anniversary Monterey Jazz Festival. Prestigious as such a commission is, no one could have expected a piece of such grave and joyous brilliance as *Theme For Monterey*. At more than three-quarters of an hour, it has a scope and simplicity of purpose which few contemporary players would have dared, and yet repeated listenings reveal a whole raft of subtle ideas, personal and musicological references. The 'encore' pieces, 'Summertime' and the brief bop exercise of 'Anthropology', offer just a glimpse of how a Wilson band attacks repertory material. Both arrangements were premiered at the Library of Congress in recognition of its archiving of Wilson's work.

The real interest lies in his suite of original themes. 'Lyons' Roar' is a dedication to Monterey Festival maven Jimmy Lyons; the main soloists are trumpeter Oscar Brashear, tenors Carl Randall and Randall Willis, and guitarist Anthony Wilson, who probably gets more space on the disc than he strictly deserves. It also features pianist Brian O'Rourke, who is the most effective presence on 'Cookin' On Cannery Row' and 'Spanish Bay'. The set is very nearly hijacked by the very first track, an exquisite thing called 'Romance', which highlights the bright, expressive soprano of Scott Mayo.

****** New York, New Sound**

Mack Avenue MAC 1009 *Clark Terry (t, flhn); Jimmy Owens, Eddie Henderson, Jon Faddis, Frank Greene, Sean Jones (t); Benny Powell, Luis Bonilla, Dennis Wilson (tb): Douglas Purviance (tb, btb); Jesse Davis (as); Jerry Dodgion (f, as); Jimmy Heath (ts); Frank Wess (f, ts); Jay Brandford (bs); Kenny Barron, Renee Rosnes (p); Anthony Wilson, Oscar Castro-Neves (g); Bob Cranshaw, Trey Henry, Larry Ridley (b); Lewis Nash, Stix Hooper (d); Lenny Castro (perc).* 02.

In his 80s, Wilson is still writing music, still visiting new places to have his work played, and it was a marvellous initiative by Stix Hooper's Mack Avenue label to record this all-star collective swinging through some of his material. The big piece is a comprehensive revision of his 1997 'Theme For Monterey', but there are other Wilson favourites such as 'Blues For Yna Yna', and the orchestra bristle through these vintage charts in a mercurial high gear. How much longer anyone will be able to assemble a band which has the likes of Jimmy Heath, Clark Terry and Frank Wess sitting alongside Jesse Davis and Renee Rosnes is impossible to say, but this is a meeting of generations working together on some of the masterpieces of modern big-band writing and creating a record any jazz lover should be delighted to hear.

Glenn Wilson

BARITONE SAXOPHONE, BASS CLARINET, ALTO FLUTE

Contemporary saxophonist specializing in baritone, heard in big-band situations and occasional small-group leadership dates.

***** Impasse**

Cadence CJR 1023 *Wilson; Harold Danko (p); Dennis Irwin (b); Adam Nussbaum (d).* 3/84.

Although, like so many baritone specialists, Wilson seems doomed to recording mainly as a section sideman, he plays with fine gusto and thoughtful intelligence on the records made under his own leadership. His debut, *Impasse*, has recently been reissued on CD. While a little rough-and-ready, it still sounds well, the baritonist getting a huge sound out of the horn, and the playing wants for nothing in ferocity. Danko, always a thinking player, keeps a clear harmonic course underneath. His later records for Sunnyside seem to have slipped away, but are worth looking for.

Matt Wilson (born 1964)

DRUMS

Came to Boston from Illinois in the late '80s and immediately won a reputation as an intelligent, subtle percussionist who could adapt his approach to any situation. Unusually for a drummer, Wilson has been able to record regularly as leader.

*****(*) As Wave Follows Wave**

Palmetto 2020 *Wilson; Dewey Redman (ts); Larry Goldings (org); Cecil McBee (b).* 4/96.

The debut album was pretty much stolen by fellow Palmetto star Dewey Redman, whose own recording opportunities have been dismayingly few over the years. Redman's muscular tenor sits well with the organ and drums and he delivers some fine playing on 'July Hymn' (a tribute to Don Cherry) and on 'Body And Soul'. Wilson mixes in originals and traditional themes ('Sweet Betsy From The Pike') and includes a couple of unaccompanied drum and percussion features ('Nice Colors' and the clever closing 'Mr Zimmerman's Farm', which does for B. Dylan what Old MacDonald did for agricultural sound effects generally). A fine debut record, even if the old timer pinched it.

*****(*) Going Once, Going Twice**

Palmetto 2032 *Wilson; Joel Frahm (ss, ts); Lee Konitz (as); Andrew D'Angelo (as, bcl); Pete McCann (bj); Yosuke Inoue (b); Ned Sublette (v).* 3/98.

****** Smile**

Palmetto 2049 *As above, except omit Konitz, McCann, Sublette.* 3/99.

The title track features an auctioneer (Ned Sublette), which is a unique credit in this book. It's a very funny, very cleverly conceived track, also featuring banjoist Pete McCann in a role that might have suited Bill Frisell. It's a set that combines intelligent jazz themes, including Herbie Nichols' rarely heard 'Chit-Chatting', with Pete Seeger's version of Ecclesiastes, 'Turn! Turn! Turn!'. By no means put off by his experience with Redman, Wilson has even more saxophonists this time.

D'Angelo is credited with the fine 'Andrew's Ditty', which rivals Wilson's own compositions, and Lee Konitz is drafted in on 'Brattleboro'. A promising sophomore performance from Wilson, who grows in range and stature each time.

Smile was a step on again, a set that mixes in the humour ever more comfortably. 'Take Me Out To The Ball Game' is hilarious, as is 'Go, Team, Go!', though what's interesting is how seamlessly Wilson and his men weave their larking into some fairly robust outside jazz. Frahm's bass clarinet work was likened to Eric Dolphy on this record's first appearance and while it's an absurd comparison at face value, you can hear what was meant. 'A Dusting Of Snow' shows what a fine impressionistic drummer Wilson can be in a more thoughtful mood, while 'Daymaker' is just great small group arranging. Of the brought-in material, Monk's rarely played 'Boo Boo's Birthday' is outstanding and there is a fine reading of 'Strangers In The Night', which is virtually unrecognizable as such until it's almost over.

*****(*) Arts And Crafts**

Palmetto 2069 *Wilson; Terell Stafford (t); Larry Goldings (p); Dennis Irwin (b).* 3/01.

For this one, Wilson alters the instrumentation considerably and comes up with yet another variation on his protean musical personality. The drafting of Stafford proves to be a key element. The trumpeter is strongly featured on a tribute to Lester Bowie and throughout sounds full-voiced, supple and warm. The inclusion of Ornette Coleman's 'Old Gospel' is another sign of Wilson's eclecticism, but the weight falls very much on his own writing here. 'Final Answer' is a buoyant post-bop idea which clinches the Dolphy connection; 'Arts And Crafts' itself is a slower and more thoughtful theme which conjures one of Golding's best moments of the set (he's on piano throughout). They close the set with 'Love Walked In' and 'All Through The Night'.

****** Humidity**

Palmetto 2089 *Wilson; John Carlson (t, pkt-t); Andrew D'Angelo (as, bcl, perc); Jeff Lederer (ts, f, perc); Felicia Wilson (vn); Yosuke Inoue (b).* 2/03.

Wilson's awareness of modern jazz history is underlined on the opening 'Thank You, Billy Higgins', a tribute to the late drummer (and possible influence) who worked with Ornette Coleman. Just occasionally it sounds as though Wilson is trying to be eclectic for eclecticism's sake. Here he does 'Don't Blame Me' alongside his own Colemanish 'Swimming In The Trees' and (mis-named) 'Raga', as well as a version of Tadd Dameron's 'Our Delight'. It's all a joyous mess, held together by the sheer force of Wilson's creative personality. Reunited with Andrew D'Angelo and a second reedman, he seems to have discovered his ideal instrumentation. The brassmen and fiddler are guests but Carlson's pocket trumpet is an important marker of the Coleman/Cherry axis Matt is exploring.

As a body of work, Wilson's Palmetto discs are among the most exciting in recent jazz; conscious of history, exploratory, funny and mournful by turns, they keep the listener guessing and, better still, thirsty for more.

Reuben Wilson (born 1935)

ORGAN

One of Blue Note's roster of soul-jazz Hammond players, Wilson was born in Oklahoma and schooled in Pasadena where he knew Bobby Hutcherson. His career faltered with his style of music, but recent years have seen him declared a cult figure.

***** Love Bug**

Blue Note 29905 *Wilson; Lee Morgan (t); George Coleman (ts); Grant Green (g); Jimmy Lewis (b); Leo Morris, Idris Muhammad (d).* 3 & 10/69.

****(*) Blue Mode**

Blue Note 29906 *Wilson; John Manning (ts); Melvin Sparks (g); Tommy Derrick (d).* 12/69.

***** Blue Breakbeats**

Blue Note 94707 *As above, except add Trevor Lawrence (ts).* 68–69.

In the '90s, it wasn't uncommon to hear Wilson's organ lines sampled by the likes of A Tribe Called Quest. His earlier celebrity wasn't quite as assured. Blue Note signed him thinking he'd be the next big organ star and threw plenty of bankable names at his first recordings. Wilson, though, wasn't quite distinctive enough to make it in a market already saturated with strong and idiosyncratic Hammond stylists. The first album is currently deleted, though some of it is available on *Blue Breakbeats*. On *Love Bug*, he dabbles with Larry Young's mixture of hot grooves and freedom, but doesn't sound as if his heart is in it. The first set included pop material – 'I'm Going To Make You Love Me', 'I Say A Little Prayer' – with funky originals 'Love Bug' and 'Hot Rod'. The CD has a bonus of 'Hold On, I'm Comin''. Of the band, Morgan is on auto-pilot, Coleman and Green are the real stars, but Idris Muhammad was to make a career out of this kind of session and it's worth checking out his moves.

The second record, minus the star names from the Blue Note stable, also saw a move into a much more straightforward and commercially minded brand of soul-jazz. The opening sequence of 'Bambu' (which hints at the earlier approach) and 'Knock On Wood' is pretty much the best of an album that freewheels from there on in. There's not much to excite a hard bop fanatic and the whole package is rather lame, though you wouldn't know it from the number of 'Bambu' samples ricocheting round DJ booths three decades later. There were to be a couple more Blue Notes, but neither *A Groovy Situation* nor *Set Us Free* are still in print; doubtless original copies change hands for silly money.

Blue Breakbeats is probably the only Wilson album anyone really needs. It includes 'Hot Rod', 'Love Bug', 'Bus Ride', 'Orange Peel' and from the first album, *On Broadway*, the attractive 'Ronnie's Bonnie'.

****(*) Organ Donor**

Jazzateria 298 *Wilson; Kenny Rampton (t); Jason Forsythe (tb); Melvin Butler (ss, f, af); Bruce Flowers (ky); Robin Macatangay (g); Chris Parks (b); Adrian Harpham (d); Starr Adkins, Saundra Williams (v).* 98.

***** Organ Blues**

Jazzateria 309 *Wilson; Melvin Butler (ts); Grant Green Jr (g); Bernard Purdie (d).* n.d.

With the upsurge of interest in rare grove and acid jazz, Wilson made a comeback in the '90s. He was never the most exciting

Hammond player on the scene even in the '60s and the later material is fairly thin. On *Organ Donor* he retreads some of his best known tunes in company with a young band who probably grew up on the Blue Notes. The results are only fair, but Reuben still knows how to grind the organ, even if his colleagues seem to be away on another riff altogether. 'Hot Rod' is a reasonable version and 'Got To Get Your Own '98' is a respectable update with a good vocal by Saundra Williams. We'll pass over 'Now's The Time' in silence; likewise the album title.

Organ Blues benefits from a better pedigree band, lead by Grant Green Jr and anchored by the fine Bernard Purdie, who can do anything from rock backbeat to free jazz. Melvin Butler honks righteously on the opening 'Blues For McDuff', one of a couple of tributes to fellow Hammond-men. Jimmy Smith is also namechecked but the straightahead approach and raw blues quality is very much Wilson's own.

Steve Wilson (born 1961)

ALTO SAXOPHONE

Played in soul bands as a teenager, then arrived in jazz as a member of Blue Note's Out of the Blue Band in the '80s. Since then has been a prolific New York sideman, with a few dates of his own.

***(*) New York Summit

Criss Cross Criss 1062 *Wilson; Tom Williams (t); Mulgrew Miller (p); James Genus (b); Carl Allen (d).* 12/91.

*** Blues For Marcus

Criss Cross Criss 1073 *Wilson; Steve Nelson (vib); Bruce Barth (p); James Genus (b); Lewis Nash (d).* 1/93.

Wilson first surfaced in the mid-'80s with Out of the Blue, a group dedicated to the classic Blue Note style. With a sound reminiscent of former Messenger Bobby Watson (a stylistic link confirmed by his sound-alike duets with vibraphonist Nelson on *Blues For Marcus*), the young Virginian acquitted himself more than respectably. Wilson is by no means an uncritical retro hard-bopper. His first two CDs as leader demonstrate impressive if marginally over-ambitious skills as a composer ('Diaspora' on the second record gets rather hung up on complex time-signatures) but also an instinct for unusual repertoire. The first record opens with Ted Curson's lovely 'Reava's Waltz' and includes material by Ron Carter, Duke Ellington, Eddie Harris, Thelonious Monk, Joe Sample and Bobby Timmons ('Damned If I Know', rather than the ubiquitous 'Moanin'') alongside a single original. By 1993, Wilson's confidence in his own work is more evident, but there is still room for Ornette Coleman's 'Jayne', Joe Chambers's 'Patterns' and Roland Kirk's 'The Haunted Melody'. Wilson hasn't as yet quite put together the band that suits his approach. Tom Williams is a competent rather than an exciting trumpeter in the Freddie Hubbard mould; he sounds clean and orderly in ensembles but lacks pep in his solos. An outing on the Wilson original 'Ujima' is little more than a warm-up effort. Ironically, he's missed on the second album, which is rather light in sound. Barth contributes an original, 'Cornerstone', but as a player he lacks Mulgrew Miller's firmly anchored chords and easy switches of register. Genus is the only common element. He may have slipped the engineers a sawbuck before the later sessions, for he's much more clearly audible than on *Summit*.

*** Step Lively

Criss Cross Criss 1096 *Wilson; Cyrus Chestnut (p); Freddie Bryant (g); Dennis Irwin (b); Gregory Hutchinson (d); Daniel Sadownick (perc).* 12/93.

Wilson's third Criss Cross is not so much a progression as an affirmation of the sound impression of the previous two. His lean, unsentimental tone on the alto blends with a rather good-humoured approach, which makes for a somewhat unusual blend of lightness and intensity. He restricts himself to two self-penned originals – the complex blues of the title-track and the jaunty 'The Epicurean' – and the presence of the admirable Chestnut lends further muscle. In the end, perhaps no more than another solid Criss Cross date, but there are plenty of rewarding things, and Wilson deserves attention.

**** Four For Time

Criss Cross 1115 *Wilson; Bruce Barth (p); Larry Grenadier (b); Leon Parker (d).* 12/94.

The key track here is 'Groovesome Twosome', a duet with drummer Parker on his minimal kit. The interplay between the two is the axis round which this working group revolves, though Barth's Monk-influenced style and compositional ideas ('By The Window') are important as well. Wilson sticks to alto and seems determined to keep matters as in-line and uncomplicated as possible. He largely succeeds. Parker is magnificent, and it's good to see his role recognized in the reappearance of his compositon 'Belief', which he used as title track for his own record. Grenadier deserves a mention as well, picking up the bare clues in some of Barth's accompaniments and giving them a rounded harmonic support.

*** Generations

Stretch 9019-2 *Wilson; Mulgrew Miller (p); Ray Drummond (b); Ben Riley (d).* 2/98.

The 'generations' refer to the players of yore who have inspired Wilson, and he brought in three of them – Riley aside, not exactly names that were prominent long ago! – to back him up. The results are pleasing, if hardly outstanding. Miller and Drummond are such seasoned pros that even their routine work has an eminence to it, but they don't do much more than create a diplomatic framework for Wilson's solos. The leader sounds fine, although if he's to make an impact as a leader on record, he's going to need a more meaningful context than this.

*** Passages

Stretch 9025-2 *Wilson; Nicholas Payton (t, flhn); Bruce Barth (ky); Ed Howard (b); Adam Cruz (d).* 12/99.

Again, too much like piece-work, not enough reason-to-be. 'Turnin' The Corner' is a strong start, but thereafter the material quickly thins out and some accomplished playing searches for a solid line to earth.

**(*) Soulful Song

Max Jazz 401 *Wilson; Bruce Barth (p); Paul Bollenback (g); James Genus, Ed Howard (b); Adam Cruz (d, perc); Billy Kilson (d); Wilson Corniel (perc); Carla Cook, Phillip Manuel, Rene Marie (v).* 5/03.

This is a very dull set, with Wilson reduced to accompanist role, backing some very ho-hum singing and some rather drab arrangements. There's no obvious rationale for this record, given the momentum Steve seemed to have from his Criss Cross and Stretch records. He indulges his multi-instrumentalism more than the music strictly demands and rarely to any dramatic or musical effect. Fans will be disappointed; newcomers will wonder what the buzz was about.

Teddy Wilson (1912–86)

PIANO

Born in Austin, Texas, Wilson visited Chicago in 1928 and fell in love with the jazz there. He formed a duo with Art Tatum in 1931, then arrived in New York to join Benny Carter, thanks to John Hammond. His studio small-group work included classic sessions with Billie Holiday and Lester Young, and he then joined Benny Goodman. A brief spell with his own big band in 1939 was suspended in favour of more small-group work, then a staff job at CBS and teaching at Juilliard. He toured as a soloist in the '60s, '70s and '80s, always the most gracious and poised of performers.

*****(*) Teddy Wilson 1934–35**
Classics 508 *Wilson; Roy Eldridge, Dick Clark (t); Benny Morton (tb); Tom Macey, Benny Goodman, Cecil Scott (cl); Hilton Jefferson, Johnny Hodges (as); Chu Berry, Ben Webster (ts); John Trueheart, Lawrence Lucie, Dave Barbour (g); John Kirby, Grachan Moncur (b); Cozy Cole (d); Billie Holiday (v).* 5/34–12/35.

*****(*) Teddy Wilson Vol. 1: Too Hot For Words**
Hep 1012 *As above.* 1–10/35.

Few jazz records have endured quite as well as Teddy Wilson's '30s music. Wilson arrived in New York as, on the basis of the four solo titles which open the first Classics CD, an enthusiastic young stride pianist, already under the spell of Earl Hines and of Art Tatum, with whom he worked as a two-man piano team. But even here there are the signs of an individual whose meticulous, dapper delivery and subtle reading of harmony would be hugely influential. Amazingly, everything is in place by the time of the first band session in July 1935: the initial line-up includes Eldridge, Goodman and Webster, and the singer is Billie Holiday, who would feature as vocalist on most of Wilson's pre-war records. Two classics were made immediately – 'What A Little Moonlight Can Do' and 'Miss Brown To You' – and the style was set: a band chorus, a vocal, and another chorus for the band, with solos and obbligatos in perfect accord with every other note and accent. All the others seem to take their cue from the leader's own poise, and even potentially unruly spirits such as Eldridge and Webster behave. The first of Classics' comprehensive seven-disc series includes 11 piano solos and 12 band sides, and it's a delight from start to finish, even though there was better to come.

The reissue of these records has been complicated by Holiday's presence, for all her tracks with Wilson are now also available on discs under her own name. Collectors will have to follow their own tastes, but we would opine that, of all the various transfers of this material, the Hep discs – which follow the Classics discs fairly closely in sequencing, if finally not quite so generously in the number of tracks – have the most truthful sound. Even so, the Classics CD, above, is consistently clean and enjoyable in sonic terms.

*****(*) Teddy Wilson 1935–36**
Classics 511 *Wilson; Dick Clark, Gordon Griffin, Frankie Newton, Roy Eldridge, Jonah Jones (t); Benny Morton (tb); Benny Goodman, Buster Bailey, Rudy Powell, Tom Macey (cl); Jerry Blake (cl, as); Vido Musso (cl, ts); Harry Carney (cl, bs); Johnny Hodges (as); Ted McRae, Chu Berry (ts); Dave Barbour, John Trueheart, Allan Reuss, Bob Lessey, Lawrence Lucie (g); Lionel Hampton (vib); Israel Crosby, Harry Goodman, Leemie Stanfield, Grachan Moncur, John Kirby (b); Gene Krupa, Big Sid Catlett, Cozy Cole (d); Helen Ward, Ella Fitzgerald, Red Harper, Billie Holiday (v).* 12/35–8/36.

****** Teddy Wilson Vol. 2: Warmin' Up**
Hep 1014 *As above.* 12/35–6/36.

***** Teddy Wilson 1936–37**
Classics 521 *Wilson; Gordon Griffin, Irving Randolph, Henry 'Red' Allen, Jonah Jones, Buck Clayton, Cootie Williams (t); Cecil Scott (cl, as, ts); Vido Musso (cl, ts); Harry Carney (cl, bs); Benny Goodman (cl); Johnny Hodges (as); Ben Webster, Prince Robinson, Lester Young (ts); Allan Reuss, Freddie Green, James McLin (g); Harry Goodman, Milt Hinton, Walter Page, John Kirby (b); Cozy Cole, Jo Jones, Gene Krupa (d); Billie Holiday, Midge Williams, Red Harper (v).* 8/36–3/37.

****** Teddy Wilson Vol. 3: Of Thee I Swing**
Hep 1020 *Largely as above.* 8/36–2/37.

Wilson hit his stride as this long series of sessions proceeded. The next two Classics CDs are laden with fine music, and Billie Holiday's contributions assume greatness; the 16 tracks she sings on Classics 521 number among her finest records, and the mixed quality of the material seems to make no difference to her. Just as Lionel Hampton began pilfering men from local big bands for his Victor sessions, so Wilson organized similar contingents for his records, and some of these bands are drawn from either the Goodman or the Basie orchestra, although one offbeat session features Henry Allen, Cecil Scott and Prince Robinson. The spotlight is off Wilson to some extent, but one of the major reasons for the success of these dates is the light, singing fluency of the rhythm section, and the pianist's unemphatic but decisive lead is the prime reason for that. Ella Fitzgerald sings on one session on Classics 511 and Midge Williams, Helen Ward and Red Harper take their turns at the microphone, but it's Holiday one remembers. Lester Young's association with the singer also starts here, but his solos are really no more memorable than the offerings by Buck Clayton, Benny Goodman or Roy Eldridge. Those collecting the Classics CDs may be dismayed by the erratic sound-quality on Classics 521 in particular, and once again we prefer the Hep series.

This might be the place to mention *Teddy Wilson & His All-Stars Vol. 1* (Columbia 501649), a disgracefully lazy reissue from a major label, which merely transfers an old '60s LP edition straight to CD, with no proper remastering and no documentation. Awful sound.

****** Teddy Wilson 1937**
Classics 531 *Wilson; Cootie Williams, Harry James, Buck Clayton (t); Buster Bailey, Benny Goodman, Archie Rosati (cl); Harry Carney (cl, bs); Johnny Hodges (as); Vido Musso, Lester Young (ts); Red Norvo (xy); Allan Reuss, Freddie Green (g); John Kirby, John Simmons, Harry Goodman, Artie Bernstein, Walter Page (b); Cozy Cole, Jo Jones, Gene Krupa (d); Helen Ward, Billie Holiday, Frances Hunt, Boots Castle (v).* 3–8/37.

****** Teddy Wilson Vol. 4: Fine & Dandy**
Hep 1029 *Largely as above.* 3–7/37.

*****(*) Teddy Wilson 1937–1938**

Classics 548 *Wilson; Harry James, Buck Clayton (t); Bobby Hackett (c); Benny Morton (tb); Pee Wee Russell, Prince Robinson (cl); Johnny Hodges, Tab Smith (as); Gene Sedric, Lester Young, Chu Berry, Vido Musso (ts); Red Norvo (xy); Allan Reuss, Freddie Green (g); Walter Page, Al Hall, John Simmons (b); Johnny Blowers, Jo Jones, Cozy Cole (d); Billie Holiday, Nan Wynn (v).* 9/37–4/38.

****** Teddy Wilson Vol. 5: Blue Mood**

Hep 1035 *As above.* 8/37–1/38.

****** Teddy Wilson 1938**

Classics 556 *Wilson; Jonah Jones, Harry James (t); Bobby Hackett (c); Trummy Young, Benny Morton (tb); Pee Wee Russell (cl); Benny Carter, Johnny Hodges, Toots Mondello, Ted Buckner, Edgar Sampson (as); Lester Young, Herschel Evans, Bud Freeman, Chu Berry, Ben Webster (ts); Allan Reuss, Al Casey (g); Al Hall, John Kirby, Milt Hinton, Walter Page (b); Johnny Blowers, Cozy Cole, Jo Jones (d); Billie Holiday, Nan Wynn (v).* 4–11/38.

****** Moments Like This**

Hep CD 1043 *As above, except add Roy Eldridge (t), Ernie Powell (c).* 3/38–1/39.

This is jazz of such a consistently high level that it seems churlish to offer criticism. The Classics CDs are mainly in pretty good, clean sound, with the occasional track sounding a little starchier: the Hep transfers continue to be our first recommendation, though the Classics 'uniform' editions may appeal more to some collectors. The first 1937 CD is magnificent, the first five sessions as strong in material as they are in performances: 'Mean To Me', 'I'll Get By', 'How Am I To Know?' and more. These are also among Holiday's greatest records. The 1937–8 disc includes the September 1937 session which offered the memorable two-part 'Just A Mood' quartet with Harry James and Red Norvo, as well as a previously rejected date. The 1938 set sees Bobby Hackett arriving to play lead, as well as six solos originally made for the 'Teddy Wilson School For Pianists'. Wilson's mixture of lyricism and vigour is almost unique in the jazz of the period and it suggests a path which jazz doctrine has seldom explored since.

***** Teddy Wilson 1939**

Classics 571 *Wilson; Roy Eldridge, Karl George, Harold 'Shorty' Baker (t); Floyd Brady (tb); Pete Clark (cl, as, bs); Rudy Powell (cl, as); Benny Carter (as, ts); Ben Webster, George Irish (ts); Danny Barker, Al Casey (g); Al Hall, Milt Hinton (b); Cozy Cole, J. C. Heard (d); Billie Holiday, Thelma Carpenter, Jean Eldridge (v).* 1–9/39.

Inevitably, Wilson went on to lead his own big band, and musicians were more than impressed by its secure power and purposeful clarity of tone, a direct extension of Wilson's own manner. But it failed commercially, and its records don't quite match its reputation, largely through charts that are only so-so but which may have come alive in person. The 1939 sides are collected here, along with four more Wilson solos, including a sparkling 'China Boy'.

***** Teddy Wilson 1939–1941**

Classics 620 *Similar to above, except add Doc Cheatham, Bill Coleman (t); Floyd Brady, Benny Morton (tb); Jimmy Hamilton (cl); George James (bs); Eddie Gibbs (g); Yank Porter (d); Helen Ward (v); omit Roy Eldridge, Powell, Barker, Carter, Hinton, Cole, Carpenter, Holiday and Jean Eldridge.* 12/39–4/41.

After two more sessions with the big band, Wilson returned to small groups and then a trio as his last sessions for Columbia. Still not quite up to the impeccable calibre of the earlier dates, but a 1940 session with Bill Coleman and Benny Morton in the front line is fine, and Wilson's solos-with-rhythm maintain his own fierce standards.

***** The Keystone Transcriptions**

Storyville STCD 8258 *Wilson (p solo).* 39–40.

An hour's worth of solo Wilson taken off surviving acetates made for a transcription service. There are 26 pieces, and Wilson fastens on to each in turn, polishes it, drops it in the slot, and moves on. His perfect economy gives a brittle, brilliant quality to the music: the pieces dissolve like ice in a glass. But if he gloves his emotions, there's still a strangely affecting quality to the more wistful melodies, as in 'You're My Favourite Memory'. A modest yet valuable survival.

*****(*) Teddy Wilson 1942–1945**

Classics 908 *Wilson; Emmett Berry, Joe Thomas, Charlie Shavers, Buck Clayton (t); Benny Morton (tb); Edmond Hall (cl); Ben Webster (ts); Remo Palmieri (g); Red Norvo (vib); Al Hall, Billy Taylor, Johnny Williams (b); J. C. Heard, Big Sid Catlett, Specs Powell (d); Helen Ward, Maxine Sullivan (v).* 1/42–8/45.

It starts with a handsome solo on 'These Foolish Things', then moves through various small-group dates for Columbia, V-Disc and his first sessions for Musicraft. The instinctual chemistry of the great '30s sessions is gone, but these are still groups full of fine players, and there are moments to savour: Berry and Morton on 'B Flat Swing', Red Norvo, Maxine Sullivan on 'This Heart Of Mine'. The final date includes Clayton and Webster on four excellent titles.

***** Teddy Wilson 1946**

Classics 997 *Wilson; Buck Clayton (t); Scoville Browne (as, cl); Don Byas, Charlie Ventura (ts); George James (bs); Remo Palmieri (g); Billy Taylor (b); J. C. Heard (d); Sarah Vaughan (v).* 5–11/46.

Wilson's Musicraft sessions are tarnished by their indifferent piano-sound, and some of his subtlety is lost. But there are nevertheless 14 handsome solos collected here, four titles by an octet with Clayton and Byas, and four by a quartet with Ventura. Sarah Vaughan sings on four tracks; 'Penthouse Serenade' is gorgeous, and the horns are splendid on 'I Want To Be Happy'.

***** The Alternative Takes Vol. 1 1934-1941**

Neatwork RP 2021 *As various discs above.* 5/34–4/41.

*****(*) The Alternative Takes Vol. 2 1938-1945**

Neatwork RP 2032 *As various discs above.* 4/38–8/45.

The first volume starts with Wilson's first solo session (in poor sound), and from there goes through various small-band dates, two sides by his orchestra, and a group of alternates from his beautiful 1941 dates for Columbia. Three alternates of Earl Hines's 'Rosetta' are among the tracks of particular interest: while his time remains pretty constant, each take is very different from the others in the detail of his playing. As fastidious as he was, Wilson was also a real improviser. The 11 April session carries over into Volume 2, where a romping 'China Boy' gets as far as take seven: it's hard to see why so many takes were made when there seems to be little wrong with any of them. Thereafter there are alternates from Commodore and Musicraft, before the chronology reverts to 1938 and takes in eight tracks from Wilson's 'School For Pianists' sessions. Reproduction is, as usual with this series, a very mixed bag indeed, but there's so much to enjoy – especially on the second disc – that Wilson admirers will certainly want to investigate.

***** And Then They Wrote... / Mr Wilson And Mr Gershwin**
Collectables COL-CD-6680 *Wilson; Major Holley, Arvell Shaw (b); Bert Dahlander (d).* 1-12/59.

Two of Wilson's Columbia albums at last given a CD reissue. The LP era and its expansive approach to performance-duration didn't seem to make much difference to the pianist: every one of these 24 tracks plays out to 78-side length (although 'I Got Rhythm' is wrongly listed on the sleeve as lasting eight minutes!), and this crisp despatch became characteristic of Wilson's diffident approach to his latter-day record-making. Columbia didn't give him a very interesting brief: the first LP is devoted to familiar jazz hits of the order of 'Rosetta' and 'Honeysuckle Rose', and the second is all Gershwin. Wilson works through it all as if he's skimming stones on water, and with the rhythm section keeping simple time, it's all quietly enjoyable and not very memorable.

**** Teddy Wilson Meets Eiji Kitamura**
Storyville STCD 4152 *Wilson; Eiji Kitamura (cl); Ichiro Masuda (vib); Masanaga Harada (b); Buffalo Bill Robinson (d).* 10/70.

***** With Billie In Mind**
Chiaroscuro CRD III *Wilson.* 5/72.

Despite the Collectables issue listed above, Columbia and Verve should be doing something about reissuing Wilson's late-'50s sessions (Mosaic has done a boxed set of some of them). Until then, there is still a significant gap in the discography, which picks up with these various dates from the late '60s onwards. Wilson's later music is frequently disappointing in the light of his earlier achievements. Lacking any commitment from a major label, he seemed to wander from session to session with a sometimes cynical approach to the occasion, careless of the company and relying on an inner light which had long since burned down to a routine. Only when a sympathetic producer was on hand did Wilson raise his game, and the solo records listed above include some of the best music of his later albums. *With Billie In Mind* is devoted to material he had recorded with Holiday in the '30s, and its graceful, characteristic atmosphere makes for a special occasion. Six titles are added to the original LP issue. The other record is eminently missable. Eiji Kitamura and his companions trade mostly in second-hand swing, and Wilson hardly raises his game.

***** Teddy Wilson And His All Stars**
Chiaroscuro CR(D) 150 *Wilson; Harry 'Sweets' Edison (t); Vic Dickenson (tb); Bob Wilber (cl, ss); Major Holley (b); Oliver Jackson (d).* 6/76.

A rare example of Wilson leading an American small group. It might have been a little classic, but something's wrong. Bobby Hackett was supposed to play on the date, but he died; Edison, his substitute, is too louche for the occasion. Wilber's arrangements are a shade too clever, and some of the tempos are too fast. But on a few slow ones, where Dickenson can stretch out, and Wilson seems to peer through from the back (the studio sound isn't very good, either), it sounds much better.

***** Masters Of Jazz Vol. 11: Teddy Wilson**
Storyville STCD 4111 *Wilson; Jesper Lundgaard, Niels-Henning Orsted Pedersen (b); Bjarne Rostvold, Ed Thigpen (d).* 12/68–6/80.

***** Alone**
Storyville STCD 8211 *Wilson (p solo).* 5/83.

Wilson carried on working into the '80s, and these are among his final recordings. He still sounds much as he did nearly 50 years before – sometimes more professionally detached, occasionally quietly enjoying his own wisdom. The material on the *Masters Of Jazz* disc – drawn from two trio dates 12 years apart – is still heavily reliant on the '30s standards which Wilson always stood by. As good as anything he recorded later in life. *Alone* was cut at a Danish concert. The normally taciturn pianist talks between some of the tunes, and he sounds in amiable spirits on some of his favourites, though the location sound and the piano itself seem no more than adequate.

Lem Winchester (1928–61)

VIBRAPHONE

Of all jazz's casualties, Winchester is one of the saddest, not because he mortgaged his life to drugs or liquor, but because he died in a pointless firearm accident on the brink of success. A Delaware police officer, he had been only an amateur player until the first of these brought him both critical acclaim and awards.

**** Winchester Special**
Original Jazz Classics OJC 1719 *Winchester; Benny Golson (ts); Tommy Flanagan (p); Wendell Marshall (b); Art Taylor (d).* 9/59.

**** Lem's Beat**
Original Jazz Classics OJC 1785 *Winchester; Curtis Peagler (as); Oliver Nelson (ts); Billy Brown (g); Roy Johnson (p); Wendell Marshall (b); Art Taylor (d).* 4/60.

****(*) Another Opus**
Original Jazz Classics OJC 1816 *Winchester; Frank Wess (f); Hank Jones (p); Johnny Hammond Smith (org); Eddie McFadden (g); Eddie Jones, Wendell Marshall (b); Bill Erskine, Gus Johnson (d).* 6–10/60.

***** With Feeling**
Original Jazz Classics OJC 1900 *Winchester; Richard Wyands (p); George Duvivier (b); Roy Haynes (d).* 10/60.

Winchester's vibes playing is vigorous enough, if sometimes flat-footed, but he is one of those players who tend to be comprehensively upstaged by their sidemen. Golson's gruff, argumentative tenor on the first record and Nelson's loamy sound on the second create most of the interest, and Wess, still an underrated exponent of the flute, is as interesting as always on *Another Opus*. The rhythm section on *Lem's Beat* and the bonus 'Lid Flippin'' on the third record hint at some of the forthcoming extroversions of soul-jazz without quite leaving hard-bop routine behind. The leader's solo spots on 'Friendly Persuasion' and 'Lady Day' are exquisite, but it's always been a little hard to be excited about a player whose moment seemed to have passed almost before anyone registered he was there.

Only the final album in the group, the most recent to make the transfer to CD, prompts any substantial reassessment. Abandoning the larger-scale arrangements he got from Oliver Nelson, Lem concentrates on a small-group blowing session and generates a joyous mood on 'Skylark' and 'But Beautiful'. Wyands is as immaculate as ever, punching out solid, blocky chords round the vibes, while Duvivier and Haynes keep the boilers stoked. Winchester's death was a loss to the music and to the truncated history of jazz vibes, but even now he sounds like a minor talent.

Kai Winding (1922–83)

TROMBONE, TROMBONIUM

Winding was born in Denmark and came to America in his early teens. He was around to see the birth of bebop and helped to devise a fast, clear-toned delivery for the trombone, a development which also had an impact on how the horn sections of big bands could sound. His long partnership with J. J. Johnson is definitive of the modern history of the instrument.

***** Kai And Jay And Bennie Green With Strings**
Original Jazz Classics OJCCD 1727 *Winding; Bennie Green, J. J. Johnson (tb); Dick Katz, John Malachi (p); Peck Morrison, Tommy Potter (b); Al Harewood, Osie Johnson (d); strings.* 8/52, 12/54.

*****(*) Nuf Said**
Rhino 75995 *Winding; J. J. Johnson (tb); Dick Katz (p); Tommy Potter (b); Al Harewood (d).* 55.

***** Jive At Five**
Status DSTS 1012 *Winding; Carl Fontana, Wayne Andre (tb, trombonium); Dick Lieb (btb, trombonium); Roy Frazee (p); Kenny O'Brien (b); Tom Montgomery (d).* 6/57.

***** Cleveland June 1957**
Storyville 8263 *As above.* 6/57.

The success of Jay and Kai was, in the end, not altogether equitably shared. J. J. Johnson's unchallenged dominance on the trombone as a bop voice was always questionable. Where J.J. brought a saxophone-like articulation to the instrument, it was Winding who showed how it could follow the woodwind players' fast vibrato and percussive attack and still retain its distinctive character. While with the Kenton band, Winding worked out ways of producing a very tight vibrato with the lip rather than using the slide, and this had a marked impact on a younger generation of players. A lot of the surviving Winding material is on discs also featuring J.J., Bennie Green and others, and more can be found under J.J.'s entry. Early on, though, the balance of innovation seemed to fall to the Dane. The sessions from 1952 and 1954 are important not so much for the lush and overcooked tracks with strings as for the later pairing of Jay and Kai in a quintet format. These cuts established a formula which was to become uniquely successful, though it may have hampered both men subsequently. Winding's compositions, 'Wind Bag' and 'Don't Argue', suggest that he was also a deft composer with a quirky approach to harmony and a fuller understanding than most of his employers and colleagues of the value of his rapid-fire attack and clean-edged delivery.

Nuf Said is a valuable reissue, capturing the partnership at its most confident, but in this format also showing how much hard work went on in the studio to perfect the elegantly choreographed sound. There are seven alternative takes, including versions of 'Lover' and 'It's All Right With Me' which seriously rival the release numbers. The quintet had a settled sound by this point, but there is no mistaking that the main action lies with the two front men, and even the agile Katz is given little of moment to do except comp and fill.

The 1957 records are under Winding's sole leadership. His stint with Kenton had convinced him that massed trombones made the noise closest to the angels and he persisted with the choral approach. Here it works very well indeed; though some will be put off by what might be thought to be Kentonisms, they should be assured that the idiom and the arrangements are Winding's own. The key tracks are an original blues and a thoroughly wonderful version of 'In A Sentimental Mood' in which the voicings could hardly be bettered. The Cleveland set is a club recording and there is a degree of background distraction, but the performances are good and, though this overlaps somewhat with the other set, it is nicely mastered and fans of Kai's approach will enjoy the experience. There remains through it all something a little cold about Winding's work. Certainly, compared to J.J., he couldn't give a ballad more than a gruff expressiveness, but that was not his forte. What he did, he did well, and he deserves more credit for it.

***** Bone Appetit: The Definitive Black & Blue Sessions**
Black & Blue BB 955 2 *Winding; Curtis Fuller (tb); Hank Jones (p); John Clayton (b); Jimmy Cobb (d).* 7/80.

This catches Winding three years from his death and in league with one of the leading trombonists of a somewhat younger generation. Fuller's association with John Coltrane on *Blue Train* has rather distorted perceptions of his stylistic debts. Here, he sounds perfectly consistent with Kai's drily swinging approach and well up to speed with the older man's ultra-fast delivery on tunes like 'Niçoise' of which two takes are included.

The disc restores all of the material recorded at Black & Blue's outdoor studio in Paris. The sound is clear and natural and the trombones are very well captured. Fuller's original title-tune is instantly appealing and beautifully played. 'La Valse Bonita' is equally delicious, with some wonderfully detailed interplay between the horns. Jones is a master in settings like this and his comping is subtle and gracious from start to finish. A valuable addition to the discography of both men and a useful document in the somewhat undersubscribed canon of modern trombone playing.

Norma Winstone (born 1941)

VOCALS

Studied in London and became associated with the new British jazz of the '60s, singing in a variety of mainstream-to-modern situations. Her coming out was at Ronnie Scott's, opening for Roland Kirk. Formed Azimuth with former husband John Taylor and Kenny Wheeler in the '70s and has continued to broaden her scope of associations. An unassuming virtuoso.

****** Edge Of Time**
Disconforme 148 *Winstone; Henry Lowther, Kenny Wheeler (t, flhn); Malcolm Griffiths, Chris Pyne, Paul Rutherford (tb); Mike Osborne (as, cl); Alan Skidmore (ts); Art Themen (bs); John Taylor (p); Gary Boyle (g); Chris Laurence (b); Tony Levin (d).* 71.

Winstone's first entry on Mike Westbrook's remarkable road-movie of an album, *Metropolis*, is one of the most breathtaking in contemporary jazz, a pure, reed-like tone that suddenly rises up out of the growling 'male' horns. One of the things that makes Winstone so exceptional as a singer is her equal confidence with pure abstraction (as in much of her work with Azimuth) and the most straightforward vocal line. Like Karin Krog in Norway, she is a fine musician in her own right, a sensitive lyricist as well as an imaginative standards singer.

Originally issued on Argo, Winstone's debut as leader is still a breathtaking experience. As on *Metropolis*, much of the drama on *Edge Of Time* comes from her crystalline voice swooping in and out of the horns. The title-track begins slow and abstractly, almost as if caught out of time itself and then the *rubato* begins to organize itself until the song runs along a big band line that would satisfy Duke Ellington. The big piece of the album is the joyous and forthright 'Enjoy This Day', where subtle dissonance brings a hint of anxiety, almost foreboding to an otherwise upbeat tune; Kenny Wheeler's solo is superb and one can clearly hear the dynamic Winstone established with the trumpeter and with pianist Taylor, later to be her husband; his harmonic awareness comes across in every bar. In contrast to 'Enjoy This Day', 'Erebus, Son of Chaos' ought to be dark and brooding, but comes across rather jolly. The only weak point is the brief 'Songs For A Child', though this pure-voice balladry has influenced some surprising artists since 1971. A terrific record and definitely the place to start investigating Winstone's wonderful work.

*****(*) Live At Roccella Jonica**

Splasc(h) 508 *Winstone; Paolo Fresu, Kenny Wheeler (t, flhn); John Taylor (p); Paolo Damiani (b); Tony Oxley (d).* 84.

Little-known, but definitely worth searching out, this powerful group offered Winstone a perfect setting: harmonically sophisticated, rhythmically strong and, given the two-trumpet front line, lots of melodic drama as well. The main piece is an astonishing 23-minute improvisation, 'Rumori Mediterranei', which sees the group working with almost telepathic understanding. Taylor and Oxley are like good and wicked angels, the one cajoling gently, the other tempting, caressing his kit and then jangling it dangerously. Damiani, one of the key figures in Italian jazz, isn't especially well recorded but he's audibly at the heart of things. Fresu and Wheeler play a similar role: Fresu rawer but also more sentimental, Wheeler outwardly soft but with an iron core – his 'The Widow In The Window', segued with 'Mark Time', is the highlight of the first half of a marvellous concert recording.

*****(*) Somewhere Called Home**

ECM 1337 *Winstone; Tony Coe (cl, ts); John Taylor (p).* 7/86.

*****(*) Well Kept Secret**

Hot House HHCD 1015 *Winstone; Stacey Rowles (flhn); Jimmy Rowles (p); George Mraz (b); Joe LaBarbera (d).* 10/93.

***** ... Like Song, Like Weather**

Enodoc ENOCD 002 *Winstone; John Taylor (p).* 3/96.

***** Manhattan In The Rain**

Enodoc ENOCD 001 *Winstone; Tony Coe (ts, cl); Steve Gray (p, syn); Chris Laurence (b).* 3/97.

Somewhere Called Home is a more-than-acceptable sample of Winstone's atmospheric approach. It takes a certain amount of brass neck to include 'Hi Lili Hi Lo' and 'Tea For Two' on a set like this. Coe and Taylor are able and sensitive partners, but one wonders whether it wouldn't have come off better with just Taylor's thoughtful accompaniments.

The title of *Well Kept Secret* just about says it all. This finds Winstone where she should be (no disrespect to Taylor *et al*), working with an international musician of Rowles's quality. 'A Timeless Place' is gorgeous, with its Winstone lyric to the celebrated 'Peacocks' melody, and 'A Flower Is A Lovesome Thing' is fragile and delicate without giving any sense that it will be easy to pull apart.

The security of the secret is underlined by the fact that little has been added to Winstone's catalogue. *Manhattan In The Rain* and ... *Like Song, Like Weather* stray perilously close to the Radio 2 strain. These seem to have been released out of chronological sequence. The duo album has a quiet grace but little dramatic tension. 'I Loves You Porgy' is perhaps too polite a reading to be quite convincing, and both Winstone and her playing partner sound easier when the material is slightly quirkier, as on 'Carla's Blues' (aka Carla Bley's 'Sing Me Softly Of The Blues') and 'Tango Beyond', the latter co-written with Tony Coe. *Manhattan* is another set of light-textured standards opening on a high with Lerner and Loewe's 'The Heather On The Hill', but rarely reaching such heights again. The album seems to be dedicated to the memory of Tom Jobim and Elis Regina; but there's little in a groove that would suggest they are a major influence, and Winstone's reading of 'Retrato Em Branco E Petro' is very much in her own voice, and not a version of someone else's. Coe is underused (his clarinet line on 'The Heather' is breathtaking) and the absence of a percussionist softens the edges almost too much. Here and there a more emphatic attack might have helped. It is time this magisterial singer was given a secure and prolific recording base.

Jens Winther (born 1960)

TRUMPET, FLUGELHORN

Danish trumpeter with wide international experience.

****(*) Looking Through**

Storyville STCD 4127 *Winther; Tomas Franck (ts); Thomas Clausen (p); Jesper Lundgaard (b); Alex Riel (d).* 4/88.

*****(*) Scorpio Dance**

Storyville STCD 4179 *Winther; Tomas Franck (ts); Ben Besiakov (p); Lennart Ginman (b); Al Foster (d).* 3/91.

***** The Four Elements**

Stunt 19802 *Winther; Michael Molhede, Andreas Pesendorfer, Duncan Mackay, Kornel Kovacs, Rich Nichols, Justin Mullens, Mick Ball (t); Peter Dahlgren, Nichol Thomson, Werner Wurm, Aurelio Santoro (tb); Mattias Jacobson (btb); David Liebman (ss); James Knight, Hagai Amir (as); Felix Petry, Bruno Brochet (ts); Idrikis Veitners (bs); Pessi Levanto (p); Tadao Tsujikawa (syn); Jacco Griekspoor (vib); Carballo Serafin (g); Jacon Jensen (b); Eric Garland (d); Agnes Heginger, Eri Matsubara, Carolina Saboia, Waltraud Kottler, Dorothy Murphy (v).* 7/96.

Winther has the confidence to play either tight, modern, hard bop or a more free-thinking, if fundamentally conservative, kind of improvisation. He can sustain long solos, but his ballad statements or flugelhorn lead on the likes of 'Ubataba', on the first record, are just as revealing. The earlier session is solid Danish jazz, but it could have lost a couple of tracks and been the better for it: Lundgaard and Riel don't sound terribly interested for once, and Clausen's frequent use of a Fender Rhodes electric piano lends a somewhat dated feel to the sound. *Scorpio Dance* is sharper all round. The sound is crisper, if a little dry, and Foster's presence (at Winther's own invitation) is inspirational, with the drummer on tirelessly inventive form. The two long tracks, 'Scorpio Dance' and 'Tree Of Life', bring out terrific solos from Winther, and there is a probing trumpet–drums duet on 'Intimy'. Ginman is lost in the mix, but otherwise the group sound very alert, and Besiakow sensibly takes much more of a back seat than Clausen did on the earlier record.

The big-band record for Stunt is hugely ambitious. It features members of the International Association Of Schools Of Jazz Orchestra, founded by Dave Liebman, which rehearsed Winther's four-part work while working on a cruise ship; it delivered this performance for the 1996 Copenhagen Festival. Winther is principal soloist, Liebman chips in with a terrific solo on 'Fire', and the music is a polymorphous assemblage of styles – Gil Evans veils of sound, Palle Mikkelborg funk, various odds and ends from the big-band tradition. The enthusiasm of the players seems boundless, and if it may not stand up to minute examination it's surely an entertaining show.

****(*) Standards**
Stunt STUCD 00062 *Winther; Lennart Ginman (b); Søren Christensen (d).* 11/99.

***** Walk The Walk Talk The Talk**
Stunt STUCD 01172 *Winther; Claus Waidtløw (saxes); Anders Lindvall (g); Kasper Vadsholt (b); Jeppe Grame (d).* 6/01.

Recorded at the Copenhagen Jazzhouse, with a reserved crowd in attendance, *Standards* is very routine. Winther brings little that's new to material which is all too familiar, and he's dangerously exposed in this setting. Ginman and Christensen sound in great heart, though.

The next one is all muscle, sweat and shouting. The rhythm section play like they're ready for the Mahavishnu revival, Lindwall is all rock over jazz, and the horns keep getting cut up on the curves. There are two enormously long pieces, 'Clear Lydian Sky' and 'The Afghan Road', which kindle the intermittent fire of old-fashioned fusion. It's a rather curious move for the trumpeter, especially since he makes only a modest impression on his surroundings, but some of the music has a heated, sometimes exhausted sense of exhilaration about it.

Christine Wodrascka

PIANO

Improvising pianist drawing on free and composed forms alike.

****** Vertical**
FMP CD 79 *Wodrascka (p solo).* 6/95.

From the interrupted cakewalk of 'Vocalises' to the prepared-piano harshness of 'Vaudevillesque', Wodrascka's 12 pieces for the keyboard have a bewitching variety and spontaneity about them, even as they seem composed and complete. Nothing here rambles or outstays its welcome: even the slow development of 'Voyage Intervisceral', full of glowering bass-register sonorities, seems to last as long as it ought to. Jazz is clearly only a part of her vocabulary, which suggests a synthesis of many strands of composition and improvisation, but Wodrascka moves confidently through her options; she can also be very funny.

***** Aux Portes Du Matin**
Leo LR 318 *Wodrascka; Ramon Lopez (d).* 11/00.

Like Sylvie Courvoisier, Wodrascka suggests several musical disciplines in her playing, but unlike Courvoisier she has no apparent struggle between them – it's just a flowing intermingling of idioms. The problem here, though, is Lopez, who instead of being a useful duet partner simply gets in the way a lot of the time, and some of the prepared-piano sections are a racket. In clearer space, Wodrascka still delivers some fascinating music.

Nils Wogram (born 1975)

TROMBONE

German trombonist who studied for three years in New York, 1992–4, now making records in various Euro-American situations.

***** New York Conversations**
Mons 874658 *Wogram; Kenny Werner (p); Brad Shoeppach (g); Doug Weiss (b); Owen Howard (d).* 4/94.

***** Speed Life**
Enja 9346-2 *Wogram; Simon Nabatov (p); Nicolas Thys (b); Jochen Rückert (d).* 12/97.

Wogram's music is like he sounds: big, brassy, confident. The groups on these dates follow as keenly as they can. He isn't afraid of free, open space: 'Newsed', on *Speed Life*, makes the most of a seemingly themeless environment, and the four-way contrapuntalism of 'Annoying Neighbour', later on the same record, is a complex idea delivered with punch and panache. His phrasing has a vocalist's touch, full of human colour, shouting interpolations, grunts and occasional snarls, but always pushing quickly onwards to the next idea: he doesn't hang around. Nabatov, who likes a challenge, is a more than suitable partner on the Enja album, and they have a rapport which is sometimes striking, sometimes a bit mysterious. The tunes here are rather oblique, though: Wogram's originals are clever, but perhaps not quite as personalized as they should be, and the record runs out of light here and there.

The Mons album was made when Wogram was still only 21. His playing is full of zing, and the solos have a boppish zip to them that he seems to have subsequently toned down in favour of a more expressionist approach. His team are splendid: Werner, who doesn't know how to play indifferently, is full of ideas from his mercurial solo on the opening 'Brazil' onwards.

*****(*) Serious Fun**
CIMP 212 *Wogram; Conrad Bauer (tb).* 9/99.

***** Serious Fun + One**
CIMP 221 *As above, except add Dominic Duval (b).* 9/99.

Wogram steps over into free playing entirely – and with one of the great trombone masters of the idiom to boot. Exploring harmonics and overtones, counterpoint, dialogue, dynamics, space, compression, melody, volume and quiet, they rattle through 16 individual pieces. Like most such records, the listener needs a taste for it, but with playing of this quality (and they even make it easier for the wary, slicing the music into small and digestible episodes), the music stands very tall.

When Duval joins in, the music gathers extra weight but loses a lot of its bite. Duval's effects cloud the air and often obscure what the trombones are doing, making the music seem a lot more difficult than it actually is. But there are still some very fetching pieces, especially the simple sonorities of 'Country Ballad'.

****** Odd And Awkward**

Enja 9416-2 2CD *Wogram; Cuong Vu (t); Hayden Chisholm (as, cl); Chris Speed (ts, cl); Steffen Schorn (bs, bcl, cbcl, af); Simon Nabatov (p); Henning Sieverts (b); Jochen Rückert (d). 6/00.*

A feast of group music, split between one disc for sextet and another for the full octet. The initial surprise is that the two 'missing' instruments are piano and bass, which leaves five horns and drums to negotiate the eventful twists and turns of the first half. Wogram continually varies the pace and weight of each piece, breaking it into solos, duets, duets plus charts, with and without drums, and the full group roaring through a thicket as dense as 'Children's Hunt' or 'Tea Time Part II' as if they were clearing it with machetes. He has a team of superbly expressive players to make it all happen and comes up with ingenious pairings: listen to Vu's snickering volleys mixed with Schorn's contrabass clarinet on 'Spring Part I'.

The second disc sounds more conventionally orchestrated and loses a degree of rasp and snap. But it's hardly any less inventive. Sometimes Wogram sounds like he's unspooling an endless melody line, often over shifting harmonic banks that have a big band's richness of tonal colour. Kudos to Rückert for keeping the whole thing swinging and the momentum flowing – a less proactive drummer might have turned a lot of the music into an overcoloured sludge. But this is a marvellous entry all round, and certainly Wogram's magnum opus so far.

****** Root 70**

2nd Floor 008 *Wogram; Hayden Chisholm (as, bcl); Matt Penman (b); Jochen Rückert (d). 11/00.*

Paring back to a quartet, Wogram continues in top form. This band is all wheeling, whizzing agility. The leader's own playing is so fast and accurate, in terms of getting notes out of the horn and getting them to hit the target, that it leaves the listener breathless. Yet he doesn't skimp on the expressive edge which gave the earlier records their pungency. Chisholm is comparably quick, a tad less vocalized, but his beautifully clear sound moves through the demanding tunes like quicksilver. Penman and the faithful Rückert spin appositely elegant rhythms around the horns, and it's often as if there are two separate teams, dancing balletically in their own right yet interacting with precise synchronicity. Oliver Bergner (working in Cologne) gives them a beautiful sound. The tunes – six by Wogram, with two pieces from Chisholm bookending either side of the record – are bright, funny and ripe with long, long melodies. Terrific!

Booty Wood (1919–87)

TROMBONE

Born Mitchell Bootie, and a Dayton, Ohio man to the core, Booty was Ellington's plunger mute specialist, a speciality act that perhaps eclipsed his charm on the open horn.

*****(*) Chelsea Bridge**

Black & Blue 914 *Wood; Cat Anderson (t); Norris Turney (as); Harold Ashby (ts); Raymond Fol (p); Aaron Bell (b); Sam Woodyard (d). 7/78.*

Booty gave himself to the Ellington band heart and soul and like many of his peers could never quite extricate himself from its heavy gravity. Here, with the exception of local man Fol, he's surrounded by Ellingtonians for a date heavily marked by the Duke's spirit. There are a dozen or more dates like this in the Black & Blue catalogue, a lifesaving gig for many players at this time, but there are few more delightful than this one. Freed from the sterner disciplines of the orchestra, everyone relaxes and plays for fun. Anderson is obviously liberated from his role as high wire man and plays some fine middle-register stuff. Turney and Ashby weave together sinuously and the rhythm section never drops the pace for a moment.

Phil Woods (born 1931)

ALTO AND SOPRANO SAXOPHONES, CLARINET, BASS CLARINET, VOCAL

Toured with big bands before much small-group work in the '50s, forming a two-alto band with Gene Quill in 1957. Then more big-band work and many, many studio sessions in the '60s. Formed European Rhythm Machine quartet while living in Paris. Returned to USA in early '70s and has since run his own quintet for many years, touring and recording regularly. A master of unadorned bebop alto, his unstinting allegiance to the Parker method has been deepened by persistence and a bottomless appetite for playing.

*****(*) Pot Pie**

Original Jazz Classics 1881 *Woods; Jon Eardley (t); George Syran (p); Teddy Kotick (b); Nick Stabulas (d). 10/54–2/55.*

***** Woodlore**

Original Jazz Classics OJC 052 *Woods; John Williams (p); Teddy Kotick (b); Nick Stabulas (d). 11/55.*

***** Pairing Off**

Original Jazz Classics OJC 092 *Woods; Donald Byrd, Kenny Dorham (t); Gene Quill (as); Tommy Flanagan (p); Doug Watkins (b); Philly Joe Jones (d). 6/56.*

****(*) The Young Bloods**

Original Jazz Classics OJC 1732 *Woods; Donald Byrd (t); Al Haig (p); Teddy Kotick (b); Charli Persip (d). 11/56.*

****(*) Four Altos**

Original Jazz Classics OJC 1734 *Woods; Gene Quill, Sahib Shihab, Hal Stein (as); Mal Waldron (p); Tommy Potter (b); Louis Hayes (d). 2/57.*

*****(*) Phil & Quill**

Original Jazz Classics OJC 215 *Woods; Gene Quill (as); George Syran (p); Teddy Kotick (b); Nick Stabulas (d). 3/57.*

***** Sugan**

Original Jazz Classics OJC 1841 *Woods; Ray Copeland (t); Red Garland (p); Teddy Kotick (b); Nick Stabulas (d). 7/57.*

Phil Woods has never seemed like a beginner. He sprang into his recording career. Tone, speed of execution and ideas were all first-hand borrowings from bebop and, inevitably, Parker; but he sounded like a mature player from the first, and he has often suffered from a degree of neglect, both as a young musician and as a senior one. A series of Prestige dates from the '50s have never exactly been collectors' pieces, but they deserve a fresh appraisal in their OJC incarnations. *Pot Pie* was his first disc as a leader, and it wears very well. Eardley contributes three angular originals and his clean, clear sound is a pleasing foil for the alto-man, who actually sounds rather less in debt to Bird than he sometimes did later. The solos on the title-track and 'Mad About The Boy' have an inquiring bent that belies Woods's rep as an inflexible speedster. *Woodlore* too is a relatively quiet business, and it's the prettiness of his sound that impresses on 'Be My Love' and 'Falling In Love All Over Again'; but 'Get Happy' is a burner. The rhythm section, with Williams sometimes barely in touch, is less impressive.

Pairing Off and *Four Altos* milk the jam-session format which was beloved by Prestige at the time, and both dates come off better than most. *Pairing Off* features a couple of crackerjack blues in the title-tune and 'Stanley The Steamer', and only Byrd's relative greenness lets the side down; Philly Joe is superbly inventive at the kit. *Four Altos* is an idea that ought to pall quickly, but the enthusiasm of Woods and Quill in particular elevates the makeshift charts into something worthwhile. They made a very fine team: *Phil & Quill* doesn't have an ounce of spare fat in the solos, and the spanking delivery on, say, 'A Night At St Nick's' is as compelling as anything Prestige were recording at the period. Quill's duskier tone and more extreme intensities are barely a beat behind Woods's in terms of quality of thought (they also have two tracks on the subsequent compilation, *Bird Feathers*, OJC 1735 CD). *The Young Bloods*, although interesting for a rare 1950s appearance by Al Haig, is beset by the familiar problem of Byrd's lack of authority, and sparks never fly between the horns the way Woods would probably have wished. *Sugan* is an attractive meeting with Red Garland and it has some gripping moments, although the reliance on bebop staples and occasionally rote delivery suggest that the date could have used more preparation.

*** At The Montreux Jazz Festival

Verve 065512-2 *Woods; George Gruntz (p); Henri Texier (b); Daniel Humair (d).* 6/69.

This was a hit group at European festivals at the time, and they played a typically boisterous set here. The long pieces sometimes get bogged down in note-spinning, but it's passionately done in its way. The live sound is okay.

*** Round Trip

Verve 559804-2 *Woods; orchestra, including Thad Jones (t), Jimmy Cleveland (tb), Jerry Dodgion, Jerome Richardson (reeds, f); Herbie Hancock, Roland Hanna (p), Richard Davis (b), Grady Tate (d); strings.* 7/69.

At least this fills part of what is a huge gap in the Woods discography. Woods himself turned his hand to many of the arrangements and, although weighed down with strings and some questionable originals ('Love Song For Dead Ché'?), the record manages to be appealingly pretty as well as regularly torched by the unfettered Woods alto. Listen to his tumultuous solo on 'Here's That Rainy Day' as one example.

*** Quartet Volume One: A Live Recording

Clean Cuts CCD 702 *Woods; Mike Melillo (p); Steve Gilmore (b); Bill Goodwin (d).* 5/79.

A huge jump in the discography: Woods was frequently in the studios in the '60s but usually for other leaders, and his '70s albums for RCA and Muse are out of print. This on-the-hoof live date from Austin, Texas, catches his then-current quartet in thoughtful form. A relaxed, almost pensive set features nearly as much Melillo and Gilmore as Woods, and the leader is a little more laid-back than usual.

CORE COLLECTION

**** Phil Woods/Lew Tabackin

Evidence ECD 22209-2 *Woods; Lew Tabackin (ts); Jimmy Rowles (p); Michael Moore (b); Bill Goodwin (d).* 12/80.

Available briefly as a Japanese vinyl release, this is a great favourite of ours and we are delighted to see it on CD at last. There can be few more rambunctious jazz records made at that time: in what is a good-natured cutting contest between two masters of bebop saxophone, they have at it for a glorious 58 minutes (there's an alternative take of 'Theme Of No Repeat'). One could argue that everything that has to be said is said in the first eight minutes, a 'Limehouse Blues' that takes the roof off – but, for the sheer ebullience of blowing on the changes, there are few better records than this. The terrific rhythm-section is, in the circumstances, a delightful bonus.

**** Integrity

Red 123177-2 2CD *Woods; Tom Harrell (t, flhn); Hal Galper (p); Steve Gilmore (b); Bill Goodwin (d).* 4/84.

This became a firm line-up, and any who heard the group in concert will surely want this live record. Harrell had worked for some years as a freelance in search of a context, and with Woods he secured a precise focus: the material here is a connoisseur's choice of jazz themes – including Neal Hefti's 'Repetition', Ellington's 'Azure', Wayne Shorter's 'Infant Eyes' and Sam Rivers's '222' – mediated through a very clear-headed approach to modern bop playing. Harrell's lucid tone and nimble, carefully sifted lines are as piquant a contrast with Woods as one could wish, without creating any clashes of temperament. Galper's pensiveness is occasionally a fraction too laid-back, but he moves as one with bass and drums. Woods himself assumes a role both paternal and sporting, stating themes and directions with unswerving authority but still taking risky routes to resolving an idea: his solo on Charlie Mariano's 'Blue Walls', for instance, is rhythmically as daring as any of his early work. Good in-concert recording.

***(*) Heaven

Evidence ECD 22148-2 *As above.* 12/84.

This was one of the great touring and recording bands of the '80s, Harrell and Woods inspiring each other and the rhythm section inquiring and swinging. Woods didn't need to change anything about his own style, but it blossoms anew in counterpoint with Harrell's lyrical fire, and each album is handsomely programmed and delivered. However, with Concord deleting all their Woods holdings, there's not much around now. *Heaven* suffers just slightly from a clattery sound, but the material – two Ellington tunes, Brubeck's 'The Duke', another skintight treatment of Sam Rivers's '222' and a completely unorthodox 'I'm Getting Sentimental Over You' – overcomes.

*** Embraceable You

Philology 214 W 25 *Woods; Marco Tamburini, Flavio Boltro, Paolo Fresu (t, flhn); Danilo Terenzi, Hal Crook, Roberto Rossi (tb); Giancarlo Maurino (ss, as); Mario Raja (ss, ts); Maurizio Giammarco (ts); Roberto Ottini (bs); Danilo Rea (ky); Enzo Pietropaoli (b); Roberto Gatto (d).* 7/88.

A passionate mess. Nothing wrong with the calibre of the band – these are some of Italy's finest. Woods, too, is in strong form and occasionally reaches exalted heights: the reading of 'Embraceable You', characterized with the purplest of prose in the sleeve-notes, is almost as good as the producer makes out. But Mario Raja's arrangements are cumbersome, the band seem under-rehearsed, and the studio sound is hopelessly ill-focused: Paolo Piangiarelli may be a great fan, but he should entrust production duties to someone else.

*** Phil On Etna

Philology W 38/39 2CD *Woods; Giovanni La Ferlita, Mario Cavallaro, Giuseppe Privitera, Enzo Gulizia (t); Camillo Pavone, Paul Zelig Rodberg, Benvenuto Ramaci (tb); Salvo Di Stefano (btb); Carlo Cattano, Umberto Di Pietro (as); Salvo Famiani, Ercole Tringale (ts); Anthony Russo (bs); Giuseppe Emmanuele (p); Nello Toscano (b); Pucci Nicosia (d); Antonella Consolo (v).* 3/89.

Another extravagant set from Philology, compiling 100 minutes of music from a concert with the Catania City Brass Orkestra, a young big band following up a week's tuition under Woods's direction. They're eager to please, and Woods himself plays with astonishing commitment as featured soloist throughout: several of the improvisations here rank with anything he's recorded in recent years. But the band lack any notable finesse and, faced with a demanding chart such as 'Pink Sunrise', they're audibly struggling. The few other soloists play with the trepidation of keen but bashful students. Good live sound, though.

*** Elsa

Philology W 206-2 *Woods; Enrico Pieranunzi (p).* 7/91.

Elsa is from an Italian concert. While Pieranunzi listens and follows intently, Woods goes his own way, so the interactive elements are all in one direction. Philology's warts-and-all presentation, intent on capturing every note, also lets the impact of the music falter, since 78 minutes is really too much of a good thing in less than perfect sound. But there is still much vivid and inimitable playing: the title-tune and the following shift into 'Some Day My Prince Will Come' are full of great alto-playing.

*** Phil's Mood

Philology W 207-2 *Woods; Enrico Pieranunzi (p); Enzo Pietropaoli (b); Alfred Kramer (d).* 90.

**(*) Live At The Corridonia Jazz Festival

Philology W 211-2 *As above, except Roberto Gatto (d) replaces Kramer.* 7/91.

Woods's partnership with Pieranunzi is a fruitful new step for him. The studio album, *Phil's Mood*, uses some of the same material as the live disc and, since there are also multiple takes – four altogether of 'New Lands' – they cover the ground with scrupulous intensity. A wider choice of material would have made the earlier record stronger, but it still stands as a persuasive Woods session, the rhythm section responding to his customary plangency. The live album is again blemished by too much material and indifferent sound: more festival versions of 'Lover Man' and 'Anthropology' are hardly the best way to encounter Woods on record today.

*** Full House

Milestone 9196 *Woods; Hal Crook (tb); Jim McNeely (p); Steve Gilmore (b); Bill Goodwin (d).* 2/91.

Cut live at Hollywood's Catalina, this set shows no sign of energy flagging, though there are no special felicities – just a top band going through its sure-footed paces.

*** Just Friends

Philology W 106 *Woods; Renato Sellani (p); Massimo Morriconi (b).* 6/94.

*** Our Monk

Philology W 78 *Woods; Franco D'Andrea (p).* 11/94.

More of Phil's Italian adventures. *Just Friends* lets him loose on standards with fresh-faced support from Sellani and Morriconi and is merely an interim report from a musician in good shape. The Monk recital with D'Andrea is the more challenging occasion, and it is absorbing for the way an initially unlikely interpreter such as Woods handles the repertoire. Actually, one can go all the way back to *Pot Pie* to discover Monkian leanings in his style, and the contours of this material offer him few problems at any level. D'Andrea tends to buff away at the tunes and flatten them a little, but it's a fair match.

*** Plays The Music Of Jim McNeely

TCB 95402 *Woods; Brian Lynch (t); Jim McNeely (p); Steve Gilmore (b); Bill Goodwin (d).* 2/95.

*** Mile High Jazz Live In Denver

Concord CCD-4739 *As above, except Bill Charlap (p) replaces McNeely.* 4/96.

Less frequently recorded in the '90s, the Woods quintet has been through some changes – McNeely has come and gone and Lynch has replaced Crook – while following a course faithful to the leader's stance. These are more good – if not quite outstanding – sessions of modern hard bop. McNeely had already left when the TCB album was made, but he returned to cut seven of his own tunes with the group. Fine material, and the performances are strong, if not quite as multifarious as the themes deserve. Concord's *Mile High Jazz* is a vigorous show, Lynch in good fettle and the leader showing that he's lost none of his chops. Perhaps the main interest is in hearing how inventive Gilmore and Goodwin are, more than 20 years after they started working with Woods. If the horns have the limelight, they're pushed and fed by a consistently imaginative rhythm that deserves more acclaim than it's received.

***(*) The Rev And I

Blue Note 494100-2 *Woods; Johnny Griffin (ts); Cedar Walton (p); Peter Washington (b); Ben Riley (d); Bill Goodwin (perc).* 1/98.

Woods loves two-sax encounters, and this session (he and Griffin, like so many other big-bandsmen who've played together, call each other 'Section') brims over with bonhomie and swagger. The old Hampton favourite, 'Red Top', is pure catnip. Griffin is no longer the terror he once was, but Woods still sounds like he could take on any comers. Producer Bill Goodwin has taken the trouble to make sure that there's enough pre-match preparation to take it above blowing-session status, and it all benefits from that finesse. And each saxophonist gets a gorgeous ballad feature.

★★★(★) Encontro (On Jobim)
Philology 301 *Woods; Irio De Paula (g).* 5/00.

★★★ Voce E Eu
Philology 302 *Woods; Stefano Bollani (p); Barbara Casini (v).* 5/00.

★★★(★) Dameronia
Philology 303 *Woods; Fabrizio Bossi (t); Rosario Giuliani (as); Franco D'Andrea (p); Massimo Moriconi (b); Lorenzo Tucci (d).* 5/00.

★★★ The Solo Album
Philology 304 *Woods (as, p, v solo).* 5/00.

★★★(★) Balladeer Supreme
Philology 305 *Woods; Franco D'Andrea (p).* 5/00.

★★★ Woods Plays D'Andrea
Philology 306 *As above, except add Massimo Moriconi (b); Ellade Bandini (d).* 5/00.

★★★(★) Woods Plays Woods
Philology 307 *Woods; Stefano Bollani (p); Ares Tavolazzi (b); Massimo Manzi (d).* 5/00.

With typical outlandishness, Paolo Piangiarelli decided to record his beloved musician over five days in seven different situations and persuaded Phil into completing seven full albums. Some of the old invincibility has gone out of his tone and phrasing, and he doesn't cut through ensembles with the effortless sting that he once mustered, but he's still a darn good saxophone player. This set makes for a long listen, and while Woodsphiles will enjoy investigating everything, the less committed may prefer to check out just one or two records. Briefly, the best: the duets with De Paula are charming, both men relishing the sweet material; *Balladeer Supreme* is a warm-hearted dialogue with Franco D'Andrea; *Dameronia* is a lively and inventive meeting with 'the new Italian generation', although D'Andrea is perhaps not quite so new; and *Woods Plays Woods* puts him with a fine trio christened 'The Italian Rhythm Machine'. The vocal set with Casini depends on how much her smooth if not especially compelling singing appeals. *Plays D'Andrea* suffers just a little from Woods's unfamiliarity with the material. *The Solo Album* has some of the most poignant music, given the light fading of his powers, and dedications to Bird and Benny Carter are marked by wistfulness as much as any jazz fire. He sings his own 'The Last Page' at the piano.

★★★(★) Play Henry Mancini
Jazzed Media JM 1002 *Woods; Carl Saunders (t, flhn); Jeff Jenkins (p); Ken Walker (b); Paul Romaine (d).* 8/03.

He may be troubled by emphysema these days, but the old warrior can't half play still: he actually sounds stronger here than he does on the Italian sessions. They took the trouble to create quintet arrangements for every tune in this set of Mancini covers, and with Saunders playing some glittering solos to match the alto-man, it's a throughly enjoyable set in Phil's classic idiom.

Daniel Woodtli

TRUMPET

Swiss trumpeter here leading an international trio.

★★★ Someday In April
Altrisuoni AS 145 *Woodtli; Nick Perrin (g); Lorenz Beyeler (b).* 11/02.

The instrumentation recalls the fine sessions by Chet Baker, Nils Pedersen and Doug Raney, and while the results are very different, there's a similar dependence on streams of melody. They're inventive players: Woodtli has a lovely open tone, though he gets decidedly funky with the mute on 'The Corn (The Eye Of The Chicken)', and Perrin shifts between counterpoint, solo parts and harmonic filler. They try and make each piece different with subtle shifts of emphasis and there's no rambling. A modest but enjoyable entry.

Reggie Workman (born 1937)

DOUBLE BASS

Played R&B as a teenager, then worked in New York hard-bop groups in the '60s before moving towards the freer styles of Archie Shepp and John Coltrane. Heavily involved in education and has latterly begun leading his own groups.

★★★(★) Synthesis
Leo CDLR 131 *Workman; Oliver Lake (reeds); Marilyn Crispell (p); Andrew Cyrille (d).* 6/86.

★★★(★) Altered Spaces
Leo CDLR 183 *Workman; Don Byron (cl); Marilyn Crispell (p); Jason Hwang (vn); Gerry Hemingway (d); Jeanne Lee (v).* 2/92.

As befits his name, Workman has clocked up an astonishing number and range of sideman credits: with Coltrane (*Olé*, the 1961 European tour, the *Africa/Brass* sessions) and with Wayne Shorter, Mal Waldron, Art Blakey, Archie Shepp and David Murray. Workman is also a forceful leader who has moved on to explore areas of musical freedom influenced by African idioms and frequently resembling the trance music of the *griots*. Of the available albums, *Synthesis*, a live performance from The Painted Bride in Philadelphia, is the most convincing. Workman bows, triple-stops and produces unreliably pitched sounds (presumably from below the bridge), leaving it to Crispell, as on *Images*, to give the performance its undoubted sense of coherence. Of the six tracks on *Synthesis*, it is her 'Chant' which sounds most like a fully articulated composition. Workman's ideas are developed less completely and, while they often lead to more adventurous solo excursions from the individual performers, they rarely do much more than peter out.

Altered Spaces is the most ambitious work the Ensemble has yet tackled. The long suite, 'Apart', explores territory very close to Don Byron's chilling *Tuskegee Experiments* yet seems closer in spirit to the revolutionary stoicism of Brecht's *Mother Courage*, which Jeanne Lee's vocal explicitly quotes. The bass-and-violin prelude serves as an introduction to Jason Hwang, author of the controversial play, *M. Butterfly*, and of the libretto for Philip Glass's *1000 Airplanes On The Roof*. A new member of the Ensemble, Hwang brings an oriental calm that takes the music ever further away from 'jazz'. Oddly, on this occasion it is

Crispell who sounds locked into a formulaic sound that seems to be pushing for resolutions that the two string players' long lines and Hemingway's open-ended patters serve to resist. Impressive, all the same, for its sheer cross-grainedness.

★★★★ Summit Conference
Postcards POST1003 *Workman; Julian Priester (tb); Sam Rivers (ts, ss); Andrew Hill (p); Pheeroan akLaff (d).* 12/93.

★★★★ Cerebral Caverns
Postcards POST1010 *Workman; Julian Priester (tb); Sam Rivers (ts, ss, f); Elizabeth Panzer (hp); Geri Allen (p); Gerry Hemingway (d, elec); Al Foster (d); Tapan Modak (tablas).*

These are cracking records, made by top-flight players. The *Summit Conference* group has a wish-list quality and delivers from the very start. Rivers and Priester are in boilingly good form, and the younger akLaff keeps the pace up. Slight quibbles about Hill's audibility; he isn't a delicate player and it worried us that he didn't seem to be coming through. Though the bulk of the session is up-tempo, often in fractured metres, there's still room for a heart-on-sleeve ballad, Rivers's 'Solace', introduced by trombone, piano and sax (in that order) before the composer goes up a gear and delivers his most magisterial solo for years. Priester's 'Breath' is pitched in a distant, sharp-ridden key that would have most players twitching; this group brings it on exactly on the button and without a hesitant moment.

Almost inevitably, *Cerebral Caverns* (now isn't that an off-putting title?) doesn't quite match up, but it's hard to mark it down, given the quality of performances. Allen is always better on other people's dates, and here she's called on to do the sort of high-intensity stuff that Marilyn Crispell brought to previous Workman groups. She's featured in two trios with Workman, one with Hemingway (superb), one with harp (fascinating, but not quite there). 'Fast Forward' reunites the earlier group, without piano, and with the more experienced but no less passionate Foster on drums. The title-piece is the most ambitious in terms of sound, with harp again, flute, and Hemingway's electronically triggered drum-pads contributing to a complex mix of textures.

World Saxophone Quartet

GROUP

No permutation of instruments can be more sheerly tedious and yet more compelling than four saxophones together. The difference lies in the players involved and, for as many years as anyone cares to remember, the World Saxophone Quartet has been the market-leader. Less self-consciously radical and avant-garde than ROVA and yet streets ahead of the average ensemble for sheer enterprise, they have always been riveting live and only slightly less compelling on record.

★★★ Steppin'
Black Saint 120027 *Hamiet Bluiett (bs, f, af, acl); Julius Hemphill (f, ss, as); Oliver Lake (ss, ts, as, f); David Murray (ts, bcl).* 12/78.

★★★★ W.S.Q.
Black Saint 120046 *As above.* 3/80.

★★★(★) Revue
Black Saint 120056 *As above.* 10/80.

★★★ Live In Zurich
Black Saint 120077 *As above.* 11/81.

★★★(★) Plays Duke Ellington
Elektra Musician 979137 *As above.* 4/86.

★★★★ Dances And Ballads
Elektra Musician 979164 *As above.* 4/87.

★★★(★) Rhythm And Blues
Elektra Musician 60864 *As above.* 11/88.

Market-leaders in the now well-attested saxophone-quartet format, the WSQ were founded in 1977. The debut album was not particularly well recorded but it helped establish the group's identity as adventurous composer-improvisers who could offer great swinging ensembles (not quite as hokey as those of the 29th Street Saxophone Quartet) and remarkable duo and trio divisions of the basic instrumentation. The armoury of reeds was pretty modest to begin with, but increasingly after 1978 all four members began to 'double' on more exotic specimens, with Bluiett's alto clarinet (rarely used in a jazz context) and Murray's bass clarinet both lending significant variations of tonality and texture. 'Scared Sheetless' from the first album gives a fair impression of its not altogether serious appropriation of free-jazz devices. 'R&B' on the second album plays with genre in a friendlier and more ironic way.

The best of the earlier records, *W.S.Q.* is dominated by a long suite that blends jazz and popular elements with considerable ingenuity and real improvisational fire. 'The Key' and 'Ballad For Eddie Jefferson' (dedicated to the inventor of jazz vocalese) are perhaps the most interesting elements, but the closing 'Fast Life' is as fine a curtain-piece as the group has recorded. With *Revue* (a significant pun), the centre of gravity shifts slightly towards rising star Murray and towards what looks like a reassessment of the group's development. Murray's 'Ming' is well known from his own records but has never been played with such fierce beauty.

The Ellington album marks a gentle, middle-market turn that did the group no harm at all. Opening and closing with 'Take The "A" Train', they check out 'Sophisticated Lady' and 'I Let A Song Go Out Of My Heart', do a wonderful 'Come Sunday', and add a raw lyricism to 'Lush Life' and 'Prelude To A Kiss'. The sound is better than usual, with no congestion round about the middle, as on some of the earlier sets. There's a broader big-band sound to *Dances And Ballads*, achieved without the addition of outsiders as on *Metamorphosis*, below, which seems to draw something from the Ellington set. Hemphill contributes only two tracks, but there's a fine version of David Murray's Pres tribute, 'For Lester' (later to appear on his octet, *HopeScope*), and Oliver Lake's 'West African Snap', 'Belly Up' and 'Adjacent' are among the best of his recorded compositions. The soul staples covered on *Rhythm And Blues* – including 'Let's Get It On', '(Sittin' On) The Dock Of The Bay' and, unforgettably, 'Try A Little Tenderness', with Murray's tenor going places Otis Redding never heard of – are done with absolute conviction and seriousness. Only *Steppin'* and the rather rough *Live In Zurich* are disappointments, though the latter has a fine reading of 'Steppin'' itself.

All four members developed highly individual careers apart, Murray most of all; along with Hemphill, he is the most distinctive and flexible composer. The durability of the group lay in the degree to which personal strengths were encouraged and exploited rather than subordinated. With so many instrumental permutations and the possibility of internal subdivisions, the WSQ's exploratory sound has never settled into a manner.

***** Metamorphosis**

Elektra Nonesuch 979258 *Oliver Lake (as, ss, f); David Murray (ts, bcl); Hamiet Bluiett (bs); Arthur Blythe (as); Melvin Gibbs (b); Chief Bey, Mar Gueye, Mor Thiam (perc).* 4/90.

The departure of Julius Hemphill and arrival of Arthur Blythe couldn't have looked altogether propitious, given (a) Hemphill's importance as a writer for the group, and (b) Blythe's stuttering fortunes in recent years. The title-track, though, is given over to the new boy and he fills the outgoing man's shoes with impressive confidence, checking in with a powerful contrapuntal weave that is lifted a notch by the (initially disturbing; the WSQ used always to go it alone) presence of the three African drummers. In the event, they add a great deal more than bassist Gibbs, who clocks on for three tracks only and might as well not have bothered. Murray's 'Ballad For The Black Man' is very much an individual feature and easily the most coherent single track; Lake's 'Love Like Sisters' has tremendous potential but might well sound better tackled by a more conventional horn-plus-inventive-rhythm outfit.

***** Breath Of Life**

Nonesuch 983124 *As above.* 92.

Even giants nod on occasion and this nondescript set has to be accounted an off-day in the WSQ's impressive progress. The playing is immaculate as ever, but there is a strange lack of focus in the writing, a bland equalization of voices, almost as if someone had called a truce on competing visions.

*****(*) Moving Right Along**

Black Saint 120127 *Oliver Lake, Eric Person (as, ss); James Spaulding (as); David Murray (ts, bcl); Hamiet Bluiett (bs, acl).* 10/93.

First indications were that the WSQ were going to be feeling their way around for some time. *Moving Right Along* sees the first recording of the group with Eric Person, who also contributes a fresh original, 'Antithesis'. He fits in immediately and well, and sounds closer to the group's overall conception than Spaulding. The emphasis this time is on sharp, tight arrangements. 'Giant Steps' is dispatched in less than three minutes and there is a superb two-part arrangement of 'Amazing Grace' by Bluiett, who also contributes 'N.T.', a hard-edged portrait of the Black insurrectionist. Bluiett's 'Astral Travels' are less convincing, but his alto clarinet has become an integral component of the group sound; opening up the lower registers previously led to the more romantically inclined Murray on his second horn.

*****(*) Four Now**

Justin Time JUST 83-2 *Hamiet Bluiett (bs, contra-acl); Oliver Lake (as); David Murray (ts, bcl); John Purcell (saxello, eng hn, f, af); Chief Bey, Mar Gueye, Mor Thiam (perc, v).* 95.

A reunion of the guest line-up that made the 1991 *Metamorphosis* record, this is the better album because the elements seem to work together rather than in strict parallel. Three of the tracks are written by Mar Gueye and the gifted Mor Thiam, and one feels that the idiom is more suited to the Senegalese percussionists than was the case on the earlier record. There are also fewer avant-garde gestures from the WSQ itself, who last time out – and this is a view marked with 20/20 hindsight – seemed anxious to demonstrate their greater sophistication by playing rugged dissonances and hard-edged melodies that excluded rather than welcomed the Africans. Purcell has established himself as a key member of the group. His composition 'Colors' may have originally been written for other forces (that is our guess) but it is beautifully arranged for the Quartet, and it coaxes some lovely playing from everyone concerned.

***** Takin' It 2 The Next Level**

Justin Time 93-2 *Oliver Lake (as); John Purcell (ts, saxello); David Murray (ts, bcl); Hamiet Bluiett (bs); Donald Blackman (ky); Calvin Jones (b); Ronnie Burrage (d).* 6/96.

Again the empty chair went to John Purcell; in addition, a full-on rhythm section. The results are typically spirited and entirely within the WSQ tradition. 'Rio' blends the quartet's multiple voices with a percolating rhythm to fine effect, and big set-pieces like 'Blues For A Warrior Spirit' and 'The Desegregation Of Our Children' are as formidable as they should be. But it's hard to avoid the feeling that the group is not continuing out of any artistic necessity, and as propulsive as the rhythm players are, their principal contribution is perhaps to rationalize the WSQ into just another band.

****** Selim Sivad: A Tribute To Miles Davis**

Justin Time JUST 119-2 *Hamiet Bluiett (bs, contra-acl); Oliver Lake (as, f); David Murray (ts, bcl); John Purcell (saxello, af); Jack DeJohnette (d, p); Okyerema Asante, Chief Bey, Titos Sompa (perc).* 98.

The curse of tribute albums – of which there are in any case too many – is a craven literalism, a wannabe mimicry of voices which were unique or idiosyncratic or plain perverse. True to form, the WSQ's take on Miles Davis's long and epochal career is cast very much in the band's own idiom. From the delicate lyricism of 'Blue In Green' to the abstract attack of 'Selim' from the violent, palindromic *Live/Evil*, Miles's music is comprehensively rethought rather than merely pastiched. Some tunes are barely recognizable, a shift that suggests creative response rather than ineptitude. 'Freddie Freeloader' becomes a sardonic African dance; 'Nefertiti', always a test-piece, is handed to kalimba and flute while the other horns spar and dodge; even the late 'Tutu' is recast and put back in time as if it were a contrafact on some forgotten theme of the '60s avant-garde. If the purpose of a tribute is to recognize the genius of a forerunner, *Selim Sivad* underlines the great genius of its dedicatee, but does something more. It takes and inverts Miles's ideas and makes them work in a musical environment far away from any the great man physically inhabited. The presence of DeJohnette is important. He helped shape the basic metres of this most unbasic of musics. He himself has moved on, but he has retained enough of his rough schooling to think himself back into that revolutionary mind-set. A brilliant, beautiful record.

***** M'Bizo**

Justin Time JUST 123 *As above; add Mario Canonge, D. D. Jackson (p); Jimane Nelson (org); James Lewis, Jaribu Shahid (b); Ronnie Burrage (d); Mabeleng Moholo (makhoyane); omit DeJohnette.* 11/97–6/98.

*****(*) Requiem For Julius**

Justin Time Just 137 *As above; omit guest musicians.* 99.

*****(*) 25th Anniversary: The New Chapter**

Justin Time JUST 149 *As above.* 5/00.

****** Steppenwolf**

Justin Time JUST 128 *As above.* 01.

WSQ quite consciously entered a new phase with these records. They attempted to put the spirit of Julius Hemphill finally and affectionately behind them, celebrated a quarter-century of activity – and in the live session at Steppenwolf Theater turned in one of their most appealing and impressive performances ever.

The earliest record of the group is the fruit of a trip to South Africa and some very happy musical associations created there. The set is, of course, dedicated to the late Johnny Dyani, a man whose spirit touched everyone he met and thousands whom he didn't. The three-part 'M'Bizo Suite' occupies the bulk of the record, though the opening 'Snanapo', which features ethnic touches, and 'Matshidiso', which calls on piano, organ and drums, are both powerful works.

The requiem for Hemphill is a lovely work, preceded by 'Ebony', Bluiett's 'Free and Independent Thought' and the delightful 'All Praise'. Not just for their connection with the WSQ's past, this and the 25th–anniversary record are perhaps the most accessible recordings by the group and they are certainly a good place to start, though listeners should certainly go back to the early discs with Hemphill to see what the great man was all about.

The Steppenwolf gig is the one we would most strongly recommend however. This was the night when Purcell finally sounded like a permanent and unmoveable component of the quartet. Sticking to soprano and clarinet on this occasion, he sets aside his eclectic multi-instrumentalism in favour of a highly focused and very accurate line, blowing cleanly and as swingingly as an old-style clarinettist. Bluiett and Lake provide the harmonic superstructure while Murray weaves his own dark magic. The group's version of 'Giant Steps' is a career highpoint.

***** Experience**

Justin Time 102 *As above; add Craig Harris (tb, didjeridu); Billy Bang (vn); Matt Garrison (b).* 03.

We wondered how long it would be before the WSQ tackled the Jimi Hendrix songbook. Here it is, fresh, brash and sophisticated in exactly the proportions you would expect. Kicking off with 'Freedom' is the only surprise. After that, all the usual suspects are included: 'Foxy Lady', 'Hey Joe', 'If 6 Was 9', 'Hear My Train A-Comin'', 'Machine Gun', 'The Wind Cries Mary' and 'Little Wing'. The augmented sound is always a plus, especially if you find the sound of four saxophones hard to handle.

World's Greatest Jazz Band

GROUP

The name was pure hubris, but it served what was really no more than a continuation of the Dixieland outfit which Yank Lawson and Bob Haggart had led for many years in the '50s and '60s.

***** Plays Cole Porter And Rodgers & Hart**

Jazzology JCD-320 *Yank Lawson, John Best (t); Carl Fontana, George Masso (tb); Peanuts Hucko (cl); Tommy Newsom, Al Klink (ts); Ralph Sutton (p); Bob Haggart (b); Gus Johnson (d).* 75.

***** Plays George Gershwin And Rodgers & Hart**

Jazzology JCD-300 *As above, except add Billy Butterfield (t), Eddie Miller (ts); Roger Kellaway (p); Nick Fatool (d); omit Newsom.* 75–6/77.

***** Plays Duke Ellington**

Jazzology JCD-340 *Yank Lawson, Billy Butterfield (t); George Masso, Sonny Russo (tb); Phil Bodner (cl); Al Klink (ts); John Bunch (p); Bob Haggart (b); Bobby Rosengarden (d).* 76.

The WGJB was something of an institution for a while, and in its heyday kept the Dixie-to-mainstream spirit alive during a dim time for that music. It predated the 'authentic' movement for this kind of jazz, so it tended to stay on the showbiz side of things, which means that the group's many LPs for the World Jazz label have a perfunctory edge which may disappoint some. It's professional, well-groomed Dixieland which is on show here. That said, these three 'songbook' collections (reissued from the World Jazz originals) have their moments, courtesy of the various soloists, and they bring back a style of playing which has to a considerable extent vanished with the group's passing.

John Wright

PIANO

Veteran Chicagoan pianist whose sequence of albums for Prestige in the early '60s was a modest blend of hard bop and gentle soul-jazz.

***** South Side Soul**

Original Jazz Classics OJC 1743 *Wright; Wendell Marshall (b); Walter McCants (d).* 8/60.

***** Mr Soul**

Original Jazz Classics OJC 1876 *Wright; Wendell Marshall (b); Walter Perkins Jr (d).* 4/62.

These are pleasant, almost harmless reminders of pianist John Wright whose Prestige albums once attracted a small following. There's little here that didn't emerge just as readily on records by Ahmad Jamal and Junior Mance, and Wright's deferential side – his ballads are carefully weighted and closer to Bill Evans than anything – has perhaps told against these discs reaching a wider audience in more recent years. The album titles and tunes of the order of 'Strut' are of their period, and one wonders what Wright felt about the bag he ended up in. He certainly finds the possibilities of 'What's New' (*Mr Soul*) at least as appealing as any down-home clichés. On their own terms, these are agreeable survivals.

Leo Wright (1933–91)

ALTO SAXOPHONE, FLUTE, CLARINET

The Texan studied music at home and began his recording career with vibraharpist Dave Pike. Other associations followed, including Dizzy Gillespie, Tom Jobim and Jimmy Witherspoon. In the '70s, he moved to Europe and worked with his wife, singer Elly Wright. Though primarily an alto-player, Wright was also a superb flautist.

***** Suddenly The Blues**

Koch International 8544 *Wright; Kenny Burrell (g); Ron Carter (b); Rudy Collins (d).* 4/62.

The two key Leo Wright documents are his classic 1960 Atlantic album *Blues Shout* and his autobiography *God Is My Booking Agent.* The former is not currently in circulation and the latter may be hard to find, but this Koch reissue is a welcome introduction to a much underrated player. The repertoire touches usefully on two of Wright's most fruitful associations, with Lalo Schifrin (the intense 'Dionysos') and Jobim ('A Felicidad'). The original themes are relatively scanty but 'The Wriggler' is a fine blowing theme and the title-track highlights the leader's soaring vocalized solo voice. 'Greensleeves' is decidedly tongue in cheek, but Wright is enough of a romantic to leave the old theme intact. To be fair, the set is very nearly stolen by Burrell, who is in cracking form throughout, but fair play too to the little-known Collins, who stokes the boilers manfully.

Richard Wyands (born 1928)

PIANO

A failsafe sideman, Wyands has been in countless bands and on numberless records, always in an easy-going but authoritative bop orthodoxy. He very occasionally gets his own gig in the studios.

***** Then, Here And Now**
Storyville STCD 8269 *Wyands; Lisle Atkinson (b); David Lee (d).* 78.

***** Reunited**
Criss Cross 1105 *Wyands; Peter Washington (b); Kenny Washington (d).* 95.

***** Get Out Of Town**
Steeplechase SCCD 31401 *As above.* 10/96.

***** Half And Half**
Criss Cross 1185 *As above.* 12/99.

Wyands is an evergreen who seems to have been around for ever. Most jazz fans will have seen or heard him with one group or another, in mainstream or post-bop environments, and been thankful that such a witty and apposite player has been on hand in the rhythm section. That he had turned fifty before making a first record under his own name may suggest that leadership isn't Richard's forte. He is a bright, clear-voiced technician, but by no means a compelling soloist. Wyands is in the venerable tradition of Wynton Kelly, Bobby Timmons and Sonny Clark and so offers few surprises – more a quietly swinging satisfaction. The brickwork is solid enough; one simply waits and hopes for something a little more rough-hewn than his symmetrical, chord-based statements.

The two later records are full of good music, but both seem rather deliberate and pre-set. It seems that the debut session, originally released on Jazzcraft, was squeezed into a hefty gigging schedule. If so, Wyands and his fans are the gainers. He sounds relaxed, not note-perfect but in tune with both material and sidemen. 'Yesterdays' is the most inventive cut, and a good example of Wyands's witty rhythmic experiments. It's a shame that there isn't an alternative of this number, as there is of Duke's 'Blue Rose' and the Latin-tinged original 'Leonora'. J. J. Johnson's 'Lament' and the show tune 'As Long As There's Music' are both given expressive readings. A drawback is the piano sound, which is disappointingly thin and tingly.

Of the later records – and note the gap in chronology – the first Criss Cross set is our marginal preference, with a more imaginative programme of tunes and a more concentrated approach. Whereas Atkinson and Lee provide not much more than foursquare support on the Storyville, Washington and Washington are more inventive on their own account.

Half And Half comes with an informative sleeve essay by Ted Panken which tells much about Wyands's career, although the most telling remark comes from Kenny Washington, discussing the pianist: 'He just knows instinctively what to do, when he's supposed to do it.' In other words, a failsafe pro, which is fine for the band, but perhaps less interesting for the listener, since Richard doesn't really strike a new note out of anything here. Something of his original favourite Teddy Wilson survives in his touch, and maybe a Garnerish chord here and there; but this is proper, elegant piano playing, which rarely stirs the blood.

Albert Wynn (1907–73)

TROMBONE

Born in New Orleans, Wynn accrued a wide range of experience: touring with Ma Rainey, then various stints in St Louis, Europe (for four years), New York and Chicago. He settled there in the '40s and worked with various revivalist bands in the city until ill-health slowed him down in the '60s.

***** Albert Wynn And His Gutbucket Seven**
Original Jazz Classics OJC 1826 *Wynn; Bill Martin (t, v); Darnell Howard (cl); Buster Moten, Blind John Davis (p, v); Mike McKendrick (g, bj); Robert Wilson (b); Booker Washington (d).* 9/61.

Wynn is on a fair number of Chicago records from the '20s, but he was something of a forgotten man by the time he made this entry in Riverside's *Living Legends* series. His solos are rather careful and circumspect, which leaves the main limelight to the formidable Howard, whose bustling work leans towards the gaspipe manner at some points but is undeniably exciting. Martin's rather mannered trumpet is a nice balance, and the only time-wasting is from bluesman Davis, whose two vocals are dispensable. Wilson and Washington keep unobtrusive time. A worthwhile survival.

Yosuke Yamashita (born 1942)

PIANO

Along with Jon Jang, Yamashita is the most significant pianist of Asian background since Toshiko Akiyoshi. His approach embraces classic piano jazz and elements of oriental harmony and rhythm. Very much a group player, he is not so much a powerful soloist as a gifted conceptualist who controls many parameters of the music.

*****(*) Fragments 1999**
Verve 543064-2 *Yamashita; Cecil McBee (b); Pheeroan akLaff (d).* 5/99.

*****(*) Resonant Memories**
Verve 549630-2 *Yamashita (p solo).* 5/00.

Verve's reluctance to keep Yamashita's catalogue in print makes it difficult for listeners to follow what has been a prodigious decade of work by his New York Trio. He is an intriguing stylist with a highly individual take on the modern-jazz tradition, exploring bop and swing staples but also delving into the turbulent sound-world of Albert Ayler, often in the company of his compatriot, Akira Sakata. With a sharp but curiously delicate touch, Yamashita prefers to play in short, apparently discontinuous blocks of sound that often do not connect in accordance with accepted harmonic or even rhythmic logic. His piano–shakuhachi duets with Hozan Yamamoto (one of a group of deleted Enjas) are particularly unusual in their approach to rhythm.

With his American players he takes a more conventional course through the literature, but harmonically he thinks through and constructs solos with a sharply individual stance, and the very long 'Fragments' is a fine example of the kind of entire, oddly ordered world which this group can create at full stretch. Titles such as 'Who's Valentine' and 'Altered Leaves' offer clues to the basis of some of his originals, but it's always Yamashita who calls the tunes. McBee and akLaff are hip to everything that's happening along the way.

The solo record is no less satisfying, even if Yamashita came to the idea a little abruptly after the abandonment of a big-band project. Even after so many 'Round Midnight's, this one is new and undiscovered. 'Greensleeves' flits in and out of waltz-time, and 'You Are Valentine' and 'Brightness' set down wonderful examples of his lyrical side. 'I'm A Fool To Want You', a request by his producer-manager G, is flinty and poignant. Marvellous music.

Keith Yaun

GUITAR

Boston-based improviser and free-bopper, with some interesting takes on modern classical repertoire.

★★★(★) Countersink
Leo Lab CD 047 *Yaun; Nathan Cook (ts); Mat Maneri (vn); John Lockwood (b); Johnny McLellan (d).* 1/98.

★★(★) Amen: Improvisations on Messiaen
Boxholder 010 *As above, except omit Lockwood; add Bern Nix (g).* 00.

A seasoned veteran of the Boston improvising scene, Yaun is a thoughtful, precise player who seems to regard improvisation as a dialectical process, advancing ideas, flatly contradicting them and then patiently synthesizing the two into musical statements of real substance. On this debut recording, an apparently new band sounds as if it has been working together for some time.

Much of the music comes from drummer McLellan, whose 'Durt Kolphy' opens the record. This is inspired by Kurt Cobain and an idea of Eric Dolphy's. It's very quiet and focused music, dominated by Yaun's reflective solo and a rather more stressed statement by Mat Maneri. 'Loner Inches' is credited to the violinist but sounds very much like a collective improvisation and is the weakest thing on the record. The group seem to play better when anchored to something even fleeting, as it is on the very beautiful 'Heavy Hand Of Love', the longest track on the record and one of the most compelling performances we've heard in this vein for years.

Two versions of 'Runup' show the group in a more free-blowing, jazz-influenced vein, reflecting the record's steady move back towards jazz idiom. 'Collide' is a waltz that might have come from the pen of Max Roach on a quiet day; no surprise that McLellan is again the composer. Saxophonist Nathan Cook doesn't establish much of a presence until the latter part of the album, but it's easy to overlook his rather dry delivery. He often sounds as if he were playing a C-melody or some other non-canonical saxophone, but in terms of development he is close cousin to Anthony Braxton in his Warne Marsh mode. Lockwood is someone we have heard and been impressed by before. His contribution here is always significant, and agreeably understated.

The Messiaen project might seem doomed from the outset, but this depends on a false assumption about the French composer, who could be as earthly and physical as he was spiritual and other-worldly. However, Yaun hasn't necessarily brought out that side in his strange and mostly unidentifiable improvisations on Messiaen themes, including 'Amen de la Création', 'La Ville qui Dormait' and some organ compositions. The results are quite gentle, almost New Age, and unlikely to stir anyone not already sold on this sub-genre of jazz–classical crossovers.

Yerba Buena Stompers

GROUP

First formed by John Gill as a homage to Lu Watters, the YBS take a respectfully irreverent approach to the traditonal repertoire.

★★★(★) Dawn Club Favorites
Stomp Off CD 1369 *Leon Oakley, Duke Heitger (t); Tom Bartlett (tb, v); Ray Cadd (tba); Larry Wright (cl); Pete Clute (p); John Gill (bj, v); Clint Baker (d).* 4/01.

★★★(★) Barbary Coast Favorites
Stomp Off CD 1375 *As above, except Marty Eggers (p) replaces Clute.* 10/01.

★★★(★) New Orleans Favorites
Stomp Off CD 1381 *As above.* 3/02.

In his sleevenotes, John Gill is a bit defensive about the rather poor time Lu Watters and his bands had at the hands of critics and historians; but that is all long ago and rather far away now, and paying tribute to him needs no real justification. The YBS certainly have that slightly disreputable and noisy approach to revivalism which was the Watters trademark, and as an antidote to the Lincoln Center variety (though that's no bad alternative) these discs make a rowdily compelling case for the continued relevance of this sort of jazz. Gill has been going at this repertoire from several directions in the past 20 years or so, and where his Dixieland Serenaders and Silver Leaf Jazz Band approach it from a rather more respectful and proper perspective, the YBS just biff their way through it. The fast tempos are a bit quicker than you'd expect, and the slow tempos are a bit quicker than you'd expect. They leave very little time for you to catch your breath: the solos fly past. Larry Wright's clarinet walks a fairly crazy line between Ted Lewis and George Lewis. Tom Bartlett sings here and there: the lyrics to 'Second Line Stomp' were written by Gill while he was working on a steamboat, so you can hardly ask for more authenticity. Maybe none of the three discs is really classic, but each offers a tremendous amount of fun.

John Young (born 1922)

PIANO

A great veteran of the local scene in Chicago for decades, John Young is an unfussy and genuine master of the post-bebop language. His few records are modest statements with no pretensions to anything beyond his own solid form.

***** Serenata**

Delmark DD 403 *Young; Victor Sproles (b); Phil Thomas (d).* 2/59.

A local legend in Chicago, where he has worked and played his whole life, John Young has done little to put his name in the history books or discographies. This short, enjoyable session – three alternative takes carry it just past the 40-minute mark – makes no case for immortality, but it is a fine example of how the music is succoured by the craftsmanship of such an accomplished player. Young hits a soulful groove on some tunes, abetted by the alert but quite spacious rhythms of Sproles and Thomas, and his naturally dancing, infectious manner has enough of the blues in it to make his swing and bebop stylings stay close to the tradition. 'Cubana Chant' is as good as any Ray Bryant or Red Garland fingersnapper, and the title-piece has an unfussy lyricism which is very attractive. Excellent remastering for CD issue.

Larry Young (1940–78)

ORGAN

Born in Newark, he studied piano and began on organ, at seventeen, in his father's nightclub. Associated with hard-bop in the '60s, then with fusion (Lifetime); but he made little public headway and was marginalized at the time of his death from pneumonia.

*****(*) Testifying**

Original Jazz Classics OJCCD 1793 *Young; Thornel Schwartz (g); Jimmie Smith (d).* 8/60

*****(*) Young Blues**

Original Jazz Classics OJCCD 1831 *As above, except add Wendell Marshall (b).* 9/60.

***** Groove Street**

Original Jazz Classics OJCCD 1853 *As above, except omit Marshall; add Bill Leslie (ts).* 2/62.

Larry Young – later known as Khalid Yasin Abdul Aziz – was the first Hammond player to shake off the pervasive influence of Jimmy Smith (not to be confused with Jimmie the drummer on the earlier of these records) and begin the assimilation of John Coltrane's harmonics to the disputed border territory between jazz and nascent rock.

Young was to achieve almost legendary status with bands like Lifetime and Love Cry Want, and on Miles Davis's electronic masterpiece, *Bitches Brew*. On all three, and on one-off sessions like John McLaughlin's *Devotion*, he traded on a wild, abstract expressionist approach, creating great billowing sheets of sound. It's unfortunate that much of what survives of his work outside these groups is a throwback to the organ–guitar–drums jazz he was leaving behind at the end of the '60s. *Testifying* and *Young Blues* are both pretty callow, squarely in the Jimmy McGriff mould; Schwartz played with Jimmy for a time. Even so, both sets show a measure of the tonal sophistication Young was to display in later years. James Blood Ulmer fans would sense a kindred spirit on tracks like 'Exercise For Chihuahuas' and 'Some Thorny Blues' and the title-number on *Testifying*.

Groove Street is a broodingly funky organ/guitar/saxophone workout that manages to make some convincing changes on what might have been a drab and over-exploited formula. It certainly isn't the most subtle of records, but it has great strengths and is well worth hearing.

*****(*) Into Something!**

Blue Note 543276-2 *Young; Sam Rivers (ts); Grant Green (g); Elvin Jones (d).* 11/64.

This record promises somewhat more than it delivers. Sam Rivers plays with concentrated brilliance without engaging the emotions and Green is a good deal drier than usual, perhaps to compensate for a more than usually high-temperature group. Young and Jones keep the temperature well up. All the compositions are by the organist, and 'Plaza De Toros' and 'Tyrone' offer a useful encapsulation of his polytonal approach.

CORE COLLECTION

♛ ** Unity**

Blue Note 56416-2 *Young; Woody Shaw (t); Joe Henderson (ts); Elvin Jones (d).* 11/65.

Quite simply a masterpiece. Whipped along by Jones's ferocious drumming and Henderson's meaty tenor, even on a soft-pedal tune like 'Softly As In A Morning Sunrise'. Young contributes nothing as a writer, which doesn't in any way diminish the impact of his performance. Woody Shaw's 'The Moontrane', 'Zoltan' and 'Beyond All Limits' are a measure of *his* under-regarded significance as a composer; the first of the three is the perfect test of Young's absorption of Coltrane's ideas, as he develops a rather obvious (if precocious – Shaw wrote it when he was just eighteen) sequence of harmonics into something that represents a genuine extension of the great saxophonist, not just a bland repetition. This is a record that has proved hard to track down over the years. Of all our highest-rated albums, it has been one of the most elusive, despite the label and Young's relative eminence. Its inclusion in Blue Note's recent Rudy van Gelder edition is testimony to two great men of music.

****(*) Mother Ship**

Blue Note 90415 *Young; Lee Morgan (t); Herbert Morgan (ts); Eddie Gladden (d).* 2/69.

Young's last album for Blue Note did not see the light of day until 1980. Three other post-*Unity* Blue Notes – *Of Love And Peace, Contrasts, Heaven On Earth* – have still not reappeared. It's a disappointing set, stuck somewhere between hard bop, soul jazz and the avant-garde. Certainly, it doesn't live up to the high expectations set up by Larry's 1985 masterpiece. Originals like 'Street Scene' and 'Love Drops' come across as heads and jamming themes rather than true compositions and the performances are shapelessly energetic. There might be one strong CD to be culled from Young's later-'60s work for the label; his reputation certainly merits it.

****(*) Lawrence Of Newark**

Sanctuary 81221 *Young; Charles McGee (t); Pharoah Sanders (ts); Cedric Lawson (p); James Blood Ulmer (g); Dierdre Johnson (clo); Juini Booth, Don Pate (b); James Flores,*

Howard King (d); Art Gore (d, perc); Armen Halburian, Abdul Hakim, Pappy Laboy, Uman Abdul Muizz, Jumma Santos (perc). 73.

Posed in Arab headdress on the cover, this latter-day Lawrence was already bound for the Empty Quarter in critical terms. After this sprawling, rhythm-dominated album, Young was to make just two more fusion records before his untimely death. The only real pointer towards anything new here is 'Khalid Of Space: Part 2 – Welcome', which has an interesting structure. For the most part, though, these tracks go the way of the opening 'Sunshine Fly Away', which begins promisingly and fails to go anywhere.

McGee is cut-price Morgan and Ulmer still sounds rather constrained, relative to what he was doing later in the decade. Dierdre Johnson's cello is an interesting component, but it is largely lost in a wash of percussion.

It's tempting to compare Young's last few years with those of Albert Ayler. There are superficial resemblances, like having his wife Althea sing on some of the records, but Larry's attempt to blend his avant-garde style with a more popular approach is nothing like as successful as Ayler's, whose last records have been the subject of a revision over the last few years. It may be that his two Arista discs, *Spaceball* and *Fuel*, reappear before our next edition, but we're not convinced they'll add anything material to the story. A disappointing end.

Lester Young (1909–59)

TENOR SAXOPHONE, CLARINET, VOCAL

A profoundly sensitive individual, in terms both of aesthetics and of a deep capacity for hurt, Pres – as Billie Holiday dubbed him – is one of the most influential saxophonists ever to play jazz. He marks a point of transition from swing to bebop. Borrowing something from Frankie Trumbauer, he first developed a style which was dry and cool and which changed dramatically after Young's traumatic time in the military, which occasioned a serious breakdown. He grew up near New Orleans and played in a family setting, but left home to start a professional career with Art Bronson and then with Walter Page's Blue Devils. Count Basie recruited the 25-year-old but Young soon left and joined Fletcher Henderson's band, where his unorthodox approach, so very different from the Coleman Hawkins orthodoxy, led him to be ostracized. He was soon back with Basie and started to record under his own name and as an accompanist for Billie Holiday, to whom he was the perfect foil. His improvisations grew ever more elegantly structured, built up from short, slightly staccato phrases, but stretched out and ambiguous. The draft was a nightmare for Young, who was court-martialled for drug abuse. The man who emerged in 1945 was at least partly broken and became increasingly dependent on drink and narcotics; his tone coarsened and his solos became ever more formulaic as the legend of Pres grew. The late recordings, like Billie Holiday's, have their admirers, but they are a pale shadow of the pre-war Young.

CORE COLLECTION

**** The Complete Aladdin Sessions

Blue Note 32787 2CD *Young; Shorty McConnell, Howard McGhee (t); Vic Dickenson (tb); Willie Smith (as); Maxwell Davis (ts); Joe Albany, Jimmy Bunn, Nat Cole, Gene DiNovi, Wesley Jones, Michael 'Dodo' Marmarosa, Argonne Thornton (p); Irving Ashby, Nasir Baraakat, Dave Barbour, Fred Lacey, Chuck Wayne (g); Ted Briscoe, Red Callender, Curtis Counce, Rodney Richardson, Junior Rudd, Curley Russell (b); Chico Hamilton, Roy Haynes, Tiny Kahn, Lyndell Marshall, Johnny Otis, Henry Tucker (d). 7/42–12/47.*

Listeners who have heard Young's classic solos – the 1936 'Lady Be Good' with Jo Jones and Carson Smith, 'Jumpin' At The Woodside' and the later 'Lester Leaps In' with Basie – will have to judge how much of a falling-off is evident in the material on the Savoy sessions, which are marked by flashes of brilliance but not distributed consistently enough. The truth is that Young's best work was nearly all done for others. The Aladdin sessions do, however, cover some of his best work as a leader, though even some of these are for another singer, Helen Humes. Young's cool, wry approach still seems slightly out of synch with prevailing expectations, though he is absolutely *simpatico* with Willie Smith, another figure now routinely overlooked in accounts of how jazz developed into its modern phase. The big pluses on this generously proportioned compilation are a rare glimpse of the 1942 Los Angeles session with Nat Cole and an instrumental 'Riffin' Without Helen', recorded as part of the Humes session, presumably while she was off powdering her nose. Michael Cuscuna has made his usual impeccable job of bringing the sound-quality up to speed for CD. Carefully declicked and with background noise reduced to a minimum, these two discs provide optimum listening.

***(*) Lester Young, 1943–1946

Classics 932 *Young; Harry 'Sweets' Edison, Al Killian, Joe Newman (t); Ted Donnelly, Dicky Wells, Eli Robinson, Lewis Taylor (tb); Jimmy Powell, Earl Warren (as); Buddy Tate (ts); Rudy Rutherford (bs); Count Basie, Johnny Guarnieri, Clyde Hart (p); Freddie Green (g); Rodney Richardson, Slam Stewart (b); Big Sid Catlett, Jo Jones, Shadow Wilson (d); other personnel as for Aladdin sessions above. 12/43–1/46.*

This Classics compilation covers at least some of the same territory as the Aladdin sessions above, and includes the same instrumental from the Humes session, of which Blue Note were making much; Anatol Schenker suggests that it was actually released in small numbers under the title 'It's Better To Give Than To Receive'. The December 1945 and January 1946 sessions overlap both formats, but the Classics set also includes the Savoy dates of April and May 1944, the former under Earl Warren's leadership, the latter a small group with the Count and the Basie band rhythm section.

*** Kansas City Sax: The Complete Kansas City Master Takes

Jasmine 2600 *Young; Buck Clayton (t); Dicky Wells (tb); Eddie Durham (tb, g); Count Basie, Sammy Benskin, Joe Bushkin (p); Freddie Green (g); Al Hall, Walter Page, Rodney Richardson, John Simmons (b); Jo Jones, Shadow Wilson (d). 38–44.*

The title is a clever fudge. When members of Count Basie's rhythm section took time off from big-band duties, they formed the *ad hoc* Kansas City Five, which became a sextet with the recruitment of Lester, and later evolved into the KC Seven. A couple of tracks are also credited to guitarist Freddie Green accompanying Sylvia Sims. Its activities have been documented on a couple of Classics compilations, but this Jasmine reissue affords a glimpse of the best of the work under Lester's name. He wasn't the only soloist, but he produced some fine work in this relaxed atmosphere and 'Way Down Yonder In New Orleans' and 'Three Little Words' remain classics of the late swing era, so worth a look.

*****(*) The Complete Savoy Recordings**
Savoy 27122 2CD *Similar to the above.* 44–52.

Lester's work for Savoy was of mixed quality, and many of the alternates included on this 46 track collection are only of interest to serious collectors. However, there's enough substance to this handsome and well-documented set to attract anyone who wants to hear the great man in some depth, well-mastered and with informative liner-notes. The personnels are easy enough to disentangle from the comments above, but while label compilations are often useful route maps through a career, for all their importance these sessions don't tell the full Young story, even from this period and it can just as easily be reconstructed by other means.

****(*) Volume 1: 1939–1947 – The Alternative Takes**
Neatwork 2035 *As for the above,* 39–47.

Depending on your point of view, the Neatwork releases are either a welcome resource for collectors or barrel-scrapings. With an artist as controversial, particularly in his later years, as Lester, they might be thought to have a resonance and value not obvious in other cases, and yet these 25 tracks, including three takes of Johnny Guarnieri's 'Exercise In Swing' and four of 'Salute To Fats' add surprisingly little to our understanding of Lester in some of his more productive years. Solos are generally taken along very similar lines on different takes and apart from flaws in articulation and occasional missed cues, as on two of the above numbers, there's not much to differentiate them, certainly not an artist who reinvents every time the red light goes on. These are limited edition releases, aimed at a specialist market. We'd recommend all but devoted collectors to steer clear.

***** Lester Young 1947–1951**
Classics 1247 *Young; Jesse Drakes, Shorty McConnell (t); Jerry Elliott (tb); Hank Jones, John Lewis, Junior Mance, Gene DiNovi, Argonne Thornton (p); Nasir Barakaat, Chuck Wayne (g); Ray Brown, LeRoy Jackson, Gene Ramey, Rodney Richardson, Curley Russell, Joe Shulman (b); Bill Clark, Roy Haynes, Jo Jones, Tiny Khan, Lyndell Marshall, Buddy Rich (d).* 4/47–1/51.

***** Lester Young 1951–1952**
Classics 1325 *Young; John Lewis, Oscar Peterson (p); Barney Kessel (g); Ray Brown, Gene Ramey (b); J. C. Heard, Jo Jones (d).* 1/51–11/52.

The beginning of Young's association with Norman Granz finds him in fairly poor shape, either physically, mentally or both. There's a sleepwalker's false clarity to some of the playing on the September 1949 and June 1950 sessions that bodes ill for the future and the saxophone is thready and insecure. Pres wasn't in the studio at all during 1948 because of the recording ban and the last date before that is a shaky, end-of-contract gig for Aladdin where DiNovi, Wayne, Russell and Khan battle their way through a set that hadn't been discussed, let alone rehearsed beforehand. Earlier in 1947, Lester had recorded the beautiful 'I'm Confessin'' with a virtually unknown group, his solo standing out like a diamond pin on a dull club tie. His first excursion as leader after the band was a June 1949 date for Savoy; it sounds unbelievably rough and ready, not much more than a blues jam over not more than two or three ideas. Lester gets off some nice, tongued phrases on 'Ding Dong' (based on the 'All Of Me' chords) but he's struggling in the main. Opinion still rages about this period in Lester's career. Some maintain he was a broken reed; others insist that like Billie Holiday's his expression moved onto a new plane. We're inclined to the former view, even though flashes of the old genius do shine through.

The following volume concludes the January 1951 date with Lewis, Ramey and Jones and marks a possible recovery from wartime trauma and the recording ban. 'Frenesi' is the best thing from that date. It swings unexpectedly and the intonation is light but accurate over Lewis's sophisticated chording. This is the kind of environment in which Lester could create wonderful things out of the flimsiest of material. Two originals, 'Pete's Café' and 'Little Pee's Blues' round out that date but the same orchestra was back in the studio in March to cut another four sides for Mercury and two for Norgran. These are test cases in the Lester Young debate. 'Lester Swings' does exactly that, while the B-side 'Slow Motion Blues' is as painfully dragged and mournful as anything Lester ever committed to disc. It would be tempting to play it as evidence of the saxophonist's mental decline except that there is a sardonic humour to its long line which suggests that something else may be in play.

Some of the later material can be found on the sets below, but suffice it to say that these two volumes are a valuable resource for anyone interested in Young's career and putative decline, *provided* they're listened to thoroughly and with due scepticism. Not every fractured performance is a sign of incipient breakdown. Nor does a smooth legato point to mental health.

*****(*) Lester Young & The Piano Giants**
Verve 835316-2 *Young; Harry 'Sweets' Edison, Roy Eldridge (t); Vic Dickenson (tb); Nat Cole, Hank Jones, John Lewis, Oscar Peterson, Teddy Wilson (p); Herb Ellis, Freddie Green (g); Ray Brown, Gene Ramey, Joe Shulman (b); Bill Clark, Jo Jones, Buddy Rich (d).* 3/46–1/56.

***** Lester Young Trio**
Verve 521650-2 *Young; Harry 'Sweets' Edison (t); Dexter Gordon (ts); Nat Cole (p); Red Callender (b); Juicy Owens, Buddy Rich (d).* 43, 4/46.

***** Masters Of Jazz: Lester Young**
Storyville STCD 4107 *Young; Jesse Drakes, Idrees Sulieman (t); John Lewis, Bill Potts, Horace Silver (p); Aaron Bell, Gene Ramey, Franklin Skeete, Norman Williams (b); Jo Jones, Connie Kay, Abram Lee, Jim Lucht (d).* 5/51–12/56.

*****(*) The President Plays**
Verve 521451-2 *Young; Oscar Peterson (p); Barney Kessel (g); Ray Brown (b); J. C. Heard (d).* 11/52.

***** Pres & Sweets**
Verve 849391-2 *Young; Harry 'Sweets' Edison (t); Oscar Peterson (p); Herb Ellis (g); Ray Brown (b); Buddy Rich (d).* 12/55.

***** Pres & Teddy**
Verve 831270-2 *Young; Teddy Wilson (p); Gene Ramey (b); Jo Jones (d).* 1/56.

*****(*) The Lester Young Story**
Proper PROPERBOX 8 4CD *As various discs above.* 10/36–9/49.

Immediately after the war there was evidence of some of the less desirable traits that crept into his '50s work (a formulaic repetition and a self-conscious and histrionic distortion of tone and phrasing akin to his friend Billie Holiday's around the same time); it's clear that he is trying to rethink harmonic progression. A new device, much noted, is his use of an arpeggiated tonic triad in first inversion (i.e. with the third rather than the root in lowest position) which, whatever its technical niceties, smoothed out chordal progression from ever shorter phrases. Some of that is evident in the 1946 trios with Rich and Cole, and on other augmented line-ups from that time. There are extra versions of 'Back To The Land' and 'I Cover The Waterfront', illustrating Pres's ability to reshape a theme and send it off in a new direction, while still using the same basic roster of melodic devices.

The 1952 session for Norman Granz (now believed to have been made in November, not in August) includes the slightly bizarre sound of Young lewdly singing the lyric to 'It Takes Two To Tango': 'Drop your drawers, take them off ...' It's a curiosity, but the rest of the session is very good indeed. The Verve compilation includes some excellent material, recorded in January 1956, with Roy Eldridge, another stylistic bridge-builder, and Teddy Wilson, together with a 1950 version of 'Up'N'Adam' with Hank Jones. The Nat Cole material is available separately on the *Trio* album.

The Lester Young Story leaves only a few gaps in its documentation of the first era of Young on record. The four CDs sound good and there's a detailed booklet.

***** Lester Young In Washington, D.C. 1956: Volume 1**
Original Jazz Classics OJC 782 *Young; Bill Potts (p); Norman Williams (b); Jim Lucht (d).* 12/56.

***** Lester Young In Washington, D.C. 1956: Volume 2**
Original Jazz Classics OJCCD 881 *As above.* 12/56.

***** Lester Young In Washington, D.C. 1956: Volume 3**
Original Jazz Classics OJCCD 901 *As above.* 12/56.

***** Lester Young In Washington, D.C. 1956: Volume 4**
Original Jazz Classics OJCCD 1043 *As above.* 12/56.

****(*) Lester Young In Washington, D.C. 1956: Volume 5**
Original Jazz Classics OJCCD 1051 *As above.* 12/56.

***** The Best Of Lester Young**
Pablo 2405420 *As above.*

The 1956 OJCs further confound the notion of a man who had given up on life and art; though drastically reconceived and hardly abetted by Potts's backward-looking accompaniments (it was often Pres's sidemen who wanted to play in the 'old style' about which he became so painfully ambivalent), 'Lester Leaps In' and 'These Foolish Things' (both on the better Volume 2) are major jazz performances. Right to the very end Young was capable of quite extraordinary things. 'There Will Never Be Another You', with Kenny Clarke, Jimmy Gourley, Harold Kauffman and Jean-Marie Ingrand (with one exception, not the company he deserved) was recorded within a fortnight of his death and still sounds vital, moving and full of musical intelligence.

Young's later years have been unhelpfully coloured by too many sorry anecdotes (about his drinking, world-weariness and increasingly restricted conversational code) and, more recently, by Bertrand Tavernier's composite anti-hero, Dale Turner, in *Round Midnight*, a character who is truer in spirit to the declining Bud Powell. Powell felt safe in the past and retreated into re-creations of his best work. Throughout his life, Young had been brutally cut off from his own past; by its end the only direction he knew was uneasily forward.

***** The Ultimate Lester Young**
Verve 539772-2 *As for Verve recordings above.* 44–55.

Another in Verve's insightful series in which younger-generation musicians – in this case, Wayne Shorter – select material by their artistic forebears. Wayne suggests that it was Pres's tragedy that after the war he wasn't given much opportunity to play with younger musicians of a more advanced disposition. The strong implication is that the modernist hints and foreshadows which can be heard in his phrasing and his harmonics throughout this thoroughly enjoyable compilation might have flowered into something new and different. We are inclined to think that this was wishful thinking. Lester was a pretty broken man in terms of straightforward physical health, and he was certainly not agile enough to cope with much in the way of mental gymnastics.

***** Jazz Masters 30**
Verve 521859-2 *Young; Nat Cole, Hank Jones, John Lewis, Oscar Peterson, Teddy Wilson (p); Barney Kessel (g); Ray Brown, Gene Ramey, Slam Stewart (b); Big Sid Catlett, J. C. Heard, Jo Jones, Buddy Rich (d).* 43–56.

A very good introduction to Young's later work, faithfully and pleasingly remastered. The *Ultimate* collection is probably our favourite of the two and, given that there is a significant overlap, it is the one to opt for.

*****(*) Laughin' To Keep From Cryin'**
Verve 543301-2 *Young; Harry 'Sweets' Edison, Roy Eldridge (t); Hank Jones (p); Herb Ellis (g); George Duvivier (b); Mickey Sheene (d).* 2/58.

Late in the day and a desperately tired act. There are moments, as when Pres switches to clarinet for 'Salute To Benny' and 'They Can't Take That Away From Me', when the music is as vivid and logical as one might hope but for the most part this is a drab curtain-call, and Young doesn't even appear on all the tracks, sitting out the first part of the 'Ballad Medley', which he finishes with the trio on 'Blue And Sentimental'. The remastering is very good, and something of the smothered passion of Pres's late recording does come across.

***** The Complete Lester Young Studio Sessions On Verve**
Verve 547087-2 8CD *Young; Harry 'Sweets' Edison, Jesse Drakes, Roy Eldridge (t); Vic Dickenson (tb); Nat Cole, John Lewis, Oscar Peterson, Teddy Wilson, Gildo Mahones, Lou Stein, Hank Jones, René Urtreger (p); Barney Kessel, Herb Ellis, Freddie Green, Jimmy Gourley (g); Joe Shulman, Ray Brown, Gene Ramey, John Ore, George Duvivier, Jamil Nasser (b); Jo Jones, Bill Clark, Buddy Rich, J. C. Heard, Connie Kay, Louie Bellson, Mickey Sheen, Kenny Clarke (d).* 3/46–3/59.

Here finally are Lester Young's closing years in all the close-up detail befitting such an important musician. Even as vinyl, these dates were scattered across many albums – the booklet reproduces no fewer than 21 different 'original' LP sleeves – and several of the tracks have been unavailable in any form for many years. A lot of it is, by the standards of most jazz, wretched music. All too often in these dates its principal is playing so poorly, with such lack of control, that if newcomers were to hear Young for the first time, in these dates, they would be astonished that he is as revered as he is. Some of the eight discs can be virtually written off altogether as pleasurable listening experiences. Others expose Young as a hollow, crippled voice surrounded by sympathetic but bewildered contemporaries, gamely trying either to hold him up or to cover him up with their own playing. The final session here, recorded in Paris in March 1959, finds Young so enfeebled that he can barely get the notes out of the horn, and to listen to this as entertainment is a stretch which we would rather not extend to.

Young's Verve story, as suggested already, is a lot more complex than mere inexorable decline. The first seven sessions are all tenor-plus-rhythm with, in succession, Nat Cole, Hank Jones, John Lewis and Oscar Peterson. The material is blues, a few workouts on familiar chords and standards, some of them rather surprising choices. None of the performances is bad, and Young contributes something fine to each of them – an unpredictable curlicue, a pale flurry of melody, a bashful beeping on a single note. Yet, at the same time, there is something wrong with all of them. Sometimes a solo will seem ready to fold up and die, and he will have to pull it round at the last moment. Other passages find him strong and hale, only to tamely crack a note or suddenly stumble, a beach jogger tripping over driftwood. It wouldn't matter so much if it happened only here and there – but it happens on every tune, to some degree.

The exceptionally handsome booklet quotes a remark made by Coleman Hawkins, the earth to Lester's air sign: 'That Lester Young, how does he get away with it? He's stoned half the time, he's always late, and he can't play.' It was and it wasn't true.

***(*) Le Dernier Message De Lester Young**
Emarcy 598557-2 *Young; René Urtreger (p); Jimmy Gourley (g); Jamil Nasser (b); Kenny Clarke (d).* 3/59.

If you love Lester's music, you won't want to hear this ghastly farewell. One wonders especially what Kenny Clarke, who must have played with Lester on many better days, thought of it all.

Bojan Z (born 1968)

PIANO

Bojan Z(ulfikarpasic) – he often reduces his name to help out tongue-tied audiences – is from Belgrade, where he switched from being a teenage fusion star to acoustic jazz. He works regularly in the Julian Lourau group and has these CDs to his name.

*****(*) Quartet**
Label Bleu LBLC 6565 *Zulfikarpasic; Julien Lourau (ss, ts); Marc BuronFosse (b); François Merville (d).* 12/93.

*****(*) Solobsession**
Label Bleu LBLC 6624 *Zulfikarpasic (p solo).* 12/00.

****** Transpacifik**
Label Bleu LBLC 6654 *Zulfikarpasic; Scott Colley (b); Nasheet Waits (d).* 6/03.

Sparkling and original music from Z (we'll call him that to save our typing fingers). *Quartet* is full of bright, ingenious themes that hopscotch between bases with rare insouciance, cunningly 'European' melodies hidden in settings which otherwise play footsie with post-bop genre moves. Try 'Mashala', which sounds vaguely exotic – an Indian march? – yet refuses to plant its feet anywhere. Lourau and Z are long-standing playing companions and they perform each other's music with fine gusto. The solo record, boiled down from hours of playing, is full of ideas. One Z trait is his concern to get the most out of both hands at the keyboard. He does fascinating essays on 'Valse Hot' and Ornette's 'Mothers Of The Veil', but his own 'Multi Don Kulti' and 'Zulfikar-Pacha' are just as strong, leavened by the kind of humour which contemporary jazz only rarely deals in.

One could muse for hours on how 'Balkan' his music is, and he invites it with titles and pieces like 'Bulgarska' on *Transpacifik*. This is a virtuoso trio session, yet, again, notably uncluttered: as many-noted as Z's music often is, his lines are often prismatically clear. Colley and Waits fall in with his sound quickly and it all goes to make up a memorable trio record.

Bobby Zankel (born 1949)

ALTO AND SOPRANO SAXOPHONES

Based in Philadelphia, Zankel is a saxophonist and composer working in an area that moves between post-bop and a conservative kind of free playing.

***** Seeking Spirit**
Cadence CJR 1050 *Zankel; Stan Slotter (t, f); Johnny Coles (t); Odean Pope (ts); Ray Wright (bs); Sumi Tonooka, Uri Caine (p); Tyrone Brown (b); Craig McIver, David Gibson (d).* 3/91–1/92.

****(*) Emerging From The Earth**
Cadence CJR 1059 *As above, except add John Blake (vn), Ralph Peterson Jr (d), Ron Howerton (perc); omit Coles, Pope, Wright, Tonooka, McIver, Gibson.* 3/94.

****(*) Human Flowers**
CIMP 103 *Zankel; Marilyn Crispell (p); Newman Baker (d).* 11/95.

Zankel seems like a talented player-composer, and it's a pity that his debut album is let down by some unwarranted flaws. The record is evenly split between sessions for quartet and octet: the former blaze along on the back of Gibson's explosive drumming, and some clever touches in the writing – the layered rhythms of 'Something Up Her Sleeve', for instance – help to concentrate the intensity of the playing. The five octet pieces are a shade more ambitious, but the sometimes ragged ensembles distract from thoughtful improvising by Pope, Coles and Tonooka. The leader's own alto works off an impassioned delivery, but he's badly served by the production, which should have him much nearer the front.

Emerging From The Earth is an ambitious continuation, involving the septet in all eight pieces, but again there are disappointing aspects. Even as Zankel crowds his compositions with incident, the sound of the group seems awry – Blake's violin doesn't really fit in, and some of the ensembles demand a coherence that eludes them – while the sound is again a drawback: too often the instruments sound like a muddle, and the rhythm section in particular is made to seem chaotic by the mix.

The trio session, *Human Flowers*, is entirely different. Performed as a continuous three-way conversation, with few changes in dynamics, this is rather wearying stuff over the long haul, and when Zankel's ingenuities are tested to the full he comes up a bit short at times. The CIMP philosophy of releasing unmixed live digital sound doesn't work very well here: piano and drums both sound too thin to give the music sufficient impact.

***** Prayer And Action**

CIMP 131 *Zankel; John Swana (t); Bryan Carrott (vib); Tyrone Brown (b); Ralph Peterson Jr (d).* 11/96.

***** Transcend And Triumph**

CIMP 240 *Zankel; Rick Iannacone (g); Craig McIver (d).* 2/01.

Zankel's a bit of an odd man out at CIMP. His jazz works when it puts its trust in some basic principles: entirely free space rarely suits him. The quintet of *Prayer And Action* looks like a Criss Cross rather than a CIMP line-up, and the label's naturalistic sound (as they see it) tends to thin out the band's impact – a surprising situation for any band with Peterson in it. The drummer's superb momentum does carry any dead spots in the solos, though, and Carrott is similarly important, playing almost continuously in support of the horns and intensifying when it's his solo. Swana sounds less content, and there are passages which feel like mere vamping.

The smaller scale of *Transcend And Triumph* puts more responsibility on Zankel as a saxophonist, but he was in good fettle for this date and his Ornette Coleman leanings score points in this context. The trio work together as a continuous force and on something as concentrated as 'Scrupulosity', a few seconds under seven minutes, there's a strong result. In the end, though, the record doesn't sustain itself – Zankel hasn't got Coleman's knack for playing the same twists and turns and making each return visit plausible.

Joe Zawinul (born 1932)

PIANO, KEYBOARDS

Born in Vienna, he studied at the Conservatory there prior to wartime evacuation. Became interested in jazz and eventually went to the USA on a Berklee scholarship. Played for Dinah Washington, then with Cannonball Adderley for the rest of the '60s. Then with Miles Davis, subsequently forming the hugely successful Weather Report, with Wayne Shorter and Miroslav Vitous, eventually disbanded in 1986. Later projects have been mixed successes, but he remains a major composer and few have been as creatively successful with electric keyboards.

***** And The Austrian All Stars / His Majesty Swinging Nephews, 1954–1957**

RST 91549 *Zawinul; Dick Murphy (t); Hans Salomon (as, ts); Karl Drewo (ts); Johnny Fischer, Rudolf Hansen (b); Victor Plasil (d).* 10/54–3/57.

***** The Beginning**

Fresh Sound FSRCD 142 *Zawinul; George Tucker (b); Frankie Dunlop (d); Ray Barretto (perc).* 9/59.

Creator of some of the classic jazz tunes of the last 40 years, from 'Mercy Mercy Mercy' and 'Country Preacher' to 'Birdland' and beyond, Joe Zawinul has managed to place himself where the action is since he arrived in the United States in 1959. These records straddle that moment of fruitful exile. In Austria, the young conservatory-trained pianist had worked with the legendary Friedrich Gulda, but he had also been involved with a number of inventive small groups who represented the accelerated development of jazz during the de-Nazification period. The RST disc covers what was probably the most advanced group in Austria at the time, formed in 1954 and sounding pretty much on a par with any similarly aged and inclined group from the United States. Originally recorded for Turicaphon's Elite Special label, it's a fascinating session for a first glimpse of Zawinul as jazz composer. Even this early, 'Mekka' is unmistakably his, a forceful pounding left hand holding the ideas together, exotic intervals and resolutions consigned to the top line. Elsewhere, Zawinul takes the least likely harmonic path, occasionally leaving the otherwise excellent Salomon and the less adroit Drewo at the starting gate.

By 1957 and his trio with Fischer and Plasil, it's clear that he needs broader horizons for his playing. The move to America seemed inevitable. There, he gigged with Maynard Ferguson and Dinah Washington before falling in with Adderley and making a record, still to be found in the secondhand trays, with Ben Webster. The Fresh Sound album – misleadingly titled, unless one chooses to think of the move Stateside as the start of his 'real' career – was made soon after his arrival, testimony to the substantial word-of-mouth reputation Zawinul acquired on an already overcrowded scene. In what was then, mercifully, not the parlance, he really goes for it, obviously trying to make an impact with a set of lyrical standards. Given the instincts of Tucker and Dunlop, the pace is medium to up, but there are affecting ballad performances as well: 'My One And Only Love' is beautiful, only slightly marred by Barretto's intrusive percussion. These records shouldn't be overvalued. To a degree, they are curiosities, because they pose the question as to how a young man from the city of serialism and the waltz acquired sufficient jazz know-how to make himself indispensable to Cannonball Adderley, catch the eye of Ben Webster and, later, Miles Davis, and go on to found one of the most successful fusion groups ever.

***** The Rise And Fall Of The Third Stream / Money In The Pocket**

Rhino R2 71675 *Zawinul; Blue Mitchell, Jimmy Owens (t); William Fischer, Joe Henderson, Clifford Jordan (ts); Pepper Adams (bs); Bob Cranshaw, Richard Davis, Sam Jones (b); Louis Hayes, Roy McCurdy, Freddie Waits (d); Warren Smith (perc); Alfred Brown, Selwart Clarke, Theodore Israel (vla); Kermit Moore (clo).* 4/66–12/67.

In 1967 the fusion revolution, in which Zawinul was to have a significant part, was still a year or two away. These two records are pretty much of their time, a mixture of funky soul-jazz on the earlier *Money* and then-fashionable classical/non-European crossovers on the '67 sessions. Third Stream seems less risibly distant now than it once did, and it was a movement that perfectly suited someone of Zawinul's background. The opening track, 'Baptismal', underlines one legitimate objection. A brooding cello solo with viola just behind (anticipating the tonality of later work like 'His Last Journey' on *Zawinul*) gives way to a medium-pace jazz tune which bears only the slightest relation to the introduction. The setting of the two-part 'Soul Of A Village' would seem, on the face of it, to be far to the east of the Tyrol (China, possibly), and the embellishments are a little intrusive. These are not Zawinul compositions; with the exception of 'From Vienna, With Love', everything is credited to William Fischer. (We take leave to doubt this: though Fischer certainly did the arrangements, surely at least some of these ideas are Zawinul's? If not, the resemblance is uncanny.)

The jazzier *Money* session is nicely done. Joel Dorn's hand at the controls was a guarantee of quality at this time. While he sounds a bit heavy-handed when balancing the strings on *Third Stream*, the horn arrangements on the remaining tracks are brightly registered, with lots of room for Adams's rich tone and a clear vantage for the neglected Mitchell. Zawinul here shares the credits with Henderson (the thoughtful 'If') and two tunes by another musician who always gets the foundations right before he does the curlicues, bassist Sam Jones. It isn't a classic session, but whenever the horns give ground to Zawinul and the rhythm section, as on the closing 'Del Sasser', his playing is absolutely riveting.

**** Zawinul

Atlantic 7567 81375 *Zawinul; Jimmy Owens, Woody Shaw (t); Wayne Shorter, Earl Turbinton (ss); George Davis, Hubert Laws (f); Herbie Hancock (p); Walter Booker, Miroslav Vitous (b); Joe Chambers, Billy Hart, David Lee (d); Jack DeJohnette (hca, perc).* 70.

The eponymous Atlantic album with its haunting sepia cover – a huge close-up of Zawinul's sombre face – was made the year that Weather Report was formed and a year after Zawinul took part in Miles Davis's epochal – or at the very least transitional – *In A Silent Way*, for which the Austrian wrote the title-track, also included here. *Zawinul* is a lovely, lovely record. Somewhat pretentiously entitled 'Music for two electric pianos, jazz flute, trumpet, soprano saxophone, two contrabasses and percussion', it nods in the direction of his conservatory past almost as much as it anticipates the experiments in fusion music. Woody Shaw's echoplexed trumpet strongly recalls Miles (who writes the liner-note) but, with Vitous handling one of the bass parts and Shorter replacing the little-known Turbinton on 'Double Image', the original Weather Report is already in place. *I Sing The Body Electric*, the group's second disc, was to include a live-in-Japan version of 'Doctor Honoris Causa', a tribute to Zawinul's keyboard twin, Herbie Hancock. Here it gets a much more measured reading, less frenetic and intense, more floating and indefinite, as in 'His Last Journey', where the electric piano's ability to imitate tolling bells (another Weather Report favourite) is exploited to great effect. Not just because Shorter is present, 'Double Image' is the track that most clearly points forward. The brief 'Arrival In New York' is an aural impression of the immigrant wharves; not far removed from Mingus's 'Foggy Day' on *Pithecanthropus Erectus*, it underlines how important sheer sound was to Zawinul and his group. There is nothing here as completely abstract as on the first two Weather Report records, and there is much that harks back to the gospelly funk of his days with Cannonball. Even so, it is a disc that looks forward more securely than back.

(***) Stories Of The Danube

Philips 454 143 *Zawinul; Amit Chatterjee (g, v); Burhan Ocal (oud, v, perc); Walter Grassman (d); Arto Tuncboyaciyan (perc, v); Czech State Philharmonic Orchestra, Brno; Caspar Richter (cond).* 11/95.

Billed as Zawinul's first symphony, this majestically proportioned progress from source to sea and through several centuries of bloody but replenishing history is certainly not a jazz record, nor is it intended to be. Zawinul's long-standing interest in orchestral writing and in finding neutral ground between improvisation and composition is well served, but the music fails to catch light. There are moments in 'Gipsy', which comes at the very heart of the piece, the middle one of its seven movements, when it all starts to make sense, but the pace is ponderous and the orchestrations far from convincing. 'Unknown Soldier' is very different from the haunting track on Weather Report's *I Sing The Body Electric*, and this is perhaps the best point of comparison with past work. Spectacularly mounted as a live piece, it may well have been impressive. As a recorded work, it simply fails to convince.

*** World Tour

ESC Records ESC/EFA 03656 2CD *Zawinul; Gary Poulson (g); Richard Bona, Victor Bailey (b); Paco Sery (d, kalimba, v); Manolo Badrena (perc, v, nolopipe); Frank Hoffman, Pape Abdou Sech (v).* 5–11/97.

Joe! Call home! Between 29 January and 14 December 1997, the Zawinul Syndicate played 126 concerts, 24 in October alone. Even by the overblown standards of stadium mega-rock, this is a pretty heroic endeavour. Sadly, the music documented is rarely more than mildly involving, a mixture of stretched-out world-music jams and tighter song-forms. The best of the material – 'Lost Tribes' on disc two, the long 'Indiscretions' and the opening 'Patriots' on disc one – is close enough to Weather Report grooves to draw in the old fans. Much of the rest, though, falls into a rather bland and formulaic delivery which must have become ever more deeply entrenched as the caravan moved on. The live mixes are generally very good, though often percussion is allowed to dominate. Richard Bona is a less jazz-orientated bassist than Victor Bailey, but in a perverse way he fits more comfortably into the mix. Badrena is a star and occasionally outshines Zawinul himself, but this is unquestionably Joe's concept and the main man's gig.

** My People

Escapade 03651 *Zawinul; Mike Mossman (t, tb); Bobby Malach (ts); Amit Chatterjee, Osmane Kouka, Gary Poulson (g); Burhan Ocal (oud); Richard Bona (b); Tal Bergmann (d, perc); Alex Acuña, Souleyman Doumbia, Trilok Gurtu, Michito Sanchez (perc); Lucho Avelleneda, Bolot, Assitan Dembele, Djeme Doumboouya, Duke Ellington, Salif Keita, Kenny O'Brien, Beto Sabala, Thomas Sanchez (v); Arto Tuncboyaciyan (v, perc).* 96.

Zawinul claims Czech, Hungarian and Sinti ancestry, and this is his attempt to create a personalized kind of world music by bringing together as many different musical traditions as possible and watching them spark off each other. Except that they don't, leaving a drab residue of common riffs, rhythms and disharmonies. A hugely disappointing record.

**** Faces and Places

ESC 03679 2 *Zawinul; Harry Kim (flhn); Lester Benedict (tb); Bob Malach (ts); Dean Brown, Amit Chatterjee (g); Etienne Mbappe, Richard Bona (b, v); Victor Bailey (b); Paco Sery (d, g); Nathaniel Townsley (d); Manolo Badrena, Zakir Hussain, Randy Regalado (perc); Maria Joao, Sabine Kabongo, Perry Sisters, Richard Page, Kitty Winter (v).* 01.

Joe's best post-Weather Report record, this draws on a typically wide range of influences, from African highlife to hardbop, West Coast cool to Eastern Europe conservatory. The key element in the group sound is Malach, who must be the most convincing and inventive reed man Joe has worked with since Wayne Shorter. Bassist Richard Bona and drummer Paco Sery complete the basic equation. As usual, there are too many Vocoder effects and too many long, bass-driven vamps, but tunes like 'The Spirit of Julian 'C' Adderley', 'Café Andalusia' and 'Rooftops of Vienna' are packed with atmosphere and not just atmosphere but also solid musical information. At 70-plus Joe is making some of the most convincing music of his career.

Don't rule out a Weather Report reunion of some sort, but be assured that even without that unpredictable umbrella of a project title, Joe Zawinul is always his own man and always capable of turning on the sunshine or delivering a lightning strike of a musical surprise.

Denny Zeitlin (born 1938)

PIANO

Studied with George Russell and has since operated parallel careers in jazz and psychiatry, though the latter seems to be the more dominant side of his work of late.

*****(*) Time Remembers Time Once**
ECM 837020-2 *Zeitlin; Charlie Haden (b).* 7/81.

***** Tidal Wave**
Quicksilver 4007 *Zeitlin; John Abercrombie (g); Charlie Haden (b); Peter Donald (d).* 1/81, 2/83.

Zeitlin is one of a select number of jazz musicians who have combined playing with a career in medicine or, in his case, psychiatry. While a student at Columbia University, he was signed by the legendary talent-spotter John Hammond and recorded a number of albums, including the excellent *Zeitgeist*, which showed off his ability to marry free improvisation with a strong sense of musical structure. Ironically, he's probably better known by film-music buffs (largely for a soundtrack to the remake of *Invasion Of The Body Snatchers*) than by jazz fans. It's curious, too, given his undoubted facility as a composer, that he usually prefers to play standards. The set with Charlie Haden is also dominated by other composers' work – Cole Porter, Luiz Eca, Coltrane, Ornette, as well as Haden, and two standards, 'As Long As There's Music' and 'How High The Moon', the latter wittily segued on to Trane's 'Satellite'. The title-piece is in Zeitlin's robust philosophical voice, a piece too secure in itself to be labelled an exercise in nostalgia but one that certainly harks back to an earlier age.

Zeitlin released only three records in the '70s, *Expansion*, *Syzygy* and *Soundings* on the obscure Arch label. He seemed to be returning to music more seriously at the start of the next decade. *Tidal Wave*, recently reissued on CD, has one solo track from 1981 – a fine version of Parker's 'Billie's Bounce' – and a set of group tracks made with Haden again, John Abercrombie and drummer Peter Donald. The results are fine and swinging, though it's the Strayhorn classic 'Chelsea Bridge' that stands out ahead of Zeitlin's atmospheric compositions.

Si Zentner (1917–2000)

TROMBONE

Played with several leading big bands in the '40s, then as a studio musician, and eventually as a bandleader himself. He was still leading a big band at Vegas resorts when in his eighties.

***** Swing Fever**
Fresh Sound FSCD 2007 *Zentner; Don Fagerquist, Uan Rasey, Joe Triscari, Ray Triscari, Vince Falzone, Jules Chalkin, Tom Scott, Ollie Mitchell (t); Vern Friley, Bob Pring, Ray Klein, Walt Maltzahn, Roger White (tb); Bernie Fleischer, (as, f); Howard Terry, Don Lodice, Modesto Briseno (ts); Teddy Lee (bs); Bruce McDonald (p); Tony Rizzi, Jack Marshall (g); Lyle Rich, Mel Pollan (b); Jackie Mills, Roy Rotan (d).* 12/58–1/59.

Mike Baillie's excellent sleevenote fills in the details of Si Zentner's mostly unsung career in big-band music – a top-notch studio pro but a man zealously dedicated to live work with a genuine, swing-styled orchestra. These sessions were some of the few opportunities he got to record one of his road bands. Baillie unsnobbishly describes it as 'superior dance band music', and although charts such as 'Little Boy Blues' give some space to soloists, the band's the thing, and each of these tunes is given a whip-smart reading, the brass sections predominating. Bones Howe engineered the sessions and gave Si's team a beautiful sound, which carries across 40-plus years with aplomb. Zentner made numerous big-band dates for Capitol which waver between swing and easy listening, and it would be good to have a decent compilation of the best of them.

Monica Zetterlund (born 1938)

VOCAL, PIANO

The leading jazz singer from Sweden – and, arguably, all of Scandinavia – Zetterlund made her first demos in 1957 and was dubbed the 'Swedish Sensation' by her first LP. Although she subsequently made some more pop-flavoured records and has followed a successful second career as an actress, she remains a jazz artist and continues to record with the Swedish jazz élite of several generations.

****** Swedish Sensation! The Complete Columbia Recordings, 1958–60**
EMI 475061-2 (Swed) 2CD *Zetterlund; Bengt-Arne Wallin, Allan Botschinsky, Pelle Bolvig, Erik Larsen, Jorgen Moller, Benny Bailey, Bernth Gustavsson, Gosta Nilsson, Donald Byrd, Sixten Erikkson, Weine Renliden, Arnold Johansson, Jan Allan (t); Ake Bjorkman (flhn); Ake Persson, Willy Clausen, John Lind, Bent Ronak, Kurt Jarnberg, Andreas Skjold, George Vernon, Jorgen Johansson, Gordon Ohlsson, Gunnar Medberg, Folke Rabe (tb); Arne Domnérus, Johannes Jorgenson, Uffe Karskov, Rolf Backman, Rolf Billberg (as); Rolf Blomqvist, Karl Leukowitz, Poul Moller, Georg Bjorklund, Johnny Ekh, Bjarne Nerem, Lennart Jansson, Carl-Henrik Noren (ts); Rune Falk (bs, bcl); Lars Gullin, Stig Gabrielsson, Gunnar Larsen (bs); Gunnar Svensson, Atli Bjorn, Lars Bagge, Bengt Hallberg, Thore Swanerud, Rolf Larsson (p); Christer Jagerhult (cel); Rune Gustafsson, Bengt Hogberg (g); Georg Riedel, Finn Ziegler, Dan Jacobsen, Lars Pettersson, Arne Wilhelmsson, Gunnar Almstedt, Claes Rindroth (b); Joe Harris, William Schiopffe, Pedro Biker, Sture Kallin, Egil Johansen, Jack Noren (d); strings.*

****(*) Nu Ar Det Skont Att Leva**
EMI 136449-2 (Swed) *Zetterlund; Maffy Falay, Bernth Gustavsson, Weine Renliden, Jan Allan, Americo Bellotto, Gunnar Gunrup, Luciano Mosetti (t); Olle Holmqvist, Lars Olofsson, Torgny Nilsson, Bengt Edwardsson (tb); Sven Larsson (btb, tba); Christer Torge (btb); Solve Klingstedt, Hans Bergman, Olle Schill, Kjell-Inge Stevensson, Lars Ahman (cl); Leif Hellmann (as); Bjarne Nerem (ts); Erik Nilsson, Lars Gullin (bs); Ulf Bergstrom, Yngve Sandstrom, Jan Kling, Christer Persson, Jerker Halldén (f); Monica Dominique (p, org); Lasse Bagge (p, cel); Carl-Axel Dominique (vib); George Wadenius, Rune Gustafsson, Lennart Nyhlen (g); Palle*

Danielsson, Bosse Hagstrom, Sture Akerberg (b); Tommy Slim Borgudd, Egil Johansen, Johan Dielemans (d). 71–75.

***** For Lester And Billie**

Phontastic PHONTCD 7562 *Zetterlund; Nisse Sandström (ts); Horace Parlan (p); Red Mitchell (b).* 8/83–1/84.

***** Topaz**

RCA 74321 164752 (Swed) *Zetterlund; Jan Allan (t); Bernt Rosengren (ts); Toots Thielemans (hca); Lasse Bagge, Stefan Nilsson, Tommy Lydell (ky); Johan Norberg, Peter Ericson (g); Hasse Larsson, Sture Akerberg (b); Christer Jansson, Johan Dielemans (d); Titiyo Jah, Henry Gibson (perc).* 93.

There is now a decent representation of this coolest of cool stylists on CD – though, since these are all Swedish releases, it will take readers outside that country a bit more effort to track them down (there are other discs available in Sweden which we have not been able to hear so far). The EMI double-CD is still the perfect introduction to her early work, converting the *Swedish Sensation!* album along with the tracks from eight EPs into a handsomely documented package. Singing mostly in English (four tracks from an EP dedicated to *My Fair Lady* songs are sung in Swedish) Zetterlund has some of the slightly fey charm of Astrud Gilberto, but she's a much more accomplished vocalist. On ballads, she makes no attempt at any breathy charm but delivers lines with a clarity and restraint that can sound unforgettably poignant from moment to moment. An incomparably lovely 'Deep In A Dream', done almost as a duet with Arne Domnérus, is one special highlight, but there are many more, from the almost artless sincerity of the first two EPs to the fine work with arranger Lars Gullin on two late tracks. Along the way are many neat cameos by most of the famous names in Swedish jazz of the period, plus Bailey and Byrd as guest-star trumpeters.

Occupied with film and TV work, Zetterlund has had something of an on-and-off career since. The second EMI disc collects all the 1975 *Hey, Man!* album with five tracks from 1971's *Monica-Monica*, though some of these are bizarrely misguided: an arrangement of Albinoni's *Adagio* is set against Frank Zappa's 'Toads Of The Short Forest'! Superior are the 1975 tracks, with a fine 'If You Could See Me Now'. Monica was a little frail and out of practice for the Phontastic sessions, but her opening duet with Mitchell on 'I Should Care' is as beguiling as ever, and the three instrumentalists (Zetterlund sings on 6 of the 15 tracks) are in top form for their trio pieces, Sandstrom relishing the situation. *Topaz* is another gentle, reflective record. The settings are updated to the '90s with keyboards and guitar, and the songs are mostly contemporary, but Zetterlund sings them with the peculiar kind of cool panache that has yet to desert her. Thielemans is a helpful presence, and Rosengren has a strong solo on 'The Zanzibar Song'.

*****(*) The Best Of Monica Zetterlund**

Emarcy 014092-2 *Zetterlund, with various (unlisted) accompaniments.* 62–76.

A fine cross-section drawn from Monica's Philips albums. It is a little sad to note that her Eurovision entry, the charming 'Once Upon A Time In Stockholm', finished last in the 1963 competition, held in London that year. We hope she doesn't hold it against us!

****** Ett Lingonris Som Satts I Cocktailglas**

RCA 74321 32989-2 6CD *Zetterlund; others as discs above, plus Bill Evans (p) and many more!* 57–93.

Gorgeous packaging for this six-disc celebration of Zetterlund's career for RCA, starting with some scratchy 1957 demos and going as far as her 1993 *Topaz* set. There are many items which will surprise even dedicated Zetterlund collectors along the way, including alternative takes from her celebrated session with Bill Evans (and a TV-show track with Evans for good measure), and the final disc is made up of rare concert and soundtrack recordings covering the breadth of her work. There are tracks from her London session of 1964, with Bill McGuffie and Jimmy Deuchar; a moving reading of Lars Gullin's 'Silhouette', with the Thad Jones–Mel Lewis Orchestra; several challenging songs by Povel Ramel, which she handles superbly; and plenty more besides. Excellent remastering of even the live tracks. There are 13 duplications with the *Swedish Sensation!* set, but that will not stop Monica's admirers from seeking out what is the outstanding collection of her work on the market (non-Swedish speakers should be warned, though, that the booklet is entirely and exclusively in her own language).

***** Det Finns Dagar**

RCA 74321 4174-2 *Zetterlund; Anders Bergcrantz (c, t, flhn); Gustavo Bergalli (t); Fredrik Norén (flhn); Bertil Strandberg, Nils Landgren (tb); Mattis Cederberg (btb); Gunnar Magnusson (cl); Ulf Andersson (ts, ss, f); Bernt Rosengren (ob); Sven Larson (tba); Helene Cort, Jerker Halldén (f); Jan Sigurd (p); Mats Asplen, Kjell Ohman (org); Hakan Andersson (acc); Magnus Persson (vib); Thomas Hallberg (g); Jan Adefeldt, Per-Ola Gadd, Marcus Wikström, Hans Backenroth (b); Rune Carlsson, Christer Sjöström (d); strings.* 97.

This recent record from the *grande dame* of Swedish jazz is full of graceful music. She was never a big-sounding singer and the voice is growing more frail, but the understated way with lyrics is all her own, and this set of originals by pianist Jan Sigurd is tailored to suit her style. A glance through the personnel shows how she's kept the faith with jazz as the music which suits her, too.

Gal Ziv

GUITAR

Young Israeli guitarist, here making his debut on the New York scene.

***** The Flow**

Cadence CJR 1125 *Ziv; Don Braden (ts); Emanuelle Somer (ob); Joris Teepe (b); Vito Lesczak (d).* 11/99.

Starting your record with an arrangement of the first movement of Shostakovich's Quartet No. 7 seems pretty audacious – especially when you give the principal solo to an oboe player – but thereafter Ziv's set settles into an amenable, familiar groove. Mostly it's the quartet (minus Somer) laying sketches on top of the guitarist's pretty if not particularly substantial themes. The leader plays everything with a clean open tone and picks his way rather carefully through the tunes. The main interest comes, perhaps inevitably, from Braden, who sounds like he's enjoying himself. He cleverly builds a solo out of the staccato feel of the 'Sanity' theme and plays an improvisation on 'Avinu Malkenu' that speaks strongly to the listener.

John Zorn (born 1954)

ALTO SAXOPHONE, DUCK CALLS

A lifelong New Yorker, Zorn studied briefly in St Louis but made his mark with the circle of improvisers based in New York in the mid-'70s. Steadily came to wider attention through relentless work, composing, performing, and eventually gaining major-label recognition, though this was soon sidelined in favour of his own label, Tzadik, which releases most of his work. Groups down the years include Naked City, Painkiller and Masada. Outspoken, furiously prolific but ruthless about quality control, Zorn has fashioned his own multiple-idiom music, of which jazz remains a buried but tangible part.

*** First Recordings 1973

Tzadik TZ 7304 *Zorn (all instruments).* 73.

***(*) The Parachute Years 1977–1980

Tzadik TZ-7316 7CD *Zorn; George E. Lewis (tb); Bruce Ackley (ss); Robert Dick (f, bf, picc); Anthony Coleman (ky); Wayne Horvitz (ky, hca, elec); Bob Ostertag (elec); Mark Miller (vib, perc); LaDonna Smith, Polly Bradfield (vn, vla); Eugene Chadbourne (g, tiple); Davey Williams (g, bj); Henry Kaiser, Bill Horvitz (g); Tom Cora (clo); David Moss, Charles Noyes (d, etc.).* 77–81.

Whatever path you take across contemporary jazz, contemporary improvisation, contemporary film music or any of the advanced sonics, it is likely that you will come across John Zorn. What follows cannot pretend to be anything more than a sketchy and partial discography and, even if the border patrols we have posted on the country called Jazz are now notoriously soporific and unvigilant, some at least of these records will offend purists.

Zorn's early work on record was for a long time available only on ultra-rare vinyl, or not at all. The debut recordings see him navigating a solitary course through the shattered columns of avant-garde jazz. 'Variations On A Theme By Albert Ayler' (as ever, difficult to be categorical about *what* Ayler theme it is) suggests where Zorn was artistically at the age of nineteen, but 'Wind Ko/La' and 'Automata Of Al-Jazari' offer useful pointers to the years ahead and their obsessions.

The seven-disc set documents his period with the independent Parachute label. There are four principal works: *Lacrosse*, in its original sextet version (1978) and in a previously unheard quartet format from a year earlier (Zorn, Chadbourne, Kaiser, Ackley); *Hockey*, played by two different trios, one acoustic, one electric; *Pool*, 50 minutes of music by the 1980 quintet of Zorn, Bradfield, Miller, Noyes and Ostertag; and *Archery*, dated 1979 but cut in 1981, with three long rehearsal-pieces as a bonus. These are all examples of the composer-leader's game of system-pieces, the mechanics of, say, an Avalon Hill wargame used as a suggestive basis for structuring an improvisation. While that sometimes oblique patterning implies a kindred music to those of Leo Smith or Anthony Braxton in the same time-frame, Zorn's meticulousness and intensity outdo even those Chicagoan masters. *Lacrosse* remains a stunning experience, the instruments recorded in glaring close-up, with the leader's squawking reeds in an almost brutal alignment with the sounds of the string players. While the free playing sometimes approximates the feel and grain of some of the more chamberish Company ensembles, the notes to some of the discs reveal how focused and fierce Zorn was about getting the results he wanted: as 'free' as this improvising is, very little is actually left to chance, at least in the accustomed manner of free playing. What is lost in spontaneity is made up for by the often furious grip which Zorn imposes on all the players and their contributions, an element which remains the constant in his discography.

Historically, this is arguably as important a set as any Blue Note or Prestige milestone, with Chadbourne, Williams, Bradfield, Smith, Kaiser, the Horvitzes and the rest all playing as significant a performing role as the leader in what was an unrepeatable slice of New York's music of that time. Burrowing through it some 20 years on, we find it a startling reminder of the small-scale earthquake which these performers instigated. Rather than mere 'prentice work, one can often hear things in this collection which echo more vividly than much of Zorn's more obviously 'outrageous' work with Naked City and the like. Remastered with great vitality, bringing the music right into the present, this is a model reissue.

***(*) Locus Solus

Tzadik TZ 7303 *Zorn; Wayne Horvitz (ky); Arto Lindsay (g); Anton Fier, Mark Miller, Ikue Mori (d); Christian Marclay (turntables); Whiz Kid (scratching); Peter Blegvad (v).* 83.

This is one of the sacred texts of '80s New York improv, a fierce, scrabbly set of associations that draw heavily on the power-trio aesthetic of rock bands like Hüsker Dü. Zorn favours the short, sharp shock approach to improvisation, steering sessions that are remarkably reminiscent of Billy Jenkins's 12 × 3-minute-round 'Big Fights', but for the fact that one player is always refereeing and sometimes even normalizing the music. *Locus Solus* is one of those records that, in one respect very much of its time, also seems to float freely without obvious stylistic or fashion anchors. It's impressively compact but sometimes rather too abrupt.

*** The Classic Guide To Strategy: Volumes 1 and 2

Tzadik TZ 7305 *Zorn (ss, as, cl, game calls).* 2/83–9/85.

Originally issued as a Lumina LP, Volume One of the *The Classic Guide* seems to have been the first chapter in a sequence of five records, all bearing the same title. There is some evidence that the history of American culture, and particularly Jewish-American culture, may be the history of huge, hubristic projects which never quite came to fruition: Norman Mailer's multi-decker novel of Hollywood, Alfred Kazin's history of the Jews, Saul Bellow's ever-receding *Meisterwerk*. It becomes easier with the passing years to see Zorn in this company and this strange, wilful record, reminiscent in its way of Braxton's solo-sax monologues though utterly different in intent, feeds a growing impression of Zorn as a jazz traditionalist who has been let down by the idiom rather than turning his back on it.

As we will doubtless repeat *ad nauseam* to the end of this section, this surviving torso of a much larger project serves notice of what an inventive saxophone player Zorn is, a quality which is easy to overlook. The basic material is tuneful free bop, oddly soulful and full of character. The *faux*-oriental titles – 'Senki' and 'The Moon In The Cold Stream Like A Mirror' – are a diversion, as are the non-Western flourishes, though the material on Volume Two, almost all of which appears on the CD issue, seems closer to Japanese music than the first sessions. This is emphatically a jazz record.

CORE COLLECTION

♛ **** The Big Gundown

Tzadik TZ 7328 *Zorn; Jim Staley (tb, btb); Tim Berne (as); Vicki Bodner (ob, eng hn); Bill Frisell, Fred Frith, Jody Harris, Robert Quine, Vernon Reid (g); Arto Lindsay, Anthony Coleman (p, ky); Wayne Horvitz (p); Big John Patton (org); Orvin Acquart (hca); Toots Thielemans (hca, whistling); Ned Rothenberg (shakuhachi, etc.); Michihiro Sato (shamisen); Guy Klucevesek (acc); Carol Emanuel (hp); Polly Bradfield (vn); Melvin Gibbs (b); Anton Fier (d); Mark Miller, Bobby Previte (d, perc); Cyro Baptista, Reinaldo Fernandes, Duduka Fonseca, Claudio Silva, Jorge Silva (perc); David Weinstein (elec); Bob James (tapes); Christian Marclay (turntables); Laura Biscotto, Diamanda Galas, Shelley Hirsch (v).* 9/84–9/85.

Utterly remarkable in every way and one of the essential records of the '80s. Ennio Morricone's soundtrack scores – to movies by Pontecorvo, Lelouch, Bertolucci, Petri and, most memorably, Sergio Leone – are among the most significant artistic collaborations of recent times, a simultaneous confirmation and dismantling of the *auteur* myth. Zorn appears to have been influenced every bit as much by Leone's weird pans, sustained close-ups and frozen poses (where a fly or a melting harmonica note on the soundtrack might command more attention than the actor), followed by bouts of violence which are ritualized rather than choreographed (as they would be in a Peckinpah movie).

Zorn assembles musicians with his usual puppet-master care, bringing on harmonica player Toots Thielemans to whistle plangently on 'Poverty' from *Once Upon A Time In America*, organist Big John Patton to grind out the 'Erotico' line from *The Burglars*, Diamanda Galas and Vernon Reid to lash up a storm on 'Metamorfosi', a theme from Petri's *La Classe Operaia Va In Paradiso*. Zorn's political concerns are engaged to the extent of his determination to raise preterite music to the gates of heaven, thereby overcoming what he considers the 'racist' compartmentalization of high and low, black and white, formal and improvised styles on which the music industry depends.

***The Big Gundown* establishes the pattern for much of Zorn's subsequent music. It is very much a 'studio' record, an artefact, and Zorn himself has adduced the example of George Martin and the Beatles, or the earlier works of another enormous, alphabetically and stylistically late-coming influence, Frank Zappa. Like Zappa, Zorn appears to trash the very musics he seems to be setting up as icons. The result is ambivalent, unsettling and utterly contemporary.**

*** Ganryu Island

Tzadik TZ 7319 *Zorn; Michihiro Sato (shamisen).* 11/84.

Originally issued on Yukon Records, which allowed cynics to grumble that listening to *Ganryu Island* is like panning for gold: seeming eternities spent plodging through muddy dross in order to turn up just a few moments of pure gold. By the oddest perversity, the very best tracks seem to be those which were excluded from the vinyl release, unless it is simply the case that one needs some time with Zorn and Sato before the music delivers up its delights. *Shamisen* rarely avoid a generic, plinky-plonky sound, but Sato is genuinely interesting.

**** Spillane

Elektra Nonesuch 79172 *Zorn; Jim Staley (tb); Anthony Coleman, Wayne Horvitz (p, ky); Big John Patton (org); Dave Weinstein (ky); Carol Emanuel (hp); Albert Collins, Bill Frisell (g); Melvin Gibbs (b); David Hofstra (b, tba); Bob James (tapes, CDs); Ronald Shannon Jackson (d); Bobby Previte (d, perc); Christian Marclay (turntables); Kronos Quartet: David Harrington, John Sherba (vn); Hank Dutt (vla); Joan Jeanrenaud (clo); Ohta Hiromi (v).* 8/86–9/87.

Zorn's own liner-notes to *Spillane* offer immensely valuable insights into his work and philosophy: his interest in Carl Stalling, composer of Bugs Bunny and other cartoon soundtracks; his Japan obsession (reflected here in 'Forbidden Fruit' for voice and string quartet); his conceptual-collage, file-card approach to 'Spillane' itself; the need for longer durations to accommodate Albert Collins's blues lines on 'Two-Lane Highway'; his overall conviction that 'the era of the composer as autonomous musical mind has just about come to an end'.

For all their apparent serendipity, Zorn's groups are selected with very great care. He approaches instrumental coloration much as a graphic artist might use a 'paintbox' package on a computer graphics screen, trying possibilities consecutively or even simultaneously, but making his gestures in a very precise, hard-edged way. 'Spillane' is a sequence of tiny sound-bites, evocative not so much of Mickey Spillane's fictional world (in the sense of dim bars, lonely roads, chalked outlines on the pavement) as of his language, which is notably fragmentary, clipped and elided, poised between literalism and the purest self-reference. Zorn has pointed to the fact that Schoenberg's earliest atonal works were given unity only by use of texts; and it's clear that Zorn's imagery works in much the same way, with Mickey Spillane's voices soundtracking the music rather than vice versa.

'Two-Lane Highway' follows a more systematic and structured groove, a concerto for bluesman and improvising orchestra, with Collins's guitar, voice, mere *presence* taking the part of the solo instrument. The final part, 'Forbidden Fruit', is actually more conventional and is by far the dullest thing Zorn has done on record, reminiscent of Ennio Morricone's non-film, squeaky-door compositions.

**** Spy Vs Spy

Elektra Musician 960844 *Zorn; Tim Berne (as); Mark Dresser (b); Joey Baron, Michael Vatcher (d).*

In some respects a more straightforward tribute than the Morricone set, Zorn's take on the music of Ornette Coleman is a headlong, hardcore thrash that approaches levels of sheer intensity never attempted by Coleman's own Prime Time band. Only one of the first dozen tracks is over three minutes in length. 'Chronology', from Coleman's classic Atlantic album, *The Shape Of Jazz To Come*, lasts exactly 68 seconds, and half a dozen others, drawn from Coleman's output between 1958 and the '80s, occupy no more than 15 minutes between them. It is these, rather than the more measured performances, which seem most faithful to the originals. The twinned altos, sharply separated by channel, scribble all over the white-noise drumming, brutal graffito effects which almost miraculously preserve Coleman's melodic outlines.

*** Filmworks VII

Tzadik TZ 7315 *Zorn; Wayne Horvitz (ky); Bill Frisell (g, bj); Carol Emanuel (hp); Kermit Driscoll (b); Bobby Previte (d).* 10/88.

Zorn's submersion in the hectic aesthetics of Japanese comics and cartoons was confirmed when he created these tracks for a children's cartoon show. This is the soundbite culture *in excelsis*, a slew of tiny programmatic gestures, most of them too brief to register as anything other than sonic blips. Even if you are cynical about the opposite extreme, John Coltrane's hour-long meditations on standard tunes, this is hard going as a continuous listen. It would make sense to programme one track every 20–30 minutes for the course of the day and treat them as if they were radio interstitials. Zorn has relocated the terms of aesthetic debate, from production to consumption.

*** Filmworks III

Tzadik TZ 7309 *Zorn; Dave Douglas (t); Keith Underwood (f); Robert Quine (g); Marc Ribot (g, bj); Arto Lindsay (g, v); Anthony Coleman (org); Peter Scherer (ky); Guy Klucevesek (acc); Carol Emanuel (hp); Jill Jaffee (vla); Erik Friedlander (clo); Greg Cohen, Kermit Driscoll, Bill Laswell, Chris Wood (b); David Hofstra (b, tba); Miguel Frasconi (glass hca); Joey Baron, Sim Cain (d); Bobby Previte (d, perc); Ikue Mori (d machine); Cyro Baptista (perc, v); Christian Marclay (turntables); David Shea (samples).* 90–95.

Another eclectic slew of material intended to accompany images but just about self-determining enough – for the first two dozen tracks, at least – to stand alone as an aural experience. Half of that number are for Joe Chapelle's *Thieves Quartet* and are played by the Masada lineup of Zorn, Douglas, Cohen and Baron. These are riveting pieces, albeit only the end-title-piece is of any great length. For Mei-Juin Chen's *Hollywood Hotel*, Zorn is joined by Marc Ribot in a sequence of surreal musical encounters which don't work quite as well out of context. For our money, the remaining material, written for Weiden and Kennedy, is dispensable, too rapid-fire to be of lasting interest and on occasion almost deliberately perverse in bringing the most elaborate instrumentation to the least substantial musical ideas. One for serious collectors only, but worth hearing once.

** Guts Of A Virgin / Buried Secrets

Earache MOSH 198 *Zorn; Justin Broadrick (g, d machine); G. C. Green, Bill Laswell (b); Mick Harris (d, v).* 4/91.

Gross-out cover; tiny, confrontational tracks; provocative titles like 'Handjob', 'Purgatory Of Fiery Vulvas' and 'One Eyed Pessary' ... like any genuinely major artist, Zorn reserves the right to pour out smoke and ash as well as genuinely creative magma; but these tracks, officially credited to Pain Killer, really do give off more heat than light. Needless to say, there are things which deserve attention. For the most part, though, *Guts/Secrets* is little more than a sequence of hostile gestures. Also released in CD single format on Zorn's own Tzadik, it perhaps makes more sense heard as random and discontinuous provocation. Genuine students and aficionados may find it profitable. Bystanders might usefully remain just that.

(***) Elegy

Tzadik TZ 7302 *Barbara Chaffe (af, bf); David Abel (vla); Scummy (g); William Winant (perc); David Shea (turntables); David Slusser (elec); Mike Patton (v).* 11/91.

(****) Kristallnacht

Tzadik TZ 7301 *Frank London (t); David Krakauer (cl, bcl); Mark Feldman (vn); Marc Ribot (g); Anthony Coleman (ky); Mark Dresser (b); William Winant (perc).* 11/92.

Zorn does not play on these remarkable records, but all the music is by him and they bear his stamp throughout. *Elegy* is a suite of four, inexplicably colour-coded pieces. The later album is a set of more expressive and more obviously programmatic ideas, from the opening 'Shtetl', with its startling echoes of Jewish folk forms, to the closing 'Gariin'. Here are the seeds of what was to be a wholesale engagement – or re-engagement – with Jewish musical culture, most clearly represented in the Masada project of future years, but retroactively evident throughout the work of the previous decade and more. A key moment, even if the man himself wasn't playing.

***(*) Live At The Knitting Factory

Knitting Factory Works KFW 124 *Zorn; Steven Bernstein (t, sampler); Frank London (t, perc); Curtis Fowlkes, Steve Swell (tb); Marcus Rojas (tba); Doug Wieselman (cl); Tim Smith (bcl); Leslie Ross (bsn, shawm, reeds); Roy Nathanson (ss, as, ts); Allan Chase, Margaret Lancaster (ss, as); Paul Shapiro (ss, ts, f); Jay Rodrigues (as); Blaise Siwula (as, t); Walter Thompson (as, bs, f); David Cast Castiglione (ts, bs, bcl); Paul Hoskin (bs); David Krakauer (cl, bcl); Evan Gallagher (ky, sample tb, c); Nick Balaban, Randy Hutton, Myra Melford, Matthew Ostrowski, Dan Rosengard (syn); Craig Flanagin, Marc Ribot, Vito Ricci, Adam Rogers, Rolf Sturm, Kiki Wada (g); David Watson (g, t); Bob Lipman (g, perc); John King (dobro); Bill Ware (vib); Andrea Parkins (acc); Zeena Parkins (hp); Fred Lonberg-Holm (hp, CD players, sampler); April Chung, Alicia Svigals (vn); Thomas Ulrich (clo); Michelle Kinney (clo, elec); Paul Morrissett (kaval, gaida, vn); Reg Anderson (strings); Ed Broms, Joe Gallant, Brad Jones, Sebastian Steinberg, Chris Wood (b); K. J. Grant (b, v); Steve Waxman (b, t, perc); Christine Bard, Louie Belogenis, Hollis Headrick, James Lo, James Perowsky (d); Michael Evans, E. J. Rodriguez (d, perc); James Pugliese (d, perc, sampler); Billy Martin, Danny Sedownik, Jane Tomkiewicz (perc); Dawn Buckholz, Anthony Coleman, Mark Degliatoni, Lee Hyla, David Shea, David Weinstein (sampler); Tim Spelios (CD players); Gisburg (v, hca, whistle); Jeff Buckley, M. Doughty, Judy Dunway, Mark Ettinger, Tamela Glen, Cassie Hoffman, Donna Jewell, Makigami Koichi, Nina Mankin, Chris Nelson, Juliet Palmer, Wilbur Pauley, Rick Porterfield, Eric Qin, Kevin Sharp, Sharon Topper (v).* 1–12/92.

Zorn plays Cecil B. DeMille. A cast of what seems like thousands wheeled on at New York's premier club over a year-long residency/workshop to generate a set of inventive variations on a snakey theme. As the personnel details should suggest, the emphasis is on multi-instrumentalism. No virtuosic playing but rather a gestural sound collage that puts the emphasis on process over product. Only Zorn could have conceived such a project and his presence as conductor, *auteur*, dramaturge is essential to its success. It isn't a record that will appeal to anyone who looks first for a settled groove or a hummable tune, but it is undoubtedly fascinating, abstract expressionism of a modern and compelling sort.

**(*) Filmworks II

Tzadik TZ 7306 *Zorn; Anthony Coleman (prepared p, ky); Marc Ribot (g, bj); Carol Emanuel (hp); Andy Haas (didjeridu); Cyro Baptista, Jim Pugliese (perc); David Shea (turntables, perc).* 5 & 6/92.

This is Zorn's *Chappaqua Suite*, originally written and recorded for a film by Walter Hill, but rejected – as Ornette Coleman was in favour of Ravi Shankar – for a more accessible Ry Cooder soundtrack. *Chappaqua* remains a classic of its kind. This sounds like occasional music which has managed to miss its occasion, which is just about right.

****** Masada: Alef**
DIW 888 *Zorn; Dave Douglas (t); Greg Cohen (b); Joey Baron (d).* 2/94.

*****(*) Masada: Beit**
DIW 889 *As above.* 2/94.

***** Masada: Gimel**
DIW 890 *As above.* 2 & 6/94.

(***) Masada: Dalet
DIW DIWS 3 *As above.* 2/94.

By the mid-'90s, the Zorn discography had become unmanageable. It is no less so now. There is in preparation a 100-CD set, marketed in Japan, where Zorn is something of a cult hero. Even a project like this one, in which the saxophonist often movingly explores aspects of his Judaism, raises questions about opportunism. Why was his interest in Hebrew culture not made known sooner? A desire for privacy? A slow awakening to his cultural roots? Or a more cynical reason?

There seems no reason to take the third course in approaching these records. They are beautifully played, folk themes with a contemporary cutting edge, performed by a razor-sharp band whose stylistic reach is almost unbelievably capacious. The first three, named after the A-B-C of the Hebrew alphabet, are almost required listening, but thereafter the series becomes almost indistinguishably repetitive, an impression reinforced by near-identical covers. Number four was not previously listed because it was issued only as a free record for those who had bought earlier CDs. Several letters, ranging from friendly to grumpy, suggest that it has since been made commercially available; not in our local emporia, alas, so we'll stick with the protective brackets.

As always, and even when ostensibly drawing his inspiration from the notorious mass suicide of the Zealots at Masada, a key moment in Jewish history, Zorn has an eye to the market strategy. He has become an ambiguous superstar of the avant-garde; the only artist one might compare him to is Laurie Anderson, except that he has never sought her brand of middle-market appeal. An astonishing musician, as these records confirm, his place in the music is no more clear-cut than before.

*****(*) Bar Kokhba**
Tzadik TZ 7108 *Zorn; Dave Douglas (t); David Krakauer, Chris Speed (cl); John Medeski (org, p); Anthony Coleman (p); Marc Ribot (g); Mark Feldman (vn); Erik Friedlander (clo); Greg Cohen, Mark Dresser (b); Kenny Wolleson (d).* 8/94–3/96.

Larger-scale versions of Masada's 'radical Jewish culture', these are exquisitely voiced folkloric essays, executed without strain. Zorn's own part in these ensembles is more distant. The music genuinely sounds as if it arises out of the culture intact and without mediation, which is considerable testimony to his powers of synthesis and persuasion. As ever, Douglas and Speed are the most effective solo performers, though Dresser's rich bass playing is a huge asset.

***** Art Of Memory**
Incus CD 20 *Zorn; Fred Frith (g).* 94.

Freely improvised, but packed with associations from both players' musical pasts. Frith is a romantic and a mnemonist, creating music like an old bluesman out of remembered shards and fragments. Zorn responds with some of his most rooted and responsive playing, and yet the music seems private, enclosed, elbows out to the world. Fascinating as it is to have such encounters on disc, it also seems intrusive. A record to hear once and then file away.

(***) Tokyo Operations '94
Avant AVAN 049 *Takei Makoto (shakuhachi); Tanaka Yumiko (gidayu); Uchihashi Kazuhisha (g); Nakamujra Hitomi (hichiriki); Maruta Miki (koto); Kinoshita Shinichi (shamisen); Isso Yukihiro (nokan, dengakubue); Ito Taeko (ortin doo); Mekken (b); Senba Kiyohiko, Uemura Masahiro (perc); Yamamoto Kyoko (v); Makigami Koichi (prompter).* 11/94.

You must have had that moment in an Oriental restaurant when your mother says, 'Yes, very nice, dear, but could I have a knife and fork?' The procedures here are at the sushi-and-fries end of the counter, a group of Japanese players working in a (non-)genre which is neither idiomatic nor completely subversive. Zorn's Cobra was always an umbrella project and only intermittently successful. This is not one of the great moments.

***** Masada: Hei**
DIW 891 *Zorn; Dave Douglas (t); Greg Cohen (b); Joey Baron (d).* 7/95.

***** Masada: Vav**
DIW 892 *As above.* 7/95.

For all but the most attentive and committed listeners, Masada started to seem like late Miles Davis. The real fans were swapping C90s and DATs of live performances, and admitting that the issued sessions were getting seriously commonplace. There were a few live bootleg recordings doing the rounds with Kenny Wollesen on drums in place of Baron. It's immediately evident from these how important Joey is to the sound of the band, and how irreplaceable. By this stage, Masada recordings are both utterly original and by-the-yard, a disconcerting collision of critical opposites that rather closes down any effort of judgement.

***** Weird Little Boy**
Avant AVAN 043 *Zorn; Chris Cochrane (g); Trey Spruance (g, ky, d); Mike Patton (d, v); William Winant (perc).* 11/95.

An amplified unit with a strong rock influence, Weird Little Boy is thirled to Dennis Cooper's unsettling texts, but very much coloured by the Zorn aesthetic. Unlike Naked City or the Sonny Clark tribute group, it's very much the saxophonist's album. There has been too little of Zorn's saxophone on recent records, so it's good to have some to take a fix on. The distinctive alto sound is heard to good effect here, but has to vie for attention with keyboards and samplers and some clutter from the other players.

***** Filmworks V**
Tzadik TZ 7307 *Zorn; Robert Quine, Marc Ribot (g); Cyro Baptista (perc); Jason Baker (v).* 10/95.

***** Filmworks VI**
Tzadik TZ 7308 *Zorn; Marc Ribot (g); Mark Feldman (vn); Erik Friedlander (clo); Greg Cohen (b); Cyro Baptista (perc); Ikue Mori (d machine); Jason Baker (v).* 1 & 7/96.

Written for Oki Hiroyuki's movie, *Tears Of Ecstasy*, forty-eight tiny musical moments of jewelled beauty and not much consequence make up Volume Five of *Filmworks*. Baker figures on only one track and it would have been interesting to have heard more. He resurfaces, again only briefly, on Volume Six, which, unusually, includes more developed pieces – including a sonic landscape for Maria Beatty's *The Black Glove* – and rather more interesting films than some of its predecessors.

***** Masada: Zayin**
DIW 893 *As above.* 4/96.

***** Masada: Het**
DIW 894 *As above.* 8/96.

Still beautiful, often moving (as on the opening 'Schechem' on *Het*, aka *Masada 8*), but by this stage in the game desperately calling out for a sensible one- or two-CD compilation. Listening to this stuff in bulk has a hypnotic inconsequence. How great it would be to encounter even one of these later records out of the blue, and without the weight of the previous six or seven or eight pressing down on one's expectations.

***** Filmworks IV – S&M + More**
Tzadik TZ 7310 *Zorn; Robert Quine (g); Kuroda Kyoko (p); Anthony Coleman (org); Jim Pugliese (vib, perc); Carol Emanuel (hp); Jill Jaffee (vla); Erik Friedlander (clo); Joey Baron (d); Cyro Baptista (perc).*

A more scattered but also more concentrated set of film-related pieces. Two of the tracks – 'Elegant Spanking' and 'A Lot Of Fun For The Evil One' – are around the quarter-hour mark and are highly developed performances. The strings are restricted to the former of these tracks and they mark Zorn's most convincingly idiomatic use of fiddles and harp on record. The sound is pretty shaky, except on the two tracks where the leader is credited with what has become his other 'instrument' – 'sound design'. His grasp of the spatial dimensions of music, its shifting masses and inertias, is as impressive as his more linear writing and playing.

(***) Angelus Novus
Tzadik TZ 7028 *Stephen Drury (p); Callithumpian Consort of New England Conservatory.* 97.

Another compositional by-way, easily overlooked but well worth hunting down. The playing is poised and confident and suggests that in future Zorn may well find himself in the same position as Anthony Braxton, making a move from improvised performance to a creator of interpretative composition.

***** Masada: Tet**
DIW 933 *Zorn; Dave Douglas (t); Greg Cohen (b); Joey Baron (d).* 4/97.

Volume Nine of the ongoing project and a few intriguing signs that the constituent personalities are beginning to secede from the original Zorn premiss, or perhaps it's simply that Masada has begun to acquire an identity as a band rather than as a Zorn concept. 'Meholalot' is magnificent and the closing 'Jachin' suggests there may yet be a few unrevealed facets to a group of real originality and expressiveness.

***** Filmworks VIII**
DIW 7318 *Zorn; Anthony Coleman (p); Marc Ribot (g); Mark Feldman (vn); Erik Friedlander (clo); Min Xiao-Fen (pipa); Greg Cohen (b); Kenny Wollesen (d, perc); Cyro Baptista (perc).* 7 & 11/97.

Zorn's film writing has been fuller in texture and in development of late, and these two projects – recorded for *The Port Of Last Resort* and *Latin Boys Go To Hell*, two films we don't know – are very much of a piece with that. One of the themes for *Port* is heard in three different versions, for *pipa*, guitar and piano. Other tracks are retreads of things that have floated around the Zorn canon for years.

***** Masada: Yod**
DIW 935 *Zorn; Dave Douglas (t); Greg Cohen (b); Joey Baron (d).* 97.

Volume Ten ends with 'Zevul' which – alphabetically at least – suggests that Masada may have reached a point of stasis, other than for the live performances which are sure to leak out, officially and unofficially, over the next few years. What a long, strange trip it has been; but, hand on heart, how often do you listen to these after the first spin?

****** Live In Jerusalem**
Tzadik TZ 7234 2CD *As above.* 97.

*****(*) Live In Taipei**
Tzadik TZ 7235 2CD *As above.* 97.

Any few remaining doubts about the durability and creative freshness of Masada were blown apart by these extraordinary releases. The sound-quality is good, the performances as good as anything Zorn has ever done as a performing musician. Inevitably, given the group's tacit manifesto, the Jerusalem concert represented an emotional high which isn't sustained in the Taipei recording. Even so, it too is a very valuable document and, it seems, there are more live sets to come from this period.

(***) The Circle Maker
Tzadik 7122 2CD *Marc Ribot (g); Mark Felman (vn); Erik Friedlander (clo); Greg Cohen (b); Joey Baron (d); Cyro Baptista (perc).* 12/97.

Two interrelated groups involved here: the Masada String Trio (Feldman, Friedlander and Cohen); and the Bar Kokhba Sextet, which adds Ribot, Baptista and Baron. Recorded over two days in New York City, and produced by Zorn, these are unexpectedly bright and affirmative pieces, as if the coming of Thanksgiving had lifted the darkness of other cultural associations. The trio tracks which occupy disc one are the more interesting. Zorn's writing for strings isn't entirely idiomatic; here and there, there are melodic lines for violin which sound as if they've been transcribed from saxophone, but this doesn't detract from the impact of almost 30 vigorously expressive pieces. Some have been heard before and Zorn/Masada enthusiasts can indulge comparative studies to their hearts' content.

****** Downtown Lullaby**
Depth Of Field DOF 2 *Zorn; Elliott Sharp (g); Wayne Horvitz (p, org, ky); Bobby Previte (d).* 1/98.

A new year and a moment to plight a renewed troth to improvisation. Horvitz emerges as the key contributor, having been out of the picture, *vis-à-vis* Zorn's music, for a little while. Named after NY addresses, the seven tracks have the buzz and excitement of the city. Previte is a very different kind of drummer from Baron, and he fights against the rhythm and the idiosyncratic melody with a jolly, combative self-possession. For a change, certainly relative to recent projects, Zorn limits himself to alto, and some of his fragmentary solos are as good as anything he's done for years.

Mark Zubek (born 1974)

DOUBLE BASS

The talented young Canadian was spotted by Betty Carter, who composed lyrics for one of his compositions, 'Love Notes', and recorded it with a group which included Dave Holland, one of Zubek's teachers. He writes fluent, harmonically vivid tunes and is an able improviser.

*****(*) Horse With A Broken Leg**
Fresh Sound New Talent FSNT 078 *Zubek; Philippe Thomas (t); Seamus Blake, Chris Cheek, Mark Turner (ts); Chander Sardjoe (d).* 11/99.

Zubek brilliantly solves the problem of writing for a group without a harmony instrument by distributing the horn voicings with great subtlety and by filling in the vacuum with his own strong presence. Both quartet (Turner on sole tenor) and quintet settings are extremely effective, but without a second saxophone on 'Petite Rosalie' and '2513' the sound becomes very spare indeed.

Lest animal lovers become alarmed, the title-track is a reference to the hobbling 9/4 metre which provides a considerable challenge to the horn soloists and drummer; Sardjoe is excellent, a real find. Zubek himself doesn't solo on it or on 'Low Down', which features the excellent Seamus Blake, but he provides strong statements on 'Yes Yes', 'No No' and on a wonderful arrangement of Hendrix's fiery 'Manic Depression'.

Zubop

GROUP

Vigorous British post-bop outfit putting an Anglicized spin on some verities in the language.

***** Cycle City**
33 Records JAZZ 006 *Will Embling/Wisbling/Embliss (t, vtb, v); Ricky Edwards (as, f, bcl, v); Jon Petters (ts, cl, v); Mark Allen (bs); Philip Clouts (p, acc, v); Duncan Noble (b, v); Lindon Donaldson, Cliff Venner (d).* 91.

***** Freewheeling**
33 Records JAZZ 015 *As above, except omit Allen, Donaldson, Venner; add Sean Randle (d), Gary Hammond (perc).* 8/93.

***** Hiptodisiac**
33 Records JAZZ 038 *As above, except add John Blackwell (g), Juldeh Camara (riti, v).* 96.

***** Tekezze**
33 Records 33JAZZ 060 *As above.* 00.

***** ZubopGambia**
33 Records 33JAZZ 102 *As above.* 01.

The only mystery here is why the trumpeter's name keeps changing. Zubop play vivacious and intelligent, Afro-tinged bop fusion with no obvious identity problems. All three albums have been marked out by strong, idiosyncratic writing, somewhere between Django Bates and Dudu Pukwana, and a vigorous group sound and, though the band conspicuously lacks a strong single soloist, there is always enough going on in the ensembles to sustain interest, though by *Hiptodisiac* one does begin to wonder where it's all leading.

The first album was a breath of fresh air, with room to stretch out on 'Cycle City', 'Bheki's Arrival' (co-written with pianist Mseleku) and 'Free Yourself', and a brash, almost callow sound that was instantly and lastingly appealing. On the well-named *Freewheeling*, '20,000 Leagues Above Peckham' is a combination of full-on jam and intricate structure, a quality that crops up again on the most recent and most playful of Zubop's discs, where 'Gamelanaskanabopolus', 'We Come From The Universe Like The Dolphins And Frogs' (two more tunes by Edwards) and the folksier 'Song Of Snape' suggest that the band may be moving in a new direction, somewhat closer to the territory carved out by Bill Bruford's Earthworks.

Tekezze and *ZubopGambia* take things back round in an African direction again. They seemed to return from African travels full of new ideas and infused with an energy that comes across most strongly on *ZubopGambia*, recorded live at Ronnie Scott's. 'Tales Of Tekezze' is probably the strongest statement on the set, but there is as always much to like. It would demand a heart of stone not to enjoy what Zubop do, but it's hard to make too serious a case for them either. Clever, enjoyable jazz.